Acronyms, Initialisms & Abbreviations Dictionary

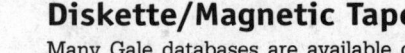

ISSN 0270-4404

Acronyms, Initialisms & Abbreviations Dictionary

A Guide to Acronyms, Abbreviations, Contractions, Alphabetic Symbols, and Similar Condensed Appellations

Covering: Aerospace, Associations, Banking, Biochemistry, Business, Data Processing, Domestic and International Affairs, Economics, Education, Electronics, Genetics, Government, Information Technology, Investment, Labor, Law, Medicine, Military Affairs, Pharmacy, Physiology, Politics, Religion, Science, Societies, Sports, Technical Drawings and Specifications, Telecommunications, Trade, Transportation, and Other Fields

25th Edition

Volume 1

Part 3

P-Z

Mary Rose Bonk,
Editor

Pamela Dear,
Associate Editor

GALE

DETROIT • LONDON

Editor: Mary Rose Bonk

Associate Editor: Pamela Dear

Contributing Editor: Mildred Hunt

Data Entry Manager: Eleanor M. Allison
Data Entry Coordinator: Kenneth Benson

Production Director: Mary Beth Trimper
Production Assistant: Carolyn Fischer

Graphic Services Manager: Barbara J. Yarrow
Graphic Artist: Gary Leach

Manager, Technical Support Services: Theresa A. Rocklin
Programmer: Charles Beaumont

Library of Congress Catalog Card Number 84-643188
ISBN 0-7876-2423-3 (Volume 1 Complete)
ISBN 0-7876-2424-1 (Part 1: A-F only)
ISBN 0-7876-2425-X (Part 2: G-O only)
ISBN 0-7876-2426-8 (Part 3: P-Z only)
ISSN 0270-4404

Printed in the United States of America

Contents

Volume 1
Part 1 A-F

Volume 1
Part 2 G-O

Volume 1
Part 3 P-Z

Gale's publications in the acronyms and abbreviations field include:

***Acronyms, Initialisms & Abbreviations Dictionary* series:**

Acronyms, Initialisms & Abbreviations Dictionary (Volume 1). A guide to acronyms, initialisms, abbreviations, and similar contractions, arranged alphabetically by abbreviation.

Acronyms, Initialisms & Abbreviations Dictionary Supplement (Volume 2). An interedition supplement in which terms are arranged alphabetically both by abbreviation and by meaning.

Reverse Acronyms, Initialisms & Abbreviations Dictionary (Volume 3). A companion to Volume 1 in which terms are arranged alphabetically by meaning of the acronym, initialism, or abbreviation.

***Acronyms, Initialisms & Abbreviations Dictionary* Subject Guide series:**

Computer & Telecommunications Acronyms (Volume 1). A guide to acronyms, initialisms, abbreviations, and similar contractions used in the field of computers and telecommunications in which terms are arranged alphabetically both by abbreviation and by meaning.

Business Acronyms (Volume 2). A guide to business-oriented acronyms, initialisms, abbreviations, and similar contractions in which terms are arranged alphabetically both by abbreviation and by meaning.

***International Acronyms, Initialisms & Abbreviations Dictionary* series:**

International Acronyms, Initialisms & Abbreviations Dictionary (Volume 1). A guide to foreign and international acronyms, initialisms, abbreviations, and similar contractions, arranged alphabetically by abbreviation.

Reverse International Acronyms, Initialisms & Abbreviations Dictionary (Volume 2). A companion to Volume 1, in which terms are arranged alphabetically by meaning of the acronym, initialism, or abbreviation.

***Periodical Title Abbreviations* series:**

Periodical Title Abbreviations: By Abbreviation (Volume 1). A guide to abbreviations commonly used for periodical titles, arranged alphabetically by abbreviation.

Periodical Title Abbreviations: By Title (Volume 2). A guide to abbreviations commonly used for periodical titles, arranged alphabetically by title.

New Periodical Title Abbreviations (Volume 3). An interedition supplement in which terms are arranged alphabetically both by abbreviation and by title.

User's Guide

The following examples illustrate possible elements of entries in *AIAD:*

① ② ③ ④ ⑤
FATAC... Force Aerienne Tactique [*Tactical Air Force*] [*French*] (NATG)
⑥ ⑦
MMT... Multiple-Mirror Telescope [*Mount Hopkins, AZ*] [*Jointly operated by Smithsonian Institution and the University of Arizona*] [*Astronomy*]
⑧

① Acronym, Initialism, or Abbreviation

② Meaning or Phrase

③ English Translation

④ Language (for non-English entries)

⑤ Source code (Allows you to verify entries or find additional information. Decoded in the List of Selected Sources)

⑥ Location or Country of origin (Provides geographic identifiers for airports, colleges and universities, libraries, military bases, political parties, radio and television stations, and others)

⑦ Sponsoring organization

⑧ Subject category (Clarifies entries by providing appropriate context)

The completeness of a listing is dependent upon both the nature of the term and the amount of information provided by the source. If additional information becomes available during future research, an entry is revised.

Arrangement of Entries

Acronyms, initialisms, and abbreviations are arranged alphabetically in letter-by-letter sequence. Spacing, punctuation, and capitalization are not considered. If the same term has more than one meaning, the various meanings are subarranged in word-by-word sequence.

Should you wish to eliminate the guesswork from acronym formation and usage, a companion volume could help. *Reverse Acronyms, Initialisms and Abbreviations Dictionary* contains essentially the same entries as *AIAD,* but arranges them alphabetically by meaning, rather than by acronym or initialism.

List of Selected Sources

Each of the sources included in the following list contributed at least 50 terms. It would be impossible to cite a source for every entry because the majority of terms are sent by outside contributors, are uncovered through independent research by the editorial staff, or surface as miscellaneous broadcast or print media references.

For sources used on an ongoing basis, only the latest edition is listed. For most of the remaining sources, the edition that was used is cited. The editors will provide further information about these sources upon request.

Unless further described in an annotation, the publications listed here contain no additional information about the acronym, initialism, or abbreviation cited.

(AABC) *Catalog of Abbreviations and Brevity Codes*. Washington, DC: U.S. Department of the Army, 1981. [Use of source began in 1969]

(AAG) *Aerospace Abbreviations Glossary*. Report Number AG60-0014. Prepared by General Dynamics/Astronautics. San Diego, CA: 1962.

(AAGC) *Acronyms and Abbreviations in Government Contracting*. 2d ed. By Patricia A. Tobin and Joan Nelson Phillips. Washington, DC: George Washington University, 1997.

(AAMN) *Abbreviations and Acronyms in Medicine and Nursing*. By Solomon Garb, Eleanor Krakauer, and Carson Justice. New York, NY: Springer Publishing Co., 1976.

(ABBR) *Abbreviations: The Comprehensive Dictionary of Abbreviations and Letter Symbols*. Vol. 1 C. By Edward Wall. Ann Arbor, MI: The Pierian Press, 1984.

(AC) *Associations Canada 1995/96*. Edited by Ward McBurney. Toronto, Canada: Canadian Almanac & Directory Publishing Co. Ltd., 1995.

(ACII) *"Acronym and Initials Index."* 7 February 1996. <http://www.ioi.ie/~readout/cl.html> (7 November 1996).

(AD) *Abbreviations Dictionary*. 8thed. By Ralph De Sola. Boca Raton, FL: CRC Press, 1992.

(ADA) *The Australian Dictionary of Acronyms and Abbreviations*. 2nd ed. Compiled by David J. Jones. Leura, NSW, Australia: Second Back Row Press Pty. Ltd., 1981.

(ADDR) *Army Dictionary and Desk Reference*. By Tim Zurick. Harrisburg, PA: Stackpole Books, 1992.

(AEBS) *Acronyms in Education and the Behavioral Sciences*. By Toyo S. Kawakami. Chicago, IL: American Library Association, 1971.

(AEE) *American Educators' Encyclopedia*. By Edward L. Dejnozka and David E. Kapel. Westport, CT: Greenwood Press, 1991.

(AF) *Reference Aid: Abbreviations in the African Press*. Arlington, VA: Joint Publications Research Service, 1979.

(AFIT) *Compendium of Authenticated Systems and Logistics*. Washington, DC: Air Force Institute of Technology, 1984.

(AFM) *Air Force Manual of Abbreviations*. Washington, DC: U.S. Department of the Air Force, 1975. [Use of source began in 1969]

(AIA) *Aviation Insurance Abbreviations, Organisations and Institutions*. By M.J. Spurway. London, England: Witherby & Co. Ltd., 1983.

(AIE) *Acronyms and Initialisms in Education*. 6th ed. Compiled by John Hutchins. Norwich, England: Librarians of Institutes and Schools of Education, 1995.

(ANA) *"Abbreviations" - U.S. Navy Dictionary*. 3rd revision. Washington DC: DCP, 1989.

(APTA) *Australian Periodical Title Abbreviations*. Compiled by David J. Jones. Leura, NSW, Australia: Second Back Row Press Pty. Ltd., 1985.

(ARC) *Agricultural Research Centres: A World Directory of Organizations and Programmes*. 2 vols. Edited by Nigel Harvey. Harlow, Essex, England: Longman Group, 1983.

A world guide to official, educational, industrial, and independent research centers which support research in the fields of agriculture, veterinary medicine, horticulture, aquaculture, food science, forestry, zoology, and botany.

(ARCH) *Dictionary of Architecture and Construction*. Edited by Cyril M. Harris. New York, NY: McGraw-Hill, Inc., 1975.

(ASF) *Guide to Names and Acronyms of Organizations, Activities, and Projects*. By Food and Agriculture Organization of the United Nations. Fishery Information, Data, and Statistics Service and U.S. National Oceanic and Atmospheric Administration. Aquatic Sciences and Fisheries Information System Reference Series, Number 10, 1982. n.p.

(BABM) *Bailliere's Abbreviations in Medicine*. 5th ed. By Edwin B. Steen. London, England: Bailliere Tindall, 1984.

(BARN) *The Barnhart Abbreviations Dictionary*. Edited by Robert K. Barnhart. New York, NY: John Wiley & Sons, Inc., 1995.

(BI) *British Initials and Abbreviations*. 3rd ed. By Ian H. Wilkes. London, England: Leonard Hill Books, 1971.

(BIB) *Bibliotech*. Ottawa, Canada: National Library of Canada, 1988-89.

(BJA) *Biblical and Judaic Acronyms*. By Lawrence Marwick. New York, NY: Ktav Publishing House, Inc., 1979.

(BRI) *Book Review Index*. 1997 Cumulation. Edited by Beverly Baer. Detroit, MI: Gale Research, 1998.

(BROA) *Broadcasting and Cable Yearbook 1997*. 2 vol. New Providence, NJ: R.R. Bowker, 1997.

(BTTJ) *Breaking Through Technical Jargon: A Dictionary of Computer and Automation Acronyms*. By Mark S. Merkow. New York, NY: Van Nostrand Reinhold, 1990.

(BUR) *Computer Acronyms and Abbreviations Handbook*. Tokyo, Japan: Burroughs Co. Ltd., 1978.

(BYTE) *Byte: The Small Systems Journal*. Peterborough, NH: McGraw-Hill Information Systems, Inc., 1987-89.

(CAAL) *CAAL COMOPTEVFOR Acronym and Abbreviation List*. Norfolk, VA: (CAAL-U) Operational Test and Evaluation Force, 1981.

(CB) *Centres & Bureaux: A Directory of Concentrations of Effort, Information and Expertise*. Edited by Lindsay Sellar. Beckenham, Kent, England: CBD Research Ltd., 1987.

A guide to British organizations which include the words "centre" or "bureau" in their names. Entries include name and address; telephone and telex numbers; chief official; and a description of the purposes, activities, and services of the organization.

(CDAI) *Concise Dictionary of Acronyms and Initialisms*. By Stuart W. Miller. New York, NY: Facts on File Publications, 1988.

(CDE) *The Computer Desktop Encyclopedia*. By Alan Freedman. New York, NY: AMACOM, 1996.

(CDI) *The Cancer Dictionary*. By Roberta Altman and Michael Sarg, M.D. New York, NY: Facts on File, 1992.

(CED) *Current European Directories*. 2nd ed. Edited by G.P. Henderson. Beckenham, Kent, England: CBD Research, 1981.

(CET) *Communications-Electronics Terminology*. AFM 11-1. Vol. 3. U.S. Department of the Air Force, 1973.

(CINC) *A CINCPAC Glossary of Commonly Used Abbreviations and Short Titles*. By Ltc. J.R. Johnson. Washington, DC: 1968.

(CMD) *Complete Multilingual Dictionary of Computer Terminology*. Compiled by Georges Nania. Chicago, IL: National Textbook Co., 1984.

Computer-related terms in Spanish, French, Italian, Portuguese, and English. Indexes in French, Italian, Spanish, and Portuguese are also provided.

(CNC) *American National Standard Codes for the Representation of Names of Countries, Dependencies, and Areas of Special Sovereignty for Information Interchange*. U.S. National Bureau of Standards. Washington, DC: Government Printing Office, 1986. [Use of source began in 1977]

These standard codes, approved by the International Organization for Standardization and the American National Standards Institute, are used in the international interchange of data in many fields.

(CPH) *The Charles Press Handbook of Current Medical Abbreviations*. 3rd ed. Philadelphia, PA: The Charles Press Publishers, Inc., 1991.

(CRD) *Computer-Readable Databases: A Directory and Data Sourcebook*. 6th ed. Edited by Kathleen Young Marcaccio. Detroit, MI: Gale Research, 1990.

A guide to online databases, offline files available in various magnetic formats, and CD-ROM files. Entries include producer name, address, telephone number, description of coverage, vendors, and contact person.

(CROSS) *Cross-Border Links: A Directory of Organizations in Canada, Mexico, and the United States*. Edited by Ricardo Hernandez and Edith Sanchez. Albuquerque, NM: Inter-Hemispheric Education Resource Center, 1992.

(CSR) *Computer Science Resources: A Guide to Professional Literature.* Edited by Darlene Myers. White Plains, NY: Knowledge Industry Publications, Inc., 1981.

Covers several types of computer-related literature including journals, technical reports, directories, dictionaries, handbooks, and university computer center newsletters. Five appendices cover career and salary trends in the computer industry, user group acronyms, university computer libraries, and trade fairs and shows.

(CTT) *Corporate TrendTrac.* Edited by A. Dale Timpe. Detroit, MI: Gale Research, 1988-89.

Covers mergers and acquisitions, stock exchange listings and suspensions, company name changes, bankruptcies, liquidations, and reorganizations.

(DA) *Dictionary of Aviation.* By R. J. Hall and R. D. Campbell. Chicago, IL: St. James Press, 1991.

(DAS) *Dictionary of Abbreviations and Symbols.* By Edward Frank Allen. London, England: Cassell and Co. Ltd., 1949.

(DAVI) *The Davis Book of Medical Abbreviations: A Deciphering Guide.* By Sarah Lu Mitchell-Hatton. Philadelphia, PA: F. A. Davis Co., 1991.

(DBA) *Directory of British Associations.* Edited by G. P. Henderson and S. P. A. Henderson. Beckenham, Kent, England: CBD Research, Ltd., 1990.

(DBQ) *A Dictionary of British Qualifications.* London, England: Kogan Page Ltd., 1985.

(DCTA) *Dictionary of Commercial Terms and Abbreviations.* By Alan E. Branch. London, England: Witherby & Co. Ltd., 1984.

(DD) *The Financial Post Directory of Directors 1997.* Toronto, Canada: The Financial Post, 1996.

(DEN) *Dictionary of Electronics and Nucleonics.* By L.E.C. Hughes, R. W. B. Stephens and L. D. Brown. New York, NY: Barnes & Noble, 1969.

(DFIT) *Dictionary of Finance and Investment Terms.* 4th ed. Edited by John Downes and Jordan Elliot Goodman. Hauppauge, NY: Barron's Educational Series, 1995.

(DGA) *Dictionary of Graphic Arts Abbreviations.* By L. W. Wallis. Rockport, MA: Rockport Publishers, Inc., 1986.

(DHSM) *Dictionary of Health Services Management.* 2nd ed. By Thomas C. Timmreck. Owings Mills, MD: Rynd Communications, 1987.

(DI) *The Dictionary of Initials-What They Mean.* Compiled and edited by Harriette Lewis. Kingswood, Surrey, England: Paper Fronts Elliot Right Way Books, 1983.

(DICI) *The Dictionary of Initials.* By Betsy M. Parks. Secaucus, NJ: Citadel Press, 1981.

(DIT) *Dictionary of Informatics Terms in Russian and English.* By G. S. Zhdanov, E. S. Kolobrodov, V. A. Polushkin, and A. I. Cherny. Moscow: Nauka, 1971.

(DLA) *Bieber's Dictionary of Legal Abbreviations.* 3rd ed. By Mary Miles Prince. Buffalo, NY: William S. Hein & Co., 1988.

(DMA) *Dictionary of Military Abbreviations: British, Empire, Commonwealth*. By B. K. C. Scott. Hastings, East Sussex, England: Tamarisk Books, 1982.

(DMAA) *Dictionary of Medical Acronyms and Abbreviations*. 3rd ed. Edited by Stanley Jablonski. Philadelphia, PA: Hanley & Belfus, Inc., 1998.

(DMC) *Webster's New World Dictionary of Media and Communications*. Revised ed. By Richard Weiner. New York, NY: Macmillan, 1996.

(DNAB) *Dictionary of Naval Abbreviations*. 3rd ed. Compiled and edited by Bill Wedertz. Annapolis, MD: Naval Institute Press, 1984.

(DOAD) *The Dictionary of Advertising*. Edited by Laurence Urdang. Lincolnwood, IL: NTC Business Books, 1986.

(DOG) *A Dictionary of Genetics*. 5th ed. By Robert C. King and William D. Stansfield. New York, NY: Oxford University Press, 1997.

(DOGT) *"List of Acronyms."* <http://www.em.doe.gov/rtc1994/loa.html> (5 March 1997).

(DOM) *The Dictionary of Multimedia: Terms & Acronyms*. By Brad Hansen. Wilsonvillee, OR: Franklin, Beedle & Associates, 1997.

(DOMA) *Dictionary of Military Abbreviations*. By Norman Polmar, Mark Warren, and Eric Wertheim. Annapolis, MD: Naval Institute Press, 1994.

(DS) *Dictionary of Shipping International Trade Terms and Abbreviations*. 3rd ed. By Alan E. Branch. London, England: Witherby & Co. Ltd., 1986.

(DSA) *Dictionary of Sigla and Abbreviations to and in Law Books before 1607*. By William Hamilton Bryson. Charlottesville, VA: University Press of Virginia, 1975.

(DSUE) *A Dictionary of Slang and Unconventional English*. 8th ed. By Eric Partridge. New York, NY: Macmillan Publishing Co., 1984.

(DUND) *Directory of United Nations Databases and Information Services*. 4th ed. Compiled by the Advisory Committee for the Coordination of Information Systems. New York, NY: United Nations, 1990.

A guide to computerized databases and information systems/services. Entries include sponsoring organization, year established, type, scope, coverage, timespan, and contact information.

(DWSG) *Defense Weapon Systems Glossary*. By David Trotz. Piscataway, NJ: Target Marketing, 1992.

(EA) *Encyclopedia of Associations*. 29th ed. Vol. 1, National Organizations of the U.S. Edited by Carol A. Schwartz and Rebecca L. Turner. Detroit, MI: Gale Research, 1995 (and supplement 1995) [Use of source began in 1960]

A guide to trade, professional, and other nonprofit associations that are national and international in scope and membership and that are headquartered in the United States. Entries include name and address; telephone and telex number; chief official; and a description of the purpose, activities, and structure of the organization.

(EAAP) *Encyclopedia of Associations: Association Periodicals*. 3 vols. Edited by Denise M. Allard and Robert C. Thomas. Detroit, MI: Gale Research, 1987.

A directory of publications issued by all types of national nonprofit organizations in the United States. Entries include title and organization name, address, telephone number; description of periodical, frequency of publication, and price.

(EAIO) *Encyclopedia of Associations: International Organizations*. 29th ed. Edited by Linda Irvin. Detroit, MI: Gale Research, 1995. [Use of source began in 1985]

A guide to trade, professional, and other nonprofit associations that are national or international in scope and membership and that are headquartered outside the United States. Entries include name and address; principal foreign language name; telephone and telex number; chief official; and a description of the purpose, activities, and structure of the organization.

(ECED) *The European Communities Encyclopedia and Directory 1992*. London, England: Europa Publications Ltd., 1991; distributed in U.S. by Gale Research, Detroit, MI.

A comprehensive guide to the European Communities. Entries explain widely-used acronyms and include address, telephone, telex, fax numbers and chief officers for EC-level organizations.

(ECII) *Electronics, Computers and Industrial Instrumentation Abbreviations and Acronyms*. Edited by Sergio Sobredo. Miami, FL: Sergio Sobredo Technical Services, 1986.

(ECON) *The Economist*. London, England: The Economist Newspaper Ltd., 1997. [Use of source began in 1988]

(EDAC) *Dictionary of Educational Acronyms, Abbreviations, and Initialisms*. 2nd ed. Edited by James C. Palmer and Anita Y. Colby. Phoenix, AZ: Oryx Press, 1985.

(EE) *Eastern Europe and the Commonwealth of Independent States 1992*. London, England: Europa Publications Ltd., 1992; distributed in U.S. by Gale Research, Detroit, MI.

(EECA) *Dictionary of Electrical, Electronics, and Computer Abbreviations*. By Phil Brown. London, England: Buttersworth, 1985.

(EG) *Environmental Glossary*. 4th ed. Edited by G. William Frick and Thomas F.P. Sullivan. Rockville, MD: Government Institutes, Inc., 1986.

(EGAO) *Encyclopedia of Governmental Advisory Organizations*. 9th ed. Edited by Donna Batten. Detroit, MI: Gale Research, 1994-95 (and supplement, 1995). [Use of source began in 1975]

A reference guide to permanent, continuing, and ad hoc U.S. presidential advisory committees, interagency committees, and other government-related boards, panels, task forces, commissions, conferences, and other similar bodies serving in a consultative, coordinating, advisory, research, or investigative capacity. Entries include name and address, telephone number, designated federal employee, history, recommendation and findings of the committee, staff size, publications, and subsidiaries. Also includes indexes to personnel, reports, federal agencies, presidential administration, and an alphabetical and keyword index.

(EMRF) *The St. James Encyclopedia of Mortgage & Real Estate Finance*. By James Newell, Albert Santi, and Chip Mitchell. Chicago, IL: St. James Press, 1991.

(EPA) *Glossary of EPA Acronyms*. Washington, DC: Environmental Protection Agency, 1987.

(ERG) *Environmental Regulatory Glossary*. 5th ed. Edited by G. William Frick and Thomas F. P. Sullivan. Rockville, MD: Government Institutes, Inc., 1990.

(EY) *The Europa World Year Book 1992*. London: Europa Publications Ltd., 1992. distributed in U.S. by Gale Research, Detroit, MI.

An annual survey containing detailed information about the political, economic, statistical, and commercial situation of the regions and countries covered.

(FAAC) *Contractions Handbook*. Changes. U.S. Department of Transportation. Federal Aviation Administration, 1993. [Use of source began in 1969]

(FAAL) *Location Identifiers*. U.S. Department of Transportation. Federal Aviation Administration. Air Traffic Service, 1982.

(FEA) *The Far East and Australasia 1987*. 18th ed. London, England: Europa Publications Ltd., 1986; distributed in U.S. by Gale Research, Detroit, MI.

An annual survey containing detailed information about the political, economic, statistical, and commercial situation of the regions and countries covered.

(FFDE) *The Facts on File Dictionary of Environmental Science*. By L. Harold Stevenson and Bruce Wyman. New York, NY: Facts on File, 1991.

Defines terms from disciplines as diverse as biology, chemistry, geology, physics, engineering, meteorology, social science, medicine, and economics.

(GAAI) *"Glossary of Abbreviations, Acronyms, and Initialisms."* 17 February 1998. <http://www.em.doe.gov/idb97/acropdf.html

(GAVI) *"Glossary of Aviation Acronyms and Abbreviations."* <http://olias.arc.nasa.gov/AFO_Acronyms_.html> (5 March 1997).

(GEA) *Government Economic Agencies of the World: An International Directory of Governmental Organisations Concerned with Economic Development and Planning*. A Keesing's Reference Publication. Edited by Alan J. Day. Harlow, Essex, England: Longman Group Ltd., 1985.

Covers over 170 countries and territories. Two introductory sections for each area cover economic data and prevailing economic and political conditions. Individual entries provide title, address, and names of chief officials of each agency. Current activities and financial structure of each agency are also detailed. An index of agency officials is provided.

(GFGA) *Guide to Federal Government Acronyms*. Edited by William R. Evinger. Phoenix, AZ: The Oryx Press, 1989.

(GNE) *The Green Encyclopedia*. By Irene Franck and David Brownstone. New York, NY: Prentice Hall General Reference, 1992.

(GPO) *Style Manual*. Washington, DC: Government Printing Office, 1984.Terms are included in Chapter 24, Foreign Languages.

(GRD) *Government Research Directory*. 8th ed. Edited by Joseph M. Palmisano. Detroit, MI: Gale Research, 1994. (and supplement, 1994).

A descriptive guide to U.S. government research and development centers, institutes, laboratories, bureaus, test facilities, experiment stations, data collection and analysis centers, and grants management and research coordinating offices in agriculture, business, education, energy, engineering, environment, the humanities, medicine, military science, and basic applied sciences.

(HCT) *Health Care Terms.* 2nd ed. By Vergil N. and Debora A. Slee. St. Paul, MN: Tringa Press, 1991.

(HGAA) *The Handy Guide to Abbreviations and Acronyms for the Automated Office.* By Mark W. Greenia. Seattle, WA: Self-Counsel Press Inc., 1986.

(IAA) *Index of Acronyms and Abbreviations in Electrical and Electronic Engineering.* Compiled by Buro Scientia. New York, NY: VCH Publishers, 1989.

(IBMDP) *IBM Data Processing Glossary.* 6th ed. White Plains, NY: IBM Corp., 1977.

(ICAO) *Aircraft Type Designators.* 13th ed. International Civil Aviation Organization, August, 1981.

(ICDA) *Designators for Aircraft Operating Agencies, Aeronautical Authorities and Services.* 49th ed. International Civil Aviation Organization, June, 1982.
Document also includes telephony designators and postal and telegraphic addresses of government civil aviation authorities.

(ICLI) *Location Indicators.* 51st ed. International Civil Aviation Organization, February, 1987.
Document also contains addresses of flight information centers.

(IDOE) *The Illustrated Dictionary of Electronics.* 6th ed. By Stan Gibilisco. New York, NY: TAB Books, 1994.

(IEEE) *IEEE Standard Dictionary of Electrical and Electronics Terms.* Edited by Frank Jay. New York, NY: The Institute of Electrical and Electronics Engineers, Inc., 1977, 1984.
Includes definitions for thousands of electrical and electronics terms. Each entry includes a numeric source code.

(IIA) *Index of Initials and Acronyms.* Compiled by Richard Kleiner. New York, NY: Auerbach Publishers, 1971.

(IID) *Information Industry Directory.* 15th ed. Edited by Annette Novallo. Detroit, MI: Gale Research, 1995. (and supplement, 1995).
An international guide to computer-readable databases, database producers, and publishers, online vendors and time-sharing companies, telecommunications networks, and many other information systems and services. Entries include name and address, telephone number, chief official, and a detailed description of the purpose and function of the system or service.

(ILCA) *Index to Legal Citations and Abbreviations.* By Donald Raistrick. Abingdon, Oxfordshire, England: Professional Books Ltd., 1981.

(IMH) *International Marketing Handbook.* 2nd ed. Edited by Frank Bair. Detroit, MI: Gale Research, 1985.
An in-depth guide to commercial and trade data on 142 countries of the world. Features include a list of European trade fairs and a report on growth markets in Western Europe.

(INF) *Infantry.* Fort Benning, GA: U.S. Army Infantry Training School, 1996. [Use of source began in 1983]

(IRC) *International Research Centers Directory 1992-93.* 6th ed. Edited by Annette Piccirelli. Detroit, MI: Gale Research, 1991.
A world guide to government, university, independent, nonprofit, and commercial research and development centers, institutes, laboratories, bureaus, test facilities,

experiment stations, and data collection and analysis centers, as well as foundations, councils, and other organizations which support research.

(IRUK) *Industrial Research in the United Kingdom.* 12th ed. Harlow, Essex, England: Longman Group UK Ltd., 1987.

A guide to all groups conducting or funding research relevant to British industrial development. Entries include name, address, telephone and telex numbers; chief officials; and scope of activities.

(IT) *Information Today: The Newspaper for Users and Producers of Electronic Information Services.* Medford, NJ: Learned Information Inc., 1988-89.

(ITD) *International Tradeshow Directory.* 5th ed. Frankfurt, Germany: M + A Publishers for Fairs, Exhibitions and Conventions Ltd., 1989.

A guide to trade fairs and exhibitions throughout the world. Entries include event name, dates, frequency, location, description of purpose, profile of exhibitors and attendees.

(IYR) *The 1989-92 International Yacht Racing Rules.* London, England: International Yacht Racing Union, 1989.

(KSC) *A Selective List of Acronyms and Abbreviations.* Compiled by the Documents Department, Kennedy Space Center Library, 1971, 1973.

(LAIN) *Latest Intelligence: An International Directory of Codes Used by Government, Law Enforcement, Military, and Surveillance Agencies.* By James E. Tunnell. Blue Ridge Summit, PA: TAB BOOKS, 1990.

(LCCP) *MARC Formats for Bibliographic Data.* Appendix II. Washington, DC: Library of Congress, 1982.

(LCLS) *Symbols of American Libraries.* 14th ed. Edited by the Enhanced Cataloging Division. Washington, DC: Library of Congress, 1992. [Use of source began in 1980]

(LWAP) *Legal Words and Phrases: Speed Abbreviations.* By Joel Larus. Boston, MA: Aurico Publishing, 1965.

(MAE) *Medical Abbreviations and Eponyms.* By Sheila B. Sloane. Philadelphia, PA: W.B. Saunders Co., 1985.

(MAH) *Medical Abbreviations Handbook.* 2nd ed. Oradell, NJ: Medical Economics Co., Inc., 1983.

(MCD) *Acronyms, Abbreviations, and Initialisms.* Compiled by Carl Lauer. St. Louis, MO: McDonnell Douglas Corp., 1989. [Use of source began in 1969]

(MDG) *Microcomputer Dictionary and Guide.* By Charles J. Sippl. Champaign, IL: Matrix Publishers, Inc., 1975.

A listing of definitions for over 5,000 microelectronics terms. Seven appendices.

(MEDA) *Medical Acronyms.* 2nd ed. By Marilyn Fuller Delong. Oradell, NJ: Medical Economic Books, 1989.

(MENA) *The Middle East and North Africa 1987.* 33rd ed. London, England: Europa Publications Ltd., 1986; distributed in U.S. by Gale Research, Detroit, MI.

An annual survey containing detailed information about the political, economic, statistical, and commercial situation of the regions and countries covered.

(MHDB) *McGraw-Hill Dictionary of Business Acronyms, Initials, and Abbreviations.* By Jerry M. Rosenberg. New York, NY: McGraw-Hill, Inc., 1992.

(MHDI) *McGraw-Hill Dictionary of Information Technology and Computer Acronyms, Initials, and Abbreviations.* By Jerry M. Rosenberg. New York, NY: McGraw-Hill, Inc., 1992.

(MHDW) *McGraw-Hill Dictionary of Wall Street Acronyms, Initials, and Abbreviations.* By Jerry M. Rosenberg. New York, NY: McGraw-Hill, Inc., 1992.

(MSA) *Military Standard Abbreviations for Use on Drawings, and in Specifications, Standards, and Technical Documents.* MIL-STD-12D. U.S. Department of Defense, 1981. [Use of source began in 1975]

(MSC) *Annotated Acronyms and Abbreviations of Marine Science Related Activities.* 3rd ed. Revised by Charlotte M. Ashby and Alan R. Flesh. Washington, DC: U.S. Department of Commerce. National Oceanographic and Atmospheric Administration. Environmental Data Service. National Oceanographic Data Center, 1976, 1981.

(MUGU) *The Mugu Book of Acronyms and Abbreviations.* Missile Range, California: Management Engineering Office, 1963, 1964.

(NADA) *The New American Dictionary of Abbreviations.* By Mary A. De Vries. New York, NY: Signet, 1991.

(NASA) *Space Transportation System and Associated Payloads: Glossary, Acronyms, and Abbreviations.* Washington, DC: U.S. National Aeronautics and Space Administration, 1985.

(NATG) *Glossary of Abbreviations Used in NATO Documents.* AAP 15(B), n.p., 1979. [Use of source began in 1976]

(NCC) *NCC The National Centre for Information Technology. Guide to Computer Aided Engineering, Manufacturing and Construction Software.* Manchester, England: NCC Publications. The National Computing Centre Ltd., 1985.

Includes software classifications and descriptions, names and addresses of suppliers, processor manufacturers, and operating systems.

(NFD) *The NSFRE Fund-Raising Dictionary.* Edited by Barbara R. Levy. New York, NY: John Wiley & Sons, Inc., 1996.

(NFPA) *Standard for Fire Safety Symbols/NFPA170.* Quincy, MA: National Fire Protection Association, 1994.

(NG) *NAVAIR Glossary of Unclassified Common-Use Abbreviated Titles and Phrases.* NAVAIRNOTE 5216 AIR-6031, n.p., July, 1969.

(NGC) *Catalogue of the National Gallery of Canada.* Compiled by National Gallery of Canada. Ottawa, Canada: National Gallery of Canada, 1998.

(NHD) *The New Hacker's Dictionary.* Edited by Eric Raymond. Cambridge, MA: MIT Press, 1991.

(NITA) *Dictionary of New Information Technology Acronyms.* 2nd ed. By Michael Gordon, Alan Singleton, and Clarence Rickards. London, England: Kogan Page, Ltd., 1986.

(NLC) *Symbols of Canadian Libraries.* 12th ed. National Library of Canada. Minister of Supply and Services Canada, 1987.

(NOAA) *NOAA Directives Manual.* 66-13 Acronyms. 1977.

(NQ) *NASDAQ Company Directory.* New York, NY: National Association of Securities Dealers, Inc., 1990. [Use of source began in 1983]
Entries include company name, SIC code, contact person's name, title, address, and telephone number.

(NRCH) *A Handbook of Acronyms and Initialisms.* Washington, DC: U.S. Nuclear Regulatory Commission. Division of Technical Information and Document Control, 1985.

(NTCM) *NTC's Mass Media Dictionary.* R. Terry Ellmore. Lincolnwood, IL: National Textbook Co., 1991.

(NUCP) *A Dictionary of Nuclear Power and Waste Management with Abbreviations and Acronyms.* Foo-Sun Lau. Letchworth, England: Research Studies Press, Ltd., 1987.

(NVT) *Naval Terminology.* NWP3. Rev. B. U.S. Department of the Navy. Office of the Chief of Naval Operations, 1980. [Use of source began in 1974]
Includes a section on definitions of naval terminology.

(OA) *Ocran's Acronyms: A Dictionary of Abbreviations and Acronyms Used in Scientific and Technical Writing.* By Emanuel Benjamin Ocran. London, England: Routledge & Kegan Paul Ltd., 1978.

(OAG) *Official Airline Guide Worldwide Edition.* Oak Brook, IL: Official Airlines Guide, Inc., 1984. [Use of source began in 1975]

(OCD) *Oxford Classical Dictionary.* 2nd ed. Edited by N.G. Hammond and H.H. Scullard. London, England: Oxford University Press, 1970.

(OCLC) *OCLC Participating Institutions Arranged by OCLC Symbol.* Dublin, OH: OCLC, 1981.

(ODBW) *The Oxford Dictionary for the Business World.* New York, NY: Oxford University Press, Inc., 1993.

(OICC) *Abbreviations and Acronyms.* Des Moines, IA: Iowa State Occupational Information Coordinating Committee, 1986.

(OLDSS) *Online Database Search Services Directory.* 2nd ed. Edited by Doris Morris Maxfield. Detroit, MI: Gale Research, 1988.
Provides detailed descriptions of the online information retrieval services offered by libraries, private information firms, and other organizations in the United States and Canada. Entries include name and address, telephone number, and key contact, as well as online systems accessed, frequently searched databases, and access hardware.

(OPSA) *"Official Postal Service Abbreviations."* <http://www.usps.gov/ncsc/lookups/abbr_suffix.txt> (17 December 1996).

(OSI) *OSI Standards and Acronyms.* 3rd ed. Compiled by Adrian V. Stokes. United Kingdom: Stokes, 1991.

(PAZ) *Parenting A to Z.* By Irene M. Franck and David M. Brownstone. New York, NY: HarperCollins Publishers, Inc., 1996.

(PCM) *PC Magazine.* New York, NY: Ziff-Davis Publishing Co., 1997. [Use of source began in 1987]

(PD) *Political Dissent: An International Guide to Dissident, Extra-Parliamentary, Guerrilla and Illegal Political Movements*. A Keesing's Reference Publication. Compiled by Henry W. Degenhardt. Edited by Alan J. Day. Harlow, Essex, England: Longman Group, 1983.

Includes the history and aims of approximately 1,000 organizations, with details of their leaderships.

(PDAA) *Pugh's Dictionary of Acronyms and Abbreviations: Abbreviations in Management, Technology and Information Science*. 5th ed. By Eric Pugh. Chicago, IL: American Library Association, 1987.

(PGP) *Peterson's Graduate Programs in the Humanities, Arts & Social Sciences*. 31st ed. Princeton, NJ: Peterson's 1997.

(PPE) *Political Parties of Europe*. 2 vols. Edited by Vincent E. McHale. The Greenwood Historical Encyclopedia of the World's Political Parties. Westport, CT: Greenwood Press, 1983.

One of a series of reference guides to the world's significant political parties. Each guide provides concise histories of the political parties of a region and attempts to detail the evolution of ideology, changes in organization, membership, leadership, and each party's impact upon society.

(PPW) *Political Parties of the World*. 2nd ed. A Keesing's Reference Publication. Compiled and edited by Alan J. Day and Henry W. Degenhardt. Harlow, Essex, England: Longman Group, 1980, 1984.

Covers historical development, structure, leadership, membership, policy, publications, and international affiliations. For each country, an overview of the current political situation and constitutional structure is provided.

(PS) *Popular Science*. New York, NY: Times-Mirror Magazines, Inc., 1995. [Use of source began in 1992]

(RCD) *Research Centers Directory*. 19th ed. Edited by Thomas J. Cichonski. Detroit, MI: Gale Research, 1994. [Use of source began in 1986]

A guide to university-related and other nonprofit research organizations carrying on research in agriculture, astronomy and space sciences, behavioral and social sciences, computers and mathematics, engineering and technology, physical and earth sciences and regional and area studies.

(RDA) *Army RD and A Magazine*. Alexandria, VA: Development, Engineering, and Acquisition Directorate, Army Materiel Command, 1997. [Use of source began in 1979]

(ROG) *Dictionary of Abbreviations*. By Walter T. Rogers. London, England: George Allen & Co. Ltd., 1913; reprinted by Gale Research, 1969.

(SAA) *Space-Age Acronyms, Abbreviations and Designations*. 2nd ed. By Reta C. Moser. New York, NY: IFI/Plenum, 1969.

(SAG) *Stock Abbreviation Guide*. New York, NY: Associated Press. [Database]

(SDI) *Report to the Congress on the Strategic Defense Initiative*. U.S. Department of Defense. Strategic Defense Initiative Organization, April, 1987.

(SEIS) *Seismograph Station Codes and Characteristics*. Geological Survey. Circular 791. By Barbara B. Poppe, Debbi A. Naab, and John S. Derr. Washington, DC: U.S. Department of the Interior, 1978.

(SLS) *World Guide to Scientific Associations and Learned Societies/Internationales Verzeichnis Wissenschaftlicher Verbande und Gesellschaften.* 4th ed. Edited by Barbara Verrel. New York, NY: K.G. Saur, 1984.

A directory of more than 22,000 societies and associations in all fields of science, culture, and technology. International, national, and regional organizations from 150 countries are also included.

(SPSG) *Security Owner's Stock Guide.* New York, NY: Standard & Poor's Corp., 1994. [Use of source began in 1988]

(SRA) *State and Regional Associations of the United States.* 9th ed. Edited by Tracey E. Chirico, Buck J. Downs and John J. Russell. Washington, DC: Columbia Books, Inc., 1997.

(SSD) *Space Station Directory and Program Guide.* Edited and compiled by Melinda Gipson, Jane Glass, and Mary Linden. Arlington, VA: Pasha Publications Inc., 1988.

(TAG) *Transportation Acronym Guide 1996.* U.S. Department of Transportation. Washington, DC: Bureau of Transportation Statistics, 1996.

(TDOB) *The Dictionary of Banking.* By Charles J. Woelfel. Chicago, IL: Probus Publishing Company, 1994.

(TEL) *Telephony's Dictionary.* 2nd ed. By Graham Langley. Chicago, IL: Telephony Publishing Corp., 1986.

Includes definitions for U.S. and international telecommunications terms. Ten appendices.

(TNIG) *Telecommunications, Networking and Internet Glossary.* By George S. Machovec. Chicago, IL: American Library Association, 1993.

(TOCD) *The Official Catholic Directory 1997.* New Providence, NJ: P.J. Kenedy & Sons, 1997.

(TSPED) *Trade Shows and Professional Exhibits Directory.* 2nd ed. Edited by Robert J. Elster. Detroit, MI: Gale Research, 1987. [Use of source began in 1986]

A guide to scheduled events providing commercial display facilities including conferences, conventions, meetings, fairs and festivals, etc. Entries include name of trade show; sponsor name, address, and telephone number; attendance figures; principal exhibits; special features; publications; and date and location of shows.

(TSSD) *Telecommunications Systems and Services Directory.* 4th ed. (and supplement). Edited by John Krol. Detroit, MI: Gale Research, 1989. [Use of source began in 1985]

An international descriptive guide to telecommunications organizations, systems, and services. Entries include name and address, telephone number, chief official, and a description of the purposes, technical structure, and background of the service or system.

(USDC) *"Glossary of Acronyms".* U.S. Department of Commerce. <http://www.pmel.noaa.gov/pubs/acronym.html> (5 March 1997).

(USGC) *"U.S. Government Commonly Used Abbreviations and Acronyms."* <http://www.fed.gov/hptext/infohwy/gov_acro.html> (5 March 1997).

(VNW) *Words of the Vietnam War.* By Gregory R. Clark. Jefferson, NC: McFarland and Co., Inc., 1990.

(VRA) *VRA Special Bulletin. No. 2, 1987: Standard Abbreviaitons for Image Descriptions for Use in Fine Arts Visual Resources Collections.* Compiled by Nancy S. Schuller. Austin, TX: Visual Resources Association, 1987.

(WDAA) *Webster's New World Dictionary of Acronyms and Abbreviations.* By Auriel Douglas and Michael Strumpf. New York, NY: Webster's New World, 1989.

(WDMC) *Webster's New World Dictionary of Media and Communications.* Revised and updated ed. By Richard Weiner. New York, NY: Webster's New World, 1996.

(WGA) *Webster's Guide to Abbreviations.* Springfield, MA: Merriam-Webster Inc., 1985.

(WYGK) *HR Words you Gotta Know!* By William R. Tracey. New York, NY: AMACOM, 1994.

Acronyms, Initialisms & Abbreviations Dictionary

P-Z

P
By Acronym

P........ Aircraft [*Wind triangle problems*]
P........ All India Reporter, Patna [*A publication*] (DLA)
P........ Armour Pharmaceutical Co. [*Research code symbol*]
P........ Assistant in Private Practice [*Chiropody*] [*British*]
P........ Asta Werke AG [*Germany*] [*Research code symbol*]
P........ Bristol Laboratories [*Research code symbol*]
P........ cis-Platinum [*Cisplatin*] [*Also, cis-DDP, CDDP, CPDD, CPT, DDP*] [*Antineoplastic drug*]
P........ Dainippon Pharmaceutical Co. [*Japan*] [*Research code symbol*]
P........ Democratic People's Republic of Korea [*Aircraft nationality and registration mark*] (FAAC)
p........ Density [*Heat transmission symbol*]
P........ Departure
p........ Difficulty [*of a test item*] [*Psychology*]
P........ Electric Dipole Moment (BARN)
P........ Farbenfabriken Bayer [*Germany*] [*Research code symbol*]
P........ Farmitalia [*Italy*] [*Research code symbol*]
P........ Faulty Punctuation [*Used in correcting manuscripts, etc.*]
P........ Force of Concentrated Load
P........ Games [*or Matches*] Played [*Sports statistics*]
P........ Hole P-Type Semiconductor Material
P........ Indian Law Reports, Patna Series [*A publication*] (DLA)
P........ Law Reports, Probate, Divorce, and Admiralty [*Since 1890*] [*England*] [*A publication*] (DLA)
P........ Lepetit [*Italy*] [*Research code symbol*]
P........ Mainsail Hoist Lenght [*IOR*]
p........ Momentum [*Symbol*] [*IUPAC*]
P........ Office of Personnel [*Coast Guard*]
p........ On Probation [*Navy British*]
P........ Orbital Period [*of a comet*] [*In years*]
P........ Pacer
P........ Pacific Coast Stock Exchange [*Later, PSE*]
p-----........ Pacific Ocean [*MARC geographic area code Library of Congress*] (LCCP)
P........ Pacific Reporter [*A publication*] (DLA)
P........ Pack [*JETDS*]
P........ Packed Lunches [*School meals*] [*British*]
P........ Pad (SAA)
P........ Paddington Railway Station (ROG)
P........ Paddle (DS)
P........ Page
p........ Page (WDMC)
p........ Page (ODBW)
P........ Paid This Year [*In stock listings of newspapers*]
P........ Pain [*Medicine*]
P........ Pair (IAA)
P........ Paired [*for or against*] [*Votes in Congress*]
P........ Paise [*Monetary unit*] [*India*]
P........ Palace (ROG)
P........ Pale (ADA)
P........ Pallet [*Spacelab*] [*NASA*] (NASA)
P........ Pamphlet
P........ Pancuronium [*A muscle relaxant*]
P........ Pandects [*A publication Authority cited in pre-1607 legal work*] (DSA)
P........ Panel (NFPA)
p........ Panel (VRA)
P........ Papa [*Phonetic alphabet*] [*International*] (DSUE)
P........ Papa [*Pope*] [*Latin*]
P........ Paper
P........ Paperback (WGA)
P........ Papilla [*Optic*] [*Medicine*]
P........ Papillate [*A type of seed*] [*Botany*]
p........ Para [*Chemistry*]
P........ Para [*Monetary unit*] [*Former Yugoslavia*]
P........ Parachutist [*Army skill qualification identifier*] (INF)
P........ Paragraph (ADA)
P........ Paralegal Program [*Association of Independent Colleges and Schools specialization code*]
P........ Parallax
P........ Parallel
P........ Paramecin [*A protozoan toxin*]
P........ Parashah (BJA)
P........ Pardon (ADA)
P........ Parenchyma [*Botany*]
P........ Parent (CPH)
P........ Parental
P........ Parietal Electrode Placement in Electroencephalography [*Medicine*] (DMAA)
P........ Parish (ROG)
P........ Parity [*Atomic physics*]
P........ Parity [*Obstetrics*] (DAVI)
P........ Park
P........ Parking Place [*Traffic sign*] [*British*]
P........ Parlophone [*Record label*] [*Great Britain, Italy, Australia, etc.*]
P........ Parson
P........ Part
p........ Part (WDMC)
P........ Parthian [*Language, etc.*]
P........ Partial [*Astronomy*]
P........ Partial Pressure (MAE)
P........ Partial Tension [*Medicine*] (DAVI)
P........ Participle [*Grammar*]
P........ Partim [*In Part*]
P........ Partnership
P........ Party
P........ Parve [*or Pareve*] [*In food labeling, indicates food is kosher and can be used with either meat or dairy products*]
P........ Passed [*Examination*]
P........ Passing Showers [*Meteorology*]
P........ Past
p........ Past (WDMC)
P........ Paste
P........ Pasteboard (DGA)
P........ Pasteurella [*Genus of bacteria*]
P........ Pastor
P........ Patent
P........ Pater [*Father*] [*Latin*]
P........ Paternally Contributing [*Genetics*] (DAVI)
P........ Patient
P........ Patrol [*Designation for all US military aircraft*]
P........ Patrol Service Gunnery Instructor [*Officer's rating*] [*British Royal Navy*]
P........ Patron
P........ Pattern
P........ Paulus de Liazaris [*Deceased, 1356*] [*Authority cited in pre-1607 legal work*] (DSA)
P........ Paused Program [*Computer science*]
P........ Paved Surface [*Aviation*] (DA)
P........ Pavilion (ROG)
P........ Pawn [*Chess*]
P........ Pax [*Peace*] [*Latin*]
P........ Pay
P........ Payee
P........ Paymaster [*Military*] (ROG)
p........ P-Doped Semiconductor [*Photovoltaic energy systems*]
P........ Peak
P........ Peak (IDOE)
P........ Peat (ROG)
P........ Pebbles [*Quality of the bottom*] [*Nautical charts*]
P........ Pectoral [*Anatomy*] (ROG)
p........ Peculiar [*Astronomy*]
P........ Pedestrian (WDAA)
P........ Peg [*Telecommunications*] (IAA)
P........ Pelagius [*Deceased, 1232*] [*Authority cited in pre-1607 legal work*] (DSA)
P........ Pen [*Sports*]
p........ Pence [*Monetary unit*] [*British*]
P........ Pencil Tube (MDG)
P........ Pengo [*Monetary unit in Hungary until 1946*]
P........ Penicillin
p........ Penni(a) [*Penny or Pence*] [*Monetary unit*] [*Finland*] (GPO)
P........ Pennsylvania (DLA)
P........ Pennsylvania State Library, Harrisburg, PA [*Library symbol Library of Congress*] (LCLS)
P........ Penny
p........ Penny (ODBW)
P........ Pentachlorophenol [*Also, PCP*] [*Wood preservative*] [*Organic chemistry*] (TEL)
P........ Pentode [*Electronics*] (OA)
P........ Peony [*Horticulture*]
P........ People
P........ Pepper (DICI)

P.................. Per
P.................. Per (IDOE)
p.................. Per (WDMC)
P.................. Percentile
P.................. Perceptual
P.................. Perceptual Speed [*A factor ability*] [*Psychology*]
P.................. Perch
P.................. Perchloroethylene [*Also, TCE*] [*Dry cleaning*]
P.................. Percussion
P.................. Pere [*Father*] [*French*]
P.................. Perforateur Honeywell Bull (IAA)
P.................. Perforation
P.................. Performance [*Army*] (INF)
P.................. Performer
P.................. Perfusionist [*Medicine*] (DAVI)
P.................. Perianth
P.................. Pericardium [*Medicine*]
P.................. Perimeter
P.................. Period
P.................. Peripheral (DAVI)
P.................. Perishable
P.................. Permanent [*Inks*] (DGA)
P.................. Permanent Stay [*in hospital*] [*British*]
P.................. Permeance (IDOE)
P.................. Permutation (NITA)
P.................. Perpetuus [*Uninterrupted*] [*Latin*]
p.................. Perseverate [*Psychology*]
P.................. Persian (DLA)
P.................. Persimmon
P.................. Persistence [*Medicine*]
P.................. Person
P.................. Personal (DA)
P.................. Personality Organization and Stability [*Eysenck*] [*Psychology*]
P.................. Personnel
P.................. Person to Person [*Telecommunications*] (TEL)
P.................. Perstetur [*Continue*] [*Pharmacy*] (ROG)
P.................. Persuasion [*Novel by Jane Austen*]
P.................. Peseta [*Monetary unit*] [*Spain and Latin America*]
P.................. Pesewa [*Monetary unit*] [*Ghana*]
P.................. Pesher (BJA)
P.................. Peshitta (BJA)
P.................. Peso [*Monetary unit*] [*Spain and Latin America*]
P.................. Peta [*A prefix meaning multiplied by* 10^{15}] [*SI symbol*]
P.................. Peter [*Phonetic alphabet*] [*World War II*] (DSUE)
P.................. Peter [*New Testament book*]
P.................. Peters' United States Supreme Court Reports [*26-41 United States*] [*A publication*] (DLA)
P.................. Petiole [*Botany*]
P.................. Petite (WGA)
P.................. Petrol [*British Waterways Board sign*]
P.................. Petrus Hispanus [*Authority cited in pre-1607 legal work*] (DSA)
P.................. Peyote
P.................. Pfizer, Inc. [*Research code symbol*]
P.................. Pharmacopoeia
P.................. Phencyclidine [*An anesthetic*]
P.................. Phenolphthalein [*Chemical indicator*]
P.................. Philadelphia [*Pennsylvania*] [*Mint mark, when appearing on US coins*]
P.................. Phillips Petroleum [*NYSE symbol*] (TTSB)
P.................. Phillips Petroleum Co. [*NYSE symbol*] (SPSG)
P.................. Phoenician (BJA)
P.................. Phon [*Unit of loudness level*]
P.................. Phone (IAA)
p.................. Phosphate [*One-letter symbol*] [*Biochemistry*]
p.................. Phosphoric Residue [*As substituent on nucleoside*] [*Biochemistry*]
P.................. Phosphorus [*Chemical element*]
P.................. Photographic Reconnaissance Capability [*When suffix to Navy aircraft designation*]
P.................. Phototropism [*Botany*]
P.................. Phrase Structure Rule [*Linguistics*]
P.................. Physics [*Secondary school course*] [*British*]
P.................. Physiology [*Medical Officer designation*] [*British*]
P.................. Phytophthora [*A fungus*]
P.................. Piaggio Rinaldo [*Industria Aeronautiche & Meccaniche SpA*] [*Italy ICAO aircraft manufacturer identifier*] (ICAO)
P.................. Pianissimo [*Very Softly*] [*Music*]
P.................. Piano [*Musical instrument*]
P.................. Piano [*Softly*] [*Music*]
P.................. Piaster [*Monetary unit*] [*Spain, Republic of Vietnam, and some Middle Eastern countries*]
P.................. Pica [*Typography*] (ADA)
p.................. Pica [*Typography*] [*Also, P*] (WDMC)
P.................. Pick (IAA)
P.................. Pickering's Massachusetts Reports [*18-41 Massachusetts*] [*A publication*] (DLA)
p.................. Pico [*A prefix meaning divided by one trillion*] [*SI symbol*]
P.................. Picot [*Crochet*] (ROG)
P.................. Pie
P.................. Pied [*Foot*] [*French*]
P.................. Pierced [*Quilting*]
P.................. Pigs (ROG)
P.................. Pilaster [*Technical drawings*]
P.................. Pillar [*Buoy*]
P.................. Pilot
P.................. Pink
P.................. Pinnule
P.................. Pint
P.................. Pip [*Phonetic alphabet*] [*Pre-World War II*] (DSUE)
P.................. Pipe
P.................. Pipe Rolls [*British*]
P.................. Pique; Inclusions [*Diamond clarity grade*]
P.................. Pitch [*or Pitcher*] [*Baseball*]
P.................. Pitch [*Technical drawings*]
P.................. Pitch (IDOE)
P.................. Pith [*Botany*]
P.................. Pitman Examination Institute [*British*]
P.................. Pitman-Moore Co. [*Research code symbol*]
P.................. Pius [*Dutiful*] [*Latin*]
P.................. Placebo [*Medicine*]
P.................. Placentinus [*Deceased, 1192*] [*Authority cited in pre-1607 legal work*] (DSA)
P.................. Placitum [*or Placita*] [*Agreeable, Agreed Upon*] [*Latin*] [*Legal term*] (DLA)
P.................. Plaintiff
P.................. Plaintiff [*Legal shorthand*] (LWAP)
P.................. Plan (CPH)
P.................. Planed
P.................. Planning
P.................. Plasma
P.................. Plasmodium [*Biology*] (MAE)
P.................. Plastid [*Botany*]
P.................. Plate [*Electron tube*] [*Technical drawings*]
P.................. Plate (IDOE)
P.................. Platform (DCTA)
P.................. Players League [*Major league in baseball, 1890*]
P.................. Pleasant
P.................. Pleinsbachian [*Geology*]
P.................. Plotter [*British military*] (DMA)
P.................. Plug
P.................. Plus [*More*]
P.................. Poco [*Somewhat*] [*Music*]
P.................. Point [*Lacrosse position*]
P.................. Point (IDOE)
P.................. Point-to-Point Radio [*FAA designator*] (CET)
P.................. Poise [*Unit of dynamic viscosity*]
P.................. Poison
P.................. Polar Distance [*Navigation*]
P.................. Polarization
P.................. Pole
P.................. Political Division [*Geography*]
P.................. Polka [*Music*]
P.................. Pollen [*Botany*]
P.................. Polymorphic [*Biology*]
P.................. Polymyxin [*An antibiotic*] (DAVI)
P.................. Polyneuropathy [*Medicine*]
P.................. Polynomial Time (IAA)
P.................. Polyphagous [*Biology*]
P.................. Polytechnic (AIE)
P.................. Pond [*Maps and charts*]
P.................. Pondere [*By Weight*] [*Latin*]
p.................. Pondus [*Weight*] [*Latin*] (MAE)
P.................. Ponendum [*To Be Placed*] [*Latin*]
P.................. Pontifex [*Bishop*] [*Latin*]
P.................. Pool
P.................. Poop [*Portion of a ship*]
P.................. Poorly Organized, Unstable Personality [*Eysenck*] [*Psychology*]
P.................. Poor Skiing Conditions
P.................. Pope
P.................. Popular Response [*Rorschach*] [*Psychology*]
P.................. Population
P.................. Populus [*People*] [*Latin*]
P.................. Porcelain
P.................. Porphyrin [*Medicine*] (DAVI)
P.................. Port [*Maps and charts*]
P.................. Portable [*JETDS nomenclature*]
P.................. Portion
P.................. Portland [*Diocesan abbreviation*] [*Oregon*] (TOCD)
P.................. Portugal [*IYRU nationality code*]
P.................. Position
p.................. Positive [*Crystal*]
P.................. Positive (IAA)
P.................. Positive Conducting [*Electronics*] (IAA)
P.................. Post [*After*] [*Latin*]
P.................. Post [*Surgery laboratory work*] (DAVI)
P.................. Postage
P.................. Posten [*Sentry*] [*German military*]
P.................. Posterior
P.................. Postpartum [*Medicine*]
P.................. Pouce [*Inch*] [*French*]
P.................. Pound (IDOE)
P.................. Pounds [*As measurement of total stress*] [*Aerospace*] (AAG)
P.................. Pour [*For*] [*French*]
P.................. Power [*Symbol*] [*IUPAC*]
P.................. Poynting Vector [*Electromagnetism*] (DEN)
P.................. Practical
P.................. Practical Intelligence
P.................. Pre-1920 [*Deltiology*]
P.................. Preceding
P.................. Precipitation Static
P.................. Precise Code [*Computer science*] (RDA)

P Predators Present [*Ecology*]
P Predicate
P Predictor [*British military*] (DMA)
P Prednisolone [*Endocrinology*]
P Prednisone [*Also, PDN, Pr, Pred, Pro*] [*Endocrinology*] [*Antineoplastic drug*]
P Preferred
P Prefix [*Indicating a private radiotelegram*]
P P-Register [*Computer science*]
P Preliminary
P Premolar [*Dentistry*]
P Presbyopia [*Ophthalmology*]
P Presbyterian
P Prescribing
P Present
P Present BIT [*Binary Digit*] [*Computer science*]
P Preset
P President
P Press [*Publishing*]
P Pressure [*or p*] [*Symbol IUPAC*]
P Pressurized Tank [*Liquid gas carriers*]
P Preview
P Prey [*Zoology*]
P Price [*Economics*]
P Pridie [*The Day Before*] [*Latin*]
P Priest
P Priestly Source [*Biblical scholarship*]
P Prilled
P Primary
P Primary (IDOE)
P Primary [*or Push*] Wave [*Earthquakes*]
P Primipara [*Woman bearing first child*] [*Medicine*] (MAE)
P Primitive
P Primus [*First*] [*Latin*]
P Prince
P Princeps [*First Edition*] [*French*]
P Princess (ROG)
P Principal
P Print
p Print [*Film*] [*Also, P*] (WDMC)
P Priority [*Telecommunications*] (TEL)
P Priory
P Prismatic Joint (IAA)
P Prisoner [*Military*]
P Private
P Private Trust [*Includes testamentary, investment, life insurance, holding title, etc.*] [*Legal term*] (DLA)
P Private Venture
P Privy (ROG)
P Pro [*For*] [*Latin*]
P Probability [*or Probability Ratio*] [*Statistics*]
P Probate
P Probe (MSA)
P Probucol [*Anticholesteremic*]
P Procarbazine [*Also, PC, PCB, Pr*] [*Antineoplastic drug*]
P Procedure
P Proceedings (IAA)
P Processor [*Computer science*]
P Proconsul
P Producer [*Films, television, etc.*]
P Product
P Production [*of Energy*]
P Profession
P Professional [*Civil Service employees designation*]
P Proficiency
P Profit
P Progesterone [*A hormone*]
P Program (KSC)
P Programmable
P Progressive
P Prohibited Area [*Followed by identification*]
P Proliferation [*Biology*]
P Proline [*One-letter symbol; see Pro*]
P Promoter [*Genetics*]
P Prompt [*i.e., the right side*] [*A stage direction*]
P Proof [*Philately*]
P Prop (DS)
P Propagation Distribution [*Broadcasting*]
P Propionic [*Bacteriology*] (DAVI)
P Proportional (IAA)
P Proportion in a Specific Class
P Propulsion (AAG)
P Protein
P Proteinuria [*Clinical chemistry*]
P Protestant
P Protet [*Protest*] [*French*]
P Proteus [*Genus of bacteria*] (MAE)
P Proto [*Linguistics*]
p Proton [*A nuclear particle*]
P Protoplasmic [*Freeze etching in microscopy*]
P Prototroch
P Prototype (AAG)
P Provisional
p Proximum [*Near*] [*Latin*] (MAE)
P Psychiatry
P Psychometrist [*Psychology*]
P Publications
P Public Houses [*Public-performance tariff class*] [*British*]
P Public Safety [*FCC*] (NTCM)
P Pudding [*Phonetic alphabet*] [*Royal Navy World War I*] (DSUE)
P Pugillus [*A Handful*] [*Pharmacy*] (ROG)
P Pula [*Monetary unit*] (ODBW)
P Pull (NFPA)
P Pulled Up [*Horse racing*]
P Pulse
P Pump (AAG)
P Punch
P Punctum Proximum [*Near Point of vision*] [*Ophthalmology*] (DAVI)
P Punic (BJA)
P Punkt [*Point*] [*German military*]
P Punter [*Football*]
P Pupil
P Purchased (AAG)
P Purified [*Animal breeding*]
P Purinethol [*Mercaptopurine*] [*Also, M, MP*] [*Antineoplastic drug*]
P Purkinje Cell [*Neuroanatomy*]
P Purl [*Knitting*]
P Purple
P Purpure [*Purple*] [*Heraldry*]
P Pursuit [*Airplane designation*]
P Put [*In options listings of newspapers*]
P Pya [*Monetary unit*] [*Myanmar*]
p Pyranose [*One-letter symbol*] [*Biochemistry*]
P Pyroxene Subgroup [*Acmite, sodium metasilicate, potassium metasilicate, diopside, wollastonite, hypersthene*] [*CIPW classification Geology*]
P RADAR [*JETDS nomenclature*]
P Reproducing [*JETDS nomenclature*]
P Single Paper [*Wire insulation*] (AAG)
P Soft Pad [*Missile launch environment symbol*]
P Warner-Lambert Pharmaceutical Co. [*Research code symbol*]
P_1 Inorganic Phosphate [*Chemistry*] (DAVI)
p-1 Page 1 [*Also, P-1*] (WDMC)
P-1 Page One [*Broadcasting*] (WDMC)
p1 Para 1 [*Unipara - having borne one child*] (DAVI)
P_1 Parental Generation (MAE)
P1 Pershing 1 [*Missile*] (GFGA)
P_1 Pulmonic First Heart Sound [*Medicine*] (DAVI)
P_1 Pulmonic First Sound [*Medicine*] (MEDA)
P1a Pershing 1a [*Missile*] (GFGA)
P1E Planed One Edge [*Technical drawings*] (DAC)
P1MG P1 [*Code*] for Multigroup [*Method*] [*Nuclear energy*] (NRCH)
P1S Planed One Side [*Technical drawings*] (DAC)
P1S2E Planed One Side and Two Edges [*Technical drawings*] (DAC)
P2 Papua New Guinea [*Aircraft nationality and registration mark*] (FAAC)
P-2 Propaganda Due [*Secret Italian Masonic organization, allegedly tied to the Roman Catholic church*]
P_2 Pulmonic Second Sound [*Medicine*]
P2 Second Pilot [*Aviation*] (AIA)
P 2d Pacific Reporter, Second Series [*A publication*] (DLA)
P2d Pacific Reporter, Second Series [*West*] [*A publication*] (AAGC)
P2I Planned Product Improvement
P^2NBC^2 Physiological and Psychological Effects of NBC [*Nuclear, Biological, and Chemical Warfare*] and Extended Operations [*Army study project*] (INF)
P3 Industry Composites and Polymer Processing Program [*Massachusetts Institute of Technology*] [*Research center*] (RCD)
P3 Phillips Post Processor
P3 Portable Plotting Package [*Nuclear energy*] (NRCH)
P/3 Proximal Third [*of bone*] [*Orthopedics*] (DAVI)
P_3I Planned Program Product Improvement [*Army*]
P^3I Preplanned Product Improvement [*DoD*]
P^3I Pre-Planned Product Improvement (DOMA)
P4 Aruba [*Aircraft nationality and registration mark*] (FAAC)
P4 Production Process Prove-Out Program
P4P Pagans for Peace Network [*Canada*] (EAIO)
P4S Planed Four Sides [*Technical drawings*] (DAC)
P4SR Predicted Four Hour Sweat Rate (PDAA)
P6ROC P6 Rover Owners Club (EAIO)
P 14 Pattern 14 Rifle [*Made in the US for Great Britain, beginning in 1914*]
P 32 Radioactive Phosphorus (DAVI)
P_{50} Partial pressure of oxygen at 50% hemoglobin saturation [*Medicine*]
P-55 Hydroxypregnanedione [*Endocrinology*] (DAVI)
P-88/ARA Project '88: Americans for the Reagan Agenda [*Defunct*] (EA)
P_A Alveolar Pressure [*Medicine*] (DAVI)
PA B. F. Jones Memorial Library, Aliquippa, PA [*Library symbol Library of Congress*] (LCLS)
PA Office of Public Affairs [*DoD*]
PA Packet Adapter [*Telecommunications*] (IAA)
PA Pad Abort [*NASA*] (KSC)
PA Paging and Area Warning (MCD)
Pa Paine's United States Circuit Court Reports [*A publication*] (DLA)
PA Paintmakers Association [*British*] (DBA)
PA Paired Associates [*Psychometrics*]
PA Pakistan Army
PA Paleopathology Association
PA Palestine Affairs [*New York*] [*A publication*] (BJA)
PA Palestinian Authority [*Political movement*] (ECON)
PA Palladium [*Chemical element*] (ROG)
PA Panama [*ANSI two-letter standard code*] (CNC)

PA .... Pan American World Airways, Inc. [See also PAA, PAN-AM, PN] [ICAO designator] (MCD)
P-A .... Pan-Atlantic Steamship Corp. (MHDW)
PA .... Panatlas Energy, Inc. [Toronto Stock Exchange symbol]
PA .... Panic Attack [Medicine] (MEDA)
PA .... Pantothenic Acid (DMAA)
pa .... Paper (VRA)
PA .... Paper (WGA)
PA .... Paper Advance (BUR)
PA .... Para-Amps (EA)
Pa .... Parachutist [British military] (DMA)
PA .... Paralysis Agitans
PA .... Parametric Amplifier
PA .... Par Amitie [By Favor] [French]
Pa .... Paranoia [Psychology]
PA .... Parapsychological Association (EA)
PA .... Par Autorite [By Authority] [French]
PA .... Parental Advisory (WDMC)
PA .... Parents Anonymous (EA)
PA .... Parents' Association
PA .... Parish
PA .... Parti Affectae [To the Affected Part] [Pharmacy]
PA .... Partial Application [Military] (AFIT)
P_A .... Partial Pressure in Arterial Blood [Medicine] (DAVI)
PA .... Participating Activity [Responsible for standardization efforts] [DoD]
PA .... Participial Adjective [Grammar]
PA .... Particular Average
PA .... Parti de l'Action [Party of Action] [Morocco] [Political party] (PPW)
PA .... Partido Andalucista [Spain] [Political party] (ECED)
PA .... Partido Arnulfista [Panama] [Political party] (EY)
PA .... Partners of the Americas (EA)
Pa .... Pascal [Symbol] [SI unit of pressure]
PA .... Passenger Address System [Aviation] (DA)
PA .... Passenger Agent
PA .... Passenger Ship
PA .... Passive Aggressive (DMAA)
PA .... Patent Assignee (NITA)
PA .... Patents (NITA)
PA .... Pathfinder Association (EAIO)
PA .... Pathology (AAMN)
PA .... Patient
PA .... Patient's Advocate [Medicine] (DMAA)
PA .... Patrol Aircraft (NATG)
PA .... Pattern Analysis [Test]
PA .... Paying Agent [Legal term] (DLA)
P/A .... Payment Authority [Business term]
PA .... Peak Amplitude [Medicine] (DMAA)
PA .... Pedestrians Association [British] (DBA)
PA .... Pending Availability
PA .... Pendulous Axis [Accelerometer] (IEEE)
PA .... Pennsylvania [Postal code]
Pa .... Pennsylvania (ODBW)
Pa .... Pennsylvania Reports [A publication] (AAGC)
PA .... Pennsylvania Supreme Court Reports [1845-date] [A publication] (DLA)
PA .... People's Alliance [Althydubandalag] [Iceland] [Political party] (PPW)
PA .... Peptide Absorption
PA .... Per Abdomen
PA .... Per Adresse [Care Of] [German]
PA .... Per Annum [By the Year] [Latin]
PA .... Per Auguri [Used on visiting cards to express congratulations, birthday wishes, etc.] [Italian]
PA .... Percentage Activity [Measurement] (DAVI)
PA .... Performance Alertness (AEBS)
PA .... Performance Analysis
PA .... Performance Appraisal Required [Civil Service]
PA .... Performance Assessment (DOGT)
PA .... Performing Arts [US Copyright Office class]
PA .... Periapical [Anatomy] (DAVI)
PA .... Periarteritis [Medicine] (DMAA)
PA .... Peridural Artery [Medicine] (DMAA)
PA .... Periodic Acid [Inorganic chemistry]
pA .... Periplanone A [Biochemistry]
PA .... Permanent Abeyance [FDA]
PA .... Permanent Address (ROG)
PA .... Permanent Appointment
PA .... Permanently Associated [Telecommunications] (TEL)
PA .... Pernicious Anemia [Hematology]
PA .... Personal Accident [Insurance] (AIA)
P/A .... Personal Account (WDAA)
PA .... Personal Affairs (AFM)
PA .... Personal Appearance
PA .... Personal Assistant [British]
PA .... Personal Audit [Psychological testing]
PA .... Personnel Administrator [American Society for Personnel Administration] [A publication Information service or system]
PA .... Personnel Area (NRCH)
PA .... Pfizer, Inc. [Research code symbol]
PA .... Phakic-Aphakic [Ophthalmology] (MAE)
PA .... Pharmacology, Clinical [Medical specialty] (DHSM)
PA .... Phase Angle (IAA)
PA .... Phenol Alcohol [Chemistry] (DAVI)
PA .... Phentolamine [Antiadrenergic]
PA .... Philippine Army
PA .... Philippine Association (EA)
PA .... Phonocardiogram Amplifier [Cardiology]
PA .... Phosphatidic Acid [Biochemistry]
PA .... Phosphoarginine [Biochemistry]
PA .... Phosphoric Acid (ECON)
PA .... Photoallergenic [Response] [Medicine]
PA .... Photodiode Amplifier
PA .... Phthalic Anhydride [Organic chemistry]
PA .... Physical Activity (MCD)
PA .... Physician Advisor (HCT)
PA .... Physician's Assistant
PA .... Physics Abstracts [Institution of Electrical Engineers] [Information service or system A publication] (CRD)
PA .... Phytoalexin [Plant pathology]
PA .... Piaster [Monetary unit] [Spain, Republic of Vietnam, and some Middle Eastern countries]
PA .... Picatinny Arsenal [New Jersey] [Later, Armament Development Center] [Army]
pA .... Picoampere [One trillionth of an ampere]
PA .... Pierre Allain [Lightweight rock-climbing boot named after its designer]
PA .... Pierre Arpels [Jewelry designer]
PA .... Pills Anonymous [Later, DA] [An association] (EA)
PA .... Pilot Approval [Automotive project management]
P/A .... Pilotless Aircraft
PA .... PIMCO Advisors'A' [NYSE symbol] (TTSB)
PA .... Pimco Advisors Ltd. [NYSE symbol] (SAG)
PA .... Pipeline Authority [Australia]
PA .... Piper Aircraft Corp. [ICAO aircraft manufacturer identifier] (ICAO)
PA .... Pirke Avot (BJA)
PA .... Pitch Angle
PA .... Pituitary-Adrenal [Endocrinology] (DAVI)
P/A .... Planetary Atmosphere (SAA)
PA .... Planning Assistance (EA)
PA .... Plasma Adsorption [Medicine] (DMAA)
PA .... Plasma Aldosterone [Endocrinology]
PA .... Plasminogen Activator [Biochemistry]
PA .... Platelet Adhesiveness [Hematology]
PA .... Platform Assembly (MCD)
PA .... Podiatry Association [British] (DBA)
PA .... Point of Aim [Military]
PA .... Points Against [Football]
PA .... Polar Atlantic [American air mass]
PA .... Polarization Approximation [Physical chemistry]
PA .... Polarographic Analyzer
P/A .... Polar to Analog (KSC)
PA .... Police Academy
PA .... Police Agent (WDAA)
PA .... Policy Analyst (GNE)
PA .... Polyacetal [Organic chemistry]
PA .... Polyacrylic [Organic chemistry]
PA .... Polyamide [Organic chemistry]
PA .... Polyanhydride [Organic chemistry]
PA .... Polyarteritis [Medicine]
PA .... Polyarthritis [Medicine] (DMAA)
PA .... Polymer Adhesive
PA .... Port Agency [Army]
PA .... Port Authority [Western Australia]
PA .... Position Angle [Astronomy]
PA .... Position Approximate [Nautical charts]
PA .... Positive Addiction [Self-improvement method developed by William Glasser, MD]
PA .... Positive Attitude
PA .... Post Adjutant
PA .... Postal Assistant (DCTA)
PA .... Post Amplifier
PA .... Post-Aural [Medicine] (DMAA)
PA .... Posterior Anterior [Medicine]
PA .... Posterior Aorta
PA .... Postmortem Aging [of meat]
PA .... Potato Agar [Microbiology]
PA .... Potsmokers Anonymous (EA)
PA .... Power Amplifier
PA .... Power Approach [Aerospace]
PA .... Power of Attorney
P/A .... Power of Authority
PA .... Practice Amendment (AAG)
PA .... Prealbumin [Biochemistry]
PA .... Preamplifier
PA .... Preapproved
PA .... Prearm
PA .... Preavailability
PA .... Precision-Acrobatics (DOMA)
PA .... Precision Angle (IAA)
PA .... Precision Architecture [Hewlett-Packard Co.] [Computer science]
PA .... Precomputed Altitude
PA .... Predictive Accuracy [Medicine] (DMAA)
PA .... Predictive Analyzer [Computer science] (DIT)
PA .... Prefect-Apostolic [Roman Catholic]
PA .... Pregnancy-Associated [Gynecology] (MAE)
PA .... Preliminary Acceptance (KSC)
PA .... Preliminary Amplifier (IAA)
PA .... Preliminary Assessment (ERG)
PA .... Preparing Activity [Responsible for Federal document and study projects]
P/A .... Presence or Absence
PA .... Present Again (ADA)

PA ... Preservation Action (EA)
PA ... Presidents Association [*New York, NY*] (EA)
PA ... Press Agent
PA ... Press Association Ltd. (IID)
PA ... Pressure Actuated [*Switch*]
PA ... Pressure Alarm [*Nuclear energy*] (NRCH)
PA ... Pressure Altitude [*Aviation*]
PA ... Pressure Angle (MSA)
PA ... Pressure Area [*Medicine*]
PA ... Price Analyst
PA ... Primary Aerospace Vehicle [*or Aircraft*]
PA ... Primary Amenorrhea [*Gynecology*] (MAE)
PA ... Primary Anemia [*Medicine*]
PA ... Prince Albert Coat [*Slang*]
PA ... Principal Assistant (NOAA)
PA ... Principal Axes
PA ... Principle of Adding [*New math*]
PA ... Priority A (MCD)
PA ... Priority Aggregate
PA ... Prior to Admission [*Medicine*]
PA ... Privacy Act
PA ... Private Account [*Banking*]
PA ... Private Architect [*British*]
Pa ... Proactinium (IDOE)
PA ... Proactivator [*Medicine*]
PA ... Pro Anno [*For the Year*] [*Latin*]
PA ... Proanthocyanidin (Assay) [*Analytical chemistry*]
PA ... Pro Applicatione [*To Be Applied*] [*Pharmacy*] (ROG)
PA ... Probability of Acceptance (KSC)
PA ... Probability of Acquisition [*Military*]
P/A ... Problem Analysis (NASA)
PA ... Probleme der Agyptologie [*A publication*] (BJA)
PA ... Procainamide [*Cardiac depressant*]
PA ... Process Allocator [*Telecommunications*] (TEL)
PA ... Process Automation (CMD)
PA ... Procurement Agency (MCD)
PA ... Procurement Appropriations [*Army*] (AABC)
PA ... Procurement, Army
PA ... Procurement Authorization
PA ... Procuring Activity [*Military*]
PA ... Product Acceptance [*Automotive engineering*]
PA ... Product Administration (HCT)
PA ... Product Analysis (IEEE)
PA ... Product Assortment (MHDB)
PA ... Product Assurance (NASA)
PA ... Production Adjustment
PA ... Production Assistant
PA ... Professional Administrator [*Australia A publication*]
PA ... Professional Agent [*Professional Insurance Agents*] [*A publication*]
PA ... Professional Association [*Telecommunications*]
PA ... Profile Analysis [*Medicine*]
PA ... Profile Angle (MSA)
PA ... Program Access
PA ... Program Account (NG)
PA ... Program Address
PA ... Program Administrator (MCD)
PA ... Program Agent (OICC)
PA ... Program Aid [*A publication*]
PA ... Program Amount (NITA)
PA ... Program Analysis [*Computer science*]
PA ... Program Application Instructions [*Telecommunications*] (TEL)
PA ... Program Assessment (MCD)
PA ... Program Attention [*Computer science*] (IAA)
PA ... Program Attention Key [*Computer science*]
PA ... Program Authorization (AFM)
PA ... Program for the Aging (OICC)
PA ... Programmable Automation
PA ... Programmed Arithmetic (IAA)
PA ... Progressive Alliance [*Defunct*] (EA)
PA ... Project Administration (MCD)
PA ... Project Analysis (MHDB)
PA ... Project Authorization
PA ... Proliferating Angioendotheliomatosis
PA ... Prolonged-Action [*Pharmacy*]
PA ... Prolotherapy Association (EA)
PA ... Property Administrator [*DoD*]
PA ... Prophylactic Antibiotic
PA ... Propionic Acid (DMAA)
PA ... Proponent Agency [*Army*]
PA ... Proportional Action (AAG)
PA ... Proposal Authorization
PA ... [*The*] Proprietary Association [*Later, NDMA*] (EA)
PA ... Propulsion Assistance (DS)
PA ... Prosecuting Attorney
PA ... Prospecting Authority [*Australia*]
PA ... Prostitutes Anonymous (EA)
Pa ... Protactinium [*or Protoactinium*] [*Chemical element*]
PA ... Protected Area [*Nuclear energy*] (NRCH)
PA ... Protective Antigen
PA ... Protestant Alliance [*British*] (DBA)
PA ... Prothonotary Apostolic
PA ... Proton Affinity [*Surface ionization*]
PA ... Protrusio Acetabuli [*Medicine*] (DMAA)
PA ... Provisional Allowance
PA ... Pseudoaneurysm [*Medicine*]
PA ... Pseudo-Astronomy
PA ... Pseudomonas aeruginosa [*Bacterium*]
PA ... Psoriasis Association [*Australia*]
PA ... Psychiatric Aide (DAVI)
PA ... Psychoanalyst
PA ... Psychogenic Aspermia [*Medicine*]
PA ... Psychological Age
PA ... Public Accountant
PA ... Public Act
PA ... Public Address [*Amplification equipment*] [*Communications*]
PA ... Public Address System (WDMC)
PA ... Public Administration
PA ... Public Advocate (EA)
PA ... Public Affairs
PA ... Public Archives [*of Canada*]
PA ... Public Assistance
PA ... Publication Announcement
PA ... Publishers' Alliance [*Defunct*] (EA)
PA ... Publishers' Association [*London, England*] (DIT)
PA ... Pull and Adjust [*Brace*] [*Medicine*]
PA ... Pulmonary Angiography [*Medicine*]
PA ... Pulmonary Artery [*Medicine*]
PA ... Pulmonary Atresia [*Medicine*]
PA ... Pulpoaxial [*Dentistry*]
PA ... Pulsating Arc (IAA)
PA ... Pulse Amplifier
PA ... Puppeteers of America (EA)
PA ... Purchasing Agent
PA ... Purge Alarm [*Nuclear energy*] (NRCH)
PA ... Puromycin Aminonucleoside [*Biochemistry*] (OA)
PA ... Purpose and Activities (NITA)
PA ... Put Away [*Papers*] [*British*]
PA ... Puumala [*Vole virus*]
PA ... Pyro Ammonia (ROG)
PA ... Pyrrolizidine Alkaloid [*Toxicology*]
PA ... Pythium aphanidermatum [*A fungus*]
PAO_2 ... Arterial Oxygen Pressure (MAE)
PAA ... Pa-An [*Myanmar*] [*Airport symbol*] (OAG)
PAA ... Pacific Arts Association (EA)
PAA ... Pan Am Corp. [*AMEX symbol*] (SAG)
PAA ... Pan American Minerals Corp. [*Toronto Stock Exchange symbol Vancouver Stock Exchange symbol*]
PAA ... Pan American World Airways, Inc. [*See also PA, PAN-AM, PN*]
PAA ... Pancretan Association of America (EA)
PAA ... Pancyprian Association of America [*Defunct*] (EA)
PAA ... Panguna [*Solomon Islands*] [*Seismograph station code, US Geological Survey*] (SEIS)
PAA ... Paper Agents Association [*British*] (DBA)
paa ... Papuan-Australian [*MARC language code Library of Congress*] (LCCP)
PAA ... Para-Azoxyanisole [*Organic chemistry*]
PAA ... Parke, Davis & Co. [*Research code symbol*]
PAA ... Parti Affectae Applicandus [*Apply to the Affected Part*] [*Pharmacy*]
PAA ... Patriot Airlines, Inc. [*ICAO designator*] (FAAC)
PAA ... Pay Adjustment Authorization
PAA ... Peracetic Acid [*Organic chemistry*]
PAA ... Peruvian American Association (EA)
PAA ... Petroleum Administration Act [*Canada*]
PAA ... Phased Array Antenna
PAA ... Phenanthrene Amino Alcohol [*Organic chemistry*]
PAA ... Phenanthrylacetamide [*Organic chemistry*]
PAA ... Phenylacetic Acid [*Organic chemistry*]
PAA ... Phonetic Alphabet Association (DGA)
PAA ... Phosphonoacetic Acid [*Antiviral compound*]
PAA ... Photographers Association of America [*Later, Professional Photographers of America*]
PAA ... Photon Activation Analysis
PAA ... Pi Alpha Alpha (EA)
PAA ... Pill Addicts Anonymous (EA)
PAA ... Planar Array Antenna
PAA ... Plasminogen Activator Activity [*Biochemistry*]
PAA ... Platelet Associated Activity [*Pharmacology*]
PAA ... Polish Association of America [*Later, NFLI*] (EA)
PAA ... Polocrosse Association of Australia
PAA ... Polyacrylamide [*Also, PAAM, PAM*] [*Organic chemistry*]
PAA ... Polyacrylic Acid [*Organic chemistry*]
PAA ... Polyaspartic Acid [*Biochemistry*]
PAA ... Polycyclic Aromatic Amine [*Organic chemistry*]
PAA ... Population Association of America (EA)
PAA ... Port Autonome d'Abidjan [*The Ivory Coast*] (EY)
PAA ... Post Award Action
PAA ... Potato Association of America (EA)
PAA ... Power Amplifier Assembly
PAA ... Pre-Apprenticeship Allowance
PAA ... Primary Aircraft Authorized [*Air Force*]
PAA ... Primary Auxiliary Area [*Nuclear energy*] (NRCH)
PAA ... Print Advertising Association [*Defunct*] (EA)
PAA ... Priority Abatement Areas [*Environment*] (GNE)
PAA ... Procurement Appropriation, Army (MCD)
PAA ... Procurement of Ammunition, Army (AABC)
PAA ... Professional Apparel Association
PAA ... Professional Archers Association (EA)
PAA ... Programme d'Aide aux Athletes [*Athlete Assistance Program*] [*Canada*]
PAA ... Purchasing Agents Association (NADA)

PAA............. Pyridineacetic Acid [*Organic chemistry*]
P/AA3........... Probationary Aircraft Artificer 3rd Class [*British military*] (DMA)
PAAA........... Premium Advertising Association of America [*Later, PMAA*] (EA)
P/AAA2........ Probationary Aircraft Artificer, Acting, 2nd Class [*British military*] (DMA)
PAAB........... PERSCOM [*Personnel Command*] Acquisition Accession Board [*Army*] (INF)
PAABA......... Para-Acetamidobenzoic Acid [*Biochemistry*]
PAABS......... PanAmerican Association of Biochemical Societies (EA)
PAAC........... Pacific and Asian Affairs Council
PAAC........... Program Analysis Adaptable Control [*Computer science*]
PAACE......... Precision Aircraft Armament Control Experiment (RDA)
PAACS......... Prior Active Army Commissioned Service
PAACT......... Patient Advocates for Advanced Cancer Treatments
PAADAR....... Passive Airborne Detection and Ranging (MSA)
PAADC......... Principal Air Aide-de-Camp [*RAF*] [*British*]
PA Admin Bull... Pennsylvania Bulletin [*A publication*] (DLA)
PA Admin Code... Pennsylvania Administrative Code [*A publication*] (DLA)
PAAECI........ Pan American Association of Educational Credit Institutions [*See also APICE*] (EAIO)
PAAES......... Prior Active Army Enlisted Service
PAAES......... Publications. American Archaeological Expedition to Syria [*A publication*] (BJA)
PAAFB......... Patrick Auxiliary Air Force Base [*Florida*] (SAA)
PAAFCS....... Prior Active Air Force Commissioned Service
PAAFES....... Prior Active Air Force Enlisted Service
PAAGE......... Panel on Alternate Approaches to Graduate Education (EA)
PAAH........... Polyacrylamide-Hydrazide [*Organic chemistry*]
PAAHA......... Para-Acetamidohippuric Acid [*Biochemistry*]
PAAM........... Physicians Association for Anthroposophical Medicine (EA)
PAAM........... Polyacrylamide [*Also, PAA, PAM*] [*Organic chemistry*]
PAAM........... Projective Assessment of Aging Method [*Personality development test*] [*Psychology*]
P/AAMHRC... Pacific/Asian American Mental Health Research Center [*University of Illinois at Chicago*] [*Research center*] (RCD)
PAAN........... Product Assurance Alert Notice (MCD)
PA & E......... Program Analysis and Evaluation
PA & F......... Percussion, Auscultation, and Fremitus [*Medicine*]
PA & I.......... Planning, Analysis, and Integration
PA & T......... Product Assurance and Test
PAANS......... Pan African Association of Neurological Sciences (EAIO)
PAANSW...... Prisoners' Aid Association of New South Wales [*Australia*]
PAAO........... Pan-American Association of Ophthalmology (EA)
P(A-a)O$_2$...... Alveolar-Arterial Pressure Difference [*For A-aDO$_2$*] [*Medicine*] (DAVI)
PAAORLBE... Pan-American Association of Oto-Rhino-Laryngology and Broncho-Esophagology [*Mexico City, Mexico*] (EAIO)
PAAP........... Peaceful Alternatives to the Atlantic Pact
PAAP........... Provisional Algal Assay Procedure [*Test measuring impact of chemicals on algal growth*]
PAAQ........... Palmer [*Alaska*] [*ICAO location identifier*] (ICLI)
PAAR........... Precision Approach Airfield RADAR [*Aviation*] (IAA)
PAAS........... Pan American Allergy Society (EA)
PAAS........... Performance Assessment and Appraisal System
PAAS........... Phased Array Analysis System
PAAS........... Phased Array Antenna System
PAASF......... Pan American Silver Corp. [*NASDAQ symbol*] (SAG)
PAASF......... Pan Amer Silver [*NASDAQ symbol*] (TTSB)
PAAT........... Parent as a Teacher Inventory [*Psychology*]
PAAT........... Personnel and Administrative Assistance Team [*Navy*] (NVT)
PAAT........... Personnel Assistance and Audit Team [*Military*]
PAAT........... Professional Association of Alexander Teachers [*British*] (DBA)
PAAT........... Programmer Analyst Aptitude Test
PAAT........... Public Affairs Assist Team [*Hazardous substance emergency response*]
PAATI......... Phased Array Antenna Technology Investigation
PAATLANT... Personnel and Administration Assistance Team, Atlantic [*Navy*] (DNAB)
PAATPAC..... Personnel and Administration Assistance Team, Pacific [*Navy*] (DNAB)
PAAWA........ Pakistan Australia Association of Western Australia
PAAWA........ Progressive Axemen's Association of Western Australia
P(A-awo)..... Pressure Gradient from Alveolus to Airway Opening [*Medicine*] (DAVI)
PAAWWW.... Pacific Asian American Women Writers West (EA)
PAAXOP...... Pan-Dodecanesian Association of America "Xanthos O Philikos" (EA)
PAb............. Abington Free Library, Abington, PA [*Library symbol Library of Congress*] (LCLS)
PAB............. Cabrini College, Library, Radnor, PA [*OCLC symbol*] (OCLC)
PAB............. PAB Bankshares, Inc. [*AMEX symbol*] (SAG)
PAB............. Pacific Air Boats Ltd. [*Canada ICAO designator*] (FAAC)
PAB............. Panair do Brasil, SA
PAB............. Para-Aminobenzoate (DMAA)
PAB............. Para-Aminobenzoic Acid [*Also, PABA*] [*Biochemistry*]
PAB............. Paramaribo [*Suriname*] [*Geomagnetic observatory code*]
PAB............. Parti des Paysans, Artisans, et Bourgeois [*Farmers', Artisans', and Burghers' Party*] [*Switzerland Political party*] (PPE)
PAB............. Patent Abstracts Bibliography [*NASA*]
PAB............. Patrick Air Force Base [*Florida*]
PAB............. Peanut Advisory Board (EA)
PAB............. Pedro Afonso [*Brazil*] [*Airport symbol*] (AD)
PAB............. Pension Appeals Board [*Canada*]
PAB............. Performance Assesment Battery [*Medicine*] (DMAA)
PAB............. Personal Address Book [*MAPI - Mail Applications Program Interface*] [*Microsoft Corp.*] [*Computer science*]
PAB............. Petroleum Administrative Board [*Terminated, 1936*]
PAB............. Pharmacologic Autonomic Block [*Medicine*] (DMAA)
PAB............. Plastic Assault Boat [*Navy*]
PAB............. Plumbing Advisory Board [*South Australia*]
PAB............. Police Administration Building
PAB............. Police Appeal Board [*South Australia*]
PAB............. Policies Allotment Board [*Navy*] (DNAB)
PAB............. Polyclonal Antibody [*Immunochemistry*]
P/AB........... Port Side Abreast (DNAB)
PAB............. Potter & Brumfield, Inc. (IAA)
PAB............. Poultry Advisory Board [*Queensland, Australia*]
PAB............. Power-Assisted Brakes
PAB............. Prealbumin [*Biochemistry*]
PAB............. Precision Aneroid Barometer (DNAB)
PAB............. Preliminary As-Built [*Nuclear energy*] (NRCH)
PAB............. Premature Atrial Beat [*Cardiology*] (AAMN)
PAB............. Price Adjustment Board
PAB............. Price Agreement Bulletin
PAB............. Primary Auxiliary Building [*Nuclear energy*] (NRCH)
PAB............. Priorities Allotment Board
PAB............. Priority Assignment Base (MCD)
PAB............. Private Activity Bond (AAGC)
PAB............. Product Application Bulletins [*A publication*] (EAAP)
PAB............. Program Advisory Board (MCD)
PAB............. Promotions Appeal Board [*Victoria, Australia*]
PAB............. Psychiatric Attitudes Battery [*Psychology*]
PAB............. Psychology of Addictive Behaviors [*An association*] (EA)
PAB............. Pulmonary Artery Banding [*Cardiology*]
PAB............. Pulsed Adsorption Bed [*Process*]
PAB............. Pulsed Air Blast
PAB............. Purple Agar Base [*Media*] [*Microbiology*]
PABA........... Barter Island [*Alaska*] [*ICAO location identifier*] (ICLI)
PABA........... Para-Aminobenzoic Acid [*Also, PAB*] [*Biochemistry*]
PA BA.......... Pennsylvania Bar Association. Reports [*A publication*] (DLA)
PABA........... Pro-Am Bowfishing Association
PABA........... Progressive Angus Breeders Association
PAB Bk........ PAB Bankshares, Inc. [*Associated Press*] (SAG)
PA B Brief... Pennsylvania Bar Brief [*A publication*] (DLA)
PABC........... Pan American Basketball Confederation [*See also CPB*] (EAIO)
PABD........... Precise Access Block Diagram
PABE........... Bethel [*Alaska*] [*ICAO location identifier*] (ICLI)
PABE........... Program and Budget Estimate (MCD)
PABF........... Precision Air-Bearing Floor (SSD)
PABFSA....... Pediatric Association of Black French-Speaking Africa (EAIO)
PABG........... Big Delta [*Alaska*] [*ICAO location identifier*] (ICLI)
PABI............ Delta Junction/Allen Army Air Field [*Alaska*] [*ICAO location identifier*] (ICLI)
PA Bk Cas... Pennsylvania Bank Cases [*A publication*] (DLA)
PABLA......... Problem Analysis by Logical Approach
PABLE......... Payable (ROG)
PABLI.......... Pages Bleues Informatisees [*Commission of the European Communities*] [*Information service or system*] (CRD)
PABLOS....... Program to Analyse the Block System [*Computer science*] (PDAA)
PABM........... Big Mountain Air Force Station [*Alaska*] [*ICAO location identifier*] (ICLI)
PABMI......... Performing Arts Biography Master Index [*A publication*]
PABN........... Pacific Capital Bancorp [*NASDAQ symbol*] (SAG)
PABP........... Poly(A)-Binding Protein
PABP........... Pulmonary Artery Ballon Pump [*Medicine*] (DMAA)
PAB-PTC...... Promotion Appeal Board, Postal and Telecommunications Commission [*Australia*]
PAB(Q)........ Poultry Advisory Board (Queensland) [*Australia*]
PABR........... Barrow [*Alaska*] [*ICAO location identifier*] (ICLI)
PABR........... Planning Appeals Board. Reports [*A publication*]
P Abr.......... Pulton's Abridgment of the Statutes [*A publication*] (DLA)
PA Browne (PA)... Browne's Reports (Pennsylvania) [*A publication*] (DLA)
PA Browne R... Browne's Reports [*Pennsylvania*] [*A publication*] (DLA)
PABS........... Pan-American Biodeterioration Society (EA)
PABS........... Para-Aminobenzensulfonamide [*Antibiotic*]
PABST......... Primary Adhesively Bonded Structural Technology [*Aviation*]
PABT........... Bettles [*Alaska*] [*ICAO location identifier*] (ICLI)
PABV........... Percutaneous Aortic Balloon Valvuloplasty [*Medicine*] (HCT)
PABV........... Pyroactuated Ball Valve
PABX........... Private Automatic Branch Exchange [*Telecommunications*] (DEN)
PAC............. cis-Platinum [*Cisplatin*], Adriamycin, Cyclophosphamide [*Antineoplastic drug regimen*]
PAC............. Pacific (AFM)
Pac.............. Pacific [*Record label*] [*France*]
PAC............. Pacific
Pac.............. Pacifica: Australian Theological Studies [*A publication*] (APTA)
PAC............. Pacific Air Command [*Air Force*]
PAC............. Pacific Command [*Military*] (GFGA)
PAC............. Pacific Ocean
PAC............. Pacific Region [*USTTA*] (TAG)
Pac.............. Pacific Reporter [*A publication*] (DLA)
PAC............. Pacific Telesis Group [*NYSE symbol*] (SPSG)
PAC............. Pacific Telesis Group Financing I [*NYSE symbol*] (SAG)
PAC............. Pacific Telesis Group Financing II [*NYSE symbol*] (SAG)
PAC............. Package Attitude Control [*NASA*]
PAC............. Packaged Assembly Circuit
PAC............. Packard Automobile Classics (EA)
PAC............. Packed Memory [*Computer science*] (IAA)
PAC............. Packet Autopiloted Cruiseway
PAC............. Pacto de Alianza de Centro [*Chile*] [*Political party*] (EY)
PAC............. Pak-Man Resources, Inc. [*Vancouver Stock Exchange symbol*]

PAC Palo Alto - Branner [*California*] [*Seismograph station code, US Geological Survey Closed*] (SEIS)

PAC Pan-Africanist Congress [*South Africa*]

PAC Panama City [*Panama*] Paitilla Airport [*Airport symbol*] (OAG)

PAC Pan American College [*Texas*]

PAC Pan-American Congress

PAC Papular Acrodermatitis of Childhood

PAC Para-Aminoclonidine [*Biochemistry*]

PAC Para-Aminosalicylic Acid Calcium Salt [*Pharmacology*]

PAC Parachute and Cable Defence [*British military*]

PAC Parallel Alternate Curriculum (EDAC)

PAC Parametric Amplifier Converter

P-A-C Parent-Adult-Child [*Transactional analysis*]

PAC Parent Advisory Committee [*Migrant education*] (AEE)

PAC Parent Advisory Council (EDAC)

PAC Parker Aircraft Corp. (MCD)

PAC Partido Autentico Constitucional [*Authentic Constitutional Party*] [*El Salvador*] [*Political party*]

PAC Parts Allocation Chart (MCD)

PAC Pascagoula, MS [*Location identifier FAA*] (FAAL)

PAC Passed the Final Examination of the Advanced Class [*Military College of Science*] [*British*]

PAC Passive Acoustic Classification (NVT)

PAC Patents Advisory Committee [*British*]

PAC Patient Airlift Center [*Aeromedical evacuation*]

PAC Patriot Advanced Capability [*Missile technology*] [*Military*] (PS)

PAC Patriot Antimissile Capability [*Army*]

PAC Payment after Closing [*Insurance*]

PAC Peace Action Center [*Defunct*] (EA)

PAC Pedagogic Automatic Computer (IEEE)

PAC Pediatric AIDS [*Acquired Immune Deficiency Syndrome*] Coalition (EA)

PAC Penalty Assessment Criteria [*Environmental Protection Agency*]

PAC Penetration Aids Deployment Concept (SAA)

PA C Pennsylvania Commonwealth Court Reports [*A publication*] (DLA)

PAC People Against Cancer

PAC People's Army Congress

PAC Peptide Acid [*Organic chemistry*]

PAC Performance Analysis and Control

PAC Performance Assured Certification

PAC Peripheral Autonomous Control (NITA)

PAC Personal Access Code

PAC Personal Analog Computer

PAC Person in Addition to Crew [*Sailing*]

PAC Personnel Action Center [*Army*] (INF)

PAC Personnel Action Code

PAC Personnel and Administration Center [*Army*] (AABC)

PAC Personnel Assistance Center [*Military*] (INF)

PAC Perturbed Angular Correlation

PAC Pesticides Advisory Committee [*Tasmania, Australia*]

PAC Petroleum Advisory Committee [*of Organization for Economic Cooperation and Development*] [*Terminated, 1976*] (EGAO)

PAC Pharmaceutical Advertising Council [*New York, NY*] (EA)

PAC Phenacetin [*Acetophenetidin*], Aspirin, Caffeine [*Pharmacology*]

PAC Photoacoustic [*Spectroscopy*]

PAC Photoactive Compound [*Chemistry*]

PAC Photo Aperture Card (SAA)

PAC Phototypesetting Automatic Controller (DGA)

PA-C Physician's Assistant-Certified (WGA)

PAC Pilotless Aircraft [*Navy*] (IAA)

PAC Piper Aircraft Corp.

PAC Place Complement of Address in Index Register (SAA)

PAC Planned Amortization Class [*Investment term*] (DFIT)

PAC Planned-Amortization-Class Bond [*Investment term*]

PAC Planned Amortization Credit [*Investment term*] (ECON)

PAC Planned Availability Concept (MHDI)

PAC Planning Advisory Committee (OICC)

PAC Plasma Aldosterone Concentration [*Hematology*] (DMAA)

PAC Plasma Arc Chamber

PAC Plasma Arc Cutting [*Welding*]

PAC Platelet-Associated Complement [*Medicine*] (DMAA)

PAC Platinol [*Cisplatin*], Adriamycin, Cyclophosphamide [*Antineoplastic drug regimen*]

PAC Plowshare Advisory Committee [*AEC*]

PAC Pneumatic Analog Computer

PAC Pneumatic Auxiliary Console (AAG)

PAC Pod Air Conditioner (AAG)

PAC Poisons Advisory Committee [*Australia*]

PAC Polar Air Cargo, Inc. [*FAA designator*] (FAAC)

PAC Policy Advisory Center

PAC Policy Advisory Committee [*National Cancer Institute*] [*Department of Health and Human Services*] (GFGA)

PAC Policy Advisory Committee [*Office of Economic Opportunity*]

PAC Polish American Congress (EA)

PAC Political Action Caucus [*Superseded by LPAC*] (EA)

PAC Political Action Committee [*Generic term*]

PAC Political Action Committee

PAC Polled Access Circuit

PAC Pollution Abatement and Control

PAC Polyaluminum Chloride [*Inorganic chemistry*]

PAC Polyanionic Cellulose [*Organic chemistry*]

PAC Polycyclic Aromatic Compound [*Organic chemistry*]

PAC Population Action Council (EA)

PAC Porterfield Airplane Club (EA)

PAC Post-Adoption Centre [*British*] (CB)

PAC Post Award Conference (MCD)

PAC Post Award Contract

PAC Powdered Activated Carbon [*Adsorbent*]

PAC Pre-Action Calibration [*Gunnery*] (NVT)

PAC Pre-Admission Certification [*Medicine*] (MEDA)

PAC Preauthorized Check Plan [*Insurance*]

PAC Pre-Authorized Chequing [*Canada*]

PAC Preauthorized Chequing [*Canadian term for an electronic funds transfer*] (NFD)

PAC Premature Atrial Contraction [*Medicine*]

PAC Premature Auricular Contraction [*Cardiology*] (AAMN)

PAC Preservation and Conservation [*IFLA Core Program*]

PAC Pressure Alpha Center (MCD)

PAC Primary Address Code (AFM)

PAC Prime [*or Principal*] Associate Contractor (MCD)

PAC Principal Associate Contractor (MCD)

PAC Printing Accountants Club (EA)

PAC Priority Area Children (AIE)

PAC Privacy Act Coordinator [*Navy*] (DNAB)

PAC Probe Aerodynamic Center [*NASA*]

PAC Problem Action Center [*NASA*] (NASA)

PAC Process Analytical Chemistry

PAC Procurement and Contract (IAA)

PAC Production Acceleration Capacity [*Manufacturing*]

PAC Product of Ambulatory Care [*Medicine*] (HCT)

PAC Professional Activities Survey [*Medicine*]

PAC Program Acquisition Cost (MCD)

PAC Program Address Counter [*Computer science*] (EECA)

PAC Program Adjustment Committee

PAC Program Advisory Committee

PAC Program Allocation Checker

PAC Program Application Code (DNAB)

PAC Program Assembly Card (NITA)

PAC Program Authorized Credentials [*Computer science*]

PAC Programmable Analogical Controller (NITA)

PAC Programmable Automatic Comparator

PAC Programme Activity Center [*Advisory Committee on Pollution of the Sea*]

PAC Progress Assessment Chart [*Psychology*]

PAC Project Advisory Committee (EGAO)

PAC Project Analysis and Control (IAA)

PAC Promoting Achievement through Communications [*Education*]

PAC Protect America's Children [*An association*] (EA)

PAC Protection Auxiliary Cabinet [*Nuclear energy*] (NRCH)

PAC Prudential Assurance Co. Ltd. [*Australia*]

PAC Public Access Catalogue (ADA)

PAC Public Access Control

PAC Public Accounts Committee [*British government*]

PAC Public Affairs Committee [*Defunct*] (EA)

PAC Public Affairs Coordinator [*Nuclear energy*] (NRCH)

PAC Public Affairs Council (EA)

PAC Public Archives of Canada

PAC Public Authority Contribution [*Australia*]

PAC Public Awareness Committee [*American Library Association*]

PAC Publishers' Ad Club [*New York, NY*] (EA)

PAC Pulmonary Artery Catheter [*Medicine*]

PAC Purchasing and Contracting [*Army*] (IAA)

PAC Pure and Applied Chemistry [*IUPAC*]

PAC Pursuant to Authority Contained In [*Army*]

PAC Put and Call [*Stock exchange term*]

Pac 2d Pacific Reporter, Second Series [*A publication*] (DLA)

PAC-10 Pacific 10 Conference (EA)

Pac A Pacific Affairs [*A publication*] (BRI)

PACA Perishable Agricultural Commodities Act, 1930

PACA Picture Agency Council of America (EA)

PACA Principal Assistant County Architect [*British*]

PACA Propulsion and Control Assembly

PACA Proyecto Ambiental para Centro America [*Environmental Project for Central America*] [*Spanish*] (ECON)

PACAACS Pacific Area Airways and Air Communications (IAA)

PacA & E Pacific Aerospace & Electronics, Inc. [*Associated Press*] (SAG)

PACADIV Pacific Fleet Advance Headquarters Division (DNAB)

PACADV Pacific Fleet Advance Headquarters [*Guam*]

PACAF Pacific Air Forces

PACAFBASECOM Pacific Air Forces Base Command

PACAF-OA Pacific Air Forces Operations Analysis

PACAF-OA Pacific Air Forces Operations Analysis Office [*Hickam Air Force Base, HI*]

PACAH Pitch Attitude Command/Attitude Hold [*Aviation*] (MCD)

PacAni Pacific Animated Imaging Corp. [*Associated Press*] (SAG)

PACAP Pituitary Adenylate Cyclase Activating Polypeptide [*Biochemistry*]

PACAP Pituitary Adenylyl Cyclase-Activating Polypeptide [*Endocrinology*]

Pacar PACCAR, Inc. [*Associated Press*] (SAG)

PacAS Pacific American Income Shares, Inc. [*Associated Press*] (SAG)

PACAS Patient Care System [*Army*] (AABC)

PA Cas Pennsylvania Supreme Court Cases (Sadler) [*A publication*] (DLA)

PACAS Personnel Access Control Accountability System [*NASA*] (MCD)

PACAS Psychological Abstracts Current Awareness Service (IID)

PACB Pan-American Coffee Bureau [*Defunct*] (EA)

PACB Poppy Advisory and Control Board [*Tasmania, Australia*]

PACBAR Pacific Barrier RADAR (MCD)

PacBB Pacific Basin Bulk Shippers Ltd. [*Associated Press*] (SAG)

PacBBS Pacific Basin Bulk Shippers Ltd. [*Associated Press*] (SAG)

PacBio Pacific Biometrics, Inc. [*Associated Press*] (SAG)

PacBiom Pacific Biometrics, Inc. [*Associated Press*] (SAG)

PACC .... Pacific Coast [*Railroad*] (MHDB)
PA CC .... Pennsylvania County Court Reports [*A publication*] (DLA)
PACC .... PERT [*Program Evaluation and Review Technique*] Associated Cost Control [*Computer science*] (IAA)
PACC .... Portable Arm Control Console (KSC)
PACC .... Primary Ambulatory Care Center [*Medicine*] (DMAA)
P(ACC) .... Probability of Acceptance
PACC .... Problem Action Control Center [*NASA*] (NASA)
PACC .... Product Administration and Contract Control (IAA)
PACC .... Products Administration Contract Control
PACC .... Professional Association of Custom Clothiers (EA)
PACC .... Programmable Array Combinatorial Circuit (NITA)
PACC .... Promoting Aphasics' Communicative Competence [*Medicine*] (DMAA)
PACC .... Propulsion and Auxiliary Control Console [*NASA*] (DNAB)
PACC .... Protected Air-Cooled Condenser [*Nuclear energy*] (NRCH)
PACC .... Protein A Immobilized in Collodion Charcoal (DAVI)
PACC .... Public Arts Advisory Council (NADA)
PACCA .... Policy Alternatives for the Caribbean and Central America (EA)
PACCALL ..... Pacific Fleet Calls [*Radio call signs*]
PacCapB ...... Pacific Capital Bancorp [*Associated Press*] (SAG)
PACCAR .... Pacific Car and Foundry
PACCE .... Providing Professional Development, Assessment, and Coordination of Competency-Based Education Project [*Illinois*] (EDAC)
PACCIOS ...... Pan American Council of International Committee of Scientific Management
PACCO .... Cisplatin, Adriamycin, Cyclophosphamide, CCNU [*Lomustine*], Oncovin [*Vincristine*] [*Antineoplastic drug regimen*]
Pac Coast Int ... Pacific Coast International [*A publication*] (ILCA)
Pac Coast LJ ... Pacific Coast Law Journal [*A publication*] (DLA)
PACCOM ...... Pacific Command [*Military*]
PACCOM ...... Pacific Communications Network [*Computer science*] (TNIG)
PACCOM ...... Pacific Fleet Communications Instructions
PACCOMOPCONCEN ... Pacific Fleet Command Operational Control Center (DNAB)
PA CCR .... Pennsylvania County Court Reports [*A publication*] (DLA)
PA CC Reps ... Pennsylvania County Court Reports [*A publication*] (DLA)
PacCrst .... Pacific Crest Capital [*Associated Press*] (SAG)
PACCS .... Pan American Cancer Cytology Society [*Defunct*] (EA)
PACCS .... Post-Attack Command and Control System [*Military*]
PACCS/ADA ... Post-Attack Command and Control System/Airborne Data Automation [*Military*]
PACCSq .... Post-Attack Command Control Squadron [*Air Force*]
PACCT .... PERT [*Program Evaluation and Review Technique*] and Cost Correlation Technique
PACCT .... Political Action Committee for Cable Television (NTCM)
PACD .... Cold Bay [*Alaska*] [*ICAO location identifier*] (ICLI)
PACD .... Pacific Division [*Military*]
PACD .... Parachute and Cable Defence [*British military*] (DMA)
PACDA .... Personnel and Administration, Combat Development Activity [*Army*] (AABC)
PA C Dec WCC ... Pennsylvania Courts, Decisions in Workmen's Compensation Cases [*A publication*] (DLA)
PACDIV .... Pacific Division [*Military*]
PacDunl .... Pacific Dunlop Ltd. [*Associated Press*] (SAG)
PACE .... Ampace Corp. [*NASDAQ symbol*] (SAG)
PACE .... Pacific Agricultural Cooperative for Export [*Corte Madera, CA*] (EA)
PACE .... Pacific Alternate Command Element (CINC)
PACE .... Pacific America Container Express (MHDB)
PACE .... Pacific Atoll Cratering Experiment [*Military*] (DNAB)
PACE .... Packaged CRAM [*Card Random-Access Memory*] Executive [*NCR Corp.*] [*Computer science*]
PACE .... Package for Architectural Computer Evaluation (PDAA)
PACE .... Packet of Accelerated Christian Education [*Educational material marketed by fundamentalist company, Accelerated Christian Education*]
PACE .... Parental Alliance for Choice in Education (AIE)
PACE .... Parents and Children's Equality [*An association*] (PAZ)
PACE .... Passive Attitude Control Experimental [*Satellite*]
PACE .... Patient Advise and Consent Encounter
PACE .... Patrol Airship Concept Evaluation
PACE .... People with Arthritis Can Exercise [*Medical program*]
PACE .... Performance Advantage with Cummins Electronics [*Automotive engineering*]
PACE .... Performance and Cost Evaluation
PACE .... Performing Arts, Culture, and Entertainment [*Proposed cable television system*]
PACE .... Peripheral Automatic Channel Emulator [*Computer science*]
PACE .... Personalized Aerobics for Cardiovascular Enhancement
PACE .... Petroleum Association for Conservation of the Canadian Environment
PACE .... Phased Array Control Electronics
PACE .... Physics and Chemistry Experiment
PACE .... Planetary Association for Clean Energy (EA)
PACE .... Plan for Action by Citizens in Education
PACE .... Planned Action with Constant Evaluation [*Computer science*]
PACE .... Planning and Control Made Easy (PDAA)
PACE .... Plant Acquisition and Construction Equipment [*Nuclear energy*] (NRCH)
PACE .... Plant and Capital Equipment (MCD)
PACE .... Plasma-Assisted Chemical Etching [*Metallurgy*]
PACE .... Platinol [*Cis-Platinum*] [*Antineoplastic drug regimen*] (DAVI)
PACE .... Police and Criminal Evidence Act [*1964*] [*British*]
PACE .... Policy Analysis for California Education [*Research center*] (RCD)
PACE .... Portable Acoustic Collection Equipment (MCD)
PACE .... Precision Analog Computing Equipment
PACE .... Preflight Acceptance Checkout Equipment
PACE .... Prelaunch Automatic Checkout Equipment [*NASA*]
PACE .... Priority Access Control Enabled [*Telecommunications*]
PACE .... Priority Activities in Cancer Education
PACE .... Prisoners Accelerated Creative Exposure [*An association*]
PACE .... Procedural Approach to the Composition of Essays [*In book title*]
PACE .... Processing and Control Element [*Computer science*] (IAA)
PACE .... Producers of Associated Components for Electronics (IAA)
PACE .... Professional Activities for Continuing Education [*AEC*]
PACE .... Professional and Administrative Career Examination [*Formerly, FSEE*] [*Civil Service*]
PACE .... Professional Application Creation Environment (NITA)
PACE .... Professional Association of Christian Educators (EA)
PACE .... Professional Association of Consulting Engineers
PACE .... Program Analysis Control and Evaluation [*Computer science*] (IAA)
PACE .... Program for Acquiring Competence in Entrepreneurship (EDAC)
PACE .... Program for Afloat College Education [*Navy*] (NVT)
PACE .... Programmable Autonomously-Controlled Electrode [*Instrumentation*]
PACE .... Programmed Automatic Communications Equipment
PACE .... Programming Analysis Consulting Education (IEEE)
PACE .... Program of All-Inclusive Care for the Elderly
PACE .... Progressive Aerobic Circuit Exercise [*Fitness training*]
PACE .... Project for the Advancement of Church Education
PACE .... Projects to Advance Creativity in Education [*HEW*]
PACE .... Promoting Aphasics Communicative Effectiveness [*Australia*]
PACE .... Providing Avenues for Continuing Encouragement [*Scholarship awarded by Fraternity of Recording Executives*]
PACE .... Provisioning Action Control Evaluation [*Military*] (AFIT)
PACE .... Public Affairs Council Education [*An association*] [*Canadian*] (NFD)
PACE .... Public Affairs Council for Education [*Canada*]
PACE .... Pulse-Synthesized Advanced Conversion Equipment
P/ACEA2 ...... Probationary Control Electrical Artificer, Acting, 2nd Class [*British military*] (DMA)
PACED .... Program for Advanced Concepts in Electronic Design
PACEE .... Propulsion and Auxiliary Control Electronic Enclosure (DNAB)
PaceHlt .... Pace Health Management Systems, Inc. [*Associated Press*] (SAG)
PACE/LV ...... Preflight Acceptance Checkout Equipment-Launch Vehicle
PACEMAKER ... Public Agency Career Employment Maker [*OEO project*]
PACEN .... Public Affairs Center [*Navy*] (DNAB)
PACENLANT ... Public Affairs Center, Atlantic [*Navy*] (DNAB)
PACENPAC .... Public Affairs Center, Pacific [*Navy*] (DNAB)
PACENS .... Patient Census
PacEnt .... Pacific Enterprises [*Associated Press*] (SAG)
PACEO .... Professional Application Creation Environment (HGAA)
PACER .... Parent Advocacy Coalition for Educational Rights [*Minnesota*] (EDAC)
PACER .... Part and Component Evaluation Report [*NASA*]
PACER .... Planning Automation and Control for Evaluating Requirements
PACER .... Portable Aircraft Condition Evaluator Recorder
PACER .... Postadoption Center for Education and Research
PACER .... Postoperational Analysis Critique and Exercise Report [*Military*] (CAAL)
PACER .... Prescriptive Analysis for Curriculum Evaluation [*Vocational guidance*]
PACER .... Priority for Allocation/Application of COMSEC Equipment Resources (MCD)
PACER .... Private Access to Court Electronic Records (AAGC)
PACER .... Process Assembly Case Evaluator Routine [*Computer science*]
PACER .... Program-Assisted Console Evaluation and Review [*Air Force*]
PACER .... Programmed Automatic Circuit Evaluator and Recorder
PACER .... Program of Active Cooling Effects and Requirements
PACER .... Public Access to Court Electronic Records
PACERS .... Pacing and Cardiac Electrophysiology Retrieval System [*Intermedics, Inc.*] [*Information service or system*] (IID)
PACES .... Parent Attitude Toward Child Experssiveness Scale (EDAC)
PACES .... Patient as Customer Evaluation Survey
PACES .... Political Action Committee for Engineers and Scientists
PACE-S/C ..... Preflight Acceptance Checkout Equipment for Spacecraft
Pace U .... Pace University (GAGS)
PAC-EX .... Canadian National Packaging Exposition [*Packaging Association of Canada*] (TSPED)
PACEX .... Pacific Exchange [*System*] [*Military*] (AFM)
PACF .... Pacific
Pacf .... PacifiCorp [*Associated Press*] (SAG)
PACF .... Partial Autocorrelation Function [*Statistics*]
PAC-FACS .... Programmed Appropriation Commitments - Fixed Asset Control System (PDAA)
PACFAST ..... Pacific Forward Area Support Team (DNAB)
PACFASTDET ... Pacific Forward Area Support Team Detachment (DNAB)
PACFASTREP ... Pacific Forward Area Support Team Representative (DNAB)
PacFIN .... Pacific Fishery Information Network [*Database*] [*National Marine Fisheries Service*]
PACFLAP ..... Pacific Fleet Augmentation Plan [*Navy*] (NVT)
PACFLT .... Pacific Fleet
PACFLTCOM ... Pacific Fleet Command
PACFLTMOPHOTOU ... Pacific Fleet Mobile Photographic Unit (MUGU)
PACFLTPROPEXAMBD ... Pacific Fleet Propulsion Examining Board (DNAB)
PACFORNET ... Pacific Coast Forest Research Information Network [*Later, WESTFORNET*] [*Forest Service*] (IID)
PACFW .... President's Advisory Committee for Women [*Terminated, 1980*] (EGAO)
PacGate .... Pacific Gateway Properties [*Associated Press*] (SAG)
PACGCS .... Prior Active Coast Guard Commissioned Service
PacGE .... Pacific Gas & Electric Co. [*Associated Press*] (SAG)
PACGEEIA .... Pacific Area Ground Environment Electronic Installation Agency (CINC)
PACGES .... Prior Active Coast Guard Enlisted Service

PACGO President's Advisory Committee on Government Organization [*Abolished, 1961*]
PACGSR Pan American Center for Geographical Studies and Research [*See also CEPEIGE*] (EAIO)
PacGul Pacific Gulf Properties, Inc. [*Associated Press*] (SAG)
PacGulf Pacific Gulf Properties [*Associated Press*] (SAG)
PACH Performing Arts Center for Health [*New York University/Bellevue Hospital, New York, NY*] [*Superseded by Center for Dance Medicine -CDM*]
PACH Pipers to After Coming Head [*Obstetrics*] (DAVI)
PACH Public Administration Clearing House [*1931-1956*]
PACH Publishers' Accounts Clearing House [*British*] (BI)
PACHACH Partizanim-Chayalim-Chalutzim (BJA)
PACHEDPEARL Pacific Headquarters, Pearl Harbor, Hawaii [*Navy*]
PACIA Particle Counting Immunoassay
PACICOM Pacific Coastal Marine Productivity [*Marine science*] (OSRA)
PACIF Pacific
Pacif PacifiCorp [*Associated Press*] (SAG)
PacifBnk Pacific Bank NA [*Associated Press*] (SAG)
PacifC PacifiCare Health Systems, Inc. [*Associated Press*] (SAG)
PacifCp PacifiCorp [*Associated Press*] (SAG)
Pacif Defence Reporter Pacific Defence Reporter [*A publication*]
Pacific CLJ Pacific Coast Law Journal [*San Francisco*] [*A publication*] (DLA)
Pacific Law Mag Pacific Law Magazine [*A publication*] (DLA)
Pacific Rep Pacific Reporter [*A publication*] (DLA)
Pacif Is Mon Pacific Islands Monthly [*A publication*]
Pacif Rep Pacific Reporter [*A publication*] (DLA)
PACIFY Parents and Alumni Committee Involved for Youth [*Brown University*]
PACIMS Passive Chemical Ionization Mass Spectrometry
PACINTCEN Pacific Intelligence Center (DNAB)
PacIntl Pacific International Services Corp. [*Associated Press*] (SAG)
PACIR Practical Approach to Chemical Information Retrieval
PACIT Passive and Active Interface Test [*Electronic warfare*]
PACK Gibraltar Packaging Group [*NASDAQ symbol*] (TTSB)
PACK Gibraltar Packaging Group, Inc. [*NASDAQ symbol*] (SAG)
PACK Packing and Allocation for a COMPOOL [*Communications Pool*] Kaleidoscope (SAA)
PACK Parents and Cataract Kids [*An association*] (PAZ)
PACK Pontoon Air Cushion Kit [*Army*] (RDA)
PACKAGE Planned Aids for Cross-Culture Knowledge, Action and Growth in Effectiveness
PackRs Packaging Research Corp. [*Associated Press*] (SAG)
PackRsh Packaging Research Corp. [*Associated Press*] (SAG)
PACL Clear [*Alaska*] [*ICAO location identifier*] (ICLI)
Pac Law Mag Pacific Law Magazine [*A publication*] (DLA)
Pac Law Reptr Pacific Law Reporter [*San Francisco*] [*A publication*] (DLA)
Pac Leg N Pacific Legal News [*A publication*] (DLA)
Pac Luth U Pacific Lutheran University (GAGS)
PACM Parts and Componenets Manual (IAA)
PACM Passive Countermeasures (MSA)
PACM Pulse Amplitude Code Modulation [*Electronics*]
PACMD Philadelphia Contract Management District (SAA)
PACMETNET Pacific Meteorological Network (AAG)
PACMI President's Advisory Committee on Management Improvement [*Terminated, 1973*]
PACMISCEN Pacific Missile Center [*Marine science*] (DNAB)
PACMISRAN Pacific Missile Range [*Later, WTR*] (MUGU)
PACMISRANFAC Pacific Missile Range Facility [*Obsolete*]
PACMISRANFACDET Pacific Missile Range Facility Detachment [*Obsolete*] (DNAB)
PACMISRANFACREP Pacific Missile Range Facility Representative [*Obsolete*] (DNAB)
PACMISTESTCEN Pacific Missile Test Center [*Navy*]
PACMISTESTCEN LO Pacific Missile Test Center Liaison Office [*Navy*] (DNAB)
PACMS Psycho-Acoustical Measuring System (PDAA)
PA Cmwlth Pennsylvania Commonwealth Court Reports [*A publication*] (DLA)
PACN Pacific Area Communicatios Network (SAA)
PACNAVCONSTFOR Pacific Naval Construction Force (DNAB)
PACNAVFACENGCOM Pacific Division Naval Facilities Engineering Command
PACNCF Pacific Naval Construction Force (DNAB)
PACNCO Personnel Assistance Center Noncommissioned Officer (INF)
PACNET OCLC Pacific Network [*Claremont, CA*] [*Information service or system*] (IID)
PACNET Plymouth Audioconferencing Network [*Plymouth Polytechnic*] [*Plymouth, England*] [*Telecommunications*] (TSSD)
PACNET POCC [*Payload Operations Control Center*] Automated Computer Network
PACNY Pawnbrokers' Association of the City of New York (EA)
PACO Accounting Policy Division (AAGC)
PacO Pacific Ocean
PACO Peak Aboriginal Community Organisation [*Australia*]
PACO Pivot Ambulating Crutchless Orthosis [*Medicine*]
PACO Polaris Accelerated Change Operation [*Missiles*]
PACO Primary Administrative Contracting Officer [*Military*] (AFIT)
PACO Principal Administrative Contracting Officer (AAGC)
PA$_{CO2}$ Alveolar Carbon Dioxide Pressure [*in blood gases*] [*Medicine*] (DAVI)
Pa$_{co_2}$ Arterial Carbon Dioxide Pressure, Tension [*Medicine*] (MAE)
PACOB Propulsion Auxiliary Control Box (AAG)
PA Co Ct Pennsylvania County Court Reports [*A publication*] (DLA)
PA Co Ct R Pennsylvania County Court Reports [*A publication*] (DLA)
PACOM Pacific Command [*Military*]
PACOM Pacific Communications Group
PACOMBPO Pacific Command Blood Program Office [*Military*] (DNAB)
PACOMDET Pacific Command Detachment [*Military*] (DNAB)
PACOMEP Pacific Command Emergency Procedures (CINC)
PACOMEW Pacific Command Electronic Warfare (CINC)
PACOMINTS Pacific Command Intelligence School (CINC)
PACOMJRO Pacific Command Joint Medical Regulating Office (DNAB)
PA Commw Pennsylvania Commonwealth Court Reports [*A publication*] (DLA)
Pa Commw Pennsylvania Commonwealth Reports [*A publication*] (AAGC)
PA Commw Ct Pennsylvania Commonwealth Court Reports [*A publication*] (DLA)
PA Com Pl Pennsylvania Common Pleas Reporter [*A publication*] (DLA)
PA Cons Stat Pennsylvania Consolidated Statutes [*A publication*] (DLA)
PA Cons Stat Ann Pennsylvania Consolidated Statutes, Annotated [*A publication*] (DLA)
PA Cons Stat Ann (Purdon) Pennsylvania Consolidated Statutes, Annotated (Purdon) [*A publication*] (DLA)
PACOPS Pacific Air Combat Operations Staff
PACOPS Pacific Air Force Operations (MCD)
PACOR Passive Correlation and Ranging
PACOR Passive Correlation and Ranging Station (IAA)
PACORE Parabolic Corner Reflector
PACORNALOG Pacific Coast Coordinator of Naval Logistics
PA Corp Pennsylvania Corp. Reporter [*A publication*] (DLA)
PA Corp R Pennsylvania Corp. Reporter [*A publication*] (DLA)
PA Corp Rep Pennsylvania Corp. Reporter [*A publication*] (DLA)
PACOS Package Operating System (PDAA)
PA County Ct Pennsylvania County Court Reports [*A publication*] (DLA)
PA CP Pennsylvania Common Pleas Reporter [*A publication*] (DLA)
PACP Photo Aperture Card Program (SAA)
PACP Propulsion Auxiliary Control Panel [*NASA*] (KSC)
PACP Pulmonary Artery Counter-Pulsation [*Cardiology*] (MAE)
PacPhy Pacific Physician Services, Inc. [*Associated Press*] (SAG)
PACPIP Public Advocate - Coalition of Public Interest Professionals (EA)
PACPrT Pac Telesis Fin I 7.56%'TOPrS' [*NYSE symbol*] (TTSB)
PACQI Probability of Acquisition [*Military*]
Pac R Pacific Reporter [*Commonly cited as P*] [*A publication*] (DLA)
PA CR Pennsylvania County Court Reports [*A publication*] (DLA)
PACR Performance and Compatibility Requirements
PACR Perimeter Acquisition RADAR (MSA)
PACRAD Practical Absolute Cavity Radiometer (PDAA)
PacR & E Pacific Research & Engineering Corp. [*Associated Press*] (SAG)
PACRAO Pacific Association of Collegiate Registrars and Admission Officers
PACRED Pacific Area Cooperative Renewable Energy Development [*University of Hawaii*]
PacRehab Pacific Rehabilitation & Sports Medicine, Inc. [*Associated Press*] (SAG)
Pac Rep Pacific Reporter [*Commonly cited as P*] [*A publication*] (DLA)
PACREP Port Activities Report [*Navy*]
PACREPCOMNAVSURFRES Pacific Representative for Commander Naval Surface Reserve Force (DNAB)
PACREPNAVRES Pacific Representative of the Chief of Naval Reserve (DNAB)
Pac Repr Pacific Reporter [*A publication*] (DLA)
PACRESFLT Pacific Reserve Fleet
PacRim Pac Rim Holding Corp. [*Associated Press*] (SAG)
PACS Cape Sarichef Air Force Station [*Alaska*] [*ICAO location identifier*] (ICLI)
PACS Pacific Area Communications System (MCD)
Pac S Pacific Studies [*A publication*] (BRI)
PACS Pan America Climate Studies [*Marine science*] (OSRA)
PACS Particle Analysis Cameras for the Shuttle [*NASA*]
PACS Patient Accounting, Census, and Statistics
PACS Patient Care and Services (DMAA)
PACS Peace and Common Security [*Defunct*] (EA)
PACS Photo Aperture Card System (SAA)
PACS Physics and Astronomy Classification Scheme
PACS Picture Archival and Communication System
PACS Pitch Augmentation Control System (PDAA)
PACS Plant Automation Communication System [*IBM Corp.*]
PACS Pointing and Attitude Control System [*Aerospace*] (NASA)
PACS Post-Attack Communication System
PACS Principal Appreciation Conversion Security [*Finance*]
PACS Process Automation & Computer Systems
PACS Program Authorization Control System (MCD)
PACS Programmable Armament Control Set (DOMA)
Pa CSA Pennsylvania Consolidated Statutes, Annotated [*A publication*] (DLA)
PACSAT Packet Satellite [*Telecommunications*]
PACSAT Passive Communications Satellite
PA/CSC Payload Accommodation/Carrier Support Center [*NASA*] (SSD)
PACSCAT Pacific Ionospheric Scatter (CINC)
PacSci Pacific Scientific Co. [*Associated Press*] (SAG)
PACS DB Picture Archiving and Communication System Data Base (DMAA)
PacSen Pacific Sentinel Gold Corp. [*Associated Press*] (SAG)
PACSUBDSEC Pacific Submarine Direct Support Element Coordinator (DNAB)
PacSun Pacific Sunwear of California, Inc. [*Associated Press*] (SAG)
PacT Pacific Telesis Group Financing I [*Associated Press*] (SAG)
PacT Pacific Telesis Group Financing II [*Associated Press*] (SAG)
PACT Pan American Commission of Tampa (EA)
PACT Pandick Computerized Typesetting (NITA)
PACT Papillary Carninoma of Thyroid [*Medicine*] (DMAA)
PACT Parents, Children, and Teachers (AIE)
PACT Participating and Assertive Consumer Training [*Health education*]
PACT Paved Concrete Track [*Railways*]
PACT Pay Actual Computer Time
PACT PCTE Added Common Tools (NITA)
PACT Performing Arts for Crisis Training [*In association name, PACT Training*] (EA)
PACT Perturbed-Anisotropic-Chain Theory [*Chemistry*]
PACT Phased Control Technique (PDAA)
PACT Philadelphia Association for Clinical Trials (DAVI)

PACT Philco Automatic Circuit Tester
PACT Plan of Action for Challenging Times (EA)
PACT Portable Aircraft Calibration Tracker [*NASA*]
PACT Poseidon Automatic Cable Tester [*Missiles*] (DNAB)
PACT Powdered Activated Carbon Treatment [*For wastewater*] [*E. I. Du Pont De Nemours & Co., Inc.*]
PACT Precision Aircraft Control Technology (MCD)
PACT Precordial Acceleration Tracing [*Medicine*] (DMAA)
PACT Predictive Analysis and Crash Testing [*Automotive safety research*]
PACT Prepaid Accountable Care Term [*Medicine*] (DMAA)
PACT Print Active Computer Tables (SAA)
PACT Private Agencies Collaborating Together (EA)
PACT Processing and Communications Terminal (MCD)
PACT Production Action Control Technique (SAA)
PACT Production Analysis Control Technique [*Navy*]
PACT Professional Association of Canadian Theatres
PACT Program for Automatic Coding Techniques [*Computer science*]
PACT Programmable Asynchronous Clustered Teleprocessing
PACT Programmed Analysis Computer Transfer (KSC)
PACT Programmed Automatic Circuit Tester
PACT Progress in Advanced Component Technology (IAA)
PACT Project for the Advancement of Coding Techniques
PACT Protective Action for Children's Television (NTCM)
PACT Provide Addict Care Today [*Later, NADAP*]
PACT Public Action Coalition on Toys [*Opposes sexist toys*]
PACTA Packed Tape Assembly
PACTCU Pacific Area Communications Message Traffic Control Unit (IAA)
PacTec Pacer Technology [*Associated Press*] (SAG)
PACTEL Pacific Telesis (NITA)
PacTel Pacific Telesis Group [*Associated Press*] (SAG)
PACTEL PA Computers & Telecommunications [*Information service or system*] (IID)
PACTEL Planning Associates for Computers and Telecommunications (NITA)
PACTEX Pacific-Texas [*Pipeline*]
PACTIV Principos Activos [*Ministerio de Sanidad y Consumo*] [*Spain Information service or system*] (CRD)
PACTO Professional, Administrative, Clerical, Technical, and Other (BARN)
PACTOA Pacific Technical Operations Area [*Military*]
PacTOP Pacific Tsunami Observation Program (USDC)
PacTOP Pacific Tsunami Observation Program [*Marine science*] (OSRA)
PACTS Parents, Administrators, Community, Teachers, and Students [*School-community groups*]
PACTS Programmer Aptitude Competence Test System
PACTS Public Access Cordless Telephone Service [*Australia*]
PACTT Planning the Australian Capital Territory Together
Pac U Pacific University (GAGS)
PACU Post-Anesthesia Care Unit (MEDA)
PACUIT Packet + Circuit (MHDI)
Pac Union C Pacific Union College (GAGS)
PACUSA Pacific Air Command, United States Army
PACV Cordova [*Alaska*] [*ICAO location identifier*] (ICLI)
PACV Patrol Air-Cushion Vehicle [*Also called Hovercraft*] [*Navy*]
PACV Personnel Air-Cushion Vehicle
PACV Post-Accident Containment Venting [*Nuclear energy*] (NRCH)
PACVD Plasma-Assisted Chemical Vapor Deposition [*Coating technology*]
PACWP Pulmonary Arterial Capillary Wedge Pressure [*Medicine*] (DMAA)
PACX Private Automatic Computer Exchange [*Telecommunications*]
PACZ Cape Romanzof Air Force Station [*Alaska*] [*ICAO location identifier*] (ICLI)
PAD Accounting Policy Division (AAGC)
PAD Anthropology of Development Programme [*McGill University*] [*Canada Research center*] (RCD)
PAD Packet Assembler/Disassembler [*Switching technique*] [*Computer science*]
PAD Packet Assembly Disassembly (NITA)
PAD Padder [*Capacitor*] [*Electronics*]
PAD Paderborn [*Germany Airport symbol*] (OAG)
PAD Padova [*Italy*] [*Seismograph station code, US Geological Survey*] (SEIS)
PAD Padstow [*Town in England*]
PAD Paducah Gaseous Diffusion Plant [*Department of Energy*] [*Paducah, KY*] (GAAI)
PAD Palestine Arab Delegation (EA)
PAD Partido Accion Democratica [*Democratic Action Party*] [*El Salvador*] [*Political party*] (PPW)
PAD Partido de Accion Democrata [*Democratic Action Party*] [*Spain Political party*] (PPW)
PAD Passenger Airbag Disable
PAD Passive Acoustic Detection [*Military*] (CAAL)
PAD Passive Air Defense [*British*]
PAD Patriot Arm Decoy [*Weaponry*] (DWSG)
PAD Payable after Death [*Insurance*] (ADA)
PAD Pedagogischer Austauschdienst [*Pedagogical Exchange Service*] [*German*]
PAD Penetration Aids Deployment [*Weaponry*] (DWSG)
PAD People Against Displacement (NADA)
PAD Percutaneous Abscess Drainage [*Surgery*] (DAVI)
PAD Percutaneous Automated Diskectomy [*Neurology*] (DAVI)
PAD Performance Analysis and Design [*Nuclear energy*] (NRCH)
PAD Performing Arts Directory [*A publication*]
PAD Peripheral Arterial Disease [*Medicine*]
PAD Permissible Accumulated Dose
PAD Personal Articulation Device [*Facetious term for pre-word-processing equipment*]
PAD Perturbed Angular Distribution [*Nuclear physics*]
PAD Peters' United States District Court Reports, Admiralty Decisions [*A publication*] (DLA)
PAD Petroleum Administration for Defense [*Abolished, 1954*]
PAD Phenacetin [*Acetophenetidin*], Aspirin, Deoxyephedrine [*Pharmacology*]
PAD Phonological Acquisition Device (DAVI)
PAD Photon Absorption Densitometry [*Medicine*] (DMAA)
pad Photoshop File [*Computer science*]
PAD Pilotless Aircraft Division [*Navy*]
PAD Pitch Angle Distribution
PAD Pitch Axis Definition
PAD Pitless Adapter Division of Water Systems Council (EA)
PAD Planning Action Directive [*Military*] (AFIT)
PAD Planning and Analysis Division [*Environmental Protection Agency*] (GFGA)
PAD Player Assessment Device
PAD Polar and Auroral Dynamics [*Meteorology*]
PAD Polyaperture Device [*NASA*] (KSC)
PAD Pontoon Assembly Depot (NVT)
PAD Pontoon Assembly Detachment
PAD Poor Acquisition Data (AAG)
PAD Port of Aerial Debarkation [*Air Force*]
PAD Positioning Arm Disk
PAD Post-Activation Diffusion (IEEE)
PAD Post Alloy Diffusion (IAA)
PAD Potential Area of Danger [*Navigation*]
PAD Power Amplifier Device [*or Driver*]
PAD Preadvisory Data (KSC)
PAD Precise Access Diagram
PAD Preferred Arrival Date (AFM)
PAD Preliminary Advisory Data (MCD)
PAD Presence and Amplitude Detector
PAD Pressure Anomaly Difference (PDAA)
PAD Preventive Aggressive Device [*Restraint*] [*Medicine*]
PAD Primary Aeronautical Designation (DNAB)
PAD Primary Affective Disorder [*Psychiatry*] (DAVI)
PAD Primary Afferent Depolarization [*Electrophysiology*]
PAD Procurement Acquisition Directive
PAD Product Assembly Document
PAD Product Assembly Drawing [*Automotive project management*]
PAD Product Assurance Directorate [*Armament, Munitions, and Chemical Command*] [*Army*]
PAD Professional Administrative Development [*Medicine*]
PAD Professional Express Courier Service, Inc. [*ICAO designator*] (FAAC)
PAD Program Action Directive (AFM)
PAD Program Analysis Division (AAGC)
PAD Program Analysis for Documentation [*Computer science*]
PAD Program Approval Document [*NASA*] (KSC)
PAD Project Approval Document [*NASA*]
PAD Propellant Acquisition Device (NASA)
PAD Propellant-Actuated Device
PAD Provisional Acceptance Date (NATG)
PAD Psychoaffective Disorder [*Psychiatry*] (DAVI)
PAD Public Affairs Division [*Military*] (AABC)
PAD Public Assistance Director [*Federal disaster planning*]
PAD Pueblo Army Depot [*Colorado*]
PAD Pulmonary Artery Diastolic [*Pressure*] [*Cardiology*]
PAD Pulsatile Assist Device [*Cardiology*]
PAD Pulse Averaging Discriminator
PAD Pulsed Activation Doppler (MCD)
PAD Pulsed Amperometric Detection [*Electroanalytical chemistry*]
PADA Payroll Automation for Department of Agriculture
PADA Pharmacists Against Drug Abuse (EA)
PADA Poly(adipicanhydride) [*Organic chemistry*]
PADA Prespin Automatic Dynamic Alignment
PADA Public Address Assembly [*Ground Communications Facility, NASA*]
PADA (Pyridylazo)dimethylaniline [*Organic chemistry*]
PADAC Professional Art Dealers Association of Canada
PADAF Pacific Command Air Defense Analysis Facility (CINC)
PADAL Pattern for Analysis, Decision, Action, and Learning
PA D & C Pennsylvania District and County Reports [*A publication*] (DLA)
PA D & C 2d Pennsylvania District and County Reports, Second Series [*A publication*] (DLA)
PA D & C 3d Pennsylvania District and County Reports, Third Series [*A publication*] (DLA)
PA D & C Rep Pennsylvania District and County Reports [*A publication*] (DLA)
PADAR Passive Airborne Detection and Ranging
PADAR Passive Detection and Ranging [*Electronics*] (IAA)
PADAR Program Approval Disposal and Redistribution [*Army*] (AABC)
PADAT Psychological Abstracts Direct Access Terminal
PADC Pennsylvania Avenue Development Corp. [*Washington, DC*] [*Federal corporatio n*]
PADC Piccole Apostole della Carita [*Ponte Lambro, Italy*] (EAIO)
PADCP Paul Andrew Dawkins Children's Project (EA)
PADD Passive Antidrown Device (DWSG)
PADD Petroleum Administration for Defense District [*Department of Energy*]
PADD Planned Active Duty Date [*Military*]
PADD Portable Acoustic Doppler Detector
PADDS Procurement Automated Data Document System [*Military*] (RDA)
PADE Pad Automatic Data Equipment (PDAA)
PADEL Pattern Description Language
PA Dep L & I Dec Pennsylvania Department of Labor and Industry Decisions [*A publication*] (DLA)
PA Dep Rep Pennsylvania Department Reports [*A publication*] (DLA)
PADER Pennsylvania Department of Environmental Resources

PADER .... Pennsylvania Department of Environmental Resources (DOGT)
PADF .... Driftwood Bay Air Force Station [*Alaska*] [*ICAO location identifier*] (ICLI)
PADF .... Pan American Development Foundation (EA)
PADGEM ...... Platelet Activation-Dependent Granulocyte External Membrane Protein [*Biochemistry*]
PADGERC .... PACOM [*Pacific Command*] Air Defense Ground Environment Requirements Committee (CINC)
PADGT .... Past Assistant Deputy Grand Treasurer [*Freemasonry*]
PADI .... Parti pour l'Avancement de la Democratie en Ituri [*Party for Democratic Advancement in Ituri*] [*Political party*]
PADI .... Professional Association of Diving Instructors (EA)
PADIA .... Patrol Diagnosis (NITA)
PADIE .... Prevention and Detection of Illegal Entry [*Military*] (DNAB)
PADIL .... Patriot Air Defense Information Language [*Army*]
Padin .... Partido de Integracion Nacional [*National Integration Party*] [*Peru*] [*Political party*] (PPW)
PADIS .... Pan-African Documentation and Information System [*Economic Commission for Africa*] [*United Nations*] (IID)
PA Dist .... Pennsylvania District Reporter [*A publication*] (DLA)
PA Dist & Co R... Pennsylvania District and County Reports [*A publication*] (DLA)
PA Dist & Co Repts... Pennsylvania District and County Reports [*A publication*] (DLA)
PA Dist & C Rep... Pennsylvania District and County Reports [*A publication*] (DLA)
PA Dist R..... Pennsylvania District Reporter [*A publication*] (DLA)
PA Dist Rep.... Pennsylvania District Reports [*A publication*] (DLA)
PADK .... Adak/Davis [*Alaska*] [*ICAO location identifier*] (ICLI)
PADL .... Dillingham [*Alaska*] [*ICAO location identifier*] (ICLI)
PADL .... Part and Assembly Description Language [*Computer science*]
PADL .... Parts and Design Language (NITA)
PADL .... Performing and Captive Animals Defence League [*British*] (BI)
PADL .... Personal Activities of Daily Living (DMAA)
PADL .... Pilotless Aircraft Development Laboratory [*Navy*]
PADLA .... Programmable Asynchronous Dual Line Adapter
PADLOC .... Passive Active Detection and Location (IEEE)
PADLOC .... Passive Detection and Location [*Air Force*] (IAA)
PADLOC .... Passive Detection and Location of Countermeasures [*Air Force*]
PADLOCC ..... Passive Detection and Location of Countermeasures [*Air Force*] (IAA)
PAdm .... Professional Administrator (DD)
PADMIS .... Patient Administration Information System [*Army*] (AABC)
PADO .... Proposed Advanced Development Objective [*Army*] (AABC)
PADOC .... Pay Adjustment Document [*Army*]
PADP .... Physicians Against the Death Penalty (EA)
PADP .... Proposal for Advanced Development Program
PADP .... Pulmonary Artery Diastolic Pressure [*Cardiology*] (AAMN)
PADQ .... Kodiak [*Alaska*] [*ICAO location identifier*] (ICLI)
PADR .... Parts and Data Record System (MCD)
PA DR .... Pennsylvania District Reports [*A publication*] (DLA)
PADR .... Production Administration Deficiency Report [*DoD*]
PADRA .... Pass to Air Defense RADAR [*Aviation*] (FAAC)
PADRE .... Particle Analysis and Data Reduction [*Environmental Protection Agency*] (GFGA)
PADRE .... Particulate Data Reduction (EPA)
PADRE .... Patient Automatic Data Recording Equipment (IEEE)
PADRE .... Portable Automatic Data Recording Equipment
PADS .... Parametric Array Doppler SONAR (PDAA)
PADS .... Passive-Active Data Simulation
PADS .... Passive Advanced Sonobuoy
PADS .... Pen Application Development System [*Computer software*] [*Slate Corp.*] (PCM)
PADS .... People Against Dioxins in Sanitary Products [*An association Australia*]
PADS .... Performance Analysis and Design Synthesis [*Computer program*] [*NASA*]
PADS .... Performance Analysis Display System (NITA)
PADS .... Peroxylaminedisulfonate [*Organic chemistry*]
PADS .... Personnel Automated Data System [*TIMMS*] [*Navy*]
PADS .... Planned Arrival and Departure System [*FAA*] (TAG)
PADS .... Plant Alarm and Display System [*Nuclear energy*] (NRCH)
PADS .... Point Air Defense System
PADS .... Position and Azimuth Determining System [*Aviation*]
PADS .... Precision Aerial Delivery System
PADS .... Precision Aerial Display System
PADS .... Precision Antenna Display System (IAA)
PADS .... Professional Application Development System [*Slate*] [*Computer science*]
PADS .... Programmer Advanced Debugging System [*Computer science*]
PADT .... Postalloy Diffusion Technique (IAA)
PADT .... Postalloy Diffusion Transistor
PADU .... Dutch Harbour [*Alaska*] [*ICAO location identifier*] (ICLI)
PADUA .... Progressive Augmentation by Dilating the Urethra Anterior [*Medicine*] (DMAA)
PADUD .... Program of Advanced Professional Development, University of Denver College of Law (DLA)
PADWSS ...... Pulsed Acoustic Doppler Wind Shear Sensing System (PDAA)
PAE .... Everett, WA [*Location identifier FAA*] (FAAL)
PAE .... Paea [*Society Islands*] [*Seismograph station code, US Geological Survey*] (SEIS)
PAE .... Paisajes Espanoles SA [*Spain ICAO designator*] (FAAC)
PAE .... Parachutust Adjustable Equipment Bag [*Army*] (VNW)
P AE .... Partes Aequales [*Equal Parts*] [*Pharmacy*]
PAE .... Passed Assistant Engineer [*British*]
PAE .... Payload Accomodations Equipment [*NASA*] (SSD)
PAE .... Payload Attach Equipment [*NASA*] (SSD)
PAE .... Peoria & Eastern Railway [*Absorbed into Consolidated Rail Corp.*] [*AAR code*]
PAE .... Personal Arms and Equipment [*Army*] (ADDR)
PAE .... Phase Angle Error
PAE .... Photo-Anodic Engraving (PDAA)
PAE .... Phthalic Acid Esters [*Organic chemistry*]
PAE .... Physical Aptitude Examination (AFM)
PAE .... Planning and Estimating (IAA)
PAE .... Polyarylether [*Organic chemistry*]
PAE .... Polyaspartic Ester [*Organic chemistry*]
PAE .... Port of Aerial Embarkation [*Air Force*]
PAE .... Post-Accident Environment [*Nuclear energy*] (IEEE)
PAE .... Preliminary Airworthiness Evaluations
PAE .... Preliminary Army Evaluation (MCD)
PAE .... Preventive Action Engineer (NASA)
PAE .... Problem Assessment Engineering (NASA)
PAE .... Projets pour une Agriculture Ecologique [*Ecological Agriculture Projects - EAP*] [*Sainte Anne De Bellevue, PQ*] (EAIO)
PAE .... Public Affairs Event (NVT)
PAEAC .... Parliamentary Association for Euro-Arab Cooperation (EA)
PAEC .... Pakistan Army Education Corps [*British military*] (DMA)
PAECI .... Pan American Association of Educational Credit Institutions [*Bogota, Colombia*] (EAIO)
PAECT .... Pollution Abatement and Environmental Control Technology [*Army*] (AABC)
PAED .... Anchorage/Elmendorf Air Force Base [*Alaska*] [*ICAO location identifier*] (ICLI)
PAED .... Paediatric [*or Paediatrics*]
PAED .... Plans, Analysis, and Evaluation Division [*Army*] (MCD)
PAEDP .... Pulmonary Artery End-Diastolic Pressure [*Cardiology*]
PAEG .... Prueba de Admisiones para Estudios Graduados (GAGS)
PAEH .... Cape Newenham Air Force Station [*Alaska*] [*ICAO location identifier*] (ICLI)
PAEI .... Fairbanks/Eielson Air Force Base [*Alaska*] [*ICAO location identifier*] (ICLI)
PAEI .... Periscope Azimuth Error Indicator
PAEI .... Purchasing Agents of the Electronic Industry [*Rosedale, NY*] (EA)
PAEK .... Polyaryletherketone [*Organic chemistry*]
PAEL .... Preliminary Allowance Equipage List [*Military*] (CAAL)
PAEM .... Program Analysis and Evaluation Model (IEEE)
PAEN .... Kenai [*Alaska*] [*ICAO location identifier*] (ICLI)
PAEP .... Preliminary Annual Engineering Plan [*Military*] (AFIT)
P AEQ .... Partes Aequales [*Equal Parts*] [*Pharmacy*]
PAES .... Phenyl(aminoethyl)sulfide [*Biochemistry*]
PAES .... Planning Analysis Evaluation System
PAET .... Planetary Atmosphere Experimental [*or Experiments*] Test [*NASA*]
PAEW .... Personnel and Equipment Working [*Aviation*] (FAAC)
PAEWCC ...... Peace Activists East and West Coordinating Committee (EA)
PAF .... Pacific Air Forces
PAF .... Pacific Aqua Foods Ltd. [*Toronto Stock Exchange symbol*]
PAF .... Page Address Field
PAF .... Panaf Airways Ltd. [*Gambia*] [*ICAO designator*] (FAAC)
PAF .... Pan American Foundation [*Defunct*] (EA)
PAF .... Paraburdoo [*Western Australia*] [*Airport symbol*] (AD)
PAF .... Paroxysmal Atrial [*or Auricular*] Fibrillation [*Medicine*] (MAE)
PAF .... Partitive Analytical Forecasting (PDAA)
PAF .... Payload Attachment Fitting [*NASA*]
PAF .... Peak Annual Funding (NASA)
PAF .... Pediatric AIDS Foundation (PAZ)
PAF .... Performing Arts Foundation (EA)
PAF .... Peripheral Address Field
PAF .... Permanent Air Force [*Australia*]
PAF .... Peroxisome Assembly Factor [*Biochemistry*]
PAF .... Personal Ancestry File [*Computer science*] (PCM)
PAF .... Personal Article Floater [*Air baggage insurance*]
PAF .... Philippine Air Force
PAF .... Phosphodiesterase-Activating Factor [*Medicine*] (DMAA)
PAF .... Photoactivated Fluorescence Molecules [*Analytical biochemistry*]
PAF .... Platelet-Activating Factor [*Hematology*]
PAF .... Platelet Aggregation Factor [*Hematology*]
PAF .... Polaris Accelerated Flight [*Chamber*] [*Missiles*]
PAF .... Pollen Adherence Factor [*Immunology*] (DMAA)
PAF .... Portable Arc Furnace
PAF .... Port-Aux-Francais [*Kerguelen Islands*] [*Seismograph station code, US Geological Survey Closed*] (SEIS)
PAF .... Portuguese Air Force
PAF .... Posterior Auditory Field
PAF .... Preadmission Assessment Form [*Health Care Financing Administration*]
PAF .... Prearranged Fire
PAF .... Preatomized Fuel [*Trademark*] [*Petroform product*]
PAF .... Premature Anti-Fascist [*World War II designation used by Army Counterintelligence Department*]
PAF .... Price Analysis File (AFIT)
PAF .... Printed and Fired Circuit
PAF .... Pro-American Forum [*Defunct*] (EA)
PAF .... Production Assembly Facility [*Manufacturing*]
PAF .... Pseudoamniotic Fluid [*Gynecology*]
PAF .... Pseudo-Archaic Forgery
PAF .... Psychoanalytic Assistance Fund (EA)
PAF .... Public Agenda Foundation (EA)
PAF .... Public Art Fund (EA)
PAF .... Publication Authority Form (AAG)
PAF .... Pulmonary Arteriovenous Fistula [*Medicine*]
PAF .... Pulse-Air Feeder [*Automotive engineering*]

PAFA .... Fairbanks/International [*Alaska*] [*ICAO location identifier*] (ICLI)
PAFA .... Pakistan Australia Friendship Association [*Australia*]
PAFA .... Pan-American Festival Association (EA)
PAFA .... Pennsylvania Academy of the Fine Arts
PAFA .... Presidential Academic Fitness Award [*Department of Education*] (GFGA)
PAFA .... Priority Based Assessment of Foot Additives [*Medicine*] (DMAA)
PAFAM .... Performance and Failure Assessment Monitor (MCD)
PAFAMS .... Pan American Federation of Associations of Medical Schools [*See also FEPAFEM*] [*Caracas, Venezuela*] (EAIO)
PAFATU .... Pan-African Federation of Agricultural Trade Unions (EA)
PAFB .... Fairbanks/Wainwright Army Air Field [*Alaska*] [*ICAO location identifier*] (ICLI)
PAFB .... Patrick Air Force Base [*Florida*]
PAFC .... Paul Anka Fan Club (EA)
PAFC .... Phase-Locked Automatic Frequency Control [*Telecommunications*]
PAFC .... Phosphoric Acid Fuel Cell [*Energy source*]
PAFCOMNET ... Pacific Air Forces Communications Network (SAA)
PAFCS .... Prior Active Foreign Commissioned Service
PAFD .... Percutaneous Abscess and Fluid Drainage [*Medicine*] (DMAA)
PAFDEFNET ... Pacific Air Forces Defense Network (SAA)
PAFE .... Place Accepted for Enlistment
PAFEC .... Program for Automatic Finite Element Calculation (IAA)
PAFES .... Prior Active Foreign Enlisted Service (DNAB)
PAFI .... Platelet-Aggregation Factor Inhibitor [*Medicine*] (DMAA)
PAFIB .... Paroxysmal Atrial [*or Auricular*] Fibrillation [*Medicine*] (MAE)
PA Fid .... Pennsylvania Fiduciary Reporter [*A publication*] (DLA)
PA Fiduc .... Pennsylvania Fiduciary Reporter [*A publication*] (DLA)
PAFMECSA ... Pan African Freedom Movement for East, Central, and Southern Africa [*Superseded in 1963 by the liberation committee of the Organization of African Unity*] (PD)
PAFP .... Photochemical Aerosol-Forming Potential of Polluted Air [*Environmental chemistry*]
PAFP .... Pre-Achilles Fat Pad [*Medicine*] (DMAA)
PAFR .... Fort Richardson/Bryant Army Air Field [*Alaska*] [*ICAO location identifier*] (ICLI)
PAFS .... Primary Air Force Specialty
PAFSC .... Primary Air Force Specialty Code
PAFT .... Polish American Folk Theatre
PAFT .... Programme for Alternative Fluorocarbon Toxicity Testing [*British*]
PAFTT .... Program for Alternative Fluorocarbon Toxicity Testing [*Environmental science*]
PAFU .... Patriot Arm Fire Unit [*Weaponry*] (MCD)
PAFU .... Propulsion Arming and Firing Unit [*Military*]
PAFVA .... Polish Air Force Veterans Association (EA)
PAFW .... Farewell [*Alaska*] [*ICAO location identifier*] (ICLI)
PAG .... I Pagliacci [*Opera*] (DSUE)
PAG .... Pacific Gulf Properties [*AMEX symbol*] (TTSB)
PAG .... Pacific Gulf Properties, Inc. [*AMEX symbol*] (SAG)
PAG .... Pagadian [*Philippines*] [*Airport symbol*] (OAG)
Pag .... Page's Three Early Assize Rolls, County of Northumberland [*Surtees Society Publications, Vol. 88*] [*A publication*] (ILCA)
PAG .... Paget Resources Ltd. [*Vancouver Stock Exchange symbol*]
Pag .... Pagoda
PAG .... Panagjuriste [*Bulgaria*] [*Geomagnetic observatory code*]
PAG .... Panjim [*India*] [*Airport symbol*] (AD)
PAG .... Pariaqueductal Grey Matter [*Neurology*] (DAVI)
PAG .... Parts Acquisition Group
PAG .... Party for the Autonomy of Gibraltar [*Political party*] (PPW)
PAG .... Pentaacetylglucose [*Laundry bleach activator*]
PAG .... Periaqueductal Gray Matter [*Brain anatomy*]
PAG .... Perimeter Aviation Ltd. [*Canada ICAO designator*] (FAAC)
PAG .... Pesticide Assessment Guideline [*Environmental Protection Agency*]
PAG .... Photoacid Generator
Pag .... Piper [*Airplane code*]
PAG .... Polyacrylamide Gel [*Analytical chemistry*]
PAG .... Polyalkylene Glycol [*Organic chemistry*]
PAg .... Poultry-Related Antigens [*Immunology*]
PAG .... Poverty Advisory Group
PAG .... Prealbumin Globulin [*Biochemistry*] (OA)
PAG .... Precision Alignment Gyrocompass
PAG .... Precursor Active Galaxies
PAG .... Pregnancy-Associated alpha-Glycoprotein [*Gynecology*]
PAG .... Preliminary Analysis Group (NATG)
PAG .... Prince Albert's Guard [*British military*] (DMA)
PAG .... Professional Activities Group
PAg .... Professional Agrologist (DD)
PAG .... Professional Auto Group, Inc.
PAG .... Program Assessment Guide [*Department of Labor*] (OICC)
PAG .... Progress Analysis Group [*Navy*] (MCD)
PAG .... Project Advisory Group [*Army*]
PAG .... Property Advisory Group [*British*] (DCTA)
PAG .... Protective Action Guide [*Nuclear energy*]
PAG .... Protein Advisory Group [*United Nations*]
pAg .... Protein A-Gold Technique [*Medicine*] (DMAA)
PAG .... Spring Garden College, Philadelphia, PA [*OCLC symbol*] (OCLC)
PAGA .... Galena [*Alaska*] [*ICAO location identifier*] (ICLI)
PAGA .... Pan American Grace Airways, Inc. [*Also, PANAGRA*]
PAGA .... Proliferation-Associated Gene A (DMAA)
PAGAD .... People Against Gangsterism and Drugs [*South Africa*]
PAGAN .... Pattern Generation Language [*Computer science*]
PAGB .... Proprietary Association of Great Britain
PAGDC .... Past Assistant Grand Director of Ceremonies [*Freemasonry*] (ROG)
PAGE .... Page Generation [*or Generator*] (PDAA)
Page .... Page's Three Early Assize Rolls, County of Northumberland [*Surtees Society Publications, Vol. 88*] [*A publication*] (DLA)
PAGE .... Paging Network [*NASDAQ symbol*] (SPSG)
PAGE .... PERT [*Program Evaluation and Review Technique*] Automated Graphical Extension (KSC)
PAGE .... Philatelic Association of Government Employees
PAGE .... Piston Arrestment Gas Entrapment System [*SPRINT launch cell*] [*Army*] (AABC)
PAGE .... Polyacrylamide Gel Electrophoresis [*Analytical chemistry*]
PAGE .... Preliminary Automated Ground Environment
PAGE .... Preview and Graphics Editing [*Computer science*] (MHDI)
PAGE .... Program for Automated Gated Evaluation [*Cardiology*] (DAVI)
PAGE .... Publish Australia Group Enterprise
PageAm .... Page America Group, Inc. [*Associated Press*] (SAG)
Page Contr ... Page on Contracts [*A publication*] (DLA)
Page Div .... Page on Divorce [*A publication*] (DLA)
PAGEL .... Priced Aerospace Ground Equipment List
PAGEOS .... Passive Geodetic Earth-Orbiting Satellite [*NASA*]
Pages .... Pages, Inc. [*Associated Press*] (SAG)
PAGES .... Past Global Changes [*Marine science*] (OSRA)
PAGES .... Program Affinity Grouping and Evaluation System
PAGI .... Penn America Group [*NASDAQ symbol*] (SAG)
PAGI .... Penn-America Group [*NASDAQ symbol*] (TTSB)
PAGICEP .... Petroleum and Gas Industry Communications Emergency Plan [*FCC*]
Paging .... Paging Network, Inc. [*Associated Press*] (SAG)
Paging .... Paging Partners Corp. [*Associated Press*] (SAG)
PagingN .... Paging Network Inc. [*Associated Press*] (SAG)
PagingP .... Paging Partners Corp. [*Associated Press*] (SAG)
PAGIS .... Performance Assessment of Geological Isolation System [*Nuclear energy*] (NUCP)
Pag Jud Puz ... Paget's Judicial Puzzles [*A publication*] (DLA)
PAGK .... Gulkana [*Alaska*] [*ICAO location identifier*] (ICLI)
PAGL .... Pulsed Argon Gas LASER
PAGMK .... Primary African Green Monkey Kidney [*Cells*]
PAGN .... Pagnall [*England*]
PAGS .... Parti de l'Avant-Garde Socialiste [*Socialist Vanguard Party*] [*Algeria*] [*Political party*] (PD)
PAGS .... Polish-American Guardian Society (EA)
PAGTU .... Pan-American Ground Training Unit
PAGZ .... Pages, Inc. [*NASDAQ symbol*] (SAG)
PAH .... Paducah [*Kentucky*] [*Airport symbol*] (OAG)
PAH .... Pahoa [*Hawaii*] [*Seismograph station code, US Geological Survey Closed*] (SEIS)
PAH .... Panorama Air Tour, Inc. [*ICAO designator*] (FAAC)
PAH .... Para-Aminohippurate [*Clearance Test*] [*Urology*] (DAVI)
PAH .... Para-Aminohippuric [*Biochemistry*]
PAH .... Parts Application Handbook
PAH .... Pathtechnics Ltd. [*Vancouver Stock Exchange symbol*]
PAH .... Patriot Amer Hospitality [*NYSE symbol*] (TTSB)
PAH .... Patriot American Hospitality, Inc. [*NYSE symbol*] (SAG)
PAH .... Payload Accommodations Handbook [*NASA*] (NASA)
PAH .... Phase Adjusting Hub
PAH .... Phenylalanine Hydroxylase [*An enzyme*]
Pah .... Piper Pressurised Prop-Jet [*Airplane code*]
PAH .... Pitch Attitude Hold [*Aviation*] (MCD)
PAH .... Polycyclic [*or Polynuclear*] Aromatic Hydrocarbon [*Organic chemistry*]
PAH .... Polycyclic Aromatic Hydrocarbon
PAH .... Polycyclic Aromatic Hydrocarbons [*Automotive emissions*] [*Organic chemistry*]
PAH .... Pulmonary Artery Hypertension [*Medicine*]
PAH .... Pulmonary Artery Hypotension [*Cardiology*] (DAVI)
PAH .... Push and Hold [*Push button*]
PAHA .... Para-Aminohippuric Acid
PAHA .... Polish American Historical Association (EA)
PAHA .... Procainamide-Hydroxylamine (DMAA)
PAHBAH .... Para-Hydroxybenzoic Acid Hydrazide [*Organic chemistry*]
PAHC .... Pan American Highway Congresses (EA)
PAHC .... Pontifical Association of the Holy Childhood (EA)
PAHCOM .... Professional Association of Health Care Office Managers
PAHEF .... Pan American Health and Education Foundation (EA)
PAHEL .... Pay Records and Health Records
PAHEO .... Particle Accelerators in High Earth Orbit [*Proposed*]
PAHEP .... Plasma and High Energy Physics (IAA)
PAHF .... Pan American Hockey Federation [*Winnipeg, MB*] (EAIO)
PAHL .... Pressure Alarm, High-Limit [*Nuclear energy*] (NRCH)
PAHO .... Homer [*Alaska*] [*ICAO location identifier*] (ICLI)
PAHO .... Pan American Health Organization (EA)
PAHR .... Post-Accident Heat Removal [*Nuclear energy*]
PAHS .... Passive Annual Heat Storage [*Housing technology*]
PAI .... Kitty Hawk Aircargo, Inc. [*ICAO designator*] (FAAC)
PAI .... Pacific Aerospace Index (DIT)
PAI .... Pacific American Income Shares, Inc. [*NYSE symbol*] (SPSG)
PAI .... Pacific American Institute (EA)
PAI .... Pacific Am'n Inc. Shrs [*NYSE symbol*] (TTSB)
PAI .... Pacoima, CA [*Location identifier FAA*] (FAAL)
Pai .... Paige's New York Chancery Reports [*A publication*] (DLA)
Pai .... Paine's United States Circuit Court Reports [*A publication*] (DLA)
PAI .... Pair Attraction Inventory [*Premarital, marital, and family counseling test*] [*Psychology*]
PAI .... Parachute Association of Ireland (EAIO)
PAI .... Paradise Airways, Inc. [*FAA designator*] (FAAC)
PAI .... Parti Africain de l'Independance [*African Independence Party*] [*Senegal*] [*Political party*] (PPW)
PAI .... Partido Aragones Independiente [*Spain Political party*] (EY)
PAI .... Parts Application Information [*Manufacturing*]

PAI............ Passive-Aggressive Index [*Psychology*]
PAI............ Patient Assesment Instrument [*Medicine*] (DMAA)
PAI............ Percent Adherence Index
PAI............ Performance Audit Inspection [*Environmental Protection Agency*] (GFGA)
PAI............ Performance Audit Inspection (GNE)
PAI............ Personal Accident Insurance
PAI............ Personal Adjustment Inventory [*Psychology*]
PAI............ Personnel Accreditation Institute (EA)
PAI............ Phosphate Adsorption Index [*Analytical chemistry*]
PAI............ Photographic Administrators, Inc. (EA)
PAI............ Piedmont Aviation, Inc. [*Air carrier designation symbol*]
PAI............ Piping and Instrumentation [*Nuclear energy*] (IAA)
PAI............ Pirchei Agudath Israel (EA)
PAI............ Place Accumulator in Indicators (IAA)
PAI............ Plasminogen-Activator Inhibitor [*Biochemistry*]
PAI............ Plunger Actuated Indexer
PAI............ Poale Agudath Israel of America (EA)
PAI............ Polish Assistance, Inc. (EA)
PAI............ Polyamide-Imide [*Organic chemistry*]
PAI............ Prearrival Inspection
PAI............ Precise Angle Indicator
PAI............ Primary Aerospace Vehicle [*or Aircraft*] Inventory
PAI............ Process Analytical Instrument
PAI............ Process Automation Interface (IAA)
PAI............ Processed Apples Institute (EA)
PAI............ Production Acceptance Inspection (IAA)
PAI............ Production Adjustment Index [*Word processing*]
PAI............ Professional Athletes International [*Later, NFLPA*] (EA)
PAI............ Programmer Appraisal Instrument [*Computer science*] (IEEE)
PAI............ Project Assignment Instruction (MCD)
PAI............ Property Agents International
PAI............ Protocol Addressing Information [*Telecommunications*] (OSI)
PAI............ Public Affairs Information, Inc. [*Sacramento, CA*] [*Database producer*] [*Information service or system*]
PAI............ Public Affairs Institute [*Defunct*] (EA)
PAI............ Public Assistance Information [*A publication*]
PAIA............ Pan American Implant Association (EA)
PAIB............ Polish-American Information Bureau [*Later, PATIB*] (EA)
PAIC............ Persia and Iraq Command [*World War II*]
PAIC............ Personal Attribute Inventory for Children (EDAC)
PAIC............ Procedures, Alternatives, Indications, and Complications [*Medicine*] (DMAA)
PAIC............ Public Address Intercom System (NRCH)
PAICC............ Professional Association of the Interstate Commerce Commission
Pai Ch............ Paige's New York Chancery Reports [*A publication*] (DLA)
PAID............ Pacific Animated Imaging [*NASDAQ symbol*] (TTSB)
PAID............ Pacific Animated Imaging Corp. [*NASDAQ symbol*] (SAG)
PAID............ Pan African Institute for Development (EAIO)
PAID............ Parked Aircraft Intrusion Detector (PDAA)
PAID............ Personnel and Accounting Integrated Data [*System*] [*Veterans Administration*]
PAID............ Piping and Instrumentation Diagram [*or Design*] [*Nuclear energy*] (IAA)
PAID............ Price and Item Display [*British*]
PAID............ Problem Areas in Diabetes [*Scale*] [*Medicine*] (DMAA)
PAID............ Programmers Aid in Debugging [*Computer science*] (MHDI)
PAIDS............ Paralyzed Academic Investigator's Disease Syndrome [*Medicine*] (DMAA)
PAIDS............ Pediatric Acquired Immune Deficiency Syndrome [*Medicine*]
PAIF............ Persia and Iraq Force [*World War II*]
PAIFORCE............ Persia and Iraq Force [*World War II*] (DMA)
PAIg............ Platelet-Associated Immunoglobulin [*Hematology*]
PAIGC............ Partido Africano da Independencia da Guine e do Cabo Verde [*African Party for the Independence of Guinea and Cape Verde*] [*Political party*] (PPW)
Paige............ Paige's New York Chancery Reports [*A publication*] (DLA)
Paige Ch............ Paige's New York Chancery Reports [*1828-45*] [*A publication*] (DLA)
Paige Ch Rep... Paige's New York Chancery Reports [*A publication*] (DLA)
Paige's Ch... Paige's New York Chancery Reports [*A publication*] (DLA)
PAIgG............ Platelet-Associated Immunoglobulin G [*Hematology*]
PAIGH............ Pan American Institute of Geography and History [*Research center Mexico*] (IRC)
PAIL............ Iliamna [*Alaska*] [*ICAO location identifier*] (ICLI)
PAIL............ Post-Attack Intercontinental Link
PAILS............ Projectile Airburst and Impact Location System
PAILS............ Publication Automated Information Locator System [*Army*]
PAIM............ Indian Mountain Air Force Station [*Alaska*] [*ICAO location identifier*] (ICLI)
PAIM............ Parti Africain pour l'Independance des Masses [*African Party for the Independence of the Masses*] [*Senegal*] [*Political party*] (PPW)
PAIM............ Primary Air Inlet Muffler (MCD)
PAIMEG............ Pan American Institute of Mining, Engineering, and Geology [*Defunct*]
Paine............ Paine's United States Circuit Court Reports [*A publication*] (DLA)
Paine & D Pr... Paine and Duer's Practice [*A publication*] (DLA)
Paine CC............ Paine's United States Circuit Court Reports [*A publication*] (DLA)
Paine CCR............ Paine's United States Circuit Court Reports [*A publication*] (DLA)
Paine Cir Ct R... Paine's United States Circuit Court Reports [*A publication*] (DLA)
PAINT............ Painting (ROG)
PAINT............ Painting
PAINT............ Post-Attack Intelligence
PainWeb............ PaineWebber Group, Inc. [*Associated Press*] (SAG)
PainWP............ Paine Webber Premier Tax Free Income [*Associated Press*] (SAG)
PAIP............ Preverbal Assessment-Intervention Profile [*Test*]
PAIP............ Production Acceleration Insurance Program
PAIP............ Public Affairs and Information Program [*Atomic Industrial Forum*] (NRCH)
PAIR............ Pairgain Technologies [*NASDAQ symbol*] (SAG)
PAIR............ Performance Accountability and Improvement Report
PAIR............ Performance and Improved Reliability
PAIR............ Performance and Integration Retrofit
PAIR............ Performance Assessment in Reading [*Educational test*]
PAIR............ Precision Approach Interferometer RADAR (MCD)
PAIR............ Preliminary Assessment Information Rule [*Environmental Protection Agency*]
PAIR............ Procurement Automated Integrated Requirements (MCD)
PAIR............ Psychological Audit for Interpersonal Relations [*Psychology*]
PAIR............ Pulse-Air Injection Reactor [*Automotive engineering*]
PAIRC............ Polish American Immigration and Relief Committee (EA)
PAIRS............ Parent Assisted Instruction in Reading and Spelling (AIE)
PAIRS............ Private Aircraft Inspection Reporting System (PDAA)
PAIRS............ Product Assurance Information Retrieval System [*Boeing*]
PAIRS............ Program for the Analysis of Infrared Spectra [*Computer program*] [*Analytical chemistry*]
PairTch............ Pairgain Technologies [*Associated Press*] (SAG)
PAIS............ Padre Island National Seashore [*National Park Service designation*]
PAIS............ Partido Amplio de Izquierda Socialista [*Chile*] [*Political party*] (EY)
PAIS............ Partido Autentico Institucional Salvadoreno [*Salvadoran Authentic Institutional Party*] [*Political party*] (PPW)
PAIS............ Personnel Authentication Identification System (MCD)
PAIS............ Petroleum Abstracts Information Services [*University of Tulsa*] [*Oklahoma*] [*Information service or system*] (IID)
PAIS............ Project Analysis Information System [*Agency for International Development*]
PAIS............ Prototype Advanced Indicator System (MCD)
PAIS............ Psychological Abstracts Information Services [*American Psychological Association*]
PAIS............ Psychosocial Adjustment to Illness Scale [*Personality development test*] [*Psychology*]
PAISA............ Partido Autentico Institucional Salvadoreno [*Salvadoran Authentic Institutional Party*] [*Political party*] (EY)
PAIS FLI............ PAIS Foreign Language Index (NITA)
PAIT............ Program for Advancement of Industrial Technology [*Canada*]
PAIVS............ Pulmonary Atresia with Intact Ventricular Septum [*Cardiology*] (DAVI)
PAIX............ Pacific Alaska Airlines [*Air carrier designation symbol*]
PAJ............ Kansas City, MO [*Location identifier FAA*] (FAAL)
PAJ............ Paralysis Agitans Juvenilis [*Medicine*] (DMAA)
PAJ............ Performing Arts Journal [*A publication*]
PAJA............ Parachute Jumping Activities [*Aviation*] (FAAC)
PAJAR............ Parti Rakyat Jati Sarawak [*Sarawak Native People's Party*] [*Malaysia*] [*Political party*] (PPW)
PAJES............ Parents of Adult Jewish Singles
PAJN............ Juneau [*Alaska*] [*ICAO location identifier*] (ICLI)
PAK............ Hanapepe, HI [*Location identifier FAA*] (FAAL)
PAK............ Pacific Alaska Airlines [*ICAO designator*] (FAAC)
PAK............ Pakistan [*ANSI three-letter standard code*] (CNC)
Pak............ Pakistan (VRA)
PAK............ Panzer Abwehr Kanone [*Cannon Against Armor*] [*German antitank gun*]
PAK............ Performance Advantage Kit [*Personal computers*]
PAK............ Polycyclic Aromatic Ketone [*Organic chemistry*]
PAK............ Power Amplifier Klystron
PAK............ Program Attention Key [*Computer science*] (BUR)
Pak Bar J............ Pakistan Bar Journal [*A publication*] (DLA)
Pak Crim LJ... Pakistan Criminal Law Journal [*A publication*] (DLA)
PAKEX............ International Packaging Exhibition [*British*] (ITD)
PakisInv............ Pakistan Investment Fund, Inc. [*Associated Press*] (SAG)
Pak LR............ Pakistan Law Reports [*India*] [*A publication*] (DLA)
Pak L Rev............ Pakistan Law Review [*A publication*] (DLA)
PAKN............ King Salmon [*Alaska*] [*ICAO location identifier*] (ICLI)
Pak Sup Ct Q... Pakistan Supreme Court Law Quarterly [*Lahore, Pakistan*] [*A publication*] (DLA)
PAKT............ Ketchikan [*Alaska*] [*ICAO location identifier*] (ICLI)
PAL............ Allegheny County Law Library, Pittsburgh, PA [*OCLC symbol*] (OCLC)
PAL............ Pacific Aeronautical Library
PAL............ Pacific Air Lines
pal............ Pahlavi [*MARC language code Library of Congress*] (LCCP)
PAL............ Paired-Associates Learning [*Task*] [*Psychology*]
PAL............ Palace
Pal............ Palamedes [*of Gorgias*] [*Classical studies*] (OCD)
pal............ Palate (DMAA)
PAL............ Palatine [*or Palatinate*] [*Genealogy*]
PAL............ Paleography (ROG)
PAL............ Paleontology
PAL............ Paleozoic [*Period, era, or system*] [*Geology*]
PAL............ Palestine
pal............ Palette (VRA)
PAL............ Palisades [*New York*] [*Seismograph station code, US Geological Survey*] (SEIS)
PAL............ Pallor (KSC)
Pal............ Palmer's Assizes at Cambridge [*England*] [*A publication*] (DLA)
Pal............ Palmer's English King's Bench Reports [*1619-29*] [*A publication*] (DLA)
Pal............ Palmer's Reports [*53-60 Vermont*] [*A publication*] (DLA)
PAL............ Paloma Petroleum Ltd. [*Toronto Stock Exchange symbol*]
PAL............ Paradox Application Language [*ANSA*] [*Computer science*]
PAL............ Parcel Air Lift [*US Postal Service*]
PAL............ Parents Anonymous Lifeline [*British*] (DI)

PAL............. Parser Assembly Language [*Computer science*]
PAL............. Parts and Assemblies Locator [*ADP/CES*]
PAL............. Parts Authorization List (KSC)
PAL............. Passive Activity Loss [*Investment term*] (DFIT)
PAL............. Patent Associated Literature
PAL............. Pathology Laboratory [*Test*]
PAL............. Pectin Acid Lyase [*An enzyme*]
PAL............. Pedagogic Algorithmic Language [*Computer science*]
PAL............. People Against Chlordane (EA)
PAL............. People-Animals-Love (EA)
PAL............. Peptidyl-Alpha-Hydroxyglycine Alpha-Amidating Lysine Phase Alteration Plane [*Medicine*] (DMAA)
PAL............. Perceptual Alternatives Laboratory [*University of Louisville*] [*Research center*] (RCD)
PAL............. Performance Assessment Logic
PAL............. Peripheral Access Lattices
PAL............. Permanent Artificial Lighting (IEEE)
PAL............. Permissive Action Link [*Army*]
PAL............. Permissive Arming Line [*or Link*]
PAL............. Peroxide Assisted Leach [*Ore processing*]
PAL............. Personal Assets Line
PAL............. Personnel Accounting Level [*Air Force*] (AFM)
PAL............. Personnel Address Listing (SAA)
PAL............. Personnel Airlock [*Nuclear energy*] (NRCH)
PAL............. Personnel Augmentation List [*Military*]
PAL............. Phase Alternate Line (NITA)
PAL............. Phase Alternation Line [*West German color television system*]
PAL............. Phase-Alternation System [*A color TV format*] [*Also, phase alternate each line*] (WDMC)
PAL............. Phenylalanine Ammonia-Lyase [*An enzyme*]
PAL............. Philippine Air Lines
PAL............. Philippine Air Lines, Inc. [*ICAO designator*] (FAAC)
PAL............. Philips Assembler Language (IAA)
PAL............. Pipe Analysis Log [*Gas well*]
PAL............. Point, Area, and Line Source Air Quality Model [*Environmental Protection Agency*] (GFGA)
PAL............. Police Athletic League
PAL............. Police Attendance Line
PAL............. Poly-DL-alanine Poly-L-lysine [*Biochemical analysis*]
PAL............. Positive Arming Link [*Military*] (DNAB)
PAL............. Postal Answer Line [*US Postal Service automated telephone information service*]
PAL............. Posterior Axillary Line [*Medicine*]
PAL............. Power and Light (IAA)
PAL............. Power Assist Lathe
PAL............. Pre-Academic Learning Inventory [*Child development test*]
PAL............. Preapproved Loan [*Business term*]
PAL............. Precision Artwork Language [*Computer science*]
PAL............. Preliminary Allowance List [*Military*] (DNAB)
PAL............. Premier Automobiles Ltd. [*India*]
PAL............. Prescribed Action Link [*DoD*]
PAL............. Present Atmospheric Level
PAL............. Price and Availability List (CINC)
PAL............. Princeton Accelerator Laboratory
PAL............. Princeton Air Link
PAL............. Prisoner-at-Large
PAL............. Privileged Architecture Library Code
PAL............. Problem Action Log (AAG)
PAL............. Process Assembler Language
PAL............. Process Audit List (MCD)
PAL............. Production and Application of Light (MCD)
PAL............. Product of Activated Lymphocytes [*Medicine*] (DMAA)
PAL............. Profile Automobile League (EA)
PAL............. Programmable Algorithm Machine Assembly Language [*Computer science*]
PAL............. Programmable Array Logic [*Computer science*] (IEEE)
PAL............. Programmed Application Library [*IBM Corp.*]
PAL............. Programmed Audit Library
PAL............. Programmer Assistance and Liaison [*Computer science*] (NRCH)
PAL............. Progressive Alliance of Liberia [*Political party*] (PPW)
PAL............. Prototype Application Loop [*Nuclear energy*] (NRCH)
PAL............. Psycho-Acoustic Laboratory [*Harvard University*] (MCD)
PAL............. Public Archives of Canada Library [*UTLAS symbol*]
PAL............. Publications Allowance List [*Military*] (CAAL)
PAL............. Pulsed Argon LASER
PAL............. Push and Latch [*Push button*]
PAL............. Pyogenic Abscess of the Liver [*Medicine*] (DMAA)
PALA............ N-(Phosphoacetyl)-L-aspartate [*Biochemistry*]
pala............ Palace (VRA)
pala............ Palazzo (VRA)
Pala............ Partido Laborista [*Labor Party*] [*Panama*] [*Political party*] (PPW)
PALA............ Partition Affinity Ligand Assay [*Analytical microbiology*]
PALA............ Passenger Acceptance and Load Accumulation [*Aviation*]
PALA............ Phosphonoacetyl-L-Aspartate [*Biochemistry*]
PALA............ Polish American Librarians Association (EA)
PALA............ Prison Atheist League of America (EA)
PALACE......... Profiling ALACE [*Autonomous Lagrangian Circulation Explorer*] [*Marine science*] (OSRA)
PALAEOB..... Palaeobotany
PALAEOG..... Palaeography
PALAEONT... Palaeontology
Pal Ag......... Paley on Principal and Agent [*3rd ed.*] [*1833*] [*A publication*] (DLA)
PALASM...... Programmable Array Logic Assembler [*Computer science*] (IEEE)
PA Law J..... Pennsylvania Law Journal [*A publication*] (DLA)
PA Law Jour... Pennsylvania Law Journal [*Philadelphia*] [*A publication*] (DLA)
PA Laws...... Laws of the General Assembly of the Commonwealth of Pennsylvania [*A publication*] (DLA)
PA Law Ser... Pennsylvania Law Series [*A publication*] (DLA)
PALC........... Palace
PALC........... Passenger Acceptance and Load Control [*Aviation*]
PALC........... Point Arguello Launch Complex
PALC........... Precastable Autoclaved Lightweight Concrete [*Residential construction*]
PAL-C......... Profile of Adaptation to Life - Clinical [*Personality development test*] [*Psychology*]
PALCO......... Pan American Liaison Committee of Women's Organizations (EA)
PALCON...... Pallet-Size Container (MCD)
Pal Conv...... Paley on Summary Convictions [*10th ed.*] [*1953*] [*A publication*] (DLA)
PALCR......... Propulsion Auxiliaries Local Control Rack (DNAB)
PALCRU....... Pay and Allowances Accrue From [*Air Force*]
PALCS......... Permissive Action Link Cypher System (MCD)
PAL-D......... Phase Alternation Line Delay (IEEE)
PALDS......... Point, Area, and Line Source with Deposition and Settling of Pollutants [*Air quality model*] [*Environmental Protection Agency*] (GFGA)
Pale............ Palestine (VRA)
PALE............ Pelvis and Legs Elevating [*Pilot seat*]
PA Leg Gaz... Legal Gazette (Pennsylvania) [*A publication*] (DLA)
PA Leg Gaz... Legal Gazette Reports (Campbell) [*Pennsylvania*] [*A publication*] (DLA)
PA Legis Serv... Pennsylvania Legislative Service (Purdon) [*A publication*] (DLA)
paleob......... Paleobotany (BARN)
PALEOECOL... Paleoecologic
paleog......... Paleography
PALEOGEOG... Paleogeographic
Paleol......... Paleolithic (VRA)
paleon......... Paleontology
PALEONT..... Paleontologic
PALEX......... Pacific Armies Look Exercise
Paley Ag...... Paley on Principal and Agent [*A publication*] (DLA)
Paley Princ & Ag... Paley on Principal and Agent [*3rd ed.*] [*1833*] [*A publication*] (DLA)
Palfed......... PALFED, Inc. [*Associated Press*] (SAG)
PA LG......... Legal Gazette (Pennsylvania) [*A publication*] (DLA)
PA LG......... Legal Gazette Reports (Campbell) [*Pennsylvania*] [*A publication*] (DLA)
Palg Ch........ Palgrave's Proceedings in Chancery [*A publication*] (DLA)
Palgrave...... Palgrave's Proceedings in Chancery [*A publication*] (DLA)
Palgrave...... Palgrave's Rise and Progress of the English Commonwealth [*A publication*] (DLA)
Palg Rise & Prog... Palgrave's Rise and Progress of the English Commonwealth [*1832*] [*A publication*] (DLA)
Palg Rise Etc... Palgrave's Rise and Progress of the English Commonwealth [*A publication*] (DLA)
PAL-H......... Profile of Adaptation to Life - Holistic [*Personality development test*] [*Psychology*]
PALI............ Pacific and Asian Linguistics Institute [*University of Hawaii*]
Pali............ Partido Liberal [*Nicaragua*] [*Political party*] (EY)
PALI............ Prince Albert's Light Infantry [*Military unit*] [*British*]
PALIKA........ Parti de Liberation Kanak [*New Caledonia*] [*Political party*] (EY)
PALINET...... Pennsylvania Area Library Network
PALINET/ULC... PALINET and Union Library Catalogue of Pennsylvania [*Philadelphia, PA*] [*Library network*]
PALIS........... Property and Liability Information System
PA LJ........... Pennsylvania Law Journal [*A publication*] (DLA)
PA LJ........... Pennsylvania Law Journal Reports [*1842-52*] [*A publication*] (DLA)
PA LJR......... Clark's Pennsylvania Law Journal Reports [*A publication*] (DLA)
PALL............ Pallet [*Freight*]
PallCp.......... Pall Corp. [*Associated Press*] (SAG)
PALLNIC....... Palladium-Nickel (EECA)
PALM........... PALFED, Inc. [*NASDAQ symbol*] (NQ)
Palm............ Palmer's Assizes at Cambridge [*England*] [*A publication*] (DLA)
Palm............ Palmer's English King's Bench Reports [*1619-29*] [*A publication*] (DLA)
Palm............ Palmer's Reports [*53-60 Vermont*] [*A publication*] (DLA)
PALM........... Palmistry (ADA)
Palm............ Palmyrene (BJA)
PALM........... Philips Automated Laboratory Management System (NITA)
PALM........... Precision Altitude and Landing Monitor [*Aircraft location*]
Palm Comp L... Palmer's Company Law [*22nd ed.*] [*1976*] [*A publication*] (DLA)
Palm Comp Prec... Palmer's Company Precedents [*17th ed.*] [*1956-60*] [*A publication*] (DLA)
Palmer......... Palmer's Assizes at Cambridge [*England*] [*A publication*] (DLA)
Palmer......... Palmer's English King's Bench Reports [*A publication*] (DLA)
Palmer......... Palmer's Reports [*53-60 Vermont*] [*A publication*] (DLA)
Palmer Co Prec... Palmer's Company Precedents [*16 eds.*] [*1877-1952*] [*A publication*] (DLA)
Palmer Pr Comp... Palmer's Private Companies [*41st ed.*] [*1950*] [*A publication*] (DLA)
PALMES........ Pulsed Appendage Large Mobile Electromagnetic-Pulse Simulator (PDAA)
PalmHH........ Palm Harbor Homes, Inc. [*Associated Press*] (SAG)
PALMNET..... Protocol for Automotive Local Area Network
Palm Pr Lords... Palmer's Practice in the House of Lords [*1830*] [*A publication*] (DLA)
PalmrMd...... Palomar Medical Technologies [*Associated Press*] (SAG)
PALMS......... Propulsion Alarm and Monitoring System (PDAA)
PALMS......... Provisioning Automated Logistics Material System (MCD)
Palm Sh........ Palmer's Shareholders [*34th ed.*] [*1936*] [*A publication*] (DLA)

Palm Wr ...... Palmer's Law of Wreck [*1843*] [*A publication*] (DLA)
PALN ...... Para-Aortic Lymph Node [*Anatomy*] (DAVI)
PALO ...... Phosphonoacetyl-L-Ornithine [*Biochemistry*]
PALO ...... Port Amenities Liaison Officer [*British*] (DSUE)
PALOS ...... Pacific Logistic Operations - Streamline [*Army*]
PALP ...... Palpable [*Medicine*]
palp ...... Palpation [*Medicine*] (DMAA)
palp ...... Palpitation [*Cardiology*] (DAVI)
PALP ...... Pyridoxal Phosphate [*Also, PLP*] [*Biochemistry*]
PALPI ...... Palpitation [*Medicine*]
palpit ...... Palpitation [*Medicine*]
PALR ...... Permissive Action Link Report [*Army*] (AABC)
PA L Rec ...... Pennsylvania Law Record [*A publication*] (DLA)
PALS ...... Paired Associate Learning Subtest [*Speech and language therapy*] (DAVI)
PALS ...... Patient Advocacy Legal Service [*An association Defunct*] (EA)
PA LS ...... Pennsylvania Law Series [*A publication*] (DLA)
PALS ...... People Against Lenient Sentences [*An association Australia*]
PALS ...... People Against Loneliness [*British*] (DI)
PALS ...... Periarteriolar Lymphocyte Sheath (AAMN)
PALS ...... Permissive Action Link System [*Army*]
PALS ...... Phase Alternation Line Simple [*TV decoding system*]
PALS ...... Photo Area and Location System (NASA)
PALS ...... Point Arguello Launch Site (AAG)
PALS ...... Positioning and Locating System [*Aviation*] (PDAA)
PALS ...... Precision Approach and Landing System (NASA)
PALS ...... Precision Approach Lighting System [*Aviation*] (FAAC)
PALS ...... Prestaged Ammunition Loading System [*Army*] (RDA)
PALS ...... Principle of the Alphabet Literacy System [*Software*] [*IBM Corp.*]
PALS ...... Principles of Adult Learning Scale (EDAC)
PALS ...... Prison-Acquired Lymphoproliferative Syndrome [*Medicine*] (DMAA)
PALS ...... Protection Against Limited Strikes [*Military defence system*]
PA L Ser ...... Pennsylvania Law Series [*A publication*] (DLA)
PALS-G ...... Passive Artillery Locating System - Ground Based (MCD)
PALSG ...... Personnel and Logistics Systems Group [*Army*] (AABC)
PA-LS-ID ...... Pernicious Anemia-Like Syndrome and Immunoglobulin Deficiency [*Hematology*] (AAMN)
PALST ...... Picture Articulation and Screening Test
PAlt ...... Altoona Area Public Library, Altoona, PA [*Library symbol Library of Congress*] (LCLS)
PALT ...... Procurement Administrative Lead Time
PALU ...... Cape Lisburne Air Force Station [*Alaska*] [*ICAO location identifier*] (ICLI)
PALU ...... Progressive Arbeiders- en Landbouwersunie [*Progressive Workers' and Farm Laborers' Union*] [*Surinam*] [*Political party*] (PPW)
Palud ...... Paludonus [*Pierre de la Palu*] [*Deceased, 1342*] [*Authority cited in pre-1607 legal work*] (DSA)
PALV ...... Passiflora Latent Virus [*Plant pathology*]
PALW ...... Plasma Arc-augmented Laser Welding
PALX ...... Private Automatic Loudspeaking Exchange [*Telecommunications*] (IAA)
PAM ...... Pacific Armies Management
PAM ...... Palermo [*California*] [*Seismograph station code, US Geological Survey*] (SEIS)
PAM ...... Pamida Holdings [*AMEX symbol*] (TTSB)
PAM ...... Pamida Holdings Corp. [*AMEX symbol*] (SPSG)
PAM ...... Pamour, Inc. [*Toronto Stock Exchange symbol*]
Pam ...... Pampa [*Record label*] [*Brazil*]
PAM ...... Pamphlet (AFM)
pam ...... Pamphlet (WDMC)
PAM ...... PAM Transportation Services, Inc. [*Associated Press*] (SAG)
PAM ...... Panama City, FL [*Location identifier FAA*] (FAAL)
PAM ...... Panel Monitor (MHDI)
PAM ...... Panoramic
PAM ...... Panvalet Access Method (IAA)
PAM ...... Parameter Adjusting Mechanism
PAM ...... Parametric Amplifier (NATG)
PAM ...... Parents Against Molesters (EA)
PAM ...... Partial Mobilization Expansion Plan [*Army*] (GFGA)
PAM ...... Partitioned Access Method [*Computer science*]
PAM ...... Payload Assist Module [*NASA*] (MCD)
PAM ...... Penetration Augmented Munition
PAM ...... Penicillin Aluminum Monostearate [*Antibiotic*]
PAM ...... People's Action Movement [*Nevis*] [*Political party*] (PPW)
PAM ...... People's Anti-War Mobilization (EA)
PAM ...... Performance Analysis Model (MCD)
PAM ...... Performance Assessment Monitoring (MCD)
PAM ...... Performing Arts Medicine
PAM ...... Peripheral Adapter Module
PAM ...... Personal Accounting Management
PAM ...... Personal Applications Manager [*Hewlett-Packard Co.*]
PAM ...... Personnel Action Memorandum [*Military*]
PAM ...... Personnel Availability Model (PDAA)
PAM ...... Phase-Amplitude Modulation
PAM ...... Phased Array Module
PAM ...... Phenylalanine Mustard (AAMN)
PAM ...... Philosophies, Ancient and Modern [*A publication*]
PAM ...... Phoenix Airborne Missile
PAM ...... Phoenix Air Service GmbH [*Germany ICAO designator*] (FAAC)
PAM ...... Pittsburgh, Allegheny & McKees Rocks Railroad Co. [*AAR code*]
PAM ...... Planning, Activation, Modification [*Army reorganization*]
PAM ...... Plasma-Arc Machining [*Manufacturing term*]
PAM ...... Pledged Account Mortgage
PAM ...... Pole Amplitude Modulation (IEEE)
PAM ...... Polyacrylamide [*Also, PAA, PAAM*] [*Organic chemistry*]
PAM ...... Portable Alpha Monitor
PAM ...... Portable Automated Mesonet [*Meteorology*]
PAM ...... Position and Altitude Monitor (MCD)
PAM ...... Postacceptance Modification
PAM ...... Post-Accident Monitoring [*Nuclear energy*] (NRCH)
PAM ...... Postauricular Myogenic [*Medicine*] (DMAA)
PAM ...... Potential Acuity Meter [*Instrumentation*]
PAM ...... Power Assist Module [*NASA*]
PAM ...... Pozzolan Aggregate Mixture (OA)
PAM ...... Pralidoxime [*Pharmacology*] (DAVI)
PAM ...... Pralidoxime Chloride [*Pharmacology*] (DAVI)
PAM ...... Pralidoxime Methiodide [*Biochemistry*]
PAM ...... Presbyterian Association of Musicians (EA)
PAM ...... Pressure-Acoustic-Magnetic [*Minesweeping system*] (DNAB)
PAM ...... Primary Access Method [*Sperry UNIVAC*]
PAM ...... Primary Acquired Melanosis [*Oncology*]
PAM ...... Primary Amoebic Meningitis [*or Meningoencephalitis*] [*Medicine*]
PAM ...... Primary Auxiliary Memory [*Unit*] [*Computer science*] (MCD)
PAM ...... Priorities and Allocations Manual [*Army*] (AABC)
PAM ...... Process Automation Monitor [*Texas Instruments, Inc.*]
PAM ...... Processor and Memory [*Computer science*]
PAM ...... Procurement Aids Man [*Marine Corps*]
PAM ...... Procurement of Aircraft and Missiles
PAM ...... Profit Analysis Model (MHDI)
PAM ...... Program Analysis Memorandum (MCD)
PA-M ...... Program Authorization - Map [*Military*] (AFIT)
PAM ...... Program Automated Method [*Computer science*]
PAM ...... Programmable Algorithm Machine [*Computer science*]
PAM ...... Propulsion Assistance Module (MCD)
PAM ...... Protopan Chloride [*Medicine*] (BARN)
PAM ...... Pulmonary Alveolar Macrophage [*Attacks inhaled particles*]
PAM ...... Pulmonary Alveolar Microlithiasis [*Medicine*] (MAE)
PAM ...... Pulse-Address MODEM
PAM ...... Pulse Amplitude Modulation [*Electronics*]
PAM ...... Pyridine Aldoxime Methiodide [*Biochemistry*]
PAM ...... Pyridine Aldoxime Methyl [*Pharmacology*]
PAM ...... University of Pennsylvania, School of Medicine, Philadelphia, PA [*OCLC symbol*] (OCLC)
PAm ...... Wissahickon Valley Public Library, Ambler, PA [*Library symbol Library of Congress*] (LCLS)
PAM-A ...... PAM [*Payload Assist Module*] Atlas-Centaur Class Spacecraft (NASA)
PAMA ...... Pan American Medical Association [*Also known as Association Medica Pan Americana*] (EA)
PAMA ...... Para-Dimethylaminophenylazopyridine [*An indicator*] [*Chemistry*]
PAMA-A ...... Payload Assist Module - Atlas Class Spacecraft (MCD)
PAMA ...... Polish Alma Mater of America (EA)
PAMA ...... Polyalkylmethacrylate (IAA)
PAMA ...... Pre-Assigned Multiple Access [*Telecommunications*] (LAIN)
PAMA ...... Press Advertisement Managers' Association (DGA)
PAMA ...... Professional Aviation Maintenance Association (EA)
PAMA ...... Pulse-Address Multiple Access [*Satellite communications*]
PAMAC ...... Parts and Materials Accountability Control
PAMAD ...... Parents Against Middle-Aged Discrimination [*British*] (DI)
PAMAI ...... Program of Action for Mediation, Arbitration, and Inquiry [*American Library Association*]
PAMAM ...... Polyamidoamine [*Organic chemistry*]
PAMB ...... Pressure Ambient (NASA)
PAmbT ...... Trinity Episcopal School, Ambridge, PA [*Library symbol*] [*Library of Congress*] (LCLS)
PAMC ...... McGrath [*Alaska*] [*ICAO location identifier*] (ICLI)
PAMC ...... Pakistan Army Medical Corps
PAMC ...... Provident American Corp. [*Norristown, PA*] [*NASDAQ symbol*] (NQ)
PAMC ...... Provisional Acceptable Means of Compliance (MCD)
PAMC ...... Pterygoarthromyodysplasia Congenital [*Medicine*] (DMAA)
PAmC ...... Temple University, Ambler Campus, Ambler, PA [*Library symbol Library of Congress*] (LCLS)
PAMCCS ...... Prior Active Marine Corps Commissioned Service
PAMCES ...... Prior Active Marine Corps Enlisted Service
PAMCI ...... Pyridinealdoxime Methochloride [*Organic chemistry*]
PAMCS ...... Phoenix Airborne Missile Control System
PAM-D ...... PAM [*Payload Assist Module*] Delta Class Spacecraft (NASA)
PAMD ...... Parallel Access Multiple Distribution (PDAA)
PAM-D ...... Payload Assist Module - Delta Class Spacecraft (MCD)
PAMD ...... Periodic Acid Mixed Diamine (OA)
PAMD ...... Price and Management Data
PAMD ...... Primary Adrenocortical Micronodular Dysplasia [*Medicine*] (DMAA)
PAM/D ...... Process Automation Monitor/Disc Version (NITA)
PAMD ...... Process Automation Monitor/Disk Version [*Texas Instruments, Inc.*]
PAMD ...... Public Access Machine Readable Documents (NITA)
PAMDS ...... Price and Management Data Section [*of a stock list*] [*Navy*]
PAME ...... Pandemokratiki Agrotikon Metapon Ellados [*Pan-Democratic Agrarian Front of Greece*] [*Political party*] (PPE)
PAME ...... Primary Amoebic Meningoencephalitis [*Medicine*]
P/AMEA2 ...... Probationary Marine Engineering Artificer, Acting, 2nd Class [*British military*] (DMA)
PAMETON ...... Paracetamol and Methionine [*Pain-relief drug*]
PAMF ...... Portable Arc Melting Furnace
PAMF ...... Programmable Analogue Matched Filter (PDAA)
PAM-FM ...... Pulse Amplitude Modulation - Frequency Modulation [*Electronics*]
PAmh ...... Amherst Papyri [*A publication*] (OCD)
PamHld ...... Pamida Holdings Corp. [*Associated Press*] (SAG)
PAMI ...... Personnel Accounting Machine Installation
PAMI ...... Prairie Agricultural Machinery Institute [*Canada*]
PAMI ...... Primary Angioplasty in Myocardial Infarction [*Cardiology study*]

PAMI ... Professional Arts Management Institute (EA)
PAMIE ... Physical and Mental Impairment of Function Evaluation [*Medicine*] (DMAA)
PAMII ... Protection and Advocacy for Mentally Ill Individuals Act [*1986*]
PAMIRASAT ... Passive Microwave Radiometer Satellite (PDAA)
PAMIRASAT ... Primary Afferent Depolarization (PDAA)
PAMIS ... Processing and Manufacturing in Space [*European Space Agency*]
PAMIS ... Psychological Operations Automated Management Information System (MCD)
PA Misc ... Pennsylvania Miscellaneous Reports [*A publication*] (DLA)
PAMLPU ... Pianoforte Action Makers' Labour Protection Union [*British*]
PAMN ... Procurement Aircraft and Missiles, Navy [*An appropriation*]
PAMO ... Pacific Airlift Management Office [*Military*]
PAMO ... Port Air Materiel Office
PAMP ... Pampero [*River Plate gale*] [*Nautical term*] (DSUE)
PAMP ... Pulmonary Artery Mean Pressure [*Medicine*] (MEDA)
PAMPA ... Pacific Area Movement Priority Agency [*Military*]
PAMPA ... Precision Aerobatics Model Pilots Association (EA)
PamPAC ... Pamela's Political Action Committee [*Nickname of "Democrats for the '80's," a committee founded by Pamela Harriman*]
PAMPER ... Practical Application of Mid-Points for Exponential Regression
PAMPH ... Pamphlet [*Freight*]
Pamph Laws ... Pamphlet Laws, Acts [*A publication*] (DLA)
Pamphl Laws ... Pamphlet Laws, Acts [*A publication*] (DLA)
PAMPS ... Poly(Acrylamidomethyl Propane) Sulphonic Acid [*Organic chemistry*]
PAMPUS ... Photons for Atomic and Molecular Processes and Universal Studies [*Physics*]
PAMR ... Anchorage/Merrill Field [*Alaska*] [*ICAO location identifier*] (ICLI)
Pamrapo ... Pamrapo Bancorp, Inc. [*Associated Press*] (SAG)
PAMRF ... Palo Alto Medical Research Foundation [*Research center*] (RCD)
PAMRS ... Parameter Adaptive Model Reference System
PAMS ... Pacific Advanced Media Studies [*Australia*]
PAMS ... Pacific Armies Management Seminar
PAMS ... Pad Abort Measuring System [*NASA*] (KSC)
PAMS ... Paging Area Memory Space [*Computer science*] (IAA)
PAMS ... Plan Analysis and Modeling System (MHDB)
PAMS ... Portable Acoustic Monitoring System
PAMS ... Post-Accident Monitoring System [*Nuclear energy*] (NRCH)
PAMS ... Predictive Aircraft Maintenance System
PAMS ... Preselected Alternate Master-Slave [*Telecommunications*] (TEL)
PAMS ... Printing Advisory and Management Service (DGA)
PAMS ... Procurement Action Management System (MCD)
PAMS ... Public Access Message System
PAMTGG ... Pan Am Makes the Going Great [*Title of ballet choreographed by George Balanchine, taken from Pan American World Airways' slogan*] [*Pronounced "pam-ti-guh-guh"*]
PAMUSA ... Post-Attack Mobilization of the United States Army
PAMUX ... Parallel Addressable Multiplexer [*Telecommunications*] (IAA)
PAMV ... Petunia Asteroid Mosaic Virus [*Plant pathology*]
PAMWA ... Pan American Medical Women's Alliance (EA)
PAMX ... Pancho's Mexican Buffet [*NASDAQ symbol*] (TTSB)
PAMX ... Pancho's Mexican Buffet, Inc. [*NASDAQ symbol*] (NQ)
PAN ... National Action Party [*Mexico Political party*] (PD)
PAN ... Pagans Against Nukes [*British*] (DI)
PAN ... Paladin Fuel Technology [*Vancouver Stock Exchange symbol*]
PAN ... Panama [*ANSI three-letter standard code*] (CNC)
Pan ... Panama (ODBW)
Pan ... Panama (VRA)
pan ... Panchromatic [*Photography*] (WDMC)
PAN ... Panchromatic (DEN)
Pan ... Panegyricus [*of Pliny the Younger*] [*Classical studies*] (OCD)
PAN ... Paneled (WGA)
PAN ... Panimavida [*Chile*] [*Seismograph station code, US Geological Survey Closed*] (SEIS)
PAN ... Panis [*Bread*] [*Pharmacy*] (ROG)
pan ... Panjabi [*MARC language code Library of Congress*] (LCCP)
PAN ... Panoramic (MSA)
Pan ... Panormitanus [*Nicholas de Tudeschis*] [*Deceased, 1445*] [*Authority cited in pre-1607 legal work*] (DSA)
Pan ... Pantheon [*Record label*] [*France, etc.*]
PAN ... Pantry (MSA)
PAN ... Partido de Accion Nacional [*Nicaragua*] [*Political party*] (EY)
PAN ... Pattani [*Thailand*] [*Airport symbol*] (OAG)
PAN ... Peace Action Network (EA)
PAN ... Pennsylvania Animal Network [*Coalition operated by Trans-Species Unlimited*]
PAN ... Pennsylvania Association of Notaries (EA)
PAN ... Performing Artists Network [*Electronic network*]
PAN ... Periarteritis Nodosa [*Also, PN*] [*Medicine*]
PAN ... Periodic Alternating Nystagmus [*Ophthalmology*]
PAN ... Peroxyacetyl Nitrate [*Lacrimator*]
PAN ... Personal Area Network [*Computer science*]
PAN ... Pesticides Action Network (EA)
PAN ... Polled Access Network
PAN ... Polska Akademia Nauk [*Polish Academy of Sciences*] [*Also, an information service or system*] (IID)
PAN ... Polyacrylonitrile [*Organic chemistry*]
PAN ... Polyacrylonitrile
PAN ... Polyarteritis Nodosa [*Medicine*]
PAN ... Positional Alcohol Nystagmus [*Physiology*]
PAN ... Primary Account Number [*Business term*]
PAN ... Project Authorization Notice (MCD)
PAN ... Propodial Anlage [*Zoology*]
PAN ... Publications Account Number [*DoD*]
PAN ... Puromycin Aminonucleoside [*Medicine*] (DMAA)
PAN ... Pyridylazonaphthol [*An indicator*] [*Chemistry*]
PAN ... Switchboard Panel [*Telecommunications*] (TEL)
PA$_{N2O}$ ... Mean Alveolar Nitrous Oxide Tension [*Medicine*] (DAVI)
PANA ... Panaco, Inc. [*NASDAQ symbol*] (SAG)
PANA ... PanAfrican News Agency (EAIO)
PANA ... Pan-Asia News Agency Ltd. [*Also, PANASIA*] [*Hong Kong*]
PANA ... Pan-Asian Newspaper Alliance [*Also, PANANEWS*] (NADA)
PANA ... Panorama (VRA)
PANA ... Polish-American Numismatic Association (EA)
PANABANK ... Banco Panamericano [*Panama*] (EY)
PanaBev ... Panamerican Beverages [*Commercial firm Associated Press*] (SAG)
Panaco ... Panaco, Inc. [*Associated Press*] (SAG)
PANAFTEL ... Pan-African Telecommunications (BARN)
PANAGRA ... Pan American Grace Airways, Inc. [*Also, PAGA*]
PANAIR ... Panama Air Lines
PANAL ... Papuan National Alliance [*Political party*] (PPW)
PANALU ... Parti National Lumumba [*Lumumba National Party*] [*Political party*]
PAN-AM ... Pan American World Airways, Inc. [*See also PA, PAA, PN*]
PANAMAC ... Pan American World Airways Communications System
PanAmC ... Pan Am Corp. [*Associated Press*] (SAG)
PanAmSat ... Pan American Satellite [*Greenwich, CT*] [*Telecommunications service*] (TSSD)
Pan-Am TS ... Pan-American Treaty Series [*A publication*] (DLA)
PANANEWS ... Pan-Asian Newspaper Alliance [*Also, PANA*] (NADA)
PANAR ... Panoramic RADAR
PANASIA ... Organization of Pan Asian American Women (EA)
PANASIA ... Pan-Asia News Agency Ltd. [*Also, PANA*] [*Hong Kong*]
PanASlv ... Pan American Silver Corp. [*Associated Press*] (SAG)
Panax ... Panax Pharmaceutical Co. Ltd. [*Associated Press*] (SAG)
PanaxP ... Panax Pharmaceutical Co. Ltd. [*Associated Press*] (SAG)
PANB ... Panic Bolt
PANC ... Anchorage/International [*Alaska*] [*ICAO location identifier*] (ICLI)
PANC ... Power Amplifier Neutralizing Capacitor (DEN)
P-ANCA ... Perinuclear Anti-Neutrophilic Cytoplasmic Antibody [*Medicine*] (DMAA)
PANCAN ... [*The*] Panama Canal
PANCANCO ... Panama Canal Co. [*Superseded by Panama Canal Commission*]
PANCAP ... Practical Annual Capacity [*FAA*]
panchr ... Panchromatic (VRA)
PancMx ... Pancho's Mexican Buffet, Inc. [*Associated Press*] (SAG)
PANCO ... Procurement Aids Noncommissioned Officer [*Marine Corps*]
Pand ... [*The*] Pandects [*A publication*] (DLA)
PAND ... Pandering [*FBI standardized term*]
PAND ... Passive Air Navigation Device
PAND ... Performing Artists for Nuclear Disarmament (EA)
PAND ... Primary Adrenocortical Nodular Dysplasia [*Endocrinology*] (DMAA)
P & A ... Page and Adams' Code [*1912*] [*A publication*] (DLA)
P & A ... Pay and Allowances
P & A ... Pennsylvania & Atlantic Railroad Co. (IIA)
P & A ... Percussion and Auscultation [*Medicine*]
PANDA ... Performance and Demand Analyser (PDAA)
P & A ... Personnel and Administration [*Army*] (AABC)
P & A ... Pioneer and Ammunition
P & A ... Plans and Analysis
PANDA ... Portable Array for Numerical Data Acquisition [*Instrumentation*]
P & A ... Prediction and Allocation
PANDA ... Prestel Advanced Network Design Architecture
P & A ... Price and Availability
P & A ... Pricing and Acceptability Claims Processing System [*Health insurance*] (GHCT)
P & A ... Print and Advertising [*Marketing*] (ECON)
P & A ... Priorities and Allocations (MUGU)
P&A ... Prizes and Awards Committee (ACII)
P & A ... Procedures and Analysis
P & A ... Procurement and Assignment
P & A ... Professional and Administrative (AAG)
PANDA ... Programmers' Analysis 'N' Development Aid (NITA)
P & A ... Protection and Advocacy [*System*] [*To protect the rights of developmentally disabled persons*]
PandaPrj ... [*The*] Panda Project, Inc. [*Associated Press*] (SAG)
P & AR ... Pacific & Arctic Railway (MHDB)
P & AW ... Paging and Area Warning
P&B ... Pain & Burning [*Medicine*] (DMAA)
P&B ... Phenobarbital and Belladonna [*Medicine*] (DMAA)
P & B ... Phenobarbital and Belladonna [*A drug regimen*]
P & B ... Planning and Budgeting [*Military*] (AFIT)
P & B ... Price and Budgeting (MCD)
P & B ... Printing and Binding [*Publishing*]
P & B ... Pugsley and Burbridge's New Brunswick Reports [*A publication*] (DLA)
P & C ... Parge and Core [*Construction*]
P & C ... Performance and Control (SSD)
P & C ... Physical and Chemical (AAG)
P & C ... Prideaux and Cole's English Reports [*4 New Sessions Cases*] [*A publication*] (DLA)
P & C ... Prism and Cover (Test) [*Ophthalmology*]
P & C ... Procurement and Contracting (AFM)
P & C ... Purchasing and Contracting
P & C ... Put and Call [*Stock exchange term*]
P & CA ... Paying and Collecting Area (AFM)
P & CO ... Plans and Combat Operations
P & CP ... Plate and Cylinder Production (DGA)
P & CR ... Performance and Compatibility Requirements
P & CR ... Planning and Compensation Reports [*British*]
P & CR ... Property and Compensation Reports [*A publication*] (DLA)

P & CYC ...... Police and Citizens' Youth Club [*Australia*]
P & D .... Law Reports, Probate and Divorce [*England*] [*A publication*] (DLA)
P & D .... Perry and Davison's English Queen's Bench Reports [*1834-44*] [*A publication*] (DLA)
P & D .... Pick Up and Delivery [*Business term*]
P & D .... Pioneer and Demolition Section [*Army*]
P & D .... Pressing and Distribution (WDMC)
P & D .... Probate and Divorce [*Legal*] [*British*]
P & D .... Procurement and Distribution [*Military*]
P & D .... Promote and Develop Fishery Products Pertaining to American Fisheries Account [*National Oceanic and Atmospheric Administration*] (GFGA)
P & DD .... Plumbing and Deck Drain (MSA)
P & DR .... Price and Delivery Request
P & DSEC .... Pioneer and Demolition Section [*Army*]
P & E .... Pike and Eel [*A pub at Cambridge University*] [*British*] (DSUE)
P & E .... Planning and Estimating (AAG)
P & E .... Privileges and Elections Subcommittee [*US Senate*]
P & E .... Procurement and Expedition
P & E .... Propellants and Explosives [*Military*] (AABC)
P & E .... Pyrotechnical and Explosive [*NASA*] (KSC)
Pandect Flor... Pandectae Florentinae [*A publication*] (DSA)
P & EE .... Proof and Experimental Establishments (RDA)
P & EML .... Personnel and Equipment Modification List [*Air Force*]
P & ESI .... Physical and Engineering Sciences Division [*Army Research Office*]
P & F .... P & F Industries, Inc. [*Associated Press*] (SAG)
P & F .... Petroleum and Fuel
P & F .... Pike and Fischer's Administrative Law [*A publication*] (DLA)
P & F .... Pike and Fischer's Federal Rules Service [*A publication*] (DLA)
P & F .... Pike and Fischer's OPA Price Service [*A publication*] (DLA)
P & F .... Planning and Forecasting (MCD)
P & F .... Plant and Facilities
Pand Flo ...... Pandectae Florentinae [*A publication*] (DSA)
P & FM .... Programs and Financial Management [*Navy*]
P & F Radio Reg... Pike and Fischer's Radio Regulation Reporter [*A publication*] (DLA)
P & FS .... Particles and Fields Subsatellite [*NASA*] (KSC)
P & G .... Post and Girder [*Lumber*] (DAC)
P & G .... Procter & Gamble Co.
P & G News... Plants and Gardens News [*A publication*]
P & H .... Patton, Jr., and Heath's Reports [*Virginia Special Court of Appeals*] [*A publication*] (DLA)
P&H .... Postage and Handling (WDMC)
P & I .... Passenger and Immigration Lists [*A publication*]
P & I .... Performance and Interface [*Specification*] [*NASA*] (NASA)
P & I .... Piping and Instrumentation [*Nuclear energy*] (NRCH)
P & I .... Postage and Insurance
P & I .... Principal and Interest [*Banking*] (ADA)
P&I .... Principal and Interest [*Finance*] (DFIT)
P & I .... Privileges and Immunities [*Legal shorthand*] (LWAP)
P & I .... Properties and Installations
P & I .... Protection and Indemnity [*Insurance*]
P & ID .... Piping and Instrumentation Diagram [*or Design or Drawing*] [*Calcomp Ltd. Software package*] [*Nuclear energy*] (NRCH)
P & ID .... Piping and Instrumentation Diagram [*Engineering*]
P & ID .... Process and Instrumentation Diagram [*Engineering*] (NRCH)
P & J .... Plaza y Janes [*Publisher*] [*Spain*]
P & K .... Perry and Knapp's English Election Cases [*1833*] [*A publication*] (DLA)
P & KI .... Promisel & Korn, Inc. [*Information service or system*] (IID)
P & L .... Paul and Lisa (EA)
P & L .... Points and Lines [*Military*] (CAAL)
P & L .... Power and Lighting (MSA)
P & L .... Pratt & Lambert, Inc.
P & L .... Profit and Loss [*Accounting*]
P&L .... Profit and Loss Statement [*Finance*] (DFIT)
PANDLCHAR... Pay and Allowances Chargeable
P & L Dig Laws... Pepper and Lewis' Digest of Laws [*Pennsylvania*] [*A publication*] (DLA)
P & LERR .... [*The*] Pittsburgh & Lake Erie Railroad Co.
P & L Laws... Private and Local Laws [*A publication*] (DLA)
P & M .... Law Reports, Probate and Matrimonial Cases [*England*] [*A publication*] (DLA)
P & M .... Pollock and Maitland's History of English Common Law [*A publication*] (DLA)
P & M .... Probate and Matrimonial [*Legal*] [*British*]
p&m .... Probate and Matrimonial (AD)
P & M .... Processes and Materials (NASA)
P & MHEL ... Pollock and Maitland's History of English Common Law [*A publication*] (DLA)
P & MP .... Paris & Mount Pleasant Railroad (IIA)
P & N .... Piedmont and Northern Railroad (AD)
p & n .... Psychiatry and Neurology (AD)
P & N .... Psychiatry and Neurology
P & O .... Paints and Oil
p & o .... Paints and Oil (AD)
P & O .... Parasites and Ova [*Gastroenterology*] (DAVI)
P & O .... Peninsular & Occidental Steamship Co. (AD)
P & O .... Peninsular & Oriental Steam Navigation Co. [*Steamship line*]
P & O .... Performance and Operational [*Test or reports*]
P & O .... Pickled and Oiled
p & o .... Pickled and Oiled (AD)
P & O .... Planning and Operations
P & O .... Planning and Organization
P & O .... Plans and Operations Division [*War Department*] [*World War II*]
P & O .... Portland & Ogdensburgh Railroad
P & O .... Positioning and Orientation
P&O .... Prosthetic and Orthotic [*Health insurance*] (GHCT)
P & OC .... Peninsular & Oriental (Steam Navigation) Co. Ltd. (ROG)
P & O Div .... Planning and Operations Division [*Military*]
p & oo .... Pianistic and Orchestral Orgasm [*Music*] (AD)
PANDORA .... Passive and Active Signal Digital Correlator Analyzer (MCD)
P & OSCC .... Plans and Operations for the Safeguard Communications Command [*Army*] (RDA)
P & OSNCo... Peninsular & Oriental Steam Navigation Co. [*Steamship line*]
P & P .... Packing and Preservation
P & P .... Pam and Peter Fisher [*Commercial firm British*]
p & p .... Parsimonious and Penurious (AD)
p&p .... Payments and Progress (AD)
P and P .... Payments and Progress Committee [*NATO*] (NATG)
P & P .... Peace and Prosperity Issue [*Politics*]
P & P .... Pins and Plaster [*Orthopedics*] (DAVI)
P & P .... Plans and Policies
P & P .... Plans and Programs
P & P .... Postage and Packing [*Shipping*]
P & P .... Pride and Prejudice [*Novel by Jane Austen*]
P & P .... Procurement and Production [*Military*]
P & P .... Production and Procurement [*Military*]
P & P/CT ..... Prothrombin and Proconvertin Control [*Hematology*] (DAVI)
P & PD .... Percussion and Postural Drainage
P & PM .... Packing and Packaging Manual (MCD)
P & PP .... Pull and Push Plate
p & pp .... Pull and Push Plate (AD)
P & PU .... Peoria and Pekin Union [*Railroad*] (AD)
P & PW .... Publicity and Psychological Warfare
P & Q .... Peace and Quiet
p & q .... Peace and Quiet (AD)
P and Q .... Prime Quality [*Slang*]
p & r .... Parallax and Refraction (AD)
P&R .... Parks & Recreation [*A publication*] (BRI)
P & R .... Pelvic and Rectal [*Medicine*]
P & R .... Performance and Resources (NASA)
P & R .... Philadelphia & Reading Railway
P & R .... Picture and Resume [*Theatre slang*]
P & R .... Pigott and Rodwell's Reports in Common Pleas [*1843-45*] [*A publication*] (DLA)
P & R .... Planning and Review (MCD)
P & R .... Post and Rail
P & R .... Pulse and Respiration [*Medicine*]
P and RD ..... Decisions of the Department of the Interior, Pension and Retirement Claims [*United States*] [*A publication*] (DLA)
P & RT .... Physical and Recreational Training [*Navy British*]
P & S .... Packers and Stockyards
P & S .... Pain and Suffering (DAVI)
P & S .... Paracentesis and Suction [*Medicine*]
P & S .... Pay and Supply [*Coast Guard*]
PANDS .... Pay and Supply [*Coast Guard*]
P & S .... Perkins & Squier [*Paper manufacturer*]
P & S .... Physicians and Surgeons (DAVI)
P & S .... [*The*] Pittsburg & Shawmut Railroad Co.
P & S .... Planking and Strutting [*Construction*]
P & S .... Port and Starboard
PANDS .... Print and Search Processor [*Computer science*]
P & S .... Purchase and Sale [*Business term*]
P & SA .... Packers and Stockyards Administration [*Department of Agriculture*]
P & SF .... Panhandle & Santa Fe Railway Co.
P & SI .... Pay and Supply Instruction [*Coast Guard*]
P & SM .... Procurement and Subcontract Management [*NASA*] (NASA)
P & SNP ...... Pay and Subsistence of Naval Personnel [*Budget appropriation title*]
P & T .... Permanent and Total [*Disability*] [*Medicine*]
P & T .... Personnel and Training [*Military*] (MUGU)
P & T .... Pharmacy and Therapeutics
P & T .... Plans and Training [*Military*] (IIA)
P & T .... Posts and Timbers [*Technical drawings*]
P & T .... Professional and Technology [*Category*] [*British*]
P & T .... Pugsley and Trueman's New Brunswick Reports [*A publication*] (DLA)
P & T .... Purge-and-Trap [*Technique*] [*Environmental Protection Agency*]
P & TD .... Parts and Tool Disposition (SAA)
P & T Div .... Plans and Training Division [*Military*]
P&U .... Pharmacia & Upjohn AB [*Commercial firm*] [*Sweden*]
P & V .... Percuss and Vibrate [*Medicine*] (DAVI)
P & V .... Pyloroplasty and Vagotomy [*Medicine*]
P & VE .... Propulsion and Vehicle Engineering [*A Marshall Space Flight Center laboratory*] (MCD)
P & VE-ADM... Propulsion and Vehicle Engineering - Administrative [*Marshall Space Flight Center Laboratory*] (SAA)
P & VE-DIR... Propulsion and Vehicle Engineering - Director [*Marshall Space Flight Center Laboratory*] (SAA)
P & VE-E ..... Propulsion and Vehicle Engineering - Vehicle Engineering [*Marshall Space Flight Center Laboratory*] (SAA)
P & VE-F ..... Propulsion and Vehicle Engineering - Advanced Flight Systems [*Marshall Space Flight Center Laboratory*] (SAA)
P & VE-M .... Propulsion and Vehicle Engineering - Engineering Materials [*Marshall Space Flight Center Laboratory*] (SAA)
P & VE-N ..... Propulsion and Vehicle Engineering - Nuclear Vehicle Projects [*Marshall Space Flight Center Laboratory*] (SAA)
P & VE-P ..... Propulsion and Vehicle Engineering - Propulsion and Mechanics [*Marshall Space Flight Center Laboratory*] (SAA)

P & VE-PC ..... Propulsion and Vehicle Engineering - Program Coordination [*Marshall Space FlightCenter Laboratory*] (SAA)
P & VE-REL... Propulsion and Vehicle Engineering - Reliability [*Marshall Space Flight Center Laboratory*] (SAA)
P & VE-S..... Propulsion and Vehicle Engineering - Structures [*Marshall Space Flight Center Laboratory*] (SAA)
P & VE-TS ..... Propulsion and Vehicle Engineering - Technical and Scientific Staff [*Marshall Space Flight Center Laboratory*] (SAA)
P & VE-V ..... Propulsion and Vehicle Engineering - Vehicle Systems Integration [*Marshall Space Flight Center Laboratory*] (SAA)
P & VIR .... Pure and Vulcanized Rubber Insulation
P & W .... Penrose and Watts' Pennsylvania Reports [*1829-32*] [*A publication*] (DLA)
P & W .... Pension and Welfare (WDMC)
P&W .... Pension and Welfare [*Payments made to talent unions for the benefit of performers*] (WDMC)
P & W .... Post and Wire (ADA)
P & W .... Pratt & Whitney [*Aircraft*]
P & WA .... Pratt & Whitney Aircraft (KSC)
P & WV .... Pittsburgh & West Virginia Railroad
PANE .... Performance Analysis of Networks, Electrical
PanEC .... Panhandle Eastern Corp. [*Associated Press*] (SAG)
Paneg .... Panegyricus [*of Isocrates*] [*Classical studies*] (OCD)
panendo .... Panendoscopy [*Medicine*]
PANES .... Prior Active Navy Enlisted Service
PANES .... Program for Analysis of Nonlinear Equilibrium and Stability [*NASA*]
PANF .... Plan Account Number File [*IRS*]
PANFI .... Precision Automatic Noise Figure Indicator
PANGCS .... Prior Active National Guard Commissioned Service
PANGES .... Prior Active National Guard Enlisted Service
PANGIS .... Pan-African Network for a Geological Information System [*UNESCO*] (DUND)
PANGLOSS... Parallel Architecture for Networking Gateways Linking OSI Systems (NITA)
PANH .... Panhandling [*FBI standardized term*]
PANH .... Picolinaldehyde Nicotinoylhydrazone [*Reagent*]
PANHONLIB... Panama, Honduras, and Liberia [*Acronym used to refer to merchant ships operating under "flags of convenience"*]
PANI .... Patriarch Athenagoras National Institute (EA)
PANIC .... Planned Attack on Nine Inner Cities [*to build education parks*]
Panj C .... Panjab Code [*India*] [*A publication*] (DLA)
Pank Jur ...... Pankhurst's Jurisprudence [*A publication*] (DLA)
PAnL .... Lebanon Valley College, Annville, PA [*Library symbol Library of Congress*] (LCLS)
PANL .... Universal Display [*NASDAQ symbol*] (TTSB)
PANL .... Universal Display Corp. [*NASDAQ symbol*] (SAG)
PANLAR .... PanAmerican League Against Rheumatism [*Canada*] (EAIO)
PANLIBHON... Panama, Liberia, and Honduras [*Acronym used to refer to merchant ships operating under "flags of convenience"*]
PANLIBHONCO... Panama-Liberia-Honduras-Costa Rica
PANLW .... Universal Display Wrrt [*NASDAQ symbol*] (TTSB)
PANMV .... Panicum Mosaic Virus [*Plant pathology*]
PANN .... Professional Association of Nursery Nurses [*British*] (DBA)
PAN NA .... Pesticides Action Network, North America (GNE)
PANNAP .... Panavia New Aircraft Project (MCD)
PANNDA .... Precedent Analysis by Nearest Neighbor Discriminant Analysis
PANNR .... Previous Applicants Need Not Reapply [*Civil Service*]
PANOR .... Panoramic (IAA)
Panor .... Panormitanus [*Nicholas de Tudeschis*] [*Deceased, 1445*] [*Authority cited in pre-1607 legal work*] (DSA)
PA NP .... Brightly's Pennsylvania Nisi Prius Reports [*A publication*] (DLA)
PANPA .... Pacific Area Newspaper Publishers Association (EAIO)
PANPRA .... Parti Nationaliste Progressiste Revolutionnaire [*Haiti*] [*Political party*] (EY)
PANPUB .... Panel Publishers (DLA)
PANR .... Panhandle Royalty Co. [*NASDAQ symbol*] (SAG)
PANRA .... Panhandle Rty [*NASDAQ symbol*] (TTSB)
PanRoyl .... Panhandle Royalty Co. [*Associated Press*] (SAG)
PANS .... Pest Articles News Summaries [*Commonwealth Mycological Institute*] [*Kew, England*] [*A publication*]
PANS .... Positioning and Navigation System
PANS .... Pretty Amazing New Services (NITA)
PANS .... Priority Admission to Nursery Schools (AIE)
PANS .... Procedures for Air Navigation Services [*ICAO*]
PANS .... Programmable Augmented Noise Source [*Military*] (CAAL)
PANS .... Puromycin Aminonucleoside [*Biochemistry*]
PANSDOC .... Pakistan National Scientific and Documentation Center [*Later, PASTIC*]
PANSDOC .... Pakistan National Scientific and Technology Documentation Centre (NITA)
PANSEAFRON... Panama Sea Frontier
PANSMET .... Procedures for Air Navigation Services - Meteorology (IEEE)
PANSS .... Positive and Negative Syndrome Scale [*Medicine*] (DMAA)
PANSW .... Playgroup Association of New South Wales [*Australia*]
PANSW .... Police Association of New South Wales [*Australia*]
PANSY .... Program Analysis System (PDAA)
PANT .... Annette Island [*Alaska*] [*ICAO location identifier*] (ICLI)
PANT .... Pantex Plant [*Department of Energy*] [*Amarillo, TX*] (GAAI)
PANT .... Pantograph (KSC)
pant .... Pantomine
PANT .... Police Association of the Northern Territory [*Australia*]
Pantch .... Panatech Research & Development Corp. [*Associated Press*] (SAG)
Pantex .... Pantex Site
Pantex EIS... Pantex Site Environmental Impact Statement
PANTHEON... Public Access by New Technology to Highly Elaborate Online Networks [*Computer science*] (PDAA)
PANTIES ...... Passive Automatic Nighttime Tracking Investigation and Evaluation Studies [*DoD*]
PAntin .... [*The*] Antinoe Papyrus of Theocritus [*Classical studies*] (OCD)
PAntinoop .... Antinoopolis Papyri [*A publication*] (OCD)
PantiP .... Peroxidase-Antiperoxidase [*Immunochemistry*]
PANTO .... Pantomime
panto .... Pantomime [*British*] [*Slang*] (WDMC)
pantrop .... Pantropical [*Botany*]
PANTS .... Pantaloons (DSUE)
PANX .... Panax Pharmaceutical [*NASDAQ symbol*] (TTSB)
PANX .... Panax Pharmaceutical Company Ltd. [*NASDAQ symbol*] (SAG)
PANXU .... Panax Pharmaceutical Unit [*NASDAQ symbol*] (TTSB)
PANXW .... Panax Pharmaceutical Wrrt [*NASDAQ symbol*] (TTSB)
PANY .... Platinumsmiths Association of New York (EA)
PANY .... Port Authority of New York [*Later, PANYNJ*]
PANYNJ .... Port Authority of New York and New Jersey [*Formerly, PANY*]
PAO .... Palo Alto, CA [*Location identifier FAA*] (FAAL)
PAO .... Paotow [*Republic of China*] [*Seismograph station code, US Geological Survey*] (SEIS)
PAO .... Paragon Group [*NYSE symbol*] (TTSB)
PAO .... Paragon Group, Inc. [*NYSE symbol*] (SAG)
PAO .... Paramount Resources, Inc. [*Vancouver Stock Exchange symbol*]
PaO .... Paranoia Obvious [*Psychology*]
PAO .... Parts Assembly Order (IAA)
PAO .... Peacetime Acquisition Objective [*DoD*] (AFIT)
PAO .... Peak Acid Output [*Physiology*]
PAO .... Penalty Appeals Officer [*IRS*]
PA/O .... Performing Arts/Omaha [*Nebraska*]
PAO .... Peripheral Airway Obstruction [*Medicine*] (DMAA)
PAO .... Phenylarsine Oxide
PAO .... Pinellas Area Office [*Energy Research and Development Administration*]
PAO .... Plasma Amine Oxidase [*Hematology*] (DMAA)
PAO .... Polyalkyleneoxide [*Organic chemistry*]
PAO .... Polyalphaolefin [*Organic chemistry*]
PAO .... Polynesian Airline Operations Ltd. [*Western Samoa*] [*ICAO designator*] (FAAC)
PAO .... Primary Action Office [*or Officer*] [*Army*]
PAO .... Prince Albert's Own [*Military unit*] [*British*]
PAO .... Principal Administrative Officer
PAO .... Pro Athletes Outreach (EA)
PAO .... Procurement Assistance Office (AAGC)
PAO .... Product Activity/Operational Code (MCD)
PAO .... Product Assurance Operations [*Army*]
PAO .... Program Action Officer [*Navy*] (CAAL)
PAO .... Project Action Officer [*Air Force*] (AFIT)
PAO .... Project Administration Officer [*Military*] (AFIT)
PAO .... Property Action Order
PAO .... Public Affairs Office [*NASA*]
PAO .... Public Affairs Officer [*Embassies*]
PAO .... Pulmonary Artery Occlusion [*Medicine*] (DMAA)
PAO .... Pulsed Avalanche Diode Oscillator [*Telecommunications*] (IEEE)
PAO .... Pustulotic Arthroosteitis [*Medicine*] (DMAA)
PA_{O2} .... Alveolar Oxygen Pressure [*in blood gases*] [*Medicine*] (DAVI)
PAO2 .... Alveolar Oxygen Pressure (WDAA)
PAO2 .... Arterial Oxygen Pressure (WDAA)
PaO_2 .... Arterial Partial Pressure of Oxygen [*Medicine*] (DAVI)
pAO_2 .... Oxygen Pressure on Room Air [*Medicine*] (DAVI)
PAOA .... Pan American Odontological Association (EA)
PAOC .... Pakistan Army Ordnance Corps [*British military*] (DMA)
PAOC .... Pan-African Ornithological Congress
PAOC .... Pentacostal Assemblies of Canada
PAOC .... Pollution Abatement Operations Center (MCD)
PAOC .... Principal Administrative Officers Committee [*Chiefs of Staff*] [*World War II*]
PAOD .... Peripheral Arteriosclerotic Occlusive Disease [*Medicine*] (MAE)
P/AOEA2 ..... Probationary Ordnance Electrical Artificer, Acting, 2nd Class [*British military*] (DMA)
PA of W .... Pentecostal Assemblies of the World (EA)
PAOL .... Poly-alpha-olefin [*Organic chemistry*]
PAOM .... Nome [*Alaska*] [*ICAO location identifier*] (ICLI)
PAOP .... Pulmonary Artery Occlusion Pressure [*Cardiology*]
PAOR .... Northway [*Alaska*] [*ICAO location identifier*] (ICLI)
PAOT .... Kotzebue [*Alaska*] [*ICAO location identifier*] (ICLI)
PAOT .... Persons at One Time
PAP .... Asia Pulp & Paper ADS [*NYSE symbol*] (TTSB)
PAP .... Asia Pulp and Paper Co. Ltd. [*NYSE symbol*] (SAG)
PAP .... Langtry Flying Group Ltd. [*British*] [*FAA designator*] (FAAC)
PAP .... Pacific Automation Products (IAA)
P/AP .... Painter/Apprentice Painter (AAG)
PAP .... Pancreatitis-Associated Protein [*Medicine*] (DMAA)
PAP .... Papain [*An enzyme*]
PAP .... Papanicolaou [*Diagnosis, smear, stain, or test*] [*Medicine*]
PAP .... Papanicolaou [*diagnosis, smear, stain, or test*] [*Gynecology*] (DAVI)
PAP .... Paper (DSUE)
PAP .... Paper Bound [*Books*] (ROG)
pap .... Papilla [*Medicine*]
Pap .... Papua [*New Guinea*] (BARN)
pap .... Papyrus (VRA)
Pap .... Papyrus (BJA)
PAP .... Para-Aminophenol [*Organic chemistry*]
PAP .... Parallel Applications Programme [*British*]

PAP .... Participatory Anthropic Principle [*Term coined by authors John Barrow and Frank Tipler in their book, "The Anthropic Cosmological Principle"*]
PAP .... Parti d'Action Paysanne [*Farmers Actions Party*] [*Burkina Faso*] [*Political party*]
PAP .... Partido Accion Popular [*Popular Action Party*] [*Peru*] [*Political party*]
PAP .... Partido Accion Popular [*Popular Action Party*] [*Ecuador*] [*Political party*]
PAP .... Password Authentication Protocol [*Computer science*] (PCM)
PAP .... Patient Assesment Program [*Medicine*] (DMAA)
PAP .... Patrol Amphibian Plane
PAP .... Paulin [*H.*] & Co. Ltd. [*Toronto Stock Exchange symbol*]
PAP .... Payload Activity Planner [*NASA*]
PAP .... Peak Airway Pressure [*Physiology*]
PAP .... Pension Administration Plan [*Insurance*]
PAP .... Pentyl-alpha-pyrone [*Organic chemistry*]
PAP .... People's Action Party [*Singapore*] [*Political party*] (PPW)
PAP .... People's Action Party [*Papua New Guinea*] [*Political party*] (EY)
PAP .... People's Action Party [*Malaya*] [*Political party*]
PAP .... People's Alliance Party [*Solomon Islands*] [*Political party*] (PPW)
PAP .... Periphery Access Processor [*Computer science*] (IAA)
PAP .... Peroxidase-Antiperoxidase [*Immunochemistry*]
PAP .... Personal Auto Policy [*Insurance*]
PAP .... Personnel Allocation Plan [*Navy*]
PAP .... Personnel Assistance Point [*Army*] (AABC)
PAP .... Phase Advance Pulse
PAP .... Phenolphthalein in Paraffin [*Emulsion*]
PAP .... Phenyl Acid Phosphate [*Organic chemistry*]
PAP .... Philippine Aid Plan
PAP .... Phosphoadenosine Phosphate [*Biochemistry*]
PAP .... Photodiode Array Processing (MCD)
PAP .... Photonic Array Processor [*Device for manipulating light beams in an optical computer*]
PAP .... Physics and Astronomy Programs [*NASA*]
PAP .... Pierced Aluminum Plank [*Technical drawings*]
PAP .... Pilotless Aircraft Program (NG)
PAP .... Plant Air Package (IAA)
PAP .... Platelet Aggregation Profiler [*Hematology*]
PAP .... Platelet Alkaline Phosphatase [*An enzyme*]
P a P .... Poco a Poco [*Little by Little*] [*Music*]
PAP .... Pokeweed Antiviral Protein [*Immunochemistry*]
PAP .... Political Asylum Project [*Defunct*] (EA)
PAP .... Politiki Aneksartitos Parataksis [*Independent Political Front*] [*Greek Political party*] (PPE)
PAP .... Polska Agencja Prasowa [*Polish Press Agency*]
PAP .... Poly(acryloylpyrrolidine) [*Organic chemistry*]
PAP .... Poly-a-polymerase [*An enzyme*]
PAP .... Port-Au-Prince [*Haiti*] [*Airport symbol*] (OAG)
PAP .... Positive Airway Pressure (MAE)
PAP .... Prearranged Payments [*Business term*]
pAP .... Presynaptic Action Potential [*Neurochemistry*]
PAP .... Primary Atypical Pneumonia [*Medicine*]
PAP .... Printer Access Protocol (BYTE)
PAP .... Prison-Ashram Project (EA)
PAP .... Procurement and Production (AFIT)
PAP .... Product Assurance Plan [*Army*] (AABC)
PAP .... Production Allocation Program
PAP .... Project Aerospace Plane (AAG)
PAP .... Projected Average Progress (NG)
PAP .... Prostatic Acid Phosphatase [*An enzyme*]
PAP .... Proton Attenuation Procedure
PAP .... Public Affairs Program [*of the American Friends Service Committee*] (EA)
PAP .... Public Assistance Program
PAP .... Public Awareness Program
PAP .... Pulmonary Alveolar Proteinosis [*Medicine*]
PAP .... Pulmonary Arterial [*or Artery*] Pressure [*Medicine*]
PAP .... Purple Acid Phosphatase [*An enzyme*]
PAPA .... Back Bay Restaurant Group, Inc. [*NASDAQ symbol*] (SAG)
PAPA .... Back Bay Restaurant Grp [*NASDAQ symbol*] (TTSB)
PAPA .... Parallax Aircraft Parking Aid (PDAA)
PAPA .... Philippines Alien Property Administration
PAPA .... Pizza and Pasta Association [*British*] (DBA)
PAPA .... Probabilistic Automatic Pattern Analyzer [*Computer science*]
PAPA .... Programmer and Probability Analyzer [*Computer science*] (IEEE)
PAPA .... Psychiatrists Against Psychiatric Abuse [*Canada*] (EAIO)
PapaJohn .... Papa Johns International, Inc. [*Associated Press*] (SAG)
Pap & Disc Vic Inst Eng... Papers and Discussions. Victorian Institute of Engineers [*Australia A publication*]
Pap & Proc Roy Soc Tas... Papers and Proceedings. Royal Society of Tasmania [*A publication*]
PAPAS .... Pin and Pellet Assay System [*Nuclear energy*] (NRCH)
PAPAV .... Papaver Poppy [*Botany*] (ROG)
PAPB .... Point Barrow [*Alaska*] [*ICAO location identifier*] (ICLI)
PAPC .... Processed Apple and Pear Committee [*Victoria, Austrial*]
PAPCA .... Pan-American Progressive Consumers Alliance [*Later, NPCA*] (EA)
PAPCAPS .... Publicly Available Price Cap Agreements (AAGC)
PapclS .... Paperclip Imaging Software, Inc. [*Associated Press*] (SAG)
PAPCNY .... Portuguese American Progressive Club of New York (EA)
PAPE .... Photoactive Pigment Electrophotography (IEEE)
PAPER .... Prairie Association of Publishers Education Representatives [*Canada*]
PAPERCHEM... Paper Chemistry [*Institute of Paper Chemistry*] [*Appleton, WI Bibliographic database*]
PAPERMAN... Payroll and Accounting, Personnel Management, Manpower Utilization [*Air Force*]
PAPF .... Platelet Adhesiveness Plasma [*Hematology*] (DMAA)
PAPH .... (Pyridinealdehyde)pyridylhydrazone [*Organic chemistry*]
Papi .... Papi [*Aemilius*] Papinianus [*Deceased, 212*] [*Authority cited in pre-1607 legal work*] (DSA)
Papi .... Papirius Justus [*Flourished, 2nd century*] [*Authority cited in pre-1607 legal work*] (DSA)
PAPI .... Precision Approach Path Indicator [*Aviation*] (FAAC)
PAPI .... Precision Approach Path Indicator [*FAA*] (TAG)
PAPI .... Professional Association of Pet Industries (EA)
PapJohn .... Papa Johns International, Inc. [*Associated Press*] (SAG)
PaPL .... Pennsylvania Power & Light Co. [*Associated Press*] (SAG)
PAPL .... Preliminary Allowance Parts List [*Military*] (CAAL)
PaPL .... W. and F. Pascoe Proprietory Ltd., Milsons Point, NSW, Australia [*Library symbol*] [*Library of Congress*] (LCLS)
PAPM .... Passed Assistant Paymaster [*British*]
PAPM .... Port Moller Air Force Station [*Alaska*] [*ICAO location identifier*] (ICLI)
PAPM .... Pulse Amplitude and Phase Modulation (PDAA)
PAPMOP .... Product Assurance Program Management Operations Plan (MCD)
PAPMV .... Papaya Mosaic Virus [*Plant pathology*]
Papo .... Partido de Accion Popular [*Popular Action Party*] [*Panama*] [*Political party*] (PPW)
PAPOC .... Parents' Alliance to Protect Our Children (EA)
PAPOILA .... Pacis Amico, Persecutionis Osore, Joanne Lockio Anglo [*Pseudonym used by John Locke*]
PAPOVA .... Papilloma Virus, Polyoma Virus, Vacuolating Virus
PAPP .... Pappenheimer Bodies [*Hematology*] (DAVI)
PAPP .... Para-Aminopropiophenone [*Pharmacology*]
PAPP .... Parametric Aircraft Performance Program (MCD)
PAPP .... Pregnancy-Associated Plasma Protein
PAPP .... Pull and Push Plate (IAA)
PAPPA .... Pulp and Paper Prepackaging Association [*Later, SSI*] (EA)
PAPPGM .... Preliminary Army Planning and Program Guidance Memorandum (MCD)
PAPR .... Powered Air Purifying Respirator (ERG)
PA Prac .... Standard Pennsylvania Practice [*A publication*] (DLA)
PAPRICAN ... Pulp and Paper Research Institute of Canada [*McGill University*] [*Research center*] (RCD)
Paps .... Papillomas [*Medicine*] (DMAA)
PAPS .... Performance Analysis and Prediction Study (PDAA)
PAPS .... Periodic Acid-Schiff with Phenylhydrazine Interposition [*A stain*]
PAPS .... Periodic Armaments Planning System (MCD)
PAPS .... Periodic Arrays of Pinning Sites [*Solid state physics*]
PAPS .... Permissive Arming and Protection System [*AEC*]
PAPS .... Phosphoadenosine Diphosphosulfate [*Phosphoadenosyl-Phosphosulfate*] [*Biochemistry*] (DAVI)
PAPS .... Phosphoadenosine Phosphosulfate [*Also, APPS*] [*Biochemistry*]
PAPS .... Phosphoadenylyl Sulfate [*Biochemistry*]
PAPS .... Procurement and Production Status System
PAPS .... Public Assistance Processing System
PA/PS .... Pulmonary Atresia/Pulmonary Stenosis [*Cardiology*] (DAVI)
PAPSB .... Patent Attorneys' Professional Standards Body [*Australia*]
PA PSC .... Pennsylvania Public Service Commission Annual Report [*A publication*] (DLA)
PA PSC Dec... Pennsylvania Public Service Commission Decisions [*A publication*] (DLA)
PAPSI .... Pregnancy-Associated Prostaglandin Synthetase Inhibitor [*Endocrinology*]
PAPT .... Palladium Print (VRA)
PAPTC .... Pakistan Army Physical Training Corps [*British military*] (DMA)
PAPTC .... Paper Tape Controller (NITA)
PAPTE .... President's Advisory Panel on Timber and the Environment
PAPUFA .... Physiologically Active Polyunsaturated Fatty Acid [*Nutrition*]
PAPVC .... Partial Anomalous Pulmonary Venous Connection (MAE)
PAPVR .... Partial Anomalous Pulmonary Venous Return
PAPW .... Papworth [*England*]
Papy .... Papy's Reports [*5-8 Florida*] [*A publication*] (DLA)
PAQ .... Palmer, AK [*Location identifier FAA*] (FAAL)
PAQ .... Partially Allocated Quotas [*Ocean fishery management*]
PAQ .... Personal Attributes Questionnaire
PAQ .... Port Authorities Queensland [*Australia*]
PAQ .... Position Analysis Questionnaire
PAQ .... Preliminary Allowance Quantity [*Military*] (CAAL)
PAQ .... Process Average Quality
PAQAB .... President's Air Quality Advisory Board [*Environmental Protection Agency*]
PAQR .... Polyacenequinone Radical [*Organic chemistry*]
PAQS .... Pacific Association of Quantity Surveyors [*Australia*]
PAR .... Coastcast Corp. [*NYSE symbol*] (SPSG)
Par .... Guiraudus Pargues [*Authority cited in pre-1607 legal work*] (DSA)
PAR .... Pacific-Antarctic Ridge [*Geology*]
PAR .... Page Address Register
PAR .... Panama Canal Commission Acquisition Regulation (AAGC)
PAR .... Parabolic Aluminized Reflector [*Lamp*]
PAR .... Parabolic Aluminized Reflector [*A spotlight*] (WDMC)
PAR .... Paracel Islands [*ANSI three-letter standard code*] (CNC)
PAR .... Parachute
par .... Paraffin [*Chemistry*] (DAVI)
PAR .... Paragon Resources Ltd. [*Vancouver Stock Exchange symbol*]
PAR .... Paragraph (AAG)
par .... Paragraph (WDMC)
Par .... Paraguay
Par .... Parah (BJA)
PAR .... Paralipomenon [*Old Testament book*] [*Douay version*]

PAR .... Parallax
PAR .... Parallax and Refraction (IAA)
PAR .... Parallel (KSC)
par .... Parallel (WDMC)
PAR .... Parallelogram [*Geometry*] (ADA)
PAR .... Parameter
PAR .... Parametric Amplifier
Par .... Paranoid [*Psychiatry*] (DAVI)
PAR .... Paraphrase (ADA)
PAR .... Parcel
PAR .... Parenthesis
par .... Parenthesis (WDMC)
Par .... Parents Magazine [*A publication*] (BRI)
PAR .... Paris [*France*] [*Airport symbol*] (OAG)
PAR .... Parish
PAR .... Paris - Parc St. Maur [*France*] [*Seismograph station code, US Geological Survey*] (SEIS)
PAR .... Parity (ADA)
Par .... Parker's English Exchequer Reports [*A publication*] (DLA)
Par .... Parker's New York Criminal Reports [*A publication*] (DLA)
PAR .... Parochial
Par .... Parsons' Reports [*65-66 New Hampshire*] [*A publication*] (DLA)
par .... Part (BARN)
PAR .... Partheite [*A zeolite*]
PAR .... Participating [*Health insurance*] (GHCT)
PAR .... Participating Provider [*Health insurance*] (DMAA)
PAR .... Participation-Achievement-Reward (PDAA)
PAR .... Partido Aragones Regionalista [*Aragonese Regional Party*] [*Spain Political party*] (PPW)
PAR .... Partito Anti-Reformista [*Anti-Reform Party*] [*Malta*] [*Political party*] (PPE)
PAR .... Parts Approval Request (MCD)
PAR .... Passive Avoidance Reaction [*Medicine*] (DMAA)
PAR .... Payload Adapter Ring
PAR .... [*The*] Payment Analysis Report [*Dun & Bradstreet Credit Services*] [*Information service or system*] (CRD)
PAR .... Peacetime Airborne Reconnaissance (AFM)
PAR .... Peak Accelerometer Recorder (IEEE)
PAR .... Peak Area Ratio [*Chromatographic analysis*]
PAR .... Peak-to-Average Ratio [*Telecommunications*]
PAR .... Pennsylvania Advanced Reactor
PAR .... People Against Racism [*Civil rights organization*]
PAR .... People Against Rape (EA)
PAR .... Per Acre Rental (WDAA)
PAR .... Perennial Allergic Rhinitis [*Medicine*]
PAR .... Performance Analysis and Review
PAR .... Performance Analysis Routine [*Computer science*]
PAR .... Performance Appraisal Report [*Nuclear energy*] (NRCH)
PAR .... Performance Assessment Report [*Small Cities Community Development Block Grant*] [*Department of Housing and Urban Development*] (GFGA)
PAR .... Performance Augmentation Ring (MCD)
PAR .... Perimeter Acquisition RADAR [*Army*]
PAR .... Perimeter Array RADAR (MCD)
PAR .... Personnel Activity Report [*Office of Management and Budget*]
PAR .... Personnel Activity Request
PAR .... Personnel Advancement Requirement [*Navy*] (NVT)
PAR .... PERT [*Program Evaluation and Review Technique*] Analysis Report (KSC)
PAR .... Phased Array RADAR
PAR .... Phosphoric Acid-Resistant
PAR .... Photosynthetically Active Radiation
PAR .... Physiological Aging Rate
PAR .... Pilot Action Request
PAR .... Plain Abdominal Radiograph [*Medicine*] (DMAA)
PAR .... Planed All Round (DAC)
PAR .... Planning Action Request [*NASA*] (MCD)
PAR .... Planning Activity Report
PAR .... Platelet Aggregate Ratio [*Hematology*]
PAR .... Police Accident Report [*NHTSA*] (TAG)
PAR .... Pollen Accumulation Rate [*Botany*]
PAR .... Polyarylate [*Resin*]
PAR .... Population at Risk (FFDE)
PAR .... Positive Acknowledgment and Retransmission [*Telecommunications*] (IAA)
PAR .... Positive Attitudinal Reinforcement [*In George Lee Walker novel "The Chronicles of Doodah"*]
PAR .... Post Adjudicative Review [*Social Security Administration*] (OICC)
PAR .... Postanesthesia [*or Postanesthetic*] Room [*Medicine*]
PAR .... Postanesthetic Recovery [*Medicine*]
PAR .... Post Attach Requirements (AAG)
PAR .... Potassium-Adsorption-Ratio
PAR .... Power Analysis Report [*Automobile testing*]
PAR .... Preadmission Review (WYGK)
PAR .... Precedent, Action, and Result
PAR .... Precision Aircraft Reference
PAR .... Precision Approach RADAR [*Aviation*]
PAR .... Preferential Arrival Route [*Aviation*] (DA)
PAR .... Price-Adjusted Rate Preferred [*Investment term*] (MHDW)
PAR .... Prime Assets Ratio
PAR .... Princeton Applied Research Corp. [*Princeton University*]
PAR .... Print Area Reader (DGA)
PAR .... Priority Action Report (AAG)
PAR .... Priority Action Request (AAG)
PAR .... Probabilistic Analysis of Risk (KSC)
PAR .... Probable Allergic Rhinitis [*Medicine*] (DAVI)
PAR .... Problem Accountability Record (NASA)
PAR .... Problem Action Record (KSC)
PAR .... Problem Action Request (NASA)
PAR .... Problem Analysis and Resolution
PAR .... Problem Analysis and Response Program (IAA)
PAR .... Problem Analysis Report (MCD)
PAR .... Process Action Request
PAR .... Product Acceptance & Research [*Commercial firm*] (WDMC)
PAR .... Product Acceptance Review (NASA)
PAR .... Production Acceptance Review
PAR .... Production Action Request (MCD)
PAR .... Production Analysis Report
PAR .... Production, Augmentation, and Reliability (NG)
PAR .... Production Automated Riveting
PAR .... Product of Antigenic Recognition [*Immunochemistry*]
PAR .... Professional Abstracts Registries [*Database Innovations, Inc.*]
PAR .... Profile of Average Reflectivity
PAR .... Program Action Request (SSD)
PAR .... Program Activity Recording [*Computer science*] (IAA)
PAR .... Program Address Register
PAR .... Program Adjustment Request [*Navy*]
PAR .... Program Administrator's [*Progress*] Report [*DoD*]
PAR .... Program-Aid Routine [*Computer science*]
PAR .... Program Allocation and Reimbursements (AFIT)
PAR .... Program Analysis and Review
PAR .... Program Appraisal and Review (IEEE)
PAR .... Program Appraisal Report
PAR .... Program Assessment Report [*or Review*] (MCD)
PAR .... Program Audience Rating
PAR .... Program for Alcohol Recovery
PAR .... Progressive Aircraft Repair [*or Rework*]
PAR .... Project Audit Report
PAR .... Project Authorization Request (IAA)
PAR .... Projected Automation Requirement
PAR .... Proposal Analysis Report (AAGC)
PAR .... Propulsion and Aeroballistics Research (SAA)
PAR .... Proximal Alveolar Region [*Medicine*] (DMAA)
PAR .... Pseudoautosomal Region [*Genetics*]
PAR .... Public Administration Review [*A publication*] (BRI)
PAR .... Public Affairs Research Council [*Research center*] (RCD)
PAR .... Publication Analysis Report (SAA)
PAR .... Pulmonary Arteriolar Resistance [*Medicine*] (MAE)
PAR .... Pulse Acquisition RADAR [*Military*] (NG)
PAR .... Purchasing Approval Request (NRCH)
PAR .... Push and Release [*Push button*]
PAR .... (Pyridylazo)resorcinol [*Organic chemistry*]
PAR .... Spair [*Russian Federation*] [*ICAO designator*] (FAAC)
PARA .... Parabolic (IAA)
para .... Paracentesis [*Medicine*] (MAE)
PARA .... Parachute
PARA .... Paragraph (AFM)
PARA .... Paraguay
PARA .... Parallel (WDAA)
PARA .... Paramount Financial [*NASDAQ symbol*] (TTSB)
PARA .... Paramount Financial Corp. [*NASDAQ symbol*] (SAG)
para .... Paraphrase (BARN)
para .... Paraplegic
para .... Parathy Roidectomy [*Medicine*] (DMAA)
para .... Parity [*Gynecology and obstetrics*] (DAVI)
para .... Parquet (BARN)
PARA .... Particle Aiding Replication of Adenovirus [*Virology*]
PARA .... Policy Analysis and Resource Allocation [*Department of State*]
PARA .... Polyarylamid [*Organic chemistry*]
PARA .... Problem Analysis and Recommended Action (IAA)
PARA .... Professional Audiovideo Retailers Association (EA)
Para 1 .... Unipara [*Having borne one child*] [*Gynecology and obstetrics*] (DAVI)
Para-A .... Paratyphoid A [*Medicine*] (DAVI)
PARAB .... Parabola [*Mathematics*] (IAA)
Para-B .... Paratyphoid B [*Medicine*] (DAVI)
PARABAT ..... Parachute Battalion [*Army*]
PARABOL ..... Parabolic (IAA)
Para-C .... Paratyphoid C [*Medicine*] (DAVI)
Paracels ...... Paracelsus Healthcare Corp. [*Associated Press*] (SAG)
paracent ...... Paracentesis [*Medicine*]
PARACOMPT ... Parameter Analysis of Respiration Agents Considering Operations Motivation Protection and Time Model (MCD)
PARACS ...... Perimeter Acquisition RADAR Attack Characterization System (MCD)
PARADA ...... Preparatory Academy for the Royal Academy of Dramatic Art [*British*] (BI)
PARADE ...... Passive-Active Range Determination
Paradl ...... Paradise, Inc. [*Associated Press*] (SAG)
PARADISE .... Phased Array RADAR and Divers Integrated Semiconductor Elements (PDAA)
Par Adm ...... Parsons on the Law of Shipping and Admiralty [*A publication*] (DLA)
PARADROP ... Airdrop by Parachute
PAR AFF ...... Pars Affecta [*The Part Affected*] [*Pharmacy*]
PARAFRAG ... Parachute Fragmentation Bomb [*Air Force*]
PARAG .... Paraguay [*or Paraguayan*] (WDAA)
ParagGg ...... Paragon Group, Inc. [*Associated Press*] (SAG)
ParagGp ...... Paragon Group, Inc. [*Associated Press*] (SAG)
ParagTr ...... Paragon Trade Brands [*Associated Press*] (SAG)
Para II .... Bipara [*Having borne two children*] [*Gynecology and Obstetrics*] (DAVI)

Para III .... Tripara [*having borne three children*] [*Gynecology and obstetrics*] (DAVI)
PARAKU .... Pasokan Rakyat Kalimantan Utara [*North Kalimantan People's Forces*] [*Malaya*]
PARAM .... Parameter (KSC)
ParaMed .... Paradigm Medical Industries, Inc. [*Associated Press*] (SAG)
Parameters... Parameters: US Army War College Quarterly [*A publication*] (BRI)
PARAMI .... Parsons Active Ring-Around Miss Indicator
PARAMIS ...... Parsons Passive Miss Distance Indicating System (SAA)
Par Am Law... Parsons' Commentaries on American Law [*A publication*] (DLA)
Par Am Law Comm... Parsons' Commentaries on American Law [*A publication*] (DLA)
Paramnt .... Paramount Financial Corp. [*Associated Press*] (SAG)
PARAMP .... Parametric Amplifier
ParamrkE ...... Paramark Enterprises, Inc. [*Associated Press*] (SAG)
Paramt .... Paramount Financial Corp. [*Associated Press*] (SAG)
PARAN .... Perimeter Array Antenna (PDAA)
Par & Fonb Med Jur... Paris and Fonblanque's Medical Jurisprudence [*A publication*] (DLA)
Par Ant .... Parochial Antiquities [*A publication*] (DLA)
PARAPSYCH... Parapsychology
PARAQUAD... Paraplegic and Quadriplegic Association of New South Wales [*Australia*]
PARARESCUE... Rescue by Individuals Parachuted to Distressed Persons [*Air Force*]
PARAS .... Parasitic (IAA)
PARASEV ..... Paraglider Research Vehicle [*NASA*]
parasit .... Parasitology [*Medicine*] (DMAA)
PARASITOL... Parasitology
parasym ...... Parasympathetic [*Division of autonomic nervous system*] [*Neurolgoy*] (DAVI)
parasym div... Parasympathetic Division [*of autonomic nervous system*] [*Neurology*] (DAVI)
PARASYN .... Parametric Synthesis [*Computer science*]
PARATHORMONE... Parathyroid Hormone [*Endocrinology*]
PARATROOPS... Parachute Infantry [*Military*]
para VIII ...... Octipara [*Having borne eight children*] [*Gynecology and obstetrics*] (DAVI)
Paravnt .... Paravant Computer Systems, Inc. [*Associated Press*] (SAG)
PARAW .... Paramount Financial Wrrt [*NASDAQ symbol*] (TTSB)
PARB .... Perimeter Acquisition RADAR Building [*Army*] (AABC)
PARB .... Public Accountants Registration Board [*Australia*]
PARBICA ...... Pacific Regional Branch of the International Council on Archives (EAIO)
Par Bills & N... Parsons on Bills and Notes [*A publication*] (DLA)
PARC .... Pacific Air Rescue Center [*or Command*] (CINC)
PARC .... Pacific-Asia Resources Center [*Japan*] (EAIO)
PARC .... Palo Alto Research Center [*Xerox Corp.*]
PARC .... Pan-African Resource Center (EA)
PARC .... Pan-African Rinderpest Campaign [*Organization of African Unity*]
PARC .... Parcelas
parc .... Parchment (VRA)
PARC .... Pennsylvania Association for Retarded Children (EDAC)
PARC .... Pericardial Fluid [*Cardiology*] (DAVI)
PARC .... Periodic Aircraft Reconditioning Cycle (DNAB)
PARC .... Predator and Rodent Control [*US Fish and Wildlife Service*] (IIA)
PARC .... President's Appalachian Regional Commission
PARC .... Princeton Applied Research Corp.
PARC .... Principal Assistant Responsible for Contracting [*Army*]
PARC .... Profile Analysis and Recording Control (PDAA)
PARC .... Progressive Aircraft Reconditioning [*or Repair*] Cycle
PARCA .... Pan American Railway Congress Association
PARCH .... Parchment (ADA)
Par Ch .... Parents' Choice [*A publication*]
Par Ch .... Parents' Choice [*A publication*] (BRI)
PARCHM ...... Parchment (ROG)
PARCHT .... Parchment
PaRCL .... Parsec Research Control Language [*Pronounced "parkul"*] [*Parsec Reseach Robotics*]
Parcls .... Paracelsian, Inc. [*Associated Press*] (SAG)
Parclsn .... Paracelsian, Inc. [*Associated Press*] (SAG)
PARCOM ...... Paris Commission [*See also CP*] (EAIO)
Par Cont ...... Parsons on Contracts [*A publication*] (DLA)
Par Costs ..... Parsons on Costs [*A publication*] (DLA)
PARCP .... PEMARS [*Procurement of Equipment and Missiles, Army Management and AccountingReporting System*] Accounting and Reporting Control Point [*Army*]
ParcPplce .... Parcplace Systems, Inc. [*Associated Press*] (SAG)
PARCS .... Perimeter Acquisition RADAR Attack Characterization System [*Army*]
PARCS .... Pesticide Analysis Retrieval and Control System (NITA)
PARD .... Parts Application Reliability Data (IEEE)
PARD .... Periodic and Random Deviation
PARD .... Personnel Actions and Records Directorate [*Military Personnel Center*] (AABC)
PARD .... Pilot Airborne Recovery Device [*A balloon-parachute*]
PARD .... Pilotless Aircraft Research Division [*Later, Applied Materials and Physics Division*] [*Langley Research Center*]
PARD .... Post-Accident Radioactivity Depletion [*Nuclear energy*] (NRCH)
PARD .... Precision Annotated Retrieval Display [*System*] [*Computer science*]
PARD .... Project Activities Relationship Diagram (PDAA)
PARDAC .... Parallel Digital-to-Analog Converter
Par Dec .... Parsons' Decisions [*2-7 Massachusetts*] [*A publication*] (DLA)
PARDENTL... Paradental
Pardgm .... Paradigm Technology, Inc. [*Associated Press*] (SAG)
Pard Lois Mar... Pardessus' Lois Maritimes [*A publication*] (DLA)
PARDON ...... Pastors' Anonymous Recovery-Directed Order for Newness [*Rehabilitation program for troubled clergymen*] [*Defunct*]
PARDOP ...... Passive Ranging Doppler
PARDP .... Perimeter Acquisition RADAR Data Processor [*Army*] (AABC)
PARDS .... Phased Array RADAR Detection System (PDAA)
Pard Serv .... Pardessus' Traites des Servitudes [*A publication*] (DLA)
PARE .... People Against Racism in Education
PARE .... Price Adjusted Rates of Exchange [*Monetary conversion rate*] (ECON)
PARE .... Program Analysis and Resouces Evaluation (IAA)
P/AREA .... Probationary Acting Radio Electrical Artificer [*British military*] (DMA)
PAREC .... Pay Record
PA Rec .... Pennsylvania Record [*A publication*] (DLA)
PAREN .... Parenthesis [*or Parentheses*] (AFM)
paren .... Parenthesis (WDMC)
PAREN .... Progressive Aircraft Engine Repair
PARENS .... Parentheses (NTCM)
PARENT .... Parenteral
PARENTS ..... People of America Responding to Educational Needs of Today's Society (EA)
Parents Cit Guide... Parents and Citizens Guide [*A publication*]
PARENTSQ... Parent Squadron Base [*Military*] (NVT)
PA Rep .... Pennsylvania Reports [*A publication*] (DLA)
Par Eq Cas... Parsons' Select Equity Cases [*1842-51*] [*Pennsylvania*] [*A publication*] (DLA)
Par Eq Cases... Parsons' Select Equity Cases [*Pennsylvania*] [*A publication*] (DLA)
PARESEV ..... Paraglider Research Vehicle [*NASA*] (MCD)
Par Ess .... Parsons' Essays on Legal Topics [*A publication*] (DLA)
PARET .... Parallel Architecture Research and Evaluation Tool [*Computer science*]
PAREX .... Programmed Accounts Receivable Extra Service [*Computer science*]
Parexel .... Parexel International Corp. [*Associated Press*] (SAG)
PARF .... Paradise, Inc. [*NASDAQ symbol*] (SAG)
PARF .... Polymorphic Amplifiable Restriction (Endonuclease) Fragment [*Genetics*]
PARF .... Practical Allergy Research Foundation (EA)
PARFAS .... Passive Radio Frequency Acquisition System
PARFR .... Program for Applied Research on Fertility Regulation [*Northwestern University*] [*Research center*]
PARG .... Polytechnic Academic Registrars' Group (AIE)
Pargs .... Guiraudus Pargues [*Authority cited in pre-1607 legal work*] (DSA)
PARGS .... Parks and Recreation Girls Service
PARI .... Parent Attitude Research Instrument [*A questionnaire*]
PARIET .... Parietal Cell Antibody [*Immunology*] (DAVI)
PARIF .... Program for Automation Retrieval Improvement by Feedback (NITA)
PARIS .... Passenger Routing and Information System [*FTA*] (TAG)
PARIS .... Pictorial and Artifact Retrieval and Information System [*Canadian Heritage Information Network*] [*Information service or system*]
PARIS .... Planning Aid for Retail Information System [*IBM Corp.*]
PARIS .... Portable Automated Remote Inspection System [*Failure Analysis Associates*] (RDA)
PARIS .... Postal Address Reader Indexer System (PDAA)
PARIS .... Pour l'Amenagement et le Renouveau Institutionel et Social [*France Political party*]
PARIS .... Pulse Analysis-Recording Information System
ParisBu .... Paris Business Forms, Inc. [*Associated Press*] (SAG)
PARK .... Park [*Postal Service standard*] (OPSA)
PARK .... Parkerized [*Metallurgy*] [*Tradename*]
Park .... Parker's English Exchequer Reports [*1743-67*] [*A publication*] (DLA)
Park .... Parker's New Hampshire Reports [*A publication*] (DLA)
Park .... Parker's New York Criminal Cases [*1823-68*] [*A publication*] (DLA)
PARK .... Parking
PARK .... Premier Parks [*NASDAQ symbol*] (TTSB)
PARK .... Premier Parks, Inc. [*NASDAQ symbol*] (SAG)
PARKA .... Pacific Acoustic Research Kaneohe-Alaska [*Navy*]
Park Arb ...... Parker on Arbitration [*1820*] [*A publication*] (DLA)
Park Ch .... Parker's Practice in Chancery [*A publication*] (DLA)
Park CR .... Parker's New York Criminal Reports [*A publication*] (DLA)
Park Cr Cas... Parker's New York Criminal Cases [*A publication*] (DLA)
Park Crim L... Parker's New York Criminal Reports [*A publication*] (DLA)
Park Crim (NY)... Parker's New York Criminal Cases [*A publication*] (DLA)
Park Crim R... Parker's New York Criminal Reports [*A publication*] (DLA)
Park Crim Rep... Parker's New York Criminal Reports [*A publication*] (DLA)
Park Cr Rep... Parker's New York Criminal Reports [*A publication*] (DLA)
Park Dig ...... Parker's California Digest [*A publication*] (DLA)
Park Dow ..... Park. Dower [*1819*] [*A publication*] (DLA)
ParkDrl .... Parker Drilling Co. [*Associated Press*] (SAG)
ParkEl .... Park Electrochemical Corp. [*Associated Press*] (SAG)
Parker .... Parker on the Laws of Shipping and Insurance [*England*] [*A publication*] (DLA)
Parker .... Parker's English Exchequer Reports [*A publication*] (DLA)
Parker .... Parker's New Hampshire Reports [*A publication*] (DLA)
Parker .... Parker's New York Criminal Reports [*6 vols.*] [*A publication*] (DLA)
Parker Cr Cas... Parker's New York Criminal Reports [*A publication*] (ILCA)
Parker Cr Cas (NY)... Parker's New York Criminal Reports [*A publication*] (ILCA)
Parker Cr R... Parker's New York Criminal Reports [*A publication*] (ILCA)
Parker Cr R (NY)... Parker's New York Criminal Reports [*A publication*] (ILCA)
Parker's Crim R... Parker's New York Criminal Reports [*A publication*] (DLA)
Parker's Crim Rep (NY)... Parker's New York Criminal Reports [*A publication*] (DLA)
Parker's Cr R... Parker's New York Criminal Reports [*A publication*] (DLA)
Park Exch .... Parker's English Exchequer Reports [*1743-67*] [*A publication*] (DLA)
Park Hist Ch... Parkes' History of Court of Chancery [*1828*] [*A publication*] (DLA)
ParkHn .... Parker-Hannifin Corp. [*Associated Press*] (SAG)

Park Ins........ Parker's Insurance [*8 eds.*] [*1787-1842 England*] [*A publication*] (DLA)
ParkMed...... Park Meditech, Inc. [*Associated Press*] (SAG)
ParkNatl...... Park National Corp. [*Associated Press*] (SAG)
Park NH........ Parker's New Hampshire Reports [*A publication*] (DLA)
ParkOh........ Park Ohio Industries [*Associated Press*] (SAG)
ParkOh........ Park-Ohio Industries, Inc. [*Associated Press*] (SAG)
ParkPar........ Parker & Parsley Petroleum [*Associated Press*] (SAG)
Park Pr Ch... Parker's Practice in Chancery [*A publication*] (DLA)
Park Rev Cas... Parker's English Exchequer Reports (Revenue Cases) [*A publication*] (DLA)
Parkrvsn...... Parkervision, Inc. [*Associated Press*] (SAG)
PARKS......... Parks [*Commonly used*] (OPSA)
ParkvF......... Parkvale Financial Corp. [*Associated Press*] (SAG)
PARKWAY.... Parkway [*Commonly used*] (OPSA)
PARKWAYS... Parkways [*Commonly used*] (OPSA)
PARKWY...... Parkway [*Commonly used*] (OPSA)
Parkwy......... [*The*] Parkway Co. [*Associated Press*] (SAG)
PARL........... Parallel
PARL........... Parliament
PARL........... Parlux Fragrances [*NASDAQ symbol*] (TTSB)
PARL........... Parlux Fragrances, Inc. [*NASDAQ symbol*] (NQ)
Par L........... Parsons' Law by Hughes [*A publication*] (DLA)
PARL........... Prince Albert RADAR Laboratory
PARLARS.... Particulars
Par Laws Bus... Parsons' Laws of Business [*A publication*] (DLA)
PARLB......... Parliamentary Borough
Parl Cas...... Parliamentary Cases [*House of Lords Reports*] [*A publication*] (DLA)
Parlex.......... Parlex Corp. [*Associated Press*] (SAG)
Parl Hist Eng... Parliamentary History of England [*Pre-1803*] [*A publication*] (DLA)
PARLIGAES... Parliamentary Liaison Group for Alternative Energy Strategies [*British*]
PARLIKDER... Partiya Litsom k Derevne [*The Party Face to Face with the Countryside*] [*Given name popular in Russia after the Bolshevik Revolution*]
PARLO......... Parlando [*Music*] (ROG)
Parl Reg...... Parliamentary Register [*England*] [*A publication*] (DLA)
PARLT......... Parliament
PARLTY....... Parliamentary
Parlux.......... Parlux Fragrances, Inc. [*Associated Press*] (SAG)
PARLV......... Parsley Latent Virus [*Plant pathology*]
PARLY......... Parliamentary
PARM.......... Parallelogram [*Geometry*] (ROG)
PARM.......... Parameter [*Computer science*]
PARM.......... Participating Manager
PARM.......... Partido Autentico de la Revolucion Mexicana [*Authentic Party of the Mexican Revolution*] [*Political party*] (PPW)
PARM.......... Persistent Antiradiation Missile (MCD)
PARM.......... Post-Attack Resource Management System (MCD)
PARM.......... Precision Anti-Radiation Missile [*Military*] (PDAA)
PARM.......... Program Analysis for Resource Management
PARMA........ Program for Analysis, Reporting, and Maintenance [*Computer science*]
PARMA........ Public Agency Risk Managers Association [*San Jose, CA*] (EA)
Par Mar Ins... Parsons on Marine Insurance and General Average [*A publication*] (DLA)
Par Mar L..... Parsons on Maritime Law [*A publication*] (DLA)
ParMd.......... Paradigm Medical Industries, Inc. [*Associated Press*] (SAG)
PARMEDL.... Paramedical
Par Merc Law... Parsons on Mercantile Law [*A publication*] (DLA)
ParmTch...... Parametric Technology Corp. [*Associated Press*] (SAG)
PARMV........ Parsnip Mosaic Virus [*Plant pathology*]
Par N & B.... Parsons' Notes and Bills [*A publication*] (DLA)
Parnassus.... Parnassus: Poetry in Review [*A publication*] (BRI)
PARO........... Patent Royalties (AAGC)
PAROCH...... Parochial (ROG)
Paroch Ant... Kennett's Parochial Antiquities [*A publication*] (DLA)
Parod Epic Gr Rel... Parodorum Epicorum Graecorum Reliquiae [*A publication*] (OCD)
PAROS......... Passive Ranging on Submarines [*Navy*]
PAROS......... Programmed Automated Replenishment Ordering System (IAA)
PAROSS....... Passive/Active Reporting Ocean Surveillance System [*Navy*] (NVT)
PAROX......... Paroxysmal [*Medicine*]
PARP........... Partially Acidulated Rock Phosphate (OA)
PARP........... Procyclic Acidic Repetitive Protein [*Biochemistry*]
PARP........... Production Assistance Report to Pricing [*DoD*]
Par Part...... Parsons on Partnership [*1889*] [*A publication*] (DLA)
ParPet......... Parallel Petroleum Corp. [*Associated Press*] (SAG)
ParPf2......... Partners Preferred Yield II [*Associated Press*] (SAG)
ParPf3......... Partners Perferred Yield III [*Associated Press*] (SAG)
ParPfd......... Partners Preferred Yield [*Associated Press*] (SAG)
PARPRO...... Peacetime Aerial Reconnaissance Program [*Military*] (NVT)
PARQ........... ParcPlace-Digitalk [*NASDAQ symbol*] (TTSB)
PARQ........... Parcplace Systems, Inc. [*NASDAQ symbol*] (SAG)
PARQ........... Parental Acceptance-Rejection Questionnaire [*Psychology*]
PARR........... Bullet Sports International, Inc. [*NASDAQ symbol*] (SAG)
PARR........... Bullet Sports Intl [*NASDAQ symbol*] (TTSB)
PARR........... Pakistan Atomic Research Reactor
Par R........... Parsons' Select Equity Cases [*Pennsylvania*] [*A publication*] (DLA)
PARR........... Performance Analysis Reliability Reporting (DNAB)
PARR........... Post-Accident Radioactivity Removal [*Nuclear energy*] (NRCH)
PARR........... Postanesthesia Recovery Room [*Medicine*] (DAVI)
PARR........... Procurement Authorization and Receiving Report [*NASA*] (KSC)
PARR........... Program Analysis and Resources Review
PARR........... Program Assessment Review Report [*Military*] (GFGA)
PARRC......... Pacific Aerospace Rescue and Recovery Center [*Air Force*]
Par Rights Cit... Parsons on the Rights of a Citizen of the United States [*A publication*] (DLA)
PARRS......... Postal Analysis Response and Reporting System [*Computer system designed to track mail through the US Postal Service*] [*R. R. Donnelley & Sons Co.*]
PARRS......... Psychological Abstracts Reference Retrieval System [*Syracuse University*]
PARS........... Parachute Altitude Recognition System (MCD)
Pars............ Parsons' Select Equity Cases [*1842-51*] [*Pennsylvania*] [*A publication*] (DLA)
PARS........... Passenger Airlines Reservation System
PARS........... Patrol Analysis Recording System [*British*]
PARS........... Pedestrians Association for Road Safety [*British*] (DI)
PARS........... Perimeter Acquisition RADAR [*Characterization*] System (MCD)
PARS........... Pershing Audio Reproduction System (PDAA)
PARS........... Personal Adjustment and Role Skills Scale [*Medicine*] (DMAA)
PARS........... Pharmos Corp. [*NASDAQ symbol*] (SAG)
PARS........... Photoacoustic Raman Spectroscopy
PARS........... Pilotless Aircraft Research Station [*NASA*]
PARS........... Precision and Accuracy Reporting System [*Environmental Protection Agency*] (GFGA)
PARS........... Preservation and Reformatting Section [*Committee of Association for Library Collections and Technical Services*]
PARS........... Preservation & Reformatting Section [*Association for Library Collections and Technical Services*] [*American Library Association*]
PARS........... Prisoner Aid and Rehabilitation Society (NADA)
PARS........... Private Aircraft Reporting System [*FAA*] (PDAA)
PARS........... Procurement Accounting and Reporting System [*Navy*] (NVT)
PARS........... Program Analysis and Review System (EDAC)
PARS........... Programmed Airline Reservation System
PARS........... Property Accountability Record System (NASA)
PARS........... Provincial Archives and Records Service [*Canada*]
PARSA......... Parasitological Society of Southern Africa (EAIO)
PARSA......... Postgraduate and Research Students' Association [*Australian National University*]
PARSAC....... Particle Size Analog Computer (IAA)
PARSAC....... Particle Size Analogue Computer (PDAA)
Pars Ans...... Parsons' Answer to the Fifth Part of Coke's Reports [*A publication*] (DLA)
PARSAVAL.... Pattern Recognition System Application Evaluation (IAA)
Pars Bills & N... Parsons on Bills and Notes [*A publication*] (DLA)
Pars Cont..... Parsons on Contracts [*A publication*] (DLA)
Pars Dec...... Parsons' Decisions [*2-7 Massachusetts*] [*A publication*] (DLA)
PARSEC....... Parallax Second [*Unit of interstellar-space measure*]
PARSEC....... Parser and Extensible Compiler [*Programming language*] (CSR)
PARSECS..... Program for Astronomical Research and Scientific Experiments Concerning Space
Pars Eq Cas... Parsons' Select Equity Cases [*1842-51*] [*Pennsylvania*] [*A publication*] (DLA)
PARSET....... Precision Askania Range System of Electronic Timing (MUGU)
PARSEV....... Paraglider Research Vehicle [*NASA*] (KSC)
Par Sh & Adm... Parsons on the Law of Shipping and Admiralty [*A publication*] (DLA)
PARSIM....... Perimeter Acquisition RADAR Simulation [*Missile system evaluation*] (RDA)
PARSIM....... Plant Appropriation Request Simulation (IAA)
PARSIP........ Point Arguello Range Safety Impact Predictor (MUGU)
Pars Mar Ins... Parsons on Marine Insurance [*A publication*] (DLA)
Pars Mar Law... Parsons on Maritime Law [*A publication*] (DLA)
Pars Merc Law... Parsons on Mercantile Law [*A publication*] (DLA)
Parsons'...... Parsons' Select Equity Cases [*Pennsylvania*] [*A publication*] (DLA)
PARSQ......... Pararescue
Pars Sel Eq Cas (PA)... Parsons' Select Equity Cases [*Pennsylvania*] [*A publication*] (DLA)
Pars S Eq Cas... Parsons' Select Equity Cases [*Pennsylvania*] [*A publication*] (DLA)
Pars Shipp & Adm... Parsons on Shipping and Admiralty [*A publication*] (DLA)
PARSYM....... Partial Symmetry
PARSYN....... Parametric Synthesis [*Computer science*]
PART........... Pan American Round Tables in the USA [*Defunct*] (EA)
PART........... Partial (MSA)
part............ Partial (VRA)
PART........... Participate (AABC)
PART........... Participle [*Grammar*]
PART........... Particle (IAA)
PART........... Particular
PART........... Partis [*A Part*] [*Pharmacy*]
PART........... Partition [*Ballistics*]
PART........... Partner (ADA)
PART........... Parts Allocation Requirements Technique
PART........... People Against Racist Terror (EA)
PART........... Performing Arts Repertory Theater
PART........... Production Allocation and Requirements Technique (MHDB)
PART........... Professional Audit Review Team (AAGC)
PARTAC....... Precision Askania Range Target Acquisition and Control (MUGU)
PART AEQ.... Partes Aequales [*Equal Parts*] [*Pharmacy*]
PART AEQUAL... Partes Aequales [*Equal Parts*] [*Pharmacy*] (ROG)
Part An........ De Partibus Animalium [*of Aristotle*] [*Classical studies*] (OCD)
ParTch......... PAR Technology Corp. [*Associated Press*] (SAG)
PART DOLENT... Partes Dolentes [*Painful Parts*] [*Pharmacy*]
PARTEI........ Purchasing Agents of the Radio, Television, and Electronics Industries [*An association*] (IAA)

PARTES .... Piece-Wise Application of Radiation through the Electromagnetic-Pulse Simulator (PDAA)
Parth .... Parthenius [*First century BC*] [*Classical studies*] (OCD)
PARTIAL ...... Participation in Architectural Layout (PDAA)
parti bd .... Particle Board (VRA)
Partic .... Participating [*or Participation*] (DLA)
PARTIC .... Participial [*Grammar*]
PARTIC .... Particle
PARTIC .... Particular
PARTICO ...... Parti d'Interets Congolais [*Party for Congolese Interests*] [*Political party*]
Partidas .... Moreau-Lislet and Carleton's Laws of Las Siete Partidas in Force in Louisiana [*A publication*] (DLA)
PARTIE .... People's Alliance to Reform, Transform and Improve Everything (EA)
PARTN .... Partnership (ADA)
PARTNER ..... Proof of Analog Results through a Numerical Equivalent Routine [*Computer science*]
PartnerR ...... PartnerRe Ltd. [*Associated Press*] (SAG)
Part Or .... Partitiones Oratoriae [*of Cicero*] [*Classical studies*] (OCD)
PARTR .... Particular (ROG)
PARTS .... Parts Assembly and Reuse Tool Set [*Computer software*] [*Digitalk, Inc.*] (PCM)
PARTS .... Precision Approach RADAR Training System (MCD)
PARTS .... Price Analysis and Review Technique for Spares
PARTSHIP .... Partnership [*Legal shorthand*] (LWAP)
PartsS .... Parts Source, Inc. (The) [*Associated Press*] (SAG)
PART VIC ..... Partitis Vicibus [*In Divided Parts*] [*Pharmacy*]
PARU .... Personnel Applied Research Unit [*Canadian military*]
PARU .... Photographic and Reproduction Unit
PARU .... Police Aerial Reinforcement [*or Resupply*] Unit [*Thailand*] (CINC)
PARU .... Postanesthetic Recovery Unit [*Medicine*]
PARV .... Paravane [*Anti-moored-mine device*] (KSC)
PARV .... Parvus [*Small*] [*Pharmacy*]
PARV3 .... Parsnip Virus 3 [*Plant pathology*]
ParVec .... Purdue Center for Parallel and Vector Computing [*Purdue University*] [*Research center*] (RCD)
Parvnt .... Paravant Computer Systems, Inc. [*Associated Press*] (SAG)
PARVSTRCRA... Paravane and Stores Crane [*Engineering*]
PARW .... Professional Association of Resume Writers (EA)
Par WC .... Parish Will Case [*A publication*] (DLA)
Par Wills ...... Parsons on Wills [*1854*] [*A publication*] (DLA)
PAS .... National Postsecondary Agriculture Student Organization (EA)
PAS .... Palestine Aid Society of America (EA)
PAS .... Para-Aminosalicylic [*Acid*] [*Organic chemistry*]
PAS .... Parametric Amplifier System
PaS .... Paranoia Subtle [*Psychology*]
PAS .... Parent Attitude Scale
PAS .... Paros [*Greece*] [*Airport symbol*] (OAG)
PAS .... Partido de Accion Socialista [*Socialist Action Party*] [*Costa Rica*] [*Political party*] (PPW)
PAS .... Parti Islam se Malaysia [*Islamic Party of Malaysia*] [*Political party*] (PPW)
PAS .... Partito de Azione de Sardegna [*Sardinian Action Party*] [*Italy Political party*] (PPW)
PAS .... Pasadena [*California*] [*Seismograph station code, US Geological Survey*] (SEIS)
PA S .... Pascal Second
PAS .... Pascal Source File [*Computer science*]
PAS .... Passage (AABC)
PAS .... Passed to the Adjacent Sector
PAS .... Passing Aid System (IAA)
Pas .... Passipoverus [*Flourished, 13th century*] [*Authority cited in pre-1607 legal work*] (DSA)
PAS .... Passive (WDAA)
PAS .... Patent Applicant Service (NITA)
PAS .... Patient Administration System [*British*]
PAS .... Patient Appointments and Scheduling [*Medicine*] (DMAA)
PAS .... Patients' Aid Society
PAS .... Payload Accommodations Studies [*NASA*] (NASA)
PAS .... Pelita Air Service PT [*Indonesia*] [*ICAO designator*] (FAAC)
PA S .... Pennsylvania Superior Court Reports [*A publication*] (DLA)
PAS .... Percussive Arts Society (EA)
PAS .... Perigee-Apogee Satellite [*Aerospace*]
PAS .... Perigee-Apogee Stage [*Aerospace*]
PAS .... Perigee-Apogee System [*Aerospace*]
PA/S .... Periodic Acid/Schiff [*A stain*]
PAS .... Peripheral Anterior Synechia [*Ophthalmology*]
PAS .... Persistent Atrial Standstill [*Medicine*] (DMAA)
PAS .... Personal Acquaintance Service
PAS .... Personal Attitude Survey (EDAC)
PAS .... Personnel Accounting Symbol [*Air Force*] (AFM)
PAS .... Personnel Accounting System [*Marine Corps*]
PAS .... Personnel Activity Sequence (AAG)
PAS .... Personnel Administration Section [*Library Administration Division of ALA*]
PAS .... Personnel Assignment Survey (MCD)
PAS .... Phase Address System
PAS .... Phase Array System
PAS .... Philanthropic Advisory Service
PAS .... Phosphoric Acid-Sensitive
PAS .... Photoabsorption Spectroscopy [*Chemistry*]
PAS .... Photoacoustic Spectrometry [*Also, OAS*]
PAS .... Physician-Assisted Suicide
PAS .... Physicians for Automotive Safety [*Defunct*] (EA)
PAS .... Pierce-Arrow Society (EA)
PAS .... Pilots Advisory Service
PAS .... Pilot's Attack Sight [*British*]
PAS .... Pioneer America Society (EA)
PAS .... Planning Advisory Service (GNE)
PAS .... Plant Alarms Sum (ECII)
PAS .... Plasma Arc System
PAS .... Plessey Assessment Services (NITA)
PAS .... Pneumatic Air Saw
PAS .... Policy Analysis Staff [*Environmental Protection Agency*] (GFGA)
PAS .... Polish Academy of Sciences
PAS .... Polish Astronautical Society [*See also PTA*]
PAS .... Poly(alkyl Sulfone) [*Organic chemistry*]
PAS .... Polyaminosiloxane [*Organic chemistry*]
PAS .... Polyarylsulfone [*Organic chemistry*]
PAS .... Positron Annihilation Spectroscopy (MCD)
PAS .... Post Abortion Syndrome
PAS .... Postacoustic Spectroscopy
PAS .... Posterior Airway Space [*Medicine*] (DMAA)
PAS .... Posterior Area of [*Loose*] Skin
PAS .... Postponed Accounting System [*Banking*]
PAS .... Power Apparatus and Systems (MCD)
PAS .... Power-Assisted Steering [*Automotive feature*]
PAS .... Power-Assist System [*Motorcycle steering*]
PAS .... Pre-Admission Screening [*Medicine*] (MEDA)
PAS .... Preadmission Screening
PAS .... Preaward Survey [*To determine a contractor's capability*] [*DoD*]
PAS .... Precise Acquisition System
PAS .... Preconscious Activity Scale (EDAC)
PAS .... Pregnancy Advisory Service [*British*]
PAS .... Premature Atrial Stimulus [*Medicine*] (DMAA)
PAS .... Presidential Appointee Subject
PAS .... President's Advisor for Science
PAS .... Pressure-Assisted Sintering [*Forging*] [*Automotive engineering*]
PAS .... Pressurized Air Subsystem
PAS .... Price Analysis Sheet
PAS .... Primary Alerting System
PAS .... Primary Ascent System [*Aerospace*] (NASA)
PAS .... Principal Assistant Secretary
PAS .... Prisoners' Aid Society [*Australia*]
PAS .... Privacy Act Statement (NRCH)
PAS .... Problem Appraisal Scales [*Personality development test*] [*Psychology*]
PAS .... Processed Array Signal
PAS .... Procurement Action System (MCD)
PAS .... Procurement Appropriation, Secondary (MCD)
PAS .... Product Acceptance Standard [*Automotive engineering*]
PAS .... Product Assurance Survey
PAS .... Product Availability Search (MCD)
PAS .... Professional Activity Study [*Later, CPHA*]
PAS .... Professor of Aerospace Studies [*Air Force*] (AFIT)
PAS .... Professor of Air Science [*Air Force*]
PAS .... Program Activity Structure
PAS .... Program Address Storage (IEEE)
PAS .... Program Allowance Schedule
PAS .... Program Alternative Simulation (IAA)
PAS .... Program of Advanced Studies
PAS .... Progressive Accumulated Stress [*Psychiatry*]
PAS .... Propulsion and Auxiliary Systems Department [*David W. Taylor Naval Ship Research and Development Center*]
PAS .... Public Address System
PAS .... Public Administration Service (EA)
PAS .... Pulmonary Artery Stenosis [*Medicine*]
PAS .... Pulsating Air System [*Automotive engineering*]
PAS .... Pump Actuator Set
PAS .... Pyrotechnics Arming Switch
Pas .... Terminus Paschae [*Easter Term*] [*Latin Legal term*] (DLA)
PASA .... Pacific American Steamship Association [*Later, AIMS*]
PASA .... Para-Aminosalicylic Acid [*Organic chemistry*]
PASA .... Participating Agency Service Agreement (GNE)
PASA .... PCR [*Polymerase Chain Reaction*] Amplification of Specific Alleles [*Genetics*]
PASA .... Personnel Administrative Services Agency [*Army*]
PASA .... Pioneers' Association of South Australia
PASA .... Pipelines Authority of South Australia
PASA .... Playgroup Association of South Australia
PASA .... Police Association of South Australia
PASA .... Primary Acquired Sideroblastic Anemia [*Medicine*]
PASA .... Proximal Articular Set Angle [*Orthopedics*] (DAVI)
PASAR .... Psychological Abstracts Search and Retrieval
PASARR ...... Preadmission Screening and Annual Resident Review [*Medicare*]
PASAT .... Particle Accelerator Science and Technology (IAA)
PASAT .... Poppleton-Allen Sales Aptitude Test
PASB .... Pan American Sanitary Bureau
PASB .... Perpetual Savings Bank FSB (MHDW)
PASb .... Predneaziatskii Sbornik Voprosy Khattologii i Khurritologii [*A publication*] (BJA)
P-as-B .... Program as Broadcast [*Radio*] (DEN)
PASB .... Public Authorities Superannuation Board [*New South Wales, Australia*]
PASBI .... Palo Alto Social Background Inventory [*Psychology*]
PASC .... Deadhorse [*Alaska*] [*ICAO location identifier*] (ICLI)
PASC .... Pacific Area Standards Congress [*American National Standards Institute*]
PASC .... Palestine Armed Struggle Command (PD)
PASC .... Pan American Sanitary Conference

PASC .... Pan American Standards Commission [*See also COPANT*] (EAIO)
PAS-C .... Para-Aminosalicylic Acid Crystallized with Ascorbic Acid [*Organic chemistry*] (MAE)
Pasc .... Paschal [*Easter Term*] [*Legal term*] (DLA)
Pasc .... Paschal's Reports [*25, 28-31 Texas*] [*A publication*] (DLA)
PASC .... Precision Adaptive Sub-Band Coding [*Electronics*]
PASC .... Primitive Art Society of Chicago (EA)
PASCA .... Positron Annihilation Spectroscopy for Chemical Analysis
PASCAL .... Philips Automatic Sequence Calculator
PASCAL .... Program Applique a la Selection et a la Compilation Automatique de la Litterature [*Centre National de la Recherche Scientifique-Informascience*] [*Bibliographic database*]
PASCALS .... Projected Antisubmarine Classification and Location System (DNAB)
PASCH .... Pascha [*Easter*] [*Church calendars*] (ROG)
Pasch .... Paschal [*Easter Term*] [*Legal term*] (DLA)
Paschal .... Paschal's Reports [*28-31 Texas*] [*Supplement to Vol. 25*] [*A publication*] (DLA)
Paschal's Ann Const ... Paschal's United States Constitution, Annotated [*A publication*] (DLA)
Pasch Dig .... Paschal's Texas Digest of Decisions [*A publication*] (DLA)
PASCOSS .... Passive and Active Control of Space Structures
PASCT .... Pan American Society for Chemotherapy of Tuberculosis [*See also SAQT*] [*Buenos Aires, Argentina*] (EAIO)
PASD .... After Diastase Digestion [*Biochemistry*] (DAVI)
p'ase .... Alkaline Phosphatase [*Biochemistry*] (DAVI)
PASE .... Post-Apollo Space Electrophoresis [*European Space Agency*]
PASE .... Power-Assisted Storage Equipment (IEEE)
PASE .... Product Acceptance Exceptions
PASE .... Programs in the Arts for Special Education Project (EDAC)
PASEP .... Passed Separately [*Military*]
PASES .... Performance Assessment of Syntax: Elicited and Spontaneous [*Educational test*]
Pas Ex .... Passive Exercise [*Physical Therapy*] (DAVI)
PASF .... Photographic Art and Science Foundation (EA)
PASFIS .... Philippines Aquatic Sciences and Fisheries Information System [*Marine science*] (OSRA)
PASG .... Patent Abstracts Section, Official Gazette [*Federal government*] [*A publication*]
PASG .... Pneumatic Antishock Garment [*Roentgenology*]
PASG .... Pulse Amplifier/Symbol Generator
PASG .... Pulse Analyzer Signal Generator
PASGT .... Personnel Armor System for Ground Troops (RDA)
PASI .... Pikunas Adult Stress Inventory [*Psychology*]
PA/SI .... Preliminary Assessment and Site Inspection [*Environmental Protection Agency*] (FFDE)
PASI .... Professional Associate, Chartered Surveyors' Institution [*Later, ARICS*]
PASI .... Psoriasis Area and Severity Index [*Medicine*]
PASI .... Sitka [*Alaska*] [*ICAO location identifier*] (ICLI)
PASIC .... Percussive Arts Society International Convention [*Percussive Arts Society*]
PasifSat .... Pasifik Satelit Nusantara (PT) [*Associated Press*] (SAG)
PAS-INAH .... Para-Aminosalicylic Acid and Isonicotinic Acid Hydrazide (BARN)
PASITAM .... Program of Advanced Studies of Institution Building and Technical Assistance Methodologies [*MUCIA*]
PASL .... Polish Americans for the Statue of Liberty [*Defunct*] (EA)
PASLA .... Programmable Asynchronous Line Adapter
PASLIB .... Pakistan Association of Special Libraries (NITA)
Pas Lux .... Pasicrisie Luxembourgeoise [*Luxembourg Law Reports*] [*A publication*] (ILCA)
PASM .... Partitionable SIMD/MIMD [*Single Instruction, Multiple Data/Multiple Instruction, Multiple Data*] (MCD)
PASM .... Periodic Acid - Silver Methenamine [*Biological stain*]
PASM .... Preaward Survey Monitor [*DoD*]
PASMA .... Prefabricated Aluminium Scaffold Manufacturers Association [*British*] (DBA)
PASN .... St. Paul Island [*Alaska*] [*ICAO location identifier*] (ICLI)
PASO .... Pan American Sanitary Organization
PASO .... Pan American Sports Organization [*See also ODEPA*] [*Mexico City, Mexico*] (EAIO)
PA/SO .... Port Antisubmarine Officer [*Navy*]
PASO .... Principal Armament Supply Officer [*British military*] (DMA)
PASOC .... Partido de Accion Socialista [*Party of Socialist Action*] [*Spain Political party*] (PPW)
PASOCO .... Parti Socialiste des Comores [*Socialist Party of Comoros*] [*Political party*] (EY)
PASOH .... Partido de Accion Socialista de Honduras [*Political party*] (EY)
PASOH .... Partido Socialista de Honduras [*Honduran Socialist Party*] [*Political party*]
PASOK .... Panellinion Sosialistikon Kinema [*Pan-Hellenic Socialist Movement*] [*Greek Political party*] (PPE)
PASOLS .... Pacific Area Senior Officer Logistics Seminar (MCD)
PASP .... Pancreas-Specific Protein [*Medicine*] (DMAA)
PASP .... Port Autonome de San Pedro [*The Ivory Coast*] (EY)
PA/SP .... Positioner Antenna and Solar Panel [*NASA*]
PASP .... Price Adjusting Sampling Plan (PDAA)
PASP .... Pulmonary Artery Systolic Pressure [*Medicine*] (DMAA)
PAS(PR) .... Principal Assistant Secretary (Priority)
PAS procedure ... Periodic Acid Schiff Procedure (DOG)
P-as-R .... Program as Recorded [*Radio*] (DEN)
PASRB .... Preaward Survey Review Board [*DoD*]
PASS .... Panic Attack Sufferers' Support Groups (EA)
PASS .... Parents Against Subliminal Seduction [*Defunct*] (EA)
PASS .... Parked Aircraft Security System (PDAA)
PASS .... Parts Analysis Summary Sheet
PASS .... Pass [*Postal Service standard*] (OPSA)
Pass .... Passage (DD)
PASS .... Passage [*Maps and charts*] (KSC)
PASS .... Passenger (KSC)
PASS .... Passenger Automated Selection System (ADA)
PASS .... Passim [*Everywhere*] [*Latin*]
PASS .... Passivate [*Metallurgy*] (IAA)
PASS .... Passive
PASS .... Passive-Active Surveillance System (MCD)
Pass .... Passover (BARN)
PASS .... Patrol Advanced Surveillance System (MCD)
PASS .... Pay/Personnel Administrative Support System (NVT)
PASS .... Penetration Aids/Strike System (NG)
PASS .... Performance Analysis Subsystem [*Military*] (CAAL)
PASS .... Personalized Automotive Security System [*In product name, PASS-Key*] [*Delco Electronics*] [*Automotive engineering*]
PASS .... Petroleum Abstracts Search Service [*Online information service*]
PASS .... Phased Array Sector Scanner [*Instrument for measuring ultrasound*] [*Trademark of General Electric Co.*]
PASS .... Phoenix Ability Survey System [*Test*]
PASS .... Pilot Aerial Survival System (PDAA)
PASS .... Pirelli Active Safety System
PASS .... Planning and Scheduling Session
PASS .... Planning and Scheduling System (NASA)
PASS .... Policyowner Attitude Survey Service [*LIMRA*]
PASS .... Polymeric Aluminum Silicate Sulfate [*Inorganic chemistry*]
PASS .... Pooled Analytical Stereoplotter System (PDAA)
PASS .... Portable Assisted Study Sequence Program [*California*] (EDAC)
PASS .... Positioning and Surveying System (MCD)
PASS .... Post-Accident Sampling Systems [*Nuclear energy*]
PASS .... Precision Autocollimating Solar Sensor
PASS .... Pressurized Air Starter System (MCD)
PASS .... Price Adjusted Single Sampling (PDAA)
PASS .... Primary Academic Sentiment Scale [*Child development test*]
PASS .... Primary Avionics Software System (NASA)
PASS .... Private Alarm Signalling System
PASS .... Private Automatic Switching System [*Telecommunications*]
PASS .... Procurement Aging and Staging System [*Army*] (AABC)
PASS .... Procurement Automated Source System [*Small Business Administration*] [*Washington, DC Information service or system*] (IID)
PASS .... Production Automated Scheduling System (IEEE)
PASS .... Professional Accounting System for Schools (AIE)
PASS .... Professional Airways Systems Specialists (EA)
PASS .... Professional Amateur Sports Systems [*Cable-television network*]
PASS .... Professional Association of Secretarial Services [*Later, NASS*] (EA)
PASS .... Program Aid Software Systems [*Computer science*] (IEEE)
PASS .... Program Alternative Simulation System (KSC)
PASS .... Program Analysis of Service Systems [*Procedure to evaluate human service programs*]
PASS .... Programmed Access/Security System [*Card Key Systems*]
PASSA .... Pacific American Steamship Association [*Later, AIMS*] (EA)
PASSAGE .... Passage [*Commonly used*] (OPSA)
PASSAT .... PASCAL Subset for Application in Test Computers (NITA)
PASSEX .... Passing Exercise (DOMA)
PASSIM .... President's Advisory Staff on Scientific Information Management
PASS-IN-REVIEW ... Priority Aircraft Subsystem Suitability Intensive Review (MCD)
PASSION .... Program for Algebraic Sequences Specifically of Input-Output Nature [*Computer science*]
PASSMAN .... Pay/Personnel Administrative Support System Manual (DNAB)
PASSR .... Passenger (DCTA)
PASSWD .... Password [*Computer science*]
PAST .... Pasteurella [*Genus of bacteria*]
PAST .... Pastillus [*A Lozenge, Troch, Pastil*] [*Pharmacy*] (ROG)
Past .... Pastoral Epistles (BJA)
PAST .... Pastorate
PA St .... Pennsylvania State Reports [*A publication*] (DLA)
PAST .... Periodic Acid-Schiff Technique [*Medicine*] (DMAA)
PAST .... Portable Arming System Trainer (MCD)
PAST .... Process Accessible Segment Table
PAST .... Professor of Air Science and Tactics
PAST .... Propulsion and Associated Systems Test (MCD)
PA Stat Ann ... Pennsylvania Statutes, Annotated [*A publication*] (DLA)
PA Stat Ann (Purdon) ... Pennsylvania Statutes, Annotated (Purdon) [*A publication*] (DLA)
PA State .... Pennsylvania State Reports [*A publication*] (DLA)
PA State R .... Pennsylvania State Reports [*A publication*] (DLA)
PASTIC .... Pakistan Scientific and Technological Information Center [*Formerly, PANSDOC*] [*Quaid-I-Azan University Campus Islamabad, Pakistan*]
PAStO .... Our Lady of Angels College, Aston, PA [*Library symbol Library of Congress*] (LCLS)
PA St R .... Pennsylvania State Reports [*A publication*] (DLA)
PASTRAM .... Passenger Traffic Management System [*Army*]
PA St Tr .... Pennsylvania State Trials (Hogan) [*A publication*] (DLA)
PASU .... Pan-African Socialist Union [*Southern Rhodesia*]
PASU .... Patrol Aircraft Service Unit
PASU .... Performing Arts Study Unit (EA)
PASU .... Polyarylsulfone [*Organic chemistry*]
PASU .... Preliminary Approval for Service Use [*Military*]
PASU .... Provisional Approval for Service Use [*Navy*] (NVT)
PA Summary ... Summary of Pennsylvania Jurisprudence [*A publication*] (DLA)
PA Super .... Pennsylvania Superior Court Reports [*A publication*] (DLA)
PA Super Ct ... Pennsylvania Superior Court Reports [*A publication*] (DLA)
PA Superior Ct ... Pennsylvania Superior Court Reports [*A publication*] (DLA)

PASUS .... Pan American Society of the United States (EA)
PASV .... Pangola Stunt Virus [*Plant pathology*]
PASV .... Sparrevohn Air Force Station [*Alaska*] [*ICAO location identifier*] (ICLI)
PASW .... Personal Assistance Service Worker [*Medicine*] (DMAA)
PASW .... Pure Atria Corp. [*NASDAQ symbol*] (SAG)
PASWEPS .... Passive Antisubmarine Warfare Environmental Protection System [*Navy*] (NATG)
PASY .... Shemya Air Force Base [*Alaska*] [*ICAO location identifier*] (ICLI)
PAt .... Allentown Public Library, Allentown, PA [*Library symbol Library of Congress*] (LCLS)
Pat .... All India Reporter, Patna Series [*A publication*] (ILCA)
PAT .... Athenaeum of Philadelphia (EA)
PAT .... Athenaeum of Philadelphia, Philadelphia, PA [*OCLC symbol*] (OCLC)
Pat .... Indian Law Reports, Patna Series [*A publication*] (DLA)
Pat .... Indian Rulings, Patna Series [*A publication*] (DLA)
PAT .... International Brotherhood of Painters and Allied Trades
PAT .... National Patents Appeal Tribunal [*England*] (DLA)
PAT .... Palleted Automated Transport (PDAA)
PAT .... Parametric Artificial Talker
PAT .... Paroxysmal Atrial [*or Auricular*] Tachycardia [*Medicine*]
PAT .... Parts Accountability Technique (MCD)
PAT .... Passive Acoustic Target [*Military*]
PAT .... Passive Acoustic Torpedo [*Military*]
PAT .... Passive Angle Track (NVT)
pa t .... Past Tense [*Grammar*] (BARN)
Pat .... Patent (AAGC)
PAT .... Patent (KSC)
PAT .... Patent Rolls [*British*]
pat .... Paternal Origin [*Medicine*] (DMAA)
PAT .... Paterson [*Diocesan abbreviation*] [*New Jersey*] (TOCD)
Pat .... Paterson's Scotch Appeals, House of Lords [*A publication*] (DLA)
Pat .... Pathe [*Record label*] [*France*]
PAT .... Patient
pat .... Patina (VRA)
PAT .... Patio
PAT .... Patna [*India*] [*Airport symbol*] (OAG)
Pat .... Paton's Scotch Appeal Cases, House of Lords [*A publication*] (DLA)
PAT .... Patras [*Greece*] [*Seismograph station code, US Geological Survey*] (SEIS)
PAT .... Patriarch [*Greek Church*] (ROG)
PAT .... Patrick Air Force Base [*Florida*] (KSC)
PAT .... Patrol
PAT .... Patten Corp. [*NYSE symbol*] (SPSG)
PAT .... Pattern
PAT .... Pattern Analysis Test [*Army*]
PAT .... People's Action Team [*South Vietnam*]
PAT .... Performance Acceptance Test (SAA)
PAT .... Performance Appraisal Team [*Nuclear energy*] (NRCH)
PAT .... Peripheral Allocation Table (NITA)
PAT .... Peripheral Assignment Table (CMD)
PAT .... Permit Assistance Team [*Environmental Protection Agency*] (GFGA)
PAT .... Personalized Array Translator (IEEE)
PAT .... Personnel Assistance Team [*Military*]
PAT .... Personnel Authorization Table [*Air Force*]
PAT .... Phenylaminotetrazole [*Psychology*]
PAT .... Phosphinothricin Acetyl Transferase [*An enzyme*]
PAT .... Photo Articulation Test
PAT .... Physics Achievement Test
PAT .... Picric Acid Turbidity Test
PAT .... Picture Arrangement Test
PAT .... Plasma Arc Tunnel
PAT .... Plastic Apply Template (MCD)
PAT .... Platoon Anti-Tank (SAA)
PAT .... Plenum Air Tread [*Army amphibian vehicle*]
PAT .... Plutonium Air Transportable [*Nuclear energy*] (NRCH)
PAT .... Point after Touchdown [*Football*]
PAT .... Polar Adjectives Test (AEBS)
PAT .... Polar Auxin Transport [*Botany*]
PAT .... Polaris Acceleration Test [*Military*] (SAA)
PAT .... Police Association of Tasmania [*Australia*]
PAT .... Political Action Teams
PAT .... Polyaminotriazole [*Organic chemistry*]
PAT .... Polyarlterephthalate [*Organic chemistry*]
PAT .... Position Adjusting Type
PAT .... Postavailability Trials
PAT .... Power Ascension Testing (IEEE)
PAT .... Preadmission Testing
PAT .... Prearranged Transfers
PAT .... Precision Aim Technique [*for helicopters*] [*Army*] (RDA)
PAT .... Prediction Analysis Techniques
PAT .... Pregnancy at Term [*Gynecology*]
PAT .... Preliminary Acceptance Trials [*Navy*]
PAT .... Prescription Athletic Turf [*Trademark for an artificial turf*]
PAT .... Pressure Assembled Thyristor
PAT .... Printer Action Table [*Computer science*] (HGAA)
PAT .... Prioirty Access Timer [*Telecommunications*] (OSI)
PAT .... Priority Air Transport [*Army*] (FAAC)
PAT .... Priority Air Travel [*Army*]
PAT .... Prism Adaptation Test [*Ophthalmology*]
PAT .... Problem Action Team [*NASA*] (NASA)
PAT .... Procedure for Automatic Testing (IAA)
PAT .... Procedures Authorized Task (MCD)
PAT .... Process Action Team [*Army*] (RDA)
PAT .... Process-Activation Table [*Computer science*]
PAT .... Process Analysis Team
PAT .... Product Acceptance Test [*Advertising*] (DOAD)
PAT .... Production Acceptance Test [*NASA*] (KSC)
PAT .... Production Assessment Test
PAT .... Professional, Administrative, and Technical (OICC)
PAT .... Professional Association of Teachers [*British*]
PAT .... Professional Association of Teachers [*British*] (DBA)
PAT .... Proficiency Analytical Testing [*National Institute on Occupational Safety and Health*]
PAT .... Program Analysis Team (KSC)
PAT .... Program Attitude Test (IEEE)
PAT .... Programmable Actuator-Transducer [*Automotive engineering*]
PAT .... Programmed Activity Transmission (MCD)
PAT .... Programmer Aptitude Test
PAT .... Project Action Team [*Acquisition Reform*] (AAGC)
PAT .... Property and Accounting Technician [*Navy*]
PAT .... Proportional to Absolute Temperature (IAA)
PAT .... Pseudoadder Tree [*Computer science*]
PAT .... Psychoacoustic Testing
PAT .... PSYOP [*Psychological Operation*] Automated Terminal (RDA)
PAT .... Public Administration Times [*A publication*] (EAAP)
PAT .... Pulsed Amplifier Tube
PAT .... Pump Algebra Tutor [*Computer program*]
PaT .... Purge-and-Trap [*Technique*] [*Environmental Protection Agency*]
PAtA .... Air Products & Chemicals, Inc., Allentown, PA [*Library symbol Library of Congress*] (LCLS)
PATA .... Pacific American Tankship Association [*Defunct*] (EA)
PATA .... Pacific Area Travel Association [*San Francisco, CA*]
PATA .... Pacific Asia Travel Association (EA)
PATA .... Patagonia [*Region of South America*] (ROG)
PATA .... Plenum Air Tread, Amphibious [*Army vehicle*]
PATA .... Pneumatic All-Terrain Amphibian (IEEE)
PATA .... Professional Aeromedical Transport Association (EA)
PATA .... Proprietary Articles Trade Association [*British*] (BI)
PATA .... Tanana [*Alaska*] [*ICAO location identifier*] (ICLI)
Pat Abr .... Paterson's Abridgment of Poor Law Cases [*1857-63*] [*A publication*] (DLA)
PAT & E .... Product Acceptance Testing and Evaluation [*Marketing*] (MCD)
Pat & H .... Patton, Jr., and Heath's Reports [*Virginia Special Court of Appeals*] [*A publication*] (DLA)
Pat & Mr ...... Paterson and Murray's Reports [*1870-71*] [*New South Wales*] [*A publication*] (DLA)
Pat App .... Craigie, Stewart, and Paton's House of Lords Appeals from Scotland [*1726-1857*] [*A publication*] (DLA)
Pat App Cas... Paterson's Scotch Appeal Cases [*A publication*] (DLA)
Pat App Cas... Paton's Scotch Appeal Cases [*Craigie, Stewart, and Paton*] [*A publication*] (DLA)
PATAS .... Portable Air-Launched Missile Telemetry Acquisition System (MCD)
PATASWDEVGRU... Patrol Antisubmarine Warfare Development Group
PATBOMRON... Patrol-Bombing Squadron
PATBX .... Private Automatic Telegraph Branch Exchange [*Telecommunications*]
PATBX .... Private Automatic Telex Branch Exchange (NITA)
PAtC .... Cedar Crest College, Allentown, PA [*Library symbol Library of Congress*] (LCLS)
PATC .... Paroxysmal Atrial [*or Auricular*] Tachycardia [*Medicine*]
PATC .... PATCLASS [*Pergamon ORBIT InfoLine, Inc.*] [*No longer available online*] [*Information service or system*] (CRD)
PATC .... Pioneer Automobile Touring Club (EA)
PAT-C .... Position, Attitude, Trajectory-Control [*Aerospace*] (AAG)
PATC .... Potomac Appalachian Trail Club (EA)
PATC .... Professional, Administrative, Technical, and Clerical [*Bureau of Labor Statistics survey*]
PATC .... Tin City Air Force Station [*Alaska*] [*ICAO location identifier*] (ICLI)
PATCA .... Panama Air Traffic Control Area
PATCA .... Phase Lock Automatic Tuned Circuit Adjustment [*Telecommunications*]
PATCA .... Printing and Allied Trades Christian Association (DGA)
PATCA .... Professional and Technical Consultants Association (EA)
Pat Cas .... Reports of Patent, Design, and Trade Mark Cases [*England, Scotland, Ireland*] [*A publication*] (DLA)
PATCENT ..... Patching Central [*Army*] (AABC)
PATCH .... People Against Toxic Chemical Hazards [*An association Australia*]
PATCH .... Planned Approach to Community Health
PA-TCH-SP... Periodic Acid-Thiocarbohydrazide-Silver Proteinate [*Test*] [*Cytology*]
PATCO .... Prednisone, ara-C [*Cytarabine*], Thioguanine, Cyclophosphamide, Oncovin [*Vincristine*] [*Antineoplastic drug regimen*]
PATCO .... Professional, Administrative, Technical, Clerical, and Other [*Bureau of Labor Statistics survey*] (DNAB)
PATCO .... Professional Air Traffic Controllers Organization [*Defunct*] (EA)
PATCOM ...... Patriot Communications Model (MCD)
Pat Comp..... Paterson's Compendium of English and Scotch Law [*A publication*] (DLA)
PATD .... Parts and Tool Disposition (IAA)
PATD .... Patented
Pat Dec......... Decisions of the Commissioner of Patents [*A publication*] (DLA)
Pat Des & TM Rev... Patent, Design, and Trade Mark Review [*India*] [*A publication*] (DLA)
Pat Dig .... Pattison's Missouri Digest [*A publication*] (DLA)
PATDPA .... Deutsche Patent Datenbank [*German Patent Database*] [*German Patent Office*] [*Information service or system*] (IID)
PATE .... Programmed Automatic Telemetry Evaluator
PATE .... Programmed Automatic Test Equipment
PATE .... Psychodynamics and Therapeutic Education
PATE .... Pulmonary Artery Thromboembolectomy [*Cardiology*] (DAVI)
PATEFA News... Printing and Allied Trades Employers' Federation. News [*A publication*]

PATELL........ Psychological Abstracts Tape Edition Lease or Licensing
PatEng......... Patterson Energy, Inc. [*Associated Press*] (SAG)
Pater........... Paterson's New South Wales Reports [*A publication*] (DLA)
Pater........... Paterson's Scotch Appeal Cases [*A publication*] (DLA)
Pater Ap Cas... Paterson's Scotch Appeal Cases [*A publication*] (DLA)
Pater App.... Paterson's Scotch Appeal Cases [*A publication*] (DLA)
Paters App... Paterson's Appeal Cases [*A publication*] (ILCA)
Paters Comp... Paterson's Compendium of English and Scotch Law [*A publication*] (DLA)
Paterson...... Paterson on the Game Laws [*A publication*] (DLA)
Paterson...... Paterson on the Liberty of the Subject [*A publication*] (DLA)
Paterson...... Paterson's Compendium of English and Scotch Law [*A publication*] (DLA)
Paterson...... Paterson's Law and Usages of the Stock Exchange [*A publication*] (DLA)
Paterson...... Paterson's Scotch Appeal Cases [*A publication*] (DLA)
Paterson Sc App Cas... Paterson's Scotch Appeal Cases [*A publication*] (DLA)
PATF........... Program Activation Task Force [*Military*] (AFIT)
PATF........... Property Accountability Task Force [*Army*] (MCD)
PATFOR........ Patrol Force
Pat Game L... Paterson on the Game Laws [*1861*] [*A publication*] (DLA)
PATGC......... Purge-and-Trap Gas Chromatography [*Environmental Protection Agency*]
PATH.......... Partnership Approach to Health (MEDA)
PATH.......... Path [*Postal Service standard*] (OPSA)
PATH.......... Pathology
PATH.......... Pathology (AABC)
PATH.......... Peer Attitudes Toward the Handicapped Scale [*Psychology*] (EDAC)
PATH.......... Performance Analysis and Test Histories (KSC)
PATH.......... Pituitary Adrenotrophic Hormone [*Endocrinology*]
PATH.......... Port Authority Trans-Hudson [*New York*]
PATH.......... Preserve American Patriotic Holidays Committee (EA)
PATH.......... Program for Appropriate Technology in Health (EA)
PATH.......... Program on Advanced Technology for the Highway
PATH.......... Prospectors and Treasure Hunters Guild (EA)
PATHAT....... Precision Aim-Technique Heliborne Antitank [*Gun system concept*] [*Ballistic Research Laboratory*] (RDA)
PATHE......... Positive Action Through Holistic Evaluation Program (EDAC)
Pat HL Sc.... Paterson's Scotch Appeal Cases [*A publication*] (DLA)
Pat HL Sc.... Paton's Scotch Appeal Cases [*A publication*] (DLA)
PathoG......... PathoGenesis Corp. [*Associated Press*] (SAG)
PATHOL........ Pathological (MSA)
PATHS......... Pacific Transport of Heat and Salt [*Canada-Japan-USA*] [*Marine science*] (OSRA)
PATHS......... Path [*Commonly used*] (OPSA)
PATHS......... Peer Attitudes Toward the Handicapped Scale [*Educational testing*]
PATHS......... Precursor above the Horizon Sensor [*Strategic Defense Initiative*]
PATI............ Passive Airborne Time-Difference Intercept [*Navy*]
PATI............ Patient Infosystems, Inc. [*NASDAQ symbol*] (SAG)
PATIA........... Pacific Area Trading and Investment Area
Patiala......... Indian Law Reports, Patiala Series [*A publication*] (DLA)
PATIB........... Polish-American Travel Information Bureau (EA)
PATINA......... Potomac Antique Tools and Industries Association (EA)
PatInfo......... Patient Infosystems, Inc. [*Associated Press*] (SAG)
Pat Ins......... Paton on Insurance [*1962*] [*A publication*] (DLA)
Pat J............ Patent Journal, Including Trademarks and Models [*South Africa*] [*A publication*] (DLA)
PATK............ Patrick Indus [*NASDAQ symbol*] (TTSB)
PATK............ Patrick Industries, Inc. [*NASDAQ symbol*] (NQ)
PATK............ Talkeetna [*Alaska*] [*ICAO location identifier*] (ICLI)
PAtL............ Lehigh County Historical Society, Allentown, PA [*Library symbol Library of Congress*] (LCLS)
PATL............ Tatalina Air Force Station [*Alaska*] [*ICAO location identifier*] (ICLI)
PATLAW....... Patent Law (NITA)
Pat Law Rev... Patent Law Review [*A publication*] (DLA)
Patlex.......... Patlex Corp. [*Associated Press*] (SAG)
Pat Licens... Paterson's Licensing Acts Annual [*A publication*] (DLA)
Pat LJ.......... Patna Law Journal [*India*] [*A publication*] (DLA)
Pat LR.......... Patent Law Review [*A publication*] (DLA)
Pat LR.......... Patna Law Reports [*India*] [*A publication*] (DLA)
Pat L Reptr... Patna Law Reporter [*India*] [*A publication*] (DLA)
Pat L Rev.... Patent Law Review [*A publication*] (DLA)
Pat LT.......... Patna Law Times [*India*] [*A publication*] (DLA)
Pat LW......... Patna Law Weekly [*A publication*] (DLA)
PAtM............ Muhlenberg College, Allentown, PA [*Library symbol Library of Congress*] (LCLS)
PAT MED..... Patent Medicine (WDAA)
PATMI.......... Powder Actuated Tool Manufacturers' Institute (EA)
PATMKG....... Patternmaking (WGA)
Pat Mort...... Patch on Mortgages [*1821*] [*A publication*] (DLA)
PATMRG....... PACOM [*Pacific Command*] Air Target Materials Review Group (CINC)
PATN........... Pattern (MDG)
PATNT......... Patent
PATNT......... Playgroup Association of the Northern Territory [*Australia*]
PATO........... Pacific-Asian Treaty Organization (NADA)
PATO........... Partial Acceptance and Takeover Date [*Telecommunications*] (TEL)
PATO........... Pattetico [*Pathetically*] [*Music*] (ROG)
PATO........... Principal Ammunition Technical Officer [*British military*] (DMA)
Pat Off......... Patent Office (DLA)
Pat Off J...... Patent Office Journal [*India*] [*A publication*] (DLA)
Pat Off Rep... Patent Office Reports [*A publication*] (DLA)
PATOLIS...... Patent Online Information System [*Database*] [*Japan*]
Paton........... Craigie, Stewart, and Paton's Scotch Appeal Cases [*1726-1821*] [*A publication*] (DLA)
Paton App Cas... Paton's Scotch Appeal Cases [*A publication*] (DLA)
Paton Sc App Cas... Paton's Scotch Appeal Cases [*A publication*] (DLA)
PATOOMB.... Phage and the Origins of Molecular Biology
PATOS......... Patent-Online-System [*Bertelsmann Datenbankdienste GmbH*] [*Database*]
PATP........... Poets and the Pub [*Programme*] [*Australia*]
PATP........... Preliminary Authority to Proceed (NASA)
PATP........... Production Acceptance Test Procedure (MCD)
PATP........... (Pyridylcarbonylamino)tetrahydropyridine [*Biochemistry*]
PATPEND..... Patent Pending
PAT-PTR...... US Patent Data Base - Patent Technology Reports [*Patent and Trademark Office*] [*Database*]
PATR........... Patriarch
PATR........... Patriotic (ROG)
PATR........... Patron
PATR........... Production Acceptance Test Requirement (MCD)
PATRA......... Printing, Packaging, and Allied Trades Research Association
PATRA......... Professional and Technical Role Analyses [*Occupational therapy*]
PatrAH......... Patriot American Hospitality, Inc. [*Associated Press*] (SAG)
PATRDL....... Pan American Tung Research and Development League [*Defunct*] (EA)
Patr Elect Cas... Patrick's Election Cases [*1824-49*] [*Upper Canada*] [*A publication*] (DLA)
PATRIC........ Pattern Recognition and Information Correlations [*Police crime-detection computer*]
PATRIC........ Pattern Recognition Interpretation and Correlation (CET)
PATRIC........ Position and Time-Resolved Ion Counting [*Detector*]
PATRICIA..... Practical Algorithm to Receive Information Coded in Alphanumeric [*Information retrieval*]
Patrick El Cas... Patrick's Election Cases [*Canada*] [*A publication*] (DLA)
PATRIOT...... Phased Array Tracking to Intercept of Target [*Air defense system unit*] [*Army*] (RDA)
PatriotB........ Patriot Bank Corp. (PA) [*Associated Press*] (SAG)
PatrkInd....... Patrick Industries, Inc. [*Associated Press*] (SAG)
PatrNBk....... Patriot National Bank CT [*Associated Press*] (SAG)
PATROL....... Program for Administrative Traffic Reports On-Line [*Computer program*] [*Bell System*]
PatrolGr....... Patrologia Graeca (BJA)
PatrolLat...... Patrologia Latina (BJA)
PATRON....... Patrol Squadron
PATS............ Payload Avionics Test Station [*NASA*] (SSD)
PATS............ Payment and Telecommunication Services Corp. [*New York, NY Telecommunications Defunct*] (TSSD)
PATS............ People Against Tobacco Smoke (EA)
PATS............ Personnel Assistance Teams [*Military*]
PATS............ Personnel in an Awaiting Training Status [*Air Force*] (AFM)
PATS............ Portable Acoustic Tracking System for Divers (MCD)
PATS............ Preacademic Training Student [*Military*]
PATS............ Preauthorized Automatic Transfer Scheme [*Banking*]
PATS............ Precise Automated Tracking System (PDAA)
PATS............ Precision Altimeter Techniques Study
PATS............ Precision Automated Tracking System [*FAA*] (TAG)
PATS............ Predicasts Abstract Terminal System [*Computer science*]
PATS............ Primary Aircraft Training System (MCD)
PATS............ Program for Analysis of Time Series (NASA)
PATS............ Programmatic and Technical Support [*Army*]
PATS............ Propulsion Analysis Trajectory Simulation [*Computer program*] [*NASA*]
PATSEARCH... Patent Search [*Computer science*]
PATSEARCH... Patent Search System (NITA)
Pat Ser......... Indian Law Reports, Patna Series [*A publication*] (DLA)
Pat St Tr...... Paton on Stoppage in Transitu [*1859*] [*A publication*] (DLA)
PATSU......... Patrol Aircraft Service Unit
PATSY......... Parametric Test Synthesis [*Computer science*]
PATSY......... Picture Animal Top Star of the Year [*or Performing Animal Television Star of the Year*] [*American Humane Association award*]
PATSY......... Programmer's Automatic Testing System
PATSY......... Pulse-Amplitude Transmission System (PDAA)
PATT............ Partial Automatic Translation Technique
PATT............ Patent (ROG)
PATT............ Pattern (AAG)
PATT............ Programmable Automatic Transistor Tester (PDAA)
PATT............ Project for the Analysis of Technology Transfer [*NASA*]
Patt & H....... Patton, Jr., and Heath's Reports [*Virginia*] [*A publication*] (DLA)
Patt & Heath R... Patton, Jr., and Heath's Reports [*Virginia*] [*A publication*] (DLA)
Patt & H (VA)... Patton, Jr., and Heath's Reports [*Virginia*] [*A publication*] (DLA)
PattDntl....... Patterson Dental Co. [*Associated Press*] (SAG)
Patten.......... Patten Corp. [*Associated Press*] (SAG)
PATTERN..... Planning Assistance Through Technical Evaluation of Relevance Numbers [*RAND Corp.*]
PATTH......... People Against Telephone Terrorism and Harassment (EA)
PATTI........... Precise and Accurate Time and Time Interval [*An experiment aboard the Spacelab*] [*NASA*] (PDAA)
PATTI........... Prompt Action to Telephone Inquiries (SAA)
PAT/TM........ Patient's Time (DAVI)
Pat TM & Copyr J of R & Educ... Patent, Trademark, and Copyright Journal of Research and Education [*A publication*] (DLA)
Patton & H... Patton, Jr., and Heath's Reports [*Virginia Special Court of Appeals*] [*A publication*] (DLA)
Patton & Heath... Patton, Jr., and Heath's Reports [*Virginia*] [*A publication*] (DLA)
Patton & H (VA)... Patton, Jr., and Heath's Reports [*Virginia Special Court of Appeals*] [*A publication*] (DLA)
Pat Trademark & Copyright J (BNA)... Patent, Trademark, and Copyright Journal (Bureau of National Affairs) [*A publication*] (DLA)
PATU........... PanAfrican Telecommunications Union (EAIO)

PATU .... Pan American Taekwondo Union (EA)
PATWA .... Playgroup Association of Western Australia
PATWA .... Professional and Technical Workers Aliyah [*British*] (BI)
PATWAS ...... Pilots Automatic Telephone Weather Answering Service
PATWING..... Patrol Wing [*Later, Fleet Air Wing*]
PATWINGDET... Patrol Wing [*Later, Fleet Air Wing*] Detachment (DNAB)
PATWINGLANTFLT... Patrol Wing [*later, Fleet Air Wing*] Atlantic Fleet
PATWINGSCOFOR... Patrol Wing [*later, Fleet Air Wing*] Scouting Force
PATX........ Private Automatic Telegraph Exchange (PDAA)
PATX........ Private Automatic Telex Exchange (NITA)
PAU .... Pacific Command Frequency Allocation and Uses (CINC)
PAU .... Pan American Union [*Central organ and permanent secretariat of the OAS*]
PAU .... Pattern Articulation Unit [*Computer science*]
PAU .... Pauk [*Myanmar*] [*Airport symbol*] (OAG)
PAU .... Paulingite [*A zeolite*]
Pau .... Paulus de Liazaris [*Deceased, 1356*] [*Authority cited in pre-1607 legal work*] (DSA)
PAU .... Pauzhetka [*Former USSR Seismograph station code, US Geological Survey*] (SEIS)
pau .... Pennsylvania [*MARC country of publication code Library of Congress*] (LCCP)
PAU .... Phenol-Acetic Acid-Urea [*Medicine*] (DMAA)
PAU .... Pilotless Aircraft Unit
PAU .... Portable Annotation Unit [*Military*] (CAAL)
PAU .... Position Analog Unit [*Manufacturing term*]
PAU .... Precision Approach - UNICOM [*Aviation*]
PAU .... Present Address Unknown
PAU .... Probe Aerodynamic Upper [*NASA*] (MCD)
PAU .... Production Assurance Unit (MCD)
PAU .... Programmes Analysis Unit [*British*] (MCD)
PAU .... University of Pennsylvania, Philadelphia, PA [*OCLC symbol*] (OCLC)
PAUBM .... Pan American Union of Baptist Men [*Defunct*] (EA)
PAUC .... Program Acquisition Unit Cost (AAGC)
PAUCA .... Providence Association of Ukrainian Catholics in America (EA)
Pau de Cast... Paulus de Castro [*Deceased, 1441*] [*Authority cited in pre-1607 legal work*] (DSA)
Pau de La.... Paulus de Liazaris [*Deceased, 1356*] [*Authority cited in pre-1607 legal work*] (DSA)
Pau de Montep... Paulus Ruinus de Montepico [*Flourished, 15th century*] [*Authority cited in pre-1607 legal work*] (DSA)
PAUDGET..... Photometer, Automated Universal Distribution Gonielectric Type
PAUH .... Harris [*Paul*] Stores [*NASDAQ symbol*] (SAG)
PAUH .... Paul Harris Stores [*NASDAQ symbol*] (SAG)
PAUH .... Paul Harris Stores [*NASDAQ symbol*] (TTSB)
Pau Hunga... Paulus Hungarus [*Deceased, 1242*] [*Authority cited in pre-1607 legal work*] (DSA)
Pau Hungar... Paulus Hungarus [*Deceased, 1242*] [*Authority cited in pre-1607 legal work*] (DSA)
PAUKO........ Pan-American Union of Karatedo Organizations [*Later, PUKO*] (EA)
PAUL .... Paullum [*A Little*] [*Pharmacy*]
Paul de Cast... Paulus de Castro [*Deceased, 1441*] [*Authority cited in pre-1607 legal work*] (DSA)
Paul de Castr... Paulus de Castro [*Deceased, 1441*] [*Authority cited in pre-1607 legal work*] (DSA)
Pau Leon..... Paulus Leonius [*Flourished, 16th century*] [*Authority cited in pre-1607 legal work*] (DSA)
Paul Liaz..... Paulus de Liazaris [*Deceased, 1356*] [*Authority cited in pre-1607 legal work*] (DSA)
PAULS .... Pennsylvania Union List of Serials
Paulson .... Paulson Capital Corp. [*Associated Press*] (SAG)
PaulSon....... Paul-Son Gaming Corp. [*Associated Press*] (SAG)
Paulus .... Julius Paulus. Sententiae Receptae [*A publication*] (DLA)
PAUMV .... Potato Aucuba Mosaic Virus [*Plant pathology*]
PAUN .... Unalakleet [*Alaska*] [*ICAO location identifier*] (ICLI)
PAUP .... Phylogenic Analysis Using Parsimony [*Biology*]
Paus .... Pausanias [*Second century AD*] [*Classical studies*] (OCD)
PAUS .... Piedmontese Association of the United States (EA)
PAUS .... Planning and Analysis for Uncertain Situations (MHDI)
PAUSE .... People Against Unconstitutional Sex Education
PAUT .... Pennsylvania & Atlantic Railroad Co. [*Absorbed into Consolidated Rail Corp.*] [*AAR code*]
PAUX .... Pauxillum [*A Little*] [*Pharmacy*]
P/AV........ Particular Average
PaV........ Pathe-Vox [*Record label*] [*France*]
PAV........ Paulo Afonso [*Brazil*] [*Airport symbol*] (OAG)
PAV........ Pavia [*Italy*] [*Seismograph station code, US Geological Survey*] (SEIS)
PAV........ Pavilion
Pav .... Pavo [*Constellation*]
PAV........ Pay Adjustment Voucher [*Military*]
PAV........ Personnel Allotment Voucher [*Army*]
PAV........ Phase Angle Voltmeter
PA(V)........ Police Association (Victoria) [*Australia*]
PAV........ Position and Velocity
PAV........ Position and Velocity Tracking (IAA)
PAV........ Poste-Avion [*Airmail*] [*French*]
PAV........ Potential Acquisition Valuation Method [*Management*]
PAV........ Potential AIDS [*Acquired Immune Deficiency Syndrome*] Victim
PAV........ Pressure-Actuated Valve (NASA)
PAV........ Pressure Altitude Variation [*Aviation*]
PAV........ Propellant-Actuated Valve
PAV........ Public Access Videotex
PAV........ Public Against Violence [*Former Czechoslovakia*] [*Political party*]
PAV........ Puella Americana Vallensis [*Valley Girl*] [*Teenaged girl who follows the fads, fashions, and slang originated among teenagers in California's San Fernando Valley*]
PAVA .... Polish Army Veterans Association of America (EA)
PAVAS .... Performing and Visual Arts Society (EA)
PAVD .... Valdez [*Alaska*] [*ICAO location identifier*] (ICLI)
PAVE........ Parents Active for Vision Education [*An association*] (EA)
PAVE........ Paving
PAVE........ Performance-Based Adult Vocational Education (EDAC)
PAVE........ Position and Velocity Extraction
PAVE........ Preparing for AIDS/HIV Vaccine Evaluation [*National Institutes of Health project*]
PAVE........ Primary Auditory Visual Experience [*National Visitor Center*]
PAVE........ Principles and Applications of Value Engineering
PAVe........ Procarbazine, Alanine Nitrogen Mustard [*L-Phenylanine mustard, L-PAM*], Velban [*Vinblastine*] [*Antineoplastic drug regimen*]
PAVE........ Professional Audiovisual Education Study
PAVE........ Programmed Analysis for Value Engineers
PAVE PAWS... Precision Acquisition of Vehicle Entry Phased Array Warning System
PAVF........ Pulmonary Arteriovenous Fistula [*Medicine*]
PAVFC .... Princeton Azimuthally-Varying-Field Cyclotron
PAVG .... Prince Albert's Volunteer Guards [*British military*] (DMA)
pavl .... Pavilion (VRA)
PAVLA .... Papal Volunteers for Latin America [*Defunct*]
PAVM........ Patrons of the Arts in the Vatican Museum (EA)
PAVM........ Phase Angle Voltmeter
PAVM........ Proximity Automatic Vehicle Monitoring (PDAA)
PAVM........ Pulmonary Arteriovenous Malformation [*Medicine*] (DMAA)
PAVMT........ Pavement
PAVN .... People's Army of Vietnam
PAVO .... Prince Albert Victor's Own [*British military*] (DMA)
PAVOC........ Prince Albert Victor's Own Cavalry [*British military*] (DMA)
PA/VR........ Public Assistance/Vocational Rehabilitation
PAVS .... Pulmonary Arterial Vasconstrictor Substance [*Medicine*]
PAVT........ Position and Velocity Tracking
PAW........ Pambwa [*Papua New Guinea*] [*Airport symbol*] (OAG)
PAW........ Panel of American Women (EA)
PAW........ Peak Airway Pressure [*Medicine*] (DAVI)
PAW........ People for the American Way (EA)
PAW........ Percussive Arc Welder
PAW........ Performance Analysis Workstation [*Computer science*]
PAW........ Peripheral Airways [*Medicine*] (DMAA)
PAW........ Petroleum Administration for War [*World War II*]
PAW........ Plant-Available Water [*Botany*]
PAW........ Plasma Arc Welding
PAW........ Poetic Allusion Watch
PAW........ Port Angeles Western Railroad (IIA)
PAW........ Powered All the Way
Paw .... Pressure in the Airway [*level to be specified*] (DAVI)
PAW........ Primary Affective Witzelsucht [*Medicine*] (CPH)
PAW........ Public Administered Whipping [*Slang*]
PAW........ Pulmonary Artery Wedge [*Pressure*] [*Cardiology*] (DAVI)
PAW........ Pulmonary Artery Wedge Pressure [*Cardiology*]
PAWA .... Pan American Women's Association (EA)
PAWA .... Pan-American World Airways (NADA)
PAWA .... Power and Water Authority [*Northern Territory, Australia*]
PAWAF .... Polish American Workmen's Aid Fund (EA)
PAWBP .... Pension and Welfare Benefit Programs [*Labor-Managment Services Administration*] (IAA)
PAWC .... Pan-American Weightlifting Confederation (EA)
PA WC Bd Dec... Pennsylvania Workmen's Compensation Board Decisions [*A publication*] (DLA)
PA WC Bd Dec Dig... Digest of Decisions, Pennsylvania Workmen's Compensation Board [*A publication*] (DLA)
PA WC Bd (Dep Rep Sup)... Workmen's Compensation Supplement to Department Reports of Pennsylvania [*A publication*] (DLA)
PAWD .... Kodiak/Municipal [*Alaska*] [*ICAO location identifier*] (ICLI)
PAWE........ Program for Analysis of the World Ecosystem
PAWES .... Performance Assessment and Workload Evaluation (GAVI)
PAWLC .... Pan-American Weightlifting Confederation (EA)
PAWN .... First Cash [*NASDAQ symbol*] (TTSB)
PAWN .... First Cash, Inc. [*NASDAQ symbol*] (SAG)
PAWN .... Photon Adjoint with Neutron (PDAA)
PAWN .... Poole, Aberley, Worthington, and Nolen [*Four early residents of Pawn, Oregon. The city derives its name from the initial letters of their surnames*]
PAWNW........ First Cash Wrrt [*NASDAQ symbol*] (TTSB)
PAWO .... Pan-African Women's Organization [*Commercial firm*] (NADA)
Pawo .... Pressure at the Airway Opening [*Medicine*] (DAVI)
PAWOS........ Portable Automatic Weather Observing Station (MCD)
PAWP .... Pulmonary Artery Wedge Pressure [*Medicine*]
PAWS .... Parachute Altitude Wind Sensor
PAWS .... Performing Animal Welfare Society (EA)
PAWS .... Pet Animal Welfare Scheme [*British*] (DI)
PAWS .... Pets Are Worth Safeguarding [*An association*]
PAWS .... Phased Array Warning System
PAWS .... Polar Automatic Weather Station (NG)
PAWS .... Portable Automatic Weather Station (MUGU)
PAWS .... Pro-Active World Suspension [*Automotive engineering*]
PAWS .... Programmed Automatic Welding System
PAWS .... Progressive Animal Welfare Society (GNE)
PAWT........ Wainwright [*Alaska*] [*ICAO location identifier*] (ICLI)
PAWW .... Wildwood [*Alaska*] [*ICAO location identifier*] (ICLI)

PAX............ OPTEVFOR [*Operational Test and Evaluation Force*] Detachment, Patuxent River, MD [*Navy*] (CAAL)
PAX............ Pan Air, Inc. [*ICAO designator*] (FAAC)
PAX............ Pan Central Explorations Ltd. [*Toronto Stock Exchange symbol*]
PAX............ Parallel Architecture Extended [*Computer science*]
PAX............ Passenger (AFM)
PAX............ Patuxent River [*Maryland*] (MCD)
PAX............ Paxson [*Alaska*] [*Seismograph station code, US Geological Survey*] (SEIS)
Pax............ Paxton [*Record label*] [*Great Britain*]
PAX............ Person-to-Person Accelerated Xerography [*Office technology*] [*British*]
PAX............ Photoemission of Adsorbed Xenon [*Physics*]
PAX............ Physical Address Extension
PAX............ Place Address in Index Register (SAA)
PAX............ Private Automatic Exchange [*Telecommunications*]
Paxar.......... Paxar Corp. [*Associated Press*] (SAG)
PAXCON........ Passenger Airlift Contract [*Military*]
PaxsnC........ Paxson Communications Corp. [*Associated Press*] (SAG)
PAY............ Pamol [*Malaysia*] [*Airport symbol*] (OAG)
PAY............ SPS Transaction Services [*NYSE symbol*] (SAG)
PAYA.......... Yakutat [*Alaska*] [*ICAO location identifier*] (ICLI)
PAYABL........ Payable
Pay & Iv Carr... Payne and Ivamy's Carriage by Sea [*10th ed.*] [*1976*] [*A publication*] (DLA)
PAYC.......... Payco American Corp. [*NASDAQ symbol*] (NQ)
Paychx......... Paychex, Inc. [*Associated Press*] (SAG)
Payco.......... Payco American Corp. [*Associated Press*] (SAG)
PAYCOM........ Payload Command [*NASA*] (MCD)
PayCsh........ Payless Cashways, Inc. [*Associated Press*] (SAG)
PAYDAT........ Payload Data [*NASA*] (MCD)
PAYE........... Pay As You Earn
PAYE........... Pay As You Enter
PAYE........... Pitch and Yaw Engine (MCD)
PAYERS....... Program Accomplishment Year to Date Evaluation Reviews
PAYES......... Program for Assessing Youth Employment Skills [*Vocational guidance test*]
PAYG.......... Pay-As-You-Go
PAYGO........ Pay as You Go [*US Congress*]
PAYLD......... Payload
PaylSh......... Payless ShoeSource, Inc. [*Associated Press*] (SAG)
PAYM.......... Paymaster [*Military British*] (ROG)
PAYMARCORPS... Paymaster, Marine Corps
PAYMR........ Paymaster
PAYMT......... Payment
PAYMTR...... Paymaster [*Military British*] (ROG)
PAYR.......... Paymaster (WGA)
PAYS.......... Patriotic American Youth Society
PAYSOP....... Payroll-Based Stock Option Plan [*Human resources*] (WYGK)
PAYSOP....... Payroll/Stock Ownership Plan
PAYSU........ P'Eylim-American Yeshiva Student Union (EA)
PAYT.......... Payment
PAYX.......... Paychex, Inc. [*NASDAQ symbol*] (NQ)
PAZ............ Palaeozoic Axial Zone [*Geophysics*]
PAZ............ Partial Annealing Zone [*Geology*]
PAZ............ PM Air, Inc. [*ICAO designator*] (FAAC)
PAZ............ Poza Rica [*Mexico*] [*Airport symbol*] (OAG)
PAZA.......... Anchorage [*Alaska*] [*ICAO location identifier*] (ICLI)
PAZA.......... Pan American Zebu Association [*Later, IZBA*] (EA)
PAZF.......... Fairbanks [*Alaska*] [*ICAO location identifier*] (ICLI)
PB.............. Air Burundi [*ICAO designator*] (AD)
PB.............. Bachelor of Philosophy (WDAA)
PB.............. Bethlehem Public Library, Bethlehem, PA [*Library symbol Library of Congress*] (LCLS)
PB.............. Dr. Karl Thomae GmbH [*Germany*] [*Research code symbol*]
Pb.............. Lead
PB.............. Lead [*BTS*] (TAG)
P/B............. Pad and Boom [*Refueling*] [*Aerospace*] (MSA)
PB.............. Page Buffer (NITA)
PB.............. Painted Base (AAG)
PB.............. Panama Basin
PB.............. Panamerican Beverages [*NYSE symbol*] (SPSG)
PB.............. Panamerican Beverages 'A' [*NYSE symbol*] (TTSB)
PB.............. Panic Bar [*Technical drawings*]
PB.............. Paperback (CDAI)
PB.............. Paper Base (MSA)
PB.............. Paperboard Industries Corp. [*Toronto Stock Exchange symbol*]
PB.............. Papua Besena [*Papua New Guinea*] [*Political party*] (FEA)
PB.............. Paraffin Bath [*Medicine*]
PB.............. Paris Bourse [*The French stock exchange*]
PB.............. Parity BIT [*Binary Digit*] [*Data communications*] (IAA)
PB.............. Parke-Bernet [*Later, SPB*] [*Manhattan art auction house*]
PB.............. Parliamentary Bill [*British*] (ROG)
PB.............. Parole Board [*Australian Capital Territory*]
PB.............. Particle-Beam Weapon
PB.............. Parts Breakdown
PB.............. Passbook [*Banking*]
PB.............. Passed Ball
PB.............. Patrol Base [*Army*] (VNW)
PB.............. Patrol Boat [*Navy symbol*]
PB.............. Patrol Bomber
PB.............. Paul-Bunnell [*Test*] [*Immunology*] (AAMN)
PB.............. Pawnbroker
PB.............. Pay Board
PB.............. Peaceful Beginnings (EA)
PB.............. Peanut Butter [*Brand name of the Red Wing Co.*]
PB.............. Pennsylvania Ballet
PB.............. Pentaborane [*Rocket fuel*]
PB.............. Pentobarbital [*Organic chemistry*]
PB.............. Peribrachialis [*Anatomy*]
PB.............. Peripheral Blood [*Medicine*] (AAMN)
PB.............. Peripheral Buffer
PB.............. Permanent Ballast (DS)
PB.............. Permanent Bunkers
PB.............. Permanently Blind
PB.............. Peroneus Brevis [*Muscle*] [*orthopedics*] (DAVI)
PB.............. Petrus Brito [*Flourished, 13th century*] [*Authority cited in pre-1607 legal work*] (DSA)
PB.............. Phalangeal Bracket [*i.e., cup handle*] [*Slang*]
PB.............. Pharmacopoeia Britannica [*British Pharmacopoeia*]
PB.............. Phenobarbital [*A drug*]
PB.............. Philosophiae Baccalaureus [*Bachelor of Philosophy*]
PB.............. Phonetically Balanced [*With reference to word lists*]
PB.............. Phosphate Buffer
PB.............. Phosphoribosyl
PB.............. Photon Barrier [*Astrophysics*]
PB.............. Physics Briefs [*Physikalische Berichte*] [*American Institute of Physics Database*] [*Information service or system*] (IID)
PB.............. Physiotherapists Board [*Australian Capital Territory*]
PB.............. Picket Boat [*Navy*]
PB.............. Piebald
PB.............. Piggyback (IAA)
PB.............. Pilotless Bomber [*Air Force*]
PB.............. Pinchbeck [*Jewelry*] (ROG)
PB.............. Pinch Biopsy [*Medicine*] (MEDA)
PB.............. Pine Bark
PB.............. Pink Bollworm [*Cotton pest*]
PB.............. Pipe Break [*Nuclear energy*] (NRCH)
PB.............. Piperonyl Butoxide [*Organic chemistry*]
PB.............. Pit Border [*Paleobotany*]
PB.............. Pitney-Bowes, Inc.
PB.............. Planning Board
PB.............. Plasminogen Binding [*Hematology*]
PB.............. Plate Block [*Philately*]
PB.............. Playback (KSC)
PB.............. Plot Board (KSC)
PB.............. Plugboard
PB.............. Plugging Back [*Computer science*] (IAA)
Pb.............. Plumbum [*Lead*] [*Chemical element*]
PB.............. Plymouth Brethren (ROG)
PB.............. Pocket Book
PB.............. Police Burgh
PB.............. Policy Board (OICC)
PB.............. Polished Buckram (DGA)
PB.............. Pollen Body [*Botany*]
PB.............. Polybenzene [*Organic chemistry*]
PB.............. Polybutylene [*Organic chemistry*]
PB.............. Polymyxin B [*An antibiotic*]
PB.............. Polystyrene Base (DGA)
PB.............. Pony Baseball (EA)
PB.............. Poop and Bridge [*of a ship*] (DS)
PB.............. Population Biology
PB.............. Ports and Beaches (NATG)
PB.............. Powder Bed (DAVI)
PB.............. Powder Board (DAVI)
PB.............. Power Boiler
PB.............. Power Box (IAA)
PB.............. Power Brakes [*Automotive engineering*]
PB.............. Power Builder [*Computer software*] (CDE)
PB.............. Prayer Book
PB.............. Preburner [*NASA*] (NASA)
PB.............. Preliminary Breakdown
PB.............. Premature Beat [*Medicine*] (CPH)
PB.............. Premium Bond (ODBW)
Pb.............. Presbyopia [*Ophthalmology*]
PB.............. Presentation Brothers [*See also FPM*] (EAIO)
PB.............. President's Budget (DOMA)
PB.............. Presiding Bishop [*Episcopal Church*]
PB.............. Pressure Breathing
PB.............. Primary Buffer [*Chemistry*]
PB.............. Primary Bus [*Computer science*] (CAAL)
PB.............. Primitive Baptist
PB.............. Prisoners' Barracks (ADA)
PB.............. Private Business [*Slang British*]
PB.............. Privately Bonded
Pb.............. Probability (PCM)
PB.............. Process Basic (ECII)
PB.............. Process Bulletin
PB.............. Production Base (MCD)
PB.............. Professional Books Ltd. (ILCA)
PB.............. Profile Block (MCD)
PB.............. Program Baseline (DOMA)
PB.............. Program Block (IAA)
PB.............. Program Breakdown
PB.............. Program Budgeting (ADA)
PB.............. Property Book [*Army*] (AABC)
PB.............. Proportional Band
PB.............. Protein-Binding (MAE)
PB.............. Protein-Bound [*Clinical chemistry*] (DAVI)
PB.............. Provisional Battalion [*Military A publication*] (ROG)

PB............... Pseudoterminal Bud [*Botany*]
PB............... Ptychodiscus brevis [*An alga, the cause of the red tide*]
PB............... Public (DSUE)
PB............... Publications (NITA)
PB............... Publications Board [*Later, CFSTI, NTIS*]
PB............... Publications Bulletin
PB............... Publisher (NITA)
PB............... Publishers' Binding (DGA)
PB............... Publisher's Name [*Online database field identifier*]
PB............... Pull Back (NTCM)
PB............... Pull Box (AAG)
PB............... Pulse Beacon (KSC)
PB............... Purl into Back of Stitch [*Knitting*] (WDAA)
PB............... Purplish Blue
PB............... Push Button
PB4............... Plate Block of Four [*Philately*]
PBa............... Academy of the New Church, Bryn Athyn, PA [*Library symbol Library of Congress*] (LCLS)
Pba............... Brachial Arterial Pressure [*Medicine*] (MAE)
PBA............... Pacific Broadcasting Association (EAIO)
PBA............... Paid by Agent [*Business term*] (DCTA)
PBA............... Partido Barrientista Autentico [*Bolivia*] [*Political party*] (PPW)
PBA............... Patrol Boat, Air Cushion (MCD)
PBA............... Patrolmen's Benevolent Association
PBA............... Pencil Beam Antenna
PBA............... Percutaneous Bladder Aspiration [*Urology*] (DAVI)
PBA............... Permanent Budget Account
PBA............... Phenylboronate Agarose [*Biochemistry*] (DAVI)
PBA............... Phenylboronic Acid [*Organic chemistry*]
PBA............... Phenylbutyric Acid [*Organic chemistry*]
PBA............... Physical Blowing Agent [*Plastics technology*]
PBA............... Pill Box Antenna
PBA............... Pine Bluff Arsenal [*Army*] (AABC)
PBA............... Plant Breeding Abstracts [*A publication*]
PbA............... Plasmodium Berghei Anka [*Bacteriology*]
PBA............... Plastic Bag Association (EA)
PBA............... Polar Bear Association (EA)
PBA............... Polish Beneficial Association (EA)
PBA............... Polybenzamide [*Organic chemistry*]
PBA............... Polybutyl Acrylate [*Organic chemistry*]
PBA............... Polyclonal B Cell Activator [*Hematology*]
PBA............... Port Blair [*Andaman Islands*] [*Seismograph station code, US Geological Survey*] (SEIS)
PBA............... Port of Bristol Authority [*British*]
PBA............... Poultry Breeders of America (EA)
PBA............... Powered Battle Armor [*A computer game*] (PCM)
PBA............... Prescott Builders Association (EA)
PBA............... President of the British Academy
PBA............... Pressure Breathing Assistor [*Medicine*]
PBA............... Principal Business Activity (GFGA)
PBA............... Printed Board Assembly (IAA)
PBA............... Printing Brokerage Association (EA)
PBA............... Production Base Analysis (MCD)
PBA............... Professional Bookmen of America [*Later, Pi Beta Alpha*] (EA)
PBA............... Professional Bowlers Association of America (EA)
PBA............... Provincetown-Boston Airlines, Inc.
PBA............... Prune Belly Anomaly [*Medicine*] (DMAA)
PBA............... Public Buildings Administration [*Functions transferred to PBS, 1949*]
PBA............... Pulpobuccoaxial [*Dentistry*]
PBA............... Pyrenebutyric Acid [*Organic chemistry*]
PBAA............... Periodical and Book Association of America (EA)
PBAA............... Poly(butadiene-acrylic Acid) [*Organic chemistry*]
PBAA............... Private Businesses Association of Australia
PBAC............... Pacific Bantam Austin Club (EA)
PBAC............... Program Budget Advisory Committee [*Army*]
PB-AESRS............... Property Book - Army Equipment Status Reporting System (AABC)
PBAL............... Protected Bronchoalveolar Lavage [*Medicine*] (DMAA)
PBAN............... Pheromone Biosynthesis-Activating Neuropeptide [*Biochemistry*]
PBAN............... Poly(butadiene-acrylonitrile) [*Organic chemistry*]
PB and J............... Peanut Butter and Jelly
PBAPRS............... Program/Budget Accounting and Progress Reporting System [*Proposed*] [*Navy*]
PBAPS............... Peach Bottom Atomic Power Station (NRCH)
PBAPS............... Pipe Break Air Piping System (IEEE)
PBAPS............... Pipe Break Automatic Protective System (IEEE)
PBAR............... Baker Island Army Air Field [*Baker Island*] [*ICAO location identifier*] (ICLI)
PBAS............... Program Budget Accounting System [*Military*] (GFGA)
PBAT............... Pyro Battery (KSC)
PBATS............... Professional Baseball Athletic Trainers Society (EA)
PBAV............... Percutaneous Balloon Aortic Valvuloplasty [*Cardiology*] (CPH)
PBAV............... Power Boat Association of Victoria [*Australia*]
PBB............... Bloomsburg State College, Bloomsburg, PA [*OCLC symbol*] (OCLC)
PBB............... Parallel by Bit
PBB............... Paranaiba [*Brazil*] [*Airport symbol*] (OAG)
PBB............... Parti Pesaka Bumiputera Bersatu Sarawak [*United Bumiputra Party*] [*Malaysia*] [*Political party*] (FEA)
PBB............... Polybrominated Biphenyl [*Flame retardant, toxic chemical*]
PBB............... Posterior Basal Body [*Botany*]
PBB............... Private Boxes and Bags
PBB............... Program Plan Budgeting (TDOB)
PBB............... Project Blue Book [*An association*] (EA)
PBBATU............... Pastrycooks, Bakers, Biscuitmakers, and Allied Trades Union [*Australia*]
PBBCAS............... Program-Based Budget Classification and Analysis System [*Pronounced "pib-kaz"*] [*Office of Management and Budget*]
PBbCHi............... Columbia County Historical Society, Bloomsburg, PA [*Library symbol Library of Congress*] (LCLS)
PBBFI............... Pearl S. Buck Birthplace Foundation, Inc. (EA)
PBBH............... Peter Bent Brigham Hospital [*Boston*]
PBbS............... Bloomsburg State College, Bloomsburg, PA [*Library symbol Library of Congress*] (LCLS)
PBBS............... Pertubuhan Bumiputera Bersatu Sarawak [*United Sarawak National Association*] [*Malaysia*] [*Political party*] (FEA)
PBBs............... Polybromated Biphenyls [*Organic chemistry*] (DAVI)
PBBSF............... Pacific Basin Bulk [*NASDAQ symbol*] (TTSB)
PBBSF............... Pacific Basin Bulk Shippers Ltd. [*NASDAQ symbol*] (SAG)
PBBWF............... Pacific Basin Blk Shipng Wrrt [*NASDAQ symbol*] (TTSB)
PBBWF............... Pacific Basin Bulk Shippers Ltd. [*NASDAQ symbol*] (SAG)
PBC............... Columbia/Mt. Pleasant, TN [*Location identifier FAA*] (FAAL)
PBC............... Pacific Bible College [*California*]
PBC............... Packed by Carrier
PBC............... Pakistan Broadcasting Corp. (IMH)
PBC............... Panamerican Badminton Confederation (EAIO)
PBC............... Parallel by Character
PBC............... Pedal Branch of Columellar [*Muscle*]
PBC............... Pen and Brush Club (EA)
PBC............... People's Bank of China (ECON)
PBC............... People's Bicentennial [*later, Business*] Commission
PBC............... Periodic Bond Chain (IAA)
PBC............... Peripheral Blood Cells [*Medicine*]
PBC............... Peripheral Bus Computer [*Bell System*]
PBC............... Personnel/Burden Carrier Manufacturers Association [*Defunct*] (EA)
PBC............... Plain Bond Copier [*Pitney Bowes*]
PBC............... Planning and the Black Community (EA)
PBC............... Point of Basal Convergence
PBC............... Practice Bomb Contained (NG)
PBC............... Prebed Care [*Medicine*] (MAE)
PBC............... Presbyterians for Biblical Concerns (EA)
PBC............... Primary Biliary Cirrhosis [*Medicine*]
PBC............... Program Booking Center [*Telecommunications*] (TEL)
PBC............... Program Budget Committee [*Military*]
PBC............... Psychometric Behavior Checklist [*Psychology*]
PBC............... Public Buildings Commission [*Functions transferred to PBA, 1939*]
PBCA............... Pacific Bible College of Azusa [*California*]
PBCA............... Paperboard Butter Chip Association
PBCA............... Professional Business Colleges of Australia
PBCB............... Pierce-Blank Die (Class B) (MCD)
PBCB............... Professional Boxing Control Board [*Victoria, Australia*]
PBCC............... Packard Bell Computer Corp. (IAA)
PBCC............... Pitney Bowes Credit Corp.
PBCCH............... Pentabromochlorocyclohexane [*Flame retardant*] [*Organic chemistry*]
PBCE............... Pine Bluff Cotton Exchange [*Defunct*] (EA)
PBCF............... Prudential-Bache Capital Funding
PBCI............... Pamrapo Bancorp [*NASDAQ symbol*] (TTSB)
PBCI............... Pamrapo Bancorp, Inc. [*NASDAQ symbol*] (NQ)
PBCMO............... Poly(bis(chloromethyl)oxetane) [*Organic chemistry*]
PBCO............... Praseodymium Barium Copper Oxide [*Inorganic chemistry*]
PB/COC............... Plymouth Barracuda/Cuda Owners Club (EA)
PbCoNA............... Publishing Co. of North America, Inc. (The) [*Associated Press*] (SAG)
PBCS............... Persian Bicolor and Calico Society (EA)
PBCS............... Post Boost Control System [*Aerospace*]
PBCT............... People's Bank [*Bridgeport, CT*] [*NASDAQ symbol*] (NQ)
PBCT............... Proposed Boundary Crossing Time [*Aviation*]
PBCTP............... People's Bank 8.5% Cv 'A' Pfd [*NASDAQ symbol*] (TTSB)
PBCU............... Predominately Black Colleges and Universities
PBC-USA............... Polar Bear Club - USA (EA)
PBC-WS............... Polar Bear Club - Winter Swimmers [*Later, PBC-USA*] (EA)
PBD............... Pacific Basin Development Corp. [*Vancouver Stock Exchange symbol*]
PBD............... Paperboard (MSA)
PBD............... Parallel Blade Damper (OA)
PBD............... Particle Board [*Technical drawings*]
PBD............... Paul-Bunnell-Davidsohn [*Test*] [*Immunology*]
PBD............... Payload Bay Door [*NASA*] (NASA)
PBD............... Percutaneous Biliary Drainage [*Gastroenterology*] (DAVI)
PBD............... Phenylbiphenylyloxadiazole [*Analytical biochemistry*]
PBD............... Pierce-Blank Die (MCD)
PBD............... Place Bearing/Distance [*Way point*] (GAVI)
PBD............... Plasterboard
PBD............... Plenum Bleed Duct [*Hovercraft*]
PBD............... Polybutadiene [*Organic chemistry*]
PBD............... Porbandar [*India*] [*Airport symbol*] (OAG)
PBD............... Postburn Day [*Medicine*] (DMAA)
PBD............... Power Building (NATG)
PBD............... Precise Block Diagram
PBD............... Pressboard (MSA)
PBD............... Program Budget Decision [*DoD*]
PBD............... Program Budget Directive (MCD)
PBD............... Program Budget Document (MCD)
PBD............... Programmer Brain Damage [*Computer hacker terminology*] (NHD)
PBD............... Proliferative Breast Disease [*Medicine*]
PBDB............... Provisional Base Defense Battalion [*Marine Corps*] (VNW)
PBDC............... Pacific Basin Development Council (EA)
PBDF............... Payload Bay Door Forward [*NASA*] (MCD)
PBDG............... Push-Button Data Generator (IEEE)
PBDI............... Position Bearing and Distance Indicator (MCD)
PBDM............... Payload Bay Door Mechanism [*NASA*] (NASA)

PBDMA........ Poly(butadiene-malic Acid) [*A polymer*]
PBDS.......... Parti Bansa Dayak Sarawak [*Malaysia*] [*Political party*] (FEA)
PBDU.......... Pancreaticobiliary Ductal Union [*Anatomy*]
PBe............ Beaver Memorial Library, Beaver, PA [*Library symbol Library of Congress*] (LCLS)
PBE............ Paint, Body, and Equipment [*Automotive engineering*]
PBE............ Paschen-Back Effect [*Spectroscopy*]
PBE............ Pemberton Exploration [*Vancouver Stock Exchange symbol*]
PBE............ Perlsucht Bacillary Emulsion [*Medicine*]
PBE............ Piggyback Experiment
PBE............ Poison-Boltzmann Equation [*Physical chemistry*]
PBE............ Polybutene [*Organic chemistry*]
PBE............ Present-Barrel-Equivalent
PBE............ Prompt Burst Experiments [*Nuclear energy*] (NRCH)
PBE............ Prompt-by-Example [*Computer science*]
PBE............ Proton Balance Equation
PBE............ Proton Binding Energy
PBE............ Puerto Berrio [*Colombia*] [*Airport symbol*] (OAG)
PBE............ Pulsed Bridge Element [*Telecommunications*] (OA)
PBEA.......... Paint, Body, and Equipment Association (EA)
PBEB.......... Pentabromoethylbenzene [*Flame retardant*] [*Organic chemistry*]
PBeC.......... Beaver County Court House, Beaver, PA [*Library symbol Library of Congress*] (LCLS)
PBEC.......... Pacific Basin Economic Council (FEA)
PBEC.......... Public Broadcasting Environment Center [*Corporation for Public Broadcasting*]
PBECL........ Performance-Based Exposure Control Limit [*Environmental science*]
PBEI.......... Performance-Based Evaluation Instrument (EDAC)
PBEIST....... Planning Board European Inland Surface Transport [*Army*] (AABC)
PBel.......... Centre County Library, Bellefonte, PA [*Library symbol Library of Congress*] (LCLS)
PBelC........ Centre County Court House, Bellefonte, PA [*Library symbol Library of Congress*] (LCLS)
PBER.......... Program Budget Execution Review [*Army*]
PBerol........ Berlin Papyri [*A publication*] (OCD)
PBf............ Carnegie Free Library, Beaver Falls, PA [*Library symbol Library of Congress*] (LCLS)
PBF............ Fast Patrol Boat [*Ship symbol*] [*NATO*] (NATG)
PBF............ Patriotic Burmese Forces [*World War II*]
PBF............ Patrol Boat, Fast [*British military*] (DMA)
PBF............ Peribronchial Fibrosis [*Medicine*]
PBF............ Pilot Bypass Filter (IAA)
PBF............ Pine Bluff [*Arkansas*] [*Airport symbol Obsolete*] (OAG)
PBF............ Plastic Bottle Feeder
PBF............ Plates for Beam Forming (DEN)
PBF............ Poop, Bridge, and Forecastle [*of a ship*] (DS)
PBF............ Portal Blood Flow [*Physiology*]
PBF............ Potential Benefit Factor (OA)
PBF............ Power Burst Facility [*Nuclear energy*]
PBF............ Pulmonary Blood Flow [*Medicine*]
PBFA.......... Particle Beam Fusion Accelerator
PBFA.......... Provincial Booksellers' Fairs Association [*British*] (DI)
PBFC.......... Peter Breck Fan Club (EA)
PBFC.......... Pierce Brosnan Fan Club (EA)
PBFD.......... Pierce Bland and Form Die (MSA)
PBFE.......... Peroxisomal Bifunctional Enzyme (DMAA)
PB-Fe......... Protein-Bound Iron (MAE)
PBfG.......... Geneva College, Beaver Falls, PA [*Library symbol Library of Congress*] (LCLS)
PBFG.......... Guided Missile Fast Patrol Boat [*Ship symbol*] (NATG)
PBFG.......... Patrol Boat, Fast, Guided Weapon [*British military*] (DMA)
PBFI.......... Paris Business Forms, Inc. [*Burlington, NJ*] [*NASDAQ symbol*] (NQ)
PBFI.......... Paris Corp. [*NASDAQ symbol*] (TTSB)
PBFL.......... Planning for Better Family Living [*UN Food and Agriculture Organization*]
PBFP.......... Provisioning Budget Forecast Procedure (MCD)
PBF/WR....... Presiding Bishop's Fund for World Relief (EA)
PBG............ Phenylbiguanide [*Biochemistry*]
PBG............ Photonic Bandgap [*Physics*]
PBG............ Plattsburgh, NY [*Location identifier FAA*] (FAAL)
PBG............ Poly(benzyl Glutamate) [*Organic chemistry*]
PBG............ Porphobilinogen [*Clinical chemistry*]
PBG............ Powszechny Bank Gospodarczy [*Poland*]
PBG............ Program and Budget Guidance [*Army*]
PBGA.......... Plastic Ball Grid Arrays
PBGC.......... Pension Benefit Guaranty Corp. [*Government agency*]
PBGD.......... Porphobilinogen Deaminase [*An enzyme*]
PBGI.......... Piedmont BankGroup, Inc. [*NASDAQ symbol*] (NQ)
PBG-QN....... Porphobilinogen - Quantitative [*Genetics*] (DAVI)
PBG-S......... Porphobilinogen Synthase [*Medicine*] (DMAA)
PBH............ Partial Bulkhead (DS)
PBH............ Patrol Boat, Hydrofoil (MCD)
PBH............ Phillips, WI [*Location identifier FAA*] (FAAL)
PBH............ Post Biblical Hebrew [*Language, etc.*] (BJA)
PBH............ Primordial Black Hole [*Astrophysics*]
PBH............ Pulling Boat Hands (DMAA)
PBHB.......... Poly-Beta-Hydroxybutyrate (DMAA)
PBHF.......... President Benjamin Harrison Foundation (EA)
PBHP.......... Pounds per Brake Horsepower
PB-HTGR..... Peach Bottom High-Temperature Gas-Cooled Reactor
PBI............ Palm Beach International Airport [*FAA*] (TAG)
PBI............ Paper Bag Institute (EA)
PBI............ Parental Bonding Instrument
PBI............ Partial Background Investigation [*Army*]
PBI............ Partial Bony Impaction [*Orthopedics*] (DAVI)
PBI............ Paving Brick Institute
PBI............ Peace Brigades International (EA)
PBI............ Pen and Brush, Inc. (EA)
PBI............ Penile-Brachial Index [*Medicine*] (DAVI)
PBI............ Phenformin [*An oral hypoglycemic*] [*Obsolete*] (DAVI)
PBI............ Philadelphia Bible Institute [*Pennsylvania*]
PBI............ Phillips Business Information, Inc. (IID)
PBI............ Pitch Boundary Indicator (MCD)
PBI............ Pitney Bowes [*NYSE symbol*] (TTSB)
PBI............ Pitney-Bowes, Inc. [*NYSE symbol*] (SPSG)
PBI............ Plant Biological Institute [*University of Saskatchewan*] [*Canada*]
PBI............ Plant Biotechnology Institute [*National Research Council of Canada*] [*Research center*] (RCD)
PBI............ Plant Breeding Institute [*British*]
PBI............ Plastic Bottle Institute (EA)
PBI............ Plumbing Brass Institute [*Later, PMI*] (EA)
PBI............ Polybenzimidazole [*Organic chemistry*] (NATG)
PBI............ Poly(phenylenebibenzimidazole) [*Organic chemistry*]
PBI............ Poor Bloody Infantry [*British military slang*]
PBI............ Process Branch Indicator
PBI............ Programme Biologique Internationale [*International Biological Program - IBP*] (MSC)
PBI............ Projected Books, Inc. [*Defunct*] (EA)
PBI............ Prophylactic Brain Irradiation [*Oncology*]
PBI............ Protein-Bound Iodine [*Clinical chemistry*]
PBI............ Public Benevolent Institution [*Australia*]
PBI............ Pupil Behavior Inventory [*Psychology*]
PBI............ Push-Button Indicator
PBI............ Puzzle Buffs International (EA)
PBI............ West Palm Beach [*Florida*] [*Airport symbol*]
PBIB.......... Partially-Balanced Incomplete Block (PDAA)
PBIC.......... Poly(butyl Isocyanate) [*Organic chemistry*]
PBIC.......... Programmable Buffer Interface Card [*Computer science*] (NASA)
PBICSGH..... Permanent Bureau of International Congresses for the Sciences of Genealogy and Heraldry (EA)
PBIF.......... Pacific Bible Institute of Fresno [*California*]
PBIL.......... Polybenzimidazolone [*Organic chemistry*]
PBIM.......... Programmable Buffer Interface Module (MCD)
PBIO.......... PerSeptive Biosystems [*NASDAQ symbol*] (TTSB)
PBIO.......... PerSeptive Biosystems, Inc. [*NASDAQ symbol*] (SAG)
PBIOZ........ PerSeptive Biosystems Wrrt [*NASDAQ symbol*] (TTSB)
PBIP.......... Paperbound Books in Print [*A publication*]
PBIP.......... Pulse Beacon Impact Predictor (AAG)
PBIPr......... Pitney Bowes $2.12 Cv Pref [*NYSE symbol*] (TTSB)
PBIS.......... Performance-Based Incentive System (AAGC)
PBISTP....... Peter Burwash International Special Tennis Programs (EA)
PBIT.......... Parity BIT [*Binary Digit*] [*Data communications*]
PB/IWT....... Ports and Beaches and Inland Waterways Transports [*Military*] (NATG)
PBIX.......... Patriot Bank [*NASDAQ symbol*] (TTSB)
PBIX.......... Patriot Bank Corp. (PA) [*NASDAQ symbol*] (SAG)
PBJ............ Paper-Braided Jute (IAA)
PBJ............ Peanut Butter and Jelly
PBJ............ Peanut Butter and Jelly Sandwich (TAG)
PBJ............ Presa Benito Juarez [*Mexico*] [*Seismograph station code, US Geological Survey*] (SEIS)
PBJC.......... Palm Beach Junior College [*Lakeworth, FL*]
PBK............ Paperback
PBK............ Payload Bay Kit [*NASA*] (NASA)
PBK............ Phi Beta Kappa [*Honorary society*]
PB (k)........ Phonetically Balanced (Kindergarten) [*Speech and language therapy*] (DAVI)
PBK............ Phosphorylase B Kinase [*An enzyme*] (MAE)
PBK............ Poncebank [*NYSE symbol*] (SAG)
PBK............ PONCEBANK [*NYSE symbol*] (TTSB)
PBKAL......... Paris, Brussels, Koln [*Cologne*], Amsterdam, London [*High-speed rail network*] (ECON)
PBKB.......... Peoples Bancshares, Inc. [*NASDAQ symbol*] (SAG)
PBKB.......... People's Savings Bank of Brockton [*Brockton, MA*] [*NASDAQ symbol*] (NQ)
PBKC.......... Premier Bankshares [*NASDAQ symbol*] (TTSB)
PBKC.......... Premier Bankshares Corp. [*NASDAQ symbol*] (NQ)
PBKS.......... Provident Bankshares [*NASDAQ symbol*] (TTSB)
PBKS.......... Provident Bankshares Corp. [*NASDAQ symbol*] (NQ)
PBKTOA....... Printing, Bookbinding, and Kindred Trades' Overseers Association [*British*] (BI)
PBL............ Bethlehem Public Library, Bethlehem, PA [*OCLC symbol*] (OCLC)
PBl............ Blairsville Public Library, Blairsville, PA [*Library symbol Library of Congress*] (LCLS)
PBL............ Lehigh University, Bethlehem, PA [*Library symbol Library of Congress*] (LCLS)
PBL............ Parachute-Braked Landing [*Military*] (IAA)
PBL............ Payload Bay Liner [*NASA*] (MCD)
PBL............ Peripheral Blood Leukocyte [*or Lymphocyte*] [*Hematology*]
PBL............ [*The*] Philadelphia Belt Line Railroad Co. [*AAR code*]
PBL............ Photo Butt Line (MSA)
PBL............ Planetary Boundary Layer [*Aerospace*]
PBL............ Potential Binding Level [*Of natural waters for metal ions*]
PBL............ Product Baseline (MCD)
PBL............ Prune Brownline [*Plant pathology*]
PBL............ Public Broadcasting Laboratory (NTCM)
PBL............ Public Broadcast Laboratory
pbl............ Publisher [*MARC relator code*] [*Library of Congress*] (LCCP)
PBL............ Pueblo [*Diocesan abbreviation*] [*Colorado*] (TOCD)
PBL............ Puerto Cabello [*Venezuela*] [*Airport symbol*] (OAG)

PBlbM.......... Montgomery County Community College, Blue Bell, PA [*Library symbol Library of Congress*] (LCLS)
PBLD.......... Progressive Base Line Dimensioning (SAA)
PBLG.......... Polybenzyl-L-glutamate [*Biochemistry*]
PBLI.......... Premature Birth, Live Infant [*neonatology*] (DAVI)
PBIP.......... Blairsville Public Library, Blairsville, PA [*Library symbol*] [*Library of Congress*] (LCLS)
PBLS.......... Production Baseline Set (MCD)
PBLSHNG.... Publishing
PBm.......... Bryn Mawr College, Bryn Mawr, PA [*Library symbol Library of Congress*] (LCLS)
PBM.......... Paramaribo [*Surinam*] [*Airport symbol*] (OAG)
PBM.......... Patrol Search Plane [*Navy designation for Mariner aircraft*]
PBM.......... Peak Bone Mass [*Medicine*] (DMAA)
PBM.......... Performance-Based Management (AAGC)
PBM.......... Performance Based Method [*Environmental Protection Agency*] [*Analytical chemistry*]
PBM.......... Peripheral Basement Membrane [*Medicine*] (DMAA)
PBM.......... Peripheral Blood Mononuclear [*Cells*] [*Hematology*]
PBM.......... Permanent Bench Mark
PBM.......... Pharmaceutical Benefit Manager [*or Management*] [*Managed health care*]
PBM.......... Pharmacy Benefit Managers (ECON)
PBM.......... PIXEL Block Mode [*Computer science*] (BYTE)
PBM.......... Placental Basement Membrane [*Medicine*] (DMAA)
PBM.......... Portable BIT [*Binary Digit*] Map [*Computer science*]
PBM.......... Potential Barrier Method (IAA)
PBM.......... Pressure Bias Modulation (MCD)
PBM.......... Principal Beach Master [*RAF*] [*British*]
PBM.......... Probability Based-Matched [*Database search techniques*]
PBM.......... Production Base Modernization (MCD)
PBM.......... Program Budget Manager (MCD)
PBM.......... Program Business Management (NASA)
PBM.......... Pulse Burst Modulation (IAA)
PBmA.......... American College of Life Underwriters, Bryn Mawr, PA [*Library symbol Library of Congress*] (LCLS)
PBMA.......... Peanut Butter Manufacturers Association [*Later, PBNPA*] (EA)
PBMA.......... Plastic Bath Manufacturers Association [*British*] (DI)
PBMA.......... Plumbers and Builders Merchants Association [*Australia*]
PBMA.......... Polybutyl Methacrylate [*Organic chemistry*]
PBMA.......... Pressed Brick Makers' Association Ltd. [*British*] (BI)
PBMASA...... Paper Bag Manufacturers' Association of South Australia
PBMC.......... Moravian College and Theological Seminary, Bethlehem, PA [*Library symbol Library of Congress*] (LCLS)
PBMC.......... Peripheral Blood Mononuclear Cells [*Hematology*]
PBMCA........ Archives of the Moravian Church, Bethlehem, PA [*Library symbol Library of Congress*] (LCLS)
PBME.......... Physiology and Biomedical Engineering [*Program*] (DAVI)
PBME.......... Physiology and Biomedical Engineering Program (BABM)
PBMI.......... Pacific Biometrics, Inc. [*NASDAQ symbol*] (SAG)
PBmL.......... Ludington Public Library, Bryn Mawr, PA [*Library symbol Library of Congress*] (LCLS)
PBMNC........ Peripheral Blood Monomuclear Cell [*Hematology*] (DAVI)
PBMR.......... Pennsylvania Bureau of Municipal Research (MCD)
PBMR.......... Provisional Basic Military Requirements (NATG)
PBMS.......... Parcel Business Machine System (NITA)
PBMS.......... Performance-Based Measurement System [*Environmental Protection Agency*]
PBMS.......... Photonburst Mass Spectrometry
PBMS.......... Pitney Bowes Management Services
PBM/STIRS... Probability Based Matching and Self-Trained Interpretive and Retrieval Systems [*Database*] [*John Wiley & Sons, Inc.*] [*Information service or system*] (CRD)
PBMW.......... Moravian College, Bethlehem, PA [*Library symbol Library of Congress*] (LCLS)
PBN.......... Northampton County Area Community College, Bethlehem, PA [*Library symbol Library of Congress*] (LCLS)
PBN.......... Paralytic Brachial Neuritis [*Medicine*] (MAE)
PBN.......... PE Ben Oilfield Services Ltd. [*Toronto Stock Exchange symbol*]
PBN.......... Peribrachialis Nuclei [*Neurology*]
PBN.......... Phenyl(butyl)nitrone [*Organic chemistry*]
PBN.......... Physical Block Number
PBN.......... Pilatus Britten-Norman Ltd. [*British ICAO designator*] (FAAC)
PBN.......... PointCast Business Network
PBN.......... Polymixin-B Sulfate/Bacitracin/Neomycin [*Antibacterial regime*]
PBN.......... Porto Amboin [*Angola*] [*Airport symbol*] (OAG)
PBN.......... Primary Block Number [*Computer science*]
PBN.......... Pyrolytic Boron Nitride [*Inorganic chemistry*]
PBNA.......... Partial Body Neutron Activation [*Radiology*]
PBNA.......... Phenyl-beta-naphthylamine [*Organic chemistry*]
PBNB.......... People's Savings Financial Corp. [*Formerly, People's Savings Bank New Britain*] [*NASDAQ symbol*] (NQ)
PBNB.......... Peoples Svgs Finl [*NASDAQ symbol*] (TTSB)
PBNE.......... Philadelphia, Bethlehem & New England Railroad Co. [*AAR code*]
PBNM.......... Parallel Bar Noise Maker [*Antiacoustic torpedo device*]
PBNP.......... Phipps Bend Nuclear Plant (NRCH)
PBNP.......... Point Beach Nuclear Plant (NRCH)
PBNP.......... Porcine Brain Natriuretic Peptide [*Biochemistry*]
PBNPA........ Peanut Butter and Nut Processors Association (EA)
PBNSW........ Pharmacy Board of New South Wales [*Australia*]
PBNSW........ Police Board of New South Wales [*Australia*]
PBNT.......... Parole Board of the Northern Territory [*Australia*]
PBO.......... Packed by Owner
PBO.......... Paleobioclimatic Operator
PBO.......... Paraburdoo [*Australia Airport symbol*] (OAG)
PBO.......... Pauling Bond Order [*Physical chemistry*]
PBO.......... Penicillin in Beeswax [*Medicine*] (DMAA)
PBO.......... Penicillin in Beeswax and Oil [*Medicine*] (DMAA)
PBO.......... Performance-Based Organization
P Bo.......... Petrus Boaterius [*Flourished, 1285-1321*] [*Authority cited in pre-1607 legal work*] (DSA)
pbo.......... Placebo [*Medicine*]
PBO.......... Plotting Board Operator (MUGU)
PBO.......... Poly(p-phenylene Benzobisoxazole) (RDA)
PBO.......... Poor Bloody Observer [*British World War I military slang*] (DSUE)
PBO.......... Print Business Opportunities [*A publication*] (EAAP)
PBO.......... Projected Benefit Obligation (TDOB)
PBO.......... Property Book Officer [*Army*] (AABC)
PBO.......... Push-Button Operation
PBoC.......... People's Bank of China
PBOCST...... Poly(butoxycarbonyloxystyrene) [*Organic chemistry*]
PBOD.......... Phytoplankton Biochemical Oxygen Demand [*Oceanography*]
PBOI.......... Public Board of Inquiry
PBOIP.......... Preliminary Basis of Issue Plan [*Military*] (MCD)
PBOS.......... Planning Board for Ocean Shipping [*Army NATO*]
PBP.......... [*The*] Paper Bag Players (EA)
PBP.......... Para-(Benzyloxy)phenol [*Organic chemistry*]
PB/P.......... Particleboard/Plywood
PBP.......... Pay-Back Period [*Finance*]
PBP.......... Pay by Phone [*Business term*]
PBP.......... Peak Blood Pressure [*Cardiology*] (DAVI)
PBP.......... Pellin-Broca Prism [*Physics*]
PBP.......... Penicillin-Binding Protein [*Biochemistry*]
PBP.......... Performance-Based Pay
PBP.......... Periplasmic Binding Protein [*Biochemistry*]
PBP.......... Person Before Place [*Library cataloguing*] (DGA)
PBP.......... Pheromonebinding Proteins [*Biochemistry*]
PBP.......... Phosphate-Binding Protein [*Biochemistry*]
PBP.......... Picnic Basket Porphyrin [*Organic chemistry*]
PBP.......... Picture-by-Picture [*Television technology*] (PS)
PBP.......... Play-by-Play (WDMC)
PBP.......... Plotting Board Plot (MUGU)
PBP.......... Point by Point
PBP.......... Porphyrin Biosynthetic Pathway [*Biochemistry*] (AAMN)
PBP.......... Power Bias Panel
PBP.......... Pregnenolone Binding Protein [*Endocrinology*]
PBP.......... Private Brand Proneness [*Marketing*]
PBP.......... Production Base Plan (MCD)
PBP.......... Program and Budget Planning
PBP.......... Program Board Panel
PBP.......... Progressive Bulbar Palsy [*Medicine*] (MEDA)
PBP.......... Provider Based Physician
PBP.......... Pulse Burst Period (PDAA)
PBP.......... Purified Brucella Protein [*Biochemistry*] (DAVI)
PBP.......... Push-Button Panel
PBPA.......... Pharmaceutical Benefits Pricing Authority [*Australia*]
PBPB.......... Para-bromophenacyl Bromide [*Organic chemistry*]
PBPB.......... Pyridinium Bromide Perbromide [*Inorganic chemistry*]
PBPC.......... Passenger and Baggage Processing Committee [*IATA*] (DS)
PBPE.......... Population Biology/Physiological Ecology [*Program*] [*National Science Foundation*]
PBPITMT...... Production Base Productivity Improvement through Manufacturing Technology (MCD)
PBPK.......... Physiologically Based Pharmacokinetics [*Biochemistry*]
PBPM.......... Poultry Byproduct Meal
PBPS.......... Painting Brushmakers' Provident Society [*A union*] [*British*]
PBPS.......... Paulist Bible Pamphlet Series [*Glen Rock, NJ*] [*A publication*] (BJA)
PBPS.......... Performance-Based Payment System
PBPS.......... Post-Boost Propulsion System [*Aerospace*]
PBPTC........ Palm Beach Psychotherapy Training Center (EA)
PBPV.......... Percutaneous Balloon Pulmonary Valvuloplasty [*Medicine*] (DMAA)
PBQ.......... Pharmacy Board of Queensland [*Australia*]
PBQ.......... Physiotherapists' Board of Queensland [*Australia*]
PBQ.......... Podiatrists' Board of Queensland [*Australia*]
PBQ.......... Poste De La Baleine [*Quebec*] [*Seismograph station code, US Geological Survey*] (SEIS)
PBQ.......... Preschool Behavior Questionnaire
PBr.......... Carnegie Public Library, Bradford, PA [*Library symbol Library of Congress*] (LCLS)
PBR.......... Pabst Blue Ribbon [*Beer*]
PBR.......... Packed Bed Reactor
PBR.......... Particle Bed Reactor [*Department of Energy*]
PBR.......... Patapsco & Back Rivers Railroad Co. [*AAR code*]
PBR.......... Patrol Boat, River [*Navy symbol*]
PBR.......... Patrol Boat Roadstead [*Navy*]
PBR.......... Payment by Results [*Payment system*]
PBR.......... Pebble-Bed Reactor [*Nuclear energy*]
PBR.......... Pembroke, NH [*Location identifier FAA*] (FAAL)
PBR.......... Pencil Beam RADAR
PBR.......... Permit by Rule [*Pollution control*]
PBR.......... Pigment-Binder Ratio [*Weight*]
PBR.......... Pittsburgh Byzantine [*Diocesan abbreviation*] [*Pennsylvania*] (TOCD)
PBR.......... Plant Breeders' Rights
PBR.......... Plum Brook Reactor [*Nuclear energy*]
PBR.......... Pole Broken [*Telecommunications*] (TEL)
PBR.......... Power Breeder Reactor (AAG)
PBR.......... Precision Bombing Range [*Army*]
PBR.......... Pressurized Ballistic Range [*NASA*]
PBR.......... Price-to-Book Value Ratio [*Investment term*] (DFIT)
PBR.......... Procedure Base Register (IAA)

PBR Professional Bull Riders [*An association*]

PBR Puerto Barrios [*Guatemala*] [*Airport symbol*] (AD)

PBR Pyridine-Butadiene Rubber

PBra Carnegie Free Library, Braddock, PA [*Library symbol Library of Congress*] (LCLS)

PBRA Practical Bomb Rack Adapter (NG)

PBRA Professional Bicycle Racers Association [*Defunct*] (EA)

PBracAL Allegheny International, Inc., Brackenridge, PA [*Library symbol Library of Congress*] (LCLS)

Pb-RBC Lead Red Blood Count [*For lead poisoning*] [*Medicine*] (DAVI)

PBRE Pebble-Bed Reactor Experiment [*Nuclear energy*]

PBRERP Permanent Board for Review of the Enlisted Retention Program

PBRERS Permanent Board for Review of the Enlisted Rating Structure

PBRESD Polar Branch, Research Environmental Science Division [*Army*]

PBRF Plant Breeding Research Forum [*Defunct*] (EA)

PBRF Plum Brook Reactor Facility [*Lewis Research Center*]

PBriR Rohm & Haas Co., Bristol, PA [*Library symbol Library of Congress*] (LCLS)

P/BRK Power Brake [*Automotive engineering*]

PBroGS Church of Jesus Christ of Latter-Day Saints, Genealogical Society Library, Philadelphia Branch, Broomall, PA [*Library symbol Library of Congress*] (LCLS)

PBRS Polybromostyrene [*Organic chemistry*]

PBRS Pupil Behavior Rating Scale [*Psychology*]

PBRS Push-Button Rotary Switch

PBRV Potato Black Ringspot Virus [*Plant pathology*]

PBS Bethlehem Steel Corp., Charles H. Herty, Jr., Memorial Library, Bethlehem, PA [*Library symbol Library of Congress*] (LCLS)

PBS Pacific Biological Station [*Department of Fisheries and Oceans*] [*Canada Research center*] (RCD)

PBS Palestine Broadcasting Service (BJA)

PBS Parenchymatous Bundle Sheath [*Botany*]

PBS Parimutuel Betting System

PBS Parti Bersatu Sabah [*Malaysia*] [*Political party*] (ECON)

PBS Particulate Biogenic Silica [*Environmental science*]

PBS Parts Breakdown Structure

PBS Peninsular Base Section [*Military*]

PBS Periscope Bombsight Stabilizer

PBS Personal Bibliographic Software, Inc. [*Information service or system*] (IID)

PBS Peterborough Board of Education [*UTLAS symbol*]

PBS Philippine Broadcasting Service (NADA)

PBS Philips Business Systems (NITA)

PBS Phosphate-Buffered Saline

PBS Phosphate-Buffered Sodium (MAE)

PBS Phycobilisome [*Biochemistry*]

PBS Picture Building System (NITA)

PBS Pigeon Bay [*South Carolina*] [*Seismograph station code, US Geological Survey*] (SEIS)

PBS Pilgrim Amer Bk & Thrift [*NYSE symbol*] (TTSB)

PBS Pilgrim American Bank & Thrift Fund, Inc. [*NYSE symbol*] (SAG)

PBS Pilgrim Regional Bank Shares, Inc. [*NYSE symbol*] (SPSG)

PBS Place Before Subject [*Library cataloguing*] (DGA)

PBS Plettenberg Bay [*South Africa*] [*Airport symbol*] (AD)

PBS Podiatry Bibliographical Society [*Defunct*] (EA)

PBS Polarization Beam Splitter

PBS Poly(butenesulfone) [*Organic chemistry*]

PBS Polysteel Building Systems Ltd. [*Toronto Stock Exchange symbol*]

PBS Potere Battericida del Sangue [*Bactericidal Property of the Blood*] [*Medicine*]

PBS Poverty Budget Share [*Bureau of the Census*] (GFGA)

PBS Power Breakfast Syndrome [*Suffered by late-risers forced to attend breakfast meetings*]

PBS Prayer Book Society [*British*] (DBA)

PBS Prefabricated Bituminous Surfacing

PBS Press-Button Signalling (PDAA)

Pbs Pressure at the Body Surface [*Medicine*] (DAVI)

PBS Pressure Boundary Subsystem [*Nuclear energy*] (NRCH)

PBS Primer Binding Site [*Genetics*]

PBS Production Base Support [*Army*] (AABC)

PBS Professional Bibliographic System [*Database manager package*] [*Personal Bibliographic Software, Inc. Ann Arbor, MI*]

PBS Professional Bowhunters Society (EA)

PBS Program and Budgeting System (OICC)

PBS Program Board Stowage

PBS Program Breakdown Structure [*Nuclear energy*]

PBS Program Buffer Storage (IAA)

PBS Project Breakdown Structure [*Nuclear energy*] (NRCH)

PBS Protestant Big Sisters

PBS Prune Belly Syndrome [*Medicine*] (DMAA)

PBS Public Brand Software (PCM)

PBS Public Broadcasting Service [*Facetious translation: Primarily British Shows*] (EA)

PBS Public Broadcasting System

PBS Public Buildings Service [*of General Services Administration*]

PBS Push-Button Switch

PBSA Parole Board of South Australia

PBSA Pastoral Board of South Australia

PBSA Pharmacy Board of South Australia

PBSA Phosphate-Buffered Saline Azide [*Culture medium*]

PBSA Phylloxera Board of South Australia

PBSA Physiotherapists' Board of South Australia

PBSAA Partially Blinded Soldiers' Association of Australia

PBSC Panelized Building Systems Council (EA)

PBSC Performance-Based Service Contracting (AAGC)

PBSC Peripheral-Blood Stem-Cell [*Biochemistry Medicine*]

PBSCMA Peanut Butter Sandwich and Cookie Manufacturers Association [*Later, PBNPA*] (EA)

PBSE Philadelphia-Baltimore Stock Exchange [*Later, Philadelphia-Baltimore-WashingtonStock Exchange*]

PBSF Pacific Bank NA [*NASDAQ symbol*] (SPSG)

PBshBrc Peoples Bancshares, Inc. [*Associated Press*] (SAG)

PBSM Plastic Bonded Starter Mix

PBSP Prognostically Bad Sign During Pregnancy [*Obstetrics*] (MAE)

PBSR Permanent Building Societies Registrar [*New South Wales, Australia*]

PB SRAM Pipeline Burst SRAM [*Static Random-Access Memory*] [*Computer science*]

PbSt9 Public Storage Properties IX [*Associated Press*] (SAG)

PbSt 10 Public Storage Properties X, Inc. [*Associated Press*] (SAG)

PbSt 11 Public Storage Properties XI, Inc. [*Associated Press*] (SAG)

PbSt 12 Public Storage Properties XII, Inc. [*Associated Press*] (SAG)

PbSt14 Public Storage Properties XIV, Inc. [*Associated Press*] (SAG)

PbSt15 Public Storage Properties XV, Inc. [*Associated Press*] (SAG)

PbSt16 Public Storage Properties XVI, Inc. [*Associated Press*] (SAG)

PbSt17 Public Storage Properties XVII, Inc. [*Associated Press*] (SAG)

PbSt18 Public Storage Properties XVIII, Inc. [*Associated Press*] (SAG)

PbSt19 Public Storage Properties XIX, Inc. [*Associated Press*] (SAG)

PbSt20 Public Storage Properties XX, Inc. [*Associated Press*] (SAG)

PBSTA Push-Button Station (IAA)

PBSteel Bethlehem Steel Corp., Charles M. Schwab Memorial Library, Bethlehem, PA [*Library symbol Library of Congress*] (LCLS)

PBSU Portable Beacon and Scoring Unit (MCD)

PBSW Push-Button Switch

PBT Pacific Ballet Theatre

PBT Para-Bandit Target

PBT Parity BIT [*Binary Digit*] Test

PBT Passband Tuning

PBT Peoria Board of Trade (EA)

PBT Permeable Base Transistor [*Electronics*]

PBT Permian Basin Royalty Trust [*NYSE symbol*] (SPSG)

PBT Permian Basin Rty Tr [*NYSE symbol*] (TTSB)

PBT Philippine Ballet Theater (ECON)

PBT Pierce-Blank Tool (MCD)

PBT Piggyback Tape [*or Twistor*] [*Computer science*]

PBT Pittsburgh Ballet Theatre

PBT Polybay Tier

PBT Polybenzothiazole [*Organic chemistry*]

PBT Polybutylene Terephthalate [*Organic chemistry*]

PBT Preferred Body Temperature [*Physiology*]

PBT Preliminary-Breath-Test [*Device used by police to determine whether or not a driver is legally intoxicated*]

PBT Professional Billiards Tour [*An association*]

PBT Profit before Tax [*Finance*] (WDAA)

PBT Push-Button Telephone

PBT Red Bluff, CA [*Location identifier FAA*] (FAAL)

PBT$_4$ Protein-Bound Thyroxine [*Endocrinology*] (DAVI)

PBTC Peoples Banctrust [*NASDAQ symbol*] (TTSB)

PBTC Peoples BancTrust Company Inc. [*NASDAQ symbol*] (SAG)

PBTC Postal Business Training Centre [*British*]

PBTE Performance-Based Teacher Education (OICC)

PBTF Pump Bearing Test Facility [*Nuclear energy*]

P/BTN Push Button [*Automotive engineering*]

PBTP Polybutylene Terephthalate [*Organic chemistry*]

PBTS Proton Beam Transport System

PBTX Ptychodiscus brevis Toxin [*Florida red-tide toxin*]

PBU Air-Burundi [*ICAO designator*] (FAAC)

PBU Bucknell University, Lewisburg, PA [*OCLC symbol*] (OCLC)

PBU Palm Beach County Utility Corp. [*Toronto Stock Exchange symbol*]

PBU Perry Basin [*Utah*] [*Seismograph station code, US Geological Survey*] (SEIS)

PBU Premature Baby Unit [*National Health Service*] [*British*] (DI)

PBU Push Button Unit (NITA)

PBU Putao [*Myanmar*] [*Airport symbol*] (OAG)

PBUP Perforated Backup Plate

PBut Butler Public Library, Butler, PA [*Library symbol Library of Congress*] (LCLS)

PButV United States Veterans Administration Hospital, Butler, PA [*Library symbol Library of Congress*] (LCLS)

PBV English Prayer Book Version (BJA)

PBV Pedal Blood Vessel

PBV Pharmacy Board of Victoria [*Australia*]

PBV Platinol [*Cisplatin*], Bleomycin, Vinblastine [*Antineoplastic drug regimen*]

PBV Post Boost Vehicle [*Missiles*] (AFM)

PBV Predicted Blood Volume [*Medicine*]

PBV Proportioning and Bypass Valve

PBV Pulmonary Blood Volume [*Medicine*]

PBVM Presentation of the Blessed Virgin Mary [*Roman Catholic women's religious order*]

PBVM Presentation of the Blessed Virgin Mary Sisters (TOCD)

PBVM Sisters of the Presentation of the B.V.M. (TOCD)

PBVM Union of the Sisters of the Presentation of the Blessed Virgin Mary (TOCD)

PBVP Post Boost Vehicle Propulsion [*Missiles*] (MCD)

PBVR [*The*] Port Bienville Railroad [*AAR code*]

PBvu Andrew Bayne Memorial Library, Bellevue, PA [*Library symbol Library of Congress*] (LCLS)

PBW Particle-Beam Weapon

PBW Parts by Weight (IEEE)

PBW Percussive Butt Welder

PBW .... Pink Bollworm [Cotton pest]
PBW .... Posterior Bite Wing [Dentistry]
PBW .... Power by Wire [Flight control]
PBW .... Proportional Bandwidth (MCD)
PBW .... Pulse Burst Wave
PBWA .... Plasma Beat Wave Accelerator [Physics]
PBWA .... Plasma Beta-Wave Accelerator [Plasma physics]
PBWAA .... Professional Basketball Writers' Association of America (EA)
PBWEE .... Pilot Boll Weevil Eradication Experiment [Department of Agriculture]
PBWF .... Pulse Burst Waveform
PBWSE .... Philadelphia-Baltimore-Washington Stock Exchange [Later, Philadelphia Stock Exchange]
PBWT .... Parts by Weight (WDAA)
PBX .... PBX Resources [Vancouver Stock Exchange symbol]
PBX .... Plastic Bonded Explosive
PBX .... Private Branch Exchange [Telecommunications]
PBXFS .... Private Branch Exchange Final Selector [Telecommunications] (IAA)
PBY .... Kayenta, AZ [Location identifier FAA] (FAAL)
PBY .... Patrol Bomber [Navy designation for Catalina aircraft]
PBY .... Pearl Air Services (U) Ltd. [Uganda] [ICAO designator] (FAAC)
PBY .... Pep Boys-Man,Mo,Ja [NYSE symbol] (TTSB)
PBY .... Pep Boys - Manny, Moe & Jack [NYSE symbol] (SPSG)
PBY .... Pillars Bay [Alaska] [Airport symbol] (AD)
PBYP .... Play-By-Play Toys&Novelties [NASDAQ symbol] (TTSB)
PBYP .... Play By Play Toys & Novelties, Inc. [NASDAQ symbol] (SAG)
PBZ .... Khortitsa-Air Ltd. [Ukraine] [FAA designator] (FAAC)
PBZ .... Phenoxybenzamine [Also, POB] [Adrenergic blocking agent]
PBZ .... Phenylbutazone [Anti-inflammatory compound]
PBZ .... Plettenberg [South Africa] [Airport symbol] (OAG)
PBZ .... Pyribenzamine [Antihistamine] [Trademark]
PBzN .... Peroxybenzoyl Nitrate [Lacrimator]
PBZT .... Poly-P-Phenylene Benzobesthiazole
PC .... All India Reporter, Privy Council [1914-50] [A publication] (DLA)
PC .... British and Colonial Prize Cases [A publication] (DLA)
PC .... Civilian Personnel Division [Coast Guard]
PC .... Coastal Escort [Ship symbol] (NATG)
PC .... Communist Party [Peru] [Political party] (PD)
PC .... Fiji Air [ICAO designator] (AD)
PC .... Indian Rulings, Privy Council [1929-47] [A publication] (DLA)
PC .... J. Lewis Crozer [Chester Public] Library, Chester, PA [Library symbol Library of Congress] (LCLS)
PC .... Judicial Committee of the Privy Council (DLA)
PC .... Pacific Coast Railroad [AAR code Terminated]
PC .... Pacific Command [Department of Defense] (BARN)
PC .... Package Control [or Controller]
PC .... Packed Cell [Hematology] (MAE)
PC .... Pad Coordinator [NASA]
PC .... Paired Comparisons [Education] (EDAC)
PC .... Palmitoyl Carnitine [Biochemistry]
PC .... [The] Panama Canal
Pc .... Pancuronium [A muscle relaxant]
PC .... Panoramic Camera
PC .... Paper Chromatography
PC .... Paper Copy
PC .... Paper Core (IAA)
PC .... Paper or Cloth [Freight]
PC .... Paracortex (DMAA)
PC .... Paracortical Hyperplasia [Oncology]
PC .... Parallax Second [Unit of interstellar-space measure]
PC .... Parameter Checkout [Computer science] (IAA)
PC .... Parametric Cubic [Computer science] (OA)
PC .... Parental Control [Channel lockout] [Video technology]
PC .... Parent Care (EA)
PC .... Parent Cells
PC .... Parents' Charter (AIE)
PC .... Parish Church [British] (ROG)
PC .... Parish Council
PC .... Parity Check [Computer science] (IAA)
PC .... Parliamentary Cases [A publication] (DLA)
PC .... PARSEC [Parallax Second] [Unit of interstellar-space measurement]
pc .... Parsec (IDOE)
PC .... Part Card [Computer science] (IAA)
PC .... Participation Certificate
PC .... Parti Communiste [Communist Party] [Luxembourg] [Political party] (PPW)
PC .... Particulate Component (DMAA)
PC .... Partido Colorado [Colorado Party] [Uruguay] [Political party] (PPW)
PC .... Partido Conservador [Conservative Party] [Ecuador] [Political party] (PPW)
PC .... Partido Conservador [Conservative Party] [Nicaragua] [Political party] (EY)
PC .... Partition Coefficient
PC .... Parts Catalog (KSC)
PC .... Passenger Certificate [Shipping] (DS)
PC .... Past Commander
PC .... Patent Cases [A publication] (DLA)
PC .... Patent Classification (NITA)
PC .... Patent Committee (MCD)
PC .... Patentee/Company Code (NITA)
PC .... Path Control [Computer science] (IBMDP)
PC .... Path Controller (NITA)
PC .... Patres Conscripti [Senators] [Latin]
PC .... Patrol Car [British military] (DMA)
PC .... Patrol Craft
PC .... Patrol Vessel, Submarine Chaser [Navy symbol]
PC .... Pay Clerk
PC .... Paymaster-Captain [Navy British]
PC .... Paymaster-Commander [Navy British]
PC .... Payment Center (MHDB)
PC .... Peace Commissioner [Ireland]
PC .... Peace Corps (EA)
PC .... Peak Capacity
PC .... Peg Count [Telecommunications] (TEL)
PC .... Penal Code [A publication] (DLA)
PC .... Penetrating Cell
PC .... Penn Central Transportation Co. [Subsidiary of Penn Central Corp.] [Absorbed into Consolidated Rail Corp.] [AAR code]
PC .... Penny Cyclopoedia [British A publication] (ROG)
PC .... Penske Car [Racing model]
PC .... Pentose Cycle [Biochemistry] (MAE)
PC .... People for a Change [An association Defunct] (EA)
PC .... People's Conference [India] [Political party] (PPW)
PC .... Percent [or Percentage] (IAA)
pc .... Percent (WDMC)
PC .... Per Centum [By the Hundred] [Latin]
PC .... Perciconia circinata [A toxin-producing fungus]
PC .... Per Compass (IAA)
PC .... Per Condoglianza [Used on visiting cards to express condolence] [Italian]
PC .... Percutaneous Cholecystostomy [Medicine]
PC .... Perfins Club (EA)
PC .... Performance Code
PC .... Performance Contract (OICC)
PC .... Pericarditis [Avian pathology]
PC .... Pericentral
PC .... Pericynthion [Perilune, or low point, in lunar orbit]
PC .... Period Contract
PC .... Peripheral Cell
PC .... Peripheral Control (BUR)
PC .... Peripheral Controller (NITA)
PC .... Peritoneal Cell (DMAA)
PC .... Permeance Coefficient (IAA)
PC .... Perpetual Curate
PC .... Personal Call (OA)
PC .... Personal Care
PC .... Personal Computer
pc .... Personal Computer (WDMC)
PC .... Personal Copier [In product name, PC-10] [Canon Inc.]
PC .... Personal Corporation (BARN)
PC .... Personal Correction
PC .... Personnel Carrier [A vehicle]
PC .... Perspective control [Photography]
PC .... Petro-Canada
PC .... Petty Cash
p/c .... Petty Cash (WDMC)
pc .... Petty Cash (WDMC)
PC .... Pharmacology [Medicine] (DMAA)
PC .... Pharmacy Corps [Army]
PC .... Phase-Change [Physics]
PC .... Phase Code (NITA)
PC .... Phase Coherent (CET)
PC .... Phase Control (IAA)
PC .... Phenol Coefficient (IIA)
PC .... Pheochromocytoma [Oncology]
PC .... Philco Corp. (IAA)
PC .... Philosophical Classics [A publication]
PC .... Phobia Clinic (EA)
PC .... Phosphate Cycle [Chemistry] (MAE)
PC .... Phosphatidylcholine [Lecithin] [Biochemistry]
PC .... Phosphocholine [Biochemistry]
PC .... Phosphocreatine [Also, PCr] [Creatine phosphate; see CP] [Biochemistry]
PC .... Phosphorylcholine [Biochemistry]
PC .... Photocell
PC .... Photoconductor
PC .... Photocounting
Pc .... Phthalocyanine [Organic chemistry]
PC .... Physicians's Corporation [Medicine] (DMAA)
PC .... Physocyanin [Biochemistry]
PC .... Phytophthora Cinnamoni [A fungus]
PC .... Pica [Typography] (WDMC)
PC .... Pick Up Cargo (AFM)
pC .... Picocoulomb [One trillionth of a coulomb]
pC .... Picocurie [Also, pCi] [One trillionth of a curie]
pc .... Picocurie (IDOE)
PC .... Picture (MDG)
PC .... Piece (AAG)
pc .... Piece (VRA)
pc .... Pied Carre [Square Foot] [French]
pc .... Pied Cube [Cubic Foot] [French]
PC .... Pierre Cardin [Fashion designer]
PC .... Pill Counter [Medicine] (DMAA)
PC .... Pilotage Charts [Air Force]
PC .... Pioneer Clubs (EA)
PC .... Pioneer Corps [British military] (DMA)
PC .... Piriform Cortex (DMAA)
pc .... Pitcairn [MARC country of publication code Library of Congress] (LCCP)
PC .... Pitch Channel
PC .... Pitch Circle [Technical drawings]

PC .... Pitch Control (KSC)
PC .... Pitch Cycle (DNAB)
PC .... Pitting Corrosion (PDAA)
PC .... Pittsburgh Commerce Institute
PC .... Plaid Cymru [*Welsh national liberation party*] [*Political party*]
P/C .... Plane Captain (MUGU)
PC .... Plane Change (MCD)
PC .... Plane Commander
PC .... Planetary Citizens (EA)
PC .... Planning Card (AAG)
PC .... Planning Concept (MCD)
PC .... Plant Computer (NRCH)
PC .... Planting Council (EA)
PC .... Plasma Cell [*Oncology*]
PC .... Plasma Chromatography
PC .... Plasmacytoma [*Medicine*]
PC .... Plastic Core
Pc .... Plastocyanin
PC .... Plate Circuit (DEN)
PC .... Platelet Concentrate [*Hematology*]
PC .... Platelet Count [*Hematology*]
PC .... Platform/Crane (DCTA)
PC .... Pleas of the Crown [*A publication*] (DLA)
P/C .... Pledges/Cost (WDMC)
p/c .... Pledges/Cost [*Fundraising*] (WDMC)
PC .... Plenum Chamber
PC .... Plug Care [*Computer science*] (IAA)
PC .... Plug Cock (AAG)
PC .... Plug Compatible [*Computer science*] (BUR)
PC .... Pneumotoxic Center (AAMN)
PC .... Pocket Computer
PC .... Poetry Criticism [*A publication*]
PC .... Point Contact (IDOE)
PC .... Point of Curve [*Technical drawings*]
PC .... Polar Component [*Food science*]
PC .... Polar Continental [*American air mass*]
PC .... Polar Crane [*Nuclear energy*] (NRCH)
P-C .... Polar to Cartesian
PC .... Pole Cell [*Insect embryology*]
P/C .... Police Car
PC .... Police Commissioner (WGA)
PC .... Police-Constable [*Scotland Yard*]
PC .... Police Court [*British*] (ROG)
PC .... Policy Control (ADA)
PC .... Political Code [*A publication*] (ILCA)
PC .... Political Correctness
PC .... Politically Correct
P/C .... Polizza di Carico [*Bill of Lading*] [*Shipping*] [*Italian*]
PC .... Pollution Control (MHDB)
PC .... Polycarbonate [*Organic chemistry*]
PC .... Polycarbosilane [*Organic chemistry*]
PC .... Polymer-Concrete (KSC)
PC .... Polyposis Coli [*Medicine*] (DMAA)
PC .... Pondus Civile [*Civil (Avoirdupois) Weight*] [*Pharmacy*] (ROG)
PC .... Poni Curavit [*Caused to Be Placed*] [*Latin*]
PC .... Poor Clares [*Roman Catholic women's religious order*]
PC .... Poor Classes [*British*] (DSUE)
PC .... Poor Condition [*Medicine*] (DMAA)
PC .... Poor Coordination [*Medicine*] (DMAA)
pc .... Pop Corn [*Crochet*]
PC .... Popular Cult
PC .... Population Census
PC .... Population Communication (EA)
PC .... Population Concern [*British*] (EAIO)
PC .... Population Council (EA)
PC .... Portable Computer
PC .... Portacaval [*Medicine*]
PC .... Portal Cirrhosis [*Medicine*] (DMAA)
PC .... Port Call [*Army*]
PC .... Port Committee (NATG)
PC .... Port Control [*Telecommunications*] (TEL)
PC .... Portion Control [*Food service*]
PC .... Portland Cement
PC .... Position Classification (GFGA)
PC .... Positive Column (IAA)
PC .... Positive Control
Pc .... Positive Wave in Children [*Neurophysiology*]
PC .... Postal Clerk [*Navy rating*]
PC .... Postcard
PC .... Post Card (ROG)
pc .... Postcard (WDMC)
pc .... Postcard (ODBW)
PC .... Post-Chlorinated (IAA)
PC .... Post Cibos [*After Meals*] [*Latin*] [*Pharmacy*] (DAVI)
PC .... Post Cibum [*After Meals*] [*Pharmacy*]
PC .... Postcode (ADA)
PC .... Postcoital [*Medicine*]
PC .... Postcoital [*Medicine*] (DMAA)
PC .... Post Commander [*Military*]
PC .... Post Consulatum [*After the Consulate*] [*Latin*]
PC .... Posterior Cervical [*Medicine*] (DMAA)
PC .... Posterior Chamber [*Ophthalmology*]
PC .... Posterior Circumflex [*Artery*] [*Anatomy*] (DAVI)
PC .... Posterior Commissure [*Neuroanatomy*]
PC .... Posterior Cortex [*Medicine*] (DMAA)
PC .... Postinflammatory Corticoid [*Medicine*]
PC .... Potential Complications [*Medicine*] (DMAA)
pc .... Pottery Cache (BJA)
PC .... Pour Condoler [*To Offer Sympathy*] [*French*]
PC .... Power Cartesian (IAA)
PC .... Power Circuit (IAA)
PC .... Power Component (IAA)
PC .... Power Contactor
PC .... Power Control [*System*] (NG)
P-C .... Power Conversion (CET)
pc .... Power Cord (BARN)
PC .... Practice Cases [*A publication*] (DLA)
PC .... Precarrier
PC .... Precast
PC .... Precaution Category [*For clinical laboratories*]
PC .... Precedents in Chancery [*A publication*] (DLA)
PC .... Pre-Chamber [*Automotive engineering*]
PC .... Precision Control [*Computer programming*] (BYTE)
PC .... Preconditioning [*Medicine*] (DMAA)
PC .... Precordia [*Anatomy*]
PC .... Pre-Emphasis Circuit (OA)
PC .... Preliminary Commitment (IMH)
PC .... Prenatal Care [*Medicine*] (DMAA)
PC .... Preparatory Commission
PC .... Preparatory Committee
PC .... Present Complaint [*Medicine*]
PC .... Presidents Club [*Commercial firm*] (EA)
PC .... Press Club (NTCM)
PC .... Press Council [*British*]
PC .... Pressure Chamber
PC .... Pressure Controller [*Nuclear energy*]
PC .... Prestressed Concrete (BARN)
pc .... Price (BARN)
PC .... Price Commission [*Cost of Living Council*]
PC .... Price Control Cases [*A publication*] (DLA)
P/C .... Price/Cost
PC .... Pricellular Corp. [*AMEX symbol*] (SAG)
PC .... PriCellular Corp.'A' [*AMEX symbol*] (TTSB)
PC .... Price per Copy [*of books*]
PC .... Prices Current
pc .... Prices Current (WDMC)
PC .... Priest Confessor
PC .... Primary Center
PC .... Primary Circuit (MCD)
PC .... Primary Closure [*Medicine*] (DMAA)
PC .... Primary Code
PC .... Primary Contributor
PC .... Primary Control (MCD)
PC .... Prime Contractor
PC .... Prime Cost
PC .... Prince Consort (IIA)
PC .... Prince Edward Island Provincial Library, Charlottetown, Prince Edward Island [*Library symbol National Library of Canada*] (NLC)
PC .... Principal Chaplain (ADA)
PC .... Principal Component
PC .... Print Club (EA)
PC .... Print Command [*Computer science*] (IAA)
PC .... Print Contrast (DGA)
PC .... Print Cycle [*Computer science*] (IAA)
PC .... Printed Card (IAA)
PC .... Printed Circuit
PC .... Printer Control
PC .... Printing Cylinder (DGA)
PC .... Print of Curve (IAA)
PC .... Prisoner of Conscience (BJA)
PC .... Privacy Commission
PC .... Private Concerns [*An association Defunct*] (EA)
PC .... Private Contract [*Tea trade*] (ROG)
PC .... Private Corporation
PC .... Privatization Council [*New York, NY*] (EA)
PC .... Privilege Car [*on a train*] [*Theatre slang*]
PC .... Privileged Character [*A favored student*] [*Teen slang*]
PC .... Privy Council [*or Councillor*] [*British*]
PC .... Prize Court (DLA)
PC .... Probable Cause [*Legal term*]
PC .... Probate Court [*British*] (ROG)
PC .... Procaer SpA [*Italy ICAO aircraft manufacturer identifier*] (ICAO)
PC .... Procarbazine [*Also, P, PCB, Pr*] [*Antineoplastic drug*]
PC .... Procerebral Lobe [*Neuroanatomy*]
PC .... Process Chemistry
PC .... Process Computer (NRCH)
PC .... Process Control (DEN)
PC .... Processing Center [*Telecommunications*] (TEL)
PC .... Processing Conditions [*Food*] (DICI)
PC .... Processor Controller [*Computer science*] (MDG)
PC .... Procollagen [*Medicine*] (DMAA)
PC .... Procurement Command [*Army*]
PC .... Procurement Communication [*Military*]
PC .... Producers' Council [*Later, CPMC*] (EA)
PC .... Product Code (NITA)
PC .... Production Certificate (MCD)
PC .... Production Company [*Films, television, etc.*]
PC .... Production Control (MCD)
PC .... Production Costs
PC .... Productive Cough [*Medicine*] (DMAA)

PC........ Professional Communication (MCD)
PC........ Professional Corporation
PC........ Professors of Curriculum (EA)
PC........ Profit Center (MHDB)
PC........ Program Card [*Computer science*] (IAA)
PC........ Program Change
PC........ Program Check [*Computer science*] (IAA)
PC........ Program Committee [*UN Food and Agriculture Organization*]
PC........ Program Communications [*Military*] (AFIT)
PC........ Program Control
PC........ Program Controller (NITA)
PC........ Program Coordination (IEEE)
PC........ Program Counter
PC........ Programmable Computer
PC........ Programmable Controller (NITA)
PC........ Programmable Controller (ACII)
PC........ Programmable Logic Control [*Computer science*] (IAA)
PC........ Programmable Machine Control (IAA)
PC........ Programmed Check (AAG)
PC........ Progressive Conservative [*Canada Political party*]
PC........ Prohormone Convertase [*Medicine*] (DMAA)
PC........ Project Censored (EA)
PC........ Project Children (EA)
PC........ Project Control (NASA)
PC........ Project Coordinator (NG)
PC........ Project Cuddle [*An association*] (EA)
PC........ Projector Charge
PC........ Proof Coins [*Numismatics*]
P/C........ Property/Casualty [*Insurance*]
PC........ Proportional Counter [*Instrumentation*]
PC........ Proposed Change
PC........ Propositional Calculus [*Logic*]
PC........ Propulsive Coefficient
PC........ Propylene Carbonate [*Organic chemistry*]
PC........ Prospectors Club [*Later, PCI*]
PC........ Prostatic Carcinoma [*Medicine*] (DMAA)
PC........ Prosthetics Center [*Veterans Administration*]
PC........ Protective Climate [*Solar heating*]
PC........ Protective Cover (MCD)
PC........ Protein C [*Medicine*] (DMAA)
PC........ Protein Convertase [*Medicine*] (DMAA)
PC........ Proto-Canaanite (BJA)
PC........ Protocol Converter (MCD)
PC........ Provincial Commissioner [*British government*]
PC........ Provisional Costs
PC........ Provisional Cut [*Television*] (NTCM)
PC........ Provocative Concentration [*Immunology*]
PC........ Pseudocode (AAG)
PC........ Pseudoconditioning Control [*Neurophysiology*]
PC........ Psychodevelopment Checklist [*Psychology*] (DAVI)
PC........ Publications in Climatology (MCD)
PC........ Public Citizen (EA)
PC........ Public Contract
PC........ [*The*] Publishers' Circular [*A publication*] (ROG)
PC........ Pubococcygeus [*Muscle*] [*Anatomy*]
PC........ Pubococcygeus [*Muscle*] [*Anatomy*] (DAVI)
PC........ Pull Chain [*Technical drawings*] (DAC)
PC........ Pulmonary Capillary [*Medicine*]
PC........ Pulmonic Closure [*Medicine*] (MAE)
PC........ Pulsating Current
PC........ Pulse Cleaned [*Dust filtration*]
PC........ Pulse Code [*Telecommunications*] (IAA)
PC........ Pulse Comparator (AAG)
PC........ Pulse Compression
PC........ Pulse Controller
PC........ Pulse Counter [*Computer science*] (MDG)
PC........ Pulverized Coal [*Fuel technology*]
PC........ Punch Card (NITA)
PC........ Punched Card [*Computer science*]
PC........ Punjab Cavalry [*British military*] (DMA)
PC........ Puns Corps (EA)
PC........ Purchase Card
PC........ Purchasing and Contracting [*Army*]
PC........ Pure Clairvoyance [*Psychical research*]
PC........ Purified Concentrate
PC........ Purkinje Cell [*Neuroanatomy*]
PC........ Pyrrolinecarboxylic Acid [*Biochemistry*]
PC........ Pyruvate Carboxylase [*An enzyme*] (MAE)
PC........ Single Paper Single Cotton [*Wire insulation*] (AAG)
PC........ Submarine Chaser [*173 foot*] [*Navy symbol Obsolete*]
PC........ Sumitomo Chemical Co. [*Japan*] [*Research code symbol*]
PC........ Veterans of the US Posse Comitatus (EA)
PC1........ Postal Clerk, First Class [*Navy rating*]
PC1........ Power Control One [*Hydraulic*] (MCD)
PC2........ Postal Clerk, Second Class [*Navy rating*]
PC2........ Power Control Two [*Hydraulic*] (MCD)
PC3........ Postal Clerk, Third Class [*Navy rating*]
PCA........ Acts of the Privy Council [*England*] [*A publication*] (DLA)
PCA........ Calgon Corp., Pittsburgh, PA [*OCLC symbol*] (OCLC)
PCA........ Pacific Communications Area [*Air Force*] (MCD)
PCA........ Panama Canal Authority
PCA........ Paper Converters Association [*Defunct*] (EA)
PCA........ Paperweight Collectors' Association (EA)
PCA........ Papillon Club of America (EA)
PCA........ Para-Chloroaniline [*Organic chemistry*]
PCA........ Parachute Club of America [*Later, USPA*] (EA)
PCA........ Para-Coumaric Acid [*Organic chemistry*]
PCA........ Parietal Cell Antibodies [*Immunology*]
PCA........ Parliamentary Commissioner for Administration [*British*]
PCA........ Parochial Clergy Association [*British*] (DBA)
PCA........ Parti Communiste Algerien [*Algerian Communist Party*] [*Political party*]
PCA........ Partido Comunista de Argentina [*Communist Party of Argentina*] [*Political party*] (PD)
PCA........ Parts Control Area [*NASA*] (KSC)
PCA........ Party of the Civic Alliance [*Romania*] [*Political party*] (EY)
PCA........ Passive Cutaneous Anaphylaxis [*Immunochemistry*]
PCA........ Patient Care Aide [*or Assistant*] (DAVI)
PCA........ Patient Care Audit (HCT)
PCA........ Patient-Controlled Analgesia
PCA........ Patient Support Associate [*Medicine*]
PCA........ Patriotic Catholic Association [*Name given to nationalized Catholic Church in China*]
PCA........ Peak Clipping Amplifier
PCA........ Pekingese Club of America (EA)
PCA........ Pentachloraniline [*Organic chemistry*]
PCA........ Pentachloroanisole [*Organic chemistry*]
PCA........ Percent Cortical Area [*Neurology*]
PCA........ Perchloric Acid [*Inorganic chemistry*]
PCA........ Percutaneous Carotid Arteriogram [*Medicine*] (MAE)
PCA........ Pericruciate Association [*Cortex, of cat*]
PCA........ Period Contract Acceptance
PCA........ Peripheral Circulatory Assist [*Medicine*]
PCA........ Peritoneal Carcinomatosis [*Oncology*]
PCA........ Permanent Change of Assignment [*Army*]
PCA........ Permanent Court of Arbitration [*See also CPA*] [*Hague, Netherlands*] (EAIO)
PCA........ Personal Care Aide [*or Assistant or Attendant*]
PCA........ Personal Cash Allowance
PCA........ Pest Control Association (NADA)
PCA........ Phenylcarboxylic Acid [*Chemistry*] (DAVI)
PCA........ Photon Counting Array [*Instrumentation*]
PCA........ Physical Configuration Audit [*Military, NASA*]
PCA........ Physicians Corp. of America (ECON)
PCA........ Pinnacle [*Alaska*] [*Seismograph station code, US Geological Survey*] (SEIS)
PCA........ Pitcairn Cierva Autogiro [*Aeronautics*]
PCA........ Pitch Control Assembly (MCD)
PCA........ Plane Circular Aperture
PCA........ Plasma Catecholamine [*Biochemistry*]
PCA........ Plasma-Covered Antenna
PCA........ Plate Count Agar [*Microbiology*]
PCA........ Pneumatic Control Assembly (NASA)
PCA........ Point of Closest Approach
PCA........ Polar Cap Absorption
PCA........ Polarizer-Compensator-Analyzer (PDAA)
PCA........ Police Complaint Authority [*British*]
PCA........ Polish Community in Australia
PCA........ Polycrystalline Alumina
PCA........ Poodle Club of America (EA)
PCA........ Pool Critical Assembly [*Nuclear reactor*]
PCA........ Popular Culture Association (EA)
PCA........ Pork Council of Australia
PCA........ Porous-Coated Anatomical [*Prosthesis*]
PCA........ Porsche Club of America (EA)
PCA........ Portacaval Anastomosis [*Animal model of chronic liver disease*]
PCA........ Portage Creek [*Alaska*] [*Airport symbol*] (OAG)
PCA........ Port Communications Area [*Telecommunications*] (TEL)
PCA........ Portland Cement Association (EA)
PCA........ Ports Canada
PCA........ Positive Control Area
PCA........ Positive Controlled Airspace
PCA........ Postconstruction Availability (NVT)
PCA........ Posterior Cerebral Artery [*Brain anatomy*]
PCA........ Posterior Communicating Artery [*Anatomy*]
PCA........ Posterior Cricoarytenoid [*A muscle of the larynx*]
PCA........ Potash Co. of America, Inc. [*Toronto Stock Exchange symbol*]
PCA........ Potato Carrot Agar [*Culture Media*]
PCA........ Potentially Contaminated Area (DNAB)
PCA........ Poultrymen's Cooperative Association (EA)
PCA........ Power Conditioning Assembly
PCA........ Power Control Assembly (NASA)
PCA........ Precipitation with a Compressed Fluid Antisolvent [*Chemical engineering*]
PCA........ Precision Clearing Agent (DNAB)
PCA........ Pre-Conditioned Air System [*Aviation*] (DA)
PCA........ Precontractual Authorization
PCA........ Prescribed Concentration of Alcohol (ADA)
PCA........ President's Council on Aging [*Inactive*]
PCA........ Prestressed Concrete Association [*British*] (DBA)
PCA........ Primary Carbon Assimilation [*Botany*]
PCA........ Primary Control Assembly [*Nuclear energy*] (NRCH)
PCA........ Primary Coolant Activity [*Nuclear energy*] (NRCH)
PCA........ Prime Candidate Alloy (MCD)
PCA........ Prime Condition Aircraft
PCA........ Principal Component Analysis
PCA........ Principal Control Authority (NATG)
PCA........ Prindle Class Association (EA)
PCA........ Print Council of America (EA)
PCA........ Printed Circuit Assembly [*Telecommunications*] (TEL)

PCA............ Printer Communications Adapter
PCA............ Printers' Costing Association [*British*] (BI)
PCA............ Printing Corp. of America
PCA............ Private Communications Association [*Later, NCA*]
PCA............ Process Control Analyzer
PCA............ Procoagulant Activity
PCA............ Procrastinators' Club of America (EA)
PCA............ Producers Commission Association (EA)
PCA............ Production Code Administration (BARN)
PCA............ Production Compliance Audit [*Automotive emissions standards*]
PCA............ Professional Chess Association (EA)
PCA............ Professional Comedians' Association (EA)
PCA............ Professional Cycling Association [*British*] (DBA)
PCA............ Program Calibration Area [*Computer science*] (DOM)
PCA............ Program Change Analysis [*DoD*]
PCA............ Program Coupler Assembly (KSC)
PCA............ Program Cumulative Audience [*Advertising*] (DOAD)
PCA............ Programmable Communications Adapter [*Computer science*]
PCA............ Progress Change Authority
PCA............ Progressive Citizens of America
PCA............ Proprietary Crematoria Association [*British*] (DBA)
PCA............ Protective Clothing Arrangement [*Telecommunications*] (TEL)
PCA............ Protective Connecting Arrangement [*Telecommunications*] (TEL)
PCA............ Prototype Protein C Activator [*Biochemistry*]
PCA............ Public Archives, Charlottetown, Prince Edward Island [*Library symbol National Library of Canada*] (NLC)
PCA............ Puli Club of America (EA)
PCA............ Pulp Chemicals Association (EA)
PCA............ Pulse Code Adaptor (NITA)
PCA............ Pulse Counter Adapter
PCA............ Putnam California Investment Grade Municipal [*AMEX symbol*] (SPSG)
PCA............ Putnam Cal Inv Grade Muni [*AMEX symbol*] (TTSB)
PCA............ Pyrotechnic Control Assembly [*NASA*]
PCA............ Pyrrolidonecarboxylic Acid [*Organic chemistry*]
PCAA.......... Pancretan Association of America (EA)
PCAA.......... Particulate Combined Amino Acid [*Marine biology*]
PCaab......... Parietal Cell Autoantibody [*Immunology*]
PcA&E......... Pacific Aerospace & Electronics, Inc. [*Associated Press*] (SAG)
PCAC.......... Partially Conserved Axial Current [*Electronics*] (IAA)
PCAC.......... Partially Conserved Axial-Vector Current
PCAC.......... Private College Admissions Center [*Later, NAAPHE*]
PCAC.......... Professional Classes Aid Council (AIE)
PC Act........ Probate Court Act [*A publication*] (DLA)
PCAD.......... Package Computer-Aided Design [*Computer science*]
PCAD.......... Program Change Approval Document (DOMA)
PCADS......... Panoramic Control and Display System (MCD)
PCAE.......... Polar Cap Absorption Event
PC-AEO........ Personal Computer - Annual Energy Outlook Forecasting Model [*Department of Energy*] (GFGA)
PCAG.......... Pentobarbital-Chlorpromazine-Alcohol Group [*Medicine*]
PCAG.......... Research Station, Agriculture Canada [*Station de Recherches, Agriculture Canada*] Charlottetown, Prince Edward Island [*Library symbol National Library of Canada*] (NLC)
PCAI.......... Parliamentary Commissioner for Administrative Investigations [*Western Australia*]
PCAI.......... PCA International, Inc. [*NASDAQ symbol*] (NQ)
PCAI.......... PCA Intl [*NASDAQ symbol*] (TTSB)
PCAI.......... Personal Care Assessment Instrument [*Australia*]
PCA Int....... PCA International, Inc. [*Associated Press*] (SAG)
P Cal......... Petrus Calvelli [*Flourished, 14th century*] [*Authority cited in pre-1607 legal work*] (DSA)
PCalS.......... California State College, California, PA [*Library symbol Library of Congress*] (LCLS)
PCAM.......... Partitioned Content Addressable Memory
PCAM.......... Physician Corp. of Amer [*NASDAQ symbol*] (TTSB)
PCAM.......... Physician Corp. of America [*NASDAQ symbol*] (SAG)
PCAM.......... Punched Card Accounting Machine [*Computer science*]
PCamA......... Alliance College, Cambridge Springs, PA [*Library symbol Library of Congress*] (LCLS)
PCAMIC........ People Concerned about MIC [*Methyl Isocyanate*] (EA)
PCAMP......... Protective Coatings and Metalizing Process (DNAB)
PCAN.......... Program Change Action Notice (DNAB)
PC & A........ Project Control and Administration [*NASA*]
PC & B........ Personnel Compensation and Benefits (GFGA)
PC & D........ Priest, Confessor, and Doctor (ROG)
PC & H........ Packing, Crating, and Handling [*Shipping*] (AFM)
PC & IC....... Polaris Control and Information Center [*Missiles*]
PC & OR....... Procurement, Commitment, and Obligation Record [*Navy*]
PC & S........ Posts, Camps, and Stations [*Military*]
PC & S........ Preliminary Command and Sequencing [*Viking lander mission*] [*NASA*]
PCANSW........ Pest Control Association of New South Wales [*Australia*]
PCAO.......... President's Commission on Americans Outdoors
PCAP.......... Physical Correlation Analysis Program [*Military*]
P-CAP......... Physically-Challenged Assistance Program [*Chrysler Motors Corp.*] [*Detroit, MI*] [*Information service or system*] (IID)
PCAP.......... Post Commercial Action Plan [*International Trade Administration*]
PCAP.......... Programmer Capacity
PC App........ Law Reports, Privy Council, Appeal Cases [*England*] [*A publication*] (DLA)
PCAPS......... Production Control and Planning System (MCD)
PCAQ.......... Pony Club Association of Queensland [*Australia*]
PCAR.......... PACCAR, Inc. [*NASDAQ symbol*] (NQ)
PCAR.......... Parent-Child Activity Rating Scale [*Education*] (EDAC)
PCAR.......... Process Characterization Analysis Package (MHDI)
P (Card)...... Personal Card [*Containing person's name, address, age, description, job, habits, haunts, movements*] [*Used in Belfast, Northern Ireland*]
PCarl.......... Bosler Free Library, Carlisle, PA [*Library symbol Library of Congress*] (LCLS)
PCarlA......... United States Army War College, Carlisle Barracks, PA [*Library symbol Library of Congress*] (LCLS)
PCarlD......... Dickinson College, Carlisle, PA [*Library symbol Library of Congress*] (LCLS)
PCarlD-L....... Dickinson School of Law, Sheeley-Lee Law Library, Carlisle, PA [*Library symbol Library of Congress*] (LCLS)
PCarlH......... Cumberland County Historical Society and Hamilton Library Association, Carlisle,PA [*Library symbol Library of Congress*] (LCLS)
PCarlMH........ United States Army, Military History Research Collection, Carlisle Barracks, PA [*Library symbol Library of Congress*] (LCLS)
PCarlPL........ United States Army, Carlisle Barracks Post Library, Carlisle Barracks, PA [*Library symbol Library of Congress*] (LCLS)
PCARS.......... Point Credit Accounting and Reporting System (AFM)
PCAS........... Patient Care Algorithm System [*Medicine*] (DMAA)
PCAS........... Persistent Chemical Agent Stimulant
PCAS........... Possible Carotid Artery System [*Medicine*]
PCAS........... Primary Central Alarm Station [*Nuclear energy*] (NRCH)
P Cas.......... Prize Cases [*1914-22*] [*England*] [*A publication*] (DLA)
P Cas.......... Prize Cases (Trehearn and Grant) [*England*] [*A publication*] (DLA)
PCAS........... Punch Card Accounting System [*Computer science*]
PCASA.......... Pony Club Association of South Australia
PCAS/CADS...... Persistent Chemical Agent Stimulant/Chemical Agent Disclosure Solution [*Army*]
PCASP.......... Passive-Cavity Aerosal Spectrometer Probe [*Meteorology*]
PCASS.......... Parts Control Automated Support System [*Database*]
PCAST.......... President's Council of Advisers on Science and Technology [*1989*]
PCAT........... Pharmacy College Admissions Test (GAGS)
PCAT........... Pharmacy College Admission Test
pCAT........... Plasmid Chloramphenicol Acetyltransferase [*An enzyme*]
PCAT........... Procedures for the Control of Air Traffic (SAA)
PCAU........... Parachute Course Administrative Unit [*Military British*] (INF)
PCAU........... Philippine Civil Affairs Unit [*Army unit which supplied emergency subsistence after end of Japanese dominance*] [*World War II*]
PCAV........... Pony Club Association of Victoria [*Australia*]
PCAV........... Principal Component Analysis with Varimax Rotation
PCAWA.......... Pony Club Association of Western Australia
PCB............ Central Pennsylvania District Library Center, Bellefonte, PA [*OCLC symbol*] (OCLC)
PcB............ Near Point of Convergence [*Ophthalmology*]
PCB............ Page Control Block [*Computer science*] (IBMDP)
PCB............ Pancuronium Bromide [*A muscle relaxant*] (DAVI)
PCB............ Paracervical Block [*Anesthesiology*]
PCB............ Parti Communiste de Belgique [*Communist Party of Belgium*] [*See also KPB*] [*Political party*] (PPE)
PCB............ Partido Comunista de Bolivia [*Communist Party of Bolivia*] [*Political party*] (PPW)
PCB............ Partido Comunista do Brasil [*Communist Party of Brazil*] [*Pro-Albanian*] [*Political party*] (PPW)
PCB............ Parts Control Board
PCB............ Patent Compensation Board [*Energy Research and Development Administration*]
PCB............ Percutaneous Biopsy [*Medicine*] (CPH)
PCB............ Petty Cash Book [*Business term*]
PCB............ Planning Change Board (AAG)
PCB............ Plenum Chamber Burning
PCB............ Polychlorinated Biphenyl [*Organic chemistry*]
PCB............ Polychlorobenzene
PCB............ Portacaval Bypass [*Cardiology*] (DMAA)
PCB............ Port Check BIT [*Binary Digit*] [*Telecommunications*] (TEL)
PCB............ Postcoital Bleeding [*Medicine*] (DMAA)
PCB............ Power Circuit Breaker (MSA)
PCB............ Power Control Box (NASA)
PCB............ Precambrian Shield Resources Ltd. [*Toronto Stock Exchange symbol*]
PCB............ Premier Commercial Bank Ltd. [*Nigeria*]
PCB............ Primary Carpet Backing
PCB............ Printed Circuit Board (MCD)
pcb............ Printed-Circuit Board (IDOE)
PCB............ Prix de Cession de Base [*Basic Wholesale Price*] [*French*]
PCB............ Procarbazine [*Also, P, PC, Pr*] [*Antineoplastic drug*]
PCB............ Process Control Block
PCB............ Processor Command Bus (NITA)
PCB............ Product Configuration Baseline (NASA)
PCB............ Program Communication Block
PCB............ Program Control Block [*Computer science*] (BUR)
PCB............ Project Change Board (AAG)
PCB............ Project Control Branch [*Social Security Administration*]
PCB............ Projected Control Board
PCB............ Property Control Branch [*of Allied Military Government*] [*Post-World War II*]
PCB............ Proprietor of Copyright on a Work by a Corporate Body
PCB............ Propulsion [*Ground*] Control Box (AAG)
PCB............ Public Coin Box [*Telecommunications*] (TEL)
PCB............ Publisher's Central Bureau
PCBA........... Para-Chlorobenzoic Acid [*Organic chemistry*]
PCBA........... Pepsi-Cola Bottlers Association (EA)
PCBA........... Pioneer Citizens Band Association (IAA)
PCBA........... Polyclonal B Cell Activation [*Hematology*]

PCBA .... Printed Circuit Board Assembly (MCD)
PCBB .... Power Conditioning Brass Board (MCD)
PCBB .... Primary Commercial Blanket Bond [*Insurance*]
PCBC .... Para-Chlorobenzyl Chloride [*Organic chemistry*]
PCBC .... Partially Conserved Baryon Current (IEEE)
PCBC .... Perry County Financial [*NASDAQ symbol*] (TTSB)
PCBC .... Perry County Financial Corp. [*NASDAQ symbol*] (SAG)
PCBC .... Polk County Biomedical Consortium [*Library network*]
PCBC .... Progressive Conservative Broadcasting Corp. [*Fictional version of the Cana dian Broadcasting Corp.*]
PCBCL .... Printed Circuit Board Configuration List (MCD)
PCBD .... Polychlorinated Benzodioxin [*Organic chemistry*]
PCBDA .... Put and Call Brokers and Dealers Association [*Inactive*] (EA)
PCBG .... Primary Care Block Grant
PCB-ML .... Partido Comunista Marxista-Leninista de Bolivia [*Marxist-Leninist Communist Party of Bolivia*] [*Political party*] (PPW)
PC-BMP .... Phosphorylcholine-Binding Myeloma Protein [*Medicine*] (DMAA)
PCBN .... Para-Chlorobenzonitrile [*Organic chemistry*]
PCBN .... Polycrystalline Cubic Boron Nitrite
PCBPA .... Personal Computer Board Panel Assembly (DWSG)
PCBR .... Printed Circuit Board Repair (MCD)
PC/BRD .... Printed Circuit Board [*Automotive engineering*]
PCBS .... Plastic Connector Backing Shell
PCBS .... Positive Control Bombardment System [*Air Force*]
PCBS .... Printed Circuit Board Socket
PCBS .... Pupil Classroom Behavior Scale
PCBTF .... Para-Chlorobenzotrifluoride [*Organic chemistry*]
PCBTS .... Portable Cesium Beam Time Standard
PCC .... Acts of the Privy Council, Colonial Series [*A publication*] (DLA)
PCC .... Chief Postal Clerk [*Navy rating*]
PCC .... Order of St. Clare (TOCD)
PCC .... Pacific Cruise Conference [*Formerly, TPPC*] [*Defunct*] (EA)
PCC .... Package Carrier Committee (EA)
PCC .... Pad Control Center [*NASA*] (NASA)
PCC .... Paid Circulation Council [*Later, ASCMP*]
PCC .... Palestinian Ceramic Chronology [*200BC-70AD*] [*A publication*] (BJA)
PCC .... Panama Canal Co. [*Superseded by Panama Canal Commission*]
PCC .... Panama Canal Commission [*Independent government agency*]
PCC .... Panamerican Cultural Circle (EA)
PCC .... Parent and Child Center [*Project Head Start*]
PCC .... Parklawn Health Library Computer Center [*Department of Health and Human Services*] (GFGA)
PCC .... Parochial Church Council [*Church of England*]
PCC .... Partial Crystal Control (IEEE)
PCC .... Partido Comunista Chileno [*Communist Party of Chile*] [*Political party*] (PD)
PCC .... Partido Comunista Cubano [*Communist Party of Cuba*] [*Political party*] (PPW)
PCC .... Partido Conservador Colombiano [*Conservative Party of Colombia*] [*Political party*] (PPW)
PCC .... Party of Catalan Communists [*Political party*] (PPW)
PCC .... Pasadena City College [*California*]
PCC .... Patient Care Coordinator [*Medicine*]
PCC .... Payload Control and Checkout [*NASA*] (NASA)
PCC .... Peak Cathode Current
PCC .... People's Caretakers' Council [*Rhodesian*]
PCC .... People's Christian Coalition [*Later, Sojourners*] (EA)
PCC .... Pepper Community [*Later, IPC*]
PCC .... Per-Command Course (MCD)
PCC .... Per Copia Conforme [*True Copy*] [*Italian*]
PCC .... Performance Certification Component [*SQT*] (MCD)
PCC .... Performance Criteria Categories (MCD)
PCC .... Peripheral Control Computer
PCc .... Periscopic Concave [*Ophthalmology*]
PCC .... Permanent Consultative Committee
PCC .... Personal Care Clinic (DAVI)
PCC .... Personal Code Calling (NITA)
PCC .... Personal Communications Controller (NITA)
PCC .... Personal Computer Coprocessor
PCC .... Personnel Control Center [*Air Force*] (AFM)
PCC .... Personnel Coordination Center [*Army*]
PCC .... Perth Chamber of Commerce [*Western Australia*]
PCC .... Peters' United States Circuit Court Reports [*A publication*] (DLA)
PCC .... Phaeochromocytoma [*Medicine*] (BABM)
PCC .... Phenylchlorocarbene [*Organic chemistry*]
PCC .... Pheochromocytoma [*Oncology*]
PCC .... Philippine Christian College (AEBS)
PCC .... Phosphate Carrier Compound
PCC .... Photoelectric Counter Chronometer (IAA)
PCC .... Physical Coal Cleaning [*Fuel technology*]
PCC .... Pilarcitos Creek [*California*] [*Seismograph station code, US Geological Survey*] (SEIS)
PCC .... Pilot Control Console
PCC .... Piperidinocyclohexanecarbonitrile [*Organic chemistry*]
PCC .... Planning Coordination Conference [*NATO*] (NATG)
PCC .... Plastics in Construction Council [*Later, CCS*]
PCC .... Platform Control Center [*NASA*] (SSD)
PCC .... Platoon Command Center [*Army*]
PCC .... Plug Compatible Computer (ADA)
PCC .... Plutonium Concentrator Concentrate [*Nuclear energy*] (NRCH)
PCC .... PMC Commercial Tr [*AMEX symbol*] (TTSB)
PCC .... PMC Commercial Trust [*AMEX symbol*] (SAG)
PCC .... Pointe Claire Public Library [*UTLAS symbol*]
PCC .... Point of Compound Curve (KSC)
PCC .... Poison Control Center
PCC .... Polarity Coincidence Correlator
PCC .... Policy Coordination Council (USDC)
PCC .... Policy Coordination Council [*Marine science*] (OSRA)
PCC .... Political Consultative Committee [*Warsaw Pact*]
PCC .... Political Consultative Council (CINC)
PCC .... Polycore Composite Construction [*Automotive engineering*]
PCC .... Polymer-Cement Concrete (KSC)
PCC .... Polynesian Cultural Center (EA)
PCC .... Pontifical Council for Culture [*Vatican City*] (EAIO)
PCC .... Poor Clares of St. Colette [*Roman Catholic women's religious order*]
PCC .... Population Crisis Committee (EA)
PCC .... Portable Cable Checker
PCC .... Portland Cement Concrete
PCC .... Positive Control Communication
PCC .... Postal and Courier Communications [*British*]
PCC .... Postal Concentration Center [*Army*]
PCC .... Pour Copie Conforme [*Certified True Copy*] [*French*]
PCC .... Power Control Console [*Diving apparatus*]
PCC .... Precast Concrete [*Technical drawings*]
PCC .... Precipitated Calcium Carbonate [*Inorganic chemistry*]
PCC .... Pre-Command Course [*Military*]
PCC .... Precompressor Cooling (MCD)
PCC .... Pregnancy Crisis Centre [*Australia*]
PCC .... Premature Chromosome Condensation [*Genetics*]
PCC .... Prerogative Court of Canterbury [*English court previously having jurisdiction over wills*]
PCC .... Presbyterian Charismatic Communion [*Later, PRR*] [*An association*] (EA)
PCC .... President of the Canteen Committee [*Military British*]
PCC .... President's Conference Committee
PCC .... Press Complaints Commission (ECON)
PCC .... Price Control Council (NADA)
PCC .... Primary Care Center [*Health care*] (HCT)
PCC .... Primary Care Clinic (DAVI)
PCC .... Primary Category Code (NITA)
PCC .... Print Collectors' Club [*British*] (DBA)
PCC .... Printed Circuit Card
PCC .... Printed Circuit Conference
PCC .... Printers' Charitable Corp. (DGA)
PCC .... Private Carrier Conference [*of ATA*] (EA)
PCC .... Privy Council Cases [*British*]
PC(C) .... Privy Councillor (Canada)
PCC .... Problem Control and Contact Unit [*IRS*]
PCC .... Process Chemistry Cell (NRCH)
PCC .... Process Control Computer
PCC .... Processor Control Cards [*Computer science*] (IAA)
PCC .... Processor Control Console [*Telecommunications*] (TEL)
PCC .... Product Control Center [*DoD*]
PCC .... Production Compression Capability
PCC .... Productivity Communication Center [*Defunct*] (EA)
PCC .... Program Control Card (IAA)
PCC .... Program Control Counter
PCC .... Program-Controlled Computer (DIT)
PCC .... Program Coordination Committee (SSD)
PCC .... Program for Cooperative Cataloging [*American Library Association*]
PCC .... Progress Control Clerk [*DoD*]
PCC .... Project Control Center
PCC .... Project Coordination Centre [*Defence Research Board*] [*Canada*]
PCC .... Propionyl CoA Carboxylase [*An enzyme*]
PCC .... Prothrombin Complex Concentrates [*Hematology*]
PCC .... Protocol Converter Concentrator [*Telecommunications*] (IAA)
PCC .... Provincial Congress Committee
PCC .... Provisioning Control Code [*Military*] (AFIT)
PCC .... Psychometric Colorimeter Chamber (MCD)
PCC .... Puerto Rico [*Colombia*] [*Airport symbol*] (AD)
PCC .... Pulse Counter Chain
PCC .... Pulverized Coal Combustion [*or Combustor*]
PCC .... Pure Car Carrier [*Shipping*] (DS)
PCC .... Pyridinium Chlorochromate [*Organic chemistry*]
PCC .... Pyroconvective Cooling
PC(C) .... Submarine Chaser (Control) [*173 foot*] [*Navy symbol Obsolete*]
PCCA .... Confederation Art Gallery and Museum, Charlottetown, Prince Edward Island [*Library symbol National Library of Canada*] (NLC)
PCCA .... Pacific Class Catamaran Association (EA)
PCCA .... Pattern-Contingent Chromatic Aftereffects
PCCA .... Pewter Collectors Club of America (EA)
PCCA .... Pipe Collectors Club of America [*Defunct*] (EA)
PCCA .... Playing Card Collectors' Association (EA)
PCCA .... Police Car Collectors Association (EA)
PCCA .... Portable Computer and Community Association
PCCA .... Postcard Collector's Club of America [*Defunct*] (EA)
PCCA .... Power and Communication Contractors Association (EA)
PCCA .... Professional Compounding Centers of America
PCCA .... Promotion of Community and Cultural Awareness [*Australia*]
PCCADS .... Panoramic Cockpit Control and Display System (MCD)
PCCAF .... Procedure Change Control Action Form (AAG)
PCCAF .... Procedure Committee Change Authorization Form (AAG)
PcCAp .... Pacific Coast Apparel Co., Inc. [*Associated Press*] (SAG)
PcCap .... Pacificorp Capital [*Associated Press*] (SAG)
PCCAP .... Physicians' Continued Competence Assessment Program [*Medicine*] (DMAA)
PcCApp .... Pacific Coast Apparel Co., Inc. [*Associated Press*] (SAG)
PCCB .... Payload Configuration Control Board [*NASA*] (MCD)
PCCB .... Program Configuration Control Board [*NASA*] (NASA)
PCCB .... Project Configuration Control Board [*Army*] (AABC)

PCCC .... Participating College Correspondence Course (MUGU)
PCCC .... Polytechnics and Colleges Computer Committee (AIE)
PCCD .... Peristaltic Charge-Coupled Device (IEEE)
PCCDS .... Patrol Craft Combat Direction System [*Navy*] (SAA)
PCCE .... Pacific Coast Coin Exchange
PCCE .... Payload Common Communication Equipment [*NASA*] (NASA)
PCCEI .... Permanent Charities Committee of the Entertainment Industries (EA)
PCCEMRSP... Permanent Commission for the Conservation and Exploitation of the Maritime Resources of the South Pacific
PCCES .... Planning and Coordinating Committee for Environmental Studies [*National Research Council*]
PCCF .... Plan Case Control File [*IRS*]
PCCF .... Prostate Cancer Cure Foundation Ltd.
PCCF .... Protein C Cofactor (DMAA)
PCCG .... PCC Group [*NASDAQ symbol*] (TTSB)
PCCG .... PCC Group, Inc. [*NASDAQ symbol*] (SAG)
PCCG .... Protestant Cinema Critics Guild [*Later, PCG*] (EA)
PCCGB .... Photographic Collectors Club of Great Britain (DBA)
PCC Gp .... PCC Group, Inc. [*Associated Press*] (SAG)
PCCh .... Partido Comunista de Chile [*Chilean Communist Party*] [*Political party*] (EY)
PCCH .... Pentachlorocyclohexene [*Organic chemistry*]
PCCI .... Pacific Crest Capital [*NASDAQ symbol*] (SAG)
PCCI .... Paper Cup and Container Institute [*Later, SSI*] (EA)
PCCI .... President's Committee on Consumer Interests [*Terminated, 1971*]
PCCL .... People's Community Civic League (EA)
PCCL .... Precontract Cost Letter [*Navy*] (NG)
PCCM .... Master Chief Postal Clerk [*Navy rating*]
PCCM .... Pediatric Critical Care Medicine (DMAA)
PCCM .... Portuguese Cultural Centre of Melbourne [*Victoria, Australia*]
PCCM .... Primary Care Case Management [*Medicine*] (DMAA)
PCCM .... Primary Care Case Manager [*Medicine*] (DMAA)
PCCM .... Private Circuit Control Module [*Telecommunications*] (TEL)
PCCM .... Program Change Control Management (NASA)
PCCM .... Program Control Contract Manager (MCD)
PCC (M-L) ... Parti Communiste Canadien (Marxiste-Leniniste) [*Marxist-Leninist Communist Party of Canada*] [*Political party*]
PCCN .... Part Card Change Notice (KSC)
PCCN .... Port Call Control Number [*Army*] (AABC)
PCCN .... Preliminary Configuration Control Number (AAG)
PCCN .... Provisioning Contract Control Number (NASA)
PCCNL .... Pacific Coast Coordinator of Naval Logistics
PCCO .... Plant Clearance Contracting Officer [*DoD*]
PCCOA .... Coles Associates Ltd., Charlottetown, Prince Edward Island [*Library symbol National Library of Canada*] (NLC)
PCCP .... Canadian Pension Commission [*Commission Canadienne des Pensions*], Charlottetown, Prince Edward Island [*Library symbol National Library of Canada*] (BIB)
PCCP .... Preliminary Contract Change Proposal [*NASA*] (KSC)
PCCP .... Private Child Care Provider (EDAC)
PCCPS .... Pacific Coast Canned Pear Service (EA)
PCCR .... Procurement Code Change Request (IAA)
PCCR .... Publishing Center for Cultural Resources [*Defunct*] (EA)
PCCS .... Parti Conservateur Chretien-Social [*Conservative Christian-Social Party*] [*Switzerland Political party*] (PPE)
PCCS .... Photographic Camera Control System (KSC)
PCCS .... Ported Coax Cable Sensor [*Military*] (DWSG)
PCCS .... Positive Control Communications System
PCCS .... Processor Common Communications System
PCCS .... Program and Cost Control System [*Army*] (RDA)
PCCS .... Program Change Control System (NG)
PCCS .... Project Cost Control System
PCCS .... Publications Contract Coverage Schedule (MCD)
PCCS .... Senior Chief Postal Clerk [*Navy rating*]
PCCT .... Percept and Concept Cognition Test [*Psychology*]
P-CCU .... Post Coronary Care Unit
PCCU .... President's Commission on Campus Unrest (EA)
PCCU .... Punched Card Control Unit [*Computer science*] (AABC)
PCCW .... Price/Costco, Inc. [*NASDAQ symbol*] (SPSG)
PCD .... Democratic Conservative Party [*Nicaragua*] [*Political party*] (PD)
PCD .... Pacific Car Demurrage Bureau, San Francisco CA [*STAC*]
PCD .... Pacific Communications Division [*Military*]
PCD .... Panama Canal Department
PCD .... Papillary Collecting Duct [*Medicine*] (DMAA)
PCD .... Parti Communiste du Dahomey [*Communist Party of Dahomey*] [*Benin*] [*Political party*]
PCD .... Partido Comunista Dominicano [*Dominican Communist Party*] [*Dominican Republic*] [*Political party*] (PPW)
PCD .... Patriotic Coalition for Democracy [*Political group*] [*Guyana*]
PCD .... PCD, Inc. [*Associated Press*] (SAG)
PCD .... Perceptual-Communicative Disorder [*Education*] (EDAC)
PCD .... Personal Communication Device [*FTA*] (TAG)
PCD .... Phenylchlorodiazirine [*Organic chemistry*]
PCD .... Phosphate-Citrate-Dextrose Polycystic Disease (MAE)
PCD .... Photo Compact Disk [*Eastman Kodak Co.*] (PCM)
PCD .... Photoconductive Decay [*Semiconductor material*]
PCD .... Pine Channel Gold [*Vancouver Stock Exchange symbol*]
PCD .... Pitch Circle Diameter [*Technical drawings*] (IAA)
PCD .... Planned Completion Date (TEL)
PCD .... Plasma Cell Dyscrasia [*Medicine*]
PCD .... Plasma-Coupled Device
PCD .... Plutonium Concentrator Distillate [*Nuclear energy*] (NRCH)
PCD .... Pneumatic Control Distributors (KSC)
PCD .... Polar Cap Disturbance (DNAB)
PCD .... Polychlorinated Dibenzo (BARN)
PCD .... Polycrystalline Diamond (ECON)
PCD .... Polycystic Disease [*of kidneys*] [*Medicine*]
PCD .... Polymeric Carrier Delivery System [*Nuclear energy*] (NUCP)
PCD .... Port Control Diagnostic [*Telecommunications*] (TEL)
PCD .... Positive Control Document (MCD)
Pcd .... Postcard (BJA)
PCd .... Post Card [*Philately*]
PCD .... Posterior Corneal Deposit [*Ophthalmology*] (MAE)
PCD .... Pounds per Capita per Day (AAG)
PCD .... Power Control and Distribution
PCD .... Power Control Device [*Nuclear energy*] (NRCH)
PCD .... Power Conversion Distributor
PCD .... Precision Course Direction [*Aerospace*] (MCD)
PCD .... Pressure Control Distributor (KSC)
PCD .... Primary Ciliary Dyskinesia [*Medicine*]
PCD .... Primary Current Distribution [*Electroplating*]
PCD .... Problem Control and Display
PCD .... Procedural Change Directive (KSC)
PCD .... Proceed [*ICAO designator*] (FAAC)
PCD .... Procurement and Contracts Division [*NASA*]
PCD .... Procurement Control Document [*NASA*] (MCD)
PCD .... Product Configuration Documentation (AAGC)
PCD .... Production Common Digitizer
PCD .... Program Change Decision [*Army*]
PCD .... Program Control Display System [*NATO Air Defense Ground Environment*] (NATG)
PCD .... Program Control Document (KSC)
PCD .... Programmed Cell Death [*Cytology*]
PCD .... Project Control Drawing (AAG)
PCD .... Projected Charge Density (PDAA)
PCD .... Protocatechuatedioxygenase [*An enzyme*]
PCD .... Pulmonary Clearance Delay [*Medicine*]
PCDA .... Post Card Distributors Association
PCDA .... Professional Currency Dealers Association (EA)
PCDA .... Protective Clothing Distributors Association [*British*] (DBA)
PCDB .... Poison Control Data Base [*Database*]
PCDC .... Diagnostic Chemicals Ltd., Charlottetown, Prince Edward Island [*Library symbol National Library of Canada*] (NLC)
PCDC .... Plasma Clot Diffusion Chamber [*Medicine*] (DMAA)
PCDC .... Plutonium Canister Decontamination Cell [*Nuclear energy*] (NRCH)
PCDD .... Pentachlorodioxin [*Organic chemistry*]
PCDD .... Polychlorinated Dibenzodioxin [*Organic chemistry*]
PCDD .... Polychlorinated Dibenzodioxins [*Automotive emissions*] [*Organic chemistry*]
PCDDS .... Private Circuit Digital Data Service [*Telecommunications*] (TEL)
PCDE .... Parent Council for Deaf Education [*Australia*]
PCDESIG ...... Plane Captain Designated [*or Designation*] (DNAB)
PCDF .... Polychlorinated Dibenzofuran [*Organic chemistry*]
PCDF .... Polychlorinated Dibenzofurans [*Automotive emissions*] [*Organic chemistry*]
PCDH .... Polychlorinated Diaromatic Hydrocarbon [*Organic chemistry*]
PCDHi .... Delaware County Historical Society, Chester, PA [*Library symbol Library of Congress*] (LCLS)
PCDI .... PCD, Inc. [*NASDAQ symbol*] (SAG)
PCDI .... PCD Inc. [*NASDAQ symbol*] (TTSB)
PCDI .... Per Capita Disposable Income [*Economics*]
PCDI .... Pierce Die
PCDI .... Printed Circuit Design Interface (NITA)
PCDJ .... Pakistan Committee for Democracy and Justice [*Defunct*] (EA)
PCDL .... Pro-Choice Defense League (EA)
PCdoB .... Partido Comunista do Brasil [*Communist Party of Brazil*] [*Political party*] (PPW)
PC DOCS ..... PC DOCS Group International [*Associated Press*] (SAG)
PC-DOS .... Personal Computer Disk Operating System [*IBM's version of Microsoft program*]
PC-DOS .... Personal Computer-Disk Operating System (DOM)
PCDP .... Parti Comorien pour la Democratie et le Progres [*Political party*] (EY)
PCDP .... Pilot Control and Display Panel
PCDP .... Punched Card Data Processing
PCD-PRP ..... Pueblo, Cambio, y Democracia - Partido Roldosista Popular [*People, Change, and Democracy - Popular Roldosista Party*] [*Ecuador*] [*Political party*] (PPW)
PCDR .... Procedure (AAG)
PCDS .... Payload Command Decoder Subunit [*NASA*] (KSC)
PCDS .... Power Conversion and Distribution System
PCDS .... Procurement Congressional Descriptive Summary [*Army*] (RDA)
PCDS .... Project Control Drawing System (AAG)
PCDU .... Payload Command Decoder Unit [*NASA*] (NASA)
PCDUS .... Plasma Cell Dyscrasias of Unknown Significance [*Medicine*]
PCE .... Page Communications Engineers, Inc. [*Canada*] (MCD)
PCE .... Painter Creek, AK [*Location identifier FAA*] (FAAL)
PCE .... Palm Island [*Queensland*] [*Airport symbol*] (AD)
PCE .... Parameter Checkout Engineer [*Computer science*] (IAA)
PCE .... Partido Comunista de Espana [*Communist Party of Spain*] [*Political party*] (PPE)
PCE .... Partido Comunista Ecuatoriano [*Communist Party of Ecuador*] [*Political party*] (PPW)
PCE .... Passenger Car Equivalence [*TRB*] (TAG)
PCE .... Patrol Escort [*Patrol Craft Escort*] [*Navy symbol*]
PCE .... Pedco Energy Ltd. [*Vancouver Stock Exchange symbol*]
PCE .... Perchloroethylene [*Organic chemistry*]
PCE .... Peripheral Control Element
PCE .... Peripheral Controller Enclosure (NITA)
PCE .... Personal Consumption Expenditure
PCE .... Petrozavodsk Commodity Exchange [*Russian Federation*] (EY)

PCE Photocell Emitter (IAA)
PCE Physical Capacities Evaluation [*Test of hand skills*]
PCE Piece [*Numismatics*]
PCE Plasma Chamber Evacuation Subsystem (MCD)
PCE Platinol [*Cis-Platinum*] Cyclophosphamide, Vindesine [*Antineoplastic drug regimen*] (DAVI)
PCE Plug Compatible Ethernet
PCE Pollution Control Equipment (GFGA)
PCE Polyarthrite Chronique Evolutive [*Chronic Evolutive Polyarthritis*] [*Medicine French*]
PCE Polychloroethylene (BARN)
PCE Polymer-Coated Erythromycin [*An antibiotic*] (DAVI)
PCE Ponce [*Diocesan abbreviation*] [*Puerto Rico*] (TOCD)
PCE Pool Control Error (IAA)
PCE Positive Continuous Engagement [*Automotive engineering*]
PCE Potentially Compensable Event (DICI)
PCE Power Conditioning Equipment
PCE Power Conversion Equipment (DNAB)
PCE Pressure to Clutch Engage [*Aerospace*] (AAG)
PCE Prince Edward Island Department of Education, Charlottetown, Prince Edward Island [*Library symbol National Library of Canada*] (NLC)
PCE Privy Councillor, England (ROG)
PCE Process [*or Processor*] Control Element [*Computer science*] (IAA)
PCE Production Check Equipment (MCD)
PCE Professional Continuing Education (DOMA)
PCE Program Cost Estimate (AFM)
PCE Prohormone-Converting Endopeptidase
PCE Pseudocholinesterase [*Same as ACAH*] [*An enzyme*]
PCE Pulmocutaneous Exchange
PCE Punch Card Equipment [*Computer science*] (AFM)
PCE Pyrometric Cone Equivalent [*Refractory industry*]
PCE Submarine Chaser Escort
PCEA Pacific Coast Electrical Association
PCEA Patient-Controlled Epidural Analgesia
PCEA Phosphate Chemicals Export Association (EA)
PCEA Presbyterian Church of Eastern Australia
P/CEA3 Probationary Control Electrical Artificer 3rd Class [*British military*] (DMA)
PCEAA Professional Construction Estimators Association of America (EA)
PCE(C) Patrol Vessel, Escort (Control) [*180 feet*] [*Navy symbol Obsolete*]
PCEDURE Procedure (ROG)
PCEEDGS Proceedings (ROG)
PCEEO President's Committee on Equal Employment Opportunity [*Later, OFCCP*] [*Department of Labor*]
PCEH President's Committee on Employment of the Handicapped [*Washington, DC*]
PCEI Prime Contract End Item (MCD)
PCEM Parliamentary Council of the European Movement
PCEM Process Chain Evaluation Model (IEEE)
PCEM Program Committee on Education for Mission (EA)
PCEM Propulsion Contamination Effects Module (NASA)
PcEn Pacific Enterprises [*Associated Press*] (SAG)
PCEN Paracentesis Fluid [*Medicine*] (DAVI)
PCEQ President's Commission on Environmental Quality (GNE)
PCE-R Partido Comunista de Espana - Reconstituido [*Reconstituted Spanish Communist Party*] [*Political party*] (PD)
PCER Patrol Rescue Escort [*Patrol Craft Escort Rescue*] [*Navy symbol*]
P Cert Ed Professional Certificate in Education
PCES Pace Health Management Systems, Inc. [*NASDAQ symbol*] (SAG)
PCES PACE Health Mgmt [*NASDAQ symbol*] (TTSB)
PCES President's Committee on Economic Security [*New Deal*]
PCET Personal Computer Extended Technology [*Computer bus*]
PCETF Power Conversion Equipment Test Facility [*Nuclear energy*]
PCEU Partido Comunista de Espana Unificado [*Unified Communist Party of Spain*] [*Political party*] (PPW)
PCEU Pulse Compression/Expansion Unit
PCF Pacific Air Express [*ICAO designator*] (FAAC)
PCF Pacific Ridge Resources [*Vancouver Stock Exchange symbol*]
PCF Pacificulture Foundation (EA)
PCF Palliative Care Foundation [*Canada*] (EAIO)
PCF Parents' Choice Foundation (EA)
PCF Parti Communiste Francais [*French Communist Party*] [*Political party*] (PPW)
PCF Patrol Craft (Fast) [*Navy symbol*]
PCF Payload Control Facility [*NASA*] (MCD)
PCF Peace Centers Foundation [*Later, UDC*] (EA)
PCF Pentagon Counterintelligence Force
PCF Peripheral Circulatory Failure [*Medicine*] (DMAA)
PCF Personal Card File
PCF Personnel Control Facility [*Army*] (AABC)
PCF Pharyngoconjunctival Fever [*Medicine*]
PCF Pharyngoconjunctival Fever (DAVI)
PCF Plan Characteristics File [*IRS*]
PCF Polycationized Ferritin [*Biochemistry*]
PCF Postcard Club Federation [*Defunct*] (EA)
PCF Posterior Carotid Foramen [*Anatomy*]
PCF Posterior Cranial Fossa [*Anatomy*] (MAE)
PCF Potential Conflict Forecasts [*Army*]
PCF Potentially Critical Failures
PCF Pounds per Cubic Foot
PCF Power Cathode Follower
PCF Power per Cubic Foot
PCF Prairie Chicken Foundation (EA)
PCF Primary Checkpoint File
PCF Probability of Consequence Factor
PCF Processed Citation File
PCF Program Change Factor
PCF Program Characteristics File [*Medicaid*] (GFGA)
PCF Program Checkout Facility
PCF Program Complex File [*Computer science*] (MHDI)
PCF Program Control Facility
PCF Programmed Cryptographic Facility [*Computer science*]
PCF Prothrombin Conversion Factor [*Hematology*]
PCF Public Concern Foundation (EA)
PCF Pulse Compression Filter
PCF Pulse-to-Cycle Fraction
PCF Pulverized Coal-Fired Plant
PCF Putnam High Income Convertible & Bond Fund [*NYSE symbol*] (SPSG)
PCF Putnam Hi Income Cv/Bd Fd [*NYSE symbol*] (TTSB)
PCFA Pin, Clip, and Fastener Association [*Later, PCFS*] (EA)
PCFA Precast Concrete Frame Association [*British*] (DBA)
PCFC Phil Collins Fan Club (EA)
PCFC Pioneer Commercial Funding Corp. [*NASDAQ symbol*] (SAG)
PCFC Polytechnics and Colleges Funding Council [*British*]
Pcfcp25 Pacificorp [*Associated Press*] (SAG)
Pcfcp35 Pacificorp [*Associated Press*] (SAG)
PCFE Polytrifluorochloroethylene [*Organic chemistry*]
PCFE Prime Contractor Furnished Equipment (MCD)
PCFFA Pacific Coast Federation of Fishermen's Associations (EA)
PC/FGD Pulverized Coal / Flue Gas Desulfurization [*Energy technology*]
PCFIA Particle Concentration Fluorescence Immunoassay
PCFM Production Control File Manager (IAA)
PCFN PC Financial Network (PCM)
PCFO Position Classification Field Office
PCFP Predicted Comparative Failure Probability
PCFR Programmatic Center for Fire Research [*National Institute of Standards and Technology*]
PCFRE Professional Council of Religious Education [*British*] (DBA)
PCFS Pin, Clip, and Fastener Services (EA)
PCFT Information Centre, Prince Edward Island Food Technology Centre, Charlottetown [*Library symbol National Library of Canada*] (BIB)
PCG Guided Missile Coastal Escort [*Ship symbol*] (NATG)
PCG Pacific Gas & Elec [*NYSE symbol*] (TTSB)
PCG Pacific Gas & Electric Co. [*AMEX symbol*] (SPSG)
PCG Pacific Gas & Electric Co. [*NYSE symbol*] (SAG)
PCG Paracervical Ganglion [*Anatomy*]
PCG Parti Communiste de Guadeloupe [*Communist Party of Guadeloupe*] [*Political party*] (PPW)
PCG PezCorona Gold Corp. [*Vancouver Stock Exchange symbol*]
PCG PG & E Capital I [*AMEX symbol*] (SAG)
PCG PG & E Corp. Holdings Co. [*NYSE symbol*] (SAG)
PCG Phonocardiogram [*Cardiology*]
pcg Picogram [*Measurement*] (DAVI)
P/CG Pilot Controller Glossary [*Aviation*] (FAAC)
PCG Plain Clothes Gratuity [*British military*] (DMA)
PCG Plains Cotton Growers (EA)
PCG Planning and Control Guide
PCG Planning Career Goals [*Vocational guidance test*]
PCG Policy Coordination Group (DOGT)
PCG Power Conditioning Group (MCD)
PCG Primate Chorionic Gonadotropin [*Medicine*] (DMAA)
PCG Printed Circuit Generator
PCG Programmable Character Generator
PCG Protestant Cinema Guild [*Formerly, PCCG*] [*Defunct*]
PCG Pubococcygeus [*Muscle*] (BABM)
PCG Pubococcygeus [*Muscle*] [*Anatomy*] (DAVI)
PCG Pulsed Coaxial Gun
PCG2 Preconditioned Conjugate Gradient
PCGD Pollution Control Guidance Document
PCGF Protein Crystal Growth Facility (SSD)
PCGM Pacific Coast Garment Manufacturers [*Later, AAMA*] (EA)
PCGN Permanent Committee of Geographical Names [*Later, BGN*]
PCGOV Port Charges Paid by Foreign Government (DNAB)
PCGPrA Pacific Gas & El 6% Pfd [*AMEX symbol*] (TTSB)
PCGPrB Pacific Gas & El 5 1/2% Pfd [*AMEX symbol*] (TTSB)
PCGPrC Pacific Gas & El 5% Pfd [*AMEX symbol*] (TTSB)
PCGPrCA PG&E Cap I 7.90%'QUIPS' [*AMEX symbol*] (TTSB)
PCGPrD Pacific Gas & El 5% Pfd [*AMEX symbol*] (TTSB)
PCGPrE Pac G&E 5%cmRed1stA Pfd [*AMEX symbol*] (TTSB)
PCGPrG Pacific Gas & El 4.80% Pfd (TTSB)
PCGPrH Pacific Gas & El 4.50% Pfd [*AMEX symbol*] (TTSB)
PCGPrI Pacific Gas & El 4.36% Pfd [*AMEX symbol*] (TTSB)
PCGPrQ Pacific Gas & El 7.44% Pfd [*AMEX symbol*] (TTSB)
PCGPrU Pacific Gas & El 7.04% Pfd [*AMEX symbol*] (TTSB)
PCGPrX Pacific Gas & El 6.875% Pfd [*AMEX symbol*] (TTSB)
PCGPrY Pacific Gas & El 6.57% Pfd [*AMEX symbol*] (TTSB)
PCGPrZ Pacific Gas & El 6.30% Pfd [*AMEX symbol*] (TTSB)
PCGRIDS Personal Computer Gridded Interactive Display and Diagnostic System [*Marine science*] (OSRA)
PCGRIDS Personal Computer Gridded Interactive Display and Diagnostic System (USDC)
PCGS Professional Coin Grading Service (BARN)
PCGS Protein Crystal Growth System
PCGU Protein Crystal Growth Unit (SSD)
PCGVB Pairwise Correlated Generalized Valence Bond [*Physics*]
PCH Cheyney State College, Cheyney, PA [*OCLC symbol*] (OCLC)
PCH Packing, Crating, and Handling [*Shipping*]
PCH Parent Compound Handbook [*Later, Ring Systems Handbook*] [*American Chemical Society*]

PCH .... Pari-Cachoeira [*Brazil*] [*Airport symbol*] (AD)
PCH .... Paroxysmal Cold Hemoglobinuria [*Medicine*]
PCH .... Partido Comunista de Honduras [*Communist Party of Honduras*] [*Political party*] (PD)
PCH .... Patrol Craft (Hydrofoil) [*Navy symbol*]
PCH .... PCH Post Career [*Vancouver Stock Exchange symbol*]
PCh .... Phosphocholine [*Biochemistry*]
PCH .... Physicochemical Hydrodynamics [*A publication*]
PCH .... Pitch
PCH .... Polycyclic Hydrocarbon (DMAA)
pch .... Porch (VRA)
PCH .... Porch (WGA)
PCH .... Porous Clay Heterostructure [*Materials science*]
PCH .... Positive Channel [*Telecommunications*] (IAA)
PCH .... Potlatch Corp. [*Formerly, PFI*] [*NYSE symbol*] (SPSG)
PCH .... Prepare Chassis
PCH .... Presbyterian Church House [*British*] (BI)
PCH .... Prince Charles Hospital [*Australia*]
Pch .... Principal Chaplain [*Navy British*]
PCH .... Punch (KSC)
PCH .... Purchase (DCTA)
PCH & T .... Packaging, Crating, Handling, and Transportation [*Shipping*] (CINC)
PCHAR .... Printing Character [*Computer science*]
PCHBD .... Patchboard (MSA)
PCHC .... Holland College, Charlottetown, Prince Edward Island [*Library symbol National Library of Canada*] (NLC)
PCHC .... People's Center for Housing Change (EA)
PChCo .... Conococheague District Library, Chambersburg, PA [*Library symbol Library of Congress*] (LCLS)
PCHCY .... Parents Campaign for Handicapped Children and Youth (EA)
PCHD .... Purchased (ROG)
PCHE .... Poor Clare Nuns of the Holy Eucharist [*Roman Catholic religious order*]
PC HE .... Pseudocholinesterase [*An enzyme*] (DAVI)
PCHE .... Purchase (ROG)
PCheS .... Cheyney State College, Cheyney, PA [*Library symbol Library of Congress*] (LCLS)
PCHG .... Punching
PCHIS .... Population Clearing House and Information System (NITA)
PCHK .... Parity Check [*Data communications*] (TEL)
PCHL .... Pacific Coast Hockey League [*Later, Western Hockey League*] (EA)
PCHLT .... Pressurized Cabin Hydraulic Leakage Tester (DWSG)
PCHM .... PharmChem Laboratories [*NASDAQ symbol*] (SPSG)
PCHMOS .... Positive-Channel Metal-Oxide Semiconductor [*Electronics*] (IAA)
PCHN .... Programmed Course, Home Nursing [*Red Cross*]
PCHR .... Panamanian Committee for Human Rights (EA)
PCHR .... Paraguay Committee for Human Rights [*British*]
PCHR .... Pentecostal Coalition for Human Rights [*Defunct*] (EA)
PCHR .... Purchaser (ROG)
PCHRG .... Public Citizen Health Research Group (EA)
P Chr N .... Post Christum Natum [*After the Birth of Christ*] [*Latin*]
PCHS .... Purchase (WGA)
PCHSR .... Purchaser
PCHT .... Packaging, Crating, Handling, and Transportation [*Shipping*] (AABC)
PCHT .... Parchment (MSA)
PChW .... Wilson College, Chambersburg, PA [*Library symbol Library of Congress*] (LCLS)
PCI .... Packet Communications, Inc.
PCI .... Panel Call Indicator
PCI .... Pantone Color Institute (EA)
PCI .... Parti Communiste Internationaliste [*Internationalist Communist Party*] [*France Political party*] (PPE)
PCI .... Partito Comunista Italiano [*Italian Communist Party*] [*Political party*]
PCI .... Paterson Candy International [*British*]
PCI .... Pattern Correspondence Index
PCI .... Pattern of Cockpit Indication
PCI .... Pavement Condition Index [*Aviation*] (DA)
PCI .... Pax Christi International (EAIO)
PCI .... PCL Industries Ltd. [*Toronto Stock Exchange symbol*]
PCI .... Pellet Clad Interaction [*Nuclear energy*] (NRCH)
PCI .... Per Column Inch [*Publishing*]
PCI .... Periodic Conformance Inspection (MCD)
PCI .... Peripheral Command Indicator
PCI .... Peripheral Component Interconnect [*Telecommunications*] (PCM)
PCI .... Peripheral Component Interface (PCM)
PCI .... Peripheral Controller Interface
PCI .... Personal Computer Interface [*Varitronics Systems, Inc.*]
PCI .... Photographic Credit Institute (EA)
PCI .... Physical Configuration Inspection (AFIT)
PCI .... Physical Configuration Item [*Military*]
Pci .... Phytophthora Citricola [*A fungus*]
pCi .... Picocurie [*Also, pC*] [*One trillionth of a curie*]
PCI .... Pilot Club International (EA)
PCI .... Pilot Controller Integration (IEEE)
PCI .... Pilots for Christ International (EA)
PCI .... Pipe Collectors International [*Later, PCCA*] (EA)
PCI .... Planning Card Index (AAG)
PCI .... Plant Control Interface
PCI .... Pneumatic Circuit Indicator
PCI .... Pneumatosis Cystoides Intestinorum [*Medicine*] (AAMN)
PCI .... Polar Circulation Index [*Climatology*]
PCI .... Political Campaign Institute [*Commercial firm*] (EA)
PCI .... Polycrystal Isolation (IAA)
PCI .... Population Communications International [*An association*] (EA)
PCI .... Portable Cesium Irradiator
PCI .... Portable Compass Indicator
PCI .... Possible Criminal Informant
PCI .... Potato Chip Institute, International [*Later, PC/SFA*] (EA)
PCI .... Powder Coating Institute (EA)
PCI .... Pre-Chamber Ignition [*Automotive engineering*]
PCI .... Precision Components, Inc. [*Addison, IL*] [*Telecommunications service*] (TSSD)
PCI .... Pre-Combat Inspection (INF)
PCI .... Pre-Counseling Inventory [*Psychology*]
PCI .... Presentation Context Identifier [*Computer science*] (TNIG)
PCI .... Press Control, Inc.
PCI .... Prestressed Concrete Institute (EA)
PCI .... Prime Ceiling Incentive
PCI .... Private Citizen, Inc. [*An association*] (EA)
PCI .... Privy Council Decisions [*India*] [*A publication*] (DLA)
PCI .... Privy Councillor, Ireland (ROG)
PCI .... Process Control Interface
PCI .... Product Change Information
PCI .... Product Configuration Identification (KSC)
PCI .... Product Cost Index
PCI .... Production Control Information [*Software supplier*] [*Sheffield, England*] (NCC)
PCI .... Program Check Interruption [*Computer science*] (MDG)
PCI .... Program Control Input (NASA)
PCI .... Program-Controlled Interruption [*Computer science*] (IBMDP)
PCI .... Program in Correctional Institutions (OICC)
PCI .... Programmable Communications Interface
PCI .... Project Concern International (EA)
PCI .... Prophylactic Cranial Irradiation [*Oncology*]
PCI .... Proportional Change Index [*Occupational therapy*]
PCI .... Prospectors Club International [*Defunct*] (EA)
PCI .... Protein C Inhibitor [*Organic chemistry*]
PCI .... Prothrombin Consumption Index (PDAA)
PCI .... Protocol Computers Inc. (NITA)
PCI .... Protocol Control Information [*Telecommunications*]
PCI .... Pupil Control Ideology Form [*Education*] (EDAC)
PCIAC .... Petro-Canada International Assistance Corp.
PCIAOH .... Permanent Commission and International Association on Occupational Health (EAIO)
PCIB .... Personal Computer Instruments Bus (NITA)
PCIC .... Poison Control Information Center
PCICP .... Primary Control Inventory Control Point [*Navy*]
PCICS .... Permanent Council of the International Convention of Stresa on Cheeses (EAIO)
PCIE .... President's Council on Integrity and Efficiency (AAGC)
PCIE .... President's Council on Integrity and Efficiency in Government (EPA)
PCIEC .... Permanent Committee for International Eucharistic Congresses (EA)
PCIF .... Printed Circuit Interconnection Federation [*British*] (DBA)
PCIFC .... Patsy Cline International Fan Club (EA)
PCIFC .... Permanent Commission of the International Fisheries Convention
PCIJ .... Permanent Court of International Justice Cases [*A publication*] (DLA)
PCIJ Ann R ..... Permanent Court of International Justice Annual Reports [*A publication*] (DLA)
pCi/L .... Picocuries per Liter [*Measure of radioactivity*]
PCIL .... Pilot-Controlled Instrument Landing [*Aviation*] (NASA)
PCILO .... Perturbative Configuration Interaction [*Based on*] Localized Orbitals [*Quantum mechanics*]
PCIM .... Packet Channel Interface Module [*Telecommunications*]
PCIM .... Parti du Congres de l'Independance de Madagascar [*Party of the Congress for Malagasy Independence*]
PCIMP .... President's Commission on Income Maintenance Programs (EA)
PCIMR .... Centre for Information and Technical Assistance, Institute of Man and Resources,Charlottetown, Prince Edward Island [*Library symbol National Library of Canada*] (NLC)
PCIMS .... Positive Chemical Ionization Mass Spectroscopy
PCIN .... Program Change Identification Number (NASA)
PCIN .... Program Change Integration (NASA)
PCI/O .... Program-Controlled Input-Output
PC-IOC .... Posterior Chamber - Intraocular Lens [*Ophthalmology*]
PCIOL .... Posterior Chamber Intraocular Lens [*Ophthalmology*] (DAVI)
PCIOMR .... Preconditioning Interim Operating Management Recommendation [*Nuclear energy*] (NRCH)
PCIOS .... Processor Common Input/Output System [*Computer science*]
PCIP .... Personal Computer, Instrument Product
PCIP .... Poseidon [*Missile*] Communication Improvement Program [*Navy*]
PCIPI .... Permanent Committee on Industrial Property [*World Intellectual Property Organization*] [*Switzerland Information service or system*] (IID)
PCIR .... Post-Contract Implementation Report (AAGC)
PCIRO .... Preparatory Commission for International Refugee Organization
PCIS .... Canton Island [*Phoenix Islands*] [*ICAO location identifier*] (ICLI)
PCIS .... Patient Care Information System (IID)
PCIS .... PCI Services [*NASDAQ symbol*] (TTSB)
PCIS .... PCI Services, Inc. [*NASDAQ symbol*] (SAG)
PCIS .... Personal Computer Information Service (NITA)
PCIS .... Primary Containment Isolation System [*Nuclear energy*] (NRCH)
PCIS .... Processed Commodities Inventory System [*Department of Agriculture*] (GFGA)
PCIS .... Production Control Information System (NVT)
PCIS .... Professional Career Information Service [*Department of Labor*]
PCI Sv .... PCI Services, Inc. [*Associated Press*] (SAG)
PCIU .... Programmable Communications Interface Unit
PC/IX .... Personal Computer / Interactive Executive (HGAA)
PCIYRA .... Pacific Coast Intercollegiate Yacht Racing Association
PCJ .... Pax Christi Institute (TOCD)

PCJ .... Peoples Jewellers Ltd. [*Toronto Stock Exchange symbol*]
PCJ .... Pontifical College Josephinum [*Worthington, OH*]
PCJ .... Pontifical College Josephinum, Worthington, OH [*OCLC symbol*] (OCLC)
PCJ .... Pulsed Combustion Jet
PCJ .... Sisters of the Poor Child Jesus [*Roman Catholic religious order*]
PCJC .... Parliamentary Criminal Justice Committee [*Queensland, Australia*]
PCJE .... Program on Criminal Justice and the Elderly (DICI)
PCJILMCC.... Philip C. Jessup International Law Moot Court Competition (EAIO)
PCjr .... Personal Computer-Junior (NITA)
PC Judg .... Privy Council Judgments [*India*] [*A publication*] (DLA)
pck .... Peacock [*Philately*]
PCK .... Peacock H.E. and Son (Thorney) Ltd. [*British*] [*FAA designator*] (FAAC)
PCK .... Peck (IAA)
PCK .... Phase Control Keyboard
PCK .... Polycystic Kidney [*Medicine*] (DMAA)
PCK .... Porcupine Creek, AK [*Location identifier FAA*] (FAAL)
PCK .... Premarital Counseling Kit [*Psychology*]
PCK .... Primary Chicken Kidney [*Cell line*]
PCK .... Printed Circuit Keyboard
PCK .... Processor Controlled Keying [*Computer science*] (DCTA)
PCKB .... Printed Circuit Keyboard
PCKD .... Polycystic Kidney Disease [*Medicine*]
PCL .... Alberta Attorney General, Provincial Court Libraries [*UTLAS symbol*]
PCl .... Clarion Free Library, Clarion, PA [*Library symbol Library of Congress*] (LCLS)
PCL .... Confederation Centre Library, Charlottetown, Prince Edward Island [*Library symbol National Library of Canada*] (NLC)
PCL .... Pachaco Lake [*California*] [*Seismograph station code, US Geological Survey*] (SEIS)
PCL .... Pacific Coast League [*Baseball*]
PCL .... Pallet Coolant Loop (NASA)
PCL .... Parallel Communications Link
PCL .... Parcel
PCL .... Parti Communiste de Luxembourg [*Communist Party of Luxembourg*] [*Political party*] (PPE)
PCL .... Parti Communiste Libanais [*Lebanese Communist Party*] [*Political party*] (PPW)
PCL .... Pencil (MSA)
PCL .... Permissible Contamination Limits [*Nuclear energy*] (NRCH)
PCL .... Persistent Corpus Luteum [*Medicine*]
PCL .... Personnel Security Clearance
P Cl .... Petrus Calvelli [*Flourished, 14th century*] [*Authority cited in pre-1607 legal work*] (DSA)
PCL .... Philippine Cultural League [*Australia*]
PCL .... Phillips Cables Ltd. [*Toronto Stock Exchange symbol*]
PCL .... Pilot Controlled Lighting [*Aviation*] (FAAC)
PCL .... Planning and Conservation League (EA)
PCL .... Planning Configuration List
PCL .... Planning Consultancy Ltd. (NITA)
PCL .... Plasma Cell Leukemia [*Oncology*]
PCL .... Playboy Club of London
PCL .... Plum Creek Timber Co., Inc. [*NYSE symbol*] (SPSG)
PCL .... Plum Creek Timber L.P. [*NYSE symbol*] (TTSB)
PCL .... Plutonium-Contaminated Liquid [*Nuclear energy*] (NUCP)
PCL .... Pocket Checklist (MCD)
PCL .... Polycaprolactone [*Organic chemistry*]
PCL .... [*The*] Polytechnic of Central London
PCL .... Positive Control Line
PCL .... Post Conference List
PCL .... Posterior Chamber Lens [*Ophthalmology*] (DAVI)
PCL .... Posterior Cruciate Ligament [*Anatomy*]
PCL .... PostScript and LASERJet-Type [*LASER printer*]
PCL .... Power Control Lever (DNAB)
PCL .... Power Control List (MCD)
PCL .... Preliminary Change Letter [*Navy*] (NG)
PCL .... Premier Cruise Lines
PCL .... Primary Coolant Line (NASA)
PCL .... Primary Coolant Loop (NASA)
PCL .... Print Control Language (NITA)
PCL .... Printed Circuit Lamp
PCL .... Printer Command Language [*Hewlett Packard*] [*Computer science*]
PCL .... Printer Control Language
PCL .... Procedural Control Language [*1971*] [*Computer science*] (CSR)
PCL .... Process Capability Laboratory
PCL .... Process Communications Link (ECII)
PCL .... Process Control Language [*Texas Instruments, Inc.*] [*Computer science*] (IAA)
PCL .... Programming Checklist (MCD)
PCL .... Programming Control Language [*Computer science*] (PCM)
PCL .... Project Control Ledgers [*Navy*] (NG)
PCL .... Pseudocleistogamous [*Botany*]
PCL .... Pucallpa [*Peru*] [*Airport symbol*] (OAG)
PCL .... Pulse Compression Loop
PCL .... Purkinje Cell Layer [*Cytology*]
PCLA .... Polish Canadian Librarians Association
PCLA .... Power Control Linkage Assembly
PCLA .... Process Control Language [*Texas Instruments, Inc.*]
PCLA .... Project Coordination and Liaison Administration (OICC)
PCLC .... Pest Control Licensing Committee [*New South Wales, Australia*]
PCLD .... Dependent Political Entity [*Board on Geographic Names*]
PCLDI .... Prototype Closed-Loop Development Installation [*Nuclear energy*] (NRCH)
PCLE .... Pinnacle Systems [*NASDAQ symbol*] (TTSB)
PCLE .... Pinnacle Systems, Inc. [*NASDAQ symbol*] (SAG)
PCLG .... Public Citizen Litigation Group (EA)
PCLI .... Independent Political Entity [*Board on Geographic Names*]
PCLI .... Parti de la Convergence pour les Libertes et l'Integration [*Burkina Faso*] [*Political party*] (EY)
PCLI .... Plasma Cell Labeling Index [*Medicine*] (DMAA)
PC-LITE .... Processor, Laptop Imagery Transmission Equipment (DOMA)
PCLJ .... Pacific Coast Law Journal [*A publication*] (DLA)
PCLK .... Pay Clerk
PCLLG .... Ollennu's Principles of Customary Land Law in Ghana [*A publication*] (DLA)
PCLLRC .... Post-Colonial Literatures and Languages Centre [*Macquarie University*] [*Australia*]
PCLMP .... President's Advisory Committee on Labor-Management Policy [*Abolished, 1973*]
PCLN .... Personalcomputer Literaturnachweis [*Datendienst Weiss*] [*Database*]
PC-LNIM ...... Personal Computer Local Network Interface Module (TSSD)
PCLO .... Passenger Control Liaison Office [*or Officer*] [*Army*] (AABC)
PCLP .... PaperClip Imaging Software [*NASDAQ symbol*] (TTSB)
PCLP .... Paperclip Imaging Software, Inc. [*NASDAQ symbol*] (SAG)
PCLPW .... Paperclip Imaging Softw'r Wrrt [*NASDAQ symbol*] (TTSB)
PCLR .... Parallel Communications Link Receiver (NITA)
P Cl R .... Parker's New York Criminal Reports [*A publication*] (DLA)
PCLR .... PR [*Public Relations*] Committee for Licensing and Registration (EA)
P Cl R .... Privy Council Reports [*A publication*] (DLA)
PClS .... Clarion State College, Clarion, PA [*Library symbol Library of Congress*] (LCLS)
PCLS .... Law Society of Prince Edward Island, Charlottetown, Prince Edward Island [*Library symbol National Library of Canada*] (NLC)
PCLS .... People's Committee for Libyan Students (EA)
PCLS .... Prototype Closed-Loop System [*Nuclear energy*] (NRCH)
PCLST .... Polychlorstyrene [*Organic chemistry*]
PCLT .... Portable Coded LASER Target
PCLT .... Prototype Closed-Loop Test [*Nuclear energy*] (NRCH)
PCLU .... Pioneer Civil Labour Unit [*British*]
PClvU .... Ursinus College, Collegeville, PA [*Library symbol Library of Congress*] (LCLS)
PCLW .... Platinum Compensating Lead Wire (PDAA)
PCLX .... Section of Independent Political Entity [*Board on Geographic Names*]
PCM .... Coastal Escort Medium [*200-500 tons*] [*Ship symbol*] (NATG)
PCM .... Pacific Comox Resources [*Vancouver Stock Exchange symbol*]
PCM .... Parabolic Collimator Mirror
PCM .... Paragraph Completion Method [*Education*] (EDAC)
PCM .... Parallel Cutter Mechanism
PCM .... Parity Check Matrix (MCD)
PCM .... Parti Communiste Marocain [*Moroccan Communist Party*] [*Political party*]
PCM .... Parti Communiste Martiniquais [*Communist Party of Martinique*] [*Political party*] (PPW)
PCM .... Parti des Classes Moyennes [*Middle Class Party*] [*Luxembourg*] [*Political party*] (PPE)
PCM .... Partido Comunista Mexicano [*Mexican Communist Party*] [*Political party*] (PPW)
PCM .... Passive Countermeasure
PCM .... Patient Care Manager
PCM .... Patient Management Category (HCT)
PCM .... Penalty Cost Model
PCM .... Pending Contractual Matters (NRCH)
PCM .... Per Calendar Month [*Business term*] (ADA)
pcm .... Per Calendar Month [*Business term*] (ODBW)
PCM .... Percentage of Completion Method (AAGC)
PCM .... Percent Milli (NRCH)
PCM .... Peregrine Capital Myanmar
PCM .... Performance Capability Measure (IAA)
PCM .... Pericentriolar Material [*Biochemistry*]
PCM .... Phase Change Material
PCM .... Phase Change Materials [*Solar energy*]
PCM .... Phase Conjugate Mirror
PCM .... Phase Contrast Microscopy
PCM .... Philippine Campaign Medal
PCM .... Photochemical Machining [*Desktop manufacturing*]
PCM .... Photoformed Ceramic Modules [*Du Pont process for making microconductors*]
PCM .... PIMCO Commercial Mortgage Security Trust [*NYSE symbol*] (SPSG)
PCM .... PIMCO Comml Mtg Sec Tr [*NYSE symbol*] (TTSB)
PCM .... PIPES Buffer with Calcium and Magnesium
PCM .... Pitch Control Motor
PCM .... Planning and Control Memorandum [*Army*]
PCM .... Plug Compatible Mainframe [*Computer science*]
PCM .... Plug Compatible Manufacturer [*Computer science*]
PCM .... Plug Compatible Memory
PCM .... Plug Compatible Module [*Computer science*] (IAA)
PCM .... Plutonium Contaminated Material
PCM .... Police Court Mission [*British*] (ROG)
PCM .... Polyimide Composite Material
PCM .... Portable Conformable Mask [*Microlithography*]
PCM .... Port Command Area [*Telecommunications*] (TEL)
PCM .... Postal [*Service*] Contracting Manual [*A publication*] (AAGC)
PCM .... Post Column Method [*Chromatography*]
PCM .... Postgraduate Committee in Medicine [*Australia*]
PCM .... Postmammillary Caudal Magnocellular Nuclei [*Neuroanatomy*]
PCM .... Power Control Mission (NASA)
PCM .... Power-Cooling Mismatch [*Nuclear energy*]
PCM .... Powertrain Control Module [*Automotive engineering*]
PCM .... Precision Condenser Microphone

PCM President's Certificate of Merit [*Military decoration*] (AFM)
PCM Primary Care Manager (HCT)
PCM Primary Code Modulation [*Computer science*] (IAA)
PCM Process Communication Monitor [*Telecommunications*] (IAA)
PCM Process Control Module [*Telecommunications*] (TEL)
PCM Productive Cost Management (ADA)
PCM Profiling Current Meter [*Oceanography*] (MSC)
PCM Program Configuration Manager
PCM Program Continuity Memorandum [*Military*]
PCM Program Cost Management (MCD)
PCM Project Cost Model [*Project Software Ltd.*] [*Software package*] (NCC)
PCM Protein-Calorie Malnutrition [*Medicine*]
PCM Protein-Carboxyl Methylase [*Medicine*] (BABM)
PCM Protein-Carboxyl Methylase [*Biochemistry*] (DAVI)
PCM Pulse Code Modulation [*Telecommunications*] (OSI)
PCM Punch Card Machine [*Computer science*]
PCM Pyrotechnic Countermeasure [*Military*] (SDI)
PCM WestAir Industries, Inc. [*ICAO designator*] (FAAC)
PCMA Pennsylvania Coal Mining Association (EA)
PCMA Personal Computer Management Association [*Orange, CA*] [*Commercial firm Information service or system*] (EA)
PCMA Phenylcyclopropanemethylamine [*Organic chemistry*]
PCMA Plaited Cordage Manufacturers Association [*British*] (BI)
PCMA Post Card Manufacturers Association [*Defunct*] (EA)
PCMA Potato Chip Manufacturers [*British*] (DBA)
PCMA Power Cooling Mismatch Accident [*Nuclear energy*] (NUCP)
PCMA Prince Edward Island Department of Municipal Affairs, Charlottetown, Prince Edward Island [*Library symbol National Library of Canada*] (NLC)
PCMA Professional Convention Management Association [*Birmingham, AL*] (EA)
PCMA Provincial Carters' and Motormen's Association [*A union*] [*British*]
PCMANSW Precast Concrete Manufacturers' Association of New South Wales [*Australia*]
PCMAV Precast Concrete Manufacturers' Association of Victoria [*Australia*]
PCMB Para-Chloromercuribenzoate [*Organic chemistry*]
PCMC Para-Chloro-meta-cresol [*Organic chemistry*]
PCMC Postal [*Service*] Contracting Manual Circular (AAGC)
PCMC Provided Chief of Mission Concurs [*Army*]
PCMCIA People Can't Memorize Computer Industry Acronyms (PS)
PCMCIA Personal Computer Memory Card International Association (PCM)
PCMCIA Portable Computer Memory Card Industry Association (DOM)
PCMD Particle Count Monitoring Device (KSC)
PCMD Passive Count Monitoring Device (KSC)
PCMD Procurement and Contracts Management Division [*Environmental Protection Agency*] (GFGA)
PCMD Pulse Code Modulation, Digital
PCMDHS Pulse Code Modulation Data Handling System [*Telecommunications*] (IAA)
PCMDI Program for Climate Model Diagnosis and Intercomparison [*Department of Energy*]
PCME Pulse Code Modulation Event
PCMF Phi Chi Medical Fraternity (EA)
PCM-FM Pulse Code Modulation - Frequency Modulation
PCM/FSK/AM Pulse Code Modulation/Frequency Shift Keying/Amplitude Modulation (SAA)
PCMGS Pulse Code Modulated Ground Station
PCMH Para-Cresol Methylhydroxylase [*An enzyme*]
PCMH Postgraduate Center for Mental Health (EA)
PCMI Photo-Chemical Machining Institute (EA)
PCMI Photochromic Microimage [*Microfiche*]
PCMI Photochromic Microimage System (IAA)
PCMI Plastic Container Manufacturers Institute [*Defunct*] (EA)
PCMI President's Council on Management Improvement [*Executive Office of the President*] (GFGA)
PCMIA Pittsburgh Coal Mining Institute of America (EA)
PCMIP Pontifical Commission for Migrants and Itinerant Peoples [*See also PCMT*] [*Vatican City, Vatican City State*] (EAIO)
PCMK Piece Mark
PC-ML Marxist-Leninist Communist Party [*Bolivia*] [*Political party*] (PPW)
PCML Parti Communiste Marxiste-Leniniste [*Marxist-Leninist Communist Party*] [*France Political party*] (PPW)
PCML Partito Comunista Marxista-Leninista [*Marxist-Leninist Communist Party*] [*San Marino*] [*Political party*] (PPE)
PCML President's Committee on Migratory Labor [*Terminated, 1964*]
PCMLF Parti Communiste Marxiste-Leniniste Francais [*French Marxist-Leninist Communist Party*] [*Dissolved, 1978*] [*Political party*] (PPW)
PC(ML)I Partito Comunista (Marxista-Leninista) de Italia [*Communist Party of Italy (Marxist-Leninist)*] [*Political party*] (PPE)
PCMM Plug Compatible Mainframe Manufacturer (NITA)
PCMMU PCM [*Punch Card Machine*] Master Unit [*Computer science*] (GFGA)
PCMMU Pulse Code Modulation Master Unit [*Electronics*] (NASA)
PCM/NRZ Pulse Code Modulation/Nonreturn to Zero (KSC)
PCMO Passenger Car Motor Oil
PCMO Principal Clinical Medical Officer [*British*]
PCMO Principal Colonial Medical Officer [*British*]
PCMOD Personal Computer Modification Program
PCMP Packed Computational (IAA)
PCMP Pennsylvania Comprehensive Mathematics Plan (EDAC)
PCMP (Phenylcyclohexyl)methylpiperidine [*Organic chemistry*]
PCMP Preliminary Configuration Management Plan (MCD)
PCMPM Pulse Code Modulation-Phase-Modulation (IAA)
PCMPN Pulse Code Modulation Pseudonoise [*Telecommunications*] (IAA)
PCMPS Para-Chloromercuriphenylsulfonic Acid [*Organic chemistry*]
PCM-PS Pulse Code Modulation - Phase-Shift
PCMR Patient Computer Medical Record
PCMR Photochromic Microreproduction (DIT)
PCMR President's Committee on Mental Retardation [*Washington, DC*]
PCMS Para-Chloromercuriphenyl Sulfonate [*or Sulfonic Acid*] [*Organic chemistry*]
PCMS Pattern Card Makers' Society [*British*] (BI)
PCMS P-Com, Inc. [*NASDAQ symbol*] (SAG)
PCMS Photographic Cabinet Makers' Society [*A union*] [*British*]
PCMS Plasma Chromatography Mass Spectroscopy
PCMS Production Control Monitoring System (NVT)
PCMS Pulse Code Modulation Shared (MCD)
PCMS Punch Card Machine System [*Computer science*]
PCMT Pontificia Commissione Migrazioni e Turismo [*Pontifical Commission for Migrants and Itinerant Peoples - PCMIP*] [*Vatican City, Vatican City State*] (EAIO)
PCMTE Pulse Code Modulation and Timing Equipment (KSC)
PCMTEA Pulse Code Modulation and Timing Electronics Assembly
PCMTS Pulse Code Modulation Telemetry System (AAG)
PCMU Physico-Chemical Measurements Unit [*British*]
PCMU Propellant Calibration Measuring Unit (KSC)
PCMV Porcine Cerebral Microvascular [*Cell line*]
PCMX Para-Chloro-meta-xylenol [*Organic chemistry*]
PCN Pacific Communications Network [*Air Force*] (IAA)
PCN Package Control Number
PCN Page Change Notice (MCD)
PCN PanCana Minerals [*Toronto Stock Exchange symbol*]
PCN Parent Country National (PDAA)
PCN Part Control Number (AAG)
PCN Partido Comunista de Nicaragua [*Communist Party of Nicaragua*] [*Political party*] (PD)
PCN Partido Conservador Nicaraguense [*Nicaraguan Conservative Party*] [*Political party*] (PPW)
PCN Partido de Conciliacion Nacional [*National Reconciliation Party*] [*El Salvador*] [*Political party*] (PPW)
PCN Parts Change Notice (MCD)
PCN Pavement Classification Number [*Aviation*] (DA)
PCN Penicillin [*Antibiotic*]
PCN Percutaneous Nephrostomy (DAVI)
PCN Permanent Control Number (MCD)
PCN Personal Communications Network [*British*]
PCN Personal Computer Network [*Telecommunications*]
PCN Personal Computer News (NITA)
PCN Piacenza [*Italy*] [*Seismograph station code, US Geological Survey Closed*] (SEIS)
PCN Pitcairn Islands [*ANSI three-letter standard code*] (CNC)
PCN Planning Change Notice
PCN PointCast Network [*Computer science*]
PCN Point Comfort & Northern Railway Co. [*AAR code*]
PCN Polychlorinated Naphthalene [*Organic chemistry*]
PCN Position Control Number (AFM)
PCN Post Christum Natum [*After the Birth of Christ*] [*Latin*] (ROG)
PCN Potato Cyst Nematode [*Plant pathology*]
PCN Pregnenolone Carbonitril [*Pharmacology*] (DAVI)
PCN Prelaunch Channel Number [*NASA*] (IAA)
PCN Primary Care Network [*Medical insurance*]
PCN Primary Care Nursing
PCN Princeton Aviation Corp. [*ICAO designator*] (FAAC)
PCN Procedure Change Notice
PCN Processing Control Number
PCN Procurement Control Number (AFM)
PCN Product Control Number (AFM)
PCN Production Change Number (KSC)
PCN Program Change Notice (MCD)
PCN Program Composition Notation [*Computer science*]
PCN Program Control Number (AFM)
PCN Project Control Number (AAG)
PCN Proposal Control Number (AAG)
PCN Publication Change Notice (MCD)
PCN Public Convenience and Necessity [*Department of Transportation*]
PCN Pulse Compression Network
PCNA Palestine Congress of North America [*Defunct*] (EA)
PCNA Porsche Cars North America, Inc.
PCNA Proliferating Cell Nuclear Antigen [*Cytology, immunology*]
PCNA Publishing Co. North Amer [*NASDAQ symbol*] (TTSB)
PCNA Publishing Co. of North America, Inc. (The) [*NASDAQ symbol*] (SAG)
PCNAC Professionals Coalition for Nuclear Arms Control (EA)
PCNB Pentachloronitrobenzene [*Agricultural fungicide*]
PCNB Permanent Control Narcotics Board
PCNE Protocol Converter for Native Equipment [*Telecommunications*] (IAA)
PCNF Pacific Central NOTAM [*Notice to Airmen*] Facility [*Military*]
PCNI Physician Computer Network [*NASDAQ symbol*] (SPSG)
PCNI Physician Computer Ntwk [*NASDAQ symbol*] (TTSB)
PCNI Physicians Computer Network [*NASDAQ symbol*] (SAG)
PCNM Polymer-Immobilised Clusters of the Noble Metals [*Catalytic chemistry*]
PCNP Personal Computer Network Program (HGAA)
PCNR Part Control Number Request (AAG)
PCNR Planning Change Notice Request
PCNS Polar Coordinates Navigation System
PCNSL Polymerised Cashew Nut Shell Liquid (PDAA)
PCNV Provisional Committee on Nomenclature of Viruses (DAVI)
PCNY Proofreaders Club of New York (EA)
P_{co} Carbon Monoxide Tension (DAVI)

PCO .... Conococheague District Library, Chambersburg, PA [*OCLC symbol*] (OCLC)
PCO .... Pacific Coastal Airline [*Canada ICAO designator*] (FAAC)
PCO .... Parcel Concentration Office [*British*]
PCO .... Parliamentary Counsel's Office [*Australia*]
PCO .... Passport Control Officer [*British*]
PCO .... Patient Complains Of [*Medicine*]
PCO .... Peacetime Contingency Operation [*Army*] (ADDR)
PCO .... Pest Control Operator
PCO .... Philadelphia College of Osteopathy [*Pennsylvania*]
PCO .... Phoenix Canada Oil Co. Ltd. [*Toronto Stock Exchange symbol*]
PCO .... Photosynthetic Carbon Oxidation [*Plant metabolism*]
PCO .... Picture Control Oscilloscope (IAA)
PCO .... Placement Contracting Officer [*Army*] (AABC)
PCO .... Plant Clearance Officer [*DoD*]
PCO .... Plant Clearance Order
PCO .... Point of Control and Observation [*Telecommunications*] (OSI)
PCO .... Police Commissioner's Office
PCO .... Polycystic Ovary [*Gynecology*]
PCO .... Ponca City [*Oklahoma*] [*Seismograph station code, US Geological Survey*] (SEIS)
PCO .... Post Checkout
PCO .... Postcheckout Operations
PCO .... Potassium Channel Opener [*Vasodilator*]
PCO .... Predicted Cardia Output [*Medicine*] (DMAA)
PCO .... Primary Communications-Oriented (IAA)
PCO .... Primary Contracting Officer (MCD)
PCO .... Prime Contracting Officer (SAA)
PCO .... Prince Consort's Own [*Military unit*] [*British*]
PCO .... Principal Careers Officer (AIE)
PCO .... Principal Coast Officer [*Customs*] [*British*] (ROG)
PCO .... Principal Contracting Officer [*Air Force*]
PCO .... Printer Control Option (SAA)
PCO .... Printing Control Officer [*Air Force*] (AFM)
PCO .... Privy Council Office [*British*]
PCO .... Procurement Change Order (MCD)
PCO .... Procurement Contracting Officer (AAGC)
PCO .... Procuring Contracting Office [*or Officer*] [*Military*]
PCO .... Procuring Contrast Offer
PCO .... Professional Conference Organizer
PCO .... Program Comparator
PCO .... Program-Controlled Output (NASA)
PCO .... Program Coordination Office (AAG)
PCO .... Project Control Office (MCD)
PCO .... Property Control Office [*of Allied Military Government*] [*Post-World War II*]
PCO .... Proposed Change Order (AFIT)
PCO .... Prospective Commanding Officer [*Navy*]
PCO .... Provisioning Contracting Officer [*Military*] (AFIT)
PCO .... Publications Control Officer [*DoD*]
PCO .... Public Call Office (DAS)
PCO .... Public Communications Office
PCO .... Purchase Change Order (MCD)
PCO_2 .... Carbon Dioxide Tension [*in blood gases*] (DAVI)
pCO_2 .... Partial Pressure of Carbon Dioxide (AAMN)
pCO_2 .... Pressure of Carbon Dioxide (HGAA)
PCoA .... Principal Co-Ordinates Analysis
PCOAS .... Permanent Council of the Organization of American States
P Coast LJ .... Pacific Coast Law Journal [*A publication*] (DLA)
PCOB(UN) .... Permanent Central Opium Board (United Nations)
PCOC .... Partit Comunista Obrero de Catalunya [*Communist Workers' Party of Catalonia*] [*Political party*] (PPW)
PCOC .... Primary Care Organization Consortium [*Health insurance*] (DMAA)
PCOD .... Permanent Change of Duty [*Navy*] (DNAB)
PCOD .... Polycystic Ovarian Disease [*Medicine*]
PCOE .... Partido Comunista Obrero de Espana [*Communist Workers' Party of Spain*] [*Political party*] (PPW)
PCOF .... Probable Cause of Failure (MCD)
PC of E .... Presbyterian Church of England
PCOGA .... Pacific Coast Oyster Growers Association (EA)
PCOI .... Preconstruction Operating Instruction [*Environmental Protection Agency*]
PCOIT .... Putnam Convertible Opportunities & Income Trust [*Associated Press*] (SAG)
PCOL .... Protocol Systems [*NASDAQ symbol*] (TTSB)
PCOL .... Protocol Systems, Inc. [*NASDAQ symbol*] (SAG)
PCOLA .... Pulse-Coded Optical Landing Aid [*Aviation*] (PDAA)
P-Com .... P-Com, Inc. [*Associated Press*] (SAG)
PCOM .... Philadelphia College of Osteopathic Medicine
PCOM .... Photocomm, Inc. [*NASDAQ symbol*] (NQ)
PCOM .... Posterior Communicating [*Artery*] [*Medicine*] (DMAA)
PCON .... Para-Chloro-ortho-nitroaniline [*Also, PCONA*] [*Organic chemistry*]
PCON .... Personnel Continuity
PCON .... Platelet Concentration [*hematology*] (DAVI)
PCON .... Primary Care Organization Network [*Health insurance*] (DMAA)
PCONA .... Para-Chloro-ortho-nitroaniline [*Also, PCON*] [*Organic chemistry*]
P Contr LJ .... Public Contract Law Journal [*A publication*] (AAGC)
PCOP .... Pharmacopeia Inc. [*NASDAQ symbol*] (TTSB)
PCOP .... Port Charges Operator (DNAB)
PCOP .... Port Charges Paid by Commercial Operator (DNAB)
PCOP .... President's Commission on Obscenity and Pornography (DGA)
PCOPF .... President's Council on Physical Fitness [*Later, PCPFS*] (KSC)
PCOR .... Pressure Compensator Over-Ride (PDAA)
PCOR .... Profit Commission on Renewal [*Insurance*] (AIA)
PCOR .... PSICOR, Inc. [*NASDAQ symbol*] (NQ)
PCoR .... Robert Morris College, Coraopolis, PA [*Library symbol Library of Congress*] (LCLS)
PCORN .... Perpetual Convertible or Redeemable Note [*Economics*]
PCOS .... Polycystic Ovarian Syndrome [*Also, POS*] [*Gynecology*]
PCOS .... Primary Communications-Oriented System (IEEE)
PCOS .... Process Control Operating System
PCOS .... Project Concern's Options Service (EA)
P-COSWA .... Pugwash Conferences on Science and World Affairs
PCOT .... Payload Center Operations Team [*NASA*] (MCD)
PCOTES .... Prototype Carrier Operational Test and Evaluation Site [*Military*] (CAAL)
PCOUNT .... Parameter Count [*Computer science*]
PCOV .... Precombustor Oxidizer Valve (KSC)
P(COV) .... Probability of No Covariate Effect [*Statistics*]
PCOYO .... President's Council on Youth Opportunity [*Defunct*] (EA)
PCP .... Centre for Personal Construct Psychology [*British*] (CB)
PCP .... Paired Cone Pigments [*Vision physiology*]
PCP .... Palestinian Communist Party [*Political party*] (PD)
PCP .... PanCanadian Petroleum [*TS, Exchange Symbol*] (TTSB)
PCP .... PanCanadian Petroleum Ltd. [*Toronto Stock Exchange symbol Vancouver Stock Exchange symbol*]
PCP .... Para-Chlorophenol [*Organic chemistry*]
PCP .... Paraguayan Communist Party
PCP .... Parallel Cascade Processor (IEEE)
PCP .... Parallel Circular Plate (IEEE)
PCP .... Parliamentary Conservative Party [*British*] (BARN)
PCP .... Partido Comunista Paraguayano [*Paraguayan Communist Party*] [*Political party*] (PD)
PCP .... Partido Comunista Peruano [*Peruvian Communist Party*] [*Political party*] (PPW)
PCP .... Partido Comunista Portugues [*Portuguese Communist Party*] [*Political party*] (PPE)
PCP .... Partido Comunista Puertorriqueno [*Puerto Rican Communist Party*] [*Political party*] (PPW)
PCP .... Passenger Control Point [*Army*] (AABC)
PCP .... Past Chief Patriarch [*Freemasonry*]
PCP .... Patient Care Publications
PCP .... Payload Control Processor [*NASA*]
PCP .... Peace Corps Physician
PCP .... Pentachlorophenate [*A topical antibacterial*] (DAVI)
PCP .... Pentachlorophenol [*Wood preservative*] [*Organic chemistry*]
PCP .... Peridinin-Chlorophyll-Protein [*Botany*]
PCP .... Peripheral Control Program
PCP .... Peripheral Control Pulse [*Computer science*]
PCP .... Peripheral Coronary Pressure [*Cardiology*] (AAMN)
PCP .... Personal Communications Programme [*British*]
PCP .... Peter Collins Publishing [*British*]
PCP .... Phencyclidine Palmitate [*Organic chemistry*] (DAVI)
PCP .... (Phenylcyclohexyl)piperidine [*or Phencyclidine*] [*Anesthetic A street drug*]
PCP .... Philadelphia College of Pharmacy and Science, Philadelphia, PA [*OCLC symbol*] (OCLC)
PCP .... Phosphor Coated Paper
PCP .... Photon-Coupled Pair (IEEE)
PCP .... Pilot Control Panel
PCP .... Planar Combat Problem
PCP .... Plastic Clad Plastic [*Materials science*]
PCP .... Platoon Command Post [*Military*] (RDA)
PCP .... Plug Compatible Peripheral [*Computer science*] (EECA)
PCP .... Pneumatics Control Panel (AAG)
PCP .... Pneumocystic Pneumonia [*Medicine*] (DAVI)
PCP .... Pneumocystis Carinii Pneumonia [*Microbiology*]
PCP .... Polaroid Color Pack Camera
PCP .... Polychloroprene [*Organic chemistry*]
PCP .... Poorly Characterized Phase [*Mineralogy*]
PCP .... Portable Code Processor
PCP .... Portuguese Communist Party
PCP .... Post-Construction Permit [*Nuclear energy*] (NRCH)
PCP .... Posted County Price [*Agriculture*]
PCP .... Postgraduate Center for Psychotherapy [*Later, Postgraduate Center for Mental Health*] (EA)
PCP .... Potential Contractor Program (MCD)
PCP .... Power Control Panel [*Aerospace*] (AAG)
PCP .... Preassembled Cable in Pipe
PCP .... Precision Castparts [*NYSE symbol*] (TTSB)
PCP .... Precision Castparts Corp. [*NYSE symbol*] (SPSG)
PCP .... Preliminary Cost Proposal (MCD)
PCP .... Pressurization Control Panel [*NASA*] (KSC)
PCP .... Primary Care Physician
PCP .... Primary Command Point [*Military*] (CAAL)
PCP .... Primary Control Program [*Computer science*]
PCP .... Primary Coolant Pump [*Nuclear energy*] (NRCH)
PCP .... Primary Cross-Connection Point (NITA)
PCP .... Principal Care Provider [*For a patient*] (DAVI)
PCP .... Printed Circuit Patchboard
PCP .... Process Control Processor (IEEE)
PCP .... Process Control Program [*Nuclear energy*] (NRCH)
PCP .... Processor Control Program
PCP .... Product Change Proposal (MCD)
PCP .... Product Chassis Package
PCP .... Production Change Point
PCP .... Program Change Procedure
PCP .... Program [*or Project*] Change Proposal
PCP .... Program Control Plan (AAG)
PCP .... Program Control Procedure [*Nuclear energy*] (NRCH)

PCP............. Programmable Communication Processor
PCP............. Progressive Conservative Party [*Australia Political party*]
PCP............. Progressive Conservative Party [*Canada Political party*] (PPW)
PCP............. Progressive Constitutionalist Party [*Malta*] [*Political party*] (PPE)
PCP............. Project Control Plan (IEEE)
PCP............. Project Cost Plan (NASA)
PCP............. Prototype Communications Processor
PCP............. Psilcybin [*Medicine*] (MEDA)
PCP............. Pulmonary Capillary Pressure [*Medicine*] (CPH)
PCP............. Pulse Comparator
PCP............. Pulse Cytophotometry [*Hematology*]
PCP............. Punched Card Punch [*Computer science*] (IEEE)
PcP............. Reflected P Wave [*Earthquakes*]
PCPA.......... Pacific Conservatory of the Performing Arts
PCPA.......... Panel of Consultants for the Performing Arts [*of CFC*]
PCPA.......... Para-Chlorophenoxyacetic Acid [*Organic chemistry*]
PCPA.......... Para-Chlorophenylacetic Acid [*Organic chemistry*]
PCPA.......... Para-Chlorophenylalanine [*Biochemistry*]
PCPA.......... Poor Clares of Perpetual Adoration [*Roman Catholic women's religious order*]
PCPA.......... Protestant Church-Owned Publishers Association (EA)
PCPAC........ Parker-Coltrane Political Action Committee [*Defunct*] (EA)
PCPAV........ Pensioners-Combined Pensioners Association of Victoria [*Australia*]
PCPBMA...... Pacific Coast Paper Box Manufacturers' Association (EA)
PCPC.......... Power Conversion Products Council [*Later, PCPCI*] (EA)
PCPCA........ Pairpoint Cup Plate Collectors of America (EA)
PCPCI......... Power Conversion Products Council International (EA)
PCPCN........ Part Card Procurement Change Notice (KSC)
PCPE.......... Partido Comunista de los Pueblos de Espana [*Communist Party of the Peoples of Spain*] [*Political party*] (EY)
PCPF.......... President's Council on Physical Fitness [*Later, PCPFS*]
PCPFS........ President's Council on Physical Fitness and Sports (EGAO)
PCPG.......... Primary Clock Pulse Generator
PCPI........... Parent Cooperative Pre-Schools International (EA)
PCPI........... Permanent Committee on Patent Information [*World Intellectual Property Organization*] [*Information service or system*] (IID)
PCPI........... President's Commission on Personnel Interchange [*Later, President's Commission on Executive Exchange*]
PCPJ........... Peoples Coalition for Peace and Justice [*Defunct*]
PCPL........... Government Services Library, Charlottetown, Prince Edward Island [*Library symbol National Library of Canada*] (NLC)
PCPL........... Planning Library, Charlottetown, Prince Edward Island [*Library symbol National Library of Canada*] (NLC)
PCPL........... Production Control Priority List (MCD)
PCPL........... Proposed Change Point Line [*NASA*] (KSC)
PCPL........... Pulmonary Capillary Protein Leakage [*Medicine*] (DMAA)
PCPM.......... PERT [*Program Evaluation and Review Technique*] Cost Performance Measurement
PCP M-L...... Partido Comunista de Portugal, Marxista-Leninista [*Marxist-Leninist Communist Party of Portugal*] [*Political party*] (PPE)
pcpn........... Precipitation (DAVI)
PCPP.......... (Para-Chlorophenoxy)propionic Acid [*Organic chemistry*]
PCPP.......... Peace Corps Partnership Program (EA)
PCPS.......... Percutaneously-Introduced Cardiopulmonary Support System [*Medicine*]
PCPS.......... Philadelphia College of Pharmacy and Science [*Pennsylvania*]
PCPS.......... Pool Cooling and Purification System [*Nuclear energy*] (NRCH)
PCPS.......... Private Companies Practice Section
PCPS.......... Proceedings of the Cambridge Philological Society [*A publication*] (OCD)
PCPS.......... Program Change Package (IAA)
PCPS.......... Pulse-Coded Processing System
PCPT.......... Para-Chlorophenylthio [*Organic chemistry*]
PCPT.......... Perception
PCPT.......... Physical Combat Proficiency Test [*Army*]
PCPT.......... Post Conference Provisioning Tape (MCD)
PCPV.......... Partido Comunista del Pais Valenciano [*Spain Political party*] (EY)
PCPV.......... Point-Contact Photo-Voltaic [*Solar cells*]
PCPV.......... Prestressed Concrete Pressure Vessel
PCQ........... Pacificorp [*NYSE symbol*] (SAG)
PCQ........... PacifiCorp 8.375% 'QUIDS' [*NYSE symbol*] (TTSB)
PCQ........... Production Control Quantometer
PCQ........... Productivity Criteria Quotient
PCQ........... Professional Capabilities Questionnaire [*Jet Propulsion Laboratory, NASA*]
PCQ........... Yuma, AZ [*Location identifier FAA*] (FAAL)
PCQEH........ Queen Elizabeth Hospital, Charlottetown, Prince Edward Island [*Library symbol National Library of Canada*] (NLC)
PCQT.......... Paper-Core Quad Trunk (PDAA)
PCQT.......... Personal Computer Query Tool [*Military software package*] (INF)
PC Quote..... PC Quote, Inc. [*Associated Press*] (SAG)
PCR............ Pacific Amber Resources [*VS, Exchange Symbol*] (TTSB)
PCR............ Page Control Register
PCR............ Parker's Criminal Reports [*New York*] [*A publication*] (DLA)
PCR............ Partial Carriage Return (IAA)
PCR............ Parti Communiste Reunionnais [*Communist Party of Reunion*] [*Political party*] (PPW)
PCR............ Partido Comunista Revolucionario [*Revolutionary Communist Party*] [*Peru*] [*Political party*] (PPW)
PCR............ Partidul Comunist Roman [*Romanian Communist Party*] [*Political party*] (PPE)
PCR............ Pass Card Reader [*Telecommunications*] (TEL)
PCR............ Patient Charge Ratio
PCR............ Patient Contact Record [*Medicine*] (DMAA)
PCR............ Payload Certification Review (SSD)
PCR............ Payload Changeout Room [*NASA*] (NASA)
PCR............ Payload Checkout Room [*NASA*] (NASA)
P Cr........... Paymaster-Commander [*Navy British*] (DMA)
PCR............ PC Resource [*A publication*]
PCR............ Pearson Aviation Corp. [*ICAO designator*] (FAAC)
PCR............ Peer Code Review (IAA)
PCR............ Peninsular Chemresearch [*Calgon Corp.*]
PCR............ Pennsylvania Corp. Reporter [*A publication*] (DLA)
PCR............ Pennsylvania County Court Reports [*A publication*] (DLA)
PCR............ Per Call Rate [*Telecommunications*] (IAA)
PCR............ Perini Corp. [*AMEX symbol*] (SPSG)
PCR............ Period Contract Request
PCR............ Periodic Current Reversal [*Electrochemistry*]
PCR............ Peripheral Control Routine (CMD)
PCR............ Personal Care Residence (DAVI)
PCR............ Personal Communications Report [*FutureComm Publications, Inc.*] [*Information service or system Defunct*] (CRD)
PCr............. Phosphocreatine [*Also, CP, PC*] [*Biochemistry*]
PCR............ Photoconductive Relay (IEEE)
PCR............ Photoconductive Resonance [*Physics*]
PCR............ Photosynthetic Carbon Reduction [*Plant metabolism*]
PCR............ Pine Creek Railroad [*An association*] (EA)
PCR............ Planned Component Replacement [*Predictive maintenance schedule*]
PCR............ Planning Change [*or Check*] Request (AAG)
PCR............ Plant Control Room [*Nuclear energy*] (IAA)
PCR............ Plasma Clearance Rate [*Medicine*] (DMAA)
P_{cr}............ Plasma Creatinine (DAVI)
PCR............ Pneumatic Checkout Rack (KSC)
PCR............ Pneumatic Control Regulator (KSC)
PCR............ Pollution Control Report [*Navy*]
PCR............ Pollution Control Revenue
PCR............ Polychromatic Color Removal [*Printing technology*]
PCR............ Polymerase Chain Reaction [*Genetics*]
PCR............ Population Census Report (OICC)
PCR............ Positive Control Route [*Aviation*] (OA)
PCR............ Post-Compression Remodeling [*Medicine*] (DMAA)
PCR............ Post-Consumer Recycle [*or Reclaim*] [*Plastics industry*]
PCR............ Post-Consumer Resin [*Plastic recycling*]
PCR............ Postconviction Remedy
PCR............ Powell Cycle Registry (EA)
PCR............ Power Change Request [*NASA*] (NASA)
PCR............ Power Control Room [*Nuclear energy*] (IAA)
PCR............ Power Conversion Room
PCR............ Pressure Check Range
PCR............ Prestressed Ceramic RADOME
PCR............ Preventative Cyclic Retransmission [*Telecommunications*] (TEL)
PCR............ Primary Chemotherapy-Radiotherapy [*Oncology*]
PCR............ Primary Cosmic Radiation
PCR............ Principal Components Regression
PCR............ Print Command Register
PCR............ Probable Causal Relationship [*Medicine*] (MEDA)
PCR............ Procedure Change Request [*NASA*]
PCR............ Procurement Center Representative [*Small Business Administration*]
PCR............ Production Capability Review [*Army*]
PCR............ Production Change Request (MCD)
PCR............ Production Control Record [*NASA*] (KSC)
PCR............ Program Change Request [*DoD*]
PCR............ Program Control Register
PCR............ Program Control Report
PCR............ Program Counter [*Computer science*] (IAA)
PCR............ Programmer in Charge of Records [*Computer science*] (IAA)
PCR............ Program to Combat Racism [*British*] (DI)
PCR............ Progress Curve Report
PCR............ Project Control Room [*NASA*] (NASA)
PCR............ Project Cost Record [*or Report*] [*NASA*] (KSC)
PCR............ Project on Corporate Responsibility (EA)
PCR............ Protein Catabolic Rate [*Biochemistry*] (DAVI)
PCR............ Proven Commercial Registration [*Advertising*] (WDMC)
PCR............ Publication Change Request (MCD)
PCR............ Publication Contract Requirements
PCR............ Puerto Carreno [*Colombia*] [*Airport symbol*] (OAG)
PCR............ Pulse Compression RADAR
PCR............ Punched Card Reader [*Computer science*] (BUR)
PCR............ Punched Card Requisition [*Computer science*] (MCD)
PCRA.......... Phantom Class Racing Association (EA)
PCRA.......... Poland China Record Association (EA)
PCRAM........ Page Composition Random Access Memory (NITA)
PCR & A....... Picked Cold, Rolled, and Annealed [*Metallurgy*] (ROG)
PCRAP........ Personal Computer Response Analysis Program
PCRB.......... Personnel and Control Room Building [*Nuclear energy*] (NRCH)
PCRB.......... Pollution Control Revenue Bond [*Environmental Protection Agency*]
PCRB.......... Program Change Review Board [*NASA*]
PCRC.......... Pacific Concerns Resource Center (EA)
PCRC.......... Paraffined Carton Research Council [*Later, Paperboard Packaging Council*]
PCRC.......... Perinatal Clinical Research Center [*Case Western Reserve University*] [*Research center*] (RCD)
PCRC.......... Poor Clergy Relief Corp. [*British*] (BI)
PCRC.......... Primary Communications Research Centre [*University of Leicester*] [*Canada*]
PCRCA........ Pickled, Cold-Rolled, and Close-Annealed [*Metal*]
PCRD.......... Primary Control Rod Driveline [*Nuclear energy*] (NRCH)
PCRDM........ Primary Control Rod Drive Mechanism [*Nuclear energy*] (NRCH)
PC Rep........ English Privy Council Reports [*A publication*] (DLA)
PCRF.......... Paralysis Cure Research Foundation (EA)

PCRF .... Parker Chiropractic Resource Foundation (EA)
PCRH .... Provincial Cities and Rural Highways Program [*Australia*]
PCRI .... Papanicolaou Cancer Research Institute [*University of Miami*] [*Research center*]
PCRM .... Physicians Committee for Responsible Medicine (EA)
PCRM .... Primary Certified Reference Material [*Nuclear energy*] (NRCH)
PCRMGPS .... Poor Clerks Regular of the Mother of God of the Pious Schools [*Rome, Italy*] (EAIO)
PCRML .... Parti Communiste Revolutionnaire - Marxiste-Leniniste [*Revolutionary Marxist-Leninist Communist Party*] [*France Political party*] (PPW)
PC-ROM .... Personal Computer Read-Only Memory
PCRP .... Pennsylvania Comprehensive Reading Program (EDAC)
Pcr/Pi .... Phosphocreatine to Inorganic Phosphate Ratio
PCRPr .... Perini Corp. Dep Cv Exch Pfd [*AMEX symbol*] (TTSB)
PCRPS .... Program for Collaborative Research in the Pharmaceutical Sciences [*University of Illinois at Chicago*] [*Information service or system*] (IID)
PCRR .... Pennsylvania Central Railroad (ROG)
PCRS .... Poor Clergy Relief Society [*British*]
PCRS .... Precision Chiropractic Research Society [*Also known as Spinal Stress Research Society*] (EA)
PCRS .... Primary Control Rod System [*Nuclear energy*] (NRCH)
PCRS .... Primary CRITICOMM [*Critical Intelligence Communications System*] Relay Station (CET)
PCRV .... Poinsettia Cryptic Virus [*Plant pathology*]
PCRV .... PowerCerv Corp. [*NASDAQ symbol*] (TTSB)
PCRV .... PowerCerv Corp. [*NASDAQ symbol*] (SAG)
PCRV .... Pressurized Concrete Reactor Vessel [*Nuclear energy*]
PCRV .... Prestressed Concrete Reactor Vessel [*Nuclear energy*]
PCS .... IEEE Professional Communication Society (EA)
PCS .... Pace Car Society [*Defunct*] (EA)
PCS .... Pacific Command Ship
PCS .... Palliative Care Service
PCS .... Paracas [*Peru*] [*Seismograph station code, US Geological Survey Closed*] (SEIS)
PCS .... Parents' Confidential Statement [*Education*]
PCS .... Parti Chretien-Social [*Christian Social Party*] [*Luxembourg*] [*Political party*] (PPW)
PCS .... Particle Counting System
PCS .... Parti Communiste Suisse [*Communist Party of Switzerland*] [*Political party*] (PPE)
PCS .... Particulates, Condensables, and Solubles [*In gases*]
PCS .... Partido Comunista Salvadoreno [*Salvadoran Communist Party*] [*Political party*] (PPW)
PCS .... Partito Comunista Sammarinese [*Communist Party of San Marino*] [*Political party*] (PPE)
PCS .... Parts, Components, Subassemblies
PCS .... Parts Control System [*DoD*]
PCS .... Passive Containment System [*Nuclear energy*] (NRCH)
PCS .... Patient Care System
PCS .... Patrol Vessel, Submarine Chaser (Control) [*136 feet*] [*Navy symbol Obsolete*]
PCS .... Patterns of Care Study [*Roentgenography*]
PCS .... Paul Claudel Society (EA)
PCS .... Payless Cashways [*NYSE symbol*] (TTSB)
PCS .... Payless Cashways, Inc. [*NYSE symbol*] (SPSG)
PCS .... Payload Checkout System [*NASA*] (NASA)
PCS .... Payload Control Supervisor [*NASA*] (MCD)
PCS .... Pergamon Compact Solution [*CD-ROM publisher*] (IT)
PCS .... Periodical Control System [*Libraries*]
PCS .... Peripheral Computer System (IAA)
PCS .... Permanent Change of Station [*Army*]
PCS .... Permanent Cruiser Service [*British military*] (DMA)
PCS .... Permit Compliance System [*Environmental Protection Agency*] (GFGA)
PCS .... Personal Care Subsidy [*Australia*]
PCS .... Personal Communications Service [*Provided by Personal Communications Network*]
PCS .... Personal Communications Services [*Telecommunications*]
PCS .... Personal Communications System
PCS .... Personal Composition System (DGA)
PCS .... Personal Computing System
pcs .... Personal Conferencing Specification [*Telecommunications*] (CDE)
PCS .... Personnel Capabilities System [*Jet Propulsion Laboratory, NASA*]
PCS .... Personnel Change of Station
PCS .... Personnel Consultancy Services Ltd. [*British*]
PCS .... Petrochemical Corp. of Singapore
PCS .... Pharmaceutical Card System (MCD)
PCS .... Pharmacogenic Confusional Syndrome [*Medicine*] (DMAA)
PCS .... Phase Combining System [*Trademark*] [*A solubilizer in scintillation counting*]
PCS .... Phase Compensator System
PCS .... Philippine Collectors Society (EA)
PCS .... Philips Car Systems
PCS .... PhonoCardioScan [*Cardiology*]
PCS .... Photoformed Ceramic Substrates [*Du Pont process for making microconductors*]
PCS .... Photon Correlation Spectroscopy
PCS .... Physical-Chemical System (SAA)
PCS .... Physical Control System
PCS .... Physically Controlled Space [*Military*] (GFGA)
PCS .... Pictorial Cancellation Society [*Defunct*] (EA)
pcs .... Picture File [*Computer science*]
PCS .... Pieces
PCS .... Pilot Control System (MCD)
PCS .... Pitch Control System (MCD)
PCS .... Planning Control Sheet
PCS .... Plant Computer System (NRCH)
PCS .... Plant Control System [*Nuclear energy*] (NRCH)
PCS .... Plastic-Clad Silica [*Optics*]
PCS .... Plastic Coated Silica (NITA)
PCS .... Plastic Connector Shell
PCS .... Platoon Combat Skills [*Army*] (INF)
PCS .... Plausible Conflict Situations [*Army*]
PCS .... Pluto-Charon System [*Planetary science*]
PCS .... Pneumatic Control System [*Gas chromatography*]
PCS .... Pointing-Control System [*Aerospace*]
PCS .... Polymer-Clad Silica [*Chemistry*]
PCS .... Portable Communications System
PCS .... Portacaval Shunt [*Medicine*]
PCS .... Port Command Store [*Telecommunications*] (TEL)
PCS .... Port Control Store [*Telecommunications*] (TEL)
PCS .... Port Control System [*Telecommunications*] (TEL)
PCS .... Position Classification Standard [*Civil Service*]
PCS .... Position Control System
PCS .... Position, Course, and Speed
PCS .... Positive Concatenation Structures [*Mathematics*]
PCS .... Postal Church Service
PCS .... Postal Commemorative Society (EA)
PCS .... Postcardiotomy Syndrome [*Medicine*]
PCS .... Postcaval [*or Portacaval*] Shunt [*Medicine*]
PCS .... Posterior Concave Side
PCS .... Posts, Camps, and Stations [*Military*]
PCS .... Potash Corp. of Saskatchewan [*Canada*]
PCS .... Power Conditioning System
PCS .... Power Conversion System
PCS .... Powered Causeway Section [*Military*] (CAAL)
PCS .... Practical Computer Solutions (NITA)
PCS .... Precedence Charting System (IAA)
PCS .... Precision Casting Standard (MCD)
PCS .... Preconscious
PCS .... Preferred Capital Stock [*Investment term*]
PCS .... Pregnancy Counselling Service [*Australia*]
PCS .... Preliminary Component Specification
PCS .... Press Computer System (DGA)
PCS .... Pressure Control System
PCS .... Pressure Cycling Switch [*Automotive engineering*]
PCS .... Primary Calibration System
PCS .... Primary Cancer Site [*Oncology*]
PCS .... Primary Conditioning Solution
PCS .... Primary Control Ship [*Navy*]
PCS .... Primary Coolant System (MSA)
PCS .... Prime Compatible Set (PDAA)
PCS .... Principal Clerk of Session
PCS .... Principal Coordinating Scientist [*NASA*] (KSC)
PCS .... Print Contrast Scale (IEEE)
PCS .... Print Contrast Signal [*Computer science*]
PCS .... Print Contrast System (BUR)
PCS .... Probability of Command Shutdown (MCD)
PCS .... Probability of Correct Selection [*Statistics*]
PCS .... Probability of Crew Survival (AAG)
PCS .... Procedure Completion Sheet [*NASA*] (MCD)
PCS .... Process Communication Supervisor (IAA)
PCS .... Process Computer System (NRCH)
PCS .... Process Control Sheet [*Nuclear energy*] (NRCH)
PCS .... Process Control System
PCS .... Pro Computer Services (NITA)
PCS .... Production Control Section
PCS .... Production Control System (BUR)
PCS .... Professional Careers Sourcebook [*A publication*]
PCS .... Professional Car Society (EA)
PCS .... Program Coordination Staff [*Environmental Protection Agency*] (GFGA)
PCS .... Program Cost Status [*Report*] (MCD)
PCS .... Program Counter Store
PCS .... Programmable Communications Subsystem
PCS .... Project Control Sheet [*Computer science*]
PCS .... Project Control System [*Computer science*]
PCS .... Project Coordination Staff [*NASA*] (KSC)
PCS .... Property Consultants Society [*British*] (DBA)
PCS .... Property Control System
PCS .... Proprietary Computer Systems, Inc. [*Information service or system*] (IID)
PCS .... Provision Coordinate Schedule (MCD)
PCS .... Pseudotumor Cerebri Syndrome [*Medicine*] (DMAA)
PCS .... Publication Control Sheet (MCD)
PCS .... Public Choice Society (EA)
PCS .... Pump Control Sensor
PCS .... Punch Card System (NITA)
PCS .... Punched Card System [*Computer science*]
PCS .... Pyrotechnics Circuit Simulator
PCS .... Sabah Chinese Party [*Malaysia*] [*Political party*] (FEA)
PCS .... Submarine Chaser
PCS .... Sun Shipbuilding & Dry Dock Co., Chester, PA [*Library symbol Library of Congress*] (LCLS)
PCSA .... Palm and Cycad Societies of Australia
PCSA .... Patrol Craft Sailors Association (EA)
PCSA .... Personal Computing Systems Architecture
PCSA .... Power Crane and Shovel Association (EA)
PCSA .... Seaman Apprentice, Postal Clerk, Striker [*Navy rating*]

PCS(A)......... Submarine Chaser (Air Cushion) (MCD)
PCsB........... Baptist Bible College of Pennsylvania, Clarks Summit, PA [*Library symbol Library of Congress*] (LCLS)
PCSC........... Control Submarine Chaser [*136 feet*] [*Navy symbol Obsolete*]
PCSC........... Plant Cell Suspension Cultures [*Biotechnology*]
PCSC........... Power Conditioning, Switching, and Control
PCSC........... Principal Commonwealth Supply Committee [*World War II*]
PCS-CSS....... Parents' Confidential Statement of the College Scholarship Service [*Education*] (IIA)
PCSD........... Partido Cristao Social Democratico [*Christian Social Democratic Party*] [*Portugal Political party*] (PPE)
PCSD........... Polychloro(chloromethylsulfonamido)diphenyl Ether [*Insectproofing agent for wool*]
PCSD........... President's Council on Sustainable Development [*1993*]
PCSE........... Pacific Coast Stock Exchange [*Later, PSE*] (EA)
PCSE........... President's Committee on Scientists and Engineers [*Expired, 1958*]
PCSE........... Printed Circuit Soldering Equipment
PC/SFA........ Potato Chip/Snack Food Association [*Formerly, NPCI, PCI*] [*Later, SFA*]
PCSFSK....... Phase Comparison Sinusoidal Frequency Shift Keying
PCSG........... Public Cryptography Study Group [*Defunct*] (EA)
PCSH........... Pierce Shell
PCS(H)......... Submarine Chaser (Hydrofoil) (MCD)
PCSIG.......... Personal Computer-Software Interest Group (EA)
PCSIR.......... Pakistan Council of Scientific and Industrial Research
PCSJ........... All-Party Parliamentary Committee for the Release of Soviet Jewry (EAIO)
PCSM........... Percutaneous Stone Manipulation [*Medicine*]
PCSN........... PC Satellite Network
PCSN........... Precision Standard [*NASDAQ symbol*] (TTSB)
PCSN........... Precision Standard, Inc. [*NASDAQ symbol*] (NQ)
PCSN........... Private Circuit-Switching Network [*Telecommunications*] (OSI)
PCSN........... Seaman, Postal Clerk, Striker [*Navy rating*]
PCSP........... Permanent Commission for the South Pacific (WDAA)
PCSP........... Programmed Communications Support Program [*Air Force*] (AFM)
PCSPS......... Principal Civil Service Pension Scheme [*British*]
PCSS........... PC Service Source [*NASDAQ symbol*] (TTSB)
PCSS........... PC Service Source, Inc. [*NASDAQ symbol*] (SAG)
PCSS........... Platform Check Subsystem
PCSS........... Princess (ROG)
PCST........... Precision Castparts Corp. (MHDW)
PCST........... President's Committee on Science and Technology
PC Svc......... PC Service Source, Inc. [*Associated Press*] (SAG)
PCSW........... Police Chiefs Spouses - Worldwide [*An association*] (EA)
PCSW........... President's Commission on the Status of Women
PCT............. Pacific Coast Tariff Bureau, San Francisco CA [*STAC*]
PCT............. Pacific Crest Trail
PCT............. Paper Crepe Tape
PCT............. Para-Chlorotoluene [*Organic chemistry*]
PCT............. Parti Communiste Tunisien [*Tunisian Communist Party*] [*Political party*] (PD)
PCT............. Parti Congolais du Travail [*Congolese Labor Party*] [*Political party*] (PPW)
PCT............. Partido Conservador Tradicional [*Traditionalist Conservative Party*] [*Nicaragua*] [*Political party*]
PCT............. Patent Cooperation Treaty [*World Intellectual Property Organization, 1978*]
PCT............. Peace Air Togo [*ICAO designator*] (FAAC)
PCT............. Peak Centerline Temperature [*Nuclear energy*] (NRCH)
PCT............. Peak Cladding Temperature [*Nuclear energy*] (NRCH)
PCT............. Percent [*or Percentage*]
PCT............. Percentage [*Used instead of "average"*] [*Baseball*]
PCT............. Perfect Crystal Technology (IAA)
PCT............. Performance Correlation Technique
PCT............. Periodic Confidence Test
PCT............. Peripheral Control Terminal
PC/T........... Personal Computer/Technology (HGAA)
PCT............. Personality Completion Test [*Psychology*]
PCT............. Pharmacy and Chemistry Technician [*Navy*]
PCT............. Philadelphia College of Textiles and Science, Philadelphia, PA [*OCLC symbol*] (OCLC)
PCT............. Photoinduced Charge Transfer [*Electrochemistry*]
PCT............. Photon-Coupled Transistor (IEEE)
PCT............. Physical Correlate Theory [*Psychophysics*]
PCT............. Picture
PCT............. Pitch Centering Torquer (SAA)
PCT............. Planning and Control Techniques
PCT............. Plasmacrit Test [*Medicine*]
PCT............. Plasmacytoma [*Medicine*]
PCT............. Platelet Count [*Hematology*]
PCT............. Point-Contact Transistor [*Electronics*] (IAA)
PCT............. Polychemotherapy [*Oncology*]
PCT............. Polychlorinated Terphenyl [*Pesticide*]
PCT............. Polychloroterphenyl [*Organic chemistry*]
PCT............. Porcine Calcitonin [*Biochemistry*] (AAMN)
PCT............. Porphyria Cutanea Tarda [*Disease*] [*Medicine*]
PCT............. Portable Camera-Transmitter
PCT............. Portable Conference Telephone [*Bell Laboratories*]
PCT............. Portacaval Transposition [*Medicine*] (MAE)
PCT............. Positron Computed Tomography
PCT............. Postcoital Test [*Medicine*] (DAVI)
PCT............. Potato Curly Top Disease [*Plant pathology*]
PCT............. Potential Current Transformer
PCT............. Precinct
PCT............. Preliminary Change Transmittal (AAG)
PCT............. Pressure Concentration Temperature
PCT............. Prime Contract Termination (AAG)
PCT............. Princeton [*New Jersey*] [*Airport symbol Obsolete*] (OAG)
PCT............. Prism Cover Test [*Ophthalmology*] (CPH)
PCT............. Private Communications Technology [*Microsoft Corp.*] [*Computer science*]
PCT............. Private Communications Technology [*Computer science*]
P Ct............. Probate Court (DLA)
PCT............. Production Confirmatory Test (MCD)
PCT............. Programa de Cooperacion Tecnica [*Program of Technical Cooperation - PTC*] [*Organization of American States*] [*Washington, DC*]
PCT............. Program Control Table [*Computer science*]
PCT............. Program Counter Timer (IAA)
PCT............. Project Control Tool (BUR)
PCT............. Property Capital Trust [*AMEX symbol*] (SPSG)
PCT............. Property Cap Tr [*AMEX symbol*] (TTSB)
PCT............. Prothrombin Consumption Time [*Hematology*] (DAVI)
PCT............. Proximal Convoluted Tubule [*of a nephron*]
PCT............. Puangchon Chao Thai [*Thai Mass Party*] [*Thailand*] [*Political party*]
PCT............. Pulse Compression Tube
PCT............. Pulse Count [*Telecommunications*] (TEL)
PCT............. Wesman Personnel Classification Test
PCTA........... Pentachlorothioanisole [*Organic chemistry*]
PCTB........... Pacific Coast Tariff Bureau
PCTC........... Penn Central Transportation Co.
PCTC........... Pure Car Truck Carrier [*Shipping*] (DS)
PCTC........... Pyrotechnic Circuit Test Console (KSC)
PCTDS......... Problem and Change Tracking Directory System
PCTE........... Portable Commercial Test Equipment (NASA)
PCTE........... Portable Common Test Environment [*British*]
PCTE........... Portable Common Tools Environment (IAA)
PCTF........... Plant Component Test Facility [*Nuclear energy*]
PCTF........... Power Conversion Test Facility (SAA)
PCTFE......... Polychlorotrifluoroethylene [*Organic chemistry*]
PCTFE......... Polychlorotrifluoroethylene [*Lubricants*]
PCTFE......... Polymonochlorotrifluorethyle [*Organic chemistry*] (IAA)
PCT-GF........ Plasmacytoma Growth Factor [*Oncology*]
PCTH........... Pacific Aerospace & Electronics, Inc. [*NASDAQ symbol*] (SAG)
PCTH........... PCT Holdings [*NASDAQ symbol*] (TTSB)
PCTH........... PCT Holdings, Inc. [*NASDAQ symbol*] (SAG)
PCTHold....... PCT Holdings, Inc. [*Associated Press*] (SAG)
PCTIS.......... Preston Commercial and Technical Information Service (NITA)
PCTL........... PictureTel Corp. [*NASDAQ symbol*] (NQ)
PCTL........... Picture Tel Corp. [*NASDAQ symbol*] (TTSB)
PC/TM......... Performance Criteria and Test Methods Task
PCTM........... Pulse-Count Modulation (MSA)
PCTO........... Payload Cost Tradeoff Optimization [*NASA*] (NASA)
PCTP........... Partido Comunista dos Trabalhadores Portugueses [*Portuguese Workers' Communist Party*] [*Political party*] (PPW)
PCTP........... Pierce Template
PCTR........... Physical Constant Test Reactor [*Nuclear energy*]
PCTR........... Program Counter
PCTR........... Property Control Transaction Report
PCTR........... Pulsed Column Test Rig [*Chemical engineering*]
PCTS........... Pentagon Consolidated Telecommunications System (MCD)
PCTS........... Portable Cesium Time Standard
PCTS........... President's Committee for Traffic Safety (EA)
PCTT........... Precommit Track Time [*DoD*]
PCTUULAW... Permanent Congress of Trade Union Unity of Latin American Workers [*See also CPUSTAL*] [*Mexico City, Mexico*] (EAIO)
PCTV........... People's Choice TV [*NASDAQ symbol*] (TTSB)
PCTV........... Peoples Choice TV Corp. [*NASDAQ symbol*] (SAG)
PCTV........... Private Channel Television
PCtvL.......... Lukens Steel Co., Coatesville, PA [*Library symbol Library of Congress Obsolete*] (LCLS)
PCtvVA........ United States Veterans Administration Hospital, Medical Library, Coatesville, PA [*Library symbol Library of Congress*] (LCLS)
PCTWin....... PC [*Personal Computer*] Tools for Windows (PCM)
PCTY........... Party City [*NASDAQ symbol*] (TTSB)
PCTY........... Party City Corp. [*NASDAQ symbol*] (SAG)
PCU............. Packet Communications Unit
PCU............. Paging Control Unit [*Telecommunications*] (TEL)
PCU............. Pain Control Unit
PCU............. Palliative Care Unit [*Medicine*] (CPH)
PCU............. Partido Conservador Unido [*Chilean Catholic political party*]
PCU............. Passenger Control Unit (MCD)
PCU............. Patient Care Unit (HCT)
PCU............. Payload Checkout Unit [*NASA*] (MCD)
PCU............. Peripheral Control Unit (CMD)
PCU............. Picayune, MS [*Location identifier FAA*] (FAAL)
pcu.............. Platinum Cobalt Unit [*Water analysis*]
PCU............. Pneumatic Checkout Unit (AAG)
PCU............. Pod Cooling Unit (AAG)
PCU............. Portable Checkout Unit
PCU............. Portable Computer Unit
PCU............. Portuguese Continental Union of the United States of America (EA)
PCU............. Post-Coronary Care Unit [*Cardiology*] (DAVI)
PCU............. Pound Centigrade Unit
PCU............. Power Conditioning Unit
PCU............. Power Control Unit
PCU............. Power Conversion Unit (IEEE)
PCU............. Pressure Control Unit (MCD)
PCU............. Price [*Utah*] [*Seismograph station code, US Geological Survey*] (SEIS)

PCU Primary Care Unit [*Medicine*] (DMAA)
PCU Primary Control Unit (IAA)
PCU Print Control Unit (SAA)
PCU Printed Control Unit [*Military*] (GFGA)
PCU Processor Control Unit
PCU Product Co-Ordination Unit [*British Overseas Trade Board*] (DS)
PCU Program Control Unit [*Computer science*]
PCU Progress Control Unit (KSC)
PCU Progressive Care Unit [*Medicine*]
PCU Propellant Control Unit (SAA)
PCU Protective Care Unit [*Medicine*]
PCU Protein-Calorie Undernutrition [*Medicine*]
PCU Pulmonary Care Unit [*Medicine*] (DMAA)
PCU Punched Card Unit (NITA)
PCU Punched Card Utility [*Computer science*]
PCU Southern Peru Copper [*NYSE symbol*] (TTSB)
PCU Southern Peru Copper Corp. [*NYSE symbol*] (SAG)
PCU University of Prince Edward Island, Charlottetown, Prince Edward Island [*Library symbol National Library of Canada*] (NLC)
PCUA Power Controller Unit Assembly (IEEE)
PCUA Pressure Control Unit, Atlas (MCD)
PCUA PROFIT Control Users Association (EA)
PCUC Positive Continuous Ullage Control
PCU/HDR Primary Control Unit, Hydraulics (AAG)
PCUI Partito Comunista Unificado de Italia [*Unified Communist Party of Italy*] [*Political party*] (PPE)
PCUR Pulsating Current
PCUS Port Charges Paid by United States Army, Navy, or Air Force (DNAB)
PCUS Propeller Club of the United States (EA)
PC-USA Pax Christi - USA (EA)
PCUSAW Pen Center USA West (EA)
PCUSEQ Pressure Control Unit Sequencer (AAG)
pcut Percutaneous [*Medicine*] (AAMN)
PCUUS Polish Council of Unity in the United States [*Defunct*] (EA)
PCV Pacific Concord Resources Corp. [*Vancouver Stock Exchange symbol*]
PCV Packed Cell Volume [*Hematology*] (CPH)
PCV Parietal Cell Vagotomy [*Medicine*] (AAMN)
PCV Partido Comunista Venezolana [*Venezuelan Communist Party*] [*Political party*] (PPW)
PCV Passenger Carrying Vehicle [*Military*] (GFGA)
PCV Passenger Control Vehicle (WDAA)
PCV Peace Corps Volunteer
PCV Peanut Clump Virus [*Plant pathology*]
PCV Penciclovir [*Antiherpetic*]
PCV Petty Cash Voucher (MCD)
PCV Phenetic Coefficient of Variation
PCV Pneumatic Control Valve
PCV Pollution Control Valve (IEEE)
PCV Polycythemia Vera [*Also, PV*] [*Hematology*]
PCV Porcine Cirovirus
PCV Positive Crankcase Ventilation [*For automotive antipollution systems*]
PCV Postcapillary Venule [*Medicine*] (DMAA)
PCV Precheck Verification [*NASA*] (NASA)
PCV Pressure [*or Pressurizer*] Control Valve (AAG)
PCV Pressure-Control Ventilation [*Medicine*] (DMAA)
PCV Primary Containment Vessel
PCV Primary Control Vessel (DNAB)
PCV Primate Calicivirus
PCV Procarbazine, CCNU [*Lomustine*], Vincristine [*Antineoplastic drug regimen*] (DAVI)
PCV Proportioning Control Valve [*Automotive brakes*]
PCV Protocol Converter [*Electronics*] (ECII)
PCV Pump Control Valve [*Hydraulics*]
PCV Purge Control Valve (NASA)
PCV Putnam Convertible Opportunities & Income Trust [*NYSE symbol*] (SAG)
PCV Putnam Cv Opp Inc. Tr [*NYSE symbol*] (TTSB)
PCV Pyrocatechol Violet [*Also, PV*] [*An indicator Chemistry*]
PCV Veterans Affairs, Canada [*Affaires des Anciens Combattants Canada*] Charlottetown, Prince Edward Island [*Library symbol National Library of Canada*] (NLC)
PCvA Allentown College of Saint Francis De Sales, Center Valley, PA [*Library symbol Library of Congress*] (LCLS)
PCVB Pyro Continuity Verification Box [*NASA*] (NASA)
PCVC Partially Conserved Vector Current (IAA)
PCVC Public Citizens Visitors Center [*An association Defunct*] (EA)
PCVD Plasma Chemical Vapor Deposition
PCVL Pilot-Controlled Visual Landing [*Aviation*] (NASA)
PCV-M Myeloid Metaplasia with Polycythemia Vera [*Hematology*] (MAE)
PCVN Precracked Charpy V-Notch (PDAA)
PCW Personal Computer World Show [*Montbuild Ltd.*] (TSPED)
PCW Plate Control Wedge [*Printing technology*]
PCW Point Calculation Worksheet [*Army*] (INF)
PCW PortaCom Wireless [*VS, Exchange Symbol*] (TTSB)
PCW Port Clinton, OH [*Location identifier FAA*] (FAAL)
PCW Post Consumer Waste (EG)
PCW Previously Complied With
PCW Primary Cooling Water [*Reactor*]
PCW Princess Charlotte of Wales [*Military unit*] [*British*]
PCW Principal Conductor of the Works [*Freemasonry*]
PCW Program Control Word
PCW Proprietor of Copyright on a Composite Work
PCW Pulmonary Capillary Wedge [*Medicine*]
PCW Pulsed Continuous Wave (IEEE)
PCW Widener College, Chester, PA [*Library symbol Library of Congress*] (LCLS)
PCWA Pharmaceutical Council of Western Australia
PCWBS Preliminary Contract Work Breakdown Structure (MCD)
PCWCA Poured Concrete Wall Contractors Association (EA)
PC-WNIM Personal Computer Wide Area Network Interface Module (TSSD)
PCWO Production Control Work Order (MCD)
PCWP Pulmonary Capillary Wedge Pressure [*Medicine*]
PCWU Port Commissioners Workers' Union [*India*]
PCX Pacificorp [*NYSE symbol*] (SAG)
PCX PacifiCorp 8.55%'QUIDS' [*NYSE symbol*] (TTSB)
PCx Periscopic Convex [*Ophthalmology*] (DAVI)
PCx Periscopic Convex [*Ophthalmology*]
PCX Plasma Confinement Experiment [*Physics*]
PCX Process Control Executive (MHDI)
PCXR Portable Chest X-Ray (CPH)
PCY Aquila Air, Inc. [*ICAO designator*] (FAAC)
PCY Pacific Cypress Minerals Ltd. [*Vancouver Stock Exchange symbol*]
PCY Pittsburgh, Chartiers & Youghiogheny Railway Co. [*AAR code*]
PCY Plastocyanin
PCY Prerogative Court of York [*English court previously having jurisdiction over wills*]
PCYC Pharmacyclics, Inc. [*NASDAQ symbol*] (SAG)
PCYF President's Council on Youth Fitness (EA)
PCYF Progressive Conservative Youth Federation of Canada
PCZ Canal Zone [*ANSI three-letter standard code Obsolete*] (CNC)
PCZ Panama Canal Zone [*Panama*] [*Airport symbol*] (AD)
PCZ Paracomp Technology, Inc. [*Vancouver Stock Exchange symbol*]
PCZ Petro-Canada [*NYSE symbol*] (SAG)
PCZ Petro-Canada Variable Vtg [*NYSE symbol*] (TTSB)
PCZ Physical Control Zone (NASA)
PCZ Positive Control Zone (DNAB)
PCZ Procarbazine [*Antineoplastic drug*] (DAVI)
PCZ Prochlorperazine [*Antiemetic*]
PCZ Waupaca, WI [*Location identifier FAA*] (FAAL)
PCZPP Petro-Canada Installm't Vtg [*NYSE symbol*] (TTSB)
PD Democratic Party [*Ecuador*] [*Political party*] (PD)
PD Doctor of Pedagogy
PD Doctor of Pharmacy
PD Doctor of Philosophy (WDAA)
Pd Dorsal Pressure Neuron [*of a leech*]
PD Dublin Pharmacopoeia
PD Interpupillary Distance
PD Law Reports, Probate, Divorce, and Admiralty Division [*1875-90*] [*England*] [*A publication*] (DLA)
p/d Packs per Day [*Cigarettes*] [*Medicine*]
PD Pad (MCD)
PD Paget's Disease [*Medicine*]
PD Paid
pd Paid (WDMC)
pd Paid (ODBW)
PD Palisade Diabase [*Geology*]
Pd Palladium [*Chemical element*]
PD Pancreatic Divisum [*Medicine*]
PD Pancreatic Duct [*Anatomy*]
PD Pants Down [*At a disadvantage*] [*Slang*] (DSUE)
pd Papilla Diameter [*Medicine*]
PD Papillary Distance
PD Paralyzing Dose [*Pharmacology*] (DAVI)
PD Parental Ditype [*Genetics*]
PD Parke-Davis [*Commercial firm*] (DAVI)
PD Parkinsonism Dementia [*Medicine*]
PD Parkinson's Disease [*Medicine*]
PD Pars Distalis [*Medicine*]
PD Part Damaged (ROG)
PD Partial Discharge [*High-voltage testing*] (IEEE)
PD Particle-Density [*Forensic science*]
PD Parti Democratique [*Democratic Party*] [*Luxembourg Political party*] (EAIO)
PD Partido Democrata [*Democratic Party*] [*Chile*] [*Political party*]
PD Partido Democrata [*Democratic Party*] [*Costa Rica*] [*Political party*] (PPW)
PD Passed
pd Passed (ODBW)
PD Passive Detection [*Electronics*]
PD Past Due
PD Paste-Down [*Album*] [*Photography*] (ROG)
PD Patent Ductus [*Cardiology*] (MAE)
PD Pay Department [*Army British*] (ROG)
PD Pay Dirt
PD Payload Diameter
PD Peak Detector
PD Pedestal (IAA)
PD Pediatric [*or Pediatrics*]
Pd Pediatrics (DMAA)
PD Pem Air [*ICAO designator*] (AD)
P/D Penetration Diameter [*Military*]
PD People's Democracy [*Ireland*] [*Political party*]
PD Pepper Dust [*An adulterating element*]
PD Percutaneous Drain [*Surgery*] (DAVI)
PD Per Diem [*By the Day*] [*Latin*]
pd Per Diem [*By the Day*] [*Latin*] (ODBW)
pd Per Diem [*By the day*] [*Latin*] (WDMC)
PD Per Diliquium [*By Deliquescence*] [*Pharmacy*] (ROG)
PD Perfect Diffuser [*Optics*]

PD .... Performance Demonstration (MCD)
PD .... Performer Diploma (PGP)
PD .... Periderm [*Botany*]
PD .... Period (AABC)
PD .... Periodic Duty (IAA)
PD .... Peripheral Device (BUR)
PD .... Periscope Depth (IAA)
PD .... Peritoneal Dialysis [*Medicine*]
PD .... Permanent Deactivation
PD .... Permits Division [*Environmental Protection Agency*] (GFGA)
PD .... Personnel Department
PD .... Personnel Development
PD .... Personnel Distribution [*Army*]
PD .... Pharmacy Director
PD .... Pharmacy Dispenser [*British military*] (DMA)
PD .... Phase Discriminator
PD .... Phelps Dodge [*NYSE symbol*] (TTSB)
PD .... Phelps Dodge Corp. [*NYSE symbol*] (SPSG)
PD .... Phenyldichlorarsine [*A war gas*]
PD .... Philosophiae Doctor [*Doctor of Philosophy*]
PD .... Phosphate Dehydrogenase
PD .... Phosphate Dextrose (DAVI)
PD .... Phosphodiester [*Organic chemistry*]
PD .... Photodiode
PD .... Photo Ditector (EECA)
PD .... Photosensitivity Dermatitis [*Medicine*] (DMAA)
PD .... Phyllis Dorothy James White [*In name P. D. James*] [*Author*]
PD .... Physical Damage [*Insurance*]
PD .... Physical Development (IAA)
PD .... Physical Disabilities
PD .... Physical Distribution (ADA)
PD .... Physics Department
PD .... Picknick Dam [*TVA*]
P/D .... Pickup and Deposit
PD .... Pictorial Display (MCD)
PD .... Pierce's Disease [*Plant pathology*]
PD .... Pilot Dogs (EA)
PD .... Piskei Din Shel Bet ha-Mishpat ha-'Elyon le-Yisrael (BJA)
PD .... Pitch Circle Diameter [*Technical drawings*] (IAA)
PD .... Pitch Diameter
PD .... Pitch Down (MCD)
PD .... Pivoted Door (AAG)
PD .... Plane Disagreement [*Telecommunications*] (TEL)
PD .... Planned Derating [*Electronics*] (IEEE)
PD .... Planning Directive (NG)
PD .... Planning Document
PD .... Plans Division [*Military*]
PD .... Plasma Defect [*Medicine*] (MAE)
PD .... Plasma Defect [*Hematology*] (DAVI)
PD .... Plasma Deposited (IAA)
PD .... Plasma Desorption [*of ions for analysis*]
PD .... Plasma Display
PD .... Plate Dissipation
PD .... Platelet Deaggregation [*Hematology*]
PD .... Plausible Deniability
PD .... Plotting Display (IAA)
PD .... Point Defense
PD .... Point Delay Fuze [*Army*]
PD .... Point Detonating [*Projectile*]
PD .... Polar Distance [*Navigation*]
PD .... Police Department
PD .... Policy Determination (GNE)
pd .... Pond [*Pound*] [*Monetary unit*] [*Afrikaans*]
PD .... Pontoon Dock
PD .... Pool Density [*Pisciculture*]
PD .... Poorly Differentiated [*Medicine*]
PD .... Population Density (NRCH)
PD .... Population Distribution (NRCH)
PD .... Population Doubling
PD .... Pore Diameter
PD .... Porphobilinogen Deaminase [*Clinical chemistry*] (MAE)
PD .... Port Director
PD .... Port Du [*Carriage Forward*] [*French*]
PD .... Port Dues
PD .... Port of Debarkation [*Navy*]
PD .... Position Description
PD .... Position Document
PD .... Position Doubtful [*Nautical charts*]
PD .... Positive Displacement
PD .... Positives and Deposition (DGA)
PD .... Postage Due
PD .... Postal District
PD .... Postdated
PD .... Post Dated (WDAA)
PD .... Post Diluvium [*After the Flood*] [*Latin*] (ROG)
PD .... Postdoctorate
PD .... Posterior Deltoid [*Myology*]
PD .... Posterior Digestive [*Gland*]
PD .... Postnasal Drainage [*Medicine*]
PD .... Postural Drainage [*Medicine*] (MAE)
PD .... Potential Difference [*Electricity*]
PD .... Pound (ROG)
PD .... Power Distribution
PD .... Power Divider (IAA)
PD .... Power Doubler (IAA)
PD .... Power Driven (IAA)
PD .... Precision Device [*British military*] (DMA)
PD .... Precision Drilling (1987) Ltd. [*Toronto Stock Exchange symbol*]
PD .... Predeployment
P/D .... Predicted [*NASA*] (KSC)
PD .... Predilute
PD .... Preference for Duty
PD .... Pregnanediol [*Biochemistry*]
PD .... Preliminary Design
PD .... Prescription Drug
PD .... Presidential Determination
PD .... Presidential Directive
PD .... Press Division [*Environmental Protection Agency*] (GFGA)
PD .... Pressor Dose [*Medicine*]
Pd .... Pressure, Diastolic [*Cardiology*]
PD .... Pressure Distillate (IAA)
PD .... Pressure Drop (KSC)
PD .... Presumptive Disability [*Title XVI*] [*Social Security Administration*] (OICC)
PD .... Prevention Detention [*Scotland Yard*]
PD .... Preventive Dentistry (DAVI)
PD .... Prime Driver
PD .... Principal Distance [*Graphic arts*] (OA)
PD .... Printer Driver
PD .... Printer's Devil (ROG)
PD .... Priority Designator [*Army*]
PD .... Priority Directive
PD .... Prism Diopter
PD .... Prisoner's Dilemma [*Psychology*]
PD .... Privatdozent [*Tutor*] [*German*]
PD .... Private Detective
PD .... Probability Density [*Statistics*] (IAA)
PD .... Probability of Damage (MCD)
PD .... Probability of Death [*Biology*]
PD .... Probability of Detection
PD .... Problem Definition [*Army*]
PD .... Process Data (NITA)
PD .... Process Descriptor [*Telecommunications*] (IAA)
PD .... Process Diagnostic [*Interpersonal skills and attitudes test*]
PD .... Procurement Data
PD .... Procurement Directive [*Army*]
PD .... Procurement District [*Air Force*] (AFIT)
PD .... Procurement Division
PD .... Procurement Document (NASA)
PD .... Procurement Drawing
pd .... Pro Defendente [*On Behalf of Defendant*] [*Latin Legal term*] (DLA)
PD .... Product Design [*Phase*]
P/D .... Product Development
PD .... Production and Deployment Phase [*Military*] (MCD)
PD .... Production Department
PD .... Production Director (NTCM)
PD .... Professional Development (ADA)
PD .... Professional Digital [*Recording*] (NTCM)
PD .... Professional Diploma [*Education*] (AEE)
PD .... Profile Descent (GAVI)
PD .... Programa Democratico [*Democratic Program*] [*Spain Political party*] (PPE)
PD .... Program Deceleration (KSC)
PD .... Program Decoder
PD .... Program Directive (NG)
PD .... Program Director [*Television*]
PD .... Progression of Disease [*Medicine*]
PD .... Progressive Democrats [*Ireland*] [*Political party*]
PD .... Project Directive (NASA)
PD .... Project Document
PD .... Projected Decision Date (NRCH)
PD .... Projected Display
PD .... Promotion Director
PD .... Propellant Dispersion (KSC)
PD .... Property Damage
PD .... Property Disposition [*FHA*] (EMRF)
PD .... Proportional Derivative (IAA)
PD .... Proportional Plus Derivative (IAA)
PD .... Proposal Development (AAG)
PD .... Prostatodynia [*Medicine*]
PD .... Protective Device (BUR)
PD .... Protein Diet (DMAA)
PD .... Prototype Demonstration
PD .... Provisioning Document
PD .... Provocation Dose [*Medicine*] (MEDA)
PD .... Proximity Detector
PD .... Prussian Dollar [*Monetary unit*] (ROG)
PD .... Pseudohomogeneous Axial Dispersion Model [*Fluid dynamics*]
PD .... Psychodynamic
Pd .... Psychopathic Deviate [*Psychology*]
PD .... Psychotic Depression [*Medicine*]
PD .... Psychotic Deviate [*Psychiatry*] (DAVI)
PD .... Publication Date [*Online database field identifier*]
PD .... Public Defender [*Australia*]
PD .... Public Domain
PD .... Publisher's Directory [*Formerly, BPD*] [*A publication*]
PD .... Pulley Drive (IAA)
PD .... Pulmonary Disease [*Medicine*]
PD .... Pulpodistal [*Dentistry*]
PD .... Pulse Detector [*Spectroscopy*]

PD............ Pulse Doppler
PD............ Pulse Driver
PD............ Pulse Duration
P-D............ Punch-Die (MSA)
PD............ Punch Driver
pd............ Pupillary Distance [*Medicine*]
PD............ Purchase Description
PD............ Pyloric Dilator [*Neuron*]
PD............ Pyramidal Decussation [*Neuroanatomy*]
PD1............ Portable Dictionary 1 [*English/Japanese electronic dictionary*] [*Sanyo Electric*]
PDA............ Pacific Dance Association (EA)
PDA............ Pacific Dermatologic Association (EA)
PDA............ Packaging Distributors Association [*British*] (DBA)
PDA............ Parallel Data Adapter
PDA............ Parametric Design Analysis (RDA)
PDA............ Parenteral Drug Association (EA)
PdA............ Partei der Arbeit [*Labor Party*] [*Switzerland Political party*] (PPE)
PDA............ Parti Democratico da Angola [*Democratic Party of Angola*] [*Political party*]
PDA............ Partido Democratico Arubano [*Democratic Party of Aruba*] [*Political party*] (EY)
PDA............ Parti Dolonti Applicandum [*Apply to Painful Part*] [*Pharmacy*] (ROG)
PDA............ Partit Democrata d'Andorra [*Andorran Democratic Party*] [*Political party*] (PPW)
Pd'A............ Partito d'Azione [*Action Party*] [*Italy Political party*] (PPE)
PDA............ Parts Disposal Area (MCD)
PDA............ Party of Democratic Action [*Bosnia-Herzegovina*] [*Political party*] (EY)
PDA............ Pasadena Energy [*Vancouver Stock Exchange symbol*]
PDA............ Patent Ductus Arteriosus [*Cardiology*]
PDA............ Patient Data Automation
PDA............ Payroll Deduction Authorization (MCD)
PDA............ Peak Distribution Analyzer
PDA............ Pediatric Allergy
PdA............ Pediatric Allergy [*Medicine*] (DMAA)
PDA............ Pentadecanoic Acid [*Organic chemistry*]
PDA............ Percent Defective Allowable (MHDB)
PDA............ Permanent Duty Assignment [*Air Force*] (AFM)
PDA............ Personal Deposit Account [*Banking*]
PDA............ Personal Digital Assistant (ECON)
PDA............ Personal Digital Assistant [*Computer science*]
PDA............ Petrol Dealers' Association [*British*]
PDA............ Phenylenediamine [*Chemistry*]
PDA............ Philadelphia Dance Alliance
PDA............ Phorbol Diacetate [*Organic chemistry*]
PDA............ Photodiode Array [*Instrumentation*]
PDA............ Photographic Dealers' Association [*British*] (BI)
PDA............ Photon Detector Assembly (MCD)
PDA............ Physical Device Address [*Computer science*] (IBMDP)
PDA............ Piperidinedicarboxylic Acid [*Organic chemistry*]
PDA............ Pisatin Demethylase [*An enzyme*]
PDA............ Point Density Analysis [*Mathematics*]
PDA............ Point Director Array
PDA............ Pointing Device Adapter [*Computer science*]
PDA............ Poise Distribution Amplifier (AFM)
PDA............ Polarization Diversity Array
PDA............ Polydiacetylene [*Organic chemistry*]
PDA............ Poly(dimethylacrylamide) [*Organic chemistry*]
PDA............ Ponta Delgada [*Azores*] [*Seismograph station code, US Geological Survey*] (SEIS)
PDA............ Population Drainage Area [*Civil Defense*]
PDA............ Portable Diagnostic Analyzer (SSD)
PDA............ Post Acceleration (IAA)
PDA............ Post-Deflection Accelerator (DEN)
PDA............ Post-Delivery Availability [*Military*] (NVT)
PDA............ Post-Design Analysis
PDA............ Posterior Descending Artery [*Anatomy*] (DAVI)
PDA............ Potato Dextrose Agar [*Culture media*]
PDA............ Pour Dire Adieu [*To Say Farewell*] [*On visiting cards*] [*French*]
PDA............ Power Distribution Assembly (KSC)
PDA............ Precision Drive Axis (KSC)
PDA............ Predelivery Acceptance Test [*NASA*]
PDA............ Predialyzed Human Albumin [*Medicine*] (MAE)
PDA............ Predicted Drift Angle [*Navigation*]
PDA............ Predocketed Application (NRCH)
PDA............ Pregnancy Discrimination Act [*An amendment to Title VII of the Civil Rights Act of 1964*] (PAZ)
PDA............ Pregnancy Discrimination Act of 1978 (WYGK)
PDA............ Preliminary Design Acceptance (NRCH)
PDA............ Preliminary Design Activity (LAIN)
PDA............ Preliminary Design Approval [*or Authorization*] (NRCH)
PDA............ Preliminary Design Assessment [*Nuclear energy*] (NRCH)
PDA............ Present Duty Assignment Option [*Military*]
PDA............ Principal Decision Authority (DOMA)
PDA............ Principal Deputy for Acquistion [*Army*] (RDA)
PDA............ Principal Development Activity [*Navy*]
PDA............ Principal Development Authority (MCD)
PDA............ Principal Diagonal Artery [*Anatomy*] (DAVI)
PDA............ Principal DOD Executive (AAGC)
PDA............ Private Doctors of America [*Defunct*] (EA)
PDA............ Probabilistic Decision Algorithm [*Artificial intelligence job performance aid*] [*Army*]
PDA............ Probability Discrete Automata (IEEE)
PDA............ Probability Distribution Analyzer [*Statistics*]
PDA............ Probably Disappointed Again (PCM)
PDA............ Probate, Divorce, and Admiralty [*British*] (DLA)
PDA............ Problem Determination Aid (EECA)
PDA............ Processor and Distribution Assembly [*Viking lander analysis equipment*] [*NASA*]
PDA............ Procurement Defense Agencies [*DoD*]
PDA............ Product Departure Authorization
PDA............ Professional Drivers Association
PDA............ Program Developing Agency [*Military*] (CAAL)
PDA............ Prolonged Depolarizing Afterpotential [*Neurophysiology*]
PDA............ Propanediamine [*Organic chemistry*]
PDA............ Propellant Drain Area (NASA)
PDA............ Property Disposal Account [*Military*] (NG)
PDA............ Property Disposal Agent [*Military*] (NG)
PDA............ Property Disposition Authorization
PDA............ Proposed Development Approach [*Navy*]
PDA............ Propylenediamine [*Organic chemistry*]
PDA............ Prospectors' and Developers' Association [*Canada*]
PDA............ Prototype Development Associate
PDA............ Public Display of Affection [*Slang*]
PDA............ Puerto Inirida [*Colombia*] [*Airport symbol*] (OAG)
PDA............ Pulse Demodulation Analysis
PDA............ Pulse Distribution Amplifier
PDA............ Pump Distributors Association [*British*] (DBA)
PDA............ Pump Drive Assembly
PDA............ Pushdown Automation [*Computer science*] (HGAA)
PDAAP............ Plume Data Analysis of Advanced Propellants (MCD)
PDAB............ Para-(Dimethylamino)benzaldehyde [*Organic chemistry*]
PDAB............ Physical Disability Appeals Board [*Military*] (AFM)
PDAC............ Professional Development Advisory Committee [*American Occupational Therapy Association*]
PDAC............ Prospectors and Developers Association of Canada (EAIO)
PDAD............ Photodiode Array Detector [*Spectrophotometry*]
PDAD............ Probate, Divorce, and Admiralty Division [*Legal*] [*British*] (ROG)
PDAFSC............ Projected Duty Air Force Specialty Code (AFM)
PDAID............ Problem Determination Aid [*Computer science*] (MDG)
PDA-KM............ Party of Democratic Action of Kosovo-Metohija [*Serbia*] [*Political party*] (EY)
PDalCM............ College Misericordia, Dallas, PA [*Library symbol Library of Congress*] (LCLS)
PDAM............ Periodontal Disease-Associated Microbiotae [*Dentistry*]
PD & C............ Postural Drainage and Clapping [*Medicine*] (DAVI)
PD & D............ Product Design & Development [*Radnor, PA*] [*A publication*]
PD & E............ Provisioning Documentation and Effort [*Military*] (AFIT)
PD & P............ Postural Drainage and Percussion [*Medicine*] (DAVI)
PD & PL............ Property Damage and Public Liability [*Insurance*] (IIA)
PD & R............ Policy Development and Research
PD & RS............ Payload Deployment and Retrieval Subsystem [*NASA*] (NASA)
PDanMHi............ Montour County Historical Society, Danville, PA [*Library symbol Library of Congress*] (LCLS)
PDanSH............ Danville State Hospital, Danville, PA [*Library symbol Library of Congress*] (LCLS)
PDAP............ Palmer Drug Abuse Program (DMAA)
PDAP............ Programmable Digital Autopilot (MCD)
PDAP............ Provincial Development Assistance Program [*Agency for International Development*]
PDAP............ Publication Design and Ad Placement (DGA)
PDAR............ Parts Drawing Approval Request (MCD)
PD/AR............ Photosensitivity Dermatitis and Actinic Reticuloid Syndrome [*Medicine*] (DMAA)
PDAR............ Preferential Departure [*Aviation*] (DA)
PDAR............ Preferential Departure and Arrival Route [*FAA*] (TAG)
PDAR............ Producibility Design Analysis Report (AAG)
PDAR............ Program Description and Requirements [*NASA*] (NASA)
PDARR............ Production Drawing and Assembly Release Record (AAG)
PDA-S............ Party of Democratic Action of the Sandjak [*Serbia*] [*Political party*] (EY)
PDAS............ Photo Data Analysis System [*Navy*]
PDAS............ Photodiode Array Spectrophotometer (USDC)
PDAS............ Photodiode Array Spectrophotometer [*Marine science*] (OSRA)
PDAS............ Plant Data Acquisition System (NRCH)
PDAS............ [*A*] Popular Dictionary of Australian Slang [*A publication*]
PDAS............ Portable Data Acquisition System (MCD)
PDAS............ Programmable Data Acquisition System (IDOE)
PDASD............ Principal Deputy Assistant Secretary of Defense
PDate............ Pay Date
PDATE............ Production Date [*Computer science*]
PDAV............ Parkinson's Disease Association of Victoria [*Australia*]
P (Day)............ Production Day [*Army*] (AABC)
Pd B............ Bachelor of Pedagogy
PDB............ Packard Data Bank (EA)
PDB............ Para-Dichlorobenzene [*Insecticide for moths, etc.*]
PDB............ Partei der Deutschsprachigen Belgier [*Party of German-Speaking Belgians*] [*Political party*] (PPW)
PDB............ Pedro Bay [*Alaska*] [*Airport symbol*] (OAG)
PDB............ Pee Dee Belemnite [*An isotopic standard for oxygen and carbon*]
PDB............ Pentadecylbenzene [*Organic chemistry*]
PDB............ Performance Data Base (GAVI)
PDB............ Performance Data Book (NASA)
PDB............ Periodical Directories and Bibliographies [*A publication*]
PDB............ Personality Data Base
PDB............ Phorbol Dibutyrate [*Also, PDBu*] [*Organic chemistry*]
PDB............ Phosphorus-Dissolving Bacteria [*Microbiology*]
PDB............ Piedmont Bancorp [*AMEX symbol*] (TTSB)
PDB............ Piedmont Bancorp, Inc. [*AMEX symbol*] (SAG)

PDB .... Pierce's Disease Bacterium [*Plant pathology*]
PDB .... Plasma Diagnostic Base
PDB .... Police Discipline Board [*New South Wales, Australia*]
PDB .... Positive Displacement Blower
PDB .... Potato Dextrose Broth [*Microbiology*]
PDB .... Power Distribution Box (NASA)
PDB .... President's Daily Brief
PDB .... Price Decontrol Board [*Post-World War II*]
PDB .... Primary Data Bus [*Computer science*]
PDB .... Process Descriptor Base [*Telecommunications*] (TEL)
PDB .... Process Display Data Base [*Computer science*] (ECII)
PDB .... Program Definition Block (NITA)
PDB .... Project Development Brochure [*Military*]
PDB .... Protein Data Bank [*Brookhaven National Laboratory*] [*Information service or system*] (CRD)
PDB .... Psychic Detective Bureau (EA)
PDBA .... Personnel Database Application (MCD)
PDBA/SIPM... Personnel Database Application / Student Instructor Performance Module (DNAB)
PDBH .... Production Broach (AAG)
PDBIN .... Processor Data Bus In (MHDI)
PDBM .... Pulse Delay Binary Modulation (MCD)
PDBMI .... Periodical Directories and Bibliographies Master Index [*A publication*]
PDBP .... Powered Disposal Bomb Pod (AAG)
PDBR .... Page-Directory Base Register [*Computer science*] (BYTE)
PDBU .... Pesticides Documentation Bulletin
PDBu .... Phorbol Dibutyrate [*Also, PDB*] [*Organic chemistry*]
PDBz .... Phorbol Dibenzoate [*Organic chemistry*]
PDC .... Community College of Philadelphia, Philadelphia, PA [*OCLC symbol*] (OCLC)
PDC .... Mueo [*New Caledonia*] [*Airport symbol*] (OAG)
PDC .... Pacific Defense College (CINC)
PDC .... Package Design Council [*New York, NY*] (EA)
PDC .... Pacte Democratica per Catalunya [*Democratic Pact for Catalonia*] [*Spain Political party*] (PPE)
PDC .... Page Description Communications [*Microsoft Corp.*] (PCM)
PDC .... Paper Distribution Centers
PDC .... Paper Distribution Council (EA)
PDC .... Parallel Data Communicator (AAG)
PDC .... Parallel Data Controller
PDC .... Parametric Defense Coverage
PDC .... Parti Democrate Chretien [*Christian Democratic Party*] [*Burundi*] [*Political party*]
PDC .... Parti Democrate-Chretien Suisse [*Christian Democratic Party of Switzerland*] [*Political party*] (PPE)
PDC .... Parti des Democrates Camerounais [*Political party*] (EY)
PDC .... Partido da Democracia Cristao [*Christian Democratic Party*] [*Portugal Political party*] (PPW)
PDC .... Partido Democracia Cristiana [*Christian Democratic Party*] [*Guatemala*] [*Political party*] (PPW)
PDC .... Partido Democrata Cristiano [*Christian Democratic Party*] [*Peru*] [*Political party*] (PPW)
PDC .... Partido Democrata Cristiano [*Christian Democratic Party*] [*Paraguay*] [*Political party*] (PPW)
PDC .... Partido Democrata Cristiano [*Christian Democratic Party*] [*Costa Rica*] [*Political party*] (PPW)
PDC .... Partido Democrata Cristiano [*Christian Democratic Party*] [*Honduras*] [*Political party*] (PPW)
PDC .... Partido Democrata Cristiano [*Christian Democratic Party*] [*Bolivia*] [*Political party*] (PPW)
PDC .... Partido Democrata Cristiano [*Christian Democratic Party*] [*Panama*] [*Political party*] (PPW)
PDC .... Partido Democrata Cristiano [*Christian Democratic Party*] [*El Salvador*] [*Political party*]
PDC .... Partido Democrata de Confianza Nacional [*Nicaragua*] [*Political party*] (EY)
PDC .... Partido Democratico Cristao [*Christian Democratic Party*] [*Brazil Political party*]
PDC .... Partido Democratico Cristiano [*Christian Democratic Party*] [*Argentina Political party*] (PPW)
PDC .... Partido Democratico Cristiano [*Christian Democratic Party*] [*Chile*] [*Political party*] (PPW)
PDC .... Partito della Democrazia Cristiana [*Christian Democratic Party*] [*Italy Political party*]
PDC .... Passive Data Collection
PDC .... Pediatric Cardiology [*Medical specialty*] (DHSM)
PDC .... Pentadecylcatechol [*An allergen*]
PDC .... Per Diem, Travel and Transportation Allowance Committee for Departments of the Army, Navy, and Air Force
PDC .... Performance Data Computer
PDC .... Personnel Data Card
PDC .... Personnel Distribution Command
PDC .... Philosophy Documentation Center (EA)
PDC .... Photo-Data Card [*Trademark*] [*Computer science*]
PDC .... Photonuclear Data Center [*National Institute of Standards and Technology*]
PDC .... Pieve Di Cadore [*Italy*] [*Seismograph station code, US Geological Survey Closed*] (SEIS)
PDC .... Piston-Driven Compaction (MCD)
PDC .... Plastic Dielectric Capacitor
PDC .... Pneumatic Damping Control
PDC .... Polaris Documentation Control [*Missiles*]
PDC .... Policy Determination Committee (AAG)
PDC .... Polycrystalline Diamond Compact [*Well drilling technology*]
PDC .... Polycrystalline Diamond Compact Drill Bit
PDC .... Polystyrene Dielectric Capacitor
PDC .... Population Documentation Center [*Food and Agriculture Organization*] [*United Nations Information service or system*] (IID)
PDC .... Portable Data Carrier
PDC .... Portable Data Communications [*British*]
PDC .... Position Depth Charge
PDC .... Power Distribution and Control
PDC .... Power Distribution Cubiale (NATG)
PDC .... Practice Depth Charge
PDC .... Prairie Du Chien, WI [*Location identifier FAA*] (FAAL)
PDC .... Predecessors and Defunct Companies (NITA)
PDC .... Predefined Command (MCD)
PDC .... Predeparture Check [*Aviation*] (AIA)
PDC .... Pre-Departure Clearance [*FAA*] (TAG)
PDC .... Pre Departure Clearance (GAVI)
PDC .... Predetection Combining (IAA)
PDC .... Predocketed Construction (NRCH)
PDC .... Preliminary Diagnostic Clinic
PDC .... Premission Documentation Change [*NASA*] (KSC)
PDC .... Premium and Dispersion Credits [*Insurance*]
PDC .... Prescott Development Corp. [*Vancouver Stock Exchange symbol*]
PDC .... Presely Cos. 'A' [*NYSE symbol*] (TTSB)
PDC .... Presley Co. [*NYSE symbol*] (SPSG)
PDC .... Pressure Die Casting [*Commercial firm British*]
PDC .... Prevention of Deterioration Center [*Defunct*] (EA)
PDC .... Price Decontrol Board [*Post-World War II*] [*A publication*] (DLA)
PDC .... Private Diagnostic Clinic
PDC .... Probability of Detection and Conversion [*Military*]
PDC .... Procurement Document Change (NASA)
PDC .... Production Decision Criteria
PDC .... Production Drawing Control
PDC .... Proficiency Data Card [*Army*]
PDC .... Program Data Cards (OICC)
PDC .... Program Data Coordinator (MCD)
PDC .... Programmable Digital Controller (PDAA)
PDC .... Programmes Directorate Committee [*British*]
PDC .... Project Data Card
PDC .... Project Data Control (MCD)
PDC .... Prolonged Detention Care (CPH)
PDC .... Prosthetic Distribution Center [*Veterans Administration*]
PDC .... Psychodevelopment Checklist [*Psychology*] (DAVI)
PDC .... Publications Distribution Center [*Military*] (AFM)
PDC .... Public Dividend Capital (PDAA)
PDC .... Public Documents Commission [*Government agency*]
PDC .... Publishers' Data Center, Inc.
PDC .... Pulse-Duration Commutator
PDC .... Pure Direct Current [*Electronics*] (IAA)
PDC .... Pyridinium Dichromate [*Organic chemistry*]
PDC .... Pyrotechnic Devices Checker
PDC .... Pyruvate Decarboxylase [*An enzyme*]
PDC .... Pyruvate Dehydrogenase Complex [*Also, PDHC*] [*Biochemistry*]
PDC .... Single Paper Double Cotton [*Wire insulation*] (AAG)
PDCA .... Painting and Decorating Contractors of America (EA)
PDCA .... Pioneer Dairymen's Club of America (EA)
PDCA .... Plan-Do-Check-Act [*Medicine*] (DMAA)
PDCA .... Pug Dog Club of America (EA)
PDCA .... Purebred Dairy Cattle Association (EA)
PDCA .... United States Professional Diving Coaches Association (EA)
PDCAU .... Pete Duel - Clube da Amizade do Universo [*Pete Duel Universal Friendship Club - PDUFC*] (EAIO)
PDCC .... Print and Drawing Council of Canada [*1976*] (NGC)
PDCD .... Primary Degenerative Cerebral Disease [*Medicine*] (DMAA)
PDCG .... Partido Democracia Cristiana Guatemalteca [*Guatemalan Christian Democratic Party*] [*Political party*] (PPW)
PDCH .... Parti Democratique Chretien d'Haiti [*Political party*] (EY)
PDCI .... Parti Democratique de la Cote-D'Ivoire [*Democratic Party of the Ivory Coast*] [*Political party*] (PPW)
Pdck .... Probability of Detection Conversion and Kill [*for an interceptor system*] [*Military*]
PDCL .... Provisioning Data Check List [*NASA*] (KSC)
PDCN .... Partido Democratico de Cooperacion Nacional [*Democratic Party of National Cooperation*] [*Guatemala*] [*Political party*]
PDCN .... Public Data Communications Network [*Library science*]
PDCO .... Patterson Dental [*NASDAQ symbol*] (TTSB)
PDCO .... Patterson Dental Co. [*NASDAQ symbol*] (SAG)
PDCO .... Property Disposal Contracting Officer [*Military*]
PDCP .... Pilot's Display Control Panel
PDCP .... Private Development Corp. of the Philippines
PDCPD .... Polydicyclopentadiene [*Organic chemistry*]
PDCR .... Project Data Compliance Report (MCD)
PDCR .... Proprietary Data Control Record (NASA)
PDCRC .... Periodontal Disease Clinical Research Center [*State University of New York at Buffalo*] [*Research center*] (RCD)
PDCS .... Parallel Digital Computing System
PDCS .... Partito Democratico Cristiano Sammarinese [*Christian Democratic Party of San Marino*] [*Political party*] (PPE)
PDCS .... Performance Data Computer System (MCD)
PDCS .... Power Distribution and Control System [*or Subsystem*] [*NASA*] (NASA)
PDCS .... Processing Distribution and Control System
PDCS .... Programmable Data Collection System [*Military*] (CAAL)
PDCS .... Propellant Development & Characterization Subcommittee [*Joint Army, Navy, NASA, Air Force*]
PDCS .... Prototype Die Casting Service

PD-CSE........ Pulsed Doppler Cross-Sectional Echocardiography [*Medicine*] (DMAA)
PDCU.......... Plotting Display Control Unit
PDCU.......... Power Distribution and Control Unit
Pd D.......... Doctor of Pedagogy
PDD........... Package Designation and Description File (DOMA)
PDD........... Pancreatic Dorsal Duct [*Anatomy*]
PDD........... Participacion Democratica de Tzquierda [*Chile*] [*Political party*] (EY)
PDD........... Past Due Date
PDD........... Pervasive Developmental Disorder [*Medicine*]
PDD........... Phenyldodecane [*Organic chemistry*]
PDD........... Phorbol Didecanoate [*Organic chemistry*]
PDD........... Physical Damage Division [*Navy*]
PDD........... Physical Defense Division [*Army*]
PDD........... Platinum Diamminodichloride [*Cisplatin and cis-platinum*] [*Antineoplastic drug*] (DAVI)
PDD........... Plotting Data Distributor (MCD)
PDD........... Post Dialing Delay [*Telecommunications*] (TEL)
PDD........... Precision Depth Digitizer [*Oceanography*]
PDD........... Preferred Delivery Date (AFM)
PDD........... Preliminary Design and Development (MCD)
PDD........... Premenstrual Dysphoric Disorder [*Proposed psychiatric diagnosis*]
PDD........... Premodulation Processor - Deep Space - Data
PDD........... Presidential Decision Directive
PDD........... Primary Degenerative Dementia [*Medicine*]
PDD........... Principal Distribution Depot [*DoD*]
PDD........... Priority Delivery Date (AFM)
PDD........... Probability Density Distribution [*Statistics*]
PDD........... Procurement Description Data [*DoD*]
PDD........... Professional Development Division [*American Occupational Therapy Association*]
PDD........... Program Description Document [*Military*] (CAAL)
PDD........... Program Design Data
PDD........... Program Dimension Drawing (MCD)
PDD........... Program Directive Document (RDA)
PDD........... Projected Data Display
PDD........... Projected Decision Date (NRCH)
PDD........... Prospective Decision Date (NRCH)
PDD........... Provisioning Description Data
PDD........... Public Documents Department [*Government Printing Office*]
PDD........... Pulse Delay Device
PDD........... Puy-De-Dome [*France*] [*Seismograph station code, US Geological Survey Closed*] (SEIS)
PDD........... Pyridoxine-Deficient Diet (MAE)
PDDA.......... Power Driver Decontamination Apparatus (NATG)
PDDAIO........ Parts for Direct Discrete Analog Input/Output (MCD)
PDDB.......... Phenododecinium [*or Phenoxyethyldimethyl-dodecylammonium*] Bromide [*Antiseptic*]
PDDB.......... Product Definition Database (MCD)
PDDC.......... Proceed Directly on Course [*Aviation*] (FAAC)
PDDD.......... Program Demonstration and Development Division [*ACTION*]
PDDF.......... Propargyl(dideaza)folic Acid [*Biochemistry*]
PDDGM......... Past District Deputy Grand Master [*Freemasonry*]
PDDI.......... Product Definition Data Interface (MCD)
PD Div'l Ct... Probate, Divorce, and Admiralty Divisional Court [*England*] (DLA)
PDDL.......... Perpendicular Diffraction Delay Line (PDAA)
PDDLS......... Post D-Day Logistic Support [*Army*] (AABC)
PDDM.......... Disciples of the Divine Master [*Roman Catholic women's religious order*]
PDDM.......... Pious Disciples of the Divine Master (TOCD)
PDD/NOS....... Pervasive Developmental Disorder, Not Otherwise Specified
PDD/RDD....... Priority Delivery Date/Required Delivery Date (AFM)
PDDS.......... Parasitic Disease Drug Service (MAE)
PDDS.......... Program Definition Data Sheet
PDE........... Page-Directory Entry [*Computer science*] (BYTE)
PDE........... Pandie Pandie [*Australia Airport symbol Obsolete*] (OAG)
PDE........... Parade
Pde........... Parade [*Record label*]
PDE........... Paroxysmal Dyspnea on Exertion [*Medicine*]
PDE........... Partei fuer Deutschland und Europa [*Party for Germany and Europe*] [*Germany Political party*] (PPW)
PDE........... Partial Differential Equation
PDE........... Paste Down Ends [*Graphic arts*] (DGA)
PDE........... Pediatric Endocrinology [*Medical specialty*] (DHSM)
PDE........... Personnel Development and Education (MCD)
PDE........... Phosphatidyl(dimethyl)ethanolamine [*Biochemistry*]
PDE........... Phosphodiesterase [*An enzyme*]
PDE........... Pilot's Discrete Encoder
PDE........... Plain Deckle Edges [*Graphic arts*] (DGA)
PDE........... Position-Determining Equipment
PDE........... Pride Resources Ltd. [*Vancouver Stock Exchange symbol*]
PDE........... Principal DOD [*Department of Defense*] Executive
PDE........... Producers' Durable Equipment (GFGA)
PDE........... Production Design Engineers
PDE........... Professional Development Education [*Military*] (RDA)
PDE........... Projectile Development Establishment [*British*]
PDE........... Propellant Disposition Effects
PDE........... Prospective Data Element [*Army*] (AABC)
PDE........... Pulsed Doppler Echocardiography [*Medicine*] (DMAA)
PDEA.......... Phenyldiethanolamine [*Organic chemistry*]
P de Ancha.... Petrus de Ancharano [*Deceased, 1416*] [*Authority cited in pre-1607 legal work*] (DSA)
P de B........ Petrus de Bellapertica [*Deceased, 1308*] [*Authority cited in pre-1607 legal work*] (DSA)
P de Bp....... Petrus de Bellapertica [*Deceased, 1308*] [*Authority cited in pre-1607 legal work*] (DSA)
PDECS......... Portable Detector and Cueing System
PDED.......... Partial Double Error Detecting (NITA)
PDED.......... Partial Double Error Detection
PDED.......... Program Development and Evaluation Division [*Environmental Protection Agency*] (GFGA)
PDEI.......... Phosphodiesterase Inhibitor [*Biochemistry*]
PDEL.......... Partial Differential Equation Language [*Computer science*]
P de L........ Paulus de Liazaris [*Deceased, 1356*] [*Authority cited in pre-1607 legal work*] (DSA)
PDELAN........ Partial Differential Equation Language [*Computer science*] (CSR)
PDELB......... Plumbers and Drainers' Examination and Licensing Board [*Queensland, Australia*]
PDEM.......... Personal Dust Exposure Monitor (PDAA)
P de Orfi..... Petrus de Orfila [*Deceased, 1307*] [*Authority cited in pre-1607 legal work*] (DSA)
PDEP.......... Preliminary Draft Equipment Publication (MCD)
PDEQ.......... Profile of DARCOM Environmental Quality (MCD)
PDES.......... Phase Image of Poly(diethylsiloxane) [*Organic chemistry*]
PDES.......... Preliminary Draft Environmental Statement (NRCH)
PDES.......... Product Data Exchange Specification (NITA)
PDES.......... Product Data Exchange using STEP [*Sequentially Timed Events Plotting*]
PDES.......... Product Definition Exchange Specification [*Army*]
PDES.......... Pulse-Doppler Elevation Scan (PDAA)
P de Sal...... Petrus de Salinis [*Flourished, 13th century*] [*Authority cited in pre-1607 legal work*] (DSA)
P de Sam...... Petrus de Sampsone [*Flourished, 1246-58*] [*Authority cited in pre-1607 legal work*] (DSA)
P de Samp..... Petrus de Sampsone [*Flourished, 1246-58*] [*Authority cited in pre-1607 legal work*] (DSA)
P Det......... Port Detachment [*British military*] (DMA)
PDET.......... Post-Diapause Eclosion Time [*Entomology*]
PDET.......... Probability of Detection, Evaluation, and Transfer (MCD)
PDEX.......... Pro-Dex, Inc. [*NASDAQ symbol*] (NQ)
PDF........... Hancock [*John*] Patriot Premium Dividend Fund I [*NYSE symbol*] (SAG)
PDF........... John Hancock Patr Prem Dv Fd [*NYSE symbol*] (TTSB)
PDF........... LAR Transregional, Linhas Aereas Regionais SA [*Portugal ICAO designator*] (FAAC)
PDF........... Paget's Disease Foundation (EA)
PDF........... Pair Distribution Function [*Physical chemistry*]
PDF........... Pakistan Democratic Front
PDF........... Panama Defense Forces [*Later, Public Forces*]
PDF........... Parkinson's Disease Foundation (EA)
PDF........... Particle Distribution Function
PDF........... Parti Democrate Francais [*French Democratic Party*] [*Political party*] (PPW)
PDF........... Passive Direction Finding
PDF........... Pavement Depth Factor (ADA)
PDF........... Peace Development Fund (EA)
PDF........... Pele Defense Fund (EA)
PDF........... People's Democratic Force [*The Bahamas*] [*Political party*] (EY)
PDF........... Peritoneal Dialysis Fluid [*Medicine*] (DMAA)
PDF........... Planar Deformation Feature [*Geology*]
PDF........... Planet Drum Foundation (EA)
PDF........... Plant Design Factor [*Nuclear energy*] (NRCH)
PDF........... Plant Design Flood [*Nuclear energy*] (GFGA)
PDF........... Platform Independent File Format [*Computer science*]
PDF........... Point Detonating Fuse (IAA)
PDF........... Point Detonating Fuze [*Army*]
PDF........... Pooled Development Funds [*Economics*]
PDF........... Popular Democratic Front [*Jordan*] [*Political party*]
PDF........... Porsche Dual-Function Transmission [*Automotive engineering*]
PDF........... Portable Document File [*Computer science*] (PCM)
PDF........... Portable Document Format [*Computer science*]
pdf........... Portable Document Format [*Computer science*]
PDF........... Post Defense Force
PDF........... Post Detection Filter [*Telecommunications*] (TEL)
PDF........... Powder Diffraction File (DICI)
PDF........... Power Diffraction File (NITA)
PDF........... Primordial Density Fluctuation [*Cosmology*]
PDF........... Principal Direction of Fire [*Military*]
PDF........... Probability Density Function [*Statistics*]
PDF........... Probability Distribution Function [*Statistics*]
PDF........... Processor Defined Function
PDF........... Production and Distribution of Foodstuffs [*British*]
PDF........... Program Data File
PDF........... Program Data Form [*Army*]
PDF........... Program Development Facility [*Computer science*] (MHDI)
PDF........... Project Design Flood (NRCH)
PDF........... Protected Difference Fat (OA)
PDF........... Pyruvate Dehydrogenase (DMAA)
PDFC.......... Premature Dead Female Child (DAVI)
PDFCS......... Pennsylvania Dutch Folk Culture Society (EA)
PDFD.......... Predemonstration Fusion Device
PDFD.......... Pulsed Doppler Frequency Diversity (NG)
PDFES......... Pitch-Synchronous Digital Feature Extraction System (PDAA)
PDFG.......... Planar Distributed Function Generator (PDAA)
PDFG.......... Platelet-Derived Growth Factor [*Endocrinology*] (DAVI)
PDFLP......... Popular Democratic Front for the Liberation of Palestine
PDFM.......... Phillips and Drew Fund Management [*England*] [*British*]
PDFRR......... Program Directors Flight Readiness Review [*NASA*] (KSC)

PDFWPR ...... Physical Disabilities Fieldwork Performance Report [*Occupational therapy*]
PDG ...... Padang [*Indonesia*] [*Airport symbol*] (OAG)
PDG ...... Padding
PDG ...... Parachute Drop Glider
PDG ...... Paradigm (WGA)
PDG ...... Parkinsonism-Dementia Complex of Guam [*Medicine*] (DMAA)
PDG ...... Parti Democratique de Guinee [*Democratic Party of Guinea*] [*Political party*] (PPW)
PDG ...... Parti Democratique Gabonais [*Gabonese Democratic Party*] [*Political party*] (PPW)
PDG ...... Passive Defense Group (MUGU)
PDG ...... Patent Documentation Group (DIT)
PDG ...... PDG Remediation, Inc. [*Associated Press*] (SAG)
PDG ...... Personalistic Discussion Group - Eastern Division (EA)
PDG ...... Phosphogluconate Dehydrogenase [*Organic chemistry*] (MAH)
PDG ...... Placer Dome, Inc. [*NYSE symbol Toronto Stock Exchange symbol Vancouver Stock Exchange symbol*] (SPSG)
PDG ...... Precision Drop Glider [*Army*]
PDG ...... Pregnanediol Glucuronide [*Endocrinology*]
PDG ...... President Directeur General [*President Director General*] [*French*]
PDG ...... Pretty Damn Good
PDG ...... Production Development Group (IAA)
PDG ...... Professional Dyers Guild [*Defunct*]
PDG ...... Program Documentation Generator [*Computer science*] (MHDI)
PDG ...... Programs Development Group (MUGU)
PDG ...... Proposal Development Group [*Aerospace*] (AAG)
PDGA ...... Professional Disc Golf Association
PDGA ...... Pteroyldiglutamic Acid [*Pharmacology*]
PDGDL ...... Plasma Dynamics and Gaseous Discharge Laboratory [*MIT*] (MCD)
PDGE ...... Partido Democratico de Guinea Ecuatorial [*Democratic Party of Equatorial Guinea*] [*Political party*] (EY)
PDGE ...... PDG Environmental [*NASDAQ symbol*] (TTSB)
PDGE ...... PDG Environmental, Inc. [*NASDAQ symbol*] (SAG)
PDG En ...... PDG Environmental, Inc. [*Associated Press*] (SAG)
PDGF ...... Platelet-Derived Growth Factor [*Genetics*]
PDGF ...... Platelet-Derived Growth Factor [*Medicine*]
PDGFA ...... Platelet-Derived Growth Factor [*Medicine*] (DMAA)
PDGFR ...... Platelet-Derived Growth Factor Receptor [*Genetics*]
PDGMS ...... Peabody Developmental Gross Motor Scale
PDGS ...... PDG Remediation [*NASDAQ symbol*] (TTSB)
PDGS ...... PDG Remediation, Inc. [*NASDAQ symbol*] (SAG)
PDGS ...... Precision Delivery Glider System
P-DGs ...... Presidents-Directeurs Generaux
PDGS ...... Probe Drill Guidance System
PDGS ...... Product Design Graphics System [*Prime Computer Ltd.*] [*Software package*] (NCC)
PDGSW ...... PDG Remediation Wrrt [*NASDAQ symbol*] (TTSB)
PDGW ...... Principle Directorate of Guided Weapons [*British*] (SAA)
PDGXT ...... Predischarge Graded Exercise Test [*Cardiology*] (DAVI)
PDH ...... Packaged Disaster Hospital [*Public Health Service*]
PDH ...... Passive Defense Handbook [*Navy*] (MCD)
PDH ...... Past Dental History
PDH ...... Phosphate Dehydrogenase (MAE)
PDH ...... Planned Derated Hours [*Electronics*] (IEEE)
PDH ...... Pocket Dosimeter-High (MCD)
PDH ...... Pyruvate Dehydrogenase [*An enzyme*]
PDH & DS ... Plant Data Handling and Display System [*Nuclear energy*] (NRCH)
PDHC ...... Pyruvate Dehydrogenase Complex [*Biochemistry*]
PDHF ...... Postdilution Hemofiltration [*Medicine*]
PDHL ...... Peak Design Heat Loss (PDAA)
PDHV-RDA ... Parti Democratique de la Haute Volta-Rassemblement Democratique Africain [*Democratic Party of Upper Volta-African Democratic Rally*]
PDI ...... Pain Disability Index [*Medicine*] (DMAA)
PDI ...... Palmer Drought Index
PDI ...... Panel Data Interface [*Computer science*] (IAA)
PDI ...... Paradise Island Airlines, Inc. [*ICAO designator*] (FAAC)
PDI ...... Partai Demokrasi Indonesia [*Indonesian Democratic Party*] [*Political party*] (PPW)
PDI ...... Partial Delivery Injection [*Materials science*]
PDI ...... Parti Democratique de l'Independance [*Democratic Independence Party*] [*Morocco*] [*Political party*]
PDI ...... Partito Democratica Italiana [*Italian Democratic Party*] [*Political party*] (PPE)
PDI ...... Payload Data Interleaver [*NASA*] (NASA)
PDI ...... Perfect Digital Invariant (OA)
PDI ...... Periodontal Disease Index [*Dentistry*] (DMAA)
PDI ...... Personal Disposable Income [*Economics*]
PDI ...... Pictorial Deviation Indicator (AAG)
PDI ...... Picture Description Instruction [*Telecommunications*]
PDI ...... Pilot Direction Indicator [*Electronic communications*]
PDI ...... Plan-Do Intergration [*Medicine*] (DMAA)
PDI ...... Plumbing and Drainage Institute (EA)
PDI ...... Porto D'Ischia [*Italy*] [*Seismograph station code, US Geological Survey Closed*] (SEIS)
PDI ...... Post Detection Integration (MCD)
PDI ...... Potential Determining Ions
PDI ...... Power Dissipation Index (IAA)
PDI ...... Powered Descent Initiation [*Aerospace*]
PDI ...... Pre-Delivery Inspection (DCTA)
PDI ...... Predeployment Inspection [*Navy*] (NVT)
PDI ...... Premdor, Inc. [*Toronto Stock Exchange symbol*]
PDI ...... Privately Developed Item (AAGC)
PDI ...... Professional Development Institute [*Canada*]
PDI ...... Program Design, Inc. [*Commercial firm*]
PDI ...... Program with Developing Institutions (EA)
PDI ...... Project Data Index [*Jet Propulsion Laboratory, NASA*]
PDI ...... Protein Dispersibility Index [*Analytical chemistry*]
PDI ...... Protein Disulfide-Isomerase [*An enzyme*]
PDI ...... Psychiatric Diagnostic Interview [*Personality development test*] [*Psychology*]
PDI ...... Psychological Distress Inventory [*Student personality test*]
PDI ...... Psychomotor Development Index [*Bayley Scales of Infant Development*]
PDI ...... Public Debt Interest (ADA)
PDI ...... Public Demographics, Inc. (IID)
PDI ...... Putnam Dividend Income [*NYSE symbol*] (SPSG)
PDI ...... Putnam Dividend Income [*NYSE symbol*] (TTSB)
Pdi ...... Transdiaphragmatic [*Pressure*]
PDIAL ...... Public Dialup Internet Access List [*Computer science*] (CDE)
PDIC ...... Periodic (AFM)
PDIC ...... Professional Driver Improvement Course
PDIE ...... Phosphodiesterase (DMAA)
PDIF ...... Putnam Dividend Income Fund [*Associated Press*] (SAG)
PDII ...... Pusat Dokumentasi dan Informasi Ilmiah [*Indonesian Center for Scientific Documentation and Information*] [*Information service or system*] (IID)
PDIIS ...... Priority Defense Items Information System
PDIL ...... Power-Dependent Insertion Limit [*Nuclear energy*] (NRCH)
PDIN ...... Pusat Dokumentasi Ilmiah Nasional (NITA)
PDIO ...... Parallel Digital Input/Output
PDIO ...... Photodiode
P-DIOL ...... Pregnanediol [*Biochemistry*]
PDIP ...... Preflight Data Insertion Program (NVT)
PDIP ...... Program Development Increment Package [*Military*]
PDIR ...... Priority Disassembly and Inspection Report
PDIR ...... Program Directive
PDIS ...... Parts Dissection Information System
PDIS ...... Payload Data Interleaver System [*NASA*] (MCD)
PDIS ...... Pressure Differential Switch (IAA)
PDIS ...... Product Description Information Standards [*or System*]
PDISCH ...... Pump Discharge
PDISPL ...... Positive Displacement [*Engineering*]
PDIT ...... Provision for Deferred Income Tax
PDIUM ...... Partito Democratico Italiano di Unita Monarchica [*Italian Democratic Party of Monarchical Unity*] [*Political party*] (PPE)
P Div ...... Law Reports, Probate Division [*England*] [*A publication*] (DLA)
PDJ ...... Plaine Des Jarres [*South Vietnam*]
PDJ ...... Precision Drill Jig
PDJB ...... Precision Drill Jig Bushing
PD/JV ...... Project Definition/Joint Validation (MCD)
PDK ...... Atlanta [*Georgia*] De Kalb/Peachtree Airport [*Airport symbol Obsolete*] (OAG)
PDK ...... PDK Labs, Inc. [*Associated Press*] (SAG)
PDK ...... Phase-Delay Keying [*Computer science*]
PDK ...... Phi Delta Kappa [*Fraternity*]
PDK ...... Phileleftheron Demokratikon Kendron [*Liberal Democratic Union*] [*Greek*] (PPE)
PDK ...... Phileleftheron Demokratikon Komma [*Liberal Democratic Party*] [*Greek Political party*] (PPE)
PDK ...... Poop Deck [*Naval engineering*]
PDK ...... Promenade Deck [*of a ship*] (DS)
PDK ...... Science Foods, Inc. [*AMEX symbol*] (SAG)
PDKL ...... PDK Labs [*NASDAQ symbol*] (TTSB)
PDKL ...... PDK Labs, Inc. [*NASDAQ symbol*] (SAG)
PDKLM ...... PDK Labs Wrrt'C' [*NASDAQ symbol*] (TTSB)
PDKLP ...... PDK Labs $0.49 Cv'A' Pfd [*NASDAQ symbol*] (TTSB)
PDL ...... Page Description Language [*Computer graphics*]
PDL ...... Partido Democrata Liberal [*Liberal Democratic Party*] [*Spain Political party*] (EY)
PDL ...... Parts Deletion List (MSA)
PDL ...... Parts Difference List (MCD)
PDL ...... Parts Documentation List (MCD)
PDL ...... Pass Down the Line [*Book*] [*Navy*] (MUGU)
PDL ...... Patent Depository Library [*Designated by the Patent and Trademark Office*]
PDL ...... People's Democracy of Laos [*Political party*] (VNW)
PDL ...... Periodontal Ligament [*Dentistry*]
PDL ...... Permanent Duty Location
PDL ...... Photodissociation Dye LASER
PDL ...... Picture Description Language [*Computer science*] (MHDI)
PDL ...... Placer Development Ltd. [*Toronto Stock Exchange symbol Vancouver Stock Exchange symbol*]
PDL ...... Pocket Dosimeter-Low (MCD)
PDL ...... Polarization Diversity LIDAR
PDL ...... Ponce De Leon
PDL ...... Ponta Delgada [*Portugal*] [*Airport symbol*] (OAG)
PDL ...... Poorly Differentiated Lymphocytic [*Oncology*]
PDL ...... Population Doubling Level [*Cytology*]
PDL ...... Portable Data Loader [*Aviation*]
pdl ...... Poundal [*Unit of force*]
PDL ...... Poverty Datum Line
PDL ...... Precision Delay Line
PDL ...... Presidential Realty Corp. [*AMEX symbol*] (SPSG)
PDL ...... Print Definition Language [*Computer science*] (EECA)
PDL ...... Procedure Definition Language [*Computer science*] (BUR)
PDL ...... Procedure Distribution List (MCD)
PDL ...... Process Design Language [*Computer science*] (MHDI)
PDL ...... Procurement Data List

PDL............ Product Disaster Loans [*Small Business Administration*]
PDL............ Professional Development League (EA)
PDL............ Program Description Language (MCD)
PDL............ Program Design Language (NASA)
PDL............ Program Device Librarian [*Computer science*]
PDL............ Programmable Data Language (NITA)
PDL............ Programmed Digital Logic
PDL............ Project Document List
PDL............ Protocol Description Language [*Telecommunications*] (IAA)
PDL............ Publishers' Databases Ltd. [*Publishing consortium*] [*British*]
pdl............ Pudendal [*Anatomy*] (MAE)
PDL............ Pulsed Dye LASER
PDL............ Pumped Dye LASER
PDL............ Push Down List [*Computer science*] (MHDI)
PDL A......... Presidential Rlty Cl'A' [*AMEX symbol*] (TTSB)
PD(LAO)...... Public Defender (Legal Aid Office) [*Australia*]
PDL B......... Presidential Rlty Cl'B' [*AMEX symbol*] (TTSB)
PDLC.......... North American Palladium [*NASDAQ symbol*] (SAG)
PDLC.......... Partido Liberal de Cataluna [*Liberal Democratic Party of Catalonia*] [*Political party*] (PPW)
PDLC.......... Polymer Dispersed Liquid Crystal [*Physical chemistry*]
PDLC.......... Polymer-Dispersed Liquid Crystal [*Electronics*]
PDLC.......... Poorly Differentiated Lung Cancer [*Medicine*] (DMAA)
PDLCF........ North Amer Palladium [*NASDAQ symbol*] (TTSB)
PDLD.......... Poorly Differentiated Lymphocytic-Diffuse [*Oncology*] (DMAA)
PDL/FT²...... Poundals per Square Foot
PDLI........... Protein Design Labs [*NASDAQ symbol*] (TTSB)
PDLI........... Protein Design Labs, Inc. [*NASDAQ symbol*] (SAG)
PDLL........... Poorly Differentiated Lymphatic [*or Lymphocytic*] Lymphoma [*Oncology*]
PDLM.......... Periodic Depot Level Maintenance
PDLM.......... Planned Depot Level Maintenance (MCD)
PDLM.......... Programmed Depot Level Maintenance [*Air Force*]
PDLN.......... Poorly Differentiated Lymphocytic-Nodular [*Oncology*] (DMAA)
PDLP.......... Pacific Dunlop Ltd. [*NASDAQ symbol*] (NQ)
PDLPY........ Pacific Dunlop Ltd. (MHDW)
PDLPY........ Pacific Dunlop Ltd. ADR [*NASDAQ symbol*] (TTSB)
PDLS.......... Party of the Democratic Left of Slovakia [*Former Czechoslovakia*] [*Political party*] (EY)
PDL S/FT².... Poundal Seconds per Square Foot
PDLT........... P-Channel Depletion-Load Triode Inverter
PD/LT.......... Program Design and Learning Tool (NITA)
Pd M........... Master of Pedagogy
PDM............ Partial Descriptive Method
PDM............ Parti Democratique Malgache [*Malagasy Democratic Party*]
PDM............ Partido de los Democratas Melillenses [*Spanish North Africa*] [*Political party*] (MENA)
PDM............ Patient Data Management
PDM............ Pendant Drop Method
PDM............ People's Democratic Movement [*Turks and Caicos Islands*] [*Political party*] (PPW)
PDM............ People's Democratic Movement [*Papua New Guinea*] [*Political party*] (FEA)
PDM............ People's Democratic Movement [*Guyana*] [*Political party*] (EY)
PDM............ Percent Deviation from the Median
PDM............ Phase Displacement (IAA)
PDM............ Physical Distribution Management
PDM............ Physiological Data Monitor
PDM............ Pilot Decision Making [*Aviation*] (DA)
PDM............ Pinch Design Method [*Heat exchange design*]
PDM............ Pitt-DesMoines Inc. [*AMEX symbol*] (TTSB)
PDM............ Pittsburgh - Des Moines, Inc. [*AMEX symbol*] (SPSG)
pdm............ Podium (VRA)
PDM............ Point Distribution Model (DMAA)
PDM............ Polynomial Discriminant Method (PDAA)
PDM............ Portable Differential Magnetometer
PDM............ Power Density Meter
PDM............ Practical Data Manager [*Hitachi Ltd.*] [*Japan*]
PDM............ Precedence Diagraming Method (MCD)
PDM............ Predictive Maintenance
PDM............ Preliminary Development Model
PDM............ Preliminary Draft Manuscript
PDM............ Presidential Decision Memorandum [*Jimmy Carter Administration*]
PDM............ Print Down Module
PDM............ Processor Data Monitor (NASA)
PDM............ Product Data Management
PDM............ Product Development Manual [*Automotive project management*]
PDM............ Production Decision Criteria Matrix
PDM............ Program Data Manager (MCD)
PDM............ Program Decision Memorandum [*Military*]
PDM............ Programmed Depot Maintenance (MCD)
PDM............ Progres et Democratie Moderne [*Progress and Modern Democracy*] [*France Political party*] (PPE)
PDM............ Project Design Memo
PDM............ Protected Difference Milk (OA)
PDM............ Publications Distribution Manager [*Military*] (AFM)
PDM............ Pulse Data Modulation [*Computer science*] (IAA)
PDM............ Pulse Delay Mechanism [*British military*] (DMA)
PDM............ Pulse Delta Modulation (IEEE)
PDM............ Pulse Duration Modulation [*Data transmission*]
PDM............ Pursuit Deterrent Munition
PDM............ Push Down Memory [*Computer science*]
PDMA.......... Peninsula Drafting Management Association
PDMA.......... Prescription Drug Marketing Act [*1987*]
PDMA.......... Product Development and Management Association [*Indianapolis, IN*] (EA)
PDMAC........ Prescription Drug Maximum Allowable Cost
PDMAMS..... Product Design Minuteman Airborne Mechanical System (SAA)
PDMC.......... Premature Dead Male Child (DAVI)
PDMC.......... Princeton Dental Management Corp. [*NASDAQ symbol*] (SAG)
PDMC.......... Princeton Dental Mgmt [*NASDAQ symbol*] (TTSB)
PDMCW....... Princeton Dental Mgmt Wrrt [*NASDAQ symbol*] (TTSB)
PDME.......... Pendant-Drop Melt Extraction [*Metal fiber technology*]
PDME.......... Precision Distance Measuring Equipment (MCD)
PDM-FM...... Pulse-Duration Modulation - Frequency Modulation (CET)
PDMLR........ Post-Development Maintainability Logistics Review (MCD)
PDMM.......... Push Down Memory MODEM [*Computer science*]
PDMMS....... Product Design Minuteman Mechanical System (IAA)
PDMNT........ Piedmont
PDMO.......... Production Mold (AAG)
PDMP.......... Positive Displacement Mechanical [*or Metering*] Pump
PDMPO........ Polydimethyl Phenylene Oxide [*Organic chemistry*]
PDMR.......... Provisioning Data Master Record (MCD)
PDMS.......... Particle Desorption Mass Spectrometry
PDMS.......... Patient Data Management Systems [*Medical records*] (DAVI)
PDMS.......... Pesticide Document Management System [*Environmental Protection Agency*] (GFGA)
PDMS.......... Pharmacokinetic Drug Monitoring Services [*Medicine*] (DMAA)
PDMS.......... Photodissociation Mass Spectrometry
PDMS.......... Physiological Data Monitoring System
PDMS.......... Plant Design and Management System [*Computer Aided Design Centre*] [*Software package*] (NCC)
PDMS.......... Plasma Desorption Mass Spectroscopy
PDMS.......... Point Defense Missile System [*NATO*] (NATG)
PDMS.......... Polydimethylsiloxane [*Organic chemistry*]
PDMS.......... Power-Plant and Process Design Management System [*Computer science*]
PDMS.......... Program Definition and Management System (MCD)
PDMT.......... Predominant [*National Weather Service*] (FAAC)
PDMU.......... Passive Data Memory Unit
PDMU.......... Production Mock-Up (AAG)
PDMV.......... Pressure Differential Monitoring Valve
PDN............ Partido Democratico Nacional [*National Democratic Party*] [*Chile*] [*Political party*]
PDN............ Partido Democratico Nacional [*National Democratic Party*] [*Venezuela Political party*]
PDN............ Partito Democratico Nazionalista [*Democratic Nationalist Party (1921-1926)*] [*Malta*] [*Political party*] (PPE)
PDN............ Partnerships Data Net [*Defunct*] (EA)
PDN............ Petition Denied
PDN............ Port Heiden, AK [*Location identifier FAA*] (FAAL)
PDN............ Power Dividing Network [*Telecommunications*] (LAIN)
PDN............ Prednisone [*Also, P, Pr, Pred, Pro*] [*Endocrinology*] [*Antineoplastic drug*]
PDN............ Private Duty Nurse (DAVI)
PDN............ Problem Documentation Number (AAG)
PDN............ Production (AFM)
PDN............ Properly Driven Net
PDN............ Public Data Network [*Packet-switching network*] [*British Telecommunications Ltd. London*]
PDNC.......... Presidents' Day National Committee (EA)
PDNES........ Pulse-Doppler Non-Elevation Scan (PDAA)
PDNF.......... Prime Disjunctive Normal Form (PDAA)
PD/NSC....... Presidential Directives/National Security Council
PDO............ Philips & Du Pont Optical Co. [*Wilmington, DE*]
PDO............ Phthalate Dioxygenase [*An enzyme*]
PDO............ Portable Distributed Objects [*Next*]
PDO............ Port Dry Out [*Nuclear energy*] (NUCP)
PDO............ Postman's Delivery Office (DCTA)
PDO............ Prado [*Brazil*] [*Airport symbol*] (AD)
PDO............ Printer Direction Optimizer (BUR)
PD-O........... Program Directive - Operations (KSC)
PDO............ Property Disposal Officer [*Army*]
PdO............ Psychopathic Deviate Obvious [*Psychology*]
PDO............ Publications Distribution Officer [*Military*]
PDO............ Public Defender's Office [*Australia*]
PDO............ Public Defender's Office (LAIN)
PDoB.......... Bucks County Free Library, Doylestown, PA [*Library symbol Library of Congress*] (LCLS)
PDoBHi........ Bucks County Historical Society, Doylestown, PA [*Library symbol Library of Congress*] (LCLS)
PDOC.......... Particulate and/or Dissolved Organic Carbon [*Chemistry*]
PDOD.......... Phytoplankton Dissolved Oxygen Deficit [*Oceanography*]
PDOF.......... Principal Direction of Force [*Mechanical engineering*]
PDOIS......... People's Democratic Organisation for Independence and Socialism [*Senegambia*] [*Political party*]
PDOL.......... Publishers Discount Option List
PDoN.......... Delaware Valley College of Science and Agriculture, Doylestown, PA [*Library symbol Library of Congress*] (LCLS)
PDOP.......... Position Dilution of Position [*Navigation systems*]
PDOP.......... Position Dilution of Precision
PDOP.......... Prospective Designated Overhaul Point (MCD)
PDOS.......... Parent Diabetes Opinion Survey [*Test*]
PDowN........ Newcomen Society in North America, Downingtown, PA [*Library symbol Library of Congress*] (LCLS)
P/DOZ......... Per Dozen (WDAA)
PDP............ Packaging Development Plan
PDP............ Pakistan Democratic Party [*Political party*] (PD)
PDP............ Parallel Detection Polychromator [*Instrumentation*]

PDP .... Parallel Distributed Processing [*A simulation of mental processes*]
PDP .... Parker & Parsley Petrol [*NYSE symbol*] (TTSB)
PDP .... Parker & Parsley Petroleum [*NYSE symbol*] (SAG)
PDP .... Parliamentary Democratic Party [*Myanmar*] [*Political party*]
PDP .... Parti Democrate Populaire [*Popular Democratic Party*] [*France Political party*] (PPE)
PDP .... Partido da Direita Portuguesa [*Party of the Portuguese Right*] [*Political party*] (PPE)
PDP .... Partido Democrata Popular [*Popular Democratic Party*] [*Spain Political party*] (PPW)
PDP .... Partido Democrata Popular [*Popular Democratic Party*] [*Dominican Republic*] [*Political party*] (PPW)
PDP .... Partido Democratico para o Progresso [*Democratic Progressive Party*] [*Guinea-Bissau*] [*Political party*] (EY)
PDP .... Partito Democratico Populare [*Popular Democratic Party*] [*San Marino*] [*Political party*] (PPE)
PDP .... Party for Democratic Prosperity [*Macedonia*] [*Political party*]
PDP .... Passive Driving Periscope [*Military*] (PDAA)
PDP .... Pattern Disruption Point [*Medicine*] (DMAA)
PDP .... Payload Distribution Panel [*NASA*] (MCD)
PDP .... Payload Distribution Plan
PDP .... Pentadecylphenol [*Organic chemistry*]
PDP .... People's Democratic [*Saint Christopher and Nevis*] [*Political party*] (EY)
PDP .... People's Democratic Party [*Sudan*] [*Political party*]
PDP .... People's Democratic Party [*South Korea Political party*] (EY)
PDP .... People's Democratic Party [*Netherlands Antilles*] [*Political party*] (EY)
PDP .... People's Democratic Party [*Sierra Leone*] [*Political party*] (EY)
PDP .... Personal Development Program (MCD)
PDP .... Pesticide Data Program [*Environmental Protection Agency*]
PDP .... Phenyl-Dichlorophosphine (PDAA)
PDP .... Philadelphia, PA [*Location identifier FAA*] (FAAL)
PDP .... Philippine Democratic Party [*Pilipino Lakas Ng Bayan*] [*Political party*] (PPW)
PDP .... Pilot District Project [*Office of Economic Opportunity*] [*Defunct*] (EA)
PDP .... Piperidino-Pyrimidine [*Biochemistry*] (MAE)
PDP .... Pitch-Depitch (AAG)
PDP .... Planning Development Program (OICC)
PDP .... Plasma Diagnostics Package [*NASA*]
PDP .... Plasma Display Panel [*Computer science*]
PDP .... Plasma Display Processor [*Computer science*]
PDP .... Polysilicon Dielectric Polysilicon [*Organic chemistry*] (IAA)
PDP .... Popular Democratic Party [*Puerto Rico*] [*Political party*]
PDP .... Positive Displacement Pump
PDP .... Post Detection Processor [*Military*] (CAAL)
PDP .... Post-Drug Potentiation
PDP .... Post-Insertion Deorbit Preparation [*NASA*] (MCD)
PDP .... Power Distribution Panel
PDP .... Power Drain Protection [*Automotive engineering*]
PDP .... Preliminary Definition Plan (NASA)
PDP .... Preliminary Design Phase
PDP .... Preliminary Design Proposal (MCD)
PDP .... Preprototype Demonstration
PDP .... Prescription Drug Plan [*Insurance*] (WYGK)
PDP .... Prescription Drug Program [*Health insurance*] (GHCT)
PDP .... Present-Day Primers [*A publication*]
PDP .... Pressure Distribution Panel (AAG)
PDP .... Principal Display Panel [*Packaging*]
PDP .... Procedure Definition Processor [*Computer science*]
PDP .... Procedure Definition Processor (NITA)
PDP .... Process Data Processing (IAA)
PDP .... Process Development Pile [*Nuclear energy*]
PDP .... Procurement Data Package [*Military*] (AABC)
PDP .... Product Development Process [*Automotive engineering*]
PDP .... Production Data Package (MCD)
PDP .... Professional Development Program [*Military*]
PDP .... Program Decision Package [*Military*]
PDP .... Program Definition Phase [*Army*]
PDP .... Program Development Paper (MCD)
PDP .... Program Development Plan [*NASA*]
PDP .... Program Development Plan (USDC)
PDP .... Programmable Data Processor (IAA)
PDP .... Programmed Data Processor
PDP .... Programmed Digital Processor
PDP .... Progressive Democratic Party [*Montserrat*] [*Political party*] (PPW)
PDP .... Progressive Democratic Party [*St. Vincent*] [*Political party*] (PPW)
PDP .... Project Definition Phase (NRCH)
PDP .... Project Development Plan
PDP .... Punta Del Este [*Uruguay*] [*Airport symbol*] (OAG)
PDPA .... People's Democratic Party of Afghanistan [*Political party*] (PPW)
PDPA .... Production Pattern (AAG)
PDPC .... Position Display Parallax Corrected
PDPC .... Post Detection Pulse Compression [*Military*] (CAAL)
PDP-CVS .... Positive Displacement Pump-Constant Volume Sampler (ERG)
PDPD .... Prolonged-Dwell Peritoneal Dialysis [*Medicine*] (DMAA)
PDPF .... Packet Data Processing Facility (MCD)
PDPGM .... Past Deputy Provincial Grand Master [*Freemasonry*]
PDPH .... Postdural Puncture Headache [*Medicine*] (DMAA)
PDPI .... Primer-Dependent Deoxynucleic Acid Polymerase Index [*Medicine*] (DMAA)
PDPIC .... Professional Development Program Improvement Center (EDAC)
PDPL .... Property Damage, Personal Liability [*Insurance*]
PDPM .... Preliminary Draft Presidential Memo
PDPOA .... Proposal Directive Plan of Action (MCD)
PDPR .... Present-Day Preachers [*A publication*]
PDPS .... Parts Data Processing System [*Bell Telephone*]
PDPS .... Problem Driver Pointer System [*NHTSA*] (TAG)
PDPS .... Program Data Processing Section (AAG)
PDPS .... Program Data Processing System (IAA)
PDPS .... Program Definition Phase Studies [*Navy*]
PDPS .... Project Data Processing System (MCD)
PDPT .... Parti Democratique des Populations Togolaises [*Togolese Democratic People's Party*] [*Political party*]
PDPUB .... Pedicel Pubescence [*Botany*]
PDPVF .... Presidential and Democratic Party Victory Fund (EA)
PDQ .... Packages Delivered Quick [*Allegheny Airlines service*]
PDQ .... Parallel Data Query [*Computer science*] (CDE)
PDQ .... Parental Diagnostic Questionnaire [*Speech evaluation test*]
PDQ .... Parodies Done Quirkily [*Humorous translation of Peter Schickele's PDQ Bach*]
PDQ .... PDQ Air Service, Inc. [*ICAO designator*] (FAAC)
PDQ .... Permanent Durable Quality [*Paper*]
PDQ .... Personal Description Questionnaire
PDQ .... Pertinent Data Quest (MCD)
PDQ .... Photo Data Quantizer
PDQ .... Physician's Data Query [*NIH*]
PDQ .... Please Draw Quickly [*Initialism used as title of TV series*]
PDQ .... Point, Digital, Qualifier [*In automobile name Opel PDQ*]
PDQ .... Prescreening Developmental Questionnaire [*Child development test*]
PDQ .... Pretty Damn Quick
PDQ .... Pretty Darn Quick (TAG)
PDQ .... Price and Delivery Quotations
PDQ .... Prime Hospitality [*NYSE symbol*] (SPSG)
PDQ .... Programmed Data Quantizer
PDQ .... Protocol Data Query [*Database*] [*National Institutes of Health*]
PDQC .... Physicians Data Query: Cancer Information File [*Database*]
PDQD .... Physicians Data Query: Directory File [*Database*]
PDQP .... Physicians Data Query: Protocol File [*Database*]
PDR .... Page Data Register
PDR .... Parent Daily Telephone Report [*Education*] (EDAC)
PDR .... Particulate Data Reduction (EPA)
PDR .... Parti Democratique Progressif [*Algeria*] [*Political party*] (EY)
PDR .... Party of Democratic Reform [*Slovenia*] [*Political party*] (EY)
PDR .... Pattern Delayed-Response [*Ophthalmology*]
PDR .... Peak Dose Rate [*Radiation*] (AAG)
PDR .... Pediatric Radiology [*Medical specialty*] (DHSM)
PDR .... Periscope Depth Range [*SONAR*]
PDR .... Periscope Detection RADAR (NG)
PDR .... Pharma-Dokumentationsring [*Pharma Documentation Ring*] [*Information service or system*] (IID)
PDR .... Phase Data Recorder (KSC)
PDR .... Phase Delay Rectifier
PDR .... Philippine Defense Ribbon [*Military decoration*]
PDR .... Photodissociation [*or Photodominated*] Region [*Galactic science*]
PDR .... Physicians' Desk Reference [*Also, an information service or system A publication*]
PDR .... Pilot's Display Recorder
PDR .... Piskei Din Shel Batei ha-Din ha-Rabaniyim be-Yisrael (BJA)
PDR .... Plasma-Developed Resist Processing [*Lithography*]
PDR .... Position Distribution Report [*DoD*]
PDR .... Pounder (MSA)
PDR .... Powder
PDR .... Power Directional Relay
PDR .... Precision Depth Recorder
PDR .... Predetection Recording
PDR .... Predetermined Demand Rate
PDR .... Pre-Determined Route [*Aviation*] (DA)
PDR .... Preferential Departure Route [*FAA*] (TAG)
PDR .... Preliminary Data Report
PDR .... Preliminary Data Requirements (NASA)
PDR .... Preliminary Design Report (NRCH)
PDR .... Preliminary Design Review (NASA)
PDR .... Pressurized Deuterium Reactor [*Nuclear energy*]
PDR .... Price Description Record [*Computer science*] (IBMDP)
PDR .... Primary Demographic Report [*A. C. Nielsen Co.*] (NTCM)
PDR .... Priority Data Reduction
PDR .... Process Dynamics Recorder
PDR .... Processed Data Recorder
PDR .... Processing Data Rate (IEEE)
PDR .... Procurement Data Reference
PDR .... Product Design Review [*Army*]
PDR .... Program Design Review (MCD)
PDR .... Program Director's Review [*NASA*] (NASA)
PDR .... Program Discrepancy Report (IEEE)
PDR .... Program Document Requirement (BUR)
PDR .... Program Drum Recording
PDR .... Proliferative Diabetic Retinopathy [*Ophthalmology*]
PDR .... Publications Data Request
PDR .... Public Document Room (NRCH)
PDR .... Pulse Doppler RADAR
PDR .... Pulse Duty Ratio
PDRA .... Professional Drag Racing Association (EA)
PDRB .... Permanent Diability Rating Board (DMAA)
PDRC .... Clinical Research Center for Periodontal Disease [*University of Florida*] [*Research center*] (RCD)
PDRC .... Personnel Despatch and Reception Centre [*British military*] (DMA)
PDRC .... Peter Duel Remembrance Club (EA)
PDRC .... Poultry Disease Research Center [*University of Georgia*] [*Research center*] (RCD)

PDRC .... Preliminary Design Review Commercial (MCD)
PDRC .... Pressure Difference Recording Controller
PDRC .... Professional Development and Recruitment Career Program [*Military*]
PDRC .... Program Development Review Committee [*Navy*] (CAAL)
PDRD .... Procurement Data Requirements Document (NASA)
PDRD .... Program Definition and Requirements Document (SSD)
PDRE .... People's Democratic Republic of Ethiopia
PDRF .... Passive Defense Recovery Force (MUGU)
PDRF .... Presbyterians for Democracy and Religious Freedom (EA)
PDRH .... Partido Democratico Revolucionario Hondureno [*Revolutionary Democratic Party of Honduras*] [*Political party*]
PdRK .... Pesikta de-Rav Kahana (BJA)
PDRL .... Permanent Disability Retired List
PDRL .... Procurement Data Requirements List (NASA)
PDRM .... Payload Deployment and Retrieval Mechanism [*NASA*]
PDRM .... Post-Depositional Remanent Magnetization [*Geophysics*]
PDRM .... Postdetrital Remanent Magnetization [*Geophysics*]
PDRMA .... Portable Drilling Rig Manufacturers Association [*Defunct*] (EA)
PDRP .... Program Data Requirement Plan [*Nuclear Regulatory Commission*] (NRCH)
PDRS .... Payload Deployment and Retrieval System [*NASA*] (GFGA)
PDRSS .... Payload Deployment and Retrieval System Simulation [*NASA*] (SSD)
PDRSTA .... Payload Deployment and Retrieval System Test Article [*NASA*] (NASA)
PDRY .... People's Democratic Republic of Yemen [*Political party*]
PDS .... Auburn/Lewiston, ME [*Location identifier FAA*] (FAAL)
PDS .... Pacific Data System (IAA)
PDS .... Package Data System (NASA)
PDS .... Packet Data Satellites [*Telecommunications*] (TSSD)
PDS .... Paid-during-Service [*Billing*]
PDS .... Pain Dysfunction Syndrome [*Medicine*] (AAMN)
PDS .... Parkinson's Disease Society [*British*]
PDS .... Paroxysmal Depolarizing Shift [*Physiology*]
PDS .... Partei des Demokratischen Sozialismus [*Party of Democratic Socialism*] [*Germany Political party*] (EAIO)
PDS .... Parti Democratique Senegalais [*Senegalese Democratic Party*] [*Political party*] (PPW)
PDS .... Partido Democrata Socialista [*Socialist Democratic Party*] [*Panama*] [*Political party*] (PPW)
PDS .... Partitioned Data Set [*or System*] [*Computer science*] (NASA)
PDS .... Partito Democratico della Sinistra [*Democratic Party of the Left*] [*Formerly, Italian Communist Party*] [*Political party*] (EY)
PDS .... Partito di Democrazia Socialista [*Socialist Democracy Party*] [*San Marino*] [*Political party*] (PPW)
PDS .... Party of Democratic Socialism [*Germany Political party*]
PDS .... Passive Detection System (NVT)
PDS .... Patient Data System [*Pharmacology*] (DAVI)
PDS .... Patient Decontamination Site [*Army*] (INF)
PDS .... Pediatric Surgery [*Medical specialty*] (DHSM)
PdS .... Pediatric Surgery [*Medicine*] (DMAA)
PDS .... Penultimate Digit Storage [*Telecommunications*] (TEL)
PDS .... Performer Design Sheet
PDS .... Perimeter Defense System (MCD)
PDS .... Periodicals Data System (NITA)
PDS .... Peritoneal Dialysis System [*nephrology*] (DAVI)
PDS .... Permanent Duty Station [*Air Force*] (AFM)
PDS .... Personal Data System (NITA)
PDS .... Personal Decision Series (HGAA)
PDS .... Personal Development Study [*Psychology*]
PDS .... Personnel Daily Summary [*Army*] (AABC)
PDS .... Personnel Data System [*Air Force*]
PDS .... Personnel Decontamination Station (MCD)
PDS .... Personnel Delivery System
PDS .... Petroleum Data System [*University of Oklahoma*] [*Databank*] (IID)
PDS .... Petroleum Data System [*Petroleum Information Corp.*] [*Information service or system*] (IID)
PDS .... Pharma-Dokumentations-Service [*Pharma Documentation Service*] [*Information service or system*] (IID)
PDS .... Phased Development Shuttle [*NASA*] (KSC)
PDS .... Phot Document Sensor [*Electronics*] (IAA)
PDS .... Photo-Digital Store
PDS .... Photodischarge Spectroscopy (MCD)
PDS .... Photothermal Deflection Spectroscopy (MCD)
PDS .... Piedras Negras [*Mexico*] [*Airport symbol*] (AD)
PDS .... Planning Data Sheet (KSC)
PDS .... Planning Data Systems [*Information service or system*] (IID)
PDS .... Plant Data System [*Nuclear energy*] (NRCH)
PDS .... Plasma-Derived Serum
PDS .... Plasma Display (MCD)
PDS .... Plotter Display System (DNAB)
PDS .... Pneumatic Distribution System
PDS .... Polydimethylsiloxane [*Organic chemistry*]
PDS .... Polydioxanone [*Organic chemistry*]
PDS .... Portable Data System (MCD)
PDS .... Portable Duress Sensor (MCD)
PDS .... Position-Determining System
PDS .... Post Design Services [*British*] (RDA)
PDS .... Power Density Spectra (IEEE)
PDS .... Power Distribution Specification (IAA)
PDS .... Power Distribution System [*or Subsystem*]
PDS .... Power Drive System
PDS .... Preadsorb-Dilute-Shake [*Phage growth method*]
PDS .... Precision Drilling Corp. [*NYSE symbol*] (SAG)
PDS .... Predialyzed Human Serum [*Medicine*] (MAE)
PDS .... Predocketed Special Project (NRCH)
PDS .... Premises Distribution System [*AT & T Corp.*]
PDS .... Priority Decision System (NITA)
PDS .... Priority Distribution System [*Military*] (AFM)
PDS .... Prisoner Detention System
PDS .... Private Database Service (NITA)
PDS .... Probability Distribution Subprogram [*Computer science*] (BUR)
PDS .... Problem Data System (MCD)
PD/S .... Problem Definition/Solution
PDS .... Problem Descriptor System
PDS .... Procedures Development Simulator (KSC)
PDS .... Processor Direct Slot [*Computer science*]
PDS .... Procurement Data Sheet
PDS .... Product Design Standard
PDS .... Production Data Sheet (MCD)
PDS .... Professional Development School
PDS .... Professional Development Seminar (HGAA)
PDS .... Professional Development System [*PC software*] [*Microsoft, Inc.*] (PCM)
PDS .... Program Data Sheets [*Army*] (AABC)
PDS .... Program Data Source (BUR)
PDS .... Program Design Specification (CAAL)
PDS .... Program Development Specialist
PDS .... Program Development System [*Computer science*]
PDS .... Program Distribution System
PDS .... Programmable Data Station [*or System*]
PDS .... Programming Documentation Standards [*Computer science*] (WDAA)
PDS .... Progressive Deterioration Scale
PDS .... Propellant Delivery System
PDS .... Propellant Dispersion System (MCD)
PDS .... Protected Distribution System [*Military*] (GFGA)
PDS .... Proximity Defense Systems [*Military*] (INF)
PdS .... Psychiatric Deviate, Subtle (DAVI)
PdS .... Psychopathic Deviate Subtle [*Psychology*]
PDS .... Pulse Doppler Seeker
PDS .... Punch Driver Selectric
PDS .... Purchasing Department Specification (MSA)
PDS .... Pyrotechnic Devices Simulator (SAA)
PDSA .... People's Dispensary for Sick Animals [*British*]
PDS-A .... Personnel Data System - Airmen [*Air Force*]
PDSA .... Predesign and Systems Analysis [*NASA*] (KSC)
PDSA .... Private Doctors' Society of South Australia
PDS-A(I) .... Personnel Data System - Airmen (Interim) [*Air Force*] (AFM)
PDSC .... PACOM [*Pacific Command*] Data Systems Center (MCD)
PDSC .... Parti Democrate et Social Chretien [*Zaire*] [*Political party*] (EY)
PDS-C .... Personnel Data System - Civilian [*Air Force*] (AFM)
PDSC .... Pressure Differential Scanning Calorimetry [*Analytical technique*]
PDSC .... Publishers Data Service Corp. [*Monterey, CA*]
PDSD .... Point Detonating Self-Destroying [*Projectile*]
PDSDD .... Plotting Display Subchannel Data Distributor (MCD)
PDSE .... Production Sample (AAG)
PDSF .... PDS Financial [*NASDAQ symbol*] (TTSB)
PDSF .... PDS Financial Corp. [*NASDAQ symbol*] (SAG)
PDS Fin .... PDS Financial Corp. [*Associated Press*] (SAG)
PDSI .... Palmer Drought Severity Index [*Meteorology*]
PDSI .... Performance Data Services, Inc. [*Falls Church, VA*] [*Software manufacture r*]
PDSI .... Portable Digital Strain Indicator
PDSK .... Petroleum Distribution System - Korea [*Army*] (MCD)
PDSM .... Powder Diffraction Search-Match System [*International Data Center*]
PDS/MAGEN .... Problem Descriptor System/Matrix Generation [*Programming language*] [*1965*] (CSR)
PDSMS .... Point Defense Surface Missile System
PDSMS .... Power Diffraction Search and Match System (PDAA)
PDS-O .... Personnel Data System - Officers [*Air Force*] (AFM)
PDSOF .... Public Domain Software on File [*Facts on File, Inc.*] [*Information service or system*] (IID)
PDSOR .... Positive Definitive Successive Over-Relaxation (PDAA)
PDSP .... Personnel Data System - Planning [*Air Force*] (AFM)
PDSPI .... Polyurethane Division, Society of the Plastics Industry (EA)
PDSQ .... Point Detonating Super-Quick Fuze (NATG)
PDS-R .... Parti Democratique Senegalais - Renovation [*Senegalese Democratic Party - Reform*] [*Political party*]
PDSS .... Particle Doppler Shift Spectrometer (PDAA)
PDSS .... Physical Disabilities Special Interest Section [*American Occupational Therapy Association*]
PDSS .... Post-Deployment Software System (MCD)
PDST .... Pacific Daylight Saving Time (KSC)
pdstl .... Pedestal (VRA)
PDSTT .... Pulse Doppler Single Target Track [*Military*] (CAAL)
PD Supp .... Per Diem Supplement (AAGC)
PDT .... Hancock [*John*] Patriot Premium Dividend, Inc. II [*NYSE symbol*] (SPSG)
PDT .... John Hancock Patr Prem Dv II [*NYSE symbol*] (TTSB)
PDT .... Pacific Daylight Time
PDT .... Panoramic Design Technique
PDT .... Parallel Data Transmission
PdT .... Parti du Travail [*Labor Party*] [*Switzerland Political party*] (PPE)
PDT .... PDT, Inc. [*Associated Press*] (SAG)
PDT .... Pendleton [*Oregon*] [*Airport symbol*] (OAG)
PDT .... Performance Demonstration Test
PDT .... Peripheral Data Transfer [*Telecommunications*] (IAA)
PDT .... Personal Data Transmitter [*From the movie "Aliens"*]
PDT .... Phenyldimethyltriazine [*Organic chemistry*] (AAMN)
PDT .... Photodynamic Therapy [*Oncology*]
PDT .... Physical Device Table (NITA)

PDT............ Picture Description Test (PDAA)
PDT............ Piedmont Airlines, Inc. [*ICAO designator*] (FAAC)
PDT............ Planned Data to Transportation [*DoD*]
PDT............ Plasma Display Terminal [*Computer science*]
PDT............ Pollable Data Terminal [*Bell System*]
PDT............ Population Doubling Time [*Cytology*]
PDT............ Post Alloy Diffused Transistor [*Electronics*] (IAA)
PDT............ Posting Data Transfer [*Air Force*] (AFM)
PDT............ Power Distribution Trailer (NATG)
PDT............ Predelivery Test (MCD)
PDT............ Predictor Display Technique
PDT............ President Mines [*Vancouver Stock Exchange symbol*]
PDT............ Processed Directional Transmission [*Military*] (NVT)
PDT............ Product Development Team [*Automotive project management*]
PDT............ Programmable Data Terminal [*Digital Equipment Corp.*] (IEEE)
PDT............ Published Data Tape [*A. C. Nielsen Co.*] [*A publication*] (WDMC)
PDT............ Pulse Delay Time
PDT............ (Pyridyl)diphenyltriazine [*Analytical chemistry*]
PDT-1......... Picatinny Arsenal Detonation Trap Number 1 [*Army*] (AABC)
PDTA.......... Production Tape (AAG)
PDTA.......... Professional Dance Teachers Association (EA)
PDTA.......... Propylenediaminetetraacetic Acid [*Organic chemistry*]
PDT & T...... Post-Delivery Test and Trials [*Military*] (CAAL)
PDTC.......... Philadelphia Depository Trust Co.
PDTF.......... Program Development and Test Facility [*Social Security Administration*]
PDTI........... PDT, Inc. [*NASDAQ symbol*] (SAG)
PDTMR....... Phalloidin Tetramethylrhodamine [*Biochemistry*]
PDTP.......... Plasma Display Touch Panel [*Computer science*]
PDTRST....... Podiatrist
PDTS.......... Procurement Document Tracking System (MCD)
PDTS.......... Program Development Tracking System [*Computer science*]
PDTS.......... Programmable Data Terminal Set [*Military*] (CAAL)
PDTTT......... Post-Delivery Test and Trial Team (MCD)
PDU............ Pacific Democrat Union (EAIO)
PDU............ Parti Dahomeen de l'Unite [*Dahomean Unity Party*] [*Benin*] [*Political party*]
PDU............ Parti Democrate Unifie [*Unified Democratic Party*] [*Name replaced by Section Voltaique de Rassemblement Burkina Faso*] [*Political party*]
PDU............ Paysandu [*Uruguay*] [*Airport symbol*] (OAG)
PDU............ Phase Demodulation Unit
PDU............ Photomultiplier Detector Unit (KSC)
PDU............ Pilot's Display Unit (MCD)
PDU............ Positive Displacement Unit [*Mechanical pumps*]
PDU............ Power Distribution Unit (AAG)
PDU............ Power Drive Unit (MCD)
PDU............ Pressure Distribution Unit
PDU............ Process Demonstration Unit [*Chemical engineering*]
PDU............ Process Development Unit [*Chemical engineering*]
PDU............ Production Distribution Unit (AAG)
PDU............ Programmable Delay Unit
PDU............ Programmable Diagnostic Unit [*TACOM*] [*Army*] (RDA)
PDU............ Project Development Unit [*Chemical engineering*]
PDU............ Projection Display Unit
PDU............ Protocol Data Unit [*Telecommunications*]
PDU............ Protocol Data Unit [*Electronic communications*]
PDU............ Pulsed Doppler Ultrasonography [*Radiology*] (DAVI)
PDU............ Pulse Detection Unit (NASA)
PDUFA........ Prescription Drug User Fee Act
PDUFC........ Pete Duel Universal Friendship Club (EAIO)
PdUP.......... Partito di Unita Proletaria per il Comunismo [*Democratic Party of Proletarian Unity for Communism*] [*Italy Political party*] (PPE)
PDur........... Papyri Durani (BJA)
PDUR.......... Predischarge Utilization Review [*Medicine*]
PDUS.......... Primary Data User Station [*Computer science*] (PDAA)
PDV............ Parcel Delivery Van
PDV............ Phocine Distemper Virus
PDV............ Polyhedra Derived Virus
PDV............ Ponderosa Ventures, Inc. [*Vancouver Stock Exchange symbol*]
PDV............ Premodulation Processor - Deep Space - Voice
PDV............ Pressure Disconnect Valve (MCD)
PDV............ Probability of Detection and Verification [*Military*] (CAAL)
PDV............ Prune Dwarf Virus
PDV............ Pyrotechnic Development Vehicle (PDAA)
PDVN.......... Power-Driven
PDVOR........ Precision Doppler VHF Omni-Range (PDAA)
PDW............ Evansville, IN [*Location identifier FAA*] (FAAL)
PDW............ Partially Delactosed Whey (OA)
PDW............ Personal Defense Weapon [*Army*] (INF)
PDW............ Personal Design Workstation (DGA)
PDW............ Platelet Distribution Width [*Hematology*]
PDW............ Priority Delayed Weather [*NWS*] (FAAC)
PDWHF........ Platelet-Derived Wound-Healing Factor [*Biochemistry*]
PDWP.......... Partially Delactosed Whey Powder (OA)
PDX............ Passive Dosimeter Experiment (KSC)
PDX............ Place Decrement in Index
PDX............ Poloidal Divertor Experiment [*Princeton University*]
PDX............ Portland [*Oregon*] [*Airport symbol*] (OAG)
PDX............ Prado Explorations Ltd. [*Toronto Stock Exchange symbol*]
PDX............ Private Digital Exchange
PDX............ Probable Diagnosis (DAVI)
PDX............ Program Development Executive (MHDI)
PDY............ Piccadilly Resources Ltd. [*Vancouver Stock Exchange symbol*]
PDY............ Principal Duty [*Military*]
PDYN.......... Prodynorphin [*Biochemistry*]
PDZ............ Ontario, CA [*Location identifier FAA*] (FAAL)
PDZ............ Pedernales [*Venezuela*] [*Airport symbol*] (OAG)
PE............... British Aircraft Corp. Ltd. [*ICAO aircraft manufacturer identifier*] (ICAO)
PE............... Easton Area Public Library, Easton, PA [*Library symbol Library of Congress*] (LCLS)
PE............... Edinburgh Pharmacopoeia [*British*] (DAVI)
PE............... Ice Pellets [*Meteorology*]
PE............... Pacific Electric Railway [*AAR code*]
PE............... Page-End Character [*Computer science*]
PE............... Paper Electrophoresis [*Medicine*] (MAE)
PE............... Parabolic Equation
PE............... Parity Error
PE............... Partes Aequales [*Equal Parts*] [*Pharmacy*]
PE............... Patrol Vessel, Eagle [*Eagle boat*] [*Navy symbol Obsolete*]
PE............... Peacetime Establishment [*Military*] (NATG)
Pe............... Peclet Number [*IUPAC*]
PE............... PECO Energy [*Formerly, Philadelphia Electric Co.*] [*NYSE symbol*] (SPSG)
PE............... Pectinesterase [*Also, PME*] [*An enzyme*]
PE............... Pediatrics (DAVI)
Pe............... Pelagius [*Deceased, 1232*] [*Authority cited in pre-1607 legal work*] (DSA)
pe............... Pen (VRA)
PE............... Penile Erection [*Medicine*] (DMAA)
PE............... Pentaeythrol (IAA)
Pe............... Pentyl [*Biochemistry*]
PE............... People Express [*ICAO designator*] (AD)
PE............... Pericardial Effusion [*Cardiology*] (DAVI)
PE............... Period Ending
PE............... Periodic (AAG)
PE............... Peripheral Equipment (AAG)
PE............... Periscope
PE............... Peritoneal Exudate [*Medicine*]
PE............... Perkin Elmer Corp.
PE............... Permanent Echo [*RADAR*]
PE............... Permanent Error (IAA)
PE............... Permissible Error (ADA)
PE............... Perry Ellis [*Fashion designer, 1940-86*]
PE............... Persistent Estrus [*Endocrinology*]
PE............... Personal Effects
PE............... Personal Equipment
PE............... Personnel, Enlisted [*or Enlisted Personnel Division*] [*Coast Guard*]
PE............... Personnel Equipment [*Air Force*] (AFM)
PE............... Personnel Equivalent [*DoD*]
PE............... Peru [*ANSI two-letter standard code*] (CNC)
pe............... Peru [*MARC country of publication code Library of Congress*] (LCCP)
Pe............... Perylene [*Organic chemistry*] (AAMN)
PE............... Peterborough [*Postcode*] (ODBW)
PE............... Petroleum Economist [*London*] [*A publication*] (BJA)
PE............... Petroleum Engineer
Pe............... Petrus de Bellapertica [*Deceased, 1308*] [*Authority cited in pre-1607 legal work*] (DSA)
Pe............... Petrus Hispanus [*Authority cited in pre-1607 legal work*] (DSA)
PE............... Phakoemulsification [*Ophthalmology*] (DAVI)
PE............... Pharmacopaeia Edinensis [*Edinburgh Pharmacopoeia*] [*A publication*] (ROG)
PE............... Pharyngoesophageal [*Medicine*]
PE............... Phase Encoding [*Magnetic tape recording*] [*Computer science*] (MDG)
PE............... Phenylephrine
PE............... Philadelphia Stock Exchange (CDAI)
PE............... Phosphatidylethanolamine [*Biochemistry*]
PE............... Photoelectric
PE............... Photoelectron (IAA)
PE............... Photoemission [*Physics*]
PE............... Photographic Effect (MAE)
PE............... Photon Echo [*Spectroscopy*]
PE............... Phycoerythrin [*Biochemistry*]
PE............... Physical Education
PE............... Physical Evaluation [*Medicine*] (MAE)
PE............... Physical Examination
PE............... Physiological Ecology
PE............... Pictorial Eleven [*Later, PES*] [*An association*] (EA)
PE............... Pigment Epithelium [*of the retina*]
PE............... Pilot Equalizer (IAA)
PE............... Pilot Error
PE............... Pinion End
PE............... Pistol Expert
PE............... Plain Edges [*Graphic arts*] (DGA)
PE............... Plain End [*Lumber*] (DAC)
PE............... Planetary Explorer [*NASA*]
PE............... Planification de l'Emploi [*Canadian Jobs Strategy - CJS*]
P/E............. Planning Economics Group, Boston [*Information service or system*] (IID)
PE............... Planning Estimate
PE............... Plant Engineering (AAG)
PE............... Plant Equipment (MCD)
PE............... Plant Extrusion (OA)
PE............... Plasma Emission [*Spectrophotometry*]
PE............... Plasma Exchange [*Medicine*]
PE............... Plastic Explosive (NATG)
PE............... Pleural Effusion [*Medicine*]
PE............... Pneumatic Equalization [*Tube*] [*Otorhinolaryngology*] (DAVI)

PE ... Pocket Edition (WDAA)
PE ... Pollen Equivalent [*Immunology*]
PE ... Polyelectrolyte [*Organic chemistry*]
PE ... Polyethylene [*Organic chemistry*]
PE ... Population Equivalent (FFDE)
PE ... Porcelain Enamel [*Technical drawings*]
PE ... Portable Executable
PE ... Portable Executable File [*Computer science*]
PE ... Port Engineer (DNAB)
PE ... Port of Embarkation [*Military*]
PE ... Position Effect [*Parapsychology*]
PE ... Position Error
PE ... Positive Expulsion (SAA)
PE ... Positives and Etching (DGA)
PE ... Post Engineer [*Army*] (AABC)
PE ... Post Exchange [*Marine Corps*]
PE ... Postexposure [*Medicine*]
PE ... Potato Eaters (EA)
PE ... Potential Energy
PE ... Potential Evapotranspiration (DICI)
PE ... Potential Excess [*of stock*] [*DoD*]
PE ... Powdered Extract [*Pharmacy*]
PE ... Power Equipment [*Military*] (IAA)
PE ... Practical Exercise
P-E ... Precipitation-Evaporation
PE ... Pre-Eclampsia [*Medicine*]
PE ... Pre-Emption [*Telecommunications*] (TEL)
PE ... Preliminary Evaluation
PE ... Preliminary Exploitation (MCD)
PE ... Prepaid Expense [*Finance*] (MHDW)
PE ... Presidential Exemption [*Environmental Protection Agency*]
PE ... Presiding Elder
PE ... Pressure Enclosure (MCD)
PE ... Pressure Equalization [*Tube*] [*Otorhinolaryngology*] (DAVI)
PE ... Pressure Equalizing [*Tube*] [*Otorhinolaryngology*] (DAVI)
Pe ... Pressure on Expiration [*Medicine*]
PE ... Priced Exhibit (MCD)
P/E ... Price [*or Profit*]/Earnings Ratio [*Relation between price of a company's stock and its annual net income*]
PE ... Price Earnings Ratio [*Investment term*] (DFIT)
PE ... Primary Education (AIE)
PE ... Primary Electricity
PE ... Prime Equipment
PE ... Primitive Endoderm [*Cytology*]
PE ... Primitive Equation
PE ... Prince Edward Island [*Canadian province*] [*Postal code*]
PE ... Principal Engineer (AAG)
PE ... Printer's Error
PE ... Probable Error [*Statistics*]
PE ... Procedures Evaluation [*DoD*]
PE ... Processing Element [*of central processing unit*]
PE ... Procurement Executive [*British*]
PE ... Production Engineering
PE ... Production Engineering Division [*Frankford Arsenal*] [*Philadelphia, PA*]
PE ... Production Executive [*British*]
P/E ... Professional and Executive [*Employment register*] [*British*]
PE ... Professional Education (AFM)
PE ... Professional Engineer
PE ... Program Element (AFM)
PE ... Program Evaluation (OICC)
PE ... Programmed Exciter
PE ... Project Engineer
PE ... Project Equality (EA)
PE ... Prometheus-Europe [*Paris, France*] (EAIO)
PE ... Proponent Evaluation (MCD)
PE ... Protected Environment
PE ... Protect Enable [*Computer science*] (PCM)
PE ... Protein Electrophoresis [*Biochemistry*] (DAVI)
PE ... Protestant Episcopal
PE ... Proteus Engine [*Hovercraft*]
PE ... Proton Event
PE ... Pseudomonas Exotoxin [*Bacterial toxin*]
PE ... Pulley End
PE ... Pulmonary Edema [*Medicine*]
PE ... Pulmonary Effusion [*Medicine*]
PE ... Pulmonary Embolism [*Medicine*]
PE ... Pulse Echo [*Materials research*]
PE ... Pulse Encoding [*Computer science*]
PE ... Purchased Equipment
PE ... Pyroelectric
Pe ... Warner-Lambert Pharmaceutical Co. [*Research code symbol*]
PEA ... Pan Europeenne Air Service [*France ICAO designator*] (FAAC)
PEA ... Papillary Eccrine Adenoma [*Oncology*]
PEA ... Parking Enforcement Aide (ECON)
PEA ... Pattern Error Analysis
PEA ... Patterson Experimental Array (MCD)
PEA ... Payload Enclosure Assembly (MCD)
Pea ... Peake's English Nisi Prius Reports [*1790-1812*] [*A publication*] (DLA)
PEA ... Pella, IA [*Location identifier FAA*] (FAAL)
PEA ... Penneshaw [*Australia Airport symbol*] (OAG)
PEA ... Pennsylvania Electric Association
PEA ... Phenethyl Alcohol [*Organic chemistry*]
PEA ... Phenylethanolamine [*Organic chemistry*]
PEA ... Phenylethylamine [*Biochemistry*]
PEA ... Phosphoethanolamine [*Organic chemistry*]
PE(A) ... Physical Education (Association) [*British*]
PEA ... Pilot's Employment Agency
PEA ... Pitch Error Amplifier
PEA ... Plant Engineering Agency
PEA ... Plastics Engineers Association [*Defunct*] (EA)
PEA ... Platform Electronics Assembly (KSC)
PEA ... Polish Ex-Servicemen's Association [*Australia*]
PEA ... Poly(ethyl Acrylate) [*Organic chemistry*]
PEA ... Portuguese East Africa [*Mozambique*]
PEA ... Potash Export Association (EA)
PEA ... Poultry Education Association [*British*] (BI)
PEA ... Power Excursion Accident [*Nuclear energy*] (NUCP)
PEA ... Preliminary Environmental Assessment (MCD)
PEA ... Primary Expense Account
PEA ... Private Employment Agency (OICC)
PEA ... Process Environmental Analysis
PEA ... Process Equipment Accessory (MCD)
PEA ... Procurement Executives Association (AAGC)
PEA ... Program Element Administrator [*Navy*] (NG)
PEA ... Progressive Education Association [*Defunct*]
PEA ... Public Education Association
PEA ... Push-Effective Address [*Computer science*] (IEEE)
PEA ... Pyridylethylamine [*Organic chemistry*]
Pea (2) ... Peake's Additional Cases Nisi Prius [*170 English Reprint*] [*1795-1812*] [*A publication*] (DLA)
PEAA ... Program Elements Activity Accounts (MCD)
P/EA(A)3 ... Probationary Electrical Artificer (Air) 3rd Class [*British military*] (DMA)
Pea Add Cas ... Peake's English Nisi Prius Reports [*Vol. 2*] [*A publication*] (DLA)
Peab L Rev ... Peabody Law Review [*A publication*] (DLA)
Peabody Inst ... Peabody Institute of The Johns Hopkins University (GAGS)
PEAC ... Pharmaceutical Education Advisory Committee [*Australia*]
PEAC ... Photoelectric Alignment Collimator (IAA)
PEAC ... Photoelectric Auto Collimator
PEAC ... Photoelectroanalytical Chemistry
PEAC ... Police Education Advisory Council [*New South Wales, Australia*]
PEACE ... People Emerging Against Corrupt Establishments [*Underground military newspaper*]
PEACE ... Project Evaluation and Assistance, Civil Engineering [*Air Force*]
PEACESAT ... Pan-Pacific Editing and Communication Experiment by Satellite (NITA)
PEACESAT ... Pan-Pacific Educational and Cultural Exchange by Satellite Program [*University of Hawaii, Manoa*] [*Research center*] (RCD)
PEACESAT ... Pan-Pacific Education and Communication Experiments by Satellites [*University of Hawaii*] [*NASA*]
PEACU ... Plastic Energy Absorption in Compression Unit (IEEE)
PEAD ... Presidential Emergency Action Document
PEADS ... Presidential Emergency Action Direction System (MCD)
PEAI ... Physical Education Association of Ireland (EAIO)
PEAK ... Peak Technologies Group, Inc. [*NASDAQ symbol*] (SAG)
PEAK ... Peak Technologies Grp [*NASDAQ symbol*] (TTSB)
Peake ... Peake's Cases [*1790-1812*] [*A publication*] (DLA)
Peake Add Cas ... Peake's Additional Cases Nisi Prius [*1795-1812*] [*A publication*] (DLA)
Peake Ev ... Peake on the Law of Evidence [*A publication*] (DLA)
Peake NP ... Peake's English Nisi Prius Cases [*170 English Reprint*] [*A publication*] (DLA)
Peake NP Add Cas ... Peake's Additional Cases Nisi Prius [*170 English Reprint*] [*England*] [*A publication*] (DLA)
Peake NP Add Cas (Eng) ... Peake's Additional Cases Nisi Prius [*170 English Reprint*] [*England*] [*A publication*] (DLA)
Peake NP Cas ... Peake's English Nisi Prius Cases [*170 English Reprint*] [*1790-1812*] [*A publication*] (DLA)
Peake NP Cas (Eng) ... Peake's English Nisi Prius Cases [*170 English Reprint*] [*A publication*] (DLA)
PeakTch ... Peak Technologies Group, Inc. [*Associated Press*] (SAG)
PEAM ... Personal Electronic Aid for Maintenance [*Military*]
Pea MS ... Peachey on Marriage Settlements [*1860*] [*A publication*] (DLA)
PEAMUSE ... Peabody Museum of Archaeology and Ethnology [*Harvard University*] [*Research center*] (RCD)
PE & M ... Plant Engineering and Maintenance (MCD)
PEAP ... Pad Emergency Air Pack [*NASA*] (KSC)
PEAP ... Pesticide Education and Action Project (EA)
PEAP ... Positive End-Airway Pressure [*Medicine*] (DMAA)
PEAP ... Principal Error Axis for Position
PEAP ... Program Evaluation Analysis Plan (MCD)
PeAR ... Die Provinzeinteilung des Assyrischen Reiches [*A publication*] (BJA)
Pearce CC ... Pearce's Reports in Dearsley's English Crown Cases [*A publication*] (DLA)
PEARL ... Committee for Public Education and Religious Liberty (EA)
PEARL ... Performance Evaluation of Amplifiers from a Remote Location
PEARL ... Periodical Enquiry Acquisition and Registration Locally (NITA)
PEARL ... Periodicals Automation, Rand Library
PEARL ... Personal Equipment and Rescue/Survivable Lowdown (MCD)
PEARL ... Process and Experiment Automation Real-Time Language [*Computer science*]
PEARL ... Program for EPS [*Electrical Power System*] Analysis and Rapid Look-Ahead [*NASA computer program*]
PEARL ... Programmed Editor and Automated Resources for Learning
PEARLA ... Pupils Equal and React to Light and Accomodation [*Medicine*]
Pears ... Pearson's Reports [*1850-80*] [*Pennsylvania*] [*A publication*] (DLA)
Pearson ... Pearson's Common Pleas [*Pennsylvania*] [*A publication*] (DLA)
Pears (PA) ... Pearson's Reports [*1850-80*] [*Pennsylvania*] [*A publication*] (DLA)
PEART ... Passive Electronic Advanced Receiver (MCD)
pearwd ... Pear Tree Wood (VRA)

PEAS Pacific's Electronics Acquisition Service (NITA)
PEAS Physical Estimation and Attraction Scales
PEAS Policy and External Affairs Staff [*Environmental Protection Agency*] (GFGA)
PEAS Practical Engineering Applications Software (NITA)
PEAS Presbyterian Educational Association of the South [*Defunct*] (EA)
Pease Pease Oil & Gas Co. [*Associated Press*] (SAG)
PeaseOG Pease Oil & Gas Co. [*Associated Press*] (SAG)
PEAT Phenylethanolaminotetralin [*Organic chemistry*]
PEAT Pricing Evaluation for Audit Technique [*Finance*]
PEAT Programme Elargi d'Assistance Technique [*Expanded Program of Technical Assistance*] [*United Nations*]
PEAT Programmer Exercised Autopilot Test (AAG)
PEAV Principal Error Axis for Velocity
PE B Bachelor of Pedagogy (ROG)
Pe B Bachelor of Pediatrics
PEB Parametric Empirical Bayes [*Statistics*]
PEB Party Election Broadcast [*British*] (BARN)
PEB PCIA Expansion Bus [*Computer science*]
PEB Pebble [*Jewelry*] (ROG)
PEB Pebble Gold Resources [*Vancouver Stock Exchange symbol*]
PEB Pensioners' Employment Bureau [*British*]
PEB Performance Evaluation Board [*NASA*] (MCD)
PEB Phosphate Ester Base (PDAA)
PEB Phototype Environment Buoy (PDAA)
PEB Phycoerythrobilin [*Biochemistry*]
PEB Physical Evaluation Board [*Military*]
PEB Plasma Electron Beam (PDAA)
PEB Population-Environment Balance (EA)
PEB Porcelain Enamel Bath [*Classified advertising*] (ADA)
PEB Positive Expulsion Bladder
PEB Postexposure Baking [*Microlithography*]
PEB Pre-Expanded Bin (DNAB)
PEB Presidential Emergency Board
PEB Production Efficiency Board [*British World War II*]
PEB Program Element Breakdown [*Computer science*] (IAA)
PEB Propulsion Examining Board [*Navy*] (NVT)
PEB Prototype Environmental Buoy [*Marine science*] (MSC)
PEB Psycho-Educational Battery [*Educational test*]
PEB Pulmonary Ectopic Beat [*Cardiology*]
PEB Pulsed Electron Beam (IEEE)
PEBA Polyether Block Amide [*Plastics technology*]
PEBA Pulsed Electron Beam Annealer [*Photovoltaic energy systems*]
PEBA Purified Extract of Brucella abortus
PEBAB Para-(Ethoxybenzylidene)aminobenzonitrile [*Also, EBCA*] [*Organic chemistry*]
PEB & B Porcelain Enamel Bath and Basin [*Classified advertising*] (ADA)
PEBB Public Employees Blanket Bond
PeBcCH Peoples Bancorp, Inc. (Ohio) [*Associated Press*] (SAG)
PEBCO Program Evaluation and Budget Committee [*American Library Association*]
PEBD Pay Entry Base Date
PEBES Personal Earning and Benefit Estimate Statement [*Social Security Administration*]
PEBG Phenethylbiguanide [*Same as PEDG*] [*Antidiabetic compound*]
PEBH Physical Evaluation Board Hospital [*Military*]
PEBK Peoples Bank [*Catawba, NC*] [*NASDAQ symbol*] (NQ)
PEBL Port Everglades Belt Line Railway [*AAR code Obsolete*]
PEBLO Physical Evaluation Board Liaison Officer [*Air Force*] (AFM)
PEBO Peoples Bancorp [*NASDAQ symbol*] (TTSB)
PEBO Peoples Bancorp, Inc. (Ohio) [*NASDAQ symbol*] (SAG)
PEBP Patient Escorted by Police (DMAA)
PEBS Pulsed Electron Beam Source (MCD)
PEBV Pea Early-Browning Virus [*Plant pathology*]
PEC American Irish Political Education Committee (EA)
PEc Ellwood City Area Public Library, Ellwood City, PA [*Library symbol Library of Congress*] (LCLS)
PEC IEEE Power Electronics Council (EA)
PEC Pacific Command Electronic Intelligence Center (MCD)
PEC Pacific East Asia Cargo Airline, Inc. [*Philippines*] [*ICAO designator*] (FAAC)
PEC Pacific Economic Community (FEA)
PEC Packaged Electronic Circuit [*Computer science*] (IAA)
PEC Palestine Economic Commission
PEC Panasonic Energy Corp. [*Vancouver Stock Exchange symbol*]
PEC Panel Electronic Circuit (EECA)
PEC Passive Equipment Cabinet [*Military*] (CAAL)
PEC Patient Evaluation Center (DAVI)
PEC Peak Electrode Current
PEC PEC Israel Economic Corp. [*Associated Press*] (SAG)
PEC Pectoral [*Lungs and Chest*] [*Medicine*] (ROG)
PEC Pedal Excretory Cell
PEC Pelican [*Alaska*] [*Airport symbol*] (OAG)
PEC Penelec Capital Ltd. [*NYSE symbol*] (SAG)
PEC Perfil de Evaluacion del Comportamiento [*Standardized test of elementary through high school students' behavior at school, at home, and with peers*]
PEC Peritoneal Exudate Cells [*Hematology*]
PEC Perkin-Elmer Corp. (MCD)
PEC Perris [*California*] [*Seismograph station code, US Geological Survey*] (SEIS)
PEC Persistent Early Curvature
PEC Personal Education Counseling (DNAB)
PEC Personal Effects Coverage [*Insurance*]
PEC Petro-Canada
PEC Phenylene Ether Copolymer [*Organic chemistry*]
PEC Photoelectric Cell
PEC Photoelectrochemical Cell [*Energy conversion device*]
PEC Photoelectrochromic [*Chemistry*]
PEC Physics, Engineering, and Chemistry (AAG)
PEC Pigmented Emulsified Creosote
PEC Pilot Error Correction (IAA)
PEC Plain English Campaign [*British*] (DBA)
PEC Planetary Entry Capsule [*Aerospace*]
PEC Plant Equipment Codes [*DoD*]
PEC Platform Electron Card [*Electronics*] (OA)
PEC Polyestercarbonate [*Organic chemistry*]
PEC Position Error Correction (DA)
PEC Positive Engagement Clutch
PEC Potasse et Engrais Chimiques
PEC Potential Enviromental Concentration [*Pollution technology*]
PEC Predicted Environmental Concentration (DCTA)
PEC Presbyterian Evangelical Coalition (EA)
PEC Previous Element Coding
PEC Production Equipment Code [*Military*]
PEC Production Executive Committee
PEC Program Element Code (AFM)
PEC Program Environment Control
PEC Program Evaluation Center [*Navy*] (AFIT)
PEC Propulsion Environmental Chamber
PEC Protestant Episcopal Church (WDAA)
PEC Prova Elementi Combustibili [*An Italian fast reactor*]
PEC Pugwash Etudiant du Canada
PEC Pyridylethylcysteine [*Biochemistry*]
PEC Pyrogenic Exotoxin C [*Medicine*]
PECA Petroleum Equipment Contractors Association (EA)
Peca Petrus de Bellapertica [*Deceased, 1308*] [*Authority cited in pre-1607 legal work*] (DSA)
PECA Process Engineers and Constructors' Association [*Australia*]
PECAM Platelet-Endothelial Cell Adhesion Molecule [*Cytology*]
PECAN Pulse Envelop Correlation Air Navigation
PE CARD Production Estimate Card (MSA)
PECBI Professional Engineers Conference Board for Industry (EA)
PECC Pacific Economic Cooperation Conference (DOMA)
PECC Panel of Experts on Climatic Change [*WMO*] (MSC)
PECC Precanceled Envelope Collectors Club (EA)
PECC Product Engineering Control Center [*Telecommunications*] (TEL)
PECDAR Palestine Economic Council for Development and Reconstruction (ECON)
PECDS Professional Engineering Career Development Series [*Book series*]
PECE Proposed Engineering Change Estimate
PECF Pseudoextracellular Fluid [*for biocompatibility testing*]
PECFA Presidential Election Campaign Fund Act of 1966
Pecho Prostatic Echogram [*Medicine*] (AAMN)
PECI Preliminary Equipment Component Index [*or Inventory*]
PECI Productivity Enhancing Capital Investment [*DoD*]
PECIACESC Permanent Executive Committee of the Inter-American Council for Education, Science, and Culture
PECIAECOSOC Permanent Executive Committee of the Inter-American Economic and Social Council
PECIP Productivity Enhancing Capital Investment Program (MCD)
Peck Peck's Reports [*24-30 Illinois*] [*A publication*] (DLA)
Peck Peck's Reports [*7 Tennessee*] [*1921-24*] [*A publication*] (DLA)
Peck Peckwell's English Election Cases [*1802-06*] [*A publication*] (DLA)
Peck El Cas Peckwell's English Election Cases [*A publication*] (DLA)
Peck Elec Cas Peckwell's English Election Cases [*1802-06*] [*A publication*] (DLA)
Peck (Ill) Peck's Reports, Illinois Supreme Court Reports [*11-22, 24-30*] [*A publication*] (DLA)
Peck (Tenn) Peck's Reports [*7 Tennessee*] [*A publication*] (DLA)
Peck Tr Peck's Trial (Impeachment) [*A publication*] (DLA)
Peckw Peckwell's English Election Cases [*A publication*] (DLA)
PECL Preliminary Engineering Configuration List
PECM Passive Electronics Countermeasures [*Military*] (NG)
PECM Preliminary Engineering Change Memorandum [*Air Force*] (CET)
PECO Pays d'Europe Centrale et Orientale (ECON)
PECO PECO Energy [*Associated Press*] (SAG)
PECO Pecos National Monument
PECO$_2$ Mixed Expired Carbon Dioxide Tension [*Medicine*] (DAVI)
PECOS Pays D'Europe Centrale et Orientale
PECOS Pentagon Computer Operations Support (MCD)
PECOS Program Environment Checkout System
PECOS Project Evaluation and Control System (MCD)
PECOS Project Evaluation and Cost Optimization System (IAA)
PECP Preliminary Engineering Change Proposal
PECPrZ Penelec Capital L.P. 'MIPS' [*NYSE symbol*] (TTSB)
PECR Program Error Correction Report
Pe Cri Petrus Crispanus [*Authority cited in pre-1607 legal work*] (DSA)
PECS Plant Engineering Check Sheet (AAG)
PECS Portable Environmental Control System [*NASA*]
PECS Printers' Estimating and Costing System (DGA)
PECT Pectori [*To the Chest*] [*Pharmacy*]
PECTFE Polyethylene-Chlorotrifluoroethylene [*Organic chemistry*]
PECUL Peculiar (ROG)
PECUS Personal Engineering Computer User's Society [*Defunct*] (EA)
PECUSA Presidential Ethics Commission (NADA)
PECUY Pecuniary (ROG)
PECVD Plasma-Enhanced Chemical Vapor Deposition [*Coating technology*]
PECWBS Proposed Extended Contract Work Breakdown Structure [*Military*]
PECWG Piaster Expenditure Control Working Group [*Military*]
PED Doctor of Physical Education (PGP)

PED.......... Patient Examined by Doctor (DMAA)
PED.......... Pedagogue
PED.......... Pedal
PED.......... Peddler [*or Peddling*] [*FBI standardized term*]
PED.......... Pedestal (AAG)
PED.......... Pedestrian
PED.......... Pediatric Emergency Department (DMAA)
PED.......... Pediatrician
PED.......... Pediatrics (AABC)
PED.......... Pedlary (ROG)
PED.......... Pedro Aguirre Cerda [*Antarctica*] [*Seismograph station code, US Geological Survey Closed*] (SEIS)
PED.......... Period End Date (MCD)
PED.......... Personal Equipment Data [*Computer science*] (IAA)
PED.......... Personnel Equipment Data [*Army*] (IAA)
PED.......... Phosphorus Enhanced Diffusion (IAA)
PED.......... Photoemission Diode
PEd.......... Physical Education
PED.......... Pink-Eyed Dilution [*Medicine*] (DMAA)
PED.......... Positive Expulsion Device
PED.......... Production Eligibility Date (MUGU)
PED.......... Production Engineering Division [*University of Wisconsin - Madison*] [*Research center*] (RCD)
PED.......... Program Element Description
PED.......... Program Element Directive
PED.......... Program Evaluation Division [*Environmental Protection Agency*] (GFGA)
PED.......... Program Execution Directive (AAG)
PED.......... Promotion Eligibility Date [*Military*]
PED.......... Proton-Enhanced Diffusion
PED.......... Public Employee Department (of AFL-CIO) (EA)
PEd.......... Pulmonary Edema [*Medicine*]
PED.......... Pulse Edge Discrimination (OA)
PED.......... Pure Edge Dislocation
PED.......... Pyramid Element Designator
PED.......... Springfield, TN [*Location identifier FAA*] (FAAL)
PEDA.......... Pedal Artery
PEDA.......... Personnel Equipment Data Analysis
Ped B.......... Bachelor of Pedagogy
PED B.......... Bachelor of Pediatrics (WDAA)
PEDB.......... Page Element Data Base [*Printing*] (DGA)
PEDB.......... Payload Engineering Data Base [*NASA*] (SSD)
PEDB.......... Process Engineering Database
PEDC.......... Personal Effects Distribution Center
PEDC.......... Professional Educational Development Corp. [*An association*] (EA)
PEDCUG....... Planning Engineers Desktop Computer Users Group (EA)
Ped D.......... Doctor of Pedagogy
PEDD.......... Program Element Descriptive Data (CAAL)
PEddyB........ Baldwin Locomotive Works, Eddystone, PA [*Library symbol Library of Congress Obsolete*] (LCLS)
Pe de Ancar... Petrus de Ancharano [*Deceased, 1416*] [*Authority cited in pre-1607 legal work*] (DSA)
Pe de Anch... Petrus de Ancharano [*Deceased, 1416*] [*Authority cited in pre-1607 legal work*] (DSA)
Pe de Ancha... Petrus de Ancharano [*Deceased, 1416*] [*Authority cited in pre-1607 legal work*] (DSA)
Pe de Bel.... Petrus de Bellapertica [*Deceased, 1308*] [*Authority cited in pre-1607 legal work*] (DSA)
Pe de Belper... Petrus de Bellapertica [*Deceased, 1308*] [*Authority cited in pre-1607 legal work*] (DSA)
Pe de Bepe... Petrus de Bellapertica [*Deceased, 1308*] [*Authority cited in pre-1607 legal work*] (DSA)
Pe de Blpti... Petrus de Bellapertica [*Deceased, 1308*] [*Authority cited in pre-1607 legal work*] (DSA)
Pe de Pal.... Pierre de la Palu [*Deceased, 1342*] [*Authority cited in pre-1607 legal work*] (DSA)
Pe de Sal.... Petrus de Salinis [*Flourished, 13th century*] [*Authority cited in pre-1607 legal work*] (DSA)
Pe de Samp... Petrus de Sampsone [*Flourished, 1246-58*] [*Authority cited in pre-1607 legal work*] (DSA)
PEDET.......... Pedetemptim [*Gradually*] [*Pharmacy*]
PEDF.......... Pigment Epithelium-Derived Factor [*Medicine*] (DMAA)
PEDF.......... Potential-Energy Distribution Function [*Physical chemistry*]
PEDG.......... Phenethyldiguanide [*Same as PEBG*] [*Antidiabetic compound*]
PEDI.......... Pediatrics [*Medicine*] (DHSM)
Pediatric...... Pediatric Services of America, Inc. [*Associated Press*] (SAG)
PEDIN.......... National Petroleum Exploration Database [*Australia*]
PEDIN.......... Peapod Dinghy
PE Dir.......... Director of Physical Education (PGP)
PE Dir.......... Physical Education Director
PEdiS.......... Edinboro State College, Edinboro, PA [*Library symbol Library of Congress*] (LCLS)
PEDL.......... Pedicel Length [*Botany*]
Ped M.......... Master of Pedagogy
pedm.......... Pediment (VRA)
PEDMAN...... PACFLT [*Pacific Fleet*] Enlisted Personnel Distribution Manual (CINC)
PEDMS.......... Portable and Extensible Data Management System (IAA)
PEDN.......... Planned Event Discrepancy Notification [*NASA*] (KSC)
PEDOL.......... Pedology
PEDP.......... Pacific Energy Development Program [*Fiji*] [*United Nations*]
PEDRA.......... Palestine Economic Development and Reconstruction Agency (ECON)
PEDRO.......... Pneumatic Energy Detector with Remote Optics
PEDRO.......... Pride, Efficiency, Dedication, Reliability, and Order (DNAB)
PEDRTC....... Pediatric
PEDS.......... Packaging Engineering Data System (AFM)
PeDS.......... Pediatric Drug Surveillance [*Program*] (DAVI)
PeDS.......... Pediatric Drug Surveillance Program (BABM)
PEDS.......... Pediatrics
PEDS.......... Peltier Effect Diffusion Separation [*Physical chemistry*]
PEDS.......... Philips Engineering and Development System (NITA)
PEDS.......... Pilgrim Edward Doty Society (EA)
PEDS.......... Program Element Descriptive Summary (CAAL)
PEDS.......... Protective Equipment Decontamination Section [*Nuclear energy*] (NRCH)
PEDSTL........ Pedestal [*Freight*]
PEDT.......... Pendant [*Jewelry*] (ROG)
PEDT.......... Peridot [*Jewelry*] (ROG)
PEDTRC........ Pediatric
PEDUC.......... Professeurs d'Economie Domestique des Universites Canadiennes [*Canadian University Teachers of Home Economics - CUTHE*]
PEDX.......... Pediatrix Medical Group [*NASDAQ symbol*] (TTSB)
PEDX.......... Pediatrix Medical Group, Inc. [*NASDAQ symbol*] (SAG)
PEE.......... Phosphate-Eliminating Enzyme (DMAA)
PEE.......... Photoelectron Emission [*Also, OSEE*]
PEE.......... Photoemission Effect
PEE.......... Pressure Environmental Equipment (NVT)
PEE.......... Program Estimating Equation
PEE.......... Proof and Experimental Establishment [*British*]
PEE.......... Talkeetna, AK [*Location identifier FAA*] (FAAL)
PEEA.......... (Phenyl)(ethyl)ethanolamine [*Organic chemistry*]
PEEC.......... Personnel Emergency Estimator Capability
PEEC.......... Programmable Electronic Engine Control [*Automotive engineering*]
PEEC.......... Project for an Energy-Enriched Curriculum [*Department of Energy*]
PEEIC.......... Programme des Economies d'Energie dans l'Industrie Canadienne
PEEK.......... Peekskill Financial [*NASDAQ symbol*] (TTSB)
PEEK.......... Peekskill Financial Corp. [*NASDAQ symbol*] (SAG)
PEEK.......... People for the Enjoyment of Eyeballing Knees [*Group opposing below-the-knee fashions introduced in 1970*]
PEEK.......... Periodically Elevated Electronic Kibitzer
PEEK.......... Polyetheretherketone (DMAA)
PEEK.......... Polyetherketone [*Organic chemistry*]
Peekskill...... Peekskill Financial Corp. [*Associated Press*] (SAG)
PEELS.......... Parallel [*Detection*] Electron Energy Loss Spectroscopy
PEEM.......... Panel of Experts on Environmental Management (GNE)
PEEM.......... Photoemission Electron Microscope
PEEM.......... Photoemission Electron Microscopy (MCD)
PEEP.......... Panel of Experts on Environmental Pollution [*WMO*] (MSC)
PEEP.......... Pilot's Electronic Eyelevel Presentation [*British*]
PEEP.......... Porous Electrode Electrostatic Precipitation
PEEP.......... Positive End Expiratory Pressure [*Medicine*]
PEEP.......... Production Electronic Equipment Procurement Status Report
Peeples & Stevens... Peeples and Stevens' Reports [*80-97 Georgia*] [*A publication*] (DLA)
PEER.......... Pediatric Examination of Educational Readiness [*Child development test*]
Peer.......... Peerless [*Record label*] [*USA, Mexico*]
PEER.......... Planned Experience for Effective Relating
PEER.......... Price Escalation Estimated Rates
PEER.......... Program of Equal Employment Opportunity Evaluation Reports
PEER.......... Project Engineer Evaluation Report (HGAA)
PEER.......... Project on Equal Education Rights [*Defunct*] (EA)
PEERAMID... Pediatric Examination of Educational Readiness at Middle Childhood [*Child development test*] [*Psychology*]
PEERC.......... Production Engineering Education and Research Center
Peere Wms... Peere-Williams' English Chancery and King's Bench Cases [*1695-1736*] [*A publication*] (DLA)
PeerMf.......... Peerless Manufacturing Co. [*Associated Press*] (SAG)
PEET.......... Printing Equipment Education Trust [*British*]
PEETPACK... Process Engineering Evaluation Techniques Package (PDAA)
PEETSA........ Parents, Educators and Environmentalists to Save Anchoives [*An association*]
PEEX.......... Pediatric Early Elementary Examination [*Child development test*] [*Psychology*]
PEF.......... Packaging Education Foundation (EA)
PEF.......... Palestine Endowment Funds [*Later, PEF Israel Endowment Funds*] (EA)
PEF.......... Palestine Exploration Fund
PEF.......... Pathway-Exposure Factor [*Environmental chemistry*]
PEF.......... Peak Expiratory Flow [*Pulmonary function*]
PEF.......... Performance Efficiency Factor (AFIT)
PEF.......... Personal Effects Floater [*Insurance*]
PEF.......... Personality Evaluation Form [*Psychology*]
PEF.......... Phil Esposito Foundation [*Defunct*] (EA)
PEF.......... Physical Electronics Facility (MCD)
PEF.......... Plastics Education Foundation (EA)
PEF.......... Polyethylene Foam
PEF.......... Potential-Energy Function [*Physical chemistry*]
PEF.......... Powerhouse Exhaust Facility (IAA)
PEF.......... Prediction Error Filter [*Wave frequency and phase modifier*]
PEF.......... Presbyterian Evangelistic Fellowship [*Defunct*] (EA)
PEF.......... Pro Ecclesia Foundation (EA)
PEF.......... Program Estimating Factor (AFM)
PEF.......... Proposal Evaluation Form (AAG)
PEF.......... Psychiatric Evaluation Form [*Psychology*]
PEF.......... Psychiatric Evaluation Form (DAVI)
PEF.......... Pulmonary Edema Fluid [*Medicine*] (DMAA)
PEF.......... Pulse Eliminating Filter (IAA)
PEFC.......... Private Export Funding Corp. (IMH)

PEFCO .... Private Export Funding Corp.
Pe Fi .... Petrus Filipi [*Authority cited in pre-1607 legal work*] (DSA)
Pe Fili .... Petrus Filipi [*Authority cited in pre-1607 legal work*] (DSA)
PEF/NET .... Public Education Fund Network (EA)
PEFO .... Payload Effects Follow-On Study [*NASA*] (NASA)
PEFO .... Petrified Forest National Park
PEFOS .... Program Evaluation and Field Operations Staff [*Environmental Protection Agency*] (GFGA)
PEFQS .... Palestine Exploration Fund. Quarterly Statement [*London*] [*A publication*] (BJA)
PEFQST .... Palestine Exploration Fund. Quarterly Statement [*London*] [*A publication*] (BJA)
PEFR .... Peak Expiratory Flow Rate
PEFR/PIFR ... Peak Expiratory Flow/Peak Inspiratory Flow Rate [*Medicine*] (DAVI)
PEFSR .... Partial Expiratory Flow-Static Recoil Curve [*Physiology*] (MAE)
PEFT .... Peripheral Equipment Functional Test (CAAL)
PEFT .... Preschool Embedded Figures Test [*Child development test*]
PEFTOK .... Philippine Expeditionary Force to Korea [*United Nations*]
PEFTP .... Parent Education Follow Through Program (EDAC)
PEFU .... Panel of Experts on Fish Utilization [*FAO*] (ASF)
PEFV .... Partial Expiratory Flow-Volume [*Physiology*]
PEG .... General Analine & Film Co., General Research Laboratory, Easton, PA [*Library symbol Library of Congress Obsolete*] (LCLS)
PEG .... Pac Engo Materials [*Vancouver Stock Exchange symbol*]
PEG .... Pacific Environmental Group [*Marine science*] (MSC)
PEG .... Patient Evaluation Grid [*Medicine*] (DMAA)
Peg .... Pegasus [*Constellation*]
PEG .... Pelangi Air Sdn. Bhd. [*Malaysia*] [*FAA designator*] (FAAC)
PEG .... Percutaneous Endoscopic Gastrostomy [*Medicine*] (CPH)
PEG .... Performance Evaluation Group (CINC)
PEG .... Petrochemical Energy Group (EA)
PEG .... Photo Exploitation Group
PEG .... Pneumatic Explosion Generator
PEG .... Pneumoencephalogram [*Medicine*]
PEG .... Polyethylene Glycol [*Organic chemistry*]
PEG .... Previous Endorsement(s) Guaranteed [*Banking*]
PEG .... Principle of the Equivalent Generator
PEG .... Prior Endorsement Guaranteed (HGAA)
PEG .... Priorities Exploitation Group
PEG .... Priorities for ELINT Guidance (MCD)
PEG .... Process Evaluation Guide [*Graphic Communications Association*]
PEG .... Production Entitlement Guarantee [*International Agricultural Trade Research Consortium*] (ECON)
PEG .... Professional Emphasis Group [*National Audience Board*] (NTCM)
PEG .... Program Evaluation Group [*Air Force*]
PEG .... Project Engineering Guide (MCD)
PEG .... Protected Employee Group [*Program*]
PEG .... Protection Engineers Group [*United States Telephone Association*] [*Telecommunications*]
PEG .... PSE & G Capital Trust [*NYSE symbol*] (SAG)
PEG .... Public, Educational, Government [*Cable television access channels*] (NTCM)
PEG .... Public Service Elec & Gas Co. [*NYSE symbol*] (SAG)
PEG .... Public Service Electric & Gas Co. (CDAI)
PEG .... Public Service Enterprise Group, Inc. [*NYSE symbol*] (SPSG)
PEG .... Public Svc Enterpr [*NYSE symbol*] (TTSB)
PEG .... Pyrotechnic Electron Generator (MCD)
PEGA .... Pegasystems, Inc. [*NASDAQ symbol*] (SAG)
PEGA .... Polyethylene Glycol Adipate [*Organic chemistry*]
PegaCm .... Pegasus Communications Corp. [*Associated Press*] (SAG)
PEG-ADA .... Polyethylene Glycol-Adenosine Deaminase [*A modified enzyme*]
PEGASUS .... People, Goods, and Services Urban System [*Texas*] [*FHWA*] (TAG)
Pegasys .... Pegasystems, Inc. [*Associated Press*] (SAG)
PEGDE .... Pentaethylene Glycol Dodecyl Ether [*Organic chemistry*]
PEGE .... Program for Evaluation of Ground Environment
PegGld .... Pegasus Gold, Inc. [*Associated Press*] (SAG)
PEGLN .... Petiole Gland Pairs, Number Of [*Botany*]
PEGPrA .... Pub Sv E&G 4.08% Pfd [*NYSE symbol*] (TTSB)
PEGPrC .... Pub Sv E&G 4.30% Pfd [*NYSE symbol*] (TTSB)
PEGPrD .... Pub Sv E&G 5.05% Pfd [*NYSE symbol*] (TTSB)
PEGPrE .... Pub Sv E&G 5.28% Pfd [*NYSE symbol*] (TTSB)
PEGPrG .... Pub Sv E&G 6.80% Pfd [*NYSE symbol*] (TTSB)
PEGPrI .... Public Sv E&G 7.40% cm Pfd [*NYSE symbol*] (TTSB)
PEGPrJ .... Pub Sv E&G 7.52% Pfd [*NYSE symbol*] (TTSB)
PEGPrV .... Pub Sv E&G 7.44% Pfd [*NYSE symbol*] (TTSB)
PEGPrW .... Pub Sv E&G 5.97% Pfd [*NYSE symbol*] (TTSB)
PEGPrX .... Public Svc E&G Cap 8.00%'MIPS' [*NYSE symbol*] (TTSB)
PEGPrY .... Pub Sv E&G 6.75% Pfd [*NYSE symbol*] (TTSB)
PEGPrZ .... Public Svc E&G Cap 9.375% 'MIPS' [*NYSE symbol*] (TTSB)
PEGR .... Proportional Exhaust Gas Recirculation [*Engines*]
Pegs .... Pegasus [*Constellation*]
PEGS .... Polyethylene Glycol Succinate [*Organic chemistry*]
PEGS .... Project Engineering Graphics System [*Computer Aided Design Centre*] [*Software package*] (NCC)
PEGS .... Project Engineering System
PEH .... Pehpei [*Republic of China*] [*Seismograph station code, US Geological Survey*] (SEIS)
PEH .... Pehuajo [*Argentina*] [*Airport symbol*] (OAG)
PEH .... Periods of European History [*A publication*]
PEH .... Planning Estimate Handbook (SAA)
PEHA .... Pentaethylenehexamine [*Organic chemistry*]
PEHA .... Pony Express Historical Association (EA)
PEHD .... Polyethylene-High Density [*Organic chemistry*]
PEHi .... Northampton County Historical and Genealogical Society, Mary Illick Memorial Library, Easton, PA [*Library symbol Library of Congress*] (LCLS)
Pe His .... Petrus Hispanus [*Authority cited in pre-1607 legal work*] (DSA)
PEI .... Patriotic Education, Inc. (EA)
PEI .... Peine [*Chile*] [*Seismograph station code, US Geological Survey Closed*] (SEIS)
pe/i .... Pen and Ink (VRA)
PEI .... Penna RE Inv Tr SNI [*AMEX symbol*] (TTSB)
PEI .... Pennsylvania Real Estate Investment Trust [*AMEX symbol*] (SPSG)
PEI .... Pereira [*Colombia*] [*Airport symbol*] (OAG)
PEI .... Petrocel Industries, Inc. [*Vancouver Stock Exchange symbol*]
PEI .... Petroleum Equipment Institute (EA)
PEI .... Phosphate Excretion Index [*Biochemistry*] (DAVI)
PEI .... Phosphorous Excretion Index [*Medicine*] (MEDA)
PEI .... Phosphorus Excretion Index [*Biochemistry*] (DAVI)
PEI .... Physical Efficiency Index [*Medicine*] (DMAA)
PEI .... Physical Efficiency Indx [*Medicine*] (DAVI)
PEI .... Planning Executives Institute [*Later, PF*]
PEI .... Plant Engineering Inspection (AAG)
PEI .... Playboy Enterprises, Inc.
PEI .... Polyetherimide
PEI .... Polyethylenimine [*Organic chemistry*]
PEI .... Porcelain Enamel Institute (EA)
PEI .... Postejaculatory Interval [*Physiology*]
PEI .... Precipitation-Efficiency Index
PEI .... Preliminary Engineering Inspection [*NASA*] (KSC)
PEI .... Prince Edward Island [*Canadian province*]
PEI .... Prince Edward Island Provincial Library [*UTLAS symbol*]
PEI .... Prince Edward Island Reports (Haviland's) [*A publication*] (DLA)
PEI .... Professional Engineers in Industry
PEI .... Pupil Evaluation Inventory [*Education*] (EDAC)
PEIA .... Poultry and Egg Institute of America (EA)
PEIC .... Periodic Error Integrating Controller
PEID .... Program Element Identifier [*Military*] (AFIT)
PEIF .... Productivity Enhancing Incentive Fund (DNAB)
PEILS .... PACOM [*Pacific Command*] Executive Intelligence Summary (MCD)
PEIP .... Presidential Executive Interchange Program [*Federal government*]
PEIR .... Performance Evaluation and Information Reduction (IAA)
PEIR .... Problem Equipment Indicator Reports (MCD)
PEIR .... Process Evaluation and Information Reduction (IAA)
PEIR .... Project Equipment Inspection Record [*NASA*] (KSC)
PEI Rep .... Prince Edward Island Reports (Haviland's) [*1850-1914*] [*A publication*] (DLA)
PEI Rev Stat ... Prince Edward Island Revised Statutes [*Canada*] [*A publication*] (DLA)
PEIS .... Polyethylene Isophthalate [*Organic chemistry*]
PEIS .... Programmatic Environmental Impact Statement (NRCH)
PEI Stat .... Prince Edward Island Statutes [*Canada*] [*A publication*] (DLA)
PEITA .... Professional Equestrian Instructors and Trainers Association [*Defunct*] (EA)
PEITV .... Preliminary Encapsulated Inert Test Vehicle (MCD)
PEJ .... Percutaneous Endoscopic Jejunostomy [*Medicine*] (DMAA)
PEJ .... Premolded Expansion Joint [*Technical drawings*]
Pe Ja .... Petrus Jacobi [*Flourished, 14th century*] [*Authority cited in pre-1607 legal work*] (DSA)
PEJO .... Plant Engineering Job Order (AAG)
PEK .... Beijing [*China*] [*Airport symbol*] (OAG)
PEK .... Jacksonville, FL [*Location identifier FAA*] (FAAL)
PEK .... Peak Aviation, PLC [*British*] [*FAA designator*] (FAAC)
PEK .... Peking [*Republic of China*] [*Seismograph station code, US Geological Survey*] (SEIS)
PEK .... Peking [*China*] [*Airport symbol*] (AD)
PEK .... Pekoe [*Tea trade*] (ROG)
PEK .... Phase-Exchange Keying [*Computer science*] (IEEE)
PEK .... Phi Epsilon Kappa [*Fraternity*]
PEK .... Polyetherketone [*Organic chemistry*]
PEKK .... Polyetherketoneketone [*Materials science*]
PEKK .... Polyether Ketone Ketone
PEL .... Aeropelican Air Services Pty Ltd. [*Australia ICAO designator*] (FAAC)
PEL .... Lafayette College, Easton, PA [*Library symbol Library of Congress*] (LCLS)
PEL .... Paid Educational Leave (AIE)
PEL .... PanEnergy Corp. [*NYSE symbol*] (TTSB)
PEL .... Panhandle Eastern Pipe Line Co. [*NYSE symbol*] (SPSG)
Pel .... Pelagius [*Deceased, 1232*] [*Authority cited in pre-1607 legal work*] (DSA)
PEL .... Pelaneng [*Lesotho*] [*Airport symbol*] (OAG)
PEL .... Peldehue [*Chile*] [*Seismograph station code, US Geological Survey*] (SEIS)
Pel .... Pelopidas [*of Plutarch*] [*Classical studies*] (OCD)
PEL .... Peritoneal Exudate Lymphocytes [*Hematology*]
PEL .... Permissible Exposure Level
PEL .... Permissible Exposure Limit [*OSHA*]
PEL .... Personal Effectiveness Inventory (AIE)
PEL .... Personal Exposure Level [*or Limit*]
PEL .... Personnel Licensing and Training [*ICAO*] (AIA)
PEL .... Philatelic Esperanto League [*See also ELF*] [*Solna, Sweden*] (EAIO)
PEL .... Photoelectron Layer
PEL .... Picture Element [*Single element of resolution in image processing*] (IBMDP)
PEL .... Precision Elastic Limit
PEL .... Priests Eucharistic League (EA)
PEL .... Primary Effusion Lymphoma [*Oncology*]
PEL .... Production Error Log (NITA)

PEL........ Professional Education Libraries [*UTLAS symbol*]
PEL........ Proportional Elastic Limit
PEL........ Public Exposure Limit (MCD)
PEIC........ Elizabethtown College, Elizabethtown, PA [*Library symbol Library of Congress*] (LCLS)
PEIC........ Elizabethtown College, Elizabethtown, PA [*Library symbol*] [*Library of Congress*] (LCLS)
PELC........ Professional Engineers' Legislative Committee
PELEC........ Photoelectric (MSA)
PEleph........ Elephantine Papyri [*A publication*] (OCD)
PELG........ Pelger Muet Anomaly [*Laboratory science*] (DAVI)
PELG........ Poly(ethyl L-Glutamate) [*Organic chemistry*]
PELI........ Production, Engineering and Logistics Information (AAGC)
PELL........ Papers on English Language and Literature [*A publication*]
PELR........ Peeler
PELR........ Pelsart Resources NL [*NASDAQ symbol*] (NQ)
PELRV........ Pea Leafroll Virus [*Plant pathology*]
PELRY........ Pelsart Resources ADR [*NASDAQ symbol*] (TTSB)
PELS........ Precision Emitter Location System [*Air Force*] (MCD)
PELS........ Propionyl Erythromycin Lauryl Sulfate [*Antimicrobial agent*]
Pelsart........ Pelsart Resources NL [*Associated Press*] (SAG)
PELSS........ Precision Emitter Location Strike System [*Air Force*]
Pelt........ Peltier's Orleans Appeals [*1917-23*] [*A publication*] (DLA)
PELT........ Princeton American [*NASDAQ symbol*] (TTSB)
PELT........ Princeton Electronic Products, Inc. [*NASDAQ symbol*] (NQ)
PELV........ Pepino Latent Virus [*Plant pathology*]
PEM........ Parametric Earth Model [*Geodynamics*]
PEM........ Parasitic Encephalitis Meningitis [*Medicine*]
PEM........ Particle Environmental Monitor (MCD)
PEM........ Partido Ecologista Mexicano [*Political party*] (EY)
PEM........ Payload Ejection Mechanism
PEM........ PEM-AIR Ltd. [*Canada ICAO designator*] (FAAC)
PEM........ Pembrokeshire [*County in Wales*] (ROG)
PEM........ Performance Evaluation Model
PEM........ Peritoneal Exudate Macrophage [*Hematology*]
PEM........ Perrot Memorial Library, Old Greenwich, CT [*OCLC symbol*] (OCLC)
PEM........ Personal-E Mailbox [*Computer software*] (PCM)
PEM........ Personal Exposure Monitor [*Environmental chemistry*]
PEM........ Petite Ensemble Model (MCD)
PEM........ Petrox Energy & Mineral Corp. [*Toronto Stock Exchange symbol*]
PEM........ Phased Equipment Modernization [*Army*] (AABC)
PEM........ Philco Electronic Module
PEM........ Photoelastic Modulator [*Instrumentation*]
PEM........ Photoelectromagnetic
PEM........ Photoelectron Microscopy
PEM........ Photoemission Microscope
PEM........ Photographic Equipment and Materials (NATG)
PEM........ Plant Engineering and Maintenance (NASA)
PEM........ Plant Engineer Mechanical (AAG)
PEM........ Plastic-Encapsulated Microcircuit [*Telecommunications*]
PEM........ Polaris Evaluation Missile
PEM........ Polymer Electrolyte Membrane [*Fuel technology*]
PEM........ Position Encoding Module (CAAL)
PEM........ Prescription-Event Monitoring
PEM........ Primary Enrichment Medium [*Microbiology*]
PEM........ Privacy-Enhanced Mail [*Software package*]
PEM........ Probable Error of Measurement
PEM........ Process Execution Module (NITA)
PEM........ Processing Element Memory [*Computer science*]
PEM........ Processing Element Module [*Computer science*] (IAA)
PEM........ Product Effectiveness Manual
PEM........ Production Engineering Measure [*Army*] (MCD)
PEM........ Production Evaluation Missile [*Military*] (CAAL)
PEM........ Program Element Manager (MCD)
PEM........ Program Element Monitor (AFM)
PEM........ Program Endorsement Memorandum (AAGC)
PEM........ Project Engineering Memorandum
PEM........ Proposal Evaluation Manager
PEM........ Protein Energy Malnutrition [*Medicine*]
PEM........ Proton Exchange Membrane [*Fuel technology*] (PS)
PEM........ Puerto Maldonado [*Peru*] [*Airport symbol*] (OAG)
PEM........ Pulmonary Embolus [*Medicine*] (DAVI)
PEMA........ Pheny(ethyl)malonamide [*Organic chemistry*]
PEMA........ Polyethyl Methacrylate [*Organic chemistry*]
PEMA........ Process Equipment Manufacturers Association (EA)
PEMA........ Procurement Equipment Maintenance, Army (MCD)
PEMA........ Procurement, Equipment, Missiles, Army
PEMA........ Procurement of Equipment and Munition Appropriations [*Military*] (AABC)
PEMA........ Production-Equipment-Missile Agency [*Army*]
PEMAP........ President's Environmental Merit Award Program [*Environmental Protection Agency*]
PEMARS........ Procurement of Equipment and Missiles, Army Management and Accounting Reporting System (AABC)
PEMB........ Pembroke College [*Oxford and Cambridge Universities*] (ROG)
PEMB........ Pembrokeshire [*County in Wales*]
Pemb Eq........ Pemberton's Practice in Equity by Way of Revivor and Supplement [*1867*] [*A publication*] (ILCA)
Pemb Judg... Pemberton's Judgments and Orders [*A publication*] (DLA)
PEMBS........ Pembrokeshire [*County in Wales*]
PEMCONS.... Photographic Equipment Management Control System
PEMD........ Program Evaluation and Methodology Division [*General Accounting Office*] [*Federal government*] (GFGA)
PEMD........ Program for Export Market Development [*Canada*]
PEME........ Pulsed Electromagnetic Energy [*Diathermy*] (CPH)
PEMF........ Pulsating Electromagnetic Field
PEMFC........ Proton Exchange Membrane Fuel Cell [*Energy source*]
PEMN........ Program Engineering Management Network [*Computer science*] (RDA)
Pe Mo........ Petrus Morini [*Authority cited in pre-1607 legal work*] (DSA)
PEMO........ Plant Engineering Maintenance Order
PEMO........ Production Engineering and Manufacturing Organization (AAG)
PE-MOCVD... Plasma-Enhanced Metalorganic Chemical Vapor Deposition [*Coating technology*]
Pe Mori........ Petrus Morini [*Authority cited in pre-1607 legal work*] (DSA)
PEMOV........ Peanut Mottle Virus [*Plant pathology*]
PEMRam........ Precision Electromagnetic Ram [*Denne Developments*] (PS)
PEMS........ Pesticide Enforcement Management System (NITA)
PEMS........ Physical, Emotional, Mental, Safety [*Model for charting procedure*] [*Medicine*]
PEMS........ Porcelain-Enamelled Metal Substrate (EECA)
PEMS........ Portable Environmental Measuring System
PEMS........ Predictive Emission Monitoring System [*Environmental science*]
PEMS........ Professional Education of the Media Specialist
PEMS........ Propulsion Energy Management Study (MCD)
PEMT........ Phosphatidylethanolamine Methyltransferase [*An enzyme*]
PEMV........ Pea Enation Mosaic Virus [*Plant pathology*]
PeMV........ Pepper Mottle Virus
PEM-West.... Pacific Exploratory Mission-West [*Western Pacific tropospheric chemistry experiment*] (USDC)
PEM-West.... Pacific Exploratory Mission-West [*Western Pacific Tropospheric Chemistry Experiment*] [*Marine science*] (OSRA)
Pem Yeo........ Pembroke Yeomanry [*British military*] (DMA)
PEN........ Astoria, OR [*Location identifier FAA*] (FAAL)
PEN........ International PEN [*Official name; PEN, never spelled out in use, is said to stand for poets, playwrights, editors, essayists, novelists*] (EAIO)
PEN........ Pacific Exchange Network (USDC)
PEN........ Pacific Exchange Network [*Marine science*] (OSRA)
PEN........ Parenteral and Enteral Nutrition [*Gastroenterology*] (DAVI)
PEN........ Peace Education Network (EA)
PEN........ PEN American Center (EA)
PEN........ Penang [*Malaysia*] [*Airport symbol*] (OAG)
PEN........ Pendeli [*Greece*] [*Geomagnetic observatory code*]
PEN........ Penetration (AFM)
PEN........ Penicillin [*Antibiotic*]
Pen........ Penicillin [*Medicine*] (DMAA)
PEN........ Peninsula [*Maps and charts*]
PEN........ Peninsula
PEN........ Peninsula Airways, Inc. [*ICAO designator*] (FAAC)
PEN........ Penitent
PEN........ Penitentiary (WDAA)
Pen........ Pennewill's Delaware Reports [*A publication*] (DLA)
Pen........ Pennington's New Jersey Reports [*2, 3 New Jersey*] [*A publication*] (DLA)
PEN........ Pensacola [*Florida*] [*Seismograph station code, US Geological Survey Closed*] (SEIS)
PEN........ Pentazocine [*An analgesic*]
PEN........ Pentobarbital [*Sedative*]
PEN........ Pentode (DEN)
PEN........ Permanent Entry Number [*Computer science*]
PEN........ Pharmacology Equivalent Name
PEN........ Pharmacy Equivalent Name [*Medicine*] (DMAA)
PEN........ Physicians Education Network (EA)
PEN........ Poets, Playwrights, Editors, Essayists, and Novelists [*AccountingPANANEWS*] (NADA)
PEN........ Polyethylene Naphthalate [*Organic chemistry*]
PEN........ Professional Enrichment News [*Portuguese*] (BJA)
PEN........ Program Element Number [*Computer science*] (KSC)
PEN........ Program Error Note [*Computer science*]
PEN........ Public Electronic Network [*Information service or system*] (IID)
PEN........ Purchasing Electronic Notebook (HGAA)
PENA........ Primary Emission Neuron Activation (IEEE)
PENAID........ Penetration Aid [*Weaponry*]
Pen & W........ Penrose and Watts' Pennsylvania Reports [*1829-32*] [*A publication*] (DLA)
PENB........ Poultry and Egg National Board [*Later, AEB*] (EA)
PENBASE..... Peninsular Base Section [*Military*]
Pen C........ Penal Code [*A publication*] (DLA)
PENC........ Pen Interconnect [*NASDAQ symbol*] (TTSB)
PENC........ Pen Interconnect, Inc. [*NASDAQ symbol*] (SAG)
Penchk........ Pennichuck Corp. [*Associated Press*] (SAG)
PENCIL........ Pictorial Encoding Language [*Computer science*] (IEEE)
PENCIL........ Portable Encoder/Illustrator [*Facetious term for pre-word-processing equipment*]
PENCIL........ Public Education Needs Civic Involvement in Learning
Pencp........ Penncorp Financial Group [*Associated Press*] (SAG)
PencpFn........ Penncorp Financial Group [*Associated Press*] (SAG)
PENCPR........ PEN [*Poets, Playwrights, Essayists, Editors, and Novelists*] Club of PuertoRico (EA)
PENCW........ Pen Interconnect Wrrt [*NASDAQ symbol*] (TTSB)
pend........ Pendant (VRA)
Pend........ Pendant (ROG)
PEND........ Pendens [*Weighing*] [*Pharmacy*]
PEND........ Pending
Pen Dec........ Pension Decisions [*Department of the Interior*] [*A publication*] (DLA)
PENDORF.... Penetrate Dorfman [*FBI investigation of Teamster leader Allen Dorfman*]
Penedrm........ Penederm, Inc. [*Associated Press*] (SAG)
Penelc........ Penelec Capital Ltd. [*Associated Press*] (SAG)

PenEM........ Penn Engineering & Manufacturing Corp. [*Associated Press*] (SAG)
PenEMA....... Penn Engineering & Manufacturing Corp. [*Associated Press*] (SAG)
P/E NEWS.... Petroleum/Energy Business News Index [*American Petroleum Institute*] [*New York, NY Bibliographic database*]
PenG.......... Penicillin G [*Antibacterial agent*]
PenG.......... Pennsylvania Gas & Water Co. [*Associated Press*] (SAG)
PENG.......... Photo-Electro-Nystagmography [*Medicine*]
PENG.......... Prima Energy [*NASDAQ symbol*] (TTSB)
PENG.......... Prima Energy Corp. [*NASDAQ symbol*] (NQ)
PEng.......... Professional Engineer
PEng.......... Registered Professional Engineer (DD)
PENGEM...... Penetrate Gray Electronics Markets [*FBI "sting" operation, 1982, where employees of Japanese computer firms were caught trying to obtain proprietary information illegally from IBM Co.*]
PENIC.......... Penicillin [*Antibiotic*]
Penic Cam... Penicillum Camelinum [*A Camel's-Hair Brush*] [*Pharmacy*]
penin.......... Peninsula
PenInt.......... Pen Interconnect, Inc. [*Associated Press*] (SAG)
PenInter....... Pen Interconnect, Inc. [*Associated Press*] (SAG)
PeninTst...... Peninsula Trust Bank, Inc. [*Associated Press*] (SAG)
PENIT.......... Penitentiary
PENJERDEL... Pennsylvania, New Jersey, Delaware
PENK.......... Proenkephalin [*Biochemistry*]
Penn.......... Pennewill's Delaware Reports [*A publication*] (DLA)
Penn.......... Pennington's New Jersey Reports [*A publication*] (DLA)
PENN.......... Penn National Gaming [*NASDAQ symbol*] (TTSB)
PENN.......... Penn National Gaming, Inc. [*NASDAQ symbol*] (SAG)
PENN.......... Pennsylvania
Penn.......... Pennsylvania (ODBW)
PENN.......... Pennsylvanian [*Period, era, or system*] [*Geology*]
Penn.......... Pennsylvania State Reports [*A publication*] (DLA)
Penn.......... Pennypacker's Unreported Pennsylvania Cases [*A publication*] (DLA)
PENNA......... Pennsylvania
Penna.......... Pennsylvania (ODBW)
Penna Law Journal... Pennsylvania Law Journal [*A publication*] (DLA)
Penna LJ..... Pennsylvania Law Journal [*A publication*] (DLA)
PennAm....... Penn America Group [*Associated Press*] (SAG)
Penna R...... Pennsylvania State Reports [*A publication*] (DLA)
Penna SR.... Pennsylvania State Reports [*A publication*] (DLA)
Penna St.... Pennsylvania State Reports [*A publication*] (DLA)
Penna State Rep... Pennsylvania State Reports [*A publication*] (DLA)
PennBc........ PennFirst Bancorp [*Associated Press*] (SAG)
PennBcp....... PennFirst Bancorp [*Associated Press*] (SAG)
Penn Co Ct Rep... Pennsylvania County Court Reports [*A publication*] (DLA)
Penn C Opt... Pennsylvania College of Optometry (GAGS)
Penn Corp Rep... Pennsylvania Corporation Reporter [*A publication*] (DLA)
Penn Del..... Pennewill's Delaware Reports [*A publication*] (DLA)
Penn Dist & Co Rep... Pennsylvania District and County Reports [*A publication*] (DLA)
Penn Dist Rep... Pennsylvania District Reports [*A publication*] (DLA)
Penne.......... Pennewill's Delaware Reports [*17-23 Delaware*] [*1897-1909*] [*A publication*] (DLA)
PennEn........ Penn Enterprises, Inc. [*Associated Press*] (SAG)
Pennew........ Pennewill's Delaware Reports [*A publication*] (DLA)
Pennewill.... Pennewill's Delaware Supreme Court Reports [*1897-1909*] [*A publication*] (DLA)
Penney........ Penney [*J. C.*] Co., Inc. [*Associated Press*] (SAG)
PennFed....... PennFed Financial Services, Inc. [*Associated Press*] (SAG)
PenNGm....... Penn National Gaming, Inc. [*Associated Press*] (SAG)
Penning....... Pennington's New Jersey Reports [*2, 3 New Jersey*] [*A publication*] (DLA)
Pen NJ......... Pennington's New Jersey Reports [*2, 3 New Jersey*] [*A publication*] (DLA)
Penn Law Jour... Pennsylvania Law Journal [*A publication*] (DLA)
Penn LG...... Pennsylvania Legal Gazette [*A publication*] (DLA)
Penn LG...... Pennsylvania Legal Gazette Reports (Campbell) [*A publication*] (DLA)
Penn LJ...... Pennsylvania Law Journal [*A publication*] (DLA)
Penn LJR..... Pennsylvania Law Journal Reports, Edited by Clark [*1842-52*] [*A publication*] (DLA)
Penn L Rec... Pennsylvania Law Record [*Philadelphia*] [*A publication*] (DLA)
Penn L Rev... Pennsylvania Law Review [*A publication*] (DLA)
PennOct....... Penn Octane Corp. [*Associated Press*] (SAG)
PENNORTH... Pennyworth [*British*] (ROG)
Penn R........ Pennsylvania State Reports [*A publication*] (DLA)
Penn Rep..... Pennsylvania State Reports [*A publication*] (DLA)
Penn Rep..... Penrose and Watts' Pennsylvania Reports [*A publication*] (DLA)
Penn St...... Pennsylvania State Reports [*A publication*] (DLA)
PENNSTAC... Penn State University Automatic Digital Computer
Penn Stat..... Pennsylvania State Reports [*A publication*] (DLA)
Penn State Rep... Pennsylvania State Reports [*A publication*] (DLA)
Penn St R..... Pennsylvania State Reports [*A publication*] (ILCA)
Penn St Rep... Pennsylvania State Reports [*A publication*] (DLA)
Penn St U.... Pennsylvania State University (GAGS)
Penn St U Harrisburg... Pennsylvania State University at Harrisburg (GAGS)
Penn Super... Pennsylvania Superior Court Reports [*A publication*] (DLA)
PENNTAP..... Pennsylvania Technical Assistance Program [*Pennsylvania State University*] [*University Park, PA*]
PennTr......... Penn Traffic Co. [*Associated Press*] (SAG)
PennTrty...... Penn Treaty American [*Associated Press*] (SAG)
PennVa........ Penn Virginia Corp. [*Associated Press*] (SAG)
Pennwd........ Pennwood Savings Bank [*Associated Press*] (SAG)
Penny.......... Pennypacker's Pennsylvania Colonial Cases [*A publication*] (DLA)
Penny.......... Pennypacker's Unreported Pennsylvania Cases [*A publication*] (DLA)
Penny Col Cas... Pennypacker's Pennsyulvania Colonial Cases [*A publication*] (DLA)
Pennyp........ Pennypacker's Unreported Pennsylvania Cases [*A publication*] (DLA)
Pennyp Col Cas... Pennypacker's Pennsylvania Colonial Cases [*A publication*] (DLA)
Pennyp (PA)... Pennypacker's Unreported Pennsylvania Cases [*A publication*] (DLA)
Pennzol........ Pennzoil Co. [*Associated Press*] (SAG)
PEN-O.......... Penner Serotype-O [*Laboratory science*] (DAVI)
Penob.......... Penobscot Shoe Co. [*Associated Press*] (SAG)
PENOL.......... Penology
Pen P.......... Penault's Prerosti de Quebec [*A publication*] (DLA)
PENR.......... Penryn [*England*]
PENRAD....... Penetration RADAR
Penr Anal.... Penruddocke's Short Analysis of Criminal Law [*2nd ed.*] [*1842*] [*A publication*] (DLA)
Penr & W.... Penrose and Watts' Pennsylvania Reports [*1829-32*] [*A publication*] (DLA)
PenRE.......... Pennsylvania Real Estate Investment Trust [*Associated Press*] (SAG)
Pen Ref....... Penal Reformer [*1934-39*] [*A publication*] (DLA)
Pen Ref League M Rec... Penal Reform League Monthly Record [*1909-12*] [*A publication*] (DLA)
Pen Ref League Q Rec... Penal Reform League Quarterly Record [*1912-20*] [*A publication*] (DLA)
PENREP....... Penetration Report [*National Security Agency*]
Penril.......... Penril Corp. [*Associated Press*] (SAG)
PENS.......... Partido Espanol Nacional Sindicalista [*Political party*] [*Spain*]
PENS.......... Percutaneous Epidural Nerve Stimulator [*neurology*] (DAVI)
PENS.......... Polymer Ejection for Noise Suppression
PENSAM...... Penetration Survivability Assessment Model (MCD)
Pens & Profit Sharing (P-H)... Pension and Profit Sharing (Prentice-Hall, Inc.) [*A publication*] (DLA)
PensCr......... Pensamiento Cristiano. Tribuna de Exposicion del Pensamiento Evangelico [*Cordoba, Argentina*] [*A publication*] (BJA)
Pension Rep... Pension Reporter [*Bureau of National Affairs*] [*A publication*] (DLA)
PenskeM....... Penske Motorsports, Inc. [*Associated Press*] (SAG)
Pens Rep (BNA)... Pension Reporter (Bureau of National Affairs) [*A publication*] (DLA)
PenST.......... Penicillin Skin Test [*Immunology*]
Pen St R...... Pennsylvania State Reports [*A publication*] (DLA)
PENT.......... Penetrate (AABC)
PENT.......... Pentagon
PENT.......... Pentameter
Pent.......... Pentateuch (BJA)
PENT.......... Pentecost
PENT.......... Pentode (AAG)
Pent.......... Pentothal [*Anesthetic*] (AAMN)
PENT.......... Phenylethanolamine N-Methyltransferase (DMAA)
PENTAC....... Penetration for Tactical Aircraft [*Air Force*]
PENTAFLUX... Fifth Flux Experiment (USDC)
Pentair........ Pentair, Inc. [*Associated Press*] (SAG)
Pentch......... Pentech International, Inc. [*Associated Press*] (SAG)
PENTE.......... Pentecostal
PENTENG..... Pentagon English [*Pseudotechnical language*]
Pentl.......... Pentelic (VRA)
PenTrt......... Penn Treaty American Corp. [*Associated Press*] (SAG)
pentu.......... Pentateuch (VRA)
PENV.......... Philip Environmental [*NASDAQ symbol*] (SAG)
PENVAL....... Penetration Evaluation [*Military*] (NVT)
Pen VK........ Penicillin V Postassium [*An antibiotic*] (DAVI)
PENW.......... Penetrating Wound
PENW.......... PENWEST Ltd. [*Bellevue, WA*] [*NASDAQ symbol*] (NQ)
PENW.......... Penwith [*England*]
Penwst........ PENWEST Ltd. [*Associated Press*] (SAG)
PENZ.......... Penzance [*City in England*] (ROG)
PEO.......... Pankypria Ergatiki Omospondia [*Pancyprian Federation of Labour*] [*The "Old Trade Unions" Cyprus*]
PEO.......... Patrol Emergency Officer [*Nuclear energy*] (NRCH)
PEO.......... People
PEO.......... Peoria [*Diocesan abbreviation*] [*Illinois*] (TOCD)
peo.......... Persian, Old [*MARC language code Library of Congress*] (LCCP)
PEO.......... Petroleum & Resources [*NYSE symbol*] (TTSB)
PEO.......... Petroleum & Resources Corp. [*NYSE symbol*] (SPSG)
PEO.......... Petrolia Oil & Gas [*Vancouver Stock Exchange symbol*]
PEO.......... Philanthropic and Educational Organization [*Facetious translation "Pop Eats Out"*]
PEO.......... Planners for Equal Opportunity [*Defunct*] (EA)
PEO.......... Plant Engineering Order
PEO.......... Plant Equipment Operator [*Nuclear energy*] (NRCH)
PEO.......... Poly(ethylene oxide) [*Acronym is trade name owned by Seitetsu Kagaku Co.*]
PEO.......... President's Export Council (AAGC)
PEO.......... Principal Executive Officer [*Civil Service*] [*British*]
PEO.......... Process Engineering Order
PEO.......... Product Engineering Office
PEO.......... Production Engineering Order
PEO.......... Program Evaluation Office [*Army*]
PEO.......... Program Executive Office [*or Officer*]
PEO.......... Progressive External Ophthalmoplegia
PEO.......... Propulsion Engineering Officer (MCD)
PEO.......... Prospective Engineer Officer
PEO.......... Protect Each Other [*An association*] (NADA)
PEO.......... Public Employment Office [*State Employee Security Agency*] (OICC)
PEO-ASM..... Program Executive Office - Armored Systems Modernization [*Army*] (RDA)

PeoBkIN....... Peoples Bank Corp. Indianapolis [*Associated Press*] (SAG)
PEOC.......... Publishing Employees Organizing Committee [*AFL-CIO*]
PEO-FAS...... Program Executive Office - Field Artillery System [*Army*] (RDA)
PEO-GPALS... Program Executive Officer, Global Protection Against Limited Strikes [*Army*] (RDA)
PEO-IEW...... Program Executive Office - Intelligence and Electronic Warfare [*Army*] (RDA)
Peo L Adv.... People's Legal Advisor [*Utica, NY*] [*A publication*] (DLA)
PEO-MD...... Program Executive Office - Missile Defense [*Military*] (RDA)
PeopBcp...... Peoples Bancorp [*Dekalb County*] [*Associated Press*] (SAG)
PeopBcT...... Peoples BancTrust Co. [*Associated Press*] (SAG)
PeopBk........ Peoples Bank [*Catawba, NC*] [*Associated Press*] (SAG)
PeopChc...... Peoples Choice TV Corp. [*Associated Press*] (SAG)
PeopCT........ Peoples Bank [*Bridgeport, CT*] [*Associated Press*] (SAG)
PeopEn........ Peoples Energy Corp. [*Associated Press*] (SAG)
PeopFin....... Peoples Financial Corp. [*Associated Press*] (SAG)
PeopFst....... People First Corp. [*Associated Press*] (SAG)
PeopHld....... Peoples Holding Co. [*Associated Press*] (SAG)
PeopHrt....... People's Heritage Financial Group, Inc. [*Associated Press*] (SAG)
Peoples........ Peoples' Reports [*77-97 Georgia*] [*A publication*] (DLA)
PeopleTel.... Peoples Telephone Co. [*Associated Press*] (SAG)
Peopsft........ Peoplesoft, Inc. [*Associated Press*] (SAG)
PeopTel....... People's Telephone Co., Inc. [*Associated Press*] (SAG)
PEOS........... Propulsion and Electrical Operating System (IEEE)
PeoSvFn...... People's Savings Financial Corp. [*Associated Press*] (SAG)
PEOX........... Polyethyleneoxide [*Organic chemistry*]
PEP............. All India Reporter, Patiala and East Punjab States Union Series [*A publication*] (ILCA)
PEP............. Charlotte, NC [*Location identifier FAA*] (FAAL)
PEP............. Cyclophosphamide, VM-26 Prednisolone [*Antineoplastic drug regimen*] (DAVI)
PEP............. Packet Exchange Protocol [*Computer science*] (CDE)
PEP............. Packetized Ensemble Protocol [*Computer science*]
PEP............. Paperless Electronic Payment [*Business term*]
PEP............. Paperless Entry Processing User Group [*Defunct*] (CSR)
PEP............. Parenting, Education, and Political Involvement [*Jack and Jill of America*]
PEP............. Parti Ecologiste pour le Progres [*Burkina Faso*] [*Political party*] (EY)
PEP............. Parti Evangelique Populaire [*Popular Protestant Party*] [*Switzerland Political party*] (PPE)
PEP............. Partitioned Emulation Program [*Computer science*] (BUR)
PEP............. Patent Examining Procedure (IAA)
PEP............. Pauli Exclusion Principle [*Physics*]
PEP............. Peak Effective Power
PEP............. Peak Energy Product
PEP............. Peak Envelope Power [*Telecommunications*]
PEP............. Peer Evaluation Program [*College of American Pathologists*]
PEP............. People for Energy Progress [*Defunct*] (EA)
PEP............. Pepitilla [*Race of maize*]
PEP............. Peppermint (DSUE)
PEP............. PepsiCo Inc. [*NYSE symbol*] (SPSG)
Pep............. Peptidase (DMAA)
PEP............. Peptide [*Biochemistry*]
PEP............. Performance Effectiveness [*or Evaluation*] Program [*Navy*]
PEP............. Performance Evaluation Procedure [*Joint Commission on Accreditation of Hospitals*] (DHSM)
PEP............. Peripheral Event Processor [*Computer science*]
PEP............. Perkin-Elmer Processor [*Computer*]
PEP............. Personal Employee Profiling [*Information service or system*] (IID)
PEP............. Personal Equity Plan [*Finance*]
PEP............. Personal Exemption Phase-Out [*Income tax*]
PEP............. Personal Exercise Programmer
PEP............. Personality-Profile Exam
PEP............. Personnel Exchange Program [*Military*] (NVT)
PEP............. Pfizer, Inc., Research Center Library, Easton, PA [*Library symbol Library of Congress*] (LCLS)
PEP............. Phenethyl Propionate [*Insect attractant*] [*Organic chemistry*]
PEP............. Phosphoenolpyruvate [*Biochemistry*]
PEP............. Photoelectric Potential
PEP............. Photoelectrophoresis
PEP............. Photographic Exploitation Products (MCD)
PEP............. Physical Education Program
PEP............. Physiological Evaluation of Primates
PEP............. Pictorial End-Papers [*Publishing*]
PEP............. Pipeline Expanding Polymer
PEP............. Piping Efficiency Program
PEP............. Planar Epitaxial Passivated
PEP............. Planetary Ephemeris Program (IEEE)
PEP............. Planetary Exploration Plan [*NASA*]
PEP............. Plant Equipment Package [*DoD*]
PEP............. Platform Electronic Package
PEP............. Platform Evaluation Program
PEP............. Plessey Electronic Payroll (DEN)
PEP............. Plume Exposure Pathway [*Nuclear emergency planning*]
PEP............. Political and Economic Planning [*A British organization*] [*Later, Policy Studies Institute*]
PEP............. Polyestradiol Phosphate [*Endocrinology*]
PEP............. Polyethylene Powder
PEP............. Polynominal Error Protection (MCD)
PEP............. Pool Exercise Program [*Arthritis Foundation*]
PEP............. Porsche Experimental Prototype [*Automotive engineering*]
PEP............. Portable Energy Provision (SSD)
PEP............. Portfolio Evaluation Plan [*Australia*]
PEP............. Positive Energy [*Vancouver Stock Exchange symbol*]
PEP............. Positron-Electron Project [*High-energy accelerator*]
PEP............. Positron Electron Proton [*Physics*]
PEP............. Postal Efficiency Plan (SAA)
PEP............. Postexposure Prophylaxis [*Medicine*]
PEP............. Power Evaluation Program
PEP............. Power Extension Package (MCD)
PEP............. Power Extension Plant (MCD)
PEP............. Practical Engineering Paperwork
PEP............. Pratt & Whitney Engine Program [*Aviation*] (NG)
PEP............. Preamplifier Extension Plug
PEP............. Pre-Ejection Period [*Cardiology*]
PEP............. Pre-Employment Program
PEP............. Preferred Equipment Package [*Automotive retailing*]
PEP............. Preschool Education Program [*Sesame Street TV program*]
PEP............. President's Economy Program
PEP............. Preventive Enforcement Patrol [*New York City police*]
PEP............. Primary Education Program [*Child development test*]
PEP............. Primate Equilibrium Platform
PEP............. Princeton Electronic Products, Inc. (IAA)
PEP............. Princeton Experiment Package [*NASA*]
PeP............. Principal of Pedagogy [*Academic degree*]
PEP............. Printer-Emulation Package [*Software*]
PEP............. Priority Energy Policy [*Environmental Protection Agency*]
PEP............. Processing Enhancing Protein [*Biochemistry*]
PEP............. Procurement Evaluation Panel [*Air Force*] (MCD)
PEP............. Procytox [*Cyclophosphamide*], Epipodophyllotoxin Derivative , Prednisolone [*VM-26*] [*Antineoplastic drug regimen*]
PEP............. Producibility Engineering and Planning [*Army*] (AABC)
PEP............. Product Engineering and Production (MCD)
PEP............. Production EAGLE [*Elevation Angle Guidance Landing Equipment*] Package
PEP............. [*The*] Production Engineering and Productivity Exhibition and Conference [*British*] (ITD)
PEP............. Production Engineering Planning
PEP............. Production Equipment Package
PEP............. [*The*] Productivity Effectiveness Program [*Title of a pamphlet by Robert Gedaliah that describes sedentary exercises for desk-bound workers*]
PEP............. Professional Enhancement Project [*American Occupational Therapy Association*]
PEP............. Professional Experience Program [*Australia*]
PEP............. Proficiency Examination Program (MCD)
PEP............. Program Element Plan (AFIT)
PEP............. Program Evaluation Procedure [*Air Force*]
PEP............. Program Evaluation Program [*Air Force*] (IAA)
PEP............. Programmable Extension Package (IAA)
PEP............. Progressive Exercise Program
PEP............. Projects and Exports Policy [*Board of Trade*] [*British*]
PEP............. Prolyl Endopeptidase
PEP............. Promoting Enduring Peace (EA)
PEP............. Promotion Evaluation Pattern
PEP............. Propellant, Explosive, and Pyrotechnic
PEP............. Property Estimation Program [*Utah Water Research Laboratory*]
PEP............. Proposal Equipment Packages (MCD)
PEP............. Proposal Evaluation Panel (MCD)
PEP............. Proposal Evaluation Plan [*or Program*] (MCD)
PEP............. Proposal Exploitation Product
PEP............. Propulsion Evaluation Plan
PEP............. Protection in Evaluation Procedures
PEP............. Protein Electrophoresis [*Medicine*] (DMAA)
PEP............. Proton Electron Positron Colliding Beams (IAA)
PEP............. Proton-Electron-Proton [*Nuclear physics*]
PEP............. Psychiatric Evaluation Profile [*Psychology*] (MAE)
PEP............. Psychoeducational Profile [*Test for autistic children*]
PEP............. Psychoepistemological Profile [*Student personality test*]
PEP............. Pulse Echo Pattern
PEP............. Pulse Effective Power [*Telecommunications*] (IAA)
PEPA........... Peptidase A [*An enzyme*]
PEPA........... Per Employee per Annum
PEPA........... Petroleum Electric Power Association [*Later, EUIPA*] (EA)
PEPA........... Pitch Fibre Pipe Association of Great Britain (BI)
PEPA........... Protected Environment plus Prophylactic Antibiotics [*Oncology*]
PEPA........... Pulse Echo Pattern Analyzer
PEPAE......... Permanent Entry Permit After Entry
PEPAG......... Physical Electronics and Physical Acoustics Group [*MIT*] (MCD)
PEPAOP....... (Phenylethyl)phenylacetoxypiperidine [*Organic chemistry*]
PEPAS......... WHO [*World Health Organization*] Western Pacific Regional Centre for the Promotion of Environmental Planning and Applied Studies (EAIO)
PEPBNC....... Peninsula Enrichment Program for Bright Needy Children [*Queensland, Australia*]
PepBoy........ Pep Boys-Manny, Moe & Jack [*Associated Press*] (SAG)
PEPC........... Peptidase C [*An enzyme*]
PEPC........... Phosphoenolpyruvate Carboxylase [*An enzyme*]
PEPC........... Polynomial Error Protection Code [*Computer science*]
PEPC........... Postsecondary Education Planning Commission [*Florida*] (EDAC)
PEPC........... Potomac Electric Power Co.
PEPCK......... Phosphoenolopyruvate Carboxykinase [*An enzyme*]
PEPCK......... Phosphoenolpyruvate Carboxykinase [*An enzyme*]
PEPCO......... Potomac Electric Power Co.
PEPCOM...... Pacific Engineering Production Company (AAGC)
PEPD........... Peptidase D [*An enzyme*]
PEPE........... Parallel Element Processing Ensemble [*Burroughs Corp.*] (BUR)
PEPE........... People Persecuted by Pablo Escobar [*Colombia*] (ECON)
PEPE........... Prolonged Elevated-Pollution Episode [*Environmental Protection Agency*]

PEP/EP Pre-Ejection Period to Ejection Period [*Cardiology*] (DAVI)
PEPES People Persecuted by Pablo Escobar
PEPG Piezoelectric Power Generation
PEPG Port Emergency Planning Group [*NATO*] (NATG)
PEPI Physical Education Public Information [*Film*]
PEPI Post-Menopausal Estrogen and Progestin Intervention [*Medicine*] (BARN)
PEPI Postmenopausal Estrogen/Progestin Interventions
PEPI Postmenopausal Estrogen Progestin Interventions
PEPI Pre-Ejection Period Index [*Cardiology*]
PEPL Preliminary Engineering Parts List
PEPLAN Polaris Executive Plan [*British*]
PEP/LVET Pre-Ejection Period/Left Ventricular Ejection Time [*Medicine*] (MEDA)
PEPMC Printing Estimators and Production Men's Club [*New York, NY*] (EA)
PEPMIS Plant Equipment Packages Management Information System (MCD)
PEPMOV Pepper Mottle Virus [*Plant pathology*]
PEPMV Pepino Mosaic Virus [*Plant pathology*]
PEPP Permanent-Equity Pension Plan [*Human resources*] (WYGK)
PEPP Planetary Entry Parachute Program [*NASA*]
PEPP Positive Expiratory Pressure Plateau [*Medicine*] (MAE)
PEPP Professional Engineers in Private Practice
PEPPA Preparedness for Emergency Plant Pest Action [*In Animal and Plant Health Inspection Service publication PEPPA Pot*]
PEPPARD Propellant, Explosive, Pyrotechnic Pollution Abatement Research and Development (DNAB)
PEPPER Photo-Electric Portable Probe Reader (PDAA)
Pepper & L Dig Pepper and Lewis' Digest of Laws [*Pennsylvania*] [*A publication*] (DLA)
Pepper & L Dig Laws Pepper and Lewis' Digest of Laws [*Pennsylvania*] [*A publication*] (DLA)
Pepperdine U Pepperdine University (GAGS)
PEPPRE Photo Electric Portable Probe Reader (IAA)
PEPR Precision Encoding and Pattern Recognition Device [*Computer science*]
PEPrA PECO Energy, $3.80 Pfd [*NYSE symbol*] (TTSB)
PEPrB PECO Energy, $4.30 Pfd [*NYSE symbol*] (TTSB)
PEPrC PECO Energy, $4.40 Pfd [*NYSE symbol*] (TTSB)
PEPrD PECO Energy, $4.68 Pfd [*NYSE symbol*] (TTSB)
PEPrF PECO Energy Dep Pfd [*NYSE symbol*] (TTSB)
PEPrY PECO En Cap Tr I 8.72% 'TOPrS' [*NYSE symbol*] (TTSB)
PEPrZ PECO Energy L.P. MIPS'A' [*NYSE symbol*] (TTSB)
PEPS National Committee on Public Employee Pension Systems (EA)
PEPS Peperomia and Exotic Plant Society (EA)
PEPS Peptidase S [*An enzyme*]
PEPS Pesticide Enforcement Policy Statement [*Environmental Protection Agency*]
PEPS Primary Earnings per Share (TDOB)
PEPS Primary Environmental Prediction System
PEPS Primary Environmental Processing Systems [*Navy*] (GFGA)
PEPS Production Engineering Productivity System [*Camtek Ltd.*] [*Software package*]
PEPS Productivity Environmental Preference Survey [*Test*]
PEPS Program Element Plan Supplement
PEP-SEP Peptide Separation [*Biochemistry*]
PEPSI Plasma Electron Profiles, Symmetric Integrals (MCD)
PepsiC PepsiCo, Inc. [*Associated Press*] (SAG)
PepsiPR Pepsi Cola Puerto Rico Bottling [*Associated Press*] (SAG)
PEPSS Preschool and Early Primary Skills Survey [*Child development test*]
PEPSS Programmable Equipment for Personnel Subsystem Simulation
PEPSU All India Reporter, Patiala and East Punjab States Union [*1950-57*] [*A publication*] (DLA)
PEPSU Patiala and East Punjab States Union
PEPSY Precision Earth-Pointing System (MCD)
PEPTP (Phenylethyl)Phenyltetrahydropyridine [*Organic chemistry*]
PEP/USA Parkinson's Educational Program - USA (EA)
PEPUSL Pepperdine University School of Law (DLA)
PEpW Westinghouse Electric Corp., East Pittsburgh, PA [*Library symbol Library of Congress*] (LCLS)
PEQ Pecos City, TX [*Location identifier FAA*] (FAAL)
PEQ Personal Experience Questionnaire [*Psychology*]
PEQ Petroquin Resources Ltd. [*Vancouver Stock Exchange symbol*]
PEQ Potomac Edison [*NYSE symbol*] (SAG)
PEQ Potomac Edison 8.00% 'QUIDS' [*NYSE symbol*] (TTSB)
PEQUA Production Equipment Agency [*Army*]
PEQUOD Pacific Equatorial Ocean Dynamics
PEQUOD Pacific Equatorial Ocean Dynamics [*Project*] [*USA*] [*Marine science*] (OSRA)
PEr Erie Public Library, Erie, PA [*Library symbol Library of Congress*] (LCLS)
PER For Each (DAVI)
PER Packed Encoding Rules (ACII)
PER Par Exchange Rate [*Business term*]
PER Parity Error Rate
PER Parole Evidence Rule [*Legal shorthand*] (LWAP)
PER Partido Estadista Republicano [*Puerto Rico*] [*Political party*]
PER Path Extension Ratio (MCD)
PER Peak Ejection Rate [*Cardiology*]
PER Peak Expiration Rate [*Medicine*]
Per Pediatric Emergency Room (DAVI)
Pe R Pennewill's Delaware Reports [*A publication*] (DLA)
per Perennial [*Botany*]
Per Perera's Select Decisions [*Ceylon*] [*A publication*] (DLA)
PER Per Exchange Rate [*Finance*] (MHDW)
PER Performance (DA)
PER Performance Evaluation Report [*DoD*]
PER Perhaps (ROG)
Per Pericles [*Shakespearean work*]
Per Pericles [*of Plutarch*] [*Classical studies*] (OCD)
PER Perigee (KSC)
per Perineal [*Gynecology*] (MAE)
Per Periochae [*of Livy*] [*Classical studies*] (OCD)
Per Period [*Record label*]
PER Period
per Period (VRA)
per Periodic (AAMN)
PER Periodical (ROG)
per Periodicity (DMAA)
PER Periodogram (DMAA)
PER Permission (AABC)
Per Perseus [*Constellation*]
PER Persia [*Obsolete*]
Per Persia (VRA)
per Persian, Modern [*MARC language code Library of Congress*] (LCCP)
PER Person
per Person (WDMC)
PER Personnel (KSC)
PER PERT [*Program Evaluation and Review Technique*] Event Report
PER Perth [*Australia Airport symbol*] (OAG)
PER Perth [*Australia Seismograph station code, US Geological Survey Closed*] (SEIS)
PER Peru [*ANSI three-letter standard code*] (CNC)
PER Pharmaceutical Evaluation Report [*Australia*]
PER Phase Engineering Report
PER Physical Examination Rate [*Military*] (AFM)
PER Planning, Evaluation, and Reporting [*Education-improvement system*]
PER Pominex Ltd. [*Toronto Stock Exchange symbol*]
PER Ponca City, OK [*Location identifier FAA*] (FAAL)
PER Port Everglades Railway [*AAR code*]
PER Postelectrophoresis Relaxation
PER Post Engineer Request
PER Post-Execution Reporting (MHDI)
PER Potential Excess Report
PER Preedited Region [*Genetics*]
PER Pre-Emptive Right (MHDW)
PER Preliminary Engineering Report (KSC)
PER PressNet Environmental Reports [*Information service or system*] (IID)
PER Price Earnings Ratio [*Relation between price of a company's stock and its annual net income*]
PER Printing Executive Register (DGA)
PER Probable Error Radial [*Statistics*] (IAA)
PER Product Engineering Recommendation [*Automotive engineering*]
PER Production Engine Remanufacturers Program [*Automotive engineering*]
PER Professional and Executive Recruitment Service [*British*]
PER Professional Employment Register [*British*] (ODBW)
PER Proficiency Evaluation Review
PER Program Error Report (MHDI)
PER Program Event Recording [*Computer science*] (MDG)
PER Program Execution Request
PER Proposal Evaluation Report (MCD)
PER Protein Efficiency Ratio [*Nutrition*]
PER Public Employees Roundtable (EA)
PER Pyrotechnical Evaluation Range [*Army*] (RDA)
PERA Planning and Engineering for Repair and Alteration [*Navy*]
PERA Production Engineering Research Association [*Research center British*] (IRC)
PERA Production Engine Remanufacturers Association (EA)
Per A J Performing Arts Journal [*A publication*] (BRI)
PERAM Personnel Action Memorandum [*Military*]
PER AN Per Annum [*By the Year*] [*Latin*]
Per & Dav Perry and Davison's English King's Bench Reports [*1838-41*] [*A publication*] (DLA)
Per & Kn Perry and Knapp's English Election Reports [*1838*] [*A publication*] (DLA)
PER ANN Per Annum [*By the Year*] [*Latin*]
PERA system Project Engineering Research Association system (NITA)
Pe Rave Petrus Ravennas [*Flourished, 1468-1508*] [*Authority cited in pre-1607 legal work*] (DSA)
PERB Public Employment Relations Board (EDAC)
PERC Parents Educational Resource Center
PERC Peace on Earth Research Center
PERC Perclose, Inc. [*NASDAQ symbol*] (SAG)
PERC Percolator (DSUE)
PERC Percussion (AAG)
PERC Pittsburgh Energy Research Center [*Later, PETC*] [*Energy Research and Development Administration*]
PERC Political & Economic Risk Consultancy [*Commercial firm*] [*Hong Kong*]
PERC Political Economy Research Center [*Research center*] (RCD)
PERC Processor Emergency Recovery Circuit [*Bell System*]
PERC Professional Engineering and Research Consultants
PERC Psoriasis Education and Research Centre [*University of Toronto*] [*Canada Research center*] (RCD)
PERC Public Employment Relations Commission (EDAC)
PERCAM Performance and Cost Analysis Model (MCD)
Per Cap Per Capita [*By the Individual*] [*Latin*]
PERCAP Persian Gulf Requirements and Capabilities [*Military*]
PERCASREPT Personnel Casualty Report [*Military*] (NVT)
PERCENT Per Centum [*By the Hundred*] [*Latin*]

PERCHLOR... Perchloride [*Chemistry*] (ROG)
PERCI .... Personnel Contamination Instrumentation
Perclose ...... Perclose, Inc. [*Associated Press*] (SAG)
PERCOM ...... Personnel Command [*Army*] (MCD)
PERCOMP.... Personal Computing Conference (MHDI)
PERCOMPASIA... South East Asian Personal Computer Hardware and Software Show
Percon .... Percon, Inc. [*Associated Press*] (SAG)
Per con .... Per Contra [*On the Other Side*] [*Latin*]
PERCOS .... Performance Coding System
Percptr......... Perceptron, Inc. [*Associated Press*] (SAG)
Per CS .... Perrault's Conseil Superieur [*Canada*] [*A publication*] (DLA)
PERCS .... Preference Equity Redemption Cumulative Stock (ECON)
PERCUSS...... Percussion [*Medicine*] (DAVI)
PERCUSS & AUSC... Percussion and Ausculation [*Medicine*] (DHSM)
PERD .... Perdendo [*or Perdendosi*] [*Softer and Slower Music*]
PERD .... Periodic (MSA)
PERD .... Perused (ROG)
PERDA .... Per Diem [*By the Day*] [*Latin*] (NOAA)
PERDDiMS... Personnel Deployment and Distribution Management System [*Military*] (AABC)
PERDEN .... Perdendo [*or Perdendosi*] [*Softer and Slower Music*]
PERDEX .... Permuted Formula Index [*Molecular formula indexing*]
PerDia .... Personal Diagnositics, Inc. [*Associated Press*] (SAG)
PEREF.......... Personal Effects
PEREF.......... Propellant Engine Research Environmental Facility
Pereg........... Peregrinus Fabius [*Authority cited in pre-1607 legal work*] (DSA)
PERF............ Peak Expiratory Flow Rate [*Medicine*] (DMAA)
PERF............ Perfect
PERF............ Perfect
PERF............ PerfectData Corp. [*NASDAQ symbol*] (NQ)
PERF............ Perforate [*or Perforator*]
PERF............ Perforation (DSUE)
perf............. Perforation (WDMC)
PERF............ Performance (KSC)
perf............. Performance (VRA)
PERF............ Perfusionist [*Medicine*] (HCT)
PerF............ Perma Fix Environmental Services [*Associated Press*] (SAG)
PERF............ Planetary Entry Radiation Facility [*Langley Research Center*] [*NASA*] (PDAA)
PERF............ Police Executive Research Forum (EA)
PERFCE........ Performance
PERFD .... Performed (ROG)
Perfdta......... PerfectData Corp. [*Associated Press*] (SAG)
PERFINS ...... Perforated Insignia [*Philately*]
PERFM......... Perform (ROG)
PerFood....... Performance Food Group [*Commercial firm Associated Press*] (SAG)
PERFORM.... Performance
PERFR .... Perforator (IAA)
PERF RM..... Perfect Ream (DGA)
PerfSys....... Performance Systems International, Inc. [*Associated Press*] (SAG)
PerfTech....... Performance Technologies, Inc. [*Associated Press*] (SAG)
Perfum......... Perfumania, Inc. [*Associated Press*] (SAG)
PERFW .... Perforating Wound
PErG .... Gannon University, Erie, PA [*Library symbol Library of Congress*] (LCLS)
PERG .... Pergola [*Classified advertising*] (ADA)
PERG .... Production Emergency Redistribution Group
PERG .... Production Equipment Redistribution Group [*Army*]
PERGO......... Project Evaluation and Review with Graphic Output (IEEE)
PERGRA........ Permission Granted [*Military*]
PERH .... Perhaps
PerHi .... Erie County Historical Society, Erie, PA [*Library symbol Library of Congress*] (LCLS)
PERI............. Pea Ridge National Military Park
PERI............. Perigee
PERI............. Perimeter (AABC)
peri.............. Perineal [*Anatomy*] (DAVI)
PERI............. Periodical
PERI............. Periphonics Corp. [*NASDAQ symbol*] (SAG)
PERI............. Periscope
PERI............. Peritoneal Fluid (DAVI)
PERI............. Platemakers Educational and Research Institute [*Later, IAP*]
PERI............. Production Equipment Redistribution Inventory [*Army*]
PERI............. Production Equipment Reserve Inventory [*Navy*] (NG)
PERI............. Protein Engineering Research Institute [*Japanese governmental and industrial consortium*] [*Later, BERI*]
PERI............. Psychiatric Epidemiology Research Interview
PERIAP .... Periapical [*Dentistry*]
peric .... Pericope (VRA)
Pericom .... Pericom Semiconductor Corp. [*Associated Press*] (SAG)
PERIF........... Peripheral
perig............ Perigee (BARN)
Pe Rigal ...... Petrus Rigaldi [*Flourished, 14th century*] [*Authority cited in pre-1607 legal work*] (DSA)
PERIM .... Perimeter (KSC)
PERI/M .... Perimortem (DAVI)
PeriniC .... Perini Corp. [*Associated Press*] (SAG)
PERINTREP... Periodic Intelligence Report (NATG)
PERINTREPT... Periodic Intelligence Report
PERINTSUM... Periodic Intelligence Summary [*Army*] (AABC)
perio............ Periodontist [*Dentistry*] (DAVI)
PERIPH .... Periphery (KSC)
Periphn........ Periphonics Corp. [*Associated Press*] (SAG)
Peripl M Eux... Periplus Maris Euxini [*of Arrian*] [*Classical studies*] (OCD)
PERIS .... Periscope (KSC)
PERJ............ Perjury [*FBI standardized term*]
PERJY.......... Perjury (ROG)
PERK .... Payroll Earnings Record Keeping
Perk............. Perkins on Conveyancing [*A publication*] (DLA)
Perk............. Perkins on Pleading [*A publication*] (DLA)
Perk............. Perkins' Profitable Book (Conveyancing) [*A publication*] (DLA)
PERK .... Perquisite
PERK .... Prospective Evaluation of Radial Keratotomy [*for eye surgery*]
PERK .... Prospective Evaluation of Radial Keratotomy [*Protocol*] [*Ophthalmology*] (DAVI)
PERKARA...... Parti Perdapuan Kebangsaan Ra'ayat Brunei [*Brunei People's National United Party*] [*Political party*] (EY)
PerkEl.......... Perkin-Elmer Corp. [*Associated Press*] (SAG)
PerkF........... Perkins Family Restaurants Ltd. [*Associated Press*] (SAG)
Perk Pr Bk... Perkins' Profitable Book (Conveyancing) [*A publication*] (DLA)
perks .... Perquisites (MHDB)
PERL............ Pathologically Eclectic Rubbish Lister
PERL............ Perkin-Elmer Robot Language
PERL............ Perle Systems Ltd. [*Scarborough, ON*] [*NASDAQ symbol*] (NQ)
PERL............ Perusal (ROG)
PERL............ Pictorial Engineering and Research Laboratory
PERL............ Portable Electronic Runway Lighting (PDAA)
PERL............ Practice Extraction and Report Language [*Facetious translation: Pathologically Eclectic Rubbish Lister*] [*Computer science*] (NHD)
PERL............ Prepositioned Equipment Requirements List [*Navy*] (MCD)
PERL............ Public Employee Relations Library [*of International Personnel Management Association*]
PERL............ Pupils Equal and Reactive to Light (DAVI)
PERL............ Pupils Equal, Regular, and Reactive to Light (DAVI)
PERLA .... Pupils Equal, React to Light and Accommodation [*Medicine*]
PERLA .... Pupils Equal, Regular and Reactive to Light and Accommodation (DAVI)
PerleSys ...... Pearle Systems Ltd. [*Associated Press*] (SAG)
PERLF........... Perle System [*NASDAQ symbol*] (TTSB)
PERLS .... Principal Exchange-Rate-Linked Securities [*Investment term*]
PERM........... Permanent
PERM........... Permanent Bancorp [*NASDAQ symbol*] (SAG)
PERM........... Permanent Employee (DSUE)
PERM........... Permeability
PERM........... Permian [*Period, era, or system*] [*Geology*]
PERM........... Permission (MSA)
PERM........... Permutation (DSUE)
PERM........... Pre-Embossed Rigid Magnetic Media [*Computer science*]
PERM........... Program Evaluation for Repetitive Manufacture (IEEE)
PERMACAP... Personnel Management and Accounting Card Processor [*Military*]
PERMACAPS... Personnel Management and Accounting Card Processing System (MCD)
PERMAFROST... Permanent Frost
PERMAS ...... Persatuan Rakyat Malaysian Sarawak [*Political party*] (EY)
PERMAS ...... Personnel Management Assistance System [*Military*] (AABC)
PERMB .... Permeability
PermBcp...... Permanent Bancorp [*Associated Press*] (SAG)
PErMC .... Mercyhurst College, Erie, PA [*Library symbol Library of Congress*] (LCLS)
PerMdw .... Perpetual Midwest Financial, Inc. [*Associated Press*] (SAG)
PERME......... Propellants, Explosives, and Rocket Motors Establishment [*British Ministry of Defense*] [*Research center*] (RDA)
PermF.......... Perma Fix Environmental Services [*Associated Press*] (SAG)
PermFix........ Perma Fix Environmental Services [*Associated Press*] (SAG)
PERMIC .... Personnel Management Information Center [*Navy*] (NVT)
PERMINVAR... Permeability Invariant
PERMIXT ..... Permixtus [*Mixed*] [*Pharmacy*] (ROG)
PERMLY ...... Permanently
PERMR .... Permanent Residence
PERMREP.... Permanent Representation to North Atlantic Council [*NATO*] (NATG)
PERMS .... Personnel Electronic Record Management System [*Army*] (RDA)
PERMS .... Process and Effluent Radiological Monitoring System [*Nuclear energy*] (NRCH)
PERMSS .... Process and Effluent Radiological Monitoring and Sampling System [*Nuclear energy*] (NRCH)
PERMT.......... Permanent (ROG)
PERMU .... Permanent Magnet Users Association [*Defunct*] (EA)
PernC........... Perini Corp. [*Associated Press*] (SAG)
PERNOGRA... Permission Not Granted [*Military*]
PERO .... President's Emergency Relief Organization (NADA)
PER OP EMET... Peracta Operatione Emetici [*When the Operation of the Emetic is Finished*] [*Pharmacy*] (ROG)
Per Or Cas... Perry's Oriental Cases [*Bombay*] [*A publication*] (DLA)
PEROX.......... Peroxidase Stain [*Biochemistry*] (DAVI)
PEROX.......... Peroxide
PERP .... Pan-Ethnic Republican Party of Australia [*Political party*]
PERP .... Perpendicular (AAG)
perp .... Perpendicular (VRA)
PERP .... Perpetrator (WDAA)
PERP .... Perpetual (ADA)
Per P .... Perrault's Prevoste de Quebec [*A publication*] (DLA)
PERP .... Personnel Processing (MUGU)
perpad......... Perineal Pad [*Gynecology*] (MAE)
PerpBnk........ Perpetual Bank Federal Savings Bank [*Associated Press*] (SAG)
Perpet.......... Perpetual (DLA)
per pro .... Per Procurationem [*By Proxy, By the Action Of*] [*Legal term*] [*Latin*] (BARN)
PER PROC ... Per Procurationem [*By Proxy, By the Action Of*] [*Legal term Latin*]
PerpSB .... Petpetual State Bank [*North Carolina*] [*Associated Press*] (SAG)

Per Psy........ Personnel Psychology [*A publication*] (BRI)
PERR........... Patter-Evoked Retinal Response [*neurology and ophthalmology*] (DAVI)
PERR........... Premature Engine Removal Rate (AAG)
Perrault....... Perrault's Conseil Superieur [*Canada*] [*A publication*] (DLA)
Perrault....... Perrault's Prevoste de Quebec [*A publication*] (DLA)
Perrault....... Perrault's Quebec Reports [*A publication*] (DLA)
Perrigo........ Perrigo Co. [*Associated Press*] (SAG)
PERRL......... Pupils Equal, Round and Reactive to Light (DAVI)
PERRL......... Pupils Equal, Round, Regular and Reactive to Light (DAVI)
PERRLA....... Pupils Equal, Round, React to Light and Accommodation [*Medicine*]
PERRLA....... Pupils Equal, Round, Regular, and Reactive to Light and Accommodation (DAVI)
PERRLA (DC)... Pupils Equal, Round, and Reactive to Light and Accommodation (Directly and Consensually) (DAVI)
Perry........... Perry's Oriental Cases [*Bombay*] [*A publication*] (DLA)
Perry & D.... Perry and Davison's English King's Bench Reports [*A publication*] (DLA)
Perry & D (Eng)... Perry and Davison's English King's Bench Reports [*A publication*] (DLA)
Perry & K.... Perry and Knapp's English Election Cases [*A publication*] (DLA)
Perry & Kn... Perry and Knapp's English Election Cases [*A publication*] (DLA)
PerryCF........ Perry County Financial Corp. [*Associated Press*] (SAG)
Perry Ins....... Perry's English Insolvency Cases [*1831*] [*A publication*] (DLA)
Perry OC...... Perry's Oriental Cases [*Bombay*] [*A publication*] (DLA)
PERS........... Patient Evaluation Rating Scale [*Medicine*] (DMAA)
PERS........... Performance Evaluation Reporting System [*DoD*]
PERS........... Periodical Source Index [*A publication*]
Pers........... Persae [*of Aeschylus*] [*Classical studies*] (OCD)
Pers........... Perseus [*Constellation*]
PERS........... Persia [*Obsolete*]
PERS........... Persian Leather [*Bookbinding*] (DGA)
Pers........... Persius [*34-62AD*] [*Classical studies*] (OCD)
PERS........... Person
PERS........... Personal
pers........... Personal (WDMC)
PERS........... Personal Emergency Response System [*Telecommunications*]
PERS........... Personnel (AFM)
pers........... Personnel (DD)
PERS........... Personnel Squadron
pers........... Persons (WDMC)
PERS........... Perspective (WDAA)
PERS........... Preliminary Engineering Reports (MUGU)
PERS........... Program for Evaluation of Rejects and Substitutions [*Computer science*] (IAA)
PERS........... Public Employees Retirement System (DICI)
PERSACLIT... Peritus in Sacred Liturgy [*Roman Catholic*]
PERSACS..... Personnel Structure and Accounting System [*Army*]
PERSACS..... Personnel Structure and Composition System [*Military*]
PERS & TRACOMD... Personnel and Training Command
PERSC......... Public Education Religion Studies Center [*Defunct*] (EA)
PERS CASREP... Personnel Casualty Report [*Navy*] (ANA)
PERSCEN..... Personnel Center
PERSCO....... Personnel Support of Contingency Operations [*Military*]
PersCom....... Personnel Command [*Army*] (INF)
PERSCON.... Personnel Control [*Military*]
PERSD......... Personnel Department [*Marine Corps*]
PERSDEP..... Personnel Deployment Report [*Military*]
PerSep......... PerSeptive Technologies II Corp. [*Associated Press*] (SAG)
PERSEP....... Pershing Survivability Evaluation Program [*Military*] (MCD)
PERSEPCOMD... Personnel and Separation Command (DNAB)
PERSERVDEPSERVS... Personal Services and Dependents' Services Support System [*Navy*] (DNAB)
PERSET....... Personnel Standardization and Evaluation Team [*Military*]
PERSEVCE... Perseverance (ROG)
PERSEXP..... Personal Expense Money [*Army*]
PersGp......... Personnel Group of America [*Associated Press*] (SAG)
PERSH......... Perishable (WGA)
Pershad....... Privy Council Judgments [*1829-69*] [*India*] [*A publication*] (DLA)
PERSIL........ Peroxide Silicate [*Detergent and bleach*]
Pers Inj Comment'r... Personal Injury Commentator [*A publication*] (DLA)
Pers Inj LJ... Personal Injury Law Journal [*A publication*] (DLA)
PERSINS...... Personnel Information System [*Army*]
PERSINSCOM... Personnel Information Systems Command [*Army*] (AABC)
PERSINSD... Personnel Information Systems Directorate [*Military Personnel Center*] (AABC)
PERSIR........ Personnel Inventory Report [*Army*] (AABC)
PERSIS........ Personnel Information System (MHDB)
PERSL......... Personal
Pers Man..... Personnel Management [*A publication*]
PERSMAR.... Personnel Manning Assistance Report (DNAB)
PERSNET..... Personnel Network [*Army*]
PersnMg....... Personnel Management, Inc. [*Associated Press*] (SAG)
PERSO......... Personnel Officer [*Air Force*]
PERSOF....... Personnel Officer [*Navy*]
PERSON....... Personnel Simulation On-Line [*Department of State*] [*Computer program*]
Persp........... Perspective [*Record label*]
PERSP......... Perspective (MSA)
persp........... Perspective (VRA)
PERSPAY..... Personnel and Pay [*Project*] [*Navy*]
Pers Prac B... Personnel Practice Bulletin [*A publication*]
PERSPROC... Personnel Processing [*Army*]
Pers PS....... Perspectives on Political Science [*A publication*] (BRI)
PerSptv........ PerSeptive Biosystems, Inc. [*Associated Press*] (SAG)
PERSRSCHSYSTM... Personnel Management and Training Research Statistical Data System [*Navy*] (DNAB)
PERSRU....... Personnel Reporting Unit
PERSSEPCENT... Personnel Separation Center
PERSSO....... Personnel System Staff Officer
PERSTAT..... Personnel Status Report [*Military*]
PERSTATREP... Personnel Status Report [*Military*]
PERSTRAN... Personal Transportation [*Navy*]
PERT........... Patients Experience of the Relationship with the Therapist Method
PERT........... Performance Evaluation Review Technique
PERT........... Perpetual Bank Federal Savings Bank [*NASDAQ symbol*] (SAG)
PERT........... Pertain (AABC)
PERT........... Pertussis [*Whooping cough*]
PERT........... Phenol Enhanced Reassociation Technique [*Clinical chemistry*]
PERT........... Program Estimation Revaluation Technique [*Computer science*] (IAA)
PERT........... Program Evaluation and Review Technique [*Computer science*]
PERT........... Program Evaluation Research Task (IEEE)
PERT........... Project Evaluation and Review Technique (DAC)
PERTCO....... Program Evaluation and Review Technique with Cost
PERT/CPM.... Program Evaluation and Review Technique/Critical Path Method [*Computer science*] (DOM)
PERT-CS...... Program Evaluation and Review Technique - Cost System (DNAB)
PERTHS....... Perthshire [*County in Scotland*]
PERT-NAP.... Program Evaluation and Review Technique - Network Automatic Plotting (SAA)
PERTO......... Pertaining To (NVT)
Per Tr.......... Perry on Trusts [*A publication*] (DLA)
PERTRAN..... Perturbation Transport [*NASA*]
PERTSIM..... Program Evaluation and Review Technique Simulation [*Game*]
PERT-TAM... Program Evaluation and Review Technique Task, Action, and Milestone Items
PERT/TIME... Program Evaluation and Review Technique/Time Analyzer [*Sperry UNIVAC*]
PERU.......... Production Equipment Records Unit (IEEE)
PERUG........ Perusing (ROG)
PERUSA...... Perspectives - United States of America [*History course*]
PERUV........ Peruvian
PERV.......... Pervert [*or Perverted*] [*FBI standardized term*]
PErV........... United States Veterans Administration Hospital, Erie, PA [*Library symbol Library of Congress*] (LCLS)
PErVM........ Villa Maria College, Erie, PA [*Library symbol Library of Congress*] (LCLS)
PERYLENE... Peri-Dinaphthalene [*A fluorophore*] [*Organic chemistry*]
Pes............. Esophageal Pressure [*Used to estimate intrapleural pressure*] (DAVI)
PES............. IEEE Power Engineering Society (EA)
PES............. Paid Educational Services [*British*]
PES............. Pan European Survey [*A publication*]
PES............. Paraendocrine Syndrome [*Endocrinology*]
PES............. Parent Egg Seed
PES............. Partial Energy Service [*Electric power*]
PES............. Partido Ecuatoriano Socialista [*Ecuadorean Socialist Party*] [*Political party*]
PES............. Parts Engineering Support
PES............. Passive Electromagnetic System (IAA)
PES............. Patent Examining System
PES............. Pecos Resources [*Vancouver Stock Exchange symbol*]
Pes............. Pesahim (BJA)
PES............. Peshawar [*Pakistan*] [*Seismograph station code, US Geological Survey Closed*] (SEIS)
PES............. Philosophy of Education Society (EA)
PES............. Photoelectric Scanner
PES............. Photoelectric Scanning [*Electronics*] (ECII)
PES............. Photoelectron Spectroscopy
PES............. Photoemission Spectroscopy
PES............. Photojet Edge Sensor
PES............. Physicians Equity Services
PES............. Pictorial Eleven Society [*Formerly, PE*] [*PCS*] [*Absorbed by*] (EA)
PES............. Pointing Error Sensor (MCD)
PES............. Polyethersulfone [*Organic chemistry*]
PES............. Polyethylene Sodium Sulfonate [*Anticoagulant*]
PES............. Post-Enumeration Survey [*Bureau of the Census*]
PES............. Postextrasystolic Potentiation [*Cardiology*]
PES............. Potential Energy Source [*Physiology*]
PES............. Potential-Energy Surface [*Chemical kinetics*]
PES............. Poultry and Egg Situation
PES............. Power Engineering Society
PES............. Power Engineering Specification
PES............. Preexcitation Syndrome [*Cardiology*]
Pes............. Pressure, End-Systole [*Cardiology*]
PES............. Pressure Equalization System [*Nuclear energy*] (NUCP)
PES............. Private Express Statutes (DICI)
P(ES).......... Probability of Equal Regressive Slopes [*Statistics*]
PES............. Probe Entry Site [*Instrumentation*]
PES............. Problem-Etiology-Signs [*or Symptoms*] [*Nursing*]
PES............. Processed Eucheuma Seaweed
PES............. Processor Enhancement Socket [*Computer science*] (PCM)
PES............. Production Engineering Service
PES............. Production Engineering Specification (NG)
PES............. Professional Examination Service
PES............. Program Element Summary
PES............. Program Emphasis Statement [*US Employment Service*] [*Department of Labor*]
PES............. Program Execution System
PES............. Programmable Electronic System [*Engineering*]
PES............. Programmed Electrical Stimulation [*Neurophysiology*]

PES .... Projected Engagement Scheduler [*Military*] (CAAL)
PES .... Public Expenditure Survey [*British*]
PESA .... Petroleum Electric Supply Association [*Defunct*] (EA)
PESA .... Petroleum Equipment Suppliers Association (EA)
PESA .... Propellant Expulsion and Storage Assembly
PESA .... Proton Elastic-Scattering Analysis
PESABC .... Permanent Executive Secretariat of the Andres Bello Convention [*See also SECAB*] (EAIO)
PESC .... Pool Energy Services [*NASDAQ symbol*] (TTSB)
PESC .... Pool Energy Services Co. [*NASDAQ symbol*] (SAG)
PESC .... Public Expenditure Survey Committee [*British*] (ODBW)
PESD .... Pacific Electronic Security Division [*Military*]
PESD .... Postsecondary Education Statistics Division [*Department of Education*] (GFGA)
PESD .... Private and Executive Secretary's Diploma (AIE)
PESD .... Program Element Summary Data [*DoD*]
PESD .... Program Execution Subdirective (AABC)
PESDC .... Properties of Electrolyte Solutions Data Center [*National Institute of Standards and Technology*]
PESDS .... Program Element Summary Data Sheet [*DoD*]
PESGB .... Petroleum Exploration Society of Great Britain
Pesh .... Peshitta [*Syriac translation of the Bible*] (BJA)
Peshawar .... All India Reporter, Peshawar [*1933-50*] [*A publication*] (DLA)
Peshawar .... Indian Rulings, Peshawar Series [*1933-47*] [*A publication*] (DLA)
PESI .... Perma Fix Environmental Services [*NASDAQ symbol*] (SAG)
PESI .... Perma Fix Enviro Svcs [*NASDAQ symbol*] (TTSB)
PESIA .... Postal Employees Salary Increase Act of 1960
PESIC .... Parti du Progres Economique et Social des Independants Congolais Luluabourg [*Party for Economic and Social Progress of the Congolese Independents in Luluabourg*] [*Political party*]
Pesik .... Pesikta de-Rav Kahana (BJA)
Pesikt .... Pesikta de-Rav Kahana (BJA)
PesiktR .... Pesikta Rabbati (BJA)
PESIS .... Photo-Electron Spectroscopy of Inner-Shell (PDAA)
PESIW .... Perma-Fix Envir'l Svcs Wrrt [*NASDAQ symbol*] (TTSB)
PESIZ .... Perma-Fix Envir'l Svcs Wrrt'B' [*NASDAQ symbol*] (TTSB)
PESM .... Photoelectron Spectromicroscope
PeSMoT .... Penn State Microoxidation Test [*Analytical chemistry*]
PESO .... Participation Enriches Science, Music, and Art Organizations [*Orlando, Florida*]
PESO .... Performance Evaluation Support Office
PESO .... Plant Engineering Shop Order (AAG)
PESO .... Product Engineering Services Office [*DoD*]
PESOS .... Perkin-Elmer Solvent Optimization System [*Chemistry*]
PESOS .... Photo-Electron Spectroscopy of Outer-Shell (PDAA)
PESOS .... Prepare, Explain, Show, Observe, Supervise [*Formula*] [*LIMRA*]
PESP .... Postextrasystolic Potentiation [*Medicine*] (DMAA)
PesR .... Pesikta Rabbati (BJA)
PESR .... Planning Element System Report (NATG)
PESR .... Precision Echo Sounder Recorder
PESR .... Pseudoequivalent Service Rounds [*Military*] (NVT)
PEsS .... East Stroudsburg State College, East Stroudsburg, PA [*Library symbol Library of Congress*] (LCLS)
PESS .... Pessus [*Pessary*] [*Pharmacy*]
PESS .... Problem, Etiology, Signs, and Symptoms [*Medicine*] (DMAA)
PESSO .... Personnel System Staff Officer
PEST .... Parameter Entity Symbol Translator [*Elstree Computing Ltd.*] [*Software package*] (NCC)
PEST .... Parameter Estimation by Sequential Testing [*Computer*]
PEST .... Patterned Elicitation Syntax Test [*Educational test*]
PEST .... Pesticide Evaluation Summary Tabulation
PEST .... Political, Environmental, Social, and Technological [*Business term*] (ODBW)
PEST .... Pressure for Economic and Social Toryism [*Tory Reform Group*] [*British*] (DI)
PEST .... Production Evaluation Surveillance Test
PESTAB .... Pesticides Abstracts (NITA)
PESTDOC .... Pest Control Literature Documentation [*Derwent Publications Ltd.*] [*Bibliographic database*] [*Information service or system*] (IID)
PESTDOC .... Pesticide Documentation (NITA)
PESTF .... Proton Event Start Forecast [*Solar weather information*]
PESTIC .... Pesticide
PESU .... Polyethersulfone [*Organic chemistry*]
PESV .... Pea Streak Virus [*Plant pathology*]
PESY .... Pheripheral Exchange Synchronization (IAA)
PET .... Aeropetrel [*Chile*] [*ICAO designator*] (FAAC)
PET .... Pacific Enterprises [*AMEX symbol*] (SAG)
PET .... Pacific Enterprises [*NYSE symbol*] (SPSG)
PET .... Panel on Educational Terminology [*Office of Education*]
PET .... Panel on Education and Training [*COSATI*]
PET .... Paper Equilibrium Tester (BARN)
PET .... Parent Effectiveness Training [*A course of study*]
PET .... Particle Electrostatic Thruster
PET .... Patterned Epitaxial Technology (IEEE)
PET .... Pelotas [*Brazil*] [*Airport symbol*] (OAG)
PET .... Pentaerythritol [*Organic chemistry*]
PET .... Pentaerythritol Tetranitrate [*Also, PETN*] [*Explosive, vasodilator*]
PET .... Penthouse Entertainment Network [*Cable television system*]
PET .... Performance Efficiency Test [*Employee screening and placement test*]
PET .... Performance Evaluation Team [*Nuclear energy*] (NRCH)
PET .... Performance Evaluation Test
PET .... Periodic Environmental Test
PET .... Periodic Evaluation Test
PET .... Peripheral Equipment Tester [*Computer science*] (BUR)
PET .... Personal Effectiveness Training (MCD)
PET .... Personal Electronic Transaction Computer (NITA)
PET .... Personal Electronic Transactor [*Computer*] [*Commodore Business Machines*]
PET .... Personal Employee Time (DHSM)
Pet .... Peter [*New Testament book*]
Pet .... Peters' Prince Edward Island Reports [*1850-72*] [*Canada*] [*A publication*] (DLA)
Pet .... Peters' United States Circuit Court Reports [*A publication*] (DLA)
Pet .... Peters' United States District Court Reports, Admiralty Decisions [*A publication*] (DLA)
Pet .... Peter's United States Reports [*1828-42*] [*A publication*] (AAGC)
Pet .... Peters' United States Supreme Court Reports [*26-41 United States*] [*A publication*] (DLA)
Pet .... Petihta (BJA)
PET .... Pet, Inc., Corporate Information Center, St. Louis, MO [*OCLC symbol*] (OCLC)
PET .... Petition
PET .... Petrine [*Of, or relating to, Peter the Apostle or Peter the Great*]
PET .... Petrolatum (WGA)
PET .... Petroleum
Pet .... Petroleum (DD)
PET .... Petropavlovsk [*Kazakhstan*] [*Seismograph station code, US Geological Survey*] (SEIS)
PET .... Petrotech, Inc. [*Toronto Stock Exchange symbol*]
Pet .... Petrus [*Authority cited in pre-1607 legal work*] (DSA)
Pet .... Petrus de Bellapertica [*Deceased, 1308*] [*Authority cited in pre-1607 legal work*] (DSA)
PET .... Phase Elapsed Time (NASA)
PET .... Philco Epoxy Transistor (IAA)
PET .... Photoelectric Transducer (PDAA)
PET .... Photoemission Tube
PET .... Photoinduced Electron Transfer
PET .... Phototropic Energy Transfer
PET .... Physical Equipment Table
PET .... Pierre Elliott Trudeau [*Canadian prime minister*] [*Acronymic designation considered derogatory*]
PET .... Point of Equal Time [*Aviation*]
PET .... Polyester
PET .... Polyethylene [*Organic chemistry*] (IAA)
PET .... Poly(ethylene Terephthalate) [*Organic chemistry*]
PET .... Portable Earth Terminal [*NASA*]
PET .... Portable Electronic Telephone
PET .... Portable Electronic Translator
PET .... Position-Event-Time
PET .... Positron-Emission Tomography
PET .... Potential Evapotranspiration
PET .... Potentially Exempt Transfer (ODBW)
PET .... Potentially Exempt Transfer (ODBW)
PET .... Prediction Error Transform (PDAA)
PET .... Pre-Eclamptic Toxemia [*Medicine*]
PET .... Pre-Employment Training (OICC)
PET .... Preliminary Evaluation Team
PET .... Preliminary Examination Team [*NASA*]
PET .... Preprimary Evaluation and Training
PET .... Pressure Equalization [*Tubes or Equalizing*] [*Otorhinolaryngology*] (DAVI)
PET .... Pressurization Events Trainer
PET .... Probe Ephemeris Tape
PET .... Process Evaluation Tester
PET .... Producibility Evaluation Task [*Army*] (RDA)
PET .... Production Environmental Tests
PET .... Production Evaluation Test
PET .... Production Experimental Test (SAA)
PET .... Program Evaluation Team
PET .... Program Evaluator and Tester [*Computer science*]
PET .... Property Enterprise Trust [*Investment term British*] (ECON)
PET .... Propulsion Experimental Test (SAA)
PET .... Prototype Evaluation Test
PET .... Psychiatric Emergency Team
PET .... Pulsed Electrothermal (MCD)
PET .... Pupil Evaluation Team [*Education*]
PETA .... Pentaerythritol Triacrylate [*Organic chemistry*]
PETA .... People for the Ethical Treatment of Animals (EA)
PETA .... Performance Evaluation and Trend Analysis (NASA)
PETA .... Plutonium Equipment Transfer Area [*Nuclear energy*] (NRCH)
PETA .... Portable Electronic Traffic Analyzer [*British*]
Pet Ab .... Petersdorff's Abridgment [*A publication*] (DLA)
Pet Abr .... Petersdorff's Abridgment [*1660-1823*] [*A publication*] (DLA)
Pet Ad .... Peters' United States District Court Reports, Admiralty Decisions [*A publication*] (DLA)
Pet Ad Dec .... Peters' United States District Court Reports, Admiralty Decisions [*A publication*] (DLA)
Pet Adm .... Peters' United States District Court Reports, Admiralty Decisions [*A publication*] (DLA)
Pet Adm App .... Peters' United States District Court Reports, Admiralty Decisions (Appendix) [*A publication*] (DLA)
Pet Ad R .... Peters' United States District Court Reports, Admiralty Decisions [*A publication*] (DLA)
PET & S .... Performance Evaluation, Test, and Simulation [*Air Force*]
Pet Aret .... Petrus Aretinus [*Flourished, 1088-91*] [*Authority cited in pre-1607 legal work*] (DSA)
PETAT .... Periodic Inspection Turn-Around Time [*Military*] (AFIT)
Pet Bail .... Petersdorff on Bail [*1824*] [*A publication*] (DLA)

Pet Br......... Bellewe's Cases Tempore Henry VIII [*Brooke's New Cases*] [*England*] [*A publication*] (DLA)
Pet Br......... Brooke's New Cases (Petit Brooke) [*1515-58*] [*A publication*] (DLA)
PETC........... Parent Effectiveness Training Course [*Australia*]
PETC........... Petco Animal Supplies [*NASDAQ symbol*] (SAG)
PETC........... Pittsburgh Energy Technology Center [*Formerly, PERC*] [*Department of Energy Pittsburgh, PA*] (GRD)
PETC........... Polyethylene Tetrachloride [*Organic chemistry*] (IAA)
PETC........... Portable Equipment Test Chamber (MCD)
Pet CC......... Peters' United States Circuit Court Reports [*A publication*] (DLA)
Pet Cir CR... Peters' Condensed United States Circuit Court Reports [*A publication*] (DLA)
PetcoAn....... Petco Animal Supplies [*Associated Press*] (SAG)
Pet Cond...... Peters' Condensed Reports, United States Supreme Court [*A publication*] (DLA)
Pet Cond Rep... Peters' Condensed United States Circuit Court Reports [*A publication*] (DLA)
PETD........... Petroleum Development [*NASDAQ symbol*] (TTSB)
PETD........... Petroleum Development Corp. [*NASDAQ symbol*] (NQ)
Pet de Anch... Petrus de Ancharano [*Deceased, 1416*] [*Authority cited in pre-1607 legal work*] (DSA)
Pet de Bel... Petrus de Bellapertica [*Deceased, 1308*] [*Authority cited in pre-1607 legal work*] (DSA)
Pet de Bellap... Petrus de Bellapertica [*Deceased, 1308*] [*Authority cited in pre-1607 legal work*] (DSA)
Pet de Belper... Petrus de Bellapertica [*Deceased, 1308*] [*Authority cited in pre-1607 legal work*] (DSA)
Pet de Mont... Petrus Piccoli de Monteforte [*Flourished, 14th century*] [*Authority cited in pre-1607 legal work*] (DSA)
Pet de Sam... Petrus de Sampsone [*Flourished, 1246-58*] [*Authority cited in pre-1607 legal work*] (DSA)
Pet de Samp... Petrus de Sampsone [*Flourished, 1246-58*] [*Authority cited in pre-1607 legal work*] (DSA)
Pet Dig........ Peters' United States Digest [*A publication*] (DLA)
Pet Dig........ Peticolas' Texas Digest [*A publication*] (DLA)
PetDv........... Petroleum Development Corp. [*Associated Press*] (SAG)
PETE........... Parliamentary Education for Teacher Education [*Australia*]
PETE........... Partnership for Environmental Technology Education [*Nonprofit organization of 400 community colleges*]
PETE........... Petersburg National Battlefield
PETE........... Pneumatic End to End
PETE........... Portable Educational Tools Environment (AIE)
PETE........... Portable Electronics Test Equipment (DNAB)
PETE........... Portable Emergency Thermal Environment
PETE........... Primary Bank [*NASDAQ symbol*] (SAG)
PETE........... Product Engineering Tribute to Excellence
PETE........... Proof and Experimental Test Establishment [*Canada*] (MCD)
Peter........... Analysis and Digest of the Decisions of Sir George Jessel, by A. P. Peter [*England*] [*A publication*] (DLA)
Peters.......... Haviland's Prince Edward Island Chancery Reports, by Peters [*1850-72*] [*Canada*] [*A publication*] (DLA)
Peters.......... Peters' United States Supreme Court Reports [*26-41 United States*] [*A publication*] (DLA)
Peters' Ad... Peters' United States District Court Reports, Admiralty Decisions [*A publication*] (DLA)
Peters Adm... Peters' United States District Courts Reports, Admiralty Decisions [*A publication*] (DLA)
Peters' Adm Dec... Peters' United States District Court Reports, Admiralty Decisions [*A publication*] (DLA)
Peters' Admiralty Dec... Peters' United States District Court Reports, Admiralty Decisions [*A publication*] (DLA)
Peters' Adm R... Peters' United States District Court Reports, Admiralty Decisions [*A publication*] (DLA)
Peters Adm Rep... Peters' United States District Court Reports, Admiralty Decisions [*A publication*] (DLA)
Peters CC.... Peters' United States Circuit Court Reports [*A publication*] (DLA)
Petersd Ab... Petersdorff's Abridgment [*A publication*] (DLA)
Petes........... Petes Brewing Co. [*Associated Press*] (SAG)
PETFE.......... Polyethylenetetrafluoroethylene [*Organic chemistry*]
PETFEM....... Postsecondary Education Task Force on Energy Management [*Canada*]
PetFood....... Pet Food Warehouse [*Commercial firm Associated Press*] (SAG)
PETG............ Phenylethyl(thiogalactoside) [*Organic chemistry*]
Petg Pr & Ag... Petgrave's Principal and Agent [*1857*] [*A publication*] (DLA)
Pet Greg...... Petrus Gregorius [*Deceased, 1617*] [*Authority cited in pre-1607 legal work*] (DSA)
PETH........... Pink-Eyed, Tan-Hooded Rat [*Medicine*] (DMAA)
Peth Dis...... Petheram's Discovery by Interrogations [*1864*] [*A publication*] (DLA)
PETI............ Portable Electronic Typewriter Interface [*Applied Creative Technology, Inc.*]
PETIA.......... Particle-Enhanced Turbidometric Immunoassay [*Clinical chemistry*]
Petit Br....... Petit Brooke, or Brooke's New Cases, English King's Bench [*1515-58*] [*A publication*] (DLA)
PETITN........ Petition
Pet L Nat..... Petersdorff's Law of Nations [*A publication*] (DLA)
PETM........... Petsmart, Inc. [*NASDAQ symbol*] (SAG)
PETMA......... Portable Electric Tool Manufacturers' Association [*British*] (BI)
Pet M & S... Petersdorff's Master and Servant [*1876*] [*A publication*] (DLA)
PETN........... Pentaerythritol Tetraniconitate [*Niceritrol*] [*Pharmacology*] (DAVI)
PETN........... Pentaerythritol Tetranitrate [*Also, PET*] [*Explosive, vasodilator*]
PETN........... Petition
PETNR......... Petitioner
PETP........... (Phenylethyl)phenyltetrahydropyridine [*Organic chemistry*]
PETP........... Poly(ethylene Terephthalate) [*Organic chemistry*]
PETP........... Preliminary Engineering Technical Proposal
Pet Peck Zir... Petrus Peckius (Ziricaeus) [*Deceased, 1589*] [*Authority cited in pre-1607 legal work*] (DSA)
Pet PM........ Petersen's Photographic Magazine [*A publication*] (BRI)
PETPrA........ Pacific Ent $4.36 Pfd [*AMEX symbol*] (TTSB)
PetPrac....... [*The*] Pet Practice, Inc. [*Associated Press*] (SAG)
PETPrB........ Pacific Ent $4.40 Pfd [*AMEX symbol*] (TTSB)
PETPrC........ Pacific Ent $4.50 Pfd [*AMEX symbol*] (TTSB)
PETPrD........ Pacific Ent $4.75 Pfd [*AMEX symbol*] (TTSB)
PetPRO........ Pet Professional Retailers Organization [*Defunct*] (EA)
PETQI.......... Patient Education Total Quality Improvement [*Medicine*] (DMAA)
PETR........... Petitioner
PETR........... PetroCorp [*NASDAQ symbol*] (TTSB)
PETR........... Petrocorp, Inc. [*NASDAQ symbol*] (SAG)
petr............. Petroleum [*Chemistry*] (DAVI)
PETRA......... Positron-Electron Tandem Ring Accelerator [*Nuclear*]
PETRA......... Program for the Vocational Training of Young People and their Preparation for Adult and Working Life [*EC*] (ECED)
PETRA......... Project for Evaluation and Treatment of Radioactive Waste [*Nuclear energy*] (NUCP)
Petr Bellug... Petrus Belluga [*Flourished, 1446-68*] [*Authority cited in pre-1607 legal work*] (DSA)
Petr de Benint... Petrus de Benintendis [*Flourished, 16th century*] [*Authority cited in pre-1607 legal work*] (DSA)
PETREL........ Professional Education and Training for Research Librarianship Program (EDAC)
PETRES........ Petroleum Reserves [*Navy*]
PETRESO..... Petroleum Reserves Office [*or Officer*]
petrgly......... Petroglyph (VRA)
Petr Greg..... Petrus Gregorius [*Deceased, 1617*] [*Authority cited in pre-1607 legal work*] (DSA)
PETRIBURG... Petriburgensis [*Signature of the Bishops of Peterborough*] [*Latin*] (ROG)
Petrie........... Petrie Stores Corp. [*Associated Press*] (SAG)
PETRL.......... Petroleum (AABC)
PetrlGeo....... Petroleum Geo Services [*Associated Press*] (SAG)
PetrLng........ Petersburg Long Distance [*Commercial firm Associated Press*] (SAG)
Petrlte......... Petrolite Corp. [*Associated Press*] (SAG)
Petrmn......... Petrominerals Corp. [*Associated Press*] (SAG)
Petr Nuni..... Petrus Nunius de Avendano [*Flourished, 16th century*] [*Authority cited in pre-1607 legal work*] (DSA)
PETRO......... Petroleum
PETRO......... Petroleum
PetroC......... Petro-Canada [*Associated Press*] (SAG)
PetroC2....... Petro-Canada [*Associated Press*] (SAG)
PETROCH..... Rock Chemical Database [*Ontario Geological Survey*] [*Canada Information service or system*] (CRD)
Petrocp........ Petrocorp, Inc. [*Associated Press*] (SAG)
PETRODEG... Petroleum Degrading [*Agent*]
PETROEX..... Petroleum Products Exchange Data Clearing House (NITA)
PETROG....... Petrographic
PETROGAL... Petroleos de Portugal, EP [*Portuguese Petroleum Co.*]
PETROGR.... Petrography
PETROL....... Petroleum
PETROL....... Petrology
PETROMIN... General Petroleum & Mineral Organization [*Saudi Arabia state-owned oil company*]
Petromt........ Petromet Resouces Ltd. [*Associated Press*] (SAG)
Petron.......... Petronius [*First century AD*] [*Classical studies*] (OCD)
PETRONET... Petroleum Network [*Distribution and interdiction model*] (MCD)
Petron Satyric... Petronius' [*Titus*] Arbiter, Satyricon, Etc. [*A publication*] (DLA)
PETROPHIL... Petroleum Philatelic Society International (EAIO)
PETROPOL... Petropolis [*St. Petersburg*] [*Imprint*] [*Latin*] (ROG)
PetroUn....... Petro Union, Inc. [*Associated Press*] (SAG)
Petr Rave.... Petrus Ravennas [*Flourished, 1468-1508*] [*Authority cited in pre-1607 legal work*] (DSA)
PetRs........... Petroleum & Resources Corp. [*Associated Press*] (SAG)
PETS............ Pacific Electronics Trade Show
PETS............ Payload Environmental Transportation System [*NASA*] (NASA)
PETS............ Peripheral Equipment Test Set
PETS............ P/L Experiment Test System [*NASA*] (GFGA)
PETS............ POCC [*Payload Operations Control Center*] Experiments Timeline System [*Ground Data Systems Division and Spacelab*] [*NASA*] (NASA)
PETS............ Polaris Engineering Technical Service [*Missiles*]
PETS............ Portable Engine Test Stand (MCD)
PETS............ Positions Equipment Task Summary (AAG)
PETS............ Prior to Expiration of Term of Service [*Reenlistments*] [*Military*]
PETS............ Programmed Extended Time Sharing [*Computer science*]
PETS............ Proximity Effect Tunneling Spectroscopy (MCD)
Pet SC......... Peters' United States Supreme Court Reports [*26-41 United States*] [*A publication*] (DLA)
PET scan..... Positron Emission Transaxial Tomography [*Also, PETT*] (PAZ)
PETSEC....... Petroleum Section [*Allied Force Headquarters*]
PetsMrt........ Petsmart, Inc. [*Associated Press*] (SAG)
Pet Suppl..... Supplement to Petersdorff's Abridgment [*A publication*] (DLA)
PETT............ Pendular Eye-Tracking Test [*Medicine*] (DMAA)
PETT............ Phototropic Energy Transfer Technique
PETT............ Positron Emission Transaxial [*or Transverse*] Tomography [*Roentgenography*]
PETT............ Purkinje Fiber [*Medicine*] (DMAA)
PETT............ Purpura Fulminans [*Medicine*] (DMAA)
PETT............ Push Fluids [*Medicine*] (DMAA)
PETV............ Planar Epitaxial Tuning Varactor
PETV............ Process Evaluation Test Vehicle
PEU.............. Paneuropa-Union [*Paneuropean Union*] (EAIO)

PEU............ Plasma Equivalent Unit [*Medicine*] (DMAA)
PEU............ Port Expander Unit
PEU............ Protected Environment Unit [*Medicine*]
PEUA.......... Pelvic Exam under Anesthesia [*Medicine*]
PEUU.......... Polyether Polyurethane Urea [*Organic chemistry*]
peV............ Peak Electron Volts
PEV............ Peak Envelope Voltage [*Telecommunications*] (TEL)
PEV............ Peak Expiratory Velocity [*Medicine*] (DMAA)
PEV............ Permanent Entry Visa
PEV............ Philip Environmental [*NYSE symbol*] (SAG)
PEV............ Philip Environmental [*NYSE symbol*] (TTSB)
PEV............ Pleasant Valley [*California*] [*Seismograph station code, US Geological Survey*] (SEIS)
PEV............ Position-Effect Variegation [*Genetics*]
PEV............ Position-Effect Variegation [*Genetics*] [*Botany*]
PEV............ Positive Expected Value
PEV............ Propeller-Excited Vibration (PDAA)
PEV............ Pyroelectric Vidicon (PDAA)
PEVCV........ Petunia Vein Clearing Virus [*Plant pathology*]
PEVE.......... Post Experience Vocational Education (AIE)
PEVE.......... Prensa Venezolana [*Press agency*] [*Venezuela*]
PEVI........... Perry's Victory and International Peace Memorial National Monument
PEVL.......... Polyethylene Expanded Video Longitudinal Cable (MCD)
PEVM.......... Personal'naia Elektronnaia Vychislitel'naia Mashina [*Personal Computer*] [*Russian*]
PEVM.......... Professional'naia Elektronnaia Vychislitel'naia Mashina [*Professional Computer*] [*Russian*]
PEVR.......... Power-Enrichment Vacuum Regulator [*Automotive engineering*]
PEW............ Passive Electronics Warfare (NG)
PEW............ Percussion Welding
PEW............ Peshawar [*Pakistan*] [*Airport symbol*] (OAG)
pew............ Pewter (VRA)
PEW............ Pulmonary Extravascular Water [*Medicine*] (DMAA)
PEWO.......... Plant Engineering Work Order (MCD)
PEWR.......... Plant Engineering Work Release (AAG)
PEWS.......... Parts Early Warning System (IAA)
PEWS.......... Platoon Early Warning System (RDA)
PEWS.......... Plutonium Equipment Warm Shop [*Nuclear energy*] (NRCH)
PEWV.......... Pulmonary Extravascular Water Volume [*Physiology*]
Pex............ Peak Exercise (DMAA)
PEX............ Per Example
PEX............ Phenazine Ethosulfate [*Biochemistry*]
PEx............ Physical Examination (MAE)
PEX............ Private Electronic Exchange [*Telecommunications*] (IAA)
PEX............ Pronto Explorations Ltd. [*Vancouver Stock Exchange symbol*]
PEX............ World Aircraft Flight Operation, Inc. [*ICAO designator*] (FAAC)
PEXA.......... Pre-Edge X-Ray Absorption [*For study of solids*]
PEXAFS...... Photoelectron Extended X-Ray Absorption Fine Structure
PEXRA........ Programmed Electronic X-Ray Automatic Diffractometer (IAA)
PEXRAD...... Programmed Electronic X-Ray Automatic Diffractometer
PEY............ Pengelly Mines Ltd. [*Vancouver Stock Exchange symbol*]
PEY............ Photoelectric Yield
PEYS.......... Photoelectron Yield Spectroscopy (MCD)
PEZ............ Pezgold Resource Corp. [*Vancouver Stock Exchange symbol*]
PEZ............ Pleasanton, TX [*Location identifier FAA*] (FAAL)
PEZV.......... Prime Equities International [*NASDAQ symbol*] (SAG)
PEZVF........ Prime Equities Intl [*NASDAQ symbol*] (TTSB)
PF.............. Amer First Prep Fd 2 L.P. [*AMEX symbol*] (TTSB)
PF.............. American First PREP [*Preferred Real Estate Participation*] Fund 2 Ltd. [*AMEX symbol*] (SPSG)
PF.............. Frankford Public Library, Frankford, PA [*Library symbol Library of Congress*] (LCLS)
PF.............. French Polynesia [*ANSI two-letter standard code*] (CNC)
PF.............. L-Phenylalanine Mustard and 5-Fluorouracil [*Antineoplastic drug regimen*] (DAVI)
PF.............. Pacifica Foundation (EA)
PF.............. Package Freighter [*Shipping*]
PF.............. Packing Factor (EECA)
PF.............. Packing Fraction (EECA)
PF.............. Paderewski Foundation [*Defunct*] (EA)
PF.............. Page Fault (IAA)
PF.............. Page Footing (BUR)
PF.............. Page Formatter (MDG)
PF.............. Pair Feeding (DMAA)
PF.............. Paling Fence
PF.............. Panchromatic Film (ADA)
pf.............. Paper and Foil [*Capacitor*] (DEN)
pf.............. Paracel Islands [*MARC country of publication code Library of Congress*] (LCCP)
PF.............. Parachute Facility (NASA)
PF.............. Parachute Flare (NVT)
PF.............. Parafascicular Nucleus [*Neuroanatomy*]
PF.............. Parallel Fiber [*Neuroanatomy*]
PF.............. Parallel Fold
PF.............. Paramount Funding Corp. [*Toronto Stock Exchange symbol*]
PF.............. Parapsychology Foundation (EA)
PF.............. Partial Function (IAA)
PF.............. Partition Factor (NRCH)
PF.............. Passage Free (ROG)
P/F............ Pass-Fail [*System*] (MAE)
PF.............. Patellofemoral Joint [*Anatomy*] (DAVI)
PF.............. Path Finder [*British military*] (DMA)
PF.............. Pathfinder Fund (EA)
PF.............. Patriotic Front [*Zimbabwe*] [*Political party*] (PPW)
PF.............. Patrol Vessel, Frigate [*Navy symbol*]
P/F............ Pattern Flight [*Also, P/FLT*] (MUGU)
PF.............. Payload Forward [*NASA*] (MCD)
PF.............. Payload Function [*NASA*] (MCD)
PF.............. Peace and Freedom Party [*Political party*] (DLA)
PF.............. Peak Flow [*Medicine*]
PF.............. Peak Frequency
PF.............. Peanut Flour
PF.............. Pedal Furrow
PF.............. Penetration Fracture (IAA)
PF.............. Pen Friends [*Defunct*] (EA)
PF.............. Pension Fund
PF.............. Peregrine Fund (EA)
PF.............. Perfect
PF.............. Performance Factor
PF.............. Perfusion Fixation [*Histology*]
PF.............. Perfusion Fluid [*Medicine*] (DMAA)
PF.............. Pericardial Fluid [*Medicine*] (DMAA)
PF.............. Periosteal Fibroblast [*Medicine*] (DMAA)
PF.............. Peritoneal Fluid [*Medicine*] (MAE)
PF.............. Permanent Fireman
PF.............. Permanent Force [*Canadian Militia before 1940*]
PF.............. Permeability Factor
pf.............. Perofskite [*CIPW classification*] [*Geology*]
PF.............. Personal Fouls [*Basketball*]
PF.............. Personality Factor
PF.............. Personal Security File Number [*British Secret Service*]
Pf.............. Pfeifferella [*Genus of bacteria*]
PF.............. Pfennig [*Penny*] [*Monetary unit*] [*German*]
PF.............. Phenol-Formaldehyde [*Organic chemistry*]
PF.............. Phenylalanine and Methotrexate [*Antineoplastic drug regimen*] (DAVI)
PF.............. Philatelic Foundation (EA)
PF.............. Photogrammetric Facility [*Army*]
PF.............. Physicians Forum (EA)
PF.............. Pianoforte [*Soft, then Loud*] [*Music*]
pF.............. Picofarad
PF.............. Picture Frustration [*Study*] (MAE)
PF.............. Pilgrim Fellowship (EA)
PF.............. Pilot Flying (GAVI)
PF.............. Pilot Stop Filter (IAA)
PF.............. Pininfarina [*Automotive coachworks*]
PF.............. [*The*] Pioneer & Fayette Railroad Co. [*AAR code*]
PF.............. Piu Forte [*A Little Louder*] [*Music*]
PF.............. Plain Face [*Construction*]
PF.............. Plane Frame [*Camutek*] [*Software package*] (NCC)
PF.............. Planning Forum (EA)
PF.............. Plantar Fasciaitis [*Medicine*]
PF.............. Plantar Flexion [*Medicine*]
PF.............. Plasma Factor (DMAA)
PF.............. Plasticity Index [*Soil*] (DICI)
PF.............. Platelet Factor [*Hematology*]
PF.............. Platform (SSD)
PF.............. Plentiful Foods [*Department of Agriculture*] [*A publication*]
PF.............. Pleural Fluid [*Medicine*] (DMAA)
PF.............. Plot Function [*Computer science*]
PF.............. Pneumatic Float
PF.............. Poco Forte [*Rather Loud*] [*Music*]
PF.............. Poe Foundation (EA)
PF.............. Point Foundation (EA)
PF.............. Point of Frog [*Electronics*] (MSA)
PF.............. Points For [*Football*]
PF.............. Polar Front [*Climatology*]
PF.............. Pole Fittings [*JETDS nomenclature*] [*Military*] (CET)
PF.............. Police Forces [*British*]
PF.............. Police Foundation (EA)
PF.............. POLISARIO [*Frente Popular para la Liberacion de Saguia El Hamra y Rio De Oro*] [*Popular Front for the Liberation of Saguia El Hamra and Rio De Oro Morocco*] (PD)
P/F............ Poll/Final [*Computer science*] (TNIG)
PF.............. Poloidal Field (MCD)
PF.............. Polyurethane Foam
PF.............. Pool Frequency [*Pisciculture*]
PF.............. Poop and Forecastle [*of a ship*] (DS)
PF.............. Popular Forces [*ARVN*]
PF.............. Pore Free (IAA)
PF.............. Por Favor [*Please*] [*Portuguese*]
PF.............. Portal Fibrosis [*Medicine*]
PF.............. Portfolio [*A publication*]
PF.............. Position Failure
PF.............. Position Finder [*British military*] (DMA)
PF.............. Postage Free (ROG)
PF.............. Posterior Fontanelle [*Anatomy*] (DAVI)
P/F............ Post Flight (AFIT)
PF.............. Postman's Federation [*A union*] [*British*]
PF.............. Posture Foundation [*Initialism is used in brand of sneaker shoe, PF Flyers*]
PF.............. Potency Factor (GNE)
PF.............. Powered Flight (NASA)
PF.............. Power Factor [*Radio*]
pf.............. Power Factor (IDOE)
PF.............. Power Focus [*Photography*]
PF.............. Power Frame [*Telecommunications*] (TEL)
P/F............ Practical Factors
PF.............. Precursor Fluid [*Medicine*] (MEDA)
PF.............. Preference
PF.............. Preferred

PF .... Prefetch [*Computer science*]
PF .... Preflight
PF .... Presbyterian Foundation [*Australia*]
PF .... Pressure Fan (AAG)
PF .... Preterm Foundation [*Australia*]
PF .... Primary Fibrinolysin [*Medicine*] (DMAA)
PF .... Prime Function (NASA)
PF .... Prison Fellowship Ministries (EA)
PF .... Probability of Failure (NASA)
PF .... Procurator Fiscal
PF .... Pro Female [*International Bowhunting Organization*] [*Class Equipment*]
PF .... Profile (KSC)
pf .... Pro Forma [*As a Matter of Form*] [*Latin*] (WGA)
PF .... Program Function [*Computer science*] (IBMDP)
PF .... Programmable Format [*Perforating keyboard*]
PF .... Programmable Function (NITA)
PF .... Progressive Foundation (EA)
PF .... Project Friend (EA)
PF .... Projectile Fragment
PF .... Proof
PF .... Prop Forward
PF .... Proposed Finding [*Nuclear energy*] (NRCH)
PF .... Prostatic Fluid [*Medicine*] (DMAA)
PF .... Protection Factor
PF .... Protein-Free
PF .... Protoplasmic Fracture [*Freeze etching in microscopy*]
PF .... Proximity Fuze [*Bomb, rocket, or shell*]
PF .... PsychoHistory Forum (EA)
PF .... Psynetics Foundation (EA)
P/F .... Pteropod/Foramifera [*Ratio in coastal waters*]
PF .... Public Funding [*Finance*] (WDAA)
PF .... Pulmonary Factor [*Medicine*]
PF .... Pulmonary Function [*Medicine*] (DMAA)
PF .... Pulse Feedback [*Telecommunications*] (IAA)
PF .... Pulse Frequency
PF .... Pulverized Fuel
P F .... Pump-Out Facilities [*Nautical charts*]
PF .... Punch Off [*Computer science*] (BUR)
PF .... Purge Fan [*Nuclear energy*] (NRCH)
PF .... Purkinje Fibers [*Cardiology*] (DAVI)
PF .... Purple Finch [*Ornithology*]
PF .... Purpura Fulminans (DMAA)
PF .... Pygmy Fund (EA)
PF .... Trans Pennsylvania Airlines [*ICAO designator*] (AD)
PF3a .... Platelet Factor 3 Availability [*Hematology*] (DAVI)
PFA .... Palmdale Final Assembly [*NASA*] (NASA)
PFA .... Panarcadian Federation of America (EA)
PFA .... Papermakers Felt Association (EA)
PFA .... Para-Fluorophenylalanine [*Biochemistry*]
PFA .... Participating Field Activity [*DoD*]
PFA .... Parti de la Federation Africaine [*African Federation Party*] [*Political party*]
PFA .... Pellet-Fired Appliance [*Heating system*]
PFA .... Pension Fund Association [*Japan*] (ECON)
PFA .... Perfluoroalkoxy [*Organic chemistry*]
PFA .... Personnel Functional Assessment [*Of the Army Acquisition Corps*] (RDA)
PFA .... Petroflame International [*Vancouver Stock Exchange symbol*]
PFA .... Phosphonoformic Acid [*Antiviral compound*]
PFA .... Pianists Foundation of America [*Defunct*] (EA)
PFA .... Pierce Ferry [*Arizona*] [*Seismograph station code, US Geological Survey Closed*] (SEIS)
PFA .... Pierre Fauchard Academy (EA)
PFA .... Pioneer Fraternal Association (EA)
PFA .... Pitch Follow-Up Amplifier
PFA .... Plan for Action (MCD)
PFA .... Polish Falcons of America (EA)
PFA .... Polyfurfuryl Alcohol [*Organic chemistry*]
PFA .... Polymeric Fatty Acid [*Food science*]
PFA .... Polyurethane Foam Association (EA)
PFA .... Pontius Family Association (EA)
PFA .... Popular Flying Association [*British*]
PFA .... Post Flight Analysis
PFA .... Power Fastenings Association [*British*] (DBA)
PFA .... Prescription Footwear Association (EA)
PFA .... Printer Font ASCII [*Computer science*] (CDE)
PFA .... Prison Families Anonymous (EA)
PFA .... Prison Fellowship of Australia
PFA .... Probability of False Alarm [*DoD*]
PFA .... Probability of False Alarm [*Criminology*] (LAIN)
PFA .... Production Flow Analysis (PDAA)
PFA .... Professional Farmers of America (EA)
PFA .... Professional Fishermen's Association [*Tasmania, Australia*]
PFA .... Professional Footballers' Association [*British*] (BI)
PFA .... Professional Fraternity Association (EA)
PFA .... Profunda Femoris Artery [*Anatomy*] (DAVI)
PFA .... Program and File Analysis
PFA .... Proportional Fluid Amplifier
PFA .... Pulverized Fuel Ash (IEEE)
PFA .... Pure Fluid Amplification
PFAA .... Prairie Farm Assistance Act
PFAB .... Prefabricated
PFAC .... Panepirotic Federation of America and Canada [*Later, PFACA*] (EA)
PFAC .... People for a Change (EA)
PFACA .... Panepirotic Federation of America, Canada, and Australia (EA)
P/FACCTL .... Pad Facility Controls [*Aerospace*] (AAG)
PFACP .... Pro-Fac Co-op 'A' Pfd [*NASDAQ symbol*] (TTSB)
PFACP .... Pro-Fac Cooperative, Inc. [*NASDAQ symbol*] (SAG)
PFAD .... Palm Fatty Acid Distillate [*Organic chemistry*]
PFAE .... Perfluoroalkyl Ether [*Organic chemistry*]
PFAM .... Programmed Frequency Amplitude Modulation
PFANZ .... Police Federation of Australia and New Zealand
PFAP .... Poly(fluoroalkoxyphosphazene) [*Organic chemistry*]
PFAR .... Popular Front for Armed Resistance [*Pakistan*]
PFAR .... Power Fail Automatic Restart [*Computer science*]
PFAR .... Preliminary Failure Analysis Report [*NASA*] (KSC)
PFAS .... Performic Acid-Schiff Reaction [*Medicine*] (MAE)
PFAS .... President of the Faculty of Architects and Surveyors [*British*] (DBQ)
PFASC .... PATRIOT [*Phased Array Tracking to Intercept Target*] Field Army Suppor t Center [*Army*]
PFAT .... Pre-First Article Test
PFAT .... Preliminary Flight Appraisal Test (MCD)
PFAT .... Private Forestry Association of Tasmania [*Australia*]
PFAVC .... Pacific Fleet Audio-Visual Command (DNAB)
PFAW .... People for the American Way (EA)
PFAWA .... Parents and Friends Association of Western Australia
PFAWA .... Poultry Farmers' Association of Western Australia
PFB .... Partei Freier Buerger [*Free Citizens' Party*] [*Germany Political party*] (PPW)
PFB .... Passo Fundo [*Brazil*] [*Airport symbol*] (OAG)
PFB .... Payload Feedback [*NASA*] (MCD)
PFB .... Payload Forward Bus [*NASA*] (MCD)
PFB .... Pentafluorobenzyl [*Organic radical*]
PFB .... Pentafluorobenzyl Bromide [*Organic chemistry*]
PFB .... Photo Flash Battery
PFB .... Plasti-Fab Ltd. [*Toronto Stock Exchange symbol*]
PFB .... Pneumatic Float Bridge
PFB .... Position Feedback (MCD)
PFB .... Prefabricated [*Technical drawings*]
PFB .... Preformed Beams [*SONAR*]
PFB .... Pressure Fed Booster (NASA)
PFB .... Pressurized Fluid-Bed [*Chemical engineering*]
PFB .... Printer Font Binary [*Computer science*] (CDE)
PFB .... Provisional Frequency Board [*ITU*]
PFB .... Pseudofollicutitis Barbae [*Medicine*]
PFBA .... Poly(perfluorobutyl Acrylate) [*Organic chemistry*]
PFBC .... Pentaflurobenzoyl Chloride [*Organic chemistry*]
PFBC .... Pressurized Fluidized-Bed Combustion
PFBHA .... Pentafluorobenzylhydroxylamine Hydrochloride [*Analytical biochemistry*]
PFBI .... Premier Financial Bancorp, Inc. [*NASDAQ symbol*] (SAG)
PFBI .... Premier Finl Bancorp [*NASDAQ symbol*] (TTSB)
PFBRG .... Pneumatic Float Bridge
PFBV .... Pelargonium Flower Break Virus [*Plant pathology*]
PFC .... Pacific City, OR [*Location identifier FAA*] (FAAL)
PFC .... Parallel-Flow Condenser [*Air conditioning systems*]
PFC .... Parti Feministe du Canada
PFC .... Passed Flying College [*British*]
PFC .... Passenger Facility Charge [*Airports*]
PFC .... Pathfinder Industries Ltd. [*Formerly, Pathfinder Financial Corporation*] [*Toronto Stock Exchange symbol*]
PFC .... Patient Focused Care [*Medicine*]
PFC .... Peak Follower Circuit
PFC .... Peculiar Facility Change (AAG)
PFC .... Pelvic Flexion Contracture [*Orthopedics*] (DAVI)
PFC .... Pen Fancier's Club (EA)
PFC .... Pennsylvania Public Library Film Center, University Park, PA [*OCLC symbol*] (OCLC)
PFC .... Perfluorocarbon [*Organic chemistry*]
PFC .... Perfluorocarbon [*Marine science*] (OSRA)
PFC .... Perfluorochemical [*Organic chemistry*]
PFC .... Performance Flight Certification [*NASA*] (NASA)
PFC .... Permanent Families for Children [*Defunct*] (EA)
PFC .... Persistent Fetal Circulation [*Medicine*]
PFC .... Personal Finance Center [*Information service or system*]
PFC .... Physicians for Choice (EA)
PFC .... Plan Filing Cabinet
PFC .... Plaque-Forming Cell [*Immunochemistry*]
PFC .... Plow-Furrow-Cover [*Waste*] (DICI)
PFC .... Pneumatic Function Controller
PFC .... Point Focusing and Centering [*Optics*]
PFC .... Police Forces [*British*]
PFC .... Positive Feedback Circuit
PFC .... Postflight Checklist (MCD)
PFC .... Power Factor Capacitor [*Radio*] (IAA)
PFC .... Power Factor Corrector (MCD)
PFC .... Prairie Fiction Collection, Alberta Culture [*UTLAS symbol*]
PFC .... Praying for Corporal [*Private First Class desirous of promotion, or female in wartime desirous of a boyfriend*]
PFC .... Preflight Console (MCD)
PFC .... Prefrontal Cortex [*Anatomy*]
PFC .... Preliminary Flight Certification [*NASA*]
PFC .... Presley-ites Fan Club (EA)
PFC .... Pressure Function Controller
PFC .... Primary Flight Control
PFC .... Priority Foreign Country [*International trade*] (ECON)
PFC .... Private, First Class [*Army*]
PFC .... Private Forestry Council [*Australia*]
PFC .... Privately Financed Consumption (MHDW)

PFC............ Processing Figure Channel [*Electronics*] (ECII)
PFC............ Programmed Fuel Computer [*Automotive engineering*]
PFC............ Progreso y Futuro de Ceuta [*Political party*] (EY)
PFC............ Pulsed Flame Combustor
PFC............ Pulse-Flow Coulometry
PFCA.......... Performance Ford Club of America (EA)
PFCA.......... Plastic Food Container Association [*Defunct*]
PFCC.......... Power Factor Corrector Capacitor [*Radio*] (IAA)
PFCCG........ Pacific Fleet Combat Camera Group (DNAB)
PFCD.......... Primary Flight Control Display
PFCE.......... Performance (WGA)
PFCE.......... Preface (ROG)
PFCE.......... Preference (AAG)
PFCF.......... Payload Flight Control Facility [*NASA*] (MCD)
PFCF.......... Producer Fixed Capital Formation (MCD)
PFCH.......... Prefilled Clutch Hydraulic Actuation [*Automotive Products, Inc.*] [*Automotive engineering*]
PFCM.......... Pittsburgh Festival of Contemporary Music [*Record label*]
PFCO.......... Position Field Classification Officer
PFCP.......... Primary Familial and Congenital Polycythemia [*Medicine*]
PFCR.......... Plaque-Forming Cell Response [*Immunochemistry*] (OA)
PFCRA........ Program Fraud Civil Remedies Act
PFCRN........ Partido del Frente Cardenista de Reconstruccion Nacional [*Mexico Political party*] (EY)
PFCS.......... Primary Flight Control System [*NASA*] (MCD)
PFCS.......... Primary Flow Control System [*Nuclear energy*] (NRCH)
PFCS.......... Program and Funds Control System (MCD)
PFCT.......... Pre-Flight Certification Test
PFCU.......... Power Flying Control Unit [*Aviation*] (DA)
PFCV.......... Patriotic Funds Council of Victoria [*Australia*]
PFCWTS..... Pogo Fan Club and Walt Kelly Society (EA)
PFD............ Particle [*or Proton*] Flux Density
PFD............ Perfluorodecalin [*Organic chemistry*]
PFD............ Personal, Fatigue, and Delay [*Work measurement factors*]
PFD............ Personal Flotation Device [*Life jacket*]
PFD............ Phase Frequency Distortion [*Telecommunications*] (IAA)
PFD............ Planned Flight Data [*Aviation*] (DA)
PFD............ Planning Factors Development (MCD)
PFD............ Policy Formulation Division (AAGC)
PFD............ Polyostotic Fibrous Dysplasia [*Medicine*] (DMAA)
PFD............ Position Fixing Device (ADA)
PFD............ Power Flux Density [*Telecommunications*] (TEL)
PFD............ Preferred (AAG)
PFD............ Preferred Income Fund [*NYSE symbol*] (SPSG)
PFD............ Preferred Stock [*Investment term*] (DFIT)
PFD............ Preliminary Functional Description (CINC)
PFD............ Present for Duty
PFD............ Primary Flash Distillate [*Chemical technology*]
PFD............ Primary Flight Display
PFD............ Probability of Failure on Demand (ACII)
PFD............ Process Flow Diagram (NRCH)
PFD............ Pseudoinflammatory Fundus Disease [*Medicine*] (DMAA)
PFD............ Puffed [*Freight*]
PFD............ Pulse-Frequency Diversity [*Electronics*] (NG)
PFDA.......... Perfluorodecanoic Acid [*Organic chemistry*]
PFDA.......... Post Flight Data Analysis
PFDA.......... Precision Frequency Distribution Amplifier
PFDA.......... Pulse-Frequency Distortion Analyzer
PFDBAD...... Pathfinder Badge [*Military decoration*] (GFGA)
PFDC.......... Peoples Bancorp (Dekalb County) [*NASDAQ symbol*] (SAG)
PFDC.......... Peoples Bancorp(IN) [*NASDAQ symbol*] (TTSB)
PFDC.......... Peoples Federal Savings Bank of DeKalb City [*NASDAQ symbol*] (NQ)
PFDCCA...... Prodemca: Friends of the Democratic Center in the Americas [*Defunct*] (EA)
PFDF.......... Pacific Fisheries Development Foundation [*Defunct*] (EA)
PfdInco........ Preferred Income Fund [*Associated Press*] (SAG)
PFDJ.......... People's Front for Democracy and Justice [*Formerly, EPLF*] [*Eritrea*] [*Political party*] (ECON)
PFDM.......... Preliminary Final Draft Manuscript
PFDR.......... Pathfinder [*Aircraft*]
PfdrBad....... Pathfinder Badge [*Military decoration*] (AABC)
PFDS.......... Pergamon Financial Data Services [*Pergamon Orbit Infoline Ltd.*] [*British Information service or system*] (IID)
PFD SP........ Preferred Spelling (WDAA)
PFDTM........ Preliminary Flightweight Demonstration Test Motor (MCD)
PFE............ Pacific Fruit Express Co. [*AAR code*]
PFE............ Partido Feminista de Espana [*Feminist Party of Spain*] [*Political party*] (PPW)
PFE............ Pelvic Floor Exercise (DMAA)
PFE............ Performance Fitness Examination [*Military*] (DNAB)
PFE............ Pfizer, Inc. [*NYSE symbol*] (SPSG)
PFE............ Photoferroelectric Effect [*Physics*]
PFE............ Physics of Failure in Electronics [*A publication*] (MCD)
PFE............ Plenum Fill Experiment [*Nuclear energy*] (NRCH)
PFE............ Popular Front of Estonia [*Political party*]
PFE............ Post Fire Evaluation [*Military*] (CAAL)
PFE............ Post Flight Evaluation
PFE............ Pressure Feedback Exhaust [*Automotive engineering*]
PFE............ Priests for Equality (EA)
PFE............ Primary Feedback Element (IAA)
PFE............ Process Fuel Equivalent (MCD)
PFE............ Pulsed Field Electrophoresis [*Analytical biochemistry*]
PFE............ Purchaser Furnished Equipment (NATG)
PFEAAC...... Posterior Fossa Extra-Axial Arachnoid Cyst [*Medicine*] (DAVI)
PFEC.......... Philatelic Friends Exchange Circuit (EA)
PFEFES...... Pacific and Far East Federation of Engineering Societies
PfeifVac...... Pfeiffer Vacuum Technology AG [*Associated Press*] (SAG)
PFEL.......... Pacific Far East Line
PFEP.......... Programmable Front-End Processor [*Computer science*]
PFES.......... Pan American Federation of Engineering Societies
PFES.......... Proposed Final Environmental Statement [*Department of Energy*]
PFES.......... Pure Fluid Encoder System
PFET.......... P-Channel Junction Field-Effect Transistor (IDOE)
PFF............ Page Fault Frequency [*Computer science*] (MHDI)
PFF............ Pathfinder Force [*British RADAR designation which became overall synonym for RADAR*] [*Military*]
PFF............ Permanent Family File [*Navy*] (NG)
PFF............ Phenolfurfural [*Organic chemistry*]
PFF............ Planning Factors File (MCD)
PFF............ Plaque-Forming Factor (PDAA)
PFF............ Pluto Fast Flyby [*NASA*] (PS)
PFF............ Police Field Force (CINC)
PFF............ Porcine Follicular Fluid [*Endocrinology*]
PFF............ Precast Flooring Federation [*British*] (DBA)
PFF............ Primary Focus Feed [*Satellite communications*]
PFF............ Proposed Fabric Flammability Standard [*Consumer Product Safety Commission*]
PFF............ Protein Fat-Free [*Food technology*]
PFF............ Punjab Frontier Force [*British military*] (DMA)
PFFB.......... PFF Bancorp [*NASDAQ symbol*] (TTSB)
PFFB.......... PFF Bancorp, Inc. [*NASDAQ symbol*] (SAG)
PFFBcp....... PFF Bancorp, Inc. [*Associated Press*] (SAG)
PFFC.......... Parallel-Flow Film Cooling
PFFC.......... Peoples Financial Corp. [*NASDAQ symbol*] (SAG)
PFFC.......... Philadelphia Flyers Fan Club (EA)
PFFD.......... Proximal Femoral Focal Deficiency [*Orthopedics*] (DAVI)
PFF Inc....... Police-FBI Fencing, Incognito [*Phony fencing ring operated by Washington, DC, law enforcement agents during 1976 to identify and arrest area thieves*]
PFFX.......... Profiling Fixture
PFG............ Pacific Rim Mining Corp. [*Vancouver Stock Exchange symbol*]
PFG............ Paeoniflorigenone [*Biochemistry*]
PFG............ Paper Flow Group [*Nuclear Regulatory Commission*] (GFGA)
PFG............ Peak Flow Gauge [*Medicine*] (AAMN)
PFG............ PennCorp Financial Group [*NYSE symbol*] (SPSG)
PFG............ Pfennig [*Penny*] [*Monetary unit*] [*German*]
PFG............ Piping and Filter Gallery [*Nuclear energy*] (NRCH)
PFG............ Primary Frequency Generator
PFG............ Pulsed-Field Gel Electrophoresis (DMAA)
PFG............ Pulsed Field Gradient [*Electroanalytical chemistry*]
PFG............ Purple Flower Gang (EA)
PFGC.......... Parameters from Group Contribution [*Equation of state*]
PFGC.......... Performance Food Group [*NASDAQ symbol*] (SAG)
PFGE.......... Pulsed Field Gel Electrophoresis
PFGE.......... Pulsed Field Gradient Gel Electrophoresis
PFGM.......... Guided Missile Patrol Escort [*Ship symbol*] (NATG)
PFGPr......... PennCorp Finl $3.375 Pfd [*NYSE symbol*] (TTSB)
PFGX.......... Pacific Fruit Growers Express
PFH............ Hudson, NY [*Location identifier FAA*] (FAAL)
PFH............ Pafco Financial Holdings Ltd. [*Toronto Stock Exchange symbol*]
PFH............ Pressurized Fluidized-Bed Hydroretorting [*Chemical engineering*]
PFHA.......... Paso Fino Horse Association (EA)
PFHM.......... Protein-Free Hybridoma Medium
PFHS.......... Precipitation from Homogeneous Solution [*Catalyst preparation process*]
PFI............ Pacific Forest Industries (EA)
PFI............ Pack File Indexer (NITA)
PFI............ People First International (EA)
PFI............ Pet Food Institute (EA)
PFI............ Photo Finishing Institute [*Defunct*] (EA)
PFI............ Photon Flow Integrating (IAA)
PFI............ Photon Flux Integration (IAA)
PFI............ Physical Fitness Index
PFI............ Picture and Frame Institute [*Defunct*] (EA)
PFI............ Pie Filling Institute [*Defunct*] (EA)
PFI............ Pipe Fabrication Institute (EA)
PFI............ Police Foundation Institute (NADA)
PFI............ Port Fuel Injector [*Automotive engines*]
PFI............ Position Finding Instrument (DS)
PFI............ Power Factor Indicator (IAA)
PFI............ Power Failure Indicator [*NASA*] (KSC)
PFI............ Prison Fellowship International (EA)
PFI............ Private Finance Initiative [*British*]
PFIA.......... Police and Firemen's Insurance Association (EA)
PFIA.......... Prevention of Fraud Investments Act [*British*]
PFIAB........ President's Foreign Intelligence Advisory Board (AFM)
PFI & R...... Part Fill In and Ram [*Construction*]
PFIB.......... Pentafluoroiodosylbenzene [*Organic chemistry*]
PFIB.......... Perfluoroisobutene [*Organic chemistry*]
PFIB.......... Perfluoroisobutylene [*Organic chemistry*] (MAE)
PFIC.......... Passive Foreign Investment Company [*IRS*]
PFIC.......... Processed Food Industry Council [*Australia*]
PFIEP........ Perfluorinated Ion-Exchange Polymer [*Organic chemistry*]
PFIM.......... Pure Fluid Impact Modulator
PfIMF......... Preferred Income Management Fund, Inc. [*Associated Press*] (SAG)
PFIN.......... P & F Industries, Inc. [*NASDAQ symbol*] (NQ)
PFINA........ P&F Indus'A' [*NASDAQ symbol*] (TTSB)
PFINP........ P & F Ind $1 Pfd [*NASDAQ symbol*] (TTSB)
PFIU.......... Plot File Import Utility [*IBM Corp.*]

Pfizer .... Pfizer, Inc. [*Associated Press*] (SAG)
PFJ .... Patreksfjordur [*Iceland*] [*Airport symbol*] (OAG)
PFJ .... Polar Front Jet Stream (ADA)
PFJR .... Patellofemoral Joint Reaction [*Physiology*]
PFK .... Payload Function Key [*NASA*] (MCD)
PFK .... Perfluorokerosene [*Heat transfer agent*]
PFK .... Phosphofructokinase [*An enzyme*]
PFK .... Programmed Function Key (NITA)
PFK .... Programmed Function Keyboard [*Computer science*]
PFKM .... Phosphofructokinase, Muscle Type [*Medicine*] (DMAA)
PFKY .... People First Corp. [*NASDAQ symbol*] (SAG)
PFKY .... Peoples First [*NASDAQ symbol*] (TTSB)
PFL .... Fort Sill, OK [*Location identifier FAA*] (FAAL)
PFL .... Pacific Cassiar Ltd. [*Toronto Stock Exchange symbol*]
PFL .... People for Life (EA)
PFL .... Pharmacists for Life (EA)
PFL .... Pol-Fly [*Poland ICAO designator*] (FAAC)
PFL .... Pounds per Lineal Foot [*Technical drawings*]
PFL .... Primary Freon Loop (NASA)
PFL .... Propulsion Field Laboratory
PFL .... Public Facility Loans
PFLA .... Popular Front for the Liberation of Ahvaz [*Iran*]
P-FLAG .... Federation of Parents and Friends of Lesbians and Gays (EA)
PFLF .... People, Food and Land Foundation (EA)
PFLL .... Phase and Frequency Locked Loop [*Telecommunications*] (IAA)
P Flo .... Pandectae Florentinae [*A publication*] (DSA)
PFLO .... Popular Front for the Liberation of Oman [*Political party*] (PD)
PFLOAG .... Popular Front for the Liberation of Oman and the Arabian Gulf [*Political party*] (PD)
PFLOLS .... Portable Fresnel-Lens Optical-Landing System (NG)
P Florent .... Pandectae Florentinae [*A publication*] (DSA)
PFLP .... Popular Front for the Liberation of Palestine [*Political party*] (PD)
PFLP-GC .... Popular Front for the Liberation of Palestine - General Command [*Political party*] (PD)
PFLT .... Paint Filter Liquids Test [*Environmental science*] (FFDE)
P/FLT .... Pattern Flight [*Also, P/F*] (MUGU)
PFLT .... People's Front of the Liberation Tigers [*Sri Lanka*] [*Political party*] (EY)
PFLTS .... Parquet Floor Layers' Trade Society [*A union*] [*British*]
PFLV .... Pressure Fed Launch Vehicle [*NASA*] (KSC)
PFM .... Little Franciscan Sisters of Mary [*Roman Catholic religious order*]
PFM .... Pacific Minesearch Ltd. [*Vancouver Stock Exchange symbol*]
PFM .... Patriots of Fort McHenry (EA)
PFM .... Peak Flow Meter [*Medicine*] (AAMN)
PFM .... Physiological Flow Model [*For simulating medical conditions*]
PFM .... Pitch Follow-Up Motor
PFM .... Plan for Maintenance [*Navy*]
PFM .... Planning Factors Management (MCD)
PFM .... Platform (NASA)
PFM .... Political Freedom Movement [*British*]
PFM .... Porcelain Fused to Metal [*Dentistry*]
PFM .... Porsche Flug Motor [*Automotive engineering*]
PFM .... Potato Futures Market [*Finance*]
PFM .... Poultry Feather Meal [*Fisheries*]
PFM .... Power Factor Meter
PFM .... Precision Frequency Multivider (KSC)
PFM .... Predictor Frame Memory
PFM .... Preferred Income Management Fund [*NYSE symbol*] (SPSG)
PFM .... Preferred Income Mgmt Fund [*NYSE symbol*] (TTSB)
PFM .... Preliminary Flight Motor (MCD)
PFM .... Pressure Flow Meter
PFM .... Printer Font Metrics [*Computer science*] (CDE)
PFM .... Prison Fellowship Ministries (EA)
PFM .... Pulse-Forming Machine
PFM .... Pulse-Frequency Modulation [*RADAR*] [*Telecommunications*]
P/FM .... Pylon/Fin Movement
PFM .... University of Pittsburgh, Falk Library - Health Professions, Pittsburgh, PA [*OCLC symbol*] (OCLC)
PFMA .... Pet Food Manufacturers Association [*British*] (DBA)
PFMA .... Phenolic Foam Manufacturers Association [*British*] (DBA)
PFMA .... Pipe Fittings Manufacturers Association [*Later, APFA*] (EA)
PFMA .... Plumbing Fixture Manufacturers Association [*Defunct*] (EA)
PFMA .... Pressed Felt Manufacturers' Association [*British*] (BI)
PFMAA .... Pet Food Manufacturers' Association of Australia
PFMC .... Pacific Fishery Management Council (EA)
PFMO .... Planning Factors Management Office
PFMPG .... Pacific Fleet Mobile Photographic Group (DNAB)
PFMR .... Pasadena Foundation for Medical Research [*California*]
PFMR .... Plug-Flow Membrane Reactor [*Chemical engineering*]
PFMR .... Project Funds Management Record (MCD)
PFN .... Panama City [*Florida*] [*Airport symbol*] (OAG)
PFN .... Pantyffynnon [*British depot code*]
PFN .... Partially Functional Neutrophil (DMAA)
PFN .... Parti des Forces Nouvelles [*New Forces Party*] [*France Political party*] (PPW)
PFN .... Passamaquoddy Ferry & Navigation Co. [*AAR code*]
PFN .... Permanent File Name
PFN .... Plasma Fibronectin [*Biochemistry*]
PFN .... PMC Corp. [*Toronto Stock Exchange symbol*]
PFN .... Prefinished [*Technical drawings*]
PFN .... Profilin (DMAA)
PFN .... Pulse-Forming Network
PFNA .... Pentecostal Fellowship of North America (EA)
PFNA .... Pulsed Fast Neutron Analysis [*for detection of explosives*] (PS)
PFNC .... Progress Financial Corp. [*Plymouth Meeting, PA*] [*NASDAQ symbol*] (NQ)
PFNC .... Progress Finl [*NASDAQ symbol*] (TTSB)
PFNP .... Partido Federalista Nacionalista Popular [*Panama*] [*Political party*] (EY)
PFNS .... Position Fixing Navigation System (AABC)
PFNT .... Police Force of the Northern Territory [*Australia*]
PFNT .... Preferred Networks [*NASDAQ symbol*] (TTSB)
PFNTU .... Pathfinder Navigation Training Unit [*Military*]
PFO .... Paphos [*Cyprus*] [*Airport symbol*] (OAG)
PFO .... Partly Filled Out [*Questionnaire*]
PFO .... Patent Foramen Ovale [*Cardiology*]
PFO .... Personal Freedom Outreach (EA)
PFO .... Physical Fitness Officer [*British military*] (DMA)
PFO .... Pitch Follow-Up Operation
PFO .... Pomona Public Library, Pomona, CA [*OCLC symbol*] (OCLC)
PFO .... Postal Finance Officer [*Army*]
PFO .... Preferred Income Opportunity Fund [*NYSE symbol*] (SAG)
PFO .... Preferred Income Oppt Fd [*NYSE symbol*] (TTSB)
PFO .... Procurement Field Office
PFO .... Pyrolysis Fuel Oil [*Petroleum refining*]
PFO .... Spofford, TX [*Location identifier FAA*] (FAAL)
PFOA .... Perfluorooctanoic Acid [*Organic chemistry*]
PFOB .... Perfluorocytylbromide (DMAA)
PFOBA .... Paso Fino Owners and Breeders Association [*Later, PFHA*] (EA)
PFOD .... Presumed Finding of Death [*DoD*]
PFol .... Ridley Township Public Library, Folsom, PA [*Library symbol Library of Congress*] (LCLS)
PFouad .... Les Papyrus Fouad I [*A publication*] (OCD)
PFP .... Partnership for Peace [*An organization of non-member countries which have established military cooperation with NATO*] (ECON)
PFP .... Partnership for Productivity International (EA)
PFP .... Peace and Freedom Party (EA)
PFP .... Pensions for Professionals, Inc.
PFP .... Pentafluoropropionate [*or Pentafluoropropionyl*] [*Organic chemistry*]
PFP .... Personal Financial Planning (ADA)
PFP .... Pet-Facilitated Psychotherapy [*Psychiatry*]
PFP .... Platelet-Free Plasma [*Hematology*]
PFP .... Pleiades Foundation for Peace [*Later, PFPSE*] (EA)
PFP .... Plutonium Finishing Plant
PFP .... Policy-Framework Paper (ECON)
PFP .... Popular Front Party [*Ghana*] [*Political party*] (PPW)
PFP .... Pore Forming Protein [*Biochemistry*]
PFP .... Postage Forward Parcels [*Shipping*]
PFP .... Post Flight Processor
PFP .... Premier Farnell PLC [*NYSE symbol*] (SAG)
PFP .... Premier Farnell PLC ADS [*NYSE symbol*] (TTSB)
PFP .... Primary Failed Part (DNAB)
PFP .... Probability of Failure, Performance [*NASA*] (SAA)
PFP .... Products for Power [*Automotive components manufacturer*]
PFP .... Program File Processor
PFP .... Program Financial Plan (NASA)
PFP .... Program Forecast Period [*Military*] (AFIT)
PFP .... Programmable Function Panel (NASA)
PFP .... Progressiewe Federale Party [*Progressive Federal Party*] [*South Africa*] [*Political party*] (PPW)
PFP .... Proton Flare Project (PDAA)
PFP .... Proving for Production (MCD)
PFP .... Publishers for Peace [*An association*]
PFPA .... Pentafluoropropionic Anhydride [*Organic chemistry*]
PFPA .... Pro-Family Press Association [*Defunct*] (EA)
PFPC .... Passenger Form and Procedures Committee [*IATA*] (DS)
PFPDBRD .... Paget Foundation for Paget's Disease of Bone and Related Disorders [*Formerly, Paget's Disease Foundation (PDF)*] (PAZ)
PFPE .... Perfluorinated Polyether [*Organic chemistry*]
PFPE .... Polyfluorinated Polyether [*Lubricants, polymers*]
PFP EIS .... Plutonium Finishing Plant Environmental Impact Statement
PFPH .... Pentafluorophenylhydrazine [*Organic chemistry*]
PFPI .... Partnership for Productivity International (EA)
PFPI .... Pentafluoropropionyl Imidazole [*Organic chemistry*]
PFPM .... Production Flight Procedures Manual (MCD)
PFPPr .... Premier Farnell $1.35 Pref ADS [*NYSE symbol*] (TTSB)
PFPS .... Patellofemoral Pain Syndrome [*Medicine*] (DMAA)
PFPS .... Potential for Foster Parenthood Scale [*Psychology*]
PFPS .... Progressive French Polishers' Society [*A union*] [*British*]
PFPSE .... Pleiades Foundation for Peace and Space Education (EA)
PFPUT .... Pension Fund Property Unit Trust [*British*]
PFQ .... Personality Factor Questionnaire (MAE)
PFQ .... Preflight Qualification
PFr .... Franklin Public Library, Franklin, PA [*Library symbol Library of Congress*] (LCLS)
PFR .... Parotid Flow Rate [*otorhinolaryngology*] (DAVI)
PFR .... Part Failure Rate
PFR .... Patriot Field Report [*Army*]
PFR .... Peak Flow Rate [*or Reading*] [*Medicine*]
PFR .... Perforator (DEN)
PFR .... Pericardial Friction Rub [*Medicine*] (MEDA)
PFR .... Perkins Family Restaurants Ltd [*NYSE symbol*] (SPSG)
PFR .... Perkins Family Rest L.P. [*NYSE symbol*] (TTSB)
PFR .... Permanent Factory Repairable (MCD)
PFR .... Permitted Flying Route [*Aviation*] (DA)
PFR .... Persistent Fat Retention [*Syndrome*]
PFR .... Personal Financial Record [*Army*] (AABC)
PFR .... Pfarrer [*Pastor*] [*German*] (EY)
PFR .... Photoflash Relay

PFR .... Pike Fry Rhabdovirus
PFR .... Plug-Flow Reactor [*Engineering*]
PFR .... Polarized Field Frequency Relay (IAA)
PFR .... Polarized Frequency Relay
PFR .... Portable Foot Restraint (NASA)
PFR .... Port Francqui [*Zaire*] [*Airport symbol*] (AD)
PFR .... Post-Fielding Review [*DoD*]
PFR .... Power Fail Recovery System [*Computer science*] (MDG)
PFR .... Power Fail/Restart
PF/R .... Power Fail/Restart (NITA)
PFR .... Power Failure Release
PFR .... Precision Fathometer Recorder [*Raytheon Co.*]
PFR .... Preferred Resources, Inc. [*Vancouver Stock Exchange symbol*]
PFR .... Preflight Review [*NASA*] (KSC)
PFR .... Preheating, Falling-Film, Rising-Film [*Sections of a concentrator*] [*Chemical engineering*]
PFR .... Preliminary Flight Rating [*Air Force*]
PFR .... Problem/Failure Report
PFR .... Programmed Film Reader [*System*]
pfr .... Proofreader [*MARC relator code*] [*Library of Congress*] (LCCP)
PFR .... Prototype Fast Reactor
PFR .... Pulmonary Blood Flow Redistribution [*Medicine*]
PFR .... Pulmonary Flow Rate [*Medicine*] (DAVI)
PFR .... Pulse Frequency (MDG)
PFR .... Punch Feed Read (CMD)
PFRA .... Percent of Females Reproductively Active [*Ecology*]
PFRA .... Prairie Farm Rehabilitation Administration [*Canada*]
PFRA .... Problem-Focused Research Applications [*of ASRA*] [*National Science Foundation*]
PFRA .... Professional Football Referees Association (EA)
PFRA .... Professional Football Researchers Association (EA)
PFRB .... Publications and Films Review Board [*Western Australia*]
PFRC .... Pacific Forest Research Centre [*Canada*] (ARC)
PFRD .... Preferred Stock [*Investment term*]
PFredY .... Joseph A. Yablonski Memorial Clinic, Fredericktown, PA [*Library symbol Library of Congress*] (LCLS)
PFRMG .... Performing (ROG)
PFRS .... Portable Field Recording System [*NASA*] (KSC)
PFRT .... Preliminary Flight Rating Test
PFRT .... Preliminary Flight Readiness Test [*NASA*] (KSC)
PFS .... Parallel Filter System
PFS .... Particles and Fields Subsatellite [*NASA*]
PFS .... Path Fault Secure (MHDI)
PFS .... Pay for Skills [*Human resources*] (WYGK)
PFS .... Percent Full Scale (KSC)
PFS .... Performance Funding System [*Department of Housing and Urban Development*] (GFGA)
PFS .... Peripheral Fixed Shim [*Nuclear energy*] (NRCH)
PFS .... Personal and Family Survival [*Civil Defense*]
PFS .... Personal Filing System [*Data-base program*] [*Software Publishing Corp.*]
PFS .... Personal Financial Specialist
PFS .... Photofragment Spectroscopy
PFS .... Physical File System (IAA)
PFS .... Pioneer Financial Services, Inc. [*NYSE symbol*] (SPSG)
PFS .... Pioneer Financial Svcs [*NYSE symbol*] (TTSB)
PFS .... Pitch Follow-Up System
PFS .... Pittsburgh, PA [*Location identifier FAA*] (FAAL)
PFS .... Plasterers' Friendly Society [*A union*] [*British*]
PFS .... Platform Functional Specification [*Computer science*]
PFS .... Porous Friction Surface [*Airfield pavement*]
PFS .... Positive Fuel Stop
PFS .... Prairie Flying Service (1976) Ltd. [*Canada ICAO designator*] (FAAC)
PFS .... Precision Frequency Source
PFS .... Preflight School [*Military*]
PFS .... Press Fit Socket
PFS .... Primary Fibromyalgia Syndrome [*Medicine*] (DMAA)
PFS .... Primary Flight System (NASA)
PFS .... Primary Frequency Supply [*Telecommunications*] (TEL)
PFS .... Probability of Failure, Stress [*NASA*] (SAA)
PFS .... Pro-Forma Statement (MHDI)
PFS .... Programmable Frequency Standard
PFS .... Propellant Feed System
PFS .... Propellant Field System
PFS .... Pulmonary Function Score [*Physiology*]
PFS .... Pure Fluid System
PFSB .... PennFed Financial Services, Inc. [*NASDAQ symbol*] (SAG)
PFSB .... PennFed Financial Svcs [*NASDAQ symbol*] (TTSB)
PFSh .... Partia Fashismit e Shqiperise [*Fascist Party of Albania*] [*Political party*] (PPE)
PFSH .... Porcine Follicle Stimulating Hormone [*Endocrinology*]
PFSL .... Pocahontas Federal Savings & Loan Association [*NASDAQ symbol*] (SAG)
PFSL .... Pocahontas Fed Svg& L A Ark [*NASDAQ symbol*] (TTSB)
PFSO .... Postal Finance and Supply Office (AFM)
PFSP .... Polyfactorial Study of Personality [*Psychology*] (AEBS)
PFS/PRS .... Patent Family Service/Patent Register Service [*Database*] [*International Patent Documentation Center*] [*Information service or system*] (CRD)
PFSR .... Program Financial Status Report (AAG)
PFSS .... Particles and Fields Subsatellite [*Telecommunications*] (OA)
PFSS .... Patellofemoral Stress Syndrome [*Medicine*]
PFT .... Pacific Asia Tech [*Vancouver Stock Exchange symbol*]
PFT .... Pacific Fisheries Technologists [*An association*]
PFT .... Page Frame Table (BUR)
PFT .... Pancreatic Function Test [*Medicine*]
PFT .... Paper, Flat Tape
PFT .... Parafascicular Thalamotomy [*Medicine*]
PFT .... Parallel Fourier Transform (MCD)
PFT .... Permanent Full-Time (GFGA)
PFT .... Pet-Facilitated Therapy [*Psychiatry*]
PFT .... Phenylalanine mustard [*Melphalan*], Fluorouracil, Tamoxifen [*Antineoplastic drug regimen*]
PFT .... Physical Fitness Test
PFT .... Pittsburgh, Fort Wayne & Chicago Railway Co. (IIA)
PFT .... Plastic Fuel Tank
PFT .... Portable Flame Thrower [*Army*]
PFT .... Positive Flight Termination (MUGU)
PFT .... Posterior Fossa Tumor [*Anatomy*] (MAE)
PFT .... Preflight Team [*Air Force*] (AFM)
PFT .... Preflight Tool (MCD)
PFT .... Prime Factor Transform (IAA)
PFT .... Professional Football Trainers (EA)
PFT .... Program Flying Training [*Air Force*] (AFM)
PFT .... Projective Field Theory
PFT .... Pulmonary Function Test [*Medicine*]
PFT .... Pulse Fourier Transform
PFTA .... Payload Flight Test Article [*NASA*] (MCD)
PFTA .... Post-Fielding Training Analysis
PFTB .... Preflight Test Bus (MCD)
PFTBE .... Progressive Form of Tick-Borne Encephalitis [*Medicine*] (DMAA)
PFTC .... Pestalozzi-Froebel Teachers College [*Illinois*]
PFTE .... Permanent Full-Time Equivalent (GFGA)
PFTE .... Pianoforte [*Soft, then Loud*] [*Music*]
PFTE .... Polytetrafluoroethylene [*Teflon*]
PFTE .... Portable Field Trainer/Evaluator (MCD)
PFTEA .... Post-Fielding Training Effectiveness Analysis
PFTM .... Preliminary Flight Test Memo
PFTR .... Preliminary Flight Test Report
PFTS .... Permanent Field Training Site
PFU .... Passive Filtration Unit
PFU .... Physical Fitness Uniform [*Army*] (INF)
PFU .... Plan for Use (DNAB)
PFU .... Plaque-Forming Unit [*Immunochemistry*]
PFU .... Please Follow Up
PFU .... Pock-Forming Unit
PFU .... Preparation for Use
PFUA .... Pitch Follow-Up Amplifier
PFUEI .... Prime Focus Universal Extragalactic Instrument [*Astronomy*]
PFUM .... Pitch Follow-Up Motor
PFUO .... Pitch Follow-Up Operation
PFUO .... Prolonged Fever of Unknown Origin [*Medicine*] (DMAA)
PFUS .... Pitch Follow-Up System
PFV .... Peak Flow Velocity [*Cardiology*]
PFV .... Peak Forward Voltage (IAA)
PFV .... Pestalozzi-Froebel-Verband [*Pestalozzi-Froebel Association*]
PFV .... Philippine Forces, Vietnam
PFV .... Physiological Full Value
PFV .... Probability of Failure, Vehicle [*NASA*] (SAA)
PFVEA .... Professional Film and Video Equipment Association (EA)
PFW .... Power, Fulcrum, Weight
PFW .... Predicted Fire Weapon
PFW .... Progressive Free Wave
PFWA .... Pet Food Warehouse [*NASDAQ symbol*] (SAG)
PFWA .... Professional Football Writers of America (EA)
PFwB .... Budd Co., Fort Washington, PA [*Library symbol Library of Congress*] (LCLS)
PFWOAD .... Place from Which Ordered to Active Duty [*Military*]
PFwR .... William H. Rorer, Inc., Fort Washington, PA [*Library symbol Library of Congress*] (LCLS)
PFWS .... Predicted Fire Weapon System [*Army*]
PFX .... Prefix (ROG)
PFX .... Proflex Ltd. [*Vancouver Stock Exchange symbol*]
PFY .... Prior Fiscal Year (AFIT)
PFYA .... Predicted First-Year Average [*Law school*]
PFZ .... Polar Front Zone [*Marine science*] (MSC)
PFZ .... Potassium Hexafluorozirconate [*Inorganic chemistry*]
PFZ .... Precipitate-Free Zone (MCD)
PF-ZAPU .... Patriotic Front - Zimbabwe African People's Union [*Political party*] (PD)
PG .... Florida Commuter [*ICAO designator*] (AD)
PG .... Glycerate-3-Phosphate [*Biochemistry*] (DAVI)
pg .... Page (VRA)
pg .... Page (WDMC)
PG .... Page [*or Pagination*] [*Online database field identifier*]
PG .... Paper Gain (MHDW)
PG .... Papua New Guinea [*ANSI two-letter standard code*] (CNC)
PG .... Paralysie Generale [*General Paralysis*] [*Medicine French*]
PG .... Paregoric [*Slang*]
PG .... Parental Guidance [*Pediatrics*] (DAVI)
PG .... Parental Guidance Suggested [*Formerly, GP*] [*Some material may not be suitable for preteenagers Movie rating*]
PG .... Paris Granite
PG .... Paris Group [*See also GP*] [*France*] (EAIO)
PG .... Parotid Gland [*Medicine*] (DMAA)
PG .... Partial Gum [*Philately*]
PG .... Paste Grain [*Bookbinding*]
PG .... Past Grand [*Freemasonry*]
PG .... Patrol Combatant [*Gunboat*] [*Navy symbol*]
PG .... Patrol Gunboat, Motorized [*Navy symbol*] (VNW)

PG............... Patrologiae Cursus. Series Graeca [*A publication*] (OCD)
PG............... Pay Grade
PG............... Pay Group
PG............... Paying Guest
PG............... PEACE [*Program for Emergency Assistance, Cooperation, and Education*] for Guatemala (EA)
PG............... Pedal Ganglion
PG............... Pedal Groove
PG............... Pelham Grenville Wodehouse [*British humorist, 1881-1975*]
PG............... Pentagastrin (DMAA)
Pg............... Pentagram [*One billion metric tons*]
PG............... Pepsinogen [*Medicine*] (MEDA)
PG............... Peptidoglycan [*Biochemistry*]
PG............... Permanent Glow [*Telecommunications*] (TEL)
PG............... Permanent Grade
PG............... Persian Gulf (MCD)
PG............... Pharmacopoeia Germanica [*German Pharmacopoeia*]
PG............... Phosphatidylglycerol
PG............... Phosphogluconate [*Biochemistry*]
PG............... Phosphogypsum [*Inorganic chemistry*]
PG............... Photogrammetry
pg............... Picogram [*One trillionth of a gram*]
PG............... Pilot Generator (IAA)
PG............... Pine Grosbeak [*Ornithology*]
PG............... Pipers Guild (EA)
PG............... Pituitary Gonadotropin [*Endocrinology*] (MAE)
PG............... Placebo Group [*Medicine*]
PG............... Planning Group [*DoD*]
PG............... Planning Guide [*HUD*]
PG............... Plasma Gastrin [*Endocrinology*] (AAMN)
PG............... Plasma Glucose [*Hematology*]
PG............... Plasma Triglyceride [*Hematology*] (DAVI)
PG............... Plate Glass
PG............... Plate-Glazed [*Paper*]
PG............... Pointer Game (AEBS)
PG............... Pollen Grain [*Botany*]
PG............... Polyethylene Glycol [*Organic chemistry*]
PG............... Polygalacturonase [*An enzyme*]
PG............... Polyglycine [*Biochemistry*]
PG............... Pontius Guillelmi [*Authority cited in pre-1607 legal work*] (DSA)
PG............... Port Group [*Telecommunications*] (TEL)
PG............... Portugal
Pg............... Portugal (ODBW)
Pg............... Portuguese (ODBW)
PG............... Portuguese [*Language, etc.*]
pg............... Portuguese Guinea [*Guinea-Bissau*] [*MARC country of publication code Library of Congress*] (LCCP)
PG............... Position Guide (MCD)
P/G............... Postagram [*British military*] (DMA)
PG............... Postgraduate [*Refers to courses or students*] [*Slang*]
PG............... Power Gain
PG............... Power Gate [*Electronics*] (OA)
PG............... Power Generation (MCD)
PG............... Preacher General
PG............... Precision Ground [*Electronics*] (IAA)
PG............... Predicted Grade [*IRS*]
PG............... Pregnanediol Glucuronide [*Endocrinology*]
PG............... Pregnant
pg............... Pregnant (DMAA)
PG............... Pregnant Guppy [*Reference to Boeing 377 aircraft*] (SAA)
PG............... Press Gallery [*US Senate*]
PG............... Pressure Gauge (KSC)
PG............... Priority Group
PG............... Prisonnier de Guerre [*Prisoner of War - POW*] [*French*]
PG............... Procter & Gamble [*NYSE symbol*] (TTSB)
PG............... Procter & Gamble Co. [*NYSE symbol*] (SPSG)
PG............... Proctor & Gamble [*Commercial firm*] (NADA)
PG............... Procureur Generaal [*Public Attorney*] [*Dutch*] (ILCA)
PG............... Producers Group (EA)
PG............... Professional Geologist
PG............... Professional Group (MCD)
PG............... Pro-German [*Prisoner of war term*] [*World War I*] (DSUE)
PG............... Program [*Telecommunications*]
PG............... Program Generator (IAA)
PG............... Program Generic [*Computer science*] (TEL)
PG............... Program Guidance
PG............... Programmer (AAG)
PG............... Programmer Group (IAA)
PG............... Project Group
PG............... Proof Gallon [*Wines and spirits*]
PG............... Propylene Glycol
PG............... Propyl Gallate [*Antioxidant*] [*Organic chemistry*]
PG............... Prostaglandin [*Also, Pg*] [*Biochemistry*]
PG............... Protective Ground [*Electronics*] (IAA)
PG............... Protein Granule
PG............... Proteoglycan [*Biochemistry*]
PG............... Prothoracic Gland [*Insect anatomy*]
PG............... Province Guard [*Cambodia*] (CINC)
PG............... Proving Ground [*Army*]
P-G............... Prudential Grace Lines [*Steamship*] (MHDB)
PG............... Public Gaol [*British*]
PG............... Pulse Gate
PG............... Pulse Generator
PG............... Pure Gum [*of envelopes*]
PG............... Pyoderma Gangrenosum [*Medicine*]
PG............... Pyrolytic Graphite (MCD)
PG............... Pyrotechnic Gyro (AAG)
PG-13.......... Parental Guidance Suggested [*Now: Parents Strongly Cautioned. Some material may be inappropriate for children under 13*] [*Movie rating*]
PGA............ Page [*Arizona*] [*Airport symbol*] (OAG)
PGA............ Paragould [*Arkansas*] [*Seismograph station code, US Geological Survey*] (SEIS)
PGA............ Pega Capital Resources Ltd. [*Toronto Stock Exchange symbol*]
PGA............ Pendulous Gyro Accelerometer
PGA............ Pepsinogen A (DMAA)
PGA............ Personnel Group of America [*NYSE symbol*] (SAG)
PGA............ PGI, Inc. [*AMEX symbol*] (SPSG)
PGA............ Phosphoglyceric Acid [*Biochemistry*]
PGA............ Pin-Grid-Array [*Motorola, Inc.*]
PGA............ Pin-Grid Arrays
PGA............ Pistachio Growers' Association [*Australia*]
PGA............ Plate Glass Association [*British*] (BI)
PGA............ Polyglandular Autoimmune Syndrome [*Medicine*] (DMAA)
PGA............ Polyglycolic Acid [*Organic chemistry*] (RDA)
PGA............ Poly(L-glutamic Acid) [*Organic chemistry*]
PGA............ Port of Geelong Authority [*Victoria, Australia*]
PGA............ Portugalia, Companhia Portuguesa de Transportes Aeros SA [*Portugal ICAO designator*] (FAAC)
PGA............ Potato Growers of Australia
PGA............ Power Gain Antenna
PGA............ Power Generating Assembly (KSC)
PGA............ Pressure Garment Assembly
PGA............ Producers Guild of America (EA)
PGA............ Professional Golfers Association (NADA)
PGA............ Professional Golfers' Association of America (EA)
PGA............ Professional Graphics Adapter [*IBM Corp.*]
PGA............ Professional Group Audio
PGA............ Programmable Gain Amplifier (MCD)
PGA............ Programmable Gate Array
PGA............ Prostaglandin A [*Biochemistry*]
PGA............ Prostaglandin Analog [*Biochemistry*]
PGA............ Pteroylmonoglutamic Acid [*Folic acid*] [*Also, FA, PteGlu*] [*Biochemistry*]
PGA............ Puppetry Guild of Australia
PGA............ Purchased Gas Adjustment
PGA............ Pure Grain Alcohol
PGA............ Pyrolysis Gas Analysis
PGA............ Upjohn Co. [*Research code symbol*]
PGAA.......... Professional Guides Association of America (EA)
PGAA.......... Prompt Gamma-Ray Activation Analysis
P-GABA........ Phenyl-gamma-aminobutryic Acid [*Tranquilizer*]
PGAC.......... Guam/Taguac [*Mariana Islands*] [*ICAO location identifier*] (ICLI)
PG-AC.......... Phenylglycine Acid Chloride [*Biochemistry*] (AAMN)
PGAC.......... Professional Group - Automatic Control
PGAH.......... Pineapple Growers Association of Hawaii (EA)
PGAM.......... Phosphoglyceromutase [*An enzyme*]
PG & E........ Pacific Gas and Electric [*Rock music group*]
PG & E........ Pacific Gas & Electric Co.
PG & E Cp.... PG & E Corp. Holdings Co. [*Associated Press*] (SAG)
PGANE.......... Professional Group on Aeronautical and Navigational Electronics
PGA-NOC...... Permanent General Assembly of National Olympic Committees
PGANSW...... Potato Growers' Association of New South Wales [*Australia*]
PGAP.......... Pilot Geriatric Arthritis Program [*Medicine*] (DMAA)
PGAP.......... Professional Group - Antennas and Propagation
PGAPL.......... Preliminary Group Assembly Parts List
PGAR.......... Provisional Government of the Algerian Republic
PGAS.......... Persisting Galactorrhea-Amenorrhea Syndrome [*Medicine*] (DMAA)
PGase.......... Polygalacturonase [*An enzyme*]
PGAWA........ Pastoralists and Graziers' Association of Western Australia
PGAWA........ Potato Growers' Association of Western Australia
Pg B............ Bachelor of Pedagogy
PGB............ Patrol Gunboat [*Navy symbol*] (NATG)
PGB............ Personal Guidance Base (AIE)
PGB............ Phoenix Global [*Vancouver Stock Exchange symbol*]
PGB............ Portland General Electric Co. [*NYSE symbol*] (SAG)
PGB............ Portland Genl Elec 8.25% 'QUIDS' [*NYSE symbol*] (TTSB)
PGB............ Prostaglandin B [*Biochemistry*]
PGB............ Protestant Guild for the Blind (EA)
PGB............ Pyrographalloy Boron
PGBA.......... Piece Goods Buyers Association [*Defunct*] (EA)
PGBA.......... Possum Growers and Breeders Association (EA)
PGBD.......... Pegboard [*Freight*]
PGBM.......... Pulse Gate Binary Modulation (MCD)
PGbSH.......... Seton Hill College, Greensburg, PA [*Library symbol Library of Congress*] (LCLS)
PGBTR.......... Professional Group - Broadcast and Television Receivers
PGBTS.......... Professional Group - Broadcast Transmission Systems
PGbU.......... University of Pittsburgh at Greensburg, Greensburg, PA [*Library symbol Library of Congress*] (LCLS)
PGC............ Geneva College, Beaver Falls, PA [*OCLC symbol*] (OCLC)
PGC............ Gettysburg College, Gettysburg, PA [*Library symbol Library of Congress*] (LCLS)
PGC............ Pacific Geoscience Centre [*Research center*] (RCD)
PGC............ Pagurian Corp. [*Toronto Stock Exchange symbol*]
PGC............ Parents of Galactosemic Children [*An association*]
PGC............ Past Grand Commander [*Freemasonry*] (ROG)
PGC............ Per Gyro Compass [*Navigation*]
PGC............ Persian Gulf Command [*World War II*]
PGC............ Phillips Gas [*NYSE symbol*] (SPSG)

PGC .... Policy Guidance Council (DOMA)
PGC .... Polynomial Generator Checker (IAA)
PGC .... Pontine Gaze Center [*Eye anatomy*]
PGC .... Poorly Graphitized Carbon [*Physical chemistry*]
PGC .... Port Group Control [*Telecommunications*] (TEL)
PGC .... Post-Graduate Certificate (PGP)
PGC .... Potassium Gold Cyanide [*Inorganic chemistry*]
PGC .... Potential Gas Committee
PGC .... Primordial Germ Cell
PGC .... Process Gas Chromatography
PGC .... Process Gas Consumers Group (EA)
PGC .... Professional Graphics Controller [*IBM Corp.*]
PGC .... Program Generation Center [*Military*] (CAAL)
PGC .... Programmable Guidance Controller [*Military*]
PGC .... Programmed Gain Control
PGC .... Prostaglandin C [*A prostoglandin endoperoxide*] [*Biochemistry*] (DAVI)
PGC .... Proving Ground Command [*Air Force*]
PGC .... Pulsed Gas Crymotography
PGC .... Pyrolysis Gas Chromatography
PGCA .... Patent Glazing Contractors Association [*British*] (DBA)
PGcC .... Grove City College, Grove City, PA [*Library symbol Library of Congress*] (LCLS)
PGCC .... Power Generation Control Complex [*Nuclear energy*] (NRCH)
PGCE .... Post Graduate Certificate of Education
PGCh .... Past Grand Chaplain [*Freemasonry*]
PGCOA .... Pennsylvania Grade Crude Oil Association (EA)
PGCP .... Professional Group - Component Parts
PGCPr .... Phillips Gas 9.32% Pfd [*NYSE symbol*] (TTSB)
PGCRA .... Professional Golf Club Repairmen's Association (EA)
PGCS .... Professional Group - Communications Systems
PGCT .... Professional Group - Circuit Theory
PGCU .... International Printing and Graphic Communications Union
PGCVS .... Postgraduate Committee in Veterinary Science [*Australia*]
PGD .... Hancock [*John*] Patriot Global Dividend Fund [*NYSE symbol*] (SPSG)
PGD .... John Hancock Patr Gl Div Fd [*NYSE symbol*] (TTSB)
PGD .... Pango Gold Mines Ltd. [*Toronto Stock Exchange symbol*]
PGD .... Past Grand Deacon [*Freemasonry*]
PGD .... Phosphogluconate Dehydrogenase [*Also, PGDH*] [*An enzyme*]
PGD .... Phosphoglyceraldehyde Dehydrogenase [*An enzyme*] (MAE)
PGD .... Pikwitonei Granulite Domain [*Geology*]
PGD .... Pinion Gear Drive
PGD .... Planar Gas Discharge (MCD)
PGD .... Planetary Gear Drive
PGD .... Policy and Grants Division [*Environmental Protection Agency*] (GFGA)
PGD .... Program for Geographical Display (IAA)
PGD .... Prostaglandin D [*Biochemistry*]
PGD .... Pulse Generator Display
PGD .... Punta Gorda [*Florida*] [*Airport symbol*] (OAG)
PGDA .... Piercing Pagoda [*NASDAQ symbol*] (TTSB)
PGDA .... Piercing Pagoda, Inc. [*NASDAQ symbol*] (SAG)
PGDB .... Propylene Glycol Dibenzoate [*Organic chemistry*]
PGDC .... Provincial Grand Director of Ceremonies [*Freemasonry*]
PGDCS .... Power Generation, Distribution, and Control Subsystem (MCD)
PGDF .... Pilot Guide Dog Foundation (EA)
PGDH .... Phosphogluconate Dehydrogenase [*Also, PGD*] [*An enzyme*]
PGDip .... Postgraduate Diploma [*Australia*]
PGDipA .... Postgraduate Diploma in Arts [*Australia*]
PGDipAgrSc... Postgraduate Diploma in Agricultural Science [*Australia*]
PGDipDevTech... Postgraduate Diploma in Development Technology [*Australia*]
PGDipEdSt... Postgraduate Diploma in Educational Studies [*Australia*]
PGDipForSc... Postgraduate Diploma in Forest Science [*Australia*]
PGDipIEM .... Postgraduate Diploma in Irrigation Engineering Management [*Australia*]
PGDipMath & MathEd... Postgraduate Diploma in Mathematics and Mathematics Education [*Australia*]
PGDipMgtSt... Postgraduate Diploma in Management Studies [*Australia*]
PGDipPhysio... Postgraduate Diploma in Physiotherapy [*Australia*]
PGDipSc ...... Postgraduate Diploma in Science [*Australia*]
PgDn .... Page Down [*Computer science*] (CDE)
PGDN .... Propylene Glycol Dinitrate [*Organic chemistry*]
PGDP .... Paducah Gaseous Diffusion Plant
PGDP .... Paducah Gaseous Diffusion Plant (DOGT)
PGDR .... Plasma-Glucose Disappearance Rate [*Hematology*] (MAE)
PGDRB .... Plumbers, Gasfitters, and Drainers Registration Board [*Victoria, Australia*]
PGDS .... Pioneer Ground Data System
PGDS .... Pulse Generator Display System
PGE .... Pacific Gas & Electric Co. [*Associated Press*] (SAG)
PGE .... Pacific Great Eastern Railway Co. [*Nicknames: Prince George Eventually, Please Go Easy*] [*Later, British Columbia Railway*] [*AAR code*]
PGE .... Page Petroleum Ltd. [*Toronto Stock Exchange symbol*] (SPSG)
PGE .... Phenyl Glycidyl Ether [*Organic chemistry*]
PGE .... Platelet Granule Extract [*Hematology*] (MAE)
PGE .... Platinum Group Element [*Chemistry*]
PGE .... Population Growth Estimation
PGE .... Pore Gradient Electrophoresis
PGE .... Portland General Electric Co., Library, Portland, OR [*OCLC symbol*] (OCLC)
PGE .... Portland Grain Exchange (EA)
PGE .... Precision Gimbal Experiment
PGE .... Prime Group Engineer (AAG)
PGE .... Professional Group - Education
PGE .... Prostaglandin E [*Biochemistry*]
PGE .... Purge (NASA)
PGEC .... Professional Group on Electronic Computers [*IEEE*]
PGECap .... PG & E Capital I [*Associated Press*] (SAG)
PGECP .... Professional Group Electronic Component Parts (IAA)
PGED .... Professional Group - Electronic Devices
PGEM .... Professional Group - Engineering Management
PGEner .... PG Energy, Inc. [*Associated Press*] (SAG)
PGeol .... Professional Geologist (DD)
PGeoph .... Professional Geophysicist (DD)
PGEWS .... Professional Group on Engineering Writing and Speech [*Institute of Radio Engineers; now IEEE*]
PGEX .... Pacific Gateway Exchange, Inc. [*NASDAQ symbol*] (SAG)
PGF .... Pacific Gamefish Foundation (EA)
PGF .... Pengrowth Gas Income Fund Trust Units [*Toronto Stock Exchange symbol*]
PGF .... Peptide Growth Factor [*Biochemistry*]
PGF .... Perpignan [*France*] [*Airport symbol*] (OAG)
PGF .... Plerocercoid Growth Factor [*Endocrinology*]
PGF .... Portugal Fund [*NYSE symbol*] (SPSG)
PGF .... Postglacial Fault [*Biology*]
PGF .... Presentation Graphic Feature [*Computer science*]
PGF .... Prostaglandin F [*Biochemistry*]
PGFC .... Periodical Guide for Computerists [*Applegate Computer Enterprises*] [*Information service or system Defunct*] (IID)
PGFEL .... Preliminary Government-Furnished Equipment List (MCD)
PGFM .... Prostaglandin F and its Metabolite [*Dihydro-keto-prostaglandin*] [*Medicine*] (BABM)
PGFM .... Prostaglandin F and Its Metabolite [*Dihydroketoprostaglandin*] [*Endocrinology*] (DAVI)
PGFR .... Power-Generating Fusion Reaction
PGFVS .... Postgraduate Federation in Veterinary Science [*Australia*]
PGFW .... Guam [*Mariana Islands*] [*ICAO location identifier*] (ICLI)
PGG .... Page America Group, Inc. [*AMEX symbol*] (SPSG)
PGG .... Petrogold Financial Corp. [*Vancouver Stock Exchange symbol*]
PGG .... Pneumatic Ground Group
PGG .... Power Generation Group [*Nuclear Regulatory Commission*] (NRCH)
PGG .... Prostaglandin G [*A prostaglandin endoperoxide*] [*Biochemistry*]
PG/GAG .... Proteoglycans/Glyosaminoglyans
PGGO .... Prescribed Goods (General) Order
PGH .... Pantnagar [*India*] [*Airport symbol*] (AD)
PGH .... Patrol Gunboat (Hydrofoil) [*Navy symbol*]
PGH .... Phosphoglycolohydroxamate [*Biochemistry*]
PGH .... Pituitary Growth Hormone [*Endocrinology*]
PGH .... Plasma Growth Hormone [*Hematology*] (MAE)
PGH .... Polymer Group [*NYSE symbol*] (TTSB)
PGH .... Polymer Group, Inc. [*NYSE symbol*] (SAG)
PGH .... Porcine Growth Hormone [*Biochemistry*]
PGH .... Port Group Highway [*Telecommunications*] (TEL)
PGH .... Prostaglandin H [*A prostaglandin endoperoxide*] [*Biochemistry*]
PGHA .... Park Gallatin Hereford Association (EA)
PGHFE .... Professional Group - Human Factors in Electronics
Pgh Leg Journal... Pittsburgh Legal Journal [*Pennsylvania*] [*A publication*] (DLA)
PGHM .... Payload Ground Handling Mechanism [*NASA*] (MCD)
PGHS .... Prostaglandin Hydrogen Synthase [*An enzyme*]
PGHS .... Public-General Hospital Section [*American Hospital Association*] (EA)
PGHTS .... Port Group Highway Timeslot [*Telecommunications*] (TEL)
PGI .... Chitato [*Angola*] [*Airport symbol Obsolete*] (OAG)
PGI .... General Information Programme [*UNESCO*] [*Acronym is based on foreign phrase*]
PGi .... Paragigantocellularis [*Neuroanatomy*]
PGI .... Parameter Group Identifier [*Computer science*] (TNIG)
PGI .... Paris Gestion Informatique [*Paris Informatics Administration*] [*France*] [*Information service or system*] (IID)
PGI .... Peripheral Graphics, Inc.
PGI .... Phosphoglucoisomerase [*An enzyme*]
PGI .... Ply-Gem, Inc. [*NYSE symbol*] (SAG)
PGI .... Ply Gem Industries Inc. [*NYSE symbol*] (TTSB)
PGI .... Polar Geophysical Institute [*Murmansk Region*] [*Russia*]
PGI .... Port Group Interface [*Telecommunications*] (TEL)
PGI .... Potassium, Glucose, and Insulin (MAE)
PGI .... Professional Group - Instrumentation
PGI .... Project Group, Inc. [*Advertising agency*] [*Acronym now used as official n ame of agency*]
PGI .... Prostaglandin I [*Biochemistry*]
PGI .... Provigo, Inc. [*Toronto Stock Exchange symbol*]
PGI .... Pyrotechnics Guild International (EA)
PGIA .... Pendulous Gyro Integrating Accelerometer (IAA)
PGIA .... Programmable Gain Instrumentation Amplifier (IAA)
PGIE .... Professional Group - Industrial Electronics
PGiess .... Griechische Papyri im Museum des Oberhessischen Geschichtsvereins zu Giessen [*A publication*] (OCD)
PGIM .... Professional Group on Instrumentation and Measurement [*National Bureau of Standards*]
PGIP .... Polygalacturonase-Inhibiting Protein [*Biochemistry*]
PGIP .... Post Graduate Intelligence Program (DOMA)
PGIS .... Project Grant Information System
PGIT .... Professional Group - Information Theory
PGJ .... Pipeline Girth Joint
PGJD .... Past Grand Junior Deacon [*Freemasonry*]
PGJN .... Pomegranate Guild of Judaic Needlework (EA)
PGJW .... Past Grand Junior Warden [*Freemasonry*] (ROG)
PGK .... Pangkalpinang [*Indonesia*] [*Airport symbol*] (OAG)
PGK .... Phosphoglycerate Kinase [*An enzyme*]

PGI.............. Glenside Free Library, Glenside, PA [*Library symbol Library of Congress*] (LCLS)
PGL.............. Lutheran Theological Seminary, Gettysburg, PA [*Library symbol Library of Congress*] (LCLS)
PGL.............. Paraglossa of Labium [*Entomology*]
PGL.............. Pascagoula, MS [*Location identifier FAA*] (FAAL)
PGL.............. Peoples Energy [*NYSE symbol*] (TTSB)
PGL.............. Peoples Energy Corp. [*NYSE symbol*] (SPSG)
PGL.............. Persistent Generalized Lymphadenopathy [*Medicine*]
PGL.............. Phenolic Glass Laminate
PGL.............. Phosphoglycolipid
PGL.............. Polyglutaraldehyde [*Organic chemistry*]
PGL.............. Portable Gas LASER
PGL.............. Professional Graphics Language [*Software*] [*IBM Corp.*] (BYTE)
PGL.............. Provincial Grand Lodge [*Freemasonry*]
PGL.............. Pulsed Gas LASER
PGladM........ Mary J. Drexel Home, Gladwyne, PA [*Library symbol Library of Congress Obsolete*] (LCLS)
PGIB........... Beaver College, Glenside, PA [*Library symbol Library of Congress*] (LCLS)
PGLC........... Pyrolysis Gas Liquid Chromatography
PGLD........... Phoenix Gold International, Inc. [*NASDAQ symbol*] (SAG)
PGLD........... Phoenix Gold Intl [*NASDAQ symbol*] (TTSB)
PGL-Hi........ Lutheran Historical Society, Gettysburg, PA [*Library symbol Library of Congress*] (LCLS)
PGIL............. Glenside Free Library, Glenside, PA [*Library symbol*] [*Library of Congress*] (LCLS)
PGLN........... Page and Line (IAA)
PGM............. Messiah College Learning Center, Grantham, PA [*OCLC symbol*] (OCLC)
PGM............. Palenque [*Mexico*] [*Airport symbol*] (AD)
PGM............. Papyri Graecae Magicae [*A publication*] (OCD)
PGM............. Past Grand Master [*Freemasonry*]
PGM............. Paternal Grandmother (MEDA)
PGM............. Paternal Grandmother (DAVI)
PGM............. Patrol Vessel, Motor Gunboat [*Navy symbol Obsolete*]
PGM............. Perron Gold Mines [*Vancouver Stock Exchange symbol*]
PGM............. Persatuan Geologi Malaysia [*Geological Society of Malaysia*] (EAIO)
PGM............. Phosphoglucomutase [*An enzyme*]
PGM............. Planetary Gearhead Motor [*Aerospace*]
PGM............. Planning Guidance Memorandum (DOMA)
PGM............. Plant Genetic Materials
PGM............. Platinum Group Metal [*In meteorites*]
PGM............. Poly-Gel Mitigator
PGM............. Port Graham, AK [*Location identifier FAA*] (FAAL)
PGM............. Precision Guided Missile
PGM............. Precision-Guided Munition (MCD)
PGM............. Program
PGM............. Program Guidance Memorandum
PGM............. Putnam Investment Grade Municipal Trust [*NYSE symbol*] (SPSG)
PGM............. Putnam Inv Grade Muni Tr [*NYSE symbol*] (TTSB)
PGMA........... Phosphoglycerate Mutase A (DMAA)
PGMA........... Poly(glyceryl Methacrylate) [*Organic chemistry*]
PGMA........... Private Grocers' Merchandising Association [*British*] (BI)
PGMA........... Pulsed Gas Metal Arc (KSC)
PGMA-EA...... Polyglycidal Methacrylate-Ethyl Acrylate [*Organic chemistry*] (PDAA)
PGMARV...... Precision Guided Maneuvering Re-Entry Vehicle (PDAA)
PGMB........... Phosphoglycerate Mutase B (DMAA)
PGME........... Professional Group - Medical Electronics
PGMEA......... Propylene Glycol Monomethyl Ether Acetate [*Organic chemistry*]
PGM-FI......... Programmed Fuel Injection [*Automotive engineering*]
PGMIL.......... Professional Group - Military Electronics (MUGU)
PGMILE........ Professional Group - Military Electronics (AAG)
PGMM.......... Precision Guided Mortar Munition
PGMOT........ Pollution Generation Multiplier from Output Table (PDAA)
PGMP........... Preliminary Guaranteed Minimum Price
PGMS........... Professional Grounds Management Society (EA)
PGMS........... Stillwater Mining [*NASDAQ symbol*] (TTSB)
PGMS........... Stillwater Mining Co. [*NASDAQ symbol*] (SAG)
PGMSJ.......... Professional Group of Mathematical Symbol Jugglers (MUGU)
PGMT........... Pigment (MSA)
PGMTT......... Professional Group - Microwave Theory and Techniques
PGMV........... Pea Green Mottle Virus [*Plant pathology*]
PGN............. Paragon Petroleum Ltd. [*Toronto Stock Exchange symbol*]
PGN............. Perigeniculate Nucleus [*Anatomy*]
PGN............. Phi Gamma Nu [*Fraternity*]
PGN............. Pigeon (ADA)
PGN............. Platinum Group Nugget [*In meteorites*]
PGN............. Portland General Corp. [*NYSE symbol*] (SPSG)
PGN............. Portland Genl Corp. [*NYSE symbol*] (TTSB)
PGN............. Proliferative Glomerulonephritis [*Medicine*]
PGN............. Pulse Generator
PGNAA......... Prompt Gamma Neutron Activation Analysis [*Analytical chemistry*]
PGNCS......... Primary Guidance, Navigation, and Control System [*or Subsystem*] [*Apollo*] [*NASA*] (MCD)
PGND........... Propaganda (AABC)
PGNS........... PathoGenesis Corp. [*NASDAQ symbol*] (SAG)
PGNS........... Primary Guidance and Navigation System [*Apollo*] [*NASA*]
PGNS........... Professional Group - Nuclear Science
PGNT........... Sabanettan, Tinian Island [*Mariana Islands*] [*ICAO location identifier*] (ICLI)
PGNW.......... Ritidian Point, Guam Island [*Mariana Islands*] [*ICAO location identifier*] (ICLI)
PGO............. Pagecorp, Inc. [*Toronto Stock Exchange symbol*]
PGO............. Page, OK [*Location identifier FAA*] (FAAL)
PGO............. Past Grand Orient [*Freemasonry*] (ROG)
PGO............. Peroxidase-Glucose Oxidase [*Also, GOD-POD*] [*Enzyme mixture*]
PGO............. Ponto-Geniculate-Occipital [*Electroencephalography*]
PGO............. Positive Grid Oscillator
PGOC........... Payload Ground Operations Contractor [*NASA*] (SSD)
PGOR........... Payload Ground Operation Requirements [*NASA*] (NASA)
PGORS......... Payload Ground Operation Requirements Study [*NASA*] (MCD)
PGP............. Pacific Gateway Prop [*AMEX symbol*] (TTSB)
PGP............. Pacific Gateway Properties [*Formerly, Perini Investment Properties, Inc.*] [*AMEX symbol*] (SPSG)
PGP............. Parti Gabonais du Progres [*Political party*] (EY)
PGP............. Peace Garden Project [*Later, NPG*] (EA)
PGP............. Phagocyte Glycoprotein [*Biochemistry*]
PGP............. Phosphoglycolate Phosphatase [*An enzyme*]
PGP............. Pico Glass Pellet
PGP............. Planning Grant Program
PGP............. Postgamma Proteinuria [*Medicine*] (MAE)
PGP............. Precision Gas Products [*Commercial firm*]
PGP............. Prepaid Group Practice [*Insurance*]
PGP............. Pretty Good Privacy [*Telecommunications*]
PGP............. Programmable Graphics Processor
PGP............. Project on Government Procurement (EA)
PGP............. Prostaglandin Production
PGP............. Puerta Galera [*Philippines*] [*Seismograph station code, US Geological Survey*] (SEIS)
PGP............. Pulsed Glide Path (IAA)
PGP............. University of Southern Maine at Portland, Portland, ME [*OCLC symbol*] (OCLC)
PGPEP......... Professional Group - Product Engineering and Production
PGPH........... Peptidylglutamyl-Peptide Hydrolyzing [*Biochemistry*]
PGPI............ Protein Grain Products International (EA)
PGPR........... Plant-Growth-Promoting Rhizobacteria
PGPS........... Packaged Gas Pressure System
PGPT........... Professional Group - Production Techniques
PGQC........... Professional Group-Quality Control (IAA)
PGR............. Paragould, AR [*Location identifier FAA*] (FAAL)
PGR............. Parental Guidance Recommended [*Movie rating*] [*Australia*]
PGR............. Paternal Grandfather (DAVI)
PGR............. Peregrine Petroleum [*Vancouver Stock Exchange symbol*]
PGR............. Petition Granted (DNAB)
PGR............. PGR. Press Gallery Report [*A publication*] (ADA)
PGR............. Plant Growth Regulator
PGR............. Polymerized Grass Extract [*Immunology*]
PGR............. Population Growth Rate
PGR............. Precision Graphic Recorder
PgR............. Progesterone Receptor [*Endocrinology*]
PGR............. Progressive Corp. [*NYSE symbol*] (SPSG)
PGR............. Progressive Corp., Ohio [*NYSE symbol*] (TTSB)
PGR............. Psychogalvanic Reflex [*or Response*] [*Psychology*]
PGR............. Pyrogallol Red [*Also, PR*] [*An indicator Chemistry*]
PGraM.......... Messiah College, Grantham, PA [*Library symbol Library of Congress*] (LCLS)
PGRC........... Plant Gene Resources of Canada [*See also RPC*]
PGRC........... Program Guidance and Review Committee [*Army*] (AABC)
PGrev........... Greenville Area Public Library, Greenville, PA [*Library symbol Library of Congress*] (LCLS)
PGrevT......... Thiel College, Greenville, PA [*Library symbol Library of Congress*] (LCLS)
PGRF........... Pacific Gamefish Research Foundation [*Later, PORF*] (EA)
PGRF........... Pulse Group Repetition Frequency
PGRFI.......... Professional Group - Radio Frequency Interference
PGRM.......... Parti Gerakan Rakyat Malaysia [*People's Action Party of Malaysia*] [*Political party*] (PPW)
P-GRN......... Progranulocytes [*Hematology*] (DAVI)
PGRO........... Pea Growing Research Organisation Ltd. [*British*] (BI)
PGRO........... Processors and Growers Research Organisation [*British*] (IRUK)
PGRO........... Rota/International [*Mariana Islands*] [*ICAO location identifier*] (ICLI)
PGRQC......... Professional Group - Reliability and Quality Control
PGRS........... Pergerakan Guerilja Rakyat Sarawak [*Sarawak People's Guerrilla Forces*] [*Malaya*]
PGRSA......... Plant Growth Regulator Society of America (EA)
PGRT........... Petroleum Gas and Revenue Tax [*Canada*]
PGRTRC....... Professional Group-Radio Telemetry and Remote Control (IAA)
PGRV........... Photogravure (VRA)
PGRV........... Precision Guided Reentry Vehicle
PGRVT......... Precisely Guided Reentry Test Vehicle (SAA)
PGRWG........ Payload Ground Requirements Working Group [*NASA*] (NASA)
PGS............. Naval Postgraduate School
PGS............. Pagosa Springs [*Colorado*] [*Seismograph station code, US Geological Survey Closed*] (SEIS)
PGS............. Papergram System [*Military*] (CAAL)
PGS............. Parallel Gap Soldering
PGS............. Passive Geodetic Satellite [*NASA*]
PGS............. Passive Gravity Stabilization
PGS............. Peach Springs, AZ [*Location identifier FAA*] (FAAL)
PGS............. Pennsylvania German Society [*Later, TPGS*] (EA)
PGS............. Pikunas Graphoscopic Scale [*Personality development test*] [*Psychology*]
PGS............. Plane Grating Spectrograph
PGS............. Plant Growth Substance
PGS............. Plasma Generator System
PGS............. Polish Genealogical Society (EA)
PGS............. Polymer Glass Sealant
PGS............. Portable Ground Station
PGS............. Power Generation Satellite (HGAA)

PGS .... Power Generation System [*or Subsystem*]
PGS .... Power Generator Section (KSC)
PGS .... Practical Guide Series (ACII)
PGS .... Precision Gunnery System [*Army training device*] (INF)
PGS .... Predicted Ground Speed [*Navigation*]
PGS .... President of the Geographical Society [*British*] (ROG)
PGS .... President of the Geological Society [*British*]
PGS .... Pressed Glassmakers Society [*British*] (DBA)
PGS .... Pressure-Gradient Single-Ended [*Microphone*] (DEN)
PGS .... Pretty Good Stuff [*Liquor*]
PGS .... Primary Guidance Subsystem (MCD)
PGS .... Professional Guidance Systems, Inc. [*Information service or system*] (IID)
PGS .... Progenitor Genealogical Society (EA)
PGS .... Program Generation System [*Computer science*] (MDG)
PGS .... Propellant Gauging System
PGS .... Prostaglandin Synthase [*An enzyme*]
PGS .... Provincial Grand Secretary [*Freemasonry*]
PGS .... Public Service Co. North Carolina [*NYSE symbol*] (SAG)
PGS .... Public Svc No Car [*NYSE symbol*] (TTSB)
PGS .... Tauranga Aero Club, Inc. [*New Zealand*] [*ICAO designator*] (FAAC)
PGSA .... Petroleum Geo Services [*NASDAQ symbol*] (SAG)
PGSAY .... Petroleum Geo-Svcs A/S ADS [*NASDAQ symbol*] (TTSB)
PGSB .... Past Grand Sword Bearer [*Freemasonry*] (ROG)
PGSB .... Provincial Grand Sword-Bearer [*Freemasonry*]
PGSC .... Payload and General Support Computer [*NASA*]
PGSC .... Persian Gulf Service Command
PGSCOL .... Naval Postgraduate School
PGSD .... Past Grand Senior Deacon [*Freemasonry*]
PGSE .... Payload Ground Support Equipment [*NASA*] (MCD)
PGSE .... Peculiar Ground Support Equipment [*DoD*]
PGSE .... Pulsed Field Gradient Spin-Echo
PGSE .... Pulsed Gradient Spin Echo [*Physics*]
PGSEL .... Priced Ground Support Equipment List (AAG)
PGSET .... Professional Group on Space Electronics and Telemetry (AAG)
PGSI .... Prostaglandin Synthetase Inhibitor (DMAA)
PGSN .... Saipan Island (Obyan)/International [*Mariana Islands*] [*ICAO location identifier*] (ICLI)
PGSR .... Psychogalvanic Skin Resistance [*Otolaryngology*]
PGSS .... Paget-Gorman Sign System (AIE)
PGSTAP .... Pressure, Gas, Start, Turbine, Auxiliary Pump-Drive Assembly [*Pronounced "pigstap"*]
PGSU .... Propellant [*or Propulsion*] Gas Supply Unit
PGSW .... Past Grand Senior Warden [*Freemasonry*]
PGT .... Page Table [*Computer science*] (IBMDP)
PGT .... Partido Guatemalteco del Trabajo [*Guatemalan Labor Party*] [*Political party*] (PD)
PGT .... Past Grand Treasurer [*Freemasonry*]
PGT .... Pegasus Hava Tasimaciligi AS [*Turkey*] [*ICAO designator*] (FAAC)
PGT .... Per Gross Ton [*Shipping*]
PGT .... Photo Glow Tube
PGT .... Pigtail (MSA)
PGT .... Planned Giving Today [*A publication*]
PGT .... Platoon Gunnery Trainer (DOMA)
PGT .... Pollen Grain Trajectory [*Botany*]
PGT .... Polymer Grid Triode [*Imaging technology*]
PGT .... Porangatu [*Brazil*] [*Airport symbol*] (AD)
PGT .... Potato Extract-Glucose-Thiamine Hydrochloride [*Growth medium*]
PGT .... Power Grid Tube
PGT .... Putnam Intermediate Government Income [*NYSE symbol*] (SPSG)
PGT .... Putnam Interm Gvt Income [*NYSE symbol*] (TTSB)
PGTO .... Portuguese Government Trade Office (EA)
PGTR .... Plasma-Glucose Tolerance Rate [*Hematology*] (MAE)
PGTRC .... Professional Group-Telemetry and Remote Control (IAA)
PGTS .... Precision Gunnery Training System [*Army*] (INF)
PGTSND .... Puget Sound (FAAC)
PGTT .... Prednisolone Glucose Tolerance Test [*Medicine*] (DMAA)
PGTTT .... Precision Gear Train Tools and Test
PGTV .... Pegasus Communications Corp. [*NASDAQ symbol*] (SAG)
PGTW .... Guam [*Mariana Islands*] [*ICAO location identifier*] (ICLI)
PGTZ .... Praegitzer Industries [*NASDAQ symbol*] (TTSB)
PGTZ .... Praegitzer Industries, Inc. [*NASDAQ symbol*] (SAG)
PGU .... Gannon University, Nash Library, Erie, PA [*OCLC symbol*] (OCLC)
PGU .... Pegasus Gold [*AMEX symbol*] (TTSB)
PGU .... Pegasus Gold, Inc. [*AMEX symbol Toronto Stock Exchange symbol*]
PGU .... Plant Growth Unit [*NASA*] (MCD)
PGU .... Postgonococcal Urethritis [*Medicine*]
PGU .... Power Generator Unit (IAA)
PGU .... Pressure Gas Umbilical (KSC)
PGU .... Propulsion Gas Umbilical
PGUA .... Andersen Air Force Base, Guam Island [*Mariana Islands*] [*ICAO location identifier*] (ICLI)
PGUE .... Professional Group - Ultrasonic Engineering
PGUM .... Agana Naval Air Station, Guam Island [*Mariana Islands*] [*ICAO location identifier*] (ICLI)
PgUp .... Page Up [*Computer science*] (BARN)
PGUT .... Phosphogalactose Uridyltransferase [*Known as Galactose-1-phosphate Uridyl yltransferase*] [*An enzyme*]
PGV .... Greenville [*North Carolina*] [*Airport symbol*] (OAG)
PGV .... Proximal Gastric Vagotomy [*Medicine*]
PGVC .... Professional Group - Vehicular Communications
PGW .... Parallel Gap Welding
PGW .... Past Grand Warden [*Freemasonry*]
PGW .... Practice Guided Weapon (MCD)
PGW .... Pressure Gas Welding
PGW .... Pressurized Stone Groundwood [*Pulp and paper technology*]
PGW .... United Plant Guard Workers of America
PGWA .... Pottery and Glass Wholesalers Association (NADA)
PGWB .... Psychological General Well Being [*Index*] (DMAA)
PGWC .... Pennsylvania Gas & Water Co. [*NASDAQ symbol*] (SAG)
PGWC .... PG Energy, Inc. [*NASDAQ symbol*] (SAG)
PGWCZ .... P G Energy $2.25 Dep Pfd [*NASDAQ symbol*] (TTSB)
PGWG .... Parliamentary Group for World Government
PGWG .... Particles and Gases Working Group [*NASA*] (NASA)
PGWR .... Pressurised Gas-Cooled Water Reactor [*Nuclear energy*] (NUCP)
PGWS .... P. G. Wodehouse Society (EA)
PGWT .... Peipeinimaru, Tinian Island [*Mariana Islands*] [*ICAO location identifier*] (ICLI)
PGwvG .... Gwynedd-Mercy College, Gwynedd, PA [*Library symbol Library of Congress*] (LCLS)
PGX .... Prostaglandin X [*or Prostacyclin*] [*Biochemistry*]
PGY .... Global Yield Fund, Inc. [*NYSE symbol*] (SPSG)
PGY .... Postgraduate Year
PGY .... San Diego, CA [*Location identifier FAA*] (FAAL)
PGYE .... Peptone, Glucose Yeast Extract [*Medium*] [*Medicine*] (BABM)
PGYE .... Peptone, Glucose Yeast Extract [*Medium*] [*Biochemistry*] (DAVI)
PGZ .... Ponta Grossa [*Brazil*] [*Airport symbol*] (OAG)
PG/ZD .... Group Propogate / Zero Detect (MHDI)
PH .... Czechoslovakia [*License plate code assigned to foreign diplomats in the US*]
pH .... Hydrogen Ion Concentration (MAE)
Ph .... [*The*] New Testament in Modern English [*1958*] [*J. B. Phillips*] [*A publication*] (BJA)
PH .... Page Heading (BUR)
PH .... Pan Head [*Screw Head*] (ECII)
PH .... Parker-Hannifin [*NYSE symbol*] (TTSB)
PH .... Parker-Hannifin Corp. [*NYSE symbol*] (SPSG)
PH .... Parotid Hormone [*Biochemistry*]
PH .... Past History [*Medicine*]
PH .... Pearl Harbor, Hawaii
PH .... Penthouse (DD)
PH .... Penthouse
pH .... Percent Hydrogen (SSD)
PH .... Performance History
PH .... Per Hour (IAA)
PH .... Period Hours (IAA)
PH .... Persistent Hepatitis [*Medicine*]
PH .... Personal History [*Medicine*] (AAMN)
PH .... Personal Hygiene (MCD)
PH .... Perth [*Postcode*] (ODBW)
Ph .... Phallacidin [*Biochemistry*]
PH .... Phantom (IAA)
PH .... Phantom Circuit [*Telecommunications*] (TEL)
Ph .... Pharmacia AB [*Sweden*] [*Research code symbol*]
Ph .... Pharmacopoeia
PH .... Phase (KSC)
ph .... Phase (WDMC)
Ph .... Phenanthrene [*Organic chemistry*] (AAMN)
Ph .... Phenyl [*Organic chemistry*]
PH .... Phiala [*Bottle*] [*Pharmacy*]
Ph' .... Philadelphia [*Chromosome*]
PH .... Philadelphia [*Diocesan abbreviation*] [*Pennsylvania*] (TOCD)
PH .... Philharmonic Hall (NADA)
Ph .... Philippians [*New Testament book*] (BJA)
ph .... Philippines [*IYRU nationality code*] [*MARC country of publication code Library of Congress*] (LCCP)
PH .... Philippines [*ANSI two-letter standard code*] (CNC)
Ph .... Philippus [*Flourished, 13th century*] [*Authority cited in pre-1607 legal work*] (DSA)
Ph .... Phillimore's English Ecclesiastical Reports [*A publication*] (DLA)
Ph .... Phillips' English Chancery Reports [*1841-49*] [*A publication*] (DLA)
Ph .... Phillips' English Election Cases [*1780-81*] [*A publication*] (DLA)
PH .... Phillips Head (DAC)
PH .... Phone (MDG)
PH .... Phone
Ph .... Phosphate
PH .... Phot [*Electronics*] (DEN)
PH .... Photographer's Mate [*Navy rating*]
PH .... Photography Program [*Association of Independent Colleges and Schools specialization code*]
Ph .... Photoreceptor
Ph .... Photostat (BJA)
PH .... Phrase (ADA)
Ph .... Physica [*of Aristotle*] [*Classical studies*] (OCD)
PH .... Physically Handicapped (OICC)
Ph .... Phytane [*Organic chemistry*]
PH .... Piano Type Hinge
PH .... Picohenry [*One trillionth of a henry*]
P/H .... Pier to House [*Classified advertising*] (ADA)
Ph .... Pilot-Helicopter [*Navy British*]
PH .... Pilot House
PH .... Pinch Hitter [*Baseball*]
PH .... Pin Hole [*Eye examination*] (CPH)
PH .... Plane Handler [*Navy*]
PH .... Plant Height [*Botany*]
PH .... Pleckstrin-Homology [*Domain*] [*Biochemistry*]
PH .... Polynesian Airlines [*Airline code*] [*Australia*]
PH .... Poor Health (DAVI)
PH .... Porta Hepatis [*Anatomy*]

PH Porter House [*Initials often used as a pattern on clothing designed by this firm*]
P/H Postage and Handling [*Shipping*]
pH Pouvoir Hydrogene [*Hydrogen Power*] [*Negative logarithm of effective H ion concentration Chemistry*]
PH Powerhouse
PH Power of Hydrogen (IAA)
PH Practitioner's Handbooks [*A publication*]
PH Precipitation Hardening
P-H Prentice-Hall, Inc. [*Publishers*]
PH Presidential Medal of Honour [*Botswana*]
PH Previous History [*Medicine*]
PH Primary Hyperparathyroidism
PH Private Hotel
PH Probability of Hit [*Military*] (MCD)
PH Professional Hydrologist
PH Project Handclasp (EA)
PH Prospect Hill [*Vole virus*]
PH Prostatic Hypertrophy [*Medicine*] (MAE)
PH Public Health
PH Public Holiday (DA)
PH Public House [*A drinking establishment*] [*British*]
PH Pulmonary Hypertension [*Medicine*] (MAE)
PH Purple Heart [*Given to personnel wounded in military service*] [*Military decoration*]
PH Purpura Hyperglobulinemia [*Medicine*] (DAVI)
pH_I Isoelectric Point [*Chemistry*] (DAVI)
Ph^1 Philadelphia Chromosome (MAE)
PH1 Photographer's Mate, First Class [*Navy rating*]
Ph^1c Philadelphia Chromosome
PH2 Photographer's Mate, Second Class [*Navy rating*]
Ph_2O Partial Pressure of Water Vapor [*Chemistry*] (DAVI)
PH3 Photographer's Mate, Third Class [*Navy rating*]
PHA Arterial pH [*Hydrogen ion concentration*] [*Medicine*] (DAVI)
PHA Chicago, IL [*Location identifier FAA*] (FAAL)
PHa Hazelton Public Library, Hazelton, PA [*Library symbol Library of Congress*] (LCLS)
PHA Pachena Industries Ltd. [*Vancouver Stock Exchange symbol*]
PHA Palomino Horse Association (EA)
PHA Parts per Hundred of Asphalt [*Chemical technology*]
PHA Passive Hemagglutination [*Immunology*]
PHA Peripheral Hyperalimentation (Solution) [*Medicine*]
PHA Peruvian Heart Association (EA)
PHA Phenylalanin [*An amino acid*] (DAVI)
PHA Phenylalanine [*Medicine*] (MEDA)
PHA Phytohemagglutinin [*Immunology*]
PHA Phytohemagglutinin Antigen [*A skin test for cellular based immunity*] (DAVI)
PHA Polyhydroxyalkanoate [*Organic chemistry*]
PHA Poly(hydroxystearic Acid) [*Organic chemistry*]
PHA Port Heiden [*Alaska*] [*Seismograph station code, US Geological Survey Closed*] (SEIS)
PHA Poultry Husbandry Adviser [*Ministry of Agriculture, Fisheries, and Food*] [*British*]
PHA Preferred Hotels Association [*Also known as Preferred Hotel Worldwide*] (EA)
PHA Prelaunch Hazard Area (MUGU)
PHA Preliminary Hazard Analyses (NASA)
PHA Primary Human Amnion [*Biology*] (BARN)
PHA Pritikin Health Association of Australia
PHA Process Hazard Analysis [*Engineering*]
PHA Process Hazard Analysis [*Environmental science*]
PHA Process Hazards Analysis [*Chemical engineering*]
PHA Professional Hairdressers' Association [*Australia*]
PHA Professional Handlers Association (EA)
PHA Professional Horsemen's Association of America (EA)
PHA Programmable Host Access [*Computer science*] (IAA)
PHA Pseudohypoaldosteronism [*Medicine*]
PHA Public Health Act (DAS)
PHA Public Health Agency (DMAA)
PHA Public Housing Administration [*or HHFA; disbanded 1965*]
PHA Public Housing Agencies (USGC)
PHA Public Housing Agency [*Department of Housing and Urban Development*] (GFGA)
PHA Pulse Height Analysis [*Spectroscopy*]
PHA State Library of Pennsylvania, Harrisburg, PA [*OCLC symbol*] (OCLC)
PHAA Airman Apprentice, Photographer's Mate, Striker [*Navy rating*]
PHAA Percheron Horse Association of America (EA)
PHAA Photographer's Airman Apprentice [*Navy*]
PHAA Positive High-Angle of Attack
PHAA Professional Horsemen's Association of America [*Later, PHA*] (EA)
PHAABO Purebred Hanoverian Association of American Breeders and Owners (EA)
PHAB Physically Handicapped and Able Bodied [*Charitable organization*] [*British*]
PHABSIM Physical Habitat Simulation Model [*Ecology*]
PHABY Pharmacia AB [*Commercial firm*] (MHDW)
PHADA Public Housing Authorities Directors Association (EA)
PHADS Phoenix Air Defense Sector (SAA)
phaeo Phaeochromocytoma [*Pheochromocytoma*] [*Endocrinology*] (DAVI)
PHAID Positive Hostile Aircraft Identification
PHAL Phalange (WDAA)
PHAL Phalanx (WDAA)
PHAL Phytohemagglutinin-Stimulated Lymphocyte [*Medicine*] (DMAA)
Phal CC Phalen's Criminal Cases [*A publication*] (DLA)
PHALCM Phytohemagglutinin Stimulated Leukocyte Conditioned Medium
PHALSE Phreakers, Hackers, and Laundry Service Employees [*East Coast group of computer trespassers raided by the FBI*]
PHAM Phamis, Inc. [*NASDAQ symbol*] (SAG)
PHAM Phase Amplitude Monopulse (PDAA)
PHA-M Phytohemagglutinin M [*Immunology*] (MAE)
PHAM Project: Hearts and Minds [*An association*] (EA)
Phamis Phamis, Inc. [*Associated Press*] (SAG)
P-H Am Lab Arb Awards American Labor Arbitration Awards (Prentice-Hall, Inc.) [*A publication*] (DLA)
P-H Am Lab Cas American Labor Cases (Prentice-Hall, Inc.) [*A publication*] (DLA)
PHAMOS Premote Hemodynamics and Metabolism in an Orbiting Satellite (KSC)
PHAN Airman, Photographer's Mate, Striker [*Navy rating*]
PH and P Peace, Health, and Prosperity
PHANT Phantom-Glass [*Theater term*] (DSUE)
PHAOMU Pianoforte, Harmonium, and American Organ Makers' Union [*British*]
PHAP Palmitoyl Hydrolyzed Animal Protein [*Organic chemistry*]
PHAP Provincial Health Assistance Program [*Vietnam*]
PHAQ Private Hospitals' Association of Queensland [*Australia*]
PHAR Pharmaceutical (WDAA)
PHAR Pharmacology
PHAR Pharmacopoeia (ROG)
PHAR Pharmacy [*or Pharmacist*] (MSA)
PHarA AMP, Inc., Harrisburg, PA [*Library symbol Library of Congress*] (LCLS)
Phar B Pharmaciae Baccalaureus [*Bachelor of Pharmacy*]
PHarC Harrisburg Area Community College, Harrisburg, PA [*Library symbol Library of Congress*] (LCLS)
PharC Pharmaceutical Chemist [*British*]
PHarD Dauphin County Library System, Harrisburg, PA [*Library symbol Library of Congress*] (LCLS)
Phar D Pharmaciae Doctor [*Doctor of Pharmacy*]
PHARE Poland and Hungary Assistance for Economic Restructuring [*EC*] (ECED)
PHARE Program for Harmonized ATC [*Air Traffic Control*] Research in Europe (GAVI)
PharER-T Pennsylvania Department of Environmental Resources, Bureau of Topographic and Geologic Survey, Harrisburg, PA [*Library symbol*] [*Library of Congress*] (LCLS)
Phar G Graduate in Pharmacy (AAMN)
PHarH Pennsylvania Historical and Museum Commission, Harrisburg, PA [*Library symbol Library of Congress*] (LCLS)
PHarH-Ar Pennsylvania Historical and Museum Commission, Division of Archives and Manuscript, Harrisburg, PA [*Library symbol*] [*Library of Congress*] (LCLS)
PharLb Pharmchem Laboratories, Inc. [*Associated Press*] (SAG)
PHARM Pharmaceutical
Phar M Pharmaciae Magister [*Master of Pharmacy*]
PHARM Pharmacist [*or Pharmacy*]
PHARM Pharmacology
PHARM Pharmacy
Pharm Pharmacy (DD)
PHARMAC Pharmacology
PHARMACOL Pharmacological (MSA)
Pharm C Pharmaceutical Chemist (MEDA)
PHARM CHEM Pharmaceutical Chemistry (WDAA)
PHARMCL Pharmaceutical
Pharm D Doctor of Pharmacy
Pharm G Graduate in Pharmacy (MEDA)
PHARML Pharmaceutical
Pharm M Master of Pharmacy
PharMor Phar-Mor, Inc. [*Associated Press*] (SAG)
PharmoS Pharmos Corp. [*Associated Press*] (SAG)
PharmP Pharmaceutical Product Development, Inc. [*Associated Press*] (SAG)
PHAROS Phased Array RADAR Operational Simulation [*Army*] (AABC)
PHAROS Plan Handling and RADAR Operating System [*Aviation*] (DA)
PHarP Harrisburg Polyclinic Hospital, Harrisburg, PA [*Library symbol Library of Congress*] (LCLS)
PHarris Paul Harris Stores [*Associated Press*] (SAG)
PharUpj Pharmacia & Upjohn, Inc. [*Associated Press*] (SAG)
PHAS Pollution Hazard Assessment System [*Environmental science*]
PHAS Pulse Height Analyzer System
PHASE Pre-Hospital Arrest Survival Evaluation [*Cardiology study*]
PHASR Personnel Hazards Associated with Space Radiation [*Satellite*]
PHatfB Biblical School of Theology, Hatfield, PA [*Library symbol Library of Congress*] (LCLS)
PHatU Union Library Co., Hatboro, PA [*Library symbol Library of Congress Obsolete*] (LCLS)
PHav Haverford Township Free Library, Havertown, PA [*Library symbol Library of Congress*] (LCLS)
PHAV Private Hospitals' Association of Victoria [*Australia*]
PHAWA Private Hospitals' Association of Western Australia
Ph B Bachelor of Pharmacy
PhB Bachelor of Philosophy (DAVI)
Ph B Bachelor of Physical Culture
PhB British Pharmacopoeia (DAVI)
PHB Para-Hexadecylaminobenzoate [*Clinical chemistry*]
PHB Para-Hydroxybenzoate [*Organic chemistry*]
PHB Parliament House Book [*Scotland*] [*A publication*] (DLA)
PHB Parnaiba [*Brazil*] [*Airport symbol*] (OAG)
Ph B Philosophiae Baccalaureus [*Bachelor of Philosophy*]
PHB Photochemical Hole Burning [*Spectrometry*]

PHB Photographic Bulletin (MCD)
PHB Pioneer Hi-Bred International [*NYSE symbol*] (SAG)
PHB Pioneer Hi-Bred Intl [*NYSE symbol*] (TTSB)
PHB Poly(hydroxybenzoate) [*Organic chemistry*]
PHB Polyhydroxybutyrate [*Organic chemistry*]
PHB Pre-Homeobox [*Genetics*]
PHB Preventive Health Behavior [*Medicine*] (DMAA)
PHB Public Health Bibliography
PHB Public Health Service Building
PHBA Palomino Horse Breeders of America (EA)
PHBA Para-Hydroxybenzoic Acid [*Organic chemistry*]
PHBB Propylhydroxybenzyl Benzimidazole [*Organic chemistry*] (MAE)
Ph BD Doctor of Bible Philosophy
PHBH Para-Hydroxybenzoate Hydroxylase [*An enzyme*]
Ph B in Arch Bachelor of Philosophy in Architecture
Ph B in Com Bachelor of Philosophy in Commerce
Ph B in Ed Bachelor of Philosophy in Education
PhBJ Bachelor of Philosophy in Journalism (NADA)
PHBK Barking Sands, Kauai Island [*Hawaii*] [*ICAO location identifier*] (ICLI)
PHBK People's Heritage Financial Group, Inc. [*NASDAQ symbol*] (NQ)
PHBK Peoples Heritage Finl Gr [*NASDAQ symbol*] (TTSB)
PHBRZ Phosphor Bronze
PhBSp Bachelor of Philosophy in Speech (NADA)
PHBV Hydroxy Butyric Valeric Acid [*Polymer*]
PHBV Poly(hydroxybutyrate-Valerate) [*Organic chemistry*]
ph bz Phosphor Bronze (BARN)
PHC Chief Photographer's Mate [*Navy rating*]
PHC Children's Hospital of Pittsburgh, Pittsburgh, PA [*OCLC symbol*] (OCLC)
PHC Haverford College, Haverford, PA [*Library symbol Library of Congress*] (LCLS)
PHC Pacific Hurricane Centers [*National Weather Service*]
PHC Palmitoyl Homocysteine [*Biochemistry*]
PHC Pathonic Network, Inc. [*Toronto Stock Exchange symbol*]
PHC Personal Health Costs [*Medicine*] (DMAA)
PHC Personal Holding Company [*Generic term*]
PHC Perturbed-Hardness Chain [*Molecular thermodynamics*]
PHC Petroleum Helicopters de Colombia SA [*ICAO designator*] (FAAC)
Ph C Pharmaceutical Chemist
PHC PHC, Inc. [*Associated Press*] (SAG)
Ph C Philosopher of Chiropractic
PHC Photographic Change (MCD)
PHC Population Housing Census (OICC)
PHC Port Harcourt [*Nigeria*] [*Airport symbol*] (OAG)
PHC Port Hardy [*British Columbia*] [*Seismograph station code, US Geological Survey*] (SEIS)
PHC Posthospital Care [*Medicine*]
PHC [*A*] Prairie Home Companion [*National Public Radio program*]
PHC Pratt Hotel Corp. [*AMEX symbol*] (SPSG)
PHC Premolar Hypodontia, Hyperhidrosis, Canities Prematura [*Syndrome*] [*Medicine*] (DMAA)
PHC Primary Health Care
PHC Primary Health Centre [*British*]
PHC Primary Hepatic Carcinoma [*Medicine*]
PHC Primary Hepatocellular Carcinoma [*Oncology*] (DAVI)
PHC Principal Hazardous Constituent (GNE)
PHC Proliferative Helper Cells [*Immunology*]
PHCA Philippine Heart Center for Asia (PDAA)
PHCA Pig Health Control Association [*British*]
PHCA Pleasure Horse Club of America (EA)
PHCAA Public Health Cancer Association of America [*Defunct*] (EA)
P-H Cas American Federal Tax Reports (Prentice-Hall, Inc.) [*A publication*] (DLA)
PHCC Patients Encountered at [*Primary*] Health Care Centers
P-HCC Piston-Hand Control Clutch (DNAB)
PHCC Primary Hepatocellular Carcinoma [*Medicine*] (DMAA)
PHCC Punjab High Court Cases [*India*] [*A publication*] (DLA)
Ph Ch Phillips' English Chancery Reports [*1841-49*] [*A publication*] (DLA)
PHCIB Plumbing-Heating-Cooling Information Bureau (EA)
PHC Inc PHC, Inc. [*Associated Press*] (SAG)
PHCLIS Protected Home Circle Life Insurance Society (EA)
PHCM Master Chief Photographer's Mate [*Navy rating*]
PHCO Peoples Holding [*NASDAQ symbol*] (TTSB)
PHCO Peoples Holding Co. [*NASDAQ symbol*] (SAG)
PHCONST Phase Constant (IAA)
P-H Corp Corporation [*Prentice-Hall, Inc.*] [*A publication*] (DLA)
PHCP Prehospital Care Provider [*Health insurance*] (DMAA)
PHCS Senior Chief Photographer's Mate [*Navy rating*]
PHCSC Piers-Harris Children's Self-Concept Scale [*Child development test*] [*Psychology*]
PHCT Perturbed Hard Chain Theory [*Equation of state*]
PHCV-SD Phase Conversion and Step-Down (MSA)
PHD Chesapeake Biological Laboratories, Inc. [*AMEX symbol*] (SAG)
PHD Dixmont State Hospital, Sewickley, PA [*OCLC symbol*] (OCLC)
Ph D Doctor of Pharmacy
PH D Doctor of Philosophy
PhD Doctor of Philosophy (GAGS)
PHD Doctor of Public Health [*British*] (DAS)
PHD Duncan Aviation, Inc. [*ICAO designator*] (FAAC)
PHD New Philadelphia, OH [*Location identifier FAA*] (FAAL)
PHD Parallel Head Disk
PhD Perfect Hard Disk [*Century Data Systems*] [*Computer science*]
Phd Phaedo [*of Plato*] [*Classical studies*] (OCD)
PhD Pharmaciae Doctor [*Doctor of Pharmacy*] (DAVI)
PHD Phase-Shift Driver (CET)
Ph D Philosophiae Doctor [*Doctor of Philosophy*] [*Facetious translation: Piled Higher and Deeper*]
PHD Photoelectron Diffraction [*Spectroscopy*]
PHD Photohydrodynamic [*Astrophysics*]
PHD Pilot's Horizontal Display [*Aviation*] (CAAL)
PHD Poly Harnstoff Dispersion [*Organic chemistry*]
PHD Port Huron & Detroit Railroad Co. [*AAR code*]
PHD Positioning-Head Drum (DNAB)
PHD Precision High Dose
PH D Pre-Pearl Harbor Dad [*A humorous wartime degree*]
PHD Pride, Hustle, and Drive
PHD Public Health Department
PHD Public Health Director
PHD Public Housing Development [*Department of Housing and Urban Development*] (GFGA)
PHD Pulsed Holograpy Development [*Department of Energy*]
PHD Pulse Height Discrimination
PHDAN Physically Dangerous (DNAB)
PHDD Personal History of Depressive Disorders (MEDA)
PHDDS PSRO [*Professional Standards Review Organization*] Hospital Discharge Data Set
PHDE Poly(heptadiester) [*Organic chemistry*]
PHDEA Public Housing Drug Elimination Act [*1988*]
PHD.EC Chesapeake Bio Labs 'A' [*ECM, Symbol*] (TTSB)
PhDEd Doctor of Philosophy in Education [*British*] (ADA)
PHDH Dillingham Air Force Base, Oahu Island [*Hawaii*] [*ICAO location identifier*] (ICLI)
PhD(Med) Doctor of Philosophy (Medicine) (ADA)
PhDMH Doctor of Philosophy in Mechanics and Hydraulics
PhD Otol Doctor of Philosophy in Otolaryngology (PGP)
PhDPM Rehab Doctor of Physical Medicine and Rehabilitation (PGP)
PHDr Doctor of Philosophy
Phdr Phaedrus [*of Plato*] [*Classical studies*] (OCD)
PHDR Preliminary Hardware Design Review
PhD(RCA) Doctor of Philosophy (Royal College of Art) [*British*] (DBQ)
PHDS Post-Harvest Documentation Service [*Kansas State University*] (IID)
PhD Surg Doctor of Philosophy in Surgery (PGP)
PHE Aviation POL [*Petroleum, Oil, and Lubrication*] Handling Equipment (NATG)
PHE Eastern State School and Hospital, Trevose, PA [*OCLC symbol*] (OCLC)
PHE Pawan Hans Ltd. [*India*] [*ICAO designator*] (FAAC)
PHE Periodic Health Examination
PHE Petroleum Handling Equipment (MCD)
Phe Phenylalanine [*Also, F*] [*An amino acid*]
phe Phenylalanine [*Also, F*] [*An amino acid*] (DOG)
PHE Phenylephrine [*Medicine*] (DMAA)
PHE Pheophytin [*Biochemistry*]
Phe Phoenix [*Constellation*]
PHE Photo Engravers & Electrotypers Ltd. [*Toronto Stock Exchange symbol*]
PHE Plate Heat Exchanger [*Chemical engineering*]
PHE Port Hedland [*Australia Airport symbol*] (OAG)
PHE Post-Heparin Esterase [*Medicine*] (MAE)
PHE Preflight Heat Exchanger [*NASA*] (KSC)
PHEA Public Health Engineering Abstracts [*A publication*]
PHEAA Pennsylvania Higher Education Assistance Agency (EDAC)
Phear Wat Phear's Rights of Water [*1859*] [*A publication*] (DLA)
PhEEM Photoemission Electron Microscopy [*Medicine*] (DMAA)
PHEI Penetrator, High-Explosive, Incendiary (MCD)
PHEL Petroleum Helicopters, Inc. [*NASDAQ symbol*] (NQ)
PHEL Petroleum Helicopters (Vtg) [*NASDAQ symbol*] (TTSB)
PHELK Petroleum Helicopters [*NASDAQ symbol*] (TTSB)
PhelpD Phelps Dodge Corp. [*Associated Press*] (SAG)
PHeM Hershey Medical Center, Hershey, PA [*Library symbol Library of Congress*] (LCLS)
PHEM Primitive Helium Mantle [*Geology*]
PHEMA Poly(hydroxyethyl Methacrylate) [*Organic chemistry*]
phen o-Phenanthroline [*Organic chemistry*]
PHEN Phenolic (AAG)
PHEN Phenotype [*Microbiology*] (DAVI)
Pheney Rep Pheney's New Term Reports [*England*] [*A publication*] (DLA)
PHENG Photoengraving (VRA)
PH Eng Public Health Engineer
PHENO Phenobarbital [*A drug*]
pheno Phenotype
PHENO Precise Hybrid Elements for Nonlinear Operation (IEEE)
PHENOB Phenobarbital [*A Drug*] (DAVI)
phenobarb Phenobarbital [*A drug*] (DAVI)
phenom Phenomenon (BARN)
PHENOS Precise Hybrid Elements for Nonlinear Operations (IAA)
PHENTH Phenothiazine [*A drug*] (DAVI)
PHENYL Phenylpropanol [*A drug*] (DAVI)
PHEO Pheochromocytoma [*Oncology*]
PHER Photographic Mechanical Equipment Repair [*Course*] (DNAB)
PHER Plate Heat Exchanger [*Chemical Engineering*] (DNAB)
PHERMEX Pulsed High-Energy Radiographic Machine Emitting X-Rays
PHET Photoetching (VRA)
Ph Ev Phillips on Evidence [*A publication*] (DLA)
PHEWA Presbyterian Health, Education, and Welfare Association (EA)
PHF Fairview State Hospital, Waymart, PA [*OCLC symbol*] (OCLC)
PHF Newport News [*Virginia*] [*Airport symbol*] (OAG)
PHF Paired Helical Filaments [*Neuroanatomy*] [*Term coined by Dr. Robert Terry to describe the components of neurofibrillary tangles in the brains of Alzheimer's Disease patients*]

PHF.............. Patrick Henry Foundation [*Liberty, NY*] (EA)
PHF.............. Patrol Hydrofoil [*Missile*] (HGAA)
PHF.............. Peak Hour Factor [*Transportation*]
PHF.............. Peanut Hull Flour
PHF.............. Pergamon Holding Foundation [*Liechtenstein*]
PHF.............. Personal Hygiene Facility [*NASA*] (NASA)
PHF.............. Phoenix House Foundation (EA)
PHF.............. Plug Handling Fixture (NRCH)
PHF.............. Process Holding Fixture (MCD)
PHF.............. Procurement History File [*DoD*]
PHF.............. Public Health Foundation [*Information service or system*] (IID)
PHF.............. USF&G Pacholder Fd [*AMEX symbol*] (TTSB)
PHF.............. USF & G Pacholder Fund, Inc. [*AMEX symbol*] (CTT)
PHFA.............. Potomac Horse Fever Agent
PHFC.............. Pittsburgh Home Finl [*NASDAQ symbol*] (TTSB)
PHFE.............. Pulsed High-Frequency Electroporation [*Analytical biochemistry*]
P-H Fed Taxes... Federal Taxes (Prentice-Hall, Inc.) [*A publication*] (DLA)
PHFF.............. Oahu [*Hawaii*] [*ICAO location identifier*] (ICLI)
PHFG.............. Primary Human Fetal Glial [*Cytology*]
PHFPrA........ USF&G $4.10cm Cv Exch A Pfd [*NYSE symbol*] (TTSB)
PHFTX.......... Prentice-Hall Federal Taxes [*Database*] (IT)
Ph G.............. Graduate in Pharmacy
PhG.............. Pharmacopoeia Germanica [*German Pharmacopeia*] (MAE)
PHG.............. Phenate-Hexamine Goggle [*British World War I anti-poison-gas helmet*]
PHG.............. Philips Electronics NV [*Formerly, Philips NV*] [*NYSE symbol*] (SPSG)
PHG.............. Phillipsburg, KS [*Location identifier FAA*] (FAAL)
PHG.............. Phosphatidylglycerol [*Test used to determine fetal lung maturity*] (DAVI)
Phg.............. Phytophthora Megasperma Glycinea [*A fungus*]
PHG.............. Postman, Higher Grade [*British*] (DI)
PHG.............. Prototype Hydrofoil Gunboat
PHG.............. Scranton State General Hospital, Scranton, PA [*OCLC symbol*] (OCLC)
PHGA.............. Pteroylhexaglutamylglutamic [*or Pteroylheptaglutamic*] Acid [*Biochemistry*]
PhGABA........ Phenyl-gamma-aminobutyric Acid [*Tranquilizer*]
PHGLTF.......... Physiological Training Flight [*Air Force*]
Phgly.............. Phenylglycine [*An amino acid*]
PHGM.............. Patrol Hydrofoil Guided Missile [*Navy*] (DNAB)
Phgn.............. Physiognomonica [*of Aristotle*] [*Classical studies*] (OCD)
PHGNDWG... Photogenic (VRA)
PHGRM.......... Photogram (VRA)
P HGT.............. Package Height [*Freight*]
PHH.............. Andrews, SC [*Location identifier FAA*] (FAAL)
PHH.............. Haverford State Hospital, Haverford, PA [*OCLC symbol*] (OCLC)
PHH.............. Phan Thiet [*South Vietnam*] [*Airport symbol*] (AD)
PHH.............. PHH Corp. [*NYSE symbol Toronto Stock Exchange symbol*] (SPSG)
PHH.............. Phillips Head [*Screw*]
PHH.............. Posthemorrhagic Hydrocephalus [*Neurology*] (DAVI)
PHH.............. Puu Huluhulu [*Hawaii*] [*Seismograph station code, US Geological Survey Closed*] (SEIS)
PHHA.............. Pearl Harbor History Associates (EA)
PHHC.............. Programmable Hand-Held Calculator (RDA)
PHHI.............. Persistent Hyperinsulinemic Hypoglycemia of Infancy [*Medicine*]
PHHI.............. Wheeler Air Force Base, Oahu Island [*Hawaii*] [*ICAO location identifier*] (ICLI)
PHHM.............. Palm Harbor Homes [*NASDAQ symbol*] (TTSB)
PHHM.............. Palm Harbor Homes, Inc. [*NASDAQ symbol*] (SAG)
PHHN.............. Hana, Maui Island [*Hawaii*] [*ICAO location identifier*] (ICLI)
PHHSA.......... Protestant Health and Human Services Assembly (EA)
PHi.............. Historical Society of Pennsylvania, Philadelphia, PA [*Library symbol Library of Congress*] (LCLS)
PhI.............. International Pharmacopoeia
PHI.............. Permanent Health Insurance [*British*]
PHI.............. Petroleum Helicopters, Inc. (MCD)
PhI.............. Pharmacopoeia Internationalis [*International Pharmacopoeia*] (DAVI)
PHI.............. Philadelphia [*Pennsylvania*] [*Seismograph station code, US Geological Survey Closed*] (SEIS)
PHI.............. Philippine Long Distance Telephone Co. [*NYSE symbol*] (SAG)
PHI.............. Philippine Long D Tel ADS [*NYSE symbol*] (TTSB)
Phi.............. Philippus [*Flourished, 13th century*] [*Authority cited in pre-1607 legal work*] (DSA)
Phi.............. Philips [*Holland & International*] [*Record label*]
PHI.............. Philips Aviation Services [*Netherlands ICAO designator*] (FAAC)
PHI.............. Philipsburg State General Hospital, Philipsburg, PA [*Inactive*] [*OCLC symbol*] (OCLC)
PHI.............. Phillipsite [*A zeolite*]
PHI.............. Philosophie Informationsdienst [*Philosophy Information Service*] [*University of Dusseldorf*] [*Information service or system*] (IID)
PHI.............. Philosophy (WGA)
PHI.............. Phosphohexose Isomerase [*An enzyme*]
Phi.............. Physeptone [*A narcotic substitute*]
PHI.............. Physiological Hyaluronidase Inhibitor [*Biochemistry*]
PHI.............. Polarity Health Institute (EA)
PHI.............. Position and Homing Indicator
PHI.............. Prentice-Hall International [*Publisher*]
PHI.............. Programme Hydrologique International [*International Hydrological Program - IHP*] [*UNESCO*] (MSC)
PHI.............. Public Health Inspector [*British*]
PHIA.............. Pharmaceutical Ingredients Asia [*Conference*]
PHIA.............. Phenylalanine (MAE)
PHIAL.............. Phiala [*Bottle*] [*Pharmacy*]
PHIB.............. Amphibious
PHib.............. Hibeh Papyri [*A publication*] (OCD)
PHIBB.............. Project for Historical Biobibliography [*A publication*]
PHIBCB.......... Amphibious Construction Battalion [*Also, ACB*] (NVT)
PHIBCORPAC... Amphibious Corps, Pacific Fleet [*Marine Corps*]
PHIBCORPS... Amphibious Corps [*Marine Corps*]
PHIBDET.......... Amphibious Detachment
PHIBDETIND... Amphibious Detachment, India
PHIBEU.......... Amphibious Forces, Europe
PHIBEX.......... Amphibious Exercise [*NATO*]
PHIBFOR.......... Amphibious Forces
PHIBGROUP... Amphibious Group
PHIBGRU.......... Amphibious Group
PHIBLANT.......... Amphibious Forces, Atlantic Fleet
PHIBLEX.......... Amphibious Landing Exercise [*Navy*] (NVT)
PHIBNAW.......... Amphibious Forces, Northwest African Waters
PHIBOPS.......... Amphibious Operations [*Navy*] (NVT)
PHIBPAC.......... Amphibious Forces, Pacific Fleet
PHIBRAIDEX... Amphibious Raid Exercise [*Navy*] (NVT)
PHIBRECONEX... Amphibious Reconnaissance Exercise [*Navy*] (NVT)
PHIBREFTRA... Amphibious Refresher Training [*Navy*] (CAAL)
PHIBRFT.......... Amphibious Refresher Training [*Navy*] (NVT)
PHIBRON.......... Amphibious Squadron [*Army*]
PHIBSEU.......... Amphibious Forces, Europe
PHIBSFORPAC... Amphibious Forces, Pacific Fleet
PHIBSKDN.......... Amphibious Ship Shakedown Cruise [*Navy*] (NVT)
PHIBSLANT... Amphibious Forces, Atlantic Fleet
PHIBSPAC.......... Amphibious Forces, Pacific Fleet
PHIBSS.......... Amphibious Schoolship [*Navy*] (NVT)
PHIBSTRAPAC... Training Command Amphibious Forces, US Pacific Fleet
PHIBSUKAY... Amphibious Bases, United Kingdom
PHIBTF.......... Amphibious Task Force [*Navy*] (NVT)
PHIBTRA.......... Training Command Amphibious Forces
PHIBTRABASE... Amphibious Training Base [*Navy*]
PHIBTRAEX... Amphibious Training Exercise [*Navy*] (NVT)
PHIBTRAINLANT... Training Command Amphibious Forces, US Atlantic Fleet
PHIBTRAINPAC... Training Command Amphibious Forces, US Pacific Fleet
PHIBTRALANT... Training Command Amphibious Forces, US Atlantic Fleet
PHIBTRANS... Amphibious Transport [*Navy*]
PHIBTRAPAC... Training Command Amphibious Forces, US Pacific Fleet
PHIBTRBASE... Amphibious Training Base [*Navy*]
PHIBUF.......... Performance Buffet Limit (GAVI)
PHIBWARTRACEN... Amphibious Warfare Training Center [*Navy*]
PHIC.............. Poly(hexyl Isocyanate) [*Organic chemistry*]
PHICB.............. Putnam High Income Convertible & Bond Fund [*Associated Press*] (SAG)
PHICT.............. Philips Inventory Control Technique [*Computer science*] (IAA)
Phi D.............. Doctor of Philanthropy
PHID.............. Positive Hostile Identification Device [*Air Force*]
PHIGS.............. Programmers Hierarchical Interactive Graphics Standards (NITA)
PHIGS.............. Programmers Hierarchical Interactive Graphics System [*IBM Corp.*]
PHII.............. Planet Hollywood International, Inc. [*NASDAQ symbol*] (SAG)
PHII.............. Planet Hollywood Intl'A' [*NASDAQ symbol*] (TTSB)
PHIK.............. Honolulu/Hickam Air Force Base, Oahu Island [*Hawaii*] [*ICAO location identifier*] (ICLI)
Phil.............. Orationes Philippicae [*of Cicero*] [*Classical studies*] (OCD)
PHIL.............. Philadelphia [*Pennsylvania*]
Phil.............. Philadelphia (ODBW)
Phil.............. Philadelphia Reports [*A publication*] (DLA)
Phil.............. Philemon [*New Testament book*]
Phil.............. Philharmonia [*Record label*]
PHIL.............. Philharmonic
Phil.............. Philippians [*New Testament book*]
Phil.............. Philippine Island Reports [*A publication*] (DLA)
PHIL.............. Philippines (AFM)
Phil.............. Philippines (VRA)
Phil.............. Phillimore's English Ecclesiastical Reports [*A publication*] (DLA)
Phil.............. Phillips' English Chancery Reports [*1841-49*] [*A publication*] (DLA)
Phil.............. Phillips' English Election Cases [*1780-81*] [*A publication*] (DLA)
Phil.............. Phillips' Illinois Reports [*152-245 Illinois*] [*A publication*] (DLA)
Phil.............. Phillips' North Carolina Law Reports [*A publication*] (DLA)
Phil.............. Phillips' Treatise on Insurance [*A publication*] (DLA)
Phil.............. Philoctetes [*of Sophocles*] [*Classical studies*] (OCD)
PHIL.............. Philology
Phil.............. Philopoemen [*of Plutarch*] [*Classical studies*] (OCD)
PHIL.............. Philosophy
Phil.............. Philosophy (DD)
PHIL.............. Potential Host Institures List [*European Commission*]
PHIL.............. Programmable Algorithm Machine High-Level Language [*Computer science*]
PHILA.............. Philadelphia [*Pennsylvania*]
Phila.............. Philadelphia Reports [*Pennsylvania*] [*A publication*] (DLA)
Phila C Pharmacy... Philadelphia College of Pharmacy and Science (GAGS)
Philad.............. Philadelphia Reports [*Pennsylvania*] [*A publication*] (DLA)
PHILADA.......... Philadelphia (ROG)
Philada R.......... Philadelphia Reports [*Pennsylvania*] [*A publication*] (DLA)
Philada Rep... Philadelphia Reports [*Pennsylvania*] [*A publication*] (DLA)
PHILADEL.......... Philadelphia (ROG)
Philadelphia Leg Int... Philadelphia Legal Intelligencer [*Pennsylvania*] [*A publication*] (DLA)
Philadelphia Rep... Philadelphia Reports [*Pennsylvania*] [*A publication*] (DLA)
PHILAGRP.......... Philadelphia Group (DNAB)
Phila Leg Int... Philadelphia Legal Intelligencer [*Pennsylvania*] [*A publication*] (DLA)
Phila LJ.......... Philadelphia Law Journal [*A publication*] (DLA)
philan.............. Philanthropical (BJA)
PHILANTHR... Philanthropic (ROG)

Phila (PA).... Philadelphia Reports [*Pennsylvania*] [*A publication*] (DLA)
Phila Reports... Philadelphia Reports [*Pennsylvania*] [*A publication*] (DLA)
philat........... Philately
Philbro......... Philipp Brothers Ltd. [*Commercial firm*]
Phil C.......... Philosophy in Chiropractic
PHILCAG...... First Philippine Civic Action Group [*Deployed in 1964 to assist South Vietnam*] (VNW)
Phil Civ & Can Law... Phillimore's Civil and Canon Law [*A publication*] (DLA)
PHILCOM..... Philippine Global Communications, Inc. [*Manila*] [*Telecommunications*]
PhilCon........ Philadelphia Consolidated Holding [*Commercial firm Associated Press*] (SAG)
PHILCON...... Philippine Contingent [*Military*]
Phil Cop...... Phillips' Law of Copyright Designs [*A publication*] (DLA)
Phil D.......... Philosophiae Doctor [*Doctor of Philosophy*] [*See also Ph D*] [*Latin*]
PHILDANCO... Philadelphia Dance Company
Phil Dec...... Philippus Decius [*Deceased circa 1537*] [*Authority cited in pre-1607 legal work*] (DSA)
Phil Dom..... Phillimore's Law of Domicil [*A publication*] (DLA)
Phil Ecc....... Phillimore's Ecclesiastical Judgments [*A publication*] (DLA)
Phil Ecc....... Phillimore's English Ecclesiastical Law [*2 eds.*] [*1873, 1895*] [*A publication*] (DLA)
Phil Ecc....... Phillimore's English Ecclesiastical Reports [*1809-21*] [*A publication*] (DLA)
Phil Ecc Judg... Phillimore's Ecclesiastical Judgments [*1867-75*] [*A publication*] (DLA)
Phil Ecc Law... Phillimore's English Ecclesiastical Law [*2 eds.*] [*1873, 1895*] [*A publication*] (DLA)
Phil Ecc R... Phillimore's English Ecclesiastical Reports [*1809-21*] [*A publication*] (DLA)
Phil El Cas... Phillips' English Election Cases [*1780-81*] [*A publication*] (DLA)
Philem......... Philemon [*New Testament book*]
PhilEnv........ Philip Environmental [*Commercial firm Associated Press*] (SAG)
Phil Eq......... Phillips' North Carolina Equity Reports [*A publication*] (DLA)
Phil Ev......... Phillips on Evidence [*A publication*] (DLA)
Phil Ev Cow & H & Edw Notes... Phillips on Evidence, Notes by Cowen, Hill, and Edwards [*A publication*] (DLA)
PHILEX........ Philadelphia Stock Exchange
Phil Fam Cas... Phillipps' Famous Cases in Circumstantial Evidence [*A publication*] (DLA)
Phil Grand... Phillips' Grandeur of the Law [*A publication*] (DLA)
PHIL I.......... Philippine Islands (WDAA)
Phili Fran.... Philippus Francus [*Deceased, 1471*] [*Authority cited in pre-1607 legal work*] (DSA)
Phil ILJ........ Philippine International Law Journal [*A publication*] (DLA)
Phil Ins........ Phillips on Insurance [*A publication*] (DLA)
Phil Insan.... Phillips on Lunatics [*1858*] [*A publication*] (DLA)
Phil Int Law... Phillimore's International Law [*A publication*] (DLA)
Phil Int LJ... Philippine International Law Journal [*A publication*] (DLA)
Phil Int Rom Law... Phillimore's Introduction to the Roman Law [*A publication*] (DLA)
Philip........... Philippines
Philip Fran... Philippus Franchus [*Deceased, 1471*] [*Authority cited in pre-1607 legal work*] (DSA)
Philipp......... Philippines (BARN)
Philippine.... Philippine Reports [*A publication*] (DLA)
Philippine Co... Philippine Code [*A publication*] (DLA)
Philippine Internat LJ... Philippine International Law Journal [*Manila, Philippines*] [*A publication*] (DLA)
Philippine Int'l LJ... Philippine International Law Journal [*A publication*] (DLA)
Philippine LJ... Philippine Law Journal [*A publication*] (DLA)
Philippine L Rev... Philippine Law Review [*A publication*] (DLA)
PhilipsEl...... Philips Electronics NV Holding Co. [*Associated Press*] (SAG)
Phil Jud........ Phillimore's Ecclesiastical Judgments [*1867-75*] [*England*] [*A publication*] (DLA)
Phil Judg..... Phillimore's Ecclesiastical Judgments [*1867-75*] [*A publication*] (DLA)
Phill............. Phillips' English Chancery Reports [*1841-49*] [*A publication*] (DLA)
Phill............. Phillips' English Election Cases [*1780-81*] [*A publication*] (DLA)
Phill............. Phillips' Illinois Reports [*152-245 Illinois*] [*A publication*] (DLA)
Phill............. Phillips' North Carolina Equity Reports [*A publication*] (DLA)
Phill............. Phillips' North Carolina Law Reports [*A publication*] (DLA)
Phil Lab Rel J... Philippine Labour Relations Journal [*A publication*] (DLA)
Phil Law...... Phillips' North Carolina Law Reports [*A publication*] (DLA)
Phill Ch....... Phillips' English Chancery Reports [*1841-49*] [*A publication*] (DLA)
Phill Ch (Eng)... Phillips' English Chancery Reports [*1841-49*] [*A publication*] (DLA)
Phil LD........ Doctor of Lithuanian Philology
Phill Ecc Judg... Phillimore's Ecclesiastical Judgments [*1867-75*] [*A publication*] (DLA)
Phill Ecc R... Phillimore's English Ecclesiastical Reports [*1809-21*] [*A publication*] (DLA)
Phill Eq (NC)... Phillips' North Carolina Equity Reports [*A publication*] (DLA)
Phil Lic....... Licentiate of Philosophy [*British*]
Phillim......... Phillimore's English Ecclesiastical Reports [*1809-21*] [*A publication*] (DLA)
Phillim Dom... Phillimore's Law of Domicil [*A publication*] (DLA)
Phillim Eccl... Phillimore's Ecclesiastical Judgments [*1867-75*] [*A publication*] (DLA)
Phillim Eccl... Phillimore's English Ecclesiastical Reports [*1809-21*] [*A publication*] (DLA)
Phillim Ecc Law... Phillimore's English Ecclesiastical Law [*A publication*] (DLA)
Phillim Int Law... Phillimore's International Law [*A publication*] (DLA)
Phill Ins....... Phillips on Insurance [*A publication*] (DLA)
Phillips........ Phillips' English Chancery Reports [*1841-49*] [*A publication*] (DLA)
Phillips........ Phillips' English Election Cases [*1780-81*] [*A publication*] (DLA)
Phillips........ Phillips' Illinois Reports [*152-245 Illinois*] [*A publication*] (DLA)
Phillips........ Phillips' North Carolina Equity Reports [*A publication*] (DLA)
Phillips........ Phillips' North Carolina Law Reports [*A publication*] (DLA)
Phillips U.... Phillips University (GAGS)
Phil Lit R..... Philatelic Literature Review [*A publication*]
Phil LJ......... Philippine Law Journal [*Manila*] [*A publication*] (DLA)
Phill L (NC)... Phillips' North Carolina Law Reports [*A publication*] (DLA)
Phil L Rev.... Philippine Law Review [*A publication*] (DLA)
Phil Lun....... Phillips on Lunatics [*1858*] [*A publication*] (DLA)
Philly........... Philadelphia
PhilM........... Master of Philosophy (GAGS)
Phil M.......... Master of Philosophy (PGP)
Phil Mech Liens... Phillips on Mechanics' Liens [*A publication*] (DLA)
PhilMr......... Philip Morris Companies, Inc. [*Associated Press*] (SAG)
philn........... Philanthropy
Phil NC........ Phillips' North Carolina Law Reports [*A publication*] (DLA)
Philo........... Philo Judaeus [*First century AD*] [*Classical studies*] (OCD)
Philol.......... Philologus [*A publication*] (OCD)
PHILOL........ Philology
Philol Suppl... Philologus. Supplement [*A publication*] (OCD)
PHILOM....... Philomathes [*Lover of Learning*] (ROG)
PHILOMATH... Philomathematicus [*Lover of Mathematics*] (ROG)
PHILOS........ Philosophy (EY)
Philostr....... Philostratus [*Second century AD*] [*Classical studies*] (OCD)
Phil (PA)...... Philadelphia Reports [*Pennsylvania*] [*A publication*] (DLA)
Phil Pat....... Phillips on Patents [*A publication*] (DLA)
PhilPet........ Phillips Petroleum Co. [*Associated Press*] (SAG)
PHILPUC...... Philippine Presidential Unit Citation Badge [*Military decoration*]
PHILQA........ Philips Question Answering System (NITA)
Phil R.......... Philadelphia Reports [*Pennsylvania*] [*A publication*] (DLA)
Phil R.......... Philosophical Review [*A publication*] (BRI)
Phil Rep...... Philadelphia Reports [*Pennsylvania*] [*A publication*] (DLA)
PhilRH......... Phillips [*R.H.*], Inc. [*Associated Press*] (SAG)
Phil Rom Law... Phillimore's Private Law among the Romans [*A publication*] (DLA)
PHILSEAFRON... Philippine Sea Frontier
PHIL SOC..... Philharmonic Society (WDAA)
PHILSOM..... Periodical Holdings in the Library of the School of Medicine [*Washington University School of Medicine*] [*Library network*]
Phil St Leg R... Phillips' Studii Legalis Ratio [*A publication*] (DLA)
Phil St Tr... Phillipps' State Trials [*Prior to 1688*] [*A publication*] (DLA)
PhilSub........ Philadelphia Suburban Corp. [*Associated Press*] (SAG)
Phil Unters... Philologische Untersuchungen [*A publication*] (OCD)
Phil US Pr... Phillips' United States Practice [*A publication*] (DLA)
Phil Wochenschr... Philologische Wochenschrift [*A publication*] (OCD)
Phil Yb Int'l L... Philippine Yearbook of International Law [*Manila, Philippines*] [*A publication*] (DLA)
PHIM............ Posthypoxic Intention Myoclonus [*Medicine*] (DMAA)
PHIN............ Position and Homing Inertial Navigator
PHIND.......... Pharmaceutical and Healthcare Industries News Database [*PJB Group Publications Ltd.*] [*Information service or system*] (IID)
P-H Ind Rel Lab Arb... Industrial Relations, American Labor Arbitration (Prentice-Hall, Inc.) [*A publication*] (DLA)
P-H Ind Rel Union Conts... Industrial Relations, Union Contracts, and Collective Bargaining (Prentice-Hall,Inc.) [*A publication*] (DLA)
PHINet......... Prentice-Hall Information Network [*Prentice-Hall Information Services*] [*Information service or system*] (IID)
Phip............ Phipson's Digest, Natal Reports [*South Africa*] [*A publication*] (DLA)
Phip............ Phipson's Reports, Natal Supreme Court [*South Africa*] [*A publication*] (DLA)
Phip Ev........ Phipson on Evidence [*12th ed.*] [*1976*] [*A publication*] (DLA)
PHIPrA........ Philippine L-D Tel Pfd GDS [*NYSE symbol*] (TTSB)
PHIPS.......... Professional Hi-Resolution Image Processing System [*TerraVision, Inc.*] (PCM)
Phipson....... Reports of Cases in the Supreme Court of Natal [*A publication*] (DLA)
PHIRB.......... Public Health Inspectors' Registration Board [*British*] (BI)
PHIS............ Physically Handicapped in Science (BABM)
PHIS............ Physically Handicapped in Science (DAVI)
PHIS............ Program Hardware Interface Specification (CAAL)
PHITAP........ Predesigned [*or Priority*] High-Interest Tactical Air Prediction [*Acoustic forecast*] (MCD)
PHITAR........ Predesignated High-Interest Tactical Area [*Navy*] (NVT)
PhIUS.......... Pharmaceutical Ingredients U.S.
PHJ............. Danville State Hospital, Danville, PA [*OCLC symbol*] (OCLC)
PHJC........... Penn Hall Junior College [*Pennsylvania*] [*Closed, 1973*]
PHJC........... Poor Handmaids of Jesus Christ [*Ancilla Domini Sisters*] [*Roman Catholic religious order*]
PHJC........... Port Huron Junior College [*Michigan*]
PH/JO.......... Photojournalist (DNAB)
PHK............. Pahokee, FL [*Location identifier FAA*] (FAAL)
PHK............. Personal Hygiene Kit (MCD)
PhK............. Phosphorylase Kinase [*An enzyme*]
PHK............. Platelet Phosphohexokinase (MAE)
PHK............. Postmortem Human Kidney [*Cells*]
PHKO........... Kona/Ke-Ahole, Hawaii Island [*Hawaii*] [*ICAO location identifier*] (ICLI)
PHKP........... Kaanapali, Maui Island [*Hawaii*] [*ICAO location identifier*] (ICLI)
PHKU........... Kunia [*Hawaii*] [*ICAO location identifier*] (ICLI)
PHKW.......... Powerhouse Resources, Inc. [*NASDAQ symbol*] (SAG)
PHKWE........ Powerhouse Resources [*NASDAQ symbol*] (TTSB)
PHL............. Allentown State Hospital, Allentown, PA [*OCLC symbol*] (OCLC)
Ph L............ Licentiate in Philosophy
Ph L............ Licentiate of Pharmacy
PHL............. Periodical Holdings List [*Libraries*]
PHL............. Philadelphia [*Pennsylvania*] [*Airport symbol*]
PHL............. Philippines [*ANSI three-letter standard code*] (CNC)

PHL .... Phillips Michigan City Flying Service, Inc. [*ICAO designator*] (FAAC)
PHL .... Pressure to Horizontal Locks [*Missiles*] (AAG)
PHL .... Public Health Law
PHLA .... Plasma Postheparin Lipolytic Activity [*Clinical chemistry*]
PHLA .... Postheparin Lipolytic Activity [*Medicine*] (DMAA)
PHLAG .... Philips Load and Go (NITA)
PHLAG .... Phillips Petroleum Load and Go [*System*]
PHLAGS .... Phillips Petroleum Load and Go System (DNAB)
Phlb .... Philebus [*of Plato*] [*Classical studies*] (OCD)
Phld .... Philodemus [*First century BC*] [*Classical studies*] (OCD)
PHLH .... Phillips Head [*Screw*]
PHLI .... Lihue, Kauai Island [*Hawaii*] [*ICAO location identifier*] (ICLI)
PHLITHO .... Photolithographic (VRA)
PhILD .... Philippine Long Distance Telephone Co. [*Associated Press*] (SAG)
Phlm .... Philemon [*New Testament book*]
PHLO .... Phloretin [*Biochemistry*]
PHLODOT .... Phase Lock Doppler Tracking [*System*] (MUGU)
PhlpGs .... Phillips Gas [*Associated Press*] (SAG)
PHLS .... Public Health Laboratory Service [*British*]
PHLSB .... Public Health Laboratory Service Board [*British*]
PhlVH .... Phillips-Van Heusen Corp. [*Associated Press*] (SAG)
PHLX .... Philadelphia Stock Exchange
PHLY .... Philadelphia Consol Hldg [*NASDAQ symbol*] (TTSB)
PHLY .... Philadelphia Consolidated Holding [*NASDAQ symbol*] (SAG)
Ph M .... Master in Pharmacy
Ph M .... Master of Philosophy
PHM .... Mayview State Hospital, Bridgeville, PA [*OCLC symbol*] (OCLC)
PHM .... Patrol Hydrofoil Missile [*Navy symbol*]
PHM .... Patterson-Harker Method [*Physics*]
PHM .... Per Hundred Million (NASA)
PHM .... Petroleum Helicopters, Inc. [*ICAO designator*] (FAAC)
PHM .... Phantom (MSA)
PhM .... Pharmaciae Magister [*Master of Pharmacy*] (DAVI)
PHM .... Pharmacist's Mate [*Navy rating*]
PHM .... Phase Meter
PHM .... Phase Modulation [*Radio data transmission*] (DEN)
Phm .... Philemon [*New Testament book*] (BJA)
PhM .... Philips Minigroove [*Record label*]
PHM .... Posterior Hyaloid Membrane [*Eye anatomy*]
PHM .... Post-Holiday Movie
PHM .... Power Hybrid Microcircuit
PHM .... Pulte Corp. [*NYSE symbol*] (SPSG)
PHMA .... Plastic Houseware Manufacturers Association
PHMA .... Polyhexyl Methacrylate [*Organic chemistry*]
Phm B .... Bachelor of Pharmacy
PHMB .... Para-Hydroxymercuribenzoate [*Biochemistry*]
PHMC .... Probe Heater Motor Controller [*NASA*] (MCD)
Phmcyc .... Pharmacyclics, Inc. [*Associated Press*] (SAG)
PHMD .... Pseudohypertrophic Muscular Dystrophy (CPH)
PHMDP .... Pharmacist's Mate, Dental Prosthetic Technician [*Navy rating*]
Phm G .... Graduate in Pharmacy
PHMK .... Molokai, Molokai Island [*Hawaii*] [*ICAO location identifier*] (ICLI)
PHMO .... Partially Hydrogenated Menhaden Oil [*Food science*]
PhMor .... Phar-Mor, Inc. [*Associated Press*] (SAG)
PHMOV .... Phleum Mottle Virus [*Plant pathology*]
PHMP .... Primordial Hot Mantle Plume (PDAA)
PhmRes .... Pharmaceutical Resources, Inc. [*Associated Press*] (SAG)
PHMS .... Para-Hydroxymercuriphenylsulfonate [*Organic chemistry*]
PHMS .... Patrol Hydrofoil Missile Ship [*Navy/NATO*]
PHMS .... Polish Historical Military Society (EA)
PHMU .... Waimea-Kohala, Kamuela, Hawaii Island [*Hawaii*] [*ICAO location identifier*] (ICLI)
PhMV .... Phleum Mottle Virus
PHMV .... Physalis Mosaic Virus [*Plant pathology*]
PHMWO .... Prospect Hill Millimeter Wave Observatory [*Waltham, MA*] [*Air Force*]
PHMX .... PhyMatrix Corp. [*NASDAQ symbol*] (TTSB)
PHMX .... PhyMatrix Corp. [*NASDAQ symbol*] (SAG)
PHN .... Norristown State Hospital, Norristown, PA [*OCLC symbol*] (OCLC)
PHN .... Passive Heymann Nephritis [*Medicine*] (DMAA)
PHN .... Phoenix Resource Companies, Inc. [*AMEX symbol*] (SAG)
PHN .... Phone (KSC)
PHN .... Port Huron [*Michigan*] [*Airport symbol*] (AD)
PHN .... Port Huron, MI [*Location identifier FAA*] (FAAL)
PHN .... Postherpetic Neuragia [*Medicine*]
PHN .... Postherpetic Neuralgia [*Medicine*] (DAVI)
PHN .... Public Health Network [*Information service or system*] (IID)
PHN .... Public Health Nurse
PHNA .... Barbers Point Naval Air Station, Oahu Island [*Hawaii*] [*ICAO location identifier*] (ICLI)
PHNC .... Pearl Harbor, Oahu Island [*Hawaii*] [*ICAO location identifier*] (ICLI)
PHNG .... Kaneohe Bay Marine Corps Air Station, Oahu Island [*Hawaii*] [*ICAO location identifier*] (ICLI)
PHNL .... Honolulu/International, Oahu Island [*Hawaii*] [*ICAO location identifier*] (ICLI)
PHNS .... Pearl Harbor Naval Shipyard
PHNS .... Pearl Harbor Naval Shipyard (DOGT)
PHNX .... Phoenix Shannon Ltd. [*NASDAQ symbol*] (SAG)
PhnxRs .... Phoenix Resource Companies, Inc. [*Associated Press*] (SAG)
PhnxShn .... Phoenix Shannon Ltd. [*Associated Press*] (SAG)
PhnxTc .... Phoenix Technologies Ltd. [*Associated Press*] (SAG)
PHNXY .... Phoenix Shannon plc ADR [*NASDAQ symbol*] (TTSB)
PHNY .... Lanai City, Lanai Island [*Hawaii*] [*ICAO location identifier*] (ICLI)
PHNY .... Pearl Harbor Navy Yard [*Later, Pearl Harbor Naval Shipyard*]
P-H NYETR .... Prentice-Hall New York Estate Tax Reports [*A publication*] (DLA)
PHO .... Pediatric Hematology-Oncology [*Medical specialty*] (DHSM)
PHO .... Peoples Telephone Co. [*AMEX symbol*] (SAG)
PHO .... Phenolic Heavy Oil
PHO .... Philco Houston Operations (SAA)
PHO .... Phoenix Airways (Pfy) [*South Africa*] [*FAA designator*] (FAAC)
Pho .... Photographer [*British military*] (DMA)
PHO .... Physician-Hospital Organization [*Information service or system*] (HCT)
PHO .... Physician-Hospital Organization
PHO .... Point Hope [*Alaska*] [*Airport symbol*] (OAG)
PHO .... Polk State School and Hospital, Polk, PA [*OCLC symbol*] (OCLC)
PHO .... Port Health Officer
PHO .... Principal House Officer [*Australia*]
PHO .... Public Hazards Office (NADA)
PHO .... Puu Honuaula [*Hawaii*] [*Seismograph station code, US Geological Survey*] (SEIS)
PHOAC .... Photographer's Mate, Combat Aircrewman [*Navy rating Obsolete*]
Phob .... Previous Highroller, on a Budget [*Lifestyle classification*]
PHOBOS .... Photometric Instrument for Biological Optical Sections
PHOC .... Photo Control [*NASDAQ symbol*] (TTSB)
PHOC .... Photo Control Corp. [*NASDAQ symbol*] (NQ)
PHOC .... Photocopy (MSA)
PHOCAS .... Photo Optical Cable Controlled Submersible (PDAA)
PHOCIS .... Photogrammetric Circulatory Survey (PDAA)
PHOD .... Philadelphia Ordnance Depot [*Military*] (AAG)
PHODEC .... Photometric Determination of Equilibrium Constants [*Computer science*]
Phoe .... Phoenix [*Constellation*]
Phoen .... Phoenician (BJA)
Phoen .... Phoenissae [*of Euripides*] [*Classical studies*] (OCD)
PHOENIX .... Plasma Heating Obtained by Energetic Neutral Injection Experiment (IEEE)
PHOFEX .... Photofragment Excitation [*Spectroscopy*]
PHOFL .... Photoflash (AAG)
PHOG .... Kahului, Maui Island [*Hawaii*] [*ICAO location identifier*] (ICLI)
PHOM .... Photographer's Mate [*Navy rating Obsolete*]
PHON .... Phoenician
PHON .... Phonetics
PHON .... Phonogram (ROG)
PHON .... Phonograph (AAG)
PHONCON .... Telephone Conversation [*or Conference*]
PHONE .... Telephone (NTCM)
PHONET .... Phonetics (ROG)
Phonetel .... Phonetel Technologies [*Commercial firm Associated Press*] (SAG)
P HONG .... Ponchong [*Tea trade*] (ROG)
Phono .... Phonocardiogram [*Cardiology*] (DAVI)
PHONO .... Phonograph (MSA)
PHONO .... Phonograph
PHONOG .... Phonography
PHONOL .... Phonology
PHOPT .... Pseudohypoparathyroidism [*Endocrinology*]
Phorm .... Phormio [*of Terence*] [*Classical studies*] (OCD)
PHOS .... Phosphate (KSC)
PHOS .... Phosphorescent (KSC)
PHOS .... Phosphorus [*Chemical symbol is P*]
PhosBro .... Phosphor Bronze
PHOSCHEM .... Phosphate Chemicals Export Association (EA)
PHOSI .... Preliminary Handbook of Operations and Service Instructions
PHOSIAC .... Photographically Stored Information Analog Comparator
PHosp .... Post Hospital [*Army*]
PHOS-S .... Phosphorus Spot [*Urine Test*] [*Chemistry*] (DAVI)
PHOST .... Poly(hydroxystyrene) [*Organic chemistry*]
Phot .... Photius [*Ninth century AD*] [*Classical studies*] (OCD)
PHOT .... Photograph
PHOT .... Photographer [*Navy rating British*]
PHOTABS .... Photographic Abstracts [*Pergamon*] [*Database*]
PHOTAC .... Phototypesetting and Composing [*AT & T*]
Photcm .... Photocomm, Inc. [*Associated Press*] (SAG)
PHOTINT .... Photographic Intelligence [*Military*]
photmur .... Photo Mural (VRA)
photo .... Photograph (VRA)
PHOTO .... Photograph (AAG)
Photo .... Photogravure [*Philately*]
PhotoC .... Photo-Control Corp. [*Associated Press*] (SAG)
PHOTOG .... Photographic
PHOTOGR .... Photographer
PHOTOGR .... Photography
PHOTOLITH .... Photolithographic
PHOTOM .... Photometry
photomon .... Photomontage (VRA)
Photon .... Photon Dynamics, Inc. [*Associated Press*] (SAG)
PHOTOTRIGULANT .... Photographic Triangulation Group, Atlantic [*Military*] (DNAB)
PHOTOTRIGUPAC .... Photographic Triangulation Group, Pacific [*Military*] (DNAB)
Photrln .... Photronic Labs [*Associated Press*] (SAG)
PHOTRIPART .... Photo Triangulation Party [*Military*]
PHOTRON .... Photographic Squadron [*Navy*]
PHOTUB .... Phototube (KSC)
PHO/TY .... Photo Type [*Deltiology*]
PHP .... Pacific Hawaiian Products Co. [*Later, PHP Co.*]
PHP .... Packing-House Products [*Food industry*]
PHP .... Parents Helping Parents [*An association*] (EA)
PHP .... Parts, Hybrids, and Packaging (MCD)
PHP .... Passive Hyperpolarizing Potential [*Neurochemistry*]
PHP .... Payload Handling Panel [*NASA*] (MCD)
PHP .... Pennhurst State School and Hospital, Spring City, PA [*OCLC symbol*] (OCLC)

PHP .... Personal Handy Phone [Telecommunications]
PHP .... Philip, SD [Location identifier FAA] (FAAL)
PHP .... Phillip Resources, Inc. [Vancouver Stock Exchange symbol]
PHP .... Philosophia Patrum [A publication] (BJA)
PHP .... PHP Healthcare Corp. [Associated Press] (SAG)
PHP .... Physician's Health Plan
PHP .... Pinane Hydroperoxide [Organic chemistry]
PHP .... Planetary Horizon Platform [Aerospace]
PHP .... Post-Heparin Phospholipase [Medicine] (MAE)
PHP .... Postheparin Plasma (DAVI)
PHP .... Post-Hostilities Planning Subcommittee of the Chiefs of Staff Committee [World War II]
PHP .... Pounds per Horsepower
PHP .... Prentice Hall Press [Publisher]
PHP .... Prepaid Health Plan [Insurance]
PHP .... Presbyterian Hunger Program (EA)
PHP .... Primary Hyperparathyroidism (MAE)
PHP .... Propeller Horsepower
PHP .... Pseudohyperbolic Particle [Astrophysics]
PHP .... Pseudohypoparathyroidism [Endocrinology]
PHP .... Pump Horsepower
PHPA .... Pacific Herring Packers Association (EA)
PHPA .... Partially-Hydrolyzed Polyacrylamide [Well drilling technology]
PHPC .... Post-Hostilities Planning Committee [Navy World War II]
PHPG .... Poly(hydroxypropylglutamine) [Organic chemistry]
PHPHB .... P-heptyl-p-hydroxy Benzoate [A preservative used in the making of American and British beer]
PHPK .... Probability of Hit to Probability of Kill (INF)
PHPL .... Parallel Hardware Processing Language [1977] [Computer science] (CSR)
PHPO .... Private Health Plan Option [Medicare] (GFGA)
PHPS .... Post-Hostilities Planning Staff [World War II]
PHPT .... Portable High-Potential Tester
PHPT .... Primary Hyperparathyroidism
PHPV .... Persistent Hyperplastic Primary Vitreous [Ophthalmology]
PHQ .... Personnel History Questionnaire (MHDB)
PHQ .... Phenylhydroquinone [Organic chemistry]
PHQ .... Postal Headquarters [British]
PHR .... Pacific Harbour [Fiji] [Airport symbol] (OAG)
PHR .... Pacific Historical Review [A publication] (BRI)
PHR .... Parts per Hundred of Rubber [Chemical technology]
PHR .... Payload Hazardous Report (NASA)
PHR .... Peak Heart Rate [Cardiology]
PHR .... Peak Height Ratio
PHR .... Phorbol [Organic chemistry]
PHR .... Photographic Reconnaissance
PHR .... Photoreactivity (DMAA)
PHR .... Phrase
Phr .... Phrenomena: an Annual Review [A publication] (APTA)
PHR .... Physical Record [Computer science]
PHR .... Physicians for Human Rights (EA)
PHR .... Pound-Force per Hour (MCD)
PHR .... Pounds per Hour (AAG)
PHR .... Preheater (KSC)
PHR .... Process Hazardous Review [Environmental science]
PHR .... Process Heat Reactor Program [Nuclear Regulatory Commission]
PHR .... Public Health Reports [A publication]
PHR .... Pulse-Height Resolution [By photomultiplier tubes]
PHR .... Retreat State Hospital, Hunlock Creek, PA [OCLC symbol] (OCLC)
PHRACT .... Print-Handicapped Radio, Australian Capital Territory
PHRC .... Palestine Human Rights Campaign (EA)
PHRED .... Public Health Risk Evaluation Data [Environmental Safety]
PHREN .... Phrenology
Ph Rep .... Philadelphia Reports [Pennsylvania] [A publication] (DLA)
PHRF .... Performance Handicap Racing Formula [Sailing]
PHRG .... Park Home Residents Guild [British] (DBA)
PHRG .... Parliamentary Human Rights Group (EAIO)
PHRHD .... Pump, Hydraulic Ram, Hand-Driven (MSA)
PHRI .... Public Health Research Institute (NADA)
PHRI .... Public Health Research Institute of the City of New York, Inc. [Research center] (RCD)
PHRIC .... Palestine Human Rights Information Center (EA)
PHRK .... Power and Heat Rejection Kit [NASA]
PhRMA .... Pharmaceutical Research and Manufacturers of America
Phrmhse .... Pharmhouse Corp. [Associated Press] (SAG)
PhrmMkt .... Pharmaceutical Marketing Services, Inc. [Associated Press] (SAG)
PHRMST .... Pharmacist
PHRR .... Parenchymal Hepatic Resection Rate [Medicine]
PHRS .... Portable Heat Rejection System
PHRT .... Procarbazine, Hydroxyurea, Radiotherapy Protocol (DAVI)
PHS .... Packaging, Handling, and Storage (MCD)
PHS .... Pallottine House of Studies
PHS .... Pan Head Steel (IAA)
PHS .... Paternal Half Sister (OA)
PHS .... Pathological Human Serum [Serology]
PHS .... Payload Handling Station [NASA] (MCD)
PHS .... Personal Handyphone System [Telecommunications]
PHS .... Personal Health Survey [Psychology]
PHS .... Personal Hygiene Subsystem [NASA] (KSC)
PhS .... Philosophical Society [British] (DBA)
PHS .... Phitsanuloke [Thailand] [Airport symbol] (OAG)
PHS .... Photographic Historical Society (EA)
PHS .... Physicians Health Services
PHS .... Physicians' Health Study
PHS .... Police History Society [British] (DBA)
PHS .... Polyhydroxystyrene [Also, PHOST] [Organic chemistry]
PHS .... Pooled Human Serum [Hematology] (DMAA)
PHS .... Postal History Society (EA)
PHS .... Postcard History Society (EA)
PHS .... Posthypnotic Suggestion [Psychology]
PHS .... Posthypnotic Suggestion [Psychiatry] (DAVI)
PHS .... Precision Hover Sensor (PDAA)
PHS .... Prepared Hessian Surfacing [Air Force]
PHS .... Presbyterian Historical Society (EA)
PHS .... Price History System (MCD)
PHS .... Printing Historical Society [British]
PHS .... Printing House Square (DGA)
PHS .... Probability of Having a Space
PHS .... Progressive Hongkong Society [Political party]
PHS .... Prostaglandin H Synthase [An enzyme] (GNE)
PHS .... Public Health Service [Department of Health and Human Services]
PHS .... Pumped Hydro Storage [Power source]
PHS .... Somerset State Hospital, Somerset, PA [OCLC symbol] (OCLC)
PHSA .... Pearl Harbor Survivors Association (EA)
PHSA .... Polyhydroxystearic Acid [Organic chemistry]
PHSA .... Polymerized Human Serum Albumin [Biochemistry]
PHSA .... Provincial Hospital Services Association [British] (DBA)
PHSA .... Public Health Service Act (GFGA)
PHS & T .... Packaging, Handling, Storage, and Transportation [Shipping]
PhSAP .... Physical Service Access Point [Telecommunications] (OSI)
PHSAR .... Public Health Service Acquisition Regulations [Department of Health and Human Services] (GFGA)
PHSC .... Pluripotent Hematopoietic Stem Cells [Cytology]
PHSC .... Postal History Society of Canada (EA)
PHSC .... Private Hospital Supplementary Charges (ADA)
PHSCS .... Pier-Harris Self-Concept Scale (EDAC)
PHSE .... Pharmhouse Corp. [NASDAQ symbol] (SAG)
PHSE .... Phase [Computer science]
PHSE .... Piedmont Health Survey of the Elderly [Department of Health and Human Services] (GFGA)
PHSF .... Bradshaw Field, Hawaii Island [Hawaii] [ICAO location identifier] (ICLI)
PHSG .... Postal History Study Group (EA)
PHSI .... Plant Health and Seeds Inspectorate [Ministry of Agriculture, Fisheries, and Food] [British]
PHSIG .... Pan Hellenic Society Inventors of Greece in USA [Defunct] (EA)
PHSNZ .... Postal History Society of New Zealand [Auckland] (EA)
PHSO .... Partially Hydrogenated Soybean Oil [Cooking fat]
PHSO .... Postal History Society of Ontario [Later, PHSC] (EA)
PHSOC .... Photographical Historical Society of Canada
P-H Soc Sec Taxes .... Social Security Taxes (Prentice-Hall, Inc.) [A publication] (DLA)
PHS of A .... Postal History Society of the Americas (EA)
PHSP .... Phase-Splitter (MSA)
PHSP .... Public Health Service Publications
PHSPS .... Preservation, Handling, Storage, Packaging, and Shipping (NRCH)
PHSS .... Physician Support Systems [NASDAQ symbol] (TTSB)
PHSS .... Physician Support Systems, Inc. [NASDAQ symbol] (SAG)
PHST .... Packaging, Handling, Storage, and Transportation [Shipping]
Ph St Tr .... Phillipps' State Trials [A publication] (DLA)
PHSV .... Physicians Health Services, Inc. [NASDAQ symbol] (SAG)
PHSV .... Physicians Health Svcs'A' [NASDAQ symbol] (TTSB)
PHSY .... PacifiCare Health Systems, Inc. [Cypress, CA] [NASDAQ symbol] (NQ)
PHSYA .... PacifiCare Health Sys'A' [NASDAQ symbol] (TTSB)
PHT .... Managed High Yield Fd [NYSE symbol] (TTSB)
PHT .... PaineWebber Premium High Income [NYSE symbol] (SPSG)
PHT .... Paired Hands Test [Education] (EDAC)
PHT .... Paris, TN [Location identifier FAA] (FAAL)
PHT .... Passive Hemagglutination Technique [Immunology]
PHT .... Phenylhydantoin [Pharmacology] (CPH)
PhT .... [The] Phoenix and the Turtle [Shakespearean work]
pht .... Photographer [MARC relator code] [Library of Congress] (LCCP)
PHT .... Phototube
Pht .... Phthaloyl [Also, Phth] [Organic chemistry]
PHT .... Physical Therapy Technician [Navy]
PHT .... Pitch, Hit, and Throw [Youth competition sponsored by professional baseball]
PHT .... Poly-Hexylthiophene [Organic chemistry]
PHT .... Portal Hypertension [Medicine]
PHT .... Preheat
PHT .... Pulmonary Hypertension [Cardiology] (CPH)
PHT .... Putting Hubby Through [College "degree" earned by some wives]
PHT .... Pyridohomotropane [Organic chemistry]
PHT .... Torrance State Hospital, Torrance, PA [OCLC symbol] (OCLC)
PHTab .... President's Hundred Tab [Military decoration] (AABC)
PHTAT .... Para-Hydroxytriamterene [Biochemistry]
PHTATS .... Para-Hydroxytriamterene Sulfate [Biochemistry]
P-H Tax .... Federal Taxes (Prentice-Hall, Inc.) [A publication] (DLA)
P-H Tax Ct Mem .... Tax Court Memorandum Decisions (Prentice-Hall, Inc.) [A publication] (DLA)
P-H Tax Ct Rep & Mem Dec .... Tax Court Reported and Memorandum Decisions (Prentice-Hall, Inc.) [A publication] (DLA)
PHTC .... Pneumatic Hydraulic Test Console (KSC)
PHTC .... Pulse Height to Time Converter (OA)
PhTD .... Physical Therapy Doctor
PHTF .... Pearl Harbor Training Facility [Navy]
Phth .... Phthaloyl [Also, Pht] [Organic chemistry]
PHTN .... Photon Dynamics [NASDAQ symbol] (TTSB)
PHTN .... Photon Dynamics, Inc. [NASDAQ symbol] (SAG)

PHTO .... Hilo/General Lyman Field, Hawaii Island [*Hawaii*] [*ICAO location identifier*] (ICLI)
PHTS .... Primary Heat Transport System [*Nuclear energy*] (NRCH)
PHTS .... Psychiatric Home Treatment Service (DAVI)
PHU .... Philadelphia Ukrainian [*Diocesan abbreviation*] [*Pennsylvania*] (TOCD)
PHU .... Pressure, Hydraulic Unit
PHuJ .... Juniata College, Huntingdon, PA [*Library symbol Library of Congress*] (LCLS)
P-H Unrep Tr Cas... Prentice-Hall Unreported Trust Cases [*A publication*] (DLA)
Phus Plu ...... Philippus Pulderlcus [*Authority cited in pre-1607 legal work*] (DSA)
PHV .... Pahlavi [*Iran*] [*Airport symbol*] (AD)
PHV .... Parallel Hybrid Vehicle
PHV .... Paramount Home Video
PHV .... Peak Height Velocity (DMAA)
PHV .... Persistent Hypertrophic Vitreous [*Ophthalmology*] (DAVI)
PHV .... Phase Velocity
PHV .... Pro Haec Vice [*For This Turn*] [*Latin*] (ROG)
PHV .... Prospect Hill Virus [*Medicine*] (DMAA)
PHV .... Wernersville State Hospital, Wernersville, PA [*OCLC symbol*] (OCLC)
PHVA .... Plasma Homovanillic Acid [*Biochemistry*]
PHVPS .... Primary High-Voltage Power Supply
PHW .... Pemberton Houston Willoughby Investment Corp. [*Toronto Stock Exchange symbol Vancouver Stock Exchange symbol*]
PHW .... Phalaborwa [*South Africa*] [*Airport symbol*] (OAG)
PHW .... Philatelic Hobbies for the Wounded (EA)
PHW .... Prime Hard Wheat
PHW .... Warren State Hospital, Warren, PA [*OCLC symbol*] (OCLC)
PHWA .... Professional Hockey Writers' Association (EA)
PHWA .... Protestant Health and Welfare Assembly [*Later, PHHSA*] (EA)
PHWC .... Polish Helsinki Watch Committee (EAIO)
PHWFJD ...... Partners in Harmony, World Family of John Denver (EA)
PHWR .... Hickam United States Air Force Automatic Weather Switch, Oahu Island [*Hawaii*] [*ICAO location identifier*] (ICLI)
PHWR .... Pressurized Heavy Water-Moderated and Cooled Reactor [*Nuclear energy*] (IAA)
PHWR .... Pressurized Heavy Water Reactor [*Nuclear energy*]
PHX .... Partial Hepectomy [*Medicine*]
PHx .... Past History [*Medicine*] (MAE)
Phx .... Pharynx [*Anatomy*] (DAVI)
PHX .... Phoenix [*Arizona*] [*Airport symbol*] (OAG)
PHX .... Phoenix 2000 Airtaxi Ltd. [*Hungary ICAO designator*] (FAAC)
PHX .... Phoenix Network [*AMEX symbol*] (TTSB)
PHX .... Phoenix Network, Inc. [*AMEX symbol*] (SPSG)
PHX .... Woodville State Hospital, Carnegie, PA [*OCLC symbol*] (OCLC)
PhxDffP ...... Phoenix Duf & Phelps Corp. [*Associated Press*] (SAG)
PhxDfP ...... Phoenix Duff & Phelps Corp. [*Associated Press*] (SAG)
PhxDuffP ...... Phoenix Duff & Phelps Corp. [*Associated Press*] (SAG)
PhxGold ...... Phoenix Gold International, Inc. [*Associated Press*] (SAG)
PhxNet ...... Phoenix Network, Inc. [*Associated Press*] (SAG)
PHY .... C. Howard Marcy State Hospital, Pittsburgh, PA [*OCLC symbol*] (OCLC)
PHY .... Norman, OK [*Location identifier FAA*] (FAAL)
PHY .... Pharyngitis
Phy .... Physalaemin [*Biochemistry*]
PHY .... Physical
PHY .... Physician
PHY .... Physics
PHY .... Physiology (DMAA)
PHY .... Phytohemagglutinin [*Immunology*] (AAMN)
PHY .... Prospect Street High Income Portfolio, Inc. [*NYSE symbol*] (SPSG)
PHY .... Prospect Street Hi Income [*NYSE symbol*] (TTSB)
PHYC .... PhyCor, Inc. [*NASDAQ symbol*] (SPSG)
PHYCOM ...... Physicians Communications Service [*Fisher-Stevens, Inc.*] [*Merged into BRS/COLLEAGUE*]
PhyCor ...... PhyCor, Inc. [*Associated Press*] (SAG)
PhyCpt ...... Physicians Computer Network [*Associated Press*] (SAG)
PHYCUS ...... Physical Custody [*of Records*] (MHDB)
PHY ED ...... Physical Education (WGA)
PHYL .... Physiological
PHYLIP ...... Phylogeny Inference Package [*Botany*]
PHYLIS ...... Physics Online Information System [*Computer science*] (PDAA)
PHYM .... Putnam High Yield Municipal Trust [*Associated Press*] (SAG)
PhyMatr ...... PhyMatrix Corp. [*Associated Press*] (SAG)
PHYN .... Physician Reliance Network [*NASDAQ symbol*] (TTSB)
PHYN .... Physician Reliance Network, Inc. [*NASDAQ symbol*] (SAG)
PHYS .... Physical (AFM)
PHYS .... Physician
PHYS .... Physician
PHYS .... Physicist [*or Physics*] (ADA)
Phys .... Physics (DD)
PHYS .... Physio-Control Intl [*NASDAQ symbol*] (TTSB)
PhyS .... Physiological Saline [*Pharmacology*] (DAVI)
PHYS .... Physiology
PhySale ...... Physician Sales & Service, Inc. [*Associated Press*] (SAG)
PHYSB .... PacifiCare Health Sys'B' [*NASDAQ symbol*] (TTSB)
PHYSBE ...... Physiological Simulation Benchmark Experiment
PHYSCL ...... Physical
PhysCpA ...... Physician Corp. of America [*Associated Press*] (SAG)
Phys Dis ...... Physical Disability (CPH)
PHYSEC ...... Physical Security (MCD)
PHYS ED ...... Physical Education
Phys Eng ..... Physical Engineer
PHYSEXAM... Physical Examination
PhysicHlt ..... Physicians Health Services, Inc. [*Associated Press*] (SAG)
PhysIn .... Physicians Insurance Co. of Ohio [*Associated Press*] (SAG)
Physio .... Physiology (DAVI)
physio .... Physiotherapy [*Medicine*] (DMAA)
PHYSIO .... Physiotherapy [*Medicine*]
PHYSIOG ...... Physiognomy [*Slang*] (DSUE)
PHYSIOG ...... Physiographic
PHYSIOL ...... Physiological (MSA)
PHYSIOL ...... Physiology (ROG)
PHYSL .... Physiological (AFM)
Phys Med ...... Physical Medicine (CPH)
Physmet .... Physiometrix, Inc. [*Associated Press*] (SAG)
PHYSN .... Physician
PHYSOG .... Physiognomy [*Slang*] (DSUE)
PhysPRC .... Physician's Payment Review Commission (HCT)
PhysPRC .... Physician's Payment Review Commission
PHYSQUAL... Physical Disqualification [*Military*] (DNAB)
PhysRel .... Physician Reliance Network, Inc. [*Associated Press*] (SAG)
PhysRs .... Physician Resources Group, Inc. [*Associated Press*] (SAG)
PHYS SC ...... Physical Science (WDAA)
PhysSup .... Physician Support Systems, Inc. [*Associated Press*] (SAG)
PHYST .... Physicist
PHYSTER ...... Physical Therapy (AABC)
Phys Ther .... Physical Therapist (DMAA)
Phys Today... Physics Today [*A publication*] (BRI)
PHYSY .... Physiology
Phytogeog ... Phytogeography (BARN)
PHYTOPATH... Phytopathology
PHYX .... Physiometrix Inc. [*NASDAQ symbol*] (TTSB)
PHYX .... Physiometrix, Inc. [*NASDAQ symbol*] (SAG)
PHZ .... Ashland State General Hospital, Ashland, PA [*OCLC symbol*] (OCLC)
PHZH .... Honolulu Air Traffic Control Center [*Hawaii*] [*ICAO location identifier*] (ICLI)
pI .... Isoelectric Point (MAE)
PI .... Pacing Impulse [*Cardiology*] (DAVI)
PI .... Pacing Item (MCD)
PI .... Package Insert [*Instructional leaflet distributed with certain prescription drugs*] [*Also, PPI*]
PI .... Packaging Institute [*Later, PI/USA*] (EA)
PI .... Paducah & Illinois Railroad [*AAR code*]
PI .... Palmaris Longus (DMAA)
PI .... Pancreatic Insufficiency [*Gastroenterology*]
PI .... Pancreatic Lipase [*Medicine*] (DMAA)
Pi .... Pandectae (Pisanae) Florentinae [*A publication*] (DSA)
PI .... Panel Input
PI .... Pansophic Institute [*Defunct*] (EA)
PI .... Pantera International (EA)
PI .... Paper Insulated
PI .... Paracel Islands [*ANSI two-letter standard code*] (CNC)
PI .... Parallel Input [*Computer science*] (BUR)
PI .... Parameter Identifier [*Computer science*] (TNIG)
PI .... Parametric Industry (IAA)
PI .... Paranoid Ideation (DAVI)
Pi .... Parental Generation [*Medicine*] (DMAA)
PI .... Parental Investment [*Biology*]
PI .... Parity Index [*EEO*]
PI .... Particle Integration (CAAL)
PI .... Partido Independente [*Independent Party*] [*Costa Rica*] [*Political party*]
PI .... Partido Intransigente [*Intransigent Party*] [*Argentina Political party*] (PD)
PI .... Parti Independantiste [*Quebec*]
PI .... Passeport International [*International Passport*] [*An association France*] (EAIO)
PI .... Patient's Interests [*Medicine*]
PI .... Patient's Interests (DAVI)
PI .... Patrol Inspector [*Immigration and Naturalization Service*]
PI .... Payload Interrogator [*NASA*] (MCD)
PI .... Pen and Ink
PI .... Penetration Index (IAA)
PI .... Pepsin Inhibitor (OA)
PI .... Perceptions, Inc. (EA)
PI .... Perceptual Isolation
PI .... Perfect Initials [*Philately*]
PI .... Performance Improvement
PI .... Performance Index
PI .... Performance Indicator (MCD)
PI .... Performance Intensity (MAE)
PI .... Perinatal Injury [*Neonatology*] (DAVI)
PI .... Per Inquiry [*Advertising*]
pi .... Per Inquiry (WDMC)
PI .... Periodical Index Term (NITA)
PI .... Periodicals Institute (EA)
PI .... Periodic Inspection [*Military*] (AFM)
PI .... Peripheral Interface [*Computer science*] (PCM)
PI .... Peripheral Iridectomy [*Medicine*]
PI .... Perlite Institute (EA)
PI .... Permaculture International [*Australia*]
PI .... Permeability Index [*Clinical chemistry*]
PI .... Personal Identification
PI .... Personal Income
PI .... Personal Injury [*Insurance*]
PI .... Personal Injury Accident [*British police term*]
PI .... Personal Investment [*A publication*] (ADA)
PI .... Personality Inventory [*Psychology*]
PI .... Petroleum Information Corp. (IID)

PI .... Petrol Injection [*British*]
PI .... Pharmacopoeia Internationalis [*International Pharmacopoeia*]
PI .... Phase-In
PI .... Phenanthroimidazole [*Organic chemistry*]
PI .... Phenyl Isocyanate [*Organic chemistry*]
PI .... Phosphate, Inorganic [*Chemistry*]
PI .... Phosphatidylinositol [*Also, PtdIns*] [*Biochemistry*]
P-I .... Photogrammetric Instrumentation (AAG)
PI .... Photographic Interpreter
PI .... Photo International [*Defunct*] (EAIO)
PI .... Photointerpretation [*or Photointerpreter*]
PI .... Photointerpreter (IAA)
PI .... Photo Interpreter
PI .... Photoionization [*Physical chemistry*]
PI .... Physical Inventory (NRCH)
PI .... Physically Impaired
PI .... Physics International
PI .... Piaster [*Monetary unit*] [*Spain, Republic of Vietnam, and some Middle Eastern countries*]
pi .... Pica [*Typesetting*] [*Also called pie*] (WDMC)
PI .... Piedmont Aviation, Inc. [*ICAO designator*] (OAG)
PI .... Pigeon Trainer [*Navy*]
PI .... Pig Iron
Pi .... Pillius Medicinensis [*Flourished, 1165-1207*] [*Authority cited in pre-1607 legal work*] (DSA)
PI .... Pilot International (EA)
PI .... Pilot Item (MCD)
PI .... Pilotless Intercepter [*Air Force*]
PI .... Pinedale [*Wyoming*] [*Seismograph station code, US Geological Survey Closed*] (SEIS)
PI .... Pink (ROG)
PI .... Pipe [*Freight*]
PI .... Plant Introduction [*Botany*]
PI .... Plaque Index [*Dentistry*]
PI .... Plasma Iron [*Hematology*]
PI .... Plastics Institute (NADA)
PI .... Plastochron Index [*Botany*]
PI .... Plug-In Instrument (IAA)
PI .... Pneumatosis Intestinalis [*Medicine*]
PI .... Point Initiating
PI .... Point Insulating
PI .... Point of Impact (AFM)
PI .... Point of Interception [*Navigation*]
PI .... Point of Intersection
PI .... Poison Ivy [*Campers' slang*]
PI .... Polyimide [*Organic chemistry*]
PI .... Polyisoprene [*Organic chemistry*]
PI .... Polymer International (NS), Inc. [*Toronto Stock Exchange symbol*]
PI .... Pompeiiana, Inc. (EA)
PI .... Ponderal Index [*Measurement*] (DAVI)
PI .... Poni Iussit [*Ordered to Be Placed*] [*Latin*]
PI .... Popcorn Institute (EA)
PI .... Population Institute (EA)
PI .... Porch Index [*Psychiatry*] (DAVI)
PI .... Portfolio Insurance [*Finance*]
PI .... Position Indicator [*Army*]
PI .... Positive Identification Feature
PI .... Positive Intelligence (LAIN)
PI .... Positive Interlace [*Television*]
PI .... Postal Instruction (IAA)
PI .... Postimpressionist Movement [*Art*]
PI .... Postinoculation [*Medicine*]
PI .... Postischemic [*Medicine*]
PI .... Potash Institute [*Later, PPI*] (EA)
PI .... Potomac Institute [*Defunct*] (EA)
PI .... Power Indicator (IAA)
PI .... Power Injection
PI .... Power Input
PI .... Power Interlock (IAA)
PI .... Precision Instrument (NVT)
PI .... Predicted Impact (MCD)
PI .... Pregnancy Induced [*Gynecology*]
PI .... Preinduction [*Medicine*]
PI .... Preliminary Incubation (OA)
PI .... Preliminary Injunction [*Legal term*] (HGAA)
PI .... Preliminary Inspection (MCD)
PI .... Preliminary Investigation (NASA)
PI .... Preliminary Issue
PI .... Premdor, Inc. [*NYSE symbol*] (SPSG)
PI .... Preparatory Interval [*Psychometrics*]
PI .... Prepositioned Instruction [*DoD*]
PI .... Present Illness [*Medicine*]
PI .... Pressure Indicator [*Nuclear energy*]
PI .... Pressure of Inspiration [*Medicine*]
Pi .... Pressure of Inspiration [*Medicine*] (DAVI)
PI .... Primacord Interstage
PI .... Primary Infarction [*Medicine*]
PI .... Primary Input (IAA)
PI .... Prime Interest Rate [*Banking*]
PI .... Principal Investigator (MCD)
PI .... Printer [*Navy*]
PI .... Print Image (IAA)
PI .... Printing Impressions [*A publication*] (DGA)
PI .... Priority Interrupt (IEEE)
PI .... Private Institution [*British*]
PI .... Private Investigator
PI .... Priviledged Information (SAA)
PI .... Proactive Inhibition [*Psychology*]
PI .... Proactive Interference (EDAC)
PI .... Problem Input (SAA)
PI .... Process Image (NITA)
PI .... Process Instrumentation [*Nuclear energy*] (NRCH)
PI .... Processor Interface [*Computer science*] (IAA)
PI .... Procurement Inspection (MCD)
PI .... Procurement Item (NASA)
PI .... Prodigy Internet
PI .... Product Improvement (MCD)
P/I .... Production Illustration (MSA)
PI .... Production Interval
PI .... Productivity Index (IEEE)
PI .... Professional Indemnity [*Insurance*]
pi .... Professional Indemnity [*Insurance*] (ODBW)
PI .... Program Indicator (IEEE)
PI .... Program Information
PI .... Program Innovations (ADA)
PI .... Program Instruction [*Computer science*] (BUR)
PI .... Program Integrator [*Military*] (RDA)
PI .... Program Interrupt
PI .... Program Introduction
PI .... Program Issuances [*Assistance Payments Administration, HEW*]
PI .... Programmed Information [*Computer science*]
PI .... Programmed Instruction
PI .... Programmed Introduction (MCD)
PI .... Program of Instrumentation (MUGU)
PI .... Project Inform (EA)
PI .... Project Intrex [*Massachusetts Institute of Technology*] (EA)
PI .... Prolactin Inhibitor [*Endocrinology*]
PI .... Property Index [*British police term*]
PI .... Propidium Iodide [*Fluorescent dye*]
PI .... Proportional-Plus Integral [*Digital control*]
PI .... Proprietary Information (SAA)
PI .... Propyl Isome (OA)
PI .... Protamine Insulin
Pi .... Protease Inhibitor
PI .... Proteinase Inhibitor [*Biochemistry*]
PI .... Protocol Internationale
PI .... Psychiatric Institute
PI .... Psychosynthesis Institute (EA)
PI .... Publication Instructions
PI .... Public Information
PI .... Puebla Institute (EA)
PI .... Pulmonary Incompetence [*Medicine*]
PI .... Pulmonary Indices [*Medicine*]
PI .... Pulmonary Infarction [*Medicine*]
PI .... Pulmonary Intervertebral Disc [*Medicine*]
PI .... Pulse Induction (ADA)
PI .... Purge Isolation [*Nuclear energy*] (NRCH)
PI .... Pyritization Index [*Geoscience*]
PI .... Sunshine Airlines [*Airline code*] [*Australia*]
PI1 .... State Correctional Institute at Camp Hill, Camp Hill, PA [*OCLC symbol*] (OCLC)
PI2 .... State Correctional Institute at Dallas, Dallas, PA [*OCLC symbol*] (OCLC)
PI3 .... State Correctional Institute at Grateford, Grateford, PA [*OCLC symbol*] (OCLC)
PI4 .... State Correctional Institute at Huntingdon, Huntingdon, PA [*OCLC symbol*] (OCLC)
PI5 .... State Correctional Institute at Muncy, Muncy, PA [*OCLC symbol*] (OCLC)
PI6 .... State Correctional Institute at Pittsburgh, Pittsburgh, PA [*OCLC symbol*] (OCLC)
PI7 .... State Regional Correctional Facility, Greensburg, PA [*OCLC symbol*] (OCLC)
PIA .... Municipal Prem Income Tr [*NYSE symbol*] (TTSB)
PIA .... Municipal Premium Income Trust [*Formerly, Allstate Municipal Premium Fund*] [*NYSE symbol*] (SPSG)
PIA .... Pacific Islands Association (EA)
PIA .... Packaged Ice Association (EA)
PIA .... Paid in Advance (WDMC)
PIA .... Pakistan International Airlines Corp. [*ICAO designator*] (FAAC)
PIA .... Panel-Information-Air Operation
PIA .... Parapsychology Institute of America (EA)
PIA .... Particle Impact Analyzer [*Astrophysics*]
PIA .... Partitioning Industry Association [*British*] (DBA)
PIA .... Passive Immunological Agglutination
PIA .... Payload Interface Adapter [*NASA*] (SSD)
PIA .... Peoria [*Illinois*] [*Airport symbol*] (OAG)
PIA .... Perfumery Importers Association [*Defunct*] (EA)
PIA .... Peripheral Interface Adapter [*Computer science*]
PIA .... Personal Information Appliance [*Telecommunications*] (PCM)
PIA .... Personal Investment Authority [*British*] (ECON)
PIA .... Personnel Inventory Analysis [*Army*]
PIA .... Perspective Inversion Algorithm [*Computer science*]
PIA .... Petervin Information Associates [*Also, an information service or system*] (IID)
PIA .... Petroleum Incentives Administration [*Canada*]
PIA .... Phenylisopropyladenosine [*Biochemistry*]
PIA .... Phosphoroimmunoassays
PIA .... Photoelectric Intravenous Angiography [*Medicine*] (DMAA)
PIA .... Photographic Importers Association [*British*] (BI)

PIA............ Piano [*Softly*] [*Music*]
PIA............ Pilots International Association (EA)
PIA............ Pitten [*Austria*] [*Seismograph station code, US Geological Survey*] (SEIS)
PIA............ Place Indicator in Accumulators (SAA)
PIA............ Plasma Insulin Activity [*Clinical chemistry*]
PIA............ Plastics Industries Association [*Ireland*]
PIA............ Plastics Institute of America (EA)
PIA............ Plug-In Amplifier
PIA............ Polycultural Institution of America
PIA............ Positive Ion Accelerator
PIA............ Positron Intensity Accumulator (MCD)
PIA............ Postal Inspectors' Association [*A union*] [*British*]
PIA............ Potentiometric Immunoassay [*Clinical chemistry*]
PIA............ Predominant Interest Agency (AAGC)
PIA............ Preinfarction Angina [*Cardiology*] (DMAA)
PIA............ Pre-Inspection Acceptance (SAA)
PIA............ Preinstallation Acceptance
PIA............ Pressure Indicating Alarm [*Engineering*]
PIA............ Primary Inspection Agency [*Federal Manufactured Housing Construction and Safety Standards*] [*Department of Housing and Urban Development*] (GFGA)
PIA............ Primary Insurance Account [*Social Security Administration*] (OICC)
PIA............ Primary Insurance Amount
PIA............ Principal Industry Activity [*IRS*]
PIA............ Printing Industries of America (EA)
PIA............ Production Inventory Analysis (AAG)
PIA............ Professional Insurance Agents [*Alexandria, VA*] (EA)
PIA............ Program Initiation Agreement (SSD)
PIA............ Project Impact Analysis (NASA)
PIA............ Project Interface Adapter (SSD)
PIA............ Proprietary Industries Association (AAGC)
PIA............ Psychiatric Institute of America [*For-profit network of private psychiatric hospitals*] (EA)
PIA............ Public and International Affairs [*USCG*] (TAG)
PIA............ Public Information Act
PIA............ Public Information Adviser [*NATO*] (NATG)
PIA............ Public Intoxication Act [*Australia*]
PIA............ Pumice Institute of America (EA)
PIA............ Purified Isophthalic Acid
PIA............ White Haven Center, White Haven, PA [*OCLC symbol*] (OCLC)
PIAA............ Physician Insurers Association of America
PIAA............ Pre-Arrangement Interment Association of America [*Later, PAA*] (EA)
PIAC............ Partido de Integracion de America Central [*Nicaragua*] [*Political party*] (EY)
PIAC............ Peak Instantaneous Airborne Count (DA)
PIAC............ Permanent International Altaistic Conference (EA)
PIAC............ Petroleum Industry Advisory Committee [*British*]
PIAC............ Problem Identification and Correction [*DoD*] (AFIT)
PIACCS........ Pacific Integrated Automatic Command and Control System [*Military*] (DNAB)
PIACS.......... Pacific Integrated Automatic Communications Systems [*Military*]
PIACT.......... Program for the Introduction and Adaptation of Contraceptive Technology (EA)
PIADC.......... Plum Island Animal Disease Center [*Formerly, PIADL*]
PIADL.......... Plum Island Animal Disease Laboratory [*of ARS, Department of Agriculture*] [*Later, PIADC*]
PIAGET........ Promoting Intellectual Adaptation Given Experiential Transforming Project (EDAC)
PIAM............ PIA Merchandising Services, Inc. [*NASDAQ symbol*] (SAG)
PIAM............ PIA Merchandising Svcs [*NASDAQ symbol*] (TTSB)
PIAMA.......... Professional Institute for the American Management Association (OICC)
PIA Mer....... PIA Merchandising Services, Inc. [*Associated Press*] (SAG)
PIANC.......... Permanent International Association of Navigation Congresses [*Brussels, Belgium*] (EAIO)
PIand........... Papyri Iandanae [*A publication*] (OCD)
PIANG.......... Piangendo [*Plaintive*] [*Music*]
PIANISS....... Pianissimo [*Very Softly*] [*Music*]
PIAP............ Psychologists Interested in the Advancement of Psychotherapy [*Later, APA*] (EA)
PIAPACS...... Psychophysiological Information Acquisition, Processing, and Control System
PIAR............ Problem Identification and Analysis Report [*Military*] (CAAL)
PIAR............ Project Impact Analysis Report (MCD)
PIARC.......... Permanent International Association of Road Congresses [*See also AIPCR*] [*Paris, France*] (EAIO)
PIAS............ Photographic Inventory and Accountancy System
PIAS............ Piaster [*Monetary unit*] [*Spain, Republic of Vietnam, and some Middle Eastern countries*]
PIAS............ Prague Institute of Advanced Studies
PIAS............ Precision Intelligence Augmentation System
PIAS............ Pressure Indicating Alarm Switching [*Engineering*]
PIAS............ Program Impact Analysis Scenario
PIASA.......... Polish Institute of Arts and Sciences of America (EA)
PIASS.......... Paris International Aviation and Space Salon (MCD)
PIAT............ Peabody Individual Achievement Test [*Education*]
PIAT............ Projector Infantry, Antitank [*British shoulder-controlled weapon*]
PIAT............ Public Information Assist Team [*Environmental Protection Agency*] (ERG)
PIAVA.......... Polydactyly-Imperforate Anus-Vertebral Anomalies [*Syndrome*] [*Medicine*] (DMAA)
PIB............ George Junior Republic, Grove City, PA [*OCLC symbol*] (OCLC)
PIB............ Laurel/Hattiesburg [*Mississippi*] [*Airport symbol*] (OAG)
PIB............ Pacific Inland Tariff Bureau, Portland OR [*STAC*]
PIB............ Papuan Infantry Battalion
PIB............ Parachute Infantry Battalion [*Army*]
PIB............ Partial Ileal Bypass [*Medicine*]
PIB............ Partido Indio de Bolivia [*Political party*]
PIB............ Payload Integration Bay [*NASA*] (KSC)
PIB............ Pender Island [*British Columbia*] [*Seismograph station code, US Geological Survey*] (SEIS)
PIB............ Periodic Information Briefing (MCD)
PIB............ Personal Information Briefing [*of returning POW's*] [*Air Force*]
PIB............ Petroleum Information Bureau
PIB............ Photo Intelligence Brief (AFM)
PIB............ Photo Interpretation Brief (MCD)
PIB............ Plug-In Blank
PIB............ Polar Ionospheric Beacon
PIB............ Polyisobutylene [*Organic chemistry*]
PIB............ Polytechnic Institute of Brooklyn [*Later, PINY*] (MCD)
PIB............ Pre-Flight Information Bulletin [*Aviation*] (DA)
PIB............ Preliminary Instruction Book
PIB............ Prices and Incomes Board [*British*]
PIB............ Processor Interface Buffer [*Telecommunications*] (TEL)
PIB............ Product Improvement Bulletin
PIB............ Program Information Block (IAA)
PIB............ Program Information Briefing
PIB............ Programmable Input Buffer
PIB............ Propellant Inspection Building [*NASA*] (KSC)
PIB............ Publishers Information Bureau [*New York, NY*] (EA)
PIB............ Pulse Interference Blanker
PIB............ Pyrotechnic Installation Building [*NASA*] (KSC)
PIBA............ Primary Industry Bank of Australia Ltd. (ADA)
PIBAC.......... Permanent International Bureau of Analytical Chemistry of Human and Animal Food
PIBAL.......... Pilot Balloon Observation
PIBAL.......... Polytechnic Institute of Brooklyn Aeronautical Laboratory (MCD)
PIBALS........ Pilot Balloon Soundings
PIBC............ Pacific Institute of Bio-Organic Chemistry
PIBC............ Percutaneous Intraaortic Balloon Counterpulsation [*Catheter*] [*Medicine*] (DMAA)
PIBD............ Point Initiating, Base Detonating Projectile [*Army*]
PIBD............ Portable Interface Bond Detector (IAA)
PIBL............ PEMA Item Baseline List [*Army*] (AABC)
PIBMM........ Permanent International Bureau of Motorcycle Manufacturers
PIBMRI........ Polytechnic Institute of Brooklyn, Microwave Research Institute (IEEE)
PIBOL.......... Pilot Back Up Control
PIBOL.......... Pilot in Booster Loop (SAA)
PIBOR.......... Paris Interbank Offered Rank (ODBW)
PIBS............ Polar Ionospheric Beacon Satellite [*NASA*]
PIBUC.......... Pilot Back Up Control
PIC............ Calverton, NY [*Location identifier FAA*] (FAAL)
PIC............ Craig House Technoma Workshop, Pittsburgh, PA [*OCLC symbol*] (OCLC)
PIC............ Pacific Airlines Holding Co. [*Vietnam*] [*ICAO designator*] (FAAC)
PIC............ Pacific Insurance Conference
PIC............ Pacific Intelligence Center (MCD)
PIC............ Paid-In Capital [*Finance*] (MHDW)
PIC............ Paired-Ion Chromatography
PIC............ Para-iodoclonidine [*Biochemistry*]
PIC............ Parent Indicator Code (DNAB)
PIC............ Partially Incinerated Compound [*Furnace technology*]
PIC............ Particle in Cell [*Gas solid*]
PIC............ Partners in Change Program [*Department of Labor*]
PIC............ Payload Integration Center [*NASA*] (MCD)
PIC............ Payload Integration Committee [*NASA*] (NASA)
PIC............ Payload Integration Contractor (MCD)
PIC............ Peak Identification Computer
PIC............ People's Involvement Corp. (EA)
PIC............ Performance Incentive Contracting (AAGC)
PIC............ Periodic Inspection Control [*Military*] (IAA)
PIC............ Peripheral Interface Controller [*Computer science*]
PIC............ Peripherie Controller [*Computer science*] (IAA)
PIC............ Pershing Instant Comment [*Donaldson, Lufkin & Jenrette*] [*Database*]
PIC............ Personal Identification Code [*Banking*]
PIC............ Personal Intelligent Communicator [*Computer science*] (PCM)
PIC............ Personal Internet Connection [*Fee-based accounts*]
PIC............ Personality Inventory for Children [*Psychology*]
PIC............ Personnel Investigations Center
PIC............ Pesticides Information Center [*National Agricultural Library*] [*Terminated, 1969*]
PIC............ Petrochemical Investing Corp.
PIC............ Phosphoinositidase C [*An enzyme*]
PIC............ Photographic Industry Council [*Defunct*] (EA)
PIC............ Photographic Interpretation Center (MCD)
PIC............ Photo Interpretation Console (IAA)
PIC............ Piccadilly Cafeterias [*NYSE symbol*] (TTSB)
PIC............ Piccadilly Cafeterias, Inc. [*NYSE symbol*] (SPSG)
PIC............ Piccadilly Saloon [*London*] (DSUE)
PIC............ Piccolo [*Music*] (ROG)
PIC............ [*The*] Pickens Railroad Co. [*Later, PICK*] [*AAR code*]
PIC............ Picos [*Brazil*] [*Airport symbol*] (AD)
Pic............ Picrotoxin [*Biochemistry*]
Pic............ Pictor [*Constellation*]
PIC............ Pictorial (WDAA)
PIC............ Picture (AABC)
PIC............ Picture
PIC............ Picture File Format [*Computer science*] (BTTJ)

PIC Picture Interactive Computer System (IAA)
pic Pictures [*Slang*] (WDMC)
PIC Pig Improvement Co. [*British*] (ECON)
PIC Pilot in Command [*Navy*] (DOMA)
PIC Pilot-Integrated Cockpit (AAG)
PIC Pine Cay [*British West Indies*] [*Airport symbol Obsolete*] (OAG)
PIC Pitch Impregnation Carbonization (MCD)
PIC Planned Insurance Coverage
PIC Plasma Insulin Concentration [*Clinical chemistry*]
PIC Plastic Igniter Cord (IAA)
PIC Plastic Insulated Cable (IAA)
PIC Plastic Insulated Conductor
PIC Policy Information Center [*Department of Health and Human Services Information service or system*] (IID)
PIC Polyethylene Insulated Conductor [*Telecommunications*]
PIC Polymer-Impregnated Concrete (KSC)
PIC Polymorphism Information Content [*Medicine*] (DMAA)
PIC Portable Imaging Computer
PIC Position Independent Code [*Telecommunications*] (TEL)
PIC Positive Immittance Converter (PDAA)
PIC Positive Impedance Converter (IAA)
PIC Positive Ion Chamber
PIC Postinflammatory Corticoid [*Medicine*]
PIC Potential Icing Category [*Meteorology*] (DA)
PIC Power Information Center [*Interagency Advanced Power Group*] [*DoD Washington, DC*]
PIC Power Integrated Circuit [*Computer science*]
PIC Predicted Intercept Contour
PIC Preinitiation Complex [*Genetics*]
PIC Preinstallation Calibration (KSC)
PIC Preinstallation Checkout (NASA)
PIC Presbyterian Interracial Council (EA)
PIC Pressure Indicator Controller
PIC Primate Information Center [*University of Washington*] [*Seattle, WA*]
pic Prince Edward Island [*Canada MARC country of publication code Library of Congress*] (LCCP)
PIC Printer Interface Cartridge [*Epson America, Inc.*]
PIC Prior Informed Consent [*For use of pesticides*]
PIC Priority Interrupt Controller
PIC Private Industry Council [*Generic term for group that helps provide job training*]
PIC Procedures for Instrument Calibration
PIC Process Interface Control
PIC Processor Input Channel (NVT)
PIC Processor Interconnection Channel (NITA)
PIC Procurement Information Center
PIC Procurement Information Circular (AAGC)
PIC Procurement Information for Contracts [*AFSC*]
PIC Product Information Center [*AgriData Resources, Inc.*] [*Information service or system*]
PIC Production Inventory Control (MHDI)
PIC Product of Incomplete Combustion [*Environmental Protection Agency*] (ERG)
PIC Professional Image Computer (NITA)
PIC Professional Instrument Course [*Aeronautics*]
PIC Professional Interfraternity Conference [*Later, PFA*] (EA)
PIC Program for Improved Contract Management [*Military*] (AFIT)
PIC Program Identification Code (MUGU)
PIC Program Information Center
PIC Program Initiations and Commitments (AAG)
PIC Program Instruction, Calibration [*Marine Corps*]
PIC Program Interrupt Control [*Computer science*]
PIC Programmable Industrial Controller (NITA)
PIC Programmable Interrupt Controller [*Computer science*]
PIC Programmable Interval Clock (NASA)
PIC Project Information Center
PIC Prolonged Illness Coverage [*Insurance*] (PAZ)
PIC Promotion Industry Club (EA)
PIC Proton Induced Cascade [*Physics*]
PIC Pseudoisocyanine [*Organic chemistry*]
PIC Pseudo-Isocytidine [*Antineoplastic compound*]
PIC Public Information Center [*Nuclear energy*] (NRCH)
PIC Public Information Committee [*of the NATO Military Committee*] (NATG)
PIC Publishers' Information Card [*Later, IBIS*] [*British*]
PIC Pulsed Ionization Chamber
PIC Purpose Identification Code
PIC Pursuant to Instructions Contained In (MUGU)
PIC Pyrotechnic Ignition Control (NASA)
PIC Pyrotechnic Initiator Capacitor (NASA)
PIC Pyrotechnic Initiator Controller (NASA)
PICA Palestine Israelite Colonisation Association
PICA Participating Interest Contingency Agreement
PICA Police Insignia Collector's Association (EA)
PICA Police Insignia Collectors Association [*British*] (DBA)
PICA Porch Index of Communicative Ability [*Psychology*]
PICA Posterior Inferior Cerebal Artery [*Cardiology*] (DAVI)
PICA Posterior Inferior Cerebellar Artery [*Anatomy*]
PICA Posterior Inferior Communicating Artery [*Cardiology*] (DAVI)
PICA Posterior Internal Cerebral Artery [*Cardiology*] (DAVI)
PICA Power Industry Computer Applications (MCD)
PICA Press Independence and Critical Ability (NTCM)
PICA Primary Inventory Control Activity (MCD)
PICA Printing Industry Computer Associates, Inc.
PICA Private Investment Co. for Asia SA
PICA Procedures for Inventory Control Afloat [*Navy*]
PICA Professional Insurance Communicators of America (EA)
PICA Programming Interpersonal Curricula for Adolescents [*Learning model*] [*Education*]
PICA Project for Integrated Catalogue Automation [*Royal Netherlands Library*] [*Cataloging cooperative*] (IID)
PICA Property Services Agency Information on Construction and Architecture [*Property Service Agency Library Service*] [*British Information service or system*]
PICA Public Interest Computer Association (EA)
PICAC Porch Index of Communicative Ability in Children [*Psychology*]
PICAC Power Industry Computer Applications Conference (MCD)
PICADAD Place Identification/Characteristics and Area/Distance and Direction [*Bureau of the Census*]
PICAO Provisional International Civil Aviation Organization [*Later, ICAO*]
PICASO Picture Algorithms-Subroutine Orientated (NITA)
PICASSO Pen Input to Computer and Scanned Screen Output [*Computer science*] (PDAA)
PICB Peabody Institute of the City of Baltimore [*Maryland*]
PICC Parts for Import Cars Coalition [*Defunct*] (EA)
PICC Peripherally-Inserted Central Catheter [*Medicine*]
PICC Philadelphia International Convention Center [*Pennsylvania*]
PICC Piccolo
PICC Plastics in Construction Council [*Later, CCS*] (EA)
PICC Professional Institutions Council for Conservation [*British*]
PICC Provisional International Computation Center
PICCA Positive Ion Cluster Composition Analyzer [*Instrumentation*]
PicCafe Piccadilly Cafeterias, Inc. [*Associated Press*] (SAG)
PICCED Pratt Institute Center for Community and Environmental Development [*Research center*] (RCD)
PICCO Pennsylvania Industrial Chemical Corp. [*Trademark*]
PICD Preliminary Interface Control Drawing
PICD Primary Irritant Contact Dermatitis [*Medicine*] (DMAA)
PICDG Polar Icebreaker Canadian Design Group
PICE Product Improved Compatibility Electronics (MCD)
PICE Programmable Integrated Control Equipment
PICEE President's Interagency Committee on Export Expansion [*Absorbed by President's Export Council in 1979*] (EGAO)
PICE/PIA Printing Industry Credit Exchange/PIA [*of the Printing Industries of America*] [*Defunct*] (EA)
PICES North Pacific Marine Science Organization (USDC)
PICESP Put It in Corporate Executives' Swimming Pools [*Waste management slang*]
PICFS Postinfective Chronic Fatigue Syndrome [*Medicine*] (DMAA)
PICG Pig Industry Consultative Group [*Queensland, Australia*]
PICG Programme International de Correlation Geologique [*International Geological Correlation Programme - IGCP*] (EAIO)
PICGC Permanent International Committee for Genetic Congresses
PicGPA Picrylated Guinea Pig Albumin [*Immunochemistry*]
PICK Part Information Correlation Key
PICK [*The*] Pickens Railroad Co. [*Formerly, PIC*] [*AAR code*]
Pick Pickering's Massachusetts Supreme Judicial Court Reports [*1822-39*] [*A publication*] (DLA)
PICK Pickwick [*Refers to an inferior quality cigar*] (DSUE)
Pickle Pickle's Reports [*85-108 Tennessee*] [*A publication*] (DLA)
PICKLE Preserving Individual Cultures and Knowledge in Lands Everywhere [*An association*]
PICKLE President's Intelligence Checklist [*Daily report prepared by CIA*]
Pick (Mass) Pickering's Massachusetts Reports [*18-41 Massachusetts*] [*A publication*] (DLA)
Pick Stat Pickering's English Statutes [*A publication*] (DLA)
PICKUP Professional, Industrial and Commercial Updating [*Vocational training*] [*British*]
PICM Master Chief Precision Instrumentman [*Navy rating*]
PICM Permanent International Committee of Mothers
PICM Picom Insurance [*NASDAQ symbol*] (TTSB)
PICM PICOM Insurance Co. [*NASDAQ symbol*] (SAG)
PICM Professionals Insurance Co. Management Group [*NASDAQ symbol*] (SAG)
PICM Gp Professionals Insurance Co. Management Group [*Associated Press*] (SAG)
PIC-MOD Purpose Identification Code - Month and Calendar Year of Detachment (DNAB)
PIC-NF Picroindigocarmine-Nuclear Fast Red [*A biological stain*]
PICO Partido Independiente de la Clase Obrera [*Panama*] [*Political party*] (EY)
PICO Person in Column One [*1980 census*]
PICO Physicians Insurance Co. of Ohio [*NASDAQ symbol*] (NQ)
PICO PICO Holdings, Inc. [*NASDAQ symbol*] (SAG)
PICO Polar Ice Core Drilling Office [*National Science Foundation*] (MSC)
PiCO Portable Interactive Computing Object
PICO Product Improvement Control Office (AFM)
PICO Purchasing Internal Change Order (MCD)
PICOA Physicians Insur Ohio [*NASDAQ symbol*] (TTSB)
PICODE Program Indicator-Code [*Computer science*] (ECII)
PICOE Programmed Initiations, Commitments, Obligations, and Expenditures [*AFSC*]
PICO Hld PICO Holdings, Inc. [*Associated Press*] (SAG)
PICOM PICOM Insurance Co. [*Associated Press*] (SAG)
PICOMM Potter Instrument Coordinated Measuring Machine
PICON Process Intelligent Control [*A data processing system from LISP Machine, Inc.*]
PicoPd Pico Products, Inc. [*Associated Press*] (SAG)
PICORNAVIRUS Pico Ribonucleic Acid Virus

PICOS Purchased Input Concept Optimization with Suppliers [*Auto industry quality and cost management program*]
PICOST Probability of Incurring Estimated Costs [*Military*] (MCD)
PICP Prime Inventory Control Point (DNAB)
PICP Program Interface Control Plan (NASA)
PICPAB Phenomena Induced by Charged Particle Beams
PICPSA Permanent International Commission for the Proof of Small-Arms (EAIO)
PICRC Pesticide and Industrial Chemicals Research Center [*Public Health Service*] (GRD)
PICRS Program Information Control and Retrieval System (NASA)
PICRS Program Information Coordination and Review Service [*NASA*] (NASA)
PICS Permit Imprint Collectors Society (EA)
PICS Perpetual Inventory Control System
PICS Personnel Information Communication [*or Control*] System [*Computer science*]
PICS Pharmaceutical Information Control System (DIT)
PICS Photographic Information Condensing System (DNAB)
PICS Photography in Community Self-Development [*Program of Master Photo Dealers and Finishers Association*]
PICS Photo Index and Cataloging System (NASA)
PICS Pioneer Image Converter System [*NASA*]
PICS Plastid Isolation Column System [*Analytical chemistry*]
PICS Platform for Internet Content Selection [*Computer science*]
PICS Platform for Internet Content Selection [*Computer science*]
PICS Platform for Internet Content Selection [*Computer science*]
PICS Platform for Internet Content Selection
PICS Platform for Internet Content Selection [*Computer science*]
PICS Platform for Internet Content Specification [*Computer science*]
PICS Platform for Internnet Content Selection [*Computer science*]
PICS Plug-In Inventory Control System [*Bell System*]
PICS Predefined Input Control Sequence (MCD)
PICS Procurement Information Control System [*NASA*]
PICS Production Information and Control System [*IBM Corp.*] [*Software package*]
PICS Production Inventory Control System
PICS Productivity Improvement and Control System (BUR)
PICS Program Information and Control System (MCD)
PICS Protocol Implementation Conformance Statement [*Computer science*] (TNIG)
PICS/DCPR Plug-In Inventory Control System/Detailed Continuing Property Record [*Telecommunications*] (TEL)
PICSEC Picture per Second (IAA)
PICSO Pressure-Controlled Intermittent Coronary Sinus Occlusion [*Medicine*] (DMAA)
PICT Perceived Instrumentality of the College Test
PICT Philips Inventory Control Technique [*Computer science*] (IAA)
Pict Pictor [*Constellation*]
PICT Pictorial (ROG)
PICT Picture File Format [*Computer science*] (BTTJ)
PICT Project on the Improvement of College Teaching
Pict Dict Rome Pictorial Dictionary of Ancient Rome [*A publication*] (OCD)
PicTel PictureTel Corp. [*Associated Press*] (SAG)
PICTEL Picture Telephone [*Telecommunications*] (EECA)
pictg Pictograph (VRA)
PICTOMAP Photographic Image Conversion by Tonal Masking Procedures (MCD)
PICU Parallel Instruction Control Unit
PICU Pediatric Intensive Care Unit [*Medicine*]
PICU Priority Interrupt Control Unit [*Computer science*] (MDG)
PICU Pulmonary Intensive Care Unit [*Medicine*]
PICUTPC Permanent and International Committee of Underground Town Planning and Construction
PIC(WA) Potato Industry Council (Western Australia)
PID D. T. Watson Home for Crippled Children, Leetsdale, PA [*OCLC symbol*] (OCLC)
PID Pain Intensity Differences [*Medicine*]
PID Parameter Identification [*Communications*]
PID Partial Initial Decision [*Nuclear energy*] (NRCH)
PID Partido de Integracion Democrata [*Democratic Integration Party*] [*Argentina Political party*] (PPW)
PID Partido Izquierda Democratica [*Democratic Left Party*] [*Political party*] (EAIO)
PID Passenger Information Display
PID Patrol Input Device (MCD)
PID Payload Insertion Device (NASA)
PID Pelvic Inflammatory Disease [*Medicine*]
PID Perfect-Gas Isentropic Decompression [*Engineering*]
PID Peripheral Interface Device [*Computer science*] (EECA)
PID Personal Identification Device (MHDI)
PID Personality and Individual Differences [*A publication*]
PID Personnel Identification Device [*Navy*] (IAA)
PID Personnel Inquiry/Death/Occupational Illness [*Report*] (DNAB)
PID Phenindione [*or Phenylindandione*] [*Anticoagulant*]
PID Photointerpretation Department [*Military*]
PID Photoionization Detector
PID Photon-Induced Dissociation [*For spectral studies*]
PID Pictorial Information Digitizer [*Computer science*] (DIT)
PID Pilot-Induced Deceleration
PID Plan Identification Number (DOMA)
PID Plasma-Iron Disappearance [*Hematology*] (MAE)
PID Political Intelligence Department [*British World War II*]
PID Port Identification [*Telecommunications*] (TEL)
PID Primary Immunodeficiency Disease [*Medicine*]
PID Prime Item Development (MCD)
PID Process & Instrument Design (ACII)
PID Process Identifier [*Computer science*] (PCM)
PID Procurement Information Digest (AFM)
PID Procurement Item/Identification Description [*DoD*]
PID Product Innovation and Design
PID Program Information Document [*NASA*] (MCD)
PID Program Introduction Document (NASA)
PID Project Implementation Directive [*Air Force*]
PID Prolapsed Intervertebral Disc [*Medicine*]
PID Proportional-Integral-Derivative (ACII)
PID Proportional-Integral Derivative [*Engineering*]
PID Proportional Integral Differential [*Digital control-algorithm*] (IAA)
PID Proportional-Plus Integral-Plus Derivative [*Digital control algorithm*]
PID Protruded Intervertebral Disc [*Medicine*]
PID Pseudo Interrupt Device
PID Public Information Division [*Army*]
PIDA Payload Installation and Deployment Aid [*NASA*] (NASA)
PIDA Pet Industry Distributors Association (EA)
PIDA Pig Industry Development Authority [*British*] (BI)
PIDAS Portable Instantaneous Display and Analysis Spectrometer
PIDC Philadelphia Industrial Development Corp.
PIDC Procurement Intern Development Center (DNAB)
PIDCOM Process Instruments Digital Communication System [*Beckman Industries*]
PIDD Passive Identification/Detection and Direction (MCD)
PI/DE Passive Identification/Direction Finding Equipment (MCD)
PI/DE Positive Identification and Direction Equipment
PIDEP Preinterservice Data Exchange Program
PIDP Pacific Islands Development Program [*East-West Center*] [*Research center*] (RCD)
PIDP Pilot Information Display Panel
PIDP Programmable Indicator Data Processor [*Military*] (CAAL)
PIDR Product Inspection Discrepancy Report (MCD)
PIDRA Portable Insulin Dosage-Regulating Apparatus [*Medicine*]
PIDRS Photographic Instrumentation Data Recording System (MCD)
PIDS Parameter Inventory Display System (DNAB)
PIDS Physical Intrusion Detection System (DWSG)
PIDS Portable Image Display System (NASA)
PIDS Primary Immunodeficiency Syndrome [*Medicine*] (DMAA)
PIDS Prime Item Development Specification
PIDS Public Investment Data System (MHDW)
PIDSA Population Information Documentation System for Africa
PIDT Plasma-Iron Disappearance Time [*Hematology*] (MAE)
PIE Air South West [*British*] [*FAA designator*] (FAAC)
PIE Clearwater-St. Petersburg [*Florida*] [*Airport symbol*] (AD)
PIE Elwyn Institute, Elwyn, PA [*OCLC symbol*] (OCLC)
PIE Pacific Information Exchange [*Information service or system*] (IID)
PIE Pacific Islands Ecosystems [*Springfield, VA*] [*Department of the Interior No longer available online*] [*Information service or system*]
PIE Pacing Item Evaluation (MCD)
PIE Paedophile Information Exchange [*British*] (ILCA)
PIE Parallel Instruction Execution [*Computer science*] (BUR)
PIE Parallel Interface Element
PIE Patent Information Exploitation [*Canadian Patent Office*]
PIE Payload Integration Equipment [*NASA*] (MCD)
PIE Payroll Audit, Indexing, and Expiration
PIE Peripheral Interface Element [*Computer science*] (IAA)
PIE Personal Interactive Electronics [*Apple Computer Inc.*]
PIE Photo-Induced Electrochromism
PIE Pietermaritzburg [*South Africa*] [*Seismograph station code, US Geological Survey Closed*] (SEIS)
PIE Pipestone Petroleums, Inc. [*Toronto Stock Exchange symbol Vancouver Stock Exchange symbol*]
PIE Plug-In Electronics
PIE Plug-In Extension
PIE Plume Interaction Experiment [*Army*] (RDA)
PIE Pocket Internet Explorer [*Microsoft Corp.*] [*Computer science*]
PIE Poly(iminoethylene) [*Organic chemistry*]
PIE Portable Information Evaluation
PIE Post-Irradiation Examination [*Nuclear energy*] (NRCH)
PIE Post-Irradiation Experiment [*Nuclear energy*] (NRCH)
PIE Preimplantation Embryo
PIE Price in Effect [*Military*]
PIE Primary Industry and Energy
PIE Program for Increased Education [*Military*]
PIE Program Interrupt Element [*Computer science*] (IAA)
PIE Program Interrupt Entry [*Computer science*]
PIE Programming and Instrumentation Environment [*Computer science*]
PIE Prolog Inference Engine [*Computer science*]
PIE Proposal Information Exchange [*Military*]
PIE Proto-Indo-European [*Language*] (BARN)
PIE Publications Indexed for Engineering [*A publication*]
PIE Public Interest Economics Foundation [*Defunct*] (EA)
PIE Pulmonary Infiltration with Eosinophilia [*Medicine*]
PIE Pulmonary Interstitial Edema [*Medicine*] (DAVI)
PIE Pulmonary Interstitial Emphysema [*Medicine*]
PIE Pulse Interference Eliminator [*RADAR*]
PIE Pulse Interference Emitting (MCD)
PIE St. Petersburg [*Florida*] [*Airport symbol*] (OAG)
PIEA Pencil Industry Export Association [*Defunct*] (EA)
PIEA Petroleum Industry Electrical Association [*Later, ENTELEC*] (EA)
PIEA Petroleum Industry Electrotechnical Association (IAA)
PIEA Pre-Arrangement Interment Exchange of America [*Later, PIAA*]

PIE-C Public Interest Economics Center (EA)
PIECOST Probability of Incurring Estimated Costs [*Military*]
PIECP Preliminary Impact Engineering Change Proposal (MCD)
PIED Piedmont Mining Co., Inc. [*NASDAQ symbol*] (NQ)
PiedBcp Piedmont Bancorp, Inc. [*Associated Press*] (SAG)
PiedBGp Piedmont Bancgroup [*Associated Press*] (SAG)
PiedmBc Piedmont Bancorp, Inc. [*Associated Press*] (SAG)
PiedMg Piedmont Managment Co., Inc. [*Associated Press*] (SAG)
PiedMn Piedmont Mining Co., Inc. [*Associated Press*] (SAG)
PiedNG Piedmont Natural Gas Co., Inc. [*Associated Press*] (SAG)
PIE-F Public Interest Economics Foundation [*Defunct*] (EA)
Piemnt Piemonte Foods, Inc. [*Associated Press*] (SAG)
PIEP Primary Irritation Evaluation Program
PIER Product Inventory Electronically Recorded (PDAA)
Pier 1 Pier 1 Imports, Inc. [*Associated Press*] (SAG)
Pierce RR Pierce on Railroad Law [*A publication*] (DLA)
PiercPag Piercing Pagoda, Inc. [*Associated Press*] (SAG)
PIERS Port Import/Export Reporting Service [*Journal of Commerce, Inc.*] [*Information service or system*]
PIES Packaged Interchangeable Electronic System
PIES Penning Ionization Electron Spectroscopy
PIES Pollution Prevention Information Exchange System [*Environmental science*]
PIES Procurement and Inventory of Equipment System (DNAB)
PIES Project Independence Evaluation System [*Energy policy*]
PIESA Parasite-Induced Erythrocyte Surface Antigen [*Immunology*]
PIF Insured Muni Income Fd [*NYSE symbol*] (TTSB)
PIF Package Information Form (IAA)
PIF PaineWebber Premium Insured Municipal Income [*NYSE symbol*] (SPSG)
PIF Pakistan Islamic Front [*Pakistan*] [*Political party*] (ECON)
PIF Paper Industry Federation (NADA)
PIF Partners in Friendship (EA)
PIF Payload Integration Facility [*NASA*] (KSC)
PIF Peak Inspiratory Flow [*Medicine*] (AAMN)
PIF Perpetual Inventory File (DNAB)
PIF Personnel Identification Feature [*Navy*] (NVT)
PIF Phase Inversion Formulation [*Chemistry*]
PIF Pilot Information File [*Army*]
PIF Place in Inactive File [*Army*]
PIF Point Initiating Fuze
PIF Positive Identification Feature (MCD)
PIF Predictive Influence Function [*Statistics*]
PIF Preparer Inventory File [*IRS*]
PIF Privatization Investment Fund Trust Units [*Toronto Stock Exchange symbol*]
PIF Productivity Investment Fund [*Program*] [*Air Force*]
PIF Program Information File
PIF Project in Foreign Language Pedagogy (AIE)
PIF Prolactin Inhibiting Factor [*Endocrinology*] (DAVI)
PIF Prolactin-Release Inhibiting Factor [*Also, PRIH*] [*Endocrinology*]
PIF Proliferation Inhibitory Factor [*Immunochemistry*]
PIF Provision of Industrial Facilities [*Army*] (AABC)
PIF Pseudo-Identification Feature (MCD)
PIF Punjab Irregular Force [*British military*] (DMA)
PIFA Packaging and Industrial Films Association [*British*] (DBA)
PIFAL Program Instruction Frequency Analyzer [*Telecommunications*] (IAA)
PIFCM Pitch Integrated Flight Control Module (MCD)
PI-FET Piezoelectric Field-Effect Transistor (PDAA)
PIFEX Programmable Image Feature Extractor [*to provide real-time machine vision for the Martian Rover robot*] [*Jet Propulsion Laboratory*] (BYTE)
PIFF Punjab Irregular Frontier Force [*British military*] (DMA)
PIFI Piedmonte Foods [*NASDAQ symbol*] (TTSB)
PIFI Piemonte Foods, Inc. [*NASDAQ symbol*] (NQ)
PIFI Pressure-Induced Intracranial Focal Ischemia [*Medicine*]
PIFL Pipe Flow (PDAA)
PIFOV Planet in Field of View [*NASA*]
PIFR Peak Inspiratory Flow Rate [*Medicine*]
PIFR Program Interrupt Flag Register [*Computer science*] (IAA)
PIFS Plume-Induced Flow Separation
PIFS Post Infection Fatigue Syndrome [*Medicine*]
PIFS Prime Item Fabrication Specification
PIFT Platelet Immunofluorescence Test [*Analytical biochemistry*]
PIFUA Powerplant and Industrial Fuel Use Act of 1978
PIG Glenn Mills School, Glenn Mills, PA [*OCLC symbol*] (OCLC)
PIG Pacific Institute of Geography
PIG Passive-Income Generator [*Investment term*]
PIG Pendulous Integrating Gyro
PIG Penning Ionization Gauge (IAA)
PIG Phillips Ionization Gauge
PIG Phosphatidylinositol Glycan [*Biochemistry*]
PIG Photo-Island Grid
pig Pigment (BARN)
Pig Pigott's Common Recoveries [*3 eds.*] [*1739-92*] [*A publication*] (DLA)
PIG Plasmatron Inert Gas (SAA)
PIG Polymeric Immunoglobulin [*Medicine*] (DMAA)
PIG Pride, Integrity, Guts [*Police alternative for the appellation applied to police by radical groups*]
PIG Process Ink Gamut [*Printing technology*]
PIG Production Image Generator (MCD)
PIG Production Installation Group [*Military*] (CAAL)
PIG Program Implementation Guideline (EG)
PIG Pulse Inert Gas
PIGA Pendulous Integrating Gyro Accelerometer
Pig & R Pigott and Rodwell's English Registration Appeal Cases [*1843-45*] [*A publication*] (DLA)
PIGIT Putnam Intermediate Government Income Trust [*Associated Press*] (SAG)
Pig Judg Pigott's Foreign Judgments [*3rd ed.*] [*1908-09*] [*A publication*] (DLA)
PIGLET Purchase Information, Gifts, Loans, Exchanges Tracking [*Suggested name for the Library of Congress computer system*]
PIGM Pigmentum [*Paint*] [*Pharmacy*]
PIGM Putnam Investment Grade Municipal Trust [*Associated Press*] (SAG)
PIGMA Pressurized Inert Gas Metal Arc (KSC)
PIGME Programmed Inert Gas Multi-Electrode (PDAA)
PIGMI Pion Generator for Medical Irradiation [*Radiology*]
PIGMI Position Indicating General Measuring Instrument
PIGMT2 Putnam Investment Grade Municipal Trust II [*Associated Press*] (SAG)
PIGMT3 Putnam Investment Grade Multiple Sectors III [*Associated Press*] (SAG)
PIGPA Pyruvate, Inosine, Glucose Phosphate, Adenine (AAMN)
PIGR Polymeric Immunoglobulin Receptor [*Biochemistry*]
Pig Rec Pigott's Recoveries [*England*] [*A publication*] (DLA)
PIGS PAFEC Interactive Graphics System [*PAFEC Ltd.*] [*Software package*] (NCC)
PIGS Passive Infrared Guidance System [*DoD*]
PIGS Pesticides in Groundwater Strategy [*Environmental Protection Agency*] (GFGA)
PIGS Poles, Italians, Greeks, and Slavs
PIGS Portable Inertial Guidance System
PIGU Pendulous Integrating Gyro Unit
PIH Passive Immune Hemolysis (PDAA)
PIH Permanent Income Hypothesis [*Economics*]
PIH Phenylisopropylhydrazine [*Pharmacology*]
PIH Pipeline Induction Heat [*Industrial firm*] [*British*]
PIH Pocatello [*Idaho*] [*Airport symbol*] (OAG)
PIH Pork Industry Handbook [*A publication*]
PIH Pregnancy-Induced Hypertension [*Gynecology*]
PIH Primary Intracerebral Hemorrhage (CPH)
PIH Prolactin-Release Inhibiting Hormone [*Endocrinology*]
PIH Public and Indian Housing [*HUD*]
PIH St. Gabriel's Hall, Phoenixville, PA [*OCLC symbol*] (OCLC)
PIHC PHC, Inc. [*NASDAQ symbol*] (SAG)
PIHC PHC Inc.'A' [*NASDAQ symbol*] (TTSB)
PIHCA Polyisohexylcyanoacrylate [*Antibacterial*]
PIHCW PHC Inc. Wrrt [*NASDAQ symbol*] (TTSB)
PIHM Polish Institute of Hydrology and Meteorology
PII Fairbanks, AK [*Location identifier FAA*] (FAAL)
PII Pershing II [*Army*]
PII Phantom II [*Model of automobile*]
PII Plasma Inorganic Iodine [*Clinical chemistry*] (MAE)
PII Polaris Industries [*NYSE symbol*] (TTSB)
PII Polaris Industries, Inc. [*NYSE symbol*] (SAG)
PII Positive Immittance Inverter (IEEE)
PII Predominant Interest Installation (AAGC)
PII Primary Irritation Indices [*for skin*]
PII Printing Industry Institute [*A graphic arts training school*]
PII Procurement Instrument Identification (NG)
PII Sleighton School, Darling, PA [*OCLC symbol*] (OCLC)
PIIC Pergamon International Information Corp. [*Information service or system*] (IID)
PIIC Public Interest Immunity Certificate [*British*] (ECON)
PIID Prediction Interval Initiation Date (DNAB)
PIIF Proteinase Inhibitor Inducing Factor [*Biochemistry*]
PIIM Planned Interdependency Incentive Method
PIIN Procurement Instruction Identification Number [*Army*] (AABC)
PIIN Procurement Instrument Identification Number [*Military*]
PI/INT'L Packaging Institute International [*Later, IoPP*] (EA)
PIIO Poultry Industry Investigation Officer [*Australia*]
PIJ Pickled-in-Jar [*Food technology*]
PIJAC Pet Industry Joint Advisory Council (EA)
PIJR Product Improvement Joint Review [*Military*]
PIK Glasgow-Prestwick [*Scotland*] [*Airport symbol*] (OAG)
PIK Pay in Kind Preferred Stock (TDOB)
PIK Payment in Kind
PIK Pic Prospectors [*Vancouver Stock Exchange symbol*]
PIK Portable Injection Kit
PIK Prestwick [*Scotland*] [*Airport symbol*] (AD)
PIK Programmer's Imaging Kernel [*Computer science*] (BTTJ)
PIKE Pike [*Postal Service standard*] (OPSA)
Pike Pike's Reports [*1-5 Arkansas*] [*A publication*] (DLA)
Pike & F Adm Law Pike and Fischer's Administrative Law [*A publication*] (DLA)
Pike & F Fed Rules Service Pike and Fischer's Federal Rules Service [*A publication*] (DLA)
Pike & Fischer Admin Law Pike and Fischer's Administrative Law [*A publication*] (DLA)
Pike H of L Pike's History of the House of Lords [*A publication*] (DLA)
PIKES Pike [*Commonly used*] (OPSA)
Pikeville Pikeville National Corp. [*Associated Press*] (SAG)
PIK Securities Payment-in-Kind Securities [*Investment term*] (DFIT)
PIL Brazos Santiago, TX [*Location identifier FAA*] (FAAL)
PIL Pair Inter Langues [*Bourg La Reine, France*] (EAIO)
PIL Parti de l'Independance et de la Liberte [*Party for Independence and Liberty*] [*Congo*] [*Political party*]
PIL Patient Information Leaflet [*Pharmacy*]
PIL Payment in Lieu
PIL Percentage Increase in Loss [*Statistics*]
PIL Pest Infestation Laboratory [*Agricultural Research Council*] (PDAA)

PIL Pilar [*Argentina*] [*Seismograph station code, US Geological Survey*] (SEIS)
pil Pilaster (VRA)
PIL Pilot (WGA)
PIL Pilula [*Pill*] [*Pharmacy*]
Pil Pilula [*Pill*] [*Pharmacology*] (DAVI)
PIL Pistol Petroleum [*Vancouver Stock Exchange symbol*]
PIL Pitt Interpretive Language [*Computer science*] (DIT)
PIL Pittsburgh Interpretive [*or Interactive*] Language [*Computer science*] (IAA)
PIL Plastic Impregnated Laminate
PIL Practice Instrument Landing (ADA)
PIL Precision In Line [*Electronics*] (EECA)
PIL Preferred Item List (RDA)
PIL Processing Information List [*Computer science*]
PIL Procurement Information Letter (MCD)
PIL Publications International Ltd.
PIL Publishing Interchange Language [*Computer science*] (CDE)
PIL Purple Indicating Light (MSA)
PIL Purpose in Life [*Personality development test*] [*Psychology*]
PILA Power Industry Laboratory Association [*Defunct*] (EA)
PILAC Pulsed Ion Linear Accelerator
PILAR Petroleum Industry Local Authority Reporting (PDAA)
PILB Passenger and Immigration Lists Bibliography [*A publication*]
PILC Paper-Insulated, Lead-Covered Cable [*Telecommunications*]
PILC Pillared Interlayered Clays [*Catalysis technology*]
PILC Pregnancy and Infant Loss Center (EA)
PILE Product Inventory Level Estimator (PDAA)
PilgAmer Pilgrim American Bank & Thrift Fund, Inc. [*Associated Press*] (SAG)
PilgAPr Pilgrim America Prime Rate Trust [*Associated Press*] (SAG)
PilgPr Pilgrims Pride Corp. [*Associated Press*] (SAG)
PilgPrm Pilgrim Prime Rate Trust [*Associated Press*] (SAG)
Pilgr [*The*] Passionate Pilgrim [*Poetry*] (BARN)
Pilgr [*The*] Pilgrim's Progress [*Bunyan*] (BARN)
PilgRg Pilgrim Regional Banc Shares, Inc. [*Associated Press*] (SAG)
PILI Passenger and Immigration Lists Index [*A publication*]
PILL Newport Dock [*British depot code*]
PILL Programmed Instruction Language Learning [*Computer science*]
PILL ProxyMed, Inc. [*NASDAQ symbol*] (SAG)
PILL ProxyMed Inc. [*NASDAQ symbol*] (TTSB)
PILL Proxymed Pharmacy [*NASDAQ symbol*] (SAG)
PILLS Particulate Instrumentation by LASER Light Scattering (PDAA)
PILM Pillared Interlayered Montmorillonite [*Catalysis technology*]
PILMS Precision Insertion Loss Measurement Set (IAA)
PILO Public Information Liaison Officer [*Military*]
PILOT Paton Lyall Tosh [*Rock music group*]
PILOT Payment in Lieu of Taxes
PILOT Permutation Indexed Literature of Technology (IEEE)
PILOT Piloted Low-Speed Test [*Aerospace*]
PILOT Printing Industry Language for Operations of Typesetting
PILOT Programmed Inquiry, Learning or Teaching [*Computer science*]
PILOT Programmed Instruction Learning on Teaching [*A simplified programming language for computer-assisted instruction*] (EDAC)
Pilowtex Pillowtex Corp. [*Associated Press*] (SAG)
PILP Parametric Integer Linear Program [*Computer science*]
PILP Program of Industry/Laboratory Projects [*National Research Council of Canada*]
PILP Pseudoinfinite, Logarithmically Periodic
PILS Payload Integration Library System [*NASA*] (SSD)
PILS Pilsener Lager (DSUE)
PILS Precision Instrument Landing System
PIL STA Pilot Station [*Nautical charts*]
PILT Payment in Lieu of Taxes Program [*Department of the Interior*]
PILTA Payment in Lieu of Taxes Act
PIm Immaculata College, Immaculata, PA [*Library symbol Library of Congress*] (LCLS)
PIM Pacem in Maribus [*Secondary name for the International Ocean Institute*] (MSC)
PIM Pacific Rim Energy [*Vancouver Stock Exchange symbol*]
PIM Parallel Inference Machine [*Computer science*]
PIM Partners-in-Mission [*Church of England*]
PIM Penalties in Minutes [*Hockey*]
PIM Peripheral Interface Module
PIM Personal Illumination Marker [*Military*] (INF)
PIM Personal Information Manager
PIM Personal Information Manager [*Computer science*]
Pi M Pillius Medicinensis [*Flourished, 1165-1207*] [*Authority cited in pre-1607 legal work*] (DSA)
PIM Pilot Machine (NITA)
PIM Pine Mountain, GA [*Location identifier FAA*] (FAAL)
PIM Planned Incremental Modernization (DOMA)
PIM Plan of Intended Movement (MUGU)
PIM Plated Interconnecting Matrix
PIM Plug-In Module (MCD)
PIM Point Indicating Machine (IAA)
PIM Point of Intended Movement [*Military*]
PIM Polyphase Induction Motor
PIM Position and Intended Movement [*or Maneuver*] (NATG)
PIM Position in Miles (MCD)
PIM Powder Injection Molding [*Metallurgy*]
PIM Precision Indicator of the Meridian
PIM Precision Instrument Mount
PIM Presa Del Infiernillo [*Mexico*] [*Seismograph station code, US Geological Survey Closed*] (SEIS)
PIM Presbyterian Inland Mission
PIM Pricing Instructions Memorandum (MCD)
PIM Processor in Memory [*Computer science*]
PIM Processor Interface Module
PIM Product Information Memoranda
PIM Program Initialization Module [*Computer science*] (ECII)
PIM Program Integration Manual
PIM Program Interface Module
PIM Pro Independence Movement [*Puerto Rico*]
PIM Provincial Institute of Mining
PIM Pulse Intensity Modulation
PIM Pulse Interval Modulation
PIM Putnam Master Intermediate Income Trust [*NYSE symbol*] (SPSG)
PIM Putnam Master Interm Income [*NYSE symbol*] (TTSB)
PIM South Mountain Restoration Center, South Mountain, PA [*OCLC symbol*] (OCLC)
PiMA Ateneo de Manila University, Manila, Philippines [*Library symbol Library of Congress*] (LCLS)
PIMA Paper Industry Management Association (EA)
PIMA Photographic Industry Marketing Association [*Australia*]
PIMA Plug-In Module Assembly (MCD)
PIMA Polyisocyanurate Insulation Manufacturers Association (EA)
PIMA Portable Intelligence Maintenance Aid [*Army*] (DOMA)
PIMA Prime Intermediate Maintenance Activity
PIMA Printing Industry Management Association (DGA)
PIMA Professional Insurance Mass-Marketing Association [*Bethesda, MD*] (EA)
PIMCC Packards International Motor Car Club (EA)
PIMCO Physicians Insurance Medical Co. (BABM)
PIMCO Physicians Insurance Medical Co. (DAVI)
PIMCO Poultry Industry Manufacturers Council [*Defunct*] (EA)
PimcoAd Pimco Advisors Ltd. [*Associated Press*] (SAG)
PimCom Pimco Commercial Mortgage [*Associated Press*] (SAG)
pime Pontifical Institute for Foreign Missions (TOCD)
PIME Pontifical Institute for Foreign Missions (TOCD)
PIME Pontifical Institute for Mission Extension [*Roman Catholic men's religious order*]
PIMI Preinactivation Material Inspection [*Military*] (NVT)
PIMIA Potentiometric Ionophore Modulated Immunoassay [*Electrochemistry*]
PIMIS Portable Integrated Maintenance Information System
PIMK Portable Injection Molding Kit
PIML Polynomial Propogation Time Immediate Language [*Computer science*] (MHDI)
PIMMA Professional Insurance Mass-Marketing Association [*Bethesda, MD*] (EA)
PIMNY Printing Industries of Metropolitan New York
PIMO Presentation of Information for Maintenance and Operation [*DoD*]
PIMOS Parallel Inference Multiprocessor Operating System [*Computer science*]
PIMP Permissible Individual Maximum Pressure (SAA)
PIMP Peroxisomal Integral Membrane Protein [*Biochemistry*]
PIMP Pimperne [*England*]
PIMP Program for Interactive Multiple Process Simulation (PDAA)
PIMRA Pirmasens Missile Repair Activity [*Germany Army*]
PIMRIS Pacific Islands Marine Resources Information System [*Marine science*] (OSRA)
PIMS Peacekeeper in Minuteman Silos (DWSG)
PIMS Personnel Inventory Management System [*AT & T*]
PIMS Photoionization Mass Spectrometry
PIMS Pontifical Institute of Mediaeval Studies [*Canada*] (IRC)
PIMS Preform In-Mold Surfacing [*Plastics technology*]
PIMS Printers Integrated Management System (DGA)
PIMS Profit Impact of Marketing Strategy
PIMS Programmable Implantable Medication System
PIMSA Prensa Independiente Mexicana Sociedad Anonima [*Press agency*] [*Mexico*]
PIMT Protein Isoaspartyl Methyltransferase [*An enzyme*]
Pim Ten Pim on Feudal Tenures [*A publication*] (DLA)
PIMV Plantago Mottle Virus [*Plant pathology*]
PIN Jasper, TX [*Location identifier FAA*] (FAAL)
PIN Pacific Island Network (USDC)
PIN Pacific Island Network [*Marine science*] (OSRA)
PIN Page and Item Number
PIN Parallel Input
PIN Parintins [*Brazil*] [*Airport symbol*] (AD)
PIN Patriots Information Network [*Defunct*] (EA)
PIN Pennsylvania School for the Deaf, Philadelphia, PA [*OCLC symbol*] (OCLC)
PIN People in Need [*Food program sponsored by family of kidnapped heiress, Patricia Hearst, 1974*]
PIN Personal Identification Name (NITA)
PIN Personal [*or Private*] Identification Number [*Banking*]
PIN Personal Information Network [*Indesys, Inc.*] [*Telecommunications service*] (TSSD)
PIN Personal Injury Notice (AAG)
PIN Personnel Increment Number (DOMA)
PIN Piece Identification Number
PIN Pinedale [*Wyoming*] [*Seismograph station code, US Geological Survey Closed*] (SEIS)
PIN Pinion (MSA)
Pin Pinney's Wisconsin Supreme Court Reports [*1839-52*] [*A publication*] (DLA)
PIN Plan Identification Number (AFM)
PIN Plant Information Network [*Fish and Wildlife Service*] [*Ceased operation*] (IID)
PIN Plastics Industry Notes [*Later, CIN*]

PIN.............. Police Information Network [*San Francisco Bay area, California*]
PIN.............. Position Indicator
PIN.............. Positive-Intrinsic-Negative [*or P-Type Intrinsic N-Type*]
PIN.............. Power Information Network [*Computer science*]
PIN.............. Preliminary Imagery Nomination File (MCD)
PIN.............. Private Intelligent Networker (NITA)
PIN.............. Processor Independent NetWare [*Computer science*]
PIN.............. Procurement Information Notice [*Environmental Protection Agency*] (ERG)
PIN.............. Product Identification Number
PIN.............. Product Information Network [*McGraw-Hill Information Systems Co.*] [*Information service or system*] (IID)
PIN.............. Program Identification Number (MUGU)
PIN.............. Program Integrated Network
PIN.............. Property Inheritance Network Computer
PIN.............. Proposal Identification Number (AAG)
PIN.............. PSI Energy, Inc. [*NYSE symbol*] (SPSG)
PIN.............. P-Type Intrinsic N-Type [*or Positive-Intrinsic-Negative*]
PIN.............. Publication Identification Number [*Military*] (INF)
P IN^2........... Parts per Square Inch (WDAA)
P IN^3........... Parts per Cubic Inch (WDAA)
PINA............ Pacific Islands News Association [*Australia*]
PINA............ Parallax in Altitude [*Navigation*]
P in A.......... Parallax in Altitude [*Navigation*]
PINA............ Parenting in a Nuclear Age (EA)
PINA............ Potash Institute of North America [*Later, PPI*] (EA)
PinBG.......... Pinnacle Bank Group, Inc. [*Associated Press*] (SAG)
P-in-C.......... Priest-in-Charge [*Church of England*]
PINC............ Property Income Certificate [*Investment term British*]
PINCCA........ Price Index Numbers for Current Cost Accounting [*Service in Information and Analysis*] [*British Information service or system*] (IID)
PinclF.......... Pinnacle Financial Services, Inc. [*Associated Press*] (SAG)
PinclFn........ Pinnacle Financial Services [*Associated Press*] (SAG)
PinclM......... Pinnacle Micro, Inc. [*Associated Press*] (SAG)
PinclMic....... Pinnacle Micro, Inc. [*Associated Press*] (SAG)
PIND............ Particle Impact Noise Detection
Pind............ Pindar [*518-438BC*] [*Classical studies*] (OCD)
PINE............ Passive Infrared Night Equipment (MCD)
PINE............ Pine [*Commonly used*] (OPSA)
PINELLAS.... Pinellas Plant [*Department of Energy*] [*Largo, FL*] (GAAI)
PINES.......... Pines [*Commonly used*] (OPSA)
PINES.......... Public Information on Nuclear Energy Service [*American Nuclear Society*]
PING............ Packet Internet Groper [*Computer program*] (PCM)
ping............ Pinguis [*Fat, Grease*] [*Latin*] (DAVI)
Ping Chat Mortg... Pingrey's Treatise of Chattel Mortgages [*A publication*] (DLA)
PINGO.......... Public Interest Nongovernmental Organization
PINGP.......... Prairie Island Nuclear Generating Plant (NRCH)
PINH............ Pyridoxal Isonicotinoylhydrazone [*Biochemistry*]
PINI............ Positive Ion Neutral Injector [*Nuclear energy*] (NUCP)
Pinktn.......... Pinkerton's, Inc. [*Associated Press*] (SAG)
PINN............ Pinnacle Banc Group [*NASDAQ symbol*] (TTSB)
PINN............ Pinnacle Banc Group, Inc. [*NASDAQ symbol*] (SAG)
PINN............ Pinnacles National Monument
Pinn............ Pinney's Wisconsin Reports [*A publication*] (DLA)
PINN............ Proposed International Nonproprietary Name [*Drug research*]
PinnclBk...... Pinnacle Bank [*Associated Press*] (SAG)
Pinney.......... Pinney's Wisconsin Reports [*A publication*] (DLA)
Pinney (sv)... Pinney's Wisconsin Reports [*A publication*] (DLA)
PinnSyst...... Pinnacle Systems, Inc. [*Associated Press*] (SAG)
PINO............ Positive Input - Negative Output [*Computer science*]
PINPrB......... PSI Energy, 4.16%cmPfd vtg [*NYSE symbol*] (TTSB)
PINPrC......... PSI Energy, 4.32% Pfd [*NYSE symbol*] (TTSB)
PINPrD......... PSI Energy, 7.15% Pfd [*NYSE symbol*] (TTSB)
PINPrJ......... PSI Energy, 6.875% Pfd [*NYSE symbol*] (TTSB)
PINPrK......... PSI Energy, 7.44% Pfd [*NYSE symbol*] (TTSB)
PinptRtl....... Pinpoint Retail Solutions [*Associated Press*] (SAG)
PINS............ Palletized Inertial Navigation System [*Military*] (LAIN)
PINS............ Personnel Information System [*Army*] (AABC)
PINS............ Persons in Need of Supervision [*Classification for delinquent children*]
PINS............ Point-in-Space (MCD)
PINS............ Political Information System [*Databank of political strategist Richard Wirthlin*]
PINS............ Portable Inertial Navigation System
PINS............ Precise Integrated Navigation System [*Offshore Systems of Vancouver*]
PINS............ Precise Integrated Navigation System [*Navy*] (DOMA)
PINSAC........ PINS [*Portable Inertial Navigation System*] Alignment Console
PINSTD........ Preinserted
PINSTECH.... Pakistan Institute of Nuclear Science and Technology
PINT............ Power Intelligence (DNAB)
PINT............ Purdue Interpretive Programming and Operating System (MCD)
PINTE.......... Processor Interrupts Enabled [*Computer science*] (MHDI)
PINTS.......... Ported-Coax Intrusion Sensor [*Military*] (INF)
PInU............ Indiana University of Pennsylvania, Indiana, PA [*Library symbol Library of Congress*] (LCLS)
PINV............ Post-Imperative Negative Variation [*Medicine*] (DMAA)
Pin (Wis)...... Pinney's Wisconsin Reports [*A publication*] (DLA)
Pin Wis R..... Pinney's Wisconsin Reports [*A publication*] (DLA)
PINWOR...... Pinworm [*Gastroenterology*] (DAVI)
PinWst......... Pinnacle West Capital Corp. [*Associated Press*] (SAG)
PINX............ Pinxit [*He, or She, Painted It*] [*Latin*]
PINXT.......... Pinxit [*He, or She, Painted It*] [*Latin*] (ROG)
PINY............ Polytechnic Institute of New York
PIO.............. Palestine Information Office (EA)
PIO.............. Parallel Input/Output
PIO.............. Peripheral Input/Output (NITA)
PIO.............. Pheniminooxazolidinone [*Pharmacology*]
PIO.............. Photocomposition Input Option (NITA)
PIO.............. Photo Interpretation Officer [*Air Force*]
PIO.............. Physical Input-Output [*Computer science*] (IAA)
PIO.............. Pielago [*Ship's rigging*] (ROG)
PIO.............. Pilot-Induced Oscillation
PIO.............. Pilot Information Office
PIO.............. Pinon, NM [*Location identifier FAA*] (FAAL)
PIO.............. Pi Omicron National Sorority (EA)
PIO.............. Pioneer Airlines, Inc. [*ICAO designator*] (FAAC)
PIO.............. Pioneer Electron ADR [*NYSE symbol*] (TTSB)
PIO.............. Pioneer Electronic Corp. [*NYSE symbol*] (SPSG)
PIO.............. Poets International Organisation [*Bangalore, India*] (EAIO)
PIO.............. Position Iterative Operation
PIO.............. Precision Interactive Operation [*Computer science*]
PIO.............. Precision Iterative Operation (IAA)
PIO.............. Preliminary Inquiry Officer (DNAB)
PIO.............. Private Input/Output [*Telecommunications*] (TEL)
PIO.............. Process Input-Output [*Computer science*] (ECII)
PIO.............. Processor Input-Output [*Computer science*] (MDG)
PIO.............. Programmed Input/Output
PIO.............. Provisioned Item Order (MCD)
PIO.............. Public Information Office [*or Officer*]
PIO.............. Western Pennsylvania School for the Deaf, Pittsburgh, PA [*OCLC symbol*] (OCLC)
PIOB............ President's Intelligence Oversight Board (DOMA)
PIOC............ Program Input-Output Cassette [*Computer science*] (IAA)
PIOCC.......... Province Intelligence and Operations Coordination Center [*Vietnam*] (VNW)
PIOCS.......... Parallel Input/Output Control System (NITA)
PIOCS.......... Physical Input-Output Control System [*Computer science*] (BUR)
PIODCA........ Peruvian Inca Orchid Dog Club of America (EA)
PIOFA.......... Petroleum Ether Insoluble Oxidized Fatty Acid [*Food science*]
PIOG............ Pioneer Group [*NASDAQ symbol*] (TTSB)
PIOG............ [*The*] Pioneer Group, Inc. [*NASDAQ symbol*] (NQ)
pion............ Pi-Meson (BARN)
PION............ Pioneer (AABC)
PIONA.......... Pioneer Companies, Inc. [*NASDAQ symbol*] (SAG)
PIONA.......... Pioneer Cos. 'A' [*NASDAQ symbol*] (TTSB)
PionCos........ Pioneer Companies, Inc. [*Associated Press*] (SAG)
PioneerC....... Pioneer Commercial Funding Corp. [*Associated Press*] (SAG)
PionF........... Pioneer Financial Services, Inc. [*Associated Press*] (SAG)
PionFS......... Pioneer Financial Services, Inc. [*Associated Press*] (SAG)
PionGp......... [*The*] Pioneer Group, Inc. [*Associated Press*] (SAG)
PionHiB........ Pioneer Hi-Bred International [*Associated Press*] (SAG)
PionInt......... Pioneer Interest Shares [*Associated Press*] (SAG)
PionrC.......... Pioneer Commercial Funding Corp. [*Associated Press*] (SAG)
PionrEl......... Pioneer Electronic Corp. [*Associated Press*] (SAG)
PionStd........ Pioneer Standard Electronics [*Associated Press*] (SAG)
PionStd........ Pioneer-Standard Electronics, Inc. [*Associated Press*] (SAG)
PIOP............ Pharmacists in Ophthalmic Practice (EA)
PIOPED........ Prospective Investigation of Pulmonary Embolism Diagnosis [*Medicine*]
PIOPIC......... Protection and Indemnity of Oil Pollution Indemnity Clause [*Insurance*] (DS)
PioRail......... Pioner Railcorp [*Associated Press*] (SAG)
PIOS............ Pioneer-Standard Electronics, Inc. [*NASDAQ symbol*] (NQ)
PIOS............ Pioneer Std Electr [*NASDAQ symbol*] (TTSB)
PIOSA.......... Pan-Indian Ocean Science Association (NOAA)
PIOSP.......... Process Input-Output Subroutine Package [*Computer science*] (MHDI)
PIOTA.......... Post-Irradiation Open Test Assembly [*Nuclear energy*] (NRCH)
PIOTA.......... Proximity Instrumented Open Test Assembly [*Nuclear energy*] (NRCH)
PIOU............ Parallel Input-Output Unit [*Computer science*] (IEEE)
PIOUS.......... Peripheral Integrated Off-Line Utility System (SAA)
PIP.............. 6-Mercaptopurin, Vincristine, Methotrexate, Citrovorum Factor [*Chemotherapy*] (DAVI)
PIP.............. Package Irradiation Plant [*Nuclear energy*] (NUCP)
PIP.............. Pan-Iranist Party [*Political party*] (PPW)
PIP.............. Paper Impact Printing (HGAA)
PIP.............. Para-Isothiocyanatephenethylamine [*Biochemistry*]
PIP.............. Parental Involvement Project (AIE)
PIP.............. Participant Instrumentation Package (MCD)
PIP.............. Participant Instrumentation Package
PIP.............. Participating Irredeemable Preference [*Shares*]
PIP.............. Participation Interest Purchase [*FNMA*] (EMRF)
PIP.............. Partido Independentista Puertorriqueno [*Puerto Rican Independence Party*] [*Political party*] (PPW)
PIP.............. Partners in Progress [*Government*] [*Civil rights*]
PIP.............. Pasuquin [*Philippines*] [*Seismograph station code, US Geological Survey*] (SEIS)
PIP.............. Path Independent Protocol
PIP.............. Payload Integration Plan [*NASA*] (NASA)
PIP.............. Payload Interface Plan [*NASA*] (NASA)
PIP.............. Payment in Part [*Business term*]
PIP.............. Peak Inspiratory Pressure [*Medicine*] (DAVI)
PIP.............. Periodic Interim Payment Program [*Medicare*] (GFGA)
PIP.............. Peripheral Interchange Program [*Computer science*]
PIP.............. Peripheral Interface Programmer [*Circuit*] [*Computer science*]
PIP.............. Persistent Internal Polarization

PIP.............. Personal Identification Project [*Computer science*]
PIP.............. Personal Innovation Program
PIP.............. Personnel Interface Processor (MCD)
PIP.............. Pesticide Information Profiles (GNE)
PIP.............. Petroleum Incentives Program [*Canada*]
PIP.............. Phosphatidylinositol Phosphate [*Biochemistry*]
PIP.............. Photo Image Processor (MCD)
PIP.............. Photo Interpretive Program (BUR)
PIP.............. Picture-in-a-Picture [*Multi-Vision Products*] [*Video technology*]
PIP.............. Pilot Point [*Alaska*] [*Airport symbol*] (OAG)
PIP.............. Piperacillin [*An antibiotic*]
PIP.............. Plant-in-Place
PIP.............. Plant Instrumentation Program
PIP.............. Policy Improvement Program
PIP.............. Policy Integration Program
PIP.............. Pollution Information Project (NITA)
PIP.............. Population Information Program [*Later, CCP*] (EA)
PIP.............. Portable Instrumentation Package [*Military*] (CAAL)
PIP.............. Position Indicating Probe (IEEE)
PIP.............. Postinspiratory Pressure [*Medicine*] (DAVI)
PIP.............. Power Input Panel
PIP.............. Prearrival Inspection Procedure
PIP.............. Precise Installation Position
PIP.............. Predicted Impact Point [*Aerospace*] (AAG)
PIP.............. Predicted Intercept Point
PIP.............. Preliminary Information Pamphlet
PIP.............. Preparatory Investment Protection [*For the consortia which invested in deep sea mining*]
PIP.............. Preparedness and Industrial Planning
PIP.............. Pretty Important Person
PIP.............. Primary Indicating Position (IAA)
PIP.............. Primary Indicating Position Data Logger (IEEE)
PIP.............. Prior Immobilization and Positioning [*Roentgenology*]
PIP.............. Probabilistic Information Processing
PIP.............. Problem Identification Program (MCD)
PIP.............. Problem Input Preparation [*Computer science*] (BUR)
PIP.............. Procedural Information Pamphlet
PIP.............. Proceedings in Print [*A bibliographic publication*]
PIP.............. Product Improvement (MCD)
PIP.............. Product Improvement Plan
PIP.............. Product Improvement Program [*Military*]
PIP.............. Product Improvement Proposal (MCD)
PIP.............. Product Introductory Presentation
PIP.............. Production Implementation Program (AAG)
PIP.............. Production Improvement Program [*Navy*] (NG)
PIP.............. Production Instrumentation Package (NASA)
PIP.............. Productivity Improvement Program [*Office of Management and Budget*] (GFGA)
PIP.............. Productivity Improvement Program [*Department of Labor*]
PIP.............. Profile Ignition Pick-Up [*Automotive engineering*]
PIP.............. Profit Improvement Program
PIP.............. Program Implementation Plan (MCD)
PIP.............. Program Information Package (AAGC)
PIP.............. Program in Process [*Computer science*] (BUR)
PIP.............. Program in Progress [*Computer science*] (IAA)
PIP.............. Program Integrating Plan [*Computer science*] (IAA)
PIP.............. Program Integration Plan
PIP.............. Programmable Integrated Processor (IEEE)
PIP.............. Programmable Interconnect Point [*Computer science*]
PIP.............. Programmed Individual Presentation (IAA)
PIP.............. Programs for the Improvement of Practice [*Washington, DC Department of Education*] (GRD)
PIP.............. Progressive Independent Party [*South Africa Political party*] (EY)
PIP.............. Progressive Inspection Plan [*Navy*] (NG)
PIP.............. Projected Impact Point [*Aviation*]
PIP.............. Project Implementation Plan
PIP.............. Project Initiation Period
PIP.............. Project Instrumentation Plan [*NASA*] (GFGA)
PIP.............. Project on Information Processing (IEEE)
PIP.............. Proof in Print
PIP.............. Proposal Instruction Package (MCD)
PIP.............. Proprietary Information Protection
PIP.............. Prototypic Inlet Piping [*Nuclear energy*] (NRCH)
PIP.............. Provabilistic Information Processing [*Computer science*] (IAA)
PIP.............. Prove in Plan (MCD)
PIP.............. Proximal Interphalangeal [*Joint*]
PIP.............. Psychotic Inpatient Profile [*Psychology*]
PIP.............. Public and Institutional Property [*Insurance*]
PIP.............. Public Involvement Program (GNE)
PIP.............. Puerto Rican Independence Party [*Political party*] (PD)
PIP.............. Pulse Input Proportional [*Electro-optical system*]
PIP.............. Pulse Integrating Pendulum
PIP.............. Western Psychiatric Institute and Clinic, University of Pittsburgh, Pittsburgh, PA [*OCLC symbol*] (OCLC)
PIPA............ Pacific Industrial Property Association (EA)
PIPA............ Pulse Integrating Pendulum Accelerometer
PIPA............ Pulse Integrating Pendulum Assembly (NASA)
PIPACE........ Peacetime Intelligence Plan, Allied Central Europe [*NATO*]
Pip & C Mil L... Pipon and Collier's Military Law [*3rd ed.*] [*1865*] [*A publication*] (DLA)
PI-PB.......... Performance Versus Intensity Function for Phonetically Balanced Words (MEDA)
PIPCST........ Piping Cost and Weight Analysis Program (DNAB)
PIPE............ Consolidated Stainless [*NASDAQ symbol*] (TTSB)
PIPE............ Consolidated Stainless, Inc. [*NASDAQ symbol*] (SAG)
PIPE............ Persistent Interstitial Pulmonary Emphysema [*Medicine*] (DMAA)
PIPE............ Pipestone National Monument
PIPE............ Plumbing Industry Progress and Education Fund
PIPECO........ Photoion-Photoelectron Coincidence [*Spectroscopy*]
PIPER.......... Pulsed Intense Plasma for Exploratory Research
PiperJaf....... Piper Jaffray, Inc. [*Associated Press*] (SAG)
PIPES.......... Piperazinediethanesulfonic Acid [*A buffer*]
PIPES.......... Program on International Politics, Economics, and Security [*University of Chicago*]
PIPICO........ Panel on International Programs and International Cooperation in Oceans Affairs [*Department of State*] (NOAA)
PIPICO........ Panel on International Programs and International Organizations [*US State Department*] (USDC)
PIPIDA........ N-Para-Isopropylacetanilide-Iminodiacetic Acid [*Scan*] [*Radiology*] (DAVI)
PIPIDA........ Para-Isopropylphenyl(iminodiacetic Acid)
PIPIT........... Peripheral Interface and Program Interrupt Translator (PDAA)
PIPJ............ Proximal Interphalangeal Joint [*Anatomy*]
PIPLC.......... Phosphatidylinositol-Specific Phospholipase C [*Biochemistry*]
PIPO............ Parallel-In Parallel-Out [*Telecommunications*] (TEL)
PIPO............ Phase-In, Phase-Out (MCD)
PIPPAP........ Pile for Producing Power and Plutonium [*Nuclear energy*] (NRCH)
PIPPS.......... Publication Information Processing and Printing System
Pippy........... Person Inheriting Parents' Property [*Lifestyle classification British*]
PIPR............ Plant-in-Place Records
PIPR............ Polytechnic Institute of Puerto Rico
PIPR............ Public Interest Public Relations (EA)
PIPRS.......... Ping Intercept Passive Ranging SONAR [*Military*]
PIPS............ Paperless Item Processing System [*Banking*]
PIPS............ Patient-Identified Physicians Survey [*Department of Health and Human Services*] (GFGA)
PIPS............ Pattern Information Processing System
PIPS............ Peabody Intellectual Performance Scale [*Education*]
PIPS............ Postinjection Propulsion Subsystem [*NASA*]
PIPS............ Preschool Interpersonal Problem Solving Test
PIPS............ Production Information Processing System (IAA)
PIPS............ Professional Improvement Points Program [*Louisiana*] (EDAC)
PIPS............ Professional Institute of the Public Service of Canada [*See also IPFP*]
PIPS............ Properties of Irregular Parts System (MCD)
PIPS............ Pulsed Integrating Pendulums [*NASA*] (QAA)
PIPS............ Science and Technology Policies Information Exchange Programme [*SPINES*] [*UNESCO*] [*Superseded by*] [*Information service or system*] (IID)
PIPSAR........ Pipe Sizing Program - Air (DNAB)
PIPSCR........ Philippine Islands Public Service Commission Reports [*A publication*] (DLA)
PIPSPK........ Pipe Sizing Program - Sprinkling (DNAB)
PIPSST........ Pipe Sizing Program - Steam (DNAB)
PIPTA.......... Panel on International Procurement in the Technology Age (AAGC)
PIPUCR........ Philippine Islands Public Utility Commission Reports [*A publication*] (DLA)
PIQ.............. Parallel Instruction Queue
PIQ.............. Performance Intelligence Quotient [*Psychology*] (DMAA)
PIQ.............. Program Idea Quotient [*Home testing measurement*] (NTCM)
PIQ.............. Property in Question
PIQ.............. State Regional Correctional Facility at Mercer, Mercer, PA [*OCLC symbol*] (OCLC)
PIQA............ Procurement Integration Quality Assurance (AAGC)
PIQA............ Proofing, Inspection, and Quality Assurance [*Military*]
PIQSY.......... Probes for the International Quiet Solar Year [*OSS*]
PIR.............. Packaging Information Record (MCD)
PIR.............. Parachute Infantry Regiment [*Military*]
PIR.............. Paragnostic Information Retrieval [*Parapsychology*]
PIR.............. Parallel Injection Readout (IAA)
PIR.............. Partido de la Izquierda Revolucionaria [*Party of the Revolutionary Left*] [*Bolivia*] [*Political party*] (PPW)
PIR.............. Passive Infrared
PIR.............. Past in Review (EA)
PIR.............. Peak Intensity Ratio [*Spectroscopy*]
PIR.............. Pennsylvania International Raceway [*Auto racing*]
PIR.............. Pennsylvania Rehabilitation Center, Johnstown, PA [*OCLC symbol*] (OCLC)
PIR.............. Periodic Incremental Release [*Physiology*]
PIR.............. Periodic Intelligence Report
PIR.............. Periodic Intelligence Review [*Supreme Allied Commander, Atlantic*] (NATG)
PIR.............. Personal Interview Record
PIR.............. Personnel Information Roster [*Military*]
PIR.............. Pesticide Ingredient Review Program [*Chemical Specialties Manufacturers Association*]
PIR.............. Petrolite Irradiation Reactor
PIR.............. Philippine Independence Ribbon [*Military decoration*]
PIR.............. Phoenix International Raceway
PIR.............. Photographic Intelligence Report [*Military*]
PIR.............. Photo Interpretation Report [*Air Force*] (AFM)
PIR.............. Pier 1 Imports [*NYSE symbol*] (SPSG)
PIR.............. Pierre [*South Dakota*] [*Airport symbol*] (OAG)
PIR.............. Pilot Request (SAA)
PIR.............. Pirmasens [*Federal Republic of Germany*] [*Seismograph station code, US Geological Survey*] (SEIS)
PIR.............. Plug-In Relay
PIR.............. Post Implementation Review
PIR.............. Postinhibitory Rebound [*Physiology*]
PIR.............. Precision Inspection Request (IAA)

PIR .... Precision Instrumentation RADAR
PIR .... Predicted Intercept Range [*Military*] (CAAL)
PIR .... Prematriculation Immunization Requirement
PIR .... Pressure Ignition Rocket (NATG)
PIR .... Pressure Indicator Recorder (ECII)
PIR .... Prim-Air Aps [*Denmark ICAO designator*] (FAAC)
PIR .... Primary Intelligence Requirement [*Military*] (INF)
PIR .... Priority Information Requirement [*Military intelligence*] (INF)
PIR .... Priority Intelligence Requirement [*Military*] (INF)
PIR .... Prisoner-Initiated Review
PIR .... Process and Indoctrinate Recruits
PIR .... Procurement Initiation Request (MCD)
PIR .... Product Improvement Review
PIR .... Product Information Release
PIR .... Production Inspection Record
PIR .... Professional Investor Report [*A publication*] (IT)
PIR .... Program Incident Report
PIR .... Program Information Report [*Head Start Program*] [*Department of Health and Human Services*] (GFGA)
PIR .... Program Interrupt Register [*Computer science*] (IAA)
PIR .... Project Independence Report
PIR .... Protein Identification Resource [*National Biomedical Research Foundation*] [*Georgetown University Medical Center*] [*Information service or system*] (IID)
PIR .... Protocol-Independent Routing [*Computer science*]
PIR .... Publication Information Register (IAA)
PIR .... Pure India Rubber [*Cables*]
PIRA .... Paper Industries Research Association (NADA)
PIRA .... Photographic Instrument Repairing Associates [*British*] (DBA)
PIRA .... Printing Industry Research Association (NADA)
PIRA .... Prison Industries Reorganization Administration [*Terminated, 1940*]
PIRA .... Provisional Irish Republican Army
PIRA .... Research Association for the Paper and Board, Printing and Packaging Industries [*Research center*] (IRC)
PIRAD .... Proximity Information, Range, and Disposition
PIRAI .... PIRA International [*British*] (EAIO)
PIRAMID .... Project: Individualized Reading and Mathematics Inter-District (EDAC)
PIRAS .... Polarized Infrared Absorption Spectroscopy
PIRATA .... Pilot Research Moored Array in the Tropical Atlantic [*Proposed project*] [*Marine science*] (OSRA)
PIRATE .... Public Information in Rural Areas Technical Experiment (NITA)
PIRATE .... Public Information in Rural Areas Technology Experiment [*British Library*] (PDAA)
PIRAZ .... Positive Identification RADAR Advisory Zone (NVT)
PIRB .... Position Indicating Radio Beacon
PIRC .... Portable Inflatable Recompression Chamber (MCD)
PIRC .... Pressure Indicator Recorder Controller (ECII)
PIRC .... Preventive Intervention Research Center for Child Health [*Yeshiva University*] [*Research center*] (RCD)
PIRC .... Protocol Implementation Review Committee [*National Institutes of Health*]
PIRCS .... Passive Infrared Confirming Sensor (MCD)
PIRD .... Program Instrumentation Requirements Document [*NASA*]
PIR databases ... Protein Information Resource Databases (DOG)
PIRE .... Pacific Institute for Research and Evaluation [*Research center*] (RCD)
PI Rep .... Philippine Island Reports [*A publication*] (DLA)
PIREP .... Pilot Report [*Pertaining to meteorological conditions*] [*FAA*]
PIREPS .... Pilot Reports [*Marine science*] (OSRA)
PIRETS .... Pittsburgh Retrieval System (NITA)
PIRF .... Perimeter-Insulated Raised Floor [*Residential construction*]
PIRF .... Petroleum Industry Research Foundation (NADA)
PIRFC .... Pilot Requests Forecast [*Aviation*] (FAAC)
PIRG .... Public Interest Research Group [*Formed by consumer-advocate Ralph Nader*]
P-IRI .... Plasma Immunoreactive Insulin [*Hematology*] (MAE)
PIRI .... Psychologists Interested in Religious Issues (EA)
PIRID .... Passive Infrared Intrusion Detector (NVT)
PIRINC .... Petroleum Industry Research Foundation (EA)
PIRL .... PRISM [*Personnel Record Information System for Management*] Information RetrievalLanguage [*Computer science*] (PDAA)
PIRN .... Preliminary Interface Revision Notice [*NASA*] (KSC)
PIRO .... People, Ideas, Resources, Objectives [*Management strategy*] (DHSM)
PIRO .... Pictured Rocks National Lakeshore [*National Park Service designation*]
PIRP .... Provisional International Reference Preparation
PIRR .... Parts Installation and Removal Record [*NASA*] (KSC)
PIRR .... Prepositioned War Reserve Interrogation and Readiness Reporting (MCD)
PIRR .... Problem Investigation and Repair Record [*NASA*] (KSC)
PIRR .... PWRS [*Prepositioned War Reserve Stock*] Interrogation and Readiness Reporting System [*Navy*]
PIRRB .... Photo Intelligence Requirements Review Board [*Military*]
PIRS .... Passive Infrared Seeker
PIRS .... Personal Information Retrieval System
PIRS .... Philosopher's Index Retrieval System (NITA)
PIRS .... Philosopher's Information Retrieval System [*Bowling Green State University*]
PIRS .... Plasma Immunoreactive Secretion [*Medicine*] (DMAA)
PIRS .... Pollution Incident Reporting System [*Coast Guard*]
PIRS .... Poseidon Information Retrieval System [*Missiles*]
PIRS .... Project Information Retrieval System [*HEW*]
PIRT .... Precision Infrared Tracking
PIRT .... Precision Infrared Triangulation
PIRT .... Pretreatment Implementation Review Task Force [*Environmental Protection Agency*] (EPA)
PIRU .... Public Information Reference Unit [*Environmental Protection Agency*] (GFGA)
Pis .... In Pisonem [*of Cicero*] [*Classical studies*] (OCD)
PIS .... Parts Identification Service
PIS .... Passenger Information System
PIS .... Passive Infrared System
PIS .... Patent Inventor Service (NITA)
PIS .... Penning Ionization Spectroscopy (PDAA)
PIS .... Photographic Interpretation Section
PIS .... Pisa [*Italy*] [*Seismograph station code, US Geological Survey Closed*] (SEIS)
PIS .... Piscivorous
PIS .... Poitiers [*France*] [*Airport symbol*] (OAG)
PIS .... Position Indicator System
PIS .... Positive Ion Source
PIS .... Postal Inspection Service
PIS .... Preinfarction Syndrome [*Cardiology*]
PIS .... Preinsert Sequencing
PIS .... Pressure-Indicating Switch [*Nuclear energy*] (NRCH)
PIS .... Prime Implicant Solution (IAA)
PIS .... Process Instrumentation System [*Nuclear energy*] (NRCH)
PIS .... Process Instrument Sheet
PIS .... Product Information Specialist
PIS .... Provisional International Standard
PIS .... Pulsed Illumination Source
PIS .... Pulse Integration System
PIS .... Stevens Trade School, Lancaster, PA [*OCLC symbol*] (OCLC)
PISA .... Persistent Information Space Architecture [*Computer science*]
PISA .... Phase Invariant Signature Algorithm [*Chemistry*] (DAVI)
PISA .... Polish Independent Student Association (EA)
PISA .... Public Interest Satellite Association [*Defunct*] (EA)
PISAB .... Pulse Interference Separation and Blanking [*RADAR*]
PISAL .... Periodicals in South African Libraries (NITA)
PISB .... People's Institute for Survival and Beyond (EA)
PISC .... Pacific International Services Corp. [*NASDAQ symbol*] (NQ)
PISC .... Parris Island, South Carolina [*Marine Corps*]
PISC .... Petroleum Industry Security Council (EA)
Pisc .... Pisces [*Constellation*]
PISCES .... Percutaneously Inserted Spinal Cord Electrical Stimulation [*Medicine*] (DMAA)
PISCES .... Production Information Stocks and Cost Enquiry System (MHDB)
PISE .... No Pilot Balloon Observation Due to Unfavorable Sea Conditions [*NWS*] (FAAC)
PISE .... Pnuematically-Impacted Stabilized Earth
PISG .... Pitcairn Islands Study Group (EA)
PISGA .... Palestinian Interim Self-Government Authority [*Proposed*] (ECON)
PISH .... Program Instrumentation Summary Handbook [*NASA*] (KSC)
PISMV .... Plantago Severe Mottle Virus [*Plant pathology*]
PISO .... No Pilot Balloon Observation Due to Snow [*Meteorology*] (FAAC)
PISO .... Parallel-In Serial-Out [*Telecommunications*] (TEL)
PISP .... Pipe Springs National Monument
PISSC .... Programme International sur la Securite des Substances Chimiques [*International Programme on Chemical Safety*] (EAIO)
PIST .... Piston [*Automotive engineering*]
Pist .... Piston's Mauritius Reports [*A publication*] (DLA)
Piston .... Piston's Mauritius Reports [*A publication*] (DLA)
PISU .... Polyimidesulfone [*Organic chemistry*]
PISUKI .... Pacific Islands Society of the United Kingdom and Ireland (EAIO)
PISW .... Process Interrupt Status Word
PISW .... Program Interrupt Status Word (NITA)
PIT .... Pacific Investment Trust [*Finance*] [*British*]
PIT .... Panair International SRL [*Italy ICAO designator*] (FAAC)
PI/T .... Parallel Interface/Timer [*Motorola, Inc.*]
PIT .... Parameter Input Tape (IAA)
PIT .... Participate in Archeology
PIT .... Parti de l'Independance et du Travail [*Party of Independence and Labor*] [*Senegal*] [*Political party*] (PPW)
PIT .... Parti Ivoirien des Travailleurs [*Ivorian Workers' Party*] [*The Ivory Coast*] [*Political party*] (EY)
PIT .... Partners in Transition [*Poland, Czechoslovakia, and Hungary*] (ECON)
PIT .... Part-Time, Intermittent, Temporary [*Nuclear energy*]
PIT .... Passive Integrated Transponder
PIT .... Patellar Inhibition Test [*Neurology*] (DAVI)
PIT .... Performance Improvement Tests
PIT .... Peripheral Input Tape [*Computer science*]
PIT .... Peripheral Interface Tests (MCD)
PIT .... Permanent Income Theory [*Econometrics*]
PIT .... Personal Income Tax
PIT .... Phase Inversion Temperature [*Physical Chemistry*]
PIT .... Photographic Interpretation Technique
PIT .... Physical Inventory Taking (MHDB)
PIT .... Picture Identification Test [*Psychology*]
PIT .... Picture Impressions Test [*Psychology*]
PIT .... Pilot Instructor Training [*Aviation*] (FAAC)
PIT .... Pirates Gold Corp. [*Vancouver Stock Exchange symbol*]
Pit .... Pitocin [*Trademark of Parke, Davis & Co. for Oxytocin, a labor-inducing drug*]
Pit .... Pitressin [*Trademark of Parke, Davis & Co. for Vasopressin, an antidiuretic hormone*]
PIT .... Pittsburgh [*Pennsylvania*] [*Seismograph station code, US Geological Survey Closed*] (SEIS)
PIT .... Pittsburgh [*Pennsylvania*] [*Airport symbol*]

PIT .... Pituitary [*Endocrinology*] (AAMN)
PIT .... Plasma Iron Transport [*Hematology*]
PIT .... Plasma Iron Turnover [*Hematology*] (DAVI)
PIT .... Polar Ionospheric Trough
PIT .... Polaris Industrial Team [*Missiles*]
PIT .... Pre-Induction Training
PIT .... Preinstallation Test [*NASA*] (KSC)
PIT .... Prevailing-In Torque [*Automotive engineering*]
PIT .... Print Illegal and Trace
PIT .... Printing and Information Technology Division (NITA)
PIT .... Processing of Indexing Terms
PIT .... Product Improvement Test
PIT .... Program Instruction Tape [*Computer science*] (IEEE)
PIT .... Programmable Interval Timer
PIT .... Programmed Instruction Text
PIT .... Projected Inactive Time [*Computer science*]
PIT .... Property Income Trust [*Investment term*]
PIT .... Provincial Institute of Textiles
PIT .... Psychological Insight Test [*Psychometrics*]
PIT .... University of Pittsburgh, Pittsburgh, PA [*OCLC symbol*] (OCLC)
PITA .... Pacific International Trapshooting Association (EA)
PITA .... Pain in the Ass
PITA .... Paper Industry Technical Association [*British*] (EAIO)
PITA .... Provincial Institute of Technology and Art
PITB .... Pacific Inland Tariff Bureau
PITB .... PUSH [*People United to Save Humanity*] International Trade Bureau (EA)
Pitblado Lect ... Isaac Pitblado's Lectures on Continuing Legal Education [*A publication*] (DLA)
PITC .... Phenylisothiocyanate [*Organic chemistry*]
PITC .... Photoinduced Tunnel Current
Pitc .... Pitcairn's Criminal Trials [*1488-1624*] [*Scotland*] [*A publication*] (DLA)
PITC .... Pittencrieff Communic [*NASDAQ symbol*] (TTSB)
PITC .... Pittencrieff Communications [*NASDAQ symbol*] (SAG)
Pitc Crim Tr ... Pitcairn's Ancient Criminal Trials [*Scotland*] [*A publication*] (DLA)
PITCOM .... Parliamentary Information Technology Committee [*Political communications*] [*British*]
Pitc Tr .... Pitcairn's Criminal Trials [*3 Scotland*] [*A publication*] (DLA)
PitDsm .... Pittsburgh-Des Moines Corp. [*Associated Press*] (SAG)
PITE .... Project on Information Technology and Education [*Defunct*] (EA)
Pitencr .... Pittencrieff Communications [*Commercial firm Associated Press*] (SAG)
PITF .... Poultry Industry Trust Fund [*Australia*]
PITFC .... Potato Industry Trust Fund Committee [*Western Australia*]
PITG .... Payload Integration Task Group [*NASA*] (NASA)
PITI .... Principal, Interest, Taxes, Insurance [*Real estate*]
Pitisc Lex .... Pitisci's Lexicon [*A publication*] (DLA)
Pitm Prin & Sur ... Pitman on Principal and Surety [*A publication*] (DLA)
PITN .... Polyisothianaphthene [*Organic chemistry*]
PitnB .... Pitney-Bowes, Inc. [*Associated Press*] (SAG)
PitnyBw .... Pitney-Bowes, Inc. [*Associated Press*] (SAG)
PITP .... Phosphatidylinositol Transfer Protein [*Biochemistry*]
PITR .... Plasma Iron Transport [*or Turnover*] Rate [*Hematology*]
PITS .... Parent-Infant Traumatic Stress (DAVI)
PITS .... Partners In Transition [*Poland, Czech, Hungary - called the Visegrad Trio*]
PITS .... Passive Intercept Tracking System
PITS .... Patriot Integration and Test System [*Army*]
PITS .... Payload Integration Test Set [*NASA*] (MCD)
PITS .... Photoinduced Transient Spectroscopy
PITS .... Primary Influent Treatment System
PITS .... Project Information Tracking System [*Environmental Protection Agency*] (GFGA)
PITS .... Propellant Injector Tube Simulator (MCD)
PITS .... Propulsion Integration Test Stand
PitstnMn .... [*The*] Pittston Co. [*Associated Press*] (SAG)
PitstnSvc .... [*The*] Pittston Co. [*Associated Press*] (SAG)
Pit Sur .... Pitman on Principal and Surety [*1840*] [*A publication*] (DLA)
Pitt .... Pittsburgh, PA (DLA)
PITT .... Polaris Integrated Test Team [*Missiles*]
Pitt Bank ...... Pitt's Bankruptcy Acts [*A publication*] (DLA)
PITTC .... Philips International Telecommunications Training Center (IAA)
Pitt CC Pr .... Pitt's County Court Practice [*A publication*] (DLA)
Pitt LJ .... Pittsburgh Legal Journal [*A publication*] (DLA)
Pitts .... Pittsburgh, PA (DLA)
Pitts .... Pittsburgh Reports [*A publication*] (DLA)
Pittsb .... Pittsburgh, PA (DLA)
Pittsb .... Pittsburgh Reports [*A publication*] (DLA)
Pittsb Leg J ... Pittsburgh Legal Journal [*Pennsylvania*] [*A publication*] (DLA)
Pittsb Leg J NS ... Pittsburgh Legal Journal, New Series [*Pennsylvania*] [*A publication*] (DLA)
Pittsb Leg J (OS) ... Pittsburgh Legal Journal, Old Series [*A publication*] (DLA)
Pittsb Leg J (PA) ... Pittsburgh Legal Journal [*Pennsylvania*] [*A publication*] (DLA)
Pittsb LJ ...... Pittsburgh Legal Journal [*Pennsylvania*] [*A publication*] (DLA)
Pittsb L Rev ... Pittsburgh Law Review [*A publication*] (DLA)
Pittsb R (PA) ... Pittsburgh Reporter [*Pennsylvania*] [*A publication*] (DLA)
Pittsburgh Leg J ... Pittsburgh Legal Journal [*Pennsylvania*] [*A publication*] (DLA)
Pittsburgh Leg Journal ... Pittsburgh Legal Journal [*Pennsylvania*] [*A publication*] (DLA)
Pittsburg St U ... Pittsburg State University (GAGS)
Pitts Leg J ... Pittsburgh Legal Journal [*Pennsylvania*] [*A publication*] (DLA)
Pitts Leg J (NS) ... Pittsburgh Legal Journal, New Series [*Pennsylvania*] [*A publication*] (DLA)
Pitts Leg Jour ... Pittsburgh Legal Journal [*Pennsylvania*] [*A publication*] (DLA)
Pitts LJ .... Pittsburgh Legal Journal [*A publication*] (DLA)
Pitts LJ (NS) ... Pittsburgh Legal Journal, New Series [*A publication*] (DLA)
Pitts R .... Pittsburgh Reports [*Pennsylvania*] [*A publication*] (DLA)
Pitts Rep ..... Pittsburgh Reports [*A publication*] (DLA)
Pitts Rep (PA) ... Pittsburgh Reports [*Pennsylvania*] [*A publication*] (DLA)
Pittway .... Pittway Corp. [*Associated Press*] (SAG)
Pittwy .... Pittway Corp. [*Associated Press*] (SAG)
PittwyA .... Pittway Corp. [*Associated Press*] (SAG)
PITU .... Pipe or Tubing [*Freight*]
PitWVa .... Pittsburgh & West Virginia Railroad [*Associated Press*] (SAG)
PITY-EM ...... Principal, Interest, Taxes, Energy, and Maintenance [*Real estate*]
PITYP .... Pinatype (VRA)
PIU .... East Pennsylvania Psychiatric Institute, Philadelphia, PA [*OCLC symbol*] (OCLC)
PIU .... Path Information Unit [*Computer science*]
PIU .... Pathological Internet Use
PIU .... Photographic Interpretation Unit [*Marine Corps*]
PIU .... Pilot Indicator Unit [*Aviation*] (IAA)
PIU .... Pilot Information Utilization
PIU .... Piura [*Peru*] [*Airport symbol*] (OAG)
PIU .... Plug-In Unit
PIU .... Polymerase-Inducing Unit
PIU .... Power Integration Unit (SSD)
PIU .... Power Intercept Unit [*Military*] (CAAL)
PIU .... Power Interface Unit (MCD)
PIU .... Private Islands Unlimited (EA)
PIU .... Process Input Unit [*Computer science*] (BUR)
PIU .... Process Interface Unit
PIU .... Programmer Interface Unit (MCD)
PIU .... Pyrotechnic Initiator Unit (MCD)
PiU .... University of the Philippines, Quezon City, Philippines [*Library symbol Library of Congress*] (LCLS)
PIUG .... Parti Independantiste de l'Unite Guyanaise [*Pro-Independence Party of Guyanese Unity*] [*Political party*] (PPW)
PIUMP .... Plug-In Unit Mounting Panel
PIUS .... Process Inherent Ultimately Safe [*Nuclear reactor*]
PI/USA .... Packaging Institute, United States of America [*Later, PI/INT'L*] (EA)
PIV .... Parainfluenza Virus
PIV .... Peak Inverse Voltage [*RADAR*]
PIV .... Peripheral Intravenous [*Line*] [*Pharmacology*] (DAVI)
PIV .... Pick Inverse Voltage [*Electronics*] (ECII)
PIV .... Piva [*Solomon Islands*] [*Seismograph station code, US Geological Survey Closed*] (SEIS)
PIV .... Pivot [*Automotive engineering*]
PIV .... Planet in View [*NASA*]
PIV .... Plug-In Valve
PIV .... Positive Infinitely Variable
PIV .... Post Indicator Valve
PIV .... Product Inspection Verification
PIV .... Propellant Isolation Valve
PIV .... Scotland School for Veterans' Children, Scotland, PA [*OCLC symbol*] (OCLC)
PIV4 .... Plantago Virus 4 [*Plant pathology*]
PIVAD .... Product Improvement Vulcan Air Defense (MCD)
PIVADS .... Product Improved Vulcan Air Defense System (MCD)
PIVD .... Protruded Intervertebral Disc [*Medicine*]
PIVED .... Plasma-Injection Vacuum Energy Diverter
PIVKA .... Protein in Vitamin K Absence (AAMN)
PIVN .... Public Interest Video Network/New Voices Radio (EA)
PIVOT .... Planning and Implementing Vocational Readiness in Occupational Therapy
PIVR .... Pacemaker-Induced Ventricular Rate [*Cardiology*] (CPH)
PIVS .... Particle-Induced Visual Sensations
PIVT .... Production Improvement Verification Test
PIVX .... Plantain Virus X [*Plant pathology*]
PIW .... Period of Incapacity for Work (DI)
PIW .... Plastic Insulated Wire
PIW .... Ports and Inland Waterways
PIW .... Program Interrupt Word
PIW .... Woodhaven Center, Philadelphia, PA [*OCLC symbol*] (OCLC)
PIWC .... Petroleum Industry War Council
PIWG .... Product Improvement Working Group [*Military*] (AFIT)
PIWI .... No Pilot Balloon Observation Due to High, or Gusty, Surface Wind [*NWS*] (FAAC)
PIWWC .... Planetary Initiative for the World We Choose (EA)
PIX .... Parallel Interface Extender [*Computer science*] (IAA)
PIX .... Pico Island [*Azores*] [*Airport symbol*] (OAG)
PIX .... Picture
PIX .... Picture Rocks, PA [*Location identifier FAA*] (FAAL)
PIX .... Pinxit [*He, or She, Painted It*] [*Latin*] (ROG)
PIX .... Proton-Induced X-Ray Analysis
PIX .... Youth Development Center, Loysville, Loysville, PA [*OCLC symbol*] (OCLC)
Pix Aud .... Pixley on Auditors [*8th ed.*] [*1901*] [*A publication*] (DLA)
PIXE .... Particle [*or Proton*]-Induced X-Ray Emission
PIXEL .... Picture Element [*Single element of resolution in image processing*]
PIXR .... Pixar [*NASDAQ symbol*] (TTSB)
PIXT .... PixTech, Inc. [*NASDAQ symbol*] (SAG)
PixTech .... PixTech, Inc. [*Associated Press*] (SAG)
PIY .... Pembroke Imperial Yeomanry [*British military*] (DMA)
PIY .... Youth Development Center, New Castle, New Castle, PA [*OCLC symbol*] (OCLC)
PIZ .... Pizaz European [*British*] [*FAA designator*] (FAAC)
PIZ .... Point Lay [*Alaska*] [*Airport symbol*] (OAG)
PIZ .... Point Lay, AK [*Location identifier FAA*] (FAAL)

PIZ............ Youth Development Center, Waynesburg, Waynesburg, PA [*OCLC symbol*] (OCLC)
PIZZ............ Pizzicato [*Plucked*] [*Music*]
PizzaInn....... Pizza Inn, Inc. [*Associated Press*] (SAG)
PJ............ Air St. Pierre [*ICAO designator*] (AD)
PJ............ Bombay High Court Printed Judgments [*1869-1900*] [*India*] [*A publication*] (DLA)
PJ............ Netherlands Antilles [*International civil aircraft marking*] (ODBW)
PJ............ Pajamas
PJ............ Panel Jack
PJ............ Parnelli Jones [*Race car driver*]
PJ............ Parteijargon [*Party Language*] [*German*]
PJ............ Participating Jurisdiction
PJ............ Peripheral Jet (AAG)
PJ............ Petajoule (ADA)
PJ............ Picojoule [*Logic gate efficiency measure*] (MDG)
PJ............ Plasma Jet (AAG)
PJ............ Plastic Jacket
PJ............ Police Justice
PJ............ Possible Jobs [*Test*] [*Psychology*]
PJ............ Presiding Judge
PJ............ Presiding Probate Judge [*British*] (ROG)
PJ............ Prince of Jerusalem [*Freemasonry*]
PJ............ Probate Judge
PJ............ Procurement Justification [*Navy*]
PJ............ Project Jonah [*Defunct*] (EA)
PJ............ Puisne Judge [*Australia*]
PJ............ Pulsejet
PJ............ Purchases Journal [*Accounting*]
PJA............ Abington Library Society, Jenkintown, PA [*Library symbol Library of Congress Obsolete*] (LCLS)
PJA............ Pipe Jacking Association [*British*] (DBA)
PJAFC............ P. J. Allman Fan Club (EA)
PJAL............ Progressive Jewish Activism List [*An association*]
PJAIG............ Alverthorpe Gallery, Rosenwald Collection, Jenkintown, PA [*Library symbol Library of Congress*] (LCLS)
PJAM............ PJ America, Inc. [*NASDAQ symbol*] (SAG)
PJ Amer...... PJ America, Inc. [*Associated Press*] (SAG)
PJB............ Pad Journal Bearing
PJB............ Premature Junctional Beat [*Cardiology*]
PJBD............ Permanent Joint Board on Defense [*US, Canada*]
PJC............ Jean Coutu Group (PJC), Inc. [*Toronto Stock Exchange symbol*]
PJC............ Paducah Junior College [*Kentucky*]
PJC............ Paris Junior College [*Texas*]
PJC............ Pensacola Junior College [*Florida*]
PJC............ Perkinston Junior College [*Mississippi*]
PJC............ Piper Jaffray Companies [*NYSE symbol*] (SPSG)
PJC............ Piper Jaffray Cos. Inc. [*NYSE symbol*] (TTSB)
PJC............ Post Junior College [*Connecticut*]
PJC............ Poteau Junior College [*Oklahoma*]
PJC............ Pratt Junior College [*Kansas*]
PJC............ Premature Junctional Contractions [*Cardiology*] (DMAA)
PJC............ University of Pittsburgh, Johnstown, Johnstown, PA [*OCLC symbol*] (OCLC)
PJCTL............ Projectile (MSA)
Pjctvs............ Projectavision, Inc. [*Associated Press*] (SAG)
Pjctvsn............ Projectavision, Inc. [*Associated Press*] (SAG)
PJD............ Pedro Dome [*Alaska*] [*Seismograph station code, US Geological Survey Closed*] (SEIS)
PJE............ Parachute Jumping Exercise
PJE............ Private Jet Expeditions, Inc. [*ICAO designator*] (FAAC)
PJE............ Project Engineer
PJE............ Pulse Jet Engine
PJES............ Photojet Edge Sensor
PJF............ Peripheral Jet (Flat-Bottom)
PJF............ Pharmaceutical Journal Formulary (ROG)
PJF............ Pin Jointed Framework
PJFS............ Philip Jose Farmer Society (EA)
PJG............ Panjgur [*Pakistan*] [*Airport symbol*] (OAG)
PJG............ Potts Junction [*Guam*] [*Seismograph station code, US Geological Survey*] (SEIS)
PJH............ Piper, Jr., H. E., Philadelphia PA [*STAC*]
PJH............ PLRS/JTIDS [*Position Location Reporting System/Joint Tactical Information Distribution System*] Hybrid (MCD)
PJHI............ PLRS/JTIDS [*Position Location Reporting System/Joint Tactical Information Distribution System*] Hybrid Interface
PJI............ Parachute Jump Instructor [*Military British*] (INF)
PJI............ Pattern Jury Instructions [*A publication*]
PJI............ Personnel Journal Index [*Personnel Journal*] [*Information service or system*] (CRD)
PJI............ Point Judith, RI [*Location identifier FAA*] (FAAL)
PJILMCC...... Philip C. Jessup International Law Moot Court Competition (EA)
PJIT............ Parts Just in Time
P JI............ Pharmaceutical Journal [*A publication*] (ROG)
PJL............ Printer Job Language [*Computer science*]
PJLB............ Lower Burma Printed Judgments [*A publication*] (DLA)
PJM............ Pennsylvania-Jersey-Maryland [*Electric power pool*]
PJM............ Polymer Jell Material
PJM............ Positive Joint Mobilization [*Medicine*] (DMAA)
PJM............ Postjunctional Membrane
PJM............ Power Jets Memorandum
PJM............ Project Manager [*Military*]
PJN............ Fort Lauderdale, FL [*Location identifier FAA*] (FAAL)
PJo............ Cambria County Library System, Johnstown, PA [*Library symbol Library of Congress*] (LCLS)
PJO............ Pioneer Jupiter Orbit [*NASA*]
PJON............ Johnston Island/Johnston Atoll [*Johnston Island*] [*ICAO location identifier*] (ICLI)
PJOP............ Preliminary Joint Operation Procedure (KSC)
PJoU............ University of Pittsburgh at Johnstown, Johnstown, PA [*Library symbol Library of Congress*] (LCLS)
PJP............ Pancreatic Juice Protein [*Medicine*] (DMAA)
PJPC............ Plug/Jack Patch Cord
PJR............ Peoria, IL [*Location identifier FAA*] (FAAL)
PJR............ Peterson, J. Robert, New York NY [*STAC*]
PJR............ Philadelphia Journalism Review [*A publication*]
PJR............ Pipe Joint Record (DNAB)
PJR............ Port Jersey [*AAR code*]
PJR............ Power Jets Report
P Jr & H...... Patton, Jr., and Heath's Reports [*Virginia Special Court of Appeals*] [*A publication*] (DLA)
PJS............ Jet Aviation, Business Jets AG [*Switzerland ICAO designator*] (FAAC)
PJS............ Newport News, VA [*Location identifier FAA*] (FAAL)
PJ's............ Pajamas [*Slang*]
PJ's............ Paramedic Jumpers
PJS............ Peripheral Jet (Skegs)
PJS............ Peritoneojugular Shunt [*Medicine*] (DMAA)
PJS............ Peutz-Jeghers Syndrome [*Oncology*]
PJ's............ Physical Jerks [*Exercise*] [*Slang British*] (DSUE)
PJS............ Piezojunction Sensor
PJS............ Plug and Jack Set
PJS............ Production Job Sheet
PJSS............ PACAF [*Pacific Air Forces*] Jungle Survival School (AFM)
PJT............ Paroxysmal Junctional Tachycardia [*Cardiology*]
PJT............ Practical Job Training (MCD)
PJT............ Pulse Jitter Tester
PJTN............ Projection (MSA)
PJTR............ Projector (MSA)
PJTV............ Projectavision, Inc. [*NASDAQ symbol*] (SAG)
PJTVP............ Projectavision $0.40 Cv'B'Pfd [*NASDAQ symbol*] (TTSB)
PJTVW............ Projectavision Inc. Wrrt [*NASDAQ symbol*] (TTSB)
PJU............ Juniata College, Huntingdon, PA [*OCLC symbol*] (OCLC)
PJU............ Physician's Journal Update [*Television program*]
PJV............ Pump Jet Vehicle
PJVT............ Paroxysmal Junctional-Ventricular Tachycardia [*Medicine*] (MEDA)
PK............ Central Parking [*NYSE symbol*] (TTSB)
PK............ Central Parking Corp. [*NYSE symbol*] (SAG)
pK............ Dissociation Constant [*Chemistry*] (DAVI)
pK'............ Negative Log of the Dissociation Constant [*Medicine*]
PK............ Pack (AAG)
PK............ Package [*Shipping*] (MCD)
pk............ Pakistan [*IYRU nationality code*] [*MARC country of publication code Library of Congress*] (LCCP)
PK............ Pakistan [*ANSI two-letter standard code*] (CNC)
PK............ Park [*or Parking*]
Pk............ Park (DD)
pk............ Park (VRA)
PK............ Peak [*Maps and charts*]
pK............ Peak Value [*Computer science*]
PK............ Peck (AAG)
pk............ Peck (DMAA)
PK............ Penetrating Keratoplasty [*Ophthalmology*] (DAVI)
PK............ Peter King [*Afro-jazz band*]
PK............ Pharmacokinetic
PK............ Phileleftheron Komma [*Liberal Party*] [*Greek Political party*] (PPE)
PK............ Pig Kidney [*Medicine*] (DMAA)
PK............ Pike
P_K............ Plasma Potassium [*Biochemistry*] (DAVI)
PK............ Pokhvala Knige [*A publication*]
PK............ Pole Cat [*Slang*]
PK............ Position Keeper
PK............ Posta Kutusu [*Postbox*] [*Turkish*] (EY)
PK............ Prausnitz-Kuestner [*Reaction*] [*Immunology*]
PK............ Prausnitz-Kunstner [*Reaction or Transfer Test*] [*Medicine*] (DAVI)
PK............ Preacher's Kid [*Slang*]
PK............ Pridie Kalendas [*The Day before the Calends*] [*Latin*]
PK............ Primary Key [*Computer science*] (PCM)
PK............ Principal Keeper [*Slang for a warden*]
PK............ Probability of Kill (MCD)
PK............ Prophets and Kings (BJA)
PK............ Protein Kinase [*Also, PKase*] [*An enzyme*]
PK............ Psychokinesis
PK............ Pyruvate Kinase [*An enzyme*]
PK............ West Irian [*Aircraft nationality and registration mark*] (FAAC)
P-K4............ Pawn to King Four [*Standard opening to a game of chess. Pawn is moved to the fourth square in front of the king*]
PKA............ Equator Airlines Ltd. [*Kenya*] [*ICAO designator*] (FAAC)
PKA............ Napaskiak [*Alaska*] [*Airport symbol*] (OAG)
PKA............ Napaskiak, AK [*Location identifier FAA*] (FAAL)
pKa............ Negative Log of Dissociation Constant [*Medicine*] (DAVI)
PKA............ Paul Kagan Associates, Inc. [*Information service or system Telecommunications*] (IID)
PKA............ Pi Kappa Alpha [*Fraternity*]
PKA............ Polk Audio [*AMEX symbol*] (SAG)
PKA............ Primary Knock-on-Atom (MCD)
PKA............ Professional Karate Association [*Defunct*] (EA)
PKA............ Prokininogenase [*An enzyme*] (MAE)
PKA............ Protein Kinase A [*An enzyme*]
PkAF............ Pakistani Air Force

PKAFA .... PKA [*Professional Karate Association*] Fighters Association [*Defunct*] (EA)
PKAR .... Protein Kinase Activation Ratio [*Medicine*] (DMAA)
PKAS .... Parti Kadazan Asli Sabah [*Malaysia*] [*Political party*] (FEA)
PKase .... Protein Kinase [*Also, PK*] [*An enzyme*]
PKAWA .... Pocket Knife Ancillary Workers' Association [*A union*] [*British*]
PKB .... Parkersburg [*West Virginia*] [*Airport symbol*] (OAG)
PKB .... Parkersburg, WV [*Location identifier FAA*] (FAAL)
PKB .... Photoelectric Keyboard
PKB .... Portable Keyboard
PKB .... Protein Kinase B [*An enzyme*]
PKC .... Cocoa, FL [*Location identifier FAA*] (FAAL)
PKC .... Peckham Road [*California*] [*Seismograph station code, US Geological Survey*] (SEIS)
PKC .... Phuket [*Thailand*] [*Airport symbol*] (AD)
PKC .... Position Keeping Computer
PKC .... Problem-Knowledge Coupler (DMAA)
PKC .... Protein Kinase C [*An enzyme*]
PKC .... Public Key Cryptography
PKD .... Pac Ed Systems Corp. [*Vancouver Stock Exchange symbol*]
PKD .... Packed (IAA)
PKD .... Parker Drilling [*NYSE symbol*] (TTSB)
PKD .... Parker Drilling Co. [*NYSE symbol*] (SPSG)
PKD .... Park Rapids, MN [*Location identifier FAA*] (FAAL)
PKD .... Partially Knocked Down [*Consignment*] [*Shipping*] (DS)
PKD .... Philip K. Dick [*Science fiction writer*]
PKD .... Pi Kappa Delta [*Society*]
PKD .... Polycystic Kidney Disease [*Medicine*]
PKD .... Programmable Keyboard and Display [*Computer science*] (NASA)
PKD .... Proliferative Kidney Disease [*Medicine*] (DMAA)
PKDB .... Partai Kebang-Saan Demokratik Brunei [*Brunei National Democratic Party*] [*Political party*] (EY)
PKDG .... Professional Knitwear Designers Guild
PKDOM .... Pack for Domestic Use
PKD PDR ...... Packed Powder (WGA)
PKDS .... Philip K. Dick Society [*Defunct*] (EA)
PKE .... Pacific Kenridge [*Vancouver Stock Exchange symbol*]
PKE .... Park Electrochemical [*NYSE symbol*] (TTSB)
PKE .... Park Electrochemical Corp. [*NYSE symbol*] (SPSG)
PKE .... Parker, CA [*Location identifier FAA*] (FAAL)
PKE .... Parkes [*Australia Airport symbol*] (OAG)
PKE .... Public-Key Encryption [*Microcomputer technology*]
PKF .... Pakistan Investment Fd [*NYSE symbol*] (TTSB)
PKF .... Pakistan Investment Fund [*NYSE symbol*] (SPSG)
PKF .... Park Falls, WI [*Location identifier FAA*] (FAAL)
PKF .... Parkfield Array [*California*] [*Seismograph station code, US Geological Survey*] (SEIS)
PKF .... Phagocytosis and Killing Function [*Immunology*] (AAMN)
PKF .... Polarity Correlation Function (IAA)
PKF .... Primary Kidney Fold
PKFC .... Princess Kitty Fan Club (EA)
PKG .... Package [*Shipping*] (AFM)
PKG .... Package
pkg .... Package (WDMC)
Pkg .... Packing (DS)
PKG .... Parking (KSC)
PKG .... Phonocardiogram [*Cardiology*]
PKGD .... Packaged (IAA)
PKGE .... Package
pkge .... Package (WDMC)
Pkg instr ...... Packing Instruction (DS)
PKGNG .... Packaging
PKG-POL ...... Packaged POL [*Petroleum, Oils and Lubricants*] (DOMA)
PKH .... Park Hill [*California*] [*Seismograph station code, US Geological Survey*] (SEIS)
PKH .... Probability of a Kill Given a Hit [*Military*] (DNAB)
PKHOW .... Pack Howitzer [*Marine Corps*]
PKI .... Parkland Industries Ltd. [*Toronto Stock Exchange symbol*]
PKI .... Partai Katolik Indonesia [*Catholic Party of Indonesia*] [*Political party*]
PKI .... Partai Komunis Indonesia [*Communist Party of Indonesia*] [*Political party*]
PKI .... Partai Kristen Indonesia [*Christian Party of Indonesia*] [*Political party*]
PKI .... Potato Kallikrein Inhibitor [*Medicine*] (DMAA)
PKI .... Protein Kinase Inhibitor [*Biochemistry*]
PKI .... Pyruvate Kinase, Liver Type [*Medicine*] (DMAA)
PKK .... Kurdish Workers' Party [*Turkey Political party*] (PD)
PKK .... Pakokku [*Myanmar*] [*Airport symbol*] (OAG)
PKK .... Porkkala [*Finland*] [*Seismograph station code, US Geological Survey*] (SEIS)
PKK .... Protein Kinase K [*An enzyme*]
PKKP .... Pakistan National Scientific and Documentation Center, Karachi, Pakistan [*Library symbol Library of Congress*] (LCLS)
PKL .... Parklane Technologies, Inc. [*Vancouver Stock Exchange symbol*]
PKL .... Pi Kappa Lambda [*Society*]
PK-LT .... Psychokinesis on Living Targets
PKM .... Packmaster [*Army*] (WGA)
PKM .... Perigee Kick Motor (MCD)
PKMA .... Eniwetok [*Marshall Islands*] [*ICAO location identifier*] (ICLI)
PK-MB .... Psychokinetic Metal-Bending [*Parapsychology*]
PKMJ .... Majuro [*Marshall Islands*] [*ICAO location identifier*] (ICLI)
PKMKCMD ... Perhaps...Kids Meeting Kids Can Make a Difference (EA)
Pkmr .... Packmaster [*Army*]
PKMS .... Pertubohan Kebangsaan Melayu Singapura [*Singapore Malays' National Organization*] [*Political party*] (FEA)
PKN .... Aspen, CO [*Location identifier FAA*] (FAAL)
PKN .... Pangkalanbuun [*Indonesia*] [*Airport symbol*] (OAG)
PKN .... Parkinsonism [*Medicine*] (DMAA)
PKN .... Pauken [*Kettledrums*]
PKN .... Perkin-Elmer [*NYSE symbol*] (TTSB)
PKN .... Perkin-Elmer Corp. [*NYSE symbol*] (SPSG)
PKNG HSE .... Packing House [*Freight*]
PKO .... Parakou [*Benin*] [*Airport symbol*] (OAG)
PKO .... Peace-Keeping Operation (MCD)
PKO .... Perdant par Knockout [*Losing by a Knockout*] [*French*]
PKOH .... Park-Ohio Indus [*NASDAQ symbol*] (TTSB)
PKOH .... Park Ohio Industries [*NASDAQ symbol*] (SAG)
PKOH .... Park-Ohio Industries, Inc. [*NASDAQ symbol*] (NQ)
PKP .... Palestiner Komunistische Partei [*Palestine Communist Party*] [*Political party*] (BJA)
PKP .... Partido Komunista ng Pilipinas [*Communist Party of the Philippines*] [*Political party*] (PPW)
PKP .... Penetrating Keratoplasty [*Ophthalmology*]
PKP .... Perustuslaillinen Kansanpuolue [*Constitutional People's Party*] [*Finland Political party*] (PPE)
PKP .... Phi Kappa Phi [*Honor society*] (AEE)
PKP .... Polskie Koleje Panstwowe [*Polish State Railways*]
PKP .... Preknock Pulse
PKP .... Pukapuka [*French Polynesia*] [*Airport symbol*] (OAG)
PKP .... Purple-K-Powder
PKPA .... Parental Kidnapping Prevention Act (BARN)
PK/PK .... Peak-to-Peak (MCD)
PKpP .... Pennwalt Corp., King Of Prussia, PA [*Library symbol Library of Congress*] (LCLS)
PKPS .... [*The*] Poughkeepsie Savings Bank FSB [*Poughkeepsie, NY*] [*NASDAQ symbol*] (NQ)
PKPS .... Poughkeepsie Svgs Bank [*NASDAQ symbol*] (TTSB)
PKQ .... Dallas-Fort Worth, TX [*Location identifier FAA*] (FAAL)
PKR .... Packer (WGA)
PKR .... Packer
PKR .... Phased Knee Rehabilitation (DMAA)
PKR .... Picker
PKR .... P. K. Le Roux Dam [*South Africa*] [*Seismograph station code, US Geological Survey*] (SEIS)
PKR .... Pokhara [*Nepal*] [*Airport symbol*] (OAG)
PKR .... Polycystic Kidney Research Foundation (PAZ)
PKRDD .... Pravitel'stvennaya Komissiya po Raketam Dalnego Deistviya [*State Commission for the Study of the Problems of Long-Range Rockets*] [*Former USSR*]
PKs .... Bayard Taylor Memorial Library, Kennett Square, PA [*Library symbol Library of Congress*] (LCLS)
PKS .... Packs of Cigarettes Smoked
PKS .... Parti Kongres Sarawak [*Malaysia*] [*Political party*] (EY)
PKS .... Phi Kappa Sigma [*Fraternity*]
PKS .... Polyketide Synthase [*An enzyme*]
PKSEA .... Pack for Overseas
PKSh .... Partia Komuniste e Shqiperise [*Communist Party of Albania*] [*Later, PPSh*] [*Political party*] (PPE)
PKsL .... Longwood Gardens Library, Kennett Square, PA [*Library symbol Library of Congress*] (LCLS)
PKSS .... Probability of Kill Single Shot (MCD)
PKT .... Packet
PKT .... Phase Keying Technique
PKT .... Phi Kappa Tau [*Fraternity*]
PKT .... Pittsburgh Theological Seminary, Pittsburgh, PA [*OCLC symbol*] (OCLC)
PKT .... Pocket (MSA)
PKTN .... Pinkerton's, Inc. [*NASDAQ symbol*] (SAG)
PKU .... Pekanbaru [*Indonesia*] [*Airport symbol*] (OAG)
PKU .... Phenylketonuria [*Congenital metabolism disorder*] [*Medicine*]
PKU .... Pianoforte Keymakers' Union [*British*]
PKU-P .... PKU [*Phenylketonuria*] Parents (EA)
PKuS .... Kutztown State College, Kutztown, PA [*Library symbol Library of Congress*] (LCLS)
PKV .... Killed Poliomyelitis Vaccine [*Immunology*] (MAE)
PkV .... Peak Kilovolts
PKV .... Port Lavaka, TX [*Location identifier FAA*] (FAAL)
PKVL .... Pikeville National [*NASDAQ symbol*] (TTSB)
PKVL .... Pikeville National Corp. [*NASDAQ symbol*] (NQ)
PKW .... Kenosha, WI [*Location identifier FAA*] (FAAL)
PKW .... Personenkraftwagen [*Automobile*] [*German*]
PKW .... Selebi-Phikwe [*Botswana*] [*Airport symbol*] (OAG)
PKWA .... Kwajalein [*Marshall Islands*] [*ICAO location identifier*] (ICLI)
PKWAY .... Parkway (MSA)
PKWY .... Parkway (KSC)
PKWY .... Parkway
PKWY .... [*The*] Parkway Co. [*NASDAQ symbol*] (NQ)
PKWYS .... Parkways [*Commonly used*] (OPSA)
PKX .... Pohang Iron & Steel ADS [*NYSE symbol*] (TTSB)
PKX .... Pohang Iron & Steel Co., Ltd. [*NYSE symbol*] (SAG)
PKY .... Pak Lay [*Laos*] [*Airport symbol*] (AD)
PKY .... Palangkaraya [*Indonesia*] [*Airport symbol*] (OAG)
PKY .... Parkway (MCD)
PKY .... Parkway
Pky .... Parkway (DD)
PKY .... Pecky (WGA)
PKZ .... Pakse [*Laos*] [*Airport symbol*] (AD)
PKZ .... Pensacola, FL [*Location identifier FAA*] (FAAL)
PL .... Aero Peru [*ICAO designator*] (AD)
PL .... Front Line [*Revolutionary group*] [*Italy*]

PL .... Lancaster County Library, Lancaster, PA [*Library symbol Library of Congress*] (LCLS)
PL .... Packing List
PL .... Padlock (AAG)
PL .... Pail
PL .... Palm Leaf [*Reaction*] [*Medicine*]
PL .... Pamphlet Laws [*A publication*] (DLA)
PL .... Panel Left [*Nuclear energy*] (NRCH)
PL .... Paperleg [*A favored student*] [*Teen slang*]
PL .... Paper Life Ltd. [*British*]
PL .... Paper Loss (MHDW)
PL .... Parish Line R. R. [*AAR code*]
PL .... Partial Loss [*Insurance*]
PL .... Partido Liberal [*Liberal Party*] [*Paraguay*] [*Political party*] (PPW)
PL .... Partido Liberal [*Liberal Party*] [*Honduras*] [*Political party*]
PL .... Partido Liberal [*Liberal Party*] [*Colombia*] [*Political party*] (EY)
PL .... Partido Liberal [*Liberal Party*] [*Peru*] [*Political party*] (EY)
PL .... Partido Liberal [*Liberal Party*] [*Panama*] [*Political party*] (PPW)
PL .... Partido Liberal [*Liberal Party*] [*Portugal Political party*] (PPE)
PL .... Partido Liberal [*Liberal Party*] [*Spain Political party*] (PPE)
PL .... Partido Libertador [*Liberating Party*] [*Brazil Political party*]
PL .... Parti Liberal [*Liberal Party (1974-1979)*] [*Belgium Political party*] (PPE)
PL .... Parting Line [*Castings*] (AAG)
PL .... Parts List
PL .... Passenger Liability [*Insurance*] (BARN)
PL .... Patent Location (NITA)
PL .... Path Loss [*Communications*]
PL .... Patrol Land [*Aviation*]
PL .... Patrologiae Cursus. Series Latina [*A publication*] (OCD)
Pl .... Paul (BJA)
PL .... Paulist League (EA)
PL .... Payload [*NASA*] (KSC)
PL .... Paymaster-Lieutenant [*Navy British*]
PL .... Peak Loss (IAA)
PL .... Peanut Leafspot [*Plant pathology*]
PL .... Pectate Lyase [*An enzyme*]
Pl .... Pelagius [*Deceased, 1232*] [*Authority cited in pre-1607 legal work*] (DSA)
PL .... Pelusium Line [*Nile delta*] [*Geology*]
pl .... Pencil (VRA)
PL .... People for Life (EA)
PL .... People's Lobby (EA)
PL .... Perceived Level [*Noise*]
PL .... Perception of Light
PL .... Peroneus Longus [*Muscle*] [*Orthopedics*] (DAVI)
P/L .... Personal Lines
PL .... Personnel Laboratory [*Air Research and Development Command*] [*Air Force*] (AAG)
PL .... Petty Larceny
PL .... Phase Line
PL .... Philosophical Library [*A publication*]
PL .... Phone Line
PL .... Phospholipid [*Biochemistry*]
PL .... Photoconductor Lamp (IAA)
PL .... Photolettering (DGA)
PL .... Photolocator (MCD)
PL .... Photoluminescence
pl .... Piazza (VRA)
pl .... Picoliter [*One trillionth of a liter*] (MAE)
PL .... Pilatus Flugzeugwerke AG [*Switzerland ICAO aircraft manufacturer identifier*] (ICAO)
PL .... Pile
PL .... Pipeline
PL .... Pipe Lines Act [*Town planning*] [*British*]
PL .... Piping Load [*Nuclear energy*] (NRCH)
PL .... Pitch Line (MSA)
PL .... Place [*Investment term*]
PL .... Place
Pl .... Place (DD)
PL .... Place
pl .... Place (ODBW)
pl .... Place (VRA)
PL .... Placebo [*Medicine*]
PL .... Placental Lactogen [*Endocrinology*]
Pl .... Plagioclase [*Lunar geology*]
PL .... Plain (MSA)
PL .... Plain Language [*As opposed to coded message*] [*Military*]
PL .... Plans
PL .... Plantagenet [*Genealogy*] (ROG)
PL .... Plantar [*Related to the sole of the foot*] (DAVI)
pl .... Plasma
Pl .... Plasmodium [*The malarial parasite*] [*Infectious diseases*] (DAVI)
PL .... Plaster (WGA)
PL .... Plastic Laboratory [*Princeton University*] (MCD)
PL .... Plastic Limit (IEEE)
PL .... Plastic Surgery [*Medicine*]
pl .... Plastid [*Botany*]
PL .... Plate (KSC)
PL .... Plateau Length
PL .... Plated (IAA)
pl .... Platelet [*Hematology*] (MAE)
PL .... Platelet Lactogen [*Hematology*] (DMAA)
PL .... Platinum [*Chemistry*] (ROG)
Pl .... Plato [*Fourth century BC*] [*Classical studies*] (OCD)
PL .... Platoon (NATG)
PL .... Platoon Leader [*Military*] (INF)
Pl .... Platz [*Square*] [*German*] (EY)
pl .... Platz (VRA)
PL .... Players League [*Major league in baseball, 1890*]
pl .... Plaza (VRA)
PL .... PLC Capital LLC, Inc. [*NYSE symbol*] (SAG)
PL .... Pleadings [*Legal shorthand*] (LWAP)
PL .... Pleasure (ROG)
PL .... [*The*] Plessey Co. Ltd. (MCD)
pl .... Pleural [*Medicine*] (MAE)
PL .... Plimsoll Line [*Shipping*] (DAS)
Pl .... Ploshchad [*Square*] [*Russian*] (EY)
Pl .... Plowden's English King's Bench Commentaries [*or Reports*] [*1550-80*] [*A publication*] (DLA)
PL .... Plug (AAG)
PL .... Plume [*Numismatics*]
PL .... Plural
pl .... Plural (ODBW)
PL .... Plymouth [*Postcode*] (ODBW)
PL .... Poet Laureate
PL .... Poetry London [*A publication British*]
Pl .... Poiseuille [*Unit of dynamic viscosity*]
pl .... Poland [*MARC country of publication code Library of Congress*] (LCCP)
PL .... Poland [*ANSI two-letter standard code*] (CNC)
PL .... Polarized Light
PL .... Policy Loan
PL .... Poly-L-lysine [*Also, PLL*] [*Biochemical analysis*]
PL .... Poor Law [*A publication*] (DLA)
PL .... Portable Low-Power [*Reactor*] (NRCH)
PL .... Port Line [*Steamship*] (MHDW)
PL .... Position Line [*Navigation*]
PL .... Position Location [*DoD*]
PL .... Post Landing [*NASA*] (KSC)
PL .... Post Laundry [*Army*]
PL .... Power Line (IAA)
PL .... Power Loading (IAA)
PL .... Power Locks (BARN)
PL .... Prayers for Life (EA)
PL .... Prelaunch (NASA)
PL .... Preliminary Leaf [*Bibliography*]
P/L .... Presentation Label [*Publishing*]
PL .... Presley Labs [*Vancouver Stock Exchange symbol*]
PL .... Pressurizer Level (IEEE)
PL .... Price Level [*Economics*]
PL .... Price List
PL .... Primary Leading [*Photography*] (DGA)
PL .... Primrose League [*British*] (DI)
PL .... Prince Line [*Steamship*] (MHDW)
PL .... Princess Louise's Sutherland and Argyll Highlanders [*Military British*] (ROG)
PL .... Private Label [*Business term*]
PL .... Private Line
PL .... Procedural Language (PCM)
PL .... Procedure Library [*Computer science*]
PL .... Production Language
PL .... Production List (AAG)
PL .... Product Liability [*Insurance*]
PL .... Product License
P/L .... Profit and Loss [*Accounting*]
PL .... Program Level (IAA)
PL .... Program Library [*Computer science*]
PL .... Program Logic [*Computer science*] (TEL)
PL .... Programming Language [*Computer science*]
PL .... Progressive Labor [*A faction of Students for a Democratic Society*]
PL .... Projection Lens [*Microscopy*]
PL .... Project Leader
PL .... Project Lighthawk [*Later, LH*] (EA)
PL .... Project Local [*Defunct*] (EA)
PL .... Prolymphocytic Leukemia [*Also, PLL*] [*Oncology*]
PL .... Promotion List (DICI)
PL .... Propagation Loss
PL .... Propellant Loading [*NASA*] (KSC)
PL .... Property Line [*Real estate*] (MSA)
PL .... Proportional Limit
P/L .... Proprietary Limited (ADA)
PL .... Propulsion Laboratory [*Army*] (GRD)
PL .... Prospective Loss
PL .... Protected Location [*Shipping*] (DS)
PL .... Protective Life Corp. [*NYSE symbol*] (SPSG)
PL .... Protectively Located [*Plant layout*]
PL .... Provisioning List (MCD)
PL .... Pseudolumina [*Anatomy*]
PL .... Psychological Laboratory (MCD)
PL .... Public Law [*An act of Congress*]
PL .... Public Liability [*Business term*]
PL .... Public Library
Pl .... Pulmonary Venous Pressure [*Medicine*] (MAE)
PL .... Pulpolingual [*Dentistry*]
PL .... Pulsatility Index [*Medicine*]
PL .... Pulse Length (NVT)
P/L .... Purchased Labor (NASA)
PL .... Pyridoxal [*Also, Pxl*] [*Biochemistry*]
PL .... Radio Positioning Land Station [*ITU designation*] (CET)

P_L .... Transpulmonary Pressure [*Cardiology*] (DAVI)
PL/1 .... Programming Language, Version One [*Computer science*] (MCD)
PLA .... Pakistan Liberation Army (PD)
PLA .... Palau [*Palau Islands*] [*Seismograph station code, US Geological Survey Closed*] (SEIS)
PLA .... Palestine Liberation Army
PLA .... Parachute Location Aid (MCD)
PLA .... Para Legal Association [*British*] (DBA)
PLA .... Parlamento Latinoamericano [*Latin American Parliament - LAP*] [*Bogota, Colombia*] (EAIO)
PLA .... Parlar Resources Ltd. [*Vancouver Stock Exchange symbol*]
PLA .... Partido Laborista Agrario [*Panama*] [*Political party*] (EY)
PLA .... Partido Liberal Autentico [*Panama*] [*Political party*] (EY)
PLA .... Party of Labor of Albania [*Political party*] (PPW)
PLA .... Passengers' Luggage in Advance [*Railway*] (ROG)
PLA .... Patriotic Liberation Army [*Myanmar*] (PD)
PLA .... Pedestrian League of America [*Later, APA*] (EA)
Pla .... Pelagius [*Deceased, 1232*] [*Authority cited in pre-1607 legal work*] (DSA)
PLA .... Pennilane Development [*Vancouver Stock Exchange symbol*]
PLA .... People's Liberation Army [*National Liberation Front*] [*North Vietnam*] (VNW)
PLA .... People's Liberation Army [*India*] (PD)
PLA .... People's Liberation Army [*China*]
PLA .... Pet Lovers Association (EA)
PLA .... Phase Locked Arrays [*Physics*]
PLA .... Philatelic Literature Association [*Later, APRL*] (EA)
PLA .... Phospholipase A [*An enzyme*] (DAVI)
PLA .... Physiological Learning Aptitude (KSC)
PLA .... Pitch Lock Actuator (MCD)
PLA .... Place (ADA)
PLA .... Placebo [*Medicine*]
Pla .... Placentinus [*Deceased, 1192*] [*Authority cited in pre-1607 legal work*] (DSA)
PLA .... Placita
PLA .... Placitum [*or Placita*] [*Agreeable, Agreed Upon*] [*Latin*] [*Legal term*] (DLA)
PLA .... Plain Language Address [*Telecommunications*] (TEL)
PLA .... Planned Labor Application [*Military*] (AFIT)
PLA .... Planned Landing Area [*NASA*]
PLA .... Plan of Launch Azimuth [*Aerospace*] (AAG)
pla .... Plaster (VRA)
PLA .... Playboy Enterprises Cl'B' [*NYSE symbol*] (TTSB)
PLA .... Playboy Enterprises, Inc. [*NYSE symbol*] (SPSG)
PLA .... Plaza (ADA)
PLA .... Poetry League of America (EA)
PLA .... Polylactic Acid [*Organic chemistry*] (RDA)
PLA .... Poly-L-arginine [*Biochemistry*]
PLA .... Polynesian Air-Ways [*ICAO designator*] (FAAC)
PLA .... Popular Library of Art [*A publication*]
PLA .... Port of London Authority [*British*]
PLA .... Posterior Left Atrial Wall [*Cardiology*] (DAVI)
PLA .... Potential Leaf Area [*Botany*]
PLA .... Potentially Lethal Arrhythmia [*Medicine*] (DMAA)
PLA .... Power Lever Angle
PLA .... Practice Landing Approach [*Aviation*]
PLA .... Price-Level-Adjusted Accounting (ADA)
PLA .... Print Load Analyzer
PLA .... Private Libraries Association [*British*]
PLA .... Product License Application [*FDA*]
PLA .... Professional Legal Assistants (EA)
PLA .... Program-Length Advertising [*Broadcasting*] (WDMC)
PLA .... Programmable Line Adapter
PLA .... Programmable Logic Array [*Computer science*]
PLA .... Programmed Logic Array (NITA)
PLA .... Project Labor Agreement (AAGC)
PLA .... Proton Linear Accelerator
PLA .... Psycholinguistic Age [*Education*]
PLA .... Psychological Learning Aptitude (MCD)
PLA .... Public Library Association (EA)
PLa .... Pulpolabial [*Dentistry*]
PLA .... Pulpolingouaxial [*Dentistry*]
PLA .... Pulsed LASER Annealing [*Semiconductor technology*]
PLA .... Pulverized Limestone Association (EA)
PLA .... University of Pittsburgh, Law School, Pittsburgh, PA [*OCLC symbol*] (OCLC)
PLA_2 .... Phospholipase A_2 [*An enzyme*]
PLAA .... Playboy Enterprises'A'(vtg) [*NYSE symbol*] (TTSB)
PLAA .... Positive Low Angle of Attack
PLA AEPS .... PLA [*Public Library Association*] Alternative Education Programs Section
PLAAF .... People's Liberation Army Air Force
PLA AFLS .... PLA [*Public Library Association*] Armed Forces Library Section
PLAAR .... Packaged Liquid Air-Augmented Rocket (MCD)
PLAAS .... Plasma Atomic Absorption System [*Spectrometry*]
PLA AV .... PLA [*Public Library Association*] Audiovisual
PLA AVC ...... PLA [*Public Library Association*] Audiovisual Committee
PLAB .... Party-Line Adapter Board [*Telecommunications*] (MHDI)
PLAB .... Photronics, Inc. [*NASDAQ symbol*] (NQ)
PLAB .... Professional and Linguistic Assessment Board (AIE)
PLAC .... Placebo [*Medicine*]
Plac .... Placentinus [*Deceased, 1192*] [*Authority cited in pre-1607 legal work*] (DSA)
PLAC .... Post-Launch Analysis of Compliance [*NASA*]
Plac Abbrev ... Placitorum Abbreviatio [*Latin A publication*] (DLA)
Plac Ang Nor ... Bigelow's Placita Anglo-Normanica [*A publication*] (DLA)
PLACE .... Place [*Commonly used*] (OPSA)
PLACE .... Positioner Layout and Cell Evaluator [*Robotics*]
PLACE .... Position Location and Aircraft Communication Equipment
PLACE .... Position Location and Communications Experiment [*NASA*]
PLACE .... Post-LANDSAT Advanced Concept Evaluation (MCD)
PLACE .... Programa Latinoamericano de Cooperacion Energetica [*Latin American Energy Cooperation Program*] (EAIO)
PLACE .... Programming Language for Automatic Checkout Equipment
PlacerD .... Placer Dome, Inc. [*Associated Press*] (SAG)
Plac Gen .... Placita Generalia [*Latin A publication*] (DLA)
PLACID .... Payload Aboard, Caution in Descent [*NASA*]
PLA CIS .... PLA [*Public Library Association*] Community Information Section
PLACO .... Planning Committee [*International Organization for Standardization*] (IEEE)
PLAD .... Parachute Low-Altitude Delivery [*Air Force*]
PLAD .... Plain Language Address Directory
PLAD .... Price-Level-Adjusted Deposit
PLAD .... Public Lands Appreciation Day [*A joint effort of Times Mirror Magazines and the Bureau of Land Management*] (PS)
PLAD .... Public Lands Appreciation Day
PLADS .... Parachute Low-Altitude Delivery System [*Military*]
PLADS .... Pulsed LASER Airborne Depth Sounding System [*Naval Oceanographic Office*]
PLAF .... People's Liberation Armed Forces [*National Liberation Front*] [*North Vietnam*] (VNW)
PLAFB .... Plattsburgh Air Force Base [*New York*] (AAG)
PLAFSEP ...... Processing Libraries - Anecdotes, Facetia, Satire, Etc., Periodicals [*A publication*]
Plag .... Plagioclase [*Lunar geology*]
PLAGM .... Placid, Louisiana Land and Exploration, Amerada Hess, Getty, and Marathon [*Oil-and gas-holding bloc in Alaska*]
PLAI .... Preschool Language Assessment Instrument [*Child development test*]
PLAIC .... Purdue Laboratory for Applied Industrial Control [*Purdue University*] [*Research center*] (RCD)
PLAID .... Professional Library Access and Information Delivery [*Information service or system*] (IID)
PLAID .... Programmed Learning Aid
PLAIN .... Plain [*Commonly used*] (OPSA)
PLAINES .... Plains [*Commonly used*] (OPSA)
PLAINS .... Plains [*Commonly used*] (OPSA)
Plaintr .... Plaintree Systems, Inc. [*Associated Press*] (SAG)
PLAL .... Pro-Life Action League (EA)
PLA LC .... PLA [*Public Library Association*] Legislative Committee
PLAM .... Plastic Laminate [*Technical drawings*]
PLAM .... Practice Limpet Assembly Modular [*Navy*] (CAAL)
PLAM .... Price-Level-Adjusted Mortgage
PLAME .... Propulsive Left Landing with Aerodynamic Maneuvering Entry (PDAA)
PLAMED .... Plantas Medicinales [*Ministerio de Sanidad y Consumo*] [*Spain Information service or system*] (CRD)
PLA MLS .... PLA [*Public Library Association*] Metropolitan Libraries Section
PLA MPLSS ... PLA [*Public Library Association*] Marketing of Public Library Services Section
PLAN .... Open Plan Systems [*NASDAQ symbol*] (TTSB)
PLAN .... Open Plan Systems, Inc. [*NASDAQ symbol*] (SAG)
PLAN .... Parts Logistics Analysis Network
PLAN .... Payload Local Area Network [*NASA*] (SSD)
PLAN .... People's Liberation Army Navy
PLAN .... People's Liberation Army of Namibia [*Political party*] (PPW)
PLAN .... Personal LAN (NITA)
PLAN .... Personal Local Area Network [*Telecommunications*] (OSI)
PLAN .... Planned Lifetime Advocacy Network
Plan .... Planning (DLA)
PLAN .... Planning
PLAN .... Positive Locator Aid to Navigation
PLAN .... Problem Language Analyzer [*Computer science*]
PLAN .... Professional Local Area Network (NITA)
PLAN .... Program for Learning in Accordance with Needs [*Westinghouse Learning Corp.*]
PLAN .... Program Language Analyzer [*Computer science*] (IEEE)
PLAN .... Programming Language Nineteen-Hundred [*Computer science*]
PLAN .... Protect Life in All Nations (EA)
PLAN .... Public Libraries Automation Network [*California State Library*] [*Sacramento, CA*]
Plan & Comp ... Planning and Compensation Reports [*British A publication*] (DLA)
PlanarSy .... Planar Systems [*Commercial firm Associated Press*] (SAG)
PLANAT .... North Atlantic Treaty Regional Planning Group
Planc .... Pro Plancio [*of Cicero*] [*Classical studies*] (OCD)
PLANCODE ... Planning, Control, and Decision Evaluation System [*IBM Corp.*]
PLand .... Professional Landman [*Canada*] (DD)
PL & PD .... Public Liability and Property Damage [*Insurance*]
Pl & Pr Cas ... Pleading and Practice Cases [*1837-38*] [*England*] [*A publication*] (DLA)
PL & R .... Postal Laws and Regulations [*Later, Postal Manual*]
PLANES .... Programmed Language-Based Enquiry System
PLANES .... Programmed Language Enquiry System (NITA)
PLANET .... Planned Logistics Analysis and Evaluation Technique [*Air Force*]
PLANET .... Planning Evaluation Technique (MCD)
PLANET .... Private Local Area Network [*Racal LAN Systems, Inc.*] [*Boca Raton, FL*] (TSSD)
PLANET .... Probing Lensing Anomalies Network [*Astronomy*]
PLANEX .... [*The*] Planning Exchange Database [*Pergamon InfoLine*] [*Database*] [*Information service or system*] (IID)
PLANEX .... Planning Exercise [*Military*] (NVT)

Pl Ang-Norm... Placita Anglo-Normannica Cases (Bigelow) [*A publication*] (DLA)
Plan Higher Ed... Planning for Higher Education [*A publication*]
PlanHlly....... Planet Hollywood International, Inc. [*Associated Press*] (SAG)
PLANIT........ Programming Language for Interaction and Teaching [*1966*] [*Computer science*]
PLANMAN.... Planned Maintenance [*Contract Data Research*] [*Software package*] (NCC)
PLANN......... Plant Location Assistance Nationwide Network
PLANNET..... Planning Network
PLANS......... Position Location and Navigation System
PLANS......... Program Logistics and Network Scheduling System (IEEE)
PLANS......... Programming Language for Allocation and Network Scheduling [*1975*] [*Computer science*] (CSR)
PlanSci....... Planning Sciences International [*Associated Press*] (SAG)
Plant........... De Plantatione [*Philo*] (BJA)
PLANT......... Program for Linguistic Analysis of Natural Plants (IEEE)
PLANT......... Programming Language for Interactive Teaching [*Computer science*] (IAA)
PLANTFACTS... Steel Plants Information System [*German Iron and Steel Engineers Association*] [*Dusseldorf*] [*Information service or system*] (IID)
plant-flex..... Plantar Flexion [*Medicine*] (BABM)
plant-flex..... Plantar Flexion [*Orthopedics*] (DAVI)
Plantron....... Plantronics, Inc. [*Associated Press*] (SAG)
PLANY......... Protestant Lawyers Association of New York (EA)
PLAO........... Parts List Assembly Order (MCD)
PLAP........... Placental Alkaline Phosphatase [*An enzyme*]
PLAP........... Power Lever Angle Position (MCD)
PLAP........... Prelaunch, Launch, and Ascent Procedures [*NASA*] (IAA)
Pla Par........ Placita Parliamentaria [*Latin A publication*] (DLA)
PLapK.......... Keystone Junior College, La Plume, PA [*Library symbol Library of Congress*] (LCLS)
PLA PLSS.... PLA [*Public Library Association*] Public Library Systems Section
PLAR........... Postal Laws and Regulations (IAA)
PLARA......... Packaged Liquid Air-Augmented (IAA)
PLARS......... Position Location and Reporting System [*Military*] (INF)
PLAS........... Plaster (AAG)
PLAS........... Plastic
plas............ Plastic (VRA)
PLas........... Premier Laser Systems, Inc. [*Associated Press*] (SAG)
PLAS........... Private Line Assured Service [*Telecommunications*] (TEL)
PLAS........... Program Logical Address Space
PLAS........... Programmable Link Adaptation System (MCD)
PLASCAMS... Plastics: Computer Aided Materials Selector [*Rapra Technology Ltd.*] [*Information service or system*] (CRD)
PLASI.......... Pulsating Visual Approach Slope Indicator [*Aviation*] (FAAC)
PLASI.......... Pulse Light Approach Slope Indicator (PDAA)
PLASMA...... Parents League of American Students of Medicine Abroad [*Defunct*] (EA)
PLASMA...... Plant Services Maintenance (PDAA)
Plasma........ Plasma & Materials Technologies, Inc. [*Associated Press*] (SAG)
PLASMEX.... International Plastics Exhibition
PLA SMLS... PLA [*Public Library Association*] Small and Medium-Sized Libraries Section
PLAST......... Propellant Loading and All Systems Test [*NASA*] (KSC)
PLASTEC...... Plastics Technical Evaluation Center [*Dover, NJ*] [*Army*]
PLASTEUROTEC... Groupement Europeen des Fabricants de Pieces Techniques Plastiques [*European Group of Fabricators of Technical Plastics Parts*] (EAIO)
PlasThrm...... Plasma-Therm, Inc. [*Associated Press*] (SAG)
PlastLn........ Plasti-Line, Inc. [*Associated Press*] (SAG)
PLAT........... Pilot-LOS [*Line of Sight*] Landing Aid Television (NG)
plat............ Plate (VRA)
PLAT........... Plateau [*Board on Geographic Names*]
PLAT........... Platelet [*Hematology*]
PLAT........... Platform (KSC)
PLAT........... Platinum [*Chemical symbol is Pt*] (AAG)
PLAT........... Platinum Technology [*NASDAQ symbol*] (SPSG)
PLAT........... Platonic
PLAT........... Platoon
PLAT........... Platt National Park
PLATF......... Platform (AAG)
PLATL......... Platelets [*Hematology*] (DAVI)
PLATLDR..... Platoon Leader [*Military*]
PLATN......... Platinum [*Chemistry*] (ROG)
platn........... Platinum [*Metal*] (VRA)
PLATO......... Pennzoil Louisiana and Texas Offshore [*Oil industry group*]
PLATO......... Platform Observables Subassembly
PLATO......... Pollution Liability Agreement Among Tanker Owners [*Insurance*] (DS)
PLATO......... Programmed Logic for Automated Learning Operation [*Computer science*] (IAA)
PLATO......... Programmed Logic for Automatic Teaching [*or Training*] Operations [*University of Illinois*] [*Programming language*]
PLATR......... Pawling Lattice Test Rig [*United Nuclear Co.*]
PLATS......... Pilot Landing and Takeoff System (IIA)
PLATS......... Precision Location and Tracking System (PDAA)
PLatS.......... Saint Vincent College, Latrobe, PA [*Library symbol Library of Congress*] (LCLS)
PlatSoft....... Platinum Software Corp. [*Associated Press*] (SAG)
PLATT......... Page Level Availability Time Test [*Computer science*]
Platt........... Platt on Leases [*A publication*] (DLA)
Platt........... Platt on the Law of Covenants [*1829*] [*A publication*] (DLA)
PlatTc......... Platinum Technology, Inc. [*Associated Press*] (SAG)
Platt Cov..... Platt on the Law of Covenants [*A publication*] (DLA)
Platt Leas.... Platt on Leases [*1847*] [*A publication*] (DLA)
PLAT/VLA.... Pilot Landing Aid Television / Visual Landing Aid [*System*] (DNAB)
Plaut........... Plautus [*Third century BC*] [*Classical studies*] (OCD)
PLAV........... Polish Legion of American Veterans (NADA)
PLAV........... Polish Legion of American Veterans, USA (EA)
PLAVA......... Polish Legion of American Veterans, USA , Ladies Auxiliary (EA)
PLAVLA....... Polish Legion of American Veterans, USA, Ladies Auxiliary (EA)
PLAWM Trough... Pockels Langmuir Adam Wilson McBain Trough [*Surface film balance*]
Plaxton........ Plaxton's Canadian Constitutional Decisions [*A publication*] (DLA)
PLAY........... Players International [*NASDAQ symbol*] (TTSB)
PLAY........... Players International, Inc. [*NASDAQ symbol*] (NQ)
PLAY........... Providing Lifetime Activity for Youth
Playby......... Playboy Enterprises, Inc. [*Associated Press*] (SAG)
PlayBy......... Play By Play Toys & Novelties, Inc. [*Associated Press*] (SAG)
PlaybyA....... Playboys Enterprises [*Associated Press*] (SAG)
PlaybyB....... Playboys Enterprises [*Associated Press*] (SAG)
PlayCo......... Play Co. Toys [*Associated Press*] (SAG)
PlayCo......... Play Co. Toys & Entertainment Corp. [*Associated Press*] (SAG)
Play Co........ Play Co. Toys & Entertainment Corp. [*Associated Press*] (SAG)
Players........ Players International Corp. [*Associated Press*] (SAG)
PlaytxPd...... Playtex Products, Inc. [*Associated Press*] (SAG)
PLAZA.......... Plaza [*Commonly used*] (OPSA)
PLB............. Payload Bay [*NASA*] (MCD)
PLB............. Per Pound [*Freight*]
PLB............. Personal Locator Beacon [*Military*] (AFM)
PLB............. Phopholipase B [*An enzyme*] (DAVI)
PLB............. Phospholamban [*Biochemistry*]
PLB............. Picture Level Benchmark [*Computer science*] (CDE)
PLB............. Plattsburgh [*New York*] [*Airport symbol*] (OAG)
PLB............. Plattsburgh, NY [*Location identifier FAA*] (FAAL)
PLB............. Plumbing Mart [*Vancouver Stock Exchange symbol*]
PLB............. Poor Law Board
PLB............. Prior-Lien Bond [*Business*] (MHDB)
PLB............. Proctolin-Like Bioactivity [*Neurobiology*]
PLB............. Public Light Bus [*British*]
PLB............. Publisher's Library Binding
PLB............. Pullbutton (AAG)
PLBB........... Patent Licensing Bulletin Board [*U.S. Department of Commerce*] (BARN)
PLBD........... Payload Bay Door [*NASA*] (MCD)
PLBD........... Plugboard (MSA)
PLBG........... Plumbing (WGA)
PLBG........... Plumbing
PLBK........... Playback (NASA)
PL-BL.......... Plate Block [*Philately*]
PLBLK......... Pillow Block
PLBOL......... Position Launch/Bearing Only Launch
PLBR........... Plumber (WGA)
PLBR........... Prototype Large Breeder Reactor [*Also, NCBR*] [*Nuclear energy*]
PLC............. Pacific Logging Congress (EA)
PLC............. Palomares Road [*California*] [*Seismograph station code, US Geological Survey*] (SEIS)
PLC............. Parti de la Liberte du Citoyen [*Belgium Political party*] (EY)
PLC............. Partido Liberal Constitucionalista [*Constitutionalist Liberal Party*] [*Nicaragua*] [*Political party*] (PPW)
PLC............. Patrice Lumumba Coalition (EA)
PLC............. Paymaster-Lieutenant-Commander [*Navy British*]
PLC............. Periventricular Leukomalacia Complex [*Medicine*]
PLC............. Perry-Link Cubmarine [*A submersible vehicle*]
PLC............. Phospholipase C [*An enzyme*]
PLC............. Phospholysine C [*Biochemistry*]
PLC............. Pilot Laboratories Corp. [*Vancouver Stock Exchange symbol*]
PLC............. Placer Development Ltd. [*AMEX symbol*] (SPSG)
Pl C............. Placita Coronae [*Pleas of the Crown*] [*Latin Legal term*] (DLA)
PLC............. Planar Chromatography
PLC............. Planeta Rica [*Colombia*] [*Airport symbol*] (AD)
PLC............. Platform Control
PLC............. Platoon Leader's Class [*Army*]
PLC............. PLC Capital LLC, Inc. [*Associated Press*] (SAG)
PLC............. PLC Systems [*AMEX symbol*] (SPSG)
PLC............. Pneumatic Lead Cutter
PLC............. Poet Laureatus Caesareus [*Imperial Poet Laureate*] [*Latin*] (ROG)
PLC............. Point Loma College [*California*]
PLC............. Police
PLC............. Police Aviation Services [*British ICAO designator*] (FAAC)
PLC............. Poor Law Commissioners [*British*]
PLC............. Power Lever Control (MCD)
PLC............. Power Line Carrier
PLC............. Power Line Communications
PLC............. Power Loading Control (IAA)
PLC............. Predictive Linguistic Constraint
PLC............. Preparative Layer Chromatography
PLC............. Presbyterian Lay Committee (EA)
PLC............. Primary Leadership Course [*Army*]
PLC............. Primary Location Code [*Computer science*]
PLC............. Prime Level Code
PLC............. Private Line Carrier [*Telecommunications*] (IAA)
PLC............. Process Liquid Chromatography
PLC............. Production Line Configured [*Military*] (CAAL)
PLC............. Product Life Cycle (ODBW)
PLC............. Products List Circular [*Patents*]
PLC............. Program-Length Commercial [*Television*]
PLC............. Program Level Change Tape [*Computer science*] (IBMDP)
PLC............. Programmable Line Controller (NITA)
PLC............. Programmable Logic Control [*Computer science*]

PLC Programmable Logic Controller
PLC Programming Language Committee [*CODASYL*]
PLC Proinsulin-Like Compound [*Endocrinology*]
PLC Provisional Legislative Council [*Hong Kong*]
PLC Pseudolymphocytic Choriomeningitis [*Medicine*] (DMAA)
PLC Pseudophase Liquid Chromatography
PLC Public Lands Council (EA)
PLC Public Liability Company (DFIT)
PLC Public Lighting Commission
PLC Public Limited Co. [*British*]
PLCA Parallel Line Communication Adaptor (NITA)
PLCA Pipe Line Contractors Association (EA)
PLCAA Professional Lawn Care Association of America (EA)
PLCAI Pipe Line Contractors Association, International (EA)
PLCB Planetary Liquid-Cooled Brake [*Off-highway equipment*]
PLCB Pseudoline Control Block [*Computer science*]
PLCC Paulson Cap [*NASDAQ symbol*] (TTSB)
PLCC Paulson Capital Corp. [*NASDAQ symbol*] (SAG)
PLCC Plastic Chip Carrier (NITA)
PLCC Plastic Leaded Chip Carrier [*Computer science*]
PLCC Plastic Leadless Chip Carrier [*Computer technology*] (PCM)
PLCC Power Line Carrier Communication (PDAA)
PLCC Primary Liver Cell Cancer [*Oncology*]
PLCC Propulsion Local Control Console (DNAB)
PLCCE Preliminary Life-Cycle Cost Estimate
PLCCE Program Life-Cycle Cost Estimate [*Army*]
PLCD Product Liability Common Defense [*Later, PLPD*] [*An association*] (EA)
PLCDR Private Line Carrier Divided Ringing [*Telecommunications*] (IAA)
PLCEA Part-Length Control Element Assembly [*Nuclear energy*] (NRCH)
PLCEDM Part-Length Control Element Drive Mechanism [*Nuclear energy*] (NRCH)
PLCH Kiritimati Island [*Christmas Islands*] [*Kiribati*] [*ICAO location identifier*] (ICLI)
PLCL Phase-Locked Control Loop [*NASA*] (IAA)
PLCL Polyclonal Gammopathy Identified [*Immunology*] (DAVI)
PLCLAS Propagation Loss Classification System [*Navy*] (NVT)
PL-CLP Plantelet Clumps [*Hematology*] (DAVI)
PLCM Polycom Inc. [*NASDAQ symbol*] (TTSB)
PLCM Polycom, Inc. [*NASDAQ symbol*] (SAG)
PLCM Propellant Loading Control Monitor [*NASA*] (KSC)
PLCMC Public Library of Charlotte and Mecklenburg County [*North Carolina*]
PLCN Parts List Change Notice (MCD)
PLCO Play Company Toys [*NASDAQ symbol*] (SAG)
PLCO Play Co. Toys & Entertainment Corp. [*NASDAQ symbol*] (SAG)
PLCO Play Co. Toys & Entmt [*NASDAQ symbol*] (TTSB)
PLCO Postoperative Low Cardiac Output [*Medicine*] (DMAA)
Pl Com Plowden's English King's Bench Commentaries [*or Reports*] [*1550-80 England*] [*A publication*] (DLA)
PL Com Poor Law Commissioner [*A publication*] (DLA)
PLCOP Prelaunch Checkout Plan [*NASA*] (KSC)
PLCOW Play Co. Toys & Entmt Wrrt [*NASDAQ symbol*] (TTSB)
PLCP Photochromic Liquid Crystal Polymer [*Organic chemistry*]
Pl Cr Con Tr Plowden's Criminal Conversation Trials [*A publication*] (DLA)
PlcrD Placer Dome [*Associated Press*] (SAG)
PLCS Propellant Loading Control System [*NASA*] (AAG)
PLC Sys PLC Systems [*Associated Press*] (SAG)
PLCU Propellant Level Control Unit [*NASA*] (KSC)
PLCU Propellant-Loading Control Unit [*NASA*] (IAA)
PLCURR Plate Current [*Electronics*] (IAA)
PLCV Pelargonium Leaf Curl Virus [*Plant pathology*]
PLCWTWU Power Loom Carpet Weavers' and Textile Workers' Union [*British*]
PLCY Policy (AFM)
PLCY Policy
PlcyMg Policy Management Systems [*Associated Press*] (SAG)
PLD All Pakistan Legal Decisions [*A publication*] (ILCA)
PLD Paid Land Diversion Program [*Department of Agriculture*] (GFGA)
PLD Partial Line Down (NITA)
PLD Partial Lipodystrophy [*Medicine*]
PLD Partido de la Liberacion Dominicana [*Dominican Liberation Party*] [*Dominican Republic*] [*Political party*] (PPW)
PLD Parti Liberal-Democrate [*Cameroon*] [*Political party*] (EY)
PLd Path Loss, Downlink [*Communications*]
PLD Payload [*NASA*]
PLD Peripheral Light Detection (DMAA)
PLD Permanently Lubricated Drivetrain
PLD Personnel Letdown Device
PLD Phase Lock Demodulator
PLD Phase-Locked Detector (IAA)
PLD Phase-Locked Discriminator (IAA)
PLD Phospholipase D [*An enzyme*]
PLD Physical Logical Description (MHDI)
PLD Plaid (ADA)
PLD Plated (MSA)
PLD Platelet Defect [*Hematology*] (MAE)
PLD Played Matches [*Cricket*] (ROG)
PLD Policy Liaison Division (AAGC)
PLD Polycystic Liver Disease [*Medicine*] (DMAA)
PLD Portland, IN [*Location identifier FAA*] (FAAL)
PLD Posterior Latissimus Dorsi [*Anatomy*]
PLD Posterolateral Dendrite [*Neurology*]
PLD Potentially Lethal Damage [*Medicine*]
PLD Precision LASER Designator (RDA)
PLD Pregnancy, Labor and Delivery (DAVI)
PLD Primary Layer Depth [*Military*] (CAAL)
PLD Principle of Limit Design
PLD Probable Line of Deployment [*Army*] (AABC)
PLD Procurement Legal Division [*Later, Office of General Counsel*] [*Navy*]
PLD Product Line Development
PLD Program Listing Document (MCD)
PLD Programmable Logic Device
PLD Protective LASER Devices (MCD)
PLD Pulsed Laser Deposition [*Coating technology*]
PLD Pulsed LASER Deposition [*Coating technology*]
PLD Pulse-Length Discriminator (IEEE)
PLD Pulse Level Detector (MCD)
PLdaC Calvary Baptist School of Theology, Lansdale, PA [*Library symbol Library of Congress*] (LCLS)
PLDAL Pro-Life Direct Action League (EA)
PLDC Preliminary List of Design Changes
PLDC Primary Leadership Development Course [*Army*] (INF)
PLDC Primary Long-Distance Carrier [*Telephone service*]
PLDD Poorly Differentiated Lymphoma, Diffuse [*Oncology and pathology*] (DAVI)
PLDD Profiled Lightly Doped Drains (NITA)
PLDF Pseudo Load Factor (IAA)
PLDG Portuguese Language Development Group [*Modern Language Association of America*] (AEBS)
PLDH Plasma Lactic Dehydrogenase [*An enzyme*] (AAMN)
PLDI Payload Data Interleaver [*NASA*] (MCD)
PLDI Petersburg Long Distance [*NASDAQ symbol*] (SAG)
PLDI Plastic Die [*Tool*] (AAG)
PLDI PLD Telekom, Inc. [*NASDAQ symbol*] (SAG)
PLDIF Petersburg Long Distance [*NASDAQ symbol*] (TTSB)
PLDIS Public Library Development Incentive Scheme [*British*]
PLDISS Plate Dissipation [*Electronics*] (IAA)
PLDK Peabody Language Development Kits [*Education*]
PLDK-P Peabody Language Development Kit: Preschool (EDAC)
PLDM Payload Management [*NASA*] (MCD)
PLDMI Precise LASER Distance Measuring Instrument
PLDP Parti Liberal Democrate et Pluraliste [*Belgium Political party*] (PPW)
PLDP Public Library Development Plan [*American Library Association, Public Library Association*]
PLD-PACOM Petroleum Logistical Data - Pacific Command (CINC)
PLDR Potentially Lethal Damage Repair [*Medicine*]
PLDS Payload Support [*NASA*] (MCD)
PLDS Public Library Data Service
PLDT Philippine Long Distance Telephone Co.
PLD Tele PLD Telekom, Inc. [*Associated Press*] (SAG)
PLDTS Propellant Loading Data Transmission System [*NASA*] (KSC)
PL DYL Placidyl [*Ethchlorvynol*] [*A hypnotic and sedative*] (DAVI)
PLE Encyclopedia of Pennsylvania Law [*A publication*] (DLA)
PLE Personal Level Encryption [*Computer science*]
PLE Phased Loading Entry [*Computer science*]
PLE Photoluminescence Excitation [*Physics*]
PLE Pinnacle Bank [*AMEX symbol*] (TTSB)
PLE Pinnacle Bank [*AMEX symbol*] (SAG)
PLE Pipeline Element (NITA)
PLE [*The*] Pittsburgh & Lake Erie Railroad Co. [*AAR code*]
PLE Planned Life Extension [*Pershing*] (MCD)
Ple Pleiade [*Record label*] [*France*]
PLE Plesetsk [*Satellite launch complex*] [*Former USSR*]
PLE Preliminary Logistics Evaluation
PLE Primary Loss Expectancy [*Insurance*]
PLE Product Limit Estimator (MHDB)
PLE Professional Land Economist [*Canada*] (DD)
PL/E Programming Language / Edit [*Computer science*] (MHDI)
PLE Protein-Losing Enteropathy [*Gastroenterology*] (DAVI)
PLE Prudent Limit of Endurance (NVT)
PLE Pulsed LASER Experiment
PLE Pulse Length Error (MCD)
PLEA Pacific Lumber Exporters Association (EA)
PLEA Poverty Lawyers for Effective Advocacy
PLEA Prototype Language for Economic Analysis [*Computer science*] (IID)
PLEAD Place of Last Entered Active Duty [*Military*]
PLEADGS Pleadings [*Legal term*] (ROG)
PLEASE Parolees, Law-Enforcement Assist Student Education [*Project to reduce drug abuse among junior and senior high school students in California*]
PLeB Bucknell University, Lewisburg, PA [*Library symbol Library of Congress*] (LCLS)
PLEB Plebeian (WGA)
PLEB Plebiscitum [*A Decree of the People*] [*Latin*] (DLA)
PLebHi Lebanon County Historical Society, Lebanon, PA [*Library symbol Library of Congress*] (LCLS)
PLebV United States Veterans Administration Hospital, Lebanon, PA [*Library symbol Library of Congress*] (LCLS)
PLED Periodic Lateralized Epileptiform Discharge [*Medicine*] (MAE)
P Leg J Pittsburgh Legal Journal [*Pennsylvania*] [*A publication*] (DLA)
P Leg Jour Pittsburgh Legal Journal [*Pennsylvania*] [*A publication*] (DLA)
PLEI Public Law Education Institute (EA)
PLEM Pipeline End Manifold (PDAA)
PLEN Plenipotentiary
PLEN Plenum Publishing [*NASDAQ symbol*] (TTSB)
PLEN Plenum Publishing Corp. [*NASDAQ symbol*] (NQ)
PLEN Public Leadership Education Network (EA)
PLENAPS Plans for the Employment of Naval and Air Forces of the Associated Powers in theEastern Theatre in the Event of War with Japan
PLENCH Pliers and Wrench [*Combination tool*]
PLENG Physical Record Length [*Computer science*] (MHDI)

Plenum .... Plenum Publishing Corp. [*Associated Press*] (SAG)
PLES .... Parallel-Line Equal Space [*Medicine*] (DMAA)
PLESA .... Programs for Persons with Limited English-Speaking Ability [*Department of Labor*]
PLEU .... Pleural Fluid [*Medicine*] (DAVI)
Pleur Fl .... Pleural Fluid [*Medicine*] (MAE)
PLEURO .... Pleuropneumonia [*Veterinary medicine*] (DSUE)
PLEVA .... Pityriasis Lichenoides et Varioliformis Acuta [*Dermatology*] (MAE)
PLEX .... Plant Experimentation (PDAA)
plexg .... Plexiglass (VRA)
Plexus .... Plexus Corp. [*Associated Press*] (SAG)
PLEYA .... Public Library Entrepreneur of the Year Award [*Sponsored by Geac Computers Ltd.*]
PLF .... Franklin and Marshall College, Lancaster, PA [*Library symbol Library of Congress*] (LCLS)
PLF .... Free Library of Philadelphia, Philadelphia, PA [*OCLC symbol*] (OCLC)
PLF .... Pacific Legal Foundation (EA)
PLF .... Page Length Field
PLF .... Pala [*Chad*] [*Airport symbol*] (AD)
PLF .... Palestine Liberation Front [*Political party*] (PD)
PLF .... Parachute Landing Fall [*Military*]
PLF .... Pastel Food [*Vancouver Stock Exchange symbol*]
PLF .... Patient Load Factor (AFM)
PLF .... People's Liberation Forces [*Ethiopia*] [*Political party*] (AF)
PLF .... Perilymphatic Fistula [*Medicine*] (DMAA)
PLF .... Perilymph Fistula [*Medicine*]
PLF .... Phase Lock Frequency
PLF .... Phone Line Formatter
PLF .... Plaintiff
PLF .... Pohjanmaan Lento OY [*Finland ICAO designator*] (FAAC)
PLF .... Polar Lipid Fraction [*Biochemistry*]
PLF .... Positive Lock Fastener
PLF .... Posterior Lung Fiber [*Medicine*] (DMAA)
PLF .... Power for Level Flight [*Aeronautics*]
PLF .... Private Line Telephone
PLF .... Proliferin [*Biochemistry*]
PLF .... Proposition Letter Formula
PLF .... Public Lands Foundation (EA)
PLFA .... Polar Lipid Fatty Acid [*Biochemistry*]
PLFA .... Primary Level Field Activity [*Defense Supply Agency*]
PLFA .... Tabueran Island [*Fanning Islands*] [*Kiribati*] [*ICAO location identifier*] (ICLI)
PLFC .... Premature Living Female Child [*Neonatology*] (DAVI)
PLFC .... Pulaski Furniture [*NASDAQ symbol*] (TTSB)
PLFC .... Pulaski Furniture Corp. [*NASDAQ symbol*] (NQ)
PLFC & A .... Peggy Lee Fan Club and Archives [*Later, OOPLFC & A*] (EA)
PLFE .... Presidential Life [*NASDAQ symbol*] (TTSB)
PLFE .... Presidential Life Corp. [*NASDAQ symbol*] (NQ)
PLFF .... Plaintiff
PLFS .... Perilymphatic Fistula Syndrome [*Medicine*] (DMAA)
PLFTR .... Please Furnish Transportation Requests (NOAA)
PLFUR .... Please Furnish (NOAA)
PLG .... Piling (MSA)
PLG .... Place Resources Corp. [*Toronto Stock Exchange symbol*]
PLG .... Plane Guard (NVT)
PLG .... Plasminogen [*An enzyme*] (DAVI)
PLG .... Pleural Ganglion [*Medicine*]
PLG .... Plug (AAG)
PLG .... Poetae Lyrici Graeci [*A publication*] (OCD)
PLG .... PolyGram NV [*NYSE symbol*] (SPSG)
PLG .... Polygyros [*Greece*] [*Seismograph station code, US Geological Survey*] (SEIS)
PLG .... Poor Law Guardian [*British*]
PLG .... Private-Label and Generic Brands
PLG .... Progressive Librarians Guild [*American Library Association*]
PLG .... Prolyl(leucyl)glycinamide [*Biochemistry*]
PLG .... Pulsed Light Generator
PLGA .... Polylacticco-Glycolic Acid [*Organic chemistry*]
PLGC .... Presbyterians for Lesbian/Gay Concerns (EA)
PLGL .... Plasminogen-Like [*Medicine*] (DMAA)
PLGL .... Plate Glass
PLGM .... NYC Parents of Lesbians and Gay Men (EA)
PLGR .... Plunger (MSA)
PLGR .... Precision Lightweight Global-Positioning-Satellite Receiver
PLGR .... Precision Lightweight GPS [*Global Positioning System*] Receiver [*Army*] (INF)
PLGR .... Precision Lightweight GPS [*Global Positioning System*] Receiver [*Navigation systems*]
PLGR .... Precision Lightweight GPS Receiver
PLGS .... Partita Liberale Giovani Somali [*Somali Liberal Youth Party*] [*Political party*]
PLGSS .... Payload Ground Support Systems [*NASA*] (NASA)
PLGT .... Prototype Lunar Geologist Tool
P-LGV .... Psittacosis-Lymphogranuloma Venereum [*Medicine*]
PLH .... Hamilton Watch Co., Lancaster, PA [*Library symbol Library of Congress Obsolete*] (LCLS)
PLH .... Palaemontes-Lightening Hormone
PLH .... Paroxysmal Localized Hyperhidrosis [*Dermatology*] (DAVI)
PLH .... Partido Liberal de Honduras [*Liberal Party of Honduras*] [*Political party*] (PPW)
PLH .... Payload Handling [*NASA*] (NASA)
PLH .... Placental Lactogenic Hormone (DMAA)
PLH .... Plaser Light [*Vancouver Stock Exchange symbol*]
PLH .... Plymouth [*England*] [*Airport symbol*] (OAG)
PLH .... Punjab Light Horse [*British military*] (DMA)
PLHi .... Lancaster County Historical Society, Lancaster, PA [*Library symbol Library of Congress*] (LCLS)
PLHR .... Power Line Harmonic Radiation
PLhS .... Lock Haven State College, Lock Haven, PA [*Library symbol Library of Congress*] (LCLS)
PLI .... Empresa de Transporte Aereo del Peru [*ICAO designator*] (FAAC)
PLI .... Ltd. Systems [*Vancouver Stock Exchange symbol*]
pli .... Pali [*MARC language code Library of Congress*] (LCCP)
PLI .... Panarea [*Lipari Islands*] [*Seismograph station code, US Geological Survey*] (SEIS)
PLI .... Partido Liberal Independiente [*Independent Liberal Party*] [*Nicaragua*] [*Political party*] (PPW)
PLI .... Partito Liberale Italiano [*Italian Liberal Party*] [*Political party*] (PPW)
PLI .... Passenger and Immigration Lists Index [*A publication*]
PLI .... Payload Interrogator [*NASA*] (MCD)
PLI .... Phone Line Interface [*IBM Corp.*] (PCM)
PLI .... Pilot Location Indicator
PLI .... Polyvision Corp. [*AMEX symbol*] (SAG)
PLI .... Power Level Indicator
PLI .... Practising Law Institute (EA)
PLI .... Preload Indicating
PLI .... Private Line Interface
PLI .... Proctolin-Like Immunoactivity [*Neurobiology*]
PLI .... Professional Liability Insurance (DMAA)
PLI .... Public Lands Institute (EA)
PLI .... Pulsed LASER Interferometry
PLIA .... Pollution Liability Insurance Association [*Defunct*] (EA)
PLIANT .... Procedural Language Implementing Analog Techniques [*Computer science*] (IEEE)
PLIB .... Pacific Lumber Inspection Bureau (EA)
PLIB .... Program Library [*Computer science*]
PLIC .... Procedural Language for Integrity Constraints [*Computer science*] (MHDI)
PLICK .... Pride, Loyalty, Integrity, Capability, Knowledge (DNAB)
PLIE .... Phase Linear Interferometer Experiment (MCD)
PLIF .... Planar Laser Induced Fluorescence
PLI F .... Polo Laico Liberali-Repubblicani Federalisti [*Italy*] [*Political party*] (ECED)
PLIF .... Postlumbar Interbody Fusion [*Neurology*] (DAVI)
PLIM .... Post Launch and Instrumentation Message [*NASA*] (IAA)
PLIM .... Post Launch Information Message [*NASA*] (KSC)
PLIMC .... Pipe Line Insurance Managers Conference [*Defunct*] (EA)
PLIMS .... Programming Language for Information Management System [*Computer science*] (MHDI)
PLimT .... Tyler Arboretum, Lima, PA [*Library symbol Library of Congress*] (LCLS)
PLIN .... Power Line Impedance Network
PLINK .... American People/Link [*American Design and Communication*] [*Information service or system*] (IID)
PLIP .... Preamplifier Limited Infrared (IAA)
PLIRRA .... Pollution Liability Insurance and Risk Retention Act (GFGA)
PLIS .... Preclinical Literature Information System [*Computer science*]
PLISN .... Parts List Item Sequence Number (MCD)
PLISN .... Provisioning List Item Sequence Number (NASA)
PLISSIT .... Permission, Limited Information, Specific Suggestions, and Intensive Therapy [*Occupational therapy*]
PLIT .... Petrolite Corp. [*NASDAQ symbol*] (NQ)
PLITTY .... Private Line Teletypewriter Service [*Telecommunications*] (TEL)
PLIUN .... Partido Liberal Independiente de Unidad Nacional [*Nicaragua*] [*Political party*] (EY)
PLIW .... Preload Indicating Washer
PLJ .... Pacific Law Journal [*A publication*] (ILCA)
PLJ .... Parliamentary Lobby Journalists [*British*]
PLJ .... Pass Lake Resources Ltd. [*Vancouver Stock Exchange symbol*]
PLJ .... Patna Law Journal [*India*] [*A publication*] (ILCA)
PLJ .... Pennsylvania Law Journal [*A publication*] (DLA)
PLJ .... Permanent Loop Junctor (NITA)
PLJ .... Philippine Law Journal [*A publication*] (ILCA)
PLJ .... Pittsburgh Legal Journal [*Pennsylvania*] [*A publication*] (DLA)
PLJ .... Punjab Law Reporter [*India*] [*A publication*] (DLA)
PLJ .... Pure Lemon Juice
PLJ NS .... Pittsburgh Legal Journal, New Series [*Pennsylvania*] [*A publication*] (DLA)
PLK .... Branson, MO [*Location identifier FAA*] (FAAL)
PLK .... Phi Lambda Kappa [*Fraternity*]
PLK .... Plank (AAG)
PLK .... Ploecker-Lee-Kesler [*Equation of state*]
PLK .... Plucky Little King [*Used by Western diplomats in Amman in reference to King Hussein of Jordan*]
PLK .... Poincare-Lighthill-Kuo [*Method*]
PLK .... Salomon, Inc. [*AMEX symbol*] (SAG)
PLK .... Salomon Inc. 6.125% PRI 'ELKS' [*AMEX symbol*] (TTSB)
PLKR .... Peacoat Locker
PLL .... Pall Corp. [*NYSE symbol*] (SAG)
PLL .... Pallet [*Building construction*]
PLL .... Parts Load List (MCD)
PLL .... Passenger Legal Liability [*Insurance*] (AIA)
PLL .... Peripheral Light Loss
PLL .... Permanent Logical Link [*Telecommunications*]
PLL .... Phase-Locked Loop [*NASA*]
Pl L .... Platt on Leases [*1841*] [*A publication*] (DLA)
PLL .... Polo, IL [*Location identifier FAA*] (FAAL)
PLL .... Poly-L-lysine [*Also, PL*] [*Biochemistry*]
PLL .... Positive Logic Level

PLL .... Prescribed Load List [*Vehicle maintenance operation*] [*Army*]
PLL .... Pressure Length Loop (DMAA)
PLL .... Prince Line Ltd. [*Steamship*] (MHDW)
PLL .... Prolymphocytic Leukemia [*Also, PL*] [*Oncology*]
PLL .... Pseudoalcoholic Liver Lesions [*Medicine*]
PLLDF .... Phase-Locked Loop with Decision Feedback [*NASA*] (IAA)
PLLE .... Prueba de Lectura y Lenguaje Escrito [*Standardized test of reading and writing in Spanish for students in grades 3 through 10*]
PLLL .... Parallel Petroleum [*NASDAQ symbol*] (TTSB)
PLLL .... Parallel Petroleum Corp. [*NASDAQ symbol*] (NQ)
PLLL .... Posterior Lateral Line Lobe [*Of electric fishes*]
PLLR .... Phase Lock Loop Receiver
PLLRC .... Public Land Law Review Commission [*Terminated, 1970*]
PLLS .... Portable Landing Light System (PDAA)
PLLT .... Pallet (NATG)
PLLTN .... Pollution
PLLVM .... Pennsylvania Farm Museum of Landis Valley, Lancaster, PA [*Library symbol Library of Congress*] (LCLS)
PLM .... Pacific Law Magazine [*A publication*] (DLA)
PLM .... Packaged Liquid Missile
PLM .... Pakistan Liberation Movement [*Political party*] (PD)
PLM .... Palembang [*Indonesia*] [*Airport symbol*] (OAG)
PLM .... Palomar [*California*] [*Seismograph station code, US Geological Survey*] (SEIS)
PLM .... Passive Line Monitor [*Datapoint*]
PLM .... Passive Lunar Marker
PLM .... Payload Management [*NASA*] (NASA)
PLM .... Payload Monitoring [*NASA*] (NASA)
PLM .... People's Liberation Movement [*Montserrat*] [*Political party*] (PPW)
PLM .... Percent Labeled Mitosis [*Cytology*]
PLM .... Periodic Leg Movement (DMAA)
PLM .... Phleomycin [*Biochemistry*]
PLM .... Phospholemman [*Biochemistry*]
PLM .... Planetary Rotation Machine (IAA)
PLM .... Plasma Level Monitoring [*Medicine*] (DMAA)
PLM .... Plastic Laminating Mold (MCD)
PLM .... PLM International [*AMEX symbol*] (TTSB)
PLM .... PLM International, Inc. [*AMEX symbol*] (SPSG)
PLM .... Plymouth Financial [*Vancouver Stock Exchange symbol*]
PLM .... Poetae Latini Minores [*A publication*] (OCD)
PLM .... Polarized Light Microscopy
PLM .... Poor Law Magazine [*A publication*] (DLA)
PLM .... Power Line Modulation (AABC)
PLM .... Prelaunch Monitor [*NASA*] (KSC)
PLM .... Preliminary (KSC)
PLM .... Private Label Merchandiser [*USCG*] (TAG)
PLM .... Production Line Maintenance [*Air Force*]
PLM .... Production Line Manufacturing
PLM .... Product Line Manager
PL/M .... Programming Language for Microprocessors (NITA)
PL/M .... Programming Language/Microcomputers [*Intel Corp.*] [*1973*] [*Computer science*] (CSR)
PLM .... Programming Logic Manual
PLM .... Progressive Labor Movement (BARN)
PLM .... Pulse-Length Modulation
PLMA .... Private Label Manufacturers Association (EA)
PLMA .... Producers Livestock Marketing Association [*Later, IPLA*] (EA)
PL Mag .... Poor Law Magazine [*1858-1930*] [*Scotland*] [*A publication*] (DLA)
PLMATH ...... Procedure Library Mathematics [*Computer science*] (IAA)
PLMB .... Plumbing (AAG)
PLMBR .... Plumber
PLMC .... Premature Living Male Child [*Neonatology*] (DAVI)
PLMD .... Payload Mating Dolly [*NASA*]
PLME .... Peak Local Mean Error (MCD)
PLMES .... Planning, Measurements & Evaluation Section [*Public Library Association*] [*American Library Association*]
PLMG .... Plumbing (WGA)
PLMG .... Publishers' Library Marketing Group [*Defunct*] (EA)
PLMHi .... Lancaster Mennonite Conference Historical Society, Lancaster, PA [*Library symbol Library of Congress*] (LCLS)
PLMN .... Partido Marxista Leninista de Nicaragua [*Political party*] (EY)
PLMP .... Program Logistic Management Plan (MCD)
PLMPA .... Permanent Labourers' Mutual Protective Association [*A union*] [*British*]
PLMR .... Paris, Lyons, and Mediterranean Railway (ROG)
PLMR .... Post Launch Memorandum Report
PlmrW .... Palmer Wireless [*Associated Press*] (SAG)
PLMS .... Palms
PLMS .... Partitioned Libraries Management System (MHDI)
PLMS .... Plastic Master [*Tool*] (AAG)
PLMS .... Preservation of Library Materials Section [*Resources and Technical Services Division*] [*American Library Association*]
PLMS .... Program Logistics Master Schedule [*NASA*] (NASA)
PLMS .... Public Land Mobile Service Data Base [*Comp Comm, Inc.*] [*Information service or system*] (CRD)
PlmSSB .... Palm Springs Savings Bank [*Associated Press*] (SAG)
PLMT .... Plasmacytoid Lymphocyte [*Hematology*] (DAVI)
PLMV .... Posterior Leaf Mitral Valve [*Cardiology*] (DMAA)
PLMX .... PL/M Extended [*Programming language*] (CSR)
PLN .... Flight Plan [*Aviation code*]
PLN .... Partido de Liberacion Nacional [*National Liberation Party*] [*El Salvador*] [*Political party*] (EY)
PLN .... Partido Liberacion Nacional [*National Liberation Party*] [*Costa Rica*] [*Political party*] (PPW)
PLN .... Partido Liberal Nacionalista [*Nationalist Liberal Party*] [*Nicaragua*]
PLN .... Pellston [*Michigan*] [*Airport symbol*] (OAG)
PLN .... Pellston, MI [*Location identifier FAA*] (FAAL)
PLN .... Pelvic Lymph Node [*Gynecology*] (DAVI)
PLN .... Phospholamban [*Biochemistry*]
PLN .... Plain
PLN .... Plain
PLN .... Plan (NASA)
PLN .... Plane (MSA)
Pln .... Platoon [*British military*] (DMA)
PLN .... Plauen [*German Democratic Republic*] [*Seismograph station code, US Geological Survey*] (SEIS)
PLN .... Polnippon [*Poland ICAO designator*] (FAAC)
PLN .... Popliteal Lymph Node [*Anatomy*]
PLN .... Posterior Lip Nerve (DAVI)
PLN .... Potassium Lithium Niobate (PDAA)
PLN .... Primary Learning Network [*Computer science*] (IAA)
PLN .... Program Line Number [*DoD*]
PLN .... Program Logic Network (NASA)
PLN .... Proteoliaisin [*Biochemistry*]
PLN .... Pump-Line-Nozzle
PLNAP .... Pro-Life Nonviolent Action Project (EA)
plnd .... Planned (DA)
PLNG .... Planning
PLNN .... Planning (MCD)
PLNR .... Planar (MSA)
PLNR .... Planar Systems [*NASDAQ symbol*] (SAG)
PLNR .... Planner
PlnRsc .... Plains Resources, Inc. [*Associated Press*] (SAG)
PLNS .... Plains (MCD)
PLNS .... Plains
PLNS .... Planning Sciences International [*NASDAQ symbol*] (SAG)
PLNSTD .... Planned Standard Equipment [*Navy*] (AFIT)
PLNSY .... Planning Sciences ADS [*NASDAQ symbol*] (TTSB)
PLNT .... Planet (MSA)
PLNT .... Plant
PLNTY .... Planetary (MSA)
PLO .... Pacific Launch Operations [*NASA*]
PLO .... Palestine Liberation Organization [*Political party*] (PD)
PLO .... Parliamentary Liaison Officer (ADA)
PLO .... Partial Lunar Orbit [*Planetary science*]
PLO .... Parts List Only (MCD)
PLO .... Passenger Liaison Office [*Military*] (AABC)
PLO .... Payload Officer [*NASA*] (MCD)
PLO .... Pentagon Liaison Office (MCD)
PLO .... Peoples Liberation Organization (NADA)
PLO .... Phase-Locked Oscillator
PLO .... Plans Officer
PLO .... Polycystic Lipomembranous Osteodysplasia [*Medicine*] (DMAA)
PLO .... Poly-L-ornithine
PLO .... Poor Law Office (ROG)
PLO .... Port Liaison Officer
PLO .... Port Lincoln [*Australia Airport symbol*] (OAG)
PLO .... Presidential Libraries Office (NADA)
PLO .... Price-Lifting Operation [*Business term*] (ECON)
PLO .... Probability of Leakage through Overlay
PLO .... Product Line Organization
PLO .... Program Line Organization
PLO .... Programmed Local Oscillator
PLO .... Project Line Organization
PLO .... Public Land Order [*Interior*]
PLO .... Pulsed LASER Oscillator
PLO .... Pulsed Locked Oscillator
PLOA .... Proposed Letter of Agreement (MCD)
PLOB .... Patrol Log Observations [*Aviation*] (DSUE)
PLOB .... Place of Birth
PLOC .... Payload Operations Contractor [*NASA*] (SSD)
PLOCAP .... Post Loss-of-Coolant Accident Protection [*Nuclear energy*] (NRCH)
PLOCSA .... Personnel Liaison Officer, Chief of Staff, Army (AABC)
PLOD .... Periodic List of Data [*Computer science*]
PLOD .... Planetary Orbit Determination (IEEE)
PLOKTA .... Press Lots of Keys to Abort [*Computer term*]
P Lom .... Petrus Lombardi [*Flourished, 1154-59*] [*Authority cited in pre-1607 legal work*] (DSA)
PLOM .... Prescribed Loan Optimization Model [*Army*] (AABC)
PLOME .... Poor Little Old Me Syndrome [*British*]
PLondon .... Greek Papyri in the British Museum [*A publication*] (OCD)
PLONEF .... Plates on Elastic Foundations [*Structures & Computers Ltd.*] [*Software package*] (NCC)
PLONG .... Present Longititude [*Aviation*] (FAAC)
PLOO .... Pacific Launch Operations Office [*NASA*]
PLOP .... Planetary Landing Observation Package [*Aerospace*]
PLOP .... Pressure Line of Position [*Air Force*]
PLor .... Saint Francis College, Loretto, PA [*Library symbol Library of Congress*] (LCLS)
PLOS .... Primary Line of Sight [*Sextants*]
PLOT .... People's Liberation Organization of Tamil Eelam [*Sri Lanka*] [*Political party*]
PLOT .... Piagetian Logical Operations Test (EDAC)
PLOT .... Plotting
PLOT .... Porous Layer, Open Tubular Column [*Gas chromatography*]
PLOT .... Probability of Launch on Time (MCD)
Plot .... Vita Plotini [*of Porphyry*] [*Classical studies*] (OCD)
PLOTE .... People's Liberation Organization of Tamil Eelam [*Sri Lanka*] [*Political party*]

PLOW .... Petunia Lovers of the World
Plow .... Plowden's English King's Bench Commentaries [*or Reports*] [*A publication*] (DLA)
Plowd .... Plowden's English King's Bench Commentaries [*or Reports*] [*A publication*] (DLA)
PLOYREP ..... Unit Deployment Report (CINC)
PLP .... La Palma [*Panama*] [*Airport symbol*] (OAG)
PLP .... Packet Layer Protocol [*Computer science*] (TNIG)
PLP .... Packet Level Procedure [*or Protocol*] [*Computer programming*] (PCM)
PLP .... Palo [*Philippines*] [*Seismograph station code, US Geological Survey*] (SEIS)
PLP .... Palpus [*Arthropod anatomy*]
PLP .... Parliamentary Labour Party [*British*]
PLP .... Parti de la Liberte et du Progres [*Party of Liberty and Progress*] [*See also PVV*] [*Belgium*] (PPE)
PLP .... Partido de los Pobres [*Poor People's Party*] [*Mexico Political party*] (PD)
PLP .... Parti Liberal Progressiste [*Liberal Progressive Party*] [*Morocco*] [*Political party*] (PPW)
PLP .... Parti pour la Liberation du Peuple [*People's Liberation Party*] [*Senegal*] [*Political party*] (PPW)
PLP .... Partners for Livable Places (EA)
PLP .... Parts List Page (KSC)
PLP .... Passive Low Pass (IAA)
PLP .... Pattern Learning Parser
PLP .... People's Liberation Party [*Pakistan*]
PLP .... Periodate Lysine-Paraformaldehyde
PLP .... Personal LASER Printer [*Computer science*]
PLP .... Phillips Petroleum Co. [*Toronto Stock Exchange symbol*]
PLP .... Phoenix Aviation [*British ICAO designator*] (FAAC)
PLP .... Photolithographic Process (IAA)
PLP .... Plastic-Lined Pipe
PLP .... Polyoma-Like Particle [*Genetics*]
PLP .... Post Launch Phase
PLP .... Preferred Lenders Program [*Small Business Administration*]
PLP .... Preformed Line Product (IAA)
PLP .... Presentation Level Protocol [*AT & T Videotex System*]
PLP .... Principal Locating Point [*Automotive engineering*]
PLP .... Procedural Language Processor
PLP .... Process Layup Procedure
PLP .... Product Liability Prevention [*Conference*]
PLP .... Progressive Labor Party (EA)
PLP .... Progressive Labour Party [*Saint Lucia*] [*Political party*] (EAIO)
PLP .... Progressive Liberal Party [*Bahamas*] [*Political party*] (PPW)
PLP .... Prolactin-Like Protein [*Biochemistry*]
PLP .... Proteolipid [*Biochemistry*]
PLP .... Proteolipid Protein [*Biochemistry*]
PLP .... Pyridoxal Phosphate [*Also, PALP*] [*Biochemistry*]
PLPA .... Pageable Link-Pack Area
PLPA .... Palmyra, Palymra Island [*Line Islands*] [*ICAO location identifier*] (ICLI)
PLPA .... Permissive Low-Pressure Alarm (IEEE)
Pl Par .... Placita Parliamentaria [*Latin A publication*] (DLA)
PLPB .... Petroleum Labor Policy Board [*Abolished, 1936*]
PLPBD .... Pulpboard
PLPD .... Product Liability Prevention and Defense [*An association*] (EA)
PLP FOR ...... Foramen of Labial Palpus [*Arthropod anatomy*]
PLPG .... Publishers' Library Promotion Group [*Later, PLMG*] (EA)
PLP GRNDG ... Pulp Grinding [*Freight*]
PLPH .... Post-Lumbar Puncture Headache [*Medicine*] (DMAA)
PlPolyT .... Planet Polymer Technologies, Inc. [*Associated Press*] (SAG)
PLPP .... Position Location Post Processor (MCD)
PLPrM .... PLC Capital LLC 'A' 'MIPS' [*NYSE symbol*] (TTSB)
PLPS .... Packaged Liquid Propellant System
PLPS .... Propellant Loading and Pressurization System [*NASA*]
PLPV .... Pelargonium Line Pattern Virus [*Plant pathology*]
PLQ .... Plaque (MSA)
PLQ .... Tallahassee, FL [*Location identifier FAA*] (FAAL)
PLR .... LaRoche College, Pittsburgh, PA [*OCLC symbol*] (OCLC)
PLR .... Northwestern Air Lease Ltd. [*Canada ICAO designator*] (FAAC)
PLR .... Pacific Law Reporter [*A publication*] (DLA)
PLR .... Pakistan Law Reports [*A publication*] (DLA)
PLR .... Pakistan Law Review [*A publication*] (DLA)
PLR .... Parlake Resources Ltd. [*Toronto Stock Exchange symbol*]
PLR .... Partido Liberal Radical [*Radical Liberal Party*] [*Paraguay*] [*Political party*] (PPW)
PLR .... Partido Liberal Radical [*Radical Liberal Party*] [*Ecuador*] [*Political party*] (PPW)
PLR .... Patent Law Review [*A publication*] (DLA)
PLR .... Patent Log Reading [*Navigation*]
PLR .... Patna Law Reporter [*India*] [*A publication*] (DLA)
PLR .... Pell City, AL [*Location identifier FAA*] (FAAL)
PLR .... Pennsylvania Law Record [*Philadelphia*] [*A publication*] (DLA)
P-LR .... Pennsylvania Legislative Reference Bureau, Harrisburg, PA [*Library symbol Library of Congress*] (LCLS)
PLR .... Periodic Logistical Report
PLR .... Philippine Liberation Ribbon [*Military decoration*]
PLR .... Pillar (MSA)
PLR .... Pliers (MSA)
PLR .... Plymouth Rubber Co., Inc. [*AMEX symbol*] (SPSG)
plr .... Poplar (VRA)
PLR .... Portable LASER Range-Finder
PLR .... Power Line Radiation [*Radioscience*]
PLR .... Presentation Loss Rate (MCD)
PLR .... Pressure Level Recorder
PLR .... Primary Language Record [*Education*] (AIE)
PLR .... Primary Loss Retention [*Insurance*]
PLR .... Private Legislation Reports [*Scotland*] [*A publication*] (DLA)
PLR .... Program Life Requirement (NG)
PLR .... Program Lock-in Register (NITA)
PLR .... Prolactin Receptor [*Biochemistry*]
PLR .... Pronation/Lateral Rotation [*Fracture*] [*Orthopedics*] (DAVI)
PLR .... Psychological Laboratories [*Harvard University*] (KSC)
PLR .... Public Law Review [*A publication*]
PLR .... Public Lending Right [*Royalty for books borrowed from public libraries*] [*British*]
PLR .... Puller (MSA)
PLR .... Pulse Link Relay [*Telecommunications*] (TEL)
PLR .... Pulse Link Repeater [*Telecommunications*] (TEL)
PLR .... Punjab Law Reporter [*India*] [*A publication*] (DLA)
PLRA .... Partido Liberal Radical Autentico [*Authentic Liberal Radical Party*] [*Paraguay*] [*Political party*] (PD)
PLRA .... Pennsylvania Learning Resources Association (EDAC)
PLRA .... Photo-Litho Reproducers' Association [*British*] (BI)
PLR. A .... Plymouth Rubber'A'vtg [*AMEX symbol*] (TTSB)
PLRACTA ..... Position Location, Reporting, and Control of Tactical Aircraft [*Military*]
PLR.B .... Plymouth Rubber Cl'B' [*AMEX symbol*] (TTSB)
PLRB .... Property Loss Research Bureau (EA)
PLRC .... Pulsed LASER Remote Crosswind Sensor (MCD)
PLRCAE .... Radio Corp. of America, Electron Tube Division, Engineering Section, Lancaster, PA [*Library symbol Library of Congress Obsolete*] (LCLS)
PLRD .... Payload Requirements Document (NASA)
PLRD .... Polaroid (VRA)
PLRD .... Procurement, Logistics, and Readiness Division (AAGC)
PLRD .... Pull Rod
PLR Dacca ... Pakistan Law Reports, Dacca Series [*A publication*] (DLA)
PLRE .... Program on Long-Range Forecasting Research [*Marine science*] (OSRA)
PLRF .... Pediatric Liver Research Foundation [*Defunct*] (EA)
pLRF .... Placental Luteinizing Hormone-Releasing Factor [*Endocrinology*]
PLRF .... Planer Fixture
PLRI .... Posterolateral Rotation Instability [*Sports medicine*]
PLRJ & K ..... Punjab Law Reporter, Jammu and Kashmir Section [*India*] [*A publication*] (DLA)
PLR Kar .... Pakistan Law Reports, Karachi Series [*1947-53*] [*A publication*] (DLA)
PLR Lah .... Pakistan Law Reports, Lahore Series [*1947-55*] [*A publication*] (DLA)
PLRPF .... Personnel Loss Rate Planning Factors (MCD)
PLRS .... Pelorus
PLRS .... Phase Lock Receiving System
PLRS .... Position Location Reporting System [*Military*]
PLRS/TIDS ... Position Location Reporting System/Tactical Information Distribution Systems [*Military*] (RDA)
PLRSTN .... Pelorus Stand
PLRT .... Polarity (MSA)
PLRV .... Payload Launch Readiness Verification [*NASA*] (MCD)
PLRV .... Potato Leafroll Virus
PLRWP .... Pakistan Law Reports, West Pakistan Series [*A publication*] (DLA)
PLS .... Page Layout System [*Graphic arts*] (DGA)
PLS .... Palio Air Service [*Italy ICAO designator*] (FAAC)
PLS .... Palletized Load System [*Army*] (RDA)
PLS .... Palomar-Leiden Survey
PLS .... Papillon-Lefevre Syndrome [*Medicine*] (DMAA)
PLS .... Paracelsus Healthcare Corp. [*NYSE symbol*] (SAG)
PLS .... Parcels (MSA)
PLS .... Parent Locator Service [*A service of the Office of Child Support Enforcement (OCSE)*] (PAZ)
PLS .... Parsons Language Sample
PLS .... Partial Least Squares
PLS .... Parti Liberal Suisse [*Liberal Party of Switzerland*] [*Political party*] (PPE)
PLS .... Patrol Locator System [*Army*]
PLS .... Payload Systems [*NASA*] (MCD)
PLS .... Peerless Tube Co. [*AMEX symbol*] (SPSG)
PLS .... Peninsula Library System [*Belmont, CA*] [*Library network*]
PLS .... People's Law School [*Defunct*] (EA)
PLS .... Peralto Resources Corp. [*Vancouver Stock Exchange symbol*]
PLS .... Periodic Log System
PLS .... Personal Library Software [*Commercial firm*]
PLS .... Physical Signalling (NITA)
PLS .... Pitch Limit Switch
PLS .... Plaisance [*Mauritius*] [*Geomagnetic observatory code*]
PLS .... Plasma Light Source
PLS .... Plates [*Classical studies*] (OCD)
PLS .... Please (AFM)
PLS .... Plugging Switch (IEEE)
PLS .... Pneumatic Limit Switch
PLS .... Polson, MT [*Location identifier FAA*] (FAAL)
PLS .... Polynomial Solution (IAA)
PLS .... Polystyrene Latex Sphere
PLS .... Popular Low-Power Schottky [*Electronics*] (MCD)
PLS .... Portable Laboratory Salinometer
PLS .... Position Location System [*Army*]
PLS .... Post Landing and Safing [*NASA*] (NASA)
PLS .... Postsecondary Longitudinal Studies Program [*Department of Education*] (GFGA)
PLS .... Precautions, Limitations, and Setpoints [*Nuclear energy*] (NRCH)
PLS .... Preliminary Landing Site (NASA)

PLS Preschool Language Scale [*Child development test*]
PLS President of the Linnaean Society [*British*]
PLS Primary Landing Site (MCD)
PLS Primary Lateral Sclerosis [*Medicine*] (DMAA)
PLS Private Line Service
PLS Product Line Simulator
PLS Professional Legal Secretary [*National Association of Legal Secretaries*] [*Designation awarded by*]
PLS Profit-and-Loss-Sharing Account [*Banking*] (IMH)
PLS Programmable Logic Sequencer [*Computer science*]
PLS Programming Language for System [*Computer science*] (IAA)
PLS Progressive Learning Systems [*Potomac, MD*] (TSSD)
PLS Propellant Loading Sequencer (AAG)
PLS Propellant Loading System
PLS Prostaglandin-Like Substance [*Biochemistry*] (MAE)
PLS Providenciales [*British West Indies*] [*Airport symbol*] (OAG)
PLS Publishers Licensing Society (DGA)
PLS Pulse (MSA)
PLS Pulsed LASER System
PLS Pulsed Light Source
PLS Purnell Library Service [*Commercial firm*]
PLSC Project Level Steering Committee (HGAA)
PLSD Post Hoc Least Significant Difference [*Statistics*]
PLSD Promotion List Service Date [*Air Force*]
PLSD Protected Least Significant Difference (DMAA)
PLSFC Part Load Specific Fuel Consumption [*Gas turbine*]
PLSGT Platoon Sergeant [*Marine Corps*]
PLSHD Polished [*Freight*]
PLSI Premier Laser Systems, Inc. [*NASDAQ symbol*] (SAG)
PLSIA Premier Laser Systems'A' [*NASDAQ symbol*] (TTSB)
PLSIW Premier Laser Systems Wrrt'A' [*NASDAQ symbol*] (TTSB)
PLSIZ Premier Laser Systems Wrrt'B' [*NASDAQ symbol*] (TTSB)
PLSL Propellants and Life Support Laboratory [*NASA*] (NASA)
PLSN Pulsation (MSA)
PL/SNSR Payload Sensor [*NASA*] (GFGA)
PLSNT Pleasant
PLSO Propellant Life Support and Ordnance [*NASA*] (KSC)
PLSP Payload Signal Processor [*NASA*] (MCD)
PLSP Prelaunch Survival Probability (CINC)
PLSPS Performance Levels of a School Program Survey [*Teacher evaluation test*]
PLSR Pulsator (MSA)
PLSS Payload Support Structure [*NASA*] (SSD)
PLSS Portable Life Support System [*or Subsystem*] [*NASA*]
PLSS Post-Landing Survival System [*NASA*]
PLSS Precision Location Strike System [*Air Force*]
PLSS Prelaunch Status Simulator
PLSS Primary Life Support System [*or Subsystem*] (NASA)
PLSS Public Library Systems Section [*Public Library Association*]
PLSSRS Plant and Soil Science Research Station [*Southern Illinois University at Carbondale*] [*Research center*] (RCD)
PLSSU Portable Life Support Stretcher Unit [*Military*] (CAAL)
PLST Plastering
PLSTC Plastic (AAG)
PLSTR Plasterer (ADA)
PLSTRER Plasterer (WGA)
PLSV Propellant Latching Solenoid Valve
PLT Columbus, NE [*Location identifier FAA*] (FAAL)
PLT Lancaster Theological Seminary of the United Church of Christ, Lancaster, PA [*Library symbol Library of Congress*] (LCLS)
PLT Lutheran Theological Seminary, Philadelphia, PA [*OCLC symbol*] (OCLC)
PLT Page Layout Terminal [*Graphic arts*] (DGA)
PLT Pallet (AABC)
Plt Parliament
PLT Partido Liberal Teete [*Teete Liberal Party*] [*Paraguay*] [*Political party*] (PPW)
PLT Patna Law Times [*India*] [*A publication*] (DLA)
Plt Peltier's Orleans Appeals Decisions [*Louisiana*] [*A publication*] (DLA)
PLT Photoluminescent Thermometer
PLT Pilot (AFM)
PLT Pilot Knob [*California*] [*Seismograph station code, US Geological Survey*] (SEIS)
PLT Pipeline Time [*Army*]
PLT Plaint [*Legal term*] (ROG)
PLT Planar Tube
PLT Plant
PLT Plantronics, Inc. [*NYSE symbol*] (SPSG)
PLT Plate
PLT Platelet [*Hematology*]
PLT Platoon [*Military*] (AABC)
PLT Port Light
PLT Post Loading Test (NG)
PLT Power Line Transient (IEEE)
PLT Primed Lymphocyte Typing [*Hematology*]
PLT Princeton Large Torus [*Nuclear reactor*]
PLT Private Line Telephone
PLT Private Line Teletypewriter
PLT Procurement Lead Time [*Army*]
PLT Production Lead Time
PLT Program Library Tape [*Computer science*] (IEEE)
PLT Programmed Learning Textbook
PLT Progressive Lowering of Temperature
PLT Psittacosis-Lymphogranuloma Venereum Trachoma [*Microbiology*]
PLT Pulsed Light Theodolite
PLT Punjab Law Times [*India*] [*A publication*] (DLA)
PLT South Carolina Aeronautics Commission [*FAA designator*] (FAAC)
PLTC Partnership for Long Term Care
PLTC Port Liner Terms Charges [*Shipping*] (DS)
PLTC Propellant Loading Terminal Cabinet (AAG)
PLTD Plated
PLTF Par Leadership Training Foundation [*Defunct*] (EA)
PLTF Plaintiff [*Legal term*] (ROG)
PLTF Purple Loosestrife Task Force [*Defunct*] (EA)
PLTFF Plaintiff
PLTFM Platform
PLT-G Giant Platelet [*Hematology*] (DAVI)
PLTG Plating
PLTG Plating
PLT GL Plate Glass [*Freight*]
PLTHS Pilothouse
PLT LT Pilot Light (MSA)
PLTN Platoon
Plt Off Pilot Officer [*British military*] (DMA)
PLTP Phospholipid Transfer Protein [*Biochemistry*]
PLTR Plan for Long-Range Technical Requirements
PLTR Plotter (MSA)
PLTR Procurement Lead Time Requirement
Pltrsq Plateresque (VRA)
PLTRY Poultry [*Freight*]
PLTS Precision LASER Tracking System (NASA)
PLTTNG Pilot Training [*Air Force*]
PLTTNGSq Pilot Training Squadron [*Air Force*]
PLTTY Private Line Teletypewriter [*Telecommunications*] (IAA)
PLTTY Private Line Teletypewriter Service (NITA)
PLTXAU Public Telex Access Unit [*Telecommunications*] (OSI)
PLTY Poultry
PLTYP Plumbeotype (VRA)
PLTZC Pulitzer Publishing Co. (MHDW)
PLU Partial Line Up (NITA)
PLU Partido Liberal Unificado [*Unified Liberal Party*] [*Paraguay*] [*Political party*] (PPW)
PLu Path Loss, Uplink [*Communications*]
PLU People Like Us (IIA)
PLU PERT [*Program Evaluation and Review Technique*] Life Cycle Unified System (IAA)
PLU Phi Lambda Upsilon [*Fraternity*]
PLU Platoon Leaders Unit [*Marine Corps*]
Pl U Plowden on Usury [*A publication*] (DLA)
PLU Pluggable Unit (SAA)
PLU Plural
plu Plural (WDMC)
PLU Plutonium [*Chemical symbol is Pu*] (AAG)
PLU Poor Law Union [*British*]
PLU Pratt & Lambert United, Inc. [*NYSE symbol*] (SAG)
PLU Preservation of Location Uncertainty [*Strategy for protecting missiles*] [*Military*]
PLU Pressure Lubrication Unit
PLU Price Look-Up (IAA)
PLU Probability of Leakage through Underlay
PLU Propellant Loading and Utilization (AAG)
PLUCON Plutonium Decontamination Emergency Team [*Army*]
PLUG Propellant Loading and Utilization Group (AAG)
PLUGE Picture Line-Up Generator [*Television*]
PLuL Lincoln University, Lincoln University, PA [*Library symbol Library of Congress*] (LCLS)
PLUM Payload Launch Module
PLUM Payload Umbilical Mast (NASA)
PLUM Priority Low-Use Minimal
PLUM Programmes Library Update and Maintenance (PDAA)
PLUM Programming Language for Users of MAVIS [*Microprocessor-Based Audio Visual Information System*] (PDAA)
PLUMB Plumbum [*Lead*] [*Pharmacy*]
Plum Contr Plumptre on Contracts [*2nd ed.*] [*1897*] [*A publication*] (DLA)
PlumCrk Plum Creek Timber Co., Inc. [*Associated Press*] (SAG)
PLUNA Primeras Lineas Uruguayas de Navegacion Aerea [*Uruguayan National Airlines*]
PLund Papyri Lundenses [*A publication*] (OCD)
PLUOT Parts Listing Used On-Line Technique [*Computer science*] (IAA)
PLUP Pluperfect [*Grammar*]
PLUPF Pluperfect [*Grammar*]
PLUR Jarvis Island [*Line Islands*] [*ICAO location identifier*] (ICLI)
PLUR Photo Lab Usage Reporting (MCD)
PLUR Plural
PLUS Parent Loans to Undergraduate Students [*Later, ALAS*] [*Department of Education*]
PLUS PERT [*Program Evaluation and Review Technique*] Lifecycle Unified System
PLUS Portable Lightweight Upper Air Sounding System (MCD)
PLUS Potential Long Supply Utilization Screening (NATG)
PLUS Precision Loading and Utilization System (AAG)
PLUS Prima Leben und Sparen [*Quality Living and Saving*] [*Brand name and discount store chain in West Germany and US*]
PLUS Procedures for Long Supply Assets Utilization Screening [*DoD*]
PLUS Program Language for User's System (NITA)
PLUS Program Library Update System
PLUS Programmed Learning under Supervision
PLUS Programming Language for UNIVAC [*Universal Automatic Computer*] Systems [*Computer science*] (CSR)

PLUS .... Project Literacy US [*Joint project of American Broadcasting Co. and Public Broadcasting Service*]
PLUS .... Prudent Laboratory Use System [*Health insurance*] (GHCT)
PLUS .... Room Plus, Inc. [*NASDAQ symbol*] (SAG)
Plut .... Plutarch [*First century AD*] [*Classical studies*] (OCD)
PLUT .... Plutchnik [*Geriatric rating scale*] (DMAA)
Plut .... Plutus [*of Aristophanes*] [*Classical studies*] (OCD)
PLUTHARCO... Plutonium, Uranium, Thorium Assembly Reactivity Code
PLUTO .... Pipeline under the Ocean [*British project*] [*World War II*]
PLUTO .... Plutonium [*Loop-Testing*] Reactor [*British*] (DEN)
PLUVUE .... Plume Visibility Model [*Environmental Protection Agency*] (GFGA)
PLUZ .... Policy Land Use Zone [*Australian Capital Territory*]
PLV .... Live Poliomyelitis Vaccine [*Immunology*] (MAE)
PLV .... Panleukopenia Virus [*Medicine*] (MAE)
PLV .... Peak Left Ventricular [*Pressure*] [*Cardiology*]
PLV .... Phenylalanine-Lysine-Vasopressin (MAE)
PLV .... Phu-Lien [*Kien-An*] [*Vietnam*] [*Seismograph station code, US Geological Survey*] (SEIS)
PLV .... Polaravia OY [*Finland ICAO designator*] (FAAC)
PLV .... Posterior Left Ventricle [*Anatomy*] (DAVI)
PLV .... Posterior Left Ventricular Wall [*Cardiology*]
PLV .... Postlanding Vent [*or Ventilation*] [*Apollo*] [*NASA*]
PLV .... Power Limiting Valve
PLV .... Presentation Level Video (PCM)
PLV .... Production Level Video
PLVC .... Post-Landing Vent Control [*NASA*] (KSC)
PLVL .... Present Level [*Aviation*] (FAAC)
PLVRZD .... Pulverized (MSA)
PLW .... Palau [*ANSI three-letter standard code*] (CNC)
PLW .... Palu [*Indonesia*] [*Airport symbol*] (OAG)
PLW .... Patna Law Weekly [*India*] [*A publication*] (DLA)
PLW .... Plastic Engineering Technology Corp. [*Toronto Stock Exchange symbol*]
PLW .... Plow Snow [*NWS*] (FAAC)
PLW .... Preload Washer
PL/WA .... Plain Washer [*Automotive engineering*]
plwd .... Plywood (BARN)
PLWG .... Photographic Laboratories Working Group [*Range Commanders Council*] [*White Sands Missile Range, NM*]
PLWHA .... People Living With HIV/AIDS [*Human Immunodeficiency Virus / Acquired Immune Deficiency Syndrome*] [*Australia*]
PLWS .... Prader-Labhart-Willi Syndrome [*Medicine*] (DMAA)
PLX .... Parallax Developments [*Vancouver Stock Exchange symbol*]
PLX .... Plains Resources [*AMEX symbol*] (TTSB)
PLX .... Plains Resources, Inc. [*AMEX symbol*] (SPSG)
PLX .... Plexus [*Medicine*]
PLX .... Position Launch [*Search mode wherein X signifies the launch mode number*] (MCD)
PLX .... Propellant Loading Exercise (MCD)
PLX .... Robinson, IL [*Location identifier FAA*] (FAAL)
PLXS .... Plexus Corp. [*NASDAQ symbol*] (NQ)
PLY .... Photoluminescence Yield [*Spectroscopy*]
Ply .... Plymouth [*Record label*]
PLY .... Plywood
ply .... Plywood (VRA)
PLY .... Polaris Energy [*Vancouver Stock Exchange symbol*]
PLY .... Polyphase Corp. [*AMEX symbol*] (SPSG)
PLY .... Polyphase Corp. [*AMEX symbol*] (TTSB)
PLY .... Prune Extract Lactose Yeast Medium [*Microbiology*]
plyc .... Polychrome (VRA)
plyes .... Polyester (VRA)
PlyGem .... Ply-Gem, Inc. [*Associated Press*] (SAG)
PLYINST .... Command Comply Current Instructions
PLYM .... Plymouth [*England*]
plym .... Polymer (VRA)
P-LYM .... Prolymphocyte [*Hematology*] (DAVI)
PLYMCHAN... Plymouth Subarea Channel [*NATO*] (NATG)
Plymouth St C... Plymouth State College (GAGS)
PLYMP .... Plympton [*England*]
PLYMT .... Plymtree [*England*]
PLYPASSPORT... Application for Passport for Self and/or Dependents Accordance BUPERS Manual [*Navy*]
plypt .... Polyptic (VRA)
PlyR .... Plymouth Rubber Co., Inc. [*Associated Press*] (SAG)
plyst .... Polystyrene (VRA)
plyur .... Polyurethane (VRA)
plyvn .... Polyvinyl (VRA)
PLYWD .... Plywood (AAG)
PLYWD .... Plywood
PLZ .... Phenelzine (DMAA)
PLZ .... Plaza
Plz .... Plaza (AD)
PLZ .... Plaza (MCD)
PLZ .... Please
PLZ .... Polarize (MSA)
PLZ .... Port Elizabeth [*South Africa*] [*Airport symbol*] (OAG)
PLZ .... Programming Languages for the Zilog [*Computer science*] (CSR)
PLZA .... Plaza [*Commonly used*] (OPSA)
PLZN .... Polarization (MSA)
PLZT .... Pb-based Lanthanum-doped Zirconate Titanates
PM .... [*The*] Chesapeake & Ohio Railway Co. (Pere Marquette District) [*AAR code*]
PM .... Cold Press Molding
PM .... Ha-Po'el ha-Mizrahi (BJA)
PM .... Pacemaker [*Medicine*] (DMAA)
PM .... Pacific Mail (ROG)
P/M .... Pacific Molasses (AD)
PM .... Pad Mechanic [*Aerospace*]
PM .... Painting Machine
PM .... Pak [*or Phak*] Mai [*New Party*] [*Political party*]
PM .... Pamphlet
PM .... Panel Maintenance (IAA)
PM .... Panel Meter (IEEE)
pm .... Papier Mache (VRA)
PM .... Parachute Mine [*British military*] (DMA)
PM .... Parameter [*Computer science*]
pm .... Paramilitary (AD)
Pm .... Paratid Midle [*Band protein*] (DMAA)
PM .... Paraxial Magnification (SAA)
P/M .... Parent-Metabolite Ratio [*Medicine*] (MEDA)
PM .... Parlor Maid
PM .... Partial Remission [*Medicine*] (CDI)
PM .... Particulate Matter
PM .... Partito Monarchico [*Monarchist Party*] [*Italy Political party*] (PPE)
P/M .... Parts per Million (IEEE)
PM .... Passed Midshipman
PM .... Passed Motion
PM .... Past Master [*Freemasonry*]
PM .... Patriotic Majority [*An association*] (EA)
PM .... Patriotikon Metopon [*Patriotic Front*] [*Greek Cyprus*] [*Political party*] (PPE)
PM .... Patternmaker [*Navy rating*]
PM .... Payload Management [*NASA*] (NASA)
PM .... Payload Midbody [*NASA*] (MCD)
PM .... Paymaster
PM .... Peabody Museum (AD)
PM .... Peace Museum (EA)
PM .... Pectoralis Major [*Anatomy*]
PM .... Peculiar Meter
PM .... Penalty Minutes [*Hockey*]
PM .... Pension Mortgage [*British*]
PM .... People Meter [*TV ratings measuring device*] [*Advertising*]
PM .... Pere Marquette Railroad
PM .... Perfect Master [*Freemasonry*]
PM .... Performance Monitor [*NASA*] (NASA)
PM .... Periodic Maintenance (AFM)
PM .... Peritoneal Macrophage [*Immunology*] (AAMN)
PM .... Permanent Magnet [*Loudspeaker*]
p-m .... Permanent Magnet (AD)
PM .... Per Million
PM .... Per Minute (IAA)
PM .... Per Month
Pm .... Petameter (IDOE)
PM .... Petit Mal [*Epilepsy*]
PM .... Petroleos Mexicanos [*Spanish*] (AD)
PM .... Phased Maintenance (MCD)
PM .... Phase Match (IAA)
PM .... Phase Modulation [*Radio data transmission*]
p-m .... Phase Modulation (AD)
PM .... Philip Morris, Inc.
PM .... Phorbol Monomyristate [*Organic chemistry*]
PM .... Phosphoramide Mustard [*Antineoplastic drug*]
PM .... Photo Marketing Magazine [*A publication*] (EAAP)
PM .... Photo Master (MCD)
PM .... Photomultiplier
PM .... Phyllosticta maydis [*A toxin-producing fungus*]
P/M .... Physical Medicine [*Medical officer designation*] [*British*]
PM .... Physical Medicine
PM .... Piae Memoriae [*Of Pious Memory*] [*Latin*]
pm .... Picometer [*One trillionth of a meter*]
pM .... Picomoler [*One trillionth of a mole*] (AAMN)
PM .... Pilgrim Airlines [*ICAO designator*] (AD)
PM .... Pilot Motor (MSA)
PM .... Pioneer Ministries (EA)
PM .... Pitching Moment [*Physics*]
PM .... Pitch Mark [*Shipfitting*]
PM .... Pit Membrane [*Paleobotany*]
PM .... Planetary Mission [*NASA*] (NASA)
PM .... Plasmalemma [*Cytology*]
PM .... Plasma Membrane [*Cytology*]
PM .... Plaster Master (MSA)
PM .... Plastic Mold (MCD)
PM .... Platelet Microsome [*Medicine*] (DMAA)
P/M .... Player/Missile [*Atari computers*]
PM .... Plus Minus [*More or less*]
PM .... Pneumomediastinum [*Medicine*] (AAMN)
pm .... Poids Moliculaire [*Molecular Weight*] [*French*] (AD)
PM .... Polarization-Maintaining [*Optical Film*]
PM .... Polarization Modulation (MCD)
PM .... Police Magistrate
PM .... Police Mutual Assurance Society [*British*]
PM .... Policy Memorandum [*Military*]
PM .... Poliomyelitis [*Medicine*]
PM .... Pollen Mass [*Botany*]
PM .... Pollution Minimum
PM .... PolyMedica Industries [*AMEX symbol*] (TTSB)
PM .... PolyMedica Industries, Inc. [*AMEX symbol*] (SAG)
PM .... Polymeric Membrane
PM .... Polymethacrylic [*Organic chemistry*]
PM .... Polymorph [*Hematology*]
PM .... Polymorphonuclear [*Leukocyte*] [*Hematology*] (DAVI)

PM Polymyositis [*Medicine*]
PM Pondus Medicinale [*Medicinal Weight*] [*Pharmacy*] (ROG)
PM Pontifex Maximus [*Supreme Pontiff*] [*Latin*]
PM Poor Metabolism [*Medicine*]
PM Pope and Martyr [*Church calendars*]
PM Popular Movement Against the European Community (ECON)
PM Portable Magnetometer [*NASA*]
PM Portable Medium Power Plant [*Nuclear energy*] (NRCH)
PM Postal Manual
PM Posterior Mitral Leaflet [*Cardiology*]
PM Postmark [*Deltiology*]
PM Postmaster
PM Postmaster
PM Postmenopausal [*Gynecology*] (DAVI)
pm Post Meridiem [*After noon*] [*Latin*] (AD)
pm Post Meridiem [*Afternoon*] [*Latin*] (WDMC)
PM Post Meridiem [*After Noon*] [*Latin*]
PM Postmodernist [*Architecture*]
PM Post Mortem [*After Death*] [*Latin*]
pm Post Mortem (AD)
PM Potentiometer (DEN)
PM Potting Mold (MCD)
PM Pounds per Minute
PM Powder Metallurgy
PM Power Module (MCD)
PM Powlesland & Mason [*Railway*] [*Wales*]
PM Precious Metal
PM Preincubation Mixture
PM Premium
pm Premium (AD)
pm Premium (ODBW)
pm Premolar [*Dentistry*] (AD)
PM Premolar [*Dentistry*]
PM Prenegotiation Memorandum (AAGC)
PM Preparation Meetings [*Quakers*]
PM Prepared Message
PM Presbyterian Men (EA)
PM Presentation Manager [*Computer science*]
PM Presidential Memo
PM Pressure, Manifold
PM Pressure Multiplier [*Nuclear energy*] (NRCH)
PM Pressurized Module (SSD)
PM Presystolic Murmur [*Cardiology*]
pm Presystolic Murmur [*Medicine*] (AD)
PM Pretibial Myxedema [*Medicine*] (DMAA)
PM Preventive Maintenance
pm Preventive Maintenance (AD)
PM Preventive Material
PM Preventive Medicine [*Also, PVNTMED*] (AFM)
PM Priest and Martyr [*Church calendars*]
PM Primary Market [*Investment term*]
PM Primary Motivation [*Psychology*] (DAVI)
PM Primary Munition
PM Prime Minister
PM Prime Mover (MCD)
PM Primitive Methodists (ROG)
PM Principal Matron [*Navy British*]
PM Principle of Multiplying [*New math*]
PM Printing Mechanism (IAA)
PM Print Matrix (IAA)
PM Prize Money
PM Procedures Manual (IEEE)
PM Processing Modflow [*Computer program*] [*Scientific Software Group*]
PM Processing Module [*Computer science*]
PM Process Manager (USDC)
PM Process Manager [*Marine science*] (OSRA)
PM Process Manual
PM Processor Module (NITA)
PM Procurement and Material
PM Procurement Manual [*US Postal Service*] [*A publication*] (AAGC)
PM Production [*or Product*] Manager
PM Production Mode
PM Production Monitor (IAA)
p/m Professional/Managerial (WDMC)
PM Profit Margin (TDOB)
PM Profit Motivated [*Housing*]
PM Program (NG)
PM Program Manager [*or Management*] (MCD)
pm Program Manager (AD)
PM Program Memorandum (MCD)
PM Program Method [*Computer science*] (IAA)
PM Program Milestone [*NASA*] (NASA)
PM Program Monitoring (MUGU)
PM Project Magic (EA)
PM Project Manager [*Military*]
PM Pro Memoria [*In Remembrance*] [*Latin*]
PM Pro Mense [*Per Month*] [*Latin*]
Pm Promethium [*Chemical symbol*]
PM Pro Mille [*Per Thousand*] [*Latin*]
PM Propellant Management (KSC)
PM Proper Motion [*Astronomy*] (BARN)
PM Property Management (OICC)
PM Propulsion Memorandum
PM Propulsion Module [*NASA*] (KSC)
PM Prostatic Massage [*Medicine*]
PM Protocol Machine [*Computer science*] (TNIG)
PM Provost Marshal [*Army*]
PM Puberal Macromastia [*Medicine*] (DMAA)
PM Publicity Man [*Slang*]
pm Publicity Man (AD)
PM Pulmonary Macrophages [*Medicine*]
PM Pulpomesial [*Dentistry*]
PM Pulse Code Modulation [*Telecommunications*] (IAA)
PM Pulse Modulation
pm Pulse Modulation (AD)
PM Pulse Modulator (IDOE)
pm Pumice (AD)
Pm Pumice [*Quality of the bottom*] [*Nautical charts*]
PM Punjabi Muslim [*Pakistan*]
PM Purchase Memo (MCD)
PM Purchase-Money Mortgage [*Real estate*]
PM Purchasing Manager
PM Purpose-Made [*Construction*]
PM Push Money [*Sales incentive*]
P/M Put of More [*Stock exchange term*]
PM Pyridoxamine [*Also, Pxm*] [*Biochemistry*]
PM Sisters of the Presentation of Mary [*Roman Catholic religious order*]
PM St. Pierre and Miquelon [*ANSI two-letter standard code*] (CNC)
PM1 Patternmaker, First Class [*Navy rating*]
PM2 Patternmaker, Second Class [*Navy rating*]
PM3 Patternmaker, Third Class [*Navy rating*]
PM10 Particulate Matter [*Less than 10 microns*]
PM-10 Particulate Matter of 10 Microns in Diameter or Smaller [*BTS*] (TAG)
PMA Allegheny College, Meadville, PA [*Library symbol Library of Congress*] (LCLS)
PMA Pacific Maritime Association (EA)
PMA Pan-Macedonian Association (EA)
PMA Pan Malaysian Air Transport [*ICAO designator*] (FAAC)
PMA Panorama Resources Ltd. [*Vancouver Stock Exchange symbol*]
PMA Papillary, Marginal, Attached [*With reference to gingivae*] [*Dentistry*]
PMA Paramethoxyamphetamine
pma Paramethoxyamphetamine (AD)
PMA Parts Manufacturer Approval [*FAA*] (MCD)
PMA Parts Manufacturing Associates (AD)
PMA Peat Moss Association (EA)
PMA Pemba Island [*Tanzania*] [*Airport symbol*] (OAG)
PMA Pencil Makers Association (EA)
PMA Performance Management Association (EAIO)
PMA Performance Monitor Annunciator [*NASA*] (MCD)
PMA Permanent Magnet Association (IAA)
PMA Permanent Mailing Address
PMA Personal Managers Association [*British*] (DBA)
PMA Personal Money Allowance
PMA Personnel Management Advisor (NOAA)
PMA Personnel Management Assistance
PMA Perth Market Authority [*Australia*]
PMA Perth Muslim Association [*Australia*]
PMA Petroleum Monitoring Agency [*Ministry of Energy, Mines, and Resources*] [*Canada*]
PMA Pharmaceutical Manufacturers Association (EA)
PMA Phased Maintenance Availability [*Navy*] (DOMA)
PMA Phenylmercuric Acetate [*Also, PMAC*] [*Herbicide and fungicide*]
PMA Philadelphia Museum of Art (AD)
PMA Philadelphia Musical Academy
PMA Philippine Mahogany Association [*Defunct*] (EA)
PMA Phonograph Manufacturers Association (EA)
PMA Phorbol Myristate Acetate [*Also, PTA, TPA*] [*Organic chemistry*]
PMA Phosphomolybdic Acid [*Organic chemistry*]
PMA Photo Marketing Association (AD)
PMA Photo Marketing Association International (EA)
PMA Photonic Multichannel Analyzer
PMA Physical Medium Attachment [*Telecommunications*] (OSI)
PMA Physical Medium Attachment (NITA)
PMA Physical Memory Address
PMA Pianoforte Manufacturers' Association Ltd. [*British*] (BI)
PMA Pine Manor College, Chestnut Hill, MA [*OCLC symbol*] (OCLC)
PMA Planetary Microbiological Assay [*Aerospace*]
PMA Plastic Mock-Up Assembly
PMA Plumbers' Merchants Association [*British*] (BI)
PMA PMI Group [*NYSE symbol*] (TTSB)
PMA PMI Group, Inc. [*NYSE symbol*] (SAG)
PMA Pole-Mounted Amplifier
PMA Police Management Association [*Defunct*] (EA)
PMA Police Marksman Association (EA)
PMA Polish Museum of America (EA)
PMA Politico-Military Affairs [*U.S. Department of State*] (BARN)
PMA Poly(methyl Acrylate) [*Organic chemistry*]
PMA Polyurethane Manufacturers Association (EA)
PMA Portable Maintenance Aid [*Army*]
PMA Port Moller [*Alaska*] [*Seismograph station code, US Geological Survey*] (SEIS)
PMA Positive Mental Attitude
pma Positive Mental Attitude (AD)
PMA Potato Marketing Authority [*Australia*]
PMA Potato Merchants' Association [*Australia*]
PMA Power Marketing Administration [*Department of Energy*]
PMA Preamplifier Module Assembly
PMA Precious Metal Adder (Cost) (MCD)
PMA Precious Metal Anode
PMA Precision Measurements Association (EA)

PMA............ Precision Metalforming Association (EA)
PMA............ Premarket Approval Application [*Food and Drug Administration*]
PMA............ Prevalence of Gingivitis [*Dentistry*] (DAVI)
PMA............ Preventive Maintenance Agreement
PMA............ Primary Market Area
PMA............ Primary Mental Abilities [*Test*] [*Education*]
PMA............ Prime Macro-Assembler (NITA)
PMA............ Prinzmetal's Angina [*Cardiology*] (DAVI)
PMA............ Priority Memory Access
PMA............ Priority Memory Address (NITA)
PMA............ Prison Mission Association (EA)
PMA............ Probability of Mission Abort [*Navy*] (ANA)
PMA............ Probationary Medical Assistant [*British military*] (DMA)
PMA............ Procurement and Management Assistance [*Small Business Administration*]
PMA............ Procurement Methods Analyst (AFM)
PMA............ Produce Marketing Association [*Newark, DE*] (EA)
PMA............ Production and Marketing Administration [*Department of Agriculture*] [*Functions dispersed, 1953*]
PMA............ Professional Managers Association (EA)
PMA............ Professional Manufacturers' Agents (EA)
PMA............ Professional Mariners Alliance [*Defunct*] (EA)
PMA............ Programa Mundial de Alimentos [*World Food Program*] [*Spanish*] (AD)
PMA............ Progressive Muscular Atrophy [*Medicine*]
PMA............ Project Manager, Air Systems Command [*Navy*]
PMA............ Project Military Adviser (NATG)
PMA............ Property Management Association of America (EA)
PMA............ Property Market Analysis [*Consulting firm*] [*British*]
PMA............ Prorated Mental Age [*Psychology*]
PMA............ Protected Memory Address
PMA............ Publishers Marketing Association (EA)
PMA............ Pulpomesioaxial [*Dentistry*]
PMA............ Pump-Motor Assembly
PMA............ Purchase Methods Analyst
PMA............ Pyridylmercuric Acetate [*Fungicide*] [*Organic chemistry*]
PMA............ Pyromellitic Acid [*Organic chemistry*]
PMAA.......... Paper Makers Advertising Association (EA)
PMAA.......... Petroleum Marketers Association of America (EA)
PMAA.......... Promotion Marketing Association of America [*New York, NY*] (EA)
PMAA.......... Property Management Association of America (EA)
PMAA.......... Proprietary Medicines Association of Australia
PM-AAH........ Project Manager, Advanced Attack Helicopter [*Military*]
PMA/ARR..... Probable Missed Approach per Arrival [*Aviation*] (PDAA)
PMAC.......... Parallel Memory Address Counter [*Computer science*]
PMAC.......... Phamaceutical Manufacturers Association of Canada
PMAC.......... Pharmaceutical Manufacturers Association of Canada
PMAC.......... Phenylmercuric Acetate [*Also, PMA*] [*Herbicide and fungicide*]
PMAC.......... PMA Communications, Inc. [*Boston, MA*] (TSSD)
PMAC.......... Preliminary Maintenance Allocation Chart (MCD)
PMAC.......... Proprietary Medicines Advisory Committee [*Australia*]
PMAC.......... Provisional Military Administrative Council [*Ethiopia*] [*Political party*] (PD)
PMAC.......... Purchasing Management Association of Canada
PMACODS.... Project Manager, Army Container Oriented Distribution System (MCD)
PM ACS....... Product Manager, Army Communications System
PMAD.......... Performance Monitor Annunciation Driver [*NASA*] (MCD)
PMAD.......... Personnel Management Authorization Document [*Army*]
PMAD.......... Power Management and Distribution (NASA)
PMadW........ Westinghouse Electric Corp., Waltz Mill Site Library, Madison, PA [*Library symbol Library of Congress*] (LCLS)
PMAE.......... Peabody Museum of Archeology and Ethnology (AD)
PMAESA...... Port Management Association of Eastern and Southern Africa (EA)
PMAF.......... Pharmaceutical Manufacturers Association Foundation (IAA)
PMAF.......... Polaris Missile Assembly Facility
PMAFS........ Public Members Association of the Foreign Service (EA)
PMAG.......... Program Manager Assistance Group [*Military*] (MCD)
PMAG.......... Provisional Military Advisory Group
PMAI.......... Piano Manufacturers Association International (EA)
P/Maj.......... Pipe-Major [*British military*] (DMA)
PMALS........ Prototype Miniature Air-Launched System
PMAN.......... Piedmont Management Co., Inc. [*NASDAQ symbol*] (NQ)
PM & ACS... Procurement Management and Acquisition Control System [*Social Security Administration*]
PM & C........ Plant Monitoring and Control [*IBM Corp.*]
PM & C-HI... Plant Monitoring and Control - Host Interface [*IBM Corp.*]
PM & OA..... Printers' Managers and Overseers Association (AD)
pm & r......... Physical Medicine and Rehabilitation (AD)
PM & R........ Physical Medicine and Rehabilitation
PM&R.......... Physical Medicine and Rehabilitation
PManM........ Mansfield State College, Mansfield, PA [*Library symbol Library of Congress*] (LCLS)
PMANY........ Pattern Makers Association of New York (EA)
PMAP.......... Performance Monitor Annunciation Panel [*NASA*] (MCD)
PMAP.......... Photomap
PMAR.......... Page Map Address Register
PMAR.......... Precious Metals Area Representative [*DoD*] (AFIT)
PMAR.......... Preliminary Maintenance Analysis Report [*Aerospace*] (AAG)
PMarhSO..... Sun Oil Co., Marcus Hook, PA [*Library symbol Library of Congress*] (LCLS)
PMARP........ Peacetime Manpower Allocation Requirements Plan (CINC)
PMARS........ Performance Management and Recognition System (MCD)
PMAS.......... Police Mutual Assurance Society [*British*]
PMAS.......... Purdue Master Attitude Scales [*Psychology*]
PMASA........ Printers' Medical Aid and Sanatoria Association [*British*] (BI)
PM-ASE....... Project Manager, Aircraft Survivability Equipment [*Military*]
PM-ASH....... Project Manager, Advanced Scout Helicopter [*Military*]
PM-ASI........ Program Management Office for Armored Systems Integration [*Army*] (RDA)
PMAT.......... Page Map Address Table [*NASA*] (NASA)
PMAT.......... Plasma & Materials Technologies [*NASDAQ symbol*] (TTSB)
PMAT.......... Plasma & Materials Technologies, Inc. [*NASDAQ symbol*] (SAG)
PMAT.......... Portable Maintenance Access Terminal [*Computer science*]
PMAT.......... Primary Mental Abilities Test [*Education*]
PMAT.......... Purdue Mechanical Adaptability Test
PMATA........ Paint Manufacture and Allied Trades' Association [*British*] (BI)
PMATA........ Paper Makers' Allied Trades Association [*British*] (DBA)
PMax.......... Peak Inspiratory Pressure [*Medicine*] (DAVI)
PMB............ Canadian Print Measurement Bureau (NITA)
PMB............ Cis-Platinum, Methotrexate, Bleomycin [*Antineoplastic drug regimen*] (DAVI)
PMB............ Pacific Motor Tariff Bureau, Inc., Oakland CA [*STAC*]
PMB............ Palm Beach [*Diocesan abbreviation*] [*Florida*] (TOCD)
PMB............ Para-Hydroxymercuribenzoate [*Biochemistry*] (MAE)
PMB............ Paranormal Metal Bending
PMB............ Pembina, ND [*Location identifier FAA*] (FAAL)
PMB............ Performance Measurement Baseline (MCD)
PMB............ Physical Metallurgy Branch
PMB............ Pilot Make Busy (IEEE)
PMB............ Plastic Media Blasting [*Coating technology*]
PMB............ Polychrome Methylene Blue
PMB............ Polymethylbenzene [*Organic chemistry*]
PMB............ Polymorphonuclear Basophilic [*Leucocytes*] [*Hematology*]
PMB............ Postmenopausal Bleeding [*Medicine*]
pmb............ Post-Menopausal Bleeding [*Medicine*] (AD)
PMB............ Potato Marketing Board [*British*]
PMB............ Practice Multiple Bomb (MCD)
PMB............ Precision Manned Bomber
PMB............ Print Measurement Bureau [*Founded in 1971*] [*Also the name of a database*] [*Canada*]
PMB............ Private Mail Bag
PMB............ Program Management Board (AFM)
PMB............ Project Management and Budgeting
PMB............ PROM [*Programmable Read-Only Memory*] Memory Board
PMBA.......... Professional Master of Business Administration (PGP)
PMBC.......... Pacific Motor Boat Club (AD)
PMBC.......... Phuket Marine Biological Center [*Marine science*] (MSC)
PMBC.......... Portland Motor Boat Club [*Oregon*] (AD)
PMBC.......... Process-Model Based Controller (ACII)
PMBIAS....... Percentage Median Bias [*Statistics*]
pmbo.......... Participative Management by Objectives (AD)
PMBOK........ Project Management Body of Knowledge
PMBR.......... Practice Multiple Bomb Rack (NG)
PMBS.......... Pelican Man's Bird Sanctuary (EA)
PMBU.......... Personal Member of the Baptist Union [*British*]
PMBX.......... Private Manual Branch Exchange [*Communications*]
pmbx.......... Private Manual Branch Exchange (AD)
PMC............ Carnegie-Mellon University, Pittsburgh, PA [*OCLC symbol*] (OCLC)
PMC............ Chief Patternmaker [*Navy rating*]
PMC............ Little Missionary Sisters of Charity [*Roman Catholic religious order*]
PMC............ Pacific Marine Center [*National Oceanic and Atmospheric Administration*]
PMC............ Pacific Medical Center (BABM)
PMC............ Pacific Missile Center [*Marine science*] (MSC)
PMC............ Pan Metal [*formerly, Patton Morgan*] Corp. [*Ammunition manufacturer*]
PMC............ Parents of Missing Children [*Australia*]
PMC............ Parents of Murdered Children [*Later, POMC*] (EA)
PMC............ Partially Mission Capable [*Maintenance and supply*] (MCD)
PMC............ Patient Management Categories [*Medicine*] (MEDA)
PMC............ Patrol/Mine Countermeasure Craft [*British*]
PMC............ Payload Monitoring and Control [*NASA*] (NASA)
PMC............ Penguin Modern Classics [*Book publishing*]
PMC............ Pennsylvania Military Academy (AD)
PMC............ Pennsylvania Military College
PMC............ Pentamethyl(hydroxy)chromane [*Organic chemistry*]
PMC............ People's Mandate Committee (EA)
PMC............ Percent Modern Carbon [*In atmosphere*]
PMC............ Performance Management Computer (PDAA)
PMC............ Peripheral Mononuclear Cell [*Cytology*]
PMC............ Peritoneal Mast Cell
PMC............ Permanently Manned Capability (SSD)
PMC............ Personnel Management Centre [*British*] (ODBW)
PMC............ Personnel Mobilization Center [*Military*]
PMC............ Phased Maintenance Checklist (MCD)
PMC............ Phenolic Molding Compound
PMC............ Phenylmercuric Chloride [*Antiseptic*]
PMC............ Philatelic Music Circle (EA)
PMC............ Piperidinomethylcyclohexane [*Organic chemistry*]
PMC............ Planning Ministers' Conference [*Australia*]
PMC............ Plaster-Molded Cornice [*Construction*]
PMC............ Plutona-Molybdenum CERMET [*Ceramic Metal Element*] (NASA)
PMC............ PMC Capital [*AMEX symbol*] (TTSB)
PMC............ PMC Capital, Inc. [*AMEX symbol*] (SPSG)
PMC............ Pollen Mother Cell [*Botany*]
PMC............ Polymer Matrix Composite [*Materials science*]
PMC............ Posterior Medial Corner of Knee [*Sports medicine*]
PMC............ Post Maintenance Check (MCD)
PMC............ Post Manufacturing Checkout (KSC)

PMC............ Post Master's Certificate (PGP)
PMC............ Powdered Metal Cathode
PMC............ Power-Mate Corp. (IAA)
PMC............ Precision Machining Commercialization (MCD)
pmc............ Precision Mirror Calorimeter (AD)
PMC............ Predictive Multisensor Correlation
PMC............ Pre-Mission Calibration (PDAA)
PMC............ Premium Merchandising Club of New York (EA)
PMC............ Premotor Cortex [*Neuroanatomy*]
PMC............ President of the Mess Committee [*Military British*]
PMC............ President's Management Council (AAGC)
PMC............ Pressurized Membrane Container
pmc............ Preventive Maintenance Contract (AD)
PMC............ Primary Mesenchyme Cell [*Cytology*]
PMC............ Prime Mover Control [*Valve*]
PMC............ Princeton Microfilm Corp.
PmC............ Princeton Microfilm Corporation, Princeton, NJ [*Library symbol Library of Congress*] (LCLS)
PMC............ Private Mailing Card [*Deltiology*]
PMC............ Private Medical Communication
PMC............ Private Meter Check [*Telecommunications*] (TEL)
PMC............ Processed Meats Committee [*Later, DPMC*] (EA)
PMC............ Procurement Committee (MCD)
PMC............ Procurement Management Code [*Military*] (AFIT)
PMC............ Procurement, Marine Corps [*An appropriation*]
PMC............ Procurement Method Coding [*DoD*]
PMC............ Professional and Managerial Class [*British*] (DI)
PMC............ Professional Musicians' Club [*Australia*]
PMC............ Programmable Machine Controller (NRCH)
PMC............ Programmable Machine Tool Controller (IAA)
PMC............ Programmable Matrix Controller (IAA)
PMC............ Program Management Control
PMC............ Program Management Course [*Army*] (RDA)
PMC............ Program Marginal Checking
PMC............ Project Management Committee (AD)
PMC............ Project Management Course [*Army*]
PMC............ Project Manufacturing Controller (MCD)
PMC............ Pro Maria Committee (EA)
PMC............ Propellant Monitor and Control (AFM)
PMC............ Pseudo Machine Code [*Computer science*] (BUR)
PMC............ Pseudomembranous Colitis [*Medicine*]
PMC............ Public Media Center (EA)
PMC............ Puerto Montt [*Chile*] [*Airport symbol*] (OAG)
PMC............ Pumice (MSA)
pMc............ Pure Mexican Cocaine (AD)
PMCA.......... Purple Martin Conservation Association (EA)
PM-CAWS..... Project Manager for Cannon Artillery Weapon Systems (RDA)
PMCB.......... Partially Mission Capable Both [*Maintenance and supply*] (MCD)
P/MCB......... Project/Miscellaneous Change Board (MCD)
PMCC.......... Peerless Motor Car Club (EA)
PMCC.......... Pensky-Martens Closed Cup [*Flash point test*]
PMCC.......... Platform Mission Control Center [*NASA*]
PMCC.......... Post Mark Collectors Club (EA)
PMCC.......... Product-Moment Correlation Co-Efficient (DMAA)
PMC CT....... PMC Commercial Trust [*Associated Press*] (SAG)
PMCD.......... Post Mortem Core Dump [*Computer science*]
PMCD.......... Process Measurement & Control Division (ACII)
PMCD.......... Program Module Connection Diagram (MHDI)
PMCF.......... Partial Mission Capability Factor
PMCF.......... Post Maintenance Check Flight (MCD)
PMCH.......... Pro-Melanin-Concentrating Hormone (DMAA)
PMCHi......... Crawford County Historical Society, Meadville, PA [*Library symbol Library of Congress*] (LCLS)
PMCHL........ Pro-Melanin-Concentrating Hormone-Like (DMAA)
PMCI.......... Phosphate Mining Corp. of Christmas Island (EY)
PMC INC...... Precision Management of Concordville, Inc. [*Media, PA*] (TSSD)
PMck.......... Carnegie Free Library of McKeesport, McKeesport, PA [*Library symbol Library of Congress*] (LCLS)
PMCL.......... Posterior Medial Collateral Ligament [*Anatomy*]
PMCL.......... Proposed MAPAD Change Letter (AAGC)
PMCL.......... Proposed MILSTRIP Change Letters
PMCM.......... Master Chief Patternmaker [*Navy rating*]
PMCM.......... Partially Mission Capable Maintenance [*Maintenance and supply*] (MCD)
PMCM.......... Permanent Mold Casting Mold (MCD)
PMCM.......... Pulse Morse Code Modulation (OA)
PMCP.......... Prime Capital Corp. [*NASDAQ symbol*] (SAG)
PMCQ.......... Paper Marketing Council of Queensland [*Australia*]
PMCS.......... Partially Mission Capable Supply [*Maintenance and supply*] (MCD)
PMCS.......... Patient Management Computer Stimulation (DMAA)
PMCS.......... Preventive Maintenance Checks and Services [*for Army vehicles*] (INF)
PMCS.......... Process Monitoring and Control System
pmcs........... Process Monitoring and Control Systems (AD)
PMCS.......... Professional Military Comptroller School
PMCS.......... Program [*or Project*] Management Control System [*Army*]
PMCS.......... Pulse-Modulated Communications System
PMCS.......... Senior Chief Patternmaker [*Navy rating*]
PMCT.......... PAL [*Permissive Action Link*] Management Control Team [*Army*] (AABC)
PMCTF........ Prime Minister's Country Task Force [*Australia*]
PMCU.......... Personal Member of the Congregational Union [*British*]
PMCU.......... Predominately Minority Colleges and Universities
PMCV.......... Programmed Multichannel Valve [*Chromatography*]
PMD............ Palmdale, CA [*Location identifier FAA*] (FAAL)
PMD............ Palmdale/Lancaster [*California*] [*Airport symbol*] (OAG)
PMD............ Palmer Industries Ltd. [*Vancouver Stock Exchange symbol*]
PMD............ Panel-Mounted Display (MCD)
PMD............ Part Manufacturing Design
PMD............ Payload Mating Dolly [*NASA*]
PMD............ Payload Module Decoder [*NASA*]
PMD............ Personnel Management Division [*Environmental Protection Agency*] (GFGA)
PMD............ Pharmaco-Medical Documentation, Inc. [*Information service or system*] (IID)
PMD............ Physical Medium Dependent [*Computer science*]
PMD............ Physical Medium Dependent Layer [*Telecommunications*] (OSI)
PMD............ Planning and Management Division [*Environmental Protection Agency*] (GFGA)
PMD............ Pontiac Motor Division [*General Motors Corp.*]
Pmd............ Portmadoc (AD)
PMD............ Post-Mortem Debugger [*Computer science*] (PCM)
PMD............ Post Mortem Dump [*Computer science*]
pmd............ Post-Mortem Dumps (AD)
PMD............ Preventive Maintenance, Daily (MCD)
PMD............ Preventive Maintenance Division [*Air Force*]
PMD............ Primary Myeloproliferative Disease [*Medicine*]
PMD............ Primary Myocardial Disease [*Medicine*]
PMD............ Private Management Domain [*Computer science*] (TNIG)
PMD............ Private Medical Doctor (DAVI)
PMd............ Private Physician
PMD............ Processing, Marketing, and Distribution
PMD............ Program for Management Development [*Harvard Business School*] (DD)
PMD............ Program Management Directive [*Air Force*]
PMD............ Program Management Documentation [*Army*]
PMD............ Programmed Multiple Development [*Analytical chemistry*]
PMD............ Program Module Dictionary
PMD............ Program Monitoring and Diagnosis
PMD............ Progressive Muscular Dystrophy [*Medicine*]
PMD............ Projected Map Display
pmd............ Projected Map Display (AD)
PMD............ Project Manager Development (MCD)
PMD............ Psychemedics Corp. [*AMEX symbol*] (SAG)
PMD............ Psychiatric Military Duty
PMDA.......... Photographic Manufacturers and Distributors Association (EA)
PMDA.......... Pianoforte Manufacturers and Distributors Association [*British*] (DBA)
PMDA.......... Plastics Machinery Distributors Association [*British*] (EAIO)
PMDA.......... Pyromellitic Dianhydride [*Organic chemistry*]
PMDAMT..... Pacific Mobile Depot Activity Maintenance Team (CINC)
PMDB.......... Program Management Decision Brief [*Defense Systems Management College*] (DOMA)
PMD/BMI..... Project Management Division/Batelle Memorial Institute (AD)
PMDC.......... Pakistan Minerals Development Corp. (AD)
PMDC.......... Project for Mathematical Development of Children [*National Science Foundation*]
PMDC.......... Project Manager Development Course [*Military*] (RDA)
PMDD.......... Personnel Management Development Directorate [*Military Personnel Center*] (AABC)
PMDD.......... Premenstrual Dysphoric Disorder [*Medicine*]
PMDD.......... Premenstrual Dysphoric Disorder [*Gynecology*] (DMAA)
PMDF.......... Project Master Data File [*For spacecraft*]
PMDG.......... Pentamethylene Diguanidine [*Organic chemistry*]
PMDL.......... Palmdale, CA (NASA)
PMDL.......... Post M-Day Deployment List [*Military*] (AABC)
PMDL.......... Provisional Military Demarcation Line (CINC)
PMDM.......... Polyhedra Molecular Demonstration Model
PMDM.......... Poly(mellitic Dianhydride Methacrylate) [*Organic chemistry*]
PM/DM........ Polymyositis/Dermatomyositis [*Rheumatology*] (DAVI)
PMDO.......... Phased Maintenance During Overhaul
PMDP.......... Pavement Marking Demonstration Program [*Federal Highway Administration*]
PMDP.......... Project Manager Development Program [*Army*] (RDA)
PMDR.......... Parametric Monotone Decreasing Ratio [*Statistics*]
PMDR.......... Phosphorescence-Microwave Double Resonance
PMDR.......... Provisioning Master Data Record
PM-DRG...... Pediatric-Modified Diagnosis-Related Group (HCT)
PMDRMU..... Paper Mould and Dandy Roll Makers' Union (DGA)
PMDS.......... Peristent Muellerian Duct Syndrome [*Medicine*] (DMAA)
PMDS.......... (Phenylmercury)dodecenyl Succinate [*Antimicrobial agent*]
PMDS.......... Pilot Map Display System
PMDS.......... Point Missile Defense System (DNAB)
PMDS.......... Portable Diver Monitoring System
PMDS.......... Primary Myelodysplastic Syndrome [*Medicine*] (DMAA)
PMDS.......... Process Monitoring and Display Software [*Computer science*] (ECII)
pmds........... Projected Map Display Set (AD)
PMDS.......... Projected Map Display System
PMDS.......... Property Management and Disposal Service [*Abolished, 1973*] [*General Services Administration*]
PMDT.......... Park Meditech, Inc. [*NASDAQ symbol*] (SAG)
PMDT.......... Pentamethyldiethylenetriamine [*Organic chemistry*]
PMDTF........ Park Meditech [*NASDAQ symbol*] (TTSB)
PMDU.......... Projected Map Display Unit (DNAB)
PMDY.......... Midway Naval Station [*Henderson Field*], Sand Island [*Midway Islands*] [*ICAO location identifier*] (ICLI)
PME............ Allstate Corp. [*NYSE symbol*] (SAG)
PME............ Allstate Cp 6.76% Exch Nts '98 [*NYSE symbol*] (TTSB)
PME............ Caltech Political Military Exercise [*International relations simulation game*]
PME............ Passive Microelectronic Element

PME............ Peace Movement of Ethiopia (EA)
PME............ Pectin Methylesterase [*Also, PE*] [*An enzyme*]
PME............ Pedal Mode Ergometer
PME............ Performance Management and Evaluation
pme............ Performance-Measuring Equipment (AD)
PME............ Performance Monitoring Equipment (NVT)
PME............ Personnel Management Evaluation (USDC)
PME............ Personnel Management Evaluation [*Marine science*] (OSRA)
PME............ Personnel Management for Executives [*Military*] (RDA)
PME............ Phosphatidylmonomethylethanolamine [*Biochemistry*]
PME............ Phosphomonoester [*Biochemistry*]
PME............ Phosphorylated Monester [*Organic chemistry*]
PME............ Photomagnetoelectric
PME............ Photomagnetoelectric Effect (IAA)
PME............ Pinosylvin Methyl Ether [*Organic chemistry*]
pme............ Planning, Management, Evaluation (AD)
PME............ Polymorphonuclear Eosinophile [*Hematology*]
P Me............ Portland, Maine (AD)
PME............ Portsmouth [*England*] [*Airport symbol*] (AD)
PME............ Postmenopausal Estrogen Therapy [*Gynecology*] (CPH)
PME............ Precision Measuring Equipment (AFM)
PME............ Primary Mission Equipment
PME............ Prime Ministers of England [*A publication*]
PME............ Process and Manufacturing Engineering (NRCH)
PME............ Processor Memory Enhancement
PME............ Professional Management for Executives [*Army*]
PME............ Professional Military Education (AFM)
PME............ Professional Military Ethic (MCD)
PME............ Project Manager, Electronics System Command [*Navy*]
PME............ Protective Multiple Earthing [*Electricity*]
pme............ Protective Multiple Earthing (AD)
PMEA............ (Phenyl)(methyl)ethanolamine [*Organic chemistry*]
PMEA............ Phosphonylmethoxyethyladenine [*Antiviral*]
PMEA............ Powder Metallurgy Equipment Association (EA)
P/MEA............ Probationary Marine Engineering Artificer [*British military*] (DMA)
PMEA............ Production and Maintenance Engineering Agent (MCD)
PMEA............ Publishing Manufacturers Executive Association (EA)
PMEAR........ Preliminary Maintenance Engineering Analysis Requirement (MCD)
PMEC............ Postgraduate Medical Education Committee [*University of Queensland, Australia*]
PMED............ Paradigm Medical Industries, Inc. [*NASDAQ symbol*] (SAG)
PMedS......... Delaware County Institute of Science, Media, PA [*Library symbol Library of Congress*] (LCLS)
PMEE............ Prime Mission Electronic Equipment [*NASA*] (KSC)
PMEF............ Petroleum Marketing Education Foundation (EA)
PMEG............ Perforated Metal Export Groups [*British*] (DBA)
PMEL............ Pacific Marine Environmental Laboratory [*Seattle, WA*] [*National Oceanic and Atmospheric Administration*] (GRD)
PMEL............ Precision Measurements Equipment Laboratory [*NASA*]
PMEL............ Precision Measuring Equipment Laboratory (AD)
PMEL............ Precision Measuring Equipment Laboratory (NADA)
PM-ENDOR... Polarization Modulated Electron Nuclear Double Resonance [*Spectroscopy*]
PMEP............ Pumping Mean Effective Pressure [*Automotive engine testing*]
PMer............ Mercer Free Library, Mercer, PA [*Library symbol Library of Congress*] (LCLS)
PMES............ Personnel Management Evaluation System [*Department of Labor*]
PMES............ Productivity Measurement and Evaluation System (MCD)
PMES............ Proposed Material Erection Schedule (MCD)
PMEST.......... Personality, Matter, Energy, Space, Time [*Colon classification, S. R. Ranganathan*] [*Library science*]
pmest.......... Personality, Matter, Energy, Space, Time (AD)
pmet............ Painted Metal (AD)
PMET............ Painter Metal (AAG)
PMEV............ Panel-Mounted Electronic Voltmeter
PMEXPO...... Property Management Exposition [*Bachner Communications*] (TSPED)
PMF............ L-Phenylalanine Mustard, 5-Fluorouracil, Methotrexate [*Antineoplastic drug regimen*] (DAVI)
PMF............ Parts Master File (MCD)
PMF............ Patriot Maintenance Facility [*Army*]
PMF............ Performance Measurement Facility (IAA)
PMF............ Performance Monitor Function [*NASA*] (NASA)
PMF............ Perigee Motor Firing [*Aerospace*] (MCD)
PMF............ Permanent Magnetic Field
PMF............ Permanent Military Force (ADA)
PMF............ Personnel Master File [*Army*] (AABC)
PMF............ Pilot Mortar Fire
PMF............ Polaris Missile Facility [*Military*] (IAA)
PMF............ Presidential Medal of Freedom (AD)
PMF............ Price Master File (MCD)
PMF............ Principle Management Facility (MCD)
PMF............ Probability Mass Function (IAA)
PMF............ Probable Maximum Flood [*Nuclear energy*] (NRCH)
pmf............ Probable Maximum Flooding (AD)
PMF............ Processed Message File (MCD)
PMF............ Product Measurement Facility (IAA)
PMF............ Professional Medical Film (AABC)
PMF............ Programmable Matched Filter (IAA)
PMF............ Program Management Facility [*NASA*] (MCD)
PMF............ Progressive Massive Fibrosis
pmf............ Progressive Massive Fibrosis [*Medicine*] (AD)
PMF............ Project Management File (MCD)
PMF............ Pro Male Fingers [*International Bowhunting Organization*] [*Class equipment*]
PMF............ Pro Media Foundation (EA)
PMF............ Proton Motive Force [*Physics*]
PMFA............ Fireman Apprentice, Patternmaker, Striker [*Navy rating*]
PM-FAC....... Prednisone, Methotrexate, Fluorouracil, Adriamycin, Cyclophosphamide [*Antineoplastic drug regimen*]
PMFC............ Pacific Marine Fisheries Commission [*Later, PSMFC*] (EA)
PMFC............ Patsy Montana Fan Club (EA)
PMFG............ Peerless Manufacturing Co. [*NASDAQ symbol*] (NQ)
PMFG............ Peerless Mfg [*NASDAQ symbol*] (TTSB)
PMFI............ Perpetual Midwest Financial [*NASDAQ symbol*] (TTSB)
PMFI............ Perpetual Midwest Financial, Inc. [*NASDAQ symbol*] (SAG)
PM/FL........... Performance Monitor/Fault Locator [*Military*] (CAAL)
PMFLT.......... Pamphlet (MSA)
PMFN............ Fireman, Patternmaker, Striker [*Navy rating*]
PMFPAC...... Polaris Missile Facility, Pacific Fleet
PMFS............ Pulsed Magnetic Field System
PMFWCMA... Paper Mill Fourdrinier Wire Cloth Manufacturers Association [*Later, FWC*] (EA)
PMG............ Pall Mall Gazette [*A publication*]
PMG............ Paymaster General [*Navy*]
PmG............ Paymaster General (AD)
PMG............ Permanent Magnet Generator
PMG............ Phase Modulation Generator
PMG............ Physiological Measurement Group
PMG............ Phytophthora Megasperma F. Sp. Glycinea [*A fungus*]
PMG............ Pinto Malartic [*Vancouver Stock Exchange symbol*]
PMG............ Polymethylgalacturonase [*An enzyme*]
PMG............ Ponta Pora [*Brazil*] [*Airport symbol*] (OAG)
PMG............ Port Moresby [*Papua New Guinea*] [*Seismograph station code, US Geological Survey*] (SEIS)
PMG............ Postmaster General
PmG............ Postmaster General (AD)
PMG............ Poultry Marketing Guide
PMG............ Power Metal Grid (PDAA)
PMG............ Prediction Marker Generator
PMG............ Primary Medical Group [*Insurance*] (DMAA)
PMG............ Propodial Mucus Gland [*Zoology*]
PMG............ Provisional Military Government [*Ethiopia*]
PMG............ Provost Marshal General [*Army*]
PMG............ Putnam Investment Grade Municipal Trade II [*NYSE symbol*] (SPSG)
PMG............ Putnam Inv Grade Muni Tr II [*NYSE symbol*] (TTSB)
PMGCT.......... Primary Mediastinal Germ-Cell Tumor [*Medicine*] (DMAA)
PMGDINYC... Production Men's Guild of the Dress Industry of New York City (EA)
PMGFEL........ Preliminary Master Government-Furnished Equipment List (MCD)
PMGI............ Prime Management Group, Inc. [*NASDAQ symbol*] (SAG)
PMGI............ Princeton Media Group, Inc. [*NASDAQ symbol*] (SAG)
PMGM............ Program Manager's Guidance Memorandum
PMGO............ Office of the Provost Marshal General [*Army*]
PM-GPV........ Project Manager, General Purpose Vehicle (SAA)
PMgr............ Professional Manager (DD)
PMGS............ Predictable Model Guidance Scheme (OA)
PMGS............ Provost Marshal General's School, United States Army
PMGW............ Primary Mission Gross Weight
PMH............ Past Medical History
pmh............ Past Medical History (AD)
PMH............ Per Man Hour (WDAA)
PMH............ Phenylmercuric Hydroxide [*Organic chemistry*]
PMH............ Portsmouth, OH [*Location identifier FAA*] (FAAL)
PMH............ Posteromedial Hypothalamus [*Medicine*] (DMAA)
pmh............ Probable Maximum Hurricane (AD)
PMH............ Probable Maximum Hurricane [*Nuclear energy*] (NRCH)
PMH............ Production per Man-Hour
PMH............ Putnam Tax-Free Health Care Fund [*NYSE symbol*] (SPSG)
PMH............ Putnam Tax-Free Hlth Care Fd [*NYSE symbol*] (TTSB)
PMHC............ Pyridinylmethylethylene(hydrazinecarbothioamide) [*Organic chemistry*]
PMHL............ Preferred Measurement Hardware List [*NASA*] (NASA)
PMH/M.......... Productive Man-Hours per Month [*Navy*] (NG)
PMHP............ Para-Menthane Hydroperoxide [*Organic chemistry*]
PMHP............ Primary Mental Health Project (AD)
PMHR............ Predicted Maximum Heart Rate [*Medicine*] (DMAA)
PMHRON...... Patrol Combatant Missile Hydrofoil Squadron (DNAB)
PMHRON MLSG... Patrol Combatant Missile Hydrofoil Squadron Mobile Logistics Support Group (DNAB)
PMHS............ Polymethylhydrosiloxane [*Organic chemistry*]
PMHS............ Poly(methyl-Hydrostyrene) [*Organic chemistry*]
PMHSA.......... Polish Military History Society of America (EA)
PMHx............ Past Medical History (DAVI)
PMHYT.......... Putnam Managed High Yield Trust [*Associated Press*] (SAG)
PMi............ Milton Public Library, Milton, PA [*Library symbol Library of Congress*] (LCLS)
PMI............ Palma [*Mallorca Island*] [*Airport symbol*] (OAG)
PMI............ Palma de Mallorca Balearic Islands, Spain (AD)
PMI............ Parmac Mines [*Vancouver Stock Exchange symbol*]
PMI............ Partai Muslimin Indonesia [*Indonesian Muslim Party*] [*Political party*] (AD)
PMI............ Past [*or Previous*] Medical Illness
PMI............ Patient Medication Instruction
PMI............ Pearlitic Malleable Iron (MCD)
PMI............ Pennsylvania Muscle Institute [*University of Pennsylvania*] [*Research center*] (RCD)
PMI............ Pensions Management Institute [*British*] (EAIO)
PMI............ Perioperative Myocardial Infarction [*Medicine*] (DMAA)
PMI............ Permanent Manufacturing Information (MSA)
PMI............ Personnel Management Information (IAA)

PMI Phenylmethylisoxazole [*Organic chemistry*]
PMI Phosphomannose Isomerase [*An enzyme*] (MAE)
pmi Photographic Micro-Image (AD)
PMI Photographic Microimage Master [*Reprography*]
PMI Plant Manager Instruction [*Nuclear energy*] (NRCH)
PMI Plasma-Materials Interactions (MCD)
PMI Plumbing Manufacturers Institute (EA)
PMI Point of Maximal Impulse [*Medicine*]
pmi Point of Maximum Impulse (AD)
PMI Point of Maximum Intensity
PMI Posterior Myocardial Infarction [*Medicine*] (DMAA)
PMI Post Mortem Interval [*Forensics*] [*Medicine*]
PMI Postmyocardial Infarction [*Syndrome*] [*Medicine*]
PMI Power Management Inventory [*Test*]
PMI Precision Monolithics Inc (NITA)
PMI Preliminary Maintenance Inspection (MCD)
PMI Pre-Marital Inventory (AD)
PMI Premark International, Inc. [*NYSE symbol*] (SPSG)
PMI Premark Intl [*NYSE symbol*] (TTSB)
PMI Prescriptive Math Inventory
PMI Present Medical Illness
PMI Presidential Management Incentives [*Office of Management and Budget*]
PMI Pressed Metal Institute [*Later, AMSA*]
PMI Preventive Maintenance Inspection (AFM)
PMI Preventive Maintenance Instruction (NASA)
PMI Previous Medical Illness (CPH)
PMI Primary Measurement Instrument
PMI Principal Maintenance Inspector (NASA)
PMI Private Mortgage Insurance [*Insurance of mortgages by private insurers*]
pmi Private Mortgage Insurance (AD)
PMI Probe Ministries International (EA)
PMI Processor Monitoring Instrument [*Computer science*] (ADA)
PMI Programmable Machine Interface (MCD)
PMI Programmable Memory Interface [*Computer science*]
PMI Programmable MODEM Interface [*Computer science*] (MCD)
PMI Program Management Instruction
PMI Project Management Institute (EA)
PMI Proposed Military Improvement (CAAL)
PMI Pseudomatrix Isolation
PMI Purchased Materials Inspection
PMIA Parallel Multiplexer Interface Adapter (MCD)
PMIA Powder Metal Industries Association [*Australia*]
PMIA Presidential Management Improvement Award
PMIC Parallel Multiple Incremental Computer
PMIC Payload Mission Integration Contract (MCD)
PMIC Periodic Maintenance Information Cards (MCD)
PMIC Personnel Management Information Center [*Air Force*] (AFM)
PMIC Poultry Meat Industry Committee [*New South Wales, Australia*]
PMIC Precious Metal Indicator Code
PMIC President's Management Improvement Council (AD)
PMIF Powder Metal Industries Federation
PMIG Political-Military Interdepartmental Group (AD)
PMIG Programmers Minimal Interface to Graphics (MCD)
PMI Gp PMI Group, Inc. [*Associated Press*] (SAG)
PMIIT Putnam Master Intermediate Income Trust [*Associated Press*] (SAG)
PMIJ Pulse-Modulated Infrared Jammer
PMilan Papiri Milanesi [*A publication*] (OCD)
PMilS Millersville State College, Millersville, PA [*Library symbol Library of Congress*] (LCLS)
PMI/MO Precedence Manual In / Manual Out (DNAB)
PMIP Paleoclimate Modeling Intercomparison Project [*Marine science*] (OSRA)
PMIP Pan Malayan Islamic Party
PMIP Postmaintenance Inspection Pilot
PMIP Presidential Management Intern Program [*Executive Office of the President*] (GFGA)
PMIPK Poly(methyl Isopropenyl Ketone) [*Organic chemistry*]
PMIPK Poly(Methyl Isopropenyl Ketone) [*Organic chemistry*]
PMIR Program Manager's Integration Review [*NASA*] (NASA)
PMIR Psi-Mediated Instrumental Response [*Parapsychology*]
PMIRD Passive Microwave Intercept Receiver Display
PMIS Passive Microwave Imaging System [*NASA*]
PMIS Patient Medical Information System (OA)
PMIS Personal Management Information System [*Computer science*] (IAA)
PMIS Personnel Management Information System
PMIS Planning Management Information System (AD)
PMIS Plant Monitoring and Information System [*Nuclear energy*] (NRCH)
PMIS Postmyocardial Infarction Syndrome [*Medicine*] (DMAA)
PMIS Precision Mechanisms in Sodium [*Nuclear energy*] (NRCH)
PMIS Premis Corp. [*NASDAQ symbol*] (SAG)
PMIS Printing Management Information Systems
PMIS Process Management Information System (ACII)
PMIS Product Management Information System (AD)
PMIS Program Management Information System [*Army*]
PMIS Program Measurement Information System [*Computer science*] (IAA)
PMIS Projects Management Information System [*UNESCO*] (DUND)
PMIS PSRO [*Professional Standards Review Organization*] Management Information System (DHSM)
PMIT Putnam Master Income Trust [*Associated Press*] (SAG)
PMITS Post Mobilization Individual Training and Support (MCD)
PMJ Porto Murtinho [*Brazil*] [*Airport symbol*] (AD)
PMJ Pulse-Modulated Jammer
PMJC Pine Manor Junior College (AD)
PMJEG Performance Measurement Joint Executive Group (DOMA)
PMJI Pardon My Jumping In [*E-Mail discussion*]
PMK Palair Macedonian [*Yugoslavia*] [*ICAO designator*] (FAAC)
PMK Panel Marking Kit
PMK Pitch Mark [*Shipfitting*] (AAG)
pmk Pitch Mark (AD)
PMK Pointe Molloy [*Kerguelen Islands*] [*Seismograph station code, US Geological Survey*] (SEIS)
PMK Portable Molding Kit
PMK Postmark
pmk Postmark (AD)
PMK Primark Corp. [*NYSE symbol*] (SPSG)
PMK Primary Monkey Kidney [*Physiology*]
PMK Primary Rhesus Monkey Kidney (AAMN)
PMKM Past Master, Knights of Malta [*Freemasonry*] (ROG)
PMKY Pittsburgh, McKeesport & Youghiogheny [*AAR code*]
PML Pacific Micronesian Line (AD)
PML Pakistan Muslim League [*Political party*]
PML Parts Material List
PML Pattern Makers' League of North America (EA)
PML Physical Memory Level
PML PI Edit's Macro Language [*Iliad Group*] [*Computer science*]
PML [*The*] Pierpont Morgan Library (BJA)
PML Plymouth Marine Laboratory [*Natural Environment Research Council*] [*British Information service or system*] (IID)
PML Polymer Microdevice Laboratory [*Case Western Reserve University*] [*Research center*] (RCD)
PML Polymorphonuclear Leukocyte [*Hematology*]
PML Port Moller [*Alaska*] [*Airport symbol*] (OAG)
PML Port Moller, AK [*Location identifier FAA*] (FAAL)
PML Posterior Mitral Leaflet [*Cardiology*]
PML Preliminary Materials List [*NASA*]
PML Probable Maximum Loss [*Insurance*]
pml Probable Maximum Loss (AD)
PML Programmable Macro Logic (NITA)
PML Progressive Multifocal Leukoencephalopathy [*Oncology*]
PML Promotion Management List [*Pronounced "pemell"*] [*Air Force*]
PML Promyelocytic Leukaemia Protein [*Biochemistry*]
PML Promyelocytic Leukemia [*Medicine*]
PML Putnam Investment Grade Multiple Sectors III [*AMEX symbol*] (SPSG)
PML Putnam Inv Grade Muni Tr III [*AMEX symbol*] (TTSB)
PML University of Windsor, Paul Martin Law Library [*UTLAS symbol*]
pmla Parmelia (AD)
PMLA Production Music Libraries Association (EA)
PMLA Publication of the Modern Language Association of America (AD)
PMLC Pooled Mixed Lymphocyte Culture [*Clinical chemistry*]
PMLC Programmed Multiline Controller
PMLD Profound and Multiple Learning Difficulties (AIE)
PMLE Polymorphous Light Eruption [*Medicine*]
PMLF Project Marketing Loan Facility [*Australia*]
PMLG Poly(methyl L-Glutamate) [*Organic chemistry*]
PMLM Photosensitive Membrane Light Modulator
PMLO Philippine Military Liaison Officer (DNAB)
PMLO Principal Military Landing Officer (AD)
PMLO Principal Military Landing Offices [*British*]
PMLPC Permanent Mass Layoffs and Plant Closings Program [*Bureau of Labor Statistics*]
PM-LSM Polarization-Modulation Laser-Scanning Microscopy
PMLV Permanent Magnet Latch Valve
PMM Military Morale Division [*Coast Guard*]
PMM Partial Matrix Multiply (IAA)
PMM Peace Mission Movement (EA)
PMM Peat Marwick McLintock [*Accounting firm*] [*British*]
PMM Pedestal-Mounted Manipulator [*Nuclear energy*] (NRCH)
PMM Penobscot Marine Museum (EA)
PMM Permanent Magnet Motor (IAA)
PMM Personnel Management Manual [*A publication*] (ADA)
PMM Petroleum Marketing Management [*Petroleum Marketers Association of America*] [*A publication*]
PMM Petroleum Marketing Monthly [*Department of Energy Information service or system*] (CRD)
PMM Physical Memory Manager [*Computer science*] (PCM)
PMM Phytophthora Megasperma F.Sp Medicaginia [*A fungus*]
PMM Poly(methyl Methacrylate) [*Also, PMMA*] [*Organic chemistry*]
PMM Pool Maintenance Module [*Telecommunications*] (TEL)
PMM Portavideo [*Vancouver Stock Exchange symbol*]
PMM Post Mast Message (IAA)
PMM Presa Malpaso [*Mexico*] [*Seismograph station code, US Geological Survey*] (SEIS)
PMM Process Monitoring Modules (ACII)
PMM Procom Emerald [*Vancouver Stock Exchange symbol*]
PMM Professional Music Men, Inc. (EA)
PMM Profile Milling Machine
PMM Programmable Microcomputer Module
PMM Property Management Manual [*NASA*] (MCD)
PMM Pullman, MI [*Location identifier FAA*] (FAAL)
PMM Pulse Mode Multiplex
pmm Pulse Mode Multiplex (AD)
PMM Purchase-Money Mortgage [*Real estate*]
PMM Putnam Managed Municipal Income [*NYSE symbol*] (SPSG)
PMM Putnam Managed Muni Income [*NYSE symbol*] (TTSB)
PMMA Pere Marquette Memorial Association (EA)
PMMA Poly(methyl Methacrylate) [*Also, PMM*] [*Organic chemistry*]
pmma Polymethylmethacrylate (AD)

PMMA Polymethyl Methacrylate [*Dentistry*] (DAVI)
PMMA Poly Methyl Methacrylate Association [*European Council of Chemical Manufacturers Federations*] [*Brussels, Belgium*] (EAIO)
PMMAP Poly(methyl Methacrylate Peroxide) [*Organic chemistry*]
PMMAPA Poly Methyl Methacrylate Producers Association [*Belgium*] (EAIO)
PMMB Parallel Memory-to-Memory Bus
PMMC Permanent Magnetic Movable Coil
PM-MCD Project Manager for Mines, Countermine, and Demolitions [*Army*] (RDA)
PM-MEP Project Manager - Mobile Electric Power [*DoD*]
PMMF Precious Metals Master File [*DoD*] (AFIT)
PMMI Packaging Machinery Manufacturers Institute (EA)
PMMI Putnam Managed Municipal Income Trust [*Associated Press*] (SAG)
PMMM Pall Mall Money Management [*Investment group*] [*British*]
PMMO Particulate Methane Monooxygenase [*Biochemistry*]
PMMP Preventive Maintenance Management Program
PMMR Panel-Mounted Microfilm Reader
PMMR Passive Multichannel Microwave Radiometer [*NASA*]
PMMS Phrenicon Metabolic Monitoring System
PMMS Plainsong and Mediaeval Music Society (EA)
PMMS Program Master Milestone Schedule (MCD)
PMMU Paged Memory Management Unit [*Computer chip*] (BYTE)
pmmu Paged Memory-Management Unit (AD)
PMMV Pea Mild Mosaic Virus [*Plant pathology*]
PMN Pacific Mountain Network [*Television*]
PMN Pahute Mesa [*Nevada*] [*Seismograph station code, US Geological Survey Closed*] (SEIS)
PMN Permian Resources Ltd. [*Vancouver Stock Exchange symbol*]
PMN Phenylmercuric Nitrate [*Antiseptic*]
PMN Polymorphonuclear [*Hematology*]
pmn Polymorphonuclear Neutrophil (AD)
PMN Polymorphonuclear Neutrophilic [*Hematology*]
PMN Polymorphonucleocyte [*Hematology*] (CPH)
PMN Postman (DCTA)
PMN Premanufacture Notification [*Environmental Protection Agency*]
PMN Pre-Manufacturing Notice [*Government regulations*]
PMN Premarket Notification [*Requirement for introducing new chemicals into the EEC*]
pmn Producto Material Neto [*Net Material Product*] [*Spain*] (AD)
PMN Program Management Network (MCD)
PMN Proposed Material Need (MCD)
PMN Pumani [*Papua New Guinea*] [*Airport symbol*] (OAG)
PMN Putnam New York Investment Grade Municipal [*AMEX symbol*] (SPSG)
PMN Putnam NY Inv Grade Muni [*AMEX symbol*] (TTSB)
PMNA Pacific Mountain Network Association (AD)
PMNA Parkers Marsh Natural Area [*Virginia*] (AD)
PM-NAVCON Project Manager, Navigation and Control [*Military*]
PMNC Peripheral Blood Mononuclear Cell [*Medicine*] (DMAA)
PMNF Premanufacture Notification Form [*Environmental Protection Agency*] (GFGA)
PMNG Polymorphonuclear Granulocyte [*Hematology*] (DAVI)
PMNH Peabody Museum of Natural History (NADA)
PMNH Peabody Museum of Natural History (AD)
pmnl Polymorphonuclear Leukocyte (AD)
PMNL Polymorphonuclear Leukocyte [*Hematology*]
PMNN Polymorphonuclear Neutrophil (DMAA)
PMNP Platform-Mounted Nuclear Plant (NRCH)
PMNR Periadenitis Mucosa Necrotica Recurrens [*Medicine*]
pmnr Periadenitis Mucosa Necrotica Recurrens (AD)
PMNR Porter McLeod National Retail [*NASDAQ symbol*] (SAG)
PMNR Porter McLeod Natl Retail [*NASDAQ symbol*] (TTSB)
PMN/SFS People's Music Network for Songs of Freedom and Struggle (EA)
PMNT Permanent (IAA)
PM-NUC Project Manager for Nuclear Munitions [*Army*] (RDA)
PMNV Project Manager, Night Vision (RDA)
PM NV/RSTA Project Manager for Night Vision/Reconnaissance Surveillance and Target Acquisition [*Military*] (RDA)
PMo Monessen Public Library, Monessen, PA [*Library symbol Library of Congress*] (LCLS)
PMO Palermo [*Italy*] [*Airport symbol*] (OAG)
PMO Palermo Resources, Inc. [*Vancouver Stock Exchange symbol*]
pmo Palomar Mountain Observatory (AD)
PMO Perroni, Martin, O'Reilly [*Commercial firm*]
PMO Personnel Management Officer [*Army*] (INF)
PMO Perturbation Molecular Orbital [*Theory*]
PMO Pianissimo [*Very Softly*] [*Music*] (ROG)
pmo Pianissimo [*Very Softly*] [*Italian*] [*Music*] (AD)
PMO Pine Mountain Observatory
PMO Polaris Material Office [*Missiles*]
PMO Polaris Missile Office
PMO Pomariorio [*Tuamotu Archipelago*] [*Seismograph station code, US Geological Survey*] (SEIS)
PMO Port Meteorological Office [*National Weather Service*]
PMO Postal Money Order [*Military*]
PMO Postmenopausal Osteoporosis [*Medicine*]
PMO Prime Minister's Office
PMO Principal Medical Officer
pmo Printed Matter Only (AD)
PMO Product Manager's Office (RDA)
PMO Product Manufacturing Organization
PMO Profit Making Organization
PMO Program Management Office [*Environmental Protection Agency*] (GFGA)
PMO Program Management Office [*NASA*] (KSC)
PMO Project Management Office [*Army*] (AABC)
PMO Property Movement Order
PMO Provisional [*Program Management*] Office [*Army*]
PMO Provost Marshal's Office
PMO Psychiatric Military Officer
PMO Putnam Municipal Opportunities Trust [*NYSE symbol*] (SPSG)
PMO Putnam Muni Opport Tr [*NYSE symbol*] (TTSB)
PMOA Prospectors and Mine Owners Association (EA)
PMOC Pioneer Mission Operations Center [*NASA*]
PMODA Phenyl(mercapto)oxadiazole [*Reagent*]
PMOF Presidential Medal of Freedom [*Military decoration*] (GFGA)
PM of F Presidential Medal of Freedom [*Military decoration*] (AABC)
PMOG Plutonium Maintenance and Operating Gallery [*Nuclear energy*] (NRCH)
PMOG Proposed Material Ordering Guide (MCD)
pmol Picomole [*One trillionth of a mole*] (WGA)
PMOLANT Polaris Material Office, Atlantic Fleet [*Missiles*]
pmole Picomole [*One trillionth of a mole*] (DAVI)
PMOM Performance Management Operations Manual [*NASA*] (NASA)
PMON Performance Management Operations Network [*NASA*] (NASA)
P-MONO Promonocytes [*hematology*] (DAVI)
PMOPAC Polaris Material Office, Pacific Fleet [*Missiles*]
PMOR Phar-Mor, Inc. [*NASDAQ symbol*] (SAG)
P Mor Port Moresby (AD)
PMORW Phar-Mor Wrrt [*NASDAQ symbol*] (TTSB)
PMOS Permanent Manned Orbital Station (AAG)
PMOS Physical Movement of Spacecraft (SAA)
PMOS Positive-Channel Metal-Oxide Semiconductor [*Telecommunications*] (TEL)
P-MOS Positive Channel Metal Oxide Semiconductor (NITA)
PMOS Primary Military Occupational Specialty [*Army*]
PMOS Program Management and Operations Staff [*Environmental Protection Agency*] (GFGA)
PMOSC Primary Military Occupational Code (AD)
PMOSC Primary Military Occupational Specialty Code [*Army*] (AABC)
PMOT Putnam Municipal Opportunities Trust [*Associated Press*] (SAG)
PMP Pacific Magazines and Printing Ltd. [*Commercial firm Australia*]
PMP Packed Main Parachute
PMP Pain Management Program [*Neurology*] (DAVI)
PMP Parallel Microprogrammed Processor [*Computer science*]
PMP Parent Mass Peak
PMP Parents' Magazine Press
PMP Partido ng Masang Pilipino [*Political party*] (EY)
PMP Parti du Mouvement Populaire de la Cote Francaise des Somalis [*Popular Movement Party of French Somaliland*] [*Political party*]
PMP Partito Monarchico Popolare [*Popular Monarchist Party*] [*Italy Political party*] (PPE)
PMP Parts, Materials, and Packaging (MCD)
PMP Parts, Materials, and Processes (MCD)
PMP Passive Measurement Program
PMP Past Menstrual Period [*Medicine*]
PMP Patient Management Problem [*Gerontology*]
PMP Performance Management Package [*NASA*] (NASA)
PmP Pergamon Press, Inc., Fairview Park, Elmsford, NY [*Library symbol Library of Congress*] (LCLS)
PMP Permanent Manned Presence (SSD)
pmp Per-Member Payment (AD)
PMP Persistent Mentoposterior [*A fetal position*] [*Obstetrics*]
PMP Peter Miller Apparel Group, Inc. [*Toronto Stock Exchange symbol*]
PMP Phenyl(methyl)pyrazolone [*An organic pigment*]
PMP Piecewise Markov Process (PDAA)
PMP Pimaga [*Papua New Guinea*] [*Airport symbol*] (OAG)
PMP Planar Metallization with Polymer (IAA)
PMP Planned Maintenance Plan (MCD)
PMP Poly(metal Phosphinate) [*Organic chemistry*]
PMP Poly(methylpentene) [*Organic chemistry*]
PMP Pompano Beach, FL [*Location identifier FAA*] (FAAL)
PMP Pompeii [*Italy*] [*Seismograph station code, US Geological Survey Closed*] (SEIS)
PMP Pontifical Mission for Palestine (EA)
PMP Position Management Program
PMP Powdered Metal Part
PMP Powder Melting Process [*Physics*]
PMP Power Management Profile [*Test*]
pmp Precious Metal Plating (AD)
PMP Preliminary Management Plan (AD)
PMP Preliminary Mission Profile (MCD)
PMP Premodulation Processor
PMP Preoperational Maintenance Plan
PMP Preoperational Monitoring Program [*Nuclear energy*] (NRCH)
PMP Pressure Measurement Package
PMP Preventive Maintenance Plan (KSC)
PMP Preventive Maintenance Procedure [*Nuclear energy*] (NRCH)
PMP Previous Menstrual Period [*Medicine*]
pmp Previous Menstrual Period [*Medicine*] (AD)
PMP Prime Mission Project [*Military*]
PMP Prime Motor Inns L.P. [*NYSE symbol*] (TTSB)
PMP Prime Motor Inns Ltd. [*NYSE symbol*] (SPSG)
PMP Prior Menstrual Period [*Gynecology*] (DAVI)
PMP Prism-Mirror-Prism [*For electron microscopy*]
PMP Probable Maximum Precipitation [*Nuclear energy*] (NRCH)
PMP Procurement Methods and Practices (AD)
PMP Product and Marketing Planning (IAA)
PMP Professor of Moral Philosophy
PMP Profit-Maximizing Price (MHDW)

PMP............ Program Management Plan [*NASA*]
PMP............ Program Monitor Panel
PMP............ Progressive Merger Procedure [*Econometrics*]
PMP............ Project Management Professional
PMP............ Project Master Plan [*Army*]
PMP............ Project on Military Procurement [*Later, PGP*] (EA)
PMP............ Property Management Plan [*Australia*]
PMP............ Protective Mobilization Plan
PMP............ Pulmonary Mean Pressure [*Medicine*]
PMP............ Pulsed Microwave Power
PMP............ Pump (KSC)
PMP............ Pyridoxamine Phosphate [*Biochemistry*]
PMPA.......... Permanent Magnet Producers Association [*Later, MMPA*] (EA)
PMPA.......... Petroleum Marketing Practices Act
PMPA.......... Phosphonylmethoxypropyladenine
PMPA.......... (Phosphonylmethoxypropyl)adenine [*Antiviral*]
PMPA.......... Proximal Main Pulmonary Artery [*Anatomy*]
PMPE.......... Punch Memory Parity Error [*Computer science*] (IAA)
PMPEA........ Professional Motion Picture Equipment Association [*Later, PFVEA*] (EA)
PMPFR........ Program Manager's Preflight Review [*NASA*] (KSC)
PMPG.......... Pumping
PMPH.......... Pamphlet (DLA)
PMPL.......... Preferred Mechanical Parts List [*NASA*] (NASA)
PMPM.......... Perpetual Motion Poetry Machine
PMPM.......... Phase Margin Performance Measure [*Manual control system*]
PMPM.......... Programmable Multiple Position Machine (MCD)
PMPM.......... Pulse Mode Performance Model (KSC)
PMPMA........ Plastic and Metal Products Manufacturers Association (EA)
PMPO.......... Postmenopausal Palpable Ovary [*Gynecology*]
PMPP.......... Program Management Phase-Out Plan [*Military*] (AFIT)
PMPPI......... Polymethylenepolyphenyl Polyisocyanate [*Organic chemistry*]
PMPQ.......... Professional and Managerial Position Questionnaire [*Test*]
PMPR.......... Program Management and Performance Review
PMPS.......... Postmastectomy Pain Syndrome [*Medicine*] (DMAA)
PMPS.......... Program Management Planning and Scheduling [*Military*] (DNAB)
PMQ............ Perito Moreno [*Argentina*] [*Airport symbol*] (OAG)
PMQ............ Permanent Married Quarters [*Canadian Forces*]
PMQ............ Phytylmenaquinone [*Vitamin K*] [*Also, K*] [*Biochemistry*]
PMQ............ Phytylmenaquinone (DMAA)
PMQ............ Prime Minister's Question [*British*] (BARN)
PMQ............ Primitive Methodist Quarterly Review [*A publication*] (ROG)
PMR............ Pacific Missile Range [*Later, WTR*]
PMR............ Palmer [*Alaska*] [*Seismograph station code, US Geological Survey*] (SEIS)
PMR............ Palmerston North [*New Zealand*] [*Airport symbol*] (OAG)
PMR............ Parabolic Microwave Reflector
PMR............ Paramagnetic Resonance (IAA)
PMR............ Partido Mariateguista Revolucionario [*Peru*] [*Political party*] (EY)
PMR............ Partidul Muncitoresc Roman [*Romanian Workers' Party*] [*Political party*]
PMR............ Parts Material Requirements File
PMR............ Payload Mass Ratio
PMR............ Paymaster
Pmr............ Paymaster (AD)
PMR............ Performance Measurement Report [*NASA*] (NASA)
PMR............ Performance Monitoring Receiver
PMR............ Perinatal Mortality Rate [*Medicine*]
PMR............ Planned Maintenance Requirements
PMR............ Point of Minimum Radius (IAA)
PMR............ Polise-Air [*Russian Federation*] [*ICAO designator*] (FAAC)
PMR............ Pollutant Mass Rate [*Environmental science*] (GFGA)
PMR............ Polymerization of Monomer Reactants [*Organic chemistry*]
PMR............ Polymorphic Reticulosis [*Ophthalmology*] (DAVI)
PMR............ Polymyalgia Rheumatica [*Medicine*]
PMR............ Portable Microfiche Reader [*DASA Corp.*]
PMR............ Posteromedial Release [*Orthopedics*] (DAVI)
PMR............ Postmaster (DCTA)
PMR............ Potential Military Relevance
PMR............ Power Monitor Relay
PMR............ Preliminary Materials Review
P/M/R......... Premakeready [*Graphic arts*] (DGA)
pmr............ Pressure-Modulated Radiometer (AD)
PMR............ Pressure Modulation Radiometer
PMR............ Preventive Maintenance and Repair [*Aviation*] (MCD)
PMR............ Primary Mission Readiness
PMR............ Prime Resources Corp. [*Vancouver Stock Exchange symbol*]
PMR............ Priority Monitor Report
PMR............ Procurement Management Review [*DoD*]
PMR............ Profoundly Mentally Retarded
PMR............ Program Management Responsibility (MCD)
PMR............ Program Manager's Review [*NASA*] (NASA)
PMR............ Programmed Mixture Ratio (KSC)
PMR............ Projection Microradiography (IAA)
PMR............ Project Management Report
PMR............ Pro Male Release [*International Bowhunting Organization*] [*Class equipment*]
PMR............ Propellant Mass Ratio (SAA)
PMR............ Property Management Regulation (AAGC)
PMR............ Property Movement Request (MCD)
PMR............ Proportionate Morbidity Ratio [*Statistics*] (DAVI)
PMR............ Proportionate Mortality Rate [*or Ratio*]
PMR............ Protein Magnetic Resonance [*Medicine*] (MAE)
PMR............ Proton Magnetic Resonance
PMR............ Provisioning Master Record (MCD)
PMR............ Public Mobile Radio (WDMC)
PMR............ Pulsational Magnetic Radiation [*Astronomy*]
PMRA.......... Percent of Males Reproductively Active [*Ecology*]
PMRA.......... Projected Manpower Requirements Account [*Navy*]
PMRAFNS.... Princess Mary's Royal Air Force Nursing Service [*British*]
PMRB.......... Preliminary Materials Review Board
PMRC.......... Pakistan Medical Research Council
PMRC.......... Parents' Music Resource Center (EA)
PMRC.......... Prepositioned Material Receipt Card [*DoD*]
PMRC.......... Proctor Maple Research Center [*University of Vermont*] [*Research center*] (RCD)
PMR Cp....... PMR Corp. [*Associated Press*] (SAG)
PMRD.......... Prepositioned Material Receipt Documents (MCD)
PMRDET...... Pacific Missile Range Detachment [*Obsolete*] (MUGU)
PMRF.......... Pacific Missile Range Facility [*Obsolete*] (MSC)
PMRFAC...... Pacific Missile Range Facility [*Obsolete*] (MUGU)
PMRG.......... Preliminary Materials Review Group [*NASA*] (KSC)
PMRI........... Porous Media Research Institute [*University of Waterloo*] [*Research center*] (RCD)
PMRI........... Posteromedial Rotation Instability [*Sports medicine*]
PMRL.......... Pulp Manufacturers' Research League
PMRM.......... Periodic Maintenance Requirements Manual [*Navy*]
PMRMO........ Protectable Mobilization Reserve Materiel Objective [*Army*] (AABC)
PMRMR........ Protectable Mobilization Reserve Materiel Requirements [*Army*]
PMRN.......... Parents' Music Resource Network (EA)
PMR/NMC.... Pacific Missile Range / Naval Missile Center (SAA)
PMRO.......... Popular Magazine Review Online [*EBSCO Subscription Services*] [*Information service or system*]
PMRP.......... Petroleum Material Requirements Plan (MCD)
PMRP.......... PMR Corp. [*NASDAQ symbol*] (SAG)
PMRP.......... Precious Metals Recovery Program [*DoD*] (AFIT)
PM-RPV...... Project Manager, Remotely Piloted Vehicle [*Military*]
PMRR.......... Pacific Missile Range Representative [*Obsolete*] (MUGU)
PMRR.......... Pre-Mate Readiness Review [*NASA*] (KSC)
PMRS.......... Parachute Medical Rescue Service (EA)
PMRS.......... Performance Management and Recognition System
PMRS.......... Physical Medicine and Rehabilitation Service
PMRSG........ Pacific Missile Range Study Group [*Obsolete*]
PMRT.......... Peabody Mathematics Readiness Test [*Educational test*]
PMRT.......... Program Management Responsibility Transfer (MCD)
PMRT.......... Progressive Muscle Relaxation Training [*Psychology*]
PMRTD........ Program Management Responsibility Transfer Date (AFIT)
PMRTF........ Pacific Missile Range Tracking Facility [*Obsolete*] (MUGU)
PMRTP........ Program Management Responsibility Transfer Plan (AFIT)
PMRX.......... Pharmaceutical Marketing Services [*NASDAQ symbol*] (SPSG)
PMRX.......... Pharmaceutical Mktg Svcs [*NASDAQ symbol*] (TTSB)
PMRY.......... Pomeroy Computer Resources [*NASDAQ symbol*] (TTSB)
PMRY.......... Pomeroy Computer Resources, Inc. [*NASDAQ symbol*] (SAG)
PMRY.......... Presidio of Monterey [*Military*] (AABC)
PMS............ Chorionic Gonadotropin in Pregnant Mare's Serum [*Veterinary medicine*] (DAVI)
PMS............ Palmer - Arctic Valley [*Alaska*] [*Seismograph station code, US Geological Survey*] (SEIS)
PMS............ Pantone Matching System [*Printing*]
PMS............ Paper Manifesting System
PMS............ Parallel Mass Spectrometer
PMS............ Para-Methylstyrene [*Organic chemistry*]
PMS............ Partial Metric System (MCD)
PMS............ Particle Measuring Systems [*Aerosol measurement device*]
PMS............ Partido Mexicano Socialista [*Political party*] (EY)
PMS............ Pavement Management System [*Australia*]
PMS............ Peabody Museum of Salem (AD)
PMS............ Pedestal-Mounted Stinger [*Army*]
PMS............ People's Medical Society (EA)
PMS............ People's Message System [*For Apple II computers*] [*Electronic bulletin board*]
PMS............ Performance Management Software (IAA)
PMS............ Performance Management System
PMS............ Performance Measurement System [*Nuclear Regulatory Commission*] (MCD)
PMS............ Performance Monitoring System [*Fort Belvoir, VA*] [*Army*] (NASA)
PMS............ Permanent Magnet Speaker
PMS............ Permanent Manual System (AD)
PMS............ Personal Mailing System (HGAA)
PMS............ Personnel Management Series [*Civil Service Commission*]
PMS............ Personnel Management Specialist (GFGA)
PMS............ Personnel Management System [*Air Force*] (AFM)
PMS............ Phenazine Methosulfate [*Biochemistry*]
pms............ Phenazine Methosulphate (AD)
PMS............ Phoenix Missile System
PMS............ Physiological Monitoring System (SAA)
PMS............ Phytophthora Megasperma Var. Sojae [*A fungus*]
PMS............ Piccola Missione per il Sordomuti [*Little Mission for the Deaf-Mute - LMDM*] [*Rome, Italy*] (EAIO)
PMS............ Picturephone Meeting Service [*AT & T*]
PMS............ Pitch Microwave System
PMS............ Planemasters Services, Inc. [*ICAO designator*] (FAAC)
PMS............ Planned Maintenance System [*SNMMS*]
PMS............ Planned Missile System
PMS............ Plant Monitoring System [*Nuclear energy*] (NRCH)
PMS............ Plasmid Maintenance Sequence [*Genetics*]
PMS............ Plastic to Metal Seal
PMS............ P-Methylstyrene [*Plastics*]
PMS............ PM Industries, Inc. [*Vancouver Stock Exchange symbol*]
PMS............ Polaris Missile System

PMS............ Polar Meteorological Satellite (SSD)
PMS............ Policy Management Systems [*NYSE symbol*] (SPSG)
PMS............ Policy Mgmt Systems [*NYSE symbol*] (TTSB)
PMS............ Pollution Monitoring Satellite
pms............ Pollution-Monitoring Satellite (AD)
PMS............ Polymethylstyrene [*Organic chemistry*]
PMS............ Poor Miserable Soul [*Medical slang*]
pms............ Poor Miserable Soul (AD)
PMS............ Popular Music and Society [*A publication*] (BRI)
PMS............ Portable Monitoring Set (MCD)
PMS............ Post-Marketing Surveillance
PMS............ Postmeiotic Segregation [*Genetics*]
PMS............ Postmenopausal Syndrome [*Medicine*]
pms............ Post-Menopausal Syndrome [*Medicine*] (AD)
PMS............ Post-Merger Syndrome [*Business term*]
PMS............ Postmitochondrial Supernatant [*Medicine*] (MAE)
PMS............ Post-Mortem Survival [*Parapsychology*]
PMS............ Power Management System
PMS............ Prang-Mark Society (EA)
PMS............ Predicted Manning System [*Military*]
PMS............ Pregnant Mare's Serum [*Endocrinology*]
pms............ Pregnant Mare's Serum (AD)
PMS............ Premature Start [*Yacht racing*] (IYR)
PMS............ Premenstrual [*Stress*] Syndrome [*Medicine*]
pms............ Pre-Menstrual Syndrome [*Medicine*] (AD)
PMS............ Pre-Midshipmen School
PMS............ President of the Meteorological Society [*British*]
PMS............ President of the Miniature Society [*British*] (DI)
PmS............ Preston Microfilming Services Ltd., Toronto, ON, Canada [*Library symbol Library of Congress*] (LCLS)
PMS............ Preventive Maintenance System
PMS............ Probability of Mission Success [*Aerospace*] (AAG)
PMS............ Probable Maximum Surge [*Nuclear energy*] (NRCH)
PMS............ Process Measurement Systems Ltd. (NITA)
PMS............ Processor Memory Switch [*Computer science*] (ECII)
PMS............ Processors, Memories, and Switches [*Programming language*] (CSR)
p-m-s............ Processors-Memories-Switches (AD)
PMS............ Production Management System [*Safe Computing Ltd.*] [*Software package*] (NCC)
PMS............ Product Management System
PMS............ Professor of Military Science
PMS............ Program Management Staff [*Environmental Protection Agency*] (GFGA)
PMS............ Program Management Support [*Army*]
PMS............ Program Management System [*Computer science*]
PMS............ Program Master Schedule (MCD)
PMS............ Programmed Mode Switch (IAA)
PMS............ Projected Map System (OA)
PMS............ Project Management System [*IBM Corp.*] [*Computer science*]
PMS............ Project Manager, Ships
PMS............ Proposal Management System
PMS............ Public Management Sources [*A publication*]
PMS............ Public Message Service [*Western Union Corp.*]
PMS............ Publisher Management System (NITA)
PMS............ Pureed, Mechanical, Soft [*Diet*] (DAVI)
PMSA............ Office of the Project Manager Selected Ammunition [*DoD*]
PMSA............ Pacific Merchant Shipping Association (AD)
PMSA............ Pacific Merchant Shipping Association (NADA)
PMSA............ Paddy's Market Stallholders' Association [*Australia*]
PMSA............ PM [*Product Management*] Materiel Systems Assessment (RDA)
PMSA............ Posterior Middle Suprasylvian Area [*Anatomy*]
PMSA............ Primary Metropolitan Statistical Area [*Census Bureau*]
PMSA............ Professional Master of Science in Accounting (PGP)
P/MSA............ Project/Major Subcontractor Affected (MCD)
PMSA............ Project Manager for Selected Ammunition
PMSA............ Project Manager's System Assessment
PMS & T...... Professor of Military Science and Tactics
PMSAT............ Pre-Medical Student Assessment Test (EDAC)
PMSC............ Pediatric Medical Special Care (DMAA)
PMSC............ Pluripotent Myeloid Stem Cell [*Cytology*] (MAE)
PMSC............ Prime Minister's Science Council [*Australia*]
PMSD............ Parti Mauricien Social-Democrate [*Mauritian Social Democratic Party*] [*Political party*] (PPW)
PMSD............ Program Management and Support Division [*Environmental Protection Agency*] (GFGA)
PMS/DOD.... Performance Measurement System/Department of Defense
PMSE............ Percentage Mean Squared Error [*Statistics*]
PMSE............ Permanent Memory with Semi-Elastic Range (MCD)
PMSE............ Program Management Simulation Exercise [*Aerospace*]
PMSF............ Phenylmethylsulfonyl Fluoride [*Analytical chemistry*]
PMSFN............ Planetary Manned Space Flight Network [*Aerospace*] (MCD)
PMSG............ Peace Movement Study Group [*Colgate University*] (EA)
PMSG............ Pregnant Mare's Serum Gonadotrophin [*Endocrinology*]
pmsg............ Pregnant Mare's Serum Gonadotrophin (AD)
PMSGT............ Paymaster Sergeant [*Marine Corps*]
PMSI............ Prime Medical Services [*NASDAQ symbol*] (TTSB)
PMSI............ Prime Medical Services, Inc. [*NASDAQ symbol*] (NQ)
PMSI............ Prime Medics [*NASDAQ symbol*] (SAG)
PMSN............ Permission (FAAC)
PMSO............ Project Management Staff Officer [*Military*] (AFIT)
PMSO............ Project Management Support Office [*Army*] (RDA)
PMSP............ Parallel Modular Signal Processor
PMSP............ Photon-Counting Microspectrophotometer
PMSP............ Plant Modelling System Program (PDAA)
PMSP............ Preliminary Maintainability and Spare Parts
pm specialists... Paramilitary Specialists (AD)
PMSPS............ Project Management Staffing Practices Study [*Navy*] (NG)
PMSR............ Patternmaker, Ship Repair [*Navy rating*]
PMSR............ Physical, Mental, Social, Religious [*"Fourfold Life" symbol of American Youth Foundation*]
PMSRC............ Pittsburgh Mining and Safety Research Center [*Bureau of Mines*]
PMSRP............ Physical and Mathematical Sciences Research Paper (IEEE)
PMSS............ Personnel Mobility Support System [*Military*]
PMSS............ Precision Measuring Subsystem (KSC)
PMSS............ Program Management Support Staff [*Environmental Protection Agency*] (GFGA)
PMSS............ Program Manager's Support System [*Defense Systems Management College*] [*Fort Belvoir, VA*] (RDA)
PMS/SMS.... Planned Maintenance System for Surface Missile Ships
PMSSMS.... Planned Maintenance System for Surface Missile Ships (AD)
PMST............ Professor of Military Science and Tactics (MUGU)
PMSV............ Pilot-to-Metro Service
PMSX............ Processor Memory Switch Matrix
PMT............ Medical Photography Technician [*Navy*]
PMT............ Page Map Table [*NASA*] (HGAA)
PMT............ Para-Methoxytoluene [*Organic chemistry*]
PMT............ Partido Mexicano de los Trabajadores [*Mexican Workers' Party*] [*Political party*] (PPW)
PMT............ Passenger-Miles Traveled [*DOE*] (TAG)
pmt............ Payment (AD)
PMT............ Payment (AFM)
PMT............ Pennsylvania Motor Truck Association, Inc., Harrisburg PA [*STAC*]
PMT............ Perceptual Maze Test [*Psychology*]
PMT............ Performance Measuring Tool (MCD)
PMT............ Periodic Maintenance Team
PMT............ Permanent Magnet Tester [*Memory*] [*Bell Laboratories*] (IAA)
PMT............ Permanent Magnet Twistor [*Memory*] [*Bell Laboratories*]
PMT............ Permit (FAAC)
PMT............ Person-Miles of Travel [*FHWA*] (TAG)
PMT............ Personnel Management Team
PMT............ Phase-Modulated Transmission
PMT............ Philip Michael Thomas [*Co-star in TV series "Miami Vice"*]
PMT............ Photomechanical Transfer [*Negative paper*] [*Eastman Kodak*]
PMT............ Photomultiplier Tube [*Electronics*]
pmt............ Photomultiplier Tubes (AD)
PMT............ Physical Master Tape (IAA)
PMT............ Physical Message Type [*Communications*]
PMT............ Pine Mountain [*Oregon*] [*Seismograph station code, US Geological Survey*] (SEIS)
PMT............ Planning/Management Team [*NASA*] (MCD)
PMT............ PMC Technologies Ltd. [*Vancouver Stock Exchange symbol*]
PMT............ Polaromicrotribometry [*Analytical chemistry*]
PMT............ Portable Magnetic Tape
PMT............ Porteus Maze Test [*Medicine*] (MAE)
pmt............ Positive Matte Technique (AD)
PMT............ Post-Maastricht Tension [*European community*] (ECON)
PMT............ Post-Market Trading
PMT............ Potteries Motor Traction Co. [*British*]
PMT............ Power Microwave Tube
PMT............ Precious Metal Tip (IAA)
PMT............ Pre-Determined Motion-Time [*Management*] (PDAA)
PMT............ Premenstrual Tension [*Medicine*]
pmt............ Premenstrual Tension [*Medicine*] (AD)
PMT............ Premillennial Tension
PMT............ Preparatory Marksmanship Training [*Military*] (INF)
PMT............ Prepare Master Tape
PMT............ Preventive Maintenance Time (MCD)
PMT............ Production Monitoring Test (NG)
PMT............ Products, Marketing, and Technology [*Bank Administration Institute*] [*A publication*]
PMT............ Program Master Tape
PMT............ Programmed Math Tutorial [*National Science Foundation*]
pmt............ Programs, Materials, Techniques (AD)
PMT............ Project Management Team (ODBW)
PMT............ Pulse-Modulator Tube
PMT............ Pure Milk Tablet (IIA)
PMT............ Putnam Master Income Tr [*NYSE symbol*] (TTSB)
PMT............ Putnam Master Income Trust [*NYSE symbol*] (SPSG)
PMTA............ Page Map Table Address Register [*NASA*] (HGAA)
PMTAS............ Pre-Menstrual Tension Advisory Service [*British*]
PMTB............ Pacific Motor Tariff Bureau (AD)
PMTB............ Pacific Motor Tariff Bureau (NADA)
PMTC............ Pacific Missile Test Center [*Point Mugu, CA*] [*Navy*]
PMTC............ Parametric Technical [*NASDAQ symbol*] (TTSB)
PMTC............ Parametric Technology Corp. [*NASDAQ symbol*] (NQ)
PMTC............ Pittsburgh Mining Technology Center [*Department of Energy*] (GRD)
PMTD............ Post Mortem Tape Dump [*Computer science*]
PMTE............ Page Map Table Entry [*NASA*] (IAA)
PMT-EM............ Project Manager, Training Devices Engineering Management [*Orlando, FL*] [*Army*]
PMTHP............ Project Mercury Technical History Program [*NASA*]
PMTI............ Palomar Medical Technologies [*NASDAQ symbol*] (SAG)
PMTI............ Palomar Med Tech [*NASDAQ symbol*] (TTSB)
PM TMDS.... Program Manager - Test, Measurement, and Diagnostic Systems [*Army*]
PMTO............ Project Manager Test Offices [*Military*]
PMTP............ Production Missile Test Program
P/MTR............ Potentiometer [*Automotive engineering*]
PM TRADE... Office of the Project Manager for Training Devices [*Military*] (RDA)
PMTS............ PMT Services [*NASDAQ symbol*] (SAG)

PMTS .... Precision Missile Tracking System [*Military*] (IAA)
PMTS .... Predetermined Motion Time Standards [*Management*] (IAA)
PMTS .... Predetermined Motion Time Systems [*Management*]
PMTS .... Premenstrual Tension Syndrome [*Medicine*]
PMT Svc .... PMT Services [*Associated Press*] (SAG)
PMTT .... Phase-Modulated Telemetry Transmission
PMTT .... Pulmonary Mean Transit Time [*Medicine*] (MAE)
PMTV .... Potato Mop-Top Virus [*Plant pathology*]
PMU .... Paimiut, AK [*Location identifier FAA*] (FAAL)
PMU .... Pattern Makers Union (AD)
PMU .... Pattern Makers Union (NADA)
pmu .... Performance Monitor Unit (AD)
PMU .... Performance Monitor Unit [*Communications*]
PMU .... Permanently Medically Unfit
PMU .... Physical Mock-Up
pmu .... Physical Mockup (AD)
PMU .... Pierce Mountain [*Vancouver Stock Exchange symbol*]
PMU .... Plant Makeup [*Nuclear energy*] (NRCH)
PMU .... Pontifical Missionary Union [*Later, PMUPR*] [*See also OPM*] (EA)
PMU .... Portable Memory Unit [*Computer science*]
PMU .... Pregnant Mare's Urine [*Veterinary medicine*] (BARN)
PMU .... Pressure Measuring Unit (KSC)
PMU .... Preventive Medicine Unit [*Navy*] (NVT)
pmu .... Productive Man Work Unit (AD)
PMU .... Program Management Unit [*Computer science*] (IAA)
PMU .... Pulse Modulation Unit (NASA)
PMUB .... Presbyterian, Methodist, and United Board [*British military*] (DMA)
PMUPR .... Pontifical Missionary Union of Priests and Religious (EA)
PMUS .... Permanently Mounted User Set [*Computer science*] (ADA)
PMUSAOAS ... Permanent Mission of the United States of America to the Organization of American States (AD)
PM-UTTAS ... Project Manager, Utility Tactical Transport Aircraft System [*Military*]
PMUX .... Programmable Multiplex [*Computer science*] (TEL)
PMUX .... Propulsion Multiplexer
PMv .... Monroeville Public Library, Monroeville, PA [*Library symbol Library of Congress*] (LCLS)
PMV .... Panicum Mosaic Virus
PMV .... Papaya Mosaic Virus
PMV .... Paramyxovirus
PMV .... Parcel Mail Vans [*British railroad term*]
PMV .... Passenger Motor Vehicle
PMV .... Peanut Mottle Virus
PMV .... Plasma Membrane Vesicle [*Cytology*]
PMV .... Plate-Motion Vector [*Geology*]
PMV .... Plattsmouth, NE [*Location identifier FAA*] (FAAL)
PMV .... Politically Motivated Violence (ADA)
PMV .... Porlamar [*Venezuela*] [*Airport symbol*] (OAG)
PMV .... Prime Mission Vehicle (MCD)
PMV .... Private Market Value [*Investment term*] (DFIT)
PMV .... Private Motor Vehicle (DNAB)
PMV .... Prolapsing Mitral Valve [*Cardiology*]
PMV .... Pro Mundi Vita [*Brussels, Belgium*] [*Defunct*] (EAIO)
PMvAC .... Community College of Allegheny County, Boyce Campus, Monroeville, PA [*Library symbol Library of Congress*] (LCLS)
PMVB .... Pocono Mountain Vacation Bureau (AD)
pmvi .... Periodic Motor Vehicle Inspection (AD)
PMVI .... Periodic Motor Vehicle Inspection (PDAA)
PMvK .... Koppers Co., Inc., Research Department, Monroeville, PA [*Library symbol Library of Congress*] (LCLS)
PMVL .... Posterior Mitral Valve Leaflet [*Anatomy*] (AAMN)
PMV-LATA ... Passenger Motor Vehicle Labour Adjustment Training Arrangements [*Australia*]
PMVMP .... Passenger Motor Vehicle Manufacturing Plan [*Australia*]
pmvp .... Precio Maximo de Venta al Publico [*Maximum Price Charged the Public*] [*Spanish*] (AD)
p mvr .... Prime Mover (AD)
PMVR .... Prime Mover [*Technical drawings*]
PMvS .... United States Steel Corp., Research Center Library, Monroeville, PA [*Library symbol Library of Congress*] (LCLS)
PMW .... Pacemaker Wire [*Cardiology*] (DAVI)
PMW .... Parts Manufacturing Workmanship
PMW .... Pole Mountain [*Wyoming*] [*Seismograph station code, US Geological Survey Closed*] (SEIS)
PMW .... Preventive Maintenance Welding (PDAA)
PMW .... Private Microwave [*System*]
PMW .... Progressive Mine Workers of America
PMW .... Project Magic Wand [*Military*] (MCD)
PMW .... Project Management Work-Bench (NITA)
PMW .... Prompt Mobilization Designation Withdrawn
PMW .... Pulse-Modulated Wave [*Telecommunications*] (IAA)
PMWCMA .... Paper Mill Wire Cloth Manufacturers' Association (DGA)
PMWIN .... Processing MODFLOW for Windows
PMWP .... Probable Maximum Winter Precipitation [*Nuclear energy*] (NRCH)
PMX .... Packet Multiplexer
PMX .... Palmer, MA [*Location identifier FAA*] (FAAL)
PMX .... Pamorex Minerals, Inc. [*Toronto Stock Exchange symbol*]
PMX .... Petroleos Mexicanos [*Mexico ICAO designator*] (FAAC)
PMX .... Physical Modelling Extension (NITA)
pmx .... Private Manual Exchange (AD)
PMX .... Private Manual Exchange
PMX .... Protected Message Exchange
PMyE .... Evangelical Congregational School of Theology, Myerstown, PA [*Library symbol Library of Congress*] (LCLS)
PMYOB .... Please Mind Your Own Business
pmyob .... Please Mind Your Own Business (AD)
PMZ .... Palmar [*Costa Rica*] [*Airport symbol*] (AD)
PMZ .... Plymouth, NC [*Location identifier FAA*] (FAAL)
PN .... Coastal Airways [*ICAO designator*] (AD)
PN .... Nacionalista [*Nationalist Party*] [*Spain*] [*Political party*] (AD)
Pn .... North Celestial Pole (AD)
pn---- .... North Pacific [*MARC geographic area code Library of Congress*] (LCCP)
PN .... North Pole [*Also, NP*]
PN .... Pacific Communications Net [*Air Force*]
PN .... Pacific Northern [*Airline*] (AD)
PN .... Pakistan Navy
PN .... Palus Nebularum [*Lunar area*]
pn .... Panama [*MARC country of publication code Library of Congress*] (LCCP)
PN .... Pan-American World Airways [*Stock exchange symbol*] (AD)
PN .... Papillary or Nodular Hyperplasia [*Medicine*]
PN .... Parenteral Nutrition [*Medicine*]
PN .... Partenavia Construzioni Aeronautiche SpA [*Italy ICAO aircraft manufacturer identifier*] (ICAO)
PN .... Particulate Nitrogen [*Chemistry*]
PN .... Partido Nacional [*National Party*] [*Honduras*] [*Political party*] (PPW)
PN .... Partido Nacional [*National Party*] [*Uruguay*] [*Political party*] (PPW)
PN .... Partido Nacional [*National Party*] [*Dominican Republic*] [*Political party*]
PN .... Partido Nacional [*National Party*] [*Spain*] [*Political party*] (AD)
PN .... Parti Nationaliste [*Canada*]
Pn .... Partition (WGA)
pn .... Partition (AD)
PN .... Partit Nazzjonalista [*Nationalist Party*] [*Malta*] [*Political party*] (EAIO)
PN .... Part Number
P/N .... Part Number (AD)
pn .... Part Number (AD)
PN .... Party Notified (IAA)
PN .... Patent Number (NITA)
PN .... Perceived Noise
PN .... Percussion Note [*Physiology*]
pn .... Percussion Note (AD)
PN .... Performance Number
PN .... Periarteritis [*or Polyarteritis*] Nodosa [*Also, PAN*] [*Medicine*]
PN .... Perigean Range
Pn .... Perigean Range (AD)
PN .... Peripheral Nerve [*Anatomy*]
PN .... Peripheral Neuropathy [*Medicine*]
PN .... Peroxide Number [*Hydrocarbon fuel specifications*]
PN .... Personal Name (NITA)
PN .... Personal Names from Cuneiform Inscriptions of the Cassite Period [*A publication*] (BJA)
PN .... Personnelman [*Navy rating*]
PN .... Personnel Navigant
PN .... Phase Name (NITA)
PN .... Phenolic Nylon
PN .... Philippine Navy
PN .... Phon [*Unit of loudness level*] (IAA)
P/N .... Phonogram [*British military*] (DMA)
pN .... Piconewton [*Unit of force*]
PN .... Piedmont & Northern Railway Co. [*AAR code*]
PN .... Pilot Navigator (IAA)
pn .... Pine (VRA)
P/N .... Pin Number (AAG)
PN .... Pitcairn Islands [*ANSI two-letter standard code*] (CNC)
PN .... Place-Name
PN .... Place of Publication Class Number (NITA)
PN .... Planners Network (EA)
PN .... Plant Normal [*Nuclear energy*] (NRCH)
PN .... Plaque Neutralization [*Dentistry*] (DMAA)
PN .... Plasticity Number (AAG)
PN .... Please Note
pn .... Please Note (AD)
P/N .... Please Note [*Copyediting*] (WDMC)
PN .... Pneumatic
PN .... Pneumonia [*Medicine*]
PN .... Point of No Return (AD)
PN .... Polish Notation [*Mathematics*]
PN .... Polyarteritis Nodosa [*Rheumatology*] (DAVI)
PN .... Pontine Nuclei [*Neuroanatomy*]
P/N .... Porter/Novelli [*A public relations firm*] [*New York, NY*] (WDMC)
pn .... Position (AD)
PN .... Position (WGA)
PN .... Positional Nystagmus [*Physiology*] (MAE)
PN .... Position Number (ADA)
PN .... Position Pennant [*Navy British*]
P/N .... Positive/Negative
PN .... Postal Note (ADA)
PN .... Postnasal [*Otorhinolaryngology*] (DAVI)
PN .... Postnatal [*Medicine*]
PN .... Practical Nurse
PN .... Preliminary Notification (NRCH)
PN .... Press Night
PN .... Princeton Aviation [*ICAO designator*] (AD)
PN .... Processing Negativity [*Computer science*]
PN .... Procurement Notice [*NASA*] (AAGC)
Pn .... Production [*Economics*]
PN .... Production Notice (KSC)
PN .... Product Name (NITA)
PN .... Programmable Network

PN............... Program Notice (KSC)
PN............... Program Number [*Horse racing*]
PN............... Progress note [*Medical records*] (DAVI)
PN............... Projection Neurons [*Neuroanatomy*]
PN............... Project Note
PN............... Project Number [*Online database field identifier*] [*Computer science*]
PN............... Promissory Note [*Business term*]
pn............... Promissory Note (AD)
PN............... Pronuclei [*Embryology*]
PN............... Proportional Navigation (IAA)
PN............... Pseudonoise
PN............... Pseudorandom Number
PN............... Psychiatric Nurse
pn............... Psychiatry-Neurology (AD)
PN............... Psychoneurologist
PN............... Psychoneurotic [*Cases, patients, etc.*]
PN............... Public Network [*Telecommunications*]
PN............... Publisher's Name [*Online database field identifier*]
PN............... Pulse Network (KSC)
PN............... Punch On
pn............... Punch-On [*Computer science*] (AD)
PN............... Pupil Nurse [*British*] (DI)
PN............... Putative Neurotransmitter [*Biochemistry*]
PN............... Pyelonephritis [*Medicine*] (MAE)
PN............... Pyridine Nucleotide [*Medicine*] (DMAA)
PN............... Pyridoxine [*or Pyridoxol*] [*Also, Pxn*] [*Biochemistry*]
PN............... Pyrrolnitrin [*Antifungal antibiotic*]
PN............... Regular Pending Transaction [*IRS*]
PN1............... Personnelman, First Class [*Navy rating*]
P_{N2}............... Partial Pressure of Nitrogen [*Medicine*] (DAVI)
PN2............... Personnelman, Second Class [*Navy rating*]
PN3............... Personnelman, Third Class [*Navy rating*]
Pn6............... Partenavia [*Airplane code*]
PNA............... Nomina Anatomica (Paris) [*Anatomical Nomenclature*] (DAVI)
PNA............... Pacific/North American [*Sector*] [*Marine science*] (OSRA)
PNA............... Pacific/North American [*Sector*] (USDC)
PNA............... Pacific North Atlantic [*Marine science*] (OSRA)
PNA............... Pacific Northern Airlines (AD)
PNA............... Packet Network Adaptor (NITA)
PNA............... Pakistan National Alliance (PD)
PNA............... Palestinian National Authority [*Political party*] (ECON)
PNA............... Pamplona [*Spain*] [*Airport symbol*] (OAG)
PNA............... Panna [*India*] [*Airport symbol*] (AD)
PNA............... Pa-O National Army [*Myanmar*] [*Political party*] (EY)
PNA............... Paper Napkin Association
PNA............... Parallel and Novel Architectures [*British*]
PNA............... Para-Nitroaniline [*Organic chemistry*]
PNA............... Parenting in a Nuclear Age (EA)
PNA............... Parisiensis Nomina Anatomica [*Paris Anatomical Nomenclature*] [*Medicine*]
PNA............... Partacoona [*Australia Seismograph station code, US Geological Survey*] (SEIS)
PNA............... Parti Nationale Africain [*African National Party*] [*Chad*] [*Political party*]
PNA............... Passed, but Not Advanced
PNA............... Peanut Agglutinin [*Immunology*]
PNA............... Pentosenucleic Acid [*Biochemistry*]
PNA............... People's News Agency [*An association*] (EA)
PNA............... Peptide Nucleic Acid [*Biochemistry*]
PNA............... Philippines News Agency (AD)
PNA............... Philippines News Agency (NADA)
PNA............... Pinedale, WY [*Location identifier FAA*] (FAAL)
PNa............... Plasma Sodium [*Organic chemistry*] (DAVI)
PNA............... Polish National Alliance of the United States of North America (EA)
PNA............... Polish Nobility Association (EA)
PNA............... Polyamide Nucleic Acid [*Biochemistry*]
PNA............... Polynuclear Aromatic [*Organic chemistry*]
PNA............... Price Not Available (DNAB)
PNA............... Processing Terminal Network Architecture [*Computer science*] (BUR)
PNA............... Professional Numismatists' Association [*British*] (BI)
PNA............... Project Network Analysis
PNA............... Universal Airlines, Inc. [*ICAO designator*] (FAAC)
PNAB............... Percutaneous Needle Aspiration Biopsy [*Medicine*]
PNAC............... President's National Advisory Committee (AD)
PNAC............... President's National Advisory Committee (NADA)
PNAC............... Psychiatric Nurses' Association of Canada
PNAF............... Plan Name and Address File [*IRS*]
PNAF............... Potential Network Access Facility
PNAF............... Primary Nuclear Airlift Force
PNAH............... Polynuclear Aromatic Hydrocarbon [*Environmental chemistry*]
PNAI............... Provincial Newspapers Association of Ireland (AD)
PNAMBIC............... Pay No Attention to the Man Behind the Curtain [*Computer hacker terminology*] (NHD)
PNAP............... Pro-Life Nonviolent Action Project (EA)
PNAS............... Palletized Night Attack System
PNAS............... Prudent No Added Salt [*Diet*] (DAVI)
PNASA............... Para-Nitroaniline-o-sulfonic Acid [*Organic chemistry*]
PnASat............... PanAmSat Corp. [*Associated Press*] (SAG)
P-NAV............... Personal Navigation
PNAV............... Precise Navigation
PNAV............... Precision Navigation Ambiguity Resolution
PNAV............... Proportional Navigation
PNAvQ............... Positive-Negative Ambivalent Quotient [*Psychology*]
pnavq............... Positive-Negative Ambivalent Quotient (AD)
PNazMHi............... Moravian Historical Society, Nazareth, PA [*Library symbol Library of Congress*] (LCLS)
PNB............... North Platte, NE [*Location identifier FAA*] (FAAL)
PNB............... Pacific Northwest Ballet
PNB............... Particle/Neutral Beam (MCD)
PNB............... Partido ng Bayan [*Party of the Nation*] [*Philippines*] [*Political party*]
PNB............... Permodalan Nasional Bank [*Malaysia*]
PNB............... Philippine National Bank (AD)
PNB............... Pomio [*New Britain*] [*Seismograph station code, US Geological Survey Closed*] (SEIS)
PNB............... Porto Nacional [*Brazil*] [*Airport symbol*] (AD)
PNB............... Premature Nodal Beat [*Cardiology*] (DAVI)
pnb............... Producto Nacional Bruto [*Gross National Product*] [*Spanish*] (AD)
PNB............... Produto Nacional Bruto [*Gross National Product*] [*Portugal*] (AD)
PNB............... Prostatic Needle Biopsy [*Oncology*] (DAVI)
PNBA............... Pacific Northwest Booksellers Association (AD)
PNBAS............... ((Para-Nitrophenyl)azo)salicylic Acid [*A dye*] [*Organic chemistry*]
PNBB............... Parc National de la Boucle du Baoule [*Baoule River Bend National Park*] [*French*] [*Mali*] (AD)
PNBC............... Pacific Northwest Bibliographic Center [*Library network*]
PNBC............... Princeton National Bancorp [*NASDAQ symbol*] (SAG)
PNBC............... Princeton Natl Bancorp [*NASDAQ symbol*] (TTSB)
PNBF............... Peak Nucleate Boiling Flux
PNBK............... Patriot National Bank CT [*NASDAQ symbol*] (SAG)
PNBK............... Patriot Natl Bk [*NASDAQ symbol*] (TTSB)
PNBMS............... Pacific Northwest Bird and Mammal Society [*Later, SNUB*] (EA)
PNBP............... Parc National de la Boucle de la Pendjari [*Penjari River Bend National Park*] [*French*] [*Dahamey*] (AD)
PNBS............... Pyridinium(nitro)benzenesulfonate [*Organic chemistry*]
PNBT............... Para-Nitroblue Tetrazolium
PNC............... Chief Personnelman [*Navy rating*]
PNc............... New Castle Free Public Library, New Castle, PA [*Library symbol Library of Congress*] (LCLS)
PNC............... Northampton County Area Community College, Bethlehem, PA [*OCLC symbol*] (OCLC)
PNC............... Pakistan National Congress [*Political party*]
PNC............... Palestine National Council (PD)
PNC............... Parque Nacional Canaima [*Canaima National Park*] [*Venezuela*] (AD)
PNC............... Partido Nacional Ceuti [*Ceuta National Party*] [*Political party*] (PPW)
PNC............... Partido Nacional Conservador [*Nicaragua*] [*Political party*] (EY)
PNC............... Partido Nacional Cristiano [*National Christian Party*] [*Colorado Political party*] (EY)
PNC............... Partido Nacionalista Ceuti [*Political party*] (EY)
PNC............... Partidual Nationale Crestine [*National Christian Party*] [*Romania*] [*Political party*] (PPE)
PNC............... Parti National Caledonien [*Caledonian National Party*] [*Political party*] (PPW)
PNC............... Passenger Name Check-In (MCD)
pnc............... Pencillin (AD)
PNC............... Pencrude Resources, Inc. [*Vancouver Stock Exchange symbol*]
PNC............... Penicillin
PNC............... People's National Congress [*Guyana*] (PD)
PNC............... Peripheral Nerve Conduction [*Neurology*] (DAVI)
PNC............... Peripheral Nucleated Cell (AAMN)
PNC............... Personal Number Calling [*Telecommunications*]
PNC............... Philatelic-Numismatic Combination [*or Commemorative*]
PNC............... Phosphonitrilic Chloride [*Inorganic chemistry*]
PNC............... Physitest Normalise Canadien [*Canadian Standardized Test of Fitness - CSTF*]
PNC............... Pine Canyon [*California*] [*Seismograph station code, US Geological Survey*] (SEIS)
PNC............... Place Names Committee [*Victoria, Australia*]
PNC............... Plate Number Coil [*Philately*]
pnc............... Plate Number Coil (AD)
PNC............... PNC Bank Corp. [*NYSE symbol*] (SPSG)
PNC............... PNC Bank Corp. [*NYSE symbol*] (TTSB)
PNC............... Pneumotaxic Center [*Medicine*] (DAVI)
PNC............... Pneumotaxic Center (BABM)
PNC............... Police National Computer [*British*]
PNC............... Ponca City [*Oklahoma*] [*Airport symbol*] (OAG)
PNC............... Ponca City, OK [*Location identifier FAA*] (FAAL)
PNC............... Postnatal Clinic
PNC............... Power Reactor and Nuclear Fuel Development Corp. [*Japan*] (PDAA)
PNC............... Premature Nodal Contraction [*Cardiology*]
pnc............... Premature Nodal Contraction (AD)
PNC............... Prenatal Care [*Obstetrics*] (DAVI)
PNC............... Prenatal Clinic [*Obstetrics*] (DAVI)
PNC............... Prenodal Contraction [*Cardiology*] (DAVI)
PNC............... PRIMENET Node Controller (NITA)
PNC............... Programmed Numerical Control
PNC............... Prohibition National Committee (EA)
PNC............... Pseudonurse Cells [*Cytology*]
PNCB............... Pakistan Narcotics Control Board
PNCB............... Para-Nitrochlorobenzene [*Organic chemistry*]
PNCC............... Partial Network Control Center
PNCC............... President's National Crime Commission (AD)
PNCC............... President's National Crime Commission (NADA)
PNCE............... Private New Capital Expenditure
PNCFN............... Permanent Nordic Committee on Food and Nutrition [*Copenhagen, Denmark*] (EAIO)
PNCH............... Partido Nacional Conservador de Honduras [*National Conservative Party of Honduras*] [*Political party*]
PNCH............... Punch
pnch............... Punch (AD)

PNCH Punch
PNCK Pancake
PNCL Pinnacle Micro [*NASDAQ symbol*] (TTSB)
PNCL Pinnacle Micro, Inc. [*NASDAQ symbol*] (NQ)
Pncla Pensacola, Florida (AD)
PNCM Master Chief Personnelman [*Navy rating*]
PNCOC Primary Noncommissioned Officer Course [*Army*] (INF)
PNCPrC PNC Bank Cp $1.60 Cv C Pfd [*NYSE symbol*] (TTSB)
PNCPrD PNC Bank Cp $1.80 Cv D Pfd [*NYSE symbol*] (TTSB)
PNCS Private Network Communication Systems (MCD)
PNCS Senior Chief Personnelman [*Navy rating*]
PNCU Police National Computer Unit [*British*]
Pnd Pandjang (AD)
pnd Paroxysmal Noctural Dyspnoea (AD)
PND Paroxysmal Nocturnal Dyspnea [*Medicine*]
PND Parti des Nationalistes du Dahomey [*Dahomean Nationalists Party*] [*Political party*]
PND Partido Nacional Democratico [*National Democratic Party*] [*Dominican Republic*] [*Political party*]
PND Partido Nacional Democratico [*National Democratic Party*] [*Costa Rica*] [*Political party*] (PPW)
PND Partidul National-Democratic [*National Democratic Party*] [*Romania*] [*Political party*] (PPE)
PND Parti National Democrate [*Morocco*] [*Political party*] (EY)
PND Passive Navigation Device
PND Pending
PND Pictorial Navigation Display (OA)
PND Postnasal Drainage [*or Drip*] [*Medicine*]
pnd Postnasal Drip [*Medicine*] (AD)
PND Postnatal Days
PND Postnatal Depression [*Medicine*] (ECON)
pnd Pound (MAE)
PND Preliminary Number Deflator [*Empirical mathematics*] (ECON)
PND Premodulation Processor - Near Earth Data (KSC)
PND Prenatal Diagnosis [*Medicine*]
PND Present Next Digit
PND Pressed Notch Depth (PDAA)
PND Primary Navigation Display (GAVI)
PND Principal Neutralizing Determinant [*Immunology*]
PND Principal Neutralizing Domain [*Medicine*]
PND Program Network Diagram [*Telecommunications*] (TEL)
PND Pseudonyms and Nicknames Dictionary [*A publication*]
PND Punta Gorda [*Belize*] [*Airport symbol*] (OAG)
PNDA Panda Project [*NASDAQ symbol*] (TTSB)
PNDA [*The*] Panda Project, Inc. [*NASDAQ symbol*] (SAG)
PNDA People for Nuclear Disarmament Australia [*An association*]
PNDB Pelerinage a Notre Dame de Beauraing [*An association*] (EAIO)
PNdB Perceived Noise Decibels
pndb Perceived Noise Decibels (AD)
PNDC Parallel Network Digital Computer (IEEE)
PNDC Partido Nacional de Democracia Centrista [*Chile*] [*Political party*] (EY)
PNDC Progressive Neuronal Degeneration of Childhood [*Medicine*]
PNDC Provisional National Defence Council [*Ghana*] (PD)
PNDD Parti National pour la Democratie et le Developpement [*Benin*] [*Political party*] (EY)
PNDG Pending (AFM)
pndg Pending (AD)
PNDI Pennsylvania Natural Diversity Inventory [*Bureau of Forestry*] [*Harrisburg*] [*Information service or system*] (IID)
PNDL Pentland Group plc [*LO Symbol*] (TTSB)
P-N-D-L-R Park-Neutral-Drive-Low-Reverse (AD)
PNDLR Pendular
PNDM Project Nondesign Memo
pndnt Pendentive (VRA)
PNDO Partial Neglect of Differential Overlap [*Physics*]
Pndo Pinedo (AD)
PNDP Para-Nitrophenyl Diphenyl Phosphate [*Organic chemistry*]
PNDR Ponder Industries [*NASDAQ symbol*] (TTSB)
PNDR Ponder Industries, Inc. [*NASDAQ symbol*] (SAG)
PNDT Parti Nationale pour la Developpement du Tchad [*National Party for the Development of Chad*]
PNE Pacific National Exchange Vancouver [*Vancouver*] (AD)
PNE Pacific National Exhibition [*Vancouver*] (AD)
PNE Pacific National Exhibition Home Show [*Southex Exhibitions*] (TSPED)
PNE Paine College, Warren A. Candler Library, Augusta, GA [*OCLC symbol*] (OCLC)
PNE Panhandle Eastern Corp. [*Toronto Stock Exchange symbol*]
PNE Peaceful Nuclear Explosion
pne Peaceful Nuclear Explosion (AD)
PNE Philadelphia [*Pennsylvania*] North Philadelphia [*Airport symbol*] (OAG)
PNE Philadelphia, PA [*Location identifier FAA*] (FAAL)
PNE Pine
PNE PINE [*Postal Service standard*] (OPSA)
PNE Plasma Norepinephrine [*Medicine*] (DMAA)
PNE Pneumoencephalography [*Medicine*] (CPH)
PNe Pointe Noire (AD)
pne Practical Nurse's Education (AD)
PNE Practical Nurse's Education
PNEA Parque Nacional El Avila [*El Avila National Park*] [*Spanish*] (AD)
PNEC Predicted No Effect Concentration [*Environmental technology*]
PNEC Primary Navy Enlisted Classification [*Code*]
PNEd Pharmacopeia Nederlandsche [*Netherlands Pharmacopoeia*]
PNEDC Programme National D'etude de la Dynamique du Climat [*France*] [*Marine science*] (OSRA)
PNEDC Programme National d'Etudes de la Dynamique du Climat (USDC)
PNEM Paraneoplastic Encephalomyelitis [*Medicine*] (DMAA)
PNEM-APROME Partido Nacionalista Espanol de Melilla - Asociacion pro Melilla [*Spanish North Africa*] [*Political party*] (MENA)
PNERL Pacific Northwest Environmental Research Laboratory [*Environmental Protection Agency*] (MSC)
PNES Pines
Pnes Pines (AD)
PNES Pines
PNET Peaceful Nuclear Explosions Treaty [*Officially, Treaty on Underground Nuclear Explosions for Peaceful Purposes*]
PNET Peripheral Neuroepithelioma [*Medicine*] (DMAA)
PNET Primitive Neuroectodermal Tumor [*Oncology*]
PNET ProNet, Inc. [*NASDAQ symbol*] (NQ)
PNEU Parents' National Educational Union [*British*]
PNEU Pneumatic (AAG)
pneu Pneumatic (AD)
pneu Pneumonia [*Medicine*] (MAE)
PNEUG Pneumatic Pressure Generator (MCD)
PNEUM Pneumatic
PNEUM Pneumonia (WDAA)
PNEUMO Pneumothorax [*Medicine*]
pneumoccon Pneumocconiosis [*Medicine*] (AD)
pneumog Pneumograph (AD)
pneumonoultra Pneumonoultra-Microscopicsilicovolcanoconiosis [*Medicine*] (AD)
PNEUROP European Committee of Manufacturers of Compressors, Vacuum Pumps, and Pneumatic Tools (EA)
PNF Pacific National Financial Corp. [*Toronto Stock Exchange symbol Vancouver Stock Exchange symbol*]
PNF Palestine National Front [*Political party*] (PD)
PNF Partito Nazionale Fascista [*National Fascist Party*] [*Italy Political party*] (PPE)
PNF Peierls-Nabarro Force [*Physics*]
PNF Penn Traffic [*NYSE symbol*] (TTSB)
PNF Penn Traffic Co. [*NYSE symbol*] (SAG)
PNF Phosphonitrilic Fluoroelastomer [*Synthetic rubber*]
PNF Pilot Not Flying (GAVI)
PNF Positive Neutral Finder [*Automotive engineering*]
PNF Postnuclear Fraction [*Biochemical tissue analysis*]
PNF Prenex Normal Form [*Logic*]
PNF Proprioceptive Neuromuscular Facilitation [*Neurology*]
pnf Proprioceptive Neuromuscular Facilitation (AD)
pnfd Present Not for Duty (AD)
PNFD Present Not for Duty [*Military*]
PNFI Petawawa National Forestry Institute [*Canadian Forestry Service*] [*Research center*] (RCD)
PNFI Pinnacle Financial Services, Inc. [*NASDAQ symbol*] (NQ)
PNFI Pinnacle Financial Svcs [*NASDAQ symbol*] (TTSB)
PNFS Peak and Northern Footpaths Society [*British*] (DBA)
PNFSO Primary Nonferrous Smelter Order [*Environmental Protection Agency*]
PNG Pacific Northern Gas Ltd. [*Toronto Stock Exchange symbol Vancouver Stock Exchange symbol*]
PNG Papua New Guinea [*ANSI three-letter standard code*] (CNC)
PNG Papua New Guinea Banking Corp.
PNG Papua Nueva Guinea [*Papua New Guinea*] [*Spanish*] (AD)
PNG Paranagua [*Brazil*] [*Airport symbol*] (OAG)
PNG Parque Nacional Guatopo [*Guatopo National Park*] [*Venezuela*] [*Spanish*] (AD)
PNG Partido Nacional Guevarista [*Ecuador*] [*Political party*] (PPW)
Png Penang (AD)
PNG Penghu [*Hokoto*] [*Republic of China*] [*Seismograph station code, US Geological Survey*] (SEIS)
PNG Penicillin G [*Medicine*] (DMAA)
png Persona Non Grata [*An Unacceptable Person*] [*Latin*] (AD)
PNG Persona Non Grata [*Unacceptable Person*] [*Latin*]
PNG Philippine Natural Gum
PNG Plant Nitrogen in Grain [*Harvest nitrogen index*]
PNG Popondetta [*New Guinea*] [*Airport symbol*] (AD)
PNG Portable Network Graphic [*Computer science*] (PCM)
PNG Portable Network Graphics [*Computer science*] (PCM)
PNG Portable Network Graphics [*Computer science*] (DOM)
PNG Professional Numismatists Guild (EA)
PNG Pseudonoise Generator
PNG Puerto Rico Air NAtional Guard [*FAA designator*] (FAAC)
PNGCS Primary Navigation, Guidance and Control System (KSC)
PNGFA Pacific Northwest Grain and Feed Association (EA)
PNGI Papua New Guinea Institute of Chemistry
PNGL Papua New Guinea Line (AD)
PNGS Primary Navigation System
PNGV Partnership for a New Generation of Vehicles [*Collaboration of government and industry*]
PNGV Partnership for a New Generation of Vehicles
PNH North Hills School District Instructional Materials Center, Pittsburgh, PA [*OCLC symbol*] (OCLC)
PNH Pan Head [*Design engineering*]
PNH Paroxysmal Nocturnal Hemoglobinuria [*Medicine*]
pnh Paroxysmal Nocturnal Hemoglobinuria (AD)
PNH Partido Nacional Hondureno [*Honduran National Party*] [*Political party*]
PNH Parti National d'Haiti [*National Party of Haiti*] [*Political party*]
PNH Phnom Penh [*Cambodia*] [*Airport symbol*] (OAG)
PNH Pitcher Mountain [*New Hampshire*] [*Seismograph station code, US Geological Survey*] (SEIS)

PNH Polynuclear Hydrocarbon (DMAA)

PNHA Physicians National Housestaff Association [*Defunct*]

PNHDL Panhandle [*NWS*] (FAAC)

PNHDL Panhandle

PNHP Parque Nacional Henri Pittier [*Henri Pittier National Park*] [*Venezuela*] [*Spanish*] (AD)

PNHS Pacific Northwest Heather Society [*Later, NAHS*] (EA)

PNI Aerovias de Poniente SA de CV [*Mexico ICAO designator*] (FAAC)

PNI Parque Nacional Iguazu [*Iguazu National Park*] [*Spanish*] (AD)

PNI Partai Nasionalis Indonesia [*Nationalist Party of Indonesia*] [*Political party*]

PNI Participate but Do Not Initiate [*Investment term*]

PNI Partido Nacional Independiente [*National Independent Party*] [*Costa Rica*] [*Political party*] (PPW)

PNI Part Number Index (MCD)

PNI Pascoe Nally International [*British*]

PNI Peer Nomination Inventory [*Psychology*]

PNI Peripheral Nerve Injury [*Medicine*]

PNI Pharmaceutical News Index [*UMI/Data Courier*] [*Information service or system A publication*]

PNI Pictorial Navigation Indicator [*Aviation*] (DA)

PNI Picture Netwok International, Ltd.

PNI Picture Network International [*Commercial firm Information service or system*]

PNI Pinerola [*Italy*] [*Seismograph station code, US Geological Survey*] (SEIS)

PNI Ponape [*Caroline Islands*] [*Airport symbol*] (OAG)

PNI Positive Noninterfering [*Alarm system*]

pni Positive Noninterfering (AD)

PNI Postnatal Infection [*Medicine*]

PNI Principal Neo-Tech, Inc. [*Toronto Stock Exchange symbol*]

PNI Prognostic Nutrition Index [*Dietetics*] (DAVI)

PNI Protease Nexin I [*Biochemistry*]

PNI Psychoneuroimmunology

pni Psychoneuroimmunology (AD)

pni Pulsed Neutron Interrogation (AD)

PNI Pulsed Neutron Interrogation (PDAA)

PNIC Pleasure Navigation International Joint Committee [*See also CINP*] [*The Hague, Netherlands*] (EAIO)

P Nic Port Nicholson (AD)

PNID Peer Nomination Inventory of Depression [*Child development test*] [*Psychology*]

P-NID Precedence Network In-Dialing [*Telecommunications*] (TEL)

PNID/NOD Priority Network In-Dial / Network Out-Dial (DNAB)

PNIE Priority National Intelligence Estimate [*CIA*] (LAIN)

PNII Prentiss Normal and Industrial Institute [*Mississippi*]

PNII Protease Nexin II [*Biochemistry*]

PNIO Priority National Intelligence Objectives (MCD)

PNIP Positive-Negative-Intrinsic-Positive [*Electron device*] (MSA)

PNIPAAM Poly-N-isopropylacrylamide [*Organic chemistry*]

PNIPAM Poly-N-Isopropylacrylamide [*Organic chemistry*]

PNITC Pacific Northwest International Trade Council (AD)

PNITC Pacific Northwest International Trade Council (NADA)

PNJ Paterson [*New Jersey*] [*Airport symbol*] (AD)

PNJ Paterson [*New Jersey*] [*Seismograph station code, US Geological Survey*] (SEIS)

PNJ Paterson, NJ [*Location identifier FAA*] (FAAL)

PNJ Polar Night Jet Stream (ADA)

PNJALBB Peter Noone Just a Little Bit Better Promotion Club (EA)

PNK Pink [*Electrical wiring*]

PNK Pinkham Creek [*Montana*] [*Seismograph station code, US Geological Survey Closed*] (SEIS)

PNK Pink Pages Publication [*Vancouver Stock Exchange symbol*]

PNK Polynucleotide Kinase [*An enzyme*]

PNK Pontianak [*Indonesia*] [*Airport symbol*] (OAG)

PNK Pyridoxine Kinase (DMAA)

PNkA Aluminum Co. of America, ALCOA Research Laboratories Library, New Kensington, PA [*Library symbol Library of Congress*] (LCLS)

PNKA Protein Induced by Vitamin K Absence and Antagonists (PDAA)

pnksh Pinkish [*Philately*]

PNL Aero Personal SA de CV [*Mexico ICAO designator*] (FAAC)

PNL Instrument Panel [*Automotive engineering*]

PNL Pacific Naval Laboratories (AD)

PNL Pacific Northwest Laboratory [*Department of Energy*] [*Richland, WA*]

PNL Pakistan National League [*Political party*]

PNL Panel (KSC)

pnl Panel (AD)

PNL Pantelleria [*Italy*] [*Airport symbol*] (OAG)

PNL Partidul National Liberal [*National Liberal Party*] [*Romania*] [*Political party*] (PPE)

PNL Parti National Liberal [*National Liberal Party*] [*Lebanon*] [*Political party*] (PPW)

PNL Passenger Name List [*Travel industry*]

PNL Peanut Lectin [*Immunochemistry*]

PNL Peninsula [*Alaska*] [*Seismograph station code, US Geological Survey*] (SEIS)

PNL Perceived Noise Level

PNL Philippine National Line (AD)

PNL Pine Bell Mines [*Vancouver Stock Exchange symbol*]

PNL Polytechnic of North London, School of Librarianship, London, England [*OCLC symbol*] (OCLC)

PNL Prescribed Nuclear Load [*Military*] (AABC)

PNL Pressure Noise Level (MCD)

PNL Pulsed Neodymium LASER

PNLA Pacific Northwest Library Association

PNLA Pacific Northwest Loggers Association (EA)

PNLA Percutaneous Needle Lung Aspiration [*Medicine*] (DMAA)

PNLAADA Programme National de Lutte Contre l'Abus de l'Alcohol et des Drogues chez les Autochtones [*Canada*]

pnlbd Panelboard [*National Electrical Code*] (IEEE)

PNLBRG Panel Bridge (MUGU)

PNLG Phase Nulling LASER Gyroscope

PNL/I Provisioning Numerical Listing/Index

PNLM Palestine National Liberation Movement [*Political party*] (BJA)

PNLO Principal Naval Liaison Officer [*British*]

PNLRM Preferred National Land Rights Model [*Australia*]

PNLT Perceived Noise Level, Tone Corrected

PNM Pan-Somali Nationalist Movement [*Political party*]

PNM Partido Nacionalista de Mexicano [*Nationalist Party of Mexico*] [*Political party*]

PNM Partito Nazionale Monarchico [*National Monarchist Party*] [*Italy Political party*] (PPE)

PNM People's National Movement [*Trinidad and Tobago*] [*Political party*] (PD)

PNM Perinatal Mortality [*Medicine*]

PNM Phenolic Nylon with Microballoon

PNM Pinnacles National Monument [*California*] (AD)

PNM Price Negotiation Memorandum (MCD)

PNM Public Service Co. of New Mexico [*NYSE symbol*] (SPSG)

PNM Public Svc New Mexico [*NYSE symbol*] (TTSB)

PNM Pulse Number Modulation

PNM-Aprome Partido Nacionalista de Melilla - Asociacion Pro Melilla [*Political party*] (EY)

PNMC Phenyl Methylcarbamate [*Organic chemistry*]

PNMF Pseudo Noise Matched Filter (IAA)

PNMG Persistent Neonatal Myasthenia Gravis [*Medicine*] (DAVI)

PNMO Provided No Military Objection Exists [*Army*]

PNMT Phenylethanolamine N-Methyltransferase [*An enzyme*]

PNMT Positive-Negative Metal Transistor [*Electronics*] (IAA)

PNN Penn Engineering & Manufacturing Corp. [*AMEX symbol*] (SPSG)

PNN Penn Engr & Mfg [*AMEX symbol*] (TTSB)

PNN Pinnacle Mountain [*Alaska*] [*Seismograph station code, US Geological Survey*] (SEIS)

PNN Princeton, ME [*Location identifier FAA*] (FAAL)

PNN.A Penn Engr & Mfg'A' [*AMEX symbol*] (TTSB)

pn nb Piano Nobile (VRA)

PNNCF Pacific Northern Naval Coastal Frontier

PNNL Pacific Northwest National Laboratory

PNNT Pennant (MSA)

PNNW Pennichuck Corp. [*NASDAQ symbol*] (SAG)

PNo Montgomery County-Norristown Public Library, Norristown, PA [*Library symbol Library of Congress*] (LCLS)

PNO Nashville, TN [*Location identifier FAA*] (FAAL)

PNO Pancontinental Oil Ltd. [*Toronto Stock Exchange symbol*]

PNO Pa-O National Organization [*Myanmar*] [*Political party*] (EY)

PNO Parque Nacional Ordesa [*Ordesa National Park*] [*Spanish*] (AD)

PNO Parti Nationaliste Occitan [*Occitanian Nationalist Party*] [*France Political party*] (PPE)

PNO Party for National Order [*Turkey Political party Defunct*] (MENA)

PNO Pendleton [*Oregon*] [*Seismograph station code, US Geological Survey*] (SEIS)

pno Pergamino [*Parchment*] [*Spanish*] (AD)

pno Piano (AD)

PNO Piano

PNO Piano [*Music*]

PNO Port of New Orleans (AD)

PNO Preliminary Notification [*Nuclear energy*] (NRCH)

PNO Premium Notice Ordinary [*Insurance*]

PNO Principal Naval Overseer [*British*]

PNO Principal Nursing Officer

PNOA Para-Nitro-ortho-anisidine [*Organic chemistry*]

pnob Pencil Note on Back [*Philately*]

PNOC Philippine National Oil Co. (AD)

PNOC Proposed Notice of Change

PNO-CI Pair Natural Orbital Configuration Interaction [*Atomic physics*]

PNoH Norristown State Hospital, Norristown, PA [*Library symbol Library of Congress*] (LCLS)

PNohM Mary Immaculate Seminary, Northampton, PA [*Library symbol Library of Congress*] (LCLS)

PNOK Primary Next of Kin [*Army*] (AABC)

PNOM Procedural Nomenclature (MCD)

PNOPO Parliament National Organisations and Public Offices [*British*]

PNortHi Historical Society of Montgomery County, Norristown, PA [*Library symbol Library of Congress Obsolete*] (LCLS)

PNOT Para-Nitro-ortho-toluidine [*Organic chemistry*]

PNOT Para-Nitro-o-toluidine [*Organic chemistry*]

PNP Pakistan National Party [*Political party*] (PD)

PNP Panache Resources, Inc. [*Vancouver Stock Exchange symbol*]

PNP Para-Nitrophenol [*or Nitrophenyl*] [*Organic chemistry*]

PNP Para-Nitrophenyl-Beta-Galactosidase [*An enzyme*] (DAVI)

PNP Partido Nacionalista del Pueblo [*Bolivia*] [*Political party*] (PPW)

PNP Partido Nacionalista ng Pilipinas [*Philippine Nationalist Party*] [*Political party*] (EY)

PNP Partido Nacionalista Popular [*Popular Nationalist Party*] [*Panama*] [*Political party*] (PPW)

PNP Partido Nashonal di Pueblo [*National People's Party*] [*Netherlands Antilles*] [*Political party*] (EY)

PNP Partido Nuevo Progresista [*New Progressive Party*] [*Puerto Rico*] [*Political party*] (PPW)

PNP .... Partidul National Poporului [*National People's Party*] [*Romania*] [*Political party*] (PPE)
PNP .... Parti National du Progres [*National Progress Party*] [*Congo*] [*Political party*]
PNP .... Parti National Populaire [*National Popular Party*] [*Canada Political party*] (PPW)
PNP .... Parti National Progressiste [*Haiti*] [*Political party*] (EY)
PNP .... Peake's English Nisi Prius Cases [*1790-1812*] [*A publication*] (DLA)
PNP .... Peak Negative Pressure [*Medicine*] (DAVI)
PNP .... Pearl Necklace Polymer [*Organic chemistry*]
PNP .... Pediatric Nephrology [*Medical specialty*] (DHSM)
PNP .... Pediatric Nurse Practitioner
PNP .... Penuelas [*Puerto Rico*] [*Seismograph station code, US Geological Survey*] (SEIS)
PNP .... People's National Party [*Ghana*] [*Political party*] (PPW)
PNP .... People's National Party [*Jamaica*] [*Political party*] (PPW)
PNP .... Peripheral Neuropathy [*Medicine*]
PNP .... Platelet Neutralization Procedure [*Medicine*] (MEDA)
PNP .... Platt National Park [*Oklahoma*] (AD)
PnP .... Plug and Play (PCM)
PNP .... Plug and Play [*Microsoft Corp.*] [*Computer auto-configuration system*] (PCM)
PNP .... Popondetta [*Papua New Guinea*] [*Airport symbol*] (OAG)
PNP .... Popular Nationalist Party [*Panama*] [*Political party*] (PD)
PNP .... Positive-Negative-Positive [*Transistor*]
pnp .... Positive Negative Positive (AD)
PNP .... Precision Navigation Project
PNP .... Preliminary Network Plan (SSD)
PNP .... Prenegotiation Position (MCD)
PNP .... Private Non-Profit
PNP .... Progressive National Party [*Turks and Caicos Islands*] [*Political party*] (PPW)
PNP .... Progressive Nuclear Palsy [*Neurology*] (DAVI)
PNP .... Prototype Nuclear Process
PNP .... Psychogenic Nocturnal Polydipsia [*Medicine*]
PNP .... P-Type, N-Type, P-Type Transistor (NITA)
PNP .... Purine-Nucleoside Phosphorylase [*An enzyme*]
PNP .... Purine Nucleotide Phosphorylase [*An enzyme*] (DAVI)
PNP .... Pyridoxine Phosphate [*Biochemistry*]
PNPA .... Para-Nitrophenyl Acetate [*Organic chemistry*]
PNPDPP .... Para-Nitrophenyl Diphenyl Phosphate [*Organic chemistry*]
PNPF .... Piqua Nuclear Power Facility
PNPG .... Para-Nitrophenylglycerine [*Biochemistry*]
PNPG .... Parti National Populaire Guyanais [*French Guiana*] [*Political party*] (EY)
PNPG .... P-Nitrophenyl-B-Galactoside [*Chemistry*] (MAE)
PNPH .... Parti National Progressiste d'Haiti [*National Progressive Party of Haiti*] [*Political party*]
PNPL .... Para-Nitrophenyl Laurate [*Organic chemistry*]
PNPLS .... Progress at NPL [*National Priorities List*] Sites [*A publication*] [*EPA*]
pnpn .... Positive-Negative Positive-Negative (AD)
PNPN .... Positive-Negative-Positive-Negative [*Transistor*] (MUGU)
P-NPNN .... Para-Nitrophenyl Nitronyl Nitroxide
PNPP .... Para-Nitrophenyl Phosphate [*Organic chemistry*]
PNPP .... Perry Nuclear Power Plant (NRCH)
PNPR .... Positive-Negative Pressure Respiration
pnpr .... Positive-Negative Pressure Respiration (AD)
PNPS .... Palisades Nuclear Power Station (NRCH)
P-NPS .... Para-Nitrophenylsulfate [*Pharmacology*] (DAVI)
PNPS .... Plant Nitrogen Purge System (IEEE)
PNPS .... Plant Nuclear Protection System (IAA)
PNQ .... Pine Crest Resources [*Vancouver Stock Exchange symbol*]
PNQ .... Poona [*India*] [*Airport symbol*] (OAG)
PNR .... Panair [*Spain ICAO designator*] (FAAC)
PNR .... Partido Nacionalista Renovador [*Nationalist Renewal Party*] [*Guatemala*] [*Political party*] (PPW)
PNR .... Partido Nacionalista Revolucionario [*Revolutionary Nationalist Party*] [*Ecuador*] [*Political party*] (PPW)
PNR .... Partido Nacional Republicano [*National Republican Party*] [*Paraguay*] [*Political party*]
PNR .... Partido Nacional Republicano [*National Republican Party*] [*Portugal Political party*] (PPE)
PNR .... Partido Nacional Revolucionario [*National Revolutionary Party*] [*Venezuela Political party*]
PNR .... Partij Nationalistische Republiek [*Nationalist Republic Party*] [*Surinam*] [*Political party*] (PPW)
PNR .... Passenger Name Record [*Airlines*]
PNR .... Pennant Resources Ltd. [*Toronto Stock Exchange symbol*]
PNR .... Penrod [*Nevada*] [*Seismograph station code, US Geological Survey Closed*] (SEIS)
PNR .... Pentair, Inc. [*NYSE symbol*] (TTSB)
PNR .... Philippine National Railways (DS)
PNR .... Pioneer
Pnr .... Pioneer (AD)
PNR .... Pioneer
PNR .... Pittsburgh Naval Reactor (AD)
PNR .... Pittsburgh Naval Reactors Office [*Energy Research and Development Administration*]
PNR .... Pointe Noire [*Congo*] [*Airport symbol*] (OAG)
PNR .... Point of No Return [*Aviation*]
pnr .... Point of No Return (AD)
PNR .... Popular News and Review [*A publication*]
PNR .... Preliminary Negotiation Reports
PNR .... Primary Navigation Reference (AAG)
PNR .... Prior Notice Required (AFM)
pnr .... Prior Notice Required (AD)
PNR .... Prisoner
PNR .... Proved Name Registraton [*Advertising*] (DOAD)
PNR .... Proximal Negative Response
PNR .... Pulletop Nature Reserve [*New South Wales*] (AD)
PNR .... Pulse Nuclear Radiation (AAG)
PNRBC .... Pacific Northwest River Basin Commission
PNRC .... Pacific Northwest Regional Commission [*Department of Commerce*]
PNRC .... Potomac Naval River Command (MCD)
PNRC .... Projet National de Coordination des Ressources dans le Domaine de la Statistiques et de l'Information Judiciaires [*Canada*]
PNRE .... Pan Atlantic Re, Inc. (MHDW)
PNRG .... Prime Energy [*NASDAQ symbol*] (SAG)
PNRG .... PrimeEnergy Corp. [*NASDAQ symbol*] (SPSG)
PNRHSL .... Pacific Northwest Regional Health Science Library [*Library network*]
PNRL .... Penril DataComm Ntwks [*NASDAQ symbol*] (TTSB)
PNRL .... Penril Data Communication Networks [*NASDAQ symbol*] (SPSG)
PNRO .... Pittsburgh Naval Reactors Office [*Department of Energy*] [*West Mifflin, PA*] (GAAI)
PNRP .... Philadelphia Pulmonary Neoplasm Research Project (AD)
PNRS .... Preliminary Natural Resources Survey (GNE)
PNRS .... Project Notification and Review System [*Department of Labor*]
PNRSV .... Prunus Necrotic Ringspot Virus
PNS .... Pacific Navigation Systems (AD)
PNS .... Pakistan Naval Ship (AD)
PNS .... Parabolized Navier-Stokes Modeling (MCD)
PNS .... Paraneoplastic Neurodegenerative Syndrome [*Medicine*]
PNS .... Parasympathetic Nervous System
pns .... Parasympathetic Nervous System (AD)
PNS .... Park-Neutral Switch [*Automotive engineering*]
PNS .... Partial Niche Separation
PNS .... Partial Nonprogressing Stroke (CPH)
PNS .... Part Number Specification (MCD)
PNS .... Peculiar and Nonstandard Items (AAG)
PNS .... Penas [*Bolivia*] [*Seismograph station code, US Geological Survey*] (SEIS)
PNS .... Pennington's Stores Ltd. [*Toronto Stock Exchange symbol*]
PNS .... Pensacola [*Florida*] [*Airport symbol*] (OAG)
PNS .... People's News Service [*British*]
PNS .... Peripheral Nerve Stimulator [*Medicine*] (MAE)
PNS .... Peripheral Nervous System [*Medicine*]
pns .... Peripheral Nervous System (AD)
PNS .... Perkins Nuclear Station (NRCH)
PNS .... Philadelphia & Norfolk Steamship [*AAR code*]
PNS .... Philadelphia Naval Shipyard (AD)
PNS .... Philippines News Service
PNS .... Plate Number Society [*Defunct*] (EA)
PNS .... Pooled Normal Serum (PDAA)
PNS .... Portable Navigation System
PNS .... Portsmouth Naval Shipyard [*New Hampshire*]
PNS .... Positive-Negative Selection [*Genetic engineering technique*]
PNS .... Posterior Nasal Spine [*Medicine*] (DMAA)
PNS .... Post Nickel Strike (PDAA)
PNS .... Postnuclear Supernatant
PNS .... Practical Nursing Student (DAVI)
PNS .... Prescribed Nuclear Stockage [*Military*] (AABC)
PNS .... Probability of Not Having a Space
PNS .... Professionals for National Security [*Defunct*] (EA)
PNS .... Professor of Naval Science
PNS .... Project of National Significance
PNS .... Publishers Newspaper Syndicate
PNS .... Survey Udara (Penas) PT [*Indonesia*] [*ICAO designator*] (FAAC)
PNSA .... Pacific Northwest Ski Association (EA)
PNSA .... Peanut and Nut Salters Association [*Later, PBNPA*] (EA)
PNSA .... Seaman Apprentice, Personnelman, Striker [*Navy rating*]
PNS & T .... Professor of Naval Science and Tactics [*Naval ROTC*]
PNSC .... Packet Network Service Centre (NITA)
PNSCP .... Plan for Navy Satellite Communications Plan
PNSD .... Parti National pour la Solidarite et le Developpement [*Algeria*] [*Political party*] (EY)
PNSI .... Polhemus Navigational Sciences, Inc. (MCD)
PNSN .... Parque Nacional Sierra Nevada [*Sierra Nevada National Park*] [*Venezuela*] [*Spanish*] (AD)
PNSN .... Pension
PNSN .... Seaman, Personnelman, Striker [*Navy rating*]
PNSO .... Pull Next Stitch Over [*Knitting*] (BARN)
PNSP .... Penicillin-Nonsusceptible S. Pneumoniae [*Clinical chemistry*]
PNSQ .... Porter Need Satisfaction Questionnaire (EDAC)
PNSS .... Pediatric Nutrition Surveillance System [*Centers for Disease Control*] (DAVI)
PNSTDC .... Pakistan National Scientific and Technical Documentation Center (AD)
PNSUS .... Placename Survey of the US (EA)
PNSY .... Portsmouth Naval Shipyard [*New Hampshire*]
PNt .... Newtown Library Co., Newtown, PA [*Library symbol Library of Congress Obsolete*] (LCLS)
PNT .... Paint (MSA)
pnt .... Paint (AD)
PNT .... Paint
Pnt .... Panart [*Record label*] [*Cuba, USA*]
PNT .... Para-Nitrotoluene [*Organic chemistry*]
PNT .... Paroxysmal Nodal Tachycardia [*Cardiology*]
PNT .... Parque Nacional Tijuca [*Tijuca National Park*] [*Brazil*] [*Portuguese*] (AD)
PNT .... Partial Nodular Transformation (DMAA)

PNT .... Partido Nacionalista de los Trabajadores [*Argentina Political party*] (EY)
PNT .... Parti National du Travail [*Haiti*] [*Political party*] (EY)
PNT .... Parti National du Travail [*Benin*] [*Political party*] (EY)
PNT .... Patient (AABC)
PNT .... Penna Enterprises [*NYSE symbol*] (TTSB)
PNT .... Penn Enterprises, Inc. [*NYSE symbol*] (SAG)
PNT .... Pentagon
Pnt .... Pentagon (AD)
PNT .... Penticton [*British Columbia*] [*Seismograph station code, US Geological Survey*] (SEIS)
PNT .... Percutaneous Nephrostomy Tube [*Nephrology*] (DAVI)
PNT .... Petromet Resources Ltd. [*Toronto Stock Exchange symbol*]
PNT .... Point
PNT .... Pontiac, IL [*Location identifier FAA*] (FAAL)
PNT .... Position-Navigation-Time
PNT .... Project Network Technique (EECA)
PNTA .... Pacific Northwest Trade Association
PNTA .... Pentair, Inc. [*NASDAQ symbol*] (NQ)
Pnt Anx .... Pentagon Annex (AD)
PNtB .... Bucks County Community College, Newtown, PA [*Library symbol Library of Congress*] (LCLS)
PNTB .... Peninsula Trust Bank [*NASDAQ symbol*] (TTSB)
PNTB .... Peninsula Trust Bank, Inc. [*NASDAQ symbol*] (SAG)
PNTBT .... Partial Nuclear Test Ban Treaty (AD)
PNtC .... Council Rock High School, Newtown, PA [*Library symbol Library of Congress*] (LCLS)
PNTC .... Panatech Res & Dev [*NASDAQ symbol*] (TTSB)
PNTC .... Panatech Research & Development Corp. [*NASDAQ symbol*] (NQ)
PNTCENS .... Patient Census Report
PNTD .... Painted
pntd .... Painted (AD)
PNTD .... Personnel Neutron Threshold Detector (IEEE)
PN/TDMA .... Pseudo Noise/Time Division Multiple Access (MCD)
PNtE .... Ellis College, Newtown, PA [*Library symbol Library of Congress Obsolete*] (LCLS)
PNTG .... Petromet Resources Ltd. [*NASDAQ symbol*] (NQ)
PNTG .... Printing (ROG)
PNTGF .... Petromet Resources [*NASDAQ symbol*] (TTSB)
PNTGN .... Pentagon (MSA)
PNTK .... Pentech International [*NASDAQ symbol*] (TTSB)
PNTK .... Pentech International, Inc. [*NASDAQ symbol*] (NQ)
PNTL .... Phonetel Technologies [*NASDAQ symbol*] (TTSB)
PNTL .... Phonetel Technologies, Inc. [*NASDAQ symbol*] (NQ)
PNTO .... Portuguese National Tourist Office (EA)
PNTO .... Principal Naval Transport Officer [*British military*] (DMA)
PNTOS .... Para-Nitrotoluene-ortho-sulfonic Acid [*Organic chemistry*]
pntr .... Painter (AD)
PNTR .... Painter
PNTR .... Pointer (MCD)
PNTRY .... Pantry
PNts .... Newtown Public Library, Newtown Square, PA [*Library symbol Library of Congress*] (LCLS)
PNTYP .... Panno Type (VRA)
PNU .... Panguitch [*Utah*] [*Airport symbol*] (OAG)
PNU .... Peasants' National Unity [*Afghanistan*] [*Political party*] (EY)
PNU .... Personennamen der Texte aus Ugarit [*A publication*] (BJA)
PNU .... Pharmacia & Upjohn [*NYSE symbol*] (TTSB)
PNU .... Pharmacia & Upjohn, Inc. [*NYSE symbol*] (SAG)
PNU .... Platinum Communication System [*Vancouver Stock Exchange symbol*]
PNU .... Pneumatic Scale Corp. [*Stock exchange symbol*] (AD)
PNU .... Protein Nitrogen Units [*Clinical chemistry*]
PNUA .... Partito Nazionale Unito Africa [*National Party of United Africans*] [*Somalia*] [*Political party*]
PNUA .... Polish National Union of America (EA)
PNUD .... Programa de las Naciones Unidas para el Desarrollo [*United Nations Development Program - UNDP*] [*Spanish*] (MSC)
PNUMA .... Programa de las Naciones Unidas para el Medio Ambiente [*United Nations Environmental Programme Regional Office for Latin America*] (EAIO)
PNUT .... Portable Nursing Unit Terminal
PNUT .... Possible Nuclear Underground Test
pnutbutsan .... Peanut-Butter Sandwich (AD)
p-nut butter .... Peanut-Butter Sandwich (AD)
pnutbutwich .... Peanut-Butter Sandwich (AD)
PNUTS .... Possible Nuclear Test Site [*Pronounced "peanuts"*] [*Air Force intelligence*]
PNV .... National Velasquista Party [*Ecuador*] [*Political party*] (PPW)
PNV .... Panavia SA [*ICAO designator*] (FAAC)
PNV .... Partido Nacionalista Vasco [*Basque Nationalist Party*] [*Spain Political party*] (PPE)
PNV .... Partido Nacional Velasquista [*National Velasquista Party*] [*Ecuador*] [*Political party*] (PPW)
PNV .... Parti National Voltaique [*Voltaic National Party*] [*Political party*]
PNV .... Patino N. V. [*Toronto Stock Exchange symbol*]
PNV .... Potential Natural Vegetation (GNE)
PNV .... Prenatal Vitamins (DAVI)
PNVAL .... Previously Not Available [*Army*] (AABC)
PNVD .... Passive Night Vision Devices [*Army*] (AABC)
PNVS .... Pilot Night Vision System [*Army*] (MCD)
PNVS .... Pilot's Night Vision Sensor
PNVTS .... Pyrotechnics No-Voltage Test Set
PNW .... Pacific Northwest
PNW .... Pacific Northwest Outport [*MTMC*] (TAG)
PNW .... Pinnacle West Capital [*NYSE symbol*] (TTSB)
PNW .... Pinnacle West Capital Corp. [*NYSE symbol*] (SPSG)
PNW .... [*The*] Prescott & Northwestern Railroad Co. [*AAR code*]
PNWC .... Pacific Northwest Writers' Conference
PNwC .... Westminster College, New Wilmington, PA [*Library symbol Library of Congress*] (LCLS)
PNWCSC .... Pacific Northwest Canadian Studies Consortium [*University of Oregon*]
PNWD/BMI .... Pacific Northwest Division/Battelle Memorial Institute (AD)
PNWL .... Pacific Northwest Laboratory [*AEC*]
PNWR .... Piedmont National Wildlife Refuge [*Georgia*] (AD)
PNWR .... Presquile National Wildlife Refuge [*Virginia*] (AD)
PNWR .... Pungo National Wildlife Refuge [*North Carolina*] (AD)
PNWRBC .... Pacific Northwest River Basins Commission [*Water Resources Council*] [*Terminated, 1981*] (NOAA)
PNX .... Imperial Airways, Inc. [*ICAO designator*] (FAAC)
PNX .... Pneumothorax [*Medicine*]
pnx .... Pneumothorax [*Medicine*] (AD)
pnxt .... Pinxit [*He or She Painted It*] [*Latin*] (AD)
PNXT .... Pinxit [*He, or She, Painted It*] [*Latin*]
PNY .... Camp Parks, CA [*Location identifier FAA*] (FAAL)
PNY .... Penny
PNY .... Piedmont Natl Gas [*NYSE symbol*] (TTSB)
PNY .... Piedmont Natural Gas Co., Inc. [*NYSE symbol*] (SPSG)
PNY .... Plattsburgh [*New York*] [*Seismograph station code, US Geological Survey*] (SEIS)
PNY .... Portuguese Navy
PNYA .... Port of New York Authority [*Later, PANYNJ*]
PNYCTC .... Pennsylvania New York Central Transportation Co. (AD)
PNZ .... Pennzoil Co., Exploration Library, Houston, TX [*OCLC symbol*] (OCLC)
Pnz .... Penzance (AD)
PNZ .... Petrolina [*Brazil*] [*Airport symbol*] (OAG)
PO .... Aeropelican Intercity Commuter Air Services [*ICAO designator*] (AD)
po---- .... Oceanica [*MARC geographic area code Library of Congress*] (LCCP)
PO .... Officer Personnel Division [*Coast Guard*]
PO .... Oil City Library, Oil City, PA [*Library symbol Library of Congress*] (LCLS)
PO .... Oscillopolarograph
PO .... Paarieto-Occipital [*Medicine*] (DMAA)
PO .... Pacific Ocean
PO .... Palomar Capital [*Vancouver Stock Exchange symbol*]
PO .... Parallel Output [*Computer science*] (BUR)
P:O .... Parent Offspring [*Genetics*]
PO .... Parieto-Occipital [*Anatomy*] (AAMN)
PO .... Parity Odd
PO .... Parking Orbit [*NASA*]
PO .... Parliamentary Officer [*Australia*]
PO .... Parole Officer
P/O .... Parole Officer (AD)
PO .... Partial Pressure of Oxygen (DAVI)
p/o .... Part of (AD)
P/O .... Part Of (KSC)
PO .... Passport Office [*Department of State*]
PO .... Patent Office [*Later, PTO*] [*Department of Commerce*]
PO .... Performance Objectives (OICC)
PO .... Performing Organization (NITA)
PO .... Period of Onset [*Medicine*]
PO .... Perioperative [*Medicine*] (DMAA)
PO .... Permit Office [*British*] (ROG)
PO .... Per Order (WDMC)
po .... Per Os [*By Mouth*] [*Latin*] (AD)
PO .... Per Os [*By Mouth*] [*Pharmacy*]
PO .... Peroxidase [*Also, POD*] [*An enzyme*]
PO .... Personnel Office [*Kennedy Space Center Directorate*] (NASA)
PO .... Personnel Officer
PO .... Pesticides Office [*Environmental Protection Agency*]
PO .... Petty Officer [*Navy*]
PO .... Phase-Out
PO .... Philharmonic Orchestra [*Music*]
P/O .... Phone Order [*Medicine*]
P/O .... Phosphate to Oxygen (BARN)
PO .... Phymatotrichum omnivorum [*A fungus*]
PO .... Pilot Officer
P/O .... Pilot Officer (AD)
P/O .... Pitch Over
PO .... Planetary Office (IAA)
PO .... Planetary Orbit
PO .... Planned Obsolescence (MHDB)
PO .... Planning Objectives
PO .... Poco [*Somewhat*] [*Music*]
po .... Poetry (AD)
PO .... Point (WGA)
PO .... Polarity (AAG)
po .... Polarity (AD)
PO .... Pole [*Unit of measurement*]
PO .... Police Officer
PO .... Political Officer [*NATO*]
P/O .... Pollen/Ovule Ratio [*Botany*]
Po .... Polonium [*Chemical element*]
PO .... Polskie Zaklady Lotnicze [*Poland ICAO aircraft manufacturer identifier*] (ICAO)
PO .... Polymerizable Oligomer (OA)
PO .... Polyolefin [*Organic chemistry*]
Po .... Polyzoa [*Quality of the bottom*] [*Nautical charts*]

PO .... Por Orden [*By Order*] [*Spanish*]
PO .... Port Flag [*Navy British*]
PO .... Portland Oregonian [*A publication*] (AD)
PO .... Port Officer
po .... Portugal [*MARC country of publication code Library of Congress*] (LCCP)
PO .... Portugal [*NATO*]
Po .... Portuguese [*Language, etc.*] (DLA)
PO .... Position Offered
Po .... Possible
PO .... Postal Officer (DCTA)
PO .... Postal Order
PO .... Posterior (MAE)
PO .... Post Flight Inspection [*Air Force*]
PO .... Post Office
po .... Post Office (WDMC)
PO .... Post Office (NITA)
PO .... Post Office Department [*Canada*]
PO .... Postoperative [*Medicine*]
p-o .... Postoperative (AD)
PO .... Post Orbit [*NASA*]
PO .... Postpay Coin Telephone [*Telecommunications*] (TEL)
PO .... Potential Officer [*British military*] (DMA)
PO .... Power-Operated
po .... Power-Operated (AD)
po .... Power Oscillator (AD)
PO .... Power Oscillator [*Electronics*]
PO .... Power Output
PO .... Pre-Authorization Order
PO .... Predominating Organism (AAMN)
PO .... Preoperational (MCD)
PO .... Preoptic [*Area of the brain*]
PO .... Presbyteri Oratorii [*Oratorians*] [*Roman Catholic religious order*]
PO .... Presbyterorum Ordinis [*Decree on the Ministry and Life of Priests*] [*Vatican II document*]
PO .... Pressure Oscillation (IAA)
PO .... Preventive Officer [*British*] (ROG)
PO .... Previous Orders [*Military*]
po .... Previous Orders (AD)
PO .... Primary Output (IAA)
PO .... Principal Officer [*Foreign Service*]
PO .... Principal Only (DFIT)
PO .... Principal Only Strip [*Mortgage security*]
PO .... Printout
PO .... Privately Owned (AFM)
PO .... Private Office [*Documents issued by the Secretary General, NATO*] (NATG)
PO .... Probation Officer
P/O .... Probation Officer (AD)
PO .... Processing Office [*Bureau of the Census*] (GFGA)
PO .... Procurement Objective (NVT)
PO .... Production Offset (AABC)
PO .... Production Order (KSC)
PO .... Professional Officer
PO .... Professor Ordinarius [*Ordinary Professor*] [*Latin*] (ROG)
PO .... Programmed Oscillator
PO .... Program Objective
PO .... Program Office [*Air Force*] (CET)
PO .... Program Originator (AFM)
PO .... Project Office [*or Officer*] [*Military*]
PO .... Project ORBIS (EA)
PO .... Project Order [*DoD*]
PO .... Project Overcome (EA)
PO .... Proposals Outstanding
PO .... Proposition One [*Defunct*] (EA)
PO .... Propylene Oxide [*Organic chemistry*]
PO .... Province of Ontario [*Canada*]
PO .... Provisioning Order (AFM)
PO .... Pseudoadiabatic Operation [*Chemical engineering*]
PO .... Psychological Operation [*Military*] (CINC)
PO .... Public Offering [*Investment term*]
PO .... Public Office [*British*] (ROG)
PO .... Public Official
PO .... Pull Out (IAA)
PO .... Pulmonary Valve Opening [*Cardiology*]
PO .... Pulsed Carrier without Any Modulation Intended to Carry Information (IEEE)
PO .... Pulse Oscillator (IAA)
PO .... Pulse Output
PO .... Punch Out [*Computer science*] (IAA)
PO .... Punted Over [*Boating*] [*British*] (ROG)
PO .... Purchase Order
PO .... Purchasing Office [*DoD*] (AFIT)
PO .... Putout [*Baseball*]
P-O .... Pyrenees-Orientales (AD)
PO .... Radio Positioning Mobile Station [*ITU designation*] [*Telecommunications*] (CET)
PO1 .... Petty Officer, First Class [*Navy*]
PO 1/C .... Petty Office First Class [*Military*] (AD)
pO_2 .... Oxygen Pressure (DAVI)
PO_2 .... Partial Pressure of Oxygen (AAMN)
PO2 .... Petty Officer, Second Class [*Navy*]
PO 2/C .... Petty Office Second Class [*Military*] (AD)
PO3 .... Petty Officer, Third Class [*Navy*]
PO 3/C .... Petty Office Third Class [*Military*] (AD)
POA .... Le Point Air [*France ICAO designator*] (FAAC)
POA .... Pacific Ocean Area [*World War II*]
POA .... Pahoa, HI [*Location identifier FAA*] (FAAL)
POA .... Pancreatic Oncofetal Antigen [*Immunochemistry*]
POA .... Panel of Americans [*Defunct*] (EA)
POA .... Pay-on-Answer [*Telecommunications British*]
POA .... Peacetime Operating Assets [*DoD*] (AFIT)
POA .... Petroleum Operating Agreement (CINC)
POA .... Petty Officer Airman [*British military*] (DMA)
POA .... Phalangeal Osteoarthritis [*Medicine*]
POA .... Phenoxyacetic Acid [*Organic chemistry*]
POA .... Place of Acceptance [*Business term*] (DCTA)
poa .... Place of Acceptance (AD)
POA .... Plan of Action (NASA)
POA .... Point Of Action (EECA)
POA .... Point of Application [*Medicine*] (MAE)
POA .... Polarized Orbital Approximation (PDAA)
POA .... Police Officers' Association [*British*] (BI)
POA .... Pontifica Opera di Assistenza [*Pontifical Relief Organization*]
POA .... Portland Opera Association [*Oregon*] (AD)
POA .... Porto Alegre [*Brazil*] [*Airport symbol*] (OAG)
POA .... Port of Arrival
POA .... Power of Attorney
PoA .... Power of Attorney (AD)
POA .... Power Open Association [*Computer science*] (CDE)
POA .... Preoptic Area [*of the brain*]
POA .... Price on Application [*Business term*] (ADA)
POA .... Primary Optic Afferents
poa .... Primary Optical Area (AD)
POA .... Primary Optic Atrophy
POA .... Prison Officers' Association [*A union*] [*British*] (DCTA)
POA .... Privately Owned Automobile
POA .... Privately-Owned Open Air-Braked [*Railway wagons*] (PDAA)
POA .... Probability of Acceptance (IAA)
POA .... Proof of Accounts
POA .... Provisional Operating Authorization [*for nuclear power plant*]
POA .... Public Order Act
POA .... Purchased on Assembly (KSC)
POA .... Purchase Order Authorization (SAA)
POA .... Purgeable Organic Analyzer
POAA .... Planetary Operations Analysis Area [*NASA*]
POAA .... Post Office Agents' Association [*Australia*]
POAA .... Property Owners Association of America [*Defunct*] (EA)
POA & M .... Plan of Action and Milestones (NVT)
POAC .... Peace Officers Association of California (AD)
POAC .... Pony of the Americas Club (EA)
POAC .... Port and Ocean Engineering Under Arctic Conditions International Committee (EAIO)
POAC .... Post Office Advisory Committee [*British*]
POAC .... Post Office Advisory Council (AD)
POAC .... Post Office Ambulance Centre [*British*] (DI)
POACH .... Prednisone, Oncovin [*Vincristine*] Cytosine Arabinoside, Cyclophospham ide, and Adriamycin [*Antineoplastic drug regimen*] (DAVI)
POACMN .... Petty Officer Aircrewman [*British military*] (DMA)
POACS .... Prior Other Active Commissioned Service [*Military*]
POADS .... Portland Air Defense Sector (SAA)
POAE .... Port of Aerial Embarkation [*Air Force*]
POAE .... Principal Officer of Aircraft Equipment [*Ministry of Aircraft Production*] [*British World War II*]
POAES .... Prior Other Active Enlisted Service [*Military*]
POAF .... Petty Officer Air Fitter [*British military*] (DMA)
POAG .... Peace Officers Association of Georgia (AD)
POAG .... Primary Open-Angle Glaucoma [*Ophthalmology*]
POA-HA .... Preoptic Anterior Hypothalamic Area [*Medicine*] (DMAA)
POAHEDPEARL ... Pacific Ocean Areas Headquarters Pearl Harbor
POALS .... Petty Officers Advanced Leadership School [*Navy*] (MUGU)
POAM .... Polar Ozone Aerosol Measurement
POAN .... Procurement of Ordnance and Ammunition - Navy
PO & CS .... Post Office and Civil Service Committee [*US Senate*] [*Obsolete*]
POANSW .... Property Owners' Association of New South Wales [*Australia*]
POAQ .... Property Owners' Association of Queensland [*Australia*]
POAR .... Postal Laws and Regulations [*Later, Postal Manual*] (IAA)
POAR .... Problem-Objective-Approach-Response [*System of planning patient care*] [*Medicine*]
POAR .... Project Order Action Request [*Navy*] (NG)
poas-- .... American Samoa [*MARC geographic area code Library of Congress*] (LCCP)
POAS .... Pankypria Omospondia Anexartiton Syntechnion [*Pancyprian Federation of Independent Trade Unions*] [*Cyprus*]
POASP .... Plans and Operations Automated Storage Program [*Military*]
POATSC .... Pacific Overseas Air Technical Service Command
POAU .... Protestants and Other Americans for Separation of Church and State (NADA)
POAU .... Protestants and Other Americans United [*for Separation of Church and State*]
POB .... Fayetteville, NC [*Location identifier FAA*] (FAAL)
POB .... Paris Opera Ballet
POB .... Parti Ouvrier Belge [*Belgian Workers' Party*] [*Later, Belgian Socialist Party*] [*Political party*] (PPE)
POB .... Penicillin, Oil, Beeswax [*Medicine*]
POB .... Perfluorooctyl Bromide [*Organic chemistry*]
POB .... Persons on Board [*Aviation*]
pob .... Persons on Board (AD)
POB .... Phenoxybenzamine [*Later, PBZ*] [*Adrenergic blocking agent*]

pob .... Pilot on Board (AD)
POB .... Place of Birth
pob .... Poblacion [*Population*] [*Spanish*] (AD)
pob .... Point of Beginning (AD)
POB .... Point of Beginning
POB .... Point of Business
PoB .... Port of Baltimore (AD)
POB .... Postal Bulletin [*A publication*]
POB .... Post Office Box
POB .... Power Outlet Box
POB .... Prevention of Blindness [*Medicine*] (MAE)
pob .... Prevention of Blindness (AD)
POB .... Public Oversight Board
POB .... Push-Out Base (IAA)
POB .... Servicios Aereos Poblanos, SA de CV [*Mexico*] [*FAA designator*] (FAAC)
POB^2 .... Prepped Out Beyond Belief [*Book title*]
POBA .... Patent Office Board of Appeals (IAA)
POBA .... Plain Old Balloon Angioplasty [*Cardiology*] [*Facetious*]
POBAL .... Powered Balloon [*System*]
POBATO .... Propellant on Board at Takeoff
POBCOST .... Probabilistic Budgeting and Forward Costing (MCD)
POBN .... (Pyridyloxide)butylnitrone [*Organic chemistry*]
POBN .... Pyridyl Oxide-N-tert-butylnitrone [*Organic chemistry*]
pobp-- .... British Solomon Islands [*MARC geographic area code Library of Congress*] (LCCP)
POBR .... Poe & Brown [*NASDAQ symbol*] (SAG)
POBR .... Problem-Oriented Basic Research [*National Science Foundation*]
pobra .... Pony and Zebra (AD)
POBS .... Portsmouth Bank Shares [*NASDAQ symbol*] (TTSB)
POBS .... Portsmouth Bank Shares, Inc. [*NASDAQ symbol*] (NQ)
POBSP .... Pacific Ocean Biological Survey Program [*Smithsonian Institution*] (GFGA)
POBY .... Prior Operating Budget Year [*Military*] (AFIT)
POC .... Clarion State College, Oil City, PA [*Library symbol Library of Congress*] (LCLS)
POC .... La Pocatiere [*Quebec*] [*Seismograph station code, US Geological Survey*] (SEIS)
POC .... La Verne, CA [*Location identifier FAA*] (FAAL)
POC .... Packaged Optimization Control [*Engineering*]
POC .... Parallel Optical Computer
POC .... Parent-Offspring Conflict
POC .... Particulate Organic Carbon
POC .... Particulate Organic Concentration [*Environmental science*]
POC .... Parti d'Opposition Congolais [*Congolese Opposition Party*] [*Political party*]
POC .... Patch Output Converter (IAA)
POC .... Payload Operations Center [*NASA*] (NASA)
POC .... Performance Optimization Code
POC .... Personnel Operations Center
POC .... Peugeot Owners' Club (EA)
POC .... Physics of Control (IAA)
POC .... Pick Off, Circuit
POC .... Pittsburgh Opera Co. (AD)
POC .... Planning Objective Coordinator
POC .... Plymouth Owners Club (EA)
POC .... Pocono Airlines, Inc. [*ICAO designator*] (FAAC)
POC .... Poco Petroleums Ltd. [*Toronto Stock Exchange symbol*]
POC .... Poculum [*Cup*] [*Pharmacy*]
POC .... Point of Care [*Medicine*]
POC .... Point of Compliance (FFDE)
POC .... Point of Contact (AABC)
poc .... Point of Contact (AD)
POC .... Porsche Owners Club (EA)
POc .... Porte-Oceane [*Record label*] [*France*]
POC .... Port of Call
POC .... Post Office Corps [*British military*] (DMA)
POC .... Post Office Counters Ltd. [*British*]
POC .... Post of the Corps
POC .... Postoperative Care [*Medicine*]
POC .... Postoral Ciliary [*Gland*]
POC .... Power Control
POC .... Power on Clear (MHDI)
POC .... Precision Oscillator Crystal
POC .... Preliminary Operational Capability [*Military*] (AFIT)
POC .... Preservation of Capital [*Investment term*]
POC .... Principal Operating Component
poc .... Principal Operating Component (AD)
POC .... Prisoners of Conscience [*File of persons imprisoned for political or religious beliefs kept by Amnesty International*]
POC .... Prison Officer's Club (AD)
poc .... Privately Owned Conveyance (AD)
POC .... Privately Owned Conveyance [*Army*]
POC .... Procarbazine, Oncovin [*Vincristine*], CCNU [*Lomustine*] [*Antineoplastic drug regimen*]
POC .... Proceeding on Course [*Aviation*] (FAAC)
POC .... Process Operator Console
POC .... Production Office Coordinator (WDMC)
POC .... Production Operational Capability
POC .... Production Order Change (KSC)
POC .... Products of Combustion (DICI)
POC .... Products of Conception [*Medicine*] (MEDA)
POC .... Products of Conception [*Obstetrics*] (DAVI)
POC .... Professional Officer Course [*AFROTC*] (AFM)
POC .... Programs of Cooperation (MCD)
POC .... Proof of Concept [*Army*]
POC .... Proopiocortin [*Biochemistry*]
POC .... Public Oil Co. (AD)
POC .... Purchase Order Closeout (NASA)
POC .... Purchase Order Contract
POC .... Purgeable Organic Carbon [*Chemistry*]
POCA .... Association of Psychiatric Outpatient Centers of America [*Psychiatric Out patient Centers of America*] [*Acronym is based on former name,*] (EA)
POCA .... Petty Officer Caterer [*British military*] (DMA)
POCA .... Post Office Clerks' Association [*A union*] [*Northern Ireland*]
POCA .... Prednisone, Oncovin [*Vincristine*], Cytarabine, Adriamycin [*Antineoplastic drug regimen*]
POCA .... Public Offender Counselors Association [*Later, IAAOC*] (EA)
POCAL .... Pre-Operational Common Age List
PO Cas .... Perry's Oriental Cases [*Bombay*] [*A publication*] (DLA)
POCASEA .... Protection of Children Against Sexual Exploitation Act of 1977
POCB .... Plain Ol' Country Boy
POCC .... Payload Operations Control Center [*NASA*] (NASA)
POCC .... Penn Octane [*NASDAQ symbol*] (TTSB)
POCC .... Penn Octane Corp. [*NASDAQ symbol*] (SAG)
POCC .... Procarbazine, Oncovin [*Vincristine*], Cyclophosphamide, CCNU [*Lomustine*] [*Antineoplastic drug regimen*]
POCC .... Program Operation Control Center [*Space science*]
Poc Costs .... Pocock on Costs [*1881*] [*A publication*] (DLA)
POCE .... Pantone Open Color Environment [*Joint venture between Pantone, Inc. and LightSource Computer Images*] [*Computer science*] (PCM)
POCE .... Proof-of-Concept Experiment [*Solar thermal conversion*]
POCEL .... Petty Officer Control Electrician [*British military*] (DMA)
POCET .... Proof-of-Concept Experiment Testbed [*Solar thermal conversion*] (MCD)
POCH .... Progressiven Organisationen der Schweiz [*Progressive Organizations of Switzerland*] [*Political party*] (PPE)
PochFdl .... Pocahontas Federal Savings & Loan Association [*Associated Press*] (SAG)
poci-- .... Caroline Islands [*MARC geographic area code Library of Congress*] (LCCP)
POCI .... Pontiac-Oakland Club International (EA)
POCI .... Precision Optics Corp. [*NASDAQ symbol*] (SAG)
POCI .... Precision Optics Mass [*NASDAQ symbol*] (TTSB)
POCIBO .... Polar Circling Balloon Observatory
POCIL .... Pocillum [*Little Cup*] [*Pharmacy*] (ROG)
Pocill .... Pocillum [*Little Cup*] [*Pharmacy*]
POCK .... Petty Officer Cook [*British military*] (DMA)
pock .... Pocket (AD)
Pocket Bks .... Pocket Books (AD)
POCL .... Power on Clear [*Navy Navigation Satellite System*] (DNAB)
POCL .... Project Office Change Letter
POCM .... Partido Obrero y Campesino de Mexico [*Mexico Political party*]
POCM .... Postal Contracting Manual [*Postal Service*]
POCN .... Purchase Order Change Notice
POCN .... Purchase Order Change Number
POCO .... European Political Cooperation [*EC*] (ECED)
POCO .... Physiology of Chimpanzees in Orbit [*NASA*]
Poco .... Politically Correct
POCO .... Position Computer (IAA)
POCO .... Power On - Clock On [*Aerospace*]
POCO .... Purchase Order Change Order (AAG)
POCO .... Purchase Order Closeout (AAG)
POCOA .... Post Office Controlling Officers' Association [*A union*] [*British*]
pocp-- .... Canton and Enderbury Islands [*MARC geographic area code Library of Congress*] (LCCP)
POCP .... Program Objectives Change Proposal
POCR .... Program Objectives Change Request [*DoD*]
POCS .... Patent Office Classification System [*later, PTO*] Classification System
Po Ct .... Police Court (DLA)
POCTA .... Prevention of Cruelty to Animals Society Member (DSUE)
POCUL .... Poculum [*Cup*] [*Pharmacy*] (ROG)
pocul .... Poculum [*Cup*] (AD)
pocw-- .... Cook Island [*MARC geographic area code Library of Congress*] (LCCP)
POD .... Pacific Ocean Division [*Army Corps of Engineers*]
pod .... Paid on Delivery (AD)
POD .... Parent Organization Designator (MCD)
POD .... Parents of Diabetics
POD .... Payable on Death [*Insurance*]
pod .... Payable on Death (AD)
POD .... Payload Operations Division [*NASA*] (MCD)
POD .... Pay on Delivery [*Shipping*]
POD .... Permissible Operating Distance [*Army*] (AFIT)
POD .... Peroxidase [*Also, PO*] [*An enzyme*]
POD .... Personal Orientation Dimensions [*Personality development test*] [*Psychology*]
POD .... Piece of Data [*Computer science*] (NHD)
POD .... Place of Death (MAE)
POD .... Place of Delivery [*Shipping*] (DS)
POD .... Place of Discharge
POD .... Plan of the Day
POD .... Pneumatically Operated Disconnect (KSC)
POD .... Pocket Oxford Dictionary [*A publication*]
POD .... Podiatry (DAVI)
POD .... Podkamennaya [*Former USSR Geomagnetic observatory code*]
POD .... Podor [*Senegal*] [*Airport symbol*] (OAG)
POD .... Point of Departure

POD .... Point of Discharge (GFGA)
POD .... Point-of-Origin Device (IEEE)
pod .... Point-of-Origin Device (AD)
POD .... Polycystic Ovarian Disease [*Medicine*]
POD .... Port of Debarkation [*Military*]
pod .... Port of Debarkation (AD)
POD .... Port of Delivery [*Shipping*]
pod .... Port of Departure (AD)
POD .... Port of Destination [*MARAD*] (TAG)
POD .... Port of Discharge [*Navy*]
POD .... Post of Duty
POD .... Post Office Department [*Later, United States Postal Service*]
POD .... Post Office Directory
POD .... Postoperative Day [*Medicine*]
POD .... Potential Ozone Depleter
POD .... Pounds-Out-the-Door [*Measure of industrial production*]
POD .... Precision Orbit Determination (MCD)
POD .... Preflight Operation Division [*NASA*]
pod .... Probability of Detection (AD)
POD .... Probability of Detection (USDC)
POD .... Probability of Detection [*Marine science*] (OSRA)
pod .... Process-Oriented Design (AD)
POD .... Professional and Organizational Development [*In association name Professional and Organizational Development Network in Higher Education*] (EA)
POD .... Programmed Operational Date (AFIT)
POD .... Program Objectives Document (AAGC)
POD .... Program Office Directive
POD .... Program Operation Description
POD .... Project Operations Director (BARN)
POD .... Proof of Debt [*Business term*] (DCTA)
POD .... Proof of Delivery [*Shipping*] (DS)
POD .... Proof of Deposit [*Banking*]
POD .... Proof of Design (MCD)
POD .... Prosthetics and Orthotics Database [*University of Strathclyde*] [*Glasgow, Scotland*] [*Information service or system*] (IID)
POD .... Protective Oceanic Device
POD .... Proton Omnidirectional Detector (USDC)
POD .... Proton Omnidirectional Detector [*Marine science*] (OSRA)
POD .... Proximity Optical Device (NASA)
POD .... Pulse Omission Detector (MCD)
POD .... Purchase Order Deviation (KSC)
PO'd .... Put Out [*i.e., angry*] [*Bowdlerized version*]
PODA .... Piloting of Office Documentation Architecture (NITA)
PODA .... Priority Oriented Demand Assignment [*Computer science Telecommunications*]
PODAF .... Post Operation Data Analysis Facility
PODAF .... Power Density Exceeding a Specified Level over an Area with an Assigned Frequency Band (IEEE)
PoDAG .... Polar DAAC [*Distributed Active Archive Center*] Advisory Group (USDC)
PoDAG .... Polar DAAC [*Distributed Active Archive Center*] Advisory Group [*Marine science*] (OSRA)
PODAPS .... Portable Data Processing System
PODAS .... Portable Data Acquisition System
PODBCA .... Post Office Department Board of Contract Appeals (AFIT)
PODCC .... Plan, Organize, Direct, Coordinate, Control [*Principles of management*]
Pod D .... Doctor of Podiatry
PODE .... Pacific Ocean Division Engineers (CINC)
podex .... Photographic Exercise (AD)
PODF .... Post of Duty File
podia .... Podiatrist (AD)
PODIM .... Poseidon Design Information Memo [*Missiles*]
PODM .... Preliminary Orbit Determination Method [*Computer*] [*NASA*]
PODO .... Profit on Day One [*Classification for new newspaper*]
PODRS .... Patent Office [*later, PTO*] Data Retrieval System [*Department of Commerce*]
PODS .... Parents of Down's Syndrome (EA)
PODS .... Perceptions of Developmental Skills Profile [*Education*] (EDAC)
PODS .... Pilot Ocean Data System (MCD)
PODS .... Portable Data Store [*Computer science*] (PDAA)
PODS .... Postoperative Destruct System (MCD)
PODSC .... Parents of Down's Syndrome Children (EA)
PODUC .... Provided [*Following Named*] Officers Have Not Departed Your Command [*Amend Assignment Instructions as Indicated*] [*Army*] (AABC)
PODx .... Postoperative Diagnosis [*Medicine*]
PODx .... Preoperative Diagnosis [*Medicine*]
POE .... Fort Polk [*Louisiana*] [*Airport symbol*] (OAG)
POE .... Fort Polk, LA [*Location identifier FAA*] (FAAL)
POE .... Pacific Orient Express (WDAA)
POE .... Panel on the Environment [*of President's Science Advisory Committee*]
POE .... Payment Option Election (MCD)
POE .... Peace on Earth [*Australia Political party*]
POE .... People of the Earth [*Also, RAN*] (EA)
POE .... Pilot Operational Equipment (MCD)
POE .... Plank-on-Edge
POE .... Pneumatically Operated Equipment (AAG)
POE .... Point of Entry [*Accounts*]
POE .... Point of Exposure [*Environmental Protection Agency*] (ERG)
POE .... Polyolefin Elastomers [*Plastics*]
POE .... Polyoxyethylene [*Organic chemistry*]
poe .... Polyoxyethylene (AD)
POE .... Port of Embarkation [*Shipping*]
POE .... Port of Embarkation (DFIT)
POE .... Port of Entry [*Shipping*]
POE .... Post-Occupancy Evaluation
POE .... Post-Operations Evaluation (MCD)
POE .... Postoperative Endophthalmitis [*Ophthalmology*]
POE .... Postoperative Exercise [*Medicine*] (DAVI)
POE .... Power Open Environment [*Computer science*]
POE .... Predicted Operational Environment [*Military*] (CAAL)
POE .... Pretesting Orientation Exercises [*US Employment Service*] [*Department of Labor*]
POE .... Primary Organization Element (NOAA)
POE .... Print Out Effect
POE .... Projected Operational Environment (NVT)
POE .... Proof of Eligibility [*Medicine*] (DMAA)
POE .... Pull-Over Enrichment [*Automotive engineering*]
POE .... Pulsar Energy/Resources [*Vancouver Stock Exchange symbol*]
POE .... Pulse Oriented Electrophoresis [*Analytical biochemistry*]
poea-- .... Easter Island [*MARC geographic area code Library of Congress*] (LCCP)
POEA .... Philippines Overseas Employment Administration (PDAA)
POEA .... Protection of Offshore Energy Assets [*Navy*] (NVT)
P/OEA3 .... Probationary Ordnance Electrical Artificer 3rd Class [*British military*] (DMA)
POEAS .... Planetary Orbiter Error Analysis Study Program
poe buoy .... Plank-on-Edge Buoy (AD)
PoeBwn .... Poe & Brown [*Commercial firm Associated Press*] (SAG)
poecrit .... Poetry Criticism (AD)
POED .... Post Office Engineering Department (IAA)
POED .... Program Organization for Evaluation and Decision
PO'ed .... Put Out [*i.e., angry*] [*Bowdlerized version*]
POEE .... Post Office Electrical Engineer (IAA)
POEER .... Pacific Oceanographic Equipment Evaluation Range (NOAA)
POEF .... Post Office Engineering Federation [*A union*] [*British*]
POEIT .... Provisional Organization for European Inland Transportation [*World War II*]
POEL(A) .... Petty Officer Electrician (Air) [*British military*] (DMA)
POEL(AW) .... Petty Officer Electrician (Air Weapon) [*British military*] (DMA)
POEMS .... Plasma Cell Dyscracia with Polyneuropathy, Organomegaly, Endocrinopathy, Monoclonal Protein [*M-protein*], Skin changes [*Medicine*] (DAVI)
POEMS .... Polyneuropathy Associated with Organomegaly Endocrine Disorders, Myeloma, and Skin Modifications
POEMS .... Polyoxyethylene Monostearate [*Organic chemistry*]
POENIT .... Poenitentia [*Penance*] [*Latin*] (ADA)
POEOP .... Polyoxyethyleneoxypropylene [*Organic chemistry*]
Poe Pl .... Poe on Pleading and Practice [*A publication*] (DLA)
POES .... Polar Operational Environmental Satellite (USDC)
POES .... Polar Orbiting Environmental Satellite
POES .... Polar-Orbiting Operational Environmental Satellite (USDC)
POES .... Polar-orbiting Operational Environmental Satellite [*Marine science*] (OSRA)
POESID .... Position of Earth Satellite in Digital Display (MCD)
Poet .... De Poetis [*of Suetonius*] [*Classical studies*] (OCD)
POET .... Petty Officer Enroute Training [*Navy*] (NVT)
Poet .... Poetica [*of Aristotle*] [*Classical studies*] (OCD)
poet .... Poetical (AD)
Poet .... Poetry [*A publication*] (BRI)
POET .... Portable Optic-Electronic Tracker (PDAA)
POET .... Portable Orders Entry Terminal (IAA)
POET .... Primed Oscillator Expendable Transponder [*Military*] (CAAL)
POET .... Program Operation and Environment Transfer (SAA)
POET .... Psychological Operations Exploitation Team [*Vietnam*]
POET .... Pulse Oximeter/End Tidal [*Carbon Dioxide*] [*Medicine*] (DAVI)
Poetics T .... Poetics Today [*A publication*] (BRI)
Poet Mel Gr... Poetae Melici Graeci [*A publication*] (OCD)
POETRI .... Programme on Exchange and Transfer of Information (NITA)
POETRI .... Programme on Exchange and Transfer of Information on Community Water Supply and Sanitation [*International Reference Center for Community Water Supply and Sanitation*] [*Information service or system*] (IID)
Poet Rom Vet... Poetarum Romanorum Veterum Reliquiae [*A publication*] (OCD)
POETS .... Phooey on Everything, Tomorrow's Saturday [*Bowdlerized version*]
POETS .... Push Off Early, Tomorrow's Saturday [*Bowdlerized version*]
POEU .... Post Office Engineering Union [*British*]
POF .... American Jurisprudence Proof of Facts [*A publication*]
POF .... Philharmonic Orchestra of Florida (AD)
POF .... Pillar of Fire Church (IIA)
POF .... Pinhole Occulter Facility (SSD)
POF .... Planned Outage Factor [*Electronics*] (IEEE)
POF .... Plastic Optical Fiber [*Automotive electronics*]
pof .... Please Omit Flowers (AD)
POF .... Point-of-Failure [*Computer science*] (IBMDP)
POF .... Police Officer, Female
POF .... Polymer Optical Fiber [*Telecommunications*]
POF .... Poplar Bluff [*Missouri*] [*Airport symbol*] (OAG)
POF .... Poplar Bluff, MO [*Location identifier FAA*] (FAAL)
POF .... Positive Opening Fin (MCD)
POF .... Postovulatory Follicle [*Endocrinology*]
POF .... Primary Ovarian Failure [*Gynecology*] (DMAA)
POF .... Priority of Fire [*Military*] (INF)
POF .... Privately Owned Firearm (MCD)
POF .... Prolific Resources [*Vancouver Stock Exchange symbol*]
POF .... Pyruvate Oxidation Factor [*Biochemistry*]
POFA .... Programmed Operational Functional Appraisal [*Navy*]

PofB............ Ponies of Britain [*An association*] (DBA)
P of E............ Portal of Entry [*Bacteriology*]
P of E............ Port of Embarkation [*Military*]
PofE............ Port of Entry [*Immigration*] (DAVI)
P of H............ Patron of Husbandry
POFI............ Pacific Oceanic Fisheries Investigations (NOAA)
pofj--............ Fiji [*MARC geographic area code Library of Congress*] (LCCP)
P of L............ Port of London (ROG)
POFOOGUSA... Protection of Foreign Officials and Official Guests of the United States Act
pofp............ French Polynesia [*MARC geographic area code Library of Congress*] (LCCP)
PO-FY............ Program Objectives for Fiscal Year (DNAB)
POG............ Pacific Oceanographic Group [*British Columbia*] (AD)
POG............ Parents of Gays (EA)
POG............ Patina Oil & Gas [*NYSE symbol*] (TTSB)
POG............ Petty Officer's Guide [*A publication Navy*]
POG............ Piping Instrumentation and Operating Gallery [*Nuclear energy*] (NRCH)
POG............ Plant Operating Guide (DNAB)
Pog............ Pogonion (DMAA)
POG............ Port Gentil [*Gabon*] [*Airport symbol*] (OAG)
POG............ Position of Germany [*British World War II*]
POG............ Post Office Guide [*Book of regulations*] [*British*]
POG............ Project Officer's Group
POG............ Propulsion Operating Guide (DNAB)
POG............ Provisional Ordnance Group [*Military*]
POG............ Psychological Operations Group (DOMA)
POGASIS...... Planetary Observation Geometry and Science Instrument Sequence Program [*Aerospace*]
POGaz............ Post Office Gazette [*British A publication*] (DCTA)
POGE............ Planning Operational Gaming Experiment [*Game*]
pogg--............ Galapagos Islands [*MARC geographic area code Library of Congress*] (LCCP)
pogn--............ Gilbert and Ellice Islands [*Tuvalu*] [*MARC geographic area code Library of Congress*] (LCCP)
POGO............ Pennzoil Offshore Gas Operators (AD)
POGO............ Personal Objectives and Goals (MCD)
Pogo............ Pogonomyrinex Occidentalis [*A genus of ants*]
POGO............ Polar Orbiting Geophysical Observatories [*Marine science*] (OSRA)
POGO............ Polar Orbiting Geophysical Observatory [*NASA*]
POGO............ Pop Your Seat Belt, Open the Window, Get Out [*Automobile safety*]
POGO............ Pre-Oxidation Gettering of the Other Side (PDAA)
POGO............ Prime's Online Graduate Opportunities (NITA)
POGO............ Privately Owned/Government Operated (GFGA)
POGO............ Programmer-Oriented Graphics Operation (IEEE)
POGO............ Program Optimizer (IAA)
PogoPd............ Pogo Producing Co. [*Associated Press*] (SAG)
POGPr............ Patina Oil & Gas 7.125% Pfd [*NYSE symbol*] (TTSB)
POGR............ Poplar Grove National Cemetery
POGS............ National Association of Post Office and General Service Maintenance Employees [*Later, APWU*] [*AFL-CIO*]
POGSI............ Policy Group on Scientific Information [*Marine science*] (MSC)
POGT............ Power-Operated Gun Turret
pogu--............ Guam [*MARC geographic area code Library of Congress*] (LCCP)
POG.WS............ Patina Oil & Gas Wrrt [*NYSE symbol*] (TTSB)
pOH............ Hydroxyl Concentration [*Organic chemistry*] (MAE)
POH............ Pilot's Operating Handbook [*Aviation*] (DA)
POH............ Placed off Hire
POH............ Planned Outage Hours [*Electronics*] (IEEE)
POH............ Pocahontas, IA [*Location identifier FAA*] (FAAL)
Poh............ Pohang (AD)
POH............ Pull-Out Harness
poh............ Pull Out of Hole (AD)
Pohang............ Pohang Iron & Steel Co., Ltd. [*Associated Press*] (SAG)
POHC............ Principal Organic Hazardous Constituent [*Environmental chemistry*]
POHI............ Physically or Otherwise Health Impaired
POHM............ Page-Oriented Holograph Memory [*Computer science*]
POHMA............ Project for the Oral History of Music in America
POHS............ Presumed Ocular Histoplasmosis Syndrome [*Ophthalmology*]
POHWARO... Pulsated, Overheated, Water Rocket [*Swiss space rocket*]
POI............ Parking Orbit Injection [*NASA*]
POI............ Parti Oubanguien de l'Independance [*Ubangi Independence Party*] [*Political party*]
POI............ Period of Interest (MCD)
POI............ Personal Orientation Inventory [*Psychology*]
POI............ Personal Outlook Inventory [*Employment test*]
POI............ Plan of Instruction
POI............ Point of Impact
POI............ Point of Interception (GNE)
POI............ Point of Interface [*Telecommunications*]
POI............ Poison
POI............ Potosi [*Bolivia*] [*Airport symbol*] (AD)
POI............ Pre-Overhaul Inspection (MCD)
POI............ Pressure-Operated Initiator (MCD)
POI............ Probability Of Intercept (LAIN)
POI............ Product of Inertia (MCD)
POI............ Program of Instruction
POI............ Public Office of Information (MCD)
POI............ Purchase Order Item (KSC)
POIC............ Petty Officer in Charge [*Navy*] (NVT)
POIC............ Poly(octyl Isocyanate) [*Organic chemistry*]
POID............ Post Office Investigation/Intelligence Department [*British*] (DI)
POIF............ Plan Organization Index File [*IRS*]
poik............ Poikilocyte [*or Poikilocytosis*] [*Medicine*] (MAE)
POIL............ Power Density Imbalance Limit (IAA)
POINT............ Pasadena Online Information Network [*Pasadena Public Library*] (OLDSS)
POINT............ Point [*Commonly used*] (OPSA)
POINT............ Pursuing Our Italian Names Together (EA)
POINTER...... Particle Orientation Interferometer [*ASD*]
POINTER...... Pre-University Orbital Information Tracker Equipment and Recorder (PDAA)
POINTERM... Appointment Will Be Regarded as Having Terminated upon This Date
Point Loma C... Point Loma Nazarene College (GAGS)
POINTMAIL... Letter Appointment in Mail
POINTS............ Points [*Commonly used*] (OPSA)
POIP............ Potential Offender Identification Program
POIPCD............ Patent Office and Industrial Property and Copyright Department [*British*]
POIQT............ Performance-Oriented Infantry Qualification Test (INF)
POIR............ Project Officers Interim Report [*Air Force*] (MCD)
POIS............ Parkland On-Line Information Systems [*Computer science*] (DMAA)
POIS............ Poison (AAMN)
pois............ Poison (AD)
POIS............ Poisoning [*FBI standardized term*]
POIS............ Post Office Insurance Society [*British*] (DI)
POIS............ Procurement Operations Information System (MCD)
POIS............ Prototype On-Line Instrument System [*Computer science*] (NRCH)
POIS............ Purchase Order Information System (MCD)
POISE............ Panel on Inflight Scientific Experiments [*NASA*]
POISE............ Photosynthetic Oxygenation Illuminated by Solar Energy
POISE............ Pointing and Stabilization Platform Element [*Army*] (MCD)
POISE............ Preoperational Inspection Services Engineering (IAA)
POIT............ Power of Influence Test [*Psychology*]
POJ............ Patent Office Journal [*India*] [*A publication*] (DLA)
POJ............ Selma, AL [*Location identifier FAA*] (FAAL)
poji--............ Johnston Atoll [*MARC geographic area code Library of Congress*] (LCCP)
POK............ Sacramento, CA [*Location identifier FAA*] (FAAL)
poki--............ Kermadec Islands [*MARC geographic area code Library of Congress*] (LCCP)
POKMV............ Pokeweed Mosaic Virus [*Plant pathology*]
POL............ Pacific Oceanographic Laboratories [*Later, Pacific Marine Environmental Laboratory*]
POL............ Pair Orthogonalized Lowdin [*Physics*]
POL............ Parents of Large Families
POL............ Patent Office Library (AD)
POL............ Paul Otchakovsky-Laurens [*Publishing imprint, named for imprint editor*]
POL............ Pemba [*Mozambique*] [*Airport symbol*] (OAG)
POL............ Petroleum, Oil, and Lubricants [*Military*]
pol............ Petroleum-Oil-and-Lubricants (AD)
POL............ Philips Optical Language (IAA)
POL............ Physician-Owned Laboratory (HCT)
POL............ Physician's Office laboratory
POL............ Pola [*Yugoslavia*] [*Seismograph station code, US Geological Survey Closed*] (SEIS)
POL............ Polacca [*Ship's rigging*] (ROG)
POL............ Poland [*ANSI three-letter standard code*] (CNC)
Pol............ Poland (VRA)
pol............ Polar (AD)
POL............ Polar International Airlines, Inc. [*ICAO designator*] (FAAC)
POL............ Polarity [*or Polarize*] (KSC)
Pol............ Polen [*Poland*] [*Norwegian*] (AD)
POL............ Police
POL............ Policy
POL............ Polish (AAG)
pol............ Polish [*MARC language code Library of Congress*] (LCCP)
pol............ Polished (VRA)
POL............ Polish Ocean Lines (AD)
POL............ Polite
Pol............ Politica [*of Aristotle*] [*Classical studies*] (OCD)
POL............ Political
POL............ Politician
Pol............ Pollexfen's English King's Bench Reports [*1669-85*] [*A publication*] (DLA)
POL............ Polling (IAA)
POL............ Pollution
POL............ Polonium [*Chemical symbol is Po*] (AAG)
Pol............ Polydor & Deutsche Grammophon [*Record label*] [*Germany, Europe, etc.*]
POL............ Polymerase [*An enzyme*]
Pol............ Polyphon [*Record label*] [*Denmark, etc.*]
POL............ Porto Amelia [*Mozambique*] [*Airport symbol*] (AD)
POL............ Port of Loading [*Shipping*]
POL............ Practical Quantification Limit [*Metallurgy*]
POL............ Premature Onset of Labor [*Obstetrics*] (DAVI)
POL............ Problem-Oriented Language [*Computer science*]
pol............ Problem-Oriented Language (AD)
POL............ Procedure-Oriented Language [*Computer science*]
POL............ Process-Oriented Language [*Computer science*] (IEEE)
POL............ Program Oriented Language [*Computer science*] (ECII)
POL............ Proudman Oceanographic Laboratory [*UK*] [*Marine science*] (OSRA)
POL............ Provisional Operating License [*for nuclear power plant*]
POL............ Public Opinion Laboratory [*Northern Illinois University*] [*Research center*] (RCD)
p-ola............ Payola (AD)
POLA............ Polymerase Alpha (DMAA)
POLA............ Project on Linguistic Analysis

POLA .... Prostitutes of Los Angeles [*An association*] (AD)
POLAC .... Problem-Oriented Language for Analytical Chemistry [*Computer science*] (PDAA)
POLAD .... Political Adviser
polad .... Political Adviser (AD)
Pol Ad .... Political Adviser (AD)
Polam LJ .... Polamerican Law Journal [*A publication*] (DLA)
POLANG .... Polarization Angle [*Telecommunications*]
polang .... Polarization Angle (AD)
polar .... Polarity (AD)
POLAR .... Polarity [*or Polarize*] (IAA)
POLAR .... Production Order Location and Reporting [*NASA*] (NASA)
POLAR .... Projected Operational Logistics Analysis Requirements
Polar BEAR ... Polar Beacon Experiments and Auroral Research (AD)
PolarE .... Polar Express Corp. [*Associated Press*] (SAG)
Polaris .... Polaris Industries, Inc. [*Associated Press*] (SAG)
POLARIS .... Polar-Motion Analysis by Radio Interferometric Surveying [*Geodetic measuring facilities*]
Polaroid .... Polaroid Corp. [*Associated Press*] (SAG)
POLARS .... Pathology On-Line Logging and Reporting System [*Computer science*] (PDAA)
POL BKM .... Polished Buckram (DGA)
Pol C .... Political Code [*A publication*] (DLA)
POLCAP .... Petroleum, Oils, and Lubricants Capabilities (MCD)
POLCATS .... Pollution Characterization by Absorption on Spectroscopy (SSD)
POLCOD .... Police Code [*INTERPOL*]
Pol Code .... Political Code [*A publication*] (DLA)
Pol Col .... Police College (AD)
Pol Com .... Police Commissaire [*Interpol*] [*British*] (AD)
Pol Com .... Police Commissioner (AD)
pol com .... Political Committee (AD)
Pol Cont .... Pollock on Contracts [*A publication*] (DLA)
polcrit .... Political Critic (AD)
POLD .... Professional and Occupational Licensing Directory [*A publication*]
POLDAM .... POL [*Petroleum, Oil, and Lubricants*] Installations Damage Report (NATG)
poldamr .... Petroleum, Oil, and Lubrication Installation Damage Report (AD)
POLDER .... Polarization and Directionality of the Earth's Reflectances [*Instrumentation*]
Pol Dig Part ... Pollock's Digest of the Laws of Partnership [*A publication*] (DLA)
POLDPS .... Pioneer Off-Line Data-Processing System [*NASA*]
POLE .... Point-of-Last-Environment [*Computer science*] (IBMDP)
POLE .... Prednisolone, Oncovin [*Vicristine*], L-Asparaginase [*Antineoplastic drug regimen*] (DAVI)
pol econ .... Political Economy (AD)
polem .... Polemic (AD)
POLEX .... Polar Experiment
POLEX .... Political Exercise [*International relations game*]
POLEX-NORTH ... Polar Experiment in the Northern Hemisphere (MSC)
POLEX-SOUTH ... Polar Experiment in the Southern Hemisphere (MSC)
polf .... Parents of Large Families (AD)
Pol Fed .... Police Federation [*London*] (AD)
Pol Fedn Newsl ... Police Federation Newsletter [*A publication*] (DLA)
POLFER .... Polizia Ferroviaria [*Railroad Police*] [*Italian*] (AD)
Pol Found .... Police Foundation [*Washington, D.C.*] (AD)
POLGEN .... Problem-Oriented Language Generator [*Computer science*] (BUR)
poli .... Politician (AD)
POLIC .... Petroleum Intersectional Command [*Army*] (AABC)
Police Fedn Newsl ... Police Federation Newsletter [*A publication*] (ILCA)
Police J Ct ... Police Justice's Court [*A publication*] (ILCA)
Police LQ .... Police Law Quarterly [*A publication*] (ILCA)
POL IND .... Pollen Index (WDAA)
pol ind .... Pollen Index (AD)
pol in the pen ... Politician in the Penitentiary (AD)
polio .... Poliomyelitis [*Medicine*] (AD)
POLIO .... Poliomyelitis [*Medicine*]
POLIS .... Parliamentary On-Line Information System [*House of Commons Library*] [*Bibliographic database*] [*Information service or system*] [*British*] (IID)
POLIS .... Petroleum Intersectional Service [*Army*]
POLIS .... Political Institutions Simulation [*Game*]
poli sci .... Political Science
PolishTel .... Polish Telephones & Microwave Corp. [*Associated Press*] (SAG)
POLIT .... Political (EY)
polit .... Political (AD)
Polit .... Politics [*A publication*]
POLITBUREAU ... Political Bureau [*of USSR*]
POLITBURO ... Politicheskoe Byuro [*Political Bureau of USSR*]
Politburo .... Politicheskoe Byuro [*Political Bureau of the Central Committee*] [*Russian*] (AD)
Pol J .... Police Journal [*A publication*] (ILCA)
POLK .... Polk Audio [*NASDAQ symbol*] (TTSB)
POLK .... Polk Audio, Inc. [*Baltimore, MD*] [*NASDAQ symbol*] (NQ)
POLKA .... Periodical On-Line Keyword Access [*Computer science*] (PDAA)
PolkAu .... Polk Audio, Inc. [*Associated Press*] (SAG)
PolkAud .... Polk Audio [*Associated Press*] (SAG)
POLK of A .... Polka Lovers Klub of America (EA)
Poll .... Pollack's Ohio Unreported Judicial Decisions Prior to 1823 [*A publication*] (ILCA)
POLL .... Pollex [*An Inch*] [*Pharmacy*]
Poll .... Pollexfen's English King's Bench Reports [*1669-85*] [*A publication*] (ILCA)
poll .... Pollution (AD)
POLL .... Public Opinion Location Library [*The Roper Center for Public Opinion Research*] [*Information service or system*] (CRD)
Pol Law of Nat ... Polson's Law of Nations [*1848*] [*A publication*] (DLA)
Poll CC Pr ... Pollock's Practice of the County Courts [*A publication*] (ILCA)
Poll Contr Guide ... Pollution Control Guide [*A publication*] (DLA)
Pollex .... Pollexfen's English King's Bench Reports [*1669-85*] [*A publication*] (ILCA)
Pollexf .... Pollexfen's English King's Bench Reports [*1669-85*] [*A publication*] (ILCA)
Pollexfen .... Pollexfen's English King's Bench Reports [*1669-85*] [*A publication*] (ILCA)
Pollock & Maitl ... Pollock and Maitland's History of English Common Law [*A publication*] (DLA)
PolloTrp .... Pollo Tropical [*Commercial firm Associated Press*] (SAG)
Poll Prod .... Pollock on the Production of Documents [*A publication*] (DLA)
Pol LQ .... Police Law Quarterly [*A publication*] (DLA)
POLLS .... Parliamentary On-Line Library Study [*Atomic Energy Authority*] [*British*]
POLLUT .... Pollution
Pollution Cont Guide (CCH) ... Pollution Control Guide (Commerce Clearing House) [*A publication*] (DLA)
Pol Mil Dig ... Poland's Digest of the Military Laws of the United States [*A publication*] (DLA)
poln-- .... Central and Southern Line Islands [*MARC geographic area code Library of Congress*] (LCCP)
poln .... polnisch [*Polish*] [*German*] (AD)
POLO .... Pacific Command Operations Liaison Office [*Army*] (AABC)
POLO .... Plant and Office Layout (MCD)
POLO .... Polar Orbiting Lunar Observatory [*Satellite*]
POLO .... Problem-Oriented Language Organizer [*Computer science*] (PDAA)
POLO .... Procurement Online Ordering System (MCD)
Polon .... Polonais [*Polish*] [*French*] (AD)
POLOPS .... Polynomial Operations [*Air Force*]
Pol Part .... Pollock's Digest of the Laws of Partnership [*A publication*] (DLA)
Pol Prod Doc ... Pollock on the Power of Courts to Compel the Production of Documents [*A publication*] (DLA)
POLPS .... Polymorphonuclear Leukocytes [*Hematology*] (DAVI)
POLR .... Polar Express Corp. [*NASDAQ symbol*] (SAG)
POLREG .... Polynomial Regression (IAA)
POLREP .... Pollution Report (GNE)
Pol Res Q .... Political Research Quarterly [*A publication*] (BRI)
PolrEx .... Polar Express Corp. [*Associated Press*] (SAG)
PolRs .... Pollution Research and Control Corp. [*Associated Press*] (SAG)
POLRW .... Polar Express Wrrt'B' [*NASDAQ symbol*] (TTSB)
Pol Rze Lud ... Polaska Rzeczpospolita Ludowa [*Polish People's Republic*] (AD)
pols .... Political Prisoners (AD)
pols .... Politicians (AD)
PolSc .... Political Science (DD)
pol sci .... Political Science (AD)
Pol Sci Quar ... Political Science Quarterly [*A publication*] (ILCA)
POLSG .... Polishing
Pols Nat .... Polson's Law of Nations [*1848*] [*A publication*] (DLA)
POLSTRADA ... Polizia Stradale [*Highway Police*] [*Italian*] (AD)
Pol Stud J .... Policy Studies Journal [*A publication*] (BRI)
PolTel .... Polish Telephones & Microwave Corp. [*Associated Press*] (SAG)
POLTHN .... Polyethylene [*Organic chemistry*]
POLTL .... Political (AFM)
POLTN .... Pollution
Pol Tr Mar ... Poland's Law of Trade Marks [*A publication*] (DLA)
POLUT .... Pollution
PolutRs .... Pollution Research and Control Corp. [*Associated Press*] (SAG)
POLWAR .... Political Warfare
polwar .... Political Warfare (AD)
POLWARADDIR ... Political Warfare Advisory Directorate
POLX .... Polydex Pharmaceuticals Ltd. [*NASDAQ symbol*] (NQ)
POLXF .... Polydex Pharmaceuticals [*NASDAQ symbol*] (TTSB)
POLY .... Planet Polymer Technologies [*NASDAQ symbol*] (TTSB)
POLY .... Planet Polymer Technologies, Inc. [*NASDAQ symbol*] (SAG)
Pol'y .... Policy (DLA)
poly .... Polydipsia [*Medicine*] (DAVI)
POLY .... Polyester
POLY .... Polyethylene (DEN)
poly .... Polyethylene (AD)
POLY .... Polygamy [*FBI standardized term*]
poly .... Polymer (AD)
POLY .... Polymorphonuclear Leukocyte [*Hematology*]
poly .... Polymorphonuclear Neutrophil Granulocyte [*Hematology*] (DAVI)
Poly .... Polynesia (AD)
poly .... Polyphagia [*Medicine*] (DAVI)
Poly .... Polytechnic (AD)
poly .... Polytechnic (AD)
POLY .... Polytechnic
poly .... Polyuria [*Medicine*] (DAVI)
poly .... Polyvinyl (AD)
PolyA .... Polyadenylated
poly(A) .... Polyadenylic Acid [*Biochemistry*] (MAE)
Polyb .... Polybius [*Second century BC*] [*Classical studies*] (OCD)
Pol YB Int'l L ... Polish Yearbook of International Law [*Warsaw*] [*A publication*] (DLA)
Pol Yb of Internat L ... Polish Yearbook of International Law [*Warsaw*] [*A publication*] (DLA)
poly bot .... Polyethylene Bottle (AD)
POLYC .... Polychromasia [*Hematology*] (DAVI)
poly-C .... Polycytidylic Acid [*Biochemistry*] (DMAA)
Polycom .... Polycom, Inc. [*Associated Press*] (SAG)
Polydex .... Polydex Pharmaceuticals Ltd. [*Associated Press*] (SAG)
POLYDOC .... Polytechnical Documentation (NITA)

POLYDOP .... Polystation Doppler Tracking System (MCD)
POLYEST ..... Polyester
polyg .... Polygraph (AD)
poly-G........... Polyguanylic Acid [*Biochemistry*] (DMAA)
POLYGON .... Oceanographic Experiment in the North-East Atlantic [*Former USSR*] [*Marine science*] (OSRA)
PolyGp......... Polymer Group, Inc. [*Associated Press*] (SAG)
Polygr.......... PolyGram NV [*Associated Press*] (SAG)
poly-I........... Polyinosinic Acid [*Biochemistry*] (DMAA)
poly I:C........ Polyinosinic Polycytidylic Acid (BARN)
Polym .... Polymusic [*Record label*]
POLYMAT .... Polymer Materials [*Deutsches Kunststoff-Institut*] [*Germany Information service or system*] (CRD)
Polymed ...... PolyMedica Industries, Inc. [*Associated Press*] (SAG)
POLYMODE... Polygon-MODE [*Mid-Ocean Dynamics Experiment*] [*Soviet-US cooperative undersea weather exploration*]
polymorph ... Polymorphonuclear [*Leukocyte*] [*Hematology*] (DAVI)
polymorph ... Polymorphous (AD)
POLYN .... Polynesia
Polyn .... Polynesia (VRA)
POLYOX....... Poly(ethylene Oxide) [*Trademark*]
Polyph .... Polyphase Instrument Corp. [*Associated Press*] (SAG)
PolyRs .... Polymer Research Corp. of America [*Associated Press*] (SAG)
poly sci........ Political Science (AD)
polysex......... Polysexual (AD)
polys (segs)... Polymorphonuclear Segmented Neutrophils [*Hematology*] (DAVI)
poly-T .... Polythymidylic Acid [*Biochemistry*] (DMAA)
polytech........ Polytechnical (BARN)
POLYTRAN... Polytranslation Analysis and Programming (IEEE)
Poly U .... Polytechnic University (GAGS)
poly(U) .... Polyuridylic Acid [*Biochemistry*] (MAE)
Polyvisn....... Polyvision Corp. [*Associated Press*] (SAG)
Polyvsn........ Polyvision Corp. [*Associated Press*] (SAG)
polywater .... Polymerized Water (AD)
POLY-WRI ... Polytechnic Institute of New York Weber Research Institute [*Farmingdale, NY*]
POM............. Aurelio y Gustavo Pompa Estrella [*Mexico*] [*FAA designator*] (FAAC)
POM............. Operation: Peace of Mind [*Later, Runaway Hotline*] [*An association*] (EA)
POM............. Pallet-Only Mode [*NASA*] (NASA)
POM............. Particulate Organic Matter [*Environmental chemistry*]
POM............. Pennysylvania-Ohio-Maryland League [*Old baseball league*]
POM............. Peritronics Med [*Vancouver Stock Exchange symbol*]
POM............. Personal Opinion Message [*Western Union*] (IIA)
POM............. Personnel, Operations, Maintenance (MCD)
POM............. Phase of the Moon [*Astronomy*] (NHD)
POM............. Phenomenon of Man [*Project*] (EA)
POM............. Police Officer, Male
POM............. Polycyclic Organic Matter
pom .... Polycyclic Organic Matter (AD)
POM............. Polymerized and Oxidized Material [*Food science*]
POM............. Polynuclear Organic Matter (FFDE)
POM............. Polyoxometalate [*Organic chemistry*]
pom .... Polyoxymethylene (AD)
POM............. Poly(oxymethylene) [*Organic chemistry*]
pom .... Pomeranian (AD)
POM............. Pomeranian Dog (DSUE)
pom .... Pomeridiano [*Afternoon*] [*Italian*] (AD)
Pom .... Pommy [*British*] (ODBW)
pom .... Pomological (AD)
POM............. Pomona [*California*] [*Seismograph station code, US Geological Survey Closed*] (SEIS)
POM............. Pomona, CA [*Location identifier FAA*] (FAAL)
pom .... Pom-Pom (AD)
Pom .... Pompon [*Horticulture*]
POM............. Pool Operational Module [*Telecommunications*] (TEL)
POM............. Port Moresby [*Papua New Guinea*] [*Airport symbol*] (OAG)
PoM .... Port of Miami (AD)
POM............. Position Modulator (NRCH)
POM............. Potential Officer Material [*British military*] (DMA)
POM............. Potomac Electric Power Co. [*NYSE symbol*] (SPSG)
POM............. Potomac Electric Pwr [*NYSE symbol*] (TTSB)
POM............. Preparation for Overseas Movement [*Military*]
pom .... Preparation for Overseas Movement (AD)
POM............. Prescription Only Medicine [*British*]
POM............. Printer Output Microfilm
POM............. Print on Metal (DGA)
POM............. Printout Microfilm (NITA)
POM............. Priority of Movements [*Military British*]
POM............. Prior to Overseas Movement [*DoD*]
POM............. Professional or Managerial (WDMC)
POM............. Professionals, Owners, and Managers [*A. C. Nielsen Co.*] [*Demographic category*] (NTCM)
POM............. Program Objectives Memorandum [*Military*]
POM............. Program Operation Mode
POM............. Project Office Memo
POM............. Project Officers Meeting
POMA .... Petty Officer Medical Assistant [*British military*] (DMA)
POMA .... Petty Officer's Military Academy [*Navy*]
POMA .... Polyoctyl Methacrylate [*Organic chemistry*]
POMAR .... Position Operational, Meteorological Aircraft Report
POMAR .... Preventive Operational Maintenance and Repair [*Military*] (NVT)
POMAS .... Procurement Office for Military Automotive Supplies
pomato .... Potato-Tomato (AD)
POMBA .... Parents of Multiple Births Associations of Canada
POM/BES ..... Program Objective Memorandum/Budget Estimate Submission (MCD)
POMC .... Parents of Murdered Children (EA)
POMC .... Pro-Opiomelanocortin [*Endocrinology*]
POMC .... Proopiomelanocortin (DMAA)
Pom Code Rem... Pomeroy on Code Remedies [*A publication*] (DLA)
Pom Const Law... Pomeroy's Constitutional Law of the United States [*A publication*] (DLA)
Pom Contr ... Pomeroy on Contracts [*A publication*] (DLA)
pomcus........ Prepositioned Material Configured in Unit Sets (AD)
POMCUS...... Prepositioning of Materiel Configured to Unit Sets [*Army*] (AABC)
POMD .... Program Operation Mode (IAA)
pome--......... Melanesia [*MARC geographic area code Library of Congress*] (LCCP)
POME........... Principal Ordnance Mechanical Engineer [*British military*] (DMA)
POME........... Prisoner of Mother England [*Nineteenth-century convict in penal colony of Australia, now a nickname for any Australian*]
POME........... Problems-Objectives-Methods-Evaluation [*Planning method*]
POMEM........ Petty Officer Marine Engineering Mechanic [*British military*] (DMA)
Pom Eq Jur... Pomeroy's Equity Jurisprudence [*A publication*] (DLA)
Pom Eq Juris... Pomeroy's Equity Jurisprudence [*A publication*] (DLA)
POMERID..... Pomeridianus [*In the Afternoon*] [*Pharmacy*]
Pomeroy...... Pomeroy Computer Resources, Inc. [*Associated Press*] (SAG)
Pomeroy...... Pomeroy's Reports [*73-128 California*] [*A publication*] (DLA)
POMF........... Polaris Missile Facility
POMFLANT... Polaris Missile Facility, Atlantic (AD)
POMFLANT... Polaris Missile Facility, Atlantic Fleet
POMFPAC .... Polaris Missile Facility, Pacific Fleet
POMGEN..... Program Objective Memorandum Generator [*Military*]
POMH .... National Association of Post Office Mail Handlers, Watchmen, Messengers, and Group Leaders [*Later, NPOMHWMGL*]
POMI .... Photochromic Microimage (IAA)
POMI .... Preliminary Operating and Maintenance Instructions [*Aerospace*] (AAG)
POMINS....... Portable Mine Neutralization System (MCD)
POMM .... Preliminary Operating and Maintenance Manual [*Military*] (AABC)
Pom Mun Law... Pomeroy on Municipal Law [*A publication*] (DLA)
POMO .... Partially Occupied Molecular Orbitals [*Physical chemistry*]
POMO .... Personnel Objectives Monitoring Operation
POMO .... Postmodern
POMO .... Production-Oriented Maintenance Organization (MCD)
POMO .... Program Operations and Management Office [*Environmental Protection Agency*] (GFGA)
POMOL .... POMCUS [*Prepositioning of Materiel Configured to Unit Sets*] Objective Levels [*Military*]
pomol .... Pomologic (AD)
POMOL .... Pomology
POMOLA...... Poor Man's Optical Landing System
Pomp .... Epistula ad Pompeium [*of Dionysius Halicarnassensis*] [*Classical studies*] (OCD)
Pomp .... Pompeius [*of Plutarch*] [*Classical studies*] (OCD)
Pomp .... Pompey (AD)
POMP .... Pomposo [*Grandly*] [*Music*] (ROG)
POMP .... Pre Coded Originating Mail Processor (PDAA)
POMP .... Prednisone, Oncovin [*Vincristine*], Methotrexate, Purinethol [*Mercaptopurine*] [*Antineoplastic drug regimen*]
POMP .... Principal Outer Membrane Protein
POMP .... Purinethol, Oncovin, Methotrexate, Prednisone [*Medicine*] (MEDA)
POMPAC .... Polaris Missile Facility, Pacific (AD)
POMPr......... Potomac Elec Pwr $2.44 Cv Pfd [*NYSE symbol*] (TTSB)
POMPrA....... Potomac El Pwr$3.89'91 Pfd [*NYSE symbol*] (TTSB)
POMPrH....... Potomac Elec Pwr $3.37cm'87 Pfd [*NYSE symbol*] (TTSB)
POMR .... Problem-Oriented Medical Record
Pom Rem .... Pomeroy on Civil Remedies [*A publication*] (DLA)
Pom Rem & Rem Rights... Pomeroy on Civil Remedies and Remedial Rights [*A publication*] (DLA)
POMR/PST... Partido Obrero Marxista Revolucionario/Partido Socialista de los Trabajadores [*Marxist Revolutionary Workers' Party/Socialist Workers' Party*] [*Peru*] [*Political party*] (PPW)
POMS .... Panel on Operational Meteorological Satellites
POMS .... Persistent Object Management System (NITA)
POMS .... Polar Operational Meteorological Satellite (USDC)
POMS .... Polar Operational Meteorological Satellite [*Marine science*] (OSRA)
POMS .... Poly-Ortho-methylstyrene [*Organic chemistry*]
POMS .... Process Operating Management System [*Manufacturing*]
POMS .... Production and Operations Management Society (EA)
POMS .... Profile of Mood States [*A questionnaire*]
POMS .... Program Operations Manual System [*Social Security Administration*]
POMSA .... Post Office Management Staffs Association [*A union*] [*British*] (DCTA)
POMS-BI...... Profile of Mood States-Bipolar Form
POMSEE .... Performance, Operating and Maintenance Standards for Electronic Equipment (NG)
pomsee......... Preparation, Operation, Maintenance, Shipboard Electronics Equipment (AD)
POMSIP .... Post Office Management and Service Improvement Program [*Obsolete*]
Pom Spec Perf... Pomeroy on Specific Performance of Contracts [*A publication*] (DLA)
POMT........... Patriot Organizational Maintenance Trainer [*Army*]
POMT........... Planning and Operations Management Team (MCD)
POMV........... National Federation Post Office Motor Vehicle Employees [*Later, APWU*] (EA)
POMV .... Privately Owned Motor Vehicle (NATG)
PON .... Paraoxonase [*An enzyme*]
PON .... Particulate Organic Nitrogen

PON Phosphorotioate Oligonucleotide [*Biochemistry*]
PON Ponce [*Puerto Rico*] [*Seismograph station code, US Geological Survey*] (SEIS)
PON Ponder Oils Ltd. [*Toronto Stock Exchange symbol*]
Pon Pontius [*Authority cited in pre-1607 legal work*] (DSA)
PON Pontoon (AAG)
pon Pontoon (AD)
PON Portuguese Navy [*ICAO designator*] (FAAC)
PON Position (IAA)
PON Pride of Newark [*Feigenspan beer*]
PON Program Opportunity Notice [*Energy Research and Development Administration*]
PON Program Opportunity Notification (AD)
pona Paraffin, Olefin, Naphthene, Aromatic (AD)
PONA Paraffins, Olefins, Naphthenes, Aromatics
Pon Ble Poncius Blegerii [*Flourished, 14th century*] [*Authority cited in pre-1607 legal work*] (DSA)
PONBRG Pontoon Bridge (MUGU)
PonBrg Pontoon Bridge (AD)
Poncebk Poncebank [*Associated Press*] (SAG)
Ponce Sch Med Ponce School of Medicine (GAGS)
PONCHO Patrons of Northwest Civic Cultural and Charitable Organizations
POND Parents of Near Drownings [*An association*] (EA)
POND Pondere [*By Weight*] [*Latin*]
pond Pondere [*By Weigh*] [*Latin*] (AD)
POND Ponderosus [*Heavy*] [*Pharmacy*]
Ponder Ponder Industries, Inc. [*Associated Press*] (SAG)
Pondo Pondoland (AD)
PONG Poet of the New Generation [*Term used to describe poets writing for entertainment value*] (ECON)
ponl-- New Caledonia [*MARC geographic area code Library of Congress*] (LCCP)
ponn-- New Hebrides [*MARC geographic area code Library of Congress*] (LCCP)
PONN Positive-on-Negative (IAA)
p-on-n Positive on Negative (AD)
PONS Platt's Oilgram News Service
PONS Profile of Nonverbal Sensitivity [*Psychology*]
pons Profile of Nonverbal Sensitivity (AD)
PONSE Personnel of the Naval Shore Establishment [*Report*] (NG)
PONSI Program of Noncollegiate Sponsored Instruction (OICC)
Pont Epistulae ex Ponto [*of Ovid*] [*Classical studies*] (OCD)
Pont Pontevedra (AD)
PONT Pontiac [*Automotive engineering*]
PONT Pontifex [*Bishop*] [*Latin*] (WGA)
Pont Pontoon (WGA)
PONTA Popular New Titles from Abroad [*Book acquisition program for libraries*]
pont b Pontoon Bridge (AD)
Ponti Pontiac (AD)
Pont Max Pontifex Maximus [*Supreme Pontiff*] [*Latin*] (AD)
ponu-- Nauru [*MARC geographic area code Library of Congress*] (LCCP)
PONUC Post Office National Users' Council [*British*]
PONVER Project on National Vocational Education Resources (EDAC)
PONY Pennsylvania, Ohio, New York Baseball League (IIA)
PONY Pennsylvania-Ontario-New York League [*Old baseball league*]
PONY Pride of the Navy Yard (DNAB)
PONY Prostitutes of New York
PONY Protect Our Nation's Youth [*Baseball league*] [*Name usually written Pony*]
PONY Purpose of Neighborhood Youth [*Foundation*]
PONYA Port of New York Authority [*Later, PANYNJ*]
POO Panel on Oceanography
POO Parents Opposed to Opting Out [*An association*] (AIE)
POO Payload Operations Office [*NASA*]
POO Platform of Opportunity Program [*National Oceanic and Atmospheric Administration*] (MSC)
POO Pocos De Caldas [*Brazil*] [*Airport symbol*] (OAG)
Poo Poole (AD)
POO Poona [*India*] [*Seismograph station code, US Geological Survey*] (SEIS)
POO Port Operations Officer (DS)
POO Post Office Order
POO Priority Operational Objective [*Military*]
POO Program Operations Officer [*Social Security Administration*]
POOD Permanent Officer of the Day [*or Deck*] [*Navy*]
pood Poodle Dog (AD)
POOD Provisioning Order Obligating Document
POOEL Petty Officer Ordnance Electrician [*British military*] (DMA)
poof Peripheral On-Line-Oriented Function [*Computer science*] (AD)
POOFF Preservation of Our Femininity and Finances [*Women's group opposing below-the-knee fashions introduced in 1970*]
POOFF Professional Oglers of Female Figures [*Men's group opposing below-the-knee fashions introduced in 1970*]
POOL SCP Pool [*NASDAQ symbol*] (TTSB)
POOL SCP Pool Corp. [*NASDAQ symbol*] (SAG)
PoolEn Pool Energy Services Co. [*Associated Press*] (SAG)
poop Nincompoop (AD)
POOP Process Oriented Observation Program [*NORPAX*] (MSC)
POOR Prevention of Over-Radiation [*Military*]
Poore Const Poore's Federal and State Constitution [*A publication*] (DLA)
Poor L & Local Gov't Poor Law and Local Government Magazine [*A publication*] (DLA)
POOS Priority Order Output System [*Japan*] (DIT)
poossIq Person of Opposite Sex Sharing Living Quarters (AD)
POOW Petty Officer of the Watch [*Navy*] (NVT)
POoW Petty Officer on Watch [*Military*] (AD)
POP Pacific Ocean Perch
POP Package for Online Programming [*Computer science*] (CDE)
POP Palletizing Optimization Potential (AD)
POP Panoramic Office Planning
POP Paperless Ordering Placement [*System*] (DOMA)
POP Parallel Output Platform
POP Parents of Punkers (EA)
POP Paroxypropione [*or Paraoxypropiophenone*] [*Endocrinology*]
POP Particle-Oriented Paper (IAA)
POP Particulate Organic Phosphorus
POP Partido de Orientacion Popular [*Popular Orientation Party*] [*El Salvador*] [*Political party*] (PPW)
POP Parti Ouvrier et Paysan du Congo [*Congolese Workers' and Peasants' Party*] [*Zaire*] [*Political party*]
POP Parti Ouvrier-Progressiste [*Canada*]
POP Patrexes of the Panopticon (EA)
POP Payload Optimized Program [*NASA*] (KSC)
POP Pay One Price
POP Peak Overpressure [*Nuclear energy*] (NRCH)
POP Perceived Outcome Potential (MHDI)
POP Performance-Oriented Packaging [*for hazardous materials*]
POP Period of Performance (MCD)
POP Perpendicular Ocean Platform [*Oceanography*]
pop Perpendicular Ocean Platform (AD)
POP Perpendicular-to-Orbit Plane [*Aerospace*] (KSC)
pop Persistent Occipito-Posterior (AD)
POP Persistent Occipit Posterior [*A fetal position*] [*Obstetrics*]
POP Persistent Organic Pollutant [*Environmental science*]
POP Persistent Organic Pollutant
POP Pharmacists in Ophthalmic Practice [*Later, PIOP*] (EA)
POP Picture-outside-Picture [*Television technology*] (PS)
POP Pipeline Outfit, Petroleum (MCD)
POP Pituitary Opioid Peptide [*Medicine*] (DMAA)
POP Plasma Oncotic Pressure [*Medicine*] (MAE)
POP Plasma Osmotic Pressure [*Medicine*]
pop Plasma Osmotic Pressure (AD)
pop Plaster of Paris (AD)
POP Plaster of Paris
POP Pneumatic Operated Piston (ECII)
PoP Point of Presence [*Telecommunications*] (PCM)
POP Point of Presence [*Telecommunications*] (DOM)
POP Point of Purchase [*Advertising*]
POP Point-of-Purchase [*Advertising*] (WDMC)
POP Polar Orbiting Platform (SSD)
POP Pollution and Overpopulation
POP Polymyositis Ossificans Progressiva [*Medicine*] (DMAA)
POP Polyolefin Plastomer [*Organic chemistry*]
POP Pope & Talbot [*NYSE symbol*] (TTSB)
POP Pope & Talbot, Inc. [*NYSE symbol*] (SPSG)
Pop Popham's English King's Bench Reports [*1592-1627*] [*A publication*] (DLA)
POP Popliteal [*Artery*] [*Anatomy*] (AAMN)
Pop Popliteal (DMAA)
pop Popliteal (AD)
POP Popondetta [*Papua New Guinea*] [*Seismograph station code, US Geological Survey Closed*] (SEIS)
Pop Poppa (AD)
pop Poppet (AD)
POP Popping [*Mining engineering*]
POP Popular
pop Popular (AD)
pop Popular (WDMC)
Pop Populare [*Record label*] [*Romania*]
Pop Population (AAG)
pop Population (WDMC)
pop Population (AD)
pop Population (ODBW)
POP Population Division [*Bureau of the Census*] (OICC)
POP Portugese Overseas Province (AD)
POP Posterior Odds Processing [*Weather forecasting*] [*National Science Foundation*]
POP Post Office Plan
POP Post Office Preferred (DCTA)
POP Post Office Protocol [*Telecommunications*]
POP Postoperative [*Medicine*]
p-op Post-Operative (AD)
POP Power On/Off Protection
POP Practical Ordered Program (OA)
POP Preburner Oxidizer Pump (MCD)
POP Preflight Operations Procedure (MCD)
POP Prelaunch Operations Plan [*NASA*] (NASA)
POP Premanagement Orientation Program [*LIMRA*]
POP Pressurizer Overpressure Protection System [*Nuclear energy*] (IEEE)
POP Primary Operation
pop Printer of Plates [*MARC relator code*] [*Library of Congress*] (LCCP)
POP Printing-Out Paper
POP Profit Option Plan [*Retailing*]
POP Programmed Operators and Primitives [*Computer science*]
POP Program Obligation Plan (KSC)
POP Program Operating Plan
POP Progressive Overload Program [*Weight training*]
POP Project Objective Plan (NG)
POP Project Optimization Procedure (IAA)

POP .... Prompt Ordering Plan
POP .... Proof-Of Principle [*Test*]
POP .... Proof of Purchase
POP .... Public Offering Price (AD)
POP .... Puerto Plata [*Dominican Republic*] [*Airport symbol*] (OAG)
POP .... Pump Optimizing Program
POP .... Purchase Outside Production (SAA)
POP3 .... Post Office Protocol 3 [*Electronic mail*]
POPA .... Patent Office Professional Association (EA)
POPA .... Payload Ordnance Processing Area (NASA)
POPA .... Pet Owners' Protective Association
Popa .... Popayan, Colombia (AD)
POPA .... Prevention of Oil Pollution Act [*1971*]
POPA .... Property Owners' Protection Association
pop advertising... Point-of-Purchase Advertising (AD)
POPAE .... Protons on Protons and Electrons [*Physics*]
POPAI .... Point-of-Purchase Advertising Institute [*Fort Lee, NJ*] (EA)
POPAL .... Pre-Operational Peculiar Age List
POP & B ..... Proposed Operating Program and Budget [*Army*]
pop art .... Popular Art (AD)
popb .... Proposed Operating Plan and Budget (AD)
POPC .... Pamitoyl-Oleoylphosphatidylcholine [*Biochemistry*]
popc-- .... Pitcairn [*MARC geographic area code Library of Congress*] (LCCP)
POP-CON ..... Populist Conservative [*Wing of the Republican Party represented by Congressmen Gingrich, Kemp, and Lott*]
POPCRU ...... Police and Prison Civil Rights Union [*Founded in 1989*] [*South Africa*] (ECON)
POPD .... Power-Operated
POPDA .... Polyoxypropylenediamine [*Organic chemistry*]
POPE .... Parents for Orthodoxy in Parochial Education [*Group opposing sex education in schools*]
POPE .... Product Oriented Procedures Evaluation (AD)
Pope Cust .... Pope on Customs and Excise [*11th ed.*] [*1828*] [*A publication*] (DLA)
POP ED .... Popular Edition [*Publishing*]
Pope Lun ...... Pope on Lunacy [*A publication*] (DLA)
PopeRes .... Pope Resources Ltd. [*Associated Press*] (SAG)
PopeTal .... Pope & Talbot, Inc. [*Associated Press*] (SAG)
popex .... Population Explosion (AD)
POPEZ .... Pope Resources L.P. [*NASDAQ symbol*] (TTSB)
POPEZ .... Pope Resources Ltd. [*NASDAQ symbol*] (SPSG)
popf .... Prepared-on-Premises Flavor (AD)
POPGUN ...... Policy and Procedure Governing the Use of Nicknames [*Army*] (AABC)
Poph .... Popham's English King's Bench Reports [*1592-1627*] [*A publication*] (DLA)
Poph (2) ...... Cases at the End of Popham's Reports [*A publication*] (DLA)
Popham .... Popham's English King's Bench Reports [*79 English Reprint*] [*1592-1626*] [*A publication*] (DLA)
Poph Insol ... Popham's Insolvency Act of Canada [*A publication*] (DLA)
POPI .... Post Office Position Indicator [*A form of long-range position indicator*] [*British*]
popi .... Post Office Position Indicator [*British*] (AD)
POPINFORM... Population Information Network [*UNESCO*]
POPINS .... Population Information System [*UNESCO*]
POPLAB .... International Program of Laboratories for Population Statistics
POPLINE ...... Population Information On-Line [*Bibliographic database*] (IID)
POPLINE ...... Population Online (NITA)
poplit .... Popliteal (AD)
POPLIT .... Popliteal [*Anatomy*]
POPMIP .... Portable Ocean Platform Motion Instrumentation Package [*Marine science*] (MSC)
Pop Mo L Tr... Popular Monthly Law Tracts [*1877-78*] [*A publication*] (DLA)
pop music .... Popular Music (AD)
POPMV .... Poplar Mosaic Virus [*Plant pathology*]
Popn .... Population
POPO .... Poured-On, Passed-Over [*Bowdlerized version*]
POPO .... Push-On, Pull-Off [*Computer science*]
pop psych.... Popular Psychiatry (AD)
popr .... Pilot Overhaul Provisioning Review (AD)
POPR .... Pilot Overhaul Provisioning Review
POPR .... Prototype Organic Power Reactor [*Nuclear energy*]
POPS .... Free-Fall Pop-Up Ocean Bottom Seismometer [*Marine science*] (MSC)
POPS .... National Beverage Corp. [*NASDAQ symbol*] (SAG)
POPS .... Pantograph Optical Projection System (IEEE)
POPS .... Parachute Opening Proximity Sensor (MCD)
POPS .... People Opposed to Pornography in Schools [*Group opposing sex education in schools*]
POPS .... Performance-Oriented Packing Standard
POPS .... Platt's Oilgram Price Service
pops-- .... Polynesia [*MARC geographic area code Library of Congress*] (LCCP)
pops .... Popular Concerts (AD)
POPS .... Positioning Orbital Propulsion System (MCD)
POPS .... Preserve Our Presidential Sites (EA)
POPS .... Pressurizer Overpressure Protection System [*Nuclear energy*] (NRCH)
POPS .... Process Operating System [*Toshiba Corp.*] [*Japan*]
POPS .... Procurers of Painted-Label Sodas [*Defunct*] (EA)
POPS .... Program for Operator Scheduling [*Bell System computer program*]
POPS .... Project Operations [*Navy*] (NVT)
POPS .... Protect Our Pelican Society [*Later, PMBS*] (EA)
POPS .... Pyrotechnic Optical Plume Simulator (MCD)
Pop Sci .... Popular Science [*A publication*] (AD)
POP SCI MO... Popular Science Monthly [*A publication*] (ROG)
POPSE .... Project Office for Physical Security Equipment [*Army*] (RDA)
POPSER .... Polaris Operational Performance Surveillance Engineering Report [*Missiles*]
POPSI .... Postulate-Based Permuted Subject Indexing (PDAA)
POPSI .... Precipitation and Off-Path Scattered Interference [*Report*] [*FCC*]
POPSIPT ...... Project Operations in Port [*Navy*] (NVT)
POPT .... Petty Officer Physical Trainer [*British military*] (DMA)
POPT .... Pretesting Orientation on the Purpose of Testing [*US Employment Service*] [*Department of Labor*]
POPU .... Push Over Pull Up (NASA)
Populuxe ..... Popular Luxury [*Coined by Thomas Hine, design critic for the Philadelphia Inquirer, to describe the period from the mid-1950's to the mid-1960's*]
POPUS .... Post Office Processing Utility Subsystem [*Telecommunications*] (TEL)
poq .... Periodic Order Quantity (AD)
POQ .... Period Order Quantity (PDAA)
POQ .... Production Offset Quantity [*Military*]
POQ .... Provided Otherwise Qualified [*Military*] (AABC)
POQ .... Public Opinion Quarterly [*A publication*] (AD)
POQ .... Push Off Quickly [*i.e., Be quick about it*] [*British*]
POQL .... Probability Outgoing Quality Limit (PDAA)
POQU .... Procedure of Questionable Usefulness [*Medicine*] (CPH)
POR .... Pacific Ocean Region
POR .... Parking Orbit Rendezvous [*NASA*] (MCD)
POR .... Partido Obrero Revolucionario [*Revolutionary Workers Party*] [*Bolivia*] [*Political party*] (PPW)
POR .... Partido Obrero Revolucionario [*Revolutionary Workers Party*] [*Peru*] [*Political party*]
POR .... Partido Obrero Revolucionario [*Revolutionary Workers Party*] [*Argentina Political party*]
POR .... Patent Office Reports [*A publication*] (DLA)
POR .... Patrol Operations Report
POR .... Payable on Receipt [*Business term*]
p-o-r .... Pay-on-Receipt (AD)
POR .... Pay on Return [*Business term*]
POR .... Peak Overshoot Ratio (IAA)
POR .... Periodic Operation Report
POR .... Personnel Occurrence Report [*RAF*] [*British*]
POR .... Physician of Record (DAVI)
POR .... Pilot Opinion Rating
POR .... Plutonium Organic Recycle [*Nuclear energy*] (NRCH)
POR .... Pola Resources Ltd. [*Vancouver Stock Exchange symbol*]
POR .... Pori [*Finland*] [*Airport symbol*] (OAG)
Por .... Porifera (AD)
Por .... Porogi [*Waterfall*] [*Russian*] (AD)
por .... Porosity (AD)
por .... Portage (BARN)
POR .... Portec, Inc. [*NYSE symbol*] (SPSG)
POR .... Portion
POR .... Portland [*Maine*] [*Seismograph station code, US Geological Survey Closed*] (SEIS)
Por .... Portland (AD)
POR .... Port of Refuge [*Shipping*]
POR .... Portrait
Por .... Portugal (AD)
Por .... Portuguese (AD)
por .... Portuguese [*MARC language code Library of Congress*] (LCCP)
POR .... Portuguese
POR .... Position of Responsibility (ADA)
POR .... Post Office Return
POR .... Post Office Rifles [*Military British*] (ROG)
POR .... Preparation of Overseas Replacement [*Military*] (RDA)
POR .... Preparation of Replacements for Oversea Movement [*MTMC*] (TAG)
POR .... Press on Regardless [*Automotive marathon*]
POR .... Price on Request
POR .... Problem-Oriented Records [*Medicine*]
POR .... Problem-Oriented Routine (IEEE)
POR .... Processing Overseas Replacement Training [*Military*] (VNW)
POR .... Production Order Records (SAA)
POR .... Production Order Request (SAA)
POR .... Project Officers Report (MCD)
POR .... Psychotherapy Outcome Research
por .... Public Opinion Research (AD)
POR .... Purchase Order Request
PORA .... Police Officers Research Association (AD)
PORA .... Police Officers Research Association (NADA)
PORAC .... Peace Officers Research Association of California
PORACC .... Principles of Radiation and Contamination Control [*Nuclear energy*]
PORAG .... Presiding Officers' Review and Advisory Group [*Commonwealth Parliament*] [*Australia*]
PORB .... Production Operations Review Board [*NASA*] (NASA)
PORC .... Partido Obrero Revolucionario-Combate [*Revolutionary Struggle Workers' Party*] [*Bolivia*] [*Political party*] (PPW)
PORC .... Peralta Oaks Research Center (AD)
PORC .... Plant Operations Review Committee [*Nuclear energy*] (NRCH)
PORC .... Porcelain (AAG)
porc .... Porcelain (AD)
PORC .... Porphyria, Chester Type (DMAA)
PORCN .... Production Order Records Change Notice (KSC)
PORCO .... Port Control Office
PORD .... Performance and Operations Requirements Document [*NASA*] (NASA)
PORDA .... Personnel Officers of Research and Development Agencies
PORDIR .... Port Director
PORE .... Point Reyes National Seashore [*National Park Service designation*]

POREA .... Post Office Regional Employees' Association [*Defunct*] (EA)
POREL(A) .... Petty Officer Radio Electrician (Air) [*British military*] (DMA)
POREP .... Position Report [*Air Force*]
PORES .... Purchase Order Receiving System (MCD)
PORF .... Pacific Ocean Research Foundation (EA)
Porg .... Person of Restricted Growth [*Slang term used to describe a person of limi ted cultural awareness*] [*Lifestyle classification*]
PORGIE .... Paperback Original [*Award for best original paperback books of the year*]
PORI .... Polaris Operational Readiness Instrumentation [*Missiles*]
PORI .... Preoperational Readiness Inspection (MCD)
PORIS .... Post Office Radio Interference Service [*British*] (DI)
PORIS .... Post Office Radio Interference Station (AD)
PORK .... Partnership for Over-Regulated Kar [*Humorous description of government-auto industry technology research program*]
porksan .... Pork Sandwich (AD)
porkwich ...... Pork Sandwich (AD)
PORL .... Peninsular/Oriental Steam Nav [*LO Symbol*] (TTSB)
porm .... Plus or Minus (AD)
PORM .... Plus or Minus
P or M .... Plus or Minus (MSA)
PORM-PST ... Partido Obrero Revolucionario Marxista-Partido Socialista de los Trabajadores [*Peru*] [*Political party*] (EY)
porn .... Pornographic (AD)
PORN .... Pornography (DSUE)
PORN .... Protect Our Responsibilities Now [*Book title*]
pornette .... Pornographic Cassette (AD)
pornfilm .... Pornographic Motion Picture Film (AD)
porno .... Pornofilm (AD)
porno .... Pornographer (AD)
PORNO .... Pornography (DSUE)
pornobio .... Pornographic Biography (AD)
pornofilm .... Pornographic Motion Picture (AD)
porno mag ... Pornographic Magazine (AD)
pornovel .... Pornographic Novel (AD)
pornovelist ... Pornographic Novelist (AD)
Porn Squad ... Pornographic Squad (AD)
pornzines .... Pornographic Magazines (AD)
PORP .... Partial Ossicular Replacement Prosthesis
PORP .... Printed on Recycled Paoer (AD)
P or P .... Publish or Perish [*Said of scholars, scientists, etc.*]
Porph .... Porphyry [*Third century AD*] [*Classical studies*] (OCD)
porph .... Porphyry (VRA)
PORR .... Preliminary Operations Requirements Review [*NASA*] (NASA)
PORR .... Purchase Order Revision Request
PORS .... Post Office Research Station (AD)
PORS .... Power-On Reset [*Electronics*]
PORS .... Product Output Reporting System
PORSE .... Post Overhaul Reaction Safeguard Examination [*Navy*] (NVT)
PORT .... Bayport Restaurant Group [*NASDAQ symbol*] (TTSB)
PORT .... Bayport Restaurant Group, Inc. [*NASDAQ symbol*] (SAG)
PORT .... Patient Outcome Research Team (PCM)
PORT .... Photo-Optical Recorder Tracker
port .... Photo-Optical Recorder Tracker (AD)
PORT .... Port [*Commonly used*] (OPSA)
port .... Portable (AD)
PORT .... Portable (KSC)
PORT .... Porter (DSUE)
Port .... Porter's Alabama Supreme Court Reports [*1834-39*] [*A publication*] (DLA)
Port .... Porter's Indiana Reports [*3-7 Indiana*] [*A publication*] (DLA)
PORT .... Portfolio (WGA)
PORT .... Portland Railroad
PORT .... Portmanteau (DSUE)
PORT .... Portrait
port .... Portrait (AD)
Port .... Portugal (ODBW)
PORT .... Portugal
Port .... Portugal (VRA)
port .... Portugiesisch [*Portuguese*] [*German*] (AD)
Port .... Portuguese (ODBW)
PORT .... Postoperative Respiratory Therapy (DAVI)
PORT .... Prescriptive Objective Reference Testing [*Vocational guidance*]
PORT .... Presentation Portfolio (VRA)
Port Ade .... Port Adelaide [*South Australia*] (AD)
Portage .... Portage Industries Corp. [*Associated Press*] (SAG)
PORTAL .... Process-Oriented Real-Time Algorithmic Language [*1978*] [*Computer science*] (CSR)
Port (Ala) ..... Porter's Alabama Reports [*A publication*] (DLA)
Port Ala R ... Porter's Alabama Reports [*A publication*] (DLA)
Port Ald .... Port Alberni [*Vancouver Island, British Columbia*] (AD)
portalet .... Portable Toilet (AD)
Port Alex ..... Port Alexander [*Alaska*] (AD)
Port Ant .... Port Antonio [*Jamaica*] (AD)
PORTAPAK ... Portable, Self-Contained, Instrument Package
Port Art .... Port Arthur (AD)
PORTAS .... Penetration of Radiation Through Aperture Simulation (PDAA)
PortBk .... Portsmouth Bank Shares, Inc. [*Associated Press*] (SAG)
PORT CEM ... Portland Cement [*Technical drawings*] (DAC)
Port Chi .... Port Chicago (AD)
Port Chi .... Portuguese China (AD)
Port Dal .... Port Dalhousie [*Ontario, Canada*] (AD)
Portec .... Portec, Inc. [*Associated Press*] (SAG)
Porter .... Porter's Alabama Reports [*A publication*] (DLA)
Porter .... Porter's Indiana Reports [*3-7 Indiana*] [*A publication*] (DLA)
Porter (Ala) ... Porter's Alabama Reports [*A publication*] (DLA)
Porter R .... Porter's Alabama Reports [*A publication*] (DLA)
Porter's Ala R ... Porter's Alabama Reports [*A publication*] (DLA)
Porter's R ..... Porter's Alabama Reports [*A publication*] (DLA)
Porter's Repts ... Porter's Alabama Reports [*A publication*] (DLA)
PortG35 .... Portland General Electric Co. [*Associated Press*] (SAG)
PortGC .... Portland General Corp. [*Associated Press*] (SAG)
PortglT .... Portugal Telecom SA [*Associated Press*] (SAG)
PORTIA .... Port Operations, Transport and Integrated Accountancy (MHDB)
Port Ind .... Portuguese India (AD)
Port Ins .... Porter's Laws of Insurance [*A publication*] (DLA)
Port Jack ..... Port Jackson Sydney [*Sydney, New South Wales, Australia*] (AD)
Portland St U ... Portland State University (GAGS)
Portland UL Rev ... Portland University. Law Review [*A publication*] (DLA)
Port Liz .... Port Elizabeth [*South Africa*] (AD)
Port Liz .... Port Elizabeth [*New Jersey*] (AD)
PORTN .... Portion (ROG)
Port Nick ..... Port Nicholson [*Wellington, New Zealand*] (AD)
PORTP .... Partido Obrero Revolucionaria Trotskista Posadista [*Bolivia*] [*Political party*] (PPW)
Port P .... Portuguese Pharmacopoeia [*A publication*]
Port Phil .... Port Phillip [*Melbourne, Victoria, Australia*] (AD)
PORTREP .... Port [*or Anchorage*] Capacity Report [*Navy*] (NVT)
Port Rich ..... Port Richmond [*Staten Island, New York*] (AD)
PORTS .... Physical Oceanographic Real-Time System (USDC)
PORTS .... Physical Oceanographic Real-Time System [*Marine science*] (OSRA)
PORTS .... Portable Remote Telecommunications System (DOMA)
PORTS .... Port Objective for Real-Time Systems (USDC)
PORTS .... Port Objective for Real-Time Systems [*Marine science*] (OSRA)
PORTS .... Ports [*Commonly used*] (OPSA)
PORTS .... Portsmouth [*City in England*]
PORTS .... Portsmouth Gaseous Diffusion Plant [*Department of Energy*] [*Portsmouth, OH*] (GAAI)
PORTS .... Portsmouth Gaseous Diffusion Plant (DOGT)
PortsBk .... Portsmouth Bank Shares [*Associated Press*] (SAG)
PORTSM .... Portsmouth [*County borough in England*]
Ports NSW Jl ... Ports of New South Wales Journal [*A publication*]
PORTSREP ... Ports Report File (MCD)
Port Sud .... Port Sudan (AD)
PORTSUM ... Port [*or Anchorage*] Summary Report [*Navy*] (NVT)
Port Swett ... Port Swettenham [*Malaysia*] (AD)
PortSys .... Porta Systems Corp. [*Associated Press*] (SAG)
Port Talb ..... Port Talbot [*Wales*] (AD)
Port Tew .... Port Tewfik [*Egypt*] (AD)
Port Tim .... Portuguese Timor (AD)
Portug .... Portugais [*Portuguese*] [*French*] (AD)
Portugl .... Portugal Fund [*Associated Press*] (SAG)
Port UL Rev ... Portland University. Law Review [*A publication*] (DLA)
Port Wash ... Port Washington [*Long Island, New York*] (AD)
Port Wel .... Port Wellen [*Ontario, CAN*] (AD)
PORV .... Pilot-Operated Relief Valve [*Nuclear energy*] (NRCH)
PORV .... Power-Operated Relief Valve [*Nuclear energy*] (NRCH)
POS .... Aeroposta SA [*Argentina ICAO designator*] (FAAC)
POS .... Catalina Marketing [*NYSE symbol*] (TTSB)
POS .... Catalina Marketing Corp. [*NYSE symbol*] (SPSG)
POS .... Pacific Ocean Ship (NASA)
POS .... Pacific Orchid Society of Hawaii (EA)
POS .... Parent Operating Service (MCD)
POS .... Parosteal Osteosarcoma [*Oncology*] (DAVI)
POS .... Partially Ordered Set (OA)
POS .... Patent Office Society (EA)
POS .... Peacetime Operating Stock [*Military*] (CINC)
POS .... Period of Service [*Military*]
POS .... Permanent Orbital Station [*NASA*] (IAA)
POS .... Photo Optic System
POS .... Pico Resources [*Vancouver Stock Exchange symbol*]
POS .... Piper Owner Society (EA)
POS .... Planar Oxygen Sensor
POS .... Plan of Service (OICC)
POS .... Plant Operating System [*Nuclear energy*] (NRCH)
PoS .... Point of Sale
pos .... Point of Sale (AD)
POS .... Point of Sale (ODBW)
p-o-s .... Point-of-Sale [*Retail*] (WDMC)
POS .... Point-of-Sale [*Retail*] (WDMC)
POS .... Point-of-Service [*Human resources*] (WYGK)
POS .... Point of Service
POS .... Point of Service [*Health plan option*]
POS .... Point of Service Option
POS .... Point-of-Service Plan [*Insurance*] (PAZ)
POS .... Polar Orbiting Satellite [*Marine science*] (OSRA)
POS .... Polar Orbiting Satellite (USDC)
POs .... Police Officers (AD)
POS .... Policy Statements [*Australian Broadcasting Tribunal*] [*A publication*]
POS .... Polycystic Ovarian Syndrome [*Also, PCOS*] [*Gynecology*]
POS .... Portable Oxygen System (MCD)
PoS .... Port of Service (AD)
PoS .... Port of Spain (AD)
POS .... Port Of Spain [*Trinidad and Tobago*] [*Airport symbol*] (OAG)
POS .... Port(s) of Support (DOMA)
pos .... Position (WDMC)
pos .... Position (AD)
POS .... Position (KSC)
POS .... Positive (AFM)
pos .... Positive (AD)

pos............ Positive (IDOE)
POS............ Possession [*or Possessive*] (WGA)
pos............ Possibility (AD)
Pos............ Possible
POs............ Postal Orders (AD)
POS............ Post Office Scheme [*Regulations*] [*British*]
POS............ Preferred Overseas Shore Duty
POS............ Pressure on Space [*Publishing*] (DGA)
POS............ Pressure-Operated Switch (IAA)
POS............ Primary Operating Stock [*DoD*]
POS............ Primary Operating System (IEEE)
POS............ Primary Oxygen System
POS............ Probability of Survival [*Automotive componant analysis*]
POS............ Problem Oriented System
POS............ Production-Oriented Survey (MCD)
pos............ Product of Sums (AD)
POS............ Products of Sums (IAA)
POS............ Professional Operating System (NITA)
POS............ Professions and Occupations Sourcebook [*A publication*]
POS............ Programmable Option Select [*Computer science*]
POS............ Programming Optimizing System (IAA)
POS............ Program of Study (AEE)
POS............ Program Operations Staff [*Environmental Protection Agency*] (GFGA)
POS............ Program Order Sequence
POS............ Protein, Oil, and Starch [*Pilot manufacturing plant established by the Canadian government*]
POS............ Pupil Observation Survey [*Education*]
POS............ Purchase Order Supplement
POSA............ Patriotic Order Sons of America (EA)
POSA............ Payment Outstanding Suspense Accounts (NATG)
posa............ Payment Outstanding Suspense Accounts (AD)
POSA............ Petty Officer Stores Accountant [*British military*] (DMA)
POSA............ Preliminary Operating Safety Analysis [*Nuclear energy*] (NRCH)
POSARS....... Plan of Service Automated Reporting System [*Employment and Training Administration*] [*Department of Labor*]
posb............ Possibly (VRA)
POSB............ Post Office Savings Bank
POSC............ Little Workers of the Sacred Heart (TOCD)
POSC............ Problem-Oriented System of Charting (AAMN)
posc--.......... Santa Cruz Islands [*MARC geographic area code Library of Congress*] (LCCP)
POSCH.......... Program of Surgical Control of Hyperlipidemia
POSCO.......... Pohang Iron & Steel Co. (ECON)
POSCOR...... Position Correct (CAAL)
POSCORB.... Planning, Organizing, Staffing, Coordinating, Reporting, and Budgeting [*Management*]
POSD............ Personnel on Station Date [*Army*] (AABC)
POSD............ Post Office Savings Department (AD)
POSD............ Program for Optical System Design
POSD............ Project Operation Support Division [*NASA*]
posdcorb...... Planning-Organization-Staffing-Directing-Coordinating-Reporting-Budgeting g (AD)
POSDCORB... Planning, Organizing, Staffing, Directing, Coordinating, Reporting, and Budgeting [*Principles of management*]
posdsplt....... Port Side Out, Starboard Side Home [*British slang*] (AD)
posdsplt....... Positive Displacement (AD)
POSDSPLT... Positive Displacement
POSE............ Parents Opposed to Sex Education
POSE............ Photogrammetric Ocean Survey Equipment
POSE............ Power Operational Support Equipment
POSE............ Promotion of Social Education [*British*] (DI)
POSER.......... Process Organization to Simplify Error Recovery (PDAA)
POSET.......... Partially Ordered Set (HGAA)
Posey............ Posey's Unreported Cases [*Texas*] [*A publication*] (ILCA)
Posey UC...... Texas Unreported Cases [*A publication*] (DLA)
Posey Unrep Cas... Posey's Unreported Cases [*Texas*] [*A publication*] (DLA)
POSF............ Port of Support File (DOMA)
POSG............ After Glucose Infusion Started [*Biochemistry*] (DAVI)
posh............ Permuted on Subject Headings (AD)
POSH............ Permuted on Subject Headings [*Indexing technique*]
POSH............ Personal & Organizational Security Handbook [*A publication*]
POSH............ Port Outwardbound, Starboard Homewardbound [*Refers to shaded cabins of British naval officers in the Far East*]
POSH............ Probability of Severe Hail (USDC)
POSH............ Probability of Severe Hail [*Marine science*] (OSRA)
posh............ Samoa Islands [*MARC geographic area code Library of Congress*] (LCCP)
POSI............ Personnel On-Site Integration (SAA)
POSI............ Positron Corp. [*NASDAQ symbol*] (SAG)
POS INIT...... Position Initialization (GAVI)
POSIP........... Portable Ship Instrumentation Package
posistor....... Positive Resistor (AD)
posit............ Position (AD)
POSIT.......... Position (NVT)
POSIT.......... Positive
posit............ Positive (AD)
POSIT.......... Positivism (ROG)
posit............ Positron (AD)
POSIT.......... Profile for Open Systems Internetworking Technologies [*Computer science*] (CDE)
POSITIVE..... Parents of Surrogate-Borne Infants and Toddlers in Verbal Exchange (EA)
Positr........... Positron Corp. [*Associated Press*] (SAG)
POSITREPS... Position Reports
POSITRON... Positive Electron
positron........ Positive Electron (AD)
Positron....... Positron Corp. [*Associated Press*] (SAG)
POSIW.......... Positron Corp. Wrrt [*NASDAQ symbol*] (TTSB)
POSIX.......... Portable Operating System Interface Exchange
POSIX.......... Portable Operating System Interface for Computer Environments (AAGC)
POSIX.......... Portable Operating System Interface for Unix [*Computer science*] (PCM)
POSIX.......... Portable Operating Systems for Computer Environments (AD)
POSIX.......... Portable Operating System Specification [*IEEE*]
POSK............ Polski Osrodek Spoleczno-Kulturalny [*Polish Social and Cultural Association - PSCA*] (EAIO)
POSKP.......... Polski Osrodek Spoleczno-Kulturalny Posk [*Polish Social and Cultural Association - PSCA*] (EAIO)
POsl............ Papyri Osloenses [*A publication*] (OCD)
POSL............ Parti Ouvrier Socialiste Luxembourgeois [*Luxembourg Socialist Workers' Party*] (EAIO)
POSM............ National Association of Post Office and General Service Maintenance Employees [*Later, APWU*] [*AFL-CIO*]
posm............ Patient-Operated Selected Mechanisms (AD)
POSM............ Patient-Operated Selector Mechanism [*Pronounced "possum"*]
POSMA.......... Postal Service Manual [*A publication*]
Posmo.......... Osmotic Permeability [*Biochemistry*] (DAVI)
POSN............ Position (AFM)
posn............ Position (AD)
posn--.......... Solomon Islands [*MARC geographic area code Library of Congress*] (LCCP)
POSNA.......... Pediatric Orthopaedic Society of North America (EA)
POS/NAV...... Position/Navigation [*System*] [*Military*] (INF)
POSNO.......... Position Number [*Military*] (ADDR)
POSNY.......... People of the State of New York (AD)
POSO............ Prosoft I-Net Solutions, Inc. [*NASDAQ symbol*] (SAG)
POSP............ Pacific Ocean Stations Program (SAA)
pos pr.......... Positive Pressure (MAE)
Pos Press.... Positive Pressure (CPH)
pos pron...... Possessive Pronoun (AD)
POSR............ Peacetime Operating Stock Requirement [*Military*] (AFIT)
POS R.......... Positive Review [*A publication*] (ROG)
POS REF...... Position Reference (GAVI)
PosResp....... Positive Response Television [*Associated Press*] (SAG)
POSRIP......... People Organized to Stop Rape of Imprisoned Persons (EA)
POSS............ Palomar Observatory Sky Survey [*NASA*]
POSS............ Passive Optical Satellite Surveillance [*System*] (NATG)
POSS............ Photo-Optical Surveillance Subsystem
P-O-S S........ Point-of-Sale System (AD)
P-O-S S........ Point-of-Service System (AD)
POSS............ Portable Oceanographic Survey System (MCD)
POSS............ Possession [*or Possessive*] (AFM)
poss............ Possession (AD)
poss............ Possessive (WDMC)
poss............ Possible (WDMC)
POSS............ Possible
poss............ Possibly (WDMC)
POSS............ Possis Medical [*NASDAQ symbol*] (TTSB)
POSS............ Possis Medical, Inc. [*NASDAQ symbol*] (NQ)
POSS............ Program Operations Support Staff [*Environmental Protection Agency*] (GFGA)
POSS............ Prototype Optical Surveillance System
POSS............ Proximal Over-Shoulder Strap [*Medicine*]
POSSE.......... Parents Opposed to Sex and Sensitivity Education [*An association*]
POSSE.......... Police Operations Systems Support System Elementary
POSSE.......... Progressive Onslaught to Stamp out Stock Errors [*Navy*] (NG)
POSSED........ Possessed (ROG)
posses.......... Possessive (AD)
POSSF.......... Post Office Staff Superannuation Fund [*British*] (DI)
Possis........... Possis Medical, Inc. [*Associated Press*] (SAG)
posslq........... Person of the Opposite Sex in Same Living Quarters (AD)
POSSLQ........ Persons of Opposite Sex Sharing Living Quarters [*Bureau of the Census*]
POSSN.......... Possession (WGA)
POSSNC........ Post Office Senior Staff Negotiating Council [*British*]
POSSON........ Possession
POSSUB........ Possible Submarine [*Navy*] (NVT)
POSSUM........ Pictures of Specific Syndromes and Unknown Malformations [*Database*]
POSSUM........ Polar Orbiting Satellite System - University of Michigan [*Designed by engineering students*]
Post............. De Posteritate Caini [*of Philo*] (BJA)
POST............ Frederick Post Drafting Equipment (AD)
POST............ International Post Ltd. [*NASDAQ symbol*] (SAG)
POST............ Intl Post Ltd [*NASDAQ symbol*] (TTSB)
POST............ Parliamentary Office of Science and Technology [*British*]
POST............ Passive Optical Scan Tracker (MCD)
POST............ Passive Optical Seeker Technique
POST............ Payload Operations Support Team [*NASA*] (MCD)
POST............ Peace Officer Standards and Training
POST............ Peritoneal Ovum Sperm Transfer [*Medicine*]
POST............ Piezoelectric-Oscillator Self-Tuned [*Electric system*]
POST............ Point-of-Sale Terminal [*Business term*]
POST............ Point-of-Sale Transaction
POST............ Polaris Operation Support Task Group [*Missiles*]
POST............ Polar Stratospheric Telescope
POST............ Police Officer Student Training (AD)
POST............ Positive (AAG)
post............ Postage (AD)

POST .... Postemergence [*Weed control*]
POST .... [*The*] Poster [*A publication*] (ROG)
post .... Poster (VRA)
post .... Posterior
post .... Posterior [*Spanish*] (AD)
post .... Post Mortem (AD)
POST .... Postmortem (AAMN)
Post .... Post's Reports [*42-64 Missouri*] [*A publication*] (DLA)
Post .... Post's Reports [*23-26 Michigan*] [*A publication*] (DLA)
POST .... Power-On Self Test [*IBM-PC feature*]
POST .... Processes of Science Test (AD)
POST .... Production-Oriented Scheduling Techniques (MCD)
POST .... Programmer Operating Standards Technique
POST .... Program to Operate Simulated Trajectories
POST .... Program to Optimize Shuttle [*or Simulated*] Trajectories [*NASA*] (KSC)
POST .... Prototype Ocean Surveillance Terminal [*Navy*] (ANA)
Post & Ins ... Postage and Insurance (ILCA)
Post & Reg... Postage and Registration (DLA)
post-Aug ...... Post-Augustan (AD)
post aur .... Post Aurem [*Behind the Ear*] [*Latin*] (AD)
POST AUR ... Post Aurem [*Behind the Ear*] [*Pharmacy*]
POSTD .... Petty Officer Steward [*British military*] (DMA)
post d .... Posterior Diameter (AD)
POSTE .... Postage (ROG)
POSTEC .... Powder Science and Technology Research Association [*Norway*] (EAIO)
poster .... Posterior (AD)
POSTER .... Post Strike Emergency Reporting
pos terminal... Point-of-Sale Terminal (AD)
Poste's Gai... Poste's Translation of Gaius [*A publication*] (ILCA)
Poste's Gaius Inst... Poste's Translation of Gaius [*A publication*] (DLA)
POSTFAT ..... Postfinal Acceptance Trials [*Navy*] (NVT)
POSTFAX ..... Post Office Facsimile [*British*]
postgangl .... Postganglionic [*Medicine*] (MEDA)
postgangl .... Postganglionic [*Neurology*] (DAVI)
PostgradDipAgr... Postgraduate Diploma in Agriculture
PostGradDipEdStud(IndArts)... Postgraduate Diploma in Educational Studies (Industrial Arts)
Postgrad Med Inst... Postgraduate Medical Institute (AD)
Postgraduate D... Postgraduate Diploma (PGP)
posth .... Posthumous (AD)
POSTH .... Posthumous
postl .... Postlude (AD)
Postl Dict..... Postlethwaite's Dictionary of Trade and Commerce [*A publication*] (DLA)
post-mort..... Post Mortem (AD)
POSTNET ..... Postnumeric Encoding Technique [*US Postal Service*]
post-obit ...... Post Obitum [*After Death*] [*Latin*]
post ofc .... Post Office (VRA)
POSTOP .... Postoperative [*Medicine*]
post-op .... Post-Operative (AD)
POSTP .... Posterior Probability [*Computations*]
POSTP .... Postprocessor [*Computer science*]
post part...... Post Partum [*Afterbirth*] [*Latin*] (AD)
PostPr.......... Post Properties, Inc. [*Associated Press*] (SAG)
POSTPRO .... Postprocessor [*Computer science*]
PostPrp........ Post Properties, Inc. [*Associated Press*] (SAG)
POSTS .... Positive Occipital Sharp Transients of Sleep [*On electroencephalogram*] [*Neurology*] (DAVI)
Post Sag D... Posterior Sagittal Diameter [*Anatomy*] (MAE)
Post Script... Post Script: Essays in Film and the Humanities [*A publication*] (BRI)
POST SING SED LIQ... Post Singulas Sedes Liquidas [*After Every Loose Stool*] [*Pharmacy*] (ROG)
post-sync..... Post-Synchronization (AD)
POSV .... Pilot-Operated Solenoid Valve [*Nuclear energy*] (IAA)
POSWG........ Poseidon Software Working Group [*Missiles*]
pot .... Dashpot (IDOE)
POT.............. Paint on Tangent (IAA)
POT.............. Parallel Output
POT.............. Pennsylvania-Ontario Transportation Co. [*AAR code*]
POT.............. Periostitis Ossificans Toxica [*Medicine*] (DMAA)
POT.............. Physical Organization Table (HGAA)
POT.............. Picture Object Table (MHDI)
POT.............. Piston Operated Transducer
POT.............. Pitch-Orthogonal Thrust
POT.............. Plain Old Telephone [*Bell System's basic model*]
pot .... Point of tangency (AD)
POT.............. Polet [*Former USSR*] [*FAA designator*] (FAAC)
pot.............. Portable Outdoor Toilet (AD)
POT.............. Portable Outside Toilet [*A unit of mobility equipment*] [*Military*]
POT.............. Port Antonio [*Jamaica*] [*Airport symbol*] (OAG)
POT.............. Post Office Telecommunications [*British*]
POT.............. Post-Operative Treatment [*Medicine*] (DMAA)
POT.............. Potable
pot.............. Potash (AD)
POT.............. Potash Corp. of Saskatchewan [*NYSE symbol*] (SPSG)
POT.............. Potash Corp. Saskatchewan [*NYSE symbol*] (TTSB)
pot.............. Potassa [*Chemistry*] (MAE)
POT.............. Potassium [*Chemical symbol is K*]
POT.............. Potato (ROG)
POT.............. Potentate
POT.............. Potential (AFM)
pot.............. Potential (AD)
pot.............. Potential (WDMC)
pot.............. Potentiometer (IDOE)
pot.............. Potentiometer (AD)
POT.............. Potentiometer [*or Potentiometric*]
Pot.............. Potion
POT.............. Potsdam [*Germany*] [*Later, NGK*] [*Seismograph station code, US Geological Survey*] (SEIS)
POT.............. Pottery
POT.............. Pottle [*Unit of measure*] (ROG)
POT.............. Pottsville Free Public Library, Pottsville, PA [*OCLC symbol*] (OCLC)
POT.............. Potus [*A Drink*] [*Pharmacy*]
POT.............. Prevailing-Out Torque [*Automotive engineering*]
POT.............. Program for Operational Trajectories (USDC)
POT.............. Program for Operational Trajectories [*Marine science*] (OSRA)
POT.............. Propeller Order Transmitter (OA)
POTAD .... Program for Operational Transport and Dispersion (USDC)
PotAGT .... Potential Abnormality of Glucose Tolerance [*Medicine*]
POT & I .... Preoverhaul Tests and Inspections [*Navy*] (NVT)
POTANN....... Potomac Annex [*Navy*]
Potash .... Potash Corp. of Saskatchewan, Inc. [*Associated Press*] (SAG)
potash alum... Potassium Aluminum Sulfate (AD)
potass.......... Potassium [*An element*] (DAVI)
POTASWG.... Poseidon Test Analysis Software Working Group [*Missiles*]
potats .... Potatoes (AD)
POTBI .... Places, Organizations, Things, Biographics, Intangibles
POTC .... PERT [*Program Evaluation and Review Technique*] Orientation and Training Center
POTCP .... Partially Oxidized Tetracyanoplatinate Compound [*Inorganic, one-dimensional conductor*]
POTD .... Player of the Decade [*Sports*]
P o TD .... Port of The Dalles (AD)
POTDIF .... Potential Difference [*Electronics*] (IAA)
Pot Dwar ..... Potter's Edition of Dwarris on Statutes [*A publication*] (DLA)
PotEd25 .... Potomac Edison [*Associated Press*] (SAG)
PotEl............ Potomac Electric Power Co. [*Associated Press*] (SAG)
POTELECTROMET... Potentiometric Electrometer (IAA)
POTEN .... Potential (AAMN)
POTF .... Polychromatic Optical Thickness Fringe (OA)
POTF............ Psychological Operations Task Force [*Army*] (INF)
Poth Cont..... Pothier's Contracts [*A publication*] (DLA)
Poth Contr Sale... Pothier's Treatise on the Contract of Sale [*A publication*] (DLA)
Poth Cont Sale... Pothier's Treatise on the Contract of Sale [*A publication*] (DLA)
Pothier Pand... Pothier's Pandectae Justinianeae, Etc. [*A publication*] (DLA)
Poth Mar Cont... Pothier's Treatise on Maritime Contracts [*A publication*] (DLA)
Poth Ob .... Pothier on the Law of Obligations [*A publication*] (DLA)
Poth Obl ...... Pothier on the Law of Obligations [*A publication*] (DLA)
Poth Oblig ... Pothier on the Law of Obligations [*A publication*] (DLA)
Poth Oeuv... Oeuvres de Pothier [*A publication*] (DLA)
Poth Pand.... Pothier's Pandects [*A publication*] (DLA)
Poth Part ..... Pothier on Partnership [*A publication*] (DLA)
Poth Proc Civ... Pothier. Procedure Civile [*A publication*] (DLA)
POTIB .... Polaris Technical Information Bulletin [*Missiles*]
POTIB .... Poseidon Technical Information Bulletin [*A publication*] (AD)
potl-- .... Tokelau Islands [*MARC geographic area code Library of Congress*] (LCCP)
Pot LD .... Pott's Law Dictionary [*3rd ed.*] [*1815*] [*A publication*] (DLA)
Potltch .... Potlatch Corp. [*Associated Press*] (SAG)
POTMC .... Protective Outfit Toxicological Microclimate Controlled (RDA)
PotmEl......... Potomac Electric Power Co. [*Associated Press*] (SAG)
POTMLD ...... Potential Mixed Layer Depth
poto--.......... Tonga [*MARC geographic area code Library of Congress*] (LCCP)
POTOMAC.... Patent Office Techniques of Mechanized Access and Classification [*Automation project, shut down in 1972*]
potosslq....... Persons of the Opposite Sex Sharing Living Quarters (AD)
potr............. Potrero [*Cattle Ranch*] [*Spanish*] (AD)
PotrSvg....... Potters Savings & Loan Co. [*Associated Press*] (SAG)
POTS .... Perials of the Sea (MHDB)
POTS .... Petty Officer Telegraphist Special (DSUE)
POTS .... Photo-Optical Terrain Simulator (MUGU)
POTS .... Plain Old Telephone Service [*or System*] [*Humorous term for Long Lines Department of AT & T See also PANS*]
pots .... Plain Old Telephone Service (AD)
POTS .... PORI [*Polaris Operational Readiness Instrumentation*] Operational Test System [*Missiles*]
pots .... Potentiometers (AD)
POTS .... Precision Optical Tracking System (KSC)
POTS .... Preoverhaul Tests [*Navy*] (NVT)
POTS .... Purchase of Telephones and Services Program (AAGC)
POTS .... Purchase of Telephone Services Contracts
pott............. Pottery (AD)
pott--.......... Trust Territory of the Pacific Islands [*MARC geographic area code Library of Congress*] (LCCP)
Pott Corp ..... Potter on Corporations [*A publication*] (DLA)
Pott Dwarris... Potter's Edition of Dwarris on Statutes [*A publication*] (DLA)
Potter.......... Potter's Reports [*4-7 Wyoming*] [*A publication*] (DLA)
PottrFinl ...... Potters Financial Corp. [*Associated Press*] (SAG)
Potts LD ...... Potts' Law Dictionary [*3rd ed.*] [*1815*] [*A publication*] (DLA)
POTUS .... President of the United States
POTV .... Personnel Orbit Transfer Vehicle (MCD)
pot w .... Portable Water (AD)
POTW .... Potable Water (KSC)
POTW .... Publically-Owned Treatment Works (DNAB)
POTW .... Publicly Owned Treatment Works (EG)
POU .... Paramount Resources Ltd. [*Toronto Stock Exchange symbol*]
POU .... Placenta, Ovary, Uterus [*Medicine*]
POU .... Point of Use

POU .... Poughkeepsie [*New York*] [*Airport symbol*] (OAG)
POU .... Poughkeepsie, NY [*Location identifier FAA*] (FAAL)
POU .... Pouilloux [*France*] [*Seismograph station code, US Geological Survey*] (SEIS)
POUCC .... Post Office Users Coordination Committee [*British*]
POUF .... Projects of Optimum Urgency and Feasibility
PoughSv ...... [*The*] Poughkeepsie Savings Bank FSB [*Associated Press*] (SAG)
POUL .... Poultry
poul .... Poultry (AD)
POUM .... Partido Obrero de Unificacion Marxista [*Workers' Party of Marxist Unification*] [*Former USSR*] (LAIN)
POUNC .... Post Office Users' National Council [*British*] (ILCA)
POUP .... Post Overhaul Upkeep Period
poup-- .... United States Miscellaneous Pacific Islands [*MARC geographic area code Library of Congress*] (LCCP)
POU/POE ...... Point-of-Use/Point-of-Entry [*Water standards*] (FFDE)
POUR .... President's Organization for Unemployment Relief (AD)
POUS .... Partido Operario de Unidade Socialista [*Workers' Party for Socialist Unity*] [*Portugal Political party*] (PPW)
POV .... Peak Operated Valve (MCD)
POV .... Peak Operating Voltage
POV .... Pend Oreille Valley Railroad (AD)
POV .... Persistence of Vision - Ray [*Computer program*]
POV .... Personally Owned Vehicle
POV .... Pinch-Off Voltage
POV .... Pittsburgh & Ohio Valley Railway Co. [*AAR code*]
POV .... Plane of Vibration
POV .... Pneumatically Operated Valve
POV .... Point of View
p-o-v .... Point-of-View (AD)
POV .... Presov [*Czechoslovakia*] [*Airport symbol*] (AD)
POV .... Pressure-Operated Valve (MCD)
POV .... Privately Owned Vehicle (NVT)
pov .... Privately Owned Vehicle (AD)
POV .... Proximity Operations Vehicle (SSD)
POV .... Purchase, Outside Vendors
POV .... Putting-On Voltage [*Doppler navigation*] (DEN)
POVC .... Probation Officers and Volunteers in Corrections [*Victoria, Australia*]
POVEU .... Program Operations Vocational Education Unit (OICC)
Pov L Rep ... Poverty Law Reporter [*Commerce Clearing House*] [*A publication*] (DLA)
POVT .... Puerperal Ovarian-Vein Thrombophlebitis [*Medicine*]
POW .... Paying Their Own Way
POW .... Pay Order of Withdrawal
POW .... Peoples of the World [*A publication*]
POW .... Perception of Ward [*Scales*] [*Psychology*]
POW .... Petty Officer of the Watch [*Navy*]
POW .... Powassan Encephalitis [*Medicine*]
POW .... Powder [*Navy*]
POW .... Power
pow .... Power (AD)
POW .... Power Corp. of Canada [*Toronto Stock Exchange symbol Vancouver Stock Exchange symbol*]
POW .... Powhatan [*Arkansas*] [*Seismograph station code, US Geological Survey*] (SEIS)
POW .... Prince of Wales
P o W .... Prince of Wales (AD)
pow .... Prisoner of War (AD)
POW .... Prisoner of War [*Also, PW*]
P o W .... Prisoner of Watergate (AD)
POW .... Progressive Order of the West [*Defunct*] (EA)
POWACO ...... Portable Water Coolant Circulator
Pow App Proc... Powell's Law of Appellate Proceedings [*A publication*] (DLA)
PoWBN .... Biblioteka Narodowa [*National Library*], Warsaw, Poland [*Library symbol Library of Congress*] (LCLS)
PoWC .... Instytut Informacji Naukowej, Technicznej, i Ekonomicznej, Warsaw, Poland [*Library symbol Library of Congress*] (LCLS)
Pow Car .... Powell's Inland Carriers [*2nd ed.*] [*1861*] [*A publication*] (DLA)
Pow Cont ..... Powell on Contracts [*A publication*] (DLA)
Pow Conv .... Powell. Conveyancing [*1810*] [*A publication*] (ILCA)
POW Country... Potash, Oil, and Wheat Country [*Saskatoon, Saskatchewan*] (AD)
powd .... Powder (AD)
POWD .... Powder [*England*]
POWD .... Powdered
Pow Dev ...... Powell's Essay upon the Learning of Devises, Etc. [*A publication*] (DLA)
POWDR .... Protect Our Wetlands and Duck Resources [*Department of the Interior*] [*Washington, DC*]
Powell .... Powell Industries, Inc. [*Associated Press*] (SAG)
POWER .... Pension Opportunities for Workers' Expanded Retirement [*Plan proposed in 1991 by the Department of Labor*]
POWER .... People Organized and Working for Economic Rebirth [*Program for black economic development*] [*Later, Nationway Ventures International Ltd.*]
POWER .... Performance Optimization with Enhanced RISC [*Reduced Instruction Set Computer*] (PCM)
POWER .... Planning Operation With Enabling Resources
POWER .... Priority Output Writers Execution Processor [*Computer science*] (IAA)
POWER .... Priority Output Writers, Execution Processors, and Input Readers (MHDI)
POWER .... Priority Output Writes Execution Process [*Computer science*] (IAA)
POWER .... Professionals Organized for Women's Equal Rights [*Feminist group*]
POWER .... PROFS [*Program for Regional Observing and Forecasting Services*] Operational Weather Education and Research (USDC)
POWER .... PROFS [*Program for Regional Observing and Forecasting Services*] Operational Weather Education and Research [*Marine science*] (OSRA)
power .... Programmed Operational Warshot Evaluation and Review (AD)
POWER .... Programmed Operational Warshot Evaluation and Review
POWER .... Promote Our Wonderful Energy Resources (EA)
Powers .... Powers' Reports, New York Surrogate Court [*A publication*] (DLA)
Power's Sur... Powers' Reports, New York Surrogate Court [*A publication*] (DLA)
Pow Ev .... Powell on Evidence [*10th ed.*] [*1921*] [*A publication*] (DLA)
powf-- .... Wallis and Futuna [*MARC geographic area code Library of Congress*] (LCCP)
POWG .... Procurement Officers Work Group (AAGC)
Pow Inl Car... Powell on the Law of Inland Carriers [*A publication*] (DLA)
POW(J) .... Prisoner of War of Japan
powk-- .... Wake Island [*MARC geographic area code Library of Congress*] (LCCP)
POWL .... Powell Indus [*NASDAQ symbol*] (TTSB)
POWL .... Powell Industries, Inc. [*NASDAQ symbol*] (NQ)
POW/MIG ..... Place of Work and Migration Sample [*Bureau of the Census*] (GFGA)
Pow Mort ..... Powell on Mortgages [*6th ed.*] [*1826*] [*A publication*] (DLA)
Pow Mortg ... Powell on Mortgages [*A publication*] (DLA)
POWO .... Prince [*or Princess*] of Wales' Own [*Military unit*] [*British*] (DMA)
PoWP .... Biblioteka Golowna Politechniki Warszawsjiej (Warsaw Technical University Central Library), Warsaw, Poland [*Library symbol Library of Congress*] (LCLS)
POWP .... Preliminary Overhaul Work Package (DNAB)
POWR .... Environmental Power [*NASDAQ symbol*] (SAG)
Pow R & D... Power, Rodwell, and Drew's English Election Cases [*1847-56*] [*A publication*] (DLA)
PowrCrv .... PowerCerv Corp. [*Associated Press*] (SAG)
POWRENAF... Petty Officer WREN [*Women's Royal Naval Service*] Air Fitter [*British military*] (DMA)
POWRENCINE... Petty Officer WREN [*Women's Royal Naval Service*] Cinema Operator [*British military*] (DMA)
POWRENCK... Petty Officer WREN [*Women's Royal Naval Service*] Cook [*British military*] (DMA)
POWRENDHYG... Petty Officer WREN [*Women's Royal Naval Service*] Dental Hygienist [*British military*] (DMA)
POWRENDSA... Petty Officer WREN [*Women's Royal Naval Service*] Dental Surgery Assistant [*British military*] (DMA)
POWRENMET... Petty Officer WREN [*Women's Royal Naval Service*] Meteorological Observer [*British military*] (DMA)
POWRENMT... Petty Officer WREN [*Women's Royal Naval Service*] Motor Transport Driver [*British military*] (DMA)
POWRENPHOT... Petty Officer WREN [*Women's Royal Naval Service*] Photographer [*British military*] (DMA)
POWRENQA... Petty Officer WREN [*Women's Royal Naval Service*] Quarters Assistant [*British military*] (DMA)
POWREN(R)... Petty Officer WREN [*Women's Royal Naval Service*] (RADAR) [*British military*] (DMA)
POWRENREL... Petty Officer WREN [*Women's Royal Naval Service*] Radio Electrician [*British military*] (DMA)
POWRENRS(M)... Petty Officer WREN [*Women's Royal Naval Service*] Radio Supervisor (Morse) [*British military*] (DMA)
POWRENSA... Petty Officer WREN [*Women's Royal Naval Service*] Stores Accountant [*British military*] (DMA)
POWRENS(C)... Petty Officer WREN [*Women's Royal Naval Service*] Stores Assistant (Clothes) [*British military*] (DMA)
POWRENS(S)... Petty Officer WREN [*Women's Royal Naval Service*] Stores Assistant (Stores) [*British military*] (DMA)
POWRENSTD... Petty Officer WREN [*Women's Royal Naval Service*] Steward [*British military*] (DMA)
POWRENS(V)... Petty Officer WREN [*Women's Royal Naval Service*] Stores Assistant (Victualling) [*British military*] (DMA)
POWRENTEL... Petty Officer WREN [*Women's Royal Naval Service*] Telephonist [*British military*] (DMA)
POWRENTSA... Petty Officer WREN [*Women's Royal Naval Service*] Training Support Assistant [*British military*] (DMA)
POWRENWA... Petty Officer WREN [*Women's Royal Naval Service*] Weapon Analyst [*British military*] (DMA)
POWRENWTR(G)... Petty Officer WREN [*Women's Royal Naval Service*] Writer (General) [*British military*] (DMA)
POWRENWTR(P)... Petty Officer WREN [*Women's Royal Naval Service*] Writer (Pay) [*British military*] (DMA)
POWRENWW... Petty Officer WREN [*Women's Royal Naval Service*] Welfare Worker [*British military*] (DMA)
Powrwv .... Powerwave Technologies, Inc. [*Associated Press*] (SAG)
POWS .... PROFS [*Program for Regional Observing and Forecasting Services*] Operational Work Station [*Marine science*] (OSRA)
POWS .... PROFS [*Program for Regional Observing and Forecasting Services*] Operational Work Station (USDC)
POWS .... Project Operating Work Statement [*NASA*] (NASA)
POWS .... Pyrotechnic Outside Warning System (IEEE)
pows-- .... Western Samoa [*MARC geographic area code Library of Congress*] (LCCP)
POW-SIG ..... Pagan/Occult/Witchcraft Special Interest Group (EA)
Pow Surr ..... Powers' Reports, New York Surrogate Court [*A publication*] (DLA)
POWTECH .... International Powder and Bulk Solids Technology Exhibition and Conference
POWTR .... Petty Officer Writer [*British military*] (DMA)
POWU .... Post Office Work Unit [*Computer performance measure*] [*British Telecom*]
PoWU .... Uniwersytet Warszawski [*University of Warsaw*], Warsaw, Poland [*Library symbol Library of Congress*] (LCLS)
POW:WE ...... Peoples of the World: Western Europeans [*A publication*]

POWWER..... Power of World Wide Energy Resources [*In organization name "Natural POWWER"*] (EA)
POX............ Partial Oxidation [*Organic chemistry*]
POX............ Point of Exit
POX............ Port Alexander [*Alaska*] [*Airport symbol*] (AD)
P-OX........... Pressure Oxidation
POX............ Purgeable Organic Halogen [*Chemistry*] (FFDE)
POX-AC........ Pox Battery, Acute [*Biochemistry*] (DAVI)
poxd--.......... Mariana Islands [*MARC geographic area code Library of Congress*] (LCCP)
poxe--.......... Marshall Islands [*MARC geographic area code Library of Congress*] (LCCP)
poxf--.......... Midway Islands [*MARC geographic area code Library of Congress*] (LCCP)
poxh--.......... Niue [*MARC geographic area code Library of Congress*] (LCCP)
POY............ Lovell-Powell [*Wyoming*] [*Airport symbol*] (AD)
POY............ Partially Oriented Yarns
POY............ Polyester Oriented Yarn (DICI)
POY............ Powell, WY [*Location identifier FAA*] (FAAL)
POY............ Prairie Oil Royalties Co. Ltd. [*AMEX symbol Toronto Stock Exchange symbol*] (SPSG)
poy............ Pre-Oriented Yarn (AD)
Poynt M & D... Poynter on Marriage and Divorce [*2nd ed.*] [*1824*] [*A publication*] (DLA)
POYO........... Pollo Tropical [*NASDAQ symbol*] (SAG)
POZ............ Poznan [*Poland*] [*Airport symbol*] (OAG)
Poz............ Poznan (AD)
PP............. Brazil [*International civil aircraft marking*] (ODBW)
PP............. Eisai Co. Ltd. [*Japan*] [*Research code symbol*]
PP............. Free Library of Philadelphia, Philadelphia, PA [*Library symbol Library of Congress*] (LCLS)
PP............. Pacific Petroleum (AD)
PP............. Page Printer (NVT)
PP............. Pages
Pp............. Pages (WDMC)
pp............. Pages (WDMC)
PP............. Pages from the Past [*Later, PIR*] [*An association*] (EA)
PP............. Palisades Plant [*Nuclear energy*] (NRCH)
PP............. Palus Putretudinis [*Lunar area*]
PP............. Pancreatic Polypeptide [*Biochemistry*]
PP............. Pandectes Periodiques [*A publication*] (ILCA)
PP............. Panel Point [*Technical drawings*]
pp............. Panel Point (AD)
PP............. Pangu Pati [*Papua New Guinea*] [*Political party*] (PPW)
PP............. Papa [*Pope*]
Pp............. Papa [*Father*] [*Latin*] (AD)
PP............. Paper Profit
pp............. Papua New Guinea [*MARC country of publication code Library of Congress*] (LCCP)
PP............. Paradigm Publishing Ltd. [*British*]
PP............. Paradoxical Pulse [*Medicine*] (DMAA)
PP............. Parallel Processor
PP............. Parcel Post
pp............. Parcel Post (AD)
PP............. Parish Priest
PP............. Paris Publications, Inc.
PP............. Parity Price (MHDW)
PP............. Parliamentary Papers [*A publication British*]
P/P............ Partial Pay [*Air Force*]
PP............. Partial Pressure
PP............. Partial Product (IAA)
PP............. Partial Program
PP............. Partia Popullore [*Popular Party*] [*Albania*] [*Political party*] (PPE)
PP............. Particular [*Named*] Port [*British*] (ROG)
PP............. Partido Panamenista [*Panamanian Party*] [*Political party*] (PPW)
PP............. Partido Popular [*Popular Party*] [*Spain Political party*] (PPE)
PP............. Partido Populista [*Populist Party*] [*Argentina Political party*]
PP............. Parti du Peuple [*People's Party*] [*Burundi*] [*Political party*]
PP............. Partners in Politics (EA)
PP............. Part Paid [*Business and trade*]
pp............. Part Paid (AD)
PP............. Parts Per
PP............. [*The*] Passionate Pilgrim [*Shakespearean work*]
PP............. Passive Participle
pp............. Passive Participle (AD)
PP............. Pastor Pastorum [*Shepherd of the Shepherds*] [*Latin*] (ROG)
PP............. Past Participle
pp............. Past Participle (WDMC)
PP............. Past Patriarch [*Freemasonry*] (ROG)
PP............. Past President
P/P............ Patch Panel (NASA)
PP............. Patent Pending (IAA)
PP............. Pater Patriae [*The Father of His Country*] [*Latin*]
PP............. Patres [*Fathers*] [*Latin*]
PP............. Patriotic Party [*British*]
PP............. Patrol Vessels [*Navy symbol*] (MUGU)
PP............. Peace PAC (EA)
PP............. Peak Power (IAA)
P_p............. Peak Power (IDOE)
PP............. Peak Pressure
PP............. Peak-to-Peak
PP............. Peanut Pals (EA)
PP............. Pedal Power
PP............. Pedal Pulse
PP............. Pellagra Preventive [*Factor*] [*See also PPF*] [*Biochemistry*]
pp............. Pellagra Preventive (AD)
P-P............ Pellagra-Preventive Factor (AD)
PP............. Pension Plan
PP............. People's Party [*Spain Political party*] (ECON)
PP............. People's Party [*Halkci Partisi*] [*Turkey Political party*] (PPW)
PP............. Pep Pill [*Slang*]
pp............. Perceptual Performance (AD)
PP............. Perfusion Pressure [*Cardiology*] (DAVI)
PP............. Periodical Publications [*British Library shelf designation*]
PP............. Peripheral Processor [*Computer science*]
PP............. Periportal [*Anatomy*]
PP............. Periproct [*Invertebrate anatomy*]
PP............. Permanent Partial [*Dentistry*] (MAE)
PP............. Permanent Party [*Military*]
pp............. Permanent Party (AD)
PP............. Permanent Pasture [*Agriculture*]
PP............. Permanent Press (ADA)
PP............. Permanent Professor
PP............. Peroxisome Proliferator [*Biochemistry*]
pp............. Per Person (AD)
PP............. Per Procurationem [*By Proxy, By the Action Of*] [*Legal term Latin*]
PP............. Personal Prelatures [*Diocesan abbreviation*] (TOCD)
PP............. Personal Property
P-P............ Person to Person [*Word processing*]
PP............. Pet Pride (EA)
PP............. Petroleum Point
PP............. Petrus Piccoli de Monteforte [*Flourished, 14th century*] [*Authority cited in pre-1607 legal work*] (DSA)
PP............. Petticoat Peeping [*From one girl to another, in reference to dress disarrangement*]
PP............. Peyer's Patch [*Immunology*]
PP............. Phillips Airlines [*ICAO designator*] (AD)
PP............. Philo-Phobe [*Psychological testing*]
P-P............ Phoenix Project [*An association*] (EA)
PP............. Phony Peach Bacteria [*Plant pathology*]
PP............. Photosynthetic Panel [*i.e., leaf*] [*Slang*]
PP............. Physical Profile
pp............. Physical Profile (AD)
pp............. Physical Properties (AD)
PP............. Physical Properties
PP............. Phytophthora Parasitica [*A fungus*]
PP............. Pianissimo [*Very Softly*] [*Music*]
pp............. Pianissimo [*Very Softly*] [*Music*] (ODBW)
PP............. Picked Ports
PP............. Pickpocket
pp............. Pickpocket (AD)
PP............. Picture Peace [*Defunct*] (EA)
pp............. Piena Pelle [*Full Leather*] [*Italian*] (AD)
PP............. Piers Plowman [*Middle English poem*]
P/P............ Pier to Pier (ADA)
PP............. Piissimus [*Most Holy*] [*Latin*]
PP............. Pilotless Plane
PP............. Pilot Parents (EA)
PP............. Pilot Punch
PP............. Pine Bark Mixed with Peat
PP............. Pink Puffer [*Emphysema*] (MAE)
PP............. Pinpoint (MAE)
PP............. Pinpoint [*Pupils*] [*Ophthalmology*] (DAVI)
PP............. Pinprick [*Medicine*] (DMAA)
PP............. Pipeline Processor (IAA)
PP............. Piping
PP............. Piscataqua Pioneers (EA)
PP............. Piu Piano [*More Softly*] [*Music*]
PP............. PIXEL-Processing [*Computer science*]
PP............. Placental Protein [*Gynecology*]
PP............. Place of Publisher (NITA)
PP............. Plane Parallel
PP............. Plane Polarized [*Telecommunications*] (TEL)
PP............. Planetary Programs [*NASA*]
PP............. Planned Parenthood
PP............. Planning Package [*NASA*] (NASA)
pp............. Planning Permission (AD)
PP............. Planning Purpose
PP............. Plan Profile
PP............. Plant Protection
PP............. Plasmapheresis [*Hematology*]
PP............. Plasma Protein
PP............. Plaster of Paris
PP............. Plate Power (IAA)
P_p............. Plate Power (IDOE)
PP............. Plate Pulse (IAA)
PP............. Play or Pay (ROG)
PP............. Please Pay (ROG)
PP............. Plethysmograph Pressure [*Measurement*] [*Medicine*] (DAVI)
PP............. Pleural Pressure [*Medicine*]
PP............. Plot Points [*Computer science*]
PP............. Pluvius Policy [*Insurance against rain*]
PP............. Pocketpiece [*A. C. Nielsen Co.*] [*Rating report*] (NTCM)
PP............. Poetry Project (EA)
P/P............ Point-to-Point [*Air Force*]
PP............. Polar Pacific [*American air mass*]
PP............. Pole Piece (DEN)
PP............. Pole Position [*Automobile racing*]
PP............. Polizei Pistole [*Police Pistol*] [*Walther Waffenfabrik, German arms manufacturer*]

PP ... Polypeptide [*Biochemistry*]
PP ... Polyphosphate [*Inorganic chemistry*] (AAMN)
PP ... Polypropylene [*Organic chemistry*]
PP ... Polypyrrole [*Photovoltaic energy systems*]
PP ... Pom-Pom [*Gun*]
PP ... Pontificum [*Of the Popes*] [*Latin*]
PP ... Popular Party [*European political movement*] (ECON)
PP ... Population Planning (DAVI)
PP ... Populist Party of America [*Political party*] (EA)
PP ... Porcelain Pavers (DICI)
PP ... Port Pipe (ADA)
PP ... Posa Piano [*Handle with Care*] [*Shipping*] [*Italian*]
PP ... Position Paper (MCD)
PP ... Postage Paid [*Shipping*]
pp ... Postage Paid (AD)
pp ... Posted Price (MENA)
PP ... Posterior Parietal Cortex [*Neuroanatomy*]
PP ... Posterior Pituitary [*Medicine*]
PP ... Post Pagado [*Postage Paid*] [*Shipping*] [*Spanish*]
pp ... Postpaid
PP ... Postpartum [*Medicine*] (CPH)
PP ... Post Partum [*After Birth*] [*Latin*] (ADA)
pp ... Post Partum [*Afterbirth*] [*Latin*] (AD)
PP ... Postpass
PP ... Postponed
PP ... Post Position [*Racing*]
PP ... Postprandial [*After Meals*] [*Pharmacy*]
PP ... Post Processing
PP ... Postprocessor [*Computer science*] (IAA)
PP ... Pounds Pressure
PP ... Pour Point [*Petroleum characteristic*]
PP ... Power Package
PP ... Power People
PP ... Power Plan (IAA)
PP ... Power Plant
PP ... Power Play [*Hockey*]
PP ... Power Pole (NASA)
PP ... Power Supplies [*JETDS nomenclature*] [*Military*] (CET)
PP ... Praemissis Praemittendis [*Omitting Preliminaries, To Whom It May Concern*] [*Latin*]
PP ... Praepter Propter [*Approximately*] [*Pharmacy*]
Pp ... Pratylenchus penetrans [*A nematode*]
PP ... Preferred Provider [*Medicine*] (DMAA)
PP ... Prentiss Properties Trust [*NYSE symbol*] (SAG)
PP ... Prepaid
PP ... Preparative Flag [*Navy British*]
PP ... Preparing, Providing [*Pharmacy*] (ROG)
PP ... Preposition [*Industrial engineering*]
PP ... Prepositional Phrase (BYTE)
PP ... Prepregnancy [*Medicine*]
PP ... Preprinted
PP ... Preprocessor
PP ... Preproduction (KSC)
PP ... Prescribed Period [*Social Security Administration*] (OICC)
PP ... Present Participle [*Grammar*]
PP ... Present Position [*Military*]
pp ... Present Position (AD)
PP ... Present Pupil (AIE)
PP ... Press Packed
PP ... Press Pressure (SSD)
PP ... Pressure Pattern (MCD)
PP ... Pressure-Proof [*Technical drawings*]
pp ... Pressure-Proof (AD)
PP ... Pretty Poor [*Slang Bowdlerized version*]
PP ... Primarily Primates [*An association*] (EA)
PP ... Primary Pressure [*Nuclear energy*] (NRCH)
PP ... Primary Producers (ADA)
PP ... Princess Pat's [*Princess Patricia of Connaught's Light Infantry*] [*Military unit*] [*Canada*]
PP ... Principal
PP ... Principal Point
PP ... Printer Page [*Computer science*]
P/P ... Printer/Plotter (NASA)
PP ... Print Positions
PP ... Print-Punch [*Computer science*] (BUR)
PP ... Priority Message Precedence [*Telecommunications*] (ADDR)
PP ... Priority Processor
PP ... Prior Permission
PP ... Private Jet Services AG [*Sweden ICAO designator*] (ICDA)
PP ... Privately Printed
pp ... Privately Printed (AD)
pp ... Privately Printed (WDMC)
P/P ... Private Passenger
PP ... Private Patient [*Medicine*]
PP ... Private Practice [*Chiropody*] [*British*]
PP ... Private Property [*Military*]
pp ... Private Property (AD)
PP ... Procurement Package (AAGC)
PP ... Procurement Plan (MCD)
PP ... Producer Price
PP ... Production Processes
PP ... Product Publication (IAA)
PP ... Professional Paper
pp ... Professional Paper (AD)
PP ... Professor Publicus [*Public Professor*] [*Latin*] (ROG)
PP ... Programming Plan (AFM)
PP ... Program Package (MCD)
PP ... Program Paper
PP ... Program Performance (NASA)
PP ... Program Product [*Computer science*]
PP ... Progress Payments [*Military procurement*]
PP ... Project Priesthood (EA)
PP ... Project Proposal (KSC)
PP ... Proletarian Party
PP ... Proodeftiki Parataxis [*Progressive Front*] [*Greek Cyprus*] [*Political party*] (PPE)
pp ... Pro Parte [*In Part*] [*Latin*]
PP ... Propeller Pitch
PP ... Proportional Part
PP ... Proposals Paper
PP ... Propria Persona [*In His or Her Own Person*] [*Latin*] (WGA)
PP ... Propulsion Power (KSC)
PP ... Protein Phosphatase [*An enzyme*]
PP ... Prothrombin-Proconvertin [*Hematology*]
PP ... Proton-Proton [*Nuclear physics*]
PP ... Protoporphyria [*Medicine*]
PP ... Protoporphyrin [*Biochemistry*]
PP ... Provisioning Procedures [*Corps of Engineers*]
PP ... Proximal Phalanx [*Anatomy*]
PP ... Pseudomyxoma Peritonei [*Medicine*] (DMAA)
PP ... Pseudoprogram (IAA)
PP ... Psychic Phenomena
PP ... Psychological Profile
PP ... Psychologists and Psychiatrists [*in service*] [*British*]
P/P ... Pterocephaliid-Ptychaspid [*Paleogeologic boundary*]
PP ... Public Property
PP ... Published Price [*of a book*]
PP ... Pulse Pair (IAA)
PP ... Pulse Polarography [*Analytical chemistry*]
PP ... Pulse Pressure [*Medicine*]
P-P ... Pulse to Pulse
PP ... Pulvis Patrum [*The Fathers' Powder (or Jesuits' Powder)*] [*Pharmacy*] (ROG)
PP ... Pump-Priming (MHDB)
PP ... Punctum Proximum [*Near Point*] [*Latin*]
pp ... Purchased Part (AD)
PP ... Purchased Parts
PP ... Purchase Power [*Commercial firm*] (EA)
PP ... Purchase Price
PP ... Pusher Plane
PP ... Push-Pull [*Technical drawings*]
p-p ... Push-Pull (AD)
PP ... Pyrophosphate [*Chemistry*]
PP1 ... Protein Phosphatase 1 [*An enzyme*]
PPA ... Athenaeum of Philadelphia, Philadelphia, PA [*Library symbol Library of Congress*] (LCLS)
PPA ... National Plant Protection Association
PPA ... Pakistan Press Association (AD)
PPA ... Pakistan Press Association (NADA)
PPA ... Paleopathology Association (EA)
PPA ... Palpation, Percussion, and Auscultation [*Medicine*]
ppa ... Palpitation, Percussion, Auscultation (AD)
PPA ... Pampa, TX [*Location identifier FAA*] (FAAL)
PPA ... Panamerican/Panafrican Association (EA)
PPA ... Paper Pail Association [*Defunct*] (EA)
PPA ... Paper Plate Association [*Later, SSI*] (EA)
PPA ... Parallel Processing Automata (PDAA)
PPA ... Parcel Post Association [*Later, PSA*] (EA)
PPA ... Parents for Private Adoption [*Defunct*] (EA)
PPA ... Partido Panamenista Autentico [*Panama*] [*Political party*] (EY)
PPA ... Partido Patriotico Arubano [*Aruban Patriotic Party*] [*Netherlands Antilles*] [*Political party*] (PPW)
PPA ... Partido Peronista Autentico [*Authentic Peronist Party*] [*Argentina Political party*] (EY)
PPA ... Pathology Practice Association (EA)
PPA ... Peat Producers Association [*British*] (EAIO)
PPA ... Pensioner Party of Australia [*Political party*]
PPA ... Pension Portability Act of 1992 (WYGK)
PPA ... Pension Protection Act (GFGA)
PPA ... People for Prison Alternatives [*An association*] (AD)
PPA ... People for Prison Alternatives [*An association*] (NADA)
PPA ... Peppa Resources [*Vancouver Stock Exchange symbol*]
PPA ... Perennial Plant Association (EA)
PPA ... Periodical Publishers Association [*Later, MCA*] (EA)
PPA ... Per Power of Attorney [*Business term*]
ppa ... Per Procura [*By Proxy*] [*Latin*]
PPA ... Personnel Pool of America [*An association*] (AD)
PPA ... Pesticide Producers Association [*Defunct*] (EA)
PPA ... Pet Producers of America (EA)
PPA ... Phenylpropanolamine [*Organic chemistry*]
ppa ... Phenylpropanolamine (AD)
PPA ... Phenylpropanolamine(hydrochloride) [*Also, PPH, PPM*] [*Decongestant*]
PPA ... Phenylpyruvic Acid [*Organic chemistry*]
PPA ... Phiala Prius Agitata [*Having First Shaken the Bottle*] [*Pharmacy*]
ppa ... Phiala Prius Agitate [*Bottle Having First Been Shaken*] [*Latin*] (AD)
PPA ... Phosphoric Acid Anodized (PDAA)
PPA ... Photo Peak Analysis (IEEE)
ppa ... Photo-Peak Analysis (AD)
PPA ... Pianoforte Publicity Association [*British*] (BI)

PPA............ Pictorial Photographers of America (EAIO)
PPA............ Pie De Palo [*Argentina*] [*Seismograph station code, US Geological Survey*] (SEIS)
PPA............ Pilot Pulse Amplitude
PPA............ Pilots and Passengers Association [*Defunct*] (EA)
PPA............ Pitch Precession Amplifier
PPA............ Pittsburgh Pneumonia Agent [*Microbiology*]
PPA............ Planned Program Accomplishment (GNE)
PPA............ Plant Patent Act [*1930*]
PPA............ Plasminogen Proactivator [*Hematology*]
PPA............ Plutonium Preparation Area [*Nuclear energy*] (GFGA)
PPA............ Policyholders Protective Association of America (EA)
PPA............ Pollution Prevention Act [*1990*]
PPA............ Polymer Permeation Analyzer
PPA............ Poly(phosphoric Acid) [*Inorganic chemistry*]
PPA............ Pool Promoters Association [*British*] (BI)
PPA............ Popcorn Processors Association [*Later, PI*]
PPA............ Popski's Private Army [*Commando force led by Vladimir Peniakoff*] [*World War II*]
PPA............ Population Planning Associates (BABM)
PPA............ Population Planning Associates [*Medicine*] (DAVI)
PPA............ Portland Port Authority [*Australia*]
PPA............ Postpartum Amenorrhea [*Medicine*]
PPA............ Post-Pill Amenorrhea [*Medicine*] (MEDA)
PPA............ Potato Processors' Association [*Australia*]
PPA............ Potato Processors Association [*British*] (DBA)
PPA............ Poultry Publishers Association (EA)
PPA............ Power Plant Automation
PPA............ Powerplant Performance Analysis
PPA............ Preferred Provider Arrangement [*Information service or system*] (HCT)
PPA............ Preferred Provider Arrangement
PPA............ Preliminary Pile Assembly (IAA)
PPA............ Preschool Playgrounds Association [*British*]
PPA............ Prescription Pricing Authority (PDAA)
PPA............ Presidents' Professional Association [*Later, Presidents Association*] (EA)
PPA............ Press and Publications Administration [*China*]
PPA............ Princeton Particle Accelerator (IAA)
PPA............ Princeton-Pennsylvania Accelerator [*Closed, 1972*] [*AEC*]
PPA............ Princeton-Pennsylvania Proton Accelerator [*Closed, 1972*] [*AEC*] (IAA)
PPA............ Principal Port Authority [*British*] (ROG)
PPA............ Printers' Provident Association (DGA)
PPA............ Printing Platemakers Association [*Later, GPA*]
PPA............ Priority Problem Areas (MCD)
PPA............ Process Plan Association [*British*] (DS)
PPA............ Process Plant Association [*British*] (DBA)
PPA............ Produce Packaging Association [*Later, PMA*] (EA)
PPA............ Professional Panhellenic Association [*Later, PFA*] (EA)
PPA............ Professional Photographers of America (AD)
PPA............ Professional Photographers of America (NADA)
PPA............ Professional Programmers Association (EA)
PPA............ Professional Putters Association (EA)
PPA............ Program Problem Area
PPA............ Progressive Party of America [*Third party in 1948 Presidential race*]
PPA............ Progress Presse Agentur GmbH [*Press agency*] [*Germany*]
PPA............ Proletarian Party of America [*Political party*] (AD)
PPA............ Proletarian Party of America (NADA)
PPA............ Prompt Payment Act (AAGC)
PPA............ Propane Phosphonic Acid Anhydride [*Organic chemistry*]
PPA............ Propane-Precipitated Asphalt [*Petroleum technology*]
PPA............ Property Protection Area
PPA............ Propheter Construction Co., Inc. [*ICAO designator*] (FAAC)
PPA............ Protected Partition Area [*Telecommunications*] (IAA)
PPA............ Protestant Press Agency [*British*]
PPA............ Prudent Purchaser Arrangement [*Medical insurance*]
PPA............ Pseudopassive Array
PPA............ Public Personnel Association [*Later, IPMA*] (EA)
PPA............ Publishers' Publicity Association (EA)
PPA............ Pulmonary Artery Pressure [*Cardiology*]
Ppa............ Pulmonary Artery Pressure [*Medicine*] (DMAA)
PPA............ Pulsed Power Amplifier
PPA............ Pulse Plasma Accelerator
PPA............ Pure Pulmonary Atresia [*Medicine*] (DMAA)
PPA............ Purple Plum Association [*Defunct*] (EA)
PPA............ Push-Pull Amplifier (IAA)
PPAA.......... Patres Amplissimi [*Cardinals*] [*Latin*]
PPAA.......... Personal Protective Armor Association (EA)
PPAAR........ Princeton University, Pennsylvania University, Army Avionics Research (PDAA)
PPAB.......... Program and Policy Advisory Board [*UN Food and Agriculture Organization*]
PPABP........ American Baptist Publication Society, Philadelphia, PA [*Library symbol Library of Congress Obsolete*] (LCLS)
PP-AC......... Air-Conditioning Power Panel (DAC)
PPAC.......... Pesticide Policy Advisory Committee [*Environmental Protection Agency*]
PPAC.......... Primary Progress Assessment Chart [*Psychology*]
PPAC.......... Private Planning Association of Canada
PPAC.......... Product Performance Agreement Center [*Military*]
PPAC.......... Progressive Political Action Committee [*Defunct*]
PPAC.......... Public Parks Advisory Committee [*South Australia*]
PPACE......... United States Army, Corps of Engineers, Philadelphia District Library, Custom House, Philadelphia, PA [*Library symbol Library of Congress*] (LCLS)
PPAChi........ American Catholic Historical Society, Philadelphia, PA [*Library symbol Library of Congress*] (LCLS)
PPADS......... Parawing Precision Aerial Delivery System (MCD)
PPAEM......... Albert Einstein Medical Center, Northern Division, Philadelphia, PA [*Library symbol Library of Congress*] (LCLS)
PPAFA......... Pennsylvania Academy of the Fine Arts, Philadelphia, PA [*Library symbol Library of Congress Obsolete*] (LCLS)
PPAG........... Personnel Profile - Age by Grade [*Army*]
PPAI............ Pinpoint Assignment Instructions [*Army*] (INF)
PPAK........... Atwater Kent Museum, Philadelphia, PA [*Library symbol Library of Congress*] (LCLS)
PPAL........... Pennsylvania Power & Light Co. (IAA)
PPAL........... Principal (ROG)
PPaIZ.......... New Jersey Zinc Co. [*of Pennsylvania*], Technical Library, Palmerton, PA [*Library symbol Library of Congress*] (LCLS)
PPAmP........ American Philosophical Society, Philadelphia, PA [*Library symbol Library of Congress*] (LCLS)
PPAmS........ American Sunday School Union, Philadelphia, PA [*Library symbol Library of Congress Obsolete*] (LCLS)
PPAmSR...... American Sugar Refining Co., Philadelphia, PA [*Library symbol Library of Congress Obsolete*] (LCLS)
PPAmSwM... American Swedish Historical Foundation, Philadelphia, PA [*Library symbol Library of Congress*] (LCLS)
PPAN........... Academy of Natural Sciences of Philadelphia, Philadelphia, PA [*Library symbol Library of Congress*] (LCLS)
PPAN........... Pyrolyzed Polyacrylonitrile [*Organic chemistry*]
PP & A........ Palpation, Percussion, and Auscultation [*Medicine*]
pp & a......... Palpitation, Percussion, and Auscultation (AD)
PP & A........ Percussion, Palpation, and Auscultation [*Medicine*] (DAVI)
pp&b........... Paper, Printing, and Binding (AD)
PP & B........ Paper, Printing, and Binding [*Publishing*]
PP & C........ Pickpocket and Confidence [*Police term*]
PP & C........ Production Planning and Control [*Military*] (AABC)
PP & C........ Project Planning and Control (NG)
PP & E........ Program Planning and Evaluation (AD)
PP&L........... Pacific Power and Light (AD)
PP&L........... Pennsylvania Power and Light (AD)
PP&L Res.... PP & L Resources, Inc. [*Associated Press*] (SAG)
PP & NA...... Private Plants and Naval Activities
PP & T......... Packaging, Preservation, and Transportation
PPAnR......... Annenberg Research Institute for Judaic and Middle Eastern Studies, Philadelphia, PA [*Library symbol*] [*Library of Congress*] (LCLS)
PPAp........... Apprentices' Free Library, Philadelphia, PA [*Library symbol Library of Congress Obsolete*] (LCLS)
PPAP........... People's Party of Arunachal Pradesh [*India*] [*Political party*] (PPW)
PPAP........... Precedents of Private Acts of Parliament [*A publication*] (DLA)
PPA pos...... Phenylpyruvic Acid Positive [*Biochemistry*] (DAVI)
PPAR........... Paging Partners [*NASDAQ symbol*] (TTSB)
PPAR........... Paging Partners Corp. [*NASDAQ symbol*] (SAG)
PPAR........... Peroxisome Proliferator-Activated Receptor [*Genetics*]
PPAR........... Priority Problem Analysis Report [*Military*] (DNAB)
PPAR........... Project Performance Audit Report
PPARA......... ARA Historical Foundation, ARA Industries, Philadelphia, PA [*Closed*] [*Library symbol*] [*Library of Congress*] (LCLS)
PPARC......... Particle Physics and Astronomy Research Council [*British*]
PPArmA....... Armstrong Association of Philadelphia, Philadelphia, PA [*Library symbol Library of Congress Obsolete*] (LCLS)
PPARW........ Paging Partners Wrrt [*NASDAQ symbol*] (TTSB)
PPAS........... Patti Page Appreciation Society (EA)
PPAS........... Peripheral Pulmonary Artery Stenosis [*Medicine*] (DMAA)
PPAS........... Portable Public Address System (MCD)
PPAS........... Potassium Picrate Active Substances [*Measure of detergent content of water*]
PPAS........... Probability Proportional to Aggregate Size [*Statistics*]
PPAtR......... Atlantic Refining Co., Philadelphia, PA [*Library symbol Library of Congress*] (LCLS)
PPATRA....... Printing, Packaging, and Allied Trades Research Association (AD)
PPATY......... Preparatory (ROG)
PPAuC......... Automobile Club of Philadelphia, Philadelphia, PA [*Library symbol Library of Congress Obsolete*] (LCLS)
PPAUS......... Peat Producers Association of the United States (EA)
PPAW........... Public Policy Affecting Women Task Force (EA)
PPAWA........ Poultry Producers' Association of Western Australia
Ppb............. Pappaband [*Hard Cover*] [*German*] (AD)
PPB............. Parachute Paraglider Building [*NASA*] (KSC)
PPB............. Parts per Billion
ppb............. Parts per Billion (AD)
ppb............. Parts per Billion 10 (IDOE)
PPB............. Petro-Canada Products, Inc. [*Toronto Stock Exchange symbol Vancouver Stock Exchange symbol*]
PPB............. Philadelphia Bar Association, Philadelphia, PA [*Library symbol Library of Congress*] (LCLS)
P-P-B.......... Planning-Programming-Budgeting [*System*] [*Army*]
PPB............. Platelet-Poor Blood [*Hematology*] (MAE)
PPB............. Platoon Patrol Base [*Military*] (VNW)
PPB............. Political Party Broadcast [*Television*] [*British*]
PPB............. Polybrominated-Biphenyl (AD)
PPB............. Poly(para-benzamide) [*Organic chemistry*]
PPB............. Positive Pressure Breathing [*Aerospace*]
PPb............. Postparotid Basic Protein (DMAA)
PPB............. Power Plant Bulletin (MCD)
PPB............. Precision Pressure Balance

PPB............ Preprophase Band [*Cytology*]
PPB............ Presidente Prudente [*Brazil*] [*Airport symbol*] (AD)
PPB............ Pres Prudente [*Brazil*] [*Airport symbol*] (OAG)
PPB............ Primary Propulsion Branch [*Manned Spacecraft Center*]
PPB............ Printing, Paper, and Binding [*Publishing*] (WDMC)
PPB............ Private Posting Box
PPB............ Procurement Policy Board [*ABA Public Contract Law Section*] (AAGC)
PPB............ Production Parts Breakdown (MCD)
PPB............ Program Performance Baseline (NASA)
PPB............ Program Planning Budget (NOAA)
PPB............ Program-Planning-Budgeting
PPB............ PROM [*Programmable Read-Only Memory*] Programmer Board
PPB............ Provisioning Parts Breakdown
PPB............ Purchasing Power Benefit (ADA)
PPB............ Push-Pull Bearing
PPBANSW...... Pasture Protection Boards' Association of New South Wales [*Australia*]
PPBAS......... Planning-Programming-Budgeting-Accounting System (AD)
PPBB........... Partai Pesaka Bumiputra Bersatu [*United Traditional Bumiputra Party*] [*Malaysia*] [*Political party*] (PPW)
PPBB........... PCI-toPCI Bridge Board (ACII)
PPBB........... Prime Power Brass Board (MCD)
PPBC........... Pittsburgh Penguins Booster Club (EA)
PPBC........... Plant Pathogenic Bacteria Committee (EA)
PPBC........... Portland Problem Behavior Checklist (EDAC)
PPBC-R........ Portland Problem Behavior Checklist - Revised [*Educational test*]
P PBD......... Paper or Paperboard [*Freight*]
PPBD........... Port of Palm Beach District [*AAR code*]
PPBE........... Passenger Protective Breathing Equipment [*Aviation*] (DA)
PPBERS....... Program Performance and Budget Execution Review System [*Army*]
PPBES......... Planning, Programming, Budgeting, and Execution System [*Army*] (RDA)
PPBES......... Program Planning and Budget Execution System [*Army*]
PPBES......... Program Planning-Budgeting-Evaluation System Project (EA)
PPBESP....... Program Planning-Budgeting-Evaluation System Project (EA)
PPBF........... Pan-American Pharmaceutical and Biochemical Federation
PPBFSPS..... Pen and Pocket Blade Forgers' and Smithers' Protective Society [*A union*] [*British*]
PPBG........... Preliminary Program and Budget Guidance
PPBH........... Pharmaceutical Partners for Better Healthcare (ECON)
PPBI........... Balch Institute, Philadelphia, PA [*Library symbol Library of Congress*] (LCLS)
PPBM........... Pulse Polarization Binary Modulation (MCD)
PPBMIS....... Planning, Programming, and Budgeting Management Information System [*Army*]
PPBP........... Pro-Platelet Basic Protein (DMAA)
PPBR........... Program Plan and Budget Request (OICC)
PPBS........... Planning, Programming, and Budgeting System [*Army*]
PPBS........... Positive Pressure Breathing System [*Aerospace*]
PPBS........... Postprandial Blood Sugar [*Clinical chemistry*]
PPBS........... Program Planning and Budgeting Staff [*Environmental Protection Agency*] (GFGA)
PPBS........... Program, Planning, and Budgeting System [*Johnson Administration*] [*Executive Office of the President*] (GFGA)
PPC............ College of Physicians of Philadelphia, Philadelphia, PA [*Library symbol Library of Congress OCLC symbol*] (LCLS)
PP-C........... Free Library of Philadelphia, Carson Collection, Philadelphia, PA [*Library symbol Library of Congress*] (LCLS)
PPC............ Pan Pacific Centers [*Defunct*] (EA)
PPC............ Paperboard Packaging Council (EA)
PPC............ Parallel Path Counter [*Electronics*] (IAA)
PPC............ Partial Pay Card
PPC............ Partido Popular Cristiano [*Christian Popular Party*] [*Peru*] [*Political party*] (PPW)
PPC............ Parting Post Calls (MCD)
PPC............ Partitu Populare Corsu [*Corsica*] [*Political party*] (PD)
PPC............ Parts Preference Code [*Military*] (AFIT)
PPC............ Patres Conscripti [*Senators*] [*Latin*] (ROG)
PPC............ Patrol Plane Commander
PPC............ Peak Power Control [*Telecommunications*] (TEL)
PPC............ Permission to Photocopy (MCD)
PPC............ Per Pupil Cost (AFM)
PPC............ Persistent Photoconductivity [*Physics*]
PPC............ Personal Portable Computer
PPC............ Personal Productivity Center
PPC............ Personal Programmable Calculator (MHDI)
PPC............ Personal Protective Clothing (GNE)
PPC............ Pet Population Control (AD)
PPC............ Petroleum Planning Committee [*Obsolete NATO*] (NATG)
PPC............ Phased Program Construction (IAA)
PPC............ Phased Provisioning Code (NASA)
PPC............ Philatelic Press Club [*Later, IPPC*]
PPC............ Photographic Processing Cells (AFM)
PpC............ Pick Publishing Corporation, New York, NY [*Library symbol Library of Congress*] (LCLS)
PPC............ Picture Postcard
ppc............ Picture Postcard (AD)
PPC............ Pierce's Perpetual Code [*1943*] [*A publication*] (DLA)
PPC............ Pine Pass [*British Columbia*] [*Seismograph station code, US Geological Survey Closed*] (SEIS)
PPC............ Plain Paper Copier [*Electrophotography*]
PPC............ Plain Plaster Cornice [*Construction*]
PPC............ Planar Postive Column (IAA)
PPC............ Plane Paper Copier (IAA)
ppc............ Plan-Paper Copier (AD)
PPC............ Plant Pest Control Division [*of ARS, Department of Agriculture*]
PPC............ Plant Process Computer
PPC............ Platform Position Computer
PPC............ Plug Patch Cord
PPC............ Plutonium Process Cell [*Nuclear energy*] (NRCH)
PPC............ Plutonium Product Cell [*Nuclear energy*] (NRCH)
PPC............ Point of Possible Collision [*Navigation*]
PPC............ Point-to-Point Correlation [*Graphing*]
PPC............ Polarizable Point Charge [*Model for the water molecule*]
PPC............ Policy Planning Council [*U.S. Department of State*] (BARN)
PPC............ Polyphthalate-Polycarbonate
PPC............ Pooled Platelet Concentrate [*Medicine*] (MEDA)
PPC............ Portable Personal Computer (DGA)
PPC............ Positive Peer Control
PPC............ Positive Peer Culture (AD)
PPC............ Posterior Parietal Cortex [*Brain anatomy*]
PPC............ Postpulmonary Complications
PPC............ Potential Points of Collision [*Navigation*]
PPC............ Potentional Performance Capability (IAA)
PPC............ Pour Prendre Conge [*To Take Leave*] [*French*]
p p c.......... Pour Prendre Conge [*To Take Leave*] [*French*] (AD)
PPC............ Power Pack Charger
PPC............ Power Plant Change (NVT)
PPC............ PPC Oil & Gas Corp. [*Toronto Stock Exchange symbol*]
PPC............ Precision Photomechanical Corp.
PPC............ Predicted Propagation Correction (PDAA)
PPC............ Preliminary Phase Correction (IAA)
PPC............ Preprocessing Center [*NASA*] (NASA)
PPC............ Pre-Proposal Conference (MCD)
PPC............ President of the Privy Council [*Canada*]
PPC............ Pressure Pulse Contour [*Cardiac computer*] (PDAA)
PPC............ Primary Power Control (MCD)
PPC............ Printers' Pension Corp. (DGA)
PPC............ Print Position Counter
PPC............ Priority Placement Certificate [*Military*] (AFM)
PPC............ Production Planning and Control
PPC............ Product Planning Committee
PPC............ Professional Personal Computer
PPC............ Program Planning and Control (AAG)
PPC............ Program Planning Coordination Office [*United Nations*]
PPC............ Progressive Patient Care
ppc............ Progressive Patient Care (AD)
PPC............ Project Parts Coordinator
PPC............ Project Physics Course [*National Science Foundation*]
PPC............ Project Planning Centre for Developing Countries [*Research center British*] (IRC)
PPC............ Pro-Personal Computer (NITA)
PPC............ Prospect Creek, AK [*Location identifier FAA*] (FAAL)
PPC............ Prospective Parliamentary Candidate [*British*]
PPC............ Proximal Palmar Crease [*Anatomy*]
PPC............ Psychorotrophic Plate Count [*Bacteriology*]
PPC............ Publishers Publicity Circle
PPC............ Pulsed Power Circuit (IEEE)
PPC............ Purchase Price Control (AD)
pPc............ Pure Peruvian Cocaine (AD)
ppca........... Plasma Prothrombin Conversion Accelerator (AD)
PPCA........... Plasma [*or Proserum*] Prothrombin Conversion Accelerator [*Factor VII*] [*Also, SPCA Hematology*]
PPCAA......... Parole and Probation Compact Administrators Association (EA)
PPCAP......... People to People Citizen Ambassador Program (EA)
PPCB........... Page Printer Control Block [*Computer science*]
PPCB........... Patrick Petroleum Co. [*NASDAQ symbol*] (SAG)
PPCC........... Carpenters' Co., Philadelphia, PA [*Library symbol Library of Congress*] (LCLS)
PPCC........... Particles per Cubic Centimeter
PPCC........... Parts per Cubic Centimeter (IAA)
PPCC........... Port Phillip Conservation Council [*Australia*]
PPCC........... Postmolded Plastic Chip Carrier [*Computer science*]
PPCCD......... Profiled Peristaltic Charge Coupled-Device [*Computer science*] (IAA)
PPCCH......... Chestnut Hill College, Philadelphia, PA [*Library symbol Library of Congress*] (LCLS)
PPCD........... Plant Pest Control Division (AD)
PPCD........... Polymorphous Posterior Corneal Dystropy [*Medicine*] (DMAA)
PPCE........... Portable Pneumatic Checkout Equipment (KSC)
PPCE........... Post-Proline Cleaving Enzyme [*Biochemistry*]
ppcf............ Plasma Prothrombin Conversion Factor (AD)
PPCF........... Plasmin Prothrombin Conversion Factor [*Factor V*] [*Hematology*]
PPCH........... People-to-People Committee for the Handicapped (EA)
PPCI........... Curtis Institute of Music, Philadelphia, PA [*Library symbol Library of Congress*] (LCLS)
PPCI........... Presentation Protocol Control Information [*Telecommunications*]
PPCiC......... Civic Club of Philadelphia, Philadelphia, PA [*Library symbol Library of Congress Obsolete*] (LCLS)
PPCIG......... Personal Property Consignment Instruction Guide (MCD)
PPCLI......... Princess Patricia of Connaught's Light Infantry [*Military unit*] [*Canada*]
PPCLI......... Princess Patricia's Canadian Light Infantry (AD)
PPCM.......... Philadelphia County Medical Society, Philadelphia, PA [*Library symbol Library of Congress Obsolete*] (LCLS)
PPCO........... Philadelphia College of Osteopathic Medicine, Philadelphia, PA [*Library symbol Library of Congress*] (LCLS)
PPCO2......... Partial Pressure Carbon Dioxide
PPCoC......... Community College of Philadelphia, Philadelphia, PA [*Library symbol Library of Congress*] (LCLS)

PPCoIP .... Colonial Penn Group, Inc., Marketing Research Library, Philadelphia, PA [*Library symbol Library of Congress*] (LCLS)
PPComm...... Commercial Museum, Philadelphia, PA [*Library symbol Library of Congress Obsolete*] (LCLS)
PPCP .... College of Physicians of Philadelphia, Philadelphia, PA [*Library symbol*] [*Library of Congress*] (LCLS)
PPCP .... Propellant Pneumatic Control Panel (KSC)
PPCPC .... Philadelphia City Planning Commission, Philadelphia, PA [*Library symbol Library of Congress*] (LCLS)
PPCPSG....... Polish POW Camps Philatelic Study Group (EA)
PPCR .... Production Planning Change Request (SAA)
PPCS .... National Carl Schurz Memorial Foundation, Philadelphia, PA [*Library symbol Library of Congress Obsolete*] (LCLS)
PPCS .... Page Printer Control System [*Computer science*]
PPCS .... Personnel Protection and Communication Services [*British*] (AD)
PPCS .... Person to Person: Collect and Special Instruction [*Telecommunications*] (TEL)
PPCS .... Precision Pointing Control System [*Engineering*]
PPCS .... Primary Producers' Cooperative Society (AD)
PPCS .... Production Planning and Control System
PPCS .... Project Planning and Control System [*Social Security Administration*]
PPCuP .... Curtis Publishing Co., Research Library, Philadelphia, PA [*Library symbol Library of Congress Obsolete*] (LCLS)
PPD .... A Posteriori Probability Distribution [*Mathematics*]
PPD .... Drexel University, Philadelphia, PA [*Library symbol Library of Congress*] (LCLS)
PPD .... Humacao-Palmas [*Puerto Rico*] [*Airport symbol*] (OAG)
PPD .... Packs per Day [*Cigarettes*] [*Medicine*]
PPD .... Panel Power Distribution (MCD)
PPD .... Papered (ROG)
PPD .... Paranoid Personality Disorder (AD)
PPD .... Para-Phenylenediamine [*Organic chemistry*]
PPD .... Partido Popular Democratico [*Popular Democratic Party*] [*Puerto Rico*] [*Political party*] (PPW)
PPD .... Partido Popular Democratico [*Popular Democratic Party of Puerto Rico*] [*Spanish*] (BARN)
PPD .... Partido por la Democracia [*Democratic Party*] [*Chile*] [*Political party*] (EY)
PPD .... Parti Populaire Djiboutien [*Djibouti People's Party*] [*Political party*] (PPW)
PPD .... Parti Progressiste Dahomeen [*Dahomey Progressive Party*] [*Political party*]
PPD .... Parts Provisioning Document
PPD .... Party for Peace and Democracy [*South Korea*] [*Political party*]
PPD .... Payload Position Data
PPD .... Pay Packets Deficiency [*British*]
PPD .... Pepsin Pancreatin Digest [*Food protein digestibility assay*]
PPD .... Permanent Partial Disability [*Dentistry*] (MAE)
PPD .... Personal Protective Device [*Toxicology*]
PPD .... Personnel Planning Data [*Navy*]
PPD .... Personnel Priority Designator [*Military*] (AFM)
PPD .... Petroleum Production Division (AD)
PPD .... Phenyldiphenyloxadiazole [*Organic chemistry*] (MAE)
PPD .... Pitch Phase Detector
PPD .... Plains Petroleum Co. [*Vancouver Stock Exchange symbol*]
PPD .... Plot Plan Drawing (SAA)
PPD .... Point Position Data
PPD .... Politieke Partij Democraten 66 [*Political Party Democrats 66*] [*Netherlands*] (EAIO)
PPD .... Portland Public Docks (AD)
PPD .... Portuguese Popular Democrats
PPD .... Posterior Polymorphous Dystrophy [*Neurology*] (DAVI)
PPD .... Postpaid
ppd .... Postpaid (WDMC)
PPD .... Postpartum Day [*Obstetrics*] (DAVI)
PPD .... Postpartum Depression (PAZ)
PPD .... PostScript Printer Description [*Computer science*] (PCM)
PPD .... Preferred Policyholders' Discount [*British*] (BARN)
PPD .... Prepaid
ppd .... Prepaid (WDMC)
PPD .... Prepaid Dental Plan [*Insurance*] (MCD)
PPD .... Pre-Paid Legal Services, Inc. [*AMEX symbol*] (SPSG)
PPD .... Pre-Paid Legal Svcs [*AMEX symbol*] (TTSB)
ppd .... Prepared (MAE)
PPD .... Preprototype Demonstration
PPD .... Presidential Protective Division [*US Secret Service*]
PPD .... Prime Power Distribution
PPD .... Principal Project Designer [*Engineering project management*]
PPD .... Printer Page Description [*Computer science*]
PPD .... Processed Payment Document (GFGA)
PPD .... Proficiency Pay Designator [*Military*] (AABC)
PPD .... Prognostic Prediction Devices
PPD .... Program Package Document
PPD .... Program Planning Directives [*NASA*] (KSC)
PPD .... Program Planning Document (NG)
PPD .... Progressive Perceptive Deafness [*Medicine*]
PPD .... Projectile Pull and Drain [*Machine*] (MCD)
PPD .... Project Planning Directive (NG)
PPD .... Prompt Payment Discount (AAGC)
PPD .... Propria Pecunia Dedicavit [*With His Own Money He Offered It*] [*Latin*] (ROG)
PPD .... Propulsion and Power Division [*Manned Spacecraft Center*] [*NASA*]
PPD .... Provisioning Procurement Data
PPD .... Pulse-Type Phase Detector
PPD .... Purchasing Power of the Dollar (MHDW)
PPD .... Purified Protein Derivative [*Tuberculin*]
ppd .... Purified Protein Derivative (AD)
PPDA .... Para-Phenylenediamine [*Organic chemistry*]
PPDA .... Phenyl Phosphorodiamidate [*Fertilizer technology*]
PPDA .... Produce Packaging Development Association (AD)
PPDB .... Personnel Planning Data Book [*Navy*]
PPDB .... Point-Positioning Data Base [*Cartography*] (RDA)
PPD-B .... Purified Protein Derivative - Battey [*Tuberculin*] (AAMN)
PPDC .... Dental Cosmos Library, Philadelphia, PA [*Library symbol Library of Congress Obsolete*] (LCLS)
PPDC .... Paraguayan People's Documentation Center [*Mestre, Italy*] (EAIO)
PPDC .... Partido Popular Democratica Cristiana [*Popular Christian Democratic Party*] [*Spain Political party*] (PPE)
PPDC .... Perfusion Program Directors Council [*Cardiology*] (DAVI)
PPDC .... Polymer Products Development Center (AD)
PP-DC .... Programming Panels and Decoding Circuits (NITA)
PPDC .... Programming Panels and Decoding Circuits
PPDD .... Pershing Physical Deception Device [*Army*]
PPDD .... Plan Position Data Display
PPDD .... Preliminary Project Design Description (NRCH)
PPDDS......... Private Practice Dental Delivery System
PPDef-M...... Defense Personnel Support Center, Directorate of Medical Material Library, Philadelphia, PA [*Library symbol Library of Congress*] (LCLS)
PPDef-M...... Defense Personnel Support Center, Directorate of Medical Material Library, Philadelphia, PA [*Library symbol*] [*Library of Congress*] (LCLS)
PPDF .... Poisson Probability Distribution Function [*Mathematics*]
PPDG........... Parti Progressiste Democratique Guadeloupeen [*Political party*] (EY)
PPDGF......... Porcine Platelet-Derived Growth Factor [*Biochemistry*]
PPDI .... Paraphenylene Diisocyanate [*Organic chemistry*]
PPDI .... Pharmaceutical Product Development, Inc. [*NASDAQ symbol*] (SAG)
PPDI .... Pharmaceutical Product Devlpmt [*NASDAQ symbol*] (TTSB)
ppdi .... Pilot's Projected-Display Indicator (AD)
PPDI .... Pre-Pre-Delivery Inspection [*Automotive project management*]
PPDIL .... Pre-Power-Dependent Insertion Limit [*Nuclear energy*] (NRCH)
PPDio .... Diocesan Library, Philadelphia, PA [*Library symbol Library of Congress Obsolete*] (LCLS)
PPDM .... E. I. Du Pont de Nemours & Co., Marshall Laboratory, Philadelphia, PA [*Library symbol Library of Congress*] (LCLS)
PPDM .... Pseudo-Pinch Design Method [*Heat exchange design*]
PPDMG........ Popular Priced Dress Manufacturers Group [*Later, AMA*] (EA)
ppdo .... Per Person, Double Occupancy (AD)
PPDO .... Personal Paid Days Off
PPDP .... Preliminary Project Development Plan [*NASA*]
PPDP .... Preprogram Definition Phase
PP-DPH........ Free Library of Philadelphia, Library for the Blind and Physically Handicapped, Philadelphia, PA [*Library symbol Library of Congress*] (LCLS)
PPDR .... Philadelphia Department of Records, Philadelphia, PA [*Library symbol*] [*Library of Congress*] (LCLS)
PPDR .... Pilot Performance Description Record
PP/DR.......... Preliminary Performance Design Requirements
PPDR .... Production Packing Depth Range (NG)
PPDrop .... Dropsie University, Philadelphia, PA [*Library symbol Library of Congress*] (LCLS)
PPDS .... Personal Printer Data Stream [*IBM Corp.*] (PCM)
PPDS .... Phonologic Programming Deficit Syndrome (DMAA)
PPDS .... Physical Property Data Service [*Institution of Chemical Engineers*] [*Databank*] [*Information service or system*] (IID)
PPDS .... Planning Production Data Sheet
PPDS .... Preservation and Packaging Data Sheet [*DoD*]
PPDS .... Publishers' Parcels Delivery Service (AD)
PPD-S.......... Purified Protein Derivative-Standard [*Tuberculin*]
PPDSE .... International Plate Printers, Die Stampers, and Engravers' Union of North America
PPDSE .... Plate Printers, Die Stampers, and Engravers [*Union*] (AD)
PPDT .... (Phenylpyridyl)diphenyltriazine [*Analytical chemistry*]
PPDT .... Poly(phenyleneterephthalamide) [*Organic chemistry*]
PPDU .... Presentation Protocol Data Unit [*Computer science*] (TNIG)
PPE.............. Independent Union of Plant Protection Employees in the Electrical and Machine Industry
PPE.............. Parti Populaire Europeen [*European Peoples' Party - EPP*] (EAIO)
PPE.............. Personal Protective Equipment [*General Motors Corp.*]
ppe .... Philosophy, Politics, and Economics (AD)
PPE.............. Philosophy, Politics, Economics [*Oxford University*]
PPE.............. Pholbe Phillips Editions [*Publisher*] [*British*]
PPE.............. Pipette [*Chemistry*]
PPE.............. Platform Position Equipment
PPE.............. Polypentene [*Organic chemistry*]
PPE.............. Polyphenylene Ether Plastic [*Materials science*]
PPE.............. Polyphenylether (IEEE)
PPE.............. Polyphosphate Ester [*Inorganic chemistry*]
PPE.............. Porcine Pancreatic Elastase [*An enzyme*]
PPE.............. Portable Purge Equipment [*NASA*]
PPE.............. Potomac Pacific Engineering, Inc.
PPE.............. Predicted Period-of-Effect [*Meteorology*]
PPE.............. Premodulation Processing Equipment
PPE.............. Preproduction Engineering
PPE.............. Preproduction Evaluation (NG)
PPE.............. Preproduction Proposal Evaluation
PPE.............. Preproenkephalin [*Biochemistry*]
PPE.............. Print-Punch Editor [*Computer science*] (SAA)
PPE.............. Problem Program Efficiency (IEEE)
PPE.............. Problem Program Evaluator

PPE............ Program Performance Evaluator (NITA)
PPE............ Program Planning and Evaluation
PPE............ Prototype Production Evaluation (NG)
PPE............ Purchasing Power Equivalent
PPE............ Pyridoxal Phosphate Effect [*Medicine*]
PPEA........... Plant Performance Evaluation Activity [*Military*] (DNAB)
PPEB........... Eastern Baptist Theological Seminary, Philadelphia, PA [*Library symbol Library of Congress*] (LCLS)
PPEB........... [*The*] Pottery of Palestine from the Earliest Times to the End of the EarlyBronze Age [*A publication*] (BJA)
PPEF........... Public Policy Education Fund (EA)
PPEFH......... E. F. Hutton & Co., Philadelphia, PA [*Library symbol Library of Congress Obsolete*] (LCLS)
PPEMA......... Portable Power Equipment Manufacturers Association (EA)
PPEN........... Purchased Parts Equipment Notice (SAA)
PPEng......... Engineers' Club, Philadelphia, PA [*Library symbol Library of Congress Obsolete*] (LCLS)
PPEP........... Eastern Pennsylvania Psychiatric Institute, Philadelphia, PA [*Library symbol Library of Congress*] (LCLS)
PPEP........... Pen Plotter Emulation Program [*Computer science*] (MHDI)
PPEP........... Plasma Physics and Environmental Perturbation (NASA)
P/PEP......... Progress Performance Evaluation Panel [*Job Corps*]
PPER........... Procurement Package Engineering Release (MCD)
PPES........... Physical Performance Evaluation System [*Army*]
PPES........... Pilot Performance Evaluation System [*Air Force*]
PPES........... Planning, Programming, and Execution System [*Army*] (AAGC)
PPeSchw..... Schwenkfelder Historical Library, Pennsburg, PA [*Library symbol Library of Congress*] (LCLS)
PPETS......... Pretreatment Permitting and Enforcement Tracking System [*Environmental Protection Agency*] (ERG)
PPF............ Franklin Institute, Philadelphia, PA [*Library symbol Library of Congress OCLC symbol*] (LCLS)
PPF............ Hancock [*John*] Patriot Preferred Dividend Fund [*NYSE symbol*] (SPSG)
PPF............ John Hancock Patr Pfd Div Fd [*NYSE symbol*] (TTSB)
PPF............ Pacific Peace Fund (EA)
PPF............ Paired-Pulse Facilitation [*Neurophysiology*]
PPF............ Panamanian Public Force (AD)
PPF............ Panels Per Facing [*Outdoor advertising*] (WDMC)
PPF............ Parsons [*Kansas*] [*Airport symbol*] (OAG)
PPF............ Parsons, KS [*Location identifier FAA*] (FAAL)
PPF............ Parti Populaire Francais [*French Popular Party*] [*Political party*] (PPE)
PPF............ Patriotic People's Front [*Hungary Political party*]
PPF............ Payload Processing Facility [*Air Force*] (NASA)
PPF............ Peacetime Planning Factors
PPF............ Peak Power Frequency
PPF............ Pellagra Preventive Factor [*See also PP*] [*Biochemistry*]
PPF............ People's Police Force
PPF............ Personal Property Floater [*Insurance*]
ppf............ Personal Property Floater [*Insurance*] (AD)
PPF............ Phagocytosis Promoting Factor [*Immunology*] (DAVI)
PPF............ Phase Pushing Factor
PPF............ Photophoretic Force [*Pressure exerted by light*]
PPF............ Plasma Protein Fraction [*Hematology*]
PPF............ Plumbers and Pipefitters [*Union*] (AD)
PPF............ Poetarum Philosophorum Graecorum Fragmenta [*A publication*] (OCD)
PPF............ Polarization-Preserving Fiber
PPF............ Poly(phenolformaldehyde) [*Organic chemistry*]
PPF............ Porous Polyurethane Foam [*Also, PUF*] [*Plastics technology*]
PPF............ Power Plant Frame [*Mazda Miata*] [*Connecting engine and transmission to final drive*]
PPF............ Presbyterian Peace Fellowship (EA)
PPF............ Primary Part Failure (DNAB)
PPF............ Principal Profile Forms [*Soil classification*]
PPF............ Privatefoeretagarnas Partioganisation i Finland [*Finnish Private Entrepreneurs' Party*] [*Political party*] (PPE)
PPF............ Production Possibility Frontier [*Economics*]
PPF............ Provision of Production Facilities [*Military*] (AABC)
PPF............ United Association of Journeymen and Apprentices of the Plumbing and Pipe Fitting Industry of the United States and Canada
PPFA........... Planned Parenthood Federation of America (EA)
PPFA........... Plastic Pipe and Fittings Association (EA)
PPFA........... Professional Picture Framers Association (EA)
PPFA........... United States Army, Frankford Arsenal Library, Philadelphia, PA [*Library symbol Library of Congress*] (LCLS)
p-p factor..... Pellagra-Preventive Factor (AD)
PPFAR......... Federal Archives and Records Center, General Services Administration, Philadelphia, PA [*Library symbol Library of Congress*] (LCLS)
PPFAS......... Past President of the Faculty of Architects and Surveyors [*British*] (DBQ)
PPF-B.......... Biochemical Research Foundation, Franklin Institute, Newark, DE [*Closed*] [*Library symbol*] [*Library of Congress*] (LCLS)
PPFC........... Philadelphia Fellowship Commission, Philadelphia, PA [*Library symbol Library of Congress Obsolete*] (LCLS)
PPFC........... Priscilla Presley Fan Club [*Defunct*] (EA)
PPFD........... Photosynthetically Active Photon Flux Density [*Botany*]
PPFF........... Poisson Probability Frequency Function [*Mathematics*]
PPF-G.......... Germantown Laboratories, Inc., Philadelphia, PA [*Library symbol Library of Congress*] (LCLS)
PPFHi.......... Historical Society of Frankford, Philadelphia, PA [*Library symbol Library of Congress Obsolete*] (LCLS)
PPFJC......... Federation of Jewish Charities, Philadelphia, PA [*Library symbol Library of Congress Obsolete*] (LCLS)
PPFML......... Fidelity Mutual Life Insurance Co., Philadelphia, PA [*Library symbol Library of Congress*] (LCLS)
PPFO........... Paris Procurement Field Office
PPFPR......... F. P. Ristine & Co., Philadelphia, PA [*Library symbol Library of Congress Obsolete*] (LCLS)
PPFr........... Friends' Free Library of Germantown, Philadelphia, PA [*Library symbol Library of Congress*] (LCLS)
PPFR........... Plutonium Product Filter Room [*Nuclear energy*] (NRCH)
PPFRB......... Federal Reserve Bank of Philadelphia, Philadelphia, PA [*Library symbol Library of Congress*] (LCLS)
PPFRT......... Prototype Preliminary Flight Rating Test
PPFS........... Pergamon Professional and Financial Services [*Commercial firm British*]
PPG............ German Society of Pennsylvania, Philadelphia, PA [*Library symbol Library of Congress*] (LCLS)
PPG............ Pacific Proving Ground [*AEC*]
PPG............ Pago Pago [*Samoa*] [*Airport symbol*] (OAG)
PPG............ Pago Pago, AQ [*Location identifier FAA*] (FAAL)
PPG............ Pediatric Pneumogram [*Radiology*] (DAVI)
PPG............ PEMA Policy and Guidance [*Military*] (AABC)
PPG............ Periodical Press Gallery [*US Senate*]
PPG............ Permanent Planning Group [*Military British*]
PPG............ Personnel Processing Group [*Army*]
PPG............ Photoplethysmography [*Medicine*]
PPG............ Picopicogram [*One trillionth of one trillionth of a gram*]
PPG............ Piezoelectric Power Generation
PPG............ Pipe Plug
PPG............ Pittsburgh Plate Glass [*Commercial firm*]
PPG............ Planned Procurement Guide
PPG............ Planning and Policy Guidance (MCD)
PPG............ Planning and Programming Guidance [*Army*] (AABC)
ppg............ Planning and Programming Guidance (AD)
PPG............ Plasma Power Generator
PPG............ Player Piano Group (EAIO)
PPG............ Points per Game (WGA)
PPG............ Policies and Procedures Guide (SAA)
PPG............ Poly(propylene Glycol) [*Organic chemistry*]
PPG............ Portal Pressure Gradient [*Medicine*] (DMAA)
ppg............ Pounds per Gallon
PPG............ Power-Play Goal [*Hockey*]
PPG............ PPG Indus [*NYSE symbol*] (TTSB)
PPG............ PPG Industries, Inc. [*Formerly, Pittsburgh Plate Glass Co.*] [*Associated Press*] (SAG)
PPG............ PPG Industries, Inc., Coatings and Resins Division, Allison Park, PA [*OCLC symbol*] (OCLC)
PPG............ Predictive Proportional Guidance
PPG............ Primary Pattern Generator [*Bell Laboratories*]
PPG............ Print Pattern Generator (IAA)
PPG............ Program for Population Genetics [*Collaboration of US and China Groups*]
PPG............ Program Planning Guide (OICC)
PPG............ Program Policy Guidelines
PPG............ Program Pulse Generator (IEEE)
PPG............ Propulsion and Power Generation
PPGA........... Pennsylvania Personnel and Guidance Association (AD)
PPGA........... Personal Producing General Agent [*Insurance*]
PPGA........... Plastic Pin Grid Array (PCM)
PPGA........... Post Pill Galactorrhea-Amenorrhea [*Medicine*]
ppga........... Post-Pill Galactorrheamenorrhea [*Medicine*] (AD)
PPGA........... Potplant Growers Association [*British*] (DBA)
PPGA........... Preschool Play-Group Association [*British*] (DI)
PPGBL......... Personal Property Government Bill of Lading (DNAB)
PPGE........... General Electric Co., Philadelphia, PA [*Library symbol Library of Congress*] (LCLS)
PPGE........... Partido del Progreso de Guinea Ecuatorial [*Progressive Party of Equatorial Guinea*] [*Political party*] (EY)
PPGE-M....... General Electric Co., Missile and Space Vehicle Department, Aerosciences Laboratory, Philadelphia, PA [*Library symbol Library of Congress*] (LCLS)
PPGen......... Genealogical Society of Pennsylvania, Philadelphia, PA [*Library symbol Library of Congress*] (LCLS)
PPGenH....... Philadelphia General Hospital Laboratories, Philadelphia, PA [*Library symbol Library of Congress Obsolete*] (LCLS)
PPGeo......... Geographical Society of Philadelphia, Philadelphia, PA [*Library symbol Library of Congress Obsolete*] (LCLS)
PPGF........... Polypeptide Growth Factor [*Endocrinology*] (DAVI)
PPGH........... Philadelphia General Hospital, Philadelphia, PA [*Library symbol Library of Congress*] (LCLS)
PPGi........... Girard College, Philadelphia, PA [*Library symbol Library of Congress Obsolete*] (LCLS)
PPGJW......... Past Pro-Grand Junior Warden [*Freemasonry*] (ROG)
PPGL........... Polished Plate Glass [*Technical drawings*] (DAC)
PPGM........... Past Provincial Grand Master [*Freemasonry*]
PPGM........... Planning-Programming Guidance Memo [*Navy*]
PPGO........... Past Pro-Grand Organist [*Freemasonry*] (ROG)
PPGO........... Past Pro-Grand Orient [*Freemasonry*] (ROG)
PPGP........... Past Pro-Grand Pursuivant [*Freemasonry*] (ROG)
PPGP........... Prepaid Group Practice [*Insurance*] (DHSM)
PPGraph...... Graphic Sketch Club, Philadelphia, PA [*Library symbol Library of Congress Obsolete*] (LCLS)
PPGratz....... Gratz College, Philadelphia, PA [*Library symbol Library of Congress Obsolete*] (LCLS)
PPGRC......... Public Policy and Government Relations Council

PPGSB .... Past Pro-Grand Sword Bearer [*Freemasonry*] (ROG)
PPGSN .... Past Provincial Grand Senior [*Freemasonry*] (ROG)
PPGSW .... Past Provincial Grand Senior Warden [*Freemasonry*]
PPGW .... Past Pro-Grand Warden [*Freemasonry*] (ROG)
PPH .... Pages per Hour
PPH .... Paid Personal Holiday
PPH .... Pamphlet
pph .... Pamphlet (AD)
pph .... Papers Per Hour [*News*] (WDMC)
PPH .... Parts per Hundred
PPH .... Peak-to-Peak Heights [*Spectrometry*]
PPH .... Persistent Pulmonary Hypertension [*Medicine*]
PPH .... Petroleum Pipehead
PPH .... Phenylpropanolamine(hydrochloride) [*Also, PPA, PPM*] [*Decongestant*]
PPH .... Phosphopyruvate Hydratase [*An enzyme*]
PPH .... PHP Healthcare [*NYSE symbol*] (TTSB)
PPH .... PHP Healthcare Corp. [*NYSE symbol*] (SPSG)
PPH .... Postpartum Hemorrhage [*Medicine*]
pph .... Post-Partum Hemorrhage [*Medicine*] (AD)
pph .... Pounds Per Hour (AD)
PPH .... Pounds per Hour (NG)
PPH .... Primary Pulmonary Hypertension [*Medicine*]
PPH .... Prophet Resources Ltd. [*Vancouver Stock Exchange symbol*]
PPH .... Protocollagen Proline Hydroxylase [*An enzyme*] (MAE)
PPH .... Pulses per Hour
pph .... Pulses Per Hour (AD)
PPHa .... Hahnemann Medical College and Hospital, Philadelphia, PA [*Library symbol Library of Congress*] (LCLS)
PPHA .... Peak Pulse Height Analysis
PPHA .... Private Proprietary Homes for Adults
PPHBA .... Peruvian Paso Half-Blood Association [*Later, PPPBR*] (EA)
PPHFC .... Holy Family College, Philadelphia, PA [*Library symbol Library of Congress*] (LCLS)
PPH/LB .... Pounds per Hour per Pound (SAA)
PPHM .... Parts per Hundred Million
P-PH-M .... Pulse Phase Modulation (DEN)
PPHN .... Persistent Pulmonary Hypertension of the Newborn [*Medicine*]
PPHOPT .... Pseudo-Pseudohypoparathyroidism [*Also, PPHP*] [*Endocrinology*]
PPHor .... Pennsylvania Horticultural Society, Philadelphia, PA [*Library symbol Library of Congress*] (LCLS)
P Php .... Port Phillip (AD)
PPHP .... Pseudo-Pseudohypoparathyroidism [*Also, PPHOPT*] [*Endocrinology*]
PPHPI .... Henry Phipps Institute, Philadelphia, PA [*Library symbol Library of Congress Obsolete*] (LCLS)
pphpm .... Parts Per Hundred Parts of Mix (AD)
pphpm .... Pints Per Hundred Parts of Mix (AD)
pphr .... Parts Per Hundred Parts of Rubber (AD)
PPHRII .... Parents of Premature and High Risk Infants International (EA)
PPHRNA .... Peruvian Paso Horse Registry of North America (EA)
PPHS .... Partisan Prohibition Historical Society (EA)
PPHSL .... Periodical Publication in Harvard Science Libraries
PPHT .... (Phenylethyl-propylamino)hydroxytetralin [*Biochemistry*]
PPHx .... Previous Psychiatric History (MEDA)
PPi .... Carnegie Library of Pittsburgh, Pittsburgh, PA [*Library symbol Library of Congress*] (LCLS)
PPI .... Institute for Psychosomatic and Psychiatric Research and Training [*Research center*] (RCD)
PPI .... Packing, Postage, and Insurance [*Shipping*]
PPI .... Padangpandjang [*Sumatra*] [*Seismograph station code, US Geological Survey*] (SEIS)
PPI .... Pages per Inch [*Publishing*]
ppi .... Pages Per Inch (AD)
ppi .... Pages Per Inch (WDMC)
PPI .... Pakistan Press International
PPI .... Pan Pacific Institute [*Flinders University, Australia*]
PPI .... Parallel Peripheral Interface [*Computer science*]
PPI .... Parcel Post, Insured [*Shipping*]
ppi .... Parcel Post Insured (AD)
PPI .... Particles per Inch
PPI .... Patient Package Insert [*Also, PI*] [*Instructional leaflet distributed with certain prescription drugs*]
PPI .... Patient Package Insert [*Pharmacy*] (DAVI)
PPI .... Pensioners for Peace International (EAIO)
PPI .... Pergamon Press, Inc.
PPI .... Personality and Personal Illness Questionnaires [*Psychology*]
PPI .... Personnel Planning Information
PPI .... Phoenix Precision Instrument Co.
PPI .... Pickle Packers International (EA)
ppi .... Picks Per Inch [*Weaving*] (DICI)
PPI .... Pico Products [*AMEX symbol*] (TTSB)
PPI .... Pico Products, Inc. [*AMEX symbol*] (SPSG)
PPI .... Pictorial Position Indicator
PPI .... Pilgrim Holdings Ltd. [*Vancouver Stock Exchange symbol*]
PPI .... PIPA [*Pulsed Integrating Pendulous Accelerometer*] Pulse Integrator
PPI .... Piston Position Indicator
PPI .... PIXEL [*Picture Element*] per Inch [*Computer science*] (PCM)
ppi .... Pixels Per Inch [*Computer graphics*] (WDMC)
PPI .... Plane Position Indicator [*RADAR*]
ppi .... Plan Position Indicator (AD)
PPI .... Plan Position Indicator Mode [*Computer science*] (ADA)
PPI .... Plasma Protein Isolate [*Food technology*]
PPI .... Plastics Pipe Institute (EA)
PPI .... Plot Position Indicator
PPI .... Point per Inch (IAA)
ppi .... Points Per Inch (WDMC)
ppi .... Policy Proof of Interest (AD)
PPI .... Policy Proof of Interest
PPI .... Polyphosphonositides
PPI .... Polyphthalimide [*Organic chemistry*]
PPI .... POM [*Program Objective Memorandum*] Preparation Instructions [*Military*]
ppi .... Pores per Inch
PPI .... Port Pirie [*Australia Airport symbol*] (OAG)
PPI .... Ports [*Harbors*] Performance Indicator [*Australia*]
PPI .... Postage Paid Impression [*Freight*] (DCTA)
PPI .... Potash and Phosphate Institute (EA)
PPI .... Pounds per Inch [*Lubrication load*]
PPI .... Preceding Preparatory Interval [*Psychometrics*]
PPI .... Preferred Parts Index
PPI .... Pre Phase-In
PPI .... Preplant Inc. [*Herbicides*] [*Agriculture*]
PPI .... Prepleading Investigation [*Law*]
PPI .... Pre-production Part Index
PPI .... Present Pain Intensity
PPI .... Present Position Indicator [*Aviation*]
PPI .... Prices Paid Index [*Economics*]
PPI .... Primary Personal Interest [*Personnel study*]
PPI .... Prince Patrick Island [*Canada*]
PPI .... Producer Price Index [*Bureau of Labor Statistics*] [*Information service or system*]
PPI .... Professional Photographers of Israel (PDAA)
PPI .... Programmable Peripheral Interface (MCD)
PPI .... Program Position Indicator
PPI .... Progressive Policy Institute [*Research center*] (RCD)
PPI .... Project Procurement Instructions [*Jet Propulsion Laboratory, NASA*]
PPI .... Project Public Information [*Department of Education*] (AEBS)
PPI .... Property Protection Insurance
PPI .... Proportional Plus Integral
PPI .... Protective Packaging, Inc. (AD)
PPI .... Public-Private Interface
PPI .... Pulse Position Indicator (MCD)
PPI .... Pulses per Inch (CMD)
ppi .... Pulses Per Inch (WDMC)
PPI .... Pyrophosphate Index [*Agronomy*]
PPi .... Pyrophosphate, Inorganic [*Chemistry*]
PPi-A .... Carnegie Library of Pittsburgh, Allegheny Regional Branch, Monroeville, PA [*Library symbol Library of Congress*] (LCLS)
PPIA .... Poultry Products Inspection Act (GFGA)
PPIA .... Programme du Pipeline des Iles de l'Arctique [*Canada*]
PPiAC .... Community College of Allegheny County, Pittsburgh, PA [*Library symbol Library of Congress*] (LCLS)
PPiAL .... Allegheny County Law Library, Pittsburgh, PA [*Library symbol Library of Congress*] (LCLS)
PPiAM .... Pittsburgh Academy of Medicine, Pittsburgh, PA [*Library symbol Library of Congress*] (LCLS)
PPIAS .... Parent-to-Parent Information on Adoption Services [*British*] (DI)
PPIB .... Programmable Protocol Interface Board
PPiC .... Carnegie-Mellon University, Pittsburgh, PA [*Library symbol Library of Congress*] (LCLS)
PPIC .... Plumbing and Piping Industry Council (AD)
PPIC .... Plumbing and Piping Industry Council (NADA)
PPIC .... Pollution Prevention Information Clearinghouse [*Environmental Protection Agency*]
PPiCa .... Carlow College, Pittsburgh, PA [*Library symbol Library of Congress*] (LCLS)
PPiCa-O .... Carlow College, Our Lady of Mercy Academy, Pittsburgh, PA [*Library symbol Library of Congress*] (LCLS)
PPiCC .... Chatham College, Pittsburgh, PA [*Library symbol Library of Congress*] (LCLS)
PPICR .... Institute for Cancer Research, Philadelphia, PA [*Library symbol Library of Congress*] (LCLS)
PPICS .... Production Planning Inventory Control System (PDAA)
PPiD .... Duquesne University, Pittsburgh, PA [*Library symbol Library of Congress*] (LCLS)
PPID .... Peak Pain Intensity Difference Score [*Medicine*] (DMAA)
PPID .... Polaris-Poseidon Intelligence Digest (MCD)
PPiD-L .... Duquesne University, School of Law, Pittsburgh, PA [*Library symbol Library of Congress*] (LCLS)
PPiE .... E. D'Appolonia Consulting Engineers, Pittsburgh, PA [*Library symbol Library of Congress*] (LCLS)
PPIE .... Prolonged Postictal Encephalopathy [*Medicine*] (DMAA)
PPIE .... Pseudophase Ion Exchange [*Chemistry*]
PPIF .... Photo Processing Interpretation Facility
ppif .... Photo-Processing Interpretation Facility (AD)
PPIFC .... Pauline Pinkney International Fan Club (EA)
PPiGulf .... Gulf Research & Development Co., Pittsburgh, PA [*Library symbol Library of Congress*] (LCLS)
PPiHB .... Carnegie-Mellon University, Hunt Institute for Botanical Documentation, Pittsburgh, PA [*Library symbol Library of Congress*] (LCLS)
PPiHi .... Historical Society of Western Pennsylvania, Pittsburgh, PA [*Library symbol Library of Congress*] (LCLS)
PPiI .... International Poetry Forum, Pittsburgh, PA [*Library symbol Library of Congress*] (LCLS)
PPiK .... Ketchum, McLeod & Grove, Inc., Pittsburgh, PA [*Library symbol Library of Congress*] (LCLS)
PPiL .... LaRoche College, Pittsburgh, PA [*Library symbol Library of Congress*] (LCLS)
PPIL .... Priced Provisioned Item List (MCD)

p-pille........ Praeventivpille [*Dano-Norwegian*] [*Contraceptive pill*] (AD)
PPiM........ Carnegie-Mellon University, Mellon Institute, Pittsburgh, PA [*Library symbol Library of Congress*] (LCLS)
PPIM........ Programmable Peripheral Interface Microcomputer (IAA)
PPiMS........ Mine Safety Appliances Co., Pittsburgh, PA [*Library symbol Library of Congress*] (LCLS)
PPIMS........ Past Performance Information Management System [*Army*]
PPIn........ Independence National Historical Park, Philadelphia, PA [*Library symbol Library of Congress*] (LCLS)
pp/in........ Pages Per Inch (AD)
PPINA........ Insurance Co., of North America, Corporate Archives, Philadelphia, PA [*Library symbol Library of Congress*] (LCLS)
PPINA........ RADAR Weather Report Not Available [*NWS*] (FAAC)
PPINE........ RADAR Weather Report Equipment No Echoes Observed [*NWS*] (FAAC)
PPINICI........ Pulsed Positive Ion-Negative Ion Chemical Ionization [*Instrumentation*]
PPINO........ RADAR Weather Report Equipment Inoperative Due to Breakdown [*NWS*] (FAAC)
PPInstHE........ Past President of the Institution of Highway Engineers [*British*] (DI)
PPIOK........ RADAR Weather Report Equipment Operation REsumed [*NWS*] (FAAC)
PPIOM........ RADAR Weather Report Equipment Inoperative Due to Maintenance [*NWS*] (FAAC)
PPIP........ Physics Post-Doctoral Information Pool [*American Institute of Physics*] (PDAA)
PPiPP........ Point Park College, Pittsburgh, PA [*Library symbol Library of Congress*] (LCLS)
PPiPPG........ PPG Industries, Inc., Glass Research Center, Information Services Library, Pittsburgh, PA [*Library symbol Library of Congress*] (LCLS)
PPiPT........ Pittsburgh Theological Seminary, Pittsburgh, PA [*Library symbol Library of Congress*] (LCLS)
PPIQ........ Personality and Personal Illness Questionnaire (AD)
PPIR........ Personnel Planning Information Report (MCD)
PPiR........ Rockwell International Corp., Pittsburgh, PA [*Library symbol Library of Congress*] (LCLS)
PPIRO........ Planned Position Indicator Readout (NVT)
PPiRP........ Reformed Presbyterian Theological Seminary, Pittsburgh, PA [*Library symbol*] [*Library of Congress*] (LCLS)
PPIS........ Pesticide Product Information System [*Environmental Protection Agency*] (GFGA)
PPIS........ Product Profile Information System [*Shell Oil Co.*]
PPIStructE........ Past President of the Institution of Structural Engineers [*British*] (DI)
PPIU........ Policy, Planning and Implementation Unit
PPIU........ Programmable Peripheral Interface Unit
PPiU........ University of Pittsburgh, Pittsburgh, PA [*Library symbol Library of Congress*] (LCLS)
PPiU-A........ University of Pittsburgh, Henry Clay Frick Fine Arts Center, Pittsburgh, PA [*Library symbol Library of Congress*] (LCLS)
PPiU-BL........ University of Pittsburgh, Blair-Lippincott Library, Eye and Ear Hospital of Pittsburgh, Pittsburgh, PA [*Library symbol Library of Congress*] (LCLS)
PPiU-H........ University of Pittsburgh, Maurice and Laura Falk Library of the Health Professions, Pittsburgh, PA [*Library symbol Library of Congress*] (LCLS)
PPiU-IS........ University of Pittsburgh, Archives of Industrial Society, Pittsburgh, PA [*Library symbol*] [*Library of Congress*] (LCLS)
PPiU-L........ University of Pittsburgh, Law School, Pittsburgh, PA [*Library symbol Library of Congress*] (LCLS)
PPiU-LS........ University of Pittsburgh, Graduate School of Library and Information Sciences, Pittsburgh, PA [*Library symbol Library of Congress*] (LCLS)
PPiU-NS........ University of Pittsburgh, Natural Sciences Library, Pittsburgh, PA [*Library symbol Library of Congress*] (LCLS)
PPiU-PH........ University of Pittsburgh, Graduate School of Public Health, Pittsburgh, PA [*Library symbol Library of Congress*] (LCLS)
PPiU-PIA........ University of Pittsburgh, Graduate School of Public and International Affairs, Pittsburgh, PA [*Library symbol Library of Congress*] (LCLS)
PPiUS........ United States Steel Corp., Pittsburgh, PA [*Library symbol Library of Congress*] (LCLS)
PPiU-SF........ University of Pittsburgh, Stephen Collins Foster Memorial [*Music*] Library,Pittsburgh, PA [*Library symbol Library of Congress*] (LCLS)
PPiUSM........ United States Department of the Interior, Bureau of Mines, Pittsburgh Research Center, Pittsburgh, PA [*Library symbol Library of Congress*] (LCLS)
PPIV........ Per Person Interview Value [*Marketing*] (WDMC)
PPIV........ Positive Personnel Identity Verification (PDAA)
PPiW........ Westinghouse Electric Corp., Research and Development Center, Pittsburgh, PA [*Library symbol Library of Congress*] (LCLS)
PPiW-N........ Westinghouse Electric Corp., Nuclear Center Library, Pittsburgh, PA [*Library symbol Library of Congress*] (LCLS)
PPiWP........ Western Psychiatric Institute and Clinic, University of Pittsburgh, Pittsburgh, PA [*Library symbol Library of Congress*] (LCLS)
PPJ........ Pressure Plane Joint
PPJ........ Pure Pancreatic Juice
PPJ........ Thomas Jefferson University, Philadelphia, PA [*Library symbol Library of Congress*] (LCLS)
PPJea........ Jeanes Hospital, Philadelphia, PA [*Library symbol Library of Congress Obsolete*] (LCLS)
PPJO........ Pli Premier Jour Officiel [*Official First Day Cover - OFDC*] [*Canada Post Corp.*]
PPJ-S........ Thomas Jefferson University, Scott Memorial Library, Philadelphia, PA [*Library symbol Library of Congress*] (LCLS)
PPJW........ Past Pro-Junior Warden [*Freemasonry*] (ROG)
PPK........ Paired Perpendicular Keratotomy [*Procedure to correct astigmatism*]
PPK........ Palmoplantar Keratoderma [*Dermatology*]
PPK........ Palmoplantar Keratosis [*Medicine*] (DMAA)
PPK........ Parametrized Post-Keplerian [*Physics*]
PPK........ Paramp Pump Klystron
PPK........ Parti Progressiste Katangais [*Political party*]
PPK........ Personal Preference Kit [*Small bag in which astronauts are allowed to take personal mementos*]
PPK........ Polizei Pistole Kriminal [*Pistol suitable for undercover police or detective use*] [*Walther Waffenfabrik, German arms manufacturer*]
PPK........ Punt, Pass, and Kick [*Youth competition sponsored by professional football*]
pPk........ Purplish Pink (AD)
PPK........ Ramp 66, Inc. [*ICAO designator*] (FAAC)
PPKB........ Partai Perpaduan Kebang-Saan Brunei [*Brunei National United Party*] [*Political party*] (EY)
PPKCA........ Pen and Pocket Knife Cutters' Association [*A union*] [*British*]
PPKG........ Power Package (MSA)
Ppl........ Intrapleural Pressure [*Medicine*] (DAVI)
PPL........ Library Co. of Philadelphia, Philadelphia, PA [*Library symbol Library of Congress*] (LCLS)
PPL........ Package Programs of London (NITA)
PPL........ Palach Press Ltd. [*British*] (EAIO)
PPL........ Palmer Physical Laboratory [*Princeton University*] (MCD)
PPL........ Pars Planus Lensectomy [*Ophthalmology*] (DAVI)
PPL........ Participle [*Grammar*] (WGA)
PPL........ PCBoard Programming Language [*Clark Development Co.*] (PCM)
PPL........ Pembina Resources Ltd. [*Toronto Stock Exchange symbol*]
PPL........ Penicilloyl Polylysine [*Pharmacology*]
PPL........ Pennsylvania Power & Light Co. [*NYSE symbol*] (SPSG)
PPL........ People
PPL........ Peripheral Blood Leukocyte [*Medicine*] (PDAA)
PPL........ Per Pupil Limitation (AFM)
PPL........ Peter Peregrinus Ltd. [*Publisher*]
PPL........ Phenylpropanolamine [*Organic chemistry*]
PPL........ Philadelphia Public Library (AD)
PPL........ Phoenix Public Library (AD)
PPL........ Phonographic Performance Ltd. [*British*]
PPL........ Photogrammetric Programming Language [*Computer science*] (PDAA)
PPL........ Physical Properties Laboratory [*Oklahoma State University*] [*Research center*] (RCD)
ppl........ Pipeline (AD)
PPL........ Pittsburgh Public Library (AD)
PPL........ Pixel per Line [*Computer science*] (IAA)
PPL........ Planned Parenthood League (AD)
PPL........ Planning Parts List
PPL........ Plan Position Landing (DEN)
PPL........ Plant Physiology Laboratory (SSD)
PPL........ Plasma Physics Laboratory [*Also known as PPPL*]
PPL........ Plasma Propulsion Laboratory (MCD)
PPL........ Plus Programming Language [*Computer science*]
PPL........ Plutonium Product Loadout [*Nuclear energy*] (NRCH)
PPL........ Police Protective League (AD)
PPL........ Police Protective League (NADA)
PPL........ Polymorphic Programming Language [*1971*] [*Computer science*] (CSR)
PPL........ Populated Place [*Board on Geographic Names*]
PPL........ Population Paper Listing [*US Census Bureau*] [*A publication*]
PPL........ Porcine Pancreatic Lipase [*An enzyme*]
PPL........ Posterior Pole Plasm [*Insect embryology*]
PPL........ Power Plant Laboratory (MUGU)
PPL........ PP&L Resources [*NYSE symbol*] (TTSB)
PPL........ PP & L Resources, Inc. [*NYSE symbol*] (SAG)
PPL........ Precise Participant Location
PPL........ Predictive Period LASER (KSC)
PPL........ Preferential Planning List
PPL........ Preferred Parts List
PPL........ Preliminary Parts List
PPL........ Preliminary Power Laboratory (IAA)
PPL........ Presbyterians Pro-Life [*An association*] (EA)
PPL........ Priced Parts List (NASA)
P/PL........ Primary Payload [*NASA*] (NASA)
PPL........ Princeton Polymer Laboratories
PPL........ Print Positions per Line [*Computer science*] (MHDI)
PPL........ Private Pilot's Licence [*British*]
PPL........ Program Production Library [*Computer science*]
PPL........ Project Priority List [*Environmental Protection Agency*]
PPL........ Protein-Polysaccharide [*Biochemistry*] (DAVI)
PPL........ Protein Preprolactin [*Biochemistry*]
PPL........ Providence Public Library (AD)
PPL........ Provisioning Parts List (AAG)
PPL........ Purchased Parts List
PPL........ Pure Prairie League [*Musical group*]
PPL........ Purple
PPL........ Puu Pili [*Hawaii*] [*Seismograph station code, US Geological Survey*] (SEIS)
PpL........ W. & F. Pascoe Proprietory Ltd., Milsons Point, Australia [*Library symbol Library of Congress*] (LCLS)
PPLA........ Practice Precautionary Landing Approach [*Aviation*]
PPLA........ Professional Photographic Laboratories Association [*British*] (DBA)

P-plane Pilotless Airplane (AD)
PPLas La Salle College, Philadelphia, PA [*Library symbol Library of Congress*] (LCLS)
PPlase Peptidylprolyl Cis-Trans Isomerase [*An enzyme*]
PPLB Postprocessor Call Library [*Computer science*] (IAA)
PPLC Patients Protection Law Commission (AD)
PPLD Pikes Peak Library District [*Internationally recognized computerized library system*]
PPLDF Professional Protector and Legal Defense Fund
PPLE Partial Preliminary Logistic Evaluation
PPLE Participle [*Grammar*]
pple Past Participle (AD)
PPLE Principle (ROG)
PPL/H Private Pilot's Licence/Helicopters [*British*] (AIA)
PPLI Precise Participant Location-Identification [*Navigation*]
PPLI Precise Position Location Information
PPLI Provisioning Parts List Index (MCD)
PPLIF Pulsed Photolysis LASER-Induced Fluorescence [*Environmental science*]
PPLL Military Order of the Loyal Legion of the United States, [*Civil*] War Library and Museum, Philadelphia, PA [*Library symbol Library of Congress*] (LCLS)
PPLLT Provisional Program Load Library Tape [*Computer science*] (MHDI)
PPLN Pipeline
pplo Pleuropneumonia-Like Organism (AD)
PPLO Pleuropneumonia-Like Organisms [*Bacteriology*]
PPLP Photopolymers Lithograph Plate
P PLPBD Paper or Pulpboard [*Freight*]
PPLPrA Penn Pwr & Lt 4.40% Pfd [*NYSE symbol*] (TTSB)
PPLPrB Penn Pwr & Lt 4.50% Pfd [*NYSE symbol*] (TTSB)
ppls Peoples [*Internet language*] [*Computer science*]
PPLS Peoples Bank Corp. (Indianapolis, IN) [*NASDAQ symbol*] (SAG)
PPLS Peoples Bank Indianapolis [*NASDAQ symbol*] (TTSB)
PPLS Precision Position Locator System [*Army*]
PPLS Preferred Parts List System (MCD)
PPLS Propellant and Pressurant Loading System [*NASA*] (KSC)
PPLT Lutheran Theological Seminary, Philadelphia, PA [*Library symbol Library of Congress*] (LCLS)
PPLV Preliminary Pollutant Limit Value (MCD)
PPLX Section of Populated Place [*Board on Geographic Names*]
PPM Aberdeen, MD [*Location identifier FAA*] (FAAL)
PPM Investment Grade Municipal Income Fund [*NYSE symbol*] (SAG)
PPM Investment Grade Muni Inc. [*NYSE symbol*] (TTSB)
PPM Mercantile Library, Philadelphia, PA [*Library symbol Library of Congress Obsolete*] (LCLS)
PPM Page-per-Minute [*Computer science*] (PCM)
PPM Pages per Minute [*Printer technology*]
ppm Papermaker [*MARC relator code*] [*Library of Congress*] (LCCP)
PPM Parallel Processing Machine [*Computer science*] (IAA)
PPM Particuliere Participatiemaatschappy [*Private Joint Stock Company*] [*Dutch*]
PPM Partido del Pueblo Mexicano [*Mexican People's Party*] [*Political party*] (PPW)
PPM Partido Proletario de Mexico [*Proletarian Party of Mexico*] [*Political party*] (AD)
PPM Parti Pekerja-Pekerja Malaysia [*Workers' Party of Malaysia*] [*Political party*] (PPW)
PPM Parti Progressiste Martiniquais [*Progressive Party of Martinique*] [*Political party*] (PPW)
PPM Partitioned-Pipe Mixer [*Engineering*]
PPM Part Program Manager
PPM Parts per Million
ppm Parts Per Million (AD)
ppm Parts per Million
ppm Parts per Million (IDOE)
PPM Parts per Minute (MCD)
PPM Pattani People's Movement [*Thailand*] [*Political party*]
PPM Peak Power Meter
PPM Peak Program Meter [*Television*]
ppm Peak Program Meter (AD)
PPM Periodic Permanent Magnet
PPM Periodic Permanent Magnet Focusing (IAA)
PPM Periodic Pulse Metering [*Telecommunications*] (TEL)
PPM Permanent Pacemaker [*Cardiology*] (MAE)
PPM Pershing Project Manager
PPM Personnel Priority Model (MCD)
PPM Personnel Program Manager [*Navy*]
PPM Persutuan Perpustakaan Malaysia [*Library Association of the Federation of Malaysia*] (AD)
PPM Phenylpropanolamine(hydrochloride) [*Also, PPA, PPH*] [*Decongestant*]
PPM Phosphopentomutase [*An enzyme*]
PPM Physician Practice Management
PPM Pictures per Minute (NTCM)
PPM Piecewise Parabolic Method [*Mathematical model of fluid flow*]
PPM Pilot Production Model [*Military*] (CAAL)
PPM Pistol Prize Money [*British military*] (DMA)
PPM Planned Preventive Maintenance (IEEE)
PPM Popocatepetl [*Mexico*] [*Seismograph station code, US Geological Survey*] (SEIS)
PPM Portable Pix Map [*Computer science*]
PPM Position and Pay Management [*Army*] (AABC)
PPM Position and Proper Motion [*Catalog of star positions*]
PPM Postage Prepaid in Money
PPM Posterior Papillary Muscle [*Image on transesophageal echocardiography*] [*Cardiology*] (DAVI)
PPM Postpass Message
PPM Post-Program Monitoring
PPM Pounds per Minute
ppm Pounds Per Minute (AD)
PPM Prairie Print Makers [*Defunct*] (EA)
PPM Prenegotiation Position Memorandum (AAGC)
PPM Presentation Protocol Machine [*Telecommunications*] (OSI)
PPM Previous Processor Mode
PPM Principal Period of Maintenance (AAGC)
PPM Problem Program Monitor (IAA)
PPM Production Planning Memorandum
PPM Program, Project Management [*Army*]
PPM Project Profile Manual
PPM Prudential Portfolio Managers Ltd. [*British*]
PPM Pulse Phase Modulation [*Telecommunications*] (IAA)
PPM Pulse Position Modulation [*Radio data transmission*]
ppm Pulse Position Modulation (AD)
PPM Pulse Power Module (RDA)
PPM Pulses per Minute
ppm Pulses per Minute (IDOE)
PPM Pyrite-Pyrrhotite-Magnetite [*Mineralogy*]
PPMA Petroleum Marketers Association of America
PPMA Petrol Pump Manufacturers Association [*British*] (DBA)
PPMA Plastic Products Manufacturers Association [*Later, Plastic and Metal Products Manufacturers Association*] (EA)
PPMA Political Products Manufacturers Association (EA)
PPMA Polypropyl Methacrylate [*Organic chemistry*]
ppma Post-Polio Muscular Atrophy [*Medicine*] (AD)
PPMA Post-Poliomyelitis Muscular Atrophy [*Medicine*]
PPMA Precision Potentiometer Manufacturers Association [*Later, Variable Resistive Components Institute*] (EA)
PPMA Produce Packaging and Marketing Association [*British*] (DBA)
PPMA Progressive Postmyelitis Muscular Atrophy [*Medicine*] (DMAA)
PPMA Pulp and Paper Manufacturers Association [*Later, PPMMA*] (EA)
PPMAP Power Planning Modeling Application Procedure [*Environmental Protection Agency*] (GFGA)
PPMC Parts per Million Carbon [*Automotive engineering*]
PPMC People to People Music Committee (EA)
PPMD Posterior Polymorphous Dystrophy of the Cornea [*Ophthalmology*] (DAVI)
PPME Pacific Plate Motion Experiment (NASA)
PPMFA Pulp and Paper Manufacturers' Federation of Australia
PPMFC Preprints on Precision Measurement and Fundamental Constants [*National Institute of Standards and Technology*]
PPMG Professional Publishers Marketing Group (EA)
PPMI Pilot Plant Meat Irradiator
PPMI Printed Paper Mat Institute (EA)
PPMIN Pulses per Minute (MSA)
PPMis Misericordia Hospital, Philadelphia, PA [*Library symbol Library of Congress Obsolete*] (LCLS)
PPML Preferred Parts and Materials List [*NASA*]
PPMM Postpolycythemia Myeloid Metaplasia [*Medicine*] (AAMN)
PPMMA Pulp and Paper Machinery Manufacturers Association [*Later, APMA*] (EA)
PPMN Preliminary Program Management Network [*Military*]
PPMO Pershing Project Manager's Office (RDA)
PPMO Provisional Program Management Office [*Army*]
PPMoI Moore College of Art, Philadelphia, PA [*Library symbol Library of Congress*] (LCLS)
PPMPC Pilot Parachute Mortar Pyrotechnic Cartridge (SAA)
PPMR Purchased Parts Material Requirements
PPMRC Pre-Positioned Materiel Receipt Card
PPMRD Pre-Positioned Material Receipt Document
PPMS Performax's Personal Matrix System (DMAA)
PPMS Pitt Press Mathematical Series [*A publication*]
PPMS Plastic Pipe Manufacturers Society [*British*] (DBA)
PPMS Poly(para-Methylstyrene) [*Organic chemistry*]
PPMS Polyphenylmethylsiloxane [*Organic chemistry*]
PPMS Professional Productivity Management System (HGAA)
PPMS Programme and Project Management System [*United Nations Development Programme*] (DUND)
PPMS Program Performance Measurement Systems (IEEE)
PPMS Purdue Perceptual-Motor Survey [*Kephart Scale*]
PPMV Parts per Million by Volume
ppmv Parts per Million by Volume [*Marine science*] (OSRA)
PPMW Parts per Million by Weight (MCD)
PPMW Primary Plant Mineralized Water (IAA)
PPN Numismatic and Antiquarian Society, Philadelphia, PA [*Library symbol Library of Congress Obsolete*] (LCLS)
PPN Papenoo [*Society Islands*] [*Seismograph station code, US Geological Survey*] (SEIS)
PPN Parameterized Post-Newtonian [*Gravity*]
PPN Parametrized Post-Newtonian [*Physics*]
PPN Partial Parenteral Nutrition [*Medicine*] (DMAA)
PPN Partido Patriotico Nobo [*New Patriotic Party*] [*Aruba*] [*Political party*] (EY)
PPN Partido Progreso Nacional [*National Progress Party*] [*Costa Rica*] [*Political party*] (PPW)
PPN Parti Progressiste Nigerien [*Nigerian Progressive Party*] [*Political party*]
PPN Patrol Plane Navigator (DNAB)
PPN Peak-to-Peak Noise [*Instrumentation*]
PPN Pedunculopontine Nucleus (DMAA)

PPN .... Peripheral Parenteral Nutrition [*Medicine*] (DAVI)
PPN .... Peroxyproprionyl Nitrate [*Organic chemistry*]
PPN .... Polyphosphonate [*Organic chemistry*]
PPN .... Popayan [*Colombia*] [*Airport symbol*] (OAG)
PPN .... Portland Public Library, Portland, ME [*OCLC symbol*] (OCLC)
PPN .... Precipitation (WGA)
PPN .... Predictive Proportional Navigation
PPN .... Procurement Program Number [*Military*]
PPN .... Project, Programmer Number
PPN .... Proportion (ROG)
ppn .... Proportion (AD)
PPN .... Public Packet Network [*Computer science*] (ODBW)
PPNA .... Peak Phrenic Nerve Activity [*Medicine*]
PPNA .... Pupil-Perceived Needs Assessment [*Education*] (EDAC)
PPNB .... Pre-Pottery Neolithic B Period [*Paleontology*]
PPNC .... Patrol Plane Navigator/Communicator (DNAB)
PPNC .... Pre-Pottery Neolithic C Phase [*Paleontology*]
PPNDG .... Petition Pending
PPNF .... Price-Pottenger Nutrition Foundation (EA)
PPNG .... Penicillinase-Producing Neisseria gonorrhoeae
PPNICI .... Pulsed Positive/Negative Ion Chemical Ionization
P/PNL .... Pocket Panel [*Automotive engineering*]
PPNMC .... United States Navy, Naval Regional Medical Center, Philadelphia, PA [*Library symbol Library of Congress*] (LCLS)
PPNP .... Point Pelee National Park [*Ontario, Canada*] (AD)
PPNSC .... Preferred Procurement Number Selector Code [*Military*] (AFIT)
PPNSCA ...... Policy Plans and National Security Council Affairs
PPNS-IE ...... Preschool and Primary Nowicki-Strickland Internal-External Control Scale (EDAC)
PPNT .... Proponent
PPNW .... Physicians for the Prevention of Nuclear War (AD)
PPNW .... Physicians for the Prevention of Nuclear War (NADA)
PPNWA .... N. W. Ayer & Son, Philadelphia, PA [*Library symbol Library of Congress Obsolete*] (LCLS)
PPO .... Diphenyloxazole [*Chemistry*] (DAVI)
PPO .... Parking Patrol Officer
PPO .... Patriot Project Office [*Army*]
PPO .... Pepsi-Cola Puerto Rico Bott'B' [*NYSE symbol*] (TTSB)
PPO .... Pepsi Cola Puerto Rico Bottling [*NYSE symbol*] (SAG)
PPO .... Permanent Paranormal Object
PPO .... Photographic Program Office [*NASA*] (KSC)
PPO .... Platelet Peroxidase [*An enzyme*]
PPO .... Pleuropneumonia Organisms [*Bacteriology*]
PPO .... Police Petty Officer (DNAB)
PPO .... Pollution Prevention Office [*Environmental Protection Agency*]
PPO .... Polyphenol Oxidase [*An enzyme*]
PPO .... Polyphenylene Oxide [*Organic chemistry*]
ppo .... Polyphenylene Oxide (AD)
PPO .... Poly(propylene Oxide) [*Organic chemistry*]
PPO .... Port Postal Office (AFM)
PPo .... Pottsville Free Public Library, Pottsville, PA [*Library symbol*] [*Library of Congress*] (LCLS)
PPO .... Power Plant Operating
PPO .... Preferred-Provided Organization [*Insurance*] (AD)
PPO .... Preferred-Provider Option [*Insurance*]
PPO .... Preferred-Provider Organization [*Insurance*]
PPO .... Pre Phase-Out
PPO .... Pressed Plutonium Oxide
PPO .... Primary Party Organization [*Politics*]
PPO .... Principal Priority Officer
PPO .... Prior Permission Only (AFM)
ppo .... Prior Permission Only (AD)
PPO .... Procurement Planning Officer
PPO .... Program Printout (MCD)
PPO .... Projected Program Objective (NG)
PPO .... Publications and Printing Office [*Army*]
PPO .... Public Pension Offset [*Federal Employees Retirement System*] (GFGA)
PPO .... Pure Plutonium Oxide
PPO .... Push-Pull Output (DEN)
PPO_2 .... Partial Pressure of Oxygen (CAAL)
PPoAr .... Schuylkill County Archives, Pottsville, PA [*Library symbol*] [*Library of Congress*] (LCLS)
PPOC .... Per Pupil Operating Cost (ADA)
PP of A .... Professional Photographers of America (EA)
PP of A .... Professional Photographers of America [*Atlanta, GA*] (WDMC)
PPOG .... Polytechnic Personnel Officers Group (AIE)
p-p-ola .... Political Plugola (AD)
ppom .... Particulate Polycyclic Organic Matter (AD)
P-POP .... Plain Paper Optimized Printing [*Canon*] [*Computer science*]
PPORT .... Prostate Patient Outcomes Research Team
PPOS .... Present Position (GAVI)
PPOS .... Saint George United Methodist Church, Philadelphia, PA [*Library symbol Library of Congress*] (LCLS)
PPOSN .... Proposition (ROG)
PPOX .... Polypropylene Oxide Plastic
PPP .... Pacific Peacemaker Project [*Defunct*] (EA)
PPP .... Pakistan People's Party [*Political party*] (PD)
PPP .... Palmoplantar Pustulosis [*Medicine*] (DMAA)
PPP .... Pan Pacific Petroleum [*Vancouver Stock Exchange symbol*]
PPP .... Paper, Printing, Publishing [*Department of Employment*] [*British*]
PPP .... Parallel Pattern Processor
PPP .... Parallel Push Pull (IAA)
PPP .... Pariser-Parr-Pople [*Physical chemistry*]
PPP .... Partai Persatuan Pembangunan [*United Development Party*] [*Indonesia*] [*Political party*] (PPW)
PPP .... Partido del Pueblo de Panama [*Panamanian People's Party*] [*Political party*] (PPW)
PPP .... Passage, Power, and Passenger [*Evaluation of labor progress*] [*Obstetrics*] (DAVI)
PPP .... Peak Pulse Power
PPP .... Pentose-Phosphate Pathway [*Metabolism*]
PPP .... Penultimate Profit [*Investment term*] (DFIT)
PPP .... Peoples Party of Pakistan (NADA)
PPP .... Peoples Party of Pakistan [*Political party*] (AD)
PPP .... People's Patriotic Party [*Myanmar*] [*Political party*] (PD)
PPP .... People's Political Party [*St. Vincent*] [*Political party*] (PPW)
PPP .... People's Progressive Party [*Gambia*] [*Political party*] (PPW)
PPP .... People's Progressive Party [*Guyana*] [*Political party*] (PD)
PPP .... People's Progressive Party [*Mauritania*] [*Political party*] (EY)
PPP .... People's Progressive Party [*Solomon Islands*] [*Political party*] (PPW)
PPP .... People's Progressive Party [*Anguilla*] [*Political party*] (PPW)
PPP .... People's Progress Party [*Papua New Guinea*] [*Political party*] (PPW)
PPP .... Permanent Party Personnel (MCD)
PPP .... Perpex Peristaltic Pump
PPP .... Personal Property Policy [*Insurance*]
PPP .... Personnel Performance Profile
PPP .... Petroleum Production Pioneers (AD)
PPP .... Phased Project Planning [*NASA*] (KSC)
PPP .... Pianississimo [*As Softly As Possible*] [*Music*]
PPP .... Pickford Projective Pictures [*Psychology*]
ppp .... Piu Pianissimo [*Very Very Softly*] [*Italian*] [*Music*] (AD)
PPP .... Planning Purpose Proposal
PPP .... Plan Position Presentation
PPP .... Platelet-Poor Plasma [*Hematology*]
PPP .... Pluripotent Progenitor [*Cytology*]
PPP .... Pogo Producing [*NYSE symbol*] (TTSB)
PPP .... Pogo Producing Co. [*NYSE symbol*] (SPSG)
PPP .... Point-to-Point Protocol [*Computer science*] (PCM)
PPP .... Polluter Pays Principle
PPP .... Poly(para-phenylene) [*Organic chemistry*]
PPP .... Polyphoretic Phosphate [*Organic chemistry*] (DAVI)
PPP .... Polypropylene-Paper-Polypropylene [*Biochemistry*]
PPP .... Popular Power Package (IAA)
PPP .... Portable Plotting Package [*Nuclear energy*] (NRCH)
PPP .... Positive Pressure Paradox
PPP .... Post-Painted Parts
PPP .... Postpartum Psychosis [*Obstetrics*] [*Psychiatry*] (DAVI)
PPP .... Powerful Permutation Procedure [*Meteorology*]
PPP .... Preferred Pharmacy Program
PPP .... Prepositional Procurement Package (DOMA)
PPP .... Prescriptive Parent Programming [*Education*]
PPP .... Prescriptive Program Plan [*Education*]
PPP .... Pretty Poor Planning
PPP .... Primary Products Promotion [*Australia*]
PPP .... Priority Placement Program (DOMA)
PPP .... Prior-Participating Preferred [*Stock*] (MHDW)
PPP .... Prison Pen Pals (EA)
PPP .... Private Patients' Plan [*British*]
PPP .... Production Part Pattern (MCD)
PPP .... Profit and Performance Planning (DCTA)
PPP .... Program Protection Plan [*DoD*] (RDA)
PPP .... Progressive People's Party [*Sierra Leone*] [*Political party*] (EY)
PPP .... Progressive People's Party [*Sudan*] [*Political party*] (EY)
PPP .... Progressive People's Party [*Liberia*] [*Political party*] (PPW)
PPP .... Propria Pecunia Posuit [*Erected at His Own Expense*] [*Latin*]
PPP .... Proserpine [*Australia Airport symbol*] (OAG)
PPP .... Province Pacification Plan (CINC)
PPP .... Provisioning Program Plan (MCD)
PPP .... Public Policy Program [*Australian National University*]
PPP .... Purchasing Power Parity [*Economics*]
PPP .... Push-Pull Power (IAA)
PPPA .... Poison Prevention Packaging Act
PPPA .... Professional Pool Players Association [*Defunct*] (EA)
PPPA .... Protein Phosphatase Alpha (DMAA)
PPPA .... Pulp and Paper Prepackaging Association [*Later, SSI*]
PPPA .... Push-Pull Power Amplifier (IAA)
PPP & M ...... Preservation, Packaging, Packing, and Marking
PPPBL .... Peripheral Pulses Palpable Both Legs [*Medicine*] (DMAA)
PPPBR .... Peruvian Paso Part-Blood Registry (EA)
PPPC .... Petroleum Pool Pacific Coast
PPPC .... Pipe Plug Producers Council (EA)
PPPCA .... Philadelphia College of Art Library, Philadelphia, PA [*Library symbol Library of Congress*] (LCLS)
PPPCity .... Philadelphia City Institute Branch Free Library, Philadelphia, PA [*Library symbol Library of Congress Obsolete*] (LCLS)
PPPCO .... Pennsylvania College of Optometry, Philadelphia, PA [*Library symbol Library of Congress*] (LCLS)
PPPCPh .... Philadelphia College of Pharmacy and Science, Philadelphia, PA [*Library symbol Library of Congress*] (LCLS)
PPPE .... Pennsylvania Economy League, Inc., Eastern Division, Philadelphia, PA [*Library symbol Library of Congress*] (LCLS)
PPPEA .... Pulp, Paper, and Paperboard Export Association of the United States (EA)
PPPEC .... Philadelphia Electric Co., Philadelphia, PA [*Library symbol Library of Congress*] (LCLS)
PPPEE .... Pulsed Pinch Plasma Electromagnetic Engine (AAG)
PPPF .... Positive Pregnancy and Parenting Fitness (EA)

PPPFM Free and Accepted Masons of Pennsylvania, Grand Lodge Library, Philadelphia, PA [*Library symbol Library of Congress*] (LCLS)

PPPG People's Progressive Party of Guyana [*Political party*]

PPPG Postprandial Plasma Glucose [*Endocrinology*] (DAVI)

PPPH Pennsylvania Hospital, Philadelphia, PA [*Library symbol Library of Congress*] (LCLS)

PPPHA Philadelphia Housing Association, Philadelphia, PA [*Library symbol Library of Congress Obsolete*] (LCLS)

PPPHC Philadelphia Tuberculosis and Health Association, Philadelphia, PA [*Library symbol Library of Congress Obsolete*] (LCLS)

PPPH-I Institute of the Pennsylvania Hospital, Philadelphia, PA [*Library symbol Library of Congress*] (LCLS)

PPPI Insurance Society of Philadelphia, Philadelphia, PA [*Library symbol Library of Congress Obsolete*] (LCLS)

PPPI Personnel Performance Problems Inventory [*Test*]

PPPI Plan Positional Plot Indicator

PPPI Precision Plan Position Indicator

PPPI Preliminary Process Potential Index

PPPI Preplanned Product Improvement [*DoD*] (MCD)

PPPI Primary Private Practice Income [*Medicine*] (MAE)

PPPI Primary Private Practice Insurance [*Medicine*] (DMAA)

PPPI Projection Plan Position Indicator

PPPI Pulp, Paper, and Paperboard Institute USA [*Later, API*]

PPPL Philadelphia Board of Public Education, Pedagogical Library, Philadelphia, PA [*Library symbol Library of Congress*] (LCLS)

PPPL Planetary Physical Processes Laboratory (SSD)

PPPL Princeton Plasma Physics Laboratory [*Also known as PPL - Plasma Physics Laboratory*] [*Princeton, NJ*] [*Department of Energy*]

PPPL Printed Planning Parts List

PPPL Program Preferred Parts List

PPPlanP Planned Parenthood of Southeast Pennsylvania, Philadelphia, PA [*Library symbol Library of Congress*] (LCLS)

PPPlay Plays and Players Club, Philadelphia, PA [*Library symbol Library of Congress Obsolete*] (LCLS)

PPPLS Public Policy for Public Libraries Section [*Public Library Association*] [*American Library Association*]

PPPM Philadelphia Museum of Art, Philadelphia, PA [*Library symbol Library of Congress*] (LCLS)

PPPM-I Philadelphia Museum of Art, College of Art, Philadelphia, PA [*Library symbol Library of Congress Obsolete*] (LCLS)

PPPP Past Performance and Present Posture (AAG)

PPPP People's Peace and Prosperity Party [*Defunct*] (EA)

pppp Piu Piu Piu Pianissimo [*Very, Very, Very Softly*] [*Italian*] [*Music*] (AD)

PPPP Porokeratosis Punctata Palmaris et Plantaris [*Medicine*] (DMAA)

PPPP Proposed Partial Package Program (MUGU)

PPPPI Photographic Projection Plan Position Indicator (DEN)

PPPPP Pain, Pallor, Pulse Loss, Paresthesia, Paralysis [*Medicine*] (MEDA)

PPPR Philadelphia Transportation Co., Philadelphia, PA [*Library symbol Library of Congress Obsolete*] (LCLS)

PPPRC Poor Richard Club, Philadelphia, PA [*Library symbol Library of Congress Obsolete*] (LCLS)

PPPres Presbyterian University of Pennsylvania, Scheie Eye Institute Library, Philadelphia, PA [*Library symbol Library of Congress*] (LCLS)

PPPRF Pan Pacific Public Relations Federation [*Thailand*] [*Defunct*]

PPPrHi Presbyterian Historical Society, Philadelphia, PA [*Library symbol Library of Congress*] (LCLS)

PPPrI Printing Institute, Philadelphia, PA [*Library symbol Library of Congress Obsolete*] (LCLS)

PPProM Provident Mutual Life Insurance Co., Philadelphia, PA [*Library symbol Library of Congress Obsolete*] (LCLS)

PPPS People's Press Printing Society [*British*]

PPPSB Philadelphia College of the Bible, Philadelphia, PA [*Library symbol Library of Congress*] (LCLS)

PPPTe Philadelphia College of Textiles and Science, Philadelphia, PA [*Library symbol Library of Congress*] (LCLS)

PPQ Abandoned Police Post [*Board on Geographic Names*]

PPQ Parts per Quadrillion

PPQ Person Perception Questionnaire [*Psychology*] (EDAC)

PPQ Pittsfield, IL [*Location identifier FAA*] (FAAL)

PPQ Planning Purpose Quote

PPQ Plant Protection and Quarantine Programs [*Department of Agriculture*] (IMH)

PPQ Polyphenylquinoxaline [*Resin*]

ppq Polyphenylquinoxaline (AD)

PPQ Possible Parliamentary Question [*Australia*]

PPQA Pageable Partition Queue Area [*Computer science*]

PPQN Parts per Quarter Note [*Computer science*] (PCM)

PPQR Priority Parts Quality Review

PPQT Preproduction Qualification Test [*Army*]

PPQT & E Pre-Production Qualification Test and Evaluation [*Army*]

PPR Paid Pensioner Recruiter [*British military*] (DMA)

PPR Palomino Pony Registry

PPR Paper

PPR Paper

PPR Partido Panamenista Republicano [*Panama*] [*Political party*] (EY)

PPR Partido Patriotico Revolucionario [*Mexico Political party*] (EY)

PPR Partido Proletariano Revolucionario [*Proletarian Revolutionary Party*] [*Portugal Political party*] (PPW)

PPR Payload Preparation Room [*VAFB*] [*NASA*] (MCD)

PPR Peak Production Rate

PPR Periodicals Publishing Record [*Alberta Public Affairs Bureau*] [*Canada Information service or system*] (CRD)

PPR Periodic Personnel Report

PPR Permanent Pay Record [*Military*]

PPR Permanent Personal Registration [*Voting*] (BARN)

PPR Peste des Petits Ruminants [*Rinderpest-like disease*] [*Veterinary medicine*]

PPR Photographic Press Review [*A publication British*]

PPR Photo-Plastic-Recording

PPR Photopolarimeter Radiometer [*Instrumentation*]

PPR Physician Payment Reform

PPR Pilgrim America Prime Rate Trust [*NYSE symbol*] (SAG)

PPR Pilgrim America Prime Rt [*NYSE symbol*] (TTSB)

PPR Pilgrim Prime Rate Trust [*NYSE symbol*] (SPSG)

PPR Pilot, Pressure Regulator (MCD)

PPR Pirapora [*Brazil*] [*Airport symbol*] (AD)

PPR Polish People's Republic

PPR Politieke Partij Radikalen [*Radical Political Party*] [*Netherlands Political party*] (PPE)

PPR Polska Partia Robotnicza [*Polish Workers' Party*] [*Political party*]

PPR Portable Propagation Recorder [*Bell System*]

PPr Port Pirie (AD)

PPR Potential Problem Report [*Navy*] (CAAL)

PPR Present Participle [*Grammar*]

ppr Present Participle (AD)

PPR Price. Procedural Regulation [*United States*] [*A publication*] (DLA)

PPR Price's Precipitation Reaction [*Medicine*]

PPR Principal Private Residence [*Income tax*] [*British*]

PPR Principal Probate Registry (DLA)

PPR Printed Paper Rate [*British*] (ILCA)

ppr Printed Paper Rate (AD)

ppr Prior Permission Required (AD)

PPR Prior Permission Required (FAAC)

PPR Procurement Problem Report (AD)

PPR Production Parts Release (KSC)

PPR Production Progress Report (MCD)

PPR Program Planning Report (IAA)

PPR Program Progress Review

PPR Program Proposal Request

PPR Progress Payment Report (AAGC)

PPR Project Progress Report (OICC)

PPR Proper [*Heraldry*]

PPR Proprietary Procurement Request (NG)

PPR Provisioning Preparedness Review [*Navy*] (CAAL)

PPR Purchase Parts Request (KSC)

PPRA Past President of the Royal Academy [*British*] (EY)

PPRA Preliminary Personnel Requirements Analysis [*Navy*]

PPRA Protection of Pupil Rights Amendment

pprbd Paperboard (AD)

PPRBD Paperboard

PPRBD Paperboard [*Freight*]

PPRC Personnel Program Review Committee [*Military*]

PPRC Physician Payment Review Commission

PPRC Pollution Prevention Research Center [*North Carolina State University*] [*Research center*] (RCD)

PPRC Prepositioned Receipt Card (AABC)

PPRCI Rittenhouse Club, Philadelphia, PA [*Library symbol Library of Congress Obsolete*] (LCLS)

PPRD Pontypool Road [*Welsh depot code*]

PPRDS Products and Process Research and Development Support (DCTA)

PPRE Peroxisome Proliferator Response Element [*Biochemistry*]

PPREC Pulp and Paper Research and Education Center [*Auburn University*] [*Research center*] (RCD)

PPREPT Periodic Personnel Report [*Military*] (AABC)

PPRETS Reformed Episcopal Seminary, Philadelphia, PA [*Library symbol Library of Congress Obsolete*]

PPRF Paramedian Pontine Reticular Formation [*Neuroanatomy*]

PPRF Postpartum Renal Failure [*Medicine*] (DMAA)

PPRF Pulse Pair Repetition Frequency (MCD)

PPRF Rosenbach Foundation, Philadelphia, PA [*Library symbol Library of Congress*] (LCLS)

PPRG Precambrian Paleobiology Research Group

PPRGF Richard Gimbel Foundation for Literary Research, Philadelphia, PA [*Library symbol Library of Congress Obsolete*] (LCLS)

PPRI PACOM [*Pacific Command*] Priority Number (CINC)

PPRIBA Past President of the Royal Institute of British Architects (EY)

PPRibP Phosphoribose Diphosphate [*Biochemistry*]

PPRIC Pulp and Paper Research Institute of Canada

PPRICA Pulp and Paper Research Institute of Canada (AD)

PPrIT Putnam Premier Income Trust [*Associated Press*] (SAG)

PPRL Poisonous Plant Research Laboratory [*Agricultural Research Service*] [*Research center*] (RCD)

PPRM Population Protection and Resources Management [*Military British*]

PPRM Pure Premium Rating Method [*Insurance*]

PPRN Preliminary Publication Revision Notice

PPRN Purchased Parts Requirement Notice (KSC)

PPRNCM Professional Performance of the Royal Northern College of Music [*British*] (DBQ)

PPRNS Pulse-Phased Radio Navigation System

PPRO Per Procuration [*Business term*]

PPROM Prolonged Premature Rupture of Membranes [*Obstetrics*] (DAVI)

PPROP Personal Property [*Legal shorthand*] (LWAP)

PPRP Polydenosine Diphosphate-Ribose Polymerase (DMAA)

PPRPF Regional Planning Federation, Philadelphia, PA [*Library symbol Library of Congress Obsolete*] (LCLS)

PPRS Perceptions of Parental Role Scales

PPRS Pharmaceutical Price Regulation Scheme [*British*]

PPRS Program Planning and Review Staff [*Environmental Protection Agency*] (GFGA)

PPRS Promotions and Placements Referral System (MCD)

PPRSA .... Past President of the Royal Society of Arts [*British*] (DI)
PPRV .... Peste des Petits Ruminants Virus [*Rinderpest-like disease*] [*Veterinary medicine*]
PPRWP .... Poor Precordial R-Wave Progression [*Cardiology*]
PPS .... Butte Aviation, Inc. [*FAA designator*] (FAAC)
PPS .... Pacific Passenger Services (AD)
PPS .... Packets per Second [*Computer science*] (PCM)
PPS .... Page Printing System [*Honeywell, Inc.*] [*Computer science*]
PPS .... Page Processing System (NITA)
PPS .... Paint, Pesticide Chemicals, and Solvents
PPS .... Paper Publications Society [*Amsterdam, Netherlands*] (EA)
PPS .... Parallel Processing System [*Computer science*] (MDG)
PPS .... Parameter Processing System (CAAL)
PPS .... Parliamentary Private Secretary [*British*]
PPS .... Partia e Punes e Shqiperise [*Party of Labor of Albania - PLA*] [*Political party*] (PPW)
PPS .... Partial Pressure Sensor
PPS .... Participating Preferred Stock (MHDW)
PPS .... Partido Popular Salvadoreno [*Salvadoran Popular Party*] [*Political party*] (PPW)
PPS .... Partido Popular Socialista [*Popular Socialist Party*] [*Argentina Political party*] (PPW)
PPS .... Partido Popular Socialista [*Popular Socialist Party*] [*Mexico Political party*]
PPS .... Parti du Progres et du Socialisme [*Party of Progress and Socialism*] [*Morocco*] [*Political party*] (PPW)
PPS .... Parti du Progres Social [*Burkina Faso*] [*Political party*] (EY)
PPS .... Parti Populaire Senegalais [*Senegalese People's Party*] [*Political party*] (PPW)
PPS .... Parti Populaire Syrien [*Syrian People's Party*] [*Political party*] (BJA)
PPS .... Parti Progressiste Soudanais [*Sudanese Progressive Party*] [*Political party*]
PPS .... Partito Populare Somalo [*Somali People's Party*]
PPS .... Parts Provisioning System (KSC)
PPS .... Patchboard Programming System
PPS .... Payload Pointing System (SSD)
PPS .... Payload Power Switch
PPS .... Pennsylvania Prison Society (AD)
PPS .... Peoples Oil Ltd. [*Vancouver Stock Exchange symbol*]
PPS .... Pepsin A [*Medicine*] (MAE)
PPS .... Performance Program Statement [*Australia*]
PPS .... Period per Second (IAA)
PPS .... Peripheral Processor System [*Computer science*] (IAA)
PPS .... Personal Plane Service [*Aircraft restoration firm*] [*British*]
PPS .... Personal Portable Shopper [*Computer science*]
PPS .... Personal Preference Scale [*Psychology*]
PPS .... Personal Printer Series [*IBM Corp.*]
PPS .... Personal Printing System [*Computer science*]
PPS .... Personal Process Service (LAIN)
PPS .... Personal Protection Squad [*of the London Metropolitan Police*]
PPS .... Personnel/Payroll System
PPS .... Personnel Processing Squadron
PPS .... Persutuan Perpustakaan Singapura [*Library Association of Singapore*] (AD)
PPS .... Petroleum Press Service
PPS .... Petroleum Production Survey [*Bureau of Mines*]
PPS .... Phantom Phanatics Society (EA)
PPS .... Phlogopite-Peridotite Solidus [*Geology*]
PPS .... Phosphorous Propellant System (KSC)
PPS .... Photophoretic Spectroscopy
PPS .... Photopolarimeter Spectrometer
PPS .... Photovoltaic Power Supply
PPS .... Pictures per Second (WDAA)
pps .... Pictures Per Second (AD)
PPS .... Piece Part Specification (MCD)
PPS .... Pierpont [*South Carolina*] [*Seismograph station code, US Geological Survey*] (SEIS)
PPS .... Pitt Press Series [*A publication*]
PPS .... Plant Parasitic Systems
PPS .... Plant Protection System [*Nuclear energy*] (NRCH)
PPS .... Plasma Power Supply
PPS .... Plutonium Product Storage [*Nuclear energy*] (NRCH)
PPS .... Pneumatic Power Subsystem (NASA)
PPS .... Point-to-Point System (IAA)
PPS .... Policy Processing Sheet [*Insurance*]
PPS .... Polonus Philatelic Society (EA)
PPS .... Polska Partia Socjalistyczna [*Polish Socialist Party*]
PPS .... Poly(para-phenylene Sulfide) [*Organic chemistry*]
PPS .... Polyphenylene Sulfide Plastic
PPS .... Polyvalance Pneumococcal Polysaccharides [*A vaccine for patients with splenectomies*] [*Medicine*] (DAVI)
PPS .... Portable Personal Shopper
PPS .... Ported Pressure Switch [*Automotive engineering*]
PPS .... Postpartum Sterilization [*Medicine*]
PPS .... Postpartum Sterilization [*Gynecology*] (DAVI)
PPS .... Postperfusion Syndrome [*Cardiology*] (DAVI)
PPS .... Postperfusion Syndrome [*Medicine*]
PPS .... Postpericardiotomy Syndrome [*Medicine*] (DMAA)
PPS .... Post-Polio Sequelae [*Medicine*]
p-ps .... Post-Polio Syndrome [*Medicine*] (AD)
PPS .... Post-Postscriptum [*Further Postscript*] [*Latin*]
PPS .... Post Production Service (AAG)
PPS .... Post Production Support (MCD)
PPS .... Post Properties [*NYSE symbol*] (TTSB)
PPS .... Post Properties, Inc. [*NYSE symbol*] (SPSG)
PPS .... Postpump Syndrome [*Medicine*] (MAE)
PPS .... Pounds per Second (AAG)
pps .... Pounds Per Second (AD)
PPS .... Precise Positioning Service [*Military*]
PPS .... Precision Positioning Service
PPS .... Precision Power Supply
PPS .... Prepositioned Stock (NG)
PPS .... Prescribed Payments System (ADA)
PPS .... Primary Paraffin Sulfonate [*Organic chemistry*]
PPS .... Primary Power Standard
PPS .... Primary Power System [*Nuclear energy*] (NRCH)
PPS .... Primary Pressure Standard
PPS .... Primary Propulsion System [*Spacecraft*]
PPS .... Primary Protection System [*Computer science*]
PPS .... Principal Private Secretary [*British*]
PPS .... Printer/Plotter System (MCD)
PPS .... Prior Preferred Stock
pps .... Private Parliamentary Secretary [*British*] (AD)
PPS .... Private Practice Section [*American Physical Therapy Association*] (EA)
PPS .... Probability Proportional to Size [*Statistics*]
PPS .... Procurement Planning Schedule [*DoD*]
PPS .... Production Planning System [*TDS Business Systems Ltd.*] [*Software package*] (NCC)
PPS .... Programmable Patch System
PPS .... Programmable Power Supply
PPS .... Programmed Processor System
PPS .... Programming Program Strela [*Computer science*]
PPS .... Program Performance Specification (CAAL)
PPS .... Program Planning Summary (OICC)
PPS .... Program Planning System [*DoD*]
PPS .... Program Policy Staff [*UN Food and Agriculture Organization*]
PPS .... Progressive Pneumonia of Sheep
PPS .... Project for Public Spaces (EA)
PPS .... Propose (FAAC)
PPS .... Propulsion and Propellant Section [*Picatinny Arsenal*] [*Dover, NJ*]
PPS .... Propulsion Pressurization Subsystem
PPS .... Prospective Payment System [*For hospital care*]
PPS .... Prospective Pricing System [*Information service or system*] (HCT)
PPS .... Prospective Pricing System
PPS .... Provisioning Parts Schedule (MCD)
PPS .... Provisioning Performance Schedule (AFM)
PPS .... Provisioning Policy Statement (MCD)
PPS .... Prudential Property Services [*Prudential Group*] [*British*]
PPS .... Public and Private [*Nongovernment*] Schools [*Public-performance tariff class*] [*British*]
PPS .... Puerto Princesa [*Philippines*] [*Airport symbol*] (OAG)
PPS .... Pulses per Second [*Data transmission*]
pps .... Pulses per Second (IDOE)
pps .... Pulses Per Second (AD)
PPSA .... Pan-Pacific Surgical Association (EA)
PPSAS .... Program Planning and Status Assessment System [*Nuclear energy*] (NRCH)
PPSAT .... Peripheral Processor Saturation (MHDI)
PPSAWA ...... Pan Pacific and Southeast Asia Women's Association (AD)
PPSAWA ...... Pan Pacific and Southeast Asia Women's Association (NADA)
PPSB .... Periodical Publishers' Service Bureau (NADA)
PPSB .... Periodical Publishers' Service Bureau (AD)
PPSB .... Prothrombin, Proconvertin, Stuart Factor, Antihemophilic B Factor [*Blood coagulation factors*] [*Hematology*]
PPSC .... Physical Profile Serial Code [*Military*]
PPSC .... Privacy Protection Study Commission [*Government commission*]
PPSC .... Processor Program State Control (NITA)
PPSCA .... Partido Popular Social Cristiano Autentico [*Political party*] (EY)
PPSCI .... Seamen's Church Institute, Philadelphia, PA [*Library symbol Library of Congress Obsolete*] (LCLS)
PPSD .... Polska Partia Socialno-Demokratyczna [*Polish Social-Democrat Party*] [*Political party*]
PPSD .... Proposed
PPSE .... Programmer Support Environment [*Computer science*] (LAIN)
PPSE .... Purpose
PPSEAWA .... Pan-Pacific and South-East Asia Women's Association [*Tokyo, Japan*] (EAIO)
PPSEAWA-USA ... Pan Pacific and Southeast Asia Women's Association of the USA (EA)
PPSF .... Palestinian Popular Struggle Front [*Political party*] (BJA)
PPS-FR .... Polska Partia Socjalistyczna - Frakcja Rewolucyjna [*Polish Socialist Party - Revolutionary Faction*] [*Political party*] (PPE)
PPSG .... Piston and Pin Standardization Group [*Later, NEPMA*] (EA)
PPSG .... Spring Garden College, Philadelphia, PA [*Library symbol Library of Congress*] (LCLS)
PPSh .... Partia e Punes e Shqiperise [*Labor Party of Albania*] [*Formerly, PKSh*] [*Political party*] (PPE)
PPSH .... Pseudovaginal Perineoscrotal Hypospadias [*Medicine*]
PPSI .... Pacific Physician Services (SPSG)
PPSI .... Pacific Physician Services, Inc. [*NASDAQ symbol*] (SAG)
PPSI .... Parent Problem-Solving Instrument (EDAC)
PPSIA .... "Personal Property Shipping Information" [*Pamphlet*] Is Applicable [*Military*] (AABC)
PPSIAD .... Past President of the Society of Industrial Artists and Designers [*British*] (DI)
PPSJ .... Pressure Plane Swivel Joint
PPSJ .... Saint Joseph's College, Philadelphia, PA [*Library symbol Library of Congress*] (LCLS)

PPSJ-AF ...... Saint Joseph's College, Academy of Food Marketing, Philadelphia, PA [*Library symbol Library of Congress*] (LCLS)
PPSKED .... Provisioning Performance Schedule (MCD)
PPSKF .... SmithKline Corp., Philadelphia, PA [*Library symbol Library of Congress*] (LCLS)
PPSL........... Program Parts Selection List
PPSL........... Provisioning Parts Selection List (MCD)
PPSMEC ...... Procurement, Precedence of Supplies, Material and Equipment Committee [*Joint Communications Board*]
PPSN .... Present Position [*Aviation*] (FAAC)
ppsn........... Present Position (AD)
PPSN .... Public Packet Switched [*or Switching*] Network [*Telecommunications*]
PPSN .... Purchased Part Shortage Notice
ppso............ Per Person, Single Occupancy (AD)
PPSO .... Personal Property Shipping Office [*Military*]
PPSOPR....... Sun Oil Co., General Office Library, Philadelphia, PA [*Library symbol Library of Congress Obsolete*] (LCLS)
PPSP .... Page Printer Spooling System [*Computer science*]
PPSP .... Ponderosa Pine or Sugar Pine [*Lumber*]
PPSP .... Power Plant Siting Program [*Environmental Protection Agency*] (GFGA)
PPSPS .... Plutonium Product Shipping Preparation Station [*Nuclear energy*] (NRCH)
PPSQ .... Principal Problem Strategy Questionnaire (EDAC)
PPSR .... Periodic Personnel Strength Report [*Army*] (AABC)
PPSS .... Foundation for the President's Private Sector Survey on Cost Control (EA)
PPSS .... Polyphenylene Sulfide Sulfone [*Organic chemistry*]
PPSS .... Public Packet Switching Service (NITA)
PPSSCC....... Foundation for the President's Private Sector Survey on Cost Control (EA)
P-PST .... Pre-Professional Skill Test (EDAC)
PPStarr........ Starr Center Association, Philadelphia, PA [*Library symbol Library of Congress Obsolete*] (LCLS)
PPStCh .... Saint Charles Borromeo Seminary, Philadelphia, PA [*Library symbol Library of Congress*] (LCLS)
PPSteph....... William B. Stephens Memorial Library, Philadelphia, PA [*Library symbol Library of Congress Obsolete*] (LCLS)
PPSTH .... Population Post-stimulus Time Histogram [*Statistics*]
PPSU .... Polyphenylene Sulfone Plastic
PPSU .... Programmable Power Supply Unit (EECA)
PPSV .... Plutonium Product Storage Vault [*Nuclear energy*] (NRCH)
PPSV .... Printing and Publishing Services, Victoria [*Australia*]
PPSWA........ Plant Protection Society of Western Australia [*Australia*]
PPS-WRN .... Polska Partia Socjalistyczna - Wolnosc, Rownosc, Niepodleglosc [*Polish Socialist Party - Freedom, Equality, Independence*] [*Political party*] (PPE)
PPT............. Palmitoyl-Protein Thioesterase [*An enzyme*]
PPT............. Pamatai [*French Polynesia*] [*Geomagnetic observatory code*]
PPT............. Papeete [*French Polynesia*] [*Seismograph station code, US Geological Survey*] (SEIS)
PPT............. Papeete [*French Polynesia*] [*Airport symbol*] (OAG)
PPT............. Papeete, Society Islands [*Airport*] (AD)
PPT............. Partial Prothrombin Time [*Hematology*]
PPT............. Parti Progressiste Tchadien [*Progressive Party of Chad*] [*Political party*]
PPT............. Parts per Thousand (DNAB)
ppt.............. Parts per Thousand (IDOE)
PPT............. Parts per Trillion
ppt.............. Parts per Trillion [*Marine science*] (OSRA)
p-p-t............ Pay-per-Transaction [*Agreement between video cassette rental stores and owners of film rights*]
PPT............. Pedunculopontine Tegmentum [*Neurology*]
PPT............. Pericles, Prince of Tyre [*A publication*] (AD)
PPT............. Periodic Programs Termination [*Computer science*]
PPT............. Period Pulse Train
PPT............. Peripheral Performance Test (CAAL)
PPT............. Permanent Part-Time (ADA)
PPT............. Personal Property Tax (MHDW)
PPT............. Phosphinothricin [*Organic chemistry*]
PPT............. Pilot's Power Tool
PPT............. Pine Point Mines Ltd. [*Toronto Stock Exchange symbol Vancouver Stock Exchange symbol*]
PPT............. Pitch Precession Torquer
PPT............. Plant Protease Test (MAE)
PPT............. Polypurine Tract [*Genetics*]
PPT............. Pooh Property Trust [*A.A. Milne estate*] [*British*]
PPT............. Poppet [*Engineering*]
PPT............. Post Production Test
PPT............. PowerPoint [*Computer science*] (PCM)
PPT............. Practical Policy Test [*Psychology*]
PPT............. Praecipitatus [*Precipitated*] [*Pharmacy*]
PPT............. Praeparata [*Prepared*] [*Pharmacy*] (ROG)
PPT............. Precipitate (MSA)
ppt.............. Precipitate (AD)
ppt.............. Precipitat Prepared [*Laboratory science*] (DAVI)
PPT............. Preproduction Test [*Army*]
PPT............. Preprotachykinin [*Biochemistry*]
PPT............. Preprototype (SAA)
PPT............. Private Purchasing Tariff [*British*]
PPT............. Probabilistic Potential Theory (PDAA)
PPT............. Process Page Table [*Telecommunications*] (TEL)
PPT............. Production Prototype
PPT............. Product Positioning Time (AFM)
PPT............. Programmer Productivity Technique (IAA)
PPT............. Project Planning Technique (MCD)
PPT............. Prompt (ROG)
PPT............. Propyl(thio)uracil [*Biochemistry*]
PPT............. Public and Private Transport
PPT............. Pulse Plasma Thruster
PPT............. Punched Paper Tape [*Computer science*]
PPT............. Putnam Premier Income Tr [*NYSE symbol*] (TTSB)
PPT............. Putnam Premier Income Trust [*NYSE symbol*] (SPSG)
PPT............. Temple University, Philadelphia, PA [*Library symbol Library of Congress*] (LCLS)
PPT............. Theosophical Society, Philadelphia, PA [*Library symbol Library of Congress Obsolete*] (LCLS)
PPTB........... Pin-Pack Test Board
PPTBA .... Pattern and Plastic Tool Builders Association [*Defunct*] (EA)
PPTC........... People-to-People Tennis Committee (EA)
PPTC........... Purchased Part Tab Card
PPTD........... Precipitated
pptd .... Precipitated (AD)
PPT-D .... Temple University, Dental-Pharmacy School, Philadelphia, PA [*Library symbol Library of Congress*] (LCLS)
PPTE........... Permanent Part-Time Employment
PPTF........... Public Policy Task Force [*Defunct*] (EA)
PPTF........... Public-Private Task Force
ppth .... Parts Per Thousand (GNE)
pPTH........... Porcine Parathyroid Hormone [*Endocrinology*]
PPTI............ Protein Polymer Technologies [*NASDAQ symbol*] (TTSB)
PPTI............ Protein Polymer Technologies, Inc. [*NASDAQ symbol*] (SAG)
PPT-ISA....... Picture Personality Test for Indian South Africans
PPTIW .... Protein Polymer Technol Wrrt [*NASDAQ symbol*] (TTSB)
PPTJ .... Theodore F. Jenkins Memorial Law Library, Philadelphia, PA [*Library symbol Library of Congress*] (LCLS)
PPTL........... Postpartum Tubal Ligation [*Medicine*]
PPTL........... Pulp and Paper Traffic League [*Defunct*] (EA)
PPT-L.......... Temple University, Law School, Philadelphia, PA [*Library symbol Library of Congress*] (LCLS)
PPT-M .... Temple University, Medical School, Philadelphia, PA [*Library symbol Library of Congress*] (LCLS)
PPTMR .... Personal Property Traffic Management Regulation
PPTN .... Precipitation
pptn .... Precipitation (AD)
PPTO .... Personal Property Transportation Officer
PPTO .... Principal Professional and Technology Officer [*British*]
PPTP........... Point-to-Point Tunneling Protocol [*Microsoft Corp.*]
PPTP........... Point-to-Point Tunneling Protocol [*Computer science*]
PPTP........... Power-Proportioning Temperature Programmer (IAA)
PPTPP .... Promulgators of Public Toilets in Public Parks (AD)
PPTR .... Punched Paper Tape Reader [*Computer science*]
PPTri .... Tri-Institutional Library, Philadelphia, PA [*Library symbol Library of Congress*] (LCLS)
PPTS........... Pianoforte Polishers' Trade Society [*A union*] [*British*]
PPTS........... Portable Perishable Tool System (MCD)
PPTS........... Pre-Planned Training System (PDAA)
PPTS........... Pre-Problem Training Situation (SAA)
PPTS........... Pyridinium Para-Toluenesulfonate [*Organic chemistry*]
PPTS........... Pyridinium-para-Tosylate [*Organic chemistry*]
PP/TSD .... Post Placement and Training Support Program for People with Disabilities [*Australia*]
PPT-T.......... Temple University, School of Theology, Philadelphia, PA [*Library symbol Library of Congress*] (LCLS)
PPTTG .... Personal Property Transit Time Guide [*MTMC*] (TAG)
PPTV........... Parts per Trillion by Volume
PPTV........... PPT Vision [*NASDAQ symbol*] (TTSB)
PPTV........... PPT Vision, Inc. [*NASDAQ symbol*] (SAG)
PPT Vis........ PPT Vision, Inc. [*Associated Press*] (SAG)
PPTW........... Permanent Part-Time Work
PPTY........... Property (AFM)
ppty .... Property (AD)
PPU .... Cocoa, FL [*Location identifier FAA*] (FAAL)
PPU .... Papun [*Myanmar*] [*Airport symbol*] (OAG)
PPU .... Parti Populaire des Ueles [*Ueles People's Party*] [*Political party*]
PPU .... Payment for Public Use [*Canada*]
PPU .... Peace Pledge Union [*British*]
PPU .... Peninsula Petroleum Corp. [*Vancouver Stock Exchange symbol*]
PPU .... Peoria & Pekin Union Railway Co. [*AAR code*]
PPU .... Peripheral Processing Unit [*Computer science*]
PPU .... Platform Position Unit
ppu .... Platform Position Unit (AD)
PPU .... Power Processing Unit (MCD)
PPU .... Pre-Processor Utility (NITA)
PPU .... Preproduction Unit (MCD)
PPU .... Primary Producers Union (AD)
PPU .... Prime Power Unit
PPU .... Professional Psychics United (EA)
PPU .... Promontory Point [*Utah*] [*Seismograph station code, US Geological Survey Closed*] (SEIS)
PPUG .... United Gas Improvement Corp., Philadelphia, PA [*Library symbol Library of Congress Obsolete*] (LCLS)
PPUI .... Pitch and Putt Union of Ireland (EAIO)
PPULC .... Union Library Catalogue of Pennsylvania, Philadelphia, PA [*Library symbol Library of Congress*] (LCLS)
PPUNA......... United States Naval Aircraft Factory, Philadelphia, PA [*Library symbol Library of Congress Obsolete*] (LCLS)
PPUnC .... University Club, Philadelphia, PA [*Library symbol Library of Congress Obsolete*] (LCLS)

PPUNH......... United States Naval Home, Philadelphia, PA [*Library symbol Library of Congress Obsolete*] (LCLS)
PPUSDA....... United States Department of Agriculture, Agricultural Research Service, Eastern Utilization Research and Development Division, Philadelphia, PA [*Library symbol*] [*Library of Congress*] (LCLS)
PPV............. Paraphenylene Vinylene [*Organic chemistry*]
PPV............. Pay-per-View [*Pay-television service*]
ppv............. Pay-Per-View (AD)
ppv............. People-Powered Vehicle (AD)
PPV............. People-Powered Vehicle [*Recreational vehicle powered by pedaling*]
PPV............. Pitch Power Valve (IAA)
PPV............. Plum Pox Virus [*Plant pathology*]
PPV............. Polarized Platen Viewer (OA)
PPV............. Poly (Phenylenevinylene) [*Organic chemistry*]
PPV............. Porcine Parvovirus [*Veterinary science*] (DMAA)
PPV............. Positive Predictive Value [*Experimentation*]
PPV............. Positive Pressure Ventilation [*Medicine*]
PPV............. Preprogrammed Vehicles (MCD)
PPV............. Primary Pressure Vessel (MCD)
P/PV............ Public/Private Ventures [*Philadelphia, PA*] [*Research center*] (RCD)
PPV............. United States Veterans Administration Hospital, Philadelphia, PA [*Library symbol Library of Congress*] (LCLS)
PPVT........... Peabody Picture Vocabulary Test [*Education*]
PPVT-R........ Peabody Picture Vocabulary Test - Revised [*Education*]
PP-W.......... Free Library of Philadelphia, H. Josephine Widener Memorial Branch, Philadelphia, PA [*Library symbol Library of Congress Obsolete*] (LCLS)
PPW............ PacifiCorp [*NYSE symbol*] (SPSG)
PPW............ Pacificorp Capital [*NYSE symbol*] (SAG)
PPW............ Papa Westray [*Scotland*] [*Airport symbol*] (OAG)
PPW............ Parts per Weight
PPW............ Petitions for Patent Waiver
PPW............ Plane-Polarized Wave
PPW............ Ponderosa Pine Woodwork Association [*NWWDA*] [*Absorbed by*] (EA)
PPW............ Potato Processing Waste
PPWA.......... Ponderosa Pine Woodwork Association [*NWWDA*] [*Absorbed by*]
PPWa.......... Wagner Free Institute of Science, Philadelphia, PA [*Library symbol Library of Congress*] (LCLS)
PPWC.......... Pulp, Paper, and Woodworkers of Canada
PPWD.......... S. S. White Co., Philadelphia, PA [*Library symbol Library of Congress Obsolete*] (LCLS)
PPWe.......... Westminster Theological Seminary, Philadelphia, PA [*Library symbol Library of Congress*] (LCLS)
PPWI........... Wistar Institute of Anatomy and Biology, Philadelphia, PA [*Library symbol Library of Congress*] (LCLS)
PPWiH......... Wills Eye Hospital, Philadelphia, PA [*Library symbol Library of Congress*] (LCLS)
PPWL........... Present Practice Waste Load (DICI)
PPWM.......... Medical College of Pennsylvania, Philadelphia, PA [*Library symbol Library of Congress*] (LCLS)
PPWP.......... Planned Parenthood - World Population [*Later, PPFA*] (EA)
PPWPr......... PacifiCorp 5% Pfd [*AMEX symbol*] (TTSB)
PPWPrE....... PacifiCorp $1.98 cm Pfd [*NYSE symbol*] (TTSB)
PPWR.......... Prepositioned War Reserves [*Army*]
PPWRS........ Prepositioned War Reserve Stocks [*Army*]
PPX............. Packet Protocol Extension
PPX............. Port Moller, AK [*Location identifier FAA*] (FAAL)
PPX............. Private Packet Exchange
PPY............. Pages per Year [*Facetious criterion for determining insignificance of Supreme Court Justices*] [*Proposed by University of Chicago professor David P. Currie*]
PPY............. Pancreatic Polypeptide [*Medicine*] (DMAA)
PPY............. Prophesy Development [*Vancouver Stock Exchange symbol*]
PPYH........... Young Men's and Young Women's Hebrew Association, Philadelphia, PA [*Library symbol Library of Congress Obsolete*] (LCLS)
PPYU........... Party of Popular Yemenite Unity [*Political party*] (PD)
PPZ............. Proton Polar Zone
PPZ............. Puerto Paez [*Venezuela*] [*Airport symbol*] (AD)
PPZ............. Zoological Society of Philadelphia, PA [*Library symbol Library of Congress Obsolete*] (LCLS)
PQ.............. Pack Quickly [*Humorous interpretation for Parti Quebecois*] [*Canada*]
PQ.............. Panic in Quebec [*Humorous interpretation for Parti Quebecois*] [*Canada*]
PQ.............. Parametric Quantron [*Physics*]
PQ.............. Parliamentary Question [*British*]
PQ.............. Parti Quebecois [*Quebec separatist political party*]
pq.............. Peculiar (AD)
PQ.............. Performance Qualification (ACII)
PQ.............. Performer Quotient [*TV-performer rating*]
PQ.............. Permeability Quotient
pq.............. Permeability Quotient (AD)
pq.............. Personality Quotient (AD)
PQ.............. Personality Quotient [*Psychology*]
p-q............. Phenol-Hydroquinone [*Photography*] (AD)
PQ.............. Philological Quarterly [*A publication*] (BRI)
PQ.............. Photo Quality (PCM)
PQ.............. Physically Qualified
PQ.............. Physician's Questionnaire (AAMN)
PQ.............. Planetary Quarantine [*NASA*]
PQ.............. Plant Quarantine Division [*of ARS, Department of Agriculture*]
PQ.............. Plasma Quad [*Instrumentation*]
PQ.............. Plastoquinone [*Biochemistry*]
PQ.............. Pollution Quotient
PQ.............. Polyquinoxaline [*Organic chemistry*]
P-Q............. Porphyrin-Quinone [*Photochemistry*]
PQ.............. PQ Corp. [*Formerly, Philadelphia Quartz Co.*]
PQ.............. Premium Quality (MUGU)
PQ.............. Preparative Quencher [*Spectroscopy*]
PQ.............. Presentation Quotient [*Business Term*]
pq.............. Previous Question (AD)
PQ.............. Previous Question [*Parliamentary law*]
Pq.............. Primaquine [*Antimalarial*]
PQ.............. Pronator Quadratus [*Muscle*] [*Anatomy*] (DAVI)
pq.............. Pro Querente [*For the Plaintiff*] [*Latin Legal term*] (DLA)
PQ.............. Province Quebec [*Quebec*] [*Canadian province Postal code*]
PQ.............. Psi Quotient [*Parapsychology*]
PQ.............. Public Quarters
PQ.............. Puerto Rico International Airlines, Inc. [*Prinair*] [*ICAO designator*] (OAG)
pq.............. Punishment Quarters (AD)
PQ.............. Pyrimethamine-Quinine [*Organic chemistry*] (MAE)
PQ.............. Quebec [*Postal code*] (CDAI)
PQ.............. South Pacific Airlines of New Zealand (AD)
PQ.............. United States Patent Quarterly [*A publication*] (DLA)
PQA............ Pacific Coast Airlines [*ICAO designator*] (FAAC)
PQA............ Parts Quality Assurance
PQA............ Petroleum Quality Assurance
PQA............ Plant Quality Assurance
PQA............ Preliminary Quantitative Analysis
PQA............ Procurement Quality Assurance [*Program*] [*DoD*]
pqa............ Procurement Quality Assurance (AD)
PQA............ Production Quality Assurance
PQA............ Project Quality Assurance
PQA............ Protected Queue Area [*Computer science*] (BUR)
PQAA.......... Province of Quebec Association of Architects [*1890, OAQ from 1974*] [*Canada*] (NGC)
PQAD.......... Plant Quality Assurance Director [*Nuclear energy*] (NRCH)
PQAI........... Procurement Quality Assurance Instruction
PQAM.......... Project Quality Assurance Manager [*Nuclear energy*] (NRCH)
PQANSW...... Paraplegic and Quadriplegic Association of New South Wales [*Australia*]
PQAP.......... Planned Quality Assurance Program [*Navy*]
PQAP.......... Procurement Quality Assurance Program [*DoD*]
PQAQ.......... Paraplegic and Quadriplegic Association of Queensland [*Australia*]
PQAR.......... Petroleum Quality Assurance Representative
PQASA........ Paraplegic and Quadriplegic Association of South Australia
PQAV.......... Paraplegic and Quadriplegic Association of Victoria [*Australia*]
PQAWA....... Paraplegic and Quadriplegic Association of Western Australia
PQB............ Quebecor Cl'A' [*AMEX symbol*] (TTSB)
PQB............ Quebecor, Inc. [*AMEX symbol*] (SPSG)
PQC............ Chieftain Airways PLC [*British ICAO designator*] (FAAC)
PQC............ Paul Quinn College [*Texas*]
PQC............ Paul Quinn College, Waco, TX [*OCLC symbol*] (OCLC)
PQC............ Phuquoc [*South Vietnam*] [*Airport symbol*] (AD)
PQC............ Precision Quartz Crystal
PQC............ Procurement Quality Control (IAA)
PQC............ Production Quality Control
PQCS.......... Process Quality Control System
PQD............ Partido Quisqueyano Democrata [*Quisqueyan Democratic Party*] [*Dominican Republic*] [*Political party*] (PPW)
PQD............ Percentage Quartile Deviation [*Statistics*]
PQD............ Plant Quarantine Division (AD)
PQD............ Predicted Quarterly Demand
PQD............ Pyroelectric Quad Detector
PQDMB........ Percentage Quartile Deviation Median Bias [*Statistics*]
PQE............ Parents for Quality Education [*Defunct*] (EA)
PQE............ Post-Qualification Education (PDAA)
pqe............ Post-Qualification Education (AD)
PQE............ Principal Quality Engineers [*British*] (RDA)
PQE............ Professional Qualification Examination [*National Security Agency*] (EDAC)
PQE............ Project Quality Engineering
PQEP.......... Product Quality Evaluation Plan [*Military*] (AABC)
PQET.......... Print Quality Enhancement Technology [*IBM*] (PCM)
PQFP.......... Plastic Quad Flat Package [*Computer science*] (PCM)
PQGS.......... Propellant Quantity Gauge [*or Gauging*] System [*Apollo*] [*NASA*]
PQI............ Presque Isle [*Maine*] [*Airport symbol*] (OAG)
PQI............ Presque Isle, ME [*Location identifier FAA*] (FAAL)
PQI............ Print Quality Improvement [*Advanced photo system*]
PQI............ Product Quality Improvement [*Program*] [*Chrysler Corp.*]
PQI............ Professional Qualification Index (AFM)
pqi............ Professional Qualification Index (AD)
PQI............ Propellant Quantity Indicator (NASA)
PQIH.......... Plant Quarantine Inspection House (AD)
PQL............ Practical Quantitation Level [*Environmental chemistry*] (ERG)
PQL............ Practical Quantitation Limit [*Environmental chemistry*]
PQL............ Prior Quarter Liability [*IRS*]
PQLI........... Physical Quality of Life Index [*Overseas Development Council*]
PQM........... Pilot Qualified in Model (NVT)
PQM........... Post Quartermaster [*Marine Corps*]
PQM........... Print Quality Monitor [*Computer science*] (IAA)
PQM........... Pulse Quaternary Modulation
PQMC......... Philadelphia Quartermaster Center [*Merged with Defense Clothing and Textile Supply Center*] [*Military*]
PQMD......... Philadelphia Quartermaster Depot [*Military*]
PQMD......... Propellant Quantity Measuring Device
PQMDO....... Proposed Quality Material Development Objective (NATG)
PQMF......... Parallel Quadrature Mirror Filter (PDAA)
PQMR......... Preliminary Quantitative Material Requirements (MCD)

PQMS .... Process Quality Measurement System [*Chemical process engineering*]
PQN .... Consolidated Petroquin [*Vancouver Stock Exchange symbol*]
PQN .... Pahaquarry [*New Jersey*] [*Seismograph station code, US Geological Survey*] (SEIS)
PQN .... Pipestone, MN [*Location identifier FAA*] (FAAL)
PQN .... Principal Quantum Number [*Atomic physics*]
PQNS .... Protein, Quantity Not Sufficient [*Laboratory science*] (DAVI)
PQO .... Phoenix, AZ [*Location identifier FAA*] (FAAL)
PQOL .... Perceived Quality of Life [*Medicine*] (DMAA)
PQOS .... Pre-Qualified Offsets Supplier
PQOSS .... Pre-Qualified Offsets Supplier Status
PQP .... Planetary Quarantine Plan [*NASA*]
PQP .... Prequalification Prototype (KSC)
PQQ .... Port Macquarie [*Australia Airport symbol*] (OAG)
PQQ .... Pyrroloquinoline Quinone [*Biochemistry*]
PQQPRI .... Provisional Qualitative and Quantitative Personnel Requirements Information [*Army*] (AABC)
PQR .... Pantan Resources [*Vancouver Stock Exchange symbol*]
PQR .... Performance Qualification Requirement
PQR .... Personnel Qualification Record [*Military*] (INF)
PQR .... Personnel Qualification Roster [*Military*] (AABC)
PQR .... Procedure Qualification Record [*Nuclear energy*] (NRCH)
PQR .... Program Quality Review (AD)
pqrs .... Productivity Increases, Quality Control, Robotization, and Savings [*Japanese formula for economic success*] (AD)
PQRST .... Personal Questionnaire Rapid Scaling Technique [*Personality development test*] [*Psychology*]
PQRST .... Product-Quality-Routing-Service-Timing [*Industrial engineering*]
PQS .... Percentage Quota System (AD)
PQS .... Personnel Qualification Standard (AD)
PQS .... Personnel Qualification Standards [*Military*] (NVT)
PQS .... Pilot Station [*Alaska*] [*Airport symbol*] (OAG)
PQS .... Production Quotation Support
PQS .... Progressive Qualification Scheme [*British*]
PQS .... Promotion Qualification Score [*Military*]
PQSF .... Preparative Quencher Stopped Flow [*Spectroscopy*]
PQT .... Parquet Resources, Inc. [*Toronto Stock Exchange symbol*]
PQT .... PC Quote [*AMEX symbol*] (TTSB)
PQT .... PC Quote, Inc. [*AMEX symbol*] (SAG)
PQT .... Performance Qualification Test (MCD)
PQT .... Polyquinazolotriazole [*Organic chemistry*]
PQT .... Preliminary Qualification Test (MCD)
PQT .... Production Qualification and Testing
PQT .... Professional Qualification Test [*of the National Security Agency*]
PQT .... Prototype Qualification Testing (RDA)
PQT & E .... Production Qualification Test and Evaluation
PQT-C .... Prototype Qualification Test - Contractor (MCD)
PQT-G .... Prototype Qualification Test - Government (MCD)
PQT/LOT .... Production Qualification Test / Limited Operational Test
PQT-SE .... Prototype Qualification Test - Service Evaluation (MCD)
PQU .... Salisbury, MD [*Location identifier FAA*] (FAAL)
PQUE .... Print Queue Processor [*Computer science*]
PQW .... Placita de Quo Warranto, Record Commission [*England*] [*A publication*] (DLA)
PQX .... Physically Qualified Except
PQZ .... Premium Quality Zinc
PR .... Abbott Laboratories [*Research code symbol*]
PR .... Aircrew Survival Equipmentman [*Navy rating*]
PR .... Pacific Reporter [*A publication*] (DLA)
P(R) .... Packet (Receive)
PR .... Painter (ADA)
PR .... Pair (KSC)
pr .... Pair (AD)
pr .... Pair (ODBW)
PR .... Pakistan Railways (DCTA)
PR .... Panama Red [*Variety of marijuana*]
Pr .... Panama-Red Marijuana (AD)
PR .... Panel Receptacle
PR .... Pangenesis Related [*Protein chemistry*]
PR .... Panthere Rose [*France*] [*An association Defunct*] (EAIO)
PR .... Paper Tape Reader
PR .... Parachute Rigger [*Navy*] (KSC)
PR .... Paradise Regained [*A publication*] (AD)
PR .... Parallax and Refraction
Pr .... Parana (AD)
pr .... Parcel Receipt (AD)
PR .... Parcel Receipt [*Shipping*]
PR .... Parental Recommendation [*Movie rating*] (CDAI)
PR .... Parents Rights (EA)
PR .... Parish Register
PR .... Park Ranger (AD)
PR .... Parliamentary Report [*British*]
PR .... Parrott Rifle
PR .... Partial Remission [*Medicine*]
PR .... Partial Response [*Oncology*]
PR .... Partial Response [*Medicine*] (DAVI)
PR .... Partido Radical [*Radical Party*] [*Spain Political party*] (PPE)
PR .... Partido Radical [*Radical Party*] [*Chile*] [*Political party*]
PR .... Partido Reformista [*Reformist Party*] [*Dominican Republic*] [*Political party*] (PPW)
PR .... Partido Republicano [*Republican Party*] [*Ecuador*] [*Political party*] (EY)
PR .... Partido Republicano [*Republican Party*] [*Panama*] [*Political party*] (EY)
PR .... Partido Revolucionario [*Revolutionary Party*] [*Guatemala*] [*Political party*] (PPW)
PR .... Partido Riojano [*Spain Political party*] (EY)
PR .... Parti Republicain [*Republican Party*] [*France Political party*] (PPW)
PR .... Parti Republicain [*Republican Party*] [*Reunion*] [*Political party*] (EY)
PR .... Parti Republicain [*Republican Party*] [*Martinique*] [*Political party*] (PPW)
PR .... Parti Republicain [*Republican Party*] [*New Caledonia*] [*Political party*] (FEA)
PR .... Partisan Review [*A publication*] (BRI)
PR .... Partito Radicale [*Radical Party*] [*Founded, 1955*] [*Italy*] [*Political party*] (PPE)
PR .... Party Raayat [*Leftist organization in Singapore*]
PR .... Passengers' Risk (ROG)
PR .... Passive Ranging [*Military*] (LAIN)
PR .... Past in Review [*Later, PIR*] (EA)
PR .... Pastor
PR .... Pathogenesis Related [*Biology*]
PR .... Patient Relations [*Medicine*]
PR .... Patient Relations (DAVI)
PR .... Patria Roja [*Red Fatherland*] [*Peru*] (PD)
PR .... Patrol Vessel, River Gunboat [*Navy symbol*]
PR .... Pattern Recognition (BUR)
PR .... Payroll
P/R .... Payroll (AD)
pr .... Payroll (AD)
PR .... Peer Review
PR .... Peking Review [*A publication*] (AD)
PR .... Pelvic Rock [*Orthopedics*] (DAVI)
PR .... Peng-Robinson [*Equation of state*]
PR .... Penicillium roqueforti [*Toxin*] [*Medicine*]
P-R .... Pennsylvania-Reading [*Seashore Lines*] (AD)
PR .... Pennsylvania Reports (Penrose and Watts) [*A publication*] (DLA)
PR .... Penny Resistance (EA)
PR .... Pen Record (SAA)
PR .... Per
PR .... Percentage Rates
PR .... Percentile Rank
pr .... Percentile Rank (AD)
PR .... Percent Recovery [*Plant pathology*]
PR .... Performance Rating (OICC)
PR .... Performance Ratio (AAG)
PR .... Performance Report (AFM)
PR .... Performance Requirement
PR .... Perfusion Rate [*Cardiology*] (DAVI)
PR .... Periodic Report (IAA)
PR .... Periodic Reversal (IAA)
PR .... Peripheral Resistance [*Medicine*]
pr .... Peripheral Resistance (AD)
PR .... Perirenal [*Nephrology*]
PR .... Permanens Rector [*Permanent Rector*]
PR .... Permeance (IAA)
PR .... Permissive Reassignment [*Air Force*] (AFM)
PR .... Per Price [*Business term*]
PR .... Per Rectum [*Medicine*]
pr .... Per Rectum [*By the Rectum*] [*Latin*] (AD)
PR .... Pershing Rifles [*Honorary military organization*]
PR .... Persistency Rater [*LIMRA*]
PR .... Personality Record [*Psychological testing*]
PR .... Personnel Resources (EA)
PR .... Pesikta Rabbati (BJA)
PR .... Pesticide Registration [*Environmental Protection Agency*]
PR .... Phenol Red
PR .... Philadelphia Reports [*Pennsylvania*] [*A publication*] (DLA)
PR .... Philanthropic Roundtable (EA)
PR .... Philippine Airlines [*ICAO designator*] (AD)
PR .... Philippine Island Reports [*A publication*] (DLA)
P-R .... Philips Roxane [*Commercial firm*] (DAVI)
PR .... Phosphate Rock [*Petrology*]
PR .... Phosphorylase-Rupturing [*Biochemistry*]
PR .... Photographic Reconnaissance [*Military*] (MCD)
PR .... Photographic Recorder
PR .... Photoreacting [*or Photoreactivation*] [*Biochemistry*]
PR .... Photo Reconnaissance [*ICAO designator*] (FAAC)
PR .... Photorecorder
PR .... Photorefractive [*Optics*]
PR .... Photoresist
P/R .... Photosynthesis/Respiration [*Biochemistry*]
PR .... Physical Record [*Computer science*]
PR .... Physican Reviewer (MEDA)
PR .... Picture Ratio (IAA)
PR .... Piezo Resistive [*Automotive electronics*]
PR .... Pilot Rating
PR .... Pinar del Rio (AD)
PR .... Pinch Runner [*Baseball*]
PR .... Pineal Recess [*Neuroanatomy*]
PR .... Pipe Rail (AAG)
PR .... Pitch Ratio
P/R .... Pitch/Roll (MCD)
PR .... Pittsburgh Reports [*1853-73*] [*Pennsylvania*] [*A publication*] (DLA)
PR .... Pityriasis [*Dermatology*]
PR .... Pityriasis Rosea [*Dermatology*] (MAE)
PR .... Planetary RADAR [*Equipment box*]
P/R .... Planned Requirements (DNAB)
PR .... Planning Reference

PR............... Plant Recovery [*Nuclear energy*] (NRCH)
PR............... Plant Report
PR............... Please Return
PR............... Plotting and RADAR
PR............... Ply Rating [*Tires*] (NATG)
PR............... Pneumatic Retinopathy [*Ophthalmology*]
PR............... Polarized Relay (IAA)
PR............... Policy Review (MCD)
PR............... Polish Register [*Polish ship classification society*] (DS)
PR............... Polskie Radio [*Polish Radio*] (AD)
PR............... Ponceau Red [*Biological stain*]
PR............... Poor Rate [*British*] (ROG)
PR............... Populus Romanus [*The Roman People*] [*Latin*]
PR............... Position Record (NASA)
PR............... Position Register (IAA)
PR............... Position Report [*Air Force*]
PR............... Postal Regulations (DLA)
PR............... Poste Recommandee [*Registered Post*]
PR............... Posterior Repair [*Gynecology*] (DAVI)
PR............... Posterior Ridge
PR............... Posterior Root [*Medicine*] (DMAA)
PR............... Post Request
PR............... Post-Resuscitation
PR............... Potency Ratio [*Medicine*] (DMAA)
PR............... Pounder [*Gun*]
PR............... Pour Remercier [*To Express Thanks*] [*French*]
PR............... Power Range [*Nuclear energy*] (NRCH)
PR............... Power Rating
PR............... Power Ratio
PR............... Power Return
Pr............... Praca [*Plaza*] [*Portuguese*] (AD)
Pr............... Practice Reports [*Various jurisdictions*] [*A publication*] (DLA)
PR............... Prairie (MCD)
Pr............... Prairie (AD)
PR............... Prairie
Pr............... Prandtl Number [*IUPAC*]
Pr............... Praseodymium [*Chemical element*]
PR............... Prayer
PR............... Preacher
Pr............... Preamble (ILCA)
Pr............... Precancelled [*Philately*]
PR............... Precedence Rating [*Military*] (AFIT)
PR............... Preconstruction Requirement [*Environmental Protection Agency*]
PR............... Predicted Rate [*Medicine*] (DAVI)
Pr............... Prednisone [*Also, P, PDN, Pred, Pro*] [*Endocrinology*] [*Antineoplastic drug*]
PR............... Preferred [*Stock exchange term*] (SPSG)
PR............... Prefix [*Indicating a private radiotelegram*] (BUR)
PR............... Pregnancy Rate [*Medicine*]
PR............... Preliminary Report
PR............... Preliminary Review [*Army*]
PR............... Premature Release [*Telecommunications*] (TEL)
PR............... Prepare Reply
PR............... Preposition
PR............... Pre-Raphaelite
PR............... Presbyopia [*Ophthalmology*]
Pr............... Presbyopia (AD)
Pr............... Presbyter [*Elder*] [*Latin*] (AD)
PR............... Presbyterian (ROG)
PR............... Present
Pr............... Presentation [*Gynecology*]
PR............... Presidency (ROG)
Pr............... Press (AD)
PR............... Pressoreceptor [*Laboratory science*] (DAVI)
PR............... Press Release
PR............... Press Revise (DGA)
PR............... Pressure
PR............... Pressure Ratio
PR............... Pressure Recorder (NRCH)
PR............... Pressure Regulator (KSC)
PR............... Preston [*Postcode*] (ODBW)
PR............... Prevention (DAVI)
pr............... Price (ODBW)
PR............... Price [*Online database field identifier*]
PR............... Price Communications [*AMEX symbol*] (TTSB)
PR............... Price Communications Corp. [*AMEX symbol*] (SAG)
PR............... Price Received
PR............... Price Redetermination [*Economics*]
PR............... Price Reduced [*of a book*]
Pr............... Price's English Exchequer Reports [*1814-24*] [*A publication*] (DLA)
PR............... Priest
PR............... Primary (NASA)
PR............... Primary RADAR (DA)
PR............... Primary Reference [*Automobile fuel*] (DICI)
PR............... Primitive
PR............... Prince
Pr............... Prince (AD)
PR............... Prince Regent (ROG)
PR............... Princess Royal's [*Military unit*] [*British*]
Pr............... Principal
PR............... Principal Register [*Computer science*]
PR............... Print [*or Printed*] (NTCM)
pr............... Print (ECII)
pr............... Print (VRA)
PR............... Printed [*or Printer*]
PR............... Printer [*Computer science*] (IAA)
PR............... Printing Request (MCD)
PR............... Print Register (IAA)
PR............... Print Restore [*Computer science*] (MHDB)
PR............... Prior
PR............... Priority Regulation
PR............... Priority Resolver
PR............... Priory
PR............... Prism
pr............... Prismatic Tank [*Liquid gas carriers*]
Pr............... Pristane [*Organic chemistry*]
pr............... Private (DLA)
PR............... Private Road [*Maps and charts*] [*British*] (ROG)
PR............... Prize Ring [*Boxing*]
PR............... Probabilistic Risk Assessment [*Computer-based technique for accident prediction*]
Pr............... Probable
PR............... Probate Reports [*A publication*] (DLA)
Pr............... Problemata [*of Aristotle*] [*Classical studies*] (OCD)
PR............... Problem Report (MCD)
Pr............... Procarbazine [*Also, P, PC, PCB*] [*Antineoplastic drug*]
PR............... Procedural Regulations [*Civil Aeronautics Board*]
PR............... Procedures Review [*DoD*]
PR............... Proceedings (IAA)
PR............... Processor [*Computer science*] (IAA)
PR............... Process-Reactive [*Scale*] [*Psychometrics*]
PR............... Proctologist
Pr............... Proctoscopy (AD)
PR............... Proctosigmoidoscopy [*Medicine*] (AD)
PR............... Procurement Regulation [*Military*]
PR............... Procurement Request [*or Requisition*]
PR............... Producing Region [*Agriculture*]
PR............... Production Rate
PR............... Production Requirements [*Military*] (AFIT)
PR............... Production Review [*Automotive project management*]
P/R............... Productivity/Respiration [*Physiology*]
PR............... Profile (DAVI)
PR............... Profile Reliability (MCD)
PR............... Profit Rate (WGA)
P-R............... Progesterone Receptor [*Endocrinology*]
PR............... Programming [*Computer science*] (IAA)
PR............... Program Register [*Computer science*] (BUR)
PR............... Program Requirements (KSC)
PR............... Progressive Resistance
PR............... Progress Report
PR............... Project Release (EA)
PR............... Project Report
PR............... Project Rover (SAA)
PR............... Prolactin [*Also, LTH, PRL*] [*Endocrinology*]
PR............... Prolonged-Release [*Pharmacy*]
Pr............... Promenade (DD)
PR............... Pronominal [*Grammar*] (ROG)
PR............... Pronoun
PR............... Pronounced
PR............... Proper
PR............... Property
PR............... Proportional Representation [*in legislatures, etc.*]
PR............... Proposed Regulation
PR............... Proposed Request
PR............... Proposed Rule [*Federal government*] (GFGA)
PR............... Propulsion Range
Pr............... Propyl [*Organic chemistry*]
PR............... Pro Rata
pr............... Prose
PR............... Prosthetic-Group Removing [*An enzyme*] (BABM)
PR............... Prosthetic-Group Removing [*Enzyme*] [*Biochemistry*] (DAVI)
PR............... Prosthion [*Medicine*] (MAE)
PR............... Protease [*Chemistry*]
PR............... Protective Reaction [*Bombing raid*] [*Vietnam*]
PR............... Protectorate Regiment [*British military*] (DMA)
PR............... Protein (MAE)
PR............... Protestant (ADA)
PR............... Prototype
PR............... Proved
PR............... Provencal [*Language, etc.*]
Pr............... Proverbs [*Old Testament book*] (BJA)
PR............... Provost (WDAA)
Pr............... Proximal
PR............... Pseudorandom
PR............... Pseudoresidual
PR............... Psychedelic Review [*A publication*]
PR............... Psychiatric Record (AD)
PR............... Publicity Release (NTCM)
PR............... Public Relations
pr............... Public Relations (AD)
PR............... Public Responsibility
PR............... Puerto Rican [*Derogatory term*]
pr............... Puerto Rico [*IYRU nationality code*] [*MARC country of publication code Library of Congress*] (LCCP)
PR............... Puerto Rico [*ANSI two-letter standard code*] (CNC)
PR............... Puerto Rico [*Postal code*]
PR............... Puerto Rico Supreme Court Reports [*A publication*] (DLA)
PR............... Pulmonic Regurgitation [*Cardiology*] (DAVI)
PR............... Pulse Rate
PR............... Pulse Ratio (IEEE)

PR............... Pulse Regenerator
PR............... Punctum Remotum [*Far Point*] [*Latin*]
pr............... Punctum Remotum [*Remote Point*] [*Latin*] (AD)
PR............... Punjab Record [*India*] [*A publication*] (DLA)
PR............... Purchase Request
PR............... Purple (AAG)
PR............... Purplish Red
pR............... Purplish Red (AD)
PR............... Pyke's Reports [*Canada*] [*A publication*] (DLA)
pr............... Pyrite [*CIPW classification*] [*Geology*]
PR............... Pyrogallol Red [*Also, PGR*] [*An indicator Chemistry*]
PR............... Pyrolytic Release
PR+............... Reactor Pressure Plus (NRCH)
PR............... Reading Public Library, Reading, PA [*Library symbol Library of Congress*] (LCLS)
PR............... River Gunboat [*Navy symbol*]
PR............... Upper Canada Practice Reports [*1850-1900*] [*Ontario*] [*A publication*] (DLA)
PR1............... Parachute Rigger, First Class [*Navy*]
PR2............... Parachute Rigger, Second Class [*Navy*]
PR3............... Parachute Rigger, Third Class [*Navy*]
PRA............... Albright College, Reading, PA [*Library symbol Library of Congress*] (LCLS)
PRA............... Division of Policy Research and Analysis [*National Science Foundation*]
PRA............... Page Replacement Algorithm [*Computer science*] (MHDI)
PRA............... Paint Research Association [*British*]
PRA............... Paperwork Reduction Act (GFGA)
PRA............... Parabolic Reflector Antenna
PRA............... Parana [*Argentina*] [*Airport symbol*] (OAG)
PRA............... Participant Record Advice
PRA............... Partido Revolucionario Autentico [*Authentic Revolutionary Party*] [*Bolivia*] [*Political party*] (PPW)
PRA............... Parti du Regroupement Africain [*African Regroupment Party*] [*Niger*] [*Political party*] (PD)
PRA............... Parti du Regroupement Africain [*African Regroupment Party*] [*Banned, 1974 Burkina Faso*] [*Political party*]
PRA............... Paymaster-Rear-Admiral [*Navy British*]
PRA............... Pay Readjustment Act [*1942*]
PRA............... Pay Record Access
pra............... Payroll Audit (AD)
PRA............... Payroll Auditor [*Insurance*]
PRA............... Peace Research Abstracts (NITA)
PRA............... Peak Recording Accelerograph [*Accelerometer*] (IEEE)
PRA............... Pendulous Reference Axis [*Accelerometer*] (IEEE)
PRA............... People's Revolutionary Army [*Grenada*]
PRA............... Permanent Restricted Area [*Former USSR*] (NATG)
PRA............... Personal Rights Association [*British*] (BI)
PRA............... Personnel Research Activity [*Later, NPTRL*] [*Navy*]
PRA............... Petrol Retailers' Association [*British*]
PRA............... Pharmacy Restructuring Authority [*Australia*]
PRA............... Phosphoribosylamine
PRA............... Pilots Rights Association (EA)
PRA............... Pitch and Roll Attitude (IAA)
PRA............... Planetary Radio Astronomy
PRA............... Planned Regulatory Action [*Federal government*] (GFGA)
PRA............... Planned Restricted Availability [*Military*] (NVT)
PRA............... Plasma Renin Activity [*Hematology*]
pra............... Plasma Renin Activity [*Medicine*] (AD)
PRA............... Plutonium Recycle Acid [*Nuclear energy*] (NRCH)
PRA............... Polar Regions Award (IAA)
PRA............... Policy Research and Analysis
PRA............... Popular Rotocraft Association (EA)
PRA............... Postal Reorganization Act (AD)
PRA............... Postal Reorganization Act of 1970 (AAGC)
PRA............... Praha [*Prague*] [*Czechoslovakia*] [*Seismograph station code, US Geological Survey*] (SEIS)
PRA............... Prairiefire Rural Action (EA)
pra............... Prakrit [*MARC language code Library of Congress*] (LCCP)
PRA............... Precision Axis (KSC)
PRA............... Premium Audit
PRA............... Prerefund Audit [*IRS*]
PRA............... Pre-Retirement Association [*British*] (DI)
PRA............... President of the Royal Academy [*British*]
PRA............... President's Re-Employment Agreement [*New Deal*]
PRA............... Primary Reviewing Authority
PRA............... Prime Responsible Authority (IAA)
PRA............... Print Alphanumerically [*Computer science*] (MDG)
pra............... Print Alphanumerically (AD)
PRA............... Probabilistic Risk Assessment [*Computer-based technique for accident prediction*]
PRA............... Probation and Rehabilitation of Airmen [*Air Force*] (AFM)
pra............... Probation and Rehabilitation of Airmen (AD)
PRA............... Production Reader Assembly (KSC)
PRA............... Production Readiness Assessment [*Army*]
PRA............... Progesterone Receptor Assay [*Clinical chemistry*]
PRA............... Program Reader Assembly [*Computer science*]
pra............... Progressive Retinal Atrophy [*Medicine*] (AD)
PRA............... Projected Requisition Authority [*Army*] (AABC)
PRA............... Prompt Radiation Analysis (MCD)
PRA............... Propionic Acid [*Organic chemistry*]
PRA............... Prospair Ltd. [*British ICAO designator*] (FAAC)
PRA............... Proust Research Association (EA)
PRA............... Psoriasis Research Association (EA)
PRA............... Psychiatric Rehabilitation Association [*British*]
PRA............... Psychological Research Associates
PRA............... Public Resources Association [*Defunct*] (EA)
PRA............... Public Roads Administration
PRA............... Puerto Rico Area Office [*AEC*]
PRA............... Puerto Rico Association (AD)
PRA............... Puerto Rico Association (NADA)
PRA............... Purchase and Resale Agreement [*Canada*] (BARN)
PRA............... US 1869 Pictorial Research Associates (EA)
PRAA............... Airman Apprentice, Parachute Rigger, Striker [*Navy rating*]
Prac............... Practical (DLA)
PRAC............... Practice (AABC)
prac............... Practice (AD)
PRAC............... Practice
PRAC............... Pressure Ratio Acceleration Control [*Gas turbine engine*]
PRAC............... Productivity Technologies Corp. [*NASDAQ symbol*] (SAG)
PRAC............... Program Resource Advisory Committee [*TRADOC*] (MCD)
PRAC............... Public Relations Advisory Committee
PRACA............... Problem Reporting and Corrective Action (MCD)
PRACA............... Puerto Rican Association for Community Affairs (EA)
Prac Act............... Practice Act [*A publication*] (DLA)
Pra Cas............... Prater's Cases on Conflict of Laws [*A publication*] (DLA)
PRaCHS............... Archbishop Carroll High School, Radnor, PA [*Library symbol*] [*Library of Congress*] (LCLS)
pracl............... Page-Replacement Algorithm and Control Logic (AD)
PRACL............... Page-Replacement Algorithm and Control Logic [*Computer science*]
PRACL............... Practical
PRACSATS... Practical Satellites
PRACT............... Practical (ROG)
pract............... Practical (AD)
pract............... Practice (AD)
PRACT............... Practice [*Legal shorthand*] (LWAP)
pract............... Practitioner (AD)
PRACT............... Practitioner
Pract Law.... Practical Lawyer [*A publication*] (DLA)
PRACTNR.... Practitioner
Pract Reg.... Practical Register in the Common Pleas [*England*] [*A publication*] (DLA)
PRAD............... Pitch Ratio Adjust Device (MCD)
PRAD............... Program Research and Development (IAA)
PRADA............... Partido Revolucionario Dominicano Autentico [*Dominican Republic*] [*Political party*]
Pr Adm Dig... Pritchard's Admiralty Digest [*3rd ed.*] [*1887*] [*A publication*] (DLA)
PRADOR...... PRF [*Pulse Repetition Frequency*] Ranging Doppler RADAR
PRADS............... Parachute Retrorocket Airdrop System (MCD)
praef............... Praefatio [*Latin*] (OCD)
Praeger............... Frederick A. Praeger (AD)
Praegtzr............... Praegitzer Industries, Inc. [*Associated Press*] (SAG)
Praem............... De Praemiis et Poenis [*of Philo*] (BJA)
praen............... Praenomen (AD)
Praep Evang... Praeparatio Evangelica [*of Eusebius*] [*Classical studies*] (OCD)
Praepo............... Praepositus [*Deceased, 1509*] [*Authority cited in pre-1607 legal work*] (DSA)
praes............... Praesens [*Present Tense*] [*Latin*]
praet............... Praeterium [*Past Tense*] [*Latin*]
PRAF............... Passenger-Reserved Air Freight
PRAG............... Pensions Research Accountants Group (MHDB)
prag............... Pragmatic (AD)
pragma............... Processing Routines Aided by Graphics for Manipulation of Arrays (AD)
PRAGMA...... Processing Routines Aided by Graphics for Manipulation of Arrays (PDAA)
Pra H & W... Prater on Husband and Wife [*2nd ed.*] [*1836*] [*A publication*] (DLA)
PrA-HPA...... Protein A Hemolytic Plaque Assay [*Medicine*] (DMAA)
PRAI............... Phosphoribosyl Anthranilate Isomerase
PRAI............... Pre-Reading Assessment Inventory [*Education*] (EDAC)
PRAIC............... President of the Royal Architectural Institute of Canada (NGC)
PRAICO............... Puerto Rican American Insurance Co. (AD)
PRAIRIE............... Prairie [*Commonly used*] (OPSA)
Prairie View A&M U... Prairie View Agricultural and Mechanical University (GAGS)
prais............... Passive-Ranging Interferometer Sensor (AD)
PRAIS............... Passive Ranging Interferometer Sensor
PRAIS............... Pesticide Residue Analysis Information Service [*British*]
PRAISE............... Pilot Records of Achievement in Schools Evaluation (AIE)
PRAISE............... Prospective Randomized Amlodipine Survival Evaluation [*Medicine*] (DMAA)
pral............... Principal [*Principal*] [*Spanish*] (AD)
PRAM............... Parallel Random Access Machine [*Computer science*]
PRAM............... Perambulator [*British*]
pram............... Perambulator (AD)
Pram............... Poseidon Random-Access Memory (AD)
PRAM............... Poseidon Random Access Memory [*Missiles*]
Pram............... Prambanam (VRA)
PRAM............... Preliminary Repair Level Decision Analysis Model (PDAA)
PRAM............... Pre-Recorded Announcement and Boarding Music Reproducer
PRAM............... Primary Report of Aircraft Mishap [*Army*] (DOMA)
pram............... Productivity, Reliability, Availability, and Maintainability (AD)
PRAM............... Productivity, Reliability, Availability, and Maintainability Office [*Air Force*]
PRAM............... Product Reliability and Maintainability
PRAM............... Programmable Random Access Memory [*Computer science*] (IAA)
PRAM............... Program Requirements Analysis Method
PRAM............... Propelled Ascent Mine
PRAM............... Propelled Rapid Ascent Mine (MCD)
PRAM............... Pseudorandom Access Memory [*Computer science*] (IAA)

PRAMPO...... Productivity, Reliability, Availability, and Maintenance Program Office [*Air Force*] (DOMA)
PRAN.......... Airman, Parachute Rigger, Striker [*Navy*]
PRAN.......... Production Analyzer (IAA)
PRAND........ Prandium [*Dinner*] [*Pharmacy*]
prand.......... Prandium [*dinner*] [*Latin*] (AD)
PR & D........ Personal Rest and Delay [*Air Force*] (AFM)
PR & D........ Power, Rodwell, and Drew's English Election Cases [*1847-56*] [*A publication*] (DLA)
PR & D........ Public Research and Development
PR & D El Cas... Power, Rodwell, and Drew's English Election Cases [*A publication*] (DLA)
Pr & Div...... Law Reports, Probate and Divorce [*England*] [*A publication*] (DLA)
PR & R........ Professional Rights and Responsibilities
PRANG......... Puerto Rico Air National Guard
PRAP.......... Patient Resident Assessment Profile [*Geriatrics*]
PRAP.......... Provincial/Regional Library Association Presidents [*Canada*]
PRAP.......... Provisions of Following Reference Apply [*Army*] (AABC)
PRAQ.......... Playground and Recreation Association of Queensland [*Australia*]
PRAR.......... Partido Revolucionario Autentico Rios [*Bolivia*] [*Political party*] (PPW)
PRARE......... Precise Range and Range-Rate Experiment
PRARIE........ Prairie [*Commonly used*] (OPSA)
PRARS......... Pitch, Roll, Azimuth Reference System (NG)
PRAS.......... Pacific Regional Advisory Service [*South Pacific Bureau for Economic Co-Operation*] (EY)
PRAS.......... Pension and Retirement Annuity System
PRAS.......... Prereduced, Anaerobically Sterilized [*Microbiology*]
PRAS.......... Pseudo-Renal Artery Syndrome [*Medicine*] (DMAA)
PRASD......... Personnel Research Activity, San Diego [*California*] [*Navy*]
PRAT.......... Parliamentary Retiring Allowances Trust [*Australia*]
PRAT.......... Platelet Radioactive Antiglobulin Test [*Hematology*] (DAVI)
PRAT.......... Prattsburgh Railroad (AD)
PRAT.......... Predicted Range Against Target [*Military*] (NVT)
PRAT.......... Pressure-Retaining Amphipod Trap [*Deep-sea biology*]
PRAT.......... Production Reliability Acceptance Test
P RAT AET... Pro Ratione Aetatis [*According to Age*] [*Pharmacy*] (ROG)
p rat aet...... Pro Ratione Aetatis [*In Proportion to Age*] [*Latin*] (AD)
P RAT AETAT... Pro Rata Aetatis [*According to Age*] [*Pharmacy*]
p rat aetat... Pro Ratione Aetatis [*In Proportion to Age*] [*Latin*] (MAE)
PratHtl......... Pratt Hotel Corp. [*Associated Press*] (SAG)
PratLm......... Pratt & Lambert United, Inc. [*Associated Press*] (SAG)
PRATRA....... Philippines Relief and Trade Rebilitation Administration (AD)
Pratt............ Pratt's Contraband-of-War Cases [*A publication*] (DLA)
Pratt............ Pratt's Supplement to Bott's Poor Laws [*1833*] [*A publication*] (DLA)
Pratt BS....... Pratt's Law of Benefit Building Societies [*A publication*] (DLA)
Pratt Cont.... Pratt's Contraband-of-War Cases [*A publication*] (DLA)
Pratt Cts Req... Pratt's Statutes Establishing Courts of Request [*A publication*] (DLA)
Pratt Fr Soc... Pratt on Friendly Societies [*15th ed.*] [*1931*] [*A publication*] (DLA)
Pratt High.... Pratt and Mackenzie on Highways [*21st ed.*] [*1967*] [*A publication*] (DLA)
Pratt Inst..... Pratt Institute (GAGS)
Pratt PL....... Pratt's Edition of Bott on the Poor Laws [*A publication*] (DLA)
Pratt Prop T... Pratt on the Property Tax Act [*A publication*] (DLA)
Pratt Sav B... Pratt on Savings Banks [*6th ed.*] [*1845*] [*A publication*] (DLA)
Pratt SL....... Pratt on Sea Lights [*2nd ed.*] [*1858*] [*A publication*] (DLA)
PRAUS......... Programme de Recherche sur l'Amiante de l'Universite de Sherbrooke [*Asbestos Research Program*] [*University of Sherbrooke Quebec*] [*Information service or system*] (IID)
PRAV.......... Planned Restricted Availability [*Navy*] (ANA)
PRAV.......... Playground and Recreation Association of Victoria [*Australia*]
PRAW.......... Personnel Research Activity, Washington, DC [*Obsolete Navy*]
PRaW.......... Wyeth Laboratories, Radnor, PA [*Library symbol Library of Congress*] (LCLS)
PRAWL........ Puerto Rican American Women's League
Prax........... Brown's Practice (Praxis) [*or Precedents*] in Chancery [*A publication*] (DLA)
Praxair......... Praxair, Inc. [*Associated Press*] (SAG)
Prax Can...... Praxis Almae Curiae Cancellariae (Brown) [*A publication*] (DLA)
PRAY.......... Paul Revere Associated Yeoman (AD)
PRAZ.......... Prazosin [*A vasodilator*]
PRB........... Basic Proline-Rich Protein (DMAA)
PRB........... Painters' Registration Board [*Western Australia*]
PRB........... Panel Review Board [*NASA*] (KSC)
PRB........... Parabola [*Mathematics*]
PRB........... Parachute Refurbishment Building [*NASA*] (NASA)
PRB........... Partido de la Revolucion Boliviana [*Bolivian Revolutionary Party*] [*Political party*] (AD)
PRB........... Partido Republicano Brasileiro [*Brazil Political party*] (EY)
PRB........... Paso Robles [*California*] [*Airport symbol*] (AD)
PRB........... Paso Robles, CA [*Location identifier FAA*] (FAAL)
PRB........... Pension Review Board [*Canada*]
PRB........... People's Republic of Benin (AD)
PRB........... Personal Reaction Blank [*Psychology*] (DAVI)
PRB........... Personnel Reaction Blank [*Psychology*]
PRB........... Personnel Records Branch [*Army*] (AABC)
PRB........... Personnel Requirements Branch (MUGU)
PRB........... Personnel Research Branch [*Army*] (MCD)
PRB........... Personnel Review Board (AD)
PRB........... Physiotherapists' Registration Board [*New South Wales, Australia*]
PRB........... Planned Requirements - Bureau Directed
PRB........... Plant Review Board [*Nuclear energy*] (NRCH)
PRB........... Podiatrists' Registration Board [*New South Wales, Australia*]
PRB........... Polar Research Board [*National Academy of Sciences*]
PRB........... Population Reference Bureau (EA)
PRB........... Post-Retirement Benefits (AAGC)
PRB........... Press-Radio Bureau (NTCM)
prb............ Principal Borehole (AD)
PRB........... Private Radio Bureau [*FCC*] (NTCM)
PRB........... Procedure Review Board [*Nuclear energy*] (NRCH)
PRB........... Procurement Review Board (MCD)
PRB........... Professional Registration Boards of the Northern Territory [*Australia*]
PRB........... Program Request Block (IAA)
PRB........... Program Review Board
PRB........... Project Review Board [*NASA*] (NASA)
PRB........... Prosthetics Research Board
PRB........... Proteus Air Systeme [*France ICAO designator*] (FAAC)
PRB........... Psychosurgery Review Board [*Victoria, Australia*]
PRB........... Public Roads Bureau
PRBA.......... Portable Rechargeable Battery Association
PRBA.......... Puerto Rican Bar Association (EA)
PRBA(AG).... Personnel Research Board of the Army, Adjutant General
PrBayA......... American Junior College of Puerto Rico, Bayamon, PR [*Library symbol Library of Congress*] (LCLS)
PrBayC......... Bayamon Central University (Universidad Central de Bayamon), Bayamon, Puerto Rico [*Library symbol Library of Congress*] (LCLS)
PRBC.......... Packed Red Blood Cells [*Medicine*]
PRBC.......... Parasitized Red Blood Cell [*Medicine*]
PRBC.......... Placental Residual Blood Volume [*Medicine*] (DMAA)
PRBC.......... Premier Bancorp, Inc. [*NASDAQ symbol*] (NQ)
PRBC.......... Prestige Bancorp, Inc. [*NASDAQ symbol*] (SAG)
PRBD.......... Paraboloid
PRBG.......... Puerto Rican Board of Guardians [*Defunct*] (EA)
PRBK.......... Provident Bancorp [*NASDAQ symbol*] (TTSB)
PRBK.......... Provident Bancorp, Inc. [*NASDAQ symbol*] (SAG)
PRBLC......... Parabolic
PRBLTY....... Probability [*NWS*] (FAAC)
PRBMECAB... Permanent Regional Bureau of the Middle East Committee for the Affairs of the Blind [*Riyadh, Saudi Arabia*] (EAIO)
PRBNT......... Prebent
PRBO.......... Position Relief Briefing Observed [*Aviation*] (FAAC)
PRBS.......... Pseudorandom Binary Sequence [*Computer science*]
PRBSG......... Pseudorandom Binary Sequence Generator [*Computer science*] (NRCH)
PRBT.......... Precision Remote Bathythermograph
PRBV.......... Placental Residual Blood Volume [*Hematology*] (MAE)
PRBV.......... Placental Residual Blood Volume [*Medicine*] (DMAA)
PRC........... Chief Aircrew Survival Equipmentman [*Formerly, Chief Parachute Rigger*] [*Navy rating*]
PRC........... Pacific Air Charter, Inc. [*ICAO designator*] (FAAC)
PRC........... Packed Red Cell [*Hematology*] (MAE)
PRC........... Pain Rehabilitation Center (AD)
PRC........... Palestine Red Crescent (AD)
PRC........... Park Ridge Center (EA)
PRC........... Partial Response Coding (IEEE)
PRC........... Partido Regionalista de Cantabria [*Spain Political party*] (EY)
PRC........... Partido Republicano Calderonista [*Calderonista Republican Party*] [*Costa Rica*] [*Political party*] (PPW)
PRC........... Partido Revolucionario Comunista [*Brazil Political party*] (EY)
PRC........... Parti Republicain Caledonien [*New Caledonia*] [*Political party*] (FEA)
PRC........... Part Requirement Card
PRC........... Parts Release Card (KSC)
PRC........... Passaic River Coalition (EA)
PRC........... Passenger Reservation Center [*Army*]
PRC........... Pay-Raise Commission (AD)
PRC........... Penrose Resources Corp. [*Vancouver Stock Exchange symbol*]
PRC........... Pension Research Council (EA)
PRC........... Pension Rights Center [*Washington, DC*] (EA)
PRC........... People's Redemption Council [*Liberia*] (PD)
PRC........... People's Republic of China [*Mainland China*]
PRC........... People's Republic of the Congo
PRC........... Periodic Reverse Current (IAA)
PRC........... Permanent Regular Commissions [*Army British*]
PRC........... Personality Research Center [*University of Texas at Austin*] [*Research center*] (RCD)
PRC........... Personnel Readiness Center [*Air Force*]
PRC........... Personnel Reception Centre [*British military*] (DMA)
PRC........... Personnel Recovery Center [*Military*]
PRC........... Personnel Reporting Code [*Army*] (AABC)
PRC........... Phase-Response Curve
PRC........... Philippine Resource Center [*An association*] (EA)
PRC........... Physical Review Council [*DoD*]
PRC........... Picatinny Research Center [*Picatinny Arsenal*] (AD)
PRC........... Pierce (MSA)
PRC........... Pitch Rate Command (MCD)
PRC........... Pitch Ratio Controller (MCD)
PRC........... Planar Random Composite (MCD)
PRC........... Planned Requirements, Conversion (NG)
PRC........... Planning Research Corp. [*Telecommunications service*] (TSSD)
PRC........... Planning Research Corporation (USDC)
PRC........... Planning Research Corporation [*Marine science*] (OSRA)
PRC........... Plant Records Center [*of the American Horticultural Society*] (IID)
PRC........... Plasma Renin Concentration [*Hematology*]
PRC........... Plastic Roller Conveyor
PRC........... Plutonium Rework Cell [*Nuclear energy*] (NRCH)
PRC........... Point of Reverse Curve (MSA)
PRC........... Point Reyes [*California*] [*Seismograph station code, US Geological Survey Closed*] (SEIS)

PRC .... Policy Review Committee [*Terminated, 1981*] [*National Security Council*] (EGAO)
PRC .... Polish Resettlement Corps [*British military*] (DMA)
PRC .... Polysulphide Rubber Compound (PDAA)
prc .... Polysulphide Rubber Compound (AD)
PRC .... Population Research Center [*University of Chicago*] [*Research center*] (RCD)
PRC .... Population Resource Center (EA)
PRC .... Postal Rate Commission [*Federal government*]
PRC .... Postconsumer Recycled Content [*Plastics technology*]
PRC .... Post Roman Conditam [*After the Founding of Rome*] [*Latin*]
PRC .... Poultry Research Centre [*of the Agricultural Research Council*] [*British*] (ARC)
PRC .... Power Reflection Coefficient [*of RADAR signals*]
PRC .... Prattsburgh Railway Corp. [*AAR code*]
PRC .... Preoral Ciliary [*Gland*]
PRC .... Pre-Ranger Course [*Army*] (INF)
PRC .... Prescott [*Arizona*] [*Airport symbol*] (OAG)
PRC .... Prescott, AZ [*Location identifier FAA*] (FAAL)
PRC .... Prescription Rate Carryover [*Health insurance*] (GHCT)
PRC .... Pressure Recorder Controller [*Nuclear energy*] (NRCH)
PRC .... Pressure Response Cell [*For chemical kinetic studies*]
PRC .... Prevention Research Center [*Pacific Institute for Research and Evaluation*] [*Research center*] (RCD)
PRC .... Price
PRC .... Price Redetermination Contract (SAA)
PRC .... Primary Routing Center [*Telecommunications*] (TEL)
PRC .... Primate Research Center
PRC .... Printer Control
PRC .... Priory Cell
Pr C .... Prize Cases [*A publication*] (DLA)
PRC .... Problem Resolution Coordinator [*IRS*]
PRC .... Procaterol [*Pharmacology*]
PRC .... Procedure Review Committee (AAG)
PRC .... Procession Register Clock
PRC .... Proconsul
PRC .... Procurement Request Code [*Military*] (AFIT)
PRC .... Production Control (IAA)
PRC .... Production Readjustments Committee [*WPB*]
PRC .... Product Regional Center [*Department of Supply and Service*] [*Canada*] (IMH)
PRC .... Professional Reference Center [*Los Angeles County Office of Education*] [*Downey, CA*] [*Library network*]
PRC .... Professional Relations Council [*American Chemical Society*]
PRC .... Programmed Rate Control (NITA)
PRC .... Program Rest Code (MCD)
PRC .... Program Review Committee (AFM)
PRC .... Prologic Management Systems, Inc. [*AMEX symbol*] (SAG)
PRC .... Propeller Change (MCD)
PRC .... Providence College, Phillips Memorial Library, Providence, RI [*OCLC symbol*] (OCLC)
PRC .... Pseudo-Range Correction
PRC .... Public Relations Club (AD)
PRC .... Pyrotechnic Rocket Container
PRC .... Revolutionary Socialist Party [*Peru*] [*Political party*] (PD)
Pr Ca .... Great War Prize Cases, by Evans [*England*] [*A publication*] (DLA)
PRCA .... Packaging Research [*NASDAQ symbol*] (TTSB)
PRCA .... Packaging Research Corp. [*NASDAQ symbol*] (SAG)
PRCA .... Palomino Rabbit Co-Breeders Association (EA)
PRCA .... Parks, Recreation and Cultural Affairs Administration [*New York City*]
PRCA .... People's Republic of China Army (MCD)
PRCA .... Pitch and Roll Channel Assembly (MCD)
PRCA .... Presbyterian Reformed Church of Australia
PRCA .... President of the Royal Canadian Academy
PRCA .... President of the Royal Canadian Academy of Arts (NGC)
PRCA .... Problem Reporting and Corrective Action (NASA)
PRCA .... Professional Rodeo Cowboys Association (EA)
PRCA .... Public Relations Consultants Association (EAIO)
PRCA .... Puerto Rico Communications Authority
PRCA .... Pure Red Cell Agenesis [*Hematology*] (MAE)
PRCA .... Pure Red Cell Aplasia [*Hematology*]
PrCaC .... Colegio Universitario de Cayey, Cayey, PR [*Library symbol Library of Congress*] (LCLS)
PRC & NW... Pierre, Rapid City & Northwestern Railroad [*Nickname: Plenty Rough Country and No Women*]
PRCAW .... Packaging Research Wrrt [*NASDAQ symbol*] (TTSB)
PRCB .... Program Requirements Change Board [*NASA*] (NASA)
PRCB .... Program Requirements Control Board [*NASA*]
PRCB .... Program Review Control Board [*NASA*] (NASA)
PRCBD .... Program Requirements Control Board Directive [*NASA*] (NASA)
PRCBD .... Program Review Control Board Directive [*NASA*] (NASA)
PRCC .... Partial Rank Correlation Coefficient [*Nuclear energy*] (NUCP)
PRCC .... Peoria Record Club [*Record label*]
PRCC .... Pollution Research and Control Corp. [*NASDAQ symbol*] (SAG)
PRCC .... Pollution Resh & Ctl CA [*NASDAQ symbol*] (TTSB)
PRCC .... Procurement Research Coordinating Counsel (AAGC)
PRCC .... Puerto Rico Cancer Center [*University of Puerto Rico*] [*Research center*] (RCD)
PRCCh .... Principal Roman Catholic Chaplain [*Navy British*]
PrcCm .... Price Communications Corp. [*Associated Press*] (SAG)
PRCCT .... Printed Circuit [*Computer science*] (IAA)
prcd .... Priced (AD)
PRCEC .... Pearce Sys Intl [*NASDAQ symbol*] (TTSB)
PR Cem .... Puerto Rican Cement Co., Inc. [*Associated Press*] (SAG)
PRCESSN..... Processing
PRCF .... Petroleum Resources Communications Foundation [*Canada*]
PRCF .... Plutonium Recycle Critical Facility [*Nuclear energy*]
Pr Ch .... Parish Church (AD)
PR Ch .... Practical Register in Chancery [*England*] [*A publication*] (DLA)
Pr Ch .... Precedents in Chancery, Edited by Finch [*1689-1722*] [*England*] [*A publication*] (DLA)
PRCH .... Precharge
PRCH .... Proprietary Chapel [*Church of England*]
PRCHNG ...... Purchasing
prchst .... Parachutist (AD)
prcht .... Parachute (AD)
PRCHT .... Parachute (AFM)
Prcht Bad..... Parachutist Badge [*Military decoration*]
PRCI .... Parti Republicain de la Cote d'Ivoire [*Republicaqn Party of the Ivory Coast*] [*Political party*] (EY)
PRCI .... Policy Review Committee Intelligence [*Military*]
PRCI .... Production Reliability Cost Improvement (DWSG)
Pr CKB .... Practice Cases, in the King's Bench [*England*] [*A publication*] (DLA)
PRCM .... Master Chief Aircrew Survival Equipmentman [*Formerly, Master Chief Parachute R igger*] [*Navy rating*]
PRCM .... Passive Radiation Countermeasure [*Military*]
PRCM .... Pericom Semiconductor Corp. [*NASDAQ symbol*] (SAG)
PRCM .... Procom Technology Inc. [*NASDAQ symbol*] (SAG)
PRCMNT...... Procurement
PRCMT .... Procurement (MSA)
PRCN .... Percon, Inc. [*NASDAQ symbol*] (SAG)
PRCN .... Precision (MSA)
PR-CNTL...... Product Control Register
PRCO .... Pacific Requisition Control Office [*Navy*]
Pr Co .... Prerogative Court (DLA)
PR/COM...... Vessel Delivered in Partially-Completed Status [*Navy*] (DNAB)
Pr Cont .... Pratt's Contraband-of-War Cases [*1861*] [*A publication*] (DLA)
PrcOptCp ..... Precision Optics Corp. [*Associated Press*] (SAG)
PRCP .... Perceptron, Inc. [*NASDAQ symbol*] (SAG)
PRCP .... Personnel Readiness Capability Program [*Navy*] (DNAB)
PRCP .... Power Remote Control Panel (AAG)
PRCP .... Practical Register in the Common Pleas [*A publication*] (DLA)
PRCP .... President of the Royal College of Physicians [*British*]
PRCP .... President of the Royal College of Preceptors [*British*] (ROG)
PRCP .... Puerto Rican Communist Party [*Political party*]
PRCPTN...... Precipitin [*Test*] [*Immunology*]
PRCR .... Protective Cover (AAG)
PrcREI .... Price REIT, Inc. [*Associated Press*] (SAG)
PRCS .... Passive and Remote Crosswind Sensor (MCD)
PRCS .... Personal Radio Communications System [*General Electric Co.*]
PRCS .... Personal Report of Confidence as a Speaker [*Psychology*]
PRCS .... Polish Red Cross Society
PRCS .... President of the Royal College of Surgeons [*British*]
PRCS .... Prevention and Removal of Corrosion and Scale [*Engineering*]
PRCS .... Process (AFM)
PRCS .... Process
prcs .... Process (AD)
PRCS .... Processing (IAA)
P/RCS .... Propulsion and Reaction Control Subsystem [*NASA*] (KSC)
PRCS .... Psychological Response Classification System
PRCS .... Purchase Requisition Change Supplement
PRCS .... Senior Chief Aircrew Survival Equipmentman [*Formerly, Senior Chief Parachute R igger*] [*Navy rating*]
PRCSG .... Processing (MSA)
PRCSG .... Processing
PRCSR .... Processor
prcst .... Precast (AD)
PRCST .... Precast (AAG)
PRCT .... Pool Repair Cycle Time (MCD)
PRCT .... Procept, Inc. [*NASDAQ symbol*] (SAG)
PRCTN .... Precaution [*ICAO designator*] (FAAC)
PRCU .... Power Regulating and Control Unit (CET)
prcu .... Power Regulation and Control Unit (AD)
PRCUA .... Polish Roman Catholic Union of America (EA)
PRCY .... ProCyte Corp. [*NASDAQ symbol*] (NQ)
PRD .... Partial Reaction of Degeneration
prd .... Partial Reaction of Degeneration (AD)
PRD .... Parti Democratique Dahomeen [*Dahomey Democratic Party*] [*Political party*]
PRD .... Partido de la Revolucion Democratica [*Mexico Political party*] (EY)
PRD .... Partido de Renovacion Democratica [*Democratic Renewal Party*] [*Costa Rica*] [*Political party*] (PPW)
PRD .... Partido Reformista Democratico [*Democratic Reformist Party*] [*Spain Political party*] (PPW)
PRD .... Partido Revolucionario Democratico [*Democratic Revolutionary Party*] [*Panama*] [*Political party*] (PPW)
PRD .... Partido Revolucionario Dominicano [*Dominican Revolutionary Party*] [*Dominican Republic*] [*Political party*] (PPW)
PRD .... Parti du Renouveau Democratique [*Benin*] [*Political party*] (EY)
PRD .... Parti Radical-Democratique Suisse [*Radical Democratic Party of Switzerland*] [*Political party*] (PPE)
PRD .... Part Reference Designator
PRD .... Party of the Democratic Revolution [*Mexico Political party*]
PRD .... Payroll Deduction
PRD .... Performance-Related Pay [*Business term*] (ECON)
PRD .... Period
PRD .... Periodontics and Restorative Dentistry
PRD .... Personal Radiation Dosimeter (KSC)
PRD .... Personnel Readiness Date [*Army*] (AABC)
PRD .... Personnel Records Division [*Army*] (AABC)

PRD .... Personnel Requirements Data (AAG)
PRD .... Personnel Research Division [*Navy*] (MCD)
PRD .... Personnel Resources Data
PRD .... Pesticides Regulation Division (AD)
PRD .... Pesticides Regulation Division (NADA)
PRD .... Physician Relations Department (DMAA)
PRD .... Piezoelectric Resonating Device
PRD .... Planned Residential Development
PRD .... Polaroid Corp. [*NYSE symbol*] (SPSG)
PRD .... Political Resource Directory [*A publication*]
PRD .... Polytechnic Research & Development Co. (AAG)
PRD .... Positive Regulatory Domain [*Genetics*]
PRD .... Postal Regulating Detachment [*Military*]
PRD .... Postradiation Dysplasia [*Medicine*]
PRD .... Potentially Reportable Deficiency [*Nuclear energy*] (NRCH)
PRD .... Power Range Detector (IEEE)
PRD .... Power Requirement Data
PRD .... Precompetitive Research and Development
PRD .... Predicted Range of the Day [*Military*] (NVT)
PRD .... Preretro Update Display
PRD .... Presidential Review Directive (USDC)
PRD .... Pressing Direction
PRD .... Pride
PRD .... Prime RADAR Digitizer (IAA)
PRD .... Princeton Reference Design (MCD)
PRD .... Printer Driver
PRD .... Printer Dump
prd .... Printer Dump (AD)
PRD .... Process Requirements Drawing (MCD)
PRD .... Procurement Regulation Directive [*NASA*] (NASA)
PRD .... Procurement Requirements Document [*NASA*] (NASA)
PRD .... Production Responsibilities Document (MCD)
PRD .... Productivity Research Division [*Office of Personnel Management*] (GRD)
PRD .... Product Research and Development [*Advertising*] (DOAD)
PRD .... Proficiency Rating Designator [*Military*]
PRD .... Program [*or Project*] Requirement Data [*NASA*] (KSC)
PRD .... Program Requirements Document
PRD .... Projected Rotation Date (NG)
PRD .... Proline-Rich Domain [*Genetics*]
prd .... Pro-Rata Distribution (AD)
PRD .... Pro Rate Distribution [*Clause*] [*Insurance*]
PRD .... Puerto Rico, Decisiones [*A publication*] (DLA)
PRD .... Push Rod [*Mechanical engineering*]
PRDA .... Pony Riding for the Disabled Association [*Australia*]
PRDA .... Program Research and Development Announcement [*Energy Research and Development Administration*]
PRDC .... Personnel Research and Development Center [*Office of Personnel Management*] (GRD)
PRDC .... Pig Research and Development Corp. [*Australia*]
PRDC .... Polar Research and Development Center [*Army*]
PRDCTVTY ... Productivity
PRDDO .... Partial Retention of Diatomic Differential Overlap [*Physics*]
PRDE .... Pride Petroleum Services, Inc. [*NASDAQ symbol*] (CTT)
PRDE .... Pride Petroleum Svcs [*NASDAQ symbol*] (TTSB)
PrdEn .... Producers Entertainment Group Ltd. [*Associated Press*] (SAG)
PrdEnt .... Producers Entertainment Group Ltd. [*Associated Press*] (SAG)
PrdePt .... Pride Petroleum Services, Inc. [*Associated Press*] (SAG)
PRDF .... Page Reference Distribution Function [*Computer science*] (IAA)
PRDF .... Political Rights Defense Fund [*Defunct*] (EA)
PRDG .... Princess Royal's Dragoon Guards [*Military unit*] [*British*] (ROG)
PRDIAG .... Primary Diagnosis [*Medicine*]
PRDL .... Personnel Research and Development Laboratory [*Navy*] (MCD)
prdl .... Predella (VRA)
PRDM .... Paradigm Technology [*NASDAQ symbol*] (TTSB)
PRDM .... Paradigm Technology, Inc. [*NASDAQ symbol*] (SAG)
PRDM .... Parti pour le Rassemblement Democratique des Mahorais [*Mayotte*] [*Political party*] (EY)
PRDN .... Partido de Reconciliacion Democratica Nacional [*Party of National Democratic Reconciliation*] [*Guatemala*] [*Political party*]
PRDNTST ..... Periodonist
PRDP .... Power Reactor Demonstration Program
PRDPEC .... Power Reactor Development Programme Evaluation Committee [*Canada*] (HGAA)
PRDR .... Preproduction Reliability Design Review [*Navy*] (CAAL)
PRDR .... Production Request Design Review
PRDS .... Paradise
PRDS .... Processed RADAR Display System (PDAA)
PRDV .... Peak Reading Digital Voltmeter
PRDX .... Prediction Program [*NASA*]
PRE .... Bureau for Private Enterprise
PRE .... Federation Europeenne des Fabricants de Produits Refractaires [*Zurich, Switzerland*] (EAIO)
PRE .... Partido Republicano Evolucionista [*Republican Evolutionist Party*] [*Portugal Political party*] (PPE)
PRE .... Partido Roldosista Ecuatoriano [*Ecuador*] [*Political party*] (EY)
PRE .... Partner-Resisted Exercise [*Army*] (INF)
PRE .... Personal Rescue Enclosure (NASA)
PRE .... Personnel Restraint Equipment (SAA)
PRE .... Petroleum Refining Engineer
PRE .... Photoreactivating
PRE .... Physical Reconditioning Exercises [*Orthopedics*] (DAVI)
PRE .... Pineridge Capital [*Vancouver Stock Exchange symbol*]
PRE .... Planetary Rotation Engine (IAA)
PRE .... Portable RADAR Equipment
pre .... Pre-Choice [*Advertising*] (WDMC)
PRE .... Precinct
PRE .... Precision Valley Aviation [*ICAO designator*] (FAAC)
PRE .... Predecessor (KSC)
pre .... Prefatory (WDMC)
PRE .... Prefect
pre .... Preferred (WDMC)
pre .... Prefix (WDMC)
PRE .... Prefix
PRE .... Preliminary
PRE .... Preliminary Amplifier (IAA)
PRE .... Premier Industrial Corp. [*NYSE symbol*] (SPSG)
pre .... Preoperative [*Surgery*] (DAVI)
PRE .... Prepayment Coin Telephone [*Telecommunications*] (TEL)
PRE .... Pre-Retirement Education (AIE)
PRE .... Presbyterian Historical Society, Philadelphia, PA [*OCLC symbol*] (OCLC)
PRE .... President of the Royal Society of Painter-Etchers and Engravers [*British*]
pre .... Pretest [*Advertising*] (WDMC)
PRE .... Pretoria [*South Africa*] [*Seismograph station code, US Geological Survey*] (SEIS)
PRE .... Problem Reproducer Equipment (SAA)
PRE .... Processing Refabrication Experiment [*Nuclear energy*] (NRCH)
PRE .... Progesterone [*A hormone*]
PRE .... Progesterone Response Element [*Endocrinology*]
PRE .... Progressive Resistive Exercise [*Medicine*]
PRE .... Protein Relaxation Enhancement (OA)
PRE .... Proton Relaxation Enhancement [*Physics*]
PRE .... Public Relations Exchange [*Later, PRXI*] (EA)
PRE .... Pulse Radiation Effect
PRE .... Spanish Catalonian Battalion (PD)
PREA .... Pension Real Estate Association (EA)
P/REA .... Probationary Radio Electrical Artificer [*British military*] (DMA)
PREAG .... Parks Residents Environmental Action Group [*Australia*]
PREAG .... Photographic Reconnaissance Equipment Advisory Group [*Military*]
PREAMP ...... Preamplifier (AAG)
PREAP .... Prison Research Education Action Project (EA)
PRE-ARM ..... People's Rights Enforced Against Riots and Murder [*Vigilante group in New Jersey*]
PREB .... Prebendary
PREB .... Pupil Record of Educational Behavior [*Aptitude test*]
Preb Dig ...... Preble. Digest, Patent Cases [*A publication*] (DLA)
Preb Pat Cas ... Preble. Digest, Patent Cases [*A publication*] (DLA)
PREC .... Palestine Research and Educational Center (EA)
p rec .... Per Rectum [*Through the rectum*] [*Pharmacology*] (DAVI)
PREC .... Precambrian [*Period, era, or system*] [*Geology*]
PREC .... Precedence (AABC)
PREC .... Preceding
PREC .... Precentor (ROG)
PREC .... Precious (ROG)
prec .... Precious (VRA)
PREC .... Precision (AABC)
Prec .... Precite [*Supra, Cited Before*] [*French*] (ILCA)
PREC .... Propulsion Research Environmental Chamber
PREC .... Public Revenue Education Council (EA)
PrecCst .... Precision Castparts Corp. [*Associated Press*] (SAG)
PRECD .... Precede (FAAC)
PrecDr .... Precision Drilling Corp. [*Associated Press*] (SAG)
PRECEDE ..... Predisposing, Reinforcing, and Enabling Causes in Educational Diagnosis and Evaluation [*Occupational therapy*]
Pre Ch .... Precedents in Chancery, Edited by Finch [*A publication*] (DLA)
Prec in Ch ... Precedents in Chancery, Edited by Finch [*24 English Reprint*] [*1689-1722*] [*A publication*] (DLA)
Prec in Ch (Eng) ... Precedents in Chancery, Edited by Finch [*24 English Reprint*] [*A publication*] (DLA)
precip .... Precipitate [*Laboratory science*] (DAVI)
PRECIP .... Precipitation
PRECIS .... Pre-Coordinate Indexing System
PRECIS .... Preserved Context Index System [*British Library*] [*London, England*] [*Information service or system*]
PRECO .... Preparatory Commission of the United Nations Organization
PRECOM ...... Precommissioning [*Military*]
PRECOM ...... Preliminary Communications Search [*Military*] (NVT)
PRECOMDET ... Precommissioning Detail [*Navy*] (NVT)
PRECOMG .... Precommissioning [*Military*] (NVT)
PRECOMM ... Preliminary Communications [*Military*] (NVT)
PRECOMMDET ... Precommissioning Detail [*Navy*]
PRECOMMSCOL ... Precommissioning School [*Navy*]
precomp ...... Precomputed Loan
PRECOMP .... Prediction of Contingency Maintenance and Parts Requirements (MCD)
PRECOMUNIT ... Precommissioning Unit [*Navy*] (DNAB)
PrecRes .... Precision Response Corp. [*Associated Press*] (SAG)
PRECSN .... Precision
PrecStd .... Precision Standard, Inc. [*Associated Press*] (SAG)
PrecSy .... Precision Systems, Inc. [*Associated Press*] (SAG)
PRED .... Predicate
PRED .... Predicted
PRED .... Prediction (AFM)
Pred .... Prednisone [*Also, P, PDN, Pr, Pro*] [*Endocrinology*] [*Antineoplastic drug*]
PRED .... Prednisone (DMAA)
PreD$_3$ .... Previtamin D3 [*A precursor to vitamin D3*] (DAVI)
PREDA .... Puerto Rico Economic Development Administration (NADA)

PREDECE ..... Predecease (ROG)
PREDICT ...... Pollution Reduction by Information and Control Technology
PREDICT ...... Prediction of Radiation Effects by Digital Computer Techniques
Pr Edw I ...... Prince Edward Island (DLA)
Pr Edw I ...... Prince Edward Island Reports [*Canada*] [*A publication*] (DLA)
Pr Edw Isl .... Prince Edward Island (DLA)
Pr Edw Isl .... Prince Edward Island Reports [*Canada*] [*A publication*] (DLA)
PREEMIE ...... Premature Baby [*Medical slang*] (WDAA)
PRE-EMPTN ... Pre-Emption (ROG)
PREF .... Preface
pref .... Preface (WDMC)
PREF .... Prefecture
PREF .... Preference [*or Preferred*] (AFM)
PREF .... Preferred (KSC)
PREF .... Preferred
PREF .... Prefix (AAG)
PREF .... Prefocused
PREF .... Propulsion Research Environmental Facility
PREFAB .... Prefabricated (KSC)
PREFACE ..... Pre-Freshman and Cooperative Education for Minorities in Engineering
PREF-AP ...... Prefect-Apostolic [*Roman Catholic*]
PREFAT .... Prepare Final Acceptance Trials [*Navy*] (NVT)
PREFCE .... Preface (ROG)
PREFD .... Preferred (WDAA)
PREFLT .... Preflight (KSC)
PREFLTSCOL ... Preflight School [*Military*]
PREFMD ...... Preformed
PREFRAM .... Prepare Fleet Rehabilitation and Modernization Overhaul [*Navy*] (NVT)
preft .... Prefecture
PREG .... Pregnancy [*or Pregnant*]
PREG .... Pregnenolone [*Endocrinology*]
pregang .... Preganglionic [*Anatomy*]
PREGN .... Pregnancy [*or Pregnant*] (AAMN)
prehis .... Prehistory [*or Prehistoric*] (BARN)
PREHIST ..... Prehistory [*or Prehistoric*] (WDAA)
PREIA .... Professional Radio and Electronics Institute of Australia
PREINACT .... Prepare Inactivation [*Navy*] (NVT)
PREINSURV ... Prepare for Board of Inspection and Survey [*Navy*] (NVT)
PreissM .... Preiss [*Byron*] Multimedia Co., Inc. [*Associated Press*] (SAG)
PREJ .... Prejudice (AABC)
PREL .... Pain Relief Level [*Medicine*]
PREL .... Preliminary
PREL .... Preliminary Evaluation [*Orbit identification*]
PREL .... Prelude [*Music*] (ROG)
PREL .... Priority Reconnaissance Exploitation List (CINC)
PREL .... Programmable Rotary Encoded Logic [*Computer science*] (MHDB)
PRELA .... Prensa Latina, Angencia Informativa Latinoamericana [*Press agency*] [*Cuba*]
PRELIM .... Preliminary (AFM)
prelim diag ... Preliminary Diagnosis [*Medicine*] (DAVI)
prelims .... Preliminary Pages [*Frontmatter*] [*Publishing*]
PRELIMY ..... Preliminary (ROG)
prelm .... Preliminary (VRA)
PRELOG .... People's Revolutionary League of Ghana [*Political party*] (PPW)
PRELORT ..... Precision Long-Range Tracking RADAR
PRELUDE .... Pre-Optimization Linearization of Undulation and Detection of Errors (PDAA)
PREM .... Preliminary Reference Earth Model [*Geology*]
PREM .... Premature [*Medicine*]
PREM .... Premier (ROG)
PREM .... Premier
prem .... Premiere (WDMC)
PREM .... Premier Financial Services, Inc. [*Freeport, IL*] [*NASDAQ symbol*] (NQ)
PREM .... Premier Financial Svcs [*NASDAQ symbol*] (TTSB)
PREM .... Premium (AFM)
prem .... Premium (WDMC)
PREM .... Probe-Microphone Real Ear Measurement [*Audiology*]
PREMA .... Pulp Refining Equipment Manufacturers Association (EA)
PremBksh .... Premier Bankshares [*Associated Press*] (SAG)
Premdr .... Premdor, Inc. [*Associated Press*] (SAG)
PREMED ...... Premedical Student (WDAA)
PRE-MED .... Previous to Appearance in MEDLINE [*Latham, NY*] [*Bibliographic database*]
PREMEDU .... Preventive Medicine Unit
Premerk .... Premark International, Inc. [*Associated Press*] (SAG)
PREMES ...... Premises (ROG)
PremFin .... Premier Financial Bancorp, Inc. [*Associated Press*] (SAG)
PremFn .... Premier Financial Services [*Associated Press*] (SAG)
premie .... Premature [*Infant*] (DAVI)
Premis .... Premis Corp. [*Associated Press*] (SAG)
PREMOD ..... Premodeling Data Output [*Environmental Protection Agency*]
PREMOD ..... Premodulation (NASA)
PREMODE .... Preliminary Mid-Ocean Dynamics Experiment [*Marine science*] (MSC)
PremrIn .... Premier Industrial Corp. [*Associated Press*] (SAG)
pre-mRNA .... Precursor-Messenger Ribonucleic Acid
PREMS .... Premises (DSUE)
PREMSS ...... Photographic Reconnaissance and Exploitation Management Support System (MCD)
PremT .... Premiere Technologies, Inc. [*Associated Press*] (SAG)
PREN .... Price Enterprises [*NASDAQ symbol*] (TTSB)
PREN .... Price Enterprises, Inc. [*NASDAQ symbol*] (SAG)
Pren Act ...... Prentice's Proceedings in an Action [*2nd ed.*] [*1880*] [*A publication*] (DLA)
prenat .... Prenatal
PrEng .... Professional Engineer
PrentPr .... Prentiss Properties Trust [*Associated Press*] (SAG)
preocc .... Preoccupied [*Biology, taxonomy*]
PREOP .... Preoperative [*Medicine*]
PRE-OPS ..... Pre-Operational Support [*Military*]
PREOS .... Predicted Range for Electrooptical Systems [*Military*] (CAAL)
PREOVHL ..... Prepare for Shipyard Overhaul [*Navy*] (NVT)
PREP .... Pacific Range Electromagnetic Platform (AAG)
PREP .... Parent Readiness Evaluation of Preschoolers [*Child development test*]
PREP .... Pattern Reversal Evoked Potential
PREP .... Peace Research and Education Project
PREP .... Peacetime Requirements and Procedures [*Strategic Air Command*] (MUGU)
PREP .... Personal Responsibility Education Process
PREP .... Persons Responsive to Educational Problems (EA)
PREP .... Plan, Rehearse, Edit, and Psych [*Public speaking preparation technique*]
PREP .... Plasma Rotating Electrode Process [*Metallurgy*]
PREP .... Population, Resources, and Environment Program [*American Association for the Advancement of Science*]
PReP .... Power PC [*Personal Computer*] Reference Platform [*Configuration standard*] (PCM)
PREP .... Predischarge Education Program [*DoD*]
PREP .... Preparation [*or Preparatory*]
PREP .... Preparation
prep .... Preparation (WDMC)
prep .... Preparatory (WDMC)
prep .... Preparatory (VRA)
prep .... Prepare (WDMC)
PREP .... Prepare (AFM)
PREP .... Preposition
prep .... Preposition (WDMC)
PREP .... Productivity Research and Extension Program [*North Carolina State University*] [*Research center*] (RCD)
PREP .... Programmed Educational Package
PREP .... Programmed Electronics Pattern (PDAA)
PREP .... Pupil Record of Educational Progress [*Education*] (AEBS)
PREP .... Purchasing, Receiving, and Payable System
PREP .... Putting Research into Educational Practice [*Information service of ERIC*]
Prepak .... People's Revolutionary Party of Kungleipak [*India*] [*Political party*] (PD)
PREPARE ..... Premarital Personal and Relationship Evaluation
PREPARE ..... Project for Retraining of Employable Persons as Relates to EDP
PREPAS .... Precise Personnel Assignment System [*Marine Corps*] (GFGA)
PrepCom ...... Preparatory Committee [*United Nations Committee on Environment and Development*]
PREPD .... Prepared
PREPE .... Prepare (ROG)
PREPG .... Preparing
PREPN .... Preparation
PREPnet ..... [*The*] Pennsylvania Research & Economic Partnership Network [*Computer science*] (TNIG)
Prepo .... Praepositus [*Deceased, 1509*] [*Authority cited in pre-1607 legal work*] (DSA)
Prepos .... Praepositus [*Deceased, 1509*] [*Authority cited in pre-1607 legal work*] (DSA)
PREPOS ...... Preposition (AABC)
PREPOSTOR ... Prepositioned Storage [*Army*] (AABC)
PREPPSA ..... Prepare Postshakedown Availability [*Navy*] (NVT)
Preppy .... Preparatory School Alumnus [*Lifestyle classification*]
PREPREG .... Pre-Impregnated Glass Fibers [*Fiberglass production*]
PREPRO ...... Prepositioning [*Ship*] [*Navy*] (DOMA)
PREPRO ...... Preprocessor [*Computer*] [*Coast Guard*]
PREPROD .... Preproduction Model [*Military*] (AFIT)
PREPS .... Predischarge Remedial Education Program [*For servicemen*]
PREPS .... Program of Research and Evaluation in Public Schools [*Mississippi State University*] [*Research center*] (RCD)
PREPSCOL ... Preparatory School
prepub .... Prepublication
PREQUAL .... Prequalified [*NASA*] (KSC)
Prer .... Prerogative Court (DLA)
PRER .... Putting Research into Educational Research
PRE-RE .... Prerefunded Municipal Note [*Investment term*] (DFIT)
PRERECPAC ... Preplanned Reconnaissance Pacific (CINC)
PREREQ ...... Prerequisite (WGA)
PRERLA ...... Pupils Round, Equal, React to Light and Accommodation [*Medicine*] (MAE)
Prerog Ct .... Prerogative Court, New Jersey (DLA)
PRES .... Premises (ROG)
PRES .... Presbyterian
PRES .... Presence
PRES .... Present (AAG)
PRES .... Preserved
PRE-S .... Preshaving (MSA)
PRES .... President (EY)
pres .... President (DD)
PRES .... President
Pres .... President (ODBW)
PRES .... President of the Royal Entomological Society [*British*]
PRES .... Pressure (FAAC)

PRES .... Preston R. R. [*AAR code*]
PRES .... Presumptive [*Grammar*]
PRES .... Prime Residential, Inc. [*NASDAQ symbol*] (SAG)
PRES .... Proton Resonance (IAA)
PRES100...... Presidential's Hundred Tab [*Military*]
Pres Abs...... Preston's Abstracts of Title [*2nd ed.*] [*1823-24*] [*A publication*] (DLA)
PRESAC....... Photographic Reconnaissance System Analysis by Computer
PRESAGE..... Program to Realistically Evaluate Strategic Anti-Ballistic Missile Gaming Effectiveness [*Military*] (PDAA)
PRESAILEDREP... Forecast Sailing Report [*Navy*] (NVT)
PRESAIR...... Pressurized Air Compressor (DNAB)
PRESB .... Presbyterian
PRESB .... Prescribe (AABC)
PresBnc....... Prestige Bancorp, Inc. [*Associated Press*] (SAG)
PRESBY....... Presbyterian
PRESBY....... Presbytery
presby .... Presbytery (VRA)
PresCasn ..... President Casinos, Inc. [*Associated Press*] (SAG)
Pres C of E Ch... Presbyterian Church of England Chaplain [*Navy British*]
PRESCOM.... Personnel Command [*Army*] (DOMA)
Pres Conv.... Preston on Conveyancing [*5th ed.*] [*1819-29*] [*A publication*] (DLA)
PRESCORE... Program for the Rapid Estimation of Construction Requirements
PRESCR....... Prescription (MSA)
PRESCR....... Prescription
Presd .... Presidio Oil Co. [*Associated Press*] (SAG)
PRESDL....... Presidential (WGA)
presen .... Presentation (VRA)
PRESERV..... Preservation
Pres Est....... Preston on Estates [*3rd ed.*] [*1829*] [*A publication*] (DLA)
PRESET....... Preset Spin Echo Technique
Pres Fal....... Falconer's Decisions, Scotch Court of Session [*1744-51*] [*A publication*] (DLA)
Pres Fal....... Gilmour and Falconer's Reports, Scotch Court of Session [*A publication*] (DLA)
Pres Falc...... President Falconer's Scotch Session Cases (Gilmour and Falconer) [*1681-86*] [*A publication*] (DLA)
PRESFR .... Pressure Falling Rapidly [*NWS*] (FAAC)
PRESIG .... Pressurizing (KSC)
PRESIGN...... Procedure Sign
PRESINSURV... Inspection and Survey Board [*Navy*]
Pres Leg...... Preston on Legacies [*1824*] [*A publication*] (DLA)
PresLf.......... Presidential Life Corp. [*Associated Press*] (SAG)
Presly .... Presley Companies [*Associated Press*] (SAG)
Pres Mer ...... Preston on Merger [*A publication*] (DLA)
PRESNAVWARCOL... Naval War College
PRES PART... Present Participle [*Grammar*] (WDAA)
PRESPROC... Presidential Proclamation
Pres Proc..... Presidential Proclamation (AAGC)
PresR........... Presidential Realty Corp. [*Associated Press*] (SAG)
PRESRR........ Pressure Rising Rapidly [*NWS*] (FAAC)
PRESS .... Pacific Range Electromagnetic Signature Studies [*or System*] [*Military*] (NG)
PRESS .... Parti Republicain Social du Senegal [*Social Republican Party of Senegal*] [*Political party*]
PRESS .... Predicted Residual Sum of Squares
PRESS .... Prereading Expectancy Screening Scale [*Educational test*]
PRESS .... Pressure (MCD)
PRESS .... Prolog Equation Solving System (BYTE)
PRESS .... Property Record for Equipment Servicing and Sharing (MCD)
PRESSAR..... Presentation Equipment for Slow Scan RADAR
PRESSDUCTOR... Pressure Inductor (IAA)
PRESSO....... Program for Elective Surgical Second Opinion [*Blue Cross/Blue Shield*]
Pres SQ .... Presidential Studies Quarterly [*A publication*] (BRI)
PRESSURS... Pre-Strike Surveillance/Reconnaissance System (MCD)
PREST .... Party on Scientific and Technical Research Policy [*European community*] (MHDB)
PREST .... Present (ROG)
PRES'T .... President
PRE-ST .... Prestart (AAG)
PREST .... Programme of Policy Research in Engineering Science and Technology [*British*]
Prest Conv... Preston on Conveyancing [*A publication*] (DLA)
Prestek .... Presstek, Inc. [*Associated Press*] (SAG)
Prest Est...... Preston on Estates [*A publication*] (DLA)
PrestFn........ Prestige Financial Corp. [*Associated Press*] (SAG)
Prest Merg... Preston on Merger [*A publication*] (DLA)
PRESTMO.... Prestissimo [*Very Fast*] [*Music*] (ROG)
PRESTO .... Personnel Response and Evaluation System for Target Obscuration [*Military*] (RDA)
PRESTO .... Prestissimo [*Very Fast*] [*Music*] (ROG)
PRESTO .... Program for Rapid Earth-to-Space Trajectory Optimization [*NASA*]
PRESTO .... Program Reporting and Evaluation System for Total Operations [*AFSC*]
PRE-STORM... Preliminary Regional Experiment for STORM [*Stormscale Operational and Research Meteorology*] (USDC)
PRE-STORM... Preliminary Regional Experiment for STORM [*Stormscale Operational and Research Meteorology*] [*Marine science*] (OSRA)
Prest Shep T... Sheppard's Touchstone by Preston [*A publication*] (DLA)
presv .... Preservation (BARN)
Presync........ Presynchronization
PRET........... Periodic Reliability Evaluation Test (MCD)
PRET........... Preterit [*Past tense*] [*Grammar*] (ROG)
PRET........... Pretoria [*South Africa*] (ROG)
PRETCHREP... Preliminary Technical Report (MCD)
PRETECHREP... Preliminary Technical Report [*Army*] (AABC)
PRETOS .... Proofreading Tests of Spelling [*Educational test*]
PRETTYBLUEBATCH... Philadelphia Regular Exchange Tea Total Young Belles Lettres Universal Experimental Bibliographical Association To Civilize Humanity [*From Edgar Allan Poe essay "How to Write a Blackwood Article"*]
PREV .... Medical and Psychological Previews [*Database*] [*BRS Information Technologies*] [*Information service or system*] (IID)
PREV .... Prevention
PREV .... Previous (AFM)
PREV .... Previous Program Selection [*In-car entertainment*] [*Electronics*]
PrevAGT ...... Previous Abnormality of Glucose Tolerance
PREVENT..... Pacific Northwest Regional Visibility Experiment using Natural Tracers [*Marine science*] (OSRA)
PREVENT..... Pacific NW Regional Visibility EXperiment using Natural Tracers (USDC)
PREVENT..... Precertification to Verify Necessary Treatment
PRevere....... Paul Revere Corp. [*Associated Press*] (SAG)
PREVLV....... Prevalve
PrevMed...... Preventive Medicine (DAVI)
PREVMEDU... Preventive Medicine Unit
pre-voc........ Prevocational [*Education*] (DAVI)
PREVT .... Preventative
PREWI .... Press Wireless [*A radio service for the transmission of news*]
Pr Exch........ Price's English Exchequer Reports [*1814-24*] [*A publication*] (DLA)
PREZ........... President Casinos [*NASDAQ symbol*] (TTSB)
PREZ........... President Riverboat Casinos [*NASDAQ symbol*] (SAG)
PRF............ Palestine Rejection Front (BJA)
PRF............ Parachute Refurbishment Facility [*NASA*] (NASA)
PRF............ Partial Reinforcement [*Training*]
PRF............ Partido Revolucionario Febrerista [*Febrerista Revolutionary Party*] [*Paraguay*] [*Political party*] (PPW)
PRF............ Patient Record Form
PRF............ Penetration Room Filtration [*Nuclear energy*] (NRCH)
prf.............. Performer [*MARC relator code*] [*Library of Congress*] (LCCP)
PRF............ Personality Research Form [*Psychology*]
PRF............ Personnel Readiness File [*Army*] (AABC)
PRF............ Petroleum Research Fund
PRF............ Phenol/Resorcinol/Formaldehyde [*Plastics technology*]
PRF............ Plant Response Fertilization [*Agriculture*]
PRF............ Plasmacytoma Repressor Factor [*Cytology*]
PRF............ Plastics Recycling Foundation (EA)
PRF............ Plutonium Reclamation Facility [*Nuclear energy*]
PRF............ Plymouth Rock Foundation (EA)
PRF............ Plywood Research Foundation (EA)
PRF............ Point Response Function [*Of a telescope*]
PRF............ Polyclonal Rheumatoid Factor [*Medicine*] (DMAA)
PRF............ Pontine Reticular Formation [*Neurophysiology*]
PRF............ Porpoise Rescue Foundation (EA)
PRF............ Potential Requirements File (NITA)
PRF............ Power Radio Frequency [*Telecommunications*] (IAA)
PRF............ Prefac Enterprises, Inc. [*Toronto Stock Exchange symbol*]
PRF............ Preformed [*Technical drawings*]
PRF............ Pride Co. $2.60cm Cv L.P. [*NYSE symbol*] (TTSB)
PRF............ Pride Companies Ltd. [*NYSE symbol*] (SPSG)
PRF............ Primary Reference Fuel [*Automotive engineering*]
PRF............ Processor Request Flag [*Telecommunications*] (TEL)
PRF............ Progressive Renal Failure [*Medicine*] (AAMN)
PRF............ Prolactin-Releasing Factor [*Endocrinology*]
PRF............ Proliferation Regulatory Factor [*Biochemistry*]
PRF............ Proof (KSC)
prf.............. Proof (WDMC)
prf.............. Proof (VRA)
PRF............ Protein Rich Fraction [*Food analysis*]
PRF............ Psychiatric Research Foundation
PRF............ Psychical Research Foundation (EA)
PRF............ Psychosynthesis Research Foundation (EA)
PRF............ Publications Reference File [*Government Printing Office*] [*Database*] [*Washington, DC*] (MCD)
PRF............ Public Relations Foundation
PRF............ Public Residential Facility
PRF............ Puerto Rico Federal Reports [*A publication*] (DLA)
PRF............ Pulse Rate Frequency (MUGU)
PRF............ Pulse Recurrence Frequency
PRF............ Pulse Repetition Frequency [*Computer science*]
prf.............. Pulse Repetition Frequency (IDOE)
PRF............ Purchase Rate Factor
PRF............ Purdue Research Foundation [*Purdue University*] [*Research center*] (MCD)
PRFA .... Plasma Recognition Factor Activity [*Hematology*] (AAMN)
Pr Falc......... President Falconer's Scotch Session Cases [*1744-51*] [*A publication*] (DLA)
PRFAW .... Personnel Research Field Activity, Washington [*Navy*] (MUGU)
PrfBcp.......... Professional Bancorp [*Associated Press*] (SAG)
PRFC .... Plymouth Rock Fanciers Club (EA)
PRFC .... Potomac River Fisheries Commission [*Maryland and Virginia*] (NOAA)
PRFCN .... Purification
PRFCS .... Pattern Recognition Feedback Control System [*Computer science*] (IAA)
PRFCS .... Prefocus
PRFD .... Pulse Recurrence Frequency Discrimination [*Telecommunications*] (TEL)
PRFE........... Polar Reflection Faraday Effect
PR Fed .... Puerto Rico Federal Reports [*A publication*] (DLA)

PRFG .... Proofing [*Freight*]
PRFI .... Portable Range-Finder/Illuminator
PRFI .... Puerto Rican Family Institute (EA)
PRFIA .... Phase-Resolved Fluoroimmunoassay
PRFIC .... Plume RADAR Frequency Interference Code (MCD)
PrfIOF .... Preferred Income Opportunity Fund [*Associated Press*] (SAG)
PRFL .... Pressure Fed Liquid (KSC)
PRFM .... Performance (MSA)
PRFM .... Perfumania, Inc. [*NASDAQ symbol*] (SAG)
PRFM .... Premature [*or Prolonged*] Rupture of Fetal Membrane [*Gynecology*] (MAE)
PRFM .... Prolonged Rupture of Fetal Membranes [*Obstetrics*] (DAVI)
PRFM .... Pseudorandom Frequency Modulated [*Computer science*]
PRFN .... Prestige Financial [*NASDAQ symbol*] (TTSB)
PRFN .... Prestige Financial Corp. [*NASDAQ symbol*] (SAG)
PRFR .... Proofer [*Freight*]
PRFRD .... Proofread (MSA)
PRFS .... Phase-Resolved Fluorescence Spectroscopy
PRFS .... Pulse Recurrence Frequency Stagger (OA)
PRFSS .... Peterborough Royal Foxhound Show Society [*British*] (DBA)
PRFT .... Partially Relaxed Fourier Transform [*Mathematics*]
PRFT .... Portable Rod-and-Frame Test (EDAC)
PRFT .... Presser Foot
PRFT .... Press Fit
PRFT .... Proffitt's, Inc. [*NASDAQ symbol*] (NQ)
PRFU .... Processor Ready for Use [*Telecommunications*] (TEL)
PRG .... Empresa Aero-Servicios Parrague Ltd. [*Chile*] [*ICAO designator*] (FAAC)
PRG .... Gilbert Associates, Inc., Reading, PA [*Library symbol Library of Congress*] (LCLS)
PRG .... Parabolic Radius Gage (MCD)
PRG .... Paris, IL [*Location identifier FAA*] (FAAL)
PRG .... Peacekeeper Rail Garrison [*Cancelled 1991*] [*Air Force*] (DOMA)
PRG .... Peerless Carpet Corp. [*Toronto Stock Exchange symbol*]
PRG .... People's Revolutionary Government [*Grenada*] (PD)
PRG .... Perennial Rye Grass [*Immunology*]
PRG .... Performance Related Gift [*Business Management*]
PRG .... Personnel Requirements Generator
PRG .... Personnel Resources Group [*Military*]
PRG .... Perugia [*Italy*] [*Seismograph station code, US Geological Survey*] (SEIS)
PRG .... Phleborrheogram [*Hematology*] (DAVI)
PRG .... Physician Resources Group, Inc. [*NYSE symbol*] (SAG)
PRG .... Physicians Resource Group [*NYSE symbol*] (TTSB)
PRG .... Pick Resources Guide [*ALLM Books*] [*England*] [*Information service or system*] (IID)
PRG .... Plastic Radial Grating
PRG .... Policy Research Group [*Australian Labor Party*]
PRG .... Powerful Radio Galaxy [*Cosmology*]
PRG .... Prague [*Former Czechoslovakia*] [*Airport symbol*] (OAG)
PRG .... Procedure Review Group [*Nuclear energy*] (NRCH)
PRG .... Program Regulation Guide
PRG .... Program Review Group [*Military*]
PRG .... Provisional Revolutionary Government [*Political arm of the Vietcong*] (VNW)
PRG .... Purge (AAG)
PRGC .... Past Royal Grand Cross [*Freemasonry*] (ROG)
PRG/I .... Pick Resources Guide/International [*ALLM Books*] [*Information service or system*] (IID)
PRGM .... Program (AFM)
PRGM .... Program
PRGMG .... Programming (MSA)
PRGMNG .... Programming
PRGMR .... Programmer (AFM)
PRGO .... Perrigo Co. [*NASDAQ symbol*] (SPSG)
PRGPrB .... Pub Sv E&G 4.18% Pfd [*NYSE symbol*] (TTSB)
PRGR .... ProGroup, Inc. [*NASDAQ symbol*] (NQ)
PRGRMR .... Programmer
PRGS .... President of the Royal Geographical Society [*British*]
PRGS .... Prognosis (AABC)
PRGS .... Progress Software [*NASDAQ symbol*] (SPSG)
PrgSoft .... Progress Software Corp. [*Associated Press*] (SAG)
PRGVN .... Provisional Revolutionary Government of South Vietnam (VNW)
PRGX .... Profit Recovery Group International, Inc. (The) [*NASDAQ symbol*] (SAG)
PRGX .... Profit Recovery Grp Intl [*NASDAQ symbol*] (TTSB)
PRH .... Partido Revolucionario Hondureno [*Honduras Revolutionary Party*] [*Political party*] (PPW)
PRH .... Petrol Railhead
PRH .... Phrae [*Thailand*] [*Airport symbol*] (OAG)
PrH .... Prepositus Hypoglossi [*Neuroanatomy*]
PRH .... Program Requirements Handbook (MUGU)
PRH .... Prolactin-Releasing Hormone [*Endocrinology*]
PRH .... Promus Hotel [*NYSE symbol*] (TTSB)
PRH .... Promus Hotel Corp. [*NYSE symbol*] (SAG)
PRH .... Psychiatric Regional Hospital [*Health insurance*] (GHCT)
PRHA .... People Refreshment House Association [*British*] (BI)
PRHA .... President of the Royal Hibernian Academy [*British*]
PRHB .... Pacific Rehabilitation & Sports Medicine, Inc. [*NASDAQ symbol*] (SAG)
PRHB .... Pacific Rehab/Sports Medicine [*NASDAQ symbol*] (TTSB)
PRHBF .... Peak Reactive Hyperemia Blood Flow [*Hematology*] (MAE)
Pr HC Ch .... Practice of the High Court of Chancery [*A publication*] (DLA)
PRHi .... Historical Society of Berks County, Reading, PA [*Library symbol Library of Congress*] (LCLS)
PRI .... Farmington, MO [*Location identifier FAA*] (FAAL)
PRI .... Institutional Revolutionary Party [*Mexico*] [*Political party*]
PRI .... Pacific Research Institute for Public Policy (EA)
PRI .... Pain Rating Index
PRI .... Paint Research Institute [*Defunct*] (EA)
PRI .... Paleontological Research Institution (EA)
PRI .... Partido Revolucionario Institucional [*Party of the Institutionalized Revolution*] [*Mexico Political party*]
PRI .... Partito Repubblicano Italiano [*Italian Republican Party*] [*Political party*] (PPW)
PRI .... Partner Relationship Inventory [*Marital relations test*] [*Psychology*]
PRI .... Partnership for Rural Improvement [*Washington*] (EDAC)
PRI .... Peace Research Institute [*Later, Institute for Policy Studies*] (EA)
PRI .... Performance Registry International
PRI .... Personal Reaction Index [*Interpersonal skills and attitudes test*]
PRI .... Personnel Research, Inc. [*Information service or system*] (IID)
PRI .... Personnel Research Institute Test (AEBS)
PRI .... Petroleum Recovery Institute [*Research center*] (RCD)
PRI .... Phosphate Rock Institute [*Defunct*] (EA)
PRI .... Phosphoribose Isomerase [*An enzyme*] (MAE)
PRI .... Photographic Reconnaissance and Interpretation (NATG)
PRI .... Photo RADAR Intelligence
PRI .... Pineapple Research Institute of Hawaii (EA)
PRI .... Plan Repeater Indicator (IAA)
PRI .... Plasticity Retention Index [*Rubber test method*]
PRI .... Plastics and Rubber Institute [*Institution of the Rubber Industry and Pla stics Institute*] [*Formed by a merger of*] (EAIO)
PRI .... Polymer Research Institute [*Polytechnic Institute of New York*] [*Research center*] (RCD)
PRI .... Polymer Research Institute [*University of Massachusetts*] [*Research center*] (RCD)
PRI .... Practice Training Index
PRI .... Praslin Island [*Seychelles Islands*] [*Airport symbol*] (OAG)
PRI .... Preliminary Rifle Instruction [*Military*]
PRI .... Prescriptive Reading Inventory
PRI .... President of the Royal Institute (of Painters in Water Colours) [*British*] (ROG)
PRI .... President of the Royal Institution (London) (ROG)
PRI .... President Regimental Institutes [*British*]
PRI .... Prevention Routiere Internationale [*International Road Safety Organization*] [*Luxembourg*] (EAIO)
Pri .... Price's English Exchequer Reports [*1814-24*] [*A publication*] (DLA)
Pri .... Price's English Mining Commissioners' Cases [*A publication*] (DLA)
PRI .... Priest [*California*] [*Seismograph station code, US Geological Survey*] (SEIS)
PRI .... Primary (KSC)
pri .... Primary (IDOE)
PRI .... Primary Rate, Inc.
PRI .... Primary Rate Interface (PCM)
PRI .... Primary Winding (IAA)
PRI .... Primate Research Institute [*New Mexico State University*] [*Hollman, NM*]
PRI .... Prime Computer Inc., Corporation Library, Framingham, MA [*OCLC symbol*] (OCLC)
PRI .... Primer (IAA)
PRI .... Princeville Airways, Inc. [*ICAO designator*] (FAAC)
PRI .... Priority (AFM)
PRI .... Priority Repair Induction [*Code*]
PRI .... Priority Requirement for Information (AFM)
Pri .... Priscianus [*Authority cited in pre-1607 legal work*] (DSA)
PRI .... Prison
PRI .... Private
PRI .... Prize [*or Prizeman*] [*British*] (ROG)
PRI .... Processing Research Institute [*Carnegie Mellon University*]
PRI .... Production Rate Index (OA)
PRI .... Production Records, Inc. (EA)
PRI .... Program Interrupt [*Computer science*] (IAA)
PRI .... Program Revision Intent
PRI .... Projection Readout Indicator [*Aviation*] (OA)
PRI .... Proteus Resources, Inc. [*Vancouver Stock Exchange symbol*]
PRI .... Psoriasis Research Institute (EA)
PRI .... Public Radio International
PRI .... Public Relations Institute of Ireland (BI)
PRI .... Puerto Rican Independence [*Later, GPRG*] [*An association*] (EA)
PRI .... Puerto Rico [*ANSI three-letter standard code*] (CNC)
PRI .... Pulse Rate Increase [*Medicine*]
PRI .... Pulse Rate Indicator
PRI .... Pulse Recurrence [*or Repetition*] Interval (NATG)
PRI .... Pulse Repetition Internal
PRI .... Pure Research Institute [*Later, BRINC*] (EA)
PRIA .... Peer Review Improvement Act of 1982
PRIA .... President of the Royal Irish Academy
PRIA .... PRI Automation [*NASDAQ symbol*] (SAG)
PRIA .... Public Rangelands Improvement Act of 1978
PRIA .... Society for Participatory Research in Asia [*India*] (EAIO)
PRIAM .... Precision Range Information Analysis for Missiles (MCD)
PRIAM .... Pre-Normative Requirements for Intelligent Actuation & Measurements (ACII)
PRIAS .... Packard's Radioimmunoassay System [*Medicine*] (DMAA)
PrIAU-SJ .... Inter-American University of Puerto Rico, San Juan Campus, San Juan, PR [*Library symbol Library of Congress*] (LCLS)
PRI Auto .... PRI Automation [*Associated Press*] (SAG)
PRIBA .... President of the Royal Institute of British Architects
PRIBAG .... Priority Baggage (DNAB)
PRI BIL .... Primary Billet (DNAB)

PRIC Dec..... Puerto Rico Industrial Commission Decisions [*A publication*] (DLA)
PRICE.......... Physicians for Research in Cost-Effectiveness (EA)
Price............ Price's English Exchequer Reports [*A publication*] (DLA)
Price............ Price's English Mining Commissioners' Cases [*A publication*] (DLA)
PRICE.......... Pricing Review to Intensify Competitive Environment [*Computer science*]
PRICE.......... Programmed Review of Information for Costing and Evaluation (MCD)
PRICE.......... Protection, Rest, Ice, Compression, Evaluation [*Medicine*]
Price & St... Price and Stewart's Trade Mark Cases [*A publication*] (DLA)
PriceCst....... Price Costco, Inc. [*Associated Press*] (SAG)
PriceEnt....... Price Enterprises, Inc. [*Associated Press*] (SAG)
Price Gen Pr... Price's General Practice [*A publication*] (DLA)
Price Liens... Price on Maritime Liens [*1940*] [*A publication*] (DLA)
Pricell.......... Pricellular Corp. [*Associated Press*] (SAG)
Price Min Cas... Price's Mining Cases [*A publication*] (DLA)
Price Notes PC... Price's Notes of Practice Cases in Exchequer [*1830-31*] [*England*] [*A publication*] (DLA)
Price Notes PP... Price's Notes of Points of Practice, English Exchequer Cases [*A publication*] (DLA)
Price PC...... Price's English Practice Cases [*1830-31*] [*A publication*] (DLA)
Price Pr Cas... Price's English Practice Cases [*A publication*] (DLA)
Price R Est... Price on Acts Relating to Real Estate [*A publication*] (DLA)
PriceTR........ Price [*T. Rowe*] Associates, Inc. [*Associated Press*] (SAG)
Prickett........ Prickett's Reports [*1 Idaho*] [*A publication*] (DLA)
PRICOM....... Prison Commission [*British*]
PRI-D........... Peace Research Institute - Dundas [*Canada*] (IRC)
PRID............ Pridie [*The Day Before*] [*Latin*]
PriD............. Princeton Datafilm, Inc., Princeton, NJ [*Library symbol Library of Congress*] (LCLS)
Prid & C...... Prideaux and Cole's English Reports [*4 New Sessions Cases*] [*1850-51*] [*A publication*] (DLA)
Prid & Co.... Prideaux and Cole's English Reports [*4 New Sessions Cases*] [*1850-51*] [*A publication*] (DLA)
Prid Ch W.... Prideaux's Directions to Churchwardens [*10th ed.*] [*1835*] [*A publication*] (DLA)
PRIDCO........ Puerto Rico Industrial Development Co.
Prid Conv..... Prideaux's Forms and Precedents in Conveyancing [*24th ed.*] [*1952*] [*A publication*] (DLA)
PRIDE.......... National Parents' Resource Institute for Drug Education (EA)
PRIDE.......... People for Rehabilitating and Integrating the Disabled through Education [*New York City*]
PRIDE.......... Perfection Requires Individual Defect Elimination
PRIDE.......... Personal Responsibility in Daily Effort [*Military Airlift Command's acronym for the Zero Defects Program*]
PRIDE.......... Preschool and Kindergarten Interest Descriptor [*Educational test*]
Pride........... Pride Companies Ltd. [*Associated Press*] (SAG)
PRIDE.......... Priority Receiving with Inter-Departmental Efficiency [*Computer science*]
PRIDE.......... Production of Reliable Items Demands Excellence [*Navy*] (NG)
PRIDE.......... Productive Rehabilitation Institute of Dallas for Ergonomics [*Research center*] (RCD)
PRIDE.......... Productivity Improvements for the Decade of the Eighties
PRIDE.......... Professional Results in Daily Effort [*Strategic Air Command's acronym for the Zero Defects Program*]
PRIDE.......... Profitable Information by Design (MHDI)
PRIDE.......... Profitable Information by Design through Phased Planning and Control (MHDB)
PRIDE.......... Programmed Reliability in Design Engineering
PRIDE.......... Promote Real Independence for the Disabled and Elderly (EA)
PRIDE.......... Prompt Response Insurance Delivery Express
PRIDE.......... Protection of Reefs and Islands from Degradation and Exploitation
PRIDE.......... Provisioning Review Input Data Evaluation (MCD)
PRIDE.......... Pulse RADAR Intelligent Diagnostic Environment [*US Army Missile Command*] (RDA)
PrideA......... Pride Automotive Group, Inc. [*Associated Press*] (SAG)
PrideAto...... Pride Automotive Group, Inc. [*Associated Press*] (SAG)
Prid Judg..... Prideaux's Judgments and Crown Debts [*4th ed.*] [*1854*] [*A publication*] (DLA)
PRIF............ Prior Year Refund Information File [*IRS*]
PRI-FLY....... Primary Flight Control [*on an aircraft carrier*] [*Navy*]
PRIH............ Prolactin-Release Inhibiting Factor [*Also, PIF*] [*Endocrinology*]
PRIISM....... Pacific Research Institute for Information Systems and Management [*University of Hawaii at Manoa*] [*Research center*] (RCD)
PRIL............ Penarth Research International Ltd. [*British*]
PRIM........... Pac Rim Holding [*NASDAQ symbol*] (SPSG)
PRIM........... Plans and Reports Improvement Memorandum [*Military*] (CAAL)
PRIM........... Plume Radiation Intensity Measurement (MUGU)
PRIM........... Primary (AFM)
PRIM........... Primase (DMAA)
PRIM........... Primate
PRIM........... Primitive
PRIM........... Program for Information Managers [*Later, AIM*] [*An association*]
PRIM........... Programmed Instruction for Management Education (HGAA)
PRIMA......... Pollutant Response in Marine Animals [*Marine science*] (MSC)
PRIMA......... Public Radio in Mid-America (NTCM)
PRIMA......... Public Risk and Insurance Management Association [*Washington, DC*] (EA)
Primadn....... Primadonna Resorts, Inc. [*Associated Press*] (SAG)
PrimaE......... Prima Energy Corp. [*Associated Press*] (SAG)
PRIM & R.... Public Responsibility in Medicine and Research (EA)
PRIMAR....... Program to Improve Management of Army Resources (AABC)
PrimaryB...... Primary Bank [*Associated Press*] (SAG)
Primary Ed... Primary Education [*A publication*]
PRIMATE..... Personal Retrieval of Information by Microcomputer and Terminal Ensemble
PRIM BIB.... Primary Bibliography (DGA)
PRIMCOM.... Pacific Rim Interactive Multimedia Computing [*Australia*]
PRIME......... Planning through Retrieval of Information for Management Extrapolation
PRIME......... Precision Integrator for Meteorological Echoes (IEEE)
PRIME......... Precision Range Integrated Maneuver Exercise [*Army*] (RDA)
PRIME......... Precision Recovery Including Maneuvering Entry [*Air Force*]
PRIME......... Prematriculation Program in Medical Education (DMAA)
PRIME......... Preparedness of Resources in Mission Evaluation (SAA)
PRIME......... Prescribed Right to Income and Maximum Equity
PRIME......... Primary Initiatives in Mathematics Education (AIE)
PRIME......... Priority Improved Management Effort (KSC)
PRIME......... Priority Improvement Effort [*DoD*]
PRIME......... Priority Management Effort [*Army*]
PRIME......... Priority Management Evaluation [*Navy*]
PRIME......... Procarbazine, Ifosfamide, Methotrexate [*Antineoplastic drug regimen*]
PRIME......... Processing, Research, Inspection, and Marine Extension Program [*National Oceanic and Atmospheric Administration*] (MSC)
PRIME......... Profession Related Intern-Mentorship Experience
PRIME......... Program Independence, Modularity, Economy
PRIME......... Programmed Instruction for Management Education [*American Management Association*]
PRIME......... Programme for International Managers in Europe [*Business program*]
PRIME......... Program Research in Integrated Multiethnic Education [*Defunct*] (EA)
PRIME BEEF... Priority Improvement Management Effort Base Engineering Emergency Force [*Air Force*] (DOMA)
PrimeCp...... Prime Capital Corp. [*Associated Press*] (SAG)
PrimeMg...... Prime Management Group, Inc. [*Associated Press*] (SAG)
PRIMENET.... Prime Network Software Package [*Prime Computer, Inc.*]
PrimEq......... Prime Equities International [*Associated Press*] (SAG)
PRIMER....... Patient Record Information for Education Requirements [*Computer science*]
PRIME RIBS... Priority Improvement Management Effort Readiness in Base Services [*Air Force*] (DOMA)
PrimeRsd.... Prime Residential, Inc. [*Associated Press*] (SAG)
PRIMES....... Preflight Integration of Munitions and Electronic Systems (MCD)
PRIMES....... Productivity Integrated Measurement System [*Army*]
PrimeSrc..... PrimeSource Corp. [*Associated Press*] (SAG)
PRIMEX....... Primary Care Extender [*Insurance*] (DMAA)
Primex......... Primex Technologies, Inc. [*Associated Press*] (SAG)
PRIMEX....... Private Message Switching [*Telecommunications British*]
PRIMIP........ Primipara [*Woman bearing first child*] [*Medicine*] (AAMN)
PRIMIR........ Product Improvement Management Information Report
PRIM LUC..... Prima Luce [*Early in the Morning*] [*Pharmacy*]
PRIM M....... Primo Mane [*Early in the Morning*] [*Pharmacy*]
PRIM METH... Primitive Methodist [*A publication*]
PRIMO......... Programmable, Realtime, Incoherent, Matrix, Optical Processor [*Computer science*]
PRIMORDIAL... Primary Order Dial (NITA)
PRIMOS....... Prime Operating System [*Prime Computer, Inc.*]
PRIMP......... Primipara [*Woman bearing first child*] [*Obstetrics*] (DAVI)
Primrk......... Primark Corp. [*Associated Press*] (SAG)
PRIMS......... Product Requirement Information Management System (MCD)
PRIMSCO...... Pilot Run Item Master Schedule Committee (IAA)
PRIMTEC...... Pacific Rim Interactive Multi-Media Technology
PRIMTRA...... Air Primary Training
PRIMUS....... Physician Reservists in Medical Universities and Schools [*Military*]
PRIMUS....... Primary Medical Care for the Uniformed Services [*DoD*]
PrimusT....... Primus Telecommunications Group, Inc. [*Associated Press*] (SAG)
PRIN........... Partido Revolucionario de la Izquierda Nacionalista [*National Leftist Revolutionary Party*] [*Bolivia*] [*Political party*] (PPW)
PRIN........... Performance Risk Index Number (NG)
PRIN........... Princeton [*New Jersey*] [*Seismograph station code, US Geological Survey*] (SEIS)
PRIN........... Principal
PRIN........... Principal
PRIN........... Principality (ROG)
PRIN........... Principally (ROG)
PRIN........... Principia [*Elements*] [*Latin*] (ROG)
PRIN........... Principle (ROG)
prin............ Principle (VRA)
PRINAIR...... Puerto Rico National Airlines
PrinAm........ Princeton American Corp. [*Associated Press*] (SAG)
PRINC......... Principal
PRINC......... Principle
PRINCE........ Parts Reliability Information Center [*NASA*]
PRINCE........ Programmed International Computer Environment [*International relations simulation game*]
PRINCE........ Programmed Reinforced Instruction Necessary to Continuing Education
PRINCE/APIC... Parts Reliability Information Center/Apollo Parts Information Center [*NASA*]
PrinceM....... Princeton Media Group, Inc. [*Associated Press*] (SAG)
Prince NML... Prince's New Mexico Laws [*A publication*] (DLA)
Princeton U... Princeton University (GAGS)
PRINCIR...... Printed Circuit (IAA)
PrincNtl....... Princeton National Bancorp [*Associated Press*] (SAG)
PRIND......... Present Indication [*Aviation*] (IAA)
PRIND......... Prolonged Reversible Ischemic Neurologic Deficit [*Medicine*] (DMAA)
PRINDUS..... Prison Industries [*Industries conducted in English prisons*]
PRINFO....... Printed Information Distribution (SAA)

PRING......... Partido Revolucionario de Izquierda Nacional Gueiler [*Revolutionary Party of the National Left - Gueiler Wing*] [*Bolivia*] [*Political party*] (PPW)
PRIN-L......... Partido Revolucionario de la Izquierda Nacional Laboral [*Political party*] (PPW)
PRINM......... Partido Revolucionario de la Izquierda Nacional Moller [*Bolivia*] [*Political party*] (PPW)
PRINMUS.... Principal Musician [*Marine Corps*]
PRINOBC/NEC... Primary Navy Officer Billet Classification and Navy Enlisted Classification
Prin PL......... Eden's Principles of Penal Law [*A publication*] (DLA)
Prins & Conderlag... Prins and Conderlag's Reports [*Ceylon*] [*A publication*] (ILCA)
PrinsRec...... Prins Recycling Corp. [*Associated Press*] (SAG)
PRINSYS...... Product Information System (IAA)
PRINT.......... Preedited Interpreter (IAA)
PRINT.......... Pre-Edited Interpretive System [*Computer science*]
print............ Printing (WDMC)
PRINT.......... Public Release of Information and Transcripts [*Student legal action organization*]
PRINTG........ Printing
printout........ Printer Output [*Computer science*] (CDE)
PRINTR........ Printer
PRINUL........ Puerto Rico International Undersea Laboratory
PRIO............ International Peace Research Institution, Oslo [*Norway*]
PRIO............ Priority [*Telecommunications*]
PRION.......... Proteinaceous Infectious Particle
PRIOR.......... Program for In-Orbital Rendezvous [*Antisatellite system*] [*Air Force*]
PRIP............ Park Restoration and Improvement Program [*National Park Service*]
PRIP............ Parts Reliability Improvement Program
PRIP............ Planned Retirement Income Program [*Institute of Financial Management*]
PRIPACSEVOCAM... Primary Pacific Secure Voice Communications [*Navy*] (CAAL)
PRIPP.......... Pacific Research Institute for Public Policy (EA)
PRIRA.......... Primary RADAR (FAAC)
PRIS............ Pacific Range Instrumentation Satellite (MUGU)
PRIS............ Pest Management Research Information System [*Agriculture Canada*] [*Information service or system*] (IID)
PRIS............ Prison (ROG)
PRIS............ Prisoner (AFM)
PRIS............ Program Resource Information System [*Department of Agriculture*]
PRIS............ Propeller Revolution Indicator System (MSA)
PRISCO........ Price Stabilization Corp.
PRISE.......... Page Reader Input System with Editing (NVT)
PRISE.......... Pennsylvania Resources and Information Center for Special Education [*Montgomery County Intermediate Unit*] [*King of Prussia*] [*Information service or system*] (IID)
PRISE.......... Pennsylvania's Regional Instruction System for Education [*Network of colleges and universities*]
PRISE.......... Program for Integrated Shipboard Electronics
PRISIC.......... Photographic Reconnaissance Interpretation Section [*Squadron*] IntelligenceCenter [*JICPOA*]
PRISM.......... Parameter Related Internal Standard Method [*Statistical procedure*]
PRISM.......... Paraxial-Ray Imaging Spectro Microscope
PRISM.......... Pattern Recognition Information Synthesis Modeling [*Market analysis*]
PRISM.......... Peace and Reconciliation Inter-Schools Movement (AIE)
PRISM.......... Pediatric Risk of Mortality [*Medicine*]
PRISM.......... Personnel Record Information Systems for Management
PRISM.......... Personnel Related Information System for Management (NITA)
PRISM.......... Personnel Requirements Information System Methodology (NVT)
PRISM.......... Photorefractive Information Storage Materials Consortium (CDE)
PRISM.......... Pittsburgh Research-Based Instructional Supervising Model (EDAC)
PRISM.......... Pliocene Research, Interpretations and Synoptic Mapping [*Climatology*]
PRISM.......... Powerful Resource for Information and System Management [*Computer science*] (IAA)
PRISM.......... Power Reactor Inherently Safe Module [*Nuclear energy*]
PRISM.......... Power Reactor Innovation Small Module [*Nuclear energy*]
PRISM.......... Priorities in School Mathematics Project (EDAC)
Prism........... Prism Group [*Associated Press*] (SAG)
PRISM.......... Programmable Integrated Scripts for MIRROR [*Management Information Reporting and review of Operational Resources Systems*] [*Computer Language*] (PCM)
PRISM.......... Programmed Integrated System Maintenance (NG)
PRISM.......... Program Reliability Information System for Management [*Polaris*]
PRISM.......... Progressive Refinement of Integrated Supply Management (AFM)
PRISM.......... Projection and Integrated Standalone Monitor [*Dolch Computer Systems*] [*Computer science*] (PCM)
PrismEnt...... Prism Entertainment Corp. [*Associated Press*] (SAG)
PrismS......... Prism Solutions [*Associated Press*] (SAG)
PRISN.......... Prime Stock Number
PRISNET...... Private Switching Network Service [*Telecommunications*]
Prison L Reptr... Prison Law Reporter [*A publication*] (ILCA)
Prison L Rptr... Prison Law Reporter [*A publication*] (DLA)
Prison Serv J... Prison Service Journal [*A publication*] (DLA)
PRISS.......... Post Deployment Software Support Real-Time Interactive Simulation System
PRISSECIMP... Primary Secondary Impedance (IAA)
PrissSys...... Peerless Systems Corp. [*Associated Press*] (SAG)
PRIST.......... Paper Radioimmunosorbent Test [*Analytical biochemistry*]
PRITAC........ Primary Tactical Radio Circuit (IAA)
Pritch Adm Dig... Pritchard's Admiralty Digest [*3rd ed.*] [*1887*] [*A publication*] (DLA)
Pritch M & D... Pritchard's Divorce and Matrimonial Causes [*3rd ed.*] [*1874*] [*A publication*] (DLA)
Pritch Quar Sess... Pritchard's Quarter Sessions [*A publication*] (DLA)
PRIV............ Private
PRIV............ Privative
PRIV............ Privilege
PRIVAUTH... Travel Authorized via Privately-Owned Vehicle with Understanding No Additional Cost to Government Involved
Priv C App... Privy Council Appeals [*England*] [*A publication*] (DLA)
Priv CDI....... Indian Privy Council Decisions [*A publication*] (DLA)
Priv Counc App... Privy Council Appeals [*England*] [*A publication*] (DLA)
Priv Counc DI... Privy Council Decisions [*India*] [*A publication*] (DLA)
PRIVE.......... Private (ROG)
Priv Hous Fin... Private Housing Finance [*A publication*] (DLA)
Priv Lond...... Privilegia Londini [*A publication*] (DLA)
Priv Maintd... Privately Maintained [*Nautical charts*]
PRIV PROP... Private Property [*Military*] (DNAB)
PRIVX.......... Private Exchange (IAA)
PRIZE.......... Program for Research in Information Systems Engineering [*University of Michigan*] [*Research center*] (RCD)
Prize CR...... Prize Court Reports [*South Africa*] [*A publication*] (DLA)
PRIZM.......... Potential Rating Index by ZIP [*Zone Improvement Plan*] Market [*Advertising*]
PRJ............ Aero Servicios Pro-Bajio, SA de CV [*Mexico*] [*FAA designator*] (FAAC)
PRJ............ American Junior College of Puerto Rico, Bayamon, PR [*OCLC symbol*] (OCLC)
PRJ............ Capri [*Italy*] [*Airport symbol*] (AD)
PRJ............ Payroll Journal [*Accounting*]
PRJ............ Port Royal [*Jamaica*] [*Seismograph station code, US Geological Survey*] (SEIS)
PRJC.......... Pearl River Junior College [*Poplarville, MS*]
PRJC.......... Puerto Rico Junior College
PRJMP........ Pressure Jump [*NWS*] (FAAC)
PRK............ Democratic People's Republic of Korea [*ANSI three-letter standard code*] (CNC)
PRK............ Paraskevi [*Lesbos*] [*Greece*] [*Seismograph station code, US Geological Survey*] (SEIS)
PRK............ Park
PRK............ Park National Corp. [*AMEX symbol*] (SAG)
PRK............ Park National Corp. [*AMEX symbol*] (TTSB)
PRK............ Parkside Petroleum, Inc. [*Toronto Stock Exchange symbol Vancouver Stock Exchange symbol*]
PRK............ People's Republic of Kampuchea [*From 1979 to 1989*] [*Formerly, Cambodia*] [*Later, SOC*] (PD)
PRK............ Phase Reversal Keying [*Computer science*] (IAA)
PRK............ Photorefractive Keratectomy [*Ophtholmology*]
PRK............ Pridie Kalendas [*The Day before the Calends*] [*Latin*]
PRK............ Primary Rabbit Kidney [*Medicine*] (DMAA)
PRK............ Primary Rabbit Kidney [*Medicine*] (DMAA)
PRK............ Primary Rat Kidney [*Cells*]
PRKC.......... Protein Kinase C (DMAA)
PRKCA........ Protein Kinase C Alpha (DMAA)
PRKG.......... Parking
PRKO.......... Progesterone Receptor Knockout [*Mouse strain*]
PRKR.......... Parkervision, Inc. [*NASDAQ symbol*] (SAG)
PRKR.......... ParkerVision Inc. [*NASDAQ symbol*] (TTSB)
PRL............ Aviaprima [*Russian Federation*] [*ICAO designator*] (FAAC)
PRL............ Pacht, Ross et Al, Los Angeles, CA [*OCLC symbol*] (OCLC)
PRL............ Page Revision Log (NASA)
PRL............ Parallel (MSA)
PRL............ Partido Radical Liberal [*Radical Liberal Party*] [*Ecuador*] [*Political party*]
PRL............ Parti Reformateur Liberal [*Liberal Reform Party*] [*Belgium Political party*] (PPW)
PRL............ Parti Republicain de la Liberte [*Republican Party for Liberty*] [*France Political party*] (PPE)
PRL............ Parti Republicain de la Liberte [*Republican Party for Liberty*] [*Burkina Faso*] [*Political party*]
PRL............ Parts Requirement List (KSC)
PRL............ Paul Revere [*NYSE symbol*] (SPSG)
PRL............ Peace Research Laboratory [*Later, LPRL*] [*An association*] (EA)
prl............. Pearl (VRA)
PRL............ Personnel Research Laboratory [*Lackland Air Force Base, TX*]
PRL............ Pesticide Research Laboratory and Graduate Study Center [*Pennsylvania State University*] [*Research center*] (RCD)
PRL............ Petroleum Refining Laboratory [*Pennsylvania State University*] (MCD)
PRL............ Philco Resources [*Vancouver Stock Exchange symbol*]
PRL............ Philips Research Laboratories (NITA)
PRL............ Photoreactivating Light
PRL............ Physiological Research Laboratories [*University of California at San Diego*] [*Research center*]
PRL............ Pioneering Research Laboratory [*Massachusetts*] [*Army*]
PRL............ Planning Requirements List (MCD)
PRL............ Plastics Research Laboratory [*MIT*] (MCD)
PRL............ Polar Research Laboratory [*USA*] [*Marine science*] (OSRA)
PRL............ Political Risk Letter [*Database*] [*Frost & Sullivan, Inc.*] [*Information service or system*] (CRD)
PRL............ Population Research Laboratory [*University of Alberta*] [*Research center*] (RCD)
PRL............ Postal Reform League (IAA)
PRL............ Preamble
PRL............ Precision Reduction Laboratory (AFM)
PRL............ Predicted Repair Level (MCD)
PRL............ Pressure Rate Limiter (MCD)
PRL............ Priority Rate Limiting (MCD)
PRL............ Progressive Republican League
PRL............ Project Research Laboratory

PRL............ Prolactin [*Also, LTH, PR*] [*Endocrinology*]
PRL............ Properties Research Laboratory [*Purdue University*] [*Lafayette, IN*]
PRL............ Propulsion Research Laboratory
PRL............ Proton Reference Level [*Chemistry*]
PRL............ Publications Requirements List (NG)
PRL............ Pulse-Reflection Logic (IAA)
PRLA.......... Prairie Religious Library Association
PrLas.......... Premier Laser Systems, Inc. [*Associated Press*] (SAG)
PR Laws Ann... Laws of Puerto Rico, Annotated [*A publication*] (DLA)
PRLC.......... Pittsburgh Regional Library Center [*Chatham College*] [*Pittsburgh, PA*] [*Library network*]
PRLCA......... Power Research Library of Contemporary Art [*University of Sydney, Australia*]
PRLDEF....... Puerto Rican Legal Defense and Education Fund (EA)
PRLI........... Purchase Request Line Item [*DoD*]
PRLINK........ Public Relations Society of America Online Information Service (IID)
PRLN.......... Paracelsian, Inc. [*NASDAQ symbol*] (SAG)
Pr Ln.......... Prior Lien [*Business term*] (MHDW)
PRLNW....... Paracelsian Inc. Wrrt [*NASDAQ symbol*] (TTSB)
PRLO.......... Prologic Management Systems, Inc. [*NASDAQ symbol*] (SAG)
PRLO.......... PROLOGIC Mgmt Sys [*NASDAQ symbol*] (TTSB)
PRLOW....... PROLOGIC Mgmt Sys Wrrt [*NASDAQ symbol*] (TTSB)
PRLP.......... Planetary Rocket Launcher Platform (AAG)
PRLP.......... Puerto Rico Legal Project [*of the National Lawyers Guild*] (EA)
PRLR.......... Parlor
PRLS.......... Peerless Systems Corp. [*NASDAQ symbol*] (SAG)
PRLS.......... Pima Regional Library Service [*Library network*]
PRLS.......... Pulsed Ruby LASER System
PRLST......... Price List
PRLTRL & M... Printer, Lithographer, and Multilith Operator [*Navy*]
PRLW.......... Parti des Reformes et de la Liberte de Wallonie [*Belgium Political party*] (PPW)
PRLX.......... Parallax (AAG)
PRLX.......... Parlex Corp. [*NASDAQ symbol*] (NQ)
PRM............ Panarim Resources, Inc. [*Vancouver Stock Exchange symbol*]
PRM............ Parameter (ECII)
PRM............ Parma Byzantine [*Diocesan abbreviation*] [*Ohio*] (TOCD)
Prm............ Parmenides [*of Plato*] [*Classical studies*] (OCD)
PRM............ Parsons Mountain [*South Carolina*] [*Seismograph station code, US Geological Survey*] (SEIS)
PRM............ Partially Reflecting Mirror
PRM............ Partially Regulated Module
PRM............ Partial Response Method
PRM............ Payload Retention Mechanism [*NASA*] (NASA)
PRM............ Period of Reduced Melting [*Climatology*]
PRM............ Personal Radiation Monitor
PRM............ Petition [*or Proposal*] for Rule Making (NRCH)
PRM............ Phosphoribomutase [*An enzyme*] (MAE)
PRM............ Photoreceptor Membrane [*Of the eye*]
PRM............ Pilots Radio Manual
PRM............ Pit Rib Meristem [*Botany*]
PRM............ Posigrade Rocket Motor (NASA)
PRM............ Power Range Monitor (IEEE)
PRM............ Precision Runway Monitor [*FAA*] (TAG)
PRM............ Preformed Road Markings [*Road markings embedded in the pavement rather than painted on street's surface*]
PRM............ Preliminary Requirements Model [*NASA*]
PRM............ Premature [*or Prolonged*] Rupture of Membranes [*Gynecology*] (MAE)
PRM............ Premium
PRM............ Presbyterian Renewal Ministries (EA)
PRM............ Presidential Review Memorandum [*Jimmy Carter Administration*]
PRM............ Pressure Monitoring Module [*Mechanical engineering*]
PRM............ Pressure Remanent Magnetization
PRM............ Preventive Medicine (MAE)
PRM............ Primary Reference Material [*Medicine*] (MAE)
PRM............ Primary Reference Material [*Library science*] (DAVI)
PRM............ Prime (AAG)
PRM............ Prime
PRM............ Prime Air, Inc. [*ICAO designator*] (FAAC)
PRM............ Primidone [*Antiepileptic drug*]
PRM............ Process Radiation Monitor [*Nuclear energy*] (NRCH)
PRM............ Programmer Reference Manual [*Computer science*]
PRM............ Programming and Resources Management [*NASA*] (MCD)
PRM............ Promote (AABC)
PRM............ Publications Requirements Manager [*DoD*]
PRM............ Puerto Lopez [*Colombia*] [*Airport symbol*] (AD)
PRM............ Pulse Rate Modulation
PRMA.......... Primadonna Resorts [*NASDAQ symbol*] (TTSB)
PRMA.......... Primadonna Resorts, Inc. [*NASDAQ symbol*] (SAG)
PrMan......... Prayer of Manasses [*Apocrypha*] (BJA)
PRMAR........ Primary Mission Area [*Military*] (CAAL)
PrmBcp........ Prime Bancorp, Inc. [*Associated Press*] (SAG)
PrmBn......... Premier Bankshares Corp. [*Associated Press*] (SAG)
PRMC.......... Periodically Replenished Magma Chambers [*Geology*]
PRMC.......... Puerto Rican Migration Consortium (EA)
PRMD.......... Private Management Domain [*Telecommunications*] (OSI)
PRME.......... Prime Retail [*NASDAQ symbol*] (TTSB)
PRME.......... Prime Retail, Inc. [*NASDAQ symbol*] (SAG)
PrmEgy........ Prime Energy [*Associated Press*] (SAG)
PrmeMd....... Prime Medics [*Associated Press*] (SAG)
PRMEP........ Prime Retail 8.5%Ptc Cv'B'Pfd [*NASDAQ symbol*] (TTSB)
PrmFar........ Premier Farnell PLC [*Associated Press*] (SAG)
PRMG.......... Piston Ring Manufacturers Group [*Later, NEPMA*] (EA)
PRM GR....... Permanent Grade (DNAB)
PRMH.......... Parti Republicain Modere Haitien [*Political party*] (EY)
PRMH.......... Profoundly Retarded Multiply Handicapped (AIE)
PrmHsp........ Prime Hospitality Corp. [*Associated Press*] (SAG)
Prmian......... Permian Basin Royalty Trust [*Associated Press*] (SAG)
Pr Min......... Printed Minutes of Evidence [*A publication*] (DLA)
PR/MIPR...... Purchase Request/Military Interdepartmental Purchase Request (AFIT)
PRMIS......... Printing Resources Management Information System (DNAB)
Prmisy......... Premisys Communications [*Associated Press*] (SAG)
Prmk........... Paramark Enterprises, Inc. [*Associated Press*] (SAG)
PRML.......... Partial Response Maximum Likelihood [*Computer science*]
PrmLasr....... Premier Laser Systems, Inc. [*Associated Press*] (SAG)
PRMLD........ Premolded [*Technical drawings*] (MSA)
PrMLtd........ Prime Motor Inns Ltd. [*Associated Press*] (SAG)
PRMO.......... Premenos Technology [*NASDAQ symbol*] (TTSB)
PRMO.......... Premenos Technology Corp. [*NASDAQ symbol*] (SAG)
PrmosT........ Premenos Technology Corp. [*Associated Press*] (SAG)
PRMP.......... Plutonium Recovery Modification Project [*Department of Energy*]
PRMP.......... Production Readiness Master Plan
PrmPks........ Premier Parks, Inc. [*Associated Press*] (SAG)
PRMR.......... Pitch Rate/Moment Ratio [*Automotive engineering*]
PRMR.......... Primer (MSA)
PrmRad........ Premier Radio Network [*Associated Press*] (SAG)
PrmrBc........ Premier Bancorp, Inc. [*Associated Press*] (SAG)
PrmRetl....... Prime Retail, Inc. [*Associated Press*] (SAG)
PrmRtl......... Prime Retail, Inc. [*Associated Press*] (SAG)
PRMS.......... Premisys Communications [*NASDAQ symbol*] (SAG)
PRM-SDX.... Pyrimethamine-Sulfadoxine [*Pharmacology*] (DAVI)
PrmsH......... Promus Hotel Corp. [*Associated Press*] (SAG)
PRMTR........ Parameter (AAG)
PRMV.......... Peach Rosette Mosaic Virus [*Plant pathology*]
PRMX.......... Primex Technologies, Inc. [*NASDAQ symbol*] (SAG)
PRN............ Greenville, AL [*Location identifier FAA*] (FAAL)
PRN............ Packet Radio Network [*Telecommunications*] (OSI)
PRN............ Pahrock Range [*Nevada*] [*Seismograph station code, US Geological Survey*] (SEIS)
PRN............ Park Reverse Neutral [*Automotive engineering*]
PRN............ Partido de la Resistencia Nicaraguense [*Political party*] (EY)
PRN............ Partido de la Revolucion Nacional [*Party of the National Revolution*] [*Bolivia*] [*Political party*] (PPW)
PRN............ Partido de Reconstrucao Nacional [*Brazil Political party*] (EY)
PRN............ Partido Republicano Nacional [*National Republican Party*] [*Costa Rica*] [*Political party*]
PRN............ Parts Requirement Notice (KSC)
PRN............ Peace Research Network [*Later, PSA*] (EA)
PRN............ Physicians Radio Network
PRN............ Previous Result Negative (IAA)
PRN............ Pridie Nonas [*The Day before the Nones*] [*Latin*]
PRN............ Princess Air [*British ICAO designator*] (FAAC)
PRN............ Printer [*Computer science*]
PRN............ Print Numerically (DEN)
PRN............ Pristina [*Former Yugoslavia*] [*Airport symbol*] (OAG)
PRN............ PR Newswire [*PR Newswire, Inc.*] [*Information service or system*] (IID)
PRN............ Procurement Reallocation Notice
PRN............ Program Release Notice [*NASA*] (NASA)
PRN............ Prominent Resources Corp. [*Vancouver Stock Exchange symbol*]
PRN............ Pronasale [*Anatomy*]
PRN............ Pro Re Nata [*Whenever Necessary*] [*Pharmacy*]
PRN............ Pseudorandom Noise
PRN............ Pseudorandom Number
PRN............ Puerto Rican Cement [*NYSE symbol*] (TTSB)
PRN............ Puerto Rican Cement Co., Inc. [*NYSE symbol*] (SPSG)
PRN............ Pulse Ranging Navigation
PRN............ Pulse Ranging Network (KSC)
PRN............ Purchase Request Number
pRNA.......... Ribonucleic Acid, Polysomal [*Biochemistry, genetics*]
PRNC.......... Potomac River Naval Command [*Washington, DC*]
PRNC.......... Prince
PRNC.......... Puerto Rico Nuclear Center
PRNDL........ Park, Reverse, Neutral, Drive, Low [*Automotive term for automatic gearshift indicator in cars; pronounced "prindle"*]
PRNDL........ Park-Reverse-Neutral-Drive-Low [*Automobile transmissions*]
PrnDn......... Princeton Dental Management Corp. [*Associated Press*] (SAG)
PrnDnt........ Princeton Dental Management Corp. [*Associated Press*] (SAG)
PRNET........ Packet Radio Network
PRNG.......... Paper Negative (VRA)
PRNG.......... Purging (MSA)
PRNI........... Premiere Radio Networks [*NASDAQ symbol*] (TTSB)
PRNI........... Premier Radio Network [*NASDAQ symbol*] (SAG)
PRNIA......... Premiere Radio Networks 'A' [*NASDAQ symbol*] (TTSB)
prnnl........... Perennial [*Botany*]
PRNP.......... Prion Protein (DMAA)
PRNS.......... Prins Recycling [*NASDAQ symbol*] (TTSB)
PRNS.......... Prins Recycling Corp. [*NASDAQ symbol*] (SAG)
PRNT.......... Plaque Reduction Neutralization Test [*Immunochemistry*]
PRNTG........ Printing (MSA)
PRNTR........ Printer
PRNTV........ Preventive
PRNU.......... Photoresponse Nonuniformity
PRO............ Pacific Research Office (CINC)
PRO............ Parallel Rod Oscillator
PRO............ Parents Reaching Out [*An association*] (EA)
PRO............ Parents Rights Organization (EA)
PRO............ Particle Reduction Oven

PRO .... Parts Release Order
PRO .... Patients' Rights Organization (EA)
PRO .... Pay and Records Office [*British military*] (DMA)
PRO .... Peer Review Organization [*Medicare*]
PRO .... Pen Recorder Output (SAA)
PRO .... Performing Rights Organization [*Formerly, BMI-Canada Ltd.*] [*Canada*]
PRO .... Perry, IA [*Location identifier FAA*] (FAAL)
PRO .... Personnel Relations Officer [*for Shore Stations*] [*Navy*]
PR/O .... Pilot Repair/Overhaul [*Military*]
PRO .... Pitch Response Operator
PRO .... Planned Requirements, Outfitting [*Navy*] (NG)
PRO .... Planning Resident Order (KSC)
PRO .... Plant Representative Officer (MCD)
PRO .... Population Renewal Office (EA)
PRO .... Precision RISC [*Reduced Instruction Set Computer*] Organization
Pro .... Prednisone [*Also, P, PDN, PR, Pred*] [*Antineoplastic drug, Endocrinology*]
PRO .... Principal Public Library [*Library network*]
PRO .... Print Octal (DEN)
PRO .... Probate
PRO .... Probation [*or Probationer*]
PRO .... Problem Resolution Office [*IRS*]
PRO .... Procedure (AABC)
Pro .... Proculus [*Flourished, 1st century*] [*Authority cited in pre-1607 legal work*] (DSA)
PRO .... Procurement Research Office [*Army*]
PRO .... Production Repair Order
PRO .... Professional
PRO .... Professional
pro .... Professional (ODBW)
PRO .... Professional Dental Technologies, Inc. [*AMEX symbol*] (SAG)
PRO .... Professional Racing Organization of America [*Later, USCF*] (EA)
PRO .... Professional Resellers Organization [*Defunct*] (EA)
PRO .... Professional Review Organization [*Medicare*]
PRO .... Proficiency
PRO .... Proflavine [*An antiseptic*]
PRO .... Programmable Remote Operation [*Computer Devices, Inc.*]
PRO .... Program Representative Office (AAGC)
PRO .... Progressive
Pro .... Proline [*Also, P*] [*An amino acid*]
pro .... Proline [*An amino acid*] (DOG)
Pro .... Prolyl [*Biochemistry*]
PRO .... Pronation [*Medicine*]
PRO .... Pronoun [*Grammar*] (WGA)
PRO .... Pronto Explorations Ltd. [*Toronto Stock Exchange symbol*]
PRO .... Propagation [*Military*]
PRO .... Propagation Prediction Report (SAA)
PRO .... Propair, Inc. [*Canada ICAO designator*] (FAAC)
PRO .... Propeller Order
PRO .... Prophylactic (AABC)
PRO .... Prostitute (ADA)
Pro .... Protein
PRO .... Protest
Pro .... Prothrombin [*Factor II*] [*Hematology*]
PRO .... Proved
pro .... Provencal [*MARC language code Library of Congress*] (LCCP)
Pro .... Proverbs [*Old Testament book*] (BJA)
PRO .... Providence [*Diocesan abbreviation*] [*Rhode Island*] (TOCD)
PRO .... Province (ROG)
PRO .... Provost
PRO .... Public Record Office [*British*]
PRO .... Public Relations Officer [*or Officer*] [*Usually military*]
PRO .... Puchase Request Order
PROA .... Polymer Research Corp. of America [*NASDAQ symbol*] (NQ)
PROA .... Polymer Resh America [*NASDAQ symbol*] (TTSB)
PROA .... Puerto Rico Operations Area
ProActiv .... ProActive Technologies, Inc. [*Associated Press*] (SAG)
PRO-AM .... Professional-Amateur (WDAA)
pro-am .... Professionals and Amateurs [*Sports*] (WDMC)
PROAP .... Principal Regional Office for Asia and the Pacific [*UNESCO*]
Prob .... English Probate and Admiralty Reports for Year Cited [*A publication*] (DLA)
Prob .... Law Reports, Probate Division [*England*] [*A publication*] (DLA)
PROB .... Probability (KSC)
prob .... Probable
PROB .... Probably
prob .... Probably (VRA)
Prob .... Probate [*Legal term*] (DLA)
PROB .... Probation [*FBI standardized term*]
PROB .... Problem
Prob .... Quod Omnis Probus Liber Sit [*of Philo*] (BJA)
PROB40 .... Probability 40 Percent [*ICAO*] (FAAC)
Prob (1891)... Law Reports, Probate Division [*1891*] [*England*] [*A publication*] (DLA)
Prob & Adm Div... Probate and Admiralty Division Law Reports [*A publication*] (DLA)
Prob & Div... Probate and Divorce, English Law Reports [*A publication*] (DLA)
Prob & Mat... Probate and Matrimonial Cases [*A publication*] (DLA)
Probat .... Probation [*Legal term*] (DLA)
Probation & Parole L Rep... Probation and Parole Law Reports [*A publication*] (DLA)
Probation & Parole L Summ... Probation and Parole Law Summaries [*A publication*] (DLA)
Probat J .... Probation Journal [*A publication*] (ILCA)
Prob C .... Probate Code [*A publication*] (DLA)
PROBCOST... Probabilistic Budgeting and Forward Costing
Prob Ct Rep... Probate Court Reporter [*Ohio*] [*A publication*] (DLA)
PROBDET..... Probability of Detection [*Navy*] (NVT)
Prob Div ...... Probate Division, English Law Reports [*A publication*] (DLA)
PROBE .... Performance Review of Base Supply Effectiveness [*Air Force*] (AFM)
PROBE .... Pilot Radiation Observation Experiment (USDC)
PROBE .... Pilot Radiation Observation Experiment [*Marine science*] (OSRA)
PROBE .... Practical Research into Organizational Behavior and Effectiveness (EDAC)
PROBE .... Profile Resolution Obtained by Excitation (PDAA)
PROBE .... Program for Research on Objectives-Based Evaluation [*UCLA*]
PROBE .... Program Optimization and Budget Evaluation [*Military*]
PROBES .... Processes and Resources of the Bering Sea Shelf [*University of Alaska*]
PROBFOR .... Probability Forecasting [*Computer program*] [*Bell System*]
PROBIT .... Probability Unit [*Statistics*]
Prob J .... Probation Journal [*A publication*] (DLA)
Prob LT .... Probyn on Land Tenure [*4th ed.*] [*1881*] [*A publication*] (DLA)
PROBO .... Product/Ore/Bulk/Oil Carrier [*Shipping*] (DS)
PROBOUT .... Proceed On or About (MUGU)
Prob Pr Act... Probate Practice Act [*A publication*] (DLA)
Prob R .... Probate Reports [*A publication*] (DLA)
Prob Rep ...... Probate Reports [*A publication*] (DLA)
Prob Rep Ann... Probate Reports, Annotated [*A publication*] (DLA)
PROBSUB .... Probable Submarine (NVT)
PROBUS ...... Program Budget System [*Military*]
Proby .... Probationary [*British military*] (DMA)
PROC .... Performing Rights Organization of Canada [*See also SDE*]
PROC .... Preliminary Required Operational Capability [*Military*]
PROC .... Procedure (AAG)
PROC .... Proceedings
proc .... Proceedings (WDMC)
PROC .... Process (AABC)
proc .... Process (VRA)
PROC .... Procession (ROG)
PROC .... Processor [*or Processing*]
Proc .... Proclamation (DLA)
PROC .... Proctor
PROC .... Procure (AABC)
PROC .... Procurement (MSA)
PROC .... Programming Computer [*Computer science*]
PROC .... Proposed Required Operational Capability [*Military*] (AABC)
PROC .... Protein C (DMAA)
PROCAL .... Programmable Calculator [*Computer science*] (IAA)
Proc Amer Soc of Internat L... Proceedings. American Society of International Law [*A publication*] (DLA)
Proc Amp..... Processing Amplifier (NTCM)
PRO CAPILL... Pro Capillis [*For the Hair*] [*Pharmacy*]
Procarb .... Procarbazine [*Antineoplastic drug*] (DAVI)
PROCAS .... Process-Oriented Contract Administration Services
Proc B & B... Proctor's Bench and Bar of New York [*A publication*] (DLA)
Proc Ch .... Proceedings in Chancery [*A publication*] (DLA)
PROCCIR ..... Procurement Circular [*Air Force*] (AFIT)
Proc Cir .... Procurement Circular (AAGC)
PROCD .... Procedure (AFM)
PROCD .... Proceed (AFM)
PROCDRE .... Procedure (ROG)
PROCED .... Procedure
Proc Elec Assoc Aust... Proceedings. Electrical Association of Australia [*A publication*]
Proc Elec Assoc NSW... Proceedings. Electrical Association of New South Wales [*Australia A publication*]
Proc Eng Assoc NSW... Proceedings. Engineering Association of New South Wales [*Australia A publication*]
Procept .... Procept, Inc. [*Associated Press*] (SAG)
PROCIEE ...... Proceedings of the Institute of Electrical Engineers [*A publication*] (IAA)
Proc Inst Criminol Univ Sydney... University of Sydney. Institute of Criminology. Proceedings [*A publication*]
Proc Instn Radio Eng Aust... Proceedings. Institution of Radio Engineers of Australia [*A publication*]
PROCLIB ...... Procedure Library [*Computer science*]
Proc Med-Leg Soc Vic... Medico-Legal Society of Victoria. Proceedings [*A publication*]
Proc Microscopical Soc Vic... Proceedings. Microscopical Society of Victoria [*Australia A publication*]
ProcmT .... Procom Technology Inc. [*Associated Press*] (SAG)
PROCO .... Procurement Officer [*Military*]
PROCO .... Programmed Combustion [*Ford Motor Co.*]
PROCO .... Projects for Continental Operations [*World War II*]
PROCOL .... Process Control Language (NITA)
PROCOL .... Process Control Oriented Language [*Computer science*] (IAA)
PROCOM ...... Procedures Committee [*Institute of Electrical and Electronics Engineers*] (IEEE)
PROCOM ...... Procurement Committee
PROCOM ...... Prognose Compiler [*Computer science*] (IAA)
PROCOMEXCHI... Mexican-Chicano Cooperative Programs on Mexican-US-Chicano Futures (EA)
PROCOMP ... Process Compiler [*Computer science*] (IAA)
PROCOMP ... Process Computer [*Computer science*]
PROCOMP ... Program Compiler [*Computer science*] (IEEE)
PROCON ...... Protocol Converter (DA)

PROCON ...... Request Diagnosis, Prognosis, Present Condition, Probable Date and Mode of Disposition of Following Patient Reported in Your Hospital [*Military*]
Procop .... Procopius [*Sixth century AD*] [*Classical studies*] (OCD)
PROCOPT ...... Processing Option [*Computer science*] (MHDB)
PROCOTIP ... Promotion Cooperative du Transport Individuel Publique [*Public cars for private use to reduce traffic congestion*] [*Also known as TIP*] [*France*]
Proc Pr .... Proctor's Practice [*A publication*] (DLA)
Proc Prac..... Proctor's Practice [*A publication*] (DLA)
Proc Roy Soc Qld... Proceedings. Royal Society of Queensland [*Australia A publication*]
Proc Roy Soc Vic... Proceedings. Royal Society of Victoria [*Australia A publication*]
PROCS .... Proceedings
Proc Sci Soc Univ Adel... Proceedings. Scientific Society. University of Adelaide [*A publication*]
PROCSD ...... Processed
PROCSEQ .... Processing Sequence [*Computer science*] (MHDB)
PROCSIM..... Processor Simulation Language [*Computer science*] (PDAA)
Proc Soc Chem Indust Vic... Proceedings. Society of Chemical Industry of Victoria [*Australia A publication*]
PROCT .... Proctology
ProctGm ...... Procter & Gamble Co. [*Associated Press*] (SAG)
PROCTO....... Proctology [*Gastroenterology*] (DAVI)
PROCTO....... Proctoscopy [*Medicine*]
PROCTOR .... Priority Routine Organizer for Computer Transfers and Operations of Registers
PROCTOT..... Priority Routine Organizer for Computer Transfers and Operations and Transfers
PROCU......... Processing Unit
PROCUP ...... Partido Revolucionario Obrerista y Clandestino de Union Popular [*Mexico Political party*] (EY)
PROCVAL..... Validation Procedures Library [*Social Security Administration*]
Proc WA Instn Eng... Proceedings. Western Australian Institution of Engineers [*A publication*]
Procyt .... ProCyte Corp. [*Associated Press*] (SAG)
PROD........... Office of Production [*National Security Agency*]
PROD........... Photographic Retrieval from Optical Disk
PROD........... Produce
PROD........... Produce
prod............ Product (WDMC)
PROD........... Product [*or Production*] (AABC)
prod............ Production (WDMC)
PROD........... Production (DOMA)
prod............ Production (DD)
Prod............ Production (AAGC)
PROD........... Professional Drivers Council for Safety and Health
PROD........... Professional Over-the-Road Drivers [*Part of Teamsters Union*]
PRODAC ...... Production Advisers Consortium (NADA)
PRODAC ...... Programmed Digital Automatic Control [*Computer science*]
PRODAM...... Production Orientated Draughting and Manufacturing (PDAA)
PRODAN ...... Propionyl(dimethylamino)naphthalene [*Organic chemistry*]
PRODASE .... Protein Database
Prod Aust..... Productivity Australia [*A publication*]
PRODC......... Production Command [*Army*]
PROD/DEPL... Production and Deployment [*Phase*] (DOMA)
Proden......... Proyecto de Desarrollo Nacional [*Project for National Development*] [*Chile*] (PPW)
ProDex......... ProDex, Inc. [*Associated Press*] (SAG)
PRODISCO... Producers Distributing Corp.
Prod Liab Int'l... Product Liability International [*A publication*] (DLA)
Prod Liab Rep... Product Liability Reporter [*Commerce Clearing House*] [*A publication*] (DLA)
Prodn.......... Production
PRODN .... Production
PRODNG....... Producing
ProDnt......... Professional Dental Technologies, Inc. [*Associated Press*] (SAG)
PRODOC ...... Procedure Documentation [*Computer science*] (MHDB)
PRODON....... Production
ProdOp .... Production Operators Corp. [*Associated Press*] (SAG)
PRO DOS..... Pro Dose [*For a Dose*] [*Pharmacy*]
ProDOS........ Professional Disk Operating System [*Computer science*]
PRODR .... Producer
PRODR .... Producer
Prods........... Products (AAGC)
Prod Safety & Liab Rep... Product Safety and Liability Reporter [*A publication*] (DLA)
PRODT......... Product
PRODUCE.... Production Distribution Using Component Evaluation (IAA)
Product........ Productivity Technologies Corp. [*Associated Press*] (SAG)
PRODUCTN.. Production
Productv ...... Productivity Technologies Corp. [*Associated Press*] (SAG)
PRODUTAS... Proceed on Duty Assigned [*Military*]
PRODVAL .... Product Validation (MCD)
PROE........... Programme Regional Oceanien de l'Environnement [*South Pacific Regional Environmental Programme - SPREP*] (EAIO)
PRO.EC........ Professional Dental Tech [*ECM, Symbol*] (TTSB)
PRO EL........ Protein Electrophoresis [*Biochemistry*] (DAVI)
Pro Ex.......... Protein Exchange [*Dietetics*]
PROF........... Peace Research Organization Fund
PROF........... Personal Radio Operators Federation [*Defunct*] (EA)
PROF........... Prediction and Optimization of Failure Rate (MHDB)
PROF........... Profanity [*FBI standardized term*]
PROF........... Profession [*or Professional*]
PROF........... Professional Office System
PROF........... Professor (EY)
PROF........... Professor
Prof............ Professor (ODBW)
Prof............ Profile
PROF........... Profile (GAVI)
prof............ Profile (VRA)
PROF........... Pupil Registering and Operational Filing [*Computer science*]
ProFac......... Pro-Fac Cooperative, Inc. [*Associated Press*] (SAG)
PROFAC....... Propulsive Fluid Accumulator
PROFACTS... Production Formulation, Accounting, and Cost System (MHDI)
Prof Admin... Professional Administrator [*A publication*]
PROFAGTRANS... Proceed by First Available Government Transportation [*Military*]
PROFAT .... Projet des Francophones de l'Atlantique [*Canada*]
pro-fax........ Production Facilities (WDMC)
Pro-Fax........ Production Facility (NTCM)
ProfBTM ...... Professional Business and Technical Management [*British*] [*An association*] (DBA)
Prof Burd..... Commemoratio Professorum Burdigalensium [*of Ausonius*] [*Classical studies*] (OCD)
Prof Corp..... Proffatt on Private Corporations in California [*A publication*] (DLA)
Prof Corp Guide (P-H)... Professional Corporation Guide (Prentice-Hall, Inc.) [*A publication*] (DLA)
PROFCY....... Proficiency
PROF-E........ Programmed Review of Operator Functions - Elementary (DNAB)
Prof Eng ...... Professional Engineer
Prof Engr..... Professional Engineer [*A publication*]
PROFESSL... Professional
PROFFIS...... Professional Filler System [*Military*]
Proffitt........ Proffitt's, Inc. [*Associated Press*] (SAG)
PROFILE ...... Programmed Functional Indices for Laboratory Evaluation [*RAND Corp.*]
PROFILES.... Personal Reflection on Family Life and Employment Stressors [*Psychology*]
PROFIS........ Programminformationssystem Sozialwissenschaften [*Informationszentrum Sozialwissenschaften*] [*Germany Defunct Information service or system*] (CRD)
PROFIT .... Program for Financed Insurance Techniques
PROFIT .... Programmed Reviewing, Ordering, and Forecasting Inventory Technique
PROFIT .... Propulsion Flight Control Integration Technology (MCD)
Prof Jur ...... Proffatt on Trial by Jury [*A publication*] (DLA)
PROFL.......... Professional
PR of MAN... [*The*] Prayer of Manasses, King of Judah [*Apocrypha*]
Prof Not....... Proffatt on Notaries [*A publication*] (DLA)
Prof Officer... Professional Officer [*A publication*]
PROFP.......... Proficiency Pay [*Military*]
ProfRec........ Profit Recovery Group International, Inc. (The) [*Associated Press*] (SAG)
PROFS .... Professional Office System [*IBM Corp.*]
PROFS .... Program for Regional Observing and Forecasting Services [*Boulder, CO*] [*Department of Commerce*] (GRD)
PROFS .... Prototype Regional Observation and Forecasting Service [*National Oceanic and Atmospheric Administration*] (GRD)
ProfStaff ...... Professional Staff [*Associated Press*] (SAG)
Prof Wills.... Proffatt on Wills [*A publication*] (DLA)
PROG........... Peer Review Oversight Group [*National Institutes of Health*]
prog............ Progesterone [*Endocrinology*] (DAVI)
prog............ Prognathism [*Dentistry*] (DAVI)
PROG........... Prognosis [*or Prognostication*] (AAG)
PROG........... Program (KSC)
PROG........... Programmer [*or Programming*]
PROG........... Programmer's Paradise [*NASDAQ symbol*] (TTSB)
PROG........... Programmers Paradise, Inc. [*NASDAQ symbol*] (SAG)
PROG........... Progress (AABC)
Prog............ Progressive [*A publication*] (BRI)
Prog Arch .... Progressive Architecture [*A publication*] (BRI)
PROG BK ..... Programmed Book [*Publishing*]
ProgBk......... Progressive Bank, Inc. [*Associated Press*] (SAG)
ProgCp......... Progressive Corp. [*Associated Press*] (SAG)
PROGDEV .... Program Device (KSC)
ProgFn......... Progress Financial Corp. [*Associated Press*] (SAG)
PROGLIB...... Production Program Library [*Social Security Administration*]
PRO GM ...... Pro Grand Master [*Freemasonry*]
PROGMG ..... Programming
PROGN .... Prognosis (AAMN)
PROGNO ...... Prognosen-Trends-Entwicklungen [*Forecasts-Trends-Developments*] [*Society for Business Information*] [*Information service or system*] (IID)
PROGOFOP... Program of Operation [*Computer science*]
ProgPar .... Programmers Paradise, Inc. [*Associated Press*] (SAG)
PROGR......... Programmer (ECII)
progr........... Progress (DAVI)
Progrp......... ProGroup, Inc. [*Associated Press*] (SAG)
PROGS......... Progressive
PROGS......... Progressive Proofs [*Graphic arts*] (DGA)
PROGVAL .... Validation Program Library [*Social Security Administration*]
PROH........... Prohibit
PROH........... Prohibition [*FBI standardized term*]
Prohib.......... Prohibited
PROI............ CFI ProServices [*NASDAQ symbol*] (TTSB)
PROI............ CFI Proservices, Inc. [*NASDAQ symbol*] (SAG)
PROI............ President of the Royal Institute of Oil Painters [*British*]
PROI............ Project Return on Investment (MHDW)
PRO-IF......... Personal Radio Operators International Federation [*Formerly, ARC*] (EA)

PROIMREP... Proceed Immediately - Report for Purpose Indicated [*Military*]
Pro Indian Soc of Internat L... Proceedings of the Conference. Indian Society of International Law [*New Delhi, India*] [*A publication*] (DLA)
PROJ.......... Project (AFM)
PROJ.......... Project
proj.......... Project (VRA)
PROJ.......... Projectile (AFM)
PROJ.......... Projector [*or Projection*]
PROJACS..... Project Analysis and Control System (MHDI)
PROJECT..... Project Engineering Control
PROJENGR... Project Engineer
PROJID........ Project Identification [*Computer science*]
PROJMGR..... Project Manager [*Military*]
PROJMGRASWS... Project Manager, Antisubmarine Warfare Systems
PROJMGRFBM... Project Manager, Fleet Ballistic Missile [*Navy*]
PROJMGRSMS... Project Manager, Surface Missile Systems [*Navy*]
ProjSft......... Project Software & Development, Inc. [*Associated Press*] (SAG)
projt............ Projector (VRA)
PROJTRNS... Project Transition [*DoD*]
PROL............ Priority Requirement Objective List (AFM)
Prol............. Prologic Management Systems, Inc. [*Associated Press*] (SAG)
PROL........... Prologue
PRO L.......... Province Laws (DLA)
PROLAC....... Prolactin [*Biochemistry*] (DAVI)
PROLAMAT... Programming Languages for Machine Tools [*Conference*]
PROLAMAT... Programming Languages for Numerically Controlled Machine Tools [*Conference*] [*Computer science*] (IAA)
PROLAN....... Processed Language [*Computer science*]
PROLE......... Proletarian (WDAA)
Proler.......... Proler International Corp. [*Associated Press*] (SAG)
Prolif........... Proliferative [*or Proliferation*]
PROLLAP..... Professional Library Literature Acquisition Program
PRO LOC et TEM... Pro Loco et Tempore [*For the Place and Time*] [*Latin*] (ROG)
PROLOG...... Production of Onshore Lower 48 Oil and Gas Model [*Department of Energy*] (GFGA)
PROLOG...... Program Logistics (NG)
PROLOG...... Programming in Logic [*Programing language*] [*1970*]
PROLOG...... Project Logic Planning (IAA)
Prolog......... Prologic Management Systems, Inc. [*Associated Press*] (SAG)
Prologc........ Prologic Management Systems, Inc. [*Associated Press*] (SAG)
Prologic...... Prologic Management Systems, Inc. [*Associated Press*] (SAG)
prolong........ Prolongatus [*Prolonged*] [*Latin*] (DAVI)
PROLT......... Procurement Lead Time
PROM.......... Passive Range of Motion [*Medicine*]
PROM.......... Pockels Readout Optical Modulator
PROM.......... Premature [*or Prolonged*] Rupture of Membranes [*Gynecology*]
PROM.......... Programmable Read-Only Memory [*Computer science*]
PROM.......... Program, Resources, Objectives, Management [*Air Force Systems Command technique*]
PROM.......... Progressive Range of Motion [*Medicine*]
PROM.......... Prolonged Rupture of Membranes [*Gynecology*] (DAVI)
PROM.......... Promenade [*Maps and charts*]
prom........... Promenade (ODBW)
prom........... Promenade (DD)
PROM.......... Prominent
PROM.......... Promise [*Legal shorthand*] (LWAP)
Prom........... Promissory [*A publication*] (DLA)
PROM.......... Promontory
PROM.......... Promote [*or Promotion*] (AFM)
PROM.......... Promotion
PROM.......... Promulgate (AABC)
Pro-MACE...... Prednisone, Methotrexate with Leucovorin, Adriamycin, Cyclophosphamide, Epipodophyllin [*Etoposide, VP-16*] [*Antineoplastic drug regimen*]
PROMACE-MOPP... Procarbazine, Methotrexate, Adriamycin, Cyclophosphamide, Etoposide, Mustargen [*Nitrogen mustard*], Oncovin , Procarbazine, Prednisone [*Vincristine*] [*Antineoplastic drug regimen*]
PROMAG...... Production Management Action Group [*British*]
PROMAP...... Program for the Refinement of the Materiel Acquisition Process [*Army*] (AABC)
PROMAR...... Program on the Promotion of Marine Sciences [*Marine science*] (OSRA)
PROMAST.... Production Master Scheduling System (PDAA)
PROMATS.... Probabilistic Materials System (PDAA)
Prom dk....... Promenade Deck [*of a ship*] (DS)
ProMED....... Program to Monitor Emerging Diseases
PROMEE...... Promisee [*Legal shorthand*] (LWAP)
PROMETHEUS... Program for European Traffic with Highest Efficiency and Unprecedented Safety (ECON)
PROMEX...... Productivity Measurement Experiment [*National Institute of Standards and Technology*]
PROMIM...... Programmable Multiple Ion Monitor
PROMIS....... Problem-Oriented Medical Information System [*Computerized patient-management system*]
PROMIS....... Process Management and Information System [*I. P. Sharp Associates Ltd.*] [*Software package*] (NCC)
PROMIS....... Project Management Integrated System (NITA)
PROMIS....... Project-Oriented Management Information System
PROMIS....... Prosecutor's Management Information System [*Law Enforcement Assistance Administration*]
PROMISE..... Programming Managers Information System (MHDI)
PROMISE..... Prospective Randomized Milrinone Survival Evaluation [*Medicine*]
PROMISS..... Packaging Requirements for Optimum Malfunction Isolation by Systematic Substitution (IAA)
PROML........ Promulgate
PROMO........ Promotion [*Slang*] (DSUE)
Promo.......... Promotional Announcement (NTCM)
PROMOR..... Promisor [*Legal shorthand*] (LWAP)
PROMPT..... Production, Reviewing, Organizing, and Monitoring of Performance Techniques (BUR)
PROMPT..... Program Monitoring and Planning Techniques (IEEE)
PROMPT..... Program Reporting, Organization, and Management Planning Technique (IAA)
PROMPT..... Program to Record Official Mail Point-to-Point Times [*Postal Service program*]
PROMPT..... Project Management and Production Team Technique [*Computer science*]
PROMPT..... Project Reporting Organization and Management Planning Technique
PROMS....... Procurement Management System (MCD)
PROMS....... Programmable Read Only Memory System [*Computer science*]
PROMS....... Program Monitoring System (MCD)
PROMS....... Projectile Measurement System [*Computer science Army*]
PROMSS..... Procedures and Relationships for the Operation of Manual Stations and Spaces (DNAB)
PROM STAT... Promotion Status (DNAB)
PROMT........ Precision Optimized Measurement Time [*Spectroscopy*]
PROMT........ Predicasts Overview of Markets and Terminology (NITA)
PROMT........ Predicasts Overviews of Marketing and Technology [*Business database*]
PROMT........ Programmable Miniature Message Terminal (MCD)
PROMUS...... Provincial-Municipal Simulator [*Computer-based urban management system*]
PROMY........ Promissory (ROG)
PRON.......... Patriotyczny Ruch Odrodzenia Narodowego [*Patriotic Movement for National Rebirth*] [*Poland*] (EY)
PRON.......... Procurement Request Order Number [*Army*] (AABC)
PRON.......... Pronation
PRON.......... Pronominal (ADA)
PRON.......... Pronoun
PRON.......... Pronounced
PRON.......... Pronunciation (ROG)
pron........... Pronunciation (WDMC)
PRONED...... Promotion of Non-Executive Directors (ODBW)
Pronet......... ProNet, Inc. [*Associated Press*] (SAG)
Pro-Nica...... Professionals - Nicaragua (EA)
PRONTO...... Program for Numeric Tool Operation [*Computer science*]
PRONTO...... Programmable Network Telecommunications Operating System
prooem........ Prooemium (BJA)
PROOF........ Precision Recording (Optical) of Fingerprints
PROOF........ Projected Return on Open Office Facilities [*Computer program*]
proOLMC..... Pro-Opiolipomelanocortin [*Endocrinology*]
PRO-OP...... Project Optimization [*Industrial engineering*]
PROP.......... Performance Review for Operating Programs (BUR)
PROP.......... Pilot Repair Overhaul and Provisioning (MUGU)
PROP.......... Planetary Rocket Ocean Platform
PROP.......... Prerelease Orientation Program [*Reformatory program*]
PROP.......... Preservation of the Rights of Prisoners [*An association British*]
PROP.......... Primary Operand Unit (IAA)
PROP.......... Prisoners' Right of Privacy [*British*] (DI)
PROP.......... Production Operators [*NASDAQ symbol*] (TTSB)
PROP.......... Production Operators Corp. [*NASDAQ symbol*] (NQ)
PROP.......... Production Planning (IAA)
PROP.......... Profit Rating of Projects
PROP.......... Proof of Purchase (WDMC)
PROP.......... Propaganda (AFM)
Prop........... Propagate [*Botany*]
PROP.......... Propellant (KSC)
PROP.......... Propeller
PROP.......... Proper
PROP.......... Propertius [*Roman poet, c. 29BC*] [*Classical studies*] (ROG)
PROP.......... Property
prop........... Property (DD)
PROP.......... Property
PROP.......... Property Release Option Program [*HUD*]
PROP.......... Proportional (KSC)
PROP.......... Proposal (AAG)
PROP.......... Proposed (AFM)
PROP.......... Proposition
PROP.......... Proprietor
PROP.......... Propulsion (AAG)
PROP.......... Propylthiouracil [*Also, PT, PTU*] [*Thyroid inhibitor*]
PROPAC...... Progressive Political Action Committee [*Defunct*] (EA)
PROPAC...... Prospective Payment Assessment Commission [*Washington, DC*] (EGAO)
PROPAKASIA... International Food Processing and Packaging Technology Exhibition and Conferencefor South East Asia
PROPAL....... Proportional
Prop & Comp... Property and Compensation Reports [*A publication*] (DLA)
Prop & Comp R... Property and Compensation Reports [*A publication*] (DLA)
PRO-PAY..... Proficiency Pay [*Military*]
PropCT........ Property Capital Trust [*Associated Press*] (SAG)
pro per........ Propria Persona [*In His or Her Own Person*] [*Latin*] (WGA)
PROPER COUNT... Property Accountability (MCD)
PROPH........ Porphyrins [*Chemistry*] (DAVI)
PROPH........ Profile of Phonology (AIE)
PROPH........ Prophylactic
Proph21....... Prophet 21, Inc. [*Associated Press*] (SAG)
PROPHET..... Proactive Rehabilitation of Outside Plant Using Heuristic Expert Techniques [*GTE computer software*]

prophy .... Prophylactic (DAVI)
PROPIN .... Proprietary Information
PROPL .... Proportional
Prop Law ..... Property Lawyer [*1826-30*] [*A publication*] (DLA)
Prop Law Bull ... Property Law Bulletin [*A publication*] (DLA)
Prop Law NS ... Property Lawyer, New Series [*England*] [*A publication*] (DLA)
PROPLING ... Propelling
PROPLOSS ... Propagation Loss (NVT)
PROPLT .... Propellant (NASA)
PROPN .... Propane
PROPN .... Proportion (MSA)
proPO .... Prophenoloxidase
PROPON .... Proportion (ROG)
PROPORICH ... Proceed to Port in Which Unit is Located [*Navy*] (DNAB)
PROPR .... Proprietary (ROG)
PROPR .... Proprietor (EY)
PROPRE .... Property Press (DLA)
PROPRSS ..... Proprietress (ROG)
PROPTRY ..... Proprietary [*Freight*]
PROPUL .... Propulsion
PROPY .... Proprietary
Pro Quer ...... Pro Querente [*For the Plaintiff*] [*Latin*] (ILCA)
PROR .... Predicted Orbit
PRORA .... Programs for Research on Romance Authors
PRORAT .... Projected Rating
PRO RAT AET ... Pro Ratione Aetatis [*According to Age*] [*Pharmacy*]
PRO RECT ... Pro Recto [*Rectal*] [*Pharmacy*]
pro rect .... pro recto [*By rectum*] [*Latin*] [*Pharmacy*] (DAVI)
PROREP .... Proceed Ship, Command Station Reporting Duty or Purpose Indicated [*Military*]
PROS .... Preventive Maintenance, Repair, and Operational Services (ODBW)
PROS .... Procurement Squadron
PROS .... Professional Reactor Operator Society (EA)
PROS .... Proscenium [*Theater term*] (DSUE)
PROS .... Prosecution (ROG)
PROS .... Prosody
PROS .... Prospect Group [*NASDAQ symbol*] (TTSB)
PROS .... [*The*] Prospect Group, Inc. [*New York, NY NASDAQ symbol*] (NQ)
pros .... Prostate [*Anatomy*] (DAVI)
PROS .... Prosthetic (AABC)
PROS .... Prostitute (DSUE)
PROS .... Prostrate
PROSA .... Programming System with Symbolic Addresses [*Computer science*] (IAA)
PROSAM ...... Programmed Single-Axis Mount [*Military camera*]
PROSAMO ..... Planned Release of Selected and Modified Organisms [*British*]
Pros Atty ...... Prosecuting Attorney (DLA)
PROSC .... Proscenium [*Theater term*] (WDAA)
PRosC .... Rosemont College, Rosemont, PA [*Library symbol Library of Congress*] (LCLS)
PROSD .... Performance Records for Optimizing System Design (IAA)
PROSE .... Personal Record of School Experiences (EDAC)
PROSE .... Problem Solution Engineering [*Programming language*] [*Computer science*] (CSR)
PROSE .... Program System Example (SAA)
PROSEA .... Plant Resources of South-East Asia [*A publication*]
PROSECON ... Prosecution (ROG)
PROSEL .... Process Control and Sequencing Language [*Computer science*] (IAA)
ProsGp .... [*The*] Prospect Group, Inc. [*Associated Press*] (SAG)
PROSI .... Public Relations Office of the Sugar Industry
PROSIG .... Procedure Signal [*Navy*]
PROSIGN ..... Procedure Sign [*Military*] (AABC)
PROSIM .... Production System Simulator [*Computer science*]
PROSIN .... Procedure Sign [*Military*] (IAA)
PROSINE ...... Procedure Sign [*Military*]
PROSMATEC ... Progressive Shift Schedule Management Technology [*Automotive engineering*]
PROSO .... Protamine Sulfate [*Biochemistry*] (DAVI)
ProSoc .... Prometheus Society (EA)
Prosoft .... Prosoft I-Net Solutions, Inc. [*Associated Press*] (SAG)
Prosop Att ... Prosopographia Attica [*A publication*] (OCD)
prosp .... Prospectively (DLA)
PROSPEC ..... PRO Specification (NITA)
PROSPECT ... Proponent Sponsored Engineer Corps Training [*Army Corps of Engineers*]
PROSPER .... Profit Simulation, Planning and Evaluation of Risk (MHDB)
ProSport ...... Professional Sports Care Management, Inc. [*Associated Press*] (SAG)
PROSPRO .... Process Systems Program
ProsSt .... Prospect Street High Income Portfolio, Inc. [*Associated Press*] (SAG)
PROST .... Pronuclear Oocyte and Sperm Transfer [*Embryology*]
prost .... Prostate (CPH)
PROST .... Prostitute [*or Prostitution*] [*FBI standardized term*]
PROSTAT ..... Prostatic (AAMN)
PROSTH ...... Prosthesis
PROSY .... People's Republic of South Yemen (BJA)
PROT .... Protect [*or Protection*] (MSA)
PROT .... Protein
PROT .... Protest (ROG)
PROT .... Protestant
PROT .... Proteus [*Bacterium*]
PROT .... Protinus [*Speedily*] [*Pharmacy*]
Prot .... Protocol (DLA)
PROT .... Prototype
PROT .... Protractor (AAG)
PROTA .... Protection Actual [*Probability for avoidance of ship*]
ProTACA ...... Procurement Technical Assistance Cooperative Agreement Program [*DoD*]
PROTAP .... Professional Opportunities through Academic Partnership [*National War College*]
PROTAP .... Protonotary Apostolic [*Roman Catholic*]
Prot CJ .... Protocol on the Statute of the European Communities Court of Justice [*A publication*] (DLA)
PROTCT .... Protective (AAG)
ProtDg .... Protein Design Labs [*Associated Press*] (SAG)
PROTEC .... Protection
PROTECON ... Process and Test Control [*Pendar Technical Association Ltd.*] [*Software package*] (NCC)
PROTECT ..... Probabilities Recall Optimizing the Employment of Calibration Time (KSC)
PROTECT ..... Protection
ProtectO ...... Protection One, Inc. [*Associated Press*] (SAG)
PRO TEM ..... Pro Tempore [*For the Time Being*] [*Latin*]
PRO TEM et LOC ... Pro Tempore et Loco [*For the Time and Place*] [*Latin*] (ROG)
Proteon .... Proteon, Inc. [*Associated Press*] (SAG)
PROTEUS ..... Profile Telemetry of Upper Ocean Currents (USDC)
PROTEUS ..... Profile Telemetry of Upper Ocean Currents [*Marine science*] (OSRA)
PROTEUS ..... Project to Research Objects Theories, Extraterrrestrials, and Unusual Sightings (EA)
PROTEUS ..... Propulsion Research and Open Water Testing of Experimental Underwater Systems (MCD)
PROTHROM ... Prothrombin [*Hematology*]
PROTIMEREP ... Proceed in Time Report Not Later Than [*Hour and/or date indicated*] [*Military*]
ProtLf .... Protective Life Corp. [*Associated Press*] (SAG)
PROTO .... Protoporphyrin [*Hematology*]
Proto .... ProtoSource Corp. [*Associated Press*] (SAG)
PROTO .... Prototype (KSC)
ProtoS .... ProtoSource Corp. [*Associated Press*] (SAG)
ProtP .... Protein Polymer Technologies, Inc. [*Associated Press*] (SAG)
Prot Pl .... Protocol on Privileges and Immunities of the European Economic Community [*A publication*] (DLA)
ProtPoly .... Protein Polymer Technologies, Inc. [*Associated Press*] (SAG)
PROTR .... Protractor (MSA)
Protr .... Protrepticus [*of Clemens Alexandrinus*] [*Classical studies*] (OCD)
ProtSy .... Protocol Systems, Inc. [*Associated Press*] (SAG)
Proud Dom Pub ... Proudhon's Domaine Public [*A publication*] (DLA)
Proudf Land Dec ... United States Land Decisions (Proudfit) [*A publication*] (DLA)
PROUS .... Proceed to a Port in Continental United States [*Military*]
PRO US EXT ... Pro Usu Externo [*For External Use*] [*Pharmacy*]
Prouty .... Prouty's Reports [*61-68 Vermont*] [*A publication*] (DLA)
Prov .... De Providentia [*of Seneca the Younger*] [*Classical studies*] (OCD)
prov .... Provenance (VRA)
PROV .... Provencal [*Language, etc.*]
PROV .... Provence [*France*] (ROG)
PROV .... Proverb
Prov .... Proverbs [*Old Testament book*]
PROV .... Provide (KSC)
PROV .... Provident Financial Holdings, Inc. [*NASDAQ symbol*] (SAG)
PROV .... Province
PROV .... Provincial
PROV .... Provinciale [*Provincial*] [*Netherlands*] (EY)
PROV .... Proving Ground [*Navy*]
PROV .... Provision [*or Provisional*] (AFM)
Prov .... Provisional Light [*Navigation signal*]
PROV .... Provost
ProvBcp .... Provident Bancorp, Inc. [*Associated Press*] (SAG)
Prov Can Stat ... Statutes of the Province of Canada [*A publication*] (DLA)
ProvCo .... Provident Companies, Inc. [*Associated Press*] (SAG)
Prov Cons .... De Provinciis Consularibus [*of Cicero*] [*Classical studies*] (OCD)
PROVCORPV ... Provisional Corps, Vietnam
PROVD .... Provided
PROVER .... Procurement for Minimum Total Cost through Value Engineering and Reliability
ProvFinl .... Provident Financial Holdings, Inc. [*Associated Press*] (SAG)
ProvGM .... Provincial Grand Master [*Freemasonry*]
PROVGR ...... Proving Grounds
PROVIB .... Propulsion System Decision and Vibration Analysis (DNAB)
Provid .... De Providentia [*of Philo*] (BJA)
Providence C ... Providence College (GAGS)
Providn .... Providian Corp. [*Formerly, Capital Holding*] [*Associated Press*] (SAG)
PROVIMI ...... Proteins, Vitamins, and Minerals (BABM)
PROVIMI ...... Proteins, Vitamins, and Minerals [*Pharmacology*] (DAVI)
PROVIS .... Provision
PROVMAAG ... Provisional Military Assistance Advisory Group (CINC)
PROVMAAG-K ... Provisional Military Assistance Advisory Group, Korea (CINC)
PROVMAIN ... Other Provisions Basic Orders Remain in Effect
PROVMAINTCO ... Provisional Maintenance Company [*Navy*] (DNAB)
PROVMUSTCO ... Provisional Medical Unit Self-Contained Company [*Navy*] (DNAB)
PROVNC ...... Province
provns .... Provisions (DLA)
PROVO .... Proviso [*Contract clause*] (ROG)
PROVO .... Provocateur (DSUE)
PROVONS .... Provisions
PROVORG .... Providing Organization (DOMA)
PROVOST .... Priority Research Objectives for Vietnam Operations Support
PROVSN ...... Provision
Prov St .... Statutes, Laws, of the Province of Massachusetts [*A publication*] (DLA)

PROWDELREP... Proceed Without Delay Report Duty or Purpose Indicated [*Military*]
PROWL........ Procedure Work Log System (IAA)
PROWLER.... Programmable Robot Observer with Logical Enemy Response [*Developed by Robot Defense Systems of Thornton, CO*]
PROWORD... Procedure Word
PRO-X.......... Prothrombin Time [*Hematology*] (CPH)
prox............. Proximal (CPH)
PROX............ Proxim, Inc. [*NASDAQ symbol*] (SAG)
PROX............ Proximity (AABC)
PROX............ Proximo [*In Next Month*] [*Latin*]
prox............. Proximo [*In Next Month*] [*Latin*] (ODBW)
PROX ACC... Proxime Accessit [*Next in Order of Merit*] [*Latin*]
PRO-XAN..... Protein-Xanthophyll [*Alfalfa protein concentrate process*]
PROXI.......... Projection by Reflection Optics of Xerographic Images (IEEE)
Proxim......... Proxim, Inc. [*Associated Press*] (SAG)
Proxima....... Proxima Corp. [*Associated Press*] (SAG)
prox luc....... Proxima Luce [*Day Before*] [*Latin*] (MAE)
Proxymd...... ProxyMed, Inc. [*Associated Press*] (SAG)
PRP............. Panretinal Photocoagulation [*Ophthalmology*]
PRP............. Parent Rule Point (MCD)
PRP............. Parti de la Revolution Populaire [*People's Revolutionary Party*] [*Zaire*] [*Political party*] (PD)
PRP............. Partido de Renovacion Puertorriqueno [*Puerto Rican Renewal Party*] [*Political party*] (EY)
PRP............. Partido de Representacao Popular [*Brazil Political party*]
PRP............. Partido Renovacion Patriotica [*Honduras*] [*Political party*] (EY)
PRP............. Partido Republicano Portugues [*Portuguese Republican Party*] [*Political party*] (PPE)
PRP............. Partido Revolucionario Popular [*Popular Revolutionary Party*] [*Portugal Political party*] (PPE)
PRP............. Parti Republicain du Progres [*Republican Progress Party*] [*Central Africa*] [*Political party*] (PD)
PRP............. Parti Republicain Progressif [*Algeria*] [*Political party*] (EY)
PRP............. Peace Resource Project (EA)
PRP............. Peak Radiated Power (CET)
PRP............. People's Redemption Party [*Nigeria*] [*Political party*] (PPW)
PRP............. People's Reform Party [*Philippines*] [*Political party*] (EY)
PRP............. People's Revolutionary Party [*Benin*] [*Political party*]
PRP............. People's Revolutionary Party [*North Vietnam*] [*Political party*]
PRP............. Peptide Recognition Protein [*Biochemistry*]
PRP............. Performance-Related Pay (ECON)
PRP............. Performance, Requirements, Practices [*Military*]
PRP............. Personnel Reliability Program [*Air Force*]
PRP............. Phantom Range Pod (MCD)
PRP............. Phase Review Package (MCD)
PRP............. Physical Readiness Program [*Navy*] (DNAB)
PRP............. Physiologic Rest Position [*Medicine*] (DMAA)
PRP............. Pickup-Zone Release Point
PRP............. Pityriasis Rubra Pilaris [*Dermatology*] (MAE)
PRP............. Placement Route and Patch [*Computer science*] (IAA)
PRP............. Platelet-Rich Plasma [*Hematology*]
PRP............. Pneumatically-Released Pilot (DNAB)
PRP............. Polymer of Ribose Phosphate [*Organic chemistry*] (MAE)
PRP............. Polyribitol Phosphate [*Organic chemistry*]
PRP............. Position Report Printout
PRP............. Postbuckled Rectangular Plate
PRP............. Potentially Responsible Party [*Environmental Protection Agency*]
PRP............. Power-Deployed Reserve Parachute (MCD)
PRP............. Premature-Removal Period (MCD)
PRP............. Prepare (FAAC)
PRP............. Prerigor Pressurization [*Meat processing*]
PR P............ Present Participle (WGA)
PRP............. President's Reorganization Project [*Carter Administration*] [*Executive Office of the President*] (GFGA)
PRP............. Pressure Rate Product [*In treadmill test*]
PRP............. Primary Raynaud's Phenomenon [*Medicine*]
PRP............. Principal Responsible Party
PRP............. Print Out [*Computer science*] (IAA)
PrP.............. Prion Protein [*Biochemistry*]
PRP............. Problem Resolution Program [*IRS*]
PRP............. Procurement Requirements Package (MCD)
PRP............. Production Readiness Plan
PRP............. Production Requirements Plan
PRP............. Production Reserve Policy
PRP............. Profit-Related Pay [*Economics*]
PRP............. Program Random Process (PDAA)
PRP............. Program Requirements Package [*Computer science*]
PRP............. Program Review Panel [*Army*] (AABC)
PRP............. Progressive Rework Plan
PRP............. Progressive Rubella Panencephalitis [*Medicine*]
PRP............. Proliferative Retinopathy Photocoagulation
PRP............. Proliferin Related Protein [*Biochemistry*]
PRP............. Proline-Rich Protein [*Biochemistry*]
PRP............. Proper Return Port [*Shipping*]
PRP............. Prospective Reimbursement Plan [*Medicaid*]
PRP............. Protease-Resistant Prion [*Medicine*]
PrP.............. Protease-Resistant Protein [*Microbiology*]
PrP.............. Protein Phosphatase [*An enzyme*]
PRP............. Pseudorandom Pulse
PRP............. Psychotic Reaction Profile [*Psychology*]
PRP............. Public Relations Personnel [*Navy*]
PRP............. Pulse Recurrence [*or Repetition*] Period (CET)
PRP............. Pulse Repetition Frequency [*Medicine*] (DAVI)
PRP............. Pulse Repetition Period [*Computer science*] (IAA)
PRP............. Purchase Request Package [*Shipping*] (MCD)
PRP............. Purple (MSA)
PRP............. Purpose (MSA)
PRP............. Reformed Presbyterian Theological Seminary, Pittsburgh, PA [*OCLC symbol*] (OCLC)
PRPA........... Professional Race Pilots Association [*Later, USARA*] (EA)
PRPB........... Parti de la Revolution Populaire du Benin [*Benin People's Revolutionary Party*] [*Political party*] (PD)
PRPC........... Parti Republicain du Peuple Camerounais [*Political party*] (EY)
PRPC........... Public Relations Policy Committee [*NATO*] (NATG)
PrPCU-L...... Catholic University of Puerto Rico, Law Library, Ponce, Puerto Rico [*Library symbol*] [*Library of Congress*] (LCLS)
PRP-D......... Polyribosylribitol Phosphate-Diptheria Toxoid [*Medicine*]
PrpdLg......... Pre-Paid Legal Services, Inc. [*Associated Press*] (SAG)
PRPF........... Planar Radial Peaking Factor [*Network analysis*] (IEEE)
PRPG........... Proportioning
PRPH........... Peripherin (DMAA)
Pr/Ph.......... Pristane/Phytane Ratio [*Environmental science*]
PRPHL......... Peripheral
PRPL........... PACOM [*Pacific Command*] Reconnaissance Priority List (CINC)
PRPL........... People's Democratic Republic of Laos
PRPL........... Procurement Repair Parts List (AAG)
PRPLN......... Propulsion (MSA)
PRPLNT....... Propellant (KSC)
PRPLT......... Propellant (MSA)
PRPNE......... Propane [*Organic chemistry*]
PRPOOS...... Plankton Rate Processes in Oligotrophic Oceans [*Cooperative research project*]
PRPP........... Phosphoribosylpyrophosphate [*Biochemistry*]
PRPP........... Phosphorylribose Pyrophosphate [*Biochemistry*]
PRPP........... Pseudoresidual Plot Program
PRPQ........... Programming Request for Price Quotation [*Computer science*]
PR PR......... Praeter Propter [*About, Nearly*] [*Latin*] (ROG)
PRPRR........ Preparer
PRPS........... Pressure Rise per Stage (MCD)
PRPS........... Program Requirement Process Specification [*NASA*] (KSC)
PRPS........... Prostatic Secretory Protein (DMAA)
PRPSA......... Personal Report of Public Speaking Apprehension (EDAC)
PRPSD......... Proposed (MSA)
PRPSL......... Proposal (MSA)
PRPT........... Parti Revolutionnaire du Peuple Tunisien [*Revolutionary Party of the Tunisian People*] [*Political party*] (PD)
PRP-T......... Polyribosylribitol Phosphate Conjugated to Tetanus Toxoid [*Medicine*]
PRPT........... Prescriptive Reading Performance Test [*Educational test*]
PRPUC........ Philippine Republic Presidential Unit Citation [*Military decoration*]
PRPUCE...... Philippine Republic Presidential Unit Citation Emblem [*Military decoration*]
prpylm......... Propylaeum (VRA)
PRQ............ Houston, TX [*Location identifier FAA*] (FAAL)
PRQ............ Personal Resources Questionnaire (DMAA)
PRQ............ Presidente Roque Saenz Pena [*Argentina*] [*Airport symbol*] (AD)
PRQA.......... Passenger Ride Quality Apparatus [*Public transportation*]
PRR............ Partner Airlines [*Former USSR*] [*FAA designator*] (FAAC)
PRR............ Parts Replacement Request (KSC)
PRR............ Passenger Reservation Request (NVT)
PRR............ Passive Ranging RADAR
PRR............ Pawling Research Reactor
PRR............ Pennsylvania Railroad Co. [*AAR code Obsolete*]
PRR............ Performance-Related Remuneration (ADA)
PRR............ Perrine, FL [*Location identifier FAA*] (FAAL)
PRR............ Perris [*California*] [*Seismograph station code, US Geological Survey Closed*] (SEIS)
PRR............ Personnel Requirements Report [*Army*]
PRR............ Philippine Research Reactor (SAA)
PRR............ Placement Revision Request
PRR............ Planning Release Record (AAG)
PRR............ Plans and Requirements Review
PRR............ Political Risk Review [*A publication*] (EAAP)
Pr R............ Practice Reports [*Quebec*] [*A publication*] (DLA)
Pr R............ Practice Reports [*Ontario*] [*A publication*] (DLA)
PRR............ Prairie [*Commonly used*] (OPSA)
PRR............ Preliminary Requirements Review [*NASA*] (KSC)
PRR............ Premature Removal Rate
PRR............ Presbyterian and Reformed Renewal Ministries International [*Formerly, PCC*] (EA)
PRR............ Pressure Rise Rate [*Nuclear energy*] (NRCH)
PRR............ Primary Production Required [*Resource management*]
PRR............ Prism Resources Ltd. [*Vancouver Stock Exchange symbol*]
PRR............ Problem Reporting and Resolution
PRR............ Producer's Reliability Risk
PRR............ Production Readiness Review
PRR............ Production Research Reports
PRR............ Program Requirements Review [*NASA*] (NASA)
PRR............ Program Revision Report (KSC)
PRR............ Proline-Rich Protein [*Biochemistry*]
PRR............ Proton Relaxation Rate
PRR............ Pseudoresident Reader (MHDB)
PRR............ Publication Revision Request (AAG)
PRR............ Puerto Rico Reactor (NRCH)
PRR............ Puerto Rico Supreme Court Reports [*A publication*] (DLA)
PRR............ Pulse Recurrence [*or Repetition*] Rate (MUGU)
PrRA........... Academia Maria Reina, Rio Piedras, PR [*Library symbol Library of Congress*] (LCLS)
PRRA.......... Puerto Rico Reconstruction Administration [*Terminated, 1955*]
PrRadA........ Premiere Radio Networks, Inc. [*Associated Press*] (SAG)

PRR & Regs... Commonwealth of Puerto Rico Rules and Regulations [*A publication*] (DLA)
PRRB .... Provider Reimbursement Review Board [*Medicare*]
PRRC .... New Mexico Petroleum Recovery Research Center [*New Mexico Institute of Mining and Technology*] [*Research center*] (RCD)
PRRC .... Pitch/Roll Rate Changer Assembly (MCD)
PRRC .... Precision Response Corp. [*NASDAQ symbol*] (SAG)
PrRe .... Evangelical Seminary, Rio Piedras, PR [*Library symbol Library of Congress*] (LCLS)
PRRE .... Pupils Round, Regular, and Equal [*Medicine*] (MAE)
Pr Reg BC ... Practical Register in the Bail Court [*A publication*] (DLA)
Pr Reg Ch.... Practical Register in Chancery [*1 vol.*] [*A publication*] (DLA)
Pr Reg CP ... Practical Register in the Common Pleas [*1705-42*] [*A publication*] (DLA)
Pr Rep .... Practice Reports [*England*] [*A publication*] (DLA)
Pr Rep .... Practice Reports [*Ontario*] [*A publication*] (DLA)
Pr Rep BC ... Lowndes, Maxwell, and Pollock's English Bail Court Practice Reports [*1850-51*] [*A publication*] (DLA)
PRRFC .... Planar Randomly Reinforced Fiber Composite
PRRI .... Puerto Rico Rum Institute [*Later, PRRPA*]
PRRM .... Presbyterian and Reformed Renewal Ministries International (EA)
PRRM .... Program Review and Resources Management [*NASA*]
PRRM .... Pulse Repetition Rate Modulation [*Data transmission*] [*Computer science*] (TEL)
PRRPA........ Puerto Rico Rum Producers Association [*Defunct*] (EA)
PRRR.......... Pioneer Railcorp [*NASDAQ symbol*] (SAG)
PRRR.......... Pioneer Railcorp [*NASDAQ symbol*] (TTSB)
PRRS .... Positioning Reporting Recording System (RDA)
PRRS .... Problem Reporting and Resolution System [*Military*] (CAAL)
PR-RSV....... Rous Sarcoma Virus, Prague Strain
PRRWO....... Puerto Rican Revolutionary Workers Organization (NADA)
PRS .... Pacific Railroad Society (EA)
PRS .... Pacific Rocket Society (EA)
PRS .... Padre Resources [*Vancouver Stock Exchange symbol*]
PRS .... Paint Research Station [*British*] (BI)
PRS .... Pairs
PRS .... Paraiso [*California*] [*Seismograph station code, US Geological Survey*] (SEIS)
PRS .... Parametric Ruled Surface (MCD)
PRS .... Parasi [*Solomon Islands*] [*Airport symbol*] (OAG)
PRS .... Parliamentary Research Services [*British*]
PRS .... Pars Systems (CRS) [*ICAO designator*] (FAAC)
PRS .... Partei fuer Renten-, Steuer-, und Soziale Gerechtigkeit [*Party for Equitable Pensions, Taxation, and Social Services*] [*Germany Political party*] (PPW)
PR's........... Partial Responders [*to medication*]
PRS .... Partial Response Signalling (NITA)
PRS .... Parti de la Revolution Socialiste [*Party of Socialist Revolution*] [*Benin*] [*Political party*]
PRS .... Parti de la Revolution Socialiste [*Party of Socialist Revolution*] [*Senegal*] [*Political party*]
PRS .... Partido de la Revolucion Socialista [*Party of the Socialist Revolution*] [*Cuba*] [*Political party*]
PRS .... Partido para a Renovacao Social [*Party for Social Renovation*] [*Guinea-Bissau*] [*Political party*] (EY)
PRS .... Partido Revolucionario Socialista [*Mexico Political party*] (EY)
PRS .... Partito Republicano Sammarinese [*Republican Party*] [*San Marino*] [*Political party*] (EY)
PRS .... Passive RADAR Surveillance [*Military*] (CAAL)
PRS .... Pattern Recognition Society (EA)
PRS .... Pattern Recognition System
PRS .... Payload Retention Subsystem [*NASA*] (NASA)
PRS .... Pennsylvania-Reading Seashore Lines [*Absorbed into Consolidated Rail Corp.*]
PRS .... Perceptual Respresentation System [*Memory*]
PRS .... Performance Rating System (OICC)
PRS .... Performing Right Society [*British*]
PRS .... Personality Rating Scale [*Psychology*]
PRS .... Personal Recording System
PRS .... Personal Relations Survey [*Managerial skills test*]
PRS .... Personnel Readiness System [*Air Force*]
PRS .... Personnel Rescue Service [*NASA*] (NASA)
PRS .... Personnel Rescue System [*NASA*] (MCD)
PRS .... Personnel Research Section [*Army*]
PRS .... Personnel Research Staff [*Department of Agriculture*]
PRS .... Philatelic Research Society
PRS .... Philosophical Research Society (EA)
PRS .... Photographic Reconnaissance System
PRS .... Photo Resist Spinner
PRS .... Physically Restricted Status [*Military*]
PRS .... Pipe Roll Society (EA)
PRS .... Planar Rider System
PRS .... Planners Referral Service [*Information service or system*] (IID)
PRS .... Planning Record Sheet
PR's........... Planning References (AAG)
PRS .... Planning Research & Systems Ltd. [*British*]
PRS .... Plasma Renin Substrate [*Hematology*]
PRS .... Pneumatic Reading System
PRS .... Pointing Reference System (KSC)
PRS .... Population Research Service [*Information service or system*] (IID)
PRS .... Positive Rolandic Spikes [*Neurology*] (DAVI)
PRS .... Power Reactant Subsystem [*NASA*] (NASA)
PRS .... Power Relay Satellite
PRS .... Prayers (ROG)
PRS .... Precipitate Reduction Sinter [*Metal*] (DICI)
PRS .... Precision Ranging System
PRS .... Precision Rotary Stripper
PRS .... Present (WGA)
PRS .... President of the Royal Society [*British*]
PRS .... Presidio Oil Co. [*AMEX symbol*] (SPSG)
PRS .... Presidio, TX [*Location identifier FAA*] (FAAL)
PRS .... Press (MSA)
PRS .... Press
PRS .... Pressure Reducing Station
PRS .... Pressure Response Spectrum [*Nuclear energy*] (NRCH)
PR/S .... Prestrike (SAA)
PRS .... Primary Recovery Ship [*NASA*]
PRS .... Primary Recovery Site [*NASA*] (KSC)
PRS .... Primary Representational System (EDAC)
PRS .... Primary Rescue Site [*NASA*] (NASA)
PRS .... Procedure Review Section [*Social Security Administration*]
PRS .... Process Radiation Sampler [*Nuclear energy*] (NRCH)
PRS .... Production Recording System
PRS .... Production Release System (MCD)
PRS .... Product Requirement Schedule (MCD)
PRS .... Programmed RADAR Simulator (IAA)
PRS .... Program Rating Summary Report [*Television ratings*] (NTCM)
PRS .... Program Requirements Summary (MUGU)
PRS .... Property Recovery Section
PRS .... Propodial Sinus [*Zoology*]
PRS .... Prospective Reimbursement System [*Health insurance*] (GHCT)
PRS .... Prospectors Air [*Vancouver Stock Exchange symbol*]
PRS .... Protestant Reformation Society (EA)
PRS .... Provide Repair Service [*Navy*] (NVT)
PRS .... Provisioning Requirements Statement
PRS .... Pseudorandom Sequence
PRS .... Psycholinguistic Rating Scale
PRS .... Public Relations Section [*Library Administration and Management Association*]
PRS .... Puerto Lempira [*Honduras*] [*Airport symbol*] (AD)
PRS .... Pure Random Search [*Optimization method*]
PRSA .... Pan-Rhodian Society of America (EA)
PRSA .... Power Reactant Storage Assembly [*NASA*] (MCD)
PRSA .... President of the Royal Scottish Academy
PRSA .... Proportional Representation Society of Australia
PRSA .... Public Relations Society of America (EA)
PRSA .... Puerto Rico Statehood Commission (EA)
PrSaC .... Colegio Universitario del Sagrado Corazon [*College of the Sacred Heart*], Santurce, PR [*Library symbol Library of Congress*] (LCLS)
PRSC .... Plutonium Rework Sample Cell [*Nuclear energy*] (NRCH)
PRSC .... Puerto Rico Solidarity Committee (EA)
PRSCHL....... Preschool
PRSCR......... Puerto Rico Supreme Court Reports [*A publication*] (DLA)
PRSD .... Portable Rectilinear Scanning Device
PRSD .... Power Reactant Storage [*or Supply*] and Distribution [*NASA*] (NASA)
PRSD .... Pressed (AAG)
PRSDS......... Power Reactant Storage and Distribution System (MCD)
PrSE........... El Mundo Publishing Co., San Juan, PR [*Library symbol Library of Congress*] (LCLS)
PRSE .... President of the Royal Society of Edinburgh
PRSEC .... Payroll Section
Prsfdr......... Pressfeeder [*Printing*]
PRSG .... Personal Radio Steering Group [*Ann Arbor, MI*] [*Telecommunications service*] (TSSD)
PRSG .... Pressing
PRSG .... Pulse-Rebalanced Strapdown Gyro (MCD)
PRSH .... President of the Royal Society for the Promotion of Health [*British*]
PRSIS .... Prospective Rate Setting Information System [*Medicine*] (DMAA)
PRSL .... Pennsylvania-Reading Seashore Lines [*Absorbed into Consolidated Rail Corp.*] [*AAR code*]
PRSM .... Prism Group [*NASDAQ symbol*] (SAG)
PR/SM .... Processor Resource/Systems Manager [*Computer science*] (CDE)
prsmc .... Prismacolor (VRA)
PRSMC......... Prism Group [*NASDAQ symbol*] (TTSB)
PRSMN......... Pressman (AABC)
PRSN .... Provisional Relative Sunspot Number [*NASA*]
PRSNG......... Pressing
PRSNL......... Personal
PRSNNL....... Personnel
PRSNT......... Present [*NWS*] (FAAC)
PRSP .... Penicillin-Resistant S. Pneumoniae [*Clinical chemistry*]
PRSP .... Puerto Rico Socialist Party (NADA)
PRSPL .... Planning and Role Setting for Public Libraries [*Public Library Association*] [*A publication*]
PRSR .... Presser (MSA)
PR/SR .... Price Redetermination/Service Reallocation (AAGC)
PRSRV .... Preservative (AAG)
PRSRZ .... Pressurize (MSA)
PRSS .... Pennsylvania-Reading Seashore Lines [*Absorbed into Consolidated Rail Corp.*]
PRSS .... Problem Report Squawk Sheet [*NASA*] (NASA)
PRSSA......... Public Relations Student Society of America (EA)
PRSSA......... Puerto Rico Mainland US Statehood Students Association (EA)
PRSSD......... Pressed
PRST .... Persist (FAAC)
PRST .... Presstek, Inc. [*NASDAQ symbol*] (NQ)
PRST .... Priest
PRST .... Probability Reliability Sequential Tests (MCD)
Pr Stat........ Private Statutes [*Legal term*] (DLA)

PRSTC .... Prosthetic
PRSTG .... Prestige
PRSU .... Police Requirements Support Unit [*Home Office*] [*British*]
PRSV .... Papaya Ringspot Virus [*Plant pathology*]
PRSV .... Preserving
PRSVN .... Preservation (AABC)
PRSW .... President of the Royal Scottish Water Colour Society
PRSW .... Pure Software [*NASDAQ symbol*] (TTSB)
PRSW .... Pure Software, Inc. [*NASDAQ symbol*] (SAG)
PrSW .... World University, San Juan, PR [*Library symbol Library of Congress*] (LCLS)
PrSW-I .... World University, International Institute of the Americas, Barbosa Esq. Guayama,San Juan, PR [*Library symbol Library of Congress*] (LCLS)
PRT .... Air Cargo Carriers, Inc. [*ICAO designator*] (FAAC)
PRT .... Parachute Radio Transmitter [*Telecommunications*] (IAA)
PRT .... Parliamentary Remuneration Tribunal [*New South Wales, Australia*]
PRT .... Parr Terminal Railroad [*AAR code*]
PRT .... Part (AAG)
PRT .... Participating Research Teams [*Department of Energy*]
PRT .... Partido Revolucionario de los Trabajadores [*Workers' Revolutionary Party*] [*Argentina Political party*] (PD)
PRT .... Partido Revolucionario de los Trabajadores [*Workers' Revolutionary Party*] [*Uruguay*] [*Political party*] (PD)
PRT .... Partido Revolucionario de los Trabajadores [*Workers' Revolutionary Party*] [*Peru*] [*Political party*] (PPW)
PRT .... Partido Revolucionario de los Trabajadores [*Revolutionary Workers' Party*] [*Costa Rica*] [*Political party*] (EY)
PRT .... Partido Revolucionario de Trabajadores [*Revolutionary Worker's Party*] [*Colorado Political party*] (EY)
PRT .... Passage Reading Test [*Education*] (EDAC)
PRT .... Patient Review Tribunal [*Queensland, Australia*]
PRT .... Patten Recognition Technology (NITA)
PRT .... Pattern Recognition Technique
PRT .... Payroll Tax (ADA)
PRT .... Periodic Reevaluation Tests
PRT .... Permanent Recording Traffic [*Telecommunications*] (IAA)
PRT .... Personal Rapid Transit [*Computer-guided transit system*]
PRT .... Personnel Research Test [*Military*]
PRT .... Petroleum Revenue Tax [*British*]
PRT .... Pharmaceutical Research and Testing [*Public Health Service*] (GRD)
PRT .... Philadelphia Reading Test [*Education*]
PRT .... Phosphoribosyltransferase [*Also, PRTase*] [*An enzyme*]
PRT .... Photoradiation Therapy [*Oncology*]
PRT .... Physical Readiness Training [*Army*] (INF)
PRT .... Pictorial Reasoning Test [*Job screening test*]
PRT .... Platinum Resistance Thermometer
PRT .... Point Retreat, AK [*Location identifier FAA*] (FAAL)
PRT .... Port
PRT .... Port
PRT .... Portable Radiation Thermometer
PRT .... Portable Radio Telephone
PRT .... Portable Remote Terminal
PRT .... Portable Router Template (MCD)
PRT .... Portable Router Tool
PRT .... Portland [*Diocesan abbreviation*] [*Maine*] (TOCD)
PRT .... Portugal [*ANSI three-letter standard code*] (CNC)
PRT .... Power Recovery Turbine
PRT .... Prato [*Italy*] [*Seismograph station code, US Geological Survey*] (SEIS)
PRT .... Precision Radiation Thermometer
PRT .... Preliminary Reference Trajectory [*NASA*] (KSC)
PRT .... Pressurized Relief Tank (NRCH)
PRT .... Primary Ranging Test (OA)
PRT .... Print
PRT .... Printer [*Computer science*] (MDG)
prt .... Printer [*MARC relator code*] [*Library of Congress*] (LCCP)
Prt .... Private [*British military*] (DMA)
PRT .... Problem Resolution Tasking System [*Army*] (INF)
PRT .... Procurement Review Team
PRT .... Procurement Round Table (EA)
PRT .... Production Reliability Test
PRT .... Production Run Tape
PRT .... Product Range Testing [*Business term*]
PRT .... Program Reference Table
PRT .... Program Review Team [*Navy*] (DNAB)
PRT .... Promotion, Transfer, and Redundancy [*Railway union agreement*] [*British*] (ECON)
PRT .... Prompt Air, Inc. [*FAA designator*] (FAAC)
PRT .... Prompt Relief Trip [*Nuclear energy*] (NRCH)
Prt .... Protagoras [*of Plato*] [*Classical studies*] (OCD)
PRT .... Prova di Restituzione Termica [*Italy*] [*Medicine*]
PRT .... Provost
PRT .... Psychiatric Rehabilitation Team (EA)
PRT .... Publications Requirements Tables (AAG)
PRT .... Pulsed RADAR Transmitter
prt .... Pulse Frequency (IDOE)
PRT .... Pulse Recurrence [*or Repetition*] Time (CET)
PRTase .... Phosphoribosyltransferase [*Medicine*] (MEDA)
PRTB .... Partido Revolucionario de Trabajadores Bolivianos [*Bolivian Workers' Revolutionary Party*] [*Political party*] (PD)
PRTBR .... Partido Revolucionario de los Trabajadores de Bolivia Romero [*Bolivia*] [*Political party*] (PPW)
PRTC .... Partido Revolucionario de los Trabajadores Centroamericanos [*Revolutionary Party of Central American Workers*] [*El Salvador*] [*Political party*] (PD)
PRTC .... Pediatric Research and Training Center [*University of Connecticut*] [*Research center*] (RCD)
PRTC .... Ports Canada
PRTC .... Professional Rate Training Course (DNAB)
PRTCD .... Puerto Rico Tax Court Decisions [*A publication*] (DLA)
PRTC-H .... Partido Revolucionario de los Trabajadores Centroamericanos - Seccion de Hondur as [*Revolutionary Party of Central American Workers - Honduras*] [*Political party*]
PRTCTV .... Protective
PRTD .... Portland Traction Co. [*AAR code*]
PRTD .... Printed (DGA)
prtd .... Printed (VRA)
PRTF .... Pheromone and Receptor Transcription Factor [*Genetics*]
PRTF .... Psychiatric Review Technique Form [*Social Security Administration*]
PRTG .... Printing (AFM)
PRTH .... Pituitary Resistance to Thyroid Hormone [*Medicine*] (DMAA)
PRTH .... Prothrombin Time [*Hematology*] (DAVI)
PRTH-C .... Prothrombin Time Control [*Hematology*] (DAVI)
PRTHS .... Pennsylvania Railroad Technical and Historical Society (EA)
PRTI .... Physical and Recreational Training Instructor [*British military*] (DMA)
PRTKT .... Parts Kit
PRTL .... Portable (DNAB)
PRTL .... Primus Telecommunications Group, Inc. [*NASDAQ symbol*] (SAG)
PRTLS .... Powered Return to Launch Site [*NASA*] (MCD)
PRTLY .... Partially
PRTM .... Printing Response-Time Monitor
PrtMcled ...... Porter McLeod National Retail [*Associated Press*] (SAG)
PRTN .... Partition
PRTN .... Proteinase (DMAA)
PRTNR .... Partner
PRTNRSHP ... Partnership
PRTO .... Preservation Research and Testing Office [*Library of Congress*] (EA)
PRTOT .... Prototype Real-Time Optical Tracker [*Computer science*]
PRTP .... Prototype (IAA)
PRTQ .... Peer Role-Taking Questionnaire [*Psychology*] (EDAC)
PRTR .... Plutonium Recycle Test Reactor [*Nuclear energy*]
PRTR .... Porter
PRTR .... Printer
PRTR .... Printer [*Navy*] (DGA)
Prt Rep .... Practice Reports [*A publication*] (DLA)
PRTRL .... Printer, Lithographer [*Navy*]
PRTRM .... Printer, Offset Process [*Navy*]
PRTRNS .... Programmable Transformer Converter (MCD)
Prtronx .... Printronix, Inc. [*Associated Press*] (SAG)
PRTS .... Personal Rapid Transit System [*Computer-guided transit system*]
PRTS .... Ports
PRTS .... Ports [*Postal Service standard*] (OPSA)
PRTS .... Pretoria Theological Series [*A publication*] (BJA)
PrtSc .... Print Screen [*Computer keyboard*]
PRTSTNT ...... Protestant
PRTV .... Positive Response Television [*NASDAQ symbol*] (SAG)
Prtw .... Propeller Twist [*Genetics*]
PRTY .... Priority
PrtyCty .... Party City Corp. [*Associated Press*] (SAG)
PRU .... Packet Radio Unit
PRU .... Paranagua [*Brazil*] [*Airport symbol*] (AD)
PRU .... Peripheral Resistance Unit [*Medicine*]
PRU .... Photographic Reconnaissance Unit [*Aircraft*] [*Marine Corps*]
PRU .... Physical Record Unit (NITA)
PRU .... Physical Research Unit (IAA)
PRU .... Pneumatic Regulation Unit (AAG)
PRU .... Polarity Reversal Unit [*Electrochemistry*]
PRU .... Polish-Russian Union (NADA)
PRU .... Primary Replacement Unit
PRU .... Prisoner's Rights Union (EA)
PRU .... Programs Research Unit (KSC)
PRU .... Prome [*Myanmar*] [*Airport symbol*] (OAG)
PRU .... Provincial Reconnaissance Unit [*Military*]
PRU .... Prudential Property & Casualty Insurance Co., Holmdel, NJ [*OCLC symbol*] (OCLC)
PRU .... Pruhonice [*Czechoslovakia*] [*Seismograph station code, US Geological Survey*] (SEIS)
PrU .... University of Puerto Rico, Rio Piedras, PR [*Library symbol Library of Congress*] (LCLS)
PRUAA .... President of the Royal Ulster Academy of Arts
PRUC .... Partido Revolucionario de Union Civico [*Revolutionary Party for Civic Union*] [*Costa Rica*] [*Political party*]
PRUC .... Practice Reports [*1848-1900*] [*Upper Canada*] [*A publication*] (DLA)
PRUD .... Partido Revolucionario de Unification Democratica [*Revolutionary Party of Democratic Unification*] [*El Salvador*]
PrudRe .... Prudential Reinsurance Holdings, Inc. [*Associated Press*] (SAG)
PrU-H .... University of Puerto Rico, Humacao Regional College, Humacao, PR [*Library symbol Library of Congress*] (LCLS)
PrU-L .... University of Puerto Rico, Law Library, San Juan, PR [*Library symbol Library of Congress*] (LCLS)
PrU-M .... University of Puerto Rico, School of Medicine, San Juan, PR [*Library symbol Library of Congress*] (LCLS)
PrU-MA .... University of Puerto Rico, Mayaguez Campus, Mayaguez, Puerto Rico [*Library symbol Library of Congress*] (LCLS)
PrU-MS .... University of Puerto Rico, Department of Marine Sciences, Mayaguez, PR [*Library symbol Library of Congress*] (LCLS)
PRUNIT .... Photo Roentgen Unit (IAA)

PrU-NS .... University of Puerto Rico, Natural Science Library, Rio Piedras, PR [*Library symbol Library of Congress*] (LCLS)
PRUS .... Prussia [*Obsolete*]
Prus .... Prussian [*Philately*]
PRUSAF ...... Puerto Rico, USA Foundation (EA)
PRV .... Papaya Ringspot Virus
PRV .... Parsley Rhabdovirus [*Plant pathology*]
PRV .... Peak Rated Voltage (IAA)
PRV .... Peak Reserve Voltage (IAA)
PRV .... Peak Reverse Voltage
PRV .... Pearl River Valley Railroad Co. [*AAR code*]
PRV .... Peugeot Renault Volvo [*Automobile joint project partners*]
PRV .... Polycythemia Rubra Vera [*Medicine*]
PRV .... Porvoo [*Finland*] [*Seismograph station code, US Geological Survey Closed*] (SEIS)
PRV .... Pour Rendre Visite [*To Make a Call*] [*French*]
PRV .... Pressure Reducing [*or Regulation or Relief*] Valve
PRV .... Princess Ventures [*Vancouver Stock Exchange symbol*]
PRV .... Prior Record Variable [*Criminal sentencing*]
prv .... Private (VRA)
PRV .... Propeller Revolution
Prv .... Proverbs [*Old Testament book*]
PRV .... Provincial
PRV .... Provincial Express, Inc. [*Canada ICAO designator*] (FAAC)
PRV .... Provisional Reconnaissance Unit
PRV .... Pseudorabies Virus
PRV .... Pseudorelative Velocity
Prv .... Pyruvenol [*Biochemistry*]
PrvAm .... Provident American Corp. [*Associated Press*] (SAG)
PrvBksh .... Provident Bankshares Corp. [*Associated Press*] (SAG)
prv coll .... Private Collection (VRA)
PRVD .... Procurement [*or Purchase*] Request for Vendor Data (AAG)
PRVDNC ...... Providence
Prvena .... Provena Foods, Inc. [*Associated Press*] (SAG)
PrvEng .... Providence Energy Corp. [*Associated Press*] (SAG)
PRVEP .... Pattern Reversal Visual Evoked Potential
PrvLf .... Provident Life & Accident Insurance Co. of America [*Associated Press*] (SAG)
PrvLLC .... Providian LLC, Inc. [*Associated Press*] (SAG)
PRVNTN ...... Prevention
PRVNTV ...... Preventive
PRVS .... Penetration Room Ventilation System [*Nuclear energy*] (IEEE)
PRVT .... Production Readiness Verification Testing (MCD)
PRVT .... Product Reliability Validation Test (MCD)
PRVW .... Preview (MSA)
PrvWor .... Providence & Worcester Railroad Co. [*Associated Press*] (SAG)
PrvWor .... Providence Worcester Railroad Co. [*Associated Press*] (SAG)
PRW .... Paired Wire [*Telecommunications*] (TEL)
PRW .... Percent Rated Wattage
PRW .... Polymerized Ragweed [*Immunology*]
PRW .... Press Relations Wire [*Commercial firm*] (EA)
PRW .... Promark Software [*Vancouver Stock Exchange symbol*]
PRW .... Prosser [*Washington*] [*Seismograph station code, US Geological Survey*] (SEIS)
PRW .... Quebecor Printing [*NYSE symbol*] (TTSB)
PRW .... Quebecor Printing, Inc. [*NYSE symbol*] (SAG)
PRW .... World University, San Juan, PR [*OCLC symbol*] (OCLC)
PRWAD .... Professional Rehabilitation Workers with the Adult Deaf [*Later, ADARA*] (EA)
PRWD .... Priority Regular World Day
PRWI .... Prince William Forest Park [*National Park Service designation*]
PRWO .... Puerto Rican Revolutionary Workers Organization
PRWP .... Poor R-Wave Progression [*On electrocardiogram*] [*Cardiology*] (DAVI)
PRWRA .... Puerto Rican Water Resources Authority
PRWS .... President of the Royal Society of Painters in Water Colours [*British*]
PRWV .... Peak Reserve Working Voltage
PRX .... Paris [*Texas*] [*Airport symbol*] (OAG)
PRX .... Paris, TX [*Location identifier FAA*] (FAAL)
PRX .... Pharmaceutical Resources [*NYSE symbol*] (SPSG)
PRX .... Pressure Regulation Exhaust
PRX .... Pseudoexfoliation (DMAA)
PRXI .... PRX [*Public Relations Exchange*] International (EA)
PRXL .... Parexel International Corp. [*NASDAQ symbol*] (SAG)
PRXL .... PAREXEL Intl [*NASDAQ symbol*] (TTSB)
PRXM .... Proxima Corp. [*NASDAQ symbol*] (SAG)
PRY .... Paraguay [*ANSI three-letter standard code*] (CNC)
PRY .... Parys [*South Africa*] [*Seismograph station code, US Geological Survey*] (SEIS)
PRY .... Pittway Corp. [*AMEX symbol*] (SPSG)
PRY.A .... Pittway Corp.'A' [*AMEX symbol*] (TTSB)
P Ryl .... Catalogue of the Greek Papyri in the John Rylands Library at Manchester [*A publication*] (OCD)
PRZ .... Portales, NM [*Location identifier FAA*] (FAAL)
PRZ .... Potential Repository Zone [*Nuclear waste storage*]
PRZ .... Prism Entertainment [*AMEX symbol*] (TTSB)
PRZ .... Prism Entertainment Corp. [*AMEX symbol*] (SPSG)
PRZ .... Przhevalsk [*Former USSR Seismograph station code, US Geological Survey*] (SEIS)
PRZF .... Pyrazofurin [*Antineoplastic drug*]
PRZF .... Pyrazofurin [*Antineoplastic drug regimen*] (DAVI)
PRZM .... Prism Solutions [*NASDAQ symbol*] (TTSB)
PRZM .... Prism Solutions [*NASDAQ symbol*] (SAG)
PS .... Abbott Laboratories [*Research code symbol*]
PS .... American Political Science Association. Quarterly [*A publication*]
PS .... Chloropicrin [*Poison gas*] [*Army symbol*]
PS .... Elementary and Early Childhood Education [*Educational Resources Information Center (ERIC) Clearinghouse*] [*University of Illinois*] (PAZ)
PS .... Pace Setter (MHDI)
PS .... Pacific Southwest Airlines [*ICAO designator*] (OAG)
PS .... Pacific Star Communication [*Vancouver Stock Exchange symbol*]
P(S) .... Packet (Send)
PS .... Packet Switching [*Telecommunications*]
PS .... Packet Switch Stream [*British*] [*Computer science*] (TNIG)
PS .... Packing Sheet (MCD)
PS .... Paddle Steamer (ADA)
PS .... Paediatric Surgery
PS .... Painting System
PS .... Pakistan Standard (IAA)
PS .... Paleontological Society (EA)
PS .... Palm Society [*Later, IPS*] (EA)
PS .... Pan Salicornia Zone [*Ecology*]
PS .... Parachute Subsystem [*NASA*] (NASA)
PS .... Paradoxical Sleep
PS .... Parallel Single [*Outdoor advertising*] (NTCM)
PS .... Parallel to Serial (NITA)
P/S .... Parallel to Serial Converter (MCD)
PS .... Paramagnetic Scheromak
PS .... Parents of Suicides (EA)
PS .... Parents' Section of the Alexander Graham Bell Association for the Deaf (EA)
PS .... Parity Switch
PS .... Parliamentary Secretary [*British*]
PS .... Parlor Snake [*Slang for "to escort visitors around post"*]
PS .... Parochial School
PS .... Parrot Society (EA)
ps .... PARSEC [*Parallax Second*] [*See PARSEC*]
PS .... Par Selling (MHDB)
PS .... Partially Sighted (AIE)
PS .... Partially Smutted [*Plant pathology*]
PS .... Partially Synergistic [*Pharmacology*]
PS .... Partido Socialista [*Socialist Party*] [*Uruguay*] [*Political party*]
PS .... Partido Socialista [*Socialist Party*] [*Chile*] [*Political party*]
PS .... Partido Socialista Portuguesa [*Portuguese Socialist Party*] [*Political party*] (PPE)
PS .... Partido Socialista - Uno [*Socialist Party - One*] [*Also, PS-1 Bolivia*] [*Political party*] (PPW)
PS .... Parti Socialiste [*Socialist Party*] [*Belgium Political party*] (PPW)
PS .... Parti Socialiste - Federation de la Reunion [*Reunion Federation of the Socialist Party*] [*Political party*] (PPW)
PS .... Parts Shipper
PS .... Part Surface (IAA)
PS .... Passed School of Instruction [*of Officers*] [*British*]
PS .... Passenger Service
PS .... Passenger Steamer
PS .... Passing Scuttle
ps .... Pastel (VRA)
PS .... Pastel Society [*British*]
PS .... Pathological (Surgical) Staging [*For Hodgkin's Disease*]
PS .... Pathologic Stage
PS .... Patient's Serum [*Medicine*]
PS .... Patrologia Syriaca (BJA)
PS .... Patrol Service [*British military*] (DMA)
PS .... Patrol Ship (CINC)
PS .... Patton Society (EA)
P/S .... Pause/Still [*Video technology*]
PS .... Payload Shroud (MCD)
PS .... Payload Specialist [*NASA*] (MCD)
PS .... Payload Station [*NASA*] (MCD)
PS .... Payload Support [*NASA*] (NASA)
PS .... Paymaster Sergeant
PS .... Pedal Sinus
PS .... Pediatric Surgery (DAVI)
PS .... Pellet Size
PS .... Penal Servitude
PS .... Penny Stock [*Investment term*]
PS .... Peperomia Society [*Later, PEPS*] (EA)
PS .... Perception Schedule
PS .... Perceptual Speed (Test) [*Psychology*]
PS .... Perfect Shuffle (MHDI)
PS .... Performance Score
PS .... Performance Standard
PS .... Performance Status [*Rehabilitation*] (DAVI)
PS .... Performing Scale [*Medicine*] (MAE)
PS .... Perimeter Surveillance (LAIN)
PS .... Periodic Syndrome [*Medicine*]
PS .... Peripheral Shock [*Psychology*]
PS .... Permanent Secretary
PS .... Permanent Signal [*Telecommunications*] (TEL)
PS .... Per Second (AAMN)
PS .... Per Ship
PS .... Personal Secretary (DCTA)
PS .... Personal Skills
PS .... Personal Survival
PS .... Personal System [*IBM computer introduced in 1987*]
PS .... Personnel Subsystem [*Army*]
PS .... Per Speculum [*Medicine*]
PS .... Peru Solidarity [*An association*] (EA)
Ps .... Peseta [*Monetary unit*] [*Andorra and Spain*] (BARN)

PS.............. Pet Switchboard [*Defunct*] (EA)
PS.............. Petty Sessions (DLA)
PS.............. Pharmaceutical Society (NADA)
P/S.............. Phaser/Subarray
PS.............. Phase Separation
PS.............. Phase-Shift
PS.............. Phasing System [*Telecommunications*] (OA)
PS.............. Phenix Society (EA)
PS.............. Phenomenally Speedy Ordinary [*Photographic plates*] (ROG)
PS.............. Philalethes Society (EA)
PS.............. Phillnathean Society (EA)
PS.............. Philolexian Society (EA)
PS.............. Philological Society (EAIO)
PS.............. Philomathean Society (EA)
PS.............. Phosphate-Saline [*A buffer*] [*Cell culture*]
PS.............. Phosphatidylserine [*Biochemistry*]
PS.............. Photochemical System
PS.............. Photoemission Scintillation (MCD)
PS.............. Photographic Service
PS.............. Photographic Squadron
PS.............. Photometer System (KSC)
PS.............. Photosystems
PS.............. Phrase Structure (WGA)
PS.............. Phylaxis Society (EA)
PS.............. Physical Sciences
PS.............. Physical Security
PS.............. Physical Sequential (HGAA)
PS.............. Physical Status [*Medicine*]
PS.............. Picket Ships [*Navy*]
ps.............. Picosecond [*One trillionth of a second*]
PS.............. Pilgrim Power Station (NRCH)
PS.............. Pilgrim Society (EA)
PS.............. Pineal Stalk [*Neuroanatomy*]
PS.............. Pine Bark Mixed with Clay Loam Soil
PS.............. Pine Siskin [*Ornithology*]
PS.............. Pink Sheet [*Investment term*]
PS.............. Pipe Size (BARN)
PS.............. Pirandello Society (EA)
PS.............. Pisosecond (IAA)
PS.............. Pistol Sharpshooter [*Army*]
PS.............. Pitot/Static Tube (MCD)
PS.............. [*The*] Pittsburg & Shawmut Railroad Co. [*AAR code*]
PS.............. Pituitary Stalk [*Neuroanatomy*]
PS.............. Planetary Society (EA)
PS.............. Planetary Surface (IAA)
PS.............. Planning and Scheduling
PS.............. Planning Study (AAG)
PS.............. Plant Stress [*Horticulture*]
PS.............. Plastic Surgery [*Medicine*]
PS.............. Plate Sunk [*Printing*] (DGA)
PS.............. Platform (Sided) (DCTA)
P/S.............. Platoon/Section [*Army*]
PS.............. Plea Side (ROG)
PS.............. Pleural Sclerite [*Entomology*]
PS.............. Plotting System
PS.............. Plus
PS.............. Pneumatic Suspension [*Automotive engineering*]
PS.............. Pneumatic System
PS.............. Poetry Society [*British*]
P/S.............. Point of Shipment
PS.............. Point of Switch
PS.............. Point of Symmetry
PS.............. Point Sparger [*Engineering*]
PS.............. Point Spread [*In visual cortex*]
PS.............. Polanyi Society (EA)
PS.............. Polaris Standard [*Missiles*]
PS.............. Polarity Scale [*Psychology*]
PS.............. Polarity Selector (IAA)
PS.............. Police Sergeant [*Scotland Yard*]
PS.............. Policy Statement
PS.............. Polio Society (EA)
Ps.............. Polyporus sulphureus [*A fungus*]
PS.............. Polystyrene [*Organic chemistry*]
PS.............. Polysulfone [*Also, PSO*] [*Organic chemistry*]
P/S.............. Polyunsaturated/Saturated [*Fatty acid ratio*]
PS.............. Population Sample (MAE)
PS.............. Porlock Society (EA)
PS.............. Porous Silicon [*Physics*]
PS.............. Porter-Silber Chromogen [*Medicine*] (MAE)
P/S.............. Port or Starboard
PS.............. Port Security
PS.............. Port Store [*Telecommunications*] (TEL)
PS.............. Port Strobe [*Telecommunications*] (TEL)
PS.............. Pos-Escrito [*Postscript*] [*Portuguese*]
PS.............. Position-Specific Antigen
PS.............. Positive Value (DA)
PS.............. Postal Satsang [*An association*] (EA)
PS.............. Postal Service [*US*]
PS.............. Poster Society (EA)
PS.............. PostScript [*Adobe printer language*]
ps.............. PostScript [*Computer science*]
PS.............. Post Scriptum [*Written Afterwards, Postscript*] [*Latin*]
PS.............. Potassium Sorbate [*Food additive*]
PS.............. Potentiometer Synchro
P/S.............. Power Section (NG)
PS.............. Power Series (IAA)
PS.............. Power Source
PS.............. Power-Specific (MCD)
PS.............. Power Spectra [*Neurophysiology*]
PS.............. Power Station (MCD)
PS.............. Power Steering [*Automobile ads*]
PS.............. Power Supply
PS.............. Powys Society (EA)
PS.............. Prairie Schooner [*A publication*] (BRI)
PS.............. Prairies Service [*Record series prefix*] [*Canada*]
PS.............. Predictive Saccades [*Ophthalmology*]
PS.............. Preduzece Soko [*Former Yugoslavia*] [*ICAO aircraft manufacturer identifier*] (ICAO)
PS.............. Preferred Stock [*Investment term*]
PS.............. Prehistoric Society (EA)
PS.............. Preliminary Study
PS.............. Preparedness Staff [*Environmental Protection Agency*] (GFGA)
Ps.............. Prescription (AAMN)
PS.............. Presentation Services [*Computer science*] (IBMDP)
PS.............. Press Secretary (ILCA)
PS.............. Press to Start (KSC)
PS.............. Pressure [*or Propellant*] Seal
P-S.............. Pressure-Sensitive
PS.............. Pressure Sensor
PS.............. Pressure Switch
Ps.............. Pressure, Systolic [*Cardiology*]
PS.............. Price Spreading [*Business term*]
PS.............. Primary School (ADA)
PS.............. Prime Select (MCD)
PS.............. Prime Sponsor
PS.............. Principal Sojourner [*Freemasonry*] (ROG)
PS.............. Principal Subject [*In a sonata or rondo*] [*Music*] (ROG)
PS.............. Print Scan [*Computer science*] (IAA)
PS.............. Prior Service [*Military*]
PS.............. Private Screenings [*Cable TV programming service*]
PS.............. Private Secretary
PS.............. Private Security Program [*Association of Independent Colleges and Schools specialization code*]
PS.............. Private Siding [*Rail*] [*Shipping*] (DS)
PS.............. Privy Seal [*British*]
PS.............. Probability of Survival (MCD)
PS.............. Problem Specification
PS.............. Problem Statement [*Computer science*] (IAA)
PS.............. Procambial Strand [*Botany*]
PS.............. Processor Status
PS.............. Process Sheet
PS.............. Process Solution (MCD)
PS.............. Process Specification
PS.............. Process Storage [*Computer science*] (IAA)
PS.............. Process Subsystem [*Telecommunications*] (TEL)
PS.............. Procurement Specification (MCD)
PS.............. Product Service (IAA)
PS.............. Product Software (MCD)
PS.............. Product Standards (MCD)
PS.............. Product Support
PS.............. Profit Sharing [*Business term*]
PS.............. Programmable Switch [*Computer science*] (IAA)
PS.............. Programmed Symbols (MEDA)
PS.............. Programming System
PS.............. Program Section [*Computer science*] (IAA)
PS.............. Program Simulation (OICC)
PS.............. Program Source [*Computer science*] (IAA)
PS.............. Program Specification (MCD)
PS.............. Program Start (KSC)
PS.............. Program Stateword [*Computer science*] (IAA)
PS.............. Program Status [*Computer science*] (IAA)
PS.............. Program Store [*Computer science*] (IEEE)
PS.............. Program Summary (NG)
PS.............. Project Slip
PS.............. Project Start [*Milestone chart*]
PS.............. Project Stock [*Military*] (AABC)
PS.............. Project Study [*British military*] (DMA)
PS.............. Proler International Corp. [*NYSE symbol*] (SPSG)
PS.............. Proler Intl [*NYSE symbol*] (TTSB)
PS.............. Prolifers for Survival [*Defunct*] (EA)
PS.............. Prometheus Society (EA)
PS.............. Prompt Side [*of a stage*] [*i.e., the right side A stage direction*]
PS.............. Proof Shot [*Ammunition*]
PS.............. Proof Stress
PS.............. Propellant Supply (KSC)
PS.............. Propellant System
PS.............. Proportional Spacing [*Typography*] (WDMC)
PS.............. Propulsion Section
PS.............. Prostaglandin Synthetase [*An enzyme*]
PS.............. Protective Service
PS.............. Protective Shelter
PS.............. Protective Subsystem [*Military*] (INF)
PS.............. Protect Status (MHDB)
PS.............. Protein Synthesis
PS.............. Proton Synchrotron [*Nuclear energy*]
PS.............. Protoplasmic Surface [*Freeze etching in microscopy*]
PS.............. Proto-Semitic (BJA)
PS.............. Provost-Sergeant
PS.............. Psalm
Ps.............. Psalms [*Old Testament book*]

PS .... Pseudo [*Classical studies*] (OCD)
Ps .... Pseudomonas [*Bacterium*] (MAE)
PS .... Pseudomonas Stutzeri [*Bacterium*]
PS .... Pseudonym (WGA)
PS .... Psychiatric (MAE)
PS .... Psychology Society (EA)
PS .... Psychometric Society (EA)
PS .... Psychonomic Society (EA)
PS .... Psychotic
PS .... Publication Standard
PS .... Public Sale
PS .... Public School
PS .... Public Service
PS .... Public Statutes [*Legal term*] (DLA)
PS .... Public Stenographer
PS .... Publishing Services [*American Library Association*]
PS .... Puget Sound [*Also, Puget Sound Naval Shipyard*] [*Washington*]
PS .... Pull Switch
PS .... Pulmonary Sequestration
PS .... Pulmonary Stenosis [*Medicine*]
PS .... Pulse per Second (IAA)
PS .... Pulse Sensor (KSC)
PS .... Pulse Shaper
PS .... Pulses per Second [*Data transmission*] (DEN)
PS .... Pulse Stretcher
PS .... Pumping Station (NATG)
PS .... Purdon's Pennsylvania Statutes [*A publication*] (DLA)
PS .... Purity-Supreme [*Supermarkets*]
PS .... Pyloric Stenosis [*Medicine*]
PS .... Serum From a Pregnant Woman (DAVI)
ps---- .... South Pacific [*MARC geographic area code Library of Congress*] (LCCP)
PS .... South Pole [*Also, SP*]
PS .... Static Pressure
PS .... Swarthmore Public Library, Swarthmore, PA [*Library symbol Library of Congress*] (LCLS)
PS .... Transport [*Russian aircraft symbol*]
PS .... US Postal Service (AAGC)
PS-1 .... Partido Socialista - Uno [*Socialist Party - One*] [*Also, PS Bolivia*] [*Political party*] (PD)
PS/2 .... Personal System/2 [*IBM Corp.*]
PS2 .... Picture System 2 [*Evans & Sutherland Computer Corp.*] (MCD)
PS^2 .... Profound Sensitivity Syndrome [*Psychology*]
PS3 .... PROBE [*Program Optimization and Budget Evaluation*] Staff Support System [*Military*]
PS2000 .... Public Service 2000 Program [*Canada*]
PSA .... Pacific Island Aviation, Inc. [*Mariana Islands*] [*ICAO designator*] (FAAC)
PSA .... Pacific Science Association (EA)
PSA .... Pacific Southwest Airlines
PSA .... Parametric Semiconductor Amplifier
PSA .... Parametric Sound Amplifier [*Blaupunkt*]
PSA .... Parcel Shippers Association (EA)
PSA .... Particle Size Analyzer
PSA .... Partido Socialista Aponte [*Bolivia*] [*Political party*] (PPW)
PSA .... Partido Socialista Argentino [*Socialist Party of Argentina*] [*Political party*]
PSA .... Parti Socialiste Autonome [*Autonomous Socialist Party*] [*France Political party*] (PPE)
PSA .... Parti Solidaire Africain [*African Solidarity Party*] [*Congo*] [*Political party*]
PSA .... Partito Socialista Autonomo [*Autonomous Socialist Party*] [*Switzerland Political party*] (PPW)
PSA .... Part Stress Analysis (MCD)
PSA .... Passenger Shipping Association [*British*] (DBA)
PSA .... Pastel Society of America (EA)
PSA .... Past Shakedown Availability [*Military*]
PSA .... Path of Steepest Ascent [*Statistical design of experiments*]
PSA .... Path Selection Algorithm [*Telecommunications*] (TEL)
PSA .... Patient Care Associate [*Medicine*]
PSA .... Payload Service Area [*NASA*] (NASA)
PSA .... Payload Support Avionics [*NASA*] (NASA)
PSA .... Peace and Solidarity Alliance (EA)
PSA .... Peace Studies Association (EA)
PSA .... People's Supreme Assembly [*Yemen*] [*Political party*] (PPW)
PSA .... Personal Service Agreements (MCD)
PSA .... Personal Statement Analyzer (HGAA)
PSA .... Personnel and Service Area [*Nuclear energy*] (NRCH)
PSA .... Personnel Support Activity (DOMA)
PSA .... Petersburg [*Alaska*] [*Seismograph station code, US Geological Survey*] (SEIS)
PSA .... Petites Soeurs de l'Assumption [*Little Sisters of the Assumption - LSA*] [*Paris, France*] (EAIO)
PSA .... Peugeot Societe Anonyme [*Peugeot Co. Ltd.*] [*French*]
PSA .... Philippine Standards Association (IAA)
PSA .... Philippine Sugar Association [*Later, PSC*] (EA)
PSA .... Philosophy of Science Association (EA)
PSA .... Phobia Society of America [*Later, ADAA*] (EA)
PSA .... Photographic Society of America (EA)
PSA .... Phycological Society of America (EA)
PSA .... Pickles and Sauces Association [*British*] (DBA)
PSA .... Pipe Stress Analysis (PDAA)
PSA .... Pirandello Society of America (EA)
PSA .... Pisa [*Italy*] [*Airport symbol*] (OAG)
PsA .... Pisces Austrinus [*Constellation*]
PSA .... Pisces Society of America
PSA .... Play Schools Association (EA)
PSA .... Pleasant Sunday Afternoons
PSA .... Plumeria Society of America (EA)
PSA .... Pneumatic Sensor Assembly
PSA .... Poe Studies Association (EA)
PSA .... Poetry Society of America (EA)
PSA .... Political Studies Association [*British*]
PSA .... Polycrystalline Silicon Self-Aligned [*Photovoltaic energy systems*] (MHDI)
PSA .... Polyethylene Sulfonic Acid [*Organic chemistry*] (MAE)
PSA .... Polysialic Acid [*Organic chemistry*]
PSA .... Polysilicic Acid [*Organic chemistry*]
PSA .... Portable Sanitation Association (EA)
PSA .... Portable Sound Analyzer
PSA .... Port Storage Area [*Telecommunications*] (TEL)
PSA .... Port Support Activity (DOMA)
PSA .... Post Shakedown Availability
PSA .... Post-Sleep Activity
PSA .... Potential Surface Analysis (ADA)
PSA .... Potters' Society of Australia
PSA .... Poultry Science Association (EA)
PSA .... Power Saw Association [*British*] (BI)
PSA .... Power Servo Amplifier (KSC)
PSA .... Power Servo Assembly (MCD)
PSA .... Power Supply Assembly
PSA .... Power Switching Amplifier
PSA .... Power Switching Assembly
PSA .... Precipitation Series Algorithm (USDC)
PSA .... Precipitation Series Algorithm [*Marine science*] (OSRA)
PSA .... Prefabricated Surfacing Aluminum
PSA .... Preferred Storage Area (MCD)
PSA .... Prefix Storage Area [*Computer science*] (OA)
PSA .... Preliminary Safety Analysis [*NASA*] (SSD)
PSA .... Pre/Post Sleep Activity (NASA)
PSA .... President of the Society of Antiquaries [*British*]
PSA .... Pressure Sensitive Adhesive [*Trademark*]
PSA .... Pressure Suit Assembly
PSA .... Pressure-Swing Adsorption [*Chemical engineering*]
PSA .... Pressure Switch Assembly (NASA)
PSA .... Pressure Switching Alarm [*Engineering*]
PSA .... Presunrise Authority
PSA .... Presunrise Service Authority (NTCM)
PSA .... Private Schools Association [*British*]
PSA .... Probabilistic Safety Analysis (NRCH)
PSA .... Problem Statement Analyzer [*Computer science*] (IAA)
PSA .... Process Service Area (IAA)
PSA .... Procurement Seminar for Auditors [*Army*]
PSA .... Product Safety Association [*Defunct*] (EA)
PSA .... Product Support Administration (MCD)
PSA .... Professional Salespersons of America [*Defunct*] (EA)
PSA .... Professional Service Association (EA)
PSA .... Professional Skills Alliance (EA)
PSA .... Professional Stringers Association [*Defunct*] (EA)
PSA .... Programmed Shutter and Aperture [*Photography*] (DICI)
PSA .... Program Study Authorization (KSC)
PSA .... Progressive Spinal Ataxia [*Medicine*] (DMAA)
PSA .... Prolonged Sleep Apnea
PSA .... Property Services Agency [*Department of the Environment*] [*British*]
PSA .... Prostate-Specific Antigen [*Immunochemistry*]
PSA .... Protective Security Attendant [*Australia*]
PSA .... Province Senior Advisor [*Army*] (VNW)
PSA .... Provisional Site Acceptance (NATG)
PSA .... Provisions Stowage Assembly (NASA)
PSA .... Psalm
Psa .... Psalms [*Old Testament book*]
PSA .... Pseudomonic Acid [*Biochemistry*]
PsA .... Psoriatic Arthritis (DAVI)
PSA .... Psychological Operations Support Activity [*Military*] (MCD)
PSA .... Psychological Semantic Analysis (NITA)
PSA .... Psychologists for Social Action [*Defunct*] (EA)
PSA .... Publication Systems Associates, Inc. [*Information service or system*] (IID)
PSA .... Public Securities Association [*Database producer*] (EA)
PSA .... Public Service Act
PSA .... Public Service Announcement
PSA .... Public Storage [*NYSE symbol*] (TTSB)
PSA .... Public Storage, Inc. [*NYSE symbol*] (SAG)
PSA .... Push Down Stack Automaton [*Computer science*]
PSA .... Storage Properties, Inc. [*AMEX symbol*] (SPSG)
PSAA .... Pacific Special Activities Area [*Military*]
PSAA .... Pakistan Students' Association of America
PSAA .... Plasma Sciences and Applications (IAA)
PSAA .... Polish Singers Alliance of America (EA)
PSAA .... Polwarth Sheepbreeders' Association of Australia
PSAA .... Poststimulatory Auditory Adaptation
PSAAV .... Provincial Sewerage Authorities Association of Victoria [*Australia*]
PSAB .... Pathology Services Accreditation Board [*Victoria, Australia*]
PSAB .... Prime Bancorp [*NASDAQ symbol*] (TTSB)
PSAB .... Prime Bancorp, Inc. [*NASDAQ symbol*] (CTT)
PSAB .... Production Systems Acceptance Branch [*Social Security Administration*]
PSAC .... Passive Satellite Attitude Control
PSAC .... Personnel Service Company [*Army*] (AABC)
PSAC .... Policy Signing and Accounting Centre [*Insurance firm*] [*British*]

PSAC .... Preferred Stock Advisory Committee [*New Deal*]
PSAC .... President's Science Advisory Committee [*Terminated, 1973*] [*Executive Office of the President*]
PSAC .... Private Security Advisory Council [*Terminated, 1977*] [*Department of Justice*] (EGAO)
PSAC .... Product Safety Advisory Council [*Consumer Product Safety Commission*]
PSAC .... Professional Skating Association of Canada
PSAC .... Public Service Alliance of Canada [*Labor union of federal government employees*]
PSACH .... Pseudoachondrodysplasia [*Medicine*] (DMAA)
PSACN .... Process Specification Advance Change Notice (SAA)
PSAcPh .... Prostate-Specific Acid Phosphatase [*An enzyme*]
PSACPOO .... President's Scientific Advisory Committee Panel on Oceanography [*Marine science*] (MSC)
PSAD .... Predicted Site Acquisition Data [*NASA*]
PSAD .... Prediction, Simulation, Adaptation, Decision [*Computer science*]
PSAD .... Procurement and Systems Acquisition Division (AAGC)
PSAF .... Private Sector Adjustment Factor [*Banking*]
PSAG .... Pelvic Sonoangiography [*Medicine*] (DMAA)
PSAGN .... Poststreptococcal Acute Glomerulonephritis [*Medicine*]
PSAI .... Pediatric Services of Amer [*NASDAQ symbol*] (TTSB)
PSAI .... Pediatric Services of America, Inc. [*NASDAQ symbol*] (SAG)
PSAIR .... Priority Specific Air Information Request [*Defense Mapping Agency*] (MCD)
PSAL .... Permanent Supplementary Artificial Lighting (IAA)
PSAL .... Programming System Activity Log [*Computer science*]
PSAL .... Public Schools Athletic League
PSALI .... Permanent Supplementary Artificial Lighting of Interiors (IEEE)
P Salin .... Petrus de Salinis [*Flourished, 13th century*] [*Authority cited in pre-1607 legal work*] (DSA)
PSALM .... Project Structured Analysis of LOGEX [*Logistical Exercise*] Methodology (MCD)
PSAM .... Partitioned Sequence Access Method
PSAM .... Point Source Ambient Monitoring [*Environmental Protection Agency*] (GFGA)
PSAMS .... Plessey Scientific-Atlanta Multistar System (NITA)
PSAN .... Phase Stabilized Ammonium Nitrate (MCD)
PSAn .... Psychoanalysis [*or Psychoanalyst*] (DAVI)
PS & A .... Pharmacy, Supply, and Administration (DOMA)
PS & B .... Power Steering and Brakes [*Automotive engineering*] (IIA)
PS & C .... Private Siding and Collected One End
PS&C .... Production Scheduling and Control (AAGC)
PS & CC .... Packaging, Storage, and Containerization Center [*DARCOM*] (MCD)
PS & D .... Private Siding and Delivered One End
PS & DS .... Program Statistics and Data Systems
PS & E .... Plans, Specifications, and Estimates [*Construction*]
PS & ER .... Production Support and Equipment Replacement [*Military*] (AABC)
PS & L .... Power Switching and Logic
PS & M .... Personnel Supervision and Management Division of ASTSECNAV's Office [*Absorbed into SECP, 1944*]
PS & T .... Pay, Subsistence, and Transportation [*Military*]
PSANDT .... Pay, Subsistence, and Transportation [*Military*]
PS & TC .... Population Studies and Training Center [*Brown University*] [*Research center*] (RCD)
PS & TN .... Pay, Subsistence, and Transportation, Navy
PS & W .... Pacific, Southern & Western Railroad [*Nickname: Play Safe and Walk*]
PSANP .... Phenol-Soluble Acidic Nuclear Protein [*s*] [*Biochemistry*]
PSAO .... Pharmacy Services Administrative Organization
PSAO .... Primary Staff Action Officer [*Military*]
PSAP .... Phenylsulfonylacetophenone
PSAP .... Plane Stress Analysis and Plot [*Computer science*]
PSAP .... Presentation Service Access Point [*Telecommunications*] (OSI)
PSAP .... Primary Public Safety Answering Point (DMAA)
PSAP .... Public Safety Answering Point [*Telecommunications*] (TEL)
PSAP .... Public Service Answering Point
PSAP .... Pulmonary Surfactant Apoprotein [*Biochemistry*]
PSAPrA .... Public Storage 10% cm'A'Pfd [*NYSE symbol*] (TTSB)
PSAPrB .... Public Storage 9.20% cm'B'Pfd [*NYSE symbol*] (TTSB)
PSAPrC .... Public Storage Adj Rt'C'Pfd [*NYSE symbol*] (TTSB)
PSAPrD .... Public Storage 9.50%'D'Pfd [*NYSE symbol*] (TTSB)
PSAPrE .... Public Storage 10%'E'Pfd [*NYSE symbol*] (TTSB)
PSAPrF .... Public Storage 9.75% 'F' Pfd [*NYSE symbol*] (TTSB)
PSAPrG .... Public Storage 8.875% Dep Pfd [*NYSE symbol*] (TTSB)
PSAPrH .... Public Storage 8.45%'H'Dep Pfd [*NYSE symbol*] (TTSB)
PSAPrX .... Public Storage 8.25%Cv Pfd [*NYSE symbol*] (TTSB)
PSAR .... Platform Shock Attenuation and Realignment System (MCD)
PSAR .... Pneumatic [*or Pressure*] System Automatic Regulator (AAG)
PSAR .... Preliminary Safety Analysis Report
PSAR .... Pressure System Automatic Regulator (IAA)
PSAR .... Process Storage Address Register [*Computer science*] (IAA)
PSAR .... Programmable Synchronous/Asynchronous Receiver (IEEE)
PSAR .... Propulsion Systems Analysis Report (SAA)
PSarg .... Pre-Sargonic (BJA)
PSAS .... Prespeech Assessment Scale [*Occupational therapy*]
PSAS .... Production Systems Acceptance Section [*Social Security Administration*]
PSAS .... Program Support and Advanced Systems (SAA)
PSASA .... Public Service Association of South Australia
PSASS .... Perishable Subsistence Automated Supply System [*DoD*]
PSASV .... Phase-Sensitive Anodic Stripping Voltammetry
PSAT .... Predicted Site Acquisition Table [*NASA*]
PSAT .... Preliminary Scholastic Aptitude Test
PSAT .... Programmable Synchronous/Asynchronous Transmitter (IEEE)
PSAT/NMSQT ... Preliminary Scholastic Aptitude/National Merit Scholarship Qualifying Test (PAZ)
PSAUK .... Political Studies Association of the United Kingdom
PSAUSA .... Polish Socialist Alliance of the United States of America (EA)
PSAX .... Pacific Southwest Airlines [*Air carrier designation symbol*]
PSB .... Bellefonte-Clearfield-Philipsburg [*Pennsylvania*] [*Airport symbol*] (AD)
PSB .... Pacific Science Board [*National Academy of Sciences*]
PSB .... Philatelic Sales Branch [*Later, PSD*] [*US Postal Service*]
PSB .... Philipsburg, PA [*Location identifier FAA*] (FAAL)
PSB .... Phosphorus-Solubilizing Bacteria [*Microbiology*]
PSB .... Plant Safety Bureau
PSB .... Plant Service Building [*Nuclear energy*] (NRCH)
PSB .... Plough, Sweeper, and Blower (DA)
PSB .... Police Superannuation Board [*Australia*]
PSB .... Polytechnic of the South Bank [*London, England*]
PSB .... Premium Savings Bond [*British*] (DCTA)
PSB .... Professional and Statutory Board (AIE)
PSB .... Program Specification Block [*IBM Corp.*]
PSB .... Program Station Basis [*Rating system*] (WDMC)
PSB .... Protected Specimen Brush [*Medicine*]
PSB .... Protein S Beta (DMAA)
PSB .... PS Business Parks, Inc. [*AMEX symbol*] (SPSG)
PSB .... Psychological Services Bureau (AEBS)
PSB .... Psychological Strategy Board [*Military*] (LAIN)
PSB .... Public Service Board (NADA)
PSBA .... Power-Specific Biological Activity [*Engine emissions testing*]
PSBA .... Public School Bursars' Association [*British*] (BI)
PSBBF .... Pearl S. Buck Birthplace Foundation (EA)
PSBBrc .... Peoples Savings Bank of Brockton [*Associated Press*] (SAG)
PSBCA .... Painted Soda Bottles Collectors Association (EA)
PSBCA .... Postal Service Board of Contract Appeals (AAGC)
PSbetaG .... Pregnancy-Specific Beta-1-Glycoprotein [*Medicine*] (DMAA)
PSBF .... Pearl S. Buck Foundation (EA)
PSBG .... Pregnancy-Specific beta-Glycoprotein [*Gynecology*]
PSBH .... Pad Safety in Blockhouse
PSBH .... Phonon Side-Band Hole [*Spectroscopy*]
PSBI .... Performance Standardization Branch Instruction (SAA)
PSBK .... Progressive Bank [*NASDAQ symbol*] (TTSB)
PSBK .... Progressive Bank, Inc. [*Pawling, NY*] [*NASDAQ symbol*] (NQ)
PSBL .... Possible (FAAC)
PSBLS .... Permanent Space Based Logistics System
PSBMA .... Professional Services Business Management Association [*Later, PSMA*] (EA)
PsbMV .... Pea Seed-Borne Mosaic Virus
PSBNAME .... Program Specification Block Name [*Computer science*] (MHDB)
PSBO .... Partial Small Bowel Obstruction [*Medicine*] (MEDA)
PSBP .... PS Business Parks, Inc. [*Associated Press*] (SAG)
PSBPrB .... Pub Sv Colo, 8.40% Pfd [*NYSE symbol*] (TTSB)
PSBR .... Pennsylvania State University Breazeale Nuclear Reactor [*Research center*] (RCD)
PSBR .... Public Sector Borrowing Requirement
PSBT .... Pilot Self-Briefing Terminal [*Aviation*] (FAAC)
PSBU .... Propeller Shaft Bearing Unit [*Truck engineering*]
PSBU .... Public Sector and Broadcasting Union [*Australia*]
PSBV .... Public Service Board Victoria [*Australia*]
PSC .... Congolese Socialist Party [*Zaire*] [*Political party*] (PD)
PSC .... Isla De Pascua [*Easter Island*] [*Seismograph station code, US Geological Survey Closed*] (SEIS)
PSC .... Pacific Salmon Commission (EA)
PSC .... Pacific Science Center
PSC .... Pacific Science Council
PSC .... Pacific South Coast Freight Bureau, San Francisco CA [*STAC*]
PSC .... Pacific Studies Center (EA)
PSC .... Palestine Solidarity Committee [*Defunct*] (EA)
PSC .... Palmer Skin Conductance
PSC .... Parallel Switch Control (MCD)
PSC .... Parallel to Serial Converter
PSC .... Parents Sharing Custody (EA)
PSC .... Partido Social Conservador Colombiano [*Colombian Social Conservative Party*] [*Political party*] (EY)
PSC .... Partido Social Cristiano [*Social Christian Party*] [*Bolivia*] [*Political party*]
PSC .... Partido Social Cristiano [*Social Christian Party*] [*Guatemala*] [*Political party*] (PPW)
PSC .... Partido Social Cristiano [*Social Christian Party*] [*Ecuador*] [*Political party*] (PPW)
PSC .... Partido Socialcristiano Nicaraguense [*Nicaraguan Social Christian Party*] [*Political party*] (PPW)
PSC .... Partido Socialista de Catalunya [*Catalan Socialist Party*] [*Spain Political party*] (PPE)
PSC .... Parti Socialiste Caledonien [*New Caledonia*] [*Political party*] (FEA)
PSC .... Parti Socialiste Camerounais [*Cameroon Socialist Party*] [*Political party*]
PSC .... Parti Socialiste Centrafricain [*Central African Socialist Party*] [*Political party*] (PD)
PSC .... Pasco [*Washington*] [*Airport symbol*] (OAG)
PSC .... Pasco, WA [*Location identifier FAA*] (FAAL)
PSC .... Passaic Byzantine [*Diocesan abbreviation*] [*New Jersey*] (TOCD)
PSC .... Passed Staff College [*British*]
PSC .... Passenger Services Conference [*IATA*] (DS)
PSC .... Patriot Steering Committee
PSC .... Paul Smiths College [*New York*]
PSC .... Peacetime Subcontract
PSC .... Pembroke State College [*North Carolina*]
PSC .... Percentage of Successful Collisions [*Obstetrics*]

PSC............ Permanent Split Capacitor (IAA)
PSC............ Personal Service Corporation (TDOB)
PSC............ Personal Supercomputer [*Culler Scientific Systems Corp.*]
PSC............ Personnel Service Center [*or Company*] [*Military*] (INF)
PSC............ Personnel Status Change (KSC)
PSC............ Personnel Subsystem Cost
PSC............ Per Standard Compass [*Navigation*]
PSC............ Petty Sessional Court [*British*] (ROG)
PSC............ Phase-Sensitive Converter
PSC............ Philadelphia Service Center [*IRS*]
PSC............ Philadelphia Suburban Corp. [*NYSE symbol*] (SPSG)
PSC............ Philander Smith College [*Little Rock, AR*]
PSC............ Phila Suburban [*NYSE symbol*] (TTSB)
PSC............ Philippine Sugar Commission (EA)
PSC............ Phonemic Spelling Council [*Defunct*] (EA)
PSC............ Photosensitive Cell (IEEE)
PSC............ Phylogenetic Species Concept [*Biology*]
PSC............ Physical Sciences Center
PSC............ Physical Sciences Committee [*Terminated, 1977*] [*NASA*] (EGAO)
PSC............ Physical Security/Pilferage Code (MCD)
Psc............ Pisces [*Constellation*]
PSC............ Pittsburgh Supercomputing Center [*National Science Foundation Research center*] (RCD)
PSC............ Pittsburgh Superconducting Center [*Pennsylvania*] (GRD)
pSC............ Plasmid Stanley Cohen [*Molecular biology*]
PSC............ Platform Support Center [*NASA*] (SSD)
PSC............ Pluripotent Stem Cell [*Cytology*]
PSC............ Plutonium Stripping Concentrate [*Nuclear energy*] (NRCH)
PSC............ Point Shipping Co. [*Steamship*] (MHDW)
PSC............ Polaroid Stereoscopic Chroncyclegraph
PSC............ Polar Science Center [*University of Washington*] [*Research center*] (RCD)
PSC............ Polar Stratospheric Cloud [*Meteorology*]
PSC............ Population Studies Center [*University of Michigan*] [*Research center*] (RCD)
PSC............ Porcelain on Steel Council [*Defunct*] (EA)
PSC............ Porter-Silber Chromogen [*Medicine*] (MAE)
PSC............ Portland Society for Calligraphy (EA)
PSC............ Postal Service Center (AFM)
PSC............ Posterior Subcapsular Cataracts [*Ophthalmology*]
PSC............ Post-Storage Checkout [*NASA*] (KSC)
PSC............ Postsynaptic Current [*Neurophysiology*]
PSC............ Potentiometer Strip Chart
PSC............ Potomac State College [*of West Virginia University*]
PSC............ Power Supply Calibrator
PSC............ Power System Communications (IAA)
PSC............ Prairie Swine Centre [*University of Saskatchewan*] [*Canada*] (IRC)
PSC............ Preferred Semiconductor Circuit [*Electronics*] (IAA)
PSC............ Pressure Suit Circuit (KSC)
PSC............ Pressure System Control (AAG)
PSC............ Prestressed Concrete (ADA)
PSC............ Presumptive Hematopoietic Stem Cell
PSC............ Price Signal Code [*Military*] (AABC)
PSC............ Primary Sclerosing Cholangitis [*Medicine*]
PSC............ Principal Subordinate Command (NATG)
PSC............ Private Secretary's Certificate [*British*] (DI)
PSC............ Private Sector Council (EA)
PSC............ PROBE [*Program Optimization and Budget Evaluation*] Steering Committee [*Military*]
PSC............ Processing and Spectral Control
PSC............ Processing Service Centers [*Social Security Administration*]
PSC............ Procurement Source Code (AFM)
PSC............ Product and Service Code (AAGC)
PSC............ Production Scheduling and Control (IAA)
PSC............ Product Safety Committee [*New South Wales, Australia*]
PSC............ Product Support Confidential (AAG)
PSC............ Professional Service Corporation [*Medicine*] (HCT)
PSC............ Professional Services Council [*Washington, DC*] (EA)
PSC............ Programmable Sample Changer [*Spectroscopy*]
PSC............ Program Schedule Chart (NASA)
PSC............ Program Sequence Control (NITA)
PSC............ Program Service Center [*Social Security Administration*] (OICC)
PSC............ Program Standards Checker [*Computer science*]
PSC............ Program Status Chart [*Computer science*]
PSC............ Program Structure Code (AFM)
PSC............ Program Support Contract (SSD)
PSC............ Program Switching Center [*Computer science*] (IAA)
PSC............ Project Systems Control (MCD)
PSC............ Propagating Space Charge (PDAA)
PSC............ Protosolar Cloud [*Astronomy*]
PSC............ Prototype System Characteristics
PSC............ PSC, Inc. [*Associated Press*] (SAG)
PSC............ Public Service Careers [*Program*] [*Department of Labor*]
PSC............ Public Service Co.
PSC............ Public Service Commission [*Usually, of a specific state*]
PSC............ Pulse Shape Control Circuit (IAA)
PSC............ Pulse Synchronized Contraction [*In the vascular system*] [*Medicine*]
PSC............ Sandoz AG [*Switzerland*] [*Research code symbol*]
PSc............ Scranton Public Library, Scranton, PA [*Library symbol Library of Congress*] (LCLS)
PSC............ Swarthmore College, Swarthmore, PA [*Library symbol Library of Congress OCLC symbol*] (LCLS)
PSCA........... Parliamentary Select Committee on Agriculture [*British*]
PscA........... Pisces Austrinus [*Constellation*]
PSCA........... Polish Social and Cultural Association [*British*] (EAIO)
PSCA........... Pressure Suit Conditioning Assembly (MCD)
PSCA........... Profit Sharing Council of America (EA)
PSCACM...... Permanent Secretariat of the Central American Common Market
PSCAN......... Purchase Order Scan
PSCAV......... Professional Squash Coaches' Association of Victoria [*Australia*]
PSCB........... Padded Sample Collection Bag [*NASA*]
PSCB........... Parliamentary Standing Committee on Broadcasting [*Australia*]
PSCBG......... Paper Shipping-Containers Buyers Group
PSCC........... Photo Systems Controller Console (KSC)
PSCC........... Power System Communications (IAA)
PSCC........... Projets de Services Communautaires du Canada
PSCD........... Plutonium Stripping Concentration Distillate [*Nuclear energy*] (NRCH)
PSCD........... Postcard (VRA)
PSCD........... Program for the Study of Crime and Delinquency [*Ohio State University*] [*Research center*] (RCD)
PSCE........... Presurgical Coagulation Evaluation [*Medicine*] (DAVI)
PSCEC......... Planning Status of Committed Engineering Changes (SAA)
PSCF........... Personal Security Clearance File
PSCF........... Processor Storage Control Function
PSCFB......... Pacific South Coast Freight Bureau
PSCG........... Power Supply and Control Gear
PSCG........... Power Supply Control Group [*Military*] (CAAL)
PSCH........... Postoperative Suprachoroidal Hemorrhage [*Medicine*]
PSC-Hi......... Friends Historical Library of Swarthmore College, Swarthmore, PA [*Library symbol Library of Congress*] (LCLS)
PSCI............ Perez Self-Concept Inventory [*Psychology*] (EDAC)
PSCI............ Plastic Shipping Container Institute (EA)
PSCI............ Primary Self-Concept Inventory [*Psychology*] (EDAC)
PSCJ............ Perseverance Society of Carpenters and Joiners [*A union*] [*British*]
PSCJ............ Progressive Society of Carpenters and Joiners [*A union*] [*British*]
PSCL............ Programmed Sequential Control Language
PSCL............ Propellants System Components Laboratory [*Kennedy Space Center*] [*NASA*]
PSCL............ Propellant Systems Cleaning Laboratory [*NASA*] (NASA)
PScL............ Scranton Public Library, Scranton, PA [*Library symbol*] [*Library of Congress*] (LCLS)
PScLL.......... Lackawanna Bar Association Law Library, Scranton, PA [*Library symbol Library of Congress*] (LCLS)
PScM........... Marywood College, Scranton, PA [*Library symbol Library of Congress*] (LCLS)
PSCM........... Process Steering and Control Module [*Telecommunications*] (TEL)
PSCM........... Professinal Sports Care Management, Inc. [*NASDAQ symbol*] (SAG)
PSCM........... Professional Sports Care Mgmt [*NASDAQ symbol*] (TTSB)
PSCN........... Partido Socialcristiano Nicaraguense [*Nicaraguan Social Christian Party*] [*Political party*] (PPW)
PSCN........... Permanent System Control Number (MCD)
PSCN........... Preliminary Specification Change Notice [*NASA*] (NASA)
PSCN........... Program Support Communications Network (SSD)
PSCN........... Proposed Specification Change Notice
PSCNET....... Pittsburgh Superconducting Center Network
PSCO........... Pennsylvania State College of Optometry
PSCO........... Personnel Survey Control Officer [*Military*] (AABC)
PSCO........... ProtoSource Corp. [*NASDAQ symbol*] (SAG)
PSCoI.......... Public Service Co. of Colorado [*Associated Press*] (SAG)
PSCOU........ ProtoSource Corp. Unit [*NASDAQ symbol*] (TTSB)
PSCOW........ ProtoSource Corp. Wrrt [*NASDAQ symbol*] (TTSB)
PSCP........... Palestine Symphonic Choir Project (EA)
P/S CP......... Platoon/Section Command Post
PSCP........... Polar Continental Shelf Project [*Canada*]
PSCP........... Posterior Subcapsular Cataractous Plaque [*Ophthalmology*] (DAVI)
PSCP........... Public Service Careers Program [*Department of Labor*]
PSC-P......... Swarthmore College Peace Collection, Swarthmore, PA [*Library symbol Library of Congress*] (LCLS)
PSCPD......... Philadelphia Signal Corps Procurement District [*Army*]
PSC-PSOE.... Partit dels Socialistes de Catalunya [*Party of Socialists of Catalonia*] [*Political party*] (PPW)
PSCPT......... Preschool Self-Concept Picture Test [*Psychology*]
PSCR........... Permanent Scratch File [*Computer science*]
PSCR........... Photo-Selective Copper Reduction [*For circuit board manufacture*]
PSCR........... Priority System Change Request
PSCR........... Production Schedule Completion Report [*DoD*]
PSCR........... Programmable Scanning Receiver (DWSG)
PSCR........... Public Service Commission Reports [*A publication*] (DLA)
PSCRD......... Program Support Communications Requirements Document (SSD)
PSCRL......... Patent Security Category Review List (AAGC)
PSCRT......... Passive Satellite Communications Research Terminal (SAA)
PSCS........... Pacific Scatter Communications System [*Air Force*] (CET)
PSCS........... Program Support Control System
PSCU........... Power Supply Control Unit (CET)
PScU........... University of Scranton, Scranton, PA [*Library symbol Library of Congress*] (LCLS)
PSCUS......... Peters' United States Surpeme Court Reports [*26-41 United States*] [*A publication*] (DLA)
PSCX........... PSC, Inc. [*Formerly, Photographic Sciences Corp.*] [*NASDAQ symbol*] (NQ)
PSD............ Destour Socialist Party [*Tunisia*] [*Political party*] (PD)
PSD............ Doctor of Political Science
Ps D............ Doctor of Psychology
Ps D............ Doctor of Psychology in Metaphysics
PSD............ Doctor of Public Service
PSD............ Packed Switched Data
PSD............ Particle Size Distribution
PSD............ Partido Socialdemocracia [*Social Democratic Party*] [*Chile*] [*Political party*] (EY)

PSD .... Partido Social Democrata [*Social Democratic Party*] [*Bolivia*] [*Political party*] (PPW)
PSD .... Partido Social Democrata [*Social Democratic Party*] [*Spain Political party*] (PPE)
PSD .... Partido Social Democrata [*Social Democratic Party*] [*Mexico Political party*] (PPW)
PSD .... Partido Social Democratico [*Social Democratic Party*] [*Brazil Political party*]
PSD .... Partido Social Democratico [*Social Democratic Party*] [*Nicaragua*] [*Political party*] (PPW)
PSD .... Partido Social Democratico [*Social Democratic Party*] [*El Salvador*] [*Political party*]
PSD .... Partido Socialista Democratico [*Social Democratic Party*] [*Argentina Political party*] (PPW)
PSD .... Partido Socialista Democratico [*Social Democratic Party*] [*Guatemala*] [*Political party*] (PD)
PSD .... Parti Social-Democrate [*Algeria*] [*Political party*] (EY)
PSD .... Parti Social-Democrate [*Social Democratic Party*] [*France Political party*] (PPW)
PSD .... Parti Social Democrate de Madagascar et des Comores [*Social Democratic Party of Madagascar and Comores*]
PSD .... Parti Social-Democratie [*Benin*] [*Political party*] (EY)
PSD .... Parti Socialiste Democratique [*Cameroon*] [*Political party*] (EY)
PSD .... Passed (ROG)
PSD .... Passing Scene Display
PSD .... Past Start Date
PSD .... Patent Search Documentation (NITA)
PSD .... Paternal Sister Dam (OA)
PSD .... Patient Symptom Diary
PSD .... Pay Supply Depot (WDAA)
PSD .... Peptone-Starch-Dextrose [*Microbiology*] (MAE)
PSD .... Permanent Signal Detection [*Telecommunications*] (TEL)
PSD .... Personal Services Department [*Navy British*]
PSD .... Personnel Services Division [*Army*]
PSD .... Personnel Support Detachment (DOMA)
PSD .... Personnel System [*or Subsystem*] Development (AAG)
PSD .... Pescadero [*California*] [*Seismograph station code, US Geological Survey*] (SEIS)
PSD .... Petroleum Safety Data [*American Petroleum Institute*]
PSD .... Petty Session Division [*Legal term*] (DLA)
PSD .... Phase-Sensitive Demodulator [*or Detector*]
PSD .... Phase Shifter Driver
PSD .... Philatelic Sales Division [*Formerly, PSB*] [*US Postal Service*]
PSD .... Photoconductive, Semiconductive Device
PSD .... Photon Stimulated Desorption [*For analysis of surfaces*]
PSD .... Pictorialized Scatter Diagram [*Botany*]
PSD .... Pitch Servo Drive
PSD .... Platform Specific Driver [*Computer science*]
PSD .... Polysilicon Diode (IAA)
PSD .... Polystyrene, Deuterated [*Organic chemistry*]
PSD .... Pore Size Distribution
PSD .... Port Said [*Egypt*] [*Airport symbol*] (AD)
PSD .... Port Security Detachment [*Military*] (GFGA)
PSD .... Position Sensitive Light Detector (IAA)
PSD .... Postal Security Device [*Computer science*]
PSD .... Post Sending Delay
PSD .... Postsynaptic Density [*Neurophysiology*]
PSD .... Power Spectral [*or Spectrum*] Density
PSD .... Power Spectrum Distribution [*Electronics*]
PSD .... Preferred Sea Duty
PSD .... Pressure-Sensitive Devices (MCD)
PSD .... Prevention of Significant Deterioration [*Environmental Protection Agency*]
PSD .... Printed Side Down [*Graphic arts*] (DGA)
PSD .... Printing Systems Division (NITA)
PSD .... Private-Sector Development (ECON)
PSD .... Procedural Support Data
PSD .... Processing Status Display [*NASA*]
PSD .... Process Specification Departure (SAA)
PSD .... Procurement Surveys Division [*NASA*] (MCD)
PSD .... Professional Service Dates [*Formerly, ADBD*]
PSD .... Professional Systems Division [*American Institute of Architects Service Corp.*] [*Information service or system*] (IID)
PSD .... Programmed Slip Differential [*Automotive engineering*]
PSD .... Programme Support and Development [*British*]
PSD .... Program Status Documents [*Computer science*]
PSD .... Program Status Doubleword
PSD .... Program Support Document (MUGU)
PSD .... Program System Description (SAA)
PSD .... Program Systems Division [*Environmental Protection Agency*] (GFGA)
PSD .... Promotion Service Date
PSD .... Propellant Slosh Dynamics
PSD .... Propellant Storage Depot [*NASA*]
PSD .... Proportional Stock Density [*Pisciculture*]
PSD .... Propulsion System Demonstrator [*Marine Corps*] (DOMA)
PSD .... Protective Serum Dilution
PSD .... Protective Structures Division [*Office of Civil Defense*]
PSD .... Pseudosingle Domain [*Behavior of grains in rocks*] [*Geophysics*]
PSD .... Pseudo Stow Document (DNAB)
PSD .... Puget Sound P&L [*NYSE symbol*] (TTSB)
PSD .... Puget Sound Power & Light Co. [*NYSE symbol*] (SPSG)
PSD .... Pulse Shape Discriminator
PSD .... Pure Screw Dislocation
PSDA .... Paper Sack Development Association [*British*] (BI)
PSDA .... Partial Source Data Automation (NVT)
PSDA .... Particle Size Distribution Analysis [*Statistics*]
PSDA .... Patient Self-Determination Act
P/SDA .... Power/Signal Distribution Assembly
PSDB .... Partido da Social Democracia Brasiliera [*Brazilian Social Democratic Party*] [*Political party*] (EY)
PSDC .... Pennsylvania State Data Center [*Middletown*] [*Information service or system*] (IID)
PSDC .... Plant Sciences Data Center [*Formerly, Plant Records Center*] [*American Horticultural Society*] [*Mt. Vernon, VA*]
PSDC .... Power Sprayer and Duster Council (EA)
PSDC .... Protective Structures Development Center [*Military*]
PSDD .... Preliminary System Design Description [*Nuclear energy*] (NRCH)
PSDDS .... Pilot [*or Public*] Switched Digital Data Service [*Telecommunications*] (TEL)
PS de G .... Partido dos Socialistas de Galicia [*Spain Political party*] (EY)
Psdepgr .... Pseudepigrapha (BJA)
PSDF .... People's Self-Defense Force [*South Vietnamese militia force*] (VNW)
PSDF .... Popular Self-Defense Force [*Local armed units protecting Vietnamese hamlets*]
PSDF .... Propulsion Systems Development Facility (KSC)
PSDI .... Partido Social Democratico Independente [*Independent Social Democratic Party*] [*Portugal Political party*] (PPE)
PSDI .... Partito Socialista Democratico Italiano [*Italian Social Democratic Party*] [*Political party*]
PSDI .... Project Software & Development, Inc. [*NASDAQ symbol*] (SAG)
PSDI .... Project Software & Dvlp [*NASDAQ symbol*] (TTSB)
PSDIAD .... Photostimulated Desorption Ion Angular Distribution [*Surface analysis*]
PSDIS .... Partito Socialista Democratico Indipendente Sammarinese [*Independent Social Democratic Party of San Marino*] [*Political party*] (PPE)
PSdM .... Mennonite Publishing House, Scottsdale, PA [*Library symbol Library of Congress*] (LCLS)
PSDM .... Presentation Services for Data Management (MHDB)
PSD(MS) .... Photon Stimulated Desorption (Mass Spectroscopy) (MCD)
PSDN .... Packet Switched Data Network [*Telecommunications*]
PSDN .... Packet-Switching Data Network [*Computer science*] (DOM)
PSDN .... Public Switched Data Network (NITA)
PSDP .... Payload Station Distribution Panel [*NASA*] (MCD)
PSDP .... Personnel Subsystem Development Plan
PSDP .... Phrase Structure and Dependency Parser (DIT)
PSDP .... Professional Skills Development Program [*Bureau of the Census*] (GFGA)
PSDP .... Programmable Signal Data Processor (MCD)
PSDPr .... Puget Sound P&L 7.875% Pfd [*NYSE symbol*] (TTSB)
PSDPrB .... Puget Sound P&L Adj Rt'B'Pfd [*NYSE symbol*] (TTSB)
PSDR .... Planning and Scheduling Document Record [*NASA*] (NASA)
PSDR .... Process Storage Data Register (IAA)
PSDR .... Program Status Doubleword Register [*Computer science*] (MHDB)
PSDR .... Public Sector Debt Repayment [*British*] (ECON)
PSDS .... Packet Switch Data System [*Information retrieval*] (IID)
PSDS .... Packet Switched Data Service [*Telecommunications*] (TEL)
PSDS .... Partito Socialista Democratico Sammarinese [*Social Democratic Party of San Marino*] [*Political party*] (PPE)
PSDS .... Passing Scene Display System
PSDS .... Permanently Separated from Duty Station [*Military*]
PSDS .... Public Switched Data Service [*Telecommunications*]
PSDS .... Public Switched Digital Service [*Computer science*] (TNIG)
PSDSP .... Pious Society of the Daughters of Saint Paul [*See also FSP*] [*Rome, Italy*] (EAIO)
PSDT .... President (ROG)
PSDTC .... Pacific Securities Depository Trust Co.
PSDU .... Polish Social Democratic Union [*Political party*]
PSDU .... Power Switching Distribution Unit
PSDU .... Presentation Service Data Unit [*Telecommunications*] (OSI)
PSDVB .... Poly(styrene-Divinylbenzene) [*Organic chemistry*]
PSE .... Aeroservicio Sipse SA de CV [*Mexico ICAO designator*] (FAAC)
PSE .... Pacific School of English [*Australia*]
PSE .... Pacific Stock Exchange (EA)
PSE .... Packet Switching Exchange [*Telecommunications*]
PSE .... Pale Soft Exudative [*Pork*]
PSE .... Paper Surface Efficiency (DGA)
PSE .... Partido Socialista de Euskadi [*Basque Socialist Party*] [*Spain Political party*] (EY)
PSE .... Partido Socialista Ecuatoriano [*Ecuadorean Socialist Party*] [*Political party*] (PPW)
PSE .... Passage
PSE .... Passive Seismic Experiment [*NASA*]
PSE .... Payload Service Equipment [*NASA*] (MCD)
PSE .... Payload Support Equipment [*NASA*] (MCD)
PSE .... Peculiar Support Equipment [*NASA*] (NASA)
PSE .... Penicillin-Sensitive Enzymes [*Biochemistry*]
PSE .... Personnel Subsystem Elements [*Army*] (AABC)
PSE .... Perth Stock Exchange [*Australia*]
PSE .... Phase-Shifter, Electronic
PSE .... Philadelphia Stock Exchange
PSE .... Photosensitive Epilepsy
PSE .... Physical Security Equipment [*Army*] (RDA)
PSE .... Phytochemical Society of Europe (EA)
PSE .... Pigin Signed English
PSE .... Pitch Steering Error
pse .... Planed and Square-Edge (DAC)
PSE .... Pleasant Saturday Evenings
PSE .... Pleasant Sunday Evenings (ROG)

PSE............. Please (MDG)
PSE............. Point of Subjective Equality [*Psychology*]
PSE............. Polestar Exploration, Inc. [*Vancouver Stock Exchange symbol*]
PSE............. Ponce [*Puerto Rico*] [*Airport symbol*] (OAG)
PSE............. Portal Systemic Encephalopathy [*Medicine*]
PSE............. Post-Separation Employment
PSE............. Postshunt Encephalopathy [*Medicine*]
PSE............. Power Spectrum Equalization [*Electronics*]
PSE............. Power System Engineering (MCD)
PSE............. Present State Examination [*Medicine*] (DMAA)
PSE............. Pressurized Subcritical Experiment [*Nuclear energy*]
PSE............. Pre-Stamped Envelope
PSE............. Prevention of Stripping Equipment (NATG)
PSE............. Principal Staff Element [*Defense Supply Agency*]
PSE............. Priority Standardization Effort [*Army*] (AABC)
PSE............. Prison Service Establishment (AIE)
PSE............. Probability of Successful Engagement [*Military*] (CAAL)
PSE............. Process Systems Engineering
PSE............. Producer Subsidy Equivalent [*OECD model for the study of farm-support policies in the EC, Japan, America, Canada, Australia, and New Zealand*]
PSE............. Product Support Engineering (MCD)
PSE............. Programmed System Evolution (MCD)
PSE............. Protein Separation Efficiency [*Food technology*]
PSE............. Proximal Sequence Element [*Genetics*]
PSE............. Psychological Stress Evaluator [*Lie detector*]
PSE............. Public Sector [*or Service*] Employment
PSE............. Public Service Electric & Gas Co., Newark, NJ [*OCLC symbol*] (OCLC)
PSE............. Pulse Sense
PSE............. Purified Spleen Extract [*Medicine*] (DMAA)
PSEA............ Pacific and Southeast Asia (DNAB)
PSEA............ Physical Security Equipment Agency [*Army*]
PSEA............ Pleaters, Stitchers, and Embroiderers Association (EA)
PSE & C...... Power Supply Engineering and Construction [*Nuclear energy*] (NRCH)
PSE & G...... Public Service Electric & Gas Co.
PSEB............ Poisoning Surveillance and Epidemiology Branch [*Defunct*] (EA)
PSEBM.......... Proceedings of the Society for Experimental Biology and Medicine [*A publication*]
P/SEC.......... Personal Secretary (DCTA)
PSEC............ Picosecond [*One trillionth of a second*]
psec............ Picosecond [*Alternative of preferred ps*] (IDOE)
PSED............ Preliminary Systems Engineering Design
PSEF............ Pennsylvania Science and Engineering Foundation
PSEF............ Plastic Surgery Educational Foundation (EA)
PSEG............ PSE & G Capital Trust [*Associated Press*] (SAG)
PSEG............ Public Service Electric & Gas Co. [*Associated Press*] (SAG)
PSEK............ Probability of Single Shot Engagement Kill [*Military*]
PSEK............ Progressive Symmetrical Erythrokeratoderma [*Medicine*] (DMAA)
PSelS........... Susquehanna University, Selinsgrove, PA [*Library symbol Library of Congress*] (LCLS)
PSEMA.......... Parti Social d'Education des Masses Africaines [*African Party for Social Education of the Masses*] [*Burkina Faso*]
PseOG.......... Pease Oil & Gas Co. [*Associated Press*] (SAG)
PSEP............ Passive Seismic Experiments Package [*NASA*]
PSEP............ Physical Security Evaluation Procedure [*US Army Construction Engineering Research Laboratory*] (RDA)
PSEQ............ Pupil Services Expectation Questionnaire
PSERC.......... Public Sector Economics Research Centre [*University of Leicester*] [*British*] (CB)
PSES............ Pretreatment Standards for Existing Sources [*Environmental Protection Agency*]
PSET............ Pre-Selection English Test [*Australia*]
PSEU............ Production Support Equipment Unit (MCD)
Pseud........... Pseudepigrapha (BJA)
PSEUD.......... Pseudonym
Pseudep........ Pseudepigrapha (BJA)
PSEUDO........ Pseudonym [*Legal shorthand*] (LWAP)
PSEW............ Project on the Status and Education of Women (EA)
PSewD.......... Dixmont State Hospital, Sewickley, PA [*Library symbol Library of Congress*] (LCLS)
PSF............. Pakistan Science Foundation
PSF............. Panama Sea Frontier
PSF............. Panhandle & Santa Fe Railway Co. [*AAR code*]
PSF............. Parti Social Francais [*French Social Party*] [*Political party*] (PPE)
PSF............. Passive Solar Foundation [*Defunct*] (EA)
PSF............. Payload Structure Fuel [*Ratio*]
PSF............. Peptide Supply Factor [*Biochemistry*]
PSF............. Performance Shaping Factor [*Engineering*]
PSF............. Permanent Signal Finder
PSF............. Personal Silicon Foundry (IAA)
PSF............. Per Square Foot (ADA)
PSF............. Philippine Sea Frontier
PSF............. Pittsfield [*Massachusetts*] [*Airport symbol*] (AD)
PSF............. Pittsfield, MA [*Location identifier FAA*] (FAAL)
PSF............. Plutonium Stripper Feed [*Nuclear energy*] (NRCH)
PSF............. Point Spread Function
PSF............. Polysulfone [*Organic chemistry*]
PSF............. Popular Struggle Front [*Palestine*] [*Political party*] (PD)
PSF............. Port Stanley [*Falkland Islands*] [*Seismograph station code, US Geological Survey Closed*] (SEIS)
PSF............. Posterior Spinal Fusion [*Medicine*] (DAVI)
PSF............. Pound-Force per Square Foot (IAA)
PSF............. Pounds per Square Foot
psf.............. Pounds per Square Foot (IDOE)
PSF............. Power Separation Filter (IAA)
PSF............. Preservation Services Fund
PSF............. Presidio of San Francisco [*Military*] (AABC)
PSF............. Prime Subframe (MCD)
PSF............. Private Source Funds (DNAB)
PSF............. Probability of Spurious Fire [*Military*] (CAAL)
PSF............. Probability Sample File [*Human Relations Area Files*] [*Information retrieval*]
PSF............. Processing and Staging Facility [*Solid rocket booster*] (NASA)
PSF............. Processing and Storage Facility [*NASA*] (NASA)
PSF............. Process Signal Former (IAA)
PSF............. Program for the Study of the Future (EA)
PSF............. Program Support Facility (USDC)
PSF............. Program Support Facility [*Marine science*] (OSRA)
PSF............. Progressive Space Forum [*Defunct*] (EA)
PSF............. Progres Social Francais [*French Social Progress*] [*Political party*] (PPE)
PSF............. Provisional Sinn Fein [*Northern Ireland*]
PSF............. Provisional System Feature [*Telecommunications*] (TEL)
PSF............. Pseudosarcomatous Fasciitis [*Medicine*]
PSF............. Saint Francis College, Loretto, PA [*OCLC symbol*] (OCLC)
PSFAM.......... Parameter Sensitive Frequency Assignment Method (MCD)
PS/FC.......... Power Supply / Frequency Converter (DWSG)
PS/FC.......... Power Supply/Fuel Cell (MCD)
PSFC............ Process Supercritical Fluid Chromatography
PSFC............ Provisional Special Forces Co. (CINC)
PSFC/HIMH... Pete Shelley Fan Club/Harmony in My Head (EA)
PSFD............ Public Sector Financial Deficit
PSFI............ PS Financial, Inc. [*NASDAQ symbol*] (SAG)
PS Fincl....... PS Financial, Inc. [*Associated Press*] (SAG)
PSFL............ Puget Sound Freight Lines [*AAR code*]
PSFQ............ Pupil Services Fulfillment Questionnaire
PSFT............ Peoplesoft, Inc. [*NASDAQ symbol*] (SAG)
PSG............. Pacific Seabird Group (EA)
PSG............. Palestine Study Group (EA)
PSG............. Parachute Study Group (EA)
PSG............. Parti Socialiste Guyanais [*Guiana Socialist Party*] [*Political party*] (PPW)
PSG............. Passage [*NWS*] (FAAC)
PSG............. Peak Systolic Gradient [*Medicine*] (MAE)
PSG............. Pershing [*Missile*] (GFGA)
PSG............. Personnel Subsystem Group (SAA)
PSG............. Petersburg [*Alaska*] [*Airport symbol*] (OAG)
PSG............. Petersburg, AK [*Location identifier FAA*] (FAAL)
PSG............. Phenol Sector Group [*European Council of Chemical Manufacturers Federations*] [*Belgium*] (EAIO)
PSG............. Phosphate-Saline-Glucose [*A buffer*] [*Cell culture*]
PSG............. Phosphosilicate Glass (IEEE)
PSG............. Phrase-Structure Grammar [*Computer science*]
PSG............. Planning Systems Generator
PSG............. Platoon Sergeant [*Army*] (AABC)
PSG............. Polysomnogram [*Medicine*] (MAE)
PSG............. Post Stall Gyration (MCD)
PSG............. Power Subsystem Group [*NASA*] (MCD)
PSG............. Pregnancy-Specific Glycoprotein [*Biochemistry*]
PSG............. Presystolic Gallop [*Cardiology*]
PSG............. Production Support Group (NITA)
PSG............. Production System Generator
PSG............. Professional Specialty Group
PSG............. Programmable Sound Generator [*Chip*] [*Atari, Inc.*]
PSG............. Programmable Symbol Generator
PSG............. Pseudomonas Syringae PV Glycinea [*Plant pathology*]
PSG............. PS Group, Inc. [*NYSE symbol*] (SPSG)
PSG............. Psychogalvanometer
PSG............. Psychological Studies Group [*Military*] (VNW)
PSG............. Public Strategies Group, Inc. [*Consulting firm hired in 1993 to improve Minneapolis school district*] (ECON)
PSG............. Publishing Systems Group [*Later, CPSUG*] (EA)
PSG............. Pulsed Strain Gauge (IAA)
PSG............. Pulse Sequence Generation [*Instrumentation*]
PSG............. Pulse Signal Generator (IAA)
PSGA............ Parkinson Support Groups of America (EA)
PSGA............ Pedal Steel Guitar Association (EA)
PSGA............ Professional Skaters Guild of America (EA)
PSGB............ Pharmaceutical Society of Great Britain
PSGB............ Primate Society of Great Britain (DBA)
PSGCU.......... Palm Springs Golf 'Unit' [*NASDAQ symbol*] (TTSB)
PSGD............ Past Senior Grand Deacon [*Freemasonry*]
PSGE............ Partido Socialdemocrata de Guinea Ecuatorial [*Social Democratic Party of Equatorial Guinea*] [*Political party*] (EY)
PSGE............ Passage [*Postal Service standard*] (OPSA)
PSGE............ Photosynthetic Gas Exchanger (SAA)
PSG-EG........ Partido Socialista Galego - Esquerda Galega [*Spain Political party*] (EY)
PSGM............ Past Supreme Grand Master [*Freemasonry*]
PSGN............ Post-Streptococcal Glomerulonephritis [*Medicine*]
PSGR............ Passenger (AFM)
PS Grp......... PS Group, Inc. [*Associated Press*] (SAG)
PSGT............ Platoon Sergeant [*Military*]
PSGTCAEI..... Permanent Secretariat of the General Treaty on Central American Economic Integration (EAIO)
PSGV............ Pacific Sentinel Gold Corp. [*NASDAQ symbol*] (SAG)
PSGVF.......... Pacific Sentinel Gold [*NASDAQ symbol*] (TTSB)
PSGW............ Past Senior Grand Warden [*Freemasonry*]

PSH .... Friends Historical Library of Swarthmore College, Swarthmore, PA [*OCLC symbol*] (OCLC)
PSH .... Parshall, ND [*Location identifier FAA*] (FAAL)
PSH .... Past Social History (CPH)
PSH .... Past Surgical History [*Medicine*] (DMAA)
PSH .... Permanent Shift of Hearing
PSH .... Peshawar [*Pakistan*] [*Seismograph station code, US Geological Survey*] (SEIS)
PSH .... Phase Shift (MSA)
PSH .... Polystyrene, Hydrogenous [*Organic chemistry*]
PSH .... Postspinal Headache (AAMN)
PSH .... Post-Stimulus Histogram [*Psychometrics*]
PSH .... Preselect Heading (NG)
PSH .... Pressure Switch, High [*Nuclear energy*] (NRCH)
PSH .... Productive Standard Hour (PDAA)
PSH .... Program Support Handbook
PSH .... Proximity Sensing Head
PSH .... Publications Statistiques Hongroises [*Hungary*]
PSH .... Public Storage Canadian Properties IIIa Ltd. [*Toronto Stock Exchange symbol*]
P Shaw .... Patrick Shaw's Justiciary Cases [*1819-31*] [*Scotland*] [*A publication*] (DLA)
PSHB .... Persistent Spectral Hole-Burning [*Spectroscopy*]
PSHC .... Permanent Secretariat of the Hemispheric Congress (EA)
PSHC .... Public Speaking and Humor Club (EA)
PSHCJ .... Philanthropic Society of House Carpenters and Joiners [*A union*] [*British*]
PSHD .... Phase-Shift Driver (MSA)
PSHD .... Port Security Harbor Defense (DOMA)
PSHF .... Polysulfone Hollow Fiber [*Filtration membrane*]
PSHFA .... Public Servants' Housing and Finance Association [*British*] (BI)
PSHR .... Pusher [*Freight*]
PShS .... Shippensburg State College, Shippensburg, PA [*Library symbol Library of Congress*] (LCLS)
PSHT .... Powys Self-Help Trust [*British*]
PSI .... Pacific Semiconductors, Inc. (MCD)
PSI .... Pacific Stratus Investigation [*Marine science*] (OSRA)
PSI .... Pacific Sulfur Investigation [*Marine science*] (OSRA)
PSI .... Pacific Sulfur/Stratus Investigation (USDC)
PSI .... Page Survival Index (PDAA)
PSI .... Paid Service Indication [*Telecommunications*] (TEL)
PSI .... Pakistan Standards Institution (IAA)
PSI .... Palmar Sweat Index (EDAC)
PSI .... Paper Stock Institute of America (EA)
PSI .... Parapat [*Sumatra*] [*Seismograph station code, US Geological Survey*] (SEIS)
PSI .... Parapsychological Services Institute (EA)
PSI .... Parenting Stress Index [*Psychology*]
PSI .... Partai Socialis Indonesia [*Socialist Party of Indonesia*]
PSI .... Participation Systems, Inc. [*Electronics Communications Co.*] [*Winchester , MA*] [*Telecommunications*] (TSSD)
PSI .... Particle-Sizing Interferometer (MCD)
PSI .... Parti Socialiste Ivoirien [*Ivorian Socialist Party*] [*The Ivory Coast*] [*Political party*] (EY)
PSI .... Partito Socialista Italiano [*Italian Socialist Party*] [*Political party*] (PPE)
PSI .... Pasni [*Pakistan*] [*Airport symbol*] (OAG)
PSI .... Passive Solar Institute [*Defunct*] (EA)
PSI .... Percent Similarity Index
PSI .... Performance Systems International, Inc.
PSI .... Peripherally Synapsing Interneuron [*Neurology*]
PSI .... Peripheral Subsystem Interface [*Computer science*] (IAA)
PSI .... Permanent Staff Instructor [*Military British*]
PSI .... Permuterm Subject Index [*Institute for Scientific Information*] [*A publication*] (IID)
PsI .... Perpetual Storage, Inc., Salt Lake City, UT [*Library symbol Library of Congress*] (LCLS)
PSI .... Personalised System of Induction (AIE)
PSI .... Personalized System of Instruction
PSI .... Personal Sequential-Inference Machine [*Computer science*]
PSI .... Personal Service Income
PSI .... Personnel Security Investigation [*Military*]
PSI .... Personnel Selection Inventory [*Test*]
PSI .... Person of Special Importance [*British military*] (DMA)
PSI .... Per Square Inch (ADA)
PSI .... Pharmaceutical Society of Ireland (BI)
PSI .... Phenomenological Systems, Inc.
PSI .... Photographic Society International (EA)
PSI .... Photographic Society of Ireland (BI)
PSI .... Photometric Sunspot Index
PSI .... Photo Services Industrial Ltd. [*British*]
PSI .... Physical, Sensitivity, Intellectual [*Biorhythmics*]
PSI .... Planned Start Installation [*Telecommunications*] (TEL)
PSI .... Plan Speed Indicator [*Military*]
PSI .... Plas Speed Indicator (IAA)
PSI .... Platoon Sector Indicator [*Army*]
PSI .... Play Skills Inventory
PSI .... Policy Studies Institute [*Research center British*] (IRC)
PSI .... Pollutant Standards Index [*Environmental Protection Agency*]
p-Si .... Polycrystalline Silicon [*Photovoltaic energy systems*]
PSI .... Porta Systems [*AMEX symbol*] (TTSB)
PSI .... Porta Systems Corp. [*AMEX symbol*] (SPSG)
PSI .... Positive Self-Image [*Psychology*]
PSI .... Posterior Sagittal Index [*Anatomy*] (AAMN)
PSI .... Posterior Superior Iliac Spine [*Posterosuperior iliac spine*] [*Anatomy*] (DAVI)
PSI .... Postpartum Support, International (EA)
PSI .... Pound-Force per Square Inch (IAA)
PSI .... Pounds per Square Inch
psi .... Pounds per Square Inch (IDOE)
psi .... Pounds per Square Inch [*Marine science*] (OSRA)
PSI .... Pounds per Square Inch Absolute (IAA)
PSI .... Power per Square Inch
PSI .... Power Static Inverter (NASA)
PSI .... Praed Street Irregulars (EA)
PSI .... Preprogrammed Self-Instruction [*Computer science*] (IEEE)
PSI .... Preschool Inventory (EDAC)
PSI .... Pre-Sentence Investigation (OICC)
PSI .... Present Serviceability Index (IEEE)
PSI .... Preservice Inspection [*Nuclear energy*] (NRCH)
PSI .... Preshipment Inspection [*International trade*]
PSI .... Pressure Sensitive Identification
PSI .... Pressurized Sphere Injection (DNAB)
PSI .... Prime System Indicator
PSI .... Probe Systems, Inc.
PSI .... Problem-Solving and Inference Machine (IAA)
PSI .... Problem-Solving Information [*Apparatus*]
PSI .... Problem-Solving Interpreter [*Computer language*]
PSI .... Process System Index
PSI .... Process Systems, Inc.
PSI .... Proctorial System of Instruction (IEEE)
PSI .... Production Stock Item (MCD)
PSI .... Product Support Instructions (AAG)
PSI .... Professional Secretaries International [*Kansas City, MO*] (EA)
PSI .... Programmed School Input (NVT)
PSI .... Program Status Information [*Computer science*] (MCD)
PSI .... Program Supply Interest (MCD)
PSI .... Project Starlight International (EA)
PSI .... Protosynthetic Indexing (NITA)
PSI .... Protosynthex Index
PSI .... PSI Energy [*Associated Press*] (SAG)
PSI .... Psychological Screening Inventory [*Personality development test*]
PSI .... Psychosomatic Inventory [*Psychology*]
PSI .... Publications Standing Instruction (AAG)
PSI .... Public Services International [*See also ISP*] [*Ferney Voltaire, France*] (EAIO)
PSI .... Pulse Sciences, Inc.
PSIA .... Paper Stock Institute of America (EA)
PSIA .... Pounds per Square Inch Absolute
psia .... Pounds per Square Inch Absolute (IDOE)
psia .... Pounds per Square Inch, Absolute [*Marine science*] (OSRA)
PSIA .... President of the Society of Industrial Artists [*British*]
PSIA .... Pressure Absolute [*AGA*] (TAG)
PSIA .... Production System Integration Area
PSIA .... Professional Ski Instructors of America (EA)
PSIA .... Public Security Investigation Agency [*Japan*] (CINC)
PSIC .... Passenger Service Improvement Corp.
PSIC .... Passive Solar Industries Council (EA)
PSIC .... Process Signal Interface Controller
PSIC .... Production Scheduling and Inventory Control
PSICOMP ..... Predicted Speech Intelligibility Computer (IAA)
Psicor .... PSICOR, Inc. [*Associated Press*] (SAG)
PSICP .... Program Support Inventory Control Point
PSID .... Partial Seismic Intrusion Device (MCD)
PSID .... Patrol Seismic Intrusion Detector [*or Device*] [*DoD*]
PSID .... Pounds per Square Inch Differential (MCD)
psid .... Pounds per Square Inch, Differential [*Marine science*] (OSRA)
PSID .... Preliminary Safety Information Document [*Nuclear energy*] (NRCH)
PS/IDS .... Physical Security/Intrusion Detection System (MCD)
PSIEP .... Project on Scientific Information Exchange in Psychology [*Superseded by Office of Communication*]
PSIFT .... Platelet Suspension Immunofluorescence Test [*Medicine*] (DMAA)
PSIG .... Per-Square-Inch Gauge (AAGC)
psig .... Pounds per Square Inch, Gauge [*Marine science*] (OSRA)
PSIG .... Pounds per Square Inch Gauge
psig .... Pounds per Square Inch Gauge (IDOE)
PSIG .... Propulsion Systems Integration Group [*NASA*] (NASA)
PSII .... Process Safety Incident Investigation [*Engineering*]
PSIL .... Potential Selected Item List (MCD)
PSIL .... Preferred Speech Interference Level
PSI-LOGO .... Listing of Oil and Gas Opportunities [*Online Resource Exchange, Inc.*] [*Database*]
PSIM .... Power System Instrumentation and Measurement (MCD)
PSIM .... Problem-Solving Instructional Material [*National Science Foundation project*]
PSINet .... PSINet, Inc. [*Associated Press*] (SAG)
PSIO .... Performance Scales Intelligence Quotient (EDAC)
PSIP .... Private Sector Initiative Program [*Department of Labor*]
PSIS .... Posterior Sacroiliac Spine [*Anatomy*] (DAVI)
PSIS .... Pounds per Square Inch Sealed (NASA)
PSIS .... Programme for Strategic and International Security Studies [*Switzerland*] (PDAA)
PSISIG .... Psychic Science International Special Interest Group (EA)
PSIT .... Property Security Investment Trust [*British*]
PSIU .... Power/Sequence Interface Unit (MCD)
PSIUP .... Partito Socialista Italiano di Unita Proletaria [*Italian Socialist Party of Proletarian Unity (1945-1947)*] [*Political party*] (PPE)
PSIV .... Passive
PSIX .... Performance Systems International, Inc. [*NASDAQ symbol*] (SAG)

PSIX............ PSINet, Inc. [*NASDAQ symbol*] (SAG)
PSIX............ PSINet Inc. [*NASDAQ symbol*] (TTSB)
PSJ............ Parallel Swivel Joint
PSJ............ Petites Soeurs de Jesus [*Little Sisters of Jesus*] [*Italy*] (EAIO)
psj............ Planed and Square-Jointed (DAC)
PSJ............ Plane Swivel Joint
PSJ............ Point Spread Junction (IAA)
PSJ............ Poso [*Indonesia*] [*Airport symbol*] (OAG)
PSJ............ Pressure Switch Joint
PSJ............ Public Service Job (OICC)
PSJS............ Pier and Span Junction Set (MCD)
PSK............ Dublin, VA [*Location identifier FAA*] (FAAL)
PSK............ Phase Shift Keying [*Computer science*]
PSK............ PostSparKasse [*Post Office Savings Bank*] [*Austria*]
PSK............ Power Supply Kit
PSK............ Private Secretary to the King [*British*]
PSK............ Program Selection Key [*Computer science*] (BUR)
PSK............ Protection Survey Kit
PSK............ Protein Serine Kinase (DMAA)
PSK............ Public Storage Properties IX, Inc. [*AMEX symbol*] (SAG)
PSK............ Pulse Shift Keying (CAAL)
PSKM............ Phase Shift Keyed Modulation (NITA)
PSKM............ Phase-Shift Keying MODEM
PSK-PCM..... Phase-Shift Keying - Pulse Code Modulation
PSL............ Palouse Silt Loam [*Agronomy*]
PSL............ Parallel Strand Lumber
PSL............ Parasternal Line [*Anatomy*] (MAE)
PSL............ Parti Social-Liberal [*Algeria*] [*Political party*] (EY)
PSL............ Paymaster-Sub-Lieutenant [*Navy British*]
PSL............ Peabody Short Line R. R. [*Army*]
PSL............ Personnel Skill Levels (AAG)
PSL............ Perth [*Scotland*] [*Airport symbol*] (AD)
PSL............ Petroleum Ether-Soluble Lipid
PSL............ Phase Sequence Logic (IAA)
PSL............ Photographic Science Laboratory [*Navy*]
PSL............ Photostimulated Luminescence [*Physics*]
PSL............ Physical Sciences Laboratory [*University of Wisconsin - Madison, New Mexico State University*] [*Research center*]
PSL............ Physical Sciences Laboratory [*Bethesda, MD*] [*National Institutes of Health*] (GRD)
PSL............ Pipe Sleeve
PSL............ Pocket Select Language [*Burroughs Corp.*]
PSL............ Polskie Stronnictwo Ludowe [*Polish Peasant Party*] [*Political party*] (PPE)
PSL............ Polystyrene Latex (PDAA)
PSL............ Portable Standard List Processing [*Computer science*]
PSL............ Potassium, Sodium Chloride, Sodium Lactate [*Solution*] (AAMN)
PSL............ Potential Source List (MCD)
PSL............ Power and Signal List [*Telecommunications*] (TEL)
PSL............ Power Source Logic
PSL............ Practical Storage Life
PSL............ Pressure Seal (NASA)
PSL............ Pressure-Sensitive Label
PSL............ Primary Standards Laboratory
PSL............ Private Sector Liquidity
PSL............ Problem-Solving Language
PSL............ Problem Specification Language
PSL............ Problem Statement Language [*Computer science*] (IAA)
PSL............ Process Simulation Language [*Computer science*] (TEL)
PSL............ Process Status Longword [*Number*] [*Computer science*] (BYTE)
PSL............ Professionnel Air Systems [*France ICAO designator*] (FAAC)
PSL............ Programming Script Language (PCM)
PSL............ Program Support Library (MCD)
PSL............ Project Support Laboratory [*Military*] (CAAL)
PSL............ Propellant Seal
PSL............ Propulsion Systems Laboratory [*USATACOM*] (RDA)
PSL............ Public School League [*Sports*]
PSL............ Public Storage Prop'A' X [*AMEX symbol*] (TTSB)
PSL............ Public Storage Properties X, Inc. [*AMEX symbol*] (SAG)
PSL............ Pycnocline Scattering Layer (DNAB)
PSL............ South Hills Library Association, Pittsburgh, PA [*OCLC symbol*] (OCLC)
PSLA............ Palaung State Liberation Army [*Myanmar*] [*Political party*] (EY)
PSLA............ Polish Sea League of America (EA)
PSLC............ Post-Schistosomal Liver Cirrhosis [*Medicine*]
PSLC............ Private Security Liaison Council (EA)
PSLI............ Packet Switch Level Interface
PSLI............ Partito Socialista dei Lavoratori Italiani [*Socialist Party of Italian Workers*] [*Political party*] (PPE)
PSLI............ Physalaemin-Like Immunoreactivity [*Medicine*]
PSL-Lewica... Polskie Stronnictwo-Lewica [*Polish Peasant Party-Left (1947-1949)*] [*Political party*] (PPE)
PSL-Lewica... Polskie Stronnictwo Ludowe-Lewica [*Polish Peasant Party-Left (1913-1920)*] [*Political party*] (PPE)
PSLLS............ Pulsed Solid-State LASER Light Source
PSL-NW....... Polskie Stronnictwo Ludowe-Nowe Wyzwolenie [*Polish Peasant Party-New Liberation*] [*Political party*] (PPE)
PSLO............ Palaung State Liberation Organization [*Myanmar*] [*Political party*] (EY)
PSL-Piast.... Polskie Stronnictwo Ludowe-Piast [*Polish Peasant Party-Piast*] [*Political party*] (PPE)
PSL/PSA...... Problem Statement Language/Problem Specification Analyzer [*Computer science*]
PSLR............ Product Safety and Liability Reporter [*A publication*]
PSLS............ Pan Stock Line Station (MCD)
PSL SOL....... Potassium, Sodium Chloride, Sodium Lactate Solution (BABM)
PSL sol....... Potassium, Sodium Chloride, Sodium Lactate Solution [*Pharmacology*] (DAVI)
PSLT............ Picture Story Language Test
PSLT............ Port Side Light (IAA)
PSLT............ Pressurized Sonobuoy Launch Tube [*Navy*] (CAAL)
pslt............ Psalter (VRA)
PSLV............ Poa Semilatent Virus
PSLV............ Polar Satellite Launch Vehicle
PSL-Wyzwolenie... Polskie Stronnictwo Ludowe-Wyzwolenie [*Polish Peasant Party-Liberation*] [*Political party*] (PPE)
PSM............ Panasystolic Murmur [*Cardiology*] (DAVI)
PSM............ Parallel Slit Map (OA)
PSM............ Parcel Sorting Machine [*Freight*] (DCTA)
PSM............ Parc Saint-Maur [*France*] [*Later, CLF*] [*Geomagnetic observatory code*]
PSM............ Particle Size Monitor [*Instrumentation*]
PSM............ Parti Socialiste Mauricien [*Mauritian Socialist Party*] [*Political party*] (EY)
PSM............ Parti Socialiste Monegasque [*Monaco Socialist Party*] [*Political party*] (PPW)
PSM............ Passenger Service Manager [*Travel industry*]
PSM............ Past Savio Movement [*Defunct*] (EA)
PSM............ Peak Selector Memory [*Computer science*]
PSM............ People for Self Management [*An association*] (NADA)
PSM............ Personal Skills Map [*Career effectiveness test*]
PSM............ Personnel Subsystem Manager [*Army*] (AABC)
PSM............ Personnel Systems Management [*Air Force*] (AFM)
PSM............ Petroleum Supply Monthly [*Database*] [*Department of Energy Information service or system*] (CRD)
PSM............ Phase-Sensitive Modulator (MCD)
PSM............ Phase-Shifter Module
PSM............ Physician and Sports Medicine [*A publication*]
PSM............ Pia Societas Missionum [*Fathers of the Pious Society of Missions, Pallottini*] [*Roman Catholic religious order*]
PSM............ Pioneer Metals Corp. [*Toronto Stock Exchange symbol Vancouver Stock Exchange symbol*]
PSM............ Platyschisma Shale Member [*Geology*]
PSM............ Please See Me
PSM............ Plymouth State College of the University of New Hampshere, Plymouth, NH [*OCLC symbol*] (OCLC)
PSM............ Point Source Monitoring [*Environmental Protection Agency*] (GFGA)
PSM............ Portsmouth [*New Hampshire*] [*Airport symbol*] (AD)
PSM............ Portsmouth, NH [*Location identifier FAA*] (FAAL)
PSM............ Postal Service Manual [*A publication*] (AFM)
PSM............ Postmitochondrial Supernatant [*Medicine*] (DMAA)
PSM............ Postsynaptic Membrane [*Neurology*]
PSM............ Power Strapping Machine
PSM............ Power Supply Module (MHDI)
PSM............ Power System Module
PSM............ Preservation Security Manager
PSM............ Pressure Switch Manifold [*Automotive transmissions*]
PSM............ Presystolic Murmur [*Cardiology*]
PSM............ Prism (MSA)
PSM............ Process Safety Management [*Chemical engineering*]
PSM............ Production Systems Management (IAA)
PSM............ Productive Standard Minute (MHDI)
PSM............ Product Support Manual (AAG)
PSM............ Professional Staff Member [*Congress*] (DOMA)
PSM............ Programming Support Monitor [*Texas Instruments, Inc.*]
PSM............ Program-Sensitive Malfunction
PSM............ Program Support Management [*NASA*] (KSC)
PSM............ Progressive Series Modulator (IAA)
PSM............ Project Safety Management
PSM............ Propellant Storage Module [*NASA*]
PSM............ Pro Sanctity Movement (EA)
PSM............ Public Service Medal
PSM............ Public Storage Prop'A' XI [*AMEX symbol*] (TTSB)
PSM............ Public Storage Properties XI, Inc. [*AMEX symbol*] (SAG)
PSM............ Pulse Slope Modulation (IAA)
PSM............ Pulse-Spacing Modulation (ECII)
PSM............ Pyro Substitute Monitor [*NASA*] (NASA)
PSm............ Thesaurus Syriacus [*R. Paine Smith*] [*A publication*] (BJA)
PSMA............ Power Saw Manufacturers Association [*Later, CSMA*] (EA)
PSMA............ Power Supply Manufacturers Association [*British*] (DBA)
PSMA............ President of the Society of Marine Artists [*British*]
PSMA............ Pressure Sensitive Manufacturers Association [*British*] (DBA)
PSMA............ Professional Services Management Association [*Alexandria, VA*] (EA)
PSMA............ Progressive Spinal Muscular Atrophy [*Medicine*]
PSMA............ Proximal Spinal Muscular [*Medicine*] (DMAA)
PSMA............ Proximal Spinal Muscular Atrophy [*Medicine*] (DMAA)
PSMA............ Pyrotechnic Signal Manufacturers Association (EA)
PSMD............ Photo Selective Metal Deposition
PSME............ Partido Socialista de Melilla [*See also PSOE*] [*Spanish North Africa*] [*Political party*] (MENA)
PSME............ Personal Social and Moral Education (AIE)
PSMed............ Psychosomatic Medicine (DAVI)
PSME-PSOE... Partido Socialista de Melilla - Partido Socialista Obrero Espanol [*Political party*] (EY)
PSMF............ Protein Sparing Modified Fast
PSMFC............ Pacific States Marine Fisheries Commission
PSMI............ Phase-Shift Modal Interference
PSMI............ Precise Ship Motion Instrument
PSMIT............ Programming Services for Multimedia Industry Terminals [*IBM Corp.*]

PSML........... Processor System Modeling Language [*1976*] [*Computer science*] (CSR)
PSMM.......... Multimission Patrol Ship [*Symbol*]
PSMMA........ Plastic Soft Materials Manufacturers Association (EA)
PSMP.......... Program on Short- and Medium-Range Weather Prediction Research [*Marine science*] (OSRA)
PSMP.......... Project Software Management Plan (SSD)
PSMPA........ Per Square Meter per Annum
PSMR.......... Parts Specification Management for Reliability
PSMR.......... Pneumatic [*or Pressure*] System Manifold Regulator [*or Manual*] (AAG)
PSMS.......... Permanent Section of Microbiological Standardization (MCD)
PSMS.......... Physical Self Maintenance Scale
PSMSL........ Permanent Service for Mean Sea Level [*of the Federation of Astronomical and Geophysical Data Analysis Services*] [*Birkenhead, Merseyside, England*] (EAIO)
PSMT.......... Paced Sequential Memory Task (PDAA)
PSMT.......... Pedestal Sight Manipulation Test (IAA)
PSMT.......... Perishable Sheet Metal Tool (MCD)
PSMU.......... Power Supply and Multiplexer Unit [*Telecommunications*] (TSSD)
PSMV.......... Paspalum Striate Mosaic Virus [*Plant pathology*]
PSMV.......... Pea Seed-Borne Mosaic Virus [*Plant pathology*]
PSN............ Package Sequence Number
PSN............ Packet Switched Network
PSN............ Packet Switching Node
PSN............ Palestine, TX [*Location identifier FAA*] (FAAL)
PSN............ Parent Support Network [*Australia*]
PSN............ Partial Shipment Number [*DoD*]
PSN............ Parti de la Solidarite Nationale [*Party of National Solidarity*] [*Luxembourg*] [*Political party*] (PPE)
PSN............ Partido Socialista Nicaraguense [*Nicaraguan Socialist Party*] [*Political party*] (PPW)
PSN............ Permanent Sort Number [*Computer science*]
PSN............ Poor Sisters of Nazareth (TOCD)
PSN............ Position
PSN............ Potosina del Aire SA de CV [*Mexico ICAO designator*] (FAAC)
PSN............ Private Satellite Network, Inc. [*New York, NY*] [*Telecommunications*] (TSSD)
PSN............ Processing Serial Number (MCD)
PSN............ Program Summary Network (MCD)
PSN............ Progressive Student Network (EA)
PSN............ Provisioning Sequence Number (MCD)
PSN............ Public Storage Prop'A' XII [*AMEX symbol*] (TTSB)
PSN............ Public Storage Properties XII, Inc. [*AMEX symbol*] (SAG)
PSN............ Public Switched Network (BUR)
PSNA.......... Phytochemical Society of North America (EA)
PSNA.......... Powys Society of North America (EA)
PSNAL........ Personal (FAAC)
PSNC.......... Pacific Steam Navigation Co. (MHDW)
PSNC.......... Parti Socialiste de la Nouvelle Caledonie [*Socialist Party of New Caledonia*] [*Political party*] (PPW)
PSNCF........ Pacific Southern Naval Coastal Frontier
PSNCO........ Personnel Staff Noncommissioned Officer [*Military*]
PSNL.......... Personnel (FAAC)
PSNP.......... Pebble Springs Nuclear Plant (NRCH)
PSNR.......... Pasifik Satelit Nusantara (PT) [*NASDAQ symbol*] (SAG)
PSNR.......... Positioner
PSNR.......... Power Signal-to-Noise Ratio
PSNRP........ Position Report [*Aviation*] (FAAC)
PSNS.......... Physical Science for Nonscience Students
PSNS.......... Pretreatment Standards for New Indirect Sources [*Environmental Protection Agency*]
PSNS.......... Programmable Sampling Network Switch
PSNS.......... Puget Sound Naval Shipyard [*Bremerton, WA*] (MCD)
PSNS-MATLABS... Puget Sound Naval Shipyard Material Laboratories [*Bremerton, WA*]
PSNSR........ Position Sensor (MCD)
PSNSW........ Philatelic Society of New South Wales [*Australia*]
PSNSY........ Puget Sound Naval Shipyard [*Bremerton, WA*]
PSNT.......... Present [*Legal term*] (ROG)
PSO............ Pad Safety Officer [*Aerospace*] (MCD)
PSO............ Paint Spray Outfit
PSO............ Paseo
PSO............ Pasto [*Colombia*] [*Airport symbol*] (OAG)
PSO............ Pasto [*Colombia*] [*Seismograph station code, US Geological Survey*] (SEIS)
PSO............ Pauli Spin Operator [*Physics*]
PSO............ Peacetime Stockage Objective [*DoD*] (AFIT)
PSO............ Penobscot Shoe [*AMEX symbol*] (TTSB)
PSO............ Penobscot Shoe Co. [*AMEX symbol*] (SPSG)
PSO............ Personal Staff Officer [*Australia*]
PSO............ Personnel Security Officer [*Military*]
PSO............ Personnel Selection Officer [*British military*] (DMA)
PSO............ Personnel Services Organisation [*Australia*]
PSO............ Piano-Shaped Object
PSO............ Pilot Systems Operator
PSO............ Planet Sensor Output
PSO............ Point Surface Origin
PSO............ Polaris Systems Officer [*British military*] (DMA)
PSO............ Policy Studies Organization (EA)
PSO............ Political Survey Officers [*Navy*]
PSO............ Polysulfone [*Also, PS*] [*Organic chemistry*]
PSO............ Port Services Office [*or Officer*] (DNAB)
PSO............ Primary Standardization Office [*Military*] (AABC)
PSO............ Principal Scientific Officer [*British*]
PSO............ Principal Staff Officer [*British military*] (DMA)
PSO............ Procurement Services Office
PSO............ Product Support Organization
PSO............ Profco Resources Ltd. [*Vancouver Stock Exchange symbol*]
PSO............ Program Staff Officer
PSO............ Progressive Supranuclear Ophthalmoplegia (CPH)
PSO............ Prospective Supply Officer (DNAB)
PSO............ Protective Security Officer
PSO............ Provisions Supply Office [*Military*]
PSO............ Proximal Subungual Onychomycosis
PSO............ Psychiatric Services Officer [*Australia*]
PSO............ Publications Supply Officer [*Military*]
PSO............ Publicity Security Officer [*Navy*]
PSO............ Public Safety Officer
PSO............ Public Service Obligation [*Australia*]
PSO............ Public Service Organisation [*Government grant*] [*British*]
PSOA.......... Postal Supervisory Officers' Association [*Australia*]
PSOA.......... Pro Stock Owners Association (EA)
PSOB.......... Paper Society for the Overseas Blind [*Defunct*] (EA)
PSOC.......... Preliminary System Operational Concept (MCD)
PSOE.......... Partido Socialista Obrero Espanol [*Spanish Socialist Workers' Party*] [*See also PSME*] [*Political party*] (PPE)
P Sol.......... Partly Soluble (WGA)
P sol.......... Partly Soluble [*Chemistry*] (DAVI)
PSOLMHT.... Pious Society of Our Lady of the Most Holy Trinity (EA)
PSom.......... Mary S. Biesecker Public Library, Somerset, PA [*Library symbol Library of Congress*] (LCLS)
PSomHi....... Somerset County Historical and Genealogical Society, Somerset, PA [*Library symbol Library of Congress*] (LCLS)
PSON.......... Paul-Son Gaming [*NASDAQ symbol*] (TTSB)
PSON.......... Paul-Son Gaming Corp. [*NASDAQ symbol*] (SAG)
PSON.......... Person (ROG)
PSONAL....... Personal (ROG)
PSOP.......... Parti Socialiste des Ouvriers et Paysans [*Socialist Party of Workers and Peasants*] [*France Political party*]
PSOP.......... Payload Systems Operating Procedures [*NASA*] (NASA)
PSOP.......... Power System Optimization Program [*Computer science*]
PSOR.......... Preliminary System of Requirements
PSOS.......... Probably Secure Operating System (MHDB)
PSP............ Pace-Setting Potential [*Physiology*]
PSP............ Pacifistische Socialistische Partij [*Pacific Socialist Party*] [*Political party Netherlands*]
PSP............ Package Size Proneness [*Marketing*]
PSP............ Packaging Shipping Procedures
PSP............ Packet Switching Processor
PSP............ Pad Safety Plan
PSP............ Palm Springs [*California*] [*Airport symbol*] (OAG)
PSP............ Palm Springs, CA [*Location identifier FAA*] (FAAL)
PSP............ Pancreatic Spasmolytic Peptide [*Biochemistry*]
PSP............ Paralytic Shellfish Poisoning [*Marine biology*]
PSP............ Parathyroid Secretory Protein [*Biochemistry*]
PSP............ Parti de la Solidarite du Peuple [*Cameroon*] [*Political party*] (EY)
PSP............ Partido Socialista del Peru [*Socialist Party of Peru*] [*Political party*] (PPW)
PSP............ Partido Socialista Popular [*Popular Socialist Party*] [*Peru*] [*Political party*] (PPW)
PSP............ Partido Socialista Popular [*Popular Socialist Party*] [*Spain Political party*] (PPE)
PSP............ Partido Socialista Popular [*Popular Socialist Party*] [*Pre-1965*] [*Cuba*] [*Political party*] (PPW)
PSP............ Partido Socialista Portuguesa [*Portuguese Socialist Party*] [*Political party*] (PPW)
PSP............ Partido Social Progresista [*Social Progressive Party*] [*Brazil Political party*]
PSP............ Parti Socialiste Polynesien [*Polynesian Socialist Party*] [*Political party*] (PPW)
PSP............ Parti Social pour le Progres [*Tunisia*] [*Political party*] (EY)
PSP............ Parti Soudanais Progressiste [*Sudanese Progressive Party*] [*Political party*]
PSP............ Parts Screening Program
PSP............ Patrol Seaplane
PSP............ Payload Signal Processor [*NASA*] (NASA)
PSP............ Payload Specialist Panel [*NASA*] (NASA)
PSP............ Payload Support Plan [*NASA*] (MCD)
PSP............ Payroll Savings Plan (GFGA)
PSP............ Peak Sideband Power (DEN)
PSP............ Perforated Steel Planking (SAA)
PSP............ Perforated Steel Plate (VNW)
PSP............ Perforated Steel Plating (DNAB)
PSP............ Performance Shaping Parameters (IEEE)
PSP............ Performance Share Plan [*Human resources*] (WYGK)
PSP............ Performance Standards Program
PSP............ Periodic Short Pulse (MAE)
PSP............ Personal Security Preview [*Psychology*] (DAVI)
PSP............ Personal Success Program
PSP............ Personnel Subsystem Process [*Army*] (AABC)
PSP............ Pharmacological Sciences Program [*Bethesda, MD*] [*National Institute of General Medical Sciences*] (GRD)
PSP............ Phenolsulfonephthalein [*Chemical indicator*]
PSP............ Pierced Steel Planking [*Military*]
PSP............ Plane Strain Plastometer
PSP............ Planet Scan Platform [*NASA*] (KSC)
PSP............ Planned Standard Programming [*Computer science*]
PSP............ Plasma Spraying [*Welding*]
PSP............ Plasmon Surface Polariton [*Physics*]

PSP............ Platform Sensor Package
PSP............ Pointed Soft Point [*Ammunition*]
PSP............ Pointed Soft Point Bullet
PSP............ Policies, Systems, and Procedures
PSP............ Polyfactorial Study of Personality [*Psychology*]
PSP............ Poly(styrene peroxide) [*Organic chemistry*]
PSP............ Portable Service Processor (IEEE)
PSP............ Positive Spike Pattern (MAE)
psp............ Posterior Subcapsular Plaque [*Ophthalmology*] (DAVI)
PSP............ Postipankki [*National savings bank*] [*Finland*]
PSP............ Post-Shoring-Polyethylene [*Method of constructing underground homes*]
PSP............ Post-Surgical Pain [*Medicine*]
PSP............ Postsynaptic Potential [*Neurophysiology*]
PSP............ Potential for Successful Performance [*Test*]
PSP............ Power System Planning
PSP............ Praja Socialist Party [*India*] [*Political party*] (PPW)
PSP............ Precision Spot Positioning
PSP............ Predictable System Performance (SAA)
PSP............ Predictive Smooth Pursuit [*Ophthalmology*]
PSP............ Pre-Season Predictor Model [*Television ratings*] (NTCM)
PSP............ Presending Pause (NITA)
PSP............ Presensitized Photoplate
PSP............ Prestart Panel [*Aerospace*] (AAG)
PSP............ Priced Spare Parts [*Military*] (AFIT)
PSP............ Primary Smog Product (PDAA)
PSP............ Primary Sodium Pump [*Nuclear energy*] (NRCH)
PSP............ Primary Supply Point [*Military*] (AFM)
PSP............ Primary Support Point [*Military*] (AFM)
PSP............ Priority Strike Program
PSP............ Problem Solving Process
PSP............ Product Service Publication [*General Motors Corp.*]
PSP............ Product Support Program (NG)
PSP............ Professional and Scholarly Publishing Division [*Association of American Publishers*] (EDAC)
PSP............ Profit Sharing Plan [*Business term*] (MHDW)
PSP............ Programmable Signal Processor (MCD)
PSP............ Program Segment Prefix [*Computer science*]
PSP............ Program Support Plan [*NASA*]
PSP............ Progressive Socialist Party [*Lebanon*] [*Political party*] (BJA)
PSP............ Progressive Supranuclear Palsy [*Neurology*]
PSP............ Project Schedule Plan (NASA)
PSP............ Project Standard Practice (DNAB)
PSP............ Protective Shielding Program
PSP............ Protocol for Specific Purpose
PSP............ Pseudopregnancy [*Gynecology*]
PSP............ Pseudostatic Spontaneous Potential (IAA)
PSP............ Public Storage Canadian Properties [*Limited Partnership Units*] [*Toronto Stock Exchange symbol*]
PSP............ Public Storage Prop'A' XIV [*AMEX symbol*] (TTSB)
PSP............ Public Storage Properties XIV, Inc. [*AMEX symbol*] (SAG)
PSP............ Puerto Rican Socialist Party [*Political party*] (PD)
PSP............ Swarthmore College Peace Collection, Swarthmore, PA [*OCLC symbol*] (OCLC)
PSPA.......... Pacific Seafood Processors Association (EA)
PSPA.......... Passive Solar Products Association (EA)
PSPA.......... Pressure Static Probe Assembly (MCD)
PSPA.......... Professional School Photographers of America (EA)
PSPA.......... Professional Sports Photographers Association [*British*] (EAIO)
PSP & E...... Product Support Planning and Estimating (AAG)
PSPC.......... Partido Socialista del Pueblo de Ceuta [*Political party*] (EY)
PSPC.......... Physical Security / Pilferage Code
PSPC.......... Polystyrene Packaging Council (EA)
PSPC.......... Position-Sensitive Proportional Counter [*Instrumentation*]
PSPC.......... President's Soviet Protocol Committee [*World War II*]
PSPD.......... Permits and State Programs Division [*Environmental Protection Agency*] (GFGA)
PSPD.......... Position-Sensitive Proportional Detector [*For X-ray diffraction*]
PSPDN........ Packet Switched Public Data Network [*Computer science*] (TNIG)
PSPEN........ Primary/Secondary Peace Education Network [*Later, PEN*] (EA)
PSPF.......... Potential Single Point Failures [*NASA*] (KSC)
PSPF.......... Prostacyclin Stimulating Plasma Factor [*Endocrinology*]
PSPFLI....... Pulsed Single Photon Fluorescence Lifetime Instrumentation
PSPGV........ Primary Sodium Pump Guard Vesel [*Nuclear energy*] (NRCH)
PSphR........ Rohm & Haas Co., Research Library Services, Spring House, PA [*Library symbol Library of Congress*] (LCLS)
PSPI........... Psychosocial Pain Inventory [*Psychology*]
PSPL........... Priced Spare Parts List
PSPL........... Progressive Socialist Party of Lebanon
PSPLR........ Priced Spare Parts List Revision
PSPM.......... Procurement Seminar for Project Management [*Army*]
PSPMW....... International Brotherhood of Pulp, Sulphite, and Paper Mill Workers [*Later, UPIU*]
PSPP.......... Preliminary System Package Plan
PSPP.......... Program System Package Plan
PSPP.......... Proposed System Package Plan [*Military*]
PSPR.......... Personnel Subsystem Products [*Army*] (AABC)
PSPR.......... Programmable Signal Processor RADAR
PSPRT........ Partial Sequential Probability Ratio Test (PDAA)
PSPS.......... Paddle Steamer Preservation Society [*British*] (BI)
PSPS.......... Pesticides Safety Precautions Scheme [*British*]
PSPS.......... Planar Silicon Photoswitch (IEEE)
PSPS.......... Power-Steering Pressure Sensor [*Automotive engineering*]
PSPS.......... Power Steering Pressure Switch [*Automotive engineering*]
PSPS.......... Product Support Procurement Summary (MCD)
PSPS.......... Program Support Plan Summary
PSPSK........ Previous Signaling Element Phase Shift Keying [*Computer science*] (IAA)
PSPT.......... Parisi Spanish Proficiency Test (EDAC)
PSPT.......... Passport (AABC)
PSPT.......... Planar Silicon Power Transistor
PSptv......... PerSeptive Biosystems, Inc. [*Associated Press*] (SAG)
PSPV.......... Partido Socialista del Pais Valenciano [*Spain Political party*] (EY)
PSQ........... Parent Symptom Questionnaire [*Medicine*] (DMAA)
PSQ........... Patient Satisfaction Questionnaire [*Medicine*] (DMAA)
PSQ........... Personnel Security Questionnaire
PSQ........... Personnel Squadron
PSQ........... Political Science Quarterly [*A publication*] (BRI)
PSQ........... Protein Sequence Query
PSQ........... Public Storage Prop'A' XV [*AMEX symbol*] (TTSB)
PSQ........... Public Storage Properties XV [*AMEX symbol*] (SPSG)
PSQA......... Pageable System Queue Area [*Computer science*] (MCD)
PSQI.......... Pittsburgh Sleep Quality Index
PSQL.......... Platinum Software [*NASDAQ symbol*] (TTSB)
PSQL.......... Platinum Software Corp. [*NASDAQ symbol*] (SAG)
PSR............ Pacific Security Region
PSR............ Pacific-Sierra Research Corp.
PSR............ Packed Snow on Runway [*NWS*] (FAAC)
PSR............ Pad Safety Report [*NASA*]
PSR............ Page Send-Receive [*Teletypewriter*]
PSR............ Pain Sensitivity Range [*Biometrics*]
PSR............ Panoramic Stereo Rectification
PSR............ Paper Stock Record (DGA)
PSR............ Parachute Status Report [*Army*] (AABC)
PSR............ Partido Socialista Revolucionario [*Revolutionary Socialist Party*] [*Mexico Political party*] (PPW)
PSR............ Partido Socialista Revolucionario [*Revolutionary Socialist Party*] [*Peru*] [*Political party*] (PPW)
PSR............ Partido Socialista Revolucionario [*Revolutionary Socialist Party*] [*Portugal Political party*] (PPE)
PSR............ Parts and Supply Requisition (IAA)
PSR............ Party Socialiste Revolutionnaire [*Socialist Revolutionary Party*] [*Lebanon*] [*Political party*] (PPW)
psr............ Paternal Sex Ratio Gene [*Genetics*]
PSR............ Paul's Scarlet Rose [*Plant cell line*]
PSR............ Pennsylvania State Reports [*A publication*] (DLA)
PSR............ Pennsylvania State University Reactor (NRCH)
PSR............ Perfectly Stirred Reactor
PSR............ Performance Summary Report (NG)
PSR............ Peripheral Shim Rod [*Nuclear energy*] (NRCH)
PSR............ Personnel Status Report [*Military*]
PSR............ Pescara [*Italy*] [*Airport symbol*] (OAG)
PSR............ Petaluma & Santa Rosa Railroad Co. [*AAR code*]
PSR............ Petrostates Resource Corp. [*Vancouver Stock Exchange symbol*]
PSR............ Pharmaceutical Sales Representative
PSR............ Phase Sensitive Rectifier (NITA)
PSR............ Phase Sequence Relay
PSR............ Philatelic Societies' Record [*A publication British*]
PSR............ Photo Scale Reciprocal (DNAB)
PSR............ Physical Sciences Research Program [*North Carolina State University*] [*Research center*] (RCD)
PSR............ Physicians for Social Responsibility (EA)
PSR............ Plow-Steel Rope
PSR............ Point of Safe Return (MCD)
PSR............ Point Source Range (IAA)
PSR............ Policy Status Report [*Insurance*]
PSR............ Political and Social Reform Movement [*British*]
PSR............ Political Science Reviewer [*A publication*] (BRI)
PSR............ Portable Seismic Recorder
PSR............ Positive Support Review, Inc. [*Telecommunications service*] (TSSD)
PSR............ Postal Service Representative [*British*] (DCTA)
PSR............ Post-Sinusoidal Resistance
PSR............ Power System Relaying (MCD)
PSR............ Predicted SONAR Range [*Military*] (NVT)
PSR............ Present Serviceability Rating [*FHWA*] (TAG)
PSR............ Presidential Special Representative (BARN)
PSR............ Price-Sales Ratio [*Economics*]
PSR............ Primary Surveillance RADAR
PSR............ Problem Status Report (MCD)
PSR............ Processor State Register
PSR............ Procurement Status Report (IEEE)
PSR............ Productivity Savings Reward (AAGC)
PSR............ Programming Status Report [*Computer science*]
PSR............ Programming Support Representative [*IBM Corp.*]
PSR............ Program Status Register
PSR............ Program Status Report [*or Review*]
PSR............ Program Status Review [*NASA*] (NASA)
PSR............ Program Study Request (AAG)
PSR............ Program Summary Record [*Military*] (AFIT)
PSR............ Program Support Representative (NITA)
PSR............ Program Support Requirements (KSC)
PSR............ Progress Summary Report
PSR............ Project Safe Run (EA)
PSR............ Project Scan Record
PSR............ Project Summary Report (MCD)
PSR............ Propeller Shaft Rate [*Navy*] (CAAL)
PSR............ Pro Seniors [*International Bowhunting Organization*] [*Class Equipment*]
PSR............ Proton Storage Ring [*Nuclear physics*]
PSR............ Prototype Systems Review

PSR .... Provisioning Support Request [*Military*] (CAAL)
PSR .... Public Service Company of Colorado [*AMEX symbol*] (SAG)
PSR .... Public Service Co. of Colorado [*NYSE symbol*] (SPSG)
PSR .... Public Social Responsibility [*Unit of the Anglican Church of Canada General Synod*]
PSR .... Public SvcColorado [*NYSE symbol*] (TTSB)
PSR .... Pulmonary Stretch Receptors [*Medicine*]
PSRA .... Problem Status Report Analysis (SAA)
PSRA .... Professional Soccer Reporter's Association (EA)
PSRAAALAA... President's Special Representative and Adviser on African, Asian, and Latin American Affairs [*Department of State*]
PSRAM .... Physical Security Requirements Assessment Methodology [*Civil Engineering Research Laboratory*] [*Navy*] (RDA)
PSRAM .... Pseudostatic Random Access Memory [*Apple Computer Inc.*]
PSRBOW...... Premature Spontaneous Rupture of Bag of Waters [*Medicine*] (MEDA)
PSRBOW...... Premature Spontaneous Rupture of Bag of Waters [*Obstetrics*] (DAVI)
PSRC .... Plastic Surgery Research Council (EA)
PSRC .... Pretrial Services Resource Center (EA)
PSRC .... PrimeSource Corp. [*NASDAQ symbol*] (SAG)
PSRC .... Public Service Research Council (EA)
PSRCA .... Professional Standards Review Council of America (EA)
PSRD .... Personnel Shipment Ready Date [*Army*] (AABC)
PSRD .... Program Support Requirements Document [*NASA*] (KSC)
PSRE .... Partido Socialista Revolucionario Ecuatoriano [*Socialist Revolutionary Party of Ecuador*] [*Political party*] (PPW)
PSRE .... Propulsion System Rocket Engine (MCD)
PSRF .... Product Support Reports and Functions
PSRF .... Profit Sharing Research Foundation (EA)
PSRI .... Particulate Solid Research Institute
PSRI .... Personnel Specialities and Record Inventory (SAA)
PSRI .... Position Subject to Return of Incumbent [*Aviation*] (FAAC)
PSRI .... Psycho-Social Rehabilitation International (EAIO)
PSRL .... Post Strike Reconnaissance List [*Military*] (CINC)
PSRM .... Parti Sosialis Rakyat Malaya [*People's Socialist Party of Malaya*]
PSRM .... Post-Scram Reactivity Monitor [*Nuclear energy*] (NRCH)
PSRM .... Pressurization Systems Regulator Manifold (AAG)
PSRM .... Processor State Register Main [*Computer science*]
PSRMA .... Pacific Southwest Railway Museum Association [*Later, SDRM*] (EA)
PSR-ML/MIR... Partido Socialista Revolucionario (Marxista-Leninista)/Movimiento de Izquierda Revolucionaria [*Revolutionary Socialist Party (Marxist-Leninist)/Mi litant Movement of the Revolutionary Left*] [*Peru*] [*Political party*] (PPW)
PSRMLS ...... Pacific Southwest Regional Medical Library [*Library network*]
PSRMT .... Piecewise-Sinusoidal Reaction Matching Technique [*Antenna*] [*Navy*]
PSRO .... Passenger Standing Route Order [*Army*] (AABC)
PSRO .... Professional Standards Review Organization [*Generic term for groups of physicians who may review the policies and decisions of their colleagues*]
PSRO .... Professional Standards Review Organization (NADA)
PSR-P .... Packed Snow on Runway - Patchy [*Aviation*] (DNAB)
PSRP .... Physical Sciences Research Papers [*Air Force*] (MCD)
PSRP .... Production Support Repair Plan (SAA)
PSRPr .... Pub Sv of Colo.,4 1/4% Pfd [*AMEX symbol*] (TTSB)
PSRPrA......... Pub Sv Colo.,7.15% Pfd [*NYSE symbol*] (TTSB)
PSRR .... Parachute Supported Radio Relay
PSRR .... Power Supply Rejection Ratio (IAA)
PSRR .... Product and Support Requirements Request [*Computer science*] (IBMDP)
PSRS .... Pictographic Self-Rating Scale [*Psychology*] (AEBS)
PSRS .... Portable Seismic Recording System
PSRS .... Position Subject to Rotating Shifts [*Aviation*] (FAAC)
PSrS .... Slippery Rock State College, Slippery Rock, PA [*Library symbol Library of Congress*] (LCLS)
PSRT .... Passive Satellite Research Terminal
PS-RTP .... Paper-Substrate Room-Temperature Phosphorescence [*Analytical chemistry*]
PSRU .... Processor State Register Utility [*Computer science*]
PSRU .... Production Support Repair Unit (SAA)
PSS............. Hastings, NE [*Location identifier FAA*] (FAAL)
PSS............. International Production, Service, and Sales Union
PSS............. Packet Switched System (NITA)
PSS............. Packet Switching Service [*Telecommunications Information service or system British*] (IID)
PSS............. Packet SwitchStream [*British Telecommunications Plc*] [*London*] [*Information service or system*] (IID)
PSS............. Pad Safety Supervision [*Aerospace*] (AAG)
PSS............. Palomar Sky Survey [*NASA*]
PSS............. Partially Sighted Society [*British*]
PSS............. Partia Socialiste e Shqiperise [*Socialist Party of Albania*] [*Political party*] (EAIO)
PSS............. Parti de Solidarite Senegalaise [*Senegalese Solidarity Party*] [*Political party*]
PSS............. Parti Socialiste Suisse [*Social Democratic Party of Switzerland*] [*Political party*] (PPE)
PSS............. Partito Socialista Sammarinese [*Socialist Party of San Marino*] [*Political party*] (PPE)
PSS............. Partito Socialista Somalo [*Somali Socialist Party*] [*Political party*]
PSS............. Passenger Service Supervisor [*Travel industry*]
PSS............. Passenger Service Systems [*Airlines*]
PSS............. Patent Search System [*Pergamon*] [*Database*] [*Computer science*] [*British*]
PSS............. Pauli Spin Susceptibility [*Physics*]
PSS............. Payless ShoeSource [*NYSE symbol*] (TTSB)
PSS............. Payless ShoeSource, Inc. [*NYSE symbol*] (SAG)
PSS............. Payload Specialist Station [*NASA*] (NASA)
PSS............. Payload Support System [*NASA*] (MCD)
PSS............. Performance Standard Sheet
PSS............. Performance Support System [*Human resources*] (WYGK)
PSS............. Periscope Simulation System [*Navy*]
PSS............. Personal Signaling System
PSS............. Personnel Service Support [*Army*] (DOMA)
PSS............. Personnel Staffing Specialist (GFGA)
PSS............. Personnel Subsystem [*Air Force*] (AFM)
PSS............. Personnel Support System [*Army*] (AABC)
PSS............. Phase-System Switching [*Physical chemistry*]
PSS............. Physical Security Subsystem
PSS............. Physiological Saline Solution [*Physiology*]
PSS............. Planetary Scan System [*or Subsystem*]
PSS............. Planned Systems Schedule (AAG)
PSS............. Planning Summary Sheets (AAG)
PSS............. Plant Science Seminar [*Later, ASP*]
PS/S............ Plumbing Supervisor/Specialist (AAG)
PSS............. Plume Suppression System [*Combustion technology*]
PSS............. Plunger Snap Switch
PSS............. Pneumatic Supply Subsystem (AAG)
PSS............. Polar Subsurface Sounder (SSD)
PSS............. Poly(styrenesulfonate) [*Organic chemistry*]
PSS............. Porcine Stress Syndrome [*Veterinary medicine*]
PSS............. Portable Simulation System (MCD)
PSS............. Port Safety and Security [*USCG*] (TAG)
PSS............. Posadas [*Argentina*] [*Airport symbol*] (OAG)
PSS............. Postal Savings System [*Terminated, 1966*]
PSS............. Postal Separation System (SAA)
PSS............. Postscripta [*Postscripts*] [*Latin*]
PSS............. Power Supply Section
PSS............. Power Supply Subsystem (IAA)
PSS............. Power System Synthesizer
PSS............. Precancel Stamp Society (EA)
PSS............. Premature Separation Switch (SAA)
PSS............. Presbyteri Sancti Sulpicii [*Sulpicians*] [*Roman Catholic men's religious order*]
P/S/S .... Price/Stern/Sloan Publishers, Inc.
PSS............. Primary Sampling System [*Nuclear energy*] (NRCH)
PSS............. Princess (ROG)
PSS............. Printer Storage System [*Computer science*] (MHDI)
PSS............. Probabilistic Safety Study [*Nuclear energy*] (NRCH)
PSS............. Process Sampling System [*Nuclear energy*] (NRCH)
PSS............. Process Standard Specification
PSS............. Process Switching Service (IAA)
PSS............. Professional Services Section (BARN)
PSS............. Professor of Sacred Scripture
PSS............. Programming Support System (SAA)
PSS............. Program Support Staff [*Environmental Protection Agency*] (GFGA)
PSS............. Progressive Science Series [*A publication*]
PSS............. Progressive Systemic Sclerosis [*Medicine*]
PSS............. Propellant Supply System [*or Subsystem*]
PSS............. Proposed Sale of Securities (GFGA)
PSS............. Proprietary Software Systems [*Computer science*] (IEEE)
PSS............. Proprietary Support System [*Computer science*] (IAA)
PSS............. Propulsion Subsystem Structure
PSS............. Propulsion Support System (KSC)
PSS............. Protective Security Service
PSS............. Protective Signature Service (MCD)
PSS............. Psalms [*Old Testament book*]
Pss.............. Pseudomonas Syringae Syringae [*Plant pathology*]
PSS............. Pseudo Spread Spectrum (MCD)
PSS............. Psychiatric Services Section [*of the American Hospital Association*] [*Later, SCSMHPS*] (EA)
PSS............. Psychiatric Status Schedules [*Psychology*]
PSS............. Psychological Saline Solution (BARN)
PSS............. Public Services Satellite
PSS............. Public Storage Canadian Properties II [*Limited Partnership Units*] [*Toronto Stock Exchange symbol*]
PSS............. Push-Button Selection Station
PSSA .... Pilot Signal Selector Adaptor (SAA)
PSSA .... Pitch Starting Synchro Assembly
PSSA .... Pseudo-Steady-State Approximation [*Chemical engineering*]
PSSAA .... Pacific Stars and Stripes Alumni Association (EA)
PSSAANDPS... Permanent Secretariat of the South American Agreement on Narcotic Drugs and Psychotropic Substances (EAIO)
PSSB .... Palm Springs Savings Bank [*Palm Springs, CA*] [*NASDAQ symbol*] (NQ)
PSSB .... Palm Springs Svgs Bk [*NASDAQ symbol*] (TTSB)
PSSB .... Passing Stopped School Bus [*Traffic offense charge*]
PSSBB .... Public School System Blanket Bond [*Insurance*]
PSSC .... Parachute Subsystem Sequence Controller [*NASA*] (SAA)
PSSC .... Personal Social Services Council [*British*] (DI)
PSSC .... Petroleum Security Subcommittee [*of Foreign Petroleum Supply Committee*] [*Terminated, 1976*] (EGAO)
PSSC .... Physical Science Study Committee [*National Science Foundation*]
PSSC .... Pious Society of Missionaries of St. Charles [*Later, CS*] [*Roman Catholic men's religious order*]
PSSC .... Public Service Satellite Consortium (EA)
PSSCC .... Peter Symonds School Cadet Corps [*British military*] (DMA)
PSSD .... Parallel-Serial Scan Design [*Electronics*]
PSSD .... Personnel Service Support Directorate (DOMA)
PSSDS .... Portable Surface Supported Diving System (PDAA)
PSSEP .... Preliminary System Safety Engineering Plan

PSSES .... Public Service Senior Executive Service [*Australia*]
PSSF .... Petites Soeurs de la Sainte-Famille [*Little Sisters of the Holy Family*] [*Sherbrooke, PQ*] (EAIO)
PSSG .... Physical Science Study Group
PSSGNR .... Passenger
PSS-I .... Peace Science Society (International) (EA)
PSSI .... Physician Sales & Service [*NASDAQ symbol*] (TTSB)
PSSI .... Physician Sales & Service, Inc. [*NASDAQ symbol*] (SAG)
PSSI .... Plasma Source Ion Implantation
PSSI .... Primary Specialty Skill Identifier [*Military*] (AABC)
PSSIIS .... Partito Socialista: Sezione Italiana del Internazionale Socialista [*Socialist Party: Italian Section of International Socialism*] [*Political party*] (PPE)
PSS(Int) .... Peace Science Society (International)
PSSJ .... Poor Sisters of St. Joseph (TOCD)
PSSK .... Probability of Single Shot Kill [*Of a guided missile*]
PSSL .... Princeton University Solid State and Materials Laboratory [*New Jersey*]
PSSM .... Preliminary Science Meeting [*NASA*]
PSSMA .... Paper Shipping Sack Manufacturers Association (EA)
PSSMLF .... Provincial Society of Spanish and Moroccan Leather Finishers [*A union*] [*British*]
PSSO .... Pass Slip Stitch Over [*Knitting*]
PsSol .... Psalms of Solomon [*Pseudepigrapha*] (BJA)
PSSP .... Partition with Self Substitution Property (IAA)
PSSP .... Payload Specialist Station Panel [*NASA*] (MCD)
PSSP .... Personnel Security and Surety Program [*Military*] (ADDR)
PSSP .... Phone Center Staffing and Sizing Program [*Telecommunications*] (TEL)
PSSR .... Parallel-Shaft Speed Reducer
PSSR .... Pre-Startup Safety Review [*Chemical engineering*]
PSSR .... Primary School Staff Relations [*Project*] (AIE)
PSSR .... Problem Status and Summary Report [*NASA*] (KSC)
PSSR .... Provisioning Supply Support Requests [*DoD*]
PSSRA .... Public Service Staff Relations Act [*Canada*]
PSSRB .... Public Service Staff Relations Board [*Canada*]
PSSS .... Philosophic Society for the Study of Sport (EA)
PSSS .... Presidential Survivability Support System
PSST .... Periodic Significant Scheduled Tasks [*NASA*] (NASA)
PSS(T) .... Pregnancy Support Service (Tasmania) [*Australia*]
PSSTA .... Port Security Station [*Coast Guard*]
PSSU .... Patch Survey and Switching Unit (MCD)
PST .... Airwork (New Zealand) Ltd. [*ICAO designator*] (FAAC)
PST .... Pacific Standard Time
PST .... Pacific Summer Time
PST .... Paired Selected Ternary (IAA)
PST .... Pair Selected Ternary [*Computer science*]
PST .... Pancreastatin [*Biochemistry*]
PST .... Pancreatic Suppression Test [*Medicine*] (AAMN)
PST .... Paroxysmal Superaventricular Tachycardia [*Medicine*] (MEDA)
PST .... Paroxysmal Supraventricular Tachycardia [*Cardiology*] (DAVI)
PST .... Partido Socialista de los Trabajadores [*Socialist Workers' Party*] [*Mexico Political party*] (PPW)
PST .... Partido Socialista de los Trabajadores [*Socialist Workers Party*] [*Panama*] [*Political party*] (EY)
PST .... Partido Socialista de los Trabajadores [*Socialist Workers' Party*] [*Colombia*] [*Political party*] (PPW)
PST .... Partition Specification Table (MHDI)
PST .... Pascal-Suttle Test [*Psychology*] (DAVI)
PST .... Pass Time [*Military*]
PST .... Paste
pst .... Paste (VRA)
PST .... Pastry (MSA)
PST .... Pasture Canyon [*Utah*] [*Seismograph station code, US Geological Survey Closed*] (SEIS)
PST .... Penicillin, Streptomycin, and Tetracycline [*Antibiotics*] (MAE)
PSt .... Pennsylvania State University, University Park, PA [*Library symbol Library of Congress*] (LCLS)
PST .... Performance Specification Tree
PST .... Periodic Self-Test [*Computer science*]
PST .... Peristimulus Time [*Neurophysiology*]
PST .... Personnel Subsystem Team [*Military*] (AFIT)
PST .... Peseta [*Monetary unit*] [*Spain and Latin America*]
PST .... Pesticide
PST .... Petrie Stores Corp. [*NYSE symbol*] (SPSG)
PST .... Phase Space Theory [*Physical chemistry*]
PST .... Phenol Sulfotransferase [*An enzyme*]
PST .... Philadelphia Suburban Transportation [*AAR code*]
PST .... Piston Shock Tunnel
PST .... Planetary Spectroscopy Telescope (SSD)
PST .... Point of Spiral Tangent (KSC)
PST .... Polaris Star Tracker [*Missiles*]
PST .... Polished Surface Technique (IEEE)
PST .... Pooled Superannuation Trust
PST .... Porcine Somatotropin [*Gene-spliced animal hormone*] [*Monsanto Co.*]
PST .... Poststenotic [*Medicine*] (DMAA)
PST .... Post-Stimulus Time
PST .... Pressure-Sensitive Tape
PST .... Preston [*Cuba*] [*Airport symbol*] (AD)
PST .... Primary Surge Tank [*Nuclear energy*] (NRCH)
PST .... Priority Selection Table [*Computer science*] (IBMDP)
PST .... Prior Service Training [*US Army Reserve*] (INF)
PST .... Production Sampling Test (IAA)
PST .... Production Special Tooling (MCD)
PST .... Production Surveillance Test (MCD)
PST .... Product Support Technician
PST .... Professional, Scientific, and Technical
PST .... Profit Sharing Trustee (DLA)
PST .... Program Status Table [*Computer science*] (IAA)
PST .... Program Synchronization Table (CMD)
PST .... Project ST [*Later, NSTA*] (EA)
PST .... Propeller STOL [*Short Takeoff and Landing*] Transport
PST .... Pro Sight Technology
PST .... Shepard's Preparing for Settlement and Trial [*A publication*]
Pst .... Static Transpulmonary Pressure at a Specific Lung Volume [*Medicine*] (DAVI)
PSTA .... Monterey Pasta [*NASDAQ symbol*] (SAG)
PSTA .... Packaging Science and Technology Abstracts [*International Food Information Service*] [*Germany Information service or system*]
PSTA .... Partido Socialista Tito Atahuichi [*Bolivia*] [*Political party*] (PPW)
PSt-A .... Pennsylvania State University, Agricultural Library, University Park, PA [*Library symbol Library of Congress*] (LCLS)
PSTA .... Pre-Sea Trial Audit (MCD)
PSTA .... Public Safety and Training Association (NADA)
PSt-All .... Pennsylvania State University, Allentown Campus, Allentown, PA [*Library symbol Library of Congress*] (LCLS)
PSt-Alt .... Pennsylvania State University, Altoona Campus, Altoona, PA [*Library symbol Library of Congress*] (LCLS)
PSt-B .... Pennsylvania State University, Berks Campus, Wyomissing, PA [*Library symbol Library of Congress*] (LCLS)
PSTB .... Perpetual State Bank (North Carolina) [*NASDAQ symbol*] (SAG)
PSTB .... Picture Story Test Blank [*Psychology*]
PSTB .... Propulsion System Test Bed [*for ABC helicopters*] (RDA)
PSTB .... Puget Sound Tug & Barge [*AAR code*]
pstbd .... Pasteboard (VRA)
PSt-Be .... Pennsylvania State University, Beaver Campus, Monaca, PA [*Library symbol Library of Congress*] (LCLS)
PSTC .... Pressure Sensitive Tape Council (EA)
PSTC .... Product Support Task Control (AAG)
PSTC .... Public Switched Telephone Circuits [*Telecommunications*] (TEL)
PStcA .... American Philatelic Research Library, State College, PA [*Library symbol Library of Congress*] (LCLS)
PSt-Ca .... Pennsylvania State University, Capitol Campus, Middletown, PA [*Library symbol Library of Congress*] (LCLS)
PSTCA .... Public Services Temporary Clerks' Association [*A union*] [*British*]
PStcH .... HRB-Singer, Inc., Science Park, State College, PA [*Library symbol Library of Congress*] (LCLS)
PSTCO .... Per Steering Compass [*Navigation*] (DNAB)
PSt-D .... Pennsylvania State University, DuBois Campus, DuBois, PA [*Library symbol Library of Congress*] (LCLS)
PSTD .... Potato Spindle Tuber Disease
PSTD .... Promotable Second-Tier Debt [*Economics*]
PStdE .... Eastern College, St. Davids, PA [*Library symbol Library of Congress*] (LCLS)
PSt-De .... Pennsylvania State University, Delaware Campus, Chester, PA [*Library symbol Library of Congress*] (LCLS)
PSt-E .... Pennsylvania State University, Behrend Campus, Erie, PA [*Library symbol Library of Congress*] (LCLS)
PSTE .... Personnel Subsystem Test and Evaluation [*Military*]
PST-E .... Priority Selection Table Extension [*Computer science*] (IBMDP)
PSTE .... Production Special Testing Equipment (MCD)
PSTEP .... Pre-Service Teacher Education Program [*National Science Foundation*]
PSTF .... Payload Spin Test Facility (MCD)
PSt-F .... Pennsylvania State University, Fayette Campus, Uniontown, PA [*Library symbol Library of Congress*] (LCLS)
PSTF .... Pioneer Station Training Facility [*NASA*]
PSTF .... Pressure Suppression Test Facility [*Nuclear energy*] (IEEE)
PSTF .... Privately-Owned Sewage Treatment Facility
PSTF .... Professional Staff [*NASDAQ symbol*] (SAG)
PSTF .... Profit Sharing Trust Fund
PSTF .... Proximity Sensor Test Facility [*Nuclear energy*] (NRCH)
PSTF .... Pump Seal Test Facility [*Nuclear energy*] (NRCH)
PSTG .... Postage (WGA)
PSTGC .... Per Steering Compass [*Navigation*]
PSt-H .... Pennsylvania State University, Hazelton Campus, Hazelton, PA [*Library symbol Library of Congress*] (LCLS)
PSTH .... Peristimulus Time Histogram
PSTH .... Posthumously
PSTH .... Poststimulus Time Histiogram [*Medical statistics*]
PSTH .... Professional Sports Teams Histories [*A publication*]
PSTI .... Pancreatic Secretory Trypsin Inhibitor [*Biochemistry*]
PSTI .... Pancreatic Secretory Trypsin Inhibitor [*Medicine*] (DMAA)
PSTIAC .... Pavements and Soil Trafficability Information Analysis Center [*Army Corps of Engineers*] (IID)
PSt-KP .... Pennsylvania State University, King of Prussia Graduate Center, King of Prussia,PA [*Library symbol Library of Congress*] (LCLS)
PSTL .... Pastoral
PSTL .... Pistol (MSA)
PSTL .... Postal (AFM)
PSTL .... Postal
PSTL .... Pressure Model Static and Transient Launch Configuration (SAA)
PSTM .... Persistent Standoff Target Marker (MCD)
PSTM .... Photon Scanning Tunnelling Microscope
PSTMA .... Paper Stationery and Tablet Manufacturers Association [*Later, PCA*] (EA)
PSt-MA .... Pennsylvania State University, Mont Alto Campus, Mont Alto, PA [*Library symbol Library of Congress*] (LCLS)

PSt-McK ...... Pennsylvania State University, McKeesport Campus, McKeesport, PA [*Library symbol Library of Congress*] (LCLS)
PSTN .... Pesticide Safety Team Network (GNE)
PSTN .... Piston (MSA)
PSTN .... Position
PSTN .... Public Switched Telephone Network
PSt-NK .... Pennsylvania State University, New Kensington Campus, New Kensington, PA [*Library symbol Library of Congress*] (LCLS)
PSt-O .... Pennsylvania State University, Ogontz Campus, Abington, PA [*Library symbol Library of Congress*] (LCLS)
PSTO .... Principal Sea Transport Officer
PSTO .... Purdue Student-Teacher Opinionaire [*Test*]
PS to PS...... Private Siding to Private Siding
PS to S........ Private Siding to Station
PSt-PiN........ Pennsylvania State University, School of Nursing, Allegheny General Hospital, Pittsburgh, PA [*Library symbol Library of Congress*] (LCLS)
PSTR .... Pastor
PSTR .... Penn State TRIGA [*Training Reactor, Isotopes General Atomic*] Reactor
P/STRG......... Power Steering [*Automotive engineering*]
PSTS............ Passive SONAR Tracking System
PSt-S .... Pennsylvania State University, Scranton Campus, Scranton, PA [*Library symbol Library of Congress*] (LCLS)
PSTS............ Primary School Teachers and Science [*Project*] (AIE)
PSt-Sk .... Pennsylvania State University, Schuylkill Campus, Schuylkill Haven, PA [*Library symbol Library of Congress*] (LCLS)
PSt-SV .... Pennsylvania State University, Shenango Valley Campus, Sharon, PA [*Library symbol Library of Congress*] (LCLS)
PSTV............ Potato Spindle Tuber Virus
PSTV............ PST Vans [*NASDAQ symbol*] (TTSB)
PSTV............ PST Vans, Inc. [*NASDAQ symbol*] (SAG)
PSTVd.......... Potato Spindle Tuber Viroid [*Plant pathology*]
PST Vn .... PST Vans, Inc. [*Associated Press*] (SAG)
PSt-WB......... Pennsylvania State University, Wilkes-Barre Campus, Wilkes-Barre, PA [*Library symbol Library of Congress*] (LCLS)
PSt-WS......... Pennsylvania State University, Worthington Scranton Campus, Dunmore, PA [*Library symbol Library of Congress*] (LCLS)
PSt-X .... Pennsylvania State University, Off-Campus Libraries [*Library symbol*] [*Library of Congress*] (LCLS)
PSt-Y .... Pennsylvania State University, York Campus, York, PA [*Library symbol Library of Congress*] (LCLS)
pstyl............. Peristyle (VRA)
P'STYL......... Pronestyl [*Procainamide*] [*Bristol-Myers Squibb Co.*] [*Pharmacology*] (DAVI)
PSTZG .... Pasteurizing [*Freight*]
PSU .... Aeropeninsular, SA de CV [*Mexico*] [*FAA designator*] (FAAC)
PSu.............. John R. Kaufman, Jr., [*Sunbury*] Public Library, Sunbury, PA [*Library symbol Library of Congress*] (LCLS)
PSU .... Package Size Unspecified
PSU .... Packet Switching Unit
PSU .... Partido Socialista Unificado [*Socialist Unification Party*] [*Argentina Political party*] (PPW)
PSU .... Partido Socialista Uruguayo [*Uruguayan Socialist Party*] [*Political party*] (PD)
PSU .... Partidul Socialist Unitar [*Unitary Socialist Party*] [*Romania*] [*Political party*] (PPE)
PSU .... Parti Socialiste Unifie [*Unified Socialist Party*] [*France Political party*] (PPW)
PSU .... Partito Socialista Unificato [*Unified Socialist Party*] [*Italy Political party*] (PPE)
PSU .... Partito Socialista Unitario [*Socialist Unity Party*] [*Italy Political party*] (PPE)
PSU .... Path Setup [*Telecommunications*] (TEL)
PSU .... Pennsylvania State University
PSU .... Pennsylvania State University, University Park (USDC)
PSU .... Pet Services, Unlimited [*Commercial firm*] (EA)
PSU .... Philatelic Sales Unit
PSU .... Photosynthetic Unit
PSU .... Plasma Spray Unit
PSU .... Polyphenylene Sulfone [*Organic chemistry*]
PSU .... Portland State University
PSU .... Port Security Unit [*Coast Guard*] (DOMA)
PSU .... Port Sharing Unit (IAA)
PSU .... Port Storage Utility [*Telecommunications*] (TEL)
PSU .... Postsurgical Unit (DAVI)
PSU .... Power Supply Unit (MSA)
PSU .... Power Switching Unit (MCD)
PSU .... Pressure Status Unit (AAG)
PSU .... Primary Sampling Unit [*Statistics*]
PSU .... Printed Side Up [*Graphic arts*] (DGA)
PSU .... Probability Sampling Unit (WDMC)
PSU .... Processor Service Unit (ECII)
PSU .... Processor Speed Up [*Computer memory core*]
PSU .... Program Storage Unit [*Computer science*] (MDG)
PSU .... Program Storage Unit (NITA)
PSU .... Public Services Unit (EERA)
PSU .... Public Storage Prop'A'XVI [*AMEX symbol*] (TTSB)
PSU .... Public Storage Properties XVI [*AMEX symbol*] (SPSG)
PSU .... Tatoo-a-Pet [*Commercial firm*] (EA)
PSUB .... Piston-Supported Upper Bearing
PSUC .... Partit Socialista Unificat de Catalunya [*Unified Socialist Party of Catalonia*] [*Spain Political party*] (PPE)
PSUD .... Psychoactive Substance Use Disorder
PSU/IRL....... Pennsylvania State University Ionosphere Research Laboratory
PSULI .... Partito Socialista Unitario de Lavoratori Italiani [*Unitary Socialist Party of Italian Workers*] [*Political party*] (PPE)
PSUN........... Pacific Sunwear of Calif [*NASDAQ symbol*] (TTSB)
PSUN........... Pacific Sunwear of California, Inc. [*NASDAQ symbol*] (SAG)
PSUP .... Pennsylvania State University Press (DGA)
PSUR .... Pennsylvania State University Reactor
PSURAO ...... Pennsylvania State University Radio Astronomy Observatory
PSurg........... Plastic Surgery [*Medicine*]
P-SURG .... Presurgery Coagulation Profile [*Hematology and surgery*] (DAVI)
PSUSAM ...... Philippine Statehood USA Movement [*An association*] (EA)
PSV............. Pair Shield Video (NITA)
PSV............. Paleosecular Variation [*Geology*]
PSV............. Peanut Stunt Virus
PSV............. Photographic-Spatial Volume (SAA)
PSV............. Pictorial Study of Values [*Psychology*]
PSV............. Planetary Space Vehicle [*NASA*] (NASA)
PSV............. Polished-Stone Value (PDAA)
PSV............. Portable Sensor Verifier (AAG)
PSV............. Positive Start Voltage
PSV............. Preserve (MSA)
PSV............. Pressure Safety Valve
PSV............. Pressure Support Ventilation [*Medicine*] (DAVI)
PSV............. Probability State Variable [*Statistics*]
PSV............. Progressieve Surinaamse Volkspartij [*Progressive Suriname People's Party*] [*Political party*] (PPW)
PSV............. Pseudo-Synthetic Video (DOMA)
PSV............. Psychological, Social, and Vocational [*Adjustment factors*]
PSV............. Public Service Vehicle
PSV............. Public Storage Prop'A'XVII [*AMEX symbol*] (TTSB)
PSV............. Public Storage Properties XVII, Inc. [*AMEX symbol*] (SAG)
PSV............. Saint Vincent College, Latrobe, PA [*OCLC symbol*] (OCLC)
PSvcBad ...... Presidential Service Badge [*Military decoration*] (AABC)
PSvCol......... Public Service Co. of Colorado [*Associated Press*] (SAG)
PSVD .... Polystyrene-Divinylbenzene Copolymer [*Organic chemistry*]
PSVER .... Pattern-Shift Visual Evoked Response [*Medicine*] (MEDA)
PSVM........... Phase-Sensitive Voltmeter
psvm............ Phase-Sensitive Voltmeter (IDOE)
PSvNM......... Public Service Co. of New Mexico [*Associated Press*] (SAG)
PSVOA .... Purse Seine Vessel Owners Association (EA)
PSVOMA...... Purse Seine Vessel Owners Marketing Association [*Later, PSVOA*] (EA)
PSVP .... Pilot Secure Voice Project [*NATO Integrated Communications System*] (NATG)
PSVT............ Paroxysmal Supraventricular Tachycardia [*Cardiology*]
PSVT............ Passivate [*Metallurgy*]
PSVTN .... Preservation (MSA)
PSVTV .... Preservative (MSA)
PSW............. Pacific Southwest Forest and Range Experiment Station [*Berkeley, CA*] [*Department of Agriculture*] (GRD)
PSW............. Peripheral Switching Unit (NITA)
PSW............. Pinetree Software Canada Ltd. [*Vancouver Stock Exchange symbol*]
PSW............. Plasma Spray Welder
PSW............. Politically Simulated World [*Computer-assisted political science game*]
PSW............. Potential Switch
PSW............. Potentiometer Slidewire
PSW............. Powerplant Specific Weight
PSW............. Primary Shield Water (DNAB)
PSW............. Processor Status Word
PSW............. Program Status Word [*Computer science*]
PSW............. Pskov State Aviation Enterprise [*Former USSR*] [*FAA designator*] (FAAC)
PSW............. Psychiatric Social Worker [*British*]
PSW............. Public Storage Prop'A'XVIII [*AMEX symbol*] (TTSB)
PSW............. Public Storage Properties XVIII [*AMEX symbol*] (SPSG)
PSWA .... Partially Smooth Water Area (DS)
PSWAD .... Perspective Study of World Agricultural Development [*FAO*] [*United Nations*] (MSC)
PSWB .... Patented Steel Wire Bureau [*British*] (BI)
PSWB .... Public School Word-Book [*A publication*]
PSWBD .... Power Switchboard
PSWBS .... Project Summary Work Breakdown Structure
PSWF .... Prolate Spheroidal Wave Function (PDAA)
PSWFRES.... Pacific Southwest Forest and Range Experiment Station [*Berkeley, CA*] (SAA)
PSWG .... Pressure Sine Wave Generator
PSWMOW.... Psychiatric Social Work in Mental Observation Wards [*British*]
PSWO .... Picture and Sound World Organization
PSWO .... Princess of Wales' Own [*Military unit*] [*British*] (ROG)
PSWO .... Product Support Work Order
PSWOPC...... Psychiatric Social Work in Out-Patient Clinics [*British*]
PSWP .... Plant Service Water Pump (IEEE)
PSWR .... Powell Sport Wagon Registry (EA)
PSWR .... Power Standing Wave Ratio
PSWR .... Program Status Word Register [*Computer science*] (MHDB)
PSWS .... Potable and Sanitary Water System [*Nuclear energy*] (NRCH)
PSwS .... Smith, Kline & French Co. [*Later, SmithKline Corp.*], Swedeland, PA [*Library symbol Library of Congress*] (LCLS)
PSWT........... Polysonic Wind Tunnel (MCD)
PSWT........... Psychiatric Social Work Training [*British*]
PSWTUF ...... Public Service Workers' Trade Union Federation [*Ceylon*]
PSX............. Pacific Scientific [*NYSE symbol*] (TTSB)
PSX............. Pacific Scientific Co. [*NYSE symbol*] (SPSG)
PSX............. Palacios, TX [*Location identifier FAA*] (FAAL)
PSX............. Pseudoexfoliation (DMAA)

PSY Port Stanley [*Falkland Islands*] [*Airport symbol*]
PSY PSM Technologies, Inc. [*Vancouver Stock Exchange symbol*]
PSY Psychiatry
PSY Psychological (CINC)
PSY Public Storage Prop'A' XIX [*AMEX symbol*] (TTSB)
PSY Public Storage Properties XIX, Inc. [*AMEX symbol*] (SAG)
PSYC Psychologist
PSYC Psychology
PsycCp Psychemedics Corp. [*Associated Press*] (SAG)
PSYCH Psychiatrist (DSUE)
PSYCH Psychiatrist
PSYCH Psychiatry
PSYCH Psychic (ROG)
PSYCH Psychology (AFM)
Psych Psychology (DD)
Psych & MLJ Psychological and Medico-Legal Journal [*A publication*] (DLA)
PSYCHC Psychiatric
PSYCHEM Psychiatric Chemistry
PSyCHES Psychiatric Case History Event System (PDAA)
psychiat Psychiatry [*or Psychiatric*] (DAVI)
PSYCHL Psychological (AFM)
PSYCHL Psychological
PSYCHO Psychoanalysis (DSUE)
psycho Psychopath [*Psychiatry*] (DAVI)
psychoan Psychoanalysis [*Medicine*] (DMAA)
PSYCHOL Psychology
psychopathol Psychopathology (DAVI)
psychophys Psychophysics [*Psychiatry*] (DAVI)
psychophysiol Psychophysiology [*Psychiatry*] (DAVI)
PsychosMed Psychosomatic Medicine [*Psychiatry*] (DAVI)
psychother Psychotherapy [*Psychiatry*] (DAVI)
PSYCHY Psychiatry
PsycINFO Psychological Abstracts Information Services [*American Psychological Association*] (IID)
PSYCINFO Psychological Information (NITA)
PSYCTRC Psychiatric
PSYCTRY Psychiatry
PSYCY Psychology
PsyD Doctor of Psychology
PsyETA Psychologists for the Ethical Treatment of Animals (EA)
Psy M Master of Psychology (PGP)
PSYOP Psychological Operation [*Military*]
PSY-OPS Psychological Warfare Operations (DNAB)
psy-path Psychopath [*Psychiatry*] (DAVI)
PSYS Precision Systems [*NASDAQ symbol*] (TTSB)
PSYS Precision Systems, Inc. [*NASDAQ symbol*] (SAG)
Psy S Specialist in Psychology (PGP)
PSY-SDIV Psychological Sciences Division [*Office of Naval Research*] (DNAB)
psy-som Psychosomatic (DAVI)
PsySR Psychologists for Social Responsibility (EA)
PSYU Public Sustained Yield Unit [*Forestry*]
PSYWAR Psychological Warfare
PSYWPN Psychological Weapon [*Military*] (AFM)
PSZ Partially-Stabilized Zirconia [*Ceramics*]
PSZ Piszkesteto [*Hungary*] [*Seismograph station code, US Geological Survey*] (SEIS)
PSZ Pressure Sealing Zipper
PSZ Pro Air Service [*ICAO designator*] (FAAC)
PSZ Public Storage Prop'A' XX [*AMEX symbol*] (TTSB)
PSZ Public Storage Properties XX [*AMEX symbol*] (SPSG)
PSZ Puerto Suarez [*Bolivia*] [*Airport symbol*] (OAG)
PSZN Pubblicazioni. Stazione Zoologica di Napoli [*A publication*]
PT Advanced Planning and Technology Office [*Kennedy Space Center Directorate*] (NASA)
PT Brazil [*International civil aircraft marking*] (ODBW)
PT Duffryn Yard [*Welsh depot code*]
PT Motor Torpedo Boat [*Navy symbol Obsolete*]
PT Pacific Time
PT Packet Terminal (NITA)
PT Page Table [*Computer science*] (IAA)
pt Paint (VRA)
PT Pain Threshold
PT Pallet Truck (DCTA)
P-T Palomero Toluqueno [*Race of maize*]
PT Paper Tape
PT Paper Title [*Business term*]
PT Paper Trooper [*One who salvaged paper for war effort*] [*World War II*]
PT Para-Terphenyl [*Organic chemistry*]
PT Parathyroid [*Medicine*]
PT Parcel Ticket [*Freight*]
PT Paroxysmal Tachycardia [*Cardiology*]
pt Part [*of a deck*] (DS)
PT Part [*Online database field identifier*]
pt Part (DAVI)
PT Partially Tested (IAA)
PT Participative Teams (MCD)
PT Partido de los Trabajadores [*Paraguay*] [*Political party*] (EY)
PT Partido Trabajador [*Mexico Political party*] (EY)
PT Partition Table [*Computer science*] (IAA)
PT Part Throttle [*Engines*]
P-T Part-Time [*Employment*]
PT Part Total [*Earnings less than weekly benefit amount*] [*Unemployment insurance*] (OICC)
PT Paschale Tempore [*Easter Time*] [*Latin*]
PT Passenger Traffic [*MTMC*] (TAG)
PT Passenger Transport
PT Passing Title [*Real estate*]
PT Passive Track [*Military*] (CAAL)
PT Past Tense
PT Pataca [*Monetary unit*] [*Macau*]
PT Patellar Tendon [*Anatomy*]
PT Patentee (NITA)
PT Patient
PT Patrol Torpedo Boat [*Later, PTF*] [*Navy symbol*]
PT Paying Teller [*Banking*]
PT Payment
pt Payment (WDMC)
PT Payout Time [*Business term*]
PT Pay Tone [*Telecommunications*] (TEL)
PT Pencil Tube
PT Penetrant Test [*Nuclear energy*] (NRCH)
PT Penetration Test (NATG)
PT Peninsula Terminal Co. [*AAR code*]
PT Pennant [*British naval signaling*]
PT Pensacola-Tallahassee [*Diocesan abbreviation*] [*Florida*] (TOCD)
PT Pension Trustee (DLA)
PT Perfect Title [*Business term*]
PT Perforated Tape [*Computer science*] (IAA)
PT Performance Technology [*Human resources*] (WYGK)
PT Performance Test
PT Pericardial Tamponade [*Medicine*] (DMAA)
PT Periodic Test [*Nuclear energy*] (NRCH)
PT Period Tapering (IAA)
PT Permeability Transition [*Biochemistry*]
PT Perpetual Traveller (ECON)
PT Persepolis Texts (BJA)
PT Persistent Tease [*Slang Bowdlerized version*]
P/T Personal Time [*Employment*]
PT Personal Trade [*Marketing and retail terminology referring to customers*]
PT Personal Transporter
PT Perstetur [*Let It Be Continued*] [*Pharmacy*]
PT Per Truck
PT Perturbation Theory [*Physical chemistry*]
PT Pertussis Toxin [*Pharmacology*]
PT Peseta [*Monetary unit*] [*Spain and Latin America*]
Pt Peter [*New Testament book*]
PT Petrol Tractor [*British*]
PT Petty Theft
PT Phase Transfer [*Physical chemistry*]
PT Phase Type (NITA)
PT Pheasant Trust (EA)
PT Phenytoin [*Pharmacology*] (DAVI)
PT Phoenix Theatre [*Defunct*] (EA)
PT Photoconductive Thermoplastic [*Materials science*]
PT Photographic Intelligenceman [*Navy rating*]
PT Phototherapy [*Medicine*]
PT Phototoxity [*Medicine*]
PT Phototransistor (NRCH)
PT Physical Teardown (MCD)
PT Physical Therapist
PT Physical Therapy [*or Therapist*]
PT Physical Training [*Military*]
PT Physiotherapy [*Medicine*]
PT Piaster [*Monetary unit*] [*Spain, Republic of Vietnam, and some Middle Eastern countries*] (IMH)
PT Picture Telegraphy [*Telecommunications*] (IAA)
PT Pine Tar [*Medicine*]
PT Pint
pt Pint (ODBW)
pt Pint (WDMC)
PT Pipe Tap (MSA)
PT Pitch Trim (MCD)
PT Placebo Treated [*Medicine*]
PT Plain Talk (EA)
PT Plain Test (MCD)
PT Planning and Timing [*of Investments*]
PT Planum Temporale [*Brain anatomy*]
P-T Plasma Thermocouple Reactor [*Nuclear energy*] (NRCH)
PT Plasticized Transparent [*Flexography*] (DGA)
PT Plastics Technology [*A publication*]
PT Plastic Tube
Pt Platinum [*Chemical element*]
PT Platoon Truck [*British*]
PT Pleno Titulo [*With Full Title*] [*Latin*]
PT Plenty Tough [*Slang*]
PT Plenty Trouble [*Slang*]
PT Plonia Technica
PT Plotting Equipment [*JETDS nomenclature*] [*Military*] (CET)
PT Plot Titles [*Test*] [*Psychology*]
PT Pneumatic Tube [*Technical drawings*]
PT Pneumothorax [*Medicine*]
PT Poetry Treasury [*An association Defunct*] (EA)
PT Point
PT Point [*Maps and charts*]
pt Point (WDMC)
pt Point (ODBW)
PT Point
Pt Point (DD)

P/T Pointer/Tracker (MCD)
PT Point of Tangency
PT Point of Turn [*Navigation*]
PT Pollen Tube [*Botany*]
PT Poll-Tax Rolls [*British*]
PT Polymeric Triglyceride [*Food science*]
PT Polythiophene [*Organic chemistry*]
PT Polyvalent Tolerance (BABM)
PT Pool Temperature [*Nuclear energy*] (NRCH)
PT Pope and Talbot [*Steamship*] (MHDW)
PT Popliteal Tendon [*Anatomy*]
PT Port
pt Port (ODBW)
pt Port (WDMC)
PT Portal Tract [*Anatomy*]
PT Port Number [*Telecommunications*] (TEL)
PT Port Talbot Railway [*Wales*]
PT Portugal [*ANSI two-letter standard code*] (CNC)
PT Portugal Telecom ADS [*NYSE symbol*] (TTSB)
PT Portugal Telecom SA [*NYSE symbol*] (SAG)
pt Portuguese Timor [*io (Indonesia) used in records cataloged after January 1978*] [*MARC country of publication code Library of Congress*] (LCCP)
PT Positional Tolerancing
PT Postal Telegraph Co. [*Terminated*]
PT Post and Telegraphy [*Telecommunications*] (IAA)
PT Poste e Telegrafi [*Post and Telegraph Service*] [*Italy*]
PT Posterior Tibial [*Anatomy*]
PT Post Town
PT Potential Transformer
PT Power Transfer (KSC)
PT Prachakorn Thai [*Thai Citizens Party*] [*Political party*]
PT Precision Teaching
PT Precision Time Fuze
PT Precision Transform [*Eastman Kodak Co.*] [*Computer science*] (PCM)
PT Preferential Treatment (OICC)
PT Preoperational Test [*Nuclear energy*] (NRCH)
PT Press Test [*Psychology*]
P/T Pressure/Temperature (KSC)
PT Pressure Test (AAG)
PT Pressure Time Fuel System [*Cummins Engine Co., Inc.*]
PT Pressure Transducer (KSC)
PT Pressure Transmitter (NRCH)
PT Pressure Tubing
PT Pretectal [*Neuroanatomy*]
pt Preterit [*Past tense*] [*Grammar*]
PT Previous Operating Time (AFIT)
PT Primal Therapy
PT Primary Target [*Army*]
PT Primary Trainer [*Aircraft*]
PT Print (MSA)
PT Printed Text
PT Printer Terminal
PT Priority Telegram
PT Prior Treatment [*Medicine*]
PT Private Terms
PT Procedure Turn [*Aviation*] (FAAC)
PT Procedure Turn [*FAA*] (TAG)
PT Processing Tax Division [*United States Internal Revenue Bureau*] (DLA)
PT Processing Time
PT Production Techniques (MCD)
PT Production Test [*Military*]
PT Productive Time [*Computer order entry*]
PT Product Team (AAGC)
PT Product Test (IAA)
PT Proficiency Testing
PT Profile Template
PT Profit Taking [*Investment term*]
PT Program (Exercise) on Treadmill
PT Programmable Terminal [*Computer science*]
PT Programmer and Timer
PT Progress in Technology [*Automotive industry*]
PT Progressive Tax (MHDW)
PT Prohibited Telegrams
PT Project Tibet (EA)
PT Project Transition [*DoD*] (OICC)
PT Project Trust (EAIO)
PT Prolong Tablets [*Pharmacy*]
PT Pronator Teres [*Musle*] [*Orthopedics*] (DAVI)
PT Proof Test (AAG)
PT Propanethiol [*Organic chemistry*]
PT Propellant Transfer
PT Propeller Torpedo [*Boat*]
PT Property Tax (MHDW)
PT Property Transfer [*Real estate*] (KSC)
PT Prophet
PT Propylthiouracil [*Also, PROP, PTU*] [*Thyroid inhibitor*]
PT Pro Tempore [*For the Time Being*] [*Latin*]
PT Prothrombin Time [*Hematology*]
PT Prototype (IAA)
PT Provascular Tissue [*Botany*]
PT Provincetown-Boston Airline [*ICAO designator*] (AD)
PT Provisioning Team (AAG)
Pt Pseudoword Target [*Psychology*]
PT Psychology Today [*A publication*] (BRI)
Pt Pteropods [*Quality of the bottom*] [*Nautical charts*]
PT PTP Resource Corp. [*Formerly, Petrologic Petroleum Ltd.*] [*Vancouver Stock Exchange symbol*]
PT Publication Type [*Online database field identifier*]
PT Public Transport (DA)
PT Public Trustee
PT Pull-Through [*Gun cleaning*]
PT Pulmonary Tuberculosis [*Medicine*]
PT Pulp Testing [*Dentistry*]
PT Pulse Timer
PT Pulse Train
PT Pulse Transformer (IAA)
PT Punched Tape [*Computer science*]
PT Punch Through [*Computer science*] (IAA)
PT Pupil Teacher
PT Purchase Tax [*British*]
PT Pure Telepathy [*Psychical research*]
PT Pyramidal Tract [*Anatomy*]
PT Pyramid Texts (BJA)
PT [*Serum Glutamic*] Pyruvic Transaminase [*Also, SGPT*] [*An enzyme*] (DAVI)
PT Total Pressure
PT1 Photographic Intelligenceman, First Class [*Navy rating*]
PT2 Photographic Intelligenceman, Second Class [*Navy rating*]
PT3 Photographic Intelligenceman, Third Class [*Navy rating*]
PTA National Postal Transport Association [*Later, APWU*]
PTA Page Table Address [*Computer science*] (IAA)
PTA Palatines to America (EA)
PTA Pantorama Industries, Inc. [*Toronto Stock Exchange symbol*]
PTA Paper and Twine Association (EA)
PTA Paper Tape Accessory (MHDI)
PTA Paper Towel Association [*British*] (BI)
PTA Parallel Tubular Array [*Cytology*]
PTA Parent-Teacher Association
PTA Part Throttle Acceleration [*Engines*] (EG)
PTA Passenger Transport Authorities [*British*]
PTA People Taking Action
PTA Percent Time Active (CAAL)
PTA Percutaneous Transluminal Angioplasty [*Medicine*]
PTA Periodical Title Abbreviations [*A publication*]
PTA Peritonsillar Abscess [*Medicine*]
PTA Persistent Truncus Arteriosus [*Medicine*] (MAE)
PTA Peseta [*Monetary unit*] [*Spain and Latin America*]
PTA Phenyltrimethylammonium [*Also, PTM, PTMA*] [*Organic chemistry*]
PTA Phorbol Tetradecanoyl Acetate [*Also, PMA, TPA*] [*Organic chemistry*]
PTA Phosphoryl Triamide [*Organic chemistry*]
PTA Phosphotransacetylase [*An enzyme*]
PTA Phosphotungstic Acid [*Inorganic chemistry*]
PTA Photographers' Telegraph Association
PTA Phototransistor Amplifier
PTA Physical Therapy Assistant
PTA Pianoforte Tuners' Association [*British*] (DBA)
PTA Picatinny Arsenal [*New Jersey*] [*Later, Armament Development Center*] [*Army*]
PTA Pilotless Target Aircraft [*Military*]
PTA Pitch Trim Adjustment
PTA Pitch Trim Angle
PTA Planar Turbulence Amplifier (IEEE)
PTA Plasma Thromboplastin Antecedent [*Factor XI*] [*Hematology*]
PTA Plasma Transferred Arc [*Metallurgy*]
PTA Platinized Titanium Anode
PTA Point of Total Assumption (MCD)
PTA Port Alsworth [*Alaska*] [*Airport symbol*] (OAG)
PTA Postcard Traders' Association [*British*] (DBA)
PTA Posterior Tibial [*Pulse*] [*Medicine*] (DAVI)
PTA Post-Test Analysis [*NASA*] (NASA)
PTA Post-Traumatic Amnesia [*Medicine*]
PTA Potential Toxic Area (NASA)
PTA Power Transfer Assembly (IAA)
PTA Preferential Trade Arrangements [*ASEAN*] (IMH)
PTA Premium Transportation Authorization (AAG)
PTA Prepaid Ticket Advice [*Travel industry*]
PTA Preparation through Acceptance
PTA Pressure Transducer Assembly
PTA Pre-Treatment Anxiety [*Medicine*] (DMAA)
PTA Prevention of Terrorism Act [*British*] (ECON)
PTA Price-Tag Awareness [*See also PTS*]
PTA Primary Target Area [*Military*]
PTA Primary Tungsten Association [*British*] (EAIO)
PTA Printing Trades Alliance [*British*] (DBA)
PTA Prior to Admission [*Medicine*]
PTA Prior to Arrival [*Medicine*] (MAE)
PTA Procrustes Target Analysis (USDC)
PTA Procrustes Target Analysis [*Marine science*] (OSRA)
PTA Programmable Translation Array
PTA Program Time Analyzer
PTA Proposed Technical Approach
PTA Propulsion Test Article [*NASA*] (NASA)
PTA Protestant Teachers Association (NADA)
PTA Prothrombin Activity [*Hematology*]
PTA Proton Target Area
PTA Ptarmigan Airways Ltd. [*Canada ICAO designator*] (FAAC)
PTA Pulse Torquing Assembly (KSC)

PTA Punta Arenas [*Chile*] [*Seismograph station code, US Geological Survey Closed*] (SEIS)
PTA Purchase Transaction Analysis
PTA Pure Terephthalic Acid (DICI)
PTA Pure Tone Average [*Otorhinolaryngology*] (DAVI)
PTA Purified Terephthalic Acid [*Organic chemistry*]
PTAA Airman Apprentice, Photographic Intelligenceman, Striker [*Navy rating*]
PTA-A Periodical Title Abbreviations: by Abbreviation [*A publication*]
PTAA Professional Tattooists Association of Australia
PTAB Photographic Technical Advisory Board [*American National Standards Institute*]
PTAB Program Status Table [*Computer science*] (IAA)
PTAC Penn Treaty American [*NASDAQ symbol*] (TTSB)
PTAC Penn Treaty American Corp. [*NASDAQ symbol*] (NQ)
PTAC Plant Transportation Advisory Committee
PTAC Professional and Technical Advisory Committee [*JCAH*]
P'TACH Parents for Torah for All Children [*Program for learning disabled children*]
PTACV Prototype Tracked Air-Cushion Vehicle
PTAD (Phenyl)triazolinedione [*Organic chemistry*]
PTAD Productivity and Technical Assistance Division [*Mutual Security Agency*] [*Abolished, 1953*]
PT AEQ Partes Aequales [*Equal Parts*] [*Pharmacy*]
PTAF Platelet Activating Factor (DMAA)
PTAF Policy Target Adjustment Factor (MEDA)
PTAFR Platelet Activating Factor Receptor (DMAA)
PTAG Professional Tattoo Artists Guild (EA)
PTAH Phosphotungstic Acid-Hematoxylin [*A stain*]
PTAL Para-Tolualdehyde [*Organic chemistry*]
PTAN Airman, Photographic Intelligenceman, Striker [*Navy rating*]
PT & E Physical Teardown and Evaluation (MCD)
PT & E Progress Tests and Examinations
PT & ER Physical Teardown and Evaluation Review (MCD)
PT & ME Physical Teardown and Maintenance Evaluation [*Army*]
PT & W Physical Training and Welfare [*British military*] (DMA)
PTANYC Protestant Teachers Association of New York City (EA)
PTAP Phenyltrimethylammonium Perbromide [*Organic chemistry*]
PTAP Profiler Triangle Analysis Package (USDC)
PTAP Profiler Triangle Analysis Package [*Marine science*] (OSRA)
PTAP Purified Diphtheria Toxoid Precipitated by Aluminum Phosphate (AAMN)
PTAR Prime Time Access Rule [*Television*]
PTASE Phosphatase [*An enzyme*] (DHSM)
PTA-T Periodical Title Abbreviations: by Title [*A publication*]
PTAT Proportional to Absolute Temperature (IAA)
PTAT Pure Tone Average Threshold (DMAA)
PTAV Percutaneous Transluminal Aortic Valvuloplasty [*Cardiology*] (CPH)
PTAVE Parents and Teachers Against Violence in Education (EA)
PTAWT Atlantic Wind Test Site, Tignish, Prince Edward Island [*Library symbol National Library of Canada*] (NLC)
PTB Page Table Base [*Computer science*] (IAA)
PTB Paragon Trade Brands [*NYSE symbol*] (SPSG)
ptB Part Bunkers [*Shipping*] (DS)
PTB Partido Trabalhista Brasileiro [*Brazilian Labor Party*] [*Political party*] (PPW)
PTB Parti du Travail de Belgique [*Belgian Labour Party*] [*Political party*] (EY)
PTB Parti du Travail du Burkina [*Burkina Faso*] [*Political party*] (EY)
PTB Patellar Tendon Bearing [*Medicine*]
PTB Payload Timing Buffer [*NASA*] (NASA)
PTB Perishables Tariff Bureau, Atlanta GA [*STAC*]
PTB Permian-Triassic Boundary [*Geology*]
PTB Personnel Test Battery
PTB Petersburg, VA [*Location identifier FAA*] (FAAL)
PTB Phosphotyrosine-Binding [*Biochemistry*]
PTB Physical Transaction Block
PTB Physikalisch Technische Bundesanstalt (ACII)
PTB Point Barrow [*Alaska*] [*Later, BRW*] [*Seismograph station code, US Geological Survey*] [*Closed*] (SEIS)
PTB Pounds per Thousand Barrels [*Petroleum technology*]
PTB Pressure Test Barrel
PTB Prior to Birth [*Medicine*]
PTB Process Technical Bulletin (MCD)
PTB Production and Test Branch (IAA)
PTB Program Time Base [*Military*] (AFIT)
PTB PT Boats, Inc. (EA)
PTBA Percutaneous Transluminal Balloon Angioplasty [*Cardiology*] (DMAA)
PTBA Proud to be Australian [*Political party*]
PTBB Para-tertiary-butylbenzaldehyde [*Organic chemistry*]
PTBBA Para-tertiary-butylbenzoic Acid [*Organic chemistry*]
PTBD Percutaneous Transhepatic Biliary Drainage [*Medicine*]
PTBD-EF Percutaneous Transhepatic Biliary Drainage - Enteric Feeding [*Medicine*] (DAVI)
PTBE Pyretic Tick-Borne Encephalitis [*Medicine*] (DMAA)
PTBF Portal Tributary Blood Flow [*Physiology*]
PTBI PT Boats, Inc. (EAIO)
PTBIPK Poly(t-Butyl Isopropenyl Ketone) [*Organic chemistry*]
PTBK Partbook [*Music*]
PTBL Portable (AABC)
PTBPD Posttraumatic Borderline Personality Disorder [*Medicine*] (DMAA)
PTBR Processing Tax Board of Review Decisions [*United States Internal Revenue Bureau*] [*A publication*] (DLA)
PTBR Punched Tape Block Reader [*Computer science*]
PtBS Poly(tertiary-butylstyrene) [*Organic chemistry*]
PTBS Posttraumatic Brain Syndrome [*Medicine*] (DMAA)
PTBT Para-tertiary-butyltoluene [*Organic chemistry*]
PTBT Partial Test-Ban Treaty
PTBT Pretransplant Blood Transfusion [*Medicine*]
PTBVK Poly(t-Butyl Vinyl Ketone) [*Organic chemistry*]
PTC Chief Photographic Intelligenceman [*Navy rating*]
PTC Motor Boat Subchaser [*Navy symbol Obsolete*]
PTC Pacific Telecommunications Council (EA)
PTC Pacific Tuna Conference
PTC PAR Technology [*NYSE symbol*] (TTSB)
PTC PAR Technology Corp. [*NYSE symbol*] (SPSG)
Ptc Participating [*Business term*]
PTC Parti Travailliste Congolais [*Congolese Labor Party*] [*Political party*]
PTC Part Through Crack [*Alloy tension*]
PTC Passive Thermal Control
PTC Patent, Trademark, and Copyright Institute [*Franklin Pierce College*] (IID)
PTC Patrol Vessel, Motor Torpedo Boat, Submarine Chaser [*Navy symbol*]
PTC Peace Tax Campaign [*Australia*]
PTC Pentagon Telecommunications Center (MCD)
PTC Peoria Terminal Co. [*AAR code*]
PTC Percutaneous Cholangiography [*Medicine*]
PTC Percutaneous Transhepatic Cholangiogram [*Medicine*]
PTC Performance Test Chamber (MCD)
PTC Performance Test Code
PTC Periscope Television Camera [*Telecommunications*] (IAA)
PTC Permission to Take Classes [*Education*]
PTC Personal Transfer Capsule
PTC Personal Typing Centre (NITA)
PTC Personnel Transfer Capsule [*Undersea technology*]
PTC Personnel Transport Carrier
PTC Phase Transfer Catalysis [*Physical chemistry*]
PTC Phenylisothiocyanate [*Organic chemistry*]
PTC Phenylthiocarbamide [*or Phenylthiocarbamyl*] [*Organic chemistry*]
PTC Pheochromocytoma, Thyroid Carcinoma Syndrome [*Oncology*] (MAE)
PTC Photographic Training Centre [*British*] (CB)
PTC Photographic Type Composition (ADA)
PTC Pipe and Tobacco Council of America [*Defunct*] (EA)
PTC Pipe Tobacco Council (EA)
PTC Pitch Trim Compensator
PTC Pitch Trim Controller (MCD)
PTC Plan to Clear [*Aviation*] (FAAC)
PTC Plasma Thromboplastin Component [*Factor IX*] [*Also, CF Hematology*]
PTC Plastic Training Cartridge [*Army*] (INF)
PTC Plugged Telescoping Catheter [*Clinical chemistry*]
PTC Pneumatic Temperature Control
PTC Pneumatic Test Console
PTC Points to Consider
PTC Police Training Centre [*British*]
PTC Portable Tele-Transaction Computer [*Telxon*]
PTC Portable Temperature Control (KSC)
PTC Porto Cannone [*Italy*] [*Seismograph station code, US Geological Survey*] (SEIS)
PTC Portuguese Trade Commission (EA)
PTC Positive Target Control [*Aviation*] (FAAC)
PTC Positive Temperature Coefficient
PTC Positive Transmitter Control
PTC Postal and Telegraphic Censorship [*Telecommunications*] (IAA)
PTC Postal Telegraph Cable
PTC Posterior Trabeculae Carneae [*Heart anatomy*]
PTC Post-Tensioned Concrete [*Technical drawings*]
PTC Post-Turnover Change [*Nuclear energy*] (NRCH)
PTC Power Testing Code (MCD)
PTC Power Transfer Coefficient
PTC Power Transmission Council
PTC Premature Tricuspid Closure [*Medicine*] (DMAA)
PTC Preoperative Testing Center
PTC Pressure and Temperature Control (KSC)
PTC Pressure Transducer Calibrator
PTC Primary Teaching Certificate [*Australia*]
PTC Primary Technical Course [*Military*]
PTC Primary Training Centre [*British military*] (DMA)
PTC Princeton Resources Corp. [*Vancouver Stock Exchange symbol*]
PTC Programmable Temperature Controls
PTC Programmable Test Console
PTC Programmed Transmission Control (BUR)
PTC Programmer Training Center
PTC Program of Technical Cooperation [*Organization of American States*]
PTC Promotional Telephone Call [*Marketing*] (OICC)
PTC Proof Test Capsule [*NASA*]
PTC Propellant Tanking Console (AAG)
PTC Propensity to Consume (MHDW)
PTC Propulsion Test Complex (KSC)
PTC Prothrombin Complex [*Hematology*]
PTC Pseudotumor Cerebri [*Medicine*] (AAMN)
PTC Psychophysical Timing Curve
PTC Publishing Technology Corp. [*Information service or system*] (IID)
PTC Pulse Time Code
PTCA Patience T'ai Chi Association (EA)
PTCA Percutaneous Transluminal Coronary Angioplasty [*Medicine*]
PTCA Plains Tribal Council of Assam [*India*] [*Political party*] (PPW)
PTCA Postal Telegraph Clerks' Association [*A union*] [*British*]
PTCA Pressure Technology Corp. of America

PTCA........... Private Truck Council of America (EA)
PTCA........... Professional Tennis Coaches' Association [*Australia*]
PTCAA......... Professional Turkey Calling Association of America (EA)
PTCAD......... Provisional Troop Carrier Airborne Division
PTCC........... Pacific Division Transport Control Center
PTCC........... PerSeptive Tech II Corp. [*NASDAQ symbol*] (SAG)
PT/CC.......... Problem Tracking and Change Control [*Computer science*]
PTCCS......... Polaris Target Card Computing System [*Missiles*]
PtcD............ Phosphatidylcholine [*Biochemistry*]
PTCD........... Private Training College for the Disabled (AIE)
PTCH........... Pacer Technology [*NASDAQ symbol*] (NQ)
PTCHY......... Patchy [*Meteorology*] (DA)
PTCI............ Programmable Telecommunications Interface (MCD)
PTCI............ Programmable Terminal Communications Interface (MCD)
PT CL.......... Part Called [*Stock exchange term*] (MHDB)
PTCL........... Peripheral T-Cell Lymphoma [*Oncology*]
PTCLD......... Part Called [*Stock exchange term*] (SPSG)
PTCM........... Master Chief Photographic Intelligenceman [*Navy rating*]
Pt Copyright & TM Cas... Patent, Copyright, and Trade Mark Cases [*United States*] [*A publication*] (DLA)
PTCP........... Parameter Test Control Program [*Computer science*] (IAA)
PTCP........... Participate (FAAC)
PTCP........... Positive Turnaround Control Point (MCD)
PTCR........... Pad Terminal Connection Room [*NASA*]
PTCR........... Payload Terminal Connector Room [*NASA*] (MCD)
PTCR........... Percutaneous Transluminal Coronary Recanalization [*Cardiology*] (DMAA)
PTCR........... Positive Temperature Coefficient Resistance [*Materials science and technology*]
PTCRA......... Percutaneous Transluminal Coronary Rotational Ablation [*Cardiology*] (DMAA)
PTCRM......... Partial Thermochemical Remanent Magnetization
PTCS........... Passive Thermal Control Section [*NASA*] (NASA)
PTCS........... Passive Thermal Control System (NASA)
PTCS........... Pax Tibi cum Sanctis [*Peace to Thee with the Saints*] [*Latin*]
PTCS........... Percutaneous Transhepatic Cholangioscopy [*Medicine*]
PTCS........... Phenyltrichlorosilane [*Organic chemistry*]
PTCS........... Planning, Training, and Checkout System [*NASA*] (MCD)
PTCS........... Powertrain Control Signal [*Automotive engineering*]
PTCS........... Pressure Transducer Calibration System
PTCS........... Propellant Tanking Computer System (KSC)
PTCS........... Senior Chief Photographic Intelligenceman [*Navy rating*]
PTCT........... Protect (MSA)
PT-CT.......... Prothrombin Time Control [*Hematology*] (DAVI)
PTCV........... Pilot-Operated Temperature Control Valve
PTCV........... Plowright Tissue Culture Vaccine [*Against rinderpest*]
PTD............. Painted (AAG)
ptd.............. Painted (VRA)
PTD............. Paper Towel Dispenser [*Technical drawings*]
PTD............. Parallel Transfer Disk [*Computer science*]
PTD............. Particle Transfer Device
PTD............. Part Throttle Deceleration [*Engines*] (EG)
PTD............. Patented (IAA)
PTD............. Percutaneous Transluminal Dilatation [*Medicine*] (DMAA)
PTD............. Period to Discharge [*Medicine*] (DAVI)
PTD............. Permanent Total Disability [*Medicine*]
PTD............. Phenyltriazolinedione [*Organic chemistry*]
Ptd.............. Phosphatidyl
PTD............. Photodiode Detector [*Instrumentation*]
PTD............. Photothermal Deflection
PTD............. Physical Teardown (MCD)
PTD............. Pilot to Dispatcher
PTD............. Plant Test Date [*Telecommunications*] (TEL)
PTD............. Pointed (WGA)
PTD............. Portland [*Oregon*] [*Seismograph station code, US Geological Survey*] (SEIS)
PTD............. Posttuning Drift
PTD............. Potsdam, NY [*Location identifier FAA*] (FAAL)
PTD............. Potter Distilleries Ltd. [*Toronto Stock Exchange symbol Vancouver Stock Exchange symbol*]
PTD............. Printed
PTD............. Prior to Discharge [*Medicine*] (MAE)
PTD............. Programmable Threshold Detector (MCD)
PTD............. Programmed Thermal Desorber
PTD............. Provisioning Technical Documentation
PTD............. Provisioning Transcript Documentation (MCD)
PTDA........... Per Task Data Area [*Computer science*] (BYTE)
PTDA........... Power Transmission Distributors Association (EA)
PTDB........... Point Target Data Base (SAA)
PTDC........... Pacific Trade and Development Conference [*OPTAD*] (FEA)
PTDDSS....... Provisioning Technical Documentation Data Selection Sheet [*NASA*] (NASA)
PTDF........... Pacific Tuna Development Foundation (EA)
PTDF........... Procurement Technical Data File [*DoD*]
Pt Dhgtr...... Patient's Daughter [*Also, Pt DTR*] (DAVI)
PTDIA......... Professional Truck Driver Institute of America (EA)
PtdIns......... Phosphatidylinositol [*Also, PI*] [*Biochemistry*]
PTDL........... Programmable Tapped Delay Line (PDAA)
PTDOS......... Processor Technology Disk Operating System
PTDP........... Preliminary Technical Development Plan (AFM)
PTDP........... Proposed Technical Development Plan
PTDQ........... Polymerized Trimethyldihydroquinoline [*Organic chemistry*]
PtdS............ Phosphatidylserine [*Biochemistry*]
PTDS........... Photo Target Detection System
PTDTL......... Pumped Tunnel Diode Transistor Logic
PT DTR........ Patient's Daughter [*Also, Pt Dhgtr*] (DAVI)
PTDU........... Pointing and Tracking Demonstration Unit (MCD)
PTe............. Indian Valley Public Library, Telford, PA [*Library symbol Library of Congress*] (LCLS)
PTE............. International Federation of Professional and Technical Engineers
PTE............. Nouadhibou [*Mauritania*] [*Airport symbol*] (AD)
PTE............. Packet Transfer Engine [*Newbridge Networks Corp.*]
PTE............. Packet Transport Equipment [*Computer science*] (PCM)
PTE............. Page Table Entry
PTE............. Parathyroid Extract [*Medicine*]
PTE............. Partido de Trabajadores Espanoles [*Spanish Workers' Party*] [*Political party*] (PPE)
PTE............. Party to Exemption [*RSPA*] (TAG)
PTE............. Passenger Transport Executive [*British*]
PTE............. Peace through Education Project [*An association*]
PTE............. Pectin transeliminase [*or Pectate Lyase*] [*An enzyme*]
PTE............. Peculiar Test Equipment
PTE............. Photographic Tasks and Equipment [*NASA*]
PTE............. Plate (ROG)
PTE............. Portable Test Equipment (AAG)
PTE............. Portage [*Alaska*] [*Seismograph station code, US Geological Survey*] (SEIS)
PTE............. Port Stephens [*Australia Airport symbol*] (OAG)
PTE............. Potential to Emit (GNE)
PTE............. Power Transport Equipment
PTE............. Pressure Test Equipment (MCD)
PTE............. Pressure-Tolerant Electronics (IEEE)
PTE............. Pretax Earnings [*Employment*]
PTE............. Pretibial Edema [*Medicine*] (DAVI)
PTE............. Primrose Technology Corp. [*Vancouver Stock Exchange symbol*]
PTE............. Private [*British*]
PTE............. Private Trade Entity
PTE............. ProActive Technologies, Inc. [*AMEX symbol*] (SAG)
PTE............. Problem Trend Evaluation (MCD)
PTE............. Production Test Equipment (MCD)
PTE............. Proximal Tibial Epiphysis [*Orthopedics*] (DAVI)
PTE............. Proxylem Tracheary Element [*Botany*]
Pte.............. Pteroyl [*Biochemistry*]
PTE............. Pulmonary Thromboembolism [*Medicine*]
PTEA........... Preliminary Training Effectiveness Analysis
PTEAR......... Physical Teardown
PTEAR......... Physical Teardown and Maintenance Allocation Review (MCD)
PTeb........... Tebtunis Papyri [*A publication*] (OCD)
PTEC........... Phoenix Technologies [*NASDAQ symbol*] (TTSB)
PTEC........... Phoenix Technologies Ltd. [*NASDAQ symbol*] (NQ)
PTEC........... Plastics Technical Evaluation Center [*Military*]
pt ed.......... Patient Education (DAVI)
PTED........... Pulmonary Thromboembolic Disease [*Medicine*]
PteGlu......... Pteroylmonoglutamic Acid [*Folic acid*] [*Also, FA, PGA*] [*Biochemistry*]
PTEK........... Premiere Technologies [*NASDAQ symbol*] (TTSB)
PTEK........... Premiere Technologies, Inc. [*NASDAQ symbol*] (SAG)
PTEL........... Peoples Telephone Co. [*NASDAQ symbol*] (TTSB)
PTEL........... People's Telephone Co., Inc. [*NASDAQ symbol*] (NQ)
PTEN........... Patterson Energy [*NASDAQ symbol*] (TTSB)
PTEN........... Patterson Energy, Inc. [*NASDAQ symbol*] (SAG)
PTEN........... Pentaerythritol Tetranitrate [*An explosive and a vasodilator*] [*Cardiology*] (DAVI)
PTEN........... Prime Time Entertainment Network [*Television broadcasting*]
PTER........... Physical Teardown and Evaluation Review (MCD)
PTES........... Productivity Trend Evaluation System (MCD)
PTES........... Purdue Teacher Evaluation Scale
PTET........... Platinum Entertainment [*NASDAQ symbol*] (TTSB)
PTETD......... Production Test Engineering Task Description (MCD)
PTETPC....... Party to Expose the Petrov Conspiracy [*Australia Political party*]
PTETS......... Pioneer Television and Electronic Technicians Society [*Defunct*] (EA)
PT EX.......... Part Exchange (WDAA)
PTF............. Malololailai [*Fiji*] [*Airport symbol*] (OAG)
PTF............. Paralemniscal Tegmental Field [*Neuroanatomy*]
PTF............. Parathyroid Fever [*Medicine*] (CPH)
PTF............. Parts Transfer Form (SAA)
PTF............. Patch and Test Facility
PTF............. Patient Treatment File [*Medicine*] (DMAA)
PTF............. Patrol Torpedo Boat, Fast [*Formerly, PT*] [*Navy symbol*]
PTF............. Payload Test Facility [*VAFB*] [*NASA*] (MCD)
PTF............. Permit to Fly [*Aviation*] (AIA)
PTF............. Petersfield Oil & Minerals [*Vancouver Stock Exchange symbol*]
PTF............. Phase Transfer Function (MCD)
PTF............. Plaintiff [*Legal term*] (ROG)
PTF............. Plasma Thromboplastin Factor [*Factor VIII*] [*Also, AHF, AHG, TPC Hematology*]
PTF............. Police Training Foundation
PTF............. Polymer Thick Film
PTF............. Port Task Force
PTF............. Power Test Fail
PTF............. Production Tabulating Form (AAG)
PTF............. Programmable Transversal Filter [*SMP*]
PTF............. Program Temporary Fix [*Computer science*]
PTF............. Proof Test Facility [*Nuclear energy*]
PTF............. Propellant Tank Flow
PTF............. Proximal Tubule Fluid [*Laboratory science*] (DAVI)
PTF............. Pulse Transfer Function
PTFA........... Preliminary Tool and Facility Analysis (MCD)
PTFA........... Prothrombin Time Fixing Agent (DMAA)
PTFC........... Pretty Things Fan Club (EA)
PTFCE......... Polytrifluorochloroethene (BARN)

PTFD........... Personnel, Training and Force Development [*Army*]
PTFDA......... Professional Travel Film Directors Association [*Later, Professional Travelogue Sponsors - PTS*] (EA)
PTFE............ Polytetrafluoroethylene [*Organic chemistry*]
PTFG............ Large Guided Missile Motorboat [*Navy symbol*] (DNAB)
PTFHA......... Physician Task Force on Hunger in America [*Defunct*] (EA)
PTFHC......... Putnam Tax Free Health Care Fund [*Associated Press*] (SAG)
PTFM............ Platform (AAG)
PTFMA......... Peacetime Force Material Assets [*Navy*] (AFIT)
PTFMA......... Public Telecommunications Financial Management Association (EA)
PTFMO......... Peacetime Force Materiel Objective [*Army*]
PTFMPO...... Peacetime Force Materiel Procurement Objective [*Army*]
PTFMR......... Peacetime Force Materiel Requirements [*Army*]
PTFMR-A..... Peacetime Force Materiel Requirements - Acquisition [*Army*] (AABC)
PTFMR-R..... Peacetime Force Materiel Requirements - Retention [*Army*] (AABC)
PTFP............ Public Telecommunications Facilities Program [*Department of Commerce*]
PTFS............ Pilot-to-Forecaster Service (NOAA)
PTFS............ Posttraumatic Fibromyalgia Syndrome [*Medicine*] (DMAA)
PTFT............ Production Temporary Facility Tool (SAA)
PTFUR......... President's Task Force on Urban Renewal (EA)
PTFX............ Plating Fixture (AAG)
ptg............... Painting (VRA)
PTG............... Parathyroid Gland [*Medicine*] (DMAA)
PTG............... Parent-Teacher Group
PTG............... Pennington Gap, VA [*Location identifier FAA*] (FAAL)
PTG............... Piano Technicians Guild (EA)
PTG............... Pietersburg [*South Africa*] [*Airport symbol*] (OAG)
PTG............... Place to Go (IAA)
PTG............... Planed, Tongued, and Grooved (DAC)
PTG............... Polaris Task Group [*Missiles*]
PTG............... Portage Industries Corp. [*AMEX symbol*] (SPSG)
PTG............... Portageville [*Missouri*] [*Seismograph station code, US Geological Survey Closed*] (SEIS)
PTG............... Portuguese (ROG)
PTG............... Precise Tone Generator [*Telecommunications*] (TEL)
PTG............... Pressure Test Gauge
PTG............... Pressure Transfer Gauge
PTG............... Printing
ptg............... Printing (WDMC)
PTG............... Professional Technical Group
PTG............... Prothoracic Gland [*Insect anatomy*]
PTG............... Pulse Target Generator
PTG............... Small Guided Missile Motorboat [*Navy symbol*] (DNAB)
PTG............... Teniposide [*Antineoplastic drug regimen*] (DAVI)
PTGA............ Pteroyltriglutamic Acid [*Pharmacology*]
PTGAP......... Professional Technical Group on Antennas and Propagation [*of the IEEE*]
PTGBD......... Percutaneous Transhepatic Gallbladder Drainage [*Medicine*]
PTGC............ Programmed Temperature Gas Chromatography
PTG CYL...... Printing Cylinder (DGA)
PTGEC......... Professional Technical Group on Electronic Computers [*Later, IEEE Computer Society*]
PT GEO........ Posted to Geographics
PTGEWS...... Professional Technical Group on Engineering Writing and Speech [*of the IEEE*]
pTGF............ Porcine Transforming Growth Factor
PTGL............ Pyrolysis to Gases and Liquids [*Chemical processing*]
PTGS............ Paper Trade Golfing Society [*British*]
PTGS............ Portable Telemetry Ground Station
PTGT............ Primary Target [*Military*]
PTH............... Hydrofoil Motor Torpedo Boat [*Ship symbol*] (NATG)
PTH............... Pallet Torque Hook
PTH............... Panther Mines Ltd. [*Vancouver Stock Exchange symbol*]
PTH............... Paper Tape Half-Duplex
PTH............... Parathormone [*Medicine*] (MAE)
PTH............... Parathyroid Hormone [*Endocrinology*]
PTH............... Path (GAVI)
PTH............... Pathology [*Medical specialty*] (DHSM)
PTH............... Peak Tanning Hours [*Supposedly occurring between 10am and 2pm*] [*See also BROTS, SROTS*]
PTH............... Phenylthiohydantoin [*Organic chemistry*]
PTH............... Plasma Thromboplastin Component [*Medicine*] (DMAA)
PTH............... Plated through Hole
Pth............... Polythiophene [*Organic chemistry*]
PTH............... Port Heiden [*Alaska*] [*Airport symbol*] (OAG)
PTH............... Port Heiden, AK [*Location identifier FAA*] (FAAL)
PTH............... Post-Transfusion Hepatitis [*Medicine*]
PTH............... Project Team Head (MHDI)
PTH............... Project Top Hat [*Defunct*] (EA)
PtHA............ Pinto Horse Association of America (EA)
P Th B......... Bachelor of Practical Theology
PThD............ Punch-Through Device (PDAA)
PtHeat......... Petroleum Heat & Power Corp. [*Associated Press*] (SAG)
PtHel............ Petroleum Helicopter, Inc. [*Associated Press*] (SAG)
PTHF............ Polytetrahydrofuran [*Organic chemistry*]
PtHg............. Partially Hearing (AIE)
PTHLGST..... Pathologist
PTH-LP........ Parathyroid Hormone-Like Peptide [*Endocrinology*]
PTHrP.......... Parathyroid Hormone-Related Protein [*Biochemistry*]
PTHS............ Parathyroid Hormone Secretion Rate [*Endocrinology*] (MAE)
PTI............... First USA Paymentech [*NYSE symbol*] (TTSB)
PTI............... First USA Paymentech, Inc. [*NYSE symbol*] (SAG)
PTI............... Package Turn In (MCD)
PTI............... Pancreatic Trypsin Inhibitor [*Biochemistry*]
PTI............... Parent Training and Information [*Centers*] [*Established under the Individuals with Disabilities Education Act (IDEA)*] (PAZ)
PTI............... Parkes-Tidbinbilla Interferometer [*Astronomy*]
PTI............... Party Identity [*Telecommunications*] (TEL)
PTI............... Pathways to Independence [*An association*] (EA)
PTI............... Pennsylvania Transportation Institute [*Pennsylvania State University*] [*Research center*] (RCD)
PTI............... Penn Telecom, Inc. [*Gibsonia, PA*] (TSSD)
PTI............... Persistent Tolerant Infection
PTI............... Personnel Tests for Industry
PTI............... Personnel Transaction Identifier [*Air Force*] (AFM)
PTI............... Philadelphia Textile Institute
PTI............... Physical-Technical Institute [*Former USSR*]
PTI............... Physical Training Instructor [*British*]
PTI............... Pictorial Test of Intelligence [*Education*]
PTI............... Pipe Test Insert [*Liquid Metal Engineering Center*] [*Energy Research and Development Administration*] (IEEE)
PTI............... Plugging Temperature Indicator [*Nuclear energy*] (NRCH)
PTI............... Poetry Therapy Institute (EA)
PTI............... Porous Tungsten Ionizer
PTI............... Post-Tensioning Institute [*Defunct*] (EA)
PTI............... Power Tool Institute (EA)
PTI............... Precision Technology, Inc. (AAG)
PTI............... Preliminary Test Information (KSC)
PTI............... [*The*] Press Trust of India
PTI............... Pretrial Intervention (BARN)
PTI............... Pre-Trial Investigation (DNAB)
PTI............... Pre-Trip Inspection [*Shipping*]
PTI............... Previously-Taxed Income
PTI............... Prinicipal-Teacher Interaction Study (EDAC)
PTI............... Production Training Indicator [*Computer science*]
PTI............... Programmed Test Input (MCD)
PTI............... Programming Tools and Information [*IBM Corp.*] [*Computer science*]
PTI............... Program Transfer Interface
PTI............... Promethean Technologies, Inc. [*Vancouver Stock Exchange symbol*]
PTI............... Publicacoes Tecnicas Internacionais Ltda. [*International Technical Publications Ltd.*] [*Information service or system*] (IID)
PTI............... Public Technology, Inc. [*Research center*] (RCD)
PTI............... Public Tool Interface [*Computer science*] (ODBW)
PTI............... Puntilla Lake, AK [*Location identifier FAA*] (FAAL)
PTIA............ Pet Trade and Industry Association (EAIO)
PTIB............ Program Testing Information Bulletin (IAA)
PTIC............ Patent and Trade Mark Institute of Canada
PTIE............ Pet Trade and Industry Exhibition [*British*] (ITD)
PTIG............ Presentation of Technical Information Group (SAA)
PTIHd.......... PTI Holding, Inc. [*Associated Press*] (SAG)
PTI Hold...... PTI Holding, Inc. [*Associated Press*] (SAG)
PTII............. PTI Holding [*NASDAQ symbol*] (TTSB)
PTII............. PTI Holding, Inc. [*NASDAQ symbol*] (SAG)
PTIIW.......... PTI Hldg Wrrt [*NASDAQ symbol*] (TTSB)
PTIL............. Parts Test Information List (KSC)
PTI-ODT...... Personnel Tests for Industry - Oral Directions Test
PTIP............ Physical Therapist in Independent Practice (GFGA)
PTIRFM....... Polarized Total Internal Reflection Fluorescence Microscopy
PTIS............ Pacific Triangle Information Services [*Information service or system*] (IID)
PTIS............ Plasma Therm [*NASDAQ symbol*] (TTSB)
PTIS............ Plasma-Therm, Inc. [*NASDAQ symbol*] (NQ)
PTIS............ Powertrain Input Signal [*Automotive engineering*]
PTIS............ Programmed Test Input System (MCD)
PTIS............ Propulsion Test Instrumentation System (KSC)
PTIWU........ Posts and Telegraphs Industrial Workers' Union [*India*]
PTIX............ Performance Technologies [*NASDAQ symbol*] (TTSB)
PTIX............ Performance Technologies, Inc. [*NASDAQ symbol*] (SAG)
PTJ............... Part-Time Job
PTJ............... Portland [*Australia Airport symbol*] (OAG)
PTJ............... Pulse Train Jitter [*Computer science*] (IAA)
PTK............... Passport to Knowledge [*Children's computer program sponsored by NASA and NSF*]
PTK............... Phototherapeutic Keratectomy [*Ophthalmology*]
PTK............... Polishing Tool Kit
PTK............... Pontiac, MI [*Location identifier FAA*] (FAAL)
PTK............... Potentiometer Tapping Kit
PTK............... Probability of Track [*Military*]
PTK............... Protein-Tyrosine Kinase [*An enzyme*]
PTKK............ Truk [*Caroline Islands*] [*ICAO location identifier*] (ICLI)
PTL............... Partial Total Loss [*Insurance*] (DS)
PTL............... Part Time Legislature
PTL............... Patrol [*or Patrolman*] (AABC)
PTL............... Patrol Boat
PTL............... Peacetime Losses [*Military*]
PTL............... Penteli [*Greece*] [*Seismograph station code, US Geological Survey*] (SEIS)
PTL............... [*Sodium*] Pentothal [*An anesthetic*] (DAVI)
PTL............... People That Love [*Of television's "PTL Club"*] [*Facetious translations: "Pass the Loot" and "Pay the Lady"*]
PTL............... Perinatal Telencephalic Leukoencephalopathy [*Medicine*]
PTL............... Peripheral T-Cell Lymphoma [*Oncology*]
PTL............... Petroleum Testing Laboratory
PTL............... Phase Tracking Loop (MCD)
PTL............... Photographic Technology Laboratory (KSC)
PTL............... Pietermaritzburg [*South Africa*] [*Airport symbol*] (AD)
PTL............... Pintle [*Design engineering*]
PTL............... Planning Test List
PTL............... Pocket Testament League (EA)

ptl .... Portal (VRA)
PTL .... Power Transmission Line (OA)
PTL .... Praise the Lord [*Of television's "PTL Club"*] [*Facetious translations: "Pass the Loot" and "Pay the Lady"*]
PTL .... Pressure, Torque, and Load
PTL .... Preterm Labor [*Obstetrics*] (DAVI)
PTL .... Pre-Test Laboratory (DNAB)
PTL .... Pretty Tough Lawyer [*Refers to Melvin Belli, attorney for Tammy and Jim Bakker of the PTL Club*]
PTL .... Primary Target Line [*Military*]
PTL .... Process and Test Language
PTL .... Providence Air Charter [*ICAO designator*] (FAAC)
PTL .... Public Television Library
PTL .... Pulse Transmission Logic (IAA)
PTLA .... Praise the Lord Anyway
PTLA .... Publishers' Trade List Annual
PTLAP .... Petroleum Test Laboratory Accreditation Program
PTLBD .... Particleboard
PTLC .... Piedmont Triad Library Council [*Library network*]
PTLC .... Precipitation Thin-Layer Chromatography [*Medicine*] (DMAA)
PT-LD .... Physical Teardown - Logistics Demonstration (MCD)
PTLD .... Post-Transfusion Liver Disease [*Medicine*]
PTLD .... Prescribed Tumor Lethal Dose [*Oncology*]
PTLEF .... Peace through Law Education Fund (EA)
PTLEN .... Petal Length [*Botany*]
PTLF .... Pressure, Temperature, Level, and Flow [*Chemical engineering*]
PTLRS .... Publications and Technical Literature Research Section [*Environmental Protection Agency*] (IID)
PTLV .... Primate T-Lymphotropic Viruses
PTLX .... Patlex Corp. [*NASDAQ symbol*] (SAG)
PTLY .... Partly [*NWS*] (FAAC)
PTM .... Palmarito [*Venezuela*] [*Airport symbol*] (OAG)
PTM .... Pancake Torquer Motor (SAA)
PTM .... Parasite Tubing Method (PDAA)
PTM .... Passenger Traffic Manager
PTM .... Pattern Transformation Memory
PTM .... Performance Test Model (OA)
PTM .... Petromac Energy, Inc. [*Vancouver Stock Exchange symbol*]
PTM .... Phase Time Modulation
PTM .... Phenyltrimethylammonium [*Also, PTA, PTMA*] [*Organic chemistry*]
PTM .... Photomultiplier (IAA)
PTM .... Photon Tunneling Microscope
PTM .... Physical Teardown and Maintenance (MCD)
PTM .... Pietermaritzburg [*South Africa*] [*Seismograph station code, US Geological Survey*] (SEIS)
PTM .... Pneumatic Telescope Mast
PTM .... Polaris Tactical Missile
PTM .... Portable Traffic Monitor [*Telecommunications*] (TEL)
PTM .... Portland Terminal Co. [*AAR code*]
PTM .... Posttransfusion Mononucleosis [*Medicine*]
PTM .... Pressure-Transmitting Medium [*Engineering*]
Ptm .... Pressure Transmural [*Pretaining to an airway or blood vessel*] [*Medicine*] (DAVI)
PTM .... Preterm Milk [*Medicine*]
PTM .... Pretuned Module [*Telecommunications*] (IAA)
PTM .... Primary Thickening Meristem [*Botany*]
PTM .... Programmable Terminal Multiplexer [*Texas Instruments, Inc.*]
PTM .... Programmable Timer Module
PTM .... Program Timing and Maintenance [*Electronics*] (IAA)
PTM .... Program Timing and Miscellaneous [*Electronics*]
PTM .... Program Trouble Memorandum [*NASA*] (IAA)
PTM .... Proof Test Model [*NASA*]
PTM .... Pulse Time Modulation [*Radio*]
PTM .... Pulse Time Multiplex
PTM .... Pulse Transmission Mode (MCD)
PTM .... Putnam Managed High Yield Trust [*NYSE symbol*] (SPSG)
PTM .... Putnam Managed Hi Yield Tr [*NYSE symbol*] (TTSB)
PTM .... Southeastern Airways Corp. [*ICAO designator*] (FAAC)
PTMA .... Phenyltrimethylammonium [*Also, PTA, PTM*] [*Organic chemistry*]
PTMA .... Phosphotungstomolybdic Acid [*Inorganic chemistry*]
PTMA .... Prothymosin Alpha (DMAA)
PTMAS .... Professional, Technical, Managerial, and Administrative Staff
PTMC .... Photomechanical (VRA)
PTMC .... Polaris Tender Management Computer [*Missiles*]
PTMC .... Polish Telephones & Microwave Corp. [*NASDAQ symbol*] (SAG)
PTMC .... Polish Tels & Microwave Corp. [*NASDAQ symbol*] (TTSB)
PTMCA .... Pit Tub and Mine Car Manufacturers' Association [*British*] (BI)
PTMCW .... Polish Tels & Microwave Wrrt [*NASDAQ symbol*] (TTSB)
PTMD .... Propellant Toxicity Monitoring Devices (KSC)
PTMDF .... Pupils, Tension, Media, Disc, Fundus [*Medicine*]
PTMEG .... Polytetramethylene Ether Glycol [*Organic chemistry*]
PTML .... PNPN [*Positive-Negative-Positive-Negative*] Transistor Magnetic Logic (IAA)
PTML .... PNP [*Positive-Negative-Positive*] Transistor Magnetic Logic (IEEE)
PTML .... Proxicom Template Markup Language [*Computer science*]
PTM/OS .... Programmable Terminal Monitor/Operating System (NITA)
PTMPY .... Per Thousand Members per Year (DMAA)
PTMS .... Parathymosin (DMAA)
PTMS .... Para-Toluidine-meta-sulfonic Acid [*Also, PTMSA*] [*Organic chemistry*]
PTMS .... Pattern Transformation Memory System
PTMS .... Precision Torque Measuring System (NASA)
PTMS .... Publication Text Management System (MCD)
PTMS .... Public Transportation Facilities and Equipment Management System [*FHWA*] (TAG)
PTMSA .... Para-Toluidine-meta-sulfonic Acid [*Also, PTMS*] [*Organic chemistry*]
PTMSP .... Poly(trimethylsilyl-propyne) [*Organic chemistry*]
PTMT .... Poly(tetramethylene Terephthalate) [*Organic chemistry*]
PTMTLG .... Pitometer-Log [*Engineering*]
PTMU .... Power and Temperature Monitor Unit (KSC)
PTMUX .... Pulse Time Multiplex (MSA)
PTMV .... Percutaneous Transvenous Mitral Valvotomy [*Cardiology*]
PTN .... Morgan City/Patterson [*Louisiana*] [*Airport symbol*] (OAG)
PTN .... Pantanal Linhas Aereas Sul-Matogrossenses SA [*Brazil*] [*ICAO designator*] (FAAC)
PTN .... Particulate Total Nitrogen [*Analytical chemistry*]
PTN .... Partido Trabalhista Nacional [*National Workers' Party*] [*Brazil*]
PTN .... Partition (KSC)
PTN .... Patterson, LA [*Location identifier FAA*] (FAAL)
PTN .... Phenotemperature Normogram [*Phenology*]
PTN .... Phenytoin [*Anticonvulsant*]
PTN .... Plant Test Number [*Telecommunications*] (TEL)
PTN .... Pluton Industries Ltd. [*Vancouver Stock Exchange symbol*]
PTN .... Potsdam [*New York*] [*Seismograph station code, US Geological Survey*] (SEIS)
PTN .... Private Telecommunication Network [*Telecommunications*] (OSI)
PTN .... Procedure Turn [*ICAO*] (FAAC)
Ptn .... Pterin [*Biochemistry*]
PTN .... Public Telephone Network (DA)
pTNM .... Postsurgical, Tumor, Nodes, and Metastases [*Classifications for postsurgical resection pathological staging of cancer*] [*Oncology*] (DAVI)
PTNR .... Partner (ROG)
PTNRSHIP ... Partnership (ROG)
PTNX .... Printronix, Inc. [*NASDAQ symbol*] (NQ)
PTNX .... Printronix Inc. [*NASDAQ symbol*] (TTSB)
PTNX .... Private Telecommunication Network Exchange [*Telecommunications*] (OSI)
PTO .... North West Geomatics Ltd. [*Canada ICAO designator*] (FAAC)
PTO .... Pacific Theater of Operations [*World War II*]
PTO .... Packard Truck Organization [*Defunct*] (EA)
PTO .... Paid Time Off (NFD)
PTO .... Participating Test Organization [*Air Force*]
PTO .... Partners Oil & Mining [*Vancouver Stock Exchange symbol*]
PTO .... Part Time Operation (DA)
PTO .... Patent and Trademark Office [*Formerly, PO*] [*Department of Commerce*]
PTO .... [*United States*] Patent and Trademark Office (AAGC)
PTO .... Pato Branco [*Brazil*] [*Airport symbol*] (OAG)
PTO .... People, Topics, Opinions [*A publication British*]
PTO .... Perlsucht Tuberculin Original [*Medicine*] (MAE)
PTO .... Permeability-Tuned Oscillator (IAA)
PTO .... Personal Time Off (DAVI)
PTO .... Please Turn Over [*the page*]
pto .... Please Turn Over (WDMC)
PTO .... Porto [*Serro Do Pilar*] [*Portugal*] [*Seismograph station code, US Geological Survey*] (SEIS)
PTO .... Port Transportation Officer
PTO .... Power Takeoff [*Automotive engineering*]
PTO .... Power Test Operations (MCD)
PTO .... Powertrain Operations [*Auto manufacturer corporate structure*]
PTO .... Professional and Technology Officer [*British*]
PTO .... Project Technical Office [*Military*] (DNAB)
PTO .... Project Type Organization (AAG)
PTO .... Proof Test Orbiter [*NASA*]
PTO .... Propellant Transfer Operation (AFM)
PTO .... Public Telecommunications Operator (NITA)
PTO .... Public Trustee Office (DLA)
PTO .... Public Trust Office [*Australia*]
PTO .... Purdue Teacher Opinionaire [*Test*]
PTO .... Pyridinethiol Oxide [*Pharmacology*]
PTOA .... Projective Tests of Attitudes
PTobA .... United States Army, Tobyhanna Army Depot Library, Tobyhanna, PA [*Library symbol Library of Congress*] (LCLS)
PTO Board ... Patent and Trademark Office Board of Patent Appeals and Interferences (AAGC)
PToG .... General Telephone & Electronics, GTE Sylvania, Inc., Towanda, PA [*Library symbol Library of Congress*] (LCLS)
PTOJ .... Passive Track-On-Jam
PTOL .... Peacetime Operating Level (AFM)
Ptol .... Ptolemaeus Mathematicus [*Second century AD*] [*Classical studies*] (OCD)
Ptol .... Ptolemaic (BJA)
PTOMAIN ..... Project to Optimize Many Individual Numbers (SAA)
PTON .... Proteon, Inc. [*NASDAQ symbol*] (SPSG)
P to P .... Plate to Plate (DEN)
P to P .... Port to Port [*Shipping*] (DS)
PTOP .... Program Test and Operations Plan
PTOPC .... Program to Program Communications (MHDI)
PTOS .... Paper Tape Oriented Operating System
PTOS .... Patent and Trademark Office Society (EA)
PTOS .... Patriot Tactical Operations Simulator [*Army*]
PTOS .... Peacetime Operating Stock [*Military*]
PTOUT .... Printout (MSA)
PTP .... Paper Tape Perforator [*or Punch*]
PTP .... Paper Tape Punch (ECII)
PTP .... Parameter Test Program (SAA)
PTP .... Parent to Parent, Inc. [*Australia*]
PTP .... Parti Togolais du Progres [*Party for Togolese Progress*]
PTP .... Peak-to-Peak [*Nuclear energy*]
PTP .... Pensions for Technical Professionals [*An association*]

PTP .... People to People International (EA)
PTP .... Percutaneous Transhepatic Selective Portography [*Roentgenography*]
PTP .... Petrologic Petroleum [*Vancouver Stock Exchange symbol*]
PTP .... Phenyltetrahydropyridine [*Biochemistry*]
PTP .... Platinum Temperature Probe
PTP .... Pointe-A-Pitre [*Guadeloupe*] [*Airport symbol*] (OAG)
PTP .... Point Park College, Pittsburgh, PA [*Inactive*] [*OCLC symbol*] (OCLC)
PTP .... Point-to-Point [*Robotics*] [*Telecommunications*]
PTP .... Pollution Transfer Program [*Marine science*] (MSC)
PTP .... Porous Tungsten Plug
PTP .... Posterior Tibial Pulse [*Cardiology*] (DAVI)
PTP .... Posto Telefonico Pubblico [*Public Telephone*] [*Italy*]
PTP .... Posttetanic Potentiation [*Neurophysiology*]
PTP .... Post-Tetanic Potentiation [*Neurology*]
PTP .... Post-Transfusion Purpura [*Medicine*]
PTP .... Potato Tuber Peroxidase [*An enzyme*]
PTP .... Preferred Target Point (KSC)
PTP .... Preliminary Task Plan (MCD)
PTP .... Pretransmission Precautionary Answer to Nature's Call [*Especially before a long program*] [*Television*]
PTP .... Pre-Turbo Pressure
PTP .... Primary Target Point [*NASA*]
PTP .... Print-to-Point [*Telecommunications*] (IAA)
PTP .... Prior to Program [*Medicine*] (MAE)
PTP .... Production Test Plan (MCD)
PTP .... Production Test Procedure (NATG)
PTP .... Professional Tax Planner
PTP .... Programmable Text Processor [*Programming language*] (CSR)
PTP .... Programmable Touch Panel [*Electronics*]
PTP .... Programmed Turn Phase
PTP .... Program Task Planning (MCD)
PTP .... Promise to Pay (MHDW)
PTP .... Protect the Planet [*Manual*]
PTP .... Protein Tyrosine Phosphatase [*An enzyme*]
PTP .... Proximity Test Plug [*Nuclear energy*] (NRCH)
PTP .... Pueblo to People (EA)
Ptp .... Transpulmonary Pressure (MAE)
PTPA .... Portal-to-Portal Act of 1947 (WYGK)
PTPase .... Protein Tyrosine Phosphatase [*An enzyme*]
PTPC .... Professional Teaching Practices Commission (OICC)
PTPC .... Protein-Tyrosine Phosphatase C (DMAA)
PTPD .... Part Paid [*Business term*]
PTPE .... Powertrain Product Engineering [*Automotive*]
PTP'er .... Prime Time Performer [*In book title, "Vitale: Just Your Average Bald, One-Eyed Basketball Wacko Who Beat the Ziggy and Became a PTP'er"*]
PTPF .... Payee TIN [*Taxpayer Identification Number*] Perfection File [*IRS*]
PTPG .... Protein-Tyrosine Phosphatase Gamma (DMAA)
PTPI .... People to People International (EAIO)
PTPI .... Professional and Technical Programs, Inc.
PTPM .... Posttraumatic Progressive Myelopathy [*Neurology*] (DAVI)
PTPN .... Peripheral [*Vein*] Total Parenteral Nutrition [*Gastroenterology*] (DAVI)
PTPN .... Ponape Island [*Caroline Islands*] [*ICAO location identifier*] (ICLI)
PTPN .... Protein-Tyrosine Phosphatase, Non-Receptor (DMAA)
PTPR .... Production Test Program Report
PTPS .... Package Test Power Supply
PTPS .... Parallel-Tuned Parallel-Stabilized (IAA)
PTPS .... Propellant Transfer Pressurization System (KSC)
PTPS .... Pumped Two-Phase System (SSD)
PTPSC .... People-to-People Sports Committee (EA)
PTPSK .... Pilot Tone Phase Shift Keying [*Computer science*] (IAA)
PTPT .... Platinum Print (VRA)
P-TPT .... Portable Tactual Performance Test [*Child development test*] [*Psychology*]
PTPU .... Program Tape Preparation Unit
PTQ .... Ludlow Aviation, Inc. [*FAA designator*] (FAAC)
PTQ .... Parent-Teacher Questionnaire (DMAA)
PTQ .... Poly(tolyquinoxaline) [*Organic chemistry*]
PTQ .... Pulse-Taking Questionnaire
PTR .... Nova Scotia Department of Lands and Forests [*Canada*] [*FAA designator*] (FAAC)
PTR .... Pacific Test Range (MUGU)
PTR .... Painter
ptr .... Painter (VRA)
PTR .... Paper Tape Reader
PTR .... Paper Towel Receptor [*Technical drawings*]
PTR .... Parr Terminal Railroad (MHDW)
PTR .... Partido Tercera Republica [*Chile*] [*Political party*] (EY)
PTR .... Partner
PTR .... Parts Tool Requirements File
PTR .... Parts Transfer Record (SAA)
PTR .... Part Throttle Reheat [*Aviation*] (OA)
PTR .... Patuxent River [*Navy*] (MCD)
PTR .... Perforated Tape Reader
PTR .... Peripheral Total Resistance [*Medicine*] (MAE)
PTR .... Perlsucht Tuberculin Rest [*Medicine*] (MAE)
P/Tr .... Permian/Triassic [*A geological period boundary*]
PTR .... Personal Technology Research [*Commercial firm*]
PTR .... Peterson [*Alabama*] [*Seismograph station code, US Geological Survey*] (SEIS)
Ptr .... Petrine [*Of, or relating to, Peter the Apostle or Peter the Great*] (BJA)
PTR .... Photoelectric Tape Reader
PTR .... Physikalisch-Technische Reichsanstalt
PTR .... Pilot Training Rate [*Navy*]
PTR .... Pleasant Harbor [*Alaska*] [*Airport symbol*] (OAG)
PTR .... Plug-Type Receptacle
PTR .... Pointer [*Computer science*]
PTR .... Polar to Rectangular (SAA)
PTR .... Pool Test Reactor [*Nuclear energy*]
PTR .... Pool Training Reactor [*Nuclear energy*]
PTR .... Poor Transmission [*Telecommunications*] (TEL)
PTR .... Portable Tape Recorder
PTR .... Port Macquarie [*New South Wales*] [*Airport symbol*] (AD)
PTR .... Position Track RADAR
PTR .... Positive Termination Rate [*Job Training and Partnership Act*] (OICC)
PTR .... Post-Trip Review
PTR .... Power Transformers (MCD)
PTR .... Precision Transmitter Receiver
PTR .... Preliminary Technical Report
PTR .... Preliminary Test Report [*NASA*] (KSC)
PTR .... Pressure Test Record
PTR .... Pressure Transmitter Recorder (ECII)
PTR .... Pressure-Tube Reactor [*Nuclear energy*]
PTR .... Pretransmit Receiving
PTR .... Pre-Trial Release (OICC)
PTR .... Printer (MSA)
P Tr .... Private Trust [*Includes testamentary, investment, life insurance, holding title, etc.*] [*Legal term*] (DLA)
PTR .... Processor Tape Read
PTR .... Production Test Record
PTR .... Production Test Requirements (KSC)
PTR .... Professional Tennis Registry, USA (EA)
PTR .... Proficiency Testing Research (EA)
PTR .... Programmer Trouble Report [*Nuclear energy*] (GFGA)
PTR .... Program Technical Review (MCD)
PTR .... Program Trouble Report [*NASA*] (KSC)
PTR .... Proof Test Reactor [*Nuclear energy*]
PTR .... Punched Tape Reader [*Computer science*]
PTR .... Pupil-Teacher Ratio
PTR .... Security Capital Pacific Trust [*NYSE symbol*] (SAG)
PTR .... Security Cap Pacific Tr [*NYSE symbol*] (TTSB)
PTRA .... Percutaneous Transluminal Renal Angioplasty [*Medicine*] (DMAA)
PTRA .... Port Terminal Railroad Association
PTRA .... Power Transmission Representatives Association (EA)
P/TRAC .... Positraction [*Automotive engineering*]
PTrB .... Betz Laboratories, Inc., Trevose, PA [*Library symbol Library of Congress*] (LCLS)
PTRC .... Personnel and Training Research Center [*Air Force*]
PTRD .... Part Redeemed [*Stock exchange term*] (SPSG)
PTRE .... PartnerRe Ltd. [*NASDAQ symbol*] (SAG)
PTRE .... Pressure Tube Reactor Experiment [*Nuclear energy*] (NUCP)
PTREF .... PartnerRe Ltd [*NASDAQ symbol*] (TTSB)
PTRF .... Peacetime Rate Factor [*Military*] (AABC)
PTRF .... Peacetime Replacement Factor [*Military*]
PTRI .... Pharmaceutical and Toxicological Research Institute [*Ohio State University*] [*Research center*] (RCD)
PTRIA .... Polystyrene-Tube Radioimmunoassay [*Medicine*] (DMAA)
PtrixMd .... Pediatrix Medical Group, Inc. [*Associated Press*] (SAG)
PTRJ .... Powered Thermocouple Reference Junction
PTRM .... Partial Thermoremanent Magnetization [*Geophysics*]
PTRN .... Photran Corp. [*NASDAQ symbol*] (TTSB)
PTRNMKR .... Patternmaker (WGA)
PTRO .... Koror [*Caroline Islands*] [*ICAO location identifier*] (ICLI)
PTRO .... Personnel Transaction Register by Originator [*Military*] (AABC)
PTRO .... Petrominerals Corp. [*NASDAQ symbol*] (NQ)
PTRO .... Preoverhaul Test Requirement Outline
PTRP .... Paper Tape Reader Punch [*Computer science*] (IAA)
PTRP .... Post-Treatment Resource Program [*Medicine*]
PTRPrA .... Security Cap Pac Cv'A'Pfd [*NYSE symbol*] (TTSB)
PTRPrB .... Security Cap Pac Tr Sr'B'Pfd [*NYSE symbol*] (TTSB)
PTRR .... Port Townsend Railroad, Inc. [*Formerly, PTS*] [*AAR code*]
PTRS .... Philosophical Transactions. Royal Society of London [*A publication*]
PTRS .... Potters Financial [*NASDAQ symbol*] (TTSB)
PTRS .... Potters Financial Corp. [*NASDAQ symbol*] (SAG)
PTRS .... Potters Savings & Loan Co. [*NASDAQ symbol*] (SAG)
ptrt .... Portrait (VRA)
PTRU .... Petro Union, Inc. [*NASDAQ symbol*] (SAG)
PT Rulings .... Pay-Roll Tax Rulings [*Australia A publication*]
PTRUQ .... Petro Union [*NASDAQ symbol*] (TTSB)
PTRV .... Peak Transient Reverse Voltage [*Electronics*] (IAA)
PTRY .... Pottery [*Freight*]
ptry .... Pottery (VRA)
PTS .... Painful Tonic Seizure (AAMN)
PTS .... Pali Text Society (EA)
PTS .... Paper Tape Sender
PTS .... Paper Tape System [*Computer science*] (IAA)
PTS .... Paper Tape-to-Magnetic Tape Conversion System (DIT)
PTS .... Papiertechnische Stiftung [*Database producer*]
PTS .... Parachute Training School [*British military*] (DMA)
PTS .... Parameter Test Setup
PTS .... Para-Toluenesulfonic Acid
PTS .... Parts
PTS .... Patellar-Tendon Supracondylar [*Anatomy*]
PTS .... Payload Test Set [*NASA*] (NASA)
PTS .... Payload Transportation System [*NASA*] (MCD)
PTS .... People's Translation Service (EA)
PTS .... Perforated Tape Subsystem [*Computer science*] (IAA)
PTS .... Performance Tracking System

PTS............ Permanent Threshold Shift [*Hearing evaluation*]
PTS............ Personal Typography System (DGA)
PTS............ Petro-Sun International, Inc. [*Toronto Stock Exchange symbol*]
PTS............ Philatelic Traders' Society Ltd. [*British*] (BI)
PTS............ Phosphotransferase System [*Organic chemistry*]
PTS............ Photogrammetric Target System [*Air Force*]
PTS............ Photogrammetric Triangulation System [*Air Force*] (IAA)
PTS............ Photothermal Spectroscopy
PTS............ Phototransmission System [*Telecommunications*] (IAA)
PTS............ Phototypesetting (DGA)
PTS............ Pilot Training Squadron [*Air Force*]
PTS............ Pi Tau Sigma [*Society*]
PTS............ Pittsburg, KS [*Location identifier FAA*] (FAAL)
PTS............ Plane Transport System (DA)
PTS............ Planning Tracking System (MCD)
PTS............ Player Trade Society [*A union*] [*British*]
PTS............ Pneumatic Test Sequencer (AFM)
PTS............ Pneumatic Test Set (KSC)
PTS............ Pneumatic Tube System
PTS............ Pod Tail Section
PTS............ Pointing and Tracking Scope
PTS............ Points [*Postal Service standard*] (OPSA)
PTS............ Points
PTS............ Points of Call Airlines Ltd. [*Canada ICAO designator*] (FAAC)
PTS............ Polar Track Structure [*Aviation*] (FAAC)
PTS............ Port Townsend Railroad, Inc. [*Later, PTRR*] [*AAR code*]
PTS............ Post and Telecommunications Service (IAA)
PTS............ Post-Traumatic Stress [*Medicine*]
PTS............ Power Transfer Switch
PTS............ Power Transient Suppressor (IEEE)
PTS............ Practical Test Standards [*FAA*] (TAG)
PTS............ Precision Timing System
PTS............ Predicasts Terminal Systems [*Predicasts, Inc.*] [*Cleveland, OH Database*]
PTS............ Predicasts Time Series [*Series of databases*] [*Predicasts, Inc. Cleveland, OH*]
PTS............ Preflight Test Set (DNAB)
PTS............ Pressure Test Station (DNAB)
PTS............ Pressurized Thermal Shock [*Nuclear energy*]
PTS............ Price-Tag Shock [*See also PTA*]
PTS............ Primary Trait System (EDAC)
PTS............ Prime Time Sunday [*TV program*]
PTS............ Princeton Theological Seminary, Princeton, NJ [*OCLC symbol*] (OCLC)
PTS............ Printing Technical School (DGA)
PTS............ Prior to Surgery (DAVI)
PTS............ Private Telecommunications Systems [*Radio-Suisse Ltd.*] [*Switzerland Telecommunications*]
PTS............ Proactive TMDE Support (RDA)
PTS............ Proceed to Select [*Telecommunications*] (TEL)
PTS............ Proceed to Send [*Telecommunications*] (TEL)
PTS............ Production Test Specification
PTS............ Professional Travelogue Sponsors (EA)
PTS............ Programmable Terminal System [*Computer science*] (IAA)
PTS............ Programmer Test Station
PTS............ Program of Technology and Society [*Later, DTS*] (EA)
PTS............ Program Test System [*Computer science*] (IEEE)
PTS............ Program Triple Store
PTS............ Project Tracking System [*Environmental Protection Agency*] (ERG)
PTS............ Propellant Transfer System
PTS............ Protestant Truth Society [*British*] (DBA)
PTS............ Provisional Technical Secretariat [*United Nations*]
PTS............ Public Telephone Service [*or System*] [*Telecommunications*] (TEL)
PTS............ Pure Time Sharing [*Computer science*] (IEEE)
PTS............ Put to Sleep [*ASPCA terminology*]
PTSA.......... Kusaie [*Caroline Islands*] [*ICAO location identifier*] (ICLI)
PTSA.......... Para-Toluenesulfonic Acid [*Organic chemistry*]
PTSA.......... Parent-Teacher-Student Association [*Nickname: "Pizza"*]
PTSA.......... Piano Trade Suppliers' Association [*British*] (BI)
PTSA.......... Professional Trucking Services Association (EA)
PTSC.......... Paper Tape Selectric Composer (DGA)
PT-S/C........ Proof Test Spacecraft [*NASA*]
PTSD.......... Pesticides and Toxic Substances Division [*Environmental Protection Agency*] (GFGA)
PTSD.......... Post-Traumatic Stress Disorder [*Psychiatry*]
PTSE.......... Paper Tape Splicing Equipment
PTSH.......... Poststimulus Time Histogram [*Medicine*] (DMAA)
PTSI........... PAM Transportation Services, Inc. [*NASDAQ symbol*] (NQ)
PTSI........... P.A.M. Transportation Svcs [*NASDAQ symbol*] (TTSB)
PTSI........... Para-Toluene Sulfonylisocyanate [*Organic chemistry*]
PTSM.......... Plant, Technology, and Safety Management (HCT)
PTSO.......... Personnel Transaction Summary by Originator [*Military*] (AABC)
PTSP.......... Paper Tape Software Package (NITA)
PTSP.......... Peacetime Support Period [*DoD*]
PT/SP......... Pressure Tube to Spool Piece [*Nuclear energy*] (NRCH)
PTS PROMT... Predicasts Overview of Markets and Technology [*Predicasts, Inc.*] [*Cleveland, OH Bibliographic database*]
PTSR.......... Performance Technical Survey Report
PTSR.......... Preliminary Technical Survey Report [*Military*] (AFIT)
PTSR.......... Pressure-Tube Superheat Reactor [*Nuclear energy*]
PTSS.......... Parallel Tuned Series Stabilized (IAA)
PTSS.......... Photon Target Scoring System (AAG)
PTSS.......... Posttraumatic Stress Syndrome [*Medicine*] (DMAA)
PTSS.......... Post-Traumatic Stress System [*Medicine*]
PTSS.......... Princeton Time Sharing Services, Inc.
ptst............ Paintstick (VRA)
PTST.......... Personnel Transaction Summary by Type Transaction [*Military*] (AABC)
PTST.......... Pretransfusion Serologic Testing
PTST.......... Prime Time School Television [*Defunct*] (EA)
PTT............ Partial Thromboplastin Time [*Hematology*]
PTT............ Particle Transport Time (MAE)
PTT............ Part Task Trainer (MCD)
PTT............ Party Test [*Telecommunications*] (TEL)
PTT............ Peak Twitch Tension [*Physiology*]
PTT............ Perth Theatre Trust [*Australia*]
PTT............ Petrotex Resources [*Vancouver Stock Exchange symbol*]
PTT............ Physical Therapist Technician
PTT............ Platform Transmitter Terminal [*Satellite-based tracking system*]
PTT............ Postal, Telegraph, and Telephone Administration (NATG)
PTT............ Postes, Telegraphes, et Telediffusion [*Post, Telegraph, and Telephone*] [*General Post Office Facetious translation: Prostitution Telematique et Telephonique*] [*France*]
PTT............ Post, Telegraph and Telephone Authority (NITA)
PTT............ Post, Telephone, and Telegraph [*Telecommunications*] (IAA)
PTT............ Post Telephone or Telex (NITA)
PTT............ Post, Telephon und Telegraphenbetriebe [*Switzerland Telecommunications*]
PTT............ Post Ten Tumblers [*Pseudonym used by William Maginn*]
PTT............ Post und Telegraphenverwaltung [*Postal and Telegraph Administration*] [*Austria Telecommunications*]
PTT............ Pratt, KS [*Location identifier FAA*] (FAAL)
PTT............ Press-to-Talk (IDOE)
PTT............ Press to Transmit
PTT............ Private Tombs at Thebes [*Oxford*] [*A publication*] (BJA)
PTT............ Processing Telecom Technologies (PCM)
PTT............ Production Type Test
PTT............ Program Technical Training (AFM)
PTT............ Program Test Tape [*Computer science*] (IEEE)
PTT............ Protein Truncation Test [*Analytical biochemistry*]
PTT............ Prothrombin Time [*Hematology*] (AAMN)
PTT............ Public Telecommunications Trust [*Proposed replacement for Corporation for Public Broadcasting*]
PTT............ Pulmonary Transit Time [*Physiology*]
PTT............ Pulse Transmission Time [*Medicine*] (DMAA)
PTT............ Push to Talk
PTT/8.......... Paper Tape Code on Eight Levels (NITA)
PTTC.......... Pacific Transportation Terminal Command [*Army*]
PTTC.......... Paper Tape and Transmission Code
PTTC.......... Perforated Tape and Transmission Code [*Telecommunications*] (IAA)
PTT-CT........ Activated Partial Thromboplastin Time, Control [*Hematology*] (DAVI)
PTTDAR....... Personnel Training and Training Devices Analysis Report (MCD)
PTTH.......... Prothoracicotropic Hormone
PTTI........... Postal, Telegraph, and Telephone International [*See also IPTT*] [*Geneva, Switzerland*] (EAIO)
PTTI........... Precise Time and Time Interval (AFM)
PTTK.......... Kosrae Island [*Caroline Islands*] [*ICAO location identifier*] (ICLI)
PTTK.......... Partial Thromboplastin Time with Kaolin [*Hematology*]
PTTL.......... Photo-Transferred Thermoluminescence (PDAA)
PTTL.......... Press-to-Test Light
PTTMC........ PACOM [*Pacific Command*] Tactical Target Materials Catalog (CINC)
PTTRN........ Pattern
PTTS.......... Pressure Temperature Test Set (DWSG)
PTTS.......... Private Telegraph and Telephone Service [*Telecommunications*] (IAA)
PTTY.......... Petty
PTU............ Package Transfer Unit
PTU............ Pallet Transporter Unit [*Military*] (CAAL)
PTU............ Parallel Transmission Unit (AAG)
PTU............ Part-Throttle Unlock [*Automotive engineering*]
PTU............ Pathology Transcription Unit
PTU............ Phenylthiourea [*Organic chemistry*]
PTU............ Pilot Test Unit [*Air Force*]
PTU............ Planning Tracking Unit (MCD)
PTU............ Platinum [*Alaska*] [*Airport symbol*] (OAG)
PTU............ Platinum, AK [*Location identifier FAA*] (FAAL)
PTU............ Plumbing Trades Union [*British*]
PTU............ Plumbing Trade Union (NADA)
PTU............ Portable Test Unit
PTU............ Power Transfer Unit
PTU............ Program Track Unit [*Telecommunications*] (LAIN)
PTU............ Propylthiouracil [*Also, PROP, PT*] [*Thyroid inhibitor*]
PTUC.......... Pacific Trade Union Community [*Australia*] (EAIO)
PTUV.......... Public Tenants' Union of Victoria [*Australia*]
PTV............ Parachute Test Vehicle
PTV............ Paratransit Vehicle
PTV............ Passenger Transfer Vehicle [*Airport transportation*]
PTV............ Passenger Transport Vehicle
PTV............ Pathfinder Test Vehicle [*NASA*] (MCD)
PTV............ Pay Television
PTV............ Peach Tree Valley [*California*] [*Seismograph station code, US Geological Survey*] (SEIS)
PTV............ Peak-to-Valley
PTV............ Penetration Test Vehicle [*Aerospace*]
PTV............ Pietas Tutissima Virtus [*Piety Is the Safest Virtue*] [*Motto of Ernst, Margrave of Brandenburg (1583-1613)*] [*Latin*]
PTV............ Pitch Thrust Vector (KSC)
PTV............ Poly(thienylenevinylene) [*Organic chemistry*]
PTV............ Porous Tungsten Vaporizer
PTV............ Porterville, CA [*Location identifier FAA*] (FAAL)

PTV .... Predetermined Time Value (IEEE)
PTV .... Programmable Temperature Vaporizer
PTV .... Programmed-Temperature Vaporizing [*Analytical chemistry*]
PTV .... Propulsion Technology Validation (MCD)
PTV .... Propulsion Test Vehicle
PTV .... Prototype Test Vehicle (MCD)
PTV .... Public Television
PTV .... Punched Tape Verifier [*Computer science*]
PTV .... Punch through Varactor [*Computer science*] (IAA)
PTV .... Puntavia Air Services [*Djibouti*] [*FAA designator*] (FAAC)
PTVA .... Propulsion Test Vehicle Assembly [*NASA*]
PTVC .... Pitch Thrust Vector Control (KSC)
PTVD .... Portable Toxic Vapor Detector
PTVE .... Propulsion Test Vehicle Engineering [*NASA*] (MCD)
PTVST .... Port Visit [*Navy*] (NVT)
PTVV .... Peak-to-Valley Variation (MCD)
PTW .... Page Table Word [*Computer science*] (IAA)
PTW .... Personal Typesetting Workstation (DGA)
PTW .... Physikalisch-Technische-Werkstatten [*Roentgenology*]
PTW .... Pilot Training Wing [*Air Force*]
PTW .... Playing to Win (EA)
PTW .... Point Target Weapon
PTW .... Pottstown, PA [*Location identifier FAA*] (FAAL)
PTW .... Pressure-Treated Wood
PTW .... Pressure-Type Window
PTWAM .... Page Table Word Associative Memory [*Computer science*] (IAA)
PTWC .... Pacific Tsunami Warning Center [*National Weather Service*] (MSC)
PTWC .... Project on Technology, Work, and Character (EA)
PT-WEX .... Part-Time Work Experience Program [*Texas*] (EDAC)
PTWF .... Pakistan Transport Workers' Federation
PTWG .... Provisioning Technical Working Group
PTWI .... Provisional Tolerable Weekly Intake [*Toxicology*]
PTWM .... Power Transformation Weighting Method [*Mathematics*]
PTWMASA .... Private Treaty Wool Merchants' Association of South Australia
PTWMAV .... Private Treaty Wool Merchants' Association of Victoria [*Australia*]
PTWMAWA .... Private Treaty Wool Merchants' Association of Western Australia
P-TWP .... Post-Township
PTWT .... Photo-Type Traveling Wave Tube (NG)
PTX .... Aereo Postal de Mexico SA de CV [*ICAO designator*] (FAAC)
PTX .... Pacific Trans-Ocean Resources Ltd. [*Toronto Stock Exchange symbol*]
PTX .... Palytoxin [*Organic chemistry*]
PTx .... Parathyroidectomy [*Medicine*]
PTX .... Pertussis Toxin [*Pharmacology*]
PTX .... Picrotoxin [*Biochemistry*]
PTX .... Pillowtex Corp. [*NYSE symbol*] (SPSG)
PTX .... Pillowtex Corp. [*NYSE symbol*] (TTSB)
PTX .... Pneumothorax [*Medicine*] (AAMN)
PTX .... Polythermalex (IAA)
PTX .... Polythiazide [*Organic chemistry*]
PTX .... Pressure-Temperature Composition
PTXA .... Parathyroidectomy and Autotransplantation [*Medicine*] (BABM)
PTXA .... Parathyroidectomy and Autotransplantation [*Endocrinology*] (DAVI)
PTXB .... Pumiliotoxin B [*Organic chemistry*]
PTY .... Panama City [*Panama*] [*Airport symbol*] (OAG)
PTY .... Parity (IAA)
PTY .... Party (AAG)
PTY .... Party
Pty .... Proprietary (DD)
PTY .... Proprietary
Pty .... Proprietary (NFD)
PTYA .... Yap [*Caroline Islands*] [*ICAO location identifier*] (ICLI)
PTZ .... Pentylenetetrazole [*CNS stimulant*]
PTZ .... Pulitzer Publishing [*NYSE symbol*] (TTSB)
PTZ .... Pulitzer Publishing Co. [*NYSE symbol*] (SPSG)
PU .... Pack Unit [*Single title, multiple orders*] [*Publishing*] [*British*]
PU .... Paid Up [*Insurance*] (EY)
pu .... Paid Up [*Insurance*] (ODBW)
PU .... Parents United (EA)
PU .... Participating Unit (NVT)
PU .... Parts Used [*Medicine*]
PU .... Passed Urine [*Medicine*]
PU .... Paste Up (ADA)
PU .... Peptic Ulcer [*Medicine*]
PU .... Perbonate Unit [*Analytical biochemistry*]
PU .... Percent Utilization [*Anesthesiology*]
PU .... Peripheral Unit [*Computers*] (MSA)
PU .... Personnel, Utility [*British military*] (DMA)
PU .... Persons Using [*Television*] (WDMC)
PU .... Peru [*IYRU nationality code*] (IYR)
PU .... Per Unit (EECA)
PU .... Per Urethra [*Medicine*]
PU .... Physical Unit [*Computer science*] (IBMDP)
PU .... Pick Up [*Business term*]
PU .... Plant Unit
PU .... Players' Union [*Football*] [*British*]
PU .... Pluggable Unit (SAA)
PU .... Pluna [*Airline flight code*] (ODBW)
Pu .... Plutonium [*Chemical element*]
PU .... Polyurethane [*Also, PUR*] [*Organic chemistry*]
PU .... Power Equipment [*JETDS nomenclature*] [*Military*] (CET)
PU .... Power Unit
PU .... Pregnancy Urine [*Medicine*]
PU .... Prilled Urea [*A fertilizer*]
PU .... Princeton University
PU .... Prisoner's Union [*Later, PRU*] (EA)
PU .... Processing Unit [*Computer science*]
PU .... Processor Utility [*Telecommunications*] (TEL)
PU .... Production Unit (CAAL)
PU .... Propellant Unit (NASA)
PU .... Propellant Utilization [*Aerospace*]
PU .... Propulsion Unit (KSC)
PU .... Propyleneurea [*Organic chemistry*]
PU .... Prostatic Urethra [*Anatomy*] [*Urology*] (DAVI)
PU .... Proutist Universal (EA)
PU .... Publications (MCD)
PU .... Publisher [*Online database field identifier*]
PU .... Puetzer [*Germany ICAO aircraft manufacturer identifier*] (ICAO)
PU .... Pump Unit (AAG)
Pu .... Punic (BJA)
Pu .... Punjab Regiment [*India*] [*Army*]
PU .... Purdue University
Pu .... Purine [*Biochemistry*]
PU .... Purple (ROG)
PU .... University of Pennsylvania, Philadelphia, PA [*Library symbol Library of Congress*] (LCLS)
PUA .... Partido de Unificacion Anticomunista [*Anti-Communist Unification Party*] [*Guatemala*] [*Political party*] (PPW)
PUA .... Patient Unit Assistant [*Medicine*] (DMAA)
PUA .... Plant-Unique Analysis [*Nuclear energy*] (NRCH)
PUA .... Polish Union of America (EA)
PUA .... Pride Users' Association [*Defunct*] (EA)
PUA .... Primeras Lineas Uruguayas de Navegacion Aerea [*Uruguay*] [*ICAO designator*] (FAAC)
PU-A .... University of Pennsylvania, Morris Arboretum, Philadelphia, PA [*Library symbol Library of Congress*] (LCLS)
PUAA .... Public Utilities Advertising Association [*Later, PUCA*] (EA)
PUAC .... Propellant Utilization Acoustical Checkout (AAG)
PU-AC .... University of Pennsylvania, Annenberg School of Communications, Philadelphia, PA [*Library symbol Library of Congress*] (LCLS)
PUAD .... Pueblo Army Depot [*Colorado*] (AABC)
PUADA .... Pueblo Army Depot Activity (AABC)
PUAID .... Parti d'Unite Arabe Islamique-Democratique [*Algeria*] [*Political party*] (EY)
PU & D .... Pick Up and Delivery [*Business term*]
PUAR .... Pulse Acquisition RADAR [*Military*] (MSA)
PU-Ar .... University of Pennsylvania Archives, Philadelphia, PA [*Library symbol*] [*Library of Congress*] (LCLS)
PUAS .... Postal Union of the Americas and Spain [*See also UPAE*] [*Montevideo, Uruguay*] (EAIO)
PUASP .... Postal Union of the Americas, Spain, and Portugal [*Uruguay*] (EAIO)
PUB .... Partido Union Boliviana [*Bolivian Unity Party*] [*Political party*] (PPW)
PUB .... Percutaneous Umbilical Blood [*Pediatrics*] (CPH)
PUB .... Phycourobilin [*Biochemistry*]
PUB .... Physical Unit Block [*Computer science*]
PUB .... Puale Bay [*Alaska*] [*Seismograph station code, US Geological Survey*] (SEIS)
PUB .... Public
pub .... Public (WDMC)
PUB .... Public
Pub .... Public (DD)
pub .... Publication (WDMC)
PUB .... Publication (AFM)
PUB .... Public House [*A drinking establishment*] [*British*]
pub .... Public House (ODBW)
PUB .... Publicity
PUB .... Public Utilities Board (NADA)
PUB .... Published (AABC)
pub .... Published (WDMC)
pub .... Publisher (WDMC)
PUB .... Publisher
PUB .... Pueblo [*Colorado*] [*Airport symbol*] (OAG)
PUB .... Pueblo, CO [*Location identifier FAA*] (FAAL)
PUBAFF .... Public Affairs (DNAB)
PUBAFFRRU .... Public Affairs Ready Reserve Unit (DNAB)
Pub Bargaining Cas (CCH) ... Public Bargaining Cases (Commerce Clearing House) [*A publication*] (DLA)
PUB BDG .... Publisher's Binding (DGA)
PUBC .... Presbyterians United for Biblical Concerns [*Later, PBC*] (EA)
Pubcaster .... Public Broadcaster [*Radio or TV station affiliated with NPR or PBS*]
PubcoC .... Pubco Corp [*Associated Press*] (SAG)
PUBD .... Published (ROG)
PUB DOC .... Public Documents (ROG)
Pub Employee Bargaining Rep (CCH) ... Public Employee Bargaining Reports (Commerce Clearing House) [*A publication*] (DLA)
Pub Employee Rel Rep ... Public Employee Relations Reports [*A publication*] (DLA)
Pub Ent Advert & Allied Fields LQ ... Publishing, Entertainment, Advertising, and Allied Fields Law Quarterly [*A publication*] (DLA)
Pub Gen Laws ... Public General Laws [*A publication*] (DLA)
PUB HA .... Public Hall [*Freemasonry*] (ROG)
Pub Health ... United States Public Health Service, Court Decisions [*A publication*] (DLA)
Pub Hist .... [*The*] Public Historian [*A publication*]
PUBINFO .... Office of Public Information [*Formerly, OPR*] [*Navy*]
Pub Int .... Public Interest [*A publication*]
PUBL .... Public (WGA)
PUBL .... Publication [*or Published or Publisher*] (EY)
PUBL .... Publish (FAAC)
Publ Admin ... Public Administration [*A publication*]
Pub Land L Rev ... Public Land Law Review [*A publication*] (DLA)

Pub Lands Dec... Department of the Interior, Decisions Relating to Public Lands [*A publication*] (DLA)
Pub Law...... Public Law (AAGC)
PUBLCTN..... Publication
PUBLD......... Published (ROG)
Pub LF......... Public Law Forum [*A publication*] (DLA)
public.......... Publicist
Publick........ Publicker Industries, Inc. [*Associated Press*] (SAG)
PUBLINX...... Public Links [*Amateur golf*]
PUBLR......... Publisher
PUBLR......... Publisher
Publ Serv Rev... Public Service Review [*A publication*]
PUBLSHG.... Publishing (DCTA)
PUBN........... Publication (MSA)
PUBNET....... American Association of Publishers' electronic ordering system
PUBO........... Pubco Corp. [*NASDAQ symbol*] (NQ)
Pub Op Q..... Public Opinion Quarterly [*A publication*] (BRI)
Pub Papers... Public Papers of the President [*A publication*] (DLA)
Pub Rel....... Public Relations
Pub Rel Bull... Public Relations Bulletin [*American Bar Association A publication*] (DLA)
Pub Rel J..... Public Relations Journal [*A publication*] (BRI)
Pub Res....... Public Resolution (AAGC)
Pub Res C.... Public Resources Code [*California*] [*A publication*] (ILCA)
Pub Res No... Public Resolution Number [*Congress*] (ILCA)
PUB RM....... Publisher's Ream (DGA)
PUBS........... Elephant & Castle Group, Inc. [*NASDAQ symbol*] (SAG)
PUBS........... Percutaneous Umbilical Blood Sampling [*Medicine*]
PUBS........... Percutaneous Umbilical Cord Sampling [*Also, Cordocentesus*] [*Medical test*] (PAZ)
PUBS........... Pop-Up Bottom Seismograph [*Marine science*] (MSC)
PUBS........... Publications (CDAI)
PUBS........... Publication Series
PUBS........... Purple Urine Bag Syndrome [*Medicine*] (DMAA)
PUBSAT....... Publications Special Assistance Team [*Military*]
Pub Ser Comm... Public Service Commission [*Usually, of a specific state*] (DLA)
PUBSF......... Elephant & Castle Group [*NASDAQ symbol*] (TTSB)
PubSNC........ Public Service Co. North Carolina [*Associated Press*] (SAG)
Pub St......... Public Statutes [*A publication*] (DLA)
PubSt........... Public Storage, Inc. [*Associated Press*] (SAG)
PubStrg........ Public Storage, Inc. [*Associated Press*] (SAG)
Pub U Rep... Public Utilities Reports [*A publication*] (DLA)
Pub Util C.... Public Utilities Code [*A publication*] (DLA)
Pub Util L Anthol... Public Utilities Law Anthology [*A publication*] (DLA)
Pub Util Rep... Public Utilities Reports [*A publication*] (DLA)
PU-BZ.......... University of Pennsylvania, Biology Library, Philadelphia, PA [*Library symbol Library of Congress*] (LCLS)
PUC............ Pacific Unicorn [*Vancouver Stock Exchange symbol*]
PUC............ Pacific Union College [*Angwin, CA*]
PUC............ Papers under Consideration
PUC............ Parti de l'Unite Congolaise [*Congolese Unity Party*] [*Political party*]
PUC............ Pediatric Urine Collector [*Medicine*]
PUC............ Permanent Unit Code (NG)
PUC............ Pick-Up Car
PUC............ Planification d'Urgence Canada [*Emergency Planning Canada - EPC*]
PUC............ Player Unit Component (MCD)
PUC............ Pontificia Universidade Catolica [*Rio de Janeiro*]
PUC............ Popular Unity of Chile [*Political party*]
PUC............ Port Utilization Committee
PUC............ Post Urbem Conditam [*After the Building of the City of Rome*] [*Latin*]
PUC............ Presidential Unit Citation [*Military decoration*]
PUC............ Price [*Utah*] [*Airport symbol*] (OAG)
PUC............ Price, UT [*Location identifier FAA*] (FAAL)
PUC............ Processing Unit Cabinet [*Computer science*]
PUC............ Production Urgency Committee [*WPB*]
PUC............ Program Under Control (NITA)
PUC............ Program Unit Code [*Military*] (AFIT)
PUC............ Provided You Concur [*Army*]
PUC............ Public Utilities Commission
PUC............ Public Utility Co.
PUC............ Punctured Uniform Code [*Computer science*] (IAA)
PU-C.......... University of Pennsylvania, Chemistry Library, Philadelphia, PA [*Library symbol Library of Congress*] (LCLS)
PUCA.......... Partido Unionista Centro Americana [*Nicaragua*] [*Political party*] (EY)
PUCA.......... Public Utilities Communicators Association [*Later, UCI*] [*New Castle, PA*] (EA)
PUCC.......... Port Utilities [*AAR code*]
PUCK.......... Florida Panthers Holdings, Inc. [*NASDAQ symbol*] (SAG)
PUCK.......... Propellant Utilization Checkout Kit (KSC)
PUCK.......... Pucklechurch [*England*]
PuCl............ Plutonium Chloride
PUCM.......... Progressive Union of Cabinet Makers [*British*]
PUCP.......... Process Unit Control Panel [*Computer science*] (IAA)
PUCS.......... Propellant Utilization Control System (KSC)
PUCU.......... Propellant Utilization Control Unit
PUD............ Parallel Undocumented Development (PDAA)
PUD............ Partido Union Democratica [*Guatemala*] [*Political party*]
PUD............ Peptic Ulcer Disease
PUD............ Physical Unit Directory [*Computer science*] (MHDI)
PUD............ Pick Up and Delivery [*Business term*]
PUD............ Planned Unit Development [*Housing*]
PUD............ Planned Urban Development
PUD............ Preretro Update Display
PUD............ Prisoner under Detention (ADA)
PUD............ Public Utility District [*Bonds*]
pud............. Pudding (BARN)
PUD............ Pudendal (DMAA)
PUD............ Puerto Deseado [*Argentina*] [*Airport symbol*] (OAG)
PUD............ Pulmonary Disease [*Medicine*]
PU-D.......... University of Pennsylvania, Evans Dental Library, Philadelphia, PA [*Library symbol Library of Congress*] (LCLS)
PUDA.......... Pueblo Depot Activity [*Colorado*] [*Army*]
PUDD.......... Programmable Universal Direct Drive
PUDG.......... Pudgie's Chicken [*NASDAQ symbol*] (TTSB)
PUDG.......... Pudgies Chicken, Inc. [*NASDAQ symbol*] (SAG)
Pudgie......... Pudgies Chicken, Inc. [*Associated Press*] (SAG)
Pudgies....... Pudgies Chicken, Inc. [*Associated Press*] (SAG)
PUDGW....... Pudgies Chicken Wrrt [*NASDAQ symbol*] (TTSB)
PUDL.......... Push Down List [*Computer science*] (IAA)
PUDN.......... Perpetuation of Unit Documentation Number (MCD)
PUDOC........ Centrum voor Landbouwpublikaties en Landbouwdocumentatie [*Center for Agricultural Publishing and Documentation*] [*Ministry of Agriculture and Fisheries*] [*Information service or system*] (IID)
PU-DPL....... Princeton University Device Physics Laboratory [*New Jersey*]
PUDT.......... Propellant Utilization Data Translator (AAG)
PUDVM....... Pulsed Ultrasound Doppler Velocity Meter
PUE............ Phosphorus Utilization Efficiency [*Ecology*]
PUE............ Physiotherapists' Union of Employees [*Australia*]
PUE............ Presidential Unit Emblem [*Military decoration*] (AABC)
PUE............ Pre-Stock Unit Equipment [*Military British*]
PUE............ Propellant Utilization Exerciser
PUE............ Puebla [*Mexico*] [*Seismograph station code, US Geological Survey Closed*] (SEIS)
PUE............ Puerto Obaldia [*Panama*] [*Airport symbol*] (OAG)
PUE............ Pyrexia of Unknown Etiology [*Medicine*]
PU-EI.......... University of Pennsylvania, Moore School of Electrical Engineering, Philadelphia, PA [*Library symbol Library of Congress*] (LCLS)
Puerto Rico... Puerto Rico Reports [*A publication*] (DLA)
Puerto Rico F... Puerto Rico Federal Reports [*A publication*] (DLA)
Puerto Rico Fed... Puerto Rico Federal Reports [*A publication*] (DLA)
Puerto Rico Rep... Puerto Rico Supreme Court Reports [*A publication*] (DLA)
PUF............ Partially Unfolded Form [*Biochemistry*]
PUF............ Partido Union Federal [*Federal Union Party*] [*Argentina Political party*]
PUF............ Pau [*France*] [*Airport symbol*] (OAG)
PUF............ People's United Front [*Bangladesh*] [*Political party*]
PUF............ People's United Front [*Papua New Guinea*] [*Political party*] (PPW)
PUF............ Percent Unaccounted For
PUF............ Polyurethane Film [*Plastics technology*]
PUF............ Polyurethane Foam
PUF............ Porous Polyurethane Foam [*Also, PPF*] [*Plastics technology*]
PUF............ Prime Underwriting Facility [*Banking*]
Puf............. Puffendorf's Law of Nature and Nations [*A publication*] (DLA)
PUF............ Pure Ultrafiltration (DMAA)
PU-F.......... University of Pennsylvania, H. H. Furness Memorial Library, Philadelphia, PA [*Library symbol Library of Congress*] (LCLS)
PUFA.......... Polyunsaturated Fatty Acid [*Nutrition*]
PU-FA......... University of Pennsylvania, School of Fine Arts, Philadelphia, PA [*Library symbol Library of Congress*] (LCLS)
PUFF.......... People United to Fight Frustrations (EA)
PUFF.......... Picofarad (MDG)
PUFF.......... Proposed Uses of Federal Funds [*Health Planning and Resource Development Act of 1974*]
PUFFS........ Passive Underwater Fire Control Feasibility Study
PUFFS........ Passive Underwater Fire Control Feasibility System
PUFFT........ Purdue University Fast FORTRAN [*Formula Translation*] Translator [*Computer science*]
PUFI........... Packed under Federal Inspection
PUFL.......... Pump Fed Liquid (KSC)
PUFO.......... Pack Up and Fade Out [*End of military exercise*] [*British*] (DSUE)
PUFS.......... Programmer's Utility Filing System (DIT)
PUFS.......... Proposed Underwater Fire Control Feasibility Study (SAA)
PUG............ Partially Underground [*Military*]
PUG............ PASCAL Users' Group [*Defunct*] (EA)
PUG............ Penta Users Group (EA)
PUG............ Port Augusta [*Australia Airport symbol*] (OAG)
PUG............ Prestel Users Group (NITA)
PUG............ PRIME Users Group (EA)
PUG............ Print under Glaze [*Ceramics*]
PUG............ Propellant Utilization and Gauging [*Apollo*] [*NASA*]
PUG............ Pugilist
PUG............ Pugillus [*A Handful*] [*Pharmacy*] (ROG)
Pug............. Pugsley's New Brunswick Reports [*14-16 New Brunswick*] [*A publication*] (DLA)
PUG............ Pulsed Universal Grid
PUG............ Pure Gold Resources, Inc. [*Toronto Stock Exchange symbol*]
PugetP........ Puget Sound Power & Light Co. [*Associated Press*] (SAG)
PUGLIG....... PUG Library Information Group (NITA)
PUGS.......... Propellant Utilization and Gauging System [*Apollo*] [*NASA*] (KSC)
Pugs............ Pugsley's New Brunswick Reports [*14-16 New Brunswick*] [*A publication*] (DLA)
Pugs & Bur... Pugsley and Burbridge's New Brunswick Reports [*17-20 New Brunswick*] [*A publication*] (DLA)
Pugs & Burg... Pugsley and Burbridge's New Brunswick Reports [*17-20 New Brunswick*] [*A publication*] (DLA)
Pugs & T..... Pugsley and Trueman's New Brunswick Reports [*A publication*] (DLA)
Pugs & Tru... Pugsley and Trueman's New Brunswick Reports [*1882-83*] [*A publication*] (DLA)
PugtP.......... Puget Sound Power & Light Co. [*Associated Press*] (SAG)

PUH .... Pauahi [*Hawaii*] [*Seismograph station code, US Geological Survey*] (SEIS)
PUH .... Pregnancy Urine Hormone [*Endocrinology*]
PUHCA .... Public Utility Holding Co. Act of 1935
PUI .... Pen User Interface [*Computer science*]
PUI .... Physical Unit of Information [*Computer science*] (IAA)
PUI .... Pilot-under-Instruction [*Navy*]
PUI .... Platelet Uptake Index [*Clinical chemistry*]
PUIC .... Project Unique Identification Code (AAGC)
PU-Ind .... University of Pennsylvania, Industrial Research Department, Philadelphia, PA [*Library symbol Library of Congress Obsolete*] (LCLS)
PUIWP .... People for a United India and World Peace (EA)
PUJ .... Punta Cana [*Dominican Republic*] [*Airport symbol*] (OAG)
PUJT .... Programmable Unijunction Transistor (IAA)
PUK .... Pack-Up Kit (MCD)
PUK .... Paducah [*Kentucky*] [*Airport symbol*] (AD)
PUK .... Parti d'Unite Katangaise [*Katanga Unity Party*] [*Political party*]
PUK .... Patriotic Union of Kurdistan [*Iraq*] [*Political party*] (PD)
PUK .... Pechiney-Ugine-Kuhlmann [*France*] [*Commercial firm*]
PUK .... Prourokinase [*Thrombolytic*] [*An enzyme*]
PUK .... Pukarua [*French Polynesia*] [*Airport symbol*] (OAG)
PUKO .... Pan-American Union of Karatedo Organizations (EA)
PUKS .... Pivotal Unknowables
PUL .... Percutaneous Ultrasonic Lithotripsy [*Medicine*]
PUL .... Preconfiguration Unit Load
PUL .... Press Union of Liberia
PUL .... Princeton University, Princeton, NJ [*Inactive*] [*OCLC symbol*] (OCLC)
PUL .... Program Update Library
PUL .... Propellant Utilization and Loading
PUL .... Publicker Indus [*NYSE symbol*] (TTSB)
PUL .... Publicker Industries, Inc. [*NYSE symbol*] (SPSG)
PUL .... Pulkovo [*Former USSR Seismograph station code, US Geological Survey*] (SEIS)
PUL .... Pulley (AAG)
PUL .... Pulmonary
PUL .... Pul. Przedsiebiorstwo Uslug Lotniczych [*Poland ICAO designator*] (FAAC)
PUL .... Pulse Resources [*Vancouver Stock Exchange symbol*]
PU-L .... University of Pennsylvania, Biddle Law Library, Philadelphia, PA [*Library symbol Library of Congress*] (LCLS)
PULA .... Public Laws
PulaskF .... Pulaski Furniture Corp. [*Associated Press*] (SAG)
PulaskiB .... Pulaski Bank, A Savings Bank [*Associated Press*] (SAG)
PULB .... Pulaski Bank, A Savings Bank [*NASDAQ symbol*] (SAG)
PULB .... Pulaski Bank A Svgs Bk MO [*NASDAQ symbol*] (TTSB)
PULHES .... Physical Capacity, Upper Extremities, Lower Extremities, Hearing, Eyes, and Psychiatric System (DNAB)
PULL .... Power for Underwater Logistics and Living
Pull Acc .... Pulling on Mercantile Accounts [*1846*] [*A publication*] (DLA)
Pull Accts ..... Pulling's Law of Mercantile Accounts [*A publication*] (DLA)
Pull Att .... Pulling on Attorneys and Solicitors [*3rd ed.*] [*1862*] [*A publication*] (DLA)
Pull Laws & Cust Lond... Pulling's Treatise on the Laws, Customs, and Regulations of the City and Port o f London [*A publication*] (DLA)
Pull Port of London... Pulling's Treatise on the Laws, Customs, and Regulations of the City and Port ofLondon [*A publication*] (DLA)
pulm .... Pulmentum [*Gruel Pulmonary*] [*Latin*] (MAE)
PULM .... Pulmonary
PULO .... Pattani United Liberation Organization [*Thailand*] [*Political party*] (PD)
PULP .... Premium Unleaded Petrol
pulpbd .... Pulpboard (VRA)
PULPP .... Peripheral Ultra-Low Power Processor (PDAA)
pulpwd .... Pulpwood (VRA)
PULS .... Poseidon Undersea Launching System (NOAA)
PULS .... Propellant Utilization Loading System (AAG)
PULS .... Pulse Bancorp [*NASDAQ symbol*] (TTSB)
PULS .... Pulse Bancorp, Inc. [*NASDAQ symbol*] (SAG)
PULSAR .... Pulsating Star
PULSAR .... Pulsed Sequencial Access Relay [*Electronics*] (ECII)
PULSAR .... Pulsed Uniform LASER-Stimulated Artificial Radiation [*Proposed acronymic designation for pulsars, in the event they are found to be artificially caused by intelligent life from outer space*]
PULSE .... Patented Uniform Lateral Stability Element
PULSE .... Public Urban Locator Service
PulseBcp ..... Pulse Bancorp, Inc. [*Associated Press*] (SAG)
PULSES .... Physical Condition, Upper Extremity Function, Lower Extremity Function, Sensory and Communication Abilities, Excretory Control, Social Support [*A neurological disability profile*]
Pulsifer (ME)... Pulsifer's Reports [*35-68 Maine*] [*A publication*] (DLA)
PULSTAR ..... Pulse Training Assembled Reactor [*Nuclear energy*] (NRCH)
Pult .... Pulton. De Pace Regis [*A publication*] (DLA)
Pulte .... Pulte Corp. [*Associated Press*] (SAG)
PultzPb .... Pulitzer Publishing Co. [*Associated Press*] (SAG)
PULV .... Pulverized
PULV .... Pulvis [*Powder*] [*Pharmacy*]
PULV CONSPER... Pulvis Conspersus [*Dusting Powder*] [*Pharmacy*]
pulv gros ..... Pulvis Grossus [*Coarse Powder*] [*Pharmacy*] [*Latin*] (MAE)
pulv subtil ... Pulvis Subtilis [*Smooth Powder*] [*Pharmacy*] [*Latin*] (MAE)
pulv tenu ..... Pulvis Tenuis [*Very fine powder*] [*Latin*] (DMAA)
PUM .... Partido Unificado Mariateguista [*Peru*] [*Political party*] (EY)
PUM .... Pennsylvania University Museum
PUM .... Per Unit Monthly (DNAB)
PUM .... Pomalaa [*Indonesia*] [*Airport symbol*] (OAG)
PUM .... President of the United Mineworkers
PUM .... Processor Utility Monitor [*Telecommunications*] (TEL)
PUMA .... Powered Ultralight Manufacturers Association [*Defunct*] (EA)
PUMA .... Processor-Upgradable Microcomputer Architecture [*DFI, Inc.*] (PCM)
PUMA .... Programmable Universal Manipulator (NITA)
PUMA .... Programmable Universal Manipulator for Assembly [*General Motors Corp. assembly robot*]
PUMA .... Programmable Universal Micro Accelerator [*Computer science*] (CDE)
PUMA .... Prostitutes' Union of Massachusetts
PUMA .... Puma Technology, Inc. [*NASDAQ symbol*] (SAG)
PumaT .... Puma Technology, Inc. [*Associated Press*] (SAG)
PU-Math ...... University of Pennsylvania, Mathematics-Physics Library, Philadelphia, PA [*Library symbol Library of Congress*] (LCLS)
PUMCODOXPURSACOMLOPAR... Pulse-Modulated Coherent Doppler-Effect X-Band Pulse-Repetition Synthetic-Array Pulse Compression Side Lobe Planar Array
PU-Med .... University of Pennsylvania, Medical School, Philadelphia, PA [*Library symbol Library of Congress*] (LCLS)
PU-Med-TS... University of Pennsylvania, Medical School, Hospital Nurses Library, Philadelphia, PA [*Library symbol Library of Congress*] (LCLS)
PUMF .... Peaceful Uses of Military Forces
PUMGC .... Pious Union of Our Mother of Good Counsel [*See also SMBC*] [*Genazzano, Italy*] (EAIO)
PUMP .... Parts Usage Maintenance Program [*Computer science*] (IAA)
PUMP .... Plant Uncoupling Mitochondrial Protein [*Biochemistry*]
PUMP .... Production Upgrade Management Program (DNAB)
PUMP .... Protesting Unfair Marketing Practices [*Student legal action organization*]
PUMS .... Permanently Unfit for Military Service [*British*]
PUMS .... Public Use Microdata Sample [*Bureau of the Census*] (GFGA)
PUMST .... Polish Underground Movement (1939-1945) Study Trust (EA)
PU-Mu .... University of Pennsylvania, University Museum, Philadelphia, PA [*Library symbol Library of Congress*] (LCLS)
PU-Music.... University of Pennsylvania, School of Music, Philadelphia, PA [*Library symbol Library of Congress*] (LCLS)
Pun .... All India Reporter, Punjab [*A publication*] (DLA)
Pun .... Indian Law Reports, Punjab Series [*A publication*] (DLA)
PUN .... Parti de l'Unite Nationale [*Party of National Unity*] [*Haiti*] [*Political party*] (PPW)
PUN .... Partido Union Nacional [*National Union Party*] [*Costa Rica*] [*Political party*]
PUN .... Plasma Urea Nitrogen (AAMN)
PUN .... Plutonyl Nitrate [*Inorganic chemistry*]
PUN .... Precision Underwater Navigation
PUN .... Punch
PUN .... Puncheon [*Unit of measurement*]
PUN .... Punia [*Zaire*] [*Airport symbol*] (AD)
Pun .... Punica [*of Silius Italicus*] [*Classical studies*] (OCD)
PUN .... Punishment (DSUE)
PUN .... Puno [*Peru*] [*Seismograph station code, US Geological Survey*] (SEIS)
PUN .... Punta [*Flamenco dance term*]
PU-N .... University of Pennsylvania, Center for the Study of the History of Nursing, Philadelphia, PA [*Library symbol*] [*Library of Congress*] (LCLS)
PUNA .... Parti de l'Unite Nationale [*National Unity Party*] [*Congo*]
PUNC .... Partido de Unidad Nacional Conservadora [*Nicaragua*] [*Political party*] (EY)
PUNC .... Practical, Unpretentious, Nomographic Computer
PUNC .... Probable Ultimate Net Cost [*Accounting*]
PUNC .... Program Unit Counter
PUNC .... Punctuation
PUNC .... Puncture (DAVI)
punceq .... Punctuated Equilibrium [*Bacteriology*]
PUNCT .... Punctuation (ROG)
PUNGA .... Parti de l'Unite Nationale Gabonaise [*Party for Gabonese National Unity*] [*Political party*]
Punj Rec ..... Punjab Record [*India*] [*A publication*] (DLA)
PUNL .... Percutaneous Ultrasonic Nephrolithotripsy [*Nephrology*] [*Radiology*] (DAVI)
PUNS .... Partido de Union Nacional del Sahara [*Western Sahara*] [*Political party*]
PUNS .... Permanently Unfit for Naval Service [*British*]
PUNSW .... Poets' Union of New South Wales [*Australia*]
PUO .... Placed under Observation [*Medicine*]
PUO .... Princeton University Observatory [*New Jersey*]
PUO .... Prudhoe Bay [*Arkansas*] [*Airport symbol*] (OAG)
PUO .... Prudhoe Bay, AK [*Location identifier FAA*] (FAAL)
Puo .... [*A*] Purine Nucleoside [*Also, R*]
PUO .... Pyrexia [*fever*] of Unknown Origin [*Commonly called Trench Fever*]
PuO2 .... Plutonium Dioxide
PUOS .... Public Understanding of Science Program (EDAC)
PUOW .... Proposed Units of Work
PUP .... Paid-Up Policy [*Insurance*] (DSUE)
PUP .... Parti de l'Unite du Peuple Gabonais [*Political party*] (EY)
PUP .... Parti de l'Unite Populaire [*Tunisia*] [*Political party*] (EY)
PUP .... Partido Union Patriotica [*Patriotic Union Party*] [*Dominican Republic*] [*Political party*] (PPW)
PUP .... Peak Underpressure [*Nuclear energy*] (NRCH)
PUP .... People's United Party [*Belize*] [*Political party*] (PPW)
PUP .... Performance Units Plan (MHDB)
PUP .... Performance Update Program [*Air Force*] (DOMA)
PUP .... Peripheral Unit Processor [*Computer science*]
PUP .... Peripheral Universal Processor (NITA)

PUP .... Pious Union of Prayer (EA)
PUP .... Plutonium Utilization Program [*Nuclear Regulatory Commission*] (NRCH)
PUP .... Po [*Upper Volta*] [*Airport symbol*] (AD)
PUP .... Popular Unity Party [*Bangladesh*] [*Political party*] (PPW)
PUP .... Power Upgrade Program
PUP .... Power Utility Pak [*Computer software*] [*Jwalk and Associates*] (PCM)
Pup .... Pre-Urban Professional [*Acronym coined by TeenAge magazine to describe it s typical reader*] [*Lifestyle classification*]
PUP .... Princeton University Press (DGA)
PUP .... Program Unit Punch (SAA)
PUP .... Progressive Unionist Party [*Northern Ireland*] [*Political party*] (PPW)
PUP .... Public Utilities Panel [*EECE*]
PUP .... Pull Up Point
PUP .... Pupakea [*Hawaii*] [*Seismograph station code, US Geological Survey Closed*] (SEIS)
PUP .... Pupil (DSUE)
Pup .... Puppis [*Constellation*]
PUPA .... Polish Union Printers Association [*Chicago*]
PU-Penn ...... University of Pennsylvania, Penniman Library of Education, Philadelphia, PA [*Library symbol Library of Congress Obsolete*] (LCLS)
PUPG .... Production Unit Price Goals (MCD)
PUPID .... Pulp and Paper Industry Division [*Instrument Society of America*]
PUPO .... Pull Up Push Over (NASA)
PUPP .... Pruritic Urticarial Papules and Plaques [*Dermatology*] (BARN)
Pupp .... Puppis [*Constellation*]
PUPPI .... Pop-Up Pore Pressure Instrument [*Oceanography*]
Puppie .... Pregnant Urban Professional [*Terminology used in "The Yuppie Handbook"*] [*Lifestyle classification*]
PUPPP .... Pruritic Urticarial Papules and Plaques of Pregnancy [*Medicine*]
PU-PSW .... University of Pennsylvania, Pennsylvania School of Social Work, Philadelphia, PA [*Library symbol Library of Congress*] (LCLS)
PUQ .... Punta Arenas [*Chile*] [*Airport symbol*] (OAG)
PUR .... Partido de Unificacion Revolucionaria [*Party of Revolutionary Unification*] [*Guatemala*] [*Political party*]
PUR .... Partido Union Revolucionaria [*Cuba*]
PUR .... Patch Unit Radio [*Bell System*]
PUR .... Persons Using Radio [*Radio ratings*] (WDMC)
PUR .... Polyurethane [*Also, PU*] [*Organic chemistry*]
PUR .... Procurement Request [*Army*] (IAA)
PUR .... Program of University Research
PUR .... Program Utility Routines [*Computer science*]
PUR .... Public Utilities Reports [*A publication Information service or system*] (IID)
PUR .... Purari [*Papua New Guinea*] [*Seismograph station code, US Geological Survey*] (SEIS)
PUR .... Purchase (AFM)
PUR .... Purchasing Receipt [*Business term*]
PUR .... Purdue University Reactor
PUR .... Purdue University Research (MCD)
PUR .... Purgative [*Medicine*] (ROG)
PUR .... Purichlor Technology Ltd. [*Vancouver Stock Exchange symbol*]
PUR .... Purifier (AAG)
Pur .... [*A*] Purine [*Biochemistry*]
PUR .... Purity [*of the Drug*] [*Pharmacy*] (ROG)
PUR .... Puromycin [*Trypanocide*] [*Antineoplastic drug*]
pur .... Purple [*Philately*]
PUR .... Purpure [*Purple*] [*Heraldry*]
PUR .... Pursuant (AABC)
PUR .... Pursuit (AABC)
pur .... Purus [*Pure*] [*Latin*]
PUR .... Spurwing Airlines (Pty) Ltd. [*South Africa ICAO designator*] (FAAC)
PUR 3d .... Public Utilities Reports, Third Series [*A publication*] (DLA)
PURA .... PACOM [*Pacific Command*] Utilization and Redistribution Agency
PURA .... Public Utilities Review Act [*1934*]
PURAC .... Personal Use Radio Advisory Committee [*FCC Defunct*] (TSSD)
PURB .... Purbeck [*District in England*]
PURC .... Pacific Utilization Research Center [*Marine science*] (MSC)
PURC .... Princeton University Research Center [*Marine science*] (MSC)
PURC .... Public Utility Research Center [*University of Florida*] [*Research center*] (RCD)
PURC .... Purchasing
PURCH .... Purchase
PURCH .... Purchase
purch .... Purchasing (DD)
PURCHG ...... Purchasing (ROG)
Purd Dig ...... Purdon's Digest of Laws [*Pennsylvania*] [*A publication*] (DLA)
Purd Dig Laws ... Purdon's Digest of Laws [*Pennsylvania*] [*A publication*] (DLA)
Purdue U ..... Purdue University (GAGS)
Purdue U (Calumet) ... Purdue University-Calumet (GAGS)
PURE .... Innovative Medical Services [*NASDAQ symbol*] (SAG)
PURE .... People United for Rural Education (EA)
PURE .... Present University Research Efforts [*Database*] [*Harperson Data Services*]
PURE .... Purepac, Inc [*NASDAQ symbol*] (SAG)
PureAtria ..... Pure Atria Corp. [*Associated Press*] (SAG)
Purepac .... Purepac, Inc. [*Associated Press*] (SAG)
PUREQ .... Purchase Requisition (NOAA)
PureSf .... Pure Software, Inc. [*Associated Press*] (SAG)
PureTc .... Pure Tech International, Inc. [*Associated Press*] (SAG)
PureWld ...... Pure World, Inc. [*Associated Press*] (SAG)
PUREX .... Plutonium Uranium Extraction [*Nuclear energy*]
purg .... Purgativus [*Cathartic, purgative*] [*Latin*] (MAE)
PURGE .... Pearson Universal Random Generator
PURIF .... Purification
PURL .... Persistent Universal Resource Locator [*Computer science*]
PURM .... Project for Utilization and Redistribution of Materiel [*Air Force*]
PUR (NS) ..... Public Utilities Reports, New Series [*A publication*] (DLA)
PURP .... Purpose (AFM)
PURP .... Purpure [*Purple*] [*Heraldry*] (ROG)
PURPA .... Public Utilities Regulatory Policy Act [*1978*]
Purple's St ... Purple's Statutes, Scates' Compilation [*A publication*] (DLA)
PurR .... Purine Repressor [*Biochemistry*]
PURRC .... Polyurethane Recycle and Recovery Council [*Plastics recycling research*]
PURS .... Partido de la Union Republicana Socialista [*Socialist Republican Union Party*] [*Bolivia*]
PURS .... Program Usage Replenishment System
PURS .... Pursuit
PURS .... Purus, Inc. [*NASDAQ symbol*] (SAG)
PURSC .... Partido Unido de la Revolucion Socialista Cubana [*Cuba*] [*Political party*] (EY)
PURSCE .... Pursuance (ROG)
PURST .... Pursuant
PURT .... PureTec Corp. [*NASDAQ symbol*] (TTSB)
PURT .... Pure Tech International, Inc. [*NASDAQ symbol*] (NQ)
Purus .... Purus, Inc. [*Associated Press*] (SAG)
PURV .... Powered Underwater Research Vehicle [*Navy*]
Purv Coll ..... Purvis' Collection of the Laws of Virginia [*A publication*] (DLA)
PURW .... Pure World, Inc. [*NASDAQ symbol*] (SAG)
PUS .... Parliamentary Under Secretary [*British*]
PUS .... Passive Ultrasonic Sensor (PDAA)
PUS .... Permanently Unfit for Service [*Military*] (ADA)
PUS .... Permanent Under Secretary [*British*]
PUS .... Personnel Utilization Sheet
PUS .... Pharmacopeia of the United States
PUS .... President of the United States
PUS .... Processor Utility Subsystem [*Telecommunications*] (TEL)
PUS .... Propellant Utilization System
PUS .... Pusan [*South Korea*] [*Seismograph station code, US Geological Survey Closed*] (SEIS)
PUS .... Pusan [*South Korea*] [*Airport symbol*] (OAG)
pus .... Pushto [*MARC language code Library of Congress*] (LCCP)
PU-S .... University of Pennsylvania, Edgar Fah Smith Memorial Library, Philadelphia, PA [*Library symbol Library of Congress*] (LCLS)
PUSAS .... Proposed United States of America Standard
PUSC .... Partido Unidad Social Cristiana [*Costa Rica*] [*Political party*] (EY)
PU-Sc .... University of Pennsylvania, Towne Scientific School, Philadelphia, PA [*Library symbol Library of Congress*] (LCLS)
PUSD .... Partido Unido Social Democratico [*United Social-Democratic Party*] [*Guinea-Bissau*] [*Political party*] (EY)
PUSD .... Polska Unia Socjaldemokratyczna [*Polish Social Democratic Union*] [*Political party*]
PUSE .... Propellant Utilization System Exerciser
PUSEC .... Polish-US Economic Council (EA)
PUSH .... People United to Save Humanity [*In organization name "Operation PUSH"*]
PUSH .... Play Units for Severely Handicapped (EDAC)
PUSH .... Public Use Sample Helper (PDAA)
PUSJD .... Pious Union of St. Joseph for the Dying [*Defunct*] (EA)
PUSJDS ...... Pious Union of St. Joseph for Dying Sinners [*Later, PUSJD*] (EA)
PUSMM .... Parti d'Union Socialiste des Musulmans Mauritaniens [*Party for Socialist Unity of Moslems of Mauritania*] [*Political party*]
PUSO .... Principal Unit Security Officer (AAG)
PU-Sp .... University of Pennsylvania, Van Pelt Library, Special Collections, Philadelphia, PA [*Library symbol*] [*Library of Congress*] (LCLS)
PU-SRS .... University of Pennsylvania, South Asia Regional Studies Library, Philadelphia, PA [*Library symbol Library of Congress*] (LCLS)
PUSS .... Pallet Utility Support Structure [*NASA*] (MCD)
PUSS .... Pilots Universal Sighting System
PUSSI .... Prostitutes United for Social and Sexual Integration [*British*] (DI)
PUST .... Panafrican Union of Science and Technology
PUT .... Aeroput [*Yugoslavia*] [*ICAO designator*] (FAAC)
PUT .... Persons Using Television [*Television ratings*]
PUT .... Persons Using Television (WDMC)
pU/T .... Pilot Under Training [*Aviation*] (DA)
PUT .... Programmable Unijunction Transistor
PUT .... Program Update Tape
PUT .... Property Unit Trust [*Finance British*]
PUT .... Provocative Use Test [*Medicine*] (DMAA)
PUT .... Punta De Talca [*Chile*] [*Seismograph station code, US Geological Survey*] (SEIS)
PUT .... Putao [*Burma*] [*Airport symbol*] (AD)
PUT .... Putnam, CT [*Location identifier FAA*] (FAAL)
PUT .... Putrescine [*Organic chemistry*]
Puter Ch ...... Puterbaugh's Illinois Chancery Pleading [*A publication*] (DLA)
Puter Pl .... Puterbaugh's Illinois Common Law Pleading [*A publication*] (DLA)
Putnam .... Putnam's Proceedings before the Justice of the Peace [*A publication*] (DLA)
PutnCA .... Putnam California Investment Grade [*Associated Press*] (SAG)
PutNY .... Putnam New York Investment Grade [*Associated Press*] (SAG)
PUTR .... Pacific Underwater Test Range (SAA)
PUTT .... Brassie Golf Corp. [*NASDAQ symbol*] (SAG)
PUTT .... Portable Underwater Tracking Transducer
PUTT .... Propellant Utilization Time Trace
PUTWS .... Put Word in String (SAA)
PUU .... Piute Reservoir [*Utah*] [*Seismograph station code, US Geological Survey*] (SEIS)
PUU .... Puerto Asis [*Colombia*] [*Airport symbol*] (OAG)

PU-UH .... University of Pennsylvania, University Hospital, Philadelphia, PA [*Library symbol Library of Congress*] (LCLS)
PU-UH-DeS ... University of Pennsylvania, University Hospital, De Schweinitz Collection of Ophthalmology, Philadelphia, PA [*Library symbol Library of Congress*] (LCLS)
PUUSNA ...... Polish Union of the United States of North America (EA)
PUV .... Posterior Urethral Valve [*Medicine*] (DMAA)
PUV .... Propellant Utilization Valve [*NASA*] (NASA)
PUV .... Pulaski [*Virginia*] [*Seismograph station code, US Geological Survey Closed*] (SEIS)
PUV .... Puumala Virus
PU-V .... University of Pennsylvania, School of Veterinary Medicine, Philadelphia, PA [*Library symbol Library of Congress*] (LCLS)
PUVA .... Photochemotherapy with Ultraviolet A [*Oncology*]
PUVA .... Psoralens and Ultraviolet A [*Therapy*] [*Medicine*]
PUVD .... Pulsed Ultrasonic Blood Velocity Detector (AAMN)
PUVEP .... Propellant Utilization Vehicle Electronic Package (MCD)
PUVLV .... Propellant Utilization Valve [*NASA*] (AAG)
PUW .... Pick-Up Walker (MEDA)
PUW .... Pullman [*Washington*] [*Airport symbol*] (OAG)
PUW .... Pullman, WA [*Location identifier FAA*] (FAAL)
PU-W .... University of Pennsylvania, Wharton School of Finance and Commerce, Philadelphia, PA [*Library symbol Library of Congress*] (LCLS)
PUWP .... Polish United Workers' Party [*See also PZPR*] [*Political party*] (PD)
PUY .... Pula [*Former Yugoslavia*] [*Airport symbol*] (OAG)
PUZ .... Puerto Cabezas [*Nicaragua*] [*Airport symbol*] (AD)
PV .... Association Quebecoise Plaidoyer-Victimes (AC)
PV .... Eastern Provincial Airways [*Labrador*] [*ICAO designator*] (OAG)
P-V .... Panton-Valentine [*Leukocidin*] [*Bacteriology*] (DAVI)
PV .... Papillomavirus
PV .... Paravane [*Anti-moored-mine device*] [*Obsolete*]
PV .... Paraventricular [*Neuroanatomy*] (MAE)
PV .... Parole Violator
PV .... Paromomycin-Vancomycin [*Blood agar*] [*Microbiology*]
PV .... Par Value [*Finance*]
pv .... Pathovar [*Microbiology*]
PV .... Path Verification
PV .... Patrol Vessel
PV .... Paving [*Technical drawings*]
P/V .... Peak-to-Valley
PV .... Pemphigus Vulgaris [*Dermatology*]
PV .... [*The*] People's Voice [*Pre-World War II publication of Adam Clayton Powell, Jr., and Charlie Buchanan*]
PV .... Peripheral Vascular [*Medicine*]
PV .... Peripheral Vein [*Anatomy*]
PV .... Peripheral Vessel [*Cardiology*] (MAE)
PV .... Peroxide Value [*Food analysis*]
PV .... Per Vaginam [*Medicine*]
PV .... Petite Vitesse [*Goods train*] [*French*]
PV .... Pfeiffer Vacuum Technology AG [*NYSE symbol*] (SAG)
PV .... Photographic Vision [*Filter*]
PV .... Photovoltaic
PV .... Physical Vulnerability [*Number*] (NATG)
pV .... Picovolt (IDOE)
PV .... Pigment Volume
PV .... Pilot Vessel
PV .... Pioneer Venus [*Spacecraft*]
PV .... Pipe Ventilated
PV .... Piston Valve [*Automotive engineering*]
PV .... Pisum Virus [*Plant pathology*]
PV .... Planetary Vehicle [*NASA*]
PV .... Planuebergang [*Grade Crossing*] [*German military - World War II*]
PV .... Plan View (MSA)
PV .... Plasma Volume [*Medicine*]
PV .... Plastic Viscosity
PV .... Playback Verifier (MCD)
PV .... Pole Vault
PV .... Polio Vaccine
PV .... Poliovirus
PV .... Polycythemia Vera [*Also, PCV*] [*Hematology*]
PV .... Polydor/Deutsche-Grammophon Variable Microgroove [*Record label*] [*Germany*]
PV .... Polyoma Virus
PV .... Polyvinyl (WGA)
PV .... Pore Volume [*Geology*]
PV .... Pornovision [*Television*]
PV .... Portal Vein [*Anatomy*]
PV .... Position Vacant (ADA)
PV .... Position Value
PV .... Positively Vet [*British*] (BARN)
PV .... Positive Volume (IEEE)
PV .... Postvaccination
PV .... Post Village
PV .... Post-Virgil
PV .... Postvoiding [*Medicine*] (MAE)
PV .... Potential Viewer [*Television ratings*] (NTCM)
PV .... Potential Vorticity [*Meteorology*] [*Fluid mechanics*]
PV .... Present Value [*Finance*]
PV .... Pressure [*or Pressurized*] Control Valve (IAA)
P/V .... Pressure/Vacuum
PV .... Pressure Velocity
PV .... Pressure Vessel (MSA)
P-V .... Pressure-Volume
PV .... Pressurization Valve
PV .... Prevailing Visibility
PV .... Prevalve (NASA)
PV .... Prevention of Violence (DICI)
P/V .... Preview
PV .... Preview Monitor [*A TV monitor*] [*Filmmaking*] (WDMC)
PV .... Priest Vicar
PV .... Primary Valve
PV .... Prime Vertical
PV .... Princess Victoria's Royal Irish Fusiliers [*Military British*] (ROG)
PV .... Private Varnish [*Privately owned railroad cars*]
PV .... Process Variable (IAA)
PV .... Production Validation [*Military*] (AABC)
PV .... Professional Virgin (DSUE)
PV .... Professional Volunteer
P/V .... Profit/Volume Ratio
PV .... Project Volunteer (EA)
PV .... Prometheus Vinctus [*of Aeschylus*] [*Classical studies*] (OCD)
PV .... Proteus Vulgaris [*Bacterium*]
PV .... Public Volunteer
PV .... Public Voucher
PV .... Pull and Void (MCD)
PV .... Pulmonary Valvotomy [*Cardiology*]
PV .... Pulmonary Vascularity [*Medicine*]
PV .... Pulmonary Vein [*Medicine*]
PV .... Pulmonic Valve [*Cardiology*] (DAVI)
PV .... Pulse Voltammetry [*Analytical chemistry*]
PV .... Pyrocatechol Violet [*Also, PCV*] [*An indicator Chemistry*]
Pv .... Ventral Pressure Neurons [*of a leech*]
PV .... Villanova University, Villanova, PA [*Library symbol Library of Congress*] (LCLS)
PV1 .... Private E-1 [*Army*]
PV-1(M) .... Poliovirus Type 1, Maloney
PV2 .... Private E-2 [*Army*]
PV-2(L) .... Poliovirus Type 2, Lansing
PV 4 .... Pickup Trucks, Vans, and Four-Wheel-Drive Vehicles [*Initialism used as title of a publication*]
PVA .... Aerotransportes Privados SA de CV [*Mexico ICAO designator*] (FAAC)
PVA .... Paralyzed Veterans of America (EA)
PVA .... Personal Values Abstract [*Scale*]
PVA .... Platinova Resources Ltd. [*Toronto Stock Exchange symbol*]
PVA .... Polyvinyl Acetate [*Organic chemistry*] (IAA)
PVA .... Poly(vinyl Alcohol) [*Also, PVAL*] [*Organic chemistry*]
PVA .... Population Viability Analysis [*Biology*]
PVA .... Portable Vehicle Analyzer [*Auto repair*] [*Electronics*]
PVA .... Positive Vorticity Advection [*NWS*] (FAAC)
PVA .... Potato Virus A [*Plant pathology*]
PVA .... Preburner Valve Actuator [*NASA*] (NASA)
PVA .... Present Value Analysis (MCD)
PVA .... Prison Visitors' Association (NADA)
PVA .... Privacy Act (MCD)
PVA .... Procedure Value Analysis (PDAA)
PVA .... Propellant Valve Actuator (MCD)
PVA .... Providencia [*Colombia*] [*Airport symbol*] (OAG)
PVA .... Provident Life Accident Insurance Co. of America [*NYSE symbol*] (SPSG)
PVAC .... Peak Volts Alternating Current (KSC)
PVAC .... Poly(vinyl Acetate) [*Organic chemistry*]
PVAC .... Present Value of Annual Charges
PVAE .... Poly(vinyl Acetate) [*Organic chemistry*]
PVAHI .... Augustinian Historical Institute, Villanova University, Villanova, PA [*Library symbol Library of Congress*] (LCLS)
PVAL .... Poly(vinyl Alcohol) [*Also, PVA*] [*Organic chemistry*]
PV & D .... Purge, Vent, and Drain (NASA)
PVAR .... Percentage Variance [*Statistics*]
PVAS .... Postvasectomy Specimen [*Urology*] (DAVI)
PVAS .... Primary Voice Alert System [*NORAD*] (MCD)
PVASI .... Pulsating/Steady Visual Approach Slope Indicator [*Aviation*] (FAAC)
PVAT .... Paravant Computer Systems, Inc. [*NASDAQ symbol*] (SAG)
PVat II .... Il Papiro Vaticano Greco II [*A publication*] (OCD)
PVB .... Platinol [*Cisplatin*], Vinblastine, Bleomycin [*Antineoplastic drug regimen*]
PVB .... Platteville, WI [*Location identifier FAA*] (FAAL)
PVB .... Poly(vinyl Butyral) [*Safety glass laminating material*] [*Organic chemistry*]
PVB .... Portametric Voltmeter Bridge
PVB .... Potentionmetric Voltmeter Bridge (IAA)
PVB .... Premature Ventricular Beat [*Cardiology*]
PVB .... Provident Life & Accident Insurance Co. of America [*NYSE symbol*] (SPSG)
PV-B .... Villanova University, Business and Finance Library, Villanova, PA [*Library symbol Library of Congress*] (LCLS)
PVBE .... Polyvinyl Butyl Ether [*Organic chemistry*]
PVBr .... Polyvinyl Bromide (PDAA)
PVBS .... Possible Vertebral-Basilar System [*Medicine*] (BABM)
PVBS .... Possible Vertebral-Basilar System [*Cardiology*] (DAVI)
PVC .... Pacvest Capital, Inc. [*Toronto Stock Exchange symbol*]
PVC .... Partido de Veteranos Civiles [*Civilian Veterans' Party*] [*Dominican Republic*] [*Political party*] (PPW)
PVC .... Peripheral Vasoconstriction [*Medicine*]
PVC .... Periscope Viewer/Controller (MCD)
PVC .... Permanent Virtual Circuit
PVC .... Photovoltaic Cell (IAA)
PVC .... Pigment Volume Concentration
PVC .... Point of Vertical Curve

PVC............ Polyvinyl Carbazol (IAA)
PVC............ Poly(vinyl Chloride) [*Organic chemistry*]
PVC............ Port Vila [*New Hebrides*] [*Seismograph station code, US Geological Survey*] (SEIS)
PVC............ Position and Velocity Computer
PVC............ Postvoiding Cystogram [*Medicine*] (MAE)
PVC............ Potential Volume Change
PVC............ Premature Ventricular Contraction [*Cardiology*]
PVC............ Pressure Vacuum Chamber
PVC............ Pressure Volume Compensator (KSC)
pvc............ Price Variation Clause (DS)
PVC............ Primary Visual Cortex [*Anatomy*]
PVC............ Private Virtual Circuit [*Telecommunications*]
PVC............ Prosthetic Valve (Disk) Closing [*Cardiology*]
PVC............ Provincetown [*Massachusetts*] [*Airport symbol*] (OAG)
PVC............ Provincetown, MA [*Location identifier FAA*] (FAAL)
PVC............ Pulmonary Venous Congestion [*Medicine*]
PVC............ Pulse Voltage Converter (OA)
PVC............ PVC Container Corp. [*Associated Press*] (SAG)
PVCA.......... Polyvinylchloride Acetate [*Organic chemistry*]
PVCBMA...... PVC [*Polyvinylchloride*] Belting Manufacturers Association [*Defunct*] (EA)
PVCC.......... PVC Container [*NASDAQ symbol*] (TTSB)
PVCC.......... PVC Container Corp. [*Eatontown, NJ*] [*NASDAQ symbol*] (NQ)
PVCCF........ Polyvinyl Chloride-Coated Fabric (PDAA)
PVCF.......... Phase Variable Canonical Form (PDAA)
PVCF.......... Present Value Cash Flow [*Finance*]
PVCI.......... Peripheral Vision Command Indicator
PVCN.......... Poly(vinyl Cinnamate) [*Organic chemistry*]
PVco₂.......... Venous Carbon Dioxide Pressure [*Medicine*] (MAE)
PVCS.......... Portable Voice Communications System
PVCV.......... Pelargonium Vein Clearing Virus [*Plant pathology*]
PVD............ Administradora de Fondos ADS [*NYSE symbol*] (TTSB)
PVD............ Administradora de Fondos de Pensiones Provida SA [*NYSE symbol*] (SAG)
PVD............ Pancreatic Ventral Duct [*Anatomy*]
PVD............ Paravisual Director [*British*]
PVD............ Parent Very Disturbed [*Pediatrics*] (DAVI)
PVD............ Percussion, Vibration, and Drainage [*Medicine*] (DAVI)
PVD............ Peripheral Vascular Disease [*Medicine*]
PVD............ Physical Vapor Deposition [*Coating technology*]
PVD............ Physical Vulnerability Division [*Air Force*]
PVD............ Planned Variations Demonstration [*HUD*]
PVD............ Plan Video Display (NITA)
PVD............ Plan [*or Planned*] View Display [*RADAR*] (AFM)
PVD............ Plan View Display (GAVI)
PVD............ Plasma Vapor Deposition (IAA)
PVD............ Portable Vapor Detector
PVD............ Posterior Vitreous Detachment [*Ophthalmology*]
PVD............ Product Verification Demonstration (MCD)
PVD............ Protective Vehicle Division [*US Secret Service*]
PVD............ Providence [*Rhode Island*] [*Airport symbol*] (OAG)
PVD............ Pulmonary Vascular Disease [*Medicine*]
PVD............ Purge, Vent, Drain System (MCD)
PVD............ Theodore Francis Green State Airport [*FAA*] (TAG)
PvdA.......... Partij van de Arbeid [*Labor Party*] [*Netherlands Political party*] (PPE)
PvdA/PTA..... Partij van de Arbeid van Belgiee/Parti du Travail de Belgique [*Belgian Labor Party*] [*Political party*] (PPW)
PVDC.......... Poly(vinylidene Chloride) [*Organic chemistry*]
PVDF.......... Poly(vinylidene Difluoride) [*Organic chemistry*]
PVDF.......... Poly(vinylidene Fluoride) [*Organic chemistry*]
PVDL.......... Precision Variable Delay Line
PVDS.......... Physical Vulnerability Data Sheets (MCD)
PvdV.......... Partij van de Vrijheid [*Party of Freedom*] [*Netherlands Political party*] (PPE)
PVE............ Perivenous Encephalomyelitis [*Neurology*] (DAVI)
PVE............ Pine Valley Explorers [*Vancouver Stock Exchange symbol*]
PVE............ Polyvinyl Ether [*Organic chemistry*]
PVE............ Porvenir [*Panama*] [*Airport symbol*] (OAG)
PVE............ Premature Ventricular Extrasystole [*Cardiology*] (AAMN)
PVE............ Process Validation Enterprise [*Army*] (RDA)
PVE............ Prolonged Vacuum Exposure
PVE............ Prosthetic Valve Echogram [*Cardiology*]
PVE............ Prosthetic Valve Endocarditis [*Medicine*]
PVE............ Provisioning Engineer
PVE............ Pulmonary Vascular Effect [*Physiology*]
PVED.......... Parity Violating Energy Difference [*Physical chemistry*]
PVED.......... Parity Violation Energy Difference [*Physics*]
PVEE.......... Polyvinyl Ethyl Ether [*Organic chemistry*]
PVEN.......... Primate Vaccine Evaluation Network
PVEP.......... Pattern Visual Evoked Potential [*neurology*] (DAVI)
PVEPP........ Preliminary Value Engineering Program Plan (MCD)
PVF............ Peak Visibility Factor
PVF............ Pension Valuation Factor
PVF............ Peripheral Visual Field [*Optics*]
PVF............ Placerville, CA [*Location identifier FAA*] (FAAL)
PVF............ Political Victory Fund [*National Rifle Association*]
PVF............ Poly(vinyl Fluoride) [*Organic chemistry*]
PVF............ Polyvinyl Formal [*Organic chemistry*]
PVF............ Portal Venous Flow [*Physiology*]
PVF............ Posterior Vitreous Face [*Ophthalmology*] (DAVI)
PVF............ Primary Ventricular Fibrillation (CPH)
PVF_2............ Poly(vinylidene Fluoride) [*Organic chemistry*]
PVFC.......... PVF Capital [*NASDAQ symbol*] (TTSB)
PVFC.......... PVF Capital Corp. [*NASDAQ symbol*] (SAG)
PVFCap........ PVF Capital Corp. [*Associated Press*] (SAG)
PVFD.......... Pipe Ventilated, Forced Draught
PVfHi.......... Valley Forge Historical Society, Valley Forge, PA [*Library symbol Library of Congress*] (LCLS)
PVFHP.......... Public Voice for Food and Health Policy (EA)
PVFM.......... Polyvinyl Formal [*Organic chemistry*]
PVfP.......... Philadelphia Quartz Co., Valley Forge, PA [*Library symbol Library of Congress*] (LCLS)
PVFS.......... Physicians for a Violence-Free Society
PVFS.......... Pinnacle Virtual File System [*Pinnacle Micro, Inc.*] [*Computer science*] (PCM)
PVFS.......... Postviral Fatigue Syndrome [*Medicine*] (DMAA)
PVG............ Periventricular Gray [*Neurobiology*]
PVG............ Portsmouth, VA [*Location identifier FAA*] (FAAL)
PVG............ Programmable Variations Generator [*Computer science*]
PVG............ Project on the Vietnam Generation [*Later, II*] (EA)
PVG............ Pulmonary Valve Gradient [*Medicine*] (DMAA)
PVGA.......... Processed Vegetable Growers Association [*British*] (DBA)
PVGC.......... Pioneer Venus Gas Chromatograph [*NASA*]
PVH............ Paraventricular Hypothalmic Nucleus [*Neuroanatomy*]
PVH............ Periventricular Hemorrhage [*Medicine*]
PVH............ Phillips-Van Heusen [*NYSE symbol*] (TTSB)
PVH............ Phillips-Van Heusen Corp. [*NYSE symbol*] (SPSG)
PVH............ Pope Valley Holding [*Vancouver Stock Exchange symbol*]
PVH............ Porto Velho [*Brazil*] [*Airport symbol*] (OAG)
PVH............ Pulmonary Venous Hypertension [*Medicine*]
PVHE.......... Polyvinyl Hexyl Ether [*Organic chemistry*]
PVHO.......... Pressure Vessel for Human Occupancy [*Deep-sea diving*]
PVHS.......... Photorefractive Volume Holographic Storage
PVI............ Pacific Vocational Institute Library [*UTLAS symbol*]
PVI............ Paranavai [*Brazil*] [*Airport symbol*] (AD)
PVI............ Peripheral Vascular Insufficiency [*Medicine*]
PVI............ Perpendicular Vegetation Index [*Botany*]
PVI............ Personal Values Inventory [*Psychology*]
PVI............ Picture Vocational Interest Questionnaire for Adults [*Vocational guidance test*]
PVI............ Pilot-Vehicle Interface [*Search technology*]
PVI............ Point of Vertical Intersection
PVI............ Poly(vinyl Isobutyl Ether) [*Organic chemistry*]
PVI............ Portal Vein Inflow [*Physiology*]
PVI............ Premature Vulcanization Inhibitor (MCD)
PVI............ Present Value Index (TDOB)
PVI............ Prevulcanization Inhibitor
PVI............ Primary Vocational Interest [*Personnel study*]
PVI............ Product Verification Inspection [*DoD*]
PVI............ Programmable Video Interface
PVID.......... Pipe Ventilated, Induced Draught
PVIF.......... Present Value Interest Factor [*Finance*]
PVIFA.......... Present Value Interest Factor of an Annuity [*Real estate*]
PVIR.......... Penn Virginia [*NASDAQ symbol*] (TTSB)
PVIR.......... Penn Virginia Corp. [*NASDAQ symbol*] (NQ)
PVIZT.......... Phenyl(vinyl)imidazolidinethione [*Organic chemistry*]
PVJ............ Pauls Valley, OK [*Location identifier FAA*] (FAAL)
PVJC.......... Palo Verde Junior College [*California*]
PVK............ Packaged Ventilation Kit [*Civil Defense*]
PVK............ Penicillin V Potassium [*Medicine*] (DMAA)
PVK............ Polyvinylcarbazol [*Organic chemistry*] (IEEE)
PVK............ Preveza/Lefkas [*Greece*] [*Airport symbol*] (OAG)
P-VL.......... Panton-Valentine Leukocidin
PVL............ Pavlikeny [*Bulgaria*] [*Seismograph station code, US Geological Survey*] (SEIS)
PVL............ Perivalvular Leakage [*Medicine*] (DMAA)
PVL............ Periventricular Leukomalacia [*Medicine*]
PVL............ Permanent Vision Loss [*Medicine*] (DMAA)
PVL............ Pressure to Vertical Locks
PVL............ Prevail (FAAC)
PV-L.......... Villanova University, Law School, Villanova, PA [*Library symbol Library of Congress*] (LCLS)
PVLR.......... Publisher/Vendor/Library Relations [*Committee of Association for Library Collections and Technical Services*]
PVLT.......... Prevalent (FAAC)
PVM............ Parallel Virtual Machine [*Software package*]
PVM............ Parasitophorous Vacuole Membrane [*Malaria*]
PVM............ Pneumonia Virus of Mice
PVM............ Poly(vinyl Methyl Ether) [*Organic chemistry*]
PVM............ Posterior Ventral Microtubule [*Anatomy*]
PVM............ Potato Virus M [*Plant pathology*]
PVM............ Potentiometric Voltmeter
PVM............ Power Vacuum Module [*Automotive engineering*]
PVM............ Pressure Vessel Material
PVM............ Progressive Minerals [*Vancouver Stock Exchange symbol*]
PVM............ Projection Video Monitor
PVM............ Protein, Vitamins, Minerals [*J. B. Williams Co. brand of liquid protein*]
PVM............ Proton Vector Magnetometer (NOAA)
PVMA.......... Pressure Vessel Manufacturers Association (EA)
PVMB.......... Potential Variation Mixed Basis [*Photovoltaic energy systems*]
PVME.......... Poly(vinyl Methyl Ether) [*Organic chemistry*]
PVMed.......... Preventative Medicine (DAVI)
PVMI.......... Parish Visitors of Mary Immaculate [*Roman Catholic women's religious order*]
PVMK.......... Polyvinyl Methyl Ketone [*Organic chemistry*] (DICI)
PVMT.......... Pavement [*Technical drawings*]
PVMTD.......... Preservation Method
PVMV.......... Pepper Veinal Mottle Virus [*Plant pathology*]
PVN............ Paraventricular Nucleus [*Brain anatomy*]

PVN .... Peters Valley [*New Jersey*] [*Seismograph station code, US Geological Survey Closed*] (SEIS)
PVN .... Poly(vinyl Nitrate) [*Organic chemistry*]
PVN .... Proven Resources Ltd. [*Vancouver Stock Exchange symbol*]
PVN .... Providian Corp. [*Formerly, Capital Holding*] [*NYSE symbol*] (SAG)
PVN .... Providian LLC [*NYSE symbol*] (SAG)
PVNGS .... Palo Verde Nuclear Generating Station (NRCH)
PVNO .... Polyvinylpyridine-N-Oxide [*Organic chemistry*]
PVNPrM .... Providian LLC'MIPS' [*NYSE symbol*] (TTSB)
PVNPS .... Post-Vietnam Psychiatric Syndrome
PVNS .... Pigmented Villonodular Synovitis [*Also, PVS*] [*Medicine*]
PVNT .... Prevent (AAG)
PVNTMED .... Preventive Medicine [*Also, PM*]
PVO .... Atlantic City, NJ [*Location identifier FAA*] (FAAL)
PVO .... Bearing Supplies Ltd. [*British ICAO designator*] (FAAC)
PVO .... Peripheral Vascular Occlusion [*Medicine*] (DAVI)
PVO .... Phosphorus Vanadium Oxide [*Inorganic chemistry*]
PVO .... Pioneer Venus Orbiter [*NASA*]
PVO .... Portoviejo [*Ecuador*] [*Airport symbol*] (OAG)
PVO .... Principal Veterinary Officer (ROG)
PVO .... Principal Visiting Officer [*Australia*]
PVO .... Private Voluntary Organization
PVO .... Project Vietnam Orphans [*British*] (DI)
PVO .... Prosthetic Valve (Disk) Opening [*Cardiology*]
PVO .... Protivo-Voxdushnaia Oborona [*Antiaircraft Defense*] [*Former USSR*]
PVO .... Pulmonary Venous Obstruction [*Medicine*] (DMAA)
PVO .... Pulmonary Venous Occlusion [*Cardiology*] (DAVI)
PvO_2 .... Partial Pressure of Venous Oxygen [*Hematology*] (CPH)
PVOA .... Passenger Vehicle Operation Association Ltd. [*British*] (BI)
PVOA .... Public Vehicle Operators' Association [*Later, CBRPT*] [*British*] (DI)
PVOD .... Peripheral Vascular Occlusive Disease [*Medicine*]
PVOD .... Pulmonary Venous Obstructive Disease [*Cardiology*] (DAVI)
PVOR .... Precision VHF [*Very High-Frequency*] Omnidirectional Range (IAA)
PVOR .... Precision VHF Omnirange
PVOUVS .... Pioneer Venus Orbiter Ultraviolet Spectrometer [*NASA*]
PV-P .... Past Vice-President
PVP .... Penicillin V Potassium [*Biochemistry*] (MAE)
PVP .... Peripheral Vein Plasma [*Cardiology*] (MAE)
PVP .... Peripheral Venous Pressure [*Cardiology*]
PVP .... Pipelined Vector Processor (NITA)
PVP .... Plant Variety Protection
PVP .... Plasma Vaporization Process
PVP .... Poly(vinylpyrrolidone) [*Organic chemistry*]
PVP .... Portal Venous Pressure [*Physiology*]
PVP .... Preferred Vision Provider
PVP .... President's Veterans Program [*Employment*]
PVP .... Professional Video Productions, Inc. [*Telecommunications service*] (TSSD)
PVP .... Pueblo Viejo [*Peru*] [*Seismograph station code, US Geological Survey Closed*] (SEIS)
PVPA .... Plant Variety Protection Act [*1970*]
PVPDC .... Poly(vinylpyridinium) Dichromate [*Organic chemistry*]
PVP-I .... Poly(vinylpyrrolidone) Iodine Complex
PVPMPC ...... Perpetual Vice-President-Member Pickwick Club [*From "The Pickwick Papers" by Charles Dickens*]
PVPO .... Plant Variety Protection Office [*Department of Agriculture*]
PVPS .... Plasma Varactor Phase Shifter
PVQ .... Deadhorse, AK [*Location identifier FAA*] (FAAL)
PVQ .... Personal Value Questionnaire [*Navy*]
PVR .... Palos Verdes [*California*] [*Seismograph station code, US Geological Survey Closed*] (SEIS)
PVR .... Peripheral Vascular Resistance [*Cardiology*]
PVR .... Personnel Vehicle Radar (LAIN)
PVR .... Phase Volume Ratio [*Physical chemistry*]
PVR .... Photo Voltaic Relay (NITA)
PVR .... Pontefract Volunteer Rifles [*British military*] (DMA)
PVR .... Portable Vehicular Ramp [*MTMC*] (TAG)
PVR .... Postvoiding Residual [*Medicine*]
PVR .... Precision Voltage Reference (MDG)
PVR .... Premature Voluntary Release [*British military*] (DMA)
PVR .... Procedure Validation Report (AAG)
PVR .... Process Variable Record
PVR .... Profit/Volume Ratio
PVR .... Proliferative Vitreoretinopathy [*Ophthalmology*]
PVR .... Proliferative Vitreoretinopathy [*Ophthalmology*] (DAVI)
PVR .... Puerto Vallarta [*Mexico*] [*Airport symbol*] (OAG)
PVR .... Pulmonary Vascular Resistance [*Physiology*]
PVR .... Pulse Volume Rate [*Physiology*]
PVR .... Pulse Volume Recording [*Medicine*]
PVR .... Pure and Vulcanized Rubber (IAA)
PVRC .... Pressure Vessel Research Committee [*National Institute of Standards and Technology*]
PVRD .... Purge, Vent, Repressurize, and Drain (NASA)
PVRI .... Pulmonary Vascular Resistance Index [*Medicine*] (DMAA)
PVRO .... Plant Variety Rights Office [*Ministry of Agriculture, Fisheries, and Food*] [*British*]
PVS .... Partner Violence Screen [*Health*]
PVS .... [*The*] Pecos Valley Southern Railway Co. [*AAR code*]
PVS .... Percussion, Vibration and Suction [*Medicine*] (DAVI)
PVS .... Performance Verification System
PVS .... Peripheral Vascular Surgery [*Cardiology*] (DAVI)
PVS .... Peritoneovenous Shunt [*Medicine*]
PVS .... Persistent Vegetative State [*Medicine*]
PVS .... Personal Videoconferencing Station [*Widcom, Inc.*] [*Los Gatos, CA*] [*Telecommunications service*] (TSSD)
PVS .... Personal Videoconferencing System (NITA)
PVS .... Photovoltaic System
PVS .... Pigmented Villonodular Synovitis [*Also, PVNS*] [*Medicine*]
PVS .... Plant Vent Stack [*Nuclear energy*] (NRCH)
PVS .... Plan-View Size (PDAA)
PVS .... Plexus Visibility Score [*Medicine*]
PVS .... Polyvinylsulfonate [*Organic chemistry*]
PVS .... Ported Vacuum Switch [*Automotive engineering*]
PVS .... Postal Vehicle Service
PVS .... Post-Vietnam Syndrome
PVS .... Potato Virus S [*Plant pathology*]
PVS .... Premature Ventricular Systole [*Cardiology*] (MAE)
PVS .... Present Value Service [*LIMRA*]
PVS .... Pressure Vacuum System
PVS .... Prime Vendor Support [*Army*]
PVS .... Principal Veterinary Surgeon [*British*]
PVS .... Priority Ventures [*Vancouver Stock Exchange symbol*]
PVS .... Private Viewdata System [*Computer science*]
PVS .... Product Verification Specification
PVS .... Professional Video Services Corp. [*Telecommunications service*] (TSSD)
PVS .... Program Validation Services [*Computer science*]
PVS .... Propellant Venting System
PVS .... Pulmonary Valve Stenosis [*Cardiology*]
PVSA .... Parkvale Financial [*NASDAQ symbol*] (TTSB)
PVSA .... Parkvale Financial Corp. [*NASDAQ symbol*] (NQ)
PVSC .... Professional Video Services Corp. [*Telecommunications service*] (TSSD)
PVSG .... Paravertebral Sympathetic Ganglion [*Neuroanatomy*]
PVSG .... Periscope Visual Scene Generation
PVSG .... Polycythemia Vera Study Group (MEDA)
PV SIg .... Polyvalent Surface Immunoglobulin [*Immunology*]
PV/ST .... Premate Verification/System Test [*NASA*] (KSC)
PVT .... Pacific Vending Technology Ltd. [*Vancouver Stock Exchange symbol*]
PVT .... Page View Terminal [*Typography*] [*Videotex terminal*]
PVT .... Page View Terminal [*A video terminal that displays a full page*] (WDMC)
PVT .... Paroxysmal Ventricular Tachycardia [*Medicine*]
PVT .... Par Voie Telegraphique [*By Telegraph*] [*French*]
PVT .... Performance Verification Test
PVT .... Personal Verifier Terminal (DA)
PVT .... Persons Viewing Television [*Television ratings*] (NTCM)
PV/T .... Photovoltaic/Thermal
PVT .... Physical Vapor Transport [*Materials processing*]
PVT .... Pivot (MSA)
PVT .... Point of Vertical Tangent
PVT .... Polyvalent Tolerance [*Immunology*]
PVT .... Poly(vinyltoluene) [*Organic chemistry*]
PVT .... Portal Vein Thrombosis [*Physiology*]
PVT .... Position Velocity-Time
PVT .... Potato Virus T [*Plant pathology*]
PVT .... Precision Verification Team
PVT .... Precision Verification Test (MCD)
PVT .... Preflight Verification Test (NASA)
PVT .... Pressure, Volume, Temperature
PVT .... Private [*Military*] (AFM)
Pvt .... Private (DD)
PVT .... Private
PVT .... Private Patient [*Medicine*] (DMAA)
PVT .... Probe Velocity Transducer (KSC)
PVT .... Product Verification Test (MCD)
PVT .... Prototype Validation Test (MCD)
PVT .... Provident Companies [*NYSE symbol*] (TTSB)
PVT .... Provident Companies, Inc. [*NYSE symbol*] (SAG)
PVT .... Provisioning Technician
PVT .... Pulse Video Thermography [*Nondestructive testing technique*]
PVT .... Pyrotechnic Verification Test [*NASA*] (NASA)
PVTAP .... Photovoltaic Transient Analysis Computer Program
PVT-C .... Production Validation Test - Contractor (MCD)
PVT-C .... Product Verification Test - Contractor (MCD)
PVT-C .... Prototype Validation Test - Contractor (MCD)
PVTE .... Private
PVT-G .... Production Validation Test - Government
PVT-G .... Prototype Validation Test - Government
PVTI .... Piping and Valve Test Insert [*Nuclear energy*] (NRCH)
PVTM .... Physical Vulnerability Technical Memorandum (MCD)
PVTOS .... Physical Vapor Transport of Organic Solutions [*Materials processing*]
PVTPr .... Provident Companies Dep Pfd [*NYSE symbol*] (TTSB)
PVTR .... Portable Video Tape Recorder
PVTS .... Pressure Vessel Thermal Shock (PDAA)
PVU .... Perimeter Ventures Ltd. [*Vancouver Stock Exchange symbol*]
PVU .... Precision Velocity Update (MCD)
PVU .... Provo [*Utah*] [*Airport symbol*] (OAG)
PVU .... Provo, UT [*Location identifier FAA*] (FAAL)
PVU .... Villanova University, Villanova, PA [*OCLC symbol*] (OCLC)
PVV .... Fondation Europeenne "Pro Venetia Viva" [*European Foundation "Pro Venetia Viva"*] (EAIO)
PVV .... Partij voor Vrijheid en Vooruitgang [*Freedom and Progress Party*] [*See also PLP*] [*Belgium*] [*Political party*] (PPW)
PVV .... Portal Venous Velocity [*Physiology*]
PVV .... Pressure, Vent, and Vacuum
PVW .... Plainview, TX [*Location identifier FAA*] (FAAL)
PVW .... Posterior Vaginal Wall [*Medicine*] (DMAA)
PVW .... Wilson College, Chambersburg, PA [*OCLC symbol*] (OCLC)

PVWA .... Planned Value of Work Accomplished
PVWA .... Plan Value Work Accounting (MCD)
PVWS .... Planned Value of Work Scheduled (MCD)
PVX .... Phosphorous-Doped Vapor-Deposited Oxide (IAA)
PVX .... Potato Virus X [*Plant pathology*]
PVY .... Pope Vanoy [*Alaska*] [*Airport symbol*] (OAG)
PVY .... Potato Virus Y
PVY .... Providence Energy [*AMEX symbol*] (TTSB)
PVY .... Providence Energy Corp. [*AMEX symbol*] (SPSG)
PVYV .... Pittosporum Vein Yellowing Virus [*Plant pathology*]
PVZ .... Painesville, OH [*Location identifier FAA*] (FAAL)
PW .... Citizens Library, Washington, PA [*Library symbol Library of Congress*] (LCLS)
PW .... Pacific Western Airlines Ltd. [*Canada ICAO designator*] (OAG)
PW .... Packed Weight
PW .... Palau [*ANSI two-letter standard code*] (CNC)
PW .... Paper Wrapper (ADA)
PW .... Paraguay Watch (EA)
PW .... Parallel With (IAA)
PW .... Passing Window (MSA)
PW .... Password [*Computer science*]
PW .... Peere-Williams' English Chancery Reports [*1695-1736*] [*A publication*] (DLA)
PW .... Pension for Wounds [*Navy British*] (ROG)
PW .... Pericardium Wall [*Medicine*]
PW .... Per Week
pw .... Per Week (ODBW)
PW .... Petroleum Week [*A publication*]
PW .... Philadelphia & Western Railroad [*AAR code Terminated*]
pW .... Picowatt
PW .... Pilot Wire (MSA)
PW .... Pine Bark Mixed with Weblite and Peat
PW .... Pitts & W Va RR SBI [*AMEX symbol*] (TTSB)
PW .... Pittsburgh & West Virginia Railroad [*AMEX symbol*] (SPSG)
PW .... Pivoted Window (AAG)
PW .... Plain Washer (MSA)
PW .... Plantar Wart [*Orthopedics*] (DAVI)
PW .... Platoon Weapons [*British military*] (DMA)
PW .... Poets and Writers (EA)
PW .... Policewoman (ODBW)
PW .... Ports and Waterways
PW .... Position Wanted [*Employment*]
PW .... Positive Women [*An association Australia*]
PW .... Postal Wire [*Telecommunications*] (IAA)
PW .... Posterior Wall [*Medicine*]
PW .... Postwar
PW .... Potable Water [*Nuclear energy*] (NRCH)
PW .... Power
PW .... Power Wagon [*Military vehicle*]
PW .... Power Windows [*Automobile ads*]
P-W .... Prader-Willi [*Syndrome*] [*Medicine*] (AAMN)
PW .... PRECIS Word (NITA)
PW .... Present Worth [*Economics*]
PW .... Pressurized Water
PW .... Prevailing Wage (MHDW)
PW .... Prime Western [*Zinc*]
PW .... Prince of Wales [*Military unit*] [*British*]
PW .... Printed Wiring (MSA)
PW .... Printing World [*A publication*] (DGA)
PW .... Prisoner of War [*Also, POW*]
PW .... Private Wire (NATG)
PW .... Progesterone Withdrawal [*Endocrinology*]
PW .... Program Word [*Computer science*] (IAA)
PW .... Projected Window (MSA)
PW .... Projection Welding
PW .... Providence & Worcester Co. [*AAR code*]
PW .... Psychological Warfare
PW .... Public Welfare
PW .... Public Works
PW .... Publishers Weekly [*A publication*] (WDMC)
PW .... Publishers Weekly [*A publication*] (BRI)
PW .... Pulpwash [*Byproduct of citrus processing*]
PW .... Pulse Width [*RADAR*]
PW .... Purlwise [*Knitting*]
PW .... Royal Warrant for Pay and Promotion [*British military*] (DMA)
Pw .... Transthoracic Pressure [*Medicine*] (DAVI)
pW0p .... Picowatts, Psophometrically Weighted at a Point of Zero Reference Level
PW2 .... Personal Workstation 2 [*Computer hardware*] [*Unisys Corp.*] (PCM)
PWA .... Oklahoma City, OK [*Location identifier FAA*] (FAAL)
PWA .... Pacific Western Airlines Ltd. [*Toronto Stock Exchange symbol Vancouver Stock Exchange symbol*]
PWA .... Palmer-Houston [*Alaska*] [*Seismograph station code, US Geological Survey*] (SEIS)
PWA .... Patient [*or Person*] with [*AIDS*] Acquired Immunodeficiency Syndrome [*Immunology*] (DAVI)
PWA .... People with AIDS Coalition (EA)
PWA .... Performance Warehouse Association (EA)
PWA .... Person with AIDS [*Acquired Immune Deficiency Syndrome*] [*Medicine*]
PWA .... Pharmaceutical Wholesalers Association [*Later, DWA*]
PWA .... Please Wait Awhile [*Humorous interpretation for Pacific Western Airlines Corp.*]
PWA .... Polish Women's Association [*Australia*]
PWA .... Portuguese West Africa [*Angola*]
PWA .... Power and Water Authority [*Northern Territory, Australia*]
PWA .... Pratt & Whitney Aircraft (MCD)
PWA .... Pray while Aloft [*Humorous interpretation for Pacific Western Airlines Corp.*]
PWA .... Printed Wire Assembly [*Computer science*]
PWA .... Prison Wardens Association (NADA)
PWA .... Private Eye Writers of America [*An association*]
PWA .... Private Write Area [*NASA*] (NASA)
PWA .... Probably Won't Arrive [*Humorous interpretation for Pacific Western Airlines Corp.*]
PWA .... Product Work Authorization (NASA)
PWA .... Professional Writers of America (NADA)
PWA .... Project Work Authorization
PWA .... Psychic Workers Association (NADA)
PWA .... Public Works Administration [*All functions transferred to office of Federal Works Agency, 1943*]
PWA .... Publishers' Weekly Announcements [*Title changed to Forthcoming Books*] [*A publication*]
PWA .... PWA Corp. [*Toronto Stock Exchange symbol Vancouver Stock Exchange symbol*]
PWa .... Warren Library Association and County Division, Warren, PA [*Library symbol Library of Congress*] (LCLS)
PWA .... Waynesburg College, Waynesburg, PA [*OCLC symbol*] (OCLC)
PWAA .... Paint and Wallpaper Association of America [*Later, NDPA*] (EA)
PWAA .... Polish Western Association of America (EA)
PWAA .... Polish Women's Alliance of America (EA)
PWAA .... Professional Women's Appraisal Association (EA)
PWAC .... Periodical Writers Association of Canada
PWAC .... Pratt & Whitney Aircraft (AAG)
PWAC .... Present Worth of Annual Charges [*Pronounced "p-wack"*] [*Bell System*]
PWacD .... David Library of the American Revolution, Washington Crossing, PA [*Library symbol Library of Congress*] (LCLS)
PWAF .... Polish Workers' Aid Fund [*Defunct*] (EA)
PWAFRR .... Present Worth of All Future Revenue Requirements [*Finance*]
PWAK .... Wake Island Air Force Base [*Wake Island*] [*ICAO location identifier*] (ICLI)
PWal .... Helen Kate Furness Free Library, Wallingford, PA [*Library symbol Library of Congress*] (LCLS)
PWalPH .... Pendle Hill Library, Wallingford, PA [*Library symbol Library of Congress*] (LCLS)
PW & B .... Philadelphia, Wilmington & Baltimore Railroad
PWAP .... Public Works of Art Projects [*New Deal*]
PWARC .... Person With AIDS-Related Complex (CPH)
PWarN .... United States Naval Air Development Center, Technical Information Library, Warminster, PA [*Library symbol*] [*Library of Congress*] (LCLS)
PWASA .... Poliomyelitis Welfare Association of South Australia
PWAV .... Powerwave Technologies, Inc. [*NASDAQ symbol*] (SAG)
PWayC .... Waynesburg College, Waynesburg, PA [*Library symbol Library of Congress*] (LCLS)
PWB .... Directorate of Post War Building [*British*] (DAS)
PWb .... Osterhout Free Library, Wilkes-Barre, PA [*Library symbol Library of Congress*] (LCLS)
PWB .... Partial Weight Bearing [*Medicine*]
PWB .... Pencil Writing on Back [*Deltiology*]
PWB .... Permanent Water Ballast (DS)
PWB .... Pilot Weather Briefing [*Aviation*] (FAAC)
PWB .... Printed Wiring Board (DOMA)
PWB .... Printed Wiring Board
PWB .... Private Wine Buyers' Society [*British*] (BI)
PWB .... Programmer's Workbench [*Microsoft, Inc.*] (PCM)
PWB .... Psychological Warfare Branch [*Allied Forces*] [*World War II*]
PWB .... Pulling Whaleboat
PWBA .... Pension and Welfare Benefits Administration [*Department of Labor*]
PWBA .... Plane-Wave Born Approximation
PWBA .... Printed Wiring Board Assembly (MCD)
PWBA .... Professional Women Bowlers Association [*Later, LPBT*] (EA)
PWBC .... PennFirst Bancorp [*NASDAQ symbol*] (SAG)
PWBC .... Peripheral White Blood Cells [*Medicine*]
PWbH .... Wyoming Historical and Geological Society, Wilkes-Barre, PA [*Library symbol Library of Congress*] (LCLS)
PWBI .... Posterior Wall of Bronchus Intermedius [*Anatomy*]
PWbK .... King's College, Wilkes-Barre, PA [*Library symbol Library of Congress*] (LCLS)
PWBK .... Pennwood Savings Bank [*NASDAQ symbol*] (SAG)
PWB/MM .... Programmer's Workbench Memorandum Macros [*Computer science*] (MHDI)
PWBP .... Pension and Welfare Benefit Programs [*Labor-Management Services Administration*]
PWBRT .... Prophylactic Whole Brain Radiation Therapy [*Medicine*] (DMAA)
PWBS .... Program Work Breakdown Structure (NASA)
PWbW .... Wilkes College, Wilkes-Barre, PA [*Library symbol Library of Congress*] (LCLS)
PWC .... Chester County District Library Center, Exton, PA [*OCLC symbol*] (OCLC)
PWC .... Pacific War Council [*World War II*]
PWC .... Parents Who Care [*An association*] (NADA)
PWC .... Paws with a Cause [*An association*] (EA)
PWC .... Peak Work Capacity
PWC .... Pentecostal World Conference [*Emmetten, Switzerland*] (EA)
PWC .... Personal Watercraft
PWC .... Physical Work Capacity
PWC .... Physicians Who Care (EA)
PWC .... Poland Watch Center [*Defunct*] (EA)

PWC............ Port Workers' Committee [*British*]
PWC............ Pratt & Whitney Canada, Inc. [*ICAO designator*] (FAAC)
PWC............ Primary Work Code (SSD)
PWC............ Printed Wiring Cards [*Telecommunications*]
PWC............ Prisoner of War Cage
PWC............ Prisoner of War Camp
PWC............ Prisoner of War Command
PWC............ Prisoner of War Compound
PWC............ Process Water Cooler (MSA)
PWC............ Professional Women in Construction (EA)
PWC............ Professional Women's Caucus (EA)
PWC............ Provincial Warning Center [*NATO*] (NATG)
PWC............ Public Works Canada [*See also TPC*]
PWC............ Public Works Center [*Navy*]
PWC............ Pulse-Width Coded
PWCA.......... Pure White Cell Aplasia [*Medicine*] (DMAA)
PWCACE....... Public Works Center Activity Civil Engineer [*Navy*] (DNAB)
PWcC........... Chester County District Library Center, West Chester, PA [*Library symbol Library of Congress*] (LCLS)
PWCC.......... Political Warfare Coordination Committee [*London*] [*World War II*]
PWCCA........ Pembroke Welsh Corgi Club of America (EA)
PWCDET...... Public Works Center Detachment [*Navy*] (DNAB)
PWCEN........ Public Works Center [*Navy*]
PWcHi......... Chester County Historical Society, West Chester, PA [*Library symbol Library of Congress*] (LCLS)
PW/CI/DET... Prisoner of War/Civilian Internees/Detainees (MCD)
PWCLANT.... Public Works Center, Atlantic [*Navy*]
PWCMIS...... Public Works Center Management Information System [*Navy*] (DNAB)
PWCMS....... Public Works Center Management System [*Navy*]
PWCOU....... Public Workers and Constructional Operatives' Union [*British*]
PWCPAC...... Public Works Center, Pacific [*Navy*]
PWCR.......... Prader-Willi Chromosome Region [*Medicine*] (DMAA)
PWcS........... West Chester State College, West Chester, PA [*Library symbol Library of Congress*] (LCLS)
PwCtlT......... Power Control Technologies, Inc. [*Associated Press*] (SAG)
PWD............ Pan World Ventures, Inc. [*Vancouver Stock Exchange symbol*]
PWD............ Participative Work Design
PWD............ People with Disabilities
PWD............ Permanent Wants Directory [*A publication*]
PWD............ Petroleum Warfare Department [*Ministry of Fuel and Power*] [*British World War II*]
PWD............ Plentywood, MT [*Location identifier FAA*] (FAAL)
PWD............ Plywood [*Technical drawings*]
PWD............ Post-Write Disturb (IAA)
PWD............ Powder (KSC)
PWD............ Power Distributor (KSC)
PWD............ Powered (IAA)
PWD............ Process Word (IAA)
PWD............ Procurement Work Directive [*Army*] (AABC)
PWD............ Proximity Warning Device (MCD)
PWD............ Psychological Warfare Division [*SHAEF*] [*World War II*]
PWD............ Public Works Department [*Navy*]
PWD............ Public Works Department (NADA)
PWD............ Pulse-Width Detector [*or Discriminator*] [*RADAR*]
PWDC.......... Philippine War Damage Commission [*Post-World War II*]
PWDCA........ Portuguese Water Dog Club of America (EA)
PWDEPT...... Public Works Department [*Navy*]
PWDG.......... Prince of Wales' Dragoon Guards [*Military British*] (ROG)
PWDI........... Program with Developing Institutions (EA)
PWDMS....... Public Works Developmental Management System [*Navy*]
PWDP.......... Powder Passing
PWDR.......... Partial Wave Dispersing Relation
pwdr............ Powder [*Pharmacy*] (DAVI)
PWDRD........ Powdered [*Freight*]
PWDS.......... Postweaning Diarrhea Syndrome [*Medicine*] (DMAA)
PWDS.......... Protected Wireline Distribution System (CET)
PWDY.......... PaineWebber Group [*Associated Press*] (SAG)
PWDY496.... PaineWebber Group [*Associated Press*] (SAG)
PWE............ Pauli-Weisskopf Equation [*Physics*]
PWE............ Pawnee City, NE [*Location identifier FAA*] (FAAL)
PWE............ Political Warfare Executive [*World War II*]
PWE............ Posterior Wall Excursion [*Anatomy*] (DMAA)
PWE............ Present Worth Expenditures [*Telecommunications*] (TEL)
PWE............ Primary Weapons and Equipment
PWE............ Prisoner of War Enclosure
PWE............ Pulse-Width Encoder
PWEA.......... Printed Wiring and Electronic Assemblies [*NASA*]
PWEA.......... Public Works Employment Act (AAGC)
PW/ED......... Pratt & Whitney Engineering Division
PWEDA........ Public Works and Economic Development Act
PWEDA........ Public Works and Economic Development Association (EA)
PWEHC........ Public Works Emergency Housing Corp. [*New Deal*]
PWES.......... Price Waterhouse Energy Solutions
PWesAC....... Community College of Allegheny County, South Campus, West Mifflin, PA [*Library symbol Library of Congress*] (LCLS)
PWesD......... Dresser Industries, Inc., Harbison-Walker Refractories Co., West Mifflin, PA [*Library symbol Library of Congress*] (LCLS)
PWF............ Pacific Whale Foundation (EA)
PWF............ Package Will Follow [*Birthday-card notation*]
PWF............ Pax World Foundation (EA)
PWF............ Permanent Wood Foundation [*Building term*]
PWF............ Personnel Working File (DOMA)
PWF............ Photoelectric Work Function
PWF............ Pop Warner Football (EA)
PWF............ Power Financial Corp. [*Toronto Stock Exchange symbol*]
PWF............ Present Worth Factor [*Real estate*]
PWF............ Private Wagon Federation [*British*] (DBA)
PWF............ Propellant Weight Fraction (NATG)
PWF............ Pulse Wave Form
PWF............ Pure Water Flux [*Engineering*]
PWFA.......... Papermakers' Woven Felt Association (DGA)
PWFG.......... Primary Waveform Generator [*Telecommunications*] (TEL)
PWFN.......... Projection Weld Flange Nut
PWFR.......... Plantwide Failure Reporting (MCD)
PWFS.......... Price Waterhouse Financial Solutions
PWG............ Panzerwagen [*Tank*] [*German military - World War II*]
PWG............ Pathology Work Group (GNE)
PWG............ Permanent Working Group (NATG)
PWG............ Photoelectric Web Guide
PWG............ Plastic Wire Guide
PWG............ Powergem Resources Corp. [*Vancouver Stock Exchange symbol*]
PWG............ Powergen PLC [*NYSE symbol*] (SAG)
PWG............ PowerGen PLC ADS [*NYSE symbol*] (TTSB)
PWG C......... PWG Capital Trust I [*Associated Press*] (SAG)
PwgnADS..... Powergan PLC [*Associated Press*] (SAG)
Pwgnlntr...... Powergan PLC [*Associated Press*] (SAG)
PWG.PP....... PowerGen PLC Interim ADS [*NYSE symbol*] (TTSB)
PWGSC........ Public Works and Government Services Canada (ACII)
PWH............ Pellet Warhead
PWH............ Poliokeawe [*Pali*] [*Hawaii*] [*Seismograph station code, US Geological Survey*] (SEIS)
PWH............ Precision Welding-Head
PWH............ Proprietor of Copyright on a Work Made for Hire
PWH............ Prototype Wave Height
PWHA.......... Plutonium Waste Handling Area [*Nuclear energy*] (NRCH)
Pwhe............ Person Who Has Everything [*Lifestyle classification*]
PWhi............ Whitehall Township Public Library, Whitehall, PA [*Library symbol Library of Congress*] (LCLS)
PWHK.......... PaineWebber Group, Inc. [*Associated Press*] (SAG)
PWHQ.......... Peace War Headquarters (NATG)
PWHS.......... Public Works Historical Society (EA)
PWHT.......... Post-Weld Heat Treatment [*Nuclear energy*] (NRCH)
PWI............. Alas Panamenas SA [*Panama*] [*ICAO designator*] (FAAC)
PWI............. PACOM [*Pacific Command*] Warning Intelligence [*Army*]
PWI............. Permanent Ware Institute [*Defunct*] (EA)
PWI............. Permanent Way Institution [*Fleet, Hampshire, England*] (EAIO)
PWI............. Physiological Workload Index [*Aviation*]
PWI............. Piecewise-Linear (IAA)
PWI............. Pilot Warning Indicator [*or Instrument*] [*Aviation*]
PWI............. Plasma Wave Instrument [*Physics*]
PWI............. Platoon Weapons Instructor [*British military*] (DMA)
PWI............. Posterior Wall Infarct [*Anatomy*] (MAE)
PWI............. Potable Water Intake
PWI............. Precedence Work Item
PWI............. Prince of Wales' Island (ROG)
PWI............. Prisoner of War Interrogation
PWI............. Projects with Industry Program [*Department of Education*]
PWI............. Proximity Warning Indicator [*or Instrument*] [*Aviation*]
PWI............. Public Windows Interface [*Computer science*] (PCM)
PWIA........... Personal Watercraft Industry Association (EA)
PWIB........... Prisoner of War Information Bureau [*Post-World War II*]
PWIC........... Prisoner of War Information Center (DOMA)
PWIF........... Plantation Workers' International Federation [*Later, IFPAAW*]
PWIFC......... Porter Wagoner International Fan Club [*Defunct*] (EA)
PWIN........... Prototype WWMCCS Intercomputer Network (MCD)
PWINO......... Precipitation Identifier Information Not Available [*NWS*] (FAAC)
PWIR........... Palmar Wireless [*NASDAQ symbol*] (SAG)
PWIR........... Palmer Wireless 'A' [*NASDAQ symbol*] (TTSB)
PWIS........... Prisoner of War Information System (DOMA)
PWJ............. Paine Webber Group [*NYSE symbol*] (TTSB)
PWJ............. PaineWebber Group, Inc. [*NYSE symbol*] (SPSG)
PWJ............. Pulsating Water-Jet Lavager [*Medicine*] (RDA)
PWJ............. PWG Capital Trust I [*NYSE symbol*] (SAG)
PWJC........... Paine, Webber, Jackson & Curtis [*Later, Paine Webber, Inc.*]
PWK............ Chicago/Wheeling, IL [*Location identifier FAA*] (FAAL)
PWK............ Prestwick BAE [*British ICAO designator*] (FAAC)
PWL............ Petroleum and Water Logistics [*Army*] (RDA)
PWL............ Piecewise-Linear
PWL............ Piecework Linear
PWL............ Port Wells [*Alaska*] [*Seismograph station code, US Geological Survey*] (SEIS)
PWL............ Poughkeepsie, NY [*Location identifier FAA*] (FAAL)
PWL............ Powell Air Ltd. [*Canada ICAO designator*] (FAAC)
PWL............ Power Level
PWL............ Printed Wiring Laboratory (MCD)
PWLB.......... Public Works Loan Board [*British*]
PWLV.......... Posterior Wall of Left Ventricle [*Anatomy*] (AAMN)
PWM........... Parentship for World Mission (NADA)
PWM........... Planar Wing Module (MCD)
PWM........... Plated Wire Memory
PWM........... Pokeweed Mitogen [*Genetics*]
PWM........... Portable Welding Machine
PWM........... Portland [*Maine*] [*Airport symbol*] (OAG)
PWM........... Portland, ME [*Location identifier FAA*] (FAAL)
PWM........... Printed Wiring Master
PWM........... Pulse Width Modulation [*Electronic instrumentation*]
PWM........... Pulse-Width Multiplier (IEEE)
PWMA......... Portable Wear Metal Analyzer [*Air Force*]
PWMAF....... Pulse-Width Modulated Audio Frequency (IAA)

PWMD .... Printed Wiring Master Drawing (NASA)
PWM-FM ..... Pulse-Width Modulation - Frequency Modulation [*RADAR*]
PWmL.......... Lycoming College, Williamsport, PA [*Library symbol Library of Congress*] (LCLS)
PWML.......... Patchy White Matter Lesion [*Medicine*]
PWMM.......... Polly Woodside Maritime Museum [*Australia*]
PWmP .... James V. Brown Library of Williamsport and Lycoming County, Williamsport, PA [*Library symbol Library of Congress*] (LCLS)
PWMR .... Periventricular White-Matter Radiolucency [*Medicine*]
P Wms......... Peere-Williams' English Chancery Reports [*1695-1736*] [*A publication*] (DLA)
PWMS .... Public Works Management System [*Navy*]
PWMSCM .... Pokeweed Mitogen-Stimulated Spleen-Cell-Conditioned Medium [*For growing cells*]
P Wms (Eng)... Peere-Williams' English Chancery Reports [*1695-1736*] [*A publication*] (DLA)
PWN .... Cash America International, Inc. [*NYSE symbol*] (SPSG)
PWN .... Cash Amer Intl [*NYSE symbol*] (TTSB)
PWN .... Patna Weekly Notes [*India*] [*A publication*] (ILCA)
PWN .... Pinewood Nematode
PWN .... Pulsar Wind Nebula [*Astronomy*]
PWN .... West Plains, MO [*Location identifier FAA*] (FAAL)
PWNBKR...... Pawnbroker
PWNDA........ Provincial Wholesale Newspaper Distributors' Association [*British*] (BI)
PW-NWLZOA... Pioneer Women/Na'amat, the Women's Labor Zionist Organization of America [*Later, MWWV*] (EA)
PWO .... Parliamentarians for World Order (EA)
PWO .... Performance Work Standard (AAGC)
PWO .... Plane-Wave Orbital [*Physics*]
PWO .... Prince of Wales' Own [*Military unit*] [*British*]
PWO .... Principal Welfare Officer [*Navy British*]
PWO .... Principle Warfare Officer [*British*]
PWO .... Production Work Order (MCD)
PWO .... Public Works Officer [*Navy*]
PWOC .... Protestant Women of the Chapel
PWOP .... Pregnant without Permission [*Military World War II*]
PWOR .... Prince of Wales' Own Royal [*Military unit*] [*British*]
PWP............ Barrio Florida [*Puerto Rico*] [*Seismograph station code, US Geological Survey*] (SEIS)
PWP............ PaineWebber Group [*NYSE symbol*] (SAG)
PWP............ Parents without Partners (EA)
PWP............ Past Worthy Patriarch
PWP............ Peasants' and Workers' Party [*India*] [*Political party*] (PPW)
PWP............ Personal Word Processor (WDMC)
PWP............ Picowatt Power (CET)
PWP............ Picowatt Psophometric (IAA)
pWp............ Picowatts, Psophometrically Weighted
PWP............ Planning Work Package (MCD)
PWP............ Plasticized White Phosphorus
PWP............ Plastic Waste Processor (DWSG)
PWP............ Polish Workers' Party
PWP............ Portable Word Processor
PWP............ Postwar Planning [*World War II*]
PWP............ Prelaunch Wind Profile (SAA)
PWP............ Preliminary Working Paper (AAGC)
P-W-P.......... Product-with-Purchase (WDMC)
p-w-p.......... Product-with-Purchase (WDMC)
PWP............ Professional Women Photographers (EA)
PWP............ Public Watering Place (ADA)
PWP............ Public Works Planning (GFGA)
PWP............ Pulmonary Wedge Pressure [*Medicine*]
PWP............ Purchase-with-Purchase [*Sales promotion*]
PWPHIT....... PaineWebber Premier High Income Trust [*Associated Press*] (SAG)
PWPIM .... PaineWebber Premier Insured Municipal Income Fund [*Associated Press*] (SAG)
PWpM.......... Merck, Sharp & Dohme [*Later, Merck & Co., Inc.*] Research Laboratories, Library Services, West Point, PA [*Library symbol Library of Congress*] (LCLS)
PWPP .... Professionwide Pension Plan [*American Chemical Society*]
PWPS .... Pure Water Preservation Society [*British*]
PWQ .... Petersburg, WV [*Location identifier FAA*] (FAAL)
PWQ .... Preferred and Well Qualified [*Candidate designation*]
PWQM .... Protection Water Quality Management
PWR .... Peak Watt Rating [*Electrical engineering*]
PWR .... Pilot Wire Regulator
PWR .... Point of Weapon Release [*Military*]
PWR .... Police War Reserve [*British*] (DAS)
PWR .... Port Walter, AK [*Location identifier FAA*] (FAAL)
PWR .... Power (KSC)
pwr .... Power (IDOE)
PWR .... Power
PWR .... Power Explorations, Inc. [*Toronto Stock Exchange symbol*]
PWR .... Power Wirewound Resistor
PWR .... Pressurized-Water Reactor [*Nuclear energy*]
PWR .... Prevailing Wage Rate [*US Employment Service*] [*Department of Labor*]
PWR .... Prince of Wales' Royal [*Military unit*] [*British*]
PWR .... Program Work Request
PWR .... Program Work Requirement (MCD)
PWR .... Project Work Review [*Army*] (AFIT)
PWR .... Publication Work Request (MCD)
PWR .... Public Worship Regulation Act [*1874*] [*British*] (ROG)
PWR .... Punjab Weekly Reporter [*India*] [*A publication*] (ILCA)
PWRCB........ President's War Relief Control Board [*World War II*]
PWRDEVELENGR... Power Development Engineer (IAA)
PWRE .... Prepositioned War Reserve Equipment [*Army*]
PWREMR...... Prepositioned War Reserve Material Requirements [*Navy*] (MCD)
PWREMS ...... Prepositioned War Reserve Material Stocks [*Navy*] (MCD)
PWR-FLECHT... Pressurized Water Ractor - Full Length Emergency Cooling Heat Transfer [*Nuclear energy*] (PDAA)
PWRH.......... Powerhouse (MSA)
PwrhsRs ...... Powerhouse Resources, Inc. [*Associated Press*] (SAG)
PWRIMC ...... Prince of Wales Royal Indian Military College [*British military*] (DMA)
PWRM .... Prepositioned War Reserve Materiel (MCD)
PWRMON .... Power Monitor (IAA)
PWRMR....... Prepositioned War Reserve Materiel Requirement (NVT)
PWRMRB...... Prepositioned War Reserve Materiel Requirement Balance (AFIT)
PWRMS .... Prepositioned War Reserve Materiel Stock (NVT)
PWRNO........ Power Failure (FAAC)
PWRO.......... Pending Work Release Order (MCD)
PWROK........ Power Restored (FAAC)
PWRPLT ...... Power Plant (IAA)
PWRPNL...... Power Panel (IAA)
PWRR.......... Prepositioned War Reserve Requirements [*Army*] (NG)
PWRR.......... Providence and Worcester Railroad Co. [*NASDAQ symbol*] (NQ)
PWRR.......... Providence & Worcester RR [*NASDAQ symbol*] (TTSB)
PWRR.......... Providence Worcester Railroad Co. [*NASDAQ symbol*] (SAG)
PWRR-MF.... Prepositioned War Reserve Requirements for Medical Facilities [*Army*] (AABC)
PWRS .... Prepositioned War Reserve Stocks [*Army*]
PWRS .... Programmable Weapons Release System (IEEE)
PWRSEMICOND... Power Semiconductor (IAA)
PWRS-MF..... Prepositioned War Reserve Stocks for Medical Facilities [*Army*] (AABC)
PWRSUP...... Power Supply (IAA)
PWRU.......... Power Unit (IAA)
PWS............ Paddle-Wheel Steamer [*Shipping*] (ROG)
PWS............ Parallel Working System
PWS............ Pattern Weavers' Society [*A union*] [*British*] (DCTA)
PWS............ Performance Work Standard
PWS............ Performance Work Statement [*DoD*]
PWS............ Peter Warlock Society (EA)
PWS............ Petrified Wood Society (EA)
PWS............ Petroleum and Water Systems [*Army*] (RDA)
PWS............ Phoenix Weapons System
PWS............ Plane-Wave Spectrum
PWS............ Plasma Wave Guide Switch (IAA)
PWS............ Plasma Wave Source [*Physics*]
PWS............ Plasma Wave System [*Instrumentation*]
PWS............ Port-Wine Stain
PWS............ Potable Water System (KSC)
PWS............ Prader-Willi Syndrome Association (EA)
PWS............ Predicted Wave Signaling
PWS............ Preliminary Work Statement (MCD)
PWS............ Pressure Wave Supercharger [*Automotive engineering*]
PWS............ Pricing Work Statement (MCD)
PWS............ Private Wire Service
PWS............ Private Wire System (AAG)
PWS............ Programmer Work Station
PWS............ Program Work Statement (MCD)
PWS............ Project Work Schedule [*Computer science*]
PWS............ Proximity Warning System (IAA)
PWS............ Psychological Warfare Service [*Allied Forces*] [*World War II*]
PWS............ Psychological Warfare Society [*Birmingham, England*] (EA)
PWS............ Public Water System (GFGA)
PWS............ Pulau-Weh [*Sumatra*] [*Seismograph station code, US Geological Survey Closed*] (SEIS)
PWSA .... Pheasant and Waterfowl Society of Australia
PWSA .... Ports and Waterways Safety Act (GFGA)
PWSA .... Professional Women Singers Association (EA)
PWSC .... Post-War Scientific Collaboration [*British*]
PWSCC .... Prince William Sound Community College [*Alaska*]
PWSO .... Pilot Weapons System Officer
PWSPMid .... PaineWebber Group, Inc. [*Associated Press*] (SAG)
PWSPP .... Payne Whitney Suicide Prevention Program [*New York Hospital*] (EA)
PWSS .... Port War Signal Station [*British military*] (DMA)
PWSS .... Public Water Supply System (GFGA)
PWST........... Protected Water Storage Tank [*Nuclear energy*] (NRCH)
PWSWA .... Processed Woodchip, Sawdust, and Woodflour Association [*British*] (BI)
PWT............ Bremerton, WA [*Location identifier FAA*] (FAAL)
PWT............ Pacific War Time (IAA)
PWT............ Pacific Winter Time (IAA)
PWT............ Penn West Petroleum Ltd. [*Toronto Stock Exchange symbol*]
PWT............ Pennyweight
PWT............ Picture World Test [*Psychology*]
PWT............ Professional Walleye Trail
PWT............ Progressive Wave Tube
PWT............ Propulsion Wind Tunnel Facility [*Arnold Air Force Base, TN*] [*Air Force*]
PWTC........... Public Works Training Center [*Navy*]
PWTC........... Public Works Transportation Center (MCD)
PWTCVA .... Procurement of Weapons and Tracked Combat Vehicles, Army (AABC)
PWTF........... Polish Workers Task Force (EA)
PWTN .... Power Train (AABC)
PWTO .... Principal Wireless Telegraphy Officer (IAA)
PWTP........... Process Waste Treatment Plant [*Engineering*]

PWTR .... Pewter (MSA)
PWTR .... Philadelphia War Tax Resistance (EA)
PWTVA .... Procurement of Weapons and Tracked Vehicles, Army (AABC)
PWU .... Political World Union (EA)
PWUSA .... Project Wolf USA (EA)
PWUSD .... PaineWebber Group, Inc. [*Associated Press*] (SAG)
PWUSJ .... PaineWebber Group [*Associated Press*] (SAG)
PWV .... Passionfruit Woodiness Virus [*Plant pathology*]
PWV .... Pittsburgh & West Virginia Railroad [*AAR code*]
PWV .... Polistes Wasp Venom [*Laboratory science*] (DAVI)
PWV .... Precipitable Water Vapor
PWV .... Pressure Wave Velocity [*Cardiology*]
PWV .... Pretoria-Witwatersrand [*South Africa*]
PWV .... Prince of Wales' Volunteers [*Military unit*] [*British*]
PWV .... Pulse Wave Velocity
PWVA .... Pacific War Veterans of America [*Defunct*]
PWVS .... Prince of Wales' Volunteer Service [*British*]
PWW .... Plannar Wing Weapon (MCD)
PWW .... Point Weather Warning
PWW .... Project West Wing (MCD)
PWW .... Washington and Jefferson College, Washington, PA [*Library symbol Library of Congress*] (LCLS)
PWWC .... Post War World Council [*Defunct*] (EA)
PW-WLZOA ... Pioneer Women, the Women's Labor Zionist Organization of America [*Later, PW-MWLZOA*] (EA)
PWWR .... Power Wirewound Resistor
PWX .... Permanent Working Staff [*NATO*] (NATG)
PWX .... Prisoners of War Executive [*Branch of SHAEF*] [*World War II*]
PWY .... PaineWebber Group [*AMEX symbol*] (SAG)
PX .... Air Niugini [*Air New Guinea*] [*ICAO designator*] (AD)
PX .... Pancreatectomized [*Medicine*]
Px .... Past History (DAVI)
PX .... Pedro Ximenez [*A blending sherry*]
PX .... Peroxidase [*Also, PO, POD*] [*An enzyme*]
PX .... Physical Examination
PX .... Piroxicam [*Anti-inflammatory*]
Px .... Plantwax [*A fungicide*]
PX .... Please Exchange
PX .... Pneumothorax [*Medicine*]
PX .... Post Exchange [*Military*]
PX .... Praxair, Inc. [*NYSE symbol*] (SPSG)
PX .... Private Examination (WDAA)
PX .... Private Exchange
PX .... Production Executive of the War Cabinet [*World War II*]
Px .... Prognosis [*Medicine*] (WGA)
PX .... Pyroxene [*Also, PYX*] [*A mineral*]
PXA .... Parana [*Brazil*] [*Airport symbol*] (AD)
PXA .... Place Index in Address (SAA)
PXA .... Pulsed Xenon Arc
PXC .... Proximity Computer (MCD)
PXCMD .... Phoenix Contract Management District (SAA)
PXD .... Place Index in Decrement
PXD .... Post-Exercise Discussion [*NATO*] (NATG)
PXD .... Price Ex-Dividend [*Stock market*]
PXE .... Pacific Research & Engineering Corp. [*AMEX symbol*] (SAG)
PXE .... Phenylxylylethane [*Organic chemistry*]
PXE .... Poly(xylenyl ether) [*Organic chemistry*]
PXE .... Provinces X Explorations [*Vancouver Stock Exchange symbol*]
PXE .... Pseudoxanthoma Elasticum [*Medicine*]
PXE.U .... Pacific Res & Engineering Unit [*AMEX symbol*] (TTSB)
PXF .... Primex Forest Industries Ltd. [*Toronto Stock Exchange symbol Vancouver Stock Exchange symbol*]
PXG .... Phoenix Gold Mines Ltd. [*Toronto Stock Exchange symbol*]
PXH .... Pacific Express Holdings Ltd. [*New Zealand*] [*ICAO designator*] (FAAC)
PXI .... Pax Christi International (EA)
PXI .... Pulsed Xenon Illuminator
PxIMP .... Peroxisomal Integral Membrane Protein [*Biochemistry*]
PX In .... Arrival Time [*Aviation*]
PXL .... Poney Explorations Ltd. [*Vancouver Stock Exchange symbol*]
PXL .... Pulsed Xenon LASER
Pxl .... Pyridoxal [*Also, PL*] [*Biochemistry*]
PXLS .... Pulsed Xenon Light Source
PXLSS .... Pulsed Xenon Light Source System
PXM .... Projection X-Ray Microscope
Pxm .... Pyridoxamine [*Also, PM*] [*Biochemistry*]
PX Me .... Report My Arrival or Departure [*Aviation slang*]
PXN .... Panoche, CA [*Location identifier FAA*] (FAAL)
PXN .... Paxson Communications 'A' [*AMEX symbol*] (TTSB)
PXN .... Paxson Communications Corp. [*AMEX symbol*] (SAG)
Pxn .... Pyridoxine [*Also, PN*] [*Biochemistry*]
PXO .... Porto Santo [*Portugal*] [*Airport symbol*] (OAG)
PXO .... Prospective Executive Officer
PX Out .... Takeoff Time [*Aviation*]
PXP .... Packet Exchange Protocol [*Computer science*] (TNIG)
PXPPL .... Pull and Push Plate
PXR .... Paxar Corp. [*NYSE symbol*] (SAG)
PXR .... Plus-X-Reversal
PXR .... Praxis Resources Ltd. [*Vancouver Stock Exchange symbol*]
PXRD .... Powder X-Ray Diffraction
PXRE .... Phoenix Re Corp. [*NASDAQ symbol*] (NQ)
PXRE .... PXRE Corp. [*NASDAQ symbol*] (TTSB)
PXRE Cp .... PXRE Corp. [*Associated Press*] (SAG)
PXS .... Plexus Resources Corp. [*Toronto Stock Exchange symbol*]
PXS .... Pulsed Xenon System
PXSC .... Proximity Sensing Computer (MCD)
PXSS .... Pulsed Xenon Solar Simulator
PXSTR .... Phototransistor (IEEE)
PXT .... Patuxent River, MD [*Location identifier FAA*] (FAAL)
PXT .... Pinxit [*He, or She, Painted It*] [*Latin*]
PXT .... Praxis Technologies Corp. [*Toronto Stock Exchange symbol*]
PXU .... Pleiku [*South Vietnam*] [*Airport symbol*] (AD)
PXU .... Portable X-Ray Unit
PXV .... Evansville, IN [*Location identifier FAA*] (FAAL)
PXV .... Pedro Ximenez Viejo [*A blending sherry*]
PXX .... Aroostook Aviation, Inc. [*FAA designator*] (FAAC)
PXX .... Porto Alfonso [*Brazil*] [*Airport symbol*] (AD)
PXXI .... Prophet 21, Inc. [*NASDAQ symbol*] (SAG)
PXY .... Milwaukee, WI [*Location identifier FAA*] (FAAL)
Pxy .... Pyridoxyl [*Biochemistry*]
PY .... Martin Memorial [*York City and County*] Library, York, PA [*Library symbol Library of Congress*] (LCLS)
PY .... Pack Year [*Cigarettes*] (MEDA)
PY .... Pack Years [*of cigarette consumption*] (DAVI)
PY .... Paraguay [*ANSI two-letter standard code*] (CNC)
py .... Paraguay [*IYRU nationality code*] [*MARC country of publication code Library of Congress*] (LCCP)
PY .... Patrol Vessel, Yacht [*Navy symbol*]
PY .... Pechiney ADS [*NYSE symbol*] (TTSB)
PY .... Pembroke Yeomanry [*British military*] (DMA)
PY .... Person Years [*After radiation exposure*]
Py .... Phosphopyridoxal [*Medicine*] (DMAA)
PY .... Physical Year
P/Y .... Pitch or Yaw
Py .... Polyoma Virus [*Medicine*] (DMAA)
PY .... Polysar Ltd. [*Toronto Stock Exchange symbol Vancouver Stock Exchange symbol*]
PY .... Prior Year (AABC)
PY .... Program Year (AFM)
PY .... Project Yedid [*Defunct*] (EA)
PY .... Proto Yiddish (BJA)
PY .... Publication Year [*Online database field identifier*]
Py .... Pyrene [*Organic chemistry*] (AAMN)
Py .... Pyridine [*Organic chemistry*]
Py .... Pyrimidine (DOG)
Py .... Pyrogen [*Medicine*]
PY .... Pyrometer (IEEE)
PY .... Pyronin Y [*A biological dye*]
PY .... Pythium [*A fungus*]
PY .... Spray [*ICAO*] (FAAC)
PY .... Surinam Airways [*ICAO designator*] (AD)
PYA .... Partners Preferred Yield [*AMEX symbol*] (SAG)
PYA .... Partners Preferred Yld'A' [*AMEX symbol*] (TTSB)
PYA .... Penn Yan, NY [*Location identifier FAA*] (FAAL)
PYA .... Pioneer Youth of America (EA)
PYA .... Pittsburgh, Youngstown & Ashland Railway Co. (IIA)
PYA .... Plan, Year, and Age [*Insurance designations*]
PYA .... Psychoanalysis [*Medicine*]
PYA .... Pyatigorsk [*Former USSR Seismograph station code, US Geological Survey*] (SEIS)
PYA .... Pyroair Tech [*Vancouver Stock Exchange symbol*]
PYAR .... Person-Years-at-Risk [*After radiation exposure*] (FFDE)
PYarE .... Electric Storage Battery Co., Yardley, PA [*Library symbol Library of Congress*] (LCLS)
Py B .... Bachelor of Pedagogy
PYB .... Borg-Warner Corp., York Division, York, PA [*Library symbol Library of Congress*] (LCLS)
PYB .... [*The*] Palestine Year Book [*New York*] [*A publication*] (BJA)
PYB .... Partners Preferred Yield II [*AMEX symbol*] (SAG)
PYB .... Partners Preferred Yld'A' II [*AMEX symbol*] (TTSB)
PYB .... Pittsburgh Youth Ballet
PYBT .... [*The*] Prince's Youth Business Trust [*British*]
PYC .... Aeropycsa SA de CV [*Mexico ICAO designator*] (FAAC)
PYC .... Kuparuk, AK [*Location identifier FAA*] (FAAL)
PYC .... Pale Yellow Candle [*Baltic coffee-house*] [*London*] (DSUE)
PYC .... Partners Preferred Yield III [*AMEX symbol*] (SAG)
PYC .... Partners Preferred Yld'A' III [*AMEX symbol*] (TTSB)
PYC .... Patrol Vessel, Yacht, Coastal [*Navy symbol Obsolete*]
PYC .... Pembroke Yeomanry Cavalry [*British military*] (DMA)
PYC .... Perishability Code [*Military*] (AFIT)
PYC .... Playon Chico [*Panama*] [*Airport symbol*] (OAG)
PYC .... Pope and Young Club (EA)
PYC .... Proteose-Yeast Castione Medium [*Microbiology*] (MAE)
PyC .... Pyogenic Culture [*Medicine*] (MAE)
PYC .... York College of Pennsylvania, York, PA [*Library symbol Library of Congress*] (LCLS)
PYCG .... Pyrochromatogram [*Analytical chemistry*]
PYCR .... Pyrroline-5-Carboxylate Reductase (DMAA)
Pyd .... [*A*] Pyrimidine Nucleoside [*Also, Y*]
PYDV .... Potato Yellow Dwarf Virus [*Plant pathology*]
PYE .... Peptone Yeast Extract [*Medium*] [*Microbiology*] (DAVI)
PYE .... Point Reyes, CA [*Location identifier FAA*] (FAAL)
PYE .... Protect Your Environment [*Groups*]
PYE .... Pryme Energy Resources [*Vancouver Stock Exchange symbol*]
PYF .... French Polynesia [*ANSI three-letter standard code*] (CNC)
PYF .... Pyrenees [*France*] [*Seismograph station code, US Geological Survey*] (SEIS)
Py-FD-MS .... Pyrolysis Field Desorption Mass Spectrometry
PYFV .... Parsnip Yellow Fleck Virus [*Plant pathology*]
PYG .... Peptone-Yeast-Glucose [*Medium*] [*Microbiology*]

PYGC .... Pyrolysis Gas Chromatography
PYGM .... Peptone-Yeast Glucose Maltose Agar [*Microbiology*] (MAE)
PYGN .... Pyrogen Unit [*Biochemistry*]
PYGS .... Church of Jesus Christ of Latter-Day Saints, Genealogical Society Library, Gettysburg Branch, York, PA [*Library symbol Library of Congress*] (LCLS)
PYH .... Puerto Ayacucho [*Venezuela*] [*Airport symbol*] (OAG)
PYH .... York Hospital, York, PA [*Library symbol Library of Congress*] (LCLS)
PYHi .... Historical Society of York County, York, PA [*Library symbol Library of Congress*] (LCLS)
Py-HRMS .... Pyrolysis High-Resolution Mass Spectrometry
PYI .... Presidential Young Investigator Program [*National Science Foundation*]
PYJ .... Louisville, KY [*Location identifier FAA*] (FAAL)
Pyke .... Pyke's Lower Canada King's Bench Reports [*1809-10*] [*A publication*] (ILCA)
Pyke LC .... Pyke's Lower Canada King's Bench Reports [*1809-10*] [*A publication*] (ILCA)
Pyke's R .... Pyke's Lower Canada King's Bench Reports [*1809-10*] [*A publication*] (ILCA)
PYL .... Perry Island, AK [*Location identifier FAA*] (FAAL)
PYLL .... Potential Years of Life Lost [*Medicine*] (DMAA)
PYLR .... Peach Yellow Leaf Roll [*Plant pathology*]
PYM .... Martin Memorial [*York City and County*] Library, York, PA [*OCLC symbol*] (OCLC)
PYM .... Pan-African Youth Movement (EA)
PYM .... Plymouth, MA [*Location identifier FAA*] (FAAL)
PYM .... Psychosomatic [*Medicine*] (DMAA)
PYM .... Psychosomatic Medicine
PYM .... Putnam High Yield Municipal [*NYSE symbol*] (SPSG)
PYM .... Putnam Hi Yield Muni [*NYSE symbol*] (TTSB)
Py-MS .... Pyrolysis Mass Spectrometry
Pymt .... Payment
PYMT .... Payment
PYMV .... Peanut Yellow Mottle Virus [*Plant pathology*]
PYN .... Chicago, IL [*Location identifier FAA*] (FAAL)
PYN .... Poneloya [*Nicaragua*] [*Seismograph station code, US Geological Survey*] (SEIS)
PYNC .... Prior Year Notice [*IRS*]
PYO .... Person-Years of Observation [*Medicine*]
PYO .... Pick Your Own [*Fruits and vegetables*] (DSUE)
PYO .... Prior Year Overhead (AAGC)
PYO .... Pyongyang [*Heizo*] [*North Korea*] [*Seismograph station code, US Geological Survey*] [*Closed*] (SEIS)
PYoW .... Westmoreland County Community College, Youngwood, PA [*Library symbol Library of Congress*] (LCLS)
PYP .... Photoactive Yellow Protein [*Biochemistry*]
PYP .... Pyrophosphate [*Scintiscanning*]
PYPER .... Promote Yard Performance Efficiency and Reliability (DNAB)
PYPH .... Polyphase
P-Y-R .... Pitch-Yaw-Roll (AAG)
PYR .... Player Resources, Inc. [*Vancouver Stock Exchange symbol*]
PYR .... Prior Year Report
PYR .... Prior Year's Return [*IRS*]
Py R .... Pyke's Lower Canada King's Bench Reports [*1809-10*] [*A publication*] (ILCA)
Pyr .... Pyralidae [*Entomology*]
PYR .... Pyramid [*California*] [*Seismograph station code, US Geological Survey*] (SEIS)
PYR .... Pyramid (MSA)
PYR .... Pyramid Air Lines [*Egypt*] [*ICAO designator*] (FAAC)
Pyr .... Pyramidal Tract [*Neuroanatomy*]
PYR .... Pyrgos [*Greece*] [*Airport symbol*] (AD)
PYR .... Pyridine [*Organic chemistry*]
Pyr .... [*A*] Pyrimidine [*Biochemistry*]
Pyr .... Pyrocap International Corp. [*Associated Press*] (SAG)
PYR .... Pyrocap International Corp. [*AMEX symbol*] (SAG)
PYR .... Pyrometer (AAG)
PYR .... Pyruvate [*Biochemistry*]
PYR.EC .... Pyrocap International [*ECM Symbol*] (TTSB)
PYRETH .... Pyrethrum [*Pellitory*] [*Pharmacology*] (ROG)
PYRKIN .... Pyruvate Kinase [*An enzyme*] (DAVI)
pyrm .... Pyramid (VRA)
PYRMD .... Pyramid [*Freight*]
PYRO .... Pyrogallic Acid (ROG)
PYRO .... Pyromaniac (WDAA)
PYRO .... Pyrotechnic
Pyrocp .... Pyrocap International Corp. [*Associated Press*] (SAG)
PYROM .... Pyrometer [*Engineering*]
PYROTECH .... Pyrotechnical (ROG)
pyrox .... Pyroxiline (VRA)
PYROX GN .... Pyroxene Gneisses [*Agronomy*]
PyrP .... Pyridoxamine Phosphate [*or Pyridoxyl Phosphate*] [*Organic chemistry*] (DAVI)
PyrP .... Pyridoxyl (Pyridoxamine) Phosphate (BABM)
PYRR .... Pyrrolidine [*Organic chemistry*]
PYRREC .... Pyrrolidinoethyl Chloride [*Organic chemistry*]
Pyrrh .... Pyrrhus [*of Plutarch*] [*Classical studies*] (OCD)
PYRS .... Pyramids [*Board on Geographic Names*]
PYRUV .... Pyruvate [*Organic chemistry*] (DAVI)
PYS .... Partial Yield Spectroscopy (MCD)
PYS .... Photoelectron Yield Spectroscopy
PYS .... Primitive Yolk Sac [*Embryology*]
PYSZ .... Partially Yttria-Stabilized Zirconia [*Industrial ceramics*]
PYT .... Payment (DCTA)
PYT .... Playitas [*Nicaragua*] [*Seismograph station code, US Geological Survey*] (SEIS)
PYT .... Prentiss, MS [*Location identifier FAA*] (FAAL)
PYT .... Pretty Young Thing [*In song title from the Michael Jackson album "Thriller"*]
PYT .... Pyng Tech [*Vancouver Stock Exchange symbol*]
Pyth .... Pythian [*of Pindar*] [*Classical studies*] (OCD)
Py-TRMS .... Pyrolysis Time-Resolved Mass Spectrometry
PYTV .... TV Filme, Inc. [*NASDAQ symbol*] (SAG)
PYV .... Payton Ventures [*Vancouver Stock Exchange symbol*]
PyV .... Polyoma Virus
PYV .... Yaviza [*Panama*] [*Airport symbol*] (OAG)
PYX .... Perryton, TX [*Location identifier FAA*] (FAAL)
PYX .... Playtex Products [*NYSE symbol*] (SPSG)
PYX .... Pyroxene [*Also, PX*] [*A mineral*]
Pyx .... Pyxis [*Constellation*]
Pyxi .... Pyxis [*Constellation*]
Pyxis .... Pyxis Corp. [*Associated Press*] (SAG)
PYXS .... Pyxis Corp. [*NASDAQ symbol*] (SAG)
PZ .... Canal Zone [*ANSI two-letter standard code Obsolete*] (CNC)
PZ .... Pancreozymin [*Also, CCK*] [*Endocrinology*]
PZ .... Panzerbrechend [*Armor-Piercing*] [*German military - World War II*]
PZ .... Pastural Zone [*Agriculture*]
PZ .... Past Z
PZ .... Paterson Zochonis [*Commercial firm*] [*British*]
PZ .... Peak-to-Zero (IAA)
PZ .... Penzance [*British depot code*]
PZ .... Peripheral Zone [*Botany*] [*Anatomy*]
PZ .... Phase Zero
Pz .... Phenylazobenzyloxycarbonyl [*Biochemistry*]
PZ .... Pick Up Zone [*Shipping*]
PZ .... Pickup Zone [*Military*] (INF)
pz .... Pieze [*Unit of pressure*]
PZ .... Pie Zeses [*May You Live Piously*] [*Italian*]
PZ .... Pizza
PZ .... Poland [*IYRU nationality code*] (IYR)
PZ .... Potez [*Etablissements Henri Potez*] [*France ICAO aircraft manufacturer identifier*] (ICAO)
PZ .... Prazosin [*A vasodilator*]
PZ .... Pregnancy Zone Protein (AAMN)
PZ .... Primary Zone [*Military*]
PZ .... Prisoner of Zion (BJA)
PZ .... Protective Zone
PZ .... Prozone Phenomenon [*Immunology*]
PZ .... Psychic Zodiac
PZ .... Pyrazine [*Organic chemistry*]
PZ .... Surinam [*Aircraft nationality and registration mark*] (FAAC)
PZA .... Patrol Zone Area (MCD)
PZA .... Paz De Ariporo [*Colombia*] [*Airport symbol*] (OAG)
PZA .... Pizzeria
PZA .... Provena Foods [*AMEX symbol*] (TTSB)
PZA .... Provena Foods, Inc. [*AMEX symbol*] (SPSG)
PZA .... Pyrazinamide [*Antibacterial compound*]
PZAA .... Polarized Zeeman Atomic Absorption
PZB .... Pietermaritzburg [*South Africa*] [*Airport symbol*] (OAG)
PZB .... Pittston Brinks Grp [*NYSE symbol*] (TTSB)
PZC .... Pezamerica Resources Corp. [*Vancouver Stock Exchange symbol*]
PZC .... Point of Zero Charge [*Electrochemistry*]
PZC .... Progressive Zionist Caucus (EA)
PZ-CCK .... Pancreozymin-Cholecystokinin [*Endocrinology*] (MAE)
PZCO .... Pickup-Zone Control Officer [*Military*] (INF)
PZD .... Partial Zona Dissection [*In-vitro fertilization*] (PAZ)
PZD .... Partial Zonal Drilling [*In vitro fertilization*] [*Medicine*] (BARN)
PZD .... Phase Zero Defense
PZDV .... Panzer-Division [*Armored Division*] [*German military*]
PZE .... Penzance [*England*] [*Airport symbol*] (OAG)
PZE .... Piezoelectric
PZFC .... Pia Zadora Fan Club (EA)
PZH .... Zhob [*Pakistan*] [*Airport symbol*] (OAG)
PZI .... Indiana University of Pennsylvania, Indiana, PA [*OCLC symbol*] (OCLC)
PZI .... Protamine Zinc Insulin
PZKPFW .... Panzerkampfwagen [*German tank*] [*World War II*]
PZKW .... Panzerkampfwagen [*German tank*] [*World War II*]
PZL .... Panstwowe Zaklady Lotnicze [*Poland ICAO designator*] (FAAC)
PZL .... Pennzoil Co. [*NYSE symbol Toronto Stock Exchange symbol*] (SPSG)
PZL .... Progressive Zionist League-Hashomer Hatzair (EA)
PZM .... Piezoelectric Mount (IAA)
PZM .... Pittston Minerals Group [*NYSE symbol*] (SPSG)
PZM .... Pressurized Zone Microphone
PZO .... Peebles, OH [*Location identifier FAA*] (FAAL)
PZO .... Puerto Ordaz [*Venezuela*] [*Airport symbol*] (OAG)
PZP .... Phase Zero Program
PZP .... Porcine Zona Pellucida [*Experimental animal contraceptive*]
PZP .... Pregnancy Zone Protein
PZPR .... Polska Zjednoczona Partia Robotnicza [*Polish United Workers' Party - PUWP*] [*Political party*] (PPW)
PZQ .... Rogers City, MI [*Location identifier FAA*] (FAAL)
PZ(R) .... Penetration Zone (Radius) (MCD)
PZR .... Pressurizer (NRCH)
PZR LCS .... Pressurizer Level Control System [*Nuclear energy*] (GFGA)
PZR PCS .... Pressurizer Pressure Control System [*Nuclear energy*] (GFGA)
PZS .... Pittston Services Group [*Formerly, The Pittston Co.*] [*NYSE symbol*] (SPSG)

PZS............. President of the Zoological Society [*British*]
PZSV........... Pelargonium Zonate Spot Virus [*Plant pathology*]
PZT............. Lead [*Plumbum*] Zirconate-Titanate [*Piezoelectric transducer*]
PZT............. Photographic Zenith Tube
PZT............. Piezoelectric Transducer [*or Translator*]
PZT............. Piezoelectric Zirconate Titanate
PZT............. Polycrystalline Lead Zirconate Titanate [*Piezoelectricity*]
PZU............. Port Sudan [*Sudan*] [*Airport symbol*] (OAG)
PZV............. New York, NY [*Location identifier FAA*] (FAAL)
PZX............. Paragould, AR [*Location identifier FAA*] (FAAL)
PZX............. Pittston Burlington Group [*NYSE symbol*] (TTSB)
PZY............. Performance Executive Airlines Ltd. [*British ICAO designator*] (FAAC)
PZY............. Piestany [*Former Czechoslovakia*] [*Airport symbol*] (OAG)
PZZ............. Pizza Patio Ltd. [*Vancouver Stock Exchange symbol*]
PZZA........... Papa Johns International, Inc. [*NASDAQ symbol*] (SAG)
PZZA........... Papa John's Intl [*NASDAQ symbol*] (TTSB)
PZZI............ Pizza Inn [*NASDAQ symbol*] (TTSB)
PZZI............ Pizza Inn, Inc. [*NASDAQ symbol*] (SAG)

Q
By Acronym

Q................. Atomic Shell of 98 Electrons per Shell (BARN)
Q................. Blood Volume (DAVI)
Q................. Cardiac Output (DAVI)
Q................. Chicago, Burlington & Quincy Railroad [*Also known as Burlington Route*] [*Slang*]
Q................. Clerical Perception [*On General Aptitude Test Battery*] (DAVI)
Q................. Codex Marchalianus (BJA)
Q................. Coefficient of Association [*Statistics*]
Q................. Coenzyme Q [*Ubiquinone*] [*Also, CoQ, U, UQ*] [*Biochemistry*]
Q................. Combination of Purpose [*JETDS nomenclature*]
Q................. Coulomb [*Unit of quality*] [*Electronics*] (WDAA)
Q................. Drone [*Designation for all US military aircraft*]
Q................. Dynamic Pressure [*NASA*]
Q................. Electrical Charge (WDAA)
q................. Electrical Quantity (IDOE)
q................. Frequency of the Rarer Allele of a Pair [*Genetics*] (DAVI)
Q................. Glutamine [*One-letter symbol; see Gln*]
Q................. Heat [*or q*] [*Symbol IUPAC*]
Q................. Kuwait [*IYRU nationality code*] (IYR)
Q................. Merit of a Coil or Capacitor [*Electronics*]
Q................. Moment of Area (BARN)
Q................. One Billion [*British thermal units*] (GNE)
Q................. Output [*Business term*]
q................. Partition Function, Particle [*Symbol*] [*IUPAC*]
Q................. Partition Function, System [*Symbol*] [*IUPAC*]
Q................. Perfusion [*Cardiology*] (DAVI)
Q................. Perihelion Distance [*Astronomy*] (BARN)
Q................. Polaris Correction [*Missiles*]
Q................. Promotional Fare [*Also, K, L, V*] [*Airline fare code*]
Q................. Proportion Not in a Specific Class
Q................. Qarar (BARN)
Q................. Q Band (IDOE)
Q................. Qere (BJA)
Q................. Q-Factor (DEN)
Q................. Q Output (IDOE)
Q................. Quaalude [*or Methaqualone*] [*A trademark*] [*Pharmacology*] (DAVI)
Q................. Quad (IAA)
Q................. Quadragesms [*Year Books of Edward III*] [*A publication*] (ILCA)
Q................. Quadrans [*A Farthing*] [*Monetary unit*] [*British*]
Q................. Quadriceps [*Anatomy*]
Q................. Quadrillion (AD)
Q................. Quadrillion BTU's [*Also known as "quads"*]
Q................. Quadruple
Q................. Quadruple Expansion Engine
Q................. Quaere [*Inquire*] [*Latin*]
Q................. Quai [*Embankment*] [*French*] (AD)
Q................. Quaker Line (AD)
Q................. Qualifier [*Linguistics*]
Q................. Quality (IAA)
Q................. Quality Factor
q................. Quality Factor (AD)
q................. Quality of Output [*Economics*]
Q................. Quantity
Q................. Quantity [*Microeconomics*] (AD)
Q................. Quantity of Electric Charge (IAA)
Q................. Quantity of Electricity [*Symbol*] [*IUPAC*]
q................. [*Value of*] Quantum (IDOE)
q................. Quaque [*Each*] [*Latin*] (AD)
Q................. Quaque [*Each or Every*] [*Latin*]
Q................. Quarantine (AD)
Q................. Quark [*Physics*]
Q................. Quart
q................. Quart (AD)
q................. Quart (WDMC)
q................. Quarter (WDMC)
q................. Quarter (AD)
q................. Quarter (ODBW)
Q................. Quarter
Q................. Quarterback [*Football*]
Q................. Quartering [*Military British*]
Q................. Quarterly
q................. Quarterly (ODBW)
q................. Quarterly [*A periodical published four times a year*] (WDMC)
Q................. Quartermaster [*Military*]
Q................. Quarternary [*Geology*]
Q................. Quarters [*Officer's rating*] [*British Royal Navy*]
Q................. Quarter Word Designator [*Computer science*]
Q................. Quartile
q................. Quartile (AD)
Q................. Quartile Variation [*Symbol*] (AD)
q................. Quarto (AD)
q................. Quarto [*Bookbinding*] (WDMC)
Q................. Quarto [*Book from 25 to 30 centimeters in height*]
Q................. Quarto Edition [*Shakespearean work*]
Q................. Quartoquadrillion (WDAA)
Q................. Quartz [*CIPW classification*] [*Geology*]
Q................. Quasi [*Almost, As It Were*] [*Latin*]
Q................. Quatrefage's Angle [*Parietal Angle*] (DAVI)
Q................. Quebec [*Phonetic alphabet*] [*International*] (DSUE)
Q................. Quebec (AD)
Q................. Queen
Q................. Queen [*Chess*]
Q................. Queen [*Phonetic alphabet*] [*Pre-World War II*] [*World War II*] (DSUE)
Q................. Queenie [*Phonetic alphabet*] [*Royal Navy World War I*] (DSUE)
Q................. Queensland [*Fever*] [*Medicine*] (BABM)
Q................. Queensland Fever [*Medicine*] (DAVI)
Q................. Queensway [*Furniture store chain*] [*British*]
Q................. Queer [*Homosexual*] [*Slang*] (DSUE)
q................. Queer (AD)
q................. Quench (AD)
Q................. Quench (IAA)
Q................. Quercetin [*Botany*]
Q................. Querwellen [*of transverse seismic waves*] (BARN)
Q................. Query
q................. Query (ODBW)
q................. Query [*Journalism*] [*Proofreading*] (WDMC)
Q................. Query Fever [*Medicine*] (DAVI)
Q................. Query Language [*1975*] (CSR)
Q................. Question
q................. Question (WDMC)
q................. Question (AD)
q................. Questioned [*Soundness of decision or reasoning in cited case questioned*] [*Used in Shepard's Citations*] [*Legal term*] (DLA)
Q................. Questionnaire
Q................. Quetzal [*Monetary unit*] [*Guatemala*]
Q................. Queue
Q................. Quick
q................. Quick (AD)
Q................. Quick [*Flashing*] Light [*Navigation signal*]
Q................. Quiescent [*Cytology*]
Q................. Quiescit [*He Rests*] [*Latin*]
Q................. Quiller-Couch [*Sir Arthur, 1863-1944, English man of letters*] [*Letter used as pen name*]
Q................. Quiller Press [*Publisher*] [*British*]
Q................. Quilting
Q................. Quinacrine [*Fluorescent method*] [*Chromosome stain*]
Q................. Quinidine [*Pharmacology*] (DAVI)
Q................. Quinone [*An oxidizing agent*] [*Chemistry*] (DAVI)
Q................. Quint [*Energy unit*] (FFDE)
Q................. Quintal [*Unit of weight*]
q................. Quintal (AD)
Q................. Quintar [*Monetary unit*] [*Albania*]
Q................. Quintus [*Fifth*] [*Latin*]
Q................. Quire [*Measure of paper*]
q................. Quire (AD)
q................. Quire [*Paper*] (WDMC)
Q................. Quisque [*Each, Every*] [*Pharmacy*]
Q................. Qumran (BJA)
Q................. Quorum (DLA)
Q................. Quotient (ADA)
Q................. Radiant Energy [*Symbol*] [*IUPAC*]
Q................. Receivership [*or Bankruptcy*] [*Designation used with NYSE symbols*] (SPSG)
Q................. Respiratory Quotient [*Also, RQ*] [*Physiology*]
Q................. San Quentin [*Prison*]
Q................. San Quentin Prison (AD)
Q................. Semi-Interquartile Range or Quartile Deviation [*Statistics*]
Q................. Sonar [*JETDS nomenclature*]
Q................. Special Purpose [*JETDS nomenclature*]
Q................. Squalls [*Meteorology*] (BARN)
Q................. Stagnation Pressure (WDAA)
Q................. Thermoelectric Power [*Physics*] (BARN)

Q .... Volume Rate [*Heat transmission symbol*]
Q1 .... First Quarto [*The earliest publication of the plays of William Shakespeare*] (WDMC)
Q1 .... Quintal [*Hundred-weight*] [*Spanish*] (AD)
Q2H .... Quaque Secunda Hora [*Every Second Hour*] [*Pharmacy*]
Q3H .... Quaque Tertia Hora [*Every Third Hour*] [*Pharmacy*]
Q4H .... Quaque Quartus Hora [*Every Fourth Hour*] [*Pharmacy*]
Q4V .... Quicker for Victory [*World War II*]
Q8 .... Quadraphonic Eight [*Tape cartridge format*] (NTCM)
Q_9 .... Ubichromanol-9 (DAVI)
Q_9 .... Ubichromenol-9 (DAVI)
Q_{10} .... Coefficient of Temperature (DAVI)
$Q1^0$ .... Every Hour around the Clock [*$Q2^0$ is evey 2 hours, etc.*] [*Pharmacy*] (DAVI)
QA .... Air Caribe [*ICAO designator*] (AD)
QA .... Bibliotheque Municipale, Alma, Quebec [*Library symbol National Library of Canada*] (NLC)
QA .... National Restaurant Association Quality Assurance Study Group (EA)
QA .... QANTAS Airways Ltd. [*Australia*] (DS)
qa .... Qatar [*MARC country of publication code Library of Congress*] (LCCP)
QA .... Qatar [*IYRU nationality code*] [*ANSI two-letter standard code*] (CNC)
QA .... Quadrans [*A Farthing*] [*Monetary unit*] [*British*] (ROG)
QA .... Quadripartite Agreement
QA .... Qualification Approval (WDAA)
QA .... Quality Acceptance (AD)
QA .... Quality Analysis (IAA)
QA .... Quality Assessment (HCT)
QA .... Quality Assurance
qa .... Quality Assurance (AD)
QA .... Quantum Access, Inc. [*Database producer*] (IID)
QA .... Quarternary Ammonium [*Chemistry*]
QA .... Quarters Allowance
QA .... Quarters Armourer [*British military*] (DMA)
QA .... Quarters Assistant [*British military*] (DMA)
QA .... Quasi Algorithm (OA)
QA .... Queen Alexandra's Imperial Military Nursing Service [*British*] (BARN)
QA .... Query Analyzer (IEEE)
QA .... Query Author [*Proofreader's notation*]
QA .... Quick-Acting
qa .... Quick-Acting (AD)
qa .... Quick Assembly (AD)
QA .... Quick Assembly [*Furniture*]
QA .... Quick Asset [*Finance*]
QA .... Quiescent Aerial [*or Antenna*]
qa .... Quiescent Aerial (AD)
QA .... Quinic Acid [*Organic chemistry*]
Q-A .... Quint-A (AD)
QA .... Quisqualic Acid [*Biochemistry*]
QAA .... ALCAN International Ltee. [*ALCAN International Ltd.*] Jonquiere, Quebec [*Library symbol National Library of Canada*] (NLC)
QAA .... Quality Assurance Assistant [*DoD*]
QAA .... Quality Assurance Audit (MCD)
QAA .... Question and Answer (IAA)
QAA .... Quinoline Amino Alcohol [*Organic chemistry*]
QA & O .... Quality Assurance and Operations [*Nuclear Regulatory Commission*] (GFGA)
QA & P .... Quanah, Acme & Pacific Railroad (AD)
QA & R .... Quality Assurance and Reliability
QAAO .... Quality Assurance and Operations (IAA)
QAAS .... Quality Assurance Acceptance Standard (IAA)
QAAS .... Quality Assurance Ammunition Specialist [*or Speciality*] (MCD)
QAB .... Quality Assurance Board (AD)
QAB .... Quality Assurance Board (NADA)
QAB .... Quality Assurance Bulletin (AD)
QAB .... Queen Anne's Bounty
QAB .... Queensland Agricultural Bank [*Australia*]
QAB .... Quick Action Button [*Military*] (CAAL)
QABA .... Biblitheque et Audiovisuel, Alma, Quebec [*Library symbol National Library of Canada*] (NLC)
QAC .... Qatar Air Cargo [*FAA designator*] (FAAC)
QAC .... Quadrant Aimable Charge Warhead (MCD)
QAC .... Quadripartite Agreements Committee [*Military*]
QAC .... Quality Assessment Coordinator (MEDA)
QAC .... Quality Assurance Chart (MCD)
QAC .... Quality Assurance Check (AD)
QAC .... Quality Assurance Checklist (NRCH)
QAC .... Quality Assurance Code
QAC .... Quality Assurance Coding (AD)
QAC .... Quality Assurance Coordinator [*Environmental Protection Agency*] (GFGA)
QAC .... Quality Assurance Criterion [*Nuclear energy*] (NRCH)
QAC .... Quarternary Ammonium Compound [*Chemistry*]
qac .... Quaternary Ammonium Compound (AD)
QAC .... Quaternary Ammonium Compound [*Chemistry*] (DAVI)
QAC .... Quebec Appeal Cases [*Maritime Law Book Co. Ltd.*] [*Canada Information service or system*] (CRD)
QAC .... Queensland Arts Council [*Australia*]
QAC .... Quick-Acting Choke [*Automotive engineering*]
QACAD .... Quality Assurance Corrective Action Document (NASA)
QACC .... Quality Assurance Coordination Committee (DMAA)
QACHL .... Centre de Documentation, Centre Hospitalier des Laurentides et Centre d'Accueil et de Readaptation des Hautes-Vallees, L'Annonciation, Quebec [*Library symbol National Library of Canada*] (BIB)
QACUE .... Quebec Association of Computer Users in Education [*Canada*] (EDAC)
Qad .... Qadmoniot [*Jerusalem*] (BJA)
QAD .... Quadriceps Active Displacement [*Sports medicine*]
QAD .... Quality Assessment Director (MEDA)
QAD .... Quality Assessment Division [*Higher Education Funding Council*] (AIE)
QAD .... Quality Assurance Data
QAD .... Quality Assurance Department (AD)
QAD .... Quality Assurance Directive
QAD .... Quality Assurance Directorate [*Materials*] [*British*]
QAD .... Quality Assurance Division [*Picatinny Arsenal*] [*Dover, NJ*]
QAD .... Quarter Amplitude Damped (ACII)
QAD .... Quick Attach-Detach [*Engine*]
qad .... Quick-Attach-Detach (AD)
QADC .... Queen's Aide-de-Camp [*Military British*]
QADI .... Quality Assurance Department Instruction (AD)
qadk .... Quick Attach-Detach-Kit (AD)
QADK .... Quick Attach-Detach Kit
QAD(MATS) .... Quality Assurance Directorate (Materials) [*British*]
QADS .... Quality Assurance Data Summary (AD)
QADS .... Quality Assurance Data System
QAE .... Quality Assurance Engineering
QAE .... Quality Assurance Evaluator [*Military*]
QAE .... Queen's Awards for Export [*British*]
QAES .... Quality Assurance and Expert Systems [*Computer science*]
QAET .... Quality Assurance Environment Testing [*Military*] (CAAL)
QAET .... Quality Assurance Evaluation Test (NG)
QAF .... Qatar Amiri Flight [*ICAO designator*] (FAAC)
QAF .... Quality Achievement Factor (RDA)
QAF .... Quality Adjustment Factor (DMAA)
qaf .... Quality-Assurance Firing (AD)
QAF .... Quality Assurance Function
QAFA .... Quality Assurance Field Activity
QAFCO .... Quatar Fertilizer Co. (AD)
QAFL .... Queensland Australian Football League (AD)
QAFM .... Quality Assurance Forms Guide Manual (SAA)
qafo .... Quality-Assurance Field Operation (AD)
QAFO .... Quality Assurance Field Operations
QAG .... Quaker Action Group (AD)
QAG .... Quality Assurance Group
QAG .... Queensland Art Gallery [*Australia*]
QAGA .... Queensland Amateur Gymnastic Association [*Australia*] (AD)
qagc .... Quiet Automatic Gain Control (AD)
QAGC .... Quiet Automatic Gain Control (IAA)
QAGTC .... Queensland Association for Gifted and Talented Children [*Australia*]
QAH .... Quick Airways Holland BV [*Netherlands ICAO designator*] (FAAC)
QAHA .... Queensland Allergy and Hyperactivity Association [*Australia*]
QAHD .... Centre de Documentation, Hotel-Dieu d'Arthabaska, Quebec [*Library symbol National Library of Canada*] (BIB)
Qahira .... El Qahira [*Cairo*] [*Egyptian Arabic*] (AD)
QAI .... Quality Assurance Index (MCD)
QAI .... Quality Assurance Inspection
QAI .... Quality Assurance Instruction (NRCH)
QAI .... Quality Assurance International
QAI .... Queen's Award to Industry [*British*] (AD)
QAIA .... Queen Alia International Airport [*Jordan*]
QAICG .... Quality Assurance Interface Coordination Group (AD)
QAID .... Queensland Association of Industries for the Disabled [*Australia*]
QAIL .... Quality Assurance Information Letter (MCD)
QAILS .... Queensland Association of Independent Legal Services [*Australia*]
QAIMNS .... Queen Alexandra's Imperial Military Nursing Service [*British*]
QAIMNSR .... Queen Alexandra's Imperial Military Nursing Service Reserve [*British military*] (DMA)
QAIP .... Quality Assurance Inspection Procedure
QAIRG .... Quality Assurance Installation Review Group [*Nuclear energy*] (NRCH)
QA + IS .... Quality Association and Inspection Service [*British*]
QAK .... Quick Attach Kit
qak .... Quick-Attach Kit (AD)
QAL .... Q Allowance List [*Aviation*] (DNAB)
QAL .... Quality Assurance Laboratory
QAL .... Quarterly Acceptance List (AFIT)
QAL .... Quarterly Accession List
QAL .... Quartz Aircraft Lamp
qal .... Quartz Aircraft Lamp (AD)
qal .... Quaternary Alluvium (AD)
QAL .... Quebec Airways Ltd. (MCD)
QAL .... Queensland Alumina Ltd. [*Australia*] (AD)
qal .... Quintal [*Hundred-weight*] [*French*] (AD)
QALAS .... Qualified Associate of the Land Agents' Society [*British*]
QALC .... College d'Alma, Lac St.-Jean, Quebec [*Library symbol National Library of Canada*] (NLC)
QALD .... Quality-Assurance Liaison Division (AD)
QALE .... Quality-Adjusted Life Expectancy [*Medicine*] (DMAA)
QALI .... Quality Assurance Letter of Instructions
QALL .... Quartz Aircraft Landing Lamp
qall .... Quartz Aircraft Landing Lamp (AD)
QALPACS .... Quality Patient Care Scale [*Medicine*] (DMAA)
QALTR .... Quality Assurance Laboratory Test Request (MCD)
QALY .... Quality-Adjusted Life Year (DMAA)
QALY's .... Quality Adjusted Life Years
QAM .... Quadrature Amplified Modulation (NITA)
qam .... Quadrature Amplitude Modulation (AD)
QAM .... Quadrature Amplitude Modulation

QAM............ Quality Assurance Manager
QAM............ Quality Assurance Manual
QAM............ Quality Assurance Monitor (HCT)
QAM............ Quality Assurance Monitor [*Medical records*] (DAVI)
QAM............ Quality Assurance Monitoring (DMAA)
QAM............ Quaque Aente Meridiem [*Every Morning*] [*Pharmacy*]
QAM............ Queensland Arts Movement [*Australia*]
QAM............ Queued Access Method [*Computer science*]
qam............ Queued Access Method (AD)
QAMDO......... Quadripartite Agreed Materiel Development Objective [*Military*]
QAMFNS...... Queen Alexandra's Military Family Nursing Service [*British military*] (DMA)
QAMIS......... Quality Assurance Management and Information System [*Environmental Protection Agency*] (GFGA)
QAMIS......... Quality Assurance Monitoring Information System (AD)
QAML........... Centre de Documentation, Musee Laurier, Arthabaska, Quebec [*Library symbol National Library of Canada*] (NLC)
QAMM.......... Quality Assurance Management Meeting [*DoD*]
QAMR.......... Quadripartite Agreed Materiel Requirement [*Military*]
QAMR.......... Quality Assurance Management Review [*DoD*]
QAMS.......... Quad-Phase Amplitude Modulation System (AD)
QAMS.......... Quality Assurance Management Staff [*Environmental Protection Agency*] (GFGA)
QAMS.......... Queensland Air Museum Society [*Australia*]
QAN............ Queensland Air Navigation Co. Ltd. [*Australia*] (ADA)
Q & A.......... Question and Answer (MSA)
Q and A....... Question and Answer (WDMC)
q & d.......... Quick and Dirty (AD)
Q & D.......... Quick and Dirty [*Computer science*]
Q & O.......... Quebec and Ontario [*Canada*] (AD)
Q & R.......... Quality and Reliability
Q & RA........ Quality and Reliability Assurance
Q & SL........ Qualifications and Standards Laboratory (WDAA)
q & t........... Quenched and Tempered (AD)
QANTAS....... Queensland & Northern Territory Aerial Service [*Later, QANTAS Airways Ltd.*] [*Australia*]
QAO............ Quality Assurance Office [*Navy*]
QAO............ Quality Assurance Officer [*Environmental Protection Agency*] (GFGA)
QAO............ Quality Assurance Operation
qao............ Quality Assurance Operation (AD)
QAO............ Quality Assurance Outline
QAO............ Queen's Awards Office [*British*]
QAOC.......... Quality Assurance Overview Contractor (AD)
QAOGR........ Queen Alexandra's Own Gurkha Rifles [*British military*] (DMA)
QAOP.......... Quality Assurance Operating Plan
QAOP.......... Quality Assurance Operating Procedure (AD)
QAP............ Quadratic Assignment Problem [*Mathematics*]
QAP............ Qualifications Appraisal Panel (OICC)
QAP............ Quality Assurance Package
QAP............ Quality Assurance Plan
QAP............ Quality Assurance Planning (AD)
QAP............ Quality Assurance Procedure
QAP............ Quality Assurance Professional (HCT)
QAP............ Quality Assurance Program [*Nuclear energy*]
QAP............ Quality Assurance Provision
QAP............ Quanah, Acme & Pacific Railway Co. [*AAR code*]
QAP............ Quinine, Atabrine, Plasmoquine [*Treatment for malaria*]
qap............ Quinine, Atebrin, Plasmoquine [*Medicine*] (AD)
QAPBS......... Queensland Association of Permanent Building Societies [*Australia*]
QAPED......... Quadripartite Agreed Plans of Engineering Design [*Military*]
QAPET......... Quadripartite Agreed Plans of Engineering Tests [*Military*]
QAPI........... Quality Assurance Program Index [*Nuclear energy*] (NRCH)
QAPL........... Queensland Airlines Party Ltd.
QAPL........... Queensland Airlines Proprietary Ltd. [*Australia*] (AD)
QAPP.......... Quality Assurance Program Plan [*Nuclear energy*] (NRCH)
QAPS.......... Queensland Association of Personnel Services [*Australia*] (AD)
QAPST......... Quadripartite Agreed Plans of Service Tests [*Military*]
QA/QC......... Quality Assurance / Quality Control (FFDE)
QAR............ Quality and Reliability (IAA)
QAR............ Quality Assurance Reagent [*Cardiology*] (DAVI)
QAR............ Quality Assurance Record
QAR............ Quality Assurance Report [*A publication*] (AD)
QAR............ Quality Assurance Representative
QAR............ Quality Assurance Requirements (NRCH)
QAR............ Quality Assurance Responsible/Witness (MCD)
QAR............ Quantitative Autoradiography [*Medicine*]
QAR............ Quasi-Adiabatic Representation
QAR............ Questionable Activity Report [*Employment and Training Administration*] [*Department of Labor*]
QAR............ Quick Access Recording
qar............ Quick-Access Recording (AD)
QARAFNS.... Queen Alexandra's Royal Air Force Nursing Service [*British*] (AD)
QARANC...... Queen Alexandra's Royal Army Nursing Corps [*British*]
QARANC...... Queen Alexandra's Royal Army Nursing Service [*British*] (AD)
QARC.......... Quality Assurance Record Center (MCD)
QARC.......... Quality Assurance Review Center [*National Cancer Institute*]
QARI........... Quality Assurance Receipt Inspection [*Military*] (DNAB)
QARM.......... Bibliotheque Municipale, Arthabaska, Quebec [*Library symbol National Library of Canada*] (NLC)
QA/RM......... Quality Assurance/Risk Management (MEDA)
QARNNS...... Queen Alexandra's Royal Navy Nursing Service [*British*]
QARNNSR.... Queen Alexandra's Royal Naval Nursing Service Reserve [*British military*] (DMA)
QAR-R......... Quality Assurance Record - Receiving (MCD)
QAR-T......... Quality Assurance Record - Tooling (MCD)
QART.......... Quality Assurance Review Technique (MHDB)
QAS............ Quality Answering System (AD)
QAS............ Quality Assurance Service [*Medicine*]
QAS............ Quality Assurance Specialist [*DoD*]
QAS............ Quality Assurance Standards [*Business*] (DAVI)
QAS............ Quality Assurance System (AD)
QAS............ Queensland Academy of Sport [*Australia*]
QAS............ Question-Answering System
qas............ Quick-Acting Scuttle (AD)
QAS............ Quick Action Shuttle
QAS............ Quisqueya Airlines SA [*Haiti*] [*ICAO designator*] (FAAC)
QASA.......... Queensland Amateur Swimming Association [*Australia*] (AD)
QASAC........ Quality Assurance Spacecraft Acceptance Center (MCD)
QASAG........ Experimental Farm, Agriculture Canada [*Ferme Experimentale, Agriculture Canada*] L'Assomption, Quebec [*Library symbol National Library of Canada*] (NLC)
QASAR........ Quality Assurance Systems Analysis Review (AD)
QASAS........ Quality Assurance Specialist, Ammunition Surveillance (MCD)
QASB.......... Bibliotheque Municipale, Asbestos, Quebec [*Library symbol National Library of Canada*] (NLC)
QASB.......... Queensland Ambulance Service Board [*Australia*]
QASC.......... Quadripartite Armaments Standardization Committee [*Military*] (AABC)
QASDM........ Quality Assurance, Sample, and Data Management
QASK.......... Quadrature Amplitude Shift Keying
QASL.......... Quality Assurance Systems List (IEEE)
QASP.......... Quality Assurance Standard Practice (MCD)
QASP.......... Quality Assurance Surveillance Plan (NITA)
QASPR........ QUALCOMM, Inc. Automatic Satellite Position Reporting
QASS.......... Queensland Academy of Space Sciences [*Australia*]
QAST.......... Quality Assurance Service [*or Serviceability*] Test [*Nuclear energy*] (NG)
QAT............ Aero Taxi [*Canada ICAO designator*] (FAAC)
Qat............ Qatabanian (BJA)
QAT............ Qatar [*ANSI three-letter standard code*] (CNC)
Qat............ Qatar (AD)
QAT............ Quaker Oats Co. [*Toronto Stock Exchange symbol*]
QAT............ Qualification Approval Test (NATG)
QAT............ Quality Action Team [*Industrial engineering*]
QAT............ Quality Assurance Team (MCD)
QAT............ Quality Assurance Technical [*Material*] (DAVI)
QAT............ Quantitative Assessment and Training Center (AD)
QATA.......... Queensland Art Teachers' Association [*Australia*]
QATB.......... Queensland Ambulance Transport Brigade [*Australia*] (AD)
QATIP......... Quality Assurance Test and Inspection Procedures (MCD)
QATP.......... Quality Assurance Technical Publications (AAG)
QATP.......... Quality Assurance Test Procedure (AD)
QATS.......... Quality Assurance and Test Service (IAA)
QATS.......... Quarterly Advanced Training Schedule [*Navy*] (DNAB)
QATT.......... Qualification for Acceptance Thermal Testing [*NASA*] (NASA)
QAU............ Quality Assurance Unit
QAUR.......... Quality Assurance and Utilization Review [*Medicine*] (DMAA)
QAVC.......... Quiet Automatic Voltage Control [*Electronics*] (ECII)
qavc........... Quiet Automatic Volume Control (AD)
QAVC.......... Quiet Automatic Volume Control
QAVP.......... Quality Assurance Verification Procedures [*Military*] (DNAB)
QAVT.......... Qualification Acceptance Vibration Test [*NASA*] (NASA)
QAW............ Quality at Work [*Quality Decision Management*] [*Computer science*] (PCM)
QAWA.......... Queensland Amateur Wrestling Association [*Australia*] (AD)
QAWT.......... Quick-Acting Water-Tight (DNAB)
QAY............ Bibliotheque Municipale, Aylmer, Quebec [*Library symbol National Library of Canada*] (NLC)
QB............. Bibliotheque Municipale, Brossard, Quebec [*Library symbol National Library of Canada*] (BIB)
qb............. Qualified Bidders (AD)
QB............. Qualified Buyer
QB............. Quantitative (Electrophysiological) Battery [*Cardiology*] (DAVI)
QB............. Quarterback [*Football*]
qb............. Quarterback (AD)
QB............. Quasi-Biennial
QB............. Quebecair, Inc. [*Airlines*] [*ICAO designator*] (OAG)
QB............. Queen's Bays [*Later, QDG*] [*Military unit*] [*British*]
QB............. Queen's Bench [*Legal*] [*British*]
QB............. Queen's Bench Reports, by Adolphus and Ellis, New Series [*A publication*] (DLA)
QB............. Queen's Bishop [*Chess*]
QB............. Queensboro Bridge [*New York City*] (AD)
QB............. Queensland Ballet [*Australia*]
QB............. Query Buffer [*Computer science*] (IAA)
QB............. Quick Batch (MHDI)
QB............. Quick Break (MSA)
qb............. Quick Break (AD)
QB............. Quickbrew [*Brand of tea*] [*British*]
QB............. Quiet Birdmen [*An association*] (EA)
Qb............. Total Body Clearance (MAE)
QB............. Whole Blood [*Hematology*] (DAVI)
QBA............ Quality Bakers of America Cooperative (EA)
QBA............ Quality Brands Associates of America [*Defunct*] (EA)
QBA............ Quantitative Budget Analysis (MCD)
QBA............ Quebecair (AD)
QBA............ Quebecair, Inc. [*Airlines*]
QBA............ Queensland Band Association [*Australia*]
QBA............ Queensland Beekeepers' Association [*Australia*]
QBA............ Queensland Bowling Association [*Australia*] (AD)

QBA Queensland Bridge Association [*Australia*]
QBAA Quality Brands Associates of America (AD)
QBAA Quality Brands Associates of America (NADA)
QBAC Quality Bakers of America Cooperative (EA)
QBAL Jillians Entertainment [*NASDAQ symbol*] (TTSB)
QBAL Jillians Entertainment Corp. [*NASDAQ symbol*] (SAG)
QBAN Qui Bixit Annos [*Who Lived ____ Years*] [*Latin*]
QBB Queen's Bad Bargain [*Undesirable serviceman*] [*Slang British*] (DSUE)
QBB Queensland Barristers' Board [*Australia*]
QBB Queensland Butter Board [*Australia*] (AD)
QBC Bella Coola [*Canada*] [*Airport symbol*] (OAG)
QBC Quality Buffy Coat [*Hematology*] (DAVI)
QBC Quantitative Buffy Coat [*Hematology*] (DAVI)
QBC Quebec [*Canada*] (WDAA)
Qbc Quebec (AD)
QBCA Quantitative Buffy-Coat Analysis (MEDA)
QBCCL Centre de Documentation, CLSC de l'Aquilon, Baie-Comeau, Quebec [*Library symbol National Library of Canada*] (BIB)
QBCH Centre de Documentation, Pavillon St.-Joseph, Centre Hospitalier Regional de Beauceville, Quebec [*Library symbol National Library of Canada*] (BIB)
QBCHS Queensland Bush Children's Health Scheme [*Australia*]
QBD Quasi-Bidirectional (MHDI)
QBD Quasi Birth and Death [*Statistics*]
QBD Queen's Bench Division [*Military unit*] [*British*]
QBD Queen's Bench Division, Law Reports [*A publication*]
QBD Queensland Book Depot [*Australia*] (AD)
QBDA Quebrada
QB Div English Law Reports, Queen's Bench Division [*1865-75*] [*A publication*] (DLA)
QBE Beaconsfield Public Library, Quebec [*Library symbol National Library of Canada*] (NLC)
QBE Query by Example [*Data processing search method*]
QBEAU Bibliotheque Municipale, Beauport, Quebec [*Library symbol National Library of Canada*] (BIB)
QBEC Bibliotheque Municipale, Becancour, Quebec [*Library symbol National Library of Canada*] (NLC)
QBEC Quebec Building Envelope Council (AC)
QBEHBI H. Bergstrom International Ltd., Beaconsfield, Quebec [*Library symbol National Library of Canada*] (NLC)
QBES Queensland Bureau of Emergency Services [*Australia*]
QBF Query-by-Forms [*Data processing search method*]
QBFJOTF [*The*] Quick Brown Fox Jumped over the Fence [*Typing exercise*]
QBFJOTLD [*The*] Quick Brown Fox Jumped over the Lazy Dogs [*Typing exercise*]
QBFP Queensland Boating and Fisheries Patrol [*Australia*]
QBG Qualified Binary Grouping [*Computer science*] (IAA)
QBG Queensland Bookbinders' Guild [*Australia*]
QBI Queen's Bureau of Investigation [*British*] (AD)
qbi Quite Bloody Impossible [*Slang*] (AD)
QBI Quite Bloody Impossible [*British slang, applied particularly to flying conditions*]
QBIC Query by Image Content [*Computer science*]
QBID Queensland Business and Industry Directory [*Australia A publication*]
QBIR Quarterly Printing Industry Business Indicator Report [*A publication*] (EAAP)
QBJ Juniorat des Freres du Sacre-Coeur, Bramptonville, Quebec [*Library symbol National Library of Canada*] (NLC)
QBL Qualified Bidders List
QBL Queensland Baseball League [*Australia*]
QBLC Queen's Bench Reports, Lower Canada [*A publication*] (DLA)
QBMS Mitel Semiconductor, Bromont, Quebec [*Library symbol National Library of Canada*] (NLC)
QBNA Queensland Bush Nursing Association [*Australia*]
QBO Bibliotheque Municipale, Boucherville, Quebec [*Library symbol National Library of Canada*] (NLC)
QBO Mail Advertising Service Association International. Quarterly Business Outlook [*A publication*]
QBO Quarterly Business Outlook [*A publication*] (EAAP)
QBO Quasi-Biennial Oscillation [*Earth science*]
QBO Quasi-Biennial Oscillation [*Marine science*] (OSRA)
QBOA Quebec Bus Owners Association (AC)
qbop Quality Basic-Oxygen Process (AD)
Q-BOP Quick Basic Oxygen Process [*Steelmaking*]
QBP Queen's Bishop's Pawn [*Chess*] (IIA)
QBPL Queens Borough Public Library [*New York, NY*]
QBR Quebecor, Inc. [*Toronto Stock Exchange symbol*]
QBR Queen's Bench Reports [*Legal*] [*British*]
QBR Queen's Bench Reports, by Adolphus and Ellis, New Series [*A publication*] (DLA)
QBRA ACS Biblio-information, Inc., Brossard, Quebec [*Library symbol National Library of Canada*] (BIB)
QBRG Centre Hospitalier Robert Giffard, Beauport, Quebec [*Library symbol National Library of Canada*] (NLC)
QBRs Queen's Bench Reports [*A publication*] (AD)
QBS Qualifications-Based Selection [*Metallurgy*]
QBSA Centre Hospitalier St.-Augustin, Beauport, Quebec [*Library symbol National Library of Canada*] (BIB)
QBSA Queensland Blinded Soldiers' Association [*Australia*]
QBSM Que Besa su Mano [*Who Kisses Your Hand*] [*Spanish*] (AD)
QBSM Que Besa Sus Manos [*Kissing Your Hands*] [*Spanish*]
QBSP Que Besa sus Pies [*Who Kisses Your Feet*] [*Spanish*] (AD)
QBSPH Centre Hospitalier de Charlevoix, Baie St.-Paul, Quebec [*Library symbol National Library of Canada*] (BIB)
QBT Quad Bus Transceiver (NITA)
qBtu Quadrillion British Thermal Units (GNE)
QBU Bibliotheque Municipale, Buckingham, Quebec [*Library symbol National Library of Canada*] (NLC)
QBUC Queen's Bench Reports, Upper Canada [*A publication*] (DLA)
Q Bull Natn Counc Women Aust ... National Council of Women of Australia. Quarterly Bulletin [*A publication*]
QBV Whole Blood Volume [*Hematology*] (DAVI)
QBWA Queensland Braille Writing Association [*Australia*]
QBWUE Queensland Blind Workers Union of Employees [*Australia*]
QBX Quick-BASIC [*Beginner's All-Purpose Symbolic Instruction Code*] Extended [*Computer science*] (PCM)
QC Air Zaire SA [*Zaire*] [*ICAO designator*] (ICDA)
QC Bibliotheque Municipale, Cowansville, Quebec [*Library symbol National Library of Canada*] (BIB)
Qc Capillary Blood Volume (DAVI)
QC Impact Pressure [*Symbol*] (WDAA)
Qc Pulmonary Capillary Blood Flow [*Medicine*] (DAVI)
QC QC Explorations [*Vancouver Stock Exchange symbol*]
QC Quad Center [*Typography*]
qc Quad Column [*Typesetting*] (WDMC)
QC Quad Crown [*Paper*] (DGA)
QC Quadrantal Correction (AD)
qc Qualcosa [*Something*] [*Italian*] (AD)
qc Qualification Course (AD)
QC Qualification Course
QC Qualifying Certificate
QC Quality Certificate
QC Quality Circle [*Labor-management team organized to increase industrial productivity*]
QC Quality Control [*or Controller*]
qc Quality Control (AD)
qc Quality Control (WDMC)
QC Quantek Corp. [*Trademark*]
QC Quantitative Chemiluminescence
QC Quantitative Command
qc Quantitative Command (AD)
QC Quantum Cascade [*LASER*] (ECON)
QC Quantum Computer [*Physics*]
qc Quantum Counter (AD)
QC Quantum Counter
QC Quarterly Credit
QC Quartermaster Corps [*Army*] (WGA)
QC Quarter of Coverage [*Social Security Administration*] (OICC)
QC Quarters of Coverage [*Social Security Administration*] (GFGA)
QC Quartz Crystal
qc Quartz Crystal (AD)
QC Quasi-Contract [*Business term*]
QC Quaternary Carrier [*Biochemistry*]
QC Quebec Central Railway Co. [*AAR code*]
QC Quebec City (AD)
QC Queen Consort [*British*] (ROG)
QC Queen's College [*Oxford and Cambridge Universities*] (ROG)
QC Queen's Counsel [*British*]
QC Quench Correction
QC Queue Control (NITA)
QC Quezon City (AD)
q/c Quick Change (AD)
QC Quick Change (IAA)
QC Quickchange [*Aviation*]
QC Quick Charge [*Airplane*] (IIA)
QC Quick Cleaning (MSA)
QC Quick Code (NITA)
qc Quick Connect (AD)
QC Quick Connect
QC Quick Curl [*Refers to Barbie doll hair*] [*Doll collecting*]
QC Quiesce-Completed [*Computer science*] (IBMDP)
QC Quiescent Center [*Plant root growth*]
QC Quincy College (AD)
QC Quinine-Colchicine [*Medicine*] (MAE)
QC Quinnipiac College (AD)
qc Quit Claim (AD)
QC Quit Claim (WDAA)
QC Quitclaim [*Legal term*] (BARN)
QC Quixote Center (EA)
QCA Bibliotheque Municipale, Candiac, Quebec [*Library symbol National Library of Canada*] (BIB)
QCA Quality Control Analysis
QCA Quantitative Coronary Angiography [*Cardiology*] (DAVI)
QCA Quantum-Dot Cellular Automata [*Microelectronics*]
QCA Quarterly Compilation of Abstracts [*A publication*]
QCA Queen Charlotte Airlines Ltd.
QCA Queensland Coal Associates [*Australia*] (AD)
QCA Queensland Coal Association [*Australia*]
QCA Queensland Colonial Association [*Australia*]
QCA Queensland Colostomy Association [*Australia*]
QCA Queensland Cricket Association [*Australia*] (AD)
QCA Queensland Croquet Association (AD)
QCA Quiet Communities Act (GFGA)
Q-cab Quiet Cab (AD)
QCAG Ministere de l'Agriculture, des Pecheries et de l'Alimentation, Chateauguay, Quebec [*Library symbol National Library of Canada*] (NLC)
QCAI Quality Conformance Acceptance Inspection (MCD)

QCAL Centre de Documentation, Centre Hospitalier Anna-Laberge, Chateauguay, Quebec [*Library symbol National Library of Canada*] (BIB)
QC & R Quality Control and Reliability (AD)
QC & T Quality Control and Techniques (SAA)
QC & T Quality Control and Test (AD)
Q CAP Quad Foolscap [*Paper*] (DGA)
QCAR Queensland Criminal Reports [*A publication*]
Q-card Qualification Card (AD)
QCAS Queensland Chamber of Agricultural Societies [*Australia*]
QCAT Quality Control and Techniques (IAA)
QCB Bibliotheque Municipale, Coaticook, Quebec [*Library symbol National Library of Canada*] (NLC)
QCB Quality Control Board (MCD)
QCB Quality Control Branch
QCB Quality Control Bulletin (AD)
QCB Queensland Coal Board [*Australia*]
QCB Queue Control Block [*Computer science*]
qcb Queue Control Block [*Data processing*] (AD)
QCBC Quaker City Bancorp [*NASDAQ symbol*] (SAG)
QCBC Queen's Commendation for Brave Conduct [*British*] (AD)
QCBC Quick Change Boost Control [*Automotive engineering*]
qcbm Quick-Connects Bulkhead Mounting (AD)
QCC Bibliotheque Gaspesienne, Cap-Chat, Quebec [*Library symbol National Library of Canada*] (NLC)
QCC Qualification Correlation Certification
qcc Qualification Correlation Certification (AD)
QCC Quality Communications Circle (MCD)
QCC Quality Control Centre (NITA)
QCC Quality Control Chain (IAA)
QCC Quality Control Committee (MCD)
QCC Queen Charlotte [*British Columbia*] [*Seismograph station code, US Geological Survey*] (SEIS)
QCC Queensland Conservation Council [*Australia*] (AD)
QCC Queensland Cotton Corp. [*Australia*]
QCC Quenched Carbonaceous Composite [*Plasma technology*]
QCC Quick Connect Coupling
qcc Quick-Connect Coupling (AD)
QCC Quinsigamond Community College [*Worchester, MA*]
QCC Qwest Commuter Corp. [*ICAO designator*] (FAAC)
QCCA Quality Control Council of America [*Defunct*] (EA)
QCCA Queensland Cleaning Contractors Association [*Australia*] (AD)
QCCARS Quality Control Collection Analysis and Reporting System
QCCB Queen's College Cadet Battalion [*Taunton*] [*British military*] (DMA)
QCCL CLSC Albert Samson, Coaticook, Quebec [*Library symbol National Library of Canada*] (NLC)
QCCR Quality Control Change Request (SAA)
QCCRS Conseil Regional de la Sante et des Services Sociaux, Chicoutimi, Quebec [*Library symbol National Library of Canada*] (NLC)
QCCS Cree School Board, Chisasibi, James Bay, Quebec [*Library symbol National Library of Canada*] (BIB)
QCCT Queensland Cultural Centre Trust [*Australia*]
QCD Quality Control Data
qcd Quality-Control Data (AD)
QCD Quality Control Directive (MCD)
QCD Quantum Chromodynamics [*Nuclear physics*]
qcd Quantum Chromodynamics (AD)
QCD Quantum Chromodynamics [*Laboratory science*] (DAVI)
QCD Query Complexity Degree (MHDB)
QCD Quick Claim Deed (MHDB)
QCD Quick Control Dial [*Photography*]
qcd Quit-Claim Deed (AD)
QCDI Quality Control Departmental Instruction (AD)
QCDP Quality Color Dithering Process [*Computer science*] (PCM)
QCDPA Quality Chekd Dairy Products Association (EA)
QCDR Quality Control Deficiency Report (AFM)
QCDSU Quality Control Directive Supplement (SAA)
QCE Quality Control and Evaluation (MCD)
QCE Quality Control Engineering (AD)
QCE Quality Control Engineers
QCEA Quaker Council for European Affairs (EA)
QCENGR Quality Control Engineer (IAA)
QCEU Queensland Colliery Employees Union [*Australia*] (AD)
QCF Quality Control [*Tabulating*] Form (AAG)
QCF Quarterly Control Contract Factor (MCD)
QCF Quartz Crystal Filter
qcf Quartz-Crystal Filter (AD)
QCF Queensland Cancer Fund [*Australia*]
QCF Quench Compensation Factor
QCFB QCF Bancorp [*NASDAQ symbol*] (TTSB)
QCFB QCF Bancorp, Inc. [*NASDAQ symbol*] (SAG)
QCF Bc QCF Bancorp, Inc. [*Associated Press*] (SAG)
QCFCLB Queensland Council of Finance Counsellors and Lease Brokers [*Australia*]
QCFO Quartz Crystal Frequency Oscillator
qcfo Quartz-Crystal Frequency Oscillator (AD)
QCG Quartz Creek Gold Mines (BC), Inc. [*Vancouver Stock Exchange symbol*]
QCGA Queensland Cane Growers' Association [*Australia*]
QCGAT Quiet, Clean, General Aviation Turbofan [*NASA*]
QCGC Queensland Cane-Growers Council [*Australia*] (AD)
QCH Hopital de Chicoutimi, Inc., Quebec [*Library symbol National Library of Canada*] (NLC)
QCH Quick Connect Handle
qch Quick-Connect Handle (AD)
QCHI Quad City Hldgs [*NASDAQ symbol*] (TTSB)
QCHI Quad City Holdings [*NASDAQ symbol*] (SAG)
QCHJC Health Sciences Information Centre, Jewish Rehabilitation Hospital [*Centre d'Information sur les Sciences de la Sante, Hopital Juif de Readaptation*] Chomedey, Quebec [*Library symbol National Library of Canada*] (NLC)
QCHM Quaker Chemical [*NASDAQ symbol*] (TTSB)
QCHM Quaker Chemical Corp. [*NASDAQ symbol*] (NQ)
QCHR Quality Control History Record
QCI Quality Conformance Inspection (MSA)
QCI Quality Control Index [*Environmental Protection Agency*] (GFGA)
QCI Quality Control Information (AABC)
qci Quality-Control Information (AD)
QCI Quality Control Inspection
QCI Quarto Castello [*Italy*] [*Seismograph station code, US Geological Survey Closed*] (SEIS)
QCI Queen's College, Ireland (ROG)
QCI Queensland Confederation of Industry [*Australia*] (AD)
QCI Quota Club International [*Later, QI*]
Q Cic Quintus Tullius Cicero (AD)
QCID Quality Control and Inspection Department [*Navy*] (DNAB)
QCIE Quality Control Inspection Element (AFIT)
QCIM Quarterly Cumulative Index Medicus [*A publication*]
QCIP Quality Control Inspection Procedure [*Nuclear energy*] (NRCH)
QCIR Queen's University at Kingston Centre for International Relations [*Canada Research center*] (RCD)
QCI's Queen Charlotte Islands
QC Isl Queen Charlotte Islands (AD)
Q City Quezon City [*Philippines*] (AD)
QCJC Queensland Criminal Justice Commission [*Australia*]
QCJJ Quaker Committee on Jails and Justice [*Canada*]
QCK Quick
qck Quick-Connect Kit (AD)
QCK Quick Connect Kit
QCL Logilab, Inc., Charlebois, Quebec [*Library symbol National Library of Canada*] (NLC)
QCL Quality Characteristics List (MSA)
QCL Quality Checklist
QCL Quality Control Level
qcl Quality-Control Level (AD)
QCLPC National Historic Park, Parks Canada [*Parc Historique National, Parcs Canada*] Coteau-du-Lac, Quebec [*Library symbol National Library of Canada*] (NLC)
QCM Bibliotheque Municipale, Chateauguay, Quebec [*Library symbol National Library of Canada*] (BIB)
QCM Quality Construction Master
QCM Quality Control Manager
QCM Quality Control Manual
QCM Quality Courts Motels [*Later, QM*]
QCM Quality of Care Measurement [*Insurance*] (WYGK)
QCM Quantitative Computer Management (IEEE)
QCM Quantum Conformal Fluctuation [*Theoretical physics*]
QCM Quartz Crystal Microbalance
QCM Quartz Crystal Monitor
QCM Queensland Chamber of Mines [*Australia*]
QCM Queensland Coal Mining [*Australia*] (AD)
QCM Quick-Connects for Bulkhead Mounting (PDAA)
QCMA Queensland Cooperative Milling Association [*Australia*] (AD)
QCMB Centre de Documentation, Musee Beaulne, Coaticook, Quebec [*Library symbol National Library of Canada*] (NLC)
QCMC Queensland Chicken Meat Council [*Australia*]
QCMM Bibliotheque Municipale, Cap-De-La-Madeleine, Quebec [*Library symbol National Library of Canada*] (NLC)
QCMP Queens' Council Member of Parliament [*British*] (AD)
QCMPE Quantum Chemistry Microcomputer Program Exchange
QCNIC Quad-Cities Nuclear Information Center (AD)
QCO Quality Completion Order (AD)
QCO Quality Control Officer (AAG)
QCO Quality Control Organization
QCO Quantity at Captain's Option [*Shipping*] (DS)
QCO Quartz Crystal Oscillator
qco Quartz-Crystal Oscillator (AD)
Q Co Queens County (AD)
QCO Quick Changeover [*Manufacturing*]
QCO_2 Microliters of Carbon Dioxide Given Off per Milligram of Tissue per Hour [*Medicine*] (DAVI)
QCOI Queensland Chamber of Industry [*Australia*]
QCOM Qualcomm, Inc. [*NASDAQ symbol*] (SPSG)
Q Conv R Queensland Conveyancing Cases [*Australia A publication*]
QCOP Quality Control Operating Procedure
QC Opt QC Optics [*Associated Press*] (SAG)
QCOTA Queensland Council on the Ageing [*Australia*]
QCP Quality Check Program [*DoD*]
QCP Quality Continuation Plan [*BMW manufacturer's warranty*]
QCP Quality Control Procedure
QCP Queens College Press [*Australia*] (AD)
QCP Quezon City [*Philippines*] [*Seismograph station code, US Geological Survey*] (SEIS)
QCP Quiet Community Program [*Environmental Protection Agency*] (GFGA)
QCPA Queensland Country Press Association [*Australia*]
QCPC Quality Control Property Clearance (SAA)
QC-PCR Quantitative Competitive Polymerase Chain Reaction [*Analytical biochemistry*]
QC-PCR Quantitative Competive Polymerase Chain Reaction [*Genetics*]

QCPE .... Quantum Chemistry Program Exchange
QCPI .... Queen's College of Physicians, Ireland (ROG)
QCPLL .... Quadrature Channel Phase-Locked Loop (IAA)
QCPM .... Quality Control Procedures Manual (SAA)
QCPMS .... Quality Control and Performance Monitoring System (MCD)
QCPP .... Quality Control Planning Procedure (IAA)
QC/PS .... Impact/Static Pressure Ratio (WDAA)
QCPSA .... Quaker Center for Prisoner Support Activities (EA)
QCPSK .... Quaternary Coherent Phase-Shift Keying
QCQ .... Quebec [*Quebec*] [*Seismograph station code, US Geological Survey*] (SEIS)
QCR .... Qualitative Construction Requirement [*Army*]
QCR .... Quality Control/Reliability
QC/R .... Quality Control/Reliability (AD)
qcr .... Quality Control/Reliability (AD)
QCR .... Quality Control Report
QCR .... Quality Control Representative [*Military*] (AABC)
QCR .... Quality Control Review
QCR .... Quality Control Room
QCR .... Quick Change Response [*System*]
qcr .... Quick-Change Response (AD)
QCR .... Quick Connect Relay
QCRC .... Quebec Central Railway Co. [*Canada*] (AD)
QCRCN .... Campus Notre-Dame-De-Foy, Cap-Rouge, Quebec [*Library symbol National Library of Canada*] (NLC)
QC Rep .... Quality-Control Representative (AD)
QC Rept .... Quality-Control Report (AD)
QCRF .... Queensland Children's Research Foundation [*Australia*]
QCRI .... Quality Control Reliability Investigator (SAA)
QCRM .... Bibliotheque Municipale, Cap-Rouge, Quebec [*Library symbol National Library of Canada*] (BIB)
QCRS .... Quality Control Reference [*Analytical chemistry*]
QCRS .... Seminaire St-Augustin, Cap-Rouge, Quebec [*Library symbol National Library of Canada*] (NLC)
QCRT .... Quick Change Real-Time (MHDI)
qcrt .... Quick-Change Real Time (AD)
QC Ry .... Quebec Central Railway [*Canada*] (AD)
QCS .... Quad-Cities Station [*Nuclear energy*] (NRCH)
QCS .... Quality Control Standard (AAG)
QCS .... Quality Control Survey (SAA)
QCS .... Quality Control System
QCS .... Quality Cost System
QCS .... Query Control Station (MCD)
QCS .... Service de la Bibliotheque de Ville de Laval, Chomedey, Quebec [*Library symbol National Library of Canada*] (BIB)
QCSB .... Queens County Bancorp [*NASDAQ symbol*] (SAG)
QCSC .... Quadripartite Chemical, Biological, Radiological Standardization Committee [*Military*] (AABC)
QCSEE .... Quiet, Clean, Short-Haul Experimental Engine [*NASA*]
QCSEL .... Quality Control Select Vendor (MCD)
QCSH .... Societe Historique du Saguenay, Chicoutimi, Quebec [*Library symbol National Library of Canada*] (NLC)
QCSHEE .... Quiet, Clean, Short-Haul Experimental Engine (DICI)
QCSM .... Quiescent Command/Service Module (MCD)
QCSO .... Quality Control Stop Order (AD)
QCSR .... Quaker Committee on Social Rehabilitation (AD)
QCSR .... Quaker Committee on Social Rehabilitation (NADA)
QCSR .... Quality Control Service Request (SAA)
QCSSO .... Queensland Council of State School Organisations [*Australia*]
QCSSP .... Quality Control Single Source Procurement (MCD)
QC Stand .... Quality-Control Standard (AD)
QCSTL .... Cote St. Luc Public Library, Quebec [*Library symbol National Library of Canada*] (NLC)
QCT .... Quality Control Technology (WDAA)
QCT .... Quantitative Computerized Tomography [*Biomedical engineering*]
QCT .... Quasiclassical Trajectory [*Chemical physics*]
QCT .... Quasi Classical Trajetory [*Physical chemistry*]
qct .... Questionable Corrective Task (AD)
QCT .... Questionable Corrective Task
QCT .... Quiescent Carrier Telephony (WDAA)
qct .... Quiescent Carrier Telephony (AD)
QCTE .... Quality Control Test Engineering (SAA)
QCTR .... Quality Control Test Report
QCTT .... Quality Control Test Team [*Military*]
QCU .... Quality Courts United [*Later, QM*] (EA)
QCU .... Quartz Crystal Unit
qcu .... Quartz Crystal Unit (AD)
qcu .... Quick-Change Unit (AD)
QCU .... Quick Change Unit (MCD)
QCU .... Universite du Quebec, Chicoutimi, Quebec [*Library symbol National Library of Canada*] (NLC)
QCUG .... Departement de Geographie, Universite du Quebec, Chicoutimi, Quebec [*Library symbol National Library of Canada*] (NLC)
QCUGC .... Cartotheque, Universite du Quebec, Chicoutimi, Quebec [*Library symbol National Library of Canada*] (NLC)
QCUS .... Quartz Crystal Unit Set
qcus .... Quartz Crystal Unit Set (AD)
qcvc .... Quick-Connect Valve Coupler (AD)
QCVC .... Quick Connect Valve Coupler
QCVTI .... Quality Control Verification Test Inspection (SAA)
QCW .... Q-Phase CW Signal [*Television*] (IDOE)
qcw .... Quadrant Continuous Wave (AD)
QCW .... Quadrant Continuous Wave
QCW .... Quality Criteria for Water (EG)
QCWA .... Quarter Century Wireless Association (EA)
QCWA .... Queensland Country Women's Association [*Australia*] (AD)
Qcy .... Quincy (AD)
QCYC .... Queensland Cruising Yacht Club [*Australia*]
QD .... Bibliotheque Municipale, Dorval, Quebec [*Library symbol National Library of Canada*] (BIB)
QD .... QData Systems, Inc. [*Vancouver Stock Exchange symbol*]
QD .... Quad Demy [*Paper*] (DGA)
QD .... Quaestiones Disputatae (BJA)
QD .... Quantity Distance [*Explosives*]
QD .... Quantum Design, Inc.
QD .... Quantum Dot [*Solid state physics*]
QD .... Quaque Die [*Every Day*] [*Pharmacy*]
QD .... Quarterdeck
qd .... Quarterdeck (AD)
QD .... Quarter Distribution [*Parapsychology*]
QD .... Quartile Deviation [*Statistics*]
qd .... Quartile Deviation (AD)
QD .... Quasi Dicat [*As If One Should Say, or As Though One Should Say*] [*Latin*]
QD .... Quasi Dictum [*As If Said, or As Though It Had Been Said*] [*Latin*]
QD .... Quasi Dixisset [*As If One Had Said*] [*Latin*]
QD .... Quater in Die [*Four Times a Day*] [*Pharmacy*]
qd .... Quater in Die [*Four Times a Day*] [*Latin*] (AD)
qd .... Questioned Document (AD)
QD .... Questioned Document [*Criminology*]
QD .... Quick Delivery (WDAA)
qd .... Quick Delivery (AD)
qd .... Quick Detachable [*Weapon*] (AD)
q-d .... Quick-Disconnect (AD)
QD .... Quick Disconnect
QD .... Quicksilver Data [*Information service or system*] (IID)
QD .... Transbrasil SA Linhas Aereas [*Brazil ICAO designator*] (ICDA)
QDA .... Quadratic Discriminant Analysis [*Mathematics*]
QDA .... Qualifying Dividend Account
QDA .... Quantitative Descriptive Analysis
QDA .... Quantity Discount Agreement
qda .... Quantity Discount Agreement (AD)
Q-DBS .... Quasi-Direct Broadcast Satellite
QDC .... Quick Dependable Communications
qdc .... Quick Detachable Communication (AD)
QDC .... Quick Die Change [*Automotive engineering*]
QDC .... Quick Disconnect Cap
qdc .... Quick-Disconnect Cap (AD)
QDC .... Quick Disconnect Connector
QDC & E .... Quartz Devices Conference and Exhibition
qdcc .... Quick-Disconnect Circular Connection (AD)
QDCC .... Quick Disconnect Circular Connector
QDCE .... College Bourgchemin (CEGEP), Drummondville, Quebec [*Library symbol National Library of Canada*] (NLC)
qdd .... Qualified for Deep Diving (AD)
QDD .... Qualified for Deep Diving Duties [*Navy British*]
QDD .... Quantized Decision Detection
qdd .... Quantized Decision Detection (AD)
QDE .... Etablissement Donnacona, Quebec [*Library symbol National Library of Canada*] (BIB)
QDE .... Qualified Designated Entities [*Independent counseling groups and churches involved with aiding aliens*] [*Immigration and Naturalization Service term*]
QDE .... Quality Data Evaluation (MCD)
QDEAS .... Quality Deficiency Evaluation and Action System (MCD)
QDEBUG .... Quick Diagnostic Debugging Program [*Computer science*] (MHDI)
QDEC .... Queensland Development Education Centre [*Australia*]
QDEC .... Queensland Distance Education College [*Australia*]
QDEK .... Quarterdeck Corp. [*NASDAQ symbol*] (TTSB)
QDEK .... Quarterdeck Corp. [*NASDAQ symbol*] (SAG)
QDEK .... Quarterdeck Office Systems [*NASDAQ symbol*] (SPSG)
QDEL .... Quidel Corp. [*NASDAQ symbol*] (SPSG)
QDELW .... Quidel Corp. Wrrt [*NASDAQ symbol*] (TTSB)
QDF .... Quantum Distribution Function
QDF .... Queensland Department of Forestry [*Australia*]
QDG .... Queen's Dragoon Guards [*Formerly, KDG, QB*] [*Military unit*] [*British*]
QD/GD .... Quincy Division/General Dynamics (AD)
Qd Govt Mining J ... Queensland Government Mining Journal [*A publication*]
Qd Graingrower ... Queensland Graingrower [*A publication*]
QDGS .... Quick-Draw Graphics System (PDAA)
QDH .... Quick Disconnect Handle
qdh .... Quick-Disconnect Handle (AD)
QDHSC .... Hopital Sainte-Croix, Drummondville, Quebec [*Library symbol National Library of Canada*] (NLC)
QDIN .... Quality Dining [*NASDAQ symbol*] (TTSB)
QDIN .... Quality Dining, Inc. [*NASDAQ symbol*] (SAG)
Qd Ind .... Queensland Industry [*A publication*]
QDISC .... Quick Disconnect
QDK .... Quick Disconnect Kit
qdk .... Quick-Disconnect Kit (AD)
Qd L .... Queensland Lawyer [*Australia A publication*]
QDL .... Quick Disconnect, Large
Qd Law Soc J ... Queensland Law Society. Journal [*A publication*]
QDM .... Centre d'Information Documentaire Come-Saint-Germain, Drummondville, Quebec [*Library symbol National Library of Canada*] (NLC)
QDM .... Quad Driver Module [*Electronics*]
QDM .... Quick Disconnect, Miniature
QDMA .... Quality Deer Management Association
QDMBPT .... Quasi-Degenerate Many-Body Perturbation Theory [*Physics*]

QDMC Quadratic Dynamic Matrix Control
QDMC Quadratic Matrix Control [*Chemical engineering*] [*Computer science*]
QDN Quick Disconnect Nipple
qdn Quick-Disconnect Nipple (AD)
qdo Quadripartite Development Objective (AD)
QDO Quadripartite Development Objective [*Military*] (AABC)
Qd'O Quai d'Orsay (AD)
QDO Quantitative Design Objective
QDO Queensland Dairyfarmers' Organisation [*Australia*]
QDO Queensland Dairymens Organisation [*Australia*] (AD)
QDO Quick Delivery Order
QDOF Queensland Department of Forests [*Australia*]
QDOPH Office des Personnes Handicapees du Quebec, Drummondville, Quebec [*Library symbol National Library of Canada*] (NLC)
QDOS Quick and Dirty Operating System [*Microsoft Corp.*] (ECON)
QDP Quick Disconnect Pivot
qdp Quick-Disconnect Pivot (AD)
Qd Police J Queensland Police Journal [*A publication*]
QDPR Quinoid Dehydropteridine Reductase [*An enzyme*] (DAVI)
QDPSK Quaternary Differential Phase-Shift Keying (TEL)
QDR Dubai Riyal [*Monetary unit*]
QDR Quadrennial Defense Review [*Army*]
QDR Qualification Design Review [*NASA*] (MCD)
QDR Quality Data and Reporting (MCD)
QDR Quality Deficiency Record [*DoD*]
QDR Quality Deficiency Report [*DoD*]
QDR Quick Disk Reformatter [*Vernon Buerg*] [*Computer utility tool*] (PCM)
Qdrax Quadrax Corp. [*Associated Press*] (SAG)
QDRI Qualitative Development Requirement Information
QDRL Questionnaire Design Research Laboratory [*Department of Health and Human Services*] (GFGA)
QDRM Banca Quadrum SA [*NASDAQ symbol*] (SAG)
QDRMY Banca QuadruADS [*NASDAQ symbol*] (TTSB)
QDRNT Quadrant (MSA)
qdrnt Quadrant (AD)
QDRO Qualified Domestic Relations Order [*Court authorization for retirement distribution*]
QDRT Quadrant
QDRTR Quadrature
QDRX Quadrax Corp. [*NASDAQ symbol*] (NQ)
QDRXZ Quadrax Corp. Wrrt 'C' [*NASDAQ symbol*] (TTSB)
QDS Quality Data System (NASA)
QDS Quantitative Decision System (AD)
QDS Quarantine Document System [*Information retrieval*] [*NASA*]
QDS Quarter Die Sumendum [*To be taken four times a day*] [*Latin*] [*Pharmacy*] (DAVI)
QDS Quick Disconnect Series
qds Quick-Disconnect Series (AD)
QDS Quick Disconnect, Small
QDS Quick Disconnect Swivel
qds Quick-Disconnect Swivel (AD)
QDSB Quadrature Double Sideband (MCD)
QDSPA Queensland Dance Studio Proprietors' Association [*Australia*]
QDT Qualified Domestic Trust
QDT Quintessence of Dental Technology
QDTA Quantitative Differential Thermal Analysis
qdta Quantitative Differential Thermal Analysis (AD)
QDTAA Queensland Dive Tourism Association of Australia
Qd Teach J Queensland Teachers' Journal [*A publication*]
QDU Dusseldorf-Main RR [*Germany Airport symbol*] (OAG)
QDV Quick Disconnect Valve
qdv Quick Disconnect Valve (AD)
QDX Quick Decision Exercise [*Training simulation*] [*Army*]
QDXR Quadriplexer
QE Bibliotheque Municipale, St.-Eustache, Quebec [*Library symbol National Library of Canada*] (BIB)
QE Journal of Quantum Electronics [*A publication*] (MCD)
QE Quadrant Elevation
qe Quadrant Elevation (AD)
QE Quadruple Expansion (DS)
QE Quaestiones et Salutationes in Exodum [*Philo*] (BJA)
QE Quality Engineer [*or Engineering*]
QE Quality Evaluation (NG)
QE Quality Excellence [*Chrysler Corp.*]
QE Quantum Efficiency
QE Quebec (AD)
QE Queen's Evidence [*British*] [*Legal term*] (BARN)
QE Queue Empty (MHDI)
QE Queue Entry
qe Quick Estimate (AD)
qe Quod Est [*Which Is*] [*Latin*] (AD)
QE Quod Est [*Which Is*] [*Latin*]
QE Quotation Estimate (MCD)
QE Quoted Exhibit (SAA)
QE 2 Queen Elizabeth 2 [*Luxury liner*]
QEA QANTAS Empire Airways Ltd. [*Later, QANTAS Airways Ltd.*]
QEA Quantum Electronics and Applications (IAA)
QEA Queensland Exporters' Association [*Australia*]
QEA Queue Element Area [*Computer science*] (IAA)
QEA Quick Electrolyte Analyzer [*Laboratory science*] (DAVI)
QEAD Quality Engineering and Assurance Division [*Navy*] (DNAB)
QEAE Quarternary Ethylaminoethyl [*Organic chemistry*]
QEAM Quick Erecting Antenna Mast [*Army*] (RDA)
QEAS Quantum Electronics and Applications Society (MCD)
QEAV Quick Exhaust Air Valve
qeav Quick-Exhaust Air Valve (AD)
QEB Quality Engineering Bulletin [*NASA*]
QEC Quantum Electronics Council
QEC Quantum Energy [*Vancouver Stock Exchange symbol*]
QEC Queen Elizabeth College [*British*]
QEC Quick Engine Change
qec Quick Engine Change (AD)
QEC Quiesce-at-End-of-Chain [*Computer science*] (IBMDP)
QECA Quick Engine Change Assembly (NG)
QECC Queen Elizabeth Chemical Center [*British*] (AD)
QECCH Compton County Historical and Museum Society [*Societe d'Histoire et du Musee du Comte de Compton*] Eaton Corner, Quebec [*Library symbol National Library of Canada*] (NLC)
QECK Quick Engine Change Kit (NG)
QECS Quick Engine Change Stand (NG)
QECU Quick Engine Change Unit
qecu Quick Engine-Change Unit (AD)
QED Quality Education Data [*Information service or system*] (IID)
QED Quality, Efficiency, Dependability (AD)
qed Quantitative Evaluative Device (AD)
QED Quantitative Evaluative Device (AEBS)
QED Quantum Electrodynamics [*Theory*]
qed Quantum Electrodynamics (AD)
QED Quantum Emission Domain [*Spectral physics*]
QED Quentin E. Deverill [*Protagonist in TV series; initialism also used as title of the series*]
QED Quick Editor [*Computer science*] (ECII)
QED Quick Erection Dome
qed Quick-Reaction Dome (AD)
QED Quick Text Editor
QED Quod Erat Demonstrandum [*Which Was the Thing to Be Proved*] [*Latin*]
qed Quod Erat Demonstrandum [*That Which Was to Be Proved*] [*Latin*] (AD)
QED Quod Erat Demonstrandum [*Which was to be demonstrated*] [*Latin*] [*Mathematics*] (WDMC)
QEDL Quality Engineering Diagnostic Laboratory (MCD)
QEE Quadriceps Extension Exercise [*Orthopedics*] (DAVI)
qee Quadruple Expansion Engine (AD)
QEEL Quality Evaluation and Engineering Laboratory [*Navy*]
QEEL/CO Quality Evaluation and Engineering Laboratory, Concord [*California*] [*Navy*]
qeev Quantum Electrodynamics Electron Volts (AD)
QEF Quail Embryo Fibroblast [*Medicine*] (DMAA)
QEF Queensland Employers Federation [*Australia*] (AD)
qef Quod Erat Faciendum [*That Which Was to Be Done*] [*Latin*] (AD)
QEF Quod Erat Faciendum [*Which Was to Be Made, or Done*] [*Latin*]
QEFD Queen Elizabeth's Foundation for the Disabled [*British*] (AD)
QEH Queen Elizabeth Hall [*London, England*]
QEH Queen Elizabeth's Hospital School [*England*]
QEI Quod Erat Inveniendum [*Which Was to Be Found Out*] [*Latin*]
qei Quod Erat Inveniendum [*That Which Was to Be Discovered*] [*Latin*] (AD)
QEIC Queensland Education Information Centre [*Australia*]
QEIC Queensland Egg Industry Council [*Australia*]
QE/K Quality Evaluation and Engineering Laboratory, Keyport [*Washington*] [*Naval Torpedo Station*]
QEKG Q-Med, Inc. [*Clark, NJ*] [*NASDAQ symbol*] (NQ)
QEL Quality Evaluation Laboratory
QEL Queue Element [*Computer science*]
QEL Quiet Extended Life
qel Quiet Extended Life (AD)
QElecSC Quadripartite Electronic Standardization Committee [*Military*] (AABC)
QELS Quantitative Evaluation of Library Searching [*Spectra matching technique*]
QELS Quasi-Elastic Light Scattering [*Also, QLS, QUELS*] [*Physics*]
QEM Quadrant Electrometer
qem Quadrant Electrometer (AD)
QEM Qualified Export Manager [*American Society of International Executives*] [*Designation awarded by*]
QEM Quality Education for Minorities (AD)
QEM Quality Education for Minorities Project (EA)
QEMH Queen Elizabeth Military Hospital [*Ministry of Defense*] [*British*] (PDAA)
QEMM Quarterdeck Expanded Memory Manager [*Computer science*]
QEN Quare Executionem Non [*Wherefore Execution Should Not Be Issued*] [*Latin Legal term*] (DLA)
QEngrSC Quadripartite Engineer Standardization Committee [*Military*] (AABC)
QENP Queen Elizabeth National Park [*Uganda*] (AD)
QENS Quasi-Elastic Neutron Scattering [*Physics*]
QEO Quality Engineering Operations
qeo Quality Engineering Operations (AD)
QEO Queen Elizabeth's Own [*British military*] (DMA)
QEONS Queen Elizabeth's Overseas Nursing Service [*British*] (DAVI)
QEOP Quartermaster Emergency Operation Plan [*Army*]
QEP Quality Evaluation Program [*College of American Pathologists*]
QEP Quality Examination Program (AFM)
QEP Queen Elizabeth Park (AD)
QEP Queen Elizabeth Planetarium (AD)
QEP Queensland Environmental Program [*Australia*] (AD)
QEPC QEP Co., Inc. [*NASDAQ symbol*] (SAG)
QEP Co QEP Co., Inc. [*Associated Press*] (SAG)
QEPL Quality Engineering Planning List (MCD)
QER Qualitative Equipment Requirements [*Army*] (AABC)
qer Qualitative Equipment Requirements (AD)

QER .... Quarterly Economic Review [*A publication*] (AD)
QER .... Quarterly Economic Review (ODBW)
QER .... Queen's Edinburgh Rifles [*British military*] (DMA)
QES .... Quadrant Eleventh-Gram Second
QES .... Quaker Esperanto Society (EA)
QESCP .... Quality Engineering Significant Control Points (MCD)
qescp .... Quality Engineering Significant Control Points (AD)
QESISB .... Queensland Electricity Supply Industry Superannuation Board [*Australia*]
QESP .... Queen Emma Summer Palace (AD)
QEST .... Quality Evaluation System Tests (NG)
QEST .... Query, Update Entry, Search, Time-Sharing System (NVT)
QESTS .... Query, Update Entry, Search, Time Sharing [*Computer science*] (AD)
QET .... Quality Expo TIME-International (ITD)
QET .... Quality in Education [*Project*] (AIE)
QET .... Quasi-Equilibrium Theory [*Physical chemistry*]
QET .... Queen Elizabeth Theatre [*Vancouver*] (AD)
QETE .... Quality Engineering Test Establishment [*Department of National Defence*] [*Canada*] (IRC)
QEV .... Quick Exhaust Valve
qev .... Quick Exhaust Valve (AD)
QEW .... Queen Elizabeth Way [*Canada*]
QEW .... Quick Early Warning Test [*Medicine*] (MAE)
QF .... Qabel Foundation (EA)
QF .... QANTAS Airways Ltd. [*Australia ICAO designator*]
QF .... Qualifying Facility [*Electric power*]
QF .... Quality Factor [*Nuclear energy*]
qf .... Quality Factor (AD)
QF .... Quality Form [*Nuclear energy*] (NRCH)
QF .... Quarterfinals (WGA)
QF .... Quench Frequency (DEN)
qf .... Quench Frequency (AD)
QF .... Queue Full
QF .... Quick-Firing [*Gun*]
QF .... Quick Fix (MCD)
QF .... Quick Freeze
qf .... Quick Freeze (AD)
QFA .... Qantas Airways Ltd. [*Australia ICAO designator*] (FAAC)
QFA .... Qualification Firings Alignment (DNAB)
qfa .... Quality per Final Article (AD)
QFA .... Quantitative Fibrinogen Assay [*Clinical chemistry*]
QFAB .... Quaker Fabric [*NASDAQ symbol*] (TTSB)
QFAB .... Quaker Fabric Corp. [*NASDAQ symbol*] (SAG)
QFB .... Quiet Fast Boat [*Navy symbol*]
QF-BH .... Quick Fix - Black Hawk
QFC .... Quantitative Flight Characteristics
qfc .... Quantitative Flight Characteristics (AD)
QFCC .... Qantas Flight Catering Centre [*Australia*]
QFCC .... Quantitative Flight Characteristics Criteria
qfcc .... Quantitative Flight Characteristics Criteria (AD)
QFCI .... Quality Food Centers [*NASDAQ symbol*] (TTSB)
QFCI .... Quality Food Centers, Inc. [*NASDAQ symbol*] (NQ)
QFCI .... Quartermaster Food and Container Institute for the Armed Forces
QFD .... Quality Function Deployment [*Automotive engineering*]
QFD .... Quality Function Development [*Failure analysis*]
QFD .... Quantum Flavor Dynamics
QFD .... Quarterly Forecast Demand
QFDA .... Queensland Funeral Directors' Association [*Australia*]
QFDO .... Queensland Film Development Office [*Australia*]
QFE .... Columbus [*Georgia*] Fort Benning [*Airport symbol*] (OAG)
QFE .... Quartz Fiber Electrometer (WDAA)
qfe .... Quartz Fiber Electrometer (AD)
QFE .... Query Formulation and Encoding
Q-fellows .... Quartermaster Fellows (AD)
Q-fellows .... Queer Fellows (AD)
Q fever .... Query Fever (AD)
QFF .... Atmospheric Pressure Converted to Mean Sea Level E levation [*Aviation code*] (AIA)
qff .... Quadruple Flip-Flop (AD)
QFF .... Quadrupole Flip-Flop [*Computer science*]
QFF .... Queensland Farmers' Federation [*Australia*]
QFGA .... Queensland Farmers and Graziers' Association [*Australia*]
QFGA .... Queensland Flower Growers' Association [*Australia*]
QFHS .... Quebec Federation of Historical Societies [*Canada*] (EAIO)
QFI .... Qualified Flight Instructor
QFI .... Qualified Flying Instructor
QFIA .... Quantitative Fluorescence Image Analysis [*Medicine*]
QFIRC .... Quick Fix Interference Reduction Capability (AFM)
qfirc .... Quick-Fix Interference-Reduction Capability (AD)
QFITC .... Queensland Fishing Industry Training Committee [*Australia*]
QFITC .... Queensland Food Industry Training Council [*Australia*]
QFITC .... Queensland Furniture Industry Training Committee [*Australia*]
QFL .... Quasi-Fermi Level
qfl .... Quasi-Fermi Level (AD)
QFLGE .... Queensland Foundation for Local Government Engineering [*Australia*]
QFM .... Quantized Frequency Modulation
qfm .... Quantized Frequency Modulation (AD)
QFM .... Quartz-Fayalite-Magnetite [*Geology*]
QFMA .... Quebec Fertilizer Manufacturers Association (AC)
QFMA .... Queensland Flour Millers' Association [*Australia*]
QFMR .... Quantized Frequency Modulation Repeater
QFN .... Quicken Financial Network (PCM)
qfo .... Quartz Frequency Oscillator (AD)
QFO .... Quartz Frequency Oscillator
QFP .... Quad Flat Pack (NITA)
qfp .... Quartz Fiber Product (AD)
QFP .... Quartz Fiber Product
QFP .... Quick Fix Program
QFPL .... Qualified Film Producers List (AAGC)
QFr .... Epistulae ad Quintum Fratrem [*of Cicero*] [*Classical studies*] (OCD)
QFR .... Quarterly Force Revision [*Military*] (NVT)
Q fract .... Quick Fraction [*Reference to membrane potentials*] (DAVI)
QFRI .... Queensland Fisheries Research Institute [*Australia*] (AD)
QFS .... Queensland Fire Service [*Australia*]
QFS .... Queensland Fisheries Service [*Australia*] (AD)
QFS .... Queensland Forest Service [*Australia*]
QFS .... Quick-Fit Sea (DNAB)
QFSM .... Queen's Fire Service Medal for Distinguished Service [*British*]
QFSM .... Queen's Fire Services Medal [*British*] (AD)
QFSR .... Quartus Foundation for Spiritual Research (EA)
QFT .... Quantized Field Theory
qft .... Quantized Field Theory (AD)
QG .... Bibliotheque Municipale, Gatineau, Quebec [*Library symbol National Library of Canada*] (NLC)
QG .... Quadrature Grid
qg .... Quadrature Grid (AD)
QG .... Quaestiones et Salutationes in Genesin [*Philo*] (BJA)
QG .... Qualified in Gunnery [*British military*] (DMA)
QG .... Quartermaster General [*Military*]
QG .... Quartier General [*Headquarters*] [*French*] (AD)
QG .... Quartier Generale [*Headquarters*] [*Italian*] (AD)
QG .... Queensland Grains [*Australia Commercial firm*]
QGA .... Queensland Graingrowers' Association [*Australia*]
QGA .... Queensland Gymnastic Association [*Australia*]
QGAH .... Hotel-Dieu de Gaspe, Quebec [*Library symbol National Library of Canada*] (NLC)
QGAP .... Centre de Documentation, Peches Maritimes, Ministere de l'Agriculture, des Pe cheries, et de l'Alimentation du Quebec, Gaspe, Quebec [*Library symbol National Library of Canada*] (NLC)
QGBES .... Queensland Government Bureau of Emergency Services [*Australia*]
QGBF .... Quasi-Grain Boundary Free [*Photovoltaic energy systems*]
QGC .... College de la Gaspesie, Gaspe, Quebec [*Library symbol National Library of Canada*] (NLC)
QGCH .... Centre Hospitalier de Gatineau, Quebec [*Library symbol National Library of Canada*] (NLC)
QGE .... Queen's Gurkha Engineers [*British military*] (DMA)
QGEN .... QIAGEN [*NASDAQ symbol*] (SAG)
QGFM .... Queensland Guild of Furniture Manufacturers [*Australia*]
QGGA .... Queensland Grain Growers Association [*Australia*] (AD)
QGI .... Grosse Ile Library, Magdalen Islands, Quebec [*Library symbol National Library of Canada*] (NLC)
QGL .... Granby Leader Mail Office, Quebec [*Library symbol National Library of Canada*] (NLC)
QGM .... Bibliotheque Municipale, Granby, Quebec [*Library symbol National Library of Canada*] (NLC)
qgm .... Quarter-Girth Measure (AD)
QGM .... Queen's Gallantry Medal [*British*]
QGMG .... Musee de la Gaspesie, Gaspe, Quebec [*Library symbol National Library of Canada*] (BIB)
QGMM .... Bibliotheque Municipale, Grand'Mere, Quebec [*Library symbol National Library of Canada*] (NLC)
QGNG .... Ecole Secondaire Nicolas-Gatineau, Gatineau, Quebec [*Library symbol National Library of Canada*] (BIB)
QGO .... Queen's Gurkha Officer [*Military British*]
QGPC .... Qatar General Petroleum Corp.
QGPO .... Qatar General Petroleum Organization (AD)
QGS .... Quantity Gauging System (NASA)
QGSH .... Societe Historique du Comte de Shefford, Granby, Quebec [*Library symbol National Library of Canada*] (NLC)
QGTB .... Queensland Government Tourist Bureau [*Australia*] (AD)
QGU .... Queensland Golf Union [*Australia*]
QGV .... Quantized Gate Video [*RADAR*]
qgv .... Quantized Gate Video (AD)
QH .... Bibliotheque Municipale, Hull, Quebec [*Library symbol National Library of Canada*] (NLC)
QH .... Quadrature Hybrid (IAA)
QH .... Quaque Hora [*Every Hour*] [*Pharmacy*]
qh .... Quaque Hora [*Every Hour*] [*Latin*] (AD)
q-h .... Quartz-Halogen (AD)
QH .... Quartz Halogen
QH .... Quartz Helix
qh .... Quartz Helix (AD)
QH .... Queen's Hall (AD)
QH .... Quorn Hounds
QH .... West African Airways [*ICAO designator*] (AD)
Q-H_2 .... Ubihydroquinone [*Ubiquinol*] [*Laboratory science*] (DAVI)
QHAC .... CEGEP [*College d'Enseignement General et Professionnel*] de Hauterive, BaieComeau, Quebec [*Library symbol National Library of Canada*] (NLC)
QHACR .... Conseil Regional de la Sante et des Services Sociaux de la Region Cote-Nord, Hauterive, Quebec [*Library symbol National Library of Canada*] (NLC)
QHB .... Economics Information Centre, Bell Canada, Hull, Quebec [*Library symbol National Library of Canada*] (NLC)
QHB .... Queen's Hard Bargain [*Undesirable serviceman*] [*Slang British*] (DSUE)
QHBC .... Bibliotheque Centrale de Pret d'Outaouais, Hull, Quebec [*Library symbol National Library of Canada*] (BIB)

QHBEER....... Headquarters Engineering Economics Reference Centre, Bell Canada, Hull, Quebec [*Library symbol National Library of Canada*] (NLC)
QHBRM........ Bell Canada Headquarters, Regulatory Matters-Regulatory Information Bank, Hull, Quebec [*Library symbol National Library of Canada*] (NLC)
QHC............ CEGEP [*College d'Enseignement General et Professionnel*] de l'Outaouais, Hull, Quebec [*Library symbol National Library of Canada*] (NLC)
QHC............ Quarter Half Circle (IAA)
QHC............ Queen's Honorary Chaplain [*British*]
QHC............ Queensland Housing Commission [*Australia*]
QHCH........... Heritage Campus, CEGEP de l'Outaouais, Hull, Quebec [*Library symbol National Library of Canada*] (NLC)
QHCL........... Centre de Documentation, CLSC de Hull, Quebec [*Library symbol National Library of Canada*] (NLC)
QHCRS.......... Conseil Regional de la Sante et des Services Sociaux de la Region Outaouais-Hull, Hull, Quebec [*Library symbol National Library of Canada*] (NLC)
QHDS........... Queen's Honorary Dental Surgeon [*British*]
QHE............ E. B. Eddy Co., Hull, Quebec [*Library symbol National Library of Canada*] (NLC)
QHE............ Quantum Hall Effect [*Physics*]
QHEA........... Queensland Horticultural Export Association [*Australia*]
Q Her.......... Queensland Heritage [*A publication*]
QHESJ.......... Ecole Secondaire St.-Joseph, Hull, Quebec [*Library symbol National Library of Canada*] (BIB)
QHGI........... Quorum Health Group [*NASDAQ symbol*] (TTSB)
QHGI........... Quorum Health Group, Inc. [*NASDAQ symbol*] (SAG)
QHI............ Qualified Helicopter Instructor
Q Hist Soc J... Queensland Historical Society. Journal [*A publication*]
QHM............ Quartz Horizontal Magnetometer (NOAA)
QHM............ Queen's Harbour Master [*British*]
QHMML.......... Micromedia Ltee., Hull, Quebec [*Library symbol National Library of Canada*] (BIB)
QHNS........... Queen's Honorary Nursing Sister [*British*]
QHO............ Queen's Hall Orchestra
QHP............ Quasi-Hydrostatic Pressure [*Physics*]
QHP............ Queen's Honorary Physician [*British*]
QHP............ Quiet Helicopter Program (RDA)
QHPJ........... Centre Hospitalier Pierre Janet, Hull, Quebec [*Library symbol National Library of Canada*] (NLC)
QHQAR.......... Centre Regional de l'Outaouais, Archives Nationales du Quebec, Hull, Quebec [*Library symbol National Library of Canada*] (BIB)
QHR............ Quality History Record [*Nuclear energy*] (NRCH)
q hr........... Quaque Hora [*Every Hour*] [*Latin Pharmacy*] (WGA)
QHRI........... Quantum Health Resources [*NASDAQ symbol*] (SPSG)
QHRI........... Quantum Hlth Resources [*NASDAQ symbol*] (TTSB)
QHS............ Qinghaosu [*Antimalarial drug*]
qhs............ Quaque Hora Somni [*Every Hour of Sleep*] [*Pharmacy*] [*Latin*] (MAE)
QHS............ Queen's Honorary Surgeon [*British*]
QHS............ Queensland Historical Society [*Australia*]
QHS............ Quick Hot-Swap [*Computer disk drive*]
QHSA........... Societe d'Amenagement de l'Outaouais, Hull, Quebec [*Library symbol National Library of Canada*] (NLC)
QHSC........... Centre Hospitalier Regional de l'Outaouais, Hull, Quebec [*Library symbol National Library of Canada*] (NLC)
QHSIA.......... Queensland Hide and Skin Industries Association [*Australia*]
QHSS........... Queensland Healthy Soil Society [*Australia*]
QHU............ Universite du Quebec, Hull, Quebec [*Library symbol National Library of Canada*] (NLC)
QHV............ Queen's Honorary Veterinarian [*British*] (AD)
QHV............ Quiet Heavy Vehicle [*Automotive engineering*]
QHY............ Quantized High Y [*Picture resolution*] (NTCM)
QI............. Cimber Air [*ICAO designator*] (AD)
QI............. Quad Imperial [*Paper*] (DGA)
QI............. Qualified Indorsement (MHDB)
QI............. Qualified Instructor [*British military*] (DMA)
QI............. Quality Improvement (HCT)
qi............. Quality Improvement (AD)
QI............. Quality Increase (AABC)
QI............. Quality Index
QI............. Quality Indices (WDAA)
qi............. Quality Indices (AD)
QI............. Quantity Indicator (KSC)
QI............. Quarterly Index [*A publication*] (AD)
QI............. Quart Imperial (DNAB)
QI............. Quartz Iodine
QI............. Quasi-Inertial
QI............. Queensland Insurance [*Australia*] (AD)
QI............. Quiet Ionosphere (IAA)
QI............. Quota International (EA)
QIA............ Quantitative Infrared Analysis
QIA............ Queensland Institute of Architects [*Australia*] (AD)
QIA............ Queensland Irish Association [*Australia*]
QIAC........... Quantimet Image Analyzing Computer (PDAA)
QIAET.......... Quartzsite Integrated Acoustic and Engine Test Site
QIAGEN......... QIAGEN [*Associated Press*] (SAG)
QIAM........... Queued Indexed Access Memory [*Computer science*] (IAA)
qiam........... Queued Indexed Access Memory [*Computer science*] (AD)
QIB............ Quarterly Information Bulletin [*Navy*] (DNAB)
QIB............ Queensland Imperial Bushmen [*British military*] (DMA)
QIB............ Quick Is Beautiful [*NASA project philosophy*]
QIC............ Aero Quick [*Mexico ICAO designator*] (FAAC)
QIC............ Quality Information Center
QIC............ Quality Inspection Criteria
qic............ Quality Inspection Criteria (AD)
QIC............ Quality Insurance Chain (IAA)
QIC............ Quarter Inch Cartridge [*Computer science*]
QIC............ Quarter-Inch Compatibility [*Format*]
QIC............ Quartz Iodine Crystal
qic............ Quartz-Iodine Crystal (AD)
QICA........... Queensland Immigration Control Association [*Australia*]
QID............ Quater in Die [*Four Times a Day*] [*Pharmacy*]
qid............ Quater in Die [*Four Times a Day*] [*Latin*] (AD)
QIDN........... Queen's Institute of District Nursing [*British*]
QIE............ Qualified International Executive (AD)
QIE............ Quantitative Immunoelectrophoresis Methods [*Analytical biochemistry*]
qie............ Qunatitative Immuno-Electrophoresis (AD)
QIE-AF......... Qualified International Executive - Air Forwarding [*American Society of I nternational Executives, Inc.*] [*Designation awarded by*]
QIE-EM......... Qualified International Executive - Export Management [*American Society o f International Executives, Inc.*] [*Designation awarded by*]
QIE-F.......... Qualified International Executive - Forwarding [*American Society of Inter national Executives, Inc.*] [*Designation awarded by*]
QIER........... Queensland Institute for Educational Research [*Australia*] (AD)
QIE-TM......... Qualified International Executive - Traffic Management [*American Society of International Executives, Inc.*] [*Designation awarded by*]
QIF............ Quantitative Immunofluorescence
QIF............ Quartz-Iron-Fayalite [*Geology*]
QIF............ Quicken Interchange File [*Computer science*] (PCM)
QIFMA.......... Archives des Freres Maristes, Iberville, Quebec [*Library symbol National Library of Canada*] (NLC)
QIG............ Quantitative Immunoglobulin [*Immunology*] (DAVI)
QIG............ Queensland Industrial Gazette [*A publication*]
QIH............ Quality International Hotels (AD)
QIK............ Quick (MSA)
QIL............ Quad In-Line
QIL............ Quartz Incandescent Lamp
qil............ Quartz Incandescent Lamp (AD)
qil............ Quartz Iodine Lamp (AD)
QIL............ Quartz Iodine Lamp
QILS........... Quantification of Integrated Logistics Support
QIMR........... Queensland Institute of Medical Research [*Australia*] (AD)
QIN............ Quality Improvement Network (DMAA)
QIO............ Queue Input/Output
QIP............ PALINET [*Pennsylvania Area Library Network*] Central, Philadelphia, PA [*OCLC symbol*] (OCLC)
QIP............ Quad-in-Line Package [*Computer science*] (IAA)
QIP............ Quality Improvement Process [*Quality control*]
QIP............ Quality Improvement Program (ACII)
QIP............ Quality Improvement Project (HCT)
QIP............ Quality Inspection Point (KSC)
QIP............ Quarterly Intercession Paper [*A publication*] (ROG)
QIP............ Quarters Improvement Program (MCD)
QIP............ Quartz Insulation Part
qip............ Quartz Insulation Part (AD)
QIP............ Query Interpretation Program (SAA)
QIP............ Quiescat in Pace [*May He, or She, Rest in Peace*] [*Latin*]
QIPA........... Queensland Institute of Public Affairs [*Australia*] (AD)
QIPS........... Qualitative Incentive Procurement Service (AD)
QIR............ Quechan Indian Reservation (AD)
QIRC........... Queensland Industrial Relations Commission [*Australia*]
QIS............ Quality Information System (IAA)
QIS............ Quality Insurance System (IAA)
QISAM.......... Queued Indexed Sequential Access Method [*IBM Corp.*] [*Computer science*]
qisam.......... Queued-Indexed Sequential-Access Method [*Computer science*] (AD)
qit............ Qualification Information and Test (AD)
QIT............ Quality Information and Test [*System*]
QIT............ Queensland Institute of Technology [*Australia*] (AD)
QITLJ.......... Queensland Institute of Technology. Law Journal [*A publication*]
QITS........... Quality Information and Test System (WDAA)
QIXX........... Quest International Resources Corp. [*NASDAQ symbol*] (SAG)
QIXXF.......... Quest Intl Res [*NASDAQ symbol*] (TTSB)
QJ............. Bibliotheque Municipale, Jonquiere, Quebec [*Library symbol National Library of Canada*] (BIB)
QJ............. Quadriceps Jerk [*Neurology*] (DAVI)
QJ............. Quick Junction [*Electronics*]
Q Japan Com'l Arb Ass'n... Quarterly. Japan Commercial Arbitration Association [*A publication*] (DLA)
QJC............ College de Joliette, Quebec [*Library symbol National Library of Canada*] (NLC)
QJC............ Quincy Junior College (AD)
QJCCI.......... Queensland Japan Chamber of Commerce and Industry [*Australia*]
QJCH........... Centre de Documentation, Departement de Sante Communautaire de Lanaudiere, Joliette, Quebec [*Library symbol National Library of Canada*] (BIB)
QJCSVA......... Archives Provinciales des Clercs de Saint-Viateur, Joliette, Quebec [*Library symbol National Library of Canada*] (NLC)
Q/JET.......... Quadrajet Carburetor [*Automotive engineering*]
QJH............ Centre Hospitalier Regional de Lanaudiere, Joliette, Quebec [*Library symbol National Library of Canada*] (NLC)
QJJ............ Seminaire de Joliette, Quebec [*Library symbol National Library of Canada*] (NLC)
QJL............ Querner, J. L., San Antonio TX [*STAC*]

QJMA.......... Musee d'Art de Joliette, Quebec [*Library symbol National Library of Canada*] (NLC)
QJMP.......... Queue Jump Command
QJOC.......... College de Jonquiere, Quebec [*Library symbol National Library of Canada*] (NLC)
QJS.......... Quarterly Journal of Speech [*A publication*] (BRI)
QJSA.......... Quarterly Journal of Studies in Alcohol [*A publication*] (AD)
qjump.......... Queue Jump (AD)
QK.......... Kirkland Municipal Library [*Bibliotheque Municipale de Kirkland*] Quebec [*Library symbol National Library of Canada*] (NLC)
QK.......... Quasi Contract [*Legal shorthand*] (LWAP)
QK.......... Queen's Knight [*Chess*]
qk.......... Quick (AD)
QK.......... Quick Kinescope [*Film replay*] (NTCM)
QKB.......... Brome County Historical Society, Knowlton, Quebec [*Library symbol National Library of Canada*] (NLC)
QKBW.......... Burroughs Wellcome & Co., Kirkland, Quebec [*Library symbol National Library of Canada*] (NLC)
QKC.......... Aero Taxi Aviation, Inc. [*ICAO designator*] (FAAC)
QKD.......... Quantum Key Distribution [*For encrypting communication*]
QKFA.......... Queensland Keep Fit Association [*Australia*]
Qk Fl.......... Quick Flashing (AD)
QKFL.......... Quick Flashing Light [*Navigation signal*]
QKITA.......... Institut de Technologie Agricole, Kamouraska, Quebec [*Library symbol National Library of Canada*] (NLC)
QKL.......... Aeromaritime (CAAA) [*France ICAO designator*] (FAAC)
QKL.......... Cologne/Bonn-Main RR [*Germany Airport symbol*] (OAG)
QKLN.......... Laboratoires Nordic, Inc., Kirkland, Quebec [*Library symbol National Library of Canada*] (BIB)
qkly.......... Quickly (AD)
qkm.......... Quadratkilometer [*Square Kilometer*] [*German*] (AD)
QKPC.......... Medical Library, Pfizer Canada, Inc., Kirkland, Quebec [*Library symbol National Library of Canada*] (NLC)
QkReily.......... Quick & Reilly Group, Inc. [*Associated Press*] (SAG)
QKT.......... Queen's Knight [*Chess*]
QKTN.......... Quickturn Design Sys [*NASDAQ symbol*] (TTSB)
QKTN.......... Quickturn Design System [*NASDAQ symbol*] (SAG)
QKTP.......... Queen's Knight's Pawn [*Chess*] (IIA)
QL.......... Ethyl 2-(Diisopropylamino)ethylmethylphosphonite [*See EDMP*] [*Army symbol*]
QL.......... Lesotho Airways [*ICAO designator*] (AD)
QL.......... Quad Left [*Typography*]
QL.......... Quality of Living
QL.......... Quantum League [*An association*] (EA)
QL.......... Quantum Leap (WDAA)
QL.......... Quantum Libet [*As Much as Is Desired*] [*Pharmacy*]
ql.......... Quantum Libet [*As Much as You Like*] [*Latin*] (AD)
Q/L.......... Quarantine Launch (AD)
ql.......... Quarrel (AD)
QL.......... Quarrel (ROG)
QL.......... Quartz-Locked
QL.......... Quebec Law [*A publication*] (DLA)
QL.......... Queen's Lancers [*Military unit*] [*British*]
QL.......... Queensland [*Airline code*] (AD)
ql.......... Query Language (AD)
QL.......... Query Language [*Computer science*] (DIT)
QL.......... Queue Length [*Telecommunications*] (TEL)
Q/L.......... Quick Look (KSC)
ql.......... Quick Look (AD)
ql.......... Quilate [*Carat*] [*Portuguese*] (AD)
ql.......... Quintal (AD)
QL.......... Quintal [*Unit of weight*]
QL.......... Qumran Literature (BJA)
QL.......... Quoc-Lo [*Main national highway in South Vietnam*] (VNW)
QL/1.......... Query Language/One [*Computer science*] (MHDI)
QLA.......... Aviation Quebec Labrador Ltd. [*Canada ICAO designator*] (FAAC)
QLA.......... Bibliotheque Municipale, Laval, Quebec [*Library symbol National Library of Canada*] (NLC)
QLA.......... Lasham [*England*] [*Airport symbol*]
QLA.......... Quebec Library Association (AC)
QLA/ABQ.......... Quebec Library Association/Association des Bibliothecaires du Quebec [*Canada*]
QLAB.......... Quick Like a Bunny
QLAC.......... CEGEP [*College d'Enseignement General et Professionnel*] Montmorency, Laval, Quebec [*Library symbol National Library of Canada*] (NLC)
QLACS.......... Cite de la Sante de Laval, Quebec [*Library symbol National Library of Canada*] (NLC)
QLACW.......... Canadian Workplace Automation Research Centre [*Centre Canadien de Recherche sur l'Informatisation du Travail*] Laval, Quebec [*Library symbol National Library of Canada*] (NLC)
QLAG.......... Research Station, Agriculture Canada [*Station de Recherches, Agriculture Canada*] Lennoxville, Quebec [*Library symbol National Library of Canada*] (NLC)
QLAH.......... Lennoxville-Ascot Historical Society Museum, Lennoxville, Quebec [*Library symbol National Library of Canada*] (NLC)
QLAID.......... Ateliers d'Ingenierie Dominion, Lachine, Quebec [*Library symbol National Library of Canada*] (NLC)
QLAP.......... Quick Look Analysis Program
QLAR.......... Canadian Arsenals Ltd. [*Arsenaux Canada Ltee.*], Le Gardeur, Quebec [*Library symbol National Library of Canada*] (BIB)
QLASC.......... College de l'Assomption, Quebec [*Library symbol National Library of Canada*] (NLC)
QLASGPT.......... Federal Training Centre, Penitentiary, Ministry of the Solicitor General [*Centre Federal de Formation, Penitencier, Ministere du Solliciteur General*] Laval, Quebec [*Library symbol National Library of Canada*] (NLC)
QLAVD.......... Centre de Documentation, Assurance-Vie Desjardins, Levis, Quebec [*Library symbol National Library of Canada*] (NLC)
QLB.......... Bishop's University, Lennoxville, Quebec [*Library symbol National Library of Canada*] (NLC)
QLBG.......... Department of Geography, Bishop's University, Lennoxville, Quebec [*Library symbol National Library of Canada*] (NLC)
QLC.......... College de Levis, Quebec [*Library symbol National Library of Canada*] (NLC)
QLC.......... Quasi-Liquid Crystal [*Organic chemistry*]
QLCCP.......... Service de Documentation et de Reference, Confederation des Caisses Populaires et d'Economie Desjardins du Quebec, Levis, Quebec [*Library symbol National Library of Canada*] (NLC)
QLCLL.......... CEGEP [*College d'Enseignement General et Professionnel*] de Levis-Lauzon, Lauzon, Quebec [*Library symbol National Library of Canada*] (BIB)
QLCRS.......... Conseil Regional de la Sante et des Services Sociaux, Longueuil, Quebec [*Library symbol National Library of Canada*] (NLC)
QLCS.......... Quick Look and Checkout System
Qld.......... Queensland (ODBW)
Qld.......... Queensland (AD)
QLD.......... Queen's Light Dragoons [*British military*] (DMA)
QLD.......... Quillo Resources, Inc. [*Vancouver Stock Exchange symbol*]
QLDC.......... Delmar Chemicals, La Salle, Quebec [*Library symbol National Library of Canada*] (NLC)
Qld Ind.......... Queensland Industry [*A publication*]
Qld Law.......... Queensland Lawyer [*A publication*]
QLDR.......... Quick Look Data Reference (NASA)
QLDS.......... Quick Look Data Station [*NASA*] (KSC)
QLE.......... Bibliotheque Municipale, Levis, Quebec [*Library symbol National Library of Canada*] (NLC)
QLFCP.......... Federation des Caisses Populaires Desjardins, Levis, Quebec [*Library symbol National Library of Canada*] (NLC)
QLFD.......... Qualified (KSC)
QLFECA.......... Archives des Freres des Ecoles Chretiennes, Ville de Laval, Quebec [*Library symbol National Library of Canada*] (NLC)
QlFood.......... Quality Food Centers, Inc. [*Associated Press*] (SAG)
qlfy.......... Qualify (AD)
qlfyg.......... Qualifying (AD)
qlfyn.......... Qualification (AD)
QLG.......... Quick-Look Guide
QLGA.......... Queensland Local Government Association [*Australia*] (AD)
QLGC.......... Qlogic Corp. [*NASDAQ symbol*] (SAG)
QLGU.......... Queensland Ladies Golf Union [*Australia*]
QLHD.......... Hotel-Dieu de Levis, Quebec [*Library symbol National Library of Canada*] (NLC)
QLI.......... Quality of Life Index
qli.......... Quality of Life Index (AD)
Q Lib.......... Quantum Libet [*As Much as You Please*] [*Pharmacy*]
qlii.......... Quais-LASER-Intensity Interferometer (AD)
Q-Link.......... QuantumLink [*Quantum Computer Services, Inc.*] [*Vienna, VA*] [*Information service or system*] (IID)
QLIT.......... Quick Look Intermediate Tape
qlit.......... Quick-Look Intermediate Tape (AD)
qll.......... Quartz Landing Lamp (AD)
QLL.......... Quartz Landing Lamp [*Aviation*]
QLLC.......... Qualified Logical Link Control [*Telecommunications*]
QLM.......... Bibliotheque Municipale de Lachine, Quebec [*Library symbol National Library of Canada*] (NLC)
QLM.......... Quasi-Lagrangian Model (USDC)
QLM.......... Quasi-Lagrangian Model [*Marine science*] (OSRA)
qlm.......... Quasi-LASER Machine (AD)
QLM.......... Quasi-Linear Machine
QLNLB.......... Institut Nazareth et Louis-Braille, Longueuil, Quebec [*Library symbol National Library of Canada*] (NLC)
QLO.......... Bibliotheque Municipale, Longueuil, Quebec [*Library symbol National Library of Canada*] (NLC)
QLOC.......... Queensland Light Opera Co. [*Australia*] (AD)
QLOCE.......... College Edouard-Montpetit, Longueuil, Quebec [*Library symbol National Library of Canada*] (NLC)
QLOCSS.......... Centre de Services Sociaux Richelieu, Longueuil, Quebec [*Library symbol National Library of Canada*] (NLC)
Qlogic.......... Qlogic Corp. [*Associated Press*] (SAG)
QLOPB.......... Centre de Documentation, Centre Hospitalier Pierre Boucher, Longueuil, Quebec [*Library symbol National Library of Canada*] (NLC)
QLOU.......... Pratt & Whitney Aircraft Ltd., Longueuil, Quebec [*Library symbol National Library of Canada*] (NLC)
QLP.......... Quality Low-Priced [*Art series*]
QLP.......... Query Language Processor [*Computer science*]
QLP.......... Quinoxaline Ladder Polymer [*Organic chemistry*]
QLPC.......... Queensland Library Promotion Council [*Australia*] (AD)
QLPED.......... Pylon Electronic Development Co. Ltd., Lachine, Quebec [*Library symbol National Library of Canada*] (NLC)
QLPS.......... Petro-Sun International, Inc., Longueuil, Quebec [*Library symbol National Library of Canada*] (NLC)
QLR.......... Quebec Law Reports
QLR.......... Queen's Lancashire Regiment [*Military unit*] [*British*]
QL(R).......... Quick Look (Report)
QLRA.......... Queensland Litter Research Association [*Australia*]
QL Rev.......... Quarterly Law Review [*A publication*] (DLA)

QLS............ Bibliotheque Municipale, La Salle, Quebec [*Library symbol National Library of Canada*] (NLC)
QLS............ Quasi-Elastic Light Scattering [*Also, QELS, QUELS*] [*Physics*]
QLS............ Quebec Land Surveyor [*Canada*] (DD)
QLS............ Queensland Law Society [*Australia*] (AD)
QLS............ Queensland Littoral Society [*Australia*] (AD)
QLS............ Quick Law Systems (AD)
QLS............ Quick Loading System (AD)
QLS............ Quick Look Station [*NASA*] (MCD)
QLSA............ Queue Line Sharing Adapter [*Computer science*]
QLSAA............ Archives des Soeurs de Sainte-Anne, Lachine, Quebec [*Library symbol National Library of Canada*] (NLC)
QLSD............ Societe de Developpement International Desjardins, Levis, Quebec [*Library symbol National Library of Canada*] (BIB)
QLSE............ ESSO Building Products of Canada Ltd., La Salle, Quebec [*Library symbol National Library of Canada*] (NLC)
QLSEA............ Queensland Livestock Exporters' Association [*Australia*]
QLSHG............ Bibliotheque Medicale, Hopital General La Salle, Quebec [*Library symbol National Library of Canada*] (NLC)
QLSI............ Quantum Learning Sys [*NASDAQ symbol*] (TTSB)
QLSI............ Quantum Learning Systems, Inc. [*NASDAQ symbol*] (SAG)
qlsm............ Quasi-LASER Sequential Machine (AD)
QLSM............ Quasi-Linear Sequential Machine
QLSO............ L'Octogone, Centre de la Culture, La Salle, Quebec [*Library symbol National Library of Canada*] (NLC)
QL Soc J............ Queensland Law Society. Journal [*A publication*]
QLSS............ Research Department, J. E. Seagram & Sons Ltd., La Salle, Quebec [*Library symbol National Library of Canada*] (NLC)
QLT............ Bibliotheque Municipale, La Tuque, Quebec [*Library symbol National Library of Canada*] (NLC)
QLT............ Quadra Logic Technologies [*Associated Press*] (SAG)
QLT............ Quadra Logic Technologies, Inc. [*Vancouver Stock Exchange symbol Toronto Stock Exchange symbol*]
QLT............ Quantitative Leak Test
qlt............ Quantitative Leak Test (AD)
QLT............ Quasi-Linear Theory
QLTA............ Queensland Lawn Tennis Association [*Australia*] (AD)
QLTI............ Quadra Logic Technologies, Inc. [*NASDAQ symbol*] (NQ)
QLTIF............ QLT Phototherapeutics [*NASDAQ symbol*] (TTSB)
QLTY............ Quality
qlty............ Quality (AD)
QLTY............ Quality (AFM)
qlty............ Quality (ODBW)
QLTYCONO............ Quality Control Officer [*Military*]
QltyDin............ Quality Dino Entertainment [*Commercial firm Associated Press*] (SAG)
qly............ Quarterly (ODBW)
Qly Land R............ Fitzgibbon's Irish Land Reports [*A publication*] (DLA)
QM............ Air Malawi [*ICAO designator*] (AD)
QM............ Bulgaria [*License plate code assigned to foreign diplomats in the US*]
QM............ Quad Medium [*Paper*] (DGA)
qm............ Quadratmeter [*Square Meter*] [*German*] (AD)
QM............ Quadrature Modulation
QM............ Qualification Motor (MCD)
QM............ Quality Management (HCT)
QM............ Quality Management
QM............ Quality Manual [*A publication*] (MCD)
QM............ Quality Memorandum
QM............ Quality Motels (EA)
QM............ Quality of Merit
QM............ Quantitative Methods
QM............ Quantum Mechanics
qm............ Quantum Mechanics (AD)
qm............ Quaque Mane [*Every Morning*] [*Latin*] (AD)
QM............ Quaque Matin [*Every Morning*] [*Pharmacy*]
QM............ Quarterly Meetings [*Quakers*]
QM............ Quarterly Memorandum
QM............ Quartermaster [*Military*] (VNW)
QM............ Quartermaster Corps (AAGC)
QM............ Quartz Manometer (ACII)
QM............ Queen Mother [*British*]
QM............ Queen's Messenger [*British*]
QM............ Queens Museum (AD)
Q-M............ Quenu-Muret Sign [*Cardiology*] (DAVI)
qm............ Query Message (AD)
QM............ Query Message (WDAA)
QM............ Query Module (MCD)
QM............ Queue Manager [*Computer science*] (CMD)
QM............ Quick-Make [*Contact*] (IAA)
QM............ Quinacrine Mustard [*Chromosome stain*]
QM............ Quinonemethide [*Organic chemistry*]
qm............ Quintal Metrico [*Metric Quintal*] [*Spain*] (AD)
QM............ Qumran Manuscripts (BJA)
QM............ Quo Modo [*In What Manner*] [*Latin*]
qm............ Quo Modo [*In What Manner*] [*Latin*] (AD)
QM1............ Quartermaster, First Class [*Navy rating*]
QM2............ Quartermaster, Second Class [*Navy rating*]
QM3............ Quartermaster, Third Class [*Navy rating*]
QMA............ Group Information Centre, Alcan Aluminum Ltd. [*Centre d'Information du Groupe, Alcan Aluminium Ltee*] Montreal, Quebec [*Library symbol National Library of Canada*] (NLC)
QMA............ Qatar Monetary Agency (AD)
qma............ Qualified Military Available (AD)
QMA............ Qualified Military Available
QMA............ Qualitative Materiel Approach [*Army*] (AABC)
QMA............ Quality Management Approach [*Business term*]
qma............ Quality Material Approach (AD)
QMA............ Quarry Masters' Association [*Australia*]
QMA............ Quarterly Moving Average
QMA............ Quartermasters Association [*Later, ALA*]
QMA............ Quebec Medical Association (AC)
QMAA............ Archives de la Chancellerie, L'Archeveche de Montreal, Quebec [*Library symbol National Library of Canada*] (NLC)
QMAAC............ Queen Mary's Army Auxiliary Corps [*The WAAC*] [*British*]
QMAB............ Montreal Association for the Blind, Quebec [*Library symbol National Library of Canada*] (NLC)
QMABB............ TECSULT, Montreal, Quebec [*Library symbol National Library of Canada*] (NLC)
QMAC............ Macdonald College Library, Ste-Anne-De-Bellevue, Quebec [*Library symbol National Library of Canada*] (NLC)
QMAC............ Quadripartite Materiel and Agreements Committee [*Military*] (AABC)
QMAC............ Quarter-Orbit Magnetic Attitude Control (PDAA)
QMACL............ Quebec Association for Children with Learning Disabilities [*Association Quebecoise pour les Enfants Souffrant de Troubles d'Apprentissage*] Montreal, Quebec [*Library symbol National Library of Canada*] (NLC)
QMACM............ Centre des Dossiers et de Documentation, Direction de Montreal, Ministere des Affaires Culturelles du Quebec [*Library symbol National Library of Canada*] (BIB)
QMACN............ Archives de la Congregation de Notre-Dame, Montreal, Quebec [*Library symbol National Library of Canada*] (NLC)
QMADMA............ Archives, Diocese of Montreal, Anglican Church of Canada, Quebec [*Library symbol National Library of Canada*] (NLC)
QMAE............ Aviation Electric Ltd., Montreal, Quebec [*Library symbol National Library of Canada*] (NLC)
QMAEC............ Atomic Energy of Canada [*L'Energie Atomique du Canada*] Montreal, Quebec [*Library symbol National Library of Canada*] (NLC)
QMAGB............ Bibliotheque Municipale, Magog, Quebec [*Library symbol National Library of Canada*] (NLC)
Q(Maint)............ Quartermaster Maintenance [*World War II*]
QMAL............ Air Liquide Canada Ltee., Montreal, Quebec [*Library symbol National Library of Canada*] (NLC)
QMALL............ Abbott Laboratories Ltd., Montreal, Quebec [*Library symbol National Library of Canada*] (NLC)
QMAM............ Allan Memorial Institute, Montreal, Quebec [*Library symbol National Library of Canada*] (NLC)
QMAMA............ Lavalin Environnement, Montreal, Quebec [*Library symbol National Library of Canada*] (NLC)
QMAMI............ Minerais LAC Ltee., Malartic, Quebec [*Library symbol National Library of Canada*] (NLC)
QMANSW............ Quarry Masters' Association of New South Wales [*Australia*]
QMAO............ Qualified for Mobilization Ashore Only [*Navy*]
qmao............ Qualified for Mobilization Ashore Only (AD)
QMAPO............ Centre de Documentation, APO Quebec, Montreal, Quebec [*Library symbol National Library of Canada*] (NLC)
QMAPS............ Quebec Aid for the Partially-Sighted [*Aide aux Insuffisants Visuels du Quebec*] Montreal, Quebec [*Library symbol National Library of Canada*] (NLC)
QMARC............ Archives Provinciales des Capucins, Montreal, Quebec [*Library symbol National Library of Canada*] (NLC)
QMAS............ Archives du Seminaire de Saint-Sulpice, Montreal, Quebec [*Library symbol National Library of Canada*] (NLC)
QMASBB............ ASEA [*Allmaenna Svenska Elektriska Aktiebolaget*] Brown Boveri, Inc., Montreal, Quebec [*Library symbol National Library of Canada*] (BIB)
QMASC............ Bibliotheque Municipale, Mascouche, Quebec [*Library symbol National Library of Canada*] (BIB)
QMASRC............ Space Research Corp., Mansonville, Quebec [*Library symbol National Library of Canada*] (NLC)
QMASSAS............ Centre de Documentation, Secteur Affaires Sociales, Association pour la Sante etla Securite du Travail, Montreal, Quebec [*Library symbol National Library of Canada*] (NLC)
QMATC............ College de Matane, Quebec [*Library symbol National Library of Canada*] (NLC)
QMAV............ Bibliotheque des Avocats, Barreau de Montreal, Quebec [*Library symbol National Library of Canada*] (NLC)
Q-max............ Quarantine Maximum (AD)
QMAY............ Ayerst, McKenna & Harrison, Inc. Montreal, Quebec [*Library symbol National Library of Canada*] (NLC)
QMB............ Information Resource Centre, Bell Canada [*Centre d'Information Specialisee, Bell Canada*], Montreal, Quebec [*Library symbol National Library of Canada*] (NLC)
QMB............ Qualified Medicare Beneficiary
QMB............ Qualified Mortgage Bond
QMB............ Quality Management Board (DOMA)
QMB............ Quarterly Management Bulletin [*A publication*] (DNAB)
QMB............ Queensbury [*England*] [*Seismograph station code, US Geological Survey*] (SEIS)
QMB............ Queensland Milk Board [*Australia*]
QMB............ Quick Make-and-Break [*Contact*] (DEN)
qmb............ Quick Make-and-Break (AD)
QMBA............ Ecole des Beaux-Arts, Montreal, Quebec [*Library symbol National Library of Canada*] (NLC)
QMBA............ Queensland Master Builders Association [*Australia*] (AD)
QMBAE............ Bristol Aero Engines Ltd., Montreal, Quebec [*Library symbol National Library of Canada*] (NLC)
QMBAN............ Centre de Documentation, Banque Nationale du Canada, Montreal, Quebec [*Library symbol National Library of Canada*] (NLC)
QMBB............ College Bois-De-Boulogne, Montreal, Quebec [*Library symbol National Library of Canada*] (NLC)

QMBBL .... Beauchemin, Beaton, Lapointe, Inc., Montreal, Quebec [*Library symbol National Library of Canada*] (NLC)
QMBC .... Byers, Casgrain, Montreal, Quebec [*Library symbol National Library of Canada*] (BIB)
QMBD .... Translation Bureau, Canada Department of the Secretary of State [*Bureau des Traductions, Secretariat d'Etat*] Montreal, Quebec [*Library symbol National Library of Canada*] (NLC)
QMBE .... Centre de Documentation, Bureau des Economies d'Energie du Quebec, Mont real, Quebec [*Library symbol National Library of Canada*] (NLC)
QMBGC .... Bibliotheque d'Ingenierie, BG Checo International Ltee., Montreal, Quebec [*Library symbol National Library of Canada*] (NLC)
QMBIM .... Bio-Mega, Inc., Montreal, Quebec [*Library symbol National Library of Canada*] (NLC)
QMBL .... Law Library, Bell Canada, Montreal, Quebec [*Library symbol National Library of Canada*] (NLC)
QMBM .... Bibliotheque de la Ville de Montreal, Quebec [*Library symbol National Library of Canada*] (NLC)
QMBMO .... Bank of Montreal [*Banque de Montreal*], Quebec [*Library symbol National Library of Canada*] (NLC)
QMBMS .... Management Sciences Library, Bell Canada, Montreal, Quebec [*Library symbol Obsolete National Library of Canada*] (NLC)
QMBN .... Bibliotheque Nationale du Quebec, Montreal, Quebec [*Library symbol National Library of Canada*] (NLC)
QMBNR .... Bell Northern Research, Montreal, Quebec [*Library symbol National Library of Canada*] (NLC)
QMBP .... Building Products Ltd., Montreal, Quebec [*Library symbol National Library of Canada*] (NLC)
QMBR .... Bio-Research Laboratories Ltd., Pointe-Claire, Quebec [*Library symbol National Library of Canada*] (NLC)
QMBT .... Montreal Board of Trade [*Chambre de Commerce du District de Montreal*] Quebec [*Library symbol National Library of Canada*] (NLC)
QMC .... Chief Quartermaster [*Navy rating*]
QMC .... College de Montreal, Quebec [*Library symbol National Library of Canada*] (NLC)
QMC .... James Carson Breckinridge Library, Quantico, VA [*OCLC symbol*] (OCLC)
QMC .... Quadripartite Materiel Committee [*Military*]
QMC .... Quartermaster Clerk [*Marine Corps*]
QMC .... Quartermaster Corps [*Army*]
QMC .... Queen Mary College [*London*]
QMC .... Queensland Mining Council [*Australia*]
QMC .... Quekett Microscopical Club [*British*] (BI)
QMC .... Quick Modification Concept (MCD)
QMCA .... Engineering Library, Canadair Ltd., Montreal, Quebec [*Library symbol National Library of Canada*] (NLC)
QMCAD .... Centre d'Animation, de Developpement, et de Recherche en Education, Montreal, Quebec [*Library symbol National Library of Canada*] (NLC)
QMCADM ..... Centre d'Accueil Domremy-Montreal, Ste.-Genevieve, Quebec [*Library symbol National Library of Canada*] (NLC)
QMCADQ ...... Conservatoire d'Art Dramatique de Montreal, Quebec [*Library symbol National Library of Canada*] (NLC)
QMCAE .... CAE Electronics Ltd., Montreal, Quebec [*Library symbol National Library of Canada*] (NLC)
QMCAG .... College Andre Grasset, Montreal, Quebec [*Library symbol National Library of Canada*] (NLC)
QMCAI .... Canadian Asbestos Information Centre [*Centre Canadien d'Information sur l'Amiante*] Montreal, Quebec [*Library symbol National Library of Canada*] (NLC)
QMC&S .... Quartermaster Center and School [*Army*] (RDA)
QMC & SO ..... Quartermaster Cataloging and Standardization Office [*Army*]
QMCAR .... Carmel de Montreal, Quebec [*Library symbol National Library of Canada*] (NLC)
QMCAT .... Commission de la Sante et de la Securite du Travail du Quebec, Montreal [*Library symbol National Library of Canada*] (NLC)
QMCAV .... Direction Generale du Cinema et de l'Audio-Visuel, Ministere des Communications du Quebec, Montreal, Quebec [*Library symbol National Library of Canada*] (NLC)
QMCB .... Canadian Broadcasting Corp. [*Societe Radio-Canada*] Montreal, Quebec [*Library symbol National Library of Canada*] (NLC)
QMCBE .... Engineering Headquarters, Canadian Broadcasting Corp. [*Service de l'Ingenierie, Societe Radio-Canada*] Montreal, Quebec [*Library symbol National Library of Canada*] (NLC)
QMCBH .... Catherine Booth Hospital, Montreal, Quebec [*Library symbol National Library of Canada*] (NLC)
QMCBM .... Music Library, Canadian Broadcasting Corp. [*Musicotheque et Discotheque, Societe Radio-Canada*], Montreal, Quebec [*Library symbol National Library of Canada*] (BIB)
QMCC .... Canada Cement Co., Montreal, Quebec [*Library symbol National Library of Canada*] (NLC)
QMCCA .... Centre Canadien d'Architecture [*Canadian Centre for Architecture*] Montreal, Quebec [*Library symbol National Library of Canada*] (NLC)
QMCCL .... Currie, Coopers & Lybrand Ltd., Montreal, Quebec [*Library symbol National Library of Canada*] (NLC)
QMCCR .... Canadian Council of Resource Ministers [*Conseil Canadien des Ministres des Ressources*] Montreal, Quebec [*Library symbol National Library of Canada*] (NLC)
QMCCS .... Centraide, Montreal, Quebec [*Library symbol National Library of Canada*] (NLC)
QMCD .... Centre Documentaire, Centrale des Bibliotheques, Montreal, Quebec [*Library symbol National Library of Canada*] (NLC)
QMCDM .... College de Maisonneuve, Montreal, Quebec [*Library symbol National Library of Canada*] (NLC)
QMCDP .... Caisse de Depot et Placement du Quebec, Montreal, Quebec [*Library symbol National Library of Canada*] (NLC)
QMCE .... Celanese Canada Ltd., Montreal, Quebec [*Library symbol National Library of Canada*] (NLC)
QMCEA .... Canadian Export Association [*Association Canadienne d'Exportation*] Montreal, Quebec [*Library symbol National Library of Canada*] (NLC)
QMCEC .... Catholic School Commission [*Commission des Ecoles Catholiques*] Montreal, Quebec [*Library symbol National Library of Canada*] (NLC)
QMCECI .... Centre Canadien d'Etudes et de Cooperation Internationale, Montreal, Quebec [*Library symbol National Library of Canada*] (NLC)
QMCED .... Centre de Documentation, Ministere du Commerce Exterieur et du Developpement Technologique du Quebec, Montreal, Quebec [*Library symbol National Library of Canada*] (BIB)
QMCF .... Merck Frosst Laboratories [*Laboratoires Merck Frosst*] Montreal, Quebec [*Library symbol National Library of Canada*] (NLC)
QMCFH .... Centre de Documentation, Charette, Fortier, Hawey, Touche, Ross, Montreal, Quebec [*Library symbol National Library of Canada*] (NLC)
QMCGW .... Clarkson, Gordon, Woods, Gordon, Montreal, Quebec [*Library symbol National Library of Canada*] (NLC)
QMCHA .... Queensland Mechanical Cane Harvesters' Association [*Australia*]
QMCHC .... Montreal Chest Hospital Centre [*Centre Hospitalier Thoracique de Montreal*]Quebec [*Library symbol National Library of Canada*] (NLC)
QMCHF .... Centre de Documentation, Centre Hospitalier Fleury, Montreal, Quebec [*Library symbol National Library of Canada*] (NLC)
QMCHL .... Centre Hospitalier de Lachine, Montreal, Quebec [*Library symbol National Library of Canada*] (NLC)
QMCICM ...... Centre Interculturel Monchanin, Montreal, Quebec [*Library symbol National Library of Canada*] (NLC)
QMCIH .... Bibliotheque de Documentation des Archives, Ville de Montreal, Quebec [*Library symbol National Library of Canada*] (NLC)
QMCIM .... Canadian Institute of Mining and Metallurgy [*Institut Canadien des Mines et de la Metallurgie*] Montreal, Quebec [*Library symbol National Library of Canada*] (NLC)
QMC-IRL .... Queen Mary College Industrial Research Ltd. [*Research center British*] (IRUK)
QMCJ .... Canadian Jewish Congress [*Congres Juif Canadien*] Montreal, Quebec [*Library symbol National Library of Canada*] (NLC)
QMCL .... CanAtom Ltd., Montreal, Quebec [*Library symbol National Library of Canada*] (NLC)
QMCLG .... College Lionel Groulx, Ste-Therese, Quebec [*Library symbol National Library of Canada*] (NLC)
QMCLK .... Quartermaster Clerk [*Navy rating*]
QMCM .... Canadian Marconi Co., Montreal, Quebec [*Library symbol National Library of Canada*] (NLC)
QMCM .... Master Chief Quartermaster [*Navy rating*]
QMCM .... Quartermaster Corporal-Major [*British military*] (DMA)
QMCN .... Canadian National Railways [*Chemins de fer Nationaux du Canada*] Montreal, Quebec [*Library symbol National Library of Canada*] (NLC)
QMCNC .... Chemical Library, Canadian National Railways [*Bibliotheque Chimique, Chemins de fer Nationaux du Canada*] Montreal, Quebec [*Library symbol Obsolete National Library of Canada*] (NLC)
QMCOM .... Conservatoire de Musique de Montreal, Quebec [*Library symbol National Library of Canada*] (NLC)
QMCP .... Canadian Pacific Ltd. [*Le Canadien Pacifique*] Montreal, Quebec [*Library symbol National Library of Canada*] (NLC)
QMCQ .... Cinematheque Quebecoise, Montreal, Quebec [*Library symbol National Library of Canada*] (BIB)
QMCR .... Canadian Copper Refiners Ltd., Montreal, Quebec [*Library symbol National Library of Canada*] (NLC)
QMCR .... Quartermaster Corps Regulations [*Army*]
QMCRI .... Centre de Recherche Industrielle du Quebec, Montreal, Quebec [*Library symbol National Library of Canada*] (NLC)
QMCRIM .... Centre de Documentation, Centre de Recherche Informatique de Montreal, Quebec [*Library symbol National Library of Canada*] (BIB)
QMCRP .... Conference des Recteurs et des Principaux des Universites du Quebec, Montreal, Quebec [*Library symbol National Library of Canada*] (NLC)
QMCS .... Christian Science Reading Room, Montreal, Quebec [*Library symbol National Library of Canada*] (NLC)
QMCS .... Quality Monitoring Control System [*Military*] (CAAL)
QMCS .... Senior Chief Quartermaster [*Navy rating*]
QMCSCA .... Archives de la Congregation de Sainte-Croix, Montreal, Quebec [*Library symbol National Library of Canada*] (NLC)
QMCSSMM ... CSSMM [*Centre de Services Sociaux du Montreal Metropolitain*], Montreal, Quebec [*Library symbol National Library of Canada*] (NLC)
QMCSSS .... Service de Reference, Conseil de la Sante et des Services Sociaux de la Region de Montreal Metropolitain, Montreal, Quebec [*Library symbol National Library of Canada*] (NLC)
QMCSVA .... Archives des Clercs de Saint-Viateur, Province de Montreal, Outremont, Quebec [*Library symbol National Library of Canada*] (NLC)
QMCT .... Commission de Transport de la Communaute Urbaine de Montreal, Quebec [*Library symbol National Library of Canada*] (NLC)
QMCTC .... Quartermaster Corps Technical Committee [*Army*]

QMCTM........ Canadian Tobacco Manufacturers' Council [*Conseil Canadien des Fabricants des Produits du Tabac*] Montreal, Quebec [*Library symbol National Library of Canada*] (NLC)
QMCVDDH... Que Me - Comite Vietnam pour la Defense des Droits de l'Homme [*Que Me - Vietnam Committee on Human Rights*] (EAIO)
QMCVM....... Commission des Valeurs Mobilieres du Quebec, Montreal, Quebec [*Library symbol National Library of Canada*] (NLC)
QMCW......... Canada Wire & Cable Co. Ltd., Montreal, Quebec [*Library symbol National Library of Canada*] (NLC)
QMD........... Institut Genealogique Drouin, Montreal, Quebec [*Library symbol National Library of Canada*] (NLC)
QMDA.......... Daniel Arbour & Associes, Montreal, Quebec [*Library symbol National Library of Canada*] (NLC)
QMDB.......... College Jean-De-Brebeuf, Montreal, Quebec [*Library symbol National Library of Canada*] (NLC)
QMDC.......... Dawson College, Montreal, Quebec [*Library symbol National Library of Canada*] (NLC)
QMDE.......... Dominion Engineering Works Ltd., Montreal, Quebec [*Library symbol National Library of Canada*] (NLC)
QMDEP........ Quartermaster Depot [*Army*]
QMDH.......... Douglas Hospital Centre [*Centre Hospitalier Douglas*] Montreal, Quebec [*Library symbol National Library of Canada*] (NLC)
QMDK.......... Quick Mechanical Disconnect Kit
qmdk........... Quick Mechanical Disconnect Kit (AD)
QMDL.......... Domtar Ltd., Montreal, Quebec [*Library symbol National Library of Canada*] (NLC)
QMDM......... Montreal Association for the Mentally Retarded [*Association de Montreal pour les Deficients Mentaux*] Quebec [*Library symbol National Library of Canada*] (NLC)
QMDMR....... Groupe DMR, Inc., Montreal, Quebec [*Library symbol National Library of Canada*] (BIB)
QMDO.......... Qualitative Materiel Development Objective [*Army*]
QMDOM....... Dominion Bridge Co. Ltd., Montreal, Quebec [*Library symbol National Library of Canada*] (NLC)
QMDPC........ Quartermaster Data Processing Center [*Army*]
QMDT.......... Dominion Textile, Montreal, Quebec [*Library symbol National Library of Canada*] (NLC)
QME............ Quantock Marine Enterprises (AD)
qme............. Queueing Matrix Evaluation (AD)
QME............ Queueing Matrix Evaluation (PDAA)
QMEA.......... Atmospheric Environment Service, Environment Canada [*Service de l'Environnement Atmospherique, Environnement Canada*] Dorval, Quebec [*Library symbol National Library of Canada*] (NLC)
QMEA.......... Queensland Meat Exporters' Association [*Australia*]
QMEC.......... Monenco Consultants Ltd., Montreal, Quebec [*Library symbol National Library of Canada*] (NLC)
QMECB........ Centrale des Bibliotheques, Services Documentaires Multimedia, Inc., Montreal, Quebec [*Library symbol National Library of Canada*] (NLC)
QMECS........ Experts-Conseils Shawinigan, Montreal, Quebec [*Library symbol National Library of Canada*] (NLC)
Q Med......... Q-Med, Inc. [*Associated Press*] (SAG)
QMED.......... Quest Medical [*NASDAQ symbol*] (TTSB)
QMED.......... Quest Medical, Inc. [*NASDAQ symbol*] (NQ)
QMEE.......... Environmental Protection Service, Environment Canada [*Service de la Protection de l'Environnement, Environnement Canada*] Montreal, Quebec [*Library symbol National Library of Canada*] (NLC)
QMEM.......... Bibliotheque Municipale de la Ville de Montreal-Est, Quebec [*Library symbol National Library of Canada*] (BIB)
QMEN.......... Ministere de l'Environnement, Montreal, Quebec [*Library symbol National Library of Canada*] (NLC)
QMENT........ National Theatre School [*Ecole Nationale de Theatre*] Montreal, Quebec [*Library symbol National Library of Canada*] (NLC)
QMEP.......... Ecole Polytechnique, Montreal, Quebec [*Library symbol National Library of Canada*] (NLC)
QMEPCC...... Quartermaster Equipment and Parts Commodity Center [*Army*]
QMERS........ E. R. Squibb & Sons Ltd., Montreal, Quebec [*Library symbol National Library of Canada*] (NLC)
QMES.......... Ecole Secondaire Saint-Stanislas, Montreal, Quebec [*Library symbol National Library of Canada*] (NLC)
QMF............ Fraser-Hickson Institute, Montreal, Quebec [*Library symbol National Library of Canada*] (NLC)
QMF............ Query Management Facility [*Database*] (BYTE)
QMFA.......... Montreal Museum of Fine Arts [*Musee des Beaux-Arts de Montreal*] Quebec [*Library symbol National Library of Canada*] (NLC)
QMFAC........ Farinon Canada, Dorval, Quebec [*Library symbol National Library of Canada*] (NLC)
QMFBD........ Federal Business Development Bank [*Banque Federale de Developpement*] Montreal, Quebec [*Library symbol National Library of Canada*] (NLC)
QMFC.......... First Church of Christ, Scientist, Montreal, Quebec [*Library symbol National Library of Canada*] (NLC)
QMFCI......... Quartermaster Food and Container Institute (AD)
QMFCIAF..... Quartermaster Food and Container Institute for the Armed Forces
QMFCJ........ Bibliotheque de Theologie, les Facultes de la Compagnie de Jesus, Montreal, Quebec [*Library symbol National Library of Canada*] (NLC)
QMFER........ Forest Engineering Research Institute of Canada [*Institut Canadien de Recherches en Genie Forestier*] Pointe-Claire, Quebec [*Library symbol National Library of Canada*] (NLC)
QMFH.......... Frank W. Horner Ltd., Montreal, Quebec [*Library symbol National Library of Canada*] (NLC)
QMFMO....... Federation des Medecins Omnipraticiens du Quebec, Montreal, Quebec [*Library symbol National Library of Canada*] (NLC)
QMFMS........ Federation des Medecins Specialistes du Quebec, Montreal, Quebec [*Library symbol National Library of Canada*] (NLC)
QMFR.......... Arctic Biological Station, Fisheries and Oceans Canada [*Station Biologique del'Arctique, Peches et Oceans Canada*] Ste-Anne-De-Bellevue, Quebec [*Library symbol National Library of Canada*] (NLC)
QMFRA........ Archives des Franciscains, Montreal, Quebec [*Library symbol National Library of Canada*] (NLC)
QMFRAN...... Studium Franciscain de Theologie, Montreal, Quebec [*Library symbol National Library of Canada*] (NLC)
QMFSGA...... Archives des Freres de Saint-Gabriel, Montreal, Quebec [*Library symbol National Library of Canada*] (NLC)
QMG............ QMG Holdings, Inc. [*Toronto Stock Exchange symbol*]
QMG............ Quartermaster General [*Army*]
QMG............ Quench Melt Growth [*Physics*]
QMG............ Sir George Williams Campus, Concordia University, Montreal, Quebec [*Library symbol National Library of Canada*] (NLC)
QMGA.......... Montreal Gazette, Quebec [*Library symbol National Library of Canada*] (NLC)
QMGB.......... Grands Ballets Canadiens, Montreal, Quebec [*Library symbol National Library of Canada*] (NLC)
QMGDH........ Grace Dart Hospital Center, Montreal, Quebec [*Library symbol National Library of Canada*] (NLC)
QM Gen....... Quartermaster General [*Military*] (GFGA)
QMGF.......... Quartermaster-General to the Forces [*Military British*]
QMGG.......... Department of Geography, Sir George Williams Campus, Concordia University, Montreal, Quebec [*Library symbol National Library of Canada*] (NLC)
QMGGM....... University Map Collection, Department of Geography, Sir George Williams Campus, Concordia University, Montreal, Quebec [*Library symbol National Library of Canada*] (NLC)
QMGH.......... Montreal General Hospital [*Hopital General de Montreal*] Quebec [*Library symbol National Library of Canada*] (NLC)
QMGHC........ Community Health Department, Montreal General Hospital [*Departement de Sante Communautaire, Hopital General de Montreal*], Quebec [*Library symbol National Library of Canada*] (NLC)
QMGHN........ Nurses' Library, Montreal General Hospital [*Bibliotheque des Infirmieres, Hopital General de Montreal*], Quebec [*Library symbol National Library of Canada*] (NLC)
QMGL.......... Genstar Ltd., Montreal, Quebec [*Library symbol National Library of Canada*] (NLC)
QMGLS........ Library Studies Program, Concordia University, Montreal, Quebec [*Library symbol National Library of Canada*] (NLC)
QMGM.......... Gaz Metropolitain, Montreal, Quebec [*Library symbol National Library of Canada*] (BIB)
QMGMC....... Quartermaster-General of the Marine Corps
QMGO.......... Quartermaster-General's Office [*Military British*] (ROG)
QMGP.......... Gerard Parizeau Ltee, Montreal, Quebec [*Library symbol National Library of Canada*] (NLC)
QMGS.......... Grand Seminaire, Montreal, Quebec [*Library symbol National Library of Canada*] (NLC)
QMH............ Hydro-Quebec, Montreal, Quebec [*Library symbol National Library of Canada*] (NLC)
QMH............ Queens Moat Houses [*Hoteller*] [*British*]
QMHC.......... Medical Library, Hoechst Canada, Inc., Montreal, Quebec [*Library symbol National Library of Canada*] (BIB)
QMHC.......... Quinhon Missionary Sisters of the Holy Cross (TOCD)
QMHCL........ Bibliotheque Medicale, Hopital Charles Lemoyne, Greenfield Park, Quebec [*Library symbol National Library of Canada*] (NLC)
QMHCLC...... Departement de Sante Communautaire, Hopital Charles Lemoyne, Greenfield Park, Quebec [*Library symbol National Library of Canada*] (NLC)
QMHD.......... Hotel-Dieu de Montreal, Quebec [*Library symbol National Library of Canada*] (NLC)
QMHDE........ Centre de Documentation, Direction de l'Environnement, Hydro-Quebec, Montreal, Quebec [*Library symbol National Library of Canada*] (NLC)
QMHE.......... Ecole des Hautes Etudes Commerciales, Montreal, Quebec [*Library symbol National Library of Canada*] (NLC)
QMHGC........ Centre Hospitalier de Verdun, Quebec [*Library symbol National Library of Canada*] (NLC)
QMHGF........ Hopital General Fleury, Montreal, Quebec [*Library symbol National Library of Canada*] (NLC)
QMHI........... Centre de Documentation, Hydro-Quebec International, Montreal, Quebec [*Library symbol National Library of Canada*] (BIB)
QMHJR........ Centre de Documentation du Personnel, Hopital de Convalescents Julius Richardson[*Staff Library, Julius Richardson Convalescent Hospital, Inc.*], Montreal, Quebec [*Library symbol National Library of Canada*] (NLC)
QMHJT......... Hopital Jean Talon, Montreal, Quebec [*Library symbol National Library of Canada*] (NLC)
QMHM.......... Centre Hospitalier Jacques Viger, Montreal, Quebec [*Library symbol National Library of Canada*] (NLC)
QMHME........ Hopital Marie-Enfant, Montreal, Quebec [*Library symbol National Library of Canada*] (NLC)
QMHMR........ Hopital Maisonneuve-Rosemont, Montreal, Quebec [*Library symbol National Library of Canada*] (NLC)
QMHND........ Hopital Notre-Dame, Montreal, Quebec [*Library symbol National Library of Canada*] (NLC)
QMHNDI...... Bibliotheque des Services Infirmiers, Hopital Notre-Dame, Montreal, Quebec [*Library symbol National Library of Canada*] (NLC)
QMHP.......... Qualified Mental Health Professional
QMHRP........ Hopital Riviere-Des-Prairies, Montreal, Quebec [*Library symbol National Library of Canada*] (NLC)

QMHRT Centre de Documentation, Redaction et Terminologie, Hydro-Quebec, Montreal, Quebec [*Library symbol National Library of Canada*] (BIB)
QMHSC Hopital du Sacre-Coeur, Montreal, Quebec [*Library symbol National Library of Canada*] (NLC)
QMHSCA Hopital Santa Cabrini, Montreal, Quebec [*Library symbol National Library of Canada*] (NLC)
QMHSJ Hopital Louis H. LaFonataine, Montreal, Quebec [*Library symbol National Library of Canada*] (NLC)
QMHSJA Hopital Ste-Jeanne-D'Arc, Montreal, Quebec [*Library symbol National Library of Canada*] (NLC)
QMHSL Hopital Saint-Luc, Montreal, Quebec [*Library symbol National Library of Canada*] (NLC)
QMHSLC Departement de Sante Communautaire, Hopital Saint-Luc, Montreal, Quebec [*Library symbol National Library of Canada*] (NLC)
QMHVG Centre de Documentation, Verification Generale, Hydro-Quebec, Montreal, Quebec [*Library symbol National Library of Canada*] (BIB)
QMI Insurance Institute of the Province of Quebec [*Insitut d'Assurance du Quebec*] Montreal, Quebec [*Library symbol National Library of Canada*] (NLC)
QMI Qualification Maintainability Inspection
QMIA International Air Transport Association [*Association du Transport Aerien International*] Montreal, Quebec [*Library symbol National Library of Canada*] (NLC)
QMIA Quartermaster Intelligence Agency [*Merged with Defense Intelligence Agency*]
QMIA Queensland Motor Industry Association [*Australia*] (AD)
QMIAA Institut des Arts Appliques, Montreal, Quebec [*Library symbol National Library of Canada*] (NLC)
QMIAG Institut des Arts Graphiques, Montreal, Quebec [*Library symbol National Library of Canada*] (NLC)
QMIAP Pavillon Albert Prevost, Montreal, Quebec [*Library symbol National Library of Canada*] (NLC)
QMIC International Civil Aviation Organization [*Organisation de l'Aviation Civile Internationale*] Montreal, Quebec [*Library symbol National Library of Canada*] (NLC)
QMICA Institute of Chartered Accountants of Quebec [*Institut Canadien des Comptables Agrees du Quebec*] Montreal, Quebec [*Library symbol National Library of Canada*] (NLC)
QMICAV Institut Culturel Avataq, Montreal, Quebec [*Library symbol National Library of Canada*] (BIB)
QMICE Canadian Institute of Adult Education [*Institut Canadien d'Education des Adultes*] Montreal, Quebec [*Library symbol National Library of Canada*] (NLC)
QMICM Institut de Cardiologie de Montreal, Quebec [*Library symbol National Library of Canada*] (NLC)
QMIF Imasco Foods Ltd., Montreal, Quebec [*Library symbol National Library of Canada*] (NLC)
QMIFQ Informatech France-Quebec, Montreal, Quebec [*Library symbol National Library of Canada*] (NLC)
QMIG Industrial Grain Products Ltd., Montreal, Quebec [*Library symbol National Library of Canada*] (NLC)
QMII Istituto Italiano di Cultura, Montreal, Quebec [*Library symbol National Library of Canada*] (NLC)
QMIIS Islamic Studies Library, McGill University, Montreal, Quebec [*Library symbol National Library of Canada*] (NLC)
QMIIST International Institute of Stress [*Institut International du Stress*] Montreal, Quebec [*Library symbol Obsolete National Library of Canada*] (NLC)
QMIKES Quadrupole Mass Analyzed Ion Kinetic Energy Spectroscopy
QMILO International Labour Office [*Bureau International du Travail*] Montreal, Quebec [*Library symbol National Library of Canada*] (NLC)
QMIM Institut Armand-Frappier, Universite du Quebc, Laval, Quebec [*Library symbol National Library of Canada*] (NLC)
QMIMM Ministere des Communautes Culturelles et de l'Immigration, Montreal, Quebec [*Library symbol National Library of Canada*] (NLC)
QMIMSO Quartermaster Industrial Mobilization Services Offices [*Army*]
QMINC Institut du Cancer de Montreal, Quebec [*Library symbol National Library of Canada*] (NLC)
QMINCA Institut National Canadien pour les Aveugles, Montreal, Quebec [*Library symbol National Library of Canada*] (NLC)
QMINP Institut National de Productivite, Montreal, Quebec [*Library symbol National Library of Canada*] (NLC)
QMIP Institute of Parasitoloy, Macdonald College, Ste-Anne-De-Bellevue, Quebec [*Library symbol National Library of Canada*] (NLC)
QMIPP Institut Philippe Pinel de Montreal, Quebec [*Library symbol National Library of Canada*] (NLC)
QMIRC Institut de Recherches Cliniques, Montreal, Quebec [*Library symbol National Library of Canada*] (NLC)
QMIRP Institute for Research on Public Policy [*Institut de Recherches Politiques*] Montreal, Quebec [*Library symbol National Library of Canada*] (NLC)
QMIRS Informatheque IRSST [*Institut de Recherche en Sante et Securite au Travail*] Montreal, Quebec [*Library symbol National Library of Canada*] (NLC)
QMIS Quality Review Management Information System [*IRS*]
QMISM Centre de Documentation, Institut Raymond-Dewar, Montreal, Quebec [*Library symbol National Library of Canada*] (NLC)
QMIST Centre d'Information, IST [*Industriel Services Techniques*], Montreal, Quebec [*Library symbol National Library of Canada*] (BIB)
QMIT Imperial Tobacco Co. of Canada Ltd., Montreal, Quebec [*Library symbol National Library of Canada*] (NLC)
QMITR Research Library, Imperial Tobacco Co. of Canada Ltd., Montreal, Quebec [*Library symbol National Library of Canada*] (NLC)
QMJ Jewish Public Library [*Bibliotheque Juive Publique, Montreal*] Quebec [*Library symbol National Library of Canada*] (NLC)
QMJB Jardin Botanique, Montreal, Quebec [*Library symbol National Library of Canada*] (NLC)
QMJES Technical Services, Joseph E. Seagram & Sons Ltd., La Salle, Quebec [*Library symbol National Library of Canada*] (NLC)
QMJG Jewish General Hospital, Montreal, Quebec [*Library symbol National Library of Canada*] (NLC)
QMJGI Institute of Community and Family Psychiatry, Jewish General Hospital, Montreal,Quebec [*Library symbol National Library of Canada*] (NLC)
QMJGL Lady Davis Institute for Medical Research, Jewish General Hospital, Montreal, Quebec [*Library symbol National Library of Canada*] (NLC)
QMJH Hopital de Mont-Joli, Inc., Quebec [*Library symbol National Library of Canada*] (NLC)
QMJHW Johnson & Higgins, Willis, Faber Ltd., Montreal, Quebec [*Library symbol National Library of Canada*] (NLC)
QMJJ Johnson & Johnson Ltd., Montreal, Quebec [*Library symbol National Library of Canada*] (NLC)
QMJL John Lovell & Son City Directories Ltd., Montreal, Quebec [*Library symbol National Library of Canada*] (NLC)
QMJLP Laboratoire de Police Scientifique, Montreal, Quebec [*Library symbol National Library of Canada*] (NLC)
QMJM Canada Department of Justice [*Ministere de la Justice*] Montreal, Quebec [*Library symbol National Library of Canada*] (NLC)
QMJRH James R. Hay & Associates, Pointe Claire, Quebec [*Library symbol National Library of Canada*] (BIB)
QMJSJ Commission des Services Juridiques du Quebec, Montreal, Quebec [*Library symbol National Library of Canada*] (NLC)
QML Loyola Campus, Concordia University, Montreal, Quebec [*Library symbol National Library of Canada*] (NLC)
QML Qayyum Moslem League [*Pakistan*] (PD)
QML Qualified Manufacturers List [*DoD*]
QMLA Laboratoires Abbott Ltee, Montreal, Quebec [*Library symbol National Library of Canada*] (NLC)
QMLAV Lavalin, Inc., Montreal, Quebec [*Library symbol National Library of Canada*] (BIB)
QMLAVE Lavalin Environment, Inc., Montreal, Quebec [*Library symbol National Library of Canada*] (BIB)
QMLBD Lafleur, Brown & De Granpre, Montreal, Quebec [*Library symbol National Library of Canada*] (BIB)
QMLCA Lower Canada Arms Collectors Association, Montreal, Quebec [*Library symbol National Library of Canada*] (NLC)
QMLCC Lower Canada College Montreal, Quebec [*Library symbol National Library of Canada*] (NLC)
QMLCPF Bibliotheque de la Faune, Ministere du Loisir, de la Chasse et de la Peche, Montreal, Quebec [*Library symbol National Library of Canada*] (NLC)
QMLF Librairies Flammarion, Montreal, Quebec [*Library symbol National Library of Canada*] (NLC)
QMLG Lakeshore General Hospital [*Hopital General du Lakeshore*] Pointe-Claire, Quebec [*Library symbol National Library of Canada*] (NLC)
QMLGC Community Health Department, Lakeshore General Hospital [*Departement de SanteCommunautaire, Hopital General du Lakeshore*], Pointe-Claire, Quebec [*Library symbol National Library of Canada*] (NLC)
QMLM Bibliotheque Municipale, Mont-Laurier, Quebec [*Library symbol National Library of Canada*] (BIB)
QMLP Centre de Documentation, La Presse Ltee., Montreal, Quebec [*Library symbol National Library of Canada*] (NLC)
QMLPT Librairie Pointe-Aux-Trembles, Quebec [*Library symbol National Library of Canada*] (NLC)
QMLQ Centre de Documentation, Loto-Quebec, Montreal, Quebec [*Library symbol National Library of Canada*] (NLC)
QMLR Constance-Lethbridge Rehabilitation Centre [*Centre de Readaptation Constance-Lethbridge*] Montreal, Quebec [*Library symbol National Library of Canada*] (NLC)
QMM Marina di Massa [*Italy*] [*Airport symbol*] (AD)
QMM McLennan Library, McGill University, Montreal, Quebec [*Library symbol National Library of Canada*] (NLC)
QMM Queensland Maritime Museum [*Australia*]
QMMAC Musee d'Art Contemporain, Montreal, Quebec [*Library symbol National Library of Canada*] (NLC)
QMMAQ La Magnetotheque, Montreal, Quebec [*Library symbol National Library of Canada*] (NLC)
QMMAR Marianapolis College, Montreal, Quebec [*Library symbol National Library of Canada*] (NLC)
QMMB Blackader/Lauterman Library of Architecture and Art, McGill University, Montreal, Quebec [*Library symbol National Library of Canada*] (NLC)
QMMBC Molson Breweries of Canada Ltd., Montreal, Quebec [*Library symbol Obsolete National Library of Canada*] (NLC)
QMMBG Botany-Genetics Library, McGill University, Montreal, Quebec [*Library symbol National Library of Canada*] (BIB)
QMMBZ Blacker-Wood Library of Zoology and Ornithology, McGill University, Montreal, Quebec [*Library symbol National Library of Canada*] (NLC)
QMMC Miron Co. Ltd., Montreal, Quebec [*Library symbol National Library of Canada*] (NLC)
QMMCH Montreal Children's Hospital, Quebec [*Library symbol National Library of Canada*] (NLC)
QMMCR Musee du Chatau de Ramezay, Montreal, Quebec [*Library symbol National Library of Canada*] (NLC)

QMMD .... Religious Studies Library, McGill University, Montreal, Quebec [*Library symbol National Library of Canada*] (NLC)
QMME .... Physical Sciences and Engineering Library, McGill University, Montreal, Quebec [*Library symbol National Library of Canada*] (NLC)
QMMG .... Map and Air Photo Library, McGill University, Montreal, Quebec [*Library symbol National Library of Canada*] (NLC)
QMMGS .... Department of Geological Sciences, McGill University, Montreal, Quebec [*Library symbol National Library of Canada*] (NLC)
QMMH .... Mental Hygiene Istitute [*Institut de l'Hygiene Mentale*] Montreal, Quebec [*Library symbol National Library of Canada*] (NLC)
QMMHH .... Maimonides Hospital Geriatric Center [*Centre Hospitalier Geriatrique Maimonides*], Montreal, Quebec [*Library symbol National Library of Canada*] (NLC)
QMMI .... Atwater Library [*Formerly, Mechanics Institute Library*] Montreal, Quebec [*Library symbol National Library of Canada*] (NLC)
QMMIQ .... Quebec Regional Office, Employment and Immigration Canada [*Bureau Regional duQuebec, Emploi et Immigration Canada*] Montreal, Quebec [*Library symbol National Library of Canada*] (NLC)
QMML .... Law Library, McGill University, Montreal, Quebec [*Library symbol National Library of Canada*] (NLC)
QMMLS .... Library Science Library, McGill University, Montreal, Quebec [*Library symbol National Library of Canada*] (NLC)
QMMM .... Medical Library, McGill University, Montreal, Quebec [*Library symbol National Library of Canada*] (NLC)
QMMMCM ... McCord Museum, McGill University, Montreal, Quebec [*Library symbol National Library of Canada*] (NLC)
QMMMDM ... Marvin Duchow Music Library, McGill University, Montreal, Quebec [*Library symbol National Library of Canada*] (NLC)
QMMMM ...... Montreal Military and Maritime Museum, Quebec [*Library symbol National Library of Canada*] (NLC)
QMMN .... Nursing/Social Work Library, McGill University, Montreal, Quebec [*Library symbol National Library of Canada*] (NLC)
QMMO .... Osler Library, McGill University, Montreal, Quebec [*Library symbol National Library of Canada*] (NLC)
QMMOC .... Monsanto Canada Ltd., Montreal, Quebec [*Library symbol National Library of Canada*] (NLC)
QMMOS .... Montreal Star, Quebec [*Library symbol National Library of Canada*] (NLC)
QMMPB .... MPB Technologies, Dorval, Quebec [*Library symbol National Library of Canada*] (NLC)
QMMRB .... Department of Rare Books and Special Collections, McGill University, Montreal, Quebec [*Library symbol National Library of Canada*] (NLC)
QMMRS .... Mendelsohn Rosentzveig Shacter, Montreal, Quebec [*Library symbol National Library of Canada*] (BIB)
QMMSC .... Howard Ross Library of Management, McGill University, Montreal, Quebec [*Library symbol National Library of Canada*] (NLC)
QMMSR .... Centre de Documentation, Ministere de la Main-d'Oeuvre et de la Securite du Revenu du Quebec, Montreal, Quebec [*Library symbol National Library of Canada*] (NLC)
QMN .... Centres Biblio-Culturels de Montreal-Nord, Quebec [*Library symbol National Library of Canada*] (NLC)
QMNA .... Canadian Pulp and Paper Asssociation [*Association Canadienne des Producteurs dePates et Papiers*] Montreal, Quebec [*Library symbol National Library of Canada*] (NLC)
QMNB .... Biotechnology Branch, CISTI , Montreal, Quebec [*Canada Institute for Scienctific and Technical Information*] [*Annexe de Biotechnologie, ICIST*] [*Library symbol*] [*National Library of Canada*] (BIB)
QMNDE .... Hopital Notre-Dame-De-L'Esperance-De-St-Laurent, Montreal, Quebec [*Library symbol National Library of Canada*] (NLC)
QMNE .... Northern Electric Co. Ltd., Montreal, Quebec [*Library symbol National Library of Canada*] (NLC)
QMNF .... National Film Board, Montreal Quebec [*Formerly, Ottawa*] [*Office National du Film, Montreal (Anciennement Ottawa)*] [*Library symbol*] [*National Library of Canada*] (NLC)
QMNFNI .... National Information/Distribution System, National Film Board [*Systeme d'Information et de Distribution pour les Produits Audio-Visuels Canadiens, Office National du film*] Montreal, Quebec [*Library symbol National Library of Canada*] (NLC)
QMNHH .... Health Protection Branch, Canada Department of National Health and Welfare [*Direction Generale de la Protection de la Sante, Ministere de la Sante Nationale et du Bien-Etre Social*] Montreal, Quebec [*Library symbol National Library of Canada*] (NLC)
QMNIH .... Montreal Neurological Institute and Hospital [*Institut et Hopital Neurologiques de Montreal*] Quebec [*Library symbol National Library of Canada*] (NLC)
QMNOT .... Northern Telecom Canada Ltd., Montreal, Quebec [*Library symbol National Library of Canada*] (NLC)
QMNR .... Noranda Research Centre, Pointe-Claire, Quebec [*Library symbol National Library of Canada*] (NLC)
QMNT .... Nesbitt, Thomson & Co. Ltd., Montreal, Quebec [*Library symbol National Library of Canada*] (NLC)
QMO .... Oratoire Saint-Joseph, Montreal, Quebec [*Library symbol National Library of Canada*] (NLC)
qmo .... Qualitative Material Objective (AD)
QMO .... Qualitative Materiel Objective [*Army*] (AABC)
QMO .... Quartz Mountain State Park [*Oklahoma*] [*Seismograph station code, US Geological Survey*] (SEIS)
QMO .... Queen Mary's Own [*British military*] (DMA)
QMO & O ..... Quebec, Montreal, Ottawa & Occidental [*Railway*]
QMOB .... Office de Biologie, Ministere du Loisir, de la Chasse et de la Peche, Montreal, Quebec [*Library symbol Obsolete National Library of Canada*] (NLC)
QMobSC ...... Quadripartite Mobility Standardization Committee [*Military*] (AABC)
QMOCP .... Canadian Livestock Feed Board [*Office Canadien des Provendes*] Montreal, Quebec [*Library symbol National Library of Canada*] (NLC)
QMOCQ .... Office de la Construction du Quebec, Montreal, Quebec [*Library symbol National Library of Canada*] (NLC)
QMOD .... Queue Modification Process
QMOF .... Ogilvie Flour Mills Co. Ltd., Montreal, Quebec [*Library symbol National Library of Canada*] (NLC)
QMOFJ .... Office Franco-Quebecois pour la Jeunesse, Montreal, Quebec [*Library symbol National Library of Canada*] (NLC)
QMOI .... Ordre des Infirmieres et Infirmiers du Quebec, Montreal, Quebec [*Library symbol National Library of Canada*] (NLC)
QMOLF .... Office de la Langue Francaise, Montreal, PQ, Canada [*Library symbol National Library of Canada*] (NLC)
QMOP .... Centre de Documentation, Office de Planification et de Developpement du Quebec, Montreal, Quebec [*Library symbol National Library of Canada*] (BIB)
QMOR .... Ogilvy, Renaud Law Library, Montreal, Quebec [*Library symbol National Library of Canada*] (BIB)
QMORC .... Quartermaster Officers' Reserve Corps [*Military*]
Q(Mov) .... Quartermaster Movements [*World War II*]
QMOW .... Quartermaster of the Watch [*Navy*] (DNAB)
QMP .... Qualitative Management Program [*Army*] (INF)
QMP .... Quezon Memorial Park [*Philippines*] (AD)
QMPA .... Centre de Documentation, Projet Archipel de Montreal, Quebec [*Library symbol National Library of Canada*] (NLC)
QMPA .... Quartermaster Purchasing Agency [*Army*]
QMPA .... Queensland Master Painters Association [*Australia*] (AD)
QMPAE .... Paramax Electronics, Montreal, Quebec [*Library symbol National Library of Canada*] (BIB)
QMPC .... Presbyterian College, Montreal, Quebec [*Library symbol National Library of Canada*] (NLC)
QMPC .... Quartermaster Petroleum Center [*Army*] (MUGU)
QMPCA .... Agriculture Canada, Montreal, Quebec [*Library symbol National Library of Canada*] (NLC)
QMPCG .... Documentation Centre, George Etienne Cartier House, Parks Canada [*Centre de Documentation, Maison George-Etienne Cartier, Parcs Canada*], Montreal, Quebec [*Library symbol National Library of Canada*] (NLC)
QMPCUSA .... Quartermaster Petroleum Center, United States Army
QMPE .... Pezaris Electronics Co., Montreal, Quebec [*Library symbol National Library of Canada*] (NLC)
QMPI .... Polish Institute of Arts and Sciences in Canada [*Institut Polonais des Arts et des Sciences au Canada*] Montreal, Quebec [*Library symbol National Library of Canada*] (NLC)
QMPM .... Peat, Marwick, Mitchell et Cie., Montreal, Quebec [*Library symbol National Library of Canada*] (NLC)
QMPM .... Quantitative Methods for Public Management [*Course*]
QMPP .... Pulp and Paper Research Institute of Canada [*Institut Canadien de Recherches sur les Pates et Papiers*] Pointe-Claire, Quebec [*Library symbol National Library of Canada*] (NLC)
QMPPM .... Montreal Branch, Pulp and Paper Research Institute of Canada [*Succursale de Montreal, Centre Canadien de Recherche sur les Pates et Papiers*], Quebec [*Library symbol National Library of Canada*] (BIB)
QMPRA .... Archives Providence, Montreal, Quebec [*Library symbol National Library of Canada*] (NLC)
QMPSB .... Protestant School Board of Greater Montreal, Quebec [*Library symbol National Library of Canada*] (NLC)
QMPSR .... P. S. Ross & Partners, Montreal, Quebec (NLC)
QMPTI .... Potton Technical Industries, Mansonville, Quebec [*Library symbol National Library of Canada*] (NLC)
QMPWQ .... Quebec Region Library, Public Works Canada [*Bibliotheque de la Region du Quebec, Travaux Publics Canada*] Montreal, Quebec [*Library symbol National Library of Canada*] (NLC)
QMQ .... Queen Mary Veterans Hospital [*Hopital Reine-Marie (Anciens combattants)*] Montreal, Quebec [*Library symbol National Library of Canada*] (NLC)
QMQAR .... Centre Regional de Montreal, Archives Nationales du Quebec, Quebec [*Library symbol National Library of Canada*] (NLC)
QMQAR .... Quebec Archives, Montreal, Quebec [*Library symbol National Library of Canada*] (NLC)
QMQB .... Quick-Make, Quick-Break
qmqb .... Quick-Make Quick-Break (AD)
QMQDP .... Commission des Droits de la Personne du Quebec, Montreal, Quebec [*Library symbol National Library of Canada*] (NLC)
QMQE .... Queen Elizabeth Hospital, Montreal, Quebec [*Library symbol National Library of Canada*] (NLC)
QMR .... Qualitative Material Report
qmr .... Qualitative Material Requirement (AD)
QMR .... Qualitative Materiel Requirement [*Army*]
QMR .... Qualitative Military Requirements [*NATO*] (NATG)
QMR .... Quartermaster
Qmr .... Quartermaster [*Military*] (AD)
QMR .... Queen Mary's Regiment [*British military*] (DMA)
QMR .... Quick Medical Reference [*Computer system*]
QMR .... Royal Bank of Canada [*Banque Royale du Canada*] Montreal, Quebec [*Library symbol National Library of Canada*] (NLC)
QMRA .... Railway Association of Canada, Montreal, Quebec [*Library symbol National Library of Canada*] (NLC)

QMRAD........ Centre de Documentation, Institut de Recherche Appliquee sur le Travail, Montreal, Quebec [*Library symbol National Library of Canada*] (NLC)
QMR & E..... Quartermaster Research and Engineering [*Military*] (AD)
QMRAQ........ Recherches Amerindiennes au Quebec, Montreal, Quebec [*Library symbol National Library of Canada*] (NLC)
QMRC.......... Quartermaster Reserve Corps [*Military*]
QMRC.......... Royal Canadian Air Force [*Corps d'Aviation Royale du Canada*] Montreal, Quebec [*Library symbol National Library of Canada*] (NLC)
QMRCH........ Richmond County Historical Society [*Societe d'Histoire du Comte de Richmond*] Melbourne, Quebec (NLC)
QMRCM....... Raymond, Chabot, Martin, Pare, Montreal, Quebec [*Library symbol National Library of Canada*] (NLC)
QMRD.......... Reader's Digest of Canada Ltd., Montreal, Quebec [*Library symbol National Library of Canada*] (NLC)
QMRE.......... Revenue Canada [*Revenu Canada*] Montreal, Quebec [*Library symbol National Library of Canada*] (NLC)
QMREC........ Quartermaster Research and Engineering Command [*Army*]
QMREFEA.... Quartermaster Research and Engineering Field Evaluation Agency [*Merged with Troop Evaluation Test*]
QMREG........ Regie de l'Electricite et du Gaz, Montreal, Quebec [*Library symbol National Library of Canada*] (NLC)
QMREX........ Canada Department of Regional Industrial Expansion [*Ministere de l'Expansion Industrielle Regionale*] Montreal, Quebec [*Library symbol National Library of Canada*] (NLC)
QMRH.......... Centre de Recherches en Relations Humaines, Montreal, Quebec [*Library symbol National Library of Canada*] (NLC)
QMRI.......... Rehabilitation Institute of Montreal [*Institut de Rehabilitation de Montreal*] Quebec [*Library symbol National Library of Canada*] (NLC)
QMRK.......... QualMark Corp. [*NASDAQ symbol*] (TTSB)
QMRL.......... Quartermaster Radiation Laboratory [*Army*]
QMRL.......... Regie du Logement, Montreal, Quebec [*Library symbol National Library of Canada*] (NLC)
QMRM.......... Reddy Memorial Hospital, Montreal, Quebec [*Library symbol National Library of Canada*] (NLC)
QMROS........ Robinson-Sheppard, Montreal, Quebec [*Library symbol National Library of Canada*] (BIB)
QMRP.......... Qualified Mental Retardation Professional
QMRP.......... Rhone-Poulenc Pharma, Inc., Montreal, Quebec [*Library symbol National Library of Canada*] (NLC)
QMRPA........ Quartermaster Radiation Planning Agency [*Army*]
QMRQ.......... Societe de Radio-Television du Quebec, Montreal, Quebec [*Library symbol National Library of Canada*] (NLC)
QMRR.......... Rolls-Royce of Canada Ltd., Montreal, Quebec [*Library symbol National Library of Canada*] (NLC)
QMRRD........ Reginald P. Dawson Library, Town of Mount Royal, Quebec [*Library symbol National Library of Canada*] (NLC)
QMRS.......... Information Centre, Canadian Security Intelligence Service [*Centre d'Information, Service Canadien du Renseignement de Securite*], Montreal, Quebec [*Library symbol National Library of Canada*] (BIB)
QMRSJA...... Archives des Religieuses Hospitalieres de Saint-Joseph, Montreal, Quebec [*Library symbol National Library of Canada*] (NLC)
QMRV.......... Royal Victoria Hospital, Montreal, Quebec [*Library symbol National Library of Canada*] (NLC)
QMRVW....... Women's Pavilion, Royal Victoria Hospital, Montreal, Quebec [*Library symbol National Library of Canada*] (NLC)
QMS............ QMS, Inc. [*Associated Press*] (SAG)
QMS............ Quadrupole Mass Spectrometer
QMS............ Quality Management System
QMS............ Quality Micro Systems [*Trademark*]
QMS............ Quality Monitoring System (MCD)
QMS............ Quarterly Meteorological Summary [*Navy*] (DNAB)
QMS............ Quartermaster School [*Army*]
QMS............ Quartermaster Sergeant [*Military*]
QMS............ Quartermaster Stores [*Military*]
QMS............ Quicksilver Messenger Service [*Pop music group*]
QMS............ Sun Life of Canada [*Sun Life du Canada*] Montreal, Quebec [*Library symbol National Library of Canada*] (NLC)
QMSA.......... Seaman Apprentice, Quartermaster, Striker [*Navy rating*]
QMSA.......... Service de la Documentation, Ministere de la Sante et des Services Sociaux du Quebec, Montreal, Quebec [*Library symbol National Library of Canada*] (NLC)
QMSAC........ Sandoz Canada, Inc., Dorval, Quebec [*Library symbol National Library of Canada*] (NLC)
QMSAP........ Societe des Artistes Professionnels du Quebec, Montreal, Quebec [*Library symbol National Library of Canada*] (NLC)
QMSC.......... Queensland Mathematical Sciences Council [*Australia*]
QMSC.......... Southern Canada Power Co., Montreal, Quebec [*Library symbol National Library of Canada*] (NLC)
QMSCA........ Statistics Canada [*Statistique Canada*] Montreal, Quebec [*Library symbol National Library of Canada*] (NLC)
QMSCC........ Queen Mary's School Cadet Corps [*British military*] (DMA)
QMSCM........ Canadian Microfilming Co. Ltd. [*Societe Canadienne du Microfilm, Inc.*] Montreal, Quebec [*Library symbol National Library of Canada*] (NLC)
QMSD.......... Information Resource Centre, Systems Development [*Centre d'Information Specialise, Systemes-Applications Pratiques*], Montreal, Quebec [*Library symbol National Library of Canada*] (BIB)
QMSDB........ Societe de Developpement de la Baie James, Montreal, Quebec [*Library symbol National Library of Canada*] (NLC)
QMSDI.......... Centre de Documentation, SOGIC [*Societe Generale des Industries Culturelles du Quebec*], Montreal, Quebec [*Library symbol National Library of Canada*] (BIB)
QMSDL......... Sidbec-Dosco Ltd./Ltee., Montreal, Quebec [*Library symbol National Library of Canada*] (NLC)
QM Segt...... Quartermaster-Sergeant [*British military*] (DMA)
QMSG.......... Queue Message [*Computer science*] (PCM)
QMSGA........ Archives Generales des Soeurs Grises, Montreal, Quebec [*Library symbol National Library of Canada*] (NLC)
QMSGE........ Office des Services de Garde a l'Enfance, Montreal, Quebec [*Library symbol National Library of Canada*] (NLC)
QMSGME..... Service General des Moyens d'Enseignement, Ministere de l'Education du Quebec, Montreal, Quebec [*Library symbol National Library of Canada*] (NLC)
QMSGT........ Quartermaster Sergeant [*Marine Corps*]
Qm Sgt........ Quartermaster Sergeant [*Military*] (AD)
QMSH.......... Societe Historique de Montreal, Quebec [*Library symbol National Library of Canada*] (NLC)
QMSHE........ Stadler Hurter, Montreal, Quebec [*Library symbol National Library of Canada*] (NLC)
QMSHQ........ Centre de Documentation, Societe d'Habitation du Quebec, Montreal, Quebec [*Library symbol National Library of Canada*] (BIB)
QMSI............ Quartermaster-Sergeant Instructor [*British military*] (DMA)
QMSI............ Scolasticat de l'Immaculee-Conception, Montreal, Quebec [*Library symbol National Library of Canada*] (NLC)
QMSIL.......... Silicart, Inc., Montreal, Quebec [*Library symbol National Library of Canada*] (NLC)
QMSJ........... St. Joseph's Teachers' College, Montreal, Quebec [*Library symbol National Library of Canada*] (NLC)
QMSMA........ St. Mary's Hospital, Montreal, Quebec [*Library symbol National Library of Canada*] (NLC)
QMSN.......... Seaman, Quartermaster, Striker [*Navy rating*]
QMSNC........ SNC, Inc., Montreal, Quebec [*Library symbol National Library of Canada*] (NLC)
QMSO.......... Quartermaster Supply Officer [*Army*]
QMSO.......... Shell Oil Co. of Canada, Montreal, Quebec [*Library symbol National Library of Canada*] (NLC)
QMSOB........ Le Groupe SOBECO, Montreal, Quebec [*Library symbol National Library of Canada*] (NLC)
QMSQC........ Squibb Canada, Inc., Montreal, Quebec [*Library symbol National Library of Canada*] (NLC)
QMSSA........ Queensland Merino Stud Sheepbreeders' Association [*Australia*]
QMST.......... Legal Department, Steinberg, Inc., Montreal, Quebec [*Library symbol National Library of Canada*] (NLC)
QMSTJ......... Centre d'Information sur la Sante de l'Enfant, Hopital Sainte-Justine, Montreal,Quebec [*Library symbol National Library of Canada*] (NLC)
QMSTJS....... Departement de Sante Communautaire, Hopital Sainte-Justine, Montreal, Quebec [*Library symbol National Library of Canada*] (NLC)
QMSU.......... Surete du Quebec, Montreal, Quebec [*Library symbol National Library of Canada*] (NLC)
QMSVM........ Centre de Service Social Ville-Marie [*Ville-Marie Social Service Centre*] Montreal, Quebec [*Library symbol National Library of Canada*] (NLC)
QMSW.......... Quartz Metal Sealed Window
qmsw........... Quartz Metal Sealed Window (AD)
QMSW.......... Sherwin-Williams Co. of Canada Ltd., Montreal, Quebec [*Library symbol National Library of Canada*] (NLC)
QMSWP........ Shawinigan Engineering Ltd. Co., Montreal, Quebec [*Library symbol National Library of Canada*] (NLC)
QMT............ Montreal Trust Co., Quebec [*Library symbol National Library of Canada*] (NLC)
QMT............ Quantitative Muscle Testing [*Medicine*] (MAE)
QM-T........... Quartermaster-Trainee [*Navy*] (DNAB)
QMT............ Queens-Midtown Tunnel (AD)
QMTA.......... Tomenson Alexander Ltd., Montreal, Quebec [*Library symbol National Library of Canada*] (NLC)
QMTC.......... Air Canada, Montreal, Quebec [*Library symbol National Library of Canada*] (NLC)
QMTD.......... Transportation Development Centre, Transport Canada [*Centre de Developpement des Transports, Transports Canada*] Montreal, Quebec [*Library symbol National Library of Canada*] (NLC)
QMTGC........ Teleglobe Canada, Montreal, Quebec [*Library symbol National Library of Canada*] (NLC)
QMTH.......... Institut de Tourisme et d'Hotellerie du Quebec, Montreal, Quebec [*Library symbol National Library of Canada*] (NLC)
QMTMO........ Centre de Documentation, Ministere du Travail du Quebec, Montreal, Quebec [*Library symbol National Library of Canada*] (NLC)
QMTOE........ Quartermaster Table of Organization and Equipment [*Units*] [*Military*]
QMTQ.......... Direction des Communications, Tourisme Quebec, Montreal, Quebec [*Library symbol National Library of Canada*] (BIB)
QMTQM........ Trans Quebec & Maritimes, Montreal, Quebec [*Library symbol National Library of Canada*] (NLC)
QMTR.......... Waterways Development, Transport Canada [*Developpement des vois Navigables, Transports Canada*] Montreal, Quebec [*Library symbol National Library of Canada*] (NLC)
QMTRA........ Centre de Documentation, Ministere des Transports du Quebec, Montreal, Quebec [*Library symbol National Library of Canada*] (NLC)
QMU............ Universite de Montreal, Quebec [*Library symbol National Library of Canada*] (NLC)
QMUA.......... Service des Archives de l'Universite de Montreal, Quebec [*Library symbol National Library of Canada*] (NLC)

QMUC.......... Union Carbide Canada Ltd., Pointe-Aux-Trembles, Quebec [*Library symbol National Library of Canada*] (NLC)
QMUDD........ Departement de Demographie, Universite de Montreal, Quebec [*Library symbol National Library of Canada*] (NLC)
QMUE.......... Bibliotheque de l'Institut d'Etudes Medievales, Universite de Montreal, Quebec [*Library symbol National Library of Canada*] (NLC)
QMUEB........ Ecole de Bibliotheconomie, Universite de Montreal, Quebec [*Library symbol National Library of Canada*] (NLC)
QMUEC........ L'Ecole de Criminologie, Universite de Montreal, Quebec [*Library symbol National Library of Canada*] (NLC)
QMUGC........ Cartotheque, Departement de Geographie, Universite de Montreal, Quebec [*Library symbol National Library of Canada*] (NLC)
QMUGL........ Cartotheque, Institut de Geologie, Universite de Montreal, Quebec [*Library symbol National Library of Canada*] (NLC)
QMUQ.......... Universite de Quebec, Montreal, Quebec [*Library symbol National Library of Canada*] (NLC)
QMUQA........ Service des Archives de l'Universite du Quebec a Montreal [*Library symbol National Library of Canada*] (BIB)
QMUQC........ Cartotheque, Universite du Quebec, Montreal, Quebec [*Library symbol National Library of Canada*] (NLC)
QMUQEN...... Ecole Nationale d'Administration Publique, Universite du Quebec, Montreal, Quebec [*Library symbol National Library of Canada*] (NLC)
QMUQET...... Ecole de Technologie Superieure, Universite de Quebec, Montreal, Quebec [*Library symbol National Library of Canada*] (NLC)
QMUQIC....... Cartotheque, INRS-Urbanisation, Montreal, Quebec [*Library symbol National Library of Canada*] (NLC)
QMUQIS....... Centre de Documentation, INRS [*Institut National de la Recherche Scientifique*]-Sante, Montreal, Quebec [*Library symbol National Library of Canada*] (NLC)
QMUQIU...... Centre de Documentation INRS [*Institut National de la Recherche Scientifique*]-Urbanisation, Montreal, Quebec [*Library symbol National Library of Canada*] (NLC)
QMUQPA...... Pavillon des Arts, Universite du Quebec, Montreal, Quebec [*Library symbol National Library of Canada*] (NLC)
QMUQS........ Bibliotheque des Sciences, Universite du Quebec, Montreal [*Library symbol National Library of Canada*] (BIB)
QMUQTM..... Tele-Universite, Universite du Quebec, Montreal, Quebec [*Library symbol National Library of Canada*] (NLC)
QMV............ Qualified Majority Voting [*Napoleonic Code*]
QMV............ RCA Victor Co. Ltd., Montreal, Quebec [*Library symbol National Library of Canada*] (NLC)
QMVC.......... Media Resource Centre, Vanier College, Montreal, Quebec [*Library symbol National Library of Canada*] (NLC)
QMVR.......... Resource Centre, VIA Rail Canada, Inc. [*Centre de Documentation, VIA Rai l Canada, Inc.*] Montreal, Quebec [*Library symbol National Library of Canada*] (NLC)
QMVRM....... Centre de Maintenance, VIA Rail, Montreal, Quebec [*Library symbol National Library of Canada*] (BIB)
QMW........... Quartz Metal Window
qmw............ Quartz Metal Window (AD)
QMW........... Warnock Hersey Co. Ltd., Montreal, Quebec [*Library symbol National Library of Canada*] (NLC)
QMWM........ William M. Mercer, Montreal, Quebec [*Library symbol National Library of Canada*] (NLC)
QMWS......... Quasi-Morphine Withdrawal Syndrome [*Medicine*] (DMAA)
QMY............ Queen Mary's Yeomanry [*British military*] (DMA)
QMY............ YWCA, Montreal, Quebec [*Library symbol National Library of Canada*] (NLC)
QMYH.......... YM - YWHA, Montreal, Quebec [*Library symbol National Library of Canada*] (NLC)
QN............... Bush Pilots Airways [*ICAO designator*] (AD)
QN............... Quantifier Negation [*Principle of logic*]
QN............... Quantum Number
QN............... Quaque Nocte [*Every Night*] [*Pharmacy*]
qn................ Quaque Nocte [*Every Night*] [*Latin*] (AD)
QN............... Quarterly Newsletter. American Bar Association [*A publication*] (DLA)
QN............... Quarterly Notes (ILCA)
QN............... Quarternote [*A publication*] (EAAP)
QN............... Queen (ADA)
QN............... Queen
Qn............... Queen (AD)
QN............... Queen's Knight [*Chess*] (IIA)
QN............... Query Normalization
QN............... Question (FAAC)
qn................ Question (WDMC)
qn................ Question (AD)
QN............... Quetzalcoatlus Northropi [*Pterosaur, a model constructed for the Smithsonian Institution and referred to by these initials*]
QN............... Quintuple Screw (DS)
QN............... Quotation [*Investment term*]
qn................ Quotation (AD)
qna.............. Quality per Next Assembly (AD)
QNA............. Quarterly National Accounts (NITA)
QNA............. Queensland Netball Association [*Australia*]
QNA............. Quinuclidinol Atrolactate [*Organic chemistry*]
QNaN........... Quiet Not a Number [*Computer programming*]. (BYTE)
QNat............ Quaestiones Naturales [*of Seneca the Younger*] [*Classical studies*] (OCD)
QNB............. Quinuclidinyl Benzilate [*Also, BZ*] [*Hallucinogen*]
QNC............. New Castle Free Public Library, New Castle, PA [*OCLC symbol*] (OCLC)
QNCH........... Quenched (MSA)
QNCHRN...... Centre Hospitalier Rouyn-Noranda, Noranda, Quebec [*Library symbol National Library of Canada*] (NLC)
QNCR........... Quarterly Noncompliance Report [*Environmental Protection Agency*] (GFGA)
QNCRS......... Conseil Regional de la Sante et des Services Sociaux Rouyn-Noranda, Noranda, Quebec [*Library symbol National Library of Canada*] (NLC)
QND............. Quantum Nondemolition [*Method of measurement*]
Qndk............ Quensk [*Language of the Quains*] (AD)
QNE............. Height Altimeter Set to 1013.2 Millibars Will Read on Landing [*Aviation code*] (AIA)
QNEC........... Qualified Non-Elective Contribution
Q Newl-Spec Comm Env L... Quarterly Newsletter. Special Committee on Environmental Law [*A publication*] (DLA)
QNF............. Queensland Newsagents' Federation [*Australia*]
QNH............. Quantity (GAVI)
QNH............. Qui Nhon [*Vietnam*] (VNW)
QNI.............. Queen's Nursing Institute [*British*]
QNIA............ Queensland Nursery Industry Association [*Australia*]
QNICA.......... Soeurs de L'Assomption, Nicolet, Quebec [*Library symbol National Library of Canada*] (NLC)
QNICS.......... Seminaire de Nicolet, Quebec [*Library symbol National Library of Canada*] (NLC)
QNIP............ Institut de Police du Quebec, Nicolet, Quebec [*Library symbol National Library of Canada*] (NLC)
QNK............. Kabo Air Travels [*Nigeria*] [*ICAO designator*] (FAAC)
QN MAG...... Quilter's Newsletter Magazine [*A publication*]
QNMC........... Quadripartite Nonmateriel Committee [*Military*] (AABC)
QNO............. Quinidine-N-oxide [*Organic chemistry*]
QNOAG......... Experimental Farm, Agriculture Canada [*Ferme Experimentale, Agriculture Canada*] Normandin, Quebec [*Library symbol National Library of Canada*] (NLC)
QNP............. Queen's Knight's Pawn [*Chess*] (IIA)
QNP............. Quezon National Park [*Philippines*] (AD)
qns.............. Quantity Not Sufficient (AD)
QNS............. Quantity Not Sufficient [*Pharmacy*]
Qns............. Queens (AD)
QNS............. Queen's Nursing Sister [*British*] (DAVI)
QNS & L....... Quebec North Shore and Labrador Railway [*Canada*] (AD)
QNSC........... Qui Nhon Support Command [*Vietnam*]
Qns Coll...... Queen's College (AD)
Qnsd............ Queensland (AD)
Qnsld........... Queensland [*Australia*] (BARN)
Qns Pk......... Queens Park (AD)
QNST........... Quick Neurological Screening Test
qnt.............. Quantisizer (AD)
QNT............. Quantizer (MDG)
QNT............. Quintet [*Music*]
qnt.............. Quintet (AD)
QNTJB......... Queensland and Northern Territory Judgements Bulletin [*Australia A publication*]
QNTM........... Quantum Corp. [*NASDAQ symbol*] (NQ)
QNTY........... Quantity (AFM)
qnty............ Quantity (AD)
QNUE........... Queensland Nurses' Union of Employees [*Australia*]
QNWR.......... Quivira National Wildlife Refuge [*Kansas*] (AD)
QNX............. Quinnex, Inc. [*FAA designator*] (FAAC)
QO............... Bar Harbor Airlines [*ICAO designator*] (AD)
QO............... Oxygen Consumption [*Biochemistry*] (DAVI)
QO............... Quaker Oats [*Trade name*]
QO............... Qualified in Ordnance [*Obsolete Navy*]
QO............... Qualified Optician [*British*]
QO............... Quartermaster Operation [*Military*]
QO............... Quarters Officer [*British military*] (DMA)
QO............... Queen's Own [*Military unit*] [*British*]
QO............... Quick Opening [*Nuclear energy*] (NRCH)
qo................ Quick Opening (AD)
QO............... Quick Outlet (WDAA)
QO............... Quinoline Oxide [*Biochemistry*] (OA)
QO_2............... Oxygen Quotient (AAMN)
QOA............. Quasi-Official Agencies (AD)
QOBV........... Quick-Opening Blowdown Valve [*Nuclear energy*] (NRCH)
QOC............. Quality of Conformance
QOC............. Quality of Contact (DAVI)
QOC............. Quasi-Optical Circuit
QOC............. Queensland Opera Company [*Australia*]
QOCG........... Queen's Own Corps of Guides [*British military*] (DMA)
QOCH........... Queen's Own Cameron Highlanders [*Military unit*] [*British*]
QOD............. Quality of Design
QOD............. Quantitative Oceanographic Data
QOD............. Quaque Otra Die [*Every Other Day*] [*Pharmacy*]
QOD............. Quebec Order of Dentists [*Canada*] (AD)
qod.............. Quick-Opening Device (AD)
QOD............. Quick-Opening Device
QOD & WSY... Queen's Own Dorset and West Somerset Yeomanry [*British military*] (DMA)
QODY........... Queen's Own Dorsetshire Yeomanry [*British military*] (DMA)
QOF............. Quaker Oats Foundation (AD)
Q of C......... Quality of Care [*Medicine*] (DAVI)
QOH............. Quantity on Hand
QOH............. Quaque Otra Hora [*Every Other Hour*] [*Pharmacy*]
QOH............. Queen's Own Hussars [*Military unit*] [*British*]
QOI.............. Quality Operating Instruction
QOIB........... Queensland Office of International Business [*Australia*]
QOIC........... Quarantine Officer in Charge [*Military*] (AD)
QOL............. Quality of Life [*Program*] [*Army*]

QOLCPF....... Bibliotheque de la Faune, Ministere du Loisir, de la Chasse, et de la Peche, Orsainville, Quebec [*Library symbol National Library of Canada*] (NLC)
QOLI........... Quality of Life Index [*Medicine*] (DMAA)
QOLP........... Queensland Open Learning Project [*Australia*]
QOLY........... Queen's Own Lowland Yeomanry [*Military unit*] [*British*] (DMA)
QOMAC........ Quarter Orbit Magnetic Attitude Control
QOMY.......... Queen's Own Mercian Yeomanry [*Military unit*] [*British*]
QON............ Quaque Otra Nocte [*Every Other Night*] [*Pharmacy*]
QON............ Quarter Ocean Net
qon............. Quarter Ocean Net (AD)
QONR.......... Queen's Own Nigeria Regiment [*British military*] (DMA)
QOOH.......... Queen's Own Oxfordshire Hussars [*British military*] (DMA)
qopri............ Qualitative Operational Requirements (AD)
Q(Ops)......... Quartermaster Operations [*World War II*]
QOR............ Qualitative Operational Requirement [*Military*]
qor.............. Qualitative Operational Requirement (AD)
QOR............ Quarterly Operating Report
QOR............ Quebec Official Reports [*A publication*] (DLA)
QOR............ Queen's Own Rifles [*Military unit*] [*British*]
QOR............ Queen's Own Royal [*Military unit*] [*British*]
QORC.......... Queen's Own Rifles, Canada [*Military*] (ROG)
QORGIY....... Queen's Own Royal Glasgow Imperial Yeomanry [*British military*] (DMA)
QORGS........ Quasi-Optimal Rendezvous Guidance System
QORGY........ Queen's Own Royal Glasgow Yeomanry [*British military*] (DMA)
QORR.......... Queen's Own Royal Regiment [*British military*] (DMA)
QORWKR..... Queen's Own Royal West Kent Regiment [*Military unit*] [*British*]
QOS............ Quality of Service [*Telecommunications*] (TEL)
QoS............ Quality of Service [*Telecommunications*]
QOS............ Quality Operating System
QOS............ Quick on System (AD)
QOT............ Quasi-Optical Technique
qot.............. Quote (AD)
QOT & E...... Qualification, Operational Test, and Evaluation
qotn............ Quotation (AD)
QOWH......... Queen's Own Worcestershire Hussars [*British military*] (DMA)
QOWVR........ Queen's Own Westminster Volunteer Rifles [*Military British*] (ROG)
QOY............ Queen's Own Yeomanry [*British military*] (DMA)
QP............... Perceptual Quotient [*Education*] (AEE)
Qp............... Pulmonary Blood Flow [*Medicine*] (DAVI)
Qp............... Quadrant Pain [*Gastroenterology*] (DAVI)
QP............... Quadratic Programming [*Computer science*] (BUR)
QP............... Quadruple Play (DEN)
QP............... Qualification Proposal
QP............... Qualified Psychiatrist (MAE)
QP............... Quality People
QP............... Quality Product (IAA)
QP............... Quanti-Pirquet [*Reaction or test for tuberculin*] (AAMN)
q-P............... Quanti-Pirquet (AD)
qp............... Quantum Placet [*At Discretion*] [*Latin*] (AD)
QP............... Quantum Placet [*As Much as You Please*] [*Pharmacy*]
QP............... Quartered Partition
Q/P............... Quartz/Phenolic
QP............... Quasiparticle [*Physics*]
QP............... Quasi-Peak
QP............... Queen Post
qp............... Queen Post (AD)
QP............... Queen's Pawn [*Chess*] (ADA)
QP............... Queen's Pleasure [*British*]
QP............... Queen's Printer [*British*] (AD)
QP............... Query Processing (MCD)
QP............... Quest for Peace (EA)
qp............... Quick Process (AD)
QP............... Quick Processing [*Chemicals*]
QP............... Quoted Price [*Investment term*]
QP............... Sunbird [*ICAO designator*] (AD)
QPA............ Bibliotheque Municipale, Port-Alfred, Quebec [*Library symbol National Library of Canada*] (NLC)
QPA............ Qualitative Point Average (WDAA)
qpa............ Qualitative Point Average (AD)
QPA............ Quality Product Assurance
Q/PA........... Quality/Productivity Assessment (MCD)
QPA............ Quantity per Application (MCD)
qpa............ Quantity per Article (AD)
qpa............ Quantity per Assembly (AD)
QPA............ Quantity per Assembly (MCD)
QPA............ Queensland Photolab Association [*Australia*]
QPA............ Queensland Police Academy [*Australia*] (AD)
QPA............ Queensland Polynesian Association [*Australia*] (AD)
QPAA.......... Quality Planning and Administration (MCD)
QPAC.......... Qualified Productivity Aid for Computing (IAA)
QPAG.......... Experimental Farm, Agriculture Canada [*Ferme Experimentale, Agriculture Canada*] La Pocatiere, Quebec [*Library symbol National Library of Canada*] (NLC)
QPAM.......... Quadrature Phase and Amplitude Modulation (NITA)
QPAM.......... Quantized Pulsed Amplitude Modulation
Q P & S....... Quaker Peace and Service (AD)
QPAT........... Quad Pulse Output Module (ACII)
QPB............ Quality Paperback Book Club [*Trademark of Book-of-the-Month Club, Inc.*]
QPBC.......... Quality Paperback Book Club [*Trademark of Book-of-the-Month Club, Inc.*] (CDAI)
QPC............ College de Ste.-Anne, La Pocatiere, Quebec [*Library symbol National Library of Canada*] (NLC)
Qpc............ Pulmonary Capillary Blood Flow [*Cardiology*] (DAVI)
QPC............ Qatar Petroleum Co. (AD)
QPC............ Quadrigeminal Plate Cistern [*Neurology*] (DAVI)
QPC............ Quality of Patient Care [*Hospital administration*] (DAVI)
QPC............ Quality Performance Chart (SAA)
QPC............ Quantity per Equipment/Component
QPC............ Quantum Point Contact [*Physics*]
QPC............ Quasi-Propulsive Coefficient (DS)
QPC............ Quasi-Public Company
QPC............ Queensland Philatelic Council [*Australia*]
QPC............ Queensland Police Club [*Australia*]
QPCAI Report... Queensland Parliamentary Commissioner for Administration. Investigations Report [*Australia A publication*]
QPCB.......... Quench Particle Collection Bomb (MCD)
QPCE.......... CEGEP [*College d'Enseignement General et Professionnel*] de La Pocatiere, Quebec [*Library symbol National Library of Canada*] (NLC)
QPCM.......... Bibliotheque Municipale, Port-Cartier, Quebec [*Library symbol National Library of Canada*] (BIB)
QPD............ Bibliotheque Intermunicipale de Pierrefonds et Dollard-Des-Ormeaux, Pierrefonds,Quebec [*Library symbol National Library of Canada*] (NLC)
QPD............ Quadrature Phase Detection [*Physics*]
QPDM.......... Quadpixel Data-Flow Manager [*Computer science*]
QPDOLL....... Quarterly Payment Demand on Legal Loan
QPEEG........ Quantitative Pharmaco-Electro-Encephalography [*Medicine*] (DMAA)
qpei............ Quality per End Item (AD)
QPEI........... Quantity per End Item (MCD)
QPES.......... Centre de Documentation, Institut de Technologie Agro-Alimentaire de La Pocatiere, Quebec [*Library symbol National Library of Canada*] (NLC)
QPF............ Quantitative Precipitation Forecast (NOAA)
qpf............. Quantitative Precipitation Forecast (AD)
QPF............ Quebec Police Force [*Canada*] (AD)
QPF............ Queensland Producers' Federation [*Australia*]
QPFC.......... Queen's Park Football Club (AD)
QPFL.......... Queensland Professional Fishermens League [*Australia*] (AD)
QPH............ Queen's Park Harriers [*British*] (ROG)
QPI............. Quadratic Performance Index
qpi............. Quadratic Performance Index (AD)
Q/PI........... Quality and Productivity Improvement (AAGC)
QPI............. Quality Productivity Improvement (MCD)
QPIMC......... Quadratic Programming Internal Model Control [*Chemical engineering*] [*Computer science*]
QPIR........... EBRI [*Employee Benefit Research Institute*] Quarterly Pension Investment Report [*A publication*]
QPIS........... Quality Performance Instruction Sheet (AD)
QPIS........... Quality Planning Instruction Sheet (MCD)
QPIT........... Quantitative Pilocarpine Ionophoresis Test
QPL............ Qualified Parts List (AAG)
QPL............ Qualified Producers List (IAA)
QPL............ Qualified Products List [*Military*]
Q PL........... Quantum Placet [*As Much as You Please*] [*Pharmacy*]
QPL............ Queensland Press Ltd. [*Australia*]
QPL............ Queens Public Library (AD)
QPL & S...... Qualified Products Lists and Sources
QPLM.......... Bibliotheque Municipale, Plessisville, Quebec [*Library symbol National Library of Canada*] (NLC)
QPLT........... Quiet Propulsion Lift Technology [*NASA*]
qplt............ Quiet Propulsion Lift Technology (AD)
QPM............ Quality Practice Manual [*A publication*]
QPM............ Quality Program Manager [*Nuclear energy*] (NRCH)
QPM............ Quality-Protein Maize
QPM............ Quantized Pulse Modulation
QPM............ Quaque Post Meridiem [*Every night*] [*Latin*] [*Pharmacy*] (DAVI)
QPM............ Quasi-Phase-Matching [*Physics*]
QPM............ Queen's Polar Medal [*British*] (AD)
QPM............ Queen's Police Medal [*British*]
QPM............ Queen's [*Victoria*] Prime Ministers [*A publication*]
QPM............ Questions of Procedure for Ministers
QPM............ Quick Printing Management [*A publication*] (DGA)
QPMV.......... Quail Pea Mosaic Virus [*Plant pathology*]
Q/PNL......... Quarter Panel [*Automotive engineering*]
QPO............ Quasi-Periodic Oscillation [*Astronomy*]
QPOC.......... Pointe-Claire Public Library [*Bibliotheque Publique de Pointe-Claire*] Quebec [*Library symbol National Library of Canada*] (NLC)
QPOCQ........ Quebec Family History Society, Pointe Claire, Quebec [*Library symbol National Library of Canada*] (BIB)
QPP............ Quality Program Plan (MCD)
QPP............ Quality Program Provision
QPP............ Quantized Pulse Position
QPP............ Quebec Pension Plan [*Canada*]
QPP............ Quebec Provincial Police [*Canada*] (AD)
QPP............ Queensland People's Party [*Australia Political party*]
QPP............ Quetico Provincial Park [*Ontario, Canada*] (AD)
QPP............ Quiescent Push-Pull [*Electronics*] (DEN)
QPPC.......... Quarterly Production Progress Conference [*Navy*] (NG)
QPPM.......... Quantized Pulse Position Modulation [*Telecommunications*] (IAA)
QPPO.......... Queensland Pork Producers' Organisation [*Australia*]
QPPR.......... Quantitative Property-Property Relationship
QPQ............ QPQ Corp. [*Associated Press*] (SAG)
QPQ............ Quench Polish Quench (PDAA)
QPQ............ Quid Pro Quid
QPQ Cp....... QPQ Corp. [*Associated Press*] (SAG)
QPQQ.......... QPQ Corp. [*NASDAQ symbol*] (SAG)

QPQQW........ QPQ Corp. Wrrt [*NASDAQ symbol*] (TTSB)
QPR........ Pittsburgh Regional Library Center - Union List, Pittsburgh, PA [*OCLC symbol*] (OCLC)
QPR........ Quadrature Partial Response (NITA)
QPR........ Qualitative Personnel Requirements [*NASA*] (KSC)
QPR........ Quality Progress Review (MCD)
QPR........ Quantity Progress Report (AD)
QPR........ Quarterly Process Review
QPR........ Quarterly Progress Report
QPR........ Quebec Practice Reports [*A publication*] (DLA)
QPR........ Queen's Park Ranger [*British*] (DI)
QPRD........ Quality Planning Requirements Document [*NASA*] (NASA)
QPRF........ Quantitative Precipitation Ratio Forecasts [*National Weather Service*]
QPRI........ Qualitative Personnel Requirements Information [*NASA*] (MCD)
QPRI........ Qualitative Personnel Requirements Inventory (MCD)
QPRM........ Bibliotheque Municipale, Princeville, Quebec [*Library symbol National Library of Canada*] (NLC)
QPRS........ Quadrature Partial-Response System [*Telecommunications*] (TEL)
QPRS........ Quarterly Project Reliability Summary [*Navy*] (NG)
QPRT........ Qualified Personal Residence Trust [*Investment term*]
QPS........ Quaker Peace and Service [*An association*] (EAIO)
QPS........ Qualified Processing Source
QPS........ Qualified Process Supplies (MCD)
QPS........ Quality Planning Specification [*NASA*] (NASA)
QPS........ Quantitative Physical Science
qps........ Quantitative Physical Science (AD)
QPS........ Quantity Planning Specification (NASA)
QPS........ Queensland Purchasing and Sales [*Australia*]
QPS........ Query Property Similarity (MHDI)
QPS........ Quick Program Search (WDAA)
QPS........ Quiescent Power Supply
QPSC........ Quiescent Power Supply Current
QPSII........ Qualified Possession Source Investment Income [*IRS*]
qpsk........ Quad-Phase Shift Key [*Computer science*] (AD)
QPSK........ Quadrature Phase Shift Key [*or Keying*] [*Telecommunications*]
QPSK........ Quaternary Phase Shift Keying (NITA)
QPSL........ Qualified Parts and Suppliers List (MCD)
QPSX........ Queued Packet Synchronous Exchange [*Telecommunications*] (OSI)
QPT........ Quadrant Power Tilt (IEEE)
QPT........ Quarterly Provisional Tax
QPT........ Quartz Pressure Transducer [*Telecommunications*] (IAA)
QPT........ Quick Prothrombin Time [*Hematology*] (DAVI)
QPTC........ Quarry Products Training Council (AIE)
QPU........ Queensland Police Union [*Australia*]
QPVT........ Quick Picture Vocabulary Test [*Speech and language therapy*] (DAVI)
QPW........ Quattro Pro for Windows [*Borland International*] [*Computer science*] (PCM)
QPX........ QPX Minerals, Inc. [*Vancouver Stock Exchange symbol*]
QQ........ Aerovias Quisqueyana [*Airlines*] [*Dominican Republic*] [*ICAO designator*] (OAG)
QQ........ Bibliotheque de Quebec, Quebec [*Library symbol National Library of Canada*] (NLC)
QQ........ Michigan Airways [*ICAO designator*] (AD)
QQ........ Potential Hijacker [*Airline notation*]
QQ........ Qara Qash [*Sinkiang province of China*] (AD)
QQ........ Qara Qum [*Sinkiang province of China*] (AD)
QQ........ Qualitate Qua [*In the Capacity Of*] [*Latin*]
Q-Q........ Quantile-Quantile [*Computer science*]
QQ........ Quaque [*Each or Every*] [*Pharmacy*]
qq........ Quaque [*Each*] [*Latin*] (AD)
qq........ Quartos (AD)
QQ........ Quartos (WDAA)
QQ........ Quasi-Quadrennial
qq........ Quelques [*Some*] [*French*] (AD)
QQ........ Que Que [*Rhodesia*] (AD)
qq........ Questionable Questionnaire (AD)
QQ........ Questionable Questionnaires
QQ........ Questions
qq........ Questions (WDMC)
qq........ Quintales [*Quintals*] [*Spanish*] (AD)
QQ........ Quisque [*Each, Every*] [*Pharmacy*]
QQ........ Quoque [*Also*] [*Pharmacy*]
qq........ Quoque [*Every*] [*Latin*] (AD)
QQA........ Archives Nationales du Quebec, Quebec [*Library symbol National Library of Canada*] (NLC)
QQA........ Quarterly Quality Assurance [*Environmental Protection Agency*]
QQAA........ Archives de l'Archeveche de Quebec, Quebec [*Library symbol National Library of Canada*] (NLC)
QQAC........ Ministere des Affaires Culturelles du Quebec, Quebec, Quebec [*Library symbol National Library of Canada*] (NLC)
QQACJ........ Archives de la Compagnie de Jesus, Province du Canada - Francais, Saint-Jerome, Quebec, Quebec [*Library symbol National Library of Canada*] (NLC)
QQAG........ Centre de Documentation du 200, Ministere de l'Agriculture, des Pecheries, et del'Alimentation, Quebec, Quebec [*Library symbol National Library of Canada*] (NLC)
QQAI........ Bibliotheque Administrative, Ministere des Affaires Inter-Gouvernementales du Quebec, Quebec, Quebec [*Library symbol Obsolete National Library of Canada*] (NLC)
QQAM........ Centre de Documentation, Ministere des Affaires Municipales du Quebec, Quebec, Quebec [*Library symbol National Library of Canada*] (NLC)
QQAND........ Archives du Monastere Notre-Dame-Des-Anges, Quebec, Quebec [*Library symbol National Library of Canada*] (NLC)
QQAPC........ Cerebral Palsy Association of Quebec, Inc. [*L'Association de Paralysie Cerebrale du Quebec, Inc.*] Quebec, Quebec [*Library symbol National Library of Canada*] (NLC)
QQAQ........ Bibliotheque des Services Diocesains, Archeveche de Quebec, Quebec [*Library symbol National Library of Canada*] (BIB)
QQAQS........ Synod Office, Diocese of Quebec, Anglican Church of Canada, Quebec, Quebec [*Library symbol National Library of Canada*] (NLC)
QQAS........ Archives du Seminaire de Quebec, Quebec, Quebec [*Library symbol National Library of Canada*] (NLC)
QQASF........ Conseil des Affaires Sociales et de la Famille, Quebec, Quebec [*Library symbol National Library of Canada*] (NLC)
QQBJNQ........ Bureau de la Baie James et du Nord Quebecois, Ste.-Foy, Quebec [*Library symbol National Library of Canada*] (NLC)
QQBL........ Bibliotheque des Freres des Ecoles Chretiennes, Quebec [*Library symbol National Library of Canada*] (NLC)
QQBMC........ Bibliotheque Municipale, Charlesbourg, Quebec [*Library symbol National Library of Canada*] (BIB)
QQBS........ Bureau de la Statistique du Quebec, Quebec, Quebec [*Library symbol National Library of Canada*] (NLC)
QQBST........ Centre de Documentation, Ministere de l'Enseignement Superieur et de la Science du Quebec, Ste.-Foy, Quebec [*Library symbol National Library of Canada*] (NLC)
QQC........ Defence Research Establishment Valcartier, Canada Department of National Defence[*Centre de Recherches pour la Defense Valcartier, Ministere de la Defense Na tionale*] Courcelette, Quebec [*Library symbol National Library of Canada*] (NLC)
QQC........ Quantitative Quality Characteristics
QQC........ Queensland Quality Centre [*Australia*]
QQCAD........ Conservatoire d'Art Dramatique du Quebec, Quebec [*Library symbol National Library of Canada*] (NLC)
QQCAI........ Centre de Documentation, Commission d'Acces a l'Information, Quebec, Quebec [*Library symbol National Library of Canada*] (NLC)
QQCAT........ Commission de la Sante et de la Securite du Travail du Quebec, Quebec, Quebec [*Library symbol National Library of Canada*] (NLC)
QQCC........ Centre de Documentation, Conseil des Colleges du Quebec, Quebec, Quebec [*Library symbol National Library of Canada*] (BIB)
QQCDP........ Commission des Droits de la Personne du Quebec, Quebec, Quebec [*Library symbol National Library of Canada*] (NLC)
QQCDT........ Centre de Documentation, Commission des Normes du Travail, Quebec, Quebec [*Library symbol National Library of Canada*] (NLC)
QQCE........ CEGEP [*College d'Enseignement General et Professionnel*] de Limoilou, Quebec, Quebec [*Library symbol National Library of Canada*] (NLC)
QQCF........ Centre Francois Charron, Quebec, Quebec [*Library symbol National Library of Canada*] (BIB)
QQCFP........ Centre de Documentation, Commission de la Fonction Publique du Quebec, Quebec, Quebec [*Library symbol National Library of Canada*] (BIB)
QQCFX........ CEGEP [*College d'Enseignement General et Professionnel*] F. X. Garneau, Sillery, Quebec [*Library symbol National Library of Canada*] (NLC)
QQCGI........ Centre de Documentation, CGI [*Conseillers en Gestion et Informatique*], I nc., Quebec [*Library symbol National Library of Canada*] (NLC)
QQCH........ Departement des Archives et Statistiques de la Ville de Quebec, Quebec, Quebec [*Library symbol National Library of Canada*] (NLC)
QQCHJH........ Centre Hospitalier Jeffery Hale, Quebec, Quebec [*Library symbol National Library of Canada*] (BIB)
QQCLF........ Conseil de la Langue Francaise, Quebec, Quebec [*Library symbol National Library of Canada*] (NLC)
QQCM........ College Merici, Quebec, Quebec [*Library symbol National Library of Canada*] (NLC)
QQCMQ........ Service de la Documentation et de l'Audiovisuel, Conservatoire de Musique de Quebec, Quebec [*Library symbol National Library of Canada*] (NLC)
QQCOC........ Centre de Documentation - DGTI [*Direction Generale des Technologies de l'Information*], Ministere des Communications du Quebec, Ste.-Foy, Quebec [*Library symbol National Library of Canada*] (BIB)
QQCOM........ Centre de Documentation, Direction Generale des Medias, Ministere des Communications du Quebec, Quebec, Quebec [*Library symbol National Library of Canada*] (BIB)
QQCPQ........ Parks Service, Environment Canada [*Service des Parcs, Environnement Canada*], Quebec [*Library symbol National Library of Canada*] (BIB)
QQCPS........ Centre de Documentation, Conseil de la Science et de la Technologie du Quebec, Ste.-Foy, Quebec [*Library symbol National Library of Canada*] (NLC)
QQCR........ Centre Hospitalier Christ-Roi, Quebec, Quebec [*Library symbol National Library of Canada*] (BIB)
QQCRS........ Conseil Regional de la Sante et des Services Sociaux, Quebec, Quebec [*Library symbol National Library of Canada*] (NLC)
QQCS........ Service de Documentation et de Bibliotheque, Complexe Scientifique, Ste.-Foy, Quebec [*Library symbol National Library of Canada*] (NLC)
QQCSF........ Consiel du Statut de la Femme, Quebec, Quebec [*Library symbol National Library of Canada*] (NLC)
QQCSS........ Centre de Documentation, Centre de Services Sociaux de Quebec, Quebec [*Library symbol National Library of Canada*] (BIB)
QQCT........ Commission de Toponymie du Quebec, Quebec, Quebec [*Library symbol National Library of Canada*] (NLC)

QQCU .... Conseil des Universites du Quebec, Ste.-Foy, Quebec [*Library symbol National Library of Canada*] (NLC)
QQCUQ .... Communaute Urbaine de Quebec [*Library symbol National Library of Canada*] (BIB)
qqd .... Quantum Quatra Die [*Every Fourth Day*] [*Latin*] (AD)
QQE .... Wildlife and Inland Waters Library, Environment Canada [*Bibliotheque de la Faune et des Eaux Interieures, Environement Canada*] Ste-Foy, Quebec [*Library symbol National Library of Canada*] (NLC)
QQED .... Centre de Documentation, Ministere de l'Education du Quebec, Quebec, Quebec [*Library symbol National Library of Canada*] (BIB)
QQEDOP .... Centre de Documentation, Office des Professions du Quebec, Quebec [*Library symbol National Library of Canada*] (NLC)
QQEN .... Ministere de l'Environnement, Ste-Foy, Quebec [*Library symbol National Library of Canada*] (NLC)
QQERE .... Centre de Documentation-Energie, Ministere de l'Energie et des Ressources du Quebec, Quebec, Quebec [*Library symbol National Library of Canada*] (NLC)
QQERM .... Centre de Documentation-Mines, Ministere de l'Energie et des Ressources du Quebec, Quebec, Quebec [*Library symbol National Library of Canada*] (NLC)
QQERT .... Centre de Documentation-Terres et Forets, Ministere de l'Energie et des Ressources du Quebec, Quebec, Quebec [*Library symbol National Library of Canada*] (NLC)
QQESE .... Centre de Documentation, Direction Generale de l'Enseignement et de la RechercheUniversitaires, Ministere de l'Enseignement Superieur et de la Science du Quebe c, Quebec, Quebec [*Library symbol National Library of Canada*] (BIB)
QQF .... Bibliotheque Franciscaine, Quebec, Quebec [*Library symbol National Library of Canada*] (NLC)
qqf .... Quelquefois [*Sometimes*] [*French*] (AD)
QQFPCE .... Direction de la Classification et de l'Evaluation des Emplois, Ministere de la Fonction Publique, Quebec, Quebec [*Library symbol National Library of Canada*] (NLC)
QQFTI .... Service du Traitement de l'Information, Ministere des Finances, Duberger, Quebec [*Library symbol National Library of Canada*] (NLC)
QQGR .... Bibliotheque Gabrielle-Roy, Quebec, Quebec [*Library symbol National Library of Canada*] (BIB)
qqh .... Quantum Quatra Hora [*Every Four Hours*] [*Latin*] (AD)
QQH .... Quaque Hora [*Every Hour*] [*Pharmacy*]
QQH .... Quaque Quarta Hora [*Every Fourth Hour*] [*Pharmacy*]
QQHA .... Queensland Quarter Horse Association [*Australia*]
QQHD .... Hotel-Dieu de Quebec, Quebec [*Library symbol National Library of Canada*] (NLC)
QQHDM .... Musee des Augustines de l'Hotel-Dieu de Quebec, Quebec [*Library symbol National Library of Canada*] (NLC)
QQHDS .... Hotel-Dieu du Sacre-Coeur, Quebec, Quebec [*Library symbol National Library of Canada*] (NLC)
QQHEJ .... Hopital de l'Enfant-Jesus, Quebec, Quebec [*Library symbol National Library of Canada*] (NLC)
QQHFA .... Hopital St-Francois d'Assise, Quebec, Quebec [*Library symbol National Library of Canada*] (NLC)
QQ HOR .... Quaque Hora [*Every Hour*] [*Pharmacy*]
qq hor .... Quaque Hora [*Every Hour*] [*Latin*] (AD)
QQHSS .... Hopital du Saint-Sacrement, Quebec, Quebec [*Library symbol National Library of Canada*] (NLC)
QQHSSC .... Centre de Documentation, Departement de Sante Communautaire, Hopital du Saint-Sacrement, Quebec, Quebec [*Library symbol National Library of Canada*] (BIB)
QQIAS .... Service de la Documentation, Ministere de la Sante et des Services Sociaux du Q uebec, Quebec, Quebec [*Library symbol National Library of Canada*] (NLC)
QQIC .... Ministere de l'Industrie, du Commerce et du Tourisme, Quebec, Quebec [*Library symbol National Library of Canada*] (NLC)
QQIF .... Inspecteur General des Institutions Financieres, Quebec, Quebec [*Library symbol National Library of Canada*] (NLC)
QQIN .... Indian and Northern Affairs Canada [*Affaires Indiennes et du Nord Canada*],Quebec [*Library symbol National Library of Canada*] (BIB)
QQIQRC .... Institut Quebecois de Recherche sur la Culture, Quebec, Quebec [*Library symbol National Library of Canada*] (NLC)
QQJ .... Ministere de la Justice du Quebec, Ste-Foy, Quebec [*Library symbol National Library of Canada*] (NLC)
QQL .... Bibliotheque de l'Assemblee Nationale, Quebec, Quebec [*Library symbol National Library of Canada*] (NLC)
QQLA .... Universite Laval, Quebec, Quebec [*Library symbol National Library of Canada*] (NLC)
QQLAAA .... Secteur Art et Architecture, Universite Laval, Quebec, Quebec [*Library symbol National Library of Canada*] (NLC)
QQLAAV .... Ecole des Arts Visuels, Universite Laval, Quebec, Quebec [*Library symbol National Library of Canada*] (NLC)
QQLACA .... Cartotheque, Universite Laval, Quebec, Quebec [*Library symbol National Library of Canada*] (NLC)
QQLACH .... Centre Hospitalier de l'Universite Laval, Quebec, Quebec [*Library symbol National Library of Canada*] (NLC)
QQLACHC .... Centre de Documentation, Departement de Sante Communautaire, Centre Hospitalier,Universite Laval, Quebec [*Library symbol National Library of Canada*] (NLC)
QQLACHR .... Centre de Recherche, Centre Hospitalier, Universite Laval, Quebec, Quebec [*Library symbol National Library of Canada*] (BIB)
QQLACHT .... Centre de Toxicologie, Centre Hospitalier, Universite Laval, Quebec, Quebec [*Library symbol National Library of Canada*] (BIB)
QQLACI .... Centre International de Recherches sur le Bilinguisme, Universite Laval, Quebec,Quebec [*Library symbol National Library of Canada*] (NLC)
QQLAD .... Faculte de Droit, Universite Laval, Quebec, Quebec [*Library symbol National Library of Canada*] (NLC)
QQLAG .... Institut de Geographie, Universite Laval, Quebec, Quebec [*Library symbol National Library of Canada*] (NLC)
QQLAGM .... Departement de Geologie et de Mineralogie, Universite Laval, Quebec, Quebec [*Library symbol National Library of Canada*] (NLC)
QQLAI .... Societa Dante Alighieri, Universite Laval, Quebec, Quebec [*Library symbol National Library of Canada*] (NLC)
QQLAS .... Bibliotheque Scientifique, Universite Laval, Quebec, Quebec [*Library symbol National Library of Canada*] (NLC)
QQLCP .... Ministere du Loisir, de la Chasse et de la Peche, Quebec, Quebec [*Library symbol National Library of Canada*] (NLC)
QQLH .... Literary and Historical Society of Quebec [*Societe Litteraire et Historique de Quebec*] Quebec [*Library symbol National Library of Canada*] (NLC)
QQLM .... Centre de Documentation, Laurentienne Mutuelle d'Assurance, Quebec, Quebec [*Library symbol National Library of Canada*] (BIB)
qqma .... Quality Qualified Military Availability (AD)
QQMAA .... Archives du Monastere des Augustines, Quebec, Quebec [*Library symbol National Library of Canada*] (NLC)
QQMAB .... Bibliotheque du Monastere des Augustines, Quebec, Quebec [*Library symbol National Library of Canada*] (NLC)
QQMAGA .... Archives des Augustines du Monastere de l'Hopital General de Quebec, Quebec [*Library symbol National Library of Canada*] (NLC)
QQM & R .... Quantitative, Qualitative, Maintainability, and Reliability
QQMC .... Forestry Canada [*Forets Canada*], Ste.-Foy, Quebec [*Library symbol National Library of Canada*] (NLC)
QQMCH .... Bibliotheque Administrative, (Edifice H), Ministere des Communications du Quebec, Quebec [*Library symbol National Library of Canada*] (NLC)
QQMF .... Laurentian Forestry Centre, Canadian Forestry Service [*Centre de Foresterie des Laurentides, Service Canadien des Forets*] Ste.-Foy, Quebec [*Library symbol National Library of Canada*] (NLC)
QQMQ .... Musee du Quebec, Quebec [*Library symbol National Library of Canada*] (NLC)
QQMR .... Le Mussee du Royal 22e Regiment et la Regie du Royal 22e Regiment, Quebec, Quebec [*Library symbol National Library of Canada*] (NLC)
QQMSRD .... Centre de Documentation, Direction Generale des Ressources Informationnelles, Ministere de la Main d'Oeuvre et de la Securite du Revenu du Quebec, Quebec, Quebec [*Library symbol National Library of Canada*] (NLC)
QQMSRP .... Centre de Documentation, Direction Generale de la Planification, Ministere de laMain-d'Oeuvre et de la Securite du Revenu du Quebec, Quebec [*Library symbol National Library of Canada*] (BIB)
QQMUC .... Centre de Documentation, Musee de la Civilisation, Quebec [*Library symbol National Library of Canada*] (BIB)
QQO .... Quasiquadrennial Oscillation [*Astronomy*]
QQOLF .... Office de la Langue Francaise, Quebec, Quebec [*Library symbol National Library of Canada*] (NLC)
QQOPC .... Office de la Protection du Consommateur, Quebec, Quebec [*Library symbol National Library of Canada*] (NLC)
QQOPD .... Direction de la Documentation, Office des Promotions du Quebec, Quebec, Quebec [*Library symbol National Library of Canada*] (NLC)
QQP .... Quick Query Program
QQPCQ .... Canadian Park Service, Environment Canada [*Service Canadien des Parcs, Environnement Canada*], Quebec, Quebec [*Library symbol National Library of Canada*] (NLC)
QQPEA .... Archives des Peres Eudistes, Charlesbourg, Quebec [*Library symbol National Library of Canada*] (NLC)
QQPR .... Quantitative and Qualitative Personnel Requirements
qqpr .... Quantitative and Qualitative Personnel Requirements (AD)
QQPRI .... Quantitative and Qualitative Personnel Requirements Information [*Military*]
QQPSM .... Maurice Lamontagne Institute, Fisheries and Oceans Canada [*Institut Maurice Lamontagne, Peches et Oceans Canada*], Mont-Joli, Quebec [*Library symbol National Library of Canada*] (NLC)
QQQE .... Centre Quebecois des Sciences de l'Eau, Universite du Quebec, Quebec, Quebec [*Library symbol National Library of Canada*] (NLC)
QQR .... Technical Information Centre, Reed Ltd., Quebec, Quebec [*Library symbol National Library of Canada*] (NLC)
QQRA .... Roche Associes Ltee., Group-Conseil, Ste.-Foy, Quebec [*Library symbol National Library of Canada*] (NLC)
QQRAA .... Regie de l'Assurance Automobile du Quebec, Sillery, Quebec [*Library symbol National Library of Canada*] (NLC)
QQRAMQ .... Regie de l'Assurance-Maladie du Quebec, Sillery, Quebec [*Library symbol National Library of Canada*] (NLC)
QQRE .... Ministere du Revenu, Ste.-Foy, Quebec [*Library symbol National Library of Canada*] (NLC)
QQRRQ .... Regie des Rentes du Quebec, Ste.-Foy, Quebec [*Library symbol National Library of Canada*] (NLC)
QQRSP .... Regie des Services Publics, Ste.-Foy, Quebec [*Library symbol National Library of Canada*] (NLC)
QQS .... Quality Quest System [*Vancouver Stock Exchange symbol*]
QQS .... Seminaire de Quebec, Quebec [*Library symbol National Library of Canada*] (NLC)

QQSAA......... Centre de Documentation, Secretariat aux Affaires Autochtones, Quebec [*Library symbol National Library of Canada*] (BIB)
QQSAJ......... Secretariat a la Jeunesse, Conseil Executif, Quebec, Quebec [*Library symbol National Library of Canada*] (NLC)
QQSC.......... Quadripartite Quartermaster Standardization Committee [*Military*] (AABC)
QQSCA......... Archives des Soeurs de la Charite de Quebec, Quebec, Quebec [*Library symbol National Library of Canada*] (NLC)
QQSCF......... Centre de Documentation, Secretariat a la Condition Feminine du Quebec, Quebec, Quebec [*Library symbol National Library of Canada*] (BIB)
QQSHQ......... Centre de Documentation, Societe d'Habitation du Quebec, Quebec [*Library symbol National Library of Canada*] (BIB)
QQSIP......... Societe Quebecoise d'Initiatives Petrolieres, Ste.-Foy, Quebec [*Library symbol National Library of Canada*] (NLC)
QQSP.......... Centre de Documentation, Syndicat de Professionnels et de Professionnelles du Gouvernement du Quebec, Quebec [*Library symbol National Library of Canada*] (BIB)
QQSS.......... Quebec Library, Translation Bureau, Secretary of State Canada [*Bibliotheque de Quebec, Bureau des Traductions, Secretariat d'Etat*], Ste.-Foy, Quebec [*Library symbol National Library of Canada*] (NLC)
QQST.......... Centre de Documentation, Conseil de la Science et de la Technologie, Quebec [*Library symbol National Library of Canada*] (NLC)
QQTCG......... Canadian Coast Guard [*Garde Cotiere Canadienne*] Quebec, Quebec [*Library symbol National Library of Canada*] (NLC)
QQTE.......... Tecrad, Inc., Ancienne-Lorette, Quebec [*Library symbol National Library of Canada*] (NLC)
QQTO.......... Ministere du Tourisme du Quebec, Quebec [*Library symbol National Library of Canada*] (NLC)
QQTQ.......... Centre de Documentation, Ministere du Travail du Quebec, Quebec [*Library symbol National Library of Canada*] (BIB)
QQTR.......... Ministere des Transports, Quebec, Quebec [*Library symbol National Library of Canada*] (NLC)
QQTRD......... Centre de Documentation, Ministere des Transports - Rue Dorchester, Quebec [*Library symbol National Library of Canada*] (NLC)
QQU........... Couvent des Ursulines, Quebec, Quebec [*Library symbol National Library of Canada*] (NLC)
QQUA.......... Archives du Monastere des Ursulines de Merici, Quebec, Quebec [*Library symbol National Library of Canada*] (NLC)
QQUIE......... Centre de Documentation, INRS [*Institut National de la Recherche Scientifique*]-Eau, Quebec, Quebec [*Library symbol National Library of Canada*] (NLC)
QQUQ.......... Universite du Quebec, Quebec, Quebec [*Library symbol National Library of Canada*] (NLC)
QQUQEN....... Ecole Nationale d'Administration Publique, Universite du Quebec, Quebec, Quebec [*Library symbol National Library of Canada*] (NLC)
QQUQT......... Tele-Universite, Universite du Quebec, Quebec, Quebec [*Library symbol National Library of Canada*] (NLC)
QQV........... Centre de Documentation, le Verificateur General du Quebec, Quebec, Quebec [*Library symbol National Library of Canada*] (BIB)
QQ V.......... Quae Vide [*Which See*] [*Plural form*] [*Latin*]
qqv........... Quae Vide [*Which See*] [*Latin*] (AD)
QQV........... Quantum Vis [*As Much as You Wish*] [*Pharmacy*] (ADA)
qqv........... Quod Vide [*Which see*] [*Latin*] (WDMC)
Q-QY.......... Question or Query (AAG)
q/qy.......... Question/Query (AD)
QQZ........... Jardin Zoologique de Quebec, Charlesbourg, Quebec [*Library symbol National Library of Canada*] (NLC)
QR............ Air Satellite [*ICAO designator*] (AD)
QR............ Qatar Riyal [*Monetary unit*] (BJA)
Qr............ Qere (BJA)
QR............ Quadrans [*A Farthing*] [*Monetary unit*] [*British*] (ROG)
QR............ Quadratic Residues (MHDB)
QR............ Quad Right [*Typography*]
QR............ Quadriradial [*Genetics*] (DAVI)
QR............ Quad Royal [*Paper*] (DGA)
QR............ Quadrupole Resonance
QR............ Qualifications Record (AEBS)
qr............ Qualifications Record (AD)
QR............ Quality Requirement (IAA)
QR............ Quality Review
QR............ Quantitative Restrictions [*International trade*]
QR............ Quantity Requested
QR............ Quantity Required
QR............ Quantum Rectum [*The Quantity Is Correct*] [*Pharmacy*]
qr............ Quantum Rectus [*Quantity is Correct*] [*Latin*] (AD)
QR............ Quantum Resources [*Vancouver Stock Exchange symbol*]
QR............ Quarantine Report [*HEW*]
QR............ Quart
QR............ Quarter
qr............ Quarter (WDMC)
qr............ Quarter (AD)
qr............ Quarterly [*A periodical published four times a year*] (WDMC)
QR............ Quarterly (ROG)
QR............ Quarterly Replenishment
QR............ Quarterly Report (OICC)
QR............ Quarter-Round [*Technical drawings*] (DAC)
QR............ Quarters Rating [*British military*] (DMA)
QR............ Quebec Official Reports [*A publication*] (DLA)
QR............ Queensland Railways [*Australia*] (AD)
QR............ Queen's Rangers [*British military*]
QR............ Queen's Regulation [*Military British*]
QR............ Queen's Rook [*Chess*] (ADA)
QR............ Queen's Royal [*Military unit*] [*British*]
Q/R........... Query/Response (MCD)
QR............ Quick Reaction
qr............ Quick Reaction (AD)
qr............ Quick Receipt (AD)
QR............ Quick Recovery (DAVI)
QR............ Quick Recovery Defibrillator [*Cardiology*] (DAVI)
QR............ Quick Response (AD)
QR............ Quieting Reflex [*In book title "Q-R: The Quieting Reflex" by Charles F. Stroebel*]
QR............ Quieting Response [*Medicine*] (DMAA)
QR............ Quinaldine Red [*Medicine*] (DMAA)
QR............ Quintana Roo (AD)
qr............ Quire (AD)
QR............ Quire [*Measure of paper*]
qr............ Quire [*Paper*] (WDMC)
QR............ Quota Restriction
QR............ Quotation Request
QR............ Sources Public Library [*Bibliotheque Municipale des Sources*] Roxboro, Quebec [*Library symbol National Library of Canada*] (NLC)
QRA........... Archeveche de Rimouski, Quebec [*Library symbol National Library of Canada*] (NLC)
QRA........... Quality and Reliability Assurance (NG)
QRA........... Quality Recording Alarm [*Engineering*]
qra........... Quality Reliability Assurance (AD)
QRA........... Quantified Risk Analysis
QRA........... Quarterly Review and Analysis
QRA........... Queensland Rifle Association [*Australia*] (AD)
QRA........... Quick Reaction Acquisition (MCD)
QRA........... Quick Reaction Aircraft (MCD)
QRA........... Quick Reaction Alert [*Military*] (AFM)
qra........... Quick Reaction Alert (AD)
QRA........... Quick Reaction Area (MCD)
QRA........... Quick Replaceable Assembly
QRAAT......... Centre de l'Abitibi-Temiscamingue, Archives Nationales du Quebec, Rouyn-Noranda,Quebec [*Library symbol National Library of Canada*] (BIB)
QRAC.......... Quality and Reliability Assessment Council
QRAC.......... Quality and Reliability Assurance Committee (AAGC)
QR Air........ Queen's Regulations and Orders for the Royal Canadian Air Force
QRAL.......... Quality and Reliability Assurance Laboratory [*NASA*] (KSC)
QRAN.......... Archives Nationales du Quebec, Rimouski, Quebec [*Library symbol National Library of Canada*] (BIB)
QR & AI....... Queen's Regulations and Admiralty Instructions [*Obsolete Navy British*]
QR & O (Can)... Queen's Regulations and Orders for the Canadian Army
QRB........... Quality Review Bulletin [*A publication*] (DMAA)
QRB........... Quarterly Review of Biology [*A publication*] (BRI)
QRBC.......... Bibliotheque Centrale de Pret d'Abitibi-Temiscamingue, Rouyn-Noranda, Quebec [*Library symbol National Library of Canada*] (NLC)
QRBM.......... Quasi-Random Band Model
qrbm.......... Quasi-Random Band Model (AD)
QRC........... Quaker Resources Canada Ltd. [*Vancouver Stock Exchange symbol*]
QRC........... Queensland Rubber Co. [*Australia*] (AD)
QRC........... Quick RAM [*Random Access Memory*] Change [*Computer science*] (IAA)
QRC........... Quick Reaction Capability [*Military*]
qrc........... Quick Reaction Capability (AD)
QRC........... Quick Reaction Change (MCD)
QRC........... Quick Reaction Communications (MHDI)
QRC........... Quick Response Capability [*Military*]
QRC........... Quick Response Controller (NITA)
QRCA.......... Qualitative Research Consultants Association (EA)
QRCB.......... College Bourget, Rigaud, Quebec [*Library symbol National Library of Canada*] (NLC)
QRCC.......... Quadripartite Research Coordination Committee [*Military*] (AABC)
QRCC.......... Query Response Communications Console
QRCC.......... Quick Reaction Combat Capability (DOMA)
QRCG.......... Quasi-Random Code Generator (CET)
qrcg.......... Quasi-Random Code Generator (AD)
QRCH.......... Centre de Documentation, Centre Hospitalier Regional de Rimouski, Quebec [*Library symbol National Library of Canada*] (NLC)
QRCN.......... College de l'Abitibi-Temiscamingue, Rouyn, Quebec [*Library symbol National Library of Canada*] (NLC)
QRCN.......... Queen's Regulations and Orders for the Royal Canadian Navy
QRCR.......... Quality Reliability Consumption Reports
QRCRS......... Conseil Regional de la Sante et des Services Sociaux, Rimouski, Quebec [*Library symbol National Library of Canada*] (NLC)
QRCUP......... Quebec Region Canadian University Press (AD)
QRD........... Quality Reliability Deployment [*Automotive engineering*]
QRD........... Quarterly Review of Doublespeak [*A publication*]
QRD........... Quick Reaction Development
QRDC.......... Quartermaster Research and Development Center [*or Command*] [*Natick, MA*]
QRDEA......... Quartermaster Research and Development Evaluation Agency [*Army*]
QRDN.......... Quality Requirement Discrepancy Notice (SAA)
QRDS.......... Quarterly Review of Drilling Statistics [*American Petroleum Institute*]
QRE........... Bibliotheque Municipale, Repentigny, Quebec [*Library symbol National Library of Canada*] (NLC)
QRE........... Quick Reaction [*or Response*] Estimate

QREC .... Quartermaster Research and Engineering Center [*or Command*] [*Natick, MA*]
QRECS .... Centre Regional de Documentation Pedagogique, Commission Scolaire de Le Gardeur,Repentigny, Quebec [*Library symbol National Library of Canada*] (BIB)
Q Rev Juris... Quarterly Review of Jurisprudence [*1887-88*] [*A publication*] (DLA)
Q Rev Rural Econ... Quarterly Review of the Rural Economy [*A publication*]
QRF .... Quadrature Rejection Frequency
QRF .... Quality Review File [*IRS*]
QRF .... Quick Reaction Force [*Military*] (CINC)
QRG .... Quadrupole Residual Gas
QRG .... Quick Reaction Grooming
QRG .... Quick Response Graphic
qrg .... Quick Response Graphic (AD)
qrga .... Quadrupole Residual Gas Analyzer (AD)
QRGA .... Quadrupole Residual Gas Analyzer
QRGAS .... Quadrupole Residual Gas Analyzer System
QRGS .... Grand Seminaire de Rimouski, Quebec [*Library symbol National Library of Canada*] (NLC)
QRH .... Rosemere High School, Quebec [*Library symbol National Library of Canada*] (BIB)
QRHD .... Bibliotheque Medicale, Hotel-Dieu de Roberval, Quebec [*Library symbol National Library of Canada*] (NLC)
QRI .... Qualitative Requirements Information [*Army*]
qri .... Qualitative Requirements Information (AD)
QRI .... Quick Reaction Integration (NASA)
QRIA .... Quick Reaction Integration Activity (NASA)
QRIB .... Haskell Free Library, Rock Island, Quebec [*Library symbol National Library of Canada*] (NLC)
QRIC .... CEGEP [*College d'Enseignement General et Professionnel*] de Rimouski, Quebec [*Library symbol National Library of Canada*] (NLC)
QRIC .... Quick Reaction Installation Capability (CET)
qric .... Quick Reaction Installation Capability (AD)
QRICC .... Quick Reaction Inventory Control Center [*Army*] (MCD)
QRIH .... Queen's Royal Irish Hussars [*Military unit*] [*British*]
QRIM .... Institut Maritime, CEGEP de Rimouski, Quebec [*Library symbol National Library of Canada*] (NLC)
QRKB .... Quebec King's Bench Reports [*A publication*] (DLA)
QRKB .... Rapports Judiciaires de Quebec, Cour du Banc du Roi [*Quebec Law Reports, King's Bench*] [*A publication*] (DLA)
QRL .... Bibliotheque Municipale, Riviere-Du-Loup, Quebec [*Library symbol National Library of Canada*] (BIB)
QRL .... Q-Switch Ruby LASER
QRL .... Quadripartite Research List [*Military*] (AABC)
QRL .... Quaternary Research Laboratory [*University of Michigan*] [*Research center*] (RCD)
QRL .... Queensland Research League [*Australia*] (AD)
QRL .... Quick Reference List
QRL .... Quick Relocate and Link
QRLC .... CEGEP [*College d'Enseignement General et Professionnel*] de Riviere-Du-Loup, Quebec [*Library symbol National Library of Canada*] (BIB)
QRLH .... Centre de Documentation DSC, Hotel-Dieu de Riviere-Du-Loup, Quebec [*Library symbol National Library of Canada*] (BIB)
QRLP .... Centre de Recherche, Tourbieres Premier Ltee., Riviere-Du-Loup, Quebec [*Library symbol National Library of Canada*] (BIB)
QRLY .... Quarterly
QRM .... Artificial Interference to Transmission or Reception [*Broadcasting*]
QRM .... Bibliotheque Municipale, Rimouski, Quebec [*Library symbol National Library of Canada*] (NLC)
QRM .... Quality and Resource Management (HCT)
QRM .... Quality and Resource Management
QRM .... Quorum Resource Corp. [*Vancouver Stock Exchange symbol*]
QRMC .... Quadrennial Review of Military Compensation [*DoD*]
QRMC .... Quick Response Multicolor Copier (MCD)
QRMF .... Quick Reacting, Mobile Force [*Military NATO*] (NATG)
QRMP .... Quick-Response Multicolor Printer (RDA)
Qr Mr .... Quartermaster [*British military*] (DMA)
Qrmr .... Quartermaster (AD)
QRN .... Soeurs de Notre-Dame du Saint-Rosaire, Rimouski, Quebec [*Library symbol National Library of Canada*] (NLC)
QRO .... Quality Review Organization (AD)
Qro .... Queretaro (AD)
qro .... Quick Reaction Operation (AD)
QRO .... Quick Reaction Operation (WDAA)
QRO .... Quick Reaction Organization (WDAA)
QROA .... Quarter Racing Owners of America (EA)
Q Roo .... Quintana Roo (AD)
QRosc .... Pro Roscio Comoedo [*of Cicero*] [*Classical studies*] (OCD)
QRP .... Queen's Rook's Pawn [*Chess*] (IIA)
QRP .... Query and Reporting Processor
QRP .... Quick Reaction Program [*Army*]
QRP .... Quick Response Proposal [*Navy*]
QRPA .... Quartermaster Radiation Planning Agency (AD)
QRPA .... Quartermaster Radiation Planning Agency (NADA)
QRPAO .... Qualified Radium Plaque Adaptometer Operator [*Navy*]
QRPS .... Quick Reaction Procurement System [*Army*] (AABC)
QRQB .... Quebec Queen's Bench Reports [*Canada*] [*A publication*] (DLA)
QRR .... Quadrature Rejection Ratio
QRR .... Quadrupole Resonance Response
QRR .... Qualitative Research Requirement for Nuclear Weapons Effects Information (AABC)
QRR .... Quality Readiness Review (MCD)
QRR .... Quarterly Research Review
QRR .... Queen's Royal Regiment [*Military unit*] [*British*]
QRR .... Queen's Royal Rifles [*British military*] (DMA)
QRR .... Quincy Railroad Co. [*AAR code*]
QRRB .... Qualified Railroad Retirement Beneficiary
QRRF .... Master Quality Review Report File [*IRS*]
QRRI .... Qualitative Research Requirements Information [*Army*]
QRRK .... Quantum Rice-Ramsperger-Kassel [*Chemical kinetics methodology*]
QRRS .... Quality Response Rating Scales (EDAC)
QRS .... Natural Interference to Transmission or Reception [*Broadcasting*]
QRS .... Qualification Review Sheet (KSC)
QRS .... Qualified Repair Source (AFIT)
QRS .... Quantum Readout System [*Method of measurement*]
QRS .... Quarters
qrs .... Quarters (AD)
QRS .... Queensland Rose Society [*Australia*]
QRS .... Queen's Row Spare
QRS .... Quick Reaction Sortie (NASA)
QRSC .... Quebec Superior Court Reports [*A publication*] (DLA)
QRSC .... Rapports Judiciaires de Quebec, Cour Superieure [*Quebec Law Reports, Superior Court*] [*A publication*] (DLA)
QRSI .... Queensland Raw Sugar Industry [*Australia*]
QRSI .... Quick Response Services [*NASDAQ symbol*] (SAG)
QRSL .... Qualified Repair Source List (AFIT)
QRSL .... Quick Reaction Space Laboratory [*NASA*] (NASA)
qrt .... Quarter (AD)
QRT .... Queue Run-Time [*Computer science*]
QRT .... Quick Reaction Task (MCD)
QRT .... Quick Reaction Team [*Military*]
QRT .... Quiet Radio Transmission (DNAB)
QRTA .... Queensland Road Transport Association [*Australia*]
qrtg .... Quartering (AD)
QRTL .... Queensland Right to Life [*An association Australia*]
QRTLY .... Quarterly (ROG)
qrtly .... Quarterly (AD)
qrtmstr .... Quartermaster (AD)
QRTP .... Quick Response Targeting Program [*Lunar*]
QRTR .... Quarter (IAA)
QRTR .... Quarter-Plate (VRA)
QRTSA .... Queensland Retail Traders and Shopkeepers' Association [*Australia*]
QRU .... Queen's Row Unit
QRU .... Universite du Quebec, Rimouski, Quebec [*Library symbol National Library of Canada*] (NLC)
QRUC .... Cartotheque, Universite du Quebec, Rimouski, Quebec [*Library symbol National Library of Canada*] (NLC)
QRUQR .... Universite du Quebec en Abitibi-Temiscamingue, Rouyn, Quebec [*Library symbol National Library of Canada*] (NLC)
QRUS .... Queen's Row Unit Spare
QRV .... Qualified Real-Estate Valuer (AD)
QRV .... Queenstown Rifle Volunteers [*British military*] (DMA)
QRV .... Quick Release Valve
qrv .... Quick-Release Valve (AD)
QRV .... Quinn River Valley [*Nevada*] [*Seismograph station code, US Geological Survey Closed*] (SEIS)
QRVB .... Queen's Rifle Volunteer Brigade [*British military*] (DMA)
QRW .... Quail Ridge Winery [*Vancouver Stock Exchange symbol*]
QRX .... Queensland Railfast Express [*Australia*] (AD)
qry .... Quality and Reliability Year (AD)
QRY .... Quality and Reliability Year
QRY .... Quarry (KSC)
QRZ .... Quaddel Reaktion Zeit [*Wheal Reaction Time*] [*German*]
QRZ .... Who is Calling [*Amateur Radio*] (BARN)
QS .... Cal Sierra [*ICAO designator*] (AD)
QS .... Every Shift [*Nursing*] (DAVI)
QS .... Les Quatre Saisons [*Record label*] [*France*]
QS .... Quadratic Sieve [*Computer science*] (BARN)
qs .... Quadrophonic Stereo (AD)
QS .... Quadrophonic Stereo (WDAA)
QS .... Quadruple Screw (IAA)
QS .... Quadrupole Splitting (OA)
QS .... Quality Standard
QS .... Quality Stock
QS .... Quality Surveillance [*Navy*] (DNAB)
QS .... Quantity Share [*Economics*]
QS .... Quantity Surveying
qs .... Quantum Satis [*Sufficient Quantity*] [*Latin*]
QS .... Quantum Sufficit [*A Sufficient Quantity*] [*Pharmacy*] (ADA)
qs .... Quantum Sufficit [*As Much as Suffices*] [*Latin*] (AD)
QS .... Quarantine Station
QS .... Quartermaster Sergeant [*Military*]
QS .... Quarternote Society (AD)
qs .... Quarter Section (AD)
QS .... Quarter Section
QS .... Quarter Sessions
Q-S .... Queckenstedt-Stookey Test [*Neurology*] (DAVI)
QS .... Quecksilbersaeule [*Mercury Column*] [*German*] (AD)
QS .... Queensland Society [*Australia*] (AD)
QS .... Queensland Society [*Australia*] (NADA)
QS .... Queen's Scarf (ADA)
QS .... Queen's Scholar [*British*]
QS .... Queen's Serjeant [*Military British*] (ROG)
Q-S .... Queneau-Schuhmann [*Lead process*]
QS .... Query Similarity [*Computer science*] (MHDI)
QS .... Query System [*Computer science*]
QS .... Question Standard (NATG)
QS .... Queueing System (AD)

QS Queue Select [*Computer science*]
QS Quickie Strike (MHDB)
QS Quick Service
QS Quick Sweep [*Construction*]
QS Quiet Sleep [*Physiology*]
QS Quota Source (AABC)
QS2 Total Electromechanical Systole [*Cardiology*] (DAVI)
QS_2I Shortened Electrochemical Systole [*Cardiology*] (DAVI)
QSA Quad Synchronous Adapter [*Perkin-Elmer*]
QSA Qualification Site Approval [*NASA*] (NASA)
QSA Qualified in Small Arms [*British military*] (DMA)
QSA Queensland Shopkeepers Association [*Australia*] (AD)
QSA Queensland Swimming Association [*Australia*]
QSA Quick Service Assistant (MCD)
QSABS Laboratoire de Sante Publique du Quebec, Ste-Anne-De-Bellevue, Quebec [*Library symbol National Library of Canada*] (NLC)
QS AD Quantum Sufficiat Ad [*To a Sufficient Quantity*] [*Pharmacy*]
QSAL Quadripartite Standardisation Agreement List [*Australia*]
QSAL Quadripartite Standardization Agreements List [*Military*]
QSAM Quadrature Sideband Amplitude Modulation [*Telecommunications*]
QSAM Queued Sequential Access Method [*IBM Corp.*] [*Computer science*]
qsam Queued Sequential Access Method (AD)
Qsan Anatomic Shunt Flow [*Medicine*] (DAVI)
qs & l Quarters, Subsistence, and Laundry (AD)
QS & L Quarters, Subsistence, and Laundry [*Military*]
(Q)SAR Quantitative Structure-Activity Relationship [*Pharmacochemistry*]
QSAT Quality Systems Acquisition Technology [*Army*] (RDA)
QSAT Queensland Scholastic Aptitude Test [*Australia*]
QSATS Quiet Short-Haul Air Transportation System
QSBC Qualified Small Business Corp.
QSBC Queensland Small Business Council [*Australia*]
QSBE Quicken Small Business Expert [*Financial software*]
qsbg Quasi-Stellar Blue Galaxies (AD)
qsbo Quasi-Stellar Blue Objects (AD)
QSBR Bio-Research Laboratory, Senneville, Quebec [*Library symbol National Library of Canada*] (NLC)
QSC African Safari Airways Ltd. [*Kenya*] [*ICAO designator*] (FAAC)
QSC Al-Ahli Bank of Qatar (MENA)
QSC College de Shawinigan, Quebec [*Library symbol National Library of Canada*] (NLC)
QSC Quality, Service, Cleanliness [*McDonald's Hamburger stands motto*]
QSC Quasi-Sensory Communication [*Parapsychology*]
QSC Quasistatic Compliance [*Measurement*] (DAVI)
QSC Quebec Securities Commission [*Canada*] (AD)
QSC Queensland Sugar Corp. [*Australia*]
QSC Queen Street Camera, Inc. [*Toronto Stock Exchange symbol*]
QSC Questionnaire Service Co. [*Information service or system*] (IID)
QSC Quick Set Compound
QSCA Queensland Specialist Contractors' Association [*Australia*]
QSCC Queensland Society for Crippled Children [*Australia*]
QSCV Quality, Service, Cleanliness, and Value [*Formula for successful fast-food restaurants as taught by McDonald's Corp. at its Hamburger University*]
QSD Quality Surveillance Division [*Navy*]
QSDC Quantitative Structural Design Criteria [*NASA*]
QSDMA Queensland Soft Drink Manufacturers' Association [*Australia*]
QSE Qualified Scientists and Engineers
qse Qualified Scientists and Engineers (AD)
QSE Quantum Size Effect (PDAA)
QSED Research Centre, Domtar Ltd., Senneville, Quebec [*Library symbol National Library of Canada*] (NLC)
QSEE Quiet STOL [*Short Takeoff and Landing*] Experimental Engine [*Aviation*] (OA)
QSEMH Missisquoi Historical Society [*Societe d'Histoire de Missisquoi*] Stanbridge-East, Quebec [*Library symbol National Library of Canada*] (NLC)
QSF Bibliotheque Municipale, Ste.-Foy, Quebec [*Library symbol National Library of Canada*] (NLC)
QSF Quasi-Static Field
qsf Quasi-Static Field (AD)
QSF Quasi-Stationary Front
QSF Queensland Soccer Federation [*Australia*] (AD)
QSFAG Research Station, Agriculture Canada [*Station de Recherches, Agriculture Canada*] Ste-Foy, Quebec [*Library symbol National Library of Canada*] (NLC)
QSFB Biorex, Ste.-Foy, Quebec [*Library symbol National Library of Canada*] (BIB)
QSFBP Maison Generalice des Soeurs du Bon Pasteur, Ste-Foy, Quebec [*Library symbol National Library of Canada*] (NLC)
QSFC Centre des Medias, CEGEP [*College d'Enseignement General et Professionnel*]de Ste.-Foy, Quebec [*Library symbol National Library of Canada*] (NLC)
QSFC College d'Enseignement, Ste.-Foy, Quebec [*Library symbol National Library of Canada*] (NLC)
QSFCAE Clinique d'Aide a l'Enfance, Ste.-Foy, Quebec [*Library symbol National Library of Canada*] (NLC)
QSFCD Societe de Cooperation pour le Developpement International, Ste.-Foy, Quebec [*Library symbol National Library of Canada*] (BIB)
QSFCM College Marguerite d'Youville, Ste.-Foy, Quebec [*Library symbol National Library of Canada*] (NLC)
QSFCP Commission de Police du Quebec, Ste.-Foy, Quebec [*Library symbol National Library of Canada*] (NLC)
QSFCR Centre de Recherche Industrielle du Quebec, Ste.-Foy, Quebec [*Library symbol National Library of Canada*] (NLC)
QSFCRO Centre de Documentation, Commission Rochon, Ste.-Foy, Quebec [*Library symbol National Library of Canada*] (BIB)
QSFCSE Centre de Documentation, Conseil Superieur de l'Education du Quebec, Ste.-Foy, Quebec [*Library symbol National Library of Canada*] (BIB)
QSFE Centre de Documentation, Directeur General des Elections du Quebec, Ste.-Foy, Quebec [*Library symbol National Library of Canada*] (BIB)
QSFHL Hopital Laval, Ste.-Foy, Quebec [*Library symbol National Library of Canada*] (NLC)
QSFIG Centre de Documentation, INRS [*Institut National de la Recherche Scientifique*]-Georessources, Ste.-Foy, Quebec [*Library symbol National Library of Canada*] (NLC)
QSFIO Institut National d'Optique, Ste.-Foy, Quebec [*Library symbol National Library of Canada*] (BIB)
QSFPC Centre de Documentation, Bureau de la Protection Civile du Quebec, Ste.-Foy, Quebec [*Library symbol National Library of Canada*] (BIB)
QSFS SOQUEM [*Societe Quebecoise d'Exploration Miniere*] Documentation, Ste.-Foy,Quebec [*Library symbol National Library of Canada*] (NLC)
QSG Quasi-Steady Glide [*NASA*]
QSG Quasi-Stellar Galaxy
qsg Quasi-Stellar Galaxy (AD)
QSGVT Quarter Scale Ground Vibration Test (MCD)
QSH Stanstead Historial Society, Quebec [*Library symbol National Library of Canada*] (NLC)
QSHAG Saint-Hyacinthe Food Research Centre, Agriculture Canada [*Centre de Recherches Alimentaires de Saint-Hyacinthe, Agriculture Canada*] Quebec [*Library symbol National Library of Canada*] (NLC)
QSHC CEGEP [*College d'Enseignement General et Professionnel*] de Shawinigan, Quebec [*Library symbol National Library of Canada*] (NLC)
QSHCH Centre Hospitalier Regional de La Mauricie, Shawinigan, Quebec [*Library symbol National Library of Canada*] (NLC)
QSHCHS Departement de Sante Communautaire, Centre Hospitalier Regional de la Mauricie, Shawinigan, Quebec [*Library symbol National Library of Canada*] (BIB)
QSHCP Hopital Communautaire du Pontiac [*Pontiac Community Hospital*], Shawville, Quebec [*Library symbol National Library of Canada*] (NLC)
QSHERAN Centre Regional de l'Estrie, Archives Nationales du Quebec, Sherbooke, Quebec [*Library symbol National Library of Canada*] (NLC)
QSHERB Bibliotheque Centrale de Pret de l'Estrie, Sherbrooke, Quebec [*Library symbol National Library of Canada*] (BIB)
QSHERC Bibliotheque des Sciences de la Sante, Universite de Sherbrooke, Quebec [*Library symbol National Library of Canada*] (NLC)
QSHERCR Conseil Regional de la Sante et des Services Sociaux des Cantons de l'Est, Sherbrooke, Quebec [*Library symbol National Library of Canada*] (NLC)
QSHERD Sherbrooke Daily Record, Quebec [*Library symbol National Library of Canada*] (NLC)
QSHERE College de Sherbrooke (CEGEP) [*College d'Enseignement General et Professionnel*], Quebec [*Library symbol National Library of Canada*] (NLC)
QSHERG Bibliotheque du Grand Seminaire, Sherbrooke, Quebec [*Library symbol National Library of Canada*] (NLC)
QSHERH Huntingdon Gleaner, Quebec [*Library symbol National Library of Canada*] (NLC)
QSHERHD Centre Hospitalier Hotel-Dieu, Sherbrooke, Quebec [*Library symbol National Library of Canada*] (NLC)
QSHERM Monastere des Peres Redemptoristes, Sherbrooke, Quebec [*Library symbol Obsolete National Library of Canada*] (NLC)
QSHERN Bibliotheque Municipale, Sherbrooke, Quebec [*Library symbol National Library of Canada*] (NLC)
QSHERS Seminaire de Sherbrooke, Quebec [*Library symbol National Library of Canada*] (NLC)
QSHERSB Les Conseillers Samson Belair, Inc., Sherbrooke, Quebec [*Library symbol National Library of Canada*] (NLC)
QSHERSC College du Sacre-Coeur, Sherbrooke, Quebec [*Library symbol National Library of Canada*] (NLC)
QSHERSF Ecole Secondaire St.-Francois, Sherbrooke, Quebec [*Library symbol National Library of Canada*] (NLC)
QSHERSG Societe de Genealogie des Cantons de l'Est, Sherbrooke, Quebec [*Library symbol National Library of Canada*] (NLC)
QSHERSH La Societe d'Histoire des Cantons de l'Est, Sherbrooke, Quebec [*Library symbol National Library of Canada*] (NLC)
QSHERSV Centre Hospitalier St.-Vincent-De-Paul, Sherbrooke, Quebec [*Library symbol National Library of Canada*] (NLC)
QSHERU Bibliotheque Generale, Universite de Sherbrooke, Quebec [*Library symbol National Library of Canada*] (NLC)
QSHERUA Galerie d'Art et Centre Culturel, Universite de Sherbrooke, Quebec [*Library symbol National Library of Canada*] (NLC)
QSHERUD Bibliotheque de Droit, Universite de Sherbrooke, Quebec [*Library symbol National Library of Canada*] (NLC)
QSHERUG Departement de Geographie, Universite de Sherbrooke, Quebec [*Library symbol National Library of Canada*] (NLC)
QSHERUGC Cartotheque, Departement de Geographie, Universite de Sherbrooke, Quebec [*Library symbol National Library of Canada*] (NLC)
QSHERURA Centre de Documentation, Programme de Recherche sur l'Amiante, Universite de Sherbrooke, Quebec [*Library symbol National Library of Canada*] (NLC)

QSHERUS .... Bibliotheque des Sciences, Universite de Sherbrooke, Quebec [*Library symbol National Library of Canada*] (NLC)
QSHERY .... Centre de Documentation et d'Audio-Visuel, Hopital d'Youville de Sherbrooke, Quebec [*Library symbol National Library of Canada*] (NLC)
QSHM .... Municipal Library [*Bibliotheque Municipale*] Shawinigan, Quebec [*Library symbol National Library of Canada*] (NLC)
QSHS .... Seminaire Ste-Marie, Shawinigan, Quebec [*Library symbol National Library of Canada*] (NLC)
QSI .... Bibliotheque Municipale, Sept-Iles, Quebec [*Library symbol National Library of Canada*] (NLC)
QSI .... Quality Salary Increase (AFM)
qsi .... Quality Salary Increase (AD)
QSI .... Quality Service Indicator
QSI .... Quality Step Increase (GFGA)
QSI .... Quantum Scalar Irradiance [*Instrumentation*]
QSI .... Quantum Systems, Inc.
QSI .... Quarterly Survey of Intentions [*Became Consumer Buying Expectations Survey*] [*Bureau of the Census*]
QSIA .... Centre Regional de la Cote-Nord, Archives Nationales du Quebec, Sept-Iles, Quebec [*Library symbol National Library of Canada*] (BIB)
QSIBCP .... Bibliotheque Centrale de Pret de la Cote-Nord, Sept-Iles, Quebec [*Library symbol National Library of Canada*] (NLC)
QSIC .... CEGEP [*College d'Enseignement General et Professionnel*] de Sept-Iles, Quebec [*Library symbol National Library of Canada*] (BIB)
QSIC .... Quality Standard Inspection Criteria
qsic .... Quality Standard Inspection Criteria (AD)
QSIH .... Hopital des Sept-Iles, Quebec [*Library symbol National Library of Canada*] (NLC)
QSII .... Quality Systems [*NASDAQ symbol*] (TTSB)
QSII .... Quality Systems, Inc. [*NASDAQ symbol*] (NQ)
QSIIOM .... Mineralogy Laboratory, Iron Ore Co., Sept-Iles, Quebec [*Library symbol National Library of Canada*] (NLC)
QSILC .... College Jesus-Marie de Sillery, Quebec [*Library symbol National Library of Canada*] (NLC)
QSIM .... Qualitative Simulation Algorithm [*Mathematics*]
QSJ .... Stanstead Journal, Quebec [*Library symbol National Library of Canada*] (NLC)
QSJHD .... Hotel-Dieu de Saint-Jerome, Quebec [*Library symbol National Library of Canada*] (NLC)
QSJM .... Queen's Silver Jubilee Medal [*British*] (AD)
QSK .... Quadriphase Shift Keying (MCD)
QSL .... Q-Switch LASER
QSL .... Qualification Status List (KSC)
QSL .... Qualified Source List [*NASA*] (NASA)
QSL .... Quality of School Life Scale [*Educational test*]
QSL .... Quarterly Stock List
QSL .... Queensland State Library [*Australia*] (AD)
QSL .... Queue Search Limit [*Computer science*]
QSLCR .... Campus 1, Champlain Regional College, St.-Lambert, Quebec [*Library symbol National Library of Canada*] (NLC)
QSLE .... Bibliotheque Municipale, Saint-Leonard, Quebec [*Library symbol National Library of Canada*] (NLC)
qsm .... Quadruple-Screw Motorship (AD)
QSM .... Quality Systems Management [*DoD*]
QSM .... Quarter Scale Model (MCD)
QSM .... Quarter Square Multiplier
qsm .... Quarter-Square Multipliers (AD)
QSM .... Quasi-Linear Sequential Machine
QSM .... Queen's Service Medal [*British*] (AD)
qsm .... Queen's Service Medal [*British*] (AD)
QSM .... South Molle Islands [*Queensland*] [*Airport symbol*] (AD)
QSMO .... Quaker State Motor Oils (AD)
QSMVMAC ... Queen Street Mall and Valley Mall Advisory Committee [*Brisbane, Australia*]
QSMVT .... Quarter Scale Model Vibration Testing (NASA)
QSND .... Qsound Labs, Inc. [*NASDAQ symbol*] (SAG)
QSNDF .... QSound Labs [*NASDAQ symbol*] (TTSB)
QSNT .... (Quinolinesulfonyl)nitrotriazole [*Organic chemistry*]
QSO .... Bibliotheque Municipale, Sorel, Quebec [*Library symbol National Library of Canada*] (NLC)
QSO .... Contact [*Amateur Radio*] (BARN)
QSO .... QUASAR [*Quasi-Stellar*] [*Astronomy*] (IAA)
QSO .... Quasi-Biennial Stratospheric Oscillation
qso .... Quasibiennial Stratospheric Oscillation (AD)
qso .... Quasistellar Object (AD)
QSO .... Quasi-Stellar [*or QUASAR*] Object
QSO .... Quebec Symphony Orchestra [*Canada*] (AD)
QSO .... Queensland Symphony Orchestra [*Australia*] (AD)
QSO .... Queen's Service Order [*British*] (AD)
QSOCS .... C. Stroemgren, Sorel, Quebec [*Library symbol National Library of Canada*] (NLC)
QSOCS .... QIT - Fer et Titane, Inc., Sorel, Quebec [*Library symbol National Library of Canada*] (NLC)
QSOP .... Quadripartite Standing Operating Procedures [*Military*]
Qsound .... Qsound Labs, Inc. [*Associated Press*] (SAG)
QSP .... Air ACG [*France*] [*FAA designator*] (FAAC)
Qsp .... Physiologic Shunt Flow [*Total venous admixture*] [*Medicine*] (DAVI)
qsp .... Quality Search Procedure (AD)
QSP .... Quench Spray Pump (IEEE)
QSP .... Quick Search Procedure
QSPA .... Queensland Secondary Principals' Association [*Australia*]
QSPP .... Quebec Society for the Protection of Plants [*Canada*] (AD)
QSPR .... Quantitative Structure-Property Relationship
QSPS .... Qualification Standards for Postal Field Service
QSPV .... Quasistatic Pressure Volume [*Measurement*] (DAVI)
Qs/Qt .... Intropulmonary Shunt Ratio [*Medicine*] (DAVI)
Qs/Qt .... Right-to-Left Shunt Ratio [*Medicine*] (DAVI)
QSR .... Quality Statistics Report [*Nuclear energy*] (NUCP)
QSR .... Quality Status Review (MCD)
QSR .... Quality Strike Reconnaissance
QSR .... Quality System Review
QSR .... Quarterly Statistical Report (NRCH)
QSR .... Quarterly Status Report
QSR .... Quarterly Summary Report
QSR .... Quartier de Securite Renforcee [*Maximum Security Prison*] [*French*] (AD)
QSR .... Quasar [*Galaxy*]
QSR .... Quasi-Stellar Radio Source
QSR .... Quebec Sturgeon River Mines Ltd. [*Toronto Stock Exchange symbol*]
QSR .... Quick Service Restaurant
QSR .... Quick-Start Recording [*Video technology*]
QSR .... Quick Strike Reconnaissance (MCD)
qsr .... Quick-Strike Reconnaissance (AD)
QSR .... Quien Sabe Ranch [*California*] [*Seismograph station code, US Geological Survey*] (SEIS)
QSR .... Quinoline Still Residue [*Coal tar technology*]
QSRA .... Queensland Smallbore Rifle Association [*Australia*]
QSRA .... Quiet Short-Haul Research Aircraft [*NASA*]
qsra .... Quiet Short-Haul Research Aircraft (AD)
Qsrel .... Relative Shunt Flow [*Medicine*] (DAVI)
QSRFC .... Queensland Sport and Recreational Fishing Council [*Australia*]
QSRIG .... Quantity Surveyors Research and Information Group (AD)
QSRMC .... Quality Scheme for Ready Mixed Concrete (EAIO)
QSRS .... Quasi-Stellar Blue Galaxies (SAA)
QSRS .... Quasi-Stellar Radio Source
qsrs .... Quasi-Stellar Radio Sources (AD)
QSRT .... QSR Ltd. [*NASDAQ symbol*] (SAG)
QSRTCG .... Queensland Sales Representatives and Commercial Travellers' Guild [*Australia*]
QSRTF .... QSR Ltd [*NASDAQ symbol*] (TTSB)
QSS .... Quadratic Score Statistic [*Test*]
QSS .... Quadruple-Screw Ship (AD)
QSS .... Quadrupole Screw Ship
QSS .... Quantitative Sacroiliac Scintigraphy [*Orthopedics*] [*Radiology*] (DAVI)
QSS .... Quasi-Steady State
QSS .... Quasi-Stellar Source
qss .... Quasi-Stellar Source (AD)
QSS .... Quench Spray Subsystem (IEEE)
QSS .... Quick Service Supervisor (MCD)
QSS .... Quick Supply Store [*Military*] (AABC)
QSS .... Quill and Scroll Society (EA)
QSS .... Quindar Scanning System (NASA)
QSS .... Quota Sample Survey (WDAA)
QSSA .... Quasi-Stationary State Approximation
qssa .... Quasi-Stationary-State Approximation (AD)
QSSCT .... Queensland Society of Sugar Cane Technologists [*Australia*] (AD)
QSSI .... Quarterly Surprise Security Inspection [*Navy*] (DNAB)
QSSP .... Quasi-Solid State Panel
qssp .... Quasi-Solid-State Panel (AD)
QSSR .... Quarterly Stock Status Report
QST .... General Call Preceding a Message [*Amateur Radio*] (BARN)
QST .... QSA Tech, Inc. [*Vancouver Stock Exchange symbol*]
QST .... Quantitative Sensory Test [*Medicine*] (DMAA)
QST .... Quebec Standard Test [*Canada*] (AD)
QST .... Questmont Mines [*Vancouver Stock Exchange symbol*]
QSTAG .... Quadripartite Standardization Agreement [*Military*]
QSTAG .... Quality Standardization Agreements (MCD)
QSTAH .... Ste-Anne's Hospital, Ste-Anne-De-Bellevue, Quebec [*Library symbol National Library of Canada*] (NLC)
QSTAJ .... John Abbott College, Ste-Anne-De-Bellevue, Quebec [*Library symbol National Library of Canada*] (NLC)
QSTAMP .... Quality Stamp
QSTAR .... Quantitative Structure-Time-Activity Relationship [*Chemistry*]
QSTAS .... Spar Technology Ltd., Ste-Anne-De-Bellevue, Quebec [*Library symbol National Library of Canada*] (NLC)
QSTB .... Bibliotheque Municipale, Saint-Bruno-De-Montarville, Quebec [*Library symbol National Library of Canada*] (BIB)
QSTBL .... Abbaye de Saint-Benoit-Du-Lac, Comte De Brome, Quebec [*Library symbol National Library of Canada*] (NLC)
QSTC .... Tioxide Canada, Inc., Sorel, Quebec [*Library symbol National Library of Canada*] (NLC)
QstDiag .... Quest Diagnostics, Inc. [*Associated Press*] (SAG)
QSTFAG .... Centre de Documentation, Ministere de l'Agriculture, des Pecheries, et de l'Alimentation, Ste.-Foy, Quebec [*Library symbol National Library of Canada*] (NLC)
QSTFCE .... Centre de Documentation, Centrale de l'Enseignement du Quebec, Ste.-Foy, Quebec [*Library symbol National Library of Canada*] (NLC)
QSTFCR .... Resource Centre, St. Lawrence Campus, Champlain Regional College, Ste.-Foy, Quebec [*Library symbol National Library of Canada*] (NLC)
QSTFP .... Protecteur du Citoyen du Quebec, Ste.-Foy [*Library symbol National Library of Canada*] (BIB)
QSTFR .... Rexfor, Ste.-Foy, Quebec [*Library symbol National Library of Canada*] (NLC)
QSTFRA .... Centre de Documentation, Roche Associes Ltee., Ste.-Foy, Quebec [*Library symbol National Library of Canada*] (NLC)

QSTHHR ...... Societe d'Histoire Regionale de St-Hyacinthe, Quebec [*Library symbol National Library of Canada*] (NLC)
QSTHS .... Seminaire de St-Hyacinthe, Quebec [*Library symbol National Library of Canada*] (NLC)
QSTHTA .... Institut de Technologie Agricole et Alimentaire de St.-Hyacinthe, Quebec [*Library symbol National Library of Canada*] (NLC)
QSTHUM ...... Headquarters Mobile Command, Canada Department of National Defence [*Quartier-General du Commandement de la Defense Nationale*] St-Hubert, Quebec [*Library symbol National Library of Canada*] (NLC)
QSTHV .... Faulte de Medecine Veterinaire de l'Universite de Montreal, Saint-Hyacinthe, Quebec [*Library symbol National Library of Canada*] (NLC)
QSTING .... Quasi-Spectral Time Integration on Nested Grids
QSTJ .... College Militaire Royal de Saint-Jean, Quebec [*Library symbol National Library of Canada*] (NLC)
QSTJA .... Bibliotheque Adelard-Berger, St.-Jean-Sur-Richelieu, Quebec [*Library symbol National Library of Canada*] (BIB)
QSTJAG .... Research Station, Agriculture Canada [*Station de Recherches, Agriculture Canada*] Saint-Jean, Quebec [*Library symbol National Library of Canada*] (NLC)
QSTJB .... Bibliotheque Municipale, Saint-Jean, Quebec [*Library symbol National Library of Canada*] (NLC)
QSTJC .... College Saint-Jean-Sur-Richelieu, Saint-Jean, Quebec [*Library symbol National Library of Canada*] (NLC)
QSTJCF .... Canadian Forces Base St. Jean [*Base des Forces Canadiennes St.-Jean*], Quebec [*Library symbol National Library of Canada*] (NLC)
QSTJE .... Bibliotheque Municipale, Saint-Jerome, Quebec [*Library symbol National Library of Canada*] (NLC)
QSTJEC .... CEGEP [*College d'Enseignement General et Professionnel*] de St.-Jerome, Quebec [*Library symbol National Library of Canada*] (BIB)
QSTJECR ..... Conseil Regional de la Sante et des Services Sociaux Laurentides-Lanaudiere, Saint-Jerome, Quebec [*Library symbol National Library of Canada*] (NLC)
QSTJEJ .... Jesuites/Bibliotheque, Saint-Jerome, Quebec [*Library symbol National Library of Canada*] (NLC)
QSTJH .... Bibliotheque Medicale, Hopital du Haut-Richelieu, St.-Jean-Sur-Richelieu, Quebec [*Library symbol National Library of Canada*] (BIB)
QSTJSC .... Centre de Documentation, Departement de Sante Communautaire du Haut-Richelieu, St.-Jean, Quebec [*Library symbol National Library of Canada*] (NLC)
QSTK .... Q Steaks, Inc. [*NASDAQ symbol*] (SAG)
QSTL .... Bibliotheque Municipale, Saint-Laurent, Quebec [*Library symbol National Library of Canada*] (NLC)
QSTLD .... Dominion Yarn Co., St. Laurent, Quebec [*Library symbol National Library of Canada*] (BIB)
QSTN .... Question (WDAA)
qstn .... Question (AD)
qstnr .... Questionnaire (AD)
qstol .... Quiet-and-Short Takeoff and Landing (AD)
QSTOL .... Quiet-Short-Takeoff-and-Landing [*Airplane*] [*Japan*]
QSTR .... Bibliotheque Municipale de Saint-Raphael-De-L'Ile-Bizard, Quebec [*Library symbol National Library of Canada*] (NLC)
qsts .... Quadruple-Screw Turbine Steamship (AD)
QSTTB .... Engineering Library, Bell Helicopter Textron, Ste. Therese, Quebec [*Library symbol National Library of Canada*] (NLC)
QSTTH .... Les Industries Harnois, St-Thomas-De-Joliette, Quebec [*Library symbol National Library of Canada*] (NLC)
QstVC .... Quest for Value Fund [*Associated Press*] (SAG)
QstVI .... Quest for Value Fund [*Associated Press*] (SAG)
qsuff .... Quantum Sufficit [*As Much As Will Suffice*] [*Latin*] (MAE)
Q-switch ...... Quantum Switch (AD)
QSWL .... Queensland Spastic Welfare League [*Australia*]
QSY .... Quiet Sun Year
qsy .... Quiet Sun Year (AD)
QSYS .... Quad Systems Corp. [*NASDAQ symbol*] (SAG)
Q-SYSTEM ... Inventory Control System With Varying Reorders (MHDB)
QT .... Bibliotheque Municipale, Trois-Rivieres, Quebec [*Library symbol National Library of Canada*] (NLC)
QT .... Blood Volume Quantity per Unit of Time [*Cardiology*] (DAVI)
QT .... Cardiac Output [*Cardiology*] (DAVI)
QT .... Quadruple Thermoplastic (SAA)
QT .... Qualification Test
QT .... Qualifier Type (NITA)
QT .... Quality Test (AD)
qt .... Quality Test (AD)
qt .... Quantitative (DAVI)
qt .... Quantity (AD)
qt .... Quantity (WDMC)
QT .... Quantity
QT .... Quarry Tile [*Technical drawings*]
qt .... Quarry Tile (AD)
qt .... Quart (AD)
QT .... Quart (AFM)
qt .... Quart (IDOE)
qt .... Quart (ODBW)
qt .... Quarter (AD)
QT .... Quarters
QT .... Quartet [*Music*]
QT .... Quasi-Triennial
QT .... Quebec-Telephone [*Toronto Stock Exchange symbol*]
QT .... Queckenstedt's Test [*Neurology*] (DAVI)
QT .... Quenched and Tempered (MCD)
QT .... Questioned Trade [*on a stock exchange*]
QT .... Queuing Theory [*Telecommunications*]
QT .... Queuing Time [*Telecommunications*] (TEL)
QT .... Quick's Test [*For pregnancy or prothrombin*] [*Laboratory science*] (DAVI)
QT .... Quick Tan [*Trademark of Plough, Inc.*]
QT .... Quick Test
QT .... Quick Test [*Medicine*] (DMAA)
qt .... Quick Test (AD)
qt .... Quiet (AD)
QT .... Quiet [*or sub rosa, as, "On the QT"*]
QT .... Qui Tam [*Who as Well*] [*Latin*] (ILCA)
QT .... Quotation Ticker [*Business term*]
QT .... Quotient
QT .... Vaengir [*ICAO designator*] (AD)
QTA .... Archives Nationales du Quebec, Trois-Rivieres, Quebec [*Library symbol National Library of Canada*] (NLC)
QTA .... Quadrant Transformer Assembly
qta .... Quadrant Transformer Assembly (AD)
QTAC .... Queensland Tertiary Admissions Centre [*Australia*] (AD)
QTAM .... Quadrature Amplitude Modulation (MCD)
qtam .... Queued Telecommunication Access Method (AD)
QTAM .... Queued Telecommunications Access Method [*IBM Corp.*] [*Computer science*]
QTAM .... Queued Terminal Access Method [*Computer science*]
QT & E .... Qualification Test and Evaluation [*Military*]
QTAT .... Quick Turn Around Time (NITA)
qtaux .... Quintaux [*Quintals*] [*French*] (AD)
QTB .... Le Boreal Express, Montreal, Quebec [*Library symbol National Library of Canada*] (NLC)
QTB .... Quarry-Tile Base [*Technical drawings*]
qtb .... Quarry-Tile Base (AD)
QTB .... Quarterly Training Briefing [*Army*] (INF)
QTB .... Queensland Timber Board [*Australia*] (AD)
QTB .... Queensland Trotting Board [*Australia*] (AD)
QTBC .... Bibliotheque Centrale de Pret de la Mauricie, Trois-Rivieres, Quebec [*Library symbol National Library of Canada*] (NLC)
QTBUE .... Queensland Timber Board Union of Employees [*Australia*]
QTC .... Quantitative Trait Loci [*Genetics*]
QTC .... Quebec Teaching Congress [*Canada*] (AD)
QTC .... Queensland Turf Club [*Australia*] (AD)
QTC .... Quick Transmission Change (MCD)
QTC .... Quick Turnaround Cell [*Engineering*] (RDA)
QTCE .... CEGEP [*College d'Enseignement General et Professionnel*], Trois-Rivieres, Quebec [*Library symbol National Library of Canada*] (NLC)
QTCHC .... Centre Hospitalier Cooke, Trois-Rivieres, Quebec [*Library symbol National Library of Canada*] (NLC)
QTCL .... College Lafleche, Trois-Rivieres, Quebec [*Library symbol National Library of Canada*] (NLC)
QTCO .... Communication-Quebec, Trois-Rivieres, Quebec [*Library symbol National Library of Canada*] (NLC)
QTCPB .... Corporation Pierre Boucher, Trois-Rivieres, Quebec [*Library symbol National Library of Canada*] (NLC)
QTCRD .... Conseil Regional de Developpement, Trois-Rivieres, Quebec [*Library symbol National Library of Canada*] (NLC)
QTCRS .... Conseil Regional de la Sante et des Services Sociaux, Trois-Rivieres, Quebec [*Library symbol National Library of Canada*] (NLC)
QTCSRV .... Commission Scolaire Regionale des Vieilles-Forges, Trois-Rivieres, Quebec [*Library symbol National Library of Canada*] (NLC)
QTCSS .... Centre de Services Sociaux, Trois-Rivieres, Quebec [*Library symbol National Library of Canada*] (NLC)
QTD .... Quadruple Terminal Digits (AABC)
QTD .... Quartered
qtd .... Quartered (AD)
QTD .... Quasi-Two-Dimensional
QTDG .... Quaker Theological Discussion Group (EA)
QT DX .... Quantitas Duplex [*Double Quantity*] [*Pharmacy*]
QTE .... Ecole Normale M. L. Duplessis, Trois-Rivieres, Quebec [*Library symbol National Library of Canada*] (NLC)
QTE .... Qualite [*Quality*] [*French*] (ROG)
QTE .... Quote
qte .... Quote (AD)
QTEC .... QuesTech Inc. [*NASDAQ symbol*] (TTSB)
QTEC .... QuesTech, Inc. [*NASDAQ symbol*] (NQ)
Q-TECH .... Quality-Technology
QTED .... Quick Text Editor (WDAA)
qted .... Quick Text Editor (AD)
qted .... Quoted (AD)
QTED .... Quoted (WDAA)
QTEF .... Queensland Tertiary Education Foundation [*Australia*]
QTEL .... Quintel Entertainment [*NASDAQ symbol*] (TTSB)
QTEL .... Quintel Entertainment, Inc. [*NASDAQ symbol*] (SAG)
QTER .... Bibliotheque Municipale, Terrebonne, Quebec [*Library symbol National Library of Canada*] (NLC)
Qtest .... Quantitative Test (NITA)
QTEV .... Quadruple Turbo-Electric Vessel (DS)
QTF .... Quarry-Tile Floor [*Technical drawings*]
qtf .... Quarry-Tile Floor (AD)
QTF .... Quebec Teachers' Federation [*Canada*] (AD)
qtfl .... Quatrefoil (VRA)
qtg .... Quoting (AD)
QTH .... Queued Transaction Handling [*Computer science*]

QTHSJ .... Hopital Saint-Joseph, Trois-Rivieres, Quebec [*Library symbol National Library of Canada*] (NLC)
QTHSM .... Hopital Sainte-Marie, Trois-Rivieres, Quebec [*Library symbol National Library of Canada*] (NLC)
QTI .... Institut Albert Tessier, Trois-Rivieres, Quebec [*Library symbol National Library of Canada*] (NLC)
QTIA .... Queensland Tourism Industry Authority [*Australia*]
QTIB .... Quebec Tourist Information Bureau [*Canada*] (AD)
QTIEA .... Queensland Timber Importers and Exporters' Association [*Australia*]
Q-TIP .... Qualified Terminable Interest Property [*Plan*] [*Tax law*]
QTIP .... Qualified Terminable Interest Property Trust [*Investment term*] (DFIT)
QTITC .... Queensland Timber Industry Training Council [*Australia*]
QTL .... Qualified Thrift Lender
QTL .... Quantitative Trait Loci [*Genetics*]
QTL .... Quantum Theory of LASERS
QTL .... Quarterly Title List
QTL .... Quintel Industries Ltd. [*Vancouver Stock Exchange symbol*]
QTLC .... Queensland Trades and Labor Council [*Australia*] (AD)
QTLMB .... Queensland Tobacco Leaf Marketing Board [*Australia*]
Qtly .... Quarterly
qtly .... Quarterly (ODBW)
qtly .... Quarterly (AD)
QTM .... Qualification Test Model
QTM .... Quechon Tribal Museum [*Yuma, Arizona*] (AD)
QTMC .... College de la Region de l'Amiante (CEGEP), Thetford-Mines, Quebec [*Library symbol National Library of Canada*] (NLC)
QTME .... Ministere de l'Energie et des Ressources du Quebec, Trois-Rivieres, Quebec [*Library symbol National Library of Canada*] (BIB)
QTMH .... Hopital General de la Regie de l'Amiante, Inc., Thetford Mines, Quebec [*Library symbol National Library of Canada*] (BIB)
QTN .... Quasithermal Noise [*Plasma physics*]
QTN .... Quotation (WDAA)
qtn .... Quotation (AD)
QTO .... Qualified Testing Officer [*British military*] (DMA)
QTO .... Quarto [*Book from 25 to 30 centimeters in height*]
qto .... Quarto (AD)
qtol .... Quiet Takeoff and Landing (AD)
QTOL .... Quiet Takeoff and Landing [*Aviation*]
QTOPDQ ...... Centre de Documentation, Office de Planification et de Developpement du Quebe c, Trois-Rivieres, Quebec [*Library symbol National Library of Canada*] (NLC)
QTP .... Qualification Test Plan [*NASA*] (NASA)
QTP .... Qualification Test Procedure
QTP .... Qualification Test Program
QTP .... Quality Test Plan [*Nuclear energy*] (NRCH)
QTP .... Quantum Theory of Paramagnetism
qtp .... Quantum Theory of Paramagnetism (AD)
QTP .... Quantum Theory Project [*University of Florida*] [*Research center*] (RCD)
QTPC .... Quadripartite Technical Procedures Committee [*Military*] (AABC)
QTPR .... Quarterly Technical Progress Report
QTPT .... Qualification Test and Proof (IAA)
QTR .... Qatar Airways [*FAA designator*] (FAAC)
QTR .... Qualification Test Report
QTR .... Qualified Tuition Reduction [*IRS*]
QTR .... Quality Technical Report (AD)
QTR .... Quality Technical Requirement (AD)
qtr .... Quarry-Tile Roof (AD)
QTR .... Quarry-Tile Roof [*Technical drawings*]
QTR .... Quarter (AFM)
qtr .... Quarter (ODBW)
QTR .... Quarter
qtr .... Quarter (AD)
QTR .... Quarterly (AFM)
QTR .... Quarterly Technical Report
QTR .... Quarterly Technical Review [*Jet Propulsion Laboratory publication*]
QTR .... Queenstake Resources [*TS Symbol*] (TTSB)
QTR .... Queenstake Resources Ltd. [*Toronto Stock Exchange symbol*]
QTRLY .... Quarterly
QTRN .... Quintiles Transnational [*NASDAQ symbol*] (TTSB)
QTRN .... Quintiles Transnational Corp. [*NASDAQ symbol*] (SAG)
QTRRSS .... Centre de Documentation, Regie de la Securite dans les Sports du Quebec, Trois-Rivieres, Quebec [*Library symbol National Library of Canada*] (NLC)
QTRS .... Quarters
QTS .... Qualification Test Specification
QTS .... Quantizer Threshold Spacing [*Telecommunications*] (MHDB)
qts .... Quarts (AD)
QTS .... Quartz Thermometer Sensor
qts .... Quick Turn Stock (AD)
QTS .... Seminaire de Trois-Rivieres, Quebec [*Library symbol National Library of Canada*] (NLC)
QTSC .... Queensland Transmission and Supply Corp. [*Australia*]
QTT .... Quartet [*Music*]
QTT .... Trois-Rivieres High School, Quebec [*Library symbol National Library of Canada*] (NLC)
QTTA .... Queensland Table Tennis Association [*Australia*]
QTTC .... Queensland Tourist and Travel Corp. [*Australia*] (AD)
qtte .... Quartette (AD)
QTTE .... Quartette [*Music*]
QTTF .... Temifibre, Inc., Temiscaming, Quebec [*Library symbol National Library of Canada*] (NLC)
QTTP .... Q-Tags Test of Personality [*Psychology*]
QTU .... Qualification Test Unit
QTU .... Queensland Teachers Union [*Australia*] (AD)
QTU .... Universite du Quebec, Trois-Rivieres, Quebec [*Library symbol National Library of Canada*] (NLC)
QTUAH .... Archives Historiques, Universite du Quebec, Trois-Rivieres, Quebec [*Library symbol National Library of Canada*] (NLC)
QTUGC .... Cartotheque, Departement de Geographie, Universite du Quebec, Trois-Rivieres, Quebec [*Library symbol National Library of Canada*] (NLC)
QTUIH .... Imprimes Historiques, Universite du Quebec, Trois-Rivieres, Quebec [*Library symbol National Library of Canada*] (NLC)
QTURA .... Archives des Ursulines, Trois-Rivieres, Quebec [*Library symbol National Library of Canada*] (NLC)
QTUTH .... Centre de Documentation en Theatre Quebecois, Trois-Rivieres, Quebec [*Library symbol National Library of Canada*] (NLC)
QTV .... Qualification Test Vehicle
Q-TWIST ..... Quality-Adjusted Time without Symptoms and Toxicity [*Medicine*] (CDI)
QTX .... Beaufort Leasing Ltd. [*Canada*] [*FAA designator*] (FAAC)
Qty .... Quality (DS)
QTY .... Quantity (KSC)
qty .... Quantity (WDMC)
QTY .... Quantity
qty .... Quantity (AD)
QTYDESREQ ... Quantity Desired as Requested [*Military*]
qtydesreq .... Quantity Desired or Requested (AD)
qtz .... Quartz (AD)
QTZ .... Quartz (AAG)
QTZ .... Quartzite [*Lithology*]
qtze .... Quartzose (AD)
qtzic .... Quartzitic (AD)
QTZN .... Quantization [*Telecommunications*] (IAA)
QTZR .... Quantizer [*Telecommunications*] (IAA)
qtzt .... Quartzite (AD)
QU .... Nicaragua [*License plate code assigned to foreign diplomats in the US*]
QU .... Quadrantectomy [*Medicine*]
QU .... Quaere [*Query*] [*Latin*]
QU .... Quail Unlimited (EA)
QU .... Quart (WGA)
qu .... Quart (AD)
qu .... Quarter (AD)
QU .... Quarter (ADA)
qu .... Quarterly (AD)
QU .... Quartermaster (ROG)
QU .... Quartern (ROG)
QU .... Quasi [*Almost, As It Were*] [*Latin*]
qu .... Quasi [*As It Were*] [*Latin*] (AD)
QU .... Quay (ROG)
QU .... Queen
Qu .... Queen (AD)
QU .... Queen's College [*Cambridge, Oxford*] (AD)
QU .... Queen's University [*Canada*]
qu .... Query (AD)
qu .... Question (AD)
QU .... Question
QU .... Questionnaire
QU .... Quina [*Quinine*] [*Pharmacy*] (ROG)
QU .... Quinto Mining [*Vancouver Stock Exchange symbol*]
QU .... Quotation (ROG)
QU .... Uganda Airlines [*ICAO designator*] (AD)
QUA .... Quabbin [*Massachusetts*] [*Seismograph station code, US Geological Survey*] (SEIS)
qua .... Quadrate (AD)
QUA .... Quassar de Mexico SA de CV [*ICAO designator*] (FAAC)
QUA .... Quinterra Resources, Inc. [*Toronto Stock Exchange symbol Vancouver Stock Exchange symbol*]
quaal .... Quaalude (AD)
QUAC .... Quadriatic Arc Computer
quack .... Quacksalver (AD)
quacks .... Quacksalvers (AD)
quackupunc ... Quackupuncture (AD)
quad .... Quaalude (AD)
QUAD .... Quadrajet Carburetor [*Automotive engineering*]
QUAD .... Quadrangle (AAG)
QUAD .... Quadrangle
quad .... Quadrangle (ODBW)
quad .... Quadrangle (AD)
quad .... Quadrant (AD)
quad .... Quadrant (DMAA)
Quad .... Quadrant [*A publication*]
QUAD .... Quadrant (KSC)
QUAD .... Quadraphonic
quad .... Quadrat (AD)
QUAD .... Quadrature (NASA)
quad .... Quadriceps [*Medicine*] (MEDA)
quad .... Quadriceps [*Muscle*] [*Anatomy*] (DAVI)
QUAD .... Quadrilateral (WGA)
QUAD .... Quadrillion
Quad .... Quadriplegic
quad .... Quadriplegic [*Medicine*] (DMAA)
QUAD .... Quadrophonic (NITA)
QUAD .... Quadruple
quad .... Quadruplet (ODBW)
quad .... Quadruplet (AD)
QUAD .... Quadruplex [*Videotape recording*] (NTCM)
Qu-AD .... Quality-Assurance Department (AD)

Qu-AD......... Quality-Assurance Division (AD)
quad c......... Quadripod Cane (AD)
QUAD CAP... Quad Foolscap [*Paper*] (DGA)
QuadCty....... Quad City Holdings [*Associated Press*] (SAG)
quad ex....... Quadriceps Exercise [*Orthopedics*] (DAVI)
QUADPAN.... Quadrilateral Element Panel Method [*Aerospace propulsion*]
quadplex..... Quadriplex (AD)
Quadr.......... Quadragesms [*Yearbooks of Edward III*] [*A publication*] (DLA)
Quadr.......... Quadrant [*A publication*]
QUADR......... Quadruple
QUADRADAR... Four-Way RADAR Surveillance
quadrap....... Quadraphonic (AD)
Quadrax....... Quadrax Corp. [*Associated Press*] (SAG)
quadrip........ Quadriplegia (AD)
quadro......... Quadroon (AD)
quadrup....... Quadruped (AD)
quadrupl...... Quadruplicato [*Four Times as Much*] [*Latin*] (AD)
Quadrupl...... Quadruplicato [*Four Times as Much*] [*Pharmacy*]
QUADS......... Quality Achievement Data System (NASA)
QuadSy........ Quad Systems Corp. [*Associated Press*] (SAG)
Quaest Conv... Quaestiones Convivales [*of Plutarch*] [*Classical studies*] (OCD)
Quaest Graec... Quaestiones Graecae [*of Plutarch*] [*Classical studies*] (OCD)
Quaest Plat... Quaestiones Platonicae [*of Plutarch*] [*Classical studies*] (OCD)
Quaest Rom... Quaestiones Romanae [*of Plutarch*] [*Classical studies*] (OCD)
quag........... Quagmire (AD)
QUAILLS...... Quick Update and Access Interlibrary Loans System
QuakCh........ Quaker Chemical Corp. [*Associated Press*] (SAG)
QuakCty....... Quaker City Bancorp [*Associated Press*] (SAG)
Quaker......... Quaker Oats (AD)
Quaker......... Quaker Press (AD)
QuakFab....... Quaker Fabric Corp. [*Associated Press*] (SAG)
QuakrOat..... Quaker Oats Co. [*Associated Press*] (SAG)
QuakSC........ Quaker State Corp. [*Associated Press*] (SAG)
QUAL........... Qualification (NG)
qual............ Qualification (AD)
qual............ Qualify (AD)
QUAL........... Qualitative
qual............ Qualitative (IDOE)
Qual............ Qualiton & MHV [*Record label*] [*Hungary*]
QUAL........... Quality (KSC)
qual............ Quality (AD)
QUAL........... Quality Semiconductor [*NASDAQ symbol*] (TTSB)
QUAL........... Quality Semiconductor, Inc. [*NASDAQ symbol*] (SAG)
QUAL ANAL... Qualitative Analysis (WDAA)
qual anal..... Qualitative Analysis (AD)
QualCert...... Qualifying Certificate [*Australia*]
Qualcom...... Qualcomm, Inc. [*Associated Press*] (SAG)
QualDin....... Quality Dining, Inc. [*Associated Press*] (SAG)
QUALENGR... Quality Engineer (IAA)
QUALGO...... Quasi-Autonomous Local Government Organisation [*British*] (DI)
QUALN........ Qualification (ROG)
QUALOD...... Quaalude [*Methaqualone*] [*A trademark*] [*Pharmacology*] (DAVI)
quals........... Qualifying Examinations (AD)
quals........... Qualifying Tests (AD)
QualSemi..... Quality Semiconductor, Inc. [*Associated Press*] (SAG)
QualSy........ Quality Systems, Inc. [*Associated Press*] (SAG)
QUALT......... Queensland University Aphasia and Language Test
QUALTA...... Quad Asynchronous Local Terminal Adapter [*Computer science*] (MHDB)
QUALTIS...... Quality Technical Information Service (NITA)
QUALTIS...... Quality Technology Information Service [*Atomic Energy Authority*] [*British*] (IID)
QUAM......... Quadrature Amplitude Modulation (IEEE)
quam.......... Quadrature-Amplitude Modulation (AD)
QUAM......... Quantized Amplitude Modulation (NITA)
QUAN.......... Quantity (KSC)
Quandary..... Quandary Peak [*Colorado*] (AD)
Quanex........ Quanex Corp. [*Associated Press*] (SAG)
QUANGO...... Quasi-Autonomous Non-Governmental [*or National Governmental*] Organisation [*British*]
quango........ Quasi-Autonomous Non-Governmental Organization (AD)
QuanRst...... Quantum Restaurant Group [*Associated Press*] (SAG)
QUANSY...... Question Answering System (MHDB)
QUANT........ Quantitative [*or Quantity*]
quant.......... Quantity (AD)
quant.......... Quantum (AD)
quant anal... Quantitative Analysis [*Laboratory science*] (DAVI)
QuantHlt...... Quantum Health Resources, Inc. [*Associated Press*] (SAG)
QuantLrn..... Quantum Learning Systems, Inc. [*Associated Press*] (SAG)
QUANTRAS... Question Analysis Transformation and Search [*Computer science*]
quantras...... Question Analysis Transformation and Search [*Data processing*] (AD)
QUANT SUFF... Quantum Sufficiat [*A Sufficient Quantity*] [*Pharmacy*]
Quant Suff... Quantum Sufficit [*A Sufficient Quantity*] [*Pharmacy*]
quant suff.... Quantum Sufficit [*Sufficient Quantity*] [*Latin*] (AD)
Quantum...... Quantum Corp. [*Associated Press*] (SAG)
QUAOPS...... Quarantine Operations [*Military*] (NVT)
quaops......... Quarantine Operations (AD)
QUAP.......... Quality Assurance Procedures
QUAP.......... Questionnaire Analysis Program (IAA)
QUAPP........ Qu'Appelle [*Canadian river*] (ROG)
QUAPS........ Quality Assurance Publications [*Navy*]
Quaq.......... Quaquero [*Quaker*] [*Spanish*] (AD)
quar........... Quarantine (AD)
QUAR.......... Quarantine (AABC)
QUAR.......... Quarry
QUAR.......... Quarter [*Business term*]
QUAR.......... Quarterly
QUARAM...... Quality and Reliability Management [*DoD*]
QUARC........ Quarterdeck Anti-Virus Research Center
Quar Crim Dig... Quarles' Tennessee Criminal Digest [*A publication*] (DLA)
QUARG........ Quality of Urban Air Review Group [*British*] (ECON)
QUARK........ Quantizer, Analyzer, and Record Keeper [*Telecommunications*] (TEL)
Quar Law Journal... Quarterly Law Journal [*Virginia*] [*A publication*] (DLA)
Quar L Rev... Quarterly Law Review [*Virginia*] [*A publication*] (DLA)
QUARLY....... Quarterly (ROG)
quar pars..... Quarta Pars [*One-Fourth Part*] [*Latin*] (AD)
quarpel........ Quartermaster Water-Repellent [*Military*] (AD)
QUARPEL..... Quartermaster Water-Repellent Clothing [*Military*]
quarr........... Quarry (AD)
QUART........ Quadrantectomy, Axillary Dissection, Radiotherapy [*Oncology*]
QUART........ Quality Assurance and Reliability Team
quart........... Quarter Gallon (AD)
Quart........... Quarterly (AD)
quart........... Quarterly (AD)
QUART........ Quarterly
quart........... Quartet (AD)
QUART........ Quartetto [*Quartet*] [*Music*] (ROG)
QUART........ Quartus [*Fourth*] [*Pharmacy*]
Quart Bull Instn Eng Aust... Quarterly Bulletin. Institution of Engineers of Australia [*A publication*]
Quart Ital..... Quartetto Italiano [*Italian Quartet*] [*Italian*] (AD)
Quart LJ (VA)... Quarterly Law Journal [*Virginia*] [*A publication*] (DLA)
Quart L Rev (VA)... Quarterly Law Review [*Virginia*] [*A publication*] (DLA)
QUARTM...... Quartermaster (ROG)
Quartrdk...... Quarterdeck Corp. [*Associated Press*] (SAG)
QUARTZ GR... Quartzite Granite [*Agronomy*]
quartzite...... Granular Quartz Rock (AD)
QUASAR...... Quasi-Stellar [*Astronomy*]
quasar......... Quasi-Stellar Radio (AD)
QUASAT....... Quasar Satellite [*Proposed observatory in space*]
QUASER....... Quantum Amplification by Stimulated Emission of Radiation
quaser......... Quantum Amplification by Stimulated-Emission of Radiation (AD)
Quash.......... Quashey (AD)
QUASS........ Quassia [*Pharmacology*] (ROG)
QUAST......... Quality Assurance Service Test (PDAA)
QUAT.......... Quater [*Four Times*] [*Pharmacy*]
QUAT.......... Quaternary [*Period, era, or system*] [*Geology*]
Quat........... Quaternary (AD)
quat............ Quaternary (AD)
QUAT.......... Quaternary Ammonium Compound [*Class of antimicrobial agents*]
QUAT.......... Quaternion (NASA)
QUAT.......... Quatrefoil [*Numismatics*]
quat............ Quattuor [*Four*] [*Latin*] (AD)
QUAT.......... Quattuor [*Four*] [*Latin*] (DAVI)
QUATIP....... Quality Assurance Test and Inspection Plan [*Military*] (CAAL)
QUB........... Queen's University, Belfast [*Ireland*]
QUBMIS....... Quantitatively Based Management Information System
quc............. Quebec [*MARC country of publication code Library of Congress*] (LCCP)
QUD........... Queen's University of Dublin (AD)
QUE........... Albuquerque Public Library, Albuquerque, NM [*OCLC symbol*] (OCLC)
QUE........... Gouvernement du Quebec, Service Aerien Gouvernemental [*Canada*] [*FAA designator*] (FAAC)
Que............ Quebec [*Canada*] (DD)
Que............ Quebec [*Canadian province*] (ODBW)
QUE........... Quebec [*Canadian province*]
QUE........... Quebecair (AD)
Que............ Quebecois (AD)
Que............ Quechua (AD)
que............ Quechua [*MARC language code Library of Congress*] (LCCP)
QUE........... Queenston Gold Mines Ltd. [*Toronto Stock Exchange symbol*]
Que............ Quenia [*Kenya*] [*Portuguese*] (AD)
QUE........... Quetta [*Pakistan*] [*Seismograph station code, US Geological Survey*] (SEIS)
Quebcor....... Quebecor, Inc. [*Associated Press*] (SAG)
Quebec L (Can)... Quebec Law Reports [*Canada*] [*A publication*] (DLA)
Quebec Pr (Can)... Quebec Practice [*Canada*] [*A publication*] (DLA)
Queb KB...... Quebec Official Reports, King's Bench [*Canada*] [*A publication*] (DLA)
QuebPr........ Quebecor Printing, Inc. [*Associated Press*] (SAG)
Queb Pr....... Quebec Practice Reports [*1897-1943*] [*A publication*] (DLA)
Que BR........ Quebec Rapports Judiciaires Officiels (Banc de la Reine, Cour Superieure) [*A publication*] (DLA)
Que C A....... Quebec Official Reports, Court of Appeals [*A publication*]
Que CA........ Rapports Judiciaires Officiels, Cour d'Appel [*1892-date*] [*Official Law Reports, Court of Appeal Quebec*] [*A publication*] (DLA)
Que CBR...... Rapports Judiciaires Officiels, Cour du Banc du Roi [*ou de la Reine*] [*Official Law Reports, Court of King's, or Queen's, Bench Quebec*] [*A publication*] (DLA)
Que CS........ Rapports Judiciaires Officiels, Cour Superieure [*Official Law Reports, Superior Court*] [*Quebec*] [*A publication*] (DLA)
QueenCB...... Queens County Bancorp [*Associated Press*] (SAG)
QueenCtB.... Queens County Bancorp [*Associated Press*] (SAG)
Queens........ Queensland [*Australia*]
Queens........ Queensway Studios [*Record label*] [*Great Britain*]
Queens B Bull... Queens Bar Bulletin [*United States*] [*A publication*] (DLA)
Queens CBA Bull... Queens County Bar Association. Bulletin [*United States*] [*A publication*] (DLA)

Queens C (CUNY)... Queens College of The City University of New York (GAGS)
Queens Intra LJ... Queen's Intramural Law Journal [*1968-70*] [*Canada*] [*A publication*] (DLA)
Queen's Intramural LJ... Queen's Intramural Law Journal [*A publication*] (DLA)
Queens JP & Loc Auth Jo... Queensland Justice of the Peace and Local Authorities' Journal [*A publication*] (DLA)
Queensl....... Queensland (AD)
Queensl Acts... Queensland Public Acts [*A publication*] (DLA)
Queens Law... Queensland Lawyer [*Australia*] [*A publication*] (DLA)
Queensl Cr Lands LR... Queensland Crown Lands Law Reports [*A publication*] (DLA)
Queensl JPR... Queensland Justice of the Peace. Reports [*A publication*] (DLA)
Queensl JP Rep... Queensland Justice of the Peace. Reports [*A publication*] (DLA)
Queensl L.... Queensland Law [*A publication*] (DLA)
Queensl LSJ... Queensland Law Society. Journal [*A publication A publication*] (DLA)
Queensl Pub Acts... Queensland Public Acts [*A publication*] (DLA)
Queensl R... Queensland State Reports [*A publication*] (DLA)
Queensl SCR... Queensland. Supreme Court. Reports [*A publication*] (DLA)
Queens L Soc'y J... Queensland Law Society. Journal [*A publication*] (DLA)
Queensl St R... Queensland State Reports [*Australia*] [*A publication*] (DLA)
Queensl St Rep... Queensland State Reports [*Australia*] [*A publication*] (DLA)
Queens Q..... Queen's Quarterly [*A publication*] (BRI)
Queens St R... Queensland State Reports [*A publication*] (DLA)
Que KB........ Quebec Official Reports, King's Bench [*A publication*] (DLA)
Que L........... Quebec Law [*A publication*] (DLA)
QUEL........... Query Language [*Computer science*] (MHDI)
Que LR........ Quebec Law Reports [*Canada*] [*A publication*] (DLA)
QUELS.......... Quasi-Elastic Light Scattering [*Also, QELS, QLS*] [*Physics*]
Quen............ Quentin (AD)
Quent........... San Quentin [*California State Prison*] (AD)
Que Pr......... Quebec Practice [*A publication*] (DLA)
Que PR........ Quebec Practice Reports [*A publication*] (DLA)
Que Prac..... Quebec Practice Reports [*A publication*] (DLA)
Que QB........ Quebec Official Reports, Queen's Bench [*A publication*] (DLA)
Quer............ Queretaro (AD)
quer............ Querulous (DAVI)
QUERC......... Quercus [*Oak*] [*Pharmacology*] (ROG)
Que Rev Jud... Quebec Revised Judicial [*A publication*] (DLA)
Que Rev Stat... Quebec Revised Statutes [*Canada*] [*A publication*] (DLA)
QUES........... Questa Oil & Gas [*NASDAQ symbol*] (TTSB)
QUES........... Questa Oil & Gas Co. [*NASDAQ symbol*] (SAG)
QUES........... Question (AAG)
ques............ Question (WDMC)
ques............ Question (AD)
QUES........... Question Mark (AABC)
Que SC........ Quebec Official Reports, Superior Court [*A publication*] (DLA)
QUEST......... Qualitative Experimental Stress Tomography
QUEST......... Quality Electrical Systems Test [*Interpreter*]
quest........... Quality Electrical System Test (AD)
QUEST......... Quality Utilization Effectiveness Statistically Qualified
QUEST......... Quantification of Uncertainty in Estimating Support Tradeoffs (PDAA)
QUEST......... Quantitative Environmental Science and Technology [*ULDECO Ltd.*] [*British*] (IRUK)
QUEST......... Quantitative Understanding of Explosive Stimulus Transfer
QUEST......... Quantitative Utility Estimates for Science and Technology [*RAND Corp.*]
QUEST......... Queens Educational and Social Team (AD)
QUEST......... Query Evaluation and Search Technique
QUEST......... Question
quest........... Questionable (DAVI)
quest........... Questioned (AD)
Questa......... Questa Oil & Gas Co. [*Associated Press*] (SAG)
QUESTA....... Questionnaire for Students, Teachers, and Administrators (EDAC)
questal........ Quiet, Experimental, Short-Takeoff-and-Landing [*NASA*] (AD)
questar........ Quantitative Utility Evaluation Suggesting Targets for the Allocations of Resources (AD)
Questar........ Questar Corp. [*Associated Press*] (SAG)
Que Stat...... Quebec Statutes [*Canada*] [*A publication*] (DLA)
Questch....... QuesTech, Inc. [*Associated Press*] (SAG)
QUESTER..... Quick and Effective System to Enhance Retrieval [*Computer science*]
quester........ Quick and Efficient System to Enhance Retrieval (AD)
QuestInt....... Quest International Resources Corp. [*Associated Press*] (SAG)
QuestM........ Quest Medical, Inc. [*Associated Press*] (SAG)
QUESTN....... Question
Questn......... Questionnaire (ADA)
questn......... Questionnaire (AD)
QUESTOL..... Quiet Experimental Short Takeoff and Landing [*Program*] [*NASA*]
Questron...... Questron Technology [*Associated Press*] (SAG)
Que Super... Quebec Official Reports, Superior Court [*A publication*] (DLA)
Que Tax Rep (CCH)... Quebec Tax Reporter (Commerce Clearing House) [*A publication*] (DLA)
QuF.............. Australian Queensland Fever (DAVI)
qufyd........... Qualified (AD)
QUGA........... Queensland United Graziers' Association [*Australia*]
QUH............. Queen's University Highland Battalion [*British military*] (DMA)
QUI............... Aero Quimmco SA de CV [*Mexico ICAO designator*] (FAAC)
QUI............... Queen's University, Ireland
QUI............... Quincy Railroad Co. [*Later, QRR*] [*AAR code*]
QUI............... Quirindi [*New South Wales*] [*Airport symbol*] (AD)
QUI............... Quito [*Ecuador*] [*Seismograph station code, US Geological Survey Closed*] (SEIS)
QUI............... Quito, Ecuador, Tracking Station [*NASA*] (NASA)
QUI............... Thomas Crane Public Library, Quincy, MA [*OCLC symbol*] (OCLC)
QUIC............ Quality Data Information and Control (NASA)
QUIC............ Quantum Information and Computing [*Consortium sponsored by DARPA*]
QUIC............ Question and Information Connection [*St. Louis Public Library*] (AD)
Quich........... Quichua (AD)
quicha......... Quantitative Inhalation Challenge Apparatus [*Medicine*] (AD)
QUICHA....... Quantitative Inhalation Challenge Apparatus [*Medicine*] (MAE)
QUICK.......... Queens University Interpretative Code (AD)
QUICK.......... Quotation Information Center KK [*Nihon Keizai Shimbun, Inc.*] [*Information service or system*] (IID)
QuickRsp..... Quick Response Services [*Commercial firm Associated Press*] (SAG)
Quicktr......... Quickturn Design System [*Commercial firm Associated Press*] (SAG)
QUICKTRAN... Quick FORTRAN [*Programming language*] [*1979*]
QUICO.......... Quality Improvement through Cost Optimization (MHDB)
quico........... Quality Improvement through Cost Optimization (AD)
QUID............ Quantified Intrapersonal Decision-Making [*In book title*]
Quidel.......... Quidel Corp. [*Associated Press*] (SAG)
QUIDS.......... Quick Interactive Documentation System (WDAA)
QUIES.......... Quiescent
QUIK............ Quiksilver, Inc. [*Costa Mesa, CA*] [*NASDAQ symbol*] (NQ)
Quikslv........ Quiksilver, Inc. [*Associated Press*] (SAG)
quiktran....... Quick Fortran [*Computer science*] (AD)
QUIL............ Quad in Line [*Electronics Telecommunications*] (TEL)
QUILL.......... Queen's University Interrogation of Legal Language (NITA)
QUILL.......... Queen's University Interrogation of Legal Literature [*Queen's University of Belfast*] [*Northern Ireland*] [*Information service or system*] (IID)
Quill & Q..... Quill & Quire [*A publication*] (BRI)
Quilmas....... San Quilmas (AD)
QUILS.......... Quarterly Index of Lubricant Sales [*Industry report*]
QUILT.......... Quantitative Intelligence Analysis Technique (PDAA)
quilwk......... Quillwork (VRA)
quim............ Quimica [*Chemistry*] [*Spanish*] (AD)
Quimigal...... Quimica de Portugal (AD)
QUIN............ Quina [*Quinine*] [*Pharmacy*] (ROG)
Quin............. Quincy (AD)
Quin............. Quincy's Massachusetts Reports [*A publication*] (DLA)
Quin............. Quinten (AD)
quin............. Quintet (AD)
Quin............. Quintilianus (AD)
Quin............. Quintilius (AD)
Quin............. Quintillian (AD)
Quin............. Quintino (AD)
Quin............. Quintius (AD)
QUIN............ Quintuple
quin............. Quintuplet (AD)
Quin Bank.... Quin on Banking [*1833*] [*A publication*] (DLA)
Quinct.......... Pro Quinctio [*of Cicero*] [*Classical studies*] (OCD)
Quincy......... Quincy's Massachusetts Reports [*A publication*] (DLA)
QUINID........ Quinidine [*Pharmacology*] (DAVI)
QUININ........ Quinine [*Pharmacology*] (DAVI)
quinq........... Quinque [*Five*] [*Latin*] (MAE)
quins........... Quintuplets (AD)
QUINT.......... Quintetto [*Quintet*] [*Music*] (ROG)
Quint........... Quintilian [*First century AD*] [*Classical studies*] (OCD)
Quint........... Quintilian (AD)
QUINT.......... Quintuple
quint........... Quintuplet [*Neonatology*] (DAVI)
quint........... Quintuplicate (AD)
quint........... Quintus [*Fifth*] [*Latin*] (AD)
QUINT.......... Quintus [*Fifth*] [*Latin*] (WGA)
Quintel......... Quintel Entertainment, Inc. [*Associated Press*] (SAG)
Quintiles...... Quintiles Transnational Corp. [*Associated Press*] (SAG)
Quinti Quinto... Year Book 5 Henry V [*England*] [*A publication*] (DLA)
Quint Smyrn... Quintus Smyrnaeus [*Classical studies*] (OCD)
quintupl....... Quintuplicate (AD)
QUIP............ Quad In-Line Package
QUIP............ Quantum-Well Infrared Photodetector [*Physics*]
QUIP............ Query Interactive Processor (IEEE)
QUIP............ Questionnaire Interpreter Program (IAA)
QUIP............ Quick-Inline Package (NITA)
QUIP............ Quipp, Inc. [*NASDAQ symbol*] (NQ)
QUIP............ QUOTA [*Query Online Terminal Assistance*] Input Processor [*Computer science*]
Quipp........... Quipp, Inc. [*Associated Press*] (SAG)
QUIS............ Queen's University Information Systems (NITA)
quis............. Quisling [*World War II*] (AD)
QUIV............ Quiver (ROG)
quix............. Quixote (AD)
QUIX............ Quixote Corp. [*NASDAQ symbol*] (NQ)
Quixte.......... Quixote Corp. [*Associated Press*] (SAG)
QUIZ............ Quizno's Corp. [*NASDAQ symbol*] (TTSB)
QUIZ............ Quizno's Franchise Corp. [*NASDAQ symbol*] (SAG)
Quiznos....... Quizno's Franchise Corp. [*Associated Press*] (SAG)
Qu Jour Int-Amer Rel... Quarterly Journal of Inter-American Relations [*A publication*] (DLA)
QUK............. Quaker Resources, Inc. [*Vancouver Stock Exchange symbol*]
QUL............. Queen's University Library (AD)
QUL............. Quillagua [*Chile*] [*Seismograph station code, US Geological Survey*] (SEIS)
Qu LJ.......... Quarterly Law Journal [*A publication*] (DLA)
QULOC........ Queensland University Libraries Office of Cooperation [*Australia*]
Qu L Rev..... Quarterly Law Review [*A publication*] (DLA)
QUM............ Queen's University, Medical Library [*UTLAS symbol*]
QUM............ Quillmana [*Peru*] [*Seismograph station code, US Geological Survey Closed*] (SEIS)

QUMDO .... Qualitative Materiel Development Objective [*Army*] (AFIT)
QUMR .... Quality Unsatisfactory Material Report (MCD)
QUN .... Qutdligssat [*Greenland*] [*Airport symbol*] (AD)
QUNO .... Quaker United Nations Office (EAIO)
QUO .... Quadex Users' Organization (EA)
QUO .... Quote Resources, Inc. [*Vancouver Stock Exchange symbol*]
QUOBIRD .... Queen's University Online Bibliographic Information Retrieval and Dissemination (NITA)
QuoBO .... Query on Business Objects [*Computer science*] (PCM)
quod .... Quodlibet [*As You Please*] [*Latin*] (AD)
Quoddy .... Passamaquoddy Bay (AD)
quok .... Quokka (AD)
Quomodo Adul ... Quomodo Adulescens Poetas Audire Debeat [*of Plutarch*] [*Classical studies*] (OCD)
QUON .... Question (ROG)
Quon Attach ... Quoniam Attachiamenta [*A publication*] (DLA)
QUONBLE .... Questionable (ROG)
Quon Pt .... Quonset Point [*Rhode Island*] (AD)
quor .... Quorom [*Of Which*] [*Latin*] (AD)
quor .... Quorum (AD)
QUOR .... Quorum [*Of Which*] [*Pharmacy*]
QuorumH .... Quorum Health Group, Inc. [*Associated Press*] (SAG)
QUOT .... Quotation
quot .... Quotation (AD)
quot .... Quoted In [*or Quoting*] [*Legal term*] (DLA)
quot .... Quotidie [*Daily*] [*Latin*] (AD)
QUOT .... Quotient (MSA)
QUOT .... Quoties [*As Often as Needed*] [*Pharmacy*]
quot .... Quoties [*As often as necessary*] [*Latin*] [*Pharmacology*] (DAVI)
QUOTA .... Query Online Terminal Assistance [*Computer science*]
QUOTID .... Quotidie [*Daily*] [*Pharmacy*]
quotid .... Quotidie [*Every Day*] [*Latin*] (AD)
QUOT OP SIT ... Quoties Opus Sit [*As Often as Necessary*] [*Pharmacy*]
quot os .... Quoties Opus Sit [*As often as necessary*] [*Latin*] [*Pharmacy*] (DAVI)
QUP .... Quality Unit Pack
qup .... Quantity per Unit Pack (AD)
QUP .... Quantity Unit Pack
QUP .... Quincemil [*Peru*] [*Airport symbol*] (AD)
QUP .... Quonset Point [*Navy*]
QUR .... Quinstar Resources [*Vancouver Stock Exchange symbol*]
Qur .... Quran [*Koran*] [*Malay*] (AD)
QuSAR .... Quantitative Structure Activity Relationships [*National Institute on Drug Abuse*]
QUST .... Questron Technology [*NASDAQ symbol*] (TTSB)
QUST .... Questron Technology [*NASDAQ symbol*] (SAG)
QUTLJ .... Queensland University of Technology. Law Journal [*A publication*]
QUX .... Quinella Exploration Ltd. [*Vancouver Stock Exchange symbol*]
QUY .... Quest Energy Corp. [*Vancouver Stock Exchange symbol*]
QV .... Bibliotheque Municipale, Victoriaville, Quebec [*Library symbol National Library of Canada*] (NLC)
QV .... Lao Aviation [*Laos*] [*ICAO designator*] (ICDA)
QV .... Qualification and Validation Board [*Army*] (RDA)
QV .... Quality Verification [*Nuclear energy*] (NRCH)
qv .... Quality Verification (AD)
QV .... Quantum Vis [*or Voleris*] [*As Much as You Wish*] [*Pharmacy*]
QV .... Quattrovalvole [*Four valves per cylinder*] [*Italian*]
QV .... Queen Victoria [*British*]
QV .... Qui Vixit [*Who Lived*] [*Latin*]
QV .... Quod Vide [*or Videte*] [*Which See*] [*Latin*]
qv .... Quod Vide [*Which see*] [*Latin*] (WDMC)
q-v .... Q-Value (AD)
QVAH .... Institut de Recherche d'Hydro-Quebec, Varennes, Quebec [*Library symbol National Library of Canada*] (NLC)
QVAI .... Centre de Documentation, INRS [*Institut National de la Recherche Scientifique*]-Energie, Varennes, Quebec [*Library symbol National Library of Canada*] (NLC)
Q Van Weyt ... Q. Van Weytson on Average [*A publication*] (DLA)
QVBFL .... Bibliotheque Felix-Leclerc, Val-Belair, Quebec [*Library symbol National Library of Canada*] (NLC)
QVC .... College de Victoriaville, Quebec [*Library symbol National Library of Canada*] (NLC)
QVC .... Qualification, Validation, and Certification Board [*Army*] (RDA)
QVC .... Quality Value Convenience Network, Inc. [*Television*]
QVCEMBO .... Ecole Quebecoise du Meuble et du Bois Ouvre, College de Victoriaville, Quebec [*Library symbol National Library of Canada*] (NLC)
QVCSF .... Queen Victoria's Clergy Sustentation Fund [*British*]
QVE .... Bibliotheque Municipale, Verdun, Quebec [*Library symbol National Library of Canada*] (BIB)
QVEC .... Cultural Centre [*Centre Culturel*] Verdun, Quebec [*Library symbol National Library of Canada*] (NLC)
QVEC .... Qualified Voluntary Employee Contribution
QVGCCQ .... Cree Regional Authority, Grand Council of the Crees (of Quebec) [*Administration Regionale Crie, Grand Conseil des Cris (du Quebec)*] Val D'Or, Quebec [*Library symbol National Library of Canada*] (NLC)
QVI .... Quality Verification Inspection
Q Vic .... Statutes of Quebec in the Reign of Victoria [*A publication*] (DLA)
QVL .... Qualified Vendors List
QVLBI .... Quasi-Very-Long-Baseline Interferometry
QVM .... Qualified Vehicle Modifier
QVM .... Queen Victoria Museum [*Launceston, Tasmania*] (AD)
QVM .... Que Viva Mexico [*Long Live Mexico*] [*Spanish*] (AD)
QVO .... Queen Victoria's Own [*British military*] (DMA)
QVP .... Quality Verification Plan
QVP .... Quick View Plus (PCM)
QVPL .... Qualified Verification Procedures List
QVR .... Quality Verification Report
QVR .... Queen Victoria's Rifles [*Military unit*] [*British*]
QVRF .... Queensland Victoria Research Foundation [*Australia*]
QVS .... Quality Verification Surveillance (AD)
QVS .... Queen Victoria's School [*British military*] (DMA)
QVSLEA .... Atmospheric Environment Service, Environment Canada [*Service de l'Environnement Atmospherique, Environnement Canada*] Ville St-Laurent, Quebec [*Library symbol National Library of Canada*] (NLC)
QVT .... Qualified Verification Testing [*NASA*]
qvt .... Quality Verification Test (AD)
QVT .... Qume Video Terminal (NITA)
QVVT .... Qualified Verification Vibration Testing [*NASA*] (NASA)
QW .... Air Turks and Caicos [*ICAO designator*] (AD)
QW .... Poland [*License plate code assigned to foreign diplomats in the US*]
QW .... Quality of Working Life (DAVI)
QW .... Quantum Well [*Physics*]
QW .... Quarter Wave
qw .... Quarter Wave (AD)
QW .... Waterloo Public Library, Quebec [*Library symbol National Library of Canada*] (NLC)
QWA .... Quarter-Wave Antenna
qwa .... Quarter-Wave Antenna (AD)
QWA .... Qwestair [*Australia ICAO designator*] (FAAC)
QWAM .... Qualified for Warrant Air Mechanic [*British military*] (DMA)
Q WAR .... Quo Warranto [*Latin Legal term*] (DLA)
QWASP .... Quebec White Anglo-Saxon Protestant
QWB .... Quality of Well-Being [*Medicine*] (DMAA)
QWBI .... Quality of Well Being Index
QWBP .... Qualification Standards for Wage Board Positions
QWC .... Queensland Writers' Centre [*Australia*]
QWC .... West Chester State College, West Chester, PA [*OCLC symbol*] (OCLC)
QWD .... Quarterly World Day
qwd .... Quarterly World Day (AD)
Q/WDO .... Quarter Window [*Automotive engineering*]
QWE .... Qualified for Warrant Engineer [*British military*] (DMA)
q-wedge .... Quartz Wedge (AD)
QWERTY .... [*The*] Standard English Language Typewriter Keyboard (BARN)
QWG .... Quadripartite Working Group [*Military*]
QWGCD .... Quadripartite Working Group for Combat Development [*American, Australian, British, and Canadian armies*] (AD)
QWG/CD .... Quadripartite Working Group on Combat Developments (MCD)
QWG/ENG .... Quadripartite Working Group on Engineering (MCD)
QWG/EW .... Quadripartite Working Group on Electronic Warfare (MCD)
QWG/LOG .... Quadripartite Working Group on Logistics [*Military*] (RDA)
QWG/PIQA ... Quadripartite Working Group on Proofing Inspection Quality Assurance (MCD)
QWG/STANO ... Quadripartite Working Group on Surveillance and Target Acquisition/Night Observation (MCD)
QWHS .... Queensland Women's Historical Society [*Australia*]
QWIKTRAN ... Quick FORTRAN [*Programming language*] [*1979*] (CSR)
QWIP .... Quantum Well Infra-red Photodetectors
qwk .... Once a Week [*Every Week*] [*Pharmacy*] (DAVI)
qwl .... Quality of Working Life (AD)
QWL .... Quality of Working Life [*Labour Canada program*]
QWL .... Quality of Work Life [*Anti-recession program of Ford Motor Co.*]
QWL .... Quick Weight Loss
qwl .... Quick Weight Loss (AD)
QWLD .... Quality of Worklife Database [*Management Directions*] [*Information service or system*] (IID)
QWM .... Qualified for Warrant Mechanician [*British military*] (DMA)
QWMP .... Quadruped Walking Machine Program [*Army*]
QWOT .... Quarter-Wave Optical Thickness (WDAA)
qwot .... Quarter-Wave Optical Thickness (AD)
qwp .... Quarter-Wave Plate (AD)
QWP .... Quarter-Wave Plate
QWR .... Quarterly Weight Report (DNAB)
QWR .... Queen's Westminster Rifles [*British military*] (DMA)
QWR .... Que West Resources Ltd. [*Toronto Stock Exchange symbol*]
QWRC .... Queensland Water Resources Commission [*Australia*]
QWRV .... Queen's Westminster Rifle Volunteers [*British military*] (DMA)
QWSH .... Congregation Shaar Hashomayim Library-Museum, Westmount, Quebec [*Library symbol National Library of Canada*] (NLC)
QWSMM .... Westmount Public Library, Quebec [*Library symbol National Library of Canada*] (NLC)
QWSSUA .... Quasi-Wide-Sense-Stationary Uncorrelated Scattering (PDAA)
QWSSUS .... Quasi-Wide Sense Stationary Uncorrelated Scattering (IAA)
QWT .... Quick Word Test [*Education*] (EDAC)
QX .... Century Airlines [*ICAO designator*] (AD)
QX .... Horizon Air [*ICAO designator*] (AD)
QX .... Qatar Amiri Flight [*Qatar*] [*ICAO designator*] (ICDA)
qx .... Quintaux [*Hundred-Weights*] [*French*] (AD)
QXE .... Horizon Airlines, Inc. [*ICAO designator*] (FAAC)
QXI .... Queue Executive Interface [*Computer science*] (MHDB)
QY .... Aero Virgin Islands [*ICAO designator*] (AD)
QY .... Quantum Yield
qy .... Quantum Yield (AD)
Qy .... Quay (AD)
QY .... Quay (ROG)
QY .... Query
qy .... Query [*Journalism*] [*Proofreading*] (WDMC)
qy .... Query (AD)

QY............... Quota Year [*Pisciculture*]
QYC............ Quincy Yacht Club (AD)
QYD............ Qi and Yin Deficiency (DMAA)
QYM............ SOLINET [*Southeastern Library Network*] Center, Atlanta, GA [*OCLC symbol*] (OCLC)
QYO............ Queensland Youth Orchestra [*Australia*] (AD)
Qz............... Quartz (AD)
qz............... Quartz (AD)
QZ............... Quartz [*Quality of the bottom*] [*Nautical charts*]
QZ............... Stockholm University Computing Center [*Sweden*] (TSSD)
QZ............... Zambia Airways [*ICAO designator*] (AD)
QZ............... Zambia Airways [*Airline flight code*] (ODBW)
Q-Zar.......... Q-Zar, Inc. [*Associated Press*] (SAG)
QZAR.......... Q-Zar, Inc. [*NASDAQ symbol*] (SAG)
QZARF........ Q-Zar Inc. [*NASDAQ symbol*] (TTSB)
QZE............ Quadratic Zeeman Effect [*Physics*]
QZM............ Quartz Mountain Gold Corp. [*Vancouver Stock Exchange symbol Toronto Stock Exchange symbol*]
QZMGF........ Quartz Mountain Gold Corp. (MHDW)
QZN............ Quan Zhou [*Republic of China*] [*Seismograph station code, US Geological Survey*] (SEIS)
QZS............ Quebec Zoological Society [*Canada*] (AD)

R

By Acronym

R................. Abstracted Reappraisement Decisions [*A publication*] (DLA)
R................. Acknowledgment of Receipt [*Message handling*] [*Telecommunications*]
R................. All India Reporter, Rajasthan [*A publication*] (DLA)
r................. Angular Yaw Velocity (AAG)
R................. Antenna with Reflector
r----- .... Arctic Ocean and Region [*MARC geographic area code Library of Congress*] (LCCP)
R................. Arginine [*One-letter symbol; see Arg*]
R................. Behnken's Unit [*Of Roentgen-Ray Exposure*] [*Radiology*] (DAVI)
R................. Carbon Stars [*Astronomy*] (BARN)
R................. [*A*] Chemical Radical (DOG)
R................. Cilag-Chemie AG [*Switzerland*] [*Research code symbol*]
R................. Correlation Coefficient [*Statistics*] (BARN)
r................. Correlation Coefficient (DAVI)
R................. Declared or Paid in the Preceding 12 Months Plus Stock Dividend [*Investment term*] (DFIT)
R................. Denver Laboratories [*Great Britain*] [*Research code symbol*]
R................. Janssen [*Belgium*] [*Research code symbol*]
R................. Kentucky Law Reporter [*A publication*] (DLA)
R................. Molar Gas Constant [*Symbol*] [*IUPAC*] (NASA)
R................. Nicolaus Rufulus [*Flourished, 13th century*] [*Authority cited in pre-1607 legal work*] (DSA)
R................. Option Not Traded [*Investment term*] (DFIT)
R................. Parti Republicain Radical et Radical-Socialiste [*France*] [*Political party*] (ECED)
R................. Product Moment Coefficient of Correlation [*Statistics*]
R................. [*A*] Purine Nucleoside [*One-letter symbol; see Puo*]
R................. Rabba (BJA)
R................. Rabbanite (BJA)
R................. Rabbi
r................. Racemic [*Also, dl, rac*] [*Chemistry*]
R................. RACON [*RADAR Beacon*]
R................. Radfahrabteilung [*Bicycle Battalion*] [*German military - World War II*]
R................. Radial [*Followed by three digits; for use on instrument approach charts*] [*Aviation*]
R................. Radian
R................. Radiancy
R................. Radiation
R................. Radical
R................. Radio
R................. Radioactive Mineral (MAE)
R................. Radiographer [*British military*] (DMA)
R................. Radiolocation (IAA)
R................. Radiology [*or Radiologist*] (ADA)
R................. Radiotelegram
R................. Radium [*Chemical symbol is Ra*] (KSC)
r................. Radius [*Symbol*] [*IUPAC*]
r................. Radius of Gyration (AAG)
R................. Rail (MSA)
R................. Railroad [*or Railway*]
R................. Rain [*Meteorology*]
R................. Raleigh [*Diocesan abbreviation*] [*North Carolina*] (TOCD)
R................. Ram
R................. Rand [*Monetary unit*] [*Botswana, Lesotho, South Africa, and Swaziland*]
R................. Random Number
R................. Range
R................. Rank
R................. Rankine [*Temperature scale*]
R................. Raphe Nucleus [*Neuroanatomy*]
R................. Rare [*Numismatics*]
R................. Rare [*When applied to species*] [*Biology*]
R................. Rate
R................. Ratio
R................. Rational Number (MDG)
R................. Rationing [*British*]
R................. Rawle's Pennsylvania Reports [*1828-35*] [*A publication*] (DLA)
R................. Rayleigh Wave [*Seismology*]
R................. Raymundus de Pennafort [*Deceased, 1275*] [*Authority cited in pre-1607 legal work*] (DSA)
R................. Raymundus de Sabanacho [*Authority cited in pre-1607 legal work*] (DSA)
R................. Rays
R................. Reaction (AAG)
R................. Read (AAG)
R................. Readability (IAA)
R................. Reader (NTCM)
R................. Readiness Count
R................. Real
R................. Ream (ADA)
R................. Rear
R................. Reasoning Factor [*or Ability*] [*Psychology*]
R................. Reaumur [*Temperature scale*] [*German*]
R................. Rebounds [*Basketball, hockey*]
R................. Receipt (ROG)
r................. Received (ODBW)
R................. Received Solid [*Amateur radio*]
R................. Receiver
R................. Receiving (IAA)
R................. Reception (IAA)
R................. Receptor [*Biochemistry*]
R................. Recessed [*Electrical outlet symbol*]
R................. Recht [*Law*] [*German*]
R................. Recipe [*Take*] [*Pharmacy*]
R................. Recipe [*Take*] [*Latin*] [*Pharmacy*] (DAVI)
R................. Reciprocating
R................. Recite [*Swell Organ*] [*Music*]
R................. Recluse
R................. Recognition [*Experimentation*]
R................. Recommendation (MHDB)
R................. Reconditioned (DCTA)
R................. Reconnaissance [*Designation for all US military aircraft*]
R................. Reconstruction Committee [*British World War II*]
R................. Record
R................. Recorder (ECII)
R................. Recovery (IAA)
R................. Recreations
R................. Recruit (ROG)
R................. Rectal [*or Rectum*] [*Medicine*]
r................. Rectangular Tank [*Liquid gas carriers*]
R................. Rectifier (IAA)
R................. Rectilinear Polarization [*Physics*] (ECON)
R................. Recto [*Also, RO*] [*Right-hand page*]
R................. Rector [*or Rectory*]
(R)............... Rectus [*Clockwise configuration*] [*See RS*] [*Biochemistry*]
R................. Rectus [*Muscle*] [*Anatomy*] (DAVI)
R................. Recurrence [*Medicine*]
R................. Red
R................. Redemption Fee [*Finance*]
R................. Redetermination
R................. Red Primary (IAA)
R................. Reducer [*Photographic processing*] (DGA)
R................. Reductase Test [*Biochemistry*] (DAVI)
R................. Redundancy [*Used in correcting manuscripts, etc.*]
R................. Reel (DGA)
R................. Referee [*Football*]
R................. Referred (OICC)
R................. Refill [*of bract liquid*] [*Botany*]
R................. Reflectance
R................. Reflection [*Angle of*]
R................. Reflector Lamp
R................. Reflexive
R................. Reform [*Judaism*]
R................. Refraction
R................. Refrigerated [*Shipping*] (DS)
R................. Refrigerated Tank [*Liquid gas carriers*]
R................. Refrigerator
R................. Refused
R................. Refuse Disposal [*British Waterways Board sign*]
R................. Regenerated [*Biology*]
R................. Regiment
R................. Regina [*Queen*] [*Latin*]
R................. Register [*Computer science*]
R................. Registered
R................. Registered Trademark (DAVI)
R................. Registrar (ROG)
R................. Regna [*Queen*] [*Latin*] (DLA)
R................. Regression Coefficient (AAMN)
R................. Regular (ADA)
R................. Regular Priority [*Wire service symbol*] (NTCM)
R................. Regulating

R................. Regulatory [*Gene*] [*Genetics*] (DAVI)
R................. Reigned
R................. Reiz [*Stimulus*] [*German Psychology*]
R................. Relapse [*Medicine*] (DMAA)
R................. Relation [*Computer science*]
R................. Relative Humidity
R................. Relative Signal Strength (IAA)
R................. Relaxed
R................. Relay (DNAB)
R................. Relevant [*Computer science*] [*Telecommunications*]
R................. Reliability (MCD)
R................. Religious (DNAB)
R................. Religious Program (NTCM)
R................. Reluctance
R................. Remote [*Telecommunications*] (TEL)
R................. Remotum [*Far Respiration*] [*Latin*] (MAE)
R................. Render (IAA)
R................. Renewed License [*FCC*] (NTCM)
R................. Repair (DNAB)
R................. Repeal [*Legal term*] (DLA)
R................. Repeat (WDMC)
R................. Repeater (IAA)
R................. Repetitive [*Electronics*]
R................. Replaceability (AAG)
R................. Replaced [*Dentistry*]
R................. Reply (ADA)
R................. Reports
R................. [*The*] Reports, Coke's English King's Bench [*A publication*] (DLA)
R................. Repressor [*Psychology*] (MAE)
R................. Repressor [*Genetics*] (DAVI)
R................. Reprint
R................. Reproducible (DNAB)
r................. Reproductive Potential [*Genetics*] (DOG)
R................. Republic
R................. Republican
R................. Request
R................. Requiescat [*He, or She Rests*] [*Latin*]
R................. Rerun [*of a television show*]
R................. Resazurin [*A pH indicator*] (DAVI)
R................. Rescinded [*Legal term*] (DLA)
R................. Research
R................. Resentment [*Psychology*]
R................. Reserve
R................. Reset (MDG)
R................. Reside [*or Resident*]
R................. Resistance [*Symbol*] [*IUPAC*]
R................. Resistor
R................. Resolution
R................. Resolved [*Legal term*] (DLA)
R................. Respectfully [*Letter closing*]
R................. Respiration
R................. Respond [*or Response*]
R................. Responder [*Strain of mice*]
R................. Responsorium [*Responsory*]
R................. Respublica [*Commonwealth*] [*Latin*]
R................. Rest [*in cell cycles*] [*Cytology*] (DAVI)
R................. Restricted [*Persons under eighteen (sixteen in some localities) not admitted unless accompanied by parent or adult guardian*] [*Movie rating*]
R................. Restricted [*Immunology*]
R................. Restricted [*Military document classification*]
R................. Restricted Area [*Followed by identification*]
R................. Retarder [*Slow*] [*On clock-regulators*] [*French*]
R................. Reticular [*Nucleus of thalamus*] [*Neuroanatomy*]
R................. Retired [*or Retiree*]
R................. Rettie's Scotch Court of Session Reports, Fourth Series [*A publication*] (DLA)
R................. Returning
R................. Reverse
R................. Reverse [*Giemsa method*] [*Chromosome stain*]
R................. Review (AAMN)
R................. Revised (MCD)
R................. Revision [*Legal term*] (DLA)
R................. Revoked [*Legal term*] (DLA)
R................. Revolute Joint (IAA)
R................. Reward
R................. Rewind
R................. Rewritten [*FAR clauses*] (AAGC)
R................. Rex [*King*] [*Latin*]
R................. Reynolds Number [*Viscosity*]
R................. Rhinitis [*Medicine*]
R................. Rhizoctonia [*A fungus*]
R................. Rho (NUCP)
R................. Rhode Island State Library, Providence, RI [*Library symbol Library of Congress*] (LCLS)
R................. Rhodesia [*Later, Zimbabwe*] (ROG)
R................. Rhodium [*Symbol is Rh*] [*Chemical element*] (ROG)
R................. Rhodopsin [*Visual purple*]
R................. Rhythm
R................. Rial [*Monetary unit*] [*Iran, Saudi Arabia, etc.*]
r................. Ribose [*One-letter symbol; see Rib*]
R................. Ricardus Anglicus [*Deceased, 1242*] [*Authority cited in pre-1607 legal work*] (DSA)
R................. Richard (King of England) (DLA)
R................. Richtkreis [*Aiming Circle*] [*Gunnery term*] [*German military - World War II*]
R................. Rickettsia
R................. Riffle
R................. Rifle
R................. Rigger [*British military*] (DMA)
R................. Right [*Direction*]
R................. Right [*Politics*]
R................. Right Edge [*Skating*]
R................. Right Eye [*Ophthalmology*] (DAVI)
R................. Right-Hand [*Music*] (DAS)
R................. Riker Laboratories, Inc. [*Research code symbol*]
R................. Rimus (BJA)
R................. Ring [*Technical drawings*]
r................. Ring Chromosome [*Medicine*] (MAE)
R................. Ring Lead [*Telecommunications*] (TEL)
R................. Ring Road [*Traffic sign*] [*British*]
R................. Rinne [*Test*] [*Hearing Test*] (DAVI)
-R................. Rinne's Test Negative [*Hearing test*]
+R................. Rinne's Test Positive [*Hearing test*]
R................. Rio [*River*] [*Spanish*] (ROG)
R................. Rise [*Electronics*]
R................. Riser [*Technical drawings*]
R................. Rises
R................. Risk
R................. River [*Maps and charts*]
R................. Riveted (DS)
R................. Road
R................. Road-Holding [*In automobile name Rolls-Royce Bentley Turbo R*]
R................. Roan (Leather) [*Bookbinding*] (ROG)
R................. Robert [*Phonetic alphabet*] [*Royal Navy World War I Pre-World War II*] (DSUE)
R................. Robertus [*Authority cited in pre-1607 legal work*] (DSA)
R................. Robin Avions [*Pierre Robin*] [*France ICAO aircraft manufacturer identifier*] (ICAO)
R................. Robotics
R................. Rock [*Maps and charts*]
R................. Rocket [*Missile vehicle type symbol*]
R................. Rod [*Measurement*]
r................. Roentgen [*Also, RU*] [*Unit measuring X and gamma radiations*]
R................. Roger [*All right or OK*] [*Communications slang*]
R................. Roger [*Phonetic alphabet*] [*World War II*] (DSUE)
R................. Roll
R................. Roller-Skating Rinks [*Public-performance tariff class*] [*British*]
R................. Rollout (KSC)
R................. Roman
R................. Roman Catholic School [*British*]
R................. Romania
R................. Romans [*New Testament book*] (BJA)
R................. Romeo [*Phonetic alphabet*] [*International*] (DSUE)
R................. Rontgen [*Measurement*] (EECA)
R................. Rood [*Unit of measurement*]
R................. Rook [*Chess*]
R................. Room (NFPA)
R................. Rorschach [*Test*] [*Psychology*] (DAVI)
R................. Rosary
R................. Roscoe's Cape Of Good Hope [*A publication*] (DLA)
R................. Rosin [*Standard material for soldering*]
R................. Rostral [*Anatomy*]
R................. Rotary Wing [*Aircraft designation*]
R................. Rotor
R................. Rough [*Appearance of bacterial colony*]
R................. Rough Sea [*Navigation*]
R................. Roussel [*France*] [*Research code symbol*]
R................. Route
R................. Routine (KSC)
R................. Royal
R................. Royalty Monthly [*A publication*]
R................. R-Register [*Computer science*]
R................. Rub [*Medicine*] (MAE)
R................. Rubber
R................. Rubidomycin [*See also D, Daunorubicin*] [*Antineoplastic drug*]
R................. Ruble [*Monetary unit*] [*Former USSR*]
R................. Rue [*Street*] [*French*]
R................. Rule
R................. Ruled [*Followed by the dates of a monarch's reign*]
r................. Ruler
R................. Rum (ROG)
R................. Run [*Distance sailed from noon to noon*] [*Navy British*] (ROG)
R................. Runic
R................. Runs [*scored*] [*Baseball or cricket*]
R................. Runway [*Aviation*] (DA)
R................. Rupee [*Monetary unit*] [*Ceylon, India, and Pakistan*]
R................. Rural (MCD)
R................. Rydberg Constant [*Spectroscopy*] [*Symbol*] (DEN)
R................. Ryder System [*NYSE symbol*] (TTSB)
R................. Ryder System, Inc. [*NYSE symbol*] (SPSG)
R................. Ryman [*Office equipment and furniture store chain*] [*British*]
R................. Ryom [*Catalog of music of Vivaldi*] (BARN)
R................. Ship [*Missile launch environment symbol*]
R................. Stauffer Chemical Co. [*Research code symbol*]
R................. Transfer Payments [*Economics*]
R................. Transport [*Naval aircraft designation*]
R................. Yaw Control Axis [*Symbol*]
$R_{(00)}$................. Rydberg Constant (IDOE)

R1 Stage Right [*Theater*] (WDMC)
R1 Cro Croke's English King's Bench Reports Tempore Elizabeth [*1582-1603*] [*A publication*] (DLA)
R 1 DIY Royal 1st Devon Imperial Yeomanry [*British military*] (DMA)
R2 Reporting Responsibility [*DoD*]
R2 Richard II [*Shakespearean work*]
R2 Cro Croke's English King's Bench Reports Tempore James [*Jacobus*] I [*A publication*] (DLA)
R2CSE Relaxed Two-Color Stimulated Echo [*Spectroscopy*]
R2DC3 Rapid Reaction, Deployable Command, Control, and Communications
R2E Realisations et Etudes Electronique [*Computer manufacturer*] [*France*]
R2P2 Rapid Retargeting and Precision Pointing [*Strategic Defense Initiative*]
R3 Rearm, Resupply, Refuel [*Army*]
R^3 Relay, Reporter, Responder [*Military*] (CAAL)
R^3 Requirements Resources Review [*Board*] [*DoD*] (DOMA)
R3 Richard III [*Shakespearean work*]
R3 Cro Croke's English King's Bench Reports Tempore Charles I [*1625-41*] [*A publication*] (DLA)
R-5-P Ribose-5-Phosphate [*Biochemistry*] (MAE)
R-19/CA Rhodes 19 Class Association (EA)
Ra Airway Resistance [*Medicine*] (MAE)
RA Antonine Sisters (TOCD)
RA Coast RADAR Station [*Maps and charts*]
RA High-Powered Radio Range (Adcock)
RA Rabbinical Assembly (EA)
Ra RADAR
RA RADAR Altimeter [*Aviation*] (KSC)
Ra RADAR Station
RA Radiation Oncology Services (MEDA)
RA Radio (WDAA)
RA Radioactive
RA Radio Altimeter
RA Radio Antenna
RA Radio Authority [*Government regulatory agency*] [*British*]
RA Radiology (DAVI)
RA Radionic Association (EA)
Ra Radium [*Chemical element*]
Ra Radius of Action (AAG)
RA Ragocyte [*Medicine*] (DMAA)
RA Ragweed Antigen [*Immunology*]
RA Rain [*ICAO*] (FAAC)
Ra Rainerius [*Authority cited in pre-1607 legal work*] (DSA)
RA Rainforest Alliance (EA)
RA Raise (AAG)
RA Ramblers' Association [*British*] (DBA)
RA Ramp Actuator
RA Random Access [*Computer science*] (AAG)
RA Range [*Aviation*]
RA Range Area (NASA)
RA Range Assessor [*British military*] (DMA)
RA Rape [*Division in the county of Sussex*] [*British*]
RA Rapid Access [*Film*] (DGA)
RA Rapid-American Corp.
RA Rapid Anastigmatic (Lens) [*Photography*] (ROG)
RA Raritan Arsenal (AAG)
Ra Rastell's Entries [*A publication*] (DSA)
RA Rate Action (AAG)
RA Rate of Application
RA Rate of Approach (IIA)
RA Ratepayers' Association [*British*] (ILCA)
RA Ratio Actuator (MCD)
RA Ration
RA Ration Allowance [*British military*] (DMA)
Ra Rayleigh Number [*IUPAC*]
Ra Raymundus de Pennafort [*Deceased, 1275*] [*Authority cited in pre-1607 legal work*] (DSA)
RA Raynaud's Phenomenon [*Medicine*]
RA Rayon (AAG)
RA Read Amplifier
RA Ready-Access [*Telecommunications*] (TEL)
RA Ready Alert [*Navy*] (NVT)
RA Rear Admiral [*Also, RADM, RADML*]
RA Rear Artillery
R/A Rear Axle [*Automotive engineering*]
RA Reasonable Alternative (GNE)
RA Rebuild America (EA)
RA Receiver Attenuation
RA Receiver Auxiliary (IAA)
RA Recipient Agency [*Federal government*] (GFGA)
RA Recipient Rights Adviser
RA Reciprocal Asymmetrical [*Medicine*] (DMAA)
RA Reckson Associates Realty [*NYSE symbol*] (TTSB)
RA Reckson Associates Realty Corp. [*NYSE symbol*] (SAG)
RA Reconnaissance Aircraft (DNAB)
RA Record Address (IAA)
R/A Recorded Announcement [*Telecommunications*] (TEL)
RA Recording Annunciator (IAA)
RA Records Administration (MCD)
RA Recreation Aide [*Red Cross*]
RA Recrystallization-Anneal (PDAA)
RA Rectifier (IAA)
RA Redevelopment Act (OICC)
RA Redstone Arsenal [*Huntsville, AL*] [*Army*]
RA Reduced Aperture (MCD)
RA Reduction of Area
RA Referees' Association [*British*] (DBA)
RA Refer to Accepter [*Banking*]
RA Refractory Anemia [*Medicine*]
RA Refractory Ascites [*Medicine*] (DMAA)
RA Refugee Agency [*NATO*] (NATG)
RA Regia Anglorum [*British*] [*An association*] (DBA)
RA Regional Administrator
RA Regional Associations [*Marine science*] (MSC)
RA Register Allocator (IAA)
RA Registered Architect (IIA)
RA Registration Act
RA Registration Appeals [*A publication*] (DLA)
RA Regular Army
RA Regulation Appeals [*A publication*] (DLA)
RA Regulatory Alternative [*Federal government*] (GFGA)
RA Regulatory Analysis [*Federal government*] (GFGA)
RA Rehabilitation Act (OICC)
RA Reimbursement Authorization (AFM)
RA Reims Aviation [*France ICAO aircraft manufacturer identifier*] (ICAO)
RA Reinforced Alert (NATG)
RA Relative Abundance [*Chemistry*]
RA Relative Activity [*Physiology*]
RA Relative Address
RA Release Authorization
RA Released-Action [*Pharmacy*]
RA Reliability Analysis (AAG)
RA Reliability Assessment (KSC)
RA Reliability Assurance (MCD)
RA Religious of the Apostolate of the Sacred Heart [*Roman Catholic women's religious order*]
RA Religious of the Assumption [*Roman Catholic women's religious order*]
RA Relocation Address
RA Relocation Assistance [*HUD*]
RA Remedial Action [*Navy*]
RA Remittance Advice (MCD)
RA Remote Access [*Telecommunications*] (IAA)
RA Remote Area
RA Renal Artery [*Anatomy*]
RA Renin Activity (AAMN)
RA Renin-Angiotensin [*Medicine*] (DMAA)
RA Rental Agreement
RA Repair Assignment (AAG)
RA Repeat Action [*Medicine*]
R/A Repeat Attempt [*Telecommunications*] (TEL)
RA Repeated Attacks [*Medicine*]
RA Replacement Algorithm
RA Reporting Activity (MCD)
RA Representative Assembly
RA Republicans Abroad (EA)
RA Requesting Agency (MUGU)
RA Requirements Analysis
RA Rescue Ambulance [*Emergency medicine*] (DAVI)
RA Reserve Affairs (DOMA)
RA Resident Agent (AFM)
RA Resident Alien
RA Resident Assistant [*College housing*]
RA Resident Assistant
RA Resident Auditor
RA Residual Air
RA Resistor Assembly
RA Resource Allocation (MCD)
RA Resource Application (ERG)
RA Resource Assistant (GNE)
RA Respiratory Allergy [*Immunology*]
RA Respiratory Arrest [*Medicine*]
R-A Response Errors [*Statistics*]
RA Restricted Account [*Banking*]
RA Resume-Accelerate [*Automotive engineering*]
RA Retinal Anlage [*Ophthalmology*]
RA Retinoic Acid [*Biochemistry*]
RA Retrograde Amnesia [*Medicine*]
RA Return Address
RA Return Air [*Technical drawings*]
R/A Return to Author [*Bookselling*]
RA Revenue Act [*1962, 1964, 1971, 1976, 1978*]
RA Revenue Agent [*IRS*]
RA Reverendus Admodum [*Very Reverend*] [*Latin*]
RA Reviewing Activity (MCD)
RA Reviewing Authority
RA Reviews in Anthropology [*A publication*] (BRI)
RA Revue Administrative [*A publication*] (ILCA)
RA Rheumatoid Agglutinins [*Clinical chemistry*]
RA Rheumatoid Arthritis [*Medicine*]
RA Rice Association [*British*] (DBA)
RA Riders Association [*Defunct*] (EA)
RA Right Accumulator (IAA)
RA Right Aft (MCD)
RA Right Angle (DEN)
RA Right Arch [*Freemasonry*]
RA Right Arm [*Medicine*]
RA Right Ascension [*Navigation*]

RA... Right Atrium [*Cardiology*]
RA... Right Auricle [*Anatomy*]
RA... Right Axilla (KSC)
RA... Ripple Adder
RA... Risk Analysis (MCD)
RA... Risk Assessment (GFGA)
RA... Road America [*Automotive raceway*]
RA... Robbery Armed
RA... Robustrus Archistriatalis [*Bird brain anatomy*]
RA... Rocket Assist (RDA)
RA... Rokitansky-Aschoff [*Sinus*] [*Gastroenterology*]
RA... Room Air (MEDA)
RA... Room Air (DAVI)
RA... Root Apex [*Botany*]
RA... Roquefort Association (EA)
RA... Rosin Acid [*Organic chemistry*]
RA... Rosin Activated [*Standard material for soldering*]
RA... Rotary Assembly
RA... Rotation Angiography [*Medicine*] (DMAA)
RA... Rotogravure Association
RA... Routing Arbiter [*Telecommunications*]
RA... Royal Academician [*or Academy*] [*British*]
RA... Royal Academy [*British*] (AIE)
RA... Royal Academy of Arts in London [*British*]
RA... Royal Arch [*Freemasonry*]
RA... Royal Armouries [*Tower of London*]
RA... Royal Art
RA... Royal Artillery [*British*]
RA... Royal Artist
RA... Royal Nepal Airlines [*ICAO designator*] (AD)
RA... Royal Regiment of Artillery [*Military British*]
RA... Rueckwaertiges Armeegebiet [*Rear area of an army*] [*German military*]
RA... Rules on Appeal [*A publication*] (DLA)
RA... Russian Air [*To distinguish call-signs and frequencies*] [*World War II British*]
RA... Russian American
RA... Thermal Resistance of Unit Area [*Heat transmission symbol*]
RAA... Blackrock CA Inv Qual Muni [*AMEX symbol*] (TTSB)
RAA... Blackrock California Investment Quality Municipal [*AMEX symbol*] (SPSG)
RAA... Rabbinical Alliance of America (EA)
RAA... RADAR Aircraft Altitude (IAA)
RAA... Random Access Array (NITA)
RAA... Reagan Alumni Association (EA)
RA(A)... Rear-Admiral of Aircraft Carriers [*Obsolete British*]
RAA... Reeve Aleutian Airways, Inc. [*Air carrier designation symbol*]
RAA... Regenerative Agriculture Association [*Later, RI*] (EA)
RAA... Regional Administrative Assistant (ADA)
RAA... Regional Airline Association (EA)
RAA... Regional Arts Association [*British*]
RAA... Reinsurance Association of America [*Washington, DC*] (EA)
RAA... Relational Algebra Accelerator [*Computer board*]
RAA... Remote Access Audio (NITA)
RAA... Remote Access Audio Device [*Computer science*] (MHDB)
RAA... Renewal Assistance Administration [*HUD*]
RAA... Renin-Angiotensin-Aldosterone [*Clinical nephrology*]
RAA... Research and Analysis (IAA)
RAA... Research Animal Alliance (EA)
RAA... Respiratory Aid Apparatus
RAA... Ricegrowers' Association of Australia
RAA... Right Angle Adapter
RAA... Right Ascension Angle
RAA... Right Atrial Appendage [*Medicine*]
RAA... Rockette Alumnae Association (EA)
RAA... Royal Academy Association [*British*] (NADA)
RAA... Royal Academy of Arts [*British*] (ROG)
RAA... Rural Assistance Authority [*New South Wales, Australia*]
RAA... Rynes Aviation, Inc. [*ICAO designator*] (FAAC)
RAAA... Red Angus Association of America (EA)
RAAA... Relocation Assistance Association of America [*Defunct*] (EA)
RAAAS... Remote Antiarmor Assault System (MCD)
RAAB... Remote Amplifier and Adaption Box (NASA)
RAAB... Remote Application and Advisory Box (MCD)
RAABF... Royal Artillery Association Benevolent Fund [*British military*] (DMA)
RAAC... Reference Areas Advisory Committee [*Victoria, Australia*]
RAAC... Rhodesian Air Askari Corps [*British military*] (DMA)
RAAC... Rome Allied Area Command [*World War II*]
RAACC... Robotics and Automation Applications Consulting Center [*Ford Motor Co.*]
RAACEF... Rear-Admiral of Aircraft Carriers, Eastern Fleet [*British*]
RAACT... Radioactive
RAAD... Radford Army Ammunition Depot [*Virginia*] (MCD)
RAAD... Restructured Air Assault Division (MCD)
RAADC... Regional Accounting and Disbursing Center (DNAB)
RAADES... Relative Antiair Defense Effectiveness Simulation [*Military*] (CAAL)
RA(A)EF... Rear-Admiral (Administration) Eastern Fleet [*British*]
RAAF... Redstone Army Airfield [*Huntsville, AL*]
RAAF... Royal Australian Air Force [*ICAO designator*] (FAAC)
RAAFA... Royal Australian Air Force Association
RAAG... Regional Aviation Assistance Group [*FAA*]
RAAM... Race Across America [*Annual cycling event*]
RAAM... Reagent Array Analysis Method [*Analytical biochemistry*]
RAAM... Remote Antiarmor Mine (RDA)
RAAM... Residual-Area-Analysis Method [*Spectrometry*]
RAAMC... Royal Australian Army Medical Corps (DAVI)
RAAMS... Remote Antiarmor Mine System [*Military*] (AABC)
RAAN... Repair Activity Accounting Number [*Navy*]
RAAP... Radford Army Ammunition Plant (AABC)
RAAP... Residue Arithmetic Associative Processor [*Computer science*] (OA)
RAAR... RAM Address Register
RAAS... Renin-Angiotensin-Aldosterone System [*Medicine*] (DMAA)
RAAS... Royal Amateur Art Society [*British*]
RAAT... Recombinant Alpha 1-Antitrypsin [*Biochemistry*]
RAATS... RCRA [*Resource Conservation and Recovery Act*] Administrative Action Tracking System (ERG)
RAAWS... RADAR Altimeter and Altitude Warning System [*Military*] (CAAL)
RAAWS... Ranger Antiarmor, Antipersonnel Weapon System [*Army*] (INF)
RAB... Rabaul [*New Britain Island*] [*Airport symbol*] (OAG)
RAB... Rabaul [*New Britain Island*] [*Seismograph station code, US Geological Survey*] (SEIS)
RAB... Rabbet (MSA)
RAB... Rabbinical
RAB... Rabbit Oil & Gas [*Vancouver Stock Exchange symbol*]
RAB... Rabelais [*French author, 1494-1553*] (ROG)
RAB... Radio Advertising Bureau [*New York, NY*] (EA)
RAB... Reactor Auxiliary Building [*Nuclear energy*] (NRCH)
RAB... Regional Advisory Board [*American Hospital Association*]
RAB... Remote Afterload Brachytherapy [*Radiology*] (DAVI)
RAB... Renewal-at-Birth [*A periodical subscription*] (WDMC)
RAB... Rent Advisory Board [*Cost of Living Council*]
RAB... Research Advisory Board (DAVI)
RAB... Rice, Applesauce, and Banana [*Diet*] (DAVI)
RAB... Richard Austen Butler [*1902-1982*] [*In book title "RAB: The Life of R. A. Butler"*]
RAB... Rotating Arm Basin
RABA... Radioantigen-Binding Assay [*Medicine*]
RABA... Re-Chargeable Air-Breathing Apparatus (PDAA)
RABAC... Real Americans Buy American Cars [*An association Defunct*]
RABAL... Radiosonde Balloon
RABAL... Radiosonde Balloon Wind Data [*Meteorology*] (FAAC)
RABAR... Raytheon Advanced Battery Acquisition RADAR
RABATS... Rapid Analytical Block Aerial Triangulation System (PDAA)
Rabb... Rabbinic [*Hebrew*] [*Language*] (BARN)
RABB... Rabbinical
RABBI... Rapid Access Blood Bank Information (MAE)
RABDF... Royal Association of British Dairy Farmers [*British*] (BI)
RABET... RADAR Beacon Transponder
RABFAC... RADAR Beacon, Forward Air Controller
RABFAC-TDC... RADAR Beacon Forward Air Controller - Target Data Communicator (MCD)
RABG... Room Air Blood Gases [*Medicine*] (DAVI)
RABH... Reported Altitude Block Height (SAA)
RABI... Royal Agricultural Benevolent Institution [*Church of England*]
RABiTS... Rolling-Assisted Biaxially Textured Substrate [*Physics*]
RABNVS... Reactor Auxiliary Building Normal Ventilation System [*Nuclear energy*] (NRCH)
RABP... Renal Artery Bypass [*Medicine*]
RABP... Retinoic Acid-Binding Protein [*Biochemistry*] (DAVI)
Rab Post... Pro Rabirio Postumo [*of Cicero*] [*Classical studies*] (OCD)
RABR... Rainbow Bridge National Monument
RABR... Right Angle Bulkhead Receptacle
RABS... Rear-Wheel Antilock Brake System [*Automotive engineering*]
RABS... Remote Air Battle Station
RABV... Reflood Assist Bypass Valve [*Nuclear energy*] (NRCH)
RABVAL... RADAR Bomb Evaluation (MCD)
R_{ac}... AC Resistance (IDOE)
RAC... IEEE Robotics and Automation Council (EA)
rac... Racemic [*Also, dl, r*] [*Chemistry*]
RAC... Racer Resources Ltd. [*Vancouver Stock Exchange symbol*]
RAC... Raciborz [*Poland*] [*Seismograph station code, US Geological Survey*] (SEIS)
RAC... Racine, WI [*Location identifier FAA*] (FAAL)
RAC... RADAR Address Counter
RAC... RADAR Area Correlator
RAC... RADAR Azimuth Converter
RAC... Radiation Advisory Committee (GNE)
RAC... Radio Adaptive Communications
RAC... Radio Advisory Committee [*Corporation for Public Broadcasting*] (NTCM)
RAC... Radiological Assessment Coordinator [*Nuclear energy*] (NRCH)
RAC... Radiometric Area Correlator (MCD)
RAC... Radio Service Code (IAA)
RAC... Raisin Administrative Committee (EA)
RAC... Ram Air Cushion [*Aerospace*] (AAG)
RAC... Ramsay's Appeal Cases [*Canada*] [*A publication*] (DLA)
RAC... Random Access Capability [*Microscopy*]
RAC... Random Access Computer (IIA)
RAC... Random Access Controller [*Computer science*] (IAA)
RAC... Rangefinder with Automatic Compensator [*Firearms*]
RAC... Rapid Action Change [*DoD*]
RAC... Ration Accessory Convenience [*World War II*]
RAC... Rational Activity Coefficient
RAC... Raw Agricultural Commodity
RAC... Reactor Accident Calculation
RAC... Read Address Counter
RAC... Reallexikon fuer Antike und Christentum [*A publication*] (OCD)
RAC... Rear-Admiral Commanding [*British*]
RAC... Receptor-Affinity Chromatography
RAC... Recessed Annular Connector

RAC .... Recombinant DNA Advisory Committee [*National Institutes of Health*]
RAC .... Reconnaissance Airplane Company [*Army*] (VNW)
RAC .... Recreation Advisory Council [*Bureau of Outdoor Recreation*]
RAC .... Rectified Alternating Current [*Radio*]
rac .... Rectified Alternating Current (IDOE)
RAC .... Rectified Alternating Current [*Electronics*] (ECII)
RAC .... Recycling Advisory Council (GNE)
RAC .... Reflect Array Pulse Compressor (RDA)
RAC .... Refrigerant-Air Condition (DNAB)
RAC .... Refueling Area Commander [*Navy*] (ANA)
RAC .... Regional Advisory Council (ACII)
RAC .... Regional Asbestos Coordinator (GNE)
RAC .... Registrar of Aboriginal Corporations [*Australia*]
RAC .... Release and Approval Center (MCD)
RAC .... Reliability Action Center [*NASA*] (NASA)
RAC .... Reliability Analysis Center [*Griffiss Air Force Base, NY*] [*DoD*] (GRD)
RAC .... Reliability Assessment of Components (KSC)
RAC .... Remote Access [*Telecommunications*] (IAA)
RAC .... Remote Access Computing System (IAA)
RAC .... Renal Arterial Constriction [*Medicine*]
RAC .... Repair, Alignment, and Calibration (NVT)
RAC .... Reparable Assets Control (AFM)
RAC .... Representation des Artistes Canadiens
RAC .... Request for Authority to Complete (DOMA)
RAC .... Request for Authority to Contract [*Military*]
RAC .... Requisition Advice Care [*Military*]
RAC .... Research Advisory Committee
RAC .... Research Advisory Council
RAC .... Research Analysis Corp. [*Nonprofit contract agency*] [*Army*]
RAC .... Response Action Contractor [*Metallurgy*]
RAC .... Response Action Coordinator [*Environmental Protection Agency*] (ERG)
RAC .... Responsibility Analysis Chart (DNAB)
RAC .... Retail Advertising Conference (EA)
RAC .... Rework After Completion (SAA)
RAC .... Rhomboidal Air Controller (PDAA)
RAC .... Right Atrial Catheter [*Medicine*] (MEDA)
RAC .... Right Atrial Catheter [*Cardiology*] (DAVI)
RAC .... Risk Assessment Code (MCD)
RAC .... River Assault Craft [*Navy*] (ANA)
RAC .... Roadside Assistance Center [*Automotive Customer Service*]
RAC .... Rotorua Aero Club [*New Zealand*] [*ICAO designator*] (FAAC)
RAC .... Royal Academician (of Canada) (ROG)
RAC .... Royal Aero Club [*British*]
RAC .... Royal Agricultural College [*British*]
RAC .... Royal Arch Chapter [*Freemasonry*]
RAC .... Royal Armoured Corps [*British*]
RAC .... Royal Artillery Committee [*British military*] (DMA)
RAC .... Royal Automobile Club [*Controlling body of motor racing in Britain*]
RAC .... Rubber Allocation Committee
RAC .... Rules of the Air and Air Traffic Control [*ICAO Air Navigation Commission*]
Ra Ca .... English Railway and Canal Cases [*A publication*] (DLA)
RACA .... Recovered Alcoholic Clergy Association (EA)
RACA .... Regroupement d'Artistes des Centres Alternatifs [*Association of National Non-Profit Artists' Centres ANNPAC*] [*Canada*]
RACA .... Requiring Activity Contract Administrator [*DoD*]
RACA .... Resource Accounting and Cost Allocation (MHDI)
RACA .... Rural Arts and Crafts Association [*Defunct*] (EA)
RACAS .... Radiation Automatic Casualty Assessment System [*Military*]
RACC .... Radiation and Contamination Control
RACC .... Regional Agricultural Credit Corp.
RACC .... Regional ASW [*Antisubmarine Warfare*] Command Center [*Navy*] (DOMA)
RACC .... Remote ARIA [*Apollo Range Instrumentation Aircraft*] Control Center [*NASA*]
RACC .... Remotely Activated Command and Control [*Military*] (CAAL)
RACC .... Reporting Activity Control Card [*Army*] (AABC)
RACC .... Research Aviation Coordinating Committee
RACC .... Rituels Accadiens [*A publication*] (BJA)
RACC .... Royal Armoured Corps Centre [*British*] (MCD)
RACC .... Royal Automobile Club of Canada
RACCA .... Refrigeration and Air Conditioning Contractors Association - National [*Later, National Environmental Systems Contractors Association*] (EA)
RACD .... Royal Army Chaplains' Department [*British*]
RACD .... Royal Army Clothing Department [*British*]
RACE .... Data Race [*NASDAQ symbol*] (TTSB)
RACE .... Date Race, Inc. [*NASDAQ symbol*] (SAG)
RACE .... Racial Attitudes and Consciousness Exam [*Two-part television program broadcast in 1989*]
RACE .... Radiation Adaptive Compression Equipment
RACE .... Random Access Card Equipment [*Computer science*] (CDE)
RACE .... Random Access Computer Equipment
RACE .... Random Access Control Equipment (IEEE)
RACE .... Rapid Amplification of CDNA [*Complementary Deoxyribonucleic Acid*] Ends [*Genetics*]
RACE .... Rapid Amplification of Cloned Ends [*Analytical biochemistry*]
RACE .... Rapid Automatic Checkout Equipment
RACE .... Regional Automatic Circuit Exchange (IAA)
RACE .... Request Altitude Changes En Route [*Aviation*]
RACE .... Research and Development in Advanced Communications for Europe [*European Community*] (MHDB)
RACE .... Research and Development in Advanced Communication Technologies for Europe (NITA)
RACE .... Research in Advanced Communications in Europe [*European Commission*]
RACE .... Research on Automatic Computation Electronics
RACE .... Resource Assessment and Conservation Engineering [*Environmental protection*]
RACE .... Response Analysis for Call Evaluation (IAA)
RACE .... Restoration of Aircraft to Combat Effectivity [*Army*]
RACE .... Results Analysis, Computation, and Evaluation (MHDI)
RACE .... Routing and Cost Estimate (IAA)
RACEL .... Record of Access/Eligibility [*DoD*]
RACEP .... Random Access and Correlation for Extended Performance [*Telecommunications*]
RACER .... Rankine-Cycle Energy Recovery [*System*] [*Navy*] (DOMA)
RACER .... Redbook Assumption Cost Estimating Request
RACER .... Runner Administration and Computerized Entry Routine [*Computer science*] (MHDI)
Race Rel L Rep ... Race Relations Law Reporter [*A publication*] (DLA)
RACES .... Radio Amateur Civil Emergency Service [*Civil defense*]
RACES .... Remote Arming Common Element System
RACF .... RAC Financial Group, Inc. [*NASDAQ symbol*] (SAG)
RACF .... RAC Fin'l Grp [*NASDAQ symbol*] (TTSB)
RACF .... Resource Access Control Facility [*IBM Corp.*]
RACFI .... Radio and Communication Facilities Inoperative
RAC Fin .... RAC Financial Group, Inc. [*Associated Press*] (SAG)
RACFO .... Radio and Communications Facilities Operative (IAA)
RACFOE .... Research Analysis Corporation Field Office, Europe [*Army*] (AABC)
RACG .... Racing
RACG .... Radiometric Area Correlation Guidance
RACGPFMP ... Royal Australian College of General Practitioners Family Medicine Program
RAChD .... Royal Army Chaplains' Department [*British*]
RACI .... Reported Altitude Change Indicator (IAA)
RACI .... Royal Australian Chemical Institute
RACIC .... Remote Area Conflict Information Center [*Battelle Memorial Institute*]
RACIS .... RADAR Computer Interaction Simulator
RACM .... Reasonable Available Control Measures [*Environmental Protection Agency*] (GFGA)
RACMD .... Radio Countermeasures and Detection (IAA)
RACMSC .... Royal Automobile Club Motor Sports Council [*British*] (DI)
RACNE .... Regional Advisory Committee on Nuclear Energy
RACNSC .... Religious Activities Committee, National Safety Council (EA)
RACO .... Racotek, Inc. [*NASDAQ symbol*] (SAG)
RACO .... RADAR-Absorbing Coating [*Military*] (RDA)
RACO .... Rear Area Combat Operations (INF)
RACOB(WA) ... Rear-Admiral Commanding Combined Operational Bases (Western Approaches) [*British*]
RACOM .... Random Communication (IAA)
RACOMS .... Rapid Combat Mapping Service [*or System*] [*Military*]
RACON .... RADAR Beacon (IAA)
Racon .... Radar Beacon (IDOE)
RACON .... RADAR Responder Beacon
Ra (Conspic) ... RADAR Conspicuous Object
RACOON .... Radiation Controlled Balloon [*Meteorology*]
Racotek .... Racotek, Inc. [*Associated Press*] (SAG)
RACP .... Royal Australasian College of Physicians
RACPAS .... RADAR Coverage Penetration Analysis
RACQ .... Radiological Advisory Council of Queensland [*Australia*]
RACR .... Resources Allocation Change Request
Rac Rel L Survey ... Race Relations Law Survey [*A publication*] (DLA)
RAC/RJ .... Religious Action Center of Reform Judaism (EA)
RACS .... Random Access Communications System
RACS .... Reactor Auxiliary Cooling System [*Nuclear energy*] (NUCP)
RACS .... Recruit Allocation Control System [*Navy*] (NVT)
RACS .... Redundant Attitude Control System (MCD)
RACS .... Regenerable Affinity Chromatography Support
RACS .... Remote Access Computing System [*Computer science*]
RACS .... Remote Automatic Calibration System (NASA)
RACS .... Remote Automatic Control System (KSC)
RACS .... Request for Approval of Contractual Support
RACS .... Road/Automobile Communication System [*Automotive engineering*]
RACS .... Rotation Axis Coordinate System (MCD)
RACS .... Royal Australasian College of Surgeons
RACT .... Reasonable Available Control Technology [*Environmental Protection Agency*]
RACT .... Remote Access Computer Technique [*Computer science*] (IEEE)
RACT .... Reverse-Acting
RACU .... Remote Acquisiton and Command Unit [*NASA*] (NASA)
RACUAHC ... Religious Action Center of the Union of American Hebrew Congregations [*Later, RAC/RJ*] (EA)
RACV .... Royal Automobile Club of Victoria
RAD .... Parti Radical [*Radical Party*] [*France*] [*Political party*] (EAIO)
RAD .... RADAR
RAD .... RADAR Approach Aid [*Aviation*] (DA)
RAD .... RADAR Augmentation Device
RAD .... Radford Army Ammunition Plant [*Virginia*]
RAD .... Radford Arsenal [*Army*] (AAG)
rad .... Radiac (IDOE)
RAD .... RADIAC [*Radiation Detection, Indication, and Computation*] Equipment (NATG)
RAD .... Radial
rad .... Radian [*Symbol*] [*SI unit of plane angle*]
RAD .... Radiation (KSC)
RAD .... Radiation Absorbed Dose [*Unit of measurement of radiation energy*]
rad .... Radiation Absorbed Dose (DOG)
RAD .... Radiator (AAG)

RAD .... Radical
rad .... Radical (IDOE)
rad .... Radio (IDOE)
RAD .... Radio (AAG)
RaD .... Radioactive Lead [*or Pb^{210}*] [*Radiology*] (DAVI)
RAD .... Radioactivity Detection
RAD .... Radiogram
RAD .... Radiographer (HCT)
Rad .... Radiola [*Record label*] [*Australia*]
RAD .... Radiologist
RAD .... Radiology [*or Radiologist*] (ADA)
Rad .... Radiotherapist (MAE)
RAD .... Radium [*Chemical symbol is Ra*]
RAD .... Radius (AAG)
rad .... Radius (IDOE)
rad .... Radix (IDOE)
RAD .... Radix [*Root*] [*Latin*]
RAD .... Radnorshire [*County in Wales*] (ROG)
RAD .... Raised Afterdeck [*of a ship*] (DS)
RAD .... Random Access Data (BUR)
RAD .... Random Access Device
RAD .... Random Access Disc (MCD)
RAD .... Rapid Access Data [*Xerox Corp.*]
RAD .... Rapid Access Data Drum (NITA)
RAD .... Rapid Access Device
RAD .... Rapid Access Disk
RAD .... Rapid Access Drive (BUR)
RAD .... Rapid Access Drum (IAA)
RAD .... Rapid Application Development [*Computer science*]
RAD .... Rapid Automatic Drill
RAD .... Ratio Adjust Device (MCD)
RAD .... Ratio Analysis Diagram [*Metallurgy*]
RAD .... Reactive Airway Disease [*Medicine*] (MAE)
RA(D) .... Rear-Admiral (Destroyers) [*Obsolete Navy British*]
RAD .... Receptor Affinity Distribution [*Biochemistry*]
RAD .... Recommendation Approval Document (MCD)
RAD .... Records Arrival Date [*Bell System*] (TEL)
RAD .... Recruiting Aids Department [*Navy*]
RAD .... Reference Attitude Display
RAD .... Reflex Anal Dilatation [*Medicine*]
RAD .... Regional Accountable Depot [*Military*]
RAD .... Regional Administrative Directors
RAD .... Relative Air Density (OA)
RAD .... Released from Active Duty [*Navy*]
RAD .... Repair at Depot (MCD)
RAD .... Reported for Active Duty [*Navy*]
RAD .... Request for Apollo Documents [*NASA*] (KSC)
RAD .... Required Availability Date [*Military*]
RAD .... Requirements Action Directive (AFM)
RAD .... Research and Advanced Development (MCD)
RAD .... Research and Development (IAA)
RAD .... Reservists on Active Duty [*Navy*]
RAD .... Resource Allocation Display [*Navy*]
RAD .... Resource Availability Determination (MCD)
RAD .... Respect voor Arbeid en Democratie [*Belgium Political party*] (EY)
RAD .... Restricted Activity Day [*Environmental medicine*]
RAD .... Restricted Activity Days [*Veterans Administration*] (GFGA)
RAD .... Restricted Shipyard Availability Requiring Drydocking [*Navy*] (NVT)
RAD .... Return to Active Duty [*Military*]
RAD .... Review and Approval Document (MCD)
RAD .... Right Angle Drive (PDAA)
RAD .... Right Anterior Descending [*Medicine*] (DAVI)
RAD .... Right Anterior Digestive [*Gland*]
RAD .... Right Axis Deviation [*Medicine*]
RAD .... Rite Aid [*NYSE symbol*] (TTSB)
RAD .... Rite Aid Corp. [*NYSE symbol*] (SPSG)
RAD .... River Assault Division [*Navy*] (VNW)
RAD .... Roentgen Administered Dose
RAD .... Royal Academy of Dancing [*British*] (EAIO)
RAD .... Royal Academy of Dancing, United States Branch (EA)
RAD .... Royal Albert Dock [*British*]
RAD .... Rural Areas Development
RAD .... Sisters of the Love of God (TOCD)
RAD .... Warroad, MN [*Location identifier FAA*] (FAAL)
RADA .... Radica Games Ltd. [*NASDAQ symbol*] (SAG)
RadA .... Radical Alliance [*British*]
RADA .... Radioactive
RADA .... Random Access Discrete Address [*Army division-level battlefield radio communications system*]
RADA .... Realignment of Airdrop Activities (MCD)
RADA .... Right Acromio-Dorsoanterior [*A fetal position*] [*Obstetrics*]
RADA .... Rosin Amine-D-Acetate [*Medicine*] (DMAA)
RADA .... Royal Academy of Dramatic Art [*British*]
RADAC .... RADAR Analog Digital Data and Control (KSC)
RADAC .... Rapid Digital Automatic Computing
RADAC .... Raytheon Automatic Drafting Artwork Compiler
RADACS .... Random Access Discrete Address Communications System [*Army*]
RadaElc .... Rada Electronics Industries Ltd. [*Associated Press*] (SAG)
RADAF .... Radica Games [*NASDAQ symbol*] (TTSB)
RADAG .... RADAR Area Correlation Guidance System (PDAA)
RaDaK .... Rabbi David Kimhi [*Biblical scholar, 1160-1235*] (BJA)
RADAL .... Radio Detection and Location
RADALT .... RADAR Altimeter [*Aviation*] (SSD)
RADAN .... RADAR Analysis System (MCD)
RADAN .... RADAR Doppler Automatic Navigator
RADAN .... RADAR Navigation
RADANT .... RADOME [*RADAR Dome*] Antenna (NVT)
Radar .... Radar's Reports [*138-163 Missouri*] [*A publication*] (DLA)
RADAR .... Radio Association Defending Airwave Rights (EA)
RADAR .... Radio Detection and Ranging
RADAR .... Radio's All-Dimension Audience Research (NTCM)
RADAR .... Random Access Dump and Reload (IAA)
RADAR .... Rassemblement des Democrates pour l'Avenir de la Reunion [*Rally of Democrats for the Future of Reunion*] [*Political party*] (PPW)
RADAR .... Receivable Accounts Data Entry and Retrieval [*Computer science*] (MHDI)
RADAR .... Reseau d'Approvisionnement et de Debouches d'Affaires [*Business Opportunities Sourcing System - BOSS*] [*Canada*]
RAD-AR .... Risk/Benefit Assessment of Drugs - Analysis and Response [*Post-marketing surveillance*]
RADAR .... Royal Association for Disability and Rehabilitation [*British*]
RADARC .... Radially Distributed Annular Rocket Chamber
RADAREVALSq ... RADAR Evaluation Squadron [*Air Force*]
RADARSAT .... RADAR Satellite [*Canada*]
RADAS .... Random Access Discrete Address System
RADAT .... RADAR Alignment Designation Accuracy Test (MCD)
RADAT .... RADAR Data Transmission
RADAT .... Radio Direction and Track
RADAT .... Radiosonde Observation Data
RADATA .... RADAR Automatic Data Transmission Assembly (IAA)
RADATA .... RADAR Data Transmission and Assembly (IEEE)
RADATAC .... Radiation Data Acquisition Chart
RADATS .... RADAR Data-Transmission System (WDAA)
RADAUS .... Radio-Austria AG
RADAY .... Radio Day (CET)
RADB .... Radiometric Age Data Bank [*Geological Survey*] [*Information service or system Defunct*] (IID)
RADBIOL .... Radiobiology
RADBN .... Radio Battalion [*Marine Corps*]
RAD(BPF) .... Rear-Admiral Commanding Destroyers (British Pacific Fleet)
RADC .... RADAR Countermeasures and Deception [*Military*] (MCD)
RADC .... Regiment Air Defense Center (NATG)
RADC .... Review, Approve or Disapprove, and Comment (MCD)
RADC .... Rome Air Development Center [*Griffiss Air Force Base, NY*] [*Air Force*]
RADC .... Royal Army Dental Corps [*British*]
RADCAP .... Research and Development Contributions to Aviation Progress [*Air Force*]
RADCAS .... Radiation Casualty [*Criteria for battlefield targets*] (MCD)
RADCAT .... RADAR Calibration Target (MCD)
RADCC .... Radiation Control Center
RADCC .... Radiological Control Center [*Army*] (KSC)
RADCC .... Rear Area Damage Control Center (AABC)
RADC/ETR .... Rome Air Development Center Deputy for Electronic Technology [*ESD*]
RADCHM .... Radiochemistry
RADCM .... RADAR Countermeasures and Deception [*Military*]
RADCOL .... RADC [*Rome Air Development Center*] Automatic Document Classification On-Line [*Air Force Information service or system*] (IID)
RADCOM .... Radio Communications (MCD)
RADCOM .... Radiometric Contrast Matching (MCD)
RADCOM .... Research and Development Command (MCD)
RADCON .... RADAR Control
RADCON .... RADAR Data Converter (AFM)
RADCON .... Radiological Control [*Military*] (AABC)
RADCOT .... Radial Optical Tracking Theodolite (MUGU)
RADCS .... RADAR Control Squadron
RADD .... Royal Association in Aid of the Deaf and Dumb [*British*] (BI)
RADDEF .... Radiological Defense [*To minimize the effect of nuclear radiation on people and resources*]
RADDOL .... Raddolcendo [*Gradually Softer*] [*Music*]
RADDS .... RADAR Display Distribution System (DWSG)
RADDS .... Raytheon Automated Digital Design System (PDAA)
RADE .... Research and Development Division [*National Security Agency*] [*Obsolete*]
RADEC .... Radiation Detection Capability (MCD)
RADEF .... Radiological Defense [*To minimize the effect of nuclear radiation on people and resources*]
Ra de Hacur ... Raoul d'Harcourt [*Deceased, 1307*] [*Authority cited in pre-1607 legal work*] (DSA)
RADELECTENG ... Radio and Electronic Engineer (IAA)
RADEM .... Random Access Delta Modulation
RADEP .... RADAR Departure [*Aviation*] (FAAC)
RADER .... Rassemblement Democratique du Ruanda [*Democratic Rally of Rwanda*]
RADES .... RADAR Evaluation Squadron [*Air Force*]
RADES .... Realistic Air Defense Engagement System [*Army*] (RDA)
RADEX .... RADAR Data Extractor (PDAA)
RADEX .... RADAR Exercise (NVT)
RADEX .... Radiation Exclusion Plot [*Chart of actual or predicted fallout*]
RADFAC .... Radiating Facility
RADFAL .... Radiological Prediction Fallout Plot
RADFET .... Radiation-Sensing Field Effect Transistor [*Instrumentation*]
RADFO .... Radiological Fallout [*Army*]
Radford U .... Radford University (GAGS)
RADHAZ .... Radiation Hazards
RADHAZ .... Radio Frequency Hazard (IAA)
RADI .... Rada Electronic Industries Ltd. [*New York, NY NASDAQ symbol*] (NQ)

RADI........ Radio Area of Dominant Influence [*Advertising*] (DOAD)
RADI........ Radiographic Inspection [*NASA*] (AAG)
Radi........ Radium [*Record label*] [*France*]
RADI........ Retail Alarm for Display and Intruder (PDAA)
RADIAC........ Radiation Detection, Indication, and Computation [*Radiological measuring instruments*]
RADIAC........ Radioactive Detection and Measurement
RADIAC........ Radio Activity Detection, Identification and Computation (IAA)
RADIAL........ Radial [*Commonly used*] (OPSA)
RADIALS........ Research and Development in Information and Library Science (NITA)
RADIAT........ Radiation
RADIC........ Radical (ROG)
RADIC........ Radio Interior Communications
RADIC........ Redifon Analog-Digital Computer [*British*]
RADIC........ Research and Development Information Center (AFM)
RadicaG........ Radica Games Ltd. [*Associated Press*] (SAG)
Radical Ed... Radical Education [*A publication*]
Radical Ed Dossier... Radical Education Dossier [*A publication*]
RADIC-LIB... Radical Liberal
RADICS........ Research and Development in Computer System (IAA)
RADIEL........ Radial [*Commonly used*] (OPSA)
RADIF........ Rada Electronics Industries [*NASDAQ symbol*] (TTSB)
RADIL........ Research Animal Diagnostic and Investigative Laboratory [*University of Missouri-Columbia*] [*Research center*] (RCD)
RADINJCLRDS... Radiation Injury Claims Record (DNAB)
RADINT........ RADAR Intelligence
RADINT........ Radio Intelligence [*Military*] (IAA)
RADIO........ Radiotherapy
RADIOBIOL... Radiobiology
RADIOCHEM... Radiochemistry
RADIOG........ Radiography (IAA)
Radio Hobbies Aust... Radio and Hobbies Australia [*A publication*]
radio-IEP........ Radioimmunoelectrophoresis [*Biochemistry*] (DAVI)
Radiol........ Radiology
Radio Rev Aust... Radio Review of Australia [*A publication*]
RADIQUAD........ Radio Quadrangle [*Military*]
RADIR........ Random Access Document Indexing and Retrieval
RADISH........ Rheumatoid Arthritis Diffuse Idiopathic Skeletal Hyperostosis (DAVI)
RAD ISO VENO BILAT... Radioactive Isotopic Venogram, Bilateral [*Nuclear Medicine*] (DAVI)
RADIST........ RADAR Distance Indicator
RadiSys........ RadiSys Corp. [*Associated Press*] (SAG)
RADIT........ Radio Teletype (IEEE)
Radius........ Radius, Inc. [*Associated Press*] (SAG)
RADIUS........ Remote Authentication Dial-In User Service [*Computer science*] (PCM)
RADIUS........ Research and Development Institute of the United States [*Research center*] (RCD)
RADIUS........ Research and Development in the United States [*Database*]
RADL........ Radial (AAG)
RADL........ Radial
RADL........ Radiological [*or Radiology*] (AAG)
RADLAB........ Radiation Laboratory (AAG)
RADLAC........ Radial Pulse Line Accelerators (MCD)
RADLCEN........ Radiological Center
RADLDEF........ Radiological Defense [*To minimize the effect of nuclear radiation on people and resources*]
RADLDEFLAB... Radiological Defense Laboratory [*NASA*]
RADLFO........ Radiological Fallout [*Army*] (AABC)
RADLGC........ Radiologic
RADLGCL........ Radiological
RADLGY........ Radiology
RADLMON... Radiological Monitor [*or Monitoring*] [*Military*]
RADLO........ Radiological Officer
RADLOPS........ Radiological Operations [*Military*] (AABC)
RADLSAFE... Radiological Safety [*Military*]
RADLSO........ Radiological Survey Officer [*Military*]
RADLSV........ Radiological Survey [*Military*]
RadLV........ Radiation Leukemia Virus [*Medicine*] (DMAA)
RADLWAR... Radiological Warfare
RADM........ RADARman (GFGA)
RADM........ Random Walk Advection and Dispersion Model [*Environmental Protection Agency*] (GFGA)
RADM........ Rear Admiral [*Also, RA, RADML*] (AAG)
RADM........ Regional Acid Deposition Model [*for acid rain*] [*Environmental Protection Agency*]
RADMAP........ Radiological Monitoring Assessment Prediction System (PDAA)
RADMIS........ Research Activities Designators Management Information System
RADMON........ Radiological Monitoring (AFM)
RADN........ Radiation (AAG)
RADN........ Radnorshire [*County in Wales*]
RADNAV........ Radio Navigation [*USCG*] (TAG)
RADNO........ Report Missing Account Radio Failure [*Meteorology*] (FAAC)
RADNORS........ Radnorshire [*County in Wales*] (ROG)
RADNOS........ No Radio [*Military*]
RADNOTE........ Radio Note [*Military*]
RADOC........ Regional Air Defense Operations Center (NATG)
RADOC........ Remote Automatic Detection Contingencies
RADOD........ Research and Development Objectives Document (MCD)
RADOME........ RADAR Dome [*NASA*]
RADON........ RADAR Beacon
RADON........ Research and Development Operational Needs (MCD)
RADOP........ RADAR Doppler [*Missile-tracking system*] (AAG)
RADOP........ RADAR Operator (CET)
RADOP........ RADAR/Optical Weapons [*Military*]
RADOP........ Radio Operator [*Navy*]
RADOPR........ Radio Operator (AAG)
RADOPWEAP... RADAR Optical Weapons (IEEE)
RADOSE........ Radiation Dosimeter Satellite [*NASA*]
RADOT........ Real-Time [*or Recording*] Automatic Digital Optical Tracker
RADP........ Right Acromio-Dorsoposterior [*A fetal position*] [*Obstetrics*]
RADPLANBD... Radio Planning Board [*Navy*]
RADPROPCAST... Radio Propagation Forecast
RADREF........ RADAR Refraction (MCD)
RADREL........ Radio Relay [*Military*]
RADRELRON... Radio Relay Squadron [*Military*] (IAA)
RADREPMN... Radio Repairman (IAA)
RADRON........ RADAR Squadron [*Air Force*]
RADRONMOB... Radio Squadron, Mobile [*Military*] (IAA)
RADRU........ Rapid Access Data Retrieval Unit [*Computer science*] (PDAA)
RADS........ RADAR Alphanumeric Display Sub-System (PDAA)
RADS........ Radar and Algorithm Display Model (USDC)
RADS........ Radar and Algorithm Display Model [*Marine science*] (OSRA)
RADS........ RADAR Squadron [*Air Force*]
RAD/S........ Radians per Second
RADS........ Radiation and Dosimetry Services (NRCH)
RADS........ Radius (AAG)
RADS........ Rapid Area Distribution Support [*Air Force*]
RADS........ Raw Data System
RADS........ Reactive Airways Dysfunction Syndrome [*Medicine*] (DMAA)
RADS........ Real-Time Analysis and Display System (USDC)
RADS........ Real-Time Analysis and Display System [*Marine science*] (OSRA)
RADS........ Retiree Activity Days [*DoD*]
RADS........ Ryukyu Air Defense System
RAD/S²........ Radians per Second Squared
RADSAFE........ Radiological Safety [*Military*]
RADSCAT........ Radiometer/Scatterometer [*Sensor*] [*Meteorology*]
RADSEC........ Radio Section (IAA)
RADSIM........ Random Access Discrete Address System Simulator [*Army*] (IAA)
RADSL........ Rate Adaptive Digital Subscriber Line (PCM)
RADSO........ Radiological Survey Officer (IEEE)
RADSOC........ Request for Authority to Develop a System or Change [*Military*] (AFIT)
RADSTA........ Radio Station
RadT........ Radiola-Telefunken [*Record label*] [*Australia*]
R/ADT........ Registration/Admission, Disposition and Transfer [*Tri-Service Medical Information System*] (DNAB)
Rad Ther........ Radiation Therapy (DAVI)
RADTR........ Radiator
RADTS........ Rabbit Antidog Thymus Serum [*Immunology*] (MAE)
RADTT........ Radiation Therapy Technologist (HCT)
RADTT........ Radio Teletypewriter (CET)
RADU........ RADAR Analysis and Detection Unit (WDAA)
RADU........ RADAR Analysis and Development Unit [*National Severe Storms Forecast Center*] (NOAA)
RADU........ Ram Air-Driven Unit
RAD-UDRT... Respect voor Arbeid en Democratie/Union Democratique pour le Respect du Travail [*Respect for Labor and Democracy/Democratic Union for the Respect of Labor*] [*Belgium Political party*] (PPE)
Rad Ul........ Radius-Ulna [*Medicine*] (MAE)
RADVS........ RADAR Altimeter and Doppler Velocity Sensor
RADWAR........ Radiological Warfare
RADWASTE... Radioactive Waste
RADY........ Radiology
RAE........ Arar [*Saudi Arabia*] [*Airport symbol*] (OAG)
RA(E)........ Engineer Rear-Admiral [*Navy British*] (DMA)
RAE........ Farnborough Rae [*British*] [*FAA designator*] (FAAC)
RAE........ RADAR Altimeter Equipment
RAE........ Radio Astronomy Explorer [*Satellite*]
RAE........ Radiodifusion Argentina al Exterior [*Broadcasting organization*] [*Argentina*]
RAE........ Range, Azimuth, and Elevation (MCD)
RAE........ Report After Execution (AAGC)
RAE........ Research and Engineering (IAA)
RAE........ Research Assessment Exercise [*Higher Education Funding Council*] (AIE)
RAE........ Review of Applied Entomology [*Database*] [*Commonwealth Institute of Entomology*] [*Information service or system*] (CRD)
RAE........ Right Arithmetic Element
RAE........ Right Ascension Encoder
RAE........ Right Atrial Enlargement [*Cardiology*]
RAE........ Royal Aeronautical Establishment [*British*] (IAA)
RAE........ Royal Aircraft Establishment [*British Ministry of Defense*] [*Research center*]
RAE........ Royal Army Establishment [*British*]
RAEA........ Regroupement des Auteurs-Editeurs Autonomes [*Canada*]
RAEB........ Refractory Anemia, Erythroblastic [*Hematology*] (DAVI)
RAEB........ Refractory Anemia with Excess of Blasts [*Hematology*]
RAEB-T........ Refractory Anemia with Excess of Blasts in Transformation [*Hematology*]
RAEC........ Rabbit Aortic Endothelial Cells
R Ae C........ Royal Aero Club [*British*] (BARN)
RAEC........ Royal Army Educational Corps [*British*]
RAECO........ Rare-Earth Cobalt
RAEDOT........ Range, Azimuth, and Elevation Detection of Optical Targets
RA EM........ Radium Emanation (WDAA)
RAEM........ Refractory Anemia with Excess Myeloblast [*Hematology*] (MAE)
RAEN........ Radio Amateur Emergency Network (IEEE)

RaeRG......... Reallexikon der Aegyptischen Religionsgeschichte [*Berlin*] [*A publication*] (BJA)
RAES.......... Radio Astronomy Experiment Selection Panel
RAES.......... Rapid Access with Extensive Search [*Algorithm*]
RAES.......... Ratios for Automotive Executives [*Computer software*]
RAES.......... Remote Access Editing System [*Computer science*] (IEEE)
RAeS.......... Royal Aeronautical Society [*British*] (EAIO)
RAET.......... Range, Azimuth, Elevation, and Time
RAETDS....... Reciprocating Aircraft Engine Type Designation System
RAETU......... Reserve Airborne Electronics Training Unit (DNAB)
RAF............. Farnas Aviation Services [*Sudan*] [*FAA designator*] (FAAC)
RAF............. Racial Awareness Facilitator [*School*] [*Navy*] (NVT)
Ra F............ Raphael Fulgosius [*Deceased, 1427*] [*Authority cited in pre-1607 legal work*] (DSA)
RAF............. Regular Air Force
RAF............. Repetitive Atrial Firing [*Medicine*] (DMAA)
RAF............. Requirements Allocation Form
RAF............. Requirements Analysis Form [*NASA*] (NASA)
RAF............. Research Aviation Facility [*National Center for Atmospheric Research*]
RAF............. Reserved Air Freight
RAF............. Resource Allocation Formula
RAF............. Reynolds Analogy Factor [*Physics*]
RAF............. Rheumatoid Arthritis Factor [*Medicine*] (MAE)
RAF............. River Assault Flotilla [*Navy*] (VNW)
RAF............. Rote Armee Faktion [*Red Army Faction (Baader-Meinhof Group)*] [*Terrorist group*] [*Germany*]
RAF............. Royal Aircraft Factory [*World War I*] [*British*]
RAF............. Royal Air Force [*British*]
RAF............. Sacramento, CA [*Location identifier FAA*] (FAAL)
RAFA........... Rank Annihilation Factor Analysis [*Computer science*]
RAFA........... Royal Air Forces Association (EAIO)
Ra Fab......... Raymundus Fabri [*Flourished, 14th century*] [*Authority cited in pre-1607 legal work*] (DSA)
RAFAC......... Radio Aids and Facilities (IAA)
Rafair.......... Royal Air Force [*Airline call sign*] [*British*]
RAFAR......... Radio Automated Facsimile and Reproduction
RAFAX......... RADAR Facsimile
RAFB........... Randolph Air Force Base [*Texas*]
RAFB........... Rickenbacker Air Force Base [*Formerly, Lockbourne Air Force Base*] [*Ohio*]
RAFB........... Royal Air Force Base [*British*]
RAFBF......... Royal Air Force Benevolent Fund [*British military*] (DMA)
RAFC........... Regional Area Forecast Center [*ICAO designator*] (FAAC)
RAFC........... Richmond Area Film Cooperative [*Library network*]
RAFC........... Royal Air Force Club [*British*]
RAFC........... Royal Air Force College [*British*]
RAFC........... Royal Artillery Flying Club [*British military*] (DMA)
RAFCC......... Royal Air Force Cinema Corp. [*British military*] (DMA)
RAFCC......... Royal Air Force Coastal Command [*British*]
RAFCWA...... Rural Adjustment and Finance Corp. of Western Australia [*Computer science*]
RAFD........... Rome Air Force Depot
RAFES......... Royal Air Force Educational Service [*British military*] (DMA)
RAFFC......... Royal Air Force Fighter Command [*British*]
Raff Pens Man... Raff's Pension Manual [*A publication*] (DLA)
RAFG........... Royal Air Force, Germany [*British military*] (DMA)
RAFHS......... Royal Air Force Historical Society [*British*] (DBA)
RAFI............ Radiosonde Observation Not Filed [*NWS*] (FAAC)
RAFI............ Rural Advancement Foundation International
RAFI............ Rural Advancement Fund International [*Later, RAFI-USA*] (EA)
RAFIAM....... Royal Air Force Institute of Aviation Medicine [*British*] (IAA)
RAFLO......... Radio Frequency Liaison Office [*Navy*] (DNAB)
RAFM........... Repair-at-Failure Maintenance (PDAA)
RAFME......... Royal Air Force, Middle East [*British military*] (DMA)
RAFMS......... Royal Air Force Medical Service [*British*]
RAFNS......... Royal Air Force Nursing Service [*British military*] (DMA)
RAFO........... Reserve Air Force Officers [*Later, RAFRO*] [*British*]
RAFO........... Resident Air Force Officer [*Australia*]
RAFR........... Royal Air Force Regiment [*British*]
RAFRC......... Revolutionary Armed Forces of the Republic of Cuba
RAFRO......... Royal Air Force Reserve of Officers [*Formerly, RAFO*] [*British*]
RAFRZ......... Radiosonde Observation Freezing Levels [*NWS*] (FAAC)
RAFS........... R. Austin Freeman Society (EA)
RAFS........... Regional Analysis and Forecast System [*National Meteorological Center*]
RAFS........... Remote Area Families Service [*Uniting Church*] [*Australia*]
RAFS........... Royal Air Force Station [*British*] (MCD)
RAFSA......... Royal Air Force Sailing Association [*British*] (BI)
RAFSAA....... Royal Air Force Small Arms Association [*British military*] (DMA)
RAFSC......... Royal Air Force Staff College [*British*]
RAFSC......... Royal Air Force Support Command [*British*]
RAFSP......... Royal Air Force Service Police [*British military*] (DMA)
RAFSTN....... Royal Air Force Air Station
RAFT........... Racial Awareness Facilitator Training [*Navy program*]
RAFT........... Radially Adjustable Facility Tube (IEEE)
RAFT........... Rear-Admiral Fleet Train [*British Pacific Fleet*]
RAFT........... Receiving Ambient Function Test (PDAA)
RAFT........... Recomp Algebraic Formula Translator [*Computer science*]
RAFT........... Reentry Advanced Fusing Test (IAA)
RAFT........... Regional Accounting and Finance Test [*Military*] (AFM)
RAFT........... Resource Allocation for Transportation (DNAB)
RAFT........... Retail Association for the Furnishing Trade [*British*] (BI)
RAFT........... Reunion des Amateurs de Fox Terriers [*An association*] (EAIO)
RAFTC......... Royal Air Forces Transport Command [*British*]

Ra Fulgo...... Raphael Fulgosius [*Deceased, 1427*] [*Authority cited in pre-1607 legal work*] (DSA)
RAFVR......... Royal Air Force Volunteer Reserve [*British*]
RAFW........... Right Atrial Free Wall [*Medicine*] (DMAA)
Rag.............. Ragland's California Superior Court Decisions [*A publication*] (DLA)
RAG............. Ragweed [*Medicine*] (DMAA)
RAG............. Rainforest Action Group [*Australia*]
RAG............. Readiness Analysis Group
RAG............. Recombination-Activating Gene
RAG............. Regimental Artillery Group [*OPFOR*] (GFGA)
RAG............. Regional Advisory Group [*Generic term*] (DHSM)
RAg............. Related Antigen [*Immunology*]
RAG............. Religious Arts Guild [*Defunct*] (EA)
RAG............. Replacement Air Group
RAG............. Requirements Advisory Group [*Air Force*] (MCD)
RAG............. Resource Appraisal Group [*US Geological Survey*]
RAG............. Retail Associates Group, Inc. [*Homesewing industry trade group*]
RAG............. Returned Ammunition Group (NATG)
RAG............. Reusable Agena [*NASA*] (NASA)
RAG............. Ring Airfoil Grenade [*Army*]
RAG............. River Assault Group [*Military*]
RAG............. ROM [*Read-Only Memory*] Address Gate [*Computer science*]
RAG............. Runway Arresting Gear [*Aviation*]
RAG-1.......... Rosenberg, Avraham, and Gutnick [*Strain of bacteria named for its researchers: Eugene Rosenberg, Avraham Reisfield, and David Gutnick*]
Ragan.......... Ragan [*Brad*], Inc. [*Associated Press*] (SAG)
RAGB........... Refractories Association of Great Britain (BI)
RAGC........... Rainbows for All God's Children [*Later, RFAGC*] (EA)
RAGC........... Relief General Communications Vessel
RAGC........... Royal and Ancient Golf Club [*Scotland*]
RAGE........... Radio Amplification of Gamma Emissions [*Antiguerrilla weapon*]
RAGE........... Rapid Gradient Echo (DMAA)
RAGE........... Receptor for Advanced Glycation End-Product [*Biochemistry*]
RAGEMS....... Radioactive Gaseous Effluent Monitoring System
RAGES......... Rail Armed Guard Escort Service [*Military Traffic Management Command*]
RAGF........... Remote Air-Ground Facility [*Aviation*]
Ragg............ Rheumatoid Agglutinator [*Immunology*]
RAGS........... Rag Shops [*NASDAQ symbol*] (TTSB)
RAGS........... Rag Shops, Inc. [*NASDAQ symbol*] (SAG)
RAGS........... Repulsive Axon Guidance Signal [*Biochemistry*]
RAGS........... Risk Assessment Guidance for Superfund [*Environmental science*]
RAGS........... Risk Assessments Guidance for Superfund [*Environmental Protection Agency*]
RagShp....... Rag Shops, Inc. [*Associated Press*] (SAG)
Rag Super Ct Dec (Calif)... Ragland's California Superior Court Decisions [*A publication*] (DLA)
RAH............. Rabbit Anti-Human [*Immunology*]
RAH............. Radiation-Anneal Hardening [*Alloy*]
RAH............. Rafha [*Saudi Arabia*] [*Airport symbol*] (OAG)
RAH............. Ralcorp Holdings [*NYSE symbol*] (SAG)
RAH............. Receipt, Excess, Adjustment, Due-In History File [*Army*]
RAH............. Receiving Array Hydrophone
RAH............. Reconnaissance Attack Helicopter
RAH............. Regent Air [*Canada ICAO designator*] (FAAC)
RAH............. Regressing Atypical Histiocytosis [*Medicine*]
RAH............. Reviews in American History [*A publication*] (BRI)
RAH............. Right Anterior Hemiblock [*Medicine*] (AAMN)
RAH............. Right Atrial Hypertrophy [*Cardiology*]
RAH............. Royal Albert Hall [*London, England*]
RAHF........... Research Animal Holding Facility [*NASA*] (NASA)
RaHGBM...... Rabbit Anti-Human Glomerular Basement Membrane [*Immunology*]
RAHLO......... Regional Aboriginal Health Liaison Officer [*Australia*]
RAHO........... Rabbit Antibody to Human Ovary [*Medicine*] (DMAA)
RAHO........... Rabbits Against Human Ovary [*Immunology*]
RAHO........... Royal Albert Hall Orchestra
RAHTG......... Rabbit Anti-Human Thymocyte Globulin [*Immunology*] (AAMN)
RAHTS......... Rabbit Anti-Human Thymocyte Serum [*Immunology*] (OA)
RAI.............. Praia [*Cape Verde Islands*] [*Airport symbol*] (OAG)
RAI.............. Racquetball Association of Ireland (EAIO)
RAI.............. RADAR Altimeter Indicator (MCD)
RAI.............. Radiation Applications, Inc.
RAI.............. Radioactive Interference [*NASA*]
RAI.............. Radioactive Iodine [*Medicine*]
RAI.............. Radioactive Isotope [*Roentgenology*]
Rai.............. Rainerius [*Authority cited in pre-1607 legal work*] (DSA)
RAI.............. Random Access and Inquiry [*Computer science*]
RAI.............. Range Azimuth Indicator
RAI.............. Raspberry Island [*Alaska*] [*Seismograph station code, US Geological Survey*] (SEIS)
RAI.............. Rassemblement Arabique-Islamique [*Algeria*] [*Political party*] (EY)
RAI.............. Receiving and Inspection (IAA)
RAI.............. Reliability Assurance Instructions (KSC)
RAI.............. Removal and Installation (IAA)
RAI.............. Repair at Intermediate (MCD)
RAI.............. Request for Additional Information (NRCH)
RAI.............. Research Advisory Institute, Inc.
RAI.............. Resource Analysts, Inc.
RAI.............. Roll Attitude Indicator [*NASA*]
RAI.............. Rounders Association of Ireland (EAIO)
RAI.............. Royal Air Inter-Compagnie d'Exploitation de Lignes Aer Interieures [*Morocco*] [*ICAO designator*] (FAAC)
RAI.............. Royal Albert Institution [*British*] (DAS)
RAI.............. Royal Anthropological Institute [*British*]

RAI .... Royal Archaeological Institute [*British*]
RAI .... Royal Artillery Institution [*British military*] (DMA)
RAI .... Runway Alignment Indicator [*Aviation*]
RAI .... Rural America, Inc. (EA)
RAIAD .... Reverse Acronyms, Initialisms, and Abbreviations Dictionary [*Formerly, RAID*] [*A publication*]
RAIAM .... Random Access Indestructive Advanced Memory [*Computer science*] (MSA)
RAIC .... Radiological Accident and Incident Control
RAIC .... Red Andina de Informacion Comercial [*Andean Trade Information Network*] (EAIO)
RAIC .... Redstone Arsenal Information Center [*Army*]
RAIC .... Royal Architectural Institute of Canada
RAICG .... Radiosonde Observation Icing At [*NWS*] (FAAC)
RAID .... RADAR Identification and Direction System (NG)
RAID .... Ram Air-Inflated Drogue [*Military*] (CAAL)
RAID .... Ram-Air Inflation Decelerator [*Munitions*] (RDA)
RAID .... Random Access Image Device [*Computer science*] (IAA)
RAID .... Random Access Interactive Debugger (IAA)
RAID .... Rapid Alerting and Identification Display (PDAA)
RAID .... Real-Time Applications Interactive Debugger (MCD)
RAID .... Recallable Airborne Infrared Display
RAID .... Reconnaissance and Interdiction Detachment [*Army*] (DOMA)
RAID .... Reduced Array of Inexpensive Drives [*Computer science*]
RAID .... Redundant Array of Independent Disks [*Computer science*] (CDE)
RAID .... Redundant Arrays of Inexpensive Disks [*Computer science*]
RAID .... Remote Access Interactive Debugger [*Computer science*] (IEEE)
RAID .... Reverse Acronyms and Initialisms Dictionary [*Later, RAIAD*] [*A publication*]
RAID .... River Assault Interdiction Division [*Navy*] (NVT)
RAIDERS .... Remote Automated Issue, Document Entry, and Register System [*Army*]
RAIDEX .... Antisurface Raiders Exercise [*NATO*] (NATG)
RAIDS .... Rapid Acquisition and Identification System
RAIDS .... Rapid Availability of Information and Data for Safety [*NASA*] (KSC)
RAIDS .... Recently Acquired Income Deficiency Syndrome
RAIDS .... Reduced Annual Income Deficiency Syndrome [*British*]
RAIF .... Reseau d'Action et d'Information pour les Femmes [*Canada*]
RAIL .... RailAmerica, Inc. [*NASDAQ symbol*] (SAG)
RAIL .... Railroad Advancement through Information and Law Foundation
RAIL .... Railway (ROG)
RAIL .... Runway Alignment Indicator Light [*or Lighting*] [*Aviation*]
RailAm .... RailAmerica, Inc. [*Associated Press*] (SAG)
Rail & Can Cas ... English Railway and Canal Cases [*A publication*] (DLA)
Rail & Can Cas ... Railway and Canal Traffic Cases [*A publication*] (DLA)
Rail Ca .... Railway and Canal Cases [*1835-54*] [*A publication*] (DLA)
Rail Cas .... Railway Cases [*A publication*] (DLA)
RailFn .... Railroad Financial Corp. [*Associated Press*] (SAG)
RAILS .... Remote Area Instrument Landing Sensor [*Army*]
RAILS .... Remote Area Instrument Landing System [*Army*]
RAILS .... Report of Assets in Long Supply
RAILS .... Runway Alignment Indicator Light [*or Lighting*] System [*Aviation*] (MCD)
Railtex .... Railtex, Inc. [*Associated Press*] (SAG)
Railway & Corp Law J ... Railway and Corporation Law Journal [*A publication*] (DLA)
Railw Cas .... Railway Cases [*A publication*] (DLA)
RAILZ .... RailAmerica Inc. Wrrt 'B' [*NASDAQ symbol*] (TTSB)
RAIM .... Receiver Autonomous Integrity Monitoring [*Computer software*]
RAIN .... Rainforest Cafe [*NASDAQ symbol*] (TTSB)
RAIN .... Rainforest Cafe, Inc. [*NASDAQ symbol*] (SAG)
RAIN .... Relational Algebraic Interpreter
RAIN .... Relief for Africans in Need (EA)
RAIN .... Reversing Acidification in Norway
RAIN .... Royal Anthropological Institute News [*Later, Anthropology Today*] [*A publication*]
RAINBO .... Research and Instrumentation for National Bio-Science Operations (MUGU)
RainCfe .... Rainforest Cafe, Inc. [*Associated Press*] (SAG)
RAINDX .... Random Acess Index Edit [*Computer science*] (IAA)
RAINIT .... Random Access Initializer [*Computer science*] (IAA)
RAINPAL .... Recursive Aided Inertial Navigation for Precision Approach and Landing [*NASA*]
RAINS .... Regional Acidification Information and Simulation [*International Institute for Applied Systems Analysis*]
RainTc .... Rainbow Technologies, Inc. [*Associated Press*] (SAG)
RAI/OP .... Repetitive Activity Input/Output Plan (PDAA)
RAIP .... Recruiting Advertising Improvement Program [*Navy*] (DNAB)
RAIP .... Requester's Approval in Principle (NRCH)
RAIR .... Ram-Augmented Interstellar Rocket (WDAA)
RAIR .... Random Access Information Retrieval [*Computer science*] (IEEE)
RAIR .... Rapid Advancement in Reading [*Education*]
RAIR .... Recordak Automated Information Retrieval [*System*]
RAIR .... Reflection Absorption Infrared Spectroscopy [*Also, IRAS, IRRAS, RAIRS, RAIS*]
RAIR .... Remote-Access Immediate Response [*Computer science*] (MHDB)
RAIRE .... Recognition Awards for the Integration of Research and Education [*National Science Foundation*]
RAIRS .... Railroad Accident/Incident Reporting System [*Department of Transportation*]
RAIRS .... Reflection Absorption Infrared Spectroscopy [*Also, IRAS, IRRAS, RAIR, RAIS*]
RAIS .... Rail Air International Service (PDAA)
RAIS .... Range Automated Information System (KSC)
RAIS .... Reflection Absorption Infrared Spectroscopy [*Also, IRAS, IRRAS, RAIR, RAIRS*]
RAISE .... Reliability Accelerated In-Service Echelon (MCD)
RAISE .... Rigorous Approach to Industrial Software Engineering [*British*]
RAIST .... Reseau Africain d'Institutions Scientifiques et Technologiques [*African Network of Scientific and Technological Institutions*] (EAIO)
RAIT .... Radioimmunotherapy [*Medicine*]
RAIT .... Reading Attitude Imagination Technique (EDAC)
Raith St .... Raithby's English Statutes at Large [*A publication*] (DLA)
Raith St .... Raithby's Study of the Law [*A publication*] (DLA)
RAI-TV .... Radio Audizioni Italiana-Televisione [*Italian Radio Broadcasting and Television Company*]
RAIU .... Radioiodide Uptake [*Endocrinology*]
RAIX .... Rosenbalm Aviation [*Air carrier designation symbol*]
Raj .... All India Reporter, Rajasthan [*A publication*] (DLA)
Raj .... Rajaratam Revised Reports [*Ceylon*] [*A publication*] (DLA)
raj .... Rajasthani [*MARC language code Library of Congress*] (LCCP)
RAJ .... Raji Airlines [*Pakistan*] [*ICAO designator*] (FAAC)
RAJ .... Rajkot [*India*] [*Airport symbol*] (OAG)
Rajasthan .... Indian Law Reports, Rajasthan Series [*A publication*] (DLA)
RAJFC .... Rex Allen, Jr. Fan Club (EA)
RAJPO .... Range Applications Joint Program Office
RAK .... Marrakech [*Morocco*] [*Airport symbol*] (OAG)
RAK .... Rakhov [*Former USSR Seismograph station code, US Geological Survey Closed*] (SEIS)
RAK .... Read Access Key
RAK .... Remote Access Key
RAK .... Riga Airclub (Latvian Professional Air Sport Center) [*FAA designator*] (FAAC)
RAKE .... Rocket Assisted Kinetic Energy [*Army*] (DOMA)
RAKO .... Rawson-Koenig [*NASDAQ symbol*] (TTSB)
RAKO .... Rawson-Koenig, Inc. [*NASDAQ symbol*] (NQ)
RAKTP .... Royal Arch Knight Templar Priest [*Freemasonry*]
RAL .... Rabalanakaia [*New Britain*] [*Seismograph station code, US Geological Survey*] (SEIS)
RAL .... Radio Annoyance Level (OA)
RAL .... Radio Astronomy Laboratory [*Research center*] (RCD)
RAL .... Ralston-Purina Group [*NYSE symbol*] (SPSG)
RAL .... Rapid Access Loop
RAL .... Rear-Admiral, Alexandria [*British*]
RAL .... Reenlistment Allowance [*Military*]
RAL .... Regional Adjunct Language [*Computer science*] (PDAA)
RAL .... Register of Additional Locations [*Library of Congress*]
RAL .... Remote Area Landing (NG)
RAL .... Reports and Analysis Letter (OICC)
RAL .... Required Average Life (MCD)
RAL .... Resorcylic Acid Lactone [*Veterinary pharmacology*]
RAL .... Responsibility Assignment List [*NASA*] (NASA)
RAL .... Reynold's Aluminum Co. of Canada Ltd. [*Toronto Stock Exchange symbol*]
RAL .... Riverband Acoustical Laboratory (KSC)
RAL .... Riverside [*California*] [*Airport symbol*] (OAG)
RAL .... Riverside, CA [*Location identifier FAA*] (FAAL)
RAL .... Robotics & Automation Research Laboratory [*University of Toronto*] [*Research center*] (RCD)
RAL .... Roswell Airlines, Inc. [*ICAO designator*] (FAAC)
RAL .... Rubber-Air-Lead [*Tile*]
RAL .... Rutherford and Appleton Laboratory [*Observatory*] [*British*]
RALAC .... RADAR Altimeter Low-Altitude Control [*Military*] (CAAL)
RALAC .... Refuse and Litter Advisory Committee [*Australia*]
RALAC .... Rehabilitation Artificial Limb, and Appliance Centre [*Australia*]
RALACS .... RADAR Altimeter Low-Altitude Control System [*Military*] (NG)
RALA-EHF .... Roycrofters-at-Large Association/Elbert Hubbard Foundation (EA)
Ralcorp .... Ralcorp Holdings [*Associated Press*] (SAG)
RALD .... Richmond Area Library Directors [*Library network*]
RALF .... Rapid Access to Literature Via Fragmentation Codes (NITA)
RALF .... Relocatable Assembly Language Floating Point
RALF .... Robotic Assistant Labor Facilitator [*In the movie "Flight of the Navigator" (1986)*]
RALFH .... Random Access Logical File Handler (MCD)
RALI .... Regimento de Artilharia Ligeira [*Light Artillery Regiment*] [*Portuguese*]
RALI .... Remarried Association of Long Island (EA)
RALI .... Resource and Land Investigation [*Program*] [*Department of the Interior*] (GRD)
RALL .... Rallentando [*Gradually Slower*] [*Music*]
RALLA .... Regional Allied Long-Lines Agency [*Formerly, RELLA*] (NATG)
RALLEN .... Rallentando [*Gradually Slower*] [*Music*] (ROG)
RALLO .... Rallentando [*Gradually Slower*] [*Music*] (ROG)
RALLOC .... Random Access Allocation [*Computer science*] (IAA)
Rallys .... Rally's, Inc. [*Associated Press*] (SAG)
RALMC .... Remote Aboriginal Language Management Committee [*Australia*]
RALPH .... Rapidly Adapting Lateral Position Handler
RALPH .... Reduction and Acquisition of Lunar Pulse Heights [*NASA*] (NASA)
RALPH .... Royal Association for the Longevity and Preservation of the Honeymooners (EA)
RALS .... Remote Augmented Lift System (MCD)
RALS .... Right Add, Left Subtract [*Army field artillery technique*] (INF)
RALS .... Robotic Ammunition Landing System
RALSA .... Restraint and Life Support Assembly (MCD)
RalsRP .... Ralston Ralston Purina Group [*Associated Press*] (SAG)
RALT .... RADAR Altimeter [*Aviation*] (NASA)
RALT .... Radio Altitude (IAA)
RALT .... Range Light (AAG)
RALT .... Ranging Airborne LASER Tracker (MCD)

RALT............ Reported Altitude (IAA)
RALT............ Routine Admission Laboratory Tests [*Medicine*]
RALU............ Register and Arithmetic/Logic Unit [*Computer science*]
RALU............ Rotary Analog Logic Unit (MCD)
RALV............ Random Access Light Valve
RaLV............ Rasheed (Rat) Leukemia Virus
RALW............ Radioactive Liquid Waste (IEEE)
Ralw & Corp LJ... Railway and Corporation Law Journal [*A publication*] (DLA)
RAM............ Rabbit Alveolar Macrophage [*Clinical chemistry*]
RAM............ Rabbit Antimouse [*Hematology*]
RAM............ RADAR-Absorbent Material [*Aviation*]
RAM............ RADAR-Absorbing Material
RAM............ Radiation Attenuation Measurement (CET)
RAM............ Radioactive Material
RAM............ Radio Attenuation Measurement [*Spacecraft for testing communications*]
RAM............ Radio Audience Measurement (NTCM)
RAM............ RAID Assessment Mode (MCD)
RAM............ Raman [*Turkey*] [*Seismograph station code, US Geological Survey*] (SEIS)
Ram............ Ramanathan's Reports [*Ceylon*] [*A publication*] (DLA)
RAM............ Ramcor Resources, Inc. [*Vancouver Stock Exchange symbol*]
RAM............ Ramenskoye [*US prefix for Soviet-Russian developmental aircraft flown at the Ramenskoye test facility*] (DOMA)
RAM............ Ramingining [*Australia Airport symbol*] (OAG)
Ram............ Ramsey's Quebec Appeal Cases [*A publication*] (DLA)
RAM............ Random Access Measurement [*System*] [*Computer science*]
RAM............ Random Access Memory [*Computer science*]
RAM............ Random Access Method [*Computer science*] (WDAA)
RAM............ Random Angle Modulation
RAM............ Range-Altitude Monitor
RAM............ Range Assessment Mode (MCD)
RAM............ Rapid Alternating Movement
RAM............ Rapid Amortization Mortgage
RAM............ Rapid Area Maintenance [*Air Force*]
RAM............ Raytheon Airborne Microwave (MCD)
RAM............ Readiness and Money (DNAB)
RAM............ Recent Advances in Manufacturing [*Information service or system*] (IID)
RAM............ Reconnaissance Air Meet (DOMA)
RAM............ Recovery Aids Material (MUGU)
RAM............ Red Artillery Model [*Military*]
RAM............ Redeye Air Missile [*System*] (RDA)
RAM............ Reentry Antimissile
RAM............ Reentry Attenuation Measurement [*NASA*]
RAM............ Reflection Anisotropy Microscopy
RAM............ Reflection Anisotropy Microscopy
RAM............ Reform the Armed Forces Movement [*Philippines*]
RAM............ Regional Audit Manager
RAM............ Registered Apartment Manager [*National Association of Home Builders*] [*Designation awarded by*]
RAM............ Regular Army and Militia [*British*]
RAM............ Relaxing Avalanche Mode (IAA)
RAM............ Releasable Asset Program [*Military*] (AFIT)
RAM............ Reliability and Maintainability (IAA)
RAM............ Reliability Assessment for Management
RAM............ Reliability, Availability, and Maintainability [*Army*]
RAM............ Religions, Ancient and Modern [*A publication*]
RAM............ Remote Access Monitor (MCD)
RAM............ Remote Area Monitoring (KSC)
RAM............ Repair and Maintenance (IAA)
RAM............ Repeater Amplitude Modulation (MCD)
RAM............ Repeating Antipersonnel Mine
RAM............ Research and Applications Module [*NASA*]
RAM............ Research Aviation Medicine [*Navy program of research into aerospace medical techniques*]
RAM............ Reserve Adjustment Magnitude
RAM............ Resident Access Methods (MCD)
RAM............ Resident Aerospace Medicine [*Physician in specialty training*] [*Military*]
RAM............ Resources Analysis and Management
RAM............ Responsibility Assignment Matrix [*NASA*] (NASA)
RAM............ Restricted Access Memory [*Computer science*] (MCD)
RAM............ Reverse Annuity Mortgage
RAM............ Revolutionary Action Movement
RAM............ Right Ascension of the Meridian [*Navigation*]
RAM............ Rocket and Missile System [*Army*]
RAM............ Rocket Assisted Motor (WDAA)
RAM............ Rolling Airframe Missile
RAM............ Royal Academy of Music [*British*]
RAM............ Royal Air Maroc [*Morocco*]
RAM............ Royal Air Maroc - Compagnie Nationale de Transports Aeriens [*Morocco*] [*ICAO designator*] (FAAC)
RAM............ Royal Appliance Manufacturing [*NYSE symbol*] (SPSG)
RAM............ Royal Appliance Mfg [*NYSE symbol*] (TTSB)
RAM............ Royal Arch Mason [*Freemasonry*]
RAM............ Royal Ark Mariners
RAMA.......... Railway Automotive Management Association [*Defunct*] (EA)
RAMA.......... Reactor Accident Mitigation Project [*Nuclear energy*] (NUCP)
RAMA.......... Recap and Movement Authorization [*NASA*] (NASA)
RAMA.......... Region of Assured Mission Abort [*Military*] (CAAL)
RAMA.......... Rome Air Materiel Area [*Deactivated*] [*Air Force*]
RAMAB........ Ready Afloat Marine Amphibious Brigade (CINC)
RAMAC........ Random Access Memory Accounting Computer [*Computer science*] (IAA)
RAMAC........ Random Access Method of Accounting and Control [*Computer science*]
RAMAC........ Random Access Method of Accounting and Control (NITA)
Ramachandrier A... Ramachandrier's Cases on Adoption [*1892*] [*India*] [*A publication*] (DLA)
Ramachandrier DG... Ramachandrier's Cases on Dancing Girls [*1892*] [*India*] [*A publication*] (DLA)
Ramachandrier HML... Ramachandrier's Cases on Hindu Marriage Law [*1891*] [*India*] [*A publication*] (DLA)
RAMADCS.... Reliability, Availability, and Maintainability Automated Data Collection System [*Army*]
RAMAIDB..... RAM [*Radioactive Materials*] Accident/Incident Database [*Nuclear energy*]
RAMAN........ Regional Atmosphere Measurement and Analysis Network [*Marine science*] (OSRA)
RAMAN........ Regional Atmospheric Measurement and Analysis Network (USDC)
Ram & Mor... Ramsey and Morin's Montreal Law Reporter [*A publication*] (DLA)
RAMARK...... RADAR Marker [*Military*]
Ram Ass...... Ram on Assets, Debts, and Incumbrances [*2nd ed.*] [*1837*] [*A publication*] (DLA)
RAMAZ........ Rabbi Moses Zacuto (BJA)
RAMB.......... Rabbit Anti-Mouse Brain (PDAA)
RAMB.......... Random Access Memory Buffer [*Computer science*]
RaM-BaM.... Rabbi Moses ben Maimon [*Maimonides*] [*Jewish philosopher, 1135-1204*]
RAMBAN...... Rabbi Moses ben Nahman [*Spanish Talmudist, 1195-1270*] (BJA)
RAMBO........ Real-Time Acquisitions Management and Bibliographic Order System [*Suggested name for the Library of Congress computer system*]
RAMBO........ Remove Aquino from Malacanang before October [*Operation proposed by rebel military leader "Gringo" Honasan*] [*1987 Philippines*]
RAMBO........ Restore a More Benevolent Order Coalition [*Later, NCAN*] (EA)
RAMC.......... Resource Allocation and Mine Costing Model [*Department of Energy*] (GFGA)
RAMC.......... Royal Army Medical College [*British*] (MCD)
RAMC.......... Royal Army Medical Corps [*Initialism also facetiously translated during World War I as "Rats after Moldy Cheese," "Rob All My Comrades," or "Run Away, Matron's Coming"*] [*British*]
Ram Cas P & E... Ram's Cases of Pleading and Evidence [*A publication*] (DLA)
RAMCEASE... Reliability, Availability, Maintainability, Cost Effectiveness and Systems Effectiveness (MHDB)
RamcoG....... Ramco Gershenson Properties Trust [*Associated Press*] (SAG)
RAMCT........ Royal Army Medical Corps, Territorials [*British*] (ROG)
RAMD.......... Random Access Memory Device [*Computer science*]
RAMD.......... Receiving Agency Materiel Division [*Military*]
RAMD.......... Reliability, Availability, and Maintainability Demonstration
RAM-D......... Reliability, Availability, Maintainability, and Durability [*Army*] (AABC)
RAMDAC...... Random Access Memory Digital to Analog Converter [*Computer science*] (CDE)
RAMEC........ Rapid Action Maintenance Engineering Change [*Navy*] (MCD)
RAMEC........ Rapid Action Minor Engineering Change
RAMECES.... Reliability, Availability, Maintainability, Enhancement of Communications-Elect ronic Systems (AAGC)
Ram F.......... Ram on Facts [*A publication*] (DLA)
RAMFAS...... Reliability Analysis of Microcircuit Failure in Avionic Systems (MCD)
RamFin......... Ramapo Financial Corp. [*Associated Press*] (SAG)
RAMHR........ Risk-Adjusted Multiple Hurdle Rates (ADA)
RAMIG......... Rabbit Antimouse Immunoglobulin G [*Immunology*]
RAMIO......... RAM Plus Input/Output (NITA)
RAMIS......... Rapid Access Management Information System [*Computer science*]
RAMIS......... Rapid Automatic Malfunction Isolation System
RAMIS......... Receive, Assemble, Maintain, Inspect, and Store (IAA)
RAMIS......... Receiving, Assembly Maintenance, Inspection, Storage [*Military*]
RAMIS......... Repair, Assemble, Maintain, Issue, and Supply (MUGU)
RAMIT......... Rate-Aided Manually Implemented Tracking (NATG)
Ram Leg J... Ram's Science of Legal Judgment [*2nd ed.*] [*1834*] [*A publication*] (DLA)
Ram Leg Judgm (Towns Ed)... Ram's Science of Legal Judgment, Notes by Townshend [*A publication*] (DLA)
RAM/LOG..... Reliability, Availability, Maintainability, and Logistics (MCD)
RAMM.......... Random Access Memory Module [*Computer science*]
RAMM.......... Random Access Metal-Oxide-Semiconductor Memory [*Computer science*] (IAA)
RAMM.......... Recording Ammeter (MSA)
RAMM.......... Regional and Mesoscale Meteorology [*Branch*] [*National Environmental Satellite, Data, and Information Service*] (USDC)
RAMM.......... Regional and Mesoscale Meteorology [*Branch*] [*Marine science*] (OSRA)
RAMMIT...... Reliability and Maintainability Management Improvement Techniques [*Army*]
RAMMIT...... Reliability, Availability, and Maintenance Management Improvements Technique
RAMMS....... Responsive Automated Materiel Management System [*Army*] (AABC)
RAMNAC..... Radio Aids to Marine Navigation Committee [*British*]
RAMOGE...... Regional Pollution Studies in the Ligurian Sea [*Marine science*] (MSC)
RAMONT...... Radiological Monitoring
RAMOS........ Reading and Mathematics Observation System (EDAC)
RAMOS........ Remote Automatic Meteorological Observing Station
RAMP.......... RADAR Mapping of Panama
RAMP.......... RADAR Masking Parameter (IAA)
RAMP.......... RADAR Modification Program (NG)
RAMP.......... Radiation Airborne Measurement Program
RAMP.......... Radio Attenuation Measurement Project
RAMP.......... Raising Achievements in Mathematics Project (AIE)

RAMP .... Ramp [*Postal Service standard*] (OPSA)
RAMP .... Random Access Mechanization of Phosphorus
RAMP .... Rapid Acquisition of Manufactured Parts [*Military*]
RAMP .... Rate and Acceleration Measuring Pendulum (PDAA)
RAMP .... Raytheon Airborne Microwave Platform [*Sky station*]
RAMP .... Records and Archives Management Programme [*UNESCO*]
RAMP .... Recovered Allied Military Personnel
RAMP .... Regional Administrative Management Plan [*Department of Labor*]
RAMP .... Reliability and Maintainability Program
RAMP .... Reliability, Availability, Maintainability Program [*Army*] (IAA)
RAMP .... Remote Access Maintenance Protocol [*Telecommunications*]
RAMP .... Research Association of Minority Professors (EA)
RAMP .... Reserve Associate Manning Program [*Military*]
RAMP .... Resource Allocation and Management Program (EDAC)
RAMP .... Review of Army Mobilization Planning (MCD)
R/AMP .... Rifampin [*Also, RF, RIF, RMP*] [*Bactericide*]
RAMP .... Ring Airfoil Munition Projectile [*Army*]
RAMP .... Rural Abandoned Mine Program [*Department of Agriculture*]
RAMPAC ...... Radioactive Materials Packaging [*Nuclear energy*]
RAMPART .... RADAR Advanced Measurements Program for Analysis of Reentry Techniques [*ARPA - Raytheon*]
RAMPART .... Route to Airlift Mobility through Partnership (MCD)
RAMPI .... Raw Material Price Index (NITA)
RAMPLAN .... Rock Mechanics Applied to Mine Planning (PDAA)
RAMPS .... Rapid Message Preparation System (NATG)
RaMPS .... Rapid Multiple Peptide System [*Biotechnology*]
RAMPS .... Repatriated American Military Personnel [*World War II*]
RAMPS .... Resources Allocation and Multiproject Scheduling
Ram Rep ..... Ramanathan's Supreme Court Reports [*Ceylon*] [*A publication*] (ILCA)
RAMS .... RADAR Target Scattering Advanced Measurement System
RAMS .... Radio Amateur Megacycle Society (IAA)
RAMS .... Random Access Measurement System [*Computer science*]
RAMS .... Random Access Memorix Storage [*Computer science*] (IAA)
RAMS .... Random Access Memory Store [*Computer science*] (TEL)
RAMS .... Rapid Munitions Assembly System (DWSG)
RAMS .... Rascal Avionics Management System (MCD)
RAMS .... Record Archival Management System (HGAA)
RAMS .... Recovery and Modification Services (MCD)
RAMS .... Recruiting Advertising Management System [*Navy*] (DNAB)
RAMS .... Reduced-Size Antenna Monopulse System
RAMS .... Regional Air Monitoring Station [*or System*] [*Environmental Protection Agency*]
RAMS .... Regional Atmospheric Modeling System (USDC)
RAMS .... Regional Atmospheric Modeling System
RAMS .... Regional Atmospheric Modeling System [*Marine science*] (OSRA)
RAMS .... Registered Australian Mortgage Securities Trust
RAMS .... Regulatory Activities Manpower System [*Nuclear energy*] (NRCH)
RAMS .... Reliability and Maintainability Studies [*Army*] (RDA)
RAM-S .... Reliability, Availability, Maintainability - Supportability (MCD)
RAMS .... Remote Area Mobility Study (MCD)
RAMS .... Remote Automatic Multipurpose Station
RAMS .... Remotely Accessible Management Systems [*Computer science*]
RAMS .... Repairables Asset Management System [*Military*] (CAAL)
RAMS .... Repair, Assembly, and Maintenance Shop (IAA)
RAMS .... Requirements Analysis Material Sheet [*or Study*] (MCD)
RAMS .... Right Ascension Mean Sun [*Navigation*]
RAMS .... Rocket and Missile System [*Army*]
RAMSA .... Radio Aeronautica Mexicana, Sociedad Anonima
Rams App .... Ramsey's Quebec Appeal Cases [*1873-86*] [*A publication*] (DLA)
Ramsay .... Ramsey Health Care, Inc. [*Associated Press*] (SAG)
Ramsay App Cas... Ramsay's Appeal Cases [*Canada*] [*A publication*] (DLA)
Ramsay App Cas (Can)... Ramsay's Appeal Cases [*Canada*] [*A publication*] (DLA)
Ram SC .... Ramanathan's Supreme Court Reports [*Ceylon*] [*A publication*] (DLA)
RAMSES ...... Reprogrammable Advanced Multimode Shipborne ECM System [*Canadian Navy*]
RAMSH .... Reliability, Availability, Maintainability, Safety, and Human Factors [*Telecommunications*] (TEL)
RAMSIM ...... Reliability, Availability, Maintenance, Simulation [*Navy*] (DNAB)
RAMSS .... Royal Alfred Merchant Seamen's Society [*British*]
RAMT .... Rabbit Antimouse Thymocyte [*Immunology*]
RAMT .... Rudder Angle Master Transmitter
RAMTAC ...... Reentry Analysis and Modeling of Target Characteristics
RAMTIP ...... Reliability and Maintainability Technology Insertion Program [*DoD*]
RAMTRA ...... Reserve Air Maintenance Training (DNAB)
Ramtrn .... Ramtron International Corp. [*Associated Press*] (SAG)
Ramtron ...... Ramtron International Corp. [*Associated Press*] (SAG)
RAMUS .... Remote Access Multi-User System (DNAB)
RAMV .... Radish Mosaic Virus [*Plant pathology*]
RAMVAN ...... Reconnaissance Aircraft Maintenance Van
Ram W .... Ram on Exposition of Wills of Landed Property [*1827*] [*A publication*] (DLA)
RAN .... Defence Products Ltd. [*British ICAO designator*] (FAAC)
RAN .... RADAR Navigation (DNAB)
RAN .... Railway Abidjan-Niger
RAN .... Rainforest Action Network (EA)
Ran .... Ranae [*Frogs*] [*of Aristophanes*] [*Classical studies*] (OCD)
RAN .... Random (DNAB)
RAN .... Rangoon [*Burma*] [*Seismograph station code, US Geological Survey Closed*] (SEIS)
RAN .... Ranitidine [*An antiulcer drug*]
RAN .... Read around Number
RAN .... Reconnaissance/Attack Navigator
RAN .... Regional Air Navigation [*ICAO*]
RAN .... Remote Area Nurse
RAN .... Renan Ltd. [*Moldova*] [*FAA designator*] (FAAC)
RAN .... Repair Activity Accounting Number [*Navy*]
RAN .... Reporting Accounting Number (NG)
RAN .... Request for Authority to Negotiate
RAN .... Requirement Action Number
RAN .... Requisition Account Number
RAN .... Resident's Admission Notes [*Medical records*] (DAVI)
RAN .... Resource-Adjacent Nation [*Ocean fishery management*]
RAN .... Revenue Anticipation Note
RAN .... Royal Australian Navy (VNW)
RAN .... Royal Australian Navy (DOMA)
RANA .... Rheumatoid Arthritis Nuclear Antigen [*Immunology*]
RANA .... Rhodesia & Nyasaland Airways
RANAS .... Rear-Admiral, Naval Air Stations [*British military*] (DMA)
RANC .... RADAR Absorption Noise and Clutter (NASA)
RANCA .... Retired Army Nurse Corps Association (EA)
RANCH .... Ranch [*Commonly used*] (OPSA)
RANCHES .... Ranch [*Commonly used*] (OPSA)
RANCID .... Real and Not Corrected Input Data [*Computer science*]
RANCIN .... Retrieval and Analysis of Navy Classified Information (DNAB)
RANCOM ..... Random Communication Satellite
Rand .... Randall's Reports [*62-71 Ohio State*] [*A publication*] (DLA)
RAND .... Rand Cap [*NASDAQ symbol*] (TTSB)
RAND .... Rand Capital Corp. [*NASDAQ symbol*] (NQ)
Rand .... Randolph's Reports [*22-27 Virginia*] [*1821-28*] [*A publication*] (DLA)
Rand .... Randolph's Reports [*7-11 Louisiana*] [*A publication*] (DLA)
Rand .... Randolph's Reports [*21-56 Kansas*] [*A publication*] (DLA)
RAND .... Random [*Sample or Specimen*] (DAVI)
RAND .... Research and Development (IAA)
RAND .... Research and No Development [*Origin of name of RAND Corporation, a nonprofit national defense research organization*]
R & A .... Rates and Allotments [*Eight-Sheet Outdoor Advertising Association*] [*A publication*]
R & A .... Reliability and Availability
R & A .... Reports and Analysis
R & A .... Rescue and Assistance
R & A .... Research and Analysis
R & A .... Responsibility and Action
R & A .... Review and Analysis
R & A .... Review and Approval
R & A .... Royal and Ancient Golf Club of St. Andrews [*Recognized as the game's legislative authority in all countries except the US*] [*British*]
R & A .... Rules and Administration Committee [*US Senate*]
R & AC .... RADAR and Air Communications
R & AD .... Research and Advanced Development
RANDAM ...... Random Access Nondestructive Advanced Memory [*Computer science*]
RANDANAL... Randomization Analyser (IAA)
Rand & Fur Poi... Rand and Furness on Poisons [*A publication*] (DLA)
Rand Ann ..... Randolph Annual [*A publication*] (DLA)
R & AT .... Research and Advanced Technology
R & B .... Red and Blue (KSC)
R & B .... Remington and Ballinger's Code [*1910*] [*A publication*] (DLA)
R & B .... Rhythm and Blues [*Music*]
R & B .... Right and Below (MEDA)
R & B .... Right and Below (DAVI)
R & B .... Room and Board
R & B Inc ..... R & B, Inc. [*Associated Press*] (SAG)
R & B Supp... Remington and Ballinger's Code, Supplement [*1913*] [*A publication*] (DLA)
R & C .... Rail and Canal
R & C .... Reasonable and Customary [*Refers to medical charges*] [*Insurance*]
R & C .... Records and Control
R & C .... Reed and Carnrick [*Commercial firm*] (DAVI)
R & C .... Requirements and Configuration
R & C .... Rest and Convalescence (ADA)
R & C .... Review and Comment [*Aerospace*]
R & C .... Rod and Custom [*A publication*]
R & C .... Russell and Chesley's Nova Scotia Equity Reports [*A publication*] (DLA)
R & C .... Russell and Chesley's Nova Scotia Reports [*A publication*] (DLA)
RandCa .... Rand Capital Corp. [*Associated Press*] (SAG)
R & Can Cas... Railway and Canal Cases [*England*] [*A publication*] (DLA)
R & Can Tr... Railway and Canal Traffic Cases [*England*] [*A publication*] (DLA)
R & Can Tr Cas... Railway and Canal Traffic Cases [*England*] [*A publication*] (DLA)
R & CC .... Railway and Canal Cases [*1835-54*] [*A publication*] (DLA)
R & CC .... Recorder and Communications Control (NASA)
R & CC .... Riot and Civil Commotion
R & C Ca ..... Railway and Canal Cases [*England*] [*A publication*] (DLA)
R & C Cas ... Railway and Canal Cases [*England*] [*A publication*] (DLA)
R & C N Sc... Russell and Chesley's Nova Scotia Reports [*A publication*] (DLA)
Rand Com Paper... Randolph on Commercial Paper [*A publication*] (DLA)
R & CS .... Radiological and Chemical Support [*Nuclear energy*] (NRCH)
R & C Tr Cas... Railway and Canal Traffic Cases (Neville) [*England*] [*A publication*] (DLA)
R & D .... Read and Destroy
R & D .... Requirements and Distribution (AFM)
R & D .... Research and Demonstration [*Labor training*]
R & D .... Research and Development
R&D .... Research and Development (IDOE)
R&D .... Research and Development (DFIT)

R & DA........ Research and Development Associates for Military Food and Packaging Systems (EA)

R & DCTE.... Research and Development Center for Teacher Education [Department of Education] (GRD)

R & DELSEC... Research and Development Electronic Security [Military] (AABC)

R & DNET.... Research and Development Network [Formerly, ARPANET]

R & DO......... Research and Development Operations [Marshall Space Flight Center] [NASA] (NASA)

R & DPP...... Research and Development Program Planning [Database] [DTIC]

R & DSoc.... Research and Development Society [British] (DBA)

R & E........... Research and Education (MAE)

R&E............ Research and Education Community

R & E........... Research and Engineering

R & E........... Restructuring and Efficiency

R & EA........ Readiness and Emergency Action [Red Cross Disaster Services]

R&EC........... Research and Engineering Council (NADA)

Rand Em Dom... Randolph on Eminent Domain [A publication] (DLA)

Rander......... Randers Group, Inc. [Associated Press] (SAG)

R & EW........ Rest and Exercise (DAVI)

R & F........... Rank and File

R & F........... Reach and Frequency [Advertising] (WDMC)

R & G........... Russell and Geldert's Nova Scotia Reports [A publication] (DLA)

R & G N Sc... Russell and Geldert's Nova Scotia Reports [A publication] (DLA)

R & H Bank... Roche and Hazlitt's Bankruptcy Practice [2nd ed.] [1873] [A publication] (DLA)

R & H Dig... Robinson and Harrison's Digest [Ontario] [A publication] (DLA)

R & I........... Radical and Intense [Extremely great] [Slang]

R & I........... Receiving and Inspection (KSC)

R & I........... Removal and Installation (NRCH)

R & IBWA.... Rural and Industries Bank of Western Australia

RANDID....... Rapid Alphanumeric Digital Indicating Device

RANDIS....... Random Disc File [Computer science] (IAA)

R & IT......... Rating and Income Tax Reports [England] [A publication] (DLA)

R & J........... Rabkin and Johnson's Federal, Income, Gift, and Estate Taxation [A publication] (DLA)

R & J........... Rafique and Jackson's Privy Council Decisions [India] [A publication] (DLA)

R & J........... Romeo and Juliet [Shakespearean work]

R & J Dig.... Robinson and Joseph's Digest [Ontario] [A publication] (DLA)

R & L........... Bureau for Reference and Loan Services [Library network]

R & L........... Rail and Lake

R & LH......... Right and Left Hands [Work-factor system]

R & LL & T... Redman and Lyon on Landlord and Tenant [8th ed.] [1924] [A publication] (DLA)

R & LO......... Reliability and Launch Operations (MCD)

R & M.......... Law Reporter, Montreal [Canada] [A publication] (DLA)

R & M.......... Redistribution and Marketing (AFM)

R & M.......... Refurbishment and Modification

R & M.......... Release and Material (MCD)

R & M.......... Reliability and Maintainability [Navy]

R & M.......... Reliability and Marketing (WDAA)

R & M.......... Repairs and Maintenance

R & M.......... Reports and Memorandum (MCD)

R & M.......... Routine and Microscopic (DAVI)

R & M.......... Russell and Mylne's English Chancery Reports [A publication] (DLA)

R & M.......... Ryan and Moody's English Nisi Prius Reports [A publication] (DLA)

R & M/2....... Averaged [Motor Octane Number] [Antiknock index Fuel technology]

R & MCC...... Ryan and Moody's English Crown Cases Reserved [A publication] (DLA)

R & MNP...... Ryan and Moody's English Nisi Prius Reports [A publication] (DLA)

R & My........ Russell and Mylne's English Chancery Reports [A publication] (DLA)

R & N.......... Rhodesia and Nyasaland Law Reports [1956] [A publication] (DLA)

R & NLR...... Rhodesia and Nyasaland Law Reports [1956-64] [A publication] (DLA)

RANDO........ Radiotherapy Analog Dosimetry

R & O.......... Rail and Ocean

R & O.......... Requirements and Objectives

RANDOLS.... Random Domain Library Screening [Genetic laboratory technique]

R & P.......... Recruitment and Placement (MCD)

R & P.......... Reserve and Process (NASA)

R & P.......... Ring and Pinion [Automotive engineering]

R & P.......... Rules and Procedures (MSA)

Rand Peak... Randall's Edition of Peake on Evidence [A publication] (DLA)

Rand Perp... Randall on Perpetuities [A publication] (DLA)

R & PI......... Rubber and Plastics Industry (MCD)

R & PM........ Resources and Program Management [NASA]

R & PP........ Recreation and Public Purposes Act

R & P SEC... Radio and Panel Section [Navy]

R & PT......... Rifle and Pistol Team [Navy]

R & QA........ Reliability and Quality Assurance

R & R.......... Rate and Rhythm [of pulse]

R & R.......... Records and Reports

R & R.......... Refueling and Rearming [Air Force]

R & R.......... Regurgitate and Reingest [Animal behavior]

R & R.......... Reinstatement and Replacement (ADA)

R & R.......... Remove and Replace (KSC)

R & R.......... Rendezvous and Recovery (NASA)

R & R.......... Repair and Return

R & R.......... Reporting and Requisitioning [Air Force]

R & R.......... Research and Reporting Committee [Interstate Conference of Employment Security Agencies] (OICC)

R & R.......... Rest and Recreation

R & R.......... Rest and Recuperation [Military]

R & R.......... Rest and Rehabilitation [Marine Corps]

R & R.......... Rich & Rare Canadian Whisky [Gooderham's]

R & R.......... Rock and Roll [Music]

R & R.......... Rock and Rye

R & R.......... Routing and Record Sheet [Air Force]

R & R.......... Russell and Ryan's English Crown Cases [A publication] (DLA)

R & RA........ Retraining and Reemployment Administration [Terminated, 1947]

R&R Bk N.... Reference & Research Book News [A publication] (BRI)

R & RC........ Reactors and Reactor Control (MCD)

R & RCC...... Russell and Ryan's English Crown Cases Reserved [A publication] (DLA)

R & RE........ Radiation and Repair Engineering [Nuclear energy] (NRCH)

R & ROTC.... Reserve and Reserve Officers' Training Corps [Army]

R & Ry CC... Russell and Ryan's English Crown Cases [A publication] (DLA)

R & S.......... Raben & Sjogren [Publisher] [Sweden]

R & S.......... Range and Safety (AAG)

R & S.......... Reconnaissance and Security [Military] (INF)

R & S.......... Reconnaissance and Surveillance (MCD)

R & S.......... Reenlistment and Separation [Military] (AFM)

R & S.......... Ren and Stimpy [Cartoon characters]

R & S.......... Renovation and Storage [Military] (AFIT)

R & S.......... Reports and Statistics Branch [US Military Government, Germany]

R & S.......... Research and Statistics (IEEE)

R & S.......... Research and Study

R & S.......... Restraints and Seclusion [Psychiatry] (DAVI)

R & SC........ Replacement and School Command [Military]

R & S SQ..... Repair and Salvage Squadron [Military]

R & T.......... Research and Technology

R & T.......... Rough and Tumble Engineers' Historical Association (EA)

R & T.......... Rush & Tomkins [Commercial firm British]

R & T WUIS... Research and Technology Work Unit Information System [Database] [Defense Technical Information Center] (CRD)

R & TWUS.... Research and Technology Work Unit Summary

R & U.......... Repairs and Upkeep [Military]

R & U.......... Repairs and Utilities [Military]

R & VR........ Rating and Valuation Reporter [A publication]

R & W.......... Rail and Water [Shipping]

R & W.......... Routing and Work [Military]

R & Z.......... Range and Zero [NASA] (KSC)

Rane........... Rainerius de Forlivio [Deceased, 1358] [Authority cited in pre-1607 legal work] (DSA)

Raney......... Raney's Reports [16-20 Florida] [A publication] (DLA)

RANG.......... Rangaire Corp. (MHDW)

RANG.......... Range Group [Military]

RANG.......... Rangoon [City in Burma] (ROG)

Rang Cr LJ... Rangoon Criminal Law Journal [A publication] (DLA)

Rang Dec..... Sparks' Rangoon Decisions [British Burma] [A publication] (DLA)

RANGECO..... Range Company (DNAB)

RangKoM..... [The] Rangkaian Komputer Malaysia [Computer science] (TNIG)

Rang LR...... Rangoon Law Reports [India] [A publication] (DLA)

RangrO........ Ranger Oil Ltd. [Associated Press] (SAG)

RANK........... Rank Group PLC (The) [NASDAQ symbol] (SAG)

RANK........... [The] Rank Organisation Ltd. [NASDAQ symbol] (NQ)

RANK........... Replacement Alpha Numeric Keyboard [Computer science] (DA)

Rank & S Comp L... Ranking and Spicer's Company Law [11th ed.] [1970] [A publication] (DLA)

RankGrp....... Rank Group PLC (The) [Associated Press] (SAG)

RankinA....... Rankin Automotive Group, Inc. [Associated Press] (SAG)

RankOrg....... [The] Rank Organisation PLC [Associated Press] (SAG)

Rank P......... Rankin on Patents [1824] [A publication] (DLA)

Rank S & P Exec... Ranking, Spicer, and Pegler on Executorship [21st ed.] [1971] [A publication] (DLA)

RANKY......... Rank Organisation ADR [NASDAQ symbol] (TTSB)

RANMOG...... Reactivity-Adjusted Non-Methane Organic Gas [Automotive emissions]

RANN........... Research Applied to National Needs [Formerly, IRRPOS] [National Science Foundation Obsolete]

RANOSP...... Radiological North Sea Project [British]

rANP........... Rat Atrial Natriuretic Peptide [Biochemistry]

RANS........... Range Squadron

RANS........... Revenue Anticipation Notes

RANSA......... Rutas Aereas Nacionales Sociedad Anonima [Cargo airline] [Venezuela]

RANSAD....... Random Access Noiselike Signal Address [Telecommunications] (IAA)

RANSW........ Ratepayers' Association of New South Wales [Australia]

RANSW........ Rationalist Association of New South Wales [Australia]

RANT........... Reentry Antenna Test

RANTE......... Royal Australian Navy Training Establishment

RANTES....... Regulated-upon-Activation, Normal T Expressed and Secreted [Immunology]

RANXPE....... Resident Army Nike-X Project Engineer (AABC)

RAO............. National Radio Astronomy Observatory, Charlottesville, VA [OCLC symbol] (OCLC)

RAO............. RADAR Operator

RAO............. Radio Astronomy Observatory [University of Michigan] [Research center]

RAO............. Rado Reef Resources [Vancouver Stock Exchange symbol]

RAO............. Raoul [Raoul Island] [Seismograph station code, US Geological Survey] (SEIS)

RAO............. Regimental Amalgamation Officer [British military] (DMA)

RAO............. Regional Accounting Office [Telecommunications] (TEL)

RAO............. Regional Administrative Office

RAO............. Regional Agricultural Officer [Ministry of Agriculture, Fisheries, and Food] [British]

RAO............. Response Amplitude Operator (PDAA)

RAO............. Retired Affairs Officers (EA)

RAO .... Ribeirao Preto [*Brazil*] [*Airport symbol*] (OAG)
RAO .... Right Anterior Oblique [*Medicine*]
RAO .... Right Anterior Occipital [*Neurology*] (DAVI)
RAO .... Rudder Angle Order (MSA)
RAOA .... Railway Accounting Officers Association [*Later, AAR*]
RAOB .... Radiosonde Observation
RAOB .... Rawindsonde Observation [*Marine science*] (OSRA)
RAOB .... Royal Antediluvian Order of Buffaloes
RAOBS .... Radiometeorograph Observation (IAA)
RAOC .... Rear Area Operations Center (MCD)
RAOC .... Regional Air Operations Center (NATG)
RAOC .... Royal Army Ordnance Corps [*Formerly, AOC*] [*British*]
RAOC(E) .... Royal Army Ordnance Corps (Engineering) [*British military*] (DMA)
Rao DHL .... Rao's Decisions on Hindu Law [*1893*] [*India*] [*A publication*] (DLA)
RAOMP .... Report of Accrued Obligations, Military Pay (AFM)
RaONC .... Radiation Oncology [*Medicine*] (DMAA)
RAOP .... Regional Air Operations Plan (NATG)
RAOT .... Rocker Arm Oiling Time (PDAA)
RAOTA .... Radio Amateur Old Timers' Association [*British*] (BI)
RAP .... I Will Call You Again [*International telex abbreviation*] (WDMC)
RAP .... RADAR-Absorbing Paint [*Military*] (RDA)
RAP .... RADAR Aim Point
RAP .... Radical Alternatives to Prison [*British*]
RAP .... Radio Access Point (MCD)
RAP .... Radio Air Play
RAP .... Radiological Assistance Plan [*AEC*]
RAP .... Radon Action Program (GNE)
RAP .... Random Access Program [*Computer science*]
RAP .... Random Access Projector
RAP .... Ranger Assessment Phase [*Army*] (INF)
RAP .... Rapid (AAG)
RAP .... Rapid Air [*France ICAO designator*] (FAAC)
RAP .... Rapid Assessment Program [*Environmental evaluation strategy*]
RAP .... Rapid City [*South Dakota*] [*Airport symbol*] (OAG)
RAP .... Rapid City, SD [*Location identifier FAA*] (FAAL)
RAP .... Rapindik [*New Britain*] [*Seismograph station code, US Geological Survey Closed*] (SEIS)
RAP .... Reactive Atmosphere Process
RAP .... Readiness Action Proposal (MCD)
RAP .... Readiness Assessment Program [*Navy*]
RAP .... Rear Area Protection [*Military*] (AABC)
RAP .... Receptor-Associated Protein [*Biochemistry*]
RAP .... Recognize All Potential (DNAB)
RAP .... Recommended Area for Protection [*Australia*]
RAP .... Recruiter Assistance [*or Assistant*] Program [*Navy*] (DNAB)
RAP .... Reduced Acreage Program [*Agriculture*]
RAP .... Redundancy Adjustment of Probability (IEEE)
RAP .... Regimental Aid Post [*British*]
RAP .... Regional Acceleratory Phenomenon [*Physiology*]
RAP .... Regional Analysis and Prediction [*Branch*] [*Marine science*] (OSRA)
RAP .... Regression Analysis Program [*Military*]
RAP .... Regression-Associated Protein [*Biochemistry*]
RAP .... Regulatory Accounting Practices [*or Principles*] [*Business term*]
RAP .... Regulatory Analysis Program [*Federal government*]
RAP .... Relational Associative Processor (IEEE)
RAP .... Relationship Anecdotes Paradigm Method [*Psychology*]
RAP .... Relative Accident Probability
RAP .... Releasable Assets Program
RAP .... Reliability Assessment Prediction
RAP .... Reliability Assessment Program
RAP .... Reliability Assurance Program (IAA)
RAP .... Reliable Acoustic Path
RAP .... Remedial Action Program [*or Project, Plan*] (MCD)
RAP .... Remote Access Point [*Telecommunications*]
RAP .... Renal Artery Pressure [*Medicine*]
RAP .... Rental Assistance Payment Program [*HUD*]
RAP .... Requirements Analysis Package [*Computer science*]
RAP .... Reset After Punch [*Computer science*] (IAA)
RAP .... Resident Assembler Program
RAP .... Resident Assessment Protocol [*Occupational therapy*]
RAP .... Resident Associate Program [*Smithsonian Institution*]
RAP .... Residual Analysis Program [*Space Flight Operations Facility, NASA*]
RAP .... Resource Access Projects [*Administration for Children, Youth and Families*] (EDAC)
RAP .... Resource Allocation Process (AAGC)
RAP .... Resource Allocation Processor (CMD)
RAP .... Response Action Plan (GNE)
RAP .... Response Analysis Program [*Computer science*] (IBMDP)
RAP .... Restricted Access Processor (SSD)
RAP .... Results Analysis Plan (MCD)
RAP .... Retained Accessory Power [*Automotive engineering*]
RAP .... Review and Analysis Process
RAP .... Revised Accounting Procedures
RAP .... Right Angle Plug
RAP .... Right Atrial Pressure [*Cardiology*]
RAP .... Ring-Around Programming (CAAL)
RAP .... Rocket-Assisted Projectile (RDA)
RAP .... "Round Up" Administration Planning Staff [*for the invasion of France*] [*World War II*]
RAP .... Rubidium Acid Phthalate [*Organic chemistry*]
RAP .... Rules for Admission to Practice [*A publication*] (DLA)
RA-P .... Rumex Acetosa Polysaccharide [*Antineoplastic drug*]
RAP .... Rupees, Annas, Pies [*Monetary units*] [*India*]
RAP .... Smithsonian Resident Associate Program (EA)
RAPAC .... Research Applications Policy Advisory Committee [*National Science Foundation*] (EGAO)
RAPAD .... Research Association for Petroleum Alternative Development
Rapal & L .... Rapalje and Lawrence's American and English Cases [*A publication*] (DLA)
Rapalje & L ... Rapalje and Lawrence's Law Dictionary [*A publication*] (DLA)
RAPAM .... Red de Accion sobre Plaguicidas y Alternativas en Mexico [*Member of the Pesticide Action Network*] (CROSS)
Rap & L .... Rapalje and Lawrence's American and English Cases [*A publication*] (DLA)
Rap & Law ... Rapalje and Lawrence's American and English Cases [*A publication*] (DLA)
Rap & L Law Dict ... Rapalje and Lawrence's Law Dictionary [*A publication*] (DLA)
RAPBPPI ...... Research Association for the Paper and Board, Printing, and Packaging Industries [*Research center British*] (IRC)
RAPC .... Radio Administration Plenipotentiary Conference
RAPC .... Right Angle Pressure Cartridge
RAPC .... Royal Army Pay Corps [*Formerly, APC*] [*British*]
RAPCAP .... RADAR Picket Combat Air Patrol (NVT)
RAPCC .... RADAR Approach Control Center (MCD)
RAPCO .... Regional Air Priorities Control Office [*Army*] (AABC)
RAPCOE .... Random Access Programming and Checkout Equipment
RAPCON .... RADAR Approach Control [*Air Force*]
Rap Contempt ... Rapalje on Contempt [*A publication*] (DLA)
RAPD .... Random Amplified Polymorphic DNA [*Deoxyribonucleic Acid*] [*Genetics*]
RAPD .... Reach Avalanche Photodiode (IAA)
RAPD .... Relatively Afferent Pupillary Defect [*Ophthalmology*]
RAPD .... Response Amplitude Probability Data
RAPE .... RADAR Arithmetic Processing Element [*Navy*]
RAPEC .... Rocket-Assisted Personnel Ejection Catapult
RAPECA .... Rassemblement du Peuple Camerounais [*Camerounese People's Rally*]
RAP-EX .... Rear Area Protection Operations Extended (MCD)
Rap Fed Ref Dig ... Rapalje's Federal Reference Digest [*A publication*] (DLA)
Raph .... Raphael Fulgosius [*Deceased, 1427*] [*Authority cited in pre-1607 legal work*] (DSA)
Raph Cum ... Raphael Cumanus [*Deceased, 1427*] [*Authority cited in pre-1607 legal work*] (DSA)
RAPI .... Radiosonde Report Already Sent in PIBAL [*Pilot Balloon Observation*] Collection [*Aviation*] (FAAC)
RAPIC .... Remedial Action Program Information Center [*Department of Energy*] [*Also, an information service or system*] (IID)
RAPID .... Rail Gun Armature Plasma Investigation Device (PDAA)
RAPID .... Random Access Personnel Information Dissemination
RAPID .... Random Access Personnel Information Disseminatora (NITA)
RAPID .... Rapid [*Commonly used*] (OPSA)
RAPID .... Rapid Access for Phoenix Intermodal Development
RAPID .... Rapid Accurate Polynomial Interpolation Device (IAA)
RAPID .... Reactor and Plant Integrated Dynamics [*Computer science*] (KSC)
RAPID .... Reader-to-Advertiser Phone Inquiry Delivery System [*Chilton Corp.*]
RAPID .... Readily Accessible Parts Information Directory [*Information service or system*] (IID)
RAPID .... Real-Time Acquisition and Processing of Inflight Data
RAPID .... Real-Time Application Program Interface to DISOSS (NITA)
RAPID .... Relative Address Programming Implementation Device [*Computer science*]
RAPID .... Reliability Assessment Program with In-Plant Data
RAPID .... Remote Access Planning for Institutional Development [*Computer science*]
RAPID .... Remote Access Procedure for Interactive Design [*General Motors Corp.*]
RAPID .... Remote Automatic Parts Input for Dealers (IAA)
RAPID .... Research in Automatic Photocomposition and Information Dissemination
RAPID .... Retrieval and Processing Information for Display
RAPID .... Retrieval and Production for Integrated Data [*Computer science*] (MHDB)
RAPID .... Retrieval through Automated Publication and Information Digest [*Computer science*] (DIT)
RAPID .... Retrorocket-Assisted Parachute in Flight Delivery
RAPID .... Rocketdyne Automatic Processing of Integrated Data [*Computer science*]
RAPID .... Ryan Automatic Plot Indicator Device
RAPIDS .... Random Access Personnel Information Dissemination System [*Army*] (AABC)
RAPIDS .... Rapid Automated Problem Identification System [*DoD*]
RAPIDS .... Rapids Commonly used (OPSA)
RAPIDS .... Real-Time Automated Personnel Identification System [*DoD*]
RAPIER .... Rapid Analysis of Products by Integrated Engineering Routines [*Computer-assisted design*]
RAPIER .... Rapid Emergency Reconstitution Team [*Military*]
RAPIT .... Record and Process Input Tables (IAA)
Rap Jud QBR ... Rapports Judiciaires de Quebec, Cour du Banc de la Reine [*Quebec Law Reports, Queen's Bench*] [*A publication*] (DLA)
Rap Jud QCS ... Rapports Judiciaires de Quebec. Cour Superieure [*Quebec Law Reports, Superior Court*] [*A publication*] (DLA)
Rap Jud Quebec CS (Can) ... Rapports Judiciaires de Quebec [*Quebec Law Reports*] [*Canada*] [*A publication*] (DLA)
Rap Jud Quebec KB (Can) ... Rapports Judiciaires de Quebec [*Quebec Law Reports*] [*Canada*] [*A publication*] (DLA)
Rap Jud Quebec QB (Can) ... Rapports Judiciaires de Quebec [*Quebec Law Reports*] [*Canada*] [*A publication*] (DLA)
Rap Lar .... Rapalje on Larceny [*A publication*] (DLA)
RAPLOC .... Rapid Passive Localization (MCD)

RAPLOC-LSI... Rapid Passive Localization - Low-Ship Impact [*Navy*] (CAAL)
RAPLOC-WAA... Rapid Passive Localization - Wide Aperture Array [*Military*] (CAAL)
RAPM......... Reliability Assessment Prediction Model
RAPM......... Risk-Adjusted Profitability Measure [*Banking*] (ECON)
Rap NY Dig... Rapalje's New York Digest [*A publication*] (DLA)
RAPO......... Rabbit Antibodies to Pig Ovary [*Immunology*]
RAPO......... Resident Apollo Project Office [*NASA*] (KSC)
RAPP......... Racial Awareness Pilot Project [*University of Cincinnati*]
RAPP......... Reconciliation and Purification Program [*Air Force*]
RAPP......... Registered Air Parcel Post
Rapp Bount... Rapp on the Bounty Laws [*A publication*] (DLA)
RAPPI......... Random Access Plan-Position Indicator [*Air Force*]
RAPPORT.... Rapid Alert Programmed, Power Management of RADAR Targets [*Military*] (PDAA)
Rapport........ Rapport: The Modern Guide to Books, Music & More [*A publication*] (BRI)
RAPP's........ Radiologists, Anesthesiologists, Pathologists, and Physiatrists
RAPR......... RADAR Processor (CET)
RAPR......... Right Angle Panel Receptacle
RAPRA......... RAPRA Technology [*Formerly, Rubber and Plastics Research Association*] (EA)
RAPRA......... Rubber and Plastics Research Association (NITA)
RAPRENOx... Rapid Reduction of Nitrogen Oxides [*Automotive engineering*]
RAPS......... RADAR-Absorbing Primary Structure (MCD)
RAPS......... RADAR Prediction System (MCD)
RAPS......... RADAR Proficiency Simulator
RAPS......... Radioactive Argon Processing System (NRCH)
RAPS......... Radiologist, Anesthesiologist, and Pathologist (HCT)
RAPS......... Rate and Position Sensor (IAA)
RAPS......... Recovery Access Presentation System (GAVI)
RAPS......... Regional Air Pollution Study [*Environmental Protection Agency*]
RAPS......... Regulated Air Pressure System (MCD)
RAPS......... Regulatory Affairs Professionals Society (EA)
RAPS......... Reliable Acoustic Path SONAR (MCD)
RAPS......... Remote Access Power Support (NITA)
RAPS......... Remote Applications Protocol Suite (ACII)
RAPS......... Remote Area Power Supply
RAPS......... Resource Analysis and Planning System [*DoD*] (DOMA)
RAPS......... Retired Annuitant Pay Statement [*DoD*]
RAPS......... Retired Army Personnel System
RAPS......... Retiree Annuitant Pay System
RAPS......... Retrieval Analysis and Presentation System [*Computer science*]
RAPS......... Right Aft Propulsion System [*Aerospace*] (GFGA)
RAPS......... Risk Appraisal of Programs System
RAPS......... Role Activity Performance Scale [*Mental health*]
RAPSAG....... Rapid Sealift Acquisition Group [*Navy*]
RAPSAT....... Ranging and Processing Satellite (DA)
RAPSG......... Rapsgate [*England*]
RAPT......... Raptor Systems [*NASDAQ symbol*] (TTSB)
RAPT......... Raptor Systems, Inc. [*NASDAQ symbol*] (SAG)
RAPT......... Reception Automatic Picture Transmission (PDAA)
RAPT......... Rehabilitation of Addicted Prisoners Trust [*British*] [*An association*]
RAPT......... Reusable Aerospace Passenger Transport (MCD)
RAPTAP....... Random Access Parallel Tape
RAPTAP....... Rapid Access Parallel Tape [*Computer science*] (IAA)
RAP-TAP...... Releasable Assets Program - Transferable Assets Program [*Navy*] (NG)
RAPTN......... RAPRA Trade Names [*RAPRA Technology Ltd.*] [*Information service or system*] (IID)
RaptorS....... Raptor Systems, Inc. [*Associated Press*] (SAG)
RAPTS......... Resource Accounting Project Tracking System (DNAB)
RAPTUS....... Rapid Thorium-Uranium System [*Nuclear energy*]
RAPUD......... Revenue Analysis from Parametric Usage Descriptions [*Telecommunications*] (TEL)
RAPWI......... Organization for the Recovery of Allied Prisoners of War and Internees [*Initially in Headquarters of Allied Land Forces, Southeast Asia*] [*World War II*]
Rap Wit....... Rapalje's Treatise on Witnesses [*A publication*] (DLA)
RAPYHT....... Retrieval and Acceleration of Promising Young Handicapped and Talented Program (EDAC)
RAQ......... Raha [*Indonesia*] [*Airport symbol*] (OAG)
RAQ......... Regional Air Quality
RAR......... Aviaross [*Russian Federation*] [*ICAO designator*] (FAAC)
RAR......... RADAR Arrival Route [*Aviation*] (DA)
RAR......... RADAR Augmentation Reliability (MCD)
RAR......... Radio Acoustic Ranging
RAR......... Random Age Replacement
RAR......... Rapid Access Recording (IEEE)
Rar......... Rare Records [*Record label*]
RAR......... Rarotonga [*Cook Islands*] [*Airport symbol*] (OAG)
RAR......... Rarotonga [*Cook Islands*] [*Seismograph station code, US Geological Survey*] (SEIS)
RAR......... Read around Ratio
RAR......... Real Aperture RADAR
RAR......... Reallexikon der Aegyptischen Religionsgeschichte [*Berlin*] [*A publication*] (BJA)
RAR......... Reasonable Assumed [*or Assured*] Resources [*Minerals*]
RAR......... Record and Report
RAR......... Redevelopment Area Resident
RAR......... Reduced Aspect Ratio
RAR......... Regular Army Reserve
RAR......... Relative Accumulation Rate [*Ecology*]
RAR......... Reliability Action Report [*or Request*]
RAR......... Remote Arm Reset (MCD)
RAR......... Remove and Replace (IAA)
RAR......... Remove Audible Ring
RAR......... Repair and Retrofix (IAA)
RAR......... Repair as Required (AAG)
RAR......... Report Authorization Record [*or Request*] (AAG)
RAR......... Reserve Asset Ratio [*Banking*] (ADA)
RAR......... Residential Appraisal Report [*Real estate*] (EMRF)
RAR......... Resource Allocation Recommendations [*Military*]
RAR......... Restricted Articles Regulation (DS)
RAR......... Retinoic Acid Receptor [*Biochemistry*]
RAR......... Return Address Register
RAR......... Revenue Agent's Report [*IRS*]
RAR......... Revenue and Retrieval (IAA)
RAR......... Revise as Required (MCD)
R-Ar......... Rhode Island State Archives, Providence, RI [*Library symbol Library of Congress*] (LCLS)
RAR......... Rhodesian African Rifles [*Military unit*]
RAR......... Right Arm Recumbent [*Medicine*] (AAMN)
RAR......... ROM [*Read-Only Memory*] Address Register
RAR......... Routing and Recording (IAA)
RAR......... Royal Army Reserve [*British*]
RAR......... Royal Australian Regiment (VNW)
RAR......... Rules and Regulations (IAA)
RAR......... Rural Area Redevelopment
RARA......... Random Access-to-Random Access [*Computer science*] (IAA)
RARA......... Retinoic Acid Receptor Alpha (DMAA)
RARA......... Rural and Remote Area
RARAD......... RADAR Advisory [*Aviation*] (FAAC)
RARAF......... Radiological Research Accelorator Facility [*Department of Energy*]
RARB......... Raritan Bancorp [*NASDAQ symbol*] (TTSB)
RARB......... Raritan Bancorp, Inc. [*NASDAQ symbol*] (NQ)
R Arb......... Recht der Arbeit [*Right to Work*] [*German*] (DLA)
RARB......... Retinoic Acid Receptor Beta (DMAA)
RARC......... Reactors and Reactor Control (IAA)
RARC......... Regional Administrative Radio Conference (NITA)
RARC......... Revoked Appointment and Returned to Civilian Status [*Navy*]
RARDE......... Royal Armament Research and Development Establishment [*British*]
RARDEN...... Royal Armament Research and Development Establishment, Enfield [*British military*] (DMA)
RARE......... Associated Networks for European Research [*EC*] (ECED)
RARE......... Bugaboo Creek Steak House [*NASDAQ symbol*] (SAG)
RARE......... Radiation and Repair Engineering [*Nuclear energy*] (IAA)
RARE......... Rail Archaeological Research Effort [*An association*]
RARE......... Ram Air Rocket Engine
RARE......... Rare Animal Relief Effort
RARE......... Rare Antigen/Antibody Resource Exchange Program [*American Association of Blood Banks*]
RARE......... Rare Hospitality Intl., Inc. [*NASDAQ symbol*] (SAG)
RARE......... Rehabilitation of Addicts by Relatives and Employers
RARE......... Reinforcement and Resupply of Europe (MCD)
RARE......... Reseaux Associes pour la Recherche Europeene [*Associated Networks for European Research*]
RARE......... Retinoic Acid Responsive Element [*Biochemistry*]
RARE......... Roadless Area Resource Evaluation
RARE......... Ronne Antarctic Research Expedition [*1947-48*]
Ra Ref......... RADAR Reflector
RAREF......... Radiation and Repair Engineering Facility [*Nuclear energy*] (NRCH)
RareHosp...... Rare Hospitality Intl., Inc. [*Associated Press*] (SAG)
RAREP......... RADAR Report [*FAA*]
RAREP......... RADAR Weather Report (IAA)
RARES......... Rotating Associative Relational Store (MHDI)
RARF......... RADOME [*RADAR Dome*], Antenna, and Radio Frequency [*Array*] [*Electronics*]
RARG......... Regulatory Analysis Review Group [*Comprising several federal agencies*]
RARI......... Reporting and Routing Instructions [*Navy*]
RarintnBc..... Raritan Bancorp [*Associated Press*] (SAG)
rariss......... Rarissimum [*Extremely Rare*] [*Latin*]
RaritnBc...... Raritan Bancorp [*Associated Press*] (SAG)
RARLS......... Rabbit Antirat Lymphocyte Serum [*Immunology*] (MAE)
RARO......... Regular Army Reserve of Officers [*British*]
RAROC......... Risk-Adjusted Return on Capital [*Economics*]
RAR OCC..... Raro Occurrit [*Rarely Occurs*] [*Latin*] (ROG)
RAROM......... RAM and ROM (NITA)
RARP......... Radio Affiliate Replacement Plan [*Canadian Broadcasting Corporation*]
RARP......... Reverse Address Resolution Protocol [*Computer science*] (PCM)
RARR......... Range and Range Rate (IAA)
RARR......... Reinstallation and Removal Record (KSC)
RARS......... Refractory Anemia with Ringed Sideroblasts [*Hematology*]
RArt......... Royal Artillery [*British*]
RARTS......... Rabbit Anti-Rat Thymocyte Serum [*Immunology*] (DMAA)
RARU......... Rackham Arthritis Research Unit [*University of Michigan*] [*Research center*] (RCD)
RARU......... Radio Range Station Reported Unreliable [*Message abbreviation*]
RAS......... Jim Ratliff Air Service, Inc. [*FAA designator*] (FAAC)
RAS......... Rabbonim Aid Society
RAS......... RADAR-Absorbing Structures
RAS......... RADAR Advisory Service
RAS......... RADAR Assembly Spares (NG)
RAS......... RADAR Augmentation System (MCD)
RAS......... Radio Astronomy Satellite (IAA)
RAS......... RADOME [*RADAR Dome*] Antenna Structure
RAS......... Radula Sinus
RAS......... Random Access Storage [*Computer science*] (IAA)
RAS......... Rapid Access Storage (NITA)

RAS .... Rasht [*Iran*] [*Airport symbol*] (OAG)
ras .... Rasurae [*Scrapings or Filings*] [*Latin*] (MAE)
RAS .... Rathus Assertiveness Scale [*Psychology*] (EDAC)
RAS .... Reaction Augmentation System
RAS .... Reactor Alarm System (IEEE)
RAS .... Reactor Analysis and Safety [*Nuclear energy*] (NRCH)
RAS .... Readers Admission System [*Online Public Access Catalog*]
RAS .... Reading Association Sydney [*Australia*]
RAS .... Rear Area Security [*Army*] (AABC)
RAS .... Recirculation Actuation Signal [*Nuclear energy*] (NRCH)
RAS .... Record Assigned System (MCD)
RAS .... Records and Analysis Subsystem (TEL)
RAS .... Recruiting Analysis Service [*LIMRA*]
RAS .... Recruitment and Assessment Services [*British Civil Service*] (ECON)
RAS .... Rectified Air Speed [*Navigation*]
RAS .... Recurrent Aphthous Stomatitis [*Medicine*]
RAS .... Reference Address for Small Core Memory (IAA)
RAS .... Reflector Antenna System
RAS .... Refractory Anemia with Ringed Sideroblasts [*Hematology*]
RAS .... Regimental Aviation Squadron [*Army*] (ADDR)
RAS .... Regional Automated Systems
RAS .... Relative Aerobic Strain (PDAA)
RAS .... Relay Antenna Subsystem [*NASA*]
RAS .... Reliability, Availability, and Serviceability [*IBM Corp. slogan*] (MCD)
RAS .... Reliability, Availability, Security (IAA)
RAS .... Remote Access Server [*Computer science*] (PCM)
RAS .... Remote Access Service [*Telecommunications*]
RAS .... Remote Access Services [*Microsoft Corp.*] [*Computer networking*] (PCM)
RAS .... Remote Acquisition Station [*Nuclear energy*] (NRCH)
RAS .... Remote Active Spectrometer
RAS .... Remote Area Support (MCD)
RAS .... Remote Arm Set (MCD)
RAS .... Renal Artery Stenosis [*Medicine*] (MAE)
RAS .... Renin-Angiotensin System [*Endocrinology*]
RAS .... Replenishment at Sea [*Navy*]
RAS .... Report Audit Summary (AAG)
RAS .... Reproduction Assembly Sheet (MCD)
RAS .... Requirements Allocation Sheet
RAS .... Requirements Analysis Sheet [*NASA*] (KSC)
RAS .... Requirements Audit System
RAS .... Reserve Advisory Squadron
RAS .... Reset and Start (IAA)
RAS .... Resource Analysis System (HGAA)
RAS .... Reticular Activating System [*Diffuse network of neurons in the brain*]
RAS .... Retiree Account Statement [*DoD*]
RAS .... Return Address Stack (ECII)
RAS .... Return of Activated Sludge (DICI)
RAS .... Rheumatoid Arthritis Serum [*Factor*] [*Medicine*]
RAS .... River Assault Squadron [*Navy*] (NVT)
RAS .... Rockhampton Aerial Services [*Australia*]
RAS .... Route Accounting Subsystem [*Telecommunications*] (TEL)
RAS .... Row Address Select (IAA)
RAS .... Row-Address Strobe (IEEE)
RAS .... Royal Accounting System [*United States Geological Survey*]
RAS .... Royal Adelaide Show [*Australia*]
RAS .... Royal Aeronautical Society [*British*]
RAS .... Royal African Society (EAIO)
RAS .... Royal Agricultural Society [*British*] (DAS)
RAS .... Royal Asiatic Society [*British*]
RAS .... Royal Astronomical Society [*British*]
RAS .... Royal International Agricultural Show [*British*] (ITD)
RAS .... Russian Academy Of Sciences
RASA .... Railway and Airline Supervisors Association [*AFL-CIO*]
RASA .... Realignment of Supply Activities (MCD)
RASA .... Redstone Arsenal Support Activity (MCD)
RASA .... Regional Aeronautical Support Activity (AFIT)
RASAU .... Reserve Antisubmarine Warfare Systems Analysis Mobilization Unit (DNAB)
RASB .... Rapid Access to Sequential Block [*Computer science*] (PDAA)
RASC .... Radiological Affairs Safety Committee (DNAB)
RASC .... Rear Area Security Controller [*Military*]
RASC .... Religious Altered State of Consciousness [*Psychology*]
RASC .... Rome Air Service Command [*Air Force*]
RASC .... Royal Agricultural Society of the Commonwealth (EAIO)
RASC .... Royal Army Service Corps [*Formerly, ASC; later, RCT*] [*British*]
RASC .... Royal Astronomical Society of Canada
RASCAL .... Random Access Secure Communications Antijam Link
RASCAL .... Rotorcraft-Aircrew Systems Concepts Airborne Laboratory (RDA)
RASCAL .... Royal Aircraft Establishment Sequence Calculator [*British*] (DEN)
RASCAL .... Rudimentary Adaptive System for Computer-Aided Learning (PDAA)
RASCAP .... Replenishment at Sea Corrective Action Program (MCD)
RASCC .... Rear Area Security Control Center [*Military*]
RASC/DC .... Rear Area Security and Area Damage Control [*Military*]
RASCOM .... Regional African Satellite Communications System (ECON)
RASCOM .... Regional African Satellite Communication System for the Development of Africa [*ITU*] [*United Nations*] (DUND)
RASCORE .... RADAR Scorer (MCD)
RASC/RCT .... Royal Army Service Corps/Royal Corps of Transport [*British*]
RASD .... Reference and Adult Services Division [*American Library Association*] (EA)
RASD .... Requirements and Specification Documentation [*Computer science*]
RASD BRASS .... RASD [*Reference and Adult Services Division*] Business Reference Services Section
RASD CODES .... RASD [*Reference and Adult Services Division*] Collection Development and Evaluation Section
RASD HS .... RASD [*Reference and Adult Services Division*] History Section
RASD ILC .... RASD [*Reference and Adult Services Division*] Interlibrary Loan Committee [*American Library Association*]
RASD MARS .... RASD [*Reference and Adult Services Division*] Machine-Assisted Reference Section
RASDS .... Regional Advisory Service in Demographic Statistics [*United Nations*] (EY)
RASE .... Rapid Acquisition by Sequential Estimation (IAA)
RASE .... Rapid Automatic Sweep Equipment [*Air Force*]
RASE .... Royal Agricultural Society of England
RASER .... Radio Amplification by Stimulated Emission of Radiation
RASER .... Random-to-Serial Converter
RASER .... Range and Sensitivity Extending Resonator [*Electronics*]
RASGN .... Reassignment
RASH .... Rain Showers [*Meteorology*]
RASHI .... Rabbi Shlomo Yitzhaqi [*Medieval Jewish commentator*]
RaSHI .... Rabbi Solomon Bar Isaac (BJA)
RASI .... Reliability, Availability, Serviceability and Improvability (NITA)
RASI .... Reliability, Availability, Service, Improvement (MHDI)
RASIDS .... Range Safety Impact Display System
RASILA .... Rannikko- ja Sisaevesiliikenteen Tvoenantajaliitto [*Employers' Federation of Coastal and Inland Waterways Transportation*] [*Finland*] (EY)
RASIS .... Reliability, Availability, Serviceability, Integrity and Security (NITA)
RASL .... Reserve Active Status List (DOMA)
RASM .... Remote Analog Submultiplexer (MCD)
rASMC .... Rat Aortic Smooth Muscle Cells
RASN .... Rain and Snow [*Sleet*] [*Meteorology*]
RASNSW .... Royal Art Society of New South Wales [*Australia*]
RASO .... Radio Allocations Study Organization (NTCM)
RASO .... Radiological Affairs Support Office [*Obsolete Navy*]
RASO .... Rear Airfield Supply Organization [*Military*]
RASO .... Regional Aviation Supply Officer [*Navy*] (AFIT)
RASONDE .... Radiosonde Observation
RASP .... Rapid Acquisition of Spare Parts (DOMA)
RASP .... Receiver Active Signal Processor [*Military*] (CAAL)
RASP .... Refined Aeronautical Support Program (NG)
RASP .... Reliability and Aging Surveillance Program [*Air Force*]
RASP .... Remote Access Switching and Patching
RASP .... Resource Allocation and Stress in Plants [*Research initiative*] [*bbscrc-Biotechnology and Biological Sciences Research Council*] [*British*]
RASP .... Retrieval and Sort Processor [*Computer science*]
RASP .... Retrieval and Statistics Processing (NITA)
RASPE .... Resident Army SENSCOM [*Sentinel Systems Command*] Project Engineer (AABC)
RASPO .... Resident Apollo Spacecraft Program Office [*NASA*] (KSC)
RASR .... Regular Army Special Reserve (ADA)
RASR .... Rodders Against Street Racing
RASS .... RADAR Acoustic Sounding System [*National Oceanic and Atmospheric Administration*]
RASS .... RADAR Attitude Sensing System (MCD)
RASS .... Radio Acoustic Sounding System
RASS .... Rapid Area Supply Support [*Military*] (AFM)
RASS .... Register, Address, Skip and Special Chip (IAA)
RASS .... Remote Activated Stores System (MCD)
RASS .... Remote Area Services Subsidy Scheme [*Australia*]
RASS .... Rheumatoid Arthritis and Sjoegren Syndrome [*Medicine*] (DMAA)
RASS .... Rock Analysis Storage System [*United States Geological Survey*] [*Information service or system*] (IID)
RASS .... ROSAT [*Roentgen Satellite*] All Sky Survey
RASS .... Rotating Acoustic Stereo-Scanner [*Telecommunications*] (OA)
RASS .... Ruggedized Airborne Seeker Simulator (MCD)
RASSAN .... RADAR Sea State Analyzer [*Marine science*] (MSC)
RASSAS .... Radio Astronomical Space System of Aperture Synthesis (MCD)
RASSH .... Radiosondes Shipped From (NOAA)
RASSR .... Reliable Advanced Solid-State RADAR
RAS-STADES .... Records Association System - Standard Data Elements System (MCD)
RASSW .... Radical Alliance of Social Service Workers (EA)
RAST .... Radioallergosorbent Test [*Immunochemistry*]
Rast .... Rastell's Entries and Statutes [*England*] [*A publication*] (DLA)
RAST .... Recovery, Assist, Secure, and Traverse System [*Navy*]
RAST .... Reliability and System Test
RASTA .... Radiant Augmented Special Test Apparatus (MCD)
RASTA .... Radiation Special Test Apparatus (IAA)
RASTA .... Radio Station [*Coast Guard*]
Rast Abr .... Rastell's Abridgment of the Statutes [*A publication*] (DLA)
RASTAC .... Random Access Storage and Control [*Computer science*]
RASTAD .... Random Access Storage and Display [*Computer science*]
RASTAS .... Radiating Site Target Acquisition System (MCD)
Rast Ent .... Rastell's Entries and Statutes [*A publication*] (DLA)
RasterG .... Raster Graphics, Inc. [*Associated Press*] (SAG)
RASTI .... Rapid Speech Transition Index [*Acoustics*]
RASTIC .... Rail, Automatic Straightening, Intrinsically Controlled [*Railroad maintenance device*] [*British*]
RASTR .... Recorded Acoustic Signal Target Repeater
RASUI .... Reliability, Availability, Serviceability, Useability, Installability (IAA)
RaSV .... Rasheed (Rat) Sarcoma Virus
RASV .... Reusable Aerodynamic Space Vehicle
RAT .... Radiatively-Active Trace [*Analytical chemistry*]
RAT .... Radiological Assessment Team [*Nuclear energy*] (NRCH)
RAT .... Ram Air Temperature

RAT............. Ram Air Turbine (MCD)
RAT............. Ranges, Ammunition, and Targets (MCD)
RAT............. Rated
RAT............. Rating (AABC)
RAT............. Ratio (AAG)
RAT............. Ratioflug Luftfahrtunternehmen GmbH [*Germany ICAO designator*] (FAAC)
RAT............. Ration (IAA)
RAT............. Rations [*Military*] (AABC)
RAT............. Rat Island [*Alaska*] [*Seismograph station code, US Geological Survey Closed*] (SEIS)
RAT............. Rat Resources [*Vancouver Stock Exchange symbol*]
RAT............. Raynaud's Association Trust (EA)
RAT............. Receipt Account Title File [*Office of Management and Budget*] (GFGA)
RAT............. Register Alias Table [*Computer science*]
RAT............. Regular Associated Troupers (EA)
RAT............. Relative Accuracy Test (GFGA)
RAT............. Reliability Assurance Test
RAT............. Remote Area Terminal
RAT............. Remote Associates Test [*Psychology*]
RAT............. Repeat Action Tablet [*Pharmacology*]
RAT............. Reseau des Amis de la Terre [*Network of Friends of the Earth*] [*France Political party*] (PPE)
RAT............. Reserve Auxiliary Transformer (IEEE)
RAT............. Resistance Armee Tunisienne [*Tunisian Armed Resistance*] (PD)
RAT............. Restricted Articles Tariff
RAT............. Right Anterior Thigh [*Anatomy*]
RAT............. Rocket-Assisted Torpedo [*Antisubmarine warfare*]
RAT............. Rocket Launched Antisubmarine Torpedo (IAA)
RAT............. Rotational Autonomic Tester
RAT............. Routing Automation Technique (PDAA)
RATA........... Rankine Cycle Air Turboaccelerator
RA/TA......... Restricted Availability/Technical Availability (NVT)
RATAC......... RADAR Analog Target Acquisition Computer
RATAC......... RADAR Coverage via Tactical Air Navigation (IAA)
RATAC......... RADAR Target Acquisition (IAA)
RATAC......... Raytheon Acoustic Telemetry and Control
RATAC......... Remote Airborne Television Display of Ground RADAR Coverage via TACAN (CET)
RATAN......... RADAR and Television Aid to Navigation
RATAN......... Radio and Television Aids to Navigation
RATAV......... RADAR Terrain Avoidance
RATBP......... Revised Appendix to Be Published (MCD)
RATC........... RADAR-Aided Tracking Computer (WDAA)
RATC........... Rate-Aided Tracking Computer
RATC........... Rhodesian Air Training Centre [*British military*] (DMA)
RATCC......... RADAR Air Traffic Control Center [*Later, RATCF*] [*Navy*]
RATCC......... Regional Air Traffic Control Center (NATG)
RATCF......... Radar Air Traffic Control Facilities [*FAA*] (TAG)
RATCHET..... Regional Atmospheric Transport Code for Hanford Emission Tracking (USDC)
RATCHET..... Regional Atmospheric Transport Code for Hanford Emission Tracking [*Marine science*] (OSRA)
RATCON....... RADAR Terminal Control
RATD........... RADAR Automatic Target Detection [*Military*] (CAAL)
RATD........... Register of Apparel and Textile Designers [*British*] (DBA)
RATD........... Russian Aviation Trade [*House*] [*Russia; established in 1991*] (DOMA)
RATDA......... Regional African Telecommunication Database [*International Telecommunication Union*] (DUND)
RATE........... Rate Analysis and Transportation Evaluation [*Student legal action organization*]
RATE........... Record and Tape Exchange [*Defunct*] (EA)
RATE........... Remote Area Teacher Education [*Australia*]
RATE........... Remote Automatic Telemetry Equipment
RATE........... Retention and Transfer Enhancement [*Military*]
RATEL......... Radiotelephone
RATEL......... Raytheon Automatic Test Equipment Language [*Computer science*] (CSR)
RATELO....... Radiotelephone Operator (AABC)
RATEP......... Remote Area Teacher Education Program [*Australia*]
RATER......... Response Analysis Tester [*NASA*]
RATES......... Rapid Access Tariff Expediting Service [*Journal of Commerce, Inc.*] [*Database*]
RATEX......... Rational Expectations [*Economics*]
RATF........... Radio Aids Training Flight [*British military*] (DMA)
RATFOR....... Rational FORTRAN [*Computer science*]
RA-TFR....... RADAR Altimeter - Terrain Following RADAR (MCD)
RATG........... Rabbit Antithymocyte Globulin [*Immunochemistry*]
RATG........... Radiotelegram [*or Radiotelegraph*]
RATG........... Radio Telegraphy
RATG........... Rhodesian Air Training Group [*British military*] (DMA)
RATHAS....... Rat Thymus Antiserum [*Biochemistry*] (MAE)
RATIG......... Robert A. Taft Institute of Government [*Later, TTI*] (EA)
RATIO......... Radio Telescope in Orbit (IEEE)
RATL........... Rational Software [*NASDAQ symbol*] (SAG)
RATLER....... Robotic All-Terrain Lunar Exploration Rover [*NASA*]
RatnSft....... Rational Software [*Associated Press*] (SAG)
RATNY......... Ratners Group PLC (MHDW)
RATO........... Rocket-Assisted Takeoff [*Aerospace*]
RATOG......... Rocket-Assisted Takeoff Gear [*Aviation*] (IEEE)
RATPAC....... RADAR Acquisition Tracking Probe for Active Calibration (DNAB)
RATR........... Reliability Abstracts and Technical Reviews [*NASA*]
RATRAN....... RADAR Triangle Navigation (IAA)
RATS........... RADAR Acquisition and Tracking System (MCD)
RATS........... RADAR Altimeter Target Simulator (MCD)
RATS........... Radio Amateur Telecommunications Society (EA)
RATS........... Ram Air Turbine System
RATS........... Rapid Area Transportation Support [*Air Force*] (MCD)
RATS........... Rate and Track Subsystem
RATS........... Rear Area Types [*Military slang for rear support troops*] (VNW)
RATS........... Reconnaissance and Tactical Security [*Teams*] [*Military*]
RATS........... Reform of the Australian Taxation System [*1985*] [*A publication*]
RATS........... Remote Alarm Transmission System
RATS........... Remote Area Tactical [*Location and Landing*] System
RATS........... Remote Area Terminal System
RATS........... Resolver Alignment Test Set
RATS........... Restricted Articles Terminal System [*IATA*] (DS)
RATSC......... Rome Air Technical Service Command [*Air Force*]
RATSCAT..... RADAR Target Scatter [*RADAR program*]
RATSEC....... Robert A. Taft Sanitary Engineering Center (AABC)
Rat Sel Cas... Rattigan's Select Hindu Law Cases [*A publication*] (DLA)
RATT........... Radio Airborne Teletype (MCD)
RATT........... Radio Telephone/Teleprinter (INF)
RATT........... Radioteletype
RATT........... Radio Teletypewriter (IAA)
RATTC......... Radio and Teletype Control Center
Rattigan....... Rattigan's Select Hindu Law Cases [*India*] [*A publication*] (DLA)
Ratt LC........ Rattigan's Leading Cases on Hindu Law [*A publication*] (DLA)
RATTLE........ Road Accident Tabulation Language (PDAA)
Rattlsnk....... [*The*] Rattlesnake Holding Co., Inc. [*Associated Press*] (SAG)
Rat Unrep Cr... Ratanlal's Unreported Criminal Cases [*India*] [*A publication*] (DLA)
RATWUS....... Research and Technology Work Unit Summary
RATx........... Radiation Therapy [*Medicine*] (MAE)
RAU............. Radioactive Uptake [*Medicine*] (DMAA)
RAU............. Radion Access Unit [*Army*]
RAU............. Rangpur [*Bangladesh*] [*Airport symbol*] (AD)
RAU............. Recurrent Aphthous Ulceration [*Medicine*]
RAU............. Regional Acquisition Unit [*NASA*] (NASA)
RAU............. Remote Acquisition Unit [*NASA*] (NASA)
RAU............. Repairs and Utilities [*Military*] (IAA)
RAU............. River Assault Unit [*Navy*]
Rauch........... Rauch Industries, Inc. [*Associated Press*] (SAG)
RA-UDAA..... Robbery Armed - Unlawful Driving Away of an Automobile [*Police code*]
RAUIC......... Repair Activity Unit Identification Code (MCD)
RAUIS......... Remote Acquisition Unit Interconnecting Station [*NASA*] (NASA)
RAUK........... Rear-Admiral of the United Kingdom [*Navy British*] (ROG)
Rauma......... Rauma Oy [*Associated Press*] (SAG)
RaumaOy..... Rauma Oy [*Associated Press*] (SAG)
RAUS........... Retired Association for the Uniformed Services (NADA)
R Aust Plan Inst J... Royal Australian Planning Institute. Journal [*A publication*]
RAUT........... Republic Automotive [*NASDAQ symbol*] (TTSB)
RAUT........... Republic Automotive Parts, Inc. [*NASDAQ symbol*] (NQ)
R Aux AF..... Royal Auxiliary Air Force [*Formerly, AAF*] [*British*]
RAV............. Cravo Norte [*Colombia*] [*Airport symbol*] (OAG)
RAV............. Ramm Venture [*Vancouver Stock Exchange symbol*]
RAV............. Random Access Viewer
RAV............. Ravensburg [*Federal Republic of Germany*] [*Seismograph station code, US Geological Survey*] (SEIS)
RAV............. Ravine, PA [*Location identifier FAA*] (FAAL)
RAV............. Receipt Authority Voucher
RAV............. Recreation-Active Vehicle
RAV............. Recreational Active Vehicle [*Toyota*] [*Concept car*]
RAV............. Recreational Active Vehicle
RAV............. Reduced Availability (MCD)
RAV............. Remotely Augmented Vehicle [*Aircraft*]
RAV............. Repackaged Asset Vehicle
RAV............. Restricted Availability (NG)
RAV............. Rogers Aviation Ltd. [*British ICAO designator*] (FAAC)
RAV............. Rous-Associated Virus (MAE)
RAV4........... Recreation-Active Vehicle 4-Wheel Drive
RAVC........... Royal Army Veterinary Corps [*Formerly, AVC*] [*British*]
RAVE........... RADAR Acquisition Visual-Tracking Equipment
RAVE........... Random Access Video Editing [*Computerized film editing*]
RAVE........... Random Access Viewing Equipment
RAVE........... Rankin Automotive Group, Inc. [*NASDAQ symbol*] (SAG)
RAVE........... Readjustment Assistance Act 74 for Vietnam Era Veterans (OICC)
RAV-E......... Recreational Active Vehicle-Electric
RAVE........... Research Aircraft for the Visual Environment [*Helicopters*] [*Army*]
RAVEC......... RADAR Vector
RAVEN......... Ranging and Velocity Navigation
Raven........... Raven Industries, Inc. [*Associated Press*] (SAG)
RAVES......... Rapid Aerospace Vehicle Evaluation System [*Grumman Corp.*]
RAVIR......... RADAR Video Recorder (NVT)
RAVN........... Raven Indus [*NASDAQ symbol*] (TTSB)
RAVN........... Raven Industries, Inc. [*NASDAQ symbol*] (SAG)
RAVPRO....... Resource Allocation and Validation Program
R-AVR......... Ruggedized Airborne Video Recorder
RAVU........... Radiosonde Analysis and Verification Unit
RAW............. Airway Resistance [*Medicine*]
RAW............. Arawa [*Papua New Guinea*] [*Airport symbol*] (OAG)
RAW............. Rapid American Withdrawal [*Antiwar march sponsored by Vietnam Veterans Against the War*] (EA)
Raw............. Rawle's Pennsylvania Reports [*5 vols.*] [*A publication*] (DLA)
RAW............. Read after Write
RAW............. Read Alter Wire
RAW............. Ready and Waiting [*or Willing*] [*Slang*]
RAW............. Rear Axle Weight [*Automotive engineering*]

RAW Reconnaissance Attack Wing [*Navy*] (NVT)
RAW Redmond, OR [*Location identifier FAA*] (FAAL)
RAW Regional Air (Pty) Ltd. [*South Africa ICAO designator*] (FAAC)
RAW Reliability Assurance Warranty (MCD)
RAW Rent-a-Wreck Industries Corp. [*Vancouver Stock Exchange symbol*]
RAW Request for Additional Work [*Navy*] (DNAB)
RAW Return America to Work [*Also translated as "Reaganomics Ain't Working"*] [*UAW bumper sticker slogan*]
RAW Revenue Anticipation Warrant
RAW Rifleman's Assault Weapon (MCD)
RAW Right Atrial Wall [*Medicine*] (DMAA)
RAW Right Attack Wing [*Women's lacrosse position*]
RAW Rural American Women (EA)
RAWA Rail-Water [*Shipping*]
RAWA Renaissance Artists and Writers Association (EA)
RAWA Rent-A-Wreck Amer Inc. [*NASDAQ symbol*] (TTSB)
RAWA Rent-a-Wreck of America, Inc. [*Los Angeles, CA*] [*NASDAQ symbol*] (NQ)
RAWA Revolutionary Association of the Women of Afghanistan
RAWARA Rail-Water-Rail [*Shipping*]
RAWARC RADAR and Warning Coordination [*Teletypewriter circuit*]
RAWB Railroad and Airline Wage Board [*Terminated, 1953*]
Raw Const Rawle on the Constitution of the United States [*A publication*] (DLA)
Raw Cov Rawle on Covenants for Title [*A publication*] (DLA)
RAWEB Refractory Anemia without Excess of Blasts [*Hematology*]
Raw Eq Rawle's Equity in Pennsylvania [*A publication*] (DLA)
RAWIE Radio Weather Intercept Element
RAWIN RADAR Wind [*Upper air observation*]
RAWIN Radar Wind Sounding [*Determination of winds by radar observation of a balloon*] [*Marine science*] (OSRA)
RAWIND RADAR Wind [*Upper air observation*]
RAWINDS RADAR Wind Sounding [*Upper air observation*] (MSA)
RAWINS RADAR Winds [*Upper air observation*]
RAWINS Radio-Winds (USDC)
RAWINSONDE RADAR Wind Sounding and Radiosonde [*Upper air observation*]
RAWINSONES Radiosonde and RAWIN [*Radar Wind Sounding*] [*Combined method*] [*Marine science*] (OSRA)
RAWINSONES Radio-Winds and Radiosondes (USDC)
RAWIT RNA [*Ribonucleic Acid*] Amplification with In/Vitro Translation [*Genetics*]
RAWL Rawlings Sporting Goods [*NASDAQ symbol*] (TTSB)
RAWL Rawlings Sporting Goods Company, Inc. [*NASDAQ symbol*] (SAG)
Rawle Rawle's Pennsylvania Supreme Court Reports [*1828-35*] [*A publication*] (DLA)
Rawle Const US Rawle on the Constitution of the United States [*A publication*] (DLA)
Rawle Cov Rawle on Covenants for Title [*A publication*] (DLA)
Rawle Pen & W Rawle, Penrose, and Watts' Pennsylvania Reports [*1828-40*] [*A publication*] (DLA)
Rawlings Rawlings Sporting Goods Co., Inc. [*Associated Press*] (SAG)
Rawl Mun Corp Rawlinson's Municipal Corporations [*10th ed.*] [*1910*] [*A publication*] (DLA)
RAWO Reliability Assurance Work Order (MCD)
RAWOOP-SNAP Ramo-Wooldridge One-Pass Assembly Program (SAA)
RAWP Resource Allocation Working Party [*British*]
RAWS RADAR Altimeter Warning Set (MCD)
RAWS RADAR Automatic Weather System
RAWS Remote Area Weather Station (MCD)
RAWS Remote Automatic Weather Station
RAWS Role Adaptable Weapons System [*Military*]
RAWSII Raw Statement of Intelligence Interest (MCD)
RawsnKo Rawson-Koenig, Inc. [*Associated Press*] (SAG)
RAWTS RNA [*Ribonucleic Acid*] Amplification with Transcript Sequencing [*Genetics*]
RAX Random Access [*Computer science*] (MHDI)
RAX Remote Access [*Computer science Telecommunications*]
RAX Rio Alto Exploration Ltd. [*Toronto Stock Exchange symbol*]
RAX Rural Automatic Exchange (DEN)
Ray Raymundus de Pennafort [*Deceased, 1275*] [*Authority cited in pre-1607 legal work*] (DSA)
Ray Raynerius de Forlivio [*Deceased, 1358*] [*Authority cited in pre-1607 legal work*] (DSA)
RAY Rayrock Yellowknife Resources, Inc. [*Toronto Stock Exchange symbol*]
RAY Raytech Corp. [*NYSE symbol*] (SPSG)
RAY Rothesay [*Scotland*] [*Airport symbol*] (OAG)
Ray B Ex Raymond's Bill of Exceptions [*A publication*] (DLA)
RAYCI Raytheon Controlled Inventory [*Computer science*]
Raycm Raychem Corp. [*Associated Press*] (SAG)
RAY-COM Raytheon Communications Equipment [*Citizens band radio*]
RAYDAC Raytheon Digital Automatic Computer (MUGU)
Ray de For Raynerius de Forlivio [*Deceased, 1358*] [*Authority cited in pre-1607 legal work*] (DSA)
Rayden Rayden on Divorce [*A publication*] (DLA)
Ray de Saba Raymundus de Sabanacho [*Authority cited in pre-1607 legal work*] (DSA)
RAYDIST Ray-Path Distance (MUGU)
Ray Ins Ray's Medical Jurisprudence of Insanity [*A publication*] (DLA)
RAYM [*The*] Raymond Corp. [*NASDAQ symbol*] (NQ)
Raym B Ex Raymond's Bill of Exceptions [*A publication*] (DLA)
Raym Ch Dig Raymond's Digested Chancery Cases [*A publication*] (DLA)
Raymd Raymond Corp. [*Associated Press*] (SAG)
Ray Med Jur Ray's Medical Jurisprudence of Insanity [*A publication*] (DLA)
Ray Men Path Ray's Mental Pathology [*A publication*] (DLA)
Raym Ld Lord Raymond's English King's Bench Reports [*3 vols.*] [*A publication*] (DLA)
Raymond Raymond's Reports [*81-89 Iowa*] [*A publication*] (DLA)
Rayn Rayner's English Tithe Cases [*3 vols.*] [*A publication*] (DLA)
RAYNET Radio Amateurs Emergency Network (EECA)
RAYNET Raytheon Data Communications Network (NITA)
RaynrInc Rayonier, Inc. [*Associated Press*] (SAG)
Rayn Ti Cas Rayner's English Tithe Cases [*1575-1782*] [*A publication*] (DLA)
RAY/RD Raytheon Co./Research Division
RAYS Risk and Youth Smoking [*Project*] (AIE)
RAYS Sunglass Hut International, Inc. [*NASDAQ symbol*] (SAG)
RAYS Sunglass Hut Intl [*NASDAQ symbol*] (TTSB)
RAYSISTOR Raytheon Resistor [*Electro-optical control device*]
RAYSPAN Raytheon Spectrum Analyzer
Raytc Raytech Corp. [*Associated Press*] (SAG)
Raytel Raytel Medical Corp. [*Associated Press*] (SAG)
RAY-TEL Raytheon Telephone [*Citizens band radio*]
Raythn Raytheon Co. [*Associated Press*] (SAG)
Ray Ti Cas Rayner's English Tithe Cases [*1575-1782*] [*A publication*] (DLA)
RayTLP Rayonier Timberlands Ltd. [*Associated Press*] (SAG)
RAZ Razoxane [*Medicine*] (DMAA)
RAZ Rijnmond Air Services BV [*Netherlands ICAO designator*] (FAAC)
RAZ Rolled Alloyed Zinc
RAZEL Range, Azimuth, and Elevation
RAZON Range and Azimuth Only
RAZPE Resident ARGMA [*Army Rocket and Guided Missile Agency*] Zeus Project Engineer (AAG)
RAZR American Safety Razor Co. [*NASDAQ symbol*] (SAG)
RAZR Amer Safety Razor [*NASDAQ symbol*] (TTSB)
RAZS Rolled Alloyed Zinc Sheet
R/B ASE [*National Institute for Automotive Service Excellence*] Test Registration Booklet [*A publication*] (EAAP)
R_B Base Resistance (IDOE)
RB Botswana [*IYRU nationality code*] (IYR)
RB RADAR Beacon
R/B Radio Beacon
RB Radio Bearing (DEN)
RB Radio Brenner [*Radio network*] [*Germany*]
RB Railroad Bond [*Business term*] (MHDW)
RB Rate Beacon (AAG)
RB Rated Boost
RB Rating Board [*Medicine*] (MAE)
RB Ration Book
RB Reactor Building [*Nuclear energy*] (NRCH)
RB Read Backward
RB Read Buffer
RB Reading & Bates [*NYSE symbol*] (TTSB)
RB Reading & Bates Corp. [*NYSE symbol*] (SPSG)
RB Reasons to Believe [*An association*] (EA)
rb Rebreathing [*Medicine*] (DAVI)
RB Recirculating Ball [*Automotive engineering*]
RB Reconnaissance Bomber
RB Recovery Beacon
RB Red Book [*Full name is "Drug Topics Red Book," a pharmacist's guide*] [*A publication*]
RB Red Brigades [*Revolutionary group*] [*Italy*]
RB Redeemable Bond [*Investment term*]
RB Reentry Body
RB Reference Burst (LAIN)
RB Regular Budget [*United Nations*]
RB Relative Bearing [*Navigation*]
RB Relay Block (MSA)
RB Remote Batch [*Computer science*] (IAA)
RB Renaut's Bodies [*Neurology*]
RB Renegotiation Board [*Terminated, 1979*] [*Federal government*]
RB Renegotiation Bulletins [*A publication*] (DLA)
RB Report Bibliography
RB Request Block
RB Research Bulletin
RB Reserve Bank (ADA)
RB Reserve Blocked (IAA)
RB Resistance Brazing
RB Respiratory Bronchiole [*Medicine*] (MAE)
RB Restiform Body [*Neuroanatomy*]
RB Restricted Bulletin
Rb Retinoblastoma [*Oncology*]
RB Retractable Boom
RB Retraining Benefits [*Employment*] (OICC)
RB Retrobulbar [*Ophthalmology*] (DAVI)
RB Return to Bias
RB Revenue Bond [*Investment term*]
RB Reverse Blocked
RB Revision Block (MSA)
RB Rich Bitch [*Slang*]
RB Rifle Brigade
RB Right Base [*Aviation*] (FAAC)
RB Right Border [*Genetics*]
RB Right Bronchus [*Anatomy*] (DAVI)
RB Right Buttock [*Anatomy*]
RB Right Fullback [*Soccer*]
RB Rigid Boat
RB Rigid Body
RB Ring Back [*Computer science*] (IAA)
RB Ripple Banking [*Electronics*] (ECII)
RB Ritzaus Bureau [*Press agency*] [*Denmark*]

RB Road Bend
RB Road Buffer (SAA)
RB Roast Beef [*Restaurant slang*]
Rb Rock Bass [*Ichthyology*]
RB Rocket Branch (AAG)
R_B Rockwell Hardness B-Scale (WDAA)
RB Rohon-Beard (Cells) [*Neurology*]
RB Rollback [*Telecommunications*] (TEL)
RB Rollback Disability Claims [*Social Security Administration*] (OICC)
RB Roller Bearing
RB Roman-British
RB Rose Bengal [*A dye*]
RB Round Bobbin [*A publication*] (EAAP)
RB Royal Burgh
RB Rubber Band (ADA)
RB Rubber Base [*Technical drawings*]
RB Rubber Bearing (DS)
RB Rubber Block (DNAB)
Rb Rubidium [*Chemical element*]
RB Ruble [*Monetary unit*] [*Former USSR*]
RB Run Back [*Typography*]
RB Running Back [*Football*]
RB Rural Bank (ADA)
RB Russell Bodies [*Medicine*]
RB Russet-Burbank Potato
RBa Barrington Public Library, Barrington, RI [*Library symbol Library of Congress*] (LCLS)
RBA Rabat [*Morocco*] [*Airport symbol*] (OAG)
RBA Rabat [*Morocco*] [*Seismograph station code, US Geological Survey*] (SEIS)
RBA RADAR Beacon Antenna
RBA Radial Blanket Assembly [*Nuclear energy*] (NRCH)
RBA Radio Beacon Array
RBA Radiobinding Assay [*Analytical chemistry*]
RBA Raisin Bargaining Association (EA)
RBA Ranger Battalions Association (EA)
RBA Rare Bird Alert [*Linnaean Society*] (BARN)
RBA Recovery Beacon Antenna [*NASA*] (KSC)
RBA Reentry Body Assembly
RBA Refined Bitumen Association [*British*] (DBA)
RBA Rehoboth Baster Association [*Namibia*] (PPW)
RBA Relative Binding Affinity [*Chemistry*]
RBA Relative Byte Address [*Computer science*] (MCD)
RBA Religious Booksellers Association (EA)
RBA Rescue Breathing Apparatus
RBA Reserve Bank of Australia
RBA Retail Bakers of America (EA)
RBA Retail, Book, Stationery, and Allied Trades Employees' Association [*A union*] [*British*]
RBA Right Brachial Artery [*Anatomy*] (DAVI)
RBA Risk-Based Audit
RBA Road Bitumen Association [*British*] (BI)
RBA Roadside Business Association (EA)
RBA Rose Bengal Antigen (MAE)
RBA Rotary Beam Antenna
RBA Rotor Blade Antenna
RBA Royal Brunei Airlines [*ICAO designator*] (FAAC)
RBA Royal Society of British Architects
RBA Royal Society of British Artists
RBAAP Riverbank Army Ammunition Plant (AABC)
RBaB Barrington College, Barrington, RI [*Library symbol Library of Congress*] (LCLS)
RBAF Royal Belgian Air Force
RBAF Royal Brunei Armed Forces
RBAL Reprocessing Building Analytical Laboratory [*Nuclear energy*] (NRCH)
RBAM Remote Batch Access Method (IAA)
RBAN Regular Best Asymptotically Normal (PDAA)
RBAP Repetitive Bursts of Action Potential [*Electrophysiology*]
RBAS Rostral Basilar Artery Syndrome [*Medicine*] (DMAA)
RBAUSC Romanian Baptist Association of United States and Canada [*Defunct*] (EA)
RBA WWII Ranger Battalions Association World War II (EA)
RBB Rabbi
RBB Rabbit-Air AG, Zurich [*Switzerland ICAO designator*] (FAAC)
RBB Remazolium Brilliant Blue [*Reactive dye composition*]
RBB Rental Bond Board [*New South Wales, Australia*]
RBB Right Breast Biopsy [*Gynecology*] (DAVI)
RBB Right Bundle Branch [*Cardiology*] (AAMN)
RBBB Right Bundle-Branch Block [*Cardiology*]
RBBP Retinoblastoma Binding Protein (DMAA)
RBBR R-B Rubber Products [*NASDAQ symbol*] (TTSB)
RBBR R-B Rubber Products, Inc. [*NASDAQ symbol*] (SAG)
RBBS Remote Bulletin Board System [*For IBM computers*] [*Telecommunications*]
RBBSB Right Bundle-Branch System Block [*Cardiology*]
RBBT Rebabbit
RBBX Right Breast Biopsy Examination [*Medicine*] (AAMN)
RBC Radio Beam Communications
RBC Radio Bureau of Canada
RBC Rail-Borne Crane [*British*]
RBC Reactive Bias Circuit (MCD)
RBC Real Estate Brokerage Council (EA)
RBC Red Badge of Courage (EA)
RBC Red Blood Cell [*or Corpuscle*] [*Medicine*]
RBC Red Blood Count [*Medicine*]
RBC Redundant Battery Charger (KSC)
RBC Regal Beloit [*AMEX symbol*] (TTSB)
RBC Regal-Beloit Corp. [*AMEX symbol*] (SPSG)
RBC Regional Blood Center [*Red Cross*]
RBC Regulations of British Columbia [*Attorney General's Ministry*] [*No longer available online*] [*Information service or system*] (CRD)
RBC Remote Balance Control
RBC Remote Black Concentrator [*Telecommunications*] (LAIN)
RBC Retortable Barrier Container [*For food*]
RBC Return Beam Camera
RBC Rhodesia Broadcasting Corp.
rbc Ribulose Bisphosphate Carboxylase/Oxygenase (DOG)
RBC Rio Blanco [*Colorado*] [*Seismograph station code, US Geological Survey Closed*] (SEIS)
RBC Roller Bearing Corp. (MCD)
RBC Ropec Industries, Inc. [*Vancouver Stock Exchange symbol*]
RBC Rotating Beam Ceilometer [*Aviation*]
RBC Rotating Biological Contractors [*Processing equipment*]
RBC Royal Bank of Canada [*UTLAS symbol*]
RBC Royal British Colonial Society of Artists
RBC Royal British-Colonial Society of Artists, London [*1886*] (NGC)
RBCA Rhodes Bantam Class Association (EA)
RBC-ADA Red Blood Cell Adenosine Deaminase [*An enzyme*] (AAMN)
RBCC Red Blood Cell Cast [*Hematology*] (DAVI)
RBCC Reentry Body Coordination Committee
RBCCW Reactor Building Closed Cooling Water [*Nuclear energy*] (NRCH)
RBCD Right Border Cardiac Dullness [*Medicine*] (DMAA)
RBC FO Red Blood Cell Fallout [*Hematology*] (DAVI)
RBCH Rod Bank Coil Unit [*Nuclear energy*] (IAA)
RBC/hpf Red Blood Cells per High Power Field [*Hematology*] (MAE)
RBCM Red Blood Cell Mass [*in circulation*]
RBCM Reference Book of Corporate Managements [*Dun's Marketing Services*] [*Information service or system*] (CRD)
RBCO Ryan Beck & Co. [*NASDAQ symbol*] (TTSB)
RBCO Ryan, Beck & Co., Inc. [*West Orange, NJ*] [*NASDAQ symbol*] (NQ)
RBCR Reprocessing Building Control Room [*Nuclear energy*] (NRCH)
RBCS Radio Beam Communications Set
RBCS Reactor Building Cooling System [*Nuclear energy*] (NRCH)
RBCTK Red Blood Cell Transketolase [*Medicine*] (PDAA)
RBCU Reactor Building Cooling Unit [*Nuclear energy*] (NRCH)
RBCV Red Blood Cell Volume [*Hematology*]
RBCWS Reactor Building Cooling Water System (IEEE)
RBD Dallas, TX [*Location identifier FAA*] (FAAL)
RBD Rapid Beam Deflector (WDAA)
RBD Recurrent Brief Depression [*Psychology*] (ECON)
RBD Refined, Bleached, and Deodorized [*Vegetable oil technology*]
RBD Reliability Block Diagram (NITA)
RBD Reliable Block Diagram (MCD)
RBD REM [*Rapid Eye Movement*] Behavior Disorder [*Medicine*]
RBD Rice Blast Disease [*Fungal disease of crop plants*]
RBD Right Border of Dullness [*Cardiology*]
RBD RNA [*Ribonucleic Acid*] Binding Domain [*Biochemistry*]
RBD Rubber Block Drive [*Mechanical power transmission*]
RBD Rubbermaid, Inc. [*NYSE symbol*] (SPSG)
RBD Trans World Express, Inc. [*ICAO designator*] (FAAC)
RBDE RADAR Bright Display Equipment [*FAA*]
RBDM Registrar of Births Deaths and Marriages [*Australia*]
RBDNRQ Received but Did Not Return Questionnaire (AABC)
RBDP Rehoboth Bevryde Demokratiese Party [*Rehoboth Free Democratic Party or Liberation Front*] [*Namibia*] [*Political party*] (EY)
RBDP Rocket Booster Development Program [*Aerospace*] (AAG)
RBDS RADAR Bomb Directing Systems
RBDS Radio Broadcast Data Service (WDMC)
RBDS Radio Broadcast Data System
RBDS Radio Broadcasting Data System
RBDS Roberds, Inc. [*NASDAQ symbol*] (SAG)
RBDT Reverse Blocking Diode Thyristor (IAA)
RBDV Raspberry Bushy Dwarf Virus [*Plant pathology*]
RBE Arbet International Ltd. [*Hungary ICAO designator*] (FAAC)
RBE Bassett, NE [*Location identifier FAA*] (FAAL)
RBE Radiation Biological Effectiveness (IAA)
RBE Radiation Biological Equivalent
RBE Red Ball Express [*Military*]
RBE Relative Biological Effectiveness [*or Efficiency*] [*of stated types of radiation*]
RBE Remain Behind Equipment [*Navy*] (ANA)
RBE Remote Batch Entry (CMD)
RBE Renabie Mines (1981) Ltd. [*Toronto Stock Exchange symbol*]
RBE Replacement Battery Equipment
RBEB Ribbon Bridge Erection Boat (MCD)
RBEC Roller Bearing Engineers Committee (EA)
RBEDT Reactor Building Equipment Drain Tank [*Nuclear energy*] (NRCH)
RB/ER Reduced Blast/Enhanced Radiation
RBES Rule-Based Expert System (LAIN)
RBESI Reactor Building Exhaust System Isolation [*Nuclear energy*] (NRCH)
RBF Raba Raba [*New Guinea*] [*Airport symbol*] (AD)
RBF Radial Basis Function [*Mathematics*]
RBF Read Bit Feedback [*Computer science*] (WDAA)
RBF Reconnaissance by Fire [*Military*] (VNW)
RBF Red Lake Buffalo Resources Ltd. [*Toronto Stock Exchange symbol*]
RBF Regional Blood Flow [*Physiology*]
RBF Remote Batch Facility
RBF Renal Blood Flow [*Medicine*]
RBF Retarded Bomb Fuze

RBF........ Roberson, Fred, Louisville KY [*STAC*]
RBFB........ Retirement Benefits Fund Board [*Australia*]
RBFC........ Razzy Bailey Fan Club (EA)
RBFC........ Retract Before Firing Contractor (NG)
RBFIT........ Retirement Benefits Fund Investment Trust [*Australia*]
RBFPP........ Rocket Booster Fuel Pod Pickup (MUGU)
RBFT........ Romanian Bank of Foreign Trade (IMH)
RBG........ British Guiana Reports of Opinions [*A publication*] (DLA)
RBG........ Right Buccal Ganglion [*Dentistry*]
RBG........ Roseburg [*Oregon*] [*Airport symbol*] (AD)
RBG........ Roseburg, OR [*Location identifier FAA*] (FAAL)
RBGDT........ Royal Botanic Gardens and Domain Trust [*Australia*]
RBGF........ Resin-Bonded Glass-Fiber (PDAA)
RBGH........ Recombinant Bovine Growth Hormone
RBGM........ Real Beam Ground Map (MCD)
RBGNH........ Royal Botanic Gardens and National Herbarium [*Australia*]
RBGS........ Radio Beacon Guidance System (AAG)
RBGS........ Royal Botanic Gardens Sydney [*Australia*]
RBH........ Regal Bahamas International Airways Ltd. [*ICAO designator*] (FAAC)
RBH........ Regimental Beachhead [*Army*]
RBH........ Royal Blind Homes [*Australia*]
RBH........ Royal Bucks Hussars [*British military*] (DMA)
RBH........ Rutherford Birchard Hayes [*US president, 1822-1893*]
RBHA........ Rotor Blade Homing Antenna
RBHB........ Red and Black Horizontal Bands [*Navigation markers*]
RBHC........ Regional Bell Holding Co. (BYTE)
RBHPC........ Rutherford B. Hayes Presidential Center (EA)
RBHPF........ Reactor Building Hydrogen Purge Fan (IEEE)
RBHS........ Reactor Building Heating System [*Nuclear energy*] (NRCH)
RBI........ Rabi [*Fiji*] [*Airport symbol*] (OAG)
RBI........ RADAR Blip Identification Message
RBI........ Radio Berlin International
RBI........ Radiographic Baseline [*Medicine*] (DMAA)
RBI........ Railway Benevolent Institution [*British*]
RBI........ Range Bearing Indicator (MCD)
RBI........ Recombinant Bio-Catalysis, Inc. [*Commercial firm*]
RBI........ Relative Bearing Indicator [*Aviation*] (DA)
RBI........ Remote Bus Isolator (SSD)
RBI........ Reply by Indorsement
RBI........ Reserve Bank of India (ECON)
RBI........ Resource-Based Industry (ODBW)
RBI........ Ripple-Blanking Input (IEEE)
RBI........ Rocketborne Instrumentation (IAA)
RBI........ Root Beer Institute [*Defunct*]
RBI........ Runs Batted In [*Baseball*]
RBiCalz........ Revista Biblica. Rafael Calzada [*Argentina*] [*A publication*] (BJA)
RBID........ Reference Burst Identification (LAIN)
RBIF........ Red Basic Intelligence File (MCD)
Rb Imp........ Rubber Base Impression [*Medicine*] (DMAA)
RBIN........ R & B, Inc. [*NASDAQ symbol*] (SPSG)
RBJ........ Aeroservicios del Bajio, SA de CV [*Mexico*] [*FAA designator*] (FAAC)
RBJ........ Rebun [*Japan*] [*Airport symbol Obsolete*] (OAG)
RBJ........ Tucson, AZ [*Location identifier FAA*] (FAAL)
RBK........ RBK NT Corp. [*Toronto Stock Exchange symbol*]
RBK........ Reebok International Ltd. [*NYSE symbol*] (SPSG)
RBK........ Reebok Intl [*NYSE symbol*] (TTSB)
RBK........ Right Bank
RBK & C........ Royal Borough of Kensington and Chelsea [*England*]
RBKV........ Resource Bank [*NASDAQ symbol*] (TTSB)
RBL........ Radiation Biology Laboratory [*Smithsonian Institution*]
RBL........ Raised Black Letters [*Automobile tires*]
RBL........ Range and Bearing Launch [*Navy*] (CAAL)
RBL........ Rat Basophilic Leukemia [*Cell line*]
RBL........ Reasonable Benefit Limit [*Superannuation*]
RBL........ Rebroadcast Link [*Aerial*]
RBL........ Recommended Buy List
RBL........ Red Bluff [*California*] [*Airport symbol*] (AD)
RBL........ Red Bluff, CA [*Location identifier FAA*] (FAAL)
RBL........ Reid's Base Line [*Neuroanatomy*]
RBL........ Resource Based Learning (ADA)
RBL........ Rheological Boundary Layer [*Physics*]
RBL........ Rifled Breech-Loading [*Gun*]
RBL........ Right Buttock Line (MCD)
RBL........ Rio Blanco Resources Ltd. [*Vancouver Stock Exchange symbol*]
RBL........ Royal British Legion [*British military*] (DMA)
RBL........ Rubblestone [*Technical drawings*]
RBL........ Ruble [*Monetary unit*] [*Former USSR*]
RBL........ Ruch Biblijny i Liturgiczny (BJA)
RBLAC........ Regional Bureau for Latin America and the Caribbean [*United Nations*] (ECON)
RBLC........ Renaissance Business and Law Center, Inc. [*Detroit, MI*] (TSSD)
RBLDR........ Rebuilder
RBLR........ Red-Banded Leaf Roller [*Entomology*]
RBLS........ River Bend Library System [*Library network*]
RBLS........ Royal British Legion of Scotland [*British*] (DBA)
rblt........ Rebuilt (VRA)
RBM........ Range Betting Method
RBM........ Readiness Based Maintenance [*Army*] (DOMA)
RBM........ Real-Time Batch Monitor [*Xerox Corp.*]
RBM........ Reasonable Benefit Multiple
RBM........ Regional Battle Manager [*DoD*]
RBM........ Regional Bone Mass
R-B-M........ Reinforced Brick Masonry
RBM........ Relative Batch Monitor [*Computer science*] (MHDB)
RBM........ Remote Batch Module
RBM........ Resistance to Bending Moment [*Automotive engineering*]
RBM........ Retractor Bulb Motoneuron [*Neurology*]
RBM........ Rifleman's Breaching Munition Program [*Military*] (INF)
RBM........ Rod-Block Monitor [*Nuclear energy*] (NRCH)
RBMA........ Radiologists Business Managers Association (EA)
RBME........ , Egon [*Keil*] [*Haydee Madsen In ballet title, "Initials RBME." Refers to the four starring dancers.*]
RBMECAB........ Regional Bureau of the Middle East Committee for the Affairs of the Blind [*An association*] (EAIO)
RBML........ Rare Books & Manuscript Librarianship [*American Library Association*]
RBMR........ Rotating Bubble Membrane Radiator [*Battelle Pacific Northwest Laboratories*]
RBMS........ Rare Books and Manuscripts Section [*Association of College and Research Libraries*]
RBMS........ Remote Bridge Management Software (HGAA)
RBMT........ Retrospective Bibliographies on Magnetic Tape (NASA)
RBMU........ Regions Beyond Missionary Union [*Later, Regions Beyond Missionary Union International*] (EA)
RBMX........ Robomatix Technologies [*NASDAQ symbol*] (SAG)
RBN........ Brown University, Providence, RI [*OCLC symbol*] (OCLC)
RBN........ PTS [*Predicasts*] Regional Business News [*Cleveland, OH*] [*Database*] [*Information service or system*] (IID)
RBN........ Radiobeacon [*Maps and charts*]
RBN........ Random Block Number [*Computer science*]
RBN........ Red Baron Aviation, Inc. [*ICAO designator*] (FAAC)
R Bn........ Red Beacon [*Nautical charts*]
RBN........ Retrobulbar Neuritis [*Medicine*]
RBN........ Ribbon (MSA)
RBN........ Rybnik [*Poland*] [*Seismograph station code, US Geological Survey*] (SEIS)
RBNA........ Royal British Nurses' Association [*British*] (BI)
RBNC........ Republic Bancorp [*NASDAQ symbol*] (TTSB)
RBNC........ Republic Bancorp, Inc. [*NASDAQ symbol*] (NQ)
RBNK........ Regent Bancshares Corp. [*NASDAQ symbol*] (NQ)
RBNKE........ Regent Bancshares [*NASDAQ symbol*] (TTSB)
RBNKP........ Ragent Bancshrs 10% Cv'A'Pfd [*NASDAQ symbol*] (TTSB)
RBNWE........ Regent Bancshares Wrrt [*NASDAQ symbol*] (TTSB)
RBNZ........ Reserve Bank of New Zealand
RBO........ Rainbow Cargo Express [*Ghana*] [*ICAO designator*] (FAAC)
RBO........ Relationship by Objective [*Management technique*]
RBO........ Ripple-Blanking Output (IEEE)
RBO........ Robore [*Bolivia*] [*Airport symbol*] (AD)
RBO........ Russian Brotherhood Organization (NADA)
RBO........ Russian Brotherhood Organization of the United States of America
RBOA........ Richardson Boat Owners Association (EA)
RBOB........ Reformulated Gasoline Blendstock for Downstream Oxygenated Blending
RBOB........ Renewable-Base Oxygenated Blend [*Automotive fuel*]
RBOC........ Rapid Bloom Offboard Chaff [*Navy ship system*]
RBOC........ Regional Bell Operating Co.
RBOC........ Report Back on Course [*Aviation*] (FAAC)
RBOD........ Required Beneficial Occupancy Data (SAA)
RBOF........ Receiving Basin for Off-Site Fuel [*Nuclear energy*]
RBOF........ Regulated Business Operations Fund (AAGC)
RBOF........ Report Back on Frequency [*Aviation*] (FAAC)
RBOK........ Rinderpest Bovine Old Kabete [*A virus*]
RBOT........ Robotics Information [*EIC/Intelligence, Inc.*] [*Information service or system*] (IID)
R-BOT........ Rotating Bomb Oxidation Test [*Lubricant testing*] [*Automotive engineering*]
RBOUSA........ Russian Brotherhood Organization of the USA (EA)
RBOW........ Rupture of the Bag of Waters [*Medicine*] (DMAA)
RBP........ Raba Raba [*Papua New Guinea*] [*Airport symbol*] (OAG)
RBP........ Ratio Balance Panel
RBP........ Ration Breakdown Point [*Military*] (AABC)
RBP........ Reactor Building Protection [*Nuclear energy*] (NRCH)
RBP........ Registered Business Programmer [*Offered earlier by Data Processing Management Association, now discontinued*] (IEEE)
RBP........ Remote Batch Processing [*Computer science*] (IAA)
RBP........ Resting Blood Pressure [*Cardiology*] (DAVI)
RBP........ Retinol-Binding Protein [*Biochemistry*]
RBP........ Retractable Bow Propeller
RBP........ Return Battery Pack (KSC)
RBP........ Riboflavin-Binding Protein [*Biochemistry*]
RBP........ Ribose Binding Protein [*Biochemistry*]
RBP........ Rocket Branch Panel (AAG)
RBP........ RUBISCO [*Ribulosebisphosphate Carboxylase/Oxygenase*] Binding Protein [*Biochemistry*]
RBPA........ Royal Bancshares of Pennsylvania [*NASDAQ symbol*] (SAG)
RBPA........ Royal Bank of Pennsylvania [*NASDAQ symbol*] (NQ)
RBPAA........ Royal Bancshares(PA)'A' [*NASDAQ symbol*] (TTSB)
RBPB........ Raffles and Bingo Permits Board [*Victoria, Australia*]
RBPC........ Revised Behavior Problem Checklist [*Test*]
RBPCA........ Rare Breeds Poultry Club of America (EA)
RBPCase........ Ribulosebisphosphate Carboxylase [*Also, RUBISCO*] [*An enzyme*]
RBPD........ Religious Book Publishing Division [*of Association of American Publishers*] [*RPG*] [*Superseded by*]
RBPP........ Rotor Burst Protection Program [*NASA*]
RBPr........ Reading & Bates $1.625 Cv Pfd [*NYSE symbol*] (TTSB)
RBPT........ Rose Bengal Plate Test [*Agriculture*] (OA)
RBQ........ Request Block Queue [*Computer science*] (IAA)
RBQ........ Rurrenabaque [*Bolivia*] [*Airport symbol*] (OAG)
RBR........ RADAR Boresight Range (KSC)
RBR........ Rambler Exploration [*Vancouver Stock Exchange symbol*]

RBR .... Refracted Bottom-Reflected Ray
RBR .... Renegotiation Board Regulation [*or Ruling*]
RBR .... Research Branch [*Naval Technical Training Command*] [*Millington, TN*]
RBR .... Rio Branco [*Brazil*] [*Airport symbol*] (OAG)
RBr .... Rogers Free Library, Bristol, RI [*Library symbol Library of Congress*] (LCLS)
RBR .... Rotor Blade RADAR
RBR .... Rubber
RBR .... Rubber
rbr .... Rubber (VRA)
rbr .... Rubricator [*MARC relator code*] [*Library of Congress*] (LCCP)
RBrHi .... Bristol Historical and Preservation Society, Bristol, RI [*Library symbol Library of Congress*] (LCLS)
RBRIZED ...... Rubberized
RBRRS .... Rhythm and Blues Rock and Roll Society [*Later, RBRRSI*] (EA)
RBRRSI .... Rhythm and Blues Rock and Roll Society, Inc. (EA)
RBrRW .... Roger Williams College, Bristol, RI [*Library symbol Library of Congress*] (LCLS)
R-B Rub .... R-B Rubber Products, Inc. [*Associated Press*] (SAG)
RBRV .... Resource-Based Relative Value [*Health insurance*]
RBRVS .... Resource-Based Relative Value Scale [*Medicare*]
RBS .... RADAR Beacon Sequencer
RBS .... RADAR Beacon Station (IAA)
RBS .... RADAR Beacon System
RBS .... RADAR Beam Sharpening
RBS .... RADAR Bombardment System (NATG)
RBS .... RADAR Bomb Scoring
RBS .... RADAR Bombsight
RBS .... Radio Beacon Station (IAA)
RBS .... Raise-Bottom-Slightly [*Definition of a gentleman*] [*Slang British*] (DI)
RBS .... Random Barrage System [*Military*]
RBS .... Random Blood Smear [*Hematology*] (DAVI)
RBS .... Random Blood Sugar [*Medicine*] (MAE)
RBS .... Rare Books Section [*Association of College and Research Libraries*]
RBS .... Rated Breaking Strength (IAA)
RBS .... Raydex Bonded Shield (NITA)
RBS .... Reactor Building Spray [*Nuclear energy*] (NRCH)
RBS .... Reactor Building Sump [*Nuclear energy*] (IAA)
RBS .... Recoverable Booster System
RBS .... Recreational Boating Safety [*USCG*] (TAG)
RBS .... Reformer's Book Shelf [*A publication*]
RBS .... Regional Briefing Station
RBS .... Remote Batch System
RBS .... Remote Battle System
RBS .... Research for Better Schools, Inc. [*Philadelphia, PA*] [*Department of Education*]
RBS .... Resources Breakdown Structure [*Computer science*] (PCM)
RBS .... Ribosome Binding Site [*Biochemistry*]
RBS .... River Bend Station [*Nuclear energy*] (NRCH)
RBS .... Roberts, IL [*Location identifier FAA*] (FAAL)
RBS .... Royal Ballet School [*British*] (DI)
RBS .... Royal Bank of Scotland [*NYSE symbol*] (SPSG)
RBS .... Royal Society of British Sculptors
RBS .... Rutherford Backscattering Spectroscopy
RBSC .... RADAR Bomb Scoring Central (NG)
RBSc .... Royal Bank of Scotland Group Ltd. [*Associated Press*] (SAG)
RBSc .... Royal Bank of Scotland Group PLC [*Associated Press*] (SAG)
RBSc .... Royal Society of British Sculptors
RBSCD .... Rare Book and Special Collections Division [*Library of Congress*]
RBSct .... Royal Bank of Scotland Group Ltd. [*Associated Press*] (SAG)
RBSDS .... Revised Bogardus Social Distance Scale (EDAC)
RBSDV .... Rice Black-Streaked Dwarf Virus [*Plant pathology*]
RBSE .... RADAR Beam Sharpening Element
RBSE .... Repository-Based Software Engineering
rBSF .... Recombinant B-Cell Stimulatory Factor [*Biochemistry*]
RBSF .... Retail Branch Stores Forum (EA)
RBSN .... Reaction Bonded Silicon Nitride [*Materials science and technology*]
RBSNSW ...... Royal Blind Society of New South Wales [*Australia*]
RBSPr .... Royal Bk Scotland Pfd ADS [*NYSE symbol*] (TTSB)
RBSPrB .... Royal Bk Scotland Pfd'B'ADS [*NYSE symbol*] (TTSB)
RBSPrC .... Royal Bk Scotland Pfd'C'ADS [*NYSE symbol*] (TTSB)
RBSPrD .... Royal Bk Scotland Pfd'D' ADS [*NYSE symbol*] (TTSB)
RBSPrX .... Royal Bk Scotland Ex Cap Sec [*NYSE symbol*] (TTSB)
RBSR .... Reprocessing Building (Cable) Spreading Room [*Nuclear energy*] (NRCH)
RBSRA .... Red Berkshire Swine Record Association (EA)
RBSS .... Recoverable Booster Space System (IAA)
RBSS .... Recoverable Booster Support System
RBST .... Rare Breeds Survival Trust [*British*]
RBST .... Remedial and Basic Skills Training (OICC)
RBT .... Rabbet [*Technical drawings*]
RBT .... Radial Beam Tube [*Electronics*]
RBT .... Rainbow Trout
RBT .... Random Breath Testing (ADA)
RBT .... Rational Behavior Therapy
RBT .... Rebate [*Technical drawings*]
RBT .... Rebuilt (DS)
RBT .... Remote Batch Terminal
RBT .... Resistance Bulb Thermometer
RBT .... Ribbon Bridge Transporter (MCD)
RBT .... Rich Best Torque [*Automotive engineering*]
RBT .... Ringback Tone [*Telecommunications*] (TEL)
RBT .... Robinton Aereo CA [*Dominican Republic*] [*ICAO designator*] (FAAC)
RBT .... Rough Blanking Template (MCD)
RBT .... Rubber Tile [*Technical drawings*]
RBT .... Rutland Biotech Ltd. [*Vancouver Stock Exchange symbol*]
RBTA .... Road Builders Training Association (EA)
RBTC .... Rational Behavior Therapy Center [*Psychology*] (DAVI)
RbtCeco .... Robertson-Ceco Corp. [*Associated Press*] (SAG)
RBTE .... Replacement Battery Terminal Equipment
RbtHalf .... Robert Half International [*Associated Press*] (SAG)
RBTIP .... Residential Building Technology Innovation Program (DICI)
RBTL .... RADAR Beacon Tracking Level [*FAA*]
RbtPhr .... Roberts Pharmaceutical Corp. [*Associated Press*] (SAG)
RBTS .... Rider Block Tagline System [*Military*] (CAAL)
RBTWT .... Radial Beam Traveling Wave Tube [*Electronics*]
RBU .... Red Butte Canyon [*Utah*] [*Seismograph station code, US Geological Survey*] (SEIS)
RBU .... Regional Business Unit
RBU .... Remote Buffer Unit (IAA)
Rbu .... Ribulose [*Biochemistry*]
RBUPC .... Research in British Universities, Polytechnics, and Colleges [*Formerly, SRBUC*] [*British Library*]
RBV .... Air Roberval [*Canada ICAO designator*] (FAAC)
RBV .... Reactor Building Vent (IEEE)
RBV .... Relative Biological Value [*Food science*]
RBV .... Return Beam Vidicon [*Satellite camera*]
RBV .... Right Brachial Vein [*Anatomy*] (DAVI)
RBV .... Robbinsville, NJ [*Location identifier FAA*] (FAAL)
RBVC .... Return Beam Vidicon Camera
RBVI .... Reactor Building Ventilation Isolation [*Nuclear energy*] (NRCH)
RBVPRM ...... Reactor Building Vent Process Radiation Monitor [*Nuclear energy*] (NRCH)
RBW .... Rainbow Group [*European political movement*] (ECON)
RBW .... Walterboro, SC [*Location identifier FAA*] (FAAL)
RBWO .... Resonant Backward Wave Oscillator (IAA)
RBX .... Manteo, NC [*Location identifier FAA*] (FAAL)
Rby .... Ribitol [*or Ribityl*] [*Biochemistry*]
RBY .... Royal Bucks Yeomanry [*British military*] (DMA)
RBY .... Ruby [*Alaska*] [*Airport symbol*] (OAG)
rby .... Ruby (VRA)
RBY .... Ruby Resources Ltd. [*Vancouver Stock Exchange symbol*]
RBYC .... Royal Berkshire Yeomanry Cavalry [*British*] (ROG)
RBZ .... Rabat Zaers [*Morocco*] [*Seismograph station code, US Geological Survey*] (SEIS)
RBZ .... Rubidazone [*An antibiotic*]
RC .... Circular Radio Beacon
RC .... Congregation de Notre Dame de la Retraite au Cenacle [*Congregation of Our Lady of the Retreat in the Cenacle*] (EAIO)
RC .... Congregation of Our Lady of the Retreat in the Cenacle [*Roman Catholic women's religious order Italy*]
RC .... Cuba [*IYRU nationality code*] (IYR)
RC .... Grupo Radio Centro [*NYSE symbol*] (SPSG)
RC .... Grupo Radio Centro ADS [*NYSE symbol*] (TTSB)
RC .... Missouri Revised Statutes [*1855*] [*A publication*] (DLA)
RC .... Nicholl, Hare, and Carrow's Railway Cases [*1835-55*] [*A publication*] (DLA)
RC .... Nondirectional Radio Beacon [*ITU designation*] (CET)
RC .... RADAR Computer (MCD)
RC .... RADAR Control (DEN)
RC .... Radio Car [*British*]
RC .... Radio Code (WDAA)
RC .... Radio Code Aptitude Area [*Military*]
R/C .... Radio Command [*or Control*] (KSC)
RC .... Radio Compass
RC .... Radio Components (IAA)
R/C .... Radio Control [*British military*] (DMA)
RC .... Radio Controlled
RC .... Radio-Controlled (IDOE)
RC .... Radix Complement [*Mathematics*]
RC .... Railway Cases [*A publication*] (DLA)
RC .... Rainbow Coalition [*Named for the 1984 political campaign of Rev. Jesse Jackson*] [*Later, NRCI*] (EA)
RC .... Rainform Compressed (MCD)
R/C .... Range Clearance [*NASA*] (KSC)
RC .... Range Command [*NASA*] (NASA)
RC .... Range Contractor [*NASA*] (KSC)
RC .... Range Control [*NASA*] (KSC)
RC .... Range Correction
RC .... Rapid Change (MCD)
RC .... Rapid City [*Diocesan abbreviation*] [*South Dakota*] (TOCD)
RC .... Rapid Curing [*Asphalt grade*]
RC .... Rate Center [*Telecommunications*] (TEL)
RC .... Rate Command
RC .... Rate of Change
R/C .... Rate of Climb [*Aviation*]
R/C .... Ratio Command (MCD)
RC .... Ray Control
RC .... Ray Control Electrode (IAA)
RC .... Rayon and Cotton [*Freight*]
RC .... Reaction Center
RC .... Reaction Chamber
RC .... Reaction Control
RC .... Reaction Coupling (IAA)
RC .... Reactor (IAA)
RC .... Reactor Cavity [*Nuclear energy*] (NRCH)
RC .... Reactor Compartment (MSA)
RC .... Reactor Coolant [*Nuclear energy*] (NRCH)
RC .... Read and Compute

RC............... Read Clock (IAA)
RC............... Reader Code
RC............... Ready Calendar
RC............... Real Circuit
RC............... Rear Commodore [*Navy*] (NVT)
RC............... Rear Connection (MSA)
RC............... Rearwin Club (EA)
RC............... Receipt
RC............... Receiver (IAA)
RC............... Receiver Card
RC............... Reception Center [*Army*]
RC............... Receptor-Chemoeffector [*Biochemistry*]
RC............... Recipient City (NITA)
RC............... Recirculating Cooler
RC............... Recirculatory Air (AAG)
R/C............... Reclining Chair (DAVI)
RC............... Recognition Context [*Computer science*] (PCM)
RC............... Reconnaissance Car [*British*]
R/C............... Reconsign
RC............... Reconstructed Communism Party [*Italy*]
RC............... Reconstruction Committee [*British World War II*]
RC............... Record Carrier (IAA)
RC............... Record Change [*or Changer*] (AAG)
RC............... Record Code (IAA)
RC............... Record Commissioners [*British*] (DLA)
RC............... Record Count [*Computer science*]
RC............... Recording Completing [*Trunk*] [*Telecommunications*] (TEL)
RC............... Recording Controller [*Nuclear energy*] (NRCH)
RC............... Records Check (AFM)
RC............... Records Communication Program [*Army*]
R/C............... Recovered
RC............... Recovery Code
RC............... Recovery Controller [*NASA*] (MCD)
R/C............... Recredited
RC............... Recruiting Center
RC............... Recurring Cost (NASA)
RC............... Red Cell [*or Corpuscle*] [*Hematology*]
RC............... Red Cell Cast [*Hematology*] (MAE)
RC............... Red China
RC............... Red Cross
RC............... Reduced Capability (MCD)
RC............... Reduced Cuing
RC............... Redundancy Check (IAA)
RC............... Reels [*JETDS nomenclature*] [*Military*] (CET)
RC............... Reference Cavity
RC............... Reference Clock [*Telecommunications*] (TEL)
RC............... Reference Configuration (SSD)
RC............... Referred Care [*Medicine*]
RC............... Reformed Church
RC............... Refrigerated Centrifuge
RC............... Regiment of Cavalry [*British military*] (DMA)
RC............... Regional Center
RC............... Regional Commandant [*Air Force British*]
RC............... Regional Commissioner [*Social Security Administration*]
RC............... Regional Council
RC............... Register Containing (SAA)
RC............... Registered Check
RC............... Registered Criminologist
RC............... Register of Copyrights [*US*]
RC............... Registration Cases [*A publication*] (DLA)
RC............... Regnecentralen Computer (NITA)
RC............... Regulatory-Catalytic Unit [*Physiology*]
RC............... Regulatory Council [*FAA*] (MCD)
RC............... Rehabilitation Center
RC............... Rehabilitation Counselor
RC............... Reinforced Concrete [*Technical drawings*]
RC............... Reinstate Card (IAA)
RC............... Relative [*Force*] Cost (MCD)
RC............... Relative Covariance [*Statistics*]
RC............... Relay Computer (BUR)
RC............... Release Card
RC............... Release Clause [*Real estate*]
RC............... Relief Claim
RC............... Remington's Code [*A publication*] (DLA)
RC............... Remote Channel (NITA)
RC............... Remote Component
RC............... Remote Computer
RC............... Remote Concentrator
RC............... Remote Control
RC............... Remote Control Authority [*FCC*] (NTCM)
RC............... Rent Charge
RC............... Rent Control (MHDB)
RC............... Reopened Claim [*Unemployment insurance*] (OICC)
RC............... Reorder Cycle
RC............... Repair Costs [*Technical drawings*]
RC............... Replacement Cost [*Insurance*]
RC............... Replication Controller [*Computer science*]
RC............... Reply Coupon [*Advertising*]
RC............... Report of Contact [*Social Security Administration*] (OICC)
RC............... Reprint with Corrections (DGA)
RC............... Republic of China (CDAI)
R/C............... Request for Checkage [*Navy*]
RC............... Requirements Contract
RC............... Rescriptum [*Counterpart*] [*Latin*]
RC............... Research Center (IEEE)
RC............... Reserve Components [*Military*]
RC............... Reserve Corps
RC............... Reserve Currency
RC............... Resin Coated (MCD)
RC............... Resistance-Capacitance
RC............... Resistance Coupled
R-C............... Resistor-Capacitor
RC............... Resistor-Capacitor Circuit (IAA)
RC............... Resolver Control
RC............... Resource Capital International Ltd. [*Toronto Stock Exchange symbol*]
RC............... Resources Council (EA)
RC............... Respiration Ceased [*Medicine*]
RC............... Respiratory Care [*Medicine*]
RC............... Respiratory Center [*Medicine*]
Rc............... Response, Conditioned [*Psychology*] (DAVI)
RC............... Responsibility Center [*Air Force*] (AFM)
RC............... Rest Camp
RC............... Rest Cure
RC............... Restrained Cursor (NITA)
RC............... Restrictive Cardiomyopathy [*Cardiology*]
RC............... Restrictive Covenant (MHDB)
RC............... Retail Consortium [*British*]
RC............... Retention Catheter [*Medicine*]
RC............... Retrograde Cystogram [*Medicine*] (MAE)
r/c............... Return Cargo [*Shipping*] (DS)
RC............... Revenue Canada
RC............... Revenue Cutter [*Coast Guard*]
RC............... Reverse Course [*Aviation*]
RC............... Reverse Current
RC............... Reversing Gear Clutch (DS)
RC............... Review Classification (NITA)
RC............... Review Cycle [*Military*] (AFIT)
RC............... Revised Code
RC............... Revue Critique de Legislation et de Jurisprudence de Canada [*A publication*] (DLA)
RC............... Ribbon-Frame Camera (MUGU)
RC............... Rib Cage [*Anatomy*]
RC............... Richard of Cashel [*Pseudonym used by Richard Laurence*]
RC............... Rider Club [*Commercial firm*] (EA)
RC............... Right Center [*Position in soccer, hockey*]
RC............... Right Center [*A stage direction*]
RC............... Right Chest [*Medicine*]
RC............... Ring Counter
RC............... Ringing Circuit [*Telecommunications*] (IAA)
RC............... Risk Capital [*Finance*]
RC............... Road Reconnaissance [*FAA*] (TAG)
RC............... Roads Corp. [*Victoria, Australia*] [*Commercial firm*]
RC............... Robert & Carriere [*France*] [*Research code symbol*]
RC............... Robot Controller (IAA)
R_C............... Rockwell Hardness C-Scale (WDAA)
RC............... Roll Center [*Automotive engineering*]
RC............... Roll Channel
RC............... Roller Chock [*Shipfitting*]
RC............... Roller Coating
RC............... Rolling Chassis [*Automotive engineering*]
RC............... Rolls Court [*Legal*] [*British*]
RC............... Roman Catholic
RC............... ROM [*Rough Order of Magnitude*] Control
RC............... Root Canal [*Dentistry*]
rc............... Root Cast [*Archaeology*]
RC............... Rosin Core [*Foundry technology*]
RC............... Rosslyn Connecting Railroad Co. [*AAR code*]
RC............... Rotary Combustion [*Automobile*]
RC............... Rotary Compression (IAA)
RC............... Rotary Converter (IAA)
RC............... Rotation Control (NASA)
RC............... Rough Cast (ADA)
RC............... Rough Cutting [*Construction*]
RC............... Round Corners [*Bookselling*]
RC............... Rounding Control [*Computer programming*] (BYTE)
R/C............... Routing and Clipping (MCD)
RC............... Royal Commission [*British*]
RC............... Royal Crest [*British*]
RC............... Royal Crown [*Soft drink brand*]
R/C............... Rubber-Capped
RC............... Rubber Covered (IAA)
RC............... Rubber Cushioned (WDAA)
RC............... Rudder Club (EA)
RC............... Rules Committee [*House of Representatives*] (OICC)
RC............... Ruling Cases [*A publication*] (DLA)
RC............... Rural Coalition (EA)
RC............... Rural Construction
RC............... Rural Education and Small Schools [*Educational Resources Information Center (ERIC) Clearinghouse*] [*Appalachia University*] (PAZ)
RC............... Rushlight Club (EA)
RC............... Taiwan [*International vehicle registration*] (ODBW)
RCA............... Rabbinical Council of America (EA)
RCA............... Racecourse Association [*British*] (DBA)
RCA............... RADAR Controlled Approach (NVT)
RCA............... Radiative-Convective-Atmospheric [*Meteorology*]
RCA............... Radio Club of America (EA)
RCA............... Radio Collectors of America (EA)
RCA............... Radio Corporation of America (NASA)
RCA............... Radio Correspondents Association (IAA)

RCA .... Radio Council of America (NADA)
RCA .... Radiological Control Area (MCD)
RCA .... Radionuclide Cerebral Angiogram [*Cardiology*] (DAVI)
RCA .... Rapid City, SD [*Location identifier FAA*] (FAAL)
RCA .... Rate Change Authorization (NVT)
RCA .... Ration Cash Allowance [*British military*] (DMA)
RCA .... Reaction Control Assembly
RCA .... Red Cell Agglutination [*Hematology*] (DAVI)
RCA .... Red Cell Aggregate [*or Aggregation*] [*Hematology*]
RCA .... Red Cross Act
RCA .... Reformed Church in America (ROG)
RCA .... Refugee Cash Assistance [*Office of Refugee Resettlement*] [*Department of Health and Human Services*] (GFGA)
RCA .... Regulator of Complement Activation [*Biochemistry*]
RCA .... Remote Control Amplifier (MCD)
RCA .... Renault Club of America [*Defunct*] (EA)
RCA .... REO [*Rawson E. Olds*] Club of America (EA)
RCA .... Replacement Cost Accounting (ADA)
RCA .... Republican Communications Association (EA)
RCA .... Request for Corrective Action (AAG)
RCA .... Resident Care Aide
RCA .... Residential Care Alternatives
RCA .... Residential Care Association [*British*]
RCA .... Retailers' Council of Australia
RCA .... Retirement Care Assoc [*NYSE symbol*] (TTSB)
RCA .... Retirement Care Associates [*NYSE symbol*] (SAG)
RCA .... Review and Concurrence Authority
RCA .... Revival Centres of Australia
RCA .... Richland Aviation [*ICAO designator*] (FAAC)
RCA .... Ricinus communis Agglutinin [*Immunology*]
RCA .... Right Coronary Artery [*Anatomy*]
RCA .... Riot Control Agent (NVT)
RCA .... Rocket Cruising Association (EA)
RCA .... Rodeo Cowboys Association [*Later, PRCA*] (EA)
RCA .... Root Canal Anterior [*Dentistry*]
RCA .... Root Cause Analysis (MCD)
RCA .... Rostrum Clubs of Australia
RCA .... Royal Cambrian Academy [*British*]
RCA .... Royal Cambrian Academy of Art [*British*]
RCA .... Royal Canadian Academy
RCA .... Royal Canadian Academy of Arts
RCA .... Royal Canadian Army (MCD)
RCA .... Royal Canadian Artillery
RCA .... Royal Choral Association [*British*] (BI)
RCA .... Royal College of Art [*British*]
RCA .... Royal Co. of Archers [*British*] (DI)
RCA .... Ruger Collectors Association (EA)
RCA .... Rural Crafts Association [*British*] (DBA)
RCA .... Soil and Water Resources Conservation Act [*1977*]
RCAA .... Rocket City Astronomical Association [*Later, VBAS*] (EA)
RCAA .... Royal Cornwall Agricultural Association [*British*] (DBA)
RCAB .... Review and Concurrence Advisory Board
RCABV .... Replacement-Cost-Adjusted Book Value (DICI)
RCAC .... Radio Corp. of America Communications (MCD)
RCAC .... Remote Computer Access Communications Service
RCAC .... Reserve Component Assistance Coordinator (MCD)
RCAC .... Royal Canadian Armoured Corps
RCACS .... USREDCOM [*United States Readiness Command*] Command and Control System (AABC)
RCADV .... Reverse Course and Advise [*Aviation*] (FAAC)
RCADXC .... Radio Club Amsterdam Dx Certificate (IAA)
RCAE .... Royal Correspondence of the Assyrian Empire [*A publication*] (BJA)
RCAF .... Rail Cost Adjustment Factor [*Interstate Commerce Commission*]
RCAF .... Returned Customer Assignment Form (IAA)
RCAF .... Royal Canadian Air Force
RCAFA .... Royal Canadian Air Force Association
RCAF(WD) .... Royal Canadian Air Force, Women's Division
RCAG .... Remote Center Air/Ground Facility [*NASA*]
RCAG .... Remote Communications Air/Ground Facility [*FAA*] (TAG)
RCAG .... Remote-Controlled Air-Ground Communication Site (MCD)
RCAG .... Replacement Carrier Air Group [*Military*] (AFIT)
RCAI .... Railroadiana Collectors Association Inc. (EA)
R/CAL .... Resistance Calibration (MCD)
RCAMC .... Royal Canadian Army Medical Corps
RCAN .... Recorded Announcement [*Telecommunications*] (TEL)
RC & CR .... Revenue, Civil, and Criminal Reporter [*Calcutta*] [*A publication*] (DLA)
RC & D .... Resource Conservation and Development [*Department of Agriculture*]
RC & L .... Rail, Canal, and Lake [*Transportation*]
RCANSW .... Registered Clubs Association of New South Wales [*Australia*]
RCANSW .... Restaurant and Caterers' Association of New South Wales [*Australia*]
RCAP .... Re Capital Corp. [*NASDAQ symbol*] (SAG)
RCAP .... Rural Community Assistance Program (EA)
RCAPC .... Royal Canadian Army Pay Corps
RCAPDR .... Revolutionary Council of the Algerian People's Democratic Republic
RCAPS .... Roosevelt Center for American Policy Studies [*Defunct*] (EA)
RCAQ .... Restaurant and Caterers' Association of Queensland [*Australia*]
RCAR .... Religious Coalition for Abortion Rights (EA)
RCAS .... Requirements for Close Air Support [*Army*] (MCD)
RCAS .... Research Center for Advanced Study [*University of Texas at Arlington*] [*Research center*] (RCD)
RCAS .... Reserve Component Automation System [*DoD*]
RCAS .... Royal Central Asian Society [*British*]
RCASC .... Royal Canadian Army Service Corps
RCASNSW .... Radio Controlled Aircraft Society of New South Wales [*Australia*]
RCAT .... Radio Code Aptitude Test
RCAT .... Radio-Controlled Aerial Target [*Military*]
RCAT .... Remote-Controlled Aerial Target (NATG)
RCAT .... Ridgetown College of Agricultural Technology [*Canada*] (ARC)
RCAV .... Restaurant and Caterers' Association of Victoria [*Australia*]
RCAVIC .... Radio Corp. of America Victor (IAA)
RCAY .... Gangshan [*China*] [*ICAO location identifier*] (ICLI)
RCB .... Radiation Control Board (AAG)
RCB .... Radio-Controlled Boat (IAA)
RCB .... Randomized Complete Block [*Statistical design*]
RCB .... Reactor Containment Building [*Nuclear energy*] (NRCH)
RCB .... Ready Crew Building (NATG)
RCB .... Reflection Coefficient Bridge
RCB .... Region Control Block [*Computer science*] (BUR)
RCB .... Regular Commissions Board [*British military*] (DMA)
RCB .... Regulations of the Civil Aeronautics Board
RCB .... Releases Control Branch [*Edison, NJ*] [*Environmental Protection Agency*] (GRD)
RCB .... Remote Circuit Breaker (MCD)
RCB .... Remote Control Bandwidth
RCB .... Representative Church Body [*Ireland*] [*Church of England*]
RCB .... Requirements Control Board (MCD)
RCB .... Resource Control Block [*Computer science*] (IBMDP)
RCB .... Retail Credit Bureau (NADA)
RCB .... Revolutionary Communist Party (NADA)
RCB .... Richards Bay [*South Africa*] [*Airport symbol*] (OAG)
RCB .... Right Cornerback [*Football*]
RCB .... Root Canal Bicuspid [*Dentistry*]
RCB .... Rubber Control Board
RCB .... Rubber-Covered Braided (IAA)
RCBA .... Ratio Changers and Boosters Assembly (MCD)
RCBA .... Relative Basal Area of Conifer Species [*Ecology*]
RCBA .... Royal Crown Bottlers Association (EA)
RC BASIC .... Regnecentralen BASIC (NITA)
RCBC .... Rapid Cycling Bubble Chamber (IAA)
RCBC .... Red Cross Blood Center
rCBF .... Regional Cerebral Blood Flow [*Medicine*]
RCBHT .... Reactor Coolant Bleed Holdup Tank [*Nuclear energy*] (NRCH)
RCBR .... Retrospective Cost-Based Reimbursement [*Health insurance*] (GHCT)
RCBR .... Rotating Catalytic Basket Reactor [*Chemical engineering*]
RCBS .... Jinmen [*China*] [*ICAO location identifier*] (ICLI)
RCBT .... Reactor Coolant Bleed Tank [*Nuclear energy*] (NRCH)
RCBV .... Regional Cerebral Blood Volume [*Medicine*] (MAE)
RCBW .... Radiological-Chemical-Biological Warfare
RCBWP .... Rubber-Covered, Braided, and Weatherproof (IAA)
RCC .... Belleville, IL [*Location identifier FAA*] (FAAL)
RCC .... International Society of Reply Coupon Collectors (EA)
RCC .... Rachel Carson Council (EA)
RCC .... Rack Clearance Center [*Association of American Publishers*]
RCC .... RADAR Control Clouds
RCC .... RADAR Control Computer (MCD)
RCC .... RADAR Control Console [*Military*] (CAAL)
RCC .... Radiation Coordinating Council [*Environmental Protection Agency*] (GFGA)
RCC .... Radio Chemical Center [*British*] (BARN)
RCC .... Radiochemical Centre [*United Kingdom*] (NRCH)
RCC .... Radio Common Carrier
RCC .... Radio Common Channels
RCC .... Radio Communications Center
RCC .... Radiological Control Center [*Army*]
RCC .... Rag Chewers' Club [*Amateur radio*]
RCC .... Range Commanders Council [*White Sands Missile Range*] (KSC)
RCC .... Range Communications Component (MCD)
RCC .... Range Control Center [*NASA*]
RCC .... Rape Crisis Center (EA)
RCC .... Ratio of Charges to Costs
RCC .... RCA Corp. Communications
RCC .... Reaction Control Center (KSC)
RCC .... Reactor Closed Cooling [*Nuclear energy*] (NRCH)
RCC .... Read Channel Continue
RCC .... Reader Common Contact
RCC .... Real-Time Computer Complex
RCC .... Recco Corp. [*Vancouver Stock Exchange symbol*]
RCC .... Receptor-Chemoeffector Complex [*Biochemistry*]
RCC .... Record Collectors' Club (EA)
RCC .... Recovery Control Center
RCC .... Rectangular Concrete Columns [*Jacys Computing Services*] [*Software package*] (NCC)
RCC .... Red Carpet Clubs [*United Airlines' club for frequent flyers*] (EA)
RCC .... Red Cell Count [*Hematology*] (MAE)
RCC .... Red Cross of Constantine (EA)
RCC .... Reduced Crude Conversion [*Petroleum refining*]
RCC .... Regional Census Center [*Bureau of the Census*] (GFGA)
RCC .... Regional Climate Center (USDC)
RCC .... Regional Climate Center [*Marine science*] (OSRA)
RCC .... Regional Control Center [*Air Force*] (DOMA)
RCC .... Regional Coordination Committee [*Department of Health and Human Services*]
RCC .... Regulated Common Carrier [*Computer science*] (TNIG)
RCC .... Regulation Communication Center [*RSPA*] (TAG)
RCC .... Reinforced Carbon-Carbon (MCD)
RCC .... Relative Casein Content [*Food analysis*]
RCC .... Remote Center Compliance [*Computer science*]
RCC .... Remote Combat Center (SAA)

RCC .... Remote Communications Central
RCC .... Remote Communications Complex
RCC .... Remote Communications Concentrator
RCC .... Remote Communications Console
RCC .... Remote Computer Center (MCD)
RCC .... Remote Control Complex (SAA)
RCC .... Renal Cell Carcinoma [*Medicine*]
RCC .... Representative Church Council [*Episcopalian*]
RCC .... Request for Contract Clearance (AAGC)
RCC .... Rescue Control Center
RCC .... Rescue Coordination Center [*Coast Guard*]
RCC .... Rescue Crew Commander (AFM)
RCC .... Research Computing Center [*University of New Hampshire*] [*Research center*] (RCD)
RCC .... Reset Control Circuit
RCC .... Residential Colleges Committee (AIE)
RCC .... Resistance-Capacitance Coupling (DNAB)
RCC .... Resistor Color Code (DEN)
RCC .... Resource Category Code [*Military*] (CAAL)
RCC .... Resource Control Center [*Military*] (AFIT)
RCC .... Resources for Community Change [*Defunct*] (EA)
RCC .... Reusable Carbon-Carbon (MCD)
RCC .... Right to Choose Coalition [*Australia*]
RCC .... Ring-Closed Circuit [*Computer science*] (IAA)
RCC .... Rio Carpintero [*Cuba*] [*Seismograph station code, US Geological Survey*] (SEIS)
RCC .... Riverside City College [*California*]
RCC .... Robotic Command Center [*Army*]
RCC .... Rochester Community College, Rochester, MN [*OCLC symbol*] (OCLC)
RCC .... Rockefeller Center Cable
RCC .... Rocket Combustion Chamber (SAA)
RCC .... Rod Cluster Control [*Nuclear energy*] (NRCH)
RCC .... Roller-Compacted Concrete
RCC .... Roman Catholic Church
RCC .... Roman Catholic Church Curate (ROG)
RCC .... Rough Combustion Cutoff [*NASA*]
RCC .... Routine Coronary Care [*Orders*] [*Cardiology*] (DAVI)
RCC .... Routing Control Center (IAA)
RCC .... Rubber Covered Cable (MSA)
RCC .... Rural Construction Cadre [*Military*]
RCC .... Russian Corps Combatants (EA)
RCCA .... Race Car Club of America [*An association*]
RCCA .... Record Carrier Competition Act [*1981*]
RCCA .... Recovery Control Center, Atlantic (DNAB)
RCCA .... Remote Control Rod Cluster Assembly (IAA)
RCCA .... Rickenbacker Car Club of America (EA)
RCCA .... Rod Cluster Control Assembly [*Nuclear energy*] (NRCH)
RCCA .... Rough Combustion Cutoff Assembly [*NASA*] (KSC)
RCCA .... Route Capacity Control Airline (DS)
RCCAM .... Remote Computer Communications Access Method [*Computer science*] (MHDB)
RCC & S ...... Riots, Civil Commotions, and Strikes [*Insurance*]
RCCB .... Remote Control Circuit Breaker (NASA)
RCCB .... Residual Current Circuit Breaker [*Electronics*] (EECA)
RCCC .... Range Communications Control Center [*Military*] (MCD)
RCCC .... Regular Common Carrier Conference (EA)
RCCC .... Reserve Component Career Counselor [*Military*] (AABC)
RCCC .... Reserve Component Coordination Council (MCD)
RC/CC .... Responsibility Center/Cost Center [*Military*] (AFIT)
RCCC .... Return Critical Control Circuit
RCCC .... Royal Caledonia Curling Club
RCCC .... Royal Commission on Corporate Concentration [*Canada*]
RCCC .... Royal Curling Club of Canada
RCCC .... Rural Cellular 'A' [*NASDAQ symbol*] (TTSB)
RCCC .... Rural Cellular Corp. [*NASDAQ symbol*] (SAG)
RC/CCI .... Resource Code/Cost Category Input (SAA)
RCCDF .... Remote Control Center Development Facility (SSD)
RCCE .... Regional Congress of Construction Employers (EA)
RC-CE .... Revenue Canada, Customs and Excise
RCCE .... Rotating Cylinder-Collector Electrode [*Electrochemistry*]
RCCES .... Research Centre for Canadian Ethnic Studies [*University of Calgary*] [*Research center*] (RCD)
RCCF .... Reserve Components Contingency Force [*Military*]
RCCh .... Roman Catholic Chaplain [*Navy British*]
RCCH .... Roman Catholic Church
RCCL .... Royal Caribbean Cruise Line
RCCLS .... Resource Center for Consumers of Legal Services [*Later, NRCCLS*] (EA)
RCCM .... Regional Committee for Community Medicine (DMAA)
RCCM .... Regional Contingency Construction Management (DOMA)
RCCM .... Research Council for Complementary Medicine [*British*] (IRUK)
RCC/MG .... Range Commanders Council Meteorological Group [*White Sands Missile Range*]
RCCO .... RADAR Control Console Operator [*Military*] (CAAL)
RCCOL .... Reinforced Concrete Column [*Camutek*] [*Software package*] (NCC)
RC COMAL ... Regnecentralen COMAL (NITA)
RCCOW .... Return Channel Control Orderwire [*Military*] (CAAL)
RCCP .... Recorder and Communications Control Panel (NASA)
RCCP .... Recovery Control Center, Pacific (DNAB)
RCCP .... Reinforced Concrete Culvert Pipe [*Technical drawings*]
RCCP .... Renal Cell Carcinoma, Papillary [*Medicine*] (DMAA)
RCCP .... Rough Cut Capacity Planning [*Manufacturing management*]
RCCPDS .... Reserve Component Common Personnel Data System [*Marine Corps*] (GFGA)
RCCPLD .... Resistance-Capacitance Coupled
RCCRA .... Rough Combustion Cutoff Replaceable Assembly [*NASA*] (KSC)
RCCS .... Rate Command Control System (AAG)
RCCS .... Reactor Cavity Cooling System [*Nuclear energy*]
RCCS .... Remote Communicatios Central Set (SAA)
RCCS .... Royal Canadian Corps of Signals
RCCT .... Randomized Controlled Clinical Trial [*Medicine*] (DMAA)
RCCT .... Reseau Canadien des Centres de Toxicologie (AC)
RCC/TG .... Range Commanders Council Telemetry Group [*White Sands Missile Range, NM*]
RCCTL .... Resistor Capacitor-Coupled Transistor Logic (IAA)
RCCUS .... Republican Citizens Committee of the United States (EA)
RCCV .... Red Clover Cryptic Virus [*Plant pathology*]
RCD .... Rabbit Calicivirus Disease
RCD .... Rabbit Calicivirus Disease
RCD .... RADAR Cloud Detection Report [*NWS*] (FAAC)
RCD .... Rapid City [*South Dakota*] [*Seismograph station code, US Geological Survey*] (SEIS)
RCD .... Rassemblement Constitutionnel Democratique [*Tunisia*] [*Political party*] (ECON)
RCD .... Rassemblement pour la Culture et la Democratie [*Algeria*] [*Political party*] (EY)
RCD .... Received
rcd .... Received (ODBW)
RCD .... Receiver-Carrier Detector
RCD .... Reconnaissance Cockpit Display
RCD .... Recontact Date [*Automotive retailing*]
RCD .... Record
RCD .... Redox Chemiluminescence Detector [*Instrumentation*] [*Sievers*]
RCD .... Reduced Crude Desulfurization [*Petroleum refining*]
RCD .... Reference Configuration Description (SSD)
RCD .... Regent's Canal Dock [*British*]
RCD .... Registered Connective Device (MHDB)
RCD .... Reinforcement Control Depot [*Air Force*]
RCD .... Relative Cardiac Dullness [*Medicine*]
RCD .... Research and Acquisition Communications Division [*Military*]
RCD .... Research Centers Directory [*A publication*]
RCD .... Residual Current Device [*Electrical circuits*]
RCD .... Retrofit Configuration Drawing (MCD)
RCD .... Reverse Circulation Drilling [*Mining technology*]
RCD .... Reverse Current Device [*Electronics*] (MSA)
RCD .... Rock Coring Device
RCD .... Rocket Cushioning Device (NG)
RCD .... Route Control Digit [*Telecommunications*] (TEL)
RCD .... Royal Canadian Dragoons [*Military*]
RCD .... Rural Civil Defense
RCD .... Sisters of Our Lady of Christian Doctrine [*Roman Catholic religious order*]
RCDA .... Recurrent Chronic Dissecting Aneurysm [*Medicine*] (DMAA)
RCDA .... Religion in Communist Dominated Areas [*A publication*]
RCDA .... Research Career Development Awards [*Department of Health and Human Services*]
RCDB .... Rubber-Covered Double-Braided (IAA)
RCDC .... Pingdong (South) [*China*] [*ICAO location identifier*] (ICLI)
RCDC .... RADAR Course-Directing Central [*Military*]
RCDC .... RADAR Course-Directing Control (MUGU)
RCDC .... Radiation Chemistry Data Center [*Notre Dame, IN*] [*Department of Commerce*]
RCDC .... Royal Canadian Dental Corps
RCDCB .... Regional Civil Defense Coordination Boards [*DoD*] (AABC)
RCDD .... Registered Communications Distribution Designer [*Building Industry Consul ting Service International*] [*Designation awarded by*] (TSSD)
RC de l'E ..... Rapports de la Cour de l'Echiquier [*Exchequer Court Reports*] [*Canada*] [*A publication*] (DLA)
RCDEP .... Rural Civil Defense Education Program
RCDG .... Recording (MSA)
RCDHS .... Rehabilitation and Chronic Disease Hospital Section [*American Hospital Association*] (EA)
RCDI .... Longtan [*China*] [*ICAO location identifier*] (ICLI)
RCDIW .... Royal Commission on the Distribution of Income and Wealth [*British*]
RCDLR .... Remote Control Door Lock Receiver
RCDM .... Regional Centre for Drama and Music [*University of New England, Australia*]
RCDMB .... Regional Civil and Defense Mobilization Boards
RCDMS .... Reliability Central Data Management System [*Air Force*] (DIT)
RCDNA .... RADAR Cloud Detection Report Not Available [*NWS*] (FAAC)
RCDNE .... RADAR Cloud Detection Report No Echoes Observed [*NWS*] (FAAC)
RCDNO .... RADAR Cloud Detector Inoperative Due to Breakdown Until [*NWS*] (FAAC)
RCDO .... Regional Case Development Officer [*Environmental Protection Agency*] (GFGA)
RCDOM .... RADAR Cloud Detector Inoperative Due to Maintenance Until [*NWS*] (FAAC)
RCDP .... Record Parallel (MCD)
RCDR .... Recorder (KSC)
RCDR .... Relative Corrected Death Rate [*Medicine*] (DMAA)
RCDS .... Records
RCDS .... Reinforced Concrete Detailing System (PDAA)
RCDS .... Royal College of Defence Studies [*British*]
RCDS .... Rural Community Development Service [*Abolished, 1970*] [*Department of Agriculture*]
RCDT .... Reactor Coolant Drain Tank [*Nuclear energy*] (NRCH)
RCE .... Aerocer SA [*Mexico ICAO designator*] (FAAC)
RCE .... Radio Communications Equipment

RCE............ Radio Control Equipment [*FAA*] (TAG)
RCE............ Railway Construction Engineer [*British military*] (DMA)
RCE............ Rapid Changing Environment (AAG)
RCE............ Rapid Circuit Etch
RCE............ Ray Control Electrode (IAA)
RCE............ Reaction Control Engine
RCE............ Reactor Compatibility Experiment [*Nuclear energy*] (NRCH)
RCE............ Reasonable Compensation Equivalent [*Medicine*] (DMAA)
rce............ Recording Engineer [*MARC relator code*] [*Library of Congress*] (LCCP)
RCE............ Reentry Control Electronics
RCE............ Reliability Control Engineering (AAG)
RCE............ Religious of Christian Education [*Roman Catholic women's religious order*]
RCE............ Remote Control Equipment (DIT)
RCE............ Repetitive Counterelectrophoresis (PDAA)
RCE............ Restricted Coulomb Energy
RCE............ Rice University, Fondren Library, Houston, TX [*OCLC symbol*] (OCLC)
RCE............ Right Center Entrance (WDAA)
RCE............ Right Center Entrance [*Theater*] (WDMC)
RCE............ Roche Harbor [*Washington*] [*Airport symbol*] (OAG)
RCE............ Ross Consumer Electronics [*British*]
RCE............ Rotary Combustion Engine (PDAA)
RCE............ Royal Canadian Engineers
RCE............ Union Restaurants Collectifs Europeens [*European Catering Association*] (EAIO)
RCEA.......... Recreational Coach and Equipment Association [*Later, MHI*]
RCEA.......... Research Council Employees' Association [*Canada*]
RCEAC........ Regional Civil Emergency Advisory Committee [*Formerly, JRCC*] [*Civil defense*]
RCEDD........ Resources, Community and Economic Development Division (AAGC)
RCEEA........ Radio Communications and Electronic Engineers Association
RCEI.......... Range Communications Electronics Instructions [*NASA*] (KSC)
RCEID........ Radio-Controlled Improvised Explosive Device [*Criminology*] (LAIN)
RCEME........ Royal Canadian Electrical and Mechanical Engineers
RCEP.......... Royal Commission on Environmental Pollution [*British*]
RCEP.......... Rural Concentrated Employment Program [*Department of Labor*]
RCERA........ Religious Committee for the ERA [*Equal Rights Amendment*] (EA)
RCERIP...... Reserve Component Equipment Readiness Improvement Program [*Military*] (AABC)
RCEUSA...... Romanian Catholic Exarchy in the United States of America (EA)
RCEVH........ Research Centre for the Education of the Visually Handicapped [*University of Birmingham*] [*British*] (CB)
RCF............ Radcliffe Resources Ltd. [*Vancouver Stock Exchange symbol*]
RCF............ Radiocommunication Failure Message [*Aviation*]
RCF............ Ratio Correction Factor
RCF............ Reader's Comment Form (IBMDP)
RCF............ Recall Finder
RCF............ Red Cell Folate [*Hematology*] (AAMN)
RCF............ Redundant Churches Fund [*British*] (EAIO)
RCF............ Refractory Ceramic Fiber [*Materials science*]
RCF............ Regenerated Cellulose Film [*Organic chemistry*]
RCF............ Relative Centrifugal Force
RCF............ Relative Cumulative Frequency
RCF............ Remote Call Forwarding [*Bell System*]
RCF............ Remote Cluster Facility (IAA)
RCF............ Remote Communication Facility [*FAA*] (TAG)
RCF............ Repair Cost Factor [*Navy*]
RCF............ Repair Cycle Float [*Military*] (AABC)
RCF............ Retail Computer Facilities
RCF............ Review of Contemporary Fiction [*A publication*] (BRI)
RCF............ River Conservation Fund [*Later, ARCC*] (EA)
RCF............ Rock Characterization Facility [*Nuclear waste storage*]
RCF............ Rosicrucian Fellowship (EA)
RCF............ Rotating Cylinder Flap
RCF............ Royal Carmarthen Fusiliers [*British military*] (DMA)
RCFA.......... Religious Communities for the Arts [*Defunct*] (EA)
RCFA.......... Royal Canadian Field Artillery [*Military*]
RCFC.......... Ray Coble Fan Club [*Defunct*] (EA)
RCFC.......... Reactor Containment Fan Cooler [*Nuclear energy*] (NRCH)
RCFC.......... Ron Craddock Fan Club (EA)
RCFC.......... Rosanne Cash Fan Club (EA)
RCFC.......... Roy Clark Fan Club (EA)
RCFC.......... Roy Clayborne Fan Club (EA)
RCFC(U)...... Reactor Core Fan Cooling (Unit) (IEEE)
RCFF.......... Repair Cycle Float Factor (MCD)
RCFM.......... Radiocommunication Failure Message [*Aviation*] (WDAA)
RCFN.......... Taidong/Fengnian [*China*] [*ICAO location identifier*] (ICLI)
RCFP.......... Reporters Committee for Freedom of the Press (EA)
RCFR.......... Red Cross Field Representative
RCFR.......... Royal Canadian Fleet Reserve
RCFS.......... Jiadong [*China*] [*ICAO location identifier*] (ICLI)
RCFT.......... Randomized Controlled Field Trial [*Statistics*]
RCFT.......... Remove Cloud From Title (MHDB)
RCFU.......... Rotary Carton Feed Unit
RCFZ.......... Fengshan [*China*] [*ICAO location identifier*] (ICLI)
RCG............ Radiation Concentration Guide [*Formerly, MPC*]
RCG............ Radioactivity Concentration Guide (KSC)
RCG............ Radio Command Guidance (AAG)
RCG............ Radioelectrocardiograph (IAA)
rCG............ Rat Chorionic Gonadotropin
RCG............ Reaction Cured Glass [*Ceramic technology*]
RCG............ Receiving (AAG)
RCG............ Recommended Concentration Guide [*Nuclear energy*] (NRCH)
RCG............ Recovery Control Group (IAA)
RCG............ Reference Concept Group (SSD)
RCG............ Restricted Categorical Grammar
RCG............ Retail Credit Group [*British*]
RCG............ Reverberation Control of Gain
RCG............ Right Cerebral Ganglion [*Anatomy*]
RCGA.......... Royal Canadian Garrison Artillery [*Military*]
RCGC.......... Royal Canberra Golf Club [*Australia*]
RCGD.......... Research Center for Group Dynamics [*University of Michigan*] [*Research center*] (RCD)
RCGI.......... Ludao [*China*] [*ICAO location identifier*] (ICLI)
RCGI.......... Renal Care Group [*NASDAQ symbol*] (TTSB)
RCGM.......... Reactor Cover Gas Monitor [*Nuclear energy*] (NRCH)
RCGM.......... Taoyuan [*China*] [*ICAO location identifier*] (ICLI)
RCGP.......... Royal College of General Practitioners [*British*]
rCGRP........ Rat Calcitonin Gene-Related Peptide [*Biochemistry*]
RCGS.......... RADAR Correlation Guidance Study
RCGS.......... Radio Command Guidance System (IAA)
RCGS.......... Recent College Graduates Survey [*Department of Education*] (GFGA)
RCGUGA...... Resistance-Capacitance Grounded Unity Gain Amplifier (IAA)
RCH............ Chile [*International vehicle registration*] (ODBW)
RCH............ Helicopter Air Service, Inc. [*ICAO designator*] (FAAC)
RCH............ Rancho
RCH............ Rauch Industries, Inc. [*AMEX symbol*] (SPSG)
RCH............ Rectocolic Hemorrhage [*Medicine*] (DMAA)
RCH............ Residential Children's Home (AIE)
RCH............ Rich Resources Ltd. [*Vancouver Stock Exchange symbol*]
RCH............ Riohacha [*Colombia*] [*Airport symbol*] (OAG)
RCH............ Rotary Clothes Hoist (ADA)
RCH............ Rural Cooperative Housing
RCHA.......... Rachel Carson Homestead Association (EA)
RCHA.......... Reference Library of Hispanic America [*A publication*]
RCHA.......... Royal Canadian Horse Artillery
RCHB.......... Reserve Cargo-Handling Battalion [*Navy*] (DOMA)
RCHCS........ Regenerable Carbon Dioxide and Humidity Control System (NASA)
RCHF.......... Richfood Hldgs [*NASDAQ symbol*] (TTSB)
RCHF.......... Richfood Holdings, Inc. [*NASDAQ symbol*] (NQ)
RCHF.......... Right Congestive Heart Failure [*Medicine*] (DMAA)
RCHG.......... Reduced Charge (AAG)
RCHI.......... Risk Capital Holdings [*NASDAQ symbol*] (TTSB)
RCHI.......... Risk Capital Holdings, Inc. [*NASDAQ symbol*] (SAG)
RCHM.......... Remote Computer-Controlled Hardware Monitor (MHDI)
RCHM.......... Royal Commission on Historical Monuments [*British*]
RCHRA........ Regional Council on Human Rights in Asia (EAIO)
RCHS.......... Railway and Canal Historical Society [*British*] (BI)
RCHS.......... Royal Caledonian Horticultural Society [*British*] (BI)
RCHT.......... Ratchet [*Design engineering*]
RCH/TCH...... Receive Channel/Transmit Channel [*Telecommunications*] (MCD)
RCHY.......... Richey Electronics [*NASDAQ symbol*] (SAG)
RCI............ RADAR Coverage Indication [*or Indicator*]
RCI............ RADAR Coverage Indicator (IAA)
RCI............ Radio Canada International
RCI............ Radiochemical Inspectorate [*British*] (NUCP)
RCI............ Radio Communications Instruction (MUGU)
RCI............ Range Communications Instruction (IAA)
RCI............ Range Communications Instructions [*NASA*] (KSC)
RCI............ Read Channel Initialize
RCI............ Reading Comprehension Interview (EDAC)
RCI............ Recommended Course Indicator
RCI............ Reggio Calabria [*Italy*] [*Seismograph station code, US Geological Survey*] (SEIS)
RCI............ Religious of Christian Instruction [*Roman Catholic religious order*]
RCI............ Remote Control Indicator (CAAL)
RCI............ Remote Control Interface
RCI............ Republique de la Cote d'Ivoire [*Republic of the Ivory Coast*] (BARN)
RC/I............ Request for Change and/or Information (SAA)
RCI............ Request for Contract Investigation (MCD)
RCI............ Resident Classification Index
RCI............ Resident Cost Inspector
RCI............ Resort Condominiums International (EA)
RCI............ Respiratory Control Index [*Biochemistry*]
RCI............ Retail Confectioners International (EA)
RCI............ Roadway Congestion Index [*BTS*] (TAG)
RCI............ ROC Communities [*NYSE symbol*] (SPSG)
RCI............ Rochester Commercial and Industrial [*Database*]
RCI............ Rogers Communications, Inc. [*Toronto Stock Exchange symbol Vancouver Stock Exchange symbol*]
RCI............ Roof Consultants Institute (EA)
RCI............ Routing Control Indicator [*Telecommunications*] (TEL)
RCI............ Royal Canadian Institute (BARN)
RCI............ Royal Channel Islands Yacht Club (BI)
RCI............ Royal Colonial Institute [*British*]
RCIA.......... Red Cell Immune Adherence [*Medicine*] (DMAA)
RCIA.......... Remote Control Interface Adapter (IAA)
RCIA.......... Retail Clerks International Association [*Later, UFCWIU*] (EA)
RCIA.......... Retail Credit Institute of America [*Later, NFCC*]
RCI.A.......... Rogers Commun Cl 'A' [*TS, Symbol*] (TTSB)
RCIADIC...... Royal Commission into Aboriginal Deaths in Custody [*Australia*]
RCIC.......... Reactor Core Isolation Cooling [*Nuclear energy*] (NRCH)
RCIC.......... Red Cross International Committee
RCIC.......... Regional Coastal Information Center [*National Marine Advisory Service*] (MSC)
RCIC.......... Reserve Component Issues Conference [*Military*] (MCD)
RCIC.......... Royal Canadian Infantry Corps
RCICS........ Reactor Core Isolation Cooling System [*Nuclear energy*] (NRCH)

RCID .... Recruiter Code Identification [*Army*] (AABC)
RCIE .... Regional Council for International Education [*University of Pittsburgh*]
RCII .... Renters Choice [*NASDAQ symbol*] (TTSB)
RCII .... Renters Choice, Inc. [*NASDAQ symbol*] (SAG)
RCIL .... Reliability Critical Item List (AAG)
RCIP .... Reseau Canadien d'Information sur le Patrimoine (AC)
RCIRF .... Radiologic Contrast-Induced Renal Failure [*Medicine*] (DMAA)
RCIRR .... Reserve Components, Individual Ready Reserve [*Military*]
RCIS .... Remote Computer Interface Subsystem (MHDB)
RCIS .... Research Conference on Instrumentation Science
RCITR .... Red Cell Iron Turnover Rate [*Hematology*] (MAE)
RCIU .... Remote Computer Interface Unit
RCIVS .... Regional Conference on International Voluntary Service [*Commercial firm*] (EAIO)
RCJ .... RCJ Resources Ltd. [*Vancouver Stock Exchange symbol*]
RCJ .... Reaction Control Jet
RCJ .... Reinforced Composite Joint
RCJ .... Reports of Certain Judgments of the Supreme Court, Vice-Admiralty Court, and Full Court of Appeal, Lagos [*1884-92*] [*Nigeria*] [*A publication*] (DLA)
RC(J) .... Rettie, Crawford, and Melville's Session Cases, Fourth Series [*1873-98*] [*Scotland*] [*A publication*] (DLA)
RCJ .... Rogationist Fathers (TOCD)
rcj .... Rogationist Fathers (TOCD)
RCJ .... Royal Courts of Justice [*British*]
RCK .... Rockdale, TX [*Location identifier FAA*] (FAAL)
RCK .... Rockford [*Diocesan abbreviation*] [*Illinois*] (TOCD)
RCKH .... Gaoxiong [*China*] [*ICAO location identifier*] (ICLI)
RCKU .... Jiayi [*China*] [*ICAO location identifier*] (ICLI)
RCKW .... Hengchun [*China*] [*ICAO location identifier*] (ICLI)
RCKY .... Rockies (FAAC)
RCKY .... Rocky
RCKY .... Rocky Shoes & Boots [*NASDAQ symbol*] (TTSB)
RCKY .... Rocky Shoes & Boots, Inc. [*NASDAQ symbol*] (SAG)
RCL .... Radial Collateral Ligament [*Anatomy*]
RCL .... Radiation Counter Laboratories, Inc.
RCL .... Radio Command Linkage (AAG)
RCL .... Radio Communications Link [*FAA*] (TAG)
RCL .... Ramp Craft Logistic [*Navy British*]
RCL .... Ramped Cargo Lighter
RCL .... Ramsey County Public Library, St. Paul, MN [*OCLC symbol*] (OCLC)
RCL .... Rationalist Concept of Logic
RCL .... Reactor Coolant Loop [*Nuclear energy*] (NRCH)
RCL .... Read Clock (IAA)
RCL .... Recall (MSA)
RCL .... Receive Clock (IAA)
RCL .... Recoil (MSA)
RCL .... Recoilless Launcher
RCL .... Redcliff [*Vanuatu*] [*Airport symbol*] (OAG)
RCL .... Reichhold Ltd. [*Toronto Stock Exchange symbol*]
RCL .... Reliability Component List (MCD)
RCL .... Reliability Control Level (KSC)
RCL .... Remote Control Location
RCL .... Repair Cycle Level
RCL .... Required Cleanliness Level [*Automobile maintenance*]
RCL .... Research Computation Laboratory [*University of Houston*] [*Research center*] (RCD)
RCL .... Reserved Commodity List [*World War II*]
RCL .... Resistance, Capacitance & Inductive (NITA)
RCL .... Ricegrowers' Cooperative Ltd. [*Australia*]
RCL .... Royal Canadian Legion
RCL .... Royal Caribbean Cruise Line [*NYSE symbol*] (SPSG)
RCL .... Royal Caribbean Cruises [*NYSE symbol*] (TTSB)
RCL .... Rubber Continuous Liner (DS)
RCL .... Ruby Crystal LASER
RCL .... Ruling Case Law
RCL .... Runway Centerline [*Aviation*]
RCLA .... Regis College Lay Apostolate [*Defunct*] (EA)
RCLB .... Revolutionary Communist League of Britain [*Political party*] (PPW)
RCLC .... Reactor Coolant Leakage Calculation (IEEE)
RCLC .... Reactor Coolant Letdown Cooler [*Nuclear energy*] (NRCH)
RCLC .... Republican Congressional Leadership Council (EA)
RCLC .... Xiao Liu Qiu [*China*] [*ICAO location identifier*] (ICLI)
RCLD .... Reclined (MSA)
RC-LDAP .... Reserve Component Leader Development Action Plan [*Army*] (INF)
RCLED .... Resonantcavity Light-Emitting Diode [*Electronics*]
RCLG .... Recoilless Gun (AABC)
RCLG .... Taizhong [*China*] [*ICAO location identifier*] (ICLI)
RCLGGL .... Royal Commission on Local Government in Greater London [*British*]
RCLJ .... Revue Critique de Legislation et de Jurisprudence [*A publication*] (DLA)
RCLL .... Runway Center Line Lights [*ICAO designator*] (FAAC)
RCLM .... Reclaim (AABC)
RCLM .... Runway Centerline Marking [*Aviation*]
RCLMG .... Reclaiming
RCLO .... Reports Control Liaison Officer [*Army*] (AABC)
RCLR .... Recoilless Rifle (AABC)
RCLS .... Lishan [*China*] [*ICAO location identifier*] (ICLI)
RCLS .... Ramapo Catskill Library System [*Library network*]
RCLS .... Recoilless
RCLS .... Runway Centerline Light System [*FAA*] (TAG)
RCLU .... Jilong [*China*] [*ICAO location identifier*] (ICLI)
RCLWUNE .... Regional Commission on Land and Water Use in the Near East (EA)
RCLY .... Lanyu [*China*] [*ICAO location identifier*] (ICLI)
RCM .... Aircam Aviation Ltd. [*British ICAO designator*] (FAAC)
RCM .... ARCO Chemical [*NYSE symbol*] (TTSB)
RCM .... ARCO Chemical Co. [*NYSE symbol*] (SPSG)
RCM .... Aviation Radio and RADAR Countermeasures Technician [*Navy*]
RCM .... La Republique des Citoyens du Monde [*Commonwealth of World Citizens*]
RCM .... RADAR [*or Radio*] Countermeasures [*Military*] (AAG)
RCM .... Radial Compression Model [*Chromatography*]
RCM .... Radiative-Convective Model [*Meteorology*]
RCM .... Radiocontrast Media [*Clinical chemistry*]
RCM .... Radio-Controlled Mine [*Military*]
RCM .... Radio Counter-Measures [*British military*] (DMA)
RCM .... Radiographic Contrast Media [*Chemistry*] (DAVI)
RCM .... Random Coefficient Model [*Mathematics*]
RCM .... Random Coincidence Monitor [*Beckman Instruments, Inc.*] [*Instrumentation*]
RCM .... Range Change Method [*Aircraft*]
RCM .... Rassemblement Chretien de Madagascar [*Christian Rally of Madagascar*]
RCM .... RCM Technologies, Inc. [*Associated Press*] (SAG)
RCM .... Reaction Control Motor (IAA)
RCM .... Reactor Materials [*A publication*]
RCM .... Read Clutch Magnet (IAA)
RCM .... Receipt of Classified Material (AAG)
RCM .... Recent Crustal Movements [*Geology*] (NOAA)
RCM .... Red Cell Mass [*Hematology*]
RCM .... Reduced Casualties and Mishaps
RCM .... Refurbished Command Module [*NASA*] (KSC)
RCM .... Regimental Corporal-Major [*British*]
RCM .... Regimental Court-Martial
RCM .... Reinforced Clostridial Medium [*Microbiology*]
RCM .... Reliability-Centered Maintenance [*DoD*]
RCM .... Reliability Centered Maintenance
RCM .... Reliability Corporate Memory (IEEE)
RCM .... Religious Conceptionist Missionaries [*Roman Catholic women's religious order*]
RCM .... Repair Cycle Monitor
RCM .... Replacement Culture Medium [*Microbiology*]
RCM .... Requirements Correlation Matrix [*Air Force*] (DOMA)
RCM .... Resource Cost Model (EDAC)
RCM .... Revised Code of Montana [*A publication*]
RCM .... Rhode Island College, Providence, RI [*OCLC symbol*] (OCLC)
RCM .... Richmond [*Australia Airport symbol*] (OAG)
RCM .... Right Costal Margin [*Medicine*]
RCM .... Rod Cell Memory (IAA)
RCM .... Root Canal Molar [*Dentistry*]
RCM .... Rosmac Resources Ltd. [*Vancouver Stock Exchange symbol*]
RCM .... Rotor Current Meter
RCM .... Rous Conditioned Medium
RCM .... Royal Canadian Mint
RCM .... Royal College of Midwives [*British*]
RCM .... Royal College of Music [*British*]
RCM .... Royal Conservatory of Music [*Leipzig*]
RCM .... Rule for Court-Martial [*Military*] (INF)
RCM .... Sisters of the Immaculate Conception (TOCD)
RCMA .... Radio Communications Monitoring Association (EA)
RCMA .... Railroad Construction and Maintenance Association [*Later, NRC/MAI*] (EA)
RCMA .... Religious Conference Management Association (EA)
RCMA .... Research Council of Makeup Artists (NTCM)
RCMA .... Reservist Clothing Maintenance Allowance [*Military*]
RCMA .... Roof Coatings Manufacturers Association (EA)
RCM and E .... Radio Control Models and Electronics [*A publication*]
RCMASA .... Russian Consolidated Mutual Aid Society of America (EA)
RCMAT .... Radio-Controlled Miniature Aerial Target [*Military*] (MCD)
RCMD .... Rice Council for Market Development (EA)
RCME .... Russian Commodity and Raw Materials Exchange [*Russian Federation*] (EY)
RCMF .... Radio Component Manufacturers' Federation (IAA)
RCMF .... Royal Commonwealth Military Forces (ADA)
RCMG .... Reseau Canadien sur les Maladies Genetiques (AC)
RCMI .... Research Centers in Minority Institutions Program [*Bethesda, MD*] [*National Institutes of Health*] (GRD)
RCMIF .... Rogers Cantel Mobile Communications [*NASDAQ symbol*] (SAG)
RCMIS .... Reserve Components Management Information System [*Army*]
RCMJ .... Donggang [*China*] [*ICAO location identifier*] (ICLI)
RCMM .... Registered Competitive Market Maker [*Stock exchange term*] (SPSG)
R + CMO .... [*The*] Rose + Croix Martinist Order (EA)
RCMP .... Recompute Last Fix [*Navy Navigation Satellite System*] (DNAB)
RCMP .... Royal Canadian Mounted Police [*Formerly, RNWMP*]
RCMPRS .... Recompression
RCMQ .... Qingquangang [*China*] [*ICAO location identifier*] (ICLI)
rCMR .... Regional Cerebral Metabolic Rate [*Brain research*]
RCMS .... Ilan [*China*] [*ICAO location identifier*] (ICLI)
RCMS .... Reliability Centered Maintenance Strategy (MCD)
RCMS .... Research Careers for Minority Scholars [*National Science Foundation*]
RCMS .... Resonator-Controlled Microwave Source (PDAA)
RCM Str .... RCM Strategic Global Government Fund [*Associated Press*] (SAG)
RCMT .... RCM Technologies [*NASDAQ symbol*] (TTSB)
RCMT .... RCM Technologies, Inc. [*NASDAQ symbol*] (NQ)
RCMTZ .... RCM Technologies Wrrt'C' [*NASDAQ symbol*] (TTSB)
RCMV .... Red Clover Mottle Virus [*Plant pathology*]
RCN .... Receipt of Change Notice
RCN .... Reconnaissance
RCN .... Record Control Number [*Military*] (AFM)

RCN ... Record Number [*Online database field identifier*]
RCN ... Recovery Communications Network
RCN ... Recreation (MSA)
RCN ... Relay-Contact Network (PDAA)
RCN ... Report Change Notice (MCD)
RCN ... Report Control Number (MCD)
RCN ... Requirements Change Notice [*NASA*] (NASA)
RCN ... Residential Communications Network [*Telecommunications service*]
RCN ... Resource Center for Nonviolence (EA)
RCN ... Reticulum-Cell Neoplasia [*Oncology*]
RCN ... Right Caudate Nucleus [*Medicine*] (DMAA)
RCN ... Rimacan Resources Ltd. [*Vancouver Stock Exchange symbol*]
RCN ... Rogers Cantel MobComm'B' [*NYSE symbol*] (TTSB)
RCN ... Rogers Cantel Mobile Communications [*NYSE symbol*] (SAG)
RCN ... Royal Canadian Navy [*Obsolete*]
RCN ... Royal College of Nursing [*British*]
RCNA ... Royal College of Nursing, Australia
RCNAS ... Royal Canadian Naval Air Station
RCNC ... Royal Canadian Naval College [*1943-1948*]
RCNC ... Royal Corps of Naval Constructors [*British*]
RCNCOES ... Reserve Components Noncommissioned Officer Education System [*Army*]
RCNDT ... Recondition
RCNLR ... Reconnaissance Long Range [*Army*]
RCNMV ... Red Clover Necrotic Mosaic Virus [*Plant pathology*]
RCNN ... Tainan [*China*] [*ICAO location identifier*] (ICLI)
RCNO ... Dongshi [*China*] [*ICAO location identifier*] (ICLI)
RCNR ... Royal Canadian Naval Reserve
RCNSC ... Reserve Component National Security Course [*National Defense University*] (INF)
RCNSS ... Reserve Component National Security Seminar (MCD)
RCNTR ... Ring Counter (MSA)
RCNV ... Resource Center for Nonviolence (EA)
RCNVR ... Royal Canadian Naval Volunteer Reserve [*1923-1945*]
RCO ... Aero Renta de Coahuila SA de CV [*Mexico ICAO designator*] (FAAC)
RCO ... Aliphatic Acyl Radical [*Biochemistry*] (DAVI)
RCO ... RADAR Control Officer
RCO ... Radio Control Operator
RCO ... Range Control Office [*or Officer*] [*NASA*] (KSC)
RCO ... Range Cutoff (MCD)
RCO ... Reactor Core (IEEE)
RCO ... Receiver Cuts Out [*Telecommunications*] (TEL)
RCO ... Reclamation Control Officer [*Military*] (AFIT)
RCO ... Recuperative Catalytic Oxidation [*Chemical engineering*]
RCO ... Regional Catering Officer [*British*] (DCTA)
RCO ... Remedy Coordination Official (AAGC)
RCO ... Remote Communication Outlet [*ATCS*]
RCO ... Remote Control Office
RCO ... Remote Control Operator
RCO ... Remote Control Oscillator
RCO ... Rendezvous Compatible Orbit [*Aerospace*]
RCO ... Reports Control Officer [*Army*] (AABC)
RCO ... Representative Calculating Operation
RCO ... Requisition Control Office
RCO ... Research Contracting Officer
RCO ... Resistance-Controlled Oscillator
RCo ... Ristocetin Cofactor
RCO ... Rococco Resources Ltd. [*Vancouver Stock Exchange symbol*]
RCO ... Royal College of Organists [*British*]
RCOA ... Radio Club of America
RCOA ... Record Club of America [*Defunct*]
RCOA ... Refugee Council of Australia
RC-OAC ... Reserve Component Infantry Officer Advance Course [*Military*] (INF)
RCOC ... Regional Communications Operations Center [*Military*] (MCD)
RC/OC ... Reverse Current/Overcurrent (KSC)
RCOC ... Royal Canadian Ordnance Corps
RC-OES ... Reserve Component Officer Education System [*Army*] (INF)
RCOG ... Royal College of Obstetricians and Gynaecologists [*British*]
RCOM ... Enroute Communications [*Aviation*] (FAAC)
RCOM ... Remote Communication Message (IAA)
RCON ... Reconfiguration [*Aviation*] (FAAC)
R/CONT ... Remote Control [*Automotive engineering*]
RCONT ... Rod Control
RCOR ... Quality Dino Entertainment [*NASDAQ symbol*] (SAG)
RCOR ... Remote Computer Output Room (MCD)
RCORF ... Quality Dino Entmt [*NASDAQ symbol*] (TTSB)
RCOT ... Recoton Corp. [*NASDAQ symbol*] (NQ)
RCOT ... Rolling Contour Optimization Theory [*Bridgestone Corp.*]
R (Count) ... Readiness Count (MCD)
RCP ... Racal Communications Processor [*Racal Datacom, Inc.*]
RCP ... RADAR Chart Protector (DNAB)
RCP ... RADAR Control Panel (MCD)
RCP ... RADAR Conversion Program
RCP ... Radiation Constraints Panel [*NASA*] (MCD)
RCP ... Radiative-Convective-Photochemical [*Meteorology*]
RCP ... Radical Caucus in Psychiatry (EA)
RCP ... Radio Control Panel [*Aviation*]
RCP ... Radiological Control Program [*Nuclear energy*] (NRCH)
RCP ... Random Chemistry Profile (DAVI)
RCP ... Random Close-Packed [*Granular physics*]
RCP ... Rapid City Public Library, Rapid City, SD [*OCLC symbol*] (OCLC)
RCP ... Reactor Characterization Program [*Nuclear energy*] (NRCH)
RCP ... Reactor Coolant Pump [*Nuclear energy*] (NRCH)
RCP ... Receive Clock Pulse
rcp ... Recipient [*MARC relator code*] [*Library of Congress*] (LCCP)
RCP ... Recognition and Control Processor [*Computer science*] (IBMDP)
RCP ... Reconciling Congregation Program (EA)
RCP ... Recording Control Panel
RCP ... Recovery Command Post
RCP ... Recruiting Command Post
RCP ... Rectangular Coordinate Plotter
RCP ... Reenlistment Control Point (DOMA)
RCP ... Reflector-cum-Periscope [*British military*] (DMA)
RCP ... Regimental Command Post
RCP ... Regional Conservation Program
RCP ... Register Clock Pulse
RCP ... Registry of Comparative Pathology (EA)
RCP ... Reinforced Concrete Pavement
RCP ... Reinforced Concrete Pipe [*Technical drawings*]
RCP ... Relative Competitive Preference [*Marketing*]
RCP ... Relative Corrector Program (IAA)
RCP ... Reliability Critical Problem (AAG)
RCP ... Remote Communication Processor (IAA)
RCP ... Remote Control Panel
RCP ... Request for Contractual Procurement
RCP ... Requirements Change Proposal
RCP ... Restartable Cryogenic Propellant
RCP ... Restoration Control Point [*Telecommunications*] (TEL)
RCP ... Retention Control Point [*Military*] (INF)
RCP ... Retrocorneal Pigmentation [*Medicine*] (DMAA)
RCP ... Returns Compliance Program [*Internal Revenue Service*]
RCP ... Revolutionary Communist Party of India [*Political party*] (PPW)
RCP ... Riboflavin Carrier Protein [*Immunology*]
RCP ... Right Circular Polarization
RCP ... Right-Hand Circular Polarization [*NASA*] (IAA)
RCP ... Rockefeller Center Properties, Inc. [*NYSE symbol*] (SPSG)
RCP ... Rockefeller Ctr Prop [*NYSE symbol*] (TTSB)
RCP ... Roll Centering Pickoff (SAA)
RCP ... Roman Catholic Priest (ROG)
RCP ... Romanian Communist Party [*Political party*]
RCP ... Rotation Combat Personnel
RCP ... Royal College of Pathologists [*British*]
RCP ... Royal College of Physicians of London [*British*]
RCP ... Royal College of Preceptors [*British*] (ROG)
RCP ... Royal College of Psychiatrists [*British*] (DAVI)
RCP ... Royal Commission on the Press [*British*]
RCP ... Rural Counselling Program [*Australia*]
RCPA ... Regional Colleges Principals' Association of Victoria [*Australia*]
RCPA ... Reserve Components Program of the Army (AABC)
RCPA ... Rural Cooperative Power Association
RCPAC ... Reserve Components Personnel and Administration Center [*Army*] (AABC)
RCPAC ... Reserve Personnel and Administrative Center [*Army*] (DOMA)
RCPath ... Royal College of Pathologists [*British*]
RCPB ... Reactor Coolant Pressure Boundary [*Nuclear energy*] (NRCH)
RCP(B) ... Romanian Communist Party (Bolshevik) [*Political party*]
RCP(b) ... Russian Communist Party (Bolsheviks) [*Political party*]
RCPC ... Regional Check Processing Centers
RCPC ... Royal Canadian Postal Corps [*Formerly, CPC*]
RCPCR ... Recombinant Circle Polymerase Chain Reaction [*Genetics*]
RCPD ... Reserve Components Personnel Directorate [*Office of Personnel Operations*] [*Army*]
RCPE ... Radiological Control Practices Evaluation (MCD)
RCPE ... Royal College of Physicians, Edinburgh
RCPEd ... Royal College of Physicians, Edinburgh
RCPG ... Regional Cooperative Physics Group [*Educational institutions in Ohio, Michigan, Illinois and Pennsylvania*] (PDAA)
RCPGlas ... Royal College of Physicians and Surgeons of Glasgow
RCPI ... Revolutionary Communist Party of India [*Political party*] (PPW)
RCPI ... Royal College of Physicians, Ireland
RCPL ... Requirements Contract Price List (AAGC)
RCPL ... Right Circularly Polarized Light
RCPL ... Royal College of Physicians, London (ROG)
RCPM ... Raven Coloured Progressive Matrices [*Psychiatry*] (DAVI)
RCPO ... Regional Contract Property Officer
RCPO ... Xinzhu [*China*] [*ICAO location identifier*] (ICLI)
RCPP ... Refrigeration, Compressor and Electrical Power, Airborne Pod Enclosure (DNAB)
RCPP ... Reinforced Concrete Pressure Pipe
RCPS ... Royal College of Physicians and Surgeons of Glasgow
RCPS ... Royal College of Physicians and Surgeons (of United States of America) (EA)
RCPS(C) ... Royal College of Physicians and Surgeons of Canada
RCPS(Glasg) ... Royal College of Physicians and Surgeons of Glasgow (DBQ)
RCPsych ... Royal College of Psychiatrists [*British*] (DAVI)
RCPT ... Receipt (AFM)
RCPT ... Receptacle (MSA)
RCPT ... Reception (AABC)
RCPT ... Refrigeration, Compressor and Electrical Power, Trailer-Mounted (DNAB)
RCPT ... Registered Cardiopulmonary Technologist [*Medicine*] (WGA)
RCPTN ... Reception (MSA)
RCPV ... Riot Control Patrol Vehicle
RCQ ... Reconquista [*Argentina*] [*Airport symbol*] (OAG)
RCQ ... Rich Capital Corp. [*Vancouver Stock Exchange symbol*]
RCQ ... Role Category Questionnaire [*Psychology*] (EDAC)
RCQC ... Magong [*China*] [*ICAO location identifier*] (ICLI)
RCQS ... Taidong/Zhihang [*China*] [*ICAO location identifier*] (ICLI)
RCR ... RADAR Control Room
RCR ... Ramsbottom Carbon Residue [*Analysis of petroleum products*]

RCR .... Randle Cliff RADAR (PDAA)
RCR .... Rated Capacity Report [*Army*]
RCR .... Reactor Control Room
RCR .... Reader Control Relay
RCR .... Receiver [*Telecommunications*] (ECII)
RCR .... Reciprocating Cryogenic Refrigerator
RCR .... Recrystallization Controlled Rolling (PDAA)
RCR .... Regenerative Cyclic Reactor [*Chemical engineering*]
RCR .... Relative Citation Rate [*Bibliography*]
RCR .... Relative Consumption Rate [*Entomology*]
RCR .... Required Carrier Return Character [*Computer science*]
RCR .... Respiratory Control Ratio [*Medicine*]
RCR .... Restitution of Conjugal Rights [*Legal*] [*British*] (ROG)
RCR .... Retrofit Configuration Record [*NASA*] (NASA)
RCR .... Reverse Contactor (IAA)
RCR .... Reverse Current Relay (IAA)
RCR .... Rochester, IN [*Location identifier FAA*] (FAAL)
RCR .... Room Cavity Ratio [*Lighting*]
RCR .... Route Contingency Reserve [*Aviation*] (DA)
RCR .... Royal Canadian Regiment [*Military*]
RCR .... Royal Canadian Rifles [*Military unit*]
RCR .... Royal College of Radiologists [*British*]
RCR .... Runway Condition Reading [*Aviation*] (FAAC)
RCR .... Runway Condition Reading [*FAA*] (TAG)
RCRA .... Radiologically-Controlled Radiation Area (DNAB)
RCRA .... Refrigeration Compressor Rebuilders Association (EA)
RCRA .... Resort and Commercial Recreation Association (EA)
RCRA .... Resource Conservation and Recovery Act [*Pronounced "rickra"*] [*1976*]
RCRA .... Rural Cooperative and Recovery Act (OICC)
RCRA .... Zouying [*China*] [*ICAO location identifier*] (ICLI)
R-CRAS .... Rogers Criminal Responsibility Assessment Scales [*Personality development test*] [*Psychology*]
RCRB .... Reseau Canadian de Recherce sur les Bacterioses (AC)
RCRBSJ .... Research Council on Riveted and Bolted Structural Joints [*Later, RCSC*] (EA)
RCRC .... Rabbinic Center for Research and Counseling (EA)
RCRC .... Reinforced Concrete Research Council (EA)
RCRC .... Revoked Commission, Returned to Civilian Status [*Navy*]
RCRD .... Record (AFM)
RCRE .... Retirement Care Associates, Inc. [*NASDAQ symbol*] (SAG)
RCRHRCS .... Research Center for Religion and Human Rights in Closed Societies (EA)
RCRIS .... Resource Conservation and Recovery Information System (ERG)
RCRL .... Reliability Critical Ranking List (AAG)
RCRP .... Regional Centers for Radiological Physics [*National Cancer Institute*]
RCRR .... Roster Chaplain - Ready Reserve [*Army*]
RCRS .... Regenerative Carbon-Dioxide Removal System (MCD)
R-CRS .... Report on Course [*Aviation*] (DA)
RCRS .... Reserve Combat Replacement Squadron (DNAB)
RCRTN .... Recreation
RCRTNL ...... Recreational
RCRTR .... Recruiter
RCS .... Rabbit Aorta Contracting Substance [*TA_2 - see TA, Thromboxane*] [*Biochemistry*]
RCS .... RADAR Calibration Sphere
RCS .... RADAR Collimator System
RCS .... RADAR Control Ship
RCS .... RADAR Cross Section
RCS .... Radio Command System
RCS .... Radio Communications Set
RCS .... Radio Communications System [*Military*] (CAAL)
RCS .... Radio Control System
RCS .... Range Calibration Satellite (SAA)
RCS .... Range Control Station [*or System*] [*Army*]
RCS .... Rapports de la Cour Supreme du Canada [*Database*] [*Federal Department of Justice*] [*Information service or system*] (CRD)
RCS .... Rate Command System (AAG)
RCS .... RCM Strategic Global Government Fund [*NYSE symbol*] (SAG)
RCS .... RCM Strategic Global Gvt Fund [*NYSE symbol*] (TTSB)
RCS .... Reaction Control System [*or Subsystem*] [*Steering system in spacecraft*] [*NASA*]
RCS .... Reactive Current Sensing (MCD)
RCS .... Reactor Coolant System [*Nuclear energy*] (NRCH)
RCS .... Rearward Communications System (MDG)
RCS .... Recurrent Change of Station (SAA)
RCS .... Recurrent Change of Status (SAA)
RCS .... Reentry Control System [*Aerospace*] (AFM)
RCS .... Reference Color Space [*Computer science*]
RCS .... Refurbishment Cost Study (KSC)
RCS .... Regional Control Station [*Military*] (MCD)
RCS .... Registrar of Cooperative Societies [*New South Wales, Australia*]
RCS .... Rehost Computer System [*Aviation*] (FAAC)
RCS .... Reliability Control Specification
RCS .... Reliable Corrective Action Summary (AAG)
RCS .... Reloadable Control Storage [*Computer science*]
RCS .... Remington's Compiled Statutes [*1922*] [*A publication*] (DLA)
RCS .... Remote Characterization System [*Remote controlled vehicle*] [*Hazardous materials control*]
RCS .... Remote Computing Service
RCS .... Remote Control Set
RCS .... Remote Control Station (NITA)
RC(S) .... Remote Control (System) (DEN)
RCS .... Rent Control System
R/CS .... Repeat Cesarean Section [*Obstetrics*] (MAE)
RCS .... Reports Control Symbol [*Military*]
RCS .... Reports Creation System
RCS .... Representative Conflict Situations [*Army*]
RCS .... Request for Consultation Service (MCD)
RCS .... Requirement Clearance Symbol [*Military*] (AFM)
RCS .... Requirements Control Symbol [*Military*] (MCD)
RCS .... Requirements Control System
RCS .... Residential Conservation Service [*Offered by major electric and gas utilities*]
Rcs .... Resources [*Army*]
RCS .... Reticulum Cell Sarcoma [*Medicine*]
RCS .... Retrofit Configuration System (MCD)
RCS .... Revenue Cutter Service [*Coast Guard*]
RCS .... Revision Control System [*Computer science*]
RCS .... Rich Coast Sulphur Ltd. [*Vancouver Stock Exchange symbol*]
RCS .... Ride-Control Segment [*or System*] [*Aviation*]
RCS .... Right Coronary Sinus [*Cardiology*] (AAMN)
RCS .... Rip-Out Control Sheet (DNAB)
RCS .... Rizzoli Corriere della Sera [*Publisher*]
RCS .... Rochester [*England*] [*Airport symbol*] (AD)
RCS .... Royal Choral Society [*British*] (EAIO)
RCS .... Royal College of Science [*British*]
RCS .... Royal College of Surgeons [*British*]
RCS .... Royal Commonwealth Society [*British*]
RCS .... Royal Corps of Signals [*British*]
RCSB .... RCSB Financial [*NASDAQ symbol*] (TTSB)
RCSB .... RCSB Financial, Inc. [*Associated Press*] (SAG)
RCSB .... [*The*] Rochester Community Savings Bank [*NASDAQ symbol*] (NQ)
RCSB .... Royal Commonwealth Society for the Blind [*British*] (DBA)
RCSBDE .... Round Corners Silver Bevelled Deckle Edges [*Bookbinding*] (DGA)
RCSBE .... Round Corners Silver Bevelled Edges [*Bookbinding*] (DGA)
RCSB Fn ..... RCSB Financial, Inc. [*Associated Press*] (SAG)
RCSBP .... RCSB Finl 7% Perp Cv 'B' Pfd [*NASDAQ symbol*] (TTSB)
RCSBP .... Reserve Components Survivor Benefits Plan [*Military*]
RCSC .... Huwei [*China*] [*ICAO location identifier*] (ICLI)
RCSC .... Radio Component Standardization Committee [*British*]
RCSC .... Reaction Control System [*or Subsystem*] Controller [*Apollo*] [*NASA*] (NASA)
RCSC .... Research Council on Structural Connections (EA)
RCSC .... Royal Canadian Sea Cadets
RCSCC .... Royal Canadian Sea Cadets Corps
RCSCJ .... Sisters of the Cross of the Sacred Heart of Jesus (Mexico) (TOCD)
RCSDE .... Reactor Coolant System Dose Equivalent (IEEE)
RCSDF .... Reconfigurable Computer System Design Facility (MHDB)
RCSDP .... League of Red Cross Societies Development Program
RCSE .... Remote Control and Status Equipment (MCD)
RCSE .... Round Corners Silver Edges [*Bookbinding*] (DGA)
RCSE .... Royal College of Surgeons, Edinburgh
RCSE .... Royal College of Surgeons, Edinburgh (DAVI)
RCSEd .... Royal College of Surgeons, Edinburgh
RCSEL .... Recommended Common Support Equipment List (MCD)
RCSEng .... Royal College of Surgeons, England
RCSG .... Restarting Computer and Symbol Generator (IAA)
RCSHSB ...... Red Cedar Shingle and Handsplit Shake Bureau [*Later, CSSB*] (EA)
RCSI .... Receipt for [*or of*] Classified Security Information (AAG)
RCSI .... Rede CONSISDATA de Servicos Integrados [*CONSISDATA Integrated Services Network*] [*Consultoria, Sistemas, e Processamento de Dados Ltda.*] [*Brazil*] [*Information service or system*] (CRD)
RCSI .... Royal College of Surgeons, Ireland
RCSIS .... Radio/Cable Switching Integration System (MCD)
RCSM .... Ri Yue Tan [*China*] [*ICAO location identifier*] (ICLI)
RCSO .... Research Contract Support Office
RCSP .... Royal Commission on Social Policy [*Australia*]
RCSQ .... Pingdong (North) [*China*] [*ICAO location identifier*] (ICLI)
RCSQ .... Royal Commonwealth Society of Queensland [*Australia*]
RCS-RF .... Rabbit Aorta Contracting Substance-Releasing Factor [*Medicine*] (PDAA)
RCSS .... Radial Compression Separation System [*Chromatography*]
RCSS .... Random Communication Satellite System
RCSS .... Recruiting Command Support System [*Navy*] (DNAB)
RCSS .... Reduced Chi-Square Statistic
RCSS .... Taibei/Songshan [*China*] [*ICAO location identifier*] (ICLI)
RCSSA .... Regional Centre for Seismology for South America (EAIO)
RCSSMRS .... Regional Centre for Services in Surveying, Mapping, and Remote Sensing [*West Africa*]
RCS Supp .... Remington's Compiled Statutes, Supplement [*A publication*] (DLA)
RCSTN .... Radio Compass Station (IAA)
RCSU .... Repair Cycle Support Unit
RCSX .... North American Car Corp. [*AAR code*]
RCT .... RADAR Control Trailer [*Military*] (AABC)
RCT .... Radiation/Chemical Technician (IEEE)
RCT .... Radiobeacon Calibration Transmitter
RCT .... Randomized Clinical Trial [*Medicine*]
RCT .... Randomized Control Trial [*Statistics*]
RCT .... Raw Cycle Time (AAGC)
RCT .... Real Estate Investment Trust [*NYSE symbol*] (SAG)
RCT .... Receipt (IAA)
RCT .... Receipts [*Stock exchange term*] (SPSG)
RCT .... Received Copy of Temporary Pay Record
RCT .... Recruit
RCT .... Reed City, MI [*Location identifier FAA*] (FAAL)
RCT .... Reference Clock Trigger [*Telecommunications*] (IAA)
RCT .... Regimental Combat Team
RCT .... Region Control Task [*Computer science*] (BUR)

RCT Registered Care Technician [*Proposed by American Medical Association to alleviate nursing shortage*]
RCT Regular Care Technologist
RCT Rehabilitation and Research Center for Torture Victims (EAIO)
RCT Remote Control [*Systems*] (MCD)
RCT Remote Control Terminal (MCD)
RCT Renal Cortical Tumor [*Oncology*]
RCT Repair Cycle Time (MCD)
RCT Repeat Cycle Timer
RCT Resistor-Capacitor Transistor (IAA)
RCT Resolver Control Transformer
RCT Resource Consulting Teacher
RCT Response Coordination Team [*Nuclear energy*] (NRCH)
RCT Retention Control Training [*Medicine*]
RCT Retrograde Conduction Time [*Medicine*] (DMAA)
RC-T Revenue Canada, Taxation
RCT Reverseconducting Thyristor (IAA)
RCT Reversible Counter
RCT Rework/Completion Tag [*Nuclear energy*] (NRCH)
RCT Ridgecrest Resources [*Vancouver Stock Exchange symbol*]
RCT Roll Call Training
RCT Root Canal Therapy [*Dentistry*]
RCT Root Canal Treatment [*Dentistry*] (DAVI)
RCT Rorschach Content Test [*Psychology*]
RCT Royal Clinical Teacher [*British*]
RCT Royal Corps of Transport [*Army British*]
RCT Royal Cosmic Theology [*British*]
RCT Ryan Air Service, Inc. [*FAA designator*] (FAAC)
RCTA Retail Confectionery and Tobacconists' Association [*British*] (DI)
RCTB Reserve Components Troop Basis [*Army*] (AABC)
RCTC Regeneratively-Cooled Thrust Chamber
RCTC Reserve Components Training Center [*Military*]
RCTC Union of Rail Canada Traffic Controllers [*See also CCFC*]
RCTDAP Reserve Components Training Development Action Plan [*Army*] (DOMA)
RCTDPOVALCAN Request Concurrent Travel of Dependents by Privately Owned Vehicle [*ALCAN Highway or Via Route Required*] [*Army*] (AABC)
RCTG Recruiting (AABC)
RCTI Rajawali Citra Televisi Indonesia (EY)
RCTL Resistance-Coupled Transistor Logic
RCTL Resistor-Capacitor Transistor Logic
RCTM Radio Technical Committee for Maritime services
RCTM Regional Center for Tropical Meteorology [*National Hurricane Center*]
RCTM Remote Control Tunnelling Machine
RCTN Reaction (MSA)
R (Ct of Sess) Rettie, Crawford, and Melville's Session Cases, Fourth Series [*1873-98*] [*Scotland*] [*A publication*] (DLA)
RCTP Reserve Components Troop Program [*Army*]
RCTP Taibei City/Taibei International Airport [*China*] [*ICAO location identifier*] (ICLI)
RCTPS Revue Canadienne de Theorie Politique et Sociale [*A publication*]
RCTRANSMOD Reserve Components Transition to Modernization
RCTS Railway Correspondence and Travel Society [*British*]
RCTS Reactor Coolant Treatment System [*Nuclear energy*] (NRCH)
RCTSR Radio Code Test, Speed of Response [*Military*]
RCTSS Regional Computerized Traffic Signal System
RCTV Radio Caracas Television [*Venezuela*] (EY)
RCTV RCA Cable and Rockefeller Center Cable Pay-TV Program Service
RCTV Remote Controlled Target Vehicle [*Military*] (INF)
RCU Atlantic, SL [*Spain*] [*FAA designator*] (FAAC)
RCU Rack Controller Unit [*Computer science*] (PCM)
RCU RADAR Calibration Unit
RCU RADAR Control Unit [*Military*] (CAAL)
RCU Rate Construction Unit [*Hypothetical basic currency unit*] (DCTA)
RCU Receiver Control Unit (IAA)
RCU Reference Control Unit (MCD)
RCU Regional Coordinating Unit [*Advisory Committee on Pollution of the Sea*]
RCU Relay Control Unit (AAG)
RCU Remote Control Unit
RCU Requisition Control Unit
R/CU Research and Curriculum Unit [*Mississippi State University*] [*Research center*] (RCD)
RCU Research Coordinating Unit [*Oklahoma State Department of Vocational and Technical Education*] [*Stillwater, OK*]
RCU Research into Chronic Unemployment [*British*]
RCU Reserve Component Unit [*Army*] (AABC)
RCU Resistor-Capacitor Unit (IAA)
RCU Respiratory Care Unit [*Medicine*]
RCU Revolution Control Unit [*Automotive engineering*]
RCU Rio Cuarto [*Argentina*] [*Airport symbol*] (OAG)
RCU Road Construction Unit (PDAA)
RCU Rocket Countermeasure Unit
RCUA Remote Checkout Umbilical Array
RCUEP Research Center for Urban and Environmental Planning [*Princeton University*]
RCUK Bakuai [*China*] [*ICAO location identifier*] (ICLI)
RCUL Reference Control Unit Launch (MCD)
RCUR Recurrent (MSA)
RCUT Rapid Carbohydrate Utilization Test (PDAA)
RCV RADAR Control Van (NATG)
RCV Radiation Control Valve [*Nuclear energy*] (NRCH)
RCV Reaction-Control Valve
RCV Receive (AFM)
rcv Receive (IDOE)
RCV Receive (IDOE)
RCV Receive
RCV Receiver
RCV Receiver/Exciter Subsystem [*Deep Space Instrumentation Facility, NASA*]
RCV Red Cell Volume [*Hematology*]
RCV Relative Conductor Volume
RCV Remote-Controlled Vehicle (MCD)
RCV Replacement Cost Valuation [*Insurance*]
RCV Restartable Cryogenic Vehicle
RCV Reversed Circular Vection [*Optics*]
RCV Revised Claim Valuation [*Insurance*]
RCV Rich Cut Virginia [*Tobacco*] (ROG)
RCV Riot Control Vehicle
RCV Robotic Combat Vehicle [*Army*] (RDA)
RCV Routine Coefficient of Variation [*Statistics*]
RCV Ryegrass Cryptic Virus [*Plant pathology*]
RCVBL Receivable
RCV-COMMZ Rear Combat Vehicle/Communications Zone (MCD)
RCVD Reactive Chemical Vapor Deposition [*Coating technology*]
RCVD Received (MSA)
RCVD Received
RCVG Receiving (MSA)
RCVG Replacement Carrier Fighter Group [*V is Navy code for Fighter*]
RCVMV Red Clover Vein Mosaic Virus
RCVNG Receiving
RCVNO Receiving Capability Out [*Aviation*] (FAAC)
RCVR Receiver (AAG)
RCVR Receiver (IDOE)
rcvr Receiver (IDOE)
RCVS Remote Control Video Switch (MCD)
RCVS Royal College of Veterinary Surgeons [*British*]
RCVSG Readiness Antisubmarine Warfare Carrier Air Wing [*Navy*] (NVT)
RCVT Registered Cardiovascular Technologist [*Medicine*] (WGA)
RCVTP Reserve Component Virtual Training Program [*Army*] (INF)
RCVTP Reserve Component Virtual Training Program [*Army*] (RDA)
RCVV Rear Compressor Variable Vane
RCVW Readiness Attack Carrier Air Wing [*Navy*] (NVT)
RCVY Recovery (MSA)
RCW Raw Cooling Water [*Nuclear energy*] (NRCH)
RCW Reactor Cooling Water [*Nuclear energy*] (NRCH)
RCW Read, Compute, Write (IAA)
RCW Record Control Word [*Computer science*]
RCW Red-Cockaded Woodpecker
RCW Reformed Church Women [*An association*] (EA)
RCW Register Containing Word
RCW Research Center on Women (EA)
RCW Resident Careworker
RCW Return Control Word
RCWA Revised Code of Washington Annotated [*A publication*] (DLA)
RCWAT Retarded Citizens' Welfare Association of Tasmania [*Australia*]
RCWI Right Ventricular Cardiac Work Index [*Cardiology*]
RCWK Xinshe [*China*] [*ICAO location identifier*] (ICLI)
RCWP Rubber Covered, Weatherproof (IAA)
RCWP Rural Clean Water Program [*Department of Agriculture*]
RCWS Remote Control Water Sampler
RCWS Research Centre for Women's Studies [*University of Adelaide, Australia*]
RCWS Russian Children's Welfare Society - Outside of Russia (EA)
RCWV Rated Continuous Working Voltage (IAA)
RCX Ladysmith, WI [*Location identifier FAA*] (FAAL)
RCX Remote Cluster Executive (IAA)
RCXY Guiren [*China*] [*ICAO location identifier*] (ICLI)
RCY Recovery (NASA)
RCY Red Cross and Red Crescent Youth [*Geneva, Switzerland*]
RCY Remaining Cycles (MCD)
RCY Rotating Coil Yoke
RCY Royal Crystal [*Vancouver Stock Exchange symbol*]
RCYRA Rooster Class Yacht Racing Association [*Defunct*] (EA)
RCYU Hualian [*China*] [*ICAO location identifier*] (ICLI)
RCZ Radiation Control Zone
RCZ Rear Combat Zone (NATG)
RCZ Rockingham, NC [*Location identifier FAA*] (FAAL)
RD Airlift International, Inc. [*ICAO designator*]
Rd Albert Rolland [*France*] [*Research code symbol*]
RD Aviona [*ICAO designator*] (AD)
RD Boots Pure Drug Co. [*Great Britain*] [*Research code symbol*]
RD Directional Radio Beacon [*ITU designation*] (CET)
R_D Drain Resistance (IDOE)
RD Indian Revenue Decisions [*A publication*] (DLA)
rd Rad [*Non-SI unit; preferred unit is Gy, Gray*]
RD RADAR (DEN)
RD RADAR Data
RD RADAR Display
RD RADARman [*Also, RDM*] [*Navy rating*]
RD Radiation Absorbed Dose [*Unit of measurement of radiation energy*] (IAA)
RD Radiation Damage [*Nucleonics*] (OA)
RD Radiation Detection
RD Radio Detector
Rd Radiolaria [*Quality of the bottom*] [*Nautical charts*]
RD Radiological Defense [*To minimize the effect of nuclear radiation on people and resources*]
Rd Rainbow Darter [*Ichthyology*]
RD Random Drift

RD .... Random Driver [*Nuclear energy*] (NRCH)
RD .... Range Development (MUGU)
RD .... Rated (IAA)
RD .... Rated Duty (IAA)
RD .... Rate Difference [*Toxicology*]
R/D .... Rate of Descent [*Aviation*] (MCD)
RD .... Ratio Detector (IAA)
RD .... Raynaud's Disease [*Medicine*]
RD .... Reaction of Degeneration [*Physiology*]
RD .... Read (AAG)
RD .... Read Data
RD .... Read Delay (IAA)
RD .... Read Direct
RD .... Reader's Digest [*A publication*]
RD .... Readiness Data
RD .... Readiness Date
RD .... Reading Disability
RD .... Reappraisement Decisions [*A publication*] (DLA)
RD .... Rear Door
RD .... Receipt Day (NRCH)
RD .... Received Data (IEEE)
RD .... Recemment Degorgee [*Recently Disgorged*] [*Refers to aging of wine*] [*French*]
RD .... Recognition Differential
RD .... Record Description [*Computer science*]
RD .... Recorder (IAA)
RD .... Recorders-Reproducers [*JETDS nomenclature*] [*Military*] (CET)
RD .... Recording Demand (DEN)
RD .... Rectifier Diode (IAA)
RD .... Red
RD .... Redirect [*Computer science*] (TNIG)
RD .... Red Pennant [*Navy British*]
Rd .... Reduce [*Army*]
RD .... Reference Designator (NASA)
RD .... Reference Document
RD .... Reference Drawing (NATG)
RD .... Refer to Drawer [*Banking*]
RD .... Regio Decreto [*Royal Decree*] [*Latin*] (DLA)
RD .... Regional Director
RD .... Register Drive (MSA)
RD .... Registered (ROG)
RD .... Registered Dietitian
RD .... Registration Division [*Environmental Protection Agency*] (EPA)
RD .... Reinforcement Designee [*Air Force*] (AFM)
RD .... Reiter's Disease [*Medicine*] (DMAA)
RD .... Relative Density
RD .... Relaxation Delay
RD .... Relay Drawer
RD .... Relay Driver
RD .... Relocatable Directory [*Computer science*] (IAA)
RD .... Remedial Design (EPA)
RD .... Remove Directory [*Computer science*]
RD .... Renal Disease [*Medicine*]
RD .... Rendered (ROG)
RD .... Replacement Detachment [*Army*]
RD .... Replenishable Demand
RD .... Reply Delay (MUGU)
RD .... Report Departing [*Aviation*] (DA)
RD .... Request Disconnect [*Telecommunications*] (OSI)
RD .... Required Date
RD .... Requirements Document [*NASA*] (KSC)
RD .... Research and Development [*Army*]
RD .... Reserve Decoration [*Navy British*]
RD .... Resistance Determinant [*Medicine*] (MAE)
RD .... Resistor Diode (IAA)
RD .... Resolver Differential (IAA)
RD .... Resource Development
RD .... Respiratory Disease
RD .... Respiratory Distress [*Medicine*] (DAVI)
RD .... Restricted Data [*Security classification*]
RD .... Retention and Disposal
RD .... Retinal Detachment [*Ophthalmology*]
RD .... Revision Directive [*Drawings*]
RD .... Revolutionary Development [*South Vietnam*]
RD .... Reye's Disease [*Medicine*]
RD .... Right Defense
RD .... Right Deltoid [*Medicine*]
RD .... Right Door [*Theater*]
RD .... Right Dorso Anterior [*Medicine*] (MAE)
RD .... Rights in Data (OICC)
RD .... Ringdown [*Telecommunications*] (TEL)
RD .... Rive Droite [*Right Bank*] [*French*]
RD .... Rix-Dollar
RD .... Road [*Maps and charts*] (AAG)
Rd .... Road (DD)
RD .... Road
Rd .... Road (ODBW)
RD .... Rod
RD .... Romanovsky Dye [*Biological stain*]
RD .... Rood [*Unit of measurement*]
RD .... Roof Diameter (IAA)
RD .... Roof Drain (AAG)
RD .... Root Diameter (MSA)
R/D .... Rotary to Digital (MCD)
RD .... Rotodrome
RD .... Round (AAG)
RD .... Routing Domain [*Computer science*] (TNIG)
RD .... Royal Dragoons [*British*]
RD .... Royal Dutch Petrol [*NYSE symbol*] (TTSB)
RD .... Royal Dutch Petroleum Co. [*NYSE symbol*] (SPSG)
RD .... Royal Naval Reserve Decoration [*British*]
RD .... Rubber Dam [*Medicine*] (DMAA)
RD .... Ruling Date [*IRS*]
RD .... Run Down [*Typography*]
RD .... Running Days
rd .... Running Days (ODBW)
RD .... Rupture Disk (KSC)
RD .... Rural Deacon [*or Deaconry*] [*Church of England*]
RD .... Rural Dean [*Church of England*]
RD .... Rural Delivery
RD .... Rural Development
RD .... Rural District
rd .... Rutherford [*Unit of strength of a radioactive source*]
RD1 .... RADARman, First Class [*Navy rating*]
RD2 .... RADARman, Second Class [*Navy rating*]
rd^2 .... Square Rod (CDAI)
RD3 .... RADARman, Third Class [*Navy rating*]
RDA .... Radioactive Dentin Abrasion [*Dentistry*]
RDA .... Railway Development Association [*British*]
RDA .... Ranging Demodulator Assembly [*Deep Space Instrumentation Facility, NASA*]
RDA .... Rassemblement Democratique Africain [*Niger*] [*Political party*] (PD)
RDA .... Rassemblement Democratique Africain [*Ivory Coast*] [*Political party*] (PPW)
RDA .... Read Data Available
RDA .... Reader's Digest Assn'A' [*NYSE symbol*] (TTSB)
RDA .... Reader's Digest Association [*NYSE symbol*] (SPSG)
RdA .... Reading Age (BABM)
RdA .... Reading Age [*Education*] (DAVI)
RDA .... Real-Time Debugging Aid
RDA .... Receive Data and Acknowledge [*Telecommunications*] (OSI)
RDA .... Recirculation Duct Assembly
RDA .... Recommended Daily Allowance [*Dietary*]
RDA .... Recommended Dietary Allowance (DAVI)
RDA .... Recommended Duty Assignment (AFM)
RDA .... Regional Dance America [*Defunct*] (EA)
RDA .... Regional Dance Association
RDA .... Regional Data Associates [*Information service or system*] (IID)
RDA .... Regional Dental Activity (AABC)
RDA .... Regional Development Authority [*Victoria, Australia*]
RDA .... Register Display Assembly
RDA .... Registered Dental Assistant (DMAA)
RDA .... Regularize Discriminant Analysis [*Mathematics*]
RDA .... Reliability Design Analysis (MCD)
RDA .... Remote Data [*or Database*] Access (NASA)
RDA .... Representational Difference Analysis [*Genetic technique*]
RDA .... Request for Deviation Approval (MCD)
RDA .... Research and Development Abstracts [*A publication*]
RDA .... Research and Development, Army
RDA .... Research, Development, and Acquisition (AAGC)
RDA .... Resent, Demand, Appreciate [*In Sidney Simon, Leland Howe, and Howard Kirschenbaum's book "Values Clarification"*]
RDA .... Resident Data Area (NASA)
RDA .... Retail Display Agreement (WDMC)
RDA .... Retail Distributors Association, Inc. [*British*] (BI)
RDA .... Reverse Diels-Alder [*Organic chemistry*]
RDA .... Riding for the Disabled Association (EAIO)
RDA .... Right Dorso Anterior [*Medicine*] (ROG)
RDA .... Rod Drop Accident (IEEE)
RDA .... Rome Daily American [*An English-language newspaper in Italy*] [*A publication*]
RDA .... Royal Danish Army (NATG)
RDA .... Royal Defence Academy [*British*]
RDA .... Royal Docks Association [*British*] (BI)
RDA .... Rules for the Discipline of Attorneys [*A publication*] (DLA)
RDA .... Run-Time Debugging Aid (MHDB)
RDA .... Run-Time Debugging Unit (NITA)
RDA .... Rural Development Abstracts [*Database*] [*Commonwealth Bureau of Agricultural Economics*] [*Information service or system*] (CRD)
RDA .... Rural Development Act [*1972*] (OICC)
RDA .... Rural Development Administration [*AEC*]
RDA .... TK Travel Ltd. [*Gambia*] [*ICAO designator*] (FAAC)
RDAA .... Range Doppler Angle Angle (IAA)
RDAA .... Riding for the Disabled Association of Australia
RDAA .... Rural Doctors' Association of Australia
RDAAC .... Research into Drug Abuse Advisory Committee [*Australia*]
RdAc .... Radioactinium [*Nuclear physics*] (WGA)
RDAC .... Recruiting District Assistance Council [*Navy*] (DNAB)
RDAC .... Research and Development Acquisition Committee [*Military*]
RDAF .... Revue de Droit Administratif et de Droit Fiscal [*Lausanne, Switzerland*] [*A publication*] (DLA)
RDAF .... Royal Danish Air Force
RDAFCI .... Research and Development Associates, Food and Container Institute (EA)
RDAISA .... Research Development and Acquisition Information Systems Activity [*Army*] (AAGC)
RDAISA .... Research, Development, and Acquisition Information Systems Agency [*Army*] (AABC)
RDAL .... Representation Dependent Accessing Language
RD & A .... Research, Development, and Acquisition [*DoD*]

RD & D........ Research, Development, and Demonstration
RD & E........ Research, Development, and Engineering
RD & ES...... Requirements Determination and Exercise System [*Military*] (MCD)
RD & P........ Research, Development, and Production [*NATO*] (NATG)
RD & S........ Research, Development, and Studies [*Marine Corps*]
RD & T........ Research, Development, and Testing
RDAR.......... Reliability Design Analysis Report (AAG)
RDARA......... Regional and Domestic Air Route Area
RDAS.......... Reflectivity Data Acquisition System
RDAT.......... Registered Designs Appeal Tribunal (DLA)
RDAT.......... Remote Data Acquisition Terminal (NRCH)
RDAT.......... Research and Development Acceptance Test
RDAT.......... Research, Development, and Test
RDAT.......... Rotary [*or Rotating*] Digital Audio Tape
RDAU.......... Remote Data Acquisition Unit
RDAV.......... Reset Data Available [*Computer science*] (MHDI)
RDAVS......... Recovered Doppler Airborne Vector Scorer
R (Day)....... Redeployment Day [*Military*]
RDB........... Racecourses Development Board [*South Australia*]
RDB........... RADAR Decoy Balloon [*Air Force*]
RDB........... Ramped Dump Barge
RDB........... Random Double-Blind Trial [*Medicine*] (DMAA)
RDB........... Rapidly Deployable Barge [*Military*] (MCD)
RDB........... Rare Disease Database [*National Organization for Rare Disorders*] [*Information service or system*] (IID)
RDB........... Reader's Digest Assn'B' [*NYSE symbol*] (TTSB)
RDB........... Readers Digest Association [*NYSE symbol*] (SAG)
RDB........... Red Data Books (GNE)
RDB........... Reference Data and Bias (SAA)
RDB........... Relational Data Base (PDAA)
RDB........... Relational Database
RDB........... Requirements and Design Branch (SAA)
RDB........... Requirements Data Bank [*Air Force*] (GFGA)
RDB........... Research and Development Board [*Abolished, 1953, functions transferred to Department of Defense*]
RDB........... Resistance Decade Box
RDB........... Round Die Bushing
RDB........... Royal Danish Ballet
RDB........... Rural Development Board [*British*]
RDBA.......... Roll Drive and Brake Assembly
RDBL.......... Readable
RDBL.......... Readable
RDBMS......... Relational Database Management System [*Computer science*] (BYTE)
RdBrick....... Red Brick Systems, Inc. [*Associated Press*] (SAG)
RDC........... Chief RADARman [*Navy rating*]
R_{dc}........... DC Resistance (IDOE)
RDC........... Racecourse Development Committee [*New South Wales*]
RDC........... RADAR Data Converter (MCD)
RDC........... RADAR Design Corp.
RDC........... RADAR Display Console
RDC........... Radiac [*Nucleonics*]
RDC........... Radiation Density Constant
RDC........... Radioactivity Decay Constant
RDC........... Rail Diesel Car
RDC........... Rand Development Corp. (IAA)
RDC........... Rapaport Diamond Corp. [*Information service or system*] (IID)
RDC........... Rapid Development Capability [*Military*] (NG)
RDC........... Rassemblement Democratique Caledonien [*Caledonian Democratic Rally*] [*Political party*] (PPW)
RDC........... Rassemblement Democratique Centrafricain [*Central African Republic*] [*Political party*]
RDC........... Rate Damping Control
RDC........... Read Data Check (CMD)
RDC........... Reading Development Continuum (AIE)
RDC........... Real Decisions Corp. [*Information service or system*] (IID)
RDC........... Recording Doppler Comparator [*Astronomy*] (OA)
RDC........... Reduce (MSA)
RDC........... Reference Designator Code (NASA)
RDC........... Reflex Digital Control
RDC........... Refugee Documentation Centre [*Information service or system*] (IID)
RDC........... Regional Data Center [*Marine science*] (MSC)
RDC........... Regional Dissemination Center [*NASA*]
RDC........... Regional Dissemination Centers [*NASA*] (PDAA)
RDC........... Regional Distribution Center [*TRW Automotive Aftermarket Group*]
RDC........... Reliability Data Center (KSC)
RDC........... Reliability Data Control (IAA)
RDC........... Remote Data Collection (MCD)
RDC........... Remote Data Concentrator
RDC........... Remote Detonation Capability
RDC........... Reply Delay Compensation (MUGU)
RDC........... Request for Document Change (NASA)
RDC........... Research and Development Command [*Military*]
RDC........... Research Diagnostic Criteria [*Medicine, psychiatry*]
RDC........... Revolutionary Development Cadre [*South Vietnam*]
RDC........... Rotary Dispersion Colorimeter
RDC........... Rotating Diffusion Cell [*Chemistry*]
RDC........... Rotating Disk Contractor [*Chemical engineering*]
RDC........... Rowan Companies, Inc. [*NYSE symbol*] (SPSG)
RDC........... Rowan Cos. [*NYSE symbol*] (TTSB)
RDC........... Royal Defence Corps [*British*]
RDC........... Rubber Development Corp. [*Expired, 1947*]
RDC........... Running-Down Clause [*Business term*]
RDC........... Rural Development and Conservation [*Department of Agriculture*]
RDC........... Rural Development Centre [*University of New England, Australia*]
RDC........... Rural District Council [*British*]
RDC........... Sisters of Divine Compassion [*Roman Catholic religious order*]
RDCA.......... Rural District Councils Association [*British*]
RDCAA......... Registered Dairy Cattle Association of Australia
RDCC.......... Regional Distributors and Carriers Conference (EA)
RD-CCSA..... Reciprocal Derivative Constant-Current Stripping Analysis [*Analytical electrochemistry*]
RDCE.......... Radio Distribution and Control Equipment [*Aviation*] (DA)
RDCEHCY.... Research and Demonstration Center for the Education of Handicapped Children and Youth [*Defunct*] (EA)
RDCEO......... Rural District Council Executive Officer [*British*]
RDCF.......... Restricted Data Cover Folder (AAG)
RDCHE......... Rene Dubos Center for Human Environments (EA)
RDCHK......... Read Check [*Computer science*] (IAA)
RDCLP......... Response Document Capability List Positive (IAA)
RDCM.......... Master Chief RADARman [*Navy rating*]
RDCM.......... Reduced Delta Code Modulation [*Digital memory*]
RDCN.......... Reduction (MSA)
RDCO.......... Reliability Data Control Office (AAG)
RDCP.......... Remote Display Control Panel (MCD)
RDCR.......... Reducer (MSA)
RDCRIT........ Read Criteria (SAA)
RDCS.......... Reconfiguration Data Collection System [*or Subsystem*] (MCD)
RDCS.......... Senior Chief RADARman [*Navy rating*]
RDCTN......... Reduction
RDCU.......... Receipt Delivery Control Unit [*Social Security Administration*]
RDD........... Random Digit Dialing [*Telecommunications*]
RDD........... Rapid Demolition Device
RDD........... Rassemblement Democratique Dahomeen [*Dahomean Democratic Rally*]
RDD........... Reactor Development Division [*of AEC*]
RDD........... Read Disconnect Delay [*Computer science*] (IAA)
RDD........... Redding [*California*] [*Airport symbol*] (OAG)
RDD........... Reference Design Document (KSC)
RDD........... Required Delivery Date (AABC)
rdd........... Required Delivery Date (ODBW)
RDD........... Requirements Definition Document [*NASA*] (NASA)
RDD........... Requisition Due Date (TEL)
RDD........... Research and Development Directorate [*Army*]
RDD........... Return Due Date [*IRS*]
RDD........... Routine Dynamic Display (MCD)
RDDA.......... Recommended Daily Dietary Allowance
RDD & E....... Research, Development, Diffusion [*or Dissemination*], and Evaluation
RDDCS......... Range Drone Data Control System [*Military*] (CAAL)
RDDM.......... Reactor Deck Development Mock-Up [*Nuclear energy*] (NRCH)
RDDMI......... Radio Digital Distance Magnetic Indicator (MCD)
RDDP.......... Polymerase [*Deoxyribonucleic Acid*] [*Formerly, RIDP*] [*An enzyme*]
RDDP.......... Response Document Discard Positive [*Computer science*] (IAA)
RDDR.......... Rod Drive
RDDS.......... RADAR Data Distribution Switchboard [*Military*] (CAAL)
RDDS.......... Range Data Distributive System [*Military*]
RDDS.......... Retail Dental Delivery System [*Dentistry*]
RDDSEM........ Real Data System Element Model [*Computer science*] (MHDB)
RDE........... RADAR Display Equipment
RDE........... Radial Defect Examination (IEEE)
RDE........... Receptor-Destroying Enzyme [*A neuraminidase*] [*Immunochemistry*]
RDE........... Recommended Distribution of Effort [*Civil defense*]
RDE........... Relational Database Engine (PCM)
RDE........... Reliability Data Extractor (MCD)
RDE........... Remote Data Entry (NITA)
RDE........... Research and Development Establishment [*British*]
RDE........... Research, Development, and Engineering (RDA)
RDE........... Research Development Exchange (OICC)
RDE........... Roating Disk Electrode
RDE........... Rotating Disc Electrode
RDE & A....... Research, Development, Engineering, and Acquisition (RDA)
RDEB.......... Recessive Dystrophic Epidermolysis Bullosa [*Also, EBDR*] [*Dermatology*]
RDEC.......... Research, Development, and Engineering Center (RDA)
R de D McGill... Revue de Droit de McGill [*A publication*] (DLA)
R de J........ Revue de Jurisprudence [*Quebec*] [*A publication*] (DLA)
R de Jur...... Revue de Jurisprudence [*Quebec*] [*A publication*] (DLA)
R de L........ Revue de Legislation et de Jurisprudence [*Canada*] [*A publication*] (DLA)
R de L et de J... Revue de Legislation et de Jurisprudence [*A publication*] (DLA)
RDEP.......... Recruit Depot [*Navy*]
RDEP.......... Response Document End Positive [*Computer science*] (IAA)
RDES.......... Remote Data Entry System (DMAA)
RDES.......... Requirement and Determination Execution System
R de S........ Ricardus Petronius de Senis [*Deceased, 1314*] [*Authority cited in pre-1607 legal work*] (DSA)
RDF........... RADAR Direction Finder [*or Finding*] (CET)
RDF........... Radial Distribution Function [*X-ray diffraction*]
RDF........... Radio Direction Finder [*or Finding*] (AABC)
RDF........... Rapid Deployment Force [*Military*]
RDF........... Recirculating Document Feeder (NITA)
RDF........... Record Definition Field [*Computer science*] (BUR)
RDF........... Recursive Digital Filter [*Computer science*] (IAA)
RDF........... Redford Resources, Inc. [*Vancouver Stock Exchange symbol*]
RDF........... Reflection Direction Finding
RDF........... Refuse-Derived Fuel (ERG)
RDF........... Repeater Distribution Frame (NATG)
RDF........... Research, Development, and Facilities (NOAA)
RDF........... Reserve Defense Fleet [*Navy*]
RDF........... Resource Data File (MCD)

RDF .... Robotech Defense Force [*Defunct*] (EA)
RDF .... Roger Wyburn-Mason and Jack M. Blount Foundation for the Eradication of Rheumatoid Disease (EA)
RDF .... Royal Dublin Fusiliers [*British*]
RDF-A .... Rapid Deployment Force - Army
RDFC .... Recurring Digital Fibroma of Childhood [*Medicine*] (DMAA)
RDFI .... Receiving Depository Financial Institution
RDFL .... Reflection Direction Finding, Low Angle (MCD)
RDF/LT .... Rapid Deployment Force/Light Tank [*Military*] (MCD)
RDFQ .... Recueil de Droit Fiscal Quebecois [*A publication*] (DLA)
RDFS .... Ratio of Decayed and Filled Surfaces [*Dentistry*] (MEDA)
RDFSTA .... Radio Direction Finder Station
RDFT .... Ratio of Decayed and Filled Teeth [*Dentistry*] (MEDA)
RDFU .... Research and Development Field Unit [*Military*]
RDFU-V .... Research and Development Field Unit - Vietnam [*Military*] (MCD)
RDFWA .... Regular Defence Force Welfare Association [*Australia*]
RDG .... Radio Directors' Guild [*Defunct*] (IAA)
RDG .... Reading
RDG .... Reading [*British depot code*]
RDG .... Reading [*Pennsylvania*] [*Airport symbol*] (OAG)
Rdg .... Reducing (WGA)
RDG .... Reference Drawing Group [*NATO*] (NATG)
RDG .... Regional Development Grant [*British*] (DCTA)
RDG .... Registrar Data Group [*Information service or system*] (IID)
RDG .... Relative Disturbance Gain [*Control engineering*]
RDG .... Research Discussion Group (EA)
RDG .... Resolver Differential Generator
RDG .... Resource Development Group Ltd. [*British*]
RDG .... Ridge (MSA)
RDG .... Ridge
RDG .... Right Digestive Gland
RDG .... Rounding
RDG .... Rover P4 Drivers Guild [*An association*] (EAIO)
RdgBate .... Reading & Bates Corp. [*Associated Press*] (SAG)
RdgBt .... Reading & Bates Corp. [*Associated Press*] (SAG)
RDGC .... Reading Co. [*NASDAQ symbol*] (NQ)
RDGCA .... Reading Co. Cl'A' [*NASDAQ symbol*] (TTSB)
RDGE .... Reading Entertainment, Inc. [*NASDAQ symbol*] (SAG)
RDGE .... Resorcinol Diglycidyl Ether [*Organic chemistry*]
RDGE .... Ridge [*Commonly used*] (OPSA)
RDGF .... Retina-Derived Growth Factor [*Biochemistry*]
RDGL .... Radiological (IAA)
RDGR .... Response Document General Reject (IAA)
RDGS .... Ridges [*Postal Service standard*] (OPSA)
RDGS .... Ridges
RDGT .... Reliability Development Growth Testing (RDA)
RDGY .... Radiology (IAA)
RDH .... Radioactive Drain Header [*Nuclear energy*] (NRCH)
RDH .... Rapid Displacement Heating [*Pulp and paper technology*]
RDH .... Red Hill Marketing Group Ltd. [*Vancouver Stock Exchange symbol*]
RDH .... Reference Datum Height [*Aviation*] (DA)
RDH .... Registered Dental Hygienist
RDH .... Remote Device Handler (IAA)
RDH .... Resource Dispersion Hypothesis [*Animal ecology*]
RDH .... Round Head
RDH .... Royal Deccan Horse [*British military*] (DMA)
RDHD .... Round Head (IAA)
RDHER .... Revolutionary Development Hamlet Evaluation Report [*South Vietnam*]
RDHM .... Royal Dental Hospital, Melbourne [*Australia*]
RDHS .... Logan's Roadhouse [*NASDAQ symbol*] (TTSB)
RdhseGr .... Roadhouse Grill, Inc. [*Associated Press*] (SAG)
RDI .... Radio Doppler Inertial
RDI .... Rassemblement Democratique pour l'Independance [*Quebec*]
RDI .... Rassemblement des Democrates Liberaux pour la Reconstruction Nationale [*Benin*] [*Political party*] (EY)
RDI .... Readicare, Inc. [*AMEX symbol*] (SAG)
RDI .... Recommended Daily Intake [*Dietary*]
RDI .... Reference Daily Intake [*FDA*]
RDI .... Reference Designation Index (MCD)
RDI .... Regulated Deficit Irrigation
RDI .... Rejection and Disposition Item
RDI .... Released Data Index
RDI .... Reliability Design Index (DNAB)
RDI .... Relief and Development Institute [*Formerly, International Disaster Institute*] [*Defunct*] (EA)
RDI .... Remote Data Input
RDI .... Research and Development Institute, Inc. [*Montana State University*] [*Research center*] (RCD)
RDI .... Research and Development of Instrumentation [*Program*] [*Army*]
RDI .... Riley's Datashare International Ltd. [*Toronto Stock Exchange symbol*]
RDI .... Route Digit Indicator [*Telecommunications*] (TEL)
RDI .... Routing Domain Identifier (TNIG)
RDI .... Royal Designer for Industry [*British*]
RDI .... Rupture Delivery Interval [*Obstetrics*]
RDIA .... Regional Development Incentives Act
RDIC .... ReadiCare, Inc. [*NASDAQ symbol*] (TTSB)
RDIF .... Rural Development Insurance Fund [*Farmers Home Administration*] [*Department of Agriculture*] (GFGA)
RDIM .... Revolving Door Identification Model (EDAC)
RDIO .... Multi-Market Radio, Inc. [*NASDAQ symbol*] (SAG)
RDIOA .... Multi-Mkt Radio'A' [*NASDAQ symbol*] (TTSB)
RDIOW .... Multi-Mkt Radio Wrrt'A' [*NASDAQ symbol*] (TTSB)
RDIOZ .... Multi-Mkt Radio Wrrt'B' [*NASDAQ symbol*] (TTSB)
RDIPP .... Rivista di Diritto Internazionale Privato e Processuale [*A publication*] (DLA)
RDIS .... Replenishment Demand Inventory System
RDIS .... Research and Development Information System [*Later, EPD/RDIS*] [*Electric Power Research Institute*] [*Information service or system*] (IID)
RDISSS .... Royal Dockyard Iron and Steel Shipbuilders' Society [*A union*] [*British*]
RDIT .... Rapid Deployment Imagery Terminal (DOMA)
RDIT .... Replication, Distribution, Installation, and Training [*Army*] (RDA)
RDIU .... Remote Device Interface Unit
RDIXS .... Research and Development Information Exchange System [*Navy*] (DOMA)
RDJ .... Readjustment
RDJ .... Rio De Janeiro [*Brazil*] [*Later, VSS*] [*Seismograph station code, US Geological Survey*] (SEIS)
RDJCT .... Register, Department of Justice and the Courts of the United States [*A publication*]
RDJTF .... Rapid Deployment Joint Task Force [*Military*] (RDA)
RDK .... Irish Air Tours [*ICAO designator*] (FAAC)
R dk .... Raised Deck [*of a ship*] (DS)
RDK .... Random-Dot Kinematogram [*For motion detection*]
RDK .... Red Oak, IA [*Location identifier FAA*] (FAAL)
RDK .... Research and Development Kit
RDK .... Ruddick Corp. [*NYSE symbol*] (SPSG)
RDL .... Radial (MSA)
RDL .... Radioactive Decay Law
RDL .... Radiological Defense Laboratory [*NASA*] (KSC)
RDL .... Rail Dynamics Laboratory
RDL .... Random Dynamic Load
RDL .... Rapid Draft Letter (DNAB)
RDL .... [*The*] Reactor Development Laboratory [*UKAEA*] [*British*]
RDL .... Rear Defence Locality [*British military*] (DMA)
RDL .... Reciprocal Detection Latency
RDL .... Recurring Document Listing (MCD)
RDL .... Redlaw Industries [*AMEX symbol*] (TTSB)
RDL .... Redlaw Industries [*AMEX symbol*] (SAG)
RDL .... Redlaw Industries, Inc. [*AMEX symbol Toronto Stock Exchange symbol*] (SPSG)
RDL .... Regional Development Laboratory [*Philadelphia, PA*]
RDL .... Reliable Detection Limit [*Analytical chemistry*]
RDL .... Remote Display Link
RDL .... Replaceable Display Light
RDL .... Report Definition Language [*Computer science*] (MHDB)
RDL .... Resistance Diode Logic (IAA)
RDL .... Resistor Diode Logic
RDL .... Rim of Dorsal Lip
RDL .... Roadair Lines IC [*Canada ICAO designator*] (FAAC)
RDL .... Rocket Development Laboratory [*Air Force*]
RDLBBB .... Rate-Dependent Left Bundle Branch Block [*Medicine*] (DMAA)
RDLGE .... Reunion Democratica para la Liberacion de Guinea Ecuatorial [*Democratic Movement for the Liberation of Equatorial Guinea*] [*Political party*] (PD)
RDLI .... Royal Durban Light Infantry [*British military*] (DMA)
RD-LMXB .... Radiation-Driven Low-Mass X-Ray Binary [*Cosmology*]
RDLN .... Retrodorsolateral Nucleus [*Neuroanatomy*]
RDLP .... Research and Development Limited Partnership [*Tax-shelter investment*]
Rdlw .... Redlaw Industries [*Associated Press*] (SAG)
RDLWS .... Redlaw Ind 2001 Wrrts [*AMEX symbol*] (TTSB)
RDLX .... Airlift International, Inc. [*Air carrier designation symbol*]
RdM .... Die Religionen der Menschheit [*A publication*] (BJA)
RDM .... RADARman [*Also, RD*]
RDM .... Radial Distribution Method
RDM .... Random (WGA)
RDM .... Random Dimer Model [*Physics*]
RDM .... Real-Time Data Manager (MCD)
RDM .... Recording Demand Meter
RDM .... Redmond [*Oregon*] [*Airport symbol*] (OAG)
RDM .... Relay Driver Module
RDM .... Remote Data Management
RDM .... Remote Digital Multiplexer (MCD)
RDM .... Respirable Dust Monitor (PDAA)
RDM .... Roadmaster Industries [*NYSE symbol*] (SAG)
RDMC .... Regional Director of Motor Carriers [*FHWA*] (TAG)
RDMC .... Research and Development Management Course [*Army*]
RDME .... Range and Distance Measuring Equipment
RDMF .... Rapidly Deployable Medical Facilities
RDMGA .... Railway Dock and Marine Grades Association [*A union*] [*British*]
RDMI .... Roof Drainage Manufacturers Institute [*Defunct*] (EA)
RDMN .... Redman Industries [*NASDAQ symbol*] (SAG)
RDMN .... Redman Industries [*NASDAQ symbol*] (TTSB)
RDMS .... Range Data Measurement Subsystem (MCD)
RDMS .... Registered Diagnostic Medical Sonologist
RDMS .... Relational Data Management System (MHDI)
RDMS .... Retail Development Management Services [*British*]
RDMS .... Retrospective Data Management System
RDMSR .... Read Machine-Specific Register [*Computer science*]
RDMSS .... Rapidly Deployable Mobile SIGINT [*Signal Intelligence*] System (MCD)
RDMTR .... Radiometer (NASA)
RDMU .... Range-Drift Measuring Unit
RDN .... Dinar SA [*Argentina ICAO designator*] (FAAC)
RDN .... Real de Minas Mine [*Vancouver Stock Exchange symbol*]
RDN .... Redundancy (IAA)

RDN............ Rejection Disposition Notice
RDN............ Relative Distinguished Name [*Telecommunications*] (OSI)
RDN............ Resource Decision Network (PDAA)
RDN............ Royal Danish Navy (NATG)
RDN............ Rural Deanery [*Church of England*]
rDNA........... Deoxyribonucleic Acid, Recombinant [*Biochemistry, genetics*]
rDNA........... Deoxyribonucleic Acid, Ribosomal [*Biochemistry, genetics*]
RDNA........... Recombinant DNA [*Deoxyribonucleic Acid*] (MCD)
rDNA........... Ribosomal DNA [*Deoxyribonucleic Acid*] (USDC)
rDNA........... Ribosomal DNA [*Deoxyribonucleic Acid*] [*Marine science*] (OSRA)
RDNG........... Reading (MSA)
RDNP........... Rassemblement Democratique Nationaliste et Progressiste [*Progressive Nationalist and Democratic Assembly*] [*Haiti*] (PD)
RDNS........... Readiness (MSA)
RDNSSA...... Royal District Nursing Society of South Australia
RDNU........... Rally for Democracy and National Unity [*Mauritania*] [*Political party*] (EY)
RDO............ Radio (AABC)
RDO............ Radio
RDO............ Radiological Defense Officer [*Civil defense*]
RDO............ Radio Readout
RDO............ Range Development Officer (MUGU)
RDO............ Readout [*Computer science*] (IAA)
RDO............ Reconnaissance Duty Officer
RDO............ Redistribution Order [*Military*] (AFM)
RDO............ Regional Defense Organization (DNAB)
RDO............ Regional Disbursing Office
RDO............ Remote Data Objects [*Computer science*]
RDO............ Remote Data Objects [*Computer science*]
RDO............ Research and Development Objectives [*Military*] (AFM)
RDO............ Research, Development, and Operation [*Military appropriation*]
RDO............ River District Office [*National Weather Service*]
RDO............ Rodeo Resources Ltd. [*Vancouver Stock Exchange symbol*]
RDO............ Runway Duty Officer [*Aviation*] (MCD)
RDOC........... Integrated Surgical Systems, Inc. [*NASDAQ symbol*] (SAG)
RDOC........... Reference Designation Overflow Code (NASA)
RDOC........... Residential Distillate Oil Combustion [*Industrial medicine*]
RDOD........... Retinal Detachment, Oculus Dexter [*Right Eye*] [*Ophthalmology*] (DAVI)
RDOINT........ Radio Intelligence [*Military*] (IAA)
RDOM........... Restructured Division Operations Manual (MCD)
RDON........... Road Octane Number [*Fuel technology*]
RDOS........... R Disc Operating System (NITA)
RDOS........... Real-Time Disk-Operating System [*Computer science*]
RDOS........... Retinal Detachment, Oculus Sinister [*Left Eye*] [*Ophthalmology*] (DAVI)
RDOSEC....... Radio Section (IAA)
RDOSTN...... Radio Service (IAA)
RDOTRANS... Radio Transmitter (IAA)
RDOUT......... Readout
RDP............ RADAR Data Processing
RDP............ RADAR Digital Probe
RDP............ Radiation Degradation Product
RDP............ Radiodifusao Portuguesa [*State Broadcasting Service*]
RDP............ Radio Distribution Point (IAA)
RDP............ Radiosonde Data Processor (IAA)
RDP............ Range Data Processor (MCD)
RDP............ Range Deflection Protractor [*Weaponry*] (INF)
RDP............ Rassemblement pour la Democratie et le Progres [*Mali*] [*Political party*] (EY)
RDP............ Ration Distributing Point [*Military*]
RDP............ Reactor Development Program [*Nuclear Regulatory Commission*] (NRCH)
RDP............ Receiver and Data Processor (MCD)
RDP............ Reconstruction and Development Program [*South Africa*]
RDP............ Recreational Dive Planner
RDP............ Rectifying-Demodulating Phonopneumograph [*Medicine*]
RDP............ Redeployment Point [*Military*] (INF)
RDP............ Regional Development Program [*Australia*]
RDP............ Remote Data Processor
RDP............ Renal Dipeptidase [*An enzyme*]
RDP............ Requirements Data Plan (NASA)
RDP............ Requirements Development Plan [*NASA*] (NASA)
RDP............ Research and Development Plan
RDP............ Research Data Publication [*Center*]
RDP............ Reunification Democracy Party [*Political party South Korea*]
RDP............ Revolutionary Development Program [*South Vietnam*]
RDP............ Ribulosediphosphate [*Also, RuBP*] [*Biochemistry*]
RDP............ Right Dorso Posterior [*Medicine*] (ROG)
RDP............ Rocca Di Papa [*Italy*] [*Seismograph station code, US Geological Survey*] (SEIS)
RDPB........... RADAR Data Plotting Board
RDPB........... Research and Development Planning and Budgeting (AFIT)
RD/PBM....... Research and Development/Programming Budget Memorandum (MCD)
RDPBN......... Response Document Page Boundary Negative [*Computer science*] (IAA)
RDPBP......... Response Document Page Boundary Positive [*Computer science*] (IAA)
RDPC........... RADAR Data Processing Center [*Military*]
RDPE........... RADAR Data Processing Equipment (AABC)
RDPE........... Reticular Degeneration of the Pigment Epithelium [*Biochemistry*] (DAVI)
RDPG........... Revolutionary Development Peoples Group [*South Vietnam*] [*Military*] (VNW)
RDPJ........... Rail Discharge Point Jet (NATG)
RDPL........... Laos [*International civil aircraft marking*] (ODBW)
RDPM........... Rail Discharge Point Mogas (NATG)
RDPM........... Revised Draft Presidential Memorandum
RDPM........... Rotary Drive Piston Motor
RDPR........... Refer to Drawer Please Represent [*Business term*] (DCTA)
RDPS........... RADAR Data Processing System
RDPS........... Remote Docking Procedures Simulator (MCD)
RDPS........... Research and Development Planning Summary
RdQ............ Reading Quotient
RDR............ Grand Forks, ND [*Location identifier FAA*] (FAAL)
RDR............ RADAR (AAG)
RDR............ RADAR Departure Route [*Aviation*] (DA)
RDR............ RADAR Diagnostic Report (IAA)
RDR............ RADAR Display Room (IAA)
RDR............ Raider
RDR............ Rapid Canadian Resource Corp. [*Vancouver Stock Exchange symbol*]
RDR............ Raw Data Recorder (NASA)
RDR............ Read Drum (IAA)
RDR............ Reader (MSA)
R/DR........... Rear Door [*Automotive engineering*]
RDR............ Receive Data Register [*Computer science*] (MDG)
RDR............ Rejection Disposition Report [*NASA*] (KSC)
RDR............ Relative Digestion Rate [*Nutrition*]
RDR............ Reliability Design Review
RDR............ Reliability Diagnostic Report (AAG)
RDR............ Remote Digital Readout
RDR............ Repeat Discrepancy Report (MCD)
RDR............ Request Data and Respond [*Telecommunications*] (OSI)
RDR............ Research and Development Report
RDR............ Research Division Report
RDR............ Restart Delay Relay (IAA)
RDR............ Ribonucleoside Diphosphate Reductase [*An enzyme*]
RDR............ Risk Data Report [*Insurance*]
RDR............ Risk-Driven Remediation
RDR............ Rudder (NASA)
RD/RA......... Remedial Design/Remedial Action [*Environmental Protection Agency*] (ERG)
RDRBCN...... RADAR Beacon (KSC)
RDRC........... Road Design and Road Costs [*British*]
RDRD........... Remote Digital Readout
RdrDB......... Readers Digest Association [*Associated Press*] (SAG)
RdrDg.......... Reader's Digest Association [*Associated Press*] (SAG)
RDR/EO....... RADAR/Electro-Optical (MCD)
RDRINT........ RADAR Intermittent (IEEE)
RDRM........... Return Data Relay Measurement (SSD)
RDRP........... Response Document Resynchronization Positive [*Computer science*] (IAA)
RDRSMTR... RADAR Transmitter (AAG)
RDRT........... Read-Rite Corp. [*NASDAQ symbol*] (SPSG)
RDRV........... Rhesus Diploid-Cell-Strain Rabies Vaccine
RDR XMTR... RADAR Transmitter
RDS............ RADAR Distribution Switchboard
RDS............ RADAUS [*Radio-Austria AG*] Data-Service [*Telecommunications*]
RDS............ Radio Data System [*Telecommunications*]
RDS............ Radio Digital System [*Telecommunications*] (TEL)
RDS............ Radio Display Service
RDS............ Railway Development Society [*British*] (DBA)
RDS............ Random Digit Sample (NTCM)
RDS............ Random Dot Stereogram
RDS............ Range Destruct System
RDS............ Rate-Determining Step [*Chemical kinetics*]
RDS............ Rate of Dispersal Success [*Ecology*]
RDS............ Raytheon Data Systems Co.
RDS............ Read Select (SAA)
RDS............ Read Strobe
RDS............ Reeds [*Music*]
RDS............ Relational Database Systems Inc. (NITA)
RDS............ Relative Detector Sensitivity [*Robotics technology*]
RDS............ Religious Drama Society of Great Britain (BI)
RDS............ Remote Data Service [*Computer science*]
RDS............ Remote Data Service [*Computer science*]
RDS............ Rendezvous Docking Simulator [*Aerospace*]
RDS............ Reperimento Documentazione Siderurgica [*Iron and Steel Documentation Service*] [*Information service or system*] (IID)
RDS............ Request for Data Services
RDS............ Required Number of Days of Stock
RDS............ Requisition Distribution System
RDS............ Research and Development Service [*Army-Ordnance*]
RDS............ Research and Development Survey
RDS............ Research Defence Society [*British*]
RDS............ Research, Development, and Standardization [*Groups*] [*Army*] (RDA)
RDS............ Research Documentation Section [*Public Health Service*] [*Information service or system*] (IID)
RDS............ Research Documents Search [*Information service or system*] (IID)
RDS............ Residuum Desulfurization [*Petroleum technology*]
Rds............ Resistance of the Airways on the Oral Side of the Point in the Airways Where Intraluminal Pressure Equals Intrapleural Pressure [*Medicine*] (DAVI)
RDS............ Resistive Divider Standard
RDS............ Resolver Differential Transmitter (IAA)
RDS............ Resource Development Services (EA)
RDS............ Respiratory Distress Syndrome [*Formerly, HMD*] [*Medicine*]
RDS............ Retail Distribution Station [*Military*] (AFM)

RDS Reticuloendothelial Depressing Substance [*Medicine*] (AAMN)
RDS Retinal Degeneration Slow [*Genetics*]
RDS Revolutionary Development Support [*South Vietnam*]
RDS Revolving Discussion Sequence
RDS Rhoades Aviation, Inc. [*ICAO designator*] (FAAC)
RDS Rhode Island Department of State Library Services, Providence, RI [*OCLC symbol*] (OCLC)
RDS Richard D. Siegrest [*Alaska*] [*Seismograph station code, US Geological Survey*] (SEIS)
RDS Rio Grande do Sul [*Brazil*] [*Airport symbol*] (AD)
RDS Roads
RDS Roads [*Postal Service standard*] (OPSA)
RDS Robotic Deriveter System
RDS Robust Detection Scheme [*Navigation*] (OA)
RDS Rocket Development Section [*Picatinny Arsenal*] [*Dover, NJ*]
RDS Rocketdyne Digital Simulator [*NASA*] (NASA)
RDS Rokeach Dogmatism Scale
RDS Rounds [*of ammunition*] [*Military*]
RDS Royal Drawing Society [*British*]
RDS Royal Dublin Society
RDS Rural Development Service [*Department of Agriculture*]
RDS Rural Development Society (NADA)
RDSA Seaman Apprentice, RADARman Striker [*Navy rating*]
RD/SB Rudder Speed Brake [*Aviation*] (MCD)
RDSD Reliability Design Support Document [*Nuclear energy*] (NRCH)
RDSD Revolutionary Development Support Division [*South Vietnam*]
RDSIM Runway Delay Simulation Model [*FAA*] (TAG)
RDSM Remote Digital Submultiplexer (KSC)
RDSM Research Development Safety Management [*Air Force*]
RDS/M Rounds per Minute [*Military*]
RDSN RADARman, Seaman [*Navy rating*]
RDSN Seaman, RADARman, Striker [*Navy rating*]
RDSO Research, Design, and Standardization Organization [*Indian Railways*] [*India*] (PDAA)
RDSP Revolutionary Development Support Plan [*or Program*] [*South Vietnam*]
RDSPA Redispatch Accepted (FAAC)
RDSS RADAR Determination Satellite System [*Aviation*] (DA)
RDSS Radio Determination Satellite Service [*Geostar Corp.*]
RDSS Rapid Deployable Surveillance Systems [*Military*] (NVT)
RDS-TMC Radio Data System - Traffic Management Channel
RDS-TMS Radio Data System - Traffic Message Channel [*Traffic and highway management*] (ECON)
RD Sup Revenue Decisions, Supplement [*India*] [*A publication*] (DLA)
RDT Radio Digital Terminal [*Bell System*]
RDT Rapid Decompression Test
RDT Reactor Development and Technology [*Nuclear energy*] (MCD)
RDT Reactor Drain Tank [*Nuclear energy*] (NRCH)
RDT Redoubt [*Alaska*] [*Seismograph station code, US Geological Survey*] (SEIS)
RDT Regular Dialysis Treatment [*Medicine*]
RDT Reliability Demonstration Test
RDT Reliability Design Test
RDT Reliability Development Testing (CAAL)
RDT Remote Data Transmitter
RDT Renal Dialysis Treatment [*Nephrology*]
RDT Repertory Dance Theatre [*Salt Lake City, UT*]
RDT Reserve Duty Training [*Military*]
RDT Resistor Diode Transistor Technique (IAA)
RDT Resource Definition Table [*Computer science*] (IBMDP)
RDT Retinal Damage Threshold [*Ophthalmology*]
RDT Revue de Droit du Travail [*A publication*] (DLA)
RDT Richard-Toll [*Senegal*] [*Airport symbol*] (OAG)
RDT Rotational Direction Transmission
RDT Routine Dialysis Therapy [*Medicine*] (DMAA)
RDT & E Research, Development, Test, and Engineering (SSD)
RDT&E Research, Development, Test, and Evaluation (AAGC)
RDT & EN Research, Development, Test, and Evaluation, Navy
RDTC Remote Distributed Terminal Controller (NITA)
RDTE Research, Development, Test, and Evaluation [*DoD*]
RDTEA Research, Development, Test, and Evaluation, Army
RDTE & E Research, Development, Test, Evaluation, and Engineering Program [*DoD*] (RDA)
RDTF Revolutionary Development Task Force [*South Vietnam*]
RdTh Radiothorium [*Nuclear physics*] (WGA)
RDTI Research, Development and Technology Investigation
RDTL Resistor Diode Transistor Logic (IEEE)
RDTLC Rotating Disc Thin-Layer Chromatography
RDTM Rated Distribution and Training Management
RDTR Radiator (MSA)
RDTR Research Division Technical Report
RDTSC Read Time Stamp Counter [*Computer science*]
RDTSR Rapid Data Transmission System for Requisitioning [*Navy*]
RDU RADAR Display Unit
RDU Raleigh/Durham [*North Carolina*] [*Airport symbol*]
RDU Receipt and Despatch Unit [*Aircraft*]
RDU Refrigerated Detector Unit (SAA)
RDU Regional Development Unit [*Manpower Services Commission*] (AIE)
RDU Remote Data Uplink [*SmartOffice*] [*Computer science*]
RDU Remote Display Unit [*American Solenoid Co.*] [*Somerset, NJ*]
RDU Rideau Resources Corp. [*Vancouver Stock Exchange symbol*]
R du B Can Revue. Barreau Canadien [*A publication*] (DLA)
RDUC Receiver Data from Unit Control (MCD)
R du D Revue du Droit [*A publication*] (DLA)
RDUS Radius, Inc. [*NASDAQ symbol*] (SAG)
RDV Recoverable Drop Vehicle (MCD)
RDV Red Devil [*Alaska*] [*Airport symbol*] (OAG)
RDV Rice Dwarf Virus [*Plant pathology*]
RDV Rotary Disk Valve [*Automotive engineering*]
RDV Rotating Dome Valve [*Military*] (RDA)
RDVT Recurrent Deep Vein Thrombosis [*Medicine*] (DAVI)
RDVT Reliability Design Verification Test
RDVU Rendezvous (AABC)
RDW Red Blood Cell Distribution Width Index [*Medicine*] (DMAA)
RDW Red Cell Size Distribution Width [*Hematology*]
RDW Redwood Resources, Inc. [*Vancouver Stock Exchange symbol*]
RDW Response Data Word (MCD)
RDW Return Data Word (MCD)
RDW Right Defense Wing [*Women's lacrosse position*]
RDWA Returned Development Workers Association (EAIO)
RDWCA Royal Dockyard Wood Caulkers' Association [*A union*] [*British*]
rdwd Redwood (VRA)
RDWND RADAR Dome Wind [*NWS*] (FAAC)
RDWS Radiological Defense Warning System
RDWW United Slate Tile and Composition Roofers, Damp and Waterproof Workers Association [*Later, UURWAW*]
RDWY Roadway
RDX Cocoa, FL [*Location identifier FAA*] (FAAL)
RDX Radixin (DMAA)
RDX Ready [*Broadcasting*] (WDMC)
RDX Research Department Explosive [*Cyclonite*]
RDY Aspen, CO [*Location identifier FAA*] (FAAL)
RDY Ready (AAG)
RDY Ready
RDY Roadway
RDY Royal Devon Yeomanry [*British military*] (DMA)
RDY Royal Dockyard [*British*]
RDYA Royal Devon Yeomanry Artillery [*British military*] (DMA)
rdymd Readymade (VRA)
RdysRst Rudys Restaurant Group [*Associated Press*] (SAG)
RDZ Radiation Danger Zone (IAA)
RDZ Ringier Dokumentationszentrum [*Ringier Documentation Center*] [*Switzerland Information service or system*] (IID)
RDZ Rodez [*France*] [*Airport symbol*] (OAG)
RE Aer Arann Teo [*ICAO designator*] (AD)
Re Earth or Geocentric Radius (AAG)
R_E Emitter Resistance (IDOE)
RE Everest Reinsurance Hldgs [*NYSE symbol*] (TTSB)
RE Everest Reinsurance Holdings, Inc. [*NYSE symbol*] (SAG)
RE Fellow of the Royal Society of Painter-Etchers and Engravers [*British*]
Re Ohio Decisions Reprint [*A publication*] (DLA)
RE Prudential Reinsurance Holdings, Inc. [*NYSE symbol*] (SAG)
RE Radiated Emission (IEEE)
RE Radiation Effects (AAG)
RE Radiation Equipment (NRCH)
RE Radio-Eireann [*Eire*] [*Record label*]
RE Radio Electrician
RE Radio Equipment (IAA)
RE Radio Exposure (AAG)
RE Radium Emanation
RE Railway Executive [*British*]
Re Rainerius [*Authority cited in pre-1607 legal work*] (DSA)
RE Rainform Expanded (MCD)
RE Ram Effect [*Mechanical engineering*] (OA)
RE Rare Earth
RE Rate Effect (IEEE)
RE Rate of Exchange
RE Rational Expectations [*Economics*] (ECON)
RE Rattus Exulans [*The Polynesian rat*]
RE Raw End (OA)
RE Reactive Evaporation [*Coating technology*]
RE Read Emitter [*Computer science*] (IAA)
RE Read Error [*Computer science*] (IAA)
RE Reading-Ease [*Score*] [*Advertising*]
Re Real [*Mathematics*]
RE Real Estate
RE Real Estate Program [*Association of Independent Colleges and Schools specialization code*]
RE Real Number (DEN)
RE Reasonable Effort (GNE)
RE Receiver/Exciter
RE Recent [*Used to qualify weather phenomena*]
RE Reconnaissance Experimental [*British military*] (DMA)
RE Recovery Equipment (IAA)
RE Rectal Examination [*Medicine*]
RE Recursively Enumerable (IAA)
RE Red Edges
RE Reel (MSA)
R/E Reentry [*Aerospace*] (KSC)
RE Reference [*Online database field identifier*]
RE Reference Equivalent [*Telecommunications*] (TEL)
RE Reflux
RE Reformed Episcopal [*Church*]
RE Refrigeration Effect
RE Regarding
RE Regional Enteritis [*Medicine*]
RE Regular Expression (IAA)
RE Rehearsal Engineer (MCD)
RE Reinforced [*Technical drawings*]

RE .... Relative Effectiveness [*or Efficiency*] (MCD)
RE .... Relay Assemblies [*JETDS nomenclature*] [*Military*] (CET)
RE .... Relay Engineer (IAA)
RE .... Release
RE .... Religious Education [*Secondary school course*] [*British*]
RE .... Religious of the Eucharist [*Roman Catholic women's religious order*]
RE .... Remote Pickup [*FCC*] (NTCM)
RE .... Renewal Registration [*US Copyright Office class*]
RE .... Renovacion Espanola [*Spanish Renovation*] (PPE)
RE .... Repair Equipment [*Navy*]
RE .... Repair Equipment for F-15 and Subsequent Programs [*Military*] (MCD)
RE .... Repayable to Either
RE .... Repetitive Extrasystole [*Cardiology*]
RE .... Reportable Event (EPA)
RE .... Republication [*NASA*]
RE .... Request for Estimate
RE .... Research and Engineering
RE .... Research and Experiments Department [*Ministry of Home Security*] [*British World War II*]
RE .... Reset (MDG)
RE .... Resolution Enhancement [*Computer graphics*]
Re .... Respiratory Exchange Ratio [*Medicine*] (MAE)
RE .... Responsible Engineer (NASA)
RE .... Rest [*or Resting*] Energy [*Medicine*]
RE .... Restriction Endonuclease [*An enzyme*]
RE .... Restriction of Extension (IAA)
RE .... Retained Earnings (TDOB)
RE .... Reticuloendothelial [*or Reticuloendothelium*] [*Medicine*]
RE .... Retinal Equivalent [*For Vitamin A*]
RE .... Retinyl Ester [*Organic chemistry*]
re .... Reunion [*MARC country of publication code Library of Congress*] (LCCP)
RE .... Reunion [*ANSI two-letter standard code*] (CNC)
RE .... Reversal of Prior Entry [*Banking*]
RE .... Revised Edition [*Publishing*]
Re .... Reynolds Number [*Viscosity*] [*IUPAC*]
Re .... Rhenium [*Chemical element*]
RE .... Rifle Expert
RE .... Right Eminent [*Freemasonry*]
RE .... Right End
RE .... Right Excellent
RE .... Right Eye
RE .... Risk Evaluation [*Insurance*]
RE .... Risk Exercise
RE .... Riviera Explorations Ltd. [*Vancouver Stock Exchange symbol*]
RE .... Rotary Engine [*Automotive engineering*]
RE .... Royal Engineers [*Military British*]
RE .... Royal Exchange [*British*]
RE .... Royal Society of Painter-Etchers and Engravers [*British*]
RE .... Royal Society of Painter-Etchers and Engravers, London [*1880*] (NGC)
RE .... Rupee [*Monetary unit*] [*Ceylon, India, and Pakistan*]
RE .... Rural Electrification
REA .... Aer Arann Teoranta [*Ireland*] [*ICAO designator*] (FAAC)
REA .... American Real Estate Investment Corp. [*AMEX symbol*] (SAG)
REA .... Amer Real Estate Investment [*AMEX symbol*] (TTSB)
REA .... RADAR Echoing Area
REA .... Radiation Emergency Area
REA .... Radiative Energy Attenuation [*Analytical chemistry*]
REA .... Radio Electrical Artificer [*British military*] (DMA)
REA .... Radioenzymatic Assay [*Analytical biochemistry*]
REA .... Railroad Evangelistic Association (EA)
REA .... Railway Express Agency [*Later, REA Express*] [*Defunct*]
REA .... Range Error Average (MUGU)
REA .... Rare-Earth Alloy
REA .... Realcap Holdings Ltd. [*Toronto Stock Exchange symbol*]
REA .... Reao [*French Polynesia*] [*Airport symbol*] (OAG)
REA .... Recycle Acid [*Nuclear energy*] (NRCH)
REA .... Reentry Angle
REA .... Regional Economic Area
REA .... Registered Environmental Assessor
REA .... Religious Education Association (EA)
REA .... Renaissance Educational Associates [*Defunct*] (EA)
REA .... Renal Anastomosis [*Medicine*]
REA .... Request for Engineering Action (IAA)
REA .... Request for Engineering Authorization
REA .... Request for Equitable Adjustment [*Navy*]
REA .... Research and Education Association
REA .... Research Engineering Authorization (AAG)
REA .... Research in Accrediting Efforts Project [*Illinois*] (EDAC)
REA .... Reserve Enlisted Association [*Defunct*] (EA)
REA .... Responsible Engineering Activity
REA .... Retirement Equity Act of 1984 (WYGK)
REA .... Rice Export Association
REA .... Ridihalgh, Eggers & Associates, Columbus, OH [*OCLC symbol*] (OCLC)
REA .... Right Ear Advantage [*Medicine*] (DMAA)
REA .... Rocket Engine Assembly
REA .... Rubber Export Association [*Defunct*] (EA)
REA .... Rural Education Association [*Later, NREA*] (EA)
REA .... Rural Electric Association (IAA)
REA .... Rural Electrification Administration [*Department of Agriculture*]
REA Bull .... Rural Electrification Administration. Bulletin [*A publication*] (DLA)
REAC .... Radiation Equipment and Accessories Corporation (SAA)
REAC .... Radiological Emergency Assessment Center [*National Science Foundation*] (NUCP)
REAC .... Reaction (AAG)
REAC .... Reactive
REAC .... Reactor (AAG)
REAC .... Real Estate Aviation Chapter (EA)
REAC .... Reeves Electronic Analog Computer
REAC .... Regional Educational Advisory Council [*British*]
ReAC .... Reinsurance Australia Corp. [*Commercial firm*]
REACCS .... Reaction Access System [*Computer program*]
REACDU .... Recalled to Active Duty
REACH .... Rape Emergency Aid and Counseling for Her [*An association*] (NADA)
REACH .... Reassurance to Each [*To help families of the mentally ill*]
REACH .... Recognizing Exceptional Achievement in Community Help Award [*Association of Personal Computer User Groups*] (PCM)
REACH .... Research, Education, and Assistance for Canadians with Herpes
REACH .... Research on the Early Abilities of Children with Handicaps Project (EDAC)
REACH .... Responsible Educated Adolescents Can Help (EA)
REACH .... Retired Executives Action Clearing House [*British*] (DI)
REACH .... Review and Analysis of Companies in Holland [*Database*] (IID)
REACH .... Rural Employment Action and Counseling Help [*Project*]
REACK .... Receipt Acknowledged
REACOT .... Remove Errors and Complete on Time (DNAB)
REACQ .... Reacquire
REACT .... RADAR Electrooptical Area Correlation Tracker [*Military*] (CAAL)
REACT .... Radio Emergency Associated Citizens Teams [*Acronym alone is now used as official association name*] (EA)
RE ACT .... Rapid Execution and Combat Targeting [*Air Force*]
RE ACT .... Reconnaissance/Reaction (MCD)
REACT .... Record Evaluate and Control Time System (IAA)
REACT .... Register Enforced Automated Control Technique [*Cash register-computing system*]
REACT .... Reliability Evaluation and Control Technique
REACT .... Requirements Evaluated against Cargo Transportation (PDAA)
REACT .... Rese Engineering Automatic Core Tester
REACT .... Resource Allocation and Control Technique [*Management*]
REAC/TS .... Radiation Emergency Assistance Center/Training Site [*Department of Energy*]
REACTS .... Reader Action Service [*ZIP code computer*]
REACTS .... Regional Educators Annual Chemistry Teaching Symposium
REACTVT .... Reactivate
READ .... RADAR Echo Augmentation Device
READ .... Readability Ease Assessment Device (MCD)
READ .... Reading [*County borough in England*]
READ .... Reading Efficiency and Delinquency [*Program*]
READ .... Real-Time Electronic Access and Display [*System*] [*Computer science*]
READ .... Relative Element Address Designate (NITA)
READ .... Remedial Education for Adults
READ .... Remote Electronic Alphanumeric Display [*Computer science*] (IEEE)
READ .... Research and Economic Analysis Division [*Office of Transportation*] (GRD)
READ .... Reserve on Extended Active Duty [*Military*]
Read Dec .... Read's Declarations and Pleadings [*A publication*] (DLA)
READE .... Reduce Errors and Decrease Expense (DNAB)
READEF .... Reason for Deficiency (SAA)
Readex .... Readex Microprint Corp., New York, NY [*Library symbol Library of Congress*] (LCLS)
Readg .... Reading Co. [*Associated Press*] (SAG)
ReadgE .... Reading Entertainment, Inc. [*Associated Press*] (SAG)
READI .... Rocket Engine Analyzer and Decision Instrumentation
READIEX .... Readiness Exercise [*Navy*] (DOMA)
READIMP .... Readiness Improvement (MCD)
Readings .... Readings: A Journal of Reviews and Commentary in Mental Health [*A publication*] (BRI)
READJ .... Readjusted
READJP .... Readjustment Pay [*Military*]
READL .... Railway Employers' Association Defence League [*British*]
readm .... Readmission [*Hospital administration*] (DAVI)
Read PL .... Read's Declarations and Pleadings [*A publication*] (DLA)
READR .... Remain in Effect after Discharge and Reenlistment [*Refers to orders*] [*Army*]
ReadRt .... Read-Rite Corp. [*Associated Press*] (SAG)
READS .... Reader Enrollment and Delivery System [*Library of Congress Washington, DC Information service or system*] (IID)
READS .... Reentry Air Data System (ADA)
READS .... Reno Air Defense Sector [*ADC*]
READSUPPGRUDET .... Readiness Support Group Detachment (DNAB)
READTRAFAC .... Readiness Training Facility (DNAB)
READU .... Ready Duty (NVT)
READU .... Ready Unit (NVT)
READYREP .... Ready-to-Sail Report [*Navy*] (NVT)
REA et A .... Rite Ecossais Ancien et Accepte [*Ancient and Accepted Scottish Rite*] [*Freemasonry*] [*French*]
REAF .... Reorganization of Engineer Active Forces (MCD)
REAF .... Resources Exchange Association Foundation [*Also known as REA Foundation*] (EA)
REAF .... Revised Engineer Active Force (MCD)
REAG .... Reproductive Effects Assessment Group [*Environmental Protection Agency*] (EPA)
ReaGld .... Rea Gold Corp. [*Associated Press*] (SAG)
ReaGold .... Rea Gold Corp. [*Associated Press*] (SAG)
R/EAL .... Reading/Everyday Activities in Life [*Educational test*]

REAL........... Realistic, Equal, Active, for Life Women of Canada [*An association*]
REAL........... Reliability, Inc. [*NASDAQ symbol*] (NQ)
REAL........... Research-Extension Analytical Laboratory [*Ohio State University*] [*Research center*] (RCD)
REAL........... Road Emulsion Association [*British*] (DBA)
REAL........... Routine Economic Air Lift [*Army*]
Realco......... Realco, Inc. [*Associated Press*] (SAG)
REALCOM.... Real-Time Communications [*RCA*]
Real Est L Rep... Real Estate Law Report [*A publication*] (DLA)
Real Est Rec... Real Estate Record [*New York*] [*A publication*] (DLA)
REAL FAMMIS... Real-Time Finance and Manpower Management Information System [*Marine Corps*] (MCD)
RealGd........ Real Goods Trading Corp. [*Associated Press*] (SAG)
Reality......... Reality Interactive, Inc. [*Associated Press*] (SAG)
REALIZN...... Realization (ROG)
REALM......... Remote Access Line Monitor [*Cornet, Inc.*]
Real Pr Cas... Real Property Cases [*England*] [*A publication*] (DLA)
Real Prop Acts... Real Property Actions and Proceedings [*A publication*] (DLA)
Real Prop Cas... Real Property Cases [*1843-47*] [*A publication*] (DLA)
Real Prop Prob & Trust J... Real Property, Probate, and Trust Journal [*A publication*] (DLA)
REAM........... Rapid Excavation and Mining [*Project*] [*Bureau of Mines*]
REAMS......... Resources Evaluation and Management System [*Army*]
REAN........... Royal East African Navy [*British military*] (DMA)
RE & D......... Research, Engineering, and Development
RE & T......... Research Engineering and Test (NASA)
REANSW...... Real Estate Association of New South Wales [*Australia*]
REAP........... Read, Encode, Annotate, Ponder [*Reading improvement method*]
REAP........... Regional Enforcement Activities Plan [*Environmental Protection Agency*] (ERG)
REAP........... Reliability Engineering Analysis and Planning (PDAA)
REAP........... Remote Entry Acquisition Package
REAP........... Research and Engineering Apprenticeship Program [*Army*] (RDA)
REAP........... Resource Center for Efficient Agricultural Production [*Macdonald College*] [*Research center*] (RCD)
REAP........... Resource Engineering & Planning Co.
REAP........... Reutilization Expedite Assets Program [*DoD*]
REAP........... Rural Environmental Assistance Program [*Department of Agriculture*]
Reap Dec..... United States Customs Court Reports, Reappraisement Decision [*A publication*] (DLA)
REAPOR....... Real Estate Accounts Payable and Operating Reports
Reapp Dec... United States Customs Court Reports, Reappraisement Decision [*A publication*] (DLA)
REAPS......... Rotary Engine Air Pollution System [*Automotive engineering*]
REAPS......... Rotary Engine Antipollution System
REAPT......... Reappoint (AFM)
REAPTD....... Reappointed (WGA)
REAR........... Reliability Engineering Analysis Report (IEEE)
REARF......... Rearm and Refuel [*Military*] (VNW)
REARM........ Renovation of Armament Manufacturing Program [*Army*] (MCD)
REARM........ Underway Rearming [*Navy*] (NVT)
REART......... Restricted Articles [*IATA*] (DS)
REAS........... Real Estate Appraisal School [*Federal Home Loan Bank Board*]
REAS........... Reasonable (ROG)
REAS........... Reasonably Expected as Safe [*Medicine*] (DMAA)
REAS........... Register of Environment Assessments and Statements (MCD)
REAS........... Resources, Entities Accounting Subsystem (MCD)
REASM......... Reassemble (AAG)
REASN......... Reason (ROG)
REASSCE..... Reassurance (ROG)
REASSEM..... Reassemble (MSA)
REASSN...... Reassign (ROG)
REASSND.... Reassigned (ROG)
REASST....... Reassignment (ROG)
REASSY....... Reassembly (MSA)
REASTAN..... Renton Electrical Analog for Solution of Thermal Analogous Networks
REAT........... Radiological Emergency Assistance Team [*AEC*]
REAUM........ Reaumur (ROG)
REAV........... Renewable Energy Authority of Victoria [*Australia*]
reax............ Reaction Shot [*TV news*] (WDMC)
REB............. RADAR Evaluation Branch [*ADC*]
REB............. Rare Earth Boride (PDAA)
REB............. Real Estate Business [*Realtors National Marketing Institute*] [*A publication*]
REB............. Reba Resources Ltd. [*Vancouver Stock Exchange symbol*]
REB............. Rebecca/Eureka [*Navigation*] (AIA)
REB............. Rebecca Eureka Beacon [*Navigation*] (IAA)
REB............. Rebel
REB............. R. E. Blake [*Record label*]
REB............. Rebounds [*Basketball, hockey*]
REB............. Rebuilt
REB............. Redwood Empire Bancorp [*AMEX symbol*] (SPSG)
REB............. Reentry Body
REB............. Reentry Body Building (IAA)
REB............. Regional Education Board of the Christian Brothers (EA)
REB............. Regional Examining Bodies [*British*] (DI)
REB............. Relativistic Electron Beam (MCD)
REB............. Research Earth Borer
REB............. Research Ethics Board [*Canada*]
REB............. Rocket Engine Band
REB............. Rod End Bearing [*Army helicopter*]
REB............. Roentgen-Equivalent-Biological [*Irradiation unit*]
REB............. Royal Exhibition Buildings [*Melbourne, Australia*]
REBA........... Relativistic Electron Beam Accelerator
REBAR......... Reinforcing Bar (AAG)
REBASB....... Real Estate and Business Agents' Supervisory Board [*Western Australia*]
REBAT......... Reference Breakdown Air Traffic Control Services Report (FAAC)
REBAT......... Restricted Bandwidth Techniques (NG)
REBC........... Real Estate Brokerage Council (EA)
R-EBD-HS.... Recessive Epidermolysis Bullosa Dystrophia-Hallopeaun Siemens [*Dermatology*]
REBE........... Recovery Beacon Evaluation
REBECCA..... RADAR Responder Beacon [*System*] (MUGU)
REBECCA..... Remote Electrical Block Energization Clock Control Arrangement (IAA)
REBEEL........ Realistic Battlefield Environment-Electronic [*Military*] (PDAA)
REBIA.......... Regional Educational Building Institute for Africa
REBK........... Repertoire des Banques de Donnees en Conversationnel [*Association Nationale de la Recherche Technique*] [*Information service or system*]
REBLT......... Rebuilt [*Automotive advertising*]
REBPr......... Redwood Empire Bcp 7.80% Cv Pfd [*AMEX symbol*] (TTSB)
REBS........... Royal Engineers Balloon School [*British military*] (DMA)
REBUD......... Rehabilitation Budgeting Program [*Telecommunications*] (TEL)
REBUS......... Reseau des Bibliotheques Utilisant SIBIL [*Library Network of SIBIL Users*] [*University of Lausanne Switzerland*] [*Information service or system*] (IID)
REBUS......... Routine for Executing Biological Unit Simulations [*Computer program*]
REC............. Clarion State College, Clarion, PA [*OCLC symbol*] (OCLC)
REC............. Radiant Energy Conversion
REC............. Radioelectrocomplexing [*Clinical chemistry*] (AAMN)
REC............. Radio Electronic Combat [*Communications*]
REC............. Radio Executives Club (NTCM)
REC............. Railway Enthusiasts' Club [*British*] (BI)
REC............. Railway Executive Committee [*British*]
REC............. Rain Erosion Coating
REC............. Rare-Earth Catalyst [*Automotive engineering*]
REC............. Reactive [*Laboratory science*] (DAVI)
REC............. Reactor Engineer Console
REC............. Real Estate Council
REC............. Receipt
REC............. Received (DS)
REC............. Receiver (AAG)
REC............. Recens [*Fresh*] [*Pharmacy*]
REC............. Recent (ROG)
REC............. Receptacle (WGA)
REC............. Reception
REC............. Recess (MSA)
REC............. Recherches sur l'Origine de l'Ecriture Cuneiforme [*A publication*] (BJA)
REC............. Recife [*Brazil*] [*Airport symbol*] (OAG)
REC............. Recipe
REC............. Reclamation (WGA)
REC............. Recommendation (AFM)
REC............. Reconnaissance and Radioelectronic Combat [*Military*] (INF)
REC............. Record (AAG)
rec.............. Record (WDMC)
REC............. Record
Rec............. Recordati [*Italy*] [*Research code symbol*]
REC............. Recorded Program (NTCM)
REC............. Recorder
rec.............. Recording (WDMC)
REC............. Recording (ECII)
REC............. Recover [*or Recovery*]
REC............. Recreation
REC............. Recreo [*Guatemala*] [*Seismograph station code, US Geological Survey*] (SEIS)
Rec............. Recruiter [*British military*] (DMA)
REC............. Rectifier (IEEE)
Rec............. Recueil (BJA)
rec.............. Recurrence [*or Recurrent*] [*Medicine*] (MAE)
REC............. Recurring (MCD)
REC............. Regiment Etranger de Cavalerie [*Foreign Cavalry Regiment*] [*French*]
REC............. Regional Electricity Co. [*British*] (ECON)
REC............. Regional Electronics Centers [*British*]
REC............. Regional Evaluation Center (NVT)
REC............. Regional Express Co. [*ICAO designator*] (FAAC)
REC............. Rehabilitation Engineering Center for the Hearing Impaired [*Gallaudet College*] [*Research center*] (RCD)
REC............. Rehabilitation Engineering Centers [*Department of Health and Human Services*]
REC............. Religious Education Centre (AIE)
REC............. REM [*Roentgen-Equivalent-Man*] Equivalent Chemical [*Irradiation unit*]
REC............. Request for Engineering Change (MCD)
REC............. Research Ethics Committee
REC............. Reserve Equalization Committee [*Military*]
REC............. Residual Evaluation Center (MCD)
REC............. Revloc, PA [*Location identifier FAA*] (FAAL)
REC............. Ripling Electrochemical
REC............. Rudge Enthusiasts Club (EA)
RECA........... Repetitive Element Column Analysis (PDAA)
RECA........... Residual Capabilities Assessment (MCD)
RECA........... Revenue and Expenditure Control Act of 1968
RECA........... Right External Carotid Artery [*Medicine*] (MEDA)
RECALC....... Recalculated
RECAP......... Real Estate Cost Analysis Program

RECAP .... Recapitulation (AABC)
RECAP .... Reliability Engineering and Corrective Action Program
RECAP .... Reliability Evaluation Continuous Analysis Program
RECAP .... Research and Education Center for Architectural Preservation [*University of Florida*] [*Research center*] (RCD)
RECAP .... Resource and Capabilities Model (KSC)
RECAP .... Review and Command Assessment of Project [*Military*]
RECAP .... Rural Enterprises Community Action Program
RECAPS .... Read Encode/Capture/Proof/Sort [*Computer science*] (MHDB)
RECAPS .... Regionalized Civilian Automated Pay System [*Air Force*]
Rec Asst ...... Recreation Assistant (MEDA)
RECAT .... Ad Hoc Committee on the Cumulative Regulatory Effects on the Cost of Automotive Transportation [*Terminated, 1972*] (EGAO)
RECAT .... Reduced Energy Consumption for Commercial Air Transportation (DICI)
RECAU .... Receipt Acknowledged and Understood
RECBAD .... United States Army Recruiter Badge [*Military decoration*] (GFGA)
RECBKS .... Receiving Barracks
RECC .... Rhine Evacuation and Control Command [*NATO*] (NATG)
RECCB .... Regional Education Committee of the Christian Brothers [*Later, REB*] (EA)
RECCE .... Reconnaissance (CINC)
RECCEN .... Reception Center [*Army*] (IAA)
RECCEXREP... Reconnaisance Exploitation Report (MCD)
RECCFO .... Received in Connection with Fitting Out (DNAB)
RECCO .... Reconnaissance (NVT)
REC COM..... Record Commissioner [*British*] (DLA)
RECD .... Received (AAG)
recd .... Received (WDMC)
recd .... Received (ODBW)
RECD .... Recorded (WDAA)
RECDC .... Regional Early Childhood Direction Centers (EDAC)
Rec Dec........ Vaux's Recorder's Decisions [*1841-45*] [*Philadelphia, PA*] [*A publication*] (DLA)
RecdSys ...... Reconditioned Systems, Inc. [*Associated Press*] (SAG)
RECDUINS ... Received for Duty under Instruction
RECDUT....... Received for Duty
RECE........... Cuban Representation of Exiles [*Also known as Representacion Cubana del Exilio*] (EA)
RECE........... Relativistic Electron Coil Experiment (MCD)
RE CEL .... Reticulum Cell [*On Differential*] [*Hematology*] (DAVI)
RECENT .... Recentis [*Fresh*] [*Pharmacy*] (ROG)
RECEP .... Reception (ADA)
RECERT .... Recertification (NASA)
RECETED ..... Receipted (ROG)
RecFIN......... Recreational Fisheries Information Network [*Database*] [*National Marine Fisheries Service*]
RECFM......... Record Format [*Computer science*]
RECG .... Radioelectrocardiograph
RECG .... Reciting
RECGA......... Research and Engineering Council of the Graphic Arts Industry
RECGAI........ Research and Engineering Council of the Graphic Arts Industry (EA)
RECGP......... Recovery Group [*Air Force*]
RECH .... Reformed Episcopal Church
RECHAR....... Recombiner Charcoal Adsorber [*Nuclear energy*] (NRCH)
RECHG .... Recharge (NASA)
RECHRG ...... Recharger
RECID .... Recidivism [*or Recidivist*] (WDAA)
RECIP .... Recipient
RECIP .... Reciprocate (AAG)
RECIP .... Reciprocating Gas-Fueled Engine
RECIPE .... Recomp Computer Interpretive Program Expediter [*Computer science*]
RECIR .... Recirculating [*Automotive engineering*]
RECIRC........ Recirculate (AAG)
RECIT.......... Recitation
RECIT.......... Recitative [*Music*]
Reckson....... Reckson Associates Realty Corp. [*Associated Press*] (SAG)
REC L .... Recent Law (DLA)
RECL........... Recital (ROG)
RECL........... Reclamation
RECL........... Reclose
Reclaim....... Reclaim, Inc. [*Associated Press*] (SAG)
RECLAIM ..... Regional Clean Air Incentive Market [*Environmental program*] (ECON)
Rec Laws..... Recent Laws in Canada [*A publication*] (DLA)
RECLR .... Recleared [*Aviation*] (FAAC)
RECM.......... Recommend (KSC)
REC MAN..... Recreation Management Exhibition [*British*] (ITD)
RECMD .... Recommend (AAG)
Recmd .... Recommissioned (DS)
RECMECH .... Recoil Mechanism (AAG)
RECMF......... Radio and Electronic Component Manufacturers' Federation
RECMFA ...... Radio and Electronic Component Manufacturers Association (IAA)
RECMN .... Recommendation
RECMOP ...... Received [*Payment under Provisions of the*] Mustering Out Payment Act [*Military*] (DNAB)
RECMPT ...... Recomputation
RECMS .... Record Maintenance Statistics (MHDB)
RECN .... Reconnaissance
RECNCLN..... Reconciliation (AABC)
RECNO .... This Office Has No Record Of [*Army*] (AABC)
RECNSTRCTV... Reconstructive
RECNUM...... Record Number [*Online database field identifier*]
RECO .... Remote Command and Control (MCD)
RECO .... Remote Control [*Of mines*] (DOMA)
RECOC .... Reading and Comprehension in Chemistry
RECODEX..... Report Collection Index [*Studsvik Energiteknik AB*] [*Database Nykoping, Sweden*]
RECOG......... Recognition [*or Recognize*] (AAG)
RECOGE....... Recognisance (ROG)
RECOGN ...... Recognizance
RECOGS....... Recognisances (ROG)
RECOGSIG ... Recognition Signal [*Navy*]
RECOL .... Retrieval Command Language [*Computer search language*]
RECOM .... Recommend (WDAA)
Recomm ...... Recommendation (DAVI)
RECOMMTRANSO... Upon Receipt of These Orders Communicate with Transportation Officer for Priority Designator via Government Air If Available to ____
RECOMP ...... Recommended Completion
RECOMP ...... Recomplement
RECOMP ...... Redstone Computer
RECOMP ...... Repairs Completed [*Military*] (NVT)
RECOMP ...... Retrieval and Composition (DIT)
RECON......... Readiness Condition [*Military*]
RECON......... Reconcentration (WDAA)
RECON......... Reconciliation
RECON......... Recondition (WDAA)
RECON......... Reconnaissance (NATG)
RECON......... Reconnoitre (WDAA)
RECON......... Reconsignment (WDAA)
recon .... Reconstruction (VRA)
RECON......... Reliability and Configuration Accountability System
RECON......... Remote Console [*NASA computer*]
RECON......... Remote Control (KSC)
RECON......... Resources Conservation (MCD)
RECON......... Retrospective Conversion (NITA)
RECON......... Retrospective Conversion of Bibliographic Records [*Library of Congress*]
RECONATKRON... Reconnaissance Attack Squadron [*Navy*] (DNAB)
RECONATKWING... Reconnaissance Attack Wing [*Navy*] (DNAB)
RECONBN .... Reconnaissance Battalion [*Navy*] (DNAB)
RECONCE..... Reconveyance (ROG)
RECONCO .... Reconnaissance Co. [*Military*]
RECOND ...... Recondition (AABC)
RECONDO.... Reconnaissance Commando Doughboy [*Military*] (AABC)
RECONEX.... Raid/Reconnaissance Exercise [*Military*] (NVT)
RECONFIG ... Reconfiguration (NASA)
RECONN ...... Reconnaissance (AAG)
R Econ S ..... Royal Economic Society [*British*]
recons denied... Reconsideration Denied (AAGC)
RECONST..... Reconstruct (AABC)
reconstr ...... Reconstruction (CPH)
RECONVCE... Reconveyance (ROG)
Recoton .... Recoton Corp. [*Associated Press*] (SAG)
RECOV .... Recovery (KSC)
RECOVER.... Remote Continual Verification [*Telephonic monitoring system*]
RECOVER.... Remote Control Verification [*Nuclear safeguards*]
RECOVY ...... Recovery
RECP .... International College of Real Estate Consulting Professionals (EAIO)
RECP .... Real Estate Consulting Professional [*International College of Real Estate Consulting Professionals*] [*Designation awarded by*]
RECP .... Receptacle
RECP .... Reception (WGA)
RECP .... Reciprocal (AAG)
RECP .... Release Engineering Change Proposal (MCD)
RECP .... Request for Engineering Change Proposal [*NASA*]
RECP .... Rural Environmental Conservation Program
Recp Cen..... Reception Center [*Army*]
RECPOM...... Resource Constrained Procurement Objectives for Munitions Model [*Army*]
RECPST....... Receptionist (WGA)
RECPT .... Receipt
RECPT .... Receipt
RECPT .... Receptacle (AAG)
RECPT .... Reception (AAG)
RECR........... Receiver
RECR........... Recreation (AABC)
RECRAS....... Retrieval System for Current Research in Agricultural Sciences [*Japan*]
RECRC......... Recirculate (NASA)
RECRE......... Recreation
Rec Rm .... Recovery Room (BARN)
RECRN......... Recreation
RECRSHIP ... Receivership (LWAP)
RECRT .... Recruit (AFM)
RECRUIT...... Recruiting
RECRYST..... Recrystallized
RECS .... Radiological Emergency Communications System [*Nuclear energy*] (NRCH)
RECS .... Rear Echelon COMINT [*Communications Intelligence*] System [*Military*] (MCD)
RecS........... Reconditioned Systems, Inc. [*Associated Press*] (SAG)
RECS .... Reconfigurable EC System (MCD)
RECS .... Reconstitutable Emergency Communications System
RECS .... Representative Shuttle Environmental Control System [*NASA*] (MCD)
RECS .... Residential Energy Consumption Survey [*Department of Energy*] (GFGA)

RECSAM Southeast Asian Regional Center for Education in Science and Mathematics [*Malaysia*]

RECSAT Reconnaissance Satellite (NVT)

RECSATSUM Reconnaissance Satellite Summary (DNAB)

rec sec Recording Secretary (WGA)

RECSG Renewable Energy Congressional Staff Group [*Defunct*] (EA)

RECSHIP Receiving Ship

Rec Spec Recreation Specialist (MEDA)

RECSQUAD Reconnaissance Squadron [*Military*]

RECSTA Receiving Station [*Military*]

RECSYS Recreation Systems Analysis [*Computer science*]

RECT Receipt

RECT Reception (IAA)

RECT Rectangle (AAG)

RECT Rectification [*or Rectifier*] (IAA)

rect Rectification (IDOE)

RECT Rectificatus [*Rectified*] [*Pharmacy*]

rect Rectified (IDOE)

rect Rectifier (IDOE)

RECT Rectify (AAG)

RECT Rector

rect Rectum [*Medicine*] (MAE)

RECT Rectus [*Muscle*] [*Anatomy*]

RECTAD Received for Temporary Additional Duty

RECTADINS Received for Temporary Additional Duty under Instruction

RECTAS Regional Centre for Training in Aerial Surveys (EAIO)

RECTD Received for Temporary Duty

RECTD Recited (ROG)

Rec Tech Recreation Technician (MEDA)

RECTEMDUINS Received for Temporary Duty under Instruction

RECTENNA Rectifying Antenna [*Microwave power transmission*]

RECTG Reciting (ROG)

RECTIFON Rectification (ROG)

RECTIL Rectilineal [*Geometry*] (ROG)

RECTON Reduction (ROG)

RECTR Recommend Transfer Of (NOAA)

RECTR Rectifier

RECTREAT Received for Treatment

RECUR Recurrence [*or Recurrent*] [*Medicine*]

RECV Receive (NASA)

rec v Recreational Vehicle (BARN)

RECVD Received

recvee Recreational Vehicle (BARN)

RecvEng Recovery Engineering, Inc. [*Associated Press*] (SAG)

RECVG Receiving

RECVR Receiver (NASA)

RECVY Recovery

RECY Recovery (AAG)

RECY Recycling Industries [*NASDAQ symbol*] (TTSB)

RECY Recycling Industries, Inc. [*NASDAQ symbol*] (SAG)

RECYCLE Recycling

Recycling Recycling Industries, Inc. [*Associated Press*] (SAG)

RED Comite International de La Croix-Rouge [*Switzerland ICAO designator*] (FAAC)

Re D Doctor of Recreation (PGP)

ReD Doctor of Recreation (GAGS)

RED New South Wales Reserved Equity Decisions [*A publication*] (DLA)

RED Radian Energy Distribution

RED Radiation Experience Data [*Food and Drug Administration*] [*Database*]

RED Radio Equipment Department [*British military*] (DMA)

RED Railroad Employees' Department [*of AFL-CIO*]

RED Range Error Detector

RED Rapid Erythrocyte Degeneration [*Medicine*] (DMAA)

RED Rapid Excess Disposal [*Military*] (AABC)

RED Rare-Earth Device

RED RCRA [*Resource Conservation and Recovery Act*] Enforcement Division [*Environmental Protection Agency*] (GFGA)

RED Redactor (WGA)

red Redeemable [*Finance*] (ODBW)

RED Redeemed

Red Redfield's New York Surrogate Reports [*A publication*] (DLA)

Red Redington's Reports [*31-35 Maine*] [*A publication*] (DLA)

RED Red Lion Inns L.P. [*AMEX symbol*] (TTSB)

RED Red Lion Inns Ltd. [*AMEX symbol*] (SPSG)

RED Red Lodge, MT [*Location identifier FAA*] (FAAL)

RED Redoubt Volcano [*Alaska*] [*Seismograph station code, US Geological Survey*] (SEIS)

RED Reduce [*or Reduction*] (AAG)

red Reduced (WDMC)

red Reduction (WDMC)

red Reduction (ODBW)

RED Redundant (KSC)

Red Redwar's Comments on Ordinances of the Gold Coast Colony [*1889-1909*] [*Ghana*] [*A publication*] (DLA)

Re-D Re-Evaluation Deadline [*Rehabilitation*] (DAVI)

RED Reflection Electron Diffraction [*For surface structure analysis*]

RED Refunding Escrow Deposit [*Finance*] (DFIT)

RED Registered Expected Death

RED Repairable Equipment Depot [*British military*] (DMA)

RED Repeat Expansion Detection [*Genetics*]

RED Restructured Expanded Data (MCD)

RED Resume Entry Device

RED Review, Evaluation, Disposition Board (AAG)

RED Ritchie's Equity Decisions (Russell) [*Canada*] [*A publication*] (DLA)

REDA Rural Educational and Development Association [*Canada*]

REDAC Racal Electronic Design and Analysis by Computer (IAA)

REDAC Real-Time Data Acquisition

Red Am R Cas Redfield's American Railway Cases [*A publication*] (DLA)

Red Am RR Cas Redfield's Leading American Railway Cases [*A publication*] (DLA)

Red & Big Cas B & N Redfield and Bigelow's Leading Cases on Bills and Notes [*A publication*] (DLA)

REDAP Reentrant Data Processing

REDAS Reduced to Apprentice Seaman [*Navy*]

REDB Redbourne [*England*]

REDB Red Brick Systems [*NASDAQ symbol*] (TTSB)

REDB Red Brick Systems, Inc. [*NASDAQ symbol*] (SAG)

Red Bail Redfield on Carriers and Bailments [*A publication*] (DLA)

REDBR Redbridge [*England*]

REDC Regional Economic Development Center [*Memphis State University*] [*Research center*] (RCD)

REDC Reinsertion of Direct Current (IAA)

REDCAP Real-Time Electromagnetic Digitally Controlled Analyser and Processor

REDCAPE Readiness Capability [*Military*]

Red Car Redfield on Carriers and Bailments [*A publication*] (DLA)

Red Cas RR Redfield's Leading American Railway Cases [*A publication*] (DLA)

Red Cas Wills Redfield's Leading Cases on Wills [*A publication*] (DLA)

REDCAT Racial and Ethnic Category [*Army*] (INF)

REDCAT Range-Extended Directionally-Controlled Antitank Missile (MCD)

REDCAT Readiness Category [*Military*]

REDCN Reducing (ROG)

REDCOM Readiness Command [*Army*]

REDCON Readiness Condition [*Military*]

REDD Reduced (ROG)

ReddiBrk Reddi Brake Supply Corp. [*Associated Press*] (SAG)

REDE Regents External Degree Examinations [*New York*] (EDAC)

Re de J Revue de Jurisprudence [*Montreal*] [*A publication*] (DLA)

Re de L Revue de Jurisprudence et Legislation [*Montreal*] [*A publication*] (DLA)

Redem Redemption (DLA)

RedEm Redwood Empire Bancorp [*Associated Press*] (SAG)

RedEmp Redwood Empire Bancorp [*Associated Press*] (SAG)

Redes Pl Redesdale's Treatise upon Equity Pleading [*A publication*] (DLA)

REDF Redfed Bancorp [*NASDAQ symbol*] (SAG)

Redf Redfield's New York Surrogate Reports [*A publication*] (DLA)

Redf Am Railw Cas Redfield's American Railway Cases [*A publication*] (DLA)

Redf & B Redfield and Bigelow's Leading Cases [*England*] [*A publication*] (DLA)

Redf Carr Redfield on Carriers and Bailments [*A publication*] (DLA)

RedfedBc Redfed Bancorp [*Associated Press*] (SAG)

RED FG Red Flint Glazed [*Paper*] (DGA)

Redf (NY) Redfield's New York Surrogate Reports [*A publication*] (DLA)

Redf Railways Redfield on Railways [*A publication*] (DLA)

Redf R Cas Redfield's Railway Cases [*England*] [*A publication*] (DLA)

Redf Sur (NY) Redfield's New York Surrogate Court Reports [*A publication*] (DLA)

Redf Surr Redfield's New York Surrogate Reports [*A publication*] (DLA)

Redf Surr (NY) Redfield's New York Surrogate Court Reports [*5 vols.*] [*A publication*] (DLA)

Redf Wills Redfield's Leading Cases on Wills [*A publication*] (DLA)

REDGF Rea Gold Corp. [*NASDAQ symbol*] (SAG)

RedhkA Redhook Ale Brewery, Inc. [*Associated Press*] (SAG)

RED HORSE Rapid Engineer Development, Heavy Operational Repair Squadron, Engineering [*Air Force*] (AFM)

RED HORSE Rapid Engineering Deployable, Heavy Operational Repair Squadron, Engineer [*Air Force*] (DOMA)

RedHot Red Hot Concepts, Inc. [*Associated Press*] (SAG)

RedHt Red Hot Concepts, Inc. [*Associated Press*] (SAG)

REDI Real Estate Data, Inc. [*Information service or system*] (IID)

REDI Reddi Brake Supply [*NASDAQ symbol*] (TTSB)

REDI Reddi Brake Supply Corp. [*NASDAQ symbol*] (SAG)

REDI Remote Electronic Delivery of Information [*Library science*]

REDICORT Readiness Improvement through Correspondence Training (MCD)

RediCr ReadiCare, Inc. [*Associated Press*] (SAG)

REDIG IN PULV Redigatur In Pulverent [*Let It Be Reduced to Powder*] [*Pharmacy*] (ROG)

Redington Redington's Reports [*31-35 Maine*] [*A publication*] (DLA)

RED in PULV Redactus in Pulverem [*Reduce to a Powder*] [*Pharmacy*]

Red Int L Reddie's Inquiries in International Law [*2nd ed.*] [*1851*] [*A publication*] (DLA)

Re Dir Director of Recreation (PGP)

REDIS Reference Dispatch (NOAA)

REDISC Rediscount [*Banking*]

REDIST Redistilled

REDISTR Redistribution (AFM)

REDL Redlane [*England*]

REDL Runway Edge Light [*ICAO designator*] (FAAC)

Redlaw Redlaw Industries, Inc. [*Associated Press*] (SAG)

REDLOG Logistic Readiness Report [*Navy*] (CINC)

Redlw Redlaw Industries, Inc. [*Associated Press*] (SAG)

Redman Redman Industries [*Associated Press*] (SAG)

Redman Redman on Landlord and Tenant [*A publication*] (DLA)

Redm Arb Redman on Arbitration [*A publication*] (DLA)

Red Mar Com Reddie's Law of Maritime Commerce [*1841*] [*A publication*] (DLA)

Red Mar Int L Reddie's Researches in Maritime International Law [*1844-45*] [*A publication*] (DLA)

REDN Reduction

REDNON Operational Readiness Report (Nonatomic) (CINC)

REDNT......... Redundant (AAG)
REDO........... RADAR Engineering Design Objectives (NG)
REDO........... Red Documental [*Ministerio de Educacion Publica*] [*Chile*] [*Information service or system*] (CRD)
REDOPS........ Ready for Operations [*Reporting system*] [*DoD*]
REDOX......... Reduction and Oxidation
REDP........... Redondo Peak [*New Mexico*] [*Seismograph station code, US Geological Survey*] (SEIS)
Red Pop...... Post Reditum ad Populum [*of Cicero*] [*Classical studies*] (OCD)
Red Pr......... Redfield's New York Practice Reports [*A publication*] (DLA)
REDR........... Redruth [*England*]
REDRAT........ Readiness Rating
REDREP........ Redeployment Report [*Military*]
Red RL......... Reddie's Roman Law [*A publication*] (DLA)
RedRoof...... Red Roof Inns, Inc. [*Associated Press*] (SAG)
Red RR......... Redfield on the Law of Railroads [*A publication*] (DLA)
Red RR Cas... Redfield's Leading American Railway Cases [*A publication*] (DLA)
REDS........... Retrovirus Epidemiology Donor Study [*Medicine*]
REDS........... Revised Engine-Delivery Schedule (DNAB)
REDS........... Royal Engineers Diving School [*British military*] (DMA)
Red Sc L...... Reddie's Science of Law [*2nd ed.*] [*A publication*] (DLA)
Red Sen...... Post Reditum in Senatu [*of Cicero*] [*Classical studies*] (OCD)
REDSG......... Redesignate (AFM)
redsh........... Reddish [*Philately*]
REDSO......... Regional Economic Development Services Office [*USAID*]
REDSOD....... Repetitive Explosive Device for Soil Displacement
REDSO/ESA... Regional Economic Development Services Office for East and Southern Africa
RED-T.......... Remote Electric Drive Turret
REDTOP....... Reactor Design from Thermal-Hydraulic Operating Parameters [*NASA*]
REDTRAIN... Readiness Training (MCD)
REDUC........ Red Latinoamericana de Documentacion en Educacion [*Latin American Education Documentation Network*] (PDAA)
REDUC........ Reduction (KSC)
REDUCE....... Reduction of Electrical Demand Using Computer Equipment [*Energy management system designed by John Helwig of Jance Associates, Inc.*]
REDUN......... Redundancy (NASA)
REDUPL....... Reduplication
REDW.......... Redwood National Park
Redwar........ Redwar's Comments on Ordinances of the Gold Coast Colony [*1889-1909*] [*Ghana*] [*A publication*] (DLA)
Redwd......... Redwood Trust, Inc. [*Associated Press*] (SAG)
Red Wills.... Redfield on the Law of Wills [*A publication*] (DLA)
REDWN......... Redrawn
REDY........... Ready (DAVI)
REDY........... Recirculating Dialyzate [*Artificial kidney dialysis system*]
REDYP......... Reentry Dynamics Program
REDZ........... Recent Drizzle [*Meteorology*] (DA)
REE............. Lubbock, TX [*Location identifier FAA*] (FAAL)
REE............. Radio Exterior Espana (EY)
REE............. Rapid Extinction Effect [*Electrophysiology*]
REE............. Rare-Earth Element [*Chemistry*]
REE............. Rational Expectations Equilibrium [*Economics*]
REE............. Red Earth Energy Ltd. [*Vancouver Stock Exchange symbol*]
REE............. Registered Export Establishment
REE............. Respiratory Energy Expenditure [*Physiology*]
REE............. Resting Energy Expenditure
REEA........... Radio and Electronics Engineering Association (IAA)
REEA........... Real Estate Educators Association [*Chicago, IL*] (EA)
Reebok........ Reebok International Ltd. [*Associated Press*] (SAG)
REEC........... Regional Export Expansion Council [*Department of Commerce*]
REECO......... Reynolds Electrical & Engineering Co.
Reed........... Reed on Bills of Sale [*A publication*] (DLA)
REED........... Reeds Jewelers [*NASDAQ symbol*] (TTSB)
REED........... Reeds Jewelers, Inc. [*Wilmington, NC*] [*NASDAQ symbol*] (NQ)
re-ed........... Re-Education (DAVI)
REED........... Resources on Educational Equity for the Disabled
REED........... Restricted Edge Emitting Diode [*Electronics*] (EECA)
Reed Am LS... Reed's American Law Studies [*A publication*] (DLA)
Reed BS...... Reed on Bills of Sale [*A publication*] (DLA)
Reed C........ Reed College (GAGS)
Reed Car..... Reed on Railways as Carriers [*A publication*] (DLA)
Reed Fraud... Reed's Leading Cases on Statute of Frauds [*A publication*] (DLA)
ReedIntl....... Reed International Ltd. [*Associated Press*] (SAG)
ReedJwl...... Reeds Jewelers, Inc. [*Associated Press*] (SAG)
Reed PA Black... Reed's Pennsylvania Blackstone [*A publication*] (DLA)
Reed Pr Sug... Reed's Practical Suggestions for the Management of Lawsuits [*A publication*] (DLA)
REEDS......... Retention of Tears, Ectrodactyly, Ectodermal Dysplasia, and Strange Hair, Skin and Teeth Syndrome [*Medicine*] (DMAA)
REEEVAC..... Renewable Energy and Energy Efficiency Joint Ventures Advisory Committee [*Department of Energy*] (EGAO)
REEF........... Rocket Exhaust Effects Facility (MCD)
REEFER........ Refrigerator, Refrigerated, or Cold Storage [*Airplane, railway car, truck*]
REEFNSW.... Real Estate Employers Federation of New South Wales [*Australia*]
REEG........... Radioelectroencephalograph
REEGT......... Registered Electroencephalographic Technician [*Medicine*] (AAMN)
REEI............ Russian and East European Institute [*Indiana University*] [*Research center*] (RCD)
REEL........... Radiation Exposure Evaluation Laboratory (DNAB)
REEL........... Recessive-Expressive Emergent Language Scores [*For the hearing-impaired*]
REELS.......... Reflected Electron Energy Loss Spectra
REEM.......... Reserves Embarked [*Navy*] (NVT)
REEN........... Regional Energy Education Network [*National Science Teachers Association*]
REENL......... Reenlist [*Military*] (AFM)
REENLA....... Reenlistment Allowance [*Military*]
REENL ALLOW... Reenlistment Allowance [*Military*] (DNAB)
REENLB....... Reenlistment Bonus [*Military*]
Reenlmt....... Re-Enlistment [*Army*]
REEP........... Range Estimating and Evaluation Procedure [*Computer science*]
REEP........... Regression Estimation of Event Probabilities (IEEE)
REEP........... Review of Environmental Effects of Pollutants [*Environmental Protection Agency*] (GFGA)
REEP........... Right End-Expiratory Pressure [*Medicine*] (DMAA)
REEP........... Role Exchange/Education-Practice (MEDA)
REES........... Center for Russian and East European Studies [*University of Pittsburgh*] [*Research center*] (RCD)
REES........... Reactive Electronic Equipment Simulator (RDA)
REES........... Regular Educator Expectancy Scale (EDAC)
REES........... Russian and East European Studies Area Program [*University of Pittsburgh*] [*Research center*] (RCD)
Reese.......... Reporter of Vols. 5 and 11, Heiskell's Tennessee Reports [*A publication*] (DLA)
REETA......... Rural Extension, Education and Training Abstracts [*Database*] [*Commonwealth Bureau of Agricultural Economics*] [*Information service or system*] (CRD)
REETS......... Radiological Effluent and Environmental Technical Specifications [*Nuclear Regulatory Commission*] (NRCH)
Reeve Des... Reeve on Descents [*A publication*] (DLA)
Reeve Dom Rel... Reeve on Domestic Relations [*A publication*] (DLA)
Reeve Eng L... Reeve's History of the English Law [*A publication*] (DLA)
Reeve Eng Law... Reeve's History of the English Law [*A publication*] (DLA)
Reeve Hist Eng Law... Reeve's History of the English Law [*A publication*] (DLA)
Reeve Sh..... Reeve on the Law of Shipping [*A publication*] (DLA)
Reeves HEL... Reeve's History of the English Law [*A publication*] (DLA)
Reeves Hist Eng Law... Reeve's History of the English Law [*A publication*] (DLA)
REF............. Range Error Function [*Aerospace*] (AAG)
REF............. Rat Embryo Fibroblast [*Cells*]
REF............. REFAC Technology Develop [*AMEX symbol*] (TTSB)
REF............. Refac Technology Development Corp. [*AMEX symbol*] (SAG)
REF............. Refectory (DSUE)
REF............. Refer (EY)
REF............. Referee
REF............. Reference [*Online database field identifier*] (NATG)
ref............... Reference (IDOE)
REF............. Reference
REF............. Referendum
REF............. Refinery [*or Refining*]
REF............. Reflection Resources [*Vancouver Stock Exchange symbol*]
REF............. Reflector
REF............. Reformation
REF............. Reformed
REF............. Refrain (WGA)
REF............. Refresher (AABC)
REF............. Refrigerant [*Cooling*] [*Medicine British*] (ROG)
REF............. Refrigerator (WGA)
REF............. Refugee Coordinator [*Department of State*] (GFGA)
REF............. Refund [*or Refunding*]
REF............. Refurbishment (NASA)
REF............. Refused (ADA)
REF............. Release of Excess Funds
REF............. Renal Erythropoietic Factor [*Medicine*]
REF............. Restriction Endonuclease Fingerprinting [*Analytical biochemistry*]
REF............. Risk Evaluation Force (DOMA)
REF............. Unclear Pronoun Reference [*Used in correcting manuscripts, etc.*]
REFA........... Real Estate Fund of America
Refac.......... Refac Technology Development Corp. [*Associated Press*] (SAG)
Re fa lo....... Recordari Facias Loquelam [*Have the Record Before the Court*] [*Latin*] [*Legal term*] (BARN)
Ref Aust...... Reference Australia [*A publication*]
Ref Bk R...... Reference Book Review [*A publication*] (BRI)
REFC........... Reference (ROG)
REFC........... Reflections of Elvis Fan Club (EA)
REFC........... Richard Eden Fan Club (EA)
REFCD......... Research and Education Foundation for Chest Disease [*Defunct*] (EA)
REFCO......... Resolution Funding Corp. [*Established by the Financial Institutions Reform , Recovery, and Enforcement Act of 1989*]
REFCON....... Reference Configuration (SSD)
RefCorp....... Resolution Funding Corp. [*Established by the Financial Institutions Reform , Recovery, and Enforcement Act of 1989*]
REFCORP..... Resolution Funding Corporation (USGC)
REFD........... Referred
REFD........... Refined
REFD........... Reformed (WGA)
REFD........... Refund (AFM)
REFD CON.... Reinforced Concrete [*Freight*]
Ref Dec....... Referee's Decision [*Legal term*] (DLA)
REF/DES...... Reference Designator Number (MCD)
REFD MTL... Reinforced Metal [*Freight*]
ref doc......... Referring Doctor [*Medicine*] (AAMN)
REFD PLYWD... Reinforced Plywood [*Freight*]
REFEC......... Refectory (DSUE)
R_{eff}........... Effective Resistance (IDOE)
REFF........... References (WGA)

REFFREQ..... Reference Frequency [*Telecommunications*] (IAA)
REFG........ Refrigerating [*or Refrigeration*]
Ref Girl........ Refractory Girl [*A publication*]
REFGR........ Refrigerator
REFI........ Regional Ejection Fraction Image [*Medicine*] (DMAA)
REFIC........ Research Fire Control (SAA)
REFIL........ Recharged from Inversion Layer (PDAA)
REFL........ Reference Line (AAG)
REFL........ Reflectance [*or Reflector*] (AAG)
REFL........ Reflection [*or Reflector*] (IAA)
REFL........ Reflex
REFL........ Reflexive
REFL........ Specimen Lost by Reference Laboratory (DAVI)
Reflctn........ Reflectone, Inc. [*Associated Press*] (SAG)
REFLD........ Reflected
REFLEC........ Reflection (IAA)
REFLECS...... Retrieval from the Literature on Electronics and Computer Sciences (PDAA)
Reflectn....... Reflectone, Inc. [*Associated Press*] (SAG)
REFLES........ Reference Librarian Enhancement System [*University of California*] [*Online microcomputer system*]
REFLEX........ Reserve Flexibility [*Military*] (MCD)
REFM........ Resource Ecology and Fisheries Management (USDC)
REFM........ Resource Ecology and Fisheries Management [*Marine science*] (OSRA)
REFMCHY.... Refrigerating Machinery
REFMS........ Recreation and Education for Multiple Sclerosis
REFMT........ Reinforcement
REFNO........ Reference Number (CINC)
Ref NRE........ Refused, Not Reversible Error [*Legal term*] (DLA)
REFONE........ Reference Our Telephone Conversation (FAAC)
REFORGER... Return of Forces to Germany [*Military*]
REFORM...... Reformatory (ROG)
REFORMA..... National Association to Promote Library Services to the Spanish-Speaking
REFORS........ Replacement Forecasting System (IAA)
REFP........ Reference Papers [*Army*] (AABC)
ref phys........ Referring Physician (DAVI)
REFR........ Refractory (AAG)
REFR........ Refractory
REFR........ Refrigerate (KSC)
REFR........ Research Frontiers [*NASDAQ symbol*] (TTSB)
REFR........ Research Frontiers, Inc. [*NASDAQ symbol*] (SAG)
REFRA........ Recent Freezing Rain [*Meteorology*] (DA)
REFRACDUTRA... Release from Active Duty for Training [*Army*] (AABC)
REFRAD........ Release from Active Duty [*Army*]
REFRADT...... Release from Active Duty for Training [*Army*] (AABC)
REFRANACDUTRA... Release from Annual Active Duty for Training [*Army*] (AABC)
REFRAT........ Release from Annual Training [*Army*] (AABC)
REFRD........ Refrigerated (AAG)
Refr G........ Refractory Girl [*A publication*]
REFRG........ Refrigerate (AAG)
REFRIG........ Refrigerated Service [*Shipping*] [*British*]
REFRIG........ Refrigeration
REFRIG........ Refrigerator
REFRIGN...... Refrigeration
REFS........ Remote Entry Flexible Security [*Computer science*] (MHDB)
REFSEARCH... Reference Materials Searching System (NITA)
REFSMMAT... Reference Stable Member Matrix (KSC)
Ref Sp........ Reformed Spelling (BARN)
REFSRV........ [*The*] Reference Service [*Mead Data Central, Inc.*] [*Information service or system*] (IID)
REFT........ Release for Experimental Flight Test (NG)
REFTEL........ Reference Telegram (NATG)
REFTEMP..... Reference Temperature (IAA)
REFTO........ Reference Travel Order (NOAA)
REFTRA........ Refresher Training (NVT)
REFTS........ Resonant Frequency Tracking System
refty........ Refectory (VRA)
REFUL........ Refueling
REFURB........ Refurbished
REFURDIS... Reference Your Dispatch
REFURLTR... Reference Your Letter
RefWID........ Refugee Women in Development (EA)
Ref WM........ Refused, Want of Merit [*Legal term*] (DLA)
REFY........ Refinery
REG........ Aircraft Nationality and Registration Marks
Reg........ Daily Register [*New York City*] [*A publication*] (DLA)
REG........ Radiation Exposure Guide
REG........ Radioencephalogram
REG........ Radioisotope Electrogenerator (IAA)
REG........ Random Event Generator [*Psychology*]
REG........ Range Extender with Gain [*Bell System*]
REG........ Reeves Entertainment Group [*Television*]
Reg........ Regal, Branch of EMI [*Record label*] [*Spain*]
REG........ Regarding
REG........ Regency Realty [*NYSE symbol*] (SPSG)
REG........ Regency Resources [*Vancouver Stock Exchange symbol*]
REG........ Regeneration (IAA)
REG........ Regent
REG........ Reggio Calabria [*Italy*] [*Airport symbol*] (OAG)
REG........ Regiment
REG........ Regina [*Queen*] [*Latin*]
REG........ Region (AAG)
reg........ Region (DD)
REG........ Regis College, Weston, MA [*OCLC symbol*] (OCLC)
REG........ Register (AAG)
REG........ Register
REG........ Registered [*Stock exchange term*] (SPSG)
REG........ Registrar (ROG)
REG........ Registration [*ICAO designator*] (FAAC)
reg........ Registration (ODBW)
Reg........ Registration Cases [*A publication*] (DLA)
Reg........ Registrum Omnium Brevium [*Register of Writs*] [*Latin A publication*] (DSA)
REG........ Registry
REG........ Regourd Aviation [*France ICAO designator*] (FAAC)
REG........ Regression Analysis [*Military*] (IAA)
REG........ Regular (AAG)
REG........ Regulate (AAG)
REG........ Regulating [*Duties*] [*Navy British*]
REG........ Regulation
REG........ Regulator (DEN)
REG........ Repair-Evacuator Group [*Former USSR*]
REG........ Rheoencephalography [*Medicine*]
REG........ Rock Eagle [*Georgia*] [*Seismograph station code, US Geological Survey*] (SEIS)
REGA........ Regional Acceptance [*NASDAQ symbol*] (TTSB)
REGA........ Regional Acceptance Corp. [*NASDAQ symbol*] (SAG)
RegAcp........ Regional Acceptance Corp. [*Associated Press*] (SAG)
REGAD........ Regenerate Address [*Computer science*] (MHDB)
REGAF........ Regular Air Force
REGAL........ Remote Generalized Application Language [*Computer science*] (PDAA)
REGAL........ Remotely Guided Autonomous Lightweight Torpedo (MCD)
RegalBel...... Regal-Beloit Corp. [*Associated Press*] (SAG)
Reg App...... Registration Appeals [*England*] [*A publication*] (DLA)
Reg Arch.... Registered Architect
REGARD...... Ruby, Emerald, Garnet, Amethyst, Ruby, Diamond [*Jewelry*]
RegBn........ Regent Bancshares Corp. [*Associated Press*] (SAG)
RegBnc........ Regent Bancshares Corp. [*Associated Press*] (SAG)
Reg Brev.... Registrum Omnium Brevium [*Register of Writs*] [*Latin A publication*] (DLA)
REGC........ Right Eminent Grand Commander [*Freemasonry*]
REG/CAN...... Registry Number/Chemical Abstracts Number [*American Chemical Society information file*]
Reg Cas....... Registration Cases [*England*] [*A publication*] (DLA)
RegCin........ Regal Cinemas, Inc. [*Associated Press*] (SAG)
REGD........ Registered (EY)
REGD........ Registered
Reg Deb...... Gales and Seaton's Register of Debates in Congress [*1824-37*] [*A publication*] (DLA)
Reg Deb (Gales)... Register of Debates in Congress (Gales) [*1789-91*] [*A publication*] (DLA)
Reg Deb (G & S)... Gales and Seaton's Register of Debates in Congress [*1824-37*] [*A publication*] (DLA)
REGE........ Regular Eight [*Motion picture*] (VRA)
REGEM........ Release of Genetically Engineered Microorganisms [*A conference*]
regen........ Regenerate [*Computer science*] (WDMC)
REGEN........ Regeneration (AAG)
REGEN........ Regenerative Generator [*Electronics*] (ECII)
regen........ Regeration [*Computer science*] (WDMC)
Regenrn........ Regeneron Pharmaceuticals, Inc. [*Associated Press*] (SAG)
REGENT........ Reduce Geography in No Time (SAA)
REGEXP........ Regular Expression [*Computer science*] (NHD)
Reg Gen...... Regulae Generales [*A publication*] (DLA)
RegHlt........ Regency Health Services, Inc. [*Associated Press*] (SAG)
REGI........ Registry, Inc. (The) [*NASDAQ symbol*] (SAG)
ReGI........ Renninger & Graves, Inc., Philadelphia, PA [*Closed*] [*Library symbol*] [*Library of Congress*] (LCLS)
REGIM........ Regimental (ROG)
REGING........ Registering (ROG)
Regional Rail Reorg Ct... Special Court Regional Railroad Reorganization Act [*A publication*] (DLA)
Regis........ Regis Corp. [*Associated Press*] (SAG)
REGIS........ Register (AABC)
REGIS........ Relational General Information System
ReGIS........ Remote Graphics Instruction Set (HGAA)
Registry........ Registry, Inc. (The) [*Associated Press*] (SAG)
Reg J Social Issues... Regional Journal of Social Issues [*A publication*]
REGL........ Regal Cinemas [*NASDAQ symbol*] (TTSB)
REGL........ Regal Cinemas, Inc. [*NASDAQ symbol*] (SAG)
REGL........ Regimental
REGL........ Regional
regl........ Regional (DD)
Regl........ Reglement [*Administrative Ordinance or Rule of Procedure*] [*French*] (ILCA)
ReglCin........ Regal Cinemas, Inc. [*Associated Press*] (SAG)
Reg Lib........ Register Book [*A publication*] (DLA)
Reg Lib........ Registrar's Book, Chancery [*A publication*] (DLA)
REGLN........ Regulation (AAG)
REGLON........ Regulation (ROG)
REGLOS........ Reserve and Guard Logistic Operations-Streamline [*Army*] (AABC)
REGM........ Register Module
Reg Maj........ Books of Regiam Majestatem [*Scotland*] [*A publication*] (DLA)
REGN........ Regeneron Pharmaceuticals [*NASDAQ symbol*] (SPSG)
REGN........ Regional
REGN........ Registry Number
REG-NEG........ Regulatory Negotiation
RegnFn........ Regions Financial Corp. [*Associated Press*] (SAG)

reg nsy Regular Nursery [*Neonatology*] (DAVI)
Regnt Regent Bancshares Corp. [*Associated Press*] (SAG)
RegntBc Regent Banchares Corp. [*Associated Press*] (SAG)
ReGo Reinventing Government [*Nickname for National Performance Review*]
Reg Om Brev Registrum Omnium Brevium [*Register of Writs*] [*Latin A publication*] (DLA)
Reg Orig Registrum Originale [*Latin A publication*] (DLA)
Reg Pl Regula Placitandi [*Rule of Pleading*] [*Latin*] [*Legal term*] (BARN)
REGPOWREN Regulating Petty Officer WREN [*Women's Royal Naval Service*] [*British military*] (DMA)
RegProf Regius Professor [*The King's Professor*] [*British*]
REGR Recent Hail [*Meteorology*] (DA)
REGR Register (ROG)
REGR Registrar
REGR Registrar
REGR Regulator (AAG)
REGRA Regression Analysis [*Military*] (IAA)
REGS Regulations
Regs Conn State Agencies Regulations of Connecticut State Agencies (AAGC)
REGSTD Registered
REGSTR Registrar
REGSTRTN Registration
REGT Regent
REGT Regiment (AABC)
REGT Regulator
RegtAsst Regent Assisted Living, Inc. [*Associated Press*] (SAG)
REGTL Regimental
Reg TM Registered Trademark (BARN)
REGUL Regular (ROG)
REGULAT Regulation
Reg Umb Regio Umbilici [*Region of the Umbilicus*] [*Pharmacy*]
regurg Regurgitation [*Medicine*] (DAVI)
Reg US Pat Off Registered at the United States Patent Office (BARN)
Reg Writ Register of Writs [*A publication*] (DLA)
REGY Registry (ROG)
REH Random Evolutionary Hits
REH Rational Expectations Hypothesis [*Economics*]
REH Rehoboth Beach [*Delaware*] [*Airport symbol*] (AD)
REH Rehoboth Beach, DE [*Location identifier FAA*] (FAAL)
REH Renin Essential Hypertension [*Medicine*] (DMAA)
REHAB Rehabilitate [*or Rehabilitation*] (AFM)
REHAB Rehabilitation
Rehab Aust Rehabilitation in Australia [*A publication*]
Rehabcre Rehabilicare, Inc. [*Associated Press*] (SAG)
RehabG RehabCare Group, Inc. [*Associated Press*] (SAG)
RehabGp RehabCare Group, Inc. [*Associated Press*] (SAG)
REHABIL Rehabilitation
REHABIT Reitan Evaluation of Hemispheric Abilities and Brain Improvement Training [*Neuropsychology test*]
Reh Allowed Rehearing Allowed [*Used in Shepard's Citations*] [*Legal term*] (DLA)
REHB Rehabilicare, Inc. [*NASDAQ symbol*] (SAG)
REHC Random Evolutionary Hits per Codon
Reh Den Rehearing Denied [*Used in Shepard's Citations*] [*Legal term*] (DLA)
Reh Dis Rehearing Dismissed [*Used in Shepard's Citations*] [*Legal term*] (DLA)
Reh'g Rehearing [*Legal term*] (DLA)
REHIS Royal Environmental Health Institute of Scotland [*British*]
REHNRAP Recreational, Entertainment, and Health Naturally Radioactive Products (NRCH)
REHT Reheat (KSC)
REHVA Representatives of European Heating and Ventilating Associations
REI Range from Entry Interface (NASA)
REI Rat der Europaeischen Industrieverbaende [*Council of European Industrial Federations*]
REI Real Estate Investment Trust of America (MHDW)
REI Real Estate Issues [*American Society of Real Estate Counselors*] [*A publication*]
REI Recognition Equipment, Inc. (IAA)
REI Recreational Equipment Inc. [*Commercial firm*]
REI Regiment Etranger d'Infanterie [*Foreign Infantry Regiment*] [*French*]
REI Reidovoe [*Former USSR Seismograph station code, US Geological Survey*] (SEIS)
REI Religion and Ethics Institute (EA)
REI Request for Engineering Information (NG)
REI Request for Engineering Investigation [*Nuclear energy*] (NRCH)
REI Research-Engineering Interaction (IEEE)
REI Reusable External Insulation [*of space shuttle*] [*NASA*]
REI Runway-End Identification [*Aviation*] (NASA)
REI Rural Economics Institute (OICC)
REIB Report Established in Block [*Aviation*] (FAAC)
REIC Radiation Effects Information Center [*Battelle Memorial Institute*] [*Defunct*]
REIC Rare Earth Information Center (NITA)
REIC Renewable Energy Info Center (EA)
REIC Research Industries Corp. [*NASDAQ symbol*] (NQ)
Reid PL Dig Reid's Digest of Scotch Poor Law Cases [*A publication*] (DLA)
REIG Rare-Earth Iron Garnet (IAA)
REIL Real Estate Investing Letter [*Harcourt Brace Jovanovich, Inc.*] [*No longer available online*] [*Information service or system*] (CRD)
REIL Runway-End Identification Lights [*Aviation*]
Reilly Reilly's English Arbitration Cases [*A publication*] (DLA)
Reilly EA Reilly's European Arbitration. Lord Westbury's Decisions [*A publication*] (DLA)
REI(M) Regiment Etranger d'Infanterie (de Marche) [*Foreign Marching Infantry Regiment*] [*French*]
REIM Reimburse (AABC)
REIMB Reimburse (MSA)
REIMBJTR Reimbursement [*in Accordance with*] Joint Travel Regulations [*Military*] (DNAB)
REIN Real Estate Information Network [*Database*]
REIN Recovery Engineering [*NASDAQ symbol*] (TTSB)
REIN Recovery Engineering, Inc. [*NASDAQ symbol*] (SAG)
REIN Reinforce
Rein Reinstated [*Regulation or order reinstated*] [*Used in Shepard's Citations*] [*Legal term*] (DLA)
REINCH Reinsch Test [*For urine mercury and arsenic*] (DAVI)
REINET Real Estate Information Network [*National Association of Realtors*] [*Information service or system*] (IID)
REINF Refund Information File [*IRS*]
REINF Reinforce (AAG)
REINFD Reinforced (AAG)
REINFG Reinforcing (AAG)
REINFM Reinforcement (AAG)
REINIT Reinitialize (MCD)
REINS RADAR-Equipped Inertial Navigation System
REINS Requirements Electronic Input System [*NASA*] (KSC)
ReinsGp Reinsurance Group of America [*Associated Press*] (SAG)
REINSR Reinsurance
REINV REfernce Invoice (FAAC)
REIQ Refrigeration Installation Equipment (SAA)
REIS Readiness Information System [*Army*]
REIS Reconstitutable and Enduring Intelligence System
REIS Regional Economic Information System [*Department of Commerce*] [*Information service or system*] (IID)
REIS Regional Energy Information System [*Minnesota State Department of Energy and Economic Development*] [*St. Paul*] [*Information service or system*] (IID)
REIS Research and Engineering Information Services [*Exxon Research & Engineering Co.*] (IID)
REIS Reseau Europeen Integre d'Image et de Services [*European Integrated Network of Image and Services*] (EAIO)
REIT Real Estate Investment Trust [*Associated Press*] (SAG)
REIT Real Estate Investment Trust [*Pooled funds that invest in income-producing residential and commerical properties*]
REIT Reiteration [*Printing*] (ROG)
REITS Racial Equality in Training Schemes (AIE)
REIV Rocket Engine Injector Valve
REJ Imperial Airlines [*British*] [*FAA designator*] (FAAC)
REJ Redig, SD [*Location identifier FAA*] (FAAL)
REJ Reject (MSA)
rej Reject (IDOE)
rej Rejection (IDOE)
REJ Religious Education Journal of Australia [*A publication*] (APTA)
REJASE Reusing Junk as Something Else [*Conversion of junk into reusable items*]
Rejasing Reusing Junk as Something Else (BARN)
REJD Rejoined (WGA)
REJEN Remote Job Entry [*Computer science*] (MHDI)
REJIS Regional Justice Information Service [*St. Louis, MO*]
REJN Rejoin (AABC)
REJO Rod Easterling and Jim Osburn [*Automobile named for designers*]
REJU Reject Unit [*IRS*]
REK Reykjavik [*Iceland*] [*Airport symbol*] (OAG)
REKY Royal East Kent Yeomanry [*Military unit*] [*British*]
REL Radiation Evaluation Loop [*Nuclear energy*] (NRCH)
REL Radio Electrician [*Navy British*]
REL Radio Engineering Laboratories
REL Rapidly Extensible Language System [*Computer science*] (CSR)
REL Rare-Earth LASER
REL Rassemblement Europeen de la Liberte [*European Liberty Rally*] [*France Political party*] (PPE)
REL Rate of Energy Loss
REL Reactor Equipment Ltd. [*Nuclear energy*] (NRCH)
REL Recommended Exposure Limit
REL Regional Education Laboratory
REL Related
REL Relation
rel Relation (DD)
REL Relations
REL Relative
rel Relative (IDOE)
REL Relativity
Rel Relatore [*Reporter*] [*Italian*] (ILCA)
REL Relay (AAG)
REL Release (AAG)
REL Reliability
REL Reliance Group Hldgs [*NYSE symbol*] (TTSB)
REL Reliance Group Holdings, Inc. [*Formerly, Leasco Corp.*] [*NYSE symbol*] (SPSG)
REL Relic
REL Relie [*Bound*] [*Publishing*] [*French*]
REL Relief (AAG)
rel Relief (VRA)
REL Religion
REL Reliquary and Illustrated Archaeologist [*A publication*] (ROG)
Rel Reliquiae [*of Suetonius*] [*Classical studies*] (OCD)
REL Reliquiae [*Remains*] [*Latin*]

REL............ Relizane [*Algeria*] [*Seismograph station code, US Geological Survey Closed*] (SEIS)
REL............ Relocatable [*Computer science*]
REL............ Reluctance (DEN)
REL............ Rescue Equipment Locker (AAG)
REL............ Resting Expiratory Level [*Medicine*] (DMAA)
REL............ Restricted Energy Loss
REL............ Trelew [*Argentina*] [*Airport symbol*] (OAG)
RELA............ Real Estate Leaders of America [*Montgomery, AL*] (EA)
RELACDU....... Released from Active Duty [*Navy*] (DNAB)
RELACS....... RADAR Emission Location Attack Control System
Rel & Pub Order... Religion and the Public Order [*A publication*] (DLA)
RELAT.......... Related
RELATN....... Relation (ROG)
RELAY.......... Relayed Correlation Spectroscopy (DMAA)
RelBcp.......... Reliance Bancorp [*Associated Press*] (SAG)
RELBL.......... Reliability
RelbLfe.......... [*The*] Reliable Life Insurance Co. [*Associated Press*] (SAG)
RELBY.......... When Relieved By [*Army*]
RELC............ Regional Language Centre [*SEAMEO*] [*Singapore*] [*Research center*] (IRC)
RELC............ Reliability Committee [*NASA*]
RELCODE..... Relative Code (NITA)
RELCT.......... Relocate (FAAC)
RELCTD....... Relocated
RELCV.......... Regional Educational Laboratory for the Carolinas and Virginia
RELD............ Rare-Earth LASER Device
RELD............ Relieved (WGA)
RELDET........ When Relieved Detached [*Duty Indicated*]
Rel d Griech... Die Religion der Griechen [*A publication*] (OCD)
RELDIRDET... When Relieved and When Directed Detached [*Duty Indicated*]
RELE............ Ariely Advertising Ltd. [*NASDAQ symbol*] (SAG)
RELE............ Radio Electrician
RELE............ Release (ROG)
RELE............ Resistive Exercise of Lower Extremities [*Medicine*] (DMAA)
Rel Ed.......... Religious Education [*A publication*] (BRI)
RELEF.......... Ariely Advertising Ltd [*NASDAQ symbol*] (TTSB)
RELET.......... Refernce Letter (FAAC)
RelGrp.......... Reliance Group Holdings, Inc. [*Formerly, Leasco Corp.*] [*Associated Press*] (SAG)
REL HUM..... Relative Humidity (WDAA)
RELI............ Real Estate Law Institute (EA)
RELI............ Reliance Bancshares [*NASDAQ symbol*] (TTSB)
RELI............ Reliance Bancshares, Inc. [*NASDAQ symbol*] (SAG)
RELI............ Religion Index [*American Theological Library Association*] [*Information service or system*]
RELIA.......... Regional European Long Lines Agency (IAA)
Reliab.......... Reliability, Inc. [*Associated Press*] (SAG)
ReliaS.......... ReliaStar Financial Co. [*Associated Press*] (SAG)
ReliaStar....... ReliaStar Financial Co. [*Associated Press*] (SAG)
ReliBsh........ Reliance Bancshares, Inc. [*Associated Press*] (SAG)
relig............ Religion (VRA)
RELIG.......... Religion [*or Religious*]
RELIP.......... Radially Extended Linear Impeller Propulsion [*Submarine technology*]
RELIPOSIS... Research Liaison Panel on Scientific Information Services (NITA)
reliq............ Reliquary (VRA)
RELIQ.......... Reliquiae [*Remains*] [*Latin*]
RELIQ.......... Reliquum [*The Remainder*] [*Pharmacy*]
Reliv............ Reliv International, Inc. [*Associated Press*] (SAG)
RELKIN........ Relativistic Kinematics (PDAA)
RELL............ Reinforced Education Learning Laboratory (EA)
RELL............ Richardson Electr [*NASDAQ symbol*] (TTSB)
RELL............ Richardson Electronics Ltd. [*NASDAQ symbol*] (NQ)
RELLA.......... Regional European Long-Lines Agency [*Later, RALLA*] (NATG)
RELLI.......... Reliable
RELMA.......... Robert E. Lee Memorial Association (EA)
RELMAP....... Regional Lagrangian Model of Air Pollution (USDC)
RELMAP....... Regional Lagrangian Model of Air Pollution [*Marine science*] (OSRA)
RELMAT....... Relative Matrix (MCD)
RELOC.......... Relocate (AAG)
RELP............ Real Estate Limited Partnership
RELPAS....... Restricted Express Lists/Physiological Activity Section [*National Science Foundation*]
REL PRON... Relative Pronoun [*Grammar*] (WDAA)
RELQ............ Release-Quiesce [*Computer science*]
REL-R.......... Reliability Report (AAG)
RELR............ Revised and Expurgated Law Reports [*India*] [*A publication*] (DLA)
RELS............ Real Estate Listing Service [*Database*] [*MDR Telecom*] [*Information service or system*] (CRD)
RELS............ Redeye Launch Simulator (MCD)
RELS............ Relations
Rel St.......... Religious Studies [*A publication*] (BRI)
RelStlAl........ Reliance Steel & Aluminum Co. [*Associated Press*] (SAG)
Rel St Rev... Religious Studies Review [*A publication*] (BRI)
RELTD.......... Related
RELV............ Reliv International, Inc. [*NASDAQ symbol*] (SAG)
RELY............ Relational Technology, Inc. (MHDW)
RELY............ Reliance Bancorp [*NASDAQ symbol*] (SAG)
REM............ Rack Entry Module (PDAA)
REM............ Radiation Equivalent Man (IAA)
REM............ Radioactivity Environmental Monitoring [*Information service or system*] (IID)
REM............ Radio Electrical Mechanic [*British military*] (DMA)
REM............ Random Entry Memory (ADA)
REM............ Range Evaluation Missile
REM............ Rapid Eye Movement
REM............ Rare Earth Metal [*Inorganic chemistry*]
REM............ Raumbildentfernungsmesser [*Stereoscopic range-finder*] [*German military - World War II*]
REM............ Reaction Engine Module [*NASA*] (KSC)
REM............ Recognition Memory [*Semionics Associates*] [*Computer science*]
REM............ Recovery Exercise Module (MCD)
REM............ Reentry Module
REM............ Reflection Electron Microscopy
REM............ Registered Environmental Manager
REM............ Registered Equipment Management [*Air Force*] (AFM)
REM............ Release-Engage [*or Engagement*] Mechanism (NASA)
REM............ Release Engine Mechanism (NASA)
REM............ Release Engine Module (MCD)
REM............ Release Escape Mechanism (MCD)
REM............ Reliability Engineering Model (KSC)
REM............ Remainder (MSA)
REM............ Remark
Rem............ Remigius [*Flourished, 841-908*] [*Authority cited in pre-1607 legal work*] (DSA)
Rem............ Remington [*Record label*] [*USA, Europe, etc.*]
REM............ Remit (AABC)
Rem............ Remittance (DLA)
REM............ Remote [*Alaska*] [*Seismograph station code, US Geological Survey*] (SEIS)
REM............ Remote Event Module [*Computer science*]
REM............ Remove [*or Removal*] (AAG)
REM............ Reserves Embarked [*Navy*] (NVT)
REM............ Reticular Erythematous Mucinosis [*Medicine*] (DMAA)
REM............ Riecam, SA [*Honduras*] [*FAA designator*] (FAAC)
REM............ Rocket Engine Module (MCD)
REM............ Roentgen-Equivalent-Mammal [*Irradiation unit*]
REM............ Roentgen-Equivalent-Man [*Later, Sv*] [*Irradiation unit*]
rem............ Roentgen Equivalent Man (IDOE)
rem............ Roentgen Equivalent Man
REMA.......... Refrigeration Equipment Manufacturers Association [*Later, ARI*] (MCD)
REMA.......... Repetitive Excess Mixed Anhydride [*Medicine*] (DMAA)
REMA.......... Rotating Electrical Machines Association [*British*] (DBA)
REMAB........ Radiation Equivalent Manikin Absorption
REMAB........ Remote Marshalling Base (MCD)
REMAC........ Remote Data Acquistion Subsystem [*Computer science*] (MHDB)
REMAD........ Remote Magnetic Anomaly Detection
Rem Am...... Remedia Amoris [*of Ovid*] [*Classical studies*] (OCD)
REMAP........ Record Extraction, Manipulation, and Print
REMAP........ Regional Environment Management Allocation Process (PDAA)
REMAP........ Rehabilitation Engineering Movement Advisory Panel (ACII)
REMARC...... Retrospective Machine Readable Catalog [*Carrollton Press, Inc.*] [*Arlington, VA Bibliographic database Online version of the US Library of Congress Shelflist*]
REMAS........ Radiation Effects Machine Analysis System (AAG)
REMAS........ Remote Energy Monitor Alarm System [*Computer science*] (MHDI)
REMAT........ Research Centre for Management of New Technology [*Wilfrid Laurier University*] [*Canada Research center*] (RCD)
REMBASS.... Remotely Monitored Battlefield Area Sensor System (MCD)
REMBJTR.... Reimbursement in Accordance with Joint Travel Regulations
REMC.......... Radio and Electronics Measurements Committee [*London, England*] (DEN)
REMC.......... REMEC Inc. [*NASDAQ symbol*] (TTSB)
REMC.......... Resin-Encapsulated Mica Capacitor
REMCA........ Reliability, Maintainability, Cost Analysis (MCD)
REMCAL...... Radiation Equivalent Manikin Calibration
REMCALC.... Relative Motion Collision Avoidance Calculator (PDAA)
REMCE........ Remittance (ROG)
REMCO........ Committee on Reference Materials [*ISO*] (DS)
REMCO........ Rear Echelon Maintenance Combined Operation [*Military*]
Rem Cr Tr... Remarkable Criminal Trials [*A publication*] (DLA)
REMD.......... Rapid Eye Movement Deprivation
Rem'd.......... Remanded [*Legal term*] (DLA)
REMDOS...... Remote Disc Operating System (NITA)
Remdy.......... Remedy Corp. [*Associated Press*] (SAG)
REME.......... Royal Electrical and Mechanical Engineers [*Military British*]
REMED........ Remedium [*Remedy*] [*Pharmacy*] (ROG)
Remedy........ Remedy Corp. [*Associated Press*] (SAG)
REMES........ Reference Message (FAAC)
REMG.......... Radioelectromyograph
Rem'g.......... Remanding [*Legal term*] (DLA)
REMI.......... Reliability Engineering and Management Institute (EA)
REMI.......... Resource Bancshares Mortgage Group [*NASDAQ symbol*] (SAG)
REMI.......... Resource Bancshares Mtg Gp [*NASDAQ symbol*] (TTSB)
REMIC........ Real Estate Mortgage Investment Conduit [*Federal National Mortgage Association*]
REMICS...... Real-Time Manufacturing Information Control System [*Computer science*] (MHDI)
REMIDS...... Remote Minefield Identification and Deployment [*or Display*] System (MCD)
Remigi.......... Remigius de Gonni [*Deceased, 1554*] [*Authority cited in pre-1607 legal work*] (DSA)
REMILOC.... Required Inservice Manyears in Lieu of Controls [*Military*]
REMIS.......... Real Estate Management Information System (BUR)
REMIS.......... Reliability and Maintainability Information System [*Air Force*] (GFGA)
REMIT.......... Remittance (DSUE)
REMIT.......... Research Effort Management Information Tabulation
Remitt.......... Remittance (DLA)
REML.......... Radiation Effects Mobile Laboratory

REML Removal (ROG)
REML Restricted Maximum Likelihood [*Statistics*]
REML Risley Engineering and Materials Laboratory (PDAA)
REM-M Rapid Eye Movement-Movement Period
Remma Reese, "Musik in the Middle Ages" [*A publication*]
REMMAN Remainderman [*Legal shorthand*] (LWAP)
REMMPS Reserve Manpower Management and Pay System [*Marine Corps*]
REMN Radio Electrical Mechanician [*British military*] (DMA)
REMN Remain (ROG)
REMOBE Readiness for Mobilization Evaluation (MCD)
REMOD Remodeling
REMON Real-Time Event Monitor [*Computer science*] (IAA)
REMOS Real-Time Event Monitor [*Computer science*] (IEEE)
REMOS Resources Management Online System (HGAA)
REMOSS Reliability Monitoring of Subcontractors/Suppliers (MCD)
REMOTE Reflective Mossbauer Technique (PDAA)
REMP Radiological Environmental Monitoring Program [*Nuclear energy*] (NRCH)
REMP Rapid Eye Movement Period (PDAA)
REMP Research and Evaluation Methods Program [*University of Massachusetts*] [*Research center*] (RCD)
REMP Research, Engineering, Mathematics, and Physics Division [*National Securi ty Agency*] [*Obsolete*]
REMP Research Group for European Migration Problems
REMP Roentgen-Equivalent-Man Period [*Irradiation Unit*] (MAE)
REMPAC Reflectivity Measurements Pacific
REMPAN Radiation Emergency Medical Preparedness and Assistance Network [*World health organization*]
REMPI Resonance Enhanced Multiple Photon Ionisation [*Physics*]
REMPI Resonant Enhanced Multiphoton Ionization [*Spectroscopy*]
REMPI Resonant Multiphoton Ionization [*Physics*]
REM-Q Rapid Eye Movement - Quiescent Period
REMR Remainder
REMR Repair, Evaluation, Maintenance, Rehabilitation
REM-RAND Remington Rand Corp. [*Later, a division of Sperry-Rand*]
REMRO Remote RADAR Operator (MCD)
REMS Rapid Excavation and Maintenance System [*for gas piping repair*]
REMS Rapid Eye Movement Sleep [*Neurology*] (DAVI)
REMS Rapid Eye Movement State
REMS Reduced Exposure Mining System
REMS Reentry Measurement System
REMS Refinery Evaluation Modeling System [*Department of Energy*] (GFGA)
REMS Registered Equipment Management System [*Air Force*]
REMS Remotely Employed Sensor [*Military*] (GFGA)
REMS Robust Expert Maintenance System [*US Army Tank-Automotive Command*] (RDA)
REMSA Railway Electrical and Mechanical Supply Association (IAA)
REMSA Railway Engineering Maintenance Suppliers Association (EA)
REMSTA Remote Electronic Microfilm Storage Transmission and Retrieval
REMSTAR Remote Electronic Microfilm in Storage Transmission and Retrieval [*Computer science*] (EECA)
REMSTAR Remote Electronic Microfilm Storage Transmission and Retrieval (NITA)
REMT Radiological Emergency Medical Team [*Military*] (AABC)
REMT Relief Electronic Maintenance Technician
REMT Remote
REMTDS Rocket Engine and Motor Type Designation System
RemTp Remedy Temp, Inc. [*Associated Press*] (SAG)
Rem Tr Cummins and Dunphy's Remarkable Trials [*A publication*] (DLA)
Rem Tr No Ch Benson's Remarkable Trials and Notorious Characters [*A publication*] (DLA)
REMUS Routine for Executive Multi-Unit Simulation (PDAA)
REMX RemedyTemp, Inc. [*NASDAQ symbol*] (SAG)
Remy Remy's Reports [*145-162 Indiana*] [*15-33 Indiana Appellate*] [*A publication*] (DLA)
REN Aero-Rent SA de CV [*Mexico ICAO designator*] (FAAC)
REN Religion and Ethics Network (EA)
REN Remote Enable (IEEE)
REN Renaissance
Ren Renaissance [*Record label*]
ren Renal [*Medicine*] (MAE)
REN Rename File [*Computer science*]
REN Rencon Mining Co. [*Vancouver Stock Exchange symbol*]
REN Renewable
REN Renewal
REN Renin [*An enzyme*]
Ren Renner's Gold Coast Colony Reports [*A publication*] (DLA)
REN Reno [*Nevada*] [*Seismograph station code, US Geological Survey Closed*] (SEIS)
ren Renovetur [*Renew*] [*Pharmacy*] [*Latin*] (MAE)
REN Ringer Equivalence Number [*Telephones*]
REN Rollins Environmental Services, Inc. [*NYSE symbol*] (SPSG)
REN Rollins Environ Sv [*NYSE symbol*] (TTSB)
RenaCap Renaissance Capital Growth & Income Fund III [*Associated Press*] (SAG)
Renais Renaissance (VRA)
RenaissRe RenaissanceRe Holdings Ltd. [*Associated Press*] (SAG)
RenalT Renal Treatment Centers, Inc. [*Associated Press*] (SAG)
RenalTrt Renal Treatment Centers, Inc. [*Associated Press*] (SAG)
RENAMO Resistencia Nacional Mocambicana [*Mozambique*]
Ren & Ref Renaissance and Reformation [*A publication*] (BRI)
RENAT Revolutsiya, Nauka, Trud [*Revolution, Science, Labor*] [*Given name popular in Russia after the Bolshevik Revolution*]
RenCm Renaissance Communications Corp. [*Associated Press*] (SAG)
REND Rendered (ADA)
RENDD Rendered (ROG)
RendeR Reversible Non-Linear Dimension Reduction
RENDOCK Rendezvous and Docking [*Aerospace*] (MCD)
RENDZ Rendezvous (KSC)
RenE Renaissance Entertainment Corp. [*Associated Press*] (SAG)
RENE Rocket Engine/Nozzle Ejector
Reneg Renegotiation (AAGC)
RenEnt Renaissance Entertainment Corp. [*Associated Press*] (SAG)
RENEW Resourcing Enabling, Network for Evangelical Women
RENFE Red Nacional de los Ferrocariles Espanoles [*Spanish National Railways*] (EY)
RENG Radio Electronic News Gathering (NTCM)
RENG Research Engineers, Inc. [*NASDAQ symbol*] (SAG)
R ENG Royal Engineers [*Military British*] (ROG)
RenHtl Renaissance Hotel Group NV [*Associated Press*] (SAG)
RENL Runway End Light [*Aviation*] (FAAC)
RENM Ready for Next Message (IAA)
RENM Request for Next Message
RENMR Reconnaissance Medium Range [*Army*]
RENN Renaissance Cap Growth & Inc Fd [*NASDAQ symbol*] (TTSB)
RENN Renaissance Capital Growth & Income Fund III [*NASDAQ symbol*] (SAG)
Renn Renner's Reports, Notes of Cases, Gold Coast Colony and Colony of Nigeria [*1861-1914*] [*A publication*] (DLA)
RENO Reno Air [*NASDAQ symbol*] (TTSB)
RENO Reno Air, Inc. [*NASDAQ symbol*] (SAG)
RenoAir Reno Air, Inc. [*Associated Press*] (SAG)
RENOT Regional Notice [*FAA*]
RENOT Regional Office Notice [*Aviation*] (FAAC)
RENOVAND Renovandus [*To Be Renewed*] [*Pharmacy*] (ROG)
RENPE Rare and Endangered Native Plant Exchange (EA)
Ren Q Renaissance Quarterly [*A publication*] (BRI)
RENRAD Rendezvous RADAR [*NASA*] (NASA)
RenRe RenaissanceRe Holdings Ltd. [*Associated Press*] (SAG)
RENS Radiation Effects on Network Systems
RENS Reconnaissance, Electronic Warfare, and Naval Intelligence System
RENS Renaissance Solutions [*NASDAQ symbol*] (TTSB)
RENS Renaissance Solutions, Inc. [*NASDAQ symbol*] (SAG)
REN SEM Renovetur Semel [*Renew Once*] [*Pharmacy*]
RenSolu RenaissanceRe Solutions, Inc. [*Associated Press*] (SAG)
RENSONIP Reconnaissance Electronic Warfare, Special Operations, and Naval Intelligence Processing (MCD)
RENT Reentry Nose Tip [*Air Force*]
RENT Rental
RENT Rentrak Corp. [*NASDAQ symbol*] (NQ)
Rentch Rentech, Inc. [*Associated Press*] (SAG)
Renters Renters Choice, Inc. [*Associated Press*] (SAG)
RentlSrv Rental Service Corp. [*Associated Press*] (SAG)
RENU Reconstruction Education for National Understanding [*An association*] (EA)
RENUNCN Renunciation (ROG)
RENV Renovate (AABC)
REO Ransom Eli Olds [*Acronym used as name of automobile manufactured by Ransom E. Olds Co.*]
REO Rare-Earth Oxide
REO Rea Gold [*AMEX symbol*] (TTSB)
REO Rea Gold Corp. [*Toronto Stock Exchange symbol Vancouver Stock Exchange symbol*]
REO Real Estate Owned [*Banking*]
REO Receptive-Expressive Observation [*Sensorimotor skills test*]
REO Regenerated Electrical Output
REO Regional Environmental Offices [*Air Force*] (DOMA)
REO Regional Executive Officer [*British*]
REO Reinforcements (DSUE)
REO Respiratory and Enteric Orphan [*Virus*] (MAE)
REO Responsible Engineering Office [*Military*] (AFIT)
REO Rio Airways, Inc. [*ICAO designator*] (FAAC)
REO Rome, OR [*Location identifier FAA*] (FAAL)
REOC Report When Established on Course [*Aviation*] (FAAC)
REOC Royal Enfield Owners Club (EA)
REON Rocket Engine Operations - Nuclear (IEEE)
REOP Reopening [*Investment term*]
ReOpt Remedial Option [*Computer science*]
REOPT Reorder Point [*Army*]
REORG Reorganize (EY)
REOS Racal Electronic Optical System [*Software package*] [*Racal Imaging Systems*]
REOS Rare-Earth Oxysulfide
REOS Reflective Electron Optical System
REOT Right-End-of-Tape
REOU Radio and Electronic Officers' Union [*British*] (DCTA)
Rep Coke's English King's Bench Reports [*1572-1616*] [*A publication*] (DLA)
Rep De Republica [*of Cicero*] [*Classical studies*] (OCD)
REP Die Republikaner [*Republican Party*] [*Germany Political party*] (PPW)
REP General system Design [*Computer science*]
Rep Knapp's Privy Council Reports [*England*] [*A publication*] (DLA)
REP RADAR Effects Processor (MCD)
REP RADAR Evaluation Pod [*Spacecraft*]
REP Radical Education Project [*Students for a Democratic Society*]
REP Radioelektronnoye Podavleniye [*Radio Electronic Suppression*] [*Soviet counterintelligence*] (LAIN)
REP Radiological Emergency Plan [*Nuclear energy*] (NRCH)
REP Railway Equipment and Publication Co., The, New York NY [*STAC*]

REP............. Range Error Probable [*Military*]
REP............. Range Estimation Program (MCD)
REP............. Rapid Electrophoresis
REP............. Reaction Energy Profile
REP............. Reasonable Efforts Program [*Environmental Protection Agency*] (EPA)
REP............. Recovery and Evacuation Program [*Marine Corps*]
REP............. Reentrant Processor [*Telecommunications*]
REP............. Reentry Physics Program
REP............. Regional Employment Premium [*British*]
REP............. Registered Environmental Professional
REP............. Rehabilitation Engineering Program [*Research center*] (RCD)
REP............. Relativistic Electron Precipitation [*Meteorology*]
REP............. Reliability Evaluation Program (IAA)
REP............. Rendezvous Evaluation Pad [*NASA*] (KSC)
REP............. Rendezvous Exercise Pod (SAA)
REP............. Repair (AAG)
REP............. Repeal (ROG)
REP............. Repeat (AAG)
rep............. Repeat (WDMC)
Rep............. Repertoire (DLA)
REP............. Repertory (ADA)
rep............. Repertory (WDMC)
rep............. Repertory (ODBW)
REP............. Repertory Theater (DSUE)
rep............. Repertory Theatre (ODBW)
REP............. Repetatur [*Let It Be Repeated*] [*Pharmacy*]
REP............. Repetition (DSUE)
rep............. Repetition (WDMC)
REP............. Repetitive Extragenic Palindrome [*or Palindromic*] [*Genetics*]
REP............. Replace (NVT)
REP............. Replication [*Telecommunications*] (TEL)
REP............. Report (AAG)
rep............. Report (WDMC)
rep............. Reporter (WDMC)
REP............. Reporter
REP............. Report Evaluation Program (SAA)
REP............. Reporting Point [*Aviation*]
REP............. Representative (AAG)
rep............. Representative (WDMC)
rep............. Representative (ODBW)
REP............. Representative
Rep............. Representing (DLA)
REP............. Reprimand (DSUE)
Rep............. Reprint (DLA)
rep............. Reprint (WDMC)
REP............. Reproducing Programs [*Computer science*]
REP............. Reproductive Endocrinology Program [*University of Michigan*] [*Research center*] (RCD)
REP............. Repsol SA ADS [*NYSE symbol*] (SPSG)
REP............. Repsol S.A. ADS [*NYSE symbol*] (TTSB)
REP............. Republic (EY)
REP............. Republican
REP............. Repulsion
REP............. Reputation (DSUE)
REP............. Request for Proposal (MUGU)
REP............. Research and Economic Programs [*Department of the Treasury*] (GRD)
REP............. Research Expenditure Proposal
REP............. Reserve Enlisted Program [*Military*]
REP............. Resonance Escape Probability [*Nuclear energy*] (NRCH)
REP............. Retrograde Pyelogram [*Medicine*]
REP............. Rework Excellence Program [*Navy*] (DNAB)
REP............. Richardson Emergency Psychodiagnostic Summary [*Psychology*]
REP............. Road Environment Pollutant [*Automotive corrosion testing*]
REP............. Rocket Engine Processor
REP............. Roentgen-Equivalent-Physical [*Irradiation unit*]
rep............. Roentgen Equivalent Physical (DOG)
REP............. Siem Reap [*Cambodia*] [*Airport symbol*] (AD)
REP............. Unnecessary Repetition [*Used in correcting manuscripts, etc.*]
Rep............. Wallace's "The Reporters" [*A publication*] (DLA)
REP 63........ Reserve Enlistment Program 1963 (MCD)
REPA........... Registered Environmental Property Assessor
REPA........... Rural Environment Planning Association [*Australia*]
REPAIR........ Reperfusion in Acute Infarction, Rotterdam [*Cardiology study*]
REPAIRS...... Readiness Evaluation Program for Avionics Intermediate Repair Simulation (MCD)
Rep & Ops Atty Gen Ind... Indiana Attorney General Reports [*A publication*] (DLA)
Repap.......... Repap Enterprises Corp., Inc. [*Associated Press*] (SAG)
REPAS......... Research, Evaluation, and Planning Assistance Staff [*AID*]
Rep Ass Y... Clayton's English Reports, York Assizes [*A publication*] (DLA)
REPAT......... Repatriate (AABC)
REPB........... Republic (MSA)
REPB........... Republic
REPB........... Republic Bancshares [*NASDAQ symbol*] (TTSB)
REPB........... Republic Bancshares, Inc. [*NASDAQ symbol*] (SAG)
REPB........... Republic Bank [*NASDAQ symbol*] (NQ)
RepBcp........ Republic Bancorp, Inc. [*Associated Press*] (SAG)
REPBX......... Reference Private Branch Exchange Message (SAA)
REPC........... Regional Economic Planning Council [*British*]
REPC........... Representation Commissioner [*Canada*]
REPC........... Research and Educational Planning Center [*University of Nevada - Reno*] [*Research center*] (RCD)
REPC........... Research and Engineering Policy Council [*DoD*]
Rep Cas Eq... Gilbert's English Chancery Reports [*1705-27*] [*A publication*] (DLA)
Rep Cas Inc Tax... Reports of Cases Relating to Income Tax [*1875*] [*A publication*] (DLA)
Rep Cas Madr... Reports of Cases, Diwani Adalat, Madras [*A publication*] (DLA)
Rep Cas Pr... Cooke's Practice Cases [*1706-47*] [*England*] [*A publication*] (DLA)
REPCAT....... Report Corrective Action Taken [*Military*]
Rep Ch........ Reports in Chancery [*1615-1710*] [*England*] [*A publication*] (DLA)
Rep Ch Pr.... Reports on Chancery Practice [*England*] [*A publication*] (DLA)
REPCO......... Replacement Parts Co.
Rep Com Cas... Commercial Cases, Small Cause Court [*1851-60*] [*Bengal, India*] [*A publication*] (DLA)
Rep Com Cas... Report of Commercial Cases [*1895-1941*] [*A publication*] (DLA)
REPCOMDESPAC... Representative of Commander Destroyers, Pacific Fleet
REPCON........ Rain Repellant and Surface Conditioner (PDAA)
Rep Const Ct... South Carolina Constitutional Court Reports [*A publication*] (DLA)
Rep Cr L Com... Reports of Criminal Law Commissioners [*England*] [*A publication*] (DLA)
REPCY......... Repair Cycle
Rep de Jur Com... Repertoire de Jurisprudence Commerciale [*Paris*] [*A publication*] (DLA)
Rep de Not... Repertoire de Notariae [*Paris*] [*A publication*] (DLA)
REPDN......... Reproduction (AFM)
REPDU......... Report for Duty [*Military*]
REPEA......... Research and Engineers Professional Employees Association
REPEET........ Reusabler Engines, Partially Enternal Expendable Tankage (PDAA)
REPEM- CEAAL... Red de Educacion Popular Entre Mujeres Afiliada al Consejo de Educacion de A dultos de America Latino [*Women's Network of the Council for Adult Education in Latin American*] [*Ecuador*] (EAIO)
RepEnv........ Republic Environmental Systems, Inc. [*Associated Press*] (SAG)
Rep Eq......... Gilbert's Reports in Equity [*England*] [*A publication*] (DLA)
REPERF....... Reperforator [*Telecommunications*] (TEL)
REPERMSG... Report in Person or by Message to Command or Person Indicated
RepEStl........ Republic Engineered Steels, Inc. [*Associated Press*] (SAG)
REPET.......... Repetatur [*Let It Be Repeated*] [*Pharmacy*]
REPET.......... Repetition (IAA)
REPFORMAINT... Representative of Maintenance Force
RepGrp........ Republic Group [*Associated Press*] (SAG)
Rep Hawaii Att'y Gen... Hawaii Attorney General Report [*A publication*] (DLA)
REPHO......... Reference Telephone Conversation (NOAA)
REPI............ Ross Educational Philosophical Inventory (EDAC)
REPIDISCA... Red Panamericana de Informacion y Documentacion en Ingenieria Sanitaria y Ciencias del Ambiente [*Pan American Network for Information and Documentation in Sanitary Engineering and Environmental Sciences*] [*WHO*] [*United Nations*] (DUND)
REPIN......... Reply If Negative [*Military*]
Rep in CA.... Court of Appeal Reports [*New Zealand*] [*A publication*] (DLA)
Rep in Can.... Reports in Chancery [*21 English Reprint*] [*A publication*] (DLA)
Rep in Ch.... Reports in Chancery [*21 English Reprint*] [*A publication*] (DLA)
Rep in Cha... Bittleston's Chamber Cases [*1883-84*] [*A publication*] (DLA)
Rep in Ch (Eng)... Reports in Chancery [*21 English Reprint*] [*A publication*] (DLA)
Rep in C of A... Reports in Courts of Appeal [*New Zealand*] [*A publication*] (DLA)
RepInd......... Republic Industries, Inc. [*Associated Press*] (SAG)
REPISIC....... Report Immediate Superior in Command [*Navy*]
Rep Jur........ Repertorium Juridicum [*Latin A publication*] (DLA)
REPL........... Replace (AAG)
repl............ Replacement (DLA)
REPL........... Replacement (ECII)
repl............ Replica (VRA)
REPLAB....... Responsive Environment Programmed Laboratory (IEEE)
RepIgn........ Repligen Corp. [*Associated Press*] (SAG)
REPLN......... Replenish (AABC)
REPLTR....... Report by Letter (NVT)
REPM.......... Rare Earth Permanent Magnet
REPM.......... Repairman (NATG)
REPM.......... Representatives of Electronic Products Manufacturers [*Later, ERA*]
RePMA......... Release Paper Manufacturers Association [*British*] (DBA)
Rep Mass Att'y Gen... Report of the Attorney General of the State of Massachusetts [*A publication*] (DLA)
Rep MC........ Reports of Municipal Corporations [*A publication*] (DLA)
REPMC........ Representative to the Military Committee [*NATO*]
REPMES...... Reply by Message (FAAC)
REPMIS....... Reserve Personnel Management Information System [*Military*]
REPML........ Reply by Mail (FAAC)
REPMSG...... Report by Message (DNAB)
REPNAVRESCEN... Report to Naval Reserve Center (DNAB)
Rep NC Att'y Gen... North Carolina Attorney General Reports [*A publication*] (DLA)
Rep Neb Att'y Gen... Report of the Attorney General of the State of Nebraska [*A publication*] (DLA)
RepNY......... Republic New York Corp. [*Associated Press*] (SAG)
REPO.......... Reporting Officer [*Navy*]
REPO.......... Repossess
REPO.......... Repurchase Agreement [*Also, RP*] [*Investment term*]
Repo........... Repurchase Agreement [*Finance*] (DFIT)
repol.......... Repolarization [*Cardiology*] (DAVI)
REP-OP...... Repetitive Operation [*Computer science*] (MDG)
Reports....... Coke's English King's Bench Reports [*1572-1616*] [*A publication*] (DLA)
REPOS........ Dealers Repurchase Agreement (TDOB)
REPPAC....... Repetitively Pulsed Plasma Accelerator
Rep Pat Cas... Reports of Patent, Design, and Trade Mark Cases [*England*] [*A publication*] (DLA)
Rep Pat Des & Tr Cas... Reports of Patent, Design, and Trade Mark Cases [*A publication*] (DLA)
Rep QA........ Reports Tempore Queen Anne [*11 Modern*] [*A publication*] (DLA)
REPR.......... Real Estate Planning Report [*Military*] (AABC)

REPR .... Repair (ROG)
REPR .... Representative
REPR .... Repressurization (MCD)
REPR .... Reprinted
reprd .... Reproduction (VRA)
repres .... Representation (VRA)
Reprint .... English Reports, Full Reprint [*A publication*] (DLA)
REPRO .... Reproduce (KSC)
repro .... Reproduction (ODBW)
REPROC .... Reprocess (MCD)
REPROD ...... Receiver Protective Device (DEN)
REPROD ...... Reproduction
REPROM ...... Reprogrammable Programmable Read-Only Memory [*Computer science*] (TEL)
REPROM ...... Reprogrammable Read-Only Memory (NITA)
REPRON ...... Representation (ROG)
REPROTOX... Reproductive Toxicology Center [*Database*] [*Washington, DC*]
REPRO TYP... Reproduction Typing (DGA)
Repr Stat NZ... Reprint of the Statutes of New Zealand [*A publication*] (DLA)
REPS .... Regional Economic Projections Series [*NPA Data Services, Inc.*] [*Information service or system*] (CRD)
REPS .... Regional Emissions Projection System [*Environmental Protection Agency*]
REPS .... Repetitive Electromagnetic Pulse Simulator [*Army*] (RDA)
REPS .... Representative
REPS .... Republic Engineered Steels [*NASDAQ symbol*] (TTSB)
REPS .... Republic Engineered Steels, Inc. [*NASDAQ symbol*] (SAG)
REPS .... Royal Engineers Postal Section [*British military*] (DMA)
RepSc .... Republic Security Financial [*Associated Press*] (SAG)
RepSec .... Republic Security Financial [*Associated Press*] (SAG)
REPSHIPS...... Reports of Shipments [*Military*]
REPSNO........ Report through Senior Naval Officer
Repsol .... Repsol SA [*Associated Press*] (SAG)
REPT............ Receipt
REPT............ Repeat (ADA)
REPT............ Repetatur [*Let It Be Repeated*] [*Pharmacy*]
REPT............ Report
REPT............ Report
REPT............ Represent (ROG)
rept............ Reprint (BJA)
REPT............ Reptron Electronics [*NASDAQ symbol*] (TTSB)
REPT............ Reptron Electronics, Inc. [*NASDAQ symbol*] (SAG)
Rep T F .... Reports, Court of Chancery Tempore Finch [*1673-81*] [*A publication*] (DLA)
Rep T Finch... Reports, Court of Chancery Tempore Finch [*1673-81*] [*A publication*] (DLA)
Rep T Finch (Eng)... Reports, Court of Chancery Tempore Finch [*1673-81*] [*England*] [*A publication*] (DLA)
Rep T Hard... Lee's English King's Bench Reports Tempore Hardwicke [*1733-38*] [*A publication*] (DLA)
Rep T Hardw... Lee's English King's Bench Reports Tempore Hardwicke [*1733-38*] [*A publication*] (DLA)
Rep T Holt... Reports Tempore Holt, English Cases of Settlement [*A publication*] (DLA)
Rept Mtg AAAS... Report. Meeting of the Australasian Association for the Advancement of Science [*A publication*]
Rept Mtg ANZAAS... Report. Meeting of the Australian and New Zealand Association for the Advancement of Science [*A publication*]
REPTO .... Rear Engine Power-Take-Off [*Automotive engineering*]
REPTO .... Reparto
Rep T O Br... Carter's English Common Pleas Reports Tempore Orlando Bridgman [*A publication*] (DLA)
REPTOF .... Reporting Officer (NATG)
Rep T QA...... Reports Tempore Queen Anne [*11 Modern*] [*A publication*] (DLA)
Reptr .... [*The*] Reporter [*Boston, Los Angeles, New York, Washington*] [*A publication*] (DLA)
REPTR .... Reporter
REPTRANS... Report for Transportation
Rept Res ...... Reporting Research [*Queensland, Department of Education, Research Branch*] [*A publication*]
Reptrn .... Reptron Electronics, Inc. [*Associated Press*] (SAG)
Rep T Talb... Reports Tempore Talbot, English Chancery [*A publication*] (DLA)
Rept T Finch... Cases Tempore Finch, English Chancery [*1673-81*] [*23 English Reprint*] [*A publication*] (DLA)
Rept T Holt... Cases Tempore Holt, English King's Bench [*A publication*] (DLA)
Rep T Wood... Manitoba Reports Tempore Wood [*Canada A publication*] (DLA)
repu .... Repousse (VRA)
REPUB .... Republican
REPUB .... Republican
RepubBk ...... Republic Bank [*Associated Press*] (SAG)
RepubBsh .... Republic Bancshares, Inc. [*Associated Press*] (SAG)
REPUD .... Repudiate
repunit .... Repeating Unit [*Mathematics*] (BARN)
REPVE .... Representative (ROG)
RepWst .... Republic Waste Industries, Inc. [*Associated Press*] (SAG)
Rep York Ass... Clayton's English Reports, York Assizes [*A publication*] (DLA)
REQ .... Request (AAG)
REQ .... Require (AAG)
REQ .... Requisition
REQAFA .... Request Advise as to Further Action [*Army*] (AABC)
REQANA .... Requirements Analysis (MCD)
REQANS .... Request Answer By [*Date*] [*Military*]
REQAURQN... Request Authority to Requisition [*Army*] (AFIT)
REQCAPS ...... Requirements and Capabilities Automated Planning System (MCD)
REQD .... Required (AAG)
REQDI .... Request Disposition Instructions [*Army*] (AABC)
REQED .... Required Execution Date (MCD)
REQF .... Wrong Test Requested - Floor Error [*Medicine*] (DAVI)
REQFOLINFO... Request Following Information Be Forwarded This Office [*Army*] (AABC)
REQIBO .... Request Item Be Placed on Back Order [*Army*]
REQID .... Request if Desired (FAAC)
REQINT .... Request Interim Reply By [*Date*] [*Military*] (AABC)
REQL .... Wrong Test Requested - Laboratory Error [*Medicine*] (DAVI)
REQMNT ...... Requirement (NVT)
REQMT .... Requirement
REQN .... Requisition (AAG)
REQNOM ...... Request Nomination
REQON .... Request Consideration (SAA)
REQP .... Recursive Equality Quadratic Program (PDAA)
REQPER ...... Request Permission [*Navy*] (NVT)
REQRCM ...... Request Your Recommendation (FAAC)
REQRE .... Require (ROG)
REQREC ...... Request Recommendation (NVT)
REQS .... Requires
REQSI .... Request Shipping Instructions [*Military*]
REQSSD ...... Request Supply Status and Expected Delivery Date [*Army*] (AABC)
REQSTD ...... Requested (FAAC)
REQSUPSTAFOL... Request Supply Status of Following [*Army*] (AABC)
REQT .... Request (ROG)
REQT .... Requirement (AAG)
REQTRAC ...... Request Tracer Be Initiated [*Military*]
REQU .... Require (IAA)
REQUAL .... Requalify
REQUCHRD... Request Unit of Issue Be Changed to Read [*Army*] (AABC)
REQUEST ...... Restricted English Question-Answering (HGAA)
REQUONS .... Requisitions
REQVER .... Requirements Verification (IEEE)
RER .... Potrerillos [*Chile*] [*Airport symbol*] (AD)
RER .... RADAR Effects Reactor
RER .... Radiation Effects Reactor [*Nuclear energy*]
RER .... Radioelektronnaya Razvedka [*Reconnaissance and Intelligence*] [*Soviet counterintelligence*] (LAIN)
RER .... Radio Expenditure Report [*A publication*] (DOAD)
RER .... Railway Equipment Register
RER .... Receiver/Exciter Ranging [*NASA*]
RER .... Redundant Element Removal (IAA)
ReR .... Remington Rand Corp., Blue Bell, PA [*Library symbol Library of Congress*] (LCLS)
RER .... Renal Excretion Rate [*Medicine*] (MAE)
RER .... Representatives for Experiment Review [*Nuclear energy*] (NRCH)
RER .... Rerun (AAG)
RER .... Residual Error Rate
RER .... Resource Evaluation Report (MCD)
RER .... Respiratory Exchange Rate
RER .... Respiratory Exchange Ratio [*Medicine*] (DAVI)
RER .... Retlaw Resources, Inc. [*Vancouver Stock Exchange symbol*]
RER .... Reusable-Expendable-Reusable
RER .... Rough [*Surfaced*] Endoplasmic Reticulum [*Cytology*]
RER .... Rubberized Equipment Repair
RERA .... Recent Rain [*Meteorology*] (DA)
RERAD .... Reference Radio
RERAD .... Reradiation
RER & D ...... Rehabilitative Engineering Research and Development Service [*Veterans Administration*] (GRD)
RERC .... Radiological Emergency Response Coordination [*Nuclear energy*] (NRCH)
RERC .... Rare Earth Research Conference (EA)
RERC .... Real Estate Research Corp.
Re/Re .... Reinforcement/Resupply [*To Europe*] (DOMA)
REREPS .... Repair and Rehabilitation of Paved Surfaces (MCD)
REREQ .... Reference Requisition (NOAA)
REREX .... Remote Readout Experiment
RERF .... Radiation Effects Research Foundation [*Formerly, ABCC*]
RERI .... Radiation Effect Research Institute
RERIC .... Regional Energy Resources Information Center [*Asian Institute of Technology*] [*British Information service or system*] (IID)
RERL .... Residual Equivalent Return Loss
Rer Nat Scr Graec Min... Rerum Naturalium Scriptores Graeci Minores [*A publication*] (OCD)
RERO .... Radiological Emergency Response Operation [*Nuclear energy*] (NRCH)
RERO .... Royal Engineers Reserve of Officers [*British*]
RERP .... Radiological Emergency Response Planning (NRCH)
RERTE .... Reroute [*Aviation*] (FAAC)
RERTR .... Reduced Enrichment in Research and Test Reactions [*Department of Energy*]
RERTR .... Research Enrichment in Research and Test Reactors Program [*Department of Energy*]
RES .... Eastman School of Music, Rochester, NY [*OCLC symbol*] (OCLC)
RES .... Office of Nuclear Regulatory Research [*Nuclear Regulatory Commission*]
RES .... Office of Research [*Bureau of Intelligence and Research*] [*Department of State*] [*Washington, DC*] (GRD)
RES .... On Reserved List [*Army British*] (ROG)
RES .... RADAR Environment Simulation (NATG)
RES .... RADAR Evaluation Squadron [*Military*]
RES .... Radiation Exposure State (NATG)
RES .... Radio-Echo Sounding [*Geophysics*]
RES .... Rapid Evaluation System (IAA)

RES............ Raytheon Electronic Systems
RES............ Readiness Estimation System (MCD)
RES............ Record Element Specification [*Computer science*]
RES............ Record Evaluation System
RES............ Reentry System (ADA)
RES............ Regional Environmental Study [*Australia*]
RES............ Rehabilitation Evolution System [*Medicine*]
RES............ Relative Electric Strength (MCD)
RES............ Relief Electronics Specialist
RES............ Remote Access Editing System [*Computer science*] (IAA)
RES............ Remote Entry Services (MCD)
RES............ Remote Entry Subsystem (IAA)
RES............ Remote Job Entry System (NITA)
RES............ Renaissance Energy Ltd. [*Toronto Stock Exchange symbol*]
RES............ Reprint Expediting Service
RES............ Resawed (WGA)
RES............ Rescue (WDAA)
RES............ Research (AAG)
res............ Research (IDOE)
RES............ Reserve (EY)
RES............ Reservoir (AAG)
RES............ Reset
RES............ Residence
RES............ Residencial
RES............ Resident
RES............ Resident
RES............ Residual (KSC)
RES............ Residue
RES............ Resigned
RES............ Resilient [*Technical drawings*]
res............ Resin (VRA)
RES............ Resistance [*or Resistor*] (AAG)
res............ Resistance (IDOE)
RES............ Resistencia [*Argentina*] [*Airport symbol*] (OAG)
RES............ Resistor
res............ Resistor (IDOE)
Res............ Resolu [*Resolved, Decided*] [*French*] (ILCA)
RES............ Resolute [*Northwest Territories*] [*Seismograph station code, US Geological Survey*] (SEIS)
RES............ Resolute Bay [*Northwest Territories*] [*Geomagnetic observatory code*]
RES............ Resolution
res............ Resolution (IDOE)
Res............ Resolved [*Legal term*] (DLA)
RES............ Resolver (IAA)
RES............ Resonator [*Automotive engineering*]
RES............ Resources
Res............ Resources (DD)
RES............ Restauraciones Aeronauticas SA de CV [*Mexico ICAO designator*] (FAAC)
RES............ Restaurant (DSUE)
RES............ Restore
Res............ Resurrection (BJA)
RES............ Reticuloendothelial Society (EA)
RES............ Reticuloendothelial System [*Medicine*]
RES............ Review of English Studies [*A publication*] (BRI)
RES............ Romance of Empire Series [*A publication*]
RES............ Royal Easter Show [*Australia*]
RES............ Royal Economic Society [*British*]
RES............ Royal Empire Society [*British*]
RES............ Royal Entomological Society [*British*]
RES............ RPC Energy Services, Inc. [*NYSE symbol*] (SPSG)
RES............ RPC Inc. [*NYSE symbol*] (TTSB)
ResA........... R & E Research Associates, Palo Alto, CA [*Library symbol Library of Congress*] (LCLS)
RESA........... Regional Education Service Agency
RESA........... Research, Evaluation, and System Analysis [*Navy*]
RESA........... Research Society of America (IAA)
RESA........... Ring-Infected Erythrocyte Surface Antigen [*Immunochemistry*]
RESA........... Runway End Safety Area [*Aviation*] (DA)
RESA........... Scientific Research Society of America (EA)
RESAF.......... Reserve of the Air Force
RESALIFT....... Reserve Airlift (NVT)
Res & Exp...... Research and Exploration [*A publication*] (BRI)
RESANTISUBCARIARGRU... Reserve Antisubmarine Warfare Carrier Air Group [*Navy*] (DNAB)
RESAR.......... Reference Safety Analysis Report [*Nuclear energy*] (NRCH)
RESASWCARAIREGRU... Reserve Antisubmarine Warfare Carrier Air Group [*Navy*] (DNAB)
RESASWTRACEN... Reserve Antisubmarine Warfare Training Center [*Navy*] (DNAB)
RESAV.......... Real Estate Salespersons' Association of Victoria [*Australia*]
RESAWA......... Real Estate Salespersons' Association of Western Australia
RESC........... Regional Educational Service Center
RESC........... Rescind (AAG)
RESC........... Rescue (AFM)
RESC........... Resource
RESC........... Resuscitation [*Medicine*] (DAVI)
RESC........... Roanoke Electric Steel [*NASDAQ symbol*] (TTSB)
RESC........... Roanoke Electric Steel Corp. [*NASDAQ symbol*] (NQ)
RESC........... Royal Engineers and Signal Corps [*Military British*] (IAA)
RescAm......... Resource America [*Commercial firm Associated Press*] (SAG)
RESCAN......... Reflecting Satellite Communication Antenna
RESCAP......... Rescue Combat Air Patrol [*Army*]
RESCAP......... Resistor-Capacitor (IAA)
ResCare........ Res Care, Inc. [*Associated Press*] (SAG)
Res Cas........ Reserved Cases [*Ireland*] [*A publication*] (DLA)
RESCD.......... Rescind [*Legal shorthand*] (LWAP)
RESCEN......... Reserve Center [*Navy*] (DNAB)
RescM.......... Resource Mortgage Capital, Inc. [*Associated Press*] (SAG)
resco.......... Resin-Coated (VRA)
RESCOMMIS... Reserve Command Management Information System (DNAB)
RESCRU......... Reserve Cruise [*Navy*] (NVT)
RESCU.......... Radio Emergency Search Communications Unit
RESCU.......... Rocket-Ejection Seat Catapult Upward [*Aviation*]
RESCUE......... Recovery Employing Storage Chute Used in Emergencies [*Inflatable aircraft wing*]
RESCUE......... Referring Emergency Service for Consumers' Ultimate Enjoyment [*Service plan of Recreational Vehicle Dealers of America*] (EA)
RESCUE......... Remote Emergency Salvage and Clean Up Equipment
RESCUER........ Rocket Escape System with Cruise Using Electric Rotor (MCD)
RESD........... Reentry Environmental Systems Division [*General Electric Co.*] (MCD)
RESD........... Resigned
RESD........... Resolved (ROG)
RESDAT......... Restricted Data [*Atomic Energy Act of 1954*]
RESDESDIV... Reserve Destroyer Division (DNAB)
RESDESRON... Reserve Destroyer Squadron (DNAB)
RESDIST........ Reserve District
Research L & Econ... Research in Law and Economics [*A publication*] (DLA)
ResEdit........ Resource Editor [*Computer science*] (DOM)
ResEngn........ Research Engineers, Inc. [*Associated Press*] (SAG)
RESEP.......... Reentry System Environmental Protection
RESER.......... Reentry Systems Evaluation RADAR [*Aerospace*]
reserva........ Reservation
Reserv Cas... Reserved Cases [*1860-64*] [*A publication*] (DLA)
RESERVE........ Reserve Training [*USCG*] (TAG)
RESERVON... Reservation (ROG)
RESET.......... Regression Specification Error Test [*Statistics*]
RESEX.......... Resource Executive (IAA)
RESF........... Research and Engineering Support Facility (MCD)
RESFAC......... Reserve Facility (DNAB)
RESFLD......... Residual Field (AAG)
RESFLY......... Respectfully (ROG)
RESFOR......... AUTODIN CRT for Secure Reserve Force (MCD)
RESFORON... Reserve Force Squadron (DNAB)
RESG........... Research Engineering Standing Group [*DoD*]
Res Gamma Eta Gamma... Rescript of Gamma Eta Gamma [*A publication*] (DLA)
RESGD.......... Resigned
RESGND......... Resigned
RESH........... Recent Shower [*Meteorology*] (DA)
RESHAPE........ Resource Self-Help/Affordability Planning Effort [*Program*] [*Federal government*] (RDA)
ReshInc........ Research, Inc. [*Associated Press*] (SAG)
ReshInd........ Research Industries Corp. [*Associated Press*] (SAG)
ReshMed........ Research Medical, Inc. [*Associated Press*] (SAG)
RESHUS......... Reseau Documentaire en Sciences Humaines de la Sante [*Network for Documentation in the Human Sciences of Health*] [*Institut de l'Information Scientifique et Technique*] [*Information service or system*] (IID)
RESI........... Republic Environmental Systems [*NASDAQ symbol*] (TTSB)
RESI........... Republic Environmental Systems, Inc. [*NASDAQ symbol*] (SAG)
RES I........... Research EMP [*Electromagnetic Pulse*] Simulator I [*Air Force*]
RESIC.......... Redstone Scientific Information Center [*Army*]
RES/IC......... Reserve - In Commission [*Vessel status*]
resid.......... Residency
RESID.......... Residual (AAG)
RESIG.......... Resignation (AFM)
RESIL.......... Resilient
RESIN.......... Resina [*Resin*] [*Pharmacy*] (ROG)
Res Ipsa....... Res Ipsa Loquitur [*The Thing Speaks for Itself*] [*Latin*] (DLA)
RES/IS......... Reserve - In Service [*Vessel status*]
RESIS.......... Resistance
RESIS.......... Resistor (IAA)
RESIST......... Replace Essential Supplies in Sufficient Time [*Navy*] (NVT)
RESIST......... Resistant
RESIST......... Resistor (WDAA)
RESIST......... Retirees to Eliminate State Income Source Tax [*An association*]
RESIST......... Reusable Surface Insulation Stresses [*NASA computer program*]
resist ex...... Resistive Exercises [*orhtopedics*] (DAVI)
RESIV.......... Real Estate and Stock Institute of Victoria [*Australia*]
Res Judic...... Res Judicatae [*A publication*] (DLA)
RESL........... Radiological and Environmental Sciences Laboratory [*Nuclear energy*] (NRCH)
RESLAB......... Research Laboratory
RESLOAD........ Resident Loader (MHDI)
RESLV.......... Resolve (KSC)
RESM........... ResMed, Inc. [*NASDAQ symbol*] (SAG)
RESMA.......... Railway Electric Supply Manufacturers Association [*Later, RSA*]
ResMed......... ResMed, Inc. [*Associated Press*] (SAG)
RESMILCON... Reserve Military Construction (DNAB)
RESN........... Recent Snow [*Meteorology*] (DA)
RESN........... Resonant
RESNA.......... RESNA [*Rehabilitation Engineering Society of North America*]: Association for the Advancement of Rehabilitation Technology [*Association retains acronym from former name*] (EA)
RESO........... Regional Environmental Support Office (DNAB)
RESO........... Resoluta [*Music*] (ROG)
RESOC.......... Research Sonobuoy Configuration (NG)
RES/OC......... Reserve - Out of Commission [*Vessel status*]
RESOJET........ Resonant Pulse Jet

RESOLN .... Resolution (MSA)
RESORS .... Remote Scanning Online Retrieval System (NITA)
RESORS .... Remote Sensing On-Line Retrieval System [*Canada Centre for Remote Sensing*] [*Department of Energy, Mines, and Resources Database*] [*Information service or system*] (IID)
RES/OS .... Reserve - Out of Service [*Vessel status*]
Resound .... Resound Corp. [*Associated Press*] (SAG)
Resp .... De Respiratione [*of Aristotle*] [*Classical studies*] (OCD)
RESP .... Registered Education Savings Plan [*Canada*]
RESP .... Regulated Electrical Supply Package
ResP .... Research Publications, Inc., New Haven, CT [*Library symbol Library of Congress*] (LCLS)
RESP .... Respectively
RESP .... Respiration (KSC)
RESP .... Respirator
Resp .... Respiratory (CPH)
RESP .... Respironics, Inc. [*NASDAQ symbol*] (NQ)
RESP .... Respondent
RESP .... Response (AAG)
Resp .... Response USA, Inc. [*Associated Press*] (SAG)
RESP .... Responsible (AFM)
RESP .... Responsible
Resp .... Respublica [*of Plato*] [*Classical studies*] (OCD)
RESPA .... Real Estate Settlement Procedures Act of 1974
RESP-A .... Respiratory Battery, Acute [*Medicine*] (DAVI)
RES PHYS .... Resident Physician (WDAA)
respir .... Respirations [*Medicine*] (DAVI)
Respirn .... Respironics, Inc. [*Associated Press*] (SAG)
RESPLY .... Respectively
RESPO .... Responsible Property Officer [*Army*] (AABC)
RespOnc .... Response Oncology, Inc. [*Associated Press*] (SAG)
RESPOND .... Respondere [*To Answer*] [*Pharmacy*] (ROG)
Respons .... Response USA, Inc. [*Associated Press*] (SAG)
RESPONSA .... Retrieval of Special Portions from Nuclear Science Abstracts (DIT)
RESPT .... Respondent
Res Pub .... Res Publica [*A publication*] (ILCA)
RESPY .... Respectfully (ROG)
RESQ .... Research Queueing (MHDB)
RESR .... Research, Inc. [*NASDAQ symbol*] (NQ)
RESR .... Resources (AABC)
RESRC .... Resource
RESRC .... Resources
RESREP .... Resident Representative (MUGU)
RESRT .... Resort
RESRT .... Resort
RESRT .... Restart [*Computer science*]
RESRV .... Reserve
RESS .... RADAR Echo Simulation Study [*or Subsystem*]
RESS .... Rapid Expansion of Supercritical Solution [*Chemical engineering*]
RESS .... Recruiting Enlisted Selection System [*Military*] (DNAB)
RESSI .... Real Estate Securities and Syndication Institute (EA)
REST .... RADAR Electronic Scan Technique
REST .... RADAR Electronic Scan Test (IAA)
REST .... Rain Erosion Seed Test
REST .... Range Endurance Speed and Time [*Computer*]
REST .... Raynaud's Phenomenon, Esophageal Motor Dysfuntion, Sclerodactyly, and Telangiectasis Syndrome [*Medicine*] (DMAA)
REST .... Reentry Environment and Systems Technology
REST .... Reentry System Test Program
REST .... Reporting System for Training [*Navy*] (NG)
REST .... Residence in Science and Technology
REST .... Respiratory Therapist (HCT)
REST .... Rest [*Commonly used*] (OPSA)
REST .... Restaurant (ROG)
REST .... Restitution [*Legal shorthand*] (LWAP)
rest .... Restorative [*Pharmacology*] (DAVI)
rest .... Restored (VRA)
REST .... Restored
REST .... Restor Industries [*NASDAQ symbol*] (TTSB)
REST .... Restor Industries, Inc. [*NASDAQ symbol*] (SAG)
REST .... Restrict (AAG)
REST .... Restricted Environmental Stimulation Technique
REST .... Restricted RADAR Electronic Scan Technique (IAA)
REST .... Routine Execution Selection Table [*Computer science*] (WDAA)
RESTA .... Reconnaissance, Surveillance, and Target Acquisition [*Military*] (AABC)
RESTAS .... Reception Station System [*Army*]
RESTAT .... Reserve Components Status Reporting [*Army*] (AABC)
RESTD .... Restricted [*Security classification*] [*Military*]
RESTO .... Restaurant
RESTOR .... Restoration
Restor .... Restor Industries, Inc. [*Associated Press*] (SAG)
RESTR .... Restaurant (WGA)
RESTR .... Restorer
RESTR .... Restrict (AABC)
RESTRACEN .... Reserve Training Center
RESTRAFAC .... Reserve Training Facility
Restric Prac .... Reports of Restrictive Practices Cases [*A publication*] (DLA)
RESTS .... Restoration Survey
RESTT .... Respiratory Therapy Technician (HCT)
RESUB .... Resublimed
RESUP .... Resupply (AABC)
RESUPSHIP .... Resident Supervisor of Shipbuilding Conversion and Repair (DNAB)
ResurP .... Resurgence Properties [*Associated Press*] (SAG)
RESURR .... Resurrection
RESUS .... Resuscitation
RESV .... Reserve Fleet [*Navy*]
RESVD .... Reserved (ROG)
RESVON .... Reservation (ROG)
RESVR .... Reservoir (AAG)
RESY .... Reconditioned Sys [*NASDAQ symbol*] (TTSB)
RESY .... Residuary (ROG)
RESYNCING .... Resynchronizing (GAVI)
RESYZ .... Reconditioned Sys Wrrt'B' [*NASDAQ symbol*] (TTSB)
RET .... Price REIT [*NYSE symbol*] (TTSB)
RET .... Price REIT, Inc. [*NYSE symbol*] (SAG)
RET .... RADAR Equipment Trailer (MCD)
RET .... Rad-Equivalent Therapy [*Radiology*]
R-ET .... Rational-Emotive Psychotherapy [*Also known as R-EP, RT*]
RET .... Readiness Enhancement Technology [*Military*]
RET .... Regional Entry Test
RET .... Registered Engineering Technologist (DD)
RET .... Reiteration [*Printers' term*] (DSUE)
RET .... Reitman's (Canada) Ltd. [*Toronto Stock Exchange symbol*]
RET .... Relay Extractor Tool
RET .... Reliability Evaluation Test
RET .... Repetitive Extrasystole Threshold [*Cardiology*]
RET .... Resolution Enhancement Technology [*Printer feature*] [*Hewlett-Packard Co.*] [*Computer science*] (PCM)
RET .... Resonance Energy Transfer [*Physical chemistry*]
RET .... Retailer
RET .... Retain (AAG)
RET .... Retard (AAG)
RET .... Reticulocyte [*Hematology*] (DAVI)
Ret .... Reticulum [*Constellation*]
RET .... Retired (AFM)
ret .... Retired (DD)
RET .... Retired after Finishing [*Yacht racing*] (IYR)
RET .... Retract
RET .... Return [*or Returnable*] (AAG)
RET .... Right Esotropia [*Ophthalmology*]
RET .... Ring Emitter Transistor
RET .... Road Equivalent Tariff [*To finance ferries*] [*British*] (DI)
RET .... Rost [*Norway*] [*Airport symbol*] (OAG)
RET .... Roster of Employees Transferred [*Army*]
RET .... Rotational Energy Transfer [*Chemical physics*]
RETA .... Reactor Environmental Test Apparatus (MCD)
RETA .... Refrigerating Engineers and Technicians Association (EA)
RETA .... Retrieval of Enriched Textual Abstracts [*Information retrieval program*]
RET-ABSTEE .... Returned Absentee (DNAB)
RETAC .... Regional Educational Television Advisory Council
RETACT .... Real-Time Advanced Core and Thermohydraulic
RETAI .... Real Estate Trainers Association, International (EA)
RETAIN .... Remote Technical Assistance and Information Network [*Computer science*]
RETAP .... Regular Education Teachers and Principals Project (EDAC)
RET BREV .... Retorna Brevium [*The Return of Writs*] [*Latin Legal term*] (DLA)
RETC .... Railroad Equipment Trust Certificate
RETC .... Rat Embryo Tissue Culture
RETC .... Regional Emergency Transportation Center [*Military*]
RETC .... Retention Curve [*U.S. EPA*]
Ret Cath .... Retention Catheter [*Medicine*] (CPH)
RETCO .... Regional Emergency Transportation Coordinator [*Military*]
RETCON .... Retroactive Continuity [*Computer science*] (NHD)
RETD .... Retained
RETD .... Retired (EY)
RETD .... Returned
RETEN .... Retention [*Insurance*] (MCD)
RETEST .... Reinforcement Testing for System Training (SAA)
RETF .... Retired Document File [*IRS*]
RETG .... Retaining
RETI .... Communaute de Travail des Regions Europeennes de Tradition Industrielle [*Association of Traditional Industrial Regions of Europe*] [*Lille, France*] (EAIO)
R et I .... Regina et Imperatrix [*Queen and Empress*] [*Latin*]
Reti .... Reticulum [*Constellation*]
R et I .... Rex et Imperator [*King and Emperor*] [*Latin*]
RETIC .... Reticulocyte [*Hematology*]
Retic Ct .... Reticulocyte Count [*Hematology*] (CPH)
RETIMP .... Raleigh-Edwards Tensile Impact Machine Pendulum
RETIREX .... Retirement Exhibition [*British*] (ITD)
Retix .... Retix, Inc. [*Associated Press*] (SAG)
RETL .... Retail
RETL .... Rocket Engine Test Laboratory [*Air Force*]
RETM .... Rare Earth Transition Metal [*Computer science*]
RETMA .... Radio-Electronics-Television Manufacturers Association [*Later, Electronic Industries Association*]
RETMOB .... Requirements for Total Mobilization Study
RETN .... Return (ROG)
RETNDU .... Return to Duty [*Military*] (DNAB)
RETNG .... Retraining
RETNN .... Retention [*Insurance*]
RETNR .... Retainer (ADA)
RETO .... Retouched (VRA)
RETO .... Review of Education and Training for Officers [*Military*] (RDA)
RETORC .... Research Torpedo Configuration (NG)
RETP .... Reliability Evaluation Test Procedure
RETP .... Reserve Entry Training Plan [*Canada*]
RETP .... Retape

RETR .... Retainer (ROG)
RETR .... Retention Register [*Computer science*]
RETR .... Retraced
RETR .... Retract (AAG)
RETR .... Retrieve (KSC)
RETRA .... Radio, Electrical, and Television Retailers' Association [*British*]
Retract .... Retractationes [*of Augustine*] [*Classical studies*] (OCD)
RETRAN .... Refined Trajectory Analysis
RETRANS .... Retransmit
RetrCre .... Retirement Care Associates, Inc. [*Associated Press*] (SAG)
RETRD .... Retarded
RETREAD .... Retiree Training for Extended Active Duty [*Military*] (MCD)
RETREP .... Regional Emergency Transportation Representative
RETRF .... Rural Electrification and Telephone Revolving Fund [*Department of Agriculture*]
RETRG .... Retracting (WGA)
RETRNG .... Retraining
RETRO .... Regional Environmental Training and Research Organization [*Retraining program for unemployed space-industry workers*]
RETRO .... Retroactive (AAG)
RETRO .... Retrofire (KSC)
RETRO .... Retrofire Officer
RETRO .... Retrofit
RETRO .... Retrograde
RETRO .... Retro-Rocket (AAG)
RETROCON .... Retroactive Conversion (WDMC)
RETROEUR .... Retrograde Europe [*Army*]
RETROF .... Retrofire (SAA)
RETRO FA .... Retroactive Family Allowance [*Military*] (DNAB)
RETROG .... Retrogressive
Retro pyelo .... Retrograde Pyelogram [*Nephrology*] (DAVI)
Retrosp .... Retrospectively (DLA)
RETROSPEC .... Retrospective Search System (NITA)
RETRV .... Retrieve (MCD)
RETS .... Radio Electronics Television School (IAA)
RETS .... Radiological Environmental Technical Specifications [*Nuclear energy*] (NRCH)
RETS .... Real-Time Sonobuoy (MCD)
RETS .... Recent Thunderstorm (DA)
RETS .... Reconfigurable Electrical Test Stand (NASA)
RETS .... Remoted Targets System (MCD)
RETS .... Renaissance English Text Society (EA)
RETSCP .... Rocket Engine Thermal Strains with Cyclic Plasticity [*Propellant*]
RETSER .... Retained in Service [*Military*] (DNAB)
RETSIE .... Renewable Energy Technologies Symposium and International Exposition [*Renewable Energy Institute*] (TSPED)
RETSPL .... Reference Equivalent Threshold Sound Pain [*or Pressure*] Level
RETT .... Relatively Easy to Test [*Audiology*]
Rett .... Rettie's Scotch Court of Session Cases, Fourth Series [*A publication*] (DLA)
Rettie .... Rettie's Scotch Court of Session Cases, Fourth Series [*A publication*] (DLA)
RETUL .... Reticulum Cells [*On differential*] [*Hematology*] (DAVI)
RETULSIGN .... Retain on Board until Ultimate Assignment Received
RETX .... Retix [*NASDAQ symbol*] (SPSG)
REU .... Air Austral [*France*] [*FAA designator*] (FAAC)
REU .... Air Reunion [*France ICAO designator*] (FAAC)
REU .... Radio Engineering Unit (IAA)
REU .... Rated Exposure Unit [*Advertising*] (NTCM)
REU .... Ready Extension Unit (MHDB)
REU .... Rectifier Enclosure Unit [*Power supply*] [*Telecommunications*] (TEL)
REU .... Requesting Expeditor Unit (DNAB)
REU .... Research Experiences for Undergraduates [*NSF grant program*]
REU .... Reunion [*ANSI three-letter standard code*] (CNC)
REU .... Reunion Island [*Seismograph station code, US Geological Survey*] (SEIS)
REU .... Reus [*Spain*] [*Airport symbol*] (OAG)
ReunInd .... Reunion Resources [*Associated Press*] (SAG)
REUNIR .... Reseau des Universites et de la Recherche [*Network of Universities and Research*] [*French*] [*Computer science*] (TNIG)
ReunRsc .... Reunion Resources [*Commercial firm Associated Press*] (SAG)
REUR .... Reference Your
REURAD .... Reference Your Radio
REURTWX .... Reference Your TWX [*Teletypewriter communications*] (AAG)
REUSE .... Revitalize Effective Utilization of Supply Excess [*Navy*] (NG)
ReutrHd .... Reuters Holdings Ltd. [*Associated Press*] (SAG)
REV .... Range Extender Vehicle [*Gasoline-electric hybrid*]
REV .... Ratio of Earth-to-Vehicle Radii
REV .... Reentry Vehicle [*Aerospace*]
REV .... Regulator of Virion-Protein Expression [*Genetics*]
REV .... Representative Elementary Volume [*Sampling for analysis*]
REV .... Reticuloendotheliosis Virus
Rev .... Revelation [*New Testament book*]
REV .... Revelstoke Companies Ltd. [*Toronto Stock Exchange symbol*]
REV .... Reventador [*Race of maize*]
REV .... Revenue
REV .... Reverend (EY)
Rev .... Reverend (DD)
REV .... Reverend
Rev .... Reverend (ODBW)
REV .... Reversal Film [*Cinematography*] (NTCM)
REV .... Reverse (AAG)
rev .... Reverse (IDOE)
rev .... Reverse (VRA)
rev .... Reversed (WDMC)
rev .... Review (WDMC)
REV .... Review (AFM)
rev .... Reviewed (WDMC)
rev .... Revise (WDMC)
REV .... Revise [*or Revision*] (AAG)
rev .... Revision (WDMC)
REV .... Revision Message [*Aviation*] (DA)
REV .... Revlon Inc'A' [*NYSE symbol*] (TTSB)
REV .... Revocable [*Business term*]
REV .... Revolution (AAG)
rev .... Revolution (WDMC)
REV .... Revolve (WDAA)
REV .... Rotor Entry Vehicle [*Aerospace*]
REVA .... Recommended Vehicle Adjustment [*Military*] (AABC)
REVAB .... Relief Valve Augmented Bypass [*Nuclear energy*] (NRCH)
REV A/C .... Revenue Account (WDAA)
Rev & TC .... Revenue and Taxation Code [*A publication*] (DLA)
REVAR .... Authorized Revisit Above-Mentioned Places and Vary Itinerary as Necessary
Rev C Abo PR .... Revista de Derecho. Colegio de Abogados de Puerto Rico [*A publication*] (DLA)
Rev Can .... Revue Canadienne [*Quebec*] [*A publication*] (DLA)
Rev C & C Rep .... Revenue, Civil, and Criminal Reporter [*Calcutta*] [*A publication*] (DLA)
Rev Can D Fam .... Revue Canadienne de Droit Familial [*A publication*] (DLA)
Rev Can Dr Com .... Revue Canadienne de Droit Communautaire [*A publication*] (DLA)
Rev Cas .... Revenue Cases [*A publication*] (DLA)
Rev Cas (Ind) .... Revised Cases [*India*] [*A publication*] (DLA)
Rev Civ Code .... Revised Civil Code [*A publication*] (DLA)
Rev Civ St .... Revised Civil Statutes [*A publication*] (DLA)
Revco .... Revco DS, Inc. [*Associated Press*] (SAG)
Rev Code Civ Proc .... Revised Code of Civil Procedure [*A publication*] (DLA)
Rev Code Cr Proc .... Revised Code of Criminal Procedure [*A publication*] (DLA)
REVCOM .... Revolutionary Committee [*China*]
REVCON .... Review Conference
Rev Contemp L .... Review of Contemporary Law [*A publication*] (DLA)
REV CPY .... Review Copy (DGA)
Rev Cr Code .... Revised Criminal Code [*A publication*] (DLA)
Rev Crit .... Revue Critique de Legislation et de Jurisprudence de Canada [*A publication*] (DLA)
Rev Crit de Leg .... Revue Critique de Legislation [*Paris*] [*A publication*] (DLA)
Rev Crit de Legis et Jur .... Revue Critique de Legislation et de Jurisprudence [*Montreal*] [*A publication*] (DLA)
Rev Cubana de Derecho .... Revista Cubana de Derecho [*Havana, Cuba*] [*A publication*] (DLA)
REVCUR .... Reverse Current (AAG)
REVD .... Reverend (ROG)
Rev'd .... Reversed [*Legal term*] (DLA)
Rev da Fac de Direito (Lisbon) .... Revista. Faculdade de Direito. Universidade de Lisboa (Lisbon) [*A publication*] (DLA)
Rev de Derecho Esp y Amer .... Revista de Derecho Espanol y Americano [*Madrid, Spain*] [*A publication*] (DLA)
Rev de Derecho Jurispr y Cienc Soc .... Revista de Derecho, Jurisprudencia, y Ciencias Sociales y Gaceta de los Tribunales [*A publication*] (DLA)
Rev de Droit Contemp .... Revue de Droit Contemporain [*Brussels, Belgium*] [*A publication*] (DLA)
Rev de Droit Hong .... Revue de Droit Hongrois [*A publication*] (DLA)
Rev de Droit Penal Mil et de Droit de la Guerre .... Revue de Droit Penal Militaire et de Droit de la Guerre [*A publication*] (DLA)
Rev de Droit Unif .... Revue de Droit Uniforme [*A publication*] (DLA)
Rev de Droit Uniforme .... Revue de Droit Uniforme [*A publication*] (DLA)
Rev de Fac de Direito (Sao Paulo) .... Revista. Faculdade de Direito. Universidade de Sao Paulo [*Sao Paulo, Brazil*] [*A publication*] (DLA)
Rev de Jur .... Revue de Jurisprudence [*Quebec*] [*A publication*] (DLA)
Rev de la Fac de Derecho (Caraboba) .... Revista. Facultad de Derecho. Universidad de Caraboba [*Valencia, Venezuela*] [*A publication*] (DLA)
Rev de la Fac de Derecho (Caracas) .... Revista. Facultad de Derecho. Universidad Catolica Andres Bello (Caracas) [*A publication*] (DLA)
Rev de la Fac de Derecho y Cienc Soc .... Revista. Facultad de Derecho y Ciencias Sociales [*Montevideo, Uruguay*] [*A publication*] (DLA)
Rev de Leg .... Revue de Legislation et de Jurisprudence [*Montreal*] [*A publication*] (DLA)
Rev de Legis .... Revue de Legislation [*Canada*] [*A publication*] (DLA)
Rev del Inst de Derecho Comparado .... Revista. Instituto de Derecho Comparado [*Barcelona, Spain*] [*A publication*] (DLA)
Rev de Sci Criminelle et de Droit Penal Compare .... Revue de Science Criminelle et de Droit Penal Compare [*Paris, France*] [*A publication*] (DLA)
REV DEV .... Revolutionary Development [*South Vietnam*]
Rev Droit Int'l Moyen-Orient .... Revue de Droit International pour le Moyen-Orient [*A publication*] (DLA)
Rev Droit Penal Militaire et Dr de la Guerre .... Revue de Droit Penal Militaire et de Droit de la Guerre [*A publication*] (DLA)
Rev du Dr .... Revue du Droit [*Quebec*] [*A publication*] (DLA)
Rev D US .... Revue de Droit. Universite de Sherbrooke [*A publication*] (DLA)
REV ED .... Revised Edition (WDAA)
REVEL .... Reverberation Elimination
REVERB .... Reverberation (NTCM)
reverb .... Reverberation [*Sound*] (WDMC)
REVERB .... Reverberator [*Automotive engineering*]
REVERSY .... Reversionary (ROG)
Rev Et Anc .... Revue des Etudes Anciennes [*A publication*] (OCD)
Rev Et Grec .... Revue des Etudes Grecques [*A publication*] (OCD)

Rev Et Lat... Revue des Etudes Latines [*A publication*] (OCD)
rev'g... Reversing [*Legal term*] (DLA)
Rev Gen... Revue Generale de Droit [*A publication*] (DLA)
Rev Gen D... Revue Generale de Droit [*A publication*] (DLA)
Rev Gen de Legis y Jurispr... Revista General de Legislacion y Jurisprudencia [*Madrid, Spain*] [*A publication*] (DLA)
Rev Gen Reg... Revised General Regulation, General Accounting Office [*United States*] [*A publication*] (DLA)
Rev Ghana L... Review of Ghana Law [*A publication*] (DLA)
Rev Hist Rel... Revue de l'Histoire des Religions [*A publication*] (OCD)
REVIEW... Recording and Video Playback of Electronic Warfare Information
Rev Internac y Diplom... Revista Internacional y Diplomatica. Publicacion Mensual [*Mexico*] [*A publication*] (DLA)
Rev Internat Franc du Droit des Gens... Revue Internationale Francaise du Droit des Gens [*A publication*] (DLA)
Rev Int'l Comm Jur... Review. International Commission of Jurists [*A publication*] (DLA)
Rev Int'l des Droits de l'Antiquite... Revue Internationale des Droits de l'Antiquite [*A publication*] (DLA)
Rev Int'l Dr Auteur... Revue Internationale du Droit d'Auteur [*A publication*] (DLA)
Rev Int'l Droit Comp... Revue Internationale de Droit Compare [*A publication*] (DLA)
Rev Int'l Dr Penal... Revue Internationale de Droit Penal [*A publication*] (DLA)
Revised Rep... Revised Reports [*England*] [*A publication*] (DLA)
Rev Ivoirienne de Droit... Revue Ivoirienne de Droit [*A publication*] (DLA)
Rev J & PJ... Revenue, Judicial, and Police Journal [*Bengal*] [*A publication*] (DLA)
Rev Jud & Police J... Revenue, Judicial, and Police Journal [*A publication*] (DLA)
Rev Jur d'Alsace et de Lorraine... Revue Juridique d'Alsace et de Lorraine [*A publication*] (DLA)
Rev Jur de Buenos Aires... Revista Juridica de Buenos Aires [*A publication*] (DLA)
Rev Jur du Congo... Revue Juridique du Congo [*A publication*] (DLA)
REVL... [*To Be*] Reviewed by Pathologist [*Laboratory science*] (DAVI)
Rev L & Soc... Review of Law and Social Change [*A publication*] (DLA)
Rev Leg... Revue de Legislation et de Jurisprudence [*Quebec*] [*A publication*] (DLA)
Rev Leg... Revue Legale [*Canada*] [*A publication*] (DLA)
Rev Legale... Revue Legale [*A publication*] (DLA)
Rev Leg NS... Revue Legale. New Series [*Canada*] [*A publication*] (DLA)
Rev Leg (OS)... Revue Legale (Old Series) [*A publication*] (DLA)
RevMex... Revolutionary Mexican Historical Society (EA)
REV/MIN... Revolutions per Minute [*e.g., in reference to phonograph records*]
REVN... Reversion (ROG)
REVNRY... Revolutionary
REVO... Revoke (AABC)
REVO... Revolution (DSUE)
REVOCN... Revocation (ROG)
REVOCON... Remote Volume Control
REVOCON... Revocation
Rev of Polish Law and Econ... Review of Polish Law and Economics [*Warsaw, Poland*] [*A publication*] (DLA)
Rev of Sym... Review of Symptoms [*Medical Records*] (DAVI)
Rev of Sys... Review of Systems [*Medical records*] (DAVI)
REVOL... Revolution (WGA)
REVON... Reversion
REVOP... Random Evolutionary Operation
Rev Ord... Revised Ordinances [*A publication*] (DLA)
Rev Ord NWT... Revised Ordinances, Northwest Territories [*1888*] [*Canada*] [*A publication*] (DLA)
Rev Pen Code... Revised Penal Code [*A publication*] (DLA)
Rev Pol Code... Revised Political Code [*A publication*] (DLA)
Rev Pol L... Review of Polish Law [*A publication*] (DLA)
REV PROC... Revenue Procedure [*Internal Revenue Service*]
REVR... Receiver (AAG)
REVR... Reversioner (ROG)
REVR... Reviewer (AFM)
Rev R... Revised Reports [*1759-1866*] [*England*] [*A publication*] (DLA)
Rev Reh... Reversed [*or Reversing*] on Rehearing [*Used in Shepard's Citations*] [*Legal term*] (DLA)
Rev Rep... Revised Reports [*England*] [*A publication*] (DLA)
Rev Rev (A)... Review of Reviews. Australian Edition [*A publication*]
REV RUL... Revenue Ruling [*Internal Revenue Service*]
REVS... Reconnaissance Electro-Optical Viewing System
REVS... Requirements Engineering and Validation System
REVS... Reverse Shot [*Photography*] (WDMC)
RevS... Reverse Shot [*Filmmaking*] (WDMC)
REV/S... Revolutions per Second
REVS... Rotor Entry Vehicle System [*Aerospace*]
Rev Sel Code Leg... Review of Selected Code Legislation [*A publication*] (DLA)
Rev St... Revised Statutes [*A publication*] (DLA)
Rev Stat... Revised Statutes [*Various jurisdictions*] [*A publication*] (DLA)
Rev Suisse Dr Int'l Concurrence... Revue Suisse du Droit International de la Concurrence [*Swiss Review of International Antitrust Law*] [*A publication*] (DLA)
Rev Sw Dig... Revision of Swift's Digest of Connecticut Laws [*A publication*] (DLA)
RevTar... Revenue Tariff [*Australia Political party*]
Rev Tax'n Indiv... Review of Taxation of Individuals [*A publication*] (DLA)
Rev Trimestr de Jurispr... Revista Trimestral de Jurisprudencia [*Rio De Janeiro, Brazil*] [*A publication*] (DLA)
Rev Tunisienne de Droit... Revue Tunisienne de Droit [*Tunis, Tunisia*] [*A publication*] (DLA)
REV VER... Revised Version (WDAA)
REVW... Review (NVT)
REVWR... Reviewer (DGA)
REVY... Reversionary (ROG)
REW... Incised Wound [*On Autopsy*] [*Pathology*] (DAVI)
REW... Read, Execute, Write [*Computer science*] (IAA)
REW... Recycle Water [*Nuclear energy*] (NRCH)
REW... Redwood Valley, CA [*Location identifier FAA*] (FAAL)
REW... Reward (AFM)
REW... Rewind (MDG)
REWARD... Reading, Writing and Arithmetic Development System (EDAC)
REWDAC... Retrieval by Title Words, Descriptors, and Classification (DIT)
REWK... Rework (MSA)
REWRC... Report When Established Well to Right of Course [*Aviation*] (FAAC)
REWS... Radio Electronic Warfare Service (MCD)
REWSON... Reconnaissance, Electronic Warfare, Special Operations, and Naval Intelligence Processing Systems
REWSONIP... Reconnaissance Electronic Warfare Special Operation and Naval Intelligence Processing (IAA)
REWTEL... Radio and Electronics World Telecommunications (NITA)
REX... Radio Exploration Satellite (PDAA)
REX... Ram Air Freight, Inc. [*ICAO designator*] (FAAC)
REX... Rapid Text Search [*Computer science*] (IT)
REX... Rare-Earth Exchanged [*Faujasite, a zeolite*]
REX... Reactor Experimental [*Former USSR*] (DEN)
REX... Real-Time Executive Routine [*Computer science*]
REX... Real-Time Executive System [*Computer science*] (MHDI)
REX... Rechtswissenschaftliche Experten und Gutachter [*NOMOS Datapool*] [*Database*]
REX... Reduced Exoatmospheric Cross Section
REX... Reentry Experiment
REX... Reflector Erosion Experiment [*NASA*]
REX... Regression Expert [*Computer science*]
REX... Related Experience (SAA)
REX... Requisition Exception Code [*Air Force*] (AFIT)
REX... Research, Evaluation, and Experimental Program [*Bureau of the Census*] (GFGA)
REX... Resonance-Enhanced X-Ray [*Physics*]
REX... Rexburg [*Idaho*] [*Seismograph station code, US Geological Survey*] (SEIS)
REX... Rex Silver Mines [*Vancouver Stock Exchange symbol*]
REX... Reynosa [*Mexico*] [*Airport symbol*] (OAG)
REX... Robot Excavation [*Carnegie-Mellon Robotics Institute*]
REX... Rolodex Electronic Express
REX... Run Executive [*Computer science*]
REXA... Radioisotope-Excited X-Ray Analyzer (PDAA)
Rexam... Rexam PLC [*Associated Press*] (SAG)
Rexel... Rexel, Inc. [*Associated Press*] (SAG)
Rexene... Rexene Corp. [*Associated Press*] (SAG)
Rexhall... Rexhall Industries [*Associated Press*] (SAG)
REXI... Resource America [*NASDAQ symbol*] (SAG)
REXI... Resource America'A' [*NASDAQ symbol*] (TTSB)
REXL... Rexhall Indus [*NASDAQ symbol*] (TTSB)
REXL... Rexhall Industries, Inc. [*NASDAQ symbol*] (NQ)
RexlSun... Rexall Sundown, Inc. [*Associated Press*] (SAG)
REXMIT... Retransmitted (AABC)
REXMY... Rexam PLC [*NASDAQ symbol*] (SAG)
REXMY... Rexam Plc ADR [*NASDAQ symbol*] (TTSB)
REXN... Rexon, Inc. [*NASDAQ symbol*] (NQ)
REXS... Radio Exploration Satellite [*Japan*]
RexStore... Rex Stores Corp. [*Associated Press*] (SAG)
REXW... Rexworks, Inc. [*NASDAQ symbol*] (NQ)
Rexwks... Rexworks, Inc. [*Associated Press*] (SAG)
REXX... Restructured Extended Executor [*IBM command language*] (PCM)
REY... Aero-Rey SA de CV [*Mexico ICAO designator*] (FAAC)
REY... Reentry
REY... Reyes [*Bolivia*] [*Airport symbol*] (OAG)
REY... Reykjavik [*Iceland*] [*Seismograph station code, US Geological Survey*] (SEIS)
REY... Reynolds & Reynolds'A' [*NYSE symbol*] (TTSB)
REY... Reynolds & Reynolds Co. [*NYSE symbol*] (SPSG)
REY... Rush Ventures, Inc. [*Vancouver Stock Exchange symbol*]
ReyMt... Reynolds Metals Co. [*Associated Press*] (SAG)
ReyMtl... Reynolds Metals Co. [*Associated Press*] (SAG)
Reyn... Reynolds, Reports [*40-42 Mississippi*] [*A publication*] (DLA)
Reyn L Ins... Reynold's Life Insurance [*A publication*] (DLA)
Reynolds... Reynolds, Reports [*40-42 Mississippi*] [*A publication*] (DLA)
Reynolds' Land Laws... Reynolds' Spanish and Mexican Land Laws [*A publication*] (DLA)
ReyPrp... Revenue Properties Co. Ltd. [*Associated Press*] (SAG)
ReyRey... Reynolds & Reynolds Co. [*Associated Press*] (SAG)
REYRTWX... Reference Your Telegraph Wire Exchange [*Telecommunications*] (IAA)
REZ... Airplanes, Inc. [*ICAO designator*] (FAAC)
REZ... Mary Esther, FL [*Location identifier FAA*] (FAAL)
REZ... Radioelektronnaya Zashchita [*Radioelectronic Defense*] [*Soviet counterintelligence*] (LAIN)
RF... Fournier [*France ICAO aircraft manufacturer identifier*] (ICAO)
RF... Franc [*Monetary unit*] [*Rwanda*]
RF... RADAR Frequency (IAA)
RF... Radial Fibers [*Ear anatomy*]
RF... Radial Flow (AAG)
RF... Radical Force (EA)
RF... Radio Facility
RF... Radio France (IAA)
RF... Radio Frequency [*Transmission*]
rf... Radio Frequency (GAVI)
RF... Rainer Foundation [*British*] (BI)
RF... Rainfed [*Agriculture*]
RF... Rainform (MCD)

RF........ Raised Face (MSA)
RF........ Range-Finder [*Gunnery*]
RF........ Rapeseed Flour [*Food technology*]
RF........ Rapid-Fire
Rf........ Rate of Flow [*Medicine*] (MAE)
RF........ Rating Factor (IEEE)
RF........ Reactive Factor (IAA)
RF........ Read Forward
RF........ Reason Foundation (EA)
RF........ Reception Fair [*Radio logs*]
RF........ Receptive Field [*of visual cortex*]
RF........ Recombination Frequency [*Genetics*] (DOG)
RF........ Reconnaissance Fighter (MUGU)
RF........ Reconnaissance Force
RF........ Recovery Forces
RF........ Recovery Forecast
RF........ Recruitment for the Armed Forces [*British*]
RF........ Rectus Femoris [*A muscle*] [*Anatomy*]
RF........ Red Fumes (NATG)
RF........ Reducing Flame
RF........ Reef
RF........ Reference [*Online database field identifier*]
RF........ Reference Fuel
RF........ Reflight
RF........ Refunding
RF........ Regional Forces [*ARVN*]
RF........ Register File
RF........ Register Finder
RF........ Reitland-Franklin Unit (AAMN)
RF........ Relative Flow [*Rate*]
RF........ Relative Fluorescence [*Analytical chemistry*] (MAE)
Rf........ Relative to the Solvent Front [*Paper chromatography*] [*Analytical chemistry*]
RF........ Release Factor (NRCH)
RF........ Releasing Factor [*Also, RH*] [*Endocrinology*]
RF........ Reliability Factor
RF........ Renal Failure [*Medicine*]
RF........ Rent Free
RF........ Replacement Factor [*Military*]
RF........ Replicative Factor [*or Form*] [*Genetics*]
RF........ Reply Finding [*Nuclear energy*] (NRCH)
RF........ Reported Frequency (NTCM)
RF........ Reporting File
RF........ Representative Fraction
RF........ Republique Francaise [*French Republic*]
RF........ Reserve Flight [*British military*] (DMA)
RF........ Reserve Force
RF........ Resistance Factor
RF........ Resorcinol-Formaldehyde [*Organic chemistry*]
RF........ Respectable Frere [*Worshipful Brother*] [*Freemasonry*] [*French*] (ROG)
RF........ Respiratory Failure [*Medicine*]
RF........ Response Factor
RF........ Retardation Factor
RF........ Retention File [*IRS*]
RF........ Reticular Formation [*Sleep*]
RF........ Retroperitoneal Fibromatosis [*Oncology*]
RF........ Reverse Free
RF........ Revolving Fund [*Finance*]
RF........ Rex Francorum [*King of the Franks*] [*Latin*]
RF........ Rheumatic Fever [*Medicine*]
RF........ Rheumatoid Factor [*Also known as IgM*] [*Immunology*]
RF........ Rhinal Fissure [*Anatomy*]
RF........ Rhodesian Front [*Later, Republican Front*]
RF........ Riboflavin [*Biochemistry*]
RF........ Rice Flour (OA)
RF........ Richmond Fellowship (EAIO)
RF........ Rifampin [*Also, R/AMP, RIF, RMP*] [*Bactericide*]
RF........ Riffle Frequency
RF........ Rigging Fixtures (MCD)
RF........ Right Field [*or Fielder*] [*Baseball*]
RF........ Right Foot
RF........ Right Forward [*Football*]
RF........ Right Front
RF........ Right Fullback [*Soccer*]
RF........ Rigid Frame [*Revolver*] (DICI)
RF........ Rinforzando [*With Special Emphasis*] [*Music*]
RF........ Ring Frame
RF........ Ripple Factor
rf........ Rise of Floor (DS)
RF........ Rockefeller Foundation
RF........ Rodeo Foundation (EA)
RF........ Roll Film [*Photography*]
RF........ Roof (WGA)
rf........ Roof (VRA)
RF........ Roof Fan (OA)
RF........ Root Canal, Filing of [*Dentistry*] (DAVI)
RF........ Rosicrucian Fellowship (EA)
RF........ Rosicrucian Fraternity (EA)
RF........ Rossair [*ICAO designator*] (AD)
RF........ Rough Finish
RF........ Routes Forestieres [*Forested Routes*] [*French*] (BARN)
RF........ Royal Fusiliers [*Military unit*] [*British*]
RF........ Royal Windsor Foresters [*British military*] (DMA)
RF........ Ruled Feint [*Paper*] (DGA)
RF........ Running Forward
Rf........ Rutherfordium [*Proposed name for chemical element 104*] [*See also Ku*]
RF........ Sisters of St. Philip Neri Missionary Teachers [*Roman Catholic religious order*]
RF........ Travelair Goteborg [*ICAO designator*] (AD)
RF1........ Federal Reserve Bank of Boston, Boston, MA [*OCLC symbol*] (OCLC)
RFA........ Blackrock FL Inv Qual Muni [*AMEX symbol*] (TTSB)
RFA........ Blackrock Florida Investment Quality Municipal [*AMEX symbol*] (SPSG)
RFA........ RADAR Filter Assembly
RFA........ Radiation Field Analyzer
RFA........ Radio Frequency Allocation (MCD)
RFA........ Radio Frequency Amplifier
RFA........ Radio Frequency Attenuator (MCD)
RFA........ Radio Frequency Authorizations [*Air Force*]
RFA........ Rainforest Foundation Australia
RFA........ Raleigh Flying Service, Inc. [*ICAO designator*] (FAAC)
RFA........ Rapid Flow Analysis
RFA........ RCRA [*Resource Conservation and Recovery Act*] Facility Assessment
RFA........ Recommendation for Acceptance (AAG)
RFA........ Recurrent Fault Analysis [*Telecommunications*] (TEL)
RFA........ Regional Financial Associates Inc.
RFA........ Registered Fitness Appraiser [*Canadian Association of Sports Sciences*]
RFA........ Register Field Address (IAA)
RFA........ Regulatory Flexibility Act
RFA........ Regulatory Flexibility Analysis (AAGC)
RFA........ Relieved from Assigned [*Military*]
RFA........ Remote File Access
RFA........ Remote Function Activator
RFA........ Renewable Fuels Association (EA)
RFA........ Request for Action (KSC)
RFA........ Request for Alteration (AAG)
RFA........ Request for Analysis
RFA........ Request for Application
RFA........ Request for Assistance (GFGA)
RFA........ Request for Grant Applications
RFA........ Reserve Forces Act
RFA........ Resident Functional Atlas (DMAA)
RFA........ Restrictive Fire Area [*Military*] (AABC)
RFA........ Retarding Field Analyzer [*Surface analysis*]
RFA........ Right Femoral Artery [*Anatomy*]
RFA........ Right Forearm [*Medicine*] (MEDA)
RFA........ Right Frontoanterior [*A fetal position*] [*Obstetrics*]
RFA........ Rimfire Adapter (MCD)
RFA........ Risley Family Association (EA)
RFA........ Rocky Flats Area Office (SAA)
RFA........ Roll Follow-Up Amplifier
RFA........ Royal Field Artillery [*Military British*]
RFA........ Royal Fleet Auxiliary [*British*]
RFA........ Rugby Fives Association [*British*] (BI)
RFA........ Rural Forestry Assistance [*Program*] [*Forest Service*]
RFAA........ Relieved from Attached and Assigned [*Army*]
RFAC........ Royal Fine Art Commission [*British*]
R factor........ Resistance Factor (DOG)
RFAD........ Released from Active Duty Not Result of Demobilization [*Navy*]
RFAD........ Request for Accelerated Delivery (MCD)
RFAED........ Readiness Forecast Authorization Equipment Data [*Air Force*] (AFM)
RFAF........ Request for Additional Fire (MCD)
RF/AFG........ Radio Frequency/Acoustic Firing Group [*Military*] (CAAL)
RFAGC........ Rainbows for All God's Children (EA)
RFALROU........ Request Follow-Up Action on Listed Requisitions Indicated Still Outstanding in Unit [*Army*] (AABC)
RF & OOA........ Railway Fuel and Operating Officers Association [*Later, IAROO*] (EA)
RFAO........ Rocky Flats Area Office [*Energy Research and Development Administration*]
RFAS........ Radio Frequency Attitude Sensor
RFASIX........ Reserve Forces Act of 1955, Six Months Trainee
RFASS........ Rapid Fire Artillery Support System (MCD)
RFAT........ Relieved from Attached [*Army*] (AABC)
RFATE........ Radio Frequency Automatic Test Equipment (MCD)
RFATHREE........ Reserve Forces Act of 1955, Three Months Trainee
RFB........ Air-Cushion Vehicle built by Rhein Flugzeugbau [*Usually used in combinati on with numerals*] [*Germany*]
RFB........ Ready for Baseline (NASA)
RFB........ Reason for Backlog [*Telecommunications*] (TEL)
RFB........ Recording for the Blind (EA)
RFB........ Recording for the Blind, Bethesda, MD [*OCLC symbol*] (OCLC)
RFB........ Registrar of Finance Brokers [*Victoria, Australia*]
RFB........ Reliability Functional Block
RFB........ Request for Bid (AFM)
RFB........ Retained Foreign Body [*Medicine*]
RFB........ Right Fullback [*Soccer*]
RFBA........ Reserve Forces Benefit Association [*Later, REA*] (EA)
RFB&D........ Recording for the Blind and Dyslexic
RFBC........ River Forest Bancorp [*NASDAQ symbol*] (NQ)
RFBD........ Recording for the Blind and Dyslexic [*An association*] (PAZ)
RFBK........ RS Financial Corp. [*Formerly, Raleigh Federal Savings Bank*] [*NASDAQ symbol*] (NQ)
RFBPA........ Raw Fat and Bone Processors Association [*British*] (BI)
RFBR........ Russian Foundation for Basic Research

RFC Radio Facility Charts (MCD)
RFC Radio Frequency Chart (AAG)
RFC Radio Frequency Choke (AAG)
RFC Radio Frequency Coil (IAA)
RFC Radio Frequency Communications
RFC Radio Frequency Compatibility
RFC Radio Frequency Controller [*Telecommunications*] (ECII)
RFC Radio Frequency Crystal
RFC Railroad Freight Classification
RFC Ranger Fan Club (EA)
RFC Rare Fruit Council [*Later, RFCI*] (EA)
RFC Ravan Fan Club [*Defunct*] (EA)
RFC Reason for Change (MCD)
RFC Recirculation Flow Control [*Nuclear energy*] (NRCH)
RFC Reconstruction Finance Corp. [*Abolished, 1957*]
RFC Reduced Function Computer [*Computer science*]
RFC Reference Concentration [*Toxicology*]
RfC Reference Concentration
RFC Regenerative Fuel Cell
RFC Relative Force Capability (NATG)
RFC Religious Formation Conference (EA)
RFC Remote Food Carriers [*Army*] (INF)
RFC Republicans for Choice (EA)
RFC Request for Change (KSC)
RFC Request for Comment [*Telecommunications*] (PCM)
RFC Request for Confirmation (MCD)
RFC Request for Connection [*Telecommunications*] (OSI)
RFC Request for Contract (GFGA)
RFC Required Functional Capability [*Navy*]
RFC Research Facilities Center [*National Oceanic and Atmospheric Administration*] (GRD)
RFC Residual Functional Capacity [*Social Security Administration*] (OICC)
RFC Residuum Fluid Cracking [*Petroleum refining*]
RFC Resolution Funding Corp. [*Established by the Financial Institutions Reform, Recovery, and Enforcement Act of 1989*]
RFC Resources for Communication [*Information service or system*] (IID)
RFC Retirement-for-Cause [*Program*] [*Air Force*]
RFC Retrograde Femoral Catheter [*Medicine*] (DMAA)
RFC RFC Resource Finance Corp. [*Toronto Stock Exchange symbol*]
RFC RFC Resources Corp. [*Vancouver Stock Exchange symbol*]
RFC River Forecast Center [*National Weather Service*] (NOAA)
RFC Rosette-Forming Cell [*Immunochemistry*]
RFC Royal Flying Corps [*Later, RAF*] [*British*]
RFC Royal Flying Cross [*British*] (IIA)
RFC Rugby Football Club
RFCA Racing Fans Club of America (EA)
RFCA Rare Fruit Council of Australia
RFCA Reconstruction Finance Corporation Act [*Obsolete*]
RFCA Residual Functional Capacity Assessment [*Social Security Administration*] (GFGA)
RFCC Regional Freight Consolidation Center (AAGC)
RFCC Resid Fluid Catalytic Cracking [*Petroleum refining*]
RFCEA Revival Fires (Christian Evangelizers Association) (EA)
RFCG Radio Frequency Command Generator (MCD)
RFCI Rare Fruit Council International (EA)
RFCI Resilient Floor Covering Institute (EA)
RFCM Radio Frequency Control Monitor [*Formerly, RFU*] (MCD)
RFCMC Reconstruction Finance Corporation Mortgage Co.
RFCO Radio Facility Control Officer [*Military*] (IAA)
RFCO Radio Frequency Checkout (AAG)
RFCO Range Facility Control Officer [*Military*] (IAA)
RFCP Radio Frequency Compatibility Program
RFCP Request for Computer Program (NASA)
RFCP Requests for Contractual Procurement (MUGU)
RFCR Refacer
RFCS Radio Frequency Carrier Shift (NVT)
RFCS Recirculation Flow Control System [*Nuclear energy*] (NRCH)
RFCS Regenerative Fuel Cell Subsystem
RFCSEUSG Retirement Federation of Civil Service Employees of the United States Government [*Defunct*] (EA)
RFCT Report of Federal Cash Transactions (OICC)
RFCV Rural Finance Council of Victoria [*Australia*]
RFD Radiation Flux Density
RFD Radio Frequency Demodulator
RFD Radio Frequency Display (MCD)
RFD Raised Face Diameter (MSA)
RFD Raised Foredeck [*of a ship*] (DS)
RFD Reactor Flight Demonstration
RFD Read for Data (IAA)
RFD Ready for Data (IEEE)
RFD Ready for Delivery (MUGU)
RFD Ready for Duty
RFD Reentry Flight Demonstration
RfD Reference Dose [*Environmental science*]
RFD Refund (WDAA)
RFD Refurbish for Delivery (MCD)
RFD Released for Delivery (NG)
RFD Remote Frequency Display (MCD)
RFD Reporting for Duty [*Air Force*]
RFD Request for Delivery
RFD Request for Deviation
RFD Request for Discussion [*Electronic newsgroups*]
RFD Request for Parts Disposition (MCD)
RFD Requirements Formulation Document [*NASA*] (NASA)
RFD Reserve Forces Duty [*Military*] (MCD)
RFD Residual Flux Density
RFD Reverse-Flow Diverter [*Engineering*]
RFD Rockford [*Illinois*] [*Airport symbol*] (OAG)
RFD Rockford Minerals, Inc. [*Toronto Stock Exchange symbol*]
RFD Rural Free Delivery [*of mail*]
RFDA Request for Deviation Approval
RFDB Red Flag Database [*Air Force*] (GFGA)
RFDL Radio Frequency Data Link (MCD)
RFDT Reliability Failure Diagnostic Team (AAG)
RFDU Reconfiguration and Fault Detection Unit
RFE Aero Fe SA [*Mexico ICAO designator*] (FAAC)
RFE Radio Free Europe
RFE Request for Effectivity (MCD)
RFE Request for Enhancement [*Computer science*] (NHD)
RFE Request for Estimate (KSC)
RFE Request for Expenditure
RFE Rotating Field Electrophoresis [*Analytical biochemistry*]
RFE Rutherfordton, NC [*Location identifier FAA*] (FAAL)
RFEA Radio Frequency Equipment Analyzer
RFEA Regional Further Education Adviser (AIE)
RFEA Regular Forces Employment Association [*British military*] (DMA)
RFECM Revised for Engineering Change Memorandum (SAA)
RFED Radio Frequency Expandable Decoy (DWSG)
RFED Research Facilities and Equipment Division [*NASA*] (MCD)
RFED Roosevelt Financial Group, Inc. [*NASDAQ symbol*] (NQ)
RFED Roosevelt Finl [*NASDAQ symbol*] (TTSB)
RFEDP Roosevelt Finl 6.5% Cv 'B' Pfd [*NASDAQ symbol*] (TTSB)
RFEHB Retired Federal Employees Health Benefits Program (MCD)
RFEI Request for Engineering Information (KSC)
RF/EMI Radio Frequency and Electromagnetic-Interference [*Telecommunications*]
RFEP Reserve Female Enlistment Program [*Military*] (DNAB)
RFER Reefer [*Military*] (DNAB)
RFE/RL Radio Free Europe/Radio Liberty (EA)
RFETS Rocky Flats Environmental Technology Site (DOGT)
RFETS Rocky Flats Environmental Technology Site [*Golden, CO*] (GAAI)
RFETS Rocky Flats Environmental Technology Site
RFETS Rocky Flats Environmental Technology Site
RFF Radio Frequency Filter
RFF Radio Frequency Finder (NVT)
RFF Radio Frequency Fuze
RFF Random Force Field
RFF Ready for Ferry [*Navy*] (NVT)
RFF Recirculative Fluid Flow
RFF REFF, Inc. [*Toronto Stock Exchange symbol*]
RFF Refuge from Flood (ADA)
RFF Regular Federal Funds [*Medicaid*] (GFGA)
RFF Relative Failure Frequency
RFF Relative Fluorescence Efficiency (DMAA)
RFF Relief from Face to Face [*Education*]
RFF Remote Fiber Fluorometer [*Instrumentation*]
RFF Request for Fire [*Military*]
RFF Request for Form
RFF Research Flight Facility [*Air Force*]
RFF Resources for the Future
RFF Rift-Fracture-Fracture [*Geology*]
RFF Royal Filling Factory [*British military*] (DMA)
RFFC Randy Floyd Fan Club (EA)
RFFD Radio Frequency Fault Detection
RFFIT Rapid Fluorescent Focus Inhibition Test [*Medicine*] (MEDA)
RFFO Request for Factory Order (MCD)
RFFS River and Flood Forecasting Service (NADA)
RFFSA Rede Ferroviaria Federal Sociedade Anonima [*Federal Railway Corporation*] [*Brazil*] (EY)
RFFT Right Front Fluid Temperature [*Automotive engineering*]
RFG RADAR Field Gradient (IEEE)
RFG Radio Frequency Generator
RFG Ramp Function Generator (IAA)
RFG Rapid-Fire Gun
RFG Rate and Free Gyro
RFG Receive Format Generator
RFG Reformulated Gasoline
RFG Refugio, TX [*Location identifier FAA*] (FAAL)
RFG Refunding [*Business term*]
RFG Register Finder Grid (IAA)
RFG Reise und Industrieflug [*Airline*] [*Germany*]
RFG Report Format Generator
RFG Rhodesian Financial Gazette [*A publication*]
RFG Rifle Fine Grain [*British military*] (DMA)
RFG Roofing (AAG)
RFG Royscot Finance Group [*Royal Bank of Scotland*]
RFGC Royal Fremantle Golf Club [*Australia*]
RFGD Radio-Frequency Glow Discharge [*Materials science*]
RFGN Refrigeration [*Charges*]
RFGT Refrigerant (MSA)
RFH Radio Frequency Head (IAA)
RFH Radio Frequency Heating
RFH Raised Face Height (MSA)
RFH Reichsfinanzhof [*Reich Finance Court*] [*German*] (ILCA)
RFH Right Femoral Hernia [*Medicine*] (DMAA)
RFH Rio Mayo [*Argentina*] [*Airport symbol*] (AD)
RFH Roof Hatch [*Technical drawings*]
RFH Royal Festival Hall [*London*]
RFH Royal Free Hospital (ROG)
RFHCO Rocket Fuel Handler Clothing Outfit [*Protective suit*]

RFHI .... Real Fire Heating International Exhibition [*British*] (ITD)
RFHT .... Radio Frequency Horn Technique
RFI .... Cohen & Steers Total Return Rt. Realty Fund [*NYSE symbol*] (SPSG)
RFI .... Cohen & Steers Total Rt Rty Fd [*NYSE symbol*] (TTSB)
RFI .... RADAR Frequency Interferometer (MCD)
RFI .... Radio Frequency Indicator
RFI .... Radio Frequency Induction [*Of plasmas*]
RFI .... Radio Frequency Interchange (MDG)
RFI .... Radio Frequency Interface (MCD)
RFI .... Radio Frequency Interference
RFI .... Rajneesh Foundation International (EA)
RFI .... RCRA [*Resource Conservation and Recovery Act*] Facility Investigation
RFI .... Ready for Installation (MCD)
RFI .... Ready for Issue [*Military*]
RFI .... Relative Fluorescent Intensity [*Analytical chemistry*]
RFI .... Release for Issue (MCD)
RFI .... Remedial Field Investigation (GNE)
RFI .... Remote Facility Inquiry [*NASA*] (KSC)
RFI .... Remote File Inquiry [*NASA*] (NASA)
RFI .... Report/File Language (HGAA)
RFI .... Representative of a Foreign Interest
RFI .... Requested for Information
RFI .... Request for Information
RFI .... Request for Inspection (IAA)
RFI .... Request for Investigation
RFI .... Request for Issue
RFI .... Retail Floorcovering Institute [*Later, AFA*] (EA)
RFI .... Richmond Fellowship International [*British*] (EAIO)
RFIC .... Radio Frequency Integrated Circuit
RFIC .... Radio Frequency Integrated Circuit
RFID .... Radio Frequency Identification
RFID .... Radio Frequency Identification
RFID .... Request for Implementation Date
RFIF .... Refund Information File [*IRS*]
RFIFO .... Receive, First-In, First-Out [*Communications engineering*]
RFIM .... Radio Frequency Interference Meter
RFIP .... Radio Frequency Impedance Probe
RF/IR .... RADAR Frequency/Infrared Frequency (IEEE)
RFIT .... Radio Frequency Interference Tests (KSC)
RFJ .... Radio Frequency Joint
RFJI .... Research Foundation for Jewish Immigration (EA)
RFK .... Anguilla, MS [*Location identifier FAA*] (FAAL)
RFK .... Radio Free Kabul [*British Defunct*] (EAIO)
RFK .... Robert Francis Kennedy [*American politician, 1925-68*]
RFKM .... Robert F. Kennedy Memorial (EA)
RFL .... Radio Frequency Laboratories
RFL .... Radio Frequency Lens
RFL .... Radio-Frequency LINAC (SDI)
RFL .... Reduced Focal Length
RFL .... Reflect (NASA)
RFL .... Reflector [*or Reflected*]
RFL .... Refuel (AAG)
RFL .... Requested Flight Level
RFL .... Reset Flux Level
RFL .... Resorcinol-Formaldehyde-Latex
RFL .... Restrictive Fire Line [*Military*] (AABC)
Rfl .... Rifle (DOMA)
RFL .... Right Frontolateral [*Anatomy*] (AAMN)
RFL .... Rotating Field Logic (IAA)
RFL .... Rough Field Landing
RFL .... Rugby Football League [*British*] (DBA)
RFLA .... Rheumatoid Factor-Like Activity [*Immunology*] (MAE)
RFLD .... Radio Frequency Leakage Detector
RFLG .... Refuelling (DA)
RFLMN .... Rifleman (AABC)
RFLP .... Restriction Fragment Length Polymorphism [*Genetics*]
R/FLR .... Rear Floor [*Automotive engineering*]
RFLS .... Rheumatoid Factor-Like Substance [*Immunology*] (MAE)
RFLT .... Right Front Lining Temperature [*Automotive engineering*]
RFLX .... Reflex (MSA)
RFM .... Radio Frequency Management (NOAA)
RFM .... Radio Frequency Monitoring [*Military*] (CAAL)
RFM .... Reactive Factor Meter
RFM .... Red Fox Minerals [*Vancouver Stock Exchange symbol*]
RFM .... Refueling Mission [*Air Force*]
RFM .... Release for Manufacture (DNAB)
RFM .... Reliability Figure of Merit (IAA)
RFM .... Reliable Flow Manager [*Computer science*]
RFM .... Reserve Forces Modernization (MCD)
RF M .... RF Management Corp. [*Associated Press*] (SAG)
RFM .... Roll Follow-Up Motor
RFM .... Roll Forming Machine
RFM .... Runway Friction Measurement [*Aviation*]
RFM .... Rural Financial Market
RFMA .... Reliability Figure of Merit Analysis
RFMC .... Regional Fishery Management Council [*National Oceanic and Atmospheric Administration*] (MSC)
RFMC .... RF Management [*NASDAQ symbol*] (TTSB)
RFMC .... RF Management Corp. [*NASDAQ symbol*] (SAG)
RFMCW .... R.F. Management Wrrt'A' [*NASDAQ symbol*] (TTSB)
RFMCZ .... R.F. Management Wrrt'B' [*NASDAQ symbol*] (TTSB)
RF Mgt .... RF Management Corp. [*Associated Press*] (SAG)
RFMI .... RF Monolithics [*NASDAQ symbol*] (TTSB)
RFMI .... RF Monolithics, Inc. [*NASDAQ symbol*] (SAG)
RFMO .... Radio Frequency Management Office (MCD)
RF Mono .... RF Monolithics, Inc. [*Associated Press*] (SAG)
RFMP .... Restriction-Fragment Melting Polymorphism [*Genetics*]
RFMS .... Remote File Management System
RFMT .... Runway Friction Measurement Test [*Aviation*]
RFMVR .... Recency-Frequency-Monetary Value Ratio (NTCM)
RFN .... Radio Frequency Noise
RFN .... Raufarhofn [*Iceland*] [*Airport symbol*] (OAG)
RFN .... Registered Fever Nurse
RFN .... Remote Filter Niche [*Nuclear energy*] (NRCH)
RFN .... Rifleman
RFNA .... Radio Frequency Noise Analyzer (DNAB)
RFNA .... Red Fuming Nitric Acid
RFNCC .... Regional Nuclear Fuel Cycle Centers
RFND .... Refined (MSA)
RFNG .... Refining
RFNG .... Roofing
RFNM .... Ready for Next Message
RFNRE .... Revolving Fund for Natural Resources Exploration [*United Nations*] (EY)
RFNRY .... Refinery
RFO .... Air Royal [*France ICAO designator*] (FAAC)
RFO .... Radio Frequency Oscillator
RFO .... Ready for Occupancy (MCD)
RFO .... Reconciling with Accounting and Finance Officer (AAGC)
RFO .... Regional Field Officer [*Civil Defense*]
RFO .... Request for Factory Order (MCD)
RFO .... Request for Orders [*Military*]
RFO .... Research Fiscal Office (SAA)
RFO .... Retrofire Officer [*NASA*] (KSC)
RFO .... Roll Follow-Up Operation
RFOA .... Reasonable Factors Other than Age [*Equal Employment Opportunity Commission*]
RFOB .... Rear Face of Block [*Automotive engineering*]
RFOFM .... Records for Our Fighting Men [*Collected phonograph records during World War II*]
RFOG .... Resonant Fiber Optic Gyroscope
RFOL .... Results to Follow (DAVI)
RFOP .... Regional Financial Operating Plan
RFP .... Radio Finger Printing [*Identification of wireless radio operators by individual keying characteristics*]
RFP .... Radio Free People [*An association Defunct*]
RFP .... Radio Frequency Plasma
RFP .... Radio Frequency Pulse (MCD)
RFP .... Raiatea [*French Polynesia*] [*Airport symbol*] (OAG)
RFP .... Rapid Filling Period [*Cardiology*]
RFP .... Reactor Feed Pump [*Nuclear energy*] (NRCH)
RFP .... Registered Financial Planner [*International Association of Registered Fin ancial Planners*] [*Designation awarded by*]
RFP .... Relative Frass Production [*Ecology*]
RFP .... Remaining Force Potential (MCD)
RFP .... Replication Fork Pause [*Genetics*]
RFP .... Reproductive Freedom Project [*ACLU*] [*Attempts to enforce the Supreme Court decisions guaranteeing a woman's right to choose abortion*] (EA)
RFP .... Republicans for Progress [*Defunct*]
RFP .... Request for Price Quotation
RFP .... Request for Programming [*Computer science*]
RFP .... Request for Proposal
RFP .... Request for Purchase
RFP .... Requirements and Formulation Phase (MCD)
RFP .... Requirements for Production [*Army*] (RDA)
RFP .... Requisition for Procurement [*DoD*]
RFP .... Retired on Full Pay [*Military British*]
RFP .... Reversed Field Pinch [*Plasma physics*] (NRCH)
RFP .... RF Power Products [*AMEX symbol*] (SAG)
RFP .... Richmond, Fredericksburg & Potomac Railroad Co. [*AAR code*]
RFP .... Right Frontoposterior [*A fetal position*] [*Obstetrics*]
RFPA .... Request for Part Approval (MCD)
RFPA .... Request for Proposal Authorization [*NASA*] (NASA)
RFPA .... Right to Financial Privacy Act
RFPB .... Reserve Forces Policy Board [*DoD*]
RFPC .... Reserve Flag Officer Policy Council [*Navy*]
RF/PF .... Regional Forces - Popular Forces [*Republic of Vietnam*] [*Army*]
RFPI .... Rapid Force Projection Initiative
RFPI .... Registered Financial Planners Institute (EA)
RFPI .... Request for Proposal Information [*Competitive bidding*]
RFPI/EFOGM .... Rapid Force Projection Initiative / Enhanced Fiber Optic Guided Missile [*Army*] (INF)
RF Pow .... RF Power Products [*Associated Press*] (SAG)
RFPP .... Radio Frequency Propagation Program (NG)
RFPR .... Radiant Flash Pyrolysis Reactor [*Chemical engineering*]
RFPR .... Reversed-Field Pinch Reactor [*Plasma physics*] (PDAA)
RFPRS .... Retail Food Price-Reporting System
RFPS .... Request for Proposal Supplement (DNAB)
RFPS .... Royal Faculty of Physicians and Surgeons of Glasgow
RFPT .... Reactor Feed Pump Turbine [*Nuclear energy*] (NRCH)
RFQ .... Radio-Frequency Quadrupole [*Accelerator for subatomic physics study*]
RFQ .... Rapid Freeze Quench
RFQ .... Request for Qualifications (OICC)
RFQ .... Request for Quotation
RFR .... Radial Flow Reactor [*Chemical engineering*]
RFR .... Radio Frequency Receiver

RFR ..... Radio Frequency Relay
RFR ..... Rear Engine, Front and Rear Drive [*Automotive design*]
RFR ..... Redfern Resources [*Vancouver Stock Exchange symbol*]
RFR ..... Reduced Frequency Response [*Telecommunications*] (OA)
RFR ..... Refraction (AAMN)
RFR ..... Reject Failure Rate
RFR ..... Required Freight Rate (DS)
RFR ..... Rio Frio [*Costa Rica*] [*Airport symbol*] (OAG)
RFR ..... Roofer (WGA)
RFR ..... Royal Air Force [*British ICAO designator*] (FAAC)
RFR ..... Royal Fleet Reserve [*British*]
RFR ..... Sisters of Our Lady of Refuge (TOCD)
RFRA ..... Religious Freedom Restoration Act
RFRC ..... Refractory (MSA)
rfrd ..... Referred (BARN)
RFRG ..... Refrigerator
RFRJ ..... Radio Frequency Rotary Joint
RFRSH ..... Refresh [*Computer graphics*]
RFS ..... Radio Frequency Seal
RFS ..... Radio-Frequency Shift (IEEE)
RFS ..... Radio Frequency Subsystem [*NASA*]
RFS ..... Raman Forward-Scattering [*Physics*]
RFS ..... Random Filing System
RFS ..... Range Frequency Synthesizer
RFS ..... Rapid Frozen Section [*Pathology and surgery*] (DAVI)
RFS ..... Ready for Sea [*Navy*]
RFS ..... Ready for Sending [*Computer science*] (IAA)
RFS ..... Ready for Service
RFS ..... Reduced Friction Strut [*Suspension system*] [*Automotive engineering*]
RFS ..... Regardless of Feature Size [*Manufacturing term*]
RFS ..... Regional Field Specialist [*Civil Defense*]
RFS ..... Regional Frequency Supplies [*Telecommunications*] (TEL)
RFS ..... Registry of Friendly Societies [*British*] (ILCA)
RFS ..... Relapse-Free Survival [*Oncology*]
RFS ..... Religion and Family Life Section (EA)
RFS ..... Remote Fiber Spectroscopy
RFS ..... Remote File Service [*or System*] [*Computer science*] (PCM)
RFS ..... Remote File Sharing [*Computer science*]
RFS ..... Renal Function Studies [*Medicine*]
RFS ..... Render, Float, and Set [*Construction*]
RFS ..... Request for Services [*Social Security Administration*]
RFS ..... Request for Shipment (MCD)
RFS ..... Resources Forecasting System
RFS ..... Response Feedback System [*NASA*]
RFS ..... R. F. Scientific, Inc. [*Telecommunications service*] (TSSD)
RFS ..... RFS Hotel Investors, Inc. [*NYSE symbol*] (SAG)
RFS ..... Roll Follow-Up System
RFS ..... Rossair Pty Ltd. [*Australia ICAO designator*] (FAAC)
RFS ..... Rossendorfer Forschungs-Reaktor [*Rossendorf Research Reactor*] [*German*]
RFS ..... Rotational Flight Simulator [*Air Force*]
RFS ..... Rover Flight Safety
RFS ..... Royal Forestry Society of England [*British*]
RFS ..... Rural Fire Service [*Australia*]
RFSAT ..... Radio Frequency Saturation (IAA)
RFSB ..... Regional Forward Scatter Branch [*Supreme Allied Commander, Europe*] (NATG)
RFSE ..... Radio Frequency Shielded Enclosure
RFS/ECM ..... Radio Frequency Surveillance/Electronic Countermeasures (MCD)
RFSH ..... Recombinant Follicle-Stimulating Hormone [*Endocrinology*]
RFSH ..... Refresh [*Computer graphics*]
RFS Htl ..... RFS Hotel Investors, Inc. [*Associated Press*] (SAG)
RFSI ..... RFS Hotel Investors [*NASDAQ symbol*] (TTSB)
RFSI ..... RFS Hotel Investors, Inc. [*NASDAQ symbol*] (SAG)
RFS/ISE ..... Ready for Sea/Individual Ship Exercise (MCD)
RFSM ..... Radio Frequency Spectrum Management (LAIN)
RFSMS ..... Radio Frequency Signal Management System [*Aviation*] (GFGA)
RFSP ..... Radioactive Fallout Study Program [*Canada*]
RFSP ..... Replacement Flight Strip Printer [*Aviation*] (DA)
RFSP ..... Request for System Proposal (MHDI)
RFSP ..... Rigid Frame Selection Program
RFSS ..... Radio Frequency Simulation System (MCD)
RFSS ..... Radio Frequency Surveillance Subsystem
RFSS ..... Reliability Failure Summary Support (SAA)
RFST ..... Rapid Frequency Settling Time (IAA)
RFST ..... Research Foundation for the Study of Terrorism [*British*]
RFSTF ..... Radio Frequency Systems Test Facility (KSC)
RFSU ..... Rugby Football Schools Union [*British*]
RFT ..... Radio Frequency Transformer (IAA)
RFT ..... Rapid Fermentation Technique
RFT ..... Ready for Training [*Military*]
RFT ..... Ready for Typesetter [*Publishing*]
RFT ..... Real Fourier Transform
RFT ..... Recursive Function Theory (IAA)
RFT ..... Reflectance, Fluorescence, Transmittance [*Densitometer*] [*Instrumentation*]
RFT ..... Refresher Training [*Navy*] (NVT)
RFT ..... Regge Field Theory [*Particle Physics*]
RFT ..... Regional Film Theatre [*British*]
RFT ..... Reinforcement
RFT ..... Repeat Formation Tester [*Well drilling*]
RFT ..... Request for Technology (DOM)
RFT ..... Request for Tender (ADA)
RFT ..... Respirator Fit Test [*Environmental science*] (FFDE)
RFT ..... Revisable Form Text [*Computer science*] (PCM)
RFT ..... Right Frontotransverse [*A fetal position*] [*Obstetrics*]
RFT ..... Rod-and-Frame Test (MAE)
RFT ..... Rotary Feed-Through
RFTA ..... Regional Fuel Tax Agreement [*FHWA*] (TAG)
RFTC ..... Radio Frequency Test Console
RFTD ..... Radial Flow Torr Deposition System (IEEE)
RFT:DCA ..... Revisable Form Text: Document Content Architecture [*IBM Corp.*] [*Computer science*]
RFTDS ..... RADAR Frequency Target Discrimination System (MCD)
RFTF ..... Radio Frequency Test Facility [*Oak Ridge National Laboratory*]
RFTF ..... Retail Fruit Trade Federation [*British*] (DBA)
RF-TK ..... Radio Frequency Tracking [*Military*] (MCD)
RFTL ..... Radio Frequency Transmission Line
RFTM ..... Radiator Fan Timer Module [*Cooling systems*] [*Automotive engineering*]
RFTN ..... Reflectone, Inc. [*NASDAQ symbol*] (NQ)
RFTO ..... Ready for Takeoff [*Aviation*]
RFTOI ..... Request for Test or Inspection (MCD)
RFTP ..... Request for Technical Proposal
RFTS ..... Radio Frequency Test Set (AABC)
RFTS ..... Request for Technical Samples (AAGC)
RFTS ..... Return Free Tax System [*Internal Revenue Service*] (GFGA)
RFTW ..... Ready for the World [*Rhythm and Blues recording group*]
RFTY ..... Reformatory (AABC)
RFU ..... Radio Frequency Unit [*Later, RFCM*] (MCD)
RFU ..... Ready-for-Use (NG)
RFU ..... Reference Frequency Unit [*Telecommunications*] (OA)
RFU ..... Reliability Field Unit
RFU ..... Remote Firing Unit (MCD)
RFU ..... Returns File Unit [*IRS*]
RFU ..... Rugby Football Union [*British*]
RFUA ..... Roll Follow-Up Amplifier
RFUDL ..... Radio Frequency Update Link
RFUM ..... Roll Follow-Up Motor
RFUO ..... Roll Follow-Up Operation
RFUS ..... Reversible Follow-Up System
RFUS ..... Roll Follow-Up System
RFV ..... RADAR Film Viewer
RFV ..... Radial Force Variation [*Automotive tire testing*]
RFV ..... Ragado Fino Virus
RFV ..... Regressing Friend Virus
RFV ..... Resonant Frequency Vibration
RFV ..... Right Femoral Vein [*Anatomy*] (DAVI)
RFVC ..... Radial Four-Valve Combustion [*Automotive engineering*]
RFVC ..... Reason for Visit Classification [*Medicine*] (DHSM)
R-FVII ..... Reading Free Vocational Interest Inventory [*Vocational guidance test*]
RFVM ..... Radio Frequency Voltmeter
RFW ..... Radio Free Women [*Defunct*] (EA)
RFW ..... Radio Frequency Wave
RFW ..... Rapid Filling Wave [*Cardiology*]
RFW ..... Reactor Feedwater [*Nuclear energy*] (NRCH)
RFW ..... Refrigerated Fresh Water Medium [*Microbiology*]
RFW ..... Request for Waiver (MCD)
RFW ..... Reserve Feed Water [*Technical drawings*]
RFW ..... Reversible Full Wave
RFW ..... Robinhood [*Queensland*] [*Airport symbol*] (AD)
RFWAC ..... Reversible Full-Wave Alternating Current
RFWAR ..... Requirements for Work and Resources (MUGU)
RFWCHS ..... Royal Far West Children's Homes Scheme [*Australia*]
RFWDC ..... Reversible Full-Wave Direct Current
RFWF ..... Radio Frequency Wave Form
RFX ..... East Hartford, CT [*Location identifier FAA*] (FAAL)
RFX ..... J.P. Hunt, Inc. [*FAA designator*] (FAAC)
RFX ..... Reversed Field Experiment [*Nuclear energy*] (NRCH)
RFX ..... Roxborough [*Queensland*] [*Airport symbol*] (AD)
RFYC ..... Royal Forth Yacht Club [*British*] (DBA)
RFZ ..... Restrictive Fire Zone [*Military*]
RFZ ..... Rinforzando [*With Special Emphasis*] [*Music*]
R_G ..... Gate Resistance (IDOE)
R_g ..... Grid Resistance (IDOE)
RG ..... RADAR Guidance (IAA)
RG ..... Radial Glial Guide [*Neurology*]
R/G ..... Radiation Guidance (MUGU)
RG ..... Radio Direction Finding Station [*ITU designation*] (CET)
RG ..... Radio Frequency Cables; Bulk [*JETDS nomenclature*] [*Military*] (CET)
RG ..... Radiogram (DEN)
RG ..... Radio Guidance (AAG)
RG ..... Radio Guide (IAA)
R-G ..... Radiologist-General
RG ..... Range (AAG)
RG ..... Ranging Gun [*British military*] (DMA)
RG ..... Rate [*Loop*] Gain
RG ..... Rate Grown
RG ..... Rate Gyroscope (KSC)
RG ..... Readiness Group [*Military*] (AABC)
RG ..... Reading [*Postcode*] (ODBW)
RG ..... Reagent Grade
RG ..... Real Gas
R/G ..... Rear Gunner [*British military*] (DMA)
RG ..... Rebuilding Grade [*Automotive engineering*] [*Polymer Steel Corp.*]
RG ..... Reception Good [*Radio logs*]
RG ..... Rechtsgeschichte [*German*] (ILCA)
RG ..... Recording (IAA)

RG .... Rectangular Guide (DEN)
R/G .... Red and Gold (Edges) [*Bookbinding*] (ROG)
RG .... Red-Green
RG .... Reduction Gear [*or Gearbox*] (NG)
RG .... Register (CET)
RG .... Regula Generalis [*General Rule or Order of Court*] [*Latin A publication*] (DLA)
RG .... Regulated Gallery [*Nuclear energy*] (NRCH)
RG .... Regulatory Guide [*Nuclear energy*] (NRCH)
RG .... Regummed [*Philately*]
RG .... Reichsgericht [*Reich Supreme Court*] [*German*] (ILCA)
RG .... Release Guard [*Telecommunications*] (TEL)
RG .... Remak's Ganglion [*Neurology*]
RG .... Remedial Gymnast [*British*]
RG .... Renabie Gold Trust [*Formerly, Barrick-Cullation Gold Trust*] [*Toronto Stock Exchange symbol*]
RG .... Report Generator (CMD)
RG .... Report Guide
RG .... Report Program Generator [*Programming language*] [*1962*] (IAA)
RG .... Reserve Grade [*Military*]
RG .... Reset Gate
RG .... Resettlement Grants [*British World War II*]
RG .... Resolving Gel [*Biochemistry*]
RG .... Reticle Generator
RG .... Reticulated Grating (AAG)
RG .... Retrograde (DAVI)
RG .... Reverse Gate
RG .... Revolutionary Government [*Vietnam*]
RG .... Right Gluteus [*Anatomy*]
RG .... Right Guard [*Football*]
RG .... Right Gun
RG .... Ringing Generator [*Telecommunications*] (TEL)
RG .... Robert Graham [*Designer's mark on US 1984 $1 Olympic commemorative coin*]
Rg .... Rodgers Antibodies [*Medicine*] (BABM)
Rg .... Rodgers Antibodies [*Immunology*] (DAVI)
RG .... Rogers CommunCl'B' [*NYSE symbol*] (TTSB)
RG .... Rogers Communications, Inc. [*NYSE symbol*] (SAG)
RG .... Rogers Group (EA)
RG .... Rogue's Gallery [*Defunct*] (EA)
RG .... Rolled Gold
RG .... Rueckgang [*Return*] [*Music*]
RG .... Varig Brazilian [*Airline flight code*] (ODBW)
RG .... VEB Fahlberg-List [*East Germany*] [*Research code symbol*]
RGA .... Range-Gemini to Agena (SAA)
RGA .... Rate Gyro Assembly
RGA .... Reduction Gearbox Assembly (DNAB)
RGA .... Regal Petroleum Ltd. [*Vancouver Stock Exchange symbol*]
RGA .... Region Air [*Seychelles*] [*ICAO designator*] (FAAC)
RGA .... Reinsurance Group of Amer [*NYSE symbol*] (TTSB)
RGA .... Reinsurance Group of America, Inc. [*NYSE symbol*] (SPSG)
RGA .... Relative Gain Array [*Control engineering*]
RGA .... Remote Gain Amplifier (IAA)
RGA .... Republican Governors Association (EA)
RGA .... Request for Graphic Arts Service
RGA .... Residual Gas Analyzer
RGA .... Ring Guild of America [*Defunct*] (EA)
RGA .... Rio Grande [*Argentina*] [*Airport symbol*] (OAG)
RGA .... Routing Accumulator (IAA)
RGA .... Royal Garrison Artillery [*British*]
RGA .... Royal Guernsey Artillery [*British military*] (DMA)
RGA .... Rubber Growers' Association [*Later, TGA*] (EAIO)
RGAA .... Radiochemical Gamma Activation Analysis
RGAL .... Rate Gyro Assembly - Left Solid Rocket Booster (MCD)
RGAL .... Reference Guide to American Literature [*A publication*]
RGAO .... Rate Gyro Assembly - Orbiter (MCD)
RGAP .... Rate Gyro Accelerometer Package (MCD)
RGAR .... Rate Gyro Assembly - Right Solid Rocket Booster (MCD)
RGAS .... Retained Gastric Antrum Syndrome [*Medicine*] (DAVI)
RGB .... Barry (R.G.) [*NYSE symbol*] (TTSB)
RGB .... Barry RG Corp. [*NYSE symbol*] (SAG)
RGB .... Barry (R.G.) Corp. [*NYSE symbol*] (SAG)
RGB .... Red-Giant Branch [*Stellar physics*]
RGB .... Red Green Blue [*Video monitor*]
RGB .... Refractory Grade Bauxite [*Geology*]
RGB .... River Gunboat
RGB Cpt .... RGB Computer & Video [*Commercial firm Associated Press*] (SAG)
RGBI .... Red Green Blue Intensity [*Video monitor*]
RGBK .... Regions Financial [*NASDAQ symbol*] (TTSB)
RGBK .... Regions Financial Corp. [*NASDAQ symbol*] (SAG)
RGB-MB .... Resistencia da Guine-Bissau Movimento Bafata [*Political party*] (EY)
RGB monitor ... Red, Green, Blue Monitor
RGBY .... Red, Green, Blue, Yellow [*Video monitor*] (IAA)
RGC .... Radio-Gas Chromatography
RGC .... Rangely [*Colorado*] [*Seismograph station code, US Geological Survey*] (SEIS)
RGC .... Reconstructed Gas Chromatogram
RGC .... Reference Gas Cell [*Instrumentation*]
RGC .... Reigate Resources (Canada) Ltd. [*Toronto Stock Exchange symbol*]
RGC .... Repair Group Category [*Military*] (AFIT)
RGC .... Repository for Germinal Choice [*A sperm bank*]
RGC .... Republic Group [*NYSE symbol*] (TTSB)
RGC .... Republic Gypsum Co. [*NYSE symbol*] (SPSG)
RGC .... Retinal Ganglion Cell [*Neurochemistry*]
RGC .... Ribosomal Gene Cluster [*Genetics*]
RGC .... Rio Grande College [*Ohio*]
RGC .... Rio Grande College, Rio Grande, OH [*OCLC symbol*] (OCLC)
RGC .... Royal Greenwich Conservatory [*British*]
RGC .... Rural Governments Coalition [*Defunct*] (EA)
RGCAS .... Remote Global Computer Access Service (MHDB)
RGCO .... Roanoke Gas [*NASDAQ symbol*] (TTSB)
RGCO .... Roanoke Gas Co. [*NASDAQ symbol*] (SAG)
RGCR .... Renner's Gold Coast Colony Reports [*1868-1914*] [*Ghana*] [*A publication*] (DLA)
RGCSP .... Review of General Concepts of Separation Panel [*FAA*] (TAG)
Rgcy .... Regency (VRA)
RgcyRlt .... Regency Realty Corp. [*Associated Press*] (SAG)
RGD .... Radiation Gasdynamics (PDAA)
RGD .... Ragged [*NWS*] (FAAC)
RGD .... Range Gate Deception [*Military*] (LAIN)
RGD .... Rarefied Gas Dynamics
RGD .... Reduction Gas Detector [*Instrumentation*]
RGD .... Regis Development Corp. [*Vancouver Stock Exchange symbol*]
RGD .... Regular Geophysical Day
RGD .... Report and Graph Designer Module [*Solomon Software*] [*Computer science*] (PCM)
RGD .... Revue de Geomorphologie Dynamique [*A publication*]
RGD .... Rigid (MSA)
RGda .... Radio Grenada
RGDAA .... Royal Guide Dogs Association of Australia
RGDAT .... Royal Guide Dogs Association of Tasmania [*Australia*]
RGDATA .... Retail Grocery, Dairy, and Allied Trades Association [*British*] (BI)
RGDT .... Reliability Growth/Development Test
RGDV .... Rice Gall Dwarf Virus [*Plant pathology*]
RGE .... Porgera [*Papua New Guinea*] [*Airport symbol*] (OAG)
RGE .... Range [*Maps and charts*] (MDG)
RGE .... Rat der Gemeinden Europas [*Council of European Municipalities*]
RGE .... Reduced Gravity Environment
RGE .... Red under Gold Edges [*Books*]
RGE .... Regroupement des Guineens a l'Exterieur [*Rally of Guineans Abroad*] (PD)
RGE .... Relative Gas Expansion (AAMN)
RGE .... Rotating Gel Electrophoresis
RGEA .... Rate Gyro Electronics Assembly (MCD)
RGEN .... Repligen Corp. [*Cambridge, MA*] [*NASDAQ symbol*] (NQ)
RGenBelge ... Revue General Belge [*A publication*] (BJA)
RGEPS .... Rucker-Gable Educational Programming Scale [*Psychology*]
RGF .... Range Gated Filter
RGF .... Rarefied Gas Field [*or Flow*]
RGF .... Royal Gun Factory [*British military*] (DMA)
RGFC .... R & G Financial Corp. [*NASDAQ symbol*] (SAG)
RGFC .... Ray Griff Fan Club (EA)
RGFC .... Remote Gas Filter Correlation (KSC)
RGFC .... Robin George Fan Club (EA)
RG Fincl .... R & G Financial Corp. [*Associated Press*] (SAG)
RGFX .... Raster Graphics, Inc. [*NASDAQ symbol*] (SAG)
RGG .... Rotating Gravity Gradiometer
RGG .... Royal Grenadier Guards [*British*]
RGH .... Rare Gas Halogen [*Inorganic chemistry*]
RGH .... Rat Growth Hormone [*Endocrinology*]
RGH .... Rough (AAG)
RghtMg .... Right Management Consultants, Inc. [*Associated Press*] (SAG)
RGI .... Randers Group, Inc. [*AMEX symbol*] (SAG)
RGI .... Rand Graduate Institute (AAGC)
RGI .... Rangiroa [*French Polynesia*] [*Airport symbol*] (OAG)
RGI .... Regional Airlines [*France ICAO designator*] (FAAC)
RGI .... Royal Glasgow Institute of Fine Arts [*Scotland*]
RGICC .... Region Internal Computer Code [*Computer science*]
RGI.EC .... Randers Group [*ECM Symbol*] (TTSB)
RGIFA .... Royal Glasgow Institute of Fine Arts [*Scotland*]
RGIS .... Regis Corp. [*NASDAQ symbol*] (NQ)
RGIS .... Route Guidance and Information System
RGIT .... Representative for German Industry and Trade [*An association*] (EA)
RGIT .... Robert Gordon Institute of Technology [*Scotland*]
RGJ .... Richmond, VA [*Location identifier FAA*] (FAAL)
RGJ .... Royal Green Jackets [*Military unit*] [*British*]
RGJLond .... Royal Green Jackets, London [*Military unit*] [*British*]
RGJTAVR .... Royal Green Jackets Territorial and Army Volunteer Reserve [*Military unit*] [*British*]
RGK .... Red Wing, MN [*Location identifier FAA*] (FAAL)
RGK .... Reserv Glavnogo Komandovaniia [*Reserve of the High Command*] [*Former USSR*]
RGL .... RADAR Gunlaying (IAA)
RGL .... Rate Gyroscope Limit
RGL .... Reading Grade Level
RGL .... Regionair Ltd. [*British ICAO designator*] (FAAC)
RGL .... Regional Resources Ltd. [*Toronto Stock Exchange symbol Vancouver Stock Exchange symbol*]
RGL .... Regulate (MSA)
RGL .... Report Generator Language [*Computer science*] (IEEE)
RGL .... Rio Gallegos [*Argentina*] [*Airport symbol*] (OAG)
RGL .... Runway Guard Light [*Aviation*] (DA)
RGL .... Wrangell, AK [*Location identifier FAA*] (FAAL)
RGLC .... Racing, Gaming, and Liquor Commission [*Northern Territory, Australia*]
RGLD .... Royal Gold, Inc. [*NASDAQ symbol*] (NQ)
RGLR .... Regular (MSA)
RGLT .... Regulating (MSA)
RGLTD .... Regulated (MSA)
RGLTR .... Regulator (MSA)

RGLTRY .... Regulatory
RGM .... Radiogas Monitor [*Nuclear energy*] (NRCH)
RGM .... Rangemile Ltd. [*British ICAO designator*] (FAAC)
RGM .... Recorder Group Monitor
RGM .... Redundant Gyro Monitor (NASA)
RGM .... Reliability Growth Management (MCD)
RGM .... Remote Geophysical Monitor (MCD)
RGM .... Reversible Gelatin Matrix
RGM .... Right Gluteus Maziums [*Muscle*] [*Anatomy*] (DAVI)
RGM .... Rounds per Gun per Minute
RGM .... Royex Gold Mining Corp. [*Toronto Stock Exchange symbol Vancouver Stock Exchange symbol*]
RGMI .... Regulations Governing the Meat Inspection [*of the USDA*]
RGMS .... Reversible Gelatin Matrix System
RGMV .... Ryegrass Mosaic Virus [*Plant pathology*]
RGN .... Ranging (IAA)
RGN .... Rangoon [*Myanmar*] [*Airport symbol*] (OAG)
RGN .... Rangoon [*Burma*] [*Airport symbol*] (AD)
RGN .... Region (AFM)
RGN .... Registered General Nurse
RG(N) .... Register (N) Stages (MCD)
RGN .... Riggins Resources [*Vancouver Stock Exchange symbol*]
RGNG .... Rigging (MSA)
RGNL .... Regional
RGNT .... Regent Assisted Living [*NASDAQ symbol*] (TTSB)
RGNT .... Regent Assisted Living, Inc. [*NASDAQ symbol*] (SAG)
RGO .... Akron, OH [*Location identifier FAA*] (FAAL)
RGO .... Argo SA [*Dominican Republic*] [*ICAO designator*] (FAAC)
RGO .... Radio Guidance Operation (DNAB)
RGO .... Ranger Oil Ltd. [*NYSE symbol Toronto Stock Exchange symbol*] (SPSG)
RGO .... Rosella Plains [*Queensland*] [*Airport symbol*] (AD)
RGO .... Royal Greenwich Observatory [*British*]
RGP .... RADAR Glider Positioning (IAA)
RGP .... Rate Gyro Package
RGP .... Regina Public Library [*UTLAS symbol*]
RGP .... Reliability Growth Program (PDAA)
RGP .... Remote Graphics Processor
RGP .... Retired Greyhounds as Pets (EA)
RGP .... Retrograde Pyelogram [*Nephrology*] (DAVI)
RGP .... Rhodesian Government Party
RGP .... Rice Genome Research Program [*Japan*]
RGP .... Rigid Gas Permeable [*Contact lens*]
RGP .... Rocketdyne Gun Propellant (MCD)
RGP .... Rolled Gold Plate [*Metallurgy*]
RGPF .... Royal Gunpowder Factory [*British*]
RG PH .... Registered Pharmacist
RGPO .... Range Gate Pull Off (NVT)
RGPS .... Razor Grinders' Protection Society [*A union*] [*British*]
RGR .... Oklahoma City, OK [*Location identifier FAA*] (FAAL)
RGR .... Range Gated Receiver
RGR .... Ranger
RGR .... Rare-Gas Recovery [*Nuclear energy*] (NRCH)
RGR .... Rassemblement des Gauches Republicaines [*Assembly of the Republican Left*] [*France Political party*]
RGR .... Receipt of Goods Received
RGR .... Region Air, Inc. [*Canada ICAO designator*] (FAAC)
RGR .... Regional Rail [*TRB*] (TAG)
RGR .... Regulus Resources, Inc. [*Vancouver Stock Exchange symbol*]
RGR .... Relative Growth Rate [*Entomology*]
RGR .... Ringer (WGA)
RGR .... Rio Grande [*Brazil*] [*Airport symbol*] (AD)
RGR .... Routing Register (IAA)
RGR .... Royal Garrison Regiment [*Military British*] (ROG)
RGR .... Royal Gurkha Regiment [*British military*] (DMA)
RGR .... Sturm Ruger [*NYSE symbol*] (TTSB)
RGR .... Sturm Ruger & Co. [*NYSE symbol*] (SPSG)
RGRDE .... Rotating Gold Ring-Disc Electrode (PDAA)
RGRMA .... Rate Gyro Redundancy Management Algorithm (NASA)
RgrT .... Ranger Tab [*Military decoration*]
RGS .... RADAR Ground Stabilization
RGS .... Radio Guidance System
RGS .... Rate Gyro System
RGS .... Reference Guides Series (ACII)
RGS .... Refined Gigabit System [*High purity hydrogen peroxide*]
RGS .... Regulators of G-Protein Signalling [*Biochemistry*]
RGS .... Release Guard Signal [*Telecommunications*] (EECA)
RGS .... Remote Ground Switching
RGS .... Rene Guyon Society (EA)
RGS .... Renown Aviation, Inc. [*ICAO designator*] (FAAC)
RGS .... Research Grants Staff [*Environmental Protection Agency*] (GFGA)
RGS .... Restructured General Support [*Military*]
RGS .... Rieger Syndrome [*Medicine*] (DMAA)
RGS .... Rifleman's Gun Shield [*Military*] (INF)
RGS .... Rio Grande Southern Railroad (IIA)
RGS .... River Gauging Station
RGS .... Rochester Gas & El [*NYSE symbol*] (TTSB)
RGS .... Rochester Gas & Electric Corp. [*NYSE symbol*] (SPSG)
RGS .... Rocket Guidance System (KSC)
RGS .... Royal Geographical Society [*British*]
RGS .... Royal Gold Enterprises, Inc. [*Toronto Stock Exchange symbol*]
RGS .... Ruffed Grouse Society. (EA)
RGS .... Sisters of Our Lady of Charity of the Good Shepherd [*Roman Catholic religious order*]
RGS .... [*The*] Sisters of the Good Shepherd (TOCD)
RGSAT .... Radio Guidance Surveillance and Automatic Tracking (AAG)
RGSC .... Ramp Generator and Signal Converter (IEEE)
RGSDLR .... Rigsdaler [*Numismatics*]
RGSF .... Reference Guide to Short Fiction [*A publication*]
RGSSA .... Royal Geographical Society of Australasia, South Australian Branch
RGSTV .... Rice Grassy Stunt Virus [*Plant pathology*]
RGSTY .... Registry
RGSU .... Restructured General Support Unit (MCD)
RGT .... Airbourne School of Flying [*British*] [*FAA designator*] (FAAC)
Rgt .... Regent [*Record label*]
RGT .... Regent College Library [*UTLAS symbol*]
RGT .... Regiment
RGT .... Rengat [*Indonesia*] [*Airport symbol*] (OAG)
RGT .... Rengat [*Sumatra, Indonesia*] [*Airport symbol*] (AD)
RGT .... Resonant Gate Transistor [*Computer science*]
RGT .... Reverse Garbage Truck (ADA)
RGT .... Rigging Template (MCD)
RGT .... Right
RGTF .... Royal General Theatrical Fund [*British*] (DI)
RGTM .... Regional Government Technical Monitor [*Department of Housing and Urban Development*] (GFGA)
RGTP .... Reseau Gouvernemental de Transmission par Paquets [*Government Packet Network - GPN*] [*Canada*]
RGTP .... Rough Template (AAG)
RGTR .... Register
RgtStrt .... Right Start, Inc. [*Associated Press*] (SAG)
RGU .... Rate Gyroscope Unit
RGU .... Regional Glucose Utilization [*Medicine*] (DMAA)
RGV .... Relative Gas Vacuolation [*In algae*]
RGV .... Rio Grande Ventures Ltd. [*Vancouver Stock Exchange symbol*]
R-GVB .... Resonating-Generalized Valence Bond [*Physical chemistry*]
RGW .... Ramp Gross Weight [*Aviation*]
RGW .... Reagent Grade Water
RGWO .... Range Gate Walk Off [*Military*] (LAIN)
RGWS .... RADAR Guided Weapon System (MCD)
RGX .... Reverse Geometry X-Ray (PS)
RGY .... Regency Airlines Ltd. [*ICAO designator*] (FAAC)
RGZ .... Recommended Ground Zero [*Military*] (AABC)
RH .... Air Zimbabwe [*Zimbabwe*] [*ICAO designator*] (ICDA)
RH .... Rabbinic Hebrew (BJA)
RH .... Radiant Heat
RH .... Radiation Homing (AAG)
RH .... Radiation Hybrid Mapping [*Biochemistry*]
RH .... Radiological Health (KSC)
r/h .... RADs [*Radiation Absorbed Doses*] per Hour (DEN)
RH .... Railhead [*British military*] (DMA)
RH .... Rankine-Hugoniot [*Physics*]
RH .... Reactive Hyperemia [*Medicine*]
RH .... Receive Hub [*Telegraph*] [*Telecommunications*] (TEL)
RH .... Receiver Hopping Mode (IAA)
RH .... Red Heat (IAA)
RH .... Red Herring [*Investment term*]
RH .... Redhill [*International vehicle registration*] (ODBW)
RH .... Reduced Haloperidol [*An antidepressant*] (DAVI)
RH .... Regal Bahamas International Airlines [*ICAO designator*] (AD)
RH .... Regional Headquarters (NOAA)
RH .... Relative Humidity
RH .... Releasing Hormone [*Also, RF*] [*Endocrinology*]
RH .... Remote-Handled [*Waste*] [*Colorado*] (GAAI)
RH .... Remotely Handled
r/h .... REMs [*Roentgen Equivalents, Man*] per Hour (DEN)
RH .... Report Heading (BUR)
RH .... Requesta Regni Hierosolymitani [*A publication*] (BJA)
RH .... Request-Response Header [*Computer science*] (BUR)
RH .... Research Highlights [*A publication*] (DIT)
RH .... Reserve Shutdown Hours (IAA)
RH .... Residential Hotels [*Public-performance tariff class*] [*British*]
RH .... Response Header (IAA)
RH .... Retinal Hemorrhage [*Medicine*] (DMAA)
RH .... Revisionist History [*Taby, Sweden*] (EAIO)
R/H .... Revolutions per Hour (DEN)
RH .... Rheostat (IEEE)
Rh .... Rhesus [*Blood factor*]
Rh .... Rhetorica [*of Aristotle*] [*Classical studies*] (OCD)
rh .... Rheumatic [*Medicine*] (MAE)
Rh .... Rheumatism [*Medicine*]
RH .... Rheumatology (DAVI)
RH .... Rhinitis [*Medicine*]
RH .... Rhinoceros (ROG)
Rh .... Rhipicephalus [*A genus of cattle tick*] (DAVI)
rh .... Rhodesia [*Southern Rhodesia*] [*MARC country of publication code Library of Congress*] (LCCP)
Rh .... Rhodium [*Chemical element*]
Rh .... Rhodopsin [*Visual Purple*]
rh .... Rhonchi [*Rales*] [*Latin*] (MAE)
RH .... Right Halfback [*Soccer*]
RH .... Right Hand
RH .... Right Hyperphoria [*Medicine*]
RH .... Road Haulage
RH .... Rockwell Hardness
r/h .... Roentgens per Hour (DEN)
RH .... Roger Houghton Ltd. [*Publisher*] [*British*]
RH .... Room Humidifier (DMAA)
RH .... Rosh Hashanah [*New Year*] (BJA)
RH .... Rotuli Hundredorum [*Latin A publication*] (DLA)

RH Round Head
RH Round Hole [*Looseleaf binding*] (DGA)
RH Round House [*Maps and charts*]
RH Royal Highlanders [*Military unit*] [*British*]
RH Royal Highness
RH Royal Hospital [*Chelsea*] [*British military*] (DMA)
RH Royal Hussars [*Military unit*] [*British*]
RH Rueckwaertiges Heeresgebiet [*Rear area of a group of armies*] [*German military*]
RH Runaway Hotline (EA)
RH Running Head [*Printing*] (WDMC)
RH Ryan's Hope [*Television program*]
RH Southern Rhodesia [*ANSI two-letter standard code Obsolete*] (CNC)
RHA Ranching Heritage Association (EA)
RHA Records Holding Area [*Military*]
RHA Regional Health Authority [*British*]
RHA Reichold [*Alabama*] [*Seismograph station code, US Geological Survey*] (SEIS)
RHA Reindeer Herders Association (EA)
RHA Religious Heritage of America (EA)
RHA Renewal and Housing Assistance Report [*HUD*]
RHA Respiratory Health Association (EA)
RHA Reykholar [*Iceland*] [*Airport symbol Obsolete*] (OAG)
RHA Rice Husk Ash (PDAA)
RHA Right Hepatic Artery [*Medicine*] (DMAA)
RHA Road Haulage Association [*British*]
RHA Rohm & Haas Co., Spring House, PA [*OCLC symbol*] (OCLC)
RHA Rolled Homogeneous Armor [*Weaponry*] (INF)
RHA Roman High Avoidance [*Behavior trait*]
RHA Rose Hybridizers Association (EA)
RHA Royal Hellenic Army (NATG)
RHA Royal Hibernian Academy
RHA Royal Horse Artillery [*British*]
RHA Rural Housing Alliance [*Later, RAI*] (EA)
RHA Rural Housing Authority [*Western Australia*]
RHAAP Rural Housing Assistance for Aborigines Program [*Australia*]
RHAB Random House AudioBooks [*Publisher*]
RHAF Royal Hellenic Air Force
RHAG Rotary Hydraulic Arresting Gear (PDAA)
RH Agglut Rheumatoid Agglutinins [*Clinical chemistry*] (CPH)
Rh Al Rhetorica ad Alexandrum [*of Aristotle*] [*Classical studies*] (OCD)
RHAM Rhammus [*Pharmacology*] (ROG)
RHAP Rhapsody (WGA)
RHAPP Rental Housing Assistance for Pensioners Program [*Australia*]
RHASS Royal Highland and Agricultural Society of Scotland [*British*]
RHA(T) Regional Health Authority (Teaching) [*British*]
RHAV Rat Hepatoma-Associated Virus
RHAW RADAR Homing and Warning (MCD)
RHAWR RADAR Homing and Warning Receiver (MCD)
RHAWS RADAR Homing and Warning System
RHB RADAR Homing Beacon [*Maps and charts*] (IAA)
RHB RADAR Homing Bomb [*Air Force*]
RHB Raise Head of the Bed [*Medicine*] (DAVI)
RHB Regional Hospital Boards [*British*]
RHB Right Halfback [*Soccer*]
RHB Right Heart Bypass [*Medicine*] (MAE)
RHB Round Head Brass [*Screw Head*] (ECII)
RHB Round Hole Broach
RHBA Racking Horse Breeders Association of America (EA)
RHBC RehabCare Corp. [*NASDAQ symbol*] (SPSG)
RHBC RehabCare Group [*NASDAQ symbol*] (TTSB)
RHBF Reactive Hyperemia Blood Flow [*Medicine*] (MAE)
RHBV Rice Hoja Blanca Virus [*Plant pathology*]
RHC Range-Height Converter (IAA)
RHC Reactive Hydrocarbon [*Environmental science*]
RHC Reactor Head Cooling [*Nuclear energy*] (NRCH)
RHC Regional Bell Holding Co. [*Computer science*] (TNIG)
RHC Regional Holding Co.
RHC Resetting Half-Cycle
RHC Resin Hemoperfusion Column
RHC Respirations Have Ceased [*Medicine*]
RHC Right-Hand Circular [*NASA*] (KSC)
RHC Right-Hand Component (IAA)
RHC Right-Hand Console
RHC Right Heart Catheterization [*Medicine*]
RHC Right Hypochondrium [*Medicine*]
RHC Rio Hotel & Casino [*NYSE symbol*] (TTSB)
RHC Riverside Methodist Hospital Library, Columbus, OH [*OCLC symbol*] (OCLC)
RHC Road Haulage Cases [*1950-55*] [*England*] [*A publication*] (DLA)
RHC Rosary Hill College [*New York*]
RHC Rotational Hand Controller [*NASA*]
RHC Royal Highlanders of Canada [*Military unit*] [*World War I*]
RHC Royal Holloway College [*British*] (DI)
RHC Rubber Hydrocarbon
RHC Rural Health Clinic [*Department of Health and Human Services*] (GFGA)
RHCA Red Hills Conservation Association (EA)
Rh CA Rhodesian Court of Appeal Law Reports [*1939-46*] [*A publication*] (DLA)
RHCA Roller Hockey Coaches Association (EA)
RHCC Reproductive Health Care Center
RHCC/PP Reproductive Health Care Center/Planned Parenthood
RHCF Residential Health Care Facility [*Medicine*] (DHSM)
RHCG Research for Health Charities Group [*British*]
RHCI Radiant Heating and Cooling Institute
RHCI Ramsay Health Care [*NASDAQ symbol*] (TTSB)
RHCI Ramsay Health Care, Inc. [*NASDAQ symbol*] (NQ)
RHCM Relative Humidity Control/Monitor (NASA)
RHCP Right-Hand Circularly Polarized [*LASER waves*]
RHCS Red Hot Concepts, Inc. [*NASDAQ symbol*] (SAG)
RHCSA Regional Hospitals Consultants' and Specialists' Association
RHCSU Red Hot Concepts Unit [*NASDAQ symbol*] (TTSB)
RHCTL Right-Hand Control (IAA)
RHD Archangelos [*Greece*] [*Seismograph station code, US Geological Survey*] (SEIS)
Rh D Doctor of Rehabilitation (PGP)
RhD Doctor of Rehabilitation (GAGS)
RHD RADAR Horizon Distance (IAA)
RHD Radiological Health Data
RHD Railhead
RHD Random House Dictionary [*A publication*]
RHD Regional Health Director [*HEW*]
RHD Relative Hepatic Dullness [*Medicine*]
RHD Renal Hypertensive Disease [*Medicine*]
RHD Required Hangar Depth (MCD)
RHD Return Head
RHD Rheumatic Heart Disease [*Medicine*]
RHD Rhodes, Inc. [*NYSE symbol*] (SPSG)
RHD Right Hand Drive [*Automotive engineering*]
RHD Rio Hondo [*Argentina*] [*Airport symbol*] (AD)
RHD Rural Housing Disaster
RHD & R Radiological Health Data and Reports [*A publication*]
RHDEL-II [*The*] Random House Dictionary of the English Language: Second Edition - Unabridged [*A publication*]
RHD-II [*The*] Random House Dictionary of the English Language: Second Edition - Unabridged [*A publication*]
RHDV Rabbit Hemorrhagic Disease Virus
RHE Radiation Hazard Effects (KSC)
RHE Random House Encyclopedia [*A publication*]
RHE Record Handling Electronics
RHE Reims [*France*] [*Airport symbol*] (OAG)
RHE Reliability Human Engineering (AAG)
RHE Remote Hellfire Electronics [*Army*]
RHE Retinohepatoendocrinologic [*Syndrome*] [*Medicine*] (DMAA)
RHE Reversible Hydrogen Electrode
RHE Rheims [*France*] [*Airport symbol*] (AD)
RHEA Reentry Heating Energies Analyzer [*Air Force*]
RHEB Right-Hand Equipment Bay [*Apollo*] [*NASA*]
RHEED Reflected High-Energy Electron Diffraction [*Spectroscopy*]
RHEED Reflection High-Energy Electron Diffraction (DMAA)
RHEED Reflective High-Energy Electron Diffraction
RHEINHYP Rheinische Hypothekenbank AG [*Germany*] (EY)
RHEL Rutherford High Energy Laboratory (MCD)
RHEM Rheometrics, Inc. [*Piscataway, NJ*] [*NASDAQ symbol*] (NQ)
RHEM Rheometrics Scientific [*NASDAQ symbol*] (TTSB)
RHEO Rheostat (AAG)
Rheomt Rheometrics, Inc. [*Associated Press*] (SAG)
Rhes Rhesus [*of Euripides*] [*Classical studies*] (OCD)
Rhet Ars Rhetorica [*of Dionysius Halicarnassensis*] [*Classical studies*] (OCD)
Rhet De Rhetoribus [*of Suetonius*] [*Classical studies*] (OCD)
Rhet Rhetores Graeci [*A publication*] (OCD)
RHET Rhetoric
Rhet Her Rhetorica ad Herennium [*First century BC*] [*Classical studies*] (OCD)
Rhet Lat Min Rhetores Latini Minores [*A publication*] (OCD)
RHEU Rheumatology (DAVI)
rheu fev Rheumatic Fever (DAVI)
rheu ht dis Rheumatic Heart Disease (DAVI)
RHEUM Rheumatism [*Medicine*]
R_{HF} High-Frequency Resistance (IDOE)
RHF Rarefied Hypersonic Flow
RHF Remembrance of the Holocaust Foundation (EA)
RHF Restricted Hartree-Fock [*Quantum mechanics*]
RHF Retired History File [*Army*]
RHF Right Heart Failure [*Medicine*]
RHF Roller Hockey Federation (EA)
RHF Royal Highland Fusiliers [*Military unit*] [*British*]
RHFC Richard Hatch Fan Club (EA)
RHFC Robyn Hitchcock Fan Club (EA)
RHFEB Right-Hand Forward Equipment Bay [*NASA*] (KSC)
RHFF Richard Hatch Fan Fellowship [*Defunct*] (EAIO)
RHFS Receiving Hospital Field Station
RHFS Round Hill Field Station [*MIT*] (MCD)
RHG Renaissance Hotel Group NV [*NYSE symbol*] (SAG)
RHG Right Hand Grip (DMAA)
RHG Royal Horse Guards [*British*]
RHG1D Royal Horse Guards and 1st Dragoons [*British military*] (DMA)
RHG-CSF Recombinant Human Granulocyte, Colony Stimulating Factor [*Hematology*]
RHGH Recombinant Human Growth Hormone [*Biochemistry*]
RHGP Russian Human Genome Project
rhGRF Rat Hypothalamus Growth Hormone-Releasing Factor [*Endocrinology*]
RHGSA Russian Historical and Genealogical Society in America [*Later, RNAA*] (EA)
RHH Right-Hand Head
RHH Right Homonymous Hemianopia [*Medicine*] (MEDA)
RHH Robertson-Ceco Corp. [*NYSE symbol*] (SPSG)
RHI RADAR Height Indicator (CET)

RHI Range-Height Indicator [*RADAR*]
RHI Real Hazard Index
RHI Relative Humidity Indicator (AAG)
RHI Responsible Hospitality Institute (EA)
RHI Rhinelander [*Wisconsin*] [*Airport symbol*] (OAG)
RHI Rhinology [*Medicine*] (DHSM)
RHI Rhode Island
RHI Rhode Island Historical Society Library, Providence, RI [*OCLC symbol*] (OCLC)
RHi Rhode Island Historical Society, Providence, RI [*Library symbol Library of Congress*] (LCLS)
Rh I Rhode Island Reports [*A publication*] (DLA)
Rh I Rhode Island Supreme Court Reports [*A publication*] (DLA)
RHI Rigid-Hull Inflatable [*US Coast Guard vessel*]
RHI Robert Half International, Inc. [*NYSE symbol*] (SPSG)
RHI Robert Half Intl [*NYSE symbol*] (TTSB)
RHI Round Hill Installation (SAA)
RHI Rural Health Initiative [*Medicine*] (DMAA)
RHIA Radiation-Hardened Interfacing Amplifier
RHIB Rain and Hail Insurance Bureau [*Defunct*] (EA)
RHIB Rigid-Hull Inflatable Boat (DOMA)
RHIC Relativistic Heavy Ion Collider [*Nuclear physics*]
RHIDEC [*The*] Restaurant/Hotel International Design Exposition (ITD)
RHIE RAND Health Insurance Experiment [*Managed care study*]
RHIF Rural Housing Insurance Fund [*Department of Agriculture*] (GFGA)
RHIFC Ray Heatherton Irish Friends Club [*Defunct*] (EA)
RHIG RH [*or Rhesus*] Immune Globulin [*Immunology*]
RHIMO Agency for Navigation on the Rhine and the Moselle (NATG)
Rhin Rhinology [*Medicine*]
RHINO RADAR Range Height Indicator Not Operating on Scan [*Meteorology*] (FAAC)
Rhino Really Here in Name Only [*Education*] [*British*]
RHINO Repeating Handheld Improved Non-Rifled Ordnance (PDAA)
RHINO Rhinoceros (DSUE)
RHINOL Rhinology [*Medicine*]
RHIO Rank Has Its Obligations [*Military slang*]
RHIP Radiation Health Information Project [*Defunct*] (EA)
RHIP Rank Has Its Privileges [*Military slang*]
RHIR Rank Has Its Responsibilities [*Military slang*]
RHi-Sh Rhode Island Historical Society, George L. Shepley Collection, Providence, RI [*Library symbol Library of Congress*] (LCLS)
RHistS Royal Historical Society [*British*]
RhITC Rhodamine Isothiocyanate [*Biochemistry*]
RHittAs Revue Hittite et Asianique [*Paris*] [*A publication*] (BJA)
Rhiz Rhizobium [*A bacterium*] (DAVI)
RHJ Rubber Hose Jacket (MSA)
RHJSC Regional Hospital Junior Staff Committee [*British*] (BABM)
RHJSC Regional Hospital Junior Staff Committee [*British*] (DAVI)
RHK Radio Hong Kong
RHK Reefing Hook
RHL Radiological Health Laboratory
RHL Rat Hepatic Lectin [*Biochemistry*]
RHL Rectangular Hysteresis Loop (PDAA)
RHL Recurrent Herpes Labialis [*Medicine*] (DMAA)
RHL Residual Hazards List [*NASA*] (NASA)
RHL Rettie's Scotch Court of Session Cases, Fourth Series [*House of Lords' Part*] [*A publication*] (DLA)
RHL Reverse Half-Line [*Feed*]
RHL Richland Mine, Inc. [*Vancouver Stock Exchange symbol*]
RHL Right Hemisphere Lesion [*Cardiology*] (DAVI)
RHL Right Hepatic Lobe [*Anatomy*]
RHL Roy Hill [*Western Australia*] [*Airport symbol*] (AD)
RHLG Radiometric Homing Level Gauge
RHLI Royal Hamilton Light Infantry [*British military*] (DMA)
Rh LJ Rhodesian Law Journal [*A publication*] (DLA)
RHLN Right Hilar Lymph Node [*Anatomy*] (MAE)
RHM Ranks Hovis McDougall [*Commercial firm British*] (ECON)
RHM Refractory Heavy Minerals [*In sands used for glass making*]
RHM Relative Humidity Monitor (GFGA)
RHM Renewal and Housing Management [*HUD*]
RHM Rhabdomyosarcoma [*Also, RMS*] [*Oncology*]
RHM Right-Hand Polarized Mode (IAA)
RHM Rio Hardy [*Mexico*] [*Seismograph station code, US Geological Survey*] (SEIS)
RHM Roentgen per Hour at One Meter
RHMII Right Hand Man II [*Computer package*] [*Futurus, Inc.*] (PCM)
RhMk Rhesus Monkey [*Medicine*] (DMAA)
RhMK Rhesus Monkey Kidney [*Medicine*] (DMAA)
RhMkK Rhesus Monkey Kidney [*Medicine*] (DMAA)
RHMS Royal Hibernian Military School [*Dublin*]
Rh Mus Rheinisches Museum fuer Philologie [*A publication*] (OCD)
RHN Rhonavia [*France ICAO designator*] (FAAC)
RHN Royal Hellenic Navy [*Obsolete*] (NATG)
Rh Neg Rhesus Factor Negative [*Hematology*] (MAE)
RhnPl Rhone-Poulenc, Inc. [*Associated Press*] (SAG)
Rh_{null} Rhesus Factor Null [*Indicates all Rhesus factors are missing*] [*Hematology*] (DAVI)
RHO Railhead Officer [*Military Obsolete*]
RHO Remanufactured High Output
RHO Rhodes [*Greece*] [*Seismograph station code, US Geological Survey Closed*] (SEIS)
RHO Rhodesia [*Later, Zimbabwe*]
RHO Rhodes Island [*Greece*] [*Airport symbol*] (OAG)
RHO Rhodopsin [*Optics*] [*Genetics*] (DOG)
RHO Rhombic [*Antenna*]
RHO Southern Rhodesia [*ANSI three-letter standard code Obsolete*] (CNC)
RHOB Rayburn House Office Building [*Washington, DC*] (DLA)
Rhod Rhodesia
RHOD Rhodium [*Chemistry*]
Rhode Island C... Rhode Island College (GAGS)
Rhode Island Rep... Rhode Island Reports [*A publication*] (DLA)
Rhode Island Sch Design... Rhode Island School of Design (GAGS)
Rhodes Rhodes, Inc. [*Associated Press*] (SAG)
Rhodesian LJ... Rhodesian Law Journal [*A publication*] (DLA)
RHOGI RADAR Homing Guidance Investigation (MCD)
RHOJ RADAR Home on Jam
Rho L Rhodian Law [*A publication*] (DLA)
rhom Rhomboid [*Muscle*] [*Anatomy*] (DAVI)
RHOM Rottlund Co. [*NASDAQ symbol*] (SAG)
RHOMB Rhomboid [*Mathematics*]
RHOSP Registered Home Ownership Savings Plan
RHOV Du Variant [*Laboratory science*] (DAVI)
RHP Radiant Heat Pump
RHP Rated Horsepower
RHP Reduced Hard Pressure (MSA)
RHP Resource Holding Potential
RHP Resource Holding Power [*Fighting ability - animal defense*]
RHP Right-Handed Pitcher [*Baseball*]
RHP Right-Hand Page (WDMC)
rhp Right-Hand Page [*Also, called Recto*] (WDMC)
RHP Right Hand Panel (MCD)
RHP Rural Health Program [*Military*] (CINC)
RHPA Reverse Hemolytic Plaque Assay [*Clinical chemistry*]
RHPC Rapid-Hardening Portland Cement
rhPF Recombinant Human Platelet Factor [*Biochemistry*]
RH PL Rhodium Plate (MSA)
RHPLC Radio-High-Performance Liquid Chromatography
Rh Pos Rhesus Factor Positive [*Hematology*] (MAE)
RhPOv Rhone Poulence Overseas Ltd. [*Associated Press*] (SAG)
RhPOv Rhone Poulenc Overseas Ltd. [*Associated Press*] (SAG)
RHPOY Rhone-Poulenc SA (MHDW)
RHPS Phillips [*R.H.*], Inc. [*NASDAQ symbol*] (SAG)
RHPS Radiation-Hardened Power Supply
RHPS Rapid Housing Payment System [*Department of Housing and Urban Development*] (GFGA)
RHPSW Phillips(R.H.)Inc. Wrrt [*NASDAQ symbol*] (TTSB)
RHQ Regimental Headquarters
RHQ Regional Headquarters (NITA)
RHR Rear Headrest
RHR Receiver Holding Register
RHR Reheater (AAG)
RHR Rejectable Hazard Rate (IEEE)
RHR Renal Hypertensive Rat [*Medicine*] (DMAA)
RHR Residual Heat Removal [*Nuclear energy*] (NRCH)
RHR Resting Heart Rate [*Cardiology*]
r/hr Roentgens per Hour (AABC)
RHR Rohr, Inc. [*NYSE symbol*] (SPSG)
RHR Roughness Height Rating (MSA)
RHR Royal Highland Regiment [*Military unit*] [*British*]
RHRP Residual Heat Removal Pump [*Nuclear energy*] (NRCH)
RHRS Residual Heat Removal System [*Nuclear energy*] (NRCH)
RHRSW Residual Heat Removal Service Water [*Nuclear energy*] (NRCH)
RHS Rectangular Hollow Section [*Metal industry*]
RHS Regency Health Services [*NYSE symbol*] (TTSB)
RHS Regency Health Services, Inc. [*NYSE symbol*] (SAG)
RHS Retirement History Survey
RHS Right-Hand Side
RHS Robin Hood Society [*British*] (DBA)
RHS Rocketdyne Hybrid Simulator [*NASA*] (NASA)
RHS Rodeo Historical Society (EA)
RHS Rolled Hollow Section
RHS Rough Hard Sphere [*Model of liquids*]
rhs Roundheaded Screw (BARN)
RHS Royal Historical Society [*British*]
RHS Royal Horticultural Society [*British*] (ARC)
RHS Royal Humane Society [*British*]
RHSA Radio Historical Society of America (NTCM)
RHSC Richmond Hill School Company [*British military*] (DMA)
RHSC Right-Hand-Side by Centroid
RHSC Right-Hand Side Console [*NASA*] (KSC)
RHSCH Rhodes Scholar
RhSh Rosh Hashanah [*New Year*] (BJA)
RHSI Royal Horticultural Society of Ireland (PDAA)
RHSI Rubber Heel and Sole Institute [*Defunct*] (EA)
RHSJ Religious Hospitallers of St. Joseph [*Roman Catholic women's religious order*]
RhSNA National Archives of Rhodesia, Salisbury, Rhodesia [*Library symbol Library of Congress*] (LCLS)
RHSNSW Royal Humane Society of New South Wales
RHSP Registered Hazardous Substances Professional [*Environmental science*]
RHSSA Royal Humane Society of South Australia [*Australia*]
RHSV Royal Horticultural Society of Victoria [*Australia*]
RHT Radiant Heat Temperature (NASA)
RHT Register Holding Time (NITA)
RHT Renal Homotransplantation [*Medicine*] (DMAA)
RHT Reynolds Hydrodynamic Theory [*Physics*]
RHT Richton International Corp. [*AMEX symbol*] (SPSG)
RHT Richton Intl [*AMEX symbol*] (TTSB)

RHT .... Right Hypertropia [*Ophthalmology*]
RHTM .... Regional Highway Traffic Model [*Database*] [*Obsolete*]
RHTPS .... Razor Hafters' Trade Protection Society [*A union*] [*British*]
RHTS .... Reactor Heat Transport System (NRCH)
RHU .... Radioisotope Heater Unit (NASA)
RHU .... Registered Health Underwriter [*NAHU*]
RHU .... Requisition Held Up (DNAB)
RHU .... Reserved for Hardware Use [*Computer science*] (IAA)
RHU .... Residuum Hydrocracking Unit [*Petroleum refining*]
RHU .... Rheumatology [*Medical specialty*] (DHSM)
rHuEPO .... Recombinant Human Erythropoietin [*Biochemistry*]
RHV .... Registered Health Visitor [*British*]
RHV .... Remnant Hepatic Volume [*Hematology*]
RHV .... RHYS Industries Ltd. [*Vancouver Stock Exchange symbol*]
RHV .... Road Haulage Vehicle (DCTA)
RHV .... San Jose, CA [*Location identifier FAA*] (FAAL)
RHW .... Required Hangar Width (MCD)
RHW .... Reversible Half-Wave
RHW .... Right Half Word
RHW .... Router Header Word (NASA)
RHWAC .... Reversible Half-Wave Alternating Current
RHWACDC ... Reversible Half-Wave Alternating Current - Direct Current
RHWB .... [*The*] Reverend Henry Ward Beecher [*American clergyman, 1813-1887*]
RHWDC .... Reversible Half-Wave Direct Current
RHWR .... RADAR Homing and Warning Receiver (MCD)
RHX .... Atlanta, GA [*Location identifier FAA*] (FAAL)
RHX .... Regenerative Heat Exchanger [*Nuclear energy*] (NRCH)
RHY .... Rhyolite Resources [*Vancouver Stock Exchange symbol*]
RHYTHM ...... Remember How You Treat Hazardous Materials [*E. I. Du Pont De Nemours & Co. program*]
Rhythm .... Rhythmica [*of Aristoxenus*] [*Classical studies*] (OCD)
RI .... Chicago, Rock Island & Pacific Railroad Co. (MHDB)
RI .... Eastern Airlines [*ICAO designator*] (AD)
RI .... Indonesia [*IYRU nationality code*] (IYR)
R_I .... Input Resistance (IDOE)
RI .... Member of the Royal Institute of Painters in Water Colours [*British*]
RI .... Morrison Restaurants, Inc. [*NYSE symbol*] (SPSG)
RI .... RADAR Input
RI .... RADAR Intercept (IAA)
RI .... RADAR Interference (LAIN)
RI .... Radiation Indicator [*Nuclear energy*] (NRCH)
RI .... Radiation Intensity (AABC)
RI .... Radicalist International [*Defunct*] (EA)
RI .... Radio Industry [*Telecommunications*] (IAA)
RI .... Radio Inertial (MCD)
RI .... Radio Influence
RI .... Radio Inspector
RI .... Radio Interference (MCD)
RI .... Radioisotope
RI .... Radix Institute (EA)
RI .... Rampart Institute (EA)
RI .... Random Interlace [*Television*]
RI .... Random Interval (AEBS)
RI .... Range Instrumentation (MCD)
RI .... Ranger Instructor [*Army*] (INF)
R/I .... Rate of Interest [*Economics*]
RI .... REACT International (EA)
RI .... Reactor Island [*Nuclear energy*] (NRCH)
RI .... Readers International [*Subscription book club*] [*British*]
RI .... Read-In (DEN)
RI .... Reallocation Inventory (AFIT)
RI .... Receiver Interface
RI .... Receiving Inspection (AAG)
RI .... Recipe Index [*A publication*]
RI .... Recombinant Inbred [*Genetics*]
RI .... Reconnaissance Inspection [*Military*] (GFGA)
RI .... Recovery, Inc.
RI .... Recruit Induction [*Military*]
RI .... Recruit Instruction [*Navy*]
RI .... Recurrent Intussusception
RI .... Redheads International (EA)
RI .... Referential Integrity [*Computer science*] (PCM)
RI .... Reflective Insulation [*Technical drawings*]
RI .... Refractive Index
RI .... Refugees International (EA)
RI .... Regimental Institute [*British military*] (DMA)
RI .... Regina Imperatrix [*Queen Empress*] [*Latin*]
RI .... Regional Ileitis [*Medicine*]
RI .... Registro Italiano [*Italian ship classification society*] (DS)
RI .... Regular Insulin [*Pharmacology*] (DAVI)
RI .... Rehabilitation International (EA)
RI .... Reimplantation [*Dentistry*]
RI .... Reinitiate (SAA)
RI .... Reinsurance (ADA)
RI .... Reissue [*of a book or periodical*] [*Publishing*]
RI .... Relative Intensity
RI .... Relaxation Instruction [*Psychology*]
RI .... Release-Inhibiting Factor [*Endocrinology*] (MAE)
RI .... Reliability Index
RI .... Religious Instruction (ADA)
RI .... Remedial Investigation [*Environmental Protection Agency*] (DOMA)
RI .... Remission Induction [*Oncology*]
RI .... Repeat Indication [*Telecommunications*] (TEL)
RI .... Replaceable Item
RI .... Replicative Intermediate [*Medicine*] (MAE)
RI .... Report of Investigation
RI .... Repulsion Induction [*Motor*]
RI .... Request for Information (MCD)
RI .... Require Identification
RI .... Rescue, Inc. (EA)
RI .... Research Institute [*Fort Belvoir, VA*] [*United States Army Engineer Topographic Laboratories*] (GRD)
RI .... Residual Income
RI .... Resistance Index
RI .... Resistance Inductance (IEEE)
RI .... Resistance International (EA)
RI .... Resolve, Inc. (EA)
RI .... Resonance Integral [*Nuclear energy*] (NRCH)
RI .... Respiratory Illness [*Medicine*]
RI .... Retention Index
RI .... Retirement Income
RI .... Retreats International (EA)
RI .... Retroactive Inhibition [*Psychology*]
RI .... Reunite, Inc. (EA)
RI .... Reverberation Index
RI .... RHEMA [*Restoring Hope through Educational and Medical Aid*] International (EA)
RI .... Rhode Island [*Postal code*]
RI .... Rhode Island Supreme Court Reports [*A publication*] (ILCA)
RI .... Ribonuclease Inhibitor
RI .... Ribosomal [*Protein*] [*Cytology*]
Ri .... Ricardus Anglicus [*Deceased, 1242*] [*Authority cited in pre-1607 legal work*] (DSA)
Ri .... Richardson Number [*Physics*]
RI .... Right Iliac [*Crest*] [*Anatomy*] (DAVI)
RI .... Rigorous Imprisonment [*British military*] (DMA)
RI .... Ring Index [*of chemical compounds*] [*A publication*]
RI .... Ring Indicator [*MODEM*] (PCM)
RI .... Rio-Sul, Servicos Aereos Regionais SA [*Brazil ICAO designator*] (ICDA)
RI .... Robotics International Association of the Society of Manufacturing Engineers (BTTJ)
RI .... Rock Island Lines [*Railroad*]
RI .... Rockwell International Corp. (MCD)
RI .... Rodale Intstitute (EA)
RI .... Rolf Institute (EA)
RI .... Room Index (PDAA)
RI .... Rotary International (EA)
RI .... Routing Identifier [*or Indicator*] (AFM)
RI .... Royal Institute of Painters in Water-Colours, London [*1831*] (NGC)
RI .... Royal Institution [*British*]
RI .... Royal Irish [*Military unit*] [*British*]
RI .... Rubber Insulation [*Technical drawings*]
RI .... Ruby Tuesday [*NYSE symbol*] (TTSB)
RI .... Ruby Tuesday, Inc. [*NYSE symbol*] (SAG)
R/I .... Rule In (DAVI)
RI .... Rulers of India [*A publication*]
RI .... Runaway Inflation (MHDB)
RI .... Rutherford Institute (EA)
RIA .... Radioimmunoassay [*Clinical chemistry*]
RIA .... Railroad Insurance Association
RIA .... Railway Industry Association [*British*] (EAIO)
RIA .... Rain in Area (ADA)
RIA .... Randomized Intervention Analysis [*Experimental design*]
RIA .... Reactivity Initiated Accident [*Nuclear energy*] (NRCH)
RIA .... Registered Industrial and Cost Accountant
RIA .... Registered Investment Adviser [*Securities*]
RIA .... Regulatory Impact Analysis [*or Assessment*]
RIA .... Religious Instruction Association [*Later, PERSC*]
RIA .... Remote Intelligence Acquisition
RIA .... Removable Instrument Assembly [*Nuclear energy*] (NRCH)
RIA .... Research Institute of America [*New York, NY*] [*Information service or system*] (IID)
RIA .... Reset Indicators from Accumulator [*Computer science*] (IAA)
RIA .... Retroactive Liability Insurance
RIA .... Reversible Ischemic Attack [*Medicine*] (DMAA)
RIA .... Rich International Airways, Inc. [*ICAO designator*] (FAAC)
RIA .... Robotic Industries Association (EA)
RIA .... Robot Institute of America (NADA)
RIA .... Rock Island Arsenal [*Illinois*] [*Army*]
RIA .... Royal Irish Academy
RIA .... Santa Maria [*Brazil*] [*Airport symbol*] (OAG)
RIAA .... Recording Industry Association of America (EA)
RIAADA .... Research Institute of African and African Diaspora Arts (EA)
RIAC .... Regional Industry Advisory Committee [*Civil Defense*]
RIAC .... Royal Irish Automobile Club (EAIO)
RIACS .... Research Institute for Advanced Computer Science [*University Space Research Association*] [*Research center*] (RCD)
RIAD .... Rencontres Internationales des Assureurs Defense [*Genoa, Italy*] (EA)
RIA-DA .... Radioimmunoassay Double Antibody [*Test*] [*Clinical chemistry*]
RIA-DA .... Radio-Immunoassay Double Antibody [*Immunology*] (DAVI)
RIAEC .... Rhode Island Atomic Energy Commission
RIAES .... Rhode Island Agricultural Experiment Station [*University of Rhode Island*] [*Research center*] (RCD)
RIAF .... Royal Indian Air Force
RIAF .... Royal Iraqi Air Force
RIAI .... Royal Institute of the Architects of Ireland

RIAIAD......... Reverse International Acronyms, Initialisms, and Abbreviations Dictionary [*A publication*]
RIAL........... Religion in American Life (EA)
RIAL........... Revised Individual Allowance List [*Navy*] (NVT)
RIAL........... Rock Island Arsenal Laboratories [*Illinois*] (MCD)
RIAL........... Runway Identifiers and Approach Lighting [*Aviation*] (IAA)
RIAM........... Royal Irish Academy of Music
RIAP........... Research Institute for Asia and the Pacific [*Australia*]
RIAR........... Requirements Inventory Analysis Report (AFM)
RIA-R.......... Rock Island Arsenal General Thomas J. Rodman Laboratory [*Army*]
RIAS........... Radio in American Sector [*of Berlin*] (SAA)
RIAS........... Readiness Information Access System (MCD)
RIAS........... Research Initiation and Support [*National Science Foundation program*]
RIAS........... Research Institute for Advanced Studies [*Martin Marietta Corp.*]
RIAS........... Roter Interactional Analysis System [*Medicine*] (DMAA)
RIAS........... Royal Incorporation of Architects in Scotland
RIAS........... Rundfunk im Amerikanischen Sektor Berlins [*Radio in American Sector*] [*Germany*]
RIASC.......... Royal Indian Army Service Corps [*British*]
RIA/SE......... Rock Island Arsenal/Science and Engineering Directorate [*Illinois*]
RIAST.......... Reitan Indiana Aphasic Screening Test [*Speech and Language Therapy*] (DAVI)
RIA Tax........ Research Institute of America Tax Coordinator [*A publication*] (DLA)
RIAX........... Rich International Airways, Inc. [*Air carrier designation symbol*]
RIB............ Racing Information Bureau [*British*] (CB)
RIB............ Railway Information Bureau
RIB............ Receiver Interface Board [*Navy Navigation Satellite System*] (DNAB)
RIB............ Recoverable Item Breakdown
RIB............ Recyclable, Incineratable, Biodegradable [*Food packaging*]
RIB............ Ribbed (AAG)
RIB............ Riberalta [*Bolivia*] [*Airport symbol*] (OAG)
Rib............ Ribose [*Also, r*] [*A sugar*]
RIB............ Right Inboard (MCD)
RIB............ Right Intermediate Bronchus [*Anatomy*]
RIB............ River Ice Breaker (PDAA)
RIB............ [*The*] Roman Inscriptions of Britain [*A publication*] (OCD)
RIB............ Rubberized Inflatable Boat (DOMA)
RIB............ Rural and Industries Bank of Western Australia [*Commercial firm*]
RIB............ Rural Industries Bureau
RIBA........... Recombinant Immunoblot Assay [*Medicine*]
RIBA........... Recombinant Immunoblot Assay (DMAA)
RIBA........... Royal Institute of British Architects (IID)
RIBA........... Royal Institute of British Architects, London [*1834*] (NGC)
RIBC........... Rigid Intermediate Bulk Container
RI Bd RC....... Rhode Island Board of Railroad Commission Reports [*A publication*] (DLA)
RIBE........... Reactive Ion Beam Etching
RIBEA.......... Rhode Island Business Educators Association (EDAC)
RIBI........... Ribi ImmunoChem Res [*NASDAQ symbol*] (TTSB)
RIBI........... Ribi Immunochem Research, Inc. [*NASDAQ symbol*] (NQ)
Ribilm......... Ribi Immunochem Research, Inc. [*Associated Press*] (SAG)
RIBIT.......... Read in Bed - It's Terrific
RIBLIM......... Reduction in Benefit Limitation
RIBMESC........ Resources Information Bank on Multicultural Education (AIE)
ribnwk......... Ribbonwork (VRA)
Ribozym........ Ribozyme Pharmaceuticals, Inc. [*Associated Press*] (SAG)
RIBS........... Readiness in Base Service [*Air Force*] (DOMA)
RIBS........... Restructured Infantry Battalion System (AABC)
RIBS........... Royal Institute of British Sculptors
RIBS........... Rutherford Ion Backscattering [*Medicine*] (DMAA)
RIBSS.......... Research Institute for the Behavioral and Social Sciences [*Army*]
rib vlt........ Ribbed Vault (VRA)
RIC............ RADAR Indicating Console [*FAA*]
RIC............ RADAR Input Control
RIC............ RADAR Intercept Calculator
RIC............ RADAR Intercept Control
RIC............ Radioimmunoconjugate
RIC............ Radio Industry Council [*British*]
RIC............ Rafter Input Converter
RIC............ Rainforest Information Centre [*Australia*] (EAIO)
RIC............ Range Instrumentation Conference (MUGU)
RIC............ Range Instrumentation Coordination (KSC)
RIC............ Raptor Information Center (EA)
RIC............ Rare-Earth Information Center (EA)
RIC............ Read-In Counter
RIC............ Receiver Impulse Characteristic (IAA)
RIC............ Reciprocal Impedance Converter (PDAA)
RIC............ Reconstituted Ion Current [*Chromatography*]
RIC............ Reconstructed Ion Chromatogram
RIC............ Record Identification Code [*Navy*]
RIC............ Recruiter Identification Code [*Military*]
RIC............ Regolamento Internazionale Carrozze [*International Carriage and Van Union*]
RIC............ Regulated Investment Company [*Business term*]
RIC............ Relocation Instruction Counter [*Computer science*] (OA)
RIC............ Remote Information Center
RIC............ Remote Interactive Communications [*Xerox Corp.*]
RIC............ Repairable Identification Code
RIC............ Repairable Item Code
RIC............ Repair Induction Code [*Module Maintenance Facility*]
RIC............ Repertoire Bibliographique des Institutions Chretiennes [*Bibliographical Repertory of Christian Institutions*] [*Centre de Recherche et de Documentation des Institutions Chretiennes*] [*France*] [*Information service or system*] (CRD)
RIC............ Replaceable Item Code
RIC............ Replacement Ion Chromatography [*Spectrometry*]
RIC............ Request for Instrumentation Clarification [*NASA*] (KSC)
RIC............ Resident Inspector-in-Charge
RIC............ Resistance, Inductance, and Capacitance (NASA)
RIC............ Resource Identification Code [*Navy*]
RIC............ Resource Information Center System [*Search system*]
RIC............ Retirement Income Credit
Ric............ Ricardus Malumbra [*Deceased, 1334*] [*Authority cited in pre-1607 legal work*] (DSA)
Ric............ Richard (King of England) (DLA)
RIC............ Richardson's Airway, Inc. [*ICAO designator*] (FAAC)
RIC............ Richmond [*Virginia*] [*Airport symbol*]
RIC............ Richmond [*Florida*] [*Seismograph station code, US Geological Survey Closed*] (SEIS)
RIC............ Richmond [*Diocesan abbreviation*] [*Virginia*] (TOCD)
RIC............ Ricks College, David O. McKay Learning Resources Center, Rexburg, ID [*OCLC symbol*] (OCLC)
RIC............ Right Iliac Crest [*Anatomy*] (DAVI)
RIC............ Right Internal Capsule [*Medicine*] (MEDA)
RIC............ Right Internal Carotid [*Artery*] [*Anatomy*] (DAVI)
RIC............ Right Internal Cartoid [*Medicine*] (MEDA)
RIC............ Road Information Center [*Arab Contractors Co.*] (IID)
RIC............ Rockwell International Corp. (NASA)
RIC............ Rodeo Information Commission (EA)
RIC............ Roman Imperial Coinage [*A publication*] (OCD)
RIC............ Routing Identification Code (NATG)
RIC............ Royal Institute of Chemistry [*Later, RSC*] [*British*]
RIC............ Royal Irish Constabulary
RIC............ Rural Information Center [*Department of Agriculture Information service or system*] (IID)
RIC............ Rural Innovation Centre [*Western Australia*]
RICA........... Costa Rica International, Inc. [*NASDAQ symbol*] (SAG)
RICA........... Railway Industry Clearance Association (EA)
RICA........... Research Institute for Consumer Affairs [*British*]
RICA........... Right Internal Cartoid Artery (MEDA)
RICA........... Rural Industry Council of Australia
RICAL.......... Research Information Center and Library [*Foster Wheeler Corp.*] [*Information service or system*] (IID)
Ric & S........ Rickards and Saunders' English Locus Standi Reports [*1890-94*] [*A publication*] (DLA)
Ricar.......... Ricardus [*Authority cited in pre-1607 legal work*] (DSA)
RICASIP........ Research Information Center and Advisory Service on Information Processing [*National Bureau of Standards - National Science Foundation*]
RICB........... Research into Child Blindness [*British*] (DI)
RICC........... Regional Interagency Coordinating Committee [*Department of Labor*]
RICC........... Remote Intercomputer Communications Interface (MCD)
RICC........... Reportable Item Control Code [*Army*] (AABC)
RICC........... Rice Industry Coordination Committee [*New South Wales, Australia*]
RICE........... American Rice, Inc. [*NASDAQ symbol*] (SAG)
RICE........... Amer Rice [*NASDAQ symbol*] (TTSB)
RICE........... Recreational Industries Council on Exporting (EA)
RICE........... Regional Information and Communications Exchange [*Rice University Library*] [*Houston, TX*]
RICE........... Relative Index of Combat Effectiveness [*Military British*]
RICE........... Research and Information Centre on Eritrea (EA)
RICE........... Research Institute on Care for the Elderly [*British*] (DBA)
RICE........... Resources in Computer Education [*Northwest Regional Educational Laboratory Microcomputer Software and Information for Teachers*] [*No longer available online*] [*Information service or system*]
RICE........... Rest, Ice, Compression, Elevation [*Medicine*]
Rice........... Rice's South Carolina Law Reports [*1838-39*] [*A publication*] (DLA)
RICE........... Right to a Comprehensive Education (EAIO)
Rice Ch........ Rice's South Carolina Equity Reports [*A publication*] (DLA)
RICE-DIETS..... Rest, Ice, Compression, and Elevation, - Drugs, Incision, Exercise Therapy, and Surgery [*Treatment for knee injuries*]
Rice Dig....... Rice's Digest of Patent Office Decisions [*A publication*] (DLA)
Rice Eq........ Rice's South Carolina Equity Reports [*1838-39*] [*A publication*] (DLA)
Rice Ev........ Rice's Law of Evidence [*A publication*] (DLA)
Rice L (SC).... Rice's South Carolina Law Reports [*A publication*] (DLA)
Rice's Code.... Rice's Code of Practice [*Colorado*] [*A publication*] (DLA)
Rice U......... Rice University (GAGS)
RICH........... Radiation-Induced Color Halo [*Physics*]
Rich........... Richard (King of England) (DLA)
Rich........... Richardson's Reports [*2-5 New Hampshire*] [*A publication*] (DLA)
RICH........... Richland, WA [*Commercial waste site*] (GAAI)
RICH........... Richmond National Battlefield Park
Rich & H....... Richardson and Hook's Street Railway Decisions [*A publication*] (DLA)
Rich & S....... Richardson and Sayles' Select Cases of Procedure without Writ [*Selden Society Publication 60*] [*A publication*] (DLA)
Rich & W....... Richardson and Woodbury's Reports [*2 New Hampshire*] [*A publication*] (DLA)
Richardson Law Practice... Richardson's Establishing a Law Practice [*A publication*] (DLA)
Rich Ch Pr..... Richardson's Chancery Practice [*1838*] [*A publication*] (DLA)
Rich CP........ Richardson's Practice Common Pleas [*England*] [*A publication*] (DLA)
RichCst........ Rich Coast Resources [*Associated Press*] (SAG)
Rich Ct Cl..... Richardson's Court of Claims Reports [*A publication*] (DLA)
Rich Dict...... Richardson's New Dictionary of the English Language [*A publication*] (DLA)
RICHE.......... Reseaud'Information et de Communication Hospitalier (OSI)

RichEl......... Richardson Electronics Ltd. [*Associated Press*] (SAG)
RICHEL........ Richmond - Cape Henry Environmental Laboratory [*NASA/USGS*]
Richfood...... Richfood Holdings, Inc. [*Associated Press*] (SAG)
Rich Land A... Richey's Irish Land Act [*A publication*] (DLA)
Rich NH........ Richardson's Reports [*3-5 New Hampshire*] [*A publication*] (DLA)
Rich PRCP... Richardson's Practical Register of English Common Pleas [*A publication*] (DLA)
Rich Pr KB... Richardson's Attorney's Practice in the Court of King's Bench [*8th ed.*] [*1792*] [*A publication*] (DLA)
Rich Pr Reg... Richardson's Practical Register of English Common Pleas [*A publication*] (DLA)
Richton........ Richton International Corp. [*Associated Press*] (SAG)
Rich Wills... Richardson's Law of Testaments and Last Wills [*A publication*] (DLA)
RichyEl......... Richey Electronics [*Associated Press*] (SAG)
RICK............ Ricks Cabaret International, Inc. [*NASDAQ symbol*] (SAG)
RICK............ Rick's Cabaret Intl [*NASDAQ symbol*] (TTSB)
RICK-A......... Rickettsial Battery [*Bacteriology*] (DAVI)
Rick & M..... Rickards and Michael's English Locus Standi Reports [*A publication*] (DLA)
Rick & S...... Rickards and Saunders' English Locus Standi Reports [*A publication*] (DLA)
RickCab....... Ricks Cabaret International, Inc. [*Associated Press*] (SAG)
Rick Eng St... Rickard's English Statutes [*A publication*] (DLA)
Ricks........... Ricks Cabaret International, Inc. [*Associated Press*] (SAG)
RICKW......... Rick's Cabaret Intl Wrrt [*NASDAQ symbol*] (TTSB)
RICL............ Receipt Inspection Checklist (DNAB)
RICM........... Reflection Interference Contrast Microscopy
RICM........... Registre International des Citoyens du Monde [*International Registry of World Citizens*]
RICM........... Right Intercostal Margin [*Medicine*]
RICMD......... Richmond Contract Management District (SAA)
RICMO......... RADAR Input Countermeasures Officer [*Air Force*]
RICMT......... RADAR Input Countermeasures Technician [*Air Force*]
RICO............ Racketeer Influenced and Corrupt Organization Act (DFIT)
RICO............ Racketeer-Influenced and Corrupt Organizations [*Nickname of a 1970 law used by federal prosecutors to indict organized crime leaders*]
RICO............ Racketeering in Interstate Commerce (DICI)
RI Comp of Rules of St Agencies... Rhode Island Compilation of Rules of State Agencies [*A publication*] (DLA)
RI Const...... Rhode Island Constitution [*A publication*] (DLA)
RICP............ Recurrent Intrahepatic Cholestasis of Pregnancy [*Obstetrics*] (DMAA)
RICRS.......... Rockford Institute Center on Religion and Society (EA)
Ric Ruf........ Ricardus Rufulus [*Authority cited in pre-1607 legal work*] (DSA)
RICS............ Range Instrumentation Control System
RICS............ Remote Image Confirming Sensor (MCD)
RICS............ Reports Index Control (MCD)
RICS............ Respiratory Intensive Care System [*Medicine*]
RICS............ Right Intercostal Space [*Anatomy*] (DAVI)
RICS............ Royal Institution of Chartered Surveyors [*British*]
RICS............ Rubber-Impregnated Chopped Strand (PDAA)
RI Ct Rec..... Rhode Island Court Records [*A publication*] (DLA)
RICU............ Respiratory Intensive Care Unit [*Medicine*]
RID.............. RADAR Input Drum
RID.............. Radial Immunodiffusion [*Analytical biochemistry*]
RID.............. Radial Immunodiffusion [*Immunology*] (DAVI)
RID.............. Radio Intelligence Division [*of the Federal Communications Commission*]
RID.............. Radioisotope Detection
RID.............. Range Instruments Development (MCD)
RID.............. Rapidate Interactive Debugger [*Computer science*] (MHDI)
RID.............. Real-Fluid Isentropic Decompression [*Engineering*]
RID.............. Recepter Interacting Domain [*Biochemistry*]
RID.............. Record Identity [*Military*] (AFIT)
RID.............. Records Issue Date [*Bell System*] (TEL)
RID.............. Reduced Ignition Relay (MCD)
RID.............. Refractive Index Detector [*Instrumentation*]
RID.............. Regimented Inmate Discipline [*Mississippi State Penitentiary*]
RID.............. Registry of Interpreters for the Deaf (EA)
RID.............. Reglement International Concernant le Transport des Marchandises Dangereuses [*International Regulation Governing the Carriage of Dangerous Goods*]
RID.............. Regulatory Integration Division [*Environmental Protection Agency*] (GFGA)
RID.............. Released to Inactive Duty
RID.............. Reliability Index Determination (MCD)
RID.............. Remission-Inducing Drug [*Medicine*]
RID.............. Remove Intoxicated Drivers [*An association*]
RID.............. Research Institutes and Divisions [*of National Institutes of Health*]
RID.............. Reset Inhibit Drive
RID.............. Reset Inhibit Drum
RID.............. Retrofit Installation Data (MCD)
RID.............. Reversible Intravas Device
RID.............. Review Item Discrepancy (MCD)
RID.............. Review Item Disposition [*NASA*] (NASA)
RID.............. Richmond, IN [*Location identifier FAA*] (FAAL)
RID.............. Rider College Library, Lawrenceville, NJ [*OCLC symbol*] (OCLC)
RID.............. Royal Irish Dragoons [*British military*] (DMA)
RIDA............ Raster Image Device Accelerator [*Printer technology*]
RIDA............ Reverse Isotope Dilution Assay [*Chemical analysis*]
RIDA............ Rural and Industrial Development Authority (NADA)
RIDAC.......... Range Interference Detecting and Control
RIDAURA..... Remission Inducing Drug, Au [*Chemical symbol for gold*], Rheumatoid Arthritis [*Gold-based drug manufactured by SmithKline Beckman Corp.*]
RIDB............ Readiness Intergrated Database
RIDC............ Ryerson International Development Centre [*Ryerson Polytechnical Institute*] [*Canada Research center*] (RCD)
RIDCSF........ Radial Immunodiffusion Cerebrospinal Fluid [*or Colloidal Gold*] [*Immunology*] (DAVI)
RIDD............ Range Instrumentation Development Division (SAA)
Riddell......... Riddell Sports, Inc. [*Associated Press*] (SAG)
Riddle's Lex... Riddle's Lexicon [*A publication*] (DLA)
RIDDOR........ Reporting of Injuries, Diseases, and Dangerous Occurrences Regulations [*British*]
RIDE............ Research Institute for Diagnostic Engineering
RIDE............ Ride Inc. [*NASDAQ symbol*] (TTSB)
RIDE............ Ride Snowboard Co. [*NASDAQ symbol*] (SAG)
RI Dec......... Rhode Island Decisions [*A publication*] (DLA)
RideInc........ Ride, Inc. [*Associated Press*] (SAG)
Rider C........ Rider College (GAGS)
RIDES.......... Rockford Infant Developmental Scales [*Child development test*]
RIDEX.......... Ridexchange (EA)
RIDF............ Random Input Describing Function [*Computer science*]
RIDG............ Ridgeview, Inc. [*NASDAQ symbol*] (SAG)
Ridg............ Ridgeway's Reports Tempore Hardwicke, Chancery and English King's Bench [*A publication*] (DLA)
RIDG............ Royal Inniskilling Dragoon Guards [*Military unit*] [*British*]
RIDG............ Royal Irish Dragoon Guards [*British military*] (DMA)
Ridg & Hard... Ridgeway's Reports Tempore Hardwicke, Chancery and English King's Bench [*A publication*] (DLA)
Ridg Ap....... Ridgeway's Irish Appeal (or Parliamentary) Cases [*A publication*] (DLA)
Ridg App..... Ridgeway's Irish Appeal (or Parliamentary) Cases [*A publication*] (DLA)
Ridg Cas...... Ridgeway's Reports Tempore Hardwicke, Chancery and English King's Bench [*A publication*] (DLA)
RIDGE.......... Ridge [*Commonly used*] (OPSA)
RIDGE.......... Ridge Interdisciplinary Global Experiments [*NOAA, NSF, ONR, and USGS*]
RIDGE.......... Ridge InterDisciplinary Global Experiments [*Program*] [*Marine science*] (OSRA)
RIDGES........ Ridges [*Commonly used*] (OPSA)
Ridgevw...... Ridgeview, Inc. [*Associated Press*] (SAG)
Ridgew........ Ridgeway's Reports Tempore Hardwicke, Chancery and English King's Bench [*A publication*] (DLA)
Ridgew Ir PC... Ridgeway's Irish Parliamentary Reports [*1784-96*] [*A publication*] (DLA)
Ridgew L & S (Ir)... Ridgeway, Lapp, and Schoales' Irish Term Reports [*A publication*] (DLA)
Ridgew L & S (Ire)... Ridgeway, Lapp, and Schoales' Irish Term Reports [*A publication*] (ILCA)
Ridgew T Hardw... Ridgeway's Reports Tempore Hardwicke, Chancery [*27 English Reprint*] [*1744-46*] [*A publication*] (DLA)
Ridgew T Hardw (Eng)... Ridgeway Tempore Hardwicke [*27 English Reprint*] [*A publication*] (DLA)
Ridg L & S... Ridgeway, Lapp, and Schoales' Irish Term Reports [*A publication*] (DLA)
Ridg Parl Rep... Ridgeway's Irish Parliamentary Reports [*1784-96*] [*A publication*] (DLA)
Ridg PC....... Ridgeway's Irish Appeal (or Parliamentary) Cases [*A publication*] (DLA)
Ridg Pr Rep... Ridgeway's Irish Appeal (or Parliamentary) Cases [*A publication*] (DLA)
Ridg Rep..... Ridgeway's Reports of State Trials in Ireland [*A publication*] (DLA)
Ridg St Tr.... Ridgeway's (Individual) Reports of State Trials in Ireland [*A publication*] (DLA)
Ridg Temp H... Ridgeway's Reports Tempore Hardwicke, Chancery [*27 English Reprint*] [*1744-46*] [*A publication*] (DLA)
Ridg T H...... Ridgeway's Reports Tempore Hardwicke, Chancery [*27 English Reprint*] [*1744-46*] [*A publication*] (DLA)
Ridg T Hard... Ridgeway's Reports Tempore Hardwicke, Chancery and English King's Bench [*27 English Reprint*] [*A publication*] (DLA)
Ridg T Hardw... Ridgeway's Reports Tempore Hardwicke, Chancery and English King's Bench [*27 English Reprint*] [*A publication*] (DLA)
Ridgw Ir PC... Ridgeway's Irish Parliamentary Cases [*A publication*] (DLA)
RIDI............ Receiving Inspection Detail Instruction [*NASA*] (NASA)
RIDIC.......... Radiopharmaceutical Internal Dose Information Center [*Oak Ridge, TN*] [*Department of Energy*] (GRD)
RIDIT........... Relative to an Identified Distribution Transformation [*Pharmacology*]
RIDL............ Radiation Instrument Development Laboratory
RIDL............ Riddell Sports [*NASDAQ symbol*] (TTSB)
RIDL............ Riddell Sports, Inc. [*NASDAQ symbol*] (SPSG)
RIDL............ Ridge Instrument Development Laboratory [*Navy*]
Ridley Civil & Ecc Law... Ridley's Civil and Ecclesiastical Law [*A publication*] (DLA)
RIDP............ Polymerase [*Deoxyribonucleic Acid*] [*Later, RDDP*] [*An enzyme*]
RIDP............ RADAR-IFF Data Processor (MCD)
RIDS............ Radio Information Distribution System (MCD)
RIDS............ Range Information Display System (MCD)
RIDS............ Receiving Inspection Data Status [*Report*] [*Nuclear energy*] (NRCH)
RIDS............ Regional Operations Control Centre Information Display System [*NORAD*]
RIDS............ Regulatory Information Distribution System [*Nuclear energy*] (NRCH)
Rid Sup Proc... Riddle's Supplementary Proceedings [*New York*] [*A publication*] (DLA)
RIE.............. RADAR Intercept Event
RIE.............. Range of Incentive Effectiveness
RIE.............. Reactive Ion Etching [*Semiconductor technology*]
RIE.............. Recognised Investment Exchange [*British*]

RIE Refrigeration Installation Equipment (SAA)
RIE Research in Education [*Monthly publication of ERIC*]
RIE Resources in Education [*Formerly, Research in Education*] [*National Institute of Education Database*]
RIE Retirement Income Endowment [*Insurance*]
RIE Rice Lake [*Wisconsin*] [*Airport symbol*] (OAG)
RIE Right Inboard Elevon [*Aviation*] (MCD)
RIE Royal Institute of Engineers [*British*]
RIEC Royal Indian Engineering College [*British*]
Ried Riedell's Reports [*68, 69 New Hampshire*] [*A publication*] (DLA)
RIEDA Reseau d'Innovations Educatives pour le Developpement en Afrique [*Network of Educational Innovation for Development in Africa*] (EAIO)
RIEDAC Research in International Economics of Disarmament and Arms Control [*A program of Columbia University School of International Affairs*]
RIEF Recycling Isoelectric Focusing [*Preparative electrophoresis*]
RIEI Roofing Industry Educational Institute (EA)
RIEM Research Institute for Environmental Medicine [*Army*] (MCD)
RIES Research Institute for Engineering Sciences [*Wayne State University*] [*Research center*] (RCD)
RIES Resonance Ionization Emission Spectroscopy
RIETCOM Regional Interagency Emergency Transportation Committee
RIF Cohen & Steers Realty Income Fund [*Formerly, Real Estate Securities Income Fund, Inc.*] [*AMEX symbol*] (CTT)
RIF Cohen & Steers Rlty Inc. Fd [*AMEX symbol*] (TTSB)
RIF Radio-Influence Field (IEEE)
RIF Radio Interference Filter
RIF Rapid Infrared Forming Technique [*Materials science*]
RIF Rate Input Form (NVT)
RIF Readiness Index Factor
RIF Reading Is Fundamental (EA)
RIF Receipt Inspection Form [*Military*] (DNAB)
RIF Reclearance in Flight [*Aviation*] (FAAC)
RIF Reconnaissance in Force [*Military*] (VNW)
RIF Reduced Injury Factor Baseball
RIF Reduction in Force [*Military*]
RIF Refund Information File [*IRS*]
RIF Relative Importance Factor (NASA)
RIF Release-Inhibiting Factor [*Endocrinology*]
RIF Reliability Improvement Factor
RIF Reportable Item File [*Military*] (AFIT)
RIF Resistance Inducing Factor (ADA)
RIF Richfield [*Utah*] [*Airport symbol*] (OAG)
RIF Richfield, UT [*Location identifier FAA*] (FAAL)
RIF Rifampicin [*An antibacterial, antibiotic, and antituberculin*] (DAVI)
RIF Rifampin [*Also, R/AMP, RF, RMP*] [*Bactericide*]
RIF Rifle
RIF Right Iliac Fossa [*Medicine*]
RIF Right Internal Fixation [*Orthopedics*] (DAVI)
RIF Rodeo Information Foundation [*Later, Rodeo News Bureau*]
RIF Royal Inniskilling Fusiliers [*Military unit*] [*British*]
RIF Royal Irish Fusiliers [*Military unit*] [*British*]
RIFA Radioiodinated Fatty Acid [*Medicine*] (MAE)
RIFC Radioactive Illuminated Fire Control (MCD)
RIFC Radio In-Flight Correction
RIFC Rat Intrinsic Factor Concentrate
RIFCM Roll Integrated Flight Control Module (MCD)
RIFF Raster Image File Format [*Computer science*] (BTTJ)
RIFF Resource Interchange File Format [*Computer science*] (PCM)
RIFF Resource Interchange File Format [*Computer science*] (CDE)
RIFFED Forced Out by a Reduction in Force
RIFFI Riksforbundet Internationella Foereningen foer Invandrarkvinnor [*Sweden*]
RIFI Radio Interference Field Intensity [*Meter*] (NG)
RIFI Radio-Interference-Free Instrument
RIFIM Radio Interference Field Intensity Meter
RIFL Random Item File Locater
RIFLIP Restriction Fragment-Length Polymorphism (BARN)
RIFM Research Institute for Fragrance Materials (EA)
RIFMA Roentgen-Isotope-Fluorescent Method of Analysis
RIFN Recombinant Interferon [*Biochemistry*]
RIFS Radioisotope Field Support
RI/FS Remedial Investigation and Feasibility Study [*Environmental Protection Agency*]
RIFT Reactor-in-Flight Test [*NASA*]
RIFT Resin Infusion Under Flexible Tooling
RIFT/S Reactor-in-Flight Test/System [*NASA*] (AAG)
RIG Rabies Immune Globulin [*Immunology*]
RIG Radio Inertial Guidance (AAG)
RIG Radio Interference Guard
RIG Rate Integrating Gyro
RIG Refractive Index Gradient [*Analytical chemistry*]
RIG Ridgeling [*Horse racing*]
RIG Riga Airlines [*Latvia*] [*ICAO designator*] (FAAC)
RIG Rigging (ROG)
RIG Rio Grande [*Brazil*] [*Airport symbol*] (OAG)
RIG Roll-Imitation Gold
RIG Royal Institue of Geology [*British*] (NUCP)
RIG Sonat Offshore Drilling [*NYSE symbol*] (TTSB)
RIG Sonat Offshore Drilling, Inc. [*NYSE symbol*] (SPSG)
RIG Transocean Offshore, Inc. [*NYSE symbol*] (SAG)
RIGB Royal Institution of Great Britain
Rigel Rigel Energy [*Associated Press*] (SAG)
RI Gen Laws General Laws of Rhode Island [*A publication*] (DLA)
RIGES Renewable Intensive Global Energy Scenario
RIGFET Resistive Insulated-Gate Field Effect Transistor
Rigg Select Pleas, Starrs, and Other Records from the Rolls of the Exchequer of the Jews, Edited by J. M. Riggs [*Selden Society Publications, Vol. 15*] [*A publication*] (DLA)
RIGGS Ross Ice Shelf Geophysical and Glaciological Survey [*Ross Ice Shelf Project*]
RIGH Rabies Immune Globulin, Human [*Immunology*] (MAE)
Rightch Rightchoice Managed Care Co. [*Associated Press*] (SAG)
RIGHTS Reforming Institutions to Guarantee Humane Treatment Standards [*Student legal action organization*]
RIGI Receiving Inspection General Instruction [*NASA*] (NASA)
rIGIF Recombinant Interferon Gamma-Inducing Factor [*Biochemistry*]
RIGR Rhode Island Government Register [*A publication*] (AAGC)
RIGS Radioimmunoguided Surgery [*Medicine*]
RIGS Radio Inertial Guidance System
RIGS Resonant Infrasonic Gauging System
RIGS Riggs National Corp. [*NASDAQ symbol*] (NQ)
RIGS Riggs Natl Corp. [*NASDAQ symbol*] (TTSB)
RIGS Runway Identifiers with Glide Slope [*Aviation*]
RigsNt Riggs National Corp. [*Associated Press*] (SAG)
RIH Rhode Island Hospital, Providence, RI [*OCLC symbol*] (OCLC)
RIH Right Inguinal Hernia [*Medicine*]
RIHANS River and Harbor Aid to Navigation System [*Coast Guard*]
RIHED Regional Institute of Higher Education and Development
RIHL Richton International Corp. (MHDW)
RiHM Riemann, "Handbuch der Musikgeschichte" [*A publication*]
RIHS Royal International Horse Show [*British*]
RIHSA Radioactive Iodinate Human Serum Albumin [*Clinical chemistry*] (AAMN)
RII RADAR Intelligence Information
RII Receiving Inspection Instruction [*Nuclear energy*] (NRCH)
RII Request for Intelligence Information [*Military*] (INF)
RII Resort Income Investors, Inc. [*AMEX symbol*] (CTT)
RIIA Royal Institute of International Affairs [*British*]
RIIC Research Institute on International Change [*Columbia University*]
RIIES Research Institute on Immigration and Ethnic Studies [*Smithsonian Institution*]
RIIS Route Integration Instrumentation System (LAIN)
RIISE Research Institute for Information Science and Engineering, Inc. [*Information service or system*] (IID)
RIISOM Research Institute for Iron, Steel, and Other Metals (MHDB)
RIIXS Remote Interrogation Information Exchange System (DNAB)
RIJ Right Internal Jugular [*Vein*] [*Anatomy*]
RIJ Rioja [*Peru*] [*Airport symbol*] (OAG)
RIJ Romano Internacionalno Jekhethanibe [*International Romani Union*] (EA)
RIJC Rhode Island Junior College [*Later, CCRI*]
RIK Eurojet Compagnie [*British ICAO designator*] (FAAC)
RIK Replacement in Kind (NG)
RIKE Raman-Induced Kerr Effect (PDAA)
RIKES Raman-Induced Kerr Effect Scattering [*Spectroscopy*]
RIL Radio Influence Level
RIL Radio Interference Level
RIL Radiolocation (IAA)
RIL Recombinant Interleukin [*Immunotherapy*]
RIL Recoverable Item List
RIL Red Indicator Light
RIL Reduction in Leadtime (MCD)
RIL Reliability Intensity Level (CAAL)
RIL Repairable Item List (CAAL)
RIL Representation Independent Language (NITA)
RIL Reset Indicators of the Left Half (IAA)
RIL Res Ipsa Loquitur [*The Thing Speaks for Itself*] [*Latin*]
RIL Res Ipsa Loquitur [*Speaks for Itself*] [*Latin*] (LWAP)
RIL Rifle, CO [*Location identifier FAA*] (FAAL)
Ril Riley's South Carolina Chancery Reports [*1836-37*] [*A publication*] (DLA)
Ril Riley's South Carolina Equity Reports [*A publication*] (DLA)
RIL University of Rhode Island, Graduate Library School, Kingston, RI [*OCLC symbol*] (OCLC)
RILAMAC Research in Laboratory Animal Medicine and Care
RILEM Reunion Internationale des Laboratoires d'Essais et de Recherches sur les Materiaux et les Constructions [*International Union of Testing and Research Laboratories for Materials and Structures*] (EAIO)
Riley Riley's Reports [*37-42 West Virginia*] [*A publication*] (DLA)
Riley Riley's South Carolina Chancery Reports [*A publication*] (DLA)
Riley Riley's South Carolina Law Reports [*A publication*] (DLA)
Riley Ch Riley's South Carolina Equity Reports [*A publication*] (DLA)
Riley Eq Riley's South Carolina Equity Reports [*A publication*] (DLA)
Riley Eq (SC) Riley's South Carolina Equity Reports [*A publication*] (DLA)
Riley L (SC) Riley's South Carolina Law Reports [*A publication*] (DLA)
RILFC Rhode Island Library Film Cooperative [*Library network*]
Ril Harp Riley's Edition of Harper's South Carolina Reports [*A publication*] (DLA)
RILKO Research into Lost Knowledge Organisation Trust (EAIO)
RILOP Reclamation in Lieu of Procurement [*Navy*] (NG)
RILPG Regenerative Injection Liquid Propellant Gun (MCD)
RILS Ranging Integration Location System
RILS Rapid Integrated Logistic Support System [*Military*] (AABC)
RILSA Resident Integrated Logistics Support Activity [*Military*] (AFIT)
RILSD Resident Integrated Logistics Support Detachment [*Military*] (MCD)
RILST Remote Integrated Logistics Support Team [*Military*] (MCD)
RILT Rabbit Ileal Loop Test [*for enterotoxins*]

RILWAS Regionalized Integrated Lake-Watershed Acidification Study [*Adirondack mountains*]
RIM Mauritania [*International vehicle registration*] (ODBW)
RIM Merrill Lynch & Co. [*AMEX symbol*] (SAG)
RIM RADAR Input Mapper
RIM RADAR Input Monitor (CET)
RIM RADAR Intelligence Map
RIM Radial Inlet Manifold
RIM Radiant Intensity Measurements (MUGU)
RIM Radioisotope Medicine
RIM Radioisotope Method [*Analytical chemistry*]
RIM Railroad Interdiction Mine [*DoD*]
RIM Rate Improvement Mortgage [*Banking*]
RIM Reaction Injection Molding [*Plastics technology*]
RIM Readiness Indicator Model (MCD)
RIM Read-In Mode
RIM Read Interrupt Mask [*Computer science*]
RIM Receipt, Inspection, and Maintenance [*Military*]
RIM Receiver Intermodulation [*Telecommunications*] (TEL)
RIM Recreation Information Management System [*Department of Agriculture Washington, DC Information service or system*] (IID)
RIM Recurrent Induced Malaria [*Medicine*] (DMAA)
RIM Refractive Index Matching [*Coal technology*]
RIM Regulation Interpretation Memorandum [*Environmental Protection Agency*]
RIM Rehabilitation Institute of Michigan
RIM Relational Information Management [*Acronym is title of a book by Wayne Erickson*] (PCM)
RIM Relative-Intensity Measure [*Medicine*] (DMAA)
RIM Relative Intensity Measures [*of nursing care*]
RIM Request Initialization Mode (IAA)
RIM Research Instrument Module (IAA)
RIM Resident Industrial Manager
RIM Resource Interface Module [*Datapoint*]
RIM Rim [*Hawaii*] [*Seismograph station code, US Geological Survey*] (SEIS)
RIM Rimrock Airlines, Inc. [*ICAO designator*] (FAAC)
RIM Rockridge Mining [*Vancouver Stock Exchange symbol*]
RIM Rotors in Motion [*Aviation*] (AIA)
RIM Royal Indian Marine
RIM RSU [*Remote Subscriber Unit*] Interface Module [*Telecommunications*]
RIM Rubber Insulation Material
RIMA Right Internal Mammary Anastomosis [*Cardiology*] (DAVI)
RIMA Right Internal Mammary Artery [*Anatomy*] (AAMN)
RIMAD Refractive Index Matched Anomalous Diffraction [*Light measurement*]
Rimage Rimage Corp. [*Associated Press*] (SAG)
RIMAS Russian Independent Mutual Aid Society (EA)
RIMAT Must Ride Company Material (FAAC)
RiMB Riemann, "Musikgeschichte in Beispielen" [*A publication*]
RIMB Roche Institute of Molecular Biology
RIMC Reparable Item Movement Control [*Military*] (AFIT)
RIMC Reportable Items of Major Combinations [*Army*] (AABC)
RIMCS Reparable Item Movement Control System [*Military*] (AFIT)
RIMD Regulation and Information Management Division [*Environmental Protection Agency*] (EPA)
RIMD Resources and Institutional Management Division [*NASA*]
RIME Radio Inertial Missile Equipment
RIME Radio Inertial Monitoring Equipment (KSC)
RIME Ranking Index for Maintenance Expenditures (PDAA)
RIME Relaynet International Message Exchange [*Information network*] [*Computer science*] (PCM)
RIME Research Institute for Management Executives [*Washington, DC*]
RIMF Reportable Item Master File [*Military*] (AFIT)
RIMG Rimage Corp. [*NASDAQ symbol*] (SAG)
RIMI Research Improvement in Minority Institutions [*Program*] [*National Science Foundation*]
RiML Riemann, "Musik Lexikon" [*A publication*]
RIMLF Rostral Interstitial Nucleus of Medial Longitudinal Fasciculus [*Neuroanatomy*]
RIMM Report on Improved Manpower Management
RIMMS RVNAF [*Republic of Vietnam Air Force*] Improvement and Modernization Management System
RIMOB Reserve Indication of Mobilization [*Army*] (AABC)
RIMP Minimum Range to Avoid Plumb Impingement (MCD)
RIMP Remote Input Message Processor
RIMP Risk Management Program (MCD)
RIMPAC Rim of the Pacific [*Naval exercise; name refers to the four participating countries: Australia, Canada, New Zealand, and the United States*]
RIMPTF Recording Industries Music Performance Trust Funds [*Later, MPTF*] (EA)
RIMR Rockefeller Institute for Medical Research
RIMRASP Reserve Intelligence Mobilization Readiness and Support Projects (MCD)
RIMS RADAR In-Flight Monitoring System
RIMS Radiant Intensity Measuring System
RIMS Radio Interference Measuring System
RIMS Record Information Movement Study (KSC)
RIMS Regional Information Management System [*FHWA*] (TAG)
RIMS Remote Information Management System
RIMS Replacement Inertial Measurement System
RIMS Requirements Inventory Management System (MCD)
RIMS Resonance Ionization Mass Spectrometry
RIMS Retarding Ion Mass Spectrometer [*Instrumentation*]
RIMS Revised Interheater Mobility Study (DOMA)
RIMS Risk and Insurance Management Society [*Database producer*] (EA)
RIMSE Relative Integrated Mean Square Error [*Statistics*]
RIMS II Regional Input-Output Modeling System
RIMSTOP Retail Inventory Management/Stockage Policy [*DoD*]
RIMTech Research Institute for the Management of Technology [*Southern California Technology Executives Network*] [*Research center*] (RCD)
R_{in} Input Resistance (IDOE)
RIN Radio Inertial (MSA)
RIN Rassemblement pour l'Independance Nationale [*Quebec separatist party, 1960-1968*] [*Canada*]
RIN Rat Insulinoma [*A cell line*]
RIN Record Identification Number
RIN Redpath Industries Ltd. [*Toronto Stock Exchange symbol*]
RIN Reference Indication Number
RIN Register in Instruction [*Computer science*] (IAA)
RIN Regular Inertial Navigator (MCD)
RIN Regulatory Identifier Number [*Environmental Protection Agency*]
RIN Report Identification Number [*Military*] (AABC)
Rin Riner's Reports [*2 Wyoming*] [*A publication*] (DLA)
RIN Ringi Cove [*Solomon Islands*] [*Airport symbol*] (OAG)
RIN Rotor Impulsive Noise [*Helicopters*]
RIN Royal Indian Navy
RIN Royal Institute of Navigation (DS)
RIN Springfield, MO [*Location identifier FAA*] (FAAL)
RINA Resident Inspector of Naval Aircraft
RINA Royal Institution of Naval Architects [*British*]
RINAL RADAR Inertial Altimeter
RINC Recruiter-in-Charge (DNAB)
RIND Research Institute of National Defense (NADA)
RIND Reversible Ischemic Neurological Deficit [*or Disability*] [*Medicine*]
Riner Riner's Reports [*2 Wyoming*] [*A publication*] (DLA)
RINEX Receiver-Independent Exchange [*Navigation systems*] [*Data communications*]
RINF Rinforzando [*With Special Emphasis*] [*Music*]
RINFZ Rinforzando [*With Special Emphasis*] [*Music*]
RING Ringer
RING Ringer Corp. [*NASDAQ symbol*] (SAG)
Ring Bank Ringwood's Principles of Bankruptcy [*18th ed.*] [*1947*] [*A publication*] (DLA)
RINGDOC Pharmaceutical Literature Documentation [*Derwent Publications Ltd.*] [*British Information service or system*] (IID)
RINGDOC Ring Documentation (NITA)
Ringer Ringer Corp. [*Associated Press*] (SAG)
RINM Resident Inspector of Naval Material
RINN Recommended International Nonproprietary Name [*Drug research*]
RINR Royal Indian Naval Reserve [*British military*] (DMA)
RINS Research Institute for the Natural Sciences
RINS Resident Inspector
RINS Rotorace Inertial Navigation System (MCD)
RINSMAT Resident Inspector of Naval Material (MUGU)
RINSORD Resident Naval Inspector of Ordnance
RINSPOW Resident Naval Inspector of Powder
RINSUL Rubber Insulation
RINT RADAR Intermittent (MSA)
RINT Radiation Intelligence
RINT Reality Interactive [*NASDAQ symbol*] (TTSB)
RINT Reality Interactive, Inc. [*NASDAQ symbol*] (SAG)
R Int'l Arb Awards United Nations Reports of International Arbitral Awards [*A publication*] (DLA)
RINTU Reality Interactive Unit [*NASDAQ symbol*] (TTSB)
RINTW Reality Interactive Wrrt [*NASDAQ symbol*] (TTSB)
RINVR Royal Indian Naval Volunteer Reserve [*British military*] (DMA)
RIO RADAR Intercept Officer [*Navy*]
RIO RADAR-Intercept Operator
RIO Radio Information Office [*National Audience Board*] (NTCM)
RIO Radio Intercept Officer (MCD)
RIO Ramus Infraorbitalis [*Anatomy*]
RIO Registry of Italian Oddities (EA)
RIO Relocatable Input/Output
RIO Remain Intact Organization (EA)
RIO Remote Input/Output (NITA)
RIO Reporting In and Out [*Military*]
RIO Research Industry Office (MCD)
RIO Reshaping the International Order [*Title of Club of Rome report*]
RIO Resident Inspector Office [*Coast Guard*]
RIO Resident Inspector of Ordnance (AAG)
RIO Resin-in-Pulp [*Process for uranium ore treatment*] (IIA)
RIO Retail Issue Outlets (NG)
RIO Ride-It-Out
RIO Right Inferior Oblique [*Medicine*] (DMAA)
RIO Right Inferior Oblique [*Projection*] [*Radiology*] (DAVI)
RIO Rio De Janeiro [*Brazil*] [*Airport symbol*] (OAG)
RIO Rio Grant [*Caja Del Rio*] [*New Mexico*] [*Seismograph station code, US Geological Survey*] [*Closed*] (SEIS)
RIO Rio Sierra Silver [*Vancouver Stock Exchange symbol*]
RIO Roll in Only (NITA)
RIO Royal Italian Opera
RioAl Rio Algom Ltd. [*Associated Press*] (SAG)
RIOC Remote Input/Output Controller [*Computer science*] (MHDB)
RIOGD Rio Grande (FAAC)
RIOH Rio Hotel & Casino [*Formerly, MarCor Resorts, Inc.*] [*NASDAQ symbol*] (SPSG)
RioHtl Rio Hotel & Casino [*Associated Press*] (SAG)

RIOJ............ Recurrent Intrahepatic Obstructive Jaundice [*Medicine*] (MAE)
RIOMETER... Relative Ionospheric Opacity Meter
RIOPR.......... Rhode Island Open Pool Reactor
RIO-RIT-RIM... Religion Index Database - Religion Index One; Religion Index Two; Research in Ministry [*American Theological Library Association*] [*Information service or system*] (CRD)
RIOS............ Joint Working Group on River Inputs to Ocean Systems [*Marine science*] (MSC)
RIOS............ Receiving Inspection Operating Sheet (MCD)
RIOS............ Remote Input-Output System [*Computer science*] (IAA)
RIOS............ ROM [*Read-Only Memory*] BIOS [*Pronounced "rye-ose"*] [*Computer science*]
RIOS............ Rotating Image Optical Scanner
RIOT............ RAM Input/Output Timer
RIOT............ Real-Time Input-Output Transducer [*or Translator*] [*Computer science*]
RIOT............ Remote Independently-Operated Transceiver
RIOT............ Remote Input/Output Terminal [*Computer science*]
RIOT............ Resolution of Initial Operational Techniques
RIOT............ Retrieval of Information by On-Line Terminal [*Atomic Energy Authority*] [*Computer science British*]
RIOTEX........ Riot Exercise (DNAB)
RIP............... RADAR Identification Point (AFM)
RIP............... RADAR Improvement Plan (NATG)
RIP............... RADAR Improvement Program
RIP............... Radioimmunoprecipitation [*Clinical chemistry*]
RIP............... Radioisotopic Pathology [*Medical specialty*] (DHSM)
RIP............... Radiological Information Plot (NATG)
RIP............... Random Input Sampling [*Computer science*]
RIP............... Rapid Ignition Propagation (MCD)
RIP............... Rapid Infusion Pump [*Chemotherapy*] (DAVI)
RIP............... Rapid Installation Plan
RIP............... Raster Image Processor [*Printer technology*]
RIP............... Rate-Invariant Path [*Economic theory*]
RIP............... Rays Initiating from a Point (MCD)
RIP............... RCRA [*Resource Conservation and Recovery Act*] Implementation Plan [*Environmental Protection Agency*] (GFGA)
RIP............... Reactive Ion Plating [*Coating technology*]
RIP............... Reactor Instrument Penetration Valve (IEEE)
RIP............... Readiness Improvement Program [*Military*] (CAAL)
RIP............... Rearrangement Induced Premeiotically [*Genetics*]
RIP............... Receiving Inspection Plan [*Nuclear energy*] (NRCH)
RIP............... Recoverable Item Program [*Marine Corps*]
RIP............... Reduction Implementation Panel [*DoD*]
RIP............... Reduction in Paperwork (SAA)
RIP............... Reenlistment Incentive Program (DNAB)
RIP............... Refractive Index Profile
RIP............... Register Indicator Panel
RIP............... Register of Intelligence Publications (MCD)
RIP............... Relationship Improvement Program (SAA)
RIP............... Reliability Improvement Program
RIP............... Remain in Place (MCD)
RIP............... Remote Image Protocol [*Computer science*]
RIP............... Remote Indicator Panel (CAAL)
RIP............... Remote Instrument Package (PDAA)
RIP............... Renin Inhibitory Peptide [*Biochemistry*]
RIP............... Repeat-Induced Point Mutation [*Genetic engineering technique*]
RIP............... Report on Individual Personnel (MCD)
RIP............... Requiescat [*or Requiescant*] in Pace [*May He (She, or They) Rest in Peace*] [*Latin*] (GPO)
RIP............... Research in Parapsychology [*A publication*]
RIP............... Research in Progress (MCD)
RIP............... Reset In Proportion [*A printing instruction*] (WDMC)
RIP............... Resin-in-Pulp [*Ore processing*]
RIP............... Respiratory Inversion Point [*Physiology*]
RIP............... Rest in Peace (TAG)
RIP............... Rest in Proportion [*Printing*] (WDMC)
RIP............... Retired in Place [*Telecommunications*] (TEL)
RIP............... Retirement Improvement Program [*Air Force*] (AFM)
RIP............... Retirement Income Plan [*Insurance*] (MCD)
RIP............... Ribosome Inactivating [*or Inhibiting*] Protein [*Biochemistry*]
RIP............... Ring Index Pointer [*Computer science*] (OA)
RIP............... Ripieno [*Additional*] [*Music*]
rip............... Ripped [*Lumber*] (BARN)
RIP............... Ripple Resources Ltd. [*Vancouver Stock Exchange symbol*]
RIP............... Rolling Injection Planter (GNE)
RIP............... Routing Information Process [*or Protocol*] [*Telecommunications*] (TEL)
RIP............... Rural Industrialization Program [*Department of Agriculture*]
RIPA............ Radioimmunoprecipitation Assay [*Clinical chemistry*]
RIPA............ Royal Institute of Public Administration [*British*]
RIPAA.......... Royal Institute of Public Administration Australia [*Australia*]
RIPC............ Regroupement des Independants et Paysans Camerounais [*Regrouping of Independents and Farmers of the Cameroons*]
RIPCO.......... Receiving Inspection and Preparation for Checkout (SAA)
RIPD............ RLG [*Research Libraries Group, Inc.*] Research-in-Progress Database [*Information service or system*] (CRD)
RIPE............ Range Instrumentation Performance Evaluation (MUGU)
RIPEM.......... Riordan's Internet Privacy Enhanced Mail [*Computer science*]
RIPFCOMTF... Rapid Item Processor to Facilitate Complex Operations on Magnetic Tape Files [*Computer science*]
RIPH & H...... Royal Institute of Public Health and Hygiene [*British*]
RIPILS.......... Recently Immigrated Professional Irish Legals [*Lifestyle classification*]
RIPIS............ Rhode Island Pupil Identification Scale [*Psychology*]
RIPL............ Representation-Independent Programming Language
RIPOM.......... Report [*command indicated*] If Present, Otherwise by Message [*Navy*]
RIPOSTE...... Restitution Incentive Program Operationalized as a Strategy Toward an Effective Learning Environment [*HEW*]
RIPP............ RADAR Intelligence Photo Producer
RIPP............ Regulatory Information on Pesticide Products [*Database*] (IT)
RIPP............ Resistive-Intermittent Positive Pressure [*Medicine*] (DMAA)
RIPP............ Russian-American Institute for President Programs [*For technology transfer*]
RIPPLE........ Radioactive Isotope-Powered Pulse Light Equipment (IEEE)
RIPPLE........ Radioisotope-Powered Prolonged Life Equipment (IEEE)
RIPPLE........ Radioisotope Power Packages for Electricity [*Nuclear energy*] (NUCP)
RIPPLE........ Ripplesmere [*England*]
RIPR............ Recommended Immediate Procurement Records (MCD)
RIPRS.......... Recovery Improvement Program Reporting System
RIPS............ RADAR Impact Prediction System (CET)
RIPS............ Radio-Isotope Power Supply [*or System*] [*Nuclear energy*] (NG)
RIPS............ Range Instrumentation Planning Study [*AFSC*]
RIPS............ Raster Image Processor System (PCM)
RIPS............ Remote Image Processing System
RIPS............ Research Institute of Pharmaceutical Sciences [*University of Mississippi*] (PDAA)
RI Pub Laws... Public Laws of Rhode Island [*A publication*] (DLA)
RIPV............ Reactor Isolation Pressure Valve (IEEE)
RIPWC.......... Royal Institute of Painters in Water-Colours [*British*]
RIQAP.......... Reduced Inspection Quality Assurance Program
RIQS............ Remote Information Query System [*Information retrieval service*] [*Computer science*]
RIR............... RADAR Interface Recorder (MCD)
RIR............... Range Illumination RADAR
RIR............... Read-Only Memory Instruction Register [*Computer science*] (IAA)
RIR............... Receiving Inspection Report
RIR............... Redgrave Information Resources Corp. [*Publisher*]
RiR............... Redgrave Information Resources Corp., Westport, CT [*Library symbol Library of Congress*] (LCLS)
RIR............... Reduction in Requirement [*Air Force*] (AFM)
RIR............... Regimental Inquiry Regulations [*British military*] (DMA)
RIR............... Rehabilitation Information Round Table (EA)
RIR............... Relative Index Register (NITA)
RIR............... Reliability Investigation Requests (KSC)
RIR............... Reportable Item Report [*NASA*] (NASA)
RIR............... Reporting Interface Record [*Computer science*] (IAA)
RIR............... Request Immediate Reply [*Business term*] (MHDB)
RIR............... Reset Indicators of the Right Half (IAA)
RIR............... Resonant Internal Reflection
RIR............... Rhode Island Red [*Poultry*]
RIR............... Ribbon-to-Ribbon (IAA)
RIR............... Richmond International Raceway [*Auto racing*]
RIR............... Right Iliac Region [*Medicine*] (MAE)
RIR............... Right Inferior Rectus [*Muscle*] [*Anatomy*] (DAVI)
RIR............... Riverside/Rubidoux, CA [*Location identifier FAA*] (FAAL)
RIR............... ROM [*Read-Only Memory*] Instruction Register
RIR............... Royal Irish Rifles [*British military*] (DMA)
RIRA............ Reports and Information Retrieval Activity (NITA)
RIRAA.......... Russian Immigrants' Representative Association In America
RIRAP.......... Recombinant Interleukin Receptor Antagonist Protein [*Biochemistry*]
RIRB............ Radioiodinated Rose Bengal [*Medicine*] (MAE)
RIRB............ Railway Insurance Rating Bureau [*Defunct*] (EA)
RIRCA.......... Rhode Island Red Club of America (EA)
RI/RD.......... Rockwell International/Rocketdyne Division
RI Rep.......... Rhode Island Reports [*A publication*] (DLA)
RIrF............. Royal Irish Fusiliers [*Military unit*] [*British*] (DMA)
RIRIG.......... Reduced-Excitation Inertial Reference Integrating Gyro
RIRJ............ Research Institute of Religious Jewry (EA)
RIRMA.......... Revisers, Ink and Roller Makers' Auxiliaries [*A union*] [*British*] (DI)
RIRMS.......... Remote Information Retrieval and Management System [*Computer science*] (BUR)
RIRO............ Roll-In/Roll-Out [*Storage allocation*] [*Computer science*]
RIRS............ Railroad Inspection Reporting System [*BTS*] (TAG)
RIRS............ Reliability Information Retrieval System (MCD)
RIRT............ Rehabilitation Information Round Table (EA)
RIRT............ Rhodium-Iron Resistance Thermometer
RIRTI.......... Recording Infrared Tracking Instrument
RIS............... Air Services Ltd. [*Czechoslovakia*] [*ICAO designator*] (FAAC)
RIS............... Kansas City, MO [*Location identifier FAA*] (FAAL)
RIS............... RADAR Information Service [*Aviation*] (DA)
RIS............... RADIAC [*Radiation Detection, Indication, and Computation*] Instrument System
RIS............... Radio Information Service (WDAA)
RIS............... Radio Interference Service [*Department of Trade*] [*British*]
RIS............... Radiology Information System [*Computer science*]
RIS............... Railway Invigoration Society [*British*] (BI)
RIS............... Ramjet Inlet System
RIS............... Range Information System [*For aircraft*] (MCD)
RIS............... Range Instrumentation Ship
RIS............... Range Instrumentation Station
RIS............... Raster Input Scanner (NITA)
RIS............... Reblooming Iris Society (EA)
RIS............... Receipt Inspection Segment (OA)
RIS............... Receiving Inspection Segment
RIS............... RECON Information System (MCD)
RIS............... Recorded Information Service [*Telecommunications*] (TEL)
RIS............... Record Input Subroutine
RIS............... Redwood Inspection Service (EA)

RIS.............. Regulatory Impact Statement
RIS.............. Regulatory Information Service [*Congressional Information Service, Inc.*] [*Information service or system Defunct*]
RIS.............. Relative Impact Strength [*Mechanical engineering*]
RIS.............. Relevent Industry Sales (PDAA)
RIS.............. Reliability Information System
RIS.............. Remote Information System
RIS.............. Reporting Identification Symbol (IAA)
RIS.............. Reports Identification Symbol
RIS.............. Requirements Planning and Inventory Control System [*Computer science*] (IAA)
RIS.............. Research Information Service [*John Crerar Library*] [*Information service or system*] (IID)
RIS.............. Research Information Services [*Georgia Institute of Technology*] [*Atlanta*] [*Information service or system*] (IID)
RIS.............. Research Information System [*Rehabilitation Services Administration*] (IID)
RIS.............. Reset Indicators Form Storage [*Computer science*] (IAA)
RIS.............. Resistor Insulator Semiconductor (IAA)
RIS.............. Resonance Ionization Spectroscopy
RIS.............. Retail Information System (BUR)
RIS.............. Retarded Infants Services [*Later, CFS*] (EA)
RIS.............. Retransmission Identity Signal [*Telecommunications*] (TEL)
RIS.............. Retroreflector in Space [*Instrumentation*]
RIS.............. Revolution Indicating System (MSA)
RIS.............. Rise Resources, Inc. [*Vancouver Stock Exchange symbol*]
RIS.............. Rishiri [*Japan*] [*Airport symbol Obsolete*] (OAG)
RIS.............. Rock Island Southern Railroad (IIA)
RIS.............. Rotatable Initial Susceptibility
RIS.............. Rotating Image Scanner
RIS.............. Routine Interest Shipping (MCD)
RIS.............. Russian Intelligence Service
RISA........... Radioactive Iodinated Serum Albumin [*Scan or Study*] [*Medicine*] (DAVI)
RISA........... Radioimmunosorbent Assay [*Clinical chemistry*]
RISA........... Radioiodinated Serum Albumin [*Medicine*]
RISA........... Railway and Industrial Spring Association [*Later, RISRI*]
RISA........... Romani Imperii Semper Auctor [*Continual Increaser of the Roman Empire*] [*Latin*]
RIS-ALEX..... Research Information Services - Alexander Library
RISB........... Rotter Incomplete Sentences Blank [*Psychology*]
RISC........... Reduced Instruction Set Chip (NITA)
RISC........... Reduced-Instruction-Set Computer (DMAA)
RISC........... Reduced Instruction Set Computer
RISC........... Reduced Instruction-Set Computing (PCM)
RISC........... Refractive Index Sounding Central
RISC........... Regulatory Information Service Center [*Office of Management and Budget*] (GFGA)
RISC........... Remote Information Systems Center
RISC........... Research Institute of Scripps Clinic [*Research center*] (RCD)
RISC........... RISCORP Inc. 'A' [*NASDAQ symbol*] (TTSB)
RISC........... Rockwell International Science Center
RISCT......... Research Institute of the Study of Conflict and Terrorism [*British*] (DBA)
RISD........... Requisition and Invoice Shipping Document
RISD........... Rhode Island School of Design
RISD........... Rural Institutions and Services Division [*FAO*]
RISE............ National Institute for Resources in Science and Engineering (EA)
RISE............ Radiation-Induced Surface Effect
RISE............ RAM [*Reliability, Availability, and Maintainability*] Improvement of Selected Equipment [*Military*] (MCD)
RISE............ Readiness Improvement Status Evaluation (MCD)
RISE............ Readiness Improvement Summary Evaluation (MCD)
RISE............ Reform of Intermediate and Secondary Education (OICC)
RISE............ Regional Initiative in Science Education
RISE............ Regional Initiatives in Science Education [*National Academy of Sciences*]
RISE............ Register for International Service in Education [*Institute of International Education*] (IID)
RISE............ Relative Integral Square Error [*Statistics*] (IAA)
RISE............ Reliability Improvement Selected Equipment (AABC)
RISE............ Research and Information Services for Education [*Montgomery County Intermediate Unit*] [*King of Prussia, PA*]
RISE............ Research and Information State Education Trust (AIE)
RISE............ Research in Science Education [*National Science Foundation*] (GRD)
RISE............ Research Institute for Studies in Education [*Iowa State University*] [*Research center*] (RCD)
RISE............ Research in Supersonic Environment
RISE............ Responsible Industry for a Sound Environment (EA)
RISE............ Reusable Inflatable Salvage Equipment
RISE............ Rulings Information System, Excise [*Revenue Canada - Customs and Excise*] [*Information service or system*] (CRD)
RISEAP........ Regional Islamic Da'Wah Council of Southeast Asia and the Pacific (EAIO)
Riser............ Riser Foods, Inc. [*Associated Press*] (SAG)
RISH........... Research Initiative into Silicon Hybrids [*British*]
RISHE.......... Research Institute for Supersensonic Healing Energies
RISI............. Resource Information Systems, Inc. (IID)
RISIC........... Rubber-Insert Sound Isolation Coupling (DNAB)
RISK........... Rock Is Stoning Kids [*Defunct*] (EA)
RISKAC........ Risk Acceptance (NASA)
RiskCap....... Risk Capital Holdings, Inc. [*Associated Press*] (SAG)
RISL............ Rand Information Systems Ltd. (NITA)
RISL............ Residual Item Selection List
RISM........... Reference Interaction Site Model [*Chemical physics*]
RISM........... Research Institute for the Study of Man [*Army*] (MCD)
RI/SME........ Robotics International of SME [*Society of Manufacturing Engineers*] (EA)
RISO........... Range Instrumentation Systems Office [*White Sands Missile Range*]
RISO........... Rocket Impacts on Stratospheric Ozone [*Air Force*]
RISOL.......... Risoluto [*Resolutely*] [*Music*] (ROG)
RISOP.......... Red Integrated Strategic Offensive Plan [*Army*] (AABC)
RISP........... Recoverable Interplanetary Space Probe (IAA)
RISP........... Regional Information Services Plan (NITA)
RISP........... Robotics and Intelligent Systems Program [*Oak Ridge National Laboratory*]
RISP........... Ross Ice Shelf Project [*International cooperative research project*]
RISQ........... [*The*] Reseau Interordinateur Scientifique Quebecois [*Canada*] [*Computer science*] (TNIG)
RI-SR.......... Removal Item - Ship's Record (MCD)
RISRI.......... Railway and Industrial Spring Research Institute [*Defunct*] (EA)
RISS........... Range Instrumentation and Support Systems
RISS........... Recommended Initial System Stockage
RISS........... Refractive Index Sounding System
RISS........... Regional Information Sharing System [*Department of Justice*]
RISS........... Rockwell International Suspension Systems Co.
RISSB......... Research Institute on the Sino-Soviet Bloc (EA)
RIST............ RADAR Installed System Tester (KSC)
RIST............ Radioimmunosorbent Technique [*or Test*] [*Clinical chemistry*]
RIST............ Radioisotopic Sand Tracer [*Marine science*] (MSC)
RISVD......... Risvegliato [*Reanimated*] [*Music*] (ROG)
RISW........... Registered Industrial Social Worker [*Designation awarded by the American Association of Industrial Social Workers*]
RISW........... Royal Institution of South Wales [*British*]
RISWR......... Regional Institute of Social Welfare Research (EA)
RIT.............. RADAR Inputs Test
RIT.............. Radio Information Test
RIT.............. Radioiodinated Triolein [*Medicine*] (MAE)
RIT.............. Radio Network for Inter-American Telecommunications
RIT.............. Railway Inclusive Tour (DCTA)
RIT.............. Rate of Information Throughput [*Computer science*] (BUR)
RIT.............. Readiness Initiative Team [*Military*]
RIT.............. Receiver Incremental Tuning
RIT.............. Receiving and Inspection Test (IAA)
RIT.............. Reclamation Insurance Type [*Military*] (AFIT)
RIT.............. Red Interamericana de Telecommunicaciones [*Inter-American Telecommunication Network*] (NTCM)
RIT.............. Refining in Transit
RIT.............. Relative Ignition Temperature
RIT.............. Remote Imagery Transceiver (DOMA)
RIT.............. Request for Interface Tool [*NASA*] (NASA)
RIT.............. Retrieval Injury Threshold
RIT.............. Reverse Income Tax (MHDW)
RIT.............. RightCHOICE Managed Care'A' [*NYSE symbol*] (TTSB)
RIT.............. Rightchoice Managed Care Co. [*NYSE symbol*] (SAG)
RIT.............. Rio Tigre [*Panama*] [*Airport symbol*] (OAG)
RIT.............. Ritardando [*Gradually Slower*] [*Music*]
rit................ Ritardando [*Gradually Slower*] [*Music*] (ODBW)
RIT.............. Ritenuto [*Immediately Slower*] [*Music*]
rit................ Ritual (BJA)
RIT.............. Rochester Institute of Technology [*New York*]
RIT.............. Rochester Institute of Technology (GAGS)
RIT.............. Rochester Institute of Technology Library [*UTLAS symbol*]
RIT.............. Rocket Interferometer Tracking
RIT.............. Rod-in-Tube
RIT.............. Rorschach Inkblot Test [*Psychiatry*] (DAVI)
RIT.............. Rosette Inhibition Titer [*Medicine*] (DMAA)
RIT.............. Rotary Indexing Table
RIT.............. Rothschild Investment Trust
RITA............ Rand Intelligent Terminal Agent
RITA............ Real-Time Integrated Ticket Administration (NITA)
RITA............ Recognition for Information Technology Achievement [*An award*] (PDAA)
RITA............ Recoverable Interplanetary Transport Approach
RITA............ Refundable Income Tax Account
RITA............ Reservation, Information, Tourist Accommodation [*Computerized system for booking hotel rooms*] [*British*]
RITA............ Resist Inside the Army [*Peace-movement slang*]
RITA............ Resistor-in-the Army [*Peace movement slang during Vietnam War*] (VNW)
RITA............ Reusable Interplanetary Transport Approach Vehicle
RITA............ Rivera and Tamayo Fault Exploration [*Marine science*] (MSC)
RITA............ Romance Is Treasured Always [*Annual award bestowed by Romance Writers of America. Acronym selected to honor cofounder, Rita Clay Estrada*]
RITA............ Rural Industrial Technical Assistance [*Latin American building program*]
RITA............ Russian Information Telegraph Agency [*Formerly, TASS*]
RITAC.......... Retail Industry Trade Action Coalition [*Washington, DC*] (EA)
RitAcc.......... Rituels Accadiens [*A publication*] (BJA)
RITAD.......... Radiation-Induced Thermally Activated Depolarization [*Radiation dosimetry technique*]
RITAL.......... Red Internacional de American Latina [*International Telecommunication Network for Latin America*] (NTCM)
RITAR.......... Ritardando [*Gradually Slower*] [*Music*]
RITARD....... Ritardando [*Gradually Slower*] [*Music*]
RITARO....... Ritardando [*Gradually Slower*] [*Music*] (ROG)
RITB............ Road Transport Industry Training Board [*British*]
RITC............ Regional Information Technology Coordinators (NITA)
RITC............ Request in Trail Climb [*Aviation*] (FAAC)

RITC............ Rhodamine Isothiocyanate [*Biochemistry*]
Ritch............ Ritchie's Cases Decided by Francis Bacon [*1617-21*] [*A publication*] (DLA)
Ritch............ Ritchie's Equity Reports [*1872-82*] [*Nova Scotia*] [*A publication*] (DLA)
Ritch Eq Dec... Ritchie's Equity Decisions [*Nova Scotia*] [*A publication*] (DLA)
Ritch Eq Rep... Ritchie's Equity Reports [*Nova Scotia*] [*A publication*] (DLA)
Ritchie......... Ritchie's Equity [*Canada*] [*A publication*] (DLA)
RITD............ Request in Trail Descent [*Aviation*] (FAAC)
RITE............ Rapidata Interactive Text Editor (IEEE)
RITE............ Rapid Information Technique for Evaluation
RITE............ Regenerative Intercooled Turbine Engine (MCD)
RITE............ Research Institute for Innovative Technolgies for the Earth
RITE............ Research Institute for Telecommunications and Economics (NITA)
RITE............ Right [*Direction of Turn*] [*ICAO designator*] (FAAC)
RiteA........... Rite Aid Corp. [*Associated Press*] (SAG)
RITEA........... Rock Island Railroad Transportation and Employee Assistance Act [*1980*]
RiteAid........ Rite Aid Corp. [*Associated Press*] (SAG)
RITEN.......... Ritenuto [*Immediately Slower*] [*Music*]
RITENA........ Reunion Internacional de Tecnicos de la Nutricion Animal [*International Meeting of Animal Nutrition Experts*] (EAIO)
RITENO........ Ritenuto [*Immediately Slower*] [*Music*] (ROG)
RITG............ Radiatively Important Trace Gas
RITI............. Resident Inspection Test Instruction
RITL............ Royal Institute of Technology Library (NITA)
RITLS.......... Rhode Island Test of Language Structure
RITOP.......... Red Integrated Tactical Operational Plan (CINC)
RITQ............ Revised Infant Temperament Questionnaire
RITR............ Rework Inspection Team Report
RITRC.......... RIT Research Corp.
RITREAD...... Rapid Iterative Reanalysis for Automated Design [*Computer program*]
RITS............ Radiatively Important Trace Species [*Program*] (USDC)
RITS............ Radiatively Important Trace Substances
RITS............ Rapid Information Transmission System
RITS............ Reconnaissance Intelligence Technical Squadron
RITS............ Remote Input Terminal System [*Computer science*] (IAA)
Rits Cts Leet... Ritson's Jurisdiction of Courts-Leet [*A publication*] (DLA)
Rits Int........ Ritso's Introduction to the Science [*A publication*] (DLA)
RITSL........... Reconfigured Integrated Two-Stage Liquefaction [*Chemical engineering*]
RITSq........... Reconnaissance Intelligence Technical Squadron [*Air Force*]
RITU............ Research Institute of Temple University (KSC)
RIU.............. Andalusia, AL [*Location identifier FAA*] (FAAL)
RIU.............. RADAR Interface Unit [*Military*] (CAAL)
RIU.............. Radioactive Iodine Uptake [*Medicine*]
RIU.............. Railroad Insurance Underwriters [*Later, RTI*] (EA)
RIU.............. Refractive Index Unit
RIU.............. Remote Interface Unit [*NASA*] (NASA)
riu............... Rhode Island [*MARC country of publication code Library of Congress*] (LCCP)
RIU.............. Ring Interface Unit [*Telecommunications*] (OSI)
RIU.............. University of Rhode Island, Kingston, RI [*OCLC symbol*] (OCLC)
RIUSA.......... Rehabilitation International USA
RIV.............. Radio Influence Voltage
RIV.............. Ramus Interventricularis [*First-order branch of coronary artery*] [*Medicine*]
RIV.............. Rapid Intervention Vehicle (DA)
RIV.............. Rapid Isolation Valve [*Analytical chemistry*]
RIV.............. Recirculation Isolation Valve (NASA)
RIV.............. Regolamento Internazionale Veicoli [*Italian generic term meaning "International Regulation of Vehicles"*] [*Initialism also refers to International Wagon Union*]
RIV.............. Right Innominate Vein [*Anatomy*] (DAVI)
RIV.............. River
RIV.............. River
RIV.............. Riverside, CA [*Location identifier FAA*] (FAAL)
RIV.............. Riverview [*Australia Seismograph station code, US Geological Survey*] (SEIS)
RIV.............. Rivet (AAG)
Riv............... Riviera [*Record label*] [*France*]
RIV.............. Riviera Holding Corp. [*AMEX symbol*] (SAG)
RIV.............. Riviera Holdings [*AMEX symbol*] (TTSB)
Riv............... Rivista [*Review*] [*Italian*] (BJA)
RIVA............ Recreational Industry Vehicle Association (IAA)
RIVAL.......... Rapid Insurance Valuation Language (IAA)
Rival............ Rival Co. [*Associated Press*] (SAG)
Riv Ann Reg... Rivington's Annual Register [*A publication*] (DLA)
RIVC............ Radionuclide Imaging of the Inferior Vena Cava [*Medicine*] (DMAA)
Riv d Arch Crist... Rivista di Archeologia Cristiana [*A publication*] (OCD)
Riv di Diritto Internaz e Comparato del Lavoro... Rivista di Diritto Internazionale e Comparato del Lavoro [*Padua, Italy*] [*A publication*] (DLA)
Riv Dir Int e Comp del Lavoro... Rivista di Diritto Internazionale e Comparato del Lavoro [*Bologna, Italy*] [*A publication*] (DLA)
Riv Dir Int'le Priv & Proc... Rivista di Diritto Internazionale Privato e Processuale [*Padova, Italy*] [*A publication*] (DLA)
RIVDIV......... River Assault Division [*Military*]
RIVE............ Resources in Vocational Education [*Database*] [*National Center for Research in Vocational Education*] [*Information service or system*] (CRD)
RIVER.......... River [*Commonly used*] (OPSA)
RIVFLOT...... River Flotilla [*Military*]
RIVFLOTONE... River Flotilla One [*Military*]
RivFor.......... River Forest Bancorp [*Associated Press*] (SAG)
Rivian.......... Riviana Foods, Inc. [*Associated Press*] (SAG)
RivianaF....... Riviana Foods, Inc. [*Associated Press*] (SAG)
Riviera......... Riviera Holding Corp. [*Associated Press*] (SAG)
Rivier C....... Rivier College (GAGS)
Riv Ital per le Sc Giur... Rivista Italiana per le Scienze Giuridiche [*A publication*] (OCD)
RIVL............ Rival Co. [*NASDAQ symbol*] (TTSB)
RIVL............ Rival Co. [*NASDAQ symbol*] (SAG)
RIVL............ Rival Manufacturing [*NASDAQ symbol*] (NQ)
RIVPATFLOT... River Patrol Flotilla [*Navy*] (DNAB)
RIVPATFOR... River Patrol Force [*Navy*] (DNAB)
RIVR............ River [*Commonly used*] (OPSA)
RIVR............ River Valley Bancorp [*NASDAQ symbol*] (SAG)
RivrNtl......... Riverside National Bank [*Associated Press*] (SAG)
RIVRON........ River Assault Squadron [*Navy*] (DNAB)
RivrVlly........ River Valley Bancorp [*Associated Press*] (SAG)
RIVS............ Ruptured Interventricular Septum [*Medicine*] (AAMN)
RIVSEC......... River Section (DNAB)
RIVSUPPRON... River Support Squadron [*Navy*] (DNAB)
RivSvgs........ Riverview Savings Bank [*Associated Press*] (SAG)
RIVT............ Rivulet (ADA)
Rivwdlnt....... Riverwood International Corp. [*Associated Press*] (SAG)
RIW.............. Reliability Improvement Warranty [*Navy*]
RIW.............. Repaired in Works [*British military*] (DMA)
RIW.............. Riverton [*Wyoming*] [*Airport symbol*] (OAG)
RIWC............ Royal Institute of Painters in Water-Colours [*British*] (ROG)
Riwt............. Rich International White Trash [*Lifestyle classification*]
RIX.............. Riga [*Former USSR Airport symbol*] (OAG)
RIX.............. University of Rhode Island, Extension Division Library, Providence, RI [*OCLC symbol*] (OCLC)
RIXOS.......... Rosat International X-Ray Optical Survey [*Cosmology*]
RIXT............ Remote Information Exchange Terminal (MCD)
RIY.............. Renaissance of Italian Youth (EA)
RIY.............. Riyan Mukalla [*South Arabia (Yemen)*] [*Airport symbol*] (AD)
RIZ.............. Radio Industry Zagreb [*Former Yugoslavia*]
RIZ.............. Rio Alzucar [*Panama*] [*Airport symbol*] (OAG)
RJ................ A'Beckett's Reserved Judgements [*Port Phillip*] [*A publication*] (ILCA)
R(J)............. Justiciary Cases [*Scotland*] [*A publication*] (DLA)
RJ................ La Reveil Juif. Sfax [*A publication*] (BJA)
RJ................ RADAR/Jimsphere
RJ................ Radial Jerk [*Reflex*] [*Neurology*] (DAVI)
RJ................ Ramjet
RJ................ Reform Judaism (BJA)
RJ................ Regional Jet [*British Aerospace/Taiwan Aerospace Corp. joint venture*] (ECON)
RJ................ Reject
RJ................ Revue de Jurisprudence [*A publication*] (DLA)
RJ................ Revue Judiciaire, by Bruzard [*1843-44*] [*Mauritius*] [*A publication*] (DLA)
RJ................ Rights and Justice [*An association British*] (EAIO)
RJ................ [*The*] River Jordan [*A publication*] (BJA)
RJ................ Rivet Joint [*RC-135 reconnaissance aircraft*] [*Air Force*] (DOMA)
RJ................ Road Junction [*Maps and charts*]
RJ................ Robert Jones [*Dressing*] [*Surgery*] (DAVI)
RJ................ Rotary Joint
RJ 500......... Rolls-Japan 500 [*Type of Rolls-Royce engine*]
RJA.............. Ramjet Addition (AAG)
RJA.............. Reform Jewish Appeal (EA)
RJA.............. Retail Jewelers of America [*Later, JA*] (EA)
RJA.............. Rotary Joint Assembly
RJA.............. Royal Jersey Artillery [*Military unit*] [*British*]
RJA.............. Royal Jordanian [*ICAO designator*] (FAAC)
RJA.............. Russko-Jewrejsky Archiw [*A publication*] (BJA)
RJAA............ Tokyo/New Tokyo International [*Japan ICAO location identifier*] (ICLI)
RJAF............ Matsumoto [*Japan ICAO location identifier*] (ICLI)
RJAF............ Royal Jordanian Air Force
RJAH............ Hyakuri [*Japan ICAO location identifier*] (ICLI)
RJAI............. Ichigaya [*Japan ICAO location identifier*] (ICLI)
RJAK............ Kasumigaura [*Japan ICAO location identifier*] (ICLI)
RJAM............ Minamitorishima [*Japan ICAO location identifier*] (ICLI)
RJamFn........ Raymond James Financial, Inc. [*Associated Press*] (SAG)
RJ & PJ......... Revenue, Judicial, and Police Journal [*Calcutta*] [*A publication*] (DLA)
RJAO............ Chichijima [*Japan ICAO location identifier*] (ICLI)
RJAT............ Takigahara [*Japan ICAO location identifier*] (ICLI)
RJAW............ Iwo Jima [*Japan ICAO location identifier*] (ICLI)
RJB.............. Rajbiraj [*Nepal*] [*Airport symbol Obsolete*] (OAG)
RJB.............. Relay Junction Box (KSC)
RJB.............. Ruby Jewel Bearing
RJBD............ Nanki-Shirahama [*Japan ICAO location identifier*] (ICLI)
RJBE............ Relative Jostle Biological Effectiveness
RJC.............. Ranger Junior College [*Texas*]
RJC.............. Reaction Jet Control [*NASA*] (NASA)
RJC.............. Robinson Jeffers Committee (EA)
RJC.............. Rochester Junior College [*Minnesota*] [*Later, Rochester Community College*]
RJCA............ Asahikawa [*Japan ICAO location identifier*] (ICLI)
RJCB............ Obihiro [*Japan ICAO location identifier*] (ICLI)
RJCC............ Sapporo/Chitose [*Japan ICAO location identifier*] (ICLI)
RJCG............ Sapporo [*Japan ICAO location identifier*] (ICLI)
RJCH............ Hakodate [*Japan ICAO location identifier*] (ICLI)
RJCK............ Kushiro [*Japan ICAO location identifier*] (ICLI)
RJCM............ New Memanbetsu [*Japan ICAO location identifier*] (ICLI)
RJCN............ Nakashibetsu [*Japan ICAO location identifier*] (ICLI)
RJCO............ Sapporo/Okadama [*Japan ICAO location identifier*] (ICLI)
RJCR............ Rebun [*Japan ICAO location identifier*] (ICLI)

RJCS .... Kushiro/Kenebetsu [*Japan ICAO location identifier*] (ICLI)
RJCT .... Tokachi [*Japan ICAO location identifier*] (ICLI)
RJCW .... Wakkanai [*Japan ICAO location identifier*] (ICLI)
RJCY .... Muroran/Yakumo [*Japan ICAO location identifier*] (ICLI)
RJD .... Reaction Jet Device [*NASA*] (NASA)
RJD .... Reaction Jet Driver [*NASA*] (NASA)
RJDA .... Rassemblement des Jeunesses Democratiques Africaines [*Rally of African Democratic Youth*]
RJDA .... Reaction Jet Driver - Aft [*NASA*] (NASA)
RJDB .... Iki [*Japan ICAO location identifier*] (ICLI)
RJDC .... Yamaguchi-Ube, Honshu Island [*Japan ICAO location identifier*] (ICLI)
RJDF .... Reaction Jet Driver - Forward [*NASA*] (NASA)
RJDG .... Fukuoka [*Japan ICAO location identifier*] (ICLI)
RJDK .... Kamigoto [*Japan ICAO location identifier*] (ICLI)
RJDM .... Metabaru [*Japan ICAO location identifier*] (ICLI)
RJDO .... Ojika [*Japan ICAO location identifier*] (ICLI)
RJDT .... Tsushima [*Japan ICAO location identifier*] (ICLI)
RJE .... Ramjet Engine
RJE .... Rayleigh-Jeans Equation [*Physics*]
RJE .... Remote Job Entry [*Computer science*]
RJEB .... Monbetsu [*Japan ICAO location identifier*] (ICLI)
RJEC .... Asahikawa [*Japan ICAO location identifier*] (ICLI)
RJ/EC .... Reaction Jet/Engine Control [*NASA*] (NASA)
RJEO .... Okushiri [*Japan ICAO location identifier*] (ICLI)
RJEP .... Remote Job Entry Protocol [*Telecommunications*] (OSI)
RJER .... Rishiri Island [*Japan ICAO location identifier*] (ICLI)
RJETS .... Remote Job Entry Terminal System [*Computer science*] (MCD)
RJF .... Les Rejaudoux [*France*] [*Seismograph station code, US Geological Survey*] (SEIS)
RJF .... Raymond James Financial, Inc. [*NYSE symbol*] (SPSG)
RJF .... Raymond James Finl [*NYSE symbol*] (TTSB)
RJFA .... Ashiya [*Japan ICAO location identifier*] (ICLI)
RJFA .... Roumanian Jewish Federation of America [*Defunct*] (EA)
RJFB .... Gannosu/Brady [*Japan ICAO location identifier*] (ICLI)
RJFC .... Yakushima [*Japan ICAO location identifier*] (ICLI)
RJFE .... Fukue [*Japan ICAO location identifier*] (ICLI)
RJFF .... Fukuoka [*Japan ICAO location identifier*] (ICLI)
RJFG .... Tanegashima [*Japan ICAO location identifier*] (ICLI)
RJFK .... Kagoshima [*Japan ICAO location identifier*] (ICLI)
RJFM .... Miyazaki [*Japan ICAO location identifier*] (ICLI)
RJFN .... Nyutabaru [*Japan ICAO location identifier*] (ICLI)
RJFO .... Oita [*Japan ICAO location identifier*] (ICLI)
RJFR .... Kitakyushu [*Japan ICAO location identifier*] (ICLI)
RJFT .... Kumamoto [*Japan ICAO location identifier*] (ICLI)
RJFU .... Nagasaki [*Japan ICAO location identifier*] (ICLI)
RJFY .... Kanoya [*Japan ICAO location identifier*] (ICLI)
RJFZ .... Tsuiki [*Japan ICAO location identifier*] (ICLI)
RJH .... Rajshahi [*Bangladesh*] [*Airport symbol*] (AD)
RJIS .... Regional Justice Information System
RJK .... Rijeka [*Former Yugoslavia*] [*Airport symbol*] (OAG)
RJKA .... Amami [*Japan ICAO location identifier*] (ICLI)
RJKB .... Okierabu [*Japan ICAO location identifier*] (ICLI)
RJKI .... Kikai/Kikaigashima Island [*Japan ICAO location identifier*] (ICLI)
RJKN .... Tokunoshima Island [*Japan ICAO location identifier*] (ICLI)
RJL .... Rigel Energy [*Formerly, Total Canada Oil & Gas Ltd.*] [*AMEX symbol*] (SPSG)
RJLI .... Royal Jersey Light Infantry [*Military unit*] [*British*]
RJM .... Reed, John M., San Antonio TX [*STAC*]
RJM .... Religious of Jesus-Mary [*Roman Catholic women's religious order*]
RJM .... Royal Jersey Militia [*Military unit*] [*British*]
RJM .... Warner Robins, GA [*Location identifier FAA*] (FAAL)
RJNF .... Fukui [*Japan ICAO location identifier*] (ICLI)
RJNG .... Gifu [*Japan ICAO location identifier*] (ICLI)
RJNH .... Hamamatsu [*Japan ICAO location identifier*] (ICLI)
RJNK .... Kanazawa/Komatsu [*Japan ICAO location identifier*] (ICLI)
RJNN .... Nagoya [*Japan ICAO location identifier*] (ICLI)
RJNO .... Oki [*Japan ICAO location identifier*] (ICLI)
RJNT .... Toyama [*Japan ICAO location identifier*] (ICLI)
RJNY .... Yaizu/Shizuhama [*Japan ICAO location identifier*] (ICLI)
RJO .... Rapports Judiciaires Officiels de Quebec [*Quebec Official Law Reports*] [*A publication*] (ILCA)
RJO .... Remote Job Output [*Computer science*]
RJO .... Revolutionary Justice Organization [*Lebanese terrorist group*]
RJOA .... Hiroshima [*Japan ICAO location identifier*] (ICLI)
RJOB .... Okayama [*Japan ICAO location identifier*] (ICLI)
RJOC .... Izumo [*Japan ICAO location identifier*] (ICLI)
RJOD .... Reaction Jet OMS [*Orbital Maneuvering Subsystem*] Driver [*NASA*] (NASA)
RJOE .... Akeno [*Japan ICAO location identifier*] (ICLI)
RJOF .... Hofu [*Japan ICAO location identifier*] (ICLI)
RJOH .... Miho [*Japan ICAO location identifier*] (ICLI)
RJOI .... Iwakuni [*Japan ICAO location identifier*] (ICLI)
RJOK .... Kochi [*Japan ICAO location identifier*] (ICLI)
RJOM .... Matsuyama [*Japan ICAO location identifier*] (ICLI)
RJOO .... Osaka/International [*Japan ICAO location identifier*] (ICLI)
RJOP .... Komatsujima [*Japan ICAO location identifier*] (ICLI)
RJOQ (BR) ... Rapports Judiciaires Officiels de Quebec, Cour du Banc du Roi [*Quebec Official Law Reports, King's Bench*] [*A publication*] (ILCA)
RJOQ (CS) ... Rapports Judiciaires Officiels de Quebec, Cour Superieure [*Quebec Official Law Reports, Superior Court*] [*A publication*] (ILCA)
RJOR .... Tottori [*Japan ICAO location identifier*] (ICLI)
RJOS .... Tokushima [*Japan ICAO location identifier*] (ICLI)
RJOT .... Takamatsu [*Japan ICAO location identifier*] (ICLI)
RJOY .... Osaka/Yao [*Japan ICAO location identifier*] (ICLI)
RJOZ .... Ozuki [*Japan ICAO location identifier*] (ICLI)
RJP .... Reaction Jet Pipe
RJP .... Realistic Job Preview
RJP .... Remote Job Processing [*Computer science*]
RJP .... Remote Job Processor (NITA)
RJP .... RJP Electronics [*Vancouver Stock Exchange symbol*]
RJP .... Rocket Jet Plume
RJPA .... Ramjet Performance Analysis (MCD)
RJQ .... Rapports Judiciaires [*Quebec Law Reports*] [*A publication*] (DLA)
RJQ BR .... Rapports Judiciaires de Quebec, Cour du Banc du Roi [*Quebec Law Reports, King's Bench*] [*A publication*] (DLA)
RJQ CS .... Rapports Judiciaires de Quebec, Cour Superieure [*Quebec Law Reports, Superior Court*] [*A publication*] (DLA)
RJR .... Mathieu's Quebec Revised Reports [*A publication*] (DLA)
RJR .... R. J. Reynolds Tobacco Co.
RJR .... RJR Nabisco Holding Corp. [*Associated Press*] (SAG)
RJR .... Rotary Joint Reed
RJRA .... Rotary Joint Reed Assembly
RJR Nab ...... RJR Nabisco Holding Corp. [*Associated Press*] (SAG)
RJRQ .... Mathieu's Quebec Revised Reports [*A publication*] (DLA)
RJS .... Reaction Jet System (KSC)
RJS .... Remote Job System [*Computer science*] (MCD)
RJS .... Richard Jeffries Society (EAIO)
RJS .... Roberta Jo Society (EA)
RJS .... Rocket and JATO [*Jet-Assisted Takeoff*] Section [*Picatinny Arsenal*] [*Dover, NJ*]
RJS .... Ruth Jackson Society (EA)
RJSA .... Aomori [*Japan ICAO location identifier*] (ICLI)
RJSC .... Yamagata [*Japan ICAO location identifier*] (ICLI)
RJSD .... Sado [*Japan ICAO location identifier*] (ICLI)
RJSFC .... R. J. Sutton Fan Club (EA)
RJSH .... Hachinohe [*Japan ICAO location identifier*] (ICLI)
RJSI .... Hanamaki [*Japan ICAO location identifier*] (ICLI)
RJSK .... Akita [*Japan ICAO location identifier*] (ICLI)
RJSM .... Misawa [*Japan ICAO location identifier*] (ICLI)
RJSN .... Niigata [*Japan ICAO location identifier*] (ICLI)
RJSO .... Ominato [*Japan ICAO location identifier*] (ICLI)
RJSS .... Sendai [*Japan ICAO location identifier*] (ICLI)
RJST .... Matsushima [*Japan ICAO location identifier*] (ICLI)
RJSU .... Kasuminome [*Japan ICAO location identifier*] (ICLI)
RJT .... Rassemblement des Jeunes Togolais [*Togolese Youth Rally*]
RJT .... Reference Jet Transport
RJT .... Royal Jubilee Trust [*Provides financial aid to start new businesses*] [*British*]
RJTA .... Atsugi [*Japan ICAO location identifier*] (ICLI)
RJTC .... Tachikawa [*Japan ICAO location identifier*] (ICLI)
RJTD .... Tokyo [*Japan ICAO location identifier*] (ICLI)
RJTE .... Tateyama [*Japan ICAO location identifier*] (ICLI)
RJTF .... Chofu [*Japan ICAO location identifier*] (ICLI)
RJTG .... Tokyo [*Japan ICAO location identifier*] (ICLI)
RJTH .... Hachijojima [*Japan ICAO location identifier*] (ICLI)
RJTI .... Tokyo [*Japan ICAO location identifier*] (ICLI)
RJTJ .... Iruma [*Japan ICAO location identifier*] (ICLI)
RJTK .... Kisarazu [*Japan ICAO location identifier*] (ICLI)
RJTL .... Shimofusa [*Japan ICAO location identifier*] (ICLI)
RJTO .... Oshima [*Japan ICAO location identifier*] (ICLI)
RJTQ .... Miyakejima [*Japan ICAO location identifier*] (ICLI)
RJTR .... Zama/Rankin [*Japan ICAO location identifier*] (ICLI)
RJTT .... Tokyo/International [*Japan ICAO location identifier*] (ICLI)
RJTU .... Utsunomiya [*Japan ICAO location identifier*] (ICLI)
RJTV .... Ramjet Test Vehicle
RJTW .... Zama [*Japan ICAO location identifier*] (ICLI)
RJTY .... Yokota [*Japan ICAO location identifier*] (ICLI)
RJTZ .... Fuchu [*Japan ICAO location identifier*] (ICLI)
RJZ .... Royal Jordanian Air Force [*ICAO designator*] (FAAC)
RK .... Air Afrique [*Ivory Coast*] [*ICAO designator*] (ICDA)
R_K .... Cathode Resistance (IDOE)
RK .... Rabbit Kidney
RK .... Rack
RK .... Radial Keratoplasty [*Ophthalmology*] (DAVI)
RK .... Radial Keratotomy [*Ophthalmology*]
RK .... Rassemblement Katangais [*Katanga Rally*]
RK .... Rat Kidney
RK .... Realkatalog der Aegyptologie [*A publication*] (BJA)
R-K .... Redlich-Kwong [*Physics*]
RK .... Republic of Korea [*IYRU nationality code*] (IYR)
RK .... Rhodopsin Kinase [*An enzyme*]
RK .... Right Kidney
RK .... Right to Know (EA)
RK .... Rock [*Maps and charts*] (MCD)
RK .... Royal Knight [*British*]
RK .... Rubbing Keel [*of a ship*] (DS)
RK .... Run of Kiln
RKA .... Air Afrique [*Ivory Coast*] [*ICAO designator*] (FAAC)
RKA .... Reaction Kinetic Analysis (PDAA)
RKA .... Rockdale, NY [*Location identifier FAA*] (FAAL)
RKAF .... Royal Khmer Air Force [*Cambodia*]
RKB .... Red Kidney Bean
RKCC .... Right to Know Committee of Correspondence [*Defunct*] (EA)
RKD .... Rockland [*Maine*] [*Airport symbol*] (OAG)
RKE .... Roskilde [*Denmark*] [*Airport symbol*] (OAG)
RKFC .... Ray Kirkland Fan Club (EA)
RKG .... Radiocardiogram
RKG .... Rockingham R. R. [*AAR code*]

RKG Royal Khmer Government [*Cambodia*]
RKH Rock Hill [*South Carolina*] [*Airport symbol*] (OAG)
RKH Rockingham Resources, Inc. [*Vancouver Stock Exchange symbol*]
RKH Rokitansky-Kuster-Hauser [*Syndrome*] [*Gynecology*] (DAVI)
RKHS Reducing Kernel Hilbert Space [*Electronics*] (OA)
RKID Right Kidney [*Urine Sample*] (DAVI)
RK II Runge-Kutta Second Order [*Mathematics*]
RkInt Rockwell International Corp. [*Associated Press*] (SAG)
RKJ Ramsey, Kenneth J., Pittsburgh PA [*STAC*]
RKJJ Kwangju [*South Korea ICAO location identifier*] (ICLI)
RKJK Kunsan [*South Korea ICAO location identifier*] (ICLI)
RKJM Mokpo [*South Korea ICAO location identifier*] (ICLI)
RKJO Hongjungri [*South Korea ICAO location identifier*] (ICLI)
RKJU Jhunju [*South Korea ICAO location identifier*] (ICLI)
RKJY Yeosu [*South Korea ICAO location identifier*] (ICLI)
RKKA Raboche-Krest'ianskaia Krasnaia Armiia [*Workers' and Peasants' Red Army*] [*Redesignated Soviety Army*] [*Former USSR*]
RKL Right Knee Left [*Guitar playing*]
RKL Ruskin Developments Ltd. [*Vancouver Stock Exchange symbol*]
RKM RADAR Keyboard Multiplexer [*Computer science*] (MHDI)
RKM Runge-Kutta Method [*Mathematics*]
RkMCh Rocky Mountain Chocolate Factory [*Associated Press*] (SAG)
RkMCn Rocky Mountain Chocolate Factory [*Associated Press*] (SAG)
RkMInet Rocky Mountain Internet, Inc. [*Associated Press*] (SAG)
RkMInt Rocky Mountain Internet, Inc. [*Associated Press*] (SAG)
RKN Root Knot Nematode [*Plant pathology*]
RKN Runge-Kutta-Nystroem [*Formula*] [*Mathematics*]
RKNC Chunchon [*South Korea ICAO location identifier*] (ICLI)
RKND Sokcho [*South Korea ICAO location identifier*] (ICLI)
RKNFSYS Rock Information System [*Carnegie Institution*] [*Databank*] [*National Science Foundation*] (IID)
RKNH Heongsung [*South Korea ICAO location identifier*] (ICLI)
RKNI Injae [*South Korea ICAO location identifier*] (ICLI)
RKNK Kwandaeri [*South Korea ICAO location identifier*] (ICLI)
RKNN Kangnung [*South Korea ICAO location identifier*] (ICLI)
RKNW Wonju [*South Korea ICAO location identifier*] (ICLI)
RKNY Yangku [*South Korea ICAO location identifier*] (ICLI)
RKO Radio-Keith-Orpheum [*Motion picture production and exhibition firm, also active in broadcasting*]
RKO Range Keeper Operator [*Navy*]
RKP Rockport, TX [*Location identifier FAA*] (FAAL)
RKP Routledge & Kegan Paul [*British publisher*]
RKPC Cheju/International [*South Korea ICAO location identifier*] (ICLI)
RKPD Chedong [*South Korea ICAO location identifier*] (ICLI)
RKPE Chinhae [*South Korea ICAO location identifier*] (ICLI)
RKPK Kimhae/International [*South Korea ICAO location identifier*] (ICLI)
RKPM Cheju/Mosulpo [*South Korea ICAO location identifier*] (ICLI)
RKPN Rooms Katholieke Partij Nederland [*Roman Catholic Party of the Netherlands*] [*Political party*] (PPE)
RKPP Busan [*South Korea ICAO location identifier*] (ICLI)
RKPS Sachon [*South Korea ICAO location identifier*] (ICLI)
RKPU Ulsan [*South Korea ICAO location identifier*] (ICLI)
RKR Poteau, OK [*Location identifier FAA*] (FAAL)
RKR Rack Register (MHDB)
RKR Rocker (AAG)
RKR Rockspan Resources [*Vancouver Stock Exchange symbol*]
RKRA Rocker Arm [*Mechanical engineering*]
RKS Reko [*Solomon Islands*] [*Seismograph station code, US Geological Survey*] (SEIS)
RKS Rock Springs [*Wyoming*] [*Airport symbol*] (OAG)
RKSA Ascom City [*South Korea ICAO location identifier*] (ICLI)
RKSB Uijeongbu [*South Korea ICAO location identifier*] (ICLI)
RKSC Cheongokri [*South Korea ICAO location identifier*] (ICLI)
RKSD Kanamni [*South Korea ICAO location identifier*] (ICLI)
RKSE Paekryoungdo Beach [*South Korea ICAO location identifier*] (ICLI)
RKSF Republic of Korea Air Force Headquarters [*South Korea ICAO location identifier*] (ICLI)
RKSG Pyongtaek [*South Korea ICAO location identifier*] (ICLI)
RKSH Kwanak [*South Korea ICAO location identifier*] (ICLI)
RKSI Chajangni [*South Korea ICAO location identifier*] (ICLI)
RKSK Susaek [*South Korea ICAO location identifier*] (ICLI)
RKSL Seoul City [*South Korea ICAO location identifier*] (ICLI)
RKSM Seoul East [*Sinchonri*] [*South Korea ICAO location identifier*] (ICLI)
RKSO Osan [*South Korea ICAO location identifier*] (ICLI)
RKSP Paekryoungdo Site [*South Korea ICAO location identifier*] (ICLI)
RKSP Rooms Katholieke Staatspartij [*Roman Catholic State Party*] [*Netherlands Political party*] (PPE)
RKSR Yeongdongri [*South Korea ICAO location identifier*] (ICLI)
RKSS Seoul/Kimpo International [*South Korea ICAO location identifier*] (ICLI)
RKST Tongoucheon [*South Korea ICAO location identifier*] (ICLI)
RKSU Yeoju [*South Korea ICAO location identifier*] (ICLI)
RKSW Suwon [*South Korea ICAO location identifier*] (ICLI)
RKSX Song San-Ri [*South Korea ICAO location identifier*] (ICLI)
RKSY Seoul/Yungsan [*South Korea ICAO location identifier*] (ICLI)
RKT Air 21, Inc. [*FAA designator*] (FAAC)
RKT Ras-al-Khaima [*Trucial Oman*] [*Airport symbol*] (AD)
RKT Ras Al Khaymah [*United Arab Emirates*] [*Airport symbol*] (OAG)
RKT Rikitea [*Tuamotu Archipelago*] [*Seismograph station code, US Geological Survey*] (SEIS)
RKT Rocket (AAG)
RKT Rock Tenn Co. [*NYSE symbol*] (SAG)
RKTA Andong [*South Korea ICAO location identifier*] (ICLI)
RKTC Chungju [*South Korea ICAO location identifier*] (ICLI)
RKTD Taejon [*South Korea ICAO location identifier*] (ICLI)
RKTH Pohang [*South Korea ICAO location identifier*] (ICLI)
RKTJ Kyungju [*South Korea ICAO location identifier*] (ICLI)
RKTM Seosan [*South Korea ICAO location identifier*] (ICLI)
RKTN Rock-Tenn 'A' [*NASDAQ symbol*] (TTSB)
RKTN Rock Tenn Co. [*NASDAQ symbol*] (SAG)
RKTN Taegu [*South Korea ICAO location identifier*] (ICLI)
RKTO Nonsan [*South Korea ICAO location identifier*] (ICLI)
RKTR Rocketeer
RKTS Sangju [*South Korea ICAO location identifier*] (ICLI)
RKTSTA Rocket Station
RKTT Taegu [*South Korea ICAO location identifier*] (ICLI)
RKTY Yechon [*South Korea ICAO location identifier*] (ICLI)
RKU Yule Island [*Papua New Guinea*] [*Airport symbol*] (OAG)
RKV Rabbit Kidney Vacuolating Virus
RKV Rose Knot Victor [*Gemini tracking ship*]
RKVA Reactive Kilovolt-Ampere
RKVAM Recording Kilovolt-Ampere Meter (MSA)
RKVP Rooms Katholieke Volkspartij [*Roman Catholic People's Party*] [*Netherlands Political party*] (PPE)
RKW Renal Potassium Wasting (MAE)
RKW Rockwood, TN [*Location identifier FAA*] (FAAL)
RKX Maxton, NC [*Location identifier FAA*] (FAAL)
Rky Rocky [*Quality of the bottom*] [*Nautical charts*]
RKY Roentgen Kymography
RKY Rokeby [*Australia Airport symbol Obsolete*] (OAG)
RL Aerolineas Nicaraguenses [*ICAO designator*] (AD)
RL Coarse Rales [*On chest ausculation*] [*Medicine*] (DAVI)
RL Crown International Airlines [*ICAO designator*] (AD)
R_L Load Resistance (IDOE)
RL Master Cross-Reference List
RL Radiation Laboratory
RL Radiation Level [*Nuclear energy*]
RL Radio Liberty [*Board for International Broadcasting*]
RL Radio Link (OA)
RL Radiolocation
RL Radioluminescent
RL Radionavigation land station using two separate loop antennas, and a single transmitter, and operating at a power of 150 watts or more [*ITU designation*] (CET)
RL Ragged Left [*Printing*] (WDMC)
rl Ragged Left [*Typesetting*] (WDMC)
RL Rahmana Litslan (BJA)
RL Rail (AAG)
RL Ralph Lauren [*Fashion designer, 1939-*]
RL Raman LASER
RL Random Lengths [*Lumber*]
RL Random Logic
RL Rated Load
R/L Rate/Limited (MCD)
RL Reactive Loss (IAA)
RL Reactor Licensing [*Nuclear energy*] (NRCH)
RL Reader's Library [*A publication*]
RL Reading List
RL Real Life (NHD)
RL Receive Leg [*Telecommunications*] (TEL)
R/L Receive Location (DOMA)
RL Receptor-Ligand Complex
RL Record Length
RL Record Librarian [*Medial records*] (DAVI)
RL Red Lamp (IAA)
R/L Redline (KSC)
RL Red Lion Hotels [*NYSE symbol*] (TTSB)
RL Red Lion Hotels, Inc. [*NYSE symbol*] (SAG)
RL Reduced [*or Reduction*] Level
RL Reel
RL Reeling Machines [*JETDS nomenclature*] [*Military*] (CET)
RL Reference Library
RL Reference Line (IAA)
RL Reference List
RL Reflection Loss [*Telecommunications*] (TEL)
RL Regent's Line [*Steamship*] (MHDW)
RL Reiz-Limen [*Stimulus threshold*] [*Psychology*]
RL Relay Logic
RL Release Load
RL Religious [*A radio station format*] (WDMC)
RL Relocation (IAA)
RL Relocation Library (HGAA)
R/L Remote/Local (NASA)
RL Remote Location (IAA)
RL Report Immediately Upon Leaving [*Aviation*] (FAAC)
RL Report Leaving [*ICAO*] (FAAC)
RL Research Laboratory
RL Reserve List (ADA)
RL Residential Lease [*Real estate*] (ADA)
RL Resistance-Inductance (IDOE)
RL Resistor Logic (IEEE)
RL Respectable Loge [*Worshipful Lodge*] [*Freemasonry*] [*French*] (ROG)
R_L Respiratory Resistance [*Medicine*] (DAVI)
RL Restaurant Liquor [*License*]
RL Restricted Line Officer
RL Retarded Learner [*Education*]
RL Reticular Lamina [*Ear anatomy*]
RL Retired List
RL Retirement Loss
R/L Return Link (MCD)

RL Return Loss
RL Revised Laws [*A publication*] (DLA)
RL Revue Legale [*Canada*] [*A publication*] (DLA)
RL Rhumb Line
RL Rial [*Monetary unit*] [*Iran, Saudi Arabia, etc.*]
RL Richland Operations Office [*Energy Research and Development Administration*]
RL Richtlinien [*Instructions, Directions*] [*German*] (ILCA)
R/L Right and Left
RL Right Lateral (DAVI)
RL Right Leg
RL Right Line
RL Right Lower [*Medicine*]
RL Right Lung
RL Right to Left
RL Ringer Lactated [*Medicine*]
RL Ring Level (BUR)
RL Rive'on Le-Khalkalah [*Tel Aviv*] (BJA)
RL River Lines, Inc. [*AAR code*]
RL Road Load [*Automotive engineering*]
RL Road Locomotive [*British*]
RL Rocket Launcher
RL Roll
RL Rolland, Inc. [*Toronto Stock Exchange symbol*]
RL Roll Lift [*NASA*] (KSC)
RL Roman Law (DLA)
RL Romeo Series L [*Alfa-Romeo*] [*Automotive model designation*]
RL Roof Leader (MSA)
RL Round Lot [*Unit of trading*]
RL Royal (ROG)
RL Royal Lancers [*British military*] (DMA)
RL Royal Licence [*British*]
RL Rugby League [*British*] (DI)
RL Run Length [*Computer science*]
RL Running Losses [*Automotive engineering*]
RL Runway Light [*Aviation*] (DA)
R_L Total Pulmonary Resistance [*Medicine*] (DAVI)
RLA Aeronautical Marker Beacon [*ITU designation*] (CET)
RLA Lar-Liniile Aeriene Romance [*Romania*] [*ICAO designator*] (FAAC)
RLA Reallexikon der Assyriologie [*Berlin*] [*A publication*] (BJA)
RLA Rebuild Los Angeles [*Commission established after 1992 riots*] (ECON)
RLA Receptive Language Age [*of the hearing-impaired*]
RLA Redevelopment Land Agency [*Washington, DC*]
RLA Regional Land Agent [*Ministry of Agriculture, Fisheries, and Food*] [*British*]
RLA Regional Letter of Acceptance [*Department of Housing and Urban Development*] (GFGA)
RLA Relay To [*ICAO*] (FAAC)
RLA Religious Leaders of America [*A publication*]
RLA Religious Liberty Association (NADA)
RLA Remote Line Adapter
RLA Remote Loop Adapter [*Telecommunications*]
RLA Repair Level Analysis [*Military*] (AFIT)
RLA Repair Line Agreement (NASA)
RLA Research Laboratory for Archeology [*British*]
RLA Responsible Local Agencies (OICC)
RLA Restricted Landing Area [*Aviation*]
RLA Roll Lock Actuator (MCD)
RLA Royal Lao [*or Laotian*] Army [*Laos*]
RLA Rui Lopes Associates, Inc. [*Sunnyvale, CA*] [*Telecommunications*] (TSSD)
RLA Run Length/Amplitude [*Computer science*]
RLA Rural Land Alliance (EA)
RLAB Royce Laboratories [*NASDAQ symbol*] (TTSB)
RLAB Royce Laboratories, Inc. [*Miami, FL*] [*NASDAQ symbol*] (NQ)
RLAC Recycling Legislation Action Coalition [*Defunct*] (EA)
RLADD RADAR Low-Angle Drogue Delivery (AFM)
RLAF Royal Laotian Air Force
RL & R Rail, Lake, and Rail
RL & S Ridgeway, Lapp, and Schoales' Irish King's Bench Reports [*1793-95*] [*A publication*] (DLA)
RL & W Roberts, Leaming, and Wallis' County Court Reports [*1849-51*] [*A publication*] (DLA)
RLANO Relay Equipment out of Operation (FAAC)
RLAOK Relay Equipment Resumed Operation (FAAC)
RLAS Rocket Lunar Attitude System
RLAss Reallexikon der Assyriologie [*Berlin*] [*A publication*] (BJA)
R LAT Right Lateral [*Medicine*] (MEDA)
RLB Air Alba Ltd. [*British ICAO designator*] (FAAC)
RLB Racecourses Licences Board [*Victoria, Australia*]
RLB RACON Station [*ITU designation*] (CET)
RLB Reliability [*or Reliable*] (AAG)
RLB Rickettsia-Like Bodies (CPH)
RLB Right Linebacker (WGA)
RLB United States Railroad Labor Board Decisions [*A publication*] (DLA)
RLBCD Right Lower Border of Cardiac Dullness [*Cardiology*]
RLB Dec Railroad Labor Board Decisions [*A publication*] (DLA)
RLBG Relative Bearing [*Aviation*] (FAAC)
RLBI Right Left Bearing Indicator [*Navigation*] (IAA)
RLBL Regional Laser and Biotechnology Laboratories [*University of Pennsylvania*] [*Research center*] (RCD)
RLBM Rearward Launched Ballistic Missile
RLC Avial (Russian Co. Ltd.) [*Former USSR ICAO designator*] (FAAC)
RLC Radio Launch Control System (IEEE)
RLC Radio Liberty Committee [*Later, RFE/RL*] (EA)
RLC Real-time Lens Error Correction [*Computer science*] (NTCM)
RLC Receive Logic Chassis
RLC Refund Litigation Coordinator [*IRS*]
RLC Regulatory Light Chain [*Physiology*]
RLC Remote Line Concentrator
RLC Remote Load Controller [*NASA*] (MCD)
RLC Remote Lock Control [*Automotive engineering*]
RLC Report Landing Completed [*Aviation*] (FAAC)
RLC Republican Liberty Caucus (EA)
RLC Residual Lung Capacity [*Medicine*]
RLC Resistance Inductance Capacitance (MSA)
RLC Revival Life Centre [*Australia*]
RLC Ribosome-Lamella Complex [*Physiology*]
RLC Right Line Contactor (MCD)
RLC Right Line Contractor
RLC Robinson Little & Co. Ltd. [*Toronto Stock Exchange symbol*]
RLC Rollins Truck Leasing [*NYSE symbol*] (SPSG)
RLC ROM [*Read-Only Memory*] Location Counter
RLC Rotating Litter Chair [*NASA*] (KSC)
RLC Run Length Coding
RLCA National Rural Letter Carriers' Association
RLCA Reaction-Limited Cluster Aggregation
RLCA Rear Lower Control Arm
RLCA Religion and Labor Council of America [*Defunct*] (EA)
RLCA Rural Letter Carriers' Association (NADA)
RLCD Relocated
RLCE Request Level Change Enroute [*Aviation*] (DA)
RLCM Rat Lung-Conditioned Medium [*Culture media*]
RLCO Realco Inc. [*NASDAQ symbol*] (TTSB)
RLCO Realco, Inc. [*NASDAQ symbol*] (SAG)
RLCOW Realco Inc. Wrrt [*NASDAQ symbol*] (TTSB)
RLCR Railcar (MSA)
RLCS Radio Launch Control System
RLCTN Relocation
RLCU Reference Link Control Unit [*Telecommunications*] (TEL)
RLD RADAR Laydown Delivery (AFM)
RLD Ready-to-Load Date [*At origin*] (DOMA)
RLD Related Living Donor [*Medicine*]
RLD Relocation Dictionary
RLD Relocation Directory (NITA)
RLD Relocation List Directory
RLD Remote Launch Demonstration [*Army*] (DOMA)
RLD Repetitive LASER Desorption
RLD Retail Liquor Dealer
RLD Rheinland Air Service [*Germany ICAO designator*] (FAAC)
RLD Richland [*Washington*] [*Airport symbol Obsolete*] (OAG)
RLD Rolled (AAG)
RLD Run Length Discriminator (MCD)
RLD Ruptured Lumbar Disc [*Medicine*]
RLDB Reference Library Data Base
RLDS Reorganized Church of Jesus Christ of Latter-Day Saints
RLDU Resources for Learning Development Unit (AIE)
RLE Raleigh Energy [*Vancouver Stock Exchange symbol*]
RLE Rate of Loss of Energy (IAA)
RLE Relative Luminous Efficiency (NATG)
RLE Request Loading Entry [*Computer science*]
RLE Research Laboratory of Electronics [*MIT*] [*Research center*]
RLE Resorts Leisure Exchange [*Commercial firm British*]
RLE Right Lower Extremity [*Medicine*]
RLE Run-Length Encoding [*Computer science*]
RLEA Railway Labor Executives' Association (EA)
RLEO Request Liaison Engineering Order [*NASA*] (NASA)
RLETFL Report Leaving Each Thousand Foot Level [*Aviation*] (FAAC)
RLEW Research Library for Edward Woodward (EA)
R_{LF} Low-Frequency Resistance (IDOE)
RLF Reactive Load Factor (IAA)
RLF Reduced Layer Formation (BARN)
RLF Relevant Labor Force (DNAB)
RLF Relief (AAG)
RLF Religion and Labor Foundation
RLF Religious Liberty Foundation [*Defunct*] (EA)
RLF Remote Lift Fan [*Aviation*]
RLF Replication Licensing Factor [*Genetics*]
RLF Retained Lund Fluid (DAVI)
RLF Retrograde Lipid Flow [*Hypothesis for biological cell movement*]
RLF Retrolental Fibroplasia [*Eye disease in premature babies*]
RLF Reverse Line Feed [*Telecommunications*] (OSI)
RLF Reverse Line Feed (NITA)
RLF Rhizoctonia-Like Fungus
RLF Right Lateral Femoral [*Site of injection*] [*Medicine*]
RLF Royal Laotian Forces
RLF Royal Literary Fund [*British*]
RLFC Rebel Lee Fan Club (EA)
RLG Glidepath [*Slope*] Station [*ITU designation*] (CET)
RLG Kremmling, CO [*Location identifier FAA*] (FAAL)
RLG Railing (AAG)
RLG Regimental Landing Group
RLG Regional Liaison Group (CINC)
RLG Release Guard [*Telecommunications*] (TEL)
RLG Relief Landing Ground [*British military*] (DMA)
RLG Research Libraries Group [*An association Also, an information service or system*] (EA)
RLG Rifle Large Grain [*British military*] (DMA)
RLG Ring LASER Gyro [*Navy*]

RLG Royal Laotian Government
RLG Royal Lepage Ltd. [*Toronto Stock Exchange symbol Vancouver Stock Exchange symbol*]
RLGD Realigned
RLGM Remote Look Group Multiplexer (MCD)
RLGM-CD Remote Look Group Multiplexer Cable Drive (MCD)
RLGN Ring LASER Gyro Navigation (MCD)
RLH Run Like Hell [*Slang*]
RLHIT Royal Life High Income Trust [*British*]
RLHP Road Load Horsepower [*Automotive engineering*]
RLHS Railway and Locomotive Historical Society (EA)
RLHTE Research Laboratory of Heat Transfer in Electronics [*MIT*] (MCD)
RLI Anniston, AL [*Location identifier FAA*] (FAAL)
RLI Radiation Level Indicator
RLI Rand Light Infantry [*British military*] (DMA)
RLI Realtors Land Institute (EA)
RLI Red Line Instrumentation (IAA)
RLI Retirement Life Item
RLI Rhodesian Light Infantry [*Military unit*]
RLI Right/Left Indicator (NVT)
RLI RLI Corp. [*NYSE symbol*] (SPSG)
RLI Rostral Length Index
RLIB Relocatable Library [*Computer science*]
RLI Cp RLI Corp. [*Associated Press*] (SAG)
RLIEVDP Request Line Items Be Expedited for Vehicles [*or Equipment*] Deadlined for Parts [*Army*] (AABC)
RLIF [*The*] Reliable Life Insurance Co. [*NASDAQ symbol*] (NQ)
RLIFA Reliable Life Ins [*NASDAQ symbol*] (TTSB)
R Lim E Roll-Limiting Engine
RLIN Research Libraries Information Network [*Pronounced "arlen"*] [*Formerly, BALLOTS Research Libraries Group, Inc. Stanford, CA*] [*Library network*] [*Information service or system*]
RLIN Royale Investments, Inc. [*NASDAQ symbol*] (SAG)
RLIN Royale Invts Inc. [*NASDAQ symbol*] (TTSB)
RLionH Red Lion Hotels, Inc. [*Associated Press*] (SAG)
RLionInn Red Lion Inns Ltd. [*Associated Press*] (SAG)
RLJ Rhodesian Law Journal [*A publication*] (DLA)
RLK Air Nelson Ltd. [*New Zealand*] [*ICAO designator*] (FAAC)
RLL Localizer Station [*ITU designation*] (CET)
RLL Rapid and Large Leakage (GNE)
RLL Relay Ladder Logic (ACII)
RLL Religion in Literature and Life [*A publication*]
RLL Relocating Linking Loader
RLL Representation-Language Language [*Computer science*]
RLL Right Lower Limb [*Medicine*]
RLL Right Lower Lobe [*Lungs*]
RLL Rim of Lateral Lip
RLL Rocket Launcher Locator
RLL Rolla, ND [*Location identifier FAA*] (FAAL)
RLL Run-Length-Limited [*Computer science*]
RLLB Right Long Leg Brace [*Medicine*]
RLLB Right Lower Leg Brace [*Medicine*]
RLLD Registered Laundry and Linen Director [*National Association of Institutio nal Linen Management*] [*Designation awarded by*]
RLLS Runway Lead-In Lighting System [*Aviation*] (FAAC)
RLLSC Right to Life League of Southern California (EA)
RLLY Rally's Hamburgers [*NASDAQ symbol*] (TTSB)
RLLY Rally's, Inc. [*NASDAQ symbol*] (NQ)
RLM Marine Radio Beacon Station [*ITU designation*] (CET)
RLM Rearward Launched Missile
RLM Reflector and Lighting Equipment Manufacturers (IAA)
RLM Reflector Lamps Manufacturer (IAA)
RLM Regional Library of Medicine [*Pan American Health Organization*]
RLM Reichsleftfahrt Ministerium [*German Air Ministry*] [*World War II*]
RLM Remote Line Module [*Telecommunications*]
RLM Return to Land and Management [*Agriculture*]
RLM Reynolds Metals [*NYSE symbol*] (TTSB)
RLM Reynolds Metals Co. [*NYSE symbol*] (SPSG)
RLM Right Lower Medial [*Medicine*] (DMAA)
RLM Royal American Airways, Inc. [*ICAO designator*] (FAAC)
RLM Royal Lancashire Militia [*British military*] (DMA)
RLM Royal London Militia
RLM Roy-L Merchant Group, Inc. [*Toronto Stock Exchange symbol*]
RLMA Roll Label Manufacturers Association (EA)
RLMD Rat Liver Mitochondria (MAE)
RLME Rapid Liquid Metal Embrittlement (MCD)
RLMM Research Laboratory for Mechanics of Materials (MCD)
RLMPrD Reynolds Metals 7%'PRIDES' [*NYSE symbol*] (TTSB)
RLMS RADAR Land Mass Simulation
RLMS Reproduction of Library Materials Section [*Resources and Technical Services Division of ALA*]
RLN LORAN Station [*ITU designation*] (CET)
RLN Recurrent Laryngeal Nerve [*Medicine*] (MAE)
RLN Regional Lymph Node [*Medicine*] (CPH)
RLN Remote LAN [*Linked Access Network*] Node [*DCA, Inc.*] (PCM)
RLN Romeo Series L Normale [*Alfa-Romeo*] [*Automotive model designation*]
RLNA Request Level Not Available [*Aviation*] (FAAC)
RLNC Regional Lymph Node Cell [*Medicine*] (DMAA)
RLND Regional Lymph Node Dissection [*Medicine*]
RLNS Revue Legale. New Series [*Canada*] [*A publication*] (DLA)
RLO Omnidirectional Range Station [*ITU designation*] (CET)
RLO RADAR Lock-On
RLO Regional Liaison Office [*Military*] (AFM)
RLO Repairs Liaison Officer [*Landing craft and barges*] [*Navy*]
RLO Residual Lymphatic Output [*Medicine*] (DMAA)
R/LO Response/Lockout (MCD)
RLO Restricted Line Officer (DNAB)
RLO Returned Letter Office
RLO Richland Operations Office [*Energy Research and Development Administration*]
RLO Rose Lookout Tower [*Oklahoma*] [*Seismograph station code, US Geological Survey*] (SEIS)
RLO Round Lot Orders [*Unit of trading*] (MHDW)
RLO Rudder Lock-Out (MCD)
RLOCK Record Lock
RLOP Reactor Licensing Operating Procedure [*Nuclear energy*] (NRCH)
RLOS Retention Level of Supply [*Navy*] (NG)
RLOS Revue Legale (Old Series) [*Canada*] [*A publication*] (DLA)
RLP Radiation-Leukemia-Protection (MAE)
RLP Rail Loading Point (NATG)
RLP Random Loose-Packed [*Granular physics*]
RLP Remote Line Printer (MCD)
RLP Ribosome-Like Particle [*Cytology*]
RLP Roads and Landscape Planning [*British*]
RLP Rosella Plains [*Australia Airport symbol Obsolete*] (OAG)
RLP Rotatable Log Periodic Antenna (MCD)
RLP Rotating Linear Polarization
RLP Ruby LASER Pulse
RLPA Retail Loss Prevention Association [*New York, NY*] (EA)
RLPA Rotating Log Periodic Antenna
RLPB Rural Land Protection Board [*Australia*]
RLPG Regenerative Liquid Propellant Gun (MCD)
RLPH Reflected Light Photohead
RLPL Railway Labor's Political League
RLPNLP Retired League Postmasters of the National League of Postmasters (EA)
RLPS Royal Liverpool Philharmonic Society [*British*] (DBA)
RLQ Right Lower Quadrant [*Medicine*] (DMAA)
RLQ Right Lower Quadrant [*of abdomen*] [*Medicine*]
RLQB Revue Legale Reports, Queen's Bench [*Canada*] [*A publication*] (DLA)
RLR Radioactive Lighting Rod [*Nuclear energy*] (NRCH)
RLR Radio Range Station [*ITU designation*] (CET)
RLR Record Length Register
RLR Red Light Running [*NHTSA*] (TAG)
RLR ReliaStar Financial [*NYSE symbol*] (TTSB)
RLR ReliaStar Financial Co. [*NYSE symbol*] (SAG)
RLR Reserves to Loans Ratio
RLR Retired Lives Reserve [*Insurance*]
RLR Reverse Locking Relay (IAA)
RLR Right Larval Retractor
RLR Right Lateral Rectus [*Eye anatomy*]
RLR Right Lateral Rotation [*Medicine*]
RLR Roller (MSA)
RLRD Register Load and Read
RLRIU Radio Logic Routing Interface Unit (MCD)
RLRPr ReliaStar Finl 10% Dep Pfd [*NYSE symbol*] (TTSB)
RLRPrA ReliaStar Fin I 8.20%'TOPrS' [*NYSE symbol*] (TTSB)
RLRS Regional Learning Resources Services [*Veterans Administration*] (GFGA)
RLS RADAR Line of Sight
RLS Radius of Landing Site [*NASA*] (KSC)
RLS Raman LASER Source
RLS Ranfurly Library Service [*An association*] (EAIO)
RLS Rate-Lock Standby [*FNMA*] (EMRF)
RLS Recursive Least Squares [*Mathematics*]
RLS Regularized Least-Squares [*Mathematics*]
RLS Remote Line Switch [*Telecommunications*] (TEL)
RLS Research in the Life Sciences Committee [*National Academy of Sciences*]
RLS Reservoir Level Sensor (MCD)
RLS Resonance Light Scattering [*Physics*]
RLS Restless Legs Syndrome [*Medicine*]
RLS Restricted Least Squares [*Statistics*]
RLS Reusable Launch System [*Aerospace*] (IAA)
RLS Rim Latch Set
RLS Ringer's Lactate Solution [*Physiology*]
RLS Riolos of Patras [*Greece*] [*Seismograph station code, US Geological Survey*] (SEIS)
RLS Robert Louis Stevenson [*Nineteenth-century Scottish author*]
RLS Rocket Launching System
RLS Roll Limit Switch
RLS Romeo Series L Sport [*Alfa-Romeo*] [*Automotive model designation*]
RLS Rotary Limit Switch
RLS Rotating Lighthouse System (IAA)
RLS Ruby LASER System
RLS Surveillance RADAR Station [*ITU designation*] (CET)
RLS Westerly, RI [*Location identifier FAA*] (FAAL)
RLSA Republican Law Students Association of New York (EA)
RLSA NY Republican Law Students Association of New York (EA)
RLSB Right Lower Scapular Border [*Medicine*] (DMAA)
RLSC Revue Legale Reports, Supreme Court [*Canada*] [*A publication*] (DLA)
RLSD Received Line Signal Detector
RLSD Research and Laboratory Services Division [*Health and Safety Executive*] [*British*] (IRUK)
RLSE Release (MSA)
RLSL Recursive Least Square Lattice (DMAA)
RLSO Regional Logistical Support Offices (DOMA)

RLSO Unit Released by Blood Bank (DAVI)
RLSP Ruby LASER Single Pulse
RLSS Regenerative Life Support System [*NASA*] (NASA)
RLSS Romeo Series L Super Sport [*Alfa-Romeo*] [*Automotive model designation*]
RLSS Royal Life Saving Society [*Studley, Warwickshire, England*] (EAIO)
RLST Read Least Significant Time [*Military*]
RLST Release Timer [*Telecommunications*] (TEL)
RLT Arlit [*Niger*] [*Airport symbol*] (OAG)
RLT Radionavigation Land Test (PDAA)
RLT Redeemable Listed Trust
RLT Regimental Landing Team [*Military*]
RLT Registered Laboratory Technician [*Medicine*] (WGA)
RLT Relating To (AABC)
RLT Reliability Life Test
RLT Reliant Airlines, Inc [*ICAO designator*] (FAAC)
RLT Remote Line Tester (PDAA)
RLT Reorder Lead Time [*Navy*] (NG)
RLT Repair Lead Time
RLT Research & Laser Technology, Inc.
RLT Return Line Tether [*NASA*] (MCD)
RLT Right Lateral Thigh [*Medicine*]
RLT Ring LASER Technique
RLT Rolling Liquid Transporter [*Army*]
RLT Romeo Series L Turismo [*Alfa-Romeo*] [*Automotive model designation*]
RLTA Reenlistment Leave Travel Allowance [*Military*]
RLTA Rhodesian Lawn Tennis Association
RLTD Related
RLTF Romeo Series L Targa Florio [*Alfa-Romeo*] [*Automotive model designation*]
RLTK Rhumbline Track [*Aviation*] (FAAC)
RLTM Research Laboratories Technical Memorandum
RLTN Relation (MSA)
RLTO Regional Lime Technical Officer [*Ministry of Agriculture, Fisheries, and Food*] [*British*]
Rltr Realtor (WGA)
RLTR Realtor
RltRef Realty Refund Trust [*Associated Press*] (SAG)
RLTS Radio Linked Telemetry System
RLTV Relative (AFM)
RLTY Realty
RltyInco Realty Income Corp. [*Associated Press*] (SAG)
RLU RADAR Logic Unit (MCD)
RLU Relative Light Units [*Analysis of light intensity*]
RLU Relay Logic Unit (IAA)
RLU Remote Line Unit [*Telecommunications*]
RLU Reserve Liaison Unit (DNAB)
RLU Waterville, ME [*Location identifier FAA*] (FAAL)
RLUD Routing Logic [*Radio Interface*] Unit Diagnostic Program [*Telecommunications*]
RLUF Refundable Life Use Fee [*Housing*] (DICI)
RLV Range Location Velocity
RLV Rauscher [*Murine*] Leukemia Virus
RLV Real Aviation Ltd. [*Ghana*] [*ICAO designator*] (FAAC)
RLV Reallexikon der Vorgeschichte [*Berlin*] [*A publication*] (BJA)
RLV Recordable LASER Videodisc [*Optical Disc Corp.*] (DOM)
RLV Relieve (AFM)
RLV Reliv' International [*AMEX symbol*] (TTSB)
RLV Reliv' International, Inc. [*AMEX symbol*] (SPSG)
RLV Reusable Launch Vehicle [*Aerospace*]
RLV Reusable Launch Vehicle [*NASA*]
RLV Roving Lunar Vehicle (AAG)
RLVD Relieved
RLVDT Rotary Linear Variable Differential Transformer
RLVL Report Level [*Aviation*] (FAAC)
RLVS Recoverable Launch Vehicle Structure (KSC)
RLW Rajasthan Law Weekly [*India*] [*A publication*] (DLA)
RLW-30 Ration Lightweight-30 Day [*Military*] (RDA)
RLWL Reactor Low-Water Level (IEEE)
RLWY Railway (AAG)
RLWY Railway
RLX Relaxin [*Biochemistry*]
RLXN Relaxation (MSA)
RLY Aerolineas Yasi, SA de CV [*Mexico*] [*FAA designator*] (FAAC)
RLY Railway
RLY Relay (AAG)
RLY Worland, WY [*Location identifier FAA*] (FAAL)
RM Lab. Roland-Marie [*France*] [*Research code symbol*]
RM Marianitas (TOCD)
RM Maritime Radionavigation Mobile Station [*ITU designation*] (CET)
R_m Meter Resistance (IDOE)
RM Office of Resource Management [*Nuclear energy*] (NRCH)
RM Rack Mounted (IAA)
RM RADAR Mapper
RM RADAR Missile (MUGU)
RM Radiation Measurement
R/M Radiation/Meteoroid [*NASA satellite*]
RM Radiation Monitor (NRCH)
RM Radical Mastectomy [*Medicine*]
RM Radioman [*Navy rating*]
RM Radioman (DOMA)
RM Radio Marker (IAA)
RM Radio Marti [*Cuba*]
RM Radio Material Officer (MCD)
RM Radio Message (IAA)
RM Radio Monitor
RM Range Marks
RM Range of Movement [*Medicine*]
RM Raven's Matrices [*Intelligence test*]
RM Raw Material
RM Reactance Meter (IAA)
RM Reaction Mass
RM Reactor Manufacturer [*Nuclear energy*] (NRCH)
RM Readiness Manager [*DARCOM*] [*Army*]
R/M Read/Mostly [*Computer science*] (TEL)
RM Read Out Material [*Computer science*] (IAA)
RM Readout Matrix
RM Ready Money (ROG)
RM Ream
rm Ream (WDMC)
RM Reasonable Man [*Legal shorthand*] (LWAP)
RM Reasoning Module [*Computer science*]
RM Receiver, Mobile
RM Receiving Memo
RM Recordimeter (NTCM)
RM Record Mark (BUR)
RM Rectangular Module (IAA)
RM Red Marrow [*Hematology*]
RM Redundancy Management (MCD)
RM Reference Manual (IAA)
RM Reference Mark (IAA)
RM Reference Material
RM Reference Memory [*Psychology*]
RM Reference Method
RM Reference Mission [*NASA*] (NASA)
RM Reflection Modulation (IAA)
RM Refresh Memory (MCD)
RM Regeneration Medium [*Biology*]
RM Regional Manager
RM Regional Meetings [*Quakers*]
RM Registered Magistrate (WDAA)
RM Registered Mail (WDAA)
RM Registered Midwife [*British*] (DBQ)
RM Register Memory
RM Reichsmark [*Later, DM*] [*Monetary unit*] [*German*]
RM Relais Musique [*Phonorecord series*] [*Canada*]
RM Relative Mobility [*of ions*] [*Chemistry*]
RM Remark [*Aviation*] (FAAC)
RM Remedial Maintenance (AFM)
Rm Remission [*Medicine*]
RM Remote (IAA)
RM Remote Manipulator [*NASA*] (NASA)
RM Remote Manual (NRCH)
RM Remote Multiplexer [*Computer science*] (CAAL)
rm Remove [*Computer science*] [*Telecommunications*]
RM Rendezvous Maneuver (MCD)
RM Repair Manual
RM Repetition Maximum [*Medicine*]
RM Replaceable Module
RM Rescue Module [*NASA*] (NASA)
RM Research Machines (NITA)
RM Research Materials [*National Institute of Standards and Technology*]
RM Research Memorandum
RM Residential Member [*American Institute of Real Estate Appraisers of the National Association of Realtors*] [*Designation awarded by*]
RM Resident Magistrate
RM Residue Manipulator (IAA)
RM Resolution Multiplier (IAA)
RM Resource Manager
RM Resource Module (SSD)
RM Respiratory Movement
RM Response Memoranda [*Jimmy Carter administration*]
RM Retail Manager
RM Retrospective Method [*Insurance*]
RM Return Material [*Navy*] (NG)
RM Review of Metaphysics [*A publication*] (BRI)
R/M Revolutions per Minute
RM Rhesus Monkey
RM Richmark Resources Ltd. [*Vancouver Stock Exchange symbol*]
RM Riding Master [*British*]
RM Right Mid
RM Ring Micrometer
RM Rocket Management (MCD)
RM Rocket Motor
RM Rocky Mountains
RM Rod Memory (IAA)
RM Rogosa SL Medium [*Microbiology*] (DAVI)
RM Rollback Module [*Telecommunications*] (TEL)
RM Rolling Moment [*Physics*]
rm Romania [*MARC country of publication code Library of Congress*] (LCCP)
RM Roman Martyrology
RM Romans [*New Testament book*]
RM Romford [*Postcode*] (ODBW)
rm Room (ODBW)
RM Room (AAG)
RM Room
Rm Room (DD)
rm Room (WDMC)

rm .... Room (VRA)
RM .... Rotating Machinery (IAA)
RM .... Roumania [*IYRU nationality code*] (IYR)
RM .... Routine Maintenance (AAG)
RM .... Routing Manager
RM .... Routing Matrix (IAA)
RM .... Rowley Mile [*Horseracing*] [*British*]
RM .... Royal Mail [*British*]
RM .... Royal Marines [*British*]
RM .... Royal Mint [*British*] (DAS)
RM .... Rubber Mold (MCD)
RM .... Rule Making [*Nuclear energy*] (NRCH)
RM .... Ruptured Membrane [*Medicine*]
RM .... Rural Municipality (DLA)
RM .... Russian Military [*World War II*]
RM .... RYMAC Mortgage Investment Corp. [*AMEX symbol*] (CTT)
RM .... RYMAC Mtge Invest [*AMEX symbol*] (TTSB)
RM .... Wings West [*ICAO designator*] (AD)
RM-1 .... Madison Chromosome [*Genetics*] (DAVI)
RM1 .... Radioman, First Class [*Navy rating*]
RM2 .... Radioman, Second Class [*Navy rating*]
RM3 .... Radioman, Third Class [*Navy rating*]
RM^3 .... Remote Multimedia Mode [*Army*]
RMA .... Racquetball Manufacturers Association [*Defunct*] (EA)
RMA .... Radio-Labeled Monoclonal Antiglobulin [*Clinical chemistry*]
RMA .... Radio Manufacturers Association [*Later, Electronic Industries Association*]
RMA .... Radiometric Microbiological Assay
RMA .... Rail Makers' Association [*British*] (BI)
RMA .... Random Multiple Access
RMA .... Rauma Oy [*NYSE symbol*] (SAG)
RMA .... Rauma Oy ADS [*NYSE symbol*] (TTSB)
RMA .... Reactive Modulation Amplifier
RMA .... Readiness Management Assembly [*Military*] (INF)
RMA .... Rear Maintenance Area [*Military British*]
RMA .... Receiver Measurement Adapter (MCD)
RMA .... Reclaim Managers Association [*Defunct*] (EA)
RMA .... Recreation Managers' Association [*British*] (DBA)
RMA .... Regiment de Marche d'Afrique [*African Marching Regiment*] [*French*]
RMA .... Regional Manpower Administration
RMA .... Registered Medical Assistants [*Later, ARMA*] (EA)
RMA .... Relative Medullary Area [*Medicine*] (DMAA)
RMA .... Relaxation Map Analysis [*Coatings*]
RMA .... Relevant Market Area [*Automotive dealership territory*]
RMA .... Reliability and Maintenance Analysis (CAAL)
RMA .... Reliability, Maintainability, and Availability [*Standards*]
RMA .... Remote Manipulator Arm [*NASA*] (MCD)
RMA .... Research and Marketing Act [*1946*]
RMA .... Reserve Military Aviator
RMA .... Retail Merchants' Association of Canada
RMA .... Retread Manufacturers Association [*British*] (DBA)
RMA .... Rhythmic Motor Activity [*Physiology*]
RMA .... Rice Millers' Association (EA)
RMA .... Right Mentoanterior [*A fetal position*] [*Obstetrics*]
RMA .... Robert Morris Associates [*National Association of Bank Loan and Credit Officers*] [*Philadelphia, PA*] (EA)
RMA .... Rockefeller Mountains [*Antarctica*] [*Seismograph station code, US Geological Survey Closed*] (SEIS)
RMA .... Rocky Mountain Airways, Inc. [*ICAO designator*] (FAAC)
RMA .... Rocky Mountain Arsenal [*Army*] (AABC)
RMA .... Rodeo Media Association [*Defunct*] (EA)
RMA .... Roma [*Australia Airport symbol*] (OAG)
RMA .... Rosin Mildly Activated [*Standard material for soldering*]
RMA .... Royal Malta Artillery [*Military unit*] [*British*]
RMA .... Royal Marine Academy [*British*]
RMA .... Royal Marine Artillery [*Obsolete British*]
RMA .... Royal Marines Association [*British military*] (DMA)
RMA .... Royal Military Academy [*For cadets of Royal Engineers and Royal Artillery; frequently referred to as Woolwich*] [*British*]
RMA .... Royal Military Asylum [*British*]
RMA .... Royal Musical Association [*British*]
RMA .... Rubber Manufacturers Association (EA)
RMA .... Rubber Manufacturers Association (NADA)
RMA .... Rusk Manufacturers Association [*British*] (DBA)
RMAA .... Rubber Manufacturers' Association of Australia
RMAAS .... Reactivity Monitoring and Alarm System [*Nuclear energy*] (NRCH)
RMAB .... Royal Marines Auxiliary Brigade [*British military*] (DMA)
RMAC .... Reactor Monitoring and Control [*Nuclear energy*] (IAA)
RMAC .... Remote Master Aircraft (MCD)
RMACHA .... Rocky Mountain Automated Clearing House Association
R-MAD .... Reactor Maintenance, Assembly, and Disassembly
RMAF .... Royal Moroccan Air Force
RMAG .... Recursive Macroactuated Generator (MHDI)
RMAG .... Rocky Mountain Association of Geologists (IAA)
RMAL .... Revised Master Allowance List [*Military*] (AFIT)
RMALAN .... Royal Malaysian Navy
RMALC .... Red Mexicana de Accion Frente al Libre Comercio [*Mexican Action Network on Free Trade*] (CROSS)
RMAN .... Recovered Materials Advisory Notice [*EPA*] (AAGC)
RM & C .... Reactor Monitoring and Control [*Nuclear energy*] (NRCH)
RM & PP .... Raw Material and Purchase Parts (MCD)
RMANOVA ... Repeated Measures Analysis of Variance [*Statistics*]
RMAO .... Resources Management and Administration Office [*Environmental Protection Agency*] (GFGA)
RMAS .... Royal Military Academy Sandhurst [*British*]
R MAST .... Radio Mast
RMAT .... Royal Marine Advisory Team [*British military*] (DMA)
RMATS-1 ..... Remote Maintenance, Administration, and Traffic System-1 [*Telecommunications*] (TEL)
RMAX .... Range, Maximum
RMB .... Radio Marker Beacon
RMB .... Radio Marketing Bureau [*British*] (CB)
RMB .... Rambler Oil Co. [*Toronto Stock Exchange symbol*]
RMB .... Rand Merchant Bank [*South Africa*]
RMB .... Raw Materials Board [*of the Reconstruction Finance Corp.*]
RMB .... Renminbi [*Monetary unit*] [*China*]
RMB .... Right Mainstem Bronchus [*Medicine*] (DMAA)
RMB .... Roadside Mailbox (ADA)
RMB .... Rocky Mountain Motor Tariff Bureau, Inc., Denver CO [*STAC*]
RMB .... Rombauer [*Missouri*] [*Seismograph station code, US Geological Survey*] (SEIS)
RMB .... ROM Memory Band (NITA)
RMB .... Royal Marine Bands [*British military*] (DMA)
RMB .... Royal Marines Badge [*British*]
RMBA .... Residual Mantle Bouguer Anomaly [*Geology*]
RMBAA .... Rocky Mountain Business Aircraft Association (IAA)
RMBC .... Regional Marine Biological Centre [*UNESCO*] (MSC)
RMBF .... Regional Myocardial Blood Flow [*Cardiology*] (DAVI)
RMBF .... Required Myocardial Blood Flow [*Cardiology*]
RMBNSW ..... Rice Marketing Board of New South Wales [*Australia*]
R-MBP-A ..... Rat-Mannose-Binding Protein A
R-MBP-C ..... Rat-Mannose-Binding Protein C
RMBPD .... Royal Marine Boom Patrol Detachment [*World War II*]
RMBQ .... Rice Marketing Board of Queensland [*Australia*]
RMBS .... Responsive Multicultural Basic Skills Approach (EDAC)
RMC .... American Restaurant Partners Ltd. [*AMEX symbol*] (SPSG)
RMC .... Amer Restaurant Ptnrs'A' [*AMEX symbol*] (TTSB)
RMC .... Captain of Royal Marines [*Military British*]
RMC .... Chief Radioman [*Navy rating*]
RMC .... Radiation Management Corp. (NRCH)
RMC .... Radiation Material Corp.
RMC .... Radioactive Materials Committee [*National Science Foundation*] (NUCP)
RMC .... Radio Management Control (MCD)
RMC .... Radio Materials Co. (IAA)
RMC .... Radio Monte Carlo [*Monaco*] (EY)
RMC .... Randolph-Macon College [*Virginia*]
RMC .... Rat Mast Cell
RMC .... Raytheon Manufacturing Co. (MCD)
RMC .... Ready Mixed Cement [*Commercial firm British*]
RMC .... Ready Mixed Concrete (ADA)
RMC .... Recursive Monte Carlo Method
RMC .... Reduced Material Condition (NVT)
RMC .... Redundancy Management Control (MCD)
RMC .... Regional Management Centre (AIE)
RMC .... Regional Media Center
RMC .... Regular Military Compensation (AABC)
RMC .... Regulated Motor Carriers
RMC .... Relative-Motion Control [*Microcopy*]
RMC .... Relay Mode Control (IAA)
RMC .... Remote Control (IAA)
RMC .... Remote Manual Control (NRCH)
RMC .... Remote Message Concentrator (IAA)
RMC .... Remote Multiplexer Combiner (MCD)
RMC .... Rendezvous Mercury Capsule [*NASA*] (AAG)
RMC .... Repair Manufacturer Codes
RMC .... Representative in Medical Council [*Royal College of Physicians*] [*British*] (ROG)
RMC .... Republican Mainstream Committee (EA)
RMC .... Republican Majority Coalition [*Republican party faction*]
RMC .... Residential Manpower Center [*Job Corps*]
RMC .... Resident Management Corp. [*Public housing*]
RMC .... Resource Management Consultants [*Salem, NH*] [*Telecommunications*] (TSSD)
RMC .... Resource Management Corp.
RMC .... [*Series*] Resources in Measurement & Control (ACII)
RMC .... Return to Military Control (AABC)
RMC .... Revolutionary Military Council [*Grenada*]
RMC .... Revue du Marche Commun [*Review of the Common Market*] [*French*]
RMC .... Revue Musicale [*A publication*]
RMC .... Rocket Motor Case
RMC .... Rocky Mountain College [*Billings, MT*]
RMC .... Rod Memory Computer [*NCR Corp.*]
RMC .... Rosemont College, Rosemont, PA [*OCLC symbol*] (OCLC)
RMC .... Rotary Mirror Camera
RMC .... Rotating Modulation Collimator
RMC .... Royal Marine Commandos [*British*]
RMC .... Royal Military College [*For army cadets; often referred to as Sandhurst*] [*British*]
RMC .... Rural Manpower Center [*Michigan State University*]
RMCA .... Right Man Coronary Artery [*Anatomy*] (DAVI)
RMCA .... Right Middle Cerebral Artery [*Anatomy*]
RMCAT .... Ralph Mayer Center for Artists' Techniques [*University of Delaware*] [*Newark*] [*Information service or system*] (IID)
RMCAT .... Right Middle Cerebral Artery Thrombosis [*Cardiology*] (DAVI)
RMCB .... Registered Mail Central Bureau [*Later, RMIA*] (EA)
RMCB .... Reserve Mobile Construction Battalion
RMCB .... Royal Marine Commando Brigade [*British*]
RMCC .... RADAR Monitor and Control Console [*Military*] (CAAL)

RMCC......... Regional Ministers Conference on Cooperatives [*Australia*]
RMCC......... Rotating Map, Cursor Centered [*Automotive engineering*]
RMCC......... Royal Military College of Canada [*British military*] (DMA)
RMCC......... Ryan and Moody's English Crown Cases [*A publication*] (DLA)
RMCCR......... Ryan and Moody's English Crown Cases [*A publication*] (DLA)
RMCCSC....... Raw Materials Committee of the Commonwealth Supply Council [*British World War II*]
RMCDC....... Rocky Mountain Child Development Center [*University of Colorado*] [*Research center*] (RCD)
RMCDE........ RADAR Message Conversion and Distribution (DA)
RM-CEAAL.... Red de Mujeres del Consejo de Educacion de Adultos de Americana Latina [*Women's Network of the Council for Adult Education in Latin America - WN-CAELA*] [*Quito, Ecuador*] (EAIO)
RMCF.......... Rocky Mountain Chocolate Factory, Inc. [*Durango, CO*] [*NASDAQ symbol*] (NQ)
RMCF.......... Rocky Mtn Choc Factory [*NASDAQ symbol*] (TTSB)
RMCI........... Right Management Consultants, Inc. [*Philadelphia, PA*] [*NASDAQ symbol*] (NQ)
RMCI........... Right Mgmt Consultants [*NASDAQ symbol*] (TTSB)
RMCL........... Recommended Maximum Contaminant Level [*Environmental Protection Agency*]
RMCL........... Right Midclavicular Line [*Anatomy*] (DAVI)
RMCM......... Master Chief Radioman [*Navy rating*]
RMCM......... Reduced Material Condition Maintenance (MCD)
RMCM......... Return Material Credit Memo
RMCM......... Rotating Map, Cursor Moving [*Automotive engineering*]
RMCM......... Royal Manchester College of Music [*British*]
RMCMI........ Rocky Mountain Coal Mining Institute (EA)
RMCO.......... Raymond Manufacturing Co.
RMCOEH...... Rocky Mountain Center for Occupational and Environmental Health [*University of Utah*] [*Research center*] (RCD)
RMCP.......... Rat Mast Cell Protease [*An enzyme*]
RMCPA........ Rocky Mountain College Placement Association (AEBS)
RMCS.......... Range Monitoring and Control Subsystem (MCD)
RMCS.......... Reactor Manual Control System [*Nuclear energy*] (NRCH)
RMCS.......... Remote Monitoring and Control System [*Telecommunications*]
RMCS.......... Royal Medical and Chirurgical Society [*British*] (ROG)
RMCS.......... Royal Military College of Science [*British*]
RMCS.......... Russian Mendeleev Chemical Society
RMCS.......... Senior Chief Radioman [*Navy rating*]
RMCSF........ Recombinant Macrophage Colony-Stimulating Factor [*Biochemistry*]
RMCT.......... Rat Mast Cell Technique [*Allergy*] (DAVI)
RMCU.......... Royal Martyr Church Union [*British*] (DBA)
RMCUSA...... Riley Motor Club USA (EA)
RMD........... Rapid Movement Disorder [*Neurology*] (DAVI)
RMD........... Raw Materials Department [*Ministry of Supply*] [*British*]
RMD........... Reaction Motors Division (SAA)
RMD........... Reading Matter Depth (DGA)
RMD........... Ready Money Down [*Immediate payment*]
RMD........... Repair and Modification Directive (AAG)
RMD........... Required Markup Declaration [*Computer science*]
RMD........... Retromanubrial Dullness [*Medicine*]
RMD........... Right Manubrial Dullness [*Anatomy*] (MAE)
RMDA.......... Request for Manufacturing Development Authorization (AAG)
RMDHS........ Regional Model Data Handling System [*Environmental Protection Agency*] (GFGA)
RMDI........... Radio Magnetic Deviation Indicator (AAG)
RM Dig......... Rapalje and Mack's Digest of Railway Law [*A publication*] (DLA)
RMDIR.......... Remove Directory [*Computer science*]
RMDL........... Remedial
RMDP.......... Resource Mothers Development Project
RMDP.......... Rural Manpower Development Program
Rmdr........... Remainder (DLA)
RMDU.......... Remote Multiplexer/Demultiplexer Unit (SSD)
RMDY.......... Remedy Corp. [*NASDAQ symbol*] (SAG)
RME............ Armenian International Airlines [*ICAO designator*] (FAAC)
RME............ Rack-Mount Extender (MHDI)
RME............ Radiation Monitoring Equipment
RME............ Rape Methyl Ester [*Fuel technology*]
RME............ Raw Materials (MCD)
RME............ Reasonable Maximum Exposure [*Toxicology*]
RME............ Receptor Mediated Endocytosis [*Biochemistry*]
RME............ Reflex Milk Ejection (OA)
RME............ Relay Mirror Experiment
RME............ Request Monitor Entry [*Computer science*]
RME............ Resident Maintenance Engineer (NATG)
RME............ Right Mediolateral Episiotomy [*Obstetrics*] (DAVI)
RME............ Rocket Mission Evaluator (MCD)
RME............ Rocky Mountain Energy [*Vancouver Stock Exchange symbol*]
RME............ Rome, NY [*Location identifier FAA*] (FAAL)
RME............ Royal Marine Engineers [*British*]
RMEC.......... Refractory Metals Electrofinishing Corp.
RMEC.......... Regional Medical Education Center [*Veterans Administration*] (GFGA)
RMED.......... Recruit, Retrain, Reemploy Medics [*Program*]
RMED.......... Research Medical [*NASDAQ symbol*] (TTSB)
RMED.......... Research Medical, Inc. [*NASDAQ symbol*] (SAG)
RMedSoc..... Royal Medical Society, Edinburgh
RMEE........... Right Middle Ear Exploration [*otorhinolaryngology*] (DAVI)
RMEF........... Rocky Mountain Elk Foundation (EA)
RMEL........... Rocky Mountain Educational Laboratory [*Closed*]
R Melb Hosp Q... Royal Melbourne Hospital. Quarterly [*A publication*]
RMER.......... Resource Management Expense Reporting System (MCD)
R Met S........ Royal Meteorological Society [*British*]
RMF............ Raw Materials Finance Department [*Ministry of Supply*] [*British*]
RMF............ RCS [*Reaction Control System*] Module Forward [*NASA*] (NASA)
RMF............ Reactivity Measurement Facility [*Nuclear energy*]
RMF............ Reamfixture (MCD)
RMF............ Reduced Magnetic Field [*Computer science*] (PCM)
RMF............ Reflectivity Measuring Facility
RMF............ Residual Master File [*Computer science*]
RMF............ Resource Measurement Facility [*Computer science*]
RMF............ Reymann Memorial Farms [*West Virginia University*] [*Research center*] (RCD)
RMF............ Right Middle Finger (DMAA)
RMF............ Rotating Magnetic Field [*Spectrometry*]
RMF............ Royal Malaysian Air Force [*ICAO designator*] (FAAC)
RMF............ Royal Munster Fusiliers [*Military unit*] [*British*]
RMFA........... Royal Malta Fencible Artillery [*British military*] (DMA)
RMFC........... Rachel Minke Fan Club (EA)
RMFC........... Ronnie McDowell Fan Club (EA)
RMFC........... Ronnie Milsap Fan Club (EA)
RMFVR........ Royal Marine Forces Volunteer Reserve [*Obsolete British*]
RMG........... RADAR Mapper Gapfiller
RMG........... RAL Marketing Group, Inc. [*Vancouver Stock Exchange symbol*]
RMG........... Ranging Machine Gun [*British military*] (DMA)
RMG........... Recommended for Medal and Gratuity [*British*]
RMG........... Relative-Motion Gauge
RMG........... Resource Management Group [*Military*]
RMG........... Right Main Gear (MCD)
RMG........... Rome [*Georgia*] [*Airport symbol Obsolete*] (OAG)
RMG........... Rome [*Georgia*] [*Seismograph station code, US Geological Survey*] (SEIS)
RMG........... Ronald Martin Groome [*Commercial firm British*]
RMG........... Royal Marine Gunner [*British*]
RMGF.......... RADAR Mapper, Gap Filler (MSA)
RMGIC......... Resin-Modified Glass-Ionomer Cement [*Dental material*]
RMGO.......... Regional Military Government Officer [*World War II*]
RMH........... Rabbit-Mouse Hybridomas [*Immunochemistry*]
RMH........... Refrigerator Mechanical Household (MSA)
RMH........... Riemann's Metrical Hypothesis [*Mathematics*]
RMHA.......... Rocky Mountain Horse Association (EA)
RMHCSDI.... Robert Maynard Hutchins Center for the Study of Democratic Institutions (EA)
RMHDDHG... Regiere Mich Herr durch Deinen Heiligen Geist [*Rule Me, Lord, Through Thy Holy Spirit*] [*Motto of Ann, Margravine of Brandenburg (1575-1612)*] [*German*]
RMHF.......... Rat, Mouse, and Hamster Fanciers (EA)
RMHI........... Religious and Mental Health Inventory
RMHT.......... RMH Teleservices, Inc. [*NASDAQ symbol*] (SAG)
RMH Tel....... RMH Teleservices, Inc. [*Associated Press*] (SAG)
RMI............ Claretian Missionary Sisters (TOCD)
RMI............ Merrell-National Laboratories [*Research code symbol*]
RMI............ Rack Manufacturers Institute (EA)
RMI............ Radiological Monitoring for Instructors [*Civil Defense*]
RMI............ Radio Magnetic Indicator
RMI............ Reactive Metals, Inc. Titanium Co. Extrusion Plant [*Department of Energy*] [*Ashtabula, OH*] (GAAI)
RMI............ Reich Ministry of Interior
RMI............ Release of Material for Issue
RMI............ Reliability Maturity Index [*Polaris*]
RMI............ Reliability Monitoring Index
RMI............ Religious of Mary Immaculate [*Roman Catholic women's religious order*]
RMI............ Remote Magnetic Indication
RMI............ Remote Method Invocation [*Computer science*]
RMI............ Remote Method Invocation [*Computer science*] (DOM)
RMI............ Renewable Materials Institute [*College of Environmental Science and Forestry at Syracuse*] [*Research center*] (RCD)
RMI............ Repair and Maintenance Instruction [*Military*]
RMI............ Repairs, Maintenance, and Improvements
RMI............ Repetitive Motion Injury
RMI............ Republic of the Marshall Islands
RMI............ Richardson-Merrell, Inc. [*Later, Richardson-Vicks, Inc.*]
RMI............ Rimini [*Italy*] [*Airport symbol*] (AD)
RMI............ Rocket Motor Igniter
RMI............ Rocky Mountain Institute (GNE)
RMI............ Roll Manufacturers Institute (EA)
RMI............ Rotonics Manufacturing [*Formerly, Koala Technologies*] [*AMEX symbol*] (SPSG)
RMI............ Route Monitoring Information [*Telecommunications*] (TEL)
RMI............ Rural Ministry Institute (EA)
RMIA.......... Rattan Manufacturers and Importers Association
RMIA.......... Registered Mail Insurance Association (EA)
RMIC.......... Research Materials Information Center [*ORNL*]
RMICBM...... Road Mobile Intercontinental Ballistic Missile
rMIF........... Recombinant Migration Inhibitory Factor [*Biochemistry*]
RMIFC......... Reba McEntire International Fan Club (EA)
RMIG.......... Royal Masonic Institution for Girls [*British*] (BI)
RMII........... Reference Method Item Identification [*DoD*]
RMII........... Rocky Mountain Internet, Inc. [*NASDAQ symbol*] (SAG)
RMIM.......... Repeater Media Interface Module [*Telecommunications*]
RMI/MO....... Routine Manual In / Manual Out [*Military*] (DNAB)
R/MIN......... Revolutions per Minute
RMIN.......... Roentgen per Minute (IAA)
RMIP.......... Reentry Measurements Instrumentation Package
RMIS.......... Readiness Management Information System [*Military*] (AABC)
RMIS.......... Resource Management Information System [*Environmental Protection Agency*]
RMIT........... Rolland Maintenance Institutional Trainer [*Army*]
RMI Ti......... RMI Titanium Co. [*Associated Press*] (SAG)

RMJ .... Ramjet (MSA)
RMJ .... Rumoi [Japan] [Seismograph station code, US Geological Survey] (SEIS)
RMJM .... Recluse Missionaries of Jesus and Mary [Roman Catholic women's religious order]
RMK .... Remark (AFM)
RMK .... Renmark [Australia Airport symbol] (OAG)
RMK .... Retrofit Modification Kit
RMK .... Rhesus Monkey Kidney [Medicine]
RMK .... Roxmark Mines Ltd. [Toronto Stock Exchange symbol]
RML .... Lieutenant, Royal Marines [Navy British] (ROG)
RML .... RADAR Mapper, Long Range
RML .... RADAR Microwave Link (IEEE)
RML .... Range Measurements Laboratory [Air Force]
RML .... Read Major Line [Computer science] (IAA)
RML .... Refresher Maintenance Lab
RML .... Regional Medical Library
RML .... Relational Machine Language
RML .... Remote Maintenance Line [Bell Laboratories]
RML .... Remote Measurements Laboratory
RML .... Rescue Motor Launch [Air/sea rescue] [Navy]
RML .... Research Machines Ltd. (NITA)
RML .... Restricted Maximum Likelihood [Statistics]
RML .... Rhizomucor Meihei Lipase [An enzyme]
RML .... Rifled Muzzle-Loading [Gun]
RML .... Right Mediolateral [Episiotomy] [Obstetrics]
RML .... Right Mentolateral [Episiotomy] [Obstetrics]
RML .... Right Middle Lobe [Lungs]
RML .... Rock Mechanics Laboratory [Pennsylvania State University] [Research center] (RCD)
RML .... Rocky Mountain Laboratories [National Institutes of Health]
RML .... Rotating Mirror LASER
RML .... Russell Corp. [NYSE symbol] (SPSG)
RMLA .... Rocky Mountain Lama Association (EA)
RMLC .... Royal Marine Labour Corps [British military] (DMA)
RMLE .... Regiment de Marche de la Legion Etrangere [Foreign Legion Marching Regiment] [French]
RMLI .... Royal Marine Light Infantry [Obsolete British]
RML IV .... Mid-Atlantic Regional Medical Library Program [Library network]
RMLO .... Reports Management Liaison Officer [Defense Supply Agency]
RMLP .... Regional Medical Library Program [Department of Health and Human Services]
RMLR .... RADAR Mapper, Long Range (MSA)
RMLR .... RADAR Microwave Link Repeater (FAAC)
RMLS .... Right Middle Lobe Syndrome [Medicine] (MEDA)
RMLT .... RADAR Microwave Link Terminal (FAAC)
RMLV .... Rauscher Murine Leukemia Virus [Medicine] (DMAA)
RMM .... Mercedarian Sisters (TOCD)
RMM .... RADAR Map Matching
RMM .... Rapid Micromedia Method [Analytical biochemistry]
RMM .... Read-Mostly Memory [Computer science]
RMM .... Read-Mostly Mode [Computer science]
RMM .... Remote Maintenance Monitor [Computer science] (MCD)
RMM .... Rifle Marksman
RMM .... Ripple Mark Meter
RMM .... Rosedale Mennonite Missions (EA)
RMMC .... Regiment Materiel Management Center [Military] (AABC)
RMMC .... Rocky Markings Mountain Mapping Center [Colorado]
RMMCA .... Road Markings Manufacturers and Contractors Association [British] (DBA)
RMMDBO ..... Royal Marine Mobile Defended Base Organisation [British military] (DMA)
RMMEA .... Rolling Mill Machinery and Equipment Association [Defunct] (EA)
RMMLA .... Rocky Mountain Modern Language Association (EDAC)
RMMLF .... Rocky Mountain Mineral Law Foundation (EA)
RMMLR .... Rocky Mountain Mineral Law Review [A publication] (DLA)
RMMP .... Riceland Mosquito Management Plan [Department of Agriculture]
RMMRA .... Rocky Mountain Midget Racing Association [Automobile competition organizer]
RMMS .... Remote Maintenance Monitoring System [FAA] (TAG)
RM/MS & C ... Redundancy Management/Moding, Sequencing, and Control (MCD)
RMMTB .... Rocky Mountain Motor Tariff Bureau, Inc.
RMMU .... Removable Media Memory Units
RMN .... Registered Mental Nurse
RMN .... Remain (FAAC)
RMN .... Reserve Material [Account] Navy
RMN .... Reuters Money Network [Reality Technologies] (PCM)
RMN .... Richard Milhous Nixon [US president, 1913-]
RMN .... RN Aviation Ltd. [British ICAO designator] (FAAC)
RMN .... Roman Corp. Ltd. [Toronto Stock Exchange symbol]
RMNS .... Royal Malayan Navy Ship [British military] (DMA)
RMNSW .... Railway Museum of New South Wales [Australia]
RMO .... RADAR Master Oscillator
RMO .... RADAR Material Office [Navy] (MCD)
RMO .... Radio Material Office [or Officer] [Navy] (IEEE)
RMO .... Records Management Office [or Officer] [Military] (AFM)
RMO .... Recruitment and Manning Organization [WSA]
RMO .... Refined Menhaden Oil [Food science]
RMO .... Regimental Medical Officer (NATG)
RMO .... Regimental Munitions Officer [Army]
RMO .... Regional Management Officer [Social Security Administration]
RMO .... Regional Medical Officer [British]
RMO .... Reports Management Officer [DoD]
RMO .... Resident Medical Officer [British]
RMO .... Resources Management Office [NASA] (KSC)
RMO .... Rochester-Mercier [New York] [Seismograph station code, US Geological Survey Closed] (SEIS)
RMO .... Rocket Management Office [Army] (RDA)
RMO .... Royal Marine Office [British]
RM Obs .... Royal Marine Observer [British military] (DMA)
RMOC .... Recommended Maintenance Operation Chart [Army] (AABC)
RMOGA .... Rocky Mountain Oil and Gas Association
RMOKHS ..... Religious and Military Order of Knights of the Holy Sepulchre (EA)
RMON .... Remote Monitoring [Computer science]
RMON .... Resident Monitor
RMON MIB ... Remote Network Monitoring Management Information Base [Telecommunications]
R MON RE(M) ... Royal Monmouthshire Royal Engineers (Militia) [British military] (DMA)
RMOS .... Real Memory Operating System [Computer science] (IAA)
RMOS .... Refractory Metal-Oxide Semiconductor (IEEE)
RMP .... Radio Management Panel (GAVI)
RMP .... Radio Motor Patrol [New York police cars]
RMP .... Rainform Message Processing (MCD)
RMP .... Raman Microprobe [Spectrometer]
RMP .... Rampart [Alaska] [Airport symbol] (OAG)
RMP .... Rampart Resources Ltd. [Vancouver Stock Exchange symbol]
RMP .... Range Maintenance Plan (MCD)
RMP .... Rapidly Miscible Pool [Medicine] (MAE)
RMP .... Rated Maximum Pressure (SAA)
RMP .... Rate Measuring Package (MCD)
RMP .... Raw Materials Processing
RMP .... Receptor-Mediated Permeabilizer [Medicine]
RMP .... Reduction of the Membrane Potential
RMP .... Reentry Measurement Program [Military]
RMP .... Refiner Mechanical Pulp [Papermaking]
RMP .... Regional Medical Program
RMP .... Registered Medical Practitioner [British] (ROG)
RMP .... Reprogrammable Microprocessor
RMP .... Research and Microfilm Publications
RMP .... Research Management Plan
RMP .... Resident Manufacturing Plan (SAA)
RMP .... Resistance Management Plans [To prevent insect adaptation to toxins]
RMP .... Resource Management Plan (GNE)
RMP .... Resting Membrane Potential [Neuroelectrochemistry]
RMP .... Resting Membrane Potential [Neurobiology]
RMP .... Revised Management Procedure
RMP .... Rifampicin [An antibacterial, Antibiotic, and antituberculin] (DAVI)
RMP .... Rifampin [Also, R/AMP, RF, RIF] [Bactericide]
RMP .... Right Mentoposterior [A fetal position] [Obstetrics]
RMP .... Risk Management Plan [Environmental Protection Agency]
RMP .... Risk Management Plan
RMP .... Risk Management Program [Environmental Protection Agency]
RMP .... Risk Management Program [Environmental Protection Agency]
RMP .... RMP: Rural Marketing and Policy [A publication]
RMP .... Rocketdyne Mortar Propellant (MCD)
RMP .... Rocket Motor Plume
RMP .... Rocket Motor Propellant (MUGU)
RMP .... Rome [Monte Porzio Catone] [Italy] [Seismograph station code, US Geological Survey] (SEIS)
RMP .... Rotorcraft Master Plan [FAA] (TAG)
RMP .... Round Maximum Pressure (NATG)
RMP .... Royal Marine Police [British military] (DMA)
RMP .... Royal Military Police [British]
RMPA .... Rocky Mountain Psychological Association (MCD)
RMPA .... Royal Medico-Psychological Association [British]
RMPCK .... Ramp Check [Aviation] (FAAC)
RMPE .... Root Mean Percentage Error [Statistics]
RMPF .... Rocky Mountain Poison Foundation
RMPI .... Remote Memory Port Interface
RMPM .... Rich Man, Poor Man [Book title]
RMPM .... Royal Mail Parcels Marketing [British Post Office]
RMPO .... Ramapo Financial [NASDAQ symbol] (TTSB)
RMPO .... Ramapo Financial Corp. [NASDAQ symbol] (NQ)
RMPP .... Risk Management and the Prevention Plan [Hazardous materials]
RMPR .... Rassemblement Mahorais pour la Republique [Mayotte Rally for the Republic] [Political party] (PPW)
RMPR .... Rated Mobilization and Professional Resource (MUGU)
RMPR .... Revised Maximum Price Regulation [World War II]
RMPS .... Regional Medical Programs Service [Health Services and Mental Health Administration, HEW]
RMPS .... Royal Melbourne Philharmonic Society [Australia]
RMPTC .... Royal Military Police Training Centre [British]
RMQ .... Air Armorique [France] [FAA designator] (FAAC)
RMQM .... Quarter-Master, Royal Marines [Navy British] (ROG)
RMR .... Air Co. Ltd. [Romania] [FAA designator] (FAAC)
RMR .... Malraux Society (EAIO)
RMR .... Rapid Memory Reload (MCD)
RMR .... Reamer [Design engineering]
RMR .... Reference Mixture Radio (KSC)
RMR .... Reflector Moderated Reactor (AAG)
RMR .... Regional Maintenance Representative [Military]
RMR .... Remote Map Reader
RMR .... Remote Meter Reading
RMR .... Reserve Minority Report [Army]
RMR .... Resource Management Review [Military]
RMR .... Resource Mortgage Capital [Formerly, RAC Mortgage Investment] [NYSE symbol] (SPSG)
RMR .... Resting Metabolic Rate [Physiology]

RMR .... Right Medial Rectus [*Eye anatomy*]
RMR .... Rock-Mass Rating [*Mining technology*]
RMR .... Rocky Mountain Review of Language & Literature [*A publication*] (BRI)
RMR .... Rotational Magnetic-Dipole Radiation [*Astronomy*]
RMR .... Rotation Magnitude Ratio
RMR .... Royal Malayan Regiment [*British military*] (DMA)
RMR .... Royal Marines Reserve [*British*]
RMR .... Royal Montreal Regiment [*Military unit*]
RMRA .... Royal Marines Rifle Association [*British military*] (DMA)
RMREL .... Rocky Mountain Regional Education Laboratory (AEBS)
RMRK .... Remark (FAAC)
RMRM .... Radioactive Materials Reference Manual (NRCH)
RMRO .... Royal Marine Routine Orders [*British military*] (DMA)
RMROCK .... Rocket Motors Records Office Center [*Navy*]
RMRPO .... Resource Mortgage Capital, Inc. [*NASDAQ symbol*] (SAG)
RMRPO .... Resource Mtg Cap cm Cv'B'Pfd [*NASDAQ symbol*] (TTSB)
RMRPP .... Resource Mtg Cap 9.75% Cv 'A' Pfd [*NASDAQ symbol*] (TTSB)
RMRS .... Remote Meter Resetting System [*Postage meter*]
RMRS .... Repeatable Maintenance and Recall System (NASA)
RMS .... RADAR Maintenance Spares (NG)
RMS .... RADAR Manual System (DNAB)
RMS .... RADAR Mapping Set [*or System*]
RMS .... Radian Means per Second (NASA)
RMS .... Radiation and Meteoroid Satellite [*NASA*]
RMS .... Radiation Monitoring Satellite (IAA)
RMS .... Radiation Monitoring System [*Nuclear energy*] (NUCP)
RMS .... Radio and Microwave Systems [*British*]
RMS .... Radiological Monitoring System
RMS .... Radiology Management System
RMS .... Radio Marker Station
RMS .... Radio Merchandise Sales (IAA)
RMS .... Radiometric Sextant Subsystem
RMS .... Rail Mail Steamer
RMS .... Railway Mail Service
RMS .... Random Mass Storage [*Computer science*]
RMS .... Random Motion Simulator [*NASA*] (NASA)
RMS .... Range Measuring System [*Air Force*]
RMS .... Range Modification System
RMS .... Rapid Multistream
RMS .... Rathkamp Matchcover Society (EA)
RMS .... Reactor Monitor System (IEEE)
RMS .... Real Market Share [*Business term*] (MHDB)
RMS .... Reconnaissance Management System
RMS .... Record Management System
RMS .... Records Management Society [*British*] (DBA)
RMS .... Recovery Management Support [*Computer science*]
RMS .... Recruiting Main Station [*Military*]
RMS .... Rectal Morphine Sulfate Suppository [*Medicine*] (DMAA)
RMS .... Redundancy Management System [*NASA*] (MCD)
RMS .... Reentry Measurement System
RMS .... Reflective Memory System (NITA)
RMS .... Regulator of Mitotic Spindle Assembly [*Cytology*]
RMS .... Regulatory Manpower System [*Nuclear energy*] (NRCH)
RMS .... Regulatory Monitoring System (NRCH)
RMS .... Rehabilitation Medicine Service [*Veterans Administration*]
RMS .... Reliability and Maintainability Simulator
RMS .... Reliability, Maintainability, Supportability [*Automotive engineering*]
RMS .... Remote Maintenance System
RMS .... Remote Manipulator Subsystem [*NASA*] (NASA)
RMS .... Remote Manipulator System [*NASA*] (IAA)
RMS .... Remote Manual Switch [*Nuclear energy*] (NRCH)
RMS .... Remote Master Station (MCD)
RMS .... Remote Missile Select
RMS .... Remote Monitor System
RMS .... Remote Multiplexer System [*Computer science*] (IAA)
RMS .... Reports Management System [*Office of Management and Budget*] [*Database*]
RMS .... Resource Management Squadron [*Military*]
RMS .... Resource Management Support (NITA)
RMS .... Resource Management System (IAA)
RMS .... Resources Management Staff [*Environmental Protection Agency*] (GFGA)
RMS .... Resources Management System [*Army*]
RMS .... Respiratory Muscle Strength [*Physiology*]
RMS .... Retromotor Simulator
RMS .... Reusable Multipurpose Spacecraft [*Aerospace*] (IIA)
RMS .... Revenue Management System (ECON)
RMS .... Revised Magnetic Standard
RMS .... Revised Management Scheme [*International Whaling Commission*]
RMS .... Rhabdomyosarcoma [*Also, RHM*] [*Oncology*]
RMS .... Rheometrics Mechanical Spectrometer
RmS .... RL Microfilm Systems, Feasterville, PA [*Library symbol*] [*Library of Congress*] (LCLS)
RMS .... Rocket Management System (MCD)
RMS .... Roll Microwave Sensor
RMS .... Romanian Missionary Society (EA)
RMS .... Root Mean Square [*Physics, statistics*]
rms .... Root Mean Square (IDOE)
rms .... Root Mean Squared (DOM)
RMS .... Rostral Migratory Stream [*Brain anatomy*]
RMS .... Royal Mail Service [*British*]
RMS .... Royal Mail Steamship [*British*]
RMS .... Royal Marine Signaller [*British military*] (DMA)
RMS .... Royal Medical Society [*British*] (DBA)
RMS .... Royal Meteorological Society [*British*]
RMS .... Royal Microscopical Society [*British*]
RMS .... Royal Museum of Scotland
RMS .... Royal Society of Miniature Painters, Sculptors, and Gravers [*British*]
RMS .... Rural Manpower Services (OICC)
RMS .... TAS Aviation, Inc. [*ICAO designator*] (FAAC)
RMSA .... Regulator of Mitotic Spindle Assembly (DMAA)
RMSA .... Rhabdomyosarcoma, Alveolar [*Medicine*] (DMAA)
RMSA .... Rural Marketing and Supply Association [*Australia*]
RMSA .... Rural Music Schools Association [*British*]
RMSA .... Seaman Apprentice, Radioman, Striker [*Navy rating*]
RM/SAD .... Remote Motor/Safe and Arming Device
RMSchMus .... Royal Marines School of Music [*British*]
RMSCR .... Rhabdomyosarcoma Chromosomal Region (DMAA)
RMSD .... Root Mean Square Deviation [*Statistics*]
RMSD .... Royal Mail Special Delivery [*British Post Office facility*] (DCTA)
RMSDS .... Reserve Merchant Ship Defense System [*Navy*] (MCD)
RMSE .... Relative Mean Square Error [*Statistics*]
RMSE .... Root Mean Square Error
RMSF .... Rocky Mountain Spotted Fever
RMSG .... Resource Management Study Group [*Military*]
RMSI .... Royal Marine Signalling Instructor [*British military*] (DMA)
RMSM .... Royal Military School of Music [*British*]
RMSN .... Seaman, Radioman, Striker [*Navy rating*]
RMSP .... Refractory Metal Sheet Program [*Navy*] (NG)
RMSP .... Resource and Mission Sponsor Plan [*Navy*]
RMSP .... Royal Mail Steam Packet Co.
RMSP .... Rubber Modified Silica Phenolie
Rmsq .... Romanesque (VRA)
RMSR .... Recovery Management Support Recorder (MHDI)
RMSS .... Range Meteorological Sounding System (MCD)
RMSS .... Religious Mercedarians of the Blessed Sacrament [*Roman Catholic women's religious order*]
RMSS .... Ruvalcaba-Myhre-Smith Syndrome [*Medicine*] (DMAA)
RMSU .... Remote Monitoring Sensor Unit (MCD)
RMSU .... Rocket Motor Switching Unit (MCD)
RMSV .... Root Mean Square Value [*Statistics*] (IAA)
RMSVP .... Remote Manipulation Subsystem Verification Plan [*NASA*] (MCD)
RMT .... Radioman Telegrapher [*Telecommunications*] (IAA)
RMT .... Radiometric Moon Tracer
RMT .... Rail, Maritime, and Transport Union [*British*] (ECON)
RMT .... Rapidly Moving Telescope [*Astronomy*]
RMT .... Rapid Mass Transfer [*Physics*]
RMT .... Rectangular Midwater Trawl (ADA)
RMT .... Registered Massage Therapist
RMT .... Registered Music Teacher
RMT .... Registered Music Therapist
RMT .... Registry of Medical Technologists
RMT .... Relative Medullary Thickness [*Of kidney*] [*Medicine*] (BABM)
RMT .... Relative Medullary Thickness [*of Kidney*] [*Nephrology*] (DAVI)
RMT .... Remote [*Telecommunications*] (MSA)
RMT .... Remount (WGA)
RMT .... Renal Mesenchymal Tumor [*Oncology*]
RMT .... Research Methods and Techniques
RMT .... Reserve Mechanical Transport [*British military*] (DMA)
RMT .... Resource Management Team (MCD)
RMT .... Retromolar Trigone [*Dentistry*] (MAE)
RMT .... Rework Monitoring Test
RMT .... Right Mentotransverse [*A fetal position*] [*Obstetrics*]
RMT .... River Management Tool
RMT .... Rocky Mount [*North Carolina*] [*Airport symbol*] (AD)
RMTB .... Reconfiguration Maximum Theoretical Bandwidth
RMTC .... RADAR Maintenance and Test Control (MCD)
RMTC .... Regional Medical Training Center
RMTC .... Rider Motorcycle Touring Club [*Later, RC*] [*Commercial firm*] (EA)
RMTE .... Remote (AAG)
RMTF .... Ready Missile Test Facility [*Military*] (CAAL)
RMTH .... Regular Member of the Third House [*Pseudonym used by Dr. Francis Bacon*]
RMTH .... River Mouth [*Board on Geographic Names*]
RMTO .... Regional Motor Transport Officer [*British*] (DCTA)
RMTR .... Ramtron International Corp. [*NASDAQ symbol*] (SAG)
RMTR .... Ramtron Int'l [*NASDAQ symbol*] (TTSB)
RMTR .... Redesigned Missile Tracking RADAR [*Army*] (AABC)
RMTR .... Repair and Maintenance Time Rate [*Automobile service*]
RMTS .... Research Member of the Technical Staff
RMU .... Radio Maintenance Unit (DEN)
RMU .... Rainbow Monument [*Utah*] [*Seismograph station code, US Geological Survey*] (SEIS)
RMU .... Reference Measuring Unit (MCD)
RMU .... Remote Maneuvering Unit [*NASA*]
RMU .... Remote Monitoring Unit [*Telecommunications*]
RMU .... Remote Multiplexer Unit [*Computer science*] (KSC)
RMU .... Romeo Series M Unificto [*Alfa-Romeo*] [*Automotive model designation*]
RMUC .... Reference Measuring Unit Computer
RMUI .... Relief Medication Unit Index [*Medicine*] (DMAA)
R-MuLV .... Rauscher Murine Leukemia Virus
RMV .... Reentry Measurement Vehicle [*Military*]
RMV .... Remotely Manned Vehicle
RMV .... Remove (AAG)
RMV .... Respiratory Minute Volume [*Physiology*]
RMV .... Ribgrass Mosaic Virus [*Plant pathology*]
RMV .... Romavia [*Romania*] [*ICAO designator*] (FAAC)
RMVBL .... Removable (AAG)

RMVD .... Removed (AAG)
RMVE .... Regiment de Marche de Volontiers Etrangers [*Foreign Volunteers Marching Regiment*] [*French*]
RMVG .... Removing (AAG)
RMVL .... Removal (AAG)
RMVM .... Review of Medical and Veterinary Mycology [*Database*] [*Commonwealth Mycological Institute*] [*Information service or system*] (CRD)
RMVT .... Repetitive Monomorphic Ventricular Tachycardia [*Cardiology*]
RMW .... Rattlesnake Mountain [*Washington*] [*Seismograph station code, US Geological Survey*] (SEIS)
RMW .... Reactor Makeup Water [*Nuclear energy*] (NRCH)
R/M/W .... Read/Modify/Write
RMW .... Read Modify Write (NITA)
RMW .... Resource Management Wing [*Military*]
RMWAA .... Roadmasters and Maintenance of Way Association of America (EA)
RMWC .... Randolph-Macon Woman's College [*Virginia*]
RMWO .... Warrant Officer, Royal Marines [*Navy British*] (ROG)
RMWR .... Religious, Morale, Welfare, and Recreation [*Military*] (AFM)
RMWS .... Reactor Makeup Water Storage [*Nuclear energy*] (NRCH)
RMWS .... Reactor Make-Up Water System [*Nuclear energy*] (IAA)
RMWT .... Reactor Makeup Water Tank [*Nuclear energy*] (NRCH)
RMX .... Remote Multiplexer (NITA)
RMX .... Resource Management Executive (MCD)
RMYC .... Royal Motor Yacht Club [*British*] (BI)
RMZ .... Right Midzone [*Medicine*] (DMAA)
R_n .... Negative Resistance (IDOE)
RN .... Neptune Radii [*Astronomy*]
RN .... Newport Public Library, Newport, RI [*Library symbol Library of Congress*] (LCLS)
RN .... Radio National [*Australian Broadcasting Corp.*]
RN .... Radio Navigation
RN .... Radio Noise (IAA)
RN .... Radionuclide [*Radiology*]
Rn .... Radon [*Chemical element*]
RN .... Random Number (IEEE)
RN .... Rassemblement National [*Canada Political party*] (PPW)
RN .... Rattus Norvegicus [*The Norway or brown rat*]
rn .... Read News [*Computer science*] (CDE)
RN .... Real Name [*British Library indexing for pseudonymous author*]
RN .... Reception Nil [*Radio logs*]
RN .... Reception Node
RN .... Recipient Name (NITA)
RN .... Record Number [*Online database field identifier*]
RN .... Red Nucleus [*Brain anatomy*]
RN .... Reference Noise [*Telecommunications*]
RN .... Reference Number
RN .... Registered Nurse
RN .... Registry Number
RN .... Rejection Notice (AAG)
RN .... Release Note [*Shipping*] (DS)
RN .... Removable Needle [*Medicine*]
RN .... Renastera Noastra [*Rumania*] [*A publication*] (BJA)
RN .... Renovacion Nacional [*National Renovation*] [*Chile*] [*Political party*] (EY)
Rn .... Renumbered [*Existing article renumbered*] [*Used in Shepard's Citations*] [*Legal term*] (DLA)
RN .... Report Number (NITA)
RN .... Research Note
RN .... Reuters News Agency (WDMC)
RN .... Revision Notice (KSC)
RN .... Revolucion Nacional [*Spain Political party*] (EY)
RN .... Reynolds Number [*Viscosity*]
RN .... Richard Nixon [*In book title "RN - The Memoirs of Richard Nixon"*]
RN .... River Name (BJA)
RN .... RJR Nabisco Holdings [*NYSE symbol*] (SPSG)
RN .... Roan (Leather) [*Bookbinding*] (ROG)
RN .... Root Tip Necrosis [*Plant pathology*]
RN .... Royal Air International [*ICAO designator*] (AD)
RN .... Royal Name (BJA)
RN .... Royal Navy [*British*]
RN .... Rubber Non-Continuous Liner (DS)
RN .... Ruin (ROG)
RN .... Ruritan National (EA)
RNA .... Radio Naval Association [*British*]
RNA .... Radio Navigational Aids (NATG)
RNA .... Radionuclide Angiography [*Medicine*]
RNA .... Rassemblement National Arabe [*Arab National Rally*] [*Tunisia*] (PD)
RNA .... Rations Not Available [*Military*] (AABC)
RNA .... Recurring Nuisances Act [*British*]
RNA .... Regina Resources [*Vancouver Stock Exchange symbol*]
RNA .... Registered Nurse Anesthetist
RNA .... Registered Nursing Assistant
RNA .... Religion Newswriters Association (EA)
RNA .... Republic of New Africa (EA)
RNA .... Research Natural Area [*National Science Foundation*]
RNA .... Ribonucleic Acid [*Biochemistry, genetics*]
RNA .... Ribonucleic Acid [*A publication*]
RNA .... Robbery Not Armed
RNA .... Romantic Novelists' Association [*British*]
RNA .... Rotatable Nozzle Assembly
RNA .... Rough, Noncapsulated, Avirulent [*With reference to bacteria*]
RNA .... Royal Naval Association [*British military*] (DMA)
RNA .... Royal Neighbors of America (EA)
RNA .... Royal Nepal Airlines Corp. [*ICAO designator*] (FAAC)
RNA .... Royal Netherlands Army
RNA .... Royal Norwegian Army (MCD)
RNAA .... Radiochemical Neutron Activation Analysis
RNAA .... Radiometric Neutron Activation Analysis
R/NAA .... Rocketdyne - North American Aviation [*Later, Rockwell International Corp.*] (AAG)
RNAA .... Russian Nobility Association in America (EA)
RNAAC .... Reference Number Action Activity Code (MCD)
RNAAF .... Royal Norwegian Army and Air Force
RNAC .... Remote Network Access Controller
RNAC .... Royal Nepal Airlines Corp.
RNAD .... Royal Naval Armament Depot [*British*]
RNAEC .... Rhodesia and Nyasaland Army Educational Corps [*British military*] (DMA)
RNAF .... Royal Naval Air Force [*British*]
RNAF .... Royal Netherlands Air Force
RNAF .... Royal Norwegian Air Force
RNAH .... Royal Naval Auxiliary Hospital [*British military*] (DMA)
RNAIA .... Royal National Agricultural and Industrial Association [*Australia*]
RNAL .... Radionuclear Applications Laboratory [*Pennsylvania State University*] [*Research center*] (RCD)
RNAM .... Regional Network for Agricultural Machinery [*Institute of Agricultural Engineering and Technology*] [*Philippines*]
RNAMY .... Royal Naval Aircraft Maintenance Yard [*British*]
RN & CR .... Ryde, Newport & Cowes Railway [*British*]
RNaNP .... National Sea Grant Depository Library, Pell Marine Science Library, Narragansett, RI [*Library symbol*] [*Library of Congress*] (LCLS)
RNAP .... Ribonucleic Acid Polymerase [*An enzyme*]
RNAPII .... Ribonucleic Acid Polymerase II [*An enzyme*]
RNAS .... Royal Naval Air Service [*Precursor of Fleet Air Arm*] [*Initialism also facetiously translated during World War I as "Really Not a Sailor"*] [*British*]
RNAS .... Royal Naval Air Station [*British*]
RNAS .... Royal Northern Agricultural Society [*British*] (DBA)
RNASBR .... Royal Naval Auxiliary Sick Berth Reserve [*British military*] (DMA)
RNase .... Ribonuclease [*An enzyme*]
RNaseP .... Ribonuclease-P [*An enzyme*]
RNasin .... Ribonuclease Inhibitor [*Biochemistry*]
RNASS .... Royal North Australian Show Society
RNATE .... Royal Naval Air Training Establishment [*British*]
RNAV .... Area Navigation
R/NAV .... Radio Navigation [*Military*] (EECA)
R-NAV .... Random Navigation
RNAV .... Remote Area Navigation [*FAA*] (TAG)
RNAV .... Royal Naval Artillery Volunteers [*British*]
RNAW .... Royal Naval Aircraft Workshop [*British*]
RNAY .... Royal Naval Aircraft Yard [*British*]
RNB .... Millville, NJ [*Location identifier FAA*] (FAAL)
RNB .... Received, Not Billed (AFM)
RNB .... Renegotiation Board [*Terminated, 1979*] [*Federal government*]
RNB .... Republic New York [*NYSE symbol*] (TTSB)
RNB .... Republic New York Corp. [*NYSE symbol*] (SPSG)
RNB .... Resonant Nuclear Battery
r'n'b .... Rhythm and Blues [*Music*] (BARN)
RNB .... RibonuCleoprotein Particle [*Biochemistry*]
RNB .... Ronneby [*Sweden*] [*Airport symbol*] (OAG)
RNB .... Royal Naval Barracks [*British*]
RNBC .... Royal Naval Beach Commando [*British*]
RNBD .... Royal North British Dragoons [*British military*] (DMA)
RNBF .... Royal North British Fusiliers [*British military*] (DMA)
RNBM .... Radio Noise Burst Monitor (MCD)
RNBM .... Royal Navy Ballistic Missile [*British*]
RNBO .... Rainbow Technologies [*NASDAQ symbol*] (TTSB)
RNBO .... Rainbow Technologies, Inc. [*NASDAQ symbol*] (NQ)
RNBPrC .... Republic NY $1.9375 cm Pfd [*NYSE symbol*] (TTSB)
RNBPrD .... Republic NY Adj Rt Dep Pfd [*NYSE symbol*] (TTSB)
RNBPrE .... Republic NY $1.8125 cm Pfd [*NYSE symbol*] (TTSB)
RNBT .... Royal Naval Benevolent Trust [*British*]
RNBW .... Rainbow
RNBWS .... Royal Naval Bird Watching Society [*British*]
RNC .... Little Raleigh [*North Carolina*] [*Seismograph station code, US Geological Survey*] (SEIS)
RNC .... McMinnville, TN [*Location identifier FAA*] (FAAL)
RNC .... Radio Noncontingent
RNC .... Rainbow Network Communications [*Floral Park, NY*] [*Telecommunications*] (TSSD)
RNC .... Registered Nurse, Certified (MEDA)
RNC .... Republican National Committee (EA)
RNC .... Request Next Character
RNC .... Ribosome-Nascent Chain [*Biochemistry*]
RNC .... Rockwood Nat'l [*PC Symbol*] (TTSB)
RNC .... Romanian National Council (EA)
RNC .... Royal Naval College [*For future officers; often spoken of as Dartmouth*] [*British*]
RNC .... Rumanian National Committee [*Later, Romanian National Tourist Office*] (EA)
RNCA .... Rhodesia and Nyasaland Court of Appeal Law Reports [*A publication*] (DLA)
RNCBC .... Reserve Naval Construction Battalion Center (DNAB)
RNCBCDET .... Reserve Naval Construction Battalion Center Detachment (DNAB)
RNCBMU .... Reserve Naval Construction Battalion Maintenance Unit (DNAB)
RNCC .... Reference Number Category Code (MCD)
RNCC .... Royal Naval College of Canada [*1911-1922*]
RNCF .... Read Natural Childbirth Foundation (EA)
RNCF .... Reserve Naval Construction Force [*Navy*] (PDAA)

RNCH.......... Ranch (MCD)
RNCH.......... Ranch
RNCHS.......... Ranch [*Commonly used*] (OPSA)
RNCM.......... Royal Northern College of Music [*British*]
RN CNAA..... Registered Nurse, Certified in Nursing Administration, Advanced (MEDA)
RNCO.......... Alrenco Inc. [*NASDAQ symbol*] (TTSB)
RNCO.......... Alrenco, Inc. [*NASDAQ symbol*] (SAG)
RNColl.......... Royal Naval College, Greenwich [*British*]
RNCR.......... Reserve Naval Construction Regiment (DNAB)
RN CS.......... Registered Nurse, Certified Specialist (MEDA)
RNCSIR.......... Royal Norwegian Council for Scientific and Industrial Research (EAIO)
RNCV.......... Radio Nacional de Cabo Verde [*National Radio of Cape Verde*] (EY)
RNCV.......... Royal Navy Coast Volunteers [*British military*] (DMA)
RNCVR.......... Royal Naval Canadian Volunteer Reserve [*World War I*]
RNCYC.......... Royal Northern and Clyde Yacht Club [*British*] (DBA)
RND.......... Radical Neck Dissection [*Medicine*]
RND.......... Railroads for National Defense [*MTMC*] (TAG)
RND.......... Random
RND.......... Rassemblement National Democratique [*National Democratic Rally*] [*Senegal*] [*Political party*] (PPW)
RND.......... Rassemblement National pour la Democratie [*Benin*] [*Political party*] (EY)
RND.......... Real-Fluid Nonisentropic Decompression [*Engineering*]
RND.......... Resistance-Nodulation-Division [*Biochemistry*]
RND.......... Round
RND.......... Round
RND.......... Royal Naval Division [*British*]
RND.......... San Antonio, TX [*Location identifier FAA*] (FAAL)
RNDH.......... Royal North Devon Hussars [*British military*] (DMA)
RNDM.......... Random (MSA)
RNDQ.......... Royal Naval Detention Quarter [*British*] (DI)
RNDr.......... Doctor of Natural Sciences
rndr.......... Rendering (VRA)
RNDZ.......... Rendezvous (KSC)
RNE.......... Aspen, CO [*Location identifier FAA*] (FAAL)
RNE.......... Morgan Stanley Russia & New Europe Fund, Inc. [*NYSE symbol*] (SAG)
RNE.......... Risley Nuclear Establishment [*British*] (NUCP)
RNE.......... Roanne [*France*] [*Airport symbol*] (OAG)
RNEC.......... Royal Naval Engineering College [*British*]
RNEColl.......... Royal Naval Engineering College [*British*]
RNEE.......... Royal Navy Equipment Exhibition [*British*]
RNEF.......... Resting (Radio-)Nuclide Ejection Fraction [*Cardiology*] (DAVI)
RNEIA.......... Royal Netherlands East Indies Army
RNEIAF.......... Royal Netherlands East Indies Air Force
RNEIN.......... Royal Netherlands East Indies Navy
RNERL.......... Radiochemistry and Nuclear Engineering Research Laboratory [*National Environmental Research Center*]
RNES.......... Royal Naval Engineering Service [*British*]
RNET.......... Remote Network (MHDB)
RNETA.......... Royal Naval Endurance Triathlon Association [*British*]
RNEW.......... Religious Network for Equality for Women (EA)
RNF.......... Radial Nerve Factor [*of sea urchin*]
RNF.......... Radio Noise Figure (CET)
RNF.......... Receiver Noise Figure
RNF.......... Refounded National Party [*South Africa Political party*] (EAIO)
RNF.......... Refracted Near Field [*Optics*]
RNF.......... Royal Naval Fund [*British*] (DAS)
RNF.......... Royal Northumberland Fusiliers [*Military unit*] [*British*]
RNF.......... Rudolf Nureyev Foundation
RNFC.......... Reference Number Format Code (MCD)
RNFC.......... Royal Naval Film Corp. [*British military*] (DMA)
RNFCC.......... Regional Nuclear Fuel Cycle Center [*National Science Foundation*] (NUCP)
rnfd.......... Reinforced (VRA)
RNFL.......... Rainfall [*NWS*] (FAAC)
RNFL.......... Retinal Nerve Fiber Layer [*Anatomy*]
RNFP.......... RADAR Not Functioning Properly [*Military*] (AFIT)
RNG.......... Radio Range
RNG.......... Random Number Generator [*Parapsychology*]
RNG.......... Range [*or Ranging*] (AAG)
RNG.......... Ranging Noise Generator
RNG.......... Reference Noise Generator
RNG.......... Regulations under the Natural Gas Act
RNG.......... Running
RNGCOMP... Range Computer (IAA)
RNGG.......... Ringing (MSA)
RNGHQ.......... Royal Navy General Headquarters [*British*]
RNGLND.......... Rangeland
RNGM.......... Royal North Gloucestershire Militia [*British military*] (DMA)
RNG RT.......... Range Rate (MCD)
RNGT.......... Renegotiate
RNH.......... New Richmond, WI [*Location identifier FAA*] (FAAL)
RNH.......... Royal Naval Hospital [*British*]
RNHA.......... Registered Nursing Home Association [*British*] (DBA)
RNHA.......... Republican National Hispanic Assembly of the United States (EA)
RNHi.......... Newport Historical Society, Newport, RI [*Library symbol Library of Congress*] (LCLS)
RN-HSG.......... Radionuclide Hysterosalpingogram [*Medicine*]
RNHU.......... Royal National Homing Union [*British*] (BI)
RNI.......... Kansas City, MO [*Location identifier FAA*] (FAAL)
RNI.......... Resident Navy Inspector
RNIB.......... Royal National Institute for the Blind [*British*]
RNIC.......... Robinson Nugent [*NASDAQ symbol*] (TTSB)
RNIC.......... Robinson Nugent, Inc. [*NASDAQ symbol*] (NQ)
RNICU.......... Regional Neonatal Intensive-Care Unit (MEDA)
RNID.......... Routine Network-In-Dial (DNAB)
RNID.......... Royal National Institute for the Deaf [*British*]
RNID/NOD.... Routine Network-In-Dial / Network-Out-Dial (DNAB)
RNIE.......... Royal Netherlands Institute of Engineers
RNIM.......... Rotors Not in Motion [*Aviation*] (AIA)
RNIO.......... Resident Naval Inspector of Ordnance
RNIP.......... Registered Nurse, Interim Permit (MEDA)
RNIR.......... Reduction to Next Inferior Rank
RNIT.......... Radio Noise Interference Test
RNJ.......... Blackrock New Jersey Investment Quality Municipal [*AMEX symbol*] (SPSG)
RNJ.......... Blackrock NJ Inv Qual Muni [*AMEX symbol*] (TTSB)
RNJ.......... Ramapo College of New Jersey, Mahwah, NJ [*OCLC symbol*] (OCLC)
RNJ.......... Rektorskommitten for de Nordiska Journalist Hogskolorna [*Committee for Nordic Universities of Journalism - CNUJ*] [*Defunct*] (EAIO)
RNJ.......... Yoron-Jima [*Japan*] [*Airport symbol*] (OAG)
RNk.......... North Kingstown Free Library, North Kingstown, RI [*Library symbol Library of Congress*] (LCLS)
RNL.......... Rainelle, WV [*Location identifier FAA*] (FAAL)
RNL.......... Renewal (MSA)
RNL.......... Rennell Island [*Solomon Islands*] [*Airport symbol*] (OAG)
RNL.......... Risley Nuclear Laboratories [*British*] (NUCP)
RNLA.......... Royal Netherlands Army
RNLAF.......... Royal Netherlands Air Force
RNLBI.......... Royal National Life-Boat Institution [*British*]
RNLC.......... Rosary Novena for Life Committee (EA)
RNLI.......... Royal National Life-Boat Institution [*British*]
RNLJ.......... Rhodesia and Nyasaland Law Journal [*A publication*] (DLA)
RNLN.......... Royal Netherlands Navy (DOMA)
RNLO.......... Royal Naval Liaison Officer [*British*]
RNLS.......... Resume Normal Speed [*Aviation*] (FAAC)
RNLT.......... Running Light
RNM.......... Radio-Navigation Mobile
RNM.......... Radionuclide Migration
RNm.......... Red Nucleus, Magnocellular [*Division*] [*Hematology*] (DAVI)
RNM.......... Resistencia Nacional Mocambicana [*Mozambican National Resistance*] (PD)
RNM.......... University of Rochester, Miner Medical Library, Rochester, NY [*OCLC symbol*] (OCLC)
RNMBR.......... Royal Naval Motor Boat Reserve [*British military*] (DMA)
RNMC.......... Regional Network Measurement Center (MHDI)
RNMC.......... Regional Nursing Midwifery Committee [*National Health Service*] [*British*] (DI)
RNMC.......... Royal Netherlands Marine Corps
RNMCB.......... Reserve Naval Mobile Construction Battalion (DNAB)
RNMCBDET... Reserve Naval Mobile Construction Battalion Detachment (DNAB)
RNMCC.......... Reference Number Mandatory Category Code [*DoD*]
RNMD.......... Registered Nurse for Mental Defectives
RNMDSF.......... Royal National Mission to Deep Sea Fishermen [*British*]
RNMH.......... Registered Nurse for the Mentally Handicapped [*British*] (DBQ)
RNMI.......... Realtors National Marketing Institute [*Chicago, IL*] (EA)
RNMS.......... Registered Nurse for the Mentally Subnormal [*British*]
RNMS.......... Royal Naval Minewatching Service [*British military*] (DMA)
RNMT.......... Registered Nuclear Medicine Technologist (DAVI)
RNMV.......... Rice Necrosis Mosaic Virus [*Plant pathology*]
RNMWS.......... Royal Naval Minewatching Service [*British*] (BI)
RNN.......... Naval War College, Newport, RI [*Library symbol Library of Congress*] (LCLS)
RNN.......... Regional NOCN [*National Ocean Communications Network*] Node (USDC)
RNN.......... Regional NOCN [*National Ocean Communications Network*] Node [*Marine science*] (OSRA)
RNN.......... Ronne [*Denmark*] [*Airport symbol*] (OAG)
RNN.......... Royal Netherlands Navy
RNN.......... Royal Norwegian Navy
RNNAS.......... Royal Netherlands Naval Air Service
RNNU.......... United States Navy, Naval Underwater Systems Center, Technical Library, Newport,RI [*Library symbol Library of Congress*] (LCLS)
RNO.......... Air Normandie [*France ICAO designator*] (FAAC)
RNO.......... Regional Nuclear Option (MCD)
RNO.......... Regional Nursing Officer [*British*]
RNO.......... Reno [*Nevada*] [*Airport symbol*] (OAG)
RNO.......... Resident Naval Officer [*Followed by place name*] (NATG)
RNO.......... Results Not Observed (DNAB)
RNO.......... Rhino Resources [*Vancouver Stock Exchange symbol*]
RNOA.......... Royal Norwegian Army (NATG)
RNOAF.......... Royal Norwegian Air Force
RNOC.......... Resistencia Nicaraguense de Organizacion Civica [*Political party*] (EY)
RNOC.......... Royal Naval Officers Club [*Defunct*] (EA)
RNODC.......... Responsible National Oceanographic Data Center [*Marine science*] (MSC)
RNON.......... Royal Norwegian Navy (NATG)
RNORA.......... Royal Norwegian Army
RNORN.......... Royal Norwegian Navy
RNP.......... Radio Navigation Point [*Military*] (MCD)
RNP.......... Rassemblement National Populaire [*National People's Rally*] [*France*]
RNP.......... Registered Nurse Practitioner (AAMN)
RNP.......... Remote Network Processor
RNP.......... Required Navigation Performance [*Aviation*] (FAAC)
RNP.......... Ribonucleoprotein [*Biochemistry*]

RNP .... RNA [*Ribonucleic Acid*] Nuclear Protein
RNP .... Rongelap [*Marshall Islands*] [*Airport symbol*] (OAG)
RNP .... Roscoe's Nisi Prius Evidence [*20th ed.*] [*1934*] [*A publication*] (DLA)
RNP .... Royal Naval Personnel Research Committee [*British*]
RNPA .... Regional Nuclear Power Authority
RNPC .... Regional Nuclear Power Co.
RNPC .... Required Navigation Performance Capability
RNPDL .... Risley Nuclear Power Development Laboratories [*British*] (NUCP)
RNPL .... Royal Naval Physiological Laboratory [*Later, AMTE (PL)*] [*British*]
RNPR .... Relative Net Protein Ratio [*Nutrition*]
RNPrB .... RJR Nabisco Sr'B'Dep Pfd [*NYSE symbol*] (TTSB)
RNPrC .... RJR Nabisco Sr'C'PERCS [*NYSE symbol*] (TTSB)
RNPRC .... Royal Naval Personnel Research Committee [*British*] (MCD)
RNPrT .... RJR Nabisco 10% 'TOPrS' [*NYSE symbol*] (TTSB)
RNPS .... Royal Naval Patrol Service [*Obsolete British*]
RNPS .... Royal Navy Polaris School [*British*]
RNQ .... Waycross, GA [*Location identifier FAA*] (FAAL)
RNR .... Rate Not Reported (DS)
RNR .... Receive Not Ready [*Computer science*] (IEEE)
RNR .... Redwood Library and Athenaeum, Newport, RI [*Library symbol Library of Congress*] (LCLS)
RNR .... RenaissanceRe Holdings Ltd. [*NYSE symbol*] (SAG)
RNR .... Renewable Natural Resources (DI)
RNR .... Renewal Not Required (AIA)
RNR .... Resonant Nuclear Reaction [*Physics*]
RNR .... Ribonucleotide Reductase [*An enzyme*]
RNR .... Ring Number Read [*Telecommunications*] (IAA)
RNR .... Robinson River [*Papua New Guinea*] [*Airport symbol*] (OAG)
r'n'r .... Rock and Roll [*Music*] (BARN)
RNR .... Royal Naval Reserve [*British*]
RNR .... Runner (MSA)
RNRA .... Resonant Nuclear Reaction Analysis [*Physics*]
RNRA .... Royal Naval Rifle Association [*British military*] (DMA)
RNRB .... Relative Navigational Reference Beacon [*Military*] (CAAL)
RNRC .... Riverside National Bank [*NASDAQ symbol*] (NQ)
RNRE .... Refused, Not Reversible Error [*Legal term*] (ILCA)
RNREF .... RenaissanceRe Holdings [*NASDAQ symbol*] (TTSB)
RNREF .... RenaissanceRe Holdings Ltd. [*NASDAQ symbol*] (SAG)
RNRF .... Renewable Natural Resources Foundation (EA)
RnRHoF&M .... Rock and Roll Hall of Fame and Museum
RNRS .... Royal National Rose Society [*British*] (EAIO)
RNR(T) .... Royal Naval Reserve (Trawlers) [*British military*] (DMA)
RNS .... Race, National Origin, and Sex (DNAB)
RNS .... RADAR Netting Station [*Military*] (AABC)
RNS .... Ransom Resources Ltd. [*Vancouver Stock Exchange symbol*]
RNS .... Reference Normal Serum [*Clincial chemistry*] (AAMN)
RNS .... Religious News Service (EA)
RNS .... Rennes [*France*] [*Airport symbol*] (OAG)
RNS .... Respiratory Nursing Society (EA)
RNS .... Reusable Nuclear Shuttle [*NASA*]
RNS .... Reusable Nuclear Stage [*Aerospace*]
RNS .... Ribonuclease S [*An enzyme*]
RNS .... Royal Naval School [*British*]
RNS .... Royal Numismatic Society [*British*]
RNS .... Russian Numismatic Society (EA)
RNS .... Services Aeronautiques Roannais [*France ICAO designator*] (FAAC)
RNSA .... Royal Naval Sailing Association [*British*]
RNSAC .... Range Surveillance Aircraft (MCD)
RNSC .... Radionuclide Superior Cavography [*Medicine*] (DMAA)
RNSC .... Reference Number Status Code (MCD)
RNSC .... Rocket/Nimbus Sounder Comparison [*NASA*]
RNSC .... Royal Naval Staff College [*British*]
RNSD .... Royal Naval Stores Depot [*British*]
RNSG .... Reserve Naval Security Group (DNAB)
RNSGC .... Reserve Naval Security Group Course (DNAB)
RNSH .... Royal National Scottish Hospital
RNS of M .... Royal Naval School of Music [*British military*] (DMA)
RNSP .... Round-Nose Soft-Point Bullet
RNSQ .... Royal Naval Sick Quarters [*British*]
RNSR .... Royal Naval Special Reserve [*British military*] (DMA)
RNSR .... Royal Nova Scotia Regiment [*Military unit*]
RNSS .... Royal Naval Scientific Service [*British*] (DEN)
RNSS .... Royal Norwegian Society of Sciences
RNSTS .... Royal Naval Supply and Transport Service [*British*]
RNSYS .... Royal Nova Scotia Yacht Squadron
RNT .... Regensburger Neues Testament [*A publication*] (BJA)
RNT .... Registered Nurse Tutor [*British*]
RNT .... Rentavion CA [*Venezuela*] [*ICAO designator*] (FAAC)
RNT .... Renton, WA [*Location identifier FAA*] (FAAL)
Rnt .... Roentgenology [*Radiology*] (DAVI)
RNTE .... Royal Naval Training Establishment [*British military*] (DMA)
RNTK .... Rentech, Inc. [*NASDAQ symbol*] (SAG)
rNTP .... Ribonucleoside Triphosphate [*Biochemistry*]
Rntrak .... Rentrak Corp. [*Associated Press*] (SAG)
RNTU .... Royal Naval Training Unit [*British military*] (DMA)
RntWay .... Rent Way, Inc. [*Associated Press*] (SAG)
RntWck .... Rent-a-Wreck of America, Inc. [*Associated Press*] (SAG)
RNTWPA .... Radio-Newsreel-Television Working Press Association (EA)
RNU .... RADAR Netting Unit [*Military*] (AABC)
RNU .... Ranau [*Malaysia*] [*Airport symbol*] (OAG)
RNV .... Cleveland, MS [*Location identifier FAA*] (FAAL)
RNV .... Radio Noise Voltage
RNV .... Radionuclide Venography [*Clinical chemistry*] (AAMN)
RNV .... Radionuclide Ventriculography [*Medicine*]
RNV .... Random Noise Voltmeter
RNV .... Relative Nutritive Value [*Nutrition*]
RNV .... Replacement Naval Vessels
RNV .... Resistive Null Voltage
RNV .... Reusable Nuclear Vehicle [*Aerospace*] (KSC)
RNV .... Royal Naval Volunteer (Reserve) [*British*] (ROG)
RNVC .... Reference Number Variation Code (MCD)
RNVG .... Radionuclide Ventriculography [*Medicine*] (DMAA)
RNVPR .... Royal Naval Volunteer Postal Reserve [*British military*] (IAA)
RN(V)R .... Royal Naval (Volunteer) Reserve [*Obsolete World War II British*]
RNVR(A) .... Royal Naval Volunteer Reserve (Air) [*British military*] (DMA)
RNVSR .... Royal Naval Volunteer Supplementary Reserve [*Obsolete World War II British*]
RNV(W)R .... Royal Naval Volunteer (Wireless) Reserve [*British military*] (DMA)
RNW .... Radio Navigational Warning (WDAA)
RNW .... Ring Number Write [*Telecommunications*] (IAA)
RNWAR .... Royal Naval Wireless Auxiliary Reserve [*British military*] (DMA)
RNWBL .... Renewable (MSA)
RNWMP .... Royal North West Mounted Police [*Later, RCMP*] [*Canada*]
RNWY .... Runway (AABC)
RNX .... Renox Creek Resources [*Vancouver Stock Exchange symbol*]
RNXS .... Royal Naval Auxiliary Service [*British*]
RNY .... Blackrock New York Investment Quality Municipal [*AMEX symbol*] (SPSG)
RNY .... Blackrock NY Inv Qual Muni [*AMEX symbol*] (TTSB)
RNY .... Rainier Energy Resources [*Vancouver Stock Exchange symbol*]
RNY .... Republic New York Corp. [*Associated Press*] (SAG)
RNY .... Required Net Yield [*Business term*] (EMRF)
RNY .... Runway Lights [*Aviation*] (AIA)
RNYPO .... Regional Navy Youth Programs Officer (DNAB)
RNZ .... Radio New Zealand
RNZ .... Royal New Zealand
RNZA .... Royal New Zealand Army (VNW)
RNZAF .... Royal New Zealand Air Force
RNZE .... Royal New Zealand Engineers
RNZIR .... Royal New Zealand Infantry Regiment (VNW)
RNZN .... Royal New Zealand Navy
RNZN(V)R .... Royal New Zealand Naval (Volunteer) Reserve
Ro .... Hoffmann-La Roche, Inc. [*Switzerland, USA*] [*Research code symbol*]
RO .... Observer (Radio) [*British military*] (DMA)
RO .... Omani Rial [*Monetary unit*] (IMH)
R_0 .... Output Resistance (IDOE)
RO .... RADAR Observer
RO .... RADAR Operator
RO .... Radiation Office [*Environmental Protection Agency*]
RO .... Radionavigation Mobile Station [*ITU designation*] (CET)
RO .... Radioopaque
RO .... Radio Operator
RO .... Radio Orchestra
RO .... Radio Orient (IAA)
RO .... Railway Office [*British*] (ROG)
RO .... Range Only (CAAL)
RO .... Range Operation (AAG)
RO .... Rank Organisation Ltd. [*Toronto Stock Exchange symbol*]
RO .... Reactor Operator [*Nuclear energy*] (NRCH)
RO .... Read Only [*Computer science*] (IBMDP)
RO .... Readout (KSC)
RO .... Reality Orientation
RO .... Receive Only
RO .... Receiving Office [*or Officer*]
RO .... Receiving Order [*Business term*] (DCTA)
RO .... Reconnaissance Officer
RO .... Recorders [*JETDS nomenclature*] [*Military*] (CET)
RO .... Records Office [*or Officer*] [*Air Force*] (AFM)
RO .... Recovery Operations [*NASA*]
RO .... Recruiting Officer [*Military*]
RO .... Recto [*Also, R*]
RO .... Reddish Orange
RO .... Redistribution Order [*Military*] (DNAB)
RO .... Reference Oscillator [*Telecommunications*] (OA)
RO .... Referral Order [*Military*] (DNAB)
RO .... Regimental Orders [*Army*]
RO .... Regional Office [*or Officer*]
RO .... Registered Office (WDAA)
RO .... Register Output
R/O .... Regular Order
RO .... Regulated Output (FAAC)
RO .... Relieving Officer (ROG)
RO .... Relocatable Output [*Computer science*]
RO .... Remote Operations [*Telecommunications*] (OSI)
RO .... Rent Officer [*British*] (ILCA)
R/O .... Repair and Overhaul (MCD)
RO .... Repair Order
RO .... Repolarization Opening [*Biochemistry*]
RO .... Reportable Occurrence [*Nuclear energy*] (NRCH)
RO .... Reporting Officer [*Army*] (AABC)
RO .... Report Over (DA)
RO .... Reproducible Ozalid (DNAB)
RO .... Requirements Objective
RO .... Requisitioning Objective [*Military*] (AABC)
R/O .... Requisitions/Objectives (CINC)
RO .... Research Objective (MCD)
RO .... Research Officer [*British*]
RO .... Reserve of Officers [*British*]
RO .... Reserve Order

RO .... Responding Officer [*Police term*]
RO .... Responsible Office (AAGC)
RO .... Restriction Orifice [*Nuclear energy*] (NRCH)
RO .... Retired Officer [*Military British*]
RO .... Retrofit Order [*Navy*] (NG)
RO .... Returning Officer (ROG)
RO .... Revenue Officer [*IRS*]
RO .... Reverse-Osmosis [*Physical chemistry*]
RO .... Rework Order (MCD)
R/O .... Rewritable/Optical
Ro .... Rhodium [*Correct symbol is Rh*] [*Chemical element*]
RO .... Right Opening (WDAA)
RO .... Right Orifice (WDAA)
RO .... Right Outboard (MCD)
RO .... Rimoil Corp. [*Toronto Stock Exchange symbol*]
RO .... Rip Out (DNAB)
RO .... Ritter-Oleson Technique [*Medicine*] (MAE)
RO .... Road (WGA)
RO .... Roan [*Thoroughbred racing*]
RO .... Rock [*Germany ICAO aircraft manufacturer identifier*] (ICAO)
Ro .... Rodoicus [*Authority cited in pre-1607 legal work*] (DSA)
Ro .... Roffredus Beneventanus [*Flourished, 1215-43*] [*Authority cited in pre-1607 legal work*] (DSA)
Ro .... Rolandus Bandinelli [*Deceased, 1181*] [*Authority cited in pre-1607 legal work*] (DSA)
RO .... Roll
Ro .... Rolle's Abridgment [*A publication*] (DLA)
RO .... Roll-On [*Trailer ship*] (DICI)
R/O .... Rollout (MCD)
R/O .... Rollover
RO .... Romania [*ANSI two-letter standard code*] (CNC)
RO .... Romans [*Old Testament book*]
RO .... Rood [*Unit of measurement*]
RO .... Room Only
RO .... Roper Organization (EA)
RO .... Rose (ROG)
RO .... Rough
RO .... Rough Opening [*Technical drawings*]
RO .... Round Off (IAA)
RO .... Route Order [*Military*]
RO .... Routine Order
RO .... Routing Office [*or Officer*] [*Navy*]
RO .... Rowed Over [*Rowing*] [*British*] (ROG)
RO .... Royal Observatory [*British*]
RO .... Royal Octavo
RO .... Royal Ordnance Factory [*British*]
R/O .... Rule Out [*Medicine*]
RO .... Runoff Election
R-O .... Run-On [*Used in correcting manuscripts, etc.*]
RO .... Runout (MSA)
RO .... Runover [*Publishing*]
RO .... Russian Obuckhoff Rifle
RO .... Rust and Oxidation (DNAB)
RO1(G) .... Radio Operator (General) 1st Class [*British military*] (DMA)
RO1(W) .... Radio Operator (Warfare) 1st Class [*British military*] (DMA)
RO2(G) .... Radio Operator (General) 2nd Class [*British military*] (DMA)
RO2(W) .... Radio Operator (Warfare) 2nd Class [*British military*] (DMA)
RO 7 R .... Rey Osterreigh and Recall [*Test*] [*Psychiatry*] (DAVI)
ROA .... Altimeter Station [*ITU designation*] (CET)
ROA .... Racehorse Owners Association [*British*] (DBA)
ROA .... Radiation Oncology Administrators [*Later, SROA*] (EA)
ROA .... Radio Operator's Aptitude Test [*Military*]
ROA .... Radius of Action (CAAL)
ROA .... Raman Optical Activity [*Spectrometry*]
ROA .... Recorder Announcement (DNAB)
ROA .... Record of Acquisition (WDAA)
ROA .... Reference Optical Alignment
ROA .... Rehabilitation of Offenders Act [*1974*] [*British*] (DCTA)
ROA .... Reinsurance Offices Association [*British*] (AIA)
ROA .... Reno Air, Inc. [*ICAO designator*] (FAAC)
ROA .... Research Opportunity Announcement (AAGC)
ROA .... Reserve Officers Association (NADA)
ROA .... Reserve Officers Association of the United States (EA)
ROA .... Retired Officers Association [*Military*]
ROA .... Return on Assets [*Business term*]
ROA .... Right Occipitoanterior [*A fetal position*] [*Obstetrics*]
ROA .... Roanoke [*Virginia*] [*Airport symbol*]
ROA .... Robert Owen Association (EA)
ROA .... Roller Owners' Association [*British*] (BI)
roa .... Romance [*MARC language code Library of Congress*] (LCCP)
ROA .... Rules of the Air (AFM)
ROA .... Russian Orchestra of the Americas
Ro Abr .... Rolle's Abridgment [*A publication*] (ILCA)
ROAD .... Inroads [*Database*] [*Australia*]
ROAD .... Reorganization Objectives, Army Division [*Military*]
ROAD .... Retires on Active Duty [*Military*] (MCD)
ROAD .... Reversible Obstructive Airway Disease (DAVI)
ROAD .... Road [*Commonly used*] (OPSA)
ROAD .... Roadway Express [*NASDAQ symbol*] (TTSB)
ROAD .... Roadway Express, Inc. [*NASDAQ symbol*] (SAG)
ROAD .... Roadway Services, Inc. [*NASDAQ symbol*] (NQ)
ROAD .... Ruch Obywatelski-Akcja Demokratyczna [*Civil Movement for Democratic Action*] [*P oland*] [*Political party*]
Roadmst .... Roadmaster Industries [*Associated Press*] (SAG)
ROADS .... Real-Time Optical Alignment and Diagnostic System [*Module*]
ROADS .... Roads [*Commonly used*] (OPSA)
ROADS .... Roadway Analysis and Design System [*Computer science*]
RoadSv .... Roadway Services, Inc. [*Associated Press*] (SAG)
RoadwyEx .... Roadway Express, Inc. [*Associated Press*] (SAG)
ROAH .... Naha [*Ryukyu Islands*] [*ICAO location identifier*] (ICLI)
ROAM .... Return on Assets Managed [*Finance*]
ROAMA .... Rome Air Materiel Area [*Deactivated*] [*Air Force*]
ROANA .... Rover Owners' Association of North America [*Defunct*] (EA)
Roan El .... Roanoke Electric Steel Corp. [*Associated Press*] (SAG)
RoanGas ...... Roanoke Gas Co. [*Associated Press*] (SAG)
ROAP .... , ara-C , Prednisone [*Vincristine*] [*Cytarabine*] [*Antineoplastic drug regimen*]
ROAR .... Radio Operated Auto Racing
ROAR .... Recovery and Overpayment Accounting and Reporting System [*Social Security Administration*] (GFGA)
ROAR .... Regional Organization for Airways Restudy
ROAR .... Restore Our Alienated Rights [*Boston antibusing group*]
ROAR .... Return of Army Repairables (AABC)
ROAR .... Royal Optimizing Assembly Routine [*Computer science*] (IAA)
ROAR .... Royal Optimizing Assembly Routing [*Royal McBee Corp.*] [*Computer science*]
ROARE .... Reduction of Attitudes and Repressed Emotions [*Treatment given to sex offenders*] [*Psychology*]
ROARS .... Rutgers Online Automated Retrieval Service [*Rutgers University*] (OLDSS)
ROAST .... Ring Out and Stress Tester (PDAA)
ROAT .... Radio Operator's Aptitude Test [*Military*]
ROATS .... Rabbit Ovarian Antitumor Serum [*Medicine*] (DMAA)
ROB .... African International Airways (West Africa) Ltd. [*Nigeria*] [*FAA designator*] (FAAC)
ROB .... Monrovia [*Liberia*] Roberts International Airport [*Airport symbol*] (OAG)
ROB .... RADAR Order of Battle
ROB .... RADAR Out of Battle (CET)
ROB .... Recovery Operations Branch [*NASA*] (KSC)
ROB .... Regional Office Building
ROB .... Relieve of Booty [*Crime term*]
ROB .... Remaining on Board
ROB .... Reorder Buffer [*Computer science*]
ROB .... Report on Board [*Navy*]
ROB .... Report on Business (IT)
ROB .... Reserveoffizier-Bewerber [*Reserve officer applicant*] [*German military - World War II*]
ROB .... Reserve on Board
ROB .... Right of Baseline (MCD)
ROB .... Right Outboard (MCD)
Rob .... Robards' Reports [*12, 13 Missouri*] [*A publication*] (DLA)
Rob .... Robards' Texas Conscript Cases [*A publication*] (DLA)
ROB .... Robert Morris College, Coraopolis, PA [*OCLC symbol*] (OCLC)
ROB .... Robertsfield [*Liberia*] [*Airport symbol*]
Rob .... Robertson's English Ecclesiastical Reports [*A publication*] (DLA)
Rob .... Robertson's Reports [*24-30 New York Superior Court*] [*1863-68*] [*A publication*] (DLA)
Rob .... Robertson's Reports [*1 Hawaii*] [*A publication*] (DLA)
Rob .... Robertson's Scotch Appeal Cases [*1707-27*] [*A publication*] (DLA)
Rob .... Roberts' Reports [*29-31 Louisiana Annual*] [*A publication*] (DLA)
ROB .... Robin International, Inc. [*Toronto Stock Exchange symbol*]
Rob .... Robinson's English Admiralty Reports [*1799-1809, 1838-1852*] [*A publication*] (DLA)
Rob .... Robinson's English Ecclesiastical Reports [*1844-53*] [*A publication*] (DLA)
Rob .... Robinson's Louisiana Reports [*1-4 Louisiana Annual*] [*1841-46*] [*A publication*] (DLA)
Rob .... Robinson's Reports [*2-9, 17-23 Colorado Appeals*] [*A publication*] (DLA)
Rob .... Robinson's Reports [*38 California*] [*A publication*] (DLA)
Rob .... Robinson's Reports [*1-8 Ontario*] [*A publication*] (DLA)
Rob .... Robinson's Reports [*40, 41 Virginia*] [*A publication*] (DLA)
Rob .... Robinson's Reports [*1 Nevada*] [*A publication*] (DLA)
Rob .... Robinson's Scotch Appeal Cases [*1840-41*] [*A publication*] (DLA)
Rob .... Robinson's Upper Canada Reports [*A publication*] (DLA)
ROB .... Roborough [*England*]
ROB .... Robotic Operating Buddy [*Nintendo video game system accessory*]
ROB .... Roburent [*Italy*] [*Seismograph station code, US Geological Survey*] (SEIS)
ROB .... Round of Beam (DS)
ROB .... Run of Book [*Advertising*] (WDMC)
ROB .... Run on Bank (MHDB)
ROB .... Waco, TX [*Location identifier FAA*] (FAAL)
RoBA .... Academia R.S. Romania [*Academy of Romania*], Bucharest, Romania [*Library symbol Library of Congress*] (LCLS)
Rob Adm & Pr... Roberts on Admiralty and Prize [*A publication*] (DLA)
ROBAMP ...... Rotational Base for Aviation Maintenance Personnel
Rob & J .... Robards and Jackson's Reports [*26, 27 Texas*] [*A publication*] (DLA)
Rob App ...... Robinson's Scotch Appeal Cases [*1840-41*] [*A publication*] (DLA)
ROBAR .... Read Only Back-Up Address Register [*Computer science*] (MHDB)
Robards .... Robards' Reports [*12, 13 Missouri*] [*A publication*] (DLA)
Robards .... Robards' Texas Conscript Cases [*1862-65*] [*A publication*] (DLA)
Robards & Jackson... Robards and Jackson's Reports [*26-27 Texas*] [*A publication*] (DLA)
ROBAT .... Robotic Obstacle-Breaching Assault Tank
Robb .... Robbins' New Jersey Equity Reports [*67-70 New Jersey*] [*A publication*] (DLA)
Robb .... Robb's United States Patent Cases [*A publication*] (DLA)
Rob Bank ..... Robertson's Handbook of Bankers' Law [*A publication*] (DLA)

Rob Bank..... Robson on Law and Practice in Bankruptcy [*7th ed.*] [*1894*] [*A publication*] (DLA)
RoBBC......... Biblioteca Centrala de Stat a R.S. Romania [*Central State Library of Romania*], Bucharest, Romania [*Library symbol Library of Congress*] (LCLS)
Robb (NJ).... Robbins' New Jersey Equity Reports [*A publication*] (DLA)
Robb Pat Cas... Robb's United States Patent Cases [*A publication*] (DLA)
Rob Cal....... Robinson's Reports [*38 California*] [*A publication*] (DLA)
Rob Car V.... Robertson's History of the Reign of the Emperor Charles V [*A publication*] (DLA)
Rob Cas....... Robinson's Scotch Appeal Cases [*1840-41*] [*A publication*] (DLA)
Rob Chr....... Robinson's Reports [*2-9, 17-23 Colorado Appeals*] [*A publication*] (DLA)
ROBCO......... Readiness Objective Code [*Military*] (AABC)
ROBCO......... Requirement Objective Code
Rob Colo..... Robinson's Reports [*2-9, 17-23 Colorado Appeals*] [*A publication*] (ILCA)
Rob Cons Cas (Tex)... Robards' Texas Conscript Cases [*A publication*] (DLA)
Rob Consc Cas... Robards' Texas Conscript Cases [*A publication*] (DLA)
Rob Dig....... Robert's Digest [*Lower Canada*] [*A publication*] (DLA)
Rob Dig....... Robert's Digest of Vermont Reports [*A publication*] (DLA)
Rob E........... Robertson's English Ecclesiastical Reports [*2 vols.*] [*1844-53*] [*A publication*] (DLA)
Rob Ecc....... Robertson's English Ecclesiastical Reports [*2 vols.*] [*1844-53*] [*A publication*] (DLA)
Rob Eccl...... Robertson's English Ecclesiastical Reports [*2 vols.*] [*1844-53*] [*A publication*] (DLA)
Rob El Law... Robinson's Elementary Law [*A publication*] (DLA)
Rob Ent....... Robinson's Book of Entries [*A publication*] (DLA)
ROBEPS....... RADAR Operating Below Prescribed Standarad [*NWS*] (FAAC)
Rob Eq......... Roberts' Principles of Equity [*A publication*] (DLA)
Rober........... Robertus [*Authority cited in pre-1607 legal work*] (DSA)
Roberds....... Roberds, Inc. [*Associated Press*] (SAG)
Rober Maran... Robertus Maranta [*Flourished, 16th century*] [*Authority cited in pre-1607 legal work*] (DSA)
Robert......... Robertson's Scotch Appeal Cases [*1707-27*] [*A publication*] (DLA)
Robert App... Robertson's Scotch House of Lords Appeals [*A publication*] (DLA)
Robert App Cas... Robertson's Scotch House of Lords Appeals [*A publication*] (DLA)
Roberts........ Roberts' Reports [*29-31 Louisiana Annual*] [*A publication*] (DLA)
Roberts Emp Liab... Roberts on Federal Liabilities of Carriers [*A publication*] (DLA)
Robertson.... Robertson's English Ecclesiastical Reports [*A publication*] (DLA)
Robertson.... Robertson's Reports [*New York Marine Court*] [*A publication*] (DLA)
Robertson.... Robertson's Reports [*24-30 New York Superior Court*] [*A publication*] (DLA)
Robertson.... Robertson's Reports [*1 Hawaii*] [*A publication*] (DLA)
Robertson.... Robertson's Scotch Appeal Cases [*1707-27*] [*A publication*] (DLA)
Robertson's Rep... Robertson's Reports [*24-30 New York Superior Court*] [*A publication*] (DLA)
Rob Forms... Robinson's Virginia Forms [*A publication*] (DLA)
Rob Fr......... Roberts on Frauds [*1805*] [*A publication*] (DLA)
Rob Fr Conv... Roberts on Fraudulent Conveyances [*A publication*] (DLA)
Rob Gav...... Robinson's Common Law of Kent, or Custom on Gavelkind [*5th ed.*] [*1897*] [*A publication*] (DLA)
Rob Hawaii... Robinson's Reports [*1 Hawaii*] [*A publication*] (DLA)
ROBIN.......... Register of Business Opportunities in New South Wales [*Australia*]
ROBIN.......... Remote On-Line Business Information Network [*Computer science*] (IEEE)
ROBIN.......... Rocket Balloon Instrument [*Air Force*]
Robin App... Robinson's Scotch House of Lords Appeals [*A publication*] (DLA)
ROBINS........ Roberts Information Services, Inc. [*Information service or system*] (IID)
Robin Sc App... Robinson's Scotch Appeal Cases [*1840-41*] [*A publication*] (DLA)
Robinson..... Robinson's English Ecclesiastical Reports [*1844-53*] [*A publication*] (DLA)
Robinson..... Robinson's Louisiana Reports [*1-12 Louisiana*] [*A publication*] (DLA)
Robinson..... Robinson's Ontario Reports [*A publication*] (DLA)
Robinson..... Robinson's Reports [*38 California*] [*A publication*] (DLA)
Robinson..... Robinson's Reports [*1 Nevada*] [*A publication*] (DLA)
Robinson..... Robinson's Reports [*17-23 Colorado*] [*A publication*] (DLA)
Robinson..... Robinson's Reports [*40-41 Virginia*] [*A publication*] (DLA)
Robinson..... Robinson's Scotch House of Lords Appeals [*A publication*] (DLA)
Robinson Sc App Cas... Robinson's Scotch Appeal Cases [*1840-41*] [*A publication*] (DLA)
Rob Jun....... William Robinson's English Admiralty Reports [*1838-52*] [*A publication*] (DLA)
Rob Jus....... Robinson's Justice of the Peace [*1836*] [*A publication*] (DLA)
Rob LA........ Robinson's Louisiana Reports [*1-4 Louisiana Annual*] [*1841-46*] [*A publication*] (DLA)
Rob (LA Ann)... Robinson's Louisiana Reports [*1-4 Louisiana Annual*] [*A publication*] (DLA)
Rob L & W... Roberts, Leaming, and Wallis' County Court Reports [*1849-51*] [*A publication*] (DLA)
Rob Leg....... Robertson's Legitimation by Subsequent Marriage [*1829*] [*A publication*] (DLA)
Rob Louis.... Robinson's Louisiana Reports [*1-12 Louisiana*] [*A publication*] (DLA)
Rob Mar (NY)... Robertson and Jacob's New York Marine Court Reports [*A publication*] (DLA)
Rob MO....... Robards' Reports [*12, 13 Missouri*] [*A publication*] (DLA)
ROBMV........ Robinia Mosaic Virus [*Plant pathology*]
RobMyr........ Robbins & Myers [*Associated Press*] (SAG)
ROBN........... Robbins & Myers [*NASDAQ symbol*] (TTSB)
ROBN........... Robbins & Myers, Inc. [*NASDAQ symbol*] (NQ)
Rob Nev...... Robinson's Reports [*1 Nevada*] [*A publication*] (DLA)
RobNug........ Robinson Nugent, Inc. [*Associated Press*] (SAG)
Rob (NY)..... Robertson's Reports [*24-30 New York Superior Court*] [*A publication*] (DLA)
ROBO........... Eshed Robotec Ltd. [*NASDAQ symbol*] (SAG)
ROBO........... Rocket Orbital Bomber
ROBOF......... Eshed Robotec 1982 Ltd [*NASDAQ symbol*] (TTSB)
ROBOMB...... Robot Bomb [*Air Force*]
Rob Ont....... Robinson's Reports [*1-8 Ontario*] [*A publication*] (DLA)
ROBOT......... Record Organization Based on Transposition (PDAA)
RobotVs....... Robotic Vision Systems, Inc. [*Associated Press*] (SAG)
Rob Pat....... Robinson on Patents [*A publication*] (DLA)
Rob Per Suc... Robertson's Law of Personal Succession [*1836*] [*A publication*] (DLA)
Rob Pr......... Robinson's Practice [*A publication*] (DLA)
Rob Prior..... Robertson's Law of Priority of Incumbrances [*A publication*] (DLA)
Robs Bank... Robson on Law and Practice in Bankruptcy [*7th ed.*] [*1894*] [*A publication*] (DLA)
Robs Bankr... Robertson's Handbook of Bankers' Law [*A publication*] (DLA)
Rob Sc App... Robinson's Scotch Appeal Cases [*A publication*] (DLA)
Rob SI......... Robertson's Sandwich Island Reports [*1 Hawaii*] [*A publication*] (DLA)
Robson........ Robson on Law and Practice in Bankruptcy [*7 eds.*] [*1870-94*] [*A publication*] (DLA)
Rob Sr Ct..... Robertson's New York Superior Court Reports [*24-30*] [*A publication*] (DLA)
Rob Succ...... Roberts on the Law of Personal Succession [*A publication*] (DLA)
Rob Super Ct... Robertson's Reports [*24-30 New York Superior Court*] [*A publication*] (DLA)
Robt Eccl..... Robertson's English Ecclesiastical Reports [*163 English Reprint*] [*1844-53*] [*A publication*] (DLA)
Robt Eccl (Eng)... Robertson's English Ecclesiastical Reports [*163 English Reprint*] [*A publication*] (DLA)
RobtHalf...... Robert Half International [*Associated Press*] (SAG)
Robt (NY).... Robertson's Reports [*24-30 New York Superior Court*] [*A publication*] (DLA)
Robt Sc App Cas... Robertson's Scotch Appeal Cases [*A publication*] (DLA)
Rob UC........ Robinson's Upper Canada Reports [*A publication*] (DLA)
ROBV........... Robotic Vision Sys [*NASDAQ symbol*] (TTSB)
ROBV........... Robotic Vision Systems, Inc. [*NASDAQ symbol*] (NQ)
Rob VA........ Robinson's Reports [*40, 41 Virginia*] [*A publication*] (DLA)
Rob W.......... Roberts. Wills and Codicils [*1826*] [*A publication*] (ILCA)
Roc.............. New Hampshire Reports [*A publication*] (DLA)
ROC............. Radius of Curvature
ROC............. Rail Operations Center [*MTMC*] (TAG)
ROC............. Railton Owners Club (EA)
ROC............. Range Operations Center [*Western Test Range*] (MCD)
ROC............. Range Operations Conference [*NASA*] (KSC)
ROC............. Rapid Omnidirectional Compaction [*Materials technology*] [*Dow Chemical Co.*]
ROC............. Rate of Climb [*Aviation*]
ROC............. Rate of Convergence (IEEE)
ROC............. Ratio of Charges [*Health insurance*] (GHCT)
ROC............. Readily-Oxidizable Carbon (PDAA)
ROC............. Receiver [*or Relative*] Operating Characteristics [*Signal detection*] [*Graph for assessing diagnostic tests*]
ROC............. Recommended Operating Condition [*Computer science*]
ROC............. Reconnaissance and Operations Center (NATG)
ROC............. Reconnaissance Optique de Caracteres [*Optical Character Recognition*] [*French*]
ROC............. Record of Changes (DNAB)
ROC............. Record of Comments (NASA)
ROC............. Redeem Our Country (EA)
ROC............. Reduced Operational Capability Program [*Navy*] (NVT)
ROC............. Reduced Oxygen Concentration (MCD)
ROC............. Reduce Operating Costs [*Air Force project*]
ROC............. Reevaluation of Capital [*Business term*] (MHDB)
ROC............. Regional Operating Center [*NATO Integrated Communications System*] (NATG)
ROC............. Region One Cooperative Library Service Unit [*Library network*]
ROC............. Regroupement des Officiers Communistes [*Burkina Faso*] [*Political party*] (EY)
ROC............. Relative Operating Characteristics (MCD)
ROC............. Reliability Operating Characteristic
ROC............. Remote Operator's Console
ROC............. Republican Organizing Committee [*Political organization in opposition to the NPL of North Dakota*]
ROC............. Republic of China
ROC............. Request of Change (NASA)
ROC............. Required Operational Capability [*Military*] (RDA)
ROC............. Requirements Document [*Army*] (RDA)
ROC............. Reserve Officer Candidate
ROC............. Residual Organic Carbon [*Organic chemistry*] (DAVI)
ROC............. Rest of Canada [*English-speaking portion of Canada*] (ECON)
ROC............. Return on Capital [*Finance*]
ROC............. Reusable Orbital Carrier [*Aerospace*] (MCD)
ROC............. Rochester [*New York*] [*Airport symbol*] (OAG)
ROC............. Rochester-Odenbach [*New York*] [*Seismograph station code, US Geological Survey*] (SEIS)
ROC............. Rochester Public Library, Rochester, MN [*OCLC symbol*] (OCLC)
Roc.............. Rochus Curtius [*Flourished, 1470-1515*] [*Authority cited in pre-1607 legal work*] (DSA)
ROC............. Rocky Mountain [*Canada ICAO designator*] (FAAC)
Roc.............. Rococo Records [*Record label*] [*Canada, USA*]
ROC............. ROC Taiwan Fund SBI [*NYSE symbol*] (SPSG)
ROC............. Rotatable Optical Cube

ROC .... Rothmans Inc. [*Formerly, Rothmans of Pall Mall Canada*] [*Toronto Stock Exchange symbol Vancouver Stock Exchange symbol*]
ROC .... Royal Observer Corps [*British civilian aircraft observers*] [*World War II*]
ROC .... Royal Ordnance Corps [*British*]
ROCAF .... Republic of China Air Force
ROCALDIS ... Routine Calls May Be Dispensed With
ROCAP .... Regional Office for Central America and Panama
ROCAP .... Regional Office [*or Officer*] for Central American Programs [*Department of State*]
ROCAPPI ...... Research on Computer Applications for the Printing and Publishing Industries
ROCAT .... Rocket Catapult
ROCC .... Range Operations Conference Circuit (MUGU)
ROCC .... Range Operations Control Center (MCD)
ROCC .... Receptor-Operated Calcium Channel [*Physiology*]
ROCC .... Regional Oil Combating Center [*United Nations Environment Programme*] (MSC)
ROCC .... Regional Operations Control Center [*AT & T*]
ROCC .... Region Operations Control Center [*NORAD*] [*ICAO designator*] (FAAC)
ROCC .... Remote Operational Control Center
Rocc .... Roccus. De Navibus et Naulo [*Maritime law*] [*A publication*] (DLA)
ROCC .... Russell's Owl Collectors Club (EA)
Rocc De Nav et Nau... Roccus. De Navibus et Naulo [*Maritime law*] [*A publication*] (DLA)
ROC Cm .... ROC Communities [*Associated Press*] (SAG)
Roccus Ins... Roccus on Insurance [*A publication*] (DLA)
ROCE .... Return on Capital Employed [*Accounting term*]
ROCF .... Rockford Industries [*NASDAQ symbol*] (TTSB)
ROCF .... Rockford Industries, Inc. [*NASDAQ symbol*] (SAG)
ROC Fd .... ROC Taiwan Fund [*Associated Press*] (SAG)
ROCH .... Rochester [*Municipal borough in England*] (ROG)
Roch .... Rochus Curtius [*Flourished, 1470-1515*] [*Authority cited in pre-1607 legal work*] (DSA)
ROCH .... Ruch Oporu Chlopskiego [*Movement of Peasant Resistance*] [*Poland Political party*] (PPE)
Roch Curt .... Rochus Curtius [*Flourished, 1470-1515*] [*Authority cited in pre-1607 legal work*] (DSA)
Roche & H Bank... Roche and Hazlitt's Bankruptcy Practice [*2nd ed.*] [*1873*] [*A publication*] (DLA)
Roche D & K... Roche, Dillon, and Kehoe's Irish Land Reports [*1881-82*] [*A publication*] (DLA)
RochG .... Rochester Gas & Electric Corp. [*Associated Press*] (SAG)
RochMed ..... Rochester Medical Corp. [*Associated Press*] (SAG)
ROCI .... Rahim Organizational Conflict Inventories [*Interpersonal skills and attitudes test*]
ROCI .... Rauschenberg Overseas Cultural Interchange [*Retrospective exhibit of artist Robert Rauschenberg's work*]
ROCI .... Rickman Owners Club International (EA)
ROCID .... Reorganization of Combat Infantry Division [*Army*] (AABC)
Roc Ins .... Roccus on Insurance [*A publication*] (DLA)
ROCK .... Gibraltar Steel [*NASDAQ symbol*] (TTSB)
ROCK .... Gibraltar Steel Corp. [*NASDAQ symbol*] (SAG)
Rock .... New Hampshire Reports [*A publication*] (DLA)
ROCK .... Rocket (MCD)
Rock .... Smith's New Hampshire Reports [*A publication*] (DLA)
RockBott ...... Rock Bottom Restaurants, Inc. [*Associated Press*] (SAG)
RockCtr .... Rockefeller Center Properties [*Associated Press*] (SAG)
Rockefeller U... [*The*] Rockefeller University (GAGS)
ROCKET .... Rand's Omnibus Calculator of the Kinetics of Earth Trajectories
ROCKEX .... Rocket Exercise [*Military*] (NVT)
ROCKF .... Rockford [*England*]
Rockford C... Rockford College (GAGS)
Rockfrd .... Rockford Industries, Inc. [*Associated Press*] (SAG)
Rockingham... Smith's New Hampshire Reports [*A publication*] (DLA)
Rock Min ..... Rockwell on Mines [*A publication*] (DLA)
ROCKOON .... Rocket Balloon [*Navy*]
RocksMiner... Rocks & Minerals [*A publication*] (BRI)
Rock Sp Law... Rockwell's Spanish and Mexican Law Relating to Mines [*A publication*] (DLA)
ROCKSTORE... Rock Storage [*Storage in excavated rock caverns*]
RockTen ...... Rock Tenn Co. [*Associated Press*] (SAG)
Rockwl .... Rockwell International Corp. [*Associated Press*] (SAG)
Rocky Mt Miner L Rev... Rocky Mountain Mineral Law Review [*A publication*] (DLA)
RockySh ...... Rocky Shoes & Boots, Inc. [*Associated Press*] (SAG)
ROCM .... Rochester Medical [*NASDAQ symbol*] (TTSB)
ROCM .... Rochester Medical Corp. [*NASDAQ symbol*] (SAG)
ROCMAGV ... Republic of China, Military Assistance Group, Vietnam
ROCMAS ...... Russian Orthodox Catholic Mutual Aid Society of USA (EA)
ROCMC .... Republic of China Marine Corps
ROCMM .... Regional Office of Civilian Manpower Management
ROCN .... Reclamation Order Control Number
ROCN .... Republic of China Navy
ROCN .... Retraining Objective Control Number [*Air Force*] (AFM)
ROCOA .... Renault Owners Club of America (EA)
ROCOB .... Rocketsonde Observation (NOAA)
ROCOCO ...... Rocailles, Coquilles, et Cordeau [*Rocks, Shells, and String*] [*French*]
ROCOMP ...... Radio or Computer Operated Mobile Platform [*Army*]
ROCOZ .... Rocket-Borne Ozonesonde (SAA)
ROCP .... RADAR Out of Commission for Parts [*ADC*]
ROCP .... Regional Occupation Center Program (OICC)
ROCP .... Remote Operator Control Panel [*Electronics*] (IAA)
ROCPEX .... Republic of China Philatelic Exhibition
ROCR .... Recovery Operations Control Room [*NASA*] (KSC)
ROCR .... Remote Optical Character Recognition [*Computer science*]
ROCS .... Railroad Operations Control System (PDAA)
ROCS .... Range Operations Control System (SAA)
ROCSIM .... Railroad Operations Computer Simulation [*FTA*] (TAG)
ROCU .... Remote Operational Control Unit [*Military*] (CAAL)
ROCWMAS... Russian Orthodox Catholic Women's Mutual Aid Society (EA)
ROD .... Aerodan, SA de CV [*Mexico*] [*FAA designator*] (FAAC)
ROD .... Railway Operating Department [*British military*] (DMA)
ROD .... Range of the Day [*Military*] (CAAL)
ROD .... Range Operations Directorate [*White Sands Missile Range*]
ROD .... Rate of Descent (KSC)
ROD .... Recorder on Demand
ROD .... Record of Decision [*Environmental Protection Agency*]
ROD .... Record of Discussion (MCD)
ROD .... Release Order Directive [*Later, ERO*] (NRCH)
ROD .... Remote Operated Door (MCD)
ROD .... Repair and Overhaul Directive (AAG)
ROD .... Repair on Demand (DA)
ROD .... Report of Discrepancies
ROD .... Required on Dock (KSC)
ROD .... Required Operational Date
ROD .... Reverse-Osmosis Desalination
ROD .... Rewritable Optical Disk [*Computer science*] (BARN)
R-O-D .... Rise-Off-Disconnect (AAG)
ROD .... Roddy Resources, Inc. [*Toronto Stock Exchange symbol*]
Rod .... Rodericus Suarez [*Flourished, 15th century*] [*Authority cited in pre-1607 legal work*] (DSA)
ROD .... Rosewood, OH [*Location identifier FAA*] (FAAL)
ROD .... Route Opening Detachment (MCD)
RODA .... Regardless of Destination Airport (FAAC)
RODA .... Sisters Oblates to Divine Love [*Roman Catholic religious order*]
RODAC .... Reorganization Objectives, Army Division, Army and Corps [*Military*] (AABC)
ROD/AC .... Rotary Dual Input for Analog Computation (SAA)
RODATA .... Registered Organization Data Bank
RODC .... Regional Oceanographic Data Center [*Marine science*] (MSC)
RODC .... Registered Organization Development Consultant [*Organization Development Institute*] [*Designation awarded by*]
RODE .... Iejima United States Air Force Base [*Ryukyu Islands*] [*ICAO location identifier*] (ICLI)
RO-DI .... Reverse Osmosis - Deionization System [*Water purification*]
RODIAC .... Rotary Dual Input for Analog Computation
R-O Dis .... Reality-Oriented Discussion
Rodm .... Rodman's Reports [*78-82 Kentucky*] [*A publication*] (DLA)
Rodman .... Rodman's Reports [*78-82 Kentucky*] [*A publication*] (DLA)
RODN .... Kadena Air Base [*Ryukyu Islands*] [*ICAO location identifier*] (ICLI)
RODO .... Range Operations Duty Officer (MUGU)
Rodo .... Rodoicus [*Authority cited in pre-1607 legal work*] (DSA)
RodRen .... Rodman & Renshaw Capital Group [*Associated Press*] (SAG)
RODS .... Real-Time Operations, Dispatching, and Scheduling [*System*] [*TRW, Inc.*]
ROE .... Birmingham, AL [*Location identifier FAA*] (FAAL)
ROE .... Rate of Exchange [*Finance*]
ROE .... Reflector Orbital Equipment
ROE .... Reflector Orbital Experiment (MCD)
ROE .... Return on Equity [*Finance*]
ROE .... Roster of Exception [*Military*] (AABC)
ROE .... Round Off Error
ROE .... Royal Observatory, Edinburgh [*Scotland*]
ROE .... Rules of Engagement [*Military*] (AABC)
ROEAP .... Regional Office for Education, Asia and Pacific [*UNESCO*] (AIE)
ROEFEX .... Rotterdam Energy Futures Exchange [*Netherlands*] (EY)
Roelk Man... Roelker's Manual for Notaries and Bankers [*A publication*] (DLA)
ROEM .... Removable, Optical, Erasable Media [*Computer science*] (BTTJ)
Roent .... Roentgenology [*Radiology*]
Roent M ...... Master of Roentgenology
ROESY .... Rotating-Frame Overhauser Enchancement Spectroscopy [*Organic chemistry*]
Roe US Com... Roe's Manual for United States Commissioners [*A publication*] (DLA)
ROEX .... Rules of Engagement Exercise (DOMA)
ROF .... Aerofrance [*France ICAO designator*] (FAAC)
ROF .... Rate of Fire [*In rounds per minute*] [*Military*]
ROF .... Reformed Ogboni Fraternity [*Nigeria*]
ROF .... Remote Operator Facility [*Honeywell, Inc.*]
ROF .... Reporting Organizational File [*Military*] (AFM)
Rof .... Roffredus Beneventanus [*Flourished, 1215-43*] [*Authority cited in pre-1607 legal work*] (DSA)
ROF .... Rose Hall [*Guyana*] [*Airport symbol*] (AD)
ROF .... Royal Oak Foundation (EA)
ROF .... Royal Ordnance Factory [*British*] (NATG)
ROFA .... Radio of Free Asia (NTCM)
ROF-B .... Royal Ordnance Factory, Bishopton [*Scotland*]
Rof Bn .... Roffredus Beneventanus [*Flourished, 1215-43*] [*Authority cited in pre-1607 legal work*] (DSA)
R of D .... Reporter of Debate [*US Senate*]
R of E .... Rate of Exchange
ROFF .... Retail Office Furniture Forum (EA)
Roffe Be ...... Roffredus Beneventanus [*Flourished, 1215-43*] [*Authority cited in pre-1607 legal work*] (DSA)
ROFFEN .... Roffensis [*Signature of Bishop of Rochester*] [*Latin*] (ROG)
ROFL .... Rolling on the Floor Laughing [*Internet language*] (PCM)
ROFL .... Rolls on Floor Laughing [*Internet language*] [*Computer science*]
ROFL .... Russian Orthodox Fraternity Lubov (EA)

RO/FLO .... Roll-On/Float-Off (DOMA)
RofnSinr ...... Rofin-Sinar Technologies, Inc. [*Associated Press*] (SAG)
R of O .... Reserve of Officers [*British*]
ROFOR .... Route Forcast [*Aviation*] (FAAC)
ROFR .... Repair of Repairables (MCD)
ROFT .... RADAR Off Target
ROFT .... Rapid Optics Fabrication Technology (MCD)
R of W .... Right of Way
ROG .... Reactive Organic Gas [*Environmental chemistry*]
ROG .... Receipt of Goods
ROG .... Recruiting Operations Group [*Military*]
ROG .... Residency Operations Group
R-O-G .... Rise-Off-Ground [*Model airplane*] (AAG)
ROG .... Rodale's Organic Gardening [*A publication*]
ROG .... Rogel [*C.C. Sergio Gonzales*], Ing. [*Mexico ICAO designator*] (FAAC)
Rog .... Rogerius Beneventanus [*Flourished, 12th century*] [*Authority cited in pre-1607 legal work*] (DSA)
ROG .... Rogers, AR [*Location identifier FAA*] (FAAL)
ROG .... Rogers Corp. [*AMEX symbol*] (SPSG)
ROG .... Roggianite [*A zeolite*]
ROG .... Rothchild Gold [*Vancouver Stock Exchange symbol*]
ROGAR .... Review of Guard and Reserve Task Force (MCD)
RogCantl ...... Rogers Cantel Mobile Communications [*Associated Press*] (SAG)
Rog CHR ...... Rogers' City Hall Recorder [*1816-22*] [*New York*] [*A publication*] (DLA)
RogCm .... Rogers Communications, Inc. [*Associated Press*] (SAG)
Rog Ecc L .... Rogers' Ecclesiastical Law [*5th ed.*] [*1857*] [*A publication*] (DLA)
Rog Ecc Law ... Rogers' Ecclesiastical Law [*A publication*] (DLA)
Rog Elec ...... Rogers on Elections and Registration [*A publication*] (DLA)
Rogers .... Rogers Corp. [*Associated Press*] (SAG)
Rogers .... Rogers on Elections [*A publication*] (DLA)
Rogers .... Rogers' Reports [*47-51 Louisiana Annual*] [*A publication*] (DLA)
Rog Hov .... Roger De Hoveden's Chronica [*A publication*] (DLA)
Rog Jud Acts ... Rogers on the Judicature Acts [*A publication*] (DLA)
Rog Min .... Rogers. Mines, Minerals, and Quarries [*A publication*] (ILCA)
Rog Min .... Rogers on Mines and Minerals [*A publication*] (DLA)
ROGOPAG .... Rossellini, Jr.; Godard, Pasolini, Gregoretti [*Title of episodic motion picture formed from surnames of its directors*]
Rog Rec .... Rogers' New City Hall Recorder [*A publication*] (DLA)
Rog Trav ...... Rogers' Wrongs and Rights of a Traveller [*A publication*] (DLA)
RogWve .... Rogue Wave Software, Inc. [*Associated Press*] (SAG)
ROH .... Rat Ovarian Hyperemia [*Test*] (MAE)
ROH .... Ray of Hope [*An association*] (EA)
ROH .... Rear Overhead [*TII*] (TAG)
R-O-H .... Receiver Off the Hook
ROH .... Regular Overhaul [*Navy*] (NG)
ROH .... Returned on Hire
roh .... Rhaeto-Romance [*MARC language code Library of Congress*] (LCCP)
ROH .... Robinhood [*Australia Airport symbol Obsolete*] (OAG)
ROH .... Rohm & Haas [*NYSE symbol*] (TTSB)
ROH .... Rohm & Haas Co. [*NYSE symbol*] (SPSG)
ROH .... Rohtak [*India*] [*Seismograph station code, US Geological Survey Closed*] (SEIS)
ROH .... Royal Opera House [*Covent Garden, London*]
RoHaas .... Rohm & Haas Co. [*Associated Press*] (SAG)
Rohr .... Rohr Industries, Inc. [*Associated Press*] (SAG)
ROI .... Member of the Royal Institute of Oil Painters [*British*]
ROI .... Radio, Optical, Inertial
ROI .... Range Operations Instruction [*NASA*] (KSC)
ROI .... Reactive Oxygen Intermediate [*Biochemistry*]
ROI .... Region of Influence
ROI .... Region of Interest [*Nuclear energy*]
ROI .... Region of Interest [*Nuclear energy*] (NRCH)
ROI .... Registration of Interest
ROI .... Relevant, Original, Impact [*Advertising*] (WDMC)
ROI .... Reliability Organization Instruction (AAG)
ROI .... Religious Observance Index (BJA)
ROI .... Remnant of Israel (EA)
ROI .... Rendezvous Orbit Insertion [*Aerospace*]
ROI .... Report of Investigation [*Military*] (AFM)
ROI .... Research Online International, Inc. [*Information service or system*] (IID)
ROI .... Resource Objectives, Inc. [*Ridgewood, NJ*] (TSSD)
ROI .... Return on Investment [*Finance*]
roi .... Return on Investment (WDMC)
ROI .... Rotating Optical Interferometer
ROI .... Royal Institute of Oil Painters [*British*]
ROI .... Royal Institute of Oil Painters, London [*1883*] (NGC)
ROIC .... Regional Officer in Charge [*CIA*] (VNW)
ROIC .... Resident Officer-in-Charge [*Military*]
ROICC .... Resident Officer-in-Charge of Construction [*Military*]
ROICM .... Resident Officer-in-Charge of Material [*Navy*] (DNAB)
ROID .... Report of Item Discrepancy [*Army*] (AABC)
ROIG .... Ishigaki Jima [*Ryukyu Islands*] [*ICAO location identifier*] (ICLI)
ROIH .... Right Oblique Inguinal Hernia [*Medicine*] (DMAA)
ROIN .... Reorganization of the Interconnection Network (MHDI)
RO in C .... Resident Officer-in-Charge [*Navy*]
ROINST .... Range Operations Instruction [*NASA*] (MUGU)
ROIP .... Remaining Oil in Place [*Petroleum industry*]
ROIS .... Radio Operational Intercom System (KSC)
ROITL .... Reports of Interest to Lawyers [*Merton Allen Associates*] [*Information service or system*] (CRD)
ROIX .... Response Oncology [*NASDAQ symbol*] (TTSB)
ROIXD .... Response Oncology, Inc. [*NASDAQ symbol*] (SAG)
ROJ .... Range of Jamming
ROJ .... Royal Order of Jagie Ilo [*Later, SHOSJ*] (EA)
ROJM .... Range of Joint Motion [*Medicine*] (DMAA)
ROK .... Republic of Korea
ROK .... Rockhampton [*Australia Airport symbol*] (OAG)
ROK .... Rockwell International Corp. [*NYSE symbol Toronto Stock Exchange symbol*] (SPSG)
ROK .... Rockwell Intl [*NYSE symbol*] (TTSB)
ROKA .... Republic of Korea Army
ROKAF .... Republic of Korea Air Force
ROKAP .... Republic of Korea Civic Action Program
ROKDTF .... Republic of Korea Division Task Force
ROKF .... Republic of Korea Forces
ROKFV .... Republic of Korea Forces in Vietnam
ROKG .... Republic of Korea Government
ROKG .... Rocking
ROKIT .... Republic of Korea Indigenous Tank Program (MCD)
ROKJ .... Kume Jima [*Ryukyu Islands*] [*ICAO location identifier*] (ICLI)
ROKMC .... Republic of Korea Marine Corps
ROKN .... Republic of Korea Navy
ROKPr .... Rockwell Intl $4.75 Cv Pfd [*NYSE symbol*] (TTSB)
ROKPrB .... Rockwell Intl $1.35 Cv PFd [*NYSE symbol*] (TTSB)
ROKPTN .... Rockhampton (ROG)
ROKPUC .... Republic of Korea Presidential Unit Citation Badge [*Military decoration*]
ROKPUCE .... Republic of Korea Presidential Unit Citation [*Military decoration*]
ROKUSCFC ... Republic of Korea and US Combined Forces Command (MCD)
ROKW .... Yomitan [*Ryukyu Islands*] [*ICAO location identifier*] (ICLI)
ROL .... Aeroel Airways Ltd. [*Israel*] [*FAA designator*] (FAAC)
ROL .... RADAR Observer License
ROL .... Record of Oral Language (ADA)
ROL .... Reduction-Option Loan [*Banking*]
ROL .... Remote Operating Location (MCD)
ROL .... Reordering Level
ROL .... Right Occipitolateral [*Obstetrics*]
ROL .... Right Occipitolateral [*Position*] (DAVI)
ROL .... Rolla [*Missouri*] [*Seismograph station code, US Geological Survey*] (SEIS)
Rol .... Rolle's Abridgment [*A publication*] (DLA)
Rol .... Rolle's English King's Bench Reports [*2 vols.*] [*A publication*] (DLA)
ROL .... Rollins, Inc. [*NYSE symbol*] (SPSG)
ROL .... Rotate Left [*Computer science*]
ROL .... Royal Oak Resources Ltd. [*Toronto Stock Exchange symbol*]
ROL .... Royal Overseas League [*British*] (EAIO)
Rol Ab .... Rolle's Abridgment [*A publication*] (DLA)
ROLAC .... Regional Office for Latin America and the Caribbean [*United Nations Environment Programme*] (EAIO)
ROLAC .... Regional Organization of Liaison for Allocation of Circuit (NATG)
ROLAC .... Registry of Life Assurance Commission [*British*]
ROLADES ..... Roland Air Defense System (MCD)
ROLC .... Our Lady of Charity of Refuge (TOCD)
ROLE .... Receive Only Link Eleven [*Naval datalink system*] [*British*]
ROLET .... Reference Our Letter (NOAA)
ROLF .... Remotely Operated Longwall Face (IEEE)
ROLFE .... Review of Law in Further Education (AIE)
Roll .... Rolle's Abridgment [*A publication*] (DLA)
Roll .... Rolle's English King's Bench Reports [*2 vols.*] [*A publication*] (DLA)
Roll Abr .... Rolle's Abridgment [*A publication*] (DLA)
Rolle .... Rolle's Abridgment [*A publication*] (DLA)
Rolle .... Rolle's English King's Bench Reports [*2 vols.*] [*1614-25*] [*A publication*] (DLA)
Rolle Abr ..... Rolle's Abridgment of the Common Law [*A publication*] (DLA)
Rolle R .... Rolle's English King's Bench Reports [*2 vols.*] [*1614-25*] [*A publication*] (DLA)
RollinE .... Rollins Environmental Services, Inc. [*Associated Press*] (SAG)
Rollins .... Rollins, Inc. [*Associated Press*] (SAG)
Rollins C ..... Rollins College (GAGS)
RollLeas ...... Rollins Truck Leasing [*Associated Press*] (SAG)
Roll Rep ...... Rolle's English King's Bench Reports [*2 vols.*] [*1614-25*] [*A publication*] (DLA)
Rolls Ct Rep ... Rolls' Court Reports [*A publication*] (DLA)
Ro/Lo .... Roll-On, Roll-Off/Lift-On, Lift-Off [*Shipping*] (DS)
ROLR .... Receiving Objective Loudness Rating [*Telephones*] (IEEE)
ROLS .... Rainbow Optical Landing System (PDAA)
ROLS .... Recoverable Orbital Launch System
ROLS .... Remote On-Line Subsystem [*Computer science*] (MHDI)
ROLS .... Remote Online System (NITA)
ROLSIM .... Roland Simulation (MCD)
ROM .... Empresa Aeromar [*Dominican Republic*] [*ICAO designator*] (FAAC)
ROM .... Priest, CA [*Location identifier FAA*] (FAAL)
ROM .... RADAR Operator Mechanic (WDAA)
ROM .... Radiopaque Contrast Material (WGA)
ROM .... Range of Motion [*or Movement*]
ROM .... Reactive Oxygen Metabolites [*Biochemistry*]
ROM .... Read-Only Memory [*Computer memory*] [*Computer science*]
ROM .... Read-Only Men [*On Board car window sign's version of the computer term, Read-Only Memory*]
ROM .... Readout Memory (IEEE)
ROM .... Reciprocal Ohmmeter [*Electronics*] (IAA)
ROM .... Recruiter of the Month [*Navy*] (DNAB)
ROM .... Refuel-On-The-Move [*Army*] (DOMA)
ROM .... Regional Oxidant Model [*Environmental Protection Agency*] (GFGA)
ROM .... Register of Merit (WGA)
ROM .... Return on Market Value [*Finance*]

ROM .... Rio Algom Ltd. [*AMEX symbol Toronto Stock Exchange symbol*] (SPSG)
Rom .... Roemisch [*Roman*] [*German*]
ROM .... Roman [*Type*] [*Publishing*]
rom .... Roman [*Type*] [*Publishing*] (ODBW)
ROM .... Romance
ROM .... Romania [*ANSI three-letter standard code*] (CNC)
Rom .... Romania (VRA)
Rom .... Romans [*New Testament book*]
rom .... Romany [*MARC language code Library of Congress*] (LCCP)
Rom .... Romany Records [*Record label*]
ROM .... Romberg [*Medicine*]
ROM .... Rome [*Italy*] [*Airport symbol*] (OAG)
ROM .... Rome [*Italy*] [*Seismograph station code, US Geological Survey Closed*] (SEIS)
Rom .... Romeo and Juliet [*Shakespearean work*]
Rom .... Romilly's Notes of English Chancery Cases [*1767-87*] [*A publication*] (DLA)
Rom .... Romulus [*of Plutarch*] [*Classical studies*] (OCD)
ROM .... Rotating Piston Machine (IAA)
ROM .... Rough Order of Magnitude [*Army*] (AABC)
ROM .... Royal Ontario Museum [*Toronto, ON*] [*Research center*]
ROM .... Run of Mine
ROM .... Rupture of Membranes [*Medicine*]
ROMA .... Return on Managed Assets [*Business term*]
ROMAC .... Range Operations Monitor Analysis Center (MCD)
ROMAC .... Range Operations Monitoring and Control
ROMAC .... Robotic Muscle Activator
Romac .... Romac Industries, Inc. [*Associated Press*] (SAG)
ROMACC .... Range Operational Monitoring and Control Center
ROMAD .... Radio Operator/Maintenance Driver
ROMAD .... Read Only Memory Automatic Design [*Computer science*] (MHDB)
Rom Adelsparteien ... Roemische Adelsparteien und Adelsfamilien [*A publication*] (OCD)
ROMAN .... Remotely-Operated Mobile Manipulator (PDAA)
Rom & Jul ... Romeo and Juliet [*Shakespearean work*] (BARN)
ROMANS .... Range-Only Multiple Aircraft Navigation System [*Air Force*]
ROMANS .... Remote Manipulation Systems [*NASA*]
RO(M)B .... Reduction of (Military) Budgets
ROMBI .... Results of Marine Biological Investigations [*Marine science*] (MSC)
ROMBUS .... Reusable Orbital Module Booster and Utility Shuttle [*Aerospace*]
ROMC .... Romac Industries, Inc. [*NASDAQ symbol*] (SAG)
ROMC .... Romac Intl [*NASDAQ symbol*] (TTSB)
Rom Cas .... Romilly's Notes of English Chancery Cases [*1767-87*] [*A publication*] (DLA)
ROMCOE .... Rocky Mountain Center on Environment (EPA)
Rom Cr Law ... Romilly's Observations on the Criminal Law [*3rd ed.*] [*1813*] [*A publication*] (DLA)
ROMD .... Minami Daito Jima [*Ryukyu Islands*] [*ICAO location identifier*] (ICLI)
ROMD .... Remote Operations and Maintenance Demonstration [*Nuclear energy*]
ROME .... Resource Organizations and Meetings for Educators [*National Center for Research in Vocational Education*] [*Information service or system Defunct*] (CRD)
ROMEMO .... Reference Our Memorandum (FAAC)
ROMES .... Reference Message from Our Office (FAAC)
Rom Forsch ... Roemische Forschungen [*A publication*] (OCD)
Rom Gesch ... Grundriss der Romischen Geschichte [*A publication*] (OCD)
Rom Gesch ... Romische Geschichte bis zum Beginn der Punischen Kriege [*A publication*] (OCD)
ROMI .... Rule Out Myocardial Infarction [*Medicine*]
Romilly NC (Eng) ... Romilly's Notes of English Chancery Cases [*A publication*] (DLA)
ROMIO .... ROM Plus Input/Output (NITA)
Rom Law .... Mackeldey's Handbook of the Roman Law [*A publication*] (DLA)
ROMM .... Read-Only Memory Module [*Computer science*]
ROMN .... Film Roman, Inc. [*NASDAQ symbol*] (SAG)
ROMO .... Rocky Mountain National Park
ROMON .... Receiving-Only Monitor
ROMOSS .... Revised Officer Military Occupational Speciality System (MCD)
ROMOTAR ... Range-Only Measurement of Trajectory and Recording
ROMP .... Radiotelephone Operator Maintenance Proficiency (DNAB)
ROMP .... Recovery of Male Potency (EA)
ROMP .... Report of Obligation Military Pay (AFM)
ROMP .... Review of Management Practices [*or Processes*]
ROMP .... Ring Opening Metathesis Polymerization [*Organic chemistry*]
Rom Pol .... Roman Politics 220-150BC [*A publication*] (OCD)
ROMPS .... Regional Office Monthly Personnel Status [*Department of Labor*]
ROMR .... Read-Only Memory Register [*Computer science*] (IAA)
Rom Rev .... [*The*] Roman Revolution [*1939*] [*A publication*] (OCD)
Rom Rule Asia Min ... Roman Rule in Asia Minor [*A publication*] (OCD)
ROMS .... Read-Only Memory Storage [*Computer science*] (IAA)
ROMS .... Remote Ocean Surface Measuring System [*Navy*] (CAAL)
Rom Staatsr ... Roemisches Staatsrecht [*A publication*] (OCD)
Rom Strafr ... Roemisches Strafrecht [*A publication*] (OCD)
Rom Stud .... Roemische Studien [*A publication*] (OCD)
ROMT .... Rom Tech [*NASDAQ symbol*] (TTSB)
ROMT .... Rom Tech, Inc. [*NASDAQ symbol*] (SAG)
RomTch .... Rom Tech, Inc. [*Associated Press*] (SAG)
ROMV .... Return on Market Value [*Finance*] (WDAA)
ROMY .... Miyako [*Ryukyu Islands*] [*ICAO location identifier*] (ICLI)
RON .... Air Nauru [*ICAO designator*] (FAAC)
RON .... Cooper Cameron [*NYSE symbol*] (TTSB)
RON .... Cooper Cameron Corp. [*NYSE symbol*] (SAG)
RON .... Remaining [*or Rest*] Overnight [*Aviation*]
RON .... Remain Overnight Position [*Military*] (VNW)
RON .... Remote [*Alaska*] [*Seismograph station code, US Geological Survey Closed*] (SEIS)
RON .... Report of NAC/ENTAC (MCD)
RON .... Research-Octane-Number [*Fuel technology*]
RON .... Rest Overnight [*or Rest-of-Night*] [*Pronounced "ron" Chance for a candidate to catch some sleep during a traveling political campaign*]
RON .... Rondon [*Colombia*] [*Airport symbol Obsolete*] (OAG)
RON .... Run Occurrence Number (IAA)
RON .... Squadron (MUGU)
RONA .... Naha United States Naval Base [*Ryukyu Islands*] [*ICAO location identifier*] (ICLI)
RONA .... Return on Net Assets
RONAG .... Reserve Officers Naval Architecture Group
RONB .... Research-Octane-Number-Barrels [*Fuel technology*]
RONC .... Ronson Corp. [*NASDAQ symbol*] (SAG)
RONCO .... Rock-Oldies-News-Commercials Operation [*Formula radio*]
RONCOM .... Ronald Como, Inc. [*Perry Como's production firm; Ronald is his son*]
RONCP .... Ronson Corp. 12% Cv Pfd [*NASDAQ symbol*] (TTSB)
ROND .... Remote Ordnance Neutralization Device (DWSG)
RONEO .... Rotary and Neostyle [*Duplicating machine*] [*Acronym is trademark*]
RONLY .... Receiver Only [*Radio*]
RONS .... Read-Only Name Store (NITA)
RONS .... Read Only Nano Store (MHDB)
RONS .... Reserve Officers of the Naval Service [*Later, ROA*]
Ronson .... Ronson Corp. [*Associated Press*] (SAG)
RONWT .... Revised Ordinances, Northwest Territories [*Canada*] [*A publication*] (DLA)
ROO .... Radio Optical Observatory
ROO .... Railhead Ordnance Officer
ROO .... Range Operations Officer
ROO .... Reserve of Officers [*British*]
ROO .... Resident Obstetric Officer [*British*]
ROO .... Richland Operations Office [*Energy Research and Development Administration*]
ROO .... Rondonopolis [*Brazil*] [*Airport symbol*] (OAG)
ROOF .... Reclaim, Inc. [*NASDAQ symbol*] (SAG)
ROOF .... Roofing
ROOI .... Return on Original Investment [*Business term*] (MHDW)
ROOM .... Hospitality Worldwide Services, Inc. [*NASDAQ symbol*] (SAG)
RoomP .... Room Plus, Inc. [*Associated Press*] (SAG)
RoomPl .... Room Plus, Inc. [*Associated Press*] (SAG)
ROOPH .... Readily Operative Overhead Protection by Hippos [*Facetious proposal for protection against nuclear attack*]
ROOSCH .... Royal Order of Sputnik Chasers
Roosevelt U ... Roosevelt University (GAGS)
ROOST .... Rapid Optical Ocean Surveillance Testbed [*Navy*] (EECA)
ROOST .... Reusable One-Stage Orbital Space Truck [*Aerospace*]
ROOT .... Relaxation Oscillator Optically Tuned
Root .... Root's Connecticut Reports [*1774-89*] [*A publication*] (DLA)
Root .... Root's Connecticut Supreme Court Reports [*1789-98*] [*A publication*] (DLA)
Root Bt Laws ... Root's Digest of Law and Practice in Bankruptcy [*1818*] [*A publication*] (DLA)
Root R .... Root's Connecticut Reports [*A publication*] (DLA)
Roots .... Root's Connecticut Reports [*A publication*] (DLA)
Root's Rep ... Root's Connecticut Reports [*A publication*] (DLA)
ROP .... Raster Operation
ROP .... Rate of Pay [*British military*] (DMA)
ROP .... Rate of Penetration [*Drilling technology*]
ROP .... Receive-Only Printer [*Computer science*]
ROP .... Receiving Operations Package [*DoD*]
ROP .... Record of Performance
ROP .... Record of Production
ROP .... Record of Purchase (NRCH)
ROP .... Recovery Operating Plan [*NASA*] (IAA)
ROP .... Refined Oil Products
ROP .... Regional Operating Plan [*Department of Labor*]
ROP .... Regional Oversight Policy [*Environmental Protection Agency*] (GFGA)
ROP .... Registered Options Principal
ROP .... Reorder Point [*Navy*] (NG)
ROP .... Reorder Price
ROP .... Repeat Offenders Project
ROP .... Republic of Panama
ROP .... Republic of the Philippines
ROP .... Requirements Objectives Period
ROP .... Retinopathy of Prematurity [*Medicine*]
ROP .... Right Occipitoposterior [*A fetal position*] [*Obstetrics*]
ROP .... Right Outside Position [*Dancing*]
ROP .... Rites of Passage
ROP .... Robson Petroleum Ltd. [*Toronto Stock Exchange symbol*]
ROP .... Roll-Over Protection Equipment (MCD)
ROP .... Rookie Orientation Program [*Automobile racing*]
Rop .... Roper on Legacies [*4 eds.*] [*1799-1847*] [*A publication*] (DLA)
ROP .... Rota [*Mariana Islands*] [*Airport symbol*] (OAG)
ROP .... Rotating Observation Platform (IAA)
ROP .... Royal Oman Police [*ICAO designator*] (FAAC)
ROP .... Royal Order of Piast (EA)
ROP .... Run of Paper [*Business term*]
ROP .... Run of Press [*i.e., on an unspecified page or plate in web press set-up*] [*Printing*]
ROP .... Run of Publication (NTCM)
ROP_3 .... Revision of Procurement Policy and Procedures
ROPA .... Regional Organ Procurement Agency [*Medicine*] (DAVI)

ROPA Reserve Officer Personnel Act of 1954
ROPAR Regional Operators Program for Aircraft Reliability
ROPB Reserve Officers Promotion Board [*Air Force*]
ROPBX Reference Our Private Branch Exchange Message (SAA)
ROPE Remotely Operated Platform Electronic [*Submarine technology*]
ROPE Respiratory-Ordered Phase Encoding [*Medicine*] (DMAA)
ROPE Reunion of Professional Entertainers (EA)
ROPER Regional Operators Program for Engine Reliability
Roper Roper Industries, Inc. [*Associated Press*] (SAG)
ROPES Regional Occupation Planning and Evaluation System (EDAC)
ROPES Remote Online Print Executive System
ROPEVAL Readiness/Operational Evaluation (NVT)
ROPEVAL Rim of the Pacific Evaluation (MCD)
ROPF Research into One-Parent Families [*British*]
Rop H & W Roper's Law of Property between Husband and Wife [*2nd ed.*] [*1826*] [*A publication*] (DLA)
ROPHO Reference Our Telephone Call (NOAA)
Rop Husb & Wife Roper's Law of Property between Husband and Wife [*A publication*] (DLA)
ROPIS Response of Plants to Interacting Stress Program [*Electric Power Research Institute*]
Rop Leg Roper on Legacies [*A publication*] (DLA)
ROPM Remote Operations Protocol Machine [*Telecommunications*] (OSI)
ROPMA Reserve Officers Personnel Management Act [*Proposed*]
ROPME Regional Organization for the Protection of the Marine Environment [*Safat, Kuwait*] (EAIO)
ROPOS Remotely Operated Platform for Ocean Science [*Marine science*] (OSRA)
ROPOS Remotely Operated Platform for Ocean Science (USDC)
ROPP Receive-Only Page Printer
ROPP Review of Plant Pathology [*Database*] [*Commonwealth Mycological Institute*] [*Information service or system*] (CRD)
Rop Prop Roper's Law of Property between Husband and Wife [*2nd ed.*] [*1826*] [*A publication*] (DLA)
ROPR Roper Industries [*NASDAQ symbol*] (TTSB)
ROPR Roper Industries, Inc. [*NASDAQ symbol*] (SAG)
ROPRA Reserve Officer Performance Recording Activity
Rop Rev Roper on Revocation of Wills [*A publication*] (DLA)
ROPS Range Operation Performance Summary
ROPS Roll-Over Protection System [*for tractors*]
ROPS Roll Over Protective Structures [*NASA*] (KSC)
ROPT Remaining Number of Operations
ROPU RADAR Overheat Protection Unit (MCD)
ROQ Houghton Lake, MI [*Location identifier FAA*] (FAAL)
ROQ Recruiter of the Quarter [*Navy*] (DNAB)
ROQ Reordering Quality
ROR Koror [*Palau Islands*] [*Airport symbol*] (OAG)
ROR Range-Only RADAR [*Military*] (AABC)
ROR Rapid-Onset-Rate [*Air Force*] (DOMA)
ROR Rate of Read
ROR Rate of Return (MCD)
ROR Released on Own Recognizance [*Law*]
ROR Repair of Repairables (MCD)
ROR Repair, Overhaul, Restoration (MCD)
ROR Residual Oil Remover [*Lens cleaner*] [*V-Vax Products*]
ROR Return of Repairables
ROR Return on Revenue
ROR Right of Rescission [*Business term*]
ROR Rochester Minerals [*Vancouver Stock Exchange symbol*]
ROR Rocket on Rotor
ROR Rockton & Rion Railway [*AAR code*]
ROR Roraima Airways [*Guyana*] [*FAA designator*] (FAAC)
ROR Rorschach [*Test*]
ROR Rotate Right [*Computer science*]
ROR Rubery Owen-Rockwell [*Automotive industry supplier*]
ror Run of Reel [*Broadcasting*] (WDMC)
RORA Aguni [*Ryukyu Islands*] [*ICAO location identifier*] (ICLI)
RORA Reliable Operate RADAR Altimeter
RORA Reserve Officer Recording Activity
RORC Royal Ocean Racing Club [*British*]
RORCE Rate of Return on Capital Employed (DS)
RORD Return on Receipt of Document [*Business term*]
RORE Iejima [*Ryukyu Islands*] [*ICAO location identifier*] (ICLI)
Ro Rep Robards' Texas Conscript Cases [*1862-65*] [*A publication*] (DLA)
Ro Rep Rolle's English King's Bench Reports [*A publication*] (DLA)
ROREQ Reference Our Requisition (NOAA)
Rorer Jud Sales Rorer on Void Judicial Sales [*A publication*] (DLA)
Rorer RR Rorer on Railways [*A publication*] (DLA)
RORET Authorized Rotational Retention [*Navy*]
RORG Naha [*Ryukyu Islands*] [*ICAO location identifier*] (ICLI)
RORH Hateruma [*Ryukyu Islands*] [*ICAO location identifier*] (ICLI)
RO/RI Redistribution Out/Redistribution In (CINC)
Ror Int St L Rorer on Inter-State Law [*A publication*] (DLA)
RORIS Remote Operated Radiographic Inspection System
Ror Jud Sal Rorer on Void Judicial Sales [*A publication*] (DLA)
RORK Kitadaito [*Ryukyu Islands*] [*ICAO location identifier*] (ICLI)
RO/RO Roll-On/Roll-Off [*Shipping*] (AFM)
RO-RO Rolls Royce [*Automobile*] [*Slang*] (DSUE)
RORQN Reference Requisition from Our Office (FAAC)
RORS Realignment of Resources and Services (MCD)
RORS Shimojishima [*Ryukyu Islands*] [*ICAO location identifier*] (ICLI)
RORSAT RADAR Ocean Reconnaissance Satellite (MCD)
RORT Report on Reimbursable Transactions [*DoD*]
RORT Tarama [*Ryukyu Islands*] [*ICAO location identifier*] (ICLI)
RORU Rest of Route Unchanged [*Aviation*] (FAAC)
RoRx Radiation Therapy (DAVI)
RORY Yoron [*Ryukyu Islands*] [*ICAO location identifier*] (ICLI)
ROS ATS-Servicii de Transport Aerian [*Italy ICAO designator*] (FAAC)
ROS RADAR Order Switch
ROS Radius of Suspension
ROS Range of Spares (MCD)
ROS Range Operations Supervisor (MUGU)
ROS Range Operation Station
ROS Rate of Speed (MCD)
ROS Rat Osteosarcoma [*Cell line*]
ROS Reactive Oxygen Species
ROS Read-Only Storage [*Computer science*]
ROS Ready Operating Status (DNAB)
ROS Reduced Operational Status [*Military*]
ROS Reed Organ Society (EA)
ROS Registration Offering Statistics System [*Securities and Exchange Commission*] (GFGA)
ROS Regulated Oxygen Supply (MCD)
ROS Regulated Oxygen System (NASA)
ROS Remote Operating System (IAA)
ROS Remote Operations Service [*Telecommunications*] (OSI)
ROS Remote Optical Sight [*Military*] (CAAL)
ROS Remote Optical System
ROS Removable Overhead Structure (MCD)
ROS Reporter on Scene (NTCM)
ROS Report Originator System [*Military*] (CAAL)
ROS Representative Observation Site [*Weather observing facility*] [*Air Force*]
ROS Requisition on Stores [*Nuclear energy*] (NRCH)
ROS Research Optical Sensor (MCD)
ROS Resident Operating System
ROS Residual Oil Saturation [*Petroleum technology*]
ROS Restored Oil Shales
ROS Return from Overseas [*Military*]
ROS Return on Sales
ROS Review of Systems [*Medicine*]
ROS Revised Occupant Simulation
ROS Rights of Stockholders [*Investment term*] (MHDW)
ROS Robotics Operating System
ROS Rod Outer Segments [*of the retina*]
ROS Rosa [*Rose*] [*Pharmacology*] (ROG)
ROS Rosario [*Argentina*] [*Airport symbol*] (OAG)
ROS Rosary
Ros Roscommon [*County in Ireland*] (WGA)
ROS Roseneath [*New Zealand*] [*Seismograph station code, US Geological Survey Closed*] (SEIS)
ROS Rose Resources Corp. [*Vancouver Stock Exchange symbol*]
ROS Roswell Public Library, Roswell, NM [*OCLC symbol*] (OCLC)
ROS Rotary on Stamps Fellowship (EA)
ROS Rotating Optical Scanner
ROS Royal Order of Scotland (EA)
ROS Run of Schedule [*Commercial announcement to be broadcast throughout the program schedule*] [*Advertising*]
ROS Run-of-Station [*Broadcasting*] (WDMC)
ROS Rush Order Service
ROSA Recording Optical Spectrum Analyzer (MCD)
ROSA Record One Stop Association [*Defunct*] (EA)
ROSA Remotely-Operated Service Arm [*Nuclear energy*] (NUCP)
ROSA Report of Student Answers [*Scoring sheet for the Scholastic Aptitude Test (SAT)*] (PAZ)
ROSA Report of Supply Activity (MCD)
ROSAR Read-Only Storage Address Register
Rosary C Rosary College (GAGS)
ROSAT RADAR Ocean Surveillance Satellite (NVT)
ROSAT Roentgen Satellite [*Space research*]
ROSC Reserve Officers Sanitary Corps
ROSC Restoration of Spontaneous Circulation
ROSC Road Operators Safety Council [*British*]
Rosc Roscoe's Reports of the Supreme Court [*1861-78*] [*South Africa*] [*A publication*] (DLA)
ROSC Roscommon [*County in Ireland*] (ROG)
Rosc Act Roscoe on Actions [*1825*] [*A publication*] (DLA)
Rosc Adm Roscoe's Admiralty Jurisdiction and Practice [*A publication*] (DLA)
Rosc Am Pro Sexto Roscio Amerino [*of Cicero*] [*Classical studies*] (OCD)
Rosc Bdg Cas Roscoe's Digest of Building Cases [*4th ed.*] [*1900*] [*A publication*] (DLA)
Rosc Bills Roscoe's Bills of Exchange [*2nd ed.*] [*1843*] [*A publication*] (DLA)
Rosc Civ Pr Roscoe's Outlines of Civil Procedure [*2nd ed.*] [*1880*] [*A publication*] (DLA)
Rosc Cr Roscoe's Law of Evidence in Criminal Cases [*16 eds.*] [*1835-1952*] [*A publication*] (DLA)
Rosc Crim Ev Roscoe's Law of Evidence in Criminal Cases [*16 eds.*] [*1835-1952*] [*A publication*] (DLA)
Rosc Ev Roscoe's Nisi Prius Evidence [*20th ed.*] [*1934*] [*A publication*] (DLA)
Rosc Jur Roscoe's Jurist [*England*] [*A publication*] (DLA)
Rosc Light Roscoe's Law of Light [*4th ed.*] [*1904*] [*A publication*] (DLA)
Rosc NP Roscoe's Law of Evidence at Nisi Prius [*20 eds.*] [*1827-1934*] [*A publication*] (DLA)
ROSCO Rotating Stratified Combustion [*Automotive engineering*]
ROSCOE RADAR and Optical Systems Code
ROSCOE Remote Operating System Conventional Operating Environment [*Computer science*] (IAA)
Roscoe Roscoe's Reports of the Supreme Court of Cape Of Good Hope [*South Africa*] [*A publication*] (DLA)

Roscoe Bldg Cas... Roscoe's Digest of Building Cases [*England*] [*A publication*] (DLA)
Roscoe Cr Ev... Roscoe's Law of Evidence in Criminal Cases [*16 eds.*] [*1835-1952*] [*A publication*] (DLA)
Roscoe's BC... Roscoe's Digest of Building Cases [*England*] [*A publication*] (DLA)
ROSCOM...... Roscommon [*County in Ireland*]
ROSCOP...... Report of Observations/Samples Collected by Oceanographic Programs [*Intergovernmental Oceanographic Commission*] (MSC)
ROSCOP...... Report on Oceanographic Cruises and Data Stations (GNE)
Rosc PC....... Roscoe's English Prize Cases [*1745-1859*] [*A publication*] (DLA)
Rosc Pl........ Roscoe's Pleading [*1845*] [*A publication*] (DLA)
ROSDAL....... Representation of Structure Diagrams Arranged Linearly [*Structure notation shorthand*] [*Chemistry*]
ROSDR........ Read-Only Storage Data Register
ROSE.......... Reconstruction by Optimized Series Expansion [*Of large molecules*]
ROSE.......... Remotely Operated Special Equipment [*Nuclear energy*]
ROSE.......... Remote Operations Service Element [*Computer science*] (TNIG)
ROSE.......... Remote Optical Sensing of Emissions [*Instrumentation*]
ROSE.......... Research Open Systems in Europe [*Computer science*] (BARN)
ROSE.......... Resident Operational Support Equipment
ROSE.......... Residuum Oil Supercritical Extraction [*Petroleum refining*]
ROSE.......... Retrieval by Online Search [*Computer science*]
ROSE.......... Rising Observational Sounding Equipment
ROSE.......... Rivera Ocean Seismic Experiment
Rose.......... Rose's English Bankruptcy Reports [*A publication*] (DLA)
ROSE.......... Rosette [*Cytology*] (DAVI)
ROSE.......... Rural Oxidants in the Southern Environment [*Marine science*] (OSRA)
ROSE.......... Rural Oxidants in the Southern Environment (USDC)
ROSE.......... T R Financial [*NASDAQ symbol*] (TTSB)
ROSE.......... TR Financial Corp. [*NASDAQ symbol*] (SAG)
Rose Bankr... Rose's English Bankruptcy Reports [*1810-16*] [*A publication*] (DLA)
Rose Bankr (Eng)... Rose's English Bankruptcy Reports [*A publication*] (DLA)
Rose BC...... Rose's English Bankruptcy Reports [*A publication*] (DLA)
ROSEBUD.... Rare Object Searches with Bolometers Underground [*Astrophysics*]
Rose Dig..... Rose's Digest of Arkansas Reports [*A publication*] (DLA)
Rose-Hulman Inst Tech... Rose-Hulman Institute of Technology (GAGS)
Rosenberger... Street Railway Law [*United States*] [*A publication*] (DLA)
Rosenberger Pock LJ... Rosenberger's Pocket Law Journal [*A publication*] (DLA)
Rose Notes... Rose's Notes on United States Reports [*A publication*] (DLA)
Rose RA...... Roscoe on Real Actions [*A publication*] (DLA)
Rose St D.... Roscoe on Stamp Duties [*A publication*] (DLA)
RoseStr....... Rose's Stores [*Associated Press*] (SAG)
ROSET......... Register of Solicitors Employing Trainees (ILCA)
Rose WC..... Rose. Will Case [*New York*] [*A publication*] (DLA)
ROSIE......... Reconnaissance by Orbiting Ship-Identification Equipment
ROSIE......... Rooters Organized to Stimulate Interest and Enthusiasm [*Women baseball fans, Cincinnati*]
ROSIE......... Rule Oriented System for Implementing Expertise (MCD)
ROSL.......... Royal Overseas League [*British*] (DI)
ROSMAR...... Rosmarinus [*Rosemary*] [*Pharmacology*] (ROG)
ROSO.......... Relay-Operated Sampling Oscilloscope
ROSP.......... Report on Syndicated Programs [*A.C. Nielsen Co.*] [*A publication*] (DOAD)
RoSPA......... Royal Society for the Prevention of Accidents [*British*]
ROSPA......... Royal Society for the Prevention of Accidents [*British*] (AIE)
ROSR.......... Radio On-Scene Report (WDMC)
ROSR.......... Real-Time On-Scene Report (NTCM)
ROSS.......... Review of Subjective Symptoms [*Medicine*] (DMAA)
ROSS.......... Ross Systems [*NASDAQ symbol*] (TTSB)
ROSS.......... Ross Systems, Inc. [*NASDAQ symbol*] (SPSG)
Ross Cont.... Ross on Contracts [*A publication*] (DLA)
Ross Conv.... Ross' Lectures on Conveyancing, Etc. [*Sc.*] [*A publication*] (DLA)
Ross LC....... Ross's Leading Cases in the Law of Scotland (Land Rights) [*1638-1840*] [*A publication*] (DLA)
Ross LC....... Ross's Leading Cases on Commercial Law [*England*] [*A publication*] (DLA)
Ross Ldg Cas... Ross's Leading Cases in the Law of Scotland (Land Rights) [*A publication*] (DLA)
Ross Ldg Cas... Ross's Leading Cases on Commercial Law [*A publication*] (DLA)
Ross Lead Cas... Ross' Leading Cases [*England*] [*A publication*] (DLA)
Ross Lead Cas... Ross's Leading Cases in the Law of Scotland (Land Rights) [*1638-1840*] [*A publication*] (DLA)
RossStr........ Ross Stores, Inc. [*Associated Press*] (SAG)
RossSy......... Ross Systems, Inc. [*Associated Press*] (SAG)
RossTch........ Ross Technology, Inc. [*Associated Press*] (SAG)
Ross V & P... Ross on Vendors and Purchasers [*2nd ed.*] [*1826*] [*A publication*] (DLA)
ROST.......... Regional Office of Science and Technology [*UNESCO*] (MSC)
ROST.......... Ross Stores [*NASDAQ symbol*] (TTSB)
ROST.......... Ross Stores, Inc. [*Newark, CA*] [*NASDAQ symbol*] (NQ)
ROSTA......... Regional Office for Science and Technology in Africa [*UNESCO*] [*See also BRUSTA*] [*Nairobi, Kenya*] (EAIO)
ROSTE......... Regional Office for Science and Technology for Europe [*UNESCO*] [*Italy*] (EAIO)
ROSTSCA..... Regional Office of Science and Technology for South and Central Asia [*UNESCO*] (IRC)
ROSTSEA..... Regional Office of Science and Technology for Southeast Asia [*UNESCO*] (IRC)
roswd........... Rosewood (VRA)
ROT........... RADAR on Target
ROT........... Range on Target
ROT........... Rate of Turn
ROT........... Read-Only Tag
ROT........... Red Oak Tannins [*in leaves*]
ROT........... Reference Our Telex (DS)
ROT........... Registered Occupational Therapist (DAVI)
ROT........... Remaining Operating Time (NASA)
ROT........... Remedial Occupation Therapy
ROT........... Reserve Oil Tank (MSA)
ROT........... Reusable Orbital Transport [*Aerospace*]
ROT........... Right Occipitotransverse [*A fetal position*] [*Obstetrics*]
ROT........... Right Outer Thigh [*Injection site*]
ROT........... Rotary (AAG)
ROT........... Rotate (AAG)
ROT........... Rotating Light [*Navigation signal*]
ROT........... Rotator [*A type of muscle*] (DAVI)
ROT........... Rotor (ADA)
ROT........... Rotorua [*New Zealand*] [*Seismograph station code, US Geological Survey Closed*] (SEIS)
ROT........... Rotorua [*New Zealand*] [*Airport symbol*] (OAG)
ROT........... Rule of Thumb
ROT........... Running Object Table [*Computer science*]
ROT........... Runway Occupancy Time [*FAA*] (TAG)
ROT........... Tarom, Romanian Air Transport [*ICAO designator*] (FAAC)
ROTAB......... Rotable Table
ROT ABCCC... Rotational Airborne Command and Control Center (CINC)
ROTAC......... Rotary Oscillating Torque Actuators
ROTAD......... Required Overseas Terminal Arrival Date (DNAB)
RotaryPw..... Rotary Power International, Inc. [*Associated Press*] (SAG)
ROTAS......... Rotate and Slide (DNAB)
Rotavapor..... Rotary Evaporator
ROT AWS..... Rotational Air Weather Squadron (CINC)
ROT BS........ Rotational Bomb Squadron (CINC)
ROTC.......... Reserve Officers' Training Corps [*Separate units for Army, Navy, Air Force*]
ROTC.......... Rotech Medical [*NASDAQ symbol*] (TTSB)
ROTC.......... RoTech Medical Corp. [*Orlando, FL*] [*NASDAQ symbol*] (NQ)
ROTCC......... Receiver-Off-Hook Tone Connecting Circuit
Rot Chart..... Rotulus Chartarum [*Charter Roll*] [*Latin A publication*] (DLA)
Rot Claus..... Rotuli Clause [*Close Roll*] [*Latin A publication*] (DLA)
ROTCM......... Reserve Officers' Training Corps Manual (AABC)
ROTCR......... Reserve Officers' Training Corps Region (AABC)
Rot Cur Reg... Rotuli Curiae Regis [*1194-99*] [*Latin A publication*] (DLA)
ROTE.......... Range Optical Tracking Equipment (AAG)
ROTE.......... Role of Occupational Therapy with the Elderly [*Project*]
ROTE AREFS... Rotating Air Refueling Squadron (CINC)
Rotech......... Rotech Medical Corp. [*Associated Press*] (SAG)
ROTEL......... Rolling Hotel [*European bus-tour system*]
ROTEL......... Rotational Telemetry
ROTERO....... Roterodamum [*Rotterdam*] (ROG)
ROTF.......... Rolling on the Floor
ROTF.......... Russian Orthodox Theological Fund (EA)
ROT FIS....... Rotating Fighter Interceptor Squadron (CINC)
ROT FIS DET... Rotating Fighter Interceptor Squadron Detachment (CINC)
ROTFL......... Rolling on the Floor Laughing [*Computer hacker terminology*] (NHD)
Rot Flor....... Rotae Florentine [*Reports of the Supreme Court of Florence*] [*Latin A publication*] (DLA)
ROTH.......... Read-Only Tape Handler
R-OTH......... Relocatable Over-The-Horizon [*Radar*] (DOMA)
ROTHR......... Relocatable Over-the-Horizon RADAR
ROTI........... CluckCorp International, Inc. [*NASDAQ symbol*] (SAG)
ROTI........... Range Optical Tracking Instrument
ROTI........... Recording Optical Tracking Instrument [*Missiles*]
ROTI........... Reinforced Oxide Throat Insert
ROTL........... Remote Office Test Line [*Bell Laboratories*]
ROTLT/BCN... Rotating Light or Beacon
ROTM.......... Futema [*Ryukyu Islands*] [*ICAO location identifier*] (ICLI)
ROTMH......... Raised Oil-Tight Manhole [*Shipfitting*]
ROTN.......... Rotation (ROG)
ROTO.......... Rotogravure [*Printing process*] (NTCM)
ROTO.......... Roto-Rooter, Inc. [*Cincinnati, OH*] [*NASDAQ symbol*] (NQ)
ROTOMT....... Rotometer
Rotonic........ Rotonics Manufacturing [*Associated Press*] (SAG)
ROTOR......... Rotorcraft Helicopter [*Pilot rating*] (AIA)
RotoRtr........ Roto Rooter, Inc. [*Associated Press*] (SAG)
ROTP.......... Regular Officer Training Plan [*Canada*]
Rot Parl....... Rotulae Parliamentariae [*Latin A publication*] (DLA)
Rot Pat........ Rotuli Patenes [*Latin A publication*] (DLA)
Rot Plac....... Rotuli Placitorum [*Latin A publication*] (DLA)
ROT PROJ.... Rotation Project (DNAB)
ROTR.......... Read-Only Typing Reperforator (NITA)
ROTR.......... Receive-Only Tape Reperforator [*Computer science*] (IAA)
ROTR.......... Receive-Only Typing Reperforator
ROTR.......... Rotator [*Electromagnetics*]
ROT RCS...... Rotational RADAR Calibration Squadron (CINC)
ROTR-S/P.... Receive-Only Typing Reperforator - Series to Parallel
ROTS.......... RADAR Observer Testing System
ROTS.......... Range on Target Signal
ROTS.......... Remote Operator Task Station [*Air Force*]
ROTS.......... Reusable Orbital Transport System [*Aerospace*] (IAA)
ROTS.......... Rotary Out Trunk Switch [*Telecommunications*] (TEL)
ROTSAL....... Rotate and Scale [*Computer science*]
ROTT.......... Rate of Turntable
ROTT.......... Reorder Tone Trunks [*Telecommunications*] (TEL)
ROT TAS...... Rotational Tactical Assault Squadron (CINC)
ROT TBS...... Rotational Tactical Bomber Squadron (CINC)
ROT TCS...... Rotational Troop Carrier Squadron (CINC)
ROTTER....... Rotterdam (ROG)

Rottlund Rottlund Co. [*Associated Press*] (SAG)
ROT TX Rotating Transformer
Rotuli Curiae Reg Rotuli Curiae Regis [*1194-99*] [*Latin A publication*] (DLA)
ROTV Reusable Orbital Transport Vehicle [*Aerospace*]
ROU Radio Officers Union [*British*]
ROU Recurrent Oral Ulcer [*Medicine*] (DMAA)
ROU Rouge Steel 'A' [*NYSE symbol*] (TTSB)
ROU Rouge Steel Co. [*NYSE symbol*] (SAG)
ROU Rougiers [*France*] [*Seismograph station code, US Geological Survey Closed*] (SEIS)
ROU Rouyn Ressources Minieres, Inc. [*Toronto Stock Exchange symbol*]
ROU Russe [*Bulgaria*] [*Airport symbol*] (OAG)
ROU Uruguay [*International vehicle registration*] (ODBW)
RougeStl Rouge Steel Co. [*Associated Press*] (SAG)
ROUL Rouleaux [*Formation Differential*] [*Cytology*] (DAVI)
ROUL Rouletted (ROG)
Roum P Roumanian Pharmacopoeia [*A publication*]
Round Dom Round's Law of Domicil [*1861*] [*A publication*] (DLA)
Round L & A Round's Right of Light and Air [*1868*] [*A publication*] (DLA)
Round Lien Round's Law of Lien [*1863*] [*A publication*] (DLA)
Roundup M Roundup Magazine [*A publication*] (BRI)
Rouse Rouse Co. [*Associated Press*] (SAG)
Rouse Conv Rouse's Practical Conveyancer [*3rd ed.*] [*1867*] [*A publication*] (DLA)
Rouse Cop Rouse's Copyhold Enfranchisement Manual [*3rd ed.*] [*1866*] [*A publication*] (DLA)
Rouse Pr Mort Rouse's Precedents and Conveyances of Mortgaged Property [*A publication*] (DLA)
R_{OUT} Output Resistance (IDOE)
R-OUT Rollout (NASA)
ROUT Routine (AABC)
ROUTE Route [*Commonly used*] (OPSA)
ROV Refined Oil of Vitriol
ROV Remotely Operated Vehicle [*Underwater robot*]
ROV Remote Operated Valve (KSC)
ROV Remote Optical Viewing
ROV Repairs to Other Vessels
ROV Report of Visit [*LIMRA*]
ROV Restricted Overhaul (MCD)
ROV Risk, Originality, and Virtuousity [*Scoring considerations in gymnastics competition*]
ROV Rostov [*Former USSR Airport symbol*] (OAG)
ROV Rover Airways International, Inc. [*ICAO designator*] (FAAC)
ROVAC Rotary Vane Air Cycle (MCD)
ROVD Relay-Operated Voltage Divider
ROVNITE Remaining Overnight
ROVS Remote Optical Viewing System
ROVS Russkiy Obshche-Voyenskiy Soyuz [*Russian Armed Forces Union*] (LAIN)
ROW Randstrom Manufacturing Corp. [*Vancouver Stock Exchange symbol*]
ROW Relocate Out of Washington [*Navy*] (NG)
ROW Rendu-Osler-Weber Syndrome [*Medicine*] (DMAA)
ROW Requisition on Warehouse [*Nuclear energy*] (NRCH)
ROW Rest of World [*Newly industrialized countries of Asia*]
ROW Right of Way
ROW Rights of Women [*British*] [*An association*] (DBA)
ROW Risk of War
ROW Roll Welding
ROW Roswell [*New Mexico*] [*Airport symbol*] (OAG)
ROW Row [*Postal Service standard*] (OPSA)
ROW Rowe Furniture [*NYSE symbol*] (TTSB)
ROW Rowe Furniture Corp. [*NYSE symbol*] (SPSG)
ROW Rowesville [*South Carolina*] [*Seismograph station code, US Geological Survey*] (SEIS)
ROWA Read Once, Write All [*Computer science*]
Rowan Rowan Companies, Inc. [*Associated Press*] (SAG)
ROW & PF Rake Out, Wedge, and Point Flashings [*Construction*]
ROWB Rowberrow [*England*]
Rowe Rowe's Interesting Cases [*England and Ireland*] [*1798-1823*] [*A publication*] (DLA)
Rowe Rowe's Interesting Parliamentary and Military Cases [*A publication*] (DLA)
RoweFrn Rowe Furniture Corp. [*Associated Press*] (SAG)
Rowell Rowell's Reports [*45-52 Vermont*] [*A publication*] (DLA)
Rowell El Cas Rowell's Contested Election Cases [*A publication*] (DLA)
Row Eng Const Rowland's Manual of the English Constitution [*1859*] [*A publication*] (DLA)
Rowe Rep Rowe's Irish Reports [*A publication*] (DLA)
Rowe Sci Jur Rowe's Scintilla Juris [*A publication*] (DLA)
ROW/FEPA Riders of the Wind, the Field Events Player's Association (EA)
ROWP Reference Overhaul Work Package (DNAB)
ROWPE Reverse Osmosis Water Purification Equipment (MCD)
ROWPS Reverse Osmosis Water Purification System (MCD)
ROWPU Reverse Osmosis Water Purification Unit [*Army*] (RDA)
ROWPVT Receptive One-Word Picture Vocabulary Test [*Educational test*]
ROWS RADAR Ocean Wave Spectrometer
ROWS Register of Weather Stations [*Meteorological Office*] (PDAA)
ROX Roseau, MN [*Location identifier FAA*] (FAAL)
ROX Roxburgh [*New Zealand*] [*Seismograph station code, US Geological Survey*] (SEIS)
ROXB Roxburghe [*Style of bookbinding*] (ROG)
ROXB Roxburghshire [*County in Scotland*]
ROXL Rotate through X Left [*Computer science*]
ROXR Rotate through X Right [*Computer science*]
ROY Conifair Aviation, Inc. [*Canada ICAO designator*] (FAAC)
ROY Moultonboro, NH [*Location identifier FAA*] (FAAL)
ROY Rest of You (IIA)
ROY Rio Mayo [*Argentina*] [*Airport symbol*] (OAG)
ROY Rookie of the Year
ROY Royal
Roy Royale & Allegro-Royale [*Record label*]
Royal Aust Hist Soc J Proc Royal Australian Historical Society. Journal and Proceedings [*A publication*]
RoyaleE Royale Energy Corp. [*Associated Press*] (SAG)
RoyalO Royal Oak Mines [*Associated Press*] (SAG)
RoyBk Royal Bank of Canada, Inc. [*Associated Press*] (SAG)
Royce Royce Value Trust, Inc. [*Associated Press*] (SAG)
RoyceMC Royce OTC Micro Capital Fund [*Associated Press*] (SAG)
RoycLab Royce Laboratories, Inc. [*Associated Press*] (SAG)
Roy Dig Royall's Digest Virginia Reports [*A publication*] (DLA)
ROYGBIV Red, Orange, Yellow, Green, Blue, Indigo, Violet [*Primary Colors*] [*Mnemonic aid*]
RoyGld Royal Gold Corp. [*Associated Press*] (SAG)
ROYL Royale Energy [*NASDAQ symbol*] (TTSB)
ROYL Royale Energy Corp. [*NASDAQ symbol*] (SAG)
RoylApl Royal Appliance Manufacturing [*Associated Press*] (SAG)
RoylD Royal Dutch Petroleum Co. [*Associated Press*] (SAG)
Royle Stock Sh Royle on the Law of Stock Shares, Etc. [*A publication*] (DLA)
RoylGrip Royal Grip, Inc. [*Associated Press*] (SAG)
RoylInv Royale Investments, Inc. [*Associated Press*] (SAG)
ROYN Yonagunijima [*Ryukyu Islands*] [*ICAO location identifier*] (ICLI)
RoyPlm Royal Palm Beach Ltd. [*Associated Press*] (SAG)
RoyPls Royal Plastics Group Ltd. [*Associated Press*] (SAG)
RP Bristol-Myers Co. [*Research code symbol*]
R_p Parallel Resistance (IDOE)
R_p Plate Resistance (IDOE)
RP Precision Airlines [*ICAO designator*] (AD)
R_p Primary Resistance (IDOE)
RP Problems of Reconstruction [*British World War II*]
RP Providence Public Library, Providence, RI [*Library symbol Library of Congress*] (LCLS)
Rp Pulmonary Resistance [*Cardiology*] (MAE)
RP RADAR Plot (DEN)
RP Radial Artery Pressure [*Medicine*]
RP Radial Pulse [*Medicine*]
RP Radiation Pressure
RP Radiation Protection
RP Radical Proverbs [*A publication*]
R-P Radiologist-Pediatric
RP Radio Phone (DS)
RP Raid Plotter
RP Rally Point [*Air Force*]
RP Ranchers for Peace (EA)
RP Range Pulse
RP Raphe Pallidus [*Anatomy*]
RP Rapid Processing [*Film*] (MAE)
RP Rappen [*Monetary unit*] [*Switzerland*]
RP Rated Pressure (NATG)
RP Rate Package (AAG)
RP Rating Pending
RP Raynaud's Phenomenon [*Medicine*]
RP Reactive Protein [*Clinical chemistry*] (MAE)
RP Reactor Pressure [*Nuclear energy*] (NRCH)
RP Reactor Project [*Nuclear energy*] (NRCH)
RP Reader Printer
RP Reader Punch
RP Readiness Potential
RP Read Printer (NITA)
RP Real Part [*of complex number*] (DEN)
RP Real Property
RP Rear Projection [*Television*]
RP Receipt Pass (AAG)
RP Received Pronunciation [*of the English language*]
RP Receive Processor
RP Reception Poor [*Radio logs*]
RP Receptor Potential
RP Recommended Practice
RP Recorded Program (IAA)
RP Recorder Point (MCD)
RP Record Position (AAGC)
RP Record Processor [*Computer science*] (OA)
RP Records of the Past [*A publication*] (BJA)
RP Recovery Phase (IEEE)
RP Reddish Purple
RP Red Phosphorus [*Military*] (RDA)
RP Reference Paper
RP Reference Pattern (NATG)
RP Reference Point
RP Reference Publication (MCD)
RP Reference Pulse
RP Refilling Point
RP Reformed Presbyterian
RP Refractory Period [*Medicine*]
RP Regeneration Project [*Later, CR*] (EA)
RP Re-Geniusing Project [*Defunct*] (EA)
RP Regimental Paymaster [*British military*] (DMA)
RP Regimental Police [*British*]
RP Registered Pharmacist (DAVI)
RP Registered Plumbers [*British*]
RP Regius Professor [*The King's Professor*] [*British*]

R-P .... Reid-Provident [*Commercial firm*] (DAVI)
RP .... Reinforced Plastic [*Packaging*]
RP .... Relative Potency (DAVI)
RP .... Relative Pressure (KSC)
RP .... Relay Panel
RP .... Release Point [*Ground traffic*] [*Military*]
RP .... Reliability Program (IAA)
RP .... Relief Pitcher [*Baseball*]
R/P .... Relief Printing (DGA)
RP .... Religious Program Specialist [*Navy*] (DNAB)
RP .... Remote Pickup
RP .... Remote Printer (BUR)
RP .... Remote Processor (NITA)
RP .... Rent Regulation (Office of Price Stabilization) [*Economic Stabilization Agency*] [*A publication*] (DLA)
RP .... Reorder Point [*Army*]
RP .... Repair Period (NASA)
RP .... Repeater
RP .... Repetitively Pulsed (MCD)
RP .... Replaceable Pad (MCD)
RP .... Replacement Pilot [*Navy*]
RP .... Replenishment Park [*British*]
RP .... Reply Paid
RP .... Reply Prepaid (IAA)
RP .... Reporting Post [*RADAR*]
RP .... Reprint
RP .... Reproducers [*JETDS nomenclature*] [*Military*] (CET)
RP .... Reproducing Punch [*Computer science*] (IAA)
RP .... Republican Party [*Iraq*] [*Political party*] (BJA)
RP .... Republic of Panama
RP .... Republic of Portugal (BARN)
RP .... Republic of the Philippines
RP .... Republikeinse Party van Suidwesafrika [*Republican Party of South West Africa*] [*Namibia*] [*Political party*] (PPW)
RP .... Repurchase Agreement [*Also, REPO*] [*Investment term*]
RP .... Research Paper
RP .... Research Publications
RP .... Reserve Personnel [*Air Force*] (AFM)
RP .... Reserve Purchase
RP .... Resistance Plate (AAG)
RP .... Resist Pressure [*Industrial engineering*]
RP .... Resolving Power [*of a lens*]
RP .... Resource Processor [*Telecommunications*] (TSSD)
RP .... Respirable Particulate [*Environmental science*] (GFGA)
RP .... Respiratory Rate:Pulse Rate [*Index*] [*Medicine*]
RP .... Responsible Party (GNE)
RP .... Resting Pressure [*Physiology*] (MAE)
RP .... Resting Pulse [*Physiology*]
RP .... Restoration Priority (CET)
RP .... Rest Pain [*Medicine*] (MAE)
RP .... Restriction of Privileges [*British military*] (DMA)
RP .... Resupply Provisions [*NASA*] (KSC)
RP .... Retained Personnel [*Military*]
RP .... Retinitis Pigmentosa [*Eye disease*] [*Ophthalmology*]
RP .... Retinitis Proliferans [*Ophthalmology*] (DAVI)
RP .... Retinyl Palmitate [*Organic chemistry*]
RP .... Retrograde Pyelography [*Medicine*]
RP .... Retroperitoneal [*Medicine*]
RP .... Return of Post
RP .... Return Premium
R/P .... Return to Port [*for Orders*] (DS)
RP .... Revealed Preference Analysis [*Economics*]
RP .... Reverend Pere [*Reverend Father*] [*French*]
RP .... Reverendus Pater [*Reverend Father*] [*Latin*]
R-P .... Reversed Phase [*Chromatography*]
RP .... Reverse Processing [*Chemical engineering*]
RP .... Revertive Pulsing
RP .... Review of Politics [*A publication*] (BRI)
RP .... Revision Proposal (NG)
Rp .... Revoked or Rescinded in Part [*Existing regulation or order abrogated in part*] [*Used in Shepard's Citations*] [*Legal term*] (DLA)
R/P .... Reward/Penalty
RP .... Rhone-Poulenc [*France*] [*Research code symbol*]
RP .... Rhone-Poulenc ADR [*NYSE symbol*] (TTSB)
RP .... Rhone-Poulenc Co. [*NYSE symbol*] (SAG)
RP .... Ribosomal Protein [*Biochemistry*]
RP .... Ribos Phosphate [*Laboratory science*] (DAVI)
R/P .... Rise/Passive (MCD)
RP .... Ristocetin-Polymyxin [*Antibacterial mixture*]
RP .... Rocket Projectile
RP .... Rocket Propellant
RP .... Rockland and Pollin [*Scale*] [*Psychology*]
RP .... Rodent Potency Dose
RP .... Rollback Process [*Telecommunications*] (TEL)
RP .... Roll Pad (MCD)
RP .... Ron Pair
RP .... Room and Pillar [*Coal mining*]
RP .... Root Primordia [*Botany*]
RP .... Rotary Pursuit [*Test for motor skill*]
RP .... Rotatable Pool Quantity
RP .... Rotuli Parliamentorum [*1278-1533*] [*Latin A publication*] (DLA)
RP .... Round Punch
RP .... Route Package (CINC)
RP .... Royal Panopticon (ROG)
RP .... Royal Provincials [*British military*] (DMA)
RP .... Rules of Procedure
RP .... Rupiah [*Monetary unit*] [*Indonesia*]
RP .... Rust Preventive
RP .... Specia [*France*] [*Research code symbol*]
RPA .... Provence Aero Service [*France ICAO designator*] (FAAC)
RPA .... Providence Athenaeum, Providence, RI [*Library symbol Library of Congress*] (LCLS)
RPA .... RADAR Performance Analyzer
RPA .... Radial Photon Absorptiometry [*Chemistry*] (DAVI)
RPA .... Radio Paging Association [*British*] (DBA)
RPA .... Radium Plaque Adaptometer [*Navy*]
RPA .... Random Phase Approximation
RPA .... Rationalist Press Association [*British*] (EAIO)
RPA .... Real Property Administrator [*Building Owners and Managers Institute*] [*Designation awarded by*]
RPA .... Record and Playback Assembly (MCD)
RPA .... Record of Procurement Action (MCD)
RPA .... Redundancy Payments Act [*1965*] [*British*] (DCTA)
RPA .... Reentrant Process Allocator [*Telecommunications*] (TEL)
RPA .... Regional Plan Association (EA)
RPA .... Regional Planning Association (NADA)
RPA .... Regional Ports Authority [*British*]
RPA .... Registered Public Accountant
RPA .... Register of Private Agents [*Victoria, Australia*]
RPA .... Relative Peak Area [*Medicine*]
RPA .... Renal Physicians Association (EA)
RPA .... Renewal Projects Administration [*HUD*]
RPA .... Replacement Price Accounting (ADA)
RPA .... Replication Protein A [*Genetics*]
RPA .... Republican Party of Australia [*Political party*]
RPA .... Request for Procurement Action [*Authorization*] [*NASA*] (NASA)
RPA .... Request Present Altitude [*Aviation*] (FAAC)
RPA .... Reserve Personnel Appropriation
RPA .... Reserve Personnel, Army
RPA .... Resident Programmer Analyst [*Computer science*]
RPA .... Resource Planning Associates, Cambridge, MA [*OCLC symbol*] (OCLC)
RPA .... Response Profile Analysis [*National Demographics & Lifestyles, Inc.*]
RPA .... Resultant Physiological Acceleration
RPA .... Retarding Potential Analyzer [*NASA*]
RPA .... Retinoylphorbolacetate [*Biochemistry*]
RPA .... Retired Philosphers Association (EA)
RPA .... Reverse Passive Anaphylazis [*Medicine*] (DMAA)
RPA .... Right Pulmonary Artery [*Medicine*]
RPA .... Rolpa [*Nepal*] [*Airport symbol*] (OAG)
RPA .... Rotorcraft Pilot's Associate [*Army*] (RDA)
RPA .... Royal Pakistan Artillery [*British military*] (DMA)
RPA .... Rubber Peptizing Agent
RPA .... Rubber Proofers' Association [*British*] (BI)
RPA .... Rural Pharmacists Association [*British*] (DBA)
RPA .... Rural Preservation Association [*British*]
RPA .... Rust Prevention Association [*Later, Crop Quality Council*]
RPAA .... Rotating Phase Array Antenna
RPAB .... Brown University, Annmary Brown Memorial Library, Providence, RI [*Library symbol Library of Congress*] (LCLS)
RPAC .... Regional Paramedic Advisory Committee [*Emergency medicine*] (DAVI)
RPAE .... Retarding Potential Analyzer Experiment [*NASA*]
RPAG .... Retired Professionals Action Group [*Later, Gray Panthers*]
RPAM .... American Mathematical Society, Providence, RI [*Library symbol Library of Congress*] (LCLS)
RPAM .... Regional Public Affairs Manager [*Nuclear energy*] (NRCH)
RPAM .... Research in Public Administration and Management [*British*]
RP & W .... Rawle, Penrose, and Watts' Pennsylvania Reports [*1828-40*] [*A publication*] (DLA)
RPAO .... Radium Plaque Adaptometer Operator [*Navy*]
RPAODS .... Remotely Piloted Aerial Observation Detection System (MCD)
RPAP .... Repap Enterprises Corp., Inc. [*NASDAQ symbol*] (NQ)
RPAPC .... Religious Press Associations Postal Coalition (EA)
RPAPF .... Repap Enterprises [*NASDAQ symbol*] (TTSB)
RPAPL .... Real Property Actions and Proceedings Law [*New York, NY A publication*]
RPAR .... Rebuttable Presumption Against Regulation [*of pesticides*] [*Environmental Protection Agency*]
RPAS .... Audubon Society of Rhode Island, Providence, RI [*Library symbol Library of Congress*] (LCLS)
RPAS .... Reactor Protection Actuating Signal [*Nuclear energy*] (NRCH)
RPASC .... Royal Pakistan Army Service Corps [*British military*] (DMA)
RPASMC .... Rubber and Plastic Adhesive and Sealant Manufacturers Council [*Later, Adhesive and Sealant Council*] (EA)
R Pat Cas .... Reports of Patent, Design, and Trade Mark Cases [*A publication*] (DLA)
RP-ATLF .... Roscoe Pound - American Trial Lawyers Foundation (EA)
RpAuto .... Republic Automotive Parts, Inc. [*Associated Press*] (SAG)
RPaw .... Pawtucket Public Library, Pawtucket, RI [*Library symbol Library of Congress*] (LCLS)
RPB .... Aerorepublica [*Columbia*] [*FAA designator*] (FAAC)
RPB .... Belleville, KS [*Location identifier FAA*] (FAAL)
RPB .... Brown University, Providence, RI [*Library symbol Library of Congress*] (LCLS)
RPB .... RADAR Plotting Board
RPB .... Recognised Professional Body [*Marketing of Investments Board Organising Committee, London Stock Exchange*] [*Finance*]
RPB .... Regional Preparedness Board [*Military*] (AABC)
RPB .... Research to Prevent Blindness (EA)

RPB .... Resources Protection Board
RPB .... River Purification Board [*British*] (DCTA)
RPB .... Royal Palm Beach Ltd. [*AMEX symbol*] (SPSG)
RPB .... Royal Protection Branch [*of the London Metropolitan Police*]
R_{pba} .... Periosteal Bone Apposition Rate [*Laboratory science*] (DAVI)
RPBG .... Revised Program and Budget Guidance [*Military*]
RPBH .... Butler Health Center, Providence, RI [*Library symbol Library of Congress*] (LCLS)
RPB-JH .... Brown University, John Hay Library of Rare Books annd Special Collections, Providence, RI [*Library symbol Library of Congress*] (LCLS)
RPB-S .... Brown University, Sciences Library, Providence, RI [*Library symbol Library of Congress*] (LCLS)
RPBSC .... Rules Peculiar to the Business of the Supreme Court [*A publication*] (DLA)
RPC .... Baltimore Regional Planning Commission [*Library network*]
RPC .... RADAR Planning Chart
RPC .... RADAR Processing Center
RPC .... Radiation Protection Committee [*South Australia*]
RPC .... Radiological Physics Center [*National Cancer Institute*]
RPC .... Rapeseed Protein Concentrate [*Food technology*]
RPC .... Readers per Copy [*Newspapers and magazines*]
RPC .... Real Property Cases [*1843-48*] [*England*] [*A publication*] (DLA)
RPC .... Real Property Commissioner's Report [*1832*] [*England*] [*A publication*] (DLA)
RPC .... Records Processing Center [*Veterans Administration*]
RPC .... Recreational Pilot Certificate [*Aviation*] (DA)
RPC .... Recruiting Publicity Center [*Military*]
RPC .... Reefed Parachute Canopy
RPC .... Refugee Processing Center (MCD)
RPC .... Regional Personnel Center
RPC .... Regional Planning Commission
RPC .... Regional Preparedness Committee [*Civil Defense*]
RPC .... Registered Protective Circuit
RPC .... Registered Publication Clerk [*or Custodian*] [*Navy*]
RPC .... Reliability Policy Committee (AAG)
RPC .... Remotely Piloted Craft [*Navy*]
RPC .... Remote Parameter Control [*Automotive engineering*]
RPC .... Remote Position Control
RPC .... Remote Power Controller
RPC .... Remote Procedure Call [*Computer science*]
RPC .... Remote Process Cell [*Nuclear energy*] (NRCH)
RPC .... Remote Processor Controller (NITA)
RPC .... Remount Purchasing Commission [*British military*] (DMA)
RPC .... Renopericardial Canal [*Medicine*]
RPC .... Repairable Provisioning Center (MCD)
RPC .... Repair Parts Catalog
RPC .... Repair Parts Cost (MCD)
RPC .... Reparable Processing Center (AFM)
RPC .... Reply Postcard
RPC .... Reported Post Coastal (NATG)
RPC .... Reports of English Patent Cases [*A publication*] (DLA)
RPC .... Reports of Patent Cases [*Legal*] [*British*]
RPC .... Reports of Patent, Design, and Trade Mark Cases [*A publication*] (DLA)
RPC .... Report to Commander [*Military*]
RPC .... Republican Policy Committee
RPC .... Request the Pleasure of Your Company [*On invitations*] (DSUE)
RPC .... Requisition Processing Cycle (MCD)
RPC .... Research and Productivity Council [*Canada*] (IRC)
RPC .... Research Planning Conference [*LIMRA*]
RPC .... Resource Policy Center [*Dartmouth College*] [*Research center*] (RCD)
RPC .... Ressources Phytogenetiques du Canada [*Plant Gene Resources of Canada - PGRC*]
RPC .... Restrictive Practices Court [*Legal*] [*British*]
RPC .... Restructured Pork Chop [*Food industry*]
RPC .... Reticularis Pontis Caudalis [*Brain anatomy*]
RPC .... Reverse-Phase Chromatography
RPC .... Reverse-Phase Column
RPC .... Rice Polishing Concentrate (OA)
RPC .... River Patrol Craft [*Military*] (CINC)
RPC .... Romanian Philatelic Club [*Defunct*] (EA)
RPC .... Rotation Planar Chromatography
RPC .... Row Parity Check (IEEE)
RPC .... Royal Parks Constabulary [*British*]
RPC .... Royal Pioneer Corps [*British*]
RPC .... RPC Energy Services, Inc. [*Associated Press*] (SAG)
RPC .... Rules of Practice in Patent Cases [*A publication*]
RPC .... Rural Political Cadre [*Vietnam*]
RPC .... Russian People's Center (EA)
RPC .... Russian Privatization Center (ECON)
RPCA .... Remotely Programmable Conference Arranger [*Telecommunications*] (TSSD)
RPCA .... Reverse Passive Anaphylaxis [*Immunology*]
RPCAS .... Requisition Priority Code Analysis System [*Army*]
RPCC .... Reactor Physics Constants Center [*Argonne National Laboratory*]
RPCC .... Remote Process Crane Cave [*Nuclear energy*] (NRCH)
RPCCA .... Red Poll Cattle Club of America [*Later, ARPA*] (EA)
RPCF .... Reiter Protein Complement Fixation [*Obsolete test for syphilis*]
RPCGN .... Rapidly Progressive Crescenting Glomerulonephritis [*Medicine*] (DMAA)
RPCH .... Reformed Presbyterian Church
RPCH .... Rural Primary Care Hospital
RPCI .... Regroupement des Partis de la Cote-D'Ivoire [*Regroupment of the Parties of the Ivory Coast*]
RP/CI .... Reinforced Plastics/Composites Institute [*Later, SPICI*] (EA)
RPCK .... Renopericardial Canal, Kidney [*Medicine*]
RP/CL .... Reporting Post, Coastal Low [*RADAR*]
RPCLF .... Revenue Properties Co. Ltd. [*NASDAQ symbol*] (SAG)
RPCLF .... Revenue Properties Ltd [*NASDAQ symbol*] (TTSB)
RPCM .... Rassemblement Populaire Caledonien et Metropolitain [*Caledonian and Metropolitan Popular Rally*] [*Political party*] (PPW)
RP/CM .... Reporting Post, Coastal Medium [*RADAR*]
RPCO .... Reclamation Program Control Officer [*Military*] (AFIT)
RPCP .... Radioisotope-Powered Cardiac Pacemaker (MCD)
RPCP .... Renopericardial Canal, Pericardium [*Medicine*]
RPCQ .... Rural Press Club [*Queensland, Australia*]
RPCR .... Rassemblement pour la Caledonie dans la Republique [*Popular Caledonian Rally for the Republic*] [*Political party*] (PPW)
RPCRAAIO ... Receive and Process Complaints and Requests for Assistance, Advice, or Information Only [*Army*] (AABC)
RPC Rep ...... Real Property Commissioner's Report [*1832*] [*England*] [*A publication*] (DLA)
RPCRS .... Reactor Protection Control Rod System (IEEE)
RPCS .... Reactor Plant Control System [*Nuclear energy*] (NRCH)
RPCS .... Reject Processing and Control System (MHDB)
RPCU .... Retropubic Cystourethropexy [*Urology*] (DAVI)
RPCV .... Returned Peace Corps Volunteer
RPCV .... Rural Press Club of Victoria [*Australia*]
RPCVCCA ..... Returned Peace Corps Volunteers Committee on Central America [*Defunct*] (EA)
RPCVD .... Remote Plasma Chemical Vapor Deposition [*Coating technology*] [*Semiconductor technology*]
RPCWA .... Rural Press Club of Western Australia
RPCX .... Roberts Pharmaceutical [*NASDAQ symbol*] (TTSB)
RPCX .... Roberts Pharmaceutical Corp. [*NASDAQ symbol*] (SAG)
RPD .... RADAR Planning Device
RPD .... RADAR Prediction Device
RPD .... Radioisotope Power Device
RPD .... Rapid (AAG)
RPD .... Rapid
RPD .... Reactive Plasma Deposition
RPD .... Reactor Plant Designer [*Nuclear energy*] (NRCH)
RPD .... Reductive Photo Dehalogenation
RPD .... Reflex Plasma Discharge
RPD .... Regius Professor of Divinity (ROG)
RPD .... Regulatory Policy Division [*Environmental Protection Agency*] (EPA)
RPD .... Relative Power Density
RPD .... Removable Partial Denture (DAVI)
RPD .... Renewal Parts Data (MSA)
RPD .... Repadre Resources Ltd. [*Vancouver Stock Exchange symbol*]
RPD .... Repatriation Pension Decisions [*Australia A publication*]
RPD .... Rerum Politicarum Doctor [*Doctor of Political Science*]
RPD .... Research Planning Diagram (PDAA)
RPD .... Reserves Available to Support Private, Noninterbank Deposits [*Federal Reserve System*]
RPD .... Resistance Pressure Detector
RPD .... Respiratory Protective Device [*Medicine*]
RPD .... Retarding Potential Difference (IEEE)
RPD .... Retired Pay Defense (NVT)
RPD .... Rhode Island School of Design, Providence, RI [*Library symbol Library of Congress*] (LCLS)
RPD .... Rocket Propulsion Department [*Royal Aircraft Establishment*] [*British*]
RPD & TM Cas ... Reports of Patent Design and Trade Mark Cases [*United Kingdom*] [*A publication*] (DLA)
RPDB .... Repertoire Pratique de Droit Belge [*A publication*] (ILCA)
RPDES .... Research Program Development and Evaluation Staff [*Department of Agriculture*]
RPDF .... Radiation Protection Design Features (NRCH)
RPDH .... Reserve Shutdown Planned Derated Hours [*Electronics*] (IEEE)
RPDL .... Radioisotope Process Development Laboratory [*ORNL*]
RPDL .... Rensselaer Polytechnic Institute Plasma Dynamics Laboratory [*Research center*] (RCD)
RPDL .... Repair Parts Decision List [*Military*] (CAAL)
RPD LMG ..... Ruchnoy Pulemyot Degtyaryov Light Machine Gun [*Soviet-made weaponry*] [*Also, RPDM, RPDM LMG*] (VNW)
RPDM .... Ruchnoy Pulemyot Degtyaryov Light Machine Gun [*Soviet-made weaponry*] [*Also, RPD LMG, RPDM LMG*] [*Military*] (VNW)
RPDM LMG ... Ruchnoy Pulemyot Degtyaryov Light Machine Gun [*Soviet-made weaponry*] [*Also, RPD LMG, RPDM*] [*Military*] (VNW)
RPDMRC .... Reference or Partial Description Method Reason Code (MCD)
RPDO .... Repair Parts Directive Order
RPDP .... Recoverable Plasma Diagnostics Package (SSD)
RPDR .... Reproducer (MSA)
RPDR .... Rotating Packed Disk Reactor [*Chemical engineering*]
RPDS .... Rapids (MCD)
RPDS .... Rapids
RPDS .... Retired Personnel Data System [*Air Force*]
RPDT .... RADAR Prediction Data Table (PDAA)
RPDt .... Registered Professional Dietitian
RPDTMC .... Reports of Patent, Design, and Trade Mark Cases [*Australia A publication*]
RPDWR .... Revised Primary Drinking Water Regulations
RPE .... Elmwood Public Library, Providence, RI [*Library symbol Library of Congress*] (LCLS)
RPE .... Radial Probable Error (IEEE)
RPE .... Radio Production Executive (IAA)
RPE .... Range Planning Estimate (MUGU)

RPE............ Range Probable Error [*Formerly, Range Error Probable*] [*Air Force*] (NATG)
RPE............ Rating of Perceived Exertion
RPE............ Record of Personal Experience (AIE)
RPE............ Reformed Protestant Episcopal
RPE............ Registered Professional Engineer (IEEE)
RPE............ Related Payroll Expense
RPE............ Related Production Equipment (SAA)
RPE............ Relative Price Effect
RPE............ Reliability Project Engineer (NASA)
RPE............ Remote Peripheral Equipment (IEEE)
RPE............ Repair Parts Estimate (MCD)
RPE............ Report of Patients Evacuated [*Aeromedical evacuation*]
RPE............ Required Page-End Character [*Computer science*]
RPE............ Resource Planning and Evaluation [*Nuclear energy*] (NRCH)
RPE............ Retinal Pigment Epithelium
RPE............ Rocket Propulsion Establishment [*British*] (KSC)
RPE............ Ron Pair Enterprises [*Division of Wilson, Inc.*]
RPE............ Rotating Platinum Electrode [*Electrochemistry*]
RPE............ Royal Pakistan Engineers [*British military*] (DMA)
RPEA.......... Regional Planning and Evaluation Agency [*California State Board of Education*]
RP/ED......... Rapid Prototyping/Evolutionary Design (MCD)
RPEN.......... Retry Pending (SSD)
RPEng......... Providence Engineering Society, Providence, RI [*Library symbol Library of Congress*] (LCLS)
RPEP.......... Rabies Post-Exposure Prophylaxis [*Medicine*] (DMAA)
RPEP.......... Register of Planned Emergency Procedures [*Military*]
RPEV.......... Roadway Powered Electric Vehicle
RPF............ RADAR Performance Figure (IAA)
RPF............ Radiometer Performance Factor
RPF............ Radio Position Finding [*A term for RADAR before early 1942*]
RPF............ Radio Proximity Fuze
RPF............ Rally for the Republic [*French Political party*] (ECON)
RPF............ Real Property Facilities [*Army*] (AABC)
RPF............ Reduced Physical Fidelity (MCD)
RPF............ Reference Point Foundation (EA)
RPF............ Reformatorische Politieke Federatie [*Reformist Political Federation*] [*Netherlands Political party*] (PPE)
RPF............ Region Peaking Factor [*Nuclear energy*] (NRCH)
RPF............ Registered Professional Forester
RPF............ Reiter Protein Complement Fixation [*Obsolete test for syphilis*] (CPH)
RPF............ Relaxed Pelvic Floor [*Medicine*]
RPF............ Remote Personnel Facility
RPF............ Remote Processing Facility (MCD)
RPF............ Renal Plasma Flow [*Medicine*]
RPF............ Repair Parts Facility (MCD)
rpf............ Reperforated [*Philately*]
RPF............ Right Panel Front [*Nuclear energy*] (NRCH)
RPF............ Rigid Plastic Foam
RPF............ Roscoe Programming Facility (NITA)
RPF............ Rotable Pool Factor (MCD)
RPF............ Royal Pacific Sea Farms Ltd. [*Toronto Stock Exchange symbol Vancouver Stock Exchange symbol*]
RPF............ Rwandan Patriotic Front [*Political party*]
RPFC.......... Ray Price Fan Club (EA)
RPFC.......... Recurrent Peak Forward Current
RPFFB........ RP [*Retinitis Pigmentosa*] Foundation Fighting Blindness (EA)
RPFMA........ Rubber and Plastic Footwear Manufacturers' Association [*British*] (BI)
RPFOD........ Reported for Duty (FAAC)
RPFS.......... Radio Position Fixing System [*Aviation*] (DA)
RPFS.......... Rudder Pedal Force Sensor (MCD)
RPFT.......... Rudder Pedal Force Transducer (MCD)
RPG............ Radar Product General [*Marine science*] (OSRA)
RPG............ Radar Product General (USDC)
RPG............ Radiation Protection Guide [*AEC*]
RPG............ Radioisotopic Power Generator [*Navy*]
RPG............ Rampage Resources Ltd. [*Vancouver Stock Exchange symbol*]
RPG............ Random Pulse Generator [*Telecommunications*] (OA)
RPG............ Rebounds per Game [*Basketball, hockey*]
RPG............ Reflection Phase Grating [*Acoustics*]
RPG............ Refugee Policy Group (EA)
RPG............ Regional Planning Group (NATG)
RPG............ Register Program Generator (HGAA)
RPG............ Religion Publishing Group [*Defunct*] (EA)
RPG............ Report Processor Generator (MCD)
RPG............ Report Program Generator [*Programming language*] [*1962*]
RPG............ Research Planning Guide (MCD)
RPG............ Retrograde Pyelogram [*Medicine*]
RPG............ Right Pedal Ganglion
RPG............ River Patrol Group [*Military*] (VNW)
RPG............ Rocket-Propelled Grenade
RPG............ Role-Playing Game [*Video game*]
RPG............ Rotary Pulse Generator
RPG............ Rounds per Gun
RPGAN........ Role-Playing Game Association Network (EA)
RPGC.......... Royal Perth Golf Club [*Australia*]
RPGG.......... Retroplacental Gamma Globulin [*Immunology*] (DAVI)
RPGMEC...... Regional Postgraduate Medical Education Committee [*Medicine*] (DMAA)
RPGN.......... Rapidly Progressive Glomerular Nephritis [*Medicine*]
RPGN.......... Rapidly Progressive Glomerulonephritis [*Nephrology*] (DAVI)
RPGPM........ Rounds per Gun per Minute
RPH............ Raypath Resources Ltd. [*Vancouver Stock Exchange symbol*]
RPH............ Registered Pharmacist
RPH............ Relative Pulse Height (OA)
RPH............ Remember Pearl Harbor [*Group*] [*World War II*]
RPH............ Remotely Piloted Helicopter
RP/H.......... Repairs, Heavy
RPH............ Retroperitoneal Hemorrhage [*Medicine*] (DAVI)
RPH............ Revolutions per Hour (MCD)
RPH............ Rhode Island Hospital, Peters House Medical Library, Providence, RI [*Library symbol Library of Congress*] (LCLS)
RPH............ Rideout Pyrohydrolysis
RPHA.......... Reverse Passive Hemagglutination [*Clinical chemistry*]
RPHAMFCA... Reversed Passive Hemagglutination by Miniature Centrifugal Fast Analysis [*Medicine*] (DMAA)
RPhilS........ Royal Philharmonic Society [*British*] (DI)
RPhO.......... Regional Pharmaceutical Officer [*National Health Service*] [*British*] (DI)
RP-HPLC..... Reversed-Phase High-Performance Liquid Chromatography
RPHST......... Research Participation for High School Teachers [*National Science Foundation*]
RPI............ Paradise Air (Pvt) Ltd. [*Sri Lanka*] [*FAA designator*] (FAAC)
RPI............ RADAR Precipitation Integrator [*National Weather Service*]
RPI............ Railway Progress Institute (EA)
RPI............ Random Procedure Information (WDAA)
RPI............ Rapeseed Protein Isolate [*Food technology*]
RPI............ Rassemblement Populaire pour l'Independance [*People's Rally for Independence*] [*Djibouti*] [*Political party*] (PPW)
RPI............ Rated Position Identifier (AFM)
RPI............ Reaction Product Imaging [*Chemistry*]
RPI............ Read, Punch, and Interpret
RPI............ Real Property Inventory [*Military*]
RPI............ Recover Processor Improvement (DWSG)
RPI............ Registro de la Propiedad Industrial [*Spanish Patent Office*] [*Information service or system*] (IID)
RPI............ Relative Position Indication (NRCH)
RPI............ Relay Position Indicator
RPI............ Remarried Parents, Inc. [*Defunct*] (EA)
RPI............ Rensselaer Polytechnic Institute [*Troy, NY*] (MCD)
RPI............ Rensselaer Polytechnic Institute (GAGS)
RPI............ Republican Party of India [*Political party*] (PPW)
RPI............ Research Price Index
RPI............ Research Publications International [*Database producer*] (IID)
RPI............ Resource Policy Institute (EA)
RPI............ Responsive Production Inventory
RPI............ Retail Prices Index [*British*]
RPI............ Reticulocyte Production Index [*Hematology*]
RPI............ Reversals per Inch (IAA)
RPI............ Revolutions per Inch (IAA)
RPI............ Rework Print Image (IAA)
RPI............ Richmond Professional Institute [*Virginia*]
RPI............ Rimpac Industries [*Vancouver Stock Exchange symbol*]
RPI............ Rod Position Indicator [*Nuclear energy*] (NRCH)
RPI............ Roller Path Inclination [*Navy*] (DOMA)
RPI............ Roll Position Indicator (MCD)
RPI............ Rose Polytechnic Institute [*Indiana*]
RPI............ Royal Polytechnic Institute (ROG)
RPIA.......... Resurgence Properties [*NASDAQ symbol*] (SAG)
RPIA.......... Rocket Propellant Information Agency (MCD)
RPIA.......... Roll Position Indicator Assembly
RPIAC........ Retail Prices Index Advisory Committee [*Department of Employment*] [*British*]
RPIC.......... Reagan Political Items Collectors (EA)
RPIC.......... Rock Properties Information Center [*Purdue University*] [*National Science Foundation*] (IID)
RPICCE....... Round Pupil Intracapsular Cataract Extraction [*Ophthalmology*] (DAVI)
RPI/CIE...... Rensselaer Polytechnic Institute/Center for Integrated Electronics [*Troy, NY*]
RPIE.......... Real Property Installed Equipment [*Air Force*] (MCD)
RPIE.......... Replacement of Photography Imagery Equipment (RDA)
RPIF.......... Real Property Industrial Fund
RPIFC........ Robert Plant International Fan Club (EA)
RPIFC........ Ronnie Prophet International Fan Club (EA)
RPII.......... Rotary Power Internationsl, Inc. [*NASDAQ symbol*] (SAG)
RPII.......... Rotary Power Intl [*NASDAQ symbol*] (TTSB)
RPI/MA....... Rensselaer Polytechnic Institute/Microwave Acoustics Laboratory [*Troy, NY*]
RPIO.......... Registered Publication Issuing Office [*Military*]
RPIPP........ Reverse Phase Ion-Pair Partition (DMAA)
RPIS.......... Regional Plant Introduction Station (GNE)
RPIS.......... Rod Position Indication System [*Nuclear energy*] (NRCH)
RPIS.......... Rod Position Information System [*Nuclear energy*] (NRCH)
RPISU........ Radon Progeny Integrating Sampling Unit (GNE)
RPIT.......... Related-Party International Transaction
RPJ............ [*The*] Rise of Provincial Jewry [*A publication*] (BJA)
RPJ............ Rotary Pressure Joint
RPJCB........ John Carter Brown Library, Providence, RI [*Library symbol Library of Congress*] (LCLS)
RPK............ Revenue Passenger Kilometer (AIA)
RPK............ Ribophosphate Pyrophosphokinase [*An enzyme*]
RPK............ Ribosephosphate Kinase (DMAA)
RPK............ Roosevelt [*Washington*] [*Seismograph station code, US Geological Survey*] (SEIS)
RPL............ RADAR Processing Language [*Computer science*] (IEEE)
RPL............ Radiation Physics Laboratory [*National Institute of Standards and Technology*] (MCD)

RPL .... Radio-Photo Luminescent [*Dosimetry*]
RPL .... Radio Physics Laboratory (IAA)
RPL .... Ramped Powered Lighter [*British military*] (DMA)
RPL .... Ram Petroleums Ltd. [*Toronto Stock Exchange symbol*]
RPL .... Ramseur Pilot Light Teaching System
RPL .... Rapid Pole Line [*A type of pole line construction*]
RPL .... Rated Power Level (NASA)
RPL .... Reactor Primary Loop
RPL .... Reading Public Library, Reading, PA [*OCLC symbol*] (OCLC)
RPL .... Receive Replenishment From [*Navy*] (NVT)
RPL .... Recommended Provisioning List
RPL .... Reemployment Priority List [*DoD*]
RPL .... Remote Program Load
RPL .... Renewal Parts Leaflet (MSA)
RPL .... Repair Parts List [*Army*] (AABC)
RP/L .... Repairs, Light
RPL .... Repeal [*Legal shorthand*] (LWAP)
RPL .... Repetitive Flight Plan [*ICAO*] (FAAC)
RPL .... Replacement (IAA)
RPL .... Replenish (NVT)
RPL .... Requested Privilege Level [*Computer science*]
RPL .... Request Parameter List [*Computer science*] (BUR)
RPL .... Resident Programming Language [*Computer science*]
RPL .... Resident Pulmonary Lymphocyte [*Immunology*]
RPL .... Reverse Polish Logic (NITA)
RPL .... Rhode Island State Law Library, Providence, RI [*Library symbol Library of Congress*] (LCLS)
RPL .... Richmond Public Library [*UTLAS symbol*]
RPL .... Ripe Pulp Liquid [*A banana substrate*]
RPL .... Ripple
RPL .... Robot Programming Language [*Computer science*]
RPL .... Rocket Propulsion Laboratory [*Air Force*]
RPL .... Rocket Propulsion Laboratory (NADA)
RPL .... Rodent and Primate Laboratory (SSD)
RPL .... Rotary Pellet Launcher [*Military*] (PDAA)
RPL .... Running Program Language [*Computer science*]
RPLAD .... Retroperitoneal Lymphoadenectomy [*Medicine*] (BABM)
RPLAD .... Retroperitoneal Lymphoadenectomy [*Oncology*] (DAVI)
RPLC .... Replace (FAAC)
RPLC .... Reversed-Phase Liquid Chromatography
RPLIND .... Retroperitoneal Lymph Node Dissection [*Medicine*] (CDI)
RPLN .... Retroperitoneal Lymph Nodes [*Medicine*]
RPLND .... Retroperitoneal Lymphadenectomy [*Oncology*] (DAVI)
RPLND .... Retroperitoneal Lymph Node Dissection [*Medicine*] (MEDA)
RPLNG .... Replenishing
RPLR .... Repeller (MSA)
RPLS .... Radionuclide Perfusion Lung Scan
RPLS .... Reactor Protection Logic System (IEEE)
RPLSN .... Repulsion (MSA)
RPLT .... Repellent (MSA)
RPLV .... Reentry Payload Launch Vehicle
rplx .... Rhoplex (VRA)
RPM .... Ngukurr [*Airport symbol*]
RPM .... RADAR Performance Monitor
RPM .... Radial-Burning Pulse Motor (MCD)
RPM .... Radiation Polarization Measurement
RPM .... Raised Pavement Marker [*Highway design*]
RPM .... Random Phase Model (OA)
RPM .... Rapid Processing Mode [*Medicine*] (MAE)
RPM .... Rate per Minute
RPM .... Raven's Proressive Matrices [*Psychiatry*] (DAVI)
RPM .... Reactive Plume Model [*Environmental Protection Agency*] (GFGA)
RPM .... Read Program Memory [*Computer science*] (MDG)
RPM .... Real Property Maintenance (DOMA)
RPM .... Real Property Management
RPM .... Reasonable Prudent Man [*Legal shorthand*] (LWAP)
RPM .... Reclamation Program Manager [*Military*] (AFIT)
RPM .... Refractory Platinum Metal
RPM .... Regional Particulate Model [*Marine science*] (OSRA)
RPM .... Regional Particulate Model (USDC)
RPM .... Registered Publications Manual [*Navy*]
RPM .... Registered Publications Memorandum
RPM .... Registrants Processing Manual [*Selective Service System*]
RPM .... Regulated Power Module
RPM .... Relative Plate Motion [*Geophysics*]
RPM .... Relaxation Potential Model [*Physics*]
RPM .... Reliability Performance Measure [*QCR*]
RPM .... Reliability Planning and Management (MCD)
RPM .... Remedial Project Manager [*Navy*]
RPM .... Remotely Piloted Munitions [*Army*]
RPM .... Remote Performance Monitoring (CET)
RPM .... Remote Program Management
RPM .... Reprogram Mode
RPM .... Resale Price Maintenance
RPM .... Research and Program Management [*NASA*]
RPM .... Resident Process Manager [*Computer science*] (PCM)
RPM .... Resistant Plant Material [*Soil science*]
RPM .... Response-per-Thousand [*Marketing*]
RPM .... Resupply Provisions Module [*NASA*] (KSC)
RPM .... Retail Price Maintenance (DCTA)
RPM .... Returns Program Manager [*IRS*]
RPM .... Revenue Passenger Mile
RPM .... Revenue per Mile
RPM .... Revolutions per Mile [*Automobile tires*]
RPM .... Revolutions per Minute [*e.g., in reference to phonograph records*]
rpm .... Revolutions per Minute (IDOE)
RPM .... Rhode Island Medical Society, Providence, RI [*Library symbol Library of Congress*] (LCLS)
RPM .... Rifle Prize Money [*British military*] (DMA)
RPM .... Rocket-Propelled Mines (NATG)
RPM .... Roll Position Mechanism (MCD)
RPM .... Rotations per Minute
RPM .... Rounds per Minute [*Military*] (INF)
RPM .... Royalty Payment Mechanism
RPM .... RPM, Inc. [*Associated Press*] (SAG)
RPM .... Runs per Minute (IAA)
RPMa .... Masonic Temple Library, Providence, RI [*Library symbol Library of Congress*] (LCLS)
RPMA .... Real Property Maintenance Activities [*or Administration*] [*Army*] (AABC)
RPMB .... Cubi Naval Air Station, Bataan [*Philippines*] [*ICAO location identifier*] (ICLI)
RPMB .... Remotely-Piloted Mini-Blimp (PDAA)
RPMC .... Cebu/Lahug, Cebu [*Philippines*] [*ICAO location identifier*] (ICLI)
RPMC .... Remote Performance Monitoring and Control
RPMC .... Reserve Personnel, Marine Corps (MCD)
RPMD .... Resources Planning and Mobilization Division [*of OEP*]
RPMD .... Rheumatic Pain Modulation Disorder [*Medicine*] (DMAA)
RPMF .... Reserve Personnel Master File [*Military*]
RPMI .... Radiant Power Measuring Instrument [*Geophysics*]
RPMI .... Revolutions-per-Minute Indicator
RPMI .... Roswell Park Memorial Institute [*State University of New York at Buffalo*] [*Research center*] (RCD)
RPMIO .... Registered Publication Mobile Issuing Office [*Military*]
RPMK .... Clark Air Base, Pampanga [*Philippines*] [*ICAO location identifier*] (ICLI)
RPML .... Laoag/International, Ilocos Norte [*Philippines*] [*ICAO location identifier*] (ICLI)
RPMM .... Manila/International [*Philippines*] [*ICAO location identifier*] (ICLI)
RPMN .... Repairman (AABC)
RPMO .... Radio Projects Management Office
RPMOR .... Rounds per Mortar
RPMORPM .... Rounds per Mortar per Minute
RPMP .... Legazpi, Albay [*Philippines*] [*ICAO location identifier*] (ICLI)
RPMP .... Register of Plan Mobilization Producers
RPMR .... Romblon, Tablas Island [*Philippines*] [*ICAO location identifier*] (ICLI)
RPMS .... Real Property Management System (MCD)
RPM/S .... Revolutions per Minute/Second (DEN)
RPMS .... Royal Postgraduate Medical School [*British*]
RPMS .... Sangley Point Naval Station, Cavite [*Philippines*] [*ICAO location identifier*] (ICLI)
RPMT .... Lapu-Lapu/Mactan International [*Philippines*] [*ICAO location identifier*] (ICLI)
RPMZ .... Zamboanga/International [*Philippines*] [*ICAO location identifier*] (ICLI)
RPN .... Registered Professional Nurse
RPN .... Renal Papillary Necrosis [*Nephrology*] (DAVI)
RPN .... Reserve Personnel, Navy [*An appropriation*]
RPN .... Reverse Polish Notation [*Arithmetic evaluation*] [*Computer science*] (IEEE)
RPN .... Rosh-Pina [*Israel*] [*Airport symbol*] (OAG)
RPN .... Royal Pakistan Navy [*British military*] (DMA)
RPND .... Reprinting, No Date [*Publishing*]
RPNSM .... Replenishment
RPNVR .... Royal Pakistan Naval Volunteer Reserve [*British military*] (DMA)
RPO .... Aeroposta, SA [*Argentina*] [*FAA designator*] (FAAC)
RPO .... Radiation Protection Officer [*NASA*] (NASA)
RPO .... Radiophare Omnidirectionnel [*Omnidirectional Radio Beacon*] (NATG)
RPO .... Railway Post Office
RPO .... Range Planning Office (MUGU)
RPO .... Rapids [*Real Time Automated Personnel Identification System*] Program Office
RPO .... Readiness Project Officer
RPO .... Regional Personnel Officer [*Social Security Administration*]
RPO .... Regional Pests Officer [*Ministry of Agriculture, Fisheries, and Food*] [*British*]
RPO .... Regional Program [*or Project*] Officer (OICC)
RPO .... Regional Purchasing Office [*Defense Supply Agency*]
RPO .... Registered Publications Officer [*Navy*] (DNAB)
RPO .... Regular Production Option [*Automotive engineering*]
RPO .... Regulating Petty Officer [*British*]
RPO .... Rejection Purchase Order (MCD)
RPO .... Repair Parts Order [*Navy*]
RPO .... Replacement Purchase Order
RPO .... Responsible Property Officer [*Military*] (AFIT)
RPO .... Retail Postal Outlet (DD)
RPO .... Retired Pay Operations [*Army*]
RPO .... Returned by the Post Office (WDMC)
RPO .... Revolution per Orbit
RPO .... Rhone-Poulenc Overseas [*NYSE symbol*] (SPSG)
RPO .... Right Posterior Oblique [*View*] [*Radiology*] (DAVI)
RPO .... Rotor Power Output
RPO .... Royal Philharmonic Orchestra [*British*]
RPOA .... Recognized Private Operating Agencies (NATG)
RPOADS ...... Remotely-Piloted Observation Aircraft Designator System (PDAA)
RPOC .... Remote Payload Operations Center [*NASA*] (MCD)
RPOC .... Report Proceeding on Course [*Aviation*] (FAAC)
RPOC .... Residual Particulate Organic Carbon [*Environmental science*]
RPOCC .... Remote Payload Operations Control Center [*NASA*] (SSD)
RPOCN .... Request for Purchase Order Change Notice (AAG)

RPOOK......... Receive Pulse On/Off Keyed (MCD)
RPOP.......... Rover Preflight Operations Procedures [*NASA*] (KSC)
RPoPrA........ Rhone-Poul Overseas 8.125% Pref [*NYSE symbol*] (TTSB)
RPorP......... Portsmouth Priory, Portsmouth, RI [*Library symbol Library of Congress*] (LCLS)
RPOW.......... RPM, Inc. [*NASDAQ symbol*] (SAG)
RPP........... RADAR Power Programmer
RPP........... Radiation Protection Plan [*Nuclear energy*] (NRCH)
RPP........... Radiochemical Processing Plant [*Oak Ridge National Laboratory*]
RPP........... Rassemblement Populaire pour le Progres [*Popular Rally for Progress*] [*Djibouti*] [*Political party*] (PPW)
RPP........... Rate Pressure Product [*Cardiology*]
RPP........... Reactor Plant Planning (DNAB)
RPP........... Rechargeable Power Pack
RPP........... Recovered Polypropylene [*Organic chemistry*]
RPP........... Recovery Pilot Plant (ACII)
RPP........... Reductive Pentose Phosphate [*Photosynthesis cycle*]
RPP........... Regional Priority Program [*Army*] (AABC)
RPP........... Registered Postal Packet
RPP........... Reinforced Pyrolytic Plastic (NASA)
RPP........... Reliability Program Plan (MCD)
RPP........... Removable Patch Panel
RPP........... Rendezvous Point Position [*Aerospace*]
RPP........... Repair Parts Provisioning
RPP........... Repap Enterprises Corp., Inc. [*Toronto Stock Exchange symbol Vancouver Stock Exchange symbol*]
RPP........... Reply Paid Postcard
RPP........... Republican People's Party [*Cumhuriyet Halk Partisi - CHP*] [*Turkey Political party*] (PPW)
RPP........... Request for Proposal Preparation (SAA)
RPP........... Requisition Processing Point [*Military*]
RPP........... Retrograde Processing Point (MCD)
RPP........... Retropubic Prostatectomy [*Medicine*]
RPP........... Reverse Pulse Polarography [*Analytical chemistry*]
RPP........... Rivers Pollution Prevention (ROG)
RPP........... Roll-Pitch Pickoff
RPP........... Rules of Practices and Procedure
RPP........... Rural Practice Project [*An association Defunct*] (EA)
RPPA.......... Repetitively-Pulsed Plasma Accelerator (IAA)
RPPA.......... Republican Postwar Policy Association [*Encouraged Republican Party to drop its isolationist viewpoint and take a stand for an American share in international collaboration after the war*] [*World War II*]
RPPC.......... Providence College, Providence, RI [*Library symbol Library of Congress*] (LCLS)
RPPDL......... Random Peptide Phage Display Library [*Biochemistry*]
RPPE.......... Research, Program, Planning, and Evaluation
RPPI.......... Remote Plan Position Indicator (MCD)
RPPI.......... Repeater Plan Position Indicator (NVT)
RPPI.......... Role Perception Picture Inventory
RPPL.......... Repair Parts Price List
RPPL.......... Repair Parts Provisioning List
RPPM.......... Park Museum Reference Library, Providence, RI [*Library symbol Library of Congress*] (LCLS)
RPPMP......... Repair Parts Program Management Plans
RPPO.......... Regional Printing Procurement Office [*Army*]
RPPP.......... Repair Parts Program Plan [*Army*]
RPPP.......... Rules of Pleading, Practice, and Procedure [*A publication*] (DLA)
RPPR.......... Red Cell Precursor Production Rate [*Hematology*] (DAVI)
RPPS.......... Reactive Perfluoroalkyl Polymeric Surfactant [*Organic chemistry*]
RPPS.......... Retired Pay / Personnel System [*Military*] (DNAB)
RPPS.......... Robotnicza Partia Polskich Socjalistow [*Workers Party of Polish Socialists*] [*Political party*] (PPE)
RPPS-Lewica... Robotnicza Partia Polskich Socjalistow - Lewica [*Workers Party of Polish Socialists - Left*] [*Political party*] (PPE)
RPPTF......... Rotatable Porous-Prism Test Fixture
RPPY.......... Reactor Plant Planning Year (DNAB)
RPQ........... Rapports de Pratique de Quebec [*Quebec Practice Reports*] [*Canada*] [*A publication*] (DLA)
RPQ........... Request for Price Quotation
RPQ........... Rutter Parent Questionnaire
RPR........... Federation Guadeloupeenne du Rassemblement pour la Republique [*Guadeloupe Federation of the Rally for the Republic*] [*Political party*] (PPW)
RPR........... Radio Physics Research
RPR........... Railway Pioneer Regiment [*British military*] (DMA)
RPR........... Raipur [*India*] [*Airport symbol*] (OAG)
RPR........... Rapid Plasma Reagin [*Card test for venereal disease*]
RPR........... Rapid Power Reduction (IEEE)
RPR........... Rassemblement pour la Republique [*Rally for the Republic*] [*France Political party*] (ECON)
RPR........... Rassemblement pour la Republique [*Rally for the Republic*] [*Wallis and Futuna Islands*] [*Political party*] (PD)
RPR........... Rassemblement pour la Republique [*Rally for the Republic*] [*Martinique*] [*Political party*] (PPW)
RPR........... Rassemblement pour la Republique [*Rally for the Republic*] [*French Guiana*] [*Political party*] (PPW)
RPR........... Rassemblement pour la Republique [*Rally for the Republic*] [*Reunion*] [*Political party*] (PPW)
RPR........... Rassemblement pour la Republique [*Rally for the Republic*] [*Mayotte*] [*Political party*] (EY)
RPR........... Rassemblement pour la Republique [*Rally for the Republic*] [*French Polynesia*] [*Political party*] (PPW)
RPR........... Rated Pressure Ratio (EG)
RPR........... Read Printer
RPR........... Rear Projection Readout
RPR........... Rectangular Parallelepiped Resonant Method [*Crystal elasticity*]
RPR........... Red Blood Cell Precursor Production Rate [*Hematology*]
RPR........... Reiter Protein Reagin [*Biochemistry*] (DAVI)
RPR........... Rent Procedural Regulation (Office of Rent Stabilization) [*Economic Stabilization Agency*] [*A publication*] (DLA)
RPR........... Repair (MSA)
RPR........... Repair
RPR........... Repair Parts Requisition
RPR........... Research Project Report [*A publication*] (EAAP)
RPR........... Reverse Phase Relay (IAA)
RPR........... Reverse Power Relay (IAA)
RPR........... Reverse Price Risk [*Finance*] (EMRF)
RPR........... Rhone-Poulenc Rorer [*NYSE symbol*] (SPSG)
RPR........... Rings Present (NITA)
RPR........... Rockport Resources Ltd. [*Vancouver Stock Exchange symbol*]
RPR........... Roger Williams College, Providence Campus, Providence, RI [*Library symbol Library of Congress*] (LCLS)
RPR........... Roll-Pitch Resolver
RPR........... Rotatable Pool Rate (MCD)
RPRA.......... Racing Public Relations Association
RPRA.......... Railroad Public Relations Association (EA)
RPRA.......... Royal Pigeon Racing Association [*British*] (DBA)
R Prac Patent Cases... Rules of Practice in Patent Cases [*A publication*] (DLA)
RPRC.......... Regional Primate Research Centers
RPRC.......... Religious Public Relations Council (EA)
RPRC.......... Retired and Pioneer Rural Carriers of United States (EA)
RPRC.......... Rhode Island College, Providence, RI [*Library symbol Library of Congress*] (LCLS)
RPR-CT........ Rapid Plasma Reagin Card Test [*Clinical chemistry*]
RPRD.......... Research Policy and Review Division [*of OEP*]
R_{pri}.......... Primary Resistance (IDOE)
RPRI.......... Radiata Pine Research Institute [*Australia*]
rPRL.......... Rat Prolactin [*Biochemistry*]
RPRL.......... Regional Parasite Research Laboratory [*US Department of Agriculture*] [*Research center*] (RCD)
RPRL.......... Regional Poultry Research Laboratory [*East Lansing, MI*] [*Department of Agriculture*] (GRD)
RPRMN......... Repairman
RPROM......... Reprogrammable Read-Only Memory [*Computer science*] (HGAA)
RPROP......... Real Property [*Legal shorthand*] (LWAP)
RPROP......... Receiving Proficiency Pay [*Military*]
RPRRB......... Real Property Resource Review Board (AFM)
RPRS.......... Random-Pulse RADAR System (AAG)
RPRS.......... Roll-Pitch Resolver System
RPRT.......... Report (AFM)
RPRT.......... Right Place at the Right Time [*A criterion for success*]
RPRV.......... Remotely Piloted Research Vehicle [*NASA*]
RPRWP......... Reactor Plant River Water Pump (IEEE)
RPS........... Racial Preservation Society [*British*]
RPS........... RADAR Plotting Sheet (OA)
RPS........... RADAR Position Symbol [*ICAO*] (FAAC)
RPS........... Radiation Protection Standards (SAA)
RPS........... Radical Philosophy Society [*British*]
RPS........... Radiological Protection Service (DEN)
RPS........... Radio Program Standard [*Australian Broadcasting Tribunal*]
RPS........... Randomized Pattern Search (PDAA)
RPS........... Range Pad Service
RPS........... Range Positioning System
RPS........... Rapid Patent Service [*Research Publications, Inc.*] [*Information service or system*] (IID)
RPS........... Rapid Photo Screening
RPS........... Rare Poultry Society [*British*]
RPS........... Reactor Protection System [*Nuclear energy*] (NRCH)
RPS........... Real-Time Processing System (NITA)
RPS........... Real-Time Programming System [*Computer science*] (IEEE)
RPS........... Record and Playback Subsystem (NASA)
RPS........... Records per Sector [*Computer science*]
RPS........... Regional Pressure Setting (DA)
RPS........... Registered Publications System
RPS........... Regulated Power Supply
RPS........... Regulatory Performance Summary [*Report*] [*Nuclear energy*] (NRCH)
RPS........... Reinforced Porcelain System [*Dentistry*]
RPS........... Relative Performance Score [*Telecommunications*] (TEL)
RPS........... Relay Power Supply (MCD)
RPS........... Remittance Processing Systems [*IRS*]
RPS........... Remote Printing System
RPS........... Remote Processing Service (BUR)
RPS........... Remote Processing System (IAA)
RPS........... Remote Programming System (MCD)
RPS........... Renal Pressor Substance [*Medicine*]
RPS........... Request for Procurement Services
RPS........... Requirements Planning System [*Computer science*]
RPS........... Response-Produced Stimulation
RPS........... Retired Persons Services (EA)
RPS........... Return Pressure Sensing (MCD)
RPS........... Reversed-Phase Series (PDAA)
RPS........... Revolutions per Second (AFM)
rps........... Revolutions per Second (IDOE)
rps........... Rhodopseudomonas Virides [*A bacterium*]
RPS........... Rhone-Poulenc Systems (NITA)
RPS........... Right Pedal Sinus
RPS........... Rigid Proctosigmoidoscopy [*Proctoscopy*]
RPS........... Ripe Pulp Solid [*A banana substrate*]
RPS........... RMS [*Remote Manipulator System*] Planning System (SSD)

RPS .... Rochester Public Schools, Library Processing Center, Rochester, MN [*OCLC symbol*] (OCLC)
RPS .... Role Performance Scale [*Occupational therapy*]
RPS .... Rotary Precision Switch
RPS .... Rotating Passing Scuttle
RPS .... Rotational Position Sensing [*Computer science*]
RPS .... Royal Philharmonic Society (EAIO)
RPS .... Royal Photographic Society of Great Britain (DEN)
RPS .... RPS Realty Trust [*NYSE symbol*] (SPSG)
RPS .... Rutile-Paper-Slurry [*Grade of titanium dioxide*]
RPSA .... Religious Program Specialist Seaman Apprentice [*Navy rating*] (DNAB)
RPSA .... Rudder Pedal Sensor Assembly (MCD)
RPSC .... Royal Philatelic Society of Canada
RPSCTDY..... Return to Proper Station Upon Completion of Temporary Duty [*Military*]
RPS-DL....... Registered Publications Section - District Library [*Navy*]
RPSEL .... Recommended Peculiar Support Equipment List (MCD)
RPSG .... Report Passing [*Aviation*] (FAAC)
RPSGB......... Royal Pharmaceutical Society of Great Britain (EAIO)
RPSGB......... Royal Photographic Society of Great Britain (EAIO)
RP (Ships)... Registered Ships' Plumbers [*British*]
RPSI .... Railway Preservation Society of Ireland (BI)
RPSI .... Roche Psychiatric Service Institute
RPSIO .... Registered Publications Subissuing Office [*Military*] (NVT)
RPSL .... Repair Parts Selective List
RPSL .... Rhode Island Department of State Library Services, Providence, RI [*Library symbol Library of Congress*] (LCLS)
RPSM .... Registered Publication Shipment Memorandum
RPSM .... Residency Program in Social Medicine (DMAA)
RPSM .... Resources Planning and Scheduling Method
RPSMG........ Reactor Protective System Motor Generator (IEEE)
RPSML .... Repair Parts Support Material List
RPSN .... Religious Program Specialist Seaman [*Navy rating*] (DNAB)
RPSP .... RADAR Programmable Signal Processor
RPSP .... Reference Preparation for Serum Proteins (DMAA)
RPS-PL........ Registered Publications Section - Personnel Library [*Navy*]
RPSS .... Ryukyu Philatelic Specialist Society (EA)
RPST .... Reaction Products Separator Tank [*Nuclear energy*] (NRCH)
RPST .... Recombinant Porcine Somatotropin
RPSTL .... Repair Parts and Special Tools List [*Army*] (AABC)
RPT.............. Congregation Sons of Israel and David, Temple Beth-El, Providence, RI [*Library symbol Library of Congress*] (LCLS)
RPT.............. Raluana Point [*New Britain*] [*Seismograph station code, US Geological Survey*] (SEIS)
RPT.............. Ramco Gershenson Properties Trust [*NYSE symbol*] (SAG)
RPT.............. Ramco-Gershenson Prop Tr [*NYSE symbol*] (TTSB)
RPT.............. Rapid Pull Through [*Gastroenterology*]
RPT.............. Rassemblement du Peuple Togolais [*Rally of the Togolese People*] [*Political party*] (PPW)
RPT.............. Reactor for Physical and Technical Investigations [*Former USSR Nuclear energy*]
RPT.............. Reactor Plant Test (DNAB)
RPT.............. Recirculation Pump Trip [*Nuclear energy*] (NRCH)
RPT.............. Recruit Performance Test (OA)
RPT.............. Reference Point Tracking
RPT.............. Registered Physical Therapist
RPT.............. Regular Public Transport (ADA)
RPT.............. Relative Prime Transform
RPT.............. Repair Parts Transporter (MCD)
RPT.............. Repeat (AAG)
rpt.............. Repeat [*International telex abbreviation and wire-service jargon*] (WDMC)
RPT.............. Repeat [*International telex abbreviation and wire-service jargon*] (WDMC)
RPT.............. Reply Paid Telegram
RPT.............. Report
RPT.............. Report (WDMC)
RPT.............. Reporting Time [*Filmmaking*] (WDMC)
RPT.............. Reprint
RPT.............. Request Programs Termination [*Computer science*]
RPT.............. Resident Provisioning Team [*NASA*]
RPT.............. Rocket-Powered Target
RPT.............. Rocket Propulsion Technician [*Air Force*]
RPT.............. Rotary Power Transformer
RPT.............. Rudder Pedal Transducer (NASA)
RPTA .... Rudder Pedal Transducer Assembly (NASA)
RPTC .... Relative Priority Test Circuit (MHDI)
RPTC .... Repeating Coil (MSA)
RPTD .... Repeated
RPTD .... Reported
RPTD .... Reprinted (WGA)
RPTD .... Ruptured
RPTF............ Republican Presidential Task Force (EA)
RPTF............ Rotatable Porro-Mirror Test Fixture
RPTL............ Real Property Tax Law [*New York, NY A publication*]
RPTLC .... Reverse Phase Thin-Layer Chromatography
RPTN .... Repetition (AAG)
RPTP .... Receptor Protein Tyrosine Phosphatase [*Biochemistry*]
RPTR .... Repeater (MSA)
RPTS .... Reactor Plant Test Section (DNAB)
RPTS .... Roadway-Powered Transporter System [*Experimental vehicle*]
RPTSO .... Reactor Plant Test Support Organization (DNAB)
RPU .... RADAR Prediction Uncertainty
RPU .... Radio Phone Unit [*Navy*]
RPU .... Radio Propagation Unit [*Army*] (MCD)
RPU .... Railway Patrolmen's International Union [*Later, BRAC*] (EA)
RPU .... Receiver Processor Unit [*Electronics*]
RPU .... Rectifier Power Unit
RPU .... Regional Planning Unit (OICC)
RPU .... Regional Processing Unit
RPU .... Registered Publication Unit
RPU .... Release Program Unit (DWSG)
RPU .... Remote Pickup Unit
RPU .... Remote Processing Unit (KSC)
RPU .... Retention Pending Use [*Air Force*]
RPU .... Retropubic Urethropexy [*Gynecology*] (DAVI)
RPU .... Rotatable Pool Unit (DNAB)
RPUA........... Aparri, Cagayan [*Philippines*] [*ICAO location identifier*] (ICLI)
RPUB........... Baguio, Benguet [*Philippines*] [*ICAO location identifier*] (ICLI)
RPUC........... Cabanatuan, Nueva Ecija [*Philippines*] [*ICAO location identifier*] (ICLI)
RPUC........... Reprint under Consideration [*Publishing*]
RPUD........... Daet, Camarines Norte [*Philippines*] [*ICAO location identifier*] (ICLI)
RPUE........... Lucena, Quezon [*Philippines*] [*ICAO location identifier*] (ICLI)
RPUF........... Floridablanca Air Base, Pampanga [*Philippines*] [*ICAO location identifier*] (ICLI)
RPUG........... Lingayen, Pangasinan [*Philippines*] [*ICAO location identifier*] (ICLI)
RPUH........... San Jose, Occidental Mindoro [*Philippines*] [*ICAO location identifier*] (ICLI)
RPUI............ Iba, Zambales [*Philippines*] [*ICAO location identifier*] (ICLI)
RPUJ............ Castillejos, Zambales [*Philippines*] [*ICAO location identifier*] (ICLI)
RPUK........... Calapan, Oriental Mindoro [*Philippines*] [*ICAO location identifier*] (ICLI)
RPUL........... Lipa/Fernando Air Base, Batangas [*Philippines*] [*ICAO location identifier*] (ICLI)
RPUM.......... Mamburao, Occidental Mindoro [*Philippines*] [*ICAO location identifier*] (ICLI)
RPUN........... Naga, Camarines Sur [*Philippines*] [*ICAO location identifier*] (ICLI)
RPUO........... Basco, Batanes Island [*Philippines*] [*ICAO location identifier*] (ICLI)
RPUP........... Jose Panganiban/PIM, Camarines Norte [*Philippines*] [*ICAO location identifier*] (ICLI)
RPUQ........... Vigan, Ilocos Sur [*Philippines*] [*ICAO location identifier*] (ICLI)
RPUR........... Baler, Aurora Sub-Province [*Philippines*] [*ICAO location identifier*] (ICLI)
RPUS........... San Fernando, La Union [*Philippines*] [*ICAO location identifier*] (ICLI)
RPUT........... Tuguegarao, Cagayan [*Philippines*] [*ICAO location identifier*] (ICLI)
RPUU........... Bulan, Sorsogon [*Philippines*] [*ICAO location identifier*] (ICLI)
RPUV........... Virac, Catanduanes [*Philippines*] [*ICAO location identifier*] (ICLI)
RPUW.......... Marinduque/Gasan, Marinduque [*Philippines*] [*ICAO location identifier*] (ICLI)
RPUX........... Plaridel, Bulacan [*Philippines*] [*ICAO location identifier*] (ICLI)
RPUY........... Cauayan, Isabela [*Philippines*] [*ICAO location identifier*] (ICLI)
RPUZ........... Bagabag, Neuva Viscaya [*Philippines*] [*ICAO location identifier*] (ICLI)
RPV .... Reactor Pressure Vessel [*Nuclear energy*] (NRCH)
RPV .... Real Program Value (CAAL)
RPV .... Recorder Processor Viewer
RPV .... Reduced Product Verification [*DoD*]
RPV .... Remotely Piloted Vehicle [*Aircraft*]
RPV .... Remote Positioning Valve
RPV .... Reserve Personnel Navy (DOMA)
RPV .... Residual Pressure Valve [*Automotive engineering*]
RPV .... Rhopalosiphum padi Virus
RPV .... Right Pulmonary Vein [*Medicine*]
RPV .... Rinderpest Virus
RPV .... Roadway Powered Vehicle [*Automotive engineering*]
RPV .... United States Veterans Administration Hospital, Davis Park, Providence, RI [*Library symbol Library of Congress*] (LCLS)
RPVA........... Tacloban/Daniel Z. Romualdez, Leyte [*Philippines*] [*ICAO location identifier*] (ICLI)
RPVB........... Bacolod, Negros Occidental [*Philippines*] [*ICAO location identifier*] (ICLI)
RPVC........... Calbayog, Western Samar [*Philippines*] [*ICAO location identifier*] (ICLI)
RPVD........... Dumaguete/Sibulan Negros Oriental [*Philippines*] [*ICAO location identifier*] (ICLI)
RPVE........... Caticlan, Aklan [*Philippines*] [*ICAO location identifier*] (ICLI)
RPVF........... Catarman, Northern Samar [*Philippines*] [*ICAO location identifier*] (ICLI)
RPVG........... Guiuan, Eastern Samar [*Philippines*] [*ICAO location identifier*] (ICLI)
RPVH........... Hilongos, Leyte Del Norte [*Philippines*] [*ICAO location identifier*] (ICLI)
RPVI............ Iloilo, Iloilo [*Philippines*] [*ICAO location identifier*] (ICLI)
RPVI-AIAF.... Remotely Piloted Vehicle Investigation - Adjustment of Indirect Artillery Fire
RPVI-ES....... Remotely Piloted Vehicle Investigation - Emerging Sensors (MCD)
RPVIO.......... Registered Publication Van Issuing Office [*Military*] (NVT)
RPV-IT......... Remotely Piloted Vehicle - Institutional Trainer [*Military*]
RPVK........... Kalibo, Aklan [*Philippines*] [*ICAO location identifier*] (ICLI)
RPVL........... Roxas/Del Pilar, Palawan [*Philippines*] [*ICAO location identifier*] (ICLI)
RPVM.......... Masbate [*Philippines*] [*ICAO location identifier*] (ICLI)
RPVN........... Medellin, Cebu [*Philippines*] [*ICAO location identifier*] (ICLI)
RPVNTV...... Rust Preventative
RPVO........... Ormoc, Leyte [*Philippines*] [*ICAO location identifier*] (ICLI)
RPVP........... Puerto Princesa, Palawan [*Philippines*] [*ICAO location identifier*] (ICLI)
RPVP........... Right Posterior Ventricular Preexcitation [*Medicine*] (DMAA)
RPVR........... Roxas, Capiz [*Philippines*] [*ICAO location identifier*] (ICLI)

RPVS .... San Jose De Buenavista/Antique [*Philippines*] [*ICAO location identifier*] (ICLI)
RPVT .... Relative Position Velocity Technique
RPVT .... Tagbilaran, Bohol [*Philippines*] [*ICAO location identifier*] (ICLI)
RPVX .... Remote-Piloted Vehicle Experiment
RPW .... Rawle, Penrose, and Watts' Pennsylvania Reports [*1828-40*] [*A publication*] (DLA)
RPW .... Resistance Projection Welding [*Manufacturing term*]
RPW .... Running Process Word (IAA)
RPWA .... Surallah/Allah Valley, Cotabato (South) [*Philippines*] [*ICAO location identifier*] (ICLI)
RPWB .... Buayan/General Santos, Cotabato (South) [*Philippines*] [*ICAO location identifier*] (ICLI)
RPWC .... Cotabato, North Cotabato [*Philippines*] [*ICAO location identifier*] (ICLI)
RPWD .... Davao/Francisco Bangoy International [*Philippines*] [*ICAO location identifier*] (ICLI)
RPWDA .... Retail Paint and Wallpaper Distributors of America [*Later, NDPA*]
RPWE .... Butuan, Agusan [*Philippines*] [*ICAO location identifier*] (ICLI)
RPW Foundation... Alberta Recreation, Parks & Wildlife Foundation (AC)
RPWG .... Dipolog, Zamboanga Del Norte [*Philippines*] [*ICAO location identifier*] (ICLI)
RPWI .... Ozamis, Misamis Oriental [*Philippines*] [*ICAO location identifier*] (ICLI)
RPWJ .... Jolo, Sulu [*Philippines*] [*ICAO location identifier*] (ICLI)
RPWK .... Tacurong/Kenram, Cotabato [*Philippines*] [*ICAO location identifier*] (ICLI)
RPWL .... Cagayan De Oro, Misamis Oriental [*Philippines*] [*ICAO location identifier*] (ICLI)
RPWM .... Malabang, Lanao Del Sur [*Philippines*] [*ICAO location identifier*] (ICLI)
RPWN .... Bongao/Sanga-Sanga, Sulu [*Philippines*] [*ICAO location identifier*] (ICLI)
RPWP .... Pagadian, Zamboanga Del Sur [*Philippines*] [*ICAO location identifier*] (ICLI)
RPWS .... Surigao, Surigao Del Norte [*Philippines*] [*ICAO location identifier*] (ICLI)
RPWT .... Del Monte, Bukidnon [*Philippines*] [*ICAO location identifier*] (ICLI)
RPWV .... Buenavista, Agusan [*Philippines*] [*ICAO location identifier*] (ICLI)
RPWW .... Tandag, Surigao Del Sur [*Philippines*] [*ICAO location identifier*] (ICLI)
RPWX .... Iligan, Lanao Del Norte [*Philippines*] [*ICAO location identifier*] (ICLI)
RPWY .... Malaybalay, Bukidon [*Philippines*] [*ICAO location identifier*] (ICLI)
RPWZ .... Bislig, Surigao Del Sur [*Philippines*] [*ICAO location identifier*] (ICLI)
RPX .... BAC Aircraft Ltd. [*British ICAO designator*] (FAAC)
RPX .... Roundup, MT [*Location identifier FAA*] (FAAL)
RPXC .... Tarlac (Crow Valley) [*Philippines*] [*ICAO location identifier*] (ICLI)
RPXG .... Lubang, Occidental Mindoro [*Philippines*] [*ICAO location identifier*] (ICLI)
RPXI .... Itbayat, Batanes [*Philippines*] [*ICAO location identifier*] (ICLI)
RPXJ .... Jomalig, Quezon [*Philippines*] [*ICAO location identifier*] (ICLI)
RPXM .... Fort Magsaysay, Nueva Ecija [*Philippines*] [*ICAO location identifier*] (ICLI)
RPXP .... Poro Point, La Union [*Philippines*] [*ICAO location identifier*] (ICLI)
RPXR .... Corregidor, Cavite [*Philippines*] [*ICAO location identifier*] (ICLI)
RPXT .... Alabat, Quezon [*Philippines*] [*ICAO location identifier*] (ICLI)
RPXU .... Sorsogon, Sorsogon [*Philippines*] [*ICAO location identifier*] (ICLI)
RPY .... Blythe, CA [*Location identifier FAA*] (FAAL)
RPY .... Roll, Pitch, and Yaw
RPZ .... Runway Protection Zone [*FAA*] (TAG)
RQ .... Maldives International Airlines [*ICAO designator*] (AD)
RQ .... RASD Quarterly [*American Library Association A publication*]
RQ .... Recovery Quotient [*Medicine*] (DMAA)
RQ .... Reportable Quantity [*Hazardous substance emergency response*]
R/Q .... Request for Quotation (AAG)
R/Q .... Resolver/Quantizer (IEEE)
RQ .... Respiratory Quotient [*Also, Q*] [*Physiology*]
RQA .... Recursive Queue Analyzer (IEEE)
RQAO .... Reliability and Quality Assurance Office [*NASA*]
RQBCHS .... Royal Queensland Bush Children's Health Scheme [*Australia*]
RQBE .... Relational Query-by-Example [*Computer interface*] [*FoxPro*] (PCM)
RQC .... RADAR Quality Control
RQC .... Receiving Quality Control (IAA)
RQC .... Reliability and Quality Control (MCD)
RQCL .... Request Clearance [*Aviation*] (FAAC)
RQD .... Raised Quarter Deck [*of a ship*] (DS)
RQD .... Rock Quality Designation [*Mining technology*] [*Nuclear energy*] (NRCH)
RQDP .... Request, Quandary and Deferment Plan
RQE .... Relative Quantum Efficiency (OA)
RQE .... Responsive Quantum Efficiency
RQG .... Reduced Quantity Generator (ERG)
RQGC .... Royal Queensland Golf Club [*Australia*]
RQI .... Rayleigh Quotient Iteration
RQIAC .... Requires Immediate Action (NOAA)
RQL .... Reference Quality Level (IEEE)
RQL .... Rejectable Quality Level
RQLTA .... Royal Queensland Lawn Tennis Association [*Australia*]
RQM .... Ride Quality Meter [*Automotive testing*]
RQMC .... Regimental Quartermaster-Corporal [*British*]
RQMD .... Richmond Quartermaster Depot [*Virginia*] [*Merged with Defense General Supply Center*]
RQMNTS .... Requirements (FAAC)
RQMS .... Regimental Quartermaster-Sergeant [*British*]
RQMT .... Requirement (AFM)
RQN .... Radial Quantum Number
RQN .... Requisition (AFM)
RQO .... River Quality Objective [*British*] (DCTA)
RQOF .... Request on File (FAAC)
RQP .... Request Flight Plan [*Aviation*] (DA)
RQP .... Resistor Qualification Program
RQPP .... Request Present Position [*Aviation*] (FAAC)
RQQPRI .... Recommended Qualitative and Quantitative Personnel Requirements Information [*Military*] (MCD)
RQR .... Require (AAG)
RQR .... Requirement (IAA)
RQRD .... Required
RQRMNT .... Requirement
RQS .... Rate Quoting System
RQS .... Ready Qualified for Standby [*Military*]
RQS .... Request Supplementary Flight Plan Message [*Aviation code*]
RQS .... River Quality Standard [*British*] (DCTA)
RQT .... Reenlistment Qualification Test [*Military*] (MCD)
RQT .... Reliability Qualification Test (CAAL)
RQT .... Resistor Qualification Test
RQTAO .... Request Time and Altitude Over [*Aviation*] (FAAC)
RQTO .... Request Travel Order (NOAA)
RQTP .... Resistor Qualification Test Program
R/QTR .... Rear Quarter [*Automotive engineering*]
RQTS .... Requirements (KSC)
RQTV .... Requirements Volatility
RQUS .... Remote Query Update System [*Computer science*]
RQX .... Air Engiadina [*Switzerland ICAO designator*] (FAAC)
RQY .... Elkins, WV [*Location identifier FAA*] (FAAL)
RQY .... Relative Quantum Yield
RQZ .... Huntsville, AL [*Location identifier FAA*] (FAAL)
RR .... Pike and Fischer's Radio Regulations [*A publication*] (DLA)
RR .... Radiation Reaction [*Cells*] [*Medicine*]
RR .... Radiation-Resistant
RR .... Radiation Response
RR .... Radiation Retinopathy [*Ophthalmology*]
R/R .... Radio and RADAR
RR .... Radio Range
RR .... Radioreceptor [*Assay method*] [*Clinical chemistry*]
RR .... Radio Receptor (IAA)
RR .... Radio Recognition
RR .... Radio Regulations
RR .... Radio Relay (CINC)
RR .... Radio Research
rr .... Ragged Right [*Typography*] (BARN)
RR .... Railroad
RR .... Railroad
RR .... Raised Ranch [*Architecture*] (BARN)
RR .... Rand Rifles [*British military*] (DMA)
RR .... Range Rate (NASA)
RR .... Range Recorder [*NASA*] (IAA)
RR .... Rapid Rectilinear
RR .... Rarely Reversed [*Decisions in law*]
rr .... Rarissime [*Very Rarely*] [*Latin*] (GPO)
RR .... Raritan River Rail Road Co. [*AAR code*]
RR .... Rated Radius [*Automotive engineering*]
RR .... Rate Ratio
RR .... Rate Rebate [*British*]
RR .... Rattus Rattus [*The ship or black rat*]
RR .... Readiness Region [*Military*]
RR .... Readiness Review (KSC)
RR .... Readout and Relay
RR .... Ready Reckoner (DGA)
RR .... Ready Reference
RR .... Rear (AABC)
RR .... Rear Engine, Rear Drive [*Automotive engineering*]
RR .... Receive Ready [*Computer science*] (IEEE)
RR .... Receiver Room [*Navy*] (CAAL)
RR .... Receiving Report (AAG)
RR .... Recipient Rights
RR .... Recoilless Rifle
RR .... Recommended for Re-Engagement [*British*]
RR .... Record Rarities [*Record label*]
R/R .... Record/Retirement
R/R .... Record/Retransmit (IEEE)
RR .... Recovery Reliability (MCD)
RR .... Recovery Room
RR .... Recruit Roll [*Navy*]
RR .... Recurrence Rate
RR .... Rediscount Rate
RR .... Red Reflex [*Ophthalmology*] (DAVI)
RR .... Redstone Resources, Inc. [*Toronto Stock Exchange symbol*]
RR .... Reduced Range
RR .... Redundancy Reduction (AAG)
RR .... Reentry Range
RR .... Reference Receiver
RR .... Reference Register [*Computer science*]
RR .... Reflectors [*JETDS nomenclature*] [*Military*] (CET)
RR .... Regional Railroad
RR .... Registered Representative [*Wall Street stock salesman*]
RR .... Register to Register (MCD)
RR .... Register-to-Register Instruction (IAA)
RR .... Register-to-Register Operation (IAA)
RR .... Regular Respirations [*Medicine*] (MEDA)
RR .... Regular Respirations [*Medicine*] (DAVI)
RR .... Regular Rhythm [*Cardiology*] (DAVI)

RR .... Rehabilitation Record
RR .... Relative Rank
RR .... Relative Response
RR .... Relative Risk [*Medicine*]
RR .... Relay Rack [*Telecommunications*] (TEL)
RR .... Relief Radii (MSA)
RR .... Religious Roundtable (EA)
RR .... Remington Rand [*Commercial firm*] (NADA)
RR .... Removal-Replacement
RR .... Rendezvous RADAR [*NASA*]
RR .... Renegotiation Regulations
RR .... Renin Release [*Endocrinology*] (MAE)
RR .... Rent Regulation (Office of Rent Stabilization) [*Economic Stabilization Agency*] [*A publication*] (DLA)
R/R .... Repair or Replacement
R/R .... Repair/Rebuild (MCD)
RR .... Repeatedly Reactive
RR .... Repetition Rate
RR .... Report Reaching [*ICAO*] (FAAC)
RR .... Republic at Romania (BARN)
RR .... Required Reserves
RR .... Requirements Review [*NASA*] (NASA)
RR .... Requisition Restriction Code (DNAB)
RR .... Reroute [*Telecommunications*] (TEL)
RR .... Research Reactor [*Nuclear energy*] (IAA)
RR .... Research Report
RR .... Reservatis Reservandis [*With All Reserve*] [*Latin*]
RR .... Reserve Regiment [*British military*] (DMA)
RR .... Residue Register (IAA)
RR .... Resonance Raman
RR .... Resource Report
RR .... Respiratory Rate [*Medicine*]
RR .... Response Rate (DAVI)
RR .... Response Regulator [*Biochemistry*]
RR .... Responsible Receiver
RR .... Retired Reserve [*Military*]
RR .... Retro-Rocket [*Army*] (AABC)
RR .... Return Rate (IEEE)
RR .... Return Register
RR .... Revenue Release [*A publication*] (DLA)
RR .... Reverse Recovery [*Electronics*]
RR .... Reverse Reduction (DS)
RR .... Review for Religious [*A publication*] (BRI)
RR .... Revised Reports [*Legal*] [*British*]
RR .... Revision Record (MSA)
RR .... Rhodesia Regiment [*British military*] (DMA)
RR .... Rhymney Railway [*Wales*]
RR .... Ridge Regression [*Statistics*]
RR .... Rifle Range
RR .... Right Rear
RR .... Right Reverend [*Of an abbot, bishop, or monsignor*]
RR .... Rights Reserved
RR .... Rigid-Rotor [*Calculations*]
RR .... Risk Ratio
RR .... Risk Reduction [*Branch*] [*Marine science*] (OSRA)
RR .... Risk Reduction [*Branch*] [*Forecast Systems Laboratory*] (USDC)
RR .... Riva-Rocci Sphygmomanometer [*Medicine*] (DMAA)
RR .... Rodman&Renshaw Cap [*NYSE symbol*] (TTSB)
RR .... Rodman & Renshaw Capital Group [*NYSE symbol*] (SPSG)
RR .... Roemische Religions-Geschichte [*A publication*] (OCD)
RR .... Rolling Resistance [*Automotive engineering*]
RR .... Roll Radius (MCD)
RR .... Roll Roofing (AAG)
RR .... Rolls-Royce [*Automobile*]
RR .... Ronald Reagan [*US president, 1911-*]
RR .... Root Rot [*Plant pathology*]
RR .... Rough Riders [*The City of London Yeomanry*] [*Military unit*] [*British*]
RR .... Round Robin (IEEE)
RR .... Routine Message Precedence [*Telecommunications*] (ADDR)
RR .... Routine Relay (KSC)
RR .... Royal Air Force [*ICAO designator*] (AD)
RR .... Running Reverse
R/R .... Run Round [*Typography*] (DGA)
RR .... Rural Resident (OICC)
RR .... Rural Route
RR .... Rush and Run (WDAA)
RR .... Rush Release
RR .... Ruthenium Red [*Inorganic chemistry*] (OA)
RR .... Very Rare [*Numismatics*]
RRA .... Dallas-Fort Worth, TX [*Location identifier FAA*] (FAAL)
RRA .... Race Relations Act [*1976*] [*British*] (DCTA)
RRA .... RADAR Recording and Analysis Equipment (DA)
RRA .... Radiation Research Associates, Inc. (NRCH)
RRA .... Radioreceptor Assay [*Clinical chemistry*]
RRA .... Radio Relay Aircraft (CET)
RRA .... Railroad Retirement Act (GFGA)
RRA .... RAM [*Reliability, Availability, and Maintainablity*] Rationale Annex [*Army*]
RRA .... Ranger Regimental Association (EA)
RRA .... Ready Reserve Agreement [*Navy*] (DOMA)
RRA .... Reclamation Reform Act [*1982*]
RRA .... Record Retention Agreement [*IRS*]
RRA .... Redmond, R. A., Los Angeles CA [*STAC*]
RRA .... Registered Record Administrator [*American Medical Record Association*] [*Medicine*]
RRA .... Religious Research Association (EA)
RRA .... Remote Record Address
RRA .... Renal Renin Activity [*Nephrology*] (DAVI)
RRA .... Reserve Recognition Accounting [*Securities and Exchange Commission*]
RRA .... Resident Research Associate
RRA .... Revenue Reconciliation Act of 1990 (WYGK)
RRA .... Rubber Reclaimers Association [*Later, NARI*] (EA)
RRA .... Rubber Recyclers Association (EA)
RRAC .... Race Relations Advisory Committee [*Trades Union Congress*] [*British*] (DCTA)
RRAC .... Reactor Review and Audit Committee [*Oak Ridge National Laboratory*]
RRAC .... Regional Resources Advisory Committee [*Army*] (AABC)
RRAD .... Red River Army Depot [*Texas*] (AABC)
RRAD .... Roll Ratio Adjust Device (MCD)
RRAF .... Ready Reserve of the Armed Forces
RRAF .... Royal Rhodesian Air Force
RRAM .... Repetitive and Rapid Alternating Movements [*Neurology*] (DAVI)
RR & C .... Records, Reports, and Control (AFM)
RR & Can Cas... Railway and Canal Cases [*England*] [*A publication*] (DLA)
RR & Cn Cas... Railway and Canal Cases [*1835-54*] [*A publication*] (DLA)
RR & D .... Rehabilitation Research and Development Program [*Veterans Administration*] (GFGA)
RR & D .... Reparations, Removal, and Demolition [*Section*] [*Industry Branch, US Military Government, Germany*]
RR & E .... Round, Regular, and Equal [*With reference to pupils of eyes*]
RRAP .... Residential Rehabilitation Assistance Program [*Canada*]
RRAR .... ROM Return Address Register
RRAS .... Radiofrequency Resonance Absorption (MCD)
RRAS .... Routing and Remote Access Service [*Microsoft Corp.*]
RRAS .... Routing and Remote Access Service [*Computer science*]
RRB .... Race Relations Board [*Military*] (VNW)
RRB .... RADAR Reflective Balloon
RRB .... Radiographers Registration Board [*Tasmania, Australia*]
RRB .... Radio Range Beacon (IAA)
RRB .... Radio Research Board (DEN)
RRB .... Railroad Retirement Board
RRB .... Rapid Response Bibliography Service [*Information retrieval*] (AEBS)
RRB .... Regular Reenlistment Bonus [*Military*]
RRB .... Requirements Review Board (SSD)
RRB .... R. R. Bowker Co. [*Publisher*]
RRB .... Rubber Reserve Board [*of the Reconstruction Finance Corp.*]
RR-BB .... Rayon-Rayon Bias-Belted (PDAA)
RRBC .... Rat Red Blood Cell
RRBFC .... Red River Boys Fan Club [*Inactive*] (EA)
RRBLB .... United States Railroad Retirement Board. Law Bulletin [*A publication*] (DLA)
RRBN .... Round Robin [*Aviation*] (FAAC)
RRB Rept..... Radio Research Board. Report. [*Australia*] [*A publication*]
RRC .... RADAR Return Code
RRC .... Radiation Recorder Controller (NRCH)
RRC .... Radiation Resistance Cable
RRC .... Radio Receptor Co.
RRC .... Radio Relay Center (NATG)
RRC .... Radio Research Co.
RRC .... Railroad Record Club [*Commercial firm*] (EA)
RRC .... Rainy River Community College, International Falls, MN [*OCLC symbol*] (OCLC)
RRC .... Ravenroc Resources Ltd. [*Vancouver Stock Exchange symbol*]
RRC .... Reactor Recirculation Cooling [*Nuclear energy*] (NRCH)
RRC .... Readiness Reportable Code (DNAB)
RRC .... Receiving Report Change (AAG)
RRC .... Recognized Rescue Center [*Navy*] (DNAB)
RRC .... Reconstructionist Rabbinical College [*Pennsylvania*]
RRC .... Recreation Resources Center [*University of Wisconsin*] [*Research center*] (RCD)
RRC .... Recruit Reception Center
RRC .... Red River Community College [*UTLAS symbol*]
RRC .... Reentry Rate Command [*NASA*]
RRC .... Refractories Research Center [*Ohio State University*] [*Research center*] (RCD)
RRC .... Refugee Resource Center [*Defunct*] (EA)
RRC .... Regional Reporting Centers [*Navy*] (DOMA)
RRC .... Regional Resource Center
RRC .... Regional Response Center [*Environmental Protection Agency*] (EG)
RRC .... Regional Review Consultants [*American Occupational Therapy Association*]
RRC .... Regular Route Carrier
R/RC .... Removal/Recertification
RRC .... Reporting Requirements Code (DNAB)
RRC .... Report Review Committee [*National Academy of Sciences*]
RRC .... Reports of Rating Cases [*Legal*] [*British*]
RRC .... Requirements Review Committee [*Navy*]
RRC .... Research Resources Center [*University of Illinois at Chicago*] [*Research center*] (RCD)
RRC .... Residency Review Committee [*Medicine*]
RRC .... Resuscitation Research Center [*University of Pittsburgh*] [*Research center*] (RCD)
RRC .... Retrograde River Crossing (MCD)
RRC .... Retrovirus Research Center [*Veterans Administration Medical Center*] [*Baltimore, MD*]
RRC .... Rheology Research Center [*University of Wisconsin - Madison*] [*Research center*] (RCD)
RRC .... Rigid Raiding Craft [*British military*] (DMA)

RRC Road Runners Club of America
RRC Rocket Research Corp. (MCD)
RRC Rodale Research Center [*Horticulture*]
RRC Rollin' Rock Club (EA)
RRC Roll Ratio Controller (MCD)
RRC Roof Research Center [*Oak Ridge, TN*] [*Oak Ridge National Laboratory*] [*Department of Energy*] (GRD)
RRC Routine Respiratory Care [*Medicine*]
RRC Royal Red Cross [*British*]
RRC Rubber Reserve Co. [*Dissolved, 1935, functions transferred to Reconstruction Finance Corporation*]
RRC Rubber Reserve Committee [*Navy*]
RRC Rural Referral Center [*Health care*]
RRC Russell Research Center [*Department of Agriculture*]
RRC Russian Research Center [*Harvard University*] [*Research center*] (RCD)
RRC Ryde's Rating Cases [*A publication*] (DLA)
RRCA Rhinelander Rabbit Club of America (EA)
RRCA Road Runners Club of America (EA)
RRCAH Roll Rate Command/Attitude Hold (MCD)
RRCC Reduced Rate Contribution Clause [*Insurance*]
RRCCC Regional Recreation and Conservation Consultative Committee [*Thames Water Authority*] [*British*]
RRCEF Redwood Records Cultural and Educational Fund (EA)
RRCEM Residency Review Committee for Emergency Medicine (EA)
RRCM Roberts Radio Current Meter (NOAA)
RRCN Receiving Report Change Notice (AAG)
RRCO Radio Research Coordination Officer [*Air Force*]
RRCOTAAOSOCOTWAOS Rollin' Rock Club of Texas and Any Other State or Country of the World and OuterSpace
RR Cr R Revised Reports, Criminal Rulings [*1862-75*] [*India*] [*A publication*] (DLA)
RRCS Railroad Communication System
RRCS Reentry RADAR Cross Section
RRCS Revenue Receipts Control Sheets [*IRS*]
RRCU Remote Range Control Unit (MCD)
RRCUS Rhodesian Ridgeback Club of the US (EA)
RRD Reactor Radiation Division [*National Institute of Standards and Technology*]
RRD Reactor Research and Development
RRD Receive, Record, Display
RRD Reliability Requirements Directive
RRD Replacement Regulating Detachment [*Army*]
RRD Requisition Received Date [*Bell System*] (TEL)
RRD Resonant Reed Decoder
RRD Retendering Receipt Day (NRCH)
RRD Roosevelt Roads [*Puerto Rico*] [*Seismograph station code, US Geological Survey*] (SEIS)
RRD Route/Route Destination [*Telecommunications*] (TEL)
RRDA Rendezvous Retrieval, Docking, and Assembly [*of space vehicle or orbital station*] [*NASA*] (AAG)
RRDA Repetitive Report Distribution Audit (AAG)
RRDB Research Results Data Base [*Department of Agriculture*] [*Information service or system*] (IID)
RRDC Railroad Data Center [*Association of American Railroad*] (PDAA)
RRDC Road Racing Drivers Club
RRDE RADAR Research and Development Establishment (IAA)
RRDE Radio Research and Development Establishment (MCD)
RRDE Rotating Ring Disk Electrode
RRDECA Roy Rogers - Dale Evans Collectors Association (EA)
RRDF RO/RO [*Roll-On/Roll-Off*] Discharge Facility [*Army*] (RDA)
RRDFCS Redundant Reconfigurable Digital Flight Control System (MCD)
RRDO Register of Rivers Discharging into the Oceans [*United Nations Environment Programme*] (MSC)
RRDR Raw RADAR Data Recorder
RRDS Relative Record Data Set
RRDTRL Resistor-Resistor Diode Transistor Logic (IAA)
RRDU Recreation Research Demonstration Unit (RDA)
RRE Marree [*Australia Airport symbol Obsolete*] (OAG)
RRE Race-Relations Education Program [*Military*] (DNAB)
RRE RADAR Research Establishment [*British*]
RRE Radiation Related Eosinophilia [*Medicine*] (AAMN)
RRE Railroad Enthusiasts (EA)
RRE Raloxifene Response Element [*Biochemistry*]
RRE Range Rate Error
RRE Ras Responsive Element [*Genetics*]
RRE Receive Reference Equivalent [*Telecommunications*] (TEL)
RRE Reg Resources Corp. [*Vancouver Stock Exchange symbol*]
RRE Rolls-Royce Enthusiasts (EA)
RRE Roster of Required Events
RRE Royal RADAR Establishment [*British Research center*]
RREA Rendezvous RADAR Electronics Assembly [*NASA*] (MCD)
R/REA Rural/Regional Education Association (AEE)
RREAC Royal RADAR Establishment Automatic Computer (IAA)
RREAS Race Relations Employment Advisory Service [*British*]
RREB Race-Relations Education Board [*Military*] (DNAB)
RREC Reading Research and Education Center [*Champaign, IL*] [*Department of Education*] (GRD)
RREC Rehabilitation Record
RREC Rice Research and Extension Center [*University of Arkansas*] [*Research center*] (RCD)
RREF Resting Radionuclide Ejection Fraction [*Medicine*] (DAVI)
RREL Risk Reduction Engineering Laboratory
RR/EO Race Relations/Equal Opportunity [*Military*] (AABC)
RRep Records Repository [*Air Force*] (AFM)
RREP Reed Reference Electronic Publishing
R_{req} Required Resistance (IDOE)
RRESA Registered Real Estate Salespersons' Association [*Australia*]
RR et AC Rosea Rubeae et Aureae Crucis [*The Order of the Rose of Ruby and the Cross of Gold*]
RREU Rendezvous RADAR Electronics Unit [*NASA*] (MCD)
RRev Records Review [*Air Force*] (AFM)
RRF Racing Research Fund [*Defunct*] (EA)
RRF Ragged Red Fibers [*Muscle pathology*]
RRF Rapid Reaction Forces [*Army*] (AABC)
RRF Raptor Research Foundation (EA)
RRF Reading Reform Foundation (EA)
RRF Ready Reserve Fleet
RRF Ready Reserve Force [*Military*]
RRF Realty Refund SBI [*NYSE symbol*] (TTSB)
RRF Realty Refund Trust SBI [*NYSE symbol*] (SPSG)
RRF Reconnaissance Reporting Facility
RRF Red Resistance Front [*Netherlands Political party*]
RRF Reed Reactor Facility [*Reed College*] [*Research center*] (RCD)
RRF Regional Relay Facility (DNAB)
RRF Rehabilitation Research Foundation (EA)
RRF Residual Renal Function [*Medicine*] (DMAA)
RRF Resonant Reed Filter
RRF Resonant Ring Filter [*Computer science*] (IAA)
RRF Retirement Register File [*Computer science*]
RRF Revised Recommended Findings
RRF Rift-Rift-Fracture [*Geology*]
RRF Riot Relief Fund (EA)
RRF Royal Regiment of Fusiliers [*Military unit*] [*British*]
RRFC Robert Redford Fan Club (EA)
RRFC Robin Right Fan Club (EA)
RRfd Risk Reference Dose (GNE)
RRFO Rhine River Field Organization [*Post-World War II*]
RRFS Range Rate Frequency Synthesizer
RRFT Right Rear Fluid Temperature [*Automotive engineering*]
RRFWG Ready Reserve Force Working Group (DOMA)
RRG Point Mugu, CA [*Location identifier FAA*] (FAAL)
RRG RADAR Range Gate
RRG Rental Rehabilitation Grant [*Department of Housing and Urban Development*] (GFGA)
RRG Requirements Review Group [*Air Staff*] [*Air Force*] (MCD)
RRG Research Review Group (NRCH)
RRG Resource Request Generator
RRG Restabilization Reset Generator (SAA)
RRG Rodrigues Island [*Mauritius*] [*Airport symbol*] (OAG)
RRG Roll Reference Gyro (AAG)
RRH Rural Rental Housing [*Loans*] [*Farmers Home Administration*]
RRHFF Rock and Roll Hall of Fame Foundation (EA)
RRHICMD Remote Reading High Intensity Constant Monitoring Device (IAA)
RRHPF Ronald Reagan Home Preservation Foundation (EA)
RR-HPO Rapid Recompression-High Pressure Oxygen [*Medicine*] (MAE)
RRI Barora [*Solomon Islands*] [*Airport symbol*] (OAG)
RRI Radio Republic Indonesia (IAA)
RRI Radio Republik Indonesia [*Radio network*]
RRI Range Rate Indicator
RRI Red Roof Inns [*NYSE symbol*] (TTSB)
RRI Red Roof Inns, Inc. [*NYSE symbol*] (SAG)
RRI Reference Roughness Index [*FHWA*] (TAG)
RRI Refugee Relief International (EA)
RRI Reimbursement Refund Indicator [*Military*] (AFIT)
RRI Rendezvous RADAR Indicator [*NASA*] (NASA)
RRI Reroute Inhibit [*Telecommunications*] (TEL)
RRI Resident Reactor Inspector [*Nuclear energy*] (NRCH)
RRI Revised Ring Index [*A publication*]
RRI Riverside Research Institute (MCD)
RRI Rocket Research Institute
RRI Romex Resources, Inc. [*Vancouver Stock Exchange symbol*]
RRI Rowett Research Institute [*British*] (BI)
RRI Rubber Research Institute (NADA)
RRI & StL Rockford, Rock Island & St. Louis Railroad
RRIC Race Relations Information Center [*Defunct*]
RRIC RADAR Repeater Indicator Console
RRID Reverse Radial Immunodiffusion (PDAA)
RRIF Registered Retirement Investment Fund [*Canada*]
RRIHS Regional Research Institute for Human Services [*Portland State University*] [*Research center*] (RCD)
RR-IM Office of Research and Reports, Intelligence Memoranda [*CIA*]
RRIM Reinforced Reaction Injection Molding [*Plastics technology*]
RRIN Readiness Risk Index Number (NG)
RRIPM Rapid Response Interference Prediction Model (MCD)
RRIS Radiological Release Information System (MCD)
RRIS Railroad Research Information Service [*National Academy of Sciences*] [*Defunct*]
RRIS Remote RADAR Integration Station [*Military*]
RRJE Range Remote Job Entry [*Telecommunications*] (OSI)
RRK Redaurum Red Lake Mines Ltd. [*Toronto Stock Exchange symbol*]
RRK Retaining Ring Kit
RRK Rourkela [*India*] [*Airport symbol*] (AD)
RRKM Rice, Ramsperger, Kassel, Marcus [*Developers of a theorem in chemical kinetics, designated by the initial letters of their last names*]
RRL Merrill, WI [*Location identifier FAA*] (FAAL)
RRL Rabbit Reticulocyte Lysate [*Biochemistry*]
RRL Radio Relay Link (NATG)
RRL Radio Research Laboratory

RRL .... Ralston Purina Co., Corporate Library, St. Louis, MO [*OCLC symbol*] (OCLC)

RRL .... Ranchmen's Resources Ltd. [*Toronto Stock Exchange symbol*]

RRL .... Rayleigh Radiation Law [*Physics*]

RRL .... Reference Repository Location

RRL .... Regimental Reserve Line

RRL .... Registered Record Librarian [*Medicine*]

RRL .... Reserve Retired List [*Military*]

RRL .... Road Research Laboratory [*British*]

RRL .... Rocket Research Laboratories (KSC)

RRL .... Rolls Royce Ltd. [*British ICAO designator*] (FAAC)

RRL .... Ruby Rod LASER

RRL .... Rudder Reference Line [*NASA*] (NASA)

RRL .... Runway Remaining Lights [*Aviation*]

RRL .... Ruthenium Red Staining Layer [*Biology*]

RRLC .... Radiation-Resistant Linear Circuit

RRLC .... Redwood Region Logging Conference (EA)

RRLC .... Rochester Regional Library Council [*Information service or system*] (IID)

RRLG .... Rocket, Radio, Longitudinal, Generator Powered (IAA)

RRLL .... Relative Rumble Loudness Level (DICI)

RRLR .... Road Race Lincoln Register (EA)

RRLT .... Right Rear Lining Temperature [*Automotive engineering*]

RRLTU .... Recruit Remedial Literacy Training Unit (DNAB)

RRM .... Acvila Air-Romanian Carrier [*FAA designator*] (FAAC)

RRM .... Rate of Return Method [*Insurance*]

RRM .... Rayleigh-Ritz Method [*Physics*]

RRM .... Red Resource Monitoring (MCD)

RRM .... Reliant Resources Ltd. [*Vancouver Stock Exchange symbol*]

RRM .... Renegotiated-Rate Mortgage

RRM .... Reports, Reviews, Meetings

RRM .... RNA [*Ribonucleic Acid*] Recognition Motif [*Genetics*]

RRM .... Rotation Remanent Magnetization (PDAA)

RRM .... Runaway Rotating Machine

RRMC .... Royal Roads Military College [*Royal Roads, BC*]

RRMF .... RADAR Reflectivity Measuring Facility

RRMG .... Reactor Recirculation Motor Generator (IEEE)

RRMRP .... Ready Reserve Mobilization Reinforcement Pool [*Army*]

RRMRS .... Ready Reserve Mobilization Reinforcement System [*Army*]

RRMS .... Reserve Readiness and Mobility Squadron

RRMS .... Revenue Requirements Modeling System [*Department of Energy*] (GFGA)

RRN .... Rapid Reinforcement of NATO (MCD)

RRN .... Relative Record Number [*Computer science*]

RRN .... Serra Norte [*Brazil*] [*Airport symbol*] (OAG)

rRNA .... Ribonucleic Acid, Ribosomal [*Biochemistry, genetics*]

RRNC .... Ranger Rick's Nature Club (EA)

RRND .... Right Radical Neck Dissection [*Surgery*] (DAVI)

RRNN .... Reproductive Rights National Network [*Defunct*] (EA)

RRNS .... Redundant Residue Number System (IEEE)

RRNS .... Related Returns Notification System [*IRS*]

RRO .... Recipient Rights Officer

RRO .... Regimental Reserve Officer (ADA)

RRO .... Renegotiation Regional Office

RRO .... Responsible Reporting Office [*Telecommunications*] (TEL)

RRO .... Richport Resources Ltd. [*Vancouver Stock Exchange symbol*]

RROA .... Railroadians of America (EA)

RROC .... Rolls-Royce Owners' Club (EA)

RROCA .... Rolls Royce Owners' Club of Australia

RROS .... Resistive Read-Only Storage

RROSP .... Race Relations and Overseas Students Panel (AIE)

RROU .... Remote Readout Unit

RRP .... Radio Relay Pod

RRP .... Radio Ripple Proximity (IAA)

RRP .... Range Ring Profile (MCD)

RRP .... Reactor Refueling Plug (NRCH)

RRP .... Reader and Reader-Printer (PDAA)

RRP .... Ready Replacement Pilot

RRP .... Recommended Retail Price

RRP .... Recoverable Repair Parts

RRP .... Refugee Resettlement Program (MEDA)

RRP .... Regional Project Research Program (EA)

RRP .... Regular Retail Price

RRP .... Relative Refractory Period [*Medicine*]

RRP .... Relay Rack Panel

RRP .... Religious Requirements and Practices [*A publication*]

RRP .... Rental Rehabilitation Program [*Department of Housing and Urban Development*] (GFGA)

RRP .... Republican Reliance Party [*Cumhuriyetci Guven Partisi - CGP*] [*Turkey Political party*] (PPW)

RRP .... Resource Referral Program (WYGK)

RRP .... Reverse Repurchase Agreement [*Investment term*]

RRP .... Rock Hill, SC [*Location identifier FAA*] (FAAL)

RRP .... Roosevelt Roads [*Puerto Rico*] [*Seismograph station code, US Geological Survey Closed*] (SEIS)

RRP .... Rotterdam-Rhine Pipeline [*Oil*]

RRP .... Rough River Petroleum Corp. [*Vancouver Stock Exchange symbol*]

RRP .... Rudder Reference Plane [*NASA*] (NASA)

RRPA .... Relativistic Random-Phase Approximation [*Electrodynamics*]

RRPA .... Ruhr Regional Planning Authority [*Post-World War II*]

RRPB .... Retraining and Reemployment Policy Board

RRPC .... Reserve Reinforcement Processing Center [*Army*] (AABC)

RRPD .... Runway Reference Point Downwind [*Aviation*] (FAAC)

RRPE .... Union for Radical Review of Radical Political Economics [*A publication*] (EAAP)

RRPG .... Regular Right Part Grammar (IAA)

RRPI .... Relative Rod Position Indication [*Nuclear energy*] (NRCH)

RRPI .... Rotary Relative Position Indicator [*Nuclear energy*] (NRCH)

RRPL .... Recommend Repair Parts List

RRPM .... Reflective Raised Pavement Marker [*Highway design*]

RRPM .... Representatives of Radio Parts Manufacturers (IAA)

RRPP .... Reverends Peres [*Reverend Fathers*] [*French*]

RRPR .... Reduced Range Practice Rocket [*Army*]

RRPS .... Ready Reinforcement Personnel Section [*Air Force*] (AFM)

RRPS .... Ronald Reagan Philatelic Society (EA)

RRPU .... Runway Reference Point Upwind [*Aviation*] (FAAC)

RRQ .... Rock Rapids, IA [*Location identifier FAA*] (FAAL)

RRR .... Exceedingly Rare [*Numismatics*]

RRR .... RADAR Radiation Receiver

RRR .... RAF-HQSTC (Air Transport) [*British ICAO designator*] (FAAC)

RRR .... Railroad Reports [*United States*] [*A publication*] (DLA)

RRR .... Raleigh Research Reactor

RRR .... RAM [*Reliability, Availability, and Maintainability*] Rationale Report [*Army*]

RRR .... Range and Range Rate

RRR .... Range Rover Register [*An association*] (EAIO)

RRR .... Rapid Runway Repair

RRR .... Reader Railroad [*AAR code*]

RRR .... Readiness Removal Rate (DNAB)

RRR .... Readin', Ritin', and Rithmetic [*Also, 3R's*]

RRR .... Records, Racing, and Rallying [*Sporting aviation*]

RRR .... Red Red Rose [*An association Defunct*] (EA)

RRR .... Reduced Residual Radiation

RRR .... Regular Rate and Rhythm [*Cardiology*] (AAMN)

RRR .... Relay, Reporter, Responder (DWSG)

RRR .... Relief, Recovery, Reform [*Elements of the New Deal*]

RRR .... Renaissance Commun [*NYSE symbol*] (TTSB)

RRR .... Renaissance Communications Corp. [*NYSE symbol*] (SAG)

RRR .... Renin-Release Rate [*Endocrinology*] (MAE)

RRR .... Repairable Return Rate (DNAB)

RRR .... Required Rate of Return [*Finance*]

RRR .... Residual Resistance Ratio [*Metal purity*]

RRR .... Resistor-Reactor Rectifier

RRR .... Resource Rent Royalty

RRR .... Resource Requirements Request [*Military*] (MCD)

RRR .... Resurfacing, Restoration, and Rehabilitation [*US Federal Highway Administration*]

RRR .... Rework Removal Rate

RRR .... Riverton Resources Corp. [*Vancouver Stock Exchange symbol*]

RRR .... Royal Rhodesia Regiment [*British military*] (DMA)

RRR .... Rum, Romanism, and Rebellion [*Phrase coined during the Presidential campaign of 1884 to describe the Democratic party*]

RRR .... Run-Time Reduction Ratio (MHDB)

RRR .... University of Rochester, Rochester, NY [*OCLC symbol*] (OCLC)

RRRC .... Regulatory Requirements Review Committee [*Nuclear energy*] (NRCH)

RRRE .... RADAR Range-Rate Error

RR Rep .... Railroad Reports [*A publication*] (DLA)

RRRLC .... Rochester Regional Research Library Council [*Rochester, NY*] [*Library network*]

RRRN .... Round, Regular, and React Normally [*Referring to the pupils of the eyes*] (DAVI)

RRRPD .... Reseau de Radio Rurale des Pays en Developpement [*Developing Countries Farm Radio Network*] (EAIO)

RRRR .... Railroad Revitalization and Regulatory Reform Act [*1976*]

RRRRR .... Receipt [*British naval signaling*]

RRRRRR .... Remedial Readin', Remedial Ritin', and Remedial Rithmetic [*Also, 6R's*] [*Humorous interpretation of the three R's*]

RRRS .... Route Relief Requirements System [*Telecommunications*] (TEL)

RRRV .... Rate of Rise of Restriking Voltage (IEEE)

RRS .... Bedford Rae [*British ICAO designator*] (FAAC)

RRS .... Dothan, AL [*Location identifier FAA*] (FAAL)

RRS .... RADAR Ranging System

RRS .... Radiation Research Society (EA)

RRS .... Radio Receiver Set

RRS .... Radio Recording Spectrophotometer

RRS .... Radio Relay Squadron

RRS .... Radio Relay Station

RRS .... Radio Relay System

RRS .... Radio Remote Set (CAAL)

RRS .... Radio Research Station [*British*]

RRS .... Range Rate Search (MCD)

RRS .... Rational Recovery Systems (EA)

RRS .... Reaction Research Society (EA)

RRS .... Reactor Recirculating System (NRCH)

RRS .... Reactor Refueling System (NRCH)

RRS .... Reactor Regulating System (NRCH)

RRS .... Readiness Reportable Status (NVT)

RRS .... Ready Reportable Status (MCD)

RRS .... Reconnaissance Reporting System

RRS .... Red River Settlement [*Canada*]

RRS .... Reed Relay Scanner

RRS .... Regulatory Reform Staff [*Environmental Protection Agency*] (EPA)

RRS .... Relay Radio Subsystem [*NASA*]

RRS .... Remaining Radiation Service (NATG)

RRS .... Reminder of Route Same (SAA)

RRS .... Remington's Revised Statutes [*A publication*] (DLA)

RRS .... Rendezvous RADAR System [*NASA*] (MCD)

RRS .... Required Response Spectrum (IEEE)

RRS .... Research Referral Service [*International Federation for Documentation*] [*Information service or system*] (IID)
RRS .... Resin Regeneration Subsystem [*Nuclear energy*] (NRCH)
RRS .... Resonance Raman Scattering [*Spectroscopy*]
RRS .... Resonance Raman Spectroscopy
RRS .... Resources and Referral Services (OICC)
RRS .... Restraint Release System (KSC)
RRS .... Retired Reserve Section
RRS .... Retransmission Request Signal [*Telecommunications*] (TEL)
RRS .... Retrograde Rocket System
RRS .... Revised Statutes of Nebraska, Reissue
RRS .... Ribs of Reinforced Shotcrete [*Engineering*]
RRS .... River and Rainfall Station [*National Weather Service*] (NOAA)
RRS .... Roll Rate Sensor
RRS .... Roo Rat Society (EA)
RRS .... Roros [*Norway*] [*Airport symbol*] (OAG)
RRS .... Royal Research Ship [*British*]
RRSA .... Radio Republic South Africa (IAA)
RRSCS .... Rate Stabilization and Control System (MCD)
RRSM .... Rough Riding Sergeant-Major [*British military*] (DMA)
RRSP .... Registered Retirement Savings Plan [*Canada*]
RRSQ .... Radio Relay Squadron [*Military*] (IAA)
RRSSM .... Rough Riding Staff Sergeant-Major [*British military*] (DMA)
RR sta .... Railroad Station (VRA)
RRSTRAF .... Ready Reserve Strategic Army Forces
RRSV .... Red Ringspot Virus [*of blueberry*]
RRSV .... Rice Ragged Stunt Virus [*Plant pathology*]
RRT .... Radio Relay Terminal
RRT .... Rail Rapid Transit [*TXDOT*] (TAG)
RRT .... Railroad Retirement Tax [*IRS*]
RRT .... Railroad Transport (NATG)
RRT .... Randomized Response Technique [*Statistics*]
RRT .... Ready Round Transporter (NATG)
RRT .... Reentry Reference Time [*NASA*]
RRT .... Reflected-Reflected-Transmitted [*Wave mechanics*]
RRT .... Regional Response Team [*Environmental Protection Agency*] (EG)
RRT .... Registered Recreation Therapist
RRT .... Registered Respiratory Therapist
RRT .... Relative Retention Time
RRT .... Rendezvous RADAR Transducer [*NASA*] (NASA)
RR/T .... Rendezvous RADAR/Transponder [*NASA*] (KSC)
RRT .... Request for Review of Tooling
RRT .... Requirements Review Team
RRT .... Requisite Remedial Technology (EPA)
RRT .... Resazurin Reduction Time [*Medicine*] (MAE)
RRT .... Ring-Ring Trip [*Telecommunications*] (TEL)
RRT .... Robert Mines Ltd. [*Vancouver Stock Exchange symbol*]
RRTA .... Railroad Retirement Tax [*IRS*]
RRTD .... Rural Rehabilitation Technologies Database [*University of North Dakota*] [*Information service or system*] (IID)
RRTIS .... Renewable Resources Technical Information System [*Forest Service*]
RRTS .... Radiometer Recording Titration System [*Experimentation*]
RRTS .... Range-Rate Tracking System
RRTS .... Remote RADAR Tracking System (MHDI)
RRTTL .... Resistor-Resistor Transistor-Transistor Logic [*Computer science*] (IAA)
RRU .... Cedar Rapids, IA [*Location identifier FAA*] (FAAL)
RRU .... Radiobiological Research Unit (IEEE)
RRU .... Radio Research Unit [*Army*] (AABC)
RRU .... Remington-Rand UNIVAC
RRU .... Remote Readout Unit
RRU .... Remote Request Unit (CAAL)
RRU .... Resource Recycling Unit
RRU .... Respiratory Resistance Unit [*Medicine*] (DMAA)
RRU .... Retro-Rocket UNIVAC (MUGU)
R RUL .... Renegotiation Rulings (DLA)
RRV .... Denver, CO [*Location identifier FAA*] (FAAL)
RRV .... Raspberry Ringspot Virus [*Plant pathology*]
RRV .... Rate of Rise of Voltage [*Electronics*] (IAA)
RRV .... Remote Reconnaissance Vehicle (NITA)
RRV .... Rhesus Rotavirus [*Medicine*]
RRV .... Rotor Reentry Vehicle
RRV & W .... Red River Valley & Western Railroad [*North Dakota*]
RRVSGA .... Red River Valley Sugarbeet Growers Association (EA)
RRW .... Jacksonville, FL [*Location identifier FAA*] (FAAL)
RRW .... Radiation-Resistant Wire
RRW .... Royal Regiment of Wales [*Military unit*] [*British*]
RRWU .... Rhodesia Railway Workers' Union
RRX .... Railroad Crossing [*Telecommunications*] (TEL)
RRX .... Ronrico Explorations Ltd. [*Vancouver Stock Exchange symbol*]
RRZ .... RADAR Regulation Zone (DA)
RS .... Aeropesca [*ICAO designator*] (AD)
RS .... IEEE Reliability Society (EA)
RS .... Rabbinical School (BJA)
RS .... Rabbinical Seminary (BJA)
RS .... Rabbinic Supervisor (BJA)
RS .... Rachmaninoff Society [*Record label*]
RS .... RADAR Scanner
RS .... RADAR Scattering
RS .... RADAR Selector (MCD)
RS .... RADAR Set
RS .... RADAR Simulator (CET)
RS .... RADAR Start (CET)
RS .... Radial Sedan [*Class of racing cars*]
RS .... Radiated Susceptibility (IEEE)
RS .... Radiation Sensitive [*Physiology*]
RS .... Radiation Source (NRCH)
RS .... Radio Communication Supervisor (IAA)
RS .... Radio Duties - Special
RS .... Radio School (IAA)
RS .... Radio Set (IAA)
RS .... Radio Simulator
RS .... Radiospare (IAA)
RS .... Radio Station [*Maps and charts*]
RS .... Radio Supervisor [*British*]
RS .... Radio Switchboard (CAAL)
RS .... Radiotelegram Service (IAA)
RS .... Radius of Safety (MCD)
RS .... Radular Sac
RS .... Ragtime Society (EA)
RS .... Railway Station (ROG)
RS .... Rain and Snow [*Sleet*] [*Meteorology*]
RS .... Raman Scattering [*Spectroscopy*]
RS .... Raman Spectroscopy
RS .... Random Saccades [*Ophthalmology*]
RS .... Random Splice [*Telecommunications*] (TEL)
RS .... Range Safety [*NASA*] (KSC)
RS .... Range Selector
RS .... Range Setter (IAA)
R/S .... Range Surveillance
RS .... Rapid Setting [*Asphalt grade*]
RS .... Ras Shamra (BJA)
RS .... Raster Suppression [*of color images*]
RS .... Rating Schedule [*Medicine*] (MAE)
RS .... Rating Sheet [*Psychometrics*]
RS .... Rauwolfia Serpentina [*A plant, the root extract of which is used medicinally*]
RS .... RAWINSONDE [*Radiosonde and RADAR Wind Sounding*] [*Upper air observation*] (NASA)
RS .... Raw Stock
RS .... Ray Society (EA)
RS .... Reactor Safeguards (NRCH)
RS .... Reader Stop [*Computer science*] (BUR)
RS .... Readiness Squadron (DNAB)
RS .... Reading of Standard
RS .... Ready Service (AAG)
RS .... Real Storage
RS .... Rearranging Sequence [*Genetics*]
RS .... Rebuild Standard [*Marine Corps*]
RS .... Receiver Station
RS .... Receiving Ship [*or Station*]
RS .... Reception Station
RS .... Recipient's Serum [*In blood matching*]
RS .... Recipient State (NITA)
RS .... Reciprocating Steam (MCD)
RS .... Reclaimed Wheat Grass/Shrub Cover [*Agriculture*]
RS .... Recognition Structure [*Immunochemistry*]
RS .... Recommended Standard [*Telecommunications*] (TEL)
RS .... Reconfiguration System (MCD)
RS .... Reconnaissance Satellite
RS .... Reconnaissance Squadron [*Military*]
RS .... Reconnaissance-Strike [*Military*]
RS .... Reconnaissance Strip [*Military*] (AFM)
RS .... Reconstitution Site (NVT)
RS .... Recording Secretary
RS .... Record Separator [*Control character*] [*Computer science*]
RS .... Recreation Supervisor [*Red Cross*]
RS .... Recruiting Service
RS .... Recruiting Station
RS .... Recruitment Surveys [*Army British*]
RS .... Rectal Sinus
RS .... Rectal Suppository [*Medicine*]
RS .... Rectified Spirits (ROG)
RS .... Rectus-Sinister [*Nomenclature system*] [*Biochemistry*]
RS .... Redeemable Stock
RS .... Reduced Smoke (MCD)
RS .... Reduced Strength (MCD)
RS .... Reducing Substance [*Laboratory science*] (DAVI)
RS .... Reducing Sugar
RS .... Redundancy Status [*NASA*] (MCD)
RS .... Redundant Set [*NASA*] (MCD)
RS .... Reed-Sternberg Cell [*Medicine*] (MAE)
RS .... Reel Sequence [*Computer science*]
RS .... Reentry System (AFM)
RS .... Reference Serum [*Clinical chemistry*]
RS .... Reference Standard
RS .... Reformed Spelling
RS .... Refrigeration System (MCD)
RS .... Refurbishment Spare (NASA)
RS .... Regional Authorities (Scotland)
RS .... Register and Storage (MCD)
RS .... Registered Sanitarian
RS .... Register of Shipping of the USSR [*Ship classification society*] (DS)
RS .... Register Select
RS .... Register to Storage (NITA)
RS .... Registration Services
RS .... Regularly Scheduled [*Red Cross Volunteer*]
RS .... Regular Savings
RS .... Regular Station [*Military*]
RS .... Regulated Substance [*Environmental Protection Agency*]

RS Regulating Station [*Military*]
RS Regulation Station [*Air Force*]
RS Reinforcing Stimulus
RS Reiter's Syndrome [*Medicine*]
R/S Rejection Slip (ADA)
RS Relative Sweetness
RS Relay Selector (IAA)
R/S Relay Set [*Telecommunications*] (TEL)
RS Reliability Standard
RS Reliability Summary (KSC)
RS Reliance Steel & Aluminum [*NYSE symbol*] (TTSB)
RS Reliance Steel & Aluminum Co. [*NYSE symbol*] (SAG)
RS Relief Stamped (DGA)
RS Religious Studies [*Secondary school course*] [*British*]
RS Relocation Site (NVT)
RS Reminder Shock
RS Remotely Settable Fuze (MCD)
R/S Remote Site [*NASA*] (KSC)
RS Remote Site (NITA)
RS Remote Station
RS Renal Specialist [*Medicine*]
RS Render and Set [*Construction*] (IAA)
RS Renin Substrate [*Biochemistry*]
RS Rephael Society (EA)
RS Report of Survey [*Military*]
RS Reproductive Success [*Genetics*]
RS Republicains Sociaux [*Social Republicans*] [*France Political party*] (PPE)
RS Request for Services [*Social Security Administration*]
RS Request for Support (MCD)
RS Request to Send
RS Research Scientist (ADA)
RS Research Summary
RS Research Systems (MCD)
RS Reserve Section [*Military*]
RS Reserve Stock (SAA)
RS Reset
RS Reset-Set [*Computer science*]
RS Reset Steering
RS Resident School (MUGU)
RS Resistance Soldering
RS Resistant Sporangia [*Botany*]
RS Resistor (IAA)
RS Re-Solv, the Society for the Prevention of Solvent and Volatile Substance Abuse [*British*] (EAIO)
RS Resonator [*Electronics*] (IAA)
RS Resorcinol-Sulfur [*Organic chemistry*] (MAE)
RS Resources Section [*Resources and Technical Services Division*] [*American Library Association*]
RS Respiratory Syncytial [*Virus*]
RS Respiratory System [*Medicine*]
RS Response-Stimulus
RS Response to Stimulus [*Ratio*] [*Neurology*] (DAVI)
RS Responsus [*To Answer*] [*Latin*]
RS Resume Sheet
RS Resynchronizing State (IAA)
RS Retail Shops and Stores [*Public-performance tariff class*] [*British*]
R-S Reticulated Siderocyte [*Cytology*] (AAMN)
RS Return to Saturation
RS Return to Situation (SAA)
RS Revenue Sharing
RS Reverberation Strength
RS Reversal Shift [*Psychometrics*]
RS Reverse Shot [*Cinematography*] (NTCM)
RS Reverse Signal (IAA)
RS Review of Symptoms [*Medicine*]
RS Review of Systems [*Medical records*] (DAVI)
RS Revised Statutes
R/S Revolutions per Second
RS Reye's Syndrome [*Medicine*]
RS Rheinflugzeugbau [*Germany ICAO aircraft manufacturer identifier*] (ICAO)
RS Rheumatoid Spondylitis [*Medicine*] (DAVI)
RS Rhythm Strip [*Electrocardiogram*] (CPH)
RS Right Sacrum [*Medicine*] (KSC)
RS Right Safety [*Sports*]
RS Right Side
RS Ringer's Solution [*Physiology*]
RS Ripon Society (EA)
R/S Road Service
RS Road Space [*Military*]
RS Roberts Syndrome [*Medicine*] (DMAA)
RS [*The*] Roberval & Saguenay Railway Co. [*AAR code*]
RS Rochelle Salt [*Potassium Sodium Tartrate*] [*Organic chemistry*]
RS Rocket Station (IAA)
RS Rocket System (MCD)
RS Roller Shutter
RS Rolls Series [*A publication*] (DLA)
RS Roll Stabilization
RS Root Mean Square Average [*Statistics*] (IAA)
RS Root Stock [*Botany*]
RS Rotary Selector (IAA)
RS Rotary Switch (IAA)
RS Rotary System (IAA)
R-S Rough-Smooth Variation [*Bacteriology*] (DAVI)
RS Route Selector
RS Route Signal (IAA)
RS Route Switching [*Telecommunications*] (TEL)
RS Routing Slip [*Military*]
RS Royal Scots [*Military unit*]
RS Royal Society [*British*]
RS Rubble Stone (AAG)
RS Rudder Station (MCD)
RS Runaway Shop (MHDB)
R_s Screen Resistance (IDOE)
R_s Secondary Resistance (IDOE)
R_s Series Resistance (IDOE)
rs Sleet [*Meteorology*] (BARN)
R_S Source Resistance (IDOE)
Rs Sri Lanka Rupee [*Monetary unit*] (IMH)
RS Syntex Laboratories, Inc. [*Research code symbol*]
RSA Air Service Affaires [*France ICAO designator*] (FAAC)
RSA American Railway and Airline Supervisors Association (EA)
RSA Rabbit Serum Albumin [*Immunology*]
RSA Rack Service Association (EA)
RSA RADAR Service Area
RSA RADAR Signature Analysis [*Air Force*]
RSA Radiation Safety Advisor [*British*] (NUCP)
RSA Railway Security Agency [*South Vietnam government security*] (VNW)
RSA Railway Supervisors Association (NADA)
RSA Railway Supply Association (EA)
RSA Random Sequential Automaton (IAA)
RSA Range Safety Approval (MUGU)
RSA Rated Sail Area [*IOR*] [*Yacht racing*]
RSA Rate-Sensitive Assets (TDOB)
RSA Rate Sensor Assembly (MCD)
RSA Rate Subsystem Analyst (MUGU)
RSA Rationalist Society of Australia
RSA Rational Self-Analysis [*Psychology*] (DHSM)
RSA Rat Serum Albumin [*Immunology*]
RSA Redstone Arsenal [*Huntsville, AL*] [*Army*]
RSA Reference Satellite A (NASA)
RSA Refined Sugar Association [*British*] (DBA)
RSA Regional Office Systems [*Computer science*]
RSA Regional Science Association (EA)
RSA Regional Studies Association [*British*] (EAIO)
RSA Regular Spiking Activity [*Electrophysiology*]
RSA Rehabilitation Services Administration [*Office of Special Education and Rehabilitive Services, Department of Education*]
RSA Relative Specific Activity
RSA Relative Standard Accuracy [*Testing methodology*]
RSA Relay Services Association of Great Britain (BI)
RSA Remote Session Access [*Telecommunications*] (OSI)
RSA Remote Session Access (NITA)
RSA Remote Station Alarm
RSA Remote Storage Activities
RSA Renaissance Society of America (EA)
RSA Rental Service Association (EA)
RSA Repair Sevice Attendant [*Telecommunications*] (TEL)
RSA Republiek van Suid-Afrika [*Republic of South Africa*] [*Afrikaans*]
RSA Requirements Statement Analyzer
RSA Research Security Administrators
RSA Research Society on Alcoholism (EA)
RSA Resource Sharing Alliance [*Library consortium*] (IT)
RSA Respiratory Sinus Arrhythmia [*Medicine*]
RSA Responsibility for Student Achievement Scale (EDAC)
RSA Reticulum Cell Sarcoma [*Pathology*] (DAVI)
RSA Retire to Staging Area [*Military*]
RSA Returned Services Association (BARN)
RSA Revest-Shamir-Adelman [*Encryption Algorithm*] [*Theoretical mathematics*] (PCM)
RSA Revised Shapley Ames [*Catalogue of Bright Galaxies*]
RSA Revised Statutes Annotated [*A publication*] (DLA)
RSA Revised Statutes of Alberta [*Canada*] [*A publication*] (DLA)
RSA Rheometrics Sound Analyzer
RSA Rhetoric Society of America (EA)
RSA Rhythmic Slow Activity [*Electroencephalography*]
RSA Ridden Standardbred Association (EA)
RSA Right Sacroanterior [*A fetal position*] [*Obstetrics*]
RSA Right Subclavian Artery [*Anatomy*] (DAVI)
RSA Rivest-Shamir-Adelman [*Cryptography*]
RSA Rivest Shamir Adleman
RSA Rotary Servo Actuator
RSA Rotary Switch Art (IAA)
RSA Royal Scottish Academician
RSA [*The*] Royal Scottish Academy
RSA Royal Scottish Academy, Edinburgh [*1826*] (NGC)
RSA Royal Society for the Encouragement of Arts, Manufactures, and Commerce [*British*] (EAIO)
RSA Royal Society of Antiquaries
RSA Royal Society of Australia (BARN)
RSA Royal Society of the Arts [*British*]
RSA Rubber Shippers Association [*Defunct*]
RSA Runway Safety Area [*FAA*] (TAG)
RSA Rural Sanitary Authority [*British*]
RSA Russian Space Agency
RSA Santa Rosa [*Argentina*] [*Airport symbol*] (OAG)
RSAA Romanian Studies Association of America (EA)
RSAA Royal Society for Asian Affairs [*British*] (DI)

RSAAF .... Royal South African Air Force
RSABA .... Royal South Australian Bowling Association
RSAC .... RADAR Significance Analysis Code
RSAC .... Radiological Safety Analysis Computer (MCD)
RSAC .... Reactor Safety Advisory Committee [*Canada*] (BARN)
RSAC .... Recreational Software Advisory Council
RSAC .... Recreational Software Advisory Council
RSAC .... Region, State, Area, County [*Code*] [*DoD*]
RSAC .... Reliability Surveillance and Control (IAA)
RSAC .... Remote Slave Aircraft (MCD)
RSAC .... Royal Scottish Automobile Club (DBA)
RSACi .... Recreational Software Advisory Council on the Internet [*Computer science*]
RSACI .... Recreational Software Advisory Council on the Internet
RSAD .... Remote Safe-and-Arm Device
RSAF .... Republic of Singapore Air Force (PDAA)
RSAF .... Royal Saudi Air Force
RSAF .... Royal Small Arms Factory [*British*]
RSAF .... Royal Swedish Air Force
RSAG .... Reserve Storage Activity, Germersheim, West Germany [*Military*]
RSAI .... Royal Society of Antiquaries of Ireland
RSAI .... Rules, Standards and Instruction (IAA)
RSAI .... Rutgers Social Attribute Inventory [*Psychology*]
RSAK .... Reserve Storage Activity, Kaiserslautern, West Germany [*Military*]
RSAL .... Reserve Storage Activity, Luxembourg [*Military*]
RSALT .... Running, Signal, and Anchor Lights
RSAM .... Real-Time Seismic Amplitude Measurement
RSAM .... Royal Scottish Academy of Music and Drama (AIE)
RSAMC .... Royal Society of Arts, Manufacturing and Commerce [*London*]
RSAND .... Reserve Systems Analysis Division [*Military*] (DNAB)
RS & C .... Reliability, Surveillance, and Control (SAA)
RS & D .... Receipt, Storage, and Delivery [*Business term*]
RS & I .... Rules, Standards, and Instructions
RS & M .... Royal Sappers and Miners [*British military*] (DMA)
RS & MD .... Riots, Strikes, and Malicious Damage [*Insurance*] (ADA)
RS & R .... Retail, Service, and Repair
RS & S .... Receiving, Shipping, and Storage (NASA)
R San I .... Royal Sanitary Institute [*Later, RSH*] [*British*]
RSAP .... Response Session Abort Positive (IAA)
RSAP .... Revolutionaire Socialistische Arbeiders Partij [*Revolutionary Socialist Workers' Party*] [*Netherlands Political party*] (PPE)
RSARR .... Republic of South Africa Research Reactor
RSAS .... Revenue Sharing Advisory Service (EA)
RSAS .... Royal Sanitary Association of Scotland
RSAS .... Royal Surgical Aid Society [*British*] (BI)
RSAT .... Raynaud's and Scleroderma Association Trust [*British*] (EAIO)
RSB .... Radiation Safety Booklet (DNAB)
RSB .... Range Safety Beacon [*NASA*] (AAG)
RSB .... Ravensbos [*Netherlands*] [*Seismograph station code, US Geological Survey*] (SEIS)
RSB .... Reactor Service Building (NRCH)
RSB .... Reconnaissance Strike Bomber
RSB .... Recycling Sourcebook [*A publication*]
RSB .... Reduced-Size Blueprint (NG)
RSB .... Reference Standards Book [*Military*]
RSB .... Regimental Stretcher-Bearer
RSB .... Regional Shipping Boards [*NATO*] (NATG)
RSB .... Registered Schools Board [*Victoria, Australia*]
RSB .... Remote System Base (MHDI)
RSB .... Repair Service Bureau [*Telecommunications*] (TEL)
RSB .... Retail Sales Battery [*Employment test*]
RSB .... Reticulocyte Standard Buffer [*Medicine*] (DMAA)
RSB .... Rhondda & Swansea Bay Railway [*Wales*]
RSB .... Right Sternal Border [*Medicine*]
RSB .... Rochester Subway Co. [*AAR code*]
RSB .... Roller Skating Business Magazine [*A publication*] (EAAP)
RSB .... Roseberth [*Australia Airport symbol Obsolete*] (OAG)
RSB .... Royal Swedish Ballet
RSB .... Rudder Speed Brake (MCD)
RSB .... Samaero SA [*Romania*] [*ICAO designator*] (FAAC)
RSBA .... Rail Steel Bar Association [*Later, SMA*] (EA)
RSBC .... Revised Statutes of British Columbia [*A publication*] (ILCA)
RSBDC .... Regional Small Business Development Center [*Rutgers University*] [*Research center*] (RCD)
RSB(E) .... Regional Shipping Board (East) [*NATO*]
RSBEI .... Registered Student of the Institution of Body Engineers [*British*] (DBQ)
RSBO .... Refined Soybean Oil
RSBRC .... Reference and Subscription Books Review Committee [*American Library Association*]
RSBS .... RADAR Safety Beacon System (MCD)
RSBT .... Recovery Storage Unit Boot Test [*Military*]
RSB(W) .... Regional Shipping Board (West) [*NATO*]
RSC .... Racing Service Center [*Motorcycle racing*]
RSC .... RADAR Scan Converter [*Military*] (CAAL)
RSC .... RADAR Sea Clutter
RSC .... RADAR Set Control
RSC .... RADAR System Console [*Military*] (CAAL)
RSC .... RADAR System Controller [*Military*] (CAAL)
RSC .... Radiation Shielding Computer Codes [*Database*] [*Oak Ridge National Laboratory*] [*Department of Energy*] [*Information service or system*] (CRD)
RSC .... Range Safety Command [*or Control*] [*NASA*]
RSC .... Rational Self-Counseling [*Psychology*] (DHSM)
RSC .... Rat Skin Collagen
RSC .... Rat Spleen Cell [*Medicine*] (DMAA)
RSC .... Raytheon Service Co.
RSC .... Reactor Safety Commission [*Germany*]
RSC .... Reactor Safety Coordinator [*Nuclear energy*] (NRCH)
RSC .... Reactor Steam Cycle
RSC .... Reader Service Card
RSC .... Record Status Code [*Military*] (AABC)
RSC .... Referee Stops Contest [*Amateur boxing*]
RSC .... Regional Safety Coordinator [*Australia*]
RSC .... Regional Service Center [*Military*] (CINC)
RSC .... Regular, Slotted, Corrugated [*Container*]
RSC .... Reinforcement Support Category [*DoD*]
RSC .... Relative System Capability
RSC .... Relaxation-Sensitive Cell (PDAA)
RSC .... Release Schedule Code (SAA)
RSC .... Religious Sisters of Charity [*Roman Catholic religious order*]
RSC .... Remote Sensing Center [*Texas A & M University*] [*Research center*] (RCD)
RSC .... Remote Store Controller
RSC .... Replacement and School Command [*Military*]
RSC .... Rescue Sub-Center [*ICAO*] (FAAC)
RSC .... Reserve Service Control [*Navy*]
RSC .... Residential Sales Council (EA)
RSC .... Residential Support Center (OICC)
RSC .... Resident Shop Control (SAA)
RSC .... Respiratory Symptoms Complex [*Medicine*]
RSC .... Restart Capability (AAG)
RSC .... Rested-State Contraction [*Obstetrics*] (MAE)
RSC .... Reversible Sickled Cell [*Hematology*]
RSC .... Revised Statutes of Canada [*Canada Department of Justice*] [*Information service or system*] (CRD)
RSC .... Rework Support Conference [*Military*] (DNAB)
RSC .... Rex Stores [*NYSE symbol*] (TTSB)
RSC .... Rex Stores Corp. [*Formerly, Audio/Video Affiliates, Inc.*] [*NYSE symbol*] (SPSG)
RSC .... Riga Skulte Airport [*Former USSR Airport symbol Obsolete*] (OAG)
RSC .... Right-Sided Colon Cancer [*Medicine*]
RSC .... Right Stage Center [*A stage direction*]
RSC .... Right Subclavian [*Medicine*] (DMAA)
RSC .... RISC Single Chip [*IBM*] [*Computer science*]
RSC .... Road Safety Committee [*British police*]
RSC .... Road Safety Council [*Australia*]
RSC .... Royal Shakespeare Company [*British*]
RSC .... Royal Society of Canada
RSC .... Royal Society of Chemistry [*Chemical Society and Royal Institute of Chemi stry*] [*Formed by a merger of*] (EAIO)
RSC .... Rules of the Supreme Court [*A publication*] (DLA)
RSC .... Runway Surface Condition [*Aviation*] (MCD)
RSC .... Rural Service Center [*Agency for International Development*]
RSC .... Russell Sage College [*New York*]
RSC .... Saint Charles Borromeo Seminary, Overbrook, PA [*OCLC symbol*] (OCLC)
RSCA .... Religious Speech Communication Association (EA)
RScA .... Right Scapulo-Anterior [*A fetal position*] [*Obstetrics*]
RSCAA .... Radio Shack Computer Alumni Association (EA)
RSCAAL .... Remote Sensing Chemical Agent Alarm [*Army*] (INF)
RSCACT .... Road Safety Council of the Australian Capital Territory
RscBnc .... Resource Bancshares Mortgage Group [*Associated Press*] (SAG)
RSCC .... Regional Sample Control Center (GNE)
RSCC .... Remote-Site Command Computer [*NASA*]
RSCC .... Remote-Site Computer Complex [*NASA*]
RSCC .... Republican Senatorial Campaign Committee
RSCCP .... Response Session Change Control Positive (IAA)
RSCD .... Report Series Codes Dictionary [*A publication*]
RSCD .... Request to Start Contract Definition
RSCD .... Runway Surface Condition [*Aviation*] (FAAC)
RSCDS .... Royal Scottish Country Dance Society (EAIO)
RSCDSA .... Religion and Socialism Commission of the Democratic Socialists of America (EA)
RSCF .... Rotating Spherical Convection Facility (SSD)
RSCG .... Radio Set Control Group
RSCG .... Roux Seguela Cayzac & Goudard [*Advertising agency*] (ECON)
RSCH .... Range Scheduling (MUGU)
RSCH .... Ready Spares Chassis
RSCH .... Research (AFM)
RschFrnt .... Research Frontiers [*Associated Press*] (SAG)
RschFrt .... Research Frontiers, Inc. [*Associated Press*] (SAG)
RSCHM .... Royal School of Church Music [*British*]
RSCHOPSDET ... Research Operations Detachment (DNAB)
RSCIE .... Remote Station Communication Interface Equipment
RSCJ .... Society of the Sacred Heart [*Roman Catholic women's religious order*]
RSCL .... Radioactive Sodium Chemistry Loop
RSCM .... Recoiling Structural Contour Map [*Surface analysis*]
RscM .... Resource Mortgage Capital, Inc. [*Associated Press*] (SAG)
RSCM .... Royal School of Church Music [*British*]
RscMtg .... Resource Mortgage Capital, Inc. [*Associated Press*] (SAG)
RscMtge .... Resource Mortgage Capital, Inc. [*Associated Press*] (SAG)
RSCN .... Registered Sick Children's Nurse [*British*]
RSCNT .... Road Safety Council of the Northern Territory [*Australia*]
RSCO .... Rules of the Supreme Court, Order [*Number*] (ILCA)
RS Comp .... Statutes of Connecticut, Compilation of 1854 [*A publication*] (DLA)
RScP .... Right Scapuloposterior [*A fetal position*] [*Obstetrics*]
RSCR .... Range Safety Command Receiver [*NASA*] (KSC)
RSCR .... Res Care, Inc. [*NASDAQ symbol*] (SAG)

RSCR .... Reserve Special Commendation Ribbon
RSCS .... Range Safety Command System [*NASA*] (AAG)
RSCS .... Rate Stabilization and Control System
RSCS .... Remote Spooling Communications Subsystem [*IBM Corp.*] [*Computer science*] (IBMDP)
RSCS .... Remote Spooling Control System [*Computer science*] (TNIG)
RSCS .... Rod Sequence Control System [*Nuclear energy*] (NRCH)
RSCSA .... Railway Signal and Communications Suppliers Association [*Later, RSS*] (EA)
RSCSS .... Range Safety Command Shutdown System (IAA)
RSCT .... Rach Sentence Completion Test [*Speech and language therapy*] (DAVI)
RSCT .... Rohde Sentence Completions Test [*Psychology*]
RSCT .... Rotter Sentence Completion Test [*Speech and language therapy*] (DAVI)
RSCW .... Research Reactor, State College of Washington (NRCH)
RSD .... RADAR System Development (IAA)
RSD .... Radiance Spectral Distribution
RSD .... Raised (MSA)
RSD .... Raised Shelter Deck (DS)
RSD .... Range Support Directive (SAA)
RSD .... Rassemblement des Socialistes et des Democrates [*Rally of Socialists and Democrats*] [*Reunion*] [*Political party*] (PPW)
RSD .... Ratoon Stunting Disease [*of sugarcane*]
RSD .... Reentry Systems Department
RSD .... Reference Services Division [*of ALA*] [*Later, RASD*] (EA)
RSD .... Reflex Sympathetic Dystrophy [*Medicine*]
RSD .... Refueling Shutdown (IEEE)
RSD .... Relative Standard Deviation [*Statistics*]
RSD .... Relative Stock Density [*Pisciculture*]
RSD .... Reliability Status Document (IAA)
RSD .... Remote Sensing Device
RSD .... Requirements and Specifications Document [*NASA*] (NASA)
RSD .... Research Services Department [*United Way of Greater Indianapolis*] [*Indiana*] [*Information service or system*] (IID)
RSD .... Research Services Directory [*A publication*]
RSD .... Resigned
RSD .... Responsible System Designer (NRCH)
RSD .... Ring System Descriptor (NITA)
RSD .... Risk-Specific Dose [*Environmental science*] (FFDE)
RSD .... Roadside Delivery (ADA)
RSD .... Rock Sound [*Bahamas*] [*Airport symbol*] (OAG)
RSD .... Rolling Steel Door [*Technical drawings*]
RSD .... Rosehaugh Stanhope Developments [*Commercial firm British*]
RSD .... Royal Society, Dublin
RSD .... Runcible System Duplexer [*Telecommunications*] (IAA)
RSDA .... Reflex Sympathetic Dystrophy Association (EA)
RSDA .... Road Surface Dressing Association [*British*] (DBA)
RSDB .... SCB [*Statistika Centralbyran*] Regional Statistical Data Base [*Sweden Information service or system*] (CRD)
RSDC .... Radiation Subprogramme Data Center [*Marine science*] (MSC)
RSDC .... Range Safety Data Coordinator (SAA)
RSDC .... Remote Secure Data Change (DNAB)
RSDG .... Raster Scan Display Generator (MCD)
RSDG .... Royal Scots Dragoon Guards [*British military*] (DMA)
RSDI .... Retirement, Survivors, or Disability Insurance [*Social Security Administration*] (GFGA)
RSDLP .... Russian Social-Democratic Labor Party [*Political party*]
RSDLP(B) .... Russian Social-Democratic Labor Party (Bolsheviks) [*Political party*]
RSDNC .... Residence
RSDNT .... Resident
RSDP .... Remote Shutdown Panel (IEEE)
RSDP .... Remote-Site Data Processor [*NASA*]
RSDP .... Rural School Development Program [*Australia*]
RSDr .... Doctor Rerum Socialium [*Doctor of Social Sciences*] [*Latin*]
RSDRP .... Rossiiskaia Sotsial-Demokraticheskaia Rabochaya Partiia [*Russian Social Democratic Workers' Party*] [*Political party*] (PPE)
RSDS .... RADAR Systems Design Section
RSDS .... Range Safety Destruct System
RSDS .... Reflex Sympathetic Dystrophy Syndrome [*Medicine*] (DMAA)
RSDT .... Regulations of Office of the Secretary, Department of Transportation
RSDT .... Remote Station Data Terminal
RSDU .... RADAR Storm Detection Unit
RSDW .... Ross Sea Deep Water [*Marine science*] (MSC)
RSDWP .... Russian Social-Democratic Workers Party
RSE .... RADAR Search Equipment
RSE .... Raid Size Estimate
RSE .... Receiving Site Equipment [*NASA*]
RSE .... Record Selection Expression (MHDI)
RSE .... Reference Sensing Element (DNAB)
RSE .... Reference Standards Equipment [*Deep Space Instrumentation Facility, NASA*]
RSE .... Relative Standard Error [*DOE*] (TAG)
RSE .... Remote Sensing of Environment [*A publication*] (DNAB)
RSE .... Request for Self Enhancement (IAA)
RSE .... Request Select Entry [*Computer science*]
RSE .... Resistance Soldering Equipment
RSE .... Reverse Sutured Eye [*Ophthalmology*] (DAVI)
RSE .... Richmond Stock Exchange (IIA)
RSE .... Right Sternal Edge [*On Examination*] [*Cardiology*] (DAVI)
RSE .... Rouse Co. [*NYSE symbol*] (SAG)
RSE .... Royal Society of Edinburgh
RSE .... Sydney-Rose Bay [*Australia Airport symbol*] (OAG)
RSEA .... Reference Sensing Element Amplifier
RSEC .... Regional Science Experience Center
RSEC .... Regional Solar Energy Center
RSEC .... Representative Shuttle Environmental Control [*System*] [*NASA*]
R_{sec} .... Secondary Resistance (IDOE)
RSECS .... Representative Shuttle Environmental Control System [*NASA*] (MCD)
RSED .... Refund Statute Expiration Date [*IRS*]
RSEP .... Response Session End Positive (IAA)
RSEP .... Restraint System Evaluation Program [*Department of Transportation*]
RSEPrA .... Rouse Co. Sr'A'Cv Pfd [*NYSE symbol*] (TTSB)
RSEPrZ .... Rouse Capital 9.25%'QUIPS' [*NYSE symbol*] (TTSB)
RSER .... Remote Sensing of Earth Resources
RSER .... Rotary Stylus Electronics Recorder
RSERV .... Relocatable Library Service Function [*Computer science*] (IAA)
RSES .... Refrigeration Service Engineers Society (EA)
RSES .... Rosenberg Self-Esteem Scale
RSET .... Receiver Signal Element Timing (IAA)
RSEU .... Remote Scanner-Encoder Unit [*Bell Laboratories*]
RSEW .... Resistance Seam Welding
RSEW-HF .... Resistance Seam Welding - High Frequency
RSEW-I .... Resistance Seam Welding - Induction
RSEXEC .... Resource Sharing Executive (MHDI)
RSF .... Radial Stress-Field [*Hypothesis describing forces in a sand-pile*]
RSF .... Radial Structure Function [*of solid catalysts*]
RSF .... Receiving-Safing Facility [*NASA*] (MCD)
RSF .... Reciprocal Cross Sterile Females [*Genetics*]
RSF .... Refurbish and Subassemblies Facilities [*NASA*] (NASA)
RSF .... Reject Suspense File [*Army*]
RSF .... Relative Sensitivity Factor [*Analytical chemistry*]
RSF .... Relative Substitution Frequency [*of amino acids in proteins*]
RSF .... Remote Service Facility (IAA)
RSF .... Remote Support Facility
RSF .... Requisition Status File (DNAB)
RSF .... Research Systems Facility
RSF .... Residual Support Force [*After main force redeployment*] [*Military*]
RSF .... Retail Stores Forum (EA)
RSF .... Rhododendron Species Foundation (EA)
RSF .... Risk Studies Foundation (EA)
RSF .... Roll Sheet Feeder
RSF .... Rough Sunk Face [*Construction*]
RSF .... Royal Scots Fusiliers [*Military unit*]
RSF .... Russian Student Fund [*Defunct*] (EA)
RSFA .... Roller Skating Foundation of America [*Defunct*] (EA)
RSFC .... Republic Security Financial Corp. [*NASDAQ symbol*] (NQ)
RSFC .... Republic Security Finl [*NASDAQ symbol*] (TTSB)
RSFC .... Ricky Skaggs International Fan Club (EA)
RSFC .... Rolling Stones Fan Club (EA)
RSFC .... Ronnie Smith Fan Club (EA)
RSFCO .... Republic Sec Finl Cv'C'Pfd [*NASDAQ symbol*] (TTSB)
RSFCP .... Republic Sec Finl 7.5% Cv 'A' Pfd [*NASDAQ symbol*] (TTSB)
RS Fnl .... RS Financial Group [*Formerly, Raleigh Federal Savings Bank*] [*Associated Press*] (SAG)
RSFPP .... Retired Servicemen's Family Protection Plan [*Military*]
RSFQ .... Rapid Single-Flux Quantum Circuit [*Physics*]
RSFS .... Real Scene Focus Sensor (PDAA)
RSFS .... Royal Scottish Forestry Society (EAIO)
RSFSR .... Russian Soviet Federated Socialist Republic
RSG .... Rabbi Saadia Gaon [*Jewish scholar, 882-942*] (BJA)
RSG .... RADAR Set Group [*HAWK missile*] (MCD)
RSG .... RADAR Signal Generator (MCD)
RSG .... RADAR Systems Group [*of General Motors Corp.*]
RSG .... Range Safety Group [*Range Commanders Council*] [*White Sands Missile Range, NM*]
RSG .... Rate Signal Generator (AAG)
RSG .... Rate Support Grant [*British*]
RSG .... Rate Switching Gyro (MCD)
RSG .... Reassign (AABC)
RSG .... Receiving Stolen Goods
RSG .... Red Supergiant [*Astronomy*]
RSG .... Reenlistment Steering Group [*Military*] (MCD)
RSG .... Reference Signal Generator
RSG .... Regional Seat of Government
RSG .... Reitan Strength of Grip [*Medicine*] (DAVI)
RSG .... Relay Switch Group
RSG .... Research Study Group (NATG)
RSG .... Resident Study Group [*Army*] (MCD)
RSG .... Resource Service Group Ltd. [*Toronto Stock Exchange symbol*]
RSG .... Revenue Support Grant (AIE)
RSG .... Rocksprings, TX [*Location identifier FAA*] (FAAL)
RSG .... Royal Scots Greys [*Military unit*]
RSGB .... Radio Society of Great Britain [*Potters Bar, Hertfordshire, England*] (EAIO)
RSGB .... Research Surveys of Great Britain Ltd.
RSGC .... Royal Sydney Golf Club [*Australia*]
RSGI .... Riverside Group, Inc. [*Jacksonville, FL*] [*NASDAQ symbol*] (NQ)
RSGMT .... Reassignment
RSGN .... Reassign
RSGS .... Ranges and Space Ground Support (AAG)
RSGS .... Royal Scottish Geographical Society
RSH .... RADAR Status History
rsh .... Remote Shell [*Computer science*] (CDE)
RSH .... Resin Sluice Header (NRCH)
RSH .... Ring Systems Handbook [*American Chemical Society*] [*A publication*]
RSH .... Royal Society of Health [*Formerly, R San I*] [*British*]
RSH .... Russian Mission [*Alaska*] [*Airport symbol*] (OAG)
RSHA .... Reichssicherheitshauptampt [*Central Security Office of the Reich*] [*NAZI Germany*]

RSHF .... Room Sensible Heat Factor
RSHI .... Rough Service, High Impact (DNAB)
RSHM .... Religious of the Sacred Heart of Mary [*Roman Catholic women's religious order*]
RSHMI .... Russian Hydrometeorological Institute [*Marine science*] (OSRA)
RSHS .... Railroad Station Historical Society (EA)
RSHX .... Recirculation Spray Heat Exchanger [*Nuclear energy*] (NRCH)
RSI .... Air Sunshine, Inc. [*ICAO designator*] (FAAC)
RSI .... East-West Resource Systems Institute [*Research center*] (RCD)
rsi .... Race Specific Incompatibility
RSI .... RADAR Scope Interpretation (AAG)
RSI .... Radiation Shielding Information Data Base [*Oak Ridge National Laboratory*] [*Department of Energy Information service or system*] (CRD)
RSI .... Rationalization, Standardization, and Integration [*or Interoperability*] [*Program*] [*Army*] (INF)
RSI .... Reactor Siting Index (NRCH)
RSI .... Receipt, Storage, and Issue [*Army*] (AABC)
R(SI) .... Reconstruction, Social Insurance [*British World War II*]
RSI .... Record Status Indicator [*Military*] (AABC)
RSI .... Reflected Signal Indication [*Air Force*]
RSI .... Refractory Reusable Surface Insulation (PDAA)
RSI .... Regional Safety Inspector [*Ministry of Agriculture, Fisheries, and Food*] [*British*]
RSI .... Register Sender Inward [*Telecommunications*] (TEL)
RSI .... Religious Science International (EA)
RSI .... Relocation Services Institute [*British*] (DBA)
RSI .... Remote Sensing Institute [*South Dakota State University*] [*Research center*] (RCD)
RSI .... Repetitive Strain Injury (PCM)
RSI .... Replacement Stream Input [*Military*]
RSI .... Repressor-Sensitizer Index [*Psychology*]
RSI .... Repubblica Sociale Italiana [*Italian Socialist Republic*] [*Founded by Mussolini 1943-1945*]
RSI .... Research Studies Institute
R-SI .... Restricted-Security Information (DNAB)
RSI .... Reusable Surface Insulation [*NASA*]
RSI .... Ring State Indicator [*Telecommunications*] (IAA)
RSI .... Rio Sidra [*Panama*] [*Airport symbol*] (OAG)
RSI .... Roll Stability Indicator [*NASA*] (KSC)
RSI .... Rotary Shaft Indicator
RSI .... Royal Sanitary Institute (ROG)
RSI .... Royal Signals Institution [*British*] (DEN)
RSIC .... Radiation Shielding Information Center [*Department of Energy*] [*Oak Ridge, TN*]
RSIC .... Redstone Scientific Information Center [*Army*]
RSIC .... Responding Superior in Command (MCD)
R-SICU .... Respiratory-Surgical Intensive Care Unit [*of a hospital*] (AAMN)
RSID .... Resource Identification Table [*Computer science*]
RSIGG .... Rocket Signal, Green (IAA)
RSIGR .... Rocket Signal, Red (IAA)
R SIGS .... Royal Corps of Signals [*British*] (DMA)
RSIHM .... Reparation Society of the Immaculate Heart of Mary (EA)
RSIM .... RADAR Simulator (MSA)
RSIM .... Retrospective Single Ion Monitoring [*Analytical chemistry*]
RSIP .... RADAR Systems Improvement Program (DWSG)
RSIP .... Reusable Software Implementation Program (SSD)
RSIPR .... Reactor System with Interstage Product Removal [*Chemical engineering*]
RSIS .... Radical Science Information Service [*News service attempting to interrelate radical politics and scientific issues*]
RSIS .... Reed Stenhouse Investment Services [*British*]
RSIS .... Rotorcraft Systems Integration Simulator [*Joint Army-NASA program*] (RDA)
RSIS .... RSI Systems [*NASDAQ symbol*] (TTSB)
RSIS .... RSI Systems, Inc. [*NASDAQ symbol*] (SAG)
RSI Sys .... RSI Systems, Inc. [*Associated Press*] (SAG)
RSITA .... Reglement du Service International des Telecommunications de l'Aeronautique
R/SITU .... Respiratory/Surgical Intensive Therapy Unit [*of a hospital*]
RSIUFL .... Release Suspension for Issue and Use of Following Lots [*Military*]
RSIVP .... Rapid Sequence Intravenous Pyelogram [*Medicine*]
RSJ .... Religious of St. Joseph of Australia (TOCD)
RSJ .... Resistively-Shunted Junction [*Physics*]
RSJ .... Rolled-Steel Joist
RSJ .... Rolling-Stock Jigsaws [*British*]
RSK .... Ransiki [*West Irian, Indonesia*] [*Airport symbol*] (AD)
RSKERL .... Robert S. Kerr Environmental Research Laboratory [*Ada, OK*] [*Environmental Protection Agency*] (GRD)
RSKU .... Reza Shah Kibur University [*Iran*]
RSL .... Radio Standards Laboratory [*National Institute of Standards and Technology*]
RSL .... Rate-Sensitive Liabilities (TDOB)
RSL .... Reading on Statute Law [*A publication*] (DLA)
RSL .... Received Signal Level [*Telecommunications*] (TEL)
RSL .... Reconnaissance and Security Line
RSL .... Red Suspender League (EA)
RSL .... Reference Standards Laboratory [*Deep Space Instrumentation Facility, NASA*]
RSL .... Relative Sea Level
RSL .... Remote Sensing Laboratory [*University of Kansas, University of Minnesota*] [*Research center*] (MCD)
RSL .... Remote Sprint Launching [*Military*]
RSL .... Requirements Statement Language
RSL .... Research Services Ltd. [*Database producer*] [*Wembley, Middlesex, England*]
RSL .... Resource Support List [*NASA*] (MCD)
RSL .... Returned Servicemen's League [*British military*] (DMA)
RSL .... Revolutionary Socialist League (EA)
RSL .... Right Sacrolateral [*Position*] [*Obstetrics*] (DAVI)
RSL .... Rio-Sul, Servicos Aereos Regionais SA [*Brazil*] [*ICAO designator*] (FAAC)
RSL .... Ripe Skin Liquid [*A banana substrate*]
RSL .... Road Service Licence [*British*] (DCTA)
RSL .... Roselend [*France*] [*Seismograph station code, US Geological Survey*] (SEIS)
RSL .... Royal Society, London [*British*]
RSL .... Royal Society of Literature [*British*]
RSL .... RSI Retail Solutions, Inc. [*Vancouver Stock Exchange symbol*]
RSL .... Rumsford Sandy Loam [*Type of soil*]
RSL .... Russell, KS [*Location identifier FAA*] (FAAL)
RSLA .... Range Safety Launch Approval (AFM)
RSLB .... Right Short Leg Brace [*Medicine*]
RSLPI .... Recombinant Secretory Leukoprotease Inhibitor [*Biochemistry*]
RSLS .... Receiver Side Lobe Suppression (MCD)
RSLS .... Redundant Set Launch Sequencer (MCD)
RSLS .... Reply Path Side Lobe Suppression (IAA)
RSLS .... Runway Status Light System [*FAA*] (TAG)
RSLSI .... Renzulli/Smith Learning Style Inventory (EDAC)
RSLT .... Result (IAA)
RSLTS .... Results
RSLV .... Resolve (NASA)
RSLVR .... Resolver (MSA)
RSM .... Diocesan Sisters of Mercy (TOCD)
RSM .... Radiation Signature Measurement
RSM .... Radiation Survey Meter [*NASA*]
RSM .... Radio Squadron Mobile (MUGU)
RSM .... Rapeseed Meal
RSM .... Rapidly Solidified Materials
RSM .... Readability, Strength, Modulation (IAA)
RSM .... Ready Service Magazine [*Military*] (DNAB)
RSM .... Real Storage Management [*Computer science*] (IBMDP)
RSM .... Reconnaissance Strategic Missile
RSM .... Reed Switching Matrix
RSM .... Regimental Sergeant Major [*Army*]
RSM .... Religious Sisters of Mercy of Alma, Michigan (TOCD)
RSM .... Remote Monitoring Services Manager [*Telecommunications*]
RSM .... Research into Site Management (MHDB)
RSM .... Resident Sector Management [*Computer science*] (IAA)
RSM .... Resident System Monitor
RSM .... Resource Management System (IAA)
RSM .... Resource Status Monitor [*Systems Center, Inc.*]
RSM .... Response Surface Methodology
RSM .... Resume (NASA)
RSM .... Revised Statutes of Manitoba [*Canada*] [*A publication*] (DLA)
RSM .... Rivet Setting Machine
RSM .... Robert Strange McNamara [*US Secretary of Defense, 1961-68*]
RSM .... Rotterdam School of Management [*Netherlands*] (ECON)
RSM .... Royal School of Mines [*British*]
RSM .... Royal School of Musketry [*Hythe*] [*Military British*] (ROG)
RSM .... Royal Society of Medicine [*British*]
RSM .... Royal Society of Musicians of Great Britain
RSM .... Royal Surrey Militia [*British military*] (DMA)
RSM .... San Marino [*International vehicle registration*] (ODBW)
RSM .... Sisters of Mercy [*Roman Catholic religious order*]
RSM .... Sisters of Mercy (TOCD)
RSM .... Sisters of Mercy (Ballyahannon, Ireland) (TOCD)
RSM .... Sisters of Mercy (Mayo, Ireland) (TOCD)
RSM .... Sisters of Mercy of Ardagh & Clonmacnois (TOCD)
RSM .... Sisters of Mercy of Portland (TOCD)
RSM .... Sisters of Mercy of the Americas (TOCD)
RSM .... Sisters of Mercy (Sligo) (TOCD)
RSMA .... Radiological Systems Microfilm Associates (EA)
RSMA .... Railway Supply Manufacturers Association [*Defunct*] (EA)
RSMA .... Railway Systems and Management Association [*Defunct*] (EA)
RSMA .... Royal Society of Marine Artists [*Formerly, SMA*] [*British*]
RSMAS .... Rosenstiel School of Marine and Atmospheric Science [*University of Miami*] [*Research center*] (RCD)
RSmB .... Bryant College, Smithfield, RI [*Library symbol Library of Congress*] (LCLS)
RSMC .... Regional Specialized Meteorological Center [*Marine science*] (OSRA)
RSMD .... Resource Systems Management Division [*Environmental Protection Agency*] (GFGA)
RSME .... Royal School of Military Engineering [*British military*] (DMA)
RSMF .... Royal Society of Medicine Foundation (EA)
RSMG .... Rotorcraft Simulator Motion Generator [*Army*] (RDA)
RSMGB .... Royal Society of Musicians of Great Britain (EAIO)
RSMIS .... Real Estate and Space Management Information System (USDC)
RSMIS .... Real Estate and Space Management Information System [*Marine science*] (OSRA)
RSMLC .... Red de Salud de las Mujeres Latinoamericanas y del Caribe [*Latin American and Caribbean Women's Health Network*] (EAIO)
RSMM .... Redundant System Monitor Model [*NASA*] (MCD)
RSMR .... Raw Stock Material Requirements
RSMR .... Rayleigh Scattering of Moessbauer Resonance [*Physics*]
RSMR .... Relative Standard Mortality Rate (DMAA)
RSMS .... Radio Spectrum Measurement System [*National Telecommunications and Information Administration*]
RSMT .... Ras Shamra Mythological Texts (BJA)

RSMT .... Red Sea Mission Team (EA)
RSMT .... Reliability Safety Margin Test
RSN .... Radiation Surveillance Network [*Public Health Service*]
RSN .... Radio Supernovae [*Astrophysics*]
RSN .... Random Sequence Number (DNAB)
RSN .... Rassemblement pour le Salut National [*Rally for National Salvation*] [*Senegal*] (PD)
RSN .... Ready, Soon, Now (Approach) [*Marketing*]
RSN .... Real Soon Now [*Internet language*] [*Computer science*]
RSN .... Reason (AFM)
RSN .... Record Sequence Number [*Computer science*] (IAA)
RSN .... Reference Sequence Number [*Online bibliographies*]
RSN .... Reject Sequence Number [*Computer science*]
RSN .... Report Serial Number [*Army*]
RSN .... Research Surveillance Network
RSN .... Resonate (KSC)
RSN .... Revised Statutes of Newfoundland [*Canada*] [*A publication*] (DLA)
RSN .... Right Substantia Nigra [*Medicine*] (DMAA)
RSN .... Royal School of Needlework [*British*]
RSN .... Royal Swazi National Airways Corp. [*Swaziland*] [*ICAO designator*] (FAAC)
RSN .... Ruston, LA [*Location identifier FAA*] (FAAL)
RSNA .... Radiological Society of North America (EA)
RSNA .... Royal Society of Northern Antiquaries (ROG)
RSNB .... Revised Statutes of New Brunswick [*Canada*] [*A publication*] (DLA)
RSNC .... Royal Society for Nature Conservation Wildlife Trusts Partnership (EAIO)
RSND .... Resound Corp. [*NASDAQ symbol*] (SAG)
RSNF .... Royal Saudi Arabian Navy Forces (MCD)
RSNGS .... Rancho Seco Nuclear Generating Station (NRCH)
RSNO .... Referral Service Network Office
RSNP .... Registered Student Nurse Program [*Military*] (AABC)
RSNS .... Revised Statutes of Nova Scotia [*Canada*] [*A publication*] (DLA)
RSNT .... Research Society for Natural Therapeutics [*British*] (DBA)
RSNT .... Revised Single Negotiating Text [*UN Law of the Sea Conference*]
RSO .... Aero Asia [*Pakistan*] [*ICAO designator*] (FAAC)
RSO .... Radiation Safety Officer [*Nuclear energy*] (NRCH)
RSO .... Radiological Safety Office [*or Officer*] (NASA)
RSO .... Radiosonde Observation (MUGU)
RSO .... Radio Symphony Orchestra
RSO .... Railway Sorting Office
RSO .... Railway Suboffice
RSO .... Ramus Supraorbitalis [*Anatomy*]
RSO .... Range Safety Officer [*Military*]
RSO .... Range Support Operation
RSO .... Reactor Standards Office [*Oak Ridge National Laboratory*]
RSO .... Reactor System Outline [*Nuclear energy*] (NRCH)
RSO .... Reconnaissance and Survey Officer [*Military*] (AABC)
RSO .... Reconnaissance System Officer (MCD)
RSO .... Rectified Skew Orthomorphic (PDAA)
RSO .... Regimental Supply Officer [*Army*]
RSO .... Regional Safety Officer [*British*] (DCTA)
RSO .... Regional Security Officer [*Foreign Service*]
RSO .... Register Sender Outward [*Telecommunications*] (TEL)
RSO .... Relativistic and Spin-Orbit (PDAA)
RSO .... Remanso [*Brazil*] [*Airport symbol*] (AD)
RSO .... Reproduction Service Order (SAA)
RSO .... Research Ship of Opportunity
RSO .... Resident Surgical Officer [*British*]
RSO .... Retirement Service Officer [*DoD*]
RSO .... Revenue Sharing Office [*Treasury*] (OICC)
RSO .... Revised Statutes of Ontario [*Canada*] [*A publication*] (DLA)
RSO .... Revolutionaere Sozialisten (Oesterreichs) [*Revolutionary Socialists (Austria)*] [*Political party*] (PPE)
RSO .... Right Salpingo-Oophorectomy [*Medicine*]
RSO .... Robert Stigwood Orginazation [*Record label*]
RSO .... Runway Supervisory Officer [*Aviation*] (MCD)
RSO .... Rural Suboffice [*British*]
RSOB .... Russell Senate Office Building [*Also, OSOB*] [*Washington, DC*] (DLA)
RSOC .... Remote Sensing Oceanography [*Navy*]
RSOG .... Reserve Special Operations Group [*Army*]
RSOI .... Reception, Staging, Onward Movement and Integration [*Military*] (INF)
RSO/MFSO .... Range Safety Officer / Missile Flight Safety Officer [*Military*] (SAA)
RSOP .... Range Safety Operational Plan (MUGU)
RSOP .... Readiness Standing Operating Procedures [*Military*] (INF)
RSOP .... Reconnaissance, Selection, and Occupation of Position [*Military*]
RSOPN .... Resumed Operation [*Aviation*] (FAAC)
RSOR .... Range Safety Operations Requirement
RS or L .... Rated Same or Lower
RSOS .... Resident Supervisor of Shipping [*Navy*] (DNAB)
RSP .... RADAR Signal Processor
RSP .... Radii of Standard Parallels
RSP .... Radio Switch Panel
RSP .... Random Smooth Pursuit [*Ophthalmology*]
RSP .... Range Solar Panel
RSP .... Range Sorting Program
RSP .... Range Support Plan (MUGU)
RSP .... Rapid Site Preparation
RSP .... Rapid Solidification Process (MCD)
RSP .... Rassemblement Socialiste Progressiste [*Tunisia*] [*Political party*] (EY)
RSP .... Rate Sensing Package (AAG)
RSP .... Reactive Soil Pool [*Agriculture*]
RSP .... Reactivity Surveillance Procedures [*Nuclear energy*] (NRCH)
RSP .... Reader/Sorter Processor
RSP .... Real-Time Signal Processor (MCD)
RSP .... Rear-Screen Projection (WDAA)
RSP .... Receiving Stolen Property
RSP .... Recirculating Single Pass [*Medicine*] (BARN)
RSP .... Reconnaissance and Security Positions [*Military*]
RSP .... Record Select Program [*Computer science*]
RSP .... Recoverable Sparoair Probe (MUGU)
RSP .... Reinforced Structural Plastic
RSP .... Relative Stopping Power [*Nuclear energy*] (NUCP)
RSP .... Remote Sensor Platoon
RSP .... Remote Shutdown Panel [*Nuclear energy*] (NRCH)
RSP .... Remote Switching Partition (HGAA)
RSP .... Render Safe Procedure [*Military*]
RSP .... Rendezvous Station Panel [*NASA*] (MCD)
RSP .... Replenishment Spare Part
RSP .... Replication Synchronization Process [*Telecommunications*] (TEL)
RSP .... Required Space Character [*Computer science*]
RSP .... Reserve Stock Point
RSP .... Resource Sharing Protocol (IAA)
RSP .... Resource Specialist Program
RSP .... Respirable Suspended Particulates
RSP .... Responder Beacon
RSP .... Response Byte [*Computer science*]
RSP .... Restoration Priority [*Telecommunications*] (TEL)
RSP .... Retail Stockage Policy
RSP .... Revolutionaire Socialistische Partij [*Revolutionary Socialist Party*] [*Netherlands Political party*] (PPE)
RSP .... Revolutionary Socialist Party [*India*] [*Political party*] (PPW)
RSP .... Rhinoseptoplasty [*Otorhinolaryngology*] (DAVI)
RSP .... Right Sacroposterior [*A fetal position*] [*Obstetrics*]
RSP .... Robotic Sample Processor [*Automation*]
RSP .... Rocky Slope Pipeline
RSP .... Roll Stabilization Platform
RSP .... Roscoe, Snyder & Pacific Railway Co. [*AAR code*]
RSP .... Rotating Shield Plug [*Nuclear energy*] (NRCH)
RSP .... Rotation in a Selected Plane
RSP .... Route Selection Program (SAA)
RSP .... Rural Satellite Program [*US Agency for International Development*] [*Washington, DC*] [*Telecommunications*] (TSSD)
RSP .... Southern Pacific Rail [*NYSE symbol*] (TTSB)
RSP .... Southern Pacific Railroad Co. [*NYSE symbol*] (SPSG)
RSPA .... Railway Systems and Procedures Association [*Later, RSMA*]
RSPA .... Research and Special Programs Administration [*Department of Transportation*] [*Washington, DC*] (GRD)
RSPA .... Royal Society for the Prevention of Accidents [*British*]
RSPAS .... [*The*] Research School of Pacific and Asian Studies [*Australian National University*] (ECON)
RSPB .... Retail Stockage Policy, Bulk Supplies (MCD)
RSPB .... Royal Society for the Protection of Birds [*British*]
RSPBA .... Royal Scottish Pipe Band Association [*British*] (DBA)
RSPCA .... Royal Society for the Prevention of Cruelty to Animals [*British*]
RSPD .... Rapid Solidification Plasma Deposition [*Metallurgy*]
RSPD .... Research and Special Project Division [*Bureau of National Affairs*] [*Information service or system*] (IID)
RSPD .... Respond (MSA)
RSPE .... RADAR Signalling Processing Equipment
RSPE .... Retail Stockage Policy, Evaluation (MCD)
RSPEI .... Revised Statutes of Prince Edward Island [*Canada*]
RSPH .... Royal Society for the Promotion of Health [*British*] (DAVI)
RSPI .... Residential Space Planners International (EA)
RSPI .... Resident-Shared Page Index [*Computer science*] (OA)
RSPK .... Recurrent Spontaneous Psychokinesis [*Poltergeist*] [*Parapsychology*]
RSPL .... RADAR Significant Power Line
RSPL .... Recommended Spare Parts List [*NASA*]
RSPM .... Random Spatial Phase Modulator
RS/PM .... Rapid Solidification/Powder Metallurgy
RSPMP .... Ready Store Positive Maintenance Program (MCD)
RSPO .... Rail Services Planning Office [*Interstate Commerce Commission*]
RSPO .... Railway Station Police Officer [*British*]
RSPP .... Radio Simulation Patch Panel (CET)
RSPP .... Royal Society of Portrait Painters [*British*]
Rspr .... Rechtspraak [*Case Law, Judicial Decisions*] [*Netherlands*] (ILCA)
Rspr .... Rechtsprechung [*Court Practice*] [*German*] (ILCA)
Rspr Arb .... Rechtsprechung in Arbeitssachen [*Labor Court Reports*] [*German*] (ILCA)
RSPRT .... Robust Sequential Probability Ratio Test [*Navy*]
RSPS .... Range Solar Panel Substrate
RSPS .... Response (MSA)
RSPS .... Royal Scottish Pipers' Society [*British*] (DBA)
RSPT .... Rayleigh-Schrodinger Perturbation Theory [*Physical chemistry*]
RSPT .... Real Storage Page Table [*Computer science*] (BUR)
RSPT .... Report Starting Procedure Turn [*Aviation*] (DA)
RSPTR .... Respirator (MSA)
RSPV .... Respective (AABC)
RSPWC .... Royal Society of Painters in Water-Colours [*British*]
RSQ .... Rescue (AAG)
RSQ .... Revised Statutes of Quebec [*Canada*] [*A publication*] (DLA)
RSQBT .... Rescue Boat
RSQC .... Reliability, Safety, and Quality Control
RSR .... Congregation of Our Lady of the Holy Rosary [*Roman Catholic women's religious order*]
RSR .... En Route Surveillance RADAR
RSR .... Radiological Safety Review [*Nuclear energy*] (NRCH)

RSR .... Raiding Support Regiment [*British Royal Marines*] [*World War II*]
RSR .... Range Safety Report [*NASA*] (AAG)
RSR .... Rapid Solidification Rate (IEEE)
RSR .... Rate Stabilization Reserve [*Health insurance*] (GHCT)
RSR .... Reactor Safety Research [*Nuclear energy*]
RSR .... Ready Service Ring (NG)
RSR .... Red Sulfhydryl Reagent
RSR .... Reference Services Review [*A publication*] (BRI)
RSR .... Refracted Surface-Reflected Ray
RSR .... Regular Sinus Rhythm [*Physiology*]
RSR .... Relative Survival Rate [*Statistics*] (DAVI)
RSR .... Relay Set Receiver [*Telecommunications*] (IAA)
RSR .... Remote Start Relay (IAA)
RSR .... Republica Socialista Romania [*Socialist Republic of Romania*] (EY)
RSR .... Request for Scientific Research (AAG)
RSR .... Required Supply Rate [*Military*] (AABC)
RSR .... Research Study Requests
RSR .... Residue Solvent Refining [*Lummus Crest, Inc. process*]
RSR .... Resorufin [*Organic chemistry*]
RSR .... Resources Status Report
RSR .... Restore [*Computer science*] (ECII)
RSR .... Reverse Switching Rectifier (IAA)
RSR .... Revised Supplementary Regulation
RSR .... Right Element Shift Right (SAA)
RSR .... Riser Foods Cl'A' [*AMEX symbol*] (TTSB)
RSR .... Riser Foods, Inc. [*AMEX symbol*] (SPSG)
RSR .... Rocket Scoring Reliability (MCD)
RSR .... Rocket Stabilized Rod
RSR .... Rod Select Relay (IEEE)
RSR .... Rotary Seal Ring
RSR .... Rotating Shadowband Radiometer (USDC)
RSR .... Rotating Shadowband Radiometer [*Marine science*] (OSRA)
RSR .... Route Surveillance RADAR
RSR .... Rover Sports Register [*An association*] (EAIO)
RSR .... Royal Sussex Regiment [*Military unit*] [*British*]
RSR .... Worcester, MA [*Location identifier FAA*] (FAAL)
RSRA .... Rotor Systems Research Aircraft [*Army/NASA*]
RSRB .... Redesigned Solid Rocket Booster
RSRCH .... Research
RSRE .... Royal Signals and RADAR Establishment [*Computer chip designer*] [*England*]
RSRE .... Royal Signals Research Establishment [*British*]
RSRM .... Raiding Squadron Royal Marines [*British military*] (DMA)
RSRM .... Redesigned Solid Rocket Motor
RSRM .... Reduced Smoke Rocket Motor (MCD)
RSRM .... Reusable Solid Rocket Motor
RSROA .... Roller Skating Rink Operators Association (EA)
RSROAA .... Roller Skating Rink Operators Association (NADA)
RSROM .... Row Select Read-Only Memory [*Computer science*] (IAA)
RSRP .... Remote Sensing Research Program [*University of California*]
RSRP .... Rossica Society of Russian Philately (EA)
RSRS .... Radio and Space Research Station [*Later, Appleton Laboratory*] [*British*] (MCD)
RSRS .... Range Safety Receiving Station
Rsrt .... Resort
RsrtIn .... Resort Income Investors, Inc. [*Associated Press*] (SAG)
RSRV .... Rotor Systems Research Vehicle
RSRW .... Remote Short Range Wind Sensor (MCD)
RSS .... RADAR Seeker Simulator [*Military*] (CAAL)
RSS .... RADAR Sensing System [*Military*] (CAAL)
RSS .... RADAR Signal Simulator
RSS .... Radiated Simulation System (MCD)
RSS .... Radio Security Service [*British*]
RSS .... Radio Subsystem
RS(S) .... Radio Supervisor (Special) [*British military*] (DMA)
RSS .... Rail Security Service [*MTMC*] (TAG)
RSS .... Rail Surveillance Service [*Military Traffic Management Command*]
RSS .... Railway Systems Suppliers (EA)
RSS .... Range Safety Switch [*NASA*] (MCD)
RSS .... Range Safety System [*NASA*]
RSS .... Range Slaving System
RSS .... Rapid Scanning of Spectra [*Instrumentation*]
RSS .... Rashtriya Swayamsevak Sangh [*National Union of Selfless Servers*] [*Militant Hindu organization India*]
RSS .... Rat Stomach Strip [*Medicine*] (DMAA)
RSS .... Reactant Service System
RSS .... Reactants Supply System [*NASA*] (KSC)
RSS .... Reactive Stream Separation (MCD)
RSS .... Reactive System Sensitivity (IAA)
RSS .... Reactor Safety Study [*Nuclear energy*]
RSS .... Reactor Shutdown System [*Nuclear energy*] (NRCH)
RSS .... Ready Service Spares
RSS .... Real-Time Switching System
RSS .... Recombination Signal Sequence [*Immunology*]
RSS .... Reed Stenhouse Companies Ltd. [*Toronto Stock Exchange symbol*]
RSS .... Reference Sound Source
RSS .... Refrigeration System [*or Subsystem*] [*Skylab*] [*NASA*]
RSS .... Refrigeration System Shield (MCD)
RSS .... Regiae Societatis Sodalis [*Fellow of the Royal Society*] [*Latin*]
RSS .... Registered Shoeing Smith [*Blacksmith*] [*Scotland*]
RSS .... Rehabilitation Service Series
RSS .... Rehabilitation Support Schedule (AFM)
RSS .... Relative System Sensitivity
RSS .... Relaxed Static Stability [*Aviation*]
RSS .... Remote Safing Switch
RSS .... Remote Sensing Society [*Nottingham, England*] (EAIO)
RSS .... Remote Shutdown System (IEEE)
RSS .... Remote Slave Station (MCD)
RSS .... Remote Switching System [*Telecommunications*]
RSS .... Repair and Storage Shelter (SAA)
RSS .... Repeat Squawk Sheet (MCD)
RSS .... Requirements Status System [*NASA*]
RSS .... Residual Sum of Squares [*Statistics*]
RSS .... Resource Survey Satellite
RSS .... Restricted Stepsize [*Statistics*]
RSS .... Retention Spermatemia Syndrome [*Medicine*]
RSS .... Retentive Substrate Shield [*i.e., saucer*] [*Slang*]
RSS .... Revised Statutes of Saskatchewan [*Canada A publication*] (DLA)
RSS .... Reye's Syndrome Society [*Later, NRSF*] (EA)
RSS .... Ribbed Smoke Sheet [*Natural rubber*]
RSS .... Rib Structure Station [*NASA*] (MCD)
RSS .... Ride Smoothing System [*Aviation*]
RSS .... Rifle Sharpshooter
RSS .... Rigid Space Structure
RSS .... Ripe Skin Solid [*A banana substrate*]
RSS .... River Support Squadron [*Navy*] (VNW)
RSS .... Road Sensing Suspension [*Automotive engineering*]
RSS .... Rockdale, Sandow & Southern Railroad Co. [*AAR code*]
RSS .... Roger Sessions Society (EA)
RSS .... Roland International Corp. Sound Space [*Electronic music*]
RSS .... Romance of Science Series [*A publication*]
RSS .... Romanche Sedimentary Sequence [*Geology*]
RSS .... Rome and the Study of Scripture [*A publication*] (BJA)
RSS .... Root Sum Square (DA)
RSS .... Roseires [*Sudan*] [*Airport symbol*] (OAG)
RSS .... Rosette Scan Seeker [*Army*] (DOMA)
RSS .... Rotary Shaft Seal
RSS .... Rotary Stepping Switch
RSS .... Rotary Symbol Switch (MCD)
RSS .... Rotating Service Structure [*Kennedy Space Center*] (MCD)
RSS .... Route Switching Subsystem (NITA)
RSS .... Routing and Switching System
RSS .... Royal Shakespeare Society [*British*] (DI)
RSS .... Royal Statistical Society [*British*] (DI)
RSS .... Rural Sociological Society (EA)
RSS .... Russian Spring-Summer Encephalitis [*Medicine*] (MAH)
RSSA .... Resource Services Support Agreement (GNE)
RSSAILA .... Returned Sailors', Soldiers', Airmen's Imperial League of Australia [*British military*] (DMA)
RSSC .... Remote-Site Simulator Console [*NASA*]
RSSE .... Russian Spring-Summer Encephalitis [*Medicine*]
RSSEL .... Recommended Special Support Equipment List
RSSF .... Retrievable Surface Storage Facility [*Nuclear energy*]
RSSF .... Roller Speed Skating Federation (EA)
RSSI .... Railway Systems Suppliers (EA)
RSSK .... Rigid Seat Survival Kit (NG)
RSSMAP .... Reactor Safety Study Methodology Application Program [*Nuclear energy*] (NRCH)
RSSN .... Reaction-Sintered Silicon Nitrate
RSSN .... Research Space Surveillance Network
RSSP .... Range Single Shot Probability [*Military*]
RSSPCC .... Royal Scottish Society for Prevention of Cruelty to Children
RSSPL .... Recommended Spares and Spare Parts List
RSSPO .... Resident Space Shuttle Project Office [*NASA*] (NASA)
RSSRT .... Russell Sage Social Relations Test [*Psychology*]
RSSS .... Rashtriya Swayamseyak Sangh [*National Union of Selfless Servers*] [*Militant Hindu organization India*] (PD)
RSSS .... Reusable Space Shuttle System [*Aerospace*] (KSC)
RSSS .... Robotic Substrate Servicing System [*Space Automation and Robotics Center*] [*NASA*]
RSST .... Reserve Station Service Transformer [*Nuclear energy*] (NRCH)
RSSU .... Remote-Site Simulation Unit [*Navy*] (NVT)
RSSU .... Remote System Support Utility [*Telematics International, Inc.*]
RS Supp .... Supplement to the Revised Statutes [*A publication*] (DLA)
RSSW .... Ross Sea Shelf Water [*Ross Ice Shelf Project*]
RSSZ .... Rung Sat Special Zone [*Vietnam*]
RST .... RADAR Start (MSA)
RST .... RADAR Systems Technician (MCD)
RST .... Radiometric Sun Tracer
RST .... Radiosensitivity Test (AAMN)
RST .... Range Search and Track (MCD)
RST .... Rapid Solidification Technology [*Metallurgy*]
RST .... Rapid Surfactant Test [*Medicine*] (MEDA)
RST .... Readability, Strength, Tone
RST .... Read Symbol Table
RST .... Reagin Screen Test [*Medicine*] (MEDA)
RST .... Reagin Screen Test [*For syphilis*] [*Medicine*] (DAVI)
RST .... Recessed Selectromatic Terminal (NASA)
RST .... Recognition Suppression Technique
RST .... Recovery Sequence Tester
RST .... Reentry System Technology [*Aerospace*]
RST .... Reflector Support Truss
RST .... Register and Self-Test
RST .... Regularly-Scheduled Training [*Military*] (ADDR)
RST .... Reinforcing Steel [*Technical drawings*]
RST .... Reliability Shakedown Test (PDAA)
RST .... Religious of St. Andrew [*Roman Catholic religious order*]
RST .... Remote Sensing Technology [*Automotive exhaust emissions*]
RST .... Remote Station [*Computer science*]
RST .... Requirements for Scheduled Test (MUGU)

RST............ Research Study Team
RST............ Reset [*Telecommunications*] (TEL)
RST............ Reset-Set Trigger
RST............ Residential Subsurface Transformer (IAA)
RST............ Resin Skived Tape
RST............ Resistance (AABC)
RST............ Resort Airline, Inc. [*ICAO designator*] (FAAC)
RST............ Rest
RST............ Rest
RST............ Restore (MSA)
RST............ Rework/Scrap Tag (MCD)
RST............ Right Sacrotransverse [*A fetal position*] [*Obstetrics*]
RST............ Right Store (SAA)
RST............ Rochester [*Minnesota*] [*Airport symbol*] (OAG)
RST............ Rodney Smith Tube [*Medicine*] (DAVI)
RST............ Rolling Stock (CINC)
RST............ Rough Saw Template (MCD)
RST............ Routine Sequence Table
RST............ Royal Scot Resources [*Vancouver Stock Exchange symbol*]
RST............ Royal Society of Tasmania [*Australia*]
RST............ Royal Society of Teachers [*British*]
R Sta.......... Radio Telegraph Station
RSTA.......... Reconnaissance, Surveillance, and Target Acquisition Center [*Fort Monmout h, NJ*] [*Army*] (MCD)
RSta............ Regulating Station [*Army*]
RSTA.......... Sunresorts Ltd. NV [*NASDAQ symbol*] (SAG)
RSTAA.......... Reconnaissance, Surveillance, and Target Acquisition Aircraft (MCD)
RSTA & E.... Reconnaissance, Surveillance, Target Acquisition, and Engagement (MCD)
RSTA/BMC3... Reconnaissance, Surveillance, and Target Acquisition/Battle Management Command, Control, and Communications (MCD)
RSTAF.......... Sunresorts Ltd NV 'A' [*NASDAQ symbol*] (TTSB)
RSTC.......... RADAR Ship Target Classification [*Military*] (CAAL)
RSTC.......... Recreational Scuba Training Council (EA)
RSTC.......... Remote-Site Telemetry Computer [*NASA*]
RSTCP.......... Remote Synchronous Terminal Control Program (MHDI)
RSTD.......... Restricted
RSTG.......... Roasting (MSA)
RSTI............ Radiological Service Training Institute (DMAA)
RSTI............ Rofin-Sinar Technologies, Inc. [*NASDAQ symbol*] (SAG)
RSTK.......... Relay Servicing Tool Kit
RSTL.......... Red Status Timeline
RSTL.......... Relaxed Skin Tension Line [*Dermatology*]
RSTMH........ Royal Society of Tropical Medicine and Hygiene [*British*] (EAIO)
RSTN.......... Radio Solar Telescope Network (MCD)
RSTN.......... Regional Seismic Test Network [*Nuclear explosion detection*]
RSTN.......... Relay Station (IAA)
RSTO.......... Rose's Stores [*NASDAQ symbol*] (SAG)
R/STOL........ Reduced/Short Takeoff and Landing [*Aircraft*]
RStorLettRel... Rivista di Storia e Letteratura Religiosa [*Florence*] [*A publication*] (BJA)
RSTOW........ Rose's Stores Wrrt [*NASDAQ symbol*] (TTSB)
RSTP.......... Real-Time Statistical and Terminal Profile [*IRS*]
RSTP.......... Remote-Site Telemetry Processor [*NASA*] (KSC)
RSTPF.......... Rustproof (MSA)
RSTR.......... Resistor
RSTR.......... Restrict (MSA)
rstrau.......... Restaurant (VRA)
RSTRD.......... Restricted
RSTRNT....... Restaurant
RSTRT.......... Restart (NASA)
RSTS.......... RADAR System Test Station (MCD)
RSTS.......... Recovery Systems Track Site (IAA)
RSTS.......... Resource Sharing Time Sharing (NITA)
RSTS.......... Resource-Sharing Time-Sharing System
RSTS.......... Retirement Systems Testing Section [*Social Security Administration*]
RSTS.......... Retropharyngeal Soft Tissue Space [*Medicine*] (DMAA)
RSTS/E........ Resource System Time Sharing/Extended [*Computer science*] (BTTJ)
RST-V.......... Reconnaissance, Surveillance, and Targeting Vehicle [*Military*]
RSTV.......... Rice Stripe Virus [*Plant pathology*]
RSU............ Radiological Sciences Unit [*Medicine*] (DMAA)
RSU............ Railway Services Unit [*MTMC*] (TAG)
RSU............ Rating Scale Unit [*Acoustics*]
RSU............ Recorder Switch Unit
RSU............ Recovery Storage Unit [*Military*]
RSU............ Register Storage Unit
RSU............ Relay Storage Unit
RSU............ Remote Service Unit (NASA)
RSU............ Remote Subscriber Unit [*Telecommunications*]
RSU............ Remote Switching Unit [*Telecommunications*]
RSU............ Repair and Salvage Unit [*British military*] (DMA)
RSU............ Rescue Support Umbilical (MCD)
RSU............ Reserved for Software Use (IAA)
RSU............ Rio Sucio [*Colombia*] [*Airport symbol*] (AD)
RSU............ Runway Supervisory [*MTMC*] (TAG)
RSU............ Runway Supervisory Unit [*Aviation*] (FAAC)
RSUA.......... Royal Society of Ulster Architects [*British*] (BI)
RSUP.......... REGIS [*Relational General Information System*] System Users' Group (EA)
RSUT.......... Remote Start Unit Trainer (DWSG)
RSV............ Armored Reconnaissance Scout Vehicle [*Army*] (RDA)
RSV............ Diesel Run Control Solenoid Valve (IEEE)
RSV............ Random Sine Vibration
RSV............ Rat Sarcoma Virus
RSV............ Rat Seminal Vesicle
RSV............ Recently Separated Veteran
RSV............ Reconnaissance Scout Vehicle (MCD)
RSV............ Red Lake & Sun Valley [*Vancouver Stock Exchange symbol*]
RSV............ Remove Shutoff Valve (KSC)
RSV............ Research Safety Vehicle [*Department of Transportation*]
RSV............ Reserve (MSA)
RSV............ Reserve (ECII)
RSV............ Reservoir [*Board on Geographic Names*]
RSV............ Respiratory Syncytial Virus
RSV............ Respiratory Syncytial Virus [*Medicine*]
RSV............ Resupply Vehicle [*Military*]
RSV............ Revised Standard Version [*of the Bible, 1952*]
RSV............ Right Subclavian Vein [*Anatomy*]
RSV............ Robinson, IL [*Location identifier FAA*] (FAAL)
RSV............ Rous Sarcoma Virus [*Same as ASV*]
RSVA.......... Randolph-Sheppard Vendors of America (EA)
RSV-Br........ Rous Sarcoma Virus, Bryan [*Strain*]
RSVC.......... Rental Service Corp. [*NASDAQ symbol*] (SAG)
RSVC.......... Resident Supervisor Call (BUR)
RSVC.......... Right Superior Vena Cava [*Medicine*] (DMAA)
RSVE.......... Reconstituted Sendai Virus Envelope [*Immunology*]
RsvltF.......... Roosevelt Financial Group, Inc. [*Associated Press*] (SAG)
RsvltFn........ Roosevelt Financial Group, Inc. [*Associated Press*] (SAG)
RSVP.......... Please Call Back [*International telex abbreviation*] (WDMC)
RSVP.......... Radiation Spectral Visual Data Distribution (IAA)
RSVP.......... Radiation Spectral Visual Photometer
RSVP.......... Random Signal Vibration Protector (PDAA)
RSVP.......... Rapid Sampling Vertical Profiler [*Oceanography*]
RSVP.......... Rapid Serial Visual Presentation [*Computer science*]
RSVP.......... Relational Structure Vertex Processor (PDAA)
RSVP.......... Remote System Verification Program
RSVP.......... Repondez, s'Il Vous Plait [*The Favor of an Answer is Requested*] [*French*]
RSVP.......... Research Selected Vote Profile [*Election poll*]
RSVP.......... Research Society for Victorian Periodicals (EA)
RSVP.......... Resource Reservation Protocol [*Computer science*]
RSVP.......... Resource Reservation Protocol [*Computer science*]
RSVP.......... ReSource ReserVation Protocol [*Computer science*]
RSVP.......... Resource Reservation Protocol [*Videoconferencing*]
RSVP.......... Response Segmentation and Validation Program [*Donnelley Marketing InformationServices*] [*Information service or system*] (IID)
RSVP.......... Response System with Variable Prescriptions (EDAC)
RSVP.......... Restartable Solid Variable Pulse [*Motor*] (MCD)
RSVP.......... Retired Senior Volunteer Program (EA)
RSVP.......... Ride Shared Vehicle Paratransit [*Transportation system*]
RSVP.......... Rotating Surveillance Vehicle Platform [*Military*] (MCD)
RSVP.......... Rural Southern Voice for Peace [*An association*] (EA)
RSVP.......... Rural Student Vocational Program [*Washington*] (EDAC)
RSVPI.......... Retired Senior Volunteer Program International (EA)
RSVR.......... Reservoir (AAG)
RSVR.......... Resolver (AAG)
RSV(RV)...... Revised Standard Version of the Bible [*A publication*] (BJA)
RSV-SR........ Rous Sarcoma Virus, Schmidt-Ruppin [*Strain*]
RSVT.......... Stetson Reading-Spelling Vocabulary Test [*Educational test*]
RSVTN.......... Reservation
RSW............ Fort Myers [*Florida*] [*Airport symbol*] (OAG)
RSW............ Fort Myers, FL [*Location identifier FAA*] (FAAL)
RS(W).......... Radio Supervisor (Warfare) [*British military*] (DMA)
RSW............ Rattlesnake Hills [*Washington*] [*Seismograph station code, US Geological Survey*] (SEIS)
RSW............ Raw Service Water [*Nuclear energy*] (NRCH)
RSW............ Refrigerated Seawater
RSW............ Repeating Slide Wire
RSW............ Residential Social Worker (AIE)
RSW............ Resistance Spot Welding
RSW............ Retarded Surface Wave
RSW............ Right-Sided Weakness [*Neurology*] (DAVI)
RSW............ Royal Scottish Society of Painters in Water Colours
RSW............ Southwest Florida International Airport [*FAA*] (TAG)
RSWB.......... Raumordnung, Stadtebau, Wohnungswesen, Bauwesen [*Fraunhofer Society*] [*Germany*] (IID)
RSWC.......... Right Side Up with Care
RSWC.......... Royal Society of Painters in Water-Colours [*British*] (ROG)
RSWD.......... Regiment South Western District [*British military*] (DMA)
RSWF.......... Radioactive Scrap and Waste Facility
RSWPS........ Repetitive Square Wave Potential Signal [*Electrochemistry*]
RSWS.......... Royal Scottish Water-Colour Society (ROG)
RSWW.......... Ross Sea Winter Water [*Marine science*] (MSC)
RSX............ Resource-Sharing Executive (NITA)
RSX............ Resource Sharing Extention [*Computer science*] (CDE)
RSY............ Lumberton, NC [*Location identifier FAA*] (FAAL)
RSY............ Rigelyn Security [*Vancouver Stock Exchange symbol*]
RSYCS.......... Rosy Cross [*Freemasonry*]
RSYN.......... Reactor Synthesis
RSYS.......... RadiSys Corp. [*NASDAQ symbol*] (SAG)
RSYS.......... Responsible System (NASA)
RSZ............ Air Service State Co. [*Hungary ICAO designator*] (FAAC)
RSZ............ Phoenix, AZ [*Location identifier FAA*] (FAAL)
RT.............. Air Tungaru (Gilbert Islands) [*British ICAO designator*] (ICDA)
RT.............. Electric Current Relay
RT.............. Norving [*ICAO designator*] (AD)
RT.............. Rachidian Tooth
RT.............. RADAR Tracking Radiotelegraphy (IAA)
RT.............. RADAR Transparency (MCD)

R/T .... RADAR Trigger (CET)
RT .... Radiation Therapy [*Medicine*]
RT .... Radiographic Test [*Nuclear energy*] (NRCH)
RT .... Radiologic Technologist
RT .... Radio Technician
RT .... Radiotelegraphy
RT .... Radio Telegraphy (ADA)
RT .... Radiotelephone
RT .... Radio Telephone (MSA)
R/T .... Radiotelephony
RT .... Radio Telephony (NTCM)
RT .... Radio/Television Repair Program [*Association of Independent Colleges and Schools specialization code*]
RT .... Radiotherapy (AAMN)
RT .... Radio Tower (IAA)
RT .... Radio Tracking (KSC)
RT .... Radio Transmitter
RT .... Radium Therapy [*Clinical chemistry*] (MAE)
RT .... Radular Teeth
RT .... Rail Tractor [*British*]
RT .... Rail Transit [*BTS*] (TAG)
RT .... Rail Transport
RT .... Raintight (MSA)
RT .... Raise Top (OA)
RT .... Randomized Trial [*Statistics*]
RT .... Ranger Tab [*Military decoration*]
RT .... Rangetaker [*British military*] (DMA)
RT .... Range Timing (AAG)
RT .... Range-to-Target (NASA)
RT .... Range Tracking
RT .... Rapid Transit (IAA)
RT .... Rate (AAG)
RT .... Rated Time (IEEE)
RT .... Rate Transmitter
RT .... Rational Therapy [*Short form for rational-emotive therapy*]
RT .... Ratio Transfer (IAA)
RT .... Ratio Transformer [*Unit*]
RT .... Reaction Time
RT .... Reactor Trip [*Nuclear energy*] (NRCH)
RT .... Reader Tape [*Contact*] (MCD)
RT .... Reading Teacher [*A publication*] (BRI)
RT .... Reading Test
RT .... Readout Technique
RT .... Read Tape [*Computer science*]
RT .... Real Time [*Computer*] [*Computer science*]
RT .... Received Text (ROG)
R/T .... Receiver/Transmitter [*Radio*] (KSC)
RT .... Receive-Transmit [*Radio*]
RT .... Receiving Terminal (IAA)
RT .... Receiving Test (DNAB)
RT .... Receiving Tube
RT .... Recipient Type (NITA)
RT .... Reconnaissance Team [*Military*] (VNW)
R/T .... Record of Trial [*Army*] (AABC)
RT .... Record Transfer
RT .... Recovery Time [*Military*] (AFIT)
RT .... Recreational Therapist [*or Therapy*]
R/T .... Rectal Temperature (DAVI)
RT .... Recueillis Temporaires [*Temporarily Taken In*] [*Of unadoptable children*] [*French*]
RT .... Red Tetrazolium [*Also, TPTZ, TTC*] [*Chemical indicator*]
RT .... Reduced Tillage System [*Agriculture*]
RT .... Reduction Tables
RT .... Reference Trajectory [*NASA*] (KSC)
RT .... Refrigerated Trap [*Biotechnology*]
RT .... Regional Treasurer [*British*]
RT .... Registered Technician [*American Registry of X-ray Technicians*]
RT .... Registered Technologist [*Radiology*] (DAVI)
RT .... Registered Trademark (CDAI)
RT .... Registered Transmitter (IAA)
RT .... Register Ton
RT .... Register Traffic [*Telecommunications*] (TEL)
RT .... Register Transfer [*Computer science*]
R/T .... Register Translator [*Telecommunications*] (TEL)
RT .... Registration Type (NITA)
RT .... Regression Testing [*Computer science*] (IEEE)
RT .... Regressive Tax (MHDW)
RT .... Rehabilitation Therapist [*or Therapy*]
RT .... Rejection Tag (AAG)
RT .... Related Term [*Indexing*]
R/T .... Related To (DAVI)
RT .... Relaxation Time
RT .... Relaxation Training [*Psychology*]
RT .... Relay Tester
RT .... Relay Transmitter
RT .... Released Time
RT .... Release Transmittal (MCD)
RT .... Reliable Transfer [*Telecommunications*] (OSI)
RT .... Relocatable Term [*Computer science*] (IAA)
RT .... Relocation Time
RT .... Remote Terminal [*Computer science*]
RT .... Renal Transplant [*Nephrology*]
RT .... Repair Time
R/T .... Reperforator/Transmitter [*Teletypewriter*] [*Computer science*]
RT .... Request Translator (SAA)
RT .... Research and Technology
RT .... Reserve Training
RT .... Reset Trigger
RT .... Residence Time [*Chemistry*]
R-T .... Resistance Test (NASA)
RT .... Resistance Thermometer [*Electronics*] (IAA)
RT .... Resistance Transfer [*Laboratory science*] (DAVI)
RT .... Resistor Tolerance
RT .... Resistor Transistor
RT .... Resolver Transformer [*Computer science*] (IAA)
RT .... Resonant Transfer (IAA)
RT .... Respiratory Therapy [*Medicine*]
RT .... Response Time [*Computer science*]
RT .... Resting Tension [*Biology*]
RT .... Restraint of Trade (MHDW)
RT .... Resuscitation Team
RT .... Resuscitation Therapy
RT .... Resynchronization Timer [*Telecommunications*] (OSI)
RT .... Retention Time [*Computer science*]
R/T .... Retouch [*Graphic arts*] (DGA)
RT .... Retraining (OICC)
RT .... Retransformation [*Medicine*] (DMAA)
RT .... Retro Table [*NASA*]
RT .... Retroviral Transcript [*Genetics*]
RT .... Return Ticket
RT .... Reverberation Time (NTCM)
RT .... Reverse Transcriptase [*An enzyme*]
RT .... Revolving Radio Beacon [*ITU designation*] (CET)
RT .... Revolving Transmitter [*Telecommunications*] (IAA)
R/T .... Rho/Theta
RT .... Rigging Tool (MCD)
RT .... Right (EY)
rt .... Right (WDMC)
rt .... Right (VRA)
RT .... Right Tackle [*Football*]
RT .... Right Thigh [*Medicine*] (MAE)
RT .... Right Time of Departure/Arrival (DS)
RT .... Ringing Tone [*Telecommunications*] (TEL)
RT .... Ring Time [*Telecommunications*] (IAA)
RT .... Ring Trip [*Telecommunications*] (TEL)
RT .... RISC [*Reduced-Instruction Set Computer*] Technology [*IBM Corp.*]
RT .... Rise Time (DEN)
RT .... [*The*] River Terminal Railway Co. [*AAR code*]
RT .... Road Traffic
RT .... Road Transport (NATG)
RT .... Road Truck [*Shipping*] (DCTA)
RT .... Robotic Telepresence
RT .... Rocket Target
RT .... Romain de Tirtoff [*Also known as ERTE*] [*Couturier*]
RT .... Room Temperature
RT .... Root [*Mathematics*] (ROG)
RT .... Rotary Transformer (IAA)
RT .... Rotation Discrete Rate
rt .... Rotten [*Quality of the bottom*] [*Nautical charts*]
Rt .... Rotundus Nucleus (DAVI)
RT .... Rough Terrain [*Military*] (AABC)
RT .... Roundtable [*Bulletin board system*] [*Computer science*] (PCM)
RT .... Round Trip
RT .... Route (AABC)
RT .... Route
RT .... Router Template
RT .... Route Treatment [*Telecommunications*] (TEL)
RT .... Routine Tag (SAA)
RT .... Routine Test (IAA)
RT .... Royalty Trust
RT .... Rubber-Tired (SAA)
RT .... Rufous-Sided Towhee [*Ornithology*]
RT .... Running Time [*Movies*] (CDAI)
RT .... Running Title
RT .... Running Total (DAVI)
RT .... Runnymede Trust [*An association*] (EAIO)
RT .... Runup and Taxi [*Air Force*]
RT .... Ruth [*Old Testament book*]
RT .... Ryerson Tull [*NYSE symbol*] (SAG)
RT .... Rye Terms
Rt .... Tetrachoric Correlation [*Psychology*]
RT .... Theatine Sisters of the Immaculate Conception (TOCD)
R_T .... Thermal Resistance (IDOE)
R_T .... Total Pulmonary Resistance [*Medicine*] (DAVI)
RT .... Total Reserves
R_t .... Total Resistance (IDOE)
rT_3 .... Reverse Triiodothyronine [*Endocrinology*]
RT_3 .... Serum Resin Triiodothyronine [*Uptake*] [*Endocrinology*] (DAVI)
RT_3U .... Resin T_3 Uptake [*Endocrinology*]
RT_4U .... Resin T_4 Uptake [*Endocrinology*]
RTA .... Racehorse Transporters Association [*British*] (DBA)
RTA .... RADAR Terrain Analysis
RTA .... Radically Tapered Antenna
RTA .... Radiology Telephone Access (DAVI)
RTA .... Radix Teachers Association (EA)
RTA .... Rail Travel Authorization [*Military*]
RTA .... Railway Tie Association (EA)
RTA .... Rapid Thermal Annealing [*Physics*]
RTA .... Rattler Resources [*Vancouver Stock Exchange symbol*]
RTA .... Reactivity Test Assembly [*Nuclear energy*]

RTA............ Ready-to-Assemble
RTA............ Real-Time Accumulator
RTA............ Real-Time Analyzer [*Electronics*]
RTA............ Reciprocal Trade Agreement
RTA............ Refrigeration Trade Association (NADA)
RTA............ Refrigeration Trade Association of America
RTA............ Reliability Test Assembly
RTA............ Reliable Test Analyzer [*Computer science*]
RTA............ Remote Technical Assistance (NITA)
RTA............ Remote Test Access [*Telecommunications*] (TEL)
RTA............ Remote Trunk Arrangement [*Telecommunications*] (TEL)
RTA............ Renal Tubule Acidosis [*Medicine*]
RTA............ Request for Technical Action (MCD)
RTA............ Required Time of Arrival (DA)
RTA............ Resident Transient Area [*Computer science*] (IAA)
RTA............ Retired Teachers Association (BARN)
RTA............ Riberalta [*Bolivia*] [*Seismograph station code, US Geological Survey Closed*] (SEIS)
RTA............ Rise-Time Analyzer
RTA............ Road Traffic Accident [*British*]
RTA............ Road Traffic Act [*1962*] [*British A publication*] (DLA)
RTA............ Rose Trade Association [*British*] (DBA)
RTA............ Rotor Test Apparatus (MCD)
RTA............ Rotuma [*Fiji*] [*Airport symbol*] (OAG)
RTA............ Royal Thai Army
RTA............ Rubber Trade Association [*British*] (DBA)
RTA............ Rubber Trade Association of New York (EA)
RTAB.......... Royal Thai Air Force Base [*Also, RTAFB*] (VNW)
RTAC.......... Real-Time Adaptive Control
RTAC.......... Real-Time Atmospheric Compensation [*Astronomy*]
RTAC.......... Regional Technical Aid Center [*Agency for International Development*]
RTAC.......... Research and Technology Advisory Council [*Terminated, 1977*] [*NASA*] (EGAO)
RTAC.......... Roads and Transportation Association of Canada [*Ottawa, ON*] [*Formerly, Canadian Good Roads Association*] [*Research center*]
RTACF........ Real-Time Auxiliary Computing Facility [*Apollo*] [*NASA*]
RTACS........ Real-Time Adaptive Control System [*Military*] (CAAL)
RTAD.......... Renal Tubular Acidification Defect [*Medicine*] (DMAA)
RTAD.......... Router Adapter
RTAF.......... Report to Armed Forces
RTAF.......... Robot Testing and Assessment Facility
RTAF.......... Royal Thai Air Force
RTAFB........ Royal Thai Air Force Base [*Also, RTAB*] (VNW)
RTAFCONV... Royal Thai Air Force Contingent, Vietnam
RTAG.......... Range Technical Advisory Group
RTAM.......... Remote Telecommunications Access Method [*Computer science*]
RTAM.......... Remote Terminal Access Method [*Computer science*] (BUR)
RTAM.......... Resident Terminal Access Method [*Computer science*]
RTAMA........ Railway Tyre and Axle Manufacturers Association [*British*] (BI)
RTAN.......... Rubber-Toughened Amorphous Nylon [*Organic chemistry*]
RT & EPS.... Rapid Transit and Electrical Power Systems
RTANG........ Right Angle
RTAP.......... Rural Technical Assistance Program [*Department of Transportation*]
RTAPS........ Real-Time Terminal Application Program System [*Computer science*]
RTAQ.......... Remedial Teachers' Association of Queensland [*Australia*]
RTARF........ Royal Thai Armed Forces (CINC)
RTARP........ Royal Thai Army Rebuild Plant (MCD)
RTAS.......... Rapid Telephone Access System (IAA)
RTASS........ Remote Tactical Airborne SIGINT [*Signals Intelligence*] System [*Air Force*] (DOMA)
RTAVF........ Royal Thai Army Volunteer Force (VNW)
RTAWA........ Retail Traders' Association of Western Australia
RTB............ Radial Time Base
RTB............ Radiodiffusion-Television Belge [*Belgian Radio Broadcasting and Television System*]
RTB............ Range and True Bearing (IAA)
RTB............ Ranger Training Brigade [*Fort Benning, GA*] [*Army*] (INF)
RTB............ Read Tape Binary [*Computer science*] (IEEE)
RTB............ Reason to Believe (ECON)
RTB............ Regional Training Brigade [*Army*] (INF)
RTB............ Resistance Temperature Bridge (SAA)
RTB............ Resistance Temperature Bulb [*NASA*]
RTB............ Resolver Tracking Bridge
RTB............ Response/Throughput Bias [*Computer science*] (BUR)
RTB............ Return to Base [*Military*]
RTB............ Return to Bias (IAA)
RTB............ Roatan [*Honduras*] [*Airport symbol*] (OAG)
RTB............ Rocket Test Base
RTB............ Rural Telephone Bank [*Department of Agriculture*]
RTBA.......... Rate to Be Agreed [*Business term*] (DCTA)
RTBF.......... Radio-Television Belge de la Communaute Culturelle Francaise [*Broadcasting organization*] [*Belgium*] (EY)
RTBISC........ Radiodiffusion-Television Belge - Institut des Services Comuns [*Belgian Radio Broadcasting and Television - Common Services Institute*]
RTBM.......... Real-Time BIT [*Binary Digit*] Mapping
RTBM.......... Recoverable Test Bed Missile
RTBT.......... Resonant Tunneling Bipolar Transistor [*Electronics*]
RTBV.......... Rice Tungro Bacilliform Virus [*Plant pathology*]
RTC............ RADAR Tracking Center [*or Control*]
RTC............ Radiodiffusion-Television Congolaise [*Congolese Radio and Television*] (AF)
RTC............ Radio Technical Committee for Aeronautics (NTCM)
RTC............ Radio Tecnica Colombiana
RTC............ Radiotelegraph Communication (IAA)
RTC............ Radiotelephone Communication (IAA)
RTC............ Radio Transmission Control (NATG)
RTC............ Radio Tuned Circuit (DEN)
RTC............ Rails-to-Trails Conservancy (EA)
RTC............ Range Telemetry Central [*Aerospace*]
RTC............ Ratchet (AAG)
RTC............ Reader Tape Contact
RTC............ Real-Time Captioning [*for the deaf*]
RTC............ Real-Time Clock [*Computer science*] (MCD)
RTC............ Real-Time Command [*Computer science*]
RTC............ Real-Time Computation [*Computer science*] (IAA)
RTC............ Real-Time Computer
RTC............ Real-Time Conference [*GEnie*] [*Telecommunications*]
RTC............ Real-Time Control [*Computer science*] (MCD)
RTC............ Real-Time Counter [*Computer science*]
RTC............ Reconstruction of Town and Country [*British World War II*]
RTC............ Recruit Training Center
RTC............ Reference Test Chart
RTC............ Reference Transfer Calibrator (OA)
RTC............ Regional Technical College (ACII)
RTC............ Regional Term Contract
RTC............ Regional Transport Commissioner
RTC............ Rehabilitation Research and Training Centers [*Department of Health and Human Services*]
RTC............ Relative Time Clock [*Computer science*] (MDG)
RTC............ Remote Terminal Controller
RTC............ Removable Top Closure [*Nuclear energy*] (NRCH)
RTC............ Replacement Training Center [*Military*]
RTC............ Reproductive Toxicology Center [*Database*] (IID)
RTC............ Required Technical Characteristic [*Military*] (CAAL)
RTC............ Requirements Type Contract [*Military*] (AABC)
RTC............ Reserve Training Center [*Army*] (DOMA)
RTC............ Reserve Training Corps
RTC............ Residential Training College [*for disabled people*] [*British*]
RTC............ Residential Treatment Center [*Department of Health and Human Services*] (GFGA)
RTC............ Resolution Trust Corp. [*Federal government instrumentality, established in 1989*]
RTC............ Resort Timesharing Council (EA)
RTC............ Responsible Training Center [*Air Training Command*] (MCD)
RTC............ Return to Clinic [*Nursing*]
RTC............ Return to Control
RTC............ Reverse Transfer Capacitance
RTC............ Ridiculous Theatrical Company
RTC............ Road Transport Commission [*Australia*]
RTC............ Rocket Technique Committee
RTC............ Room Temperature Cure (NASA)
RTC............ Round the Clock (DAVI)
RTC............ Royal Tank Corps [*Military unit*] [*British*]
RTC-30........ Rehabilitation Research and Training Center in Blindness and Low Vision [*Mississippi State University*] [*Research center*] (RCD)
RTCA.......... Race Track Chaplaincy of America (EA)
RTCA.......... Radio Technical Commission for Aeronautics (EA)
RTCA.......... Radio-Television Correspondents Association (EA)
RTCA.......... Real-Time Casualty Assessment (MCD)
RTCA.......... Real-Time Control Area (NTCM)
RTCA.......... Ribofuranosyltriazolecarboxamide [*Ribavirin*] [*Antiviral compound*]
RTCA.......... Rural Training Council of Australia
RTCAC........ Regional Transport Coordination Advisory Committee [*New South Wales, Australia*]
RTCAD........ Register Transfer Computer-Aided Design (MHDI)
RTCANI........ Rav Tov Committee to Aid New Immigrants [*Later, RTIJRO*] (EA)
RTCB.......... ROTI [*Recording Optical Tracking Instrument*] Tracker - Cocoa Beach [*NASA*] (KSC)
RTCB.......... Run to Cladding Breach [*Nuclear energy*] (NRCH)
RTCC.......... Real-Time Command Controller [*Computer science*] (NASA)
RTCC.......... Real-Time Communications Control (NITA)
RTCC.......... Real-Time Computer Center [*NASA*] (NASA)
RTCC.......... Real-Time Computer Command [*NASA*] (NASA)
RTCC.......... Real-Time Computer Complex [*NASA*]
RTCC.......... Rolling Thunder Coordinating Committee [*Joint US Navy and Air Force group operating in Vietnam*] (VNW)
RTCDS........ Real-Time Cinetheodolite Data System
RtCE.......... Right to a Comprehensive Education [*British*]
RTCE.......... Rotation/Translation Control Electronics (NASA)
RTCF.......... Real-Time Combined File [*IRS*]
RTCF.......... Real-Time Computer Facility
RTCH.......... Rough Terrain Container Handler (MCD)
RTCIL.......... Research and Training Center on Independent Living (EA)
RTCIP.......... Real-Time Cell-Identification Processor (PDAA)
RTCL.......... Reticle [*Optics*]
RTCM.......... Radio Technical Commission for Maritime [*or Marine*] Services (TSSD)
RTCM.......... Reasonable Transportation Control Measure (GNE)
RTCMS........ Radio Technical Commission for Marine Services (IAA)
RTCO.......... Record Time Compliance Order
RTCOD........ [*The*] Research and Technology Coordinating Document [*Army*] (RDA)
RTCOMN...... Radiotelephone Communication (IAA)
RTCP.......... Radio Transmission Control Panel (NATG)
RTCP.......... Real-Time Communications Processor (NASA)
RTCP.......... Real-Time Control Program [*Computer science*] (IAA)
RTCP.......... Resident Training and Counseling Programs (OICC)
RTCS.......... Real-Time Calling Standards [*Chromatography*]

RTCS .... Real-Time Communication System
RTCS .... Real-Time Composition System (NITA)
RTCS .... Real-Time Computation System [*Computer science*] (IAA)
RTCS .... Real-Time Computer System
RTCTO .... Record Time Compliance Technical Order (AAG)
RTCU .... Real-Time Control Unit
RTCU .... Router Cutter [*Tool*] (AAG)
RTCV .... Rural Training Council of Victoria [*Australia*]
RTCVD .... Rapid Thermal Chemical Vapor Deposition [*Coating technology*] [*Semiconductor technology*]
RTC(W) .... Recruit Training Command (Women) (DNAB)
RTCWA .... Rural Training Council of Western Australia
RTD .... Radiodiffusion-Television de Djibouti
RTD .... Range Time Decoder
RTD .... Rate Damping (NASA)
RTD .... Rate Dumping (MCD)
RTD .... Read Tape Decimal
RTD .... Ready-to-Drink [*Bottled and canned beverages*]
RTD .... Real-Time Decoder
RTD .... Real Time Developments [*Commercial firm British*]
RTD .... Real-Time Display
RTD .... Reliability Technical Directive (AAG)
RTD .... Remote Temperature Detector
RTD .... Renal Tubular Defect [*Medicine*] (DMAA)
RTD .... Replacement Task Distribution
RTD .... Replacement Training Detachment (MCD)
RTD .... Research and Technology Division [*Air Force*]
RTD .... Research Thrust Division [*Washington, DC DoD*] (GRD)
RTD .... Residence Time Distribution [*Chemical engineering*]
RTD .... Resident Training Detachment [*Army*] (INF)
RTD .... Resistance Temperature Detector [*Nuclear energy*]
RTD .... Resistance Temperature Device [*Nuclear energy*] (NRCH)
RTD .... Resistance Thermometer Device (ACII)
RTD .... Resonant-Tunnelling Diode [*Solid state physics*]
RTD .... Resubmission Turnaround Documents (MEDA)
RTD .... Retard (MSA)
rtd .... Retarded (MAE)
RTD .... Retired
RTD .... Returned [*Medicine*] (DHSM)
RTD .... Return to Duty [*Military*]
RTD .... Rights in Technical Data (AAGC)
RTD .... Road Traffic Division [*British police*]
RTD .... Routine Test Dilution [*Analysis*]
RTD .... Run-Time Debugger [*Computer science*] (PCM)
RTDA .... Radio and Television Dealers' Association
RTDA .... Retail Tobacco Dealers of America (EA)
RTDA .... Returned Absentees
RTD & E ...... Research, Test, Development, and Evaluation (SSD)
RTDAP .... RADAR Target Data Analog Processor (MCD)
RTDB .... Research Training and Development Branch [*Bethesda, MD*] [*National Heart, Lung, and Blood Institute*] (GRD)
RTDBUG .... Real-Time Debug [*Computer science*] (MHDI)
RTDC .... Real-Time Data Channel (IEEE)
RTDC .... Retardation Coil (MSA)
RTDC .... Rocket-Thrown Depth Charge (NG)
RTDD .... Real-Time Data Distribution
RTDD .... Remote Timing and Data Distribution
RTDDAS .... Real-Time Digital Data Acquisition System (PDAA)
RTDDC .... Real-Time Digital Data Correction (MUGU)
RTDE .... Range Time Data Editor [*NASA*] (KSC)
RTDF .... Real-Time Data File (NOAA)
RTDG .... Radio and Television Directors Guild [*Later, DGA*]
RTDHS .... Real-Time Data Handling System
RTDP .... RADAR Target Data Processor (MCD)
RTDP .... Robotics Technology Development Program
RTDR .... Reliability Test Data Report
RTDS .... Rapid Thermal Decomposition in Solution [*Powder processing*]
RTDS .... Real-Time Data System
RTDT .... Real-Time Data Translator
RTDTL .... Resistor Tunnel Diode Transistor Logic (IAA)
RTDVHPEP ... Rural Texas Domestic Violence Health Professionals Education Program (EDAC)
RTE .... Aeronorte - Transportes Aereos Lda. [*Portugal ICAO designator*] (FAAC)
RTE .... Radiative Transfer Equation
RTE .... Radio Telefis Eireann [*Radio and television network*] [*Ireland*]
RTE .... Radio Trans-Europe
RTE .... Radio Trunk Extension (NATG)
RTE .... RADOME [*RADAR Dome*] Test Equipment
RTE .... Railway Transport Establishment [*British military*] (DMA)
RTE .... Ready to Eat [*Cereals*]
RTE .... Real-Time Engine (MCD)
RTE .... Real-Time Event [*Computer science*] (IAA)
RTE .... Real-Time Executive [*Computer science*]
RTE .... Receiver Test Equipment
RTE .... Reciprocal Thermal Efficiency (PDAA)
RTE .... Recovery Techniques Evaluation [*NASA*] (KSC)
RTE .... Regenerative Turboprop Engines
RTE .... Reliability Test Evaluation (AAG)
RTE .... Remote Terminal Emulator [*For teleprocessing validation*]
RTE .... Repairs-to-Extend [*Marine science*] (OSRA)
RTE .... Repairs-to-Extend (USDC)
RTE .... Repair Test Equipment [*Aviation*]
RTE .... Request to Expedite
RTE .... Research Training and Evaluation (OICC)
RTE .... Resident Training Equipment (MCD)
RTE .... Residual Total Elongation [*Nuclear energy*] (NRCH)
RTE .... Responsible Test Engineer [*NASA*] (NASA)
RTE .... Return from Exception [*Computer science*]
RTE .... Return to Earth [*NASA*]
RTE .... Robotic Tele-Excavation [*University of Southern California*]
RTE .... Route (AFM)
RTE .... Route
rte .... Route (DD)
RTE .... Royal Trust Energy Income Fund Trust Units [*Toronto Stock Exchange symbol*]
RTEB .... Radio Trades Examination Board [*British*] (BI)
RTE-B .... Real-Time Basic [*Computer science*] (MDG)
RTEC .... Residential Transportation Energy Consumption [*DOE*] (TAG)
RTEC .... Ross Technology [*NASDAQ symbol*] (TTSB)
RTEC .... Ross Technology, Inc. [*NASDAQ symbol*] (SAG)
RTech .... Radiology Technician [*or Technologist*] (AAMN)
RTECS .... Registry of Toxic Effects of Chemical Substances [*Department of Health and Human Services Information service or system A publication*]
RTECS .... Residential Transportation Energy Consumption Survey [*Department of Energy*] (GFGA)
RTED .... Return-to-Earth Digital [*NASA*]
RTEG .... River Transport Escort Group (CINC)
RTel .... Radio Telemetry
RTEL .... Radio Telephony (MSA)
RTEL .... Raytel Medical [*NASDAQ symbol*] (TTSB)
RTEL .... Raytel Medical Corp. [*NASDAQ symbol*] (SAG)
RTEM .... RADAR Tracking Error Measurement
RTES .... Radio and Television Executives' Society [*Later, IRTS*]
RTES .... Radio and Television Executives Society (NADA)
RTES .... Real-Time Engine Simulation (MCD)
RTES .... Real-Time Executive System [*SEMIS*]
RTEX .... Railtex, Inc. [*NASDAQ symbol*] (SAG)
RTEX .... Real-Time Executive [*Computer science*] (IAA)
RTEX .... Real-Time Telecommunications Executive (IAA)
RTF .... Radiodiffusion-Television Francaise [*French Radio Broadcasting and Television System*]
RTF .... Radiotelephone
RTF .... Radio Transmission Facility
RTF .... Razor Trade Federation [*A union*] [*British*]
RTF .... Readiness Task Force
RTF .... Ready to Fire (MCD)
RTF .... Real-Time FORTRAN [*Computer science*]
RTF .... Reconnaissance Task Force (AFM)
RTF .... Reconnaissance Technical Flight [*Air Force*]
RTF .... Refilled, Tapped, and Fractionated [*Rock formation*] [*Geology*]
RTF .... Refrigerated Transportation Foundation (EA)
RTF .... Reliability Task Force (MCD)
RTF .... Religious Task Force [*Defunct*] (EA)
RTF .... Replication and Transfer [*Medicine*] (MAE)
RTF .... Reports Tempore Finch, English Chancery [*A publication*] (DLA)
RTF .... Resistance Task Force [*Defunct*] (EA)
RTF .... Resistance Transfer Factor [*of microorganisms to drugs*]
RTF .... Respiratory Tract Fluid [*Medicine*]
RTF .... Rich Text Format [*Computer science*] (BYTE)
rtf .... Rich Text Format [*Computer science*]
RTF .... Rocket Test Facility
RTF .... Room Temperature Fluorescence [*Physics*]
RTF .... Rotational Test Facility [*NASA*]
RTF .... Rubber-Tile Floor [*Technical drawings*]
RTF .... Rutherford [*New Jersey*] [*Airport symbol*] (AD)
RTFAQ .... Read the Frequently Asked Questions [*Computer hacker terminology*] (NHD)
RTFC .... Randy Travis Fan Club (EA)
RTFC .... Retired Teamsters Fellowship Club (EA)
RTFCA .... Religious Task Force on Central America (EA)
RTFES .... Religious Task Force on El Salvador (EA)
RTFFRJ .... Research Task Force for the Future of Reform Judaism [*Defunct*] (EA)
RTFL .... Rough Terrain Fork Lift
RTFL .... Rough Terrain Front Loader (MCD)
RTFLFT .... Rough Terrain Forklift [*Military*]
RTFLT .... Rough Terrain Forklift Truck (MCD)
RTFM .... Read the Fabulous Manual [*Internet language*] [*Computer science*]
RTFM .... Read the Fascinating Manual [*You can substitute a common profane verbal adjective for the third word*] [*Internet*]
RTFM .... Read the Fine Manual [*Computer science*] (DOM)
RTFM .... Read the Flaming Manual [*Bowdlerized version*] (CDE)
RTFM .... Router Form
RTFMS .... Radio Transmission Frequency Measuring System
RTFO .... Rolling Thin Film Oven [*For testing asphaltic binders*]
RTFR .... Reliability Trouble and Failure Report
RTFS .... Razor Trade Forgers' Society [*A union*] [*British*]
RTFT .... Rough Terrain Forklift Truck
RTFV .... RADAR Target Folder Viewer
RTG .... Radioactive Thermoelectric Generator [*Nuclear energy*] (NRCH)
RTG .... Radiodiffusion-Television Gabonaise [*Gabonese radio and television network*]
RTG .... Radiodiffusion-Television Guineenne [*Guinean radio and television network*]
RTG .... Radioisotope Thermoelectric Generator
RTG .... Radiotelegraph
RTG .... Range to Go
RTG .... Range to Ground (MCD)

RTG .... Rare Tube Gas
RTG .... Rating (MUGU)
RTG .... Real Time Geometry
RTG .... Reconnaissance Technical Group [*Air Force*]
RTG .... Reglement Telegraphique [*Telegraph Regulations*] [*French*]
RTG .... Requirements Tape Generator [*NASA*]
RTG .... Reusable Training Grenade
RTG .... River Transport Group [*South Vietnamese Navy*] (VNW)
RTG .... Routing
RTG .... Royal Thai Government
RTG .... Ruteng [*Indonesia*] [*Airport symbol*] (OAG)
RTGB .... Reactor Turbine Generator Board [*Nuclear energy*] (NRCH)
RTGD .... Real-Time Graphic Display
RTGD .... Room Temperature Gamma Detector
RTG DOM .... Routing Domain [*Computer science*] (TNIG)
RTGF .... Rat Transforming Growth Factor [*Biochemistry*]
RTGp .... Reconnaissance Technical Group [*Air Force*] (AFM)
RTGp .... Reconnaissance Training Group [*Air Force*] (AFM)
RTGp .... Retraining Group [*Air Force*] (AFM)
RTGS .... Real-Time Gross Settlement [*Banking*] (ECON)
RTGS .... Return to Government Stores (SAA)
RTGU .... Router Guide
RTGV .... Real-Time Generation of Video
RTH .... New York, NY [*Location identifier FAA*] (FAAL)
RTh .... Radio-Telephone (High Frequency) [*Telecommunications*] (DS)
RTH .... Radio Thailand (FEA)
RTH .... Regional Telecommunications Hub [*Telecommunications*] (TEL)
RTH .... Relay Transformer Header
RTH .... Reports of Cases Concerning Settlements Tempore Holt [*England*] [*A publication*] (DLA)
RTH .... Reports Tempore Hardwicke [*England*] [*A publication*] (DLA)
RTH .... Ridgeway's Reports Tempore Hardwicke, Chancery and English King's Bench [*A publication*] (DLA)
RtH .... Right-Handed (DAVI)
R T Hardw ... Reports Tempore Hardwicke, English King's Bench [*A publication*] (DLA)
RTHC .... Rotation Translation Hand Controller (NASA)
RTHK .... Radio Television Hong Kong
RTHL .... Runway Threshold Light [*Aviation*] (FAAC)
R T Holt ...... Reports Tempore Holt, English King's Bench [*A publication*] (DLA)
RtHon .... Right Honourable (EY)
RThQr .... Revue de Theologie et des Questions Religieuses [*A publication*] (BJA)
RTHS .... Real-Time Hybrid System (NASA)
RTI .... RADAR Target Identification
RTI .... Radiation Transfer Index
RTI .... Radiodiffusion-Television Ivoirienne [*Ivory Coast Radio and Television*] (AF)
RTI .... Railroad Transportation Insurers [*Defunct*] (EA)
RTI .... Real-Time Interface [*Computer science*]
RTI .... Real-Time Interference [*Computer science*] (IAA)
RTI .... Referred-to-Input
RTI .... Related Technical Instruction [*Bureau of Apprenticeship and Training*] [*Department of Labor*]
RTI .... Relational Technology Inc. (NITA)
RTI .... Relaxation Time Index [*Cardiology*]
RTI .... Remnant Tumor Index [*Surgery*]
RTI .... Remote Telephone Interface
RTI .... Renault Truck Industries [*British subsidiary of Renault Vehicules Industriels*]
RTI .... Renewable Term Insurance (MHDB)
RTI .... Request for Technical Information [*Military*]
RTI .... Research Triangle Institutes [*Duke University, University of North Carolina at Chapel Hill, and North Carolina State University at Raleigh*] [*Research center*]
RTI .... Resilient Tile Institute [*Later, RFCI*] (EA)
RTI .... Respiratory Tract Infection [*Medicine*]
RTI .... Return from Interrupt [*Computer science*] (NHD)
RTI .... Reverse Transcriptase Inhibitor [*Medicine*]
RTI .... Ridge/Transform Intersection [*Geology*]
RTI .... Ridge Transform Intersection [*Geology*]
RTI .... Right Turn, International (EA)
RTI .... Rise-Time Indicator
RTI .... RMI Titanium [*NYSE symbol*] (SPSG)
RTI .... Role Taking Inventory
RTI .... Room, Tax, and Incidentals
RTI .... Root Tolerance Index [*Botany*]
RTI .... Roti [*Indonesia*] [*Airport symbol*] (OAG)
RTI .... Round Table International (EA)
RTI .... RTI, Inc. [*Associated Press*] (SAG)
Rti .... Tissue Resistance [*Laboratory science*] (DAVI)
RTIC .... Rotor Temperature Indicator and Control [*Instrumentation*]
RTIC .... RT Inds Inc. [*NASDAQ symbol*] (TTSB)
RTIC .... RT Industries, Inc. [*NASDAQ symbol*] (SAG)
RTIF .... Real-Time Interface [*Computer science*] (NASA)
RTII .... RTI, Inc. [*NASDAQ symbol*] (NQ)
RTIJRO .... Rav Tov International Jewish Rescue Organization (EA)
RT Ind .... RT Industries, Inc. [*Associated Press*] (SAG)
RTIO .... Real-Time Input/Output (NITA)
RTIO .... Real-Time Input/Output Interface Subsystem [*Space Flight Operations Facility, NASA*]
RTIO .... Remote Terminal Input/Output
RTI/OC .... Real-Time Input/Output Controller [*Computer science*] (IEEE)
RTIP .... RADAR Target Identification Point (AFM)
RTIP .... Real-Time Interactive Processor (MCD)
RTIP .... Remote Terminal Interactive Processor (MCD)
RTIP .... Remote Terminal Interface Package
RTIR .... Real-Time Infrared [*Spectroscopy*]
RTIR .... Reliability and Trend Indicator Reports (AAG)
RTIRS .... Real-Time Information Retrieval System
RTIS .... Real-Time Information Retrieval System [*Computer science*] (HGAA)
RTIS .... Rockwell Technical Information System [*Rockwell International Corp.*] [*Information service or system*] (IID)
RTISC .... River Torrens Improvement Standing Committee [*Australia*]
RTITB .... Road Transport Industry Training Board [*British*] (DCTA)
RTIV .... Rice Tungro Isometric Virus [*Plant pathology*]
RTJ .... Return Jump [*Computer science*] (MHDI)
RTK .... Range Tracker (KSC)
RTK .... Receptor Tyrosine Kinase [*Biochemistry*]
RTK .... Record Test Kit
RTK .... Right to Know [*Laws*]
RTK .... Roanoke Rapids, NC [*Location identifier FAA*] (FAAL)
RTKP .... Radiothermokeratoplasty [*Ophthalmology*] (DAVI)
RTL .... RADAR Threshold Lobe Limit (CET)
RTL .... Radial Transmission Line
RTL .... Radioisotope Transport Loop [*Nuclear energy*] (NRCH)
RTL .... Radiomaritime Telex Letter
RTL .... Radio Television Luxembourgeoise [*Radio Television Luxembourg*] [*French*]
RTL .... Reactive to Light [*Referring to the pupils of the eyes*] [*Ophthalmology*] (DAVI)
RTL .... Real-Time Language [*Computer science*] (IEEE)
RTL .... Real-Time Link [*Computer science*] (MHDI)
rtl .... Rectal (DAVI)
RTL .... Refrigerated Transmission Line
RTL .... Regeneration Thermoluminescence
RTL .... Regimental Training Line [*Army*]
RTL .... Register Transfer Language [*Computer science*] (CSR)
RTL .... Register Transfer Level
RTL .... Register-Transistor Logic [*Computer science*]
RTL .... Reinforced Tile Lintel [*Technical drawings*]
RTL .... Relative Transcription Level [*Genetics*]
RTL .... Research and Technology Laboratories [*Army*] (RDA)
RTL .... Resin-Treated Liner
RTL .... Resistor-Transistor Logic [*Computer science*] (BUR)
RTL .... Resource Tie Line [*An association*]
RTL .... Responsible Task Leader (SSD)
RTL .... Retail
RTL .... Rheintalflug-Rolf Seewald [*Austria ICAO designator*] (FAAC)
RTL .... Right-to-Life (WDAA)
RTL .... Run-Time Library [*Interdata*]
rt lat .... Right Lateral [*Medicine*] (MAE)
RT LAT .... Right Lateral (DAVI)
Rt Law Rep ... Rent Law Reports [*India*] [*A publication*] (DLA)
RTLF .... Association of Railway Trainmen and Locomotive Firemen
RTLG .... Radio Telegraph (MSA)
RTLO .... Regional Training Liaison Officer [*Ministry of Agriculture, Fisheries, and Food*] [*British*]
RTLOC .... Root Locus (IAA)
RTLP .... Reference Transmission Level Point [*Telecommunications*]
RTLS .... Return to Launch Site [*NASA*]
RTLT .... Round-Trip Light Time
RTM .... RADAR Target Materiel (AFM)
RTM .... Radiation Test Model
RTm .... Radio-Telephone (Medium Frequency) [*Telecommunications*] (DS)
RTM .... Radio Television Malaysia
RTM .... Radio-Television Malgache [*Malagasy Radio and Television*] (AF)
RTM .... Radio-Television Marocaine [*Moroccan Radio and Television*] (AF)
RTM .... Radio Thrust Misalignment
RTM .... [*The*] Railway Transfer Co. of the City of Minneapolis [*AAR code*]
RTM .... Rapid Tuning Magnetron
RTM .... Rassemblement des Travaillistes Mauriciens [*Mauritius*] [*Political party*] (EY)
RTM .... Read the Manual
RTM .... Real-Time Management (MHDB)
RTM .... Real-Time Metric
RTM .... Real-Time Module (NITA)
RTM .... Real-Time Monitor [*Systems Engineering Labs*]
RTM .... Receiver-Transmitter-Modulator
RTM .... Reconnaissance Tactical Missile
RTM .... Recording Tachometer (IEEE)
RTM .... Recovery Termination Management [*Computer science*]
RTM .... Refrigerant Transport Module [*Air-conditioning*] (PS)
RTM .... Regional Transport Model [*Environmental Protection Agency*] (GFGA)
RTM .... Registered Trademark (DEN)
RTM .... Register Transfer Module [*Computer science*] (MDG)
RTM .... Regulatory Technical Memorandum [*Nuclear energy*] (NRCH)
RTM .... Representative Town Meeting
RTM .... Requirements Traceability Matrix
RTM .... Research Technical Memorandum
RTM .... Resin Transfer Molding [*Plastics technology*]
RTM .... Response Time Module
RTM .... Revenue Ton-Miles
RTM .... Room-Temperature Metallizing (SAA)
RTM .... Rotterdam [*Netherlands*] [*Airport symbol*] (OAG)
RTM .... Routine Medical Care (DAVI)
RTM .... Royal Trust Co. Mortgage Corp. [*Toronto Stock Exchange symbol*]
RTM .... Running Time Meter (AAG)
RTM .... Runtime Manager [*Computer science*] (PCM)
RTM .... Trans Am Compania Ltda. [*Ecuador*] [*ICAO designator*] (FAAC)

RTMA.......... Radio and Television Manufacturers Association [*Later, EIA*]
RTMAGV....... Royal Thai Military Assistance Group, Vietnam
RTMBEP....... Real-Time Minimal Byte Error Probability [*Computer science*] (MHDI)
RTMC.......... Royal Thai Marine Corps (CINC)
RTMD.......... Real-Time Multiplexer Display
R_{tmf}.......... Total Matrix Formation Rate (DAVI)
RTMLA......... Round Table for the Management of Library Associations
RTMON........ Real-Time Executive Monitor [*Computer science*] (IAA)
RTMOS........ Real-Time Multiprogramming Operating System [*Computer science*] (IEEE)
RTMP.......... Rapid Thermal Melt Processed [*Inorganic chemistry*]
RTMP.......... Routing Maintenance Protocol (BYTE)
RTMP.......... Routing Table Maintenance Protocol [*Computer science*]
RTMS.......... RADAR Target Measuring System (MCD)
RTMS.......... Real-Time Memory System
RTMS.......... Real-Time Multiprogramming System
RTMS.......... Rocket Thrust Measuring System
RTMSW........ Real-Time DSN [*Deep Space Network*] Monitor Software Assembly [*NASA*]
RTMTR........ Remote Transmitter (FAAC)
RTN............ North Country Library System, Watertown, NY [*OCLC symbol*] (OCLC)
RTN............ Radial, Tangential, Normal
RTN............ Radio Telescope Network
RTN............ Raton, NM [*Location identifier FAA*] (FAAL)
RTN............ Raytheon Co. [*NYSE symbol*] (SPSG)
RTN............ Recompression Thermonuclear
RTN............ Recursive Transition Network [*Language analysis*] (BYTE)
RTN............ Registered Technologist, Nuclear Medicine (MEDA)
RTN............ Registered Trade Name
RTN............ Relative Threat Number [*Military*] (CAAL)
RTN............ Remote Terminal Network
RTN............ Remote Tracking Network
RTN............ Renal Tubule Necrosis [*Medicine*]
RTN............ Report Test Number [*NASA*]
RTN............ Resistor Terminating Network
RTN............ Retain (KSC)
RTN............ Return (AAG)
rtn............ Return (ODBW)
RTN............ Return to Neuter
RTN............ Rota [*Nicaragua*] [*Seismograph station code, US Geological Survey*] (SEIS)
RTN............ Routine
RTN............ Routing Transit Number [*Telecommunications*]
RTN............ Royal Thai Navy (CINC)
RTN............ Russian Television Network
RTNA.......... Radio and Television (NADA)
RTNA.......... Regional Television News Australia
RTN(ARRT)... Registered Technologist in Nuclear Medicine Technology (American Registry of Radiologic Technologists) (MAE)
RTNB.......... Radio-Television Nationale du Burundi (EY)
RTNC.......... Radio-Television Nationale Congolaise
RTND.......... Returned
RTNDA......... Radio-Television News Directors Association (EA)
RTNE.......... Radio Technical New Entrant [*Telecommunications*] (OA)
RTNEE......... Returnee [*Military*]
R/T Net........ Radio/Telephone Network [*Nuclear energy*] (GFGA)
RTNF.......... Recombinant Tumor Necrosis Factor [*Biochemistry*]
RTNG.......... Retaining (MSA)
RT(NM)........ Radiology Technologist (Nuclear Medicine) (DAVI)
rTNM.......... Retreatment Tumor, Nodes and Metastasis [*Staging of cancer*] (DAVI)
RTNOBE....... Round Table of National Organizations for Better Education [*Defunct*] (EA)
RTNP.......... Red Tag News Publications [*Later, RTNPA*] (EA)
RTNPA......... Red Tag News Publications Association (EA)
RTNR.......... Retainer (MSA)
RTNR.......... Ringing Tone No Reply (NITA)
RTNR.......... Ringtone No Reply [*Telecommunications*] (TEL)
RTNS.......... Rotating Target Neutron Source [*Nuclear physics*]
RTO............ Radiotelephone Operator
RTO............ Rail Transportation Officer [*Military*]
RTO............ Railway Traffic Officer [*Military*]
RTO............ Range Training Officer (MCD)
RTO............ Reactor Trip Override [*Nuclear energy*] (NRCH)
RTO............ Real-Time Operation
rto............ Recto (BJA)
RTO............ Referred-to-Output
RTO............ Regenerative Thermal Oxidation [*Metallurgy*]
RTO............ Regional Team of Officers [*British*]
RTO............ Regional Telecommunications Office [*DoD*]
RTO............ Regional Training Officer (OICC)
RTO............ Rejected Takeoff [*Aviation*] (MCD)
RTO............ Reliability Test Outline (AAG)
RTO............ Report Time Over (FAAC)
RTO............ Request to Off-Load [*Shipping*] (DS)
RTO............ Responsible Test Organization [*NASA*] (MCD)
RTO............ Responsible Test Organization
RTO............ Return to Office (DAVI)
RTO............ Road Traffic Officer [*British police*]
RTOAA......... Rejected Takeoff Area Available [*Aviation*] (DA)
RTOG.......... Radiation Therapy Oncology Group (EA)
RTOK.......... Retest OK (MCD)
RTOL.......... Reduced Takeoff and Landing [*Aviation*]
RTOL.......... Rotary Takeoff and Landing [*Aviation*] (AIA)
RTOP.......... Real-Time Optional Processing (NITA)
RTOP.......... Research and Technology Objectives and Plans [*NASA*] (NASA)
RTOP.......... Research and Technology Operating [*or Operations*] Plan [*NASA*]
RTOP.......... Research and Technology Operations and Plans [*NASA*] (AAGC)
RTOPS......... Research and Technology Objectives and Plans Summary [*NASA Information service or system*] (CRD)
R to R.......... Reach to Recovery (DAVI)
RTOR.......... Right Turn on Red [*i.e., on red traffic signal*]
RTOS.......... Real Time Operating System [*Computer science*]
RTOS.......... Real-Time Optical System (MCD)
RTOT.......... Range Track on Target [*Air Force*]
RTOW.......... Regulated [*or Restricted*] Takeoff Weight (MCD)
RTP............ Radio Televisao Portuguesa [*Portuguese Radio-Television System*]
RTP............ Rapid Thermal Processing [*Semiconductor technology*]
RTP............ Reactor Thermal Power (IEEE)
RTP............ Real-Time Peripheral (IEEE)
RTP............ Real-Time Position (AAG)
RTP............ Real-Time Processing [*Computer science*] (IAA)
RTP............ Real-Time Profiler [*Instrumentation*]
RTP............ Real-Time Program [*Computer science*] (IAA)
RTP............ Real Time Protocol [*Telecommunications*] (OSI)
RTP............ Recruitment and Training Program
RTP............ Reebok Tennis Professional [*Shoes*]
RTP............ Reference Telephonic Power (DEN)
RTP............ Reinforced Theatre Plan [*Military British*]
RTP............ Reinforced Thermoplastic
RTP............ Reinforced Thermoplastics
RTP............ Relative Threat Priority [*Military*] (CAAL)
RTP............ Reliability Test Plan (MCD)
RTP............ Remote Transfer Point
RTP............ Replication-Terminator Protein [*Genetics*]
RTP............ Republican Turkish Party [*Cyprus*] [*Political party*]
RTP............ Request for Technical Proposal [*Military*]
RTP............ Request to Purchase
RTP............ Requirement and Test Procedures
RTP............ Research Triangle Park [*North Carolina*]
RTP............ Resistor Test Program
RTP............ Resource Teaching Program (OICC)
RTP............ Restrictive Trade Practice
RTP............ Returned to Produce [*Scrapping of automotive prototypes*]
RTP............ Reverse Tie Point (KSC)
RTP............ Room-Temperature Phosphorimetry [*Spectrometry*]
RTP............ Rotex Turret Punch
RTP............ Routing Update Protocol [*Telecommunications*] (PCM)
RTP............ Rutland Plains [*Australia Airport symbol Obsolete*] (OAG)
RTPA.......... Rail Travel Promotion Agency [*Defunct*] (EA)
r-tPA.......... Recombinant Tissue Plasminogen Activator (BARN)
rtPA.......... Recombinant Tissue Plasminogen Activator [*Biochemistry*]
RTPA.......... Recombinant Tissue-Type Plasminogen Activator [*Genetics*] (DAVI)
RTPC.......... Real-Time Process Control
RTPC.......... Restrictive Trade Practices Commission
RT-PCR........ Reverse Transcription-Polymerase Chain Reaction
RTPCVD....... Rapid Thermal Processing Chemical Vapor Deposition [*Coating technology*] [*Semiconductor technology*]
RTPF.......... Round Tube-Plate Fin [*Heat exchanger*]
RTPG.......... Rubinstein-Taybi Parent Group (EA)
RTPH.......... Round Trips per Hour (MSA)
RTPI.......... Royal Town Planning Institute [*British*]
RTPL.......... Real-Time Procedural Language [*Computer science*] (MDG)
RTPLRS....... Real-Time Position Location Reporting System (MCD)
RTPM.......... Real-Time Program Management
RTPMMA....... Rubber-Toughened Polymethyl Methacrylate [*Organic chemistry*]
RTPR.......... Reference Theta Pinch Reactor
RTPR.......... Ribonucleoside Triphosphate Reductase [*An enzyme*]
RTPS.......... Real-Time Telemetry Processing System (PDAA)
RTPU.......... Reinforced Thermoplastic Polyurethane [*Plastics*]
RTPU.......... Rigid Thermoplastic Polyurethane [*Organic chemistry*]
RTQ............ Real-Time Quotes [*Information retrieval*]
RTQ............ Rutter Teacher Questionnaire
RTQA.......... Reports Tempore Queen Anne [*11 Modern*] [*England*] [*A publication*] (DLA)
RTQC.......... Real-Time Quality Control
RTR............ Le Regiment de Trois-Rivieres [*British military*] (DMA)
R TR........... Radio Tower
RTR............ Real-Time Readout
RTR............ Real-Time Record (NTCM)
RTR............ Real-Time Reliability (NITA)
RTR............ Recovery Temperature Ratio
RTR............ Recreational Therapist Registered
RTR............ Recruit Training Regiment [*Marine Corps*] (DOMA)
RTR............ Red Blood Cell Turnover Rate [*Hematology*]
RTR............ Registered Technologist, Radiography (MEDA)
RT(R).......... Registered Technologist (Radiology) (DAVI)
RTR............ Reliability Test Requirements (AAG)
RTR............ Reliable Transaction Router [*Digital Equipment Corp.*]
RTR............ Remote Transmitter
RTR............ Repair Time Ratio
RTR............ Repeater Test Rack (DEN)
RTR............ Resonance Test Reactor
RTR............ Response Time Reporting
RTR............ Return and Restore Status Register [*Computer science*]
RTR............ Returning to Ramp [*Aviation*] (FAAC)
RTR............ Ribbon-to-Ribbon Regrowth [*of silicon for photovoltaic cells*]
RTR............ Road Traffic Reports [*A publication*] (DLA)
RTR............ Rotor (MSA)

RTR .... Royal Tank Regiment [*Military unit*] [*British*]
Rtr .... Ruth Rabbah (BJA)
RTR .... Ryder Truck Rental
RTR .... Sociedade Brazileira de Turismo (ROTATUR) [*Brazil*] [*ICAO designator*] (FAAC)
RTRA .... Radio and Television Retailers' Association (NADA)
RTRA .... Road Traffic Regulation Act [*Town planning*] [*British*]
RTR(ARRT) ... Registered Technologist in Radiography (American Registry of Radiologic Technologists) (MAE)
RTRC .... Radio and Television Research Council (EA)
RTRC .... Radiotelemetry and Remote Control (MCD)
RTRC .... Regional Teacher Resource Center [*NASA*]
RTRC .... Regional Technical Report Centers [*Department of Commerce*]
RTRCDS .... Real-Time Reconnaissance Cockpit Display System [*or Subsystem*]
RTRD .... Retard [*Aviation*] (FAAC)
RTRD .... Retired
RTRDTN .... Retardation
R Tren .... Right Trendelenburg [*Position*] [*Surgery*] (DAVI)
RTREV .... Right Reverend [*Of an abbot, bishop, or monsignor*]
RTRI .... Real-Time Record Interpreter (NTCM)
RTRMNT .... Retirement
RTRN .... Return (FAAC)
RTRO .... Real-Time Readout
RTRP .... Remote Terminal Routine Package [*Computer science*] (IAA)
RTRR .... Return to Recovery Room [*Medicine*] (DAVI)
RTRRM .... Response Type Road Roughness Meter [*FHWA*] (TAG)
RTRS .... Real-Time Rescheduling Subsystem
RTRS .... Reuters Holdings Ltd. [*New York, NY NASDAQ symbol*] (NQ)
RTRSOC .... Real-Time Reporting System on Oceanic Conditions (SSD)
RTRSW .... Rotary Switch (MSA)
RTRSY .... Reuters Hldgs ADS [*NASDAQ symbol*] (TTSB)
RTRV .... Retrieve (MSA)
RT RV .... Right Reverend [*Of an abbot, bishop, or monsignor*]
RTRY .... Rotary
RTS .... RADAR Target Simulator
RTS .... RADAR Test Set
RTS .... RADAR Test Station (MCD)
RTS .... RADAR Test System
RTS .... RADAR Tracking Station [*Military*]
RTS .... RADAR Tracking System
RTS .... Radial Tuned Suspension (ADA)
RTS .... Radioactive Waste Treatment System [*Nuclear energy*] (NUCP)
RTS .... Radiodiffusion-Television du Senegal [*Radio and television network*] [*Senegal*]
RTS .... Radiotelemetry Subsystem
RTS .... Radioteletypewriter Set
RTS .... Radio-Television Scolaire [*French*]
RTS .... Radio Television Seychelles
RTS .... Radio-Television Singapore
RTS .... Radio Wire Broadcasting Network
RTS .... Rail Transfer System (KSC)
RTS .... Range Time Signal
RTS .... Range Timing System
RTS .... Rapid Transit System (DCTA)
RTS .... Rapid Transmission and Storage [*Goldmark Corp.*] [*TV system*]
RTS .... Ratio Test Set
RTS .... Reactive Terminal Service [*International Telephone & Telegraph computer*]
RTS .... Reactor Trip System [*Nuclear energy*] (NRCH)
RTS .... Readiness Training Squadron [*Military*] (NVT)
RTS .... Ready to Send [*Computer command*] (PCM)
RTS .... Real Time Scan [*Medicine*] (DMAA)
RTS .... Real-Time Simulation
RTS .... Real-Time Subroutines
RTS .... Real-Time Supply [*NASA*] (MCD)
RTS .... Real-Time System
RTS .... Reconnaissance Technical Squadron [*Air Force*] (CINC)
RTS .... Recorded Time Signal
RT/S .... Refrigeration Technician/Specialist (AAG)
RTS .... Refueling Water Transfer and Storage [*Nuclear energy*] (NRCH)
RTS .... Regional Technical Support [*Military*]
RTS .... Relay Telemetry Subsystem [*NASA*]
RTS .... Relay Test System
RTS .... Reliable Transfer Server [*Telecommunications*] (OSI)
RTS .... Relief Transport Services Ltd. [*British ICAO designator*] (FAAC)
RTS .... Religious Tract Society [*British*]
RTS .... Remember That Song (EA)
RTS .... Remote Targeting System
RTS .... Remote Terminal Scanning System [*Computer science*] (IAA)
RTS .... Remote Terminal Site [*MTMC*] (TAG)
RTS .... Remote Terminal Supervisor (CMD)
RTS .... Remote Terminal System [*Computer science*] (IAA)
RTS .... Remote Testing System (NITA)
RTS .... Remote Test System [*Bell System*]
RTS .... Remote Tracking Site [*Military*]
RTS .... Remote Tracking Station [*NASA*]
RTS .... Repaired This Station (AFM)
RTS .... Reparatur-Technische Station [*Repair and Technical Station*] [*German*]
RTS .... Request to Send
RTS .... Research and Technical Services [*Military*]
RTS .... Research Test Site (AAG)
RTS .... Resolute Resources [*Vancouver Stock Exchange symbol*]
RTS .... Resolve through Sharing (EA)
RTS .... Return from Subroutine [*Computer science*]
RTS .... Return to Search
RTS .... Return to Sender
RTS .... Return to Service [*Aviation*]
RTS .... Return to Stores
RTS .... Return to Supplier (MCD)
RTS .... Rights [*Stock market term*]
RTS .... River Thames Society [*British*]
RTS .... Rosner Television Systems, Inc. [*New York, NY*] [*Telecommunications*] (TSSD)
RTS .... Rotary Thumbwheel Switch
RTS .... Rottnest Island [*Australia Airport symbol*] (OAG)
RTS .... Royal Television Society [*British*]
RTS .... Royal Toxophilite Society [*British*]
RTS .... Rubber Traders Society (NADA)
RTS .... Rubinstein-Taybi Syndrome [*Medicine*]
RTS .... Rural Telephone System [*Telecommunications*] (OA)
RTSA .... RADAR Target Signature Analysis
RTSA .... Radio Tracking System Analyst (MUGU)
RTSA .... Remote Telephone Subscribers' Association [*Australia*]
RTSA .... Retail Trading Standards Association (WDAA)
RTSC .... Recommended Test Sequence Chart (MCD)
RTSC .... Replacement and Training School Command [*Military*]
RTSD .... Resources and Technical Services Division [*Later, ALCTS*] [*American Library Association*] (EA)
RTSD .... Royal Thai Survey Department (CINC)
RTSD CCS ... RTSD [*Resources and Technical Services Division*] Cataloging and Classification Section
RTSD PLMS ... RTSD [*Resources and Technical Services Division*] Preservation of Library Materials Section
RTSD RLMS ... RTSD [*Resources and Technical Services Division*] Reproduction of Library Materials Section
RTSD RS ..... RTSD [*Resources and Technical Services Division*] Resources Section
RTSDS .... Real-Time Scheduling Display System
RTSD SS .... RTSD [*Resources and Technical Services Division*] Serials Section
RTSE .... Reliable Transfer Service Element [*Telecommunications*] (OSI)
RTSF .... Real-Time Simulation Facility [*NASA*] (MCD)
RTSM .... Return to Stock Memo
RTSP .... Real-Time Signal Processor (NVT)
RTSP .... Real Time Streaming Protocol (PCM)
RTSq .... Reconnaissance Technical Squadron [*Air Force*] (AFM)
RTSRS .... Real-Time Simulation Research System (WDAA)
RTSS .... Real-Time Scientific System
RTSS .... Returning to School Syndrome
RTST .... Radio Technician Selection Test [*Military*]
RTST .... Right Start [*NASDAQ symbol*] (TTSB)
RTST .... Right Start, Inc. [*NASDAQ symbol*] (SPSG)
RTSV .... Real-Time Synthetic Video (DOMA)
RTSW .... Real-Time Software [*Computer science*] (MHDI)
RTT .... Radet for Teknisk Terminologi [*Norwegian Council for Technical Terminology*] [*Oslo*] [*Information service or system*] (IID)
RTT .... Radiation Therapy Technician
RTT .... Radiation Tracking Transducer
RTT .... Radiotelemetric Theodolite
RTT .... Radioteleprinter (DA)
RTT .... Radioteletype (IAA)
RTT .... Radioteletypewriter
RTT .... Radio Television Tunisien [*Tunisian Radio and Television*] (AF)
RTT .... Rate of Turntable
RTT .... Real-Time Telemetry (IAA)
RTT .... Receiver Threshold Test (CET)
RTT .... Rectangular Tongue Terminal
RTT .... Regie des Telegraphes et des Telephones [*Belgium Telecommunications service*] (TSSD)
RTT .... Regional Training Teams [*Army*]
RT(T) .... Registered Technologist (Therapy) (DAVI)
RTT .... Remote Tuning Technique
RTT .... Requirements Traceability Tool [*Computer science*]
RTT .... Resonant Tunneling Transistor [*Electronics*]
RTT .... Return Trip Time
RTT .... Revised Token Test (EDAC)
RTT .... Ring Tongue Terminal
RTT .... Rocket-Thrown Torpedo
RTT .... Role-Taking Task
RTTA .... Range Tower Transfer Assembly (KSC)
RTTA .... Ranging Tone Transfer Assembly
RTTAA .... Railway Telegraph and Telephone Appliance Association
RTT(ARRT) ... Registered Technologist in Radiation Therapy Technology (American Registry of Radiologic Technologists) (MAE)
RTTC .... Redstone Technical Test Center [*Army*] (RDA)
RTTC .... Road Time Trials Council [*Bicycle racing competition*] [*British*]
RTTD .... Real-Time Telemetry Data (MCD)
RTTDS .... Real-Time Telemetry Data System
RTTI .... Runtime Type Information [*Computer science*] (PCM)
RTTL .... Rattail [*Metallurgy*]
RTTL .... Rattlesnake Hldg Co. [*NASDAQ symbol*] (TTSB)
RTTL .... [*The*] Rattlesnake Holding Co., Inc. [*NASDAQ symbol*] (SAG)
RTTL .... Real-Time Temporal Logic [*Computer science*]
RTTL .... Running Telltale Light (MSA)
RTTM .... Real-Time Transient Model [*Computer science*]
RTTOS .... Real-Time Tactical Operating System (MCD)
RTTP .... Radiation Therapy Treatment Planning [*Medicine*] (DMAA)
RTTP .... Router Template (AAG)
RT-TRACS .... Real-Time Traffic Adaptive Signal Control [*FHWA*] (TAG)
RT-TRACS .... Real-Time Traffic Control System

RTTS .... RADAR Telephone Transmission System
RTTS .... Reaction Torque Temperature Sensitivity
RTTS .... Real-Time Telemetry System
RTTS .... Rover Tester Test Set
RTTV .... Real-Time Television
RTTV .... Research Target and Test Vehicle
RTTW .... Radioteletypewriter (IAA)
RTTY .... Radioteletype (IAA)
RTTY .... Radioteletypewriter
RTU .... RADAR Timing Unit
RTU .... Railroad Telegraphers Union
RTU .... Range Transfer Unit (MCD)
RTU .... Rate of a Transfer Unit (IAA)
RTU .... Ready to Use
RTU .... Real-Time Ultrasound [*Medicine*] (DMAA)
RTU .... Receiver/Transmitter Unit
RTU .... Recovery Task Unit
RTU .... Reinforcement Training Unit [*Army*] (AABC)
RTU .... Remote Telemetry Unit
RTU .... Remote Terminal Unit
RTU .... Renal Transplant Unit [*National Health Service*] [*British*] (DI)
RTU .... Replacement Training Unit [*Military*]
RTU .... Reserve Training Unit (MCD)
RTU .... Response Test Unit
RTU .... Return to Unit [*Military British*]
RTU .... Right to Use [*Telecommunications*] (TEL)
rTU .... rRNA[*Ribonucleic Acid*] Transcription Unit [*Genetics*] (DOG)
RTUA .... Recognition Technologies Users Association (EA)
RTUM .... Revolutionary Trade Union Movement [*Czechoslovakia*]
RTV .... Radiodiffusion-Television (Upper Volta) [*Radio and television network*]
RTv .... Radio-Telephone (Very-High Frequency) [*Telecommunications*] (DS)
RTV .... Real-Time Video
RTV .... Recovery Test Vehicle
RTV .... Reentry Test Vehicle [*Air Force*]
RTV .... Research Test Vehicle
RTV .... Retrieve Resources Ltd. [*Vancouver Stock Exchange symbol*]
RTV .... Returned to Vendor (AAG)
RTV .... Rhodesian Television (AF)
RTV .... Rice Tungro Virus
RTV .... Rocket Test Vehicle (MCD)
RTV .... Room Temperature Vulcanizing (MCD)
RTV .... Rough Terrain Vehicle
RTVA .... Radio Television de Andalucia [*Spain*] (EY)
RTVB .... Rumbo Tools for Visual Bask [*Computer science*]
RTVD .... Radiotelevision Dominicana [*Dominican Radio and Television*] [*Dominican Republic*]
RTVE .... Radiotelevision Espanola [*Spanish*]
RTVM .... Radio Television Madrid [*Spain*] (EY)
RTVM .... Real-Time Virtual Memeory [*Computer science*] (IAA)
RTVMU .... Radiotelevision Murciana [*Spain*] (EY)
RTVOS .... Real-Time Virtual Operating System (NITA)
RTVP .... Real-Time Video Processing
RTVS .... Radio/Television Services [*Washington State University*] [*Pullman*] [*Telecommunications service*] (TSSD)
RTVS .... Real Time Velocimeter System [*Army*] (RDA)
RTVS .... Relay Test and Verification System (MCD)
RTVV .... Radiotelevision Valencia [*Spain*] (EY)
RTW .... Manitoba Reports Tempore Wood [*Canada A publication*] (DLA)
RTW .... Railway Tank Wagon [*British military*] (DMA)
RTW .... Ready-to-Wear [*Clothing*]
RTW .... Return to Work (DAVI)
RTW .... Right to Work
RTW .... Right Worshipful
RTW .... Road Tank Wagon (WDAA)
RTW .... Round the World
RTW .... RTW, Inc. [*Associated Press*] (SAG)
RTWB .... Richardson's Theological Word Book [*A publication*] (BJA)
RTWI .... RTW, Inc. [*NASDAQ symbol*] (SAG)
RTWS .... Raw Type Write Submodule
RTWUS .... Research and Technology Work Unit Summary
RTx .... Radiation Therapy (DAVI)
RTX .... Rapid Transit Experimental [*Gas-turbine bus*]
RTX .... Real-Time Executive
RTX .... Resiniferatoxin [*Organic chemistry*]
RTX .... Revenue Canada Taxation Library [*UTLAS symbol*]
RTXE .... Real-Time Executive Extended (PDAA)
RTY .... Merty [*Australia Airport symbol Obsolete*] (OAG)
RTY .... Muscatine, IA [*Location identifier FAA*] (FAAL)
RTY .... Rarity (WGA)
RTY .... Ross Air Training [*British ICAO designator*] (FAAC)
RTYC .... Royal Thames Yachting Club [*British*]
RTYV .... Rice Transitory Yellowing Virus [*Plant pathology*]
RTZ .... Radio Tanzania Zanzibar
RTZ .... Retail Trading Zone (WDMC)
RTZ .... Return-to-Zero [*Recording scheme*]
RTZ .... Ritz Resources Ltd. [*Vancouver Stock Exchange symbol*]
RTZ .... RTZ Corp. [*NYSE symbol*] (SPSG)
RTZ .... RTZ Corp. ADR [*Associated Press*] (SAG)
RTZ .... RTZ Corp. plc ADS [*NYSE symbol*] (TTSB)
RTZL .... Runway Touchdown Zone Light [*Aviation*] (FAAC)
RU .... Are You [*Communication*]
RU .... Britt Airways [*ICAO designator*] (AD)
Ru .... Gosudarstvennaia Biblioteka SSR Imeni V. I. Lenina [*Lenin State Library of the USSR*], Moscow, Soviet Union [*Library symbol Library of Congress*] (LCLS)
RU .... RADAR Unit (MCD)
RU .... Radioactive Uptake [*Radiology*] (DAVI)
RU .... Railway Underwriter
RU .... Rain Umbrella [*An association*] (EA)
RU .... Range Unit
RU .... Range User
RU .... Rat Unit
RU .... Readers Union Rugby Union (NADA)
RU .... Reading of Unknown
RU .... Ready Use [*British*]
R/U .... Record/Update
RU .... Rectourethral (DAVI)
RU .... Refrigeration Unit (KSC)
RU .... Regular Unleaded [*Shell Oil Co.*]
RU .... Reinforcement Unit [*British military*] (DMA)
RU .... Relative Unit [*Typography*]
RU .... Release Unit [*Army*] (AABC)
RU .... Remote Unit (NASA)
RU .... Renaissance Universal (EA)
RU .... Repeat Unit [*Genetics*]
RU .... Replaceable Unit
RU .... Replacement Unit
RU .... Reproducing Unit
RU .... Request/Response Unit [*Computer science*]
RU .... Reserve Unit [*Equal to one US dollar*] [*International finance*] [*Former USSR*]
RU .... Resin Uptake [*Endocrinology*]
RU .... Resistance Unit (MAE)
RU .... Respiratory Unit [*Medicine*]
RU .... Retransmission Unit [*RADA*] [*Army*] (RDA)
RU .... Retrograde Urogram [*Medicine*] (MAE)
RU .... Right Upper [*Medicine*]
RU .... Right Upstage [*Theater*] (WDMC)
RU .... Roentgen Unit [*Also, r*] [*Measuring X and gamma radiations*]
RU .... Roussel [*France*] [*Research code symbol*]
Ru .... Rufinus [*Flourished, 1150-86*] [*Authority cited in pre-1607 legal work*] (DSA)
RU .... Rugby Union [*Controlling body of British rugby football*]
Ru .... Ruins
RU .... Runic [*Language, etc.*] (ROG)
RU .... Run Unit (NITA)
Ru .... Rural
RU .... Rutgers-[*The*] State University [*New Brunswick, NJ*] (PDAA)
Ru .... Ruth [*Old Testament book*]
Ru .... Ruthenium [*Chemical element*]
ru .... Rutile [*CIPW classification*] [*Geology*]
RU .... Rutin [*Organic chemistry*]
RU .... Unborrowed Reserves
RU .... University of Rhode Island, Kingston, RI [*Library symbol Library of Congress*] (LCLS)
RU .... Ursuline Nuns of the Congregation of Tildonk, Belgium [*Roman Catholic religious order*]
RU-486 .... Roussel Uclaf "Once-a-Month" Pill [*Contraceptive*]
RUA .... Arua [*Uganda*] [*Airport symbol*] (OAG)
RUA .... Reduced Under Anesthesia [*Medicine*] (DMAA)
RUA .... Retailer's Uniform Agency
RUA .... Right Upper Arm [*Medicine*]
RUA .... Routine Urinalysis (DAVI)
RUA .... Royal Ulster Academy of Painting, Sculpture, and Architecture [*Ireland*]
RUAC .... Remote User Access System [*Telecommunications*]
RUAT .... Report upon Arrival Thereat [*Army*] (AABC)
RUB .... Rich Urban Biker [*Lifestyle classification*]
RUB .... Rubber (AAG)
rub .... Rubbing (VRA)
RUB .... Rubefacient [*Producing Heat and Redness of the Skin*] [*Medicine*] (ROG)
RUB .... Ruber [*Red*] [*Pharmacy*]
RUB .... Ruble [*Monetary unit*] [*Former USSR*]
RUB .... Rubric (DLA)
RUB .... Ruby Mountain Mines [*Vancouver Stock Exchange symbol*]
RUBAC .... Relative Universal Business Automation Code
RUBB .... Great Amer BackRub [*NASDAQ symbol*] (TTSB)
RUBB .... Great American Backrub Store, Inc. [*NASDAQ symbol*] (SAG)
Rub Conv .... Rubinstein on Conveyancing [*5th ed.*] [*1884*] [*A publication*] (DLA)
RUBD .... Rubberized (AAG)
RuBeMiA .... Akademiia Nauk Belorusskaia SSR, Fundamemtalnaia Biblioteka Imeni Ia. Kolasa [*Academy of Sciences of the Belorussian SSR, J. Kolasa Fundamental Library*], Minsk, Belorussian SSR, Soviet Union [*Library symbol Library of Congress*] (LCLS)
RUBIDIC .... Rubidazone [*Zorubicin*]/DIC [*Dacarbazine*] [*Antineoplastic drug regimen*]
RUBISCO .... Ribulosebisphosphate Carboxylase/Oxygenase [*An enzyme*]
RUBN .... Russian, Ukrainian, and Belorussian Newspapers [*A bibliographic publication*]
RuBP .... Ribulosebisphosphate [*Also, RDP*] [*Biochemistry*]
RuBPCase .... Ribulosebisphosphate Carboxylase [*An enzyme*]
RuBPC/O .... Ribulosebisphosphate Carboxylase/Oxygenase [*Also, RUBISCO*] [*An enzyme*]
Rubrmd .... Rubbermaid, Inc. [*Associated Press*] (SAG)
RUBSG .... Recovery Unit and Base Support Group [*Air Force*]
RUBSH .... Rubbish

RUBSSO ...... Rossendale Union of Boot, Shoe, and Slipper Operatives [*British*] (DCTA)
RubyTu .... Ruby Tuesday, Inc. [*Associated Press*] (SAG)
RUC .... Rapid Update Cycle [*Marine science*] (OSRA)
RUC .... Rapid Update Cycle (USDC)
RUC .... Reporting Unit Code [*Computer science*]
RUC .... Riverine Utility Craft [*Vehicle for transporting through shallow water and snow*] [*Navy symbol*]
RUC .... Royal Ulster Constabulary [*British*]
RUC .... Rutas Aereas, CA [*Venezuela*] [*FAA designator*] (FAAC)
RUCA .... Rear Upper Control Arm
RUCA .... Russell Cave National Monument
RUCAG .... Residential Utility Consumer Action Group
RUCAPS .... Really Universal Computer-Aided Production System (PDAA)
RUCATSE .... Runway Capacity to Serve the South East [*Airport planning group*] [*British*] (ECON)
Rucker .... Rucker's Reports [*43-46 West Virginia*] [*A publication*] (DLA)
RUCS .... Racial Unconscious [*Psychiatry*]
Rucus .... Run Cutting and Scheduling (DICI)
RUD .... Recently Used Directory [*Computer science*] (MHDI)
RUD .... Recurrent Ulcer of the Duodenal Bulb [*Medicine*] (DMAA)
RUD .... Rudder (AAG)
RUDAEE .... Report of Unsatisfactory or Defective Airborne Electronic Equipment [*Navy*]
RUDAOE .... Report of Unsatisfactory or Defective Aviation Ordnance Equipment [*Navy*]
R/UDAT .... Regional/Urban Development Assistance Team (DICI)
RUDD .... Remote Underwater Detection Device [*Navy*]
Ruddick .... Ruddick Corp. [*Associated Press*] (SAG)
RUDH .... Reserve Shutdown Unplanned Derated Hours [*Electronics*] (IEEE)
RUDI .... Regional Urban Defense Intercept
RUDI .... Report of Unsatisfactory or Defective Instrumentation [*Navy*]
RUDI .... Restricted Use Digital Instrument (OA)
RUDIM .... Rudimentary (ROG)
RUDIS .... Reference Your Dispatch (NOAA)
RUDM .... Report of Unsatisfactory or Defective Material [*Aircraft*] [*Navy*]
RUDMIN .... Report of Unsatisfactory or Defective Mine [*Navy*] (NG)
RUDMINDE... Report of Unsatisfactory or Defective Mine, Depth Charge, or Associated Equipment [*Navy*] (NG)
RUDS .... Reflectance Units of Dirt Shade (PDAA)
RUDTORPE... Report of Unsatisfactory or Defective Torpedo Equipment [*Navy*] (NG)
RUDY .... Rudys Restaurant Group [*NASDAQ symbol*] (SAG)
RUE .... Right Upper Entrance [*A stage direction*]
RUE .... Right Upper Extremity [*Medicine*]
RUE .... Rue [*Postal Service standard*] (OPSA)
RUE .... Russellville, AR [*Location identifier FAA*] (FAAL)
Ruegg Emp L... Ruegg on Employer's Liability [*9th ed.*] [*1922*] [*A publication*] (DLA)
RUER .... SSRC [*Social Science Research Council*] Research Unit on Ethnic Relations [*Research center British*] (IRC)
RUF .... Minocqua-Woodruff, WI [*Location identifier FAA*] (FAAL)
RUF .... Radiation Usage Factor (MCD)
RUF .... Refractory Users Federation [*British*] (BI)
RUF .... Resource Utilization Factor
RUF .... Revolutionary United Front [*Sierra Leone*] [*Political party*] (EY)
RUF .... Revolving Underwriting Facility [*Finance*]
RUF .... Rigid Urethane Foam
Ruf .... Rufinus [*Flourished, 1150-86*] [*Authority cited in pre-1607 legal work*] (DSA)
RUFAS .... Remote Underwater Fisheries Assessment System [*National Oceanic and Atmospheric Administration*]
RUFC .... Rugby Union Football Club [*British*] (DAS)
RUFE .... Zeitschrift fuer Rundfunk und Fernsehen [*Journal for Radio and Television*] [*NOMOS Datapool*] [*Information service or system*]
Ruff .... Ruffhead's Edition of the Statutes, by Serjeant Runnington [*1235-1785*] [*A publication*] (DLA)
Ruff .... Ruffin and Hawks' Reports [*8 North Carolina*] [*A publication*] (DLA)
Ruff .... Statutes at Large, Ruffhead's Edition [*England*] [*A publication*] (DLA)
Ruff & H ...... Ruffin and Hawks' Reports [*8 North Carolina*] [*A publication*] (DLA)
Ruffh St .... Ruffhead's English Statutes [*A publication*] (DLA)
Ruff St .... Ruffhead's English Statutes [*A publication*] (DLA)
RUFP .... Regulations under the Federal Power Act
RUG .... Coronet Carpets, Inc. [*Toronto Stock Exchange symbol*]
RUG .... Recomp Users Group [*Computer science*]
RUG .... Regional User Group [*Computer science*]
RUG .... Report and Update Program Generator (IAA)
RUG .... Resource Utilization Group (DHSM)
RUG .... Restricted Users Group [*Computer science*] (ODBW)
RUG .... Retrograde Ureterogram [*Medicine*]
RUG .... ROSCOE User Group [*Princeton, NJ*] (CSR)
RUG .... Rugby, ND [*Location identifier FAA*] (FAAL)
RUG .... Rutgers-[*The*] State University, Graduate School of Library and InformationScience, New Brunswick, NJ [*OCLC symbol*] (OCLC)
RUH .... Range Users Handbook
RUH .... Riyadh [*Saudi Arabia*] [*Airport symbol*] (OAG)
RUHBC .... Research Unit in Health and Behavioral Change [*University of Edinburgh*] [*Scotland*] (IRC)
RUHP .... Rescue Unit Home Port [*Navy*] (NVT)
RUI .... Research in Undergraduate Institutions [*A National Science Foundation program*]
RUI .... Royal University of Ireland
RUI .... Ruidoso [*New Mexico*] [*Airport symbol*] (OAG)
RUI .... Ruidoso, NM [*Location identifier FAA*] (FAAL)
RUIA .... Railroad Unemployment Insurance Act (GFGA)
RUIN .... Regional and Urban Information Network [*Washington, DC*]
RUK .... Reed International Ltd. [*NYSE symbol*] (SAG)
RUK .... Reed Intl P.L.C. ADS [*NYSE symbol*] (TTSB)
RUKBA .... Royal United Kingdom Benevolent Institution
RuKiFrA .... Akademiia Nauk Kirgizskoi SSR, Tsentralnaia Nauchaia Biblioteka [*Academy of Sciences of the Kirghiz SSR, Central Scientific Library*], Frunze, Kirghiz SSR,Soviet Union [*Library symbol Library of Congress*] (LCLS)
RuL .... Gosudarstvennaia Publichnaia Biblioteka Imeni Saltykova-Shchedrina [*State Saltikov-Shchedrin Public Library*], Leningrad, Soviet Union [*Library symbol Library of Congress*] (LCLS)
RUL .... Refractoriness under Load (IAA)
RUL .... Representative of the Senate of the University of London (ROG)
RUL .... Right Upper Eyelid [*Medicine*]
RUL .... Right Upper Limb [*Medicine*]
RUL .... Right Upper Lobe [*of lung*] [*Medicine*]
RUL .... Right Upper Lung [*Medicine*] (MAE)
RUL .... Rikkyo University Library [*UTLAS symbol*]
RUL .... Ruled
RUL .... Rule Resources Ltd. [*Vancouver Stock Exchange symbol*]
RuLA .... Akademiia Nauk SSSR [*Academy of Sciences of the USSR*], Leningrad, Soviet Union [*Library symbol Library of Congress*] (LCLS)
Rul Cas .... Campbell's Ruling Cases [*England*] [*A publication*] (DLA)
RULE .... Restructuring the Undergraduate Learning Environment [*National Science Foundation*]
RULE .... Rule Industries, Inc. [*NASDAQ symbol*] (NQ)
RULEG .... Rule Then Example [*Computer science*] (BARN)
RuleInd .... Rule Industries, Inc. [*Associated Press*] (SAG)
RULER .... Remaining Useful Life Evaluation Rig [*Lubricant testing*]
Rules Sup Ct... Rules of the Supreme Court [*A publication*] (DLA)
RULET .... Reference Your Letter (NOAA)
RULPA .... Revised Uniform Limited Partnership Act (AAGC)
RuLU-N .... Leningradskii Universitet, Nauchnaia Biblioteka Imeni Gor'kogo [*Leningrad State University, Gor'kii Scientific Library*], Leningrad, Soviet Union [*Library symbol Library of Congress*] (LCLS)
RUM .... Railwaymen's Union of Malaya
RUM .... Ranger Uranium Mines [*Commercial firm Australia*]
RUM .... Remote Underwater Manipulator [*Oceanography*]
RUM .... Remote Unit Monitor (MCD)
RUM .... Resource and Unit Monitoring (DOMA)
RUM .... Resource Unit Management
RUM .... Resource Utilization Monitor
rum .... Romanian [*MARC language code Library of Congress*] (LCCP)
RUM .... Rotary Ultrasonic Machining [*Manufacturing term*]
RUM .... Rumangabo [*Zaire*] [*Seismograph station code, US Geological Survey*] (SEIS)
RUM .... Rumania
Rum .... Rumania (VRA)
RUM .... Rumjartar [*Nepal*] [*Airport symbol Obsolete*] (OAG)
RUM .... San Marcos, TX [*Location identifier FAA*] (FAAL)
RUMAC .... Rubber-Modified Asphalt Concrete
RUMAS .... Reserve Unit Manpower Authorization System (MCD)
RUMEM .... Reference Your Memorandum (NOAA)
RUMEMO ..... Reference Your Memorandum (FAAC)
RUMES .... Reference Message from Your Office (FAAC)
RuMG .... Gosudarstvennaia Publichnaia Nauchno-Tekhnicheskaia Biblioteka SSSR [*State Public Scientific and Technical Library*], Moscow, Soviet Union [*Library symbol Library of Congress*] (LCLS)
RuMHi .... State Public Historical Library, Moscow, Soviet Union [*Library symbol Library of Congress*] (LCLS)
RUMIC .... Remote Underwater Mine Countermeasure (PDAA)
RuMIN .... Institut Nauchnoi Informatsii po Obshchestvennym Naukam, Akademiia Nauk SSSR [*Institute of Scientific Information on Social Sciences, Academy of Sciences of the USSR*], Moscow, Soviet Union [*Library symbol Library of Congress*] (LCLS)
RUMIN .... Ruminant
RUMINT .... Rumor Intelligence
RuMLit .... Vsesoiuznaia Gosudarstvennaia Biblioteka Inostrannoi Literatury [*All-Union State Library of Foreign Literature*], Moscow, Soviet Union [*Library symbol Library of Congress*] (LCLS)
RUMOD .... Regional Underground Monolith Disposal [*Hazardous wastes*]
RuMoKisA.... Akademiia Nauk Moldavskoi SSR, Tsentralnaia Nauchnaia Biblioteka [*Academy of Sciences of the Moldavian SSR, Central Scientific Library*], Kishivev, Moldavian SSR, Soviet Union [*Library symbol Library of Congress*] (LCLS)
RUMP .... Radio-Controlled Ultraviolet Measurement Program (MUGU)
RUMP .... Remote Underwater Marine Probe (SAA)
RUMPS .... Raw Umber and Maize Preservation Society [*An association*]
RUMR .... Routine Unsatisfactory Material Report (MCD)
RuMVKP ...... Vsesoiuznaia Knizhnaia Palata [*All-Union Book Chamber*], Ulitsa Oktiab r Skaia, Moscow, Soviet Union [*Library symbol*] [*Library of Congress*] (LCLS)
RUN .... Rassemblement pout l'Unite Nationale [*Cameroon*] [*Political party*] (EY)
RUN .... Reduction Unlimited
RUN .... Reunion Island [*Airport symbol*] (OAG)
RUN .... Rewind and Unload
RUN .... Rockmaster Resources [*Vancouver Stock Exchange symbol*]
RUN .... Run [*Postal Service standard*] (OPSA)
run .... Rundi [*MARC language code Library of Congress*] (LCCP)
RUN .... Runstream [*Computer science*]
RUN .... Ruthven [*California*] [*Seismograph station code, US Geological Survey*] (SEIS)

RUn .... University of Rhode Island, Kingston, RI [*Library symbol*] [*Library of Congress*] (LCLS)
RUNCIBLE.... Revised Unified New Compiler with Its Basic Language Extended [*Computer science*]
RUNDH .... Reserve Shutdown Unit Derated Hours [*Electronics*] (IEEE)
RUNEL .... Runway-End Lighting [*Aviation*]
RUNI .... Reunion Industries [*NASDAQ symbol*] (TTSB)
RUNI .... Reunion Resources [*NASDAQ symbol*] (SAG)
RUNID .... Run Identification [*Computer science*]
Runn .... Runnell's Reports [*38-56 Iowa*] [*A publication*] (DLA)
Runn .... Statutes at Large, Runnington's Edition [*England*] [*A publication*] (DLA)
Runn Eject... Runnington on Ejectment [*2nd ed.*] [*1820*] [*A publication*] (DLA)
Runnell .... Runnell's Reports [*38-56 Iowa*] [*A publication*] (DLA)
Runn Stat .... Runnington on Statutes [*A publication*] (DLA)
RUNR............ Reunion Resources [*NASDAQ symbol*] (SAG)
RUNT .... Russian Underground Nuclear Test (MCD)
RUO .... Right Upper Outer [*Quadrant*] [*Anatomy*] (DAVI)
RUO .... Right Ureteral Orifice [*Medicine*]
RUOK............ Are You OK? [*Internet language*] [*Computer science*]
RUOK............ Response USA [*NASDAQ symbol*] (TTSB)
RUOK............ Response USA, Inc. [*NASDAQ symbol*] (SAG)
RUOKW........ Response USA Wrrt'A' [*NASDAQ symbol*] (TTSB)
RUOKZ......... Response USA Wrrt'B' [*NASDAQ symbol*] (TTSB)
RUOQ........... Right Upper Outer Quadrant [*Site of injection*] [*Medicine*]
RUP .... Rat Urine Protein [*Biochemistry*] (DAVI)
RUP .... Raza Unida Party (EA)
RUP .... Restricted Use Pesticide [*Environmental Protection Agency*] (GFGA)
RUP .... Right Upper Pole [*Medicine*] (DMAA)
RUP .... Rockefeller University Press (DGA)
RUP .... Rupertsland Resources Co. Ltd. [*Toronto Stock Exchange symbol*]
RUP .... Rupsi [*India*] [*Airport symbol*] (AD)
RUPBX......... Reference Your Public Branch Exchange Message (SAA)
Rupert J ...... Rupert Journal [*A publication*]
Rupert Newsl... Rupert Newsletter [*A publication*]
RUPHO .... Reference Your Telephone Call (NOAA)
RUPPERT...... Reserve Unit Personnel Performance Report
Ruppie......... Republican Urban Professional [*Lifestyle classification*]
RUPT .... Interrupt (NASA)
RUPT .... Rupture (NASA)
RUQ .... Rifle Unqualified [*Military*]
RUQ .... Right Upper Quadrant [*of abdomen*] [*Medicine*]
RUQ .... Salisbury, NC [*Location identifier FAA*] (FAAL)
RUR .... Reference Update Review (SSD)
RUR .... Resin Uptake Ratio [*Endocrinology*]
RUR .... Rossum's Universal Robots [*Acronym is title of play by Karel Capek*]
RUR .... Royal Ulster Rifles [*Military unit*] [*British*]
RUR .... Rural
RUR .... Rurutu Island [*French Polynesia*] [*Airport symbol*] (OAG)
rur............... Russian SFSR [*MARC country of publication code Library of Congress*] (LCCP)
RuralCel ...... Rural Cellular Corp. [*Associated Press*] (SAG)
RuralMet ..... Rural Metro Corp. [*Associated Press*] (SAG)
RURALS....... Range Utilization Resources and Allocation Listings (SAA)
RURAX......... Rural Automatic Exchange [*Telecommunications*] (TEL)
RUREQ......... Reference Your Requisition (NOAA)
RURESA....... Revised Uniform Reciprocal Enforcement of Support Act (PAZ)
RURL .... Rural Metro Corp. [*NASDAQ symbol*] (SAG)
RURLAM...... Replacement Unit Repair Level Analysis Model
RURP........... Realised Ultimate Reality Piton [*Mountain climbing*]
RURPOP ...... Rural Population File (MCD)
RURTI......... Recurrent Upper Respiratory Tract Infection [*Medicine*] (ADA)
RUS .... Air Russia Airlines [*Russian Federation*] [*ICAO designator*] (FAAC)
RUS .... Marau [*Solomon Islands*] [*Airport symbol*] (OAG)
RUS .... Radioulnar Synostosis [*Medicine*] (DMAA)
RUS .... Rapid City, SD [*Location identifier FAA*] (FAAL)
Rus .... Resistance of the Airways on the Alveolar Side of the Point in the Airways whereIntraluminal Pressure Equals intrapleural Pressure [*Medicine*] (DAVI)
RUS .... Rest of the United States [*Government's official term for its system of determining federal salaries*]
RUS .... Rural Uplook Service [*Ithaca, NY*]
RUS .... Russ Berrie & Co. [*NYSE symbol*] (SPSG)
Rus .... Russell's Election Cases [*1874*] [*Nova Scotia*] [*A publication*] (DLA)
Rus .... Russell's English Chancery Reports [*A publication*] (DLA)
RUS .... Russia
Rus .... Russia (VRA)
rus .... Russian [*MARC language code Library of Congress*] (LCCP)
RUS .... Rust College, Holly Springs, MS [*OCLC symbol*] (OCLC)
RUSA........... Reference and User Services Association [*Formerly, RASD*]
RUSAF......... Russell Metals Cv'A' [*NASDAQ symbol*] (TTSB)
RUSAF......... Russell Metals, Inc. [*NASDAQ symbol*] (SAG)
Rus & C Eq Cas... Russell and Chesley's Nova Scotia Equity Cases [*A publication*] (DLA)
RUSB .... Right Upper Sternal Border [*Anatomy*] (DMAA)
RUSDIC........ Russian Dictionary [*A publication*]
RUSEC .... Romanian-US Economic Council (EA)
Rus EC......... Russell's Contested Election Cases [*Massachusetts*] [*A publication*] (DLA)
Rus EC......... Russell's Irish Election Reports [*A publication*] (DLA)
RUSEF .... Rational Use of the Sea Floor Program [*National Oceanic and Atmospheric Administration*] (MSC)
Rus Elec Rep... Russell's Election Cases [*1874*] [*Nova Scotia*] [*A publication*] (DLA)
Rus Eq Rep... Russell's Nova Scotia Equity Decisions [*A publication*] (DLA)
Rus ER .... Russell's Election Cases [*1874*] [*Nova Scotia*] [*A publication*] (DLA)
RUSH........... Remote User Shared Hardware [*Computer science*]
RUSH........... Rudder Shaped Hull (PDAA)
RUSH........... Rush Enterprises, Inc. [*NASDAQ symbol*] (SAG)
RushEnt....... Rush Enterprises, Inc. [*Associated Press*] (SAG)
Rush Med C... Rush Medicine College (GAGS)
Rushw .... Rushworth's Historical Collections [*A publication*] (DLA)
RUSI .... Royal United Services Institute for Defence Studies [*British*]
RUSI .... Royal United Services Institute for Defence Studies [*British*] (DBA)
RUSM .... Royal United Service Museum [*British military*] (DMA)
RUSNO .... Resident United States Naval Officer
Rus P........... Russian Pharmacopoeia [*A publication*]
RUSPAND.... Russian-Spanish Dictionary [*A publication*] (SAA)
RUSS .... Remote User Service Station (MCD)
Russ .... Russell's Contested Election Cases [*Massachusetts*] [*A publication*] (DLA)
Russ .... Russell's Election Cases [*1874*] [*Nova Scotia*] [*A publication*] (DLA)
Russ .... Russell's English Chancery Reports [*A publication*] (DLA)
RUSS............ Russet
RUSS............ Russia
Russ & C..... Russell and Chesley's Nova Scotia Reports [*10-12 Nova Scotia Reports*] [*1875-79*] [*A publication*] (DLA)
Russ & C Eq Cas... Russell and Chesley's Nova Scotia Equity Cases [*A publication*] (DLA)
Russ & Ches... Russell and Chesley's Nova Scotia Reports [*A publication*] (DLA)
Russ & Ches Eq... Russell and Chesley's Nova Scotia Equity Reports [*A publication*] (DLA)
Russ & Eq ... Russell and Chesley's Nova Scotia Equity Reports [*A publication*] (DLA)
Russ & G..... Russell and Geldert's Nova Scotia Reports [*13-27 Nova Scotia Reports*] [*1879-95*] [*Canada*] [*A publication*] (DLA)
Russ & Geld... Russell and Geldert's Nova Scotia Reports [*A publication*] (DLA)
Russ & Jap PC... Russian and Japanese Prize Cases [*London*] [*A publication*] (DLA)
Russ & M .... Russell and Mylne's English Chancery Reports [*1829-33*] [*A publication*] (DLA)
Russ & My... Russell and Mylne's English Chancery Reports [*1829-33*] [*A publication*] (DLA)
Russ & R..... Russell and Ryan's English Crown Cases Reserved [*1799-1823*] [*A publication*] (DLA)
Russ & RCC... Russell and Ryan's English Crown Cases Reserved [*168 English Reprint*] [*1799-1823*] [*A publication*] (DLA)
Russ & RCC (Eng)... Russell and Ryan's English Crown Cases Reserved [*1799-1823*] [*A publication*] (DLA)
Russ & R Cr Cas... Russell and Ryan's English Crown Cases Reserved [*A publication*] (DLA)
Russ & Ry ... Russell and Ryan's English Crown Cases Reserved [*A publication*] (DLA)
Russ Arb...... Russell on Arbitrators [*A publication*] (DLA)
RussBer....... Russ Berrie & Co., Inc. [*Associated Press*] (SAG)
Russ Ch....... Russell's English Chancery Reports [*A publication*] (DLA)
Russ Con El (Mass)... Russell's Contested Election Cases [*Massachusetts*] [*A publication*] (DLA)
Russ Cr....... Russell on Crimes and Misdemeanors [*A publication*] (DLA)
Russ Crim ... Russell on Crime [*12th ed.*] [*1964*] [*A publication*] (DLA)
Russ Crimes... Russell on Crimes and Misdemeanors [*A publication*] (DLA)
Russ El Cas... Russell's Election Cases [*1874*] [*Nova Scotia*] [*A publication*] (DLA)
Russ Elect Cas... Russell's Contested Election Cases [*Massachusetts*] [*A publication*] (DLA)
Russ Elect Cas... Russell's Election Cases [*Nova Scotia*] [*A publication*] (DLA)
Russell .... Russell Corp. [*Associated Press*] (SAG)
Russell .... Russell's Nova Scotia Equity Decisions [*A publication*] (DLA)
Russell NS... Russell's Nova Scotia Equity Decisions [*A publication*] (DLA)
Russ Eq ...... Russell's Nova Scotia Equity Cases [*A publication*] (DLA)
Russ Eq Cas... Russell's Nova Scotia Equity Cases [*A publication*] (DLA)
Russ Eq Rep... Russell's Nova Scotia Equity Decisions [*A publication*] (DLA)
Russ Fact .... Russell on Factors and Brokers [*A publication*] (DLA)
RUSSICA..... Russian Information and Communications Agency (IID)
Russ Merc Ag... Russell on Mercantile Agency [*A publication*] (DLA)
RussMtl .... Russell Metals, Inc. [*Associated Press*] (SAG)
Russ N Sc ... Russell's Nova Scotia Equity Cases [*A publication*] (DLA)
Russ Rev..... Russian Review [*A publication*] (BRI)
Russ T Eld... Russell's English Chancery Reports Tempore Elden [*A publication*] (DLA)
RUSSWO ..... Revised Uniform Summary of Surveyed Weather Observations (MCD)
Rust............ De Re Rustica [*of Varro*] [*Classical studies*] (OCD)
RUSTAN...... Russian Text Analyzer
rustc .... Rustication (VRA)
RUSTIC........ Regional and Urban Studies Information Center [*Department of Energy*] (IID)
RUT .... Remote User Terminal [*Computer science*] (CAAL)
RUT .... Resource Utilization Time (NASA)
RUT .... Rooms Using Television [*Television ratings*]
RUT .... Room Usage Time
RUT .... Routair Aviation Services [*Nigeria*] [*FAA designator*] (FAAC)
RUT .... Ruta [*Rue*] [*Pharmacy*] (ROG)
RUT .... Ruth [*Nevada*] [*Seismograph station code, US Geological Survey Closed*] (SEIS)
RUT .... Rutland [*Vermont*] [*Airport symbol*] (OAG)
RUT .... Rutland Railway Corp. [*AAR code Terminated*]
RUTD........... Rutlandshire [*County in England*] (ROG)
RUTEL .... Reference Telegram from Your Office (FAAC)
Rutg Cas...... Rutger-Waddington Case [*1784*] [*New York City*] [*A publication*] (DLA)

Rutgers U .... Rutgers University (GAGS)
Rutgers UL Rev... Rutgers University. Law Review [*A publication*] (DLA)
Ruth Inst...... Rutherford's Institutes of Natural Law [*A publication*] (DLA)
RuthR .... Ruth Rabbah (BJA)
RUTLDS....... Rutlandshire [*County in England*]
RUTOP......... Rutowski Optimization [*Computer program*]
RuTuAsA....... Akademiia Nauk Turkmenskoi SSR, Tsentralnaia Nauchnaia Biblioteka [*Academy ofSciences of Turkmen SSR, Central Scientific Library*], Ashkhabad, Turkmen, SS R, Soviet Union [*Library symbol Library of Congress*] (LCLS)
RuUk............ Gosudartsvennaia Publichnaia Biblioteka Ukrainskoi SSR [*State Public Library of the Ukrainian SSR*], Kiev, Soviet Union [*Library symbol Library of Congress*] (LCLS)
RUUR........... Regrade Unclassified Upon Receipt [*Air Force*]
RUUWS........ Research Underwater-Unmanned Weapons Sensor (DNAB)
RUV............. Bellefontaine, OH [*Location identifier FAA*] (FAAL)
RUV............. Rauvai [*Tuamotu Archipelago*] [*Seismograph station code, US Geological Survey*] (SEIS)
RUWS........... Remote Unmanned Work System [*Navy*]
RUX............. Baltimore, MD [*Location identifier FAA*] (FAAL)
RUY............. Ruinas de Copan [*Honduras*] [*Airport symbol*] (AD)
RV............... Israel Aircraft Industries Ltd. [*ICAO aircraft manufacturer identifier*] (ICAO)
RV............... Rabies Virus
RV............... RADAR Vector (SAA)
RV............... Radikale Venstre [*Radical Liberals*] [*Denmark Political party*] (PPE)
RV............... Radio Vatican [*Vatican State*] (PDAA)
RV............... Radio Vehicle (DEN)
RV............... Rahway Valley R. R. [*AAR code*]
RV............... Random Variable [*Statistics*]
R/V.............. Range to Velocity [*Ratio of the RADAR platform*]
RV............... Raphanus Virus [*Plant pathology*]
RV............... Rateable Value [*Property value*] [*British*]
RV............... Rated Voltage
RV............... Rat Virus [*Immunology*] (MAE)
RV............... Reaction Voltage
RV............... Reactor Vessel [*Nuclear energy*]
RV............... Reading and Vocabulary Test [*Also, RVT*] [*Military*]
RV............... Realizable Value (ADA)
R/V.............. Rear View (AAG)
RV............... Rear View [*Technical drawings*]
RV............... Recipient Value (GFGA)
RV............... Recirculation Valve (MCD)
RV............... Recovery Vehicle [*NASA*] (NASA)
RV............... Recovery Vessel [*NASA*] (NASA)
RV............... Recreational Vehicle
RV............... Rectovaginal [*Gynecology*] (DAVI)
RV............... Recycling Valve
RV............... Reduced Voltage (IAA)
RV............... Reed Valve [*Automotive engineering*]
RV............... Reentry Vehicle [*Aerospace*]
RV............... Reeve Aleutian Airways, Inc. [*ICAO designator*] (OAG)
RV............... Reeves MacDonald Mines [*Vancouver Stock Exchange symbol*]
RV............... Reference Voltage
RV............... Refugee Voices, a Ministry with Uprooted Peoples (EA)
RV............... Reinforcement Value [*Psychology*]
RV............... Relaxation Volume (MAE)
RV............... Released Value [*Freight*]
RV............... Release Valve [*Nuclear energy*] (NRCH)
RV............... Relief Valve
RV............... Remaining Velocity [*Ballistics*]
RV............... Renal Vessel [*Medicine*]
RV............... Rendezvous
RV............... Rendezvous Vehicle [*NASA*] (KSC)
RV............... Rescue Vessel
RV............... Research Vehicle
RV............... Research Vessel
R/V.............. Research Vessel [*Marine science*] (OSRA)
RV............... Residual Variance
RV............... Residual Volume [*Physiology*]
RV............... Respiratory Volume [*Medicine*] (MAE)
RV............... Retrieval Vessel (NASA)
RV............... Retroversion
RV............... Retrovirus
RV............... Return Visit (DAVI)
Rv............... Revelation [*New Testament book*]
RV............... Reverberation Time
Rv............... Revised [*Regulation or order revised*] [*Used in Shepard's Citations*] [*Legal term*] (DLA)
RV............... Revised Version [*of the Bible, 1881*]
RV............... Rifle Volunteers
RV............... Right Ventricle [*of heart*] [*Cardiology*]
RV............... Riser Valve [*NFPA pre-fire planning symbol*] (NFPA)
RV............... Robotic Vehicle (RDA)
RV............... Rod Valgallianse [*Red Electoral Alliance*] [*Norway*] (PPE)
RV............... Routine Verification (SSD)
RV............... Roving Vehicle [*NASA*]
RV............... Rubella Vaccine (DAVI)
RV............... Rubella Virus
RV............... Runway Visibility [*Aviation*] (AFM)
RV............... Russell Viper [*Time*] (MAE)
RV............... Ryom-Vivaldi [*Catalog of music of Vivaldi*] (BARN)
RVA .... Farafangana [*Madagascar*] [*Airport symbol*] (OAG)
RVA .... RADAR Vectoring Area [*Aviation*] (DA)
RVA .... Rating and Valuation Association [*British*] (DBA)
RVA .... Raven Air, Inc. [*ICAO designator*] (FAAC)
RVA .... Reactive Volt-Ampere Meter
RVA .... Recorded Voice Announcement [*Telecommunications*] (IBMDP)
RVA .... Regular Veterans Association (NADA)
RVA .... Regular Veterans Association of the United States (EA)
RVA .... Relative Virtual Address [*Computer science*] (PCM)
RVA .... Relative Volt-Ampere
RVA .... Reliability Variation Analysis
RVA .... Remote Voltage Adjustment
RVA .... Returned Volunteer Action [*British*] [*An association*] (DBA)
RVA .... Rib-Vertebra Angle [*Anatomy*]
RVA .... Right Ventricular Assistance [*Cardiology*]
RVA .... Right Visual Acuity [*Medicine*]
RVA .... Roberts Wesleyan College, K. B. Keating Library, Rochester, NY [*OCLC symbol*] (OCLC)
RVAAP .... Ravenna Army Ammunition Plant (AABC)
RVACS .... Reactor Vessel Auxiliary Cooling System
RVAD .... Rib-Vertebra Angle Difference [*Anatomy*]
RVAH .... Reconnaissance Attack Squadron [*Navy*] (NVT)
RVANCS........ Remote View Airborne Night Classification System
RVANSW....... Retirement Village Association of New South Wales [*Australia*]
RVARM .... Recording Varmeter (MSA)
RVAT .... Retinal Visual Acuity Tester [*Ophthalmology*]
RVAV .... Regulating Valve Actuating Valve (KSC)
RVAW .... Readiness Patrol Squadron [*Navy*] (NVT)
RVB .... RADAR Video Buffer
RVB .... Rear Vacuum Break [*Automotive engineering*]
RVB .... Red Venous Blood [*Hematology*] (MAE)
RVB .... Resonating Valence Bond [*Physical chemistry*]
RVB .... Rochester Gas & Electric Corp., TIC Library, Rochester, NY [*OCLC symbol*] (OCLC)
RVB .... Royal Veteran Battalion [*British military*] (DMA)
RVBR .... Riveting Bar [*Tool*] (AAG)
RVC .... RADAR Video Controller [*Military*] (CAAL)
RVC .... Ramakrishna - Vivekananda Center (EA)
RVC .... Random Vibration Control
RVC .... Rectovaginal Constriction [*Gynecology*] (DMAA)
RVC .... Relative Velocity Computer
RVC .... Remote-Voice Control
RVC .... Reticulated Vitreous Carbon
RVC .... Retired Volunteer Coordinator
RVC .... Richards Aviation, Inc. [*ICAO designator*] (FAAC)
RVC .... Rifle Volunteer Corps [*Military unit*] [*British*]
RVC .... River Cess [*Liberia*] [*Airport symbol*] (AD)
RVC .... RNA [*Ribonucleic Acid*] Virus Capsid
RVC .... Rochester General Hospital Library, Rochester, NY [*OCLC symbol*] (OCLC)
RVC .... Rockville Centre [*Diocesan abbreviation*] [*New York*] (TOCD)
RVC .... Rotary Voice Coil [*Computer technology*]
RVC .... Royal Veterinary College [*British*]
RVC .... Royal Victorian Chain
RVCDA......... Recreational Vehicle Club Directors of America (EA)
RVCF .... Remote Vehicle Checkout Facility [*NASA*] (NASA)
RVCI .... Royal Veterinary College of Ireland
RVCM .... Recent Vertical Crustal Movement [*Geology*]
RVCM .... Republic of Vietnam Campaign Medal [*Military decoration*]
RVCV .... Raspberry Vein Chlorosis Virus [*Plant pathology*]
RVD .... Dutchess County Mental Health Center, Poughkeepsie, NY [*Inactive*] [*OCLC symbol*] (OCLC)
RVD .... RADAR Video Digitizer
RVD .... Regulatory Volume Decrease [*Cytology*]
RVD .... Relative Vertebral Density
RVD .... Remote Virtual Disk [*Computer science*]
RVD .... Residual Vapor Detector (NATG)
RVD .... Right Ventricular Dimension [*Cardiology*]
RVD .... Right Ventricular Dysfunction [*Medicine*]
RVD .... Royal Victoria Dock [*British*] (ROG)
RVDA .... Recreation Vehicle Dealers Association of North America (EA)
RVDANA ...... Recreational Vehicle Dealers Association of North America
RVDO .... Right Ventricular Diastolic Overload [*Cardiology*] (AAMN)
RVDP .... RADAR Video Data Processor
RVDP .... Relief Valve Discharge Piping [*Nuclear energy*] (NRCH)
RVDT .... Rotary Variable Differential Transducer [*or Transformer*]
RVDT .... Rotational Voltage Displacement Transmitter
RVDV .... Right Ventricular Diastolic Volume [*Cardiology*] (DAVI)
RVE............. Airventure, BVBD [*Belgium*] [*FAA designator*] (FAAC)
RVE............. RADAR Video Extractor
RVE............. Representative Volume Element
RVE............. Right Ventricular Enlargement [*Cardiology*]
RVE............. Rochester Institute of Technology, Wallace Memorial Library, Rochester, NY [*OCLC symbol*] (OCLC)
RVE............. Royce Ventures Ltd. [*Vancouver Stock Exchange symbol*]
RVE............. Saravena [*Colombia*] [*Airport symbol*] (OAG)
RVECP .... Right Ventricular Endocardial [*Cardiology*] (DMAA)
RVED-CMP... Right Ventricular End-Diastolic Compliance [*Cardiology*]
RVEDD .... Right Ventricular End-Diastolic Diameter [*Medicine*] (DMAA)
RVEDP .... Right Ventricular End-Diastolic Pressure [*Cardiology*]
RVEDPI........ Right Ventricular End-Diastolic Pressure Index [*Cardiology*]
RVEDV .... Right Ventricle End-Diastolic Volume [*Cardiology*]
RVEE........... Holiday RV Superstores [*NASDAQ symbol*] (TTSB)
RVEE........... Holiday RV Superstores, Inc. [*NASDAQ symbol*] (NQ)
RVEF .... Right Ventricular Ejection Fraction [*Cardiology*] (DAVI)
RVER .... Regional Veterans Employment Representative [*Department of Labor*]
RVESP .... Right Ventricular End-Systolic Pressure [*Cardiology*] (DAVI)

RVESV Right Ventricular End-Systolic Volume [*Cardiology*]
RVET Right Ventricular Ejection Time [*Medicine*] (MEDA)
RVET Right Ventricular Ejection Time [*Cardiology*] (DAVI)
RVF Rate Variance Formula [*Air Force*]
RVF Rift Valley Fever
RVF Right Visual Field [*Psychometrics*]
RVF Rochester Psychiatric Center Library, Rochester, NY [*OCLC symbol*] (OCLC)
RVFD Riviana Foods [*NASDAQ symbol*] (TTSB)
RVFD Riviana Foods, Inc. [*NASDAQ symbol*] (SAG)
RVFN Report of Visit of Foreign Nationals (AAG)
RVFP Right Ventricular Filling Pressure [*Medicine*] (MEDA)
RVFV Rift Valley Fever Virus [*Medicine*]
RVFX Rivet Fixture (AAG)
RVG Chicago, IL [*Location identifier FAA*] (FAAL)
RVG Radionuclide Ventriculography [*Cardiology*] (CPH)
RVG Reference-Voltage Generator
RVG Right Ventral Gluteal [*Injection site*]
RVG Right Visceral Ganglion [*Medicine*]
RVG Rotating Vertical Gradiometer
RVG Rumrill-Hoyt Corp., Library, Rochester, NY [*OCLC symbol*] (OCLC)
RV/GC Reentry Vehicle and Ground Control [*NASA*] (KSC)
RVGG Rotating Vertical Gravity Gradiometer
RVH Renovascular Hypertension [*Medicine*]
RVH Reserve Veterinary Hospital [*British military*] (DMA)
RVH Right Ventricular Hypertrophy [*Cardiology*]
RVH St. Bernard's Seminary and College Library, Rochester, NY [*OCLC symbol*] (OCLC)
RVHD Rheumatic Valvular Heart Disease [*Medicine*] (DMAA)
RVI Recorded Video Imaging (MCD)
RVI Recreational Vehicle Institute
RVI Regulatory Volume Increase [*Cytology*]
RVI Relative Value Index [*Medicine*] (MAE)
RVI Renault Vehicules Industriels [*Renault Industrial Vehicles*] [*Finland*]
RVI Reverse Interrupt [*Telecommunications*] (IAA)
RVI Reverse Interrupt Character [*Keyboard*]
RVI RV-Aviation [*Finland ICAO designator*] (FAAC)
RVI Saint Mary's Hospital, Medical Library, Rochester, NY [*OCLC symbol*] (OCLC)
RVIA Recreation Vehicle Industry Association (EA)
RVIAJ Royal Victorian Institute of Architects. Journal [*A publication*]
RVID Right Ventricular Internal Dimension [*Medicine*] (MEDA)
RVID Right Ventricular Internal Dimension [*Cardiology*] (DAVI)
RVIDP Right Ventricular Initial Diastolic Pressure [*Medicine*] (MEDA)
RVIMI Rubella Virus-Induced Mitotic Inhibitor
RVIS Reactor and Vessel Instrumentation System [*Nuclear energy*] (NRCH)
RVIT Rotary Variable Inductive Transducer [*Electronics*]
RVJ Reidsville, GA [*Location identifier FAA*] (FAAL)
RVJ Sear-Brown Associates Information Center Library, Rochester, NY [*OCLC symbol*] (OCLC)
RVJS Reentry Vehicle Jamming Simulator [*Army*]
RVK Rorvik [*Norway*] [*Airport symbol*] (AD)
RVK Sybron Corp., Medical Products Division Library, Rochester, NY [*OCLC symbol*] (OCLC)
RVL Airvallee SpA-Services Aeriens de Val d'Aoste [*Italy ICAO designator*] (FAAC)
RVL Reedsville, PA [*Location identifier FAA*] (FAAL)
RVL Revere Resources [*Vancouver Stock Exchange symbol*]
rvl Revival (VRA)
RVL Right Vastus Lateralis [*Muscle*] [*Anatomy*] (DAVI)
RVL Rolling Vertical Landing (MCD)
RVL Royal Viking Line [*Kloster Cruises of Norway*]
RVL Sybron Corp., Pfaudler Division Technical Library, Henrietta, NY [*OCLC symbol*] (OCLC)
RVLA Roanoke Valley Library Association [*Library network*]
RVLG Revolving
RVLG Right Ventrolateral Gluteal [*Site of injection*] [*Medicine*]
RVLIS Reactor Vessel Water Level Indication System (IEEE)
RVLR Revolver [*Military*] (AABC)
RVLR Road Vehicles Lighting Regulation (IAA)
RVLV Revolve (MSA)
RVM Reactive Voltmeter
RVM Reentry Vehicle Module [*NASA*] (KSC)
RVM Religious of the Blessed Virgin Mary (TOCD)
RVM Repertoire de Vedettes-Matiere [*Laval Subject Authority Records*] [*UTLAS symbol*]
RVM Residual Volatile Matter [*Chemistry*]
RVm Revised Version [*of the Bible*], Margin
RVM Right Ventricular Mean [*Medicine*] (DMAA)
RVM Rio Vista Mine [*California*] [*Seismograph station code, US Geological Survey*] (SEIS)
RVM Sybron Corp., Taylor Division Research Library, Rochester, NY [*OCLC symbol*] (OCLC)
RVMR Routine Unsatisfactory Material Report
RVMYC Royal Victorian Motor Yacht Club [*Australia*]
RVN Republic of Vietnam
RVN Requirements Verification Network [*NASA*] (NASA)
RVN Retrolabyrinthine Vestibular Neurectomy [*Medicine*]
RVN Rogersville, TN [*Location identifier FAA*] (FAAL)
RVN Rovaniemi [*Finland*] [*Airport symbol*] (OAG)
RVN Women's Career Center Library, Rochester, NY [*OCLC symbol*] (OCLC)
RVNAF Republic of Vietnam Air Force
RVNAF Republic of Vietnam Armed Forces
RVNAFHMFC Republic of Vietnam Armed Forces Honor Medal, First Class [*Military decoration*]
RVNAFHMSC Republic of Vietnam Armed Forces Honor Medal, Second Class [*Military decoration*]
RVNCAMFC Republic of Vietnam Civil Actions Medal, First Class [*Military decoration*]
RVNCAMSC Republic of Vietnam Civil Actions Medal, Second Class [*Military decoration*]
RVNCAMUC Republic of Vietnam Civil Actions Medal, Unit Citation [*Military decoration*] (GFGA)
RVNCM Republic of Vietnam Campaign Medal [*Military decoration*]
RVNF Republic of Vietnam Forces
RVNGCUC Republic of Vietnam Gallantry Cross, Unit Citation [*Military decoration*] (GFGA)
RVNGCUCW/P Republic of Vietnam Gallantry Cross Unit Citation with Palm [*Military decoration*]
RVNMC Republic of Vietnam Marine Corps
RVNN Republic of Vietnam Navy
RVNT Reentry Vehicle Nosetip [*Aerospace*] (MCD)
RVO Aquinas Institute Library, Rochester, NY [*OCLC symbol*] (OCLC)
RVO Lubbock, TX [*Location identifier FAA*] (FAAL)
RVO Rabaul Volcano Observatory [*Papua New Guinea*]
RVO Regional Veterinary Officer [*British*]
RVO Relaxed Vaginal Outlet [*Medicine*]
RVO Retinal Vein Occlusion [*Ophthalmology*] (DAVI)
RVO Right Ventricular Outflow [*Medicine*] (MEDA)
RVO Right Ventricular Overactivity [*Medicine*] (MEDA)
RVO Right Ventricular Overactivity [*Cardiology*] (DAVI)
RVO Royal Victorian Order
RVOA Right Ventricular Overactivity [*Cardiology*] (DAVI)
RVOC Research Vessel Operators Council [*Defunct*] [*Marine science*] (OSRA)
RVOC Research Vessel Operators Council [*Defunct*] (USDC)
RVOG Radio Voice of the Gospel (DICI)
RVOT Right Ventricular Outflow Tract [*Cardiology*]
RVP Avon Junior/Senior High School Library, Avon, NY [*OCLC symbol*] (OCLC)
RVP RADAR Video Processor [*Military*] (CAAL)
RVP Raster-to-Vector Processor [*Computer graphics technology*]
RVP RCA Video Productions
RVP Red Veterinary Petrolatum (MAE)
RVP Reid Vapor Pressure
RVP Renal Venous Plasma [*Biochemistry*] (DAVI)
RVP Renal Venous Pressure (OA)
RVP Resting Venous Pressure [*Medicine*] (DMAA)
RVP Reutilization Value Percentage [*DoD*]
RVP Right Ventricular Pressure [*Medicine*] (DMAA)
RVP Roll Vertical Pendulum (SAA)
RVP Rotary Vacuum Pump
RVPA Rivet Pattern (AAG)
RVPAFS Register of Veterinary Preparations and Animal Feeding Stuffs [*Australia*]
RVPER Right Ventricular Peak Filling Rate [*Medicine*] (DMAA)
RVPFR Right Ventricular Peak Filling Rate [*Medicine*] (DMAA)
RVPRA Renal Vein Plasma Renin Activity [*Medicine*] (DMAA)
RVQ Benjamin Franklin High School Library, Rochester, NY [*OCLC symbol*] (OCLC)
RVQ Recursive Vector Quantization [*Software compression program*] (PCM)
RVQ Review of Vocational Qualifications (AIE)
RVR Bishop Kearney High School Library, Rochester, NY [*OCLC symbol*] (OCLC)
RVR Cruise America [*AMEX symbol*] (TTSB)
RVR Cruise America, Inc. [*AMEX symbol*] (SPSG)
RVR RADAR Video Recorder
RVR Rapid Ventricular Response [*Cardiology*] (DAVI)
RVR Rapid Virtual Reality (PCM)
RVR Raven Air Ltd. [*British ICAO designator*] (FAAC)
RVR Reactor Visual Range (HGAA)
RVR Renal Vascular Resistance [*Medicine*]
RVR Resistance to Venous Return [*Medicine*] (MAE)
RVR Response Vacuum Reducer [*Mechanical engineering*]
RVR Reverse Velocity Rotor
RVR Rim Vent Release [*Safety device for aerosol containers*]
RVR River [*Commonly used*] (OPSA)
RVR Riverside [*California*] [*Seismograph station code, US Geological Survey*] (SEIS)
RVR Runway Visual Range [*Aviation*]
RVRA Recreation Vehicle Rental Association (EA)
RV/RA Renal Vein/Renal Activity [*Ratio*] [*Medicine*]
RVRA Renal Venous Renin Assay [*Medicine*] (MAE)
RVRC Renal Vein Renin Concentration [*Medicine*]
RVRC Runway Visual Range Center [*Aviation*] (DA)
RVRM Runway Visual Range Midpoint [*Aviation*]
RVRME Rift Valley Research Mission in Ethiopia [*Anthropology*]
RvrOaks River Oaks Furniture, Inc. [*Associated Press*] (SAG)
RVRR Runway Visual Range Rollout [*Aviation*] (FAAC)
RVRRNO Runway Visual Range Rollout Not Available [*Aviation*] (FAAC)
RVRS Runway Vision Range System [*Aviation*] (DWSG)
RvrsGp Riverside Group, Inc. [*Associated Press*] (SAG)
RVRT Runway Visual Range Touchdown [*Aviation*] (FAAC)
RVRTNQ Runway Visual Range Touchdown Not Available [*Aviation*] (FAAC)
RVRU RADAR Video Recorder Unit
RVS Brighton High School Library, Rochester, NY [*OCLC symbol*] (OCLC)
RVS Rabies Vector Species

RVS ... Radius Vector Subroutine
RVS ... Reentry Vehicle Separation [*Aerospace*] (MUGU)
RVS ... Reentry Vehicle Simulator [*Aerospace*] (AAG)
RVS ... Relative Value Scale [*or Schedule or Study*] [*Medicine*]
RVS ... Remote Viewing System
RVS ... Reported Visual Sensation [*Medicine*] (MAE)
RVS ... Requirements Validation Study (MCD)
RVS ... Research Vessel Service [*British*] (IRUK)
RVS ... Reverse (MSA)
RVS ... Riverside Mountains [*California*] [*Seismograph station code, US Geological Survey*] (SEIS)
RVS ... Rocketborne Vacuum System
RVS ... Tulsa, OK [*Location identifier FAA*] (FAAL)
RVSB ... Riverview Savings Bank [*NASDAQ symbol*] (SAG)
RVSB ... Riverview Svgs Bk FSB Camas [*NASDAQ symbol*] (TTSB)
RVSBL ... Reversible (MSA)
RVSE ... Reverse (AABC)
RVSFC ... Ricky and Vince Smith Fan Club (EA)
RVSN ... Revision [*Legal shorthand*] (LWAP)
RVSNY ... Reversionary [*Legal shorthand*] (LWAP)
RVSS ... Reactor Vessel Support System (IEEE)
RVSSC ... Reverse Self Check (AAG)
RVST ... Russel Viper Serum Time [*Clinical chemistry*]
RVSVP ... Repondez Vite, s'Il Vous Plait [*Please Reply at Once*] [*French*]
RVSW ... Right Ventricular Stroke Work [*Cardiology*]
RVSWI ... Right Ventricular Stroke Work Index [*Cardiology*]
RVSZ ... Riveting Squeezer [*Tool*] (AAG)
RVT ... Brockport High School Library, Brockport, NY [*OCLC symbol*] (OCLC)
RVT ... Reading and Vocabulary Test [*Also, RV*] [*Military*]
RVT ... Registered Vascular Technologist (DAVI)
RVT ... Reliability Verification Tests
RVT ... Renal Vein Thrombosis [*Medicine*]
RVT ... Resource Vector Table [*Computer science*] (IBMDP)
RVT ... Rivet (MSA)
RVT ... Royce Value Trust [*NYSE symbol*] (TTSB)
RVT ... Royce Value Trust, Inc. [*NYSE symbol*] (SPSG)
RVTC ... Rochester Volunteer Training Corps [*British military*] (DMA)
RVTD ... Riveted (MSA)
RVTE ... Recurring Venous Thromboembolism [*Medicine*] (DMAA)
RV/TLC ... Residual Volume per Total Lung Compliance [*Pulmonary function test*] (CPH)
RV/TLC ... Residual Volume/Total Lung Capacity Ratio [*Physiology*] (MAE)
RVTO ... Reentry Vehicle Test and Observables [*Air Force*]
RVTOL ... Rolling Vertical Takeoff and Landing [*Aviation*] (MCD)
RVTV ... Rear Vision Television [*Driver safety systems*] [*Automotive engineering*]
RVU ... Caledonia-Mumford Junior/Senior High School Library, Caledonia, NY [*OCLC symbol*] (OCLC)
RVU ... Relative Value Unit
RVU ... Relief Valve Unit
RVV ... Cardinal Mooney High School Library, Rochester, NY [*OCLC symbol*] (OCLC)
rVV ... Recombinant Vaccinia Virus
RVV ... Reeve Aleutian Airways, Inc. [*ICAO designator*] (FAAC)
RVV ... Regional Vascular Volume [*Hematology*]
RVV ... Rubella Vaccine-Like Virus (AAMN)
RVV ... Rubella Virus Vaccine [*Immunology*] (DAVI)
RVV ... Runway Visibility Values [*Aviation*]
RVV ... Russell Viper Venom [*Medicine*] (DMAA)
RVVNO ... Runway Visual Range Not Available [*Aviation*] (FAAC)
RVVO ... Right Ventricular Volume Overload [*Medicine*] (DMAA)
RVVT ... Russell Viper Venom Time [*Medicine*] (DMAA)
RVW ... Charles H. Roth High School Library, Henrietta, NY [*OCLC symbol*] (OCLC)
RVW ... Ralph Vaughan Williams [*British composer, 1872-1958*]
RVW ... Right Ventricular Weight [*Cardiology*]
RVW ... Riverwood International Corp. [*NYSE symbol*] (SPSG)
RVWT ... Right Ventricle Wall Thickness [*Medicine*] (DMAA)
RVX ... Charlotte Junior/Senior High School Library, Rochester, NY [*OCLC symbol*] (OCLC)
RVX ... Reentry Vehicle, Experimental [*Aerospace*]
RVX ... Robot Vehicle Expressway
RVY ... Churchville-Chili Senior High School Library, Rochester, NY [*OCLC symbol*] (OCLC)
RVY ... Rivera [*Uruguay*] [*Airport symbol*] (OAG)
RVYC ... Royal Victorian Yacht Club [*Australia*]
RVZ ... Dansville Senior High School Library, Dansville, NY [*OCLC symbol*] (OCLC)
RW ... Hughes Air Corp. [*ICAO designator*] (ICDA)
RW ... Race Weight [*of a horse*]
RW ... Radiation Weapon (AAG)
RW ... Radical Women (EA)
RW ... Radiological Warfare
RW ... Radiological Warhead
RW ... Radiological Weapons
RW ... Ragweed [*Immunology*]
RW ... Rail and Water [*Shipping*]
RW ... Railway
RW ... Ramo Wooldridge [*Later, TRW, Inc.*]
R/W ... Ramo-Wooldridge-Thompson Corp. [*Later, TRW, Inc.*] (AAG)
RW ... Random Walk
RW ... Random Widths [*Lumber*]
RW ... RAWINSONDE [*Radiosonde and RADAR Wind Sounding*] [*Upper air observation*]
RW ... Raw Water [*Nuclear energy*]
R-W ... Read-Write [*Computer science*] (MSA)
R/W ... Read/Write (NITA)
RW ... Real Wages [*Economics*]
RW ... Ream Wrapped (WDMC)
RW ... Rechtswissenschaft [*Jurisprudence*] [*German*] (ILCA)
RW ... Reclaimed Wheat Grass Cover [*Agriculture*]
RW ... Reconnaissance Wing [*Military*]
R(W) ... Reconstruction, Workmen's Compensation [*British World War II*]
RW ... Recreation and Welfare [*Navy*]
RW ... Recruiting Warrant
RW ... Red-Bellied Woodpecker [*Ornithology*]
RW ... Reduced Weight (DCTA)
RW ... Reel and Wheel [*Freight*]
RW ... Regions of the World [*A publication*]
RW ... Region Wide [*Forestry*]
RW ... Relative Worth (MCD)
R/W ... Report Writer [*Computer science*]
RW ... Republic [*ICAO designator*] (AD)
RW ... Resistance Welding (IEEE)
RW ... Response Word (NASA)
RW ... Restaurant Wine [*License*]
RW ... Retail World [*A publication*]
R/W ... Returned to Work
RW ... Reverse Work (WGA)
RW ... Reverse Wound (MCD)
RW ... Review
RW ... Rewind
RW ... Richardsons Westgarth [*Commercial firm British*]
RW ... Rideal-Walter Coefficient [*Pharmacy*]
RW ... Right Ear, Warm Stimulus [*Medicine*] (MEDA)
RW ... Right of Way
RW ... Right Wing
RW ... Right Worshipful
RW ... Right Worthy
RW ... River Water [*Nuclear energy*] (NRCH)
RW ... Riveted and Welded [*Shipping*] (DS)
RW ... Rotary Wing [*Aircraft designation*]
RW ... Rowa-Wagner KG [*Germany*] [*Research code symbol*]
RW ... Royal Warrant [*British*] (ADA)
RW ... Royal Warwickshire Regiment [*Military unit*] [*British*]
RW ... Runway [*Aviation*]
rw ... Rwanda [*MARC country of publication code Library of Congress*] (LCCP)
RW ... Rwanda [*ANSI two-letter standard code*] (CNC)
RW ... R. Warren [*Pseudonym used by Charles Ashton*]
RWA ... Aligiulia SpA [*Italy ICAO designator*] (FAAC)
RWA ... E. J. Wilson High School Library, Spencerport, NY [*OCLC symbol*] (OCLC)
RWa ... George Hail Free Library, Warren, RI [*Library symbol Library of Congress*] (LCLS)
RWA ... Race Walking Association [*British*] (DBA)
RWA ... RADWASTE [*Radioactive Waste*] Area [*Nuclear energy*] (NRCH)
RWA ... Railway Wheel Association [*Defunct*] (EA)
RWA ... Raoul Wallenberg Association [*See also RWF*] (EA)
RWA ... Reaction Wheel Assembly (MCD)
RWA ... Ready, Willing and Able [*Legal shorthand*] (LWAP)
RWA ... Rectangular Wave-Guide Assembly
RWA ... Regional Water Authority [*British*]
RWA ... Rippled Wall Amplifier
RWA ... Romance Writers of America (EA)
RWA ... Rotary Wing Aircraft
RWA ... Royal West of England Academy
RWA ... Rwanda [*ANSI three-letter standard code*] (CNC)
RWAAC ... Rural Workers Accommodation Advisory Committee [*New South Wales, Australia*]
RWABA ... Royal Western Australian Bowling Association
RWAFF ... Royal West African Frontier Force [*Military unit*] [*British*]
RWAGE ... Ragweed Antigen E [*Immunology*]
RWAH ... Rotor Wing Agricultural Hours [*Aviation*] (AIA)
RWAIB ... Royal Western Australian Institute for the Blind [*Australia*]
R/W & L ... Random Width and Length (DAC)
RWar ... Warwick Public Library, Warwick, RI [*Library symbol Library of Congress*] (LCLS)
RWARF ... Royal Warwickshire Fusiliers [*British military*] (DMA)
RWarR ... Rhode Island Junior College, Knight Campus, Warwick, RI [*Library symbol Library of Congress*] (LCLS)
R War R ... Royal Warwickshire Regiment [*Military unit*] [*British*] (DMA)
RWAS ... Royal Welsh Agricultural Society (BI)
RWASG ... Radiation Weapons Analysis Systems Group (SAA)
RWAV ... Rogue Wave Software, Inc. [*NASDAQ symbol*] (SAG)
RWAW ... United Union of Roofers, Waterproofers, and Allied Workers
RWAY ... Rent-Way [*NASDAQ symbol*] (TTSB)
RWAY ... Rent Way, Inc. [*NASDAQ symbol*] (SAG)
RWB ... RADWASTE [*Radioactive Waste*] Building [*Nuclear energy*] (NUCP)
RWB ... Rear Wheel Brake
RWB ... Rod Withdrawal Block [*Nuclear energy*] (NRCH)
RWB ... Roger Williams College, Bristol, RI [*OCLC symbol*] (OCLC)
RWB ... Royal Winnipeg Ballet
RWBH ... Records Will Be Handcarried [*Army*] (AABC)
RWBN ... Red and White Beacon [*Nautical charts*]
RWC ... East Junior/Senior High School Library, Rochester, NY [*OCLC symbol*] (OCLC)
RWC ... Radioactive Waste Campaign (EA)
RWC ... Rainwater Conductor (AAG)

RWC .... Raw Water Cooling
RWC .... Reactor Water Cleanup [*Nuclear energy*] (NRCH)
RWC .... Read, Write and Compare (ECII)
RWC .... Read, Write, and Compute
RWC .... Read-Write-Continue [*Computer science*]
RWC .... Relative Water Content
RWC .... Remote Workcenter
RWC .... Residential Wood Combustion
RWC .... Roberts Wesleyan College [*Rochester, NY*]
RWCH .... Republican Women of Capitol Hill (EA)
RWCP .... Real World Computing Partnership [*Japan*] [*Agreement for conducting cooperative global research*]
RWCS .... Reactor Water Cleanup System [*Nuclear energy*] (NRCH)
RWCS .... Red Wing Collectors Society (EA)
RWCS .... Report Writer Control System [*COBOL*] [*Computer science*]
RWCTF .... Radioactive Waste Consultation Task Force [*National Science Foundation*] (NUCP)
RWCU .... Reactor Water Cleanup [*Nuclear energy*] (NRCH)
RWCU .... Reactor Water Cleanup Unit [*Nuclear energy*] (IAA)
RWCUS .... Raoul Wallenberg Committee of the United States (EA)
RWD .... Air Rwanda [*ICAO designator*] (FAAC)
RWD .... Eastridge High School Library, Rochester, NY [*OCLC symbol*] (OCLC)
RWD .... Reaction with Distillation [*Koch Engineering Co.*] [*Chemical engineering*]
RWD .... Rear Wheel Drive
RWD .... Regional WIN [*Work Incentive*] Director [*Department of Health and Human Services*] (GFGA)
RWD .... Regular Way Delivery
RWD .... Regular World Day
RWD .... Rewind
RWD .... Right Wing Down [*Aviation*]
RWDCA .... Red and White Dairy Cattle Association (EA)
RWDGM .... Right Worshipful Deputy Grand Master [*Freemasonry*]
R/WDO .... Rear Window [*Automotive engineering*]
RWDS .... RADWASTE [*Radioactive Waste*] Disposal System [*Nuclear energy*] (NRCH)
RWDSU .... Retail, Wholesale, and Department Store Union (EA)
RWE .... Aero West Airlines, Inc. [*ICAO designator*] (FAAC)
RWE .... Edison Technical and Occupational Educational Center Library, Rochester, NY [*OCLC symbol*] (OCLC)
RWE .... Radio Warfare Establishment [*British military*] (DMA)
RWE .... Ralph Waldo Emerson [*Initials used as pseudonym*]
RWE .... Rheinisch-Westfaelisches Elektrizitaetswerk AG [*Rheine-Westphalian Electricity Co.*] [*Germany*]
RWe .... Westerly Public Library, Westerly, RI [*Library symbol Library of Congress*] (LCLS)
RWEA .... Royal West of England Academy
RWED .... Read/Write Extend Delete
RWEMA .... Ralph Waldo Emerson Memorial Association (EA)
RWES .... Ralph Waldo Emerson Society (EA)
RWF .... Fairport High School Library, Fairport, NY [*OCLC symbol*] (OCLC)
RWF .... Radio Wholesalers Federation [*British*] (BI)
RWF .... Raoul Wallenberg Foreningen [*Raoul Wallenberg Association - RWA*] (EAIO)
RWF .... Redwood Falls, MN [*Location identifier FAA*] (FAAL)
RWF .... Roundtable for Women in Foodservice [*Later, RWFBH*] (EA)
RWF .... Roush, W. F., Miami FL [*STAC*]
RWF .... Royal Welch [*or Welsh*] Fusiliers [*Military unit*] [*British*]
RwF .... Rwandan Franc [*Monetary unit*] (IMH)
RWFBH .... Roundtable for Women Food-Beverage-Hospitality (EA)
RWFC .... Randy Wade Fan Club (EA)
RWFC .... Red Wings For'Em Club (EA)
RWG .... Gates-Chili Senior High School Library, Rochester, NY [*OCLC symbol*] (OCLC)
RWG .... Radio Writers' Guild [*Later, WGA*]
RWG .... Redwing Airways, Inc. [*ICAO designator*] (FAAC)
RWG .... Redwing Resources, Inc. [*Vancouver Stock Exchange symbol*]
RWG .... Reliability Working Group (AAG)
RWG .... Rigid Waveguide
RWG .... Roebling Wire Gauge
RWGM .... Right Worshipful Grand Master [*Freemasonry*]
RWGR .... Right Worthy Grand Representative [*Freemasonry*]
RWGS .... Right Worthy Grand Secretary [*Freemasonry*] (ADA)
RWGT .... Right Worthy Grand Templar [*Freemasonry*]
RWGT .... Right Worthy Grand Treasurer [*Freemasonry*]
RWGW .... Right Worthy Grand Warden [*Freemasonry*]
RWGW .... Right Worthy Grand Worshipful [*Freemasonry*] (ROG)
RWH .... Geneseo Junior/Senior High School Library, Geneseo, NY [*OCLC symbol*] (OCLC)
RWH .... RADAR Warning and Homing
RWH .... Rainwater Head
RWH .... Rotor Wing Hours [*Aviation*] (AIA)
RWHD .... Rawhide (MSA)
rwhi .... Rawhide (VRA)
RWI .... Greece-Arcadia Junior/Senior High School Library, Rochester, NY [*OCLC symbol*] (OCLC)
RWI .... RADAR Warning Installation (NATG)
RWI .... Radio Wire Integration [*Military*]
RWI .... Read-Write-Initialize [*Computer science*]
RWI .... Real World Interval (WDAA)
RWI .... Regular World Interval
RWI .... Remote Weight Indicator
RWI .... Rocky Mount [*North Carolina*] [*Airport symbol*] (OAG)
RWIB .... Rioja Wine Information Bureau (EA)
RWIN .... Republic Industries [*NASDAQ symbol*] (TTSB)
RWIN .... Republic Industries, Inc. [*NASDAQ symbol*] (SAG)
RWIN .... Republic Waste Industries, Inc. [*NASDAQ symbol*] (SAG)
RWIS .... Restraint and Water Immersion Stress [*Medicine*] (DMAA)
RWIY .... Royal Wiltshire Imperial Yeomanry [*British military*] (DMA)
RWJ .... Greece-Athena Junior/Senior High School Library, Rochester, NY [*OCLC symbol*] (OCLC)
RWJ .... Robert Wood Johnson Medical School [*New Jersey*]
RWJF .... Robert Wood Johnson Foundation
RWJGW .... Right Worthy Junior Grand Warden [*Freemasonry*]
RWK .... Greece-Olympia High School Library, Rochester, NY [*OCLC symbol*] (OCLC)
RWK .... Queen's Own Royal West Kent Regiment [*Military unit*] [*British*]
RWK .... Remaining Work
RWK .... Renwick Explorations Ltd. [*Vancouver Stock Exchange symbol*]
RWK .... Rework (AAG)
RWkEPA ...... United States Environmental Protection Agency, National Marine Water Quality Laboratory, West Kingston, RI [*Library symbol Library of Congress*] (LCLS)
RWL .... H. W. Schroeder Junior/Senior High School Library, Webster, NY [*OCLC symbol*] (OCLC)
RWL .... Raised White Letters [*Tire design*] [*Automotive engineering*]
RWL .... Rawlins [*Wyoming*] [*Airport symbol*] (AD)
RWL .... Rawlins, WY [*Location identifier FAA*] (FAAL)
RWL .... Recommended Weight Limit [*Ergonmetrics*]
RWL .... Relative Water Level
RWL .... Revolutionary Workers League [*Canada*]
RWL .... Richwell Resources Ltd. [*Vancouver Stock Exchange symbol*]
RWLB .... Regional War Labor Board
RWLR .... Relative Water-Level Recorder
RWM .... Hilton High School Library, Hilton, NY [*OCLC symbol*] (OCLC)
RWM .... Radioactive Waste Management
RWM .... Read-Write Memory [*Computer science*] (MCD)
RWM .... Rectangular Wave Modulation (IEEE)
RWM .... Regional Wall Motion [*Medicine*] (DMAA)
RWM .... Resistance Welding Machine
RWM .... Right Worshipful Master [*Freemasonry*] (ROG)
RWM .... Rod Worth Minimizer [*Nuclear energy*] (NRCH)
RWM .... Roll Wrapping Machine
RWMA .... Resistance Welder Manufacturers Association (EA)
RWMAC .... Radioactive Waste Management Advisory Committee
RWMC .... Radioactive Waste Management Center
RWMS .... Radioactive Waste Management Site
RWN .... Holly Junior/Senior High School Library, Holly, NY [*OCLC symbol*] (OCLC)
RWN .... Rawdon Resources Ltd. [*Vancouver Stock Exchange symbol*]
RWN .... Winamac, IN [*Location identifier FAA*] (FAAL)
RWNBH .... Records Will Not Be Handcarried [*Army*] (AABC)
RWND .... Rewind (MSA)
RWNF .... Ryan White National Fund (EA)
RWO .... Honeoye Falls-Lima Senior High School Library, Honeoye Falls, NY [*OCLC symbol*] (OCLC)
RWO .... Kodiak, AK [*Location identifier FAA*] (FAAL)
RWO .... Reconnaissance Watch Officer (MCD)
RWO .... Regional Works Officer [*British*]
RWO .... Reimbursable Work Order [*Navy*] (NG)
RWO .... Riddare af Wasa Order [*Knight of the Order of Vasa*] [*Sweden*]
RWO .... Right Wrong Omit (IAA)
RWO .... Routine Work Order (KSC)
RWoH .... Harris Institute, Woonsocket, RI [*Library symbol Library of Congress*] (LCLS)
RWoU .... Union Saint-Jean-Baptiste d'Amerique, Woonsocket, RI [*Library symbol Library of Congress*] (LCLS)
RWP .... James Madison High School Library, Rochester, NY [*OCLC symbol*] (OCLC)
RWP .... Radiation Work Permit [*Nuclear energy*] (NRCH)
RWP .... Radio Wave Propagation
RWP .... Radio Working Party
RWP .... RADWASTE [*Radioactive Waste*] Work Permit [*Nuclear energy*] (NRCH)
RWP .... Rainwater Pipe [*Construction*]
RWP .... Rawalpindi/Islamabad [*Pakistan*] [*Airport symbol Obsolete*] (OAG)
RWP .... Reactor Work Permit (IEEE)
RWP .... Regiment Western Province [*British military*] (DMA)
RWP .... Rifle and Weapons Platoon [*Army Obsolete*] (AABC)
RWP .... Romanian Workers' Party [*Political party*]
RWP .... R-Wave Progression [*On Electrocardiograms*] [*Cardiology*] (DAVI)
RWPC .... RADWASTE [*Radioactive Waste*] Process Cell [*Nuclear energy*] (NRCH)
RWPG .... Real World Problem Generation
RWPH .... River Water Pumphouse [*Nuclear energy*] (NRCH)
RWQ .... James Monroe High School Library, Rochester, NY [*OCLC symbol*] (OCLC)
RWR .... James Sperry High School Library, Henrietta, NY [*OCLC symbol*] (OCLC)
RWR .... RADAR Warning Receiver (MCD)
RWR .... Radioactive Waste Reduction [*Nuclear energy*] (NRCH)
R-W-R .... Rail-Water-Rail [*Shipping*]
RWR .... Read/Write Register
RWR .... Relative Weight Response
RWR .... Reward Resources Ltd. [*Vancouver Stock Exchange symbol*]
RWR .... Romance Writers Report [*A publication*] (EAAP)
RWR .... Ronald Wilson Reagan [*US president, 1911-*]
RWRAT .... Replacement Weather Reconnaissance Aircraft (DNAB)
RWRC .... Remain Well to Right of Course [*Aviation*] (FAAC)

RWRSq .... Rescue and Weather Reconnaissance Squadron [*Air Force*]
RWRT .... Real World Reading Test (EDAC)
RWRW .... Rescue and Weather Reconnaissance Wing [*Air Force*]
RWS .... Air Whitsunday [*Australia ICAO designator*] (FAAC)
RWS .... Camp Springs, MD [*Location identifier FAA*] (FAAL)
RWS .... John Marshall High School Library, Rochester, NY [*OCLC symbol*] (OCLC)
RWS .... RADAR Warning System (MCD)
RWS .... Radioactive Waste System [*Nuclear energy*] (NRCH)
RWS .... Range While Search
RWS .... Reaction Wheel Scanner
RWS .... Reaction Wheel Systems (AAG)
RWS .... Receiver Waveform Simulation [*Telecommunications*] (OA)
RWS .... Regional Warning System
RWS .... Regional Weather Service (NOAA)
RWS .... Release with Service (OICC)
RWS .... Royal Society of Painters in Water-Colours [*British*]
RWS .... Royal Society of Painters in Water-Colours, London [*1804*] (NGC)
RWS .... Royal Watercolour Society [*British*] (EAIO)
RWS .... Royal West Surrey [*Regiment*] [*Military unit*] [*British*]
RWS .... Royal West Sussex [*Regiment*] [*Military unit*] [*British*]
RWSF .... RADWASTE [*Radioactive Waste*] Solidification Facility [*Nuclear energy*] (NRCH)
RWSF .... Revolutionary War Studies Forum (EA)
RWSF .... Roosevelt Warm Springs Foundation (EA)
RWSGW .... Right Worshipful Senior Grand Warden [*Freemasonry*]
RWSS .... RADWASTE [*Radioactive Waste*] Sample Station [*Nuclear energy*] (NRCH)
RWSS .... River Water Supply System (IEEE)
RWST .... Refueling Water Storage Tank [*Nuclear energy*] (NRCH)
RWT .... Kendall High School Library, Kendall, NY [*OCLC symbol*] (OCLC)
RWT .... RADAR Warning Trainer (MCD)
RWT .... Read-Write Tape [*Computer science*]
RWT .... Refueling Water Tank [*Nuclear energy*] (NRCH)
RWT .... Right When Tested (NITA)
RWTA .... River Water Treatment Area [*Nuclear energy*] (NRCH)
RWTF .... RAAF [*Royal Australian Air Force*] Welfare Trust Fund [*Australia*]
RWTH .... Rotary Wing Turbine Hours [*Aviation*] (AIA)
RWTI .... Redwood Trust [*NASDAQ symbol*] (TTSB)
RWTI .... Redwood Trust, Inc. [*NASDAQ symbol*] (SAG)
RWTIW .... Redwood Trust Wrrt [*NASDAQ symbol*] (TTSB)
RWTS .... Regenerant Waste Treatment Subsystem [*Nuclear energy*] (NRCH)
RWU .... Keshequa Junior/Senior High School Library, Nunda, NY [*OCLC symbol*] (OCLC)
RWV .... L. C. Obourn High School Library, East Rochester, NY [*OCLC symbol*] (OCLC)
RWV .... Radial Wall Variation [*Tire design*] [*Automotive engineering*]
RWV .... Radioactive Waste Vent [*Nuclear energy*] (NRCH)
RWV .... Read-Write-Verify [*Computer science*]
RWV .... Rubbery Wood Virus
RWV .... Rustad/Wickhem/Video, Inc. [*Madison, WI*] (TSSD)
RWVD .... Real World Visual Display
RWVR .... Real World Vehicular Rate
RWVRC .... Read-Write Vertical Redundancy Check [*Computer science*] (IAA)
RWW .... Lester B. Forman Central Library, Fairport, NY [*OCLC symbol*] (OCLC)
RWW .... Read while Write [*Computer science*] (IAA)
RWW .... Rear Window Wiper [*Automotive engineering*]
RWX .... Letchworth Junior/Senior High School Library, Gainesville, NY [*OCLC symbol*] (OCLC)
RWY .... Livonia High School Library, Livonia, NY [*OCLC symbol*] (OCLC)
RWY .... Railway
RWY .... Royal Wiltshire Yeomanry [*Military unit*] [*British*]
RWY .... Runway (AAG)
RWZ .... McQuaid Jesuit High School Library, Rochester, NY [*OCLC symbol*] (OCLC)
RX .... British Independent Airways [*ICAO designator*] (AD)
RX .... Capitol Air Service [*ICAO designator*] (AD)
RX .... Excess Reserves
RX .... Rank Xerox
rx .... Reaction [*Laboratory science*] (DAVI)
RX .... Receive (NITA)
RX .... Receiver [*or Reception*] [*Radio*] (NATG)
Rx .... Recipe [*Used as a symbol for medical prescriptions*]
RX .... Reconnaissance-Experimental Aircraft
RX .... Register and Indexed Storage (MCD)
RX .... Remote Exchange [*Telecommunications*] (TEL)
RX .... Repairable Exchange
RX .... Resolver-Transmitter
RX .... Rix-Dollar [*British*] (ROG)
RX .... Rupees [*Monetary unit*] [*Ceylon, India, and Pakistan*] (ROG)
RX .... Rush [*on teletype messages*]
Rx .... Therapy (DAVI)
R_x .... Unknown Resistance (IDOE)
RXA .... Arax Airlines Ltd. [*Nigeria*] [*ICAO designator*] (FAAC)
RXA .... Mount Morris Junior/Senior High School Library, Mount Morris, NY [*OCLC symbol*] (OCLC)
RXA .... Raudha [*South Arabia*] [*Airport symbol*] (AD)
RXA .... Repairable Exchange Activity [*Army*]
RXA .... Roxana Resources Ltd. [*Vancouver Stock Exchange symbol*]
RXB .... Nazareth Academy Library, Rochester, NY [*OCLC symbol*] (OCLC)
RXC .... Our Lady of Mercy High School Library, Rochester, NY [*OCLC symbol*] (OCLC)
RXD .... Penfield High School Library, Penfield, NY [*OCLC symbol*] (OCLC)
RXD .... Research or Exploratory Development (PDAA)
RXE .... Perry Junior/Senior High School Library, Perry, NY [*OCLC symbol*] (OCLC)
RXF .... Pittsford-Medon High School Library, Pittsford, NY [*OCLC symbol*] (OCLC)
RXF .... Rexford [*Montana*] [*Seismograph station code, US Geological Survey*] (SEIS)
RXG .... Pittsford-Sutherland High School Library, Pittsford, NY [*OCLC symbol*] (OCLC)
RXH .... R. L. Thomas High School Library, Webster, NY [*OCLC symbol*] (OCLC)
RXI .... Rexplore Resources International Ltd. [*Vancouver Stock Exchange symbol*]
RXI .... St. Agnes High School Library, Rochester, NY [*OCLC symbol*] (OCLC)
RXJ .... Thomas Jefferson Junior/Senior High School Library, Rochester, NY [*OCLC symbol*] (OCLC)
RXK .... Newark, OH [*Location identifier FAA*] (FAAL)
RXK .... Warsaw High School Library, Warsaw, NY [*OCLC symbol*] (OCLC)
RXL .... Air Exel [*France ICAO designator*] (FAAC)
RXL .... Rank Xerox Ltd. [*Xerox subsidiary*]
RXL .... Rexel, Inc. [*NYSE symbol*] (SAG)
RXL .... Wayland Senior High School Library, Wayland, NY [*OCLC symbol*] (OCLC)
RXLI .... Recessive X-Linked Ichthyosis [*Medicine*]
RXM .... Rexford Minerals Ltd. [*Vancouver Stock Exchange symbol*]
RXM .... RX Medical Services [*AMEX symbol*] (SPSG)
RXM .... RX Medical Services [*AMEX symbol*] (TTSB)
RXM .... West Irondequoit High School Library, Rochester, NY [*OCLC symbol*] (OCLC)
RX Med .... RX Medical Services Corp. [*Associated Press*] (SAG)
RXN .... Islip, NY [*Location identifier FAA*] (FAAL)
RXN .... Reaction [*Medicine*]
RXN .... Rexene Corp. [*NYSE symbol*] (SPSG)
RXN .... Wheatland-Chili Junior/Senior High School Library, Scottsville, NY [*OCLC symbol*] (OCLC)
RX(NP) .... Return-to-Zero Recording (Non-Polarized) [*Computer science*] (MHDB)
RXO .... York High School Library, Retsof, NY [*OCLC symbol*] (OCLC)
RXOS .... Rank Xerox Operating System [*Computer science*] (IAA)
RXP .... American Baptist Historical Society Library, Rochester, NY [*OCLC symbol*] (OCLC)
RXP .... Radix Point
RXQ .... Lincoln First Bank of Rochester Library Service, Rochester, NY [*OCLC symbol*] (OCLC)
RXQ .... Washington, DC [*Location identifier FAA*] (FAAL)
RXR .... Rainex Industries [*Formerly, Rainex Resources Ltd.*] [*Vancouver Stock Exchange symbol*]
RXR .... Revco D.S. [*NYSE symbol*] (TTSB)
RXR .... Revco DS, Inc. [*NYSE symbol*] (SPSG)
RXS .... RADAR Cross Section
RXS .... Real-Time Executive System [*SEMIS*] (IAA)
RXS .... Roxas City [*Philippines*] [*Airport symbol*] (OAG)
RXSD .... Rexall Sundown [*NASDAQ symbol*] (TTSB)
RXSD .... Rexall Sundown, Inc. [*NASDAQ symbol*] (SAG)
RXT .... Renal Treatment Centers, Inc. [*NYSE symbol*] (SAG)
RXT .... Renal Treatment Ctrs [*NYSE symbol*] (TTSB)
RXT .... Right Exotropia [*Ophthalmology*]
RXTC .... Renal Treatment Center, Inc. [*NASDAQ symbol*] (SAG)
RXTE .... Rossi X-ray Timing Explorer [*A satellite*]
RxTV .... Prescription Television
RXW .... Roxwell Gold Mines [*Vancouver Stock Exchange symbol*]
RXW .... Watersmeet, MI [*Location identifier FAA*] (FAAL)
RXX .... Reako Exploration [*Vancouver Stock Exchange symbol*]
RXY .... Roxy Petroleum Ltd. [*Toronto Stock Exchange symbol*]
RXZ .... Chicago, IL [*Location identifier FAA*] (FAAL)
RY .... Air Rwanda [*ICAO designator*] (AD)
RY .... Perkiomen Airways [*ICAO designator*] (AD)
RY .... Railway (AFIT)
RY .... Redcoat Air Cargo Ltd. [*British ICAO designator*] (ICDA)
RY .... Relative Yield [*Agriculture*]
RY .... Relay (DEN)
RY .... Residual Yield [*Agriculture*] (OA)
RY .... Riley Aeronautics Corp. [*ICAO aircraft manufacturer identifier*] (ICAO)
RY .... Roll Yoke
RY .... Royal (ROG)
RY .... Royal Bank Canada [*MS Symbol*] (TTSB)
RY .... Royal Bank of Canada [*Toronto Stock Exchange symbol Vancouver Stock Exchange symbol*]
RY .... Royal Bank of Canada, Inc. [*NYSE symbol*] (SAG)
RY .... Royal Yeomanry [*Military unit*] [*British*]
ry .... Rydberg [*Unit of energy*] [*Atomic physics Symbol*]
ry .... Ryukyu Islands, Southern [*ja (Japan) used in records cataloged after January 1978*] [*MARC country of publication code Library of Congress*] (LCCP)
RYA .... Railroad Yardmasters of America (EA)
RYA .... Royal Yachting Association [*British*] (BI)
RYA .... Ryan Air Services, Inc. [*ICAO designator*] (FAAC)
RYALM .... Relay Alarm (AAG)
RYAN .... Ryan's Family Steak Houses, Inc. [*NASDAQ symbol*] (NQ)
RYAN .... Ryan's Family Stk Hse [*NASDAQ symbol*] (TTSB)
Ryan & M .... Ryan and Moody's English Nisi Prius Reports [*171 English Reprint*] [*A publication*] (DLA)
Ryan & M (Eng) ... Ryan and Moody's English Nisi Prius Reports [*171 English Reprint*] [*A publication*] (DLA)
RyanBck .... Ryan Beck Co., Inc. [*Associated Press*] (SAG)

Ry & Can..... Reports of Railway and Canal Traffic Cases [*1855-1950*] [*A publication*]
Ry & Can Cas... Railway and Canal Cases [*England*] [*A publication*] (DLA)
Ry & Can Traf Ca... Railway and Canal Traffic Cases [*A publication*] (DLA)
Ry & Can Traf Cas... Reports of Railway and Canal Traffic Cases [*1855-1950*] [*A publication*] (ILCA)
Ry & Can Traffic Cas... Railway and Canal Traffic Cases [*England*] [*A publication*] (DLA)
Ry & Can Tr Cas... Reports of Railway and Canal Traffic Cases [*1855-1950*] [*A publication*] (DLA)
Ry & C Cas (Eng)... Railway and Canal Cases [*England*] [*A publication*] (DLA)
Ry & Corp Law J... Railway and Corporation Law Journal [*A publication*] (DLA)
Ry & Corp Law Jour... Railway and Corporation Law Journal [*A publication*] (DLA)
Ry & C Traffic Cas (Eng)... Railway and Canal Traffic Cases [*England*] [*A publication*] (DLA)
Ry & M........ Ryan and Moody's English Nisi Prius Reports [*A publication*] (DLA)
Ry & MCC ... Ryan and Moody's English Crown Cases Reserved [*A publication*] (DLA)
Ry & MNP ... Ryan and Moody's English Nisi Prius Reports [*A publication*] (DLA)
Ry & Moo.... Ryan and Moody [*1823-26*] [*A publication*] (DLA)
RyanF.......... Ryans Family Steak Houses, Inc. [*Associated Press*] (SAG)
RYB .... Raymond, MS [*Location identifier FAA*] (FAAL)
RYB .... Rybachye [*Former USSR Seismograph station code, US Geological Survey*] (SEIS)
RyBPA .... Royal Bancshares of Pennsylvania [*Associated Press*] (SAG)
RYC .... Raychem Corp. [*NYSE symbol*] (SPSG)
RYC .... Raymac Oil Corp. [*Vancouver Stock Exchange symbol*]
RYC .... Rural Youth Corps [*Defunct*] (EA)
Ry Cas......... Reports of English Railway Cases [*A publication*] (DLA)
Ry Cas......... Reports of Railway and Canal Traffic Cases [*1855-1950*] [*A publication*]
Ry Corp Law Jour... Railway and Corporation Law Journal [*A publication*] (DLA)
RYD .... Real Year Dollars (NASA)
Ryde .... Ryde's Rating Appeals [*1871-1904*] [*A publication*] (DLA)
Ryde & K..... Ryde and Konstam's Reports of Rating Appeals [*1894-1904*] [*A publication*] (DLA)
Ryde & K Rat App... Ryde and Konstam's Reports of Rating Appeals [*1894-1904*] [*A publication*] (DLA)
Ryder........... Ryder Systems, Inc. [*Associated Press*] (SAG)
Ryde Rat App... Ryde's Rating Appeals [*1871-1904*] [*A publication*] (DLA)
Rydges Mgmt Serv... Rydge's Management Service [*A publication*]
RYDMAR...... Reaction-Yield-Detected Magnetic Resonance [*Also, RYDMR*] [*Spectroscopy*]
RYDMR........ Reaction-Yield-Detected Magnetic Resonance [*Also, RYDMAR*] [*Spectroscopy*]
RYE............. Retirement Year Ending [*Army*] (AABC)
RYE............. Royalon Petroleum [*Vancouver Stock Exchange symbol*]
RyerTull....... Ryerson Tull [*Associated Press*] (SAG)
RYEV .... Radish Yellow Edge Virus [*Plant pathology*]
Ry F............. Rymer's Foedera [*20 vols.*] [*1704-35*] [*A publication*] (DLA)
RYFL............ Family Steak Houses Fla [*NASDAQ symbol*] (TTSB)
RYFL............ Family Steak Houses of Florida, Inc. [*Neptune Beach, FL*] [*NASDAQ symbol*] (NQ)
RYFO .... Ryan Foundation International [*India*] (EAIO)
RYG .... Royal Plastics Group [*NYSE symbol*] (TTSB)
RYG .... Royal Plastics Group Ltd. [*NYSE symbol*] (SAG)
RYK .... Rahimyar Kahn [*Pakistan*] [*Airport symbol*] (AD)
RYK .... Relay Creek Resources Ltd. [*Vancouver Stock Exchange symbol*]
RYK .... Romulus, NY [*Location identifier FAA*] (FAAL)
RYK .... Rykoff-Sexton, Inc. [*NYSE symbol*] (SPSG)
Rykoff .... Rykoff-Sexton, Inc. [*Associated Press*] (SAG)
ryl .... Royal [*Philately*]
RYL............. Royal
RYL............. Royal Trustco Ltd. [*Toronto Stock Exchange symbol Vancouver Stock Exchange symbol*]
RYL............. Ryland Group [*NYSE symbol*] (TTSB)
RYL............. Ryland Group, Inc. [*NYSE symbol*] (SPSG)
Ryland......... Ryland Group, Inc. [*Associated Press*] (SAG)
RylCarb........ Royal Caribbean Cruises [*Associated Press*] (SAG)
Ryl Plac Parl... Ryley's Placita Parliamentaria [*1290-1307*] [*England*] [*A publication*] (DLA)
RYM............ Reference Your Message [*Military*] (AABC)
RYM............ Revolutionary Youth Movement [*Factions of Students for a Democratic Society. See RYM-I and RYM-II*]
Rymac .... Rymac Mortgage Investment Corp. [*Associated Press*] (SAG)
Ry MCC .... Ryan and Moody's English Crown Cases [*A publication*] (DLA)
Ry Med Jur... Ryan's Medical Jurisprudence [*A publication*] (DLA)
Rymer.......... Rymer Foods, Inc. [*Associated Press*] (SAG)
Rym F.......... Rymer's Foedera [*20 vols.*] [*1704-35*] [*A publication*] (DLA)
RYM-I .... Revolutionary Youth Movement I [*Also known as "Weatherman"*] [*A faction of Students for a Democratic Society*]
RYM-II .... Revolutionary Youth Movement II [*A faction of Students for a Democratic Society*]
RYMSA .... Rural Youth Movement of South Australia
RYMV .... Rice Yellow Mottle Virus [*Plant pathology*]
RYN .... Rayon
RYN .... Rayonier, Inc. [*NYSE symbol*] (SAG)
RYN .... Ryan Aviation Corp. [*ICAO designator*] (FAAC)
RYN .... Tucson, AZ [*Location identifier FAA*] (FAAL)
RYNA .... Railroad Yardmasters of North America [*Absorbed by RYA*] (EA)
RYNV .... Rubust Yellow Net Virus [*Plant pathology*]
RYO .... Rio Turbio [*Argentina*] [*Airport symbol*] (OAG)
RYO .... Royal Oak Mines [*AMEX symbol*] (SPSG)
RYONSW ..... Rural Youth Organisation of New South Wales [*Australia*]
RYOQ.......... Rural Youth Organisation of Queensland [*Australia*]
RYOT .... Rural Youth Organisation of Tasmania [*Australia*]
RYP .... Cumberland, MD [*Location identifier FAA*] (FAAL)
R-Y-P.......... Roll, Yaw, Pitch (MCD)
RYQ .... Royalstar Resources [*Vancouver Stock Exchange symbol*]
RYR .... Radyr Junction [*Cardiff*] [*Welsh depot code*]
RYR .... Royal Yeomanry Regiment [*British military*] (DMA)
RYR .... Ryanair [*Ireland*] [*ICAO designator*] (FAAC)
RYR .... Ryanodine Receptor [*Genetics*]
RYR .... Rymer Foods [*NYSE symbol*] (TTSB)
RYR .... Rymer Foods, Inc. [*NYSE symbol*] (SPSG)
RyRC .... Ryanodine Receptor Channel [*Biochemistry*]
RYRQD .... Reply Requested (NOAA)
RYS .... Railway Stations [*Public-performance tariff class*] [*British*]
RYS .... Royal Yacht Squadron [*British*]
RYS .... Ryan Resources Ltd. [*Vancouver Stock Exchange symbol*]
RYT............. Ray-Net Communications Systems, Inc. [*Vancouver Stock Exchange symbol*]
RYT............. Reference Your Telegram (WDAA)
RYT............. Reference Your Telex (WDAA)
RYT............. Relative Yield Total [*Agriculture*]
Ryt............... Rytmi [*Record label*] [*Finland*]
RYU .... Rosanky, TX [*Location identifier FAA*] (FAAL)
RYU .... Ryukoku University [*UTLAS symbol*]
RYV .... Watertown, WI [*Location identifier FAA*] (FAAL)
RYY .... Marietta, GA [*Location identifier FAA*] (FAAL)
RZ............... Arabia [*ICAO designator*] (AD)
RZ............... Reaction Zone
RZ............... Reconnaissance Zone
RZ............... Recovery Zone (MCD)
RZ............... Regal-Zonophone [*Record label*] [*Great Britain*]
RZ............... Regiment de Zouaves
RZ............... Resistance Zone
RZ............... Return to Zero (IDOE)
RZ............... Return-to-Zero Recording [*Computer science*]
Rz................ Retzius [*Neuron*]
RZ............... Revolutionary Cells [*Revolutionary group*] [*West Germany*]
Rz .... Rhizome [*Botany*]
RZ............... Rueckenfallschirm mit Zwangsausloesung [*Static-line, backpack parachute*] [*German military - World War II*]
RZA............. Religious Zionists of America (EA)
RZA............. Santa Cruz [*Argentina*] [*Airport symbol*] (OAG)
RZB............. Roseberth [*Queensland*] [*Airport symbol*] (AD)
RZC............. Fayetteville, AR [*Location identifier FAA*] (FAAL)
RZE............. Rzeszow [*Poland*] [*Airport symbol*] (OAG)
RZF............. Riemann Zeta Function [*Mathematics*]
RZI.............. Aero Zambia Ltd. [*FAA designator*] (FAAC)
RZL............. Rensselaer, IN [*Location identifier FAA*] (FAAL)
RZL............. Return-to-Zero Level
RZM............ Return-to-Zero Mark
RZMA.......... Rolled Zinc Manufacturers Association [*Defunct*] (EA)
RZ(NP)........ Nonpolarized Return-to-Zero Recording [*Computer science*] (IBMDP)
RZ(NP)........ Return to Zero (Non-Polarized) (NITA)
RZO .... Demopolis, AL [*Location identifier FAA*] (FAAL)
RZ(P)........... Polarized Return-to-Zero Recording [*Computer science*] (IBMDP)
RZP............. Provincetown, MA [*Location identifier FAA*] (FAAL)
RZ(P) .... Return to Zero (Polarized) (NITA)
RZR .... Ramsar [*Iran*] [*Airport symbol*] (AD)
RZR .... Zephyr Aviation Services, Inc. [*ICAO designator*] (FAAC)
RZS............. Rolled Zinc Sheet
RZS............. Royal Zoological Society [*British*]
RZSI............ [*The*] Royal Zoological Society of Ireland (DI)
RZSS .... Royal Zoological Society of Scotland (EAIO)
RZT............. Chillicothe, OH [*Location identifier FAA*] (FAAL)
RZY............. Rezayeh [*Iran*] [*Airport symbol*] (AD)
RZYM........... Ribozyme Pharmaceuticals [*NASDAQ symbol*] (TTSB)
RZYM........... Ribozyme Pharmaceuticals, Inc. [*NASDAQ symbol*] (SAG)
RZZ............. Roanoke Rapids, NC [*Location identifier FAA*] (FAAL)

S

By Acronym

S .... Aerospatiale [*Societe Nationale Industrielle Aerospatiale*] (Sud Aviation) [*France ICAO aircraft manufacturer identifier*] (ICAO)

S .... Antisubmarine [*Designation for all US military aircraft*]

S .... Apparent Power [*Symbol*] (DEN)

S .... Boltzmann Constant [*Statistical mechanics*]

S .... Codex Sinaiticus (BJA)

S .... Condensation [*Physics*] (BARN)

S .... Deflection Sensitivity (IDOE)

S .... Detecting [*JETDS nomenclature*]

S .... Displacement [*Physics*] (BARN)

s .... Distance (DAVI)

S .... Elastance [*Electricity*] (BARN)

S .... Entropy [*Symbol*] [*IUPAC*]

s .... Esophoria [*Ophthalmology*] (DAVI)

S .... Esses [*Phonetic alphabet*] [*Pre-World War II*] (DSUE)

S .... Expenditure Saved [*Economics*]

S .... Fun Fairs [*Public-performance tariff class*] [*British*]

S .... Isis-Chemie KG [*Germany*] [*Research code symbol*]

S .... Magnetic Solar Daily Variation

S .... Mean Dose Per Unit Cumulated Activity (DAVI)

S .... New York Supplement [*A publication*] (DLA)

S .... No Option Offered [*Investment term*] (DFIT)

s .... Path, Length of Arc [*Symbol*] [*IUPAC*]

(S) .... Paymaster [*Navy British*]

S .... Permissible Working Stress

S .... Pitman-Moore Co. [*Research code symbol*]

S .... Pounds per Square Inch (AAG)

S .... Poynting Vector [*Symbol*] [*Electromagnetism*] (DEN)

S .... Range Bearing [*JETDS nomenclature*]

S .... Reluctance [*Symbol*] (DEN)

S .... Sabbath

S .... Sabin [*Unit of acoustic measurement*] (DEN)

S .... Sable [*Heraldry*]

S .... Sacral

S .... Sacred

S .... Sacrifice [*Baseball*]

S .... Sacrum

S .... Sadism [*or Sadist*] (CDAI)

S .... Saduccus [*Flourished, 13th century*] [*Authority cited in pre-1607 legal work*] (DSA)

S .... Saeculum

(S) .... Safe [*Task classification*] [*NASA*] (NASA)

S .... Safety [*Football*]

S .... Sailing Ship

S .... Saint

S .... Saline

S .... Saline [*Pharmacology*] (DAVI)

S .... Salmonella [*Bacteriology*] (MAE)

S .... Salvageable (AAG)

S .... Same Case [*Same case as case cited*] [*Used in Shepard's Citations*] [*Legal term*] (DLA)

S .... Sample

S .... Samuel [*Old Testament book*] (BJA)

S .... San (VRA)

S .... Sand [*Quality of the bottom*] [*Nautical charts*]

S .... Sandra [*Genotype of Phlox paniculata*]

S .... San Francisco [*California*] [*Mint mark, when appearing on US coins*]

S .... Sankt (VRA)

S .... Santa (VRA)

S .... Santo (VRA)

S .... Sapwood [*Forestry*]

S .... Satang [*Monetary unit in Thailand*]

S .... Satellite (IAA)

s .... Satellite [*Chromosomal*] [*Medicine*] (MAE)

S .... Saturation (MAE)

S .... Saturation in the Blood Phase [*Medicine*] (DAVI)

S .... Saturday

S .... Saturn

S .... Savanna Zone Soil [*Agriculture*]

s .... Save [*Computer science*] [*Telecommunications*]

S .... Savings [*Economics*]

S .... Saxon

S .... Saybolt Second (IAA)

S .... Scalar [*Mathematics*] (ROG)

S .... Scanning

S .... Scarce [*Numismatics*]

S .... Scattering Coefficient [*Photometry*]

S .... Schedule

S .... Schilling [*Monetary unit*] [*Austria*]

S .... Schistosoma [*A parasitic fluke*] (MAE)

S .... School

S .... Science (WGA)

S .... Scilicet [*Namely*] [*Latin*] (DLA)

S .... Scot

S .... Scott's Standard Postage Stamp Catalogue [*A publication*]

S .... Scouting [*Naval aircraft designation*]

S .... Screen (IAA)

s .... Screen (IDOE)

S .... Scribe

S .... Scruple [*Medicine*] (DMAA)

S .... Scuttle

S .... Scythian [*Geology*]

S .... Sea (ADA)

S .... Sea-Air Temperature Difference Correction

S .... Seaman [*Navy*]

S .... Seamless (DAC)

S .... Seaplane [*Navy*]

S .... Search

S .... Searle's Cape Of Good Hope Reports [*South Africa*] [*A publication*] (DLA)

S .... Searle's Cases in the Supreme Court [*1850-67*] [*South Africa*] [*A publication*] (DLA)

S .... Sears,Roebuck [*NYSE symbol*] (TTSB)

S .... Sears, Roebuck & Co. [*NYSE symbol*] (SPSG)

S .... Seasonal [*Business term*] (OICC)

S .... Seat (WGA)

s .... Second [*Symbol*] [*SI unit of time*]

S .... Second [*or Secondary*]

s .... Secondary [*Preferred form is sec*] [*Chemistry*]

S .... Secondary Modern School [*British*]

S .... Secondary [*or Shake*] Wave [*Earthquakes*]

S .... Secondary Winding (IAA)

S .... Secret [*Security classification*]

S .... Secretary

S .... Secretin [*Endocrinology*]

S .... Secretory Substance [*Botany*]

S .... Section

S .... Section (WDMC)

S .... Sector (IAA)

S .... Security (IAA)

S .... Sedentary [*Biology*]

S .... Seder of Triennial Cycle (BJA)

s .... Sedimentation Coefficient [*Physical chemistry*]

S .... See

S .... Seelenlaenge [*Barrel length*] [*German military - World War II*]

S .... Seguente [*And Following*] [*Italian*] (ILCA)

S .... Seite [*Page*] [*German*]

s .... Selection Coefficient (DOG)

S .... Self-Pollinated [*Botany*]

S .... Selvi [*Italy*] [*Research code symbol*]

S .... Semi

S .... Semiannually

S .... Semilente [*Insulin*] [*Pharmacology*] (DAVI)

S .... Semi-Registered Tank [*Liquid gas carriers*]

S .... Semis [*One-Half*] [*Pharmacy*]

S .... Sen [*Monetary unit in Japan*]

S .... Senate

S .... Senate Bill [*with number*] (GPO)

S .... Senor [*Mister*] [*Spanish*]

S .... Sensation [*Psychology*]

S .... Sensitivity (DEN)

S .... Sentence [*Linguistics*]

S .... Senza [*Without*] [*Music*]

S .... Separation

S .... September

S .... Septum [*Anatomy*] (DAVI)

S .... Sepulchrum [*Sepulchre*] [*Latin*]

S .... Sepultus [*Buried*] [*Latin*]

S .... Serial

S .... Series

S .... Serine [*One-letter symbol; see Ser*]

S .... Sermon

S .... Serum
S .... Servant [*Legal shorthand*] (LWAP)
S .... Service [*Military document classification*] (INF)
S .... Servicing
S .... Servier [*France*] [*Research code symbol*]
S .... Sesquiplane [*Navy*]
S .... Set
S .... Set Meals [*School meals*] [*British*]
S .... Seven (ROG)
S .... Seventy (ROG)
S .... Severity
S .... Sewage Disposal [*British Waterways Board sign*]
S .... SGOT [*Surface Serum Glutamic-Oxaloacetic*] (DAVI)
S .... Shaft Horsepower
S .... Shaft Main Engine
S .... Shape Descriptor [*S-curve, for example. The shape resembles the letter for which it is named*]
S .... Shape Factor of a Structure [*Heat transmission symbol*]
S .... Sharing Time (NTCM)
S .... Sharp
s .... Sharpshooter [*Army*]
S .... Shaw, Dunlop, and Bell's Scotch Court of Session Reports, First Series [*A publication*] (DLA)
S .... Shaw's Scotch Appeal Cases, House of Lords [*A publication*] (DLA)
S .... Shaw's Scotch Court of Session Cases [*A publication*] (DLA)
S .... Shear [*Type of seismic wave*]
S .... Sheep (ROG)
S .... Sheet [*Genetics*]
S .... Shell
S .... Shelter [*Bureau of the Census*]
S .... Sheltered [*Takeoff area for seaplanes*] [*For chart use only*]
S .... Shelters [*JETDS nomenclature*] [*Military*] (CET)
S .... Shilling [*Monetary unit in Britain*] [*Obsolete*]
S .... Ship
S .... Shire (ADA)
S .... Short Circuit
S .... Shrub [*Botany*]
S .... Shunt Ahead [*Railroad signal arm*] [*British*]
S .... Sick
S .... Side
S .... Siderocyte [*Hematology*] (AAMN)
S .... Side Signal (IAA)
S .... Sidrah (BJA)
S .... Siecle [*Century*] [*French*]
S .... Siemens [*Symbol*] [*SI unit of electric conductance*]
S .... Sierra [*Phonetic alphabet*] [*International*] (DSUE)
S .... Sigma (NUCP)
S .... Sigma Mines (Quebec) Ltd. [*Toronto Stock Exchange symbol*]
S .... Sign [*or Signed*]
S .... Signa [*Write*] [*Pharmacy*]
S .... Signal [*Telecommunications*] (TEL)
S .... Signaller [*British military*] (DMA)
S .... Signal Strength [*Broadcasting*]
S .... Signature
s .... Signature (WDMC)
/S/ .... Signed [*Before signature on typed copy of a document, original of which was signed*]
S .... Signed (DFIT)
S .... Signetur [*Let It Be Entitled*] [*Pharmacy*] (ROG)
S .... Signor [*Mister*] [*Italian*]
S .... Silent [*Dance terminology*]
S .... Silicate
S .... Silk (AAG)
S .... Silurian [*Geology*] (DOG)
S .... Silver
S .... Silversmith
S .... Simes [*Italy*] [*Research code symbol*]
S .... Similarity Index
S .... Simon de Bisignano [*Flourished, 1174-79*] [*Authority cited in pre-1607 legal work*] (DSA)
S .... Simon de Paris [*Deceased, 1273*] [*Authority cited in pre-1607 legal work*] (DSA)
S .... Simplex
S .... Simultaneous Transmission of Range Signals and Voice
S .... Sine [*Without*] [*Latin*]
S .... Single [*One way fare*] [*British*]
S .... Single
S .... Single Silk [*Wire insulation*]
S .... Singular
S .... Sinister [*Left*] [*Latin*]
(S) .... Sinister [*Counterclockwise configuration*] [*Biochemistry*]
S .... Sinistra [*Left Hand*] [*Music*]
S .... Sink
S .... Sire
S .... Sister
S .... Site [*Archaeology*]
S .... Situs [*Placed*] [*Latin*]
S .... Sixteenmo [*Book from 15 to 17-1/2 centimeters in height*]
S .... Sixth Word Designator [*Computer science*]
S .... Sized (NTCM)
S .... Skid (AAG)
S .... Slate (KSC)
S .... Slave [*LORAN stations*]
S .... Sleeping [*Medicine*]
S .... Slewed [*Antenna*]
s .... Slides (WDMC)
S .... Slip
S .... Slipped Up [*Horse racing*]
S .... Slope [*Technical drawings*]
S .... Slow
S .... Slow Muscle [*Skeletal muscle pharmacology*]
S .... Small [*Size designation for clothing, etc.*]
s .... Small (WDMC)
S .... Smoke (NFPA)
S .... Smooth [*Appearance of bacterial colony*]
S .... Smooth Sea [*Navigation*]
S .... Snack (CDAI)
S .... Sniper [*British military*] (DMA)
S .... Snow [*Meteorology*]
S .... Socialist
S .... Socialist Group [*EC*] (ECED)
S .... Societas [*Society*] [*Latin*]
S .... Socius [*or Sodalis*] [*Fellow*]
S .... Soft
S .... Software [*Computer science*]
S .... Soiled [*Deltiology*]
S .... Sol [*Monetary unit in Peru*]
S .... Solar (ADA)
S .... Solco Basel AG [*Switzerland*] [*Research code symbol*]
S .... Soldering
S .... Solicitor's Opinion [*A publication*] (DLA)
(s) .... Solid [*Chemistry*]
S .... Solid
S .... Solidus [*Shilling*] [*Latin*]
S .... Solitary [*Biology*]
S .... Solo [*Music*]
S .... Solubility
S .... Solute (DAVI)
S .... Somaliland Scouts [*Military unit*] [*British*]
S .... Son
S .... SONAR [*Sonic Azimuth and Ranging*] [*British military*] (DMA)
S .... Song (ROG)
S .... Soprano
S .... Sou [*Monetary unit in France*]
S .... Sough (AAG)
S .... Sound [*Audiology*]
S .... Sound Tape [*Films, television, etc.*]
S .... Source
S .... South [*or Southern*]
S .... South (VRA)
s----- .... South America [*MARC geographic area code Library of Congress*] (LCCP)
S .... Southern (VRA)
S .... Southern Reporter [*A publication*] (DLA)
S .... Space (IAA)
S .... Spacer
S .... Spade (ADA)
S .... Spar [*Buoy*]
S .... Spares
S .... Spatial Ability [*Psychology*]
S .... Speak
S .... Special
s .... Special Abilities of an Individual [*Symbol*] [*Psychology*]
S .... Specialist [*Ecology*]
S .... Special Preparations Necessary for Test [*Laboratory science*] (DAVI)
S .... Special Types [*JETDS nomenclature*]
S .... Species
S .... Specification
S .... Specific Factor
S .... Specific Surface
S .... Speech
S .... Speed
S .... Sphere [*or Spherical*]
S .... Spherical Joint (IAA)
S .... Spherical Lens [*Ophthalmology*] (DAVI)
s .... Spin Quantum Number [*Atomic physics*] (DEN)
S .... Spinster
S .... Spirillum [*Bacteriology*] (MAE)
S .... Split [*In stock listings of newspapers*]
S .... Spoilers in Nozzle
S .... Sponsored
S .... Spontaneous
S .... Spool
S .... Sport [*In automobile model name "Honda Civic S"*]
S .... Sports Program (NTCM)
S .... Spring-Burned [*Ecology*]
S .... Spurs [*Horse racing*]
S .... Squadron
S .... Stack
S .... Stackable Container (DCTA)
S .... Staff
S .... Staff [*License plate code assigned to foreign diplomats in the US*]
S .... Stand
S .... Standard
s .... Standard Deviation [*Also, SD*] [*Statistics*]
S .... Staphylococcus [*Medicine*] (MAE)
S .... Star (NASA)
S .... Starboard
S .... Start (KSC)
s .... Stat [*Unit of radioactive disintegration rate*]

S ..... State [*Telecommunications*]
S ..... Static
S ..... Station
S ..... Stationary
S ..... Statue (ADA)
S ..... Status Required [*Civil Service*]
S ..... Statute
S ..... Steamer
S ..... Steamship (DS)
S ..... Steel
S ..... Stem
S ..... Stephanus Provincialis [*Flourished, 1290-97*] [*Authority cited in pre-1607 legal work*] (DSA)
S ..... Stere [*Metric measure of volume*]
S ..... Stereo (CDAI)
S ..... Stereo Broadcast [*British*]
S ..... Stimulus
S ..... Stock
S ..... Stockbroker
S ..... Stoke (IAA)
S ..... Stolen Base [*Baseball*]
S ..... Stopping Power
S ..... Storage
S ..... Store (IAA)
S ..... Stores [*British military*] (DMA)
S ..... Straight
s ..... Strange [*Quark*] [*Atomic physics*]
S ..... Stratum (BJA)
S ..... Stratus [*Meteorology*]
S ..... Street [*Bureau of the Census*]
S ..... Strength (DS)
S ..... Streptococcus [*Medicine*] (MAE)
S ..... Streptomycin [*An antibiotic*]
S ..... Streptozocin [*Antineoplastic drug*]
S ..... Stroke of Piston in Inches [*Railroad term*]
S ..... Stung [*by bees*] [*Medicine*]
S ..... Subcompact [*Car size*]
S ..... Subcutaneous [*Pharmacology*] (DAVI)
S ..... Subito [*Immediately; Suddenly*] [*Music*]
S ..... Subject [*Psychology*]
S ..... Subject [*of a proposition in logic*]
S ..... Subject [*of an Experiment*] (DAVI)
S ..... Subjective [*findings*] (DAVI)
S ..... Subluxation [*Chiropractic*]
S ..... Submarine
s ..... Submerged Pump [*Liquid gas carriers*]
S ..... Substantive
S ..... Substrate (IAA)
S ..... Substrate, Free [*Enzyme kinetics*]
S ..... Succeeded
S ..... Successor
S ..... Suckling [*Medicine*] (DMAA)
S ..... Sucre [*Monetary unit*] [*Ecuador*]
S ..... Sud [*South*] [*French*] (ROG)
S ..... Sugar [*Phonetic alphabet*] [*Royal Navy World War I Pre-World War II*] [*World War II*] (DSUE)
S ..... Suit
S ..... Suitability (CAAL)
S ..... Sulfamethoxazole [*Also, SMX, SMZ*] [*Antibacterial compound*]
S ..... Sulfate
S ..... Sulfur [*Chemical element*]
S ..... Sum (MAE)
S ..... Sumendus [*To Be Taken*] [*Pharmacy*]
S ..... Summary
S ..... Summer [*Vessel load line mark*]
S ..... Summit Books [*Publisher's imprint*]
S ..... Sun
S ..... Sunday
S ..... Sunny [*Meteorology*] (ADA)
S ..... Super
S ..... Superb
S ..... Superficial
S ..... Superior
S ..... Supernatant [*Protein*] [*Cytology*]
S ..... Superseded [*New regulation or order substituted for an existing one*] [*Used in Shepard's Citations*] [*Legal term*] (DLA)
S ..... Supervisor (IAA)
S ..... Supplementary Frequency (DA)
S ..... Supply [*Department aboard a carrier*] [*Navy*]
S ..... Supply [*Economics*]
S ..... Supravergence (AAMN)
S ..... Supreme Court Reporter [*A publication*] (DLA)
S ..... Sur [*On*] [*French*]
S ..... Surface Area
S ..... Surfaced
S ..... Surgeon [*Navy British*] (ROG)
S ..... Surgery [*Medical Officer designation*] [*British*]
S ..... Surpine (DAVI)
S ..... Surplus
S ..... Surrogate
S ..... Survey
S ..... Survival
S ..... Susceptible
S ..... Suus [*His*] [*Latin*]
S ..... Svedberg Unit [*Physical chemistry*]
S ..... Sweden [*IYRU nationality code*]
S ..... Swiss Mouse [*Medicine*] (DMAA)
S ..... Switch
S ..... Switchboard [*Telecommunications*] (TEL)
s ..... Symmetrical [*Also, sym*] [*Chemistry*]
S ..... Symmetrically Substituted (IAA)
s ..... Symmetry Number [*Symbol*] [*IUPAC*]
S ..... Sync (IDOE)
S ..... Synchronized Sleep
S ..... Synchronous
S ..... Synoptic [*Meteorology*]
S ..... Synthesis [*Phase in mitosis*] [*Cytology*]
S ..... Syria (BARN)
S ..... System
s ..... Systolic [*Cardiology*] (DAVI)
s ..... Thio [*or Mercapto*] [*As substituent on nucleoside*] [*Biochemistry*]
S ..... Thiouridine [*One-letter symbol; see Srd*]
S ..... Water Surface Craft [*JETDS nomenclature*]
S ..... Wyeth Laboratories [*Research code symbol*]
S-1 ..... Personnel Section [*Military*]
S1 ..... Sacral Nerve, First [*S2 is second sacral nerve, etc., through S5*] [*Anatomy*] [*Medicine*] (DAVI)
S1 ..... Sacral Vertebra, First [*S2 is second sacral vertabra, etc., through S5*] [*Anatomy*] (DAVI)
S1 ..... Systolic, First Heart Sound [*S2 is second heart sound, etc., through S4*] [*Cardiology*] (DAVI)
S1C ..... Seaman, First Class [*Navy*]
S1E ..... Surfaced One Edge [*Technical drawings*]
S1S ..... Surfaced or Dressed One Side [*Technical drawings*]
S1S1E ..... Surfaced or Dressed One Side and One Edge [*Technical drawings*]
S1S2E ..... Surfaced One Side and Two Edges [*Lumber*] (DAC)
S1W ..... Security of the First World [*Rap music group*]
S2 ..... Bangladesh [*Aircraft nationality and registration mark*] (FAAC)
S-2 ..... Intelligence Section [*in Army brigades or smaller units, and in Marine Corps units smaller than a brigade; also, the officer in charge of this section*]
S 2d ..... New York Supplement, Second Series [*A publication*] (DLA)
S2d ..... Southern Reporter, Second Series [*West*] [*A publication*] (AAGC)
S2E ..... Surfaced Two Edges [*Lumber*] (DAC)
S2 Glf ..... STwo Golf, Inc. [*Associated Press*] (SAG)
S2H2 ..... Short, Straight Hollow Hosel [*Golf clubs*]
S2S ..... Surfaced or Dressed Two Sides [*Technical drawings*]
S2S1E ..... Surfaced Two Sides and One Edge [*Lumber*] (DAC)
S2S & CM ..... Surfaced Two Sides and Center Matched [*Lumber*] (DAC)
S2S & SL ..... Surfaced Two Sides and Shiplapped [*Technical drawings*] (DAC)
S-3 ..... Operations and Training Section [*in Army brigades or smaller units, and in Marine Corps units smaller than a brigade; also, the officer in charge of this section*]
S3 ..... Signal Selection Switchboard (CAAL)
S3 ..... Simulation in the Service of Society
S^3 ..... Small Scientific Satellite [*NASA*]
S3 ..... Synergistic Strike System
S3 ..... Systems and Software Simulator
S3E ..... Safety Emissions Energy Economics [*Automotive research*]
S3 Inc ..... S3, Inc. [*Associated Press*] (SAG)
S3T ..... Sequentially Sampling Sediment Trap [*Marine science*] (OSRA)
S3T ..... Sequentially Sampling Sediment Trap (USDC)
S-4 ..... Logistics Section [*in Army brigades or smaller units, and in Marine Corps units smaller than a brigade; also, the officer in charge of this section*]
S4 ..... Stanford School Scheduling System
S4 ..... Supply Officer [*Army*]
S4S ..... Surfaced or Dressed Four Sides [*Technical drawings*]
S4S & CS ..... Surfaced Four Sides and Caulking Seam [*Lumber*] (DAC)
S5 ..... Civil Affairs Officer [*Army*] (AABC)
S7 ..... Seller's Delivery in Seven Days [*Stock exchange term*]
S7 ..... Seychelles [*Aircraft nationality and registration mark*] (FAAC)
S9 ..... Sao Tome and Principe [*Aircraft nationality and registration mark*] (FAAC)
SA ..... Air-Cushion Vehicle built by Societe National Industrielle Aerospatiale [*France*] [*Usually used in combination with numerals*]
sa---- ..... Amazon River and Basin [*MARC geographic area code Library of Congress*] (LCCP)
SA ..... Arsine [*Medicine*] (ADDR)
sa ..... Franciscan Friars of the Atonement (TOCD)
SA ..... Franciscan Friars of the Atonement (TOCD)
SA ..... Franciscan Sisters of the Atonement (TOCD)
SA ..... Le Syllabaire Accadien [*A publication*] (BJA)
SA ..... Missionary Sisters of Our Lady of Africa [*White Sisters*] [*Roman Catholic religious order*]
SA ..... Sable [*Heraldry*]
SA ..... Sacrum Anterior [*A fetal position*] [*Obstetrics*] (DAVI)
S/A ..... Safe Arm
S/A ..... Safe Arrival
sa ..... Safe Arrival (ODBW)
SA ..... Safety Altitude [*Aviation*] (DA)
SA ..... Safety Analysis [*Nuclear energy*] (NRCH)
SA ..... Safety Assessment
SA ..... Safing Area [*NASA*] (NASA)
SA ..... Sail Area
SA ..... Sales Aid (IAA)
SA ..... Salicylic Acid [*Organic chemistry*]
SA ..... Salt Acid
SA ..... Salt Added
SA ..... Salvation Army (EA)

Sa .... Samarium [*Obsolete form; see Sm*] [*Chemical element*]
SA .... Sample Array
SA .... Sample Assembly (MCD)
SA .... Sandstorm
Sa .... Sanguinarine [*Biochemistry*]
SA .... Sanitary Authority [*British*] (ROG)
SA .... Sarcastics Anonymous (EA)
SA .... Sarcoma [*Medicine*]
SA .... Saturday
SA .... Saturn Apollo [*NASA*] (KSC)
SA .... Saudi Arabia [*ANSI two-letter standard code*] (CNC)
SA .... Saunders Aircraft Corp. Ltd. [*Canada ICAO aircraft manufacturer identifier*] (ICAO)
SA .... Sausage Aerial [*Radio*]
SA .... Savannah & Atlanta Railway Co. [*AAR code*]
SA .... Savings Account
SA .... Sawmakers' Association [*A union*] [*British*]
SA .... Scaling Amplifier
SA .... Scenic America (EA)
S/A .... Scheduled/Actual (NASA)
SA .... Schizophrenics Anonymous (EA)
SA .... Scholarship Amount (NITA)
SA .... Science Advisors [*Army*] (RDA)
SA .... Scientific American [*A publication*] (BRI)
SA .... Scientific Assistant [*Ministry of Agriculture, Fisheries, and Food*] [*British*]
SA .... Scleroderma Association (EA)
SA .... Scoliosis Association (EA)
SA .... Scout Association (EAIO)
SA .... Seaman Apprentice [*Navy rating*]
SA .... Seasonally Adjusted (WGA)
SA .... Secondary Amenorrhea [*Medicine*] (MAE)
SA .... Secondary Anemia [*Medicine*] (MAE)
SA .... Second Attack [*Men's lacrosse position*]
SA .... Secretary of the Army
SA .... Secundum Artem [*According to the Art*] [*Latin*]
SA .... Security Alarm Technician Program [*Association of Independent Colleges and Schools specialization code*]
SA .... Security Assistance (MCD)
SA .... See Also [*Indexing code*]
SA .... Seiners Association [*Later, PSVOA*]
SA .... Select Address
SA .... Selected Ammunition (RDA)
SA .... Selective Availability
SA .... Self-Administered [*Drugs*]
SA .... Self-Analysis [*Psychology*] (DAVI)
SA .... Semen Analysis
SA .... Semiannual
SA .... Semiannual (WDMC)
SA .... Semiautomatic
SA .... Senior Advisor [*Military*]
SA .... Sensation [*Unit*] (DAVI)
SA .... Sense Amplifier
SA .... Sensible Atmosphere (SAA)
SA .... Sensitized Activated
SA .... Separat-Abdruck (BJA)
SA .... Separated Atom [*Atomic physics*]
SA .... Sequential Access (IAA)
SA .... Sequential Automated
SA .... Serendipity Association (EA)
SA .... Serra
SA .... Serum Albumin [*Serology*]
SA .... Servant Allowance [*British military*] (DMA)
S/A .... Service Action (AAG)
SA .... Service Adviser [*or Attache*] [*British*]
SA .... Service Agreement (MCD)
SA .... Service Aid (IAA)
SA .... Service Air [*Nuclear energy*] (NRCH)
S/A .... Service Application [*Military*] (AFIT)
SA .... Service Area (IAA)
SA .... Service Arm (KSC)
SA .... Service Assistant [*Telecommunications*] (TEL)
SA .... Serviced Apartment
SA .... Servo Amplifier
SA .... Seventh Avenue [*New York City*]
SA .... Sexaholics Anonymous (EA)
SA .... Sexaholics Anonymous (PAZ)
SA .... Sex Appeal [*Slang*]
SA .... Sexual Abuse
SA .... Shaft Angle [*Technical drawings*]
SA .... Shell Analysis
SA .... Shift Advance Driver
SA .... Ship Abstracts [*Helsinki University of Technology*] [*Bibliographic database*]
S/A .... Ship Alteration (MCD)
S/A .... Shipped Assembled
SA .... Shipping Annual Data [*Department of Commerce*] (GFGA)
SA .... Shipping Authority
SA .... Ship to Aircraft (DEN)
SA .... Shipyard Agreement [*MARAD*] (TAG)
SA .... Shock Attenuation (AAG)
SA .... Shop Accessory [*Drawing*] (NG)
SA .... Shops Act [*1950*] [*British*] (ILCA)
SA .... Shortening Allowance [*Carpentry*]
SA .... Sicanna Industries Ltd. [*Vancouver Stock Exchange symbol*]
SA .... Sideroblastic Anemia [*Hematology*]
SA .... Siegfried AG [*Switzerland*] [*Research code symbol*]
SA .... Sierra
SA .... Signal Access
SA .... Signal Analysis
SA .... Signal Analyzer
SA .... Signal Attenuation (AAG)
SA .... Signature Analysis
SA .... Simple-Adjoint [*Method*] (USDC)
SA .... Simple Alert (NATG)
SA .... Simulated Annealing [*Physics*]
sa .... Sin Ano [*Without Year*] [*Publishing*] [*Spanish*]
SA .... Sine Anno [*Without Date of Publication*] [*Latin*]
SA .... Single Access (MCD)
SA .... Single Action [*Firearm*]
SA .... Single Amplitude (IAA)
SA .... Single Armor [*Telecommunications*] (TEL)
SA .... Sinoatrial [*Medicine*]
SA .... Sinoauricular [*Medicine*]
SA .... Sinus Aestuum [*Bay of Billows*] [*Lunar area*]
SA .... Sinus Arrhythmia [*Cardiology*] (MAE)
SA .... Sister of Arts
SA .... Site Activation [*NASA*] (MCD)
SA .... Situational Awareness [*Navy*] (DOMA)
SA .... Situation Audit (MCD)
SA .... Sleep Apnea [*Medicine*] (DMAA)
SA .... Slide Agglutination (PDAA)
SA .... Slightly Active (MAE)
SA .... Slovenian Association [*Australia*]
SA .... Slow-Acting [*Pharmacy*]
SA .... Slow-Acting Relay (IAA)
SA .... Slugging Average [*Baseball*]
SA .... Small Arms [*All firearms other than cannon*]
SA .... Smithsonian Associates [*Later, Smithsonian Resident Associate Program*]
SA .... Snap Action
SA .... Socialist Action [*An association*] (EA)
S/A .... Societa Anonima [*Stock company*] [*Italian*]
SA .... Societas Adunationis [*Franciscan Friars or Sisters of the Atonement*] [*Roman Catholic religious order*]
SA .... Societe Anonyme [*French*] (WDMC)
SA .... Society of Actuaries
SA .... Society of Alexandria [*Defunct*] (EA)
SA .... Society of Antiquaries [*British*]
SA .... Society of Archivists [*British*]
SA .... Society of Arts [*British*]
SA .... Society of Authors (DGA)
SA .... Software Applications
SA .... Soil Association [*Bristol, England*] (EAIO)
SA .... Solar Array (KSC)
SA .... Soluble in Alkaline Solution
SA .... Solution Annealed (MCD)
SA .... Son Altesse [*His or Her Highness*] [*French*]
SA .... Sonderabdruck (BJA)
SA .... Soprano, Alto
SA .... Soul Asylum [*Rock-music group*]
SA .... Source Address
SA .... South Africa [*IYRU nationality code*]
sa .... South Africa [*MARC country of publication code Library of Congress*] (LCCP)
SA .... South African Airways [*ICAO designator*]
SA .... South America
SA .... South Arabian (BJA)
SA .... South Atlantic
SA .... South Australia [*State in Australia*] (BARN)
SA .... Southbank Aviation [*Australia*]
SA .... Southern Association [*Baseball league*]
SA .... Space Aeronautics [*A publication*]
S/A .... Space Available (ADA)
SA .... Spacecraft Adapter [*NASA*]
SA .... Spaced Antenna (USDC)
SA .... Spaced Antenna [*Marine science*] (OSRA)
SA .... Spanish-American (DAVI)
SA .... Speaker Amplifier
SA .... Special Access
SA .... Special Action [*Military*] (AFM)
S/A .... Special Activities [*Air Force*]
SA .... Special Agent (AFM)
SA .... Special Application [*Lift truck*]
SA .... Special Area [*RADAR*]
SA .... Special Artificer [*Navy*]
SA .... Special Assignment [*Navy*]
SA .... Special Assistant (GFGA)
SA .... Specialty Advertising Business [*A publication*] (EAAP)
SA .... Species-Area [*Ecology*]
SA .... Specific Activity
SA .... Specific Antigen [*Immunology*]
SA .... Spectrograph Assembly (KSC)
SA .... Spectrum Analysis
SA .... Speech Amplifier (IAA)
SA .... Sperm Aster [*Cytology*]
SA .... Speronara [*Ship's rigging*] (ROG)
SA .... Spiking Activity [*Medicine*] (DMAA)
SA .... Spin Axis (AAG)
SA .... Spiritualist Association of Great Britain (BI)

SA.......... Splice Acceptor [*Genetics*]
SA.......... Splitting Amplifier (AFM)
SA.......... Sponsored [*or Sponsoring*] Agency (MCD)
SA.......... Sports Ambassadors (EA)
SA.......... Spouse's Allowance [*Canada*]
SA.......... Springfield Armory [*Army*]
SA.......... Squash Australia
SA.......... Stack Access (MHDI)
SA.......... Stage II Apparel [*AMEX symbol*] (TTSB)
SA.......... Stage II Apparel Corp. [*AMEX symbol*] (SPSG)
SA.......... Standard Accuracy [*Analytical chemistry*]
SA.......... Standard Addition
SA.......... Standard Agena [*NASA*] (KSC)
SA.......... Standards Australia
SA.......... Staphylococcus Aureus [*Microbiology*]
sA.......... Statampere [*Also, statA*] [*Unit of electric current*]
SA.......... State Agency [*Formerly, the Disability Determination Services*] [*Social Security Administration*] (OICC)
S/A.......... State Agent [*Insurance*]
SA.......... State Archives [*Australia*]
SA.......... State's Attorney
SA.......... Station Address [*Computer science*] (BUR)
SA.......... Stationary Afterglow [*Chemical kinetic*]
SA.......... Statocyst Anlage
S/A.......... Status and Alert (AAG)
SA.......... Statutes of Alberta [*Canada Information service or system*] (IID)
SA.......... Sternal Angie [*Anatomy*] (DAVI)
SA.......... Stokes-Adams [*Syndrome*] [*Medicine*]
SA.......... Stone Arch [*Bridges*]
SA.......... Storage Activity
SA.......... Storage Allocator [*Telecommunications*] (TEL)
S/A.......... Storage Area (KSC)
SA.......... Store Address
SA.......... Store Automation
SA.......... Stores Accountant [*British military*] (DMA)
SA.......... Stores Assistant [*British military*] (DMA)
SA.......... Stress Anneal (KSC)
SA.......... Stretch-Activated Ion Channel
SA.......... String Analysis (IAA)
SA.......... Structured Analysis [*Programming language*] [*1977*] (CSR)
SA.......... Students for America (EA)
SA.......... Studio Address (WDMC)
SA.......... Studio Address (WDMC)
SA.......... Sturmabteilung [*German Political party*] (PPE)
SA.......... Styrene-Acrylonitrile [*Also, SAN*] [*Organic chemistry*]
SA.......... Subaccount (NASA)
SA.......... Sub Anno [*Under the Year*] [*Latin*]
SA.......... Subarachnoid [*Medicine*]
SA.......... Subassembly
SA.......... Subcontract Agreement (MCD)
SA.......... Subject to Approval
SA.......... Submerged Arc (OA)
SA.......... Subsequent Access (BYTE)
SA.......... Subsistence Allowance
SA.......... Substitution Authorization (AAG)
SA.......... Successive Approximation (IEEE)
SA.......... Succinylacetone [*Organic chemistry*]
S/A.......... Such As
SA.......... Sugar Association
SA.......... Sulfonamide
Sa.......... Summa [*or Summe*] [*Sum or Total*] [*Latin*]
SA.......... Summing Amplifier
SA.......... Sunshine Act (GNE)
SA.......... Super America [*Automobile model, Ferrari Motors*]
SA.......... Supervisory Authority
SA.......... Superwomen Anonymous [*Later, Overachievers Anonymous*] (EA)
SA.......... Supplemental Agreement (NG)
SA.......... Supply Accountant [*Navy British*]
SA.......... Supply Activity
SA.......... Supply Assistant (WDAA)
SA.......... Support Activity (MCD)
SA.......... Support Agency [*NASA*] (KSC)
SA.......... Support Area [*NASA*] (MCD)
SA.......... Supporting Arms [*Navy A publication*]
SA.......... Surface/Air (NATG)
SA.......... Surface Antigen [*Immunology*] (DAVI)
SA.......... Surface Area
SA.......... Surgeon's Assistant [*Medicine*]
SA.......... Surgical Anastomosis [*Medicine*]
SA.......... Surgical and Anesthesia Service (HCT)
SA.......... Surveillance Approach (FAAC)
S/A.......... Survivorship Agreement [*Legal term*] (DLA)
SA.......... Sustained Action [*Pharmacy*]
SA.......... Sweep, Acoustic [*British military*] (DMA)
SA.......... Sweet Adelines (EA)
SA.......... Swept Area [*Automotive engineering*]
SA.......... Swing Arm (KSC)
SA.......... Switching Assembly (IAA)
SA.......... Switching Devices [*JETDS nomenclature*] [*Military*] (CET)
SA.......... Symbolic Assembler (IEEE)
SA.......... Sympathetic Activity [*Physiology*]
SA.......... Synchro Amplifier
SA.......... System Administrator [*Computer science*]
SA.......... System Assessment
SA.......... Systemic Antibiotic [*Medicine*]
SA.......... Systemic Aspergillosis [*Medicine*] (DMAA)
SA.......... Systems Address
SA.......... Systems Analysis
SA.......... Systems Analyst
SA.......... Systems Architecture [*British*]
SA.......... VEB Farbenfabrik Wolfen [*East Germany*] [*Research code symbol*]
SAA.......... Safety Assurance Analysis (NASA)
SAA.......... Sakai [*Japan*] [*Seismograph station code, US Geological Survey Closed*] (SEIS)
SAA.......... Sales Automation Association (EA)
SAA.......... Santiago Capital [*Vancouver Stock Exchange symbol*]
SAA.......... Saratoga, WY [*Location identifier FAA*] (FAAL)
SAA.......... Satellite Active Archive (USDC)
SAA.......... Satellite Active Archive [*Marine science*] (OSRA)
SAA.......... Satellite Attitude Acquisition
SAA.......... Saturn Apollo Applications [*NASA*] (KSC)
SAA.......... Saudia Arabia Airlines
SAA.......... S-Band Acquisition Antenna [*Deep Space Instrumentation Facility, NASA*]
SAA.......... Science and Applications [*NASA*] (SSD)
SAA.......... Scottish Aeromodellers Association (DBA)
SAA.......... Scottish Archery Association (DBA)
SAA.......... Scottish Assessors' Association (DBA)
SAA.......... Scout Association of Australia
SAA.......... Screen Advertising Association Ltd. [*British*] (BI)
SAA.......... Secretaries' Association of Australia
SAA.......... Senior Army Advisor
SAA.......... Serum Amyloid A [*Clinical chemistry*]
SAA.......... Service Action Analysis (AAG)
SAA.......... Servo-Actuated Assembly
SAA.......... Severe Aplastic Anemia [*Hematology*]
SAA.......... Sex Addicts Anonymous (EA)
SAA.......... Sexual Abuse Anonymous (EA)
SAA.......... Shakespeare Association of America (EA)
SAA.......... Shelter Advertising Association [*Minneapolis, MN*] (EA)
SAA.......... Sherman Anti-Trust Act (MHDB)
SAA.......... Signal Appliance Association [*Later, RSS*]
SAA.......... Simulated Accelerometer Assembly
SAA.......... Single Article Announcement [*American Chemical Society publication*]
SAA.......... Sisters Auxiliaries of the Apostolate (TOCD)
SAA.......... Slot Array Antenna
SAA.......... Small Arms Ammunition
SAA.......... Social Administration Association [*British*]
SAA.......... Society for Academic Achievement (EA)
SAA.......... Society for American Archaeology (EA)
SAA.......... Society for Applied Anthropology (AEBS)
SAA.......... Society for Asian Art (EA)
SAA.......... Society of American Archivists (EA)
SAA.......... Society of Animal Artists (EA)
SAA.......... Society of Archer-Antiquaries (EA)
SAA.......... Society of Architectural Administrators (EA)
SAA.......... Society of Automotive Analysts (EA)
SAA.......... Some American Artists [*An association*] (EA)
SAA.......... South African Airways [*ICAO designator*] (FAAC)
SAA.......... South African Alliance (PPW)
SAA.......... South Atlantic Anomaly [*NASA*] (KSC)
SAA.......... South Australian Artillery [*British military*] (DMA)
SAA.......... Southern Africa Association [*British*] (EAIO)
SAA.......... Southern Arts Association [*British*] (DBA)
SAA.......... Southern Ash Association [*Defunct*] (EA)
SAA.......... Special Arbitrage Account
SAA.......... Special Assignment Airlift [*Air Force*] (AFM)
SAA.......... Specialty Advertising Association [*Later, SAAI*]
SAA.......... Speech Association of America [*Later, SCA*] (EA)
SAA.......... Sri Aurobindo Association (EA)
SAA.......... Staff Administrative Assistant [*Army*] (AABC)
SAA.......... Standards Association of Australia (BARN)
SAA.......... State Aboriginal Affairs [*South Australia*]
SAA.......... State Administrative Agency (GFGA)
SAA.......... State Applicant Agency (GFGA)
SAA.......... State Approving Agency [*Bureau of Apprenticeship and Training*] [*Department of Labor*]
SAA.......... Static Allegation Analyzer [*Computer science*]
SAA.......... Step Adjustable Antenna
SAA.......... Stepfamily Association of America (EA)
SAA.......... Stokes-Adams Attack [*Medicine*] (MAE)
SAA.......... Sub-Aqua Association [*British*] (DBA)
SAA.......... Summary Activity Account [*Army*] (AABC)
SAA.......... Sunflower Association of America [*Later, NSA*] (EA)
SAA.......... Sunglass Association of America (EA)
SAA.......... Supima Association of America (EA)
SAA.......... Surety Association of America [*Iselin, NJ*] (EA)
SAA.......... Surface Active Agents (ADA)
SAA.......... Survival Air-to-Air (MCD)
SAA.......... Suzuki Association of the Americas (EA)
SAA.......... Swedish-American Association (NADA)
SAA.......... Syrian Arab Airlines
SAA.......... System Application Architecture [*IBM Corp.*]
SAAA.......... Salvation Army Association of America (NADA)
SAAA.......... San Antonio De Areco [*Argentina ICAO location identifier*] (ICLI)
SAAA.......... Scottish Amateur Athletic Association
SAAABB.......... Subcommittee on Accreditation of the American Association of Blood Banks (DAVI)
SAAARNG.......... Senior Army Advisor, Army National Guard (AABC)

SAAB Selected and Amplified Binding [*Sequence or site*] [*Genetics*]
SAAB South African Archaeological Bulletin [*A publication*]
SAAB Svenska Aeroplan Aktiebolaget [*Swedish automobile manufacturer; acronym used as name of its cars*]
SAAC Concordia/Commodoro Pierrest Egui [*Argentina ICAO location identifier*] (ICLI)
SAAC Schedule Allocation and Control (NASA)
SA/AC Scientific Adviser to the Army Council [*World War II*]
SAAC Security Assistance Accounting Center [*Military*] (AFIT)
SAAC Seismic Array Analysis Center [*IBM Corp.*]
SAAC Shelby American Automobile Club (EA)
SAAC Simulator for Air-to-Air Combat [*Air Force*]
SAAC Society for the Advancement of Ambulatory Care [*Defunct*] (EA)
SAAC South American Athletic Confederation (EAIO)
SAAC Space Applications Advisory Committee
SAAC Special Assistant for Arms Control [*Military*]
SAAC Swiss-American Aircraft Corp. (IAA)
SAACCA South Australian Aboriginal Child Care Agency
SAACI Salesmen's Association of the American Chemical Industry [*Later, SACI*] (EA)
SAACONS Standard Army Automated Contracting System (RDA)
SAACT Surveillance and Accountability Control Team (MCD)
SAA/CUA Systems Application Architecture / Common User Access [*Computer science*]
SAAD Sacramento Army Depot [*California*] (AABC)
SAAD San Antonio Air Depot [*Air Force*]
SAAD Small Arms Ammunition Depot
SAAD Societe des Amis d'Alexandre Dumas (EA)
SAAD Society for the Advancement of Anaesthesia in Dentistry (EAIO)
SAAD Sperry Air Arm Division
SAAEB South African Atomic Energy Board
SAAF Saudi Arabian Air Force
SAAF Sherman Army Airfield [*Fort Leavenworth, KS*]
SAAF Sino-American Amity Fund (EA)
SAAF Small Arms Alignment Fixture [*Weaponry*] (INF)
SAAF Small Austere Air Field (MCD)
SAAF South African Air Force
SAAG Gualeguaychu [*Argentina ICAO location identifier*] (ICLI)
SAAG Science and Applications Advocacy Group
SAAG Steroid Action Aid Group [*British*] (DBA)
SAAGS Semi-Automated Artwork Generator System (PDAA)
SAAGTC South Australian Association for Gifted and Talented Children
SAAHS Stability Augmentation Attitude Hold System [*Aviation*]
SAAI Punta Indio [*Argentina ICAO location identifier*] (ICLI)
SAAI Specialty Advertising Association International [*Irving, TX*] (EA)
SAAJ Junin [*Argentina ICAO location identifier*] (ICLI)
SAAL Single Address Assembly Machine Language [*Computer science*] (MCD)
SAAL Single-Axis Acoustic Levitator
SAAL South Australian Athletic League
SA-ALC San Antonio Air Logistics Center [*Formerly, SAAMA*] [*Air Force*] (NASA)
SAALCK State Assisted Academic Library Council of Kentucky [*Library network*]
SAALC/MM San Antonio Air Logistics Center, Directorate of Materiel Management [*Kelly Air Force Base, TX*]
SAAM Mazaruca [*Argentina ICAO location identifier*] (ICLI)
SAAM Simulation Analysis and Modeling
SAAM Small-Animal Anesthesia Machine [*Instrumentation*]
SAAM Special Air Force Airlift Mission (NASA)
SAAM Special Assignment Airlift & Mission [*MTMC*] (TAG)
SAAM Special Assignment Airlift Movement [*Army*] (AABC)
SAAM Special Assignment Air Mission [*Navy*] (NVT)
SAAMA San Antonio Air Materiel Area [*Later, SA-ALC*] [*Air Force*]
SAAMI Sporting Arms and Ammunition Manufacturers Institute (EA)
SAAMS Special Airlift Assignment Missions [*Military*]
SAAMS Special Application Alarm Monitoring System
SAAN Pergamino [*Argentina ICAO location identifier*] (ICLI)
SAAN South African Associated Newspapers
SA & F Southern Airlines and Freighters [*Australia*]
SA & MGS Small Arms and Machine Gun School [*British military*] (DMA)
SAAO South African Astronomical Observatory
SAAOC System of Analysis and Assignment of Operations according to Capacities (MHDI)
SAAP Parana/Gral Urquiza [*Argentina ICAO location identifier*] (ICLI)
SAAP Saranton Army Ammunition Plant (AABC)
SAAP Saturn Apollo Applications Program [*NASA*]
SAAP Selective Aortic Arch Perfusion [*Medicine*] (DMAA)
SAAP Society for the Advancement of American Philosophy (EA)
SAAP South Atlantic Anomaly Probe [*NASA-CNAE*]
SAAP South Australian Adoption Panel
SAAPBS South Australian Association of Permanent Building Societies
SAAPCC South African Administrative Pay and Clerical Corps [*British military*] (DMA)
SAAPE Scottish Association of Advisers in Physical Education (DBA)
SAAPSA South Australian Apple and Pear Shippers' Association
SAAR Rosario [*Argentina ICAO location identifier*] (ICLI)
SAAR Saw Arbor [*Tool*]
SAAR Seasonally Adjusted Annual Retail [*Automotive sales*]
SAAR Solar Aureole Almucantar Radiance (PDAA)
SAARC South Asian Association for Regional Cooperation
SAARD Slow-Acting Antirheumatic Drug [*Pharmacy*]
SAARD's Slow-Acting Antirheumatic Drugs [*Medicine*]
SAARF Special Allied Airborne Reconnaissance Force [*Teams parachuted into POW areas to take supplies to prisoners or to help them get out*] [*World War II*]
SAAS School of Applied Aerospace Sciences [*Air Force*]
SAAS Science Achievement Awards for Students
SAAS Scottish Agricultural Statistics Service [*University of Edinburgh*] (IRC)
SAAS Shuttle Aerosurface Actuator Simulator [*NASA*] (MCD)
SAAS Society for the Advancement of Agricultural Studies [*British*]
SAAS Society of African and Afro-American Students
SAAS Soldier as a System [*Symposium*] (RDA)
SAAS Something about the Author Autobiography Series [*A publication*]
SAAS Southern Association of Agricultural Scientists (EA)
SAAS Special Ammunition and Analysis Section [*Picatinny Arsenal*] [*Dover, NJ*]
SAAS Standard Army Ammunition System (AABC)
SAAS Stress Analysis of Axisymmetric Solids (MCD)
SAASC San Antonio Air Service Command [*Air Force*]
SAASRA South Australian Aboriginal Sports and Recreation Association
SAAST Self-Administered Alcoholism Screening Test
SAASW Sub-Antarctic Surface Water [*Marine science*] (MSC)
SAAT Satellite Attitude Acquisition Technique
SAAT Society of Architects and Associated Technicians [*British*] (BI)
SAAT Systems Analyst Aptitude Test
SAATE South Australian Association for the Teaching of English
SAATMS Satellite-Based Advanced Air Traffic Management System [*Department of Transportation*]
SAATSC San Antonio Air Technical Service Command [*Air Force*]
SAAU Selfreliance Association of American Ukrainians (EA)
SAAU Swiss Association of Autonomous Unions
SAAU Villaguay [*Argentina ICAO location identifier*] (ICLI)
SAAUSAR Senior Army Advisor, United States Army Reserve (AABC)
SAAV Santa Fe/Sauce Viejo [*Argentina ICAO location identifier*] (ICLI)
SAAVQ Societe des Artistes en Arts Visuels du Quebec [*1980, founded 1966 as SAPQ, CPQ from 1978, CAPQ from 1982*] [*Canada*] (NGC)
SAAVS Submarine Acceleration and Velocity System
SAAWC Sector Antiair Warfare Coordinator [*Center*] (NVT)
SAAWPA South Australian Amateur Water Polo Association
SAAX Saturn Airways, Inc. [*Air carrier designation symbol*]
SAB Saba [*Netherlands Antilles*] [*Airport symbol*] (OAG)
SAB Saba Petroleum [*AMEX symbol*] (TTSB)
SAB Saba Petroleum Co. [*AMEX symbol*] (SAG)
SAB Sabbath
SAB SABENA [*Societe Anonyme Belge d'Exploitation de la Nav Aerienne*] [*Belgium ICAO designator*] (FAAC)
SAB Sabhawala [*India*] [*Geomagnetic observatory code*]
Sab Sabinus [*Flourished, 5th or 6th century*] [*Authority cited in pre-1607 legal work*] (DSA)
SAB Sabotage [*FBI standardized term*]
SAB Sabouraud Dextrose Agar [*Microbiology*]
SAB Safety Advisory Board [*National Science Foundation*] (NUCP)
SAB Same as Above
SAB Same as Basic (KSC)
SAB Satellite Assembly Building (MCD)
SAB School of American Ballet [*New York*]
SAB Science Advisory Board [*Environmental Protection Agency*]
SAB Scientific Advisory Board [*Air Force*]
SAB Sealed Argon Bubbling [*Steelmaking*]
SAB Shuttle Avionics Breadboard [*NASA*] (NASA)
SAB Signal Aviation Branch
SAB Significant Asymptomatic Bacteriuria [*Medicine*] (MAE)
SAB Silk Association of Great Britain (EAIO)
SAB Sisters of St. Anne Bangalone (TOCD)
SAB Site Activation Board [*NASA*] (KSC)
SAB Snap Action Bimetal [*Automotive engineering*]
SAB Societe Anonyme Belge d'Exploitation de la Navigation Aerienne [*Sabena Belgian World Airlines*]
SAB Society for Applied Bacteriology (EA)
SAB Society of American Bacteriologists [*Later, ASM*]
SAB Solar Alignment Bay (OA)
SAB Solar Array Batteries
SAB Solid Assembly Building
SAB Soprano, Alto, Bass
SAB South African Breweries
SAB South African Breweries [*Commercial firm*]
SAB South Atlantic Bight [*A region off the southeastern coast of the United States*] [*Geography*]
SAB Space Applications Board [*National Academy of Engineering*]
SAB Spacecraft Assembly Building [*NASA*] (MCD)
SAB Special Antarctic Blend [*Fuel*]
SAB Special Assessment Bond
SAB Specific Adaptive Strategy (EDAC)
SAB Speech Adaptor Box (NITA)
SAb Spontaneous Abortion [*Medicine*] (DMAA)
SAB Spontaneous Abortion (DAVI)
SAB Stack Access Block
SAB Staff Accounting Bulletins (TDOB)
SAB Statistics and Analysis Branch [*Public Health Service*] [*Information service or system*] (IID)
SAB Storage and Assembly Building [*NASA*] (NASA)
SAB Strategic Assessment Branch [*Office of Oceanography and Marine Assessment*] [*National Oceanic and Atmospheric Administration*]
SAB Structural Adhesive Bond
SAB Subarachnoid Bleed [*Neurology*] (DAVI)
SAB Subarachnoid Block [*Medicine*] (MAE)
SAB Subject as Above [*Military*] (AABC)

SAB .... Support Activities Building [*National Security Agency*]
SAB .... Supporting Assistance Bureau [*Agency for International Development*]
SAB .... Sync Address Bus (IAA)
SAB .... System Advisory Board
SAB .... Systems Analysis Branch (IAA)
SABA .... Buenos Aires [*Argentina ICAO location identifier*] (ICLI)
SABA .... Scottish Amateur Boxing Association [*British*] (DBA)
SABA .... Serbian-American Bar Association (EA)
SABA .... Small, Able Battlefield Aircraft [*Military British*]
SABA .... Small Agile Battlefield Aircraft [*British Aerospace Ltd.*]
SABA .... Society for the Advancement of Behavior Analysis (EA)
SABA .... South African Black Alliance [*Political party*] (PPW)
SABA .... South Australian Badminton Association
SABA .... South Australian Bowling Association
SABA .... Swimmer's Air Breathing Apparatus [*Deep-sea diving*]
SabaPet .... Saba Petroleum [*Associated Press*] (SAG)
SABAR .... Satellites, Balloons, and Rockets [*Air Force program*]
SABB .... Santa Barbara Bancorp [*NASDAQ symbol*] (TTSB)
SABB .... Santa Barbara Bancorp [*NASDAQ symbol*] (SAG)
SABBA .... System Analysis - Building Block Approach [*Ge Cae International and Gen-Red Ltd.*] [*Software package*] (NCC)
SABC .... Buenos Aires (Edificio Condor) [*Argentina ICAO location identifier*] (ICLI)
SABC .... South African Broadcasting Corp.
SABC .... South Alabama Bancorp [*NASDAQ symbol*] (SAG)
SABC .... South Australia Brewing Co. [*Commercial firm*]
SABCO .... Society for the Area of Biological and Chemical Overlap
SABDR .... South Australian Birth Defects Registry
SABE .... Buenos Aires/Aeroparque, Jorge Newbery [*Argentina ICAO location identifier*] (ICLI)
SABE .... Society for Automating Better Education (IAA)
SABE .... Society for Automation in Business Education [*Later, SDE*] (EA)
SABENA .... Societe Anonyme Belge d'Exploitation de la Navigation Aerienne [*Belgian World Airlines*] [*Facetious translation: Such a Bad Experience, Never Again*]
SABER .... SECNAV [*Secretary of the Navy*] Advisory Board on Educational Requirements (NG)
SABER .... Simplified Acquisition of Base Engineering Requirements [*Air Force*]
SABER .... Surface-to-Air Beam Rider (MCD)
SABER .... Swing-Arm Beam Erector (MCD)
SABET .... SECNAV [*Secretary of the Navy*] Advisory Board on Education and Training [*Pensacola, FL*] (EGAO)
SABEU .... Scottish Adult Basic Education Unit (AIE)
SABEW .... Society of American Business Editors and Writers [*Columbia, MO*] (EA)
SABF .... Subarray Beam Former [*Computer science*] (MHDI)
SABFV .... Secondary Air Anti-Backfire Valve [*Automotive engineering*]
SABH .... South Australian Brewing Holdings [*Commercial firm*]
SABHI .... Sabouraud Dextrose Agar and Brain-Heart Infusion [*Microbiology*]
SaBi .... La Sacra Bibbia [*Turin*] [*A publication*] (BJA)
SABI .... Swiss Army Brands [*NASDAQ symbol*] (TTSB)
SABINE .... Systeme d'Acces a la Banque Informatique des Nomenclatures Europeennes [*Database*] [*EC*] (ECED)
SABINET .... South African Bibliographical and Information Network (NITA)
SABIR .... Semiautomatic Bibliographic Information Retrieval
SABIRS .... Semiautomatic Bibliographic Information Retrieval System (DIT)
SABL .... Serialized Assembly Breakdown List (SAA)
SABL .... South Australian Bookmakers' League
SABLE .... Semiautomatic BOMARC Local Environment (MCD)
SABM .... Buenos Aires (Servicio Meteorologico Nacional) [*Argentina ICAO location identifier*] (ICLI)
SABM .... Set Asynchronous Balanced Mode
SA/BM .... Systems Analysis and Battle Management [*Military*] (RDA)
SABMAR .... Service-Craft and Boats Machine Accounting Report [*Navy*] (NG)
SABME .... Set Asynchronous Balanced Mode Extended [*Telecommunications*] (OSI)
SABMIS .... Sea-Based Antiballistic Missile (IAA)
SABMIS .... Seaborne [*or Ship-Launched*] Antiballistic Missile Intercept System [*Navy*]
SABMS .... Safeguard Antiballistic Missile System [*Military*] (WDAA)
SabnR .... Sabine Royalty Trust [*Associated Press*] (SAG)
SABO .... Sense Amplifier Blocking Oscillator
SABOC .... SAGE [*Semiautomatic Ground Environment*] BOMARC [*Boring-Michigan Aeronautical Research Center*] (IAA)
SABOD .... Same as Basic Operations Directive (KSC)
SABOR .... Same as Basic Or (MUGU)
SABOSE .... SECNAV [*Secretary of the Navy*] Advisory Board on Scientific Education (DNAB)
SABP .... Salicylic Acid Binding Protein [*Biochemistry*]
SABP .... Skeletal Axis of Basal Piece
SABP .... Spontaneous Acute Bacterial Peritonitis [*Medicine*]
SABR .... Society for American Baseball Research (EA)
SABR .... Symbolic Assembler for Binary Relocatable Programs
SABRAC .... Sabra Computer (DNAB)
Sabratek .... Sabratek Corp. [*Associated Press*] (SAG)
SABRE .... SAGE [*Semiautomatic Ground Environment*] Battery Routing Equipment
SABRE .... Sales and Business Reservations Done Electronically
SABRE .... Secure Airborne RADAR Bombing Equipment (IAA)
SABRE .... Secure Airborne RADAR Equipment
SABRE .... Self-Aligning Boost and Reentry [*Air Force*]
SABRE .... Semiautomated Business Research Environment [*Computerized reservation network*] [*American Airlines*]
SABRE .... Single Army Battlefield Requirements Evaluator [*Army*]
SABRE .... South Atlantic Bight Recruitment Experiment (USDC)
SABRE .... South Atlantic Bight Recruitment Experiment [*Marine science*] (OSRA)
SABRE .... Steerable Adaptive Broadcast Reception Equipment (PDAA)
SABRE .... Store Access Bus Recording Equipment [*Telecommunications*] (TEL)
SABRE .... Sweden and Britain RADAR Auroral Experiment [*Ionospheric physics*]
SABRE .... System for Autonomous Bodies Reporting and Evaluation [*Joint project of the Government of Bangladesh and United Nations Department of Technical Co-operation for Development*] [*Information service or system*]
SabreGr .... Sabre Group Holdings, Inc. (The) [*Associated Press*] (SAG)
SABRF .... Skeletal Axis of Branchial Filament
SABRI .... Serikat Buruh Rokok Indonesia [*Cigarette Workers' Union of Indonesia*]
SABRITA .... South Africa - Britain Trade Association (DBA)
SABRS .... Standard Accounting, Budgeting, and Reporting System [*Military*] (GFGA)
SABS .... Congregation of the Sisters of the Adoration of the Blessed Sacrament [*Kerala, India*] (EAIO)
S/ABS .... Shock Absorber [*Automotive engineering*]
SABS .... South African Bureau of Standards [*National standards organization*]
SABS .... Stabilizing Automatic Bomb Sight
SABS .... Stanford Automated Bibliographic Systems (NITA)
SABSA .... South Australian Brake Specialist Association
SABU .... SAGE [*Semiautomatic Ground Environment*] Back-Up (IAA)
SABU .... Self-Adjusting Ball-Up [*A state of confusion which may, or may not, clear up of itself*] [*Military slang*]
SABU .... Semi-Automatic Back-Up [*Military*] (IAA)
SABV .... Secondary Air Bypass Valve [*Automotive engineering*]
SABW .... Society of American Business Writers [*Later, SABEW*]
Sac .... De Sacrificiis Abelis et Caini [*Philo*] (BJA)
SAC .... Pallotine Missionary Sisters Queen of Apostles Prov (TOCD)
SAC .... Saccharin [*Sweetening agent*]
SAC .... Sacramento [*California*] [*Airport symbol*] (AD)
SAC .... Sacramento, CA [*Location identifier FAA*] (FAAL)
SAC .... Sacrifice [*Baseball*]
SAC .... Sacristan
SAC .... Safety Advisory Committee (MCD)
SAC .... Sahali Resources, Inc. [*Vancouver Stock Exchange symbol*]
SAC .... Saint Ambrose College [*Davenport, IA*]
SAC .... Saint Anselm's College [*Manchester, NH*]
SAC .... Saint Anselm's College, Manchester, NH [*OCLC symbol*] (OCLC)
SAC .... Saint Augustine's College [*Raleigh, NC*]
SAC .... Salute America Committee (EA)
SAC .... San Andreas Lake [*California*] [*Seismograph station code, US Geological Survey*] (SEIS)
SAC .... San Antonio College [*Texas*]
SAC .... Santa Ana College [*California*]
SAC .... Scene-of-Action Commander [*Navy*] (NVT)
SAC .... School of Army Co-Operation [*Air Force British*]
SAC .... Scientific Advisory Committee [*Presidential*] [*Terminated*]
SAC .... Scientific Advisory Council [*Ministry of Supply*] [*British World War II*]
SAC .... Scottish Arts Council (EAIO)
SAC .... Scottish Automobile Club (DI)
SAC .... Scriptomatic Addressing Computer (HGAA)
SAC .... Secondary Accountability Center (AAG)
SAC .... Secondary Address Code
SAC .... Sectional Aeronautical Chart (NOAA)
SAC .... Security Access Control [*Computer science*]
SAC .... Self-Adjusting Clutch
SAC .... Semiautomatic Coding
SAC .... Semiautomatic Controller (CAAL)
SAC .... Senate Appropriations Committee (NVT)
SAC .... Senior Aircraftman [*British military*] (DMA)
SAC .... Service Application Code [*Navy*]
SAC .... Service Area Computer (IAA)
SAC .... Serving Area Concept [*Bell System*]
SAC .... Servo Adapter Coupler
SAC .... Shipbuilding Advisory Council [*British*]
SAC .... Ships Air Coordinator (MCD)
SAC .... Short Arm Cast [*Medicine*] (MEDA)
SAC .... Short-Arm Cast [*Orthopedics*] (DAVI)
SAC .... Side-Arm Controller [*Aviation*]
SAC .... Signal Analysis Course [*Navy*] (DNAB)
SAC .... Signature Authorization Card [*or Chart*] (AAG)
SAC .... Single Acting Cylinder
SAC .... Single Address Code (AAG)
SAC .... Sisters of the Holy Guardian Angels [*Roman Catholic religious order*]
SAC .... Soaring Association of Canada
SAC .... Social and Athletic Club
SAC .... Sociedad Anglo-Chilena [*Anglo-Chilean Society*] (EAIO)
SAC .... Societe Africaine de Culture [*Society of African Culture*]
SAC .... Society for American Cuisine [*Later, SCA*] (EA)
SAC .... Society for Analytical Chemistry [*British*]
SAC .... Society for Analytical Cytology (EA)
SAC .... Society of African Culture [*France*] (EAIO)
SAC .... Society of the Catholic Apostolate [*Pallottines*] [*Roman Catholic men's religious order*]
sac .... Society of the Catholic Apostolate, Pallottine Fathers (TOCD)
SAC .... South-African Constabulary [*Military British Defunct*] (ROG)
SAC .... South Atlantic Coast
SAC .... South Australian Club
SAC .... South Carolina Electric & Gas Co. [*NYSE symbol*] (SPSG)
SAC .... Southern Africa Committee (EA)

SAC............. Southwest Athletic Conference (EA)
SAC............. Special Accounting Class [*Navy*] (DNAB)
SAC............. Special Advisory Committee [*Navy*] (DNAB)
SAC............. Special Agent in Charge [*FBI*]
SAC............. Special Analysis Center [*Marine science*] (OSRA)
SAC............. Special Area Code [*Bell System*]
SAC............. Specialty Aromatic Compound [*Organic chemistry*]
SAC............. Specific Acoustic Capacitance
SAC............. Spectrum Analyzer Component (MCD)
SAC............. Spiritual Advisory Council (EA)
SAC............. Sport for All Clearinghouse [*Belgium*] (EAIO)
SAC............. Sprayed Acoustical Ceiling [*Technical drawings*]
S/AC............. Stabilization/Attitude Control [*NASA*] (NASA)
SAC............. Standard Agena Clamshell [*NASA*] (KSC)
SAC............. Standard Aircraft Characteristics
SAC............. Standing Armaments Committee [*NATO*] (NATG)
SAC............. Staphylococcus Aureus Cervan [*Microbiology*]
SAC............. Starptautiskas Apmainas Centrs [*International Exchange Center*] [*Latvia*] (EAIO)
SAC............. Starting Air Compressor (CAAL)
SAC............. State Advisory Committee [*Department of Education*]
SAC............. State Apprenticeship Council [*Bureau of Apprenticeship and Training*] [*Department of Labor*]
SAC............. Statistical Advisory Committee [*UN Food and Agriculture Organization*]
SAC............. Statistical Analysis Center (OICC)
SAC............. Storage Access Channel (CMD)
SAC............. Storage Access Control [*Computer science*]
SAC............. Storage Access Counter (IAA)
SAC............. Storage Address Counter (IAA)
SAC............. Store Access Controller (NITA)
SAC............. Store and Clear
SAC............. Store and Clear Accumulator [*Computer science*]
SAC............. Storeman's Action Copy (DNAB)
SAC............. Strategic Air Command [*Air Force*]
SAC............. Strategic Alert Cadre (NVT)
SAC............. Student Access Centre [*Australia*]
SAC............. Subarea Advisory Council [*Generic term*] (DHSM)
SAC............. Submitting Activity Code
SAC............. Substance Abuse Coordinator [*Navy*] (DNAB)
SAC............. Sudanese Aeronautical Services Co. Ltd. [*Sudan*] [*ICAO designator*] (FAAC)
SAC............. Sudanese African Congress [*Political party*] (MENA)
SAC............. Sudania Aviation Co. [*Sudan*] [*ICAO designator*] (FAAC)
SAC............. Sugar Association of the Caribbean [*Port Of Spain, Trinidad*] (EAIO)
SAC............. Sulfuric Acid Concentrate (MCD)
SAC............. Sunbeam Alpine Club (EA)
SAC............. Suore Missionarie dell'Apostolato Cattolico [*Missionary Sisters of the Catholic Apostolate*] [*Rome, Italy*] (EAIO)
SAC............. Supplemental Air Carrier (MCD)
SAC............. Supply Administration Center [*DoD*] (MCD)
SAC............. Supply Availability Card (MCD)
SAC............. Support Action Center [*NASA*] (MCD)
SAC............. Support Assessment Capability
SAC............. Supporting Arms Coordinator [*Air Force*] (NVT)
SAC............. Supreme Allied Command [*or Commander*] [*Headquarters in London*] [*World War II*]
SAC............. Surface-Area-Center [*Mechanical engineering*]
SAC............. Surveillance Airplane Company [*Army*] (VNW)
SAC............. Surveyors Appointments Consultancy [*Royal Institute of Chartered Surveyors*] [*British*]
SAC............. Suspended and Canceled Pesticides [*Environmental Protection Agency*] (GFGA)
SAC............. Sustained Abdominal Compression [*Gastroenterology*]
SAC............. Sveriges Arbetares Centralorganisation [*Central Organization of Swedish Workers*]
SAC............. Synchro Azimuth Converter
SAC............. Synchronous Astro Compass (SAA)
SAC............. System Assessment Capability
SAC............. System Automation Corp. [*Information service or system*] (IID)
SAC............. Systems Acquisition Career
SAC............. Systems Auditability and Control [*Computer science*]
SACA........... Cordoba/Area de Material [*Argentina ICAO location identifier*] (ICLI)
SACA........... Service Action Change Analysis (AAG)
SACA........... South Australian Council on the Ageing
SACA........... Special Assistant for Consumer Affairs [*White House*] [*Obsolete*]
SACA........... Steam Automobile Club of America (EA)
SACA........... Studebaker Automobile Club of America (EA)
SACA........... Student Action Corps for Animals (EA)
SACA........... Study Advisory Committee on Aeronautics [*National Academy of Engineering*]
SACA........... Subversive Activities Control Act of 1950
SAC(A)......... Supporting Arms Coordinator (Airborne) [*Marine Corps*] (DOMA)
SACACCS..... Strategic Air Command Automated Command Control System (AFM)
SACAD......... Stress Analysis and Computer-Aided Design [*Computer science*] (WDAA)
SACAM......... Ship Acquisition Contract Administration Manual (MCD)
SACAM......... South Australian Committee on Access and Mobility
SACAY......... SECNAV [*Secretary of the Navy*] Advisory Commission on Youth (NG)
SACB........... Subversive Activities Control Board [*Later, Federal Internal Security Board*]
SACBA......... South Australian Cat Breeders' Association
SACBC......... South Australian Children's Ballet Company
SACBC......... Southern African Catholic Bishops' Conference (EAIO)
SACBC-JPC... Southern African Catholic Bishops' Conference - Justice and Peace Commission (EAIO)
sacc............. Cogwheel [*Respiration*] [*Medicine*] (DAVI)
SACC........... La Cumbre [*Argentina ICAO location identifier*] (ICLI)
SACC........... San Antonio Contracting Center [*Air Force*]
S/ACC......... Scientific/Academic Computing Center [*State University of New York Health Science Center at Brooklyn*] [*Research center*] (RCD)
SACC........... Shore ASW [*Antisubmarine Warfare*] Command Center (DOMA)
SACC........... Slovak-American Cultural Center (EA)
SACC........... Society for Anthropology in Community Colleges (EA)
SACC........... Society of All Cargo Correspondents [*British*] [*An association*] (DBA)
SACC........... State Auditors Coordinating Committee (EA)
SACC........... Supplemental Air Carrier Conference [*Defunct*] (EA)
SACC........... Supporting Arms Coordination Center [*Air Force*]
SACC........... Systems Acquisition Contracting Course (AAGC)
SACCAR....... Southern African Centre for Co-Operation in Agricultural Research (EY)
SACCEI........ Strategic Air Command Communications-Electronics Instruction
SACCH......... Saccharatae [*Sugar-Coated*] [*Pharmacy*]
SACCHS....... Scottish Advisory Committee on Computers in the Health Service
SACCI.......... Swiss-Australian Chamber of Commerce and Industry [*Australia*]
SACCM......... Slow Access Charge-Coupled Memory [*Computer science*] (PDAA)
SACCOM....... Strategic Air Command Communications (MCD)
SACCOMNET... Strategic Air Command Communications Network
SACCON....... Strategic Air Command Command Control Network
SACCP......... Strategic Air Command Command Post
SACCS......... Schedule and Cost-Control System (MHDB)
SACCS......... Shipping and Air Cargo Commodity Statistics [*Australia*]
SACCS......... Strategic Air Command Communications [*or Control*] System [*Military*]
SACCS......... Strategic Army Command and Control Software [*Computer science Army*] (RDA)
SACCS-DPS.... SAC [*Strategic Air Command*] Automated Command Control System - Data Processing System (MCD)
SACD........... Coronel Olmedo [*Argentina ICAO location identifier*] (ICLI)
SACD........... Societe des Auteurs et Compositeurs Dramatiques [*Society of Dramatic Authors and Composers*] [*Paris, France*] (EAIO)
SACD........... Society of Americans of Colonial Descent [*Defunct*] (EA)
SACD........... Subacute Combined Degeneration [*of spinal cord*] [*Medicine*] (AAMN)
SACDA......... Surplus Agricultural Commodities Disposal Act of 1982
SACDEF....... Strategic Avionics Crewstation Design Evaluation Facility
SACDIN........ Strategic Air Command Digital Information Network (MCD)
SACDM......... Study and Action Course in District Management [*LIMRA*]
SACDNU....... Sudan African Closed Districts National Union
SAC(DP)...... Scientific Advisory Committee, Defence Services Panel [*British World War II*]
SACDRS....... Standard Air Carrier Delay Reporting System
SACDU......... Switch and Cable Distribution Unit (IAA)
SACE........... Cordoba [*Argentina ICAO location identifier*] (ICLI)
SACE........... Semiautomatic Checkout Equipment [*DoD*]
SACE........... Serum Angiotensin Converting Enzyme [*Activity*] [*Serology*]
SACE........... Shore-Based Acceptance Checkout Equipment
SACEA......... Sino-American Cultural and Economic Association
SACEM......... Society for the Advancement of Continuing Education for Ministry (EA)
SACEM......... Society of Authors, Composers, and Editors of Music (NADA)
SACEP......... South Asian Cooperative Environment Programme (GNE)
SACEUR....... Supreme Allied Commander, Europe [*NATO*]
SACEUR....... Supreme Allied Command, Europe [*World War II*] (NADA)
SACEUREP... Supreme Allied Commander, Europe Representative [*NATO*] (NATG)
SACEX......... Supporting Arms Coordination Exercise (DOMA)
SACF........... Cordoba [*Argentina ICAO location identifier*] (ICLI)
SACF........... Single Association Control Function [*Telecommunications*] (OSI)
SACF........... South Australian Cycling Federation
SACFA......... South Australian Canning Fruitgrowers' Association
SACFI.......... Scholars and Citizens for Freedom of Information (EA)
SACFS......... South Australian Country Fire Service
SACFVI........ South Australian Chamber of Fruit and Vegetable Industries
SACG........... Cordoba [*Argentina ICAO location identifier*] (ICLI)
SACG........... Senior Arms Control Group [*National Security Council*]
SACH........... Small Animal Care Hospital [*Medicine*] (DMAA)
SACH........... Solid Ankle Cushion Heel [*Foot prosthesis*]
SACHC......... Soviet-American Committee on Health Cooperation
SACHD......... South Australian Centre for Human Development
SACHQ......... Strategic Air Command Headquarters (AAG)
Sachse NM... Sachse's Minutes, Norwich Mayoralty Court [*A publication*] (DLA)
SACI........... Pilar [*Argentina ICAO location identifier*] (ICLI)
SACI........... Sales Association of the Chemical Industry (EA)
SACI........... Secondary Address Code Indicator
SACI........... South Atlantic Cooperative Investigations [*Military*]
SACI........... Special Assistant for Contracting Integrity (AAGC)
SACIM......... Society in Aid of Children Inoperable in their Motherland [*Australia*]
SACIM......... Southern African Center for Ivory Marketing
SACK........... Scientific Advisory Committee on Kangaroos [*Australia*]
SACK........... Selection Acknowledge [*Computer science*] (MHDB)
SACL........... Laguna Larga [*Argentina ICAO location identifier*] (ICLI)
SACL........... South African Confederation of Labour
SACL........... Space and Component Log
SACL........... Standards and Calibration Laboratory (KSC)
SACL........... Stress and Arousal Adjective Checklist (PDAA)
SACLAMP..... Strategic Air Command Low-Altitude Missile Program [*Air Force*]
SACLANT..... Supreme Allied Commander, Atlantic [*NATO*]
SACLANTCEN... Supreme Allied Atlantic Command Anti-Submarine Warfare Research Centre [*NATO*] [*Italy*]

SACLANTCEN... Supreme Allied Commander, Atlantic, Antisubmarine Warfare Research Center [*NATO*]
SACLANTREPEUR... Supreme Allied Commander, Atlantic, Representative in Europe [*NATO*]
SACLAU .... SACLANT [*Supreme Allied Commander, Atlantic*] Authentification System [*NATO*] (NATG)
SACLEX........ SACLANT [*Supreme Allied Commander, Atlantic*] Standing Exercise Orders [*NATO*] (NATG)
Sac Lit D ..... Doctor of Sacred Literature
SACLO .... Strategic Air Command Liaison Officer
SACLOS .... Semiautomatic Command to Line of Sight [*Military*]
SACM........... School of Acquisition Management [*Army*]
SACM........... Simulated Aerial Combat Maneuver
SACM........... South Australian Centre for Manufacturing
SACM........... Statistical Adiabatic Channel Model [*Physical chemistry*]
SACM........... Strategic Air Command Manual (IAA)
SACM........... Strategic Air Command Missile (IAA)
SACM........... Villa Gral, Mitre [*Argentina ICAO location identifier*] (ICLI)
SACMA .... Suppliers of Advanced Composite Materials
SACMA .... Suppliers of Advanced Composite Materials Association [*Arlington, VA*] (EA)
SACMAP ...... Selective Automatic Computational Matching and Positioning (MCD)
SACMAPS .... Selective Automatic Computational Matching and Positioning System
SACMC .... South Australian Chicken Meat Council
SACMDR...... Site Activation Commander [*Army*] (AABC)
SACME......... South Australian Chamber of Mines and Energy
SACMED ...... Supreme Allied Commander, Mediterranean [*World War II*]
SAC/MEP ..... Strategic Air Command/Minuteman Education Program (AFM)
SACMFCS .... Small Arms Common Module Fire Control System [*Army*]
SACMP .... South African Corps of Military Police [*British military*] (DMA)
SACMPC ...... Systems Acquisition Career Management Personnel Center [*DoD*]
SACMPC ...... Systems Acquisition Career Management Program for Civilians (AAGC)
SACN .... Ascochinga [*Argentina ICAO location identifier*] (ICLI)
SACNA .... South Africa Club of North America [*Defunct*] (EA)
SACNAS....... Society for Advancement of Chicanos and Native Americans in Science (EA)
SACNET .... Secure Automatic Communications Network
SACNSW...... Society for Arts and Crafts New South Wales [*Australia*]
SACO .... Cordoba [*Argentina ICAO location identifier*] (ICLI)
SACO .... Select Address and Contract Operate
SACO .... Service Administratif Canadien aux Organismes (AC)
SACO .... Service Administratif Canadien Outre-Mer [*Canadian Executive Service Overseas - CESO*]
SACO .... Sino American Cooperative Organization (EA)
SACO .... Subject Authority Cooperative Program [*American Library Association*]
SACO .... Supporting Administrative Contracting Officer (AFIT)
SACO .... Sveriges Akademikers Centralorganisation [*Swedish Confederation of Professional Associations*]
SACOA .... Southern Appalachian Coal Operators Association (EA)
SAC-OA....... Strategic Air Command Office of Operations Analysis
SACOD .... South African Congress of Democrats
SACOM .... SECNAV [*Secretary of the Navy*] Advisory Commission on Manpower (NG)
SACOM .... Senior Aircraft Communicator (IAA)
SACOM .... Ship's Advanced Communications (IAA)
SACOM .... Southern Area Command [*Military*] (AABC)
SACON .... Shock-Absorbing Concretes (RDA)
SACON .... Shock Attenuating Cellular Concrete [*Army*]
SACON .... Structural Analysis Consultant (MCD)
SACOPD....... Smoking-Attributable Chronic Obstructive Pulmonary Disease
SACOPS....... Strategic Air Command Operational Planning System (MCD)
SACP .... Chepes [*Argentina ICAO location identifier*] (ICLI)
SACP .... Sacrificial Anode Cathodic Protection (MCD)
SACP .... Scottish Association of Children's Panels (DBA)
SACP .... Selected Area Channelling Pattern (MCD)
SACP .... Society for Asian and Comparative Philosophy (EA)
SACP .... South African Communist Party
SACP .... Special Assistant for Civilian Personnel [*Navy*] (DNAB)
SACP .... Strategic Air Command Project Office (AAG)
SACPAN....... Stemming and Closure Panel [*Terminated, 1975*] [*DoD*] (EGAO)
SACP/EEO .... Special Assistant for Civilian Personnel / Equal Employment Opportunity [*Navy*] (DNAB)
SACPG .... Senior Arms Control Planning Group [*Pronounced "sack pig"*] [*DoD*]
SACPMC ...... Systems Acquisition Career Management Program for Civilians [*Air Force*] (DOMA)
SACPO .... Saigon Area Civilian Personnel Office [*Vietnam*]
SACPO .... South African Colored People's Organization
SACPPL .... Standing Advisory Committee on Private Pilot Licensing [*British*] (AIA)
SACPr .... So.Carolina E&G 5% cmPfd [*NYSE symbol*] (TTSB)
SACQ .... Monte Quemado [*Argentina ICAO location identifier*] (ICLI)
SACR .... Sacrament (ROG)
SACR .... Sacred (ROG)
SACR .... Sacrifice (ROG)
SACR .... Sacrist
SACR .... Semiautomatic Coordinate Reader (DNAB)
SACR .... Strategic Air Command Regulations (AAG)
SACRA......... Student Alliance for Christian Renewal in America
SACRE .... Standing Advisory Council for Religious Education (AIE)
SACRO .... Scottish Association of Care and Resettlement Offenders (DBA)
SACROC....... Scurry Area Canyon Reef Operators Committee
SACS .... Satellite Attitude-Control Simulator [*NASA*]
SACS .... Satellite Control Squadron
SACS .... Scheduling Activity Control System [*PA Computers & Telecommunications Ltd.*] [*Software package*] (NCC)
SACS .... Secondary Anticoagulation System [*Medicine*] (DMAA)
SACS .... Selective High-Frequency Antenna Coupler System [*Military*] (CAAL)
SACS .... Sensor Accuracy Check Site (MCD)
SACS .... Services After-Care Scheme [*British*]
SACS .... Ship Alteration Completion System
SACS .... Shipyard Accuracy Checksite (MCD)
SACS .... Sino-American Cultural Society (EA)
SACS .... Software Avionics Command Support (NASA)
SACS .... Solar Altitude Control System
SACS .... SONAR Accuracy Check Site (NVT)
SACS .... Southern Association of Colleges and Schools (EA)
SACS .... Structure and Composition System [*Military*] (AABC)
SACS .... Synchronous Altitude Communications Satellite
SACS .... Systems Software Avionics Command Support (MCD)
SACS .... Villa De Soto [*Argentina ICAO location identifier*] (ICLI)
SACSA .... Special Assistant for Counterinsurgency and Special Activities [*Military*] (AFM)
SACSA .... Standing Advisory Committee for Scientific Advice [*Oslo Commission*] (DCTA)
SACSDAC..... South Australian Conference of the Seventh-Day Adventist Church
SACSEA .... Supreme Allied Command [*or Commander*], Southeast Asia
SACSIR........ South African Council for Scientific and Industrial Research
SACSS .... South Australian Council of Social Service
SACSS .... Staff Association of Catholic Secondary Schools [*Australia*]
SAC/SSW..... Special Assistant to the Chief of Staff for Special Warfare [*Army*]
SACT............ Gobernador Gordillo [*Argentina ICAO location identifier*] (ICLI)
SACT............ Sinoatrial Conduction Time [*Cardiology*]
SACT............ Special Advisory Committee on Telecommunications (NTCM)
SACT............ System Availability Calculation Tool [*Science Applications International Corp.*] (MCD)
SACTO .... Sacramento Test Operations (MCD)
SACTTYNET... Strategic Air Command Teletype Network
SACTU .... South African Congress of Trade Unions
SACTW .... South African Council of Transport Workers
SACU .... Cordoba [*Argentina ICAO location identifier*] (ICLI)
SACU .... Scottish Auto-Cycle Union (DBA)
SACU .... Service for Admission to College and University [*Canada*] (AEBS)
SACU .... Society for Anglo-Chinese Understanding [*British*] (EAIO)
SACU .... South African Customs Union
SACU .... Stand-Alone Digital Communications Unit (MCD)
SACUBO....... Southern Association of College and University Business Officers (AEBS)
SACUS .... Southern Association on Children under Six (EA)
SACV .... Villa Maria Del Rio Seco [*Argentina ICAO location identifier*] (ICLI)
SACVAR....... Ship Alteration Cost Variance Account Report
SACVE .... State Advisory Councils for Vocational Education (EDAC)
SACW .... Senior Aircraftwoman [*British military*] (DMA)
SAD .... Saddle (AAG)
SAD .... Saddleback Community College District, Mission Viejo Campus, Mission Viejo, CA [*OCLC symbol*] (OCLC)
SAD .... Saddlery
Sad .... Sadler's Pennsylvania Cases [*A publication*] (DLA)
SAD .... Safe-and-Arm Device
SAD .... Safety Analysis [*or Assurance*] Diagram [*Nuclear energy*] (NRCH)
SAD .... Safety and Arming Device [*Military*] (AABC)
SAD .... Safety, Arming, and Destruct (MCD)
SAD .... Safford [*Arizona*] [*Airport symbol*] (AD)
SAD .... Safford, AZ [*Location identifier FAA*] (FAAL)
sad............... Sandawe [*MARC language code Library of Congress*] (LCCP)
SAD .... Scottish Association for the Deaf (DBA)
SAD .... Sealed and Delivery (MHDI)
SAD .... Search and Destroy (MCD)
SAD .... Seasonal Affective Disorder [*Type of depression caused by long nights, short days*]
SAD .... Selected Area [*Electron*] Diffraction [*Also, SAED*] [*Analysis of solids*]
SAD .... Self-Assessment Depression Scale (AAMN)
SAD .... Semiconductor Anticoincidence Detector
SAD .... Sentence Appraiser and Diagrammer
SAD .... Serial Analysis Delay [*Computer science*] (ECII)
SAD .... Service Action Drawing (AAG)
SAD .... Servicios Aereos de La Capital [*Colombia*] [*ICAO designator*] (FAAC)
SAD .... Ship Acoustics Department [*David W. Taylor Naval Ship Research and Development Center*]
SAD .... Shuttle Authorized Document [*NASA*] (NASA)
SAD .... Silicon Alloy Diffused (IAA)
SAD .... Silverado Mines Ltd. [*Vancouver Stock Exchange symbol*]
SAD .... Simple, Average, or Difficult (AAG)
SAD .... Single Administrative Document [*European trade contract*] [*1986*] (DCTA)
SAD .... Sinoaortic Deafferentation [*Medicine*]
SAD .... Sinoaortic Denervation [*Physiology*]
SAD .... Situation Attention Display
S-A-D........... Sleep Disturbance with Anxiety and Depression [*Combat behavior disorder*] [*Military*] (INF)
S/AD .... Small Advertisement (DGA)
SAD .... Small Airway Disease [*Medicine*] (DAVI)
SAD .... Social Avoidance Distress [*Scale*]
SAD .... Society of the Ark and the Dove (EA)
SAD .... Source-to-Axis Distance (MAE)
SAD .... South American Datum
SAD .... South Atlantic Division [*Army Corps of Engineers*]
SAD .... Soviet Air Defense
SAD .... Soviet Air Demonstration

SAD .... Space Antennae Diversity [*Telecommunications*] (TEL)
SAD .... Spacecraft Attitude Display (MCD)
SAD .... Special Adapter Device (IAA)
SAD .... Special Artificer, Special Synthetic Training Devices [*Navy*]
SAD .... Standard American Diet (DAVI)
SAD .... Station Address Directory [*Army*]
SAD .... Status Advisory Display (MCD)
SAD .... Store Access Director (NITA)
SAD .... Store Address Director
SAD .... Submarine Anomaly Detection [*Navy*] (NVT)
SAD .... Sugar, Acetone, Diacetic Acid [*Test*] [*Medicine*]
SAD .... Sugar and Acetone Determination [*Endocrinology*] (DAVI)
SAD .... Supervisory Aptitude Development [*In George Lee Walker novel "The Chronicles of Doodah"*]
SAD .... Support Acronym Definition [*Computer science*]
SAD .... Support Air Direction [*Navy*]
SAD .... Supporting Arms Department [*Navy*] (DNAB)
SAD .... Surface Area Decay [*Plant pathology*]
SAD .... Survival Assistance Director [*Federal disaster planning*]
SAD .... Sympathetic Aerial Detonation [*Air Force*]
SAD .... System Allocation Document [*NASA*] (NASA)
SAD .... System Amendment Detail(s) (NITA)
SAD .... System Analysis Drawing
SAD .... Systems Analysis and Design (NITA)
SAD .... Systems Analysis Document (MCD)
SAD .... Systems Automation Division [*Navy*] (DNAB)
SADA .... Seismic Array Data Analyzer (IEEE)
SADA .... South Australian Darts Association
SADA .... South Australian Debating Association
SADA .... Southern Appalachian Dulcimer Association (EA)
SADA .... Standard Advanced Dewar Assembly [*Army*]
SADAP .... Simplified Automatic Data Plotter
SADAP .... State Alcoholism and Drug Abuse Profile [*Public Health Service*] [*Information service or system*] (IID)
SADAR .... Satellite Data Reduction [*Processor system*]
SADARM ...... Search and Destroy Armor Munition (MCD)
SADARM ...... Selected Armor Defeating Artillery Munitions (MCD)
SADARM ...... Sense and Destroy Armor [*Army*] (RDA)
SADARM ...... Sense [*or Search*] and Destroy Armor Munition
SADAS .... Sperry Airborne Data Acquistion System (IAA)
SADBA .... South Australian Deer Breeders' Association
SADBE .... Squaric Acid Dibutylester [*Medicine*] (MEDA)
SAD Beng .... Select Cases, Sadr Diwani [*Bengal*] [*A publication*] (DLA)
SAD Bom ..... Sadr Diwani Adalat Reports [*Bombay, India*] [*A publication*] (DLA)
SADBU .... Small and Disadvantaged Business Utilization [*Department of Commerce*]
SADBUO ...... Small and Disadvantaged Business Utilization Office [*Army*] (RDA)
SADBUS ...... Small and Disadvantaged Business Utilization Specialist [*Federal government*] (GFGA)
SADC .... Sector Aid Defense Commander (NATG)
SADC .... Sequential Analog-Digital Computer (DIT)
SADC .... Sneak Attack Defense Coordinator [*Military*] (CAAL)
SADC .... Southern African Development Community (ECON)
SADCC .... South African Development Coordination Committee [*Australia*]
SADD .... Buenos Aires/Don Torcuato [*Argentina ICAO location identifier*] (ICLI)
SADD .... Semiautomatic Detection Device
SADD .... Short-Alcohol Dependence Data [*Medicine*] (DMAA)
SADD .... Standardized Assessment of Depressive Disorders [*Medicine*] (DMAA)
SADD .... Students Against Driving Drunk (EA)
SaDDC .... Durban City Council, Durban, South Africa [*Library symbol Library of Congress*] (LCLS)
SADE .... Sensitive Acoustic Detection Equipment (PDAA)
SADE .... Solar Array Drive Electronics (LAIN)
SADE .... Specialized Armoured Development Establishment [*British military*] (DMA)
SADE .... Structural Assembly Demonstration Experiment (MCD)
SADE .... Superheat Advanced Demonstration Experiment [*Nuclear energy*]
SADE .... Symbolic Application Debugging Environment
SADEC .... Spin Axis Declination [*Aerospace*] (MCD)
SADELCA ...... Sociedad Aerea del Caqueta [*Airline*] [*Colorado*]
SADEMS ...... Salt Dome Experimental Monitoring System (GFGA)
SADEYA ...... Sociedad Astronomica de Espana y America [*Hispano-American Astronomical Society*] (EAIO)
SADF .... San Fernando [*Argentina ICAO location identifier*] (ICLI)
SADF .... Semi-Automatic Document Feed (NITA)
SADF .... Semi-Automatic Document Feeder (HGAA)
SADF .... South African Defence Forces
SADF .... Statistical Analysis of Documentation Files (PDAA)
SADG .... Monte Grande [*Argentina ICAO location identifier*] (ICLI)
SADGE .... SAGE [*Semiautomatic Ground Environment*] Data Generator (IAA)
SADH .... Succinic Acid - Dimethylhydrazide [*Plant growth retardant*]
SADI .... Secretarial Automated Data Index
SADI .... Selling-Areas Distribution Index (WDMC)
SADIC .... Solid-State Analog-to-Digital Computer
SADIE .... Scanning Analog-to-Digital Input Equipment [*National Institute of Standards and Technology*]
SADIE .... Secure Automatic Data Information Exchange [*System*]
SADIE .... Semiautomatic Decentralized Intercept Environment [*Air Force*]
SADIE .... Sterling and Decimal Invoicing Electronically (IEEE)
SADIS .... Shipboard Automated Decoy Integration System [*Navy*]
SADJ .... Jose C. Paz/Dr. Mariano More [*Argentina ICAO location identifier*] (ICLI)
SADL .... La Plata [*Argentina ICAO location identifier*] (ICLI)
SADL .... Sadlier [*William H.*], Inc. [*NASDAQ symbol*] (NQ)
SADL .... Sadlier (William H.) [*NASDAQ symbol*] (TTSB)
SADL .... Ships Authorized Data List
SADL .... Significant Activities of Daily Living (WYGK)
SADL .... Significant Activity of Daily Living [*Insurance*]
SADL .... Simulated Activities of Daily Living (DMAA)
SADL .... Spares Application Data List
SADL .... Special Automated Distribution List (AFIT)
SADL .... Sterilization Assembly Development Laboratory [*NASA*]
SADL .... Synchronous Automatic Dial Language
Sadler .... Sadler's Pennsylvania Cases [*A publication*] (DLA)
Sadler (PA)... Sadler's Pennsylvania Cases [*A publication*] (DLA)
Sadlier .... Sadlier [*William H.*], Inc. [*Associated Press*] (SAG)
SADM .... Moron [*Argentina ICAO location identifier*] (ICLI)
SADM .... Secretary of the Army Decision Memorandum [*Army*] (RDA)
SADM .... Solar Array Drive Motor
SADM .... Special Atomic Demolition Munitions [*Military*] (AABC)
SADM .... System Acquisition Decision Memorandum (MCD)
SADMG .... Special Artificer, Special Devices, Machine Gun Trainer [*Navy*]
SADNWF ...... Sadr Diwani Adalat Cases, Northwest Frontier [*Pakistan*] [*A publication*] (DLA)
SADOPS ...... Ships Angle Tracking and Doppler System (IAA)
SADOT .... Structures Assembly Deployment and Operations Technology (SSD)
SADP .... El Palomar [*Argentina ICAO location identifier*] (ICLI)
SADP .... Scales of Attitudes toward Disabled Persons [*Occupational therapy*]
SADP .... Scandinavian Association of Directory Publishers (EAIO)
SADP .... Selected Area Electron Diffraction Pattern [*Analysis of solids*]
SADP .... Small Area Direct Path [*Military*] (CAAL)
SADP .... Structured Analysis, Design, and Programming [*Computer science*]
SADP .... Synthetic Array Data Processor
SADP .... System Architecture Design Package
Sad PA Cas... Sadler's Pennsylvania Cases [*1885-88*] [*A publication*] (DLA)
Sad PA Cs ... Sadler's Pennsylvania Cases [*1885-88*] [*A publication*] (DLA)
SADPMA ...... South Australian Dairy Products Manufacturers' Association
SADPO .... Senior ADP Policy Officer (AAGC)
SADPO .... Systems Analysis and Data Processing Office
SADQ .... Quilmes [*Argentina ICAO location identifier*] (ICLI)
SADQ .... Severity of Alcohol Dependence Questionnaire
SADR .... Merlo [*Argentina ICAO location identifier*] (ICLI)
SADR .... Saharan Arab Democratic Republic [*Morocco*] (PD)
SADR .... Secure Acoustic Data Relay (NVT)
SADR .... Severity Adjusted Death Rate [*Medicine*] (DHSM)
SADR .... Six Hundred Megacycle Air Defense RADAR
SADRA .... South Australian Drag Racers' Association
SADRAM ...... Seek and Destroy RADAR-Assisted Mission (MCD)
SADRCB ...... South Australian Dog Racing Control Board
SADRI .... Social and Demographic Research Institute [*University of Massachusetts*] [*Research center*] (RCD)
SADRT .... Secure Acoustic Data Relay Terminal (MCD)
SADS .... San Justo/Aeroclub Argentino [*Argentina ICAO location identifier*] (ICLI)
SADS .... Schedule for Affective Disorders and Schizophrenia [*Psychological interview*]
SADS .... Seasonal Affective Disorder Syndrome [*Psychiatry*] (DAVI)
SADS .... Semiautomatic Defense System (NG)
SADS .... Semiconductor Anticoincidence Detection System
SADS .... Senate Appropriations Defense Subcommittee
SADS .... Simulated Air Defense System [*RADAR*]
SADS .... Single Application Data Sheet
SADS .... Social Avoidance and Distress Scale [*Psychology*]
SADS .... Solar Array Drive System
SADS .... Submarine Active Detection System
SADS .... Swiss Air Defense System
SADS .... System Architecture Development Study [*NATO Integrated Communications System*] (NATG)
SADSAC ...... Sampled Data Simulator and Computer
SADSAC ...... Seiler ALGOL Digitally Simulated Analog Computer
SADSAC ...... Small Acoustic Device Simulating Aircraft Carrier (NVT)
SADSACT ..... Self-Assigned Descriptors from Self and Cited Titles [*Automatic indexing*]
SADSC .... San Antonio Data Services Center [*Military*]
SADS-C ...... Schedule for Affective Disorders and Schizophrenia - Change Version [*Personality development test*] [*Psychology*]
SADS-L ...... Schedule for Affective Disorders and Schizophrenia - Lifetime Version [*Personality development test*] [*Psychology*]
SADSSC ...... South Australian Deaf Sports and Social Club
SADS-TG ..... Submarine Active Detection System - Transmit Group [*Navy*]
SADT .... Same Direction Traffic (FAAC)
SADT .... Self-Accelerating Decomposition Temperature
SADT .... Special Active Duty for Training [*Military*] (AABC)
SADT .... Structured Analysis and Design Technique [*Programming language*] [*1978*]
SADT .... Surface Alloy Diffused-Base Transistor
SADTAC ...... Selective Automatic Decade Turnover, Absolute Control (IAA)
SADTC .... SHAPE [*Supreme Headquarters Allied Powers Europe*] Air Defense Technology Center [*Later, STC*] [*NATO*]
SADTS .... Safety and Arming Detection Test Set (DWSG)
SADU .... Sea Search Attack Development Unit
SADV .... Semiannual Density Variation [*Geophysics*]
SADZ .... Matanza/Aeroclub Universita Rio [*Argentina ICAO location identifier*] (ICLI)
SAE .... Ogallala, NE [*Location identifier FAA*] (FAAL)
SAE .... Sable Resources Ltd. [*Vancouver Stock Exchange symbol*]
SaE .... Sanguinarine Extract [*Biochemistry*]
SAE .... Self-Addressed Envelope
SAE .... Self-Aligned Emitter (IAA)

SAE............ Semi-Actuator Ejector (MCD)
SAE............ Senior Assistant Editor [*Publishing*]
SAE............ Service Acquisition Executive [*DoD*]
SAE............ Shaft Angle Encoder (KSC)
SAE............ Simple Arithmetic Expression
SAE............ Site Acceptance Evaluation [*Army*] (AABC)
SAE............ Skyways Africa Ltd. [*Kenya*] [*ICAO designator*] (FAAC)
SAE............ Society for Aerospace Engineers (AAGC)
SAE............ Society for the Advancement of Education (EA)
SAE............ Society for the Anthropology of Europe (EA)
SAE............ Society of American Etchers (NADA)
SAE............ Society of Association Executives [*British*] (EAIO)
SAE............ Society of Automotive Engineers [*Acronym is now organization's official name*] (EA)
SAE............ Society of Automotive Engineers, Inc. (AAGC)
SAE............ Solar Array Experiment (SSD)
SAE............ Son Altesse Electorale [*His Highness the Elector*] [*French*] (ROG)
SAE............ Soviet Antarctic Expedition
SAE............ Specialized Armoured Establishment [*British military*] (DMA)
SAE............ Spiral Aftereffect [*Aerospace*]
SAE............ Stamped Addressed Envelope
sae............ Stamped Addressed Envelope (ODBW)
SAE............ Stand Alone Executive (MHDI)
SAE............ Standard Australian English
SAE............ Standard Average European
SAE............ Standard of Automotive Engineers (IAA)
SAE............ Steering Angle Error
SAE............ Stop at Expiration [*Magazine subscriptions*]
SAE............ Student Action for Education [*Defunct*] (EA)
SAE............ Subcortical Arteriosclerotic Encephalopathy [*Medicine*]
SAE............ Supersonic Aircraft Engine
SAEA........... South Australian Exporters Association
SAEA........... Southeastern Adult Education Association (AEBS)
SAEA........... Southwest Atomic Energy Associates
SAE abstracts... Society of Automotive Engineers abstracts (NITA)
SAEB........... Self-Adjusting Electric Brake
SAEB........... Special Army Evaluation Board (AABC)
SAEC........... Saeculum [*Age, Century, Generation, Lifetime*] [*Latin*] (ROG)
SAEC........... South American Explorers Club (EA)
SAEC........... South Australian Equestrian Centre
SAEC........... Southern Agricultural Energy Center
SAEC........... State Administration of Exchange Control [*China*]
SAEC........... Sumitomo Atomic Energy Commission [*Japan*]
SAECG.......... Signal Averaged Electrocardiography [*Medicine*]
SAED........... Selected Area Electron Diffraction [*Also, SAD*] [*Surface analysis*]
SAED........... Societe des Amis d'Eugene Delacroix (EAIO)
SAED........... Systems Analysis and Engineering Development [*Naval Air Development Center*] (MCD)
SAEDA.......... Subversion and Espionage Directed Against US Army and Deliberate Security Violations (AABC)
SAEDE.......... Sensory Aids Evaluation and Development Center [*MIT*]
SAEDFR......... Scholars Against the Escalating Danger of the Far Right (EA)
SAEF........... Ezeiza [*Argentina ICAO location identifier*] (ICLI)
SAEF........... SEAQ Automated Execution Facility [*Software package*]
SAEF........... Small-Order Automatic Execution Facility [*London Stock Exchange*] [*British*]
SAEF........... Spacecraft Assembly and Encapsulation Facility [*NASA*] (NASA)
SAEF........... State Administrative Expense Funds
SAEF........... Stock Exchange Automatic Execution Facility
SAEH........... Society for Automation in English and the Humanities [*Later, SDE*]
SAEI........... Sumitomo Atomic Energy Industries Ltd. [*Japan*]
SAEMA.......... Scottish Association for Educational Management and Administration (AIE)
SAEMA.......... Suspended Access Equipment Manufacturers Association [*British*] (DBA)
SAEMR.......... Small Arms Expert Marksmanship Ribbon [*Military decoration*] (AFM)
SAEP........... South African Education Program [*New York, NY*]
SAES........... SAES Getters SPA [*NASDAQ symbol*] (SAG)
SAES........... Scanning Auger Electron Spectroscopy
SAES........... Special Assistant for Environmental Services [*Military*]
SAES........... Sputter Auger Electron Spectroscopy (IAA)
SAES........... Stand-Alone Engine Simulator (NASA)
SAES........... State Agricultural Experiment Station
SAESA.......... Compania de Servicios Aereos SA [*Spain ICAO designator*] (FAAC)
SAESGet........ SAES Getters SPA [*Associated Press*] (SAG)
SAESIP......... Saturn Apollo Electrical Systems Integration Panel (IAA)
SAESY.......... SAES Getters S.p.A ADS [*NASDAQ symbol*] (TTSB)
SAET........... Society for the Advancement of Economic Theory (EA)
SAET........... Society of Automotive-Electrical Technicians [*British*] (DBA)
SAET........... South Australian Electricity Trust
SAET........... Spiral Aftereffect Test [*Psychology*] (AEBS)
SAETA.......... SA Ecuatoriana de Transportes Aereos [*Airline*] [*Ecuador*]
SAEV........... Ezeiza [*Argentina ICAO location identifier*] (ICLI)
SAEW........... Ship's Advanced Electronic Warfare (MCD)
SAEWG.......... Standing Air Emissions Work Group [*Environmental Protection Agency*] (GFGA)
SAEWS.......... Ship's Advanced Electronic Warfare System (NVT)
SAEZ........... Buenos Aires [*Argentina*]/Ezeiza [*Argentina ICAO location identifier*] (ICLI)
SAF............ Republic of Singapore Air Force [*ICAO designator*] (FAAC)
SAF............ Safe, Arm, and Fuze
SAF............ Safed [*Israel*] [*Seismograph station code, US Geological Survey Closed*] (SEIS)
SAF............ Safety (KSC)
SAF............ SAF [*Society of American Florists*]- The Center for Commercial Floriculture (EA)
SAF............ Sample Air Filter
SAF............ San Andreas Fault
SAF............ Santa Fe [*New Mexico*] [*Airport symbol*] (OAG)
SAF............ Save America's Forests [*An association*] (EA)
SAF............ Scandinavian American Fraternity (EA)
SAF............ School of Aerial Fighting [*British military*] (DMA)
SAF............ Scrapie-Associated Fibrils [*Neuroanatomy*]
SAF............ Scudder New Asia Fd [*NYSE symbol*] (TTSB)
SAF............ Scudder New Asia Fund [*NYSE symbol*] (SPSG)
SAF............ Second Amendment Foundation (EA)
SAF............ Secretary of the Air Force
SAF............ Secure Automated Fabrication [*Line*] [*Nuclear energy*]
SAF............ Segment Address Field
SAF............ Self-Articulating Femoral [*Medicine*]
SAF............ Service to the Armed Forces
SAF............ Shark Attack File (DNAB)
SAF............ Shielding Analysis Form [*Civil Defense*]
SAF............ Short Address Form (NITA)
SAF............ Side and Face Milling [*Cutter*] (IAA)
SAF............ Single Action [*Maintenance*] Form (NVT)
SAF............ Small Arms Fire [*Military*] (VNW)
SAF............ Societe des Artistes Francais, Paris [*1880*] [*French*] (NGC)
SAF............ Society of American Florists (EA)
SAF............ Society of American Foresters (EA)
SAF............ Sound and Flash (IAA)
SAF............ Source Acquisitions File (MCD)
SAF............ South Africa (EY)
SAF............ South Africa Foundation (EA)
SAF............ Southern Attack Force [*Navy*]
SAF............ Soviet Air Forces (DOMA)
SAF............ Spacecraft Assembly Facility [*NASA*]
SAF............ Spanish Air Force
SAF............ Special Action Force [*Military*]
SAF............ Specification Approval Form (MCD)
SAF............ Spin Armed Fuze
SAF............ Star Alliance Foundation (EA)
SAF............ Stem Cell Activating Factor [*Biochemistry*]
SAF............ Sterilization Assembly Facility
SAF............ Strategic Air Force
SAF............ Structural Adjustment Facility [*Finance*]
SAF............ Students Against Fires [*International student engineering project for 1972-73 sponsored by Student Competitions on Relevant Engineering - SCORE*]
SAF............ Subject Authority File, Washington, DC [*UTLAS symbol*]
SAF............ Subject to the Availability of Funds (MCD)
SAF............ Super Abrasion Furnace [*Carbon black manufacture*]
SAF............ Support Action Form (MCD)
SAF............ Suppressor Activating Factor [*Immunology*]
SAF............ Svenska Arbetsgivareforeningen [*An employers' confederation*] [*Sweden*]
SAF............ Swedish Air Force
SAF............ Switchable Acoustic Filter
SAF............ Symmetry-Adapted Function
SAF............ Symposium on Applications of Ferroelectrics [*IEEE*]
SAF............ Syrian Air Force (BJA)
SAFA........... School Assistance in Federally Affected Areas
SAFA........... Service d'Aide aux Forces Alliees [*World War II*]
SAFA........... Society for Automation in the Fine Arts [*Later, SDE*]
SAFA........... Society of Air Force Anesthesiologists [*Later, DMEF*] (EA)
SAFA........... Socttish Amateur Football Association (DBA)
SAFA........... Solar Array Failure Analysis
SAFA........... Soluble Antigen Fluorescent-Antibody [*Immunology*]
SAFA........... South Australian Football Association
SAFAA.......... Secretary of the Air Force, Administrative Assistant
SAFAD.......... Small Arms for Air Defense (MCD)
SAFAD.......... Swedish Agency for Administrative Development (NITA)
SAFAH.......... Supplemental Assistance for Facilities to Assist the Homeless [*Department of Housing and Urban Development*] (GFGA)
SAF/AL......... Assistant Secretary of the Air Force (Research, Development, and Logistics)
SAF/AQ......... Assistant Secretary of the Air Force for Acquisition (AAGC)
SAFARI......... Semiautomatic Failure Anticipation Recording Instrumentation
SAFARI......... South African Fundamental Atomic Reactor Installation
SAFARI......... Spiro Agnew Fans and Rooters, Inc.
SAFB........... Scott Air Force Base [*Illinois*]
SAFB........... Shaw Air Force Base [*South Carolina*]
SAFB........... Sheppard Air Force Base [*Texas*] (AAG)
SAFBITC........ South Australian Food and Beverage Industry Training Council
SAFC........... SAFECO Corp. [*NASDAQ symbol*] (NQ)
SAFC........... Swiss Association for Friendship with China (EAIO)
SAFCA.......... Safeguard Communications Agency [*Army*]
SAFCB.......... Secretary of the Air Force Correction Board
SAFCMD......... Safeguard Command [*Army*] (AABC)
SAFCO.......... Standing Advisory Committee on Fisheries of the Caribbean Organization
SAFCOM......... Safeguard System Command [*Obsolete Army*]
SAFCOS......... Scottish Association of Family Conciliation Services (DBA)
SAFCPM......... Safeguard Communications Program Manager [*Army*] (AABC)
SAFCPMO........ Safeguard Communications Program Management Office [*Army*] (AABC)
SAFCS.......... Steam and Feedwater Rupture Control System (IAA)
SAFCTF......... Safeguard Central Training Facility [*Army*] (AABC)
SAFD........... Society of American Fight Directors (EA)

SAFDL .... Specified Acceptable Fuel Design Limit [*Nuclear energy*] (NRCH)
SAFE .... Invivo Corp. [*NASDAQ symbol*] (SAG)
SAFE .... Safe Access to Files of Estate [*Howrex Corp.*] [*Information service or system*] (IID)
SAFE .... Safe Areas for Evasion (DOMA)
SAFE .... Safeguards Analysis for Effluents
SAFE .... Safeguards Automated Facility Evaluation [*Nuclear energy*] (NRCH)
SAFE .... Safety and Functional Evaluation [*Occupational therapy*]
SAFE .... SafetyTek Corp. [*NASDAQ symbol*] (SPSG)
SAFE .... San Andreas Fault Experiment
SAFE .... Santa Fe [*Argentina ICAO location identifier*] (ICLI)
SAFE .... Satellite Alert Force Employment
SAFE .... Save Animals from Extinction [*Later, WPTI*] [*An association*]
SAFE .... Security and Freedom through Encryption [*Proposed legislative bill*]
SAFE .... Security, Aptitude, Fitness Evaluation [*Test*]
SAFE .... Security Audit and Field Evaluation (IAA)
S/AFE .... Seismic/Acoustic Feature Extraction (MCD)
SAFE .... Selected Areas for Evasion [*Military*] (MCD)
SAFE .... Self-Acceptance, Faulty Information, Effectiveness Counselling or Training [*Sex therapy*]
SAFE .... Sequential Analysis for Force Development (MCD)
SAFE .... Settlement and Accelerated Funds Exchange [*Chicago, IL*]
SAFE .... Shelter Available for Emergency
SAFE .... Simulation-Aided Fault Evaluation (MCD)
SAFE .... Society for the Advancement of Fission Energy [*Defunct*] (EA)
SAFE .... Society for the Application of Free Energy (EA)
SAFE .... Society of Associated Financial Executives
SAFE .... Society to Advance Foreclosure Education [*Defunct*] (EA)
SAFE .... Software Abstracts for Engineers [*CITIS Ltd.*] [*Ireland*] [*Information service or system*] (CRD)
SAFE .... Solar Array Flight Experiment (MCD)
SAFE .... Solvent Abuse Foundation for Education (EA)
SAFE .... Source and Application Inspection Equipment
SAFE .... South America and Far East
SAFE .... Spectronix Automatic Fire Extinguishing [*System*] [*For armored vehicles*]
SAFE .... Stationary Attachment and Flexible Endoskeleton
SAFE .... Stock Assessment and Fishery Investigations [*National Marine Fisheries Service*] (NOAA)
SAFE .... Store and Forward Element [*Telecommunications*] (TEL)
SAFE .... Straits Air Freight Express [*Australia*]
SAFE .... Strategy and Force Evaluation (MCD)
SAFE .... Students Against Famine Everywhere [*Defunct*] (EA)
SAFE .... Suntanning Association for Education (EA)
SAFE .... Support for the Analysts' File Environment (MCD)
SAFE .... Survival [*formerly, Space*] and Flight Equipment Association [*Later, SAFE Association*]
SAFE .... System, Area, Function, Equipment
SAFE .... System for Automated Flight Efficiency (PDAA)
SAFEA .... Space and Flight Equipment Assoication (IAA)
SAFEA .... Survival and Flight Equipment Association [*Later, SAFE Association*] (EA)
SAFE-BAR .... Safeland Barrier (DNAB)
SAFECEN ..... Safety Center (DNAB)
Safeco .... Safeco Corp. [*Associated Press*] (SAG)
SAFEPLAN ... Submarine Air Frequency Plan (DNAB)
SAFER .... Safety and Fitness Electronic Records System [*FHWA*] (TAG)
SAFER .... Sequential Action Flow Routine [*Military British*]
SAFER .... Simplified Aid for EVA Rescue [*NASA*]
SAFER .... Special Application of Finite Element Representation [*Marine science*] (OSRA)
SAFER .... Special Aviation Fire and Explosion Reduction (EGAO)
SAFER .... Spectral Application of Finite Element Representation (USDC)
SAFER .... Structural Analysis, Frailty Evaluation and Redesign (MHDB)
SAFER .... Systematic Aid to Flow on Existing Roads [*Traffic-control system*]
SAFER .... System for Aircrew Flight Extension and Return (PDAA)
Safeskin ...... Safeskin Corp. [*Associated Press*] (SAG)
SAFE TRIP ... Students Against Faulty Tires Ripping in Pieces [*Student legal action organization*]
SAFETY .... Safety Always Follows Everything You Do [*Sign*]
Safeway .... Safeway, Inc. [*Associated Press*] (SAG)
SAFF .... Safing, Arming, Fusing, and Firing [*Military*] (MCD)
SAFF .... Store and Forward Facsimile
SAFFE .... Society of Americans for Firearms Elimination (EA)
SAFFI .... Special Assembly for Fast Installations [*Telecommunications*] (TEL)
SAFFM .... Secretary of the Air Force, Financial Management
SAFFUC .... Sudan African Freedom Fighters' Union of Conservatives
SAFFWALD ... Saffron Walden [*Municipal borough in England*]
SAFGA .... South Australian Flower Growers' Association
SAFGAR .... Semi-Arid Grain Research and Development (GNE)
SAFGC .... Secretary of the Air Force General Counsel
SafHlt .... Safeguard Health Enterprises, Inc. [*Associated Press*] (SAG)
SAFI .... Semiautomatic Flight Inspection [*FAA*]
SAFI .... Semiautomatic Flight Inspection Aircraft (FAAC)
SAFI .... Senior Air Force Instructor
SAFI .... Sholem Aleichem Folk Institute (EA)
SAFI .... Stock Assessment and Fishery Investigations Program [*National Oceanic and Atmospheric Administration*] (GFGA)
SAFIAC .... South Australian Film Investment Advisory Committee
SAFIC .... South Australian Fishing Industry Council
SAFIE .... Secretary of the Air Force, Special Assistant for Installations
SAFIL .... Secretary of the Air Force (Installations and Logistics)
SAFIM .... Separated Associated Fluid Interaction Model [*Chemical engineering*]
SAFIMDA ..... School Aid to Federally Impacted and Major Disaster Areas (OICC)
SAFIN .... Secretary of the Air Force, Special Assistant for Intelligence
SAFIRE .... Systems Analysis for Integrated Relief Variation [*Engineering*]
SAFIS .... Secretary of the Air Force, Office of Information Services
SAFIS .... Substance Abuse Facility Information System [*Department of Health and Human Services*] (GFGA)
SAFISY .... Space Agency Forum on International Space Year
SAFITC .... South Australian Fishing Industry Training Council
SAFITP .... Safeguard Integrated Training Plan [*Army*] (AABC)
SAFLL .... Secretary of the Air Force, Office of Legislative Liaison
SAFLOG .... Safeguard Logistics Command [*Army*] (AABC)
SAFM .... Sanderson Farms [*NASDAQ symbol*] (TTSB)
SAFM .... Sanderson Farms, Inc. [*NASDAQ symbol*] (NQ)
SAFMP .... Assistant Secretary of the Air Force (Manpower and Personnel)
SAFMR .... Secretary of the Air Force, Manpower and Reserve Affairs
SAFMS .... Secretary of the Air Force, Missile and Satellite Systems (SAA)
SAFMSC ...... Safeguard Materiel Support Command [*Army*] (AABC)
SAFNGS ...... Small Arms Flash, Noise Gunfire Simulator [*Army*]
SAFO .... Safe Altitude Fuzing Option (SAA)
SAFO .... Secretary of the Air Force Order (AFM)
SAFO .... Self-Adhesive Foreign Object (PDAA)
SAFO .... Senior Acting Field Officer [*Military British*] (ROG)
SAFO .... Senior Air Force Officer [*Present*] (AFM)
SAFOC .... Semiautomatic Flight Operations Center
SAFOC .... Syndicat Autonome des Fonctionnaires d'Oubangi-Chari [*Autonomous Union of the Workers of Ubangi-Shari*]
SAFOH .... Society of American Florists and Ornamental Horticulturists [*Later, SAF*]
SAFOI .... Secretary of the Air Force, Office of Information
SAFOR .... Semi-Automated Forces [*Army*] (RDA)
SAFP .... Society of Air Force Physicians (EA)
SAFPACC ..... Safeguard Public Affairs Coordinating Committee [*Army*] (AABC)
SAFPC .... Secretary of the Air Force Personnel Council
SAFPLAN ..... Submarine Area Frequency Plan [*Navy*]
SAFPO .... Safeguard Project Office (MCD)
SAFR .... Senior Air Force Representative (AFM)
SAFR .... Social Assessment of Fisheries Resources
SAFR .... Sodium Advanced Fast Reactor
SAFR .... Source Application of Funds Report (MCD)
S Afr .... South Africa
S Afr .... South Africa (VRA)
SAFR .... Supplementary Application Forms Required [*Civil Service*]
SAFRAS .... Self-Adaptive Flexible Format Retrieval and Storage System [*Computer science*] (IID)
S Afr Bankers J ... South African Bankers' Journal [*Cape Town, South Africa*] [*A publication*] (DLA)
SAFRD .... Assistant Secretary of the Air Force (Research and Development)
SAFRD .... Secretary of the Air Force for Research and Development (IAA)
S Afr LR App ... South African Law Reports, Appellate [*A publication*] (DLA)
S Afr L Rev ... South African Law Review [*A publication*] (DLA)
S Afr LT .... South African Law Times [*A publication*] (DLA)
SAFRR .... Secretary of the Air Force, Requirements Review
S Afr Tax ..... South African Tax Cases [*A publication*] (DLA)
S Afr Tax Cas ... South African Tax Cases [*A publication*] (DLA)
SAFS .... Safing, Arming, and Fusing System [*Military*] (MCD)
SAFS .... Secondary Air Force Specialty
SAFS .... Society for Academic Freedom and Scholarship [*Canada*]
SAFSC-D ...... Safeguard System Command-RDT & E [*Research, Development, Test, and Evaluation*] Directorate [*Obsolete Army*] (MCD)
SAFSCOM .... Safeguard System Command [*Obsolete Army*] (AABC)
SAFSEA .... Safeguard System Evaluation Agency [*Army*] (AABC)
SAFSIM .... Safeguard System Simulation [*Missile system evaluation*] [*Army*] (RDA)
SAFSL .... Secretary of the Air Force Space Liaison (MCD)
SAFSM .... Safeguard System Manager [*Army*]
SAFSO .... Safeguard System Office [*Army*] (AABC)
SAFSP .... Secretary of the Air Force, Special Projects
SAFSR .... Society for the Advancement of Food Service Research (EA)
SAFT .... Safety
SAFT .... Safety 1st, Inc. [*NASDAQ symbol*] (SAG)
SAFT .... Society for the Advancement of the Field Theory (EA)
SAFT .... Spark Analysis for Traces [*Spectrometry*]
SAFT .... Synthetic Aperture Focusing Technique [*Computer imaging*]
SAFTAC .... Semiautomatic Facility for Terminal Area Control
SAFTCP .... Safeguard Tactical Communications Plan [*Army*] (AABC)
SAFTCS .... Safeguard Tactical Communications System [*Army*] (AABC)
SAF-TE .... SCSI Accessed Fault-Tolerant Enclosures [*Computer science*]
SaftKl .... Safety-Kleen Corp. [*Associated Press*] (SAG)
SAFTO .... South African Foreign Trade Organisation
SAFTRANS ... Safeguard Transportation System [*Army*] (AABC)
SAFTU .... South African Federation of Trade Unions
Saftytk .... Safetytek Corp. [*Associated Press*] (SAG)
SAFUS .... Under Secretary of the Air Force
SAFV .... Separator Assembly Fuel-Vacuum [*Automotive engineering*]
SAFWA .... Southeastern Association of Fish and Wildlife Agencies (EA)
Safwy .... Safeway, Inc. [*Associated Press*] (SAG)
SAFX .... Saw Fixture [*Tool*] (AAG)
SAFZ .... San Andreas Fault Zone [*Geology*]
s-ag-- .... Argentina [*MARC geographic area code Library of Congress*] (LCCP)
SAG .... Saga [*Japan*] [*Seismograph station code, US Geological Survey*] (SEIS)
SAG .... Saginaw [*Diocesan abbreviation*] [*Michigan*] (TOCD)
SAG .... Sagitta [*Mathematics*]
sag .... Sagittal [*Anatomy*] (DAVI)
SAG .... Sagittarius [*Constellation*]
SAG .... Sagwon, AK [*Location identifier FAA*] (FAAL)
SAG .... Saint Anthony's Guild

SAG .... Salicyl Acyl Glucuronide [*Organic chemistry*]
sag .... Sango [*MARC language code Library of Congress*] (LCCP)
SAG .... Schweizerische Afrika-Gesellschaft [*Swiss Society of African Studies*] (EAIO)
SAG .... Screen Actors Guild (EA)
SAG .... Secretaria de Agricultura y Ganaderia [*Mexico*]
SAG .... Seismic Air Gun
SAG .... Self-Agglomerator (PDAA)
SAG .... Self-Aligned Gate (IAA)
SAG .... Semiactive Guidance [*Military*] (IIA)
SAG .... Semiautogenous Grinding System [*Ore-crushing process*]
SAG .... Senescence-Associated Gene [*Biochemistry*]
SAG .... Senior Advisory Group [*Policymakers who advised President Johnson, especially regarding Vietnam*] (VNW)
SAG .... Senior Advisory Group [*Nuclear Regulatory Commission*] (GFGA)
SAG .... Service Advisory Group (NATG)
SAG .... Signal Actuated Gate
SAG .... Significant Air Gap
SAG .... Society of Arthritic Gardeners
SAg .... Soluble Antigen [*Immunochemistry*]
SAG .... Sonoangiography [*Medicine*] (DMAA)
SAG .... South Australian Gas Co. [*Commercial firm*]
SAG .... Sowjetische Aktiengesellschaften [*Soviet Corporations*] [*Germany*]
SAG .... Special Activities Group [*Air Force*]
SAG .... Standard Address Generator (IEEE)
SAG .... St. Apollonia Guild (EA)
SAG .... Strategic Communications Ltd. [*Vancouver Stock Exchange symbol*]
SAG .... Study Advisory Group [*Army*]
SAG .... Submarine Analysis Group [*Navy*] (CAAL)
SAG .... Superantigen [*Immunology*]
S/Ag .... Supervised Agency (DLA)
SAG .... Surface Action Group [*Military*] (NVT)
SAG .... Surface Attack Group [*Navy*] (CAAL)
SAG .... Swedish Air Ambulance [*ICAO designator*] (FAAC)
SAG .... Swiss Agammaglobulinemia [*Medicine*] (MAE)
SAG .... Syntax Analyzer Generator (PDAA)
SAG .... System Application Group (SAA)
SAG .... Systems Analysis Group
SAGA .... Saint-Gaudens National Historic Site
SAGA .... Sand and Gravel Association of Great Britain
SAGA .... Scottish Amateur Gymnastics Association (DBA)
SAGA .... Short-Arc Geodetic Adjustment [*Geophysics*]
SAGA .... Smocking Arts Guild of America (EA)
SAGA .... Society of American Graphic Artists (EA)
SAGA .... South Australian Gymnastic Association
SAGA .... Soviet-American Gas and Aerosol [*Experiment*] (USDC)
SAGA .... Stage and Arena Guild of America
SAGA .... Studies, Analysis, and Gaming Agency [*Military*]
SAGA .... System for Automatic Generation and Analysis
SAGA-3 .... Third Soviet-American Gas and Aerosol [*Experiment*] [*Marine science*] (OSRA)
SAGA-3 .... Third Soviet-American Gas and Aerosol [*Experiment*] (USDC)
SagaCm .... Saga Communications, Inc. [*Associated Press*] (SAG)
SAGAGB .... Sand and Gravel Association of Great Britain (BI)
SAGAN .... Scientific Apprehension of God's Awesome Nature
SagaP .... Saga Petroleum AS [*Associated Press*] (SAG)
SAGB .... Schizophrenia Association of Great Britain
SAGB .... Senior Advisory Group on Biotechnology [*British*]
SAGB .... Skibob Association of Great Britain (DBA)
SAGB .... Spiritualist Association of Great Britain
SAGC .... Saint Andrews Golf Corp. [*NASDAQ symbol*] (SAG)
SAGCI .... Semiautomatic Ground Control of Interceptors [*Military*] (IAA)
SAGCW .... Saint Andrews Golf Wrrt [*NASDAQ symbol*] (TTSB)
Sag D .... Sagittal Diameter [*Radiology*] (DAVI)
SagDEG .... Sagittarius Dwarf Elliptical Galaxy [*Astrophysics*]
SAGE .... Sagebrush Inc. [*NASDAQ symbol*] (TTSB)
SAGE .... Science and Geography Education [*Database*]
SAGE .... Scientific Advisory Group on Effects [*DoD Washington, DC*] (EGAO)
SAGE .... Semiautomatic Ground Environment [*Military*]
SAGE .... Senior Action in a Gay Environment (EA)
SAGE .... Serial Analysis of Gene Expression [*Genetics*]
SAGE .... Skylab Advisory Group for Experiments [*NASA*]
SAGE .... Society for the Advancement of Good English [*Defunct*] (EA)
SAGE .... Society for the Advancement of the George Economy [*Defunct*] (EA)
SAGE .... Solar-Assisted Gas Energy [*Water heating*] [*NASA*]
SAGE .... South African General Electric Co.
SAGE .... South Australian Group of Chief Executives of Tertiary Institutions
SAGE .... Soviet-American Gallium Experiment [*Particle physics*]
SAGE .... Special Assistant for Growing Enterprises [*Division of National American Wholesale Grocer's Association*]
SAGE .... Spoiler Assisted Ground Effect (MCD)
SAGE .... Statistical Analysis Group in Education (EDAC)
SAGE .... Sterilization Aerospace Ground Equipment (KSC)
SAGE .... Strategic Analysis Guidance and Estimate (MCD)
SAGE .... Stratospheric Aerosol Gas Experiment
SAGE .... Styrene/Allyl Glycidyl Ether [*Organic chemistry*]
Sage C .... Sage Colleges (GAGS)
SAGEE .... Surface-Air-Generated Electronic Environment (SAA)
SageLb .... Sage Laboratories, Inc. [*Associated Press*] (SAG)
SAGEM .... Societe d'Applications Generals d'Electricite et de Mecanique [*France*]
SAGES .... Society American Gastrointestinal Endoscopic Surgeons (EA)
SAGFC .... Southeastern Association of Game and Fish Commissioners [*Later, SAFWA*] (EA)
SAGG .... South Australian Government Gazette [*A publication*]
SAGGA .... Scout and Guide Graduate Association [*British*] (BI)
SAGGA .... South Australian Grape Growers' Association
SAGGBS .... Salvation Army Guides and Guards, Brownies, and Sunbeams (EAIO)
SAGGE .... Synchronous Altitude Gravity Gradient Experiment
SAGI .... South-African Garrisons Institutes [*Military British*] (ROG)
SAGI .... Specialty Advertising Guild International [*Later, SAA*] (EA)
SAGJ .... South African Geographical Journal [*A publication*]
SAGM .... Separate Absorption, Grading, and Multiplication Layers [*Semiconductor technology*]
SAGMI .... Surface Attack Guided Missile (MCD)
SAGMOS .... Self-Aligning Gate Metal Oxide Semiconductor (IEEE)
SAGO .... Latin America Center [*Acronym is based on foreign phrase Belgium*]
SA-GOR .... Security Assistance - General Operational Requirement [*Military*] (AFIT)
SAGP .... Saturable Absorber Giant Pulsing (IAA)
SAGP .... Society for Ancient Greek Philosophy (EA)
SAGP .... Streptococcal Acidic Glycoprotein [*Antineoplastic drug*]
SAGPGG .... Sheep Anti-Guinea Pig Gamma Globulin (OA)
SAGRCB .... South Australian Greyhound Racing Control Board
SAGS .... Scandinavian-American Genealogical Society (EA)
SAGS .... Semiactive Gravity-Gradient System [*NASA*]
SAGSET .... Society for Academic Gaming and Simulation in Education and Training
SAGSET .... Society for the Advancement of Games and Simulation in Education and Training [*British*] (DBA)
SAGT .... Scottish Association of Geography Teachers [*British*]
SAGT .... Solarized Advanced Gas Turbine (MCD)
SAGT .... Systematic Approach to Group Technology (PDAA)
SAGTA .... School and Group Travel Association (EAIO)
SAGU .... Saguaro National Monument
Sag Val St C ... Saginaw Valley State College (GAGS)
SAGW .... Surface-to-Air Guided Weapon [*British*]
SaH .... Saat auf Hoffnung (BJA)
SAH .... Sachem Exploration [*Vancouver Stock Exchange symbol*]
SAH .... S-Adenosylhomocysteine [*Biochemistry*]
Sah .... Sahara
SAH .... Sample and Hold (IAA)
SAH .... Sanaa [*Yemen Arab Republic*] [*Airport symbol*] (OAG)
SaH .... Sandoz Pharmaceuticals [*Research code symbol*]
SAH .... Sayakhat [*Kazakhstan*] [*ICAO designator*] (FAAC)
SAH .... School of Applied Health [*University of Texas*]
SAH .... Security Archives Holdings [*Data storage company*] [*British*]
SAH .... Semiactive Homer [*Missiles*]
SAH .... Society of Aeronautical Historians [*Netherlands*] (EAIO)
SAH .... Society of American Historians [*Defunct*] (EA)
SAH .... Society of Architectural Historians (EA)
SAH .... Society of Automotive Historians (EA)
SAH .... Standard Allowed Hours
SAH .... Standard Average Hour (HGAA)
SAH .... Subarachnoid Hemorrhage [*Medicine*]
SAH .... Supreme Allied Headquarters [*World War II*]
SAH .... Systemic Arterial Hypertension [*Cardiology*] (DAVI)
SAHA .... Society of American Historical Artists (EA)
SahaG .... Sahara Gaming [*Associated Press*] (SAG)
SAHAND .... Society Against Have a Nice Day (NADA)
SAHARA .... Synthetic Aperture High Altitude RADAR (AAG)
SAHC .... Chosmadal [*Argentina ICAO location identifier*] (ICLI)
SAHC .... S-Adenosylhomocysteine [*Biochemistry*]
SAHC .... Scottish Australian Heritage Council
SAHC .... Scottish Australian Horse Council
SAHC .... Self-Aligning Hydraulic Cylinder
SAHC .... Sleep Analyzing Hybrid Computer (PDAA)
SAHCTL .... South Australian Hard Court Tennis League
SAHDA .... South Australian Huntingtons Disease Association
SAHF .... Semiautomatic Height Finder
SahGam .... Sahara Gaming [*Associated Press*] (SAG)
SAH(GB) .... Society of Architectural Historians (of Great Britain)
SAHH .... Society for Austrian and Habsburg History (EA)
SAHI .... Sagamore Hill National Historic Site
SAHL .... Salvation Army Home League [*See also LF*] (EAIO)
SaHMI .... Sachs, "History of Musical Instruments" [*A publication*]
SAHP .... Solar-Assisted Heat Pump (PDAA)
SAHPS .... Solar Energy Assisted Heat Pump System
SAHR .... Fuerte Gral Roca [*Argentina ICAO location identifier*] (ICLI)
SAHR .... Semi-Active Homing RADAR [*Military*] (RDA)
SAHR .... Society of Army Historical Research [*British*] (BI)
SAHR .... Spring Apply, Hydraulic Release [*Truck brakes*]
SAHRA .... South Australian Herd Recorders' Association
SAHRC .... South Australian Harness Racing Club
SAHRS .... Standard Attitude Heading Reference System (MCD)
SAHS .... Sleep Apnea-Hypersomnolence Syndrome [*Medicine*] (DMAA)
SAHS .... Swedish-American Historical Society (EA)
SAHS .... Swiss-American Historical Society (EA)
SAHSA .... Servicio Aereo de Honduras Sociedad Anonima
SAHSPA .... South Australian High School Principals' Association
SAHT .... South Australian Housing Trust
SAHYB .... Simulation of Analog and Hybrid Computers
SAI .... Saigo [*Japan*] [*Seismograph station code, US Geological Survey*] (SEIS)
SAI .... Sales Activity Index [*Business*] (MHDB)
SAI .... Schizophrenics Anonymous International [*Later, Canadian Schizophrenia Foundation*] (EA)
SAI .... Science Applications, Inc. (NRCH)
SAI .... Science Associates/International [*Publisher*] (EA)

SAI .... Scientific Aid to Indochina [*Task force established 1973 by Scientists' Institute for Public Information*]
SAI .... Scientific Associates, Inc. (AAG)
SAI .... Scottish Agricultural Industries [*Commercial firm*]
SAI .... Scriptwriters' Association International [*Defunct*] (EA)
SAI .... Secondary Air Injection [*Automotive engineering*]
SAI .... Self-Actualization Inventory [*Test*]
SAI .... Self-Analysis Inventory [*Psychology*]
SAI .... Senior Advocates International [*Defunct*] (EA)
SAI .... Senior Army Instructor
SAI .... Shaheen Air International [*Pakistan*] [*ICAO designator*] (FAAC)
SAI .... Shoplifters Anonymous International (EA)
SAI .... Sigma Alpha Iota [*International professional music fraternity for women*] (EA)
SAI .... Social Adequacy Index
SAI .... Societa Anonima Italiana [*Stock company*] [*Italian*]
SAI .... Society of American Inventors (EA)
SAI .... Software Access International, Inc. [*Information service or system*] (IID)
SAI .... Sold as Is [*Philately*]
SAI .... Son Altesse Imperiale [*His or Her Imperial Highness*] [*French*]
sai .... South American Indian [*MARC language code Library of Congress*] (LCCP)
SAI .... Southern Alberta Institute of Technology [*UTLAS symbol*]
SAI .... Special Accident Insurance (MCD)
SAI .... Specific Acoustic Impedance
SAI .... Spherical Attitude Indicator (MCD)
SAI .... Standby Airspeed [*or Attitude*] Indicator (MCD)
SAI .... State Agency Issuance [*Employment and Training Administration*] (OICC)
SAI .... Statement of Additional Information [*Finances*] (BARN)
SAI .... Steering Axis Inclination [*Automotive engineering*]
SAI .... Stern Activities Index [*Psychology*]
SAI .... Storage and Inspection (IAA)
SAI .... Student Aid Index [*Department of Education*] (GFGA)
SAI .... Subarchitectural Interface
SAI .... Suburban Action Institute [*Later, MAI*] (EA)
SAI .... Sudden Auroral Intensity
SAI .... Sugar Association, Inc. (EA)
SAI .... Sunamerica Capital Trust [*NYSE symbol*] (SAG)
SAI .... Sunamerica Capital Trust II [*NYSE symbol*] (SAG)
SAI .... Sunamerica Capital Trust III [*NYSE symbol*] (SAG)
SAI .... SunAmerica, Inc. [*Formerly, Broad, Inc.*] [*NYSE symbol*] (SPSG)
SAI .... Surveillance Aided Intercept (NVT)
SAI .... Surveillance and Inspection (IAA)
SAI .... System Analysis Indicator (MCD)
SAIA .... Survival of American Indians Association (EA)
SAIAN .... Survey of American Indians and Alaska Natives [*Department of Health and Human Services*] (GFGA)
SAIAS .... Ship Aircraft Inertial Alignment System (NG)
SAIB .... Safe Area Intelligence Brief (MCD)
SAIB .... Sucrose Acetate Isobutyrate [*Organic chemistry*]
SAIC .... School of the Art Institute of Chicago
SAIC .... Science Applications International Corp.
SAIC .... Science Applications International Corporation [*Marine science*] (OSRA)
SAIC .... Ship Acquisition and Improvement Council [*Navy*] (ANA)
SAIC .... Small Arms Interpost Competition [*Military*]
SAIC .... South African Indian Congress (PD)
SAIC .... Special Agent in Charge [*Department of the Treasury*]
SAIC .... State Actuary and Insurance Commissioner [*Queensland, Australia*]
SAIC .... Switch Action Interrupt Count
SAICAR .... Succinoaminoimidazolecarboxamide Ribonucleotide [*Biochemistry*]
SAICETT .... South African Institute of Civil Engineering Technicians and Technologists (EAIO)
SAICIC .... South Australian Industrial Court and Industrial Commission
SAIC-WG .... Ship Acquisition and Improvement Council-Working Group [*Navy*] (ANA)
SAID .... Safe Area Intelligence Description (MCD)
SAID .... Safety Analysis Input Data [*Nuclear energy*] (NRCH)
SAID .... Semiautomatic Integrated Documentation
SAID .... Shuttle Avionics Integration Division [*NASA*] (SSD)
SAID .... Specific Adaptation to Improved Demands [*Sports medicine*]
SAID .... Speech Auto-Instructional Device
SAID .... Supplementary Aviation Information Display
SAIDA .... Spaced Antenna Imaging Doppler Interferometer [*Marine science*] (OSRA)
SAIDET .... Single-Axis Inertial Drift Erection Test
SAIDI .... Spaced Antenna Imaging Doppler Interferometer (USDC)
SAIDS .... Simian Acquired Immunodeficiency Syndrome [*Animal pathology*]
SAIDS .... Space Analyst Intervention Display System (MCD)
SAIE .... Source and Application Inspection Equipment
SAIE .... Special Acceptance Inspection Equipment
SAIER .... South Australian Institute of Educational Research
SAIF .... Savings Association Insurance Fund [*Functions transferred from FSLIC, 1989*] [*Pronounced "safe"*]
SAIF .... Southern Africa Institute of Fundraising (NFD)
SAIF .... Standard Avionics Integrated Fuzing [*Air Force*]
SAIFER .... Safe Arm Initiation from Electromagnetic Radiation
SAIH .... Studentenes og Akademikernes Internasjonale Hjelpefond [*Norway*]
SAIIC .... South and Central American Indian Information Center (EA)
SAIL .... Charter Bancshares [*NASDAQ symbol*] (SPSG)
SAIL .... Sea-Air Interaction Laboratory [*Oceanography*]
SAIL .... Serial ASCII Instrument Loop [*Computer science*] (OSI)
SAIL .... Ship Active Item Listing (DNAB)
SAIL .... Ship's Armament Inventory List [*Navy*]
SAIL .... Shuttle Avionics Integration Laboratory [*NASA*]
SAIL .... Simple Analytical Interactive Language [*Computer science*]
SAIL .... Staged Assessment in Learning (AIE)
SAIL .... Stanford Artificial Intelligence Laboratory [*Stanford University*]
SAIL .... Stanford Artificial Intelligence Language (NITA)
SAIL .... Steel Authority of India Ltd. [*Commercial firm*]
SAILA .... Sail Assist International Liaison Associates (EA)
SAILA .... Sault Area International Library Association [*Library network*]
SAILA .... Simplified Aircraft Instrument Landing System (PDAA)
SAILEDREP .... Sailing Report [*Navy*] (NVT)
SAILER .... Staffing of African Institutions for Legal Education and Research [*Later, I nternational Legal Center*] [*An association*]
SAILORD .... Sailing Order [*Navy*] (NVT)
SAILREP .... Sailing Report [*Navy*]
SAILS .... Seagoing Assembly-Integration-Launch System
SAILS .... Simplified Aircraft Instrument Landing System
SAILS .... Standard Army Intermediate Level Supply System [*or Subsystem*]
SAILS .... Swets Automated Independant Library System (NITA)
SAIM .... Scottish Amicable Investment Managers [*Finance*]
SAIM .... Semiautomatic Inserting Machine (SAA)
SAIM .... South America Indian Mission [*Later, SAM*] (EA)
SAIM .... System Analysis and Integration Model (IAA)
SAIM .... Systems Analysis and Integration Model (MCD)
SAIMA .... Selected Acquisitions Information and Management System (PDAA)
SAIMI .... Societe des Amis de l'Institut Metapsychique International [*Society of Friends of the International Metaphysical Institute*] (EAIO)
SAIMR .... South African Institute for Medical Research
SAIMS .... Selected Acquisitions, Information, and Management System
SAIMS .... Supersonic Airborne Infrared Measurement System (MCD)
SAIN .... Society for Advancement in Nursing (EA)
Sainan-G-D .... Sainan-Gakuin-Daigaku (BJA)
SAINET .... Science Applications, Inc. Global Computer Network (MCD)
Saint .... Saint's Digest of Registration Cases [*England*] [*A publication*] (DLA)
SAINT .... Salzburg Assembly: Impact of the New Technology
SAINT .... Satellite Array for International and National Telecommunications (MCD)
SAINT .... Satellite Inspection Technique (MCD)
SAINT .... Satellite Inspector and Satellite Interceptor [*Air Force spacecraft program*]
SAINT .... Satellite Interceptor (KSC)
SAINT .... Self-Aligning Implantation of N-Layer Technology (MCD)
SAINT .... Strategic Artificially Intelligent Nuclear Transport [*Robot series designation in 1986 movie "Short Circuit"*]
SAINT .... Symbolic Automatic Integrator
SAINT .... Systems Analysis of an Integrated Network of Tasks [*Air Force*]
SAINTS .... Single Attack Integrated System
SAIORG .... Supreme Assembly, International Order of Rainbow for Girls [*Freemasonry*] (EA)
SAIP .... Service Aircraft Instrumentation Package (MCD)
SAIP .... Ship Acquisition and Improvement Panel [*Navy*] (CAAL)
SAIP .... Societe d'Applications Industrielle de la Physique
SAIP .... Spares Acquisition Integrated with Production
SAIP .... Submarine Antenna Improvement Program [*Military*]
SAIP .... Systems Acquisition and Implementation Program [*Environmental Protection Agency*] (GFGA)
SAIPL .... Spares Acquisition Incorporated with Production List (MCD)
SAIPMS .... Science Applications Incorporated Plan Monitoring System
SAIPrB .... SunAmerica 9 1/4% cm'B'Pfd [*NYSE symbol*] (TTSB)
SAIPrE .... SunAmerica Dep'E'Pfd [*NYSE symbol*] (TTSB)
SAIPrT .... SunAmer Cap 9.95% 'TOPrS' [*NYSE symbol*] (TTSB)
SAIPrV .... SunAmer Cap II 8.35%'TOPrS' [*NYSE symbol*] (TTSB)
SAIR .... Saugus Ironworks National Historic Site
SAIR .... Semiannual Inventory Report [*Military*] (AFM)
SAIR .... Southern Association for Institutional Research (EDAC)
SAIRI .... Supreme Assembly for the Islamic Revolution in Iraq [*Political party*] (ECON)
SAIRR .... South African Institute of Racial Relations
SAIRS .... Standardized Advanced Infrared System [*Army*]
SAIS .... School of Advanced International Studies
SAIS .... School of Advanced International Studies [*Johns Hopkins University*]
SAIS .... Science and Applications Information System (SSD)
SAIS .... Societa Agricola Italo-Somala [*Italo-Somali Agricultural Society*]
SAIS .... Society for American Indian Studies (EA)
SAIS .... Southwestern American Indian Society [*Later, SAISR*] (EA)
SAISA .... South Atlantic Intercollegiate Sailing Association
SAISAC .... Ship's Aircraft Inertial System Alignment Console
SAISB .... South African Individual Scale for the Blind [*Intelligence test*]
SAISB .... South Australian Independent Schools' Board
SAI-SDDL .... Science Applications, Inc. - Software Design and Documentation Language (MCD)
SAISR .... Society for American Indian Studies and Research [*Formerly, SAIS*] (EA)
SAIT .... Southern Alberta Institute of Technology [*Calgary, AB*]
SAITR .... Special Artificer, Instruments, Typewriter, and Office Equipment Repairman [*Navy*]
SAIW .... Sun Artificial Intelligence Workstation
SAIWR .... Special Artificer, Instruments, Watch Repairman [*Navy*]
SAJ .... Golden Eagle Air Services Ltd. [*Canada ICAO designator*] (FAAC)
SAJ .... Saint Joseph Light & Power [*NYSE symbol*] (SAG)
SAJ .... Saints Alive in Jesus (EA)
SAJ .... Salon Resources Corp. [*Vancouver Stock Exchange symbol*]
SAJ .... Sirajgang [*Bangladesh*] [*Airport symbol*] (AD)
SAJ .... Society for the Advancement of Judaism (EA)
SAJ .... St. Joseph Light & Power Co. [*NYSE symbol*] (SPSG)

SAJ St. Joseph Lt & Pwr [*NYSE symbol*] (TTSB)
SAJA Special Approaches to Juvenile Assistance [*Defunct*] (EA)
SAJAA South African Journal of African Affairs [*A publication*]
SAJC Southern Association of Junior Colleges (AEBS)
SAJH San Juan Island National Historic Park
SAJI Saw Jig [*Tool*]
SAJIB Societe d'Animation du Jardin et de l'Institut Botaniques [*Canada*]
SAJMMC San Antonio Joint Military Medical Command
SAJS School for Advanced Jewish Studies (BJA)
SAJS South African Journal of Science [*A publication*]
SAK Die Sumerischen und Akkadischen Koeningsinschriften [*A publication*] (BJA)
SAK Kalispell, MT [*Location identifier FAA*] (FAAL)
SAK Red Arrows Display Squadron [*British ICAO designator*] (FAAC)
SAK Sakata [*Japan*] [*Seismograph station code, US Geological Survey*] (SEIS)
SAK Saudarkrokur [*Iceland*] [*Airport symbol*] (OAG)
SAK Stall Lake Mines [*Vancouver Stock Exchange symbol*]
SAK Stop Acknowledge (CMD)
SAK Sveriges Arbetarepartiet Kommunisterna [*Swedish Workers' Communist Party*] [*Political party*] (PPW)
SAK University of Saskatchewan Libraries [*UTLAS symbol*]
SAKB Suider Afrikaanse Katolieke Biskopsraad [*Southern African Catholic Bishops' Conference - SACBC*] (EAIO)
SAKI Saudi Arabia - Kuwait - Iraq
SAKI Solatron Automatic Keyboard Instructor
SAL Anderson County Library, Anderson, SC [*OCLC symbol*] (OCLC)
SAL Caspair Ltd. [*Kenya*] [*ICAO designator*] (FAAC)
SAL Saharan Air Layer [*Meteorology*]
SAL Salad (WGA)
SAL Salary (ADA)
SAL Sale and Leaseback (MHDW)
sal Salicylate [*Medicine*]
SAL Salina [*Diocesan abbreviation*] [*Kansas*] (TOCD)
SAL Saline
Sal Salinger's Reports [*88-117 Iowa*] [*A publication*] (DLA)
SAL Salinometer (KSC)
sal Salishan [*MARC language code Library of Congress*] (LCCP)
sal Saliva (MAE)
SAL Salivation [*Treatment for syphilis*] [*Slang British*] (DSUE)
sal Salmon [*Philately*]
Sal Salmonella [*Bacteriology*]
SAL Salo [*Italy*] [*Seismograph station code, US Geological Survey*] (SEIS)
sal Salt (MAE)
SAL Saluting (MSA)
SAL Salvation Army Shelter (DSUE)
SAL Salvex Resources Ltd. [*Vancouver Stock Exchange symbol*]
SAL Sandhills Agriculture Laboratory [*University of Nebraska - Lincoln*] [*Research center*] (RCD)
SAL San Salvador [*El Salvador*] [*Airport symbol*] (OAG)
SAL Saperstein & Associates Ltd. [*Vancouver, BC*] [*Telecommunications*] (TSSD)
SAL Saskatchewan Accelerator Laboratory [*University of Saskatchewan*] [*Canada*] (IRC)
SAL Savings and Loan (IAA)
SAL Scientific Airlock (MCD)
SAL Sea-Animal Locomotion (SAA)
SAL Seaboard Air Line Railroad [*Later, SCL*] [*AAR code*]
SAL Secundum Artis Leges [*According to the Rules of the Art*] [*Latin*] (ADA)
SAL Selected Altitude Layer [*Decoder*]
SAL Semiactive LASER [*Military*]. (CAAL)
SAL Senior High Income Portfolio II [*NYSE symbol*] (SPSG)
SAL Sensorineural Acuity Level [*Medicine*]
SAL Sequential Analysis of Chemistry Constituents (DAVI)
SAL Service Action Log (AAG)
SAL Ship Authorized Leave (NG)
SAL Ship Authorized Level (MCD)
SAL Shipboard Allowance List (MSA)
SAL Short Approach Light [*Aviation*]
SAL Shuttle Avionics Laboratory [*NASA*] (NASA)
SAL Solar Arc Lamp
SAL Solar Array Leaf
SAL Sons of the American Legion (EA)
SAL South American Program Library (IAA)
SAL South Atlantic League [*Nickname: Sally*] [*Baseball*]
SAL Southern Airlines [*Australia*]
SAL Space Astronomy Laboratory [*University of Florida*] [*Research center*] (RCD)
SAL Special Ammunition Load [*Army*] (AABC)
SAL SQL [*Structured Query Language*] Windows Application Language [*Computer science*]
SAL Standard Acceptance Limits
SAL Station Allowance Unit (NATG)
SAL Strategic Arms Limitation
SAL Strong Acid Leach (PDAA)
SAL Structural Adjustment Loan [*World Bank*]
SAL Structured Assembly Language
SAL Subject Authority List [*NASA*]
SAL Submarine Alerting and Loading System
SAL Submarine Alerting and Locating [*Navy*]
SAL Suid-Afrikaanse Lugmag [*South African Air Force*] [*See also SALM, SAAF*]
SAL Supersonic Aerophysics Laboratory (MCD)
SAL Supply and Logistics (IAA)
SAL Surface Mail Air Lifted (ADA)
SAL Symbolic Assembly Language [*Computer science*] (DIT)
SAL System Access Layer [*Computer science*]
SAL Systems and Logistics (IAA)
SAL Systems Assembly Language [*Computer science*] (IEEE)
SALA Scientific Assistant Land Agent [*Ministry of Agriculture, Fisheries, and Food*] [*British*]
SALA Secret Army for the Liberation of Armenia
SALA Servicios Aeronauticos Latina America
SALA Solar Arc Lamp Assembly
SALA Southwest Alliance for Latin America [*Defunct*] (EA)
SALALM Seminar on the Acquisition of Latin American Library Materials (EA)
SalAMGN Salomon, Inc. [*Associated Press*] (SAG)
Salant Salant Corp. [*Associated Press*] (SAG)
SA Law Reports CP South African Law Reports, Cape Provincial Division [*1910-46*] [*A publication*] (DLA)
SA Law Reports CPD South African Law Reports, Cape Provincial Division [*1910-46*] [*A publication*] (DLA)
SA Law Reports NPD South African Law Reports, Natal Province Division [*1910-46*] [*A publication*] (DLA)
SA Law Reports SWA Reports of the High Court of South-West Africa [*A publication*] (DLA)
SALC Sacramento Air Logistics Center (NASA)
SALC Secret Army for the Liberation of Corsica
SALC Special Associated Logistics Course (MCD)
Sal Comp Cr Salaman's Liquidation and Composition with Creditors [*2nd ed.*] [*1882*] [*A publication*] (DLA)
SALCV Solanum Apical Leaf-Curling Virus
SALD Fresh Choice [*NASDAQ symbol*] (TTSB)
SALD Fresh Choice, Inc. [*NASDAQ symbol*] (SAG)
SalDEC Salomon, Inc. [*Associated Press*] (SAG)
SALDRI Semiautomatic Low-Data-Rate Input (SAA)
SALDV Salvage Dive [*Military*] (MUGU)
SALE Safeguards Analytical Laboratory Evaluation [*Nuclear energy*]
SALE Silicon Avalanche Light Emitter
SALE Simple Algebraic Language for Engineers [*Computer science*]
SALE Simulated Air Launch Environment (MCD)
SALE Society for Airline Meteorologists (IAA)
SALE Special Ammunition Logistical Element
SALEA South Australian Livestock Exporters' Association
Salem Salem Corp. [*Associated Press*] (SAG)
Salem St C Salem State College (GAGS)
SALES Ship Aircraft Locating Equipment
SALF Society of American Legion Founders [*Defunct*] (EA)
SALF Somali Abo Liberation Front [*Ethiopia*] [*Political party*] (PD)
SALF Sudan African Liberation Front
SALFAS Stand-Alone Low-Frequency Active Sonar (DOMA)
SALG South American Liaison Group (CINC)
SALGEP Scottish Association of Local Government to Educational Psychologists [*British*]
SALGGC South Australian Local Government Grants Commission
SAL-GP Semiactive LASER-Guided Projectile (MCD)
SALH South Alberta Light Horse (DMA)
SalHWP Salomon, Inc. [*Associated Press*] (SAG)
SALI Selected Abstracts: Library, Information [*Australia A publication*]
SALI Surface Analysis by LASER Ionization
SALIC Salicional [*Music*]
Salick Salick Health Care, Inc. [*Associated Press*] (SAG)
salicyl Salicylate (BABM)
salicyl Salicylate [*Pharmacology*] (DAVI)
SALINET Satellite Library Information Network
SAL/IR Semiactive LASER/Infrared (DWSG)
SALIS Salisbury [*England*]
SALIS Substance Abuse Librarians and Information Specialists (EA)
Salisbury St U Salisbury State University (GAGS)
Saliva Saliva Diagnostic Systems [*Commercial firm Associated Press*] (SAG)
Salk Salkeld's English King's Bench Reports [*91 English Reprint*] [*A publication*] (DLA)
Salk (Eng) Salkeld's English King's Bench Reports [*91 English Reprint*] [*A publication*] (DLA)
SALL Sallust [*Roman historian, 86-34BC*] [*Classical studies*] (ROG)
SALL Shore Activity Load List
SALLB South Australian Law Librarians Bulletin [*A publication*]
SallieM Student Loan Marketing [*Associated Press*] (SAG)
SALLIE MAE Student Loan Marketing Association [*See also SLMA*]
SallM Student Loan Marketing Association [*Sallie Mae*] [*Associated Press*] (SAG)
Salm Salmagundi [*A publication*] (BRI)
Salm Salmanassar (BJA)
SALM Salvation Army League of Mercy [*British*] (EAIO)
SALM Single Anchor Leg Mooring [*Oil platform*]
SALM Society of Air Line Meteorologists
SALMA South American Land Mammal Age [*Geological epoch*]
Salm Abr Salmon's Abridgment of State Trials [*A publication*] (DLA)
Salmant Salmanticensis [*Salamanca, Spain*] [*A publication*] (BJA)
SalmHIF Salomon Brothers High Income Fund [*Associated Press*] (SAG)
Salmn Salomon, Inc. [*Associated Press*] (SAG)
SalmSBF Salomon Brothers Fund [*Associated Press*] (SAG)
SalMSFT Salomon, Inc. [*Associated Press*] (SAG)
Salm St R Salmon's Edition of the State Trials [*A publication*] (DLA)
Salnt Salant Corp. [*Associated Press*] (SAG)
SALO State Aviation Liaison Official (NOAA)
SALO Stop Authorization and Lift Order (AAG)

Sal08Ww..... Salomon Brothers 2008 Worldwide Dollar Government Term Trust [*Associated Press*] (SAG)
SALOA......... Special Arc Light Operation Area (DNAB)
Salomn........ Salomon, Inc. [*Associated Press*] (SAG)
SALON......... Satellite Balloon (IAA)
SALOON...... Satellite Launched from a Balloon (IAA)
SALOP......... Shrewsbury [*British depot code*]
SALOP......... Shropshire [*County in England*]
SalORCL...... Salomon, Inc. [*Associated Press*] (SAG)
SALORS....... Structural Analysis of Layered Orthotropic Ring-Stiffened Shells [*Computer program*] [*NASA*]
SALP............ Sodium Aluminum Phosphate [*Inorganic chemistry*]
SALP............ South African Labour Party
SALP............ Systematic Assessment of Licensee Performance [*Nuclear energy*] (NRCH)
SALPA......... Special Adult Learning Programmes Association (AIE)
SalPage....... Salomon Page Group Ltd. [*Associated Press*] (SAG)
SalPge......... Salomon Page Group Ltd. [*Associated Press*] (SAG)
SalPge......... Solomon Page Group Ltd. [*Associated Press*] (SAG)
SalPhib....... Salomon Phibro Oil Trust [*Associated Press*] (SAG)
SalPRI......... Salomon, Inc. [*Associated Press*] (SAG)
SALR........... Saturation Adiabatic Lapse Rate [*Meteorology*] (ADA)
SALR........... Synthetic Aperture LASER RADAR
SALRC......... Society for the Assistance of Ladies in Reduced Circumstances [*British*] (DI)
SALRCP....... South African Law Reports, Cape Provincial Division [*1910-46*] [*A publication*] (DLA)
SAL Reports OPD... South African Law Reports, Orange Free State Provincial Division [*1910-46*] [*A publication*] (DLA)
SALR SWA... South African Law Reports, South West African Reports [*A publication*] (DLA)
SALS........... Separate Access Landing System [*Aviation*] (DA)
SALS........... Short Approach Light System [*Aviation*]
SALS........... Simple Approach Lighting System [*Aviation*] (FAAC)
SALS........... Single Anchor Leg Storage (PDAA)
SALS........... Small-Angle Light Scattering
SALS........... Solid-State Acoustoelectric Light Scanner
SALS........... Southern Adirondack Library System [*Library network*]
SALS........... Southern African Literature Society [*Botswana*] (EAIO)
SALS........... Standard Army Logistics System
SALSC......... Scottish Association of Local Sports Councils (DBA)
SALSF......... Short Approach Light System with Sequenced Flashers [*Aviation*]
SALS-K........ Single Ammunition Logistics System - Korea (MCD)
SalSNPL...... Salomon, Inc. [*Associated Press*] (SAG)
SALSU......... Singapore Admiralty Local Staff Union
SaLSUA....... Sierra Leone Students Union of the Americas (EA)
Salt............. De Saltatione [*of Lucian*] [*Classical studies*] (OCD)
SALT........... Saltash [*England*]
SALT........... Salton/Maxim Housewares [*NASDAQ symbol*] (SPSG)
SALT........... Salvation and Laughter Together [*Defunct*] (EA)
SALT........... Self-Contained All-Weather Landing and Taxiing (MCD)
SALT........... Serum Alanine Aminotransferase [*An enzyme*]
SALT........... Signal and Homing Light (IAA)
SALT........... Sisters All Learning Together [*Feminist group*]
SALT........... Size, Activity, Location, Type Report [*Military*] (INF)
SALT........... Skin-Associated Lymphoid Tissue [*Dermatology*]
SALT........... Society for Applied Learning Technology (EA)
SALT........... Society of American Law Teachers (EA)
SALT........... South African Law Times [*A publication*] (DLA)
SALT........... Speech and Language Technology [*British*]
SALT........... Stand Alone Terminal (IAA)
SALT........... State Agency Libraries of Texas [*Library network*]
SALT........... Strategic Arms Limitation Treaty (MCD)
SALT........... Subscribers' Apparatus Line Tester [*Telecommunications*] (TEL)
SALT........... Suggestive-Accelerative Learning and Teaching (EDAC)
SALT........... Supporting Arms Liaison Team [*Army*] (INF)
SALT........... Swedish Aspirin Low-Dose Trial
SALT........... Symbolic Algebraic Language Translator [*Computer science*]
SALTE......... Semiautomatic Line Test Equipment (NG)
SalTerz........ Sal Terrae. Revista Hispanoamericana de Cultura Ecclesiastica [*Santander, Spain*] [*A publication*] (BJA)
SALTHQ....... Strike Command Alternate Headquarters [*Military*] (AABC)
SALTI........... Summary Accounting for Low-Dollar Turnover Items [*Army*]
SALTIRE...... Scottish Academic Live Television Interconnect and Research Environment (AIE)
SaltMax....... Salton Maxim Housewares, Inc. [*Associated Press*] (SAG)
SALT-P........ Slosson Articulation, Language Test with Phonology [*Child development test*]
SALTS......... Streamlined Alternative Logistics Transmission System (DOMA)
SALTS......... Streamlined Automated Logistics Transmission System
SALTS......... Systems Alterations Status
SALUT......... Sea, Air, Land, and Underwater Targets [*Navy*]
SALUTE....... Size, Activity, Location, Unit, Time, Equipment (MCD)
SALV........... Duty Salvage Ship [*Navy*] (NVT)
SALV........... Saliva Diagnostic Systems [*NASDAQ symbol*] (SAG)
SALV........... Salvador [*Brazil*] (ROG)
SALV........... Salvage [*Military*] (AFM)
SALVDIVB.... Salvage Diver Badge [*Military decoration*] (GFGA)
Salv Div Bad... Salvage Diver Badge [*Military decoration*]
SALVDV....... Salvage Dives [*Army*]
SALVEX....... Salvage Exercise (MCD)
SALVOPS..... Salvage Operations [*Navy*] (NVT)
SALVTNG..... Salvage Training [*Navy*] (NVT)
SALVW........ Saliva Diagnostic Sys Wrrt [*NASDAQ symbol*] (TTSB)
SALWIS....... Shipboard Air-Launched Weapons Installation System (NG)
SalWw......... Salomon Brothers Worldwide Income Fund [*Associated Press*] (SAG)
SALX........... Shamrock Airlines [*Air carrier designation symbol*]
SALX........... Synergistic Holding Corp. [*NASDAQ symbol*] (SAG)
SALY........... Salary (ROG)
SAM............ Boston Beer 'A' [*NYSE symbol*] (TTSB)
SAM............ Boston Beer Co. [*NYSE symbol*] (SAG)
SAM............ Eparchy of St. Maron of Brooklyn [*Diocesan abbreviation*] [*United States of America*] (TOCD)
SAM............ Saba [*Netherlands Antilles*] [*Airport symbol*] (AD)
SAM............ S-Adenosylmethionine [*Also, AdoMet, SAMe*] [*Biochemistry*]
SAM............ Safety Activation Monitor (IEEE)
SAM............ Salamo [*Papua New Guinea*] [*Airport symbol*] (OAG)
SAM............ Salicylamide [*Analgesic compound*]
Sam............. Samaria (BJA)
Sam............. Samaritan (BJA)
sam............. Samaritan Aramaic [*MARC language code Library of Congress*] (LCCP)
SAM............ Samarkand [*Former USSR Seismograph station code, US Geological Survey*] (SEIS)
Sam............. Samoa (BARN)
SAM............ Sample and Analysis Management System [*Computer science*]
SAM............ Sampling and Analytical Method
Sam............. Samson (BJA)
SAM............ Samsville, IL [*Location identifier FAA*] (FAAL)
Sam............. Samuel [*Old Testament book*]
SAM............ Scanning Acoustic Microscope
SAM............ Scanning Auger Microprobe (IAA)
SAM............ Scanning Auger Microscopy
SAM............ School-Aged Maternity (EDAC)
SAM............ School Apperception Method [*Psychology*]
SAM............ School Attitude Measure [*Test*] [*Canadian Comprehensive Assessment Program*]
SAM............ School in Agency Management [*LIMRA*]
SAM............ School of Aerospace Medicine [*Formerly, School of Aviation Medicine*]
SAM............ School of Assets Management [*Later, School of Materiel Readiness*] [*Army*]
SAM............ Scottish Association of Metals (DBA)
SAM............ Screen Activated Machine [*Parimutuel wagering*]
SAM............ Script Applier Mechanism [*Programming language*] [*1975*] (CSR)
SAM............ Sea Air Mariner
SAM............ Selective Automatic Monitoring
SAM............ Selective Automonitoring Tracing Routine (IAA)
SAM............ Self Addressing Memory (IAA)
SAM............ Self-Administered Medication [*Medicine*] (MEDA)
SAM............ Self-Administered Medication (DAVI)
SAM............ Self-Assembled Monolayer [*Physical chemistry*]
SAM............ Self-Propelled Anthropomorphic Manipulator [*Moon machine*]
SAM............ Semantic Analyzing Machine
SAM............ Semiautomatic Active Memory (SAA)
SAM............ Semiautomatic Film Mounter (SAA)
SAM............ Semiautomatic Mathematics (IEEE)
SAM............ Semiautomatic Mounter [*3M Co.*]
SAM............ Semiautonomous Acoustic/Magnetic [*Vehicle*] (DOMA)
SAM............ Semiconductor Active Memory [*Computer science*] (IAA)
SAM............ Semiconductor Advanced Memory [*Computer science*] (IAA)
SAM............ Send-a-Message (MCD)
SAM............ Sensing with Active Microwave
SAM............ Sequence and Monitor (IAA)
SAM............ Sequential Access Memory [*Computer science*] (IEEE)
SAM............ Sequential Access Method [*IBM Corp.*] [*Computer science*]
SAM............ Serial Access Memory [*Computer science*]
SAM............ Service Aggregated Module
SAM............ Service Attitude Measurement [*Bell System*]
SAM............ Sex Arousal Mechanism [*Medicine*]
SAM............ Shared Appreciation Mortgage [*Banking*]
SAM............ Shoot Apical Meristem [*Botany*]
SAM............ Shuttle Attachment Manipulator [*NASA*]
SAM............ Signal Analyzing Monitor (KSC)
SAM............ Signal [*System*] for Assessment and Modification [*of behavior*] [*Patented*]
SAM............ Simple Architecture Microprocessor
SAM............ Simulated Assignment Model
SAM............ Simulation of Analog Methods [*Computer science*]
SAM............ Single Application Method [*College admissions*]
SAM............ Sinusoidal Amplitude Modulation [*Physics*]
SA/M........... Site Assessment and Mitigation
SAM............ Six-Axis Manipulator (PDAA)
SAM............ Sociedad Aeronautica de Medellin [*Colombia*] [*ICAO designator*] (FAAC)
SAM............ Sociedad Aeronautica de Medellin Consolidada [*Colorado*]
SAM............ Societe des Americanistes
SAM............ Society for Adolescent Medicine (EA)
SAM............ Society for Advancement of Management [*Cincinnati, OH*] (EA)
SAM............ Society for Asian Music (EA)
SAM............ Society of Aerospace Medicine (NADA)
SAM............ Society of Americanists [*Paris, France*] (EA)
SAM............ Society of American Magicians (EA)
SAM............ Society of Antique Modelers (EA)
SAM............ Software Acquisition Manager (AAGC)
SAM............ Soldier, Sailor, Airman, Marine [*A publication*]
SAM............ Soluble Adhesion Molecule [*Biochemistry*]
SAM............ Something About Myself Inventory (EDAC)
SAM............ Sort and Merge
SAM............ Sound Absorption Material [*Aviation*]

SAM............ Sound-Activated Mobile (PDAA)
SAM............ Sourcebook in Applied Mathematics [*National Science Foundation project*]
S Am............ South America (VRA)
SAM............ South America Mission (EA)
SAM............ South American
SAM............ South American Region [*USTTA*] (TAG)
SAM............ Southern Appalachian Migrant [*Cincinnati slang*]
SAM............ Space Age Microcircuits (IAA)
SAM............ Space Assemble and Maintenance (SSD)
SAM............ Space Available Mail [*Military*] (AABC)
SAM............ Special Advisory Message
SAM............ Special Air Mission [*Aircraft*] [*Military*]
SAM............ Spills, Accidents, and Mixtures [*of Exxon Corp.'s "Stop SAM" safety program*]
SAM............ Spinal Analysis Machine
SAM............ Squarewave Amplitude Modulation
SAM............ Stabilized Assay Meter (NRCH)
SAM............ Stage Assembly and Maintenance [*Building*]
SAM............ Standard Addition Method [*Mathematics*]
SAM............ Standard Analysis Method
SAM............ Standard Assembly Module [*Eastman Kodak Co.*]
SAM............ Standard Avionics Module (MCD)
SAM............ Station Acquisition Marketing Plan [*PBS*] (NTCM)
SAM............ Stationing Analysis Model [*Military*] (GFGA)
SAM............ Stimuli and Measurements (KSC)
SAM............ Strachey and McIlroy [*in SAM/76, a programming language named after its authors and developed in 1976*] (CSR)
SAM............ Stratospheric Aerosol Measurement [*or Monitor*] [*Meteorology*]
SAM............ Strela Antiaircraft Missiles
SAM............ Streptozocin, Adriamycin, Methyl-CCNU [*or Semustine*] [*Antineoplastic drug regimen*] (DAVI)
SAM............ Stroboscopic Analyzing Monitor [*Instrumentation*]
SAM............ Strong Absorption Model [*Nuclear physics*] (OA)
SAM............ Structural Acoustic Monitor
SAM............ Structural Assembly Model [*NASA*]
SAM............ Student Achievement Monitoring [*Vocational guidance*]
SAM............ Study of American Markets [*US News and World Report*]
SAM............ Subject Activity Monitor [*Device used in biological research*]
SAM............ Subsequent Address Message [*Telecommunications*] (TEL)
SAM............ Substitute Alloy Material [*Nuclear energy*]
SAM............ Substrate Adhesion Molecule [*Cytology*]
SAM............ Substrate-Attached Material [*Cytology*]
SAM............ Subsynoptic Advection Model
SAM............ Subsystem Action Message [*Military*]
SAM............ Subtraction, Addition, Multiplication
SAM............ Sulfated Acid Mucopolysaccharide [*Medicine*] (MAE)
SAM............ Sulfur-Asphalt Module [*Road-paving technology*]
SAM............ Surface-Active Material
SAM............ Surface-to-Air Missile
SAM............ Symantec Antivirus for Macintosh [*Computer science*] (CDE)
SAM............ Symbolic and Algebraic Manipulation (IEEE)
SAM............ Synchronous Amplitude Modulation
SAM............ System Accuracy Model
SAM............ System Activity Monitor [*Computer science*]
SAM............ System Administration Manager [*Hewlett-Packard Co.*] (PCM)
SAM............ System Administration Menu [*Hewlett-Packard Co.*]
SAM............ System Analysis Machine (IAA)
SAM............ System for Automatic Message Switching [*Telecommunications*] (TSSD)
SAM............ Systems Acquisition Management (DOMA)
SAM............ Systems Acquisition Management (AAGC)
SAM............ Systems Adapter Module
SAM............ Systems Adaptor Module (NITA)
SAM............ Systems Analysis Module (IEEE)
SAM............ Systolic Anterior Motion [*Cardiology*]
SAMA.......... Gral Alvear [*Argentina ICAO location identifier*] (ICLI)
SAMA.......... Sacramento Air Materiel Area
SAMA.......... Salem Maritime National Historic Site
SAMA.......... Saudi Arabian Monetary Agency [*Riyadh*]
SAMA.......... Scientific Apparatus Makers Association [*Later, SAMAGA*] (EA)
SAMA.......... Scottish Amateur Music Association (DBA)
SAMA.......... Serum Agar Measuring Aid
SAMA.......... Site Approval and Market Analysis [*FHA*]
SAMA.......... Sociedad de Amistad Mexico Albania [*Mexico-Albania Friendship Society*] (EAIO)
SAMA.......... Specialty Automotive Manufacturers Association [*Newport Beach, CA*] (EA)
SAMA.......... Student American Medical Association [*Later, AMSA*] (EA)
SAMA.......... Survey of Adults and Markets of Affluence [*Monroe Mendelsohn Research, Inc.*] [*Information service or system*] (CRD)
SAMAA........ Special Assistant for Military Assistance Affairs [*Army*] (AABC)
SAMAC........ Scientific and Management Advisory Committee [*Terminated, 1973*] [*Army Computer Systems Command*]
SAMAC........ Swedish American Museum Association of Chicago (EA)
SAMADB...... State and Metropolitan Area Data Book [*Bureau of the Census*] (GFGA)
SAMAE........ Southern Air Materiel Area, Europe
SAMAGA...... SAMA [*Scientific Apparatus Makers Association*] Group of Associations (EA)
SAM & R..... Ship Activation, Maintenance, and Repair
SAMANTHA... System for the Automated Management of Text from a Hierarchical Arrangement
SAMAP........ Southern Air Materiel Area, Pacific [*Army*] (AFIT)
SAM-APD..... Separate Absorption and Multiplication Region Avalanche Photodiode
SAMAR........ Ship Activation, Maintenance, and Repair
SAMAR........ Surface-to-Air Missile Availability Report (NG)
SAMAS........ Security Assistance Manpower Accounting System (MCD)
SAMAS........ Service-Craft and Boats Machine Accounting System [*Navy*] (DNAB)
SA Mast Build... South Australian Master Builder [*A publication*]
SAM-B......... School of Aviation [*later, Aerospace*] Medicine - Brooks
SAMB.......... [*UK Liaison Committee for*] Sciences Allied to Medicine and Biology (ACII)
SAMB.......... Scottish Association of Master Bakers (DBA)
SAMB.......... Secondary Aircraft Maintenance Base
SAMBA........ Saudi American Bank
SAMBA........ Special Agents Mutual Benefit Association [*FBI standardized term*]
SAMBA........ Systems Approach to Managing BUSHIPS [*Bureau of Ships; later, NESC or ESC*]Acquisition [*Navy*] (MCD)
SAMBO........ Strategic Antimissile Barrage Objects
SAMBUD...... System for Automation of Materiel Plan for Army Materiel/Budget (AABC)
SAMC.......... Cristo Redentor [*Argentina ICAO location identifier*] (ICLI)
SAMC.......... Samsonite Corp. [*NASDAQ symbol*] (SAG)
SAMC.......... South African Medical Corps
SAMC.......... Southern Africa Media Center (EA)
SAMC.......... Surface Ammunition Malfunction Control (DNAB)
SAMCAP...... Surface-to-Air Missile Capability (PDAA)
SAM-CD...... Scientific American Medicine - Compact Disc [*Electronic publication*]
SAMCEP...... Self-Protected Air-to-Air Missile Concept Evaluation Program [*Army*]
SamChron.... Samaritan Chronology (BJA)
SAMCO........ Sales Associates Management Corp. [*Palm Springs, CA*] (EA)
SAMCOS...... Senior Army Materiel Command Orientation Seminar
SAMCTT...... School of Aerospace Medicine Color Threshold Test
SAMCU........ Special Airborne Medical Care Unit (MCD)
SAMD.......... Surface-to-Air Missile Development
SAMDA........ Standard Asset Management and Disposition Agreement [*Resolution Trust Corp.*]
SAM-DC...... S-Adenosylmethionine Decarboxylase [*An enzyme*]
SAM-D/CDP... Surface-to-Air Missile-Development, Contract Definition (SAA)
SAME.......... Mendoza/El Plumerillo [*Argentina ICAO location identifier*] (ICLI)
SAMe.......... S-Adenosylmethionine [*Also, AdoMet, SAM*] [*Biochemistry*]
SAME.......... Sensory-Afferent/Motor-Efferent [*Neurology*]
SAME.......... Society of American Military Engineers (EA)
SAME.......... Spanish Association for Medical Education [*British*] (EAIO)
SAME.......... Students Against Misleading Enterprises [*Student legal action organization*]
SAMEA........ South Australian Meat Exporters' Association
SAMEAC...... South Australian Multicultural and Ethnic Affairs Commission
SAMECS...... Structural Analysis Method for Evaluation of Complex Structures (PDAA)
SAMED........ South African Medical Literature [*South African Research Council*] [*Information service or system*] (CRD)
SAMEM........ Sustained-Attrition Minefield Evaluation Model (DNAB)
S Amer........ South America
SAMEX........ Shuttle Active-Microwave Experiments (MCD)
SAMEX........ Surface-to-Air Missile Exercise (NVT)
SAMF.......... Mendoza [*Argentina ICAO location identifier*] (ICLI)
SAMF.......... Salvation Army Medical Fellowship (EAIO)
SAMF.......... Seaborne Army Maintenance Facilities
SAMF.......... Ship's Air Maintenance Facility [*Navy*] (NVT)
SAMF.......... Switchable Acoustic Matched Filter
Samford U... Samford University (GAGS)
SAMFS........ South Australian Metropolitan Fire Service
SAMFU........ Self-Adjusting Military Foul-Up [*Slang*]
SAMH.......... Scottish Association for Mental Health [*British*]
SAMH.......... Valle Hermoso [*Argentina ICAO location identifier*] (ICLI)
SAMHO........ Society of Administrative Mental Health Offices [*British*] (BI)
Sam Houston St U... Sam Houston State University (GAGS)
SAMHSA...... Substance Abuse and Mental Health Services Administration [*Formerly, ADAMHA*] [*Department of Health and Human Services*]
SAMHSJ...... South Australian Methodist Historical Society. Journal [*A publication*] (ADA)
SAMI........... Sales and Marketing Information Ltd. [*Database producer*] (IID)
SAMI........... Sales Areas Marketing, Inc. (DOAD)
SAMI........... San Martin [*Argentina ICAO location identifier*] (ICLI)
SAMI........... Selling Areas-Marketing, Inc. [*Originator and database*] [*New York, NY Information service or system*] (IID)
SAMI........... Sequential Assessment of Mathematics Inventory
SAMI........... Single Action Maintenance Instruction (NG)
SAMI........... Socially Acceptable Monitoring Instrument (BABM)
SAMI........... Socially Acceptable Monitoring Instruments [*Medicine*]
SAMI........... Speed of Approach Measurement Indicator (PDAA)
SAMI........... Systems Acquisition Management Inspection
SAMICS...... Solar Array Manufacturing Industry Costing Standards
SAMICS...... Systems Applications of Millimeter Wave Contact Seeker (MCD)
SAMID........ Ship Antimissile Integrated Defense [*Program*] [*Navy*]
SAMID........ Surface-to-Air Missile Intercept Development
SAMIDS...... Ships Anti-Missile Integrated Defense System (PDAA)
SAMIP........ Surface-to-Air Missile Improvement Program (MCD)
SAMIPAC.... Societe Auxiliare et Miniere du Pacifique [*France*] (PDAA)
SAMIS........ Safety Management Information Statistics [*FTA*] (TAG)
SAMIS........ Security Assistance Management Information System (MCD)
SAMIS........ Ship Alteration Management Information System [*Discontinued*] [*Navy*]
SAMIS........ Solar Array Manufacturing Industry Simulation
SAMIS........ Standard Army Management Information System (MCD)
SAMIS........ Structural Analysis and Matrix Interpretive System (IAA)

SAMIS .... Structural Analysis and Matrix Inversion System [*Nuclear energy*] (NRCH)
SAMJ .... Jachal [*Argentina ICAO location identifier*] (ICLI)
SAML .... Nationella Samlingspartiet [*National Coalition Party*] [*Finland Political party*] (PPE)
SAML .... Sam & Libby, Inc. [*NASDAQ symbol*] (SPSG)
Saml .... Samuel [*Old Testament Book*] (WGA)
SAML .... Sinus Histiocytes with Massive Lymphadenopathy [*Clinical chemistry*]
SAML .... Standard Army Management Language (AABC)
SAMLA .... Southern Atlantic Modern Language Association
SamLby .... Sam & Libby, Inc. [*Associated Press*] (SAG)
SAMM .... Malargue [*Argentina ICAO location identifier*] (ICLI)
SAMM .... Security Assistance Management Manual [*A publication*] (AAGC)
SAMM .... South Australian Maritime Museum
SAMM .... Standard Automated Material Management System [*DoD*]
SAMM .... Systematic Activity Modeling Method (MHDB)
SAMMA .... Stores Account Material Management Afloat (NG)
SAMMA/SAL ... Stores Account Material Management Afloat / Ship Authorization Level (DNAB)
SAMMI .... Signature Analysis Methods for Mission Identification
SAMMIE .... Scheduling Analysis Model for Mission Integrated Experiments [*NASA*] (KSC)
SAMMIE .... System for Aiding Man-Machine Interaction [*Prime Computer (UK) Ltd. and Prime Computers CAD/CAM Ltd.*] [*Software package*] (NCC)
SAMMS .... Ship Alteration Material Management System
SAMMS .... Standard Automated Materiel Management System [*DoD*]
SAMNAM ..... Samradet for Nordisk Amatormusik [*Arhus, Denmark*] (EAIO)
SAM-NIS ...... Screen for Aeronautical Material - Not in Stock (DNAB)
SAMO .... Senior Administrative Medical Officer (DMAA)
SAMO .... Simulated Ab Initio Molecular Orbitals [*Atomic physics*]
SAMOA .... Systematic Approach to Multidimensional Occupational Analysis (MCD)
Samoan PLJ ... Samoan Pacific Law Journal [*A publication*] (DLA)
SAMOD .... Secretary of the Army's Mobility, Opportunity, and Development Program (MCD)
SAMOS .... Satellite-Missile Observation Satellite [*or System*]
SAMOS .... Silicon and Aluminum Metal-Oxide Semiconductor (ADA)
SAMOS .... Spot Accumulation and Melting of Snow (PDAA)
SAMOS .... Stacked-Gate Avalanche Injection Type Metal-Oxide Semiconductor (IAA)
SAMOS .... Surveillance and Missile Observation System [*Military*] (IAA)
SAMP .... La Paz [*Argentina ICAO location identifier*] (ICLI)
SAMP .... Salary Administration and Manpower Planning (PDAA)
SAMP .... Sample (AAG)
SAMP .... Sense Amplifier (NITA)
SAMP .... Shuttle Automated Mass Properties [*NASA*] (MCD)
SAMP .... Small Arms Master Plan [*Military document*] (INF)
SAMP .... Stuntmen's Association of Motion Pictures (EA)
SAMP .... Stuntwomen's Association of Motion Pictures (EA)
SAMPAC ...... Society of Advertising Musicians, Producers, Arrangers, and Composers
SAMPAM ..... System for Automation of Materiel Plans for Army Material (MCD)
SAMPAP ...... Security Assistance Master Planning and Phasing
SAMPD .... Science Analysis and Mission Planning Directorate [*NASA*]
SAMPE .... Society for the Advancement of Material and Process Engineering (EA)
SAMPE .... Society of Aerospace Material and Process Engineers (AEBS)
SAMPEX ...... Solar Anomalous and Magnetospheric Particle Explorer
SAM-PEX ..... Solar, Anomalous, and Magnetospheric Particle Explorer Satellite
SAMPF .... Sampford [*England*]
SAMPLE .... Single Assignment Mathematical Programming Language [*1971*] [*Computer science*] (CSR)
SAMPM .... Scottish Association of Milk Product Manufacturers (DBA)
SAMPS .... Shore Activity Manpower Planning System (DNAB)
SAMPS .... Subdivision and Map Plotting System (MHDB)
SAMPSP ...... Security Assistance Master Planning and Phasing (MCD)
SAMQ .... Mendoza Aeroparque [*Argentina ICAO location identifier*] (ICLI)
SAMR .... San Rafael [*Argentina ICAO location identifier*] (ICLI)
SAMR .... Special Assistant for Material Readiness [*Army*]
SAMRA .... Sino-American Medical Rehabilitation Association
SAMRAF ...... South African Military Refugee Aid Fund [*Defunct*] (EA)
SAMRT .... Shared Aperture Medium-Range Tracker (MCD)
SAMS .... Sample Method Survey [*for family housing requirements*] [*Military*] (AABC)
SAMS .... Sampling Analog Memory System
SAMS .... San Carlos [*Argentina ICAO location identifier*] (ICLI)
SAMS .... Sandia Air Force Material Study (MCD)
SAMS .... Satellite Automatic Monitoring System [*Programming language*]
SAMS .... Satellite Auto-Monitor System (NITA)
SAMS .... School for Advanced Military Studies [*Army*]
SAMS .... Scottish Association for Marine Science
SAMS .... Security Assistance Management Squadron
SAMS .... Semiautomatic Meteorological Station (SAA)
SAMS .... Ship Alteration Material Survey (DNAB)
SAMS .... Ship's Alteration Management System [*Navy*]
SAMS .... Shore Activity Management Support [*Navy*] (NVT)
SAMS .... Shuttle Attachment Manipulator System [*NASA*]
SAMS .... Shuttle Automated Management System (SSD)
SAMS .... Six Axis Motion System (PDAA)
SAMS .... Society for Advanced Medical Systems [*Later, AMIA*]
SAMS .... Society of Advanced Motorists Sydney [*Australia*]
SAMS .... Space Assembly, Maintenance, and Servicing (SSD)
SAMS .... Stand-Alone Mudmixing System
SAMS .... Standard Army Maintenance System (AABC)
SAMS .... Stratospheric and Mesospheric Sounder
SAMS .... Study Attitudes and Methods Survey [*Study skills test*]
SAMS .... Surface-to-Air Missle System [*Military*]
SAMSA .... Silica and Moulding Sands Association [*British*] (BI)
SAMSA .... Standard Army Management System - Supply Support Arrangement
SAM-SAC ..... Specialized Aircraft Maintenance - Strategic Air Command (AAG)
SAM/SAR ..... South America/South Atlantic Region [*DoD*]
SAMSARS .... Satellite-Based Maritime Search and Rescue System [*Telecommunications*] (TEL)
SAMSAT ...... Solar Activity Monitoring Satellite (MCD)
SAM/SAT ..... South America/South Atlantic Region [*Aviation*]
SAMSAT ...... Surface-to-Air Missile Servicing, Assembly, and Test
SAMSEM ..... Ship Antimissile System Engagement Model [*Navy*] (CAAL)
SAMSI .... Spacecraft Array for Michelson Spectral Inferometry
SAMSIM ...... Surface-to-Air Missile Simulation Model (MCD)
SAMS/MAMS ... Special Airspace Management System/Military Airspace Management System [*FAA*] (TAG)
Samsnte ...... Samsonite Corp. [*Associated Press*] (SAG)
SAMSO .... Space and Missile Systems Office [*Air Force*]
SAMSO .... Space and Missile Systems Organization [*Merger of Ballistic Systems Division and Space Systems Division*] [*Air Force*]
SAMSO .... Systems Analysis of Manned Space Operations (MCD)
SAMSOM ..... Support Availability Multisystem Operational Model
SAMSON ...... Sources of Ambient MicroSeismic Oceanic Noise Experiment [*Office of Naval Research*]
SAMSON ...... Strategic Automatic Message-Switching Operational Network [*Canada*] (MCD)
SAMSON ...... System Analysis of Manned Space Operations (MCD)
SAMSOR ...... Space and Missile Systems Organization Regulation [*Later, SDR*] [*Air Force*] (NASA)
SAMSOT ...... SAMID [*Ship Antimissile Integrated Defense*] System Operational Test [*Navy*] (NVT)
SAMSq .... Special Air Mission Squadron [*Vietnam Air Force*] (AFM)
SAMS-USA ... South American Missionary Society of the Episcopal Church (EA)
SAMT .... Semiautomated Mechanical Transmission [*Automotive engineering*]
SAMT .... Simulated Aircraft Maintenance Trainer (MCD)
SAMT .... State-of-the-Art Medium Terminal
SAMTEC .... Space and Missile Test and Evaluation Center [*Air Force*] (DOMA)
SAMTEC .... Space and Missile Test Center [*Air Force*]
SAMTEC/DET 1 ... Space and Missile Test Center Detachment 1 [*Patrick Air Force Base, FL*]
SAMTECM .... Space and Missile Test Center Manual [*Air Force*] (MCD)
SAMTO .... Space and Missile Test Organization [*Vandenberg Air Force Base, CA*] [*Air Force*]
SAMTS .... Simulated A/C Maintenance Training System (MCD)
SAMU .... Uspallata [*Argentina ICAO location identifier*] (ICLI)
SAMUX .... Serial Addressable Multiplexer (IAA)
SAMV .... Mendoza [*Argentina ICAO location identifier*] (ICLI)
SAMW .... Subantarctic Mode Water [*Marine science*] (OSRA)
SAMWG .... Standing Air Monitoring Work Group [*Environmental Protection Agency*] (GFGA)
S-AMY .... Serum Amylase [*Medicine*] (DMAA)
SAN .... Banco De Santiago [*NYSE symbol*] (SAG)
SAN .... Gato, CA [*Location identifier FAA*] (FAAL)
SAN .... San Angelo [*Diocesan abbreviation*] [*Texas*] (TOCD)
SAN .... Sanatorium
SAN .... San Carlos Milling [*AMEX symbol*] (TTSB)
SAN .... San Carlos Milling Co., Inc. [*AMEX symbol*] (SPSG)
SAN .... Sandersville Railroad Co. [*AAR code*]
SAN .... San Diego [*California*] [*Airport symbol*] (OAG)
SAN .... Sandwich (MSA)
San .... Sanford's Reports [*59 Alabama*] [*A publication*] (DLA)
SAN .... San Francisco Helicopter Airlines [*Air carrier designation symbol*]
SAN .... San Francisco Operations Office [*Energy Research and Development Administration*]
SAN .... Sanitary (AAG)
SAN .... Sanitation (WGA)
san .... Sanskrit [*MARC language code Library of Congress*] (LCCP)
SAN .... Santiago [*Chile*] [*Seismograph station code, US Geological Survey*] (SEIS)
SAN .... Satellite Access Nodes
SAN .... School of Air Navigation [*British*]
SAN .... Servicios Aereos Nacionales [*Ecuador*] [*ICAO designator*] (FAAC)
SAN .... Severe Acoustic Noise
SAN .... Ship Account Number [*Navy*]
SAN .... Shipping Accumulation Numbers (AAG)
SAN .... Sinoatrial Node [*Medicine*]
SAN .... Sinoauricular Node [*Medicine*] (DMAA)
SAN .... Slept All Night [*Medicine*] (DMAA)
SAN .... Society for Ancient Numismatics (EA)
SAN .... Solitary Autonomous Nodule [*Medicine*] (DMAA)
SAN .... Sonic Arts Network [*An association British*] (EAIO)
SAN .... Space Age News (AAG)
SAN .... Srpska Akademija Nauka i Umetnosti [*Belgrade, Yugoslavia*]
SAN .... Standard Address Number [*Publishing*]
SAN .... Strong Acid Number (IAA)
SAN .... Styrene-Acrylonitrile [*Also, SA*] [*Organic chemistry*]
SAN .... Subsidiary Account Number
SAN .... System Advisory Notice
SANA .... Scientists Against Nuclear Arms [*British*] [*An association*] (DBA)
SANA .... Scottish Anglers National Association (DBA)
SANA .... Slavic American National Association (EA)
SANA .... Societa Anonima Navigazione Aerea [*Italy*]
SANA .... Soycrafters Association of North America (EA)
SANA .... Soyfoods Association of North America (EA)

SANA .... Specialty Advertising National Association [*Later, SAA*] (EA)
SANA .... State, Army, Navy, Air (AABC)
SANA .... Syrian Arab News Agency
SANAA .... Servicio Autonomo Nacional de Acueductos y Alcantarillados [*Honduras*]
SANACC .... State-Army-Navy-Air Force Coordinating Committee [*Terminated, 1949*] (EGAO)
SANAE .... South African National Antarctic Expedition
SANAFREQ... Safety/NATOPS Frequency (MCD)
SANAT .... Sanatorium
Sanb .... Sanborn, Inc. [*Associated Press*] (SAG)
SANB .... South African National Bibliography
Sanb & B Ann St... Sanborn and Berryman's Annotated Statutes [*Wisconsin*] [*A publication*] (DLA)
SANBAR....... Sanders Barotropic
SANC .... Catamarca [*Argentina ICAO location identifier*] (ICLI)
SANC .... Sanctuary [*Naval cadet's hiding place for smoking*] [*Slang British*] (DSUE)
SANC .... Short-Arm Navicular Cast [*Orthopedics*] (DAVI)
SANC .... Slovak-American National Council (EA)
SANCAD....... Scottish Association for National Certificates and Diplomas
SanCarlo...... San Carlos Milling Co., Inc. [*Associated Press*] (SAG)
San Ch.......... Sandford's New York Chancery Reports [*A publication*] (DLA)
SANCIP........ SACLANT [*Supreme Allied Commander, Atlantic*] Approved NATO Common Infrastructure Program (NATG)
sanct............ Sanctuary (VRA)
SancWod ..... Sanctuary Wood Multimedia [*Commercial firm Associated Press*] (SAG)
San D .... Doctor of Sanitation
SAND .... Sampling Aerospace Nuclear Debris
SAND .... Sandata, Inc. [*NASDAQ symbol*] (NQ)
Sand .... Sandford's New York Superior Court Reports [*3-7 New York*] [*A publication*] (DLA)
SAND .... Shelter Analysis for New Designs (DNAB)
SAND .... Site Activation Need Date [*NASA*] (NASA)
SAND .... Sorting and Assembly of New Data
S & A........... Bureau of Supplies and Accounts [*Later, NSUPSC*] [*Navy*]
S & A........... Safe-and-Arm (KSC)
S & A........... Safety and Arming Device
S & A........... Saunders and Austin's Locus Standi Reports [*1895-1904*] [*A publication*] (DLA)
S & A........... Science and Application (NASA)
S & A........... Sickness and Accident [*Insurance*]
S & A........... Study and Analysis Center (AAGC)
S & A........... Sugar and Acetone [*Medicine*]
S & A........... Supplies and Accounts
SANDA......... Supplies and Accounts
S & A........... Surveillance and Accountability (NRCH)
S & A........... Surveillance and Analysis [*Environmental Protection Agency*] (GFGA)
SANDAC....... Sandia Airborne Computer
S & AD .... Science and Applications Directorate [*NASA*]
Sand & H Dig... Sandels and Hill's Digest of Statutes [*Arkansas*] [*A publication*] (DLA)
Sandars Just Inst... Sandars' Edition of Justinian's Institutes [*A publication*] (DLA)
SANDASO .... Bureau of Supplies and Accounts Shipment Order [*Obsolete Navy*]
Sandata .... Sandata, Inc. [*Associated Press*] (SAG)
S & B........... Saunders and Bidder's Locus Standi Reports [*1905-19*] [*A publication*] (DLA)
S & B........... Smith and Batty's Irish King's Bench Reports [*1824-25*] [*A publication*] (DLA)
S & B........... Sterilization and Bath
S & C........... Saunders and Cole's English Bail Court Reports [*A publication*] (DLA)
S & C........... Search and Clear [*Military*]
S & C........... Shipper and Carrier [*Business term*]
S & C........... Signal and Conditioning (KSC)
S & C........... Singh & Choudry [*Publisher*] [*British*]
S & C........... Sized and Calendered [*Paper*]
S & C........... Stabilization and Control [*Aerospace*] (KSC)
S & C........... Standards and Control
S & C........... Star and Crescent [*Steamship*] (MHDW)
S & C........... Strategic and Critical Raw Material [*Military*]
S & C........... Swan and Critchfield's Revised Statutes [*Ohio*] [*A publication*] (DLA)
S & CDU....... Switch and Cable Distribution Unit (AAG)
Sand Ch....... Sandford's New York Chancery Reports [*A publication*] (DLA)
Sand Ch R.... Sandford's New York Chancery Reports [*A publication*] (DLA)
Sand Chy..... Sandford's New York Chancery Reports [*A publication*] (DLA)
S & CM......... Strategic and Critical Materials [*Military*]
S and COH... Son and Coheir [*Genealogy*]
SandCop....... Sandwich Cooperative Bank [*Associated Press*] (SAG)
S & CP Dec... Ohio Decisions [*A publication*] (DLA)
S & C Rev St... Swan and Critchfield's Revised Statutes [*Ohio*] [*A publication*] (DLA)
S & D .... Search and Destroy [*Army*] (AABC)
S & D .... Shaw, Dunlop, and Bell's Scotch Court of Session Reports, First Series [*1821-38*] [*A publication*] (DLA)
s&d............. Signed & Dated (VRA)
S & D .... Single and Double [*Reduction gears*]
S & D .... Song and Dance Act [*Slang*]
S & D .... Stomach and Duodenum (CPH)
S & D .... Storage and Distribution
S & DJR .... Somerset & Dorset Joint Railway [*British*]
S & DR......... Somerset & Dorset Joint Railway [*British*] (ROG)
S & E........... Salaries and Expenses
S & E........... Scientific and Engineering
S & E........... Scientists and Engineers (RDA)
S & E........... Sensor and Effector (SSD)
S & E........... Services and Equipment
S & E........... Supplies and Equipage [*Military*] (CINC)
S & E........... Surfaced One Side and Edge [*Lumber*] (DAC)
S & E........... Surveillance and Entry
S & EC......... Science & Engineering Consultants [*Reston, VA*] (TSSD)
S & EPS ...... Safety & Environmental Protection Subcommittee [*Joint Army, Navy, NASA, Air Force*]
Sand Essays... Sanders' Essays on Uses and Trusts [*5th ed.*] [*1844*] [*A publication*] (DLA)
S & EV......... Saratoga & Encampment Valley Railroad (IIA)
Sandf........... Sandford's New York Superior Court Reports [*3-7 New York*] [*A publication*] (DLA)
S & F........... Security and Facilities [*DoD*]
S & F........... Staff and Faculty
S & F........... Stock and Fixtures
S & FA......... Shipping and Forwarding Agent
Sandf Ch...... Sandford's New York Chancery Reports [*A publication*] (DLA)
Sandf Ch (NY)... Sandford's New York Superior Court Reports [*3-7 New York*] [*A publication*] (DLA)
Sandf Ch Rep... Sandford's New York Chancery Reports [*A publication*] (DLA)
SandFm....... Sanderson Farms, Inc. [*Associated Press*] (SAG)
Sandf (NY)... Sandford's New York Superior Court Reports [*3-7 New York*] [*A publication*] (ILCA)
Sandf (NY) R... Sandford's New York Superior Court Reports [*A publication*] (DLA)
S & FO .... Supply and Fiscal Officer
Sandford...... Sandford's New York Superior Court Reports [*A publication*] (DLA)
Sandford's SCR... Sandford's New York Superior Court Reports [*A publication*] (DLA)
Sandford's Sup Ct R... Sandford's New York Superior Court Reports [*A publication*] (DLA)
Sandf R .... Sandford's New York Superior Court Reports [*A publication*] (DLA)
S & FR .... Stability and Frequency Response
S and FRAN... San Francisco [*California*] [*Navy*]
Sandf SC ..... Sandford's New York Superior Court Reports [*A publication*] (DLA)
Sandf SCR.... Sandford's New York Superior Court Reports [*A publication*] (DLA)
S & FSD ...... Sea and Foreign Service Duty [*A Navy pay status*]
S & FSD(A)... Sea and Foreign Service Duty (Aviation) [*A Navy pay status*]
S & FSD(S)... Sea and Foreign Service Duty (Submarine) [*A Navy pay status*]
SANDFSO .... Sea and Foreign Service Office (DNAB)
Sandf Suc.... Sandford's Heritable Succession in Scotland [*A publication*] (DLA)
Sandf Sup CR... Sandford's New York Superior Court Reports [*A publication*] (DLA)
Sandf Sup Ct... Sandford's New York Superior Court Reports [*A publication*] (DLA)
Sandf Superior Court R... Sandford's New York Superior Court Reports [*A publication*] (DLA)
S & G .... Smale and Giffard's English Vice-Chancery Reports [*A publication*] (DLA)
S & G .... Stone and Graham's Court of Referees Reports [*England*] [*A publication*] (DLA)
S & G .... Stone and Graham's Private Bills Reports [*England*] [*A publication*] (DLA)
S & G .... Stud and Girt (DAC)
S & H .... Sherratt & Hughes [*Commercial firm British*]
S and H....... Shipping and Handling (WDMC)
S and H....... Son and Heir [*Genealogy*]
S & H .... Speech and Hearing [*Medicine*]
S & H .... Sperry & Hutchinson Co.
S & H .... Steering and Hydroplane [*British*]
S & H .... Sundays and Holidays
S & H .... Survivability and Hardening (MCD)
S & H/exct... Sundays and Holidays Excepted in Lay Days (DS)
S & I............ Stocked and Issued (AFM)
S & I............ Suction and Irrigation [*Surgery*] (DAVI)
S & I............ Surveillance and Inspection (AAG)
S & I............ Surveys and Investigation
S&I .... Surveys and Investigations of the House Appropriations Committee (AAGC)
S & ID .... Surveillance and Identification
Sand Inst Just Introd... Sandars' Edition of Justinian's Institutes [*A publication*] (DLA)
Sand I Rep... Sandwich Islands Reports [*Hawaii*] [*A publication*] (DLA)
S & IS .... Survey and Investigation Staff [*Navy*] (NVT)
SanDisk....... SanDisk Corp. [*Associated Press*] (SAG)
Sand Isls..... Sandwich Islands
S & K........... Skills and Knowledges
S & L........... Sale and Leaseback
S&L............. Sale and Leaseback (DFIT)
S&L............. Savings and Loan (DFIT)
S & L........... Savings and Loan [*Association*]
S & L........... Schoales and Lefroy's Irish Chancery Reports [*1802-06*] [*A publication*] (DLA)
S & L........... Signed and Limited Edition [*Publishing*]
S & L........... Standards and Limits
S & L........... Supply and Logistics
S & L........... System and Logistics
S & LB......... Sale and Lease-Back [*Business term*] (MHDB)
Sandl St Pap... Sandler's State Papers [*A publication*] (DLA)
S & M........... Sadism and Masochism
S & M........... Sappers and Miners [*British military*] (DMA)
S & M........... September and March [*Denotes semiannual payments of interest or dividends in these months*] [*Business term*]
S & M........... Sequencer and Monitor (KSC)
S & M........... Sexton and Malone [*Comic book*] [*CBC TV series*]

S & M.......... Shaw and Maclean's House of Lords Cases [*A publication*] (DLA)
S & M.......... Smedes and Marshall's Mississippi Chancery Reports [*A publication*] (DLA)
S & M.......... Smedes and Marshall's Mississippi Reports [*9-22 Mississippi*] [*1843-50*] [*A publication*] (DLA)
S & M.......... Stock and Machinery
S & M.......... Structures and Materials (MCD)
S & M.......... Supply and Maintenance [*Army*] (AABC)
S & M.......... Surfaced and Matched [*Lumber*]
S & M.......... SYNCH [*Synchronize*] and MUX [*Multiplex*] (MCD)
S & MA.......... Supply and Maintenance Agency [*System*] [*Army*]
S & Mar...... Smedes and Marshall's Mississippi Reports [*9-22 Mississippi*] [*A publication*] (DLA)
S & Mar Ch... Smedes and Marshall's Mississippi Chancery Reports [*A publication*] (DLA)
S & M Ch.... Smedes and Marshall's Mississippi Chancery Reports [*A publication*] (DLA)
S & M Ch R... Smedes and Marshall's Mississippi Chancery Reports [*A publication*] (DLA)
S & M Ch Rep... Smedes and Marshall's Mississippi Chancery Reports [*A publication*] (DLA)
S & M Chy... Smedes and Marshall's Mississippi Chancery Reports [*A publication*] (DLA)
S & MMIS...... Supply and Maintenance Management Information System [*Army*]
S & N.......... Scottish & Newcastle Breweries [*Commercial firm British*]
S & OC.......... Signed and On Chart [*Hospital administration*] (DAVI)
SANDOCC.... San Diego Oceanic Coordinating Committee
S & P.......... Salt and Pepper
S & P.......... Save & Prosper [*Financial services group*] [*British*]
S & P.......... Stake and Platform [*Technical drawings*]
S&P.......... Standard & Poor's (DFIT)
S & P.......... Standard & Poor's Corp.
S&P.......... Standards & Practices Division (ACII)
S & P.......... Strategy and Policy Group [*War Department*] [*World War II*]
S & P (Ala) Rep... Stewart and Porter's Alabama Reports [*A publication*] (DLA)
S & PCS...... Silver and Pewter Collectors Society [*Defunct*] (EA)
S & P RES DIS... Severn and Potomac Reserve District [*Marine Corps*]
S & PTS...... Standard & Poor's Trading Systems [*Standard & Poor's Corp.*] [*Information service or system*] (IID)
Sand R........ Sandford's New York Superior Court Reports [*A publication*] (DLA)
S & R.......... Sergeant and Rawle's Pennsylvania Reports [*1824-28*] [*A publication*] (DLA)
S & R.......... Storage and Retrieval [*Computer science*]
S & R.......... Stowage and Repair
SANDRA...... Structure and Reference Analyzer [*IBM Corp.*] [*Chemistry*]
SandReg...... Sands Regent [*Associated Press*] (SAG)
S & R Neg... Shearman and Redfield on the Law of Negligence [*A publication*] (DLA)
S & R on Neg... Shearman and Redfield on the Law of Negligence [*A publication*] (DLA)
S & RP........ Spares and Repair Parts [*Navy*]
S & S.......... Saratoga & Schuylerville Railroad (IIA)
S & S.......... Sausse and Scully's Irish Rolls Court Reports [*1837-40*] [*A publication*] (DLA)
S & S.......... Schleicher & Schuell [*Filter-paper company*]
S&S.......... Science & Society [*A publication*] (BRI)
S & S.......... Searle and Smith's English Probate and Divorce Reports [*1859-60*] [*A publication*] (DLA)
S & S.......... Sense and Sensibility [*Novel by Jane Austen*]
S & S.......... Sex and Shopping [*Themes of Judith Krantz's novels*]
S & S.......... Shipping and Storage
S & S.......... Signs and Symptoms [*Medicine*]
S & S.......... Simon & Schuster [*Publisher*]
S & S.......... Simons and Stuart's English Vice-Chancellors' Reports [*1822-26*] [*A publication*] (DLA)
S & S.......... Spigot and Socket
SANDS........ Stillbirth and Neonatal Death Society [*British*] (EAIO)
SANDS........ Structural Analysis Numerical Design System
S & S.......... Supply and Service [*Army*] (AABC)
S & S.......... Support and Stimulation [*Medicine*] (DAVI)
S & S.......... Swan and Sayler's Revised Statutes of Ohio [*A publication*] (DLA)
S & S.......... Sword and Sorcery
Sand SC...... Sandford's New York Superior Court Reports [*A publication*] (DLA)
S & Sc........ Sausse and Scully's Irish Rolls Court Reports [*A publication*] (DLA)
S & SC........ Sized and Supercalendered [*Paper*]
Sands Ch..... Sandford's New York Chancery Reports [*A publication*] (DLA)
Sand SCR.... Sandford's New York Superior Court Reports [*A publication*] (DLA)
S & SD........ Sewerage and Sewage Disposal (DCTA)
S & Sm........ Searle and Smith's English Probate and Divorce Reports [*A publication*] (DLA)
sandst.......... Sandstone (VRA)
Sandst......... Sandstone [*Lithology*]
Sand Sup Ct Rep... Sandford's New York Superior Court Reports [*A publication*] (DLA)
Sand Supr Ct R... Sandford's New York Superior Court Reports [*A publication*] (DLA)
S & Sx Yeo... Surrey and Sussex Yeomanry [*British military*] (DMA)
S & T.......... Science and Technology (NATG)
S&T.......... Science and Technology (EERA)
S & T.......... Selection and Training [*Military*] (LAIN)
S & T.......... Simulation and Training
S&T.......... Sky & Telescope [*A publication*] (BRI)
S & T.......... Stenographer and Typist [*Examination*] [*Civil Service Commission*]
S & T.......... Storm and Tempest (ADA)
S & T.......... Supply and Transport [*Military*]
S & T.......... Supply and Transport Corps [*British*] (DMA)
S & T.......... Swabey and Tristram's Probate and Divorce Reports [*1858-65*] [*A publication*] (DLA)
S & TA......... Salmon and Trout Association (DBA)
S & T Bc...... S & T Bancorp [*Associated Press*] (SAG)
S & T Bcp.... S & T Bancorp [*Associated Press*] (SAG)
SandTc........ Sand Technology Systems International, Inc. [*Associated Press*] (SAG)
S & TI.......... Scientific and Technical Intelligence [*Military*] (RDA)
S & U.......... Supine and Upright (DAVI)
S & U.......... Supine and Upright (MEDA)
Sand Uses and Trusts... Sanders' Essays on Uses and Trusts [*A publication*] (DLA)
S & V.......... Shock and Vibration
SANDW........ Sandwiched (IAA)
S & W.......... Smith and Wesson (MCD)
S & W.......... Soap and Water [*Enema*] [*Medicine*]
Sandy.......... Sandy Corp. [*Associated Press*] (SAG)
SANE.......... National Committee for a Sane Nuclear Policy [*"SANE" alone now used as organization name*] (EA)
San E.......... Sanitary Engineer [*Academic degree*]
SANE.......... Santiago Del Estero [*Argentina ICAO location identifier*] (ICLI)
SANE.......... Schizophrenia: a National Emergency [*An association British*]
SANE.......... Scientific Applications of Nuclear Explosions (SAA)
SANE.......... Severe Acoustic Noise Environment
SANE.......... Standard Apple Numerics Environment [*Software*] [*Apple Computers, Inc.*]
SANE.......... Sulfur and Nitrogen Emissions (GNE)
SANF.......... Salvation Army Nurses' Fellowship (EAIO)
SANF.......... Sanford Recreation Area
Sanf.......... Sanford's Reports [*59 Alabama*] [*A publication*] (DLA)
SANF.......... South African Naval Forces
SanFeFn...... Santa Fe Financial Corp. [*Associated Press*] (SAG)
Sanfilp......... Sanfilippo [*John*] & Son, Inc. [*Associated Press*] (SAG)
San FLJ........ San Francisco Law Journal [*A publication*] (DLA)
SANFM........ Source Range Neutron Flux Monitor (IAA)
Sanf (NY)...... Sandford's New York Superior Court Reports [*3-7 New York*] [*A publication*] (DLA)
Sanford's Ch R... Sandford's New York Chancery Reports [*A publication*] (DLA)
San Fran...... San Francisco [*California*] (BARN)
San Fran Art Inst... San Francisco Art Institute (GAGS)
San Fran Conserv Music... San Francisco Conservatory of Music (GAGS)
San Fran Law Bull... San Francisco Law Bulletin [*A publication*] (DLA)
San Fran LB... San Francisco Law Bulletin [*A publication*] (ILCA)
San Fran LJ... San Francisco Law Journal [*A publication*] (DLA)
San Fran St U... San Francisco State University (GAGS)
San Fr LB.... San Francisco Law Bulletin [*A publication*] (DLA)
San Fr LJ..... San Francisco Law Journal [*A publication*] (DLA)
SANG.......... SangStat Medical [*NASDAQ symbol*] (TTSB)
SANG.......... SangStat Medical Corp. [*NASDAQ symbol*] (SAG)
sang.......... Sanguineous [*Hematology*] (DAVI)
SANG.......... Saudi Arabian National Guard (RDA)
SANG.......... Standardized Aeronautical Navigation/Guidance [*Program*] [*Air Force*]
SANGB......... Selfridge Army/Air National Guard Base (MCD)
SANGFPT...... Spherical Angles from Points (MCD)
Sangstat...... SangStat Medical Corp. [*Associated Press*] (SAG)
sangu.......... Sanguine (VRA)
SANH.......... Rio Hondo/Las Termas [*Argentina ICAO location identifier*] (ICLI)
Sanh.......... Sanhedrin (BJA)
Sanh.......... Sanherib (BJA)
SANI.......... Sanitary
SANI.......... Tinogasta [*Argentina ICAO location identifier*] (ICLI)
Sanifil.......... Sanifill, Inc. [*Associated Press*] (SAG)
SANINSP...... Sanitation Inspector [*Military*] (AABC)
Sanit.......... Sanitarium
Sanit.......... Sanitary
sanit.......... Sanitation (DAVI)
SANITN........ Sanitation
SAnitRt........ Santa Anita Realty Enterprises, Inc. [*Associated Press*] (SAG)
San Just...... Sandars' Edition of Justinian's Institutes [*A publication*] (DLA)
SANKA......... Sans Caffeine [*Acronym used as brand name*]
SANL.......... La Rioja/Cap. V. Almandos Almonacid [*Argentina ICAO location identifier*] (ICLI)
SANLF......... Saudi Arabian National Liberation Front [*Political party*] (BJA)
SANM.......... Sanmina Corp. [*NASDAQ symbol*] (SAG)
SANM.......... Synthetic Algal Nutrient Medium
SAN MIG....... San Miguel Beer (DSUE)
Sanmina....... Sanmina Corp. [*Associated Press*] (SAG)
SANO.......... Chilecito [*Argentina ICAO location identifier*] (ICLI)
SANO.......... Sano Corp. [*NASDAQ symbol*] (SAG)
SANO.......... South African Astronomical Observatory
SanoCo........ Sano Corp. [*Associated Press*] (SAG)
SANOVA....... Simultaneous Analysis of Variance
SANP.......... Secondary Auxiliary Nuclear Power
SANPRM....... Supplemental Advance Notice of Proposed Rulemaking [*RSPA*] (TAG)
SANR.......... Subject to Approval No Risk
SANROC....... South African Non-Racial Olympic Committee (EAIO)
SANS.......... Scale for the Assessment of Negative Symptoms [*Medicine*] (DMAA)
SANS.......... Schedule for the Assessment of Negative Symptoms [*Psychometrics*]
SANS.......... Simplified Account - Numbering System
SANS.......... Small-Angle Neutron Scattering
SANS.......... South African Naval Service
SANS.......... Students Against Nuclear Suicide [*Defunct*] (EA)

SANS .... Swimmer and Navigation System [*Navy*] (CAAL)
SANSAN ...... San Francisco, San Diego [*Proposed name for possible "super-city" formed by growth and mergers of other cities*]
SANSC .... Sanscrit
SANSET ...... Seaman Apprentice, Nuclear Submarine Engineering Technician [*Navy rating*] (DNAB)
SANSK .... Sanskrit [*Language, etc.*]
SANSS .... Structure and Nomenclature Search System [*Formerly, SSS*] [*Chemical Information Systems, Inc.*] [*Information service or system*]
SANSW .... Shires Association of New South Wales [*Australia*]
SANT .... Tucuman/Teniente Benjamim Matienzo [*Argentina ICAO location identifier*] (ICLI)
SANTA .... Souvenir and Novelty Trade Association (EA)
Santa Clara LR ... Santa Clara Law Review [*A publication*] (ILCA)
SantCrz .... Santa Cruz Operation, Inc. [*Associated Press*] (SAG)
SantF .... Santander Finance Ltd. [*Associated Press*] (SAG)
Santos .... Santos Ltd. [*Associated Press*] (SAG)
SANU .... San Juan [*Argentina ICAO location identifier*] (ICLI)
SANU .... Sudan African National Union [*Political party*]
SANUM .... South Africa National Union for Mineworkers
SANW .... Ceres [*Argentina ICAO location identifier*] (ICLI)
SANWFZ ...... South Asia Nuclear Weapons-Free Zone
SANWS .... Sinoatrial Node Weakness Syndrome [*Medicine*] (DMAA)
SANY .... Sanyo Electric Co. Ltd. [*NASDAQ symbol*] (NQ)
Sanyal .... Sanyal's Criminal Cases between Natives and Europeans [*1796-1895*] [*India*] [*A publication*] (DLA)
Sanyo .... Sanyo Electric Co. Ltd. [*Associated Press*] (SAG)
SANYY .... SANYO Electric Ltd ADS [*NASDAQ symbol*] (TTSB)
SAO .... Saharan Air Outbreak [*Meteorology*]
SAO .... Sahel Aviation Service [*Mali*] [*ICAO designator*] (FAAC)
SAO .... San Andreas Geological Observatory [*California*] [*Seismograph station code, US Geological Survey*] (SEIS)
SAO .... Sandia Area Office [*Energy Research and Development Administration*]
SAO .... Sao Paulo [*Brazil*] [*Airport symbol*] (OAG)
SAO .... Scottish Association of Opticians (DAS)
SAO .... Secret Army Organization [*English initialism for OAS, terrorist group in Algeria and metropolitan France*]
SAO .... Secretin-Stimulated Acid Output [*Clinical chemistry*]
SAO .... Security Assistance Office
SAO .... Security Assistance Organizations (DOMA)
SAO .... Select Address and Operate
SAO .... Selected Attack Option (MCD)
SAO .... Semiannual Oscillation [*Astronomy*]
SAO .... Senior Administrative Officer [*British military*] (DMA)
SAO .... Single Airlift Organization (CINC)
SAO .... Single Association Object [*Telecommunications*] (OSI)
SAO .... Single Attack Option
SAO .... Small Airway Obstruction [*Medicine*] (DMAA)
SAO .... Smithsonian Astrophysical Observatory [*Cambridge, MA*]
SAO .... Smooth Approach Orifice [*Mechanical engineering*]
SAO .... Social Actions Office [*or Officer*] [*Air Force*] (AFM)
SAO .... Sonobuoy Acoustic Operator [*Navy*] (CAAL)
SAO .... Special Access Only (MCD)
SAO .... Special Action Office [*Phased out, 1975*] [*Department of Justice*]
SAO .... Special Activities Office [*Air Force*] (AFM)
SAO .... Special Air Operations
SAO .... Special Analysis Office
SAO .... Special Artificer, Optical [*Navy*]
SAO .... Special Astrophysics Observatory
SAO .... Splanchnic Artery Occlusion [*Medicine*]
SAO .... Squadron Accountant Officer [*Navy British*]
SAO .... Staff Administrative Office [*Military*]
SAO .... Subsidiary/Affiliate Order (MCD)
SAO .... Subvalvular Aortic Obstruction [*Medicine*] (DMAA)
SAO .... Support Air Observation [*Navy*]
SAO .... Survey of Agency Opinion [*LIMRA*]
SAO .... Survival Assistance Officer [*Army*] (AABC)
SAO .... Systems Acquisition Officer [*Military*] (AFIT)
SAO .... Systems Analysis Office
SaO_2 .... Saturation Arterial Oxygen [*Medicine*] (DAVI)
SAOA .... Semi-Ascending Order Arrangement (PDAA)
SAOAS .... Secretary of the Army, Office of the Assistant Secretary
SAOAS .... Staff Association of the Organization of American States (EA)
SAOC .... Rio Cuarto/Area de Material [*Argentina ICAO location identifier*] (ICLI)
SAOC .... Scottish Association of Operative Coachmakers [*A union*]
SAOC .... South Australian Olympic Council
SAOC .... Space and Astronautics Orientation Course (NG)
SAOCS .... Submarine Air Optical Communications System (MCD)
SAOD .... Villa Dolores [*Argentina ICAO location identifier*] (ICLI)
SAODAP ...... Special Action Office for Drug Abuse Prevention [*Terminated, 1975*] [*FDA*]
SAOE .... Embalse Rio Tercero [*Argentina ICAO location identifier*] (ICLI)
SAOG .... Satellite Operations Group [*Military*]
SAOHSC ...... South Australian Occupational Health and Safety Commission
SAOL .... Laboulaye [*Argentina ICAO location identifier*] (ICLI)
SAOM .... Marcos Juarez [*Argentina ICAO location identifier*] (ICLI)
SAO/MEX ..... Special Action Office for Mexico [*Drug Enforcement Administration*]
SAOR .... Villa Reynolds [*Argentina ICAO location identifier*] (ICLI)
SAOS .... Scottish Agricultural Organisation Society (DBA)
SAOS .... Select Address [*and Provide*] Output Signal
SAOT .... Semiactive on Target
SAOTA .... Shrimp Association of the Americas (EA)
SAOU .... San Luis [*Argentina ICAO location identifier*] (ICLI)
SAOUG .... South African Online User Group (NITA)
SAP .... Sampling and Analysis Plan
SAP .... San Antonio Public Library, San Antonio, TX [*OCLC symbol*] (OCLC)
SAP .... San Pedro Sula [*Honduras*] [*Airport symbol*] (OAG)
sap .... Saponification [*or Saponify*] [*Analytical chemistry*] (AAMN)
SAP .... Sapporo [*Japan*] [*Seismograph station code, US Geological Survey*] (SEIS)
sap .... Sapwood [*Lumber*] (BARN)
SAP .... Scampton FTU [*British ICAO designator*] (FAAC)
SAP .... Scientific Advisory Panel [*Arlington, VA*] [*Environmental Protection Agency*] (EGAO)
SAP .... Scorched Aluminum Powder
SAP .... Scouting and Amphibian Plane [*Coast Guard*]
SAP .... Scruple Apothecaries
SAP .... Seaborne Aircraft Platform (ADA)
SAP .... Secondary Audio Program
SAP .... Second Audio Program
SAP .... Security Assistance Program (MCD)
SAP .... Semi-Armor-Piercing [*Projectile*] [*Nickname: Sex-Appeal Pete*] [*Military*]
SAP .... Seminal Acid Phosphatase [*An enzyme*]
SAP .... Separate Audio Program [*Television broadcasting*]
SAP .... Serum Alkaline Phosphatase [*Clinical chemistry*]
SAP .... Serum Amyloid P [*Clinical chemistry*]
SAP .... Service Access Point
SAP .... Service Advertising Protocol [*Computer science*] (PCM)
SAP .... Seychelles Agence de Presse [*News agency*] (EY)
SAP .... Share Assembly Program [*Computer science*]
SAP .... Ship Acquisition Plan [*Navy*]
SAP .... Ship Alteration Package [*Navy*] (DNAB)
SAP .... Shipboard Acoustic Processor [*Navy*] (CAAL)
SAP .... Shipboard Antenna Pedestal
SAP .... Simple Assembly Plan
SAP .... Simplified Acquisition Procedure (AAGC)
SAP .... Single-Axis Platform
SAP .... Sintered Aluminium Product [*Nuclear energy*] (NUCP)
SAP .... Sintered Aluminum Powder
SAP .... Site Activation Phase
SAP .... Situs Ambiguus with Polysplenia [*Medicine*] (DMAA)
SAP .... Skeletal Axis of Pinnule
SAP .... Social Action Party [*Thailand*] [*Political party*] (FEA)
SAP .... Socialistische Arbeiderspartij [*Socialist Workers' Party*] [*Netherlands Political party*] (PPW)
SAP .... Societe des Arts Plastiques de la Province de Quebec, Quebec City [*1955*] [*Canada*] (NGC)
SAP .... Society for Adolescent Psychiatry (EA)
SAP .... Society for American Philosophy [*Defunct*] (EA)
SAP .... Society of Analytical Psychology (AIE)
SAP .... Sodium Acid Pyrophosphate [*Also, SAPP*] [*Leavening agent, meat additive*]
SAP .... Soon as Possible
SAP .... South African Party [*Political party*] (PPW)
SAP .... South African Police (ECON)
SAP .... Soysal Adelet Partisi [*Social Justice Party*] [*Turkish Cyprus*] [*Political party*] (PPE)
SAP .... Special Access Program (DOMA)
SAP .... Special and Administrative Provisions [*of the Tariff Act of 1930*]
SAP .... Special Attention Personnel [*US VIP troops*] (VNW)
SAP .... Sphingolipid Activator Protein [*Biochemistry*]
SAP .... Spot Authorization Plan [*WPB*] [*Obsolete*]
SAP .... Spy Against Pollution [*An association*]
SAP .... Squadron Aid Post (ADA)
SAP .... Staphylococcus aureus Protease [*An enzyme*]
SAP .... Start of Active Profile (PDAA)
SAP .... State Association President [*American Occupational Therapy Association*]
SAP .... Statement on Auditing Procedure
SAP .... Steroidogenesis Activator Polypeptide
SAP .... Strain Arrestor Plate [*NASA*] (NASA)
SAP .... Strategic Advantages Profile
SAP .... Strategic Audit Plan
SAP .... Strong Anthropic Principle [*Term coined by authors John Barrow and Frank Tipler in their book, "The Anthropic Cosmological Principle"*]
SAP .... Structural Adjustment Package [*Australia*]
SAP .... Structural Analysis Program (MCD)
SAP .... Student Aid Project
SAP .... Subassembly Precision (MCD)
SAP .... Subject Access Project
SAP .... Substituted Accounting Period
SAP .... Sumerian Animal Proverbs (BJA)
SAP .... Superabsorbent Polymer [*Organic chemistry*]
SAP .... Supervisory Airplane Pilot
SAP .... Supplier-Allied-Price [*Automobile content legislation*]
SAP .... Supportability Assurance Program
SAP .... Surface Aligned Photochemistry [*Physics*]
SAP .... Sveriges Socialdemokratiska Arbetareparti [*Swedish Social Democratic Labor Party*] [*Political party*] (PPW)
SAP .... Symbolic Address Program
SAP .... Symbolic Assembly Program [*Computer science*]
SAP .... System Alignment Procedure (NATG)
SAP .... Systemic Arterial Pressure [*Medicine*]
SAP .... Systems Assurance Program [*IBM Corp.*]
SAPA .... Sciences - A Process Approach [*National Science Foundation*]

SAPA .... Sino-American Pharmaceutical Association
SapA .... Societa in Accomandita per Azioni [*Limited Partnership with Shares*] [*Italian*] (IMH)
SAPA .... South African Press Association
SAPAI .... Salesmen's Association of Paper and Allied Industries (EA)
SAPAS .... Semiautomatic Population Analysis System (MCD)
SAPAT .... South African Picture Analysis Test [*Psychology*]
SAPB .... South Australian Psychological Board
SAPC .... Shipowners Association of the Pacific Coast [*Defunct*] (EA)
SAPC .... Small Arms Post Competition
SAPC .... South Australian Philatelic Council
SAPC .... South Australian Planning Commission
SAPC .... Substance Abuse Problem Checklist
SAPC .... Supported Aqueous-Phase Catalysis [*Chemistry*]
SAPC .... Suspended Acoustical-Plaster Ceiling [*Technical drawings*]
SAPCH .... Semiautomatic Program Checkout (IAA)
SAPCHE .... Semiautomatic Program Checkout Equipment (AAG)
SAPCO .... Security Assistance Policy Coordinating Office [*Military*]
SAPCO .... Single-Asset Property Company [*British*]
SAPCO .... Sudanese African People's Congress [*Political party*] (EY)
SAPD .... Self-Administration of Psychotropic Drugs (AAMN)
SAPD .... South Australia. Parliamentary Debates [*A publication*]
SAPDF .... Social Activist Professors Defense Foundation [*Defunct*] (EA)
SAPDO .... Special Accounts Property Disposal Officer [*Military*]
SAPE .... Sapient Corp. [*NASDAQ symbol*] (SAG)
SAPE .... Sapient Corp. [*NASDAQ symbol*] (TTSB)
SAPE .... Society for Automation in Professional Education [*Later, SDE*]
SAPE .... Solenoid Array Pattern Evaluator
SAPEC .... Savings Associations Political Education Committee
SAPENF .... Societe Americaine pour l'Etude de la Numismatique Francaise (EA)
SAPF .... Suider-Afrika Padfederasie [*Southern Africa Road Federation - SARF*] (EAIO)
SAPFE .... Seaman Apprentice, Polaris Field Electronics [*Navy rating*] (DNAB)
SAPFL .... Seaman Apprentice, Polaris Field Launcher [*Navy rating*] (DNAB)
SAPFT .... Special Adviser to the President on Foreign Trade [*New Deal*]
SAPFU .... Surpassing All Previous Foul Ups [*Military slang*] [*Bowdlerized version*]
saph .... Sapphire [*Philately*]
SAPhA .... Student American Pharmaceutical Association [*Later, APhA-ASP*] (EA)
SAPHE .... Semi-Armor-Piercing High Explosive [*Projectile*] (MCD)
SAPHYDATA ... Panel on the Acquisition, Transmission, and Processing of Hydrological Data [*Marine science*] (MSC)
SAPI .... Sales Association of the Paper Industry [*New York, NY*] (EA)
SAPI .... Semi-Armor-Piercing Incendiary [*Projectile*] (NATG)
SAPI .... Service Access Point Identifier [*Telecommunications*] (OSI)
SAPI .... Speech Application Programming Interface (PCM)
SAPI .... Speech Application Programming Interface [*Microsoft Corp.*]
Sapiens .... Sapiens International Corp. [*Associated Press*] (SAG)
SAPIENS .... Spreading Activation Processor for Information Encoded in Network Structure [*Department of Education*]
Sapient .... Sapient Corp. [*Associated Press*] (SAG)
SAPIR .... System of Automatic Processing and Indexing of Reports
SAPIS .... State Alcoholism Profile Information System [*Public Health Service*] (IID)
SAPK .... Stress-Activated Protein Kinase [*An enzyme*]
SAPK .... Stress-Activated Protein Kinases [*An enzyme*]
sapl .... Sailed as Per List (ODBW)
SAPL .... Seacoast Anti-Pollution League (EA)
SAPL .... Service Action Parts List (AAG)
SAPL .... Society for Animal Protective Legislation (EA)
SAPL .... Spartan-Approved Parts List [*Missiles*] (MCD)
SAPLA .... Standing Advisory Panel on Library Automation (NITA)
SAPLIC .... Small Arms Projected Line Charge [*Military*] (INF)
SAPM .... Scottish Association of Plane Makers [*A union*]
SAPM .... Society for thr Aid of Psychological Minorities (NADA)
SAPMS .... Short Arm Posterior Molded Splint [*Medicine*] (MEDA)
SAPNA .... Succinyl-Alanyl-para-Nitroanilide [*Biochemistry*]
SaPNFB .... National Film Board, Pretoria, South Africa [*Library symbol Library of Congress*] (LCLS)
SAPO .... Sarawak People's Organization [*Malaysia*] [*Political party*] (PPW)
SAPO .... Silicoaluminophosphate [*Inorganic chemistry*]
SAPO .... Special Aircraft Project Office (AAG)
SAPO .... Subarea Petroleum Office [*Military*]
SAPOAD .... Systems Applications Project Operation Action Detail (IAA)
SAPON .... Saponaria [*Soapwort*] [*Pharmacology*] (ROG)
SAPON .... Saponification [*Analytical chemistry*]
SAPOS .... Satellite Positioning Service
SAPOV .... Subarea Petroleum Office, Vietnam [*Military*]
SAPP .... Security, Accuracy, Propriety, and Policy
S App .... Shaw's Scotch Appeal Cases, House of Lords [*1821-24*] [*A publication*] (DLA)
SAPP .... Skeletal Axis of Palp
SAPP .... Sodium Acid Pyrophosphate [*Also, SAP*] [*Leavening agent, meat additive*]
SAPP .... Soul Assurance Prayer Plan (EA)
SAPP .... South Australian Parliamentary Papers [*A publication*]
SAPP .... Special Airfield Pavement Program (NATG)
SAPPHIRE .... Synthetic Aperture Precision Processor High Reliability (MCD)
SAPPMA .... San Antonio Procurement and Production Materiel Area [*Air Force*]
SAPPRAD .... Southeast Asian Program for Potato Research and Development (GNE)
SAPQ .... Societe des Artistes Professionnels du Quebec [*1966, CPQ from 1978, SAAVQ from 1980, CAPQ from 1982*] [*Canada*] (NGC)
SAPR .... Semiannual Progress Report
SAPR .... Summary Area Problem Report (AAG)
SAPRC .... Security Assistance Program Review Commission
SAPRITC .... South Australian Plastics and Rubber Industry Training Committee
SAPS .... Scandinavian Association of Paediatric Surgeons (EAIO)
SAPS .... Scandinavian Association of Plastic Surgeons [*See also NPF*] (EAIO)
SAPS .... Secondary Audio Program Services [*Television*] (BARN)
SAPS .... Selected Alternate Processing Separation (MCD)
SAPS .... Servico de Alimentacao da Providencia Social [*Brazil*]
SAPS .... Shippingport Atomic Power Station (NRCH)
SAPS .... Signal Algorithmic Processing System [*Navy*]
SAPS .... Simplified Acute Physiology Score [*Medicine*]
SAPS .... Small Area Plotting Sheet
SaPS .... South African Council for Scientific and Industrial Research, Pretoria, South Africa [*Library symbol Library of Congress*] (LCLS)
SAPS .... Standalone Prediction System
SAPS .... Surety Agents Promotional Society [*Defunct*] (EA)
SAPSFA .... South Australian Professional Shark Fishermen's Association
SaPSL .... State Library, Pretoria, South Africa [*Library symbol Library of Congress*] (LCLS)
SA/PSP .... Site Activation/Phased Support Plan [*Military*] (MCD)
SAPST .... Special Assistant to the President for Science and Technology
SAPT .... Scottish Association of Public Transport (DBA)
SAPT .... South Africa Department of Posts and Telecommunications (TSSD)
SAPT .... Symmetry-Adapted Perturbation Theory [*Physical chemistry*]
SAPU .... South African Police Union (ECON)
SAPUC .... Sintered Aluminum Powder-Clad Uranium Carbide
SAPV .... Secondary Air Pulse Valve [*Automotive engineering*]
SAPW .... United Stone and Allied Products Workers of America [*Later, USWA*]
SAPX .... Salivary Peroxidase [*Medicine*] (DMAA)
SAQ .... Pittsburgh, PA [*Location identifier FAA*] (FAAL)
SAQ .... San Andros [*Bahamas*] [*Airport symbol*] (OAG)
SAQ .... Short Arc Quads [*Medicine*]
SAQ .... South Atlantic Quarterly [*A publication*] (BRI)
SAQ .... Springbank Aviation Ltd. [*Canada ICAO designator*] (FAAC)
SAQAD .... Submarine Antenna Quality Assurance Directory [*Navy*] (DNAB)
SAQAF .... Submarine Antenna Quality Assurance Facility [*Navy*] (DNAB)
SAQC .... Statistical Analysis and Quality Control
SAQM .... Standardized Air Quality Monitoring [*Environmental Protection Agency*]
SAQR .... Substance Abuse Quarterly Report [*Navy*] (DNAB)
SAQT .... Sociedad Panamericana de Quimioterapia de la Tuberculosis [*Pan American Society for Chemotherapy of Tuberculosis - PASCT*] (EA)
SAR .... National Society, Sons of the American Revolution (EA)
SAR .... Safety Analysis Report [*Nuclear energy*]
SAR .... Safety Assessment Report (MCD)
SAR .... Sales Authorization Request
SAR .... Sample Acceptance Rate [*Statistics*]
SAR .... Santa Anita Realty Enterprises, Inc. [*NYSE symbol*] (SPSG)
SAR .... Santa Anita Rlty(UNIT) [*NYSE symbol*] (TTSB)
SAR .... Santa Rosa Junior College, Santa Rosa, CA [*OCLC symbol*] (OCLC)
SAR .... Sarajevo [*Yugoslavia*] [*Seismograph station code, US Geological Survey*] (SEIS)
SAR .... Sarcoidosis [*Medicine*]
Sar .... Sarcosine [*Biochemistry*]
Sar .... Sarcosyl [*Biochemistry*]
SAR .... Sardinia [*Italy*] (ROG)
Sar .... Sarswati's Privy Council Judgments [*India*] [*A publication*] (DLA)
SAR .... Saturation Alleviation Rules
SAR .... Saudi Arabian Riyal [*Monetary unit*] (DS)
SAR .... Save Address Register (IAA)
SAR .... Scaffold Attachment Region [*Genetics*]
SAR .... Schedule Allocation Requirements (AAG)
SAR .... Schedule and Request (MCD)
SAR .... School Achievement Record [*Australia*]
SAR .... School of American Research [*Research center*] (RCD)
SAR .... Sea-Air Rescue
SAR .... Search and Release (AAG)
SAR .... Search and Rescue (FAAC)
SAR .... Search and Rescue [*Marine science*] (OSRA)
SAR .... Search and Rescue Program [*Military*]
SAR .... Segment Address Register [*Telecommunications*]
SAR .... Selected Acquisition Report [*Military*]
SAR .... Semiactive RADAR (MCD)
SAR .... Semiannual Report
SAR .... Semiautomatic Rifle [*Army*]
SAR .... Senior Army Representative
SAR .... Service Analysis Report [*Telecommunications*] (TEL)
SAR .... Service Analysis Request [*Telecommunications*] (TEL)
SAR .... Service Aptitude Rating [*Military*] (NVT)
SAR .... Service Assigned Requests (MCD)
SAR .... Servicios Aereos de Pilotos Ejecutivos [*Colombia*] [*ICAO designator*] (FAAC)
SAR .... Sexual Attitude Reassessment [*Medicine*]
SAR .... Siemens Agronaut Reactor [*Germany*]
SAR .... Significant Action Report [*Military*] (MCD)
SAR .... Silver Acorn Developments [*Vancouver Stock Exchange symbol*]
SAR .... Simulated Acid Rain
SAR .... Single-Axis Reference
SAR .... Single-BIT [*Binary Digit*] Alternation Recording
SAR .... Site Acceptance Review [*Military*]
SAR .... Society for Animal Rights [*Later, ISAR*] (EA)
SAR .... Society for Application Research [*British*] (DBA)
SAR .... Society of Authors' Representatives (EA)
SAR .... Sodium-Adsorption-Ratio

SAR .... Software Acceptance Review
SAR .... Son Altesse Royale [*His or Her Royal Highness*] [*French*]
SAR .... SONAR Acoustique Remorque [*Acoustic imaging system*] [*French*]
SAR .... Sons of the American Revolution
SAR .... Source Address Register [*Telecommunications*]
SAR .... South African Railways
SAR .... South African Republic
SAR .... South African Republic High Court Reports [*A publication*] (DLA)
SAR .... South Australian Government Railways
SAR .... Spacecraft Acceptance Review (MCD)
SAR .... Sparta, IL [*Location identifier FAA*] (FAAL)
SAR .... Special Access Required
SAR .... Special Administrative Region [*Hong Kong*]
SAR .... Special Aeronautical Requirement [*Navy*] (NG)
SAR .... Special Appaaratus Rack (IAA)
SAR .... Specific Absorption Rate
SAR .... Specific Acoustic Resistance
SAR .... Specific Activity Report
SAR .... Specific Air Range [*Military*] (LAIN)
SAR .... Specifically Authorized Representative [*Air Force*]
SAR .... Specification Approval Record (MCD)
SAR .... Stable Auroral Red [*Arc*] [*Geophysics*]
SAR .... Stack Address Register (IAA)
SAR .... Standardized Abnormality Ratio (WDAA)
SAR .... Standardized Admissions Ratios [*Hospital activity analysis*]
SAR .... Standing Authority Release [*For perishables*] [*Business term*]
SAR .... Start Action Request [*Environmental Protection Agency*]
SAR .... Starting Address Register (ECII)
SAR .... Starting Air Receiver (AAG)
SAR .... Stock Appreciation Relief [*British*]
SAR .... Stock Appreciation Rights [*Method of compensation for top executives*]
SAR .... Stock Appreciation Rights (TDOB)
SAR .... Storage Address Register [*Telecommunications*]
SAR .... Street Address Record [*Telecommunications*] (TEL)
SAR .... Structure Activity Relationship
SAR .... Student Aid Report [*Department of Education*]
SAR .... Students at Risk [*Australia*]
SAR .... Study and Review [*Reports*] (RDA)
SAR .... Subauroral Red [*Arc*] [*Geophysics*]
SAR .... Submarine Advanced Reactor
SAR .... Subsequent Application Review
SAR .... Substance Abuse Report [*Navy*] (DNAB)
SAR .... Substitution Approval Request (MCD)
SAR .... Successive Accelerated Replacement
SAR .... Successive Approximation Register [*Computer science*]
Sar............. Sulfarsphenamine [*or Sulpharsphenamine*] [*Chemistry*] (DAVI)
SAR .... Sulfuric Acid Regenerator (MCD)
SAR .... Summary Analysis Report (NASA)
SAR .... Summary Annual Report
SAR .... Sum of Absolute Residuals [*Mathematics*]
SAR .... Super-Abrasion-Resistant [*Lucite glazing material*]
SAR .... Support Air Request [*Net*] [*Navy communications*]
SAR .... Symbol Acquisition Routine
SAR .... Synthetic Aperture RADAR
SAR .... Synthetic Aperture RADAR [*Computer imaging*]
SAR .... Synthetic Aperture RADAR
SAR .... Syrian Arab Republic
SAR .... System Acquisition Report
SAR .... System Analysis Report
SAR .... System Array RADAR (KSC)
SAR .... System Availability Report
SAR .... Systemic Acquired Resistance [*Biology*]
SAR .... Systemic Arterial Resistance [*Medicine*]
SAR .... Systemic Availability Ratio [*Physiology*]
SAR .... Systems Assessment Review [*NASA*] (KSC)
SARA .... Saralasin [*Antihypertensive*]
SARA .... Saratoga National Historical Park
SARA .... Saratoga Trunk (DSUE)
SARA .... Satellite Angular Radiometer (NOAA)
SARA .... Saturates, Aromatics, Resins, and Asphaltenes [*Crude oil analysis*]
SARA .... Scottish Amateur Rowing Association (DBA)
SARA .... Search and Replace Automatically [*Computer science*] (DGA)
SARA .... Search and Rescue Aid
SARA .... Sequential Automatic Recorder and Annunciator
SARA .... Sexual Assault Research Association (EA)
SARA .... Sexually-Acquired Reactive Arthritis [*Medicine*] (PDAA)
SARA .... Ship Angle and Range (SAA)
SARA .... Sleep Apnoea Research Association [*Australia*]
SARA .... Society for the Advancement of Research into Anorexia [*British*] (DBA)
SARA .... Society of American Registered Architects (EA)
SARA .... South Australian Restaurant Association
SARA .... South Australian Rowing Association
SARA .... Southeastern Association for Research in Astronomy [*University of Georgia*] [*Research center*] (RCD)
SARA .... Still Another Response Averager
SARA .... Student Admission Records Administration (IAA)
SARA .... Superfund Amendment and Reauthorization Act [*1986*]
SARA .... System Availability and Reliability Analysis (MHDB)
SARA .... System for Anesthetic and Respiratory Analysis
SARA .... Systems Analysis and Resource Accounting [*Data processing system*]
S Arab .... Saudi Arabia (VRA)
SARAC .... South Australian Rural Advisory Council
SARAC .... Steerable Array for RADAR and Communications (CET)
SARAD .... South African Rates and Data [*A publication*] (IMH)
SARAH .... Search and Range Homing
SARAH .... Search and Rescue and Homing
SARAH .... Semiactive RADAR Alternate Head
SARAH .... Semiautomatic Range Azimuth and Height [*Subsystem*]
Sarah Lawrence C... Sarah Lawrence College (GAGS)
SaraLee .... Sara Lee Corp. [*Associated Press*] (SAG)
SARARC .... Subauroral Red Arc [*Geophysics*]
Sarat Ch Sent... Saratoga Chancery Sentinel [*1841-47*] [*New York*] [*A publication*] (DLA)
SaratgB .... Saratoga Brands, Inc. [*Associated Press*] (SAG)
SaratgBrd ...... Saratoga Brands, Inc. [*Associated Press*] (SAG)
SaratgBv .... Saratoga Beverage Group [*Associated Press*] (SAG)
SARAW .... Sarawak [*Malaysia*] (ROG)
SARB .... State Air Resources Board
Sarbah .... Sarbah's Fanti Law Reports [*Gold Coast*] [*A publication*] (DLA)
Sarbah FC ...... Sarbah's Fanti Customary Laws [*Ghana*] [*A publication*] (DLA)
SARBE .... Search and Rescue-Beacon Equipment (MCD)
SARBICA .... Southeast Asian Regional Branch of the International Council on Archives (EAIO)
SARC .... Corrientes [*Argentina ICAO location identifier*] (ICLI)
SARC .... Sarcasm (DSUE)
sarc .... Sarcoma [*Medicine*] (MAE)
sarc .... Sarcophagi (VRA)
sarc .... Sarcophagus (VRA)
SARC .... Search and Rescue Center (CINC)
SARC .... Secure Airborne RADAR Control
SARC .... Split Armature Receiver Capsule (PDAA)
SARC .... Sutton Avian Research Center
SAR-C .... Synthetic Aperture RADAR - C-Band (SSD)
SARC .... System Acquisition Review Council [*Army*]
SARC .... Systems Analysis and Research Corp.
SARCA .... Senior Army Reserve Commanders Association
SARCALM .... Synthetic Array RADAR Command Air-Launched Missile
SARCAP .... Search and Rescue - Civil Air Patrol (MCD)
SARCAP .... Search and Rescue Combat Air Patrol (IAA)
SARCAR .... Smithsonian Archaeometric Research Collection and Records [*Facility*]
SARCC .... Search and Rescue Coordination Center [*Air Force*]
SARCCUS .... South African Regional Committee for Conservation and Utilization of Soil
SARCEN .... Search and Rescue Central [*Navy*]
Sar Ch Sen... Saratoga Chancery Sentinel [*New York*] [*A publication*] (DLA)
SARCOM .... Search and Rescue Communicator [*Navy*]
SARCUP .... Search and Rescue Capability Upgrade Project [*Canadian Navy*]
SARD .... Resistencia (Ciudad) [*Argentina ICAO location identifier*] (ICLI)
SARD .... Sardinia
Sard .... Sardinia (VRA)
SARD .... Simulated Aircraft RADAR Data
SARD .... Solar Array Release and Deployment (MCD)
SARD .... Special Airlift Requirement Directive [*Air Force*] (AFM)
SARD .... Special Airlift Requirement Document [*Army*]
SARD .... Statistical Analysis and Reports Division [*Administrative Office of the U S Courts*] [*Washington, DC*] (GRD)
SARD .... Support and Range Development (MUGU)
SARD .... Synchronized Accumulating Radioisotope Detection
SARDA .... Society for Aid and Rehabilitation of Drug Addicts [*Hong Kong*]
SARDA .... State and Regional Defense Airlift Plan [*FAA, Civil Defense*]
SARDC .... Small Arms Research and Development Center [*Army*]
SARDEC .... Societe des Auteurs, Recherchistes, Documentalistes, et Compositeurs [*Canada*]
SARDET .... Search and Rescue Detachment [*Navy*] (NG)
SARDIP .... Stricken Aircraft Reclamation and Disposal Program [*Navy*] (NG)
SARDPO .... San Antonio Research and Development Procurement Office [*Air Force*]
SARDS .... Special Air Route Designators (CINC)
SARDX .... Sardonyx [*Gemstone*] (ROG)
SARE .... Resistencia [*Argentina ICAO location identifier*] (ICLI)
SARE .... Safety Review [*A publication*]
SAREA .... Sinus Area of Leaf [*Botany*]
SARED .... Supporting Applied Research and Exploratory Development [*National Weather Service*]
SAREF .... Safety Research Experiment Facility [*Nuclear energy*]
SAREP .... Speech and Reading Enrichment Program
SAREX .... Search and Rescue Exercise (MCD)
SAREX .... Search and Rescue Exercise [*Navy*] (DOMA)
SAREX .... Shuttle Amateur Radio Experiment [*NASA*]
SARF .... Formosa [*Argentina ICAO location identifier*] (ICLI)
SARF .... Semiautomated Reconstruction Facility [*Military*] (CAAL)
SARF .... Southeast Asia Rescue Foundation (EA)
SARF .... Southern Africa Road Federation [*See also SAPF*] (EAIO)
Sar FCL .... Sarbah's Fanti Customary Laws [*Ghana*] [*A publication*] (DLA)
Sar FLR .... Sarbah's Fanti Law Cases [*1845-1903*] [*Ghana*] [*A publication*] (DLA)
Sar FNC .... Sarbah's Fanti National Constitution [*Ghana*] [*A publication*] (DLA)
SARFS .... Subordinate Army Field Services
Sarg .... Sargonic (BJA)
SARG .... Self-Adapting Report Generator [*Computer science*] (MHDI)
SARG .... Synthetic Aperture RADAR Guidance (MCD)
SARG .... Synthetic Aperture Retransmission Guidance (MCD)
SARGE .... Surveillance and Reconnaissance Ground Equipment
SARGUN .... Synthetic Aperture RADAR Gun [*NASA*]
SARI .... Iguazu/Cataratas Del Iguazu [*Argentina ICAO location identifier*] (ICLI)

SARI .... Share-a-Ride International (EA)
SARI .... Silicon Architectures Research Initiative [*British*]
SARI .... Small Airport Runway Indicator (IAA)
SARI .... South Australian Recreation Institute
SARI .... Standby Altitude Reference Indicator (MCD)
SARIE .... Semiautomatic RADAR Identification Equipment (MCD)
SARIHHWP... Serendipity Association for Research and Implementation of Holistic Health and World Peace (EA)
SARIMS .... Swept Angle Retarding Ion Mass Spectrometer (PDAA)
SARIPADI .... Serikat Pamong Desa Indonesia [*Village Officials' Union of Indonesia*]
SARIS .... South African Retrospective Information System (NITA)
SARIS .... Synthetic Aperture RADAR Interpretation System [*NASA*] (MCD)
SARISA .... Surface Analysis by Resonance Ionization of Sputtered Atoms
SARITC .... South Australian Retail Industry Training Council
SARK .... Saville Advanced Remote Keying (MCD)
SARL .... Paso De Los Libres [*Argentina ICAO location identifier*] (ICLI)
SARL .... Societe a Responsabilite Limitee [*Private Limited Company*] [*French*]
SARL .... Subtropical Agricultural Research Laboratory [*Weslaco, TX*] [*Department of Agriculture*] (GRD)
SARLA .... South African Rock Lobster Association [*Defunct*]
SARLANT ..... Search and Rescue, Atlantic [*Coast Guard*]
SARM .... Monte Caseros [*Argentina ICAO location identifier*] (ICLI)
SARM .... Set Asynchronous Response Mode
SARM .... Standard Analytical Reference Material (MCD)
SARM .... Standard Antiradiation Missile (MCD)
SARM .... System Acquisition Review Memorandum [*Army*]
SARMC .... Search and Rescue Mission Coordinator [*Australia*]
SARME .... Set Asychronous Response Mode Extended [*Telecommunications*] (OSI)
SARMIS .... Search and Rescue Management Information System [*BTS*] (TAG)
SARMIT .... Sport and Recreation Association of RMIT [*Royal Melbourne Institute of Techn ology*] Union
SARNI .... Serikat Nelajan Indonesia [*Sailors' Union of Indonesia*]
SARO .... Ituzaingo [*Argentina ICAO location identifier*] (ICLI)
SARO .... Special Applications Routine (IAA)
SAROA .... Salvation Army Retired Officers Association
SAROAD ...... Storage and Retrieval of Aerometric Data [*Database*] [*Sigma Data Services Corp.*] [*Information service or system*] (CRD)
SARP .... Posadas [*Argentina ICAO location identifier*] (ICLI)
SARP .... Safety Analysis Report for Packaging [*NASA*] (NASA)
SARP .... Sardine-Anchovy Recruitment Project [*Marine science*] (OSRA)
SARP .... Schedule, Analysis, and Review Procedure [*NASA*] (KSC)
SARP .... Schedule and Resources Procedure [*NASA*] (KSC)
SARP .... Scheduling and Reporting [*or Review*] Procedure [*NASA*] (KSC)
SARP .... Scramble and Recovery Procedure (SAA)
SARP .... Severe Accident Research Plan [*Nuclear energy*] (NRCH)
SARP .... Ship Alteration and Repair Package [*Navy*] (CAAL)
SARP .... Shuttle Astronaut Recruitment Program [*NASA*] (MCD)
SARP .... Signal Automatic RADAR Processing
SARP .... Small Autonomous Research Package
SARP .... Sophisticated Automatic RADAR Processing (PDAA)
SARP .... Space Allocation and Reservation Program (MCD)
SARP .... Space Allocation Requirement Procedures (MCD)
SARP .... Standards and Recommended Practices
SARP .... Storage and Retrieval Processor (MCD)
SARPAC .... Search and Rescue, Pacific [*Coast Guard*] (DNAB)
SARPF .... Strategic Air Relocatable Photographic Facility (CINC)
SARPMA ...... San Antonio Real Property Maintenance Agency [*Military*]
SARPS .... Standards and Recommended Practices [*International Civil Aviation Organization*]
SARR .... Resistencia [*Argentina ICAO location identifier*] (ICLI)
SARRA .... Short-Arc Reduction of RADAR Altimetry
SARRP .... Severe Accident Risk Reduction Program [*Nuclear energy*] (NRCH)
SARS .... Presidencia R. Saenz Pena [*Argentina ICAO location identifier*] (ICLI)
SaRS .... Safety and Reliability Society [*British*]
SARS .... Scots Ancestry Research Society [*British*] (DBA)
SARS .... Secretary of the Army Research and Study [*Fellowship*]
SARS .... Semi-Active RADAR Simulator [*Military*]
SARS .... Semiautomated Reconstruction System [*Military*] (CAAL)
SARS .... Sensor Analog Relay System
SARS .... Ship Attitude Record System
SARS .... Simulated Airborne RADAR System (MCD)
SARS .... Single Allocation and Reservation Study (MCD)
SARS .... Single-Axis Reference System
SARS .... Solar Array Reorientation System
SARS .... Spares Accounting Replenishment System [*NASA*] (KSC)
SARS .... Standardized Army Refueling System (DOMA)
SARS .... Static Automatic Reporting System (MCD)
SARS .... Stellar Attitude Reference Study
SARS .... Student Association for the Rights of Students [*Australia*]
SARS .... Synthetic Array RADAR System
SARSA .... Social Affairs Recreation and Sports Association
SARSAT .... Search and Rescue Satellite [*Navy*]
SARSAT .... Search and Rescue Satellite-Aided Tracking [*NASA*]
SARSAT .... Synthetic Aperture RADAR Satellite [*NASA*] (SSD)
SARSEP .... Salary Reduction Simplified Employee Pension
SARSEX .... Synthetic Aperture RADAR Signature Experiment [*Oceanography*]
SARSIM .... Search and Rescue Simulation [*Coast Guard*]
SARSN .... Southern Appalachian Regional Seismic Network [*Geology*]
SARSS .... Search and Rescue Satellite System [*Navy*] (MCD)
SARSS .... Standard Army Retail Supply System
SARSS/OSC... Standard Army Retail Supply System/Objective Supply Capability (RDA)
SART .... Seattle Army Terminal
SART .... Society for Assisted Reproductive Technology (EA)
SART .... Special Army Review Team (MCD)
SART .... St. Alban's Repertory Theater [*Washington, DC*]
SART .... Standard Acid Reflux Test [*Clinical chemistry*]
SART .... Stimuli Analog Refresh Table [*NASA*] (MCD)
SART .... Stop All Racist Tours [*An association British*]
SART .... Strategic Aircraft Reconstitution Team [*Air Force*] (DOMA)
SARTACK ...... Search AntiRADAR Tactical Aircraft, K-Band
SARTAF .... Search and Rescue Task Force [*Military*] (VNW)
SARTEL .... Search and Rescue, Telephone [*Coast Guard*]
SARTOC .... Southern Africa Regional Tourism Council (EAIO)
SARTS .... Satisfaction of Army Requirements through Space (MCD)
SARTS .... Small Arms Readiness Training Section [*National Guard*]
SARTS .... Small Arms Remote Target System (MCD)
SARTS .... Switched Access Remote Test System [*Bell System*]
SARU .... Resistencia [*Argentina ICAO location identifier*] (ICLI)
SARU .... South Australian Rugby Union
SARU .... System Analysis Research Unit
SARUM .... Bishop of Salisbury [*British*]
SARUS .... Search and Rescue Using Satellites [*Air Force*]
SARV .... Satellite Aeromedical Research Vehicle
SARVIP .... Survival Army Recovery Vest, Insert, and Pockets
SAS .... Lithuanian Catholic Students' Association "Ateitis" (EA)
SAS .... Salicylazosulfapyridine [*Antibacterial*]
SAS .... Salton City, CA [*Location identifier FAA*] (FAAL)
SAS .... Sample Array System (KSC)
SAS .... Sand-Asphalt-Sulfur [*Road paving material*]
SAS .... Saskatoon [*Saskatchewan*] [*Seismograph station code, US Geological Survey Closed*] (SEIS)
SAS .... Satellite Attack Sensor
SAS .... Scandinavian Airlines System [*Sweden ICAO designator*] (FAAC)
SAS .... Schiapparelli [*Italy*] [*Research code symbol*]
SAS .... School Administrator and Supervisor (GAGS)
SAS .... SEAL [*Subsea Equipment Associates Ltd.*] Atmospheric System
SAS .... Sealed Authentication System [*Military*]
SAS .... Seasonal Agricultural Service
SAS .... Secondary Alarm Station [*Nuclear energy*] (NRCH)
SAS .... Secondary Alerting System (IAA)
SAS .... Secondary Alkane Sulfonate [*Surfactant*] [*Organic chemistry*]
SAS .... Secondary Assistance Scheme [*Australia*]
SAS .... Sections Administratives Specialisees [*French Army*]
SAS .... Secure Authentication System (IIA)
SAS .... Security Agency Study [*Nuclear energy*] (NRCH)
SAS .... Security Assistance and Sales [*DoD*]
SAS .... Segment Arrival Storage Area (KSC)
SAS .... Selected Applicant Service (NITA)
SAS .... Self-Adaptive System
SAS .... Semi-Airspace (NITA)
SAS .... Senior Assistant Secretary
SAS .... Sensor and Source
SAS .... Service Activity System
SAS .... Service Air System (NRCH)
SAS .... Service Annual Survey [*Bureau of the Census*] (GFGA)
SAS .... Sex Attitudes Survey [*Psychology*]
SAS .... Shakespearean Authorship Society [*Later, SAT*] (EA)
SAS .... Sherwood Anderson Society (EA)
SAS .... Shift Accumulator Left, Including Sign (IAA)
SAS .... Ship Alteration Suite [*Navy*] (CAAL)
SAS .... Short-Arm Splint [*Orthopedics*] (DAVI)
SAS .... Side-Angle-Side (Rule) [*Geometry*]
SAS .... Signal Airways Service
SAS .... Signal Analysis System [*Electronics*]
SAS .... Silicon Avalanche Suppressor [*Telecommunications*]
SAS .... Single Angle Scattering
SAS .... Single Anomalous Scattering [*Crystallography*]
SAS .... Single Attached Stations [*Computer science*] (TNIG)
SAS .... Single Audio System (CAAL)
SAS .... Single-Award Schedule (AAGC)
SAS .... Sklar Aphasia Scale [*Psychology*]
SAS .... Sleep Apnea Syndrome [*Medicine*]
SAS .... Small-Angle Scattering (OA)
SAS .... Small Applications Satellite (KSC)
SAS .... Small Arms School [*British military*] (DMA)
SAS .... Small Astronomy Satellite
SAS .... Small-Probe Atmospheric Structure [*NASA*]
SAS .... Smart Armor System [*Army*]
SAS .... Snake Approach Scale [*Psychology*]
SAS .... Snap Action Switch
SAS .... Societatis Antiquariorum Socius [*Fellow of the Society of Antiquaries*] [*British*]
SAS .... Society for Applied Sociology (EA)
SAS .... Society for Applied Spectroscopy (EA)
SAS .... Society for Armenian Studies (EA)
SAS .... Society of American Silversmiths (EA)
SAS .... Society of Antiquaries of Scotland (EAIO)
SAS .... Society of Australasian Specialists [*Later, SASO*]
SAS .... Sodium Alkane Sulfonate [*Detergent intermediate*]
SAS .... Sodium Aluminum Sulfate [*Organic chemistry*]
SAS .... Solar Array Structure
SAS .... Solar Array System (MCD)
SAS .... Solar Aspect Sensor
SAS .... Solomons Ano Sagufenua [*Solomon Islands*] [*Political party*] (FEA)
SAS .... Son Altesse Serenissime [*His or Her Serene Highness*] [*French*]
SAS .... Sound Amplification System
SAS .... South American Series [*A publication*]

SAS.......... South Asian Seas
SAS.......... Southern Anthropological Society
SAS.......... Southern Appalachian Studies [*Defunct*] (EA)
SAS.......... Soviet Academy of Sciences
SAS.......... Space Activity Suit
SAS.......... Space Adaptation Syndrome [*NASA*]
SAS.......... Spacecraft Antenna System
SAS.......... Special Access Space (CAAL)
SAS.......... Special Activities Squadron [*Air Force*]
SAS.......... Special Airlift Summary [*MTMC*] (TAG)
SAS.......... Special Air Service [*British commando unit*]
SAS.......... Special Air Services [*Australia*] (VNW)
SAS.......... Special Ammunition Section [*Picatinny Arsenal*] [*Army*]
SAS.......... Special Ammunition Site [*Army*]
SAS.......... Special Ammunition Stockage [*Army*] (AABC)
SAS.......... Special Ammunition Storage (RDA)
SAS.......... Special Army Squadron [*British*] (DI)
SAS.......... Stability Augmentation System [*or Subsystem*] [*FAA*]
SAS.......... Staff Activity System (IAA)
SAS.......... Staff Administrative Specialist [*Military*]
SAS.......... St. Andrew Goldfields Ltd. [*Toronto Stock Exchange symbol*]
SAS.......... St. Andrew Society [*Edinburgh, Scotland*] (EAIO)
SAS.......... Statement of Auditing Standards
SAS.......... Station Air System [*Nuclear energy*] (NRCH)
SAS.......... Statistical Analysis System [*Programming language*] [*1966*]
SAS.......... Sterile Aqueous Suspension
SAS.......... Storage Address Switch (IAA)
SAS.......... Storage Aids Systems [*Air Force*] (DOMA)
SAS.......... Strategic Aerospace Summary
SAS.......... Strategic Area Study (MCD)
SAS.......... Subaortic Stenosis [*Medicine*] (DMAA)
SAS.......... Sulfasalazine [*Pharmacology*] (DAVI)
SAS.......... Sum of Adjacent Spans
SAS.......... Super Accuracy Simplex (IAA)
SAS.......... Supercritical Antisolvent [*Chemical engineering*]
SAS.......... Superior Atrial Septum [*Anatomy*]
SAS.......... Supersonic Attack Seaplane
SAS.......... Support Amplifier Station [*Telecommunications*] (OA)
SAS.......... Supravalvular Aortic Stenosis [*Cardiology*]
SAS.......... Surface Active Substances (IEEE)
SAS.......... Survival Avionics System [*Military*] (CAAL)
SAS.......... Suspended Aluminosilicate
SAS.......... Suspended Array System [*To detect submarines*]
SAS.......... SverigeAmerika Stiftelsen [*Sweden-American Foundation*] (EAIO)
SAS.......... Switched Access System [*Telecommunications*] (TEL)
SAS.......... Synthetic Amorphous Silicas [*Inorganic Chemistry*]
SAS.......... System Acquisition School (MCD)
SAS.......... System Analysis Study
SAS.......... System Application Software [*Computer science*] (BUR)
SASA.......... Salta [*Argentina ICAO location identifier*] (ICLI)
SASA.......... Scottish Amateur Swimming Association (DBA)
SASA.......... Severe Accident Sequence Analysis [*Nuclear energy*] (NRCH)
SASA.......... Ski Area Suppliers Association (EA)
SASA.......... Small Arms Systems Agency [*Army*] (RDA)
SASA.......... Soil Association of South Australia
SASA.......... South Asian Studies Association of Australia and New Zealand
SASA.......... South Australian Sawmillers' Association
SASA.......... Special Ammunition Supply Activity (MCD)
SASAR.......... Segmented Aperture-Synthetic Aperture RADAR
SASAS.......... Southern Africa Society of Aquatic Scientists (EAIO)
SASAT.......... Shipboard Antisubmarine Attack Teacher [*Navy*]
SASB.......... South Australian Superannuation Board
SASB.......... Structural Analysis of Social Behavior
SASBFIT.......... South Australian Superannuation Board Fund Investment Trust
SASBO.......... Southeastern Association of School Business Officials (AEBS)
SASC.......... Salta [*Argentina ICAO location identifier*] (ICLI)
SASC.......... Semiautomatic Stock Control
SASC.......... Senate Armed Services Committee
SASC.......... Senior Appointments Selection Committee [*British*]
SASC.......... Small Arms School Corps [*Military British*]
SASC.......... Subject Analysis Systems Collection [*University of Toronto*] [*Information service or system*] (IID)
SASC.......... Sydney Anglican Schools Corp. [*Commercial firm*]
SASCL.......... St. Ansgar's Scandinavian Catholic League (EA)
SASCO.......... Sudanese Aeronautical Services Co. Ltd. [*Sudan*] [*ICAO designator*] (FAAC)
SASCOM.......... Southern Atlantic Satellite Communication
SASCOM.......... Special Ammunition Support Command [*Army*] (AABC)
SASCON.......... Southern African Solidarity Congress [*Zimbabwe*] [*Political party*] (PPW)
SAS/CSS.......... Stability Augmentation System with Control Stick Steering (PDAA)
SASD.......... Static Adjustable Speed Drive
SASD.......... Strategies and Air Standards Division [*Environmental Protection Agency*] (GFGA)
SA/SD.......... Structured Analysis/Structured Design (MCD)
SASDT.......... Ships and Aircraft Supplemental Data Tables [*Navy*]
SASE.......... Self-Addressed Stamped Envelope
sase.......... Self-Addressed Stamped Envelope (ODBW)
SASE.......... Small Arms Suppression Evaluation (MCD)
SASE.......... Space Adaptation Syndrome Experiment [*Pronounced "Sassy"*] [*Space shuttle experiment developed in Canada*]
SASE.......... Specific Application Service Element [*Telecommunications*] (OSI)
SASE.......... Statistical Analysis of a Series of Events (PDAA)
SASES.......... South Australian State Emergency Services
SASF.......... SIDPERS [*Standard Installation/Division Personnel System*] Authorized Strength File [*Military*] (AABC)
SASFA.......... South Australian Shark Fishermen's Association
SASG.......... Security Assistance Steering Group [*Military*]
SASG.......... Smoke/Aerosol Steering Group [*DARCOM*] (RDA)
SASH.......... Symmetry-Adapted Spherical-Harmonic [*Mathematics*]
SASHEP.......... Study of Accreditation of Selected Health Educational Programs
SASI.......... Ships and Air Systems Integration [*Navy*]
SASI.......... Shugart Associates Systems Interface
SASI.......... Society of Air Safety Investigators [*Later, ISASI*]
SASI.......... Southern Association of Science and Industry (EA)
SASI.......... Surface Air System Integration
SASI.......... System Automation Software, Inc.
SASI.......... System on Automotive Safety Information [*General Motors Corp.*] [*Information service or system*]
SASIDS.......... Stochastic Adaptive Sequential Information Dissemination System
SASIS.......... Semi-Automatic Speaker Identification System (PDAA)
SASITS.......... Submarine Advanced Signal Training System (DNAB)
SASJ.......... Jujuy [*Argentina ICAO location identifier*] (ICLI)
SASJ.......... Self-Aligning Swivel Joint
SASK.......... Saskatchewan [*Canadian province*]
Sask.......... Saskatchewan [*Canadian province*] (ODBW)
Sask.......... Saskatchewan [*Canada*] (DD)
Sask.......... Saskatchewan Law Reports [*Canada*] [*A publication*] (DLA)
Sask L.......... Saskatchewan Law [*A publication*] (DLA)
Sask LR.......... Saskatchewan Law Reports [*Canada*] [*A publication*] (DLA)
Sask R.......... Saskatchewan Law Reports [*A publication*] (DLA)
Sask Rev Stat... Saskatchewan Revised Statutes [*Canada*] [*A publication*] (DLA)
Sask Stat.......... Saskatchewan Statutes [*Canada*] [*A publication*] (DLA)
SaskTel.......... Saskatchewan Telecommunications [*Regina*] [*Information service or system*] (IID)
SASL.......... Service Approved Status List [*Navy*] (DNAB)
SASLA.......... South Australian Salaried Lawyers' Association
SASLIC.......... Surrey and Sussex Libraries in Cooperation (NITA)
SASM.......... Smithsonian Air and Space Museum
SASM.......... Society for Automation in the Sciences and Mathematics
SASM.......... Special Assistant for Strategic Mobility [*Military*] (AFM)
SASM.......... Supersonic Antiship Missile (MCD)
SASMB.......... South Australian Stock Medicines Board
SASMC.......... South Australian Sports Medicine Centre
SASMS.......... Special Assistant for Surface Missile System
SASMSA.......... South Australian Stud Merino Sheepbreeders' Association
SASN.......... Special Assistant to the Secretary of the Navy
SASO.......... Oran [*Algeria*] [*ICAO location identifier*] (ICLI)
SASO.......... Sasol Ltd. [*NASDAQ symbol*] (NQ)
SASO.......... Senior Air Staff Officer [*British*]
SASO.......... Society of Australasian Specialists/Oceania (EA)
SASO.......... South African Students' Organization (PD)
SASO.......... Superintending Armament Supply Officer [*British military*] (DMA)
SASOC.......... School Administrators and Supervisors Organizing Committee [*Later, AFSA*] (EA)
Sasol.......... Sasol Ltd. [*Associated Press*] (SAG)
SASOY.......... Sasol Ltd ADR [*NASDAQ symbol*] (TTSB)
SASP.......... Salicylazosulfapyridine (DMAA)
SASP.......... Science and Application Space Platform (MCD)
SASP.......... Shortest Activity from Shortest Project
SASP.......... Single Advanced Signal Processor [*Military*] (CAAL)
SASP.......... Site Activation and Support Plan (MCD)
SASP.......... Society for the Advancement of Social Psychology (EA)
SASP.......... Society of Sales Professionals [*Automotive sales certification program*]
SASP.......... Special Ammunition Supply Point [*Army*]
SASP.......... Specialized Acid-Soluble Spore Protein [*Bacteriology*]
SASP.......... Stand Alone Support Program
SASP.......... State Agency for Surplus Property
SASP.......... State Airport System Plan [*Department of Transportation*]
SASP.......... Submarine Analytic Search Program [*Navy*] (CAAL)
SA-SPM.......... Socialist Alliance - Socialist Party of Macedonia [*Political party*] (EY)
SASPS.......... SAMMS [*Standard Automated Materiel Management System*] Automated Small Purchase System
SASQ.......... La Quiaca [*Argentina ICAO location identifier*] (ICLI)
SASq.......... Strategic Aerospace Squadron [*Air Force*]
SASQUA.......... Southern African Society for Quaternary Research (EAIO)
SASR.......... Rivadavia [*Argentina ICAO location identifier*] (ICLI)
SASR.......... Sandy Spring Bancorp [*NASDAQ symbol*] (TTSB)
SASR.......... Sandy Spring Bancorp, Inc. [*NASDAQ symbol*] (SAG)
SASR.......... Semi-Annual Status Report (MHDI)
SASR.......... Subaqueous Sound Ranging (IAA)
SASRDI.......... Subaqueous Sound Ranging Development Installation (IAA)
SASRS.......... Satellite-Aided Search and Rescue System [*Telecommunications*]
SASS.......... SAGE [*Semiautomatic Ground Environment*] Atabe Simulation System (IAA)
SASS.......... Saturn Automatic Software System [*NASA*]
SASS.......... Schedules and Status Summary [*NASA*] (KSC)
SASS.......... School and Staffing Survey [*Department of Education*] (GFGA)
SASS.......... SEASAT [*Sea Satellite*]- A Scatterometer System [*NASA*]
SASS.......... Sir Arthur Sullivan Society [*British*] (DBA)
SASS.......... Small Aerostat Surveillance System [*Army*] (DOMA)
SASS.......... Small Airbreathing System Synthesis (MCD)
SASS.......... Society for Automation in the Social Sciences [*Later, SDE*]
SASS.......... Society for the Advancement of Scandinavian Study (EA)
SASS.......... Source Assessment Sampling System [*Environmental Protection Agency*]
SASS.......... Spark Chamber Automatic Scanning System (DNAB)
SASS.......... Special Aircraft Service Shop (NG)

SASS .... Special Army Signal Service (IAA)
SASS .... SPEEDEX [*Systemwide Project for Electronic Equipment at Depots Extended*] Automatic Scheduling System [*Military*]
SASS .... Spreadsheet Anthropometric Scaling System [*Army*] (RDA)
SASS .... Standard Analysis Software System [*Astronomy*]
SASS .... Standard Army Supply System
SASS .... Strategic Airborne Surveillance System [*Military*]
SASS .... Strategic Alerting Sound System (AAG)
SASS .... Supplement Aviation Spares Report (MCD)
SASS .... Suspended Array Surveillance System [*To detect submarines*]
SASS .... Swath-Sounding Sonar (BARN)
SASS .... Systems and Services Section [*Library Administration and Management Association*]
SASSA .... South Australian Stock Salesmen's Association
SASSC .... Senate Aeronautical and Space Sciences Committee (AAG)
SASSE .... Synchronous Altitude Spin-Stabilized Experiment
SASSI .... Synthetic Amorphous Silica and Silicates Industry Association (EA)
SASSIA .... Synthetic Amorphous Silica and Silicates Industry Association (EA)
SASSIF .... Self-Adjusting System of Scientific Information Flow
SASS LITE ... Small Airship Surveillance System, Low Intensity Target Exploitation [*Army*]
SASSM .... Surface-to-Air, Surface-to-Surface Missile (MCD)
SASSTIXS .... Satellite Air, Surface, Subsurface Tactical Information Exchange System [*Navy*] (CAAL)
SASSY .... Small Angle Separator System [*Superheavy element research*]
SASSY .... Supported Activities Supply System [*Marine Corps*]
SAST .... Safety Standards
SAST .... Selective Arterial Secretin Injection Test [*Medicine*] (DMAA)
SAST .... Self-Administered Alcoholism Screening Test [*Medicine*] (DMAA)
SAST .... Serum Aspartate Aminotransferase [*Medicine*] (DMAA)
SAST .... Serum Aspartate Aminotransferase [*An enzyme*]
SAST .... Service Announcements in Science and Technology [*National Technical Information Service*] (EA)
SAST .... Single Asphalt Surface Treatment
SAST .... Society for the Advancement of Space Travel [*Defunct*] (MCD)
SAST .... Tartagal/Gral Mosconi [*Argentina ICAO location identifier*] (ICLI)
SASTA JI ...... SASTA [*South Australian Science Teachers Association*] Journal [*A publication*]
SASTAR .... Support Activities Staffing Review (MCD)
SASTE .... Semiautomatic Shop Test Equipment (NG)
SASTP .... Stand-Alone Self-Test Program [*NASA*] (MCD)
SASTRO .... SAGE [*Semiautomatic Ground Environment*] Strobe Training Operator (IAA)
SASTU .... Signal Amplitude Sampler and Totalizing Unit (IEEE)
SASU .... Saturn Apollo Systems Utilization [*NASA*]
SASUTA .... Southern African Society of University Teachers of Accounting (EAIO)
SASV .... Secondary Air Switching Valve [*Automotive engineering*]
SASV .... Sisters of the Assumption (TOCD)
SASV .... Sisters of the Assumption of the Blessed Virgin [*Roman Catholic religious order*]
SASV .... Snap Action Spool Valve
SASVRC .... Sir Albert Sakzewski Virus Research Centre [*Australia*]
SASVRC .... Sir Albert Sakzewski Virus Research Centre [*Austria*]
SASW .... Situational Attitude Scale-Women (EDAC)
SASWREC .... SACLANT [*Supreme Allied Commander, Atlantic*] Antisubmarine Warfare Research Center (NATG)
SAT .... Asia Satellite Telecommunications Holdings Ltd. [*NYSE symbol*] (SAG)
SAT .... Canadian Satellite Communications, Inc. [*Toronto Stock Exchange symbol*]
SAT .... Safe Arming Time
SAT .... Salamaua Aerial Transport [*Australia*]
SAT .... Salaries and Allowances Tribunal [*Australia*]
SAT .... Salt Aggregation Test [*Clinical chemistry*]
SAT .... Sampler Address Translator
SAT .... San Antonio [*Texas*] [*Airport symbol*]
SAT .... Sang-Tuda [*Former USSR Seismograph station code, US Geological Survey Closed*] (SEIS)
SAT .... Satellite
SAT .... Satellite
sat .... Satin (VRA)
Sat .... Satirae [*or Sermones*] [*of Horace*] [*Classical studies*] (OCD)
SAT .... Satisfactory (AABC)
Sat .... Satura [*of Petronius*] [*Classical studies*] (OCD)
SAT .... Saturate (AAG)
sat .... Saturate (IDOE)
sat .... Saturation (IDOE)
SAT .... Saturatus [*Saturated*] [*Pharmacy*]
SAT .... Saturday (EY)
Sat .... Saturday (ODBW)
SAT .... Saturn [*Rocket*] (KSC)
Sat .... Saturn [*Record label*] [*France*]
SAT .... Saturn
Sat .... Saturnalia [*of Macrobius*] [*Classical studies*] (OCD)
SAT .... Scholastic Aptitude Test [*Trademark of the College Entrance Examination Board*]
SAT .... Scholastic Assessment Test [*Formerly, Scholastic Aptitude Test*]
SAT .... School Ability Test [*Psychology*]
SAT .... School of Applied Tactics [*AAFSAT*]
SAT .... Scientific Advisory Team [*Navy*] (MCD)
SAT .... Scientific and Technical (MCD)
SAT .... Sea Acceptance Trial
SAT .... Security Alert Team [*Military*] (AFM)
SAT .... Security Appeals Tribunal [*Australia*]
SAT .... Security Assistance Team [*Military*] (AABC)
SAT .... SEMA [*Specialty Equipment Manufacturers Association*] Action Team
SAT .... Semiarid Tropics [*Geography*]
SAT .... Semiautomatic Test Equipment [*NASA*]
SAT .... Senior Apperception Technique [*Personality development test*] [*Psychology*]
SAT .... Senior Aptitude Tests [*Educational test*]
SAT .... Sennacieca Asocio Tutmonda [*Nationless Worldwide Association*] (EAIO)
SAT .... Serial Accountability Transmittal
SAT .... Serum Agglutination Test (OA)
SAT .... Service Acceptance Trials (NVT)
SAT .... Servico Acoriana de Transportes Aereos [*Portugal ICAO designator*] (FAAC)
SAT .... Shakespearean Authorship Trust [*England*] (EAIO)
SAT .... Ship Acceptance Test [*Navy*] (CAAL)
SAT .... Ship's Apparent Time [*Navigation*]
SAT .... Silicon Annular Transistor
SAT .... Simplified Acquisition Threshold (AAGC)
SAT .... Sine Acido Thymonucleico [*Without Thymonucleic Acid*]
SAT .... Site Acceptance Test [*Military*] (AABC)
SAT .... Site Alteration Tests
SAT .... Site Assignment Time
SAT .... Sitting Atop [*Molecular configuration*]
SAT .... Small Angle Tagger (MCD)
SAT .... Small Arms Transmitter [*Army*] (INF)
SAT .... Snap Action Thermostat
SAT .... Social Assessment of Technology (PDAA)
SAT .... Socially-Appropriate Technology (PDAA)
SAT .... Societa Anonima Transadriatica [*Italy*]
SAT .... Society of Acoustic Technology (IAA)
SAT .... Software Acceptance Test
SAT .... Solar Atmospheric Tide (IAA)
SAT .... Sound-Apperception Test [*Psychology*]
SAT .... South Atlantic
SAT .... Southern African Territories
SAT .... Southern Air Transport, Inc.
SAT .... Space Available Travel
SAT .... Speaker Authentication Technique
SAT .... Special Assistance Team [*Navy*] (NG)
SAT .... Specific Aptitude Test
SAT .... Specified Actions Table [*Military*]
SAT .... Speeck Awareness Threshold [*Otorhinolaryngology*] (DAVI)
SAT .... Spiral Aftereffect Test [*Psychology*]
SAT .... Stabilization Assurance Test (IEEE)
SAT .... Standard Area of Tinplate [*100,000 square inches*]
SAT .... Stanford Achievement Test [*Education*]
SAT .... Staphylococcus Adherence Test [*Clinical chemistry*]
SAT .... Static Air Temperature
SAT .... Stepped Atomic Time [*National Institute of Standards and Technology*]
SAT .... Strategic American Traveler
SAT .... Structural Analysis Technologies, Inc.
SAT .... Study of Appeal Tribunals [*British*]
SAT .... Subacute Thyroiditis [*Medicine*]
SAT .... Subassembly Template (MCD)
SAT .... Subscriber Access Terminal
SAT .... Substance Abuse Treatment [*Health insurance*] (GHCT)
SAT .... Subsumed Abilities Test [*Student attitudes test*]
SAT .... Successive Approximation Technique (NOAA)
SAT .... Sufuric Acid Terrahydrate [*Inorganic chemistry*]
SAT .... Support Analysis Test
SAT .... Surface Aerospace Technology
SAT .... Surface Air Temperature [*Climatology*]
SAT .... Surface Alloy Transistor (IAA)
SAT .... Surface Antenna Terminal (MCD)
SAT .... Surveillance, Acquisition, and Tracking [*Military*] (RDA)
SAT .... Sustained Airborne Training [*Army*] (INF)
SAT .... Symptomless Autoimmune Thyroiditis [*Medicine*] (DMAA)
SAT .... System Access Technique [*Sperry UNIVAC*]
SAT .... System Access Terminal AT&T (NITA)
SAT .... System Alignment Test (NVT)
SAT .... System Analysis Table (IAA)
SAT .... Systematic Assertiveness Training
SAT .... Systematized Assertive Therapy [*Psychology*] (DAVI)
SAT .... Systems Acceptance Tests (KSC)
SAT .... Systems Approach to Training [*NASA*] (MCD)
SATA .... Alliance of Canadian Travel Associations - Saskatchewan (AC)
SATA .... Safety and Arming Test Aid (MCD)
SATA .... Satellite Automatic Tracking Antenna (MCD)
SATA .... Servicios Auxiliares de Transportes [*ICAO designator*] (FAAC)
SATA .... Sherman Anti-Trust Act (MHDB)
SATA .... Sociedade Acoriana de Transportes Aereos Ltda. [*Airline*] [*Portugal*]
SATA .... Something about the Author [*A publication*]
SATA .... South Australian Tennis Association
SATA .... Spatial Average, Temporal Average [*Medicine*] (DMAA)
SATA .... Student Air Travel Association
SATA .... Subsonic Aerodynamic Testing Association (MCD)
SATA .... Supervisory, Administrative, and Technical Association [*Union of Ship Distribution and Allied Workers*] [*British*] (DCTA)
SATAB .... South Australian Totalisator Board
SATAF .... Shuttle Activation Task Force [*NASA*] (NASA)
SATAF .... Site Activation Task Force [*Military*]
SATAF .... Site Activity [*or Alternation*] Task Force [*NASA*] (KSC)

SATAM......... Syndicat Autonome des Travailleurs de la Alimentation de Madagascar [*Autonomous Union of Food Workers of Madagascar*]
SATAN......... Satellite Active Nullifier [*Antisatellite weapon*]
SATAN......... Satellite Automatic Tracking Antenna
Sat An......... Satellite Receiving Antenna (NITA)
SATAN......... Security Administrator Tool for Analyzing Networks
SATAN......... Security Analysis Tool for Auditing Networks [*Computer science*] (CDE)
SATAN......... Self-Contained Automatic Tactical Air Navigation (IAA)
SATAN......... Sensor for Airborne Terrain Analysis
SATAN......... Speed and Throtte Automatic Network (PDAA)
SATAN......... Storage Array Tester and Analyzer (PDAA)
SATAN......... Strobes Against Troops at Night (MCD)
SATAN......... System Administrator Tool for Analyzing Networks
SATANAS..... Semiautomatic Analog Setting (IEEE)
SATANS....... Static and Transient Analysis, Nonlinear, Shells [*Computer program*] [*Navy*]
SATANT....... Satellite Antenna (DWSG)
SATAR......... Satellite for Aerospace Research [*NASA*]
SA Tax Cas... South African Tax Cases [*A publication*] (DLA)
SATB........... Simulated Air Training Bundle (MCD)
SATB........... Soprano, Alto, Tenor, Bass
SATB........... South African Tourism Board
SATB........... Specific Aptitude Test Battery
SATBC......... South Australian Trailer Boat Club
SATC........... Clorinda [*Argentina ICAO location identifier*] (ICLI)
SATC........... SatCon Technology [*NASDAQ symbol*] (TTSB)
SATC........... Satcon Technology Corp. [*NASDAQ symbol*] (SAG)
SATC........... Ship Automatic Torpedo Countermeasures (MCD)
SATC........... South African Tax Cases [*A publication*] (DLA)
SATC........... South Australian Timber Corp. [*Commercial firm*]
SATC........... Students Army Training Corps
SATC........... Suspended Acoustical-Tile Ceiling [*Technical drawings*]
SATCA......... Sino-American Technical Cooperation Association
SATCAMS.... Semiautomatic Tactical Control and Airspace Management System (MCD)
SATCC......... Southern Air Traffic Control Centre [*British*]
SATCH......... Salicylaldehyde Thiocarbohydrazone [*Organic chemistry*]
SATCHMO.... Satchel Mouth [*Nickname of late trumpeter Louis Armstrong*]
SATCO......... Semiautomatic Air Traffic Control (IAA)
SATCO......... Senior Air Traffic Control Officer (NATG)
SATCO......... Signal Automatic Air Traffic Control System
SATCO......... Supervisory Air Traffic Control Organization [*FAA*]
SATCOM...... Satellite Command
SATCOM...... Satellite Communication (NTCM)
SATCOM...... Satellite Communication Agency [*Army*] (IAA)
SATCOM...... Satellite Communications [*Military*]
SATCOM...... Scientific and Technical Communication
SATCOMA.... Satellite Communications Agency [*AEC/DCA*]
SATCOM AGEN... Satellite Communications Agency [*Army*]
Satcon......... Satcon Technology Corp. [*Associated Press*] (SAG)
SATCON....... Satellite Condition [*Military*] (AABC)
SATCRIS...... Semi-Arid Tropical Crops Information Service (IID)
SATCS......... Scandinavian Association for Thoracic and Cardiovascular Surgery (EA)
SATD........... El Dorado [*Argentina ICAO location identifier*] (ICLI)
SATD........... Saturated
satd............ Saturated (IDOE)
SATD........... Seattle Army Terminal Detachment (AABC)
SATD........... Simulation and Training Device [*Army*]
SATD........... Strike Aircraft Test Directorate [*Military*] (CAAL)
SATDAT....... Satellite Data (MCD)
SATDPI........ Salesmen's Association of the Textile Dyeing and Printing Industry (EA)
SATE........... Semiautomatic Test Equipment [*NASA*]
SATE........... Special Acceptance Test Equipment (MCD)
SATE........... Study of Army Test and Evaluation (MCD)
SATEC......... Semiautomatic Technical Control
SATEC......... Societe d'Aide Technique et de Cooperation [*An independent French company*]
SATEFL........ Scottish Association for the Teaching of English as a Foreign Language (AIE)
SATEL......... Satellite (IAA)
SA Telcm..... SA Telecommunications, Inc. [*Associated Press*] (SAG)
SATELCO..... Satellite Telecommunications Co. [*Japanese-American firm*]
SATELDATA... Satellite Databank [*European Space Agency*] [*Database*]
SATELLAB.... Satellite Laboratory (IAA)
SATELLITE... Scientific and Technological Library Literature [*Conference*]
SATELLORB... Satellite Simulation Observation and Research Balloon [*Military*] (DNAB)
SATEMM....... Sectorial Association Transportation Equipment & Machinery Manufacturing (AC)
SATENA....... Servicio de Aeronavegacion a Territorios Nacionales [*Colombian airline*]
SATEX......... Semiautomatic Telegraph Exchange (WDAA)
SATF........... Shiyan Automotive Transmission Factory [*China*]
SATF........... Shortest Access Time First
SATF........... Site Activation Task Force (BARN)
SATF........... Strategic Area Task Force (SAA)
SATF........... Strike and Terrain Following RADAR [*Military*] (PDAA)
SATF........... Substituted Anilines Task Force (EA)
SATFAL........ Satellite Data for Fallout (MCD)
SATFN......... Satisfaction [*Legal shorthand*] (LWAP)
SATFOR....... Special Air Task Force [*Navy*]
SAT for TEE... System Approach to Training for Transfer Effectiveness Evaluation (DNAB)
SATFY......... Satisfactory (AFM)
SATG........... Goya [*Argentina ICAO location identifier*] (ICLI)
SATG........... Saturating (WGA)
SATGA......... Societe Aerienne de Transport Guyane Antilles [*French Guiana Air Transport*]
SAT GCI....... Satellite Ground Controlled Interception (NATG)
SATH........... Shop at Home [*NASDAQ symbol*] (TTSB)
SATH........... Shop at Home, Inc. [*NASDAQ symbol*] (SAG)
SATH........... Society for the Advancement of Travel for the Handicapped (EA)
SATH........... St. Thomas National Historic Site
SAT-HI........ Stanford Achievement Test, Special Edition for Hearing Impaired Students (EDAC)
SATI............ Bernardo De Irigoyen [*Argentina ICAO location identifier*] (ICLI)
SATI............ Selective Access to Tactical Information (PDAA)
SATI............ Society for the Advancement of the Tourism Industry
SATIATER.... Statistical Approach to Investment Appraisal to Evaluate Risk (MHDW)
SATIF.......... Scientific and Technical Information Facility [*NASA*]
SATIN......... SAC [*Strategic Air Command*] Automated Total Information Network (MCD)
SATIN......... SAGE [*Semiautomatic Ground Environment*] Air Traffic Integration
SATIN......... Satellite Inspection (IAA)
SATIN......... Satellite Inspector System (AAG)
SATIPS........ Society of Assistants Training in Preparatory Schools [*British*]
SATIR......... System for Evaluation of Tactical Information on Missile Destroyers
SATIRE........ Scientific and Technical Information Reviewed and Exploited [*A publication*] (RDA)
SATIRE........ Semiautomatic Technical Information Retrieval
SATIS.......... Satisfactory (AAG)
SATIS.......... Science and Technology in Society (AIE)
SATIS.......... Scientific and Technical Information Service (NITA)
SATIS.......... Southern Africa - The Imprisoned Society [*An association British*]
SATISFN...... Satisfaction (ROG)
SATISFY...... Satisfactory (ROG)
SATITC........ South Australian Timber Industry Training Council
SATIVA........ Society for Agricultural Training through Integrated Voluntary Activities (EA)
SATK........... Las Lomitas [*Argentina ICAO location identifier*] (ICLI)
SATK........... Strike Attack [*Military*]
SATKA......... Surveillance, Acquisition, Tracking, and Kill Assessment [*Section of SDI - Strategic Defense Initiative*]
SATL........... Satellite (AABC)
SATL........... Science and Advanced Technology Laboratory [*Army*] (RDA)
SATL........... South Atlantic
SATL........... Surgical Achilles Tendon Lengthening [*Medicine*]
SATLAB........ Simulation and Training Laboratory (SSD)
SATLCONO... Satellite Control Officer [*Air Force*]
SATM........... Mercedes [*Argentina ICAO location identifier*] (ICLI)
SAT-M......... Scholastic Aptitude Test - Mathematics [*College Entrance Examination Board*]
SATM........... Sodium Aurothiomalate [*Organometallic chemistry*]
SATM........... Supply and Training Mission [*Military*] (CINC)
Sat Men........ Saturae Menippeae [*of Varro*] [*Classical studies*] (OCD)
SATMO......... Security Assistance Training Management Office [*Army*]
SATN........... Saturation
SATNAV....... Satellite Navigation (AABC)
SATNET........ Satellite Data Broadcast Networks, Inc. [*New York, NY*] [*Telecommunications*] (TSSD)
SATO........... Obera [*Argentina ICAO location identifier*] (ICLI)
SATO........... Scheduled Airlines Ticket Office
SATO........... Scheduled Airlines Traffic Office [*Military*]
SATO........... Self-Aligning Thick Oxide [*Process*]
SATO........... Shuttle Attached Teleoperator [*NASA*] (NASA)
SATO........... South American Travel Organization
SATO........... Southern African Treaty Organization (NADA)
SATO........... Station Airline Ticket Office (MCD)
SATO........... Supply and Transportation Operations [*NASA*] (NASA)
SATO........... Synthetic Aircraft Turbine Oil
SATOBS....... Satellite Observation (IAA)
SATOBS....... Satellite Observations (SAA)
SATODP....... Satellite Tracking Orbit Determination Program
SATON......... Satisfaction (ROG)
SATO-OS..... Schedule Airlines Tour Office - Overseas
SATOUR....... South African Tourism Board (EA)
SATP........... Security Assistance Training Program [*Military*]
SATP........... Single Aircraft Tracking Program (IAA)
SATP........... Small Arms Target Practice [*Navy*]
SATP........... Software Acceptance Test Procedures
SATP........... Spatial Average Temporal Peak [*Medicine*] (DMAA)
SATP........... Stabilization, Acquisition, Tracking, and Pointing
SATP........... Supplier Assurance Test Procedures
SATPATT..... Satellite Paper Tape Transfer
SATR........... Reconquista [*Argentina ICAO location identifier*] (ICLI)
SATR........... Scheduled Air Transport Rating
SATRA......... Science and Technology Research Abstracts [*A publication*]
SATRA......... Shoe and Allied Trades Research Association [*Later, Footwear Technology Centre*] [*British*] (EA)
SATRA......... Soviet-American Trade Association
SATRAC....... Satellite Automatic Terminal Rendezvous and Coupling (MCD)
SATRACK..... Satellite Tracking (MCD)
SATRAM....... Systeme d'Atterrissage a Trajectoires Multiples [*Aviation*]
SATRAN....... Satellite Reconnaissance Advance Notice (MCD)
SATROS....... Science and Technology Regional Organizations [*British*]

SATS........... S. Allan Taylor Society (EA)
SATS........... Satellite Antenna Test System [*NASA*]
SATS........... Selected Abstract Test Suite [*Telecommunications*] (OSI)
SATS........... Short Airfield for Tactical Support [*Marine Corps*]
SATS........... Shuttle Avionics Test System [*NASA*] (NASA)
SATS........... Simulated Airborne Transpondent System (MCD)
SATS........... Single Array Test System (MCD)
SATS........... Small Applications Technology Satellite (MCD)
SATS........... Small Arms Target System [*British military*] (DMA)
SATS........... Social and Technical Sciences
SATS........... Station Accommodation Test Set (SSD)
SATS........... Surrogate Acquilla Training System [*Army*]
SATS........... Synthetic Armed Aircraft Training System (SAA)
SATSA......... Signal Aviation Test and Support Activity
SATSERV..... Services by Satellite, Inc. [*Defunct*]
SATSIM........ Satellite Simulation [*Military*] (CAAL)
SATSIM........ Saturation Countermeasures Simulator
SATSLAM.... Satellite-Tracked Submarine-Launched Antimissile (MCD)
sat sol......... Saturated Solution [*Pharmacy*] (WGA)
SATSTREAM... Satellite Switchstream (NITA)
SATT........... Science, Applications, Technology Transfer, and Training [*System*] [*National Institutes of Health*]
SATT........... Semiautomatic Transistor Tester [*NASA*]
SATT........... Shear Area Transition Temperature (PDAA)
SATT........... Society of Architects and Allied Technicians (NADA)
SATT........... Strowger Automatic Toll Ticketing [*Telecommunications*]
SATTA.......... South Australian Table Tennis Association
SatTech....... Satellite Technology Management, Inc. [*Associated Press*] (SAG)
SATTR......... Satisfactory to Transfer (NOAA)
SATU.......... Curuzu Cuatia [*Argentina ICAO location identifier*] (ICLI)
SATU.......... Singapore Association of Trade Unions
SATU.......... South African Typographical Union
SATUCC....... Southern African Trade Union Coordination Council [*Gaborone, Botswana*] (EAIO)
SatUK......... Satellite United Kingdom
SATUR......... Saturate (AAG)
SATURN....... Simulation and Assignment of Traffic to Urban Road Networks [*Kins Developments Ltd.*] [*Software package*] (NCC)
SAT-V......... Scholastic Aptitude Test - Verbal [*College Entrance Examination Board*]
SATW.......... Society of American Travel Writers (EA)
satwd.......... Satinwood (VRA)
SATX........... Satellite Express [*Telecommunications*]
Sau............. All India Reporter, Saurashtra [*1950-57*] [*A publication*] (DLA)
SAU............ Saltair [*Utah*] [*Seismograph station code, US Geological Survey*] (SEIS)
SAU............ Samarkano Resources [*Vancouver Stock Exchange symbol*]
SAU............ Saudi Arabia [*ANSI three-letter standard code*] (CNC)
SAU............ Saugeen Ontario Library Service [*UTLAS symbol*]
SAU............ Sausalito, CA [*Location identifier FAA*] (FAAL)
SAU............ Sawu [*Indonesia*] [*Airport symbol*] (OAG)
SAU............ Scandinavian Association of Urology (EA)
SAU............ Scientific Arithmetic Unit
SAU............ Search Attack Unit
SAU............ Secure Access Unit (HGAA)
SAU............ Separate Administrative Unit [*Work Incentive Program*]
SAU............ Signal Acquisition Unit (NASA)
SAU............ Smallest Addressable Unit
SAU............ Social Affairs Unit [*British*]
SAU............ Spectrum Analysis Unit
SAU............ Squadron Augmentation Unit [*Navy*] (DOMA)
SAU............ Standard Advertising Unit [*System introduced to make national newspaper advertising pages uniform in size and format*]
SAU............ Statistical Analysis Unit
SAU............ Strap-Around Unit [*NASA*] (NASA)
SAU............ Substance Abuse Technology, Inc. [*AMEX symbol*] (SAG)
SAU............ Surface Attack Unit
SAU............ System [*or Subsystem*] Availability Unit
SAU............ United Aviation Services SA [*Spain ICAO designator*] (FAAC)
SAUAC......... South Australian Uranium Advisory Committee
SAU & G....... San Antonio, Uvalde & Gulf Railroad Co.
Sau & Sc..... Sausse and Scully's Irish Rolls Court Reports [*1837-40*] [*A publication*] (DLA)
SAUCERS..... Space and Unexplained Celestial Events Research Society [*Defunct*] (EA)
SAUFI.......... Sindacato Autonomo Unificato Ferrovieri Italiani [*Autonomous Union of Italian Railroad Workers*]
SAUK........... Scoliosis Association of the United Kingdom (EAIO)
SaulCntr...... Saul Centers [*Associated Press*] (SAG)
Sau LR........ Saurastra Law Reports [*India*] [*A publication*] (DLA)
Sauls........... Reports Tempore Saulsbury [*5-6 Delaware*] [*A publication*] (DLA)
SAULT......... South Australian Urban Land Trust
Saund.......... Saunders' King's Bench Reports [*1666-73*] [*A publication*] (DLA)
Saund & A... Saunders and Austin's Locus Standi Reports [*1895-1904*] [*A publication*] (DLA)
Saund & Aust... Saunders and Austin's Locus Standi Reports [*A publication*] (DLA)
Saund & B... Saunders and Bidder's Locus Standi Reports [*England*] [*A publication*] (DLA)
Saund & BC... Saunders and Cole's English Bail Court Reports [*1846-48*] [*A publication*] (DLA)
Saund & C... Saunders and Cole's English Bail Court Reports [*1846-48*] [*A publication*] (DLA)
Saund & M... Saunders and Macrae's English County Courts and Insolvency Cases [*County Courts Cases and Appeals, II-III*] [*A publication*] (DLA)
Saund & Mac... Saunders and Macrae's English County Court Cases [*A publication*] (DLA)
Saund Ass... Saunders on Assault and Battery [*1842*] [*A publication*] (DLA)
Saund Bast... Saunders on Affiliation and Bastardy [*11th ed.*] [*1915*] [*A publication*] (DLA)
Saund BC..... Saunders and Cole's English Bail Court Reports [*82 RR*] [*1846-48*] [*A publication*] (DLA)
Saund Mag Pr... Saunders' Magistrates' Courts Practice [*6th ed.*] [*1902*] [*A publication*] (DLA)
Saund Mil L... Saunders' Militia Law [*4th ed.*] [*1855*] [*A publication*] (DLA)
Saund Mun Reg... Saunders' Municipal Registration [*2nd ed.*] [*1873*] [*A publication*] (DLA)
Saund Neg... Saunders on Negligence [*2nd ed.*] [*1878*] [*A publication*] (DLA)
Saund Pl & Ev... Saunders' Pleading and Evidence [*A publication*] (DLA)
Saund Prec... Saunders' Precedents of Indictments [*3rd ed.*] [*1904*] [*A publication*] (DLA)
Saund War... Saunders on Warranties and Representations [*1874*] [*A publication*] (DLA)
SAUOS......... St. Andrews Ukrainian Orthodox Society (EA)
SAUR........... Small Auxin Up RNA [*Ribonucleic Acid*] [*Botany*]
SAUS........... Sausage (DSUE)
SAUS........... Soccer Association of the United States (EA)
S AUS.......... South Australia (BARN)
Sausse & Sc... Sausse and Scully's Irish Rolls Court Reports [*1837-40*] [*A publication*] (DLA)
S Aust.......... South Australia
S Aust Indus R... South Australia Industrial Reports [*A publication*] (DLA)
S Austl Acts... South Australia Acts [*1866-1936*] [*A publication*] (DLA)
S Austl Stat... South Australian Statutes [*1837-1975*] [*A publication*] (DLA)
S Austrl LR... South Australian Law Reports [*A publication*] (ILCA)
S Aust Teach J... South Australian Teachers' Journal [*A publication*]
S Aust Wheatgr... South Australian Wheatgrower [*A publication*]
SAUT........... Scottish Association of University Teachers [*A union*]
SAUV........... Semiautonomous Underwater Vehicle (DOMA)
SaV............. Saguaro Cactus Virus
SAV............. Sale at Valuation (WDAA)
SAV............. Sanair [*Ukraine*] [*FAA designator*] (FAAC)
SAV............. Savannah [*Tasmania*] [*Seismograph station code, US Geological Survey*] (SEIS)
SAV............. Savannah [*Georgia*] [*Airport symbol*] (OAG)
SAV............. Savannah Electric & Power Co. [*NYSE symbol*] (SPSG)
SAV............. Saveloy (DSUE)
Sav............. Savile's English Common Pleas Reports [*A publication*] (DLA)
Sav............. Savings (DLA)
SAV............. Savior
SAV............. Sequential Atrioventricular [*Pacing*] [*Medicine*] (DMAA)
SAV............. Service Availability [*AT & T*]
SAV............. Small Affluent Variable [*Moko disease of banana*] [*Plant pathology*]
SAV............. Society Against Vivisection (EA)
SAV............. Society of American Ventriloquists [*Defunct*] (EA)
SAV............. Space Air Vehicle (IAA)
SAV............. Spectra Ventures Ltd. [*Vancouver Stock Exchange symbol*]
SAV............. Standard Acceptance Value
SAV............. Statens Avtalsverk [*Sweden*]
SAV............. State-of-the-Atmosphere Variables (USDC)
sav............. Stock at Valuation (ODBW)
SAV............. Stock at Valuation
SAV............. Strike Attack Vector [*Navy*] (ANA)
SAV............. Strollad ar Vro [*Country Party*] [*France Political party*] (PPW)
SAV............. Student Alternatives to Violence [*Defunct*] (EA)
SAV............. Submerged Aquatic Vegetation
SAV............. Sudania Aviation Co. [*Sudan*] [*ICAO designator*] (FAAC)
SAV............. System Assistance Visit [*Army*]
SAVA........... Piedra Del Aguila [*Argentina ICAO location identifier*] (ICLI)
SAVA........... Servicios do Aerotaxisa e Abastecimento do Vale Amazonica [*Airline*] [*Brazil*]
SAVA........... Sexual Abuse Victims Anonymous [*Canada*]
SAVA........... Standard Army Vetronics Architecture (RDA)
SAVAC......... Simulates, Analyzes, Visualizes, Activated Circuitry (DNAB)
SAVAK......... Sazemane Attalat Va Anmiyate Keshvar [*Iranian security and intelligence organization*]
SAVAS......... Six-Factor Automated Vocational Assessment System [*Vocational guidance test*]
SAVASI........ Simple [*or Simplified*] Abbreviated Visual Approach Slope Indicator [*FAA*]
SAVB........... El Bolson [*Argentina ICAO location identifier*] (ICLI)
SAVB........... Savannah Bancorp [*NASDAQ symbol*] (TTSB)
SAVB........... Savannah Bancorp, Inc. [*NASDAQ symbol*] (SAG)
SavBcp........ Savannah Bancorp, Inc. [*Associated Press*] (SAG)
SAVBOND.... War Savings Bond [*Allotment for purchase*] [*Navy*]
SAVC........... Air-Cushion Vehicle built by Sealand Air Cushion Vehicles [*US*] [*Usually used in combination with numerals*]
SAVC........... Comodoro Rivadavia/Gral Mosconi [*Argentina ICAO location identifier*] (ICLI)
SAVC........... Society for the Anthropology of Visual Communication (EA)
Sav Conf Law... Savigny's Conflict of Laws [*2nd ed.*] [*1880*] [*A publication*] (DLA)
SAVD........... El Maiten [*Argentina ICAO location identifier*] (ICLI)
SAVD........... Spontaneous Assisted Vaginal Delivery [*Medicine*] (DMAA)
SAVDAT....... Save Data (IAA)
SAVDEP....... Savings Depot [*Military*] (DNAB)
SAV-DEP-SYS... Savings Deposit System [*Military*] (DNAB)
SAVE............ Esquel [*Argentina ICAO location identifier*] (ICLI)
SAVE............ Self-Learning Audio Visual Education [*National Foundation for the Prevention of Oral Disease*]
SAVE............ Sensitive Activity Vulnerability Estimate

SAVE........... Service Activities of Voluntary Engineers
SAVE........... Shoppers Association for Value Economy (EA)
SAVE........... Shortages and Valuable Excesses [*Navy*] (NG)
SAVE........... Situation Analysis and Vulnerability Estimate (MCD)
SAVE........... Society of Americans for Vashchenko Emigration (EA)
SAVE........... Society of American Value Engineers (EA)
SAVE........... Society of American Vintage-Radio Enthusiasts
SAVE........... South Atlantic Ventilation Experiment (USDC)
SAVE........... South Atlantic Ventilation Experiment [*Marine science*] (OSRA)
SAVE........... Spray Aeration Vacuum Extraction System [*Navy*]
SAVE........... Stop Addiction through Voluntary Effort
SAVE........... Student Action Voters for Ecology
SAVE........... Students Against Volvo Exaggerations [*Student legal action organization*]
SAVE........... Survival and Ventricular Enlargement [*Medicine*]
SAVE........... System Analysis of Vulnerability and Effectiveness (IAA)
SAVE........... Systematic Alien Verification for Entitlements [*Immigration and Naturalization Service*]
SAVE........... System Availability Estimator
SAVE........... System Avionics Value Estimation
SAVE........... System for Automatic Value Exchange [*Computer science*]
SAVED......... State-of-the-Art Vehicle Engineering Documentation (MCD)
SAVER......... Shuttle Avionics Verification and Evaluation [*NASA*] (NASA)
SAVER......... Stowable Aircrew Vehicle Escape Rotoseat (MCD)
SAVER......... Study to Assess and Validate Essential Reports [*Military*] (AABC)
SAVES......... Sizing Aerospace Vehicle Structures [*NASA*]
SAVES......... States Audiovisual Education Study
SAVF........... Comodoro Rivadavia [*Argentina ICAO location identifier*] (ICLI)
SAVH........... Las Heras [*Argentina ICAO location identifier*] (ICLI)
SAVI............ Science Activities for the Visually Impaired (AIE)
SAVI............ Students Audio Visual Interface (PDAA)
SAVICOM..... Society for the Anthropology of Visual Communication
Savigny Hist Rom Law... Savigny's History of the Roman Law [*A publication*] (DLA)
Savile.......... Savile's English Common Pleas Reports [*123 English Reprint*] [*1580-94*] [*A publication*] (DLA)
Saville......... Saville Systems [*Associated Press*] (SAG)
SAVIM......... Survivability and Vulnerability Improvement Modification [*Army*] (RDA)
SAVING........ Students Against Violence, Injustice, and Guns
SAVITAR...... Sanders Associates Video Input/Output Terminal Access Resource [*Computer science*] (IEEE)
SAVLY......... Saville Systems [*NASDAQ symbol*] (SAG)
SAVLY......... Saville Systems ADS [*NASDAQ symbol*] (TTSB)
SAVM........... Lago Musters [*Argentina ICAO location identifier*] (ICLI)
SAVMO........ Service Audiovisual Management Office [*Army*]
SavnEl......... Savannah Electric & Power Co. [*Associated Press*] (SAG)
SavnFd........ Savannah Foods & Industries, Inc. [*Associated Press*] (SAG)
SAVO........... San Antonio Oeste [*Argentina ICAO location identifier*] (ICLI)
SAVO........... Schultz Sav-O Stores [*NASDAQ symbol*] (TTSB)
SAVO........... Schultz Sav-O Stores, Inc. [*NASDAQ symbol*] (CTT)
SAVOR......... Single-Actuated Voice Recorder
Savoy.......... Savoy Pictures Entertainment, Inc. [*Associated Press*] (SAG)
SAVP........... Paso De Indios [*Argentina ICAO location identifier*] (ICLI)
Sav Pos....... Savigny on Possessions [*6th ed.*] [*1848*] [*A publication*] (DLA)
SAVPrB........ Savannah El & Pwr 6.64% Pfd [*NYSE symbol*] (TTSB)
Sav Priv....... Trial of the Savannah Privateers [*A publication*] (DLA)
SAVQ........... Maquinchao [*Argentina ICAO location identifier*] (ICLI)
SAVR........... Alto Rio Senguerr [*Argentina ICAO location identifier*] (ICLI)
SAVS........... Safeguards Area Ventilation System [*Nuclear energy*] (NRCH)
SAVS........... Scottish Anti-Vivisection Society (DI)
SAVS........... Sierra Grande [*Argentina ICAO location identifier*] (ICLI)
SAVS........... Status and Verification System [*NASA*] (KSC)
SAVT........... Save Area Table [*Computer science*] (IBMDP)
SAVT........... Secondary Address Vector Table [*Computer science*] (IBMDP)
SAVT........... Trelew/Almirante Zar [*Argentina ICAO location identifier*] (ICLI)
SAVU........... Comodoro Rivadavia [*Argentina ICAO location identifier*] (ICLI)
SAVV........... Viedma/Gobernador Castello [*Argentina ICAO location identifier*] (ICLI)
SAVY........... Puerto Madryn [*Argentina ICAO location identifier*] (ICLI)
Sav Zeitschr... Zeitschrift der Savigny-Stiftung fuer Rechtsgeschichte. Romanistische Abteilung [*A publication*] (OCD)
SAW............ Gwinn, MI [*Location identifier FAA*] (FAAL)
SAW............ Sample Assignment Word
SAW............ Satellite Attack Warning
Saw............ Sawyer's United States Circuit Court Reports [*A publication*] (DLA)
SAW............ Scottish Association of Writers [*British*]
SAW............ Search-a-Word [*Neuropsychology test*]
SAW............ Seasonal Agricultural Worker
SAW............ Seeking, Asking, and Written [*Questionnaire*] (PDAA)
SAW............ Selectively Aimable Warhead (MCD)
SAW............ Semiautomatic Weapons
SAW............ Signal Aircraft Warning
SAW............ Signal Air Warning (IAA)
SAW............ Simulate Antiaircraft Weapons (SAA)
SAW............ Small Arms Weapon
SAW............ Society of American Wars (EA)
SAW............ Solar Array Wing (MCD)
SAW............ South Albuquerque Works [*AEC*]
SAW............ Southern Army Worm [*Agronomy*]
SAW............ Special Agricultural Worker
SAW............ Special Air Warfare (AFM)
SAW............ Squad Assault Weapon [*Marine Corps*] (DOMA)
SAW............ Squad Automatic Weapon [*Army*]
SAW............ St. Andrews [*Washington*] [*Seismograph station code, US Geological Survey*] (SEIS)
SAW............ Statistical Abstract of the World [*A publication*]
SAW............ Sterling Airways Ltd. [*Denmark ICAO designator*] (FAAC)
SAW............ Strategic Aerospace Wing [*Air Force*]
SAW............ Strike Anywhere [*Match*]
SAW............ Subantarctic Water
SAW............ Submerged Arc Weld
SAW............ Surface Acoustic Wave [*Microwave system*]
SAW............ Surface Acoustic Wave [*Engineering*]
SAWA.......... Lago Argentino [*Argentina ICAO location identifier*] (ICLI)
SAWA.......... Scottish Amateur Wrestling Association (DBA)
SAWA.......... Screen Advertising World Association [*British*] (EAIO)
SAWA.......... Society of Anaesthetists of West Africa [*Nigeria*] (EAIO)
SAWA.......... Soil and Water Management Association (NADA)
SawakoC...... Sawako Corp. [*Associated Press*] (SAG)
SAWANS...... South African Women's Auxiliary Naval Service [*British military*] (DMA)
SAWAS........ South African Women's Auxiliary Services
SAWB.......... Base Marambio [*Argentina ICAO location identifier*] (ICLI)
SAWBET...... Supply Action Will Be Taken
SAWC.......... South Australian Writers' Centre
SAWC.......... Special Air Warfare Center
SAWD.......... Puerto Deseado [*Argentina ICAO location identifier*] (ICLI)
SAWD.......... Solid Amine Water Desorbed (NASA)
SAWD.......... Surface Acoustic Wave Device (PDAA)
SAWDLO...... Surface Acoustic Wave Delay Line Oscillator (PDAA)
sawdu.......... Sawdust (VRA)
SAWE.......... Rio Grande [*Argentina ICAO location identifier*] (ICLI)
SAWE.......... Simulated Area Weapons Effects
SAWE.......... Society of Aeronautical Weight Engineers (IAA)
SAWE.......... Society of Allied Weight Engineers (EA)
SAWE-IF...... Simulated Area Weapons Effects - Indirect Fire
SAWE-NBC-CAS... Simulated Area Weapons Effects - Nuclear, Biological, Chemical - Casualty Assesment System [*Army*]
SAWES........ Small Arms Weapons Effects Simulator [*Military*] (PDAA)
SAWF.......... Special Air Warfare Forces (AFM)
SAWFD........ South Australian Woods and Forests Department
SAWG.......... Rio Gallegos [*Argentina ICAO location identifier*] (ICLI)
SAWG.......... Schedule and Allocations Working Group [*NASA*] (KSC)
SAWG.......... Special Advisory Working Group (NATG)
SAWg.......... Strategic Aerospace Wing [*Air Force*] (AFM)
SAWGUS...... Standoff/Attack Weapons Guidance Utility Study (MCD)
SAWH.......... Ushuaia [*Argentina ICAO location identifier*] (ICLI)
SAWI........... Society for Animal Welfare in Israel (EAIO)
SAWIC......... South African Water Information Centre [*Information service or system*] (IID)
SAWID......... Shipboard Acoustic Warfare Integrated Defense (NVT)
SAWJ.......... San Julian/Cap. D. J. D. Vasquez [*Argentina ICAO location identifier*] (ICLI)
SAWLT......... South African Written Language Test [*Educational test*]
SAWM.......... Rio Mayo [*Argentina ICAO location identifier*] (ICLI)
SAWMA........ Soil and Water Management Association [*British*]
SAWMA........ Southern African Wildlife Management Association [*See also NVSA*] (EAIO)
SAWMARCS... Standard Aircraft Weapon Monitor and Release Control System (NG)
SAWMC........ South Australian Waste Management Commission
SAWO.......... Surface Acoustic Wave Oscillator [*Telecommunications*] (TEL)
SAWP.......... Perito Moreno [*Argentina ICAO location identifier*] (ICLI)
SAWP.......... Socialist Alliance of the Working People [*Serbia*] [*Political party*]
SAWP.......... Society of American Wood Preservers [*Defunct*] (EA)
SAWPY........ Socialist Alliance of the Working People of Yugoslavia [*Political party*] (EY)
SAWR.......... Gobernador Gregores [*Argentina ICAO location identifier*] (ICLI)
SAWRC........ South Australian Water Resources Council
SAWRS........ Supplementary Aviation Weather Reporting Station (FAAC)
SAWS.......... Jose De San Martin [*Argentina ICAO location identifier*] (ICLI)
SAWS.......... Satellite Attack Warning System
SAWS.......... Sawtek Inc. [*NASDAQ symbol*] (TTSB)
SAWS.......... Seventh-Day Adventist World Service [*ADRA*] [*Superseded by*] (EA)
SAWS.......... Silent Attack Warning System (MCD)
SAWS.......... Small Arms Weapons System (NATG)
SAWS.......... Small Arms Weapon Study [*Army*]
SAWS.......... Solar Array Wing Simulator (MCD)
SAWS.......... Special Airborne Weapon Subsystem (MCD)
SAWS.......... Squad Automatic Weapon System [*Army*]
SAWS.......... Subacoustic Warfare System
SAWS.......... Submarine Acoustic Warfare System [*Navy*] (MCD)
SAWT.......... Rio Turbio [*Argentina ICAO location identifier*] (ICLI)
SAWTOC...... Special Asian Warfare Training and Orientation Center [*Located on the Hawaiian island of Oahu*] (VNW)
SAWU.......... Santa Cruz [*Argentina ICAO location identifier*] (ICLI)
Sawy........... Sawyer's United States Circuit Court Reports [*A publication*] (DLA)
Sawyer Circt... Sawyer's United States Circuit Court Reports [*A publication*] (DLA)
Sawyer US Ct Rep... Sawyer's United States Circuit Court Reports [*A publication*] (DLA)
SAX............ Sabah Air [*Malaysia*] [*ICAO designator*] (FAAC)
SAX............ Sambu [*Panama*] [*Airport symbol*] (OAG)
SAX............ Saxon
Sax............ Saxony
SAX............ Saxophone [*Music*]
sax............ Saxophone (ODBW)
Sax............ Saxton's New Jersey Chancery Reports [*A publication*] (DLA)
SAX............ Short Axis [*Medicine*] (DMAA)

SAX............. Small-Angle X-ray [*Instrumentation*]
SAX............. Small Automatic Exchange [*Telecommunications*] (TEL)
SAX............. Sparta, NJ [*Location identifier FAA*] (FAAL)
SAX............. States Exploration Ltd. [*Toronto Stock Exchange symbol*]
SAX............. Strong Anion Exchanger [*Chemistry*]
SAX............. Surface Antigen [*Medicine*] (DMAA)
SAXA........... Slotted Array X-Band Antenna
SAXAS......... Scanning Automated X-Ray Analysis Spectrometer (DICI)
SAXD........... Small-Angle X-Ray Diffraction
SAXL........... Short-Arc Xenon Lamp
SAXLE.......... Single Cantilevered Axle
SAXS........... Small-Angle X-Ray Scattering
SAXS........... Small-Angle X-Ray Scattering
Saxt............ Saxton's New Jersey Chancery Reports [*A publication*] (DLA)
Saxt Ch........ Saxton's New Jersey Chancery Reports [*A publication*] (DLA)
SAY............. Salisbury [*Zimbabwe*] [*Airport symbol Obsolete*] (OAG)
Say............. Sayer's English King's Bench Reports [*96 English Reprint*] [*A publication*] (DLA)
SAY............. Severe Aster Yellows [*Plant pathology*]
SAY............. Soccer Association for Youth (EA)
SAY............. Speaking to American Youth (AEBS)
SAY............. Stanley Resources [*Vancouver Stock Exchange symbol*]
SAY............. Suckling Airways [*British ICAO designator*] (FAAC)
SAYE........... Save as You Earn [*National Savings Plan*] [*British*]
Sayer........... Sayer's English King's Bench Reports [*96 English Reprint*] [*1751-56*] [*A publication*] (DLA)
Sayer (Eng)... Sayer's English King's Bench Reports [*96 English Reprint*] [*A publication*] (DLA)
Sayett.......... Sayett Group, Inc. [*Associated Press*] (SAG)
SAYFC.......... Scottish Association of Young Farmers' Clubs (EAIO)
Sayles' Ann Civ St... Sayles' Annotated Civil Statutes [*Texas*] [*A publication*] (DLA)
Sayles' Civ St... Sayles' Revised Civil Statutes [*Texas*] [*A publication*] (DLA)
Sayles' Rev Civ St... Sayles' Revised Civil Statutes [*Texas*] [*A publication*] (DLA)
Sayles' St.... Sayles' Revised Civil Statutes [*Texas*] [*A publication*] (DLA)
Sayles' Supp... Supplement to Sayles' Annotated Civil Statutes [*Texas*] [*A publication*] (DLA)
SAYOS......... Salvation Army Youth Outreach Service [*Australia*]
Sayre Adm Cas... Sayre's Cases on Admiralty [*A publication*] (DLA)
SAYT........... Sayett Group [*NASDAQ symbol*] (SAG)
SAYTA......... Say Time Able [*Aviation*] (FAAC)
SAZ............. Sasstown [*Liberia*] [*Airport symbol*] (OAG)
SAZ............. Staples, MN [*Location identifier FAA*] (FAAL)
SAZ............. Swiss Air-Ambulance Ltd. [*ICAO designator*] (FAAC)
SAZA........... Azul [*Argentina ICAO location identifier*] (ICLI)
SAZB........... Bahia Blanca/Comdte. Espora [*Argentina ICAO location identifier*] (ICLI)
SAZC........... Cnel. Suarez [*Argentina ICAO location identifier*] (ICLI)
SAZD........... Dolores [*Argentina ICAO location identifier*] (ICLI)
SAZE........... Pigue [*Argentina ICAO location identifier*] (ICLI)
SAZF........... Olavarria [*Argentina ICAO location identifier*] (ICLI)
SAZG........... General Pico [*Argentina ICAO location identifier*] (ICLI)
SAZH........... Tres Arroyos [*Argentina ICAO location identifier*] (ICLI)
SAZI............ Bolivar [*Argentina ICAO location identifier*] (ICLI)
SAZJ........... Benito Juarez [*Argentina ICAO location identifier*] (ICLI)
SAZK........... Cerro Catedral [*Argentina ICAO location identifier*] (ICLI)
SAZL........... Santa Teresita [*Argentina ICAO location identifier*] (ICLI)
SAZM.......... Mar Del Plata [*Argentina ICAO location identifier*] (ICLI)
SAZN........... Neuquen [*Argentina ICAO location identifier*] (ICLI)
SAZO........... Necochea [*Argentina ICAO location identifier*] (ICLI)
SAZO........... Seeker Azimuth Orientation [*Air Force*]
SAZP........... Pehuajo/Comodoro P. Zanni [*Argentina ICAO location identifier*] (ICLI)
SAZQ........... Rio Colorado [*Argentina ICAO location identifier*] (ICLI)
SAZR........... Santa Rosa [*Argentina ICAO location identifier*] (ICLI)
SAZS........... San Carlos De Bariloche [*Argentina ICAO location identifier*] (ICLI)
SAZT........... Tandil [*Argentina ICAO location identifier*] (ICLI)
SAZU........... Puelches [*Argentina ICAO location identifier*] (ICLI)
SAZV........... Villa Gesell [*Argentina ICAO location identifier*] (ICLI)
SAZW.......... Cutral-Co [*Argentina ICAO location identifier*] (ICLI)
SAZX........... Nueve De Julio [*Argentina ICAO location identifier*] (ICLI)
SAZY........... San Martin De Los Andes/Chapelco [*Argentina ICAO location identifier*] (ICLI)
SB............... Air Caledonie International [*ICAO designator*] (AD)
Sb............... Antimony [*Chemical element*] (DOG)
SB............... Automotive Engine Rebuilders Association. Service Bulletin [*A publication*] (EAAP)
SB............... Bachelor of Science
SB............... Beauval Public Library, Saskatchewan [*Library symbol National Library of Canada*] (NLC)
SB............... International Standard Book Number [*Online database field identifier*]
SB............... La Sacra Bibbia [*Turin*] [*A publication*] (BJA)
SB............... La Sainte Bible [*A publication*] (BJA)
SB............... SAAB-Scania AB [*Sweden ICAO aircraft manufacturer identifier*] (ICAO)
SB............... Safety Bulletin
SB............... Salary Band [*British*] (DCTA)
SB............... Sales Book
SB............... Salomon, Inc. [*NYSE symbol*] (SPSG)
SB............... San Bernadino [*Diocesan abbreviation*] [*California*] (TOCD)
SB............... Santa Barbara [*Television program*]
SB............... Sarah Bernhardt [*French actress, 1844-1923*]
SB............... Savannah Bank of Nigeria
SB............... Save a Baby [*Later, LGM*] (EA)
SB............... Savings Bank
SB............... Savings Bond [*Treasury Department security*]
SB............... S-Band (KSC)
SB............... Schistosoma Bovis [*Parasitic fluke*]
SB............... Science Books & Films [*A publication*] (BRI)
SB............... Scissors Bridge (DWSG)
SB............... Scleral Buckling [*Ophthalmalogy*] (CPH)
SB............... Scoring Booklet (MCD)
SB............... Scouting-Bombing Plane [*When prefixed to Navy aircraft designation*]
SB............... Scrieve Board
SB............... Sea Base (MCD)
SB............... Seaboard World Airlines, Inc. [*ICAO designator*]
SB............... Secondary Battery [*Military*]
SB............... Secondary Buffer [*Chemistry*]
SB............... Section Base [*Military*]
SB............... Securing Bands
SB............... Selection Board [*Military*]
SB............... Selective Bibliography (MCD)
SB............... Semi-Balance [*Model*] (USDC)
SB............... Semi-Balance [*Model*] [*Marine science*] (OSRA)
SB............... Senate Bill [*in state legislatures*]
SB............... Sengstaken-Blakemore [*Tube*] [*Medicine*] (MEDA)
SB............... Sengstaken-Blakemore [*Tube*] [*Gastroenterology*] (DAVI)
SB............... Senior Beadle [*Ancient Order of Foresters*]
SB............... Senior Bond (MHDW)
SB............... Sense Byte [*Computer science*] (IAA)
SB............... Separately Binned
SB............... Serial Binary (CET)
SB............... Serial Block (MSA)
SB............... Serum Bilirubin [*Clinical chemistry*]
SB............... Service Bulletin
SB............... Service Bureau (IAA)
SB............... Serving Brother [*Church of England*]
SB............... Shanti Bahini [*Peace Force*] [*Bangladesh*] [*Political party*]
SB............... Shaper Block (MCD)
SB............... Shipbuilding [*Navy*]
SB............... Shipping Board
SB............... Shoot Bud [*Botany*]
SB............... Short Bill
SB............... Shortness of Breath [*Cardiology*]
S/B.............. Should Be
SB............... Shrunk Back-to-Back [*Packaging of volumes*] [*Publishing*]
SB............... Sick Bay
SB............... Sideband [*Radio frequency*] (AAG)
SB............... Sideroblast [*Hematology*] (AAMN)
SB............... Signal Band
SB............... Signal Battalion [*Army*]
SB............... Signal Boatswain
SB............... Signal to Background
SB............... Signature Book (ROG)
SB............... Silver Braze (MSA)
SB............... Simultaneous Broadcast
SB............... Single Bayonet [*Lamp base*] (NTCM)
SB............... Single Blind [*Experimental condition*]
SB............... Single Braid (CET)
SB............... Single-Breasted
SB............... Single Breath
SB............... Single-Ended Boiler (DS)
SB............... Sink Beater (ADA)
SB............... Sinus Bradycardia [*Cardiology*]
SB............... Sitzungsbericht [*Transaction*] [*German*]
SB............... Sleeve Bearing (KSC)
SB............... Slow Blowing (IAA)
SB............... Slow Burning
SB............... Small Block [*Automotive engineering*]
SB............... Small Bonds
SB............... Small Bore (ADA)
SB............... Small Bowel
SB............... Small Business
Sb............... Small-Mouth Bass [*Ichthyology*]
SB............... Smooth Bore [*Ballistics*]
SB............... Snow Biz [*An association*] (EA)
SB............... Social Biology Films [*National Science Foundation project*]
SB............... Society for Biomaterials (EA)
SB............... Sociologists in Business (EA)
SB............... Sodium Bicarbonate [*Inorganic chemistry*]
SB............... Sodium Bisulfite [*Inorganic chemistry*]
SB............... Sodium Borate [*Inorganic chemistry*]
SB............... Solicitors' Board [*Queensland, Australia*]
SB............... Solid Base Bullet
SB............... Solid Body [*Technical drawings*]
SB............... Solomon Islands [*ANSI two-letter standard code*] (CNC)
SB............... Sonobuoy (NVT)
SB............... Soot Blower (AAG)
SB............... Sound Blaster [*Computer science*] (DOM)
SB............... Southbound
SB............... South Britain [*England and Wales*]
SB............... South Buffalo Railway Co. [*AAR code*]
SB............... Soybean [*Medicine*] (DMAA)
SB............... Space Base [*NASA*] (KSC)
SB............... Space Booster (SAA)
SB............... Space Branch (IAA)
SB............... Special Bibliography
SB............... Special Billing [*Telecommunications*] (TEL)
SB............... Special Branch [*British police*]
SB............... Special Bulletin. New York Department of Labor [*A publication*] (DLA)
SB............... Speed Brake (MCD)

SB.............. Spina Bifida [*Medicine*]
SB.............. Spin Block (MSA)
Sb.............. Spiral Having Nuclear Regions Less Conspicuous than Sa Class and Greater than Scwith Arms Wider Open than Sa Class [*Astronomy*] (BARN)
SB.............. Splash Block
SB.............. Spontaneous Blastogenesis [*Medicine*] (DMAA)
SB.............. Sports Bribery [*FBI standardized term*]
SB.............. Spring Back (ADA)
SB.............. Stabilized Breakdown
SB.............. Standard Babylonian (BJA)
SB.............. Standard Bead
SB.............. Standby
SB.............. Standby Base [*Air Force*] (AFM)
SB.............. Stanford-Binet [*Intelligence test*] [*Education*]
SB.............. Statement of Billing
SB.............. Statistical Bulletin
SB.............. Status Board [*Automated*] (MCD)
SB.............. Statute Book (ADA)
SB.............. Steamboat
SB.............. Stereotyped Behavior [*Medicine*] (DMAA)
SB.............. Sternal Border [*Anatomy*]
Sb.............. Stibium [*Antimony*] [*Chemical element*]
sb.............. Stilb [*Unit of luminance*]
SB.............. Stillborn [*Medicine*]
SB.............. Stockbroker
SB.............. Stolen Base [*Baseball*]
SB.............. Stop Bath [*Photography*] (DGA)
SB.............. Stove Bolt
Sb.............. Strabismus [*Medicine*]
SB.............. Straight Binary
SB.............. Straw Boss (MHDB)
SB.............. Stretcher-Bearer
SB.............. Strike Benefits (MHDB)
SB.............. Stuffing Box
SB.............. Styrene Butadiene [*Organic chemistry*]
SB.............. Subbituminous
SB.............. Sub Branch [*Banking*]
SB.............. Submarine Base [*Navy*]
SB.............. Submarine Boat [*British*] (ROG)
SB.............. Submarine Fog Bell [*Mechanical*] [*Maps and charts*]
SB.............. Substantive
SB.............. Substitute Blank (IAA)
SB.............. Superbananas
SB.............. Supplementary Benefits
SB.............. Supply Bulletin [*Military*]
SB.............. Support Box
SB.............. Supreme Bench [*Legal term*] (DLA)
SB.............. Surety Bond (MHDB)
S/B.............. Surface Based (WDAA)
SB.............. Surface Binding [*Immunochemistry*]
SB.............. Surplus Budget
SB.............. Sustained Breakdown (IAA)
sb.............. Svalbard and Jan Mayen [*MARC country of publication code Library of Congress*] (LCCP)
SB.............. Switchboard
SB.............. Switchboard Operator [*Navy*]
SB.............. Symbiotic Bacteria [*Ecology*]
SB.............. Synchronization Base [*NASA*] (NASA)
SB.............. Synchronization Bit (MSA)
SBA.............. Saabruecker Beitraege zur Altertumskunde [*Bonn*] [*A publication*] (BJA)
SBA.............. Santa Barbara [*California*] [*Airport symbol*] (OAG)
SBA.............. Satellite Broadcasters Association (EA)
SBA.............. Sbarro, Inc. [*NYSE symbol*] (SAG)
SBA.............. Scene Balance Algorithm [*Color-correction look-up tables for Photo CDs*] (PCM)
SBA.............. School Band of America (AEBS)
SBA.............. School Bookshop Association [*British*] (DI)
SBA.............. Scott Base [*Antarctica*] [*Seismograph station code, US Geological Survey*] (SEIS)
SBA.............. Scottish Basketball Association (DBA)
SBA.............. Seat Back Assembly [*Aerospace*] (MCD)
SBA.............. Secondary Butyl Alcohol [*Organic chemistry*]
SBA.............. Second Bombardment Association (EA)
SBA.............. Sequential Boolean Analyzer (PDAA)
SBA.............. Serum Bile Acid [*Medicine*] (DMAA)
SBA.............. Service Brake Activator [*Automotive engineering*]
SBA.............. Setback Axle [*Truck engineering*]
SBA.............. Shaped Beam Antenna
SBA.............. Shared Batch Area [*Computer science*] (IBMDP)
SBA.............. Show Business Association [*New York, NY*] (EA)
SBA.............. Siamese Breeders of America [*Later, GSCC*] (EA)
SBA.............. Sick Bay Attendant [*Navy*]
SBA.............. Sideband Address (PCM)
SBA.............. Singapore Badminton Association (EAIO)
SBA.............. Singapore Broadcast Authority
SBA.............. Small Business Administration
SBA.............. Small Businesses' Association [*British*] (DCTA)
SBA.............. Social Behavior Assessment [*Social skills test*]
SBA.............. Society of Batik Artists [*Defunct*] (EA)
SBA.............. Sovereign Base Area (DNAB)
SBA.............. Soybean Agglutinin [*Immunology*]
SBA.............. Spina Bifida and Anencephaly [*Medicine*]
SBA.............. Spina Bifida Aperta [*Medicine*] (DMAA)
SBA.............. Spirit and Breath Association (EA)
SBA.............. STA-Mali [*ICAO designator*] (FAAC)
SBA.............. Standard Beam Approach [*British aircraft landing method*]
SBA.............. Stand-By Assistance [*Medicine*] (MEDA)
SBA.............. Stand-By Assistance (DAVI)
SBA.............. Standing British Army
SBA.............. Steamboat Association [*British*] (DBA)
SBA.............. Steroid-Binding Assay [*Clinical chemistry*]
SBA.............. Structural Board Association (EA)
SBA.............. Structure Borne Acoustics (KSC)
SBA.............. Support Base Activation (AAG)
SBA.............. Susan B. Anthony Dollar
SBA.............. Sustaining Base Automation [*Army*] (RDA)
SBA.............. Sweet Bugger All [*An exclamation*] [*Slang British*] (DSUE)
SBA.............. System for Business Automation (IAA)
SBA.............. Systems Builders Association (EA)
SBA.............. Welsh Bowling Association (DBA)
SBAA.............. Conceicao Do Araguaia [*Brazil ICAO location identifier*] (ICLI)
SBAA.............. Ships-in-Bottles Association of America (EA)
SBAA.............. Small Business Association of Australia
SBAA.............. Spina Bifida Association of America (EA)
SBAAM.............. Small Business Association of Apparel Manufacturers (EA)
SBAC.............. Small Business Assistance Center [*Worcester, MA*] (EA)
SBAC.............. Society of British Aerospace Companies (MCD)
SBAC.............. Society of British Aircraft Constructors
SBAE.............. Stabilized Bombing Approach Equipment [*Navy*]
SBAEDS.............. Satellite-Based Atomic Energy Detection System (IAA)
SBAF.............. Rio De Janeiro/Afonsos [*Brazil ICAO location identifier*] (ICLI)
SBAFWP.............. Standby Auxiliary Feed Water Pump (IEEE)
SBAH.............. Sodium Bis(methoxyethoxy)aluminum Hydride [*Organic chemistry*]
S-Bahn.............. Schnellbahn [*High-Speed Railway*] [*German*]
SBAkWissWien... Sitzungsberichte der Oesterreichischen Akademie der Wissenschaften in Wien [*A publication*] (BJA)
SBAM.............. Amapa [*Brazil ICAO location identifier*] (ICLI)
SBAM.............. Space-Based Antimissile
SBAMA.............. San Bernardino Air Materiel Area
SBAMP.............. Sea-Based Air Master Plan (MCD)
SBAN.............. Anapolis (Base Aerea) [*Brazil ICAO location identifier*] (ICLI)
SB & CR.............. Stock Balance and Consumption Report (AFM)
SBANE.............. Smaller Business Association of New England [*Waltham, MA*] (EA)
SBAP.............. Simple Bin Assignment Problem
SBAP.............. Small Business Assistance Program
SBAP.............. Society of Business Advisory Professions (EA)
SBAR.............. Aracaju/Santa Maria [*Brazil ICAO location identifier*] (ICLI)
SBarbBc.............. Santa Barbara Bancorp [*Associated Press*] (SAG)
S Bar J.............. State Bar Journal of California [*A publication*] (DLA)
Sbarro.............. Sbarro, Inc. [*Associated Press*] (SAG)
SBAS.............. S-Band Antenna Switch (MCD)
SBAS.............. Starbase Corp. [*NASDAQ symbol*] (SAG)
SBASA.............. Spina Bifida Association of South Australia
SBASI.............. Single Bridgewire Apollo Standard Initiator [*Explosive*]
SBAT.............. Spina Bifida Association of Tasmania [*Australia*]
SBAU.............. Aracatuba [*Brazil ICAO location identifier*] (ICLI)
SBAV.............. Spina Bifida Association of Victoria [*Australia*]
SBAV.............. Teodoro Sampaio/Usina Porto Primavera [*Brazil ICAO location identifier*] (ICLI)
SBAWA.............. Spina Bifida Association of Western Australia
SBAWSEF.............. Susan B. Anthony Women's Spirituality Education Forum (EA)
SBB.............. Sabina Resources Ltd. [*Vancouver Stock Exchange symbol*]
SBB.............. Saddle Back Butte [*California*] [*Seismograph station code, US Geological Survey*] (SEIS)
SBB.............. Santa Barbara-Barinas [*Venezuela*] [*Airport symbol*] (AD)
SBB.............. Satellite Busy Box (SSD)
SBB.............. Saudi-British Bank
SBB.............. Schweizerische Bundesbahnen [*Swiss Federal Railways*]
SBB.............. Self-Balancing Bridge
SBB.............. Serikat Buruh Batik [*Batik Workers' Union*] [*Indonesia*]
SBB.............. Silicon Borne Bond (IAA)
SBB.............. Silicon-Borne Bonds (SAA)
SBB.............. Single-Band Beaconry [*RADAR*]
SBB.............. Soncino Books of the Bible [*London*] [*A publication*] (BJA)
SBB.............. Specialist Blood Banking (DAVI)
SBB.............. Specialist in Blood Bank Technical (DAVI)
SBB.............. Steinman Aviation, Inc. [*FAA designator*] (FAAC)
SBB.............. Stimulation-Bound Behavior [*Medicine*] (DMAA)
SBB.............. Subtract with Borrow [*Computer science*] (PCM)
SBB.............. System Building Block [*Computer science*]
SBBA.............. Boca Do Acre [*Brazil ICAO location identifier*] (ICLI)
SBBA.............. Spanish-Barb Breeders Association (EA)
SBBE.............. Belem/Val-De-Caes [*Brazil ICAO location identifier*] (ICLI)
SBBF.............. Silicone-Based Brake Fluid [*Automotive engineering*]
SBBG.............. Baje/Cmt. Gustavo Kraemer [*Brazil ICAO location identifier*] (ICLI)
SBBH.............. Belo Horizonte/Pampulha [*Brazil ICAO location identifier*] (ICLI)
SBBI.............. Curitiba/Bacacheri [*Brazil ICAO location identifier*] (ICLI)
SBBI.............. Stocks, Bonds, Bills, and Inflation [*Investment term*]
SBBL.............. Belem [*Brazil ICAO location identifier*] (ICLI)
SBBN.............. Standard Big Bang Nucleosynthesis [*Cosmology*]
SBBO.............. Strontium Beryllium Boron Oxide [*Inorganic chemistry*]
SBBQ.............. Barbacena [*Brazil ICAO location identifier*] (ICLI)
SBBR.............. Brasilia/Internacional [*Brazil ICAO location identifier*] (ICLI)
SBBS.............. Brasilia [*Brazil ICAO location identifier*] (ICLI)
SBBT.............. Barretos [*Brazil ICAO location identifier*] (ICLI)
SBBT.............. Short Basic Battery Test (NVT)
SBBT.............. Specialist in Blood Bank Technology (HCT)
SBBU.............. Bauru [*Brazil ICAO location identifier*] (ICLI)

SBBV .... Boa Vista/Internacional [*Brazil ICAO location identifier*] (ICLI)
SBBW .... Barra Do Garcas [*Brazil ICAO location identifier*] (ICLI)
SBC .... Baptist College at Charleston, Charleston, SC [*OCLC symbol*] (OCLC)
SBC .... Ferrocarril Sonora Baja California SA de CV [*AAR code*]
SBC .... Saint Basil's College [*Stamford, CT*]
SBC .... Saint Benedict College [*Indiana*]
SBC .... Saint Bernard College [*Alabama*]
SBC .... Sam Browne's Cavalry [*British military*] (DMA)
SBC .... Santa Barbara [*California*] [*Seismograph station code, US Geological Survey*] (SEIS)
SBC .... Save the Battlefield Coalition (EA)
SBC .... SBC Communications [*NYSE symbol*] (TTSB)
SBC .... SBC Communications, Inc. [*NYSE symbol*] (SAG)
SBC .... Schmidt-Baker Camera (IIA)
SBC .... Senate Budget Committee
SBC .... Service Bureau Corp.
SBC .... Sibasa [*South Africa*] [*Airport symbol*] (OAG)
SBC .... Signal Board Computer (HGAA)
SBC .... Simpson Bible College [*Later, Simpson College*] [*California*]
SBC .... Single Board Computer
SBC .... Single Board Computer
SBC .... Single Burst Correcting
SBC .... Small Bayonet Cap
SBC .... Small Business Centre [*British*]
SBC .... Small Business Computer (BUR)
SBC .... Small Business Council (NADA)
SBC .... Societe Bibliographique du Canada (AC)
SBC .... Soleil-Babinet Compensator [*Optics*]
SBC .... Solid Bowl Centrifuge
SBC .... SONAR Breakout Cable
SBC .... Southeastern Bible College [*Lakeland, FL*]
SBC .... Southern Baptist College [*Walnut Ridge, AR*]
SBC .... Southern Baptist Convention
SBC .... Spaceborne Computer
SBC .... Special Back Care [*Medicine*]
SBC .... Speed Brake Command (NASA)
SBC .... Standard Bicarbonate [*Pharmacology*] (DAVI)
SBC .... Standard Boundary Condition
SBC .... Standard Buried Collector [*Circuit*]
SBC .... Standing Balance: Eyes Closed [*Test*] [*Occupational therapy*]
SBC .... Start Breguet Cruise [*SST*]
SBC .... Statutes of British Columbia [*British Columbia Attorney General's Ministry*] [*Information service or system A publication*] (CRD)
SBC .... Strict Bed Confinement [*Medicine*]
SBC .... Styrene Block Copolymer [*Plastics technology*]
SBC .... Subtract Contents (NITA)
SBC .... Sue Bennett College [*London, KY*]
SBC .... Summary Billing Card (AFM)
SBC .... Supplementary Benefits Commission [*Department of Employment*] [*British*]
SBC .... Surrogates by Choice (EA)
SBC .... Survey of Basic Competencies [*Achievement test*]
SBC .... Sweet Briar College [*Virginia*]
SBC .... Swiss Bank Corp.
SBC .... Swiss Broadcasting Corp.
SBC .... Sydney Basketball Council [*Australia*]
SBC .... System Bus Controller (NITA)
SBCA .... Cascavel [*Brazil ICAO location identifier*] (ICLI)
SBCA .... Saint Bernard Club of America (EA)
SBCA .... Satellite Broadcasting and Communications Association (EA)
SBCA .... SBC [*Swiss Bank Corp.*] Australia
SBCA .... Scottish Building Contractors Association (DBA)
SBCA .... Seat Belt Control Apparatus
SBCA .... Sensor-Based Control Adapter
SBCA .... Small Business Combined Association [*Australia*]
SBCA .... Small Business Council of America (EA)
SBCA .... Soybean Council of America [*Defunct*]
SBCAO .... State Business and Corporate Affairs Office [*South Australia*]
SBCC .... Cachimbo [*Brazil ICAO location identifier*] (ICLI)
SBCC .... Senate Bonding and Currency Committee (OICC)
SBCC .... Separate Bias, Common Control
SBCC .... Southern Building Code Congress, International
SBCC .... St. Brendan Cup Committee in America [*Defunct*] (EA)
SBCCA .... Still Bank Collectors Club of America (EA)
SBCCI .... Southern Building Code Congress, International (EA)
SBC Com .... SBC Communications, Inc. [*Associated Press*] (SAG)
SBCCS .... Single Byte Command Code Set Mapping [*Computer science*]
SBCD .... Campo Grande [*Brazil ICAO location identifier*] (ICLI)
SBCD .... School-Based Curriculum Development (ADA)
SB/CD .... Short Bed/Continuous Development [*Chamber for thin-layer chromatography*] [*Analytical biochemistry*]
SBCD .... Special Business and Contract Directories [*A publication*]
SBCD .... Subtract BCD [*Binary Coded Decimal*] Number [*Computer science*]
SBCDP .... Small Business Competitiveness Demonstration Program (AAGC)
SBCE .... Bachelor of Science in Civil Engineering
SBCE .... Concordia [*Brazil ICAO location identifier*] (ICLI)
SBCF .... Belo Horizonte/Confins [*Brazil ICAO location identifier*] (ICLI)
SBCF .... Seacoast Banking Corp. of Florida [*Stuart, FL*] [*NASDAQ symbol*] (NQ)
SBCF .... Southern Baptist Convention Flyers [*Defunct*] (EA)
SBCFA .... Seacoast Banking FL'A' [*NASDAQ symbol*] (TTSB)
SBCG .... Campo Grande/Internacional [*Brazil ICAO location identifier*] (ICLI)
SBCH .... Chapeco [*Brazil ICAO location identifier*] (ICLI)
SBCI .... Carolina [*Brazil ICAO location identifier*] (ICLI)
SBCI .... Solar Box Cookers International [*An association*] (EA)
SBCI .... Swiss Bank Corp. International
SBCIC .... Standard Buried Collector Integrated Circuit (IAA)
SBCJ .... Maraba/Carajas [*Brazil ICAO location identifier*] (ICLI)
SBCJ .... Store Block Control Journal [*Military*] (AABC)
SBCL .... Cruz Alta/Carlos Ruhl [*Brazil ICAO location identifier*] (ICLI)
SBCL .... SmithKline Beecham Clinical Laboratories
SBCL .... Special Buyer Credit Limit (MHDW)
SBCLS .... South Bay Cooperative Library System [*Library network*]
SBCM .... Criciuma [*Brazil ICAO location identifier*] (ICLI)
SBCM .... Security Bank Corp. [*NASDAQ symbol*] (SAG)
SBCN .... Suburban Bancorp [*NASDAQ symbol*] (SAG)
SBCN .... Suburban Bancorp Inc. [*NASDAQ symbol*] (TTSB)
SBCO .... Porto Alegre/Canoas [*Brazil ICAO location identifier*] (ICLI)
SBCO .... Shipbuilding Company
SBCO .... Southside Bancshares [*NASDAQ symbol*] (SAG)
SBC/OC .... Swiss Bank Corp./O'Connor & Associates Services (ECON)
SBCORP .... Shipbuilding Corp.
SBCP .... Campos/Bartolomeu Lisandro [*Brazil ICAO location identifier*] (ICLI)
SBCP .... Spanish Base Construction Program
SBCPO .... Sick Bay Chief Petty Officer [*British military*] (DMA)
SBCR .... Corumba/Internacional [*Brazil ICAO location identifier*] (ICLI)
SBCR .... Stock Balance and Consumption Report (NASA)
SBCS .... Satellite-Based Communication System
SBCS .... Series Book Collectors' Society (EA)
SBCS .... Shore-Based Correlation Subsystem [*Navy*] (CAAL)
SBCS .... Steam Bypass Control System [*Nuclear energy*] (NRCH)
SBCSA .... Small Business Corp. of South Australia [*Commercial firm*]
SBCT .... Curitiba/Afonso Pena [*Brazil ICAO location identifier*] (ICLI)
SBCT .... Schilling Body Coordination Test (EDAC)
SBCT .... Schottky Barrier Collector Transistor (IAA)
SBCU .... Sensor-Based Control Unit [*Computer science*]
SBCU .... Sensor Board Control Unit (NITA)
SBCUK .... School Broadcasting Council for the United Kingdom (BI)
SBCV .... Caravelas [*Brazil ICAO location identifier*] (ICLI)
SBCW .... Curitiba [*Brazil ICAO location identifier*] (ICLI)
SBCY .... Cuiaba/Marechal Rondon [*Brazil ICAO location identifier*] (ICLI)
SBCZ .... Cruzeiro Do Sul/Internacional [*Brazil ICAO location identifier*] (ICLI)
SBD .... San Bernardino, CA [*Location identifier FAA*] (FAAL)
SBD .... San Bernardino Public Library, San Bernardino, CA [*OCLC symbol*] (OCLC)
SBD .... Savings Bond Division [*Navy*]
S-BD .... S-Band (NASA)
SBD .... Schematic Block Diagram [*NASA*] (NASA)
SBD .... Schottky Barrier Diode [*Electronics*]
S-BD .... Seizure-Brain Damage [*Medicine*] (DMAA)
SBD .... Senile Brain Disease [*Medicine*] (DMAA)
SBD .... Shipboard Decoy (DWSG)
SBD .... Smart Battery Data
SBD .... Southeast Aviation Group, Inc. [*ICAO designator*] (FAAC)
SBD .... Special Business Directories [*A publication*]
SBD .... Standard Bibliographic Description
SBD .... Steel Beam Design [*Modray Ltd.*] [*Software package*] (NCC)
SBD .... Straight Bag Drainage [*Medicine*] (MAE)
SBD .... Strawboard [*Shipping*]
SBD .... Structured Block Diagram [*Computer science*] (MHDB)
SBD .... Subcontractor Bid Document (MCD)
SBD .... Surface Barrier Detector
SBDA .... Structural Biology and Design Applications [*bbscrc-Biotechnology and Biological Sciences Research Council*] [*British*]
SBDAD .... Surveillance and Battle Damage Assessment Device [*Military*]
SbdBcp .... Seaboard Bancorp [*Associated Press*] (SAG)
SBDC .... Shipbuilding and Drydock Company
SBDC .... Small Business Development Center [*Lehigh University, University of Alabama in Birmingham*] [*Research center*]
SBDC .... Small Business Development Corp.
SbdCp .... Seaboard Corp. [*Associated Press*] (SAG)
SBDD .... Structure-Based Drug Design [*Organic chemistry*]
SBDE .... Silver Bevelled Deckle Edges [*Bookbinding*] (DGA)
SBDET .... Switchboard Detachment (IAA)
SBDH .... Sociedade Brasileira de Discos Historicos J. Leon [*Record label*] [*Brazil*]
SBDK .... Sound Bytes Developer's Kit [*Computer science*]
SBDL .... Solid Blank Delay Line
SBDM .... School-Based Decision Making (ADA)
SBDN .... Presidente Prudente [*Brazil ICAO location identifier*] (ICLI)
SBDO .... Space Business Development Operation (AAG)
SBDP .... Serikat Buruh Djawatan Perindustrian [*Department of Industry Workers' Union*] [*Indonesia*]
SBDPU .... Serikat Buruh Djawantan Pekerdjaan Umun [*Public Works' Union*] [*Indonesia*]
SBDQ .... Supervisory Behavior Description Questionnaire (EDAC)
SBDT .... Schottky Barrier Diode Transistor (IAA)
SBDT .... Surface Barrier Diffused Transistor
SBDTTL .... Schottky Barrier Diode Transistor-Transistor Logic (IAA)
SBE .... Sabre Airways Ltd. [*British*] [*FAA designator*] (FAAC)
SBE .... Sacred Books of the East [*A publication*] (BJA)
SBE .... S-Band Exciter [*System*] [*Also, SBES*]
SBE .... SBE, Inc. [*Associated Press*] (SAG)
SBE .... Screen-Based Equipment
SBE .... Selebi-Pikwe [*Botswana*] [*Later, PKW*] [*Airport symbol*] (OAG)
SBE .... Self Breast Examination [*for cancer*]
SBE .... Shortness of Breath on Exertion [*Cardiology*]
SBE .... Silver Bevelled Edges [*Bookbinding*] (DGA)
SBE .... Simple Boolean Expression [*Mathematics*]

SBE.......... Small Business Edition [*Microsoft Corp.*] [*Computer software*] (PCM)
SBE.......... Smithkline Beecham Ltd. [*NYSE symbol*] (SAG)
SBE.......... Societe de Biologie Experimentale [*Society for Experimental Biology*] (EAIO)
SBE.......... Society for Business Ethics [*Santa Clara, CA*] (EA)
SBE.......... Society of Broadcast Engineers (EA)
SBE.......... Society of Business Economists (EAIO)
SBE.......... Solar Beam Experiment
SbE.......... South by East
SBE.......... Sporadic Bovine Encephalomyelitis [*Veterinary medicine*]
SBE.......... State Board of Education (OICC)
SBE.......... Strategic Bomber Enhancement (MCD)
SBE.......... Subacute Bacterial Endocarditis [*Medicine*]
SBE.......... Sub BIT [*Binary Digit*] Encoder (MCD)
SBE.......... Supertwisted Birefringence Effect (NITA)
SBE.......... System Buffer Element (NITA)
SBEA.......... Small Business Exporters Association (EA)
SBEC.......... Single-Board Engine Controller [*Automotive engineering*]
SBED.......... Serial BIT [*Binary Digit*] Error Detector
SBEE.......... Bachelor of Science in Electrical Engineering
SBEED.......... Storage Battery Electric Energy Demonstration
SBEG.......... Manaus/Eduardo Gomes [*Brazil ICAO location identifier*] (ICLI)
SBEI.......... SBE, Inc. [*NASDAQ symbol*] (NQ)
SBEI.......... Starch-Branching Enzyme I [*Plant genetics*]
SBEK.......... Jacare-Acanga [*Brazil ICAO location identifier*] (ICLI)
S Bell.......... Bell's House of Lords Scotch Appeal Cases [*1842-50*] [*A publication*] (DLA)
SBEN.......... Campos/Plataforma SS-17 [*Brazil ICAO location identifier*] (ICLI)
SBEP.......... Somatosensory Brain Stem Evoked Potential [*Neurology*] (DAVI)
SBER.......... Eirunepe [*Brazil ICAO location identifier*] (ICLI)
SBER.......... Self-Balancing Electronics Recorder
Sber.......... Sitzungsbericht [*Transaction*] [*German*] (BJA)
SBER.......... Subbit Error Rate
SBES.......... Sao Pedro Da Aldeia [*Brazil ICAO location identifier*] (ICLI)
SBES.......... S-Band Exciter System [*Also, SBE*]
SBET.......... Pedregulho/Estreito [*Brazil ICAO location identifier*] (ICLI)
SBET.......... Screen-Based Electronic Typewriter (WDMC)
SBET.......... Society for Biomedical Engineering Technicians (DMAA)
SBET.......... Society of Biomedical Equipment Technicians (EA)
SBETC.......... Small Business Export Trade Corp.
SBEU.......... Singapore Bank Employees' Union
SBEUA.......... Small Business and Economic Utilization Advisor [*Army*] (AABC)
SBF.......... Salomon Bros Fund [*NYSE symbol*] (TTSB)
SBF.......... Salomon Brothers Fund [*NYSE symbol*] (SPSG)
SBF.......... Scientific Balloon Facility
SBF.......... Serologic Blocking Factor [*Cardiology*]
SBF.......... Seven Bar Flying Service, Inc. [*ICAO designator*] (FAAC)
SBF.......... Short Backfire [*Antenna*]
SBF.......... Silicone Brake Fluid (MCD)
SBF.......... Single Barrier Failure (SSD)
SBF.......... Single Black Female [*Classified advertising*] (CDAI)
SBF.......... Small Business Funding
SBF.......... Societe Burundaise de Financement [*Development bank*] (EY)
SBF.......... Society of Business Folk [*Defunct*] (EA)
SBF.......... Southern Baptist Foundation (EA)
SBF.......... Soy Base Formula [*Nutrition*]
SBF.......... Splanchnic Blood Flow [*Physiology*]
SBF.......... Standby Flying [*British military*] (DMA)
SBF.......... Stonebridge, Inc. [*Toronto Stock Exchange symbol*]
SBF.......... Subic Bay Freeport
SBF.......... Support by Fire [*Military*] (INF)
SBF.......... Surface Burst Fuze
SBFA.......... Set Back Front Axle [*Automotive engineering*]
SBFA.......... Small Business Foundation of America [*Boston, MA*] (EA)
SBFC.......... Franca [*Brazil ICAO location identifier*] (ICLI)
SBFC.......... Sawyer Brown Fan Club (EA)
SBFD.......... Society of British Fight Directors (DBA)
SBFET.......... Schottky Barrier Gate Field Effect Transistor (IAA)
SBFI.......... Foz Do Iguacu/Cataratas [*Brazil ICAO location identifier*] (ICLI)
SBFI.......... Specialised Banking Furniture International [*Manufacturer*] [*British*]
SB FingL.......... Savings Bank of the Finger Lakes FSB [*Associated Press*] (SAG)
SBFL.......... Florianopolis/Hercilioluz [*Brazil ICAO location identifier*] (ICLI)
SBFL.......... Savings Bank of the Finger Lakes FSB [*NASDAQ symbol*] (SAG)
SBFL.......... Savings Bk of Finger Lakes [*NASDAQ symbol*] (TTSB)
SBFL.......... Super Buffer FET Logic (NITA)
SBFLA.......... Studii Biblici Franciscani. Liber Annuus [*A publication*] (BJA)
SBFM.......... Silver-Band Frequency Modulation (IEEE)
SBFM.......... Small Business Financial Manager [*Microsoft*] [*Computer science*]
SBFN.......... Fernando De Noronha [*Brazil ICAO location identifier*] (ICLI)
SBFT.......... Fronteira [*Brazil ICAO location identifier*] (ICLI)
SBFT.......... Small Bowel Follow-Through [*Medicine*] (MAE)
SBFU.......... Alpinopolis/Furnas [*Brazil ICAO location identifier*] (ICLI)
SBFU.......... Standby Filter Unit (IEEE)
SBFZ.......... Fortaleza/Pinto Martins [*Brazil ICAO location identifier*] (ICLI)
SBG.......... Salomon Bros 2008 WW Dlr Gvt [*NYSE symbol*] (TTSB)
SBG.......... Salomon Brothers 2008 World-Wide Direct Government Fund [*NYSE symbol*] (SPSG)
SBG.......... Scottish Bus Group Ltd. (DCTA)
SBG.......... Selenite Brilliant Green (MAE)
SBG.......... Southern Business Group [*Commercial firm*] [*British*]
SBG.......... Staatsbibliothek Preuss. Kulturbesitz - Gesamtkat. U. Dok., Berlin, Federal Republic of Germany [*OCLC symbol*] (OCLC)
SBG.......... Standard Battery Grade
SBG.......... Starburst Galaxy [*Astronomy*]
SBG.......... Steinberg, Inc. [*Toronto Stock Exchange symbol*]
SBG.......... Strategic Bomber Group
SBG.......... Submarine Basaltic Glasses [*Geology*]
SBG.......... Universite de Sherbrooke, Publications Officielles [*UTLAS symbol*]
SBGA.......... Brasilia/Gama [*Brazil ICAO location identifier*] (ICLI)
SBGA.......... Serum Beta-Glucuronidase Activity [*Serology*]
SBGA.......... Summit Bank Corp. [*NASDAQ symbol*] (SAG)
SBG GEDD.......... Schottky-Barrier Gate Gunn-Effect Digital Device [*Electronics*] (PDAA)
SBGI.......... Serikat Buruh Gelas Indonesia [*Glass Workers' Union of Indonesia*]
SBGI.......... Sinclair Broadcast Group'A' [*NASDAQ symbol*] (TTSB)
SBGI.......... Sinclair Broadcast Group, Inc. [*NASDAQ symbol*] (SAG)
SBGI.......... Society of British Gas Industries (BI)
SBGL.......... Rio De Janeiro/Internacional Galeao [*Brazil ICAO location identifier*] (ICLI)
SBGM.......... Guajara-Mirim [*Brazil ICAO location identifier*] (ICLI)
SBGM.......... Self Blood Glucose Monitoring [*Endocrinology*] (DAVI)
SBGMS.......... Shipbuilders', Boiler, and Gasometer Makers' Society [*A union*] [*British*]
SBGO.......... Goiania/Santa Genoveva [*Brazil ICAO location identifier*] (ICLI)
SBGP.......... Campos/Plataforma PNA-1 [*Brazil ICAO location identifier*] (ICLI)
SBGP.......... Serikat Buruh Gula Proklamasi [*Sugar Workers' Union*] [*Indonesia*]
SBGP.......... Strategic Bomber Group
SBGR.......... Sao Paulo/Internacional Guarulhos [*Brazil ICAO location identifier*] (ICLI)
SBGS.......... Ponta Grossa [*Brazil ICAO location identifier*] (ICLI)
SBGSN.......... Serikat Buruh Garam dan Soda Negeri [*Salt Workers' Association*] [*Indonesia*]
SBGT.......... Standby Gas Treatment [*Nuclear energy*] (GFGA)
SBGTS.......... Standby Gas Treatment System [*Nuclear energy*] (NRCH)
SBGW.......... Guaratingueta [*Brazil ICAO location identifier*] (ICLI)
SBH.......... Sea Blue Histiocytosis [*Medicine*]
SBH.......... Sequencing by Hybridization [*Genetics*]
SBH.......... SmithKline Beecham ADS [*NYSE symbol*] (TTSB)
SBH.......... SmithKline Beecham Ltd. ADS [*NYSE symbol*] (SPSG)
SBH.......... Sodium Borohydride [*Inorganic chemistry*]
SBH.......... Southern Blot Hybridization [*Biochemistry*]
SBH.......... State Board of Health (MAE)
SBH.......... State University of New York, Health Sciences Library, Buffalo, NY [*OCLC symbol*] (OCLC)
SBH.......... St. Barthelemy [*Leeward Islands*] [*Airport symbol*] (OAG)
SBH.......... Strip-Buried Heterostructure [*Telecommunications*] (TEL)
SBH.......... Sumerisch-Babylonische Hymnen [*A publication*] (BJA)
SBH.......... Supermassive Black Hole [*Cosmology*]
SBH.......... Switch Busy Hour [*Telecommunications*] (IEEE)
SBHC.......... Security Bank Holding Co. [*NASDAQ symbol*] (SAG)
SBHC.......... Society of the Bible in the Hands of Its Creators [*Defunct*] (EA)
SBHC.......... Speed Brake Hand Control (NASA)
SBHEU.......... Singapore Business Houses Employees' Union
SBHRG.......... Space-Based Hypervelocity Rail Gun [*Military*] (SDI)
SBHRT.......... Serikat Buruh Hotel, Rumah-Makan dan Toko [*Hotel, Restaurant and Shops' Workers' Union*] [*Indonesia*]
SBHS.......... Strict Baptist Historical Society [*British*] (DBA)
SBHT.......... Altamira [*Brazil ICAO location identifier*] (ICLI)
SBI.......... Columbia Bible College, Columbia, SC [*OCLC symbol*] (OCLC)
SBI.......... Sabine Pass, TX [*Location identifier FAA*] (FAAL)
SBI.......... Santa Barbara Island (MUGU)
SBI.......... Satellite-Borne Instrumentation (SAA)
SBI.......... Scientific Bureau of Investigation [*In radio series "Armstrong of the SBI"*]
SBI.......... Serikat Buruh Industri [*Industrial Workers' Union*] [*Indonesia*]
SB-I.......... Service de Bibliographie sur l'Informatique [*Paris Gestion Informatique*] [*France Information service or system*] (CRD)
SBI.......... Shared Bibliographic Input
SBI.......... Shares of Beneficial Interest [*Stock exchange term*]
SBI.......... Shriners Burn Institute
SBI.......... Signal Band Indication
SBI.......... Significant Business Issue (MCD)
SBI.......... Single Byte Interleaved
SBI.......... Small Business Institute [*Small Business Administration*]
SBI.......... Smith Barney Intermediate Quality Municipal Fund [*AMEX symbol*] (SAG)
SBI.......... Smith Barney Inter Muni Fd [*AMEX symbol*] (TTSB)
SBI.......... Soil Brightness Index
SBI.......... Somerville Belkin Industries Ltd. [*Toronto Stock Exchange symbol*]
SBI.......... Sound Blaster Instrument [*PC sound format*]
SBI.......... Soviet Bureau of Information
SBI.......... Soybean (Trypsin) Inhibitor [*Biochemistry*]
SBI.......... Space-Based Interceptor [*Military*] (SDI)
SBI.......... Special Background Investigation (NVT)
SBI.......... State Bank of India (PDAA)
SBI.......... Steel Boiler Institute [*Defunct*]
SBI.......... Sterol Biosynthesis Inhibitors [*Chemotherapeutic agent*]
SBI.......... Study Behavior Inventory (EDAC)
SBI.......... Sun Belt Institute (EA)
SBI.......... Sustainable Biosphere Initiative (GNE)
SBI.......... Synchronous Bus Interface [*Computer science*] (HGAA)
SBI.......... Synfuels Bibliography and Index [*A publication*]
SBI.......... Systemic Bacterial Infection (DAVI)
SBIA.......... Small Business Innovation Development Act [*1982*]
SBIB.......... Sterling Bancshares [*NASDAQ symbol*] (TTSB)
SBIB.......... Sterling Bancshares, Inc. [*NASDAQ symbol*] (SAG)
SBIBD.......... Symmetrical Balanced Incomplete Block Designs (MCD)
SBIC.......... Small Business Investment Company [*Generic term*]
SBIC.......... Small Business Investment Corp. (DFIT)
SBIC.......... Small Business Investment Corporation (AAGC)

SBICo.......... Small Business Investment Company [*Generic term*]
SBIE.......... Shared Bibliographic Input Experiment [*Special Libraries Association*]
SBIG.......... [*The*] Seibels Bruce Group, Inc. [*NASDAQ symbol*] (NQ)
SBIGE.......... Seibels Bruce Group [*NASDAQ symbol*] (TTSB)
SBIL.......... Ilheus [*Brazil ICAO location identifier*] (ICLI)
SBILS.......... Scanning Beam Instrument Landing System (KSC)
SBIN.......... Fort Battleford National Historic Park, Parks Canada [*Parc Historique National Fort Battleford, Parcs Canada*] Battleford, Saskatchewan [*Library symbol National Library of Canada*] (NLC)
SBIO.......... Synbiotics Corp. [*NASDAQ symbol*] (NQ)
SBIP.......... Ipatinga/Usiminas [*Brazil ICAO location identifier*] (ICLI)
SBIR.......... Small Business Innovation Research (AAGC)
SBIR.......... Small Business Innovation Research Program [*Small Business Administration*]
SBIR.......... Small Business Innovative Research (USDC)
SBIR.......... Small Business Innovative Research [*Program*]
SBIR.......... Small Business Innovative Research [*Marine science*] (OSRA)
SBIR.......... Storage Bus in Register
SBIRS.......... Space-Based Infrared System [*Military*]
SBIR/STTR... Small Business Innovation Research/Small Business Technology Transfer [*Army*] (RDA)
SBIS.......... Satellite-Based Interceptor System (IAA)
SBIS.......... Stanford-Binet Intelligence Scale [*Psychology*] (DAVI)
SBIS.......... Sustaining Base Information Service [*or System*] [*Army*] (RDA)
SBIT.......... Itumbiara/Hidroelectrica [*Brazil ICAO location identifier*] (ICLI)
SBIT.......... Summit Bancshares [*NASDAQ symbol*] (TTSB)
SBIT.......... Summit Bancshares Texas [*NASDAQ symbol*] (SAG)
SBIZ.......... Imperatriz [*Brazil ICAO location identifier*] (ICLI)
SBJ.......... Journal. State Bar of California [*A publication*] (DLA)
SBJ.......... Schottky Barrier Junction [*Electronics*]
SBJ.......... Simla [*India*] [*Airport symbol*] (AD)
SBJ.......... Solberg, NJ [*Location identifier FAA*] (FAAL)
SBJ.......... Subjunctive [*Grammar*] (WGA)
SBJC.......... Belem/Julio Cesar [*Brazil ICAO location identifier*] (ICLI)
SBJF.......... Juiz De Fora/Francisco De Assis [*Brazil ICAO location identifier*] (ICLI)
SBJP.......... Joao Pessoa/Presidente Castro Pinto [*Brazil ICAO location identifier*] (ICLI)
SBJR.......... Rio De Janeiro/Jacarepagua [*Brazil ICAO location identifier*] (ICLI)
SBJV.......... Joinville [*Brazil ICAO location identifier*] (ICLI)
SBK.......... Signet Banking [*NYSE symbol*] (TTSB)
SBK.......... Signet Banking Corp. [*NYSE symbol*] (SPSG)
SBK.......... Single-Beam Klystron (MSA)
SBK.......... Society for Behavioral Kinesiology
SBK.......... Softwood Bleached Kraft [*Pulp and paper technology*]
SBK.......... South Brooklyn Railway Co. [*AAR code*]
SBK.......... St. Brieuc [*France*] [*Airport symbol*] (OAG)
sbk.......... Subangular Blocky Soil [*Agriculture*]
SBK.......... System Builder Kit [*Digital Research, Inc.*] [*Computer science*] (PCM)
SBK.......... Universite de Sherbrooke, Bibliotheque [*UTLAS symbol*]
SBKEW.......... Space-Based Kinetic Energy Weapon [*Military*] (MCD)
SBKG.......... Campina Grande/Joao Suassuna [*Brazil ICAO location identifier*] (ICLI)
SBKKV.......... Space-Based Kinetic Kill Vehicle [*Military*]
SBKP.......... Sao Paulo (Campinas)/Viracopos [*Brazil ICAO location identifier*] (ICLI)
SBKU.......... Cucui [*Brazil ICAO location identifier*] (ICLI)
s-bl--.......... Brazil [*MARC geographic area code Library of Congress*] (LCCP)
SBL.......... Santa Ana [*Bolivia*] [*Airport symbol Obsolete*] (OAG)
SBL.......... Sealed Beam Lamp
SBL.......... Serrated Black Letters [*Tire design*] [*Automotive engineering*]
SBL.......... Short Brothers PLC [*British ICAO designator*] (FAAC)
SBL.......... Society of Biblical Literature (EA)
SBL.......... Soybean Lecithin [*Biochemistry*]
SBL.......... Space-Based LASER
SBL.......... Sporadic Burkitt's Lymphoma [*Medicine*]
SBL.......... Staphylococcal Bacteriophage Lysate
SBL.......... State University of New York at Buffalo, Law Library, Buffalo, NY [*OCLC symbol*] (OCLC)
SBL.......... Strong Black Liquor [*Pulp and paper technology*]
SBL.......... Structure Building Language (PDAA)
SBL.......... Styrene-Butadiene Latexes [*Organic chemistry*]
SBL.......... Surface Boundary Layer (MCD)
SBL.......... Symbol Technologies [*NYSE symbol*] (TTSB)
SBL.......... Symbol Technologies, Inc. [*NYSE symbol*] (SPSG)
SBLA.......... Shore-Based Landing Aids (MCD)
SBLA.......... Small Business Loans Act [*Canada*]
SBLB.......... Labrea [*Brazil ICAO location identifier*] (ICLI)
SBLC.......... Shallow Bed Liquid Chromatography
SBLC.......... Small Business Legislative Council [*Washington, DC*] (EA)
SBLC.......... Standby Liquid Control [*Nuclear energy*] (NRCH)
SBLE.......... Society of Biblical Literature and Exegesis [*Later, SBL*] (EA)
SBLI.......... Savings Bank Life Insurance
SBLI.......... Staff Builders 'A' [*NASDAQ symbol*] (TTSB)
SBLI.......... Staff Builders, Inc. [*NASDAQ symbol*] (NQ)
SBLJ.......... Lajes [*Brazil ICAO location identifier*] (ICLI)
SBLMC.......... Styrene Butadiene Latex Manufacturers Council (EA)
SBLN.......... Lins [*Brazil ICAO location identifier*] (ICLI)
SBLO.......... Londrina [*Brazil ICAO location identifier*] (ICLI)
SBLO.......... Strong Black Liquor Oxidation [*Pulp and paper technology*]
SBLOCA.......... Small-Break Loss of Coolant Accident [*Nuclear energy*] (NRCH)
SBLP.......... Bom Jesus Da Lapa [*Brazil ICAO location identifier*] (ICLI)
SBLP.......... Simplified Bank Loan Participation Plan [*Small Business Administration*]
SBLS.......... Lagoa Santa [*Brazil ICAO location identifier*] (ICLI)
SBLS.......... Spaceborne LASER Ranging
SBLSA.......... Small Business and Labor Surplus Advisor (AABC)
SBLT.......... Sunbelt Companies [*NASDAQ symbol*] (SAG)
SBM.......... College of Charleston, Charleston, SC [*OCLC symbol*] (OCLC)
SBM.......... SBM Industries [*Formerly, Speed-O-Print Business Machines Corp.*] [*AMEX symbol*] (SPSG)
SBM.......... School in Basic Management [*LIMRA*]
SBM.......... Science-by-Mail (EA)
SBM.......... Send a Block Message [*Computer science*] (ECII)
SBM.......... Sheboygan [*Wisconsin*] [*Airport symbol*] (OAG)
SBM.......... Sheboygan, WI [*Location identifier FAA*] (FAAL)
SBM.......... Single Black Male [*Classified advertising*]
SBM.......... Single-Buoy Mooring [*Oil tanker*]
SBM.......... Single-Point Mooring Buoy [*Navy*]
SBM.......... Societe des Bains de Mer [*Monte Carlo*]
SBM.......... Society of Behavioral Medicine (EA)
SBM.......... Solomon-Bloembergen-Morgan Equation [*Medicine*] (DMAA)
SBM.......... St. Louis, Brownsville & Mexico [*AAR code*]
SBM.......... Submerge [*or Submersible*] (KSC)
SBM.......... Submit (AABC)
SBM.......... Subtract Magnitude (IAA)
SBM.......... Super Bit Mapping [*Compact-disc technology*] (PS)
SBM.......... System Balance Measure (BUR)
SBMA.......... Maraba [*Brazil ICAO location identifier*] (ICLI)
SBMA.......... Sand and Ballast Merchants' Alliance [*British*] (BI)
SBMA.......... Service Business Marketing Association (EA)
SBMA.......... SINS [*Ship Inertial Navigational System*] Bedplate Mirror Assembly
SBMA.......... Spinal and Bulbar Muscular Atrophy [*Medicine*]
SBMA.......... Spino-Bulbar Muscular Atrophy [*Medicine*]
SBMA.......... Steel Bar Mills Association [*Later, SMA*] (EA)
SBMA.......... Stock Brick Manufacturers Association [*British*] (BI)
SBMA.......... Subic Bay Metropolitan Authority [*Philippines*]
SBMD.......... Stochastic Boundary Molecular Dynamics [*Force energy simulation method*]
SBMDL.......... Submodel
SBME.......... Macae [*Brazil ICAO location identifier*] (ICLI)
SBME.......... Society of Business Magazine Editors [*Later, ASBPE*]
SBME.......... State Board of Medical Examiners (NADA)
SBMG.......... Maringa [*Brazil ICAO location identifier*] (ICLI)
SBMG.......... Scottish Book Marketing Group
SBMI.......... School Bus Manufacturers Institute (EA)
SBM Ind.......... SBM Industries [*Associated Press*] (SAG)
SBMK.......... Montes Claros [*Brazil ICAO location identifier*] (ICLI)
SBML.......... Marilia [*Brazil ICAO location identifier*] (ICLI)
SBML.......... Signal Band Mainlobe
SBML.......... Smooth Bore Muzzle Loading [*British military*] (DMA)
SBMLCNT.... Signal Band (Energy) in Mainlobe Count [*Military*]
SBMN.......... Manaus/Ponta Pelada [*Brazil ICAO location identifier*] (ICLI)
SBMO.......... Maceio/Palmares [*Brazil ICAO location identifier*] (ICLI)
SBMP.......... Safety Base Motion Picture (VRA)
SBMPL.......... Simultaneous Binaural Midplane Localization [*Audiometry*]
SBMQ.......... Macapa/Internacional [*Brazil ICAO location identifier*] (ICLI)
SBMR.......... Manoel Ribas [*Brazil ICAO location identifier*] (ICLI)
SBMS.......... Mocoro/Dix-Sept Rosado [*Brazil ICAO location identifier*] (ICLI)
SBMSI.......... Serikat Buruh Minjak Shell Indonesia [*Union of Oil Workers for Shell of Indonesia*]
SBMSS.......... Shore-Based Message Service System (DNAB)
SBMSTE.......... Space and Ballistic Missile System Training Equipment (SAA)
SBMT.......... Sao Paulo/Marte [*Brazil ICAO location identifier*] (ICLI)
SBMU.......... Manaus [*Brazil ICAO location identifier*] (ICLI)
SBMV.......... Southern Bean Mosaic Virus
SBMV-B.......... Southern Bean Mosaic Virus - Strain B
SBMV-C.......... Southern Bean Mosaic Virus - Cowpea Strain
SBMW.......... Serikat Buruh Maclaine, Watson [*Maclaine Watson Co. Workers' Union*] [*Indones ia*]
SBMY.......... Manicore [*Brazil ICAO location identifier*] (ICLI)
SBMZ.......... Porto De Moz [*Brazil ICAO location identifier*] (ICLI)
SBN.......... Buffalo Narrows Public Library, Saskatchewan [*Library symbol National Library of Canada*] (NLC)
SBN.......... Sheridan Broadcasting Network
SBN.......... Single-Breath Nitrogen [*Test*] (DAVI)
SBN.......... Sino Business Machine [*Vancouver Stock Exchange symbol*]
SBN.......... Small Business Network [*Baltimore, MD*] (EA)
SBN.......... South Bend [*Indiana*] [*Airport symbol*] (OAG)
SBN.......... Spaceborne (KSC)
SBN.......... Standard Book Number
SBN.......... Strong Base Number (IAA)
SBN.......... Strontium-Barium-Niobidium [*Inorganic chemistry*]
SBN.......... Subic Bay News [*A publication*] (DNAB)
SBN.......... Sunbelt Nursery Group [*AMEX symbol*] (TTSB)
SBN.......... Sunbelt Nursery Group, Inc. [*AMEX symbol*] (SPSG)
SBN_2.......... Single Breath Nitrogen [*Test*] [*Medicine*]
SBNF.......... Navegantes [*Brazil ICAO location identifier*] (ICLI)
SBNH.......... Society for the Bibliography of Natural History (EA)
SBNK.......... Suburban Bancshares, Inc. [*NASDAQ symbol*] (SAG)
SBNK.......... Suburban Bancshares [*NASDAQ symbol*] (TTSB)
SBNL.......... Submarine Base, New London [*Connecticut*] [*Navy*]
SBNM.......... Santo Angelo [*Brazil ICAO location identifier*] (ICLI)
SBNO.......... Senior British Naval Officer
SBNOWA.......... Senior British Naval Officer, Western Atlantic
SBNPB.......... Space-Based Neutral Particle Beam [*Military*] (SDI)
SBNS.......... Society of British Neurological Surgeons
SBNSW.......... State Bank of New South Wales [*Australia*]
SBNT.......... Natal/Augusto Severo [*Brazil ICAO location identifier*] (ICLI)
SBNT.......... Single-Breath Nitrogen Test [*Physiology*]

s-bo--........ Bolivia [*MARC geographic area code Library of Congress*] (LCCP)
SBO........ Classification of Galactic Nebulae Between Elliptical and Spiral Types Having a Bright Nucleus and Dark Bands of Matter But No Distinguishable Arms [*Astronomy*] (BARN)
SBO........ Salina [*Utah*] [*Airport symbol*] (OAG)
SBO........ Secure Base of Operation (WDAA)
SBO........ Showboat, Inc. [*NYSE symbol*] (SPSG)
SBO........ Sidebands Only (IAA)
SBO........ Silver Box Resources [*Vancouver Stock Exchange symbol*]
SBO........ Small Bowel Obstruction [*Medicine*] (MAE)
SBO........ Small Business Office
SBO........ Small Business Ombudsman [*Federal government*] (GFGA)
SBO........ Soybean Oil
SBO........ Specific Behavioral Objectives [*Aviation*]
SBO........ Specified Bovine Offal [*Animal feed regulation*]
SBO........ Stabo Air Ltd. [*Zambia*] [*FAA designator*] (FAAC)
SBO........ Standing Balance: Eyes Open [*Test*] [*Occupational therapy*]
SBO........ Studia Biblica et Orientalia [*Rome*] [*A publication*] (BJA)
SBO........ Swainsboro, GA [*Location identifier FAA*] (FAAL)
SBOA........ Specialty Bakery Owners of America (EA)
SB of A........ Smaller Business of America [*Defunct*] (EA)
SBOI........ Oiapoque [*Brazil ICAO location identifier*] (ICLI)
SBOLS........ Shadow Box Optical Landing System
SBOM........ Soybean Oil Meal
SBOOM........ Sonic Boom [*Computer program*] [*NASA*]
SBOPERDET... Switchboard Operation Detachment (IAA)
SBOR........ Successive Block Overrelaxation (IAA)
SBOS........ Boston Bancorp [*Formerly, South Boston Savings Bank*] [*NASDAQ symbol*] (NQ)
SBOS........ Silicon-Borne Oxygen System (SAA)
SBOSI........ Serikat Buruh Obat Seluruh Indonesia [*All Indonesian Medicinal Factory Workers' Union*]
SBOST........ Slavonic Benevolent Order of the State of Texas [*Temple, TX*] (EA)
SBOT........ Sacred Books of the Old Testament [*The "Rainbow Bible"*] [*A publication*] (BJA)
SBOU........ Ourinhos [*Brazil ICAO location identifier*] (ICLI)
S/BOY........ Secondary Boycott [*Legal shorthand*] (LWAP)
SBP........ San Luis Obispo [*California*] [*Airport symbol*] (OAG)
SBP........ Scleral Buckling Procedure [*Medicine*] (MAE)
SBP........ Sec-Butyl Percarbonate [*Organic chemistry*]
SBP........ Serikat Buruh Pegadaian [*Pawnshop Workers' Union*] [*Indonesia*]
SBP........ Serikat Buruh Penerbangan [*Airways' Unions*] [*Indonesia*]
SBP........ Service Benefit Plan [*Military*] (AABC)
SBP........ Shop Procedure Bulletin [*A publication*] (EAAP)
SBP........ Shore-Based Prototype [*Nuclear energy*] (OA)
SBP........ Simulated BOMARC [*Boeing-Michigan Aeronautical Research Center*] Program (IAA)
SBP........ Societe Beneluxienne de Phlebologie [*Benelux Phlebology Society - BPS*] (EA)
SBP........ Society for Behaviorial Pediatrics (EA)
SBP........ Society of Biological Psychiatry (EA)
SBP........ Sonic Boom Panel [*Aerospace*] (MCD)
SBP........ Sosyalist Birlik Partisi [*Socialist Unity Party*] [*Turkey Political party*] (EY)
SBP........ Soziale Buergerpartei [*Social Citizen's Party*] [*Germany Political party*] (PPW)
SBP........ Spaceborne Programmer
SBP........ Special Block Purchase
SBP........ Special Boiling Point (IAA)
SBP........ Special Businessowners Policy [*Insurance*]
SBP........ Spontaneous Bacterial Peritonitis [*Medicine*]
SBP........ Squalene-Binding Protein [*Biochemistry*]
SBP........ Standard Brands Paint Co. [*NYSE symbol*] (SPSG)
SBP........ Standard Businessowners Policy [*Insurance*]
SBP........ State Bank of Pakistan
SBP........ Steroid-Binding Plasma Protein
SBP........ Subacute Bacterial Peritonitis (DAVI)
SBP........ Subic Bay [*Philippines*] [*Seismograph station code, US Geological Survey Closed*] (SEIS)
SBP........ Sugar Beet Pulp (PDAA)
SBP........ Sulfate-Binding Protein [*Biochemistry*]
SBP........ Sumerian and Babylonian Psalms [*A publication*] (BJA)
SBP........ Survivor Benefit Plan [*For survivors of retired military personnel*]
SBP........ Systemic Blood Pressure [*Medicine*] (MAE)
SBP........ Systolic Blood Pressure [*Medicine*]
SBPA........ Porto Alegre/Salgado Filho [*Brazil ICAO location identifier*] (ICLI)
SBPA........ Southern Baptist Press Association (EA)
SBPB........ Parnaiba [*Brazil ICAO location identifier*] (ICLI)
SBPB........ Space-Based Particle Beam [*Military*] (SDI)
SBPC........ Pocos De Caldas [*Brazil ICAO location identifier*] (ICLI)
SBPD........ Society of Business Publication Designers [*Later, SPD*] (EA)
SBPE........ Standard Battle Plan Emplacement [*Military*]
SBPF........ Passo Fundo/Lauro Kurtz [*Brazil ICAO location identifier*] (ICLI)
SBPG........ Paranagua [*Brazil ICAO location identifier*] (ICLI)
SBPG........ Serikat Buruh Perusahaan Gula [*Sugar Workers' Union*] [*Indonesia*]
SBPH........ Porto Velho [*Brazil ICAO location identifier*] (ICLI)
SBPH........ Single Burst Probability of Hit [*Military*] (AABC)
SBPH........ Submarine Base, Pearl Harbor [*Navy*] (DNAB)
SBPI........ Petropolis/Pico do Couto [*Brazil ICAO location identifier*] (ICLI)
SBPI........ Serikat Buruh Pelabuhan Indonesia [*Dockworkers' Union of Indonesia*]
SBPI........ Serikat Buruh Pendjahit Indonesia [*Tailors' Union of Indonesia*]
SBPIM........ Society of British Printing Ink Manufacturers (BI)
SBPK........ Pelotas [*Brazil ICAO location identifier*] (ICLI)
SBPKB........ Serikat Buruh Persuahaan Kaju dan Bangunan [*Building, Road and Irrigation Workers' Union*] [*Indonesia*]
SBPL........ Petrolina [*Brazil ICAO location identifier*] (ICLI)
SBPN........ Porto Nacional [*Brazil ICAO location identifier*] (ICLI)
SBPP........ Ponta Pora/Internacional [*ICAO location identifier*] (ICLI)
SBPP........ Serikat Buruh Pelabuhan dan Pelajaran [*Dockworkers' Union*] [*Indonesia*]
SBPPK........ Serikat Buruh Pendidikan, Pengadjaran dan Kebudjaan [*Department of Education Workers' Union*] [*Indonesia*]
SBPR........ Piracaba [*Brazil ICAO location identifier*] (ICLI)
SBPR........ Society for Back Pain Research [*British*]
SBPrC........ Salomon Inc. 9.50% Dep Pfd [*NYSE symbol*] (TTSB)
SBPrD........ Salomon Inc. 8.08% Dep Pfd [*NYSE symbol*] (TTSB)
SBPrE........ Salomon Inc. 8.40% Dep Pfd [*NYSE symbol*] (TTSB)
SBPT........ Serikat Buruh Perhubungan dan Transport [*Communications and Transportation Workers' Union*] [*Indonesia*]
SBPT........ Serikat Buruh Pertambangan Timah [*Tin Mine Labor Union*] [*Indonesia*]
SBPT........ Societe Beninoise pour la Promotion du Tourisme (EY)
SBPU........ Serikat Buruh Pekerdjaan Umum [*Public Workers' Ministry Union*] [*Indonesia*]
SBPV........ Porto Velho [*Brazil ICAO location identifier*] (ICLI)
SBPW........ Pindamonhangaba/Visaba [*Brazil ICAO location identifier*] (ICLI)
SBPW........ Special Board for Public Works [*New Deal*]
SBQ........ Grenada, MS [*Location identifier FAA*] (FAAL)
SBQ........ Sao Borja [*Brazil*] [*Airport symbol*] (AD)
SBQ........ Serikat Buruh Qantas [*Qantas Labor Union*] [*Indonesia*]
SBQ........ Smithkline Beacham Clincal Labs [*ICAO designator*] (FAAC)
SBQ........ Surveyors' Board of Queensland [*Australia*]
SBQV........ Vitoria Da Conquista [*Brazil ICAO location identifier*] (ICLI)
SBR........ Saber Aviation, Inc. [*ICAO designator*] (FAAC)
SBR........ Sabine Royalty Tr UBI [*NYSE symbol*] (TTSB)
SBR........ Sabine Royalty Trust [*NYSE symbol*] (SPSG)
SBR........ Sale by Reference
SBR........ Santa Barbara [*Monagas, Venezuela*] [*Airport symbol*] (AD)
SBR........ Scripps-Booth Register [*An association*] (EA)
SBR........ Seat Bucket Read (NG)
SBR........ Segment Base Register (BUR)
SBR........ Sequencing Batch Reactor [*Chemical engineering*]
SBR........ Service Billing Record
SBR........ Signal to Background Ratio [*Instrumentation*]
SBR........ Small Box-Respirator [*British military*] (DMA)
SBR........ Society for Biological Rhythm
SBR........ Society of Bead Researchers (EA)
SBR........ Soviet Breeder Reactor
SBR........ Space-Based RADAR (MCD)
SBR........ Standard Busy Rate (NATG)
SBR........ Starburst Energy [*Vancouver Stock Exchange symbol*]
SBR........ Stimulus-Bound Repetition [*Medicine*]
SBR........ Storage Buffer Register
SBR........ Strand Burning Rate (MCD)
SBR........ Strict Bed Rest [*Medicine*]
SBR........ Styrene-Butadiene Rubber [*Also, GR-S*] [*Synthetic rubber*]
SBR........ Supplemental Budget Request
SBRB........ Rio Branco/Presidente Medici [*Brazil ICAO location identifier*] (ICLI)
SBRC........ Santa Barbara Research Center [*Hughes Aircraft Co.*]
SBRC........ Single-Braided Rubber-Covered (IAA)
SBRC........ Southwest Border Regional Commission [*Department of Commerce*]
SBRD........ Seaboard Oil [*NASDAQ symbol*] (TTSB)
SBRD........ Seaboard Oil Co. [*NASDAQ symbol*] (SAG)
SBRE........ Recife [*Brazil ICAO location identifier*] (ICLI)
SBRF........ Recife/Guararapes [*Brazil ICAO location identifier*] (ICLI)
SBRI........ Serikat Buruh Rokok Indonesia [*Cigarette Workers' Union of Indonesia*]
SBRI........ Southwest Biomedical Research Institute [*Arizona State University*] [*Research center*] (RCD)
SBRI........ Space Biomedical Research Institute [*Houston, TX*] [*NASA*]
SBRIMCD.... Sun Bay Recovery - International Missing Children's Division (EA)
SBRJ........ Rio De Janeiro/Santos Dumont [*Brazil ICAO location identifier*] (ICLI)
SB-RK........ Bomber [*Russian aircraft symbol*]
SBRP........ Ribeirao Preto/Leite Lopes [*Brazil ICAO location identifier*] (ICLI)
SBRP........ Sonic Boom Research Program
SBRP........ Special Bridge Replacement Program 1970 [*MTMC*] (TAG)
SBRP........ Submarine Reportback Processor Unit (DWSG)
SBRQ........ Sao Roque [*Brazil ICAO location identifier*] (ICLI)
SBRRI........ Serikat Buruh Radio Republik Indonesia [*Broadcasting Workers' Association of Indonesia*]
SBRS........ Resende [*Brazil ICAO location identifier*] (ICLI)
SBRS........ Side and Back Rack System (PDAA)
SBRS........ Social Behavior Rating Scale
SBrSP01..... Smith Barney Holdings [*Associated Press*] (SAG)
SBRV........ Small Ballistic Reentry Vehicle
SBRZ........ Sanborn, Inc. [*NASDAQ symbol*] (SAG)
SBS........ Salem Corp. [*AMEX symbol*] (SPSG)
SBS........ Samuel Butler Society [*Defunct*] (EA)
SBS........ Satellite Business Systems [*McLean, VA*] [*Telecommunications*] (MCD)
SBS........ Save British Science [*An association*] (AIE)
SBS........ Save British Science Society (DBA)
SBS........ Scandinavian Broadcast System
SBS........ Scarborough Board of Education [*UTLAS symbol*]
SBS........ Scientific Business Systems (NITA)
SBS........ See Before Setting [*Typography*] (DGA)
SBS........ Semiconductor Bilateral Switch (MSA)
SBS........ Sensor Based System (BUR)

SBS .... Serially Balanced Sequence [*Statistics*]
SBS .... Servicios Aereos Barsa SA de CV [*Mexico ICAO designator*] (FAAC)
SBS .... Shaken Baby Syndrome (CPH)
SBS .... Shipboard Simulators [*Navy*] (DOMA)
SBS .... Short Baseline SONAR (PDAA)
SBS .... Short Beam Shear
SBS .... Sick Building Syndrome [*Medicine*]
SBS .... Sidi-Bou-Said [*Tunisia*] [*Seismograph station code, US Geological Survey*] (SEIS)
SBS .... Silicon Bidirectional Switch (IAA)
SBS .... Silicon Bilateral Switch
SBS .... Simultaneous Buying and Selling Arrangement
SBS .... Single-Business Service
SBS .... Sisters of the Blessed Sacrament [*Roman Catholic religious order*]
SBS .... [*The*] Sisters of the Blessed Sacrament for Indians and Colored People (TOCD)
SBS .... Small-Bowel Syndrome (DAVI)
SBS .... Small Business Server [*Microsoft Corp.*]
SBS .... Small Business Sourcebook [*A publication*]
SBS .... Small Business Specialist [*DoD*]
SBS .... Small Business System (ADA)
SBS .... Smart Business Supersite [*Internet resource*] [*Computer science*]
SBS .... Social Behavior Standards
SBS .... Social-Breakdown Syndrome (MAE)
SBS .... Society for Biomolecular Screening
SBS .... Soeurs de Bon Sauveur [*France*] (EAIO)
SBS .... Solid Bleached Sulphate [*Fiber for paperboard packaging*]
SBS .... Southern Base Section [*England*]
SBS .... Spaniel Breeders Society (EA)
SBS .... Spanish Benevolent Society "La Nacional" (EA)
SBS .... Spanish Broadcasting System
SBS .... Special Block Sale
SBS .... Special Boat Section [*British military*] (DMA)
SBS .... Special Boat Squadron [*British commando unit*]
SBS .... Staff Burn-Out Scale [*Medicine*] (MEDA)
SBS .... Standby Status (AAG)
SBS .... Steamboat Springs [*Colorado*] [*Airport symbol*] (OAG)
SBS .... Steel Building System
SBS .... Stimulated Brillouin Scattering
SBS .... Straight Binary Second
SBS .... Strategic Balkan Services [*World War II*]
SBS .... Strategic Bombing Survey
SBS .... Strategic Business Segment
SBS .... Stuttgarter Bibelstudien. Katholisches Bibelwerk [*Stuttgart*] [*A publication*] (BJA)
SBS .... Styrene-Butadiene-Styrene [*Copolymer*]
SBS .... Subscript Character [*Computer science*]
SBS .... Superburn Systems Ltd. [*Vancouver Stock Exchange symbol*]
SBS .... Surveyed Before Shipment [*Business term*] (MHDB)
SBS .... Survey of Basic Skills [*Achievement test*]
SBS .... Swedish Behavioural Sciences [*Database*] [*National Library for Psychology and Education*] [*Information service or system*] (CRD)
SBS .... Sweep Back Station (MCD)
SBS .... Swiss Benevolent Society of New York (EA)
SBS .... System Breakdown Structure [*Military*] (AFIT)
SBSA .... Sao Carlos/Francisco Pereira Lopez [*Brazil ICAO location identifier*] (ICLI)
SBSA .... Show and Breed Secretaries' Association [*British*] (BI)
SBSA .... Society of Basque Studies in America (EA)
SBSA .... Standard Business Software Award (NITA)
SBSA .... State Bank of South Australia
SBSanE .... Bachelor of Science in Sanitary Engineering
SBSB .... Small Business Service Bureau [*Worcester, MA*] (EA)
SBSB .... Society of British Snuff Blenders (EAIO)
SBSBA .... Scottish Blackface Sheep Breeders Association (EA)
SBSBS .... Smith Benevolent Sick and Burial Society [*British*]
SBSC .... Rio De Janeiro/Santa Cruz [*Brazil ICAO location identifier*] (ICLI)
SBSC .... Saint Bernardine of Siena College [*New York*]
SBSC .... Saint Bernard's Seminary and College [*New York*]
SBSC .... Schottky Barrier Solar Cell [*Electronics*] (PDAA)
SBSC .... Separate Bias, Single Control
SBSCA .... Small Business Support Center Association [*Houston, TX*] (EA)
SB/SDB .... Small Business / Small Disadvantaged Business (SSD)
SBSE .... SBS Engineering, Inc. [*NASDAQ symbol*] (SAG)
SBSE .... SBS Technologies [*NASDAQ symbol*] (TTSB)
SBSE .... SBS Technologies, Inc. [*NASDAQ symbol*] (SAG)
SBSG .... Small Business Systems Group [*Westford, MA*] [*Telecommunications*] (TSSD)
SBSI .... Seabrook Sea Island Cotton
SBSI .... Serikat Buruh Seluruh Indonesia [*All Indonesian Laborers' Union*]
SBSI .... Small Business Start-Up Index [*A publication*]
SBSJ .... Sao Jose Dos Campos [*Brazil ICAO location identifier*] (ICLI)
SBSK .... Samodzielna Brygada Strzelcow Karpackich [*Poland*]
SBSKK .... Serikat Buruh Sepatu Keradjinan Kulit Karet [*Shoe Workers' Union*] [*Indonesia*]
SBSL .... Sao Luis/Marechal Cunha Machado [*Brazil ICAO location identifier*] (ICLI)
SBSL .... Single-Bubble Sonoluminescence [*Physics*]
SBSM .... Santa Maria [*Brazil ICAO location identifier*] (ICLI)
SBSM .... Sisterhood of Black Single Mothers (EA)
SBSN .... Santarem/Internacional [*Brazil ICAO location identifier*] (ICLI)
SBSP .... Sao Paulo/Congonhas [*Brazil ICAO location identifier*] (ICLI)
SBSP .... Single Base Solid Propellant (MSA)
SB Sqn .... Special Boat Squadron [*British commando unit*] (DMA)
SBSR .... Sao Jose Do Rio Preto [*Brazil ICAO location identifier*] (ICLI)
SBSRT .... Spreen-Benton Sentence Repetition Test [*Speech and language therapy*] (DAVI)
SBSS .... Seligmann's Buffered Salt Solution [*Medicine*] (DMAA)
SBSS .... Space-Based Space Surveillance (MCD)
SBSS .... Spare Band Surveillance System (MCD)
SBSS .... Standard Base Supply System [*Military*] (AFIT)
SBST .... Santos [*Brazil ICAO location identifier*] (ICLI)
SBSTA .... Sound Bearing Station (IAA)
SBS Tech ...... SBS Technologies, Inc. [*Associated Press*] (SAG)
SBStJ .... Serving Brother, Order of St. John of Jerusalem [*British*]
SBSTNC .... Substance
SBSTR .... Substrate [*Electronics*]
SBSUSA .... Sport Balloon Society of the United States of America (EA)
SBSV .... Salvador/Dois de Julho [*Brazil ICAO location identifier*] (ICLI)
SBSY .... Cristalandia/Santa Isabel do Morro [*Brazil ICAO location identifier*] (ICLI)
SBT .... Safe Break Terminator (IAA)
SBT .... Salina Board of Trade (EA)
SBT .... San Benito [*California*] [*Seismograph station code, US Geological Survey*] (SEIS)
SBT .... San Bernardino [*California*] [*Airport symbol*] (AD)
SBT .... San Bernardino, CA [*Location identifier FAA*] (FAAL)
SBT .... Schools Board of Tasmania [*Australia*]
SBT .... Screening Breath Tester [*Drunken driving*]
SBT .... Seabright Resources, Inc. [*Toronto Stock Exchange symbol*]
SBT .... Segregated Ballast Tank [*Shipping construction*]
SBT .... Serikat Buruh Tambang [*Mine Workers' Union*] [*Indonesia*]
SBT .... Serikat Buruh Teknik [*Technicians' Union*] [*Indonesia*]
SBT .... Serikat Buruh Textil [*Textile Workers' Union*] [*Indonesia*]
SBT .... Serum Bactericidal Titer [*Clinical chemistry*]
SBT .... Shakespeare Birthplace Trust (EA)
SBT .... Shanghai Book Traders
SBT .... Sheet, Bar, Tubing (IAA)
SBT .... Shipboard Test [*Navy*] (DNAB)
SBT .... Side Buoyancy Tank
SBT .... Simultaneous Baseband Transmission [*of information*]
SBT .... Single-Breath Test (MAE)
SBT .... Six BIT [*Binary Digit*] Transcode (CMD)
SBT .... Small Boat
SBT .... Smith Barney Municipal Fund [*AMEX symbol*] (SPSG)
SBT .... Smith Barney Muni Fund [*AMEX symbol*] (TTSB)
SBT .... Sodium Bitartrate [*Inorganic chemistry*]
SBT .... Southern Bluefin Tuna [*Fish*]
SBT .... Space-Based Tug [*NASA*]
SBT .... Submarine Bathythermograph
SBT .... Submarine Bubble Target [*British military*] (DMA)
SBT .... Sulbactam (DMAA)
SBT .... Surface Barrier Transistor
SBT .... System Burning Time
SBTA .... Small Business Technical Adviser (AAGC)
SBTC .... Sino-British Trade Council (DS)
SBTC .... Speedbrake Thrust Control [*Aerospace*] (MCD)
SBTC .... Tapuruquara [*Brazil ICAO location identifier*] (ICLI)
SBTD .... Society of British Theatre Designers (DBA)
SBTE .... Teresina [*Brazil ICAO location identifier*] (ICLI)
SBTF .... Tefe [*Brazil ICAO location identifier*] (ICLI)
SBTG .... Sabotage (AABC)
SBTI .... Soybean Trypsin Inhibitor
SBTK .... Sabratek Corp. [*NASDAQ symbol*] (SAG)
SBTK .... Tarauaca [*Brazil ICAO location identifier*] (ICLI)
SBTM .... S-Band Telemetry Modification Kit (SAA)
SBTOW .... Standby Towship [*Navy*] (NVT)
SBTP .... Serikat Buruh Teknik dan Pelabuhan [*Technical and Harbour Workers' Union*] [*Indonesia*]
SBTPE .... State Boards Test Pool Examination [*Medicine*] (DMAA)
SBTS .... Shore-Based Tracking System
SBTS .... Strategic Bombardment Training Squadron
SBTS .... Stretch Block Template Set (MCD)
SBTT .... Serikat Buruh Tambang Timah [*Tin Mine Laborers' Union*] [*Indonesia*]
SBTT .... Small Bowel Transit Time [*Medicine*] (DMAA)
SBTT .... Small Business Technology Transfer (AAGC)
SBTT .... Southern Bell Telephone & Telegraph Co. (KSC)
SBTT .... Tabatinga/Internacional [*Brazil ICAO location identifier*] (ICLI)
SBTTL .... Schottky Barrier Transistor-Transistor Logic (IAA)
SBTU .... Serikat Buruh Teknik Umum [*Indonesia*]
SBTU .... Tucurui [*Brazil ICAO location identifier*] (ICLI)
SBTV .... Scandinavian Broadcasting [*NASDAQ symbol*] (SAG)
SBTVF .... Scandinavian Broadcstg Sys [*NASDAQ symbol*] (TTSB)
SBU .... Blue Earth, MN [*Location identifier FAA*] (FAAL)
SBU .... Saint Bonaventure University [*New York*]
SBU .... Scottish Badminton Union (EAIO)
SBU .... Secondary Building Unit [*Physical chemistry*]
SBU .... Silver Brazing Union (MSA)
SBU .... Skirt Buildup (SAA)
SBU .... Small Base Unit [*Telecommunications*]
SBU .... Small Battle Unit [*Navy*] (NVT)
SBU .... Small Boat Unit (DOMA)
SBU .... Small Business United [*Later, NSBU*] (EA)
SBU .... Sociedades Biblicas Unidas [*United Bible Societies*] [*British*] (EAIO)
SBU .... Software Block Update [*Army*]
SBU .... Special Business Unit
SBU .... Springbok [*South Africa*] [*Airport symbol*] (OAG)

SBU .... Stansbury Island [*Utah*] [*Seismograph station code, US Geological Survey Closed*] (SEIS)
SBU .... Starwelt Airways [*Burundi*] [*ICAO designator*] (FAAC)
SBU .... Station Buffer Unit [*Computer science*]
SBU .... Strategic Business Unit
SBU .... Svensk Biblisk Uppslagverk [*A publication*] (BJA)
SBU .... System Billing Unit (NITA)
SBUA .... Sao Gabriel Da Cachoeira [*Brazil ICAO location identifier*] (ICLI)
SBUE .... Switch-Backup Entry [*NASA*] (KSC)
SBUF .... Paulo Afonso [*Brazil ICAO location identifier*] (ICLI)
SBUF .... Staceys Buffet [*NASDAQ symbol*] (SAG)
SBUFW .... Staceys Buffet Wrrt [*NASDAQ symbol*] (TTSB)
SBUG .... Uruguaiana/Rubem Berta [*Brazil ICAO location identifier*] (ICLI)
SBUI .... Carauari [*Brazil ICAO location identifier*] (ICLI)
SBUL .... Uberlandia [*Brazil ICAO location identifier*] (ICLI)
SBUP .... Castilho/Urubupunga [*Brazil ICAO location identifier*] (ICLI)
SBUR .... Uberaba [*Brazil ICAO location identifier*] (ICLI)
SBURCS ...... Six-BIT [*Binary Digit*] Universal Random Character Set [*Computer science*]
SBUV .... Solar and Backscatter Ultraviolet Spectrometer (MCD)
SBUV .... Solar Backscatter Ultraviolet [*Ozone measurement*]
SBUV .... Solar BAckscatter Ultraviolet (USDC)
SBUV .... Solar Backscatter Ultraviolet Experiment (IAA)
SBUV/TOMS ... Solar and Backscattered Ultraviolet and Total Ozone Mapping System
SBUX .... Starbucks Corp. [*NASDAQ symbol*] (SAG)
SBV .... Sabah [*Papua New Guinea*] [*Airport symbol*] (OAG)
SBV .... Semiautomatic Bleeder Valve
SBV .... Shield Building Vent [*Nuclear energy*] (IAA)
SBV .... Single Binocular Vision
SBV .... South Boston, VA [*Location identifier FAA*] (FAAL)
SBV .... Space Biospheres Venture [*Commercial firm*] (ECON)
SBV .... State Bank of Victoria [*Australia*]
SBVC .... San Bernardino Valley College [*California*]
SBVE .... State Board of Vocational Education [*State Board of Education*] (OICC)
SBVG .... Varginha/Jam Brigadeiro Trompowsky [*Brazil ICAO location identifier*] (ICLI)
SBVH .... Vilhena [*Brazil ICAO location identifier*] (ICLI)
SBVM .... Societe de la Bourse de Valeurs Mobilieres de Bruxelles [*Stock exchange*] [*Belgium*] (EY)
SBVS .... Shield Building Ventilation System [*Nuclear energy*] (NRCH)
SBVT .... Vitoria/Goiabeira [*Brazil ICAO location identifier*] (ICLI)
SBW .... Salomon Bros W W Income Fd [*NYSE symbol*] (TTSB)
SBW .... Salomon Brothers Worldwide Income Fund [*NYSE symbol*] (SPSG)
SBW .... Shebandowan Resources [*Vancouver Stock Exchange symbol*]
SBW .... Sibu [*Malaysia*] [*Airport symbol*] (OAG)
SbW .... South by West
SBW .... Space Bandwidth Product (IAA)
SBW .... Spectral Bandwidth
SBW .... Spruce Budworm
SBW .... Steel Basement Window
SBW .... Submarine Warfare (MCD)
SBW .... Surety Bond Waiver [*SBA program*] (AAGC)
SBWAS .... Space-Based Wide-Area Surveillance [*Air Force*] (DOMA)
SBWC .... Stepped-Bore Wheel Cylinder [*Automotive brake systems*]
SBWG .... Strategic Bomb Wing [*Military*]
SBWM/F ...... Southern Baptist Women in Ministry/Folio (EA)
SBWMV .... Soilborne Wheat Mosaic Virus
SBWR .... Simplified Boiling Water Reactor [*Developed by General Electric Co.*] [*Nuclear energy*]
SBWU .... Singapore Bus Workers' Union
SBWX .... Seaboard World Airlines, Inc. [*Air carrier designation symbol*]
SBWY .... Subway
SBX .... S-Band Transponder
SBX .... Seabright Explorations, Inc. [*Toronto Stock Exchange symbol*]
SBX .... Shelby, MT [*Location identifier FAA*] (FAAL)
SBX .... Student Book Exchange
SBX .... Subsea Beacon/Transponder
SBXG .... Barra Do Garcas/Xingu [*Brazil ICAO location identifier*] (ICLI)
SBXV .... Xavantina [*Brazil ICAO location identifier*] (ICLI)
SBY .... BFS [*Berliner Spezial Flug*], Luftahrtunternehmen GmbH [*Germany ICAO designator*] (FAAC)
SBY .... Salisbury [*Maryland*] [*Airport symbol*] (OAG)
SBY .... Salisbury, MD [*Location identifier FAA*] (FAAL)
SBY .... Sand Bay [*Alaska*] [*Seismograph station code, US Geological Survey Closed*] (SEIS)
SBY .... Shapiro, Barney, Newark NJ [*STAC*]
SBY .... Standby [*Airlines*]
SBYA .... Iauarete [*Brazil ICAO location identifier*] (ICLI)
SBYen .... Salomon, Inc. [*Associated Press*] (SAG)
SBYS .... Piracununga/Campo Fontenelle [*Brazil ICAO location identifier*] (ICLI)
SBYT .... Spectrum HoloByte [*NASDAQ symbol*] (TTSB)
SBYT .... Spectrum HoloByte, Inc. [*NASDAQ symbol*] (SAG)
SBZ .... Scibe Airlift [*Zaire*] [*ICAO designator*] (FAAC)
SBZ .... Sibiu [*Romania*] [*Airport symbol*] (OAG)
SBZ .... Sowjetische Besatzungszone [*Soviet Occupation Zone*] [*East Germany*]
SBZ .... Sulfabromomethazine [*Antibacterial*] [*Veterinary medicine*]
SC .... All India Reporter, Supreme Court Reports [*A publication*] (DLA)
sc .... Brothers of the Sacred Heart (TOCD)
SC .... Brothers of the Sacred Heart (TOCD)
SC .... Cape Of Good Hope Reports [*South Africa*] [*A publication*] (DLA)
SC .... Catalan Solidarity [*Political party*] (PPW)
SC .... Christian Scientist
SC .... Closure of Semilunar Valves [*Gastroenterology*] (DAVI)
SC .... Congregation of the Servants of Christ [*Anglican religious community*]
SC .... Court of Session Cases [*Scotland*] [*A publication*] (DLA)
SC .... Cruiser Submarine [*Navy symbol Obsolete*]
SC .... Cruzeiro do Sul [*ICAO designator*] (AD)
SC .... Juta's Supreme Court Reports [*1880-1910*] [*Cape Of Good Hope, South Africa*] [*A publication*] (DLA)
SC .... Manetti Roberts [*Italy*] [*Research code symbol*]
SC .... Quebec Official Reports, Superior Court [*A publication*] (DLA)
SC .... Sabra Connection [*An association*] (EA)
SC .... Saccharomyces Cerevisiae [*Bacterium*]
SC .... Sacra Congregatio [*Sacred Congregation*] [*Latin*]
SC .... Sacrococcygeal [*Anatomy*]
SC .... Sacrosanctam Concilium [*Constitution on the Sacred Liturgy*] [*Vatican II document*]
SC .... Sad Case [*An unpopular person*] [*Teen slang*]
SC .... Safe Custody [*Banking*]
SC .... Saffery Champness International [*British accounting firm*]
S/C .... Sales Code
SC .... Sales Costs
SC .... Salesianorum Congregatio [*Congregation of St. Francis of Sales*] [*Salesian Fathers*] [*Roman Catholic religious order*]
SC .... Salmagundi Club (EA)
SC .... Salvage Charges
sc .... Salvage Charges (ODBW)
SC .... Same Case [*Law*]
SC .... Same Coupling [*Music*]
SC .... Sandia Corp.
SC .... Sanitary Corps
SC .... Sanitation Center [*Food Service*] [*Army*]
sc .... Sans Correction [*Without correction or without spectacles*] [*Ophthalmology*] (DAVI)
SC .... Satellite Carrier (IAA)
SC .... Satellite Communications [*Military*]
SC .... Satellite Computer
SC .... Saturable Core (MSA)
SC .... Saturn Coupe [*An automobile*] (ECON)
Sc .... Scaccaria [*Exchequer*] [*Latin*] (DLA)
SC .... Scale
sc .... Scale (IDOE)
Sc .... Scammon's Reports [*2-5 Illinois*] [*A publication*] (DLA)
SC .... Scandinavian
Sc .... Scandium [*Chemical element*]
SC .... Scanner (IAA)
SC .... Scapula
SC .... Scarce [*Bookselling*] (ROG)
SC .... Scavenge (AAG)
SC .... Scene
sc .... Scene [*Script notation*] (WDMC)
SC .... Scented Cape [*Tea trade*] (ROG)
SC .... Schilling [*Monetary unit*] (ROG)
S/C .... Schmidt-Cassegrain [*Telescope*]
Sc .... Schmidt Number [*IUPAC*]
SC .... School Certificate
SC .... School Construction (OICC)
SC .... Schools Council [*British*]
SC .... Schooner (ROG)
SC .... Schwann Cell [*Biology*]
SC .... Sciatic [*Nerve*] [*Anatomy*] (DAVI)
SC .... Science
sc .... Science (IDOE)
sc .... Scilicet [*Scire Licet*] [*It is permitted to know*] [*Latin*] (WDMC)
SC .... Scilicet [*Namely*] [*Legal term Latin*]
SC .... Scintillation Counter [*Instrumentation*]
SC .... Scleral Cautery [*Ophthalmology*] (CPH)
SC .... Sclerocorneall [*Ophthalmology*] (DAVI)
SC .... Scope Change (MCD)
SC .... Score (AABC)
Sc .... Scoriae [*Quality of the bottom*] [*Nautical charts*]
SC .... Scoring Criteria (MCD)
SC .... Scots
SC .... Scottish Aviation Ltd. [*ICAO aircraft manufacturer identifier*] (ICAO)
SC .... Scottish Constitution (ADA)
Sc .... Scott's English Common Pleas Reports [*A publication*] (DLA)
SC .... Scrap Carriage [*British military*] (DMA)
SC .... Screen Coordinator [*Military*] (CAAL)
SC .... Screen Flag [*Navy British*]
SC .... Screw
S/C .... Screwed and Coupled
SC .... Script [*Films, television, etc.*]
SC .... Scruple
SC .... Scrupulus [*Scruple*] [*Latin*] [*Pharmacy*] (DAVI)
SC .... Sculpsit [*He, or She, Engraved It*] [*Latin*]
SC .... Sculptor
SC .... Sculpture Center (EA)
Sc .... Scutum [*of Hesiod*] [*Classical studies*] (OCD)
SC .... [*The*] Seal Cylinders of Western Asia [*A publication*] (BJA)
SC .... Seamen's Center [*Later, Seamen and International House*] (EA)
SC .... Search Control (IEEE)
SC .... Searchlight Carrier [*British*]
SC .... Searle [*G. D.*] & Co. [*Research code symbol*]
SC .... Seat Cabs
SC .... Seco-Cemp Ltd. [*Toronto Stock Exchange symbol*]
SC .... Secondary Code

SC .... Secondary Confinement [*or Containment*] [*Nuclear energy*] (IEEE)
S-C .... Secret and Confidential Files [*Navy*]
SC .... Secretory Coil [*Medicine*] (MEDA)
SC .... Secretory Component [*Supersedes SP, TP*] [*Immunology*]
SC .... Sectional Center (EECA)
SC .... Section Code (NITA)
SC .... Secular College
SC .... Security Call [*Economics*]
SC .... Security Council (NADA)
SC .... Security Council of the United Nations
SC .... See Comments [*Routing slip*]
SC .... See Copy
SC .... Seed Coat [*Botany*]
SC .... Segment Control (SSD)
SC .... Select Cases [*Oudh, India*] [*A publication*] (DLA)
SC .... Select Committee
SC .... Selector Channel
SC .... Self-Care [*Medicine*]
SC .... Self-Check (AAG)
SC .... Self-Closing
SC .... Self Compatible
S/C .... Self-Contained [*Housing*] [*British*]
SC .... Self-Contained
SC .... Semicactus [*Horticulture*]
SC .... Semicircular (MAE)
SC .... Semiclosed [*Anatomy*]
SC .... Semiconductor
SC .... Senatus Consulto [*By the Decree of the Senate*] [*Latin*]
SC .... Senatus Consultum [*Classical studies*] (OCD)
SC .... Send Common [*Computer science*] (MHDI)
SC .... Sending Complete [*Telecommunications*] (TEL)
SC .... Senior Cameraman
SC .... Senior Counsel [*Ireland*]
S/C .... Sensor Controller (MCD)
SC .... Separate Cover
SC .... Sequence Charts (AAG)
SC .... Sequence Controller
SC .... Sequence Counter
SC .... Serum Complement [*Medicine*] (DMAA)
SC .... Servants of Charity [*Roman Catholic men's religious order*]
sc .... Servants of Charity (TOCD)
S/C .... Service Ceiling
SC .... Service Center [*IRS*]
SC .... Service Certificate [*Military British*]
SC .... Service Change
SC .... Service Charge [*Banking*]
SC .... Service Club [*Military enlisted men's club*]
SC .... Service Code [*Telecommunications*] (TEL)
SC .... Service Command [*Marine Corps*]
SC .... Service Connected [*Medicine*]
SC .... Service Corporation [*Medicine*] (HCT)
SC .... Session Cases [*Legal term British*]
SC .... Session Control [*Computer science*] (IBMDP)
SC .... Set/Clear [*Flip-flop*] [*Computer science*]
SC .... Set Clock
S/C .... Set Course [*Navigation*]
SC .... Severest Critic [*Initialism used by E. B. White to describe his wife*]
SC .... Sex Change [*Biology*]
SC .... Sex Chromatin (MAE)
SC .... Seychelles [*ANSI two-letter standard code*] (CNC)
SC .... Sezary Cell [*Medicine*] (DMAA)
SC .... Shaft Center (MSA)
SC .... Shakespearean Criticism [*A publication*]
SC .... Shaped Charge [*of explosive*]
SC .... Shaping Circuit [*Electronics*] (OA)
SC .... Sharp Cash [*Prompt payment*]
SC .... Shell Transport & Trading Co. Ltd. [*NYSE symbol*] (SPSG)
SC .... Shell Transp/Trad ADR [*NYSE symbol*] (TTSB)
SC .... Shift Control [*Computer science*] (IAA)
SC .... Shift Control Counter [*Computer science*] (MDG)
SC .... Ship Casualty Library [*Maritime Data Network, Inc.*] [*Information service or system*] (CRD)
SC .... Shipping Container
SC .... Shipping Contract (MCD)
SC .... Ship's Cook [*Navy*]
SC .... Shop Call (MCD)
SC .... Shop Carpenter
SC .... Shopping Center (MHDW)
SC .... Shopping Concourses [*Public-performance tariff class*] [*British*]
SC .... Short Circuit
SC .... Short Course [*of instruction*]
SC .... Should Cost (MCD)
S/C .... Show Cause [*Legal shorthand*] (LWAP)
SC .... Shunt Capacitor (IAA)
SC .... Sick Call [*Medicine*] (DMAA)
SC .... Sickle Cell [*Medicine*]
S-C .... Sickle-Cell Hemoglobin C [*Disease*] (DAVI)
SC .... Side Cabin
Sc .... Side Car [*Army*]
SC .... Side Contact [*Valves*] (DEN)
SC .... Sierra Club (EA)
SC .... Sieving Coefficient [*Laboratory science*] (DAVI)
SC .... Signal Comparator
SC .... Signal Conditioner
SC .... Signal Corps [*Later, Communications and Electronics Command*] [*Army*]
S/C .... Signal-to-Clutter
SC .... Significant Characteristics (MCD)
SC .... Silicone Coated
SC .... Silk Covered (IAA)
SC .... Silver Certificate
SC .... Silver Crown [*Class of racing cars*]
SC .... Silvered Copper [*Wire*] (IEEE)
SC .... Simulation Coordinator
SC .... Simulation Council (IAA)
SC .... Simulator Control (MCD)
SC .... Sine Correction [*Without lenses*] [*Ophthalmology*]
SC .... Sine-Cosine
sc .... Sine-Cosine (IDOE)
SC .... Single Carburetor [*Automotive engineering*]
SC .... Single Case
SC .... Single Cell
SC .... Single Chemical (MAE)
SC .... Single Circuit [*Electricity*]
SC .... Single Column
SC .... Single Comb
SC .... Single Contact [*Switch*]
SC .... Single Counter
SC .... Single Crochet
SC .... Single Crystal
sc .... Single Crystal (IDOE)
SC .... Single Current (IAA)
SC .... Sinusoidal Collagen [*Anatomy*]
SC .... Sioux City [*Diocesan abbreviation*] [*Iowa*] (TOCD)
SC .... Sisters of Charity [*Anglican religious community*]
SC .... Sisters of Charity of Cincinnati, Ohio (TOCD)
SC .... Sisters of Charity of Saint Vincent de Paul (EA)
SC .... Sisters of Charity of Seton Hill, Greensburg, PA (TOCD)
SC .... Sisters of St. Elizabeth, Convent Station (TOCD)
SC .... Site Contingency [*Nuclear energy*] (NRCH)
SC .... Situation Console (IAA)
SC .... Sized and Calendered [*Paper*]
SC .... Skill Component
SC .... Skin Conductance
SC .... Slave Clock (IAA)
SC .... Slip Coupling (DS)
SC .... Slow Call (WDAA)
SC .... Slow Component
SC .... Slow Curing [*Asphalt grade*]
SC .... Small Cap (WDAA)
SC .... Small Capitals [*Typography*]
SC .... Small Compact [*Car size*]
SC .... Small Craft
SC .... Smooth Contour [*Technical drawings*]
SC .... Snellen Chart [*Ophthalmology*]
SC .... Snow Cover [*Meteorology*]
SC .... So-Called
SC .... Social Credit Party [*British*]
SC .... Societas Fratrum Sacris Cordis [*Brothers of the Sacred Heart*] [*Roman Catholic religious order*]
SC .... Society for Cryobiology (EA)
SC .... Society of the Cincinnati (EA)
S/C .... Software Contractor [*NASA*] (NASA)
SC .... Soil Characteristics
SC .... Solar Cell
SC .... Solar Coil (IAA)
SC .... Solar Constant (IAA)
SC .... Soldier Capabilities
SC .... Sole Charge [*Ecclesiastical*] [*British*] (ROG)
SC .... Solid Core [*Technical drawings*]
SC .... Solid-State Circuit (MCD)
SC .... SONAR Channel [*Navy*] (CAAL)
SC .... Soncino Chumash [*A publication*] (BJA)
S/C .... Son Compte [*His, or Her, Account*] [*French*]
SC .... Songwriters Club [*Later, SLC*] (EA)
SC .... Sons of Charity [*France*] (EAIO)
SC .... Sound Channel [*Navy*] (CAAL)
SC .... Source Code
SC .... South Carolina [*Postal code*]
SC .... South Carolina Reports [*A publication*] (DLA)
Sc .... South Carolina State Library, Columbia, SC [*Library symbol Library of Congress*] (LCLS)
SC .... Southern California
SC .... Southern Classification
SC .... Southern Command [*British military*] (DMA)
SC .... Southern Conference (EA)
SC .... Southwark College [*London, England*]
SC .... Space Capsule (IAA)
SC .... Space Council [*NASA*] [*Marine science*] (OSRA)
SC .... Space Council [*National Aeronautics and Space Administration*] (USDC)
SC .... Spacecraft (MCD)
S/C .... Spacecraft/Capsule
SC .... Spacecraft Communicator (IAA)
SC .... Spark Control [*Automotive engineering*]
SC .... Special Access, Compartmented (MCD)
SC .... Special Care [*Medicine*]
SC .... Special Circuit
SC .... Special Circular

S/C.............. Special Conditions (MCD)
SC.............. Special Constable
SC.............. Specialty Code
SC.............. Specification Change
SC.............. Specification Control (IAA)
SC.............. Specific Cueing
SC.............. Speech Communication (IAA)
SC.............. Speed Controller [*Nuclear energy*] (NRCH)
SC.............. Spermatocyte
Sc.............. Spiral Having the Least Conspicuous Nuclear Regions and with Arms Very Loosely Coiled [*Astronomy*] (BARN)
SC.............. Spiroplasmavirus citri [*Bacteriology*]
SC.............. Splat Cooled (OA)
SC.............. Splenic Collateral [*Gastroenterology*] (DAVI)
S/C.............. Splitter/Combiner (NASA)
SC.............. Sponsor Code (NITA)
SC.............. Sports Council [*British*] (EAIO)
SC.............. Sporulation Capacity [*of fungi*]
SC.............. Spot Check (AAG)
SC.............. Spray Calciner [*Nuclear energy*] (NUCP)
SC.............. Spread Correlation
SC.............. Spreading Coefficient
SC.............. Spring Conditions [*Skiing*]
SC.............. Squamous Cell Carcinoma [*Also, SCC*] [*Medicine*]
SC.............. Square Corners [*Bookbinding*] (DGA)
SC.............. Squirrel Cage (IAA)
S/C.............. Stabilization and Control [*Aerospace*] (GFGA)
SC.............. Stack (Pipe) Cut [*Sanitation*] [*British*] (ROG)
SC.............. Staff Captain [*Military British*]
SC.............. Staff Car [*British*]
SC.............. Staff College [*Military*]
SC.............. Staff Corps
SC.............. Stage Center [*A stage direction*]
SC.............. Standard Candle [*Power*]
SC.............. Standard Channel (IAA)
SC.............. Standard Conditions
SC.............. Standing Committee (ADA)
SC.............. Standing Crop
SC.............. Starfleet Command [*An association*] (EA)
SC.............. Star of Courage [*Award*] [*British*]
SC.............. Start Computer
SC.............. Start Conversion [*Computer science*]
SC.............. Starting Charge [*Bookbinding*] (DGA)
sC.............. Statcoulomb [*Also, Fr, statC*] [*Unit of electric charge*]
SC.............. Statement of Capability [*NASA*]
S/C.............. Statement of Charges [*Army*]
SC.............. Statement of Compatibility [*NASA*] (MCD)
SC.............. Statistical Control
SC.............. Statistics Canada
SC.............. Status Statement [*Online database field identifier*]
SC.............. Statutes of Canada
SC.............. Steel Casting
SC.............. Steel Cored [*Conductors*]
SC.............. Steering Committee (NATG)
Sc.............. Stellacyanin
SC.............. Stellar Camera
SC.............. Stepchild [*or Children*] (DNAB)
S/C.............. Step Climb (GAVI)
SC.............. Step Counter (IAA)
SC.............. Stepped Care [*Medicine*]
SC.............. Sternoclavicular [*Joint*] [*Anatomy*]
SC.............. Stimulus, Conditioned (AAMN)
SC.............. Stock Certificate [*Investment term*]
Sc.............. Stonecat [*Ichthyology*]
SC.............. Stopcock
SC.............. Stop-Continue (DEN)
SC.............. Storage Capacity (AAG)
SC.............. Storage Circuit (IAA)
SC.............. Stored Command
S/C.............. Stowage Container
SC.............. Stratified Charge [*Automotive engineering*]
SC.............. Stratocumulus [*Cloud*] [*Meteorology*]
SC.............. Stratum Corneum [*Skin membrane*]
SC.............. Stress Cracking [*Metallurgy*]
SC.............. Strike Command [*Military*]
S/C.............. Strip Chart [*Recorder*] [*NASA*] (NASA)
SC.............. Stronnictwo Chlopskie [*Peasants' Party*] [*Poland Political party*] (PPE)
S/C.............. Subcable (KSC)
S/C.............. Subcarrier (AAG)
SC.............. Subchannel (IAA)
SC.............. Subclavian [*Anatomy*]
SC.............. Subcommittee
S/C.............. Subcontract
SC.............. Subcontractor (NATG)
SC.............. Subcorneal [*Ophthalmology*] (AAMN)
SC.............. Subcours
SC.............. Subcutaneous [*Beneath the Skin*] [*Medicine*]
SC.............. Subject Classification [*Library science*]
SC.............. Subject Code (NITA)
SC.............. Submarine Chaser [*110 foot*]
S/C.............. Submarine Coxswain [*British military*] (DMA)
SC.............. Subscriber Computer (MHDI)
SC.............. Subsidiary Company (MHDB)
SC.............. Succinylcholine [*Biochemistry*] (MAE)
SC.............. Su Cuenta [*Your Account*] [*Business term Spanish*]
SC.............. Sudden Commencement
SC.............. Suffolk and Cambridgeshire Regiment [*British military*] (DMA)
SC.............. Sugar-Coated [*Pharmacy*]
SC.............. Sulfur Colloid [*Chemistry*] (DAVI)
SC.............. Summary Court [*Navy*]
SC.............. Sumter & Choctaw Railway Co. [*AAR code*]
SC.............. Sunburn Cell [*For measuring phototoxicity*]
SC.............. Supercalendered [*Paper*]
SC.............. Super Caster [*Monotype*] (DGA)
SC.............. Supercharger [*Automotive engineering*]
SC.............. Super Computer (IAA)
S/C.............. Superconducting Magnetic (MCD)
SC.............. Super Coupe [*Model of automobile*]
SC.............. Supercritical Chromatography
SC.............. Super Current (IAA)
SC.............. Superimposed Coding [*Computer science*] (DIT)
SC.............. Superimposed Current
SC.............. Superintending Cartographer [*Navy British*]
SC.............. Superior Colliculus [*Brain anatomy*]
SC.............. Superior Court (DLA)
SC.............. Supervisor Call (IAA)
SC.............. Supervisor's Console
SC.............. Supervisory Control
SC.............. Supplemental Contract (AAG)
SC.............. Supplementary Information [*Telecommunications*] (TEL)
SC.............. Supply Catalog [*Military*] (AABC)
SC.............. Supply Control [*Military*]
SC.............. Supply Corps
SC.............. Supply Cost (AAGC)
SC.............. Support Center
SC.............. Support Chief
SC.............. Support Command [*Army*]
SC.............. Support Concept Manual [*Marine Corps*]
SC.............. Support Contractor (MCD)
SC.............. Support Controller [*NASA*] (KSC)
SC.............. Support Coordinator (AAG)
SC.............. Supporting Cells [*Zoology*]
SC.............. Suppressed Carrier (IEEE)
SC.............. Supreme Council [*Freemasonry*] (ROG)
SC.............. Supreme Court
SC.............. Supreme Court Reporter [*National Reporter System*] [*A publication*] (DLA)
SC.............. Surface Combustion [*Reducing gas process*]
SC.............. Surface Command [*NASA*] (MCD)
SC.............. Surgeon-Captain [*British military*]
SC.............. Surgeon-Commander [*British military*]
SC.............. Surgical Capsule [*of prostate gland*]
SC.............. Surrogates by Choice [*Defunct*] (EA)
SC.............. Surveillance Compliance [*Nuclear energy*] (NRCH)
SC.............. Sweetheart Contract [*Business term*] (MHDB)
SC.............. Swimmer-Canoeist [*British military*] (DMA)
SC.............. Swimming Club
SC.............. Switched Capacitor [*Electronics*] (IAA)
SC.............. Switching Cell (IEEE)
SC.............. Sylvania Central Railroad (IIA)
SC.............. Symbolic Code (AAG)
SC.............. Synanon Church (EA)
SC.............. Synaptonemal Complex [*Botanical cytology*]
SC.............. Synchro-Cyclotron
SC.............. Synchronization Coefficient
SC.............. Synclinal [*Geology*]
SC.............. System Capability
SC.............. System Category Code (NITA)
SC.............. System Controller
SC.............. System Controller [*Military*] (CAAL)
SC.............. Systems Command [*Air Force*]
SC.............. Systolic Click [*Cardiology*]
SCA.............. Air Weather Service, Technical Library, Scott AFB, IL [*OCLC symbol*] (OCLC)
SCA.............. Archibald Library, Caronport, Saskatchewan [*Library symbol National Library of Canada*] (NLC)
SCA.............. La Societe Canadienne d'Aerophilatelie (AC)
SCA.............. SAAB Club of North America [*SAAB Clubs of America*] [*Acronym is based on former name,*] (EA)
SCA.............. Sag-Control Agent [*Automotive painting and finishing*]
SCA.............. Sako Collectors Association (EA)
SCA.............. Saluki Club of America (EA)
SCA.............. Samoyed Club of America (EA)
SCA.............. Santa Catalina [*Colombia*] [*Airport symbol*] (AD)
SCA.............. Santa Cruz [*Argentina*] [*Seismograph station code, US Geological Survey Closed*] (SEIS)
SCA.............. Satellite Committee Agency [*Army*] (MCD)
SCA.............. Satellite Communications Agency [*Army*]
SCA.............. Save the Children Alliance [*Gentofte, Denmark*] (EAIO)
Sca.............. Scala [*Record label*]
SCA.............. Scarborough Public Library [*UTLAS symbol*]
SCA.............. Schedule Change Authorization [*NASA*] (NASA)
SCA.............. Schipperke Club of America (EA)
SCA.............. School and College Ability [*Test*] [*of ETS*]
SCA.............. Science Clubs of America (EA)
SCA.............. Scientific Computing and Automation
SCA.............. Scottish Canoe Association (DBA)
SCA.............. Scottish Cashmere Association (DBA)
SCA.............. Scottish Chess Association (DBA)

SCA .... Scottish Courts Administration (ILCA)
SCA .... Scottish Croquet Association (DBA)
SCA .... Screen Composers Association (NADA)
SCA .... Screen Composers of America (EA)
SCA .... Sea Cadet Association (EAIO)
SCA .... Sebright Club of America (EA)
SCA .... Secondary Communications Authorization (IEEE)
SCA .... Secondary Control Assembly [*Nuclear energy*] (NRCH)
SCA .... Sectional Chamber Association [*British*] (DBA)
SCA .... Security Capital Atlantic, Inc. [*NYSE symbol*] (SAG)
SCA .... Selective Coronary Angiogram (DAVI)
SCA .... Selectivity Clear Accumulator
SCA .... Self-Controlled Analgesia [*Medicine*] (CDI)
SCA .... Senior Citizens of America [*Defunct*] (EA)
SCA .... Sequence Chart Analyzer (IAA)
SCA .... Sequence Control Area [*NASA*] (KSC)
SCA .... Sequencer Control Assembly
S_{ca} .... Serum Calcium [*Biochemistry*] (DAVI)
SCA .... Service and Compliance Administration [*US wage/price controls agency*]
SCA .... Service Cinematographique des Armees [*France*]
SCA .... Service Contract Act [*1965*]
SCA .... Service Cryptologic Agencies [*Military*]
SCA .... Sex Chromosome Abnormality
SCA .... Shadow Communications Agency [*British Labour Party*]
SCA .... Shareholder Credit Accounting
SCA .... Sheepmeat Council of Australia
SCA .... Shelby Can-Am [*Racing car*]
SCA .... Shepherd's Center of America
SCA .... Shields Class Association (EA)
SCA .... Shipbuilders Council of America (EA)
SCA .... Ship Constructive Association [*A union*] [*British*]
SCA .... Ship Cost Adjustment [*Navy*]
SCA .... Shipping Control Authority (NVT)
SCA .... Shooters Club of America [*Defunct*]
SCA .... Short Circuit Ampere (IAA)
SCA .... Short Code Address (NITA)
SCA .... Should Cost Analysis (MCD)
SCA .... Shuttle Carrier Aircraft [*NASA*] (NASA)
SCA .... Sickle Cell Anemia [*Medicine*]
SCA .... Signal Conditioning Assembly [*NASA*] (KSC)
SCA .... Simulated Core Assembly [*Nuclear energy*] (NRCH)
SCA .... Simulation Control Area [*NASA*] (MCD)
SCA .... Simulation Conversion Assembly [*Deep Space Instrumentation Facility, NASA*]
SCA .... Single Camshaft Type A [*Cosworth racing engines*] [*Automotive engineering*]
SCA .... Single Channel Analyzer
SCA .... Ski Council of America [*Defunct*] (EA)
SCA .... Small-Caliber Ammunition (MSA)
SCA .... Smoke Control Association [*Defunct*] (EA)
SCA .... Sneak Circuit Analysis [*NASA*] (NASA)
SCA .... Social Care Association [*British*] (DBA)
SCA .... Societe Canadienne d'Astronomie
SCA .... Societe Canadienne des Anesthesistes [*Canadian Anaesthetists' Society*] (EAIO)
SCA .... Society for Commercial Archeology (EA)
SCA .... Society for Coptic Archaeology (EA)
SCA .... Society for Creative Anachronism (EA)
SCA .... Society for Cultural Anthropology (EA)
SCA .... Society of Canadian Artists [*Formerly, Society of Co-Operative Artists*]
SCA .... Society of Canadian Artists, Montreal [*1868-72*] (NGC)
SCA .... Society of Cardiovascular Anesthesiologists (EA)
SCA .... Society of Consumer Affairs (NADA)
SCA .... Software Control Authorization [*NASA*] (KSC)
SCA .... Soldiers Christian Association [*British military*] (DMA)
SCA .... Sonar Class Association (EA)
S Ca .... South Carolina Reports [*A publication*] (DLA)
SCA .... South Central Air, Inc. [*ICAO designator*] (FAAC)
SCA .... Southern Communications Area [*Military*]
SCA .... Southern Cotton Association (EA)
SCA .... Soybean Council of America [*Defunct*] (EA)
SCA .... Spacecraft Adapter [*NASA*] (KSC)
SCA .... SPALTRA [*Special Projects Alterations, Training*] Control Activity
SCA .... Special Competition Advocate (AAGC)
SCA .... Specification Compliance Agreement (MCD)
SCA .... Specific Collection Area [*Environmental science*] (FFDE)
SCA .... Specific Combining Ability
SCA .... Speech Communication Association (EA)
SCA .... Speed Coaches Association (EA)
SCA .... Sperm-Coating Antigen
SCA .... Spinach Carbonic Anhydrase [*An enzyme*]
SCA .... Spinocerebellar Ataxia [*Genetics*]
SCA .... Sprayed Concrete Association [*British*] (EAIO)
SCA .... Stamp Collectors' Association [*British*] (BI)
SCA .... Standard Consolidated Area [*Bureau of Census*]
SCA .... Stealth Club of America (EA)
SCA .... Steel Castings Association [*British*] (BI)
SCA .... Steel-Cored-Aluminium
SCA .... Sterba Curtain Antenna
SCA .... Stevengraph Collectors' Association (EA)
SCA .... Stock Company Association [*Defunct*] (EA)
SCA .... Stock Control Activity (AFIT)
SCA .... Storecast Carrier Authorization [*Broadcasting*] (WDMC)
SCA .... Student Conservation Association (EA)
SCA .... Subcarrier Authorization (MSA)
SCA .... Subcarrier Channel [*Telecommunications*]
SCA .... Subchannel Adapter
SCA .... Subclavian Artery [*Medicine*] (DMAA)
SCA .... Subcontract Authorization (AAG)
SCA .... Subcritical Assembly (DEN)
SCA .... Subcutaneous Abdominal [*Block*] [*Anesthesiology*] (DAVI)
SCA .... Subsequent Coupons Attached
SCA .... Subsidiary Channel Authorization (IAA)
SCA .... Subsidiary Communications Allocation (IAA)
SCA .... Subsidiary Communications Authorization [*Facilities used to transmit background music to subscribing customers*]
SCA .... Summary Cost Account [*Military*] (AABC)
SCA .... Superior Cerebellar Artery [*Anatomy*]
SCA .... Supersonic Cruise Aircraft (PDAA)
SCA .... Supervising Customs Agent [*U.S. Customs Service*] (BARN)
SCA .... Support Centers of America [*An association*] (EA)
SCA .... Suppressor Cell Activity [*Medicine*] (DMAA)
SCA .... Supreme and Exchequer Courts Act [*Canada*] (ILCA)
SCA .... Supreme Court Appeals [*India*] [*A publication*] (ILCA)
SCA .... Surface Coatings Abstracts [*Paint Research Association of Great Britain*] [*Bibliographic database*]
SCA .... Surgical Care Affiliates, Inc. [*NYSE symbol*] (SPSG)
SCA .... Suspended Ceilings Association [*British*] (DBA)
SCA .... Swedish Council of America (EA)
SCA .... Switch Control Assembly
SCA .... Switzerland Cheese Association [*Defunct*] (EA)
SCA .... Synagogue Council of America (EA)
SCA .... Synchronous Communications Adapter
SCA .... System Communication Area (ECII)
SCA .... System Comparison Analysis [*Bell System*]
SCA .... System Control Adapter (IAA)
SCA .... System Control Area
SCA-1 .... Type-1 Spinocerebellar Ataxia [*Medicine*] (ECON)
SCAA .... Skin Care Association of America (EA)
SCAA .... Specialty Coffee Association of America (EA)
SCAA .... Spill Control Association of America (EA)
SCAA .... Sporadic Cerebral Amyloid Angiopathy [*Medicine*] (DMAA)
SCAA .... Superconductor Applications Association (EA)
SCAA .... Sussex Cattle Association of America (EA)
SCAAN .... System for Computerized Application Analysis [*Automotive engineering*]
SCA & I .... Society for Cardiac Angiography and Interventions (EA)
SCAAP .... Special Commonwealth African Assistance Plan
SCAAP .... Super Computer Automotive Applications Partnership
SCAAS .... Strategic Communication and Alerting System
SCAB .... Single Chain Antibody Fragment [*Botany*] (ECON)
SCAB .... Streptozocin, CCNU [*Lomustine*], Adriamycin, Bleomycin [*Antineoplastic drug regimen*]
SCABG .... Single Coronary Artery Bypass [*Cardiology*] (DMAA)
SCABG .... Single Coronary Artery Bypass Graft [*Cardiology*]
SCABT .... South Carolina Association of Biology Teachers (EDAC)
SCAC .... Ancud/Pupelde [*Chile*] [*ICAO location identifier*] (ICLI)
Scac .... Scaccaria Curia [*Court of Exchequer*] [*Latin*] (DLA)
SCAC .... School and College Advisory Center [*Later, EGASCAC*] (EA)
SCAC .... Scottish Countryside Activities Council (DBA)
SCAC .... Self-Cleaning Air Cleaner
SCAC .... Standard Carriers Alpha Code (MCD)
SCAC .... Support Careers Advisory Committee [*Environmental Protection Agency*] (EPA)
SCAC .... Syntax-Controlled Acoustic Classifier [*Computer science*] (MHDI)
SCACT .... Supreme Court of the Australian Capital Territory
SC Acts .... Acts and Joint Resolutions of the State of South Carolina [*A publication*] (DLA)
SCAD .... Savannah College of Art and Design [*Georgia*]
SCAD .... Scan Converter and Display [*Systems*]
SCAD .... Schenectady Army Depot (AABC)
SCAD .... Short Chain Acyl-Coenzyme A Dehydrogenase (DMAA)
SCAD .... Small Current Amplifying Device
SCAD .... Societe Canadienne pour l'Analyse de Documents [*Indexing and Abstracting Society of Canada*]
SCAD .... State Commission Against Discrimination
SCAD .... Strategic Bomber Penetration Decoy [*Air Force*]
SCAD .... Subprogram Change Affect Diagram (MHDB)
SCAD .... Subsonic Cruise Armed Decoy [*Air Force*]
SCAD .... Systeme Communautaire d'Acces a la Documentation [*Database*] [*EC*] (ECED)
SCADA .... Student Coalition Against Drug Abuse
SCADA .... Supervisory Control and Data (IAA)
SCADA .... Supervisory Control and Data Acquisition (IEEE)
SCADA .... Supervisory Control And Data Acquisition [*Industrial engineering*] [*Computer science*]
SCADAR .... Scatter Detection and Ranging
SCADC .... Standard Central Air Data Computer
SCADE .... Signal Conditioning and Detection Electronics (MCD)
SCADEU .... Scottish Adult Basic Education Unit
SCADS .... SAS Census Access and Display System [*Information service or system*] (IID)
SCADS .... Scanning Celestial Attitude Determination System
SCADS .... Shipborne Containerized Air Defense System
SCADS .... Simulation of Combined Analog Digital Systems [*Computer science*] (IEEE)
SCADS .... Sioux City Air Defense Sector [*ADC*]
SCADS .... Speech Command Auditory Display System (MCD)

SCAE........... Scottish Center for Agricultural Engineering
SCAE........... Scottish Centre of Agricultural Engineering [*British*] (IRUK)
SCAE........... Society for Computer-Aided Engineering (EA)
SCAEC......... Submarine Contact Analysis and Evaluation Center (NVT)
SCAEF......... Supreme Commander, Allied Expeditionary Force [*World War II*]
Scaen Rom Frag... Scaenicorum Romanorum Fragmenta [*A publication*] (OCD)
SCAEPA....... Society for Computer Applications in Engineering, Planning, and Architecture [*Later, CEPA*] (EA)
SCAF........... Self-Centered-Altruism Fad
SCAF........... Supersonic Cruise Attack Fighter (MCD)
SCAF........... Suppressor Cell Activating Factor [*Biochemistry*]
SCAF........... Supreme Commander of Allied Forces (ADA)
SCAFA......... Scottish Child and Family Alliance (DBA)
SCAFB......... Schilling Air Force Base (AAG)
SCAFEDS..... Space Construction Automated Fabrication Experiment Definition Study (MCD)
SCAG........... Sandoz Clinical Assessment of Geriatrics [*Psychometrics*]
SCAG........... Southern California Association of Governments
SCAG........... Special COMSEC Advisory Group [*US Army Communications Command*] (MCD)
SCAGES....... Standing Conference of Associations for Guidance in Education Settings (AIE)
SC/AH.......... System Coordinator / Anomaly Handler (SSD)
SCAHR......... School of Community and Allied Health Resources
ScAi............. Aiken-Bamberg-Barnwell-Edgefield Regional Library, Aiken, SC [*Library symbol Library of Congress*] (LCLS)
SCAI............ Societe des Comptables en Administration Industrielle du Canada
SCAI............ Switch-to-Computer Applications Interface (CDE)
ScAiD........... E. I. Du Pont de Nemours & Co., Aiken, SC [*Library symbol Library of Congress*] (LCLS)
SCAIF........... Sertoli-Cell Androgenic Inhibitory Factor [*Endocrinology*]
ScAiTC......... Aiken Technical College, Aiken, SC [*Library symbol*] [*Library of Congress*] (LCLS)
SCAJAP........ Shipping Control Administrator Japan
SCAJAP........ Shipping Control Authority, Japan (DNAB)
ScAl............. Allendale-Hampton-Jasper Regional Library, Allendale, SC [*Library symbol*] [*Library of Congress*] (LCLS)
SCAL............ Health o meter Products [*NASDAQ symbol*] (TTSB)
SCAL............ Health O Meter Products, Inc. [*NASDAQ symbol*] (SAG)
SCAL............ Silver City Airways Ltd.
SCAL............ Skin Diver Contact Air Lenses
SCAL............ STAR [*Self Testing and Reporting*] Computer Assembly Language
SCAL............ Steel-Cored Aluminum (IAA)
SCALA......... Society of Chief Architects of Local Authorities [*British*]
SCALC......... Steel-Cored Aluminum Conductor (IAA)
SCALD......... Structural Computer-Aided Logic Design
SCALE.......... Scalable Architecture for Large Enterprises [*Computer software*] [*Symantec Corp.*] (PCM)
SCALE.......... Scales of Creativity and Learning Environment [*Educational test*]
SCALE.......... Space Checkout and Launch Equipment
SCALE.......... Symmetrically Configured AC [*Alternating Current*] Light-Emitting [*Device*]
SCALER....... Statistical Calculation and Analysis of Engine Removal [*Navy*]
SCALO......... Scanning Local Oscillator (NG)
SCALP......... Small Card Automated Layout Program (IAA)
SCALP......... Students Concerned about Legal Prices [*Student legal action organization*]
SCALP......... Suit, Contamination Avoidance, and Liquid Protection [*Army*]
SCALPEL...... Scattering With Aperture Limited Projection Electron Lithography [*AT&T development*]
SCALRA....... Scottish Adult Literacy Resource Agency
SCalWat....... Southern California Water Co. [*Associated Press*] (SAG)
Scam........... Scammon's Reports [*2-5 Illinois*] [*A publication*] (DLA)
SCAM........... SCSI [*Small Computer System Interface*] Configuration Auto Magically [*Computer science*] (PCM)
SCAM........... Selection Classification Age Maturity Program [*Medical screening procedure for athletes*]
SCAM........... Soil Classification and Mapping Branch [*Department of Agriculture*] (IID)
SCAM........... Source-Coder's Cost Analysis Model (PDAA)
SCAM........... Soviet Cost Analysis Model [*CIA*]
SCAM........... Spectrum Characteristics Analysis and Measurement [*FAA*]
SCAM........... Standing Conference for Amateur Music [*British*]
SCAM........... Station Control and Monitoring
SCAM........... Strike Camera (MCD)
SCAM........... Study Course in Agency Management [*LIMRA*]
SCAM........... Subcarrier Amplitude Modulation (IAA)
SCAM........... Subsonic Cruise Armed Missile/Decoy [*Air Force*] (MCD)
SCAM........... Synchronous Communications Access Method
SCAMA......... Service Central des Approvisionements et Materiels Americains [*Central Office of American Supplies and Equipment*] [*World War II*]
SCAMA......... Skewed Circular Arc Method of Analysis
SCAMA......... Station Conferencing and Monitoring Arrangement [*NASA*]
SCAMA......... Switching, Conferencing, and Monitoring Arrangement [*NASA*]
SCAMC......... Symposium on Computer Applications in Medical Care [*Baltimore, MD*]
SCAM/D....... Subsonic Cruise Armed Missile/Decoy [*Air Force*]
SCAMIN....... Self-Concept and Motivation Inventory (DMAA)
SCAMM........ Specimen Coordinate Automated Measuring Machine [*Defunct*]
SCAMP......... Scholarships for Children of American Military Personnel (DNAB)
SCAMP......... Schools Computers Administration and Management Project (AIE)
SCAMP......... Sectionalized Carrier and Multipurpose Vehicle [*Military*]
SCAMP......... Self-Contained Airborne Multipurpose Pod (MCD)
SCAMP......... Self-Contained Ancillary Modular Platform [*Woods Hole Oceanographic Institution*]
SCAMP......... Self-Propelled Crane for Aircraft Maintenance and Positioning (MCD)
SCAMP......... Sensor Control and Management Platoon [*Marine Corps*]
SCAMP......... Signal Conditioning Amplifier
SCAMP......... Single Channel Amplitude Monopulse Processing
SCAMP......... Small-Caliber Ammunition Modernization Program [*Army*] (RDA)
SCAMP......... Space-Controlled Army Measurements Probe
SCAMP......... Sperry Computer-Aided Message Processor [*British*]
SCAMP......... Standard Configuration and Modification Program [*Military*]
SCAMP......... Succinyl CAMP [*Biochemistry*]
SCAMP......... Summer Campus, Advanced Mathematics Program [*Institute for Defense Analysis*]
SCAMP......... System/Command Accounting/Monitoring of Projects (DNAB)
SCAMPERS... Standard Corps-Army-MACOM [*Major Army Command*] Personnel System (AABC)
SCAMPS....... Small Computer Analytical and Mathematical Programming System (IEEE)
SCAMPTME... Succinyl CAMP Tyrosine Methyl Ester [*Biochemistry*]
SCAMS......... Scanning Microwave Spectrometer
SCAN........... Alliance Imaging [*NASDAQ symbol*] (TTSB)
SCAN........... Alliance Imaging, Inc. [*NASDAQ symbol*] (SPSG)
ScAn........... Anderson County Library, Anderson, SC [*Library symbol Library of Congress*] (LCLS)
SCAN........... Satellite Cable Audio Networks [*Cable-television service*]
SCAN........... Savings Comparative Analysis [*Federal Home Loan Bank Board*] [*Database*]
SCAN........... Scandinavian
SCAN........... Scanfile [*Database*] [*Australia*]
SCAN........... Scanner Association of North America (EA)
SCAN........... Scanning (IAA)
SCAN........... Schedule for Classroom Activity Norms (EDAC)
SCAN........... Scintiscan [*Medicine*]
SCAN........... Screening Test for Identifying Central Auditory Disorders
SCAN........... Seismic Computerized Alert Network [*For warning of an earthquake*]
SCAN........... Selected Current Aerospace Notices [*NASA*]
SCAN........... Self-Containing Automatic Navigation (IAA)
SCAN........... Self-Correcting Automatic Navigator
SCAN........... Seniors Cooperative Alert Network [*An association*] (EA)
SCAN........... Sensor Controller Alert Network
SCAN........... Service Center Advantage Network [*Federal-Mogul Corp.*]
SCAN........... Service Center for Aging Information [*Department of Health and Human Services*] [*Information service or system*] (IID)
SCAN........... Shipboard Communication Area Network (DWSG)
SCAN........... Short Current Abstracts and Notes (DIT)
SCAN........... Signal Corps Administrative Network [*Obsolete Army*]
SCAN........... Silent Communication Alarm Network [*NASA*]
SCAN........... Simplified Colorimetric Analysis (MCD)
SCAN........... Small Computers in the Arts Network [*Defunct*] (EA)
SCAN........... Southern California Answering Network [*Los Angeles Public Library*] [*Information service or system*]
SCAN........... Spares Change Advance Notice (MCD)
SCAN........... State of California Answering Network [*Information service or system*] (IID)
SCAN........... Stock Control and Analysis (BUR)
SCAN........... Stock Market Computer Answering Network [*British*]
SCAN........... Student Career Automated Network (IEEE)
SCAN........... Supermarket Computer Answering Service (OA)
SCAN........... Surface Condition Analyzer (MCD)
SCAN........... Suspected Child Abuse and Neglect [*Medicine*] (DMAA)
SCAN........... Suspected Child Abuse and Neglect (DAVI)
SCAN........... Switched Circuit Automatic Network [*Army*]
SCAN........... System for Collection and Analysis of Near-Collision Reports (AAG)
SCANA......... SCANA Corp. [*Associated Press*] (SAG)
SCANA......... Self-Contained Adverse-Weather Night Attack
ScAnC......... Anderson College, Anderson, SC [*Library symbol*] [*Library of Congress*] (LCLS)
SCANCAP..... System for Comparative Analysis of Community Action Programs [*Information service or system*] (AEBS)
SCAND......... Scandinavia
SCAND......... Single Crystal Automatic Neutron Diffractometer
SCANDAL..... Select Committee to Arrange a New Deal to Avoid Litigation [*Toledo, OH, group formed in 1973 to humorously protest results of the Michigan-Toledo "War of 18 35"*]
ScandC......... Scandinavia Fund [*Associated Press*] (SAG)
SC & D......... Stock Control and Distribution (AFM)
Sc & Div....... Law Reports, Scotch and Divorce Appeals [*A publication*] (DLA)
Sc & Div App... Scotch and Divorce Appeals [*English Law Reports*] [*A publication*] (DLA)
SCANDEFA... Scandinavian Dental Fair [*Danish Dental Association*]
SC & FE....... Sierra Club and Friends of the Earth [*Marine science*] (MSC)
SCANDI........ Surveillance Control and Driver Information [*Traffic system*]
SC & J......... Signal Collection and Jamming
SCANDOC.... Scandinavian Documentation Center [*Washington, DC*]
SC & RA....... Specialized Carriers and Rigging Association (EA)
SC & S......... Strapped, Corded, and Sealed [*As, of a package or bale*]
Scand Stud Criminol... Scandinavian Studies in Criminology [*A publication*] (DLA)
SC & T......... Science and Technology (WDAA)
Scanfrm....... Scanforms, Inc. [*Associated Press*] (SAG)
ScanGr......... Scan-Graphics, Inc. [*Associated Press*] (SAG)
ScaniaA....... Scania AB [*Associated Press*] (SAG)
ScaniaB....... Scania AB [*Associated Press*] (SAG)
SCANIIR....... Surface Composition by Analysis of Neutral and Ion Impact Radiation [*Qualitative analysis*]
SCAN MAG... Scandalum Magnatum [*Defamation of Dignity*] [*Latin*] (ROG)

SCANNET..... Scandinavian Network (NITA)
SCANO......... Automatic Scanning Unit Out of Service (FAAC)
ScanOp........ Scan-Optics, Inc. [*Associated Press*] (SAG)
SCANP......... Scandinavian Periodicals Index in Economics and Business [*Helsinki School of Economics Library*] [*Information service or system*]
SCANPED..... System for Comparative Analysis of Programs For Educational Development [*Information service or system*] (AEBS)
SCANS......... Scheduling and Control by Automated Network System
SCANS......... Secretary's Commission on Achieving Necessary Skills [*Department of Labor*]
SCANS......... Spectra Calculation from Activated Nuclide Sets (PDAA)
SCANS......... System Checkout Automatic Network Simulator
SCANSAR.... Scanning Synthetic Aperture RADAR
ScanSrce..... ScanSource, Inc. [*Associated Press*] (SAG)
SCAN-Test... Scandinavian Pulp, Paper and Board Testing Committee [*Sweden*] (EAIO)
SCANTIE...... Submersible Craft Acoustic Navigation and Track Indication Equipment (PDAA)
ScanVec...... ScanVec Co. Ltd. [*Associated Press*] (SAG)
SCAO.......... Senior Civil Affairs Officer
SCAO.......... Standing Committee on Army Organization [*British*]
SCAO.......... Standing Conference of Atlantic Organisations [*British*] (EAIO)
SCAOK........ Automatic Scanning Unit Returned to Service (FAAC)
SCAO(P)...... Senior Civil Affairs Office, Police [*British*]
SCAP.......... Alto Palena/Alto Palena [*Chile*] [*ICAO location identifier*] (ICLI)
SCAP.......... Scapula (DMAA)
SCAP.......... Service Center Audit Program [*IRS*]
SCAP.......... Silent Compact Auxiliary Power
SCAP.......... Silicon Capacitance Absolute Pressure Sensor
SCAP.......... Slow Component Axonal Particulate [*Neurology*]
SCAP.......... Small Communications Augmentation Package (MCD)
SCAP.......... Space Charge Atomizing Precipitaters (KSC)
SCAP.......... Superfund Comprehensive Accomplishment Plan [*Environmental Protection Agency*] (GFGA)
SCAP.......... Supreme Commander, Allied Powers [*World War II*] (MUGU)
SCAP.......... Systems Concepts and Procedures
SCAPA........ Society for Checking the Abuses of Public Advertising [*British*]
SCAPE........ Self-Contained Atmospheric Personnel [*or Protective*] Ensemble [*Suit*] [*Aerospace*]
SCAPE........ System Compatibility and Performance Evaluation [*Military*] (CAAL)
SCAPS........ Site Characterization and Analysis Penterometer System [*Army*] (RDA)
s caps.......... Small Capital Letters (WDMC)
SCAPS........ Small Capitals [*Typography*]
SCAR.......... Arica/Internacional Chacalluta [*Chile*] [*ICAO location identifier*] (ICLI)
SCAR.......... Satellite Capture and Retrieval (AFM)
SCAR.......... Scandinavian Council for Applied Research
scar............ Scarlet [*Philately*]
SCAR.......... Schools' Campaign Against Racism [*British*] (DI)
SCAR.......... Scientific Committee on Antarctic Research [*ICSU*] [*Cambridge, England*] (EAIO)
SCAR.......... Signal Conditioner Assembly Request (MCD)
SCAR.......... Signal Conditioner Assembly Review (MCD)
S Car.......... South Carolina Reports [*A publication*] (DLA)
SCAR.......... Spacecraft Assessment Report [*NASA*] (KSC)
SCAR.......... Special Committee on Atlantic Research
SCAR.......... Special Committee on Atomic Research [*Pugwash Conference*]
SCAR.......... Special International Committee on Antarctic Research
SCAR.......... Status Control Alert and Reporting (MCD)
SCAR.......... Strike Control and Reconnaissance [*Aircraft*]
SCAR.......... Structure-Carcinogenic Activity Relationship [*Biochemistry*]
SCAR.......... Subcaliber Aircraft Rocket
SCAR.......... Subcell Address Register [*Computer science*] (MHDB)
SCAR.......... Submarine Celestial Altitude Recorder [*Navy*]
SCAR.......... Submerged Celestial Altitude Recorder (IAA)
SCAR.......... Subsequent Contrast Application Review (MCD)
SCAR.......... Supersonic Cruise Aircraft [*or Airplane*] Research [*NASA*]
SCAR.......... Supplier Corrective Action Request
SCAR.......... Supplier Corrective Action Request
SCARA........ Selective Compliance Assembly Robot Arm [*IBM Corp.*]
SCARAB...... Submersible Craft Assisting Repair and Burial [*Autonomous underwater vehicle*]
SCAR-B....... Smoke, Cloud, and Radiation in Brazil
SCARDE...... Study Committee on Analysis of Research, Development, and Engineering
SCARE........ Sensor Control Anti-Anti-Radiation Missile RADAR Evaluation (PDAA)
SCARE........ Structural Ceramic Analysis and Reliability Evaluation [*NASA*]
SCAReU...... Stanford Community Against Reagan University [*Group opposed to proposed Ronald Reagan presidential library at Stanford University*]
SCARF........ Santa Cruz Acoustic Range Facility [*Navy*]
SCARF........ Self-Contained Automated Robotic Factory
SCARF........ Side-Looking Coherent All-Range Focused
SCARF........ Special Committee on the Adequacy of Range Facilities (MUGU)
SCARF........ Strategic Cislunar Advanced Retaliatory Force (IAA)
SCARF........ Survey of Change and Residential Finance [*Census Bureau*]
SCARF........ System Control Audit Review File [*Computer science*]
SCARMD...... Severe Childhood Autosomal Recessive Muscular Dystrophy [*Medicine*]
SCARP........ Society for Comic Art Research and Preservation
S Car R........ South Carolina Law Reports [*A publication*] (DLA)
SCARS........ SACEUR [*Supreme Allied Commander, Europe*] Command Alerting Reporting System [*Army*]
SCARS........ Serialized Control and Record [*or Reporting*] System (NASA)
SCARS........ Sneak Circuit Analysis Report Summary [*NASA*] (GFGA)
SCARS........ Software Configuration Accounting and Reporting System
SCARS........ Southern's Computer-Assisted Retrieval Service [*University of Southern Mississippi*] (OLDSS)
SCARS........ Status Control Alert Reporting System (NATG)
SCARS........ System Control and Receiving Station [*Air Force*]
SCART......... Sperry Continuity and Resistance Tester
SCARWAF.... Special Category Army with Air Force
SCAS.......... Semicontinuous Activated Sludge [*Test*] [*Environmental Protection Agency*] (FFDE)
SCAS.......... Signal Corps Aviation School [*Obsolete Army*]
SCAS.......... Society for Companion Animal Studies (EAIO)
SCAS.......... Southwest Center for Advanced Studies [*Later, University of Texas at Dallas*]
SCAS.......... Spacecraft Adapter Simulator (IAA)
SCAS.......... Stability Control Augmentation System (NVT)
SCAS.......... State Cost Accounting System (OICC)
SCAS.......... Subsystem Computer Application Software (MCD)
SCASA........ Straight Chiropractic Academic Standards Association (EA)
SCASG........ SONAR Calibration and Alignment Steering Group
SCASH........ Scottish Committee Action on Smoking and Health (EAIO)
SCASP........ Sequence of Coverage and Speed (SAA)
SCASS........ Signal Corps Aircraft Signal Service [*Obsolete Army*]
SCASS........ Standing Conference of Arts and Social Sciences [*British*] (DBA)
SCAT.......... Scatterometer
SCAT.......... Scatula [*Package*] [*Pharmacy*]
SCAT.......... School and College Ability Test [*of ETS*]
SCAT.......... Schottky Cell Array Technology
SCAT.......... Science College Ability Test (EDAC)
SCAT.......... Scout/Antitank Mission [*Army*] (INF)
SCAT.......... Scout-Attack [*Helicopter*] (MCD)
SCAT.......... Security Control of Air Traffic [*FAA*]
SCAT.......... Selected Calibration and Alignment Test (MCD)
SCAT.......... Self-Contained Automatic Transmitter (MCD)
SCAT.......... Sequential Component Automatic Testing (MSA)
SCAT.......... Service Code Automatic Tester [*Automotive engineering*]
SCAT.......... Service Command Air Transportation
SCAT.......... Severe Combined Anaemia and Thrombocytopenia (ECON)
SCAT.......... Share Compiler-Assembler, Translator
SCAT.......... Sheep Cell Agglutination Test
SCAT.......... Sickle Cell Anemia Test [*Medicine*] (AAMN)
SCAT.......... Silicon Controlled Avalanche Transistor [*Electronics*] (BARN)
SCAT.......... Simulated Catalyst Activity Test [*Analytical chemistry*]
SCAT.......... Small Car Automatic Transit [*System*]
SCAT.......... Societa Ceirano Automobili Torino [*Early Italian auto manufacturer*]
SCAT.......... Solid Catalysts (KSC)
SCAT.......... Solution to Customer Aircraft Troubles (MCD)
SCAT.......... South Pacific Combat Air Transport [*World War II*]
SCAT.......... Space Communications and Tracking
SCAT.......... Special Advisory Committee on Telecommunications
SCAT.......... Speed Command Attitude/Target [*FAA*]
SCAT.......... Speed Command of Attitude/Thrust (IAA)
SCAT.......... Speed Control Approach/Takeoff
SCAT.......... Sperry Canada Automatic Tester
SCAT.......... State Change Algorithm Translator
SCAT.......... Storage, Checkout, and Transportation [*Rack*] [*Aerospace*]
SCAT.......... Submarine Classification and Tracking
SCAT.......... Supersonic Commercial Air Transport [*NASA*]
SCAT.......... Surface-Controlled Avalanche Transistor
SCAT.......... System Commonality Analysis Tool (SSD)
SCAT.......... System Configuration Acceptance Test (IAA)
SCAT.......... System for Computer Automated Typesetting (PDAA)
SCAT.......... Systems Consolidation of Accessions and Trainees [*Military*] (AABC)
SCATA........ Survival Sited Casualty Treatment Assemblage (AFM)
SCATANA..... Security Control of Air Traffic and Air Navigation Aids [*FAA*]
SCATE......... Self-Checking Automatic Testing Equipment
SCATE......... Space Chamber Analyzer - Thermal Environment [*NASA*]
SCATE......... Stromberg-Carlson Automatic Test Equipment
SCATER....... Security Control of Air Traffic and Electromagnetic Radiations [*During an air defense emergency*] [*FAA*]
Scates' Comp St... Treat, Scates, and Blackwell's Compiled Illinois Statutes [*A publication*] (DLA)
SCATHA....... Satellite Charging at High Altitude (MCD)
SCATHA....... Spacecraft Charging at High Altitudes [*Satellite*]
SCATMINWARIN... Scatterable Minefield Warning [*Army*] (ADDR)
SCAT ORIG... Scatula Originalis [*Original Package*] [*Pharmacy*]
SCATS......... Scheduling and Tracking System (MCD)
SCATS......... Self-Contained Automatic Test System
SCATS......... Sequential Controlled Automatic Transistor Start (NITA)
SCATS......... Sequentially Controlled Automatic Transmitter Start
SCATS......... Simulation, Checkout, and Training System
SCATS......... Simulation Control and Training System (NASA)
SCATS......... Standing Conference for the Advancement of Training and Supervision [*British*] (DBA)
SCATS......... Surface Combatant Airborne Tactical System (MCD)
SCATS......... Sydney Coordinated Adaptive Traffic System [*FHWA*] (TAG)
SCATSD....... Signal Corps Aviation Test and Support Detachment [*Military*] (IAA)
SCATT......... Scatterometer (USDC)
SCATT......... Scientific Communication and Technology Transfer [*System*] [*University of Pennsylvania*]
SCATT......... Shared Catalog Accessed Through Terminals [*Data processing system*]
SCATTOR..... Small Craft Assets, Training, and Turnover of Resources (DNAB)
SCAUL......... Standing Conference of African University Libraries [*Lagos, Nigeria*]
SCAULWA.... Standing Conference of African University Libraries (EAIO)
SCA(UN)...... Department of Security Council Affairs of the United Nations

Scaur.......... Pro Scauro [*of Cicero*] [*Classical studies*] (OCD)
SCAV.......... Scavenge (AAG)
SCAW.......... Scientists' Center for Animal Welfare (EA)
SCAW.......... Supreme Camp of the American Woodmen (EA)
SCAWD........ Scottish Churches Action for World Development (EAIO)
SCAWD........ Service Contract Act Wage Determination (AAGC)
SCAWH-SAWRH... Signal Company Aircraft Warning Hawaii - Signal Aircraft Warning Regiment HawaiiAssociation (EA)
SCAWNA...... Self-Contained Adverse-Weather Night Attack (MCD)
SCAWU........ Singapore Clerical and Administrative Workers' Union
SCAZ.......... South Atlantic Convergence Zone [*Marine science*] (OSRA)
Sc B.......... Bachelor of Science
ScB.......... Beaufort County Library, Beaufort, SC [*Library symbol Library of Congress*] (LCLS)
SCB.......... Sample Collection Bag [*NASA*]
SCB.......... Santa Cruz Basin [*California*] (GAAI)
SCB.......... Scarborough [*Ontario*] [*Seismograph station code, US Geological Survey Closed*] (SEIS)
SCB.......... Schedule Change Board [*NASA*] (NASA)
SCB.......... Scholarly Book Center [*ACCORD*] [*UTLAS symbol*]
SCB.......... School of Classical Ballet [*American Ballet Theater Foundation*]
Sc B.......... Scientiae Baccalaureus [*Bachelor of Science*] [*Latin*]
SCB.......... Scorpion Resources [*Vancouver Stock Exchange symbol*]
SCB.......... Scribner, NE [*Location identifier FAA*] (FAAL)
SCB.......... Secondary Carpet Backing
SCB.......... Segment Control BIT [*Binary Digit*]
SCB.......... Selection Control Board [*NASA*] (NASA)
SCB.......... Selector Control Box [*Aerospace*] (MCD)
SCB.......... Selenite Cystine Broth (OA)
SCB.......... Semiconductor Bridge
SCB.......... Session Control Block [*Computer science*] (BUR)
SCB.......... Shallow Cathode Barrier (IAA)
SCB.......... Ship Characteristics Board
SCB.......... Shipowners Claims Bureau [*New York, NY*] (EA)
SCB.......... Ships Characteristics Board
SCB.......... Ship's Cook, Butcher [*Navy*]
SCB.......... Silicon Cell Bridge
SCB.......... Silicon Circuit Board
SCB.......... Silver Cadmium Battery
SCB.......... Single-Cell Biosensor [*Analytical biochemistry*]
SCB.......... Site Control Block [*Computer science*] (OA)
SCB.......... Society for Conservation Biology (EA)
SCB.......... Society of Craftsmen Bakers [*British*] (BI)
SCB.......... Soeurs de la Charite de Besancon [*Sisters of Charity*] [*France*] (EAIO)
SCB.......... Software Control Board [*Apollo*] [*NASA*]
SCB.......... Specification Control Board [*NASA*] (NASA)
SCB.......... Stack Control Block
SCB.......... State Capacity Building (EDAC)
SCB.......... Station Control Block [*Computer science*] (IBMDP)
SCB.......... Strictly Confined to Bed [*Medicine*]
SCB.......... Student Contact Book [*A publication*]
SCB.......... Supervisory Circuit Breaker (IAA)
SCBA.......... Balmaceda/Balmaceda [*Chile*] [*ICAO location identifier*] (ICLI)
ScBa.......... Lexington County Circulating Library, Batesburg, SC [*Library symbol Library of Congress*] (LCLS)
SCBA.......... Self-Contained Breathing Apparatus
SCBA.......... Supreme Circle Brotherhood of America (EA)
SCBAL........ Standard Chartered Bank Australia Ltd. (ADA)
Sc BAM........ Bachelor of Science in Applied Mathematics
Sc BC.......... Bachelor of Science in Chemistry
SCBC.......... Small-Cell Bronchogenic Carcinoma [*Oncology*] (DAVI)
SCBCA........ Small Claims Board of Contract Appeals
SCBCL-C...... Societe Commerciale de Banque Credit Lyonnais-Cameroun (EY)
SCBCmp...... SCB Computer Technology, Inc. [*Associated Press*] (SAG)
SC Bcp........ SC Bancorp [*Associated Press*] (SAG)
SCBD.......... Scan Conversion and Bright Display
SCBD.......... Seller's Approved Configuration Baseline Document [*NASA*] (NASA)
SCBD.......... Signal Corps Base Depot [*Military*] (IAA)
Sc BE.......... Bachelor of Science in Engineering
SCBE.......... Societe Canadienne des Brevets et d'Exploitation
ScBen.......... Marlboro County Public Library, Bennettsville, SC [*Library symbol*] [*Library of Congress*] (LCLS)
SCBF.......... Sacred Cat of Burma Fanciers (EA)
SCBF.......... Spinal Cord Blood Flow
ScBi.......... Lee County Public Library, Bishopville, SC [*Library symbol*] [*Library of Congress*] (LCLS)
SCBI.......... SCB Computer Technology [*NASDAQ symbol*] (TTSB)
SCBI.......... SCB Computer Technology, Inc. [*NASDAQ symbol*] (SAG)
SCBL.......... Quilpue/Mil el Belloto [*Chile*] [*ICAO location identifier*] (ICLI)
SCBL.......... Scotts Bluff and Agate Fossil Beds National Monuments
SCBNP........ Society for the Collection of Brand-Name Pencils [*Inactive*] (EA)
Sc BP.......... Bachelor of Science in Physics
SCBQ.......... Santiago/Mil el Bosque [*Chile*] [*ICAO location identifier*] (ICLI)
SCBQ.......... Science Classroom Behavior Q-Sort (EDAC)
SCBR.......... Serum Cholesterol-Binding Reserve [*Medicine*]
SCBR.......... Stationary Catalytic Basket Reactor [*Chemical engineering*]
SCBR.......... Steam-Cooled Breeder Reactor [*Nuclear energy*]
SCBS.......... Saint Charles Borromeo Seminary [*Pennsylvania*]
SCBS.......... Society for the Conservation of Bighorn Sheep (EA)
SCBS.......... Southern Community Bancshares, Inc. [*NASDAQ symbol*] (SAG)
SC/BSE........ Scientific Co-Operation Bureau for the European and North American Region [*United Nations*] (EA)
SCBT.......... Society of Computed Body Tomography (EA)
ScBTC.......... Beaufort Technical College, Beaufort, SC [*Library symbol*] [*Library of Congress*] (LCLS)
SCBU.......... Special Care Baby Unit [*Medicine*]
SCBW.......... Society of Children's Book Writers (EA)
SCC.......... Cameron's Supreme Court Cases [*Canada*] [*A publication*] (DLA)
ScC.......... Charleston Library Society, Charleston, SC [*Library symbol Library of Congress*] (LCLS)
SCC.......... Deadhorse [*Alaska*] [*Airport symbol*] (OAG)
SCC.......... Deadhorse, AK [*Location identifier FAA*] (FAAL)
SCC.......... Sacra Congregatio Concilii [*Sacred Congregation of the Council*] [*Latin*]
SCC.......... Safety Control Center (NASA)
SCC.......... SAGE [*Semiautomatic Ground Environment*] Control Center
SCC.......... Salivary Caffeine Clearance [*Physiology*]
SCC.......... Santa Cruz [*California*] [*Seismograph station code, US Geological Survey Closed*] (SEIS)
SCC.......... Satellite Communication Concentrator
SCC.......... Satellite Communications Controller
SCC.......... Satellite Control Center
SCC.......... Satellite-Controlled Clock
SCC.......... Scandinavian Collectors Club (EA)
SCC.......... Scarborough Campus, University of Toronto [*UTLAS symbol*]
SCC.......... Schools Councils Classics Committee [*British*]
SCC.......... Science Council of Canada
SCC.......... Sea Cadet Corps [*Navy British*]
SCC.......... Sears Canada [*TS Symbol*] (TTSB)
SCC.......... Sears Canada, Inc. [*Toronto Stock Exchange symbol*]
SCC.......... Secondary Category Code (NITA)
SCC.......... Secondary Combustion Chamber [*Furnace technology*]
SCC.......... Secondary Containment Cooling (IEEE)
SCC.......... Sectional Classification Code (NITA)
SCC.......... Security Commodity Code (AAG)
SCC.......... Security Control Center [*NASA*] (KSC)
SCC.......... Security Coordination Committee (NATG)
SCC.......... Seed Certification Committee [*Queensland, Australia*]
SCC.......... Select Cases in Chancery [*Legal*] [*British*]
SCC.......... Select Cases in Chancery Tempore King, Edited by Macnaghten [*England*] [*A publication*] (DLA)
SCC.......... Self-Contained Canister (MCD)
SCC.......... Senate Children's Caucus (EA)
SCC.......... Senate Copper Caucus (EA)
SCC.......... Senior Command Course [*British military*] (DMA)
SCC.......... Sequence Control Chart
SCC.......... Sequence Controlled Calculator (IAA)
SCC.......... Sequential Control Counter [*Computer science*] (BUR)
scc.......... Serbo-Croatian (Cyrillic) [*MARC language code Library of Congress*] (LCCP)
SCC.......... Serial Communications Controller
SCC.......... Service Change Committee [*Military*]
SCC.......... Services for Crippled Children
SCC.......... Servo Control Cabinet [*Military*] (CAAL)
SCC.......... Set Conditionally [*Computer science*]
SCC.......... Sexual Concerns Checklist [*Premarital and marital relations test*]
SCC.......... Ship Control Center
SCC.......... Short-Circuit Current
SCC.......... Short-Course Chemotherapy [*Medicine*]
SCC.......... Sickle-Cell Crisis [*Hematology*] (DAVI)
SCC.......... Signaling Conversion Circuit [*Telecommunications*] (TEL)
SCC.......... Simplified Computer Code
SCC.......... Simulation Control Center [*NASA*] (KSC)
SCC.......... Single Conductor Cable (MSA)
SCC.......... Single Copy Complexity [*Genetics*]
SCC.......... Single Cotton-Covered [*Wire insulation*]
scc.......... Single Cotton Covered (IDOE)
SCC.......... Sisters of Christian Charity (TOCD)
SCC.......... Slice Control Central (SAA)
SCC.......... Slidell Computer Complex [*Slidell, LA*] [*NASA*]
SCC.......... Small Cell Cancer [*Oncology*]
SCC.......... Small Center Contact
SCC.......... Small Claims Court [*Northern Territory, Australia*]
SCC.......... Small Cleaved Cell [*Medicine*] (DMAA)
SCC.......... Small Compressor Colorimeter (MCD)
SCC.......... Societe Canadienne de Cardiologie [*Canadian Cardiovascular Society*] (EAIO)
SCC.......... Societe Canadienne de Criminologie
SCC.......... Societe Chimique des Charbonnages [*France*]
SCC.......... Society for Children with Craniosynostosis (EA)
SCC.......... Society for the Christian Commonwealth
SCC.......... Society of Cheese Connoisseurs [*British*] (DBA)
SCC.......... Society of Cosmetic Chemists (EA)
SCC.......... Soeurs de la Croix de Chavanod [*Sisters of the Cross of Chavanod*] [*France*] (EAIO)
SCC.......... Software Checkout Console [*Army*]
SCC.......... Soil Conservation Council [*South Australia*]
SCC.......... Somatic Cell Concentration (OA)
SCC.......... Source Classification Code [*Environmental Protection Agency*]
SCC.......... Southern Connecticut State College, Division of Library Science, New Haven, CT [*OCLC symbol*] (OCLC)
SCC.......... Space Chamber Complex (MCD)
SCC.......... Space Control Station
SCC.......... Spacecraft Control Center [*NASA*] (KSC)
SCC.......... Spark Control Computer [*Automotive engineering*]
SCC.......... Special Coordinating Committee [*National Security Council*] [*Terminated, 1981*]
SCC.......... Specialist Computer Centres (NITA)

SCC............ Specialized Common Carrier [*Telecommunications*] (NRCH)
SCC............ Specification for Contract Change (DNAB)
SCC............ Specific Clauses and Conditions (NATG)
SCC............ Speed Control Circuit (DNAB)
SCC............ Splenium of the Corpus Callosum [*Anatomy*]
SCC............ Squadron Control Center (AAG)
SCC............ Squamous Cell Carcinoma [*Also, SC*] [*Medicine*]
SCC............ Stabilized Core Composite [*Materials science*]
SCC............ Stamford [*Connecticut*] [*Airport symbol*] (AD)
SCC............ Standard Commodity Classification [*Military*]
SCC............ Standard Commodity Codes (MCD)
SCC............ Standard Consultative Commission [*for resolving compliance disputes arising from SALT 1 accord*]
SCC............ Standard Cubic Centimeter (KSC)
SCC............ Standardized Cost Categories
SCC............ Standards Council of Canada [*See also CCNO*]
SCC............ Standing Consultative Commission [*SALT agreements*] [*US/USSR*]
SCC............ Standing Interdepartmental Committee on Censorship [*War Cabinet*] [*British*]
SCC............ Starcraft Campers Club (EA)
SCC............ State Coordination Committee [*Responsible for administering the Work Incentive Program at the state level*]
SCC............ State Corporation Commission
SCC............ State/Territories Consultative Committee [*Australia*]
SCC............ Status Change Character (IAA)
SCC............ Steel Carriers Conference [*Later, RDCC*] [*An association*] (EA)
SCC............ Steering Control Console (DNAB)
SCC............ Stock Clearing Corp. [*NYSE*]
SCC............ Stock Control Center [*Army*]
SCC............ Storage Connecting Circuit [*Teletype*]
SCC............ Strapped, Corded and Sealed (MHDB)
SCC............ Strategic Communications Command [*Army*] (MCD)
SCC............ Stress Corrosion Cracking [*Metals*]
SCC............ Structural Concrete Consortium [*British*] (DBA)
SCC............ Student of Codrington College [*Barbados*]
SCC............ Studio Collector's Club (EA)
SCC............ Sub-Carrier Channels (NITA)
SC(C).......... Submarine Chaser (Control) [*110 foot*] [*Obsolete*]
SCC............ Submission Control Code (MCD)
SCC............ Sunbeam Car Club [*Defunct*] (EA)
SCC............ Suore della Carita Cristiana [*Sisters of Christian Charity*] [*Italy*] (EAIO)
SCC............ Super-Critical Cryogenics (SAA)
SCC............ Super Sonic Car
SCC............ Supervisor Control Console
SCC............ Supervisory Control Conference (KSC)
SCC............ Supply Control Center [*Military*]
SCC............ Supreme Court Cases [*India*] [*A publication*] (DLA)
SCC............ Supreme Court Circular [*Ceylon*] [*A publication*] (ILCA)
SCC............ Supreme Court of Canada
SCC............ Surface Combat Condition (DNAB)
SCC............ Surveillance Coordination Center (NATG)
SCC............ Switching Control Center [*Bell System*]
SCC............ Synchronous Communications Controller
SCC............ Syndicat des Communications Canada
SCC............ System Communication Controller
SCC............ System Control Code (MCD)
SCC............ System Control Console (MCD)
SCC............ System Coordinate Center [*Military*] (CAAL)
SCC............ Systems Control Center
SCCA.......... Saab Car Club of Australia
SCCA.......... Semiclosed Circle Absorber (DAVI)
SCCA.......... Single Cell Cytotoxicity Assay [*Clinical chemistry*]
SCCA.......... Society of Canadian Cine Amateurs
SCCA.......... Society of Company and Commercial Accountants [*Edgbaston, Birmingham, England*] (EAIO)
SCCA.......... Somali Cat Club of America
SCCA.......... Southeastern Cottonseed Crushers Association (EA)
SCCA.......... Specification Compliance Concept Agreements (MCD)
SCCA.......... Sports Car Club of America (EA)
SCCa.......... Squamous-Cell Carcinoma [*Oncology*] (DAVI)
SCCA.......... Subcontract Change Authorization (AAG)
SCCAC........ Society for Conceptual and Content Analysis by Computer (EA)
SCC-ACO..... Strategic Communications Command Advanced Concepts Office [*Army*]
SCCAIC....... Societe Canadienne pour la Couleur dans les Arts, l'Industrie et la Science (EAIO)
ScCam......... Kershaw County Library, Camden, SC [*Library symbol*] [*Library of Congress*] (LCLS)
SCCAM........ Standing Committee of Consumer Affairs Ministers
ScCap.......... Security Capital Industrial Trust [*Associated Press*] (SAG)
SC Cas........ Supreme Court Cases [*A publication*] (DLA)
ScCB........... Baptist College at Charleston, Charleston, SC [*Library symbol Library of Congress*] (LCLS)
SCCB........... Safety Change Control Board (MCD)
SCCB........... Site Configuration Control Board [*NASA*] (NASA)
SCCB........... Small-Cell Carcinoma of the Bronchus [*Medicine*] (DMAA)
SCCB........... Software Configuration Control Board (KSC)
SCCB........... South Carolina Cmnty Banc [*NASDAQ symbol*] (TTSB)
SCCB........... South Carolina Community Bancshare [*NASDAQ symbol*] (SAG)
SCCB........... State Contracts Control Board [*New South Wales, Australia*]
SCCBcsh...... South Carolina Community Bancshares, Inc. [*Associated Press*] (SAG)
SCCC........... Chile Chico/Chile Chico [*Chile*] [*ICAO location identifier*] (ICLI)
ScCC........... College of Charleston, Charleston, SC [*Library symbol Library of Congress*] (LCLS)
SCCC........... Satellite Communications Control Centre [*British*]
SCCC........... Shared Contingency Computer Center (MHDI)
SCCC........... Single Channel Communications Controller (NITA)
SCCC........... Squamous Cell Cervical Carcinoma [*Medicine*] (DMAA)
SCCC........... System Casualty Control Console [*Military*] (CAAL)
SCCCE......... Society of Certified Consumer Credit Executives (EA)
ScCCit......... Citadel, Charleston, SC [*Library symbol Library of Congress*] (LCLS)
SCCD........... Iquique/Los Condores [*Chile*] [*ICAO location identifier*] (ICLI)
SCCDEST..... Steering Committee on Crossborder Data Exchange in Science and Technology (NITA)
ScCDHHi...... Dalcho Historical Society of the Episcopal Diocese of South Carolina, Charleston, SC [*Library symbol Library of Congress*] (LCLS)
ScCDHi........ Dalcho Historical Society of the Episcopal Diocese of South Carolina, Charleston, SC [*Library symbol*] [*Library of Congress*] (LCLS)
SCCE........... Satellite Configuration Control Element (MCD)
SCCE........... School and College Conference on English
SCCE........... Scottish Council for Community Education
SCCE........... Society of Certified Credit Executives [*St. Louis, MO*] (EA)
SCCE........... Staged Combustion Compound Engine [*Automotive engineering*]
SCCEA......... Strategic Communications Command Equipment Applications Directorate [*Army*]
ScCenW....... Central Wesleyan College, Central, SC [*Library symbol*] [*Library of Congress*] (LCLS)
SCCF........... Calama/El Loa [*Chile*] [*ICAO location identifier*] (ICLI)
ScCF........... Charleston County Library, Charleston, SC [*Library symbol Library of Congress*] (LCLS)
SCCF........... Satellite Communication Control Facility
SCCF........... Security Clearance Case Files [*Military*] (AABC)
SCCF........... Service Center Control File [*IRS*]
SCCFF......... Second Check Character Flip-Flop [*Computer science*] (MHDB)
SCCG........... Station Communications Control Group [*Ground Communications Facility, NASA*]
ScCh........... Chester County Library, Chester, SC [*Library symbol*] [*Library of Congress*] (LCLS)
SCCH........... Chillan/Gral, Bernardo O'Higgins [*Chile*] [*ICAO location identifier*] (ICLI)
SCCH........... Society of Cinema Collectors and Historians (EA)
SCCH........... Standard Cubic Centimeters per Hour (MCD)
SCCH........... Sternocostoclavicular Hyperostosis [*Medicine*] (DMAA)
ScChf.......... Chesterfield County Library, Chesterfield, SC [*Library symbol*] [*Library of Congress*] (LCLS)
SCCHO......... Sternocostoclavicular Hyperostosis [*Medicine*] (DMAA)
ScChwC....... Chesterfield-Marlboro Technical College, Cheraw, SC [*Library symbol Library of Congress*] (LCLS)
SCCI............ Punta Arenas/Internacional Carlos Ibanez Del Campo [*Chile*] [*ICAO location identifier*] (ICLI)
SCCI............ Smurf Collectors' Club International (EA)
SCC(I)......... Special Coordination Committee (Intelligence) (MCD)
SCCI............ Supreme Court of Christmas Island [*Australia*]
SCCJ............ Supreme Court of Canada Judgements [*Canada Department of Justice*] [*Information service or system*] (CRD)
SCC(K)I....... Supreme Court of Cocos (Keeling) Islands [*Australia*]
SCCL........... Safety Compliance Certification Label [*Automotive engineering*]
SCCL........... Scottish Council for Civil Liberties (DI)
SCCL........... Scottish Council of Civil Liberties (DBA)
SCCL........... Small Cell (Anaplastic) Carcinoma of the Lung [*Oncology*]
SCCL........... Supply Catalog Components List [*Military*]
ScCleU........ Clemson University, Clemson, SC [*Library symbol Library of Congress*] (LCLS)
ScCliJ......... Jacobs Library, Clinton, SC [*Library symbol Library of Congress Obsolete*] (LCLS)
ScClP.......... Presbyterian College, Clinton, SC [*Library symbol Library of Congress*] (LCLS)
ScClTO........ Thornwell Orphanage, Clinton, SC [*Library symbol Library of Congress*] (LCLS)
ScCM.......... Medical University of South Carolina, Charleston, SC [*Library symbol Library of Congress*] (LCLS)
SCCM.......... Sertoli-Cell Culture Medium [*Clinical chemistry*]
SCCM.......... Short Circuit Conductance Matrix (PDAA)
SCCM.......... Single Chamber Controllable Motor (MCD)
SCCM.......... Society of Critical Care Medicine (EA)
SCCM.......... Standard Cubic Centimeters per Minute (NASA)
SCCM.......... Standing Commission on Church Music (EA)
SCCML........ Scottish Central Committee on Modern Languages (AIE)
ScCMP........ Middleton Place, Charleston, SC [*Library symbol Library of Congress*] (LCLS)
ScCMu........ Charleston Museum Library, Charleston, SC [*Library symbol Library of Congress*] (LCLS)
SCCN.......... Subcontract [*or Subcontractor*] Change Notice (KSC)
SCCNC........ Society of Critical Care Nurses of Canada
SCC NR....... Special Cryptologic Control Number (DNAB)
SCC(NSW)... State Chamber of Commerce [*New South Wales*] [*Australia*]
SCCO.......... Security Classification Control Officer [*Military*]
SCCO.......... Steel-Cored Copper (IAA)
ScCoA......... Allen University, Columbia, SC [*Library symbol*] [*Library of Congress*] (LCLS)
ScCoAH....... South Carolina Department of Archives and History, Columbia, SC [*Library symbol Library of Congress*] (LCLS)
ScCoB......... Benedict College, Columbia, SC [*Library symbol Library of Congress*] (LCLS)
ScCoB......... Columbia Bible College, Columbia, SC [*Library symbol Library of Congress*] (LCLS)

ScCoBC........ Columbia Bible College, Columbia, SC [*Library symbol*] [*Library of Congress*] (LCLS)
ScCoC......... Columbia College, Columbia, SC [*Library symbol Library of Congress*] (LCLS)
SCCOC......... Steel-Cored Copper Conductor (IAA)
SC Code...... Code of Laws of South Carolina [*A publication*] (DLA)
SC Code Ann... Code of Laws of South Carolina, Annotated [*A publication*] (DLA)
ScCoGS........ Church of Jesus Christ of Latter-Day Saints, Genealogical Society Library, Columbia Branch, Columbia, SC [*Library symbol Library of Congress*] (LCLS)
ScCoHE........ South Carolina Department of Health and Environmental Control, Columbia, SC [*Library symbol*] [*Library of Congress*] (LCLS)
ScCoM......... Midlands Technical College, Columbia, SC [*Library symbol*] [*Library of Congress*] (LCLS)
ScCoM-A...... Midland Technical College, Airport Campus, Library and Information Center, Columbia, SC [*Library symbol*] [*Library of Congress*] (LCLS)
ScCoM-B...... Midlands Technical College, Beltline Campus, Columbia, SC [*Library symbol*] [*Library of Congress*] (LCLS)
ScCon.......... Horry County Memorial Library, Conway, SC [*Library symbol Library of Congress*] (LCLS)
ScConH........ Horry-Georgetown Technical College, Conway, SC [*Library symbol*] [*Library of Congress*] (LCLS)
ScCoR.......... Richland County Library, Columbia, SC [*Library symbol Library of Congress*] (LCLS)
Sc Costs...... Scott's ABC Guide to Costs [*2nd ed.*] [*1910*] [*A publication*] (DLA)
ScCoT.......... Lutheran Theological Southern Seminary, Columbia, SC [*Library symbol Library of Congress*] (LCLS)
ScCoV.......... United States Veterans Administration Hospital, Columbia, SC [*Library symbol Library of Congress*] (LCLS)
SCCP........... Sabah Chinese Consolidated Party [*Malaysia*] [*Political party*] (FEA)
SCCP........... Signaling Connection Control Part [*Telecommunications*]
SCCP........... Systems Change Control Procedure [*Social Security Administration*]
SCCPG......... Satellite Communications Contingency Planning Group (NATG)
ScCPT.......... Security Capital Pacific Trust [*Associated Press*] (SAG)
SCC(Q)......... State Chamber of Commerce [*Queensland*] [*Australia*]
SCCR........... Society for Cross-Cultural Research (EA)
SCCR........... Stanford Center for Chicano Research [*Stanford University*] [*Research center*] (RCD)
SCCR........... Subcontractor Change Request (MCD)
ScCRC......... Charleston Diocesan Archives, Roman Catholic Church, Charleston, SC [*Library symbol Library of Congress*] (LCLS)
SCCRI.......... Swedish Cement and Concrete Research Institute (MCD)
SCCS........... Satellite Communications Control System (MCD)
SCCS........... Secondary Chemical Control System [*Nuclear energy*] (NRCH)
SCCS........... Sodium Chemistry Control System [*Westinghouse Corp.*] (IEEE)
SCCS........... Software Controlled Communication Services (MCD)
SCCS........... Source Code Control System [*Computer science*]
SCCS........... Souvenir Card Collectors Society (EA)
SCCS........... Souvenir China Collectors Society (EA)
SCCS........... Special Consultative Committee on Security [*OAS*]
SCCS........... Standard Commodity Classification System (NG)
SCCS........... Standard Cross-Cultural Sample [*Human Relations Area Files*] [*Information retrieval*]
SCCS........... Standard Cubic Centimeters per Second (NASA)
SCCS........... Standby Core Cooling System [*Nuclear energy*] (NRCH)
SCCS........... Straight Cut Control System (IAA)
SCCS........... STRICOM [*Strike Command*] Command and Control System [*Army*] (AABC)
SCCS........... Switching Control Center System [*Telecommunications*] (TEL)
SCCSA......... Sports Car Collectors Society of America [*Defunct*] (EA)
SCCSIAMRNASNPWPPPPPP... Select Committee to Conduct a Study and Investigation of All Matters Relating tothe Need for Adequate Supplies of Newsprint, Printing and Wrapping Paper, Paper Products, Paper, Pulp and Plywood [*US Congress*] [*World War II*]
ScCSM......... Old Slave Mart Museum, Charleston, SC [*Library symbol Library of Congress*] (LCLS)
SCCT........... Specialist in Community College Teaching (GAGS)
ScCT........... Trident Technical College, Palmer Campus, Charleston, SC [*Library symbol Library of Congress*] (LCLS)
SCC-TED...... Strategic Communications Command - Test and Evaluation Directorate [*Army*]
SCCTR......... Standing Committee for Controlled Thermonuclear Research [*Terminated, 1973*] [*AEC*] (EGAO)
SCCTSD....... Society of Catholic College Teachers of Sacred Doctrine [*Later, CTS*] (EA)
SCCU........... Scottish Cross Country Union (DBA)
SCCU........... Single Channel Control Unit
SCCU........... Spacecraft Command Control Unit (KSC)
SCCU........... Specialist Claims Control Unit [*British*]
SCCUK......... Swedish Chamber of Commerce for the United Kingdom (DS)
SCCUS......... Swedish Chamber of Commerce of the United States [*Later, Swedish-American Chamber of Commerce*]
ScCV........... United States Veterans Administration Hospital, Charleston, SC [*Library symbol Library of Congress*] (LCLS)
SCCW........... Scarritt College for Christian Workers [*Tennessee*]
SCCWRP....... Southern California Coastal Water Research Project (NOAA)
SCCY........... Coyhaique/Teniente Vidal [*Chile*] [*ICAO location identifier*] (ICLI)
SCCZ........... Punta Arenas [*Chile*] [*ICAO location identifier*] (ICLI)
SCD............ Darlington County Library, Darlington, SC [*OCLC symbol*] (OCLC)
SCD............ Doctor of Commercial Science
Sc D........... Doctor of Science
ScD............ Doctor of Science (GAGS)
SCD............ Satellite Control Department
SCD............ S-Band Cassegrain Diplexer
SCD............ Schedule (AABC)
SCD............ Schneider Corp. [*Toronto Stock Exchange symbol*]
SCD............ Science Communication Division [*George Washington University Medical Center*] [*Information service or system*] (IID)
Sc D........... Scientiae Doctor [*Doctor of Science*] [*Latin*]
SCD............ Scientific Computer Division [*Army Tank-Automotive Command*]
ScD............ Scintillation Detector (IEEE)
SCD............ Scottish Council of Dance (DBA)
SCD............ Screen Door
SCD............ Screwed (MDG)
SCD............ Secondary Current Distribution [*Electroplating*]
SCD............ Security Coding Device (NATG)
SCD............ Semiconductor Device (IAA)
SCD............ Senile Cognitive Decline [*Medicine*]
SCD............ Senior Citizen Discount
SCD............ Serial Cryptographic Device (MHDB)
SCD............ Service Computation Date [*Military*] (AFM)
SCD............ Service Connected Disability [*Medicine*] (AAMN)
SCD............ Service Control Drawing
SCD............ Servo Chart Drive
SCD............ Ship's Center Display [*Navy*] (NVT)
SCD............ Sickle Cell Disease [*Medicine*]
SCD............ Signal Canceling Device
SCD............ Significant Construction Deficiency [*Nuclear energy*] (NRCH)
SCD............ Simulated Communications Deception [*Army*] (INF)
SCD............ Slovenian Christian Democrats [*Political party*]
SCD............ Society of Craft Designers (EA)
SCD............ Software Conceptual Design [*Computer science*]
SCD............ Soil Conservation District [*Agriculture*]
SCD............ Source Control Document (NASA)
SCD............ Source Control Drawing
SCD............ Space Control Document [*NASA*] (KSC)
SCD............ Specification Control Document [*or Drawing*] [*NASA*] (NASA)
SCD............ Spinal Cord Disease [*Neurology*] (DAVI)
SCD............ Spreading Cortical Depression
SCD............ State Civil Defense
SCD............ Static Column Decode [*Computer science*]
SCD............ Sterile Connection Device [*Medicine*]
SCD............ Stored-Charge Diode (IAA)
SCD............ Strategic Communications Division [*Military*]
SCD............ Streaming Current Detector
SCD............ Structure-Chart Diagramer [*Computer science*]
SCD............ Subacute Combined Degeneration [*of spinal cord*] [*Medicine*]
SCD............ Subcarrier Discriminator
SCD............ Subcontract Deviation
SCD............ Sudden Cardiac Death [*Medicine*]
SCD............ Sudden Coronary Death (MAE)
SCD............ Sulaco [*Honduras*] [*Airport symbol*] (AD)
SCD............ Sulfur Chemiluminescence Detector
SCD............ Supply, Commissary, and Disbursing [*Navy*]
SCD............ Surrey Commercial Dock [*British*]
SCD............ Surveillance Criticality Designator [*DoD*]
SCD............ Sylacauga, AL [*Location identifier FAA*] (FAAL)
SCD............ System Contents Directory [*Computer science*] (MHDB)
SCD............ System Coordination Document
SCD............ Systems, Components, and Displays
ScDa........... Darlington County Library, Darlington, SC [*Library symbol Library of Congress*] (LCLS)
SCDA........... Iquique/Gral Diego Aracena [*Chile*] [*ICAO location identifier*] (ICLI)
SCDA........... Safing, Cool Down, and Decontamination Area [*NASA*] (NASA)
ScDA........... Scapulodextra Anterior [*A fetal position*] (AAMN)
SCDA........... SEATO [*Southeast Asia Treaty Organization*] Central Distribution Agency (NATG)
SCDA........... Situational Control of Daily Activities
SCDA........... Small Card Design Automation (IAA)
SCDA........... Societe Canadienne des Directeurs d'Association [*Formerly, Institute of Canadian Trade Association Executives*] (AC)
SCDA........... Sullivans Cove Development Authority [*Tasmania, Australia*]
SCDAA......... Sickle Cell Disease Association of America [*Formerly the National Association for Sickle Cell Disease (NASCD)*] (PAZ)
SCDAP......... Severe Core Damage Analysis Package [*Nuclear energy*] (NRCH)
SCDAuto...... Sub Carrier Demodulation, Automatic (PDAA)
SCDC........... Schools Computer Development Centre (AIE)
SCDC........... Scottish Cooperative Development Committee
SCDC........... Service Coding and Data Collection (AAG)
SCDC........... Single Commutation Direct Current (IAA)
SCDC........... Societe Canadienne de Droit Canonique (AC)
SCDC........... Societe des Comptables de Direction au Canada [*Society of Management Accountants of Canada - SMAC*]
SCDC........... Source Coding and Data Collection
SCDC........... Strategic Concepts Development Center [*National Defense University*]
SCDC........... Supreme Court Reports, District of Columbia [*A publication*] (DLA)
SCDC........... System Control Distribution Computer (MHDB)
SCDCNS....... Supreme Court Reports, District of Columbia, New Series [*A publication*] (DLA)
SCDCU......... Section Chief, Display Control Unit [*Army*]
SC/DDS........ Sensor Control/Data Display Set (MCD)
SCDE........... School, College, Department of Education (AEE)
ScDeTC........ Denmark Technical College, Denmark, SC [*Library symbol*] [*Library of Congress*] (LCLS)
ScDeV.......... Voorhees College, Denmark, SC [*Library symbol Library of Congress*] (LCLS)
SCDF........... Skin Condition Data Form [*Medicine*] (DMAA)

SCDFGNY .... Sickle Cell Disease Foundation of Greater New York (EA)
Sc D Govt .... Doctor of Science in Government
SCDHEC .... South Carolina Department of Health and Environmental Control (DOGT)
SCDHEC .... South Carolina Department of Health and Environmental Control
SCDI .... Scottish Council of Development and Industry (DI)
SCDI .... Serious Chemical Distribution Incident
SCDI .... Short Children's Depression Inventory [*Psychology*]
SC Dig .... Cassel's Supreme Court Digest [*Canada*] [*A publication*] (DLA)
Sc D in Ed ... Doctor of Science in Education
Sc D in Hyg ... Doctor of Science in Hygiene
SC Div Bad ... Second Class Diver Badge [*Military decoration*]
SCDL .... Saturated Current Demand Logic
SCDL .... Ship Configuration Detail List [*Navy*]
SCDL .... Stabilized Carbon Dioxide LASER
SCDL .... Surveillance and Control Data Link [*Military*]
SCDM .... Solar Corona Diagnostic Mission [*NASA*] (SSD)
Sc D (Med) ... Doctor of Medical Science
SCDMR .... Steam-Cooled Deuteriated Water-Moderated Reactor [*Nuclear energy*]
ScdNE .... Scudder New Europe Fund [*Associated Press*] (SAG)
SCD OC of SA ... Staff Communications Division, Office, Chief of Staff, Army (AABC)
SCD OCSA ... Staff Communications Division, Office, Chief of Staff, Army (AABC)
Sc DP .... Right Scapuloposterior Position [*of the fetus*] [*Obstetrics*]
ScDP .... Scapulodextra Posterior [*A fetal position*] (AAMN)
SCDP .... Sedimentary Chlorophyll Degradation Product [*Paleontology*]
SCDP .... Simulation Control Data Package [*NASA*] (NASA)
SCDP .... Society of Certified Data Processors [*AICCP*] [*Superseded by*] (EA)
SCDP .... Southern Cooperative Development Program [*Sponsored by Southern Consumers Education Foundation*]
SCDP .... Steel Cadmium Plated
SCDR .... Screwdriver (MSA)
SCDR .... Seller Critical Design Review [*NASA*] (NASA)
SCDR .... Shuttle Critical Design Review [*NASA*] (NASA)
SCDR .... Software Critical Design Review [*NASA*] (NASA)
SCDR .... Subcontractor Critical Design Review [*NASA*]
SCDR .... Subsystem Controller Definition Record [*Computer science*] (IBMDP)
SCDRL .... Subcontractor Data Requirements List (DNAB)
SCDS .... Scan Converter Display System (MCD)
SCDS .... Sensor Communication and Display System (MCD)
SCDS .... Shipboard Chaff Decoy System [*Navy*]
SCDS .... Signal Circuits Design Section
SCDS .... Staff of Chief of Defence Staff [*British*]
SCDSB .... Suppressed Carrier Double Sideband [*Transmission*] (IAA)
SCDSD .... Scientific Clearinghouse and Documentation Services Division [*National Science and Technology Authority*] [*Information service or system*] (IID)
SCD (St V) ... Supreme Court Decisions (St. Vincent) [*1928-36*] [*A publication*] (DLA)
SCDU .... Signal Conditioning and Display Unit [*NASA*] (NASA)
ScDunG .... W.R. Grace & Co., Cryovac Division Technical Library, Duncan, SC [*Library symbol*] [*Library of Congress*] (LCLS)
SCDW .... Surface Charge Density Wave [*Physics*]
ScDwE .... Erskine College, Due West, SC [*Library symbol Library of Congress*] (LCLS)
ScDwE-T ...... Erskine College, Erskine Theological Seminary, Due West, SC [*Library symbol Library of Congress*] (LCLS)
SCDWG .... System Concept Development Working Group
ScE .... Edgefield County Library, Edgefield, SC [*Library symbol Library of Congress*] (LCLS)
SCE .... Saturated Calomel Electrode [*Electrochemistry*]
SCE .... Scan Conversion Equipment [*Television*]
SCE .... SCEcorp [*NYSE symbol*] (SAG)
SCE .... Schedule Compliance-Evaluation [*Polaris*]
SCE .... Schellex Gold [*Vancouver Stock Exchange symbol*]
SCE .... Schlegeis [*Austria*] [*Seismograph station code, US Geological Survey*] (SEIS)
SCE .... Scottish Certificate of Education
SCE .... Scribe Ezra [*Freemasonry*]
SCE .... Secondary Chemical Equilibria [*Chromatography*]
SCE .... Secretory Carcinoma of Endometrium
SCE .... Select Cases Relating to Evidence (Strange) [*A publication*] (DLA)
SCE .... Selection Control Element
SCE .... Sentence Combining Exercise [*Education*] (EDAC)
SCE .... Separated Career Employee
SCE .... Service Checkout Equipment (IAA)
SCE .... Service Cryptologic Elements [*Army*]
SCE .... Short Channel Effect (IAA)
SCE .... Siberia Commodity Exchange [*Russian Federation*] (EY)
SCE .... Signal Conditioning Equipment
SCE .... Signal Conversion Equipment [*Telecommunications*]
SCE .... Signal Conversion Equivalent (NITA)
SCE .... Significant Combat Equipment [*Army*]
SCE .... Single-Charge Exchange [*Physics*] (OA)
SCE .... Single Cotton-Covered Enameled [*Wire insulation*] (DEN)
sce .... Single Cotton Enameled (IDOE)
SCE .... Single Cycle Execute
SCE .... Sister Chromatic Exchange Analysis (DAVI)
SCE .... Sister Chromatid Exchange [*Cytology*]
SCE .... Situationally Caused Error
SCE .... Sky Care Ltd. [*New Zealand*] [*ICAO designator*] (FAAC)
SCE .... Slope-Clearing Events [*Geology*]
SCE .... Small Current Element
SCE .... Societe Canadienne d'Esthetique [*Canadian Society for Aesthetics - CSAC*]
SCE .... Society for Clinical Ecology [*Later, AAEM*] (EA)
SCE .... Society for Creative Ethics [*Later, SPC*] (EA)
SCE .... Society of Carbide Engineers [*Later, SCTE*] (EA)
SCE .... Society of Christian Engineers (EA)
SCE .... Society of Christian Ethics (EA)
SCE .... Software Capability Evaluation (RDA)
SCE .... Solar Corona Explorer [*Project*] [*NASA*]
SCE .... Solder Circuit Etch
SCE .... Source (MSA)
SCE .... Southern California Edison Co. [*AMEX symbol*] (SAG)
SCE .... Space Cabin Environment [*Skylab*] [*NASA*]
SCE .... Spacecraft Command Encoder (MCD)
SCE .... Special Conditioning Equipment
SCE .... Spectrum Communications & Electronics Corp. [*Telecommunications service*] (TSSD)
SCE .... Stabilization Control Electronics
SCE .... Staff Civil Engineer [*Military*] (DNAB)
SCE .... Stage Calibration Equipment (SAA)
SCE .... Standard Calomel Electrode
SCE .... Standard Card Enclosure [*Business term*] (MHDI)
SCE .... Standard Communication Environment (DOMA)
SCE .... State College [*Pennsylvania*] [*Airport symbol*] (OAG)
SCE .... State College, PA [*Location identifier FAA*] (FAAL)
SCE .... Station Cable Equalizer (IAA)
SCE .... Stored Controlled Energy
SCE .... St. Petersburg Commodity Exchange [*Russian Federation*] (EY)
SCE .... Stratified-Charge Engine [*Auto engine*]
SCE .... Supercritical Extract [*Separation technology*]
SCE .... Superintending Civil Engineer [*British*]
SCE .... United States Air Force, Armament Laboratory, Technical Library, Eglin AFB, FL [*OCLC symbol*] (OCLC)
ScEA .... John R. Abney Collection, Edgefield County Library, Edgefield, SC [*Library symbol Library of Congress*] (LCLS)
ScEa .... Pickens County Library, Easley, SC [*Library symbol Library of Congress*] (LCLS)
SCEA .... Service Children's Education Authority [*Ministry of Defence*] [*British*]
SCEA .... Side Cutting Edge Angle (IAA)
SCEA .... Signal Conditioning Electronics Assembly
SCEA .... Societe Canadienne d'Education par l'Art (AC)
SCEA .... Society of Communications Engineers and Analysts
SCEA .... Society of Cost Estimating and Analysis (EA)
SCE & PWD ... Staff Civil Engineer and Public Works Department (DNAB)
SCEAR .... Scientific Committee on the Effects of Atomic Radiation
SCEB .... SHAPE [*Supreme Headquarters Allied Powers Europe*] Communications Electronics Board [*NATO*] (NATG)
SCEB .... Societe Canadienne des Etudes Bibliques [*Canadian Society of Biblical Studies - CSBS*]
SCEB .... Syndicat Canadien des Employes de Bureau [*Canadian Office Employees Union - COEU*]
SCEC .... Scottish Community Education Council (EAIO)
SCEC .... Societe Canadienne des Eleveurs de Chevres
SCEC .... Societe Canadienne des Etudes Classiques [*Classical Association of Canada - CAC*]
SCEC .... Southern California Earthquake Center
SCEC .... Spaceborne Computer Engineering Conference (MCD)
SCEC .... Student Council for Exceptional Children (AEBS)
SCECC .... Societe Canadienne pour l'Etude Comparee des Civilisations [*Canadian Society for the Comparative Study of Civilizations - CSCSC*]
SCECI .... Societe Canadienne d'Education Comparee et Internationale
SCEcp .... SCEcorp [*Formerly, Southern California Edison Co.*] [*Associated Press*] (SAG)
SCED .... Schedule (IAA)
SCEd .... Southern California Edison Co. [*Associated Press*] (SAG)
SCED .... Standing Conference on Education Development (AIE)
SCEd44 .... Southern California Edison Co. [*Associated Press*] (SAG)
Sc Ed D .... Doctor of Science in Education
SCEDS .... Societe Canadienne d'Etude du Dix-Huitieme Siecle (AC)
SCEE .... Societe Canadienne d'Etudes Ethniques (AC)
SCEE .... Societe Canadienne pour l'Etude de l'Education [*Canadian Society for the Study of Education - CSSE*]
SCEE .... Southern Coalition for Educational Equity (EA)
SCEE .... Student Committee for Economic Education (EA)
SCEEB .... Scottish Certificate of Education Examination Board
SCEEE .... Southeastern Center for Electrical Engineering Education [*Air Force*]
SCEERR .... Sacra Congregatio Episcoporum et Regularium [*Sacred Congregation of Bishops and Regulars*] [*Latin*]
SCEES .... Service Central des Enquetes et Etudes Statistiques [*Central Service for Statistical Inquiries and Studies*] [*Ministry of Agriculture Paris, France*]
SCEES .... Societe Canadienne pour l'Etude de l'Enseignement Superieur [*Canadian Society for the Study of Higher Education - CSSHE*]
SCEET .... Support Concept Economic Evaluation Technique (MCD)
SCEF .... Isla Rey Jorge/Centro Meteorologico Antartico Presidente Frei [*Chile*] [*ICAO location identifier*] (ICLI)
SCEF .... Southern Conference Educational Fund (EA)
SC/EFC .... Spoiler Control/Elevator Feel Computer (MCD)
SC/EFC CP ... SC/EFC [*Spoiler Control/Elevator Feel Computer*] Control Panel (MCD)
SCEFS .... Spoiler Control Elevator Feel System (MCD)
SCEH .... Society for Clinical and Experimental Hypnosis (EA)
ScEHi .... Edgefield County Genealogical and Historical Society, Edgefield, SC [*Library symbol*] [*Library of Congress*] (LCLS)

SCEI............ Safe Car Educational Institute
SCEI............ Serial Carry Enable Input (IAA)
SCEI............ Societe Canadienne pour les Etudes Italiennes [*Canadian Society for Italian Studies - CSIS*]
SCEI............ Special Committee on Environmental Information [*Special Libraries Association*]
SCEIBF......... Standing Conference for Europe of the International Basketball Federation (EAIO)
SCEIL.......... Service Ceiling
SCEIO.......... Societe Canadienne pour Etudes d'Intelligence par Ordinateur
SCEIU.......... Standing Conference on Education for International Understanding [*British*] (DBA)
SCEKS.......... Spectrum Clear Except Known Signals (MUGU)
SCEL............ Santiago/Internacional Arturo Merino Benitez [*Chile*] [*ICAO location identifier*] (ICLI)
scel.............. Scellino [*Shilling*] [*Monetary unit*] [*Italian*]
SCEL............ Signal Corps Engineering Laboratories [*Obsolete Army*]
SCEL............ Small Components Evaluation Loop [*Nuclear energy*] (NRCH)
SCEL............ Standing Committee on Education in Librarianship
SCELBAL...... Scientific Elementary Basic Language [*1963*] [*Computer science*] (CSR)
SCEM........... Santiago/Arturo Merino Benitez (Edificio Direccion Meteorologica) [*Chile*] [*ICAO location identifier*] (ICLI)
SCEN........... Santiago/Edificio Navegacion Aerea Arturo Merino Benitez [*Chile*] [*ICAO location identifier*] (ICLI)
SCEN........... Societe Canadienne pour l'Etude des Noms [*Canadian Society for the Study of Names - CSSN*]
SCEN........... South Central
SCENE......... Studies of Coastal and Estuarine Environments [*National Oceanic and Atmospheric Administration*] (MSC)
SCENIC........ Scientific Engineering Information Center (KSC)
SCEO........... Satellite Control Engineering Office (IAA)
SCEO........... Scottish Centre for Education Overseas (AIE)
SCEO........... Senior Chief Executive Officer [*Civil Service*] [*British*]
SCEO........... Station Construction Engineering Officer
SCEP............ Sandwich Counterelectrophoresis [*Medicine*] (DMAA)
SCEP............ Secure Communications Equipment Program [*Air Force*] (CET)
SCEP............ Significant Criminal Enforcement Project [*Bureau of Alcohol, Tobacco, and Firearms*]
SCEP............ Societe Canadienne d'Enseignement Postscolaire
SCEP............ Special Committee on Antarctic Research [*International Council of Scientific Unions*] (USDC)
SCEP............ Special Committee on Antarctic Research [*Marine science*] (OSRA)
SCEP............ Spinal Cord Evoked Potential [*Medicine*] (DMAA)
SCEP............ Study of Critical Environmental Problems [*MIT*]
SCEP............ Syndicat Canadien des Communications, de l'Energie et du Papier (AC)
SCEPC.......... Senior Civil Emergency Planning Committee [*NATO*] (NATG)
SCEPrB........ South'n Cal Ed 4.08% Pfd [*AMEX symbol*] (TTSB)
SCEPrC........ South'n Cal Ed 4.24% Pfd [*AMEX symbol*] (TTSB)
SCEPrD........ So'n Cal Ed 4.32% cm Pfd [*AMEX symbol*] (TTSB)
SCEPrE........ South'n Cal Ed 4.78% Pfd [*AMEX symbol*] (TTSB)
SCEPrG........ South'n Cal Ed 5.80% Pfd [*AMEX symbol*] (TTSB)
SCEPrP........ South'n Cal Ed 7.36% Pfd [*AMEX symbol*] (TTSB)
SCEPS.......... Solar Cell Electric Power System (RDA)
SCEPS.......... Stored Chemical Energy Propulsion System
SCEPT.......... Syndicat Canadien des Employes Professionnels et Techniques (AC)
SCEPTR........ Suitcase Emergency Procedures Trainer (MCD)
Sceptre........ Sceptre Resources Ltd. [*Associated Press*] (SAG)
SCEPTRE...... Software-Controlled Electronic-Processing Traffic-Recording Equipment (PDAA)
SCEPTRE...... System Computerized for Economical Performance, Tracking, Recording and Evaluation [*North Central Airlines*]
SCEPTRE...... System for Circuit Evaluation and Prediction of Transient Radiation Effect (MCD)
SCEPTRE...... System for Constant Elevation Precipitation Transmission and Recording
SCEPTRON... Spectral Comparative Pattern Recognizer
SCE.Q.......... So Cal Edison 8.375%'QUIDS' [*AMEX symbol*] (TTSB)
SC Eq........... South Carolina Equity Reports [*A publication*] (DLA)
SCER........... Quintero [*Chile*] [*ICAO location identifier*] (ICLI)
SCER........... Sheffield Centre for Environmental Research [*British*] (CB)
SCER........... Societe Canadienne d'Etudes de la Renaissance [*Canadian Society for Renaissance Studies - CSRS*]
SCER........... Societe Canadienne pour l'Etude de la Religion [*Canadian Society for the Study of Religion - CSSR*]
SCER........... Standing Commission on Ecumenical Relations of the Episcopal Church (EA)
SCERGA....... Societe Canadienne d'Economie Rurale et Gestion Agricole [*Canadian Agricultural Economics and Farm Management Society - CAEFMS*]
SCERP.......... Stratospheric Cruise Emissions Reduction Program (DICI)
SCERT.......... System and Computer Evaluation Revision Technique
SCERT.......... Systems and Computers Evaluation and Review Technique [*Computer science*]
SCES............ State Cooperative Extension Service
SCES............ Successories, Inc. [*NASDAQ symbol*] (SAG)
SCESB.......... State Casual Employees Superannuation Board [*Victoria, Australia*]
SCESOM....... Service Canadien pour les Etudiants et les Stagiaires d'Outre-Mer
SCESWUN.... Standing Committee on the Economic and Social Work of the United Nations
SCET............ Scottish Council for Educational Technology (IID)
SCET............ Society of Civil Engineering Technicians [*British*] (DBA)
SCET............ Spacecraft Event Time
SCET............ Standing Committee on Education and Training (ACII)
SCETA.......... Societe de Controle et d'Exploitation de Transports Auxiliaires [*France*]
SCETV.......... South Carolina Educational Television [*Columbia*] [*Telecommunications*] (TSSD)
SCEU........... Selector Channel Emulation Unit
SCEU........... Selector Channel Emulator Unit (NITA)
SCEWA........ Society for Citizen Education in World Affairs [*Later, CEA*]
SCEZ............ Santiago [*Chile*] [*ICAO location identifier*] (ICLI)
SCF.............. Florence County Library, Florence, SC [*OCLC symbol*] (OCLC)
SCF.............. Phoenix [*Arizona*] Scottsdale [*Airport symbol*] (OAG)
SCF.............. Samoth Capital Corp. [*Toronto Stock Exchange symbol*]
SCF.............. Sampled Channel Filter
SCF.............. Satellite Control Facility [*Sunnyvale, CA*] [*NASA*]
SCF.............. Save the Children Federation (EA)
SCF.............. Save the Children Fund [*British*] (EAIO)
SCF.............. S-Band Composite Feed
SCF.............. Scandinavia Co. [*Formerly, Scandinavia Fund, Inc.*] [*AMEX symbol*] (SPSG)
SCF.............. Schedule Control File
SCF.............. Schematic Concept Formation
SCF.............. Scientific Committee for Food [*European union*]
SCF.............. Scientific Computing Facility
SCF.............. Scientific Computing Feature (NITA)
SCF.............. Secondary Checkpoint File
SCF.............. Sectional Center Facility [*Air Force*] (AFM)
SCF.............. Sectional Center Facility [*First three digits of the ZIP code*] [*US Postal Service*]
SCF.............. Self-Consistent Field [*Quantum mechanics*]
SCF.............. Senior Chaplain to the Forces [*British*]
SCF.............. Sequential Compatibility Firing [*Aerospace*]
SCF.............. Signature Characterization Facility (MCD)
SCF.............. Single Catastrophic Failure (AAG)
SCF.............. Single Cost Factor
SCF.............. Single Crystal Filament
SCF.............. Skin Cancer Foundation (EA)
SCF.............. Skywings AB [*Sweden ICAO designator*] (FAAC)
SCF.............. Slovak Catholic Federation (EA)
SCF.............. Small Company Fund [*Phillips and Drew Fund Management*] [*British*]
SCF.............. SNAP [*Systems for Nuclear Auxiliary Power*] Critical Facility (NRCH)
SCF.............. Sociedad Centroamericana de Farmacologia [*Central American Society of Pharmacology - CASP*] (EAIO)
SCF.............. Society of the Compassionate Friends [*Later, TCF*] (EA)
SCF.............. Sodium Cleaning Facility [*Nuclear energy*] (NRCH)
SCF.............. Solution Crystal Facility (SSD)
SCF.............. Spacecraft Checkout Facility
SCF.............. Spacecraft Control Facility [*NASA*] (MCD)
SCF.............. Spherical Cavity Flow
SCF.............. Spinning Continuous Filament
SCF.............. Spinning Crucible Furnace
SCF.............. Standard Cascade Form (IAA)
SCF.............. Standard Charge Factor (NASA)
SCF.............. Standard Cubic Foot
SCF.............. Station Code File
SCF.............. Statistical Collection File (NASA)
SCF.............. Steinbeck Center Foundation (EA)
SCF.............. Stem Cell Factor [*Genetics*]
SCF.............. Stress Concentration Factor (MCD)
SCF.............. Subchorionic Fibrin [*Obstetrics*]
SCF.............. Sunnyvale Control Facility [*California*] [*NASA*] (NASA)
SCF.............. Supercritical Fluid
SCF.............. Support Carrier Force
SCF.............. System Change Failure (SAA)
SCFA............ Antofagasta/Internacional Cerro Moreno [*Chile*] [*ICAO location identifier*] (ICLI)
SCFA............ Segmented Continuous Flow Analysis [*Analytical chemistry*]
SCFA............ Short-Chain Fatty Acids [*Biochemistry*]
SCFA............ Skin and Cancer Foundation of Australia
SCFA............ Slovak Catholic Federation of America [*Later, SCF*] (EA)
SCFB............ Swirling Circulating Fluidized Bed
SCFBC.......... Staged-Cascade Fluidized Bed Combustion
SCFBR.......... Steam-Cooled Fast Breeder Reactor [*Nuclear energy*]
SCFC............ Southern California Film Circuit [*Library network*]
SCFC............ Steve Cochran Fan Club (EA)
SCFCS.......... Standing Committee on the Free Circulation of Scientists [*International Council of Scientific Unions*]
SCFD............ Standard Cubic Feet per Day
S/CFDR........ Survivability/Crash Flight Data Recorder (MCD)
SCFE............ Slipped Capital Femoral Epiphysis [*Orthopedics*] (DAVI)
SCFE............ Supercritical Fluid Extraction [*Also, SFE*] [*Chemical engineering*]
SCFEL.......... Standard COMSEC [*Communications Security*] Facility Equipment List
SCFF............ Scotopic Critical Flicker Frequency [*Magnetic environment*]
SCFG............ Stochastic Context-Free Grammar (PDAA)
SCFGVPT..... Southern California Figure-Ground Visual Perception Test
SCFH............ Standard Cubic Feet per Hour (AAG)
SCFI............ Streptococcal Chemotactic Factor Inhibitor [*Immunochemistry*]
ScFI............. Florence County Library, Florence, SC [*Library symbol Library of Congress*] (LCLS)
SCFL............ Source Coupled FET Logic (NITA)
ScFIM.......... Francis Marion College, Florence, SC [*Library symbol Library of Congress*] (LCLS)
ScFIT........... Florence-Darlington Technical College Library, Florence, SC [*Library symbol Library of Congress*] (LCLS)
SCFM........... Porvenir/Capitan Fuentes Martinez [*Chile*] [*ICAO location identifier*] (ICLI)

SCFM.......... Scanforms, Inc. [*NASDAQ symbol*] (NQ)
SCFM.......... Standard Cubic Feet per Minute
SCFM.......... Subcarrier Frequency Modulation [*Telecommunications*] (TEL)
SCFMA......... Summer and Casual Furniture Manufacturers Association (EA)
scf/min......... Standard Cubic Feet per Minute (DAVI)
SCFMO......... Self-Consistent Field Molecular Orbital (OA)
SCFP.......... Science Career Facilitation Project [*National Science Foundation*]
SCFP.......... Syndicat Canadien de la Fonction Publique [*Canadian Union of Public Employees - CUPE*]
SCFPA......... Structural Cement-Fiber Products Association [*Defunct*] (EA)
SCFRS......... Surface Combatant Force Requirements Study [*Navy*] (DOMA)
SCFS.......... S-Band Composite Feed System
SCFS.......... Slip-Cast-Fused Silica (RDA)
SCFS.......... Standard Cubic Feet per Second (AAG)
SCFS.......... Subcarrier Frequency Shift (IAA)
SCFSEC........ Standing Committee of French-Speaking Ethnical Communities (EA)
SCFT.......... Futaleufu/Futaleufu [*Chile*] [*ICAO location identifier*] (ICLI)
SCFTS......... Small Card Final Test System (SAA)
SCFZ.......... Antofagasta [*Chile*] [*ICAO location identifier*] (ICLI)
SCG........... Air Force Geophysics Laboratory Research Library, Hanscom AFB, MA [*OCLC symbol*] (OCLC)
ScG........... Greenville County Library, Greenville, SC [*Library symbol Library of Congress*] (LCLS)
SCG........... SCANA Corp. [*NYSE symbol*] (SPSG)
SCG........... Scientific Computing Group [*University of Toronto*] [*Research center*] (RCD)
SCG........... Scoring (ADA)
SCG........... Screen Cartoonists Guild [*Defunct*] (EA)
SCG........... Search for Common Ground (EA)
SCG........... Security Classification Guide (AFM)
SCG........... Seismocardiography [*Medicine*]
SCG........... Self Changing Gear (DCTA)
SCG........... SEMMS [*Solar Electric Multiple-Mission Spacecraft*] Coordinating Group [*NASA*]
SCG........... Sequential Control Guidance (KSC)
SCG........... Serum Chemistry Graft (MAE)
SCG........... Shipcraft Guild (EA)
SCG........... Sight Current Generator
SCG........... Sigma Science [*Vancouver Stock Exchange symbol*]
SCG........... Sitra Cargo Systems [*Peru*] [*ICAO designator*] (FAAC)
SCG........... Sliding-Coil Gauge (RDA)
SCG........... Social Credit Group [*British*] (DAS)
SCG........... Societe Canadienne de Geotechnique [*Canadian Geotechnical Society*] (EAIO)
SCG........... Society of the Classic Guitar (EA)
SCG........... Sodium Cromoglycate [*Pharmacology*]
SCG........... Solution Crystal Growth
SCG........... Space and Communications Group [*of General Motors Corp.*]
SCG........... Space Charge Grid
SCG........... Special Consultative Group [*NATO*]
SCG........... Specialist Certificate in Gerontology (GAGS)
SCG........... Specification Control Group (IAA)
SCG........... St. Claude [*Guadeloupe*] [*Seismograph station code, US Geological Survey*] (SEIS)
SCG........... Steel Carriers Group [*Later, RDCC*] [*Defunct*] (EA)
SCG........... Stored Cold Gas
SCG........... Supercritical Gas Extraction
SCG........... Superior Cervical Ganglion [*Anatomy*]
ScGa.......... Cherokee County Public Library, Gaffney, SC [*Library symbol Library of Congress*] (LCLS)
SCGA.......... Sodium-Cooled Graphite Assembly [*Nuclear energy*]
SCGA.......... Southern Cotton Ginners Association (EA)
Sc Gael........ Scotch Gaelic [*Language*] (BARN)
ScGaL.......... Limestone College, Gaffney, SC [*Library symbol Library of Congress*] (LCLS)
SCGB.......... Ski Club of Great Britain (DI)
ScGBJ.......... Bob Jones University, Greenville, SC [*Library symbol Library of Congress*] (LCLS)
SCGC.......... Societe Canadienne de Genie Civil
SCGC.......... Society of Carnival Glass Collectors
SCGCh......... Societe Canadienne du Genie Chimique
SCGD.......... Specification Control Group Directive (KSC)
SCGDL......... Signal Corps General Development Laboratory [*Obsolete Army*]
SCGE.......... Sioux City Grain Exchange (EA)
SCGE.......... Societe Canadienne de Genie Electrique
SCGEI......... Societe Canadienne de Genie Electrique et Informatique [*Canadian Society for Electrical and Computer Engineering*] [*Canada*] (EAIO)
ScGeo......... Georgetown County Memorial Library, Georgetown SC [*Library symbol Library of Congress*] (LCLS)
ScGF.......... Furman University, Greenville, SC [*Library symbol Library of Congress*] (LCLS)
SCGGA......... Sonoma County Grape Growers Association (EA)
SCGI.......... Small College Goals Inventory [*Test*]
SCGM.......... Senior Cook General Mess [*British military*] (DMA)
SCGM.......... Societe Canadienne de Genie Mecanique
SCGMB......... Societe Canadienne de Genie Medical et Biologique
SCGN.......... SciGenetics, Inc. [*NASDAQ symbol*] (SAG)
SCGO.......... Strontium Chromium Gallium Oxide [*Inorganic chemistry*]
SCGP.......... Scrabble Crossword Game Players [*Later, NSA*] (EA)
SCGP.......... Self-Contained Guidance Package (AAG)
SCGR.......... Societe Canadienne du Genie Rural
SCGRL......... Signal Corps General Research Laboratory [*Military*] (IAA)
ScGrw......... Abbeville-Greenwood Regional Library, Greenwood, SC [*Library symbol Library of Congress*] (LCLS)
ScGrwL........ Lander College, Greenwood, SC [*Library symbol Library of Congress*] (LCLS)
ScGrwP........ Piedmont Technical College, Greenwood, SC [*Library symbol Library of Congress*] (LCLS)
SCGSA......... Signal Corps Ground Signal Agency [*Military*] (IAA)
SCGSS......... Signal Corps Ground Signal Service [*Obsolete Army*]
SCGSS......... Super-Critical Gas Storage System [*NASA*] (KSC)
SCGT.......... Stanford's Compendium of Geography and Travel [*A publication*]
ScGTC......... Greenville Technical College, Greenville, SC [*Library symbol*] [*Library of Congress*] (LCLS)
SCGZ.......... Puerto Williams/Guardia-Marina Zanartu [*Chile*] [*ICAO location identifier*] (ICLI)
SCH........... AFSC Technical Information Center, Washington, DC [*OCLC symbol*] (OCLC)
SCH........... Schedule (AAG)
Sch........... Schedule (ODBW)
SCH........... Schefferville [*Quebec*] [*Seismograph station code, US Geological Survey*] (SEIS)
SCH........... Scheme (ADA)
SCH........... Schenectady, NY [*Location identifier FAA*] (FAAL)
SCH........... Schering [*Italy*] [*Research code symbol*]
SCH........... Schering-Plough Corp. [*Research code symbol*]
SCH........... Schiller [*German poet, 1759-1805*] (ROG)
SCH........... Schilling [*Monetary unit*] [*Austria*]
Sch........... Schist [*Quality of the bottom*] [*Nautical charts*]
SCH........... Schoenaur Rifle
SCH........... Scholar
SCH........... Scholarship
SCH........... Scholium [*Note*] [*Latin*]
SCH........... School (AFM)
sch........... School (VRA)
SCH........... Schooner
SCH........... Schreiber Resources Ltd. [*Vancouver Stock Exchange symbol*]
SCH........... Schreiner Airways BV [*Netherlands ICAO designator*] (FAAC)
Sch........... Schultz Number
SCH........... Schwab [*Charles*] Corp. [*NYSE symbol*] (SPSG)
SCH........... Search (MCD)
SCH........... Sector Command Headquarters (SAA)
SCH........... Seizures per Circuit per Hour [*Telecommunications*] (TEL)
SCH........... Sequencer Chassis
SCH........... Shelter Complex Headquarters [*Civil Defense*]
SCH........... Sisters of Charity of St. Vincent de Paul, Halifax [*Roman Catholic religious order*]
SCH........... Societe Canadienne d'Hermeneutique [*Canadian Society for Hermeneutics - CSH*]
SCH........... Society for Calligraphy and Handwriting (EA)
SCH........... Society for Colonial History [*Defunct*] (EA)
SCh........... Society of Christ [*Roman Catholic men's religious order*]
sch........... Society of Christ (TOCD)
SCH........... Society of Classical Homeopathy [*Australia*]
SCH........... Socket Head (AAG)
SCH........... Sole Community Hospital
SCH........... Square Cartridge Heater
SCH........... Store Channel (SAA)
SCH........... Student Contact Hours (EDAC)
SCH........... Student Credit Hours
SCH........... Studia ad Corpus Hellenisticum Novi Testamenti (BJA)
SCh........... Succinylcholine [*Biochemistry*]
SCH........... Supporting Checkout
SCHA.......... Copiapo/Chamonate [*Chile*] [*ICAO location identifier*] (ICLI)
SCHA.......... St. Croix Hotel and Tourism Association [*Virgin Islands*] (EAIO)
ScHaC......... Coker College, Hartsville, SC [*Library symbol Library of Congress*] (LCLS)
Schalk......... Schalk's Jamaica Reports [*A publication*] (DLA)
Sch & Lef...... Schoales and Lefroy's Irish Chancery Reports [*A publication*] (DLA)
Sch Aq R....... Schultes' Aquatic Rights [*1811*] [*A publication*] (DLA)
Sch Arts....... School Arts [*A publication*] (BRI)
SCHASE........ Steeplechase
SCHAVMED...... School of Aviation Medicine [*Later, School of Aerospace Medicine*] (MCD)
Schawk........ Schawk, Inc. [*Formerly, Filtertek Inc.*] [*Associated Press*] (SAG)
SChB.......... Small Chemical Businesses [*American Chemical Society*]
Sch Bailm...... Schouler on Bailments [*A publication*] (DLA)
SC-HC......... Scattered-to-Heavy Clouds [*Meteorology*] (DNAB)
SCHC.......... Society of the Companions of the Holy Cross (EA)
SCHCR......... Stanford Center for Health Care Research [*Closed, 1978*]
SCHD.......... Scheduling
SCHDL......... Schedule (ECII)
Sch Dom Rel... Schouler on Domestic Relations [*A publication*] (DLA)
SCHE.......... Scheme (ROG)
SChE.......... Serum Cholinesterase [*An enzyme*]
SCHE.......... Societe Canadienne de l'Histoire de l'Eglise [*Canadian Society of Church History - CSCH*]
SCHEC......... Societe Canadienne de l'Histoire de l'Eglise Catholique [*Canadian Catholic History Association - CCHA*]
SCHED......... Schedule (KSC)
SCHEDE........ Schedule (ROG)
Scheib......... Scheib [*Earl*], Inc. [*Associated Press*] (SAG)
Scheif Pr...... Scheiffer's Practice [*A publication*] (DLA)
SCHEM......... Schematic
Scher.......... Scherer's New York Miscellaneous Reports [*22-47*] [*A publication*] (DLA)
Scherer........ Scherer [*R.P.*] Corp. [*Associated Press*] (SAG)
SCHERZ........ Scherzando [*Playful*] [*Music*]
SchfEx......... Scheffield Explorations [*Associated Press*] (SAG)

SchG........... Schiedsgericht [*Arbitration Court*] [*German*] (ILCA)
SCHG........... Supercharge
Sch H & W... Schouler on Husband and Wife [*A publication*] (DLA)
SchHi........... South Carolina Historical Society, Charleston, SC [*Library symbol Library of Congress*] (LCLS)
SCHIS.......... Schistocytes [*Hematology*] (DAVI)
SCHIZ.......... Schizophrenia [*Medicine*]
schizo.......... Schizophrenia [*Psychology*]
SCHJ........... Societe Canadienne de l'Histoire Juive [*Canadian Jewish Historical Association - CJHS*]
SCHL........... Court of Session Cases, House of Lords [*Scotland*] [*A publication*] (DLA)
SCHL........... Scholastic Corp. [*NASDAQ symbol*] (SAG)
SCHL........... School (WGA)
SCHL........... School
SC(HL)......... Sessions Cases (House of Lords) [*Legal*] [*British*]
SCHL........... Societe Canadienne d'Hypotheques et de Logement [*Central Mortgage and Housing Corp. - CMHC*]
SCHLA......... School for Latin America [*Military*] (AFM)
Sch Leg Rec... Schuylkill's Pennsylvania Legal Record [*A publication*] (DLA)
Sch Lib........ School Librarian [*A publication*] (BRI)
Schlmb........ Schlumberger Ltd. [*Associated Press*] (SAG)
Sch LR......... Schuylkill's Pennsylvania Legal Record [*A publication*] (DLA)
SCHLS......... Schluszsatz [*Finale*] [*Music*]
SCHLSHIP..... Schoolship [*Navy*] (NVT)
SCHLSHP..... Scholarship
SCHLT......... Searchlight (MSA)
Schltzk........ Schlotzskys, Inc. [*Associated Press*] (SAG)
schm........... Schematic (VRA)
SCHM........... Schematic (AAG)
Schm........... Schoolmaster [*Navy British*]
SCHM........... Societe Canadienne d'Histoire de la Medecine [*Canadian Society for the History of Medicine - CSHM*]
SchMau........ Schweitzer Mauduit International Inc. [*Associated Press*] (SAG)
SCHMC......... Society of Catering and Hotel Management Consultants [*British*] (DBA)
Schm Civil Law... Schmidt's Civil Law of Spain and Mexico [*A publication*] (DLA)
Schm Exp...... Schmitthoff. Export Trade [*A publication*] (ILCA)
Schmidt Civ Law... Schmidt's Civil Law of Spain and Mexico [*A publication*] (DLA)
SCHMILSCIO... School of Military Sciences Officer [*Air Force*]
Schmitt........ Schmitt Industries, Inc. [*Associated Press*] (SAG)
Schm LJ....... Schmidt's Law Journal [*New Orleans*] [*A publication*] (DLA)
SCHMOO...... Space Cargo Handler and Manipulator for Orbital Operations
SCHMR......... Schoolmaster (ROG)
Sch Mus B... Bachelor of School Music
SCHN........... Schnitzer Steel Ind'A' [*NASDAQ symbol*] (TTSB)
SCHN........... Schnitzer Steel Industries, Inc. [*NASDAQ symbol*] (SAG)
Schnitzr....... Schnitzer Steel Industries, Inc. [*Associated Press*] (SAG)
SCHO........... Scholar [*or Scholarship*] (ROG)
SCHO........... Societe Canadienne d'Histoire Orale [*Canadian Oral History Association - COHA*]
SCHO........... Standard Controlled Heteroydne Oscillator
Schoales & L... Schoales and Lefroy's Irish Chancery Reports [*A publication*] (DLA)
Schol........... Scholar
SCHOL......... Scholarship
Schol........... Scholia [*Classical studies*] (OCD)
Schol........... Scholiast [*Classical studies*] (OCD)
SCHOL......... Scholium [*Note*] [*Latin*] (ROG)
SCHOLAR.... Schering-Oriented Literature Analysis and Retrieval System [*Schering-Plough Corp.*] [*Information service or system*] (IID)
Schol Bern... Scholia Bernensia ad Vergilii Bucolica et Georgica [*A publication*] (OCD)
Schol Bob.... Scholia Bobiensia [*Classical studies*] (OCD)
ScholCp....... Scholastic Corp. [*Associated Press*] (SAG)
Schol Cruq... Scholia Cruquiana [*Classical studies*] (OCD)
Schol Flor Callim... Scholia Florentina in Callimachum [*Classical studies*] (OCD)
Schomberg Mar Laws Rhodes... Schomberg's Treatise on the Maritime Laws of Rhodes [*A publication*] (DLA)
School Libs Aust... School Libraries in Australia [*A publication*]
School L Rep (Nat'l Org on Legal Probs in Educ)... School Law Reporter. National Organization on Legal Problems in Education [*A publication*] (DLA)
School of Advanced Studies Rev... School of Advanced International Studies. Review [*A publication*] (DLA)
School of LR... School of Law. Review. Toronto University [*Canada*] [*A publication*] (DLA)
Schouler Bailm... Schouler on Bailments [*A publication*] (DLA)
Schouler Dom Rel... Schouler on Domestic Relations [*A publication*] (DLA)
Schouler Pers Prop... Schouler on the Law of Personal Property [*A publication*] (DLA)
Schouler US Hist... Schouler's History of the United States under the Constitution [*A publication*] (DLA)
SchP........... Ordo Clericorum Regularium Pauperum Matris Dei Scholarum Piarum [*Roman Catholic men's religious order*]
schp............ Piarist Fathers (TOCD)
SchP........... Piarist Fathers (TOCD)
SchP........... Sisters of the Pious Schools (TOCD)
Sch Per Prop... Schouler on the Law of Personal Property [*A publication*] (DLA)
SCHPM........ Societe Canadienne d'Histoire et de Philosophie des Mathematiques [*Canadian Society for the History and Philosophy of Mathematics - CSHPM*]
SCHPS......... Societe Canadienne d'Histoire et de Philosophie des Sciences [*Canadian Society for the History and Philosophy of Science - CSHPS*]
SCHR........... Cochrane/Cochrane [*Chile*] [*ICAO location identifier*] (ICLI)
SCHR........... Scherer Healthcare [*NASDAQ symbol*] (TTSB)
SCHR........... Scherer Healthcare, Inc. [*NASDAQ symbol*] (CTT)
SCHR........... Schooner
SCHR........... Societe Canadienne d'Histoire de la Rhetorique [*See also CSHR*] [*Canada*]
SCHR........... Supervisory Change Relations Test
Sch Reg....... Schuylkill's Pennsylvania Register [*A publication*] (DLA)
SchrHl......... Scherer Healthcare, Inc. [*Associated Press*] (SAG)
SchroAsn..... Schroder Asian Growth [*Associated Press*] (SAG)
SchrPl......... Schering-Plough Corp. [*Associated Press*] (SAG)
SCHRUB...... Schmidt Rubin Rifle
SCHS........... School Squadron [*Air Force*]
SCHS........... Scottish Church History Society (EAIO)
SCHS........... Small Component Handling System [*Nuclear energy*] (NRCH)
SCHS........... Supreme Court Historical Society (EA)
SCHSIS........ South Carolina Handicapped Services Information System (EDAC)
schst........... Schist (VRA)
Schuler........ Schuler Homes, Inc. [*Associated Press*] (SAG)
Schuller....... Schuller Corp. [*Associated Press*] (SAG)
Schullr........ Schuller Corp. [*Associated Press*] (SAG)
Schulmn...... Schulman [*A.*], Inc. [*Associated Press*] (SAG)
Schult.......... Schult Homes Corp. [*Associated Press*] (SAG)
Schultz........ Schultz Sav-O-Stores, Inc. [*Associated Press*] (SAG)
Schupo......... Schutzpolizist [*Policeman*] [*German*]
Schuy Leg Rec (PA)... Schuylkill's Pennsylvania Legal Record [*A publication*] (DLA)
Schuyl Legal Rec... Schuylkill's Pennsylvania Legal Record [*A publication*] (DLA)
Schuyl Leg Rec... Schuylkill's Pennsylvania Legal Record [*A publication*] (DLA)
Schuyl Leg Reg... Schuylkill's Legal Register [*Pennsylvania*] [*A publication*] (ILCA)
Schuy Reg (PA)... Schuylkill's Pennsylvania Register [*A publication*] (DLA)
Schwab........ Schwab [*Charles*] Corp. [*Associated Press*] (SAG)
Schwarz Int L... Schwarzenberger's Manual of International Law [*A publication*] (DLA)
Schwarz Man Int L... Schwarzenberger's Manual of International Law [*A publication*] (ILCA)
Schweiz Jb f Internat Recht... Schweizerisches Jahrbuch fuer Internationales Recht/Annuaire Suisse de Droit In ternational [*Zurich, Switzerland*] [*A publication*] (DLA)
Schweiz Z f Strafrecht... Schweizerische Zeitschrift fuer Strafrecht/Revue Penale Suisse [*Berne, Switzerland*] [*A publication*] (DLA)
SCHWR........ Steam-Cooled Heavy-Water Reactor
Schwtz......... Schwitzer, Inc. [*Associated Press*] (SAG)
SCI.............. Council for the Securities Industry [*Levy*] [*British*]
SCI.............. Sacra Congregatio Indicis [*Sacred Congregation of the Index*] [*Latin*]
SCI.............. Safari Club International (EA)
SCI.............. San Clemente Island [*California*] [*Seismograph station code, US Geological Survey*] (SEIS)
SCI.............. Sand Collectors International (EAIO)
SCI.............. Santa Cruz Island (MUGU)
SCI.............. Savio Club International [*Defunct*] (EA)
SCI.............. Scale (ECII)
SCI.............. Scaleable Coherent Interface [*Computer science*]
SCI.............. Schedule-Cost Index (MCD)
SCI.............. Science (AFM)
SCI.............. Science
Sci.............. Science [*A publication*] (BRI)
SCI.............. Science Curriculum Improvement [*Study*] [*Education*]
SCI.............. Science of Creative Intelligence [*Transcendental meditation*]
SCI.............. Scientific Computers, Inc. (MCD)
SCI.............. SCI Satellite Conferencing International Corp. [*Formerly, Valclair Resources, Ltd.*] [*Vancouver Stock Exchange symbol*]
SCI.............. Seabee Club International (EA)
SCI.............. Sea Containers Inc. [*Steamship*] (MHDW)
SCI.............. Sealable Coherent Interface [*Computer science*]
SCI.............. Seamen's Church Institute of New York/New Jersey (EA)
SCI.............. Security Container Institute [*Defunct*] (EA)
SCI.............. Selected Configured Item (MCD)
SCI.............. Seminar Clearinghouse International, Inc. [*Information service or system*] (IID)
SCI.............. Sensitive Compartmented Information [*Military*]
SCI.............. Sequential Comparison Index [*Measures effect of chemical pollution in lakes and streams*]
SCI.............. Serial Communication Interface [*Computer science*]
SCI.............. Service Change Information (MCD)
SCI.............. Service Civil International [*Australia*]
SCI.............. Service Civil International [*International Voluntary Service*] [*India*]
SCI.............. SES [*Shuttle Engineering System*] Cockpit Interface [*NASA*] (SSD)
SCI.............. Sexual Communications Inventory [*Marital relations test*] [*Psychology*]
SCI.............. Ship Controlled Intercept [*RADAR*] [*Navy*]
SCI.............. Shipping Container Institute
SCI.............. Shipping Corp. of India Ltd.
SCI.............. Ship's Capability Impaired [*Navy*]
SCI.............. Short Circuit
SCI.............. Signal Corps Item [*Obsolete Army*] (NATG)
SCI.............. Simulation Councils, Inc.
SCI.............. Single-Channel Interface [*Computer science*]
SCI.............. Single Column Inch (ADA)
SCI.............. Sister Cities International (EA)
SCI.............. Slot Cell Inserter
SCI.............. Small Craft Instructor [*Red Cross*]
SCI.............. Smoke Curtain Installation [*British military*] (DMA)
SCI.............. Societe de Chimie Industrielle (EA)
SCI.............. Society of Chemical Industries (NADA)

SCI.............. Society of Chemical Industry (EA)
SCI.............. Society of Composers (EA)
SCI.............. Society of Computer Intelligence (IAA)
SCI.............. Society of the Chemical Industry (NADA)
SCI.............. Soft Cast Iron
SCI.............. Software Configuration Item [*Computer science*]
SCI.............. Source Code Indicator (MCD)
SCI.............. Special Cargo Airlines [*Russian Federation*] [*ICAO designator*] (FAAC)
SCI.............. Special Compartmented Intelligence [*DoD*] (MCD)
SCI.............. Special Control Item [*Code*]
SCI.............. Special Customs Invoice
SCI.............. Spinal Cord Injury [*Medicine*]
SCI.............. Spinal Cord-Insured (MCD)
SCI.............. Sponge and Chamois Institute (EA)
SCI.............. Staging Connections, Inc. [*Telecommunications service*] (TSSD)
SCI.............. Stampe Club International (EA)
SCI.............. Steel Construction Institute [*British*] (IRUK)
SCI.............. Stein Collectors International (EA)
SCI.............. Stem Cell Inhibitor [*Cytology*]
SCI.............. Stratospheric Circulation Index [*Geophysics*]
SCI.............. Stroke Club International (EA)
SCI.............. Structured Clinical Interview
SCI.............. Supervisor Call Instruction (IAA)
SCI.............. Supervisory Cost Inspector [*Navy*]
SCI.............. Switch Closure In (MCD)
SCI.............. Switched Collector Impedance [*Electronics*] (OA)
SCI.............. System Control Interface
SCIA............ Signal Corps Intelligence Agency [*Obsolete Army*]
SCIA............ Simultaneous Converging Instrument Approaches [*FAA*] (TAG)
SCIA............ Smart Card Industry Association (EA)
SCIA............ Social Competence Inventory for Adults [*Psychology*]
SCIA............ Society of Chief Inspectors and Advisers [*British*] (AIE)
SCIA............ Systems Change Impact Analysis [*Social Security Administration*]
SCIAPS........ Senate Comprehensive Integrated Automated Printing System
SCIAS.......... Society of Chemical Industry, American Section (EA)
SCIAS.......... Supreme Council of the Independent Associated Spiritualists [*Defunct*] (EA)
SciAtl.......... Scientific-Atlanta, Inc. [*Associated Press*] (SAG)
SCIATS........ Small Craft Instruction and Training School [*Navy*]
SCIB............ Ship Characteristics Improvement Board [*Navy*] (DOMA)
SCIB............ Significant Counterintelligence Briefs (AFM)
SCIBP.......... Special Committee for the International Biological Program [*National Research Council*]
SCIC............ Curico/General Freire [*Chile*] [*ICAO location identifier*] (ICLI)
SCIC............ Secretariat des Conferences Intergouvernementales Canadiennes
SCIC............ Semiconductor Integrated Circuit
SCIC............ Single-Column Ion Chromatography
SCIC............ Sisters of Charity of the Immaculate Conception of Ivrea (TOCD)
SCIC............ Special Control Item Code
SCICC.......... Service Center Internal Computer Code [*Computer science*]
SCICF.......... Safari Club International Conservation Fund (EA)
SCICFNDT.... Standing Committee for International Cooperation within the Field of Non-Destructive Testing (EA)
SciClone...... SciClone Pharmaceuticals, Inc. [*Associated Press*] (SAG)
SCICLOPS.... Systems Control, Incorporated Computerized Library Operations [*Information service or system*] (IID)
SCICS.......... Spinal Cord Injury Care System [*University of Alabama in Birmingham*] [*Research center*] (RCD)
Sci D........... Doctor of Science
SCID............ Severe Combined Immune Deficiency [*Immunology*]
SCID............ Small Column Insulated Delays (MCD)
SCID............ Structured Clinical Interview for DSM-III
SCID............ Subcommutator Identification [*NASA*]
SciDCom...... Doctor of Science in Commerce (NADA)
SCIDE.......... Servicio Cooperative Interamericano de Educacion
SciDMet....... Doctor of Science in Metallurgy (NADA)
SCIDNT........ System Control Incorporated Identification Program [*Navy*]
SCIDS.......... Small Container Intermodal Distribution System (PDAA)
SciDyn......... Science Dynamics Corp. [*Associated Press*] (SAG)
SCIE............ Concepcion/Carriel Sur [*Chile*] [*ICAO location identifier*] (ICLI)
SCIE............ Stolen Children Information Exchange (EA)
SCIEC.......... Southern California Industry-Education Council (SAA)
SCIENCE...... Stimulation des Cooperations Internationaux et des Echanges Necessaires aux Chercheurs Europeennes [*Stimulation of International Cooperation and the Necessary Exchanges of European Scientists*] [*EEC*]
SCIENT........ Scientific
SCIF............ Daughters of the Sacred Heart of Jesus [*Bethlehemite Sisters*] [*Roman Catholic religious order*]
SciF............ Science Foods, Inc. [*Associated Press*] (SAG)
SCIF............ Sound and Communications Industries Federation [*British*] (DBA)
SCIF............ Special Compartmented Intelligence Facility [*DoD*]
SCIF............ Static Column Isoelectric Focusing [*Materials processing*]
SCIF............ Systems Certification and Integration Facility
SCI FA......... Scire Facias [*Please make known*] [*A writ to enforce, annul, or vacate a judgment, patent, charter or other matter of record*] [*Legal term*] [*Latin*]
SCI FA......... Scire Facias [*Make Him Know*] [*Latin*] (LWAP)
Sci Fa ad Dis Deb... Scire Facias ad Disprobandum Debitum [*Latin*] (DLA)
SCIFC.......... Sandy Croft International Fan Club [*Defunct*] (EA)
SCI-FI.......... Science Fiction [*Also, SF*]
SCI Fn......... SCI Finance LLC, Inc. [*Associated Press*] (SAG)
Sci Freedom... Science and Freedom [*A publication*]
SciGen......... SciGenetics, Inc. [*Associated Press*] (SAG)
SciGm.......... Scientific Games Holding Corp. [*Associated Press*] (SAG)
SCIGY.......... Special Committee for the International Geophysical Year
SCIH............ Societe Canadienne de l'Heritage Industriel (AC)
SCIH............ Societe Canadienne d'Ingenierie Hospitaliere
SCII............. Strong-Campbell Interest Inventory [*Vocational guidance*]
SCII............. Strong-Campbell Interest Inventory (DMAA)
SCIIA........... Sudden Changes in the Integrated Intensity of Atmospherics (PDAA)
SCI-IVS........ SCI-International Voluntary Service (EA)
SCIL............. Scilicet [*Namely*] [*Legal term Latin*]
SCIL............. Selected Configuration Item List (MCD)
SCIL............. Ship's Construction Item List (MCD)
SCIL............. Soft Consumable Item List
SCIL............. Support Center International Logistics [*Army*]
SCILL........... Southern California Interlibrary Loan Project [*Library network*]
SCIM............ Congregation des Soeurs Servantes du Coeur Immaculae de Marie [*Servants of the Immaculate Heart of Mary*] [*Good Shepherd Sisters*] [*Roman Catholic religious order*]
SCIM............ Savage's Cognitive Impairment Model
SCIM............ Selected Categories in Microfiche [*National Technical Information Service*]
SCIM............ Silicon Coating by Inverted Meniscus (PDAA)
SCIM............ Speech Communications Index Meter
SCIM............ Standard Cubic Inches per Minute (AAG)
SCIM............ Subject Codes for Intelligence Management (MCD)
SCIMITAR.... System for Countering Interdiction Missiles and Targets RADARs (MCD)
SCIMP.......... Selective Cooperative Indexing of Management Periodicals [*Database*] [*European Business School Librarians Group*] [*Information service or system*] (CRD)
SCIMP.......... Self-Contained Imaging Micro-Profiler [*Instrumentation*]
SCIMPEX..... Syndicat des Commercants Importateurs et Exportateurs de l'Ouest African [*Union of Commercial Importers and Exporters of West Africa*]
SCIN............ Self-Canceling Installment Note
SC in Banco... Supreme Court in Banco [*Canada*] [*A publication*] (DLA)
SCINS.......... Self-Contained Inertial Navigation System (DOMA)
SCINSET...... Scottish Colleges In-Service Education of Teachers (AIE)
SCINT.......... Scintillator [*Nucleonics*]
SCIO............ Scios Inc. [*NASDAQ symbol*] (TTSB)
SCIO............ Scios, Inc. [*NASDAQ symbol*] (SAG)
SCIO............ Scios Nova, Inc. [*NASDAQ symbol*] (SPSG)
SCIO............ Staff Counterintelligence Officer [*Military*] (NVT)
SCIOP.......... Social Competence Inventory for Older Persons [*Psychology*]
Scios........... Scios, Inc. [*Associated Press*] (SAG)
Scios........... Scios Nova, Inc. [*Associated Press*] (SAG)
SciosNov...... Scios Nova, Inc. [*Associated Press*] (SAG)
SCIOZ.......... Scios Inc. Wrrt'D' [*NASDAQ symbol*] (TTSB)
SCIP............ Isla De Pascua/Mataveri [*Easter Island*] [*Chile*] [*ICAO location identifier*] (ICLI)
SCIP............ Sampling Close to the Injector
SCIP............ Scanning for Information Parameters
SCIP............ School Curriculum Industry Partnership [*British*] (ECON)
SCIP............ Sea Counterinfiltration Patrol (CINC)
SCIP............ Self-Contained Instrument Package (KSC)
SCIP............ Ship's Capability Impaired for Lack of Parts [*Navy*]
SCIP............ Society of Competitor Intelligence Professionals (EA)
SCIP............ Solid Cast Iron Propeller (DS)
SCIP............ Special Crisis Intervention Program (OICC)
SCIP............ Stanford Center for Information Processing [*Stanford University*] [*Later, CIT*]
SCIP............ Stanford Computer Industry Project
SCIP............ System Control Interface Package [*Computer science*] (MHDI)
SCIPHE........ Sparkman Centre for International Public Health Education (AIE)
SCIPIO......... Sales Catalog Index Project Input On-Line [*Cleveland Museum of Art*] [*Information service or system*] (IID)
SCIPMIS...... Standard Civilian Personnel Management Information System [*Army*]
SCIPP.......... Sacrococcygeal to Inferior Pubic Point [*Anatomy*] (MAE)
SCIPP.......... Santa Cruz Institute for Particle Physics [*University of California, Santa Cruz*] [*Research center*] (RCD)
SCIPP.......... Silicon-Computing Instrument Patch-Programmed (SAA)
SCIPP.......... Silicon Computing Instrument, Patch Programmed (IAA)
SCIPPY........ Social Competence Intervention Package for Preschool Youngsters (EDAC)
SCIR............ Society of Cardiovascular and Interventional Radiology (EA)
SCIR............ Subsystem Capability Impact Reporting [*Military*] (NVT)
SCIRA.......... Snipe Class International Racing Association (EA)
SCIRA.......... Stable Carbon Isotope Ratio Analysis [*For determining material source*]
SCIRA.......... State Central Information Reception Agency
SCIRC.......... Spinal Cord Injury Research Center [*Ohio State University*] [*Research center*] (RCD)
SCIRP.......... Semiconductor Infrared Photography (PDAA)
SCIRT.......... Supplier Capability Information Retrieval Technique (PDAA)
SCIS............ Safety Containment Isolation System (IEEE)
SCIS............ Science Curriculum Improvement Study [*Education*]
SCIS............ SCI Systems [*NASDAQ symbol*] (TTSB)
SCIS............ SCI Systems, Inc. [*NASDAQ symbol*] (NQ)
SC Is........... Selected Judgments of the Supreme Court of Israel [*A publication*] (DLA)
SCIS............ Spacecraft Interface Specification (MCD)
SCIS............ Spinal Cord Injury Service [*Medicine*]
SCIS............ Standard Cubic Inches per Second (NASA)
SCIS............ Survivable Communications Integration System
SCISCM........ Single Carrier Initiated Single Carrier Multiplication (MCD)
SCISD.......... Signal Corps Intermediate Supply Deport [*Army*] (IAA)

SCISEARCH... Science Citation Index Search [*Institute for Scientific Information*] [*Philadelphia, PA Bibliographic database*]
SCISO.......... Supreme Court, Individual Slip Opinions
SCISOR........ System for Conceptual Information Summarization, Organization, and Retrieval [*Software package*] (IT)
SCI/SR......... Shakaichosa-Kenkyusho Consumer Index Summary Report [*Marketing Intelligence Corp.*] [*Japan Information service or system*] (CRD)
SCISR.......... Societe Canadienne des Infirmieres en Sante Respiratoire (AC)
SCISRS........ Sigma Center Information Storage and Retrieval System
SCI Sys........ SCI Systems, Inc. [*Associated Press*] (SAG)
SCIT............ Small Craft Instructor Trainer [*Red Cross*]
SCIT............ Smaller Companies International Trust [*British*]
SCIT............ Special Commissions of Income Tax [*British*]
SCIT............ Standard Change Integration and Tracking (NASA)
SCIT............ Standardization Control of Industry Quality Tools [*Military*] (INF)
SCIT............ Storm Cell Identification and Tracking [*Algorithm*] (USDC)
SCIT............ Storm Cell Identification and Tracking [*Algorithm*] [*Marine science*] (OSRA)
SCIT............ Subcommittee on Interzonal Trade [*Allied German Occupation Forces*]
SciTch......... Scientific Technology, Inc. [*Associated Press*] (SAG)
SCITEC........ [*The*] Association of the Scientific, Engineering, and Technological Community of Canada
SciTech........ SciTech Book News [*A publication*] (BRI)
SCITEC-PAC... Science and Technology Political Action Committee (EA)
SCITEF......... Software and Interoperability Test Facility [*Fort Huachuca, AZ*] [*United States Army Electronic Proving Ground*] (GRD)
Scitex.......... Scitex Corp. Ltd. [*Associated Press*] (SAG)
SCIU............ SDPC [*Shuttle Data Processing Complex*] Configuration/Isolation Unit [*NASA*]
SCIU............ Selector Control Interface Unit (MCD)
SCIU............ Spacecraft Interface Unit (NASA)
SCI-USA....... Service Civil International - United States of America (EA)
SCIV............ Subclavian Intravenous Injection [*Medicine*]
SCIV............ Subcutaneous Intravenous [*Medicine*] (DMAA)
SCIWE......... Synthesis Center of the Institute for Wholistic Education (EA)
SCIX............ Scitex Corp. Ltd. [*NASDAQ symbol*] (NQ)
SCIX............ Signal Conditioning Index (ECII)
SCIXF.......... Scitex Corp. Ord [*NASDAQ symbol*] (TTSB)
SCIZ............ Isla De Pascua [*Easter Island*] [*Chile*] [*ICAO location identifier*] (ICLI)
scj.............. Congregation of the Priests of the Sacred Heart of Jesus (TOCD)
SCJ............. Congregatio Sacerdotum a Corde Jesu [*Congregation of the Priests of the Sacred Heart of Jesus*] [*Roman Catholic religious order*]
SC J............ Nebraska Supreme Court Journal [*A publication*] (DLA)
SCJ............. Scanjet AB [*Sweden ICAO designator*] (FAAC)
SCJ............. Science Council of Japan (MCD)
SCJ............. Sclerocorneal Junction [*Ophthalmology*] (DAVI)
SCJ............. Section of Criminal Justice [*American Bar Association*] (EA)
SC(J)........... Sessions Cases (Judiciary Reports) [*Legal*] [*British*]
SCJ............. Shaped Charge Jet (MCD)
SCJ............. Sisters of the Child Jesus [*Roman Catholic religious order*]
SCJ............. Society for Collegiate Journalists (EA)
SCJ............. Spertus College of Judaica [*Chicago, IL*] (BJA)
SCJ............. Squamocolumnar Junction [*Medicine*] (MAE)
SCJ............. Sternoclavicular Joints [*Anatomy*] (DAVI)
SCJ............. Stretch Chuck Jaws (MCD)
SCJ............. Super Cobra Jet [*Automotive engineering*]
SC J............ Supreme Court Journal [*India*] [*A publication*] (DLA)
SCJ............. Supreme Court of Justice [*British*] (ROG)
SCJA........... Senior Conformation Judges Association (EA)
SCJAEF........ Senior Conformation Judges Association Education Fund (EA)
SCJB........... Jamaica Supreme Court Judgment Books [*A publication*] (DLA)
SCJC........... Saint Catharine Junior College [*Kentucky*]
SCJM........... Sisters of Charity of Jesus and Mary [*See also ZLJM*] [*Belgium*] (EAIO)
SCJO........... Osborno/Canal Bajo [*Chile*] [*ICAO location identifier*] (ICLI)
SCJS........... Seminary College of Jewish Studies (BJA)
Sc Jur......... Scottish Jurist [*A publication*] (DLA)
SCK............. Air Force Weapons Laboratory, Kirtland AFB, NM [*OCLC symbol*] (OCLC)
SCK............. Air Sinclair Ltd. [*British ICAO designator*] (FAAC)
s-ck--.......... Colombia [*MARC geographic area code Library of Congress*] (LCCP)
SCK............. SC Bancorp [*AMEX symbol*] (SPSG)
SCK............. Serum Creatine Kinase [*An enzyme*]
SCK............. Set Clock (IAA)
SCK............. Sisters of Christ the King [*Roman Catholic religious order*]
SCK............. Stockton [*California*] [*Airport symbol*] (OAG)
SCK............. Stockton, CA [*Location identifier FAA*] (FAAL)
SCK............. Studiecentrum voor Kernenergie [*Also, CEEN, NERC*] [*Center for Nuclear Energy Studies*] [*Belgium*] (NRCH)
ScK............. Williamsburg County Library, Kingstree, SC [*Library symbol*] [*Library of Congress*] (LCLS)
SCKD........... Society of Certified Kitchen Designers (EA)
SCKLS......... South Central Kansas Library System [*Library network*]
SCKSJ.......... Supreme Commandery Knights of St. John (EA)
SCKT........... Socket Communications [*NASDAQ symbol*] (TTSB)
SCKT........... Socket Communications, Inc. [*NASDAQ symbol*] (SAG)
SCKTPT........ Southern California Kinesthesia and Tactile Perception Tests
SCKTW......... Socket Communications Wrrt [*NASDAQ symbol*] (TTSB)
ScKW........... Williamsburg Technical College, Kingstree, SC [*Library symbol Library of Congress*] (LCLS)
s-cl--.......... Chile [*MARC geographic area code Library of Congress*] (LCCP)
SCL............. Great Falls, MT [*Location identifier FAA*] (FAAL)
SCL............. Santa Clara - Ricard [*California*] [*Seismograph station code, US Geological Survey Closed*] (SEIS)
SCL............. Santiago [*Chile*] [*Airport symbol*] (OAG)
SCL............. Save a Cat League (EA)
SCL............. Scale
SCL............. Scarlet (ROG)
SCL............. Scleroderma [*Medicine*] (DAVI)
SCL............. Scottish Central Library (PDAA)
SCL............. Scrap Classification List [*DoD*]
scl.............. Scroll (VRA)
Scl............. Sculptor [*Constellation*]
SCL............. Seaboard Coast Line Railroad Co. [*Subsidiary of Seaboard Coast Line Industries*] [*Later, CSX Corp.*] [*AAR code*]
SCL............. Secondary Coolant Line [*or Loop*] [*NASA*] (NASA)
SCL............. Select Cases in Chancery Tempore King [*25 English Reprint*] [*1724-33*] [*A publication*] (DLA)
SCL............. Selectively Cross Linked
SCL............. Semiconductor Complex, Ltd. [*Commercial firm*] [*India*]
SCL............. Senior Citizens League [*Defunct*] (EA)
SCL............. Sequential Control Logic
SCL............. Serum Cholesterol Level [*Clinical chemistry*] (OA)
SCL............. Serum Copper Level [*Clinical chemistry*] (AAMN)
SCL............. Service Control Layer [*Computer science*]
SCL............. Shaped Charge Liner
SCL............. Shaw Cablesystems Ltd. [*Toronto Stock Exchange symbol*]
SCL............. Ship Configuration List [*Navy*] (CAAL)
SCL............. Signal Corps Laboratory [*Obsolete Army*]
SCL............. Signal Corps Letter (MCD)
SCL............. Simmons College, Boston, MA [*OCLC symbol*] (OCLC)
SCL............. Single Channel Monitoring (NITA)
SCL............. Single Composition Lathe-Cut [*Dental alloy*]
SCL............. Sinus Cycle Length [*Cardiology*]
SCL............. Sisters of Charity (of Leavenworth) [*Roman Catholic religious order*]
SCL............. Site Concurrence Letter (AFM)
SCL............. Skin Conductance Level [*Physiology*]
SCL............. Social
SCL............. Society for Caribbean Linguistics [*St. Augustine, Trinidad*] (EAIO)
SCL............. Society for Computers and Law [*Abingdon, Oxfordshire, England*] (EAIO)
SCL............. Society of Construction Law [*British*] (DBA)
SCL............. Society of County Librarians [*British*]
SCL............. Sofati Container Line [*Shipping line*]
SCL............. Soft Contact Lens
SCL............. Software Career Link [*Database producer*] [*Burlington, MA*]
SCL............. Sola International, Inc. [*NYSE symbol*] (SAG)
SCL............. South Carolina Law Reports [*Pre-1868*] [*A publication*] (DLA)
SCL............. South Central Regional Library System [*UTLAS symbol*]
SCL............. Southeastern Composers' League (EA)
SCL............. Southern Copper Ltd. [*Commercial firm Australia*]
SCL............. Space Charge Limited
SCL............. Space Component Lifetime (SSD)
SCL............. Specification Change Log [*NASA*] (NASA)
SCL............. Spontaneous Cycle Length
SCL............. Standard Chartered Leasing (NITA)
SCL............. Standard Classification List [*Military*]
SCL............. Standard Conventional Load
SCL............. Static Complementary Logic (ECII)
SCL............. St. Cloud [*Diocesan abbreviation*] [*Minnesota*] (TOCD)
SCL............. Stem Cell Leukaemia [*Hematology*]
SCL............. Stepan Chemical Co. [*AMEX symbol*] (SPSG)
SCL............. Stepan Co. [*NYSE symbol*] (TTSB)
SCL............. Stock Corporation Law [*A publication*] (DLA)
SCL............. String Control Language [*Computer science*]
SCL............. Student of the Civil Law
SCL............. Super Chevys Limited [*Defunct*] (EA)
SCL............. Supervisory Control Language [*Computer science*] (MHDI)
SCL............. Swiftair Cargo Ltd. [*Canada ICAO designator*] (FAAC)
SCL............. Switch-to-Computer Link (CDE)
SCL............. Symbolic Correction Loader
SCL............. Symmetric Clipper
SCL............. Symphony Command Language [*Computer science*]
SCL............. Symptom Checklist [*Medicine*] (DMAA)
SCL............. Synthetic Combinatorial Library [*Biochemistry*]
SCL............. System Command Language [*Computer science*]
SCL............. Systems Component List (KSC)
SCL............. Systems Control Language [*Computer science*]
Sc LA.......... Left Scapuloanterior Position [*of the fetus*] [*Obstetrics*]
SCLA........... Section Carry Look Ahead (MHDB)
ScLan.......... Lancaster County Library, Lancaster, SC [*Library symbol*] [*Library of Congress*] (LCLS)
ScLangU...... United Merchants Research Center, Langley, SC [*Library symbol Library of Congress*] (LCLS)
Sc La R....... Scottish Land Court Reports [*Supplement to Scottish Law Review*] [*A publication*] (DLA)
Sc La Rep... Report by the Scottish Land Court [*A publication*] (DLA)
Sc La Rep Ap... Appendices to the Report of the Scottish Land Court [*A publication*] (DLA)
Sc La Rep App... Appendices to the Report of the Scottish Land Court [*A publication*] (DLA)
ScLat.......... Dillon County Library, Latta, SC [*Library symbol*] [*Library of Congress*] (LCLS)
SCLAT......... Service Central de la Lutte Anti-terroriste [*Central Anti-Terrorist Service*] [*France*] (ECON)
ScLau.......... Laurens County Library, Laurens, SC [*Library symbol Library of Congress*] (LCLS)

SCLAV .... Sclavonic [*Language, etc.*] (ROG)
SCLB .... Southern Corn Leaf Blight (OA)
SCLC .... Small-Cell Lung Cancer [*Oncology*]
SCLC .... Southern Christian Leadership Conference (EA)
SCLC .... Space-Charge-Limited Current
SCLCP .... Side-Chain Liquid Crystalline Polymer [*Organic chemistry*]
SCLCS .... Ship Command-Launch Control Subsystem [*Navy*] (CAAL)
SCLD .... Sickle-Cell Chronic Lung Disease [*Medicine*] (DMAA)
SCLD .... Space Charge Limited Diode (IAA)
SCLDF .... Sierra Club Legal Defense Fund (EA)
SCLE .... Santiago/Los Leones [*Chile*] [*ICAO location identifier*] (ICLI)
SCLE .... Subacute Cutaneous Lupus Erythematosus [*Medicine*]
SCLE .... Subcutaneous Lupus Erythematosus [*Medicine*] (DAVI)
SCLEC .... Signal Corps Logistics Evaluation Committee [*Obsolete Army*] (KSC)
SCLER .... Scleroscope
SCLER .... Sclerosis [*Medicine*]
SCLERA .... Santa Catalina Laboratory for Experimental Relativity by Astrometry [*University of Arizona*] [*Research center*] (RCD)
SCLERO .... Scleroderma [*Medicine*]
SCLF .... Single Crystal LASER Fusion [*For dating of geological material*]
SCLFM .... Society of Chain Link Fencing Manufacturers [*British*] (DBA)
SCLI .... Somerset and Cornwall Light Infantry [*British military*] (DMA)
SCLIGFET .... Space-Charge-Limited Insulated-Gate Field Effect Transistor (PDAA)
Sc LJ .... Scottish Law Journal and Sheriff Court Record [*A publication*] (DLA)
SCLJ .... South Carolina Law Journal [*A publication*] (DLA)
SCLK .... Ship's Clerk
SCLL .... Sandia Corporation, Livermore Laboratory
SCLL .... Supreme Committee for the Liberation of Lithuania [*Defunct*] (EA)
SCLL .... Vallenar/Vallenar [*Chile*] [*ICAO location identifier*] (ICLI)
SC LM .... Scottish Law Magazine and Sheriff Court Reporter [*A publication*] (DLA)
SCLM .... Stability, Control, and Load Maneuvers [*Aerospace*] (MCD)
SCLM .... Sub-Continental Lithospheric Mantle
SCLN .... SciClone Pharmaceuticals [*NASDAQ symbol*] (TTSB)
SCLN .... SciClone Pharmaceuticals, Inc. [*NASDAQ symbol*] (SAG)
SCLO .... Self-Consistent Local Orbital [*Method*] [*Mathematics*]
SCLO .... Statistical Clearance Liaison Officer [*Army*] (AABC)
SCLOG .... Security Log [*Telecommunications*] (TEL)
Sc LP .... Left Scapuloposterior Position [*of the fetus*] [*Obstetrics*]
SCLP .... Santiago/Lo Prado [*Chile*] [*ICAO location identifier*] (ICLI)
SCLPr .... Stepan Co. 5.50% Cv Pfd [*NYSE symbol*] (TTSB)
SCLR .... Santa Clara Law Review [*A publication*] (ILCA)
Sc LR .... Scottish Law Reporter [*A publication*] (DLA)
Sc LR .... Scottish Law Review and Sheriff Court Reports [*A publication*] (DLA)
Sc L Rep ...... Scottish Law Reporter [*Edinburgh*] [*A publication*] (DLA)
SCLS .... Serra Cooperative Library System [*Library network*]
SCLS .... Shipboard Command and Launch Subsystem (MCD)
SCLS .... South Central Library System [*Library network*]
SCLS .... Study of Children's Learning Styles (EDAC)
SCLS .... Systemic Capillary Leak Syndrome [*Medicine*] (DMAA)
Sc LT .... Scots Law Times [*A publication*] (DLA)
SCLTFT .... Space Charge Limited Thin Film Triode (DICI)
SCLV .... Subclavian Vein [*Anatomy*]
SCLWR .... Scientific Computing Laboratory Work Request (IAA)
SCLY .... Scullery (MSA)
SCM .... Aero Servicio de Carga Mexicana SA de CV [*Mexico ICAO designator*] (FAAC)
Sc M .... Master of Science
SCM .... Sacra Caesarea Majestas [*Sacred Imperial Majesty*] [*Latin*]
SCM .... Samarium Cobalt Magnet
SCM .... Sanctae Memoriae [*Of Holy Memory*] [*Latin*]
SCM .... S-Band Cassegrain Monopulse
SCM .... Scammon Bay [*Alaska*] [*Airport symbol*] (OAG)
SCM .... Scammon Bay, AK [*Location identifier FAA*] (FAAL)
SCM .... Scientific Calculator Machine (NITA)
SCM .... Scratch Pad Memory (IAA)
SCM .... ScreenCam Movie [*Computer software*] (CDE)
SCM .... Segment Control Module (IAA)
SCM .... Selective Complement Accumulator
SCM .... Self-Contained Munitions
SCM .... Sender's Composition Message [*Cable*]
SCM .... Service Command Module [*Aerospace*] (MCD)
SCM .... Service Control Manager [*Computer science*]
SCM .... Shaft Cutting Machine [*Mining technology*]
SCM .... Sheep Creek Mountain [*Alaska*] [*Seismograph station code, US Geological Survey*] (SEIS)
SCM .... Shorthaul Customer Modem (NITA)
SCM .... Signal Conditioning Module
SCM .... Simulated Command Module (IAA)
SCM .... Simulated Core Mock-Up [*or Model*] [*Nuclear energy*] (NRCH)
SCM .... Sine Cosine Multiplier (IAA)
SCM .... Single-Channel MODEM [*Telecommunications*] (TEL)
SCM .... Single Chip Module [*Electronics*] (CDE)
SCM .... Single Column Model [*Marine science*] (OSRA)
SCM .... Single Column Model (USDC)
SCM .... Single Crystal Meteorite
SCM .... Siscoe Callahan [*Vancouver Stock Exchange symbol*]
SCM .... Site Configuration Message [*NASA*]
SCM .... Skill Centre Manager (AIE)
SCM .... Small Capacity Memory [*Computer science*] (IAA)
SCM .... Small-Core Memory [*Computer science*]
SCM .... Smaller Companies Market [*Business term*]
SCM .... Social Change Media [*Australia*]
SCM .... Societe Canadienne des Microbiologistes [*Canadian Society of Microbiologists*] (EAIO)
SCM .... Society for Computer Medicine [*Later, AMIA*] (EA)
SCM .... Society of Clinical Masseurs [*Australia*]
SCM .... Society of Community Medicine [*Later, SPH*] (EAIO)
SCM .... Software Configuration Management (IEEE)
SCM .... Solar Cell Module
SCM .... Soluble Cytotoxic Mediator [*Immunology*]
SCM .... Spacecraft Material [*NASA*] (SSD)
SCM .... Spares Calculation Model
SCM .... Special Court-Martial
SCM .... Specification Change Memorandum
SCM .... Spleen Concanavalin A Medium [*Immunoassay*]
SCM .... Spondylitic Caudal Myelopathy [*Medicine*] (DMAA)
SCM .... Squadron Corporal-Major [*British military*] (DMA)
SCM .... Stamp Cancelling Machine (DCTA)
SCM .... Standard Cubic Meter
SCM .... STARAN [*Stellar Attitude Reference and Navigation*] Control Module (OA)
SCM .... State-Certified Midwife [*British*]
SCM .... Steam Condensing Mode [*Nuclear energy*] (NRCH)
SCM .... Sternocleidomastoid [*Anatomy*]
SCM .... Stillman College, Tuscaloosa, AL [*OCLC symbol*] (OCLC)
SCM .... Strategic Cruise Missile (MCD)
SCM .... Streamline Curvature Method [*Computer program*]
SCM .... Streptococcal Cell Membrane [*Microbiology*]
SCM .... Strouds Creek & Muddlety Railroad [*AAR code*]
SCM .... Student Christian Movement [*British*]
SCM .... Subscribers' Concentration Module [*Telecommunications*] (TEL)
SCM .... Subsystem Configuration Management [*or Monitoring*] [*NASA*] (NASA)
SCM .... Summary Court-Martial [*Army*]
SCM .... Superconducting Magnet (IEEE)
SCM .... Supervision Control Module [*Telecommunications*] (TEL)
SCM .... Supply Categories of Material (MCD)
SCM .... Suppressed-Carrier Modulation
SCM .... Surface Contamination Module (DWSG)
SCM .... Sustained Competitive Motivation
SCM .... Sydney Conservatorium of Music [*Australia*]
SCM .... Symmetrically Cyclically Magnetized (IAA)
SCM .... System Control and Monitor [*Telecommunications*] (TSSD)
SCM .... System Control Module [*NASA*] (GFGA)
SCM .... Systems Control Microprocessor
SCMA .... Scottish Carpet Manufacturers Association (DBA)
SCMA .... Scottish Cement Merchants Association (DBA)
SCMA .... Silk Commission Manufacturers Association [*Defunct*] (EA)
SCMA .... Southern Cypress Manufacturers Association (EA)
SCMA .... Sterilised Cat Gut Manufacturers' Association [*British*] (BI)
SCMA .... Stilton Cheese Makers Association [*British*] (DBA)
SCMA .... Systems Communications Management Association (IAA)
SCMAI .... Staff Committee on Mediation, Arbitration, and Inquiry [*American Library Association*]
ScMan .... Clarendon County Public Library, Manning, SC [*Library symbol*] [*Library of Congress*] (LCLS)
ScMar .... Marion County Library, Marion, SC [*Library symbol*] [*Library of Congress*] (LCLS)
SCMAT .... Southern California Motor Accuracy Test
ScMb .... Chapin Memorial Library, Myrtle Beach, SC [*Library symbol*] [*Library of Congress*] (LCLS)
SCMB .... Standard Chartered Merchant Bank [*Singapore*]
SCMB .... Subsystem Configuration Management Board [*NASA*] (GFGA)
SCMB .... System Configuration Management Board (SSD)
SCMBCR ...... Simulated Countercurrent Moving-Bed Chromatographic Reactor [*Chemical engineering*]
ScMc .... McCormick County Library, McCormick, SC [*Library symbol*] [*Library of Congress*] (LCLS)
SCMC .... S-Carboxymethylcysteine [*An amino acid*]
SCMC .... Sisters of Charity of Our Lady, Mother of the Church [*Roman Catholic religious order*]
SCMC .... Societe de Construction des Musees du Canada
SCMC .... Sodium(carboxymethyl)cellulose [*Organic chemistry*]
SCMC .... Spontaneous Cell-Mediated Cytotoxicity [*Medicine*] (DMAA)
SCMC .... Strategic Cruise Missile Carrier
SCMC .... Supply Category of Material Code
SCMCR .... Simulated Countercurrent Moving-Bed Chromatographic Reactor [*Chemical engineering*]
SCMD .... Santiago/Ministerio de Defensa Nacional [*Chile*] [*ICAO location identifier*] (ICLI)
SCMD .... Selectively Conductive Molding Device
SCMDBMC ... Standing Committee of the Murray-Darling Basin Ministerial Council [*Australia*]
SCME .... American Federation of State, County, and Municipal Employees
SCME .... Service Center Math Error [*IRS*]
SCME .... Society of Clinical and Medical Electrologists (EA)
SCME .... Surgut Commodity and Raw Materials Exchange [*Russian Federation*] (EY)
SCMF .... Single Contact Midge Flange
SCMF .... Societe Canadienne de Musique Folklorique
SCMG .... Sierra Carriers and Mountaineering Group (EA)
SCMI .... Society to Conquer Mental Illness [*Defunct*] (EA)
Sc M in Hyg ... Master of Science in Hygiene
SCMM .... Medical Mission Sisters (TOCD)
SCMM .... Sisters of Charity of Our Lady, Mother of Mercy [*Roman Catholic religious order*]
SCMM .... Society of Catholic Medical Missionaries, Inc. [*Medical Mission Sisters*] [*Roman Catholic religious order*]
SCMO .... Senior Clerical Medical Officer (DMAA)

SCMO .... Senior Clinical Medical Officer [*British*]
SCMO .... Societe Canadienne de Meteorologie et d'Oceanographie [*Canadian Meteorological and Oceanographic Society - CMOS*]
SCMO .... Societe pour une Confederation au Moyen-Orient [*Society for Middle East Confederation - SMEC*] [*Israel*] (EAIO)
SCMO .... Studie- en Informatiecentrum TNO voor Milieu-Onderzoek [*TNO Study and Information Center on Environmental Research*] [*Information service or system*] (IID)
SCMO .... Subsidiary Communications Multiplex Operation [*FM radio frequency unused portion*]
SCMO .... Summary Court-Martial Order [*Army*]
ScMoc .... Berkeley County Library, Moncks Corner, SC [*Library symbol*] [*Library of Congress*] (LCLS)
SCMOD .... Scale Model
SCMOV .... Subterranean Clover Mottle Virus [*Plant pathology*]
SCMP .... Scottish Computers in Schools Project (AIE)
SCMP .... Second-Class Mail Publications [*Later, ASCMP*] (EA)
SCMP .... Service Craft Modernization Program [*Navy*] (CAAL)
SCMP .... Simple Cost-Effective Microprocessor (MHDI)
SCMP .... Society of Company Meeting Planners (EA)
SCMP .... Software Configuration Management Plan [*Computer science*]
SCMP .... Software Configuration Management Plan (DOMA)
SCMP .... Sulfonated Chemimechanical Pulp [*Pulp and paper technology*]
SCMP .... Support Center Management Plan (AAG)
SCMP .... System Contractor Management Plan [*NASA*] (NASA)
SCMPT .... Sperm Cervical Mucus Penetration Test [*Clinical chemistry*]
SCMR .... Secretary's Committee on Mental Retardation [*Department of Health and Human Services*]
SCMR .... South Canterbury Mounted Rifles [*British military*] (DMA)
SCMR .... Special Committee on Migration and Resettlement [*Department of State*] [*World War II*]
SCMR .... Surface Composition Mapping Radiometer [*NASA*]
SCMS .... Serial Copy Management System [*for digital audio tape recording machines*]
SCMS .... Serial Copy Master System (DOM)
SCMS .... Signal Command Management System [*Military*] (AABC)
SCMS .... Somali Current Monitoring System [*Marine science*] (MSC)
SCMS .... Standard Configuration Management Systems [*Military*] (AFIT)
SCMT .... Single-Cause Mortality Tape [*National Center for Health Statistics databank*]
SCMT .... Subcontract Management Team [*NASA*] (SSD)
SCMTVS ...... Signal Corps Mobile Television System [*Military*] (IAA)
SCMU .... Species Conservation Monitoring Unit (GNE)
Sc Mun App Rep ... Scotch Munitions Appeals Reports [*Edinburgh and Glasgow*] [*A publication*] (DLA)
SCMV .... Santa Cruz Mountain Vintners (EA)
SCMV .... Sugar Cane Mosaic Virus
SCN .... Citadel, Daniel Library, Charleston, SC [*OCLC symbol*] (OCLC)
ScN .... Newberry-Saluda Regional Library, Newberry, SC [*Library symbol*] [*Library of Congress*] (LCLS)
SCN .... Potassium Thiocyanate [*or KSCN*] [*Organic chemistry*] (DAVI)
SCN .... Saarbrucken [*Germany Airport symbol*] (OAG)
SCN .... Satellite Communications Network, Inc. [*Edison, NJ*] [*Telecommunications*] (TSSD)
SCN .... Satellite Control Network
SCN .... Scan (IAA)
SCN .... Scanner [*Computer science*]
SCN .... Schematic Change Notice
SCN .... Screen [*Technical drawings*]
SCN .... Scribe Nehemiah [*Freemasonry*]
SCN .... Search Control Number (MCD)
SCN .... Secretary's Commission on Nursing [*Department of Health and Human Services*]
SCN .... Securities Communications Network, Inc. [*Englewood, CO*] (TSSD)
SCN .... Security Capital Ind Tr [*NYSE symbol*] (TTSB)
SCN .... Security Capital Industrial Trust Co. [*NYSE symbol*] (SAG)
SCN .... Self-Checking Number
SCN .... Self-Compensating Network [*Telecommunications*] (TEL)
SCN .... Self-Contained Navigation [*NASA*]
SCN .... Sensitive Command Network
SCN .... Shipbuilding and Conversion, Navy
SCN .... Ships Construction, Navy [*Funding*]
SCN .... Shop Control Number (DNAB)
SCN .... Shortest Connected Network
SCN .... Show Cause Notice
SCN .... Silent Canyon Resources Ltd. [*Vancouver Stock Exchange symbol*]
SCN .... Single Crystal Needle
SCN .... Sisters of Charity (of Nazareth) [*Roman Catholic religious order*]
SCN .... Software Change Notice (DOMA)
SCN .... Sonoco Products Corp. [*NYSE symbol*] (SAG)
SCN .... Sorting Code Number (DCTA)
SCN .... South American Airlines [*Peru*] [*ICAO designator*] (FAAC)
SCN .... Southern Command Network [*Military*] (GFGA)
SCN .... Soybean Cyst Nematode [*Botany*]
SCN .... Special Care Nursery
SCN .... Special Change Notice (KSC)
SCN .... Specification Change Notice [*NASA*]
SCN .... Specific Control Number
SCN .... Stock Control Number
SCN .... Strategic Communications Network [*Military*] (LAIN)
SCN .... Summary and Charge Number
SCN .... Sunset Crater National Monument [*Arizona*] [*Seismograph station code, US Geological Survey*] (SEIS)
SCN .... Supply Corps, Navy
SCN .... Suprachiasmatic Nucleus [*or Nuclei*] [*of the hypothalamus Anatomy*]
SCN .... Sylvania-Corning Nuclear Corp.
SCN .... System Change Notice
SCN .... System Control Number
SCNA .... Self-Contained Night Attack (MCD)
SC_{Na} .... Sieving Coefficient for Sodium [*Organic chemistry*] (DAVI)
SCNA .... Sikh Council of North America [*Defunct*] (EA)
SCNA .... Sudden Cosmic-Noise Absorption
SCNAWAF .... Special Category Navy with Air Force
SCNB .... Societe Nationale des Chemins de Fer Belges [*Belgian National Railways*]
ScNC .... Newberry College, Newberry, SC [*Library symbol Library of Congress*] (LCLS)
SCNCM .... Standing Committee of Nature Conservation Ministers [*Australia*]
SCND .... Thiocyanate [*Organic chemistry*] (DAVI)
ScndBdc ...... Scandinavian Broadcasting [*Commercial firm Associated Press*] (SAG)
scnDNA .... Deoxyribonucleic Acid, Single Copy Nuclear [*Biochemistry, genetics*]
SCNDVA .... Standing Committee on National Defence and Veterans Affairs [*Canada*]
SCNG .... Scan Graphics [*NASDAQ symbol*] (TTSB)
SCNG .... Scan-Graphics, Inc. [*NASDAQ symbol*] (NQ)
SCNG .... Scanning (MSA)
SCNI .... Select Committee on Nationalised Industries [*British*]
SCNI .... Supreme Court of Norfolk Island [*Australia*]
SC (Nig) ...... Judgments of the Supreme Court of Nigeria [*A publication*] (DLA)
SCNMV .... Sweet Clover Necrotic Mosaic Virus [*Plant pathology*]
SCNO .... Savio Club National Office (EA)
SCNO .... Senior Canadian Naval Officer [*British military*] (DMA)
ScNoaSH ..... North Augusta Senior High School, North Augusta, SC [*Library symbol Library of Congress*] (LCLS)
SCNPrA .... Security Cap Ind Tr 9.40% Pfd [*NYSE symbol*] (TTSB)
SCNPrB .... Security Cap Ind Tr 7% Cv Pfd [*NYSE symbol*] (TTSB)
SCNPWC ...... Standing Committee for Nobel Prize Winners' Congresses (EA)
SCNR .... Scanner (MSA)
SCNR .... Scientific Committee of National Representatives [*NATO*]
Sc NR .... Scott's New English Common Pleas Reports [*A publication*] (DLA)
SCNR .... Sequence Control Number Register [*Computer science*]
SCNR .... Solid-Core Nuclear Rocket [*NASA*]
SCNR .... Supreme Council for National Reconstruction [*South Korea*]
SCNS .... Self-Contained Navigation System [*NASA*]
SCNS .... Self-Contained Navigation System
SCNS .... Statewide Course Numbering System [*Florida*] (EDAC)
SCNS .... Subcutaneous Nerve Stimulation [*For treatment of pain*]
SCN/SIN ...... Sensitive Command Network/Sensitive Information Network (CET)
SCNSW .... Spastic Centre of New South Wales [*Australia*]
SCNSW .... Supreme Court of New South Wales [*Australia*]
SCNT .... Supreme Court of the Northern Territory [*Australia*]
SCNTFC .... Scientific
SCNTN .... Self-Contained
SCNTST .... Scientist
SCNUL .... Standing Conference on National and University Libraries [*British*]
SCO .... Converse College, Spartanburg, SC [*OCLC symbol*] (OCLC)
SCO .... Euro Air Helicopter Service AB [*Sweden ICAO designator*] (FAAC)
SCO .... Manetti Roberts [*Italy*] [*Research code symbol*]
SCO .... Sales Contracting Officer [*Army*]
SCO .... Santa Cruz Operation [*Computer manufacturer*] (PCM)
SCO .... Sarawak Communist Organization [*Malaya*]
ScO .... Scientific Officer [*Also, SO*] [*Ministry of Agriculture, Fisheries, and Food*] [*British*]
SCO .... Scobey, MT [*Location identifier FAA*] (FAAL)
SCO .... Score Resources [*Vancouver Stock Exchange symbol*]
SCO .... Scoresbysund [*Greenland*] [*Seismograph station code, US Geological Survey Closed*] (SEIS)
Sco .... Scorpius [*Constellation*]
SCO .... Scottish (ROG)
Sco .... Scott's English Common Pleas Reports [*A publication*] (DLA)
SCO .... Scout [*or Scouting*] (DNAB)
SCO .... Selective Conscientious Objection
SCO .... Senior Chief Officer [*British military*] (DMA)
SCO .... Service Cryptologic Organizations (MCD)
SCO .... Show Cause Order [*Legal shorthand*] (LWAP)
SCO .... Signal Company [*Military*] (IAA)
SCO .... Single Crystal Orthoferrites
SCO .... Sisters of Charity of Ottawa [*Grey Nuns of the Cross*] [*Roman Catholic religious order*]
SCO .... Sisters of Charity of Quebec (Grey Nuns) (TOCD)
SCO .... Smith Corona Corp. [*NYSE symbol*] (SPSG)
SCO .... Societe Canadienne d'Onomastique (AC)
SCO .... Society of Commissioned Officers (EA)
SCO .... Software Change Order (MCD)
SCO .... Somatic Crossing-Over [*Medicine*] (DMAA)
SCO .... Southern College of Optometry [*Tennessee*]
S/CO .... Spacecraft Observer (KSC)
SCO .... Spacecraft Operations [*NASA*] (KSC)
SCO .... Squadron Command Officer (AAG)
SCO .... Squadron Constructor Officer [*Navy British*]
SCO .... Staff Communications Office [*Army*]
SCO .... Start Checkout [*NASA*] (NASA)
SCO .... State Coordinating Officer [*Federal disaster planning*]
SCO .... State Coroners' Office [*Australia*]
SCO .... Statistical Control Office [*or Officer*] [*Military*]
SCO .... Subcarrier Oscillator
sco .... Subcarrier Oscillator (IDOE)
SCO .... Subcommissural Organ [*Neuroanatomy*]
SCO .... Subcontract Consignment Order

SCO .... Successor Contracting Officer (MCD)
SCO .... Supercritical Oxygen (MCD)
SCO .... Switch Closure Out (MCD)
SCO .... Synthetic Crude Oil [*Fuel technology*]
SCO .... System Check-Out Computer (PDAA)
SCO .... System Counterpart Officer [*Military*] (AFIT)
SCOA .... Saluki Club of America (EA)
SCOA .... Sample Cave Operating Area [*Nuclear energy*] (NRCH)
SCOA .... Supreme Council Order of the Amaranth (EA)
SCOA .... Sydney College of the Arts [*Australia*]
SCOAL .... Short-Term Coal Analysis System [*Department of Energy*] (GFGA)
Sco & J Tel... Scott and Jarnigan on the Law of Telegraphs [*A publication*] (DLA)
SCOAP .... Scandia Controllability and Observability Analysis Program (NITA)
SCOB .... Scattered Clouds or Better (SAA)
SCOB .... Scheduled-Controlled Operant Behavior [*Environmental Protection Agency*]
SCOBA .... Standing Conference of the Canonical Orthodox Bishops in the Americas (EA)
SCOBBS .... School of Combined Operations, Beach and Boat Section [*Military British*]
SCOBO .... Satellite Collection Buoy Observations
SCOBOL .... Structured Common Business-Oriented Language
SCOC .... Santa Cruz Operation [*NASDAQ symbol*] (TTSB)
SCOC .... Santa Cruz Operation, Inc. [*NASDAQ symbol*] (SAG)
SCOC .... Sediment Community Oxygen Consumption [*Marine biology*]
SCOC .... Senior Commanders Orientation Course (MCD)
SCOC .... Short-Circuit Output Current
SCOC .... Societe Canadienne d'Orientation et de Consultation
SCOC .... Spanish Chamber of Commerce [*Taiwan*] (EAIO)
SCOC .... Support Command Operations Center [*Military*]
SCOCE .... Special Committee on Compromising Emanations [*Military*] (AABC)
SCOCLIS ...... Standing Conference of Co-Operative Library and Information Services [*British*]
Sco Costs .... Scott's Costs in the High Court [*4th ed.*] [*1880*] [*A publication*] (DLA)
SCOD .... Societe Cooperative Oecumenique de Developpement [*Ecumenical Development Cooperative Society - EDCS*] [*Netherlands*] (EAIO)
SCOD .... South Coast One Design [*Cruising boat*]
SCOD .... Specific Chemical Oxygen Demand Value [*for Complete Oxidation*]
SCOD .... Surface Crack Opening Displacement (PDAA)
SCODA .... Scan Coherent Doppler Attachment
SCODHE .... Standing Conference on Dance in Higher Education [*British*] (DBA)
SCODL .... Scan Conversion Object Description Language [*Computer science*] (PCM)
SCODS .... Study Commission on Ocean Data Stations [*Marine science*] (MSC)
SCOE .... Special Checkout Equipment [*NASA*] (NASA)
SCOEG .... Standing Conference of Employers of Graduates [*British*]
SCOFA .... Shipping Control Office, Forward Area [*Navy*]
SCOFF .... Simplified Combustion Form Function (MCD)
SCOFOR .... Scottish Forces [*World War II*]
SCOFOR .... Scouting Force [*Navy*]
SCOH .... Staff Corporal of Horse [*British military*] (DMA)
SCOHR .... Students Committee on Human Rights
Sco Int .... Scott's Intestate Laws [*A publication*] (DLA)
SCOL .... School (NVT)
SCOL .... Scottish Committee on Open Learning (AIE)
SCOLA .... Second Consortium of Local Authorities
SCOLAG Bull... Scottish Legal Action Group. Bulletin [*A publication*] (DLA)
Scol Anon .... Scolia Anonyma [*Classical studies*] (OCD)
SCOLAR .... Schools and Colleges Online Accounting and Registration System (NITA)
SCOLAR .... Standard Costing of Laboratory Resources
Scol Att .... Scolia Attica [*Classical studies*] (OCD)
SCOLAVNMED... School of Aviation Medicine [*Later, School of Aerospace Medicine*]
SCOLCAP ..... Scottish Libraries Cooperative Automation Project
SCOLD .... Small Company Online Data [*Computer science*] (PDAA)
SCOLE .... Spacecraft Control Laboratory Experiment (MCD)
SCOLE .... Standing Committee on Library Education [*American Library Association*]
SCOLMA ...... Standing Conference on Library Materials on Africa [*British*]
SCOLSHIP.... Schoolship [*Navy*] (NVT)
SCOLT .... Southern Conference on Language Teaching, Inc. (EDAC)
SCOM .... Scientific Committee [*NATO*] (NATG)
SCOM .... Site Cutover Manager [*Telecommunications*] (TEL)
SCOM .... Spacecraft Communicator
SCOM .... Supervisory Communication Relations Test
SCOM .... System Communication (MHDI)
SCOMA .... Shipping Control Office, Marianas [*Navy*]
SCOMC .... SCS/Compute, Inc. [*NASDAQ symbol*] (SAG)
ScoMIA .... Scottish Marine Industries Association (DBA)
SCOMO .... Satellite Collection of Meteorological Observations
SCOMP .... Secure Communications Processor (NITA)
S/COMPT ..... Side Compartment [*Automotive engineering*]
SCON .... Quellon/Ad Quellon [*Chile*] [*ICAO location identifier*] (ICLI)
SCON .... Santiago/Quinta Normal [*Chile*] [*ICAO location identifier*] (ICLI)
SCON .... Superconductor Technologies [*NASDAQ symbol*] (SAG)
Sco NR .... Scott's New English Common Pleas Reports [*A publication*] (DLA)
SCONRES .... Senate Concurrent Resolution (AFIT)
SCONS .... Shipment Control System [*Military*]
SCONT .... Ship Control
SCONUL .... Standing Conference on National and University Libraries [*British*]
SCOOP .... Scientific Computation of Optimal Programs (IEEE)
SCOOP .... Scientific Computation of Optimum Procurement [*Air Force*]
SCOOP .... Self-Coupled Optical Pickup (NITA)
SCOOP .... Strategic Confirmation of Optical Phenomenology
SCOOP .... Support Plan to Continuity of Operations Plan [*Military*]
SCOOP .... System for Computerization of Office Processes (MHDI)
SCOOT .... Split Cycle and Offset Optimization Technique [*FHWA*] (TAG)
SCOOT .... Support Cambodia Out of Thailand [*Military operation*] (VNW)
SCOP .... Ferrocarril del Sureste [*AAR code*]
SCOP .... Scopolamine [*Anticholinergic compound*]
SCOP .... Scopus Technology [*NASDAQ symbol*] (TTSB)
SCOP .... Scopus Technology, Inc. [*NASDAQ symbol*] (SAG)
SCOP .... Single Copy Order Plan [*Later, STOP*] [*Bookselling*]
SCOP .... Steering Committee on Pilotage (DS)
SCOPE .... Microscopic (DAVI)
SCOPE .... San Clemente Ocean Probing Experiment [*Marine science*] (OSRA)
SCOPE .... San Clemente Ocean Probing Experiment (USDC)
SCOPE .... Schedule-Cost-Performance (IEEE)
SCOPE .... Scholarly Communication: Online Publishing and Education (NITA)
SCOPE .... Scientific Committee on Problems of the Environment [*ICSU*] (EA)
Scope .... Scope Industries [*Associated Press*] (SAG)
SCOPE .... Scripps Cooperative Oceanic Productivity Expedition [*1956*]
SCOPE .... Second Chance Opportunities and Education for Women (AIE)
SCOPE .... Selected Contents of Periodicals for Educators (AEBS)
SCOPE .... Senior Citizens' Opportunities for Personal Enrichment [*Federal antipoverty program*]
SCOPE .... Sequential Customer Order Processing Electronically
SCOPE .... Service Center of Private Enterprise
SCOPE .... Simple Checkout-Oriented Program Language
SCOPE .... Simple Communications Programming Environment [*Computer science*]
SCOPE .... Smart Contract Preparation Environment [*Computer science*] (RDA)
SCOPE .... Southern Coastal Plains Expedition [*National Oceanic and Atmospheric Administration*] (MSC)
SCOPE .... Special Committee on Paperless Entries [*California interbank group*]
SCOPE .... Special Committee on Problems of the Environment [*of International Council of Scientific Unions*]
SCOPE .... Specifiable Coordinating Positioning Equipment (PDAA)
SCOPE .... Standardized Curriculum Oriented Pupil Evaluation (EDAC)
SCOPE .... Standing Committee on Professional Education (NITA)
SCOPE .... Standing Conference of Institutions of Printing Education (DGA)
SCOPE .... Stromberg Central Operations Panel - Electric
SCOPE .... Student Council on Pollution and the Environment [*Association conceived in late 1969 by then Secretary of the Interior Walter J. Hickel*]
SCOPE .... Subsystem for the Control of Operations and Plan Evaluation
SCOPE .... Summer Community Organization and Political Education Program
SCOPE .... Supervisory Control of Program Execution (MCD)
SCOPE .... Supportive Council on Preventive Effort [*Ohio*]
SCOPE .... System for Capacity and Orders Planning and Enquiries (PDAA)
SCOPE .... System to Coordinate the Operation of Peripheral Equipment
SCOPES .... Squad Combat Operations Exercise, Simulation [*Military*]
SCOPLT .... Scope Plot (IAA)
SCOPP .... School-College Orientation Program of Pittsburgh
SCOPS .... Select Committee on Ocean Policy Study [*Federal Council for Science and Technology*]
SCOPT .... Subcommittee on Programming Technology (NITA)
Scopus .... Scopus Technology, Inc. [*Associated Press*] (SAG)
ScOr .... Orangeburg County Free Library, Orangeburg, SC [*Library symbol*] [*Library of Congress*] (LCLS)
SCOR .... Scientific Committee on Oceanic Research [*ICSU*] [*Halifax, NS*] (EAIO)
Scor .... Scorpius [*Constellation*]
SCOR .... Self-Calibrating Omnirange
SCOR .... Small Cycle Observation Recording
SCOR .... Special Center of Research [*HEW*]
SCOR .... Special Committee on Oceanographic Research
SCOR .... Specialized Center of Research in Atherosclerosis [*University of Chicago*] [*Research center*] (RCD)
SCOR .... Specialized Center of Research in Ischemic Heart Disease [*University of Alabama at Birmingham*] [*Research center*] (RCD)
SCOR .... Standing Conference on Refugees [*British*]
SCOR .... Status Control of Rejections (MCD)
SCOR .... Syncor International Corp. [*NASDAQ symbol*] (NQ)
SCOR .... Syncor Int'l [*NASDAQ symbol*] (TTSB)
SCORAN .... Scorer and Analyzer [*Computerized educational testing*]
ScOrC .... Claflin College, Orangeburg, SC [*Library symbol Library of Congress*] (LCLS)
SCORDES ..... Sferics Correlation Detection System
SCORE .... Satellite Computer-Operated Readiness Equipment [*SSD*]
SCORE .... Scenario-Oriented Recurring Evaluation (PDAA)
SCORE .... Scientific Cooperative Operational Research Expedition [*National Oceanic and Atmospheric Administration*] (MSC)
SCORE .... Select Concrete Objectives for Research Emphasis (PDAA)
SCORE .... Selection Copy and Reporting (IEEE)
SCORE .... Selective Conversion and Retention [*Navy*]
SCORE .... Service Corps of Retired Executives (NADA)
SCORE .... Service Corps of Retired Executives Association [*Washington, DC*] (EA)
SCORE .... Short Course Off-Road Event [*Off-road vehicle racing*]
SCORE .... Signal Communication by Orbiting Relay Equipment [*Radio*]
Score .... Simulated Combat Operations Range Equipment (MCD)
SCORE .... Solving Community Obstacles and Restoring Employment [*Occupational therapy*]
SCORE .... Southern California Off-Road Event [*An association*]
SCORE .... Space Communications for Orbiting Relay Equipment (MCD)
SCORE .... Special Claim on Residual Equity
SCORE .... Spectral Combinations for Reconnaissance Exploitation [*Photography*]

SCORE......... Standing Committee on Regulatory Effectiveness [*Nuclear Regulatory Commission*] (NRCH)
SCORE......... Stratified Charge, Omnivorous Rotary Engine [*Automotive engineering*]
SCORE......... Street Corner Offense Reduction Experiment
SCORE......... Student Competitions on Relevant Engineering
SCORE......... Subsystem Control of Required Equipment (MCD)
SCORE......... Supervisory Coaching Relations Test
SCORE......... Supplier Cost Reduction Effort [*Auto industry, project management*]
SCORE......... Systematic Communications of Range Effectiveness (MUGU)
SCORE......... Systematic Control of Range Effectiveness (IAA)
SCORE......... System Cost and Operational Resource Evaluation (MCD)
SCORE......... System for Computerized Olympic Results and Events [*Texas Instruments, Inc.*]
SCORE......... Systems Coordinative Reporting (MCD)
ScoreBd....... Score Board, Inc. [*Associated Press*] (SAG)
SCORES....... Scenario-Oriented Recurring Evaluation System [*Military*]
SCORES....... Standard Combat Oriented Recurring Evaluation System [*Military*]
SCORES....... Steering Column and Occupant Response Simulation [*Automotive safety*] [*Computer-aided design*]
SCORN......... Special Committee Opposing Resurgent Nazism
SCORON...... Scouting Squadron
SCOROR...... Secretary's Committee on Research on Reorganization [*Navy*]
S/Corp......... Staff Corporal [*British military*] (DMA)
SCORP......... Statewide Comprehensive Outdoor Recreation Plan
SCORPI........ Subcritical Carbon-Moderated Reactor Assembly for Plutonium Investigations (MCD)
SCORPIO..... Sub Critical Carbon-Moderated Reactor Assembly for Plutonium Investigations [*British*] (NUCP)
SCORPIO..... Subject-Content-Oriented Retriever for Processing Information On-Line [*Congressional Research Service*]
SCORPIO..... Submarine Craft for Ocean Repair, Positioning, Inspection, and Observation (PDAA)
ScOrS.......... South Carolina State College, Orangeburg, SC [*Library symbol Library of Congress*] (LCLS)
ScOrSM....... Southern Methodist College, Orangeburg, SC [*Library symbol*] [*Library of Congress*] (LCLS)
ScOrTC........ Orangeburg-Calhoune Technical College, Orangeburg, SC [*Library symbol*] [*Library of Congress*] (LCLS)
SCOR U....... SCOR US Corp. [*Associated Press*] (SAG)
SCORU......... Statistical Control and Operations Records Unit [*Air Force*]
SCOS........... Scottish Certificate in Office Studies
SCOS........... Small Computer and Office Systems [*Honeywell, Inc.*]
SCOS........... Subsystem Computer Operating System [*NASA*] (NASA)
SCOSA......... Spastic Centres of South Australia
SCOSE......... Standing Committee on Submarine Escape [*British military*] (DMA)
SCOSS......... Senior Chief Officer, Shore Signal Service (IAA)
SCOST......... Special Committee on Space Technology (KSC)
SCOSTEP..... Scientific Committee on Solar Terrestrial Physics (EA)
SCOSWS...... Senior Chief Officer, Shore Wireless Service (IAA)
SCOT........... Satellite Communications Overseas Transmission
SCOT........... Satellite Communication Terminal [*Navy British*] (MCD)
SCOT........... Scotland [*or Scottish*] (EY)
Scot............ Scotland (VRA)
Scot............ Scotland [*or*] Scottish (ODBW)
SCOT........... Scott & Stringfellow Financial, Inc. [*Richmond, VA*] [*NASDAQ symbol*] (NQ)
SCOT........... Scottish [*or Scotsman*] (ROG)
SCOT........... Scottish Confederation of Tourism (DBA)
SCOT........... Scott/Stringfellow Finl [*NASDAQ symbol*] (TTSB)
SCOT........... Semi-Automated Computer-Oriented Text (PDAA)
SCOT........... Shaken and Circulatory Oxidation Test (PDAA)
SCOT........... Shell Claus Offgas Treating [*Chemical engineering*]
SCOT........... Shipborne SATCOM Terminal [*British*]
SCOT........... Shippers for Competitive Ocean Transportation [*Washington, DC*] (EA)
SCOT........... Standby Compatible One-Tape [*System*]
SCOT........... Steel Car of Tomorrow
SCOT........... Stepper Central Office Tester (NITA)
SCOT........... Subcostal Right Ventricle Outflow View [*Medicine*] (DMAA)
SCOT........... Supplementary Checkout Trailer
SCOT........... Support-Coated Open-Tubular [*Column*] [*Chromatography*]
SCOTA......... Scottish Offshore Training Association (DBA)
SCOTAC....... Speech-Compatible Tactile Communicant (MCD)
SCOTAPLL.... Standing Conference on Theological and Philosophical Libraries in London
Scot App Rep... Scottish Appeal Reports [*A publication*] (DLA)
ScotBcp........ Scotland Bancorp, Inc. [*Associated Press*] (SAG)
SCOTBEC...... Scottish Business Education Council (DCTA)
SCOTBUILD... Scottish Building and Public Works Exhibition [*Scottish Exhibitions Ltd.*] (TSPED)
SCOTCAT...... Scottish Credit Accumulation and Transfer (AIE)
SCOTCH....... Summer Cultural Opportunities for Teams and Children [*National music program*]
SCOTEC....... Scottish Technical Education Council [*British*]
SCOTENG..... Scottish Engineering Exhibition for Design, Production, and Automation [*Scottish Exhibitions Ltd.*] (TSPED)
SCOTHOT..... Scottish Hotel, Catering, and Licensed Trade Exhibition [*Scottish Exhibitions Ltd.*] (TSPED)
SCOTICE...... Scotland Iceland (IAA)
SCOTICE...... Scotland to Iceland Submarine Cable System [*Telecommunications*] (TEL)
Scot Jur....... Scottish Jurist [*A publication*] (DLA)
SCOTL......... Scotland (ROG)
Scot Law J... Scottish Law Journal [*Glasgow*] [*A publication*] (DLA)
ScotLiq........ Scotts Liquid Gold Co. [*Associated Press*] (SAG)
Scot LJ........ Scottish Law Journal and Sheriff Court Record [*A publication*] (DLA)
Scot LM....... Scottish Law Magazine and Sheriff Court Reporter [*A publication*] (DLA)
Scot L Mag... Scottish Law Magazine [*Edinburgh, Scotland*] [*A publication*] (DLA)
Scot LR........ Scottish Law Reporter [*A publication*] (DLA)
Scot L Rep... Scottish Law Reporter [*A publication*] (DLA)
Scot LT........ Scots Law Times [*A publication*] (DLA)
SCOTMET...... Scottish Metropolitan [*Property developer*]
Scotmn........ Scotsman Industries, Inc. [*Associated Press*] (SAG)
ScotNAE....... Scottish National Antarctic Expedition [*1902-04*]
SCOTNATS... Scottish Nationalists
Scot Parl Acts... Acts of the Parliaments of Scotland (DLA)
SCOTRACEN... Scouting Training Center [*Navy*]
SCOTS......... Surveillance and Control of Transmission Systems [*Bell Laboratories*]
SCOTS......... System Checkout Test Set (MCD)
Scots LTR.... Scots Law Times Reports [*A publication*] (DLA)
Scots RR..... Scots Revised Reports [*1707-1873*] [*A publication*] (DLA)
ScotSt......... Scott & Stringfellow Financial, Inc. [*Associated Press*] (SAG)
ScotStrng..... Scott & Stringfellow Financial [*Associated Press*] (SAG)
Scott........... Scott's English Common Pleas Reports [*A publication*] (DLA)
Scott........... Scott's Reports [*25, 26 New York Civil Procedure*] [*A publication*] (DLA)
SCOTT......... Single Channel Objective Tactical Terminal [*Army*] (RDA)
SCOTT......... Synchronous Continuous Orbital Three-Dimensional Tracking
Scott (Eng)... Scott's English Common Pleas Reports [*A publication*] (DLA)
Scott J........ Reporter, English Common Bench Reports [*A publication*] (DLA)
Scott NR...... Scott's New English Common Pleas Reports [*A publication*] (DLA)
ScottP......... Scott Paper Ltd. [*Associated Press*] (SAG)
SCOTT-R...... Super-Critical, Once-Thru Tube Reactor [*Experiment*] [*General Electric Co.*]
Scotts.......... Scotts Co. [*Associated Press*] (SAG)
SCOTTSU..... Scottish Open Tech Training Support Unit (AIE)
SCOTUS....... Supreme Court of the United States (WDAA)
SCOTVEC..... Scottish Technician and Vocational Educational Council (ACII)
SCOTVEC..... Scottish Vocational Education Council (ODBW)
SCOTVIC...... Standing Conference of Principals of Tertiary and Sixth Form Colleges [*British*] (AIE)
SCOU........... Ship Course
SC Oudh....... Oudh Select Cases [*India*] [*A publication*] (DLA)
SCOUG........ Southern California Online User Group (NITA)
SCOUS......... Spectrum Clear of Unknown Signals (MUGU)
SCOUT......... Shared Currency Option Under Tender (ODBW)
SCOUT......... Surface-Controlled Oxide Unipolar Transistor
SCOW.......... Scottish Convention of Women (DI)
SCOWAH...... Schmulowitz Collection of Wit and Humor [*San Francisco Public Library*]
SCOWR........ Special Committee on Water Research [*International Council of Scientific Unions*]
SCOYO......... Standing Conference of Youth Organisations (AIE)
SCP............. Brotherhood of Sleeping Car Porters [*Later, BRAC*] (EA)
SCP............. SAGE [*Semiautomatic Ground Environment*] Change Proposal (IAA)
SCP............. SAGE [*Semiautomatic Ground Environment*] Computer Program
SCP............. SAGE [*Semiautomatic Ground Environment*] Computer Project [*Military*] (IAA)
SCP............. Satellite Cloud Photograph
SCP............. Satin Chrome Plated
SCP............. Scanner Control Power (MCD)
SCP............. Scanning Phased Array
SCP............. Schematic Change Proposal
SCP............. Scope Indus [*AMEX symbol*] (TTSB)
SCP............. Scope Industries [*AMEX symbol*] (SPSG)
SCP............. Scottish Conservative Party [*Political party*]
SCP............. Scrip (ROG)
SCP............. Script [*Films, television, etc.*]
SCP............. Secondary Control Point
SCP............. Secondary Cross-Connection Point (NITA)
SCP............. Sector Command Post [*Military*]
SCP............. Secure Conferencing Project
SCP............. Security Classification Procedure [*Military*]
SCP............. Self-Consistent Phonon
SCP............. Semiconductor Products (IAA)
SCP............. Senior Companion Program (EA)
SCP............. Serial Character Printer (OA)
SCP............. Sertoli-Cell Protein [*Immunology*]
SCP............. Service Control Point [*DoD*] (AFIT)
SCP............. Servo-Controlled Positioner
SCP............. Session Control Properties [*Computer science*]
SCP............. Sheep Choroid Plexus
SCP............. Short-Circuit Protection
SCP............. Silver Cup Resources Ltd. [*Vancouver Stock Exchange symbol*]
SCP............. Simplified Clearance Procedure [*Customs*] (DS)
SCP............. Simulation Control Program [*Military*] (CAAL)
SCP............. Simulator Control Panel [*NASA*]
SCP............. Sindbis Core Protein [*Virology*]
SCP............. Single-Cell Protein
SCP............. Single Component Peak [*Spectra*]
SCP............. Sleeping Car Porters Union (MHDB)
SCP............. Small Cardioactive Peptide [*Biochemistry*]
SCP............. Small Computer Program [*Army*] (RDA)
SCP............. Smaller Communities Program [*Department of Labor*]
SCP............. Social Credit Party (NADA)
SCP............. Social Credit Party of Canada [*Parti Credit Social du Canada*] (PPW)
SCP............. Societe Canadienne de la Population [*Canadian Population Society - CPS*]

SCP.......... Societe Canadienne de Pedatrie [*Canadian Paediatric Society*] (EAIO)
SCP.......... Societe Culinaire Philanthropique [*New York, NY*] (EA)
SCP.......... Society for Czechoslovak Philately (EA)
SCP.......... Society of California Pioneers (EA)
SCP.......... Society of Christian Philosophers (EA)
SCP.......... Sodium Cellulose Phosphate [*Kidney-stone drug*]
SCP.......... Software Change Proposal (MCD)
SCP.......... Solar Cell Panel
SCP.......... Sonobuoy Control Panel
SCP.......... Spacecraft Platform [*NASA*]
SCP.......... Spanish Communist Party
SCP.......... Special Category Patient [*Aeromedical evacuation*]
SCP.......... Specialist Component Producer
SCP.......... Specific Candlepower (NASA)
SCP.......... Specific Cleavage Product [*Biochemistry*]
SCP.......... Spherical Candlepower
SCP.......... Spiritual Counterfeits Project (EA)
SCP.......... Standard Corporate Protocol [*Telecommunications*]
SCP.......... Standardized Care Plans [*for hospitals*]
SCP.......... Standards Completion Program [*Analytical method procedure, OSHA and NIOSH requirements*]
SCP.......... State College [*Pennsylvania*] [*Seismograph station code, US Geological Survey*] (SEIS)
SCP.......... Stationary Combustion Process [*Automotive engineering*]
SCP.......... Station Communications Processor
SCP.......... St. Catharines Public Library [*UTLAS symbol*]
SCP.......... Sterol Carrier Protein
SCP.......... Storage-Command Pulse [*Computer science*] (ECII)
SCP.......... Storage Control Processor (NOAA)
SCP.......... Stromberg-Carlson Practices [*Telecommunications*] (TEL)
SCP.......... Structural Ceramic Panel
SCP.......... Subcontract Proposal (AAG)
SCP.......... Sudanese Communist Party [*Political party*] (PD)
SCP.......... Sulfachloropyridazine [*Antibacterial*]
SCP.......... Supervisor's Control Panel
SCP.......... Supervisory Control Program [*Burroughs Corp.*]
SCP.......... Supplier Change Proposal (MCD)
SCP.......... Supplier's Contract Property (MCD)
SCP.......... Supply Cataloging Program
SCP.......... Supply Control Plan [*World War II*]
SCP.......... Support Control Program (IAA)
SCP.......... Surrounding Combustion Process [*Automotive engineering*]
SCP.......... Surveillance Communication Processor [*Aviation*] (OA)
SCP.......... Survey Control Point [*Military*]
SCP.......... Symbol Conversion Program (NITA)
SCP.......... Symbolic Conversion Program (BUR)
SCP.......... Synthetic Fuels Commercialization Program [*Also, SFCP*] [*Energy Resources Council*]
SCP.......... Syrian Communist Party [*Political party*] (PPW)
SCP.......... System Change Package
SCP.......... System Communication Pamphlet (IEEE)
SCP.......... System Concept Paper [*Army*] (RDA)
SCP.......... System Control Panel (IAA)
SCP.......... System Control Processor [*Honeywell, Inc.*]
SCP.......... System Control Program (NITA)
SCP.......... System Control Programming [*Computer science*]
SCP.......... Systems Change Proposal (AFM)
SCP.......... Waukegan Avionics, Inc. [*ICAO designator*] (FAAC)
sCP.......... Without Chest Pain [*Medicine*]
SCPA.......... Scottish Cashmere Producers Association (DBA)
SCPA.......... Scottish Clay Pigeon Association (DBA)
SCPA.......... Semiconductor Chip Protection Act of 1984
SCPA.......... Societe Canadienne de Peintres en Aquarelle (AC)
SCPA.......... Solar Cell Panel Assembly
SCPA.......... Southern Coal Producers Association [*Defunct*] (EA)
SCPA.......... Southern College Personnel Association (AEBS)
SCPA.......... Spacecraft Payload Adapter (MCD)
SCPA.......... Stabilization and Control System Control Panel (IAA)
SCPC.......... Signal Corps Pictorial Center [*Obsolete Army*]
SCPC.......... Single-Channel-per-Carrier [*Telecommunications*]
SCPCE.......... Societe Canadienne pour la Prevention de Cruaute aux Enfants
SCPCU.......... Society of Chartered Property and Casualty Underwriters (EA)
SCPD.......... Scratch Pad [*Computer science*]
Sc-PD.......... Silicon Photodiode
SCPD.......... Staff Civilian Personnel Division [*Army*]
SCPDCIHE.......... Standing Conference of Principals and Directors of Colleges and Institutes of Higher Education (AIE)
SCPD OCSA... Staff Civilian Personnel Division, Office, Chief of Staff, Army (AABC)
SCPE.......... Simplified Chemical Protective Equipment [*Army*] (DOMA)
SCPE.......... Simplified Collective Protection Equipment [*Military*] (RDA)
SCPE.......... Societe Canadienne de Physiologie de l'Exercice [*Formerly, Canadian Association of Sport Sciences*] (AC)
SCPE.......... Specialized Customer Premises Equipment [*for the handicapped*]
SCPE.......... Square Corners Plain Edges [*Bookbinding*] (DGA)
SCPF.......... Sacra Congregatio de Propaganda Fide [*Sacred Congregation for the Propagation of the Faith*] [*Latin*]
SCPH.......... Societe Canadienne des Pharmaciens d'Hopitaux [*Canadian Society of Hospital Pharmacists*] (EAIO)
SCPI.......... Scientists' Committee for Public Information [*Defunct*]
SCPI.......... Sequential Central Port Injection
SCPI.......... Small Computer Program Index [*No longer published*] [*ALLM Books*] (IID)
SCPI.......... Standard Commands for Programmable Controllers (ACII)
SCPI.......... Standing Committee on Professional Institutions (ACII)
SCPI.......... Structural Clay Products Institute [*Later, BIA*] (EA)
SCPK.......... Serum Creatine Phosphokinase [*An enzyme*] (AAMN)
SCPL.......... Senior Commercial Pilot's Licence [*British*] (DBQ)
SCPL.......... Signal Corps Photographic Laboratory [*Obsolete Army*]
S/Cpl.......... Staff Corporal [*British military*] (DMA)
SCPL.......... Staff of Chief of Personnel and Logistics [*British military*] (DMA)
SCPL/H.......... Senior Commercial Pilot's Licence/Helicopters [*British*] (AIA)
SCPM.......... Sample Collection and Preparation Module [*X-ray spectrometry*]
SCPM.......... Scanning Chemical Potential Microscope
SCPM.......... Semiautomatic Circuit Performance Monitor [*Navy*] (MCD)
SCPM.......... Silwood Centre for Pest Management [*Imperial College*] [*British*] (CB)
SCPMT.......... Southern California Perceptual Motor Tests
SCPNT.......... Southern California Postrotary Nystagmus Test
SCPO.......... Second-Class Post Office
SCPO.......... Senior Chief Petty Officer [*Navy rating*]
SCPP.......... Seasonal-to-Interannual Climate Prediction Program [*Marine science*] (OSRA)
SCPP.......... Seasonal-to-Interannual Climate Prediction Program (USDC)
SCPP.......... Sierra Cooperative Pilot Project [*Department of the Interior*]
SCPP.......... Supreme Court, Preliminary Prints
SCPP.......... Surveyor Command Preparation Program [*Aerospace*]
SCPPool.......... SCP Pool Corp. [*Associated Press*] (SAG)
SCPPS.......... Secondary Containment Purge and Pressure Control System [*Nuclear energy*] (NRCH)
SCPR.......... Semiconductor Parameter Retrieval [*Information Handling Services*] [*Database*]
SCPR.......... Social & Community Planning Research [*British*]
SCPR.......... Sri Chinmoy Oneness-Home Peace Run [*An association*] (EA)
SCPR.......... Standard Cardiopulmonary Resuscitation
SCPRF.......... Structural Clay Products Research Foundation [*BIA*] [*Absorbed by*] (EA)
SCPS.......... Servo-Controlled Positioning System
SCPS.......... Society of Civil and Public Servants [*A union*] [*British*] (DCTA)
SCP(S).......... Subscribers' Call Processing (Subsystem) [*Telecommunications*] (TEL)
SCPS.......... Survivable Collective Projected System
SCPS.......... Survivable Collective Protection System [*Air Force*] (DOMA)
SCPS.......... Survivable Collision Protection System (DWSG)
SCPSC.......... South Carolina Public Service Commission Reports [*A publication*] (DLA)
SCPT.......... SAGE [*Semiautomatic Ground Environment*] Computer Programming Training
SCPT.......... Schizophrenic Chronic Paranoid Type [*Medicine*] (DMAA)
SCPT.......... Security Control Point [*Military*] (MUGU)
SCPT.......... Self-Consistent Perturbation Theory [*Physics*]
ScPT.......... Tri-County Technical College, Pendleton, SC [*Library symbol*] [*Library of Congress*] (LCLS)
SCPTR.......... Standing Committee on Personnel Training and Readiness [*Navy*]
SCPV.......... Silkworm Cytoplasmic Polyhedrosis Virus (PDAA)
SCPV.......... Societe Canadienne de Physiologie Vegetale (AC)
SCQ.......... Hanscom Air Force Base, Base Library, Hanscom AFB, MA [*OCLC symbol*] (OCLC)
SCQ.......... Saco Resources [*Vancouver Stock Exchange symbol*]
SCQ.......... Santiago De Compostela [*Spain*] [*Airport symbol*] (OAG)
SCQ.......... Sisters of Charity of Quebec [*Grey Nuns*] [*Roman Catholic religious order*]
SCQ.......... Sociedad Chilena de Quimca
SCQC.......... Scout Crew Qualification Course [*Army*]
SCQE.......... Squad Combat Qualification Exercise [*Army*] (INF)
SCR.......... Cape Colony Supreme Court Reports [*A publication*] (DLA)
SCR.......... Chinook Regional Library, Swift Current, Saskatchewan [*Library symbol National Library of Canada*] (NLC)
SCR.......... Juta's Supreme Court Cases [*1880-1910*] [*Cape Of Good Hope, South Africa*] [*A publication*] (DLA)
SCR.......... Law Reports of Supreme Court of Sarawak, North Borneo, and Brunei [*A publication*] (DLA)
SCR.......... San Cristobal [*Chile*] [*Seismograph station code, US Geological Survey Closed*] (SEIS)
SCR.......... Scan Control Register (NITA)
SCR.......... Scanning Control Register
SCR.......... Schedule Change Report
SCR.......... Schedule Change Request [*NASA*] (NASA)
SCR.......... Score (ROG)
SCR.......... Scourer [*s*] [*or Scouring Freight*]
SCR.......... Scranton [*Diocesan abbreviation*] [*Pennsylvania*] (TOCD)
SCR.......... Scranton Public Library, Scranton, PA [*OCLC symbol*] (OCLC)
Scr.......... Scrapie [*Animal pathology*]
SCR.......... Scratch
SCR.......... Screen (WGA)
SCR.......... Screw (AAG)
scr.......... Scribe [*MARC relator code*] [*Library of Congress*] (LCCP)
SCR.......... Scrip (ADA)
Scr.......... Scripture (BJA)
SCR.......... Scruple
SCR.......... Scruple [*Pharmacology*] (DAVI)
SCR.......... Scurry-Rainbow Oil Ltd. [*Toronto Stock Exchange symbol*]
SCR.......... Sea Containers Ltd. [*NYSE symbol*] (SPSG)
SCR.......... Section Cross Reference (MCD)
SCR.......... Security Change Request [*Military*] (GFGA)
SCR.......... Selective Catalytic [*or Catalyst*] Reduction
SCR.......... Selective Catalytic Reduction
SCR.......... Selective Chopper Radiometer
SCR.......... Selenium Control Rectifier [*Nuclear energy*] (NRCH)
SCR.......... Self-Consistent Renormalization Theory [*Quantum mechanics*]

SCR .... Semiconductor
SCR .... Semiconductor-Controlled Rectifier
SCR .... Senate Concurrent Resolution (CDAI)
SCR .... Senior Common Room [*in British colleges and public schools*]
SCR .... Senior Contractor Representative
SCR .... Sequence Checking Routine
SCR .... Sequence-Control Register [*Computer science*] (EECA)
scr .... Serbo-Croatian (Roman) [*MARC language code Library of Congress*] (LCCP)
SCR .... Series Control Relay
SCr .... Serum Creatinine [*Hematology*]
SCR .... Set Complete Radio
SCR .... Shift Count Register
SCR .... Shipboard Census Report [*FHWA*] (TAG)
SCR .... Ship to Component Record [*Navy*]
SCR .... Short-Circuit Ratio
SCR .... Short Consensus Repeat [*Biochemistry*]
SCR .... Si-Chang Flying Service Co. Ltd. [*Thailand*] [*ICAO designator*] (FAAC)
SCR .... Signal Conditioner (IAA)
SCR .... Signal Conditioning Rack
SCR .... Signal Conversion Relay [*Telecommunications*] (TEL)
SCR .... Signal Corps Radio [*Followed by model number*] [*Obsolete Army*]
SCR .... Silicon-Controlled Rectifier [*Electronics*]
SCR .... Simulation and Control Rack
SCR .... Single Card Reader [*Computer science*] (IAA)
SCR .... Single-Channel Reception (DEN)
SCR .... Single Character Recognition
SCR .... Skin Conductance Reading [*on Biofeedback*] [*Psychiatry*] (DAVI)
SCR .... Skin Conductance Response
SCR .... Sneak Circuit Report [*NASA*] (NASA)
SCR .... Societe Collective de Retransmission du Canada (AC)
SCR .... Society for Cultural Relations between the Peoples of the British Commonwealth and the USSR
SCR .... Society of Cardiovascular Radiology [*Later, SCVIR*] (EA)
SCR .... Sodium-Cooled Reactor [*Nuclear energy*]
SCR .... Software Change Request [*NASA*]
SCR .... Software Correction Report (CAAL)
SCR .... Software Cost Reduction [*Computer science*]
SCR .... Solar Corpuscular Radiation (IAA)
SCR .... Solar Cosmic Radiation [*or Ray*]
SCR .... SONAR Control Room
SCR .... South Carolina Reports [*A publication*] (DLA)
SCR .... Space Charge Recombination (IAA)
SCR .... Spacecraft Received Time
SCR .... Spanish Communication Region [*Air Force*] (MCD)
SCR .... Spares Coordination Record (SAA)
SCR .... Special Certification Roster
SCR .... Specification Clarification Request (MCD)
SCR .... Specific Commodity Rates (DS)
SCR .... Speed Change Rate
SCR .... Spondylitic Caudal Radiculopathy [*Medicine*] (DMAA)
SCR .... Stable Continental Region [*Geology*]
SCR .... Static Card Reader
SCR .... Stock Car Racing [*A publication*]
SCR .... Strip Chart Recorder [*NASA*]
SCR .... Structurally Conserved Region [*Biochemistry*]
SCR .... Sub-Chief Ranger [*Ancient Order of Foresters*]
SCR .... Subcontractor (SAA)
SCR .... Summary Control Report [*Planning and Production*] [*Navy*]
SCR .... Supersonic Combustion Ramjet
SCR .... Support Control Room [*NASA*] (KSC)
SCr .... Supreme Court Reports [*India*] [*A publication*] (DLA)
SCR .... Supreme Court Reports [*1928-41, 1946-51*] [*Sarawak*] [*A publication*] (DLA)
SCR .... Supreme Court Reports [*Canada Department of Justice*] [*Information service or system*] (CRD)
SCR .... Surface-Contour RADAR
SCR .... Syrene-Chloroprene Rubber
SCR .... System Change Request
SCR .... System Conceptual Requirement (SSD)
SCR .... System Control Record (NITA)
SCR .... System Control Registers [*Computer science*]
SCR .... System Control Routine
SCRA .... Scottish Countryside Rangers Association (DBA)
SCRA .... Sea Containers Ltd Cl'A' [*NYSE symbol*] (TTSB)
SCRA .... Single Channel Radio Access Subsystem (MCD)
SCRA .... Specialized Carriers & Rigging Association
SCRA .... Stanford Center for RADAR Astronomy
SCRA .... Steel Can Recycling Association (EA)
SCRA .... Supreme Council of the Royal Arcanum [*Boston, MA*] (EA)
SCRAA .... Standing Conference of Regional Arts Associations [*British*] (DI)
SCRAC .... Standing Conference of Regional Advisory Councils for Further Education
SCRAG .... Senior Civilian Representative, Attorney General [*Department of Justice civil disturbance unit*]
SCRAM .... Safety Control Rod Axe Man [*Nuclear energy*] (IEEE)
SCRAM .... Scottish Campaign to Resist the Atomic Menace
SCRAM .... Selective Combat Range Artillery Missile
SCRAM .... Self-Corrected Remedial Aid and Media [*Teaching method*]
SCRAM .... Service Change Release and Manufacture (MCD)
SCRAM .... Several Compilers Reworked and Modified
SCRAM .... Short-Range Attack Missile
SCRAM .... Signal Corps Random-Access Memory (DNAB)
SCRAM .... Space Capsule Regulator and Monitor
SCRAM .... Spares Components Reidentification and Modification [*Program*] [*DoD*]
SCRAM .... Spares Control, Release, and Monitoring
SCRAM .... Special Criteria for Retrograde of Army Materiel (AABC)
SCRAM .... Speech-Controlled Respirometer for Ambulation Measurement [*Medicine*] (DMAA)
SCRAM .... Static Column Dynamic Random-Access Memory [*Computer science*] (EECA)
SCRAM .... Supersonic Combustion Ramjet Missile
SCRAM .... Synanon Committee for Responsible American Media [*Later, SCRAP*]
SCRAMJET... Supersonic Combustion Ramjet
SCRAMM ..... System Calibration, Repair, and Maintenance Model [*Military*] (CAAL)
SCRAP .... Selective Curtailment of Reports and Paperwork [*Navy*]
SCRAP .... Series Computation of Reliability and Probability [*Computer science*]
SCRAP .... Simple Complex Reaction-Time Apparatus
SCRAP .... Society for Completely Removing All Parking Meters
SCRAP .... South Coast Recycled Auto Project [*Air pollution controls credits from mobile sources for stationary sources*]
SCRAP .... Students Challenging Regulatory Agency Proceedings [*Student legal action organization*]
SCRAP .... Super-Caliber Rocket-Assisted Projectile (IEEE)
SCRAP .... Synanon Committee for a Responsible American Press (EA)
SCRAPE .... Screening Country Requirements Against Plus Excess [*DoD*]
SCRATA .... Steel Castings Research and Trade Association [*Sheffield, England*] (EAIO)
Scrat & Bra... Scratchley and Brabook's Building Societies [*2nd ed.*] [*1882*] [*A publication*] (DLA)
Scrat Bdg Soc... Scratchley's Building Societies [*5th ed.*] [*1883*] [*A publication*] (DLA)
Scrat Life Ass... Scratchley's Life Assurance [*13th ed.*] [*1887*] [*A publication*] (DLA)
SCR B .... Sea Containers Ltd Cl'B' [*NYSE symbol*] (TTSB)
SC-RB .... Separable Costs-Remaining Benefits (PDAA)
SCRB .... Software Configuration Review Board (CAAL)
SCRB .... Structured Case Review Blank
SCRBA .... Student Committee for the Right to Bear Arms [*Defunct*] (EA)
SCRC .... Spanish Colonial Research Center [*University of New Mexico*] [*Research center*] (RCD)
SCRC .... Study Circles Resource Center (EA)
SCRC .... Superfund Community Relations Coordinator [*Environmental Protection Agency*] (GFGA)
SCRD .... Secondary Control Rod Driveline [*Nuclear energy*] (NRCH)
SCRD .... Student Coalition for the Right to Drink [*Defunct*] (EA)
SCRD .... Vina Del Mar/Rodelillo [*Chile*] [*ICAO location identifier*] (ICLI)
SCRDB .... Screwed Bonnet
SCRDC .... Silicon Controlled Rectifier Regulated Direct Current (PDAA)
SCRDE .... Stores and Clothing Research and Development Establishment [*British*]
SCR dimmer... Silicon-Controlled Rectifier [*Dimmer*] [*Television*] (WDMC)
SCRDM .... Secondary Control Rod Drive Mechanism [*Nuclear energy*] (NRCH)
SCRDN .... Screw Down
SCRE .... Scottish Council for Research in Education
SCrE .... South Carolina Electric & Gas Co. [*Associated Press*] (SAG)
SCRE .... Stratified Charge Rotary Engine (DWSG)
SCRE .... Supreme Cossack Representation in Exile (EA)
SCREAM ...... Society for the Registration of Estate Agents and Mortgage Brokers (MHDB)
SCREENEX... Screening Exercise [*Military*] (NVT)
SC Regs ...... South Carolina State Register [*A publication*] (AAGC)
SCREN .... Screen [*Laboratory science*] (DAVI)
SC Rep .... Juta's Supreme Court Cases [*1880-1910*] [*Cape Of Good Hope, South Africa*] [*A publication*] (DLA)
SC Res .... Senate Concurrent Resolution (DLA)
Sc Rev Rept... Scots Revised Reports [*A publication*] (DLA)
SCREWS ...... Solar Cosmic Ray Early Warning System (MUGU)
SCRF .... Small Craft Repair Facility [*Navy*] (NVT)
SCRF .... Stanford Center for Reservoir Forecasting [*Stanford University*] [*Research center*] (RCD)
SCRF .... Surface Coil Rotating Frame [*Medicine*] (DMAA)
SCRG .... Rancagua/De La Independencia [*Chile*] [*ICAO location identifier*] (ICLI)
SCRG .... Societe Canadienne de Recherche en Geriatrie
SCRG .... Stationary Cosmic Ray Gas
SCRG .... System Change Review Group [*George C. Marshall Space Flight Center*] (NASA)
SCRH .... Sisters of Charity of Rolling Meadows (TOCD)
ScRh .... York County Library, Rock Hill, SC [*Library symbol*] [*Library of Congress*] (LCLS)
ScRhM .... Clinton Junior College, Rock Hill, SC [*Library symbol*] [*Library of Congress*] (LCLS)
ScRhW .... Winthrop College, Rock Hill, SC [*Library symbol Library of Congress*] (LCLS)
ScRhY .... York Technical College, Rock Hill, SC [*Library symbol*] [*Library of Congress*] (LCLS)
SCRI .... Science Court and Research Institute (EA)
SCRI .... Scientists' Committee for Radiation Information (EA)
SCRI .... Scottish Crop Research Institute [*Research center*] (IRC)
SCRI .... Scottish Crop Research Institute
SCRI .... South Central Reservoir Investigation [*Department of the Interior*] (GRD)
SCRI .... Southern Center for Research and Innovation, Inc. [*University of Southern Mississippi*] [*Research center*] (RCD)
SCRI .... Supercomputer Computations Research Institute [*Florida State University*] [*Research center*] (RCD)

Scrib Dow.... Scribner on the Law of Dower [*A publication*] (DLA)
SCRIBE........ System for Computerized Reporting of Information for Better Education (MHDI)
SCRIBE........ System for Correspondence Recording and Interrogation by EDP [*Electronic Data Processing*]
SCRICI........ Selected Reagent Ion Chemical Ionization [*Spectroscopy*]
SCRID.......... Silicon-Controlled Rectifier Indicator Driver (IAA)
SCRIM.......... Sideway Force Coefficient Routine Investigating Machine [*Department of Transport*] [*British*]
SCRIM.......... Supersonic Cruise Intermediate Range Missile (MCD)
SCRIMP........ Save Cash, Reduce Immediately Meat Prices [*Boston, MA, group protesting high cost of food, 1973*]
SCRIMP........ Seeman Composite Resin Infusion Molding Process
SCRIP.......... Scriptum [*Something Written*] [*Latin*] (ROG)
SCRIP.......... Scripture
SCRIP.......... Select Commission on Immigration and Refugee Policy (NADA)
SCRIP.......... Single-Chain Ribosome-Inactivating Protein [*Biochemistry*]
SCRIP.......... Statine Congener of Renin Inhibitory Peptide [*Biochemistry*]
SCRIP.......... System for Controlling Returns in Inventory and Production Data [*IRS*]
Scripps........ Scripps [*E. W.*] Co. [*Associated Press*] (SAG)
SCRIPPS...... Scripps Coronary Radiation to Inhibit Proliferation Post-Stenting
SCRIPT........ Scientific and Commercial Interpreter and Program Translator (IAA)
SCRIPT........ Scientific and Commercial Subroutine Interpreter and Program Translator
SCRIPT........ Screenwriting Coalition for Industry Professionals and Teachers (EDAC)
SCRIPT........ Scripture
script........... Scripture (VRA)
SCRIPT........ Support for Creative Independent Production Talent [*EC*] (ECED)
SCRIPT........ System Controlling Research Image Processing Tasks (MCD)
SCRIS.......... Southern California Regional Information Study [*Bureau of Census*]
Scriv Cop..... Scriven on the Law of Copyholds [*7th ed.*] [*1896*] [*A publication*] (DLA)
Scriven........ Scriven on the Law of Copyholds [*A publication*] (DLA)
SCRJ............ Supersonic Combustion Ramjet
SCRL............ Sensory Communication Research Laboratory [*Gallaudet College*] [*Research center*] (RCD)
SCRL............ Signal Corps RADAR Laboratory [*Obsolete Army*]
SCRL............ Signal Corps Radio Laboratory [*Army*] (IAA)
SCRL............ Skill Components Research Laboratory [*Air Force*] (MCD)
SCRL............ Split-Level Charge-Recovery Logic [*Computer science*]
SCRL............ Station Configuration Requirement List [*NASA*] (MCD)
SCRLC.......... South Central Research Library Council [*Library network*] (IID)
Scr LT.......... Scranton Law Times [*Pennsylvania*] [*A publication*] (DLA)
SCRLV.......... Subterranean Clover Red Leaf Virus
SCRM............ Isla Rey Jorge/Base Aerea Teniente R. Marsh Martin [*Chile*] [*ICAO location identifier*] (ICLI)
SCRM............ Secondary Certified Reference Material [*Nuclear energy*] (NRCH)
SCRMV.......... Scrophularia Mottle Virus [*Plant pathology*]
SCRN............ Screen [*s*] [*or Screening Freight*]
scrn............. Screen (VRA)
SCRN............ Screen
scRNA.......... Small Cytoplasmic RNA [*Ribanucleic Acid*] (BARN)
scRNP.......... Ribonucleoprotein, Small Cytoplasmic
scrnpr.......... Screenprint (VRA)
SCRNSW...... New South Wales Supreme Court Reports [*A publication*] (DLA)
SCRO............ Scottish Criminal Records Office [*Office of Population Census and Surveys*] [*British*]
SCRO............ Societe Canadienne de la Recherche Operationnelle
SCROLL........ String and Character Recording Oriented Logogrammatic Language [*1970*] [*Computer science*] (CSR)
SC ROM....... Scotch Roman [*Typography*] (DGA)
SCROOGE.... Society to Curtail Ridiculous, Outrageous, and Ostentatious Gift Exchange (EA)
SCROPT....... Scientific and Commercial Subroutine Interpreter and Program Translator (IAA)
SC/ROSTENA... Bureau Regional de Science et de Technologie pour l'Europe et l'Amerique du Nord [*Regional Office for Science and Technology for Europe and North America*] (EAIO)
SCRP............ Small Card Release Processing [*Computer science*] (IAA)
SCRP............ Societe Canadienne des Relations Publiques
SCRP............ Superfund Community Relations Program [*Environmental Protection Agency*] (GFGA)
SCRP............ Supplemental Conventional Reading Program [*Education*]
SCRPC.......... Societe de Physiotherapie Cardiorespiratoire du Canada (AC)
SCRPr.......... Sea Cont Ltd $1.46 1/4cmPfd [*NYSE symbol*] (TTSB)
SCRPrC........ Sea Cont Ltd. $2.10'82 Pfd [*NYSE symbol*] (TTSB)
SCRPrD........ Sea Cont Ltd. $4.125cm Cv Pfd [*NYSE symbol*] (TTSB)
SCRPrE........ Sea Cont Ltd. $4 cm Cv Pfd [*NYSE symbol*] (TTSB)
Sc RR........... Scotch Revised Reports [*A publication*] (DLA)
SCRR............ Solar Central Receiver Reformer (PDAA)
SCRR............ Standard Compliance Review Report (AAGC)
SCRR............ Supercircular Reentry Research (IAA)
SCRS............ Secondary Control Rod System [*Nuclear energy*] (NRCH)
SCRS............ Self-Control Rating Scale
SCRS............ Service Center Replacement System [*Computer science*]
SCRS............ Society of Collision Repair Specialists (EA)
SCRS............ Strip Chart Recorder System [*NASA*]
SCRT............ Sealed Cathode Ray Tube
SCRT............ Subscribers' Circuit Routine Tester [*Telecommunications*] (TEL)
SCRTA.......... Steel Castings Research and Trade Association [*British*]
SCRTC.......... Signal Corps Replacement Training Center [*Obsolete Army*]
SCRTERM..... Screw Terminal
SCRTY.......... Security
SCRUMPie... Socially Concerned Upwardly Mobile Professional [*Lifestyle classification*]
Scrut Charter... Scrutton on Charter-Parties [*18th ed.*] [*1974*] [*A publication*] (DLA)
Scrutton....... Scrutton on Charter-Parties [*16 eds.*] [*1886-1955*] [*A publication*] (DLA)
SCRV............ Spill Control Recovery Valve (PDAA)
SCRWC......... Sierra Club Radioactive Waste Campaign [*Later, RWC*] (EA)
ScS.............. Reflected S Wave [*Earthquakes*]
SCS.............. Safety Control Switch
SCS.............. Safety-Critical Systems/Software [*British*]
SCS.............. Saint Charles Seminary [*Later, SCBS*] [*Pennsylvania*]
SCS.............. Santa Clara Systems, Inc. [*San Jose, CA*] [*Telecommunications service*] (TSSD)
SCS.............. Satellite Communications Subsystem
SCS.............. Satellite Control Satellite [*Telecommunications*] (TEL)
SCS.............. Satellite Control Section (SSD)
SCS.............. Satellite Control Squadron
SCS.............. Satellite Test Center Communications Subsystem (MCD)
SCS.............. Scan Converter [*or Counter*] System
SCS.............. Scheduled Cargo Service (IIA)
SCS.............. Scientific Certification Systems (EA)
SCS.............. Scientific Civil Service [*British*]
SCS.............. Scientific Control Systems (DIT)
SCS.............. Scottish Combined Societies [*Australia*]
SCS.............. Screening and Costing Staff [*NATO*] (NATG)
SCS.............. Sea Control Ship [*Navy*] (NVT)
SCS.............. Secondary Control Ship [*Navy*] (NVT)
SCS.............. Secondary Control System (MCD)
SCS.............. Secondary Coolant System [*Nuclear energy*] (NRCH)
SCS.............. Secret Control Station [*NASA*] (KSC)
SCS.............. Secret Cover Sheet (AAG)
SCS.............. Section Control Station [*RADAR*]
SCS.............. Secure Communications System [*Military*] (CAAL)
SCS.............. Security Container System [*Army*] (AABC)
SCS.............. Security Control System (IAA)
SCS.............. Selected Cancers Study [*Centers for Disease Control*]
SCS.............. Selected Classification Service (NITA)
SCS.............. Semiconductor Controlled Switch (MSA)
SCS.............. Senior Citizen's Services [*A publication*]
SCS.............. Separate Channel Signalling (NITA)
SCS.............. Septuagint and Cognate Studies (BJA)
SCS.............. Sequence Coding System (IAA)
SCS.............. Sequence Control System (KSC)
SCS.............. Sequencing and Command Systems Specialist [*NASA*]
SCS.............. Shaken Child Syndrome (CPH)
SCS.............. Ship Control Station [*Navy*] (CAAL)
SCS.............. Short-Circuit-Stable
SCS.............. Shutdown Cooling System [*Nuclear energy*] (NRCH)
SCS.............. Sicasica [*Bolivia*] [*Seismograph station code, US Geological Survey Closed*] (SEIS)
SCS.............. Sidewinder Control System (DWSG)
SCS.............. Sigmacom Systems [*Vancouver Stock Exchange symbol*]
SCS.............. Signal Center and School [*Army*] (MCD)
SCS.............. Signal Communications System [*Air Force*]
SCS.............. Signal Conditioning System (KSC)
SCS.............. Silicon-Controlled Switch
SCS.............. Simulation Control Subsystem (KSC)
SCS.............. Simultaneous Color System (IAA)
SCS.............. Single Change of Station (IAA)
SCS.............. Single Channel Simplex
SCS.............. Single Composition Spherical [*Dental alloy*]
SCS.............. Single Control Support (BUR)
SCS.............. Slovak Catholic Sokol [*An association*] (EA)
SCS.............. Slow Code Scanner
SCS.............. Small Components Structural
SCS.............. Small Computer System
SCS.............. Social Competence Scale
SCS.............. Societe Canadienne du Sida (AC)
SCS.............. Societe Canadienne du Sommeil (AC)
SCS.............. Societe en Commandite Simple [*Simple Partnership*] [*Belgium*]
SCS.............. Society for Carribean Studies (EAIO)
SCS.............. Society for Ch'ing Studies (EA)
SCS.............. Society for Cinema Studies (EA)
SCS.............. Society for Computer Simulation [*Later, SCSI*] (EA)
SCS.............. Society for Conservative Studies [*Later, YAF*] (EA)
SCS.............. Society of Civil Servants [*British*]
SCS.............. Society of Clinical Surgery [*Defunct*] (EA)
SCS.............. Society of Construction Superintendents (EA)
SCS.............. Society of Cosmetic Scientists (EAIO)
SCS.............. Society of County Secretaries [*British*]
SCS.............. Sodium Cellulose Sulfate [*Organic chemistry*]
SCS.............. Sodium Characterization System [*Nuclear energy*] (NRCH)
SCS.............. Software Communications Service
SCS.............. Soil Conservation Service [*Department of Agriculture*]
SCS.............. Solar Collector Subassembly (MCD)
SCS.............. Solent Container Service [*British*] (DS)
SCS.............. Solid Combustion Synthesis [*Physics*]
SCS.............. SONAR Calibration Set
SCS.............. SONAR Communications Set
SCS.............. Soybean Corn Silage (OA)
SCS.............. Space Cabin Simulator (IEEE)
SCS.............. Space Command Station (AAG)
SCS.............. Space Communication System (IAA)
SCS.............. Spacecraft Control System (NASA)
SCS.............. Spacecraft System [*NASA*] (KSC)

SCS.......... Spanish Colonial Style [*Cigars*]
SCS.......... Special Communications System (MCD)
SCS.......... Special Computer Service (IAA)
SCS.......... Special Contingency Stockpile [*Military*] (AABC)
ScS.......... Specialist in Science (GAGS)
SCS.......... Speed Class Sequencing
SCS.......... Speed-Controlled Spark [*Automotive engineering*]
SCS.......... Speed Control System (PDAA)
SCS.......... Spinal Cord Society (EA)
SCS.......... Stabilization and Control System [*or Subsystem*] [*NASA*]
SCS.......... Standard Coordinate System (KSC)
SCS.......... Stationing Capability System [*Army*] (AABC)
SCS.......... Statistical Control System
SCS.......... Stiffened Cylindrical Shell
SCS.......... Stimulated Compton Scattering [*Spectroscopy*]
SCS.......... Stop Control Braking System [*Lucas Girling*]
SCS.......... Storage Computer Corp. [*AMEX symbol*] (SAG)
SCS.......... Student's Confidential Statement [*Education*]
SCS.......... Suit Communication System [*for spacesuits*] [*NASA*]
SCS.......... Superintendent of Car Service
SCS.......... Supervisory Control System (MCD)
SCS.......... Supplementary Control Strategy [*System*] [*Environmental*] (GNE)
SCS.......... Supply Control Study
SCS.......... Surface Composition Strengthened
SCS.......... Suspect Chemicals Sourcebook [*Roytech Publications*] [*Information service or system*] (CRD)
SCS.......... Sussex Cattle Society (EAIO)
SCS.......... Swedish Colonial Society (EA)
SCS.......... Sweeping Current Supply
SCS.......... Sweetens Computer Services [*British*]
SCS.......... System Conformance Statement [*Telecommunications*]
SCS.......... University of South California, School of Library Science, Los Angeles, CA [*OCLC symbol*] (OCLC)
SCSA.......... Secondary Colleges Staff Association [*Tasmania, Australia*]
SCSA.......... Ship Constructive and Shipwrights' Association [*A union*] [*British*]
SCSA.......... Siamese Cat Society of America (EA)
SCSA.......... Soil Conservation Society of America (EA)
SCSA.......... Spastic Centres of South Australia
SCSA.......... Sports Car Collectors Society of America [*Later, SCCSA*] (EA)
SCSA.......... Standard Consolidated Statistical Area [*Census Bureau*]
SCSA.......... Steering Committee for Sustainable Agriculture [*Later, CSA*] (EA)
SCSA.......... Supreme Council for Sport in Africa [*See also CSSA*] [*Yaounde, Cameroon*] (EAIO)
SCSB.......... Standard Capital Superannuation Benefit [*British*]
SCSBCVG.......... Suore di Carita delle Sante Bartolomea Capitanio e Vincenza Gerosa [*Sisters of Charity of Saints Bartholomew Capitanio And Vincent Gerosa*] [*Italy*] (EAIO)
SCSBDE.......... Square Corners Silver Bevelled Deckle Edges [*Bookbinding*] (DGA)
SCSBE.......... Square Corners Silver-Bevelled Edges [*Bookbinding*] (DGA)
SCSBM.......... Society for Computer Science in Biology and Medicine
SCSC.......... Santiago/Ciudad [*Chile*] [*ICAO location identifier*] (ICLI)
SCSC.......... ScanSource, Inc. [*NASDAQ symbol*] (SAG)
SCSC.......... Secondary Curriculum Study Center [*of NASSP*]
SCSC.......... Sorores a Caritate Sanctae Crucis [*Sisters of Mercy of the Holy Cross*] [*Roman Catholic religious order*]
SCSC.......... South Carolina State College
Sc-SC.......... South Carolina Supreme Court, Columbia, SC [*Library symbol Library of Congress*] (LCLS)
SCSC.......... Southern Connecticut State College [*New Haven*]
SCSC.......... Strategic Conventional Standoff Capability (MCD)
SCSC.......... Summer Computer Simulation Conference
SCSCB.......... Sisters of Charity of St. Charles Borromeo [*See also LCB*] (EAIO)
SCSCCL.......... Sellin Center for Studies in Criminology and Criminal Law (EA)
SCSCLC.......... Single-Carrier Space-Charge-Limited Current
SCSCmp.......... SCS Compute, Inc. [*Associated Press*] (SAG)
SCSCO.......... Secure Submarine Communications (KSC)
SC (Scot).......... Scottish Court of Session Cases, New Series [*A publication*] (DLA)
SCSCP.......... System Coordination for SAGE [*Semiautomatic Ground Environment*] Computer Programming [*Military*] (IAA)
SCSCW.......... Scancource Inc. Wrrt [*NASDAQ symbol*] (TTSB)
Sc SD.......... Doctor of Social Sciences
SCSD.......... School Construction Systems Development [*Project*] [*of Educational Facilities Laboratories*]
SCSD.......... Simulation and Control Systems Division [*General Electric Co.*] (MCD)
SCSE.......... La Serena/La Florida [*Chile*] [*ICAO location identifier*] (ICLI)
SCSE.......... Smooth Curve - Smooth Earth
SCSE.......... Society of Casual Safety Engineers
SCSE.......... Square Corners Silver Edges [*Bookbinding*] (DGA)
SCSE.......... State Commission for Space Exploration [*Former USSR*]
SCSEP.......... Senior Community Service Employment Program (EA)
Sc Sess Cas... Scotch Court of Session Cases [*A publication*] (DLA)
SCSFA.......... Sunset Coast Sub-tropical Fruits Association [*Queensland, Australia*]
SCSG.......... SAGE [*Semiautomatic Ground Environment*] Computer Support Group [*Military*] (IAA)
SCSG.......... Signal Conditioning Subsystem Group (MCD)
SCSG.......... Superior Cervical Sympathetic Ganglia [*Anatomy*]
SCSGIG.......... Supreme Council Sovereign Grand Inspectors General [*Freemasonry*]
SCSH.......... Scottish Council for Single Homeless (DBA)
SCSH.......... Sisters of Charity of St. Hyacinthe [*Grey Nuns*] [*Roman Catholic religious order*]
SCSH.......... Structural Carbon Steel Hard
SCSH.......... Survey of the Chronic Sick and Handicapped [*British*]
SCSHX.......... Shutdown Cooling System Heat Exchange [*Nuclear energy*] (NRCH)
SCSI.......... Sensors and Control Systems Institute [*Beltsville, MD*] [*Department of Agriculture*] (GRD)
SCSI.......... Small Computer System Interface [*Pronounced "scuzzy"*]
SCSI.......... Societe Canadienne de la Surete Industrielle
SCSI.......... Society for Computer Simulation International (EA)
SCSIT.......... Southern California Sensory Integration Test [*Ayres*] [*Education*]
SCSJA.......... Sisters of Charity of St. Joan Antida (TOCD)
SCSJAT.......... Sisters of Charity of St. Jeanne Antide Thouret [*Italy*] (EAIO)
SCSL.......... Sandia Corporation, Sandia Laboratory (AABC)
SCSL.......... Scientific Continuous Simulation Language (IAA)
SCSL.......... Sisters of Charity of St. Louis [*Roman Catholic religious order*]
SCSL.......... Suncoast S & L Assn FSA [*NASDAQ symbol*] (TTSB)
SCSL.......... Suncoast Savings & Loan Association [*Hollywood, FL*] [*NASDAQ symbol*] (NQ)
SCSLP.......... Smithsonian Center for Short-Lived Phenomena
SCSLP.......... Suncoast S&L 8% Cv Pfd [*NASDAQ symbol*] (TTSB)
SCS(LS).......... Sea Control Ship (Lead Ship) [*Navy*] (MCD)
SCSM.......... Small Caliber Smart Munition [*Army*] (RDA)
SCSM.......... Spacecraft Systems Monitor (IAA)
SCSM.......... Structural Carbon Steel Medium
SCSMHPS.......... Special Constituency Section for Mental Health and Psychiatric Services (EA)
SCSN.......... Santo Domingo/Santo Domingo [*Chile*] [*ICAO location identifier*] (ICLI)
SCSN.......... Southern California Seismic Network
SCSN.......... Standard Computer Software Number
SCSO.......... Space Communications Station Operation
SCSO.......... Superconducting Cavity Stabilized Oscillator [*For clocks*]
ScSocD.......... Doctor of Social Science
ScSocL.......... Licence in Social Science [*British*]
SCSP.......... Schools Cultural Studies Project (AIE)
SCSP.......... Scottish Council for Single Parents (DBA)
SCSP.......... Secretariat of the Council for Scientific Policy [*British*]
SCSP.......... Serum Cancer-Suppressive Peptide [*Oncology*]
SCSP.......... Smaller Communities Services Program [*Department of Labor*]
SCSP.......... Solid Cast Steel Propeller (DS)
SCSP.......... South China Sea Fisheries Development and Coordinating Program [*Marine science*] (OSRA)
ScSp.......... Spartanburg County Public Library, Spartanburg, SC [*Library symbol Library of Congress*] (LCLS)
SCSP.......... Storm and Combined Sewer Program (GNE)
SC/SP.......... Supracondylar/Suprapatellar [*Prosthesis*]
SCSP.......... System Calibration Support Plan [*Air Force*] (CET)
ScSpC.......... Converse College, Spartanburg, SC [*Library symbol Library of Congress*] (LCLS)
ScSpM.......... Milliken Research Corp., Research Library, Spartanburg, SC [*Library symbol Library of Congress*] (LCLS)
ScSpS.......... Sherman College of Straight Chiropractic, Spartanburg, SC [*Library symbol*] [*Library of Congress*] (LCLS)
SCSPS.......... Standing Committee on the Safeguard of the Pursuit of Science [*International Council of Scientific Unions*]
ScSpSM.......... Spartanburg Methodist College, Spartanburg, SC [*Library symbol*] [*Library of Congress*] (LCLS)
ScSpTC.......... Spartanburg Technical College, Spartanburg, SC [*Library symbol*] [*Library of Congress*] (LCLS)
ScSpW.......... Wofford College, Spartanburg, SC [*Library symbol Library of Congress*] (LCLS)
ScSpW-MHi... Methodist Historical Society, South Carolina Conference of the Methodist Church,Wofford College, Spartanburg, SC [*Library symbol Library of Congress*] (LCLS)
SCSR.......... Segundo Corral/Segundo Corral Alto [*Chile*] [*ICAO location identifier*] (ICLI)
SCSR.......... Self-Contained Self-Rescuer [*Breathing device*]
SCSR.......... Ship Construction Subsidy Regulations [*Canada*]
SCSRMA.......... Surface Coating Synthetic Resin Manufacturers Association [*British*] (BI)
SCSRS.......... Shoe Cove Satellite Receiving Station [*Canada*]
SCSRS-S.......... Standard Command Supply Review System - SAILS
SCSS.......... Satellite Communications System Control (NATG)
SCSS.......... School Child Stress Scale [*Child development test*] [*Psychology*]
SCSS.......... Scottish Council of Social Service (DI)
SCSS.......... Self-Contained Starting System [*NASA*]
SCSS.......... Sequence Coding and Search System
SCSS.......... State Controller and System Services [*NASA*]
SCSS.......... Structural Carbon Steel Soft
SCSST.......... Standing Conference on School Science and Technology [*British*]
SCST.......... Castro/Gamboa [*Chile*] [*ICAO location identifier*] (ICLI)
SCST.......... Scan Converter Storage Tube
SCST.......... Society of Commercial Seed Technologists (EA)
SCSTC.......... Senior Citizen Ski Touring Committee (EA)
Sc St Crim... Scandinavian Studies in Criminology [*1965*] [*A publication*] (DLA)
ScStg.......... Dorchester County Library, St. George, SC [*Library symbol*] [*Library of Congress*] (LCLS)
Sc St L.......... Scandinavian Studies in Law [*A publication*] (DLA)
ScStm.......... Calhoun County Public Library, St. Matthews, SC [*Library symbol*] [*Library of Congress*] (LCLS)
SCSTR.......... Segregated Continuous Stirred Tank Reactor [*Chemical engineering*]
Sc Stud Criminol... Scandinavian Studies in Criminology [*1965*] [*A publication*] (DLA)
SCSU.......... St. Cloud State University
ScSu.......... Sumter County Library, Sumter, SC [*Library symbol Library of Congress*] (LCLS)
SCSU.......... System Control Signal Unit (NITA)
ScSuM.......... Morris College, Sumter, SC [*Library symbol Library of Congress*] (LCLS)

ScSum......... Timrod Library, Summerville, SC [*Library symbol Library of Congress*] (LCLS)
ScSumL....... Timrod Library, Summerville, SC [*Library symbol*] [*Library of Congress*] (LCLS)
ScSuTC........ Sumter Technical College, Sumter, SC [*Library symbol*] [*Library of Congress*] (LCLS)
SCSW.......... Stolt Comex Seaway SA [*NASDAQ symbol*] (SAG)
SCSW.......... Super-Chilled Seawater
SCSWF........ Stolt Comex Seaway [*NASDAQ symbol*] (TTSB)
SCT............. Air Force Institute of Technology, Wright-Patterson AFB, OH [*OCLC symbol*] (OCLC)
SCT............. Saab Aircraft AB [*Sweden ICAO designator*] (FAAC)
SCT............. Sacrococcygeal Teratoma [*Oncology*]
S-C-T........... Salinity-Conductivity-Temperature
SCT............. Salmon Calcitonin [*Endocrinology*]
SCT............. Sample Control Tape [*Computer science*]
SCT............. Satellite Communication Terminal (MCD)
SCT............. S-Band Cassegrain Transmit
SCT............. Scan Conversion Tube
SCT............. Scanning Telescope (KSC)
SCT............. Scattered
SCT............. Schottky Clamped Transistor
SCT............. Scintrex Ltd. [*Toronto Stock Exchange symbol*]
SCT............. Scorpion Toxin [*Immunology*]
SCT............. Scotsman Industries [*NYSE symbol*] (TTSB)
SCT............. Scotsman Industries, Inc. [*NYSE symbol*] (SPSG)
SCT............. Scotty Lake [*Alaska*] [*Seismograph station code, US Geological Survey*] (SEIS)
SCT............. Scout (AABC)
SCT............. Screen Capture Test [*Computer science*]
Sct............. Scutum [*Constellation*]
SCT............. Semiconductor Curve Tracer
SCT............. Sentence Completion Technique [*or Test*]
SCT............. Sequence Checking Tape
SCT............. Service Counter Terminal [*Banking*]
SCT............. Sex Chromatin Test (MAE)
SCT............. Sickle Cell Trait (AAMN)
SCT............. Signal Corps Training [*Military*] (IAA)
SCT............. Single-Cell Test (MCD)
SCT............. Single Channel Transponder (MCD)
SCT............. Sioux City Terminal Railway [*AAR code*]
SCT............. Skylab Communication Terminal [*NASA*] (KSC)
SCT............. Societe Canadienne de Theologie [*Canadian Theological Society - CTS*]
SCT............. Society for Clinical Trials (EA)
SCT............. Society of Cardiological Technicians [*British*]
SCT............. Society of Cleaning Technicians (EA)
SCT............. Society of Commercial Teachers (EAIO)
SCT............. Society of County Treasurers [*British*]
SCT............. Soldier Crew Tent [*Army*] (INF)
SCT............. SONAR Certification Test
SCT............. Source Coding Team (SAA)
SCT............. Sous-Commission des Cartes Tectoniques [*Subcommittee for Tectonic Maps of the Commission for the Geological Map of the World - STMCGMW*] (EAIO)
SCT............. Space Combat Tactics (SAA)
SCT............. Special Characters Table [*Computer science*] (IBMDP)
SCT............. Special Committee on Trade
SCT............. Special Crew Time (DNAB)
SCT............. Spectral Control Technique
SCT............. Spectrographic Telescope
SCT............. Staphylococcal Clumping Test [*Medicine*] (AAMN)
SCT............. Step Control Table (CMD)
SCT............. Structural Clay Tile [*Technical drawings*]
SCT............. Student Coalition for Truth (EA)
SCT............. Subroutine Call Table [*Computer science*]
SCT............. Subscriber Carrier Terminal [*Telecommunications*] (TEL)
SCT............. Sugar-Coated Tablet
S Ct............ Supreme Court Reporter [*A publication*] (DLA)
SCt............. Supreme Court Reports
SCT............. Surface Charge Transistor [*Electronics*] (OA)
SCT............. Surface-Controlled Transistor (IAA)
SCT............. Swap Control Table [*Computer science*] (BYTE)
SCT............. System Circuit Test
SCT............. System Compatibility Tests
SCT............. System Component Test (IAA)
SCT............. System Configuration Table (IAA)
SCT............. Systems and Computer Technology (IAA)
S Ct............ US Supreme Court Reporter [*West*] [*1882-present*] [*A publication*] (AAGC)
SCTA........... Scottish Commercial Travellers Association (DBA)
SCTA........... Scottish Corn Trade Association (DBA)
SCTA........... Secondary Container Transfer Area [*Nuclear energy*] (NRCH)
SCTA........... Ships' Clerk Trade Association [*A union*] [*British*]
SCTA........... Southern California Timing Association (EA)
SCTA........... Steel Carriers Tariff Association, Inc. [*Riverdale, MD*]
SCTA........... Stone Carvers Trade Association [*A union*] [*British*]
SCTA........... Syndicat Canadien des Travailleurs Agricoles (AC)
SC (T & C)... Thompson and Cook's New York Supreme Court Reports [*A publication*] (DLA)
SCTAT......... Sex Cord Tumor with Annular Tubules [*Medicine*] (DMAA)
SCTB........... Santa Cruz Test Base (MCD)
SCTB........... Santiago/Eulogio Sanchez [*Chile*] [*ICAO location identifier*] (ICLI)
ScTB........... Scottish Tourist Board (DCTA)
S Ct Bull (CCH)... United States Supreme Court Bulletin (Commerce Clearing House) [*A publication*] (DLA)
SCTC........... Self-Contained Training Capability (DNAB)
SCTC........... Signal Corps Training Center [*Military*] (IAA)
SCTC........... Small Craft Training Center
SC/TC.......... Spacecraft Test Conductor (SAA)
SCTC........... Submarine Chaser Training Center [*Navy*]
SCTC........... Systems & Computer Tech [*NASDAQ symbol*] (TTSB)
SCTC........... Systems & Computer Technology Corp. [*NASDAQ symbol*] (NQ)
SCTC........... Temuco/Maquehue [*Chile*] [*ICAO location identifier*] (ICLI)
SCTCA......... SAC [*Strategic Air Command*] Channel and Traffic Control Agency (SAA)
SCTCA......... Strategic Air Command Channel and Traffic Control Agency (IAA)
SctCHt......... Scout Car, Half Track [*Army*]
SCTD........... Scattered
SCTD........... Scottish Centre for the Tuition of the Disabled [*Queen Margaret College*] (CB)
SCTD........... Subcaliber Training Device [*Military*] (AABC)
SCTE........... Puerto Montt/Internacional El Tepual [*Chile*] [*ICAO location identifier*] (ICLI)
SCTE........... Society of Cable Television Engineers (EA)
SCTE........... Society of Carbide and Tool Engineers (EA)
SCTE........... Spacecraft Central Timing Equipment [*NASA*]
SCTF........... Santa Cruz Test Facility (SAA)
SCTF........... SHAPE [*Supreme Headquarters Allied Powers Europe*] Centralized Training Facility [*NATO*] (NATG)
SCTF........... Sodium Chemical Technology Facility [*Nuclear energy*] (NRCH)
SCTFR......... Short-Contact-Time Fluidized Reactors [*Chemical engineering*]
SCTH........... Service Center for Teachers of History (EA)
SCTI............ Santiago/Internacional Los Cerillos [*Chile*] [*ICAO location identifier*] (ICLI)
SCTI............ SC&T Intl [*NASDAQ symbol*] (TTSB)
SCTI............ Sodium Components Test Installation [*Nuclear energy*]
SCTI............ Solid Carbide Tool Institute (EA)
SCTI............ University of Southern California Tax Institute (DLA)
SCTIW......... SC&T Intl Wrrt [*NASDAQ symbol*] (TTSB)
SCTL........... Schottky Coupled Transistor Logic (IAA)
SCTL........... Short-Circuited Terminating Line (IAA)
SCTL........... Short-Circuited Transmission Line
SCTL........... Small Components Test Loop [*Nuclear energy*]
SCTL........... Societe Canadienne des Technologistes de Laboratoire [*Canadian Society of Laboratory Technologists*] (EAIO)
SCTN........... Chaiten/Chaiten [*Chile*] [*ICAO location identifier*] (ICLI)
SCTN........... Service Center Taxpayer Notice [*IRS*]
SCTO........... Societe Canadienne des Technologistes en Orthopedie [*Canadian Society of Orthopaedic Technologists*] (EAIO)
SCTO........... Soft Carrier Turn Off (HGAA)
SCTOC......... Satellite Communications Test Operations Center
SCTP........... Ship Construction Test Plan [*Navy*] (CAAL)
SCTP........... Straight Channel Tape Print [*Computer science*] (KSC)
SCTP........... Syndicat Canadien des Travailleurs du Papier [*Canadian Paperworkers Union - CPU*]
SCTP........... Systems and Control Technology Panel (ACII)
SCTPP......... Straight Channel Tape Print Program [*Computer science*] (KSC)
SCTR........... Scooter (AAG)
SCTR........... Secretin Receptor [*Medicine*] (DMAA)
SCTR........... Sector (MSA)
SCTR........... Signal Corps Technical Requirements (MCD)
SCTR........... Single Channel Transponder (DWSG)
SCTR........... [*La*] Societe Canadienne des Therapeutes Respiratoires (AC)
SCTR........... Specialty Teleconstructioners [*NASDAQ symbol*] (SAG)
SCTR........... Specialty Teleconstructors [*NASDAQ symbol*] (TTSB)
SCTR........... Standing Conference on Telecommunications Research (IAA)
SCTRACEN... Submarine Chaser Training Center [*Navy*]
SCTRW......... Specialty Telecnstrctrs Wrrt [*NASDAQ symbol*] (TTSB)
SCTS........... SFOF [*Space Flight Operations Facility*] Communications Terminal Subsystem [*NASA*]
SCTS........... System Components Test Station (MCD)
SCTT........... Scotts Co. [*NASDAQ symbol*] (SAG)
SCTTU......... Scottish Council of Textile Trade Unions (DCTA)
SCTV........... Second City Television [*Television program, the title of which was later changed to its initialism*]
SCTV........... Standing Conference on Television Viewing [*British*]
ScTvC......... North Greenville College, Tigerville, SC [*Library symbol*] [*Library of Congress*] (LCLS)
SCTV-GDHS... Spacecraft Television - Ground Data Handling System [*NASA*]
scty............ Secretary (BARN)
SCTY........... Security (AFM)
SCTY........... Society
SCTYG......... Security Group [*Military*]
SCTYPOLICESq... Security Police Squadron [*Air Force*]
SCTYSERSCH... Security Service School [*Air Force*]
SCTYSq........ Security Squadron [*Air Force*]
SCTZ........... Puerto Montt [*Chile*] [*ICAO location identifier*] (ICLI)
SCU............ Santiago [*Cuba*] [*Airport symbol*] (OAG)
SCU............ S-Band Cassegrain Ultra
SCU............ Scan Control Unit (IAA)
SCU............ Scanner Control Unit
SCU............ Scottish Church Union
SCU............ Scottish Cricket Union (DBA)
SCU............ Scottish Crofters Union (DBA)
SCU............ Scottish Cyclists Union (DBA)
SCU............ Secondary Control Unit [*Aerospace*] (AAG)
SCU............ Selector Checkout Unit
SCU............ Sensor Control Unit (MCD)

SCU .... Sequence Control Unit [*Aerospace*] (KSC)
SCU .... Service and Cooling Umbilical [*Aerospace*] (MCD)
SCU .... Service Command Unit
SCU .... Servicing Control Unit [*Telecommunications*] (TEL)
SCU .... Sheep Canyon [*Utah*] [*Seismograph station code, US Geological Survey Closed*] (SEIS)
SCU .... Signal Conditioning Unit (NASA)
SCU .... Signal Control Unit (NASA)
SCU .... Single Conditioning Unit
scu .... South Carolina [*MARC country of publication code Library of Congress*] (LCCP)
SCU .... Special Care Unit
SCU .... Stable Control Unit
SCU .... Stand-Alone Computer Unit
SCU .... Static Checkout Unit (KSC)
SCU .... Station Control Unit
SCU .... Statistical Control Unit [*Military*]
SCU .... Steering Control Unit
SCU .... Storage Control Unit
SCU .... Street Crime Unit [*Criminology*] (LAIN)
SCU .... Subscriber Channel Unit (IAA)
SCU .... Subscribers' Concentrator Unit [*Telecommunications*] (TEL)
SCU .... Suit Cooling Unit (IAA)
SCU .... Sulfur-Coated Urea [*Chemical technology*]
SCU .... Surface Control Unit
SCU .... Switch Control Unit (MCD)
SCU .... Synchronous Controller Unit
SCU .... System Configuration Unit (MCD)
SCU .... System Control Unit
SCU .... System/Memory Control Unit (NITA)
ScU .... University of South Carolina, Columbia, SC [*Library symbol Library of Congress*] (LCLS)
SCUA .... Suez Canal Users Association (NATG)
SCUAE .... State Committee on the Utilization of Atomic Energy [*Former USSR*]
ScU-Ai .... University of South Carolina-Aiken, Aiken, SC [*Library symbol*] [*Library of Congress*] (LCLS)
SCUAS .... Standing Conference of University Appointments Services [*British*]
ScU-B .... University of South Carolina-Beaufort, Beaufort, SC [*Library symbol*] [*Library of Congress*] (LCLS)
scuba .... Self-Contained Underwater Breathing Apparatus (ODBW)
SCUBA .... Self-Contained Underwater Breathing Apparatus
SCUBA .... Submillimeter Common-User Bolometer Array [*Instrumentation*]
SCUBADIV ... Scuba Diver Badge [*Military decoration*] (GFGA)
SCUC .... Satellite Communications Users Conference [*Convention*] (TSSD)
ScU-C .... University of South Carolina-Coastal Carolina, Conway, SC [*Library symbol*] [*Library of Congress*] (LCLS)
SCUCC Dec... South Carolina Unemployment Compensation Commission Decisions [*A publication*] (DLA)
SCUCCR .... South Carolina Unemployment Compensation Commission Reports of Hearings [*A publication*] (DLA)
SCUD .... Scunner [*Missile*]
SCUD .... Subsonic Cruise Unarmed Decoy [*Air Force*] (MCD)
SCUDD .... Standing Conference of University Drama Departments (AIE)
ScudNA .... Scudder New Asia Fund [*Associated Press*] (SAG)
SCUDS .... Simplification, Clarification, Unification, Decimalization, Standardization
ScudWld ...... Scudder World Income Opportunities Ltd. [*Associated Press*] (SAG)
SCUE .... Standing Conference on University Entrance [*British*] (DI)
SCUF .... Slow Continuous Ultrafiltration [*Medicine*] (DMAA)
SCUGA .... Schools, Curriculum, Unusual, Geography, and Alumni [*University admisssion rating system*]
SCUIO .... Standing Conference of University Information Officers [*British*]
Scul .... Sculptor [*Constellation*]
SCUL .... Simulation of the Columbia University Libraries [*Data processing research*]
ScU-L .... University of South Carolina, Law School, Columbia, SC [*Library symbol Library of Congress*] (LCLS)
ScU-Lan .... University of South Carolina-Lancaster, Lancaster, SC [*Library symbol*] [*Library of Congress*] (LCLS)
SCULL .... Serial Communication Unit for Long Links
SCULP .... Sculpsit [*He, or She, Engraved It*] [*Latin*]
SCULP .... Sculptor
SCULP .... Sculpture (ROG)
sculp .... Sculpture (VRA)
SCULPS .... Sculpsit [*He, or She, Engraved It*] [*Latin*]
SCULPT .... Sculptor [*or Sculpture*]
Sculpt Hellenist Age... Sculpture of the Hellenistic Age [*A publication*] (OCD)
Sculpt R ...... Sculpture Review [*A publication*] (BRI)
SCUM .... Society for Cutting Up Men
ScU-M .... University of South Carolina, School of Medicine, Columbia, SC [*Library symbol Library of Congress*] (LCLS)
SCUMRA ...... Societe Central de l'Uranium et des Minerals et Metaux Radioactifs [*France*]
SC(UN) .... Security Council of the United Nations
ScUn .... Union County Library, Union, SC [*Library symbol*] [*Library of Congress*] (LCLS)
SCUP .... School, College, and University Partnerships Program [*Department of Education*] (GFGA)
SCUP .... School Computer Use Plan (IEEE)
SCUP .... Scupper
SCUP .... Service Center Unpostable [*IRS*]
SCUP .... Society for College and University Planning (EA)
SCUPA .... Single-Chain Urokinase-Like Plasminogen Activator [*Anticlotting agent*]
SCUPU .... Self-Contained Underwater Pinger Unit [*SONAR*]
SCUR .... Secure Computing [*NASDAQ symbol*] (TTSB)
SCUR .... Secure Computing Corp. [*NASDAQ symbol*] (SAG)
SCUR .... Selected Command Unit Review (MCD)
SCUS .... Supreme Court of the United States
ScU-S .... University of South Carolina, Science Library, Columbia, SC [*Library symbol Library of Congress*] (LCLS)
SCUSA .... Student Conference on United States Affairs
ScU-Sa .... University of South Carolina-Salkehatchie, Allendale, SC [*Library symbol*] [*Library of Congress*] (LCLS)
SCUSE .... Special Committee for United States Exports [*Washington, DC*] (EA)
ScU-Sp .... University of South Carolina-Spartanburg, Spartanburg, SC [*Library symbol*] [*Library of Congress*] (LCLS)
ScU-Su .... University of South Carolina at Sumter, Sumter, SC [*Library symbol Library of Congress*] (LCLS)
SCUT .... Schizophrenia, Chronic Undifferentiated Type [*Psychiatry*] (DAVI)
Scut .... Scutum [*Constellation*]
Scut .... Scutum [*of Hesiod*] [*Classical studies*] (OCD)
SCUTG .... Signal Corps Unit Training Group [*Military*] (IAA)
SCUTREA ..... Standing Conference on University Teaching and Research in the Education of Adults [*British*] (DI)
SCUU .... Southern College University Union
ScU-Un .... University of South Carolina-Union, Union, SC [*Library symbol*] [*Library of Congress*] (LCLS)
SCV .... Eglin Regional Hospital Library, Eglin AFB, FL [*OCLC symbol*] (OCLC)
SCV .... Saguaro Cactus Virus [*Plant pathology*]
SCV .... Scania AB [*NYSE symbol*] (SAG)
SCV .... Seaclutter Visibility [*Navy*] (CAAL)
SCV .... Selective Control Valve [*Hydraulics*]
SCV .... Side Control Valves
SCV .... Simultaneous Chest Compression and Ventilation [*Medicine*]
SCV .... Smooth, Capsulated, Virulent [*Bacteriology*]
SCV .... Solar Constant Variations
SCV .... Sons of Confederate Veterans (EA)
SCV .... South Atlantic Ltd. [*Vancouver Stock Exchange symbol*]
SCV .... Speed-Controlled Volume
SCV .... Speed Control Valve
SCV .... St. Croix [*Virgin Islands*] [*Seismograph station code, US Geological Survey*] (SEIS)
SCV .... Steam-Conditioning Valve
SCV .... Steel Containment Vessel [*Nuclear energy*] (NRCH)
SCV .... Stock Change Voucher [*Military*] (AFIT)
SCV .... Strip Chart Viewer
SCV .... Sub Center Visibility (MCD)
SCV .... Sub Clutter Visibility
SCV .... Subcutaneous Vaginal [*Block*] [*Anesthesiology*] (DAVI)
SCV .... Suceava [*Romania*] [*Airport symbol*] (OAG)
SCV .... Supersonic Cruise Missile
SCV .... Swirl Control Valve [*Automotive engine design*]
SCV .... System Compatibility Vehicle
SCV .... System Component Verification
SCV.A .... Scania AB'A'ADS [*NYSE symbol*] (TTSB)
SCV.B .... Scania AB'B'ADS [*NYSE symbol*] (TTSB)
SCVD .... Valdivia/Pichoy [*Chile*] [*ICAO location identifier*] (ICLI)
SCVE .... Spacecraft Vicinity Equipment (IAA)
SCVF .... Single Channel Voice Frequency [*Telecommunications*] (OSI)
SCVF .... Single Channel Voice Frequency (NITA)
SCVIR .... Society of Cardiovascular and Interventional Radiology (EA)
SCVL .... Shoe Carnival [*NASDAQ symbol*] (TTSB)
SCVL .... Shoe Carnival, Inc. [*NASDAQ symbol*] (SAG)
SCVM .... Shuttle Command and Voice Multiplexer (MCD)
SCVO .... Scottish Council for Voluntary Organisations (DBA)
SCVP .... Society of Clerks of Valuation Panels [*British*] (DBA)
SCVT .... Suzuki Continuously-Variable Transmission [*Automotive powertrain*]
SCVTR .... Scan Converting Video Tape Recorder (MCD)
SCVWD .... Santa Clara Valley Water District
SCW .... AFWAL [*Air Force Wright Aeronautical Laboratories*] Technical Information Center, Wright-Patterson AFB, OH [*OCLC symbol*] (OCLC)
ScW .... Collection County Memorial Library, Walterboro, SC [*Library symbol*] [*Library of Congress*] (LCLS)
SCW .... Malmo Aviation AB [*Sweden ICAO designator*] (FAAC)
SCW .... Sherman Crater - Mount Baker [*Washington*] [*Seismograph station code, US Geological Survey Closed*] (SEIS)
SCW .... Silicone Carbide Whisker
SCW .... Silk-Covered Wire (IAA)
SCW .... Slow Cyclotron Wave (IAA)
SCW .... Society of Colonial Wars
SCW .... Southern California Water Co. [*NYSE symbol*] (SAG)
SCW .... Southern Cal Water [*NYSE symbol*] (TTSB)
SCW .... Space Charge Wave (PDAA)
SCW .... State College of Washington
SCW .... St. Clair Paint & Wallpaper Corp. [*Toronto Stock Exchange symbol*]
SCW .... Substorm Current Wedge
SCW .... Supercritical Water
SCW .... Super-Critical Wing
SCW .... Superintendent of Contract Work [*Navy*]
SCWA .... South Carolina Waterfowl Association
SCWA .... Supreme Court of Western Australia
ScWal .... Oconee County Library, Walhalla, SC [*Library symbol Library of Congress*] (LCLS)
SCWC .... Special Commission on Weather Modification
SC/WCA .... Sneak Circuit/Worst Case Analysis (MCD)
SCWCU .... Supreme Council of the Western Catholic Union [*Later, Western Catholic Union*] (EA)

SCWDS Southeastern Cooperative Wildlife Disease Study [*University of Georgia*] [*Research center*] (RCD)
SCWEP Spinnable Cotton Waste Equalization Program
SCWG Satellite Communications Working Group [*NATO*] (NATG)
SCWGA Sonoma County Wineries Association [*Sonoma County Wine Growers Associatio n*] [*Acronym is based on former name,*] (EA)
ScWL Single-Comb White Leghorn [*Poultry*]
SCWM Subcortical White Matter [*Medicine*] (DMAA)
ScWn Fairfield County Library, Winnsboro, SC [*Library symbol*] [*Library of Congress*] (LCLS)
SCWO Supercalendered Web-Offset [*Paper*] (DGA)
SCWO Supercritical Water Oxidation [*Waste disposal technology*]
SCWPH Students Concerned with Public Health [*Defunct*] (EA)
SCWPLR Special Committee for Workplace Product Liability Reform (EA)
SCWR Standing Committee on Water Resources [*Australia*]
SCWR Supercritical Water Reactor
SCWS Scottish Co-Operative Wholesale Society
SCWS Space Combat Weapon System (IAA)
SCWSL Small Caliber Weapon Systems Laboratory (MCD)
SCWT Stroop Color-Word Test [*Psychology*] (DAVI)
SCWT System Cold Wire Tests
SCX Oneida, TN [*Location identifier FAA*] (FAAL)
SCX Single-Charge Exchange
SCX Solar Coronal X-Ray
SCX Starrett [*L. S.*] Co. [*NYSE symbol*] (SPSG)
SCX Starrett (L.S.)'A' [*NYSE symbol*] (TTSB)
SCX Strong Cation Exchanger [*Chemistry*]
SCX Sun Country Airlines, Inc. [*ICAO designator*] (FAAC)
SCY Scan Converter Yoke
SCY Scurry, TX [*Location identifier FAA*] (FAAL)
SCY Sports Club [*AMEX symbol*] (TTSB)
SCY Sports Club Co., Inc. [*AMEX symbol*] (SAG)
SCYL Single-Cylinder
Scyt Scythia (VRA)
SCZ Santa Cruz [*Solomon Islands*] [*Airport symbol*] (OAG)
SCZ Schwitzer, Inc. [*NYSE symbol*] (SPSG)
SCZ State Coastal Zone (NOAA)
SD Decisions of the Sadr Court [*1845-62*] [*Bengal, India*] [*A publication*] (DLA)
SD Diamant [*France*] [*Research code symbol*]
SD Diploma in Statistics (WDAA)
SD Doctor of Science (PGP)
SD Safe Deposit [*Business term*]
SD Safety Destructor (NG)
SD Said (ROG)
SD Sailed
S/D Sailing Date (DS)
SD Sailing Directions [*British*]
S/D Salaried Direct [*Ratio*]
SD Salt Depletion
SD Salutem Dicit [*Sends Greetings*] [*Latin*]
SD Same Day
SD Sample Data (NG)
SD Sample Delay
SD Sand (WGA)
SD San Diego [*Diocesan abbreviation*] [*California*] (TOCD)
SD Sash Door
SD Saturation Deficit
SD Scaling and Display (NASA)
SD Scan Data (IAA)
SD Scandinavian Delegation [*British*]
SD Scanning Densitometer [*Instrumentation*]
SD Schematic Diagram
SD Schottky Diode (IAA)
SD Scientiae Doctor [*Doctor of Science*] (ADA)
SD Scientific Design [*Group*]
SD Scleroderma [*Medicine*] (DAVI)
SD Scottish District [*Council*]
SD Scram Discharge [*Nuclear energy*] (NRCH)
SD Scrip Department (MHDB)
SD Sea Damaged
S/D Seadrome
SD Search Date (NITA)
SD Search Depth [*Navy*] (NVT)
SD Seasonal Derating (IEEE)
SD Seasoned (WGA)
SD Secchi Disk
SD Secondary Distribution [*Investment term*]
SD Second Defense [*Men's lacrosse position*]
SD Second Difference [*Statistics*] (OA)
SD Secretary of Defense
SD Section Definition (IAA)
SD Security Disconnect [*Computer science*] (ECII)
SD Sedan
SD Seed (WGA)
SD Segregation Distorter [*Genetics*]
SD Segregation Distortion (DOG)
SD Sehr Dringend [*Very urgent, used preceding German coded messages*]
SD Seismic Detector (MCD)
SD Seize Detector
SD Selenium Diode
SD Selenoid Driver (IAA)
SD Self-Destroying [*Projectile*]
SD Self-Destruct
SD Self Dual (IAA)
SD Semantic Differential
SD Semiconductor Device (IAA)
SD Semi-Darkness (DNAB)
SD Semidetached (ADA)
SD Semidiameter
SD Seminars Directory [*A publication*]
SD Senate Document
SD Senatus Decreto [*By Decree of the Senate*] [*Latin*]
SD Send Data [*Computer science*]
SD Send Digits [*Telecommunications*] (TEL)
SD Senile Dementia [*Medicine*]
SD Senior Deacon [*Freemasonry*]
SD Septal Defect [*Medicine*]
SD Sequential Disk (IAA)
SD Serializer/Deserializer
SD Serine Dehydratase [*An enzyme*]
SD Serologically Defined [*Immunology*]
SD Serologically Determined [*Medicine*]
SD Serum Defect [*Medicine*] (MAE)
SD Service Dated (ROG)
SD Service Dress
SD Servicing Diagram
SD Servus Dei [*Servant of God*] [*Latin*]
SD Settlement Date [*Business*] (MHDB)
SD Several Dates
SD Severe Duty [*Truck*]
SD Severely Diabetic
SD Sewed
SD Sewer Drain
SD Shakedown [*Nuclear energy*] (NRCH)
SD Share Distribution (ECII)
SD Shell-Destroying [*Device*]
SD Shelter Deck (DNAB)
SD Shield of David (BJA)
SD Ship Destination Test [*Intelligence test*]
SD Shop Drawing (AAG)
SD Short Day [*Botany*]
SD Short Delay
SD Short Delivery
sd Short Delivery (ODBW)
SD Short Duration
SD Shoulder Disarticulation [*Medicine*] (MAE)
SD Shoulder Dislocation
SD Shower Drain (AAG)
S/D Shut Down
SD Sicherheitsdienst [*Police Duty*] [*NAZI Germany*]
S-D Sickle Cell Hemoglobin D [*Disease*] [*Medicine*]
SD Side Deck
SD Side Door
SD Side Drum
SD Siegfried AG [*Switzerland*] [*Research code symbol*]
SD Sight Draft [*Business term*]
SD Signal Digit (IAA)
SD Signals Division [*British military*] (DMA)
SD Signal-to-Distortion (IAA)
SD Signed (WGA)
SD Signed Digit (IAA)
SD Significant Digit [*Mathematics*]
SD Simple Design
SD Simplex Drop Out (IAA)
SD Sine Dato [*Undated book*] [*Latin*]
SD Sine Die [*Without Day*] [*Latin*]
SD Single Deck [*Navigation*]
SD Single Density [*Computer science*] (IAA)
SD Single Determination
SD Single Diaphragm [*Automotive engineering*]
SD Single Distilled
SD Single Domain [*Grains in rocks*] [*Geophysics*]
S/D Sit and Dangle [*Orthopedics*] (DAVI)
SD Site Defense [*Military*] (AABC)
SD Situation Display
SD Skid
SD Skin Destruction [*Medicine*]
SD Skin Dose
SD Sleep Deprivation (PDAA)
SD Sliding Door
SD Slope Difference [*Statistics*]
SD Slowdown
s/d Small Damage (DS)
SD Small-Scale Disturbance Field
SD Smoke Detector (NASA)
SD Social Democratic Party [*Germany*]
SD Socialdemokratiet i Danmark [*Social Democratic Party of Denmark*] [*Political party*] (PPE)
SD Societas Docta (EA)
SD Soft Drawn
SD Soft Drug [*One that is metabolized to an inactive compound*]
SD Software Dynamics [*Buena Park, CA*] (TSSD)
SD Solar Dynamic (SSD)
SD Solenoid Driver (IAA)
SD Solicitation Document
SD Solid Drawn
SD Sort File Description [*Computer science*]
SD Sorties per Day [*Air Force*] (AFIT)

SD Sound [*Board on Geographic Names*]
SD Sound [*Films, television, etc.*]
sd Sound (WDMC)
SD Sounding Doubtful [*Nautical charts*]
SD Source/Destination [*Inspection/Acceptance Point*] (MCD)
SD Source Document [*Computer science*]
SD South Dakota [*Postal code*]
SD South Dakota Compiled Laws, Annotated [*A publication*] (DLA)
SD South Dakota Reports [*A publication*] (DLA)
Sd South Dakota State Library Commission, Pierre, SD [*Library symbol Library of Congress*] (LCLS)
SD South Division (ROG)
SD Southern District (DLA)
SD Spaced Doublet (IAA)
SD Space Division [*Los Angeles, CA*] [*Air Force*]
SD Spare Disposition (MCD)
SD Special Delivery
SD Special Document
SD Special Duty [*Military*]
SD Specialist Degree (PGP)
SD Specially Denatured
SD Specification Document [*NASA*] (NASA)
SD Specification for Design
SD Spectacle Dispenser [*Navy technician*]
SD Spectral Distribution
SD Speech Plus Duplex (IAA)
SD Speed Density
SD Speed Disk [*Computer program*] (PCM)
SD Sphere Drake Holdings [*NYSE symbol*] (SPSG)
SD Spin Device
SD Spin-Dipolar [*Physics*]
SD Splice Donor [*Genetics*]
SD Splitter Damper (OA)
SD Spontaneous Delivery [*Obstetrics*]
SD Sporadic Depression [*Medicine*] (DMAA)
SD Spreading Depression [*Medicine*] (DMAA)
SD Square Law Detector [*Telecommunications*] (OA)
SD Staff Development (ADA)
SD Staff Duties [*Military British*]
SD Stage Direction
SD Stage Door [*Theatrical slang*]
SD Stamp Duty
sd Stamped [*Stocks*] (MHDW)
SD Standard Decision (MCD)
SD Standard Deduction
SD Standard Definition [*Electronics*]
SD Standard Design [*of a vessel*] (DS)
SD Standard Deviation [*Also, s*]
SD Standard Dress [*Military British*]
SD Standardization Data
SD Standardization Directory
SD Standards Development (IEEE)
SD Stands Detached [*Freight*]
SD Stars of David (EA)
SD Start Date (NITA)
SD Start Delimiter [*Computer science*] (TNIG)
SD State Department
SD State Director
SD State Disability (DAVI)
S/D Statement of Differences
SD Station Director [*Deep Space Instrumentation Facility, NASA*]
SD Statutory Declaration
SD Steel Deck (ADA)
SD Stein & Day [*Publishers*]
SD Stereo Directional
SD Sterile Dressing [*Medicine*] (MEDA)
SD Sterile Dressing [*Surgery*] (DAVI)
SD Stern Discharge
SD Steward [*Navy rating*]
Sd Stimulus, Discriminative (MAE)
Sd Stimulus Drive (MAE)
SD Stock Dividend [*Investment term*]
SD Stone Disintegration [*Urology*]
S/D Storage or Distribution
SD Stores Depot [*British military*] (DMA)
SD Storm Deck [*Naval engineering*]
SD Storm Detection [*RADAR*]
SD Storm Drain [*Technical drawings*]
SD Stowage Drawer
SD Straight Drainage [*Medicine*] (MEDA)
SD Straight Duty
SD Strength Differential [*Steel*]
SD Strength-Duration (Curve) [*Prosthesis*]
SD Streptodornase [*An enzyme*]
SD Stronnictwo Demokratyczne [*Democratic Party*] [*Poland Political party*] (PPE)
SD Structural Detail (AAG)
SD Structural Dynamics (KSC)
SD Studia et Documenta ad Iura Orientis Antiqui Pertinenta [*Leiden*] [*A publication*] (BJA)
SD Study Director (MCD)
SD Subcontractor Data
SD Subdural [*Anatomy*]
SD Submarine Detector (ADA)
SD Subtotal Discectomy [*Medicine*]
SD Sudan [*ANSI two-letter standard code*] (CNC)
SD Sudan Airways [*ICAO designator*] (AD)
SD Sudden Death [*Medicine*]
S-D Sudden Death [*Tiebreaking in sports*]
SD Sugar Determination
SD Sum of Digits (SAA)
SD Sun's Declensions [*Astronomy*] (ROG)
SD Super Density [*Computer science*]
SD Super Diesel [*Automotive engineering*]
SD Super Duty [*Automotive engineering*]
SD Superintendent of Documents [*US Government Printing Office*]
SD Supplier Documentation (NASA)
SD Supply Department [*Navy*]
SD Supply Depot
SD Supply Detachment [*British military*] (DMA)
SD Supply Duct [*Nuclear energy*] (NRCH)
SD Support Directive (KSC)
SD Support [*or Supporting*] Document (KSC)
SD Surface Duct [*Navy*] (CAAL)
SD Surgical Drain (DAVI)
SD Surridge Dawson [*Commercial firm British*]
SD Surveillance Drone [*Air Force*]
SD Survival Dose
Sd Suspended [*Regulation or order suspended*] [*Used in Shepard's Citations*] [*Legal term*] (DLA)
SD Suspended Dust (DICI)
SD Swaziland
SD Sweep Driver
SD Switch Driver
SD Syllable Duration [*Entomology*]
SD Synchronous Detector [*Electronics*] (OA)
SD Synthetic Dextrose [*Biochemistry*]
SD System Demonstration [*Military*]
SD System Description
SD System Designator (AFIT)
SD System Drawer
SD Systems Designers [*Software manufacturer*] [*British*]
SD Systems Development (MCD)
SD Systems Directorate [*Army*] (RDA)
SD Systems Division [*Department of Commerce*] [*Information service or system*] (IID)
SD Systolic Discharge [*Cardiology*]
S/D Systolic to Diastolic [*Cardiology*] (MAE)
SD1 Steward, First Class [*Navy rating*]
SD2 Steward, Second Class [*Navy rating*]
SD3 Steward, Third Class [*Navy rating*]
SDA Augustana College, Sioux Falls, SD [*OCLC symbol*] (OCLC)
SDA Baghdad-Saddam [*Iraq*] [*Airport symbol*] (OAG)
SDA Sacrodextra Anterior [*A fetal position*] [*Obstetrics*]
SDA Sadr Diwani Adalat Reports [*India*] [*A publication*] (DLA)
SDA Satellite Data Area (IAA)
SDA Saw Diamond Abrasive (PDAA)
SDA Schweizerische Depeschenagentur AG [*Swiss News Agency*] (EY)
SDA Scottish Darts Association (DBA)
SDA Scottish Development Agency (DS)
SDA Scottish Diploma in Agriculture
SDA Screen Design Aid [*Computer science*] (HGAA)
SDA Screw Displacement Axis
SDA Section Department Authority
SDA Seismic Data Analysis
SDA Self-Defence Agency [*Japan*] (ECON)
SDA Semidehydroascorbate [*Biochemistry*]
SDA Sequential Degradation Analysis
SDA Service Delivery Area [*Job Training and Partnership Act*] (OICC)
SDA Seventh-Day Adventist
SDA Sex Discrimination Act [*1975*] [*British*] (DCTA)
SDA Shaft Drive Axis [*Aerospace*] (KSC)
SDA Shenandoah, IA [*Location identifier FAA*] (FAAL)
SDA Ship's Destination Authority (NVT)
SDA Shoulder Disarticulation [*Medicine*]
SDA Shut Down Amplifier (IAA)
SDA Significant Digit Arithmetic
SDA Simple Doublet Antenna
SDA Sleeve Dipole Antenna
SDA Slowdown Area
SDA Soap and Detergent Association (EA)
SDA Social Democratic Alliance [*British*]
SDA Social-Democratic Association [*Political party*] (EAIO)
SDA Solvent Deasphalting
SDA Somali Democratic Alliance [*Political party*] (EY)
SDA Source Data Acquisition (BUR)
SDA Source Data Automation [*Military*]
SDA Special Disbursing Agent, Bureau of Indian Affairs [*United States*] (DLA)
SDA Special Duty Assignment (AFM)
SDA Specially Denatured Alcohol
SDA Specific Dynamic Action [*of foods*] [*Physiology*]
SDA Spectral Distribution Analyzer
SDA Spontaneous Divergent Academic [*Test*] [*Education*]
SDA Stacked Dipole Array
SDA Standard Gold Mines Ltd. [*Vancouver Stock Exchange symbol*]
SDA St. Andrews Ltd. [*Canada ICAO designator*] (FAAC)
SDA Statistical Distribution Analyzer
SDA Step Down Amplifier
SDA Stepwise Discriminant Analysis

SDA .... Stereo Dimensional Array
SDA .... Steroid-Dependent Asthmatic [*Medicine*]
SDA .... Stevens-Duryea Associates (EA)
SDA .... Stirrer Drive Assembly
SDA .... Stranka Demokratske Akcije [*Party of Democratic Action*] [*Bosnia-Herzegovina*] [*Political party*] (EY)
SDA .... Students for Democratic Action
SDA .... Studies in the Decorative Arts [*A publication*] (BRI)
SDA .... Subcarrier Demodulator Assembly [*Deep Space Instrumentation Facility, NASA*]
SDA .... Succinic Dehydrogenase Activity
SDA .... Sulfadiazine [*Antibiotic*]
SDA .... Superficial Distal Axillary [*Lymph node*]
SDA .... Supplier Data Approval [*Nuclear energy*] (NRCH)
SDA .... Supporting Data Analysis
SDA .... Surface Design Association (EA)
SDA .... Sweet Damn All [*Nothing At All*] [*Slang*]
SDA .... Symbolic Device Address
SDA .... Symbolic Disk Address (AFM)
SDA .... Symbols-Digits-Alphabetics
SDA .... System Design Agency [*Bell Telephone Laboratory*] (MCD)
SDA .... Systems Data Analysis
SDA .... Systems Dynamic Analyzer
SDAA .... Salt Distributors Association of America (EA)
SDAA .... Scottish Dancing Association of Australia
SDAA .... Servicemen's Dependents Allowance Act
SDAA .... Skein Dyers Association of America [*Later, SRPDAA*] (EA)
SDAA .... Stacked Dipole Aerial Array
SdAbA .... Alexander Mitchell Library, Aberdeen, SD [*Library symbol Library of Congress*] (LCLS)
SdAbN .... Northern State College, Aberdeen, SD [*Library symbol Library of Congress*] (LCLS)
SdAbP .... Presentation College, Aberdeen, SD [*Library symbol Library of Congress*] (LCLS)
SDAC .... Seismic Data Analysis Center
SDAC .... Shelby Dodge Automobile Club [*Defunct*] (EA)
SDAC .... Shipping Defence Advisory Committee [*General Council of British Shipping*] (DS)
SDACMG .... Seventh-Day Adventist Church Musicians Guild [*Defunct*] (EA)
SDAD .... Satellite Digital and Analog Display
SDAD .... Special Domestically Available Documents [*NASA*] (KSC)
SDADA .... Seventh-Day Adventist Dietetic Association (EA)
SD Admin R ... Administrative Rules of South Dakota [*A publication*] (DLA)
SD Admin Reg ... South Dakota Register [*A publication*] (DLA)
SDADS .... Satellite Digital and Display System
SDAE .... San Diego & Arizona Eastern Railway Co. [*AAR code*]
SDAE .... Source Data Automation Equipment
SDAEA .... Shop, Distributive and Allied Employees' Association [*Australia*]
SDAF .... Solid-Rocket Booster Disassembly Facility [*NASA*] (NASA)
SDAF .... Special Defense Acquisition Fund [*Military*]
SDAF .... Special Development Assistance Fund
SDAFRS .... Source Data Automated Fitness Report System [*Military*] (DNAB)
SDAID .... System Debugging Aids (NITA)
S DAK .... South Dakota
S Dak .... South Dakota Reports [*A publication*] (DLA)
SDAKC .... Seventh-Day Adventist Kinship Canada [*Defunct*] (EAIO)
SDAKI .... Seventh Day Adventist Kinship International (EA)
SdAl .... Alcester Public Library, Alcester, SD [*Library symbol Library of Congress*] (LCLS)
SDAL .... Switched Data Access Line
SD Ala .... United States District Court for the Southern District of Alabama (DLA)
SdAle .... Alexandria Public Library, Alexandria, SD [*Library symbol Library of Congress*] (LCLS)
SDAM .... Social Democratic Alliance of Macedonia [*Political party*] (EY)
SDAM .... Standard Deviation above the Mean [*Statistics*]
SDA Mad .... Madras Sadr Diwani Adalat Reports [*India*] [*A publication*] (DLA)
SDAML .... Send by Airmail (NOAA)
SDANA .... Shrine Directors Association of North America (EA)
SD & A .... San Diego & Arizona Railway
SD & B .... Shaw, Dunlop, and Bell's Scotch Court of Session Reports, First Series [*1821-38*] [*A publication*] (DLA)
SD & BBA .... Soft Drink and Beer Bottlers Association [*British*] (DBA)
SD & B Sup ... Shaw, Dunlop, and Bell's Supplement, Containing House of Lords Decisions [*A publication*] (DLA)
SD & B Supp ... Shaw, Dunlop, and Bell's Supplement, Containing House of Lords Decisions [*Scotland*] [*A publication*] (DLA)
SD & I .... System Development and Integration (MCD)
SD & T .... Staff Development and Training
SD & T .... Staff Duties and Training [*British military*] (DMA)
SDAP .... Sociaal-Democratische Arbeiders Partij [*Social Democratic Workers' Party*] [*Netherlands Political party*] (PPE)
SDAP .... Special Duty Assignment Pay [*Army*] (INF)
SDAP .... System Development and Performance
SDAP .... Systems Development Analysis Program
SDAP .... Systems Development and Acquisition Plan (MCD)
SDAPP .... Special Duty Assignment Proficiency Pay [*Air Force*]
SdAr .... Arlington Public Library, Arlington, SD [*Library symbol Library of Congress*] (LCLS)
SDAR .... Submarine Departure Approval Request (DNAB)
SdArm .... Armour Public Library, Armour, SD [*Library symbol Library of Congress*] (LCLS)
SDAS .... Scientific Data Automation System (IEEE)
SDAS .... Shared Demand Assignment Signaling (MCD)
SDAS .... Simplified Directional Approach System [*Aviation*]
SDAS .... Sound Data Acquisition System [*Automotive engineering*]
SDAS .... Source Data Automation System [*Military*] (AABC)
SDA-S .... System Design Agency-Subcontractor Design Direction (MCD)
SDAS .... Systems Data Analysis Section
SDAT .... Safe Driver Attitude Test [*Educational test*]
SDAT .... Sector Design and Analysis Tool [*FAA*] (TAG)
SDAT .... Senile Dementia of the Alzheimer Type [*Medicine*]
SDAT .... Spacecraft Data Analysis Team [*NASA*]
SDAT .... Stanford Diagnostic Arithmetic Test
SDAT .... Stationary Digital Audio Tape
SDAU .... Safety Data and Analysis Unit [*British*] (DA)
SDAU .... Subscriber Digital Access Unit [*Telecommunications*]
SDAUG .... SDA [*Software Design Associates*] Users' Groups [*Later, IUG*] (EA)
SDAV .... Sialodacryoadenitis [*Virology*]
SDAVF .... Spinal Dural Arteriovenous Fistula [*Medicine*] (DMAA)
SDAVP .... Sinsinawa Dominican Apostolic Volunteer Program (EA)
SDB .... Sa Da Bandeira [*Angola*] [*Seismograph station code, US Geological Survey*] (SEIS)
SDB .... Safe Deposit Box (MHDB)
SDB .... Salesians of Don Bosco [*Roman Catholic men's religious order*]
sdb .... Salesians of Don Bosco (TOCD)
SDB .... Sandberg, CA [*Location identifier FAA*] (FAAL)
SDB .... Seaward Defence Boat [*British military*] (DMA)
SDB .... Securities Data Base System [*Information service or system*] (IID)
SDB .... Segment Descriptor Block
SDB .... Shakespeare Data Bank, Inc. [*Information service or system*] (IID)
SDB .... Shallow Draft Barge (MCD)
SDB .... Shallow Draft Board (NASA)
SDB .... Silver-Dye-Bleach (PDAA)
SDB .... Skill Development Base [*Army*] (AABC)
SDB .... Sleep-Disordered Breathing [*Medicine*] (DMAA)
SDB .... Small Disadvantaged Business [*Department of Commerce*]
SDB .... Sociaal-Democratische Bond [*Social Democratic League*] [*Netherlands Political party*] (PPE)
SDB .... Society for Developmental Biology (EA)
SDB .... Software Development Board [*Computer science*] (MHDI)
SdB .... South Dakota State University, Brookings, SD [*Library symbol Library of Congress*] (LCLS)
SDB .... Spacecraft Design Book
SDB .... Special District Bond
SDB .... Square Die Bushing
SDB .... Standard Device Byte (IAA)
SDB .... Standard Dress Blue [*Navy*] (DOMA)
SDB .... State Development Bank [*Hungary*]
SDB .... Storage Data Bus
SDB .... Strength and Dynamics Branch [*Air Force*]
SDB .... Sulfur-Disproportionating Bacteria
sdb .... Symbolic Debugger [*Also, SOLD, SYMDEB*] [*Computer science*] (BYTE)
SDB .... System Database
SDB .... System Data Buffer (MCD)
SDB .... Systems Development Branch [*Marine science*] (OSRA)
SDB .... Systems Development Branch [*Space Environmental Laboratory*] (USDC)
SDBC .... Small Disadvantaged Business Concerns
SDBCS .... Steam Dump Bypass Control System [*Nuclear energy*] (NRCH)
SDBD .... Software Data Base Document [*Computer science*] (MHDI)
SdBer .... Beresford Public Library, Beresford, SD [*Library symbol Library of Congress*] (LCLS)
SdBf .... Belle Fourche Public Library, Belle Fourche, SD [*Library symbol Library of Congress*] (LCLS)
SDBF .... System Development Breadboard Facility
SDBGC .... Seventh Day Baptist General Conference (EA)
SDBHS .... Seventh Day Baptist Historical Society (EA)
SDBI .... Specifications Drawing Baseline Index (DNAB)
SDBI .... Storage Data Bus-In [*Computer science*] (MHDB)
SDB Jo .... South Dakota Bar Journal [*A publication*] (DLA)
SDBL .... Sight Draft Bill of Lading Attached [*Business term*]
SdB-M .... South Dakota State University, Minuteman Graduate Center Library, Ellsworth AFB,Rapid City, SD [*Library symbol Library of Congress*] (LCLS)
SDBMS .... Seventh Day Baptist Missionary Society (EA)
SDBN .... Software-Defined Broadband Network (CDE)
SdBo .... Bonesteel Public Library, Bonesteel, SD [*Library symbol Library of Congress*] (LCLS)
SDBO .... Societe de Banque Occidentale [*France*] (EY)
SDBO .... Storage Data Bus-Out [*Computer science*] (MHDB)
SDBP .... Small Database Project (NITA)
SDBP .... Supine Diastolic Blood Pressure [*Medicine*]
Sd-BPH .... South Dakota State Library for the Handicapped, Pierre, SD [*Library symbol Library of Congress*] (LCLS)
SdBro .... Brookings Public Library, Brookings, SD [*Library symbol Library of Congress*] (LCLS)
SdBrS .... Bristol Independent School District Library, Bristol, SD [*Library symbol Library of Congress*] (LCLS)
SDBS .... Samson Database Services (NITA)
SDBS .... Sodium Dodecylbenzene Sulfonate [*Organic chemistry*]
SdBu .... Burke Public Library, Burke, SD [*Library symbol Library of Congress*] (LCLS)
SDBUP .... Small Disadvantaged Business Utilization Program (DOMA)
SDBWF .... Seventh Day Baptist World Federation (EA)
SDBY .... Standby
SDC .... Chief Steward [*Later, MSC*] [*Navy rating*]
SDC .... SAGE [*Semiautomatic Ground Environment*] Direction Center [*Military*] (IAA)

SDC .... SAGE [*Semiautomatic Ground Environment*] Division Commander [*Military*] (IAA)
SDC .... Salivary Duct Carcinoma [*Oncology*]
SDC .... Salt Data Centre [*British*]
SDC .... Same Distribution Center Service Area [*US Postal Service*]
SDC .... Sample Data Collection
SDC .... San Diego - Robinson [*California*] [*Seismograph station code, US Geological Survey Closed*] (SEIS)
SDC .... Sands Minerals [*Vancouver Stock Exchange symbol*]
SDC .... Scientific Data Center (MCD)
SDC .... Scientific Documentation Center Ltd. [*Dunfermline, Fife, Scotland*]
SDC .... Seaward Defense Craft (NATG)
SDC .... Secondary Distribution Center (AAG)
SDC .... Secure Data Cartridge (BYTE)
SDC .... Seismological Data Center [*Environmental Science Services Administration*]
SDC .... Seize Detector Control
SDC .... Self-Defense Corps [*Vietnam*]
SDC .... Self-Destruct Circuit (SAA)
SDC .... Semiconductor Devices Council [*Joint Electronic Device Engineering Council*] (MCD)
SDC .... September Days Club (EA)
SDC .... Serum Digoxin Concentration [*Clinical chemistry*]
SDC .... Setpoint Digital Control (IAA)
SDC .... Several Dancers Core [*Houston, TX and Atlanta, GA*]
SDC .... Shaft-Driven Compressor (DOMA)
SDC .... Shaft-Driven Counter
SDC .... Shield Design Code [*Nuclear energy*] (NRCH)
SDC .... Shipment Detail Card [*Military*]
SDC .... Shutdown Cooling [*Nuclear energy*] (NRCH)
SDC .... Signal Data Converter
SDC .... Single Drift Correction
SDC .... Situation Display Console (DOMA)
SDC .... Situation Display Converter
SDC .... Society of Daily Communicants [*Defunct*] (EA)
SD-C .... Society of Designer-Craftsmen [*British*] (EAIO)
SDC .... Society of Dyers and Colourists (EAIO)
SDC .... Society of the Divine Compassion [*Anglican religious community*]
SDC .... Sodium Deoxycholate [*Organic chemistry*]
SDC .... Software Development Computer [*NASA*] (NASA)
SDC .... Solenoidal Detector Collaboration [*Particle detection*]
SDC .... Solenoid Detector Collaboration [*Physics*]
SDC .... Solid Dielectric Cable
SDC .... SONAR Data Computer [*Navy*] (CAAL)
SDC .... Southern Defense Command [*Army*]
SDC .... Spacecraft Data Simulator [*NASA*] (KSC)
SDC .... Space Data Corp.
SDC .... Space Defense Center [*Military*] (MCD)
SDC .... Space Defense Corp. (MCD)
SDC .... Space Development Corp.
SDC .... Spares Disposition Code [*NASA*] (NASA)
SDC .... Special Day Class [*Education*]
SDC .... Special Devices Center [*Navy*]
SDC .... Specific Damping Capacity [*Metals*]
SDC .... Spiral-Defect Chaos [*Physics*]
SDC .... Square Dance Callers Club [*British*] (DBA)
SDC .... Stabilization Data Computer
SDC .... Standard Data Chain
SDC .... State Data Center [*Bureau of the Census*] (GFGA)
SDC .... State Defense Council
SDC .... State Development Company (AAGC)
SDC .... State Disasters Committee [*Australia*]
SDC .... Static Dielectric Constant
SDC .... Station Directory Control (SAA)
SDC .... Strategic Defense Command [*Military*] (SDI)
SDC .... Strategic Direction Center (MCD)
SDC .... Structural Design Criteria [*Nuclear energy*]
SDC .... Studebaker Driver's Club (EA)
SDC .... Subcontractor's Data Catalog (MCD)
SDC .... Submersible Decompression Chamber [*Underwater tank*]
SDC .... Submersible Diving Capsule [*Oceanography*]
SDC .... Succinyldicholine [*Biochemistry*] (MAE)
SDC .... Supply Distribution Center [*Military*] (AFIT)
SDC .... Support Design Change
SDC .... Swedish Airforce [*ICAO designator*] (FAAC)
SDC .... System Designator Code (AFM)
SDC .... System Design Confirmation
SDC .... System Development Corp. [*Information service or system*] (IID)
SDC .... System for Data Calculation [*Information retrieval*]
SDC .... Systems Development District (AAG)
SDC .... Yankton College, Yankton, SD [*OCLC symbol*] (OCLC)
SdCa .... Canton Carnegie Public Library, Canton, SD [*Library symbol Library of Congress*] (LCLS)
SDCA .... Scottish Deerhound Club of America (EA)
SDCA .... Square Dance Callers Association [*Australia*]
SD Cal .... United States District Court for the Southern District of California (DLA)
SdCan .... Canova Public Library, Canova, SD [*Library symbol Library of Congress*] (LCLS)
SdCar .... Carthage Public Library, Carthage, SD [*Library symbol Library of Congress*] (LCLS)
SDCC .... Simulation Data Conversion Center [*Space Flight Operations Facility, NASA*]
SDCC .... Small-Diameter Component Cask [*Nuclear energy*] (NRCH)
SDCC .... Society of the Descendants of the Colonial Clergy (EA)
SDCE .... Scientific Data Collection Exercise
SDCE .... Society of Die Casting Engineers (EA)
SDCF .... Sampled Data Channel Filter
SDCF .... Software Development Computer Facility
SdCh .... Chamberlain Public Library, Chamberlain, SD [*Library symbol Library of Congress*] (LCLS)
SDCH .... Society of Descendants of Colonial Hispanics (EA)
SDCI .... Singles and Doubles Configuration Interaction [*Quantum chemistry*] (MCD)
SDCIS .... Supplier Data Control Information System (MCD)
SdCl .... Clark Public Library, Clark, SD [*Library symbol Library of Congress*] (LCLS)
SDCL .... South Dakota Codified Laws [*A publication*]
SDCL .... Supplier Documentation Checklist (NASA)
SDCL .... Symptom Distress Check List [*Medicine*] (MAE)
SdCla .... Claremont Public Library, Claremont, SD [*Library symbol Library of Congress*] (LCLS)
SDCM .... Master Chief Steward [*Later, MSCM*] [*Navy rating*]
SdCo .... Colome Public Library, Colome, SD [*Library symbol Library of Congress*] (LCLS)
SD CO .... Safe Deposit Company (MHDW)
SD Codified Laws... South Dakota Codified Laws [*A publication*] (DLA)
SD Codified Laws... South Dakota Codified Laws Annotated [*A publication*] (AAGC)
SD Codified Laws Ann... South Dakota Codified Laws, Annotated [*A publication*] (DLA)
SDCOI .... Sector Direction Center Operating Instruction (SAA)
SD Comm .... Doctor of Science in Commerce
SD Compiled Laws Ann... South Dakota Compiled Laws, Annotated [*A publication*] (DLA)
SD Comp Laws Ann... South Dakota Compiled Laws, Annotated [*A publication*] (DLA)
SDCP .... Sample Data Collection Plan (MCD)
SDCP .... Slug Discharge Control Plan [*Pollution prevention*]
SDCP .... Summary Development Cost Plan [*NASA*] (NASA)
SDCP .... Supply Demand Control Point [*Military*]
SDCR .... Source Data Communication Retrieval
SDCS .... SAIL [*Shuttle Avionics Integration Laboratory*] Data Communications System [*NASA*] (NASA)
SDCS .... Sample Data Control System (MCD)
SDCS .... Science Data Conditioning System
SDCS .... Senior Chief Steward [*Later, MSCS*] [*Navy rating*]
SDCS .... Shutdown Cooling System [*Nuclear energy*] (NRCH)
SDCS .... Simulation Data Conversion System [*Space Flight Operations Facility, NASA*]
SDCS .... Single Differential Cross Section
SDCS .... Space Borne Data-Conditioning System (IAA)
SDCS .... Station Digital Command System (IAA)
SDCT .... Slosson Drawing Coordination Test
SdCu .... Custer County Library, Custer, SD [*Library symbol Library of Congress*] (LCLS)
SDCU .... Satellite Delay Compensation Unit [*Telecommunications*] (LAIN)
SDCW .... San Diego College for Women [*California*]
SDD .... Lubango [*Angola*] [*Airport symbol*] (OAG)
SDD .... RIC, Inc. [*ICAO designator*] (FAAC)
SDD .... Sa da Bandiera [*Angola*] [*Airport symbol*] (AD)
SDD .... Santo Domingo [*Ciudad Trujillo*] [*Dominican Republic*] [*Seismograph station code, US Geological Survey*] (SEIS)
SDD .... Scientific Discoveries and Discoverers [*A publication*]
SDD .... Scottish Development Department (DCTA)
SDD .... Scottish Diploma in Dairying
SDD .... Second Development Decade [*United Nations*]
SDD .... Selected Dissemination of Documents
SDD .... Selective Dissemination of Documentation (NITA)
SD/D .... Service Deputy/Director (MUGU)
SDD .... Shuttle Design Directive [*NASA*] (NASA)
SDD .... Sierra Nevada Gold [*Vancouver Stock Exchange symbol*]
SDD .... Signal Data Demodulator
SDD .... Silicon Disk Drive [*Computer science*]
SDD .... Single Diaphragm Distributor [*Automotive engineering*]
SDD .... Sioux Falls Public Library, Sioux Falls, SD [*OCLC symbol*] (OCLC)
SDD .... Slowdown Density
SDD .... Sodium Dimethyldithiocarbamate [*Also, SDDC*] [*Organic chemistry*]
SDD .... Software Description Document [*NASA*] (NASA)
SDD .... Software Design Description [*Computer science*] (IEEE)
SDD .... Software Design Document [*NASA*] (NASA)
SDD .... Spark Delay Device [*Automotive engineering*]
SDD .... Specially Designated Distributor [*Liquor*]
SDD .... Speed-Dependent Damping [*Automotive engineering*]
SDD .... Spin-Dependent Delocalization [*Physical chemistry*]
SDD .... Sporadic Depressive Disease [*Medicine*] (DMAA)
SDD .... Stacy Design and Development, Inc. [*Telecommunications service*] (TSSD)
SDD .... Standard Delivery Date [*Military*]
SDD .... Sterile Dry Dressing [*Surgery*] (DAVI)
SDD .... Stored Data Description
SDD .... Store Door Delivery
SDD .... Stress Degree Day [*Crop inventory*]
SDD .... Subchannel Data Distributor (KSC)
SDD .... Subsystem Design Description (MCD)
SDD .... Synthetic Dynamic Display [*Aviation*] (OA)
SDD .... System Design Description [*Nuclear energy*] (NRCH)
SDD .... System Design Document [*NASA*] (MCD)
SDD .... Systems Definition Directive [*Military*] (AFM)
SDD .... Systems Development Department [*David W. Taylor Naval Ship Research and Development Center*]

SDD .... Systems Development Dictionary (NITA)
SDD .... Systems Development Division [*Marine science*] (OSRA)
SDDAA .... School Dropout Demonstration Assistance Act
SDDC .... Self Determination for DC [*District of Columbia*] (EA)
SDDC .... Silver Diethyldithiocarbamate [*Organic chemistry*]
SDDC .... Sodium Dimethyldithiocarbamate [*Also, SDD*] [*Organic chemistry*]
SDDC .... Speed-Dependent Damping Control [*Automotive engineering*]
SDDC .... Sterile Disposable Device Committee [*Defunct*]
SDDD .... Software Detailed Design Document [*Army*]
SDDE .... Surface Demand Diving Equipment
SDDE .... System Design and Development Environment
SdDel .... Dell Rapids Carnegie Public Library, Dell Rapids, SD [*Library symbol Library of Congress*] (LCLS)
SDDL .... Stored Data Definition Language
SDDM .... Secretary of Defense Decision Memorandum
SDDP .... Sight Draft Documents Against Payment [*Business term*]
SdDr .... Draper Public Library, Draper, SD [*Library symbol Library of Congress*] (LCLS)
SDDR .... Standard Digital Data Recorder (DWSG)
SDDRL .... Self-Loading Disk Dump and Reload (IAA)
SdDs .... De Smet Public Library, De Smet, SD [*Library symbol Library of Congress*] (LCLS)
SDDS .... Satellite Data Distribution System
SDDS .... Scientific Document Delivery System
SDDS .... Secondary Data Display System (MCD)
SDDS .... Signal Data Demodulator Set [*or System*]
SDDS .... Single-Dimensional Deflection System (IAA)
SDDS .... Solid Discharge Data System [*Environmental Protection Agency*] (GFGA)
SDDS .... Sony Dynamic Digital Sound [*Surround-sound technology*] (PS)
SDDS .... Switched Digital Data Service [*Southern New England Telephone*]
SD/DS .... Synchro-Digital/Digital-Synchro (CAAL)
SDDTTG .... Stored Data Definition and Translation Task Group
SDDU .... Simplex Data Distribution Unit
SDE .... Santiago Del Estero [*Argentina*] [*Airport symbol*] (OAG)
SDE .... Self-Disinfecting Elastomer
SDE .... Simple Designational Expression
SDE .... Simultaneous Distillation-Extraction [*Chemical engineering*]
SDE .... Societe de Droits d'Execution du Canada [*Performing Rights Organization of Canada - PROC*]
SDE .... Society of Data Educators (EA)
SDE .... Software Development Environment [*NCR Corp.*]
SDE .... Source Data Entry
SDE .... Space Division Evaluator [*NASA*] (NASA)
SDE .... Spatial Database Engine
SDE .... Specific Dynamic Effect [*Medicine*]
SDE .... Standard Data Element [*Army*] (AABC)
SDE .... Standard-Dose Epinephrine [*Medicine*]
SDE .... Standard Etac Corp. [*Toronto Stock Exchange symbol*]
SDE .... State Department of Education (DAVI)
SDE .... State Difference Equation (IAA)
SDE .... Steam Distillation Extracton
SDE .... Students for Data Education (IEEE)
SDE .... Subdural Empyema [*Medicine*] (DMAA)
SDE .... Submission and Delivery Entity [*Telecommunications*] (OSI)
SDE .... Support Data Engineering (MCD)
SDE .... Syntax Directed Editor (NITA)
SDE .... System Development Engine (NITA)
SDEA .... Shop and Display Equipment Association [*British*] (EAIO)
SDE & C .... Standard Data Element and Codes [*Air Force*]
SDEC .... Sequential Detection of Emerging Competitive Target
SDECE .... Service de Documentation Exterieure et de Contre-Espionnage [*Pronounced "suh-deck"*] [*Intelligence organization France Later, DGSE*]
SdEd .... Edgemont Public Library, Edgemont, SD [*Library symbol Library of Congress*] (LCLS)
SdEdH .... Edgemont High School, Edgemont, SD [*Library symbol Library of Congress*] (LCLS)
S/DEFL .... Stone Deflector [*Automotive engineering*]
SDEG .... Special Doctrine Equipment Group [*Army*]
SDE/GWIS .... Sigma Delta Epsilon, Graduate Women in Science (EA)
SDE-IS .... State Department of Education-Information System [*Minnesota*] (EDAC)
SdEl .... Elkton Public Library, Elkton, SD [*Library symbol Library of Congress*] (LCLS)
S de M .... Sisters Servants of Mary [*Roman Catholic religious order*]
SDEO .... Second Division of Executive Officers [*A union*] [*British*]
SdeP .... Sister Servants of the Poor (TOCD)
SDEP .... Source Data Entry Package [*Computer science*] (MHDI)
SDER .... Standardized Distributed Energy Release (MCD)
SdEs .... Estelline Public Library, Estelline, SD [*Library symbol Library of Congress*] (LCLS)
S de S .... Simon de Southwell [*Flourished, 1184-1209*] [*Authority cited in pre-1607 legal work*] (DSA)
SDES .... Submarine Data Extraction System [*Navy*] (CAAL)
SDES .... Symptomatic Diffuse Esophageal Spasm [*Medicine*] (DMAA)
SDESG .... Strapdown Electrically Suspended Gyro (KSC)
SdEu .... Eureka Public Library, Eureka, SD [*Library symbol Library of Congress*] (LCLS)
SDEV .... Sequential Deviation
S de V .... Sicardus Fabri de Vauro [*Deceased, 1323*] [*Authority cited in pre-1607 legal work*] (DSA)
SDEV .... Software Developers [*NASDAQ symbol*] (TTSB)
SDEV .... [*The*] Software Developer's Co., Inc. [*NASDAQ symbol*] (NQ)
SDF .... Louisville [*Kentucky*] [*Airport symbol*] (OAG)
SDF .... Safing and Deservicing Facility [*NASA*] (NASA)
SDF .... Sanatana Dharma Foundation [*Defunct*] (EA)
SDF .... Sans Domicile Fixe [*No Fixed Address*] [*French*]
SDF .... Satellite Distribution Frame [*Telecommunications*] (TEL)
SDF .... Scottish Decorators Federation (EAIO)
SDF .... Screen Definition Facility [*Computer science*]
SDF .... Seasonal Derating Factor (IEEE)
SDF .... Self-Defense Force [*Japan*]
SDF .... Self-Defense Force [*Vietnam*] (VNW)
SDF .... Ship Description File (DNAB)
SDF .... Ship Design File (OA)
SDF .... Simplified Directional Facility [*Aviation*]
SDF .... Simultaneous Double Fire [*Automotive engineering*]
SDF .... Single Degree of Freedom [*Also, SDOF*] [*Acoustics*]
SDF .... Sioux Falls College, Sioux Falls, SD [*OCLC symbol*] (OCLC)
SDF .... Slow Death Factor [*Medicine*]
SDF .... Social Democratic Federation [*Later, SDP*] [*Early British political party, members of which were sometimes referred to as "Silly Damn Fools"*]
SDF .... Social Democratic Federation [*Japan Political party*] (PPW)
SDF .... Social Democratic Federation [*Iceland*] [*Political party*] (PPW)
SDF .... Social Democratic Front [*Ghana*] [*Political party*] (PPW)
SDF .... Social Democratic Front [*Cameroon*] [*Political party*] (EY)
SDF .... Software Development Facility [*Military*] (CAAL)
SDF .... Software Development File
SDF .... Software Development Folder (MCD)
SDF .... Software Development Framework (RDA)
SDF .... Sonic Depth Finder
SDF .... Source Development Fund [*Supply and Services Canada*]
SDF .... Source Document Folders [*IRS*]
SDF .... Southern Development Foundation (EA)
SDF .... Spatial Distribution Functions [*Of molecules*]
SDF .... Special Denatured Formula [*Applied to alcohol*]
SDF .... Spectral Density Function
SDF .... Standard Data Format [*Computer science*] (CDE)
SDF .... Standard Distance File (DOMA)
SDF .... Standard Distribution Format [*Computer science*]
SDF .... Standard Drug File [*Derwent Publications Ltd.*] [*Database*]
SDF .... Standiford Field [*FAA*] (TAG)
SDF .... Static Design Factor
SDF .... Static Direction Finder
SDF .... Step Down Fix [*Aviation*] (DA)
SDF .... Stopping Distance Factor (MCD)
SDF .... Stowe-Day Foundation (EA)
SDF .... Strategic Defensive Forces [*Army*] (AABC)
SDF .... Stress Distribution Factor [*Medicine*] (DMAA)
SDF .... Stromal Cell-Derived Factor [*Biochemistry*]
SDF .... Structural Dynamics Malfunction
SDF .... Student Description Form [*Psychology*]
SDF .... Sudan Defence Force [*British*]
SDF .... Sundorph Aeronautical, Corp. [*ICAO designator*] (FAAC)
SDF .... Supergroup Distribution Frame [*Telecommunications*] (TEL)
SDF .... Surface Direct Fire [*Navy*] (CAAL)
SDF .... Swedish Defense Forces
SDF .... System Data Format [*Computer science*]
SDF .... System Development Facility [*NASA*] (KSC)
SDFAUS .... State Defense Force Association of the United States (EA)
SDFC .... Space Disturbance Forecast Center [*Environmental Science Services Administration*] (IEEE)
SDFC .... Standardized Discriminant Function Coefficient
SDFD .... System Data Flow Diagram (IAA)
SDFG .... Single-Degree-of-Freedom Gyroscope (SAA)
SDFL .... Schottky Diode FET [*Field Effect Transistor*] Logic
SD Fla .... United States District Court for the Southern District of Florida (DLA)
SDFN .... SONAR Dome Flow Noise
SDFOV .... Simultaneous Dual Field of View
SD-FP .... Solvent Detergent Treated Frozen Plasma
SdFr .... Freeman Public Library, Freeman, SD [*Library symbol Library of Congress*] (LCLS)
SDFS .... Same-Day Funds Settlement [*Securities and Exchange Commission*]
SD/FS .... Smoke Detector/Fire Suppression (GFGA)
SDFS .... Standard Disk Filing System
SDFSNM .... Sons and Daughters of the First Settlers of Newbury, Massachusetts (EA)
SDFT .... Schottky Diode Field Effect Transistor Logic (MHDI)
SDFT .... System Demonstration Flight Test [*DoD*]
SDFTN .... Soda Fountain
SDFU .... Sanitary Drainage Fixture Unit (DAC)
SDG .... Aerosierra de Durango [*Mexico ICAO designator*] (FAAC)
SDG .... Sacred Dance Guild (EA)
SDG .... San Diego [*California*] (GAAI)
SDG .... Sao Domingos [*Brazil*] [*Airport symbol*] (AD)
SDG .... Scan Display Generator
SDG .... Screen Directors' Guild of America [*Later, DGA*]
SDG .... Siding (AAG)
SDG .... Signed, Directed Graph [*Mathematics*]
SDG .... Simulated Data Generation (IAA)
SDG .... Simulated Data Generator
SDG .... Situation Display Generator
SDG .... Sofamar Danek Group [*NYSE symbol*] (SPSG)
SDG .... Soli Deo Gloria [*Glory to God Alone*] [*Latin*]
SDG .... Special Development Groups [*Navy*]
SDG .... Stormont, Dundas and Glengarry Highlanders [*British military*] (DMA)
SDG .... Strapdown Gyroscope (SAA)
SDG .... Subminiature Displacement Gyroscope

SDG .... Sucrose Density Gradients
SDG .... Sundance Gold Mining Ltd. [*Vancouver Stock Exchange symbol*]
SDG .... Supplier Documentation Group [*NASA*] (NASA)
SDG .... System Design Group (MCD)
SDGA .... Single Conductor, Degaussing, Armored (IAA)
SDGA .... Single Degaussing Cable
SDGA .... Sucrose Density Gradient Analysis [*Clinical chemistry*]
SD GA .... United States District Court for the Southern District of Georgia (DLA)
SDGC .... Simulated Distillation Gas Chromatography
SDGC .... Sun-Diamond Growers of California (EA)
SDGE .... Situation Display Generator Element
SdGe .... Sully-Potter County Library, Gettysburg, SD [*Library symbol Library of Congress*] (LCLS)
SDGF .... Schwannoma-Derived Growth Factor [*Biochemistry*]
SDGH .... Sweet Dough
SDgo .... San Diego Gas & Electric Co. [*Associated Press*] (SAG)
SDGW .... Structural Design Gross Weight
SDH .... Scottish Diploma in Horticulture
SDH .... Seasonal Derated Hours (IEEE)
SDH .... Serine Dehydrase [*An enzyme*] (MAE)
SDH .... Servicio de Helicopteros SL [*Spain ICAO designator*] (FAAC)
SDH .... Single Dad's Hotline [*Defunct*] (EA)
SDH .... Software Development Handbook [*NASA*] (NASA)
SDH .... Sorbitol Dehydrogenase [*Also, Sorb D*] [*An enzyme*]
SDH .... South Dakota Historical Resource Center, Pierre, SD [*OCLC symbol*] (OCLC)
SDH .... Spinal Dorsal Horn [*Anatomy*]
SDH .... Structured Document Handbook [*Computer science*]
SDH .... Styling Data Handling
SDH .... Subdural Hematoma [*Medicine*]
SDH .... Succinic Dehydrogenase [*An enzyme*]
SDH .... Support Dogs for the Handicapped (EA)
SDH .... Synchronous Digital Hierarchy [*Computer science*]
SDH .... System Development Handbook [*NASA*] (NASA)
SDHACU ...... Sodium-Dependent High-Affinity Choline Uptake [*Biochemistry*]
SDHBS .... South Devon Herd Book Society [*British*] (DBA)
SDHD .... Society of Daughters of Holland Dames (EA)
SDHD .... Sudden-Death Heart Disease [*Medicine*]
SDHE .... Spacecraft Data Handling Equipment
SdHi .... South Dakota Department of Cultural Affairs, Historical Resources Center, Pierre, SD [*Library symbol Library of Congress*] (LCLS)
SdHig .... Hyde County Library, Highmore, SD [*Library symbol Library of Congress*] (LCLS)
SDHIRS .... Subdistrict Headquarters Induction and Recruiting Station [*Navy*]
SdHM .... Minnehaha County Rural Library, Hartford, SD [*Library symbol Library of Congress*] (LCLS)
SdHow .... Howard Public Library, Howard, SD [*Library symbol Library of Congress*] (LCLS)
SDHP .... Sosyal Demokrasi Halkci Partisi [*Social Democratic Populist Party*] [*Turkey Political party*] (MENA)
SDHS .... Satellite Data Handling System
SDHS .... Society of Dance History Scholars (EA)
SdHsV .... United States Veterans Administration Center, Hot Springs, SD [*Library symbol Library of Congress*] (LCLS)
SDHT .... Selectively Doped Heterojunction Transistor (NITA)
SDHT .... Selectively Doped Heterostructure Transistor
SdHuro .... Huron Public Library, Huron, SD [*Library symbol Library of Congress*] (LCLS)
SdHuroC ...... Huron College, Huron, SD [*Library symbol Library of Congress*] (LCLS)
SDHW .... Solar Domestic Hot Water
SDHyg .... Doctor of Science in Hygiene (GAGS)
SDI .... Saab Direct Ignition [*Automotive engineering*]
SDI .... Saidor [*Papua New Guinea*] [*Airport symbol*] (OAG)
SDI .... Saudi Arabian
SDI .... Saudi Arabian Airlines
SDI .... Selected Descriptive Item
SDI .... Selective Dissemination of Information [*System*] [*Computer science*]
SDI .... Self-Description Inventory [*Vocational guidance test*]
SDI .... Serial Data Interface [*Computer science*] (CDE)
SDI .... Serial Dilution Indicator [*Clinical chemistry*]
SDI .... Service de Documentation Interministerielle [*Interministerial Documentation Service*] [*National Telecommunications Research Center*] [*Information service or system*] (IID)
SDI .... Ship's Drawing Index (DNAB)
SDI .... Single Document Interface [*Computer science*] (CDE)
SDI .... Situation Display Indicator [*Aviation*] (OA)
SDI .... Society of Designers in Ireland (EAIO)
SDI .... Source Data Information
SDI .... Specifications Drawing Index (DNAB)
SDI .... Standard Data Interface [*Computer science*]
SDI .... Standard Deviation Interval [*Medicine*]
SDI .... Standard Drive Interface [*Computer science*] (CDE)
SDI .... Standardized Discharge Instructions [*for hospital patients*]
SDI .... Stars of David International (EAIO)
SDI .... State Disability Insurance
SDI .... Steel Deck Institute (EA)
SDI .... Steel Door Institute (EA)
SDI .... Strategic Defense Initiative [*Commonly known as "Starwars"*] [*Facetiously translated as "Silly Damn Idea"*]
SDI .... Subcontractor Data Item
SDI .... Submarine Detector Instructor [*British military*] (DMA)
SDI .... Super Data Interchange [*Computer science*] (HGAA)
SDI .... Supplier Data Item (MCD)
SDI .... Support Directive Instruction (KSC)
SDI .... Switched Digital International [*AT&T*] (CDE)
SDI .... Symbolic Displays, Inc. (MCD)
SDI .... System Diagram Index (IAA)
SDI .... Systems Designers International Ltd. [*British*] (IRUK)
SDIA .... Small Defense Industries Association [*Later, Strategic Industries Association*]
SDIA .... Soap and Detergent Industry Association [*British*] (DBA)
SDIAC .... Strategic Defense Initiative Advisory Council [*Military*] (SDI)
SDIC .... STC Communications Subsystem Distribution Interface Cabinet (MCD)
SDICC .... Societe de Developpement de l'Industrie Cinematographique Canadienne [*Canadian Film Development Corp. - CFDC*]
SDID .... Supplier Data Item Description (MCD)
SDIE .... Special Defense Intelligence Estimate (MCD)
SDieGs .... San Diego Gas & Electric Co. [*Associated Press*] (SAG)
SDIF .... Schistosome-Derived Immunosuppressive Factor [*Immunology*]
SDIF .... Software Development and Integration Facility [*NASA*] (NASA)
SDIF .... Standard Document Interchange Format [*Telecommunications*]
SDIG .... Screen Directors International Guild [*Absorbed by Directors Guild of America*] (EA)
SDIHD .... Sudden-Death Ischemic Heart Disease [*Medicine*]
SDII .... Special Devices [*NASDAQ symbol*] (TTSB)
SDII .... Special Devices, Inc. [*NASDAQ symbol*] (SPSG)
SDII .... Strategic Defense Initiative Institute [*Military*] (SDI)
SDI-KWOC ... Selected Dissemination of Information - Key Word Out of Context (DNAB)
SDILINE .... Selective Dissemination of Information Online [*National Library of Medicine*] [*Bethesda, MD Bibliographic database*]
SD Ill .... United States District Court for the Southern District of Illinois (DLA)
SDIM .... System for Documentation and Information in Metallurgy [*Fachinformationszentrum Werkstoffe eV*] [*Information service or system*] (IID)
SDIMU .... Strapdown Inertial Measuring Unit (MCD)
SDIN .... Special Defence Intelligence Notice (MCD)
SD Ind .... United States District Court for the Southern District of Indiana (DLA)
SDIO .... Serial Digit Input/Output [*Computer science*]
SDIO .... Strategic Defense Initiative Office [*DoD*]
SDIO .... Strategic Defense Initiative Organization [*Washington, DC DoD*] (GRD)
SD Iowa .... United States District Court for the Southern District of Iowa (DLA)
SDIP .... Specifically Designated Intelligence Position (AFM)
SDIP .... Strengthening Developing Institutions Program [*HEW*]
SDIP .... System Description and Implementation Plan [*Navy*]
SDIS .... Ship Distance
SDIS .... Ship Draft Indicating System (MSA)
SDISEM .... Strategic Defense Initiative System Evaluation Model
SDISM .... Strategic Defense Initiative System Effectiveness Model [*Military*]
SDIT .... Service de Documentation et d'Information Techniques de l'Aeronautique
SDIT .... Ship Draft Indicator Transmitter (MSA)
SDIT .... Sons and Daughters in Touch [*An association*]
SDI/UC .... State Disability Insurance - Unemployment Compensation
SDIX .... Strategic Diagnostics, Inc. [*NASDAQ symbol*] (SAG)
SDIZ .... Submarine Defense Identification Zone
SDJ .... Greensboro, NC [*Location identifier FAA*] (FAAL)
SDJ .... Sanada [*Japan*] [*Seismograph station code, US Geological Survey*] (SEIS)
SDJ .... Sendai [*Japan*] [*Airport symbol*] (OAG)
SDJ .... Senn d'Or [*Vancouver Stock Exchange symbol*]
SDJ .... Society of the Devotees of Jerusalem (EA)
SDK .... Grupo Sidek SA de CV [*NYSE symbol*] (SAG)
SDK .... Grupo Sidek S.A.'L'ADS [*NYSE symbol*] (TTSB)
SDK .... Sandakan [*Malaysia*] [*Airport symbol*] (OAG)
SDK .... Seljacko-Demokratska Koalicija [*Peasant-Democratic Coalition*] [*Former Yugoslavia*] [*Political party*] (PPE)
SDK .... Shelter Deck
SDK .... Si De Ka Quarterly [*Ann Arbor, MI*] [*A publication*] (DLA)
SDK .... Sigma Delta Kappa [*Fraternity*]
SDK .... Sociedad Aerea del Caqueta Ltd. [*Colombia*] [*ICAO designator*] (FAAC)
SDK .... Software Developer's Kit [*Computer science*] (BYTE)
SDK .... Software Development Kit [*Computer science*] (PCM)
SDK .... Studebaker's Resource Development Ltd. [*Formerly, Rio Blanco Resources Ltd.*] [*Vancouver Stock Exchange symbol*]
SDK .... System Design Kit
SDK .... System Developers' Kit [*Computer hardware*] [*Microsoft, Inc.*] (PCM)
SDK.B .... Grupo Sidek S.A.'B' ADS [*NYSE symbol*] (TTSB)
SdKJ .... Jackson-Washabaugh County Library, Kadoka, SD [*Library symbol Library of Congress*] (LCLS)
SdL .... Hearst Free Library, Lead, SD [*Library symbol Library of Congress*] (LCLS)
SDL .... National Council, Sons and Daughters of Liberty (EA)
SDL .... Saddle (MSA)
SDL .... Scenario Development Language [*Military*] (CAAL)
SDL .... Scientific DataLink [*Comtex Scientific Corp.*] [*Information service or system*] (IID)
SDL .... Scottie Gold Mines Ltd. [*Vancouver Stock Exchange symbol*]
SDL .... Scottsdale, AZ [*Location identifier FAA*] (FAAL)
SDL .... Screw Dislocation Line [*Crystullography*]
SDL .... Security Devices Laboratory (SAA)
SDL .... Seedling (WGA)
SDL .... Seismic Data Laboratory [*Teledyne Geotech*]
SDL .... Self-Directed Learning (ADA)
SDL .... Semiconductor Diode LASER [*Also, TDL*]
SDL .... Sensory Distal Latency [*Medicine*]

SDL............. Serum Digoxin Level [*Cardiology*] (DAVI)
SDL............. Shaft Driver, Left
SDL............. SHORAD [*Short Range Air Defense*] Data Link [*Army*]
SDL............. Side Discharge Loader [*Mining*]
SDL............. Simulation Data Language
SDL............. Single Driver's License [*Law*]
SDL............. Slowdown Length
SDL............. Software Design Language
SDL............. Software Development Laboratory [*NASA*] (NASA)
SDL............. Software Development Language [*Burroughs Corp.*]
SDL............. Software Development Library
SDL............. Sonic Delay Line
SDL............. Space Disturbances Laboratory [*Boulder, CO*]
SDL............. Space Dynamics Laboratories [*Utah State University*] [*Research center*] (RCD)
SDL............. Specification and Description Language [*Telecommunications*] (TEL)
SDL............. Standard Deviation of the Logarithm [*Statistics*]
SDL............. Standard Distribution List [*NASA*]
SDL............. Stark County District Library, Canton, OH [*OCLC symbol*] (OCLC)
SDL............. State-Dependent Learning [*Psychology*]
SDL............. Strip Delay Line
SDL............. Sundsvall [*Sweden*] [*Airport symbol*] (OAG)
SDL............. Supporting Document List
SDL............. Surplus Distribution List (AAG)
SDL............. Systematic Design Language [*Computer science*]
SDL............. System Descriptive Language [*Computer science*] (IEEE)
SDL............. System Design Language
SDL............. System Development Language [*1971*] [*Computer science*] (CSR)
SDL............. System Directory List [*Computer science*] (BUR)
SDL............. Systems Designers Ltd. [*Research center British*]
SDL............. Systems Designers Ltd. (NITA)
SDL............. Systems Design Laboratory (IAA)
SDL............. Systems Development Laboratories (MCD)
SDLC........... Single-Level Data Link Control (IAA)
SDLC........... Synchronous Data Link Control [*Telecommunications*]
SDLC........... System Data Link Control [*Telecommunications*]
SDLC........... System Development Life Cycle
SdLeH.......... Lennox High School Library, Lennox, SD [*Library symbol Library of Congress*] (LCLS)
SdLem.......... Lemmon Public Library, Lemmon, SD [*Library symbol Library of Congress*] (LCLS)
SdLemH....... Lemmon High School Library, Lemmon, SD [*Library symbol Library of Congress*] (LCLS)
SDLI............. SDL, Inc. [*NASDAQ symbol*] (SAG)
SDL Inc......... SDL, Inc. [*Associated Press*] (SAG)
SDLM........... Scheduled Depot Level Maintenance [*Navy*]
SDLM........... Special Depot Level Maintenance
SDLM........... Standard Depot Level Maintenance (MCD)
SDLO........... State, Defense Liaison Office [*Federal government*] (AABC)
SDLP........... Social Democratic and Labour Party [*Northern Ireland*] [*Political party*] (PPW)
SDLP........... Social Democratic and Liberal Party [*British Political party*]
SDLP........... Societe de Developpement du Livre et du Periodique [*Society for the Development of Books and Periodicals*] [*Canada*]
SDLRS......... Self-Directed-Learning Readiness Scale (MEDA)
SDLS........... Satellite Data Link Standard (DOMA)
SDLT........... Static/Dynamic Load Technology (SSD)
SDLV........... Shuttle-Derived Launch Vehicle [*NASA*] (SSD)
SdM............. Mitchell Public Library, Mitchell, SD [*Library symbol Library of Congress*] (LCLS)
SDM............. National Association of Special Delivery Messengers [*Later, APWU*] [*AFL-CIO*]
SDM............. Samsonov Density Meter [*Gravimetrics*]
SDM............. San Diego, CA [*Location identifier FAA*] (FAAL)
SDM............. Santiago De Maria [*El Salvador*] [*Seismograph station code, US Geological Survey*] (SEIS)
SDM............. School in District Management [*LIMRA*]
SDM............. Schwarz Differential Medium (OA)
SDM............. Selective Dissemination of Microfiche
SDM............. Semiconductor Disk Memory
SDM............. Sensory Detection Method [*for measuring blood pressure*]
SDM............. Sequency-Division Multiplexing (IEEE)
SDM............. Ship Design Manager
SDM............. Short-Delay Monostable [*Circuitry*]
SDM............. Shutdown Margin [*Nuclear energy*] (NRCH)
SDM............. Shutdown Mode (IEEE)
SDM............. Shuttle Data Management [*NASA*] (MCD)
SDM............. Signal Density Model (MCD)
SDM............. Simulated Dynamic Missile [*Military*] (CAAL)
SDM............. Site Defense of Minuteman [*Missiles*] (MCD)
SDM............. Site-Directed Mutagenesis [*Biochemistry*]
SDM............. Situation Display Matrix (IAA)
SDM............. Slowdown Model
SDM............. Software Development Methodology (IAA)
SDM............. Soma Dendrite Membrane
SDM............. Somali Democratic Movement [*Political party*] (EY)
SDM............. Sons and Daughters of Malta (EA)
SDM............. Space Division Multiplexing [*Physics*]
SDM............. Spares Determination Method [*Bell System*]
SDM............. Sparse Distributed Memory [*Computer science*]
SDM............. Specially Designated Merchant [*Liquor sales*]
SDM............. Standard Deviation of the Mean (AAMN)
SDM............. Standardization Design Memoranda (IEEE)
SDM............. STARAN Debug Module
SDM............. Statistical Delta Modulation
SDM............. Statistical-Dynamical Model
SDM............. Structural Development Model
SDM............. Structural Dynamics Modification
SDM............. Structures, Structural Dynamics, and Materials (MCD)
SDM............. Subdivision Manager
SDM............. Subsystem Design Manual [*NASA*] (MCD)
SDM............. Sugar Cane Downy Mildew [*Plant pathology*]
SDM............. Sulfadimethoxine [*Antibacterial*] [*Veterinary medicine*]
SDM............. Synchronous Digital Machine
SDM............. System Data Module (IAA)
SDM............. System Decision Manager (IAA)
SDM............. System Definition Manual [*NASA*] (NASA)
SDM............. Systems Design Methodology [*Computer science*] (HGAA)
SDM............. Systems Development Methodology [*Computer science*] (HGAA)
SdMa........... Bennett County Library, Martin, SD [*Library symbol Library of Congress*] (LCLS)
SDMA........... Sam Davis Memorial Association (EA)
SDMA........... Shared Direct Memory Access [*Sperry UNIVAC*]
SDMA........... Sodium Dihydrobis(methoxyethoxy)aluminate [*Organic chemistry*]
SDMA........... Space Division Multiple Access
SDMA........... Surgical Dressing Manufacturers Association [*British*] (BI)
SDMAC........ Shared Direct Memory Access Contoller [*Computer science*] (MHDI)
SdMadT....... Dakota State College, Madison, SD [*Library symbol Library of Congress*] (LCLS)
SdMar.......... Dakota Wowapipahi Library, Marty, SD [*Library symbol Library of Congress*] (LCLS)
SDMA/SS-TDMA... Space Division Multiple Access/Spacecraft Switched-Time Division Multiple Access (PDAA)
SDMD........... Sequential Decision Making Device (IAA)
SDME........... Synchronous Data Modem Equipment
SdMeS......... Menno Public School Library, Menno, SD [*Library symbol Library of Congress*] (LCLS)
SD (Met)...... Doctor of Science in Metallurgy
SDMH........... Symmetrical-Dimthylhydrazine [*Organic chemistry*]
SdMi............ Hand County Library, Miller, SD [*Library symbol Library of Congress*] (LCLS)
S-DMICC...... State-Defense Military Information Control Committee (AFM)
SdMil........... Milbank Carnegie Library, Milbank, SD [*Library symbol Library of Congress*] (LCLS)
SDMIS......... Standard Depot Management Information System [*Army*]
SDMIS......... Standardization Data Management Information System
SD Miss....... United States District Court for the Southern District of Mississippi (DLA)
SDMIX......... South Dakota Medical Information Exchange [*University of South Dakota*] [*Sioux Falls*] [*Telecommunications*] (TSSD)
SDMJ........... September, December, March, and June [*Denotes quarterly payments of interest or dividends in these months*] [*Business term*]
SdMo........... A. H. Brown Public Library, Mobridge, SD [*Library symbol Library of Congress*] (LCLS)
SDMO........... Specifications and Data Management Office [*Military*]
SDMO........... Subcommand Data Management Office [*Military*] (AFIT)
SDMS........... Shipboard Data Multiplex System (MCD)
SDMS........... Society of Diagnostic Medical Sonographers (EA)
SDMS........... Spatial Data Management System (MCD)
SDMS........... Staff Development Management System (AIE)
SDMS........... Supplier Data Management System (MCD)
SDMSS......... Software Development and Maintenance Suppport System [*Computer science*] (MHDI)
SDMT........... Stanford Diagnostic Mathematics Test [*Education*]
SDMT........... Stress and Degraded Mode Test (CAAL)
SdMW.......... Dakota Wesleyan University, Mitchell, SD [*Library symbol Library of Congress*] (LCLS)
SDN............. North American Baptist Seminary, Sioux Falls, SD [*OCLC symbol*] (OCLC)
SDN............. Sandane [*Norway*] [*Airport symbol*] (OAG)
SDN............. Satellite Data Network [*AgriData Resources, Inc.*] [*Telecommunications service Defunct*] (TSSD)
SDN............. Secret Document Number
SDN............. Separation Designation Number
SDN............. Service Dealer's Newsletter [*Lynott Associates*] [*A publication*] (IID)
SDN............. Sexually Dimorphic Nucleus [*Brain anatomy*]
SDN............. Societe Demographique Nordique [*Nordic Demographic Society - NDS*] (EAIO)
SDN............. Societe des Nations [*League of Nations*]
SDN............. Sodisco, Inc. [*Toronto Stock Exchange symbol*]
SDN............. Software Defined Network [*Telecommunications*]
SDN............. Software Development Note [*NASA*] (NASA)
SDN............. Solution-Dyed Nylon
SDN............. Strapdown Navigator
SDN............. Subdeacon
SDN............. Subscriber's Directory Number [*Telecommunications*] (TEL)
SDN............. Sudan [*ANSI three-letter standard code*] (CNC)
SDN............. Swindon [*British depot code*]
SDN............. Synchronized Digital Network [*Telecommunications*] (TEL)
SDN............. System Development Notification
SDN & SU... Step-Down and Step-Up (MSA)
SDNB........... SDNB Financial [*Associated Press*] (SAG)
SDNB........... SDNB Financial [*NASDAQ symbol*] (TTSB)
SDNB........... SDNB Financial Corp. [*NASDAQ symbol*] (NQ)
SDNCO......... Staff Duty Noncommissioned Officer [*Army*]
SdNe............ Newell Public Library, Newell, SD [*Library symbol Library of Congress*] (LCLS)
SdNeu.......... New Underwood Public Library, New Underwood, SD [*Library symbol Library of Congress*] (LCLS)

SDNF .... Shortened Disjuctive Normal Form (PDAA)
SDNM .... Sampled-Data Nonlinearity Matrix (PDAA)
SDNR .... Screw Down Non-Return Valve (DS)
SDNRIU .... Secure Digital Net Radio Interface Unit [*Army*] (RDA)
SDNS .... Scottish Daily Newspaper Society (DBA)
SDNS .... Secure Data Network System [*Computer science*]
SDNT .... Student
SDNY .... United States District Court for the Southern District of New York (DLA)
SDO .... Oglala Sioux Community College, Learning Resources Center, Pine Ridge, SD [*OCLC symbol*] (OCLC)
SdO .... Onida Public Library, Onida, SD [*Library symbol Library of Congress*] (LCLS)
SDO .... Salado [*Chile*] [*Seismograph station code, US Geological Survey Closed*] (SEIS)
SDO .... San Diego Gas & Electric Co. [*AMEX symbol*] (SPSG)
SDO .... San Diego Gas & Electric Co. [*NYSE symbol*] (SAG)
SDO .... Scan Data Out (IAA)
SDO .... Schedules Duty Officer (KSC)
SDO .... Senior Duty Officer [*Air Force British*]
SDO .... Shielded Diatomic Orbitals [*Atomic physics*]
SDO .... Shipboard Distribution Only [*Navy*] (CAAL)
SDO .... Ship Development Objective [*Navy*]
SDO .... Signal Distributing Office [*British military*] (IAA)
SDO .... Signal Distribution Officer [*British military*] (DMA)
SDO .... Singlet Delta Oxygen
SDO .... Sod House, NV [*Location identifier FAA*] (FAAL)
SDO .... Software Distribution Operation (IAA)
SDO .... SONAR Detection Opportunity [*Navy*] (CAAL)
SDO .... Source Data Operation (MDG)
SDO .... Spatial Data Option
SDO .... Special Duty Officer (MCD)
SDO .... Special Duty Only [*Military*]
SDO .... Specialist Duty Only [*Navy personnel designation*]
SDO .... Squadron Duty Officer [*Navy*] (NVT)
SDO .... Staff Duty Officer [*Army*]
SDO .... Standards Developing Organization
SDO .... Standards Development Organization
SDO .... Station Duty Officer [*Navy*]
SDO .... Synthetic Drying Oil
SDO .... Systems Development Office [*National Weather Service*]
SDOB .... Scaled Depth of Burst (MCD)
S Doc .... Senate Document (DLA)
SDOC .... Specific Direct Operating Costs
S DOC .... State Document (WDAA)
SDOE .... State Department of Education (OICC)
SDOF .... Single Degree of Freedom [*Also, SDF*] [*Acoustics*]
SD Ohio .... United States District Court for the Southern District of Ohio (DLA)
SDOM .... Society of Dirty Old Men [*Defunct*] (EA)
SDOM .... Standard Deviation of Means [*Statistics*]
SDOP .... Ship Doppler (IAA)
SDOP .... Sons and Daughters of Oregon Pioneers (EA)
SDOPR .... Sound Operator [*Navy*]
SDOPrA .... San Diego G&E 5% Pfd [*AMEX symbol*] (TTSB)
SDOPrB .... San Diego G&E 4.50% Pfd [*AMEX symbol*] (TTSB)
SDOPrC .... San Diego G&E 4.40% Pfd [*AMEX symbol*] (TTSB)
SDOPrH .... San Diego Gas & El $1.82 Pref [*AMEX symbol*] (TTSB)
SDOS .... Source Data Operating System (IAA)
SDOSD .... Standard Deviation of Standard Deviation [*Statistics*]
SDP .... Aero Sudpacifico SA [*Mexico ICAO designator*] (FAAC)
SDP .... National Society of Sons and Daughters of the Pilgrims (EA)
SDP .... Sacrodextra Posterior [*A fetal position*] [*Obstetrics*]
SDP .... Sand Point [*Alaska*] [*Airport symbol*] (OAG)
SDP .... Sand Point, AK [*Location identifier FAA*] (FAAL)
SDP .... Scottish Diploma in Poultry Husbandry
SDP .... Sea Duty Pay [*Navy*]
SDP .... Selective Data Processing (IAA)
SDP .... Sentry Dog Patrol (AFM)
SDP .... Serb Democratic Party [*Croatia*] [*Political party*] (EY)
SDP .... Serbian Democratic Party [*Bosnia-Herzegovina*] [*Political party*] (EY)
SDP .... Set-Down Pool [*Nuclear energy*] (NRCH)
SDP .... Seychelles Democratic Party
SDP .... Shelf Dynamics Program [*CUE*] (MSC)
SDP .... Ship Development Plan [*Navy*]
SDP .... Ship Discharge Package [*Military*] (INF)
SDP .... Short-Day Plant [*Botany*]
SDP .... Shuttle Data Processor [*NASA*] (MCD)
SDP .... Signal Data Processor
SDP .... Signal Dispatch Point [*Telecommunications*] (TEL)
SDP .... Silicon Diode Pellet
SDP .... Singapore Democratic Party [*Political party*] (PPW)
SDP .... Single Department Purchasing [*Agency*] [*Military*]
SDP .... Single Dry Plate (IAA)
SDP .... Sirotherm Demineralization Process
SDP .... Site Data Processor
SDP .... Site Development and Facilities Utilization Plan [*Oak Ridge National Laboratory*]
SDP .... Skill Development Program [*Australia*]
SDP .... Slowdown Power
SDP .... Small Distribution Phenomena
SDP .... Smoke Dispersion Pod
SDP .... Social Democratic Party [*Hungary*] [*Political party*]
SDP .... Social Democratic Party [*Nigeria*] [*Political party*]
SDP .... Social Democratic Party [*Albania*] [*Political party*] (EY)
SDP .... Social Democratic Party [*Philippines*] [*Political party*] (PPW)
SDP .... Social Democratic Party [*Thailand*] [*Political party*] (PPW)
SDP .... Social Democratic Party [*Germany Political party*]
SDP .... Social Democratic Party [*Trinidad and Tobago*] [*Political party*] (PPW)
SDP .... Social Democratic Party [*British Political party*]
SDP .... Social Democratic Party [*Australia Political party*]
SDP .... Social Democratic Party [*Iceland*] [*Political party*] (PPW)
SDP .... Social-Democrat Party [*Zambia*] [*Political party*] (EY)
SDP .... Socialist Democratic Party [*South Korea Political party*] (EY)
SDP .... Software Development Plan [*NASA*] (NASA)
SDP .... Software Development Processor (NITA)
SDP .... Solar Desalination Plant
SDP .... Sosyal Demokrat Partisi [*Social Democratic Party*] [*Turkish Cyprus*] [*Political party*] (EY)
SDP .... Source Data Processing
SDP .... Sozial Demokratesch Partei [*Social Democratic Party*] [*Luxembourg*] [*Political party*] (PPE)
SDP .... Spectral Dependence Photocurrent
SDP .... Sports Development Program [*Australia*]
SDP .... Standard Data Processor (SSD)
SDP .... Standard Distance Package (DOMA)
SDP .... State Data Program [*Information service or system*] (IID)
SDP .... Station Data Processing
SDP .... Steyr-Daimler-Puch [*Manufacturing firm*] [*Automotive engineering*]
SDP .... Storage and Distribution Point [*Military*] (AFM)
SDP .... Stornaway Central Development [*Vancouver Stock Exchange symbol*]
SDP .... Stranka Democratskih Reformi [*Party of Democratic Reform*] [*Slovenia*] [*Political party*] (EY)
SDP .... Stratospheric Dust Particle
SDP .... Streaming Data Procedure [*Computer science*] (CDE)
SDP .... Sub-Seabed Disposal Program [*National Science Foundation*] (NUCP)
SdP .... Sudetendeutsche Partei [*Sudeten German Party*] [*Former Czechoslovakia*] [*Political party*] (PPE)
SDP .... Sulfonyldiphenol [*Organic chemistry*]
SDP .... Sun Distributors Ltd. Class A [*NYSE symbol*] (SPSG)
SDP .... Sunsource L.P. [*NYSE symbol*] (SAG)
SDP .... Sunsource L.P.'A' [*NYSE symbol*] (TTSB)
SDP .... Suomen Sosialidemokraattinen Puolue [*Finnish Social Democratic Party*] [*Political party*] (EAIO)
SDP .... Supplementary Development Plan
SDP .... Supplier Data Package (NASA)
SDP .... Supply Distribution Point
SDP .... Surface Deformation Pattern
SDP .... Survey Data Processing
Sdp .... Suspended in Part [*Regulation or order suspended in part*] [*Legal term*] (DLA)
SDP .... Swaziland Democratic Party
SDP .... System Decision Paper
SDP .... System Design Proposal [*Navy*]
SDP .... Systems Development Package [*or Plan*] [*Military*] (NG)
SdPa .... Parker Public Library, Parker, SD [*Library symbol Library of Congress*] (LCLS)
SDPA .... Small Defense Plants Administration [*Terminated, 1953*]
SDP.B .... Sunsource L.P.'B' [*NYSE symbol*] (TTSB)
SDPC .... Shuttle Data Processing Complex [*NASA*] (MCD)
SDPC .... Social Democratic Party of Canada
SDPC .... Social Democratic Party of Croatia [*Political party*]
SDPD .... Special Defense Projects Department
SDPDA .... Special Defense Property Disposal Account [*DoD*]
SdPEC .... South Dakota Department of Education and Cultural Affairs, Historical Resources Center, Pierre, SD [*Library symbol Library of Congress*] (LCLS)
SDPF .... Science Data Processing Facility (SSD)
SDPF .... Sensor Data Processing Facility (MCD)
SDPF .... Social-Democratic Party of Finland
SDPH .... Social Democratic Party of Hungary [*Political party*] (EAIO)
SdPiO .... Oglala Sioux Community College, Pine Ridge, SD [*Library symbol Library of Congress*] (LCLS)
SDPJ .... Social Democratic Party of Japan [*Political party*] (EAIO)
SdPl .... Plankinton City Library, Plankinton, SD [*Library symbol Library of Congress*] (LCLS)
SDPL .... Safeguard Data Processing Laboratory [*Army*] (AABC)
SDPL .... Sensor Data Processing Laboratory (MCD)
SDPL .... Servomechanisms and Data Processing Laboratory [*Massachusetts Institute of Technology*] (MCD)
SDPO .... Site Defense Project Office [*Military*] (AABC)
SDPO .... Space Defense Project Office [*AMC*]
SDPP .... Social Democracy Popularist Party [*Turkey Political party*]
SDPP .... Succinimidyl Diphenyl Phosphate [*Organic chemistry*]
SDP-PDR .... Social Democratic Party - Party of Democratic Reform [*Croatia*] [*Political party*]
SdPr .... Presho Public Library, Presho, SD [*Library symbol Library of Congress*] (LCLS)
SDPR .... Sons and Daughters of Pioneer Rivermen (EA)
SDPR .... System Design and Performance Requirements
SDPS .... Signal Data Processing System
SDPS .... Social Democratic Party of Slovenia [*Political party*] (EY)
SDPT .... Structured Doll Play Test [*Psychology*]
SDPU .... Socialist and Democratic People's Union [*Mauritania*] [*Political party*] (EY)
SDQ .... Santo Domingo [*Dominican Republic*] [*Airport symbol*] (OAG)
SDQ .... Self-Description Questionnaire
SDQ .... Student Description Questionnaire

SDQA .... SAFSCOM [*Safeguard System Command*] Document Quality Audit (MCD)
SDQFC .... Sir Douglas Quintet Fan Club (EA)
SDR .... New York State Department Reports [*A publication*] (DLA)
SdR .... Rapid City Public Library, Rapid City, SD [*Library symbol Library of Congress*] (LCLS)
SDR .... Santander [*Spain*] [*Airport symbol*] (OAG)
SDR .... Schlumberger-Doll Research Center, Ridgefield, CT [*OCLC symbol*] (OCLC)
SDR .... Scientific Data Recorder
SDR .... Search Decision Rule [*Computer science*]
SDR .... Search, Detection and Recognition [*Military*]
SDR .... Seismic Detection and Ranging
SDR .... Self-Decoding Readout
SDR .... Sender (KSC)
SDR .... Sensor Data Record [*For spacecraft*]
SDR .... Service Difficulty Report (MCD)
SDR .... Shaft Driver, Right
SDR .... Sheffield District Railway (ROG)
SDR .... Ship Destination Room (NATG)
SDR .... Ship Diversion Room (NATG)
SDR .... Shipment Document Release [*Military*] (AFIT)
SDR .... Signal Data Recorder [*or Reproducer*] (MCD)
SDR .... Signal Distribution Room [*NASA*] (KSC)
SDR .... Signal to Distortion Ratio (NITA)
SDR .... Significant Deficiency Report [*Nuclear energy*] (IEEE)
SDR .... Simple Detection Response
SDR .... Single-Drift Region (IEEE)
SDR .... Single Drug Resistance
SDR .... Sisters of the Divine Redeemer [*Roman Catholic religious order*]
SDR .... Site Defense RADAR
SDR .... Sloane, Donald R., New York NY [*STAC*]
SDR .... Small Development Requirement [*Military*]
SDR .... SNAP [*Systems for Nuclear Auxiliary Power*] Development Reactor
SDR .... Snyder, TX [*Location identifier FAA*] (FAAL)
SDR .... Society for Drug Research (EAIO)
SDR .... Society of Dance Research [*British*] (DBA)
SDR .... Sodium Deuterium Reactor
SDR .... Software Design Requirement [*NASA*] (NASA)
SDR .... Software Design Review [*NASA*] (MCD)
SDR .... Solid Ducted Rocket (MCD)
SDR .... Solution Development Record
SDR .... SONAR Data Recorder
SDR .... Sophisticated Data Research, Inc. [*Information service or system*] (IID)
SDR .... Sounder (MSA)
SDR .... South Dakota Register [*A publication*] (AAGC)
SDR .... South Devon Railway (ROG)
SDR .... Space Division Regulation [*NASA*] (NASA)
SDR .... Spacelab Disposition Record [*NASA*] (NASA)
SDR .... Spatial Delayed-Response [*Ophthalmology*]
SDR .... Special Dispatch Rider
SDR .... Special Drawing Rights [*International Monetary Fund*]
SDR .... Special Drawing Rights [*Investment term*] (DFIT)
SDR .... Special Drawing Rights (TDOB)
SDR .... Spin Dependent Resonance [*Physics*]
SDR .... Splash Detection RADAR [*Military*]
SDR .... Standard Deviation of the Regression [*Statistics*]
SDR .... Standard Dimension Ratio (DAC)
SDR .... State-Dependent Retrieval [*Psychology*]
SDR .... Statistical Data Recorder [*Computer science*] (MDG)
SDR .... Storage Data Recorder (NITA)
SDR .... Storage Data Register (MCD)
SDR .... Strip Domain Resonance
SDR .... Stroud Resources Ltd. [*Toronto Stock Exchange symbol*]
SDR .... Subcontract Data Requirement
SDR .... Succession Duties Reports [*A publication*] (ILCA)
SDR .... Successive Discrimination Reversal
SDR .... Sueddeutscher Rundfunk [*South German Radio Network*]
SDR .... Surgical Dressing Room (DAVI)
SDR .... Survey of Doctorate Recipients [*National Research Council*] [*Database*]
SDR .... Syder [*Bulgaria*] [*ICAO designator*] (FAAC)
SDR .... System Data Record
SDR .... System Definition Record [*Computer science*] (IBMDP)
SDR .... System Definition Requirements
SDR .... System Design Report [*NATO*] (NATG)
SDR .... System Design Review [*NASA*] (NASA)
SDR .... System Development Requirement [*Air Force*]
SDR .... System Discrepancy Report
SDR .... System for Data Retrieval [*Information retrieval*]
S DRAKE .... Second Dynamic Response and Kinematics Experiment [*Marine science*] (MSC)
SDRAM .... Synchonous Dynamic Random Access Memory [*Computer science*]
SDR & C .... Shipment Document Release and Control [*Military*] (AFIT)
SDRB .... Software Design Review Board [*NASA*] (NASA)
SDRB .... Supplier Documentation Review Board [*NASA*] (NASA)
SDRC .... Structural Dynamics Res [*NASDAQ symbol*] (TTSB)
SDRC .... Structural Dynamics Research Corp. [*NASDAQ symbol*] (NQ)
SDRC Ops .... South Dakota Board of Railroad Commissioners Opinions [*A publication*] (DLA)
SDRD .... Supplier Data Requirements Description (NASA)
SDRD .... Supplier Documentation Review Data (NASA)
SdRe .... Redfield Carnegie Library, Redfield, SD [*Library symbol Library of Congress*] (LCLS)
SDRL .... Seller Data Requirements List (MCD)
SDRL .... Subcontractor Data Requirements List
SDRL .... Supplier Data Requirements List (NASA)
SDRM .... San Diego Railroad Museum (EA)
SdRM .... South Dakota School of Mines and Technology, Rapid City, SD [*Library symbol Library of Congress*] (LCLS)
SdRN .... National College of Business, Rapid City, SD [*Library symbol Library of Congress*] (LCLS)
SDRN .... Supplier Data Review Notice (DNAB)
SDRNG .... Sound Ranging (MUGU)
SDRP .... Simulated Data Reduction Program
SDRP .... Socjaldemokracja Rzeczypospolitej Polskiej [*Social Democracy of the Republic of Poland*] [*Political party*] (EY)
SdRS .... Saint Martins Academy, Rapid City, SD [*Library symbol Library of Congress*] (LCLS)
SDRS .... Signal Data Recording Set (MCD)
SDRS .... Spache's Diagnostic Reading Scales (EDAC)
SDRS .... Splash Detection RADAR System (MCD)
SDRS .... Standardized Delay Reporting System [*FAA*] (TAG)
SDRT .... Slot Dipole Ranging Test (OA)
SDRT .... Spadafore Diagnostic Reading Test [*Educational test*]
SDRT .... Stanford Diagnostic Reading Test [*Education*]
SDRT .... Technical Research Sub-Department [*French Acronym is based on foreign phrase*]
SD Rulings .... Stamp Duties Rulings [*Australia A publication*]
SDRW .... SONAR Dome Rubber Window (NVT)
S-DRY .... Surfaced Dry [*Lumber*]
SDS .... CAA Training Standards [*British ICAO designator*] (FAAC)
SDS .... Safety Data Sheet (KSC)
SDS .... Same Day Surgery [*Medicine*]
SDS .... Samostalna Demokratska Stranka [*Independent Democratic Party*] [*Former Yugoslavia*] [*Political party*] (PPE)
SDS .... Sample Display Service [*Department of Commerce*]
SDS .... Samson Data Systemen (NITA)
SDS .... Sanatorio Duran [*Costa Rica*] [*Seismograph station code, US Geological Survey*] (SEIS)
SDS .... Satellite Data System [*Air Force*]
SDS .... School Dental Service
SDS .... Scientific Data System [*Later, XDS*]
SDS .... Scientific Data Systems Corporation (NITA)
SDS .... Secret Delivery Station (SAA)
SDS .... Select Drive System [*Automotive engineering*]
SDS .... Self-Defense Suite [*Air Force*] (DOMA)
SDS .... Self-Directed Search
SDS .... Self-Rating Depression Scale [*Psychology*]
SDS .... Senior Direction Station (SAA)
SDS .... Sensory Deprivation Syndrome [*Medicine*]
SDS .... Serondela [*Botswana*] [*Airport symbol*] (AD)
SDS .... Servo Drive System
SDS .... Sexual Differentiation Scale [*Psychometrics*]
SDS .... Shared Data Set (OA)
SDS .... Ship Defense System
SDS .... Shop Distribution Standards (KSC)
SDS .... Short Distance Swimmer
SDS .... Shuttle Dynamic Simulation [*NASA*] (NASA)
SDS .... Side Detection System [*Delco*] (RDA)
SDS .... Signal Distribution System
SDS .... Signals Dispatch Service (IAA)
SDS .... Sign-Digit Subtractor
SDS .... Significant Digit Scanner (IAA)
SDS .... Simulating Digital Systems
SDS .... Simulation Data Subsystem (KSC)
SDS .... Sisters of the Divine Saviour [*Roman Catholic religious order*]
SDS .... Slowing Down Spectrometer (PDAA)
SDS .... Small Digital Switch (NITA)
SDS .... Smart Distributed Systems (ACII)
SDS .... Smoke Destruction System
SDS .... Social Desirability Scale (EDAC)
sds .... Society of the Divine Savior (TOCD)
SDS .... Society of the Divine Savior (TOCD)
SDS .... Sodium Dodecyl Sulfate [*Also, SLS*] [*Organic chemistry*]
SDS .... Software Design Specification [*NASA*] (NASA)
SDS .... Software Development Specification (IAA)
SDS .... Software Development System
SDS .... Solar Disk Simulator
SDS .... Sons and Daughters of the Soddies (EA)
SDS .... Sound-Deadened Steel (PDAA)
SDS .... South Dakota State Library Commission, Pierre, SD [*OCLC symbol*] (OCLC)
SDS .... Sozialistischer Deutscher Studentenbund [*Student political organization*] [*Germany*]
SDS .... Spacecraft Design Specification
SDS .... Space Defense System (AAG)
SDS .... Space Division Switching [*Telecommunications*]
SDS .... Space Documentation Service [*NASA/ESRO*] (DIT)
SDS .... Special Distress Signal (DEN)
SDS .... Special Docking Simulator [*NASA*] (KSC)
SDS .... Specific Diagnosis Service [*Medicine*] (DMAA)
SDS .... Spectrometer Digital System
SDS .... Splash Detection System
SDS .... Srpska Demokratska Stranka [*Serb Democratic Party*] [*Political party*]
SDS .... Standard Depot System [*Army*]
SDS .... State Disability Service (DAVI)
SDS .... Status Display Support (MCD)
SDS .... St. David's Society of the State of New York (EA)

SDS .... Steam Dump System [*Nuclear energy*] (NRCH)
SDS .... Steering Damping System [*Aerospace*] (MCD)
SDS .... Stimulator of DNA Synthesis [*Immunochemistry*]
SDS .... Strategic Defense System [*DoD*]
SDS .... Structured Design Strategy (NITA)
SDS .... Structured Development Strategy (NITA)
SDS .... Students for a Democratic Society [*Defunct*] (EA)
SDS .... Submerged Demineralizer System [*Water purification*]
SDS .... Subvent Datenbank Systeme [*Innovationstechnik GmbH & Co.*] [*Hamburg, Federal Republic of Germany*] [*Information service or system*] (IID)
SDS .... Sudden Death Syndrome [*in children*] [*Medicine*]
SDS .... Sudden Drowning Syndrome
SDS .... Supplemental Data Sheet
SDS .... Supplier Data Sheet
SDS .... Supplier Delivery Schedules [*Chrysler Corp.*]
SDS .... Support Data Sheet [*Military*]
SDS .... Surveillance Direction System (DOMA)
SDS .... Sweet Dough Stabilizer [*Brand of bakery product from H. C. Brill Co., Inc.*]
SDS .... Swimmer Distress Signal [*Navy*] (CAAL)
SDS .... Synchronous Data Set (NOAA)
SDS .... Syntactic Density Score (EDAC)
SDS .... Systematic Design Language [*Computer science*]
SDS .... System Data Synthesizer (KSC)
SDS .... System Design Specification
SDS .... Systems and Data Service (IAA)
SDSAM .... Specifically Designated Special Air Mission [*Aircraft*] [*Air Force*]
SDS & RU ... Soil Data Storage and Retrieval Unit [*Department of Agriculture*] (IID)
SDSBE .... San Diego Symposium for Biomedical Engineering
SDSC .... San Diego State College [*California*]
SDSC .... San Diego Supercomputer Center [*California*] [*National Science Foundation*]
Sd-SC .... South Dakota Supreme Court Library, Pierre, SD [*Library symbol Library of Congress*] (LCLS)
SDSD .... Saco Defense Systems Division [*Maremont Corp.*] (RDA)
SDSD .... Satellite Data Services Division [*National Oceanic and Atmospheric Administration Information service or system*] (IID)
SDSD .... Single Disk Storage Device [*Computer science*] (BUR)
SDSE .... Society of the Descendants of the Schwenkfeldian Exiles (EA)
SDSEM .... Spinocerebellar Degeneration-Slow Eye Movements Syndrome [*Medicine*] (DMAA)
SD Sess Laws... South Dakota Session Laws [*A publication*] (DLA)
SDSH .... Society Devoted to the Sacred Heart [*Roman Catholic women's religious order*]
SDSI .... Shared Data Set Integrity
SdSi .... Sisseton Library, Sisseton, SD [*Library symbol Library of Congress*] (LCLS)
SDSI .... Staff Development for School Improvement Program (EDAC)
SdSif .... Sioux Falls Carnegie Free Public Library, Sioux Falls, SD [*Library symbol Library of Congress*] (LCLS)
SdSifA .... Augustana College, Sioux Falls, SD [*Library symbol Library of Congress*] (LCLS)
SdSifB .... North American Baptist Seminary, Sioux Falls, SD [*Library symbol Library of Congress*] (LCLS)
SdSifC .... Sioux Falls College, Sioux Falls, SD [*Library symbol Library of Congress*] (LCLS)
SdSifH .... Coolidge High School Library, Sioux Falls, SD [*Library symbol Library of Congress*] (LCLS)
SdSifV .... United States Veterans Administration Center, Sioux Falls, SD [*Library symbol Library of Congress*] (LCLS)
SDSK .... Softdesk, Inc. [*NASDAQ symbol*] (SAG)
SDSL .... Sail Dynamics Simulation Laboratory (MCD)
SDSL .... Site-Directed Spin Labeling [*Physical chemistry*]
SDSL .... Subject Directory of Special Libraries and Information Centers [*A publication*]
SDSL .... Symmetrical Digital Single Line (DMAA)
SDSM .... Socijaldemokratski Savez Makedonije [*Social Democratic Alliance of Macedonia*] [*Political party*] (EY)
SD SMS CLSD... Side Seams Closed [*Freight*]
SDSP .... Space Defense Systems Program (DNAB)
SDS/PAGE.... Sodium Didecylsulfate-Poly-Acrylamide Gel Electrophoresis [*Medicine*] (DMAA)
SdSpe .... Grace Balloch Memorial Library, Spearfish, SD [*Library symbol Library of Congress*] (LCLS)
SdSpen .... Hanson-McCook County Regional Library, Spencer, SD [*Library symbol Library of Congress*] (LCLS)
SdSpeT .... Black Hills State College, Spearfish, SD [*Library symbol Library of Congress*] (LCLS)
SdSpU .... University of South Dakota at Springfield, Springfield, SD [*Library symbol Library of Congress*] (LCLS)
SDSRS .... Subcontractor Data Status Reporting System (MCD)
SDSS .... San Diego Shrinkers Society (EA)
SDSS .... Satellite Data System Spacecraft [*Air Force*]
SDSS .... Satellite Data System Study [*Air Force*] (SSD)
SDSS .... Self-Deploying Space Station
SDSS .... Single and Double Simultaneous Stimulation [*Neuropsychology test*]
SDSS .... Sloan Digital Sky Survey [*Astronomy*]
SDSS .... Space Division Shuttle Simulator [*NASA*] (NASA)
SDSS .... STS [*Space Transportation System*] Data Select Switch (MCD)
SDSSE .... Science Data System Support Equipment
SDSST .... Single and Double Simultaneous Stimulation Test [*Neuropsychology test*]
SdSt .... Sturgis Public Library, Sturgis, SD [*Library symbol Library of Congress*] (LCLS)
SD St BJ....... South Dakota State Bar Journal [*A publication*] (DLA)
SDSU .... San Diego State University [*California*]
SDSU .... San Diego State University (GAGS)
SDSU .... South Dakota State University [*Brookings, SD*]
SDSU .... Switched Data Service Unit [*Computer science*] (MHDI)
SDSVF .... State Dependent State Variable Feedback [*Rocket engine*] [*NASA*]
SDSW .... Sense Device Status Word
SDT .... National College Library, Rapid City, SD [*OCLC symbol*] (OCLC)
SDT .... Sacrodextra Transversa [*A fetal position*] [*Obstetrics*]
SDT .... Saidu Sharif [*Pakistan*] [*Airport symbol*] (OAG)
SDT .... Sanderson Tech, Inc. [*Vancouver Stock Exchange symbol*]
SDT .... Sandy Point [*Great Abaco Island, Bahamas*] [*Airport symbol*] (AD)
SDT .... Satellite Development Trust (NITA)
SDT .... Saturated Discharge Temperature [*Refrigeration*]
SDT .... Scaling and Display Task (NASA)
SDT .... Science Data Team
SDT .... Scientific Distribution Technique
SDT .... Sea Depth Transducer
SDT .... Second Destination Transportation (MCD)
SDT .... Self-Development Test [*Military*] (INF)
SDT .... Senior Director Technician (SAA)
SDT .... Serial Data Transmission
SDT .... Serum Dilution Test [*Clinical chemistry*]
SDT .... Shell-Destroying Tracer [*Ammunition*]
SDT .... Shipboard Data Terminal (MCD)
SDT .... Shock-to-Detonation Transition (MCD)
SDT .... Shoot Down Test (SAA)
SDT .... Shuttle Data Tape (NASA)
SDT .... Side Door Trim [*Automotive engineering*]
SDT .... Side Tank [*on a ship*] (DS)
SDt .... Sifre on Deuteronomy [*A publication*] (BJA)
SDT .... Signal Detection Theory
SDT .... Simplified Drive Train [*Navistar International Corp.*] [*Truck engineering*]
SDT .... Simulated Data Tape
SDT .... Simulated Dynamic Target [*Military*] (CAAL)
SDT .... Skylab Data Task [*NASA*]
SDT .... Society of Dairy Technology [*British*]
SDT .... Soldier Data Tag
SDT .... Source Distribution Technique
SDT .... Space Detection and Tracking (IAA)
SDT .... Spache Diagnostic Test [*Psychiatry*] (DAVI)
SDT .... Spatial Disorientation Trainer [*Military*]
SDT .... Speech Detection Threshold [*Otorhinolaryngology*] (DAVI)
SDT .... Speedy Drill Template (MCD)
SDT .... Standard Data Terminal
SDT .... Start-Data-Traffic [*Computer science*] (IBMDP)
SDT .... Steered Directional Transmission (MCD)
SDT .... Step-Down Transformer
SDT .... Stromberg Dexterity Test [*Education*]
SDT .... Structural Dynamic Test [*NASA*] (NASA)
SDT .... Subpoena Duces Tecum [*Legal term Latin*] (HGAA)
SDT .... Supplier Data Transmittal (MCD)
SD/T .... Surface Detector/Tracker [*Navy*] (CAAL)
SDT .... Surveillance Data Transmission
SDT .... Syntax-Directed Translation [*Computer science*] (MHDI)
SDT .... System Dynamic Tester
SDT .... Terrain SDP SA [*Spain ICAO designator*] (FAAC)
SDTA .... Scottish Dance Teacher's Alliance [*Glasgow, Scotland*] (EAIO)
SDTA .... Stewardsman Apprentice, Steward, Striker [*Navy rating*]
SDTA .... Structural Dynamic Test Article [*NASA*] (NASA)
SDTAQ .... Speech and Drama Teachers Association of Queensland [*Australia*]
SDTDL .... Saturated-Drift Transistor-Diode Logic (IAA)
SD Tex......... United States District Court for the Southern District of Texas (DLA)
SDTF .... Scottish Dairy Trade Federation (DBA)
SDTI .... Security Dynamics Technologies [*NASDAQ symbol*] (TTSB)
SDTI .... Security Dynamics Technologies, Inc. [*NASDAQ symbol*] (SAG)
SDTI .... Selective Dissemination of Technical Information [*Computer science*]
SDTI .... Student Developmental Task Inventory [*Educational test*]
SDTIM .... Society for the Development of Techniques in Industrial Marketing [*British*]
SDTK .... Supported Drift Tube Klystron
SDTL .... Schottky Diode Transistor Logic (IAA)
SDTN .... Space and Data Tracking Network (SSD)
SDTN .... Stewardsman, Steward, Striker [*Navy rating*]
SDTP .... Startover Data Transfer and Processing [*Program*]
SDTP PROGRM... Startover Data Transfer and Processing Program
SDTR .... Serial Data Transmitter/Receiver [*Telecommunications*] (TEL)
SDTS .... Satellite Data Transmission System (DIT)
SDTS .... Self-Defense Test Ship
SDTS .... Spatial Data Transfer Standard [*Computer science*]
SDTS .... Syntax-Directed Translation Scheme [*Computer science*] (MHDI)
SDTT .... Silicon Diode Target Tube
SDTU .... Sign and Display Trades Union [*British*] (BI)
SDU .... Huron College, Huron, SD [*OCLC symbol*] (OCLC)
SDU .... Memphis, TN [*Location identifier FAA*] (FAAL)
SDU .... Rio De Janeiro-Dumont [*Brazil*] [*Airport symbol*] (OAG)
SDU .... Satellite Data Unit (DA)
SDU .... Self-Destruct Unit
SDU .... Service Data Unit (TNIG)
SDU .... Shelter Decontamination Unit
SDU .... Short Double Upright Brace [*Orthopedics*] (DAVI)
SDU .... Signal Distribution Unit (AAG)
SDU .... Source Data Utility

sdu.............. South Dakota [*MARC country of publication code Library of Congress*] (LCCP)
SDU.............. Soziale Demokratische Union [*Social Democratic Union*] [*Germany Political party*] (PPW)
SDU.............. Spectrum Display Unit
SDU.............. Stand-Alone Diplay Unit
SDU.............. Standard Deviation Unit [*Statistics*] (MAE)
SDU.............. Station Display Unit
SDU.............. Step Down Unit [*Medicine*] (CPH)
SDU.............. Students for a Democratic University [*Canada*]
SDU.............. Subcarrier Delay Unit
SDU.............. Surface Drone Unit [*Navy*] (CAAL)
SdU.............. University of South Dakota, Vermillion, SD [*Library symbol Library of Congress*] (LCLS)
SDU.............. Westair Commuter Airlines, Inc. [*ICAO designator*] (FAAC)
SDUB.............. Short Double Upright Brace [*Medicine*] (DMAA)
SDUK.............. Society for the Diffusion of Useful Knowledge
SdU-L.............. University of South Dakota, Law Library, Vermillion, SD [*Library symbol Library of Congress*] (LCLS)
SdU-M.............. University of South Dakota, Medical School, Vermillion, SD [*Library symbol Library of Congress*] (LCLS)
SDU-NDP..... Slovenian Democratic Union - National Democratic Party [*Political party*] (EY)
SD Uniform Prob Code... South Dakota Uniform Probate Code [*A publication*] (DLA)
SDUSA.............. Social Democrats, USA (EA)
SDV.............. Santo Domingo [*Venezuela*] [*Seismograph station code, US Geological Survey*] (SEIS)
SDV.............. Satsuma Dwarf Virus [*Plant pathology*]
SDV.............. Scram Discharge Volume [*Nuclear energy*] (NRCH)
SDV.............. Servicios Aereos del Vaupes Ltd. [*Colombia*] [*ICAO designator*] (FAAC)
SDV.............. Shuttle Derived Vehicle (MCD)
SDV.............. Slowed-Down Video [*RADAR*]
SDV.............. Society of Divine Vocations [*Vocationist Fathers*] [*Roman Catholic religious order*]
SDV.............. Solar Daily Variation
SDV.............. Soybean Dwarf Virus [*Plant pathology*]
SDV.............. Spark Delay Valve [*Automotive engineering*]
SDV.............. Specially Designated Vehicle
SDV.............. Specific Desensitizing Vaccine [*Medicine*] (ADA)
SDV.............. Start Device (IAA)
SDV.............. Swimmer Delivery Vehicle [*Navy symbol Obsolete*] (MCD)
SDV.............. Tel Aviv/Yafo [*Israel*] [*Airport symbol*] (OAG)
SdV.............. Vermillion Public Library, Vermillion, SD [*Library symbol Library of Congress*] (LCLS)
SDV.............. Vocationist Fathers (TOCD)
sdv.............. Vocationist Fathers, Society of the Divine Vocations (TOCD)
SDV.............. Vocationist Sisters (TOCD)
S-DVB.............. Styrene-Divinylbenzene [*Organic chemistry*]
SDVF.............. Software Development and Verification Facilities [*NASA*] (NASA)
SDVI.............. Service Disabled Veterans Insurance
SDW.............. Dakota Wesleyan University, Layne Library, Mitchell, SD [*OCLC symbol*] (OCLC)
SDW.............. Sandwip [*Bangladesh*] [*Airport symbol*] (AD)
SDW.............. S. D. Warren [*Paper manufacturer*]
SDW.............. Segment Descriptor Word
SDW.............. Side Wheel (DS)
SDW.............. Six-Day War [*Arab-Israeli War, 1967*] (BJA)
SDW.............. Southdown, Inc. [*NYSE symbol*] (SPSG)
SDW.............. Spin-Density Wave [*Physics*]
SDW.............. Spin Density-Weighted (DMAA)
SDW.............. Standing Detonation Wave
SDW.............. Sterile Distilled Water
SDW.............. Swept Delta Wing
SdW.............. Watertown Regional Library, Watertown, SD [*Library symbol Library of Congress*] (LCLS)
SDWA.............. Safe Drinking Water Act [*1974*]
SdWa.............. Wagner Public Library, Wagner, SD [*Library symbol Library of Congress*] (LCLS)
SdWau.............. Waubay Public Library, Waubay, SD [*Library symbol Library of Congress*] (LCLS)
SdWe.............. Webster Public Library, Webster, SD [*Library symbol Library of Congress*] (LCLS)
SdWes.............. Wessington Springs Carnegie Public Library, Wessington Springs, SD [*Library symbol Library of Congress*] (LCLS)
SdWinT.............. Tripp County Library, Winner, SD [*Library symbol Library of Congress*] (LCLS)
SDWPrD.............. Southdown $2.875cm Cv'D' Pfd [*NYSE symbol*] (TTSB)
SDWRF.............. Stochastic Dominance with Respect to Function [*Statistics*]
SD W Va...... United States District Court for the Southern District of West Virginia (DLA)
SDX.............. Satellite Data Exchange
SDX.............. Sedona [*Arizona*] [*Airport symbol*] (OAG)
SDX.............. Sigma Delta Chi [*Fraternity*] (NTCM)
S + DX.............. Speech with Duplex Telegraph
SDX.............. Stampeder Exploration Ltd. [*NYSE symbol*] (SAG)
SDX.............. Storage Data Acceleration [*Computer science*]
SDX.............. Storage Data Acceleration [*Computer science*]
SDY.............. Mount Marty College, Yankton, SD [*OCLC symbol*] (OCLC)
SDY.............. Safe Air International, Inc. [*ICAO designator*] (FAAC)
SDY.............. Sandy Corp. [*AMEX symbol*] (SPSG)
SDY.............. Sidney [*Montana*] [*Airport symbol*] (OAG)
SDY.............. Sidney, MT [*Location identifier FAA*] (FAAL)
sdy.............. Study (VRA)
SdY.............. Yankton Community Library, Yankton, SD [*Library symbol Library of Congress*] (LCLS)
SdYC.............. Yankton College, Yankton, SD [*Library symbol Library of Congress*] (LCLS)
SdYM.............. Mount Marty College, Yankton, SD [*Library symbol Library of Congress*] (LCLS)
SDYN.............. Staodyn, Inc. [*NASDAQ symbol*] (NQ)
SDYNZ.............. Staodyn Inc. Wrrt'II' [*NASDAQ symbol*] (TTSB)
SDYS.............. Simpson Dysmorphia Syndrome [*Medicine*] (DMAA)
SDZ.............. Southern Pines, NC [*Location identifier FAA*] (FAAL)
SDZ.............. Stardust Ventures [*Vancouver Stock Exchange symbol*]
SDZ.............. Stimmen der Zeit (BJA)
SDZ.............. Surface Danger Zone [*Military*] (INF)
SE.............. British Charter [*British ICAO designator*] (ICDA)
SE.............. Ferrocarriles Unidos del Sureste, SA de CV [*AAR code*]
SE.............. Herself (DAVI)
SE.............. Himself (DAVI)
SE.............. Safety Equipment [*British military*] (DMA)
SE.............. Safety Evaluation (NRCH)
SE.............. Sales Engineer
SE.............. Saline Enema [*Medicine*]
SE.............. Sanford & Eastern Railroad [*AAR code Terminated*]
SE.............. Sanitary Engineer [*Academic degree*]
SE.............. Santos Dumont Experimental [*British military*] (DMA)
SE.............. Saorstat Eireann [*Irish Free State*]
SE.............. Saponification Equivalent [*Analytical chemistry*]
SE.............. Schleicher-Bruns [*Germany ICAO aircraft manufacturer identifier*] (ICAO)
SE.............. School of Engineering (MCD)
SE.............. Science, Mathematics, and Environmental Education [*Educational Resources Information Center (ERIC) Clearinghouse*] [*Ohio State University*] (PAZ)
SE.............. Scouting Experimental [*British*] (DMA)
SE.............. Sea [*Maps and charts*]
SE.............. Seasonal Employee [*Business term*] (MHDB)
SE.............. Secondary Education (AIE)
SE.............. Secondary Electron (MCD)
SE.............. Secondary Electron Multiplier (IAA)
SE.............. Secondary Emission (IAA)
SE.............. Second Entrance [*Theatrical slang*]
SE.............. Secretarial, Word Processing, and/or Medical Office Assistant Programs [*Association of Independent Colleges and Schools specialization code*]
SE.............. Securities Transaction [*Banking*]
SE.............. Seeing Eye [*An association*] (EA)
SE.............. Selenium [*Chemical element*]
Se.............. Selenium [*Chemical element*] (DOG)
SE.............. Seleucid Era (BJA)
SE.............. Self (DAVI)
SE.............. Self Employment [*Social Security Administration*] (OICC)
SE.............. Self-Evident Statement [*Used in correcting manuscripts, etc.*]
SE.............. Self-Extinguishing (IAA)
SE.............. Selling Expense (AAGC)
SE.............. Senegal [*IYRU nationality code*] (IYR)
SE.............. Senior Editor [*Publishing*]
SE.............. September (ADA)
SE.............. Sequence of Events
SE.............. Series
SE.............. Series Statement [*Online database field identifier*]
SE.............. Service Element (TNIG)
SE.............. Service Engineer
SE.............. Service Entrance (IAA)
SE.............. Service Equipment (AAG)
SE.............. Set
se.............. Seychelles [*bi (British Indian Ocean Territory) used in records cataloged before January 1978*] [*MARC country of publication code Library of Congress*] (LCCP)
SE.............. Shareholders' Equity [*Business term*]
SE.............. Shelter Equipment
SE.............. Sherritt Gordon Mines Ltd. [*Toronto Stock Exchange symbol*]
SE.............. Shielding Effectiveness (IEEE)
SE.............. Shift Engineer (NRCH)
SE.............. Shoot Emergence [*Botany*]
SE.............. Side Effect [*Medicine*]
SE.............. Signal Excess (NVT)
SE.............. Sign Extended (IAA)
SE.............. Silver Edge [*Bookbinding*] (DGA)
SE.............. Simultaneous Engineering
SE.............. Single End
SE.............. Single-Ended, Cylindrical Boiler [*Navy*]
SE.............. Single Engine
SE.............. Single Entry [*Bookkeeping*]
SE.............. Sisters of Emanuel (TOCD)
SE.............. Site Engineer (NITA)
S-E.............. Skandinaviska Enskilda Banken [*Scandinavian Private Bank*] [*Sweden*]
SE.............. Slip End (OA)
SE.............. Small End (OA)
SE.............. Smoke Extract
SE.............. Social Education [*A publication*] (BRI)
SE.............. Social Emotional
SE.............. Society of Engineers
SE.............. Society of Ethnobiology (EA)
SE.............. Socioeconomic
SE.............. Software Engineering (MCD)

SE .... Soil Extract
SE .... Solanaceae Enthusiasts [*Defunct*] (EA)
SE .... Solar Ecliptic
SE .... Solar Explorer [*NASA*]
SE .... Solidaridad Espanola [*Spanish Solidarity*] [*Political party*] (PPW)
SE .... Solid Extract [*Pharmacy*]
SE .... Sonic Extract [*Cytology*]
SE .... Sound Effect (NTCM)
SE .... Sounding Equipment (IAA)
SE .... Southeast
SE .... Southeastern Reporter [*National Reporter System*] [*A publication*] (DLA)
SE .... Southeast Skyways [*ICAO designator*] (AD)
SE .... Southern Europe (NATG)
SE .... Space Equivalent (IAA)
SE .... Space Exploration (AAG)
SE .... Spatial Emotional (Stimuli)
SE .... Special Edition [*Car model designation*]
SE .... Special Equipment
SE .... Specialized Exhibition (IMH)
SE .... Spectral Edge [*Cardiology*]
SE .... Sphenoethmoidal [*Suture*] [*Medicine*]
SE .... Spherical Equivalent
SE .... Spherical Eyeball [*Aviation*] (OA)
SE .... Spin-Echo Scan [*Roentgenology*]
SE .... Split End [*Football*]
SE .... Sprinkled Edge [*Bookbinding*] (DGA)
SE .... Stable Element
SE .... Stack Empty (MHDI)
SE .... Staff Engineer [*Navy British*] (ROG)
SE .... Stage of Exhaustion [*of gas*] [*Medicine*]
SE .... Stamped Envelope
SE .... Standard English
SE .... Standard Error
S/E .... Standardization/Evaluation (AFM)
SE .... Starch Equivalent
S-E .... Starr-Edwards [*Prosthesis*] (AAMN)
SE .... Starter Electrode
SE .... Stationary Eddy
SE .... Status Enquiry [*British*]
SE .... Status Epilepticus [*Medicine*]
SE .... Steam Emulsion
SE .... Sterling Commerce [*NYSE symbol*] (TTSB)
SE .... Sterling Electronics (IAA)
SE .... Stock Exchange
SE .... Stop Element [*Computer science*] (EECA)
SE .... Storage Element (MCD)
SE .... Straight Edge [*Philately*]
SE .... Subcontract Engineers (MCD)
SE .... Subcritical Experiment [*Nuclear energy*]
SE .... Successful Effort (DICI)
se .... Sugary Enhancer [*A gene in sweet corn*]
SE .... Summer Emergency [*Vessel load line mark*]
SE .... Super Einspritz [*Super, Injection*] [*Mercedes-Benz automotive model designation*]
SE .... Superintending Engineer (ADA)
SE .... Superior Electric (IAA)
SE .... Support Equipment (AFM)
SE .... Sustainer Engine (AAG)
SE .... Sustaining Engineering
SE .... Sweden [*ANSI two-letter standard code*] (CNC)
SE .... Switching Element (IAA)
SE .... Synthetic Environment
SE .... System Effectiveness [*Army*] (AABC)
SE .... System Element (NASA)
SE .... System Engineering (IAA)
SE .... System Equalizer (IAA)
SE .... System Expansion [*In "Macintosh SE"*] [*Apple Computer, Inc.*]
SE .... Systems Engineer [*or Engineering*] [*Computer science*]
SE .... Systems Engineer (NITA)
SE .... Wings of Alaska [*ICAO designator*] (AD)
SE2 .... Scientists and Engineers for Secure Energy (EA)
SE2d .... South Eastern Reporter, Second Series [*West*] [*A publication*] (AAGC)
SE 2d .... Southeastern Reporter, Second Series [*A publication*] (DLA)
SEA .... Clemson University, Clemson, SC [*OCLC symbol*] (OCLC)
SEA .... Marine Manufacturers Safety Equipment Association (EA)
SEA .... Safety Engineering Analysis (AFM)
SEA .... Sailing Education Association
SEA .... Scandinavian Endodontic Association [*Sweden*] (EAIO)
SEA .... Scanning Electrostatic Analysis (NASA)
SEA .... Science and Education Administration [*Department of Agriculture*]
SEA .... Scientific Exchange Agreement
SEA .... Seaboard World Airlines, Inc. (MCD)
SEA .... Sea Echelon Area [*Navy*] (NVT)
SEA .... Sea Education Association (EA)
SEA .... Seashore Environmental Alliance
SEA .... Seasonal Employees in Agriculture
SEA .... Seattle [*Washington*] [*Seismograph station code, US Geological Survey Closed*] (SEIS)
SEA .... Seattle/Tacoma [*Washington*] [*Airport symbol*] (OAG)
SEA .... Securities Exchange Act [*1934*]
SEA .... Selective Early Annuity [*Army*]
SEA .... Selective Enforcement Audit [*Automotive engineering*]
SEA .... Self-Extracting Archive [*Computer science*] (DOM)
SEA .... Senior Enlisted Academy [*Navy*]
SEA .... Senior Enlisted Advisor [*Navy*]
SEA .... Senior Executives Association (EA)
SEA .... Service Educational Activities [*Military*] (AABC)
SEA .... Service Employers Association (EA)
SEA .... Sheep Erythrocyte Agglutination [*Test*]
SEA .... Shipbuilding Exports Association [*British*] (BI)
SEA .... Ship/Equipment/Alterations [*Navy*] (NG)
SEA .... Ships Editorial Association [*Navy*]
SEA .... Silicon Elastimeter Ablator (NASA)
SEA .... Sindicato de Escritores y Artistas [*Ecuador*]
SEA .... Single European Act [*EEC*]
SEA .... Slag Employers Association [*British*] (DBA)
SEA .... Small Earth-Approacher [*Asteroid*]
SEA .... Socialist Educational Association [*British*]
SEA .... Societe d'Electronique et d'Automatique [*Became part of Compagnie Internationale d'Informatique*]
SEA .... Society for Education through Art [*British*]
SEA .... Society for Engineering in Agriculture [*Australia*]
SEA .... Society for the Elimination of Acronyms
SEA .... Society of Electronics and Automation (IAA)
SEA .... Society of Engineering Associates [*Australia*]
SEA .... Society of Equestrian Artists [*British*] (DBA)
SEA .... Society of Evangelical Agnostics [*Defunct*] (EA)
SEA .... Sociology of Education Association (EA)
SEA .... Soluble Egg Antigen [*Medicine*] (DMAA)
SEA .... SONAR Evaluation and Assistance [*Teams*]
SEA .... Sound Effects Amplifier (IIA)
SEA .... Southeast Air, Inc. [*ICAO designator*] (FAAC)
SEA .... Southeast Asia
SEA .... Southern Economic Association (EA)
SEA .... Space Energy Association (EA)
SEA .... SPALT [*Special Projects Alterations*] Evaluation Area
SEA .... Special Equipment Authorization (AAG)
SEA .... Specific Energy Absorption
SEA .... Spherical Electrostatic Analyzer
SEA .... Spontaneous Electrical Activity [*Physiology*] (AAMN)
SEA .... Standard Electronic Assembly
SEA .... Staphylococcal Enterotoxin A [*Medicine*]
SEA .... State Earthquake Administration [*China*] [*Marine science*] (OSRA)
SEA .... State Economic Area [*Bureau of Economic Analysis*] [*Department of Commerce*]
SEA .... State Education Agency [*Department of Education*]
SEA .... State Enforcement Agreement [*Environmental Protection Agency*] (GFGA)
SEA .... State-EPA [*Environmental Protection Agency*] Agreements (EG)
SEA .... Static Error Analysis
SEA .... Statistical Energy Analysis [*or Approach*] [*Vibration analysis*]
SEA .... Storage Trust Realty [*NYSE symbol*] (SAG)
SEA .... Students for Ecological Action
SEA .... Styrene and Ethylbenzene Association (EA)
SEA .... Subterranean Exploration Agency
SEA .... Sudden Enhancement of Atmospherics [*NASA*]
SEA .... Sulfated Ethoxylated Alcohol [*Surfactants*]
SEA .... Sulphur Extended Asphalt [*Paving material*]
SEA .... Support Electronics Assembly [*Military*]
SEA .... Survival Education Association [*Defunct*] (EA)
SEA .... Susquehanna Environmental Advocates (NRCH)
SEA .... System Engineering Analysis
SEA .... System Error Analysis
SEA .... Systems Effectiveness Analyzer (IEEE)
SEAAC .... Southeast Asian Art and Culture [*Foundation*]
SEAADSA .... Sea Automated Data Systems Activity [*Navy*]
Sea & Sm .... Searle and Smith's English Probate and Divorce Reports [*A publication*] (DLA)
SEAB .... Seaboard Bancorp [*NASDAQ symbol*] (NQ)
SEA/B .... Sea Energy Absorber/Bumper Barge (SAA)
SEAB .... Secretary of Energy Advisory Board [*Department of Energy*] (EGAO)
SEABASS .... Ships Emergency Automatic Buoyancy and Stability System [*Seabass Ltd.*]
SeabdOil .... Seaboard Oil Co. [*Associated Press*] (SAG)
SEABEE .... Construction Battalion [*CB*] [*Acronym is a phonetic reference to a member of this Naval unit*]
SEABEE .... Sea Barge Carrying Ships [*MARAD*] [*MTMC*] (TAG)
SEABIRD .... Ship-Design Engineering-Aided by Interactive Remote Display (PDAA)
SEABOARD .... Seaboard World Airways (MHDB)
SEABT .... SEABEE Team [*Navy*] (NVT)
SEABU .... Southeast Asia Buildup (CINC)
Seab Vend .... Seaborne on Vendors and Purchasers [*9th ed.*] [*1926*] [*A publication*] (DLA)
SEAC .... Seacoast
SeaC .... Sea Containers Ltd. [*Associated Press*] (SAG)
SEAC .... Single-Engined Aircraft (IAA)
SEAC .... Social and Economic Archive Centre [*British*]
SEAC .... Society for Economic, Social, Cultural Study and Expansion in Central Africa
SEAC .... Society for Electroanalytical Chemistry
SEAC .... Southeast Archeological Center [*US Department of the Interior*] [*Research center*] (RCD)
SEAC .... Southeast Asia Center (EA)
SEAC .... Southeast Asia Command
SEAC .... Southern Examining Accreditation Council (AIE)
SEAC .... Specialized Employability Assistance to Claimants (OICC)
SEAC .... Spongiform Encephalopathy Advisory Committee [*British*]

SEAC Standard Electronic Automatic Computer (IAA)
SEAC Standards Eastern [or Electronic] Automatic Computer [*National Institute of Standards and Technology*]
SEAC Submarine Exercise Area Coordinator [*Navy*] (NVT)
SEACAD Sea Cadet Cruise [*Navy*] (NVT)
SEACALMIS Sea Systems Calibration Management Information System (DNAB)
SEACAT SeaBird Conductivity and Temperature Recorder [*Marine science*] (OSRA)
SEACAT SeaBird Conductivity and Temperature Recorder (USDC)
SeacBk Seacoast Banking Corp. Florida [*Associated Press*] (SAG)
SEACDT Southeast Asia Collective Defense Treaty (AABC)
SEACF Support Equipment Assembly and Checkout Facility [*NASA*] (NASA)
SEACO Senior Enlisted Advisor, Communications/Operations [*Navy*] (DNAB)
SEACOM Southeast Asia Commonwealth
SEACOM South-East Asia Commonwealth Cable (NITA)
SEACOM Southeast Asia Communications (MCD)
SEACON Seafloor Construction Experiment [*Navy*]
SeaCont Sea Containers Ltd. [*Associated Press*] (SAG)
SEACOORD Southeast Asia Coordination Council [*Military*]
SEACOP Strategic Sealift Contingency Planning System [*Army*] (AABC)
Seacor Seacor Holdings [*Associated Press*] (SAG)
SEACORE Southeast Asia Communications Research (MCD)
SEACOST Systematic Equipment Analysis and Cost Optimization Scanning Technique (MHDB)
SEACS Search of Enemy Air Defense (MCD)
SEACS Ship Equipment Accounting System (MCD)
SeaCt Sea Containers Ltd. [*Associated Press*] (SAG)
SeaCt Sea Containers Ltd. [*Associated Press*] (SAG)
SE/ACT Southern Europe - ACTISUD [*Authority for the Coordination of Inland Transport in Southern Europe*] [*NATO*] (NATG)
SEAD Scottish Education and Action for Development (EAIO)
SEAD Seneca Army Depot [*New York*] (AABC)
SEAD Suppression of Enemy Air Defenses (AABC)
SEAD Survivable Electronic Air Defense
SEADAB Southeast Asia DataBase (MCD)
SEADAC Seakeeping Data Analysis Center [*Navy*]
SEADAG Southeast Asia Development Advisory Group [*Department of State*]
SeaDas SeaWiFS [*Sea-Viewing Wide Field-of-View Sensor*] Data Analysis System (USDC)
SEADCUG NAVSEA Data Communications Users Group [*Navy*]
SEADD South-East Asia Development Division [*Overseas Development Administration*] [*British*] (DS)
SEADEX Seaward Defense Exercise [*NATO*] (NATG)
SEADRM Seadrome [*Aviation*] (FAAC)
SEADROP Small Expendable Air-Dropped Remote Ocean Platform [*Marine science*] (MSC)
SEADS Shuttle Entry Air Data Sensor [*NASA*] (MCD)
SEADS Shuttle Entry Air Data System [*or Subsystem*] (NASA)
SEADS Survivable and Effective Airbreathing Defense [*Study*] (MCD)
SEADU Sea Duty
SEA-EX Sealift Express [*Military*]
SEAFAC System Engineering Analysis Facility (MCD)
SEAFAR Search and Automatic Track Fixed Array RADAR
SEAFD Seafood
SEAFDC South East Asian Fisheries Development Centre (EAIO)
SEAFDEC South East Asian Fisheries Development Centre
SEAFIS South-East Asian Fisheries Information System [*Marine science*] (OSRA)
Seafld Seafield Capital Corp. [*Associated Press*] (SAG)
SEAFLOE Southeast Florida Outfalls Experiment [*Marine science*] (OSRA)
SEAFLOE Southeast Florida Outfalls Experiment (USDC)
SEAFRON Sea Frontier
SeaFront Sea Frontiers [*A publication*] (BRI)
Seagate Seagate Technology, Inc. [*Associated Press*] (SAG)
SEAgel Safe Emulsion Agar Gel [*Organic chemistry*]
Seag Parl Reg Seager on Parliamentary Registration [*A publication*] (DLA)
Seagram [*The*] Seagram Co. Ltd. [*Associated Press*] (SAG)
Sea Grant L & Pol'y J Sea Grant Law and Policy Journal [*A publication*] (DLA)
Sea Grant LJ Sea Grant Law Journal [*A publication*] (DLA)
SEAGS Southeast Asian Geotechnical Society (EAIO)
SeagullE Seagull Energy Corp. [*Associated Press*] (SAG)
Sea H Sea History [*A publication*] (BRI)
SEAIC Southeast Asia Information Center (NG)
SEAID Support Equipment Abbreviated Items Description [*NASA*] (NASA)
SEAIG Southeast Asia Information Group (AFM)
SEAIMP Solar Eclipse Atmospheric and Ionospheric Measurements Project (IEEE)
SEAIR Southeast Asia Airlift System [*Vietnam*] [*Also, SEAAS*] [*Air Force*] (VNW)
SEAISI South East Asia Iron and Steel Institute (EA)
SEAITACS Southeast Asia Integrated Tactical Air Control System (CINC)
SEAL Los Alamos [*Ecuador*] [*ICAO location identifier*] (ICLI)
SEAL Sea, Air, and Land
SEAL Sea, Air, and Land Team [*Refers to Navy personnel trained in unconventional warfare*]
SEAL Ship's Electronics Allowance List [*Navy*]
SEAL Signal Evaluation Airborne Laboratory [*FAA*]
SEAL Society of English and American Lawyers [*British*] (DBA)
SEAL Solar Energy Applications Laboratory [*Colorado State University*] [*Research center*] (RCD)
SEAL South-East Area Libraries (NITA)
SEAL Southeast Asian Learners (MEDA)
SEAL Standard Electronic Accounting Language [*Computer science*] (BUR)
SEAL Subsea Equipment Associates Ltd. [*Bermuda*]
SEALAB Sea Laboratory
SealdAir Sealed Air Corp. [*Associated Press*] (SAG)
SEALF Semiempirical Absorption Loss Formula [*Radio*]
SEALF Southeast Asia Land Forces [*British*]
SEALITE Systematic Evaluation and Analysis of a LASER in a Test Environment (MCD)
SEALLINC Southeast Louisiana Library Network Cooperative [*Library network*]
SEALOB Sealift Obligation Report [*Army*]
SEALOCK Search, Locate, Communications, or Kill (MCD)
SEALR Southeast Asia Logistic Requirement (AFM)
Sealrgt Sealright Co., Inc. [*Associated Press*] (SAG)
SEALS Severe Environmental Air Launch Study (KSC)
SEALS Stored Energy Actuated Lift System
SEAM Ambato [*Ecuador*] [*ICAO location identifier*] (ICLI)
SEAM Saber Enterprise Applications Manager [*Computer software*] [*Saber Software Corp.*] (PCM)
SEAM Scanning Electro-Acoustic Microscopy (MCD)
SEAM Seaman Furniture [*NASDAQ symbol*] (TTSB)
SEAM Seaman Furniture Co., Inc. [*Uniondale, NY*] [*NASDAQ symbol*] (NQ)
SEAM Sidewinder Expanded Acquisition Mode (MCD)
SEAM Society for the Emancipation of the American Male
SEAM Sociology and Economic Aspects of Medicine [*American Medical Association Information service or system*] (CRD)
SEAM Software Engineering and Management
SEAM Software Enhancement and Maintenance [*Contract*]
SEAM Southeast Asia Microfilm Project [*Library network*]
SEAM Subset Extraction and Association Measurement
SEAM Surface Environment and Mining Program
SEAMA Small Electrical Appliance Marketing Association [*British*] (DBA)
SeamanF Seaman Furniture Co., Inc. [*Associated Press*] (SAG)
SEAMAP Southeast Area Monitoring and Assessment Program [*Marine science*] (OSRA)
SEAMAP Southeast Area Monitoring and Assessment Program (USDC)
SEAMAP Systematic Exploration and Mapping Program [*National Oceanic and Atmospheric Administration*] (MSC)
SeaMARCI Sea Mapping and Remote Characterization I [*Oceanography*]
SEAMARF Southeast Asia Military Air Reservation Facility (CINC)
SEAMES South East Asian Ministers of Education Secretariat [*Australia*]
SEAMEX Seamanship Exercise (NVT)
SEAMIC Southeast Asia Management Information Center [*Navy*]
SEAMINFO Surface Mining and Environment Information System [*University of Arizona*] (IID)
SEAMIST Seavan Management Information System
SEAMO Southeast Asian Ministers of Education Organization
SEAMOD Sea Systems Modification and Modernization by Modularity [*Program*] (DNAB)
SEAMORE Southeast Asia Mohawk Revision Program [*Army aviation*]
SEAMS Southeast Asian Mathematical Society [*Singapore, Singapore*]
SEAMS Special Electronics Air Mobility System [*Army*]
SEAMS Support Equipment Asset Management Subsystem (MCD)
SEAMS System Effectiveness Assurance Management System (MCD)
SEAMUS Society for Electro-Acoustic Music in the United States (EA)
SEAN Ana Maria [*Ecuador*] [*ICAO location identifier*] (ICLI)
SEAN Scientific Event Alert Network [*Smithsonian Institution*] [*Washington, DC*] (MCD)
SEAN Senior Enlisted Advisor, Navy (DNAB)
SEAN Strapdown Electrically Suspended Gyro Aerospace Navigation [*System*]
SEAN Syndicat des Enseignants Africains du Niger [*African Union of Teachers of Niger*]
SEANC Southeast Asia NOTAM [*Notice to Airmen*] Center [*Military*]
SE & CR Southeastern & Chatham Railway [*Nickname: Seldom Ever Caught Running*]
SE & I Systems Engineering and Integration
SE & O Salvo Errore et Omission [*Errors or Omissions Excepted*] [*Latin*]
SE & T Supplies, Equipment, and Training [*Civil Defense*]
SE & TD Systems Engineering and Technical Direction (AAG)
SE & W Start Early and Walk [*Fictitious railroad initialism used to indicate one of the most reliable modes of rural transportation*]
SEANITEOPS Southeast Asia Night Operations [*Army*]
SEANWFZ Southeast Asian Nuclear Weapons Free Zone
SEANZ Small Enterprise Association of Australia and New Zealand
SEAOC Structural Engineers Association of California (EA)
SEAOPS Safe Engineering and Operations [*Program*] [*Marine Corps*] (DOMA)
SEAOPSS Southeast Asia Operational Sensor System (MCD)
SEAOR Southeast Asia Operational Requirements (MCD)
SEAP Arapicos [*Ecuador*] [*ICAO location identifier*] (ICLI)
SEAP SEATO [*Southeast Asia Treaty Organization*] Administrative Publication
SEAP Secreted Alkaline Phosphatase [*Biochemistry*]
SEAP Southeast Asia Program [*Cornell University*] [*Research center*] (RCD)
SEAP Special Economic Acquisition Provision [*Procurement*]
SEAPA Spectrothermal Emission Aerosol Particle Analyzer
SEAPAC Sea Activated Parachute Automatic Crew Release (MCD)
SEAPADS Sea Planning Automated Data System
SEAPEX Southeast Asia Petroleum Exploration Society
SEAPG Support Equipment Acquisition Planning Group [*NASA*] (NASA)
SEAPRO Southeast Asia Programs Directorate
SEAPT Seaport
SEAQ Stock Exchange Automated Quotation (NITA)
SEAQ Stock Exchange Automated Quotation System [*British*]
SEAR Arajuno [*Ecuador*] [*ICAO location identifier*] (ICLI)
SEAR Safeguard Emergency Action Report [*Army*] (AABC)
SEAR Safety Evaluation Audit Report [*Nuclear energy*] (NRCH)
SEAR Southeast Asian Refugees (MEDA)

SEAR .... Summary Engineering Assessment Report (MCD)
SEAR .... Systematic Effort to Analyze Results
SEAR .... System Engineering Analysis Report
SEARA .... Stockpile Evaluation and Reliability Assessment Program
SEARAM ..... Semiactive RADAR Missile
SEA RARE.... Sea Reinforcement and Resupply of Europe (MCD)
SEARC .... Southeast Asia Regional Council
SEARCA .... SEAMEO [*Southeast Asia Ministers of Education Organization*] Regional Center for Graduate Study and Research in Agriculture [*Philippines*] [*Research center*] (IRC)
SEARCC .... Southeast Asia Regional Computer Confederation (EA)
SEARCH .... Science, Engineering, and Related Career Hints [*Scientific Manpower Commi ssion*] [*A publication*]
SEARCH .... Scientific Evaluation and Research of Charismatic Healing [*An association*] (EA)
SearcH .... Siberian Husky Eye Anomaly Research Committee (EA)
SEARCH .... System Evaluation and Reliability Checker
SEARCH .... System for Electronic Analysis and Retrieval of Criminal Histories [*Project succeeded by National Crime Information Center*] [*Department of Justice*]
SEARCH .... System for Exploring Alternative Resource Commitments in Higher Education [*Computer science*]
SEARCH .... Systemized Excerpt Abstracts and Reviews of Chemical Headlines (NITA)
Search & Seizure Bull... Search and Seizure Bulletin [*A publication*] (DLA)
SEARCHEX... Sea/Air Search Exercise [*NATO*] (NATG)
SEARCHS.... Shuttle Engineering Approach/Rollout Control Hybrid Simulation (NASA)
SEAREQ .... Sea Requirement [*Canadian Navy*]
SEAREX .... Sea/Air Chemical Exchange [*Marine science*] (MSC)
SEAREX .... Study on Sea-Air Exchanges [*USA*] [*Marine science*] (OSRA)
Searle.......... Searle's Supreme Court Reports [*1850-67*] [*Cape Colony*] [*A publication*] (DLA)
Searle & Sm... Searle and Smith's English Probate and Divorce Reports [*1859-60*] [*A publication*] (DLA)
Searle Dig .... Searle's Minnesota Digest [*A publication*] (DLA)
Searle Sm .... Searle and Smith's English Probate and Divorce Reports [*A publication*] (DLA)
SEARNG....... South East Asian Region Network for Geosciences [*International Council of Scientific Unions*]
Sears .... Sears, Roebuck & Co. [*Associated Press*] (SAG)
SEAS........... Ascazubi [*Ecuador*] [*ICAO location identifier*] (ICLI)
SEAS........... Centre of South-East Asian Studies [*University of Hull*] [*British*] (CB)
SEAS........... Sea School [*Marine Corps*]
SEAS........... Selected Effects Armament Subsystem [*Army*] (RDA)
SEAS........... Share European Association (HGAA)
SEAS........... Shipboard Environmental Data Acquisition System [*National Oceanic and Atmospheric Administration*] (MSC)
SEAS........... Ship/Equipment/Alterations Summary [*Navy*] (NG)
SEAS........... Shoreline Erosion Advisory Service [*Bureau of Flood Protection*]
SEAS........... Spiral-Ecological Approach to Supervision (EDAC)
SEAS........... State Estimation Algorithm for Small-Scale System (PDAA)
SEAS........... Strategic Environmental Assessment System [*Environmental Protection Agency*]
SEAS........... Support Equipment Avionics System
SEAS........... Surveillance Environmental Acoustic Support [*Military*] (CAAL)
SEAS........... Surveillance Environmental Acoustic Support Project [*Naval Ocean Research and Development Activity*] [*Mississippi*]
SEAS........... System Enhancement and Support [*Military*] (CAAL)
SEASA .... Science and Engineering Academy of South Africa
SEASAME .... Southeast Asian Science and Mathematics Experiment [*RECSAM*]
SEASAR .... Sea Synthetic Aperture RADAR
SEASAT....... Sea Satellite [*NASA*]
SEASC .... Scientific Exploration of the Atlantic Shelf Committee
SEASCO .... Southeast Asia Science Cooperation Office
SEASEE....... Southeast Asia Association on Seismology and Earthquake Engineering
SEASET....... Separate Effects and Systems Effects Tests [*Nuclear energy*] (NRCH)
SEASIA .... Southeast Asia (NG)
SEASS .... Southeast Asia Airlift System [*Vietnam*] [*Also, SEAIR*] [*Air Force*] (VNW)
SEASTAG..... Southeast Asia Treaty Organization Standardization Agreement
SEAT........... Atacames [*Ecuador*] [*ICAO location identifier*] (ICLI)
SEAT........... Sheep Erythrocyte Agglutination Test [*Medicine*] (DMAA)
SEAT........... Sociedad Espanol de Automoviles de Turismo [*Spanish automobile manufacturer; acronym used as name of its cars*]
SEAT........... Standardization and Evaluation Assistance Team [*Military*]
SEAT........... Stock Exchange Automated Trading
SEA/TAC ...... Seattle/Tacoma International Airport (GAVI)
SEATAC....... Southeast Asian Agency for Regional Transport and Communications Development (EAIO)
SEATAF....... Southern European Atomic Task Force [*Military*]
SEATAR .... Search and Automatic Track Array RADAR
SEATAR .... Studies on East Asia Tectonics and Resources [*Marine science*] (MSC)
SEATEC....... Sea Test and Evaluation Capability [*Navy*] (CAAL)
SEATELCOM... Southeast Asia Telecommunications System [*Military*] (AABC)
Seat F Ch .... Seaton's Forms in Chancery [*A publication*] (DLA)
SEATIC......... Southeast Asia Translation and Interrogation Center [*Navy*]
SEATICC ...... Southeast Asia Tactical Information Communications Center (DNAB)
SeatlF.......... Seattle Film Works, Inc. [*Associated Press*] (SAG)
SEATO .... Southeast Asia Treaty Organization [*International organization formed to combat the spread of Communism*] (VNW)
SEATRAD..... Southeast Asia Tin Research and Development Center [*Malaysia*] (IRC)
SEATS.......... Shubert Entertainment and Arts Ticketing System [*National computerized theatre-ticket selling system*]
SEATS.......... Special Education Administration Task Simulation Game
SeattleF....... Seattle Film Works [*Associated Press*] (SAG)
Seattle Pac U... Seattle Pacific University (GAGS)
Seattle U ..... Seattle University (GAGS)
SEA-URICA... South East Asia Universal Realtime Information Cataloging and Administration System
Sea Vend..... Seaborne on Vendors and Purchasers [*9th ed.*] [*1926*] [*A publication*] (DLA)
SEAVEY........ Sea-to-Shore Rotation Survey (DNAB)
SEAWARS.... Seawater Activated Release System [*Navy*] (CAAL)
SEAWBS ...... Southeast Asia Wideband System [*Military*]
SEAWEA ...... Sea and Weather Observations [*Navy*] (NVT)
SeawFd........ Seaway Food Town, Inc. [*Associated Press*] (SAG)
SeaWiFS...... Sea-Viewing Wide Field-of-View Sensor [*Marine science*] (OSRA)
SeaWiFS...... Sea-Viewing Wide-Field Sensor [*Oceanography*] (ECON)
SEA/W/O MEPS... South Eastern Alaska/Washington/Oregon Minimum Earned Premium Scale [*Aviation*] (AIA)
SEAX............ Span East Airlines, Inc. [*Air carrier designation symbol*]
SEB............. Scientific Equipment Bay [*NASA*] (KSC)
SEB............. Scottish Examining Board (DCTA)
SEB............. Seaboard Corp. [*AMEX symbol*] (SPSG)
SEB............. Sebenico [*Yugoslavia*] [*Seismograph station code, US Geological Survey Closed*] (SEIS)
SEB............. Sebha [*Libya*] [*Airport symbol*] (OAG)
Seb.............. Sebir [*or Sebirin*] (BJA)
SEB............. Secondary Education Board
SEB............. Security Equipment Building
SEB............. Selective Enlistment Bonus [*Navy*] (NVT)
SEB............. Single-Ended Boiler (DS)
SEB............. Skandinaviska Enskilda Banken [*Sweden*]
SEB............. Social and Emotional Behavior
SEB............. Societe des Etudes Bloyennes [*France*] (EAIO)
SEB............. Society for Economic Botany (EA)
SEB............. Society for Experimental Biology (EAIO)
SEB............. Socio-Economic Benefit
SEB............. Software Engineering Bibliographic Database [*Air Force Systems Command*] [*Information service or system*] (CRD)
SEB............. Solo Events Board [*Auto racing*]
SEB............. Source Evaluation Board [*NASA*]
SEB............. Southeastbound [*ICAO designator*] (FAAC)
SEB............. South Equatorial Belt [*Planet Jupiter*]
SEB............. Southern European Broadcasting Service [*DoD*] (GFGA)
SEB............. Special Enlistment Bonus (MCD)
SEB............. Staphylococcal Enterotoxin B [*Medicine*]
SEB............. Strip Electron Beam
SEB............. Structural Engineering Bulletin [*Department of Housing and Urban Development*] [*A publication*] (GFGA)
SEB............. Support Equipment Building [*NASA*] (NASA)
SEB............. Support Equipment Bulletin (MCD)
SEB............. System Error Bridge
SEB............. Systems Engineering Branch [*NASA*] (NASA)
SEBA........... Babahoyo [*Ecuador*] [*ICAO location identifier*] (ICLI)
SEBA........... Staphylococcal Enterotoxin B Antisera [*Medicine*]
Sebast Med... Sebastianus Medices [*Flourished, 16th century*] [*Authority cited in pre-1607 legal work*] (DSA)
Sebast Sap... Sebastianus Sapia [*Deceased, 1523*] [*Authority cited in pre-1607 legal work*] (DSA)
Sebast Vant... Sebastianus Vantius [*Flourished, 16th century*] [*Authority cited in pre-1607 legal work*] (DSA)
SEBBETSI .... Serikat Buruh Beras dan Seluruh Indonesia [*Rice and Tapioca Workers' Union of Indonesia*]
SEBC........... Bahia De Caraquez [*Ecuador*] [*ICAO location identifier*] (ICLI)
SEBC........... Societe des Eleveurs de Bovins Canadiens (AC)
SEBC........... South-Eastern Bible College [*Florida*]
SEBD .... Bola De Oro [*Ecuador*] [*ICAO location identifier*] (ICLI)
SEBD .... Software Engineering Bibliographic Data Base [*Data and Analysis Center for Software*] [*Information service or system*]
SEBDA .... Serikat Buruh Daehrah Autonoom [*Civil Servants' Union*] [*Indonesia*]
SEBE........... La Beata [*Ecuador*] [*ICAO location identifier*] (ICLI)
SEbE........... Southeast by East
SEBECC........ Scanning Electron Beam Excited Charge Collection (IAA)
SEBH .... Balao Chico [*Ecuador*] [*ICAO location identifier*] (ICLI)
SEBI........... Boliche [*Ecuador*] [*ICAO location identifier*] (ICLI)
SEBI........... Securities and Exchange Board of India (ECON)
SEBIC.......... Sustained Electron Bombardment-Induced Conductivity
SEBL........... Self-Emptying Blind Loop [*Gastroenterology*]
SEBL........... Siebel Systems, Inc. [*NASDAQ symbol*] (SAG)
SEBL........... Single European Banking Licence
SEBM........... Society for Experimental Biology and Medicine (EA)
SEBQ .... Senior Enlisted Bachelor Quarters [*Army*] (AABC)
SEBS........... Single-Ended Boiler Survey (DS)
SEbS........... Southeast by South
SEBS........... Submarine Emergency Buoyancy System
Seb Sapi...... Sebastianus Sapia [*Deceased, 1523*] [*Authority cited in pre-1607 legal work*] (DSA)
SEBSCC .... Southeast Bering Sea Carrying Capacity [*Study*] [*Marine science*] (OSRA)
SEBT........... El Batan [*Ecuador*] [*ICAO location identifier*] (ICLI)
Seb Trade-Marks... Sebastian on Trade-Marks [*A publication*] (DLA)
Seb Tr M..... Sebastian on Trade-Marks [*5th ed.*] [*1911*] [*A publication*] (DLA)

SEBUMI .... Serikat Buruh Minjak, Stanvac [*Oil Workers' Union, Stanvac*] [*Indonesia*]
SEBV............ Solder End Ball Valve
Seb Vant...... Sebastianus Vantius [*Flourished, 16th century*] [*Authority cited in pre-1607 legal work*] (DSA)
s-ec--........... Ecuador [*MARC geographic area code Library of Congress*] (LCCP)
SEC............. Safeguards Equipment Cabinet (IEEE)
SEC............. Sanitary Engineering Center
SEC............. Scientific and Engineering Computation
SEC............. Scientific Estimates Committee [*Military*] (AABC)
SEC............. Scottish Evangelistic Council (DBA)
sec.............. Secant (IDOE)
SEC............. Secant
SEC............. Second (AFM)
sec.............. Second (IDOE)
sec.............. Second (ODBW)
sec.............. Secondary (IDOE)
Sec............. Secondary [*Chemistry*]
SEC............. Secondary
SEC............. Secondary Electron Conduction [*Television camera system*]
SEC............. Secondary Emission Conductivity
SEC............. Secret (AFM)
SEC............. Secretariat
SEC............. Secretary (EY)
Sec............. Secretary (ODBW)
sec.............. Secretary (DD)
SEC............. Secretin [*Biochemistry*]
SEC............. Section
sec.............. Section (IDOE)
Sec............. Section (AAGC)
SEC............. Sector
SEC............. Secular
SEC............. Secundum [*According To*] [*Latin*]
SEC............. Secure (KSC)
SEC............. Securities [*or Security*] (AAG)
SEC............. Securities and Exchange Commission
SEC............. Securities and Exchange Commission Decisions and Reports [*A publication*] (DLA)
SEC............. Securities and Exchange Commission, Washington, DC [*OCLC symbol*] (OCLC)
SEC............. Security
Sec............. Secus [*Otherwise*] [*Latin*] (ILCA)
SEC............. Sensor and Engagement Controller [*Army*]
SEC............. Sensormatic Canada Ltd. [*Toronto Stock Exchange symbol*]
SEC............. Sequential Events Controller [*NASA*] (NASA)
SEC............. Shaftless Expander-Compressor
SEC............. Simple Electronic Computer [*Birkbeck College*] [*London, England*] (DEN)
SEC............. Single-Edge Contact (PCM)
SEC............. Single Error Correcting
SEC............. Sisters of the Eucharistic Covenant (TOCD)
SEC............. Size Exclusion Chromatography
SEC............. Social Economic Council [*Sociaal Economische Raad*] [*Netherlands*]
SEC............. Social Education Centre (AIE)
SEC............. Societe des Ecrivains Canadiens [*Society of Canadian Writers*]
SEC............. Societe Europeenne de Culture [*European Society of Culture - ESC*] (EAIO)
SEC............. Society for Educative Communication (EA)
SEC............. Society of Exchange Counselors (EA)
SEC............. Soft Elastic Capsule [*Pharmacy*]
SEC............. Solar Energy Collector
SEC............. Solar Energy Concentrator
SEC............. Solid Electrolyte Capacitor
SEC............. Source Evaluation Committee [*NASA*] (NASA)
SEC............. South East College of Air Training [*British ICAO designator*] (FAAC)
SEC............. Southeastern Command
SEC............. Southeastern Conference (EA)
SEC............. South Equatorial Current [*Oceanography*] (MSC)
SEC............. Southern Electronics Corp. (IAA)
SEC............. Space Environmental Chamber (AAG)
SEC............. Space Environment Center
SEC............. Space Environment Center [*Marine science*] (OSRA)
SEC............. Special Emergency Campaign [*Red Cross fund-raising*]
SEC............. Special Event Charter Flight [*Aviation*] (DA)
SEC............. Specific Energy Consumption [*Automotive engineering*]
SEC............. Spectroelectrochemistry
SEC............. Squamous Epithelial Cells [*Medicine*] (MEDA)
SEC............. Staff Evaluation Coordinators (MCD)
SEC............. Standard Error of Calibration
SEC............. Standard Evaluation Cylinder (MCD)
SEC............. Standards and Ethics Commission [*American Occupational Therapy Association*]
SEC............. Standing with Eyes Closed [*Equilibrium test*]
SEC............. Sterling Electronics [*NYSE symbol*] (TTSB)
SEC............. Sterling Electronics Corp. [*NYSE symbol*] (SAG)
SEC............. Stevens Creek [*California*] [*Seismograph station code, US Geological Survey*] (SEIS)
SEC............. Stock Exchange Council [*British*]
SEC............. Structural Engineers Councils (KSC)
SEC............. Submarine Element Coordinator (NVT)
SEC............. Sulfite Evaporator Condensate [*Pulp and paper technolgy*]
SEC............. Sulphur Export Corp. [*An association*] (EA)
SEC............. Supply Executive Committee [*NATO*] (NATG)
SEC............. Support Equipment Change (MCD)
SEC............. Supr Einspritz Coupe [*Super, Fuel Injection, Coupe*] [*Mercedes-Benz automotive model designation*]
SEC............. Switch Element Controller [*Telecommunications*]
SEC............. Switching Equipment Congestion [*Telecommunications*] (TEL)
SEC............. Sydney Entertainment Centre [*Australia*]
SECA........... Catarama [*Ecuador*] [*ICAO location identifier*] (ICLI)
SECA........... Self-Employment Contributions Act of 1954 [*under which self-employed persons contribute to OASDI coverage for themselves*]
SECA........... Shiatsu Education Center of America [*Later, Ohashi Institute - OI*] (EA)
SECA........... Societe d'Eco-Amenagement [*Commercial firm France*] (ECON)
SECA........... Solar Energy Construction Association [*Defunct*] (EA)
SECA........... Southern Educational Communications Authority [*Television network*] [*Obsolete*]
SECA........... Sportbike Enthusiast Club of America (EA)
SECAB .... Secretaria Ejecutiva Permanente del Convenio Andres Bello [*Permanent Executive Secretariat of the Andres Bello Convention*] (EAIO)
SECAC .... Sectional Aeronautical Chart
SECAD .... Services Engineering Computer-Aided Design [*Pierce Management Services*] [*Software package*] (NCC)
SECAD .... Support Equipment Concept Approval Data
SECAL.......... Sectoral Adjustment Loan [*World Bank*]
SECAL.......... Selected Calling System [*Military*] (AFM)
SECAL.......... Separate Engineering Control Air Limits [*Environmental science*]
SECAM......... Sequence Electronique Couleur avec Memoire [*Color Sequence with Memory*] [*French color television system*]
SECAM......... Sequential Color and Memory (IAA)
SECAM......... Systeme Electronique Couleur avec Memoire [*French broadcast color standard*]
SECAN .... Science and Engineering Committee on Advisory to NOAA [*National Oceanic and Atmospheric Administration*] [*Defunct*] (USDC)
SECAN .... Science and Engineering Committee on Advisory to NOAA [*National Oceanic and Atmospheric Administration*] [*Marine science*] (OSRA)
SECAN .... Standing Group Communication Security and Evaluation Agency Washington
Sec & Ex C... Securities and Exchange Commission (DLA)
SECANT .... Separation and Control of Aircraft Using Nonsynchronous Techniques [*Collision avoidance*] [*RCA*]
SECAP .... System Experience Correlation and Analysis Program (IAA)
SECAP .... Systems Experiment Correlation and Analysis Program (MCD)
SECAR .... Secondary RADAR (IEEE)
SECARMY.... Secretary of the Army
SEC ART....... Secundum Artem [*According to the Art*] [*Latin*]
SECAS .... Ship Equipment Configuration Accounting System (NVT)
SECBASE ..... Section Base [*Navy*] (DNAB)
SecBcp .... Security Bancorp [*Associated Press*] (SAG)
SecBHld....... Security Bank Holding Co. [*Associated Press*] (SAG)
Sec Bk Judg... Second Book of Judgments (Huxley) [*England*] [*A publication*] (DLA)
SecBn .... Second Bancorp, Inc. [*Associated Press*] (SAG)
SECC........... Condorcocha [*Ecuador*] [*ICAO location identifier*] (ICLI)
SECC........... Safe Energy Communication Council (EA)
SECC........... Scientific and Engineering Computing Council (MCD)
SECC........... South Equatorial Countercurrent [*Oceanography*] (MSC)
SECC........... State Emergency Communications Committee [*National Oceanic and Atmospheric Administration*] (GFGA)
SECC........... Survivable Enduring Command and Control
SECCA .... Southeastern Center for Contemporary Art [*North Carolina*]
SecCap .... Security Capital Corp. [*Associated Press*] (SAG)
SecCapA....... Security Capital Atlantic, Inc. [*Associated Press*] (SAG)
SecCaPT....... Security Capital Pacific Trust [*Associated Press*] (SAG)
SecCapTr..... Security Capital Industrial Trust Co. [*Associated Press*] (SAG)
SecComp..... Secure Computing Corp. [*Associated Press*] (SAG)
SEC Compl (P-H)... Securities and Exchange Commission Compliance (Prentice-Hall, Inc.) [*A publication*] (DLA)
SECD .... Secondary (AABC)
SECD .... Second Bancorp [*NASDAQ symbol*] (TTSB)
SECD .... Second Bancorp, Inc. [*NASDAQ symbol*] (SPSG)
SECD .... Secured (ROG)
SECDA .... Southeastern Community Development Association [*Defunct*] (EA)
SECDED....... Single-BIT [*Binary Digit*] Error Correction and Double-BIT Error Detection [*Binary Digit*]
SecDef......... Secretary of Defense [*DoD*] (VNW)
SECDEF........ Secretary of Defense
SEC Docket... Securities and Exchange Commission Docket [*A publication*] (DLA)
SECDP .... Second Bncp $1.50 Cv Pfd'A' [*NASDAQ symbol*] (TTSB)
Secd Pt Edw III... Year Books, Part III [*England*] [*A publication*] (DLA)
Secd Pt H VI... Year Books, Part VIII [*England*] [*A publication*] (DLA)
SECDY .... Secondary
SecDyn......... Security Dynamics Technologies, Inc. [*Associated Press*] (SAG)
SECE........... Santa Cecilia [*Ecuador*] [*ICAO location identifier*] (ICLI)
SECE........... Selfhelp of Emigres from Central Europe (EA)
SECED .... Society for Earthquake and Civil Engineering Dynamics [*British*]
SECEM......... Support Equipment Cost Effectiveness Model (MCD)
SECF........... Somali Eastern and Central Front [*Political party*] (EY)
SECF........... Surface Effect Cruiser Escort (DNAB)
SECFLT........ Second Fleet [*Atlantic*] [*Navy*]
SecFstNt...... Security First Network Bank [*Associated Press*] (SAG)
SECFT.......... Second Foot (IAA)
SECG .... Stress Electrocardiography [*Cardiology*] (DMAA)
SEC GEN...... Secretary General (WDAA)
SECGRUHQ... Security Group Headquarters
SECH .... Chone [*Ecuador*] [*ICAO location identifier*] (ICLI)

sech............ Hyperbolic Secant (IDOE)
SECH............ Secant, Hyperbolic
SECHT......... Scoping Emergency Cooling Heat Transfer [*Nuclear energy*] (KSC)
SECI............ Support Equipment Critical Item (MCD)
SECIMP....... Secondary Impedance (IAA)
SECINSP..... Security Inspection [*Military*] (NVT)
Sec Int......... Secretary of the Interior (DLA)
SECIR.......... Semiautomatic Encoding of Chemistry for Information Retrieval (DIT)
SECIT........... Syndicat des Employes Indigenes du Commerce du Togo [*Union of Indigenous Employees of Commerce of Togo*]
SEC Jud Dec... Securities and Exchange Commission Judicial Decisions [*A publication*] (DLA)
SECL............ Chiles [*Ecuador*] [*ICAO location identifier*] (ICLI)
secl.............. Secretarial (WGA)
SECL............ Secretarial
SECL............ Sequential Emitter Coupled Logic (IAA)
SECL............ Ship Equipment Configuration List (MCD)
SECL............ Symmetrical Emitter Coupled Logic (IAA)
SECL............ Symmetrically-Operated Emitter Coupled Logic (IAA)
SECLA.......... Southeastern Connecticut Library Association [*Library network*]
SEC LEG...... Secundum Legem [*According to Law*] [*Latin*]
SECLT.......... Second Lieutenant [*Army*]
SECM........... Clementina [*Ecuador*] [*ICAO location identifier*] (ICLI)
SECM........... Scanning Electrochemical Microscope
SECM........... School of English Church Music [*Later, RSCM*]
SECM........... Secom General [*NASDAQ symbol*] (TTSB)
SECM........... Secom General Corp. [*NASDAQ symbol*] (NQ)
SECMA......... Stock Exchange Computer Managers Association (MHDW)
SECMID....... Scanning Electrochemical Microscope-Induced Desorption
SECN........... Section (ROG)
SECNA......... Secretary of the Navy (NOAA)
SEC NAT...... Secundum Naturam [*According to Nature*] [*Latin*]
SECNAV....... Secretary of the Navy
SECNAVINST... Secretary of the Navy Instruction
SecndB......... Second Bancorp, Inc. [*Associated Press*] (SAG)
SecNtl.......... Security National Financial Corp. [*Associated Press*] (SAG)
SECNY......... Sales Executives Club of New York (EA)
SECO........... Coca [*Ecuador*] [*ICAO location identifier*] (ICLI)
SECO........... Securities and Exchange Commission
SECO........... Securities and Exchange Commission Organization
SECO........... Self-Regulating Error-Correct Coder-Decoder
SECO........... Sequential Coding
SECO........... Sequential Control [*Teletype*] [*Computer science*]
SECO........... Sequential Encoder-Decoder (IAA)
SECO........... Station Engineering Control Office [*Telecommunications*] (TEL)
SECO........... Steam and Electric Cogeneration [*Power source*]
SECO........... Sustainer-Engine Cutoff [*Aerospace*]
SECOBI........ Servicio de Consulta a Bancos de Informacion [*Database Consultation Service*] [*Information service or system Mexico*] (IID)
SECOF......... Shipboard Environmental Checkout Facility (DNAB)
SECOFF....... Section Office
SECOFI........ Secretaria de Comercio y Fomento Industrial [*Secretariat of Trade and IndustrialPromotion*] [*Mexico*] (CROSS)
SECOIN....... Security Consultants International
SECOL......... Southeastern Conference on Linguistics
SECOLAS..... Southeastern Conference on Latin American Studies [*United States*]
SECOM........ School Emergency Communication
Secom.......... Secom General Corp. [*Associated Press*] (SAG)
SECOM........ Security Committee
SECOM........ System Engineering Communication (IAA)
SECOMO...... Software [*or System*] Engineering Cost Model
SECON......... Secondary Electron Conduction [*Television camera system*]
Second Ed... Secondary Education [*A publication*]
Second Teach... Secondary Teacher [*A publication*]
SECONNS.... Satellite ECCM [*Electronics Counter Countermeasure*] Communications Neural Network Syster
SECOR......... Sequential Collation [*or Collection*] of Ranges [*Army*]
SECOR......... Sequential Correlation
SECOR......... Sequential Correlation of Range (IAA)
SECOR......... Sequential Cosine Ranging [*System*] (MUGU)
SECORD....... Secure Voice Cord Board [*Telecommunications*] (TEL)
SECP........... Security Capital [*NASDAQ symbol*] (TTSB)
SECP........... Security Capital Corp. [*NASDAQ symbol*] (SAG)
SECP........... Software Engineering Change Proposal (MCD)
SECP........... Solar Energy Conservation Program [*Department of Energy*]
SECP........... State Energy Conservation Program
SECP........... Subcontractor Engineering Change Proposal (MCD)
SecPac........ Security Pacific [*Bank*] (ECON)
SecPac........ Security Pacific Bank [*Hong Kong*]
SECPDED..... Single Error Correcting and Partial Double Error Detecting [*Computer science*] (MHDI)
SECPR......... Standard External Cardiopulmonary Resuscitation
SECPS......... Secondary Propulsion System [*NASA*] (KSC)
SECPS......... SEC Practice Section (TDOB)
SECR........... Curaray [*Ecuador*] [*ICAO location identifier*] (ICLI)
SECR........... Secretariat
SECRA......... Secondary RADAR [*RADAR beacon*]
SECRAC....... System Engineering Cost Reduction Assistance Contractor (PDAA)
SEC REG...... Secundum Regulam [*According to Rule*] [*Latin*]
Sec Reg Guide... Securities Regulation Guide [*Prentice-Hall, Inc.*] [*A publication*] (DLA)
SECREP....... Regional Representative of the Secretary of Transportation
SECRG......... Securing
SECRL......... Secretarial
SECS........... Seagrass Ecosystems Component Study [*Marine science*] (MSC)
SECS........... Selective Electron-Capture Sensitization [*Analytical chemistry*]
SECS........... Semiconductor Equipment Communications Standard (NITA)
SECS........... Sequential Events Control System [*NASA*] (KSC)
SECS........... Shuttle Events Control Subsystem [*NASA*] (NASA)
SECS........... Simulation and Evaluation of Chemical Synthesis [*Computer science*]
SECS........... Single-Electron Capacitance Spectroscopy
SECS........... Single-Engine Control Speed (DNAB)
SECS........... Solar Electric Communication Satellite
SECS........... Space Environmental Control System (AAG)
SECS........... Stem Elevated Camera System
SECSA......... Single Engine Control System Application (MCD)
SECSTA....... Naval Security Station
SECSW........ Science and Engineering Committee for a Secure World (EA)
SECSY......... Spin-Echo Correlated Spectroscopy
SECT........... Firing Field Equipment Service [*French Acronym is based on foreign phrase*]
SECT........... Secretariat
SECT........... Section (KSC)
SECT........... Section
sect............. Section (VRA)
SECT........... Skin Electric Tracing (IAA)
SECT........... South East Cultural Trust [*South Australia*]
SECT........... Submarine Emergency Communications Transmitter
SECTAM....... Sterile Environmental Control Technology Applications to Medicine
SECTASKFLT... Second Task Fleet
SECTBASE... Section Base [*Navy*]
SECTL.......... Secretarial
SECTL.......... Sectional
SECTLZD...... Sectionalized
SECTRANS... Secretary of Transportation (DOMA)
SEC-TREAS... Secretary-Treasurer (DNAB)
sec-treas..... Secretary-Treasurer (DD)
SECTY......... Secretary
SECU........... Cuenca [*Ecuador*] [*ICAO location identifier*] (ICLI)
SECU........... Slave Emulator Control Unit
SecuBk......... Security Bank Corp. [*Associated Press*] (SAG)
SEC(UN)...... Secretariat of the United Nations
SecurCT....... Security Connecticut Corp. [*Associated Press*] (SAG)
SECURE....... Systems Evaluation Code Under Radiation Environment
SecurFst...... Security First Corp. [*Associated Press*] (SAG)
SECUS......... Sex Information and Education Council of the United States
SECUS......... Supreme Emblem Club of the United States (EA)
SECUTC....... Southeastern Consortium of University Transportation Centers [*MTMC*] (TAG)
SECWAR...... Secretary of War [*Obsolete*]
SECWND...... Secondary Winding (IAA)
SECX........... Southern Electronics [*NASDAQ symbol*] (TTSB)
SECX........... Southern Electronics Corp. [*Tucker, GA*] [*NASDAQ symbol*] (NQ)
SECY........... Secretary
SECY........... Secretary
SECY........... Security
SED............. Sale/Engineering/Development [*Honda*] [*Automotive engineering*]
SED............. Sanitary Engineering Division [*MIT*] (MCD)
SED............. Saturn Electrostatic Discharges [*Planetary science*]
SED............. Scarborough Board of Education [*Professional Education Library*] [*UTLAS symbol*]
SED............. Scottish Education Department
SED............. Sedan (AAG)
SED............. Sedative [*Medicine*] (ROG)
SED............. Seddin [*German Democratic Republic*] [*Later, NGK*] [*Geomagnetic observatory code*]
Sed.............. Sedes [*A Stool*] [*Medicine*]
SED............. Sediment [*or Sedimentation*]
SED............. Sedition [*FBI standardized term*]
SED............. Sedona Air Center, Inc. [*ICAO designator*] (FAAC)
SED............. Segmented Expanding Die (MCD)
SED............. Semiequilibrium Dialysis [*Physical chemistry*]
SED............. Sensor Evolutionary Development (MCD)
SED............. Sequence Event Diagram (DNAB)
SED............. Seriously [*or Severely*] Emotionally Disturbed
SED............. SFS Bancorp, Inc. [*NASDAQ symbol*] (SAG)
SED............. Shipper's Export Declaration [*Customs Service*]
SED............. Shipper's Export Document [*FHWA*] (TAG)
SED............. Shore Establishments Division [*Navy*]
SED............. Signal Equipment Depot (IAA)
SED............. Simulative Electronic Deception [*Army*] (ADDR)
SED............. Skin Erythema Dose [*Medicine*]
SED............. Smoke-Emitting Diode [*Computer hacker terminology*] (NHD)
SED............. Software Engineering Data [*Data and Analysis Center for Software*] [*Information service or system*]
SED............. Software Engineering Design [*Army*]
SED............. Software Engineering Directorate [*Army*] (RDA)
SED............. Solar Energy Density
SED............. Sound Energy Density
SED............. Sozialistische Einheitspartei Deutschlands [*Socialist Unity Party of Germany*] [*Political party*] (PPW)
SED............. Soziolistische Linheitspartei Deutschlands [*Socialist Unity Party*] [*German*] (BARN)
SED............. Space Engineering Document [*NASA*] (IAA)
SED............. Space Environment Division [*NASA*]
SED............. Special Electrical Devices (AABC)
SED............. Special Expanded Display (IAA)
SEd.............. Specialist in Education (GAGS)
SED............. Spectral Energy Distribution

SED.......... Spondyloepiphysial Dysplasia [*Medicine*]
SED.......... Staphylococcal Enterotoxin D [*Medicine*]
SED.......... State Executive Director
SED.......... Status Entry Device [*Telecommunications*] (TEL)
SED.......... Stochastic Electrodynamics [*Quantum physics*]
SED.......... Stray Energy Detector
sed.......... Stream Editor [*Computer science*] (CDE)
SED.......... Strong Exchange Degeneracy [*Physics*] (OA)
SED.......... Students for Economic Democracy (EA)
SED.......... Sun Entertainment [*Vancouver Stock Exchange symbol*]
SED.......... Suppressed Electrical Discharge (IAA)
SED.......... Swansea East Dock [*Welsh depot code*]
SED.......... System Engineering Division [*Apollo Spacecraft Program Office*]
SED.......... System Entry Date [*Military*] (AFIT)
SED.......... Systems Effectiveness Demonstration (NG)
SEDA.......... Safety Equipment Distributors Association (EA)
SEDA.......... South Eastern Discotheque Association [*British*] (DBA)
SEDA.......... Staff and Educational Development Association (AIE)
SEDA.......... State Emergency Defense Airlift
SEDA.......... Structured Exploratory Data Analysis
SEDACS.......... Support Equipment Data Acquisition and Control System (MCD)
SEDAR.......... Shipborne Electronic Deflection Array RADAR (MCD)
SEDAS.......... Spurious Emission Detection Acquisition System (MCD)
SedaSpc.......... Seda Speciality Packaging [*Commercial firm Associated Press*] (SAG)
SEDC.......... Society for Emotional Development in Children [*Canada*]
SEDC.......... Steam Engine Direct Connected (MSA)
SEDCOR.......... Specialty Electronics Development Corp.
SEDD.......... Special Extra Deep Drawing (MCD)
SEDD.......... Systems Evaluation and Development Division [*NASA*]
SEDEPAC.......... Servicio, Desarrollo y Paz [*Service, Development, and Peace*] [*An association Mexico*] (CROSS)
SEDES.......... Societe d'Etudes pour le Developpement Economique et Social [*Society for the Study of Economic and Social Development*] [*Information service or system France*] (IID)
SEDFC.......... Steve Earle and Dukes Fan Organization (EA)
SEDFRE.......... Scholarship, Education, and Defense Fund for Racial Equality
Sedg & W Tit... Sedgwick and Wait on the Trial of Title to Land [*A publication*] (DLA)
Sedg & W Tr Title Land... Sedgwick and Wait on the Trial of Title to Land [*A publication*] (DLA)
Sedg Dam... Sedgwick on the Measure of Damage [*A publication*] (DLA)
SEDGE.......... SAGE [*Semiautomatic Ground Environment*] Experimental Display Generator [*Military*] (IAA)
SEDGE.......... Special Experimental Display Generation (IAA)
SEDGE.......... Special Experimental Display Generation Program (SAA)
Sedg L Cas... Sedgwick's Leading Cases on Damages [*A publication*] (DLA)
Sedg L Cas... Sedgwick's Leading Cases on Real Property [*A publication*] (DLA)
Sedg St & Const Law... Sedgwick on Statutory and Constitutional Law [*A publication*] (DLA)
Sedg Stat Law... Sedgwick on Statutory and Constitutional Law [*A publication*] (DLA)
SEDI.......... Semi-Empirical Design of Impellers [*Hydraulics*] [*Computer-aided design*]
SEDI.......... Software Engineering Demonstrator Initiative [*British*]
SEDI.......... Spondyloepiphyseal Dysplasia, Late [*Medicine*] (DMAA)
SEDIC.......... Sociedad Espanola de Documentacion e Informacion Cientifica [*Spanish Society for Documentation and Information Sciences*] [*Information service or system*] (IID)
SEDIS.......... Service Information-Diffusion [*Information Dissemination Office*] [*National Institute for Research in Informatics and Automation*] [*Information service or system*] (IID)
SEDIS.......... Surface Emitter Detection, Identification System [*Navy*]
SEDIT.......... Sophisticated String Editor (IEEE)
SEDIT.......... Source Program Editor (MHDB)
SEDL.......... Southwest Educational Development Laboratory (EA)
SEDM.......... Society for Experimental and Descriptive Malacology (EA)
SEDM.......... Status Entry Device Multiplexer [*Telecommunications*] (TEL)
SEDME.......... Survey Electronics Distance Measuring Equipment (MCD)
SEDME.......... Surveying Equipment Distance Measuring Electronic (MCD)
SEDOC.......... European System for the International Clearing of Vacancies and Applications forEmployment [*EC*] (ECED)
SEDOR.......... Spin Echo Double Resonance [*Physics*]
SEDP.......... Support for Engineer Development Priorities (MCD)
SEDPC.......... Scientific and Engineering Data Processing Center
SEDR.......... Science Education Development and Research Division [*National Science Foundation*] (GRD)
SEDR.......... Service Engineering Department Report
SEDR.......... Supplementary Experiment Data Record [*Aerospace*]
SEDR.......... System Effective Data Rate (BUR)
SEDR.......... Systems Engineering Department Report (IEEE)
sed rt.......... Sedimentation Rate [*Hematology*] (DAVI)
SEDS.......... Social and Economic Development Strategy
SEDS.......... Social-Emotional Dimension Scale [*Behavior problems test*]
SEDS.......... Society for Educational Data Systems [*Later, SDE*]
SEDS.......... Space Electronics Detection System (KSC)
SEDS.......... State Energy Data System [*Department of Energy*] [*Database*]
SEDS.......... Students for the Exploration and Development of Space (EA)
SEDS.......... Support Equipment Data System
SEDS.......... System Effectiveness Data System [*Air Force*]
SEDS.......... Systems Engineering Detailed Schedule
SEDSCAF.......... Standard ELINT Data System Codes and Format (NVT)
SEDSDR.......... Support Equipment Delivery Schedule Delinquency Report (MCD)
SEDT.......... Spondyloepiphyseal Dysplasia Tarda [*Medicine*] (DMAA)
SEE.......... SAGE [*Semiautomatic Ground Environment*] Evaluation Exercise [*Military*] (IAA)
SEE.......... San Diego/Santee, CA [*Location identifier FAA*] (FAAL)
SEE.......... Sealed Air [*NYSE symbol*] (TTSB)
SEE.......... Sealed Air Corp. [*NYSE symbol*] (SPSG)
SEE.......... Secondary Electron Emission
SEE.......... Seeing Essential English [*Sign language system for the hearing impaired*]
SEE.......... Senior Electronic Engineer (IAA)
SEE.......... Senior Environmental Employment
SEE.......... Senior Environmental Employment Program [*Environmental Protection Agency*]
SEE.......... Signals Experimental Establishment [*British military*] (DMA)
SEE.......... Signed Exact English
SEE.......... Significant Emotional Events
SEE.......... Signing Exact English [*Sign language system for the hearing impaired*]
SEE.......... Small Emplacement Excavations [*or Excavator*] [*Army*]
SEE.......... Societe d'Etudes et d'Expansion [*Studies and Expansion Society - SES*] [*Later, Et Ex*] (EAIO)
SEE.......... Societie pour l'Expansion des Exportations [*Export Development Corp.*] [*Canada*]
SEE.......... Society of Earthbound Extraterrestrials (EA)
SEE.......... Society of Electronics Engineers
SEE.......... Society of Environmental Engineers [*Later, Institute of Environmental Sciences*]
SEE.......... Society of Explosives Engineers (EA)
SEE.......... South East Air [*British ICAO designator*] (FAAC)
SEE.......... Southeastern Electric Exchange
SEE.......... Space Environmental Experiment [*NASA*] (IAA)
SEE.......... Special Purpose End Effector (MCD)
SEE.......... Standard End Effector (NASA)
SEE.......... Standard Error of Estimate
SEE.......... Staphylococcal Enterotoxin E [*Medicine*]
SEE.......... Summer Educational Enrichment
SEE.......... Sun Earth Explorer [*Satellite*] [*NASA*]
SEE.......... Support Equipment Exhibit (MCD)
SEE.......... Surgical Eye Expeditions International (EAIO)
SEE.......... Survival, Evasion, and Escape [*Military*]
SEE.......... Systems Effectiveness Engineering (MCD)
SEE.......... Systems Effectiveness Evaluation (NG)
SEE.......... Systems Efficiency Expert
SEE.......... Systems Equipment Engineer [*Telecommunications*] (TEL)
SEEA.......... Societe Europeenne d'Energie Atomique
SEEA.......... Software Error Effects Analysis
SEEA.......... Southeast European Airlines [*Greece*] [*ICAO designator*] (FAAC)
SEE/AN.......... Systems Effectiveness Evaluation/Analyzer (DNAB)
SEEAPAC.......... Shore Electronic Engineering Activity, Pacific
SEEB.......... Seeburg Industries, Inc. [*NASDAQ symbol*]
SEECA.......... Solar Energy and Energy Conservation Act of 1980
SEECA.......... State Environmental Education Coordinators Association [*Defunct*] (EA)
SEECCIASDI.......... Standing EEC [*European Economic Community*] Committee of the International Association of the Soap and Detergent Industry [*See also CPCEAISD*] [*Brussels, Belgium*] (EAIO)
SEECL.......... Solar Energy and Energy Conversion Laboratory [*University of Florida*] [*Research center*] (RCD)
SEED.......... DeKalb Genetics [*NASDAQ symbol*] (SAG)
SEED.......... DeKalb Genetics [*NASDAQ symbol*] (SAG)
SEED.......... Safe Eye Exposure Distance [*Air Force*]
SEED.......... Schoolhouse Energy Efficiency Demonstration Project (EDAC)
SEED.......... Scientists and Engineers in Economic Development [*National Science Foundation*]
SEED.......... Self-Electro-Optic Effect [*Computer imaging*]
SEED.......... Self Electrooptic Effect Device [*Optical analog of a transistor*]
SEED.......... Sewall Early Education Developmental Profiles
SEED.......... Skill Escalation Employment Development (EA)
SEED.......... Special Elementary Education for the Disadvantaged
SEED.......... Structured Environment for the Emotionally Disturbed Project (EDAC)
SEED.......... Strumech Engineering Electronic Developments (NITA)
SEED.......... Supply of Essential Engineering Data
SEED.......... Support for East European Democracies Act [*1989*]
SEED.......... Sustainable Energy and Environment Division [*United Nations*]
SEEDB.......... DEKALB Genetics'B' [*NASDAQ symbol*] (TTSB)
SEEDC.......... South East Economic Development Council [*Australian Capital Territory*]
SEEDIS.......... Socio-Economic Demographic Information System [*Lawrence Berkeley Laboratory*] [*Database*]
SEEDS.......... Shipboard Equipments Environmental Design Study (PDAA)
SEEDS.......... Ship's Electrical and Electronic Data System (DNAB)
SEEDS.......... Space Exposed Experiment Developed for Students
SEEEE.......... Societe Europeenne d'Etudes et d'Essais d'Environnment [*France*] (PDAA)
SEEF.......... Scientists and Engineers Emigrant Fund
SEEHRL.......... Sanitary Engineering and Environmental Health Research Laboratory [*Research center*] (RCD)
SEEI.......... Special Essential Elements of Information (MCD)
SEEI.......... Support Equipment End Item (MCD)
SEE-IN.......... Significant Events Evaluation and Information Network
SEEK.......... Infoseek Corp. [*NASDAQ symbol*] (SAG)
SEEK.......... Search for Education, Elevation, and Knowledge [*Program*]
SEEK.......... Sooner Exchange for Educational Knowledge [*Oklahoma*] (EDAC)
SEEK.......... Survival, Escape, and Evasion Kit [*Navy*] (NG)
SEEK.......... Systems Evaluation and Exchange of Knowledge [*Computer science*]
SEEL.......... Sex Equity in Educational Leadership Project [*Oregon*] (EDAC)

SEEL .... Singapore Electronic and Engineering, Ltd. (IAA)
SEEN .... Seeing-Eye Elephant Network [*A computer-assisted instruction program*] (EDAC)
SEEN .... Syndicat d'Etudes de l'Energie Nucleaire [*Belgium*]
SEEO .... Salvis Erroribus et Omissis [*Errors and Omissions Excepted*] [*Latin*]
SEEO .... Shore Electronic Engineering Office [*Navy*]
SEEP .... Sex Equity in Education Program (EA)
SEEP .... Shelf Edge Exchange Processes [*Oceanography*] (NOAA)
SEEP .... Sixth Fleet Escort Evaluation Program [*Navy*]
SEEP .... Small End-Expiratory Pressure [*Medicine*] (DAVI)
SEEP .... Stimulated Emission of Energetic Particles [*Experiment for study of radio waves*]
SEEPZ .... Santacruz Electronics Export Processing Zone
SEEQ .... SEEQ Technology [*NASDAQ symbol*] (TTSB)
SEEQ .... SEEQ Technology, Inc. [*NASDAQ symbol*] (NQ)
SEEQ .... Side-Effects Expectancy Questionnaire [*Psychology*]
SEER .... Seasonal Energy Efficiency Rating (AAGC)
SEER .... Seasonal Energy-Efficiency Ratio [*of heat pumps, air conditioners, etc.*]
SEER .... Seer Tech [*NASDAQ symbol*] (TTSB)
SEER .... Seer Technologies, Inc. [*NASDAQ symbol*] (SAG)
SEER .... Sensor Experimental Evaluation and Review [*Strategic Defense Initiative*]
SEER .... Service des Etudes Ecologiques Regionales [*Canada*]
SEER .... Steam Electric Evaluating and Recording (IAA)
SEER .... Student Exposition on Energy Resources [*Project*]
SEER .... Submarine Explosive Echo Ranging
SEER .... Supervisory Electronic Engineer [*Radio*]
SEER .... Surveillance, Epidemiology, and End-Results [*Program*] [*National Cancer Institute*]
SEER .... Sustainable Equilibrium Exchange Rate [*Economics*]
SEER .... System for Electronic Evaluation and Retrieval [*Computer science*]
SEER .... Systems Engineering, Evaluation, and Research (MCD)
SEEREP .... Ships' Essential Equipment Requisition Expediting Program [*Navy*] (NVT)
SEERS .... Senior Enlisted Evaluation Reports [*Military*] (INF)
SeerTc .... Seer Technologies, Inc. [*Associated Press*] (SAG)
SEES .... Esmeraldas/General Rivadeneira [*Ecuador*] [*ICAO location identifier*] (ICLI)
SEES .... Slavic and East European Section [*Association of College and Research Libraries*]
SEES .... Standard Entry/Exit System [*Army*]
SEES .... System Effectiveness Engineering Section
SEET .... Science End-to-End Test [*Space*]
SEET .... Scottish, English, and European Textiles [*Commercial firm*]
SEETB .... South East England Tourist Board (DCTA)
SEETEC .... Sight Enhancement, Education, and Technology
SEEX .... Systems Evaluation Experiment (MCD)
SEF .... Aero Servicios Ejecutivas del Pacifico, SA de CV [*Mexico*] [*FAA designator*] (FAAC)
SEF .... SALT Education Fund [*Defunct*] (EA)
SEF .... Sebring, FL [*Location identifier FAA*] (FAAL)
SEF .... Self-Extinguishing Fiber [*Monsanto Co. trademark*]
SEF .... Sequential Excitation Fluorescence [*Aviation Navy*]
SEF .... Shielding Effectiveness Factor
SEF .... Shock Excited Filter (IAA)
SEF .... Simple Environment Factor
SEF .... Simulated Engine Failure (ADA)
SEF .... Single Equivalent Formant (IAA)
SEF .... Small-End Forward [*of command module*]
SEF .... Software Engineering Facility
SEF .... Solar Energy Flux
SEF .... Somatically Evoked Field [*Neurophysiology*]
SEF .... Sound Energy Flux
SEF .... Southern Education Foundation (EA)
SEF .... Space Education Foundation [*Later, AEF*]
SEF .... Space Environmental Facility (SAA)
SEF .... Special Entry Flying List [*Navy British*]
SEF .... Stability Enhancement Function [*Aviation*] (GFGA)
SEF .... Standard External File
SEF .... Staphylococcus Aureus Enterotoxin F [*Toxic shock toxin*]
SEF .... Storage Extension Frame (NITA)
SEF .... Surface Effect Ship
SEF .... Systems Engineering Facility [*Defense Communications Agency*] (RDA)
SE/FAC .... Support Equipment/Facility [*NASA*] (NASA)
SEFACAN .... Segregator, Facer, Canceller Machine
SEFAR .... Sonic End Fire for Azimuth and Range
SEFC .... Southeast Fisheries Center [*Miami, FL*] [*National Marine Fisheries Service*] (MSC)
SEFCAR .... Southeast Florida and Caribbean Recruitment (USDC)
SEFCAR .... Southeast Florida and Caribbean Recruitment [*Marine science*] (OSRA)
SEFCL .... Southeastern Fish Control Station [*Department of the Interior*] (GRD)
SEFD .... Solar Energy Flux Density
SEFE .... Societe Europenne pour la Formation des Ingenieurs (ACII)
SEFE .... Standardization Evaluation Flight Examiner
SEFEL .... Secretariat Europeen des Fabricants d'Emballages Metalliques Legers [*European Secretariat of Manufacturers of Light Metal Packages*] (EA)
SEFES .... Southeastern Forest Experiment Station [*Asheville, NC*] [*Department of Agriculture*] (GRD)
SEFEWS .... Scientists and Engineers Field Experience with Soldiers (RDA)
SEFF .... Snakeye Free-Fall [*Navy*] (DNAB)
SEFI .... Sequential Electric Fuel Injection [*Automotive engineering*]
SEFI .... Societe Europeenne pour la Formation des Ingenieurs [*European Society for Engineering Education*] (EA)
SEFIC .... Seventh Fleet Intelligence Center [*Navy*]
SEFIC .... Spoken English for Industry and Commerce (AIE)
SEFIP .... Statistical Estimation Fault Isolation Procedure (MCD)
SEFIS .... Small Engine Fuel Injection System
SEFLO .... Sequence Flow [*Tracing technique*]
SEFM .... Support Equipment Field Modification (AAG)
SEFOR .... Southwest Experimental Fast Oxide Reactor [*Nuclear energy*]
SEFR .... Shielding Experiment Facility Reactor [*Nuclear energy*]
SEFR .... Support Equipment for Robot (DWSG)
SEFR .... System Effectiveness Forecast Report
SEFRL .... Southeastern Field Research Laboratory [*Pennsylvania State University*]
SEFS .... Special Elite Forces Society (EA)
SefT .... Sefer Torah. Post-Talmudic Tractate (BJA)
SEFT .... Single Engine Flight Training
SEFT .... Society for Education in Film and Television [*British*]
SEFT .... Spin-Echo Fourier Transform [*Physics*]
SEG .... Saturday Evening Girls [*Decorators of Arts and Crafts pottery*]
SEG .... Scientific Ecology Group Inc. (GAAI)
SEG .... Screen Extras Guild (EA)
SEG .... Seagate Technology [*NYSE symbol*] (TTSB)
SEG .... Seagate Technology, Inc. [*NYSE symbol*] (SAG)
SEG .... Sealing
SEG .... Segment (AAG)
SEG .... Segno [*Sign*] [*Music*]
SEG .... Segue [*Follows*] [*Music*]
SEG .... Selective Epitaxial Growth [*Semiconductor technology*]
SEG .... Selinsgrove, PA [*Location identifier FAA*] (FAAL)
SEG .... Sequence of Events Generator
SEG .... Side Entry Goniometer
SEG .... Skyline [*Norway ICAO designator*] (FAAC)
SEG .... Sliding Electron Gun
SEG .... Society of Economic Geologists (EA)
SEG .... Society of Exploration Geophysicists (EA)
SEG .... Socio-Economic Grade (ODBW)
SEG .... Soft Elastic Gelatin [*Medicine*] (DMAA)
SEG .... Solartron Electronic Group (IAA)
SEG .... Sonoencephalogram (AAMN)
SEG .... Special Effect Generator [*Video technology*]
SEG .... Special-Effects Generator [*Filmmaking*] (WDMC)
SEG .... Standardization Evaluation Group (AFM)
SEG .... Subesophageal Ganglion [*Anatomy*]
SEG .... System Engineering Groundrule [*NASA*] (NASA)
SEG .... Systems Engineering Group [*Air Force*]
SEG .... Systems Evaluation Group
SEGBA .... Servicios Electricos del Gran Buenos Aires, SA [*Electrical utility*] [*Argentina*]
SEGD .... Society of Environmental Graphics Designers (EA)
SEGE .... Guale [*Ecuador*] [*ICAO location identifier*] (ICLI)
SEGH .... Society for Environmental Geochemistry and Health (EA)
SEGL .... Gul [*Ecuador*] [*ICAO location identifier*] (ICLI)
SEGM .... Segment
SEGMOS .... Service Goods Movement System (IAA)
SEGR .... Guarumal [*Ecuador*] [*ICAO location identifier*] (ICLI)
SEG/R & T ...... Systems Engineering Group/Research and Technology [*Air Force*]
SEGS .... Galapagos (Baltra) [*Ecuador*] [*ICAO location identifier*] (ICLI)
segs .... Segmented Neutrophils [*Also, polymorphonuclear leukocytes and segmented white cells*] [*Immunochemistry*] (DAVI)
SEGS .... Solar Electric Generating System
SEGS .... Solar Energy Generating System (IAA)
SEGSYS .... Segmentation System (IAA)
SEGU .... Guayaquil/Simon Bolivar [*Ecuador*] [*ICAO location identifier*] (ICLI)
SEGU .... Segue Software [*NASDAQ symbol*] (TTSB)
SEGU .... Segue Software, Inc. [*NASDAQ symbol*] (SAG)
SegueS .... Segue Software, Inc. [*Associated Press*] (SAG)
SEGV .... Segmentation Violation [*Computer science*] (NHD)
SEGZ .... Gualaquiza [*Ecuador*] [*ICAO location identifier*] (ICLI)
SEH .... Sehore [*India*] [*Seismograph station code, US Geological Survey*] (SEIS)
SEH .... Shuttle Electronic Hardware [*NASA*]
SEH .... Single-Engined Helicopter (MCD)
SEH .... Societe Europeenne d'Hematologie
SEH .... Solar Equivalent Hours
SEH .... Spartech Corp. [*NYSE symbol*] (SAG)
SEH .... Standard Electrik Hellas (NITA)
SEH .... Star/Earth Horizon Sightings
SEH .... Strobel, E. H., Saint Louis MO [*STAC*]
SEH .... Subependymal Hemorrhage [*Medicine*]
SEH .... Waglisla Air, Inc. [*Canada ICAO designator*] (FAAC)
SEHAB .... Sea Rehabilitation [*Navy*] (NVT)
SEHI .... Cotacachi [*Ecuador*] [*ICAO location identifier*] (ICLI)
SEHI .... Southern Energy Homes [*NASDAQ symbol*] (TTSB)
SEHI .... Southern Energy Homes, Inc. [*NASDAQ symbol*] (SAG)
SEHK .... Swedish Export Credit Corp. [*Associated Press*] (SAG)
SE-HPLC .... Size Exclusion-High Performance Liquid Chromatography
SEHPP .... Science and Environmental Health Policy Project
SEHT .... Hacienda Taura [*Ecuador*] [*ICAO location identifier*] (ICLI)
SEI .... Safety Equipment Institute (EA)
SEI .... Seitel, Inc. [*NYSE symbol*] (SPSG)
SEI .... Self Employment Income [*Social Security Administration*] (OICC)
SEI .... Self-Esteem Inventory [*Coopersmith*] (EDAC)
SEI .... Senhor Do Bonfim [*Brazil*] [*Airport symbol*] (OAG)
SEI .... Shane Resources [*Vancouver Stock Exchange symbol*]

SEI .... Societa Editrice Internazionale [*Italy*] [*Publisher*]
SEI .... Societas Ergophthalmologica Internationalis [*International Ergophthalmological Society*] [*Stockholm, Sweden*] (EAIO)
SEI .... Society of Engineering Illustrators (EA)
SEI .... Society of Environmental Improvement [*British*] (DBA)
SEI .... Software Engineering Institute [*DoD*]
SEI .... Solid Electrolyte Interphase [*Battery technology*]
SEI .... Space Exploration Initiative [*NASA*]
SEI .... Special Engineering Investigation (MCD)
SEI .... Special Equipment Item (MCD)
SEI .... Special Experience Identifier [*Military*]
SEI .... Statistical Engineering Institute (MCD)
SEI .... Stern Environment Indexes [*Psychology*]
SEI .... Stockholm Environment Institute
SEI .... Stockpile Entry Inspection [*Navy*] (NG)
SEI .... Stray Energy Indicator
SEI .... Stress Evaluation Inventory [*Test*]
SEI .... Sumitomo Electric Industries [*Auto inudustry supplier*]
SEI .... Superficial Epithelial Infiltrates [*Ophthalmology*] (DAVI)
SEI .... Support Equipment Illustration (MCD)
SEI .... Support Equipment Installation [*NASA*] (NASA)
SEI .... Sykes Enterprises, Inc. (PCM)
SEI .... System Engineering Instrumentation (NASA)
SEI .... System/Equipment Inventory
SEIA .... Security Equipment Industry Association (EA)
SEIA .... Solar Energy Industries Association (EA)
SEIA .... Solar Energy Institute of America [*Later, SEINAM*] (MCD)
SEIAC .... Science Education Information Analysis Center [*ERIC*]
SEIB .... Ibarra [*Ecuador*] [*ICAO location identifier*] (ICLI)
SEIB .... Service des Etudes et Inventaires Bio-Physiques [*Quebec*]
SEIB .... Statistical and Economic Information Bulletin for Africa [*A publication*]
Seibel .... Seibels [*Bruce*] Group, Inc. [*Associated Press*] (SAG)
SEIC .... SEI Corp. [*NASDAQ symbol*] (NQ)
SEIC .... SEI Investments Co. [*NASDAQ symbol*] (SAG)
SEIC .... Solar Energy Information Center
SEIC .... Syndicat de l'Emploi et de l'Immigration du Canada
SEIC .... System Effectiveness Information Central
SEICO .... Science and Engineering Information Center Co. (IID)
SEICO .... Support Equipment Installation and Checkout [*NASA*] (NASA)
SEICorp .... SEI Corp. [*Associated Press*] (SAG)
SEID .... Support Equipment Illustration Data (MCD)
SEIDB .... Solar Energy Information Data Bank [*Department of Energy*]
SEIE .... Submarine Escape Immersion Equipment
SEIF .... Speak Easy International Foundation (EA)
SEIFR .... Support Equipment End Item Funding Report (MCD)
SEIG .... Intag [*Ecuador*] [*ICAO location identifier*] (ICLI)
Seign Rep ... Lower Canada Seignorial Questions Reports [*A publication*] (DLA)
SEI Inv .... SEI Investments Co. [*Associated Press*] (SAG)
SEIL .... Science Experiments Integration Laboratories
SEIL .... Southeastern Educational Improvement Laboratory [*Research Triangle Park, NC*] [*Department of Education*] (GRD)
SEIM .... Isla San Miguel [*Ecuador*] [*ICAO location identifier*] (ICLI)
SEIMC .... Special Education Instructional Materials Centers [*Office of Education*] [*Database producer*] (IID)
SEIMS .... State Economic Information Management System [*State Department*] [*Database*]
SEINAM .... Solar Energy Institute of North America [*Defunct*] (EA)
SEIOD .... Spogli Elettronici dell'Italiano delle Origini e del Duecento [*A lexical, morphological, and syntactical inventory of Old Italian texts*]
SEIP .... Strategy for Exploration of the Inner Planets (IAA)
SEIP .... System Engineering Implementation Plan
SEIR .... Solar Energy Intelligence Report [*Business Publishers Inc.*] [*No longer available online*] [*Information service or system*] (CRD)
SEIR .... Southeast Indian Ridge [*Antarctica*] [*Geology*]
SEIR .... Susceptible, Exposed, Infected or Immune, Recovered [*Epidemiological model*]
SEIRS .... Suppliers and Equipment Information Retrieval System [*International Civil Aviation Organization*] [*Databank*] [*Information service or system*] (IID)
SEIS .... Solar Energy Information Services (IID)
SEIS .... Submarine Emergency Identification Signal (NG)
SEIS .... Supplemental Environmental Impact Statement [*Department of Agriculture*]
SEISA .... South Eastern Intercollegiate Sailing Association
SEISMOG ..... Seismographic
SEISMOL ..... Seismologic
SEIT .... Satellite Educational and Informational Television
SEIT .... Supervisory Electronic Installation Technician
SEIT .... System Engineering Integration and Test (MCD)
SEIT .... System Evaluation, Integration, and Test (MCD)
Seitel .... Seitel, Inc. [*Associated Press*] (SAG)
SEIU .... Service Employees International Union (EA)
SEIWG .... Security Equipment Integration Working Group
SE/IWT .... Southern Europe - Inland Waterways Transport [*NATO*] (NATG)
SEJ .... Sliding Expansion Joint [*Technical drawings*]
SEJ .... Southeastern Jurisdictional Conference [*United Methodist Church*]
SEJA .... Jaramillo [*Ecuador*] [*ICAO location identifier*] (ICLI)
SEJCR .... Societe Europeenne des Jeunes de la Croix-Bleue [*European Society for Blue Cross Youth - ESBCY*] (EAIO)
SEJI .... Jipijapa [*Ecuador*] [*ICAO location identifier*] (ICLI)
SEK .... Salomon, Inc. [*AMEX symbol*] (SAG)
SEK .... Salomon Inc. 7.625% SNPL'ELKS' [*AMEX symbol*] (TTSB)
SEK .... Standard Electric Kirk (NITA)
SEK .... Synomospondia Ergaton Kyprou [*Cyprus Workers' Confederation*] [*"Free Labour Syndicats"*]
SEKE .... Sosialistikon Ergatikon Komma tis Elladas [*Socialist Labor Party of Greece*] [*Forerunner of Greek Communist Party (KKE)*] (PPE)
SEKF .... Sister Elizabeth Kenny Foundation [*Later, SKI*]
SEKLS .... Southeast Kansas Library System [*Library network*]
SEKRLC .... Southeastern Kentucky Regional Library Cooperative [*Library network*]
Sel .... Ducretet-Thomson [*Formerly, Ducretet Selmer*] [*Record label*] [*France*]
SEL .... Safety Engineering Laboratory [*British*] (IRUK)
SEL .... Satellite Experiment Laboratory [*National Oceanic and Atmospheric Administration*] (GRD)
SEL .... School of Electric Light [*British military*] (DMA)
SEL .... Scouts' Esperanto League (EA)
SEL .... Select [*or Selection*] (AAG)
SEL .... Selectair Ltd. [*British ICAO designator*] (FAAC)
SEL .... Selected Equipment List (NVT)
sel .... Selection [*Literature*]
SEL .... Selective (IAA)
SEL .... Selector (IAA)
Sel .... Seleucid Era (BJA)
SEL .... Seligman Select Municipal Fund [*NYSE symbol*] (SPSG)
SEL .... Seligman Select Muni Fund [*NYSE symbol*] (TTSB)
SEL .... Selkirk College Library [*UTLAS symbol*]
sel .... Selkup [*MARC language code Library of Congress*] (LCCP)
SEL .... Semi-Effective List [*British military*] (DMA)
SEL .... Semlyachik [*Former USSR Seismograph station code, US Geological Survey*] (SEIS)
SEL .... Sensitized-Erythrocyte-Lysis (PDAA)
SEL .... SENTEL Corp. [*FAA designator*] (FAAC)
SEL .... Seoul [*South Korea*] [*Airport symbol*] (OAG)
SEL .... Signal Engineering Laboratories (AAG)
SEL .... Single Engine Land [*Pilot rating*] (AIA)
SEL .... Skolta Esperanto-Ligo [*Scouts' Esperanto League*] (EAIO)
SEL .... Socialist Electoral League [*Norway*] (PPW)
SEL .... Software Engineering Laboratory [*NASA*] (MCD)
SEL .... Solar Environmental Laboratory [*National Oceanic and Atmospheric Administration*]
SEL .... Southeastern Educational Laboratory
SEL .... Space Environment Laboratory [*Boulder, CO*] [*Department of Commerce National Oceanic and Atmospheric Administration*]
SEL .... Spontaneously Emitted Light
SEL .... Standard Elektrik Lorenz AG [*Germany*]
SEL .... Stanford Electronics Laboratory [*Stanford University*] [*Research center*] (MCD)
SEL .... Star/Earth Landmark Sightings
SEL .... Super Einspritz Lang [*Fuel-injection, long wheelbase*] [*As in 450 SEL, the model number of a Mercedes-Benz automobile*]
SEL .... Support Equipment List [*Navy*]
SEL .... Surface Emitting LASER
SEL .... System Electronics Laboratory (MCD)
SEL .... System Engineering Laboratories (MCD)
SELA .... Lago Agrio [*Ecuador*] [*ICAO location identifier*] (ICLI)
SELA .... Select Appointments Holdings [*NASDAQ symbol*] (SAG)
SELA .... Southeastern Library Association (AEBS)
SELA .... Systeme Economique Latino-Americain [*Latin American Economic System - LAES*] [*French*]
SELACJ .... Secretariado Latinoamericano de la Compania de Jesus [*Latin American Bureau of Society of Jesus*] (EAIO)
SELANE .... Secure Local-Area Network [*Computer science*]
Sel App Beng ... Selected Appeals, Sadr Diwani Adalat [*Bengal, India*] [*A publication*] (DLA)
Selas .... Selas Corp. of America [*Associated Press*] (SAG)
SELAVIP ..... Servicio Latinoamericano y Asiatico de Vivienda Popular [*Latin American and Asian low Income Housing Service*] [*Chile*] (EAIO)
SELB .... Sel-Leb Marketing [*NASDAQ symbol*] (TTSB)
SELB .... Sel-Leb Marketing, Inc. [*NASDAQ symbol*] (SAG)
SELB .... Southern Education and Library Board [*Northern Ireland*] (AIE)
SelBab .... Babylonian Seleucid Era (BJA)
SELBUS .... Systems Engineering Laboratories Data Bus (NITA)
SELBW .... Sel-Leb Marketing Wrrt [*NASDAQ symbol*] (TTSB)
SELC .... La Cecilia [*Ecuador*] [*ICAO location identifier*] (ICLI)
SELC .... South East London College [*London, England*]
SELC .... Synod of Evangelical Lutheran Churches (IIA)
SELCAL .... Selective Calling [*Radio*]
Sel Cas .... Select Cases, Central Provinces [*India*] [*A publication*] (DLA)
Sel Cas Ch ... Select Cases in Chancery [*England*] [*A publication*] (DLA)
Sel Cas Ch (T King) ... Select Cases in Chancery Tempore King [*25 English Reprint*] [*1724-33*] [*A publication*] (DLA)
Sel Cas DA ... Select Cases, Sadr Diwani Adalat [*India*] [*A publication*] (DLA)
Sel Cas Ev ... Select Cases in Evidence (Strange) [*England*] [*A publication*] (DLA)
Sel Cas KB Edw I ... Select Cases in King's Bench under Edward I (Sayles) [*England*] [*A publication*] (DLA)
Sel Cas NF ... Select Cases, Newfoundland [*A publication*] (DLA)
Sel Cas NWP ... Select Cases, Northwest Provinces [*India*] [*A publication*] (DLA)
Sel Cas NY ... Yate's Select Cases [*1809*] [*New York*] [*A publication*] (DLA)
Sel Cas SDA ... Select Cases, Sadr Diwani Adalat [*Bengal, Bombay, India*] [*A publication*] (DLA)
Sel Cas T King ... Select Cases in Chancery Tempore King [*England*] [*A publication*] (DLA)
Sel Cas T Nap ... Select Cases Tempore Napier [*Ireland*] [*A publication*] (DLA)
Sel Cas with Opin ... Select Cases with Opinions by a Solicitor [*A publication*] (DLA)
Sel Ca T King ... Select Cases in Chancery Tempore King [*25 English Reprint*] [*1724-33*] [*A publication*] (DLA)
SELCH .... Selector Channel

Sel Ch Cas... Select Cases in Chancery Tempore King, Edited by Macnaghten [*England*] [*A publication*] (DLA)
SELCIR .... Systems Engineering Laboratory Circuit-Drawing Program (PDAA)
Sel Col Cas... Select Collection of Cases [*England*] [*A publication*] (DLA)
SELCOM ...... Select Committee [*Army Materiel Command*]
Selctln .... Selective Insurance Group [*Associated Press*] (SAG)
SELCTV .... Selected Television [*Commercial firm British*]
Seld .... Selden's New York Reports [*5-10 New York*] [*A publication*] (DLA)
SELD .... Snakeye Low-Drag [*Navy*] (DNAB)
SELDADS ..... SEL [*Space Environmental Laboratory*] Data Acquisition and Display System (USDC)
SELDADS ..... Space Environment Laboratory Data Acquisition and Display System [*National Oceanic and Atmospheric Administration*]
SELDAM ...... Selective Data Management System (MHDI)
Sel Dec Bomb... Select Cases, Sadr Diwani Adalat [*Bombay, India*] [*A publication*] (DLA)
SEL DECK .... Select Decking [*Lumber*]
Sel Dec Madr... Select Decrees, Sadr Adalat [*Madras, India*] [*A publication*] (DLA)
Selden .... Selden's New York Court of Appeals Reports [*A publication*] (DLA)
Selden Notes... Selden's New York Court of Appeals Notes of Cases [*1st ed.*] [*1853*] [*A publication*] (DLA)
Seld Fl .... Selden's Dissertatio ad Fletam [*A publication*] (ILCA)
Seld J .... Selden's Jani Anglorum [*A publication*] (ILCA)
Seld JP .... Selden's Judicature in Parliaments [*1681*] [*A publication*] (DLA)
Seld Mar Cl... Selden's Mare Clausum [*A publication*] (ILCA)
Seld Mare Claus... Selden's Mare Clausum [*A publication*] (DLA)
Seld Notes... Selden's New York Court of Appeals Notes [*A publication*] (DLA)
Seld Off Ch... Selden's Office of Lord Chancellor [*1671*] [*A publication*] (DLA)
SELDOM ...... Selected Dissemination of MARC (NITA)
Seld R .... Selden's New York Court of Appeals Reports [*A publication*] (DLA)
Seld Soc .... Selden Society (DLA)
Seld Soc Yrbk... Selden Society Yearbook [*United States*] [*A publication*] (DLA)
Seld Tit Hon... Selden's Titles of Honor [*A publication*] (DLA)
SELEC .... Select (ROG)
SElec .... Society of Electroscience [*British*] (DBA)
SELEC .... Superelastic LASER Energy Conversion (MCD)
SELECTAVISION... Selected Television Video Disc System (NITA)
SELENE .... Selenological and Engineering Explorer
SELEX .... Systematic Evolution of Ligands by Exponential Enrichment [*Genetics*]
SELF .... National Citizens Committee to Save Education and Library Funds
SELF .... Self-Eject Launch Facility [*NASA*] (MCD)
SELF .... Short Expeditious Landing Field (CINC)
SELF .... Simplicity, Efficiency, Lower Rates, and Fairness Tax Plan
SELF .... Societe des Ecrivains Luxembourgeois de Langue Francaise
SELF .... Student Education Loan Fund [*Minnesota*]
SELF .... Submarine Extremely Low Frequency Radio [*Navy*]
Selfcare .... Selfcare, Inc. [*Associated Press*] (SAG)
Selfix .... Selfix, Inc. [*Associated Press*] (SAG)
SELFOC .... Self Focusing [*Optics*] (EECA)
SELFTAV ...... Self-Conducted Tender Availability [*Navy*] (NVT)
Self Tr .... Selfridge's Trial [*A publication*] (DLA)
SELGEM .... Self-Generating Master [*Information management system*] [*Computer science*]
SELI .... Limoncocha [*Ecuador*] [*ICAO location identifier*] (ICLI)
SeligQual .... Seligman Quality Municipal Fund [*Associated Press*] (SAG)
SeligSel .... Seligman Select Municipal Fund [*Associated Press*] (SAG)
SELJ .... La Julia [*Ecuador*] [*ICAO location identifier*] (ICLI)
SELK .... Selkirkshire [*County in Scotland*]
SELL .... Llurimaguas [*Ecuador*] [*ICAO location identifier*] (ICLI)
SELL .... Sales Environment Learning Laboratory [*Computer-based marketing game*]
SELL .... Suomi, Eesti, Latvija, Lietuva [*Finland, Estonia, Latvia, Lithuania*]
Sel L Cas ...... Select Law Cases [*England*] [*A publication*] (DLA)
Sel-Leb .... Sel-Leb Marketing, Inc. [*Associated Press*] (SAG)
Sell Pr .... Sellon's Practice in the King's Bench [*A publication*] (DLA)
Sell Prac ...... Sellon's Practice in the King's Bench [*A publication*] (DLA)
SellrPol .... Seller Pollution Control [*Associated Press*] (SAG)
SELM .... Loma Larga [*Ecuador*] [*ICAO location identifier*] (ICLI)
SE/LM .... Systems Engineering/Logistics Management (MCD)
SelMac .... Macedonian Seleucid Era (BJA)
SEL MERC .... Select Merchantable [*Lumber*]
SELMOUS .... Special English Language Materials for Overseas University Students
SELN .... Limon [*Ecuador*] [*ICAO location identifier*] (ICLI)
SELN .... Selection (AAG)
Sel NP .... Selwyn's Law of Nisi Prius [*A publication*] (DLA)
SELO .... Loja (La Toma) [*Ecuador*] [*ICAO location identifier*] (ICLI)
SELO .... Some Essential Learner Outcomes [*Minnesota*] (EDAC)
Sel Off Ch.... Selden's Office of Lord Chancellor [*1671*] [*A publication*] (DLA)
SELOR .... Ship Emitter Location Report [*Navy*] (CAAL)
SELP .... Senior Executive Leadership Program [*Australia*]
SELPA .... Special Eduation Local Planning Agency (EDAC)
Sel Pr .... Sellon's Practice [*A publication*] (DLA)
S/ELPS .... Spanish/English Language Performance Screening (EDAC)
SELR .... Saturn Engineering Liaison Request [*NASA*] (KSC)
SELR .... Selector (AAG)
SELR .... Support Equipment List Requirement (MCD)
SELRAS .... SEL [*Space Environmental Laboratory*] Research and Analysis System (USDC)
SELREC .... Shore Electronics Reconnaissance System
SELRECT ..... Selenium Rectifier (IAA)
SELREFTRA... Selected Refresher Training [*Navy*] (NVT)
SELRES .... Selected Reserve [*Military*]
SELRFT .... Selected Refresher Training [*Navy*] (NVT)
SELS .... Selective Service
sels .... SELSYN [*Military*] (BARN)
SELS .... Severe Local Storm [*National Weather Service*]
SELS .... Space Environment Laboratory Simulation [*NASA*]
SELSA .... Southeast Library Service Area [*Library network*]
Sel Serv L Rep... Selective Service Law Reporter [*A publication*] (DLA)
Sel Serv L Rptr... Selective Service Law Reporter [*A publication*] (DLA)
SEL STR ...... Select Structural [*Lumber*]
SELSW .... Selector Switch (MCD)
SELSYN .... Self-Synchronizing [*or Synchronous*] (IAA)
SELSYN .... Self-Synchronous [*Trade name*] [*Motor*]
SELT .... Latacunga [*Ecuador*] [*ICAO location identifier*] (ICLI)
SELT .... SAGE [*Semiautomatic Ground Environment*] Evaluation Library Tape
SELT .... Self-Eject Launch Technique [*NASA*] (KSC)
SELT .... Sheet Explosive Loading Technique
SELTA .... Swedish-English Literary Translators Association [*British*] (DBA)
SELTEC .... South East London Technical College [*British*] (DI)
SELV .... Safety Extra Low Voltage (IAA)
Selvac .... Selvac Corp. [*Associated Press*] (SAG)
SELW .... Selwyn College [*Cambridge*] [*British*] (ROG)
Selw .... Selwyn's Law of Nisi Prius [*England*] [*A publication*] (DLA)
Selw & Barn... Barnewall and Alderson's English King's Bench Reports [*1st part*] [*A publication*] (DLA)
Selw NP ...... Selwyn's Law of Nisi Prius [*England*] [*A publication*] (DLA)
SEM .... Cape Central Airways, Inc. [*ICAO designator*] (FAAC)
SEM .... Satellite to Earth Missile (IAA)
SEM .... Scanning Electron Microscope [*or Microscopy*]
SEM .... Scanning Electron Microscope (DOG)
SEM .... Scanning Electron Microscopy [*Later, SMI*] [*An association*] (EA)
SEM .... Schedule Evaluation Model
SEM .... Secondary Electron Multiplier [*Detector*]
SEM .... Secondary Emission Material (IAA)
SEM .... Secondary Emission Microscope
SEM .... Secondary Emission Monitor
SEM .... Secondary Enrichment Medium [*Microbiology*]
SEM .... Security Environmental Systems, Inc. [*Vancouver Stock Exchange symbol*]
SEM .... Seller's Engineering Memo [*NASA*] (NASA)
SEM .... Selma, AL [*Location identifier FAA*] (FAAL)
Sem .... Semahoth (BJA)
SEM .... Semaphore
SEM .... Semble [*It Seems*]
SEM .... Semel [*Once*]
SEM .... Semen (WGA)
SEM .... Semester
SEM .... Semi [*One-Half*] [*Pharmacy*]
SEM .... Semicolon
sem .... Semicolon (WDMC)
SEM .... Semiconductor Electronic Memory (IAA)
SEM .... Semiconductor Packaging Materials [*AMEX symbol*] (SAG)
SEM .... Semienriched Minimal [*Agar*]
SEM .... Semimobile (WGA)
SEM .... Seminal (WGA)
SEM .... Seminary
SEM .... Semipalatinsk [*Former USSR Seismograph station code, US Geological Survey*] (SEIS)
SEM .... Semitic [*Language, etc.*]
sem .... Semitic [*MARC language code Library of Congress*] (LCCP)
SEM .... Sempre [*Throughout*] [*Music*]
SEM .... Shared Equity Mortgage
SEM .... Single European Market
SEM .... Singularity Expansion Method (IEEE)
SEM .... Society for Ethnic Missions [*Australia*]
SEM .... Society for Ethnomusicology (EA)
SEM .... Society for Experimental Mechanics (EA)
SEM .... Society of Engineers and Machinists [*A union*] [*British*]
SEM .... Soft Ejection Murmur [*Cardiology*] (DAVI)
SEM .... Software Encapsulation Methodologies
SEM .... Solar Environment Monitor
SEM .... Solvent Extraction Milling (BARN)
SEM .... Somatosensory Evoked Potential [*Neurology*] (DAVI)
SEM .... Sortie Effectiveness Model [*NASA*] (MCD)
SEM .... Southeast Missouri State University, Cape Girardeau, MO [*OCLC symbol*] (OCLC)
SEM .... Southeast Monsoon
SEM .... Southern Illinois University at Carbondale Center for Electron Microscopy [*Research center*] (RCD)
SEM .... Space Environment Monitor [*NASA*]
SEM .... Special Electric Motors [*Manufacturing company*] [*British*]
SEM .... Standard Electronic Module (CAAL)
SEM .... Standard Equipment Modules [*Navy*] (DOMA)
SEM .... Standard Error of Measurement [*Testing*]
SEM .... Standard Error of the Mean
SEM .... Standard Estimating Module (IEEE)
SEM .... State-Event Matrix [*Computer science*]
SEM .... Station Engineering Manual [*Telecommunications*] (TEL)
SEM .... Stereoscan Electron Microscope
SEM .... Stray Energy Monitor
SEM .... Structural Econometric Model [*Statistics*]
SEM .... Stupid Error Message [*Computer science*]
SEM .... Subarray Electronics Module [*Computer science*]
SEM .... Subcontractor Engineering Memorandum (MCD)
SEM .... System Effectiveness Measure (IAA)
SEM .... System Effectiveness Model (CAAL)
SEM .... System Engineering Management [*NASA*]
S-E-M .... Systems/Equipment/Munitions [*Army*] (AFIT)

SEM............ Systolic Ejection Murmur [*Cardiology*]
SEMA........... Macara [*Ecuador*] [*ICAO location identifier*] (ICLI)
SEMA........... Semiotic Abstracts [*A publication*]
SEMA........... Societe d'Etudes de Mathematiques Appliquees [*France*]
SEMA........... Special Electronic Mission Aircraft (RDA)
SEMA........... Specialty Equipment Manufacturers Association
SEMA........... Specialty Equipment Market Association [*Later, SFI*] (EA)
SEMA........... Spray Equipment Manufacturers' Association [*British*] (BI)
SEMA........... Storage Equipment Manufacturers Association [*British*] (DBA)
SEMAA......... Safety Equipment Manufacturers Agents Association (EA)
SEMANOL.... Semantics-Oriented Language [*Computer science*] (PDAA)
SEMAT......... Ship Electronic Module Assembly Test (DNAB)
SEMATECH... Semiconductor Manufacturing Technology (DOMA)
SEMATECH... Semiconductor Manufacturing Technology Consortium
SEMBEGS.... Simply Extended and Modified Batch Environmental Graphical System (MHDI)
SEMBRAT.... Single Echelon Multi-Base Resource Allocation Technique (PDAA)
SEMC........... Macas [*Ecuador*] [*ICAO location identifier*] (ICLI)
SEMC........... Semi-Tech Corp. [*NASDAQ symbol*] (SAG)
SEMC........... State Emergency Management Committee [*New South Wales, Australia*]
SEMCA......... Shipboard Electromagnetic Computability Analysis (DNAB)
SEMCC......... Southeastern Massachusetts Health Sciences Libraries Consortium [*Library network*]
SEMCF......... Semi-Tech Corp. 'A' [*NASDAQ symbol*] (TTSB)
SEMCIP........ Shipboard Electromagnetic Capability Improvement Program [*Navy*] (NVT)
SEMCOG...... Southeast Michigan Council of Governments [*Detroit, MI*]
SEMCOR...... Semantic Correlation [*Machine-aided indexing*]
SEMD........... Spondyloepimetaphyseal Dysplasia [*Medicine*] (DMAA)
SEMD........... Stray Energy Monitor Device
SEMDJL....... Spondylo-Epimetaphyseal Dysplasia with Joint Laxity [*Medicine*] (DMAA)
SEMDP........ Senior Executive/Management Development Plan (DNAB)
SEM-E......... Standard Electronic Module-E Format (MCD)
SEMEL in D... Semel in Die [*Once a Day*] [*Pharmacy*]
SEMET......... Self-Evident Meteorological Code (NATG)
SEMG........... Scanning Electron Micrograph
SEMG........... Semenogelin (DMAA)
SEMH........... Machala [*Ecuador*] [*ICAO location identifier*] (ICLI)
SEMH........... Service Engineering Man-Hours
SEMHI......... Southeastern Manufactured Housing Institute [*Later, Manufactured Housing Institute*] (EA)
SEMI........... All American Semiconductor, Inc. [*NASDAQ symbol*] (NQ)
SEMI........... All Amer Semiconductor [*NASDAQ symbol*] (TTSB)
SEMI........... Self-Evacuating Multilayer Insulation [*System*]
SEMI........... Semiconductor Equipment and Materials Institute (EA)
semi........... Semis [*One-Half*] [*Latin Pharmacy*] (MAE)
semi........... Semitrailer [*Truck and trailer rigs*] (DAVI)
SEMI........... Shipboard Electromagnetic Interference [*Navy*] (CAAL)
SEMI........... Societe d'Etudes de Marche et d'Informatique [*Society for the Study of Marketing and Informatics*] [*Information service or system Defunct*] (IID)
SEMI........... Special Electromagnetic Interference (MCD)
SEMI........... Subendocardial Myocardial Infarction [*Cardiology*] (MAE)
SEMI........... Subendorcardial Myocardial Injury [*Cardiology*] (MAE)
SEMIAUT..... Semiautomatic (IAA)
SEMICON..... Semiconductor (IAA)
SEMICOND... Semiconductor
semid.......... Semidrachma [*Half a Drachm*] [*Latin Pharmacy*] (MAE)
SEMIDR........ Semidrachma [*Half a Drachma*] [*Pharmacy*]
SEMIH.......... Semihora [*Half an Hour*] [*Pharmacy*]
SEMIKON..... Seminare/Konferenzen [*Seminars/Conferences*] [*Society for Business Information*] [*Information service or system*] [*Defunct*] (IID)
SemiLas...... Semiconductor Laser International Corp. [*Associated Press*] (SAG)
SEMINEX..... Seminary in Exile [*Liberal-oriented Lutheran seminary*]
SEMIRA....... System of Electronic Marks' Interrogation, Registration, and Administration [*Database*] [*WIPO*] [*United Nations*] (DUND)
SEMIRAD..... Secondary Electron-Mixed Radiation Dosimeter (IEEE)
SEMIROX..... Semi-Recessed Oxide (PDAA)
SEMIS......... Solar Energy Monitor in Space [*NASA*] (MCD)
SEMIS......... State Extension Management Information System [*Department of Agriculture*]
SemiTch...... Semi-Tech Corp. [*Associated Press*] (SAG)
Semitool...... Semitool, Inc. [*Associated Press*] (SAG)
SEML........... Manglaralto [*Ecuador*] [*ICAO location identifier*] (ICLI)
SEMLAM...... Semiconductor LASER Amplifier
SEMLAT....... Semiconductor LASER Array Techniques
SEMLSB....... Systolic Ejection Murmur, Left Sternal Border [*Cardiovascular*] (DAVI)
SEMM........... Scanning Electron Mirror Microscope (IAA)
SEMM........... Single Electron MOS [*Metal Oxide Semiconductor*] Memory
SEMM........... Smoke Effectiveness Manual Model (MCD)
SEMM........... Societe Europeenne de Materials Mobiles [*France*] (PDAA)
SEMM........... Solar Electric Multiple-Mission (MCD)
SEMMS......... Solar Electric Multiple-Mission Spacecraft
SEMN........... Slow Extension Motoneuron [*Neurology*]
SEMN........... Superficial Extensor Motoneuron [*Neurology*]
SEMO........... Montalvo [*Ecuador*] [*ICAO location identifier*] (ICLI)
SEMO........... State Emergency Management Organisation [*New South Wales, Australia*]
SEMO........... Supply and Equipment Management Officer (AAGC)
SEMO........... Systems Engineering and Management Operations [*Military*]
Semon.......... Semonides [*Seventh century BC*] [*Classical studies*] (OCD)
SEMOPS...... Sequential Multiobjective Problem Solving
SEMP........... Mopa [*Ecuador*] [*ICAO location identifier*] (ICLI)
SEMP........... Self-Erecting Marine Platform (PDAA)
SEMP........... Sempre [*Throughout*] [*Music*]
SEMP........... Simplified Early Maturities Participation Plan [*Small Business Administration*]
SEMP........... Societe d'Editions Medico-Pharmaceutiques [*Medical-Pharmaceutical Publishing Co.*] [*France*] [*Information service or system*] (IID)
SEMP........... Socioeconomic Military Program (CINC)
SEMP........... Standard Electronics Module Program (MCD)
SEMP........... Superconducting Electromagnetic Propulsion (ECON)
SEMP........... System Engineering Management Plan
SEMPA......... Scanning Electron Microscope and Particle Analyzer
SEMPA......... Scanning Electron Microscopy with Polarization Analysis
SEMPB......... Schiffli Embroidery Manufacturers Promotion Board (EA)
SemPck........ Semiconductor Packaging Materials [*Associated Press*] (SAG)
SEMPE......... Socio-Economic Model of the Planet Earth (PDAA)
SEMR........... Standard Electronic Module RADAR (PDAA)
SEMR........... Support Equipment Management Report (MCD)
SEMRE......... SPRINT Electromagnetic Radiation Evaluation [*Army*] (AABC)
SEMRFL....... Michigan Regional Libraries Film Program at Monroe [*Library network*]
SEMS........... Monjas Sur [*Ecuador*] [*ICAO location identifier*] (ICLI)
SEMS........... Science and Education Management Staff [*Department of Agriculture*] (GFGA)
SEMS........... Severe Environment Memory Series [*or System*] [*Computer science*]
SEMS........... Space Environment Monitor System [*NASA*] (NASA)
SEMS........... Steam Engine Makers' Society [*A union*] [*British*]
SEMS........... Stray Energy Monitor System
SEMS........... Support Engineering Manhour Summary (MCD)
SEMS........... System Engineering Management Standard
SEMS........... Systems Engineering and Management Support [*Air Force*]
SEMS........... Systems Engineering Master Schedule
SEMT........... Manta [*Ecuador*] [*ICAO location identifier*] (ICLI)
SEMT........... SIGINT/EW [*Signal Intelligence/Electronic Warfare*] Maintenance Trainer [*Army*]
Semtch........ Semtech Corp. [*Associated Press*] (SAG)
SEMTEC....... Southeastern Marine Trades Exhibit and Conference [*National Marine Manufacturers Association*] (TSPED)
SEMTR......... SPRINT Early Missile Test RADAR [*Army*] (AABC)
SEMTR......... Supervisory Electronic Maintenance Technician [*Relief*]
SEMTSA....... Structural Econometric Modeling Time Series Analysis [*Statistics*]
sem ves....... Seminal Vesicle [*Anatomy*] (WGA)
SEMX........... Semiconductor Pkg Materials [*NASDAQ symbol*] (TTSB)
SEMY........... Seminary
Sen............. De Senectute [*of Cicero*] [*Classical studies*] (OCD)
SEN............. Lexington, KY [*Location identifier FAA*] (FAAL)
SEN............. Sacred Earth Network [*An association*] (EA)
SEN............. Scanning Encoding [*Computer science*] (MHDI)
SEN............. Science Engineering News [*National Oceanic and Atmospheric Administration*]
SEN............. Semienclosed
SEN............. Senair Charter Ltd. [*British ICAO designator*] (FAAC)
SEN............. Senate
SEN............. Senator
Sen............. Senator (ODBW)
SEN............. Senator
Sen............. Senator (DFIT)
SEN............. Sendai [*Mukaiyama*] [*Japan*] [*Seismograph station code, US Geological Survey*] (SEIS)
Sen............. Seneca [*the Younger*] [*First century AD*] [*Classical studies*] (OCD)
Sen............. Seneca [*the Elder*] [*First century BC*] [*Classical studies*] (OCD)
SEN............. Senegal [*ANSI three-letter standard code*] (CNC)
SEN............. Senior (EY)
Sen............. Senior (ODBW)
SEN............. Senlac Resources, Inc. [*Toronto Stock Exchange symbol*]
SEN............. Sennae [*Of Senna*] [*Pharmacy*] (ROG)
SEN............. Sense (IAA)
SEN............. Sensitive
SEN............. Sensor (AAG)
SEN............. Senza [*Without*] [*Music*]
SEN............. Single Edge Notched
SEN............. Small Extension Node [*Telecommunications*] (LAIN)
SEN............. Societe Europeenne de Neuro+radiologie [*European Neuroradiological Association*] [*France*] (EAIO)
SEN............. Societe Europeenne de Neuroscience [*European Neuroscience Association - ENA*] (EA)
SEN............. Software Error Notification [*Computer science*]
SEN............. Southend [*Scotland*] [*Airport symbol*] (AD)
SEN............. Southern European Network (DNAB)
SEN............. Space Engagement Node
SEN............. Special Educational Needs (AIE)
SEN............. Sports Exchange Network [*Cable TV programming service*]
SEN............. State Enrolled Nurse [*British*]
SEN............. Statement of Essential Need (AAGC)
SEN............. Steam Emulsion Number
SEN............. Strike Energy, Inc. [*Vancouver Stock Exchange symbol*]
SEN............. Successor Event Number (DNAB)
SEN............. System Error Notification [*Computer science*]
SEN............. Systems Engineering Notice
Sen............. United States Senate (AAGC)
SENA........... Nor Antizana [*Ecuador*] [*ICAO location identifier*] (ICLI)
SENA........... Seaport Navigation Co. [*Later, SNCO*] [*AAR code*]
SENA........... Societe d'Energie Nucleaire Franco-Belge des Ardennes [*Belgian-French power consortium*]
SENA........... Sympathetic Efferent Nerve Activity
SENAV......... Senior Naval Aviator (NVT)

SENAVAV..... Senior Naval Aviator
SENAVOMAC... Senior Naval Officer, Military Airlift Command (MCD)
SENB.......... Single Edge Notched Beam [*Materials science and technology*]
SENC.......... Nor Cayambe [*Ecuador*] [*ICAO location identifier*] (ICLI)
S en C......... Sociedad en Comandita [*Limited partnership company*] [*Spanish*]
SenCh.......... Senior Chaplain [*Navy British*]
SEND.......... Scientists and Engineers for National Development [*Scholarship program*]
SEND.......... Securities and Exchange Commission News Digest [*A publication*]
SEND.......... Shared Equipment Need Date (NASA)
SEND.......... Southend [*County borough in England*]
SENDENTALO... Senior Dental Officer [*Navy*] (DNAB)
Sen Doc....... Senate Document (DLA)
SENE.......... Seneca Foods Corp. [*NASDAQ symbol*] (NQ)
SENEA......... Seneca Foods Cl'A' [*NASDAQ symbol*] (TTSB)
SENEAM...... Servicios a la Navegacion en el Espacio Aereo Mexicano [*Mexico ICAO designator*] (FAAC)
SENEB......... Seneca Foods Cl'B' [*NASDAQ symbol*] (TTSB)
SENECA....... Semantic Networks for Conceptual Analysis (NITA)
Seneca........ Seneca Foods Corp. [*Associated Press*] (SAG)
Seneg.......... Senegal
SENEGAMBIA... Senegal and Gambia
SENEL.......... Single Noise Exposure Level
SENET.......... Scientific and Engineering Computer Network (MCD)
SENET.......... Slotted Envelope Network (MHDI)
Senetek....... Senetek PLC [*Associated Press*] (SAG)
SENG.......... Single Engine
SEngFInstSMM... Qualified Sales Engineer of the Institute of Sales and Marketing Management [*British*] (DBQ)
SenHgh........ Senior High Income Portfolio [*Associated Press*] (SAG)
SenHgh2...... Senior High Income Portfolio II [*Associated Press*] (SAG)
SENI........... Nor Iliniza [*Ecuador*] [*ICAO location identifier*] (ICLI)
SENIC.......... Study on the Efficacy of Nosocomial Infection Control (MEDA)
SeniorTP...... Senior Tour Players Development [*Associated Press*] (SAG)
Sen J.......... Senate Journal [*A publication*] (DLA)
SENJIT......... Special Educational Needs Joint Initiative for Training (AIE)
Sen Jo......... Senate Journal [*A publication*] (DLA)
SENL........... Standard Equipment Nomenclature List [*Military*]
SENLOG....... Sentinel Logistics Command
SEN(M)........ State Enrolled Nurse (Mental Nursing) [*British*] (DBQ)
SENMEDO..... Senior Medical Officer [*Military*] (DNAB)
SENMEM...... Senior Member (DNAB)
SEN(MS)...... State Enrolled Nurse (Mental Subnormal Nursing) [*British*] (DBQ)
Senn........... Sennaherib (BJA)
SE'NNIGHT... Seven Nights [*A week*] (ROG)
SENO.......... Steam Emulsion Number
SENPO......... Sentinel Project Office [*Army*] (MCD)
SENR.......... Senior
Sen Rep...... Senate Report [*A publication*] (DLA)
Sen Rep...... United States Senate Committee Report [*A publication*] (DLA)
SenrStrat..... Senior Strategic Income Fund [*Associated Press*] (SAG)
Sens........... De Sensu [*of Aristotle*] [*Classical studies*] (OCD)
SENS.......... Sensitive (MSA)
SENS.......... Sensitivity (IAA)
SENS.......... Sensor [*Automotive engineering*]
SENS.......... Sensorium [*Neurology*] (DAVI)
SENS.......... Sensory
SENS.......... Sentex Sensing Technologies [*NASDAQ symbol*] (TTSB)
SENS.......... Sentex Sensing Technology, Inc. [*Ridgefield, NJ*] [*NASDAQ symbol*] (NQ)
SENS.......... Social England Series [*A publication*]
SENS.......... Stewart Evaluation of Nursing Scale (DMAA)
SENSCOM.... Sentinel Systems Command [*Army*] (MCD)
SENSE......... Society for Ending Needless and Silly Expenditure [*British*] (DI)
SENSE......... Sommers' Equivocation Network for Significant Expressions (SAA)
SENSEA....... Sentinel System Evaluation Agency [*DoD*]
SENSIM........ Sensor System Simulation
SENSO......... Sensor Operator (MCD)
SENSO......... Sentinel Systems Office [*Military*]
SENSOR....... Sentinel Event Notification System for Occupational Risks [*Medicine*]
Sensormt..... Sensormatic Electronics Corp. [*Associated Press*] (SAG)
SENT........... Sentence (AABC)
Sent............ Sentenza [*Decision, Judgment*] [*Italian*] (ILCA)
SENTA......... Societe d'Etudes Nucleaires et de Techniques Avancees [*France*]
SENTAC....... Society for Ear, Nose, and Throat Advances in Children (EA)
SENT CONF... Sentence to be Confined [*Navy*] (DNAB)
SENTD......... Sentenced (WGA)
SenTechWeldI... Senior Technician of the Welding Institute [*British*] (DBQ)
Sentex........ Sentex Sensing Technologies [*Associated Press*] (SAG)
SENT LP...... Sentence to Lose Pay [*Navy*] (DNAB)
SENTOS....... Sentinel Operating System (IEEE)
SentoTch..... Sento Technical Innovations Corp. [*Associated Press*] (SAG)
SenTP......... Senior Tour Players Development [*Associated Press*] (SAG)
SENTRAB..... Syndicat des Travailleurs des Entreprises, Privees, Travaux Publics et Batiments [*Union of Workers of Private Enterprises, Public Works and Buildings*] [*Togo*]
SENTRE....... Sensor of Tail Region Emitters (MCD)
SENTRY....... Survey Entry
SENU.......... Neuvo Rocafuerte [*Ecuador*] [*ICAO location identifier*] (ICLI)
SENU.......... Spectrum Efficient Network Unit (MCD)
SENUSNAVOFFNAVBALTAP... Senior United States Naval Officer, Commander Allied Naval Forces, Baltic Approaches (DNAB)
SenWO........ Senior Warrant Officer [*British*] (DI)
SENYLRC..... Southeastern New York Library Resources Council [*Highland, NY*] [*Library network*]
SEO............. Salvage Engineering Order (MCD)
SEO............. Satellite for Earth Observation
SEO............. Seguela [*Ivory Coast*] [*Airport symbol*] (OAG)
SEO............. Senior Engineer Officer [*Navy*]
SEO............. Senior Executive Officer [*Civil Service*] [*British*]
SEO............. Senior Experimental Officer [*Also, SExO, SXO*] [*Ministry of Agriculture, Fisheries, and Food*] [*British*]
SEO............. Seoul [*Keizyo*] [*South Korea*] [*Seismograph station code, US Geological Survey*] (SEIS)
SEO............. Serial Engineering Order (MCD)
SEO............. Shoulder-Elbow Orthosis [*Medicine*]
SEO............. Sin Errores y Omisiones [*Errors and Omissions Excepted*] [*Business term Spanish*]
SEO............. Society of Education Officers [*British*]
SEO............. Special Engineering Order [*NASA*] (NASA)
SEO............. Special Equipment Option [*Automotive assembly*]
SEO............. State Energy Office
SEO............. Surgical Emergency Officer (MEDA)
SEO............. Surgical Emergency Officer (DAVI)
SEO............. Synchronous Equatorial Orbit [*or Orbiter*] [*NASA*] (KSC)
SEOA........... Pasochoa [*Ecuador*] [*ICAO location identifier*] (ICLI)
SEOC........... State Emergency Operations Centre [*New South Wales, Australia*]
SEOC........... Submarine Extended Operating Cycle (NVT)
SEOCS......... Sun-Earth Observatory and Climatology Satellite
SEODSE....... Special Explosive Ordnance Disposal Supplies and Equipment [*Army*] (AABC)
SEOG........... Supplemental Educational Opportunity Grant [*Department of Education*]
SEOL............ Olmedo [*Ecuador*] [*ICAO location identifier*] (ICLI)
SEON........... Solar Electro-Optical Network (MCD)
SEON........... Solar Electro-Optical Observing Network (USDC)
SEON........... Solar Electro-Optical Observing Network [*Marine science*] (OSRA)
SEOO........... Sauf Erreur ou Omission [*Errors and Omissions Excepted*] [*French*]
SEOO........... State Economic Opportunity Office
SEOP........... Secondary Operand Unit (IAA)
SEOP........... Segment End of Pulse
SEOP........... SHAPE [*Supreme Headquarters Allied Powers Europe*] Emergency Operating Procedures [*NATO*] (NATG)
SEOP........... Siecor Electro-Optic Products [*Research Triangle Park, NC*] (TSSD)
SEOP........... System Employment and Organizational Plan [*Army*]
SEOPSN....... Select-Operate-Sense
SEOR........... Oro [*Ecuador*] [*ICAO location identifier*] (ICLI)
SEOS........... SIGINT Equipment Operator Simulator [*Military*]
S/EOS.......... Standard Earth Observation Satellite (MCD)
SEOS........... Strategic Earth Orbit System (IAA)
SEOS........... Symmetric Exchange of Symmetry [*Spectrometry*]
SEOS........... Synchronous Earth Observatory Satellite [*NASA*]
SEOSS......... Slewable Electro-Optical Sensor System
Seoul LJ...... Seoul Law Journal [*A publication*] (DLA)
SEOW.......... Society of Engineering Office Workers (EA)
SEP............. Salmonid Enhancement Program [*Canada*]
SEP............. Samenwerkende Elektriciteit Produktie Bedrijven [*Electric utility*] [*Netherlands*]
SEP............. Saturday Evening Post [*A publication*] (BRI)
SEP............. Scientific and Engineering Personnel [*Military*]
SE(P).......... Security Executive, Control at Ports [*British World War II*]
SEP............. Segment End Pulse
SEP............. Selective Employment Payments [*British*]
SEP............. Selective Employment Plan
SEP............. Self-Elevating Platform
SEP............. Self-Employed Pension [*British*]
SEP............. Semi-Engineered Prototype [*Automotive engineering*]
SEP............. Sensory Evoked Potential [*Neurophysiology*]
SEP............. Sepal [*Botany*] (WGA)
SEP............. Separate (AFM)
sep............. Separate (WDMC)
sep............. Separation (WDMC)
SEP............. Separation (IAA)
SEP............. Separation Parameter
SEP............. Sepia [*Stamp collecting*] (ROG)
sep............. Sepia (VRA)
SEP............. September (AFM)
SEP............. Septuagint [*Version of the Bible*]
SEP............. Sepultus [*Buried*] [*Latin*]
SEP............. Serial Entry Printer
SEP............. Shepherd Products Ltd. [*Toronto Stock Exchange symbol*]
SEP............. Simplified Employee Pension
SEP............. Simplified Employee Pension Plan (DFIT)
SEP............. Site Emergency Plan [*Nuclear energy*] (NRCH)
SEP............. Slow Electrical Process [*Human brain*]
SEP............. Slug Ejector Punch
SEP............. Society for Exact Philosophy (EA)
SEP............. Society of Engineering Psychologists [*Later, DAEEP*] (EA)
SEP............. Society of Experimental Psychologists (EA)
SEP............. Software End Product [*Army*]
SEP............. Software Engineering Practice
SEP............. Software Enhancement Proposal
SEP............. Solar Electric Power [*or Propulsion*]
SEP............. Solar Energetic Particle
SEP............. Soldier Enhancement Program [*Army*] (INF)
SEP............. Solid Electrolyte Potentiometry
SEP............. Somatically Evoked Potential [*Neurophysiology*]
SEP............. Somatosensory Evoked Potential [*Neurology*] (DAVI)
SEP............. SOSUS Estimated Position (NVT)
SEP............. Source Evaluation Panel [*NASA*] (NASA)

SEP Southern Education Program [*Defunct*] (EA)
SEP Space Electronic Package
SEP Special Education Programs [*Department of Education*] [*Formerly, BEH*]
SEP Special Emphasis Program [*DoD*]
SEP Special Enrollment Period [*Department of Health and Human Services*] (GFGA)
SEP Specific Excess Power (MCD)
SEP Sperm Entry Point [*into egg*]
SEP Spherical Error Precision [*or Probability*]
SEP Stable Element Panel
SEP Standard Electric Puhelinteollisius (NITA)
SEP Standard Electronic Package
SEP Standard Engineering Practice (AAG)
SEP Standard Error of Prediction
SEP Standard Evaluation Procedure [*Environmental Protection Agency*]
SEP Star Epitaxial Planar (MSA)
SEP Stephenville, TX [*Location identifier FAA*] (FAAL)
SEP Stimulated Emission Pumping [*Spectroscopy*]
SEP Strong Equivalence Principle [*Thermodynamics*]
SEP Student Enhancement Program [*Army*]
SEP Student Expense Program [*Civil Defense*]
SEP Studiegroup voor Europese Politiek (EA)
SEP Supervisor Executive Program [*NASA*] (KSC)
SEP Supplemental Environmental Projects [*Policy*] [*Environmental Protection Agency*]
SEP Support Equipment Package [*NASA*] (NASA)
SEP Surface Electrical Property [*Apollo*] [*NASA*]
SEP Surface Experiments [*NASA*]
SEP Surrendered Enemy Personnel
SEP Survey of Eastern Palestine [*A publication*] (BJA)
SEP Swedish Export Credit Corp. [*NYSE symbol*] (SAG)
SEP Symbolic Equations Program (IAA)
SEP Syringe Exchange Program [*To prevent infectious disease*]
SEP Systematic Evaluation Program [*Nuclear Regulatory Commission*]
SEP Systems Effectiveness Plan
SEP Systems Engineering Process
SEP Systems Extension Plan
SEP Systolic Ejection Period [*Cardiology*]
SEPA Pastaza [*Ecuador*] [*ICAO location identifier*] (ICLI)
SEPA Soft Enhancement of Percutaneous Absorption [*Pharmacy*]
SEPA Southeastern Power Administration [*Department of Energy*]
SEPA Southeastern Psychological Association (MCD)
SEPA Southeast Pacific Area
SEPA Soviet Extended Planning Annex (MCD)
SEPA Spanish Evangelical Publishers Association (EA)
SEPA System Evaluation Planning and Assessment Model (MCD)
SEPA Systems Engineering, Policy Analysis and Management [*Delft University of Technology, Netherlands*]
SEPAA Sheepskin Export Packers' Association of Australia
SEPAC Space Experiments with Particle Accelerators [*Spacelab mission*]
SEPACFOR Southeast Pacific Force [*later, Command*] [*Navy*]
SEPACS Sheltered Employment Procurement and Consultancy Service (AIE)
SEPAK Suspension of Expendable Penetration Aids by Kite [*Military*]
SEP & A Special Equipment Parts and Assemblies Section (AAG)
SEPAP Shuttle Electrical Power Analysis Program [*NASA*]
separ Separatum [*Separately*] [*Latin*] (MAE)
SEPAR Shuttle Electrical Power Analysis Report [*NASA*] (NASA)
SEPARON Separation (ROG)
SEPAWG Save EPA [*Environmental Protection Agency*] Working Group (EA)
SE/PB Southern Europe - Ports and Beaches [*NATO*] (NATG)
SEP Btry Separate Battery [*Army*]
SEPC Seiler Pollution Ctl Sys [*NASDAQ symbol*] (TTSB)
SEPC Seller Pollution Control [*NASDAQ symbol*] (SAG)
SEPC Space Exploration Program Council [*NASA*]
SEPCEN Separation Center [*Navy*]
SEPCOR Separate Correspondence (MCD)
SEPD Scottish Economic Planning Department [*British*]
SEPD Separated
SEPD Special-Environment Powder Diffractometer [*Crystallography*]
SEPD Special Environment Powder Diffractometer
SEPD State Emergency Planning Director [*Civil Defense*]
SEPE Pechichal [*Ecuador*] [*ICAO location identifier*] (ICLI)
SEPE Seattle Port of Embarkation
SEPE Separate (ROG)
SEPE Single Escape Peak Efficiency [*Nuclear science*] (OA)
SEPE Societe d'Edition et de Publications en Exlusivite
SEPEA Societe Europeene de Psychiatrie de l'Enfant et de l'Adolescent [*European Society of Child and Adolescent Psychiatry - ESCAP*] (EAIO)
SEPEL Southeastern Plant Environment Laboratories [*Duke University and North Carolina State University*]
SEPEMIAG Societe d'Etudes pour l'Equipement Miniere, Agricole, et Industrial du Gabon [*Gabon Society for Study of Mining, Agricultural, and Industrial Equipment*]
SEPESCA Secretariat of Fisheries [*Mexico*] (USDC)
SEPESCA Secretariat of Fisheries [*Mexico*] [*Marine science*] (OSRA)
SEPFA South East Professional Fishermen's Association [*Australia*]
SEPG Separating
SEPGA Southeastern Pecan Growers Association (EA)
Seph Sephardic [*Jews from Spain, Portugal, North Africa, and the Mediterranean*] (BJA)
SEPHA Special Emergency Programme for the Horn of Africa [*World Food Programme*] [*United Nations*]
SEPI Pichincha [*Ecuador*] [*ICAO location identifier*] (ICLI)
SEPI Society for the Exploration of Psychotherapy Integration (EA)
SEPI Sylvania Electric Products, Inc. (KSC)
SEPIL Selective Excitation of Probe Ion Luminescence [*Analytical chemistry*]
SEPL Playas [*Ecuador*] [*ICAO location identifier*] (ICLI)
SEPL South European Pipeline [*Oil*]
SEPLIS Secretariat Europeen des Professions Liberales, Independantes et Sociales [*European Secretariat of the Liberal, Independant and Social Professions*] [*EC*] (ECED)
SEPM Society for Sedimentary Geology [*Formerly, Society of Economic Paleontologists a nd Mineralogists*] (EA)
SEPMAG Separate Magnetic (NTCM)
SEPN Separation (AAG)
SEPO Posorja [*Ecuador*] [*ICAO location identifier*] (ICLI)
SEPO Space Electric Power Office [*AEC*]
SEPOL Settlement Problem-Oriented Language [*Computer science*] (IEEE)
SEPOL Soil Engineering Problem-Oriented Language [*Computer science*]
SEPORT Supply and Equipment Report [*Army*] (AABC)
SEPOS Selected Enlisted Personnel for Overseas Service [*Military*] (AABC)
SEPP Safety Engineering Program Plan [*Military*] (DNAB)
SEPP Secure Electronic Payments Protocol [*Telecommunications*]
SEPP Secure Encryption Payment Protocol [*Computer science*]
SEPP Simplified Employee Pension Plan
SEPPA Single Employer Pension Plan Amendments Act of 1986 (WYGK)
SEPPAA Single-Employer Pension Plan Amendments Act [*1986*] (GFGA)
SEPPr AB Svensk Exp Cap Sec [*NYSE symbol*] (TTSB)
SEPQUES Separation Questionnaire [*Military*] (DNAB)
SEPR Sepracor, Inc. [*NASDAQ symbol*] (SPSG)
Sepracr Sepracor, Inc. [*Associated Press*] (SAG)
Sepragn Sepragen Corp. [*Associated Press*] (SAG)
SEPRL Southeast Poultry Research Laboratory [*University of Georgia*] [*Research center*] (RCD)
SEPROS Separation Processing [*Military*]
SEPS Pasaje [*Ecuador*] [*ICAO location identifier*] (ICLI)
SEPS Secondary Electric Power System (IAA)
SEPS Service Environment Power System (IAA)
SEPS Service Module Electrical Power System [*NASA*] (KSC)
SEPS Severe Environment Power System (IEEE)
SEPS Smithsonian Earth Physics Satellite
SEPS Solar Electric Propulsion System [*NASA*]
SEPS System/Equipment Population Summary
SEPSA Society of Educational Programmers and Systems Analysts [*Later, SDE*]
SEPSC Spontaneous Excitatory Postsynaptic Current [*Neurophysiology*]
SEPSIT Solar Electric Propulsion Integration Technology (PDAA)
SEPSME Social Economic and Political Studies of the Middle East [*A publication*] (BJA)
SEPST Solar Electric Propulsion System Technology
SEPSU Science and Engineering Policy Studies Unit (AIE)
SEPT Putumayo [*Ecuador*] [*ICAO location identifier*] (ICLI)
SEPT Separate
sept Septem [*Seven*] [*Latin*] (MAE)
SEPT September (EY)
Sept Septem Contra Thebas [*of Aeschylus*] [*Classical studies*] (OCD)
Sept Septuagint [*Version of the Bible*] (BJA)
sept Septum [*Medicine*] (CPH)
SEPT Silicon Epitaxial Planar Transistor (IAA)
SEPTA Southeastern Pennsylvania Transportation Authority
SEPTAR Seaborne Powered Target [*Navy*] (NVT)
SEPTD Separated
SEPTEL Separate Telegram
SEPTG Separating
SEPTLA Southeastern Pennsylvania Theological Library Association [*Library network*]
SEPTR Separator
SEPTR September (ROG)
SEPU Puna [*Ecuador*] [*ICAO location identifier*] (ICLI)
SEPULT Sepultus [*Buried*] [*Latin*] (ROG)
SEPUP Science Education for Public Understanding Project [*Australia*]
SEPV Portoviejo [*Ecuador*] [*ICAO location identifier*] (ICLI)
SEPY Puyo [*Ecuador*] [*ICAO location identifier*] (ICLI)
SEQ Scientific Equipment (KSC)
SEQ Seguin, TX [*Location identifier FAA*] (FAAL)
SEQ Self-Esteem Questionnaire [*Personality development test*] [*Psychology*]
SEQ Sequel
seq Sequel (WDMC)
seq Sequence (WDMC)
SEQ Sequencer (IAA)
SEQ Sequens [*Sequence*] [*Latin*] (AABC)
SEQ Sequente [*And in What Follows*] [*Latin*]
SEQ Sequential Pulse Counting [*Spectrometry*]
seq Sequestration [*Orthopedics*] (DAVI)
SEQ Sequestrum [*Medicine*]
SEQ Sequitur [*It Follows*] [*Latin*]
SEQ Side Effects Questionnaire [*Medicine*] (DMAA)
SEq Spatial Equalization
SEQ DEV EX Sequential Developmental Exercises [*Occupational therapy*] (DAVI)
SEQE Quevedo [*Ecuador*] [*ICAO location identifier*] (ICLI)
SEQ-IC Sequencer-Iteration Control [*Computer science*] (MHDI)
SEQL Sequential (IAA)
SEQ LUCE Sequenti Luce [*The Following Day*] [*Latin*] (ADA)
SEQN Quininde [*Ecuador*] [*ICAO location identifier*] (ICLI)
SEQOPT Sequential Optimization (MCD)
SEQQ Sequentes [*or Sequentia*] [*The Following Plural form*] [*Latin*]
SEQQ Sequentibus [*In the Following Places*] [*Latin*] (ADA)

SEQR .... Sequencer (AAG)
SEQREC .... Sequence Recall [*Neuropsychology test*]
SEQS .... Sequoia Systems [*NASDAQ symbol*] (TTSB)
SEQS .... Sequoia Systems, Inc. [*NASDAQ symbol*] (SAG)
SEQS .... Simultaneous Equation Solver [*Computer program*]
SEQT .... System Environment Qualification Test
SEQU .... Quito/Mariscal Sucre [*Ecudaor*] [*ICAO location identifier*] (ICLI)
sequ .... Sequitur [*It Follows*] [*Latin*] (WGA)
SEQU .... Sequoia and Kings Canyon National Parks
SEQU .... SEQUUS Pharmaceuticals [*NASDAQ symbol*] (TTSB)
SEQU .... Sequus Pharmaceuticals, Inc. [*NASDAQ symbol*] (SAG)
Sequa .... Sequa Corp. [*Associated Press*] (SAG)
SequaA .... Sequa Corp. [*Associated Press*] (SAG)
SequaB .... Sequa Corp. [*Associated Press*] (SAG)
SEQUAL .... Seasonal Equatorial Atlantic Experiment
SEQUEL .... Structured English Query Language [*1974*] [*Computer science*] (CSR)
SEQUIN .... Sequential Quadrature Inband [*Television system*] (DEN)
SEQUIP .... Study of Environmental Quality Information Programs (KSC)
Sequnt .... Sequent Computer Systems, Inc. [*Associated Press*] (SAG)
Sequoi .... Sequoia Systems, Inc. [*Associated Press*] (SAG)
SEQUR .... Safety Equipment Requirements
SequTh .... Sequana Therapeutics, Inc. [*Associated Press*] (SAG)
Sequus .... Sequus Pharmaceuticals, Inc. [*Associated Press*] (SAG)
SER .... Aerocalifornia SA [*Mexico ICAO designator*] (FAAC)
SER .... Cataloging Services Department, OCLC [*Online Computer Library Center*], Inc., Columbus, OH [*OCLC symbol*] (OCLC)
SER .... Safety Evaluation Report [*Nuclear energy*] (NRCH)
SER .... Sandia Engineering Reactor [*Nuclear energy*]
SER .... Sebum Excretion Rate (OA)
SER .... Seder Eliyahu Rabbah (BJA)
SER .... Selective Early Retirement [*Army*]
SER .... Sensory Evoked Response [*Medicine*] (DMAA)
SER .... Sequential Events Recorder
SER .... Serial (AFM)
SER .... Serial
ser .... Serial (WDMC)
ser .... Series (IDOE)
SER .... Series (AAG)
Ser .... Serine [*Also, S*] [*An amino acid*]
ser .... Serine [*An amino acid*] (DOG)
SER .... Sermon
Ser .... Serpens [*Constellation*]
SER .... Servant
SER .... Service (NATG)
SER .... Service, Employment, Redevelopment [*Operation for Mexican-Americans*] [*Later, SER - Jobs for Progress*]
SER .... Servico, Inc. [*AMEX symbol*] (SPSG)
SER .... Servico Inc. [*AMEX symbol*] (TTSB)
SER .... Seymour, IN [*Location identifier FAA*] (FAAL)
SER .... Shore Establishment Realignment [*Navy*] (NVT)
SER .... Significant Event Report (IEEE)
SER .... Sikorsky Engineering Report
SER .... Silver Eagle Resources [*Vancouver Stock Exchange symbol*]
SER .... Simultaneous Evoked [*Cortical*] Response [*Neurophysiology*]
SER .... Single Electron Response [*Electronics*] (OA)
SER .... Site Evaluation Report (MCD)
SER .... Smooth [*Surfaced*] Endoplasmic Reticulum [*Cytology*]
SER .... SNAP [*Systems for Nuclear Auxiliary Power*] Experimental Reactor
SER .... Sociedad Espanola de Radiodifusion [*Broadcasting organization*]
SER .... Society for Ecological Restoration (EA)
SER .... Society for Educational Reconstruction (EA)
SER .... Society for Epidemiologic Research (EA)
SER .... Software Engineering Requirement [*Army*]
SER .... Somatosensory Evoked Response [*Neurophysiology*]
SER .... South-Eastern Railway [*British*]
SER .... Space Electric [*or Electronic*] Rocket (DNAB)
SER .... Stem End Rot [*Plant pathology*]
SER .... Student Eligibility Report (EDAC)
SER .... Sua Eccellenza Reverendissima [*His Eminence*] (EY)
SER .... Summary Earnings Record [*Social Security Administration*] (GFGA)
SER .... Support Equipment Requirement
SER .... Surface Electrical Resistivity
SER .... System Environment Recording (BUR)
SER .... Systolic Ejection Rate [*Cardiology*] (MAE)
SERA .... Sierra Railroad Co. [*AAR code*]
SERA .... Sierra Semiconductor [*NASDAQ symbol*] (SPSG)
SERA .... Society for Entrepreneurship Research and Application [*Defunct*] (EA)
SERA .... Solar and Electric Racing Association
SERA .... Special Emphasis Reliability Area (MCD)
SERA .... Stop Equal Rights Amendment [*An association Defunct*] (EA)
SERAC .... Southeastern Regional Arts Council
SERAC .... State Energy Research Advisory Committee [*Australia*]
Seragen .... Seragen, Inc. [*Associated Press*] (SAG)
SERANAK ..... Serge and Natalie Koussevitzky [*Acronym was name of summer home of Boston Symphony Orchestra conductor and his first wife*]
SERANDA .... Service Record, Health Record, Pay Account, and Personal Effects [*Military*]
SERAPE .... Simulator Equipment Requirements for Accelerating Procedural Evolution
SERAPHIM ... Systems Engineering Respecting Acquisition and Propagation of Heuristic Instructional Materials [*Chemistry*]
SERB .... Riobamba [*Ecuador*] [*ICAO location identifier*] (ICLI)
SERB .... Selective Early Retirement Board [*Army*] (INF)
SERB .... Serbia
SERB .... Shuttle Engineering Review Board [*NASA*] (NASA)
SERB .... Societe Europeene de Radiobiologie [*European Society for Radiation Biology - ESRB*] (EAIO)
SERB .... Study of the Enhanced Radiation Belt [*NASA*]
SERB .... Systems Engineering Review Board [*NASA*] (NASA)
SERBAUD .... Serikat Buruh Angkutan Udara [*Airways' Union*] [*Indonesia*]
SERBB .... State Employees' Retirement Benefits Board [*Australia*]
SERBIS .... Southeastern Regional Biomedical Information System (AEBS)
SERBIUM ..... Serikat Buruh Industri dan Umum [*Industrial and General Workers' Union*] [*Indonesia*]
SERBU .... Serikat Buruh Umum [*General Workers' Union*] [*Indonesia*]
SERBUHI ...... Serikat Buruh Harian Indonesia [*Newspaper Employees' Union of Indonesia*]
SERBUMAMI ... Serikat Buruh Makanan dan Minuman [*Food Workers' Union*] [*Indonesia*]
SERBUMIKSI ... Serikat Buruh Minjak Kelapa Seluruh [*Coconut Oil Workers' Union*] [*Indonesia*]
SERBUMIT ... Serikat Buruh Minjak dan Tambang [*Oil and Minerals Workers' Union*] [*Indonesia*]
SERBUMUSI ... Serikat Buruh Muslimin Indonesia [*Moslem Workers' Union of Indonesia*]
SERBUNI ...... Serikat Buruh Unilever Indonesia [*Unilever Employees' Union of Indonesia*]
SERBUPI ...... Serikat Buruh Perkebunan Indonesia [*Plantation Workers' Union of Indonesia*]
SERBUPRI ... Serikat Buruh Pertambangan Indonesia [*Mining Workers' Union of Indonesia*]
SERC .... Industry/University Cooperative Research Center for Software Engineering [*University of Florida, Purdue University*] [*Research center*] (RCD)
SERC .... Science and Engineering Research Council [*British Defunct*]
SERC .... Smithsonian Environmental Research Center
SERC .... Southeastern Electric Reliability Council [*Regional power council*]
SERC .... Special Education in the Regular Classroom Project [*U.S. Office of Special Educ ation and Rehabilitation Services*] (EDAC)
SERC .... State Emergency Response Commission [*Environmental science*]
SERC .... State Emergency Response Committee [*Environmental Protection Agency*]
SERC .... Sussex European Research Centre [*Research center British*] (IRC)
SERCA .... Servicios de Carga Aerea [*National Airlines*] [*Costa Rica*] (EY)
SERCH .... State Education Research Clearinghouse [*California*] (EDAC)
SERCNET ..... SERC Network (NITA)
SERD .... Stored Energy Rotary Drive
SERD .... Support Equipment Recommendation Data [*NASA*] (KSC)
SERD .... Support Equipment Requirements Data
SERDA .... Signals and Electronic Warfare Research and Development Act
SERDES .... Serializer/Deserializer
SERDES CRC ... Serializer-Deserializer Cyclic Redundancy Check (PDAA)
SERDF .... State Energy Research and Development Fund [*New South Wales, Australia*]
SERDP .... Strategic Environmental Research and Development Program [*National Center for Atmospheric Research*]
SERE .... Services Electronic Research Establishment [*British*] (DEN)
SERE .... Solar Electromagnetic Radiation Flux [*Model*] (USDC)
SERE .... Survival, Evasion, Resistance, and Escape [*Military*] (AFM)
SERENDIP .... Search for Extraterrestrial Radio Emission from Nearby Developed Intelligent Populations
SERENE .... Special Engineering Review of Events Nobody Envisioned
Serenpet ...... Serenpet, Inc. [*Associated Press*] (SAG)
Serenpt .... Serenpet, Inc. [*Associated Press*] (SAG)
SEREP .... System Environment Recording and Edit Program [*Computer science*] (IAA)
SEREP .... System Environment Recording, Editing, and Printing [*Computer science*]
SEREP .... System Error Record Editing Program [*Computer science*]
SERET .... Snakeye Retarded [*Navy*] (DNAB)
SERF .... Sandia Engineering Reactor Facility [*Nuclear energy*]
SERF .... Solar and Energy Research Facility [*University of Arizona*] [*Research center*] (RCD)
SERF .... Solar Electromagnetic Radiation Flux [*Model*] [*Marine science*] (OSRA)
SERF .... Space Environmental Research Facility
SERF .... Special Emergency Reaction Team Facility
SERF .... Special Environmental Radiometallurgy Facility [*Nuclear energy*] (NRCH)
SERF .... Special Extensive Routine Functions (NITA)
SERF .... Study of Energy Release in Flares [*International Council of Scientific Unions*]
SERF .... System for Equipment Requirements Forecasting (MHDB)
SERFACE ..... South East Regional Forum for Adult and Continuing Education [*British*] (DI)
SERFE .... Selection of Exempt Organization Returns for Examination [*IRS*]
SERFORSOPACSUBCOM ... Service Force, South Pacific, Subordinate Command
SERG .... Sergeant
SERG .... Serving (MSA)
Serg & Lowb ... English Common Law Reports, Edited by Sergeant and Lowber [*A publication*] (DLA)
Serg & Lowb Rep ... English Common Law Reports, Edited by Sergeant and Lowber [*A publication*] (DLA)
Serg & R ...... Sergeant and Rawle's Pennsylvania Reports [*A publication*] (DLA)
Serg & Raw ... Sergeant and Rawle's Pennsylvania Reports [*A publication*] (DLA)
Serg & Rawl ... Sergeant and Rawle's Pennsylvania Supreme Court Reports [*1814-28*] [*A publication*] (DLA)

Serg Att....... Sergeant on Attachment [*A publication*] (DLA)
Serg Const L... Sergeant's Constitutional Law [*A publication*] (DLA)
SERGE......... Socially and Ecologically Responsible Geographers [*Defunct*] (EA)
Serg Land Laws PA... Sergeant on the Land Laws of Pennsylvania [*A publication*] (DLA)
Serg LL........ Sergeant's Land Laws of Pennsylvania [*A publication*] (DLA)
Serg Mech L... Sergeant on Mechanics' Lien Law [*A publication*] (DLA)
SERGRAD.... Selected and Retained Graduate (DNAB)
SERGT......... Sergeant
SERH.......... Secretaria de Estado de Recursos Hidricos [*Argentina*]
SERHL......... Southeastern Radiological Health Laboratory (SAA)
SERI............ Aguarico [*Ecuador*] [*ICAO location identifier*] (ICLI)
seri............. Serigraph (VRA)
SERI............ Society for the Encouragement of Research and Invention [*Defunct*] (EA)
SERI............ Solar Energy Research Institute [*Golden, CO*] [*Department of Energy*]
SER-IV......... Supination, External Rotation - Type IV Fracture
SERIX......... Swedish Environmental Research Index [*Swedish National Environmental Protection Board*] [*Database*] (IID)
SERJ........... Serjeant [*Military British*] (ROG)
SERJ........... Space Electric Ramjet [*Air Force*]
SERJ........... Supercharged Ejector Ramjet [*Aircraft engine*]
Serjt............ Serjeant [*Military British*] (DMA)
SERJT-MAJ... Serjeant-Major [*Military British*] (ROG)
SERL............ Sanitary Engineering Research Laboratory [*University of California*] (MCD)
SERL............ Services Electronic Research Laboratory [*British*]
SERLANT..... Service Forces, Atlantic [*Navy*]
SERLINE...... Serials On-Line [*National Library of Medicine*] [*Bethesda, MD Database*]
SERM........... Selective Estrogen-Receptor Modulator [*Medicine*]
SERM........... Sermon (ROG)
SERM........... Society of Early Recorded Music (EA)
SERM........... Solar and Earth Radiation Monitor (NOAA)
SERMCE....... Amalgamated Association of Street, Electric Railway, and Motor Coach Employees of America [*Later, ATU*]
SERME......... Sign Error Root Modulus Error
SERMIS........ Support Equipment Rework Management Information System [*Navy*] (GFGA)
SERMLP....... Southeastern Regional Medical Library Program [*Emory University*] [*Library network*] (IID)
SERMS......... Selective Estrogen Receptor Modulators
SERNO......... Serial Number
SERNO......... Service Number [*Military*]
SERO........... Santa Rosa [*Ecuador*] [*ICAO location identifier*] (ICLI)
sero............ Serological [*Examination*] [*Immunology*] (DAVI)
SERO........... Serologicals Corp. [*NASDAQ symbol*] (SAG)
SERO........... Serologicals Inc. [*NASDAQ symbol*] (TTSB)
SERO........... Service Employment Redevelopment Operation (OICC)
SERO........... System Engineering Release Order (MCD)
SERODS....... Surface-Enhanced Raman Optical Data Storage Technology [*Developed at Oak Ridge National Laboratory*]
Serolog......... Serologicals Corp. [*Associated Press*] (SAG)
SERON......... Service Squadron [*Navy*]
SERP........... Self-Employed Retirement Plan [*Keogh plan*]
Serp............ Serpens [*Constellation*]
SERP........... Simulated Ejector Ready Panel
SERP........... Software Engineering Research Projects [*Data and Analysis Center for Software*] [*Database*]
SERP........... Standardization/Evaluation Review Panel (AFIT)
SERP........... Strategic Environmental Research Program [*DoD Department of Energy*]
SERP........... Supervisor's Evaluation of Research Personnel (AEBS)
SERP........... Supplemental Executive Retirement Plan [*Human resources*] (WYGK)
SERPA......... Southeastern Resource Policy Association (EA)
SERPAC....... Service Forces, Pacific [*Navy*]
SERPIN........ Serine Proteinase Inhibitor [*Biochemistry*]
SERPS......... Service Propulsion System [*or Subsystem*] [*NASA*] (KSC)
SERPS......... State Earnings-Related Pension Scheme [*British*]
SERR........... Semiannual RADWASTE [*Radioactive Waste*] Effluent Release (GFGA)
Ser R........... Serials Review [*A publication*] (BRI)
SERR........... Serrate (MSA)
SERRON....... Service Squadron [*Navy*]
SERRS......... Surface-Enhanced Resonance Raman Scattering [*Spectroscopy*]
SE/RRT........ Southern Europe - Railroad Transport [*NATO*] (NATG)
SERS........... Rio Saloya [*Ecuador*] [*ICAO location identifier*] (ICLI)
SERS........... Seaborne Environmental Reporting System
SERS........... Shuttle Equipment Record System [*NASA*] (NASA)
SERS........... Southern Education Reporting Service
SERS........... State Employees Retirement System
SERS........... Stimulus Evaluation/Response Selection Test [*Medicine*] (DMAA)
SERS........... Support Equipment Requirements Sheet
SERS........... Surface-Enhanced Raman Scattering [*Spectroscopy*]
ser sect....... Serial Sections (BABM)
ser sect....... Serial Sections [*Pathology*] (DAVI)
Sert............ Sertorius [*of Plutarch*] [*Classical studies*] (OCD)
SERT........... Shipboard Electronic Readiness Team [*Navy*] (CAAL)
SERT........... Shipboard Electronic Repair Team [*Navy*] (DOMA)
SERT........... Single-Electron Rise Time [*Scintillation counting*] (IEEE)
SERT........... Society of Electronic and Radio Technicians (IAA)
SE/RT.......... Southern Europe - Road Transport [*NATO*] (NATG)
SERT........... Space Electric [*or Electronic*] Rocket Test
SERT........... Special Education Resource Teacher
SERT........... Special Education Review Team
SERT........... Special Emergency Reaction Team
SERT........... Spinning Satellite for Electric Rocket Test
SERT........... Sustained Ethanol Release Tube [*Pharmacology*]
SERTEL....... Servicios Telereservacios SA de CV [*ICAO designator*] (FAAC)
SERTH......... Satisfactory Evidence Received This Headquarters
SERTOG....... Space Experiment on Relativistic Theories of Gravitation (PDAA)
SERTOMA.... Service to Mankind [*Meaning of name of Sertoma International Organization*]
SERTS......... Screaming Eagle Replacement Training School [*Vietnam*] [*Army*] (VNW)
SERTS......... Solar Extreme Ultraviolet Telescope and Spectrograph (MCD)
SERUG......... SII [*Systems Integrators, Incorporated*] Eastern Regional Users Group [*Defunct*] (EA)
SERV........... Serva [*Preserve*] [*Latin*] (WGA)
SERV........... Servant
SERV........... Servian (ROG)
SERV........... Service (AAG)
SERV........... Single-Stage Earth-Orbital Reusable Vehicle (MCD)
SERV........... Space Emergency Reentry Vehicle [*NASA*]
SERV........... Surface Effect Rescue Vessel [*Coast Guard*]
ServC........... Service Command [*Army*]
SERVCOMFMFPAC... Service Command, Fleet Marine Force, Pacific
SERVDIV...... Service Division [*Navy*]
SERVE......... Serve and Enrich Retirement by Volunteer Experience [*Staten Island, NY, project*]
SERVE......... Service (ROG)
SERVFOR..... Service Force [*Navy*]
SERVHEL..... Service and Health Record (DAVI)
SERVHEL..... Service Record and Health Record [*Military*]
Servico......... Servico, Inc. [*Associated Press*] (SAG)
SERVIVENSA... Empresa Servicicious Avensa SA [*Venezuela*] [*ICAO designator*] (FAAC)
SERVLANT... Service Force, Atlantic Fleet
SERVLANTSUBORDCOMD... Service Force, Atlantic Fleet, Subordinate Command
SERVMART... Service Mart
SERVNO....... Service Number [*Navy*]
SERVO......... Service Office
SERVO......... Servomechanism
SERVON....... Service Squadron [*Navy*]
Servotr......... Servotronics, Inc. [*Associated Press*] (SAG)
SERVPA....... Service Record and Pay Record [*Military*]
SERVPAC..... Service Force, Pacific Fleet
SERVPAHEL... Service Record, Pay Record, and Health Record [*Military*]
SERVREC..... Service Record
SERVS......... Spanish/English Reading and Vocabulary Screening Test
SERVSCOLCOM... Service School Command [*Navy*]
SERVSCOLCOMDET... Service Schools Command Detachment [*Navy*] (DNAB)
SERVSOWESPAC... Service Force, Southwest Pacific Fleet
SERVT......... Servant
SERY........... Sarayacu [*Ecuador*] [*ICAO location identifier*] (ICLI)
SES............. Group Psychotherapy Suitability Evaluation Scale [*Psychology*]
SES............. Samarbetsorganisationen for Emballagefragor i Skandinavien [*Scandinavian Packaging Association*] [*Sweden*] (EA)
SES............. Satellite Earth Station
SES............. Science Ethic Society (EA)
SES............. Scientific Exploration Society (EA)
SES............. Scottish Economic Society [*British*]
SES............. Seafarers Education Service [*British*]
SES............. Seagrass Ecosystem Study [*Marine science*] (MSC)
SES............. Seasonal Energy Syndrome [*Psychology*] (DAVI)
SES............. Seaward Extension Simulator (SAA)
SES............. Secondary Electron Scattering
SES............. Section d'Eclaireurs-Skieurs [*of Chasseurs Alpins, French Army*]
SES............. Seismic Electric Signal
SES............. Selma [*Alabama*] [*Airport symbol*] (AD)
SES............. Senior Executive Service [*Civil Service*]
SES............. Senior Executive Staff (AAGC)
SES............. Sequential Environmental Stress
SES............. Service Engine Soon [*Automotive engineering*]
SES............. Service Evaluation System [*Telecommunications*] (TEL)
SES............. Sesone [*Herbicide*] [*Trademark of Union Carbide Corp.*]
SES............. Shared Energy Savings
SES............. Ship Earth Station [*INMARSAT*]
SES............. Shorted Emitter Switch (IAA)
SES............. Shuttle Engineering Simulation [*NASA*] (NASA)
SES............. Shuttle Engineering System [*NASA*] (SSD)
SES............. Sight Erection Support
SES............. Signal Enhancement Seismograph
SES............. Signals Exploitation Space (MCD)
SES............. Singapore Stock Exchange (ODBW)
SES............. Single Engine Sea [*Pilot rating*] (AIA)
SES............. Small Edison Screw
SES............. Smart Energy System [*IBM Corp.*] [*Computer science*] (PCM)
SES............. Societe des Etudes Socialistes [*Society for Socialist Studies - SSS*]
SES............. Society for Environmental Stabilization [*Defunct*] (EA)
SES............. Society of Educators and Scholars (EA)
SES............. Society of Engineering Science (EA)
SES............. Society of Eye Surgeons (EA)
SES............. Socioeconomic Status [*or Strata*]
SES............. Soil Erosion Service [*Became Soil Conservation Service, 1935*]
SES............. Solar Eclipse Sensor (MCD)
SES............. Solar Energy Society [*Later, International Solar Energy Society*] (EA)
SES............. Solar Environment Simulator
SES............. SONAR Echo Simulator

SES.......... Space Environment Simulator [*NASA*]
SES.......... Space Erectable Structure
SES.......... Special Emphasis Study (NASA)
SES.......... Special Exchange Service [*Telecommunications*] (TEL)
SES.......... Special Exploitation Service [*South Vietnamese studies and observations group*] [*Military*] (VNW)
SES.......... SPRINT Engagement Simulation [*Missile system evaluation*] [*Army*] (RDA)
SES.......... Standards Engineering Society (EA)
SES.......... State Experiment Stations Division [*of ARS, Department of Agriculture*]
SES.......... Stationary Engine Society (EA)
SES.......... Steam Electric Station [*Nuclear energy*] (NRCH)
SES.......... Steam Engine Systems Corp.
SES.......... Stimulated Emission Spectroscopy
SES.......... Story of Exploration Series [*A publication*]
SES.......... Strategic Engineering Survey [*Navy*]
SES.......... Student Evaluation Scale [*Student attitudes test*]
SES.......... Studies and Expansion Society [*See also SEE*] (EAIO)
SES.......... Study of Education at Stanford [*Stanford University*]
SES.......... Subendothelial Space [*Medicine*] (DMAA)
SES.......... Suffield [*Alberta*] [*Seismograph station code, US Geological Survey*] (SEIS)
SES.......... Suffield Experimental Station [*Canada*]
SES.......... Superexcited Electronic State [*Chemistry*] (OA)
SES.......... Supervisory Electronics Specialist
SES.......... Support Equipment Subsystem
SES.......... Surface Effects Ship [*Navy symbol*]
SES.......... Sustaining Engineering Services
SES.......... Sydney Esperanto Society [*Australia*]
SES.......... Sylvania Electronic Systems (SAA)
SES.......... Symptom Evaluation Survey (EDAC)
SES.......... Synergist Erection System [*Medicine*]
SES.......... System Evaluation System (MCD)
SES.......... System External Storage
SES.......... Systems Engineering Study
SES.......... Systems Engineering Support
SES.......... Systems Engineering Work Statement
SES.......... Systems Evaluation Squadron [*Air Force*]
SESA.......... Salinas [*Ecuador*] [*ICAO location identifier*] (ICLI)
SESA.......... Signal Equipment Support Agency
SESA.......... Single End Strip Adhesion (PDAA)
SESA.......... Social and Economic Statistics Administration [*Terminated, 1975*] [*Department of Commerce*]
SESA.......... Society for Environmental Stress Analysis (IAA)
SESA.......... Society for Experimental Stress Analysis [*Later, SEM*] (EA)
SESA.......... Solar Energy Society of America (EA)
SESA.......... Southeast Singles Association
SESA.......... Standard Electrica, Sociedad Anonima [*Brazilian affiliate of ITT*]
SESA.......... State Employment Security Agency
SESA.......... Story of the Empire Series [*A publication*]
SESAC.......... Society of European Stage Authors and Composers
SESAC.......... Space and Earth Science Advisory Committee [*NASA*]
SESAC Inc........... Society of European Stage Authors and Composers [*Nashville, TN*] (WDMC)
SESAM.......... System for Emission Sampling and Measurement [*Automotive engineering*]
SESAME.......... Search for Excellence in Science and Mathematics Education [*Graduate program at University of California at Berkeley*]
SESAME.......... Selected Essential Stockage Availability Method
SESAME.......... Service, Sort and Merge [*Computer science*]
SESAME.......... Severe Environmental Storms and Mesoscale Experiment [*National Science Foundation/National Oceanic and Atmospheric Administration*]
SESAME.......... Systems Engineering Study on Atmospheric Measurements and Equipment (NOAA)
SESAT.......... Stanford Early School Achievement Test [*Educational test*]
SESB.......... Sibambe [*Ecuador*] [*ICAO location identifier*] (ICLI)
SESC.......... Selective Elution Solvent Chromatography
SESC.......... Sequential Elution Solvent Chromatography
SESC.......... Shuttle Events Sequential Control [*NASA*] (MCD)
SESC.......... South Eastern State College [*Oklahoma*]
SESC.......... Space Environment Services Center [*Boulder, CO*] [*National Oceanic and Atmospheric Administration*] (KSC)
SESC.......... Special Environmental Sample Container [*NASA*] (PDAA)
SESC.......... Sucua [*Ecuador*] [*ICAO location identifier*] (ICLI)
SESC.......... Surface Environmental Sample Container [*Apollo*] [*NASA*]
SESCI.......... Solar Energy Society of Canada, Inc. [*Societe d'Energie Solaire du Cana da*]
SESCO.......... Secure Submarine Communications
SESD.......... Santo Domingo De Los Colorados [*Ecuador*] [*ICAO location identifier*] (ICLI)
SESD.......... Space Electronic Security Division [*Military*]
SESDA.......... Scottish Electro-Static Discharge Association (EAIO)
SESDA.......... Serikat Sekerdja Departemen Agama [*Brotherhood of Employees of Department of Religious Affairs*] [*Indonesia*]
SESDA.......... Small Engine Servicing Dealers Association (EA)
SESDAQ.......... Stock Exchange of Singapore Dealing and Automated Quotation System
SE Sdg.......... Square-Edge Siding (DAC)
SESE.......... Search for Excellence in Science Education [*National Science Teacher Association*] (EDAC)
SESE.......... Secadal [*Educador*] [*ICAO location identifier*] (ICLI)
SESE.......... Secure Echo-Sounding Equipment [*SONAR*] [*Navy*]
SESE.......... Shuttle Experiment Support Equipment
SE/SE.......... Single Entry/Single Exit
SESE.......... Space Electronics Support Equipment (MCD)
SESEF.......... Ship Electronics System Evaluation Facility [*Navy*] (CAAL)
SESG.......... Sangay [*Ecuador*] [*ICAO location identifier*] (ICLI)
SESG.......... Southern Europe Shipping Group [*NATO*] (NATG)
SESGA.......... Show of Equipment and Supplies for the Graphic Arts (DGA)
SESH.......... San Honorato [*Ecuador*] [*ICAO location identifier*] (ICLI)
SESI.......... Socio-Economic-Status-Indicator (WDMC)
SESI.......... Solar Energy Society of Ireland [*International Solar Energy Society*]
SESI.......... Stock Exchange of Singapore Index (ODBW)
SESI.......... Superior Energy Services, Inc. [*NASDAQ symbol*] (SAG)
SESI.......... Superior Energy Svcs [*NASDAQ symbol*] (TTSB)
SESI.......... Sur Iliniza [*Ecuador*] [*ICAO location identifier*] (ICLI)
SE/SI.......... Systems Engineering/Systems Integration (SDI)
SESIP.......... Systems Engineering Summary of Installation and Program Planning (IAA)
SESIW.......... Superior Energy Svcs Wrrt [*NASDAQ symbol*] (TTSB)
SESIZ.......... Superior Energy Svcs Wrrt'B' [*NASDAQ symbol*] (TTSB)
SESJ.......... San Jose [*Ecuador*] [*ICAO location identifier*] (ICLI)
SESK.......... Silok [*Ecuador*] [*ICAO location identifier*] (ICLI)
SESL.......... San Lorenzo [*Ecuador*] [*ICAO location identifier*] (ICLI)
SESL.......... Self-Erecting Space Laboratory (AAG)
SESL.......... Space Environment Simulation Laboratory [*NASA*]
SESLP.......... Sequential Explicit Stochastic Linear Programming [*Computer science*]
SESM.......... Samborondon [*Ecuador*] [*ICAO location identifier*] (ICLI)
SESM.......... Strategies and Errors in Secondary Mathematics [*Project*] (AIE)
SESMA.......... Special Event Search and Master Analysis (GAVI)
SESMI.......... Systems Engineering Support and Management Integration (MCD)
SESN.......... San Carlos [*Ecuador*] [*ICAO location identifier*] (ICLI)
SESO.......... La Estrella [*Ecuador*] [*ICAO location identifier*] (ICLI)
SESO.......... Senior Equipment Staff Officer [*Air Force British*]
SESOC.......... Surface Effect Ship for Ocean Commerce
SESOME.......... Service, Sort, and Merge [*Computer science*] (IEEE)
SESP.......... Society of Experimental Social Psychology [*Defunct*] (EA)
SESP.......... Space Experimental Satellite Program [*NASA*] (SSD)
SESP.......... Space Experiment Support Program (MCD)
SESPA.......... Scientists and Engineers for Social and Political Action [*Later, SFTP*] (EA)
SESPENDO.......... Serikat Buruh Pegawai Negeri dan Daeran Otonom [*Civil Servants Workers' Union*] [*Indonesia*]
SESPO.......... Surface Effect Ships Project Office [*Navy*]
SESPROJ.......... Surface Effect Ship Project [*Navy*] (DNAB)
SESQUIH.......... Sesquihora [*An Hour and a Half*] [*Pharmacy*] (ROG)
SESQUIHOR.......... Sesquihora [*An Hour and a Half*] [*Pharmacy*]
SESR.......... San Rafael [*Ecuador*] [*ICAO location identifier*] (ICLI)
SESR.......... Segment Entry Save Register [*Computer science*] (MHDI)
SESR.......... Selected Equipment Status Report [*Navy*] (NG)
SESR.......... Societe Europeenne de Sociologie Rurale [*European Society for Rural Sociology*]
SESR.......... Special Environmental Storage Requirements (MCD)
SESRTCIC.......... Statistical, Economic, and Social Research and Training Center for Islamic Countries [*Research center Turkey*] (IRC)
SESS.......... Session
SESS.......... Society of Ethnic and Special Studies (EA)
SESS.......... Space Environmental Support System
SESS.......... Summer Employment for Science Students
Sess Ca.......... Scotch Court of Session Cases [*A publication*] (DLA)
Sess Ca.......... Sessions Cases, King's Bench [*1710-48*] [*England*] [*A publication*] (DLA)
Sess Cas.......... Scotch Court of Session Cases [*A publication*] (DLA)
Sess Cas.......... Session Cases, High Court of Justiciary Section [*1906-16*] [*Scotland*] [*A publication*] (DLA)
Sess Cas.......... Sessions Cases, King's Bench [*England*] [*A publication*] (DLA)
Sess Cas KB.......... Sessions Settlement Cases, King's Bench [*England*] [*A publication*] (DLA)
Sess Cas Sc.......... Scotch Court of Session Cases [*A publication*] (DLA)
Sess N.......... Session Notes [*Scotland*] [*A publication*] (DLA)
Sess Pap CC.......... Central Criminal Court Cases, Sessions Papers [*1834-1913*] [*England*] [*A publication*] (ILCA)
Sess Pap CCC.......... Central Criminal Court Cases, Sessions Papers [*1834-1913*] [*England*] [*A publication*] (DLA)
Sess Pap OB.......... Old Bailey's Sessions Papers [*A publication*] (DLA)
Sest.......... Pro Sestio [*of Cicero*] [*Classical studies*] (OCD)
SEST.......... San Cristobal (Galapagos) [*ICAO location identifier*] (ICLI)
SEST.......... Swedish-ESO Submillimetre Telescope [*Observatory*]
SESTF.......... Surface Effect Ship Test Facility [*Navy*] (DNAB)
SESTM.......... Societe Europeenne de la Science et de la Technologie des Membranes [*European Society of Membrane Science and Technology - ESMST*] (EA)
SestThr.......... Southeastern Thrift and Bank Fund [*Associated Press*] (SAG)
SESUNC.......... Sesuncia [*An Ounce and a Half*] [*Pharmacy*] (ROG)
SESUPP.......... Safety Evaluation Supplement (IAA)
SESY.......... Sur Cayambe [*Ecuador*] [*ICAO location identifier*] (ICLI)
SESZ.......... Sur Antizana [*Ecuador*] [*ICAO location identifier*] (ICLI)
Set.......... English Settlement and Removal Cases [*Burrow's Settlement Cases*] [*A publication*] (DLA)
SET.......... Safety Education and Training
SET.......... San Esteban [*Honduras*] [*Airport symbol*] (AD)
SET.......... Satellite Experimental Terminal (NATG)
SET.......... Scaling Erythema and Thickness [*Dermatology*]
SET.......... Scientists, Engineers, Technicians
SET.......... Secure Electronic Transactions (PCM)
SET.......... Secure Electronic Transactions [*Computer science*]
SET.......... Secure Exchange Technology

SET .... Securities Exchange of Thailand
SET .... Security Escort Team [*Military*]
SET .... Selective Electronic Training [*Navy*] (NG)
SET .... Selective Employment Tax [*British*]
SET .... Self-Employment Tax [*IRS*]
SET .... Self-Extending Translator (IEEE)
SET .... Senior Electronic Technician [*National Weather Service*]
SET .... Sensory Evaluation Test [*Army*]
SET .... Serial Endosymbiotic Theory [*Evolution*]
SET .... Service Evaluation Telemetry (AAG)
SET .... Setif [*Algeria*] [*Seismograph station code, US Geological Survey*] (SEIS)
SET .... Setting (MSA)
SET .... Settlement (ROG)
SET .... Settling
SET .... Sheraton Executive Traveler [*Sheraton Corp.*]
SET .... Siemont Resources, Inc. [*Vancouver Stock Exchange symbol*]
SET .... Simplified Engineering Technique
SET .... Simulated Emergency Test
SET .... Single-Electron-Transfer [*Organic chemistry*]
SET .... Single Electron Transistor [*Physics*]
SET .... Single-Electron Tunneling [*Physics*]
SET .... Single Escape Tower
SET .... Skin Endpoint Titration [*Medicine*] (MEDA)
SET .... Sociedad Ecuatoriana de Transportes Aereos Ltda. [*Ecuador*] [*ICAO designator*] (FAAC)
SET .... Society for Environmental Therapy [*British*]
SET .... Society for Environmental Truth (EA)
SET .... Society for the Eradication of Television (EA)
SET .... Software Encapsulation Template
SET .... Software Engineering Technology
SET .... Software Engineering Terminology [*Computer science*] (IEEE)
SET .... Solar Energy Thermionic [*Program*] [*NASA*]
SET .... Source Evaluation Team [*Army*]
SET .... Spacecraft Elapsed Time
SET .... Space Electronics and Telemetry (MCD)
SET .... Special Engineering Test (IAA)
SET .... Sports Emotion Test [*Research test*] [*Psychology*]
SET .... Stack Entry Time [*Aviation*] (FAAC)
SET .... Standard d'Exchange et de Transfert [*Computer graphics*] [*French*]
SET .... Stepped Electrode Transistor
SET .... Stock Exchange of Thailand [*Thailand*]
SET .... Stored-Energy Transmission (PDAA)
SET .... Student Empowerment Training Project (EA)
SET .... Submarine Engineering Technical
SET .... Suitability Evaluation Team (MCD)
SET .... Surrogate Embryo Transfer [*Gynecology*] (CPH)
SET .... Symbol Elaboration Test [*Psychology*]
SET .... Synchro Error Tester
SET .... Syndicat des Enseignants du Togo [*Union of Togolese Teachers*]
SET .... System Evaluation Technique (IAA)
SET .... System Extension Test
SET .... Systems Effects Test [*Nuclear energy*] (GFGA)
SET .... Systems Engineering Test (CET)
SET .... Systolic Ejection Time [*Cardiology*] (MAE)
SETA .... Satellite Electrostatic Triaxial Accelerometer
SETA .... Scottish Egg Trade Association (DBA)
SETA .... Simplified Electronic Tracking (IAA)
SETA .... Simplified Electronic Tracking Apparatus [*Air Force*]
SETA .... Systems Engineering and Technical Assistance (MCD)
SETA .... Taura [*Ecuador*] [*ICAO location identifier*] (ICLI)
SETAB .... Sets Tabular Material [*Phototypesetting computer*]
SETAC .... Sector TACAN [*Tactical Air Navigation*] System
SETAC .... Society of Environmental Toxicology and Chemistry (EA)
SETAC .... Specially Equipped Traffic Accident Car [*British police*]
SETAC .... Systems Engineering and Technical Assistance Contract
SETAD .... Secure Encryption of Tactical Analog Data
SETAD .... Secure Transmission of Acoustic Data (NVT)
SETAF .... Southern European Task Force [*NATO*]
SETAR .... Serial Event Timer and Recorder
SETA-UITA ... Syndicat Europeen des Travailleurs de l'Alimentation, de l'Hotellerie, et des Branches Connexes dans l'UITA [*European Committee of Food, Catering, and Allied Workers' Unions within the IUF - ECF-IUF*] (EAIO)
SETB .... Secondary Education Text-Books [*A publication*]
SETB .... Set Theoretic Language - BALM [*1973*] [*Computer science*] (CSR)
SETB .... Timbre [*Ecuador*] [*ICAO location identifier*] (ICLI)
SETBGT .... Set Ballistic Gain Table
SETC .... Solid Electrolyte Tantalum Capacitor
SETC .... Southeastern Theatre Conference (EA)
SETC .... Submarine Escape Training Centre [*British military*] (DMA)
SETD .... Scheduled Estimated Time of Departure [*Aviation*] (DA)
SETD .... Sledborne Event Time Digitizer
SETD .... Space Environment Test Division [*NASA*]
SE/TD .... Systems Engineering and Technical Direction (AAGC)
SETE .... Secretariat for Electronic Test Equipment [*DoD*]
SETE .... Status of Electronic Test Equipment (MCD)
SETE .... Supersonic Expendable Turbojet Engine (MCD)
SETE .... Support and Electronic Test Equipment
SETE .... System Evaluation Test Equipment [*Military*] (CAAL)
SETE .... Tena [*Ecuador*] [*ICAO location identifier*] (ICLI)
SETEL .... Societe Europeenne de Teleguidage [*Five European firms organized in 1958 under French law to act as European prime contractor for production of HAWK missiles*] [*NATO*]
SETEP .... Science and Engineering Technician Education Program [*National Science Foundation*]
SETF .... SNAP [*Systems for Nuclear Auxiliary Power*] Experimental Test Facility
SETF .... STARAN Evaluation and Training Facility
SETFIA .... South East Trawl Fishing Industry Association [*Australia*]
SETG .... Tenguel [*Ecuador*] [*ICAO location identifier*] (ICLI)
SET-GO .... Support and Encouragement for Talent - Gateway to Opportunity [*Project*] (EA)
SETH .... Taisha [*Ecudaor*] [*ICAO location identifier*] (ICLI)
SETI .... Search for Extraterrestrial Intelligence
SETI .... Societe Europeenne pour le Traitement de l'Information [*European Society for the Processing of Information*]
SETI .... Tiputini [*Ecuador*] [*ICAO location identifier*] (ICLI)
SETID .... Set Identification
SETINA .... Southeast Texas Information Network Association
SETIS .... Societe Europeenne pour l'Etude et l'Integration des Systemes Spatiaux
SETL .... Science Experiment Test Laboratory [*NASA*]
SETL .... Set Theoretic Language [*1971*] [*Computer science*] (CSR)
SETLG .... Settling (MSA)
SETO .... Pacto [*Ecuador*] [*ICAO location identifier*] (ICLI)
SETOLS .... Surface Effect Takeoff and Land System [*Naval aviation*]
Seton .... Seton's Forms of Decrees, Judgments, and Orders in Equity [*7 eds.*] [*1830-1912*] [*A publication*] (DLA)
Seton Dec .... Seton's Forms of Decrees, Judgments, and Orders in Equity [*7th ed.*] [*1912*] [*A publication*] (DLA)
Seton Hall U ... Seton Hall University (GAGS)
SETP .... Society of Experimental Test Pilots (EA)
SETP .... Tandapi [*Ecuador*] [*ICAO location identifier*] (ICLI)
SETR .... Setter (MSA)
SETR .... Tarapoa [*Ecuador*] [*ICAO location identifier*] (ICLI)
SETS .... Scottish Electrical Training Scheme Ltd. [*British*]
SETS .... Seeker Evaluation Test System [*Military*]
SETS .... Set Equation Transformation System [*1970*] [*Computer science*] (CSR)
SETS .... Site Enforcement Tracking System [*Environmental Protection Agency*] (GFGA)
SETS .... Skylab End-to-End Test System [*NASA*]
SETS .... Solar Electric Test Satellite
SETS .... Solar Energy Thermionic Conversion System [*NASA*]
SETS .... Special Electron Tube Section
SETS .... Squad Engagement Training System [*Army*] (INF)
SETS .... Standardized Environmental Technical Specifications [*Nuclear energy*] (NRCH)
SETS .... Stereo Electro-Optical Tracking System (MCD)
Sett .... Settlement Cases [*A publication*] (DLA)
SETT .... Submarine Escape Training Tank
SETT .... Teniente Ortiz [*Ecuador*] [*ICAO location identifier*] (ICLI)
SETTA .... Southeastern Test and Training Area [*Military*] (MCD)
Sett & Rem ... Settlement and Removal Cases in English King's Bench [*A publication*] (DLA)
Sett Cas .... Burrow's English Settlement Cases [*A publication*] (DLA)
Sett Cas .... Settlement and Removal Cases in English King's Bench [*A publication*] (DLA)
SETTL .... Settler [*Genealogy*]
SETTLET ...... Settlement (ROG)
SETTT .... Settlement (ROG)
SETU .... Tulcan [*Ecuador*] [*ICAO location identifier*] (ICLI)
SETWEG ...... Statistical Engine Test Work Group [*Lubricants testing*] [*Automotive engineering*]
SEU .... Saint Edward's University [*Texas*]
SEU .... Sales Education Units
SEU .... Scottish European Airways Ltd. [*British ICAO designator*] (FAAC)
SEU .... Seronera [*Tanzania*] [*Airport symbol*] (AD)
SEU .... Single Event Upset (SSD)
SEU .... Small End-Up (IAA)
SEU .... Solar Energy Update [*A publication*]
SEU .... Source Entry Utility
SEU .... Southeastern University [*Washington, DC*]
SEU .... Spiral Optics [*Vancouver Stock Exchange symbol*]
SEU .... Subjective Expected Utility [*Concept*] [*Theory used for decision making*]
SEU .... Surgery Expandable Unit (SAA)
SEUG .... Screaming Eagles Users Group [*Defunct*] (EA)
SEUL .... Servicio Europeo de Universitarios Latinoamericanos [*Belgium*]
SEUL .... Support Equipment Utilization List (NASA)
SEURE .... Systems Evaluation Code Under Radiation Environment (IEEE)
SEUS .... Southeastern United States
SEUSSN .... Southeastern United States Seismic Network (NRCH)
SEUY .... Chanduy [*Ecuador*] [*ICAO location identifier*] (ICLI)
SEV .... Scout Evaluation Vehicle
SEV .... Sensor Equivalent Visibility
SEV .... Service City, AK [*Location identifier FAA*] (FAAL)
SEV .... Sevastopol [*Former USSR Seismograph station code, US Geological Survey Closed*] (SEIS)
SEV .... Seven
SEV .... Several
SEV .... Severe [*Used to qualify weather phenomena*]
SEV .... Severed
Sev .... Severus [*of Scriptores Historiae Augustae*] [*Classical studies*] (OCD)
SEV .... Sevres [*China*] (ROG)
SEV .... Shelter Equipment Vault
SEV .... Ship Exercise Vehicle
SEV .... Simcoe Erie Investors Ltd. [*Toronto Stock Exchange symbol*]

SEV .... Small Earlywood Vessel [*Tree-ring property*]
SEV .... Societe d'Ethologie Veterinaire [*Society for Veterinary Ethology - SVE*] [*Edinburgh, Scotland*] (EAIO)
SEV .... Special Equipment Vehicle [*Military*]
SEV .... Split End Vector [*System for plant cell transformation*]
SEV .... SRAM Equivalent Volume (MCD)
SEV .... State Equalized Value [*Real estate*]
SEV .... Stockpile Emergency Verification [*DoD*]
SEV .... Surface Effects Vehicle [*Military*]
SEVA .... Skylab Extravehicular Visor Assembly [*NASA*]
SEVA .... Standup Extravehicular Activity [*Aerospace*]
SEVA .... Surface Extravehicular Activity [*Lunar exploration*]
SEVA .... System Evaluation Program (IAA)
SEVA .... Valdez [*Ecuador*] [*ICAO location identifier*] (ICLI)
SEVAC .... Secure Voice Access Console [*Army*] (AABC)
SEVAL .... Senior Evaluator (MCD)
Sev App Cas... Sevestre's Bengal High Court Appeal Cases [*1864-68*] [*India*] [*A publication*] (DLA)
SEVAS .... Secure Voice Access Systems [*Army*] (AABC)
Sev Cent N... Seventeenth-Century News [*A publication*] (BRI)
SEVEC .... Society for Educational Visits and Exchanges in Canada [*Societe Educative de Visites et d'Echanges au Canada*]
SEVENTHFLT... Seventh Fleet [*Navy*]
SevEnv .... Sevenson Environmental Services, Inc. [*Associated Press*] (SAG)
Sevestre ...... Calcutta Reports of Cases in Appeal [*A publication*] (DLA)
SEVFLT .... Seventh Fleet [*Pacific*] [*Navy*]
Sev HC .... Sevestre's Bengal High Court Reports [*India*] [*A publication*] (DLA)
SEVI .... Villano [*Ecuador*] [*ICAO location identifier*] (ICLI)
SEVL .... 7th Level Inc. [*NASDAQ symbol*] (TTSB)
SEVL .... Seventh Level, Inc. [*NASDAQ symbol*] (SAG)
SEVL .... Several (ROG)
SEVN .... Sevenson Environmental Services, Inc. [*NASDAQ symbol*] (NQ)
SEVN .... Sevenson Enviro Svcs [*NASDAQ symbol*] (TTSB)
SEVN .... Vinces [*Ecuador*] [*ICAO location identifier*] (ICLI)
SevnHil .... Seven Hills Financial Corp. [*Associated Press*] (SAG)
SEVOCOM ..... Secure Voice Communications (AFM)
SEVP .... Severance Pay [*Military*]
Sev SDA ...... Sevestre's Sadr Diwani Adalat Reports [*Bengal, India*] [*A publication*] (DLA)
SEVT .... Ventanas [*Ecuador*] [*ICAO location identifier*] (ICLI)
SEW .... Sewage [*or Sewer*] (AAG)
SEW .... Seward [*Alaska*] [*Seismograph station code, US Geological Survey*] (SEIS)
SEW .... Sewing
SEW .... Shipboard Electronics Warfare [*Navy*]
SEW .... Silicon Epitaxial Wafer
SEW .... Singer Co. NV [*NYSE symbol*] (SPSG)
SEW .... SONAR Early Warning
SEW .... Sozialistische Einheitspartei Westberlins [*Socialist Unity Party of West Berlin*] [*Germany Political party*] (PPW)
SEW .... Space and Electronic Warfare (DOMA)
SEW .... Special Effects Warhead (MCD)
SEW .... Surface Electromagnetic Wave
SEWA .... Self-Employed Women's Association [*India*]
SEWAC .... South East Wales Access Consortium (AIE)
SEWACO ...... Sensor Weapons Control and Command
SEWC .... SIGINT/Electronic Warfare Coordination Element (MCD)
S/EWCC .... Signal Intelligence/Electronic Warfare Coordination Center (NVT)
Sew Cor .... Sewell on Coroners [*1843*] [*A publication*] (DLA)
Sewell Sheriffs... Sewell on the Law of Sheriffs [*A publication*] (DLA)
SEWG .... Sewing (WGA)
SEWHO .... Shoulder-Elbow-Wrist-Hand Orthosis [*Medicine*]
SEWL .... Southeast Water Laboratory [*Environmental Protection Agency*]
SEWMA .... Simple Exponentially-Weighted Moving-Average (PDAA)
SEWMRPG... Southern European Western Mediterranean Regional Planning Group [*NATO*] (NATG)
SEWO .... Shoulder-Elbow-Wrist Orthosis [*Medicine*]
SEWPS .... Safety Weather Probability Study (MCD)
Sew R .... Sewanee Review [*A publication*] (BRI)
SEWS .... Satellite Early Warning System
SEWS .... Sun-End Work Station [*NASA*] (KSC)
SEWS .... Surface Electromagnetic Wave Spectroscopy
Sew Sh .... Sewell on the Law of Sheriffs [*1842*] [*A publication*] (DLA)
SEWT .... Simulated Electronic Warfare Training [*Army*]
SEWT .... Simulator for Electronic Warfare Training
SEWY .... Seaway Food Town [*NASDAQ symbol*] (TTSB)
SEWY .... Seaway Food Town, Inc. [*NASDAQ symbol*] (NQ)
Sex .... Sextans [*Constellation*]
sex .... Sexual (DAVI)
SEX .... Shipment Exception Code [*Military*] (AFIT)
SEX .... Sign Extend [*Computer science*] (NHD)
SEX .... Size Exclusion [*Analytical chemistry*]
SEX .... Sodium Ethyl Xanthate [*Organic chemistry*]
SEX .... Software Exchange [*Computer science*] (NHD)
SEX .... Summer Experiment Group [*Summer work for engineering undergraduates*]
SEXAFS .... Surface-Extended X-Ray Absorption Fine Structure
S Exec Doc... Senate Executive Document [*A publication*] (DLA)
S Exec Rep... Senate Executive Report [*A publication*] (DLA)
S/EXH .... Single Exhaust [*Automotive engineering*]
Sex LR .... Sexual Law Reporter [*A publication*] (DLA)
Sex L Rep ... Sexual Law Reporter [*A publication*] (DLA)
SExO .... Senior Experimental Officer [*Also, SEO, SXO*] [*Ministry of Agriculture, Fisheries, and Food*] [*British*]
SeXO .... Serum Xanthine Oxidase [*Clinical chemistry*] (AAMN)
Sex Pomp .... Sextus Pomponius [*Flourished, 2nd century*] [*Authority cited in pre-1607 legal work*] (DSA)
SEXPOT .... SPRINT [*Solid-Propellant Rocket Intercept*] Extra Pulse Out of Tail [*Army*]
s expr .... Sine Expressione [*Without Expressing*] [*Latin*] (MAE)
Sex Prob Ct Dig... Sex Problems Court Digest [*A publication*] (DLA)
SEXR .... Shoulder External Rotation [*Sports medicine*]
SEXRAT .... Sex Ratio [*Biology*]
Sext .... Liber Sextus Decretalium [*A publication*] (DSA)
Sext .... Sextans [*Constellation*]
SEXT .... Sextant (WDAA)
SEXT .... Shoulder Extension [*Sports medicine*]
Sext Emp ..... Sextus Empiricus [*Third century AD*] [*Classical studies*] (OCD)
SEY .... Air Seychelles [*ICAO designator*] (FAAC)
SEY .... Block Island, RI [*Location identifier FAA*] (FAAL)
SEY .... Secondary Electron Yield
SEY .... Selibaby [*Mauritania*] [*Airport symbol*] (OAG)
SEY .... Seymchan [*Former USSR Seismograph station code, US Geological Survey*] (SEIS)
SEY .... Southeastern Yiddish (BJA)
SEY .... Starlight Energy [*Vancouver Stock Exchange symbol*]
SEY .... Summer Employment Youth [*DoD*]
SEYA .... Yaupi [*Ecuador*] [*ICAO location identifier*] (ICLI)
Seych LR ..... Seychelles Law Reports [*A publication*] (DLA)
SEYF .... Scottish Episcopal Youth Fellowship
SEYM .... Secondary Electron Yield Measurement
Sey Merch Sh... Seymour's Merchant Shipping Acts [*2nd ed.*] [*1857*] [*A publication*] (DLA)
SEYMS .... Secondary Electron Yield Measurement System
SEYS .... Secondary Electron Yield System
SEZ .... Mahe Island [*Seychelles Islands*] [*Airport symbol*] (OAG)
SEZ .... Sedona, AZ [*Location identifier FAA*] (FAAL)
SEZ .... Servicio Especializado de Carga Aerea [*Columbia*] [*FAA designator*] (FAAC)
Sez .... Sezione [*Division*] [*Italian*] (ILCA)
SEZ .... Special Economic Zone
SEZA .... Zamora [*Ecuador*] [*ICAO location identifier*] (ICLI)
SEZP .... Zumba-Pucupamba [*Ecuador*] [*ICAO location identifier*] (ICLI)
SF .... E. R. Squibb & Sons [*Research code symbol*]
SF .... Fleet Submarine [*Navy symbol Obsolete*]
SF .... Meiji Seika Kaisha Ltd. [*Japan*] [*Research code symbol*]
SF .... Provisional Sinn Fein [*Northern Ireland*] [*Political party*] (PPW)
SF .... Royal Scots Fusiliers [*Military unit*] (DMA)
SF .... Sabre Foundation (EA)
SF .... Sacrifice Fly [*Baseball*]
SF .... Safe (NASA)
SF .... Safety (IAA)
SF .... Safety Factor
SF .... Safety, Reliability, and Quality Assurance, and Protective Services [*Kennedy Space Center*] [*NASA*] (NASA)
SF .... Salt Free [*Diet*]
SF .... Sampled Filter (IEEE)
SF .... San Francisco [*California*]
sf .... Sao Tome and Principe [*MARC country of publication code Library of Congress*] (LCCP)
SF .... Satiety Factor [*Physiology*]
SF .... Saw Fixture (MCD)
SF .... Scale Factor
SF .... Scarlet Fever [*Medicine*]
SF .... Scheduling Forecast
SF .... Scheibe-Flugzeugbau GmbH [*Germany ICAO aircraft manufacturer identifier*] (ICAO)
SF .... School of Chiropody Full Time [*British*]
SF .... Science Fiction [*Also, SCI-FI*]
sf .... Science Fiction (WDMC)
SF .... Science Frontiers [*An association*] (EA)
SF .... Scleroderma Federation (EA)
SF .... Scouting Force [*Navy*]
SF .... Scruse Air [*ICAO designator*] (AD)
SF .... Sea Flood
SF .... Seasonal Fluctuation (MHDB)
SF .... Seasonal Food [*Department of Employment*] [*British*]
SF .... Secondary Failure [*NASA*] (KSC)
SF .... Secure Facility (MCD)
SF .... Security Forces [*Japanese army*]
SF .... Security Forecast [*Control Risks Information Services - CRIS*] [*British Information service or system*] (IID)
Sf .... Sefire Inscriptions (BJA)
SF .... Select Frequency
SF .... Selection Filter (MCD)
SF .... Selous Foundation (EA)
SF .... Semifinished [*Steel or other material*]
SF .... Semifixed [*Ammunition*] (NATG)
SF .... Semi-Floating [*Automotive engineering*]
SF .... Semi-Fowler's [*Position*] [*Surgery*] (DAVI)
SF .... Seminal Fluid [*Medicine*]
SF .... Senate File (OICC)
SF .... Senior Fellow
SF .... Separation Factor [*Chemical analysis*]
SF .... Serum Fibrinogen [*Medicine*] (MAE)
SF .... Service Factor (MSA)
SF .... Servicing Flight [*British military*] (DMA)
SF .... Seva Foundation (EA)
SF .... Sexagesimo-quarto [*Book up to 7-1/2 centimeters in height*] [*Bibliography*]

Sf............... Sforzando [*With Additional Accent*] [*Music*]
SF............... Sham Feeding [*Medicine*] (DMAA)
SF............... Shell Fragment (MAE)
SF............... Sherwood Foresters [*Military unit*] [*British*]
SF............... Shift Forward
SF............... Shipfitter [*Navy*]
SF............... Shock Front (SAA)
SF............... Shortening Fraction [*Cardiology*]
SF............... Short Format
SF............... Shrapnel Fragment (MAE)
SF............... Side Frequency (DEN)
SF............... Signal Frequency
SF............... Significant Figure (IAA)
SF............... Silicia Fume [*Inorganic chemistry*]
SF............... Simian Foam-Virus [*Medicine*] (DMAA)
S/F............... Single Face
SF............... Single Feeder
S/F............... Single Flow (NASA)
SF............... Single Frequency [*Telecommunications*]
SF............... Single-Fronted (ADA)
SF............... Sinking Fund [*Finance*]
SF............... Sinn Fein [*Political front of the Irish Republican Army*]
SF............... Skin Fibroblast [*Clinical chemistry*]
SF............... Skip Flag [*Computer science*] (MDG)
SF............... Sliding Filter (NASA)
SF............... Slip Factor
SF............... Slip Fit (MSA)
SF............... Slot Format [*Microfiltration*]
SF............... Slow Fire [*Military*]
SF............... Slow Initial Function (AAMN)
SF............... Social Forces [*A publication*] (BRI)
SF............... Society Farsarotul (EA)
SF............... Sodium Azide, Fecal [*Medium*] [*Microbiology*] (DAVI)
SF............... Soft [*Horse racing*]
SF............... Soft Focus [*Cinematography*] (NTCM)
SF............... Solar Flare [*Astronomy*]
SF............... Soldiers of Freedom (EA)
SF............... Solid Fuel (ADA)
SF............... Soluble Factor (DAVI)
SF............... SONAR Frequency [*Military*] (CAAL)
SF............... Sons of the Holy Family [*Roman Catholic men's religious order*]
sf............... Sons of the Holy Family (TOCD)
SF............... Sosialistisk Folkepartiet [*Socialist People's Party*] [*Norway Political party*] (PPE)
SF............... Sound and Flash [*Military*]
SF............... Source and Fissionable [*Material*] [*Obsolete; see SS*] [*Nuclear energy*]
SF............... Source Factor [*Nuclear energy*] (NRCH)
SF............... Southern Forest Products Association
SF............... South Following [*Astronomy*]
SF............... Space Filler [*Philately*]
SF............... Space Flight [*A publication*]
SF............... Spacial Factor
SF............... Sparing Fitting [*Cargo battens*] [*Shipping*] (DS)
SF............... Special Facilities
SF............... Special Features (NITA)
SF............... Special Fixtures (MCD)
SF............... Special Forces [*Military*]
SF............... Special Fraction [*Typography*] (WDMC)
SF............... Spent Fuel [*Nuclear energy*] (NRCH)
SF............... Spinal Fluid [*Medicine*]
SF............... Spiritus Frumenti [*Whisky*] [*Pharmacy*] (ROG)
SF............... Splicing Factor [*Genetics*]
SF............... Spontaneous Fission [*Radioactivity*]
SF............... Sports Foundation (EA)
SF............... Spot Face
SF............... Sprocket Feed (ECII)
SF............... Spruce-Fast [*Forestry*]
SF............... Squadron or Flotilla Flag [*Navy British*]
SF............... Square Foot
SF............... Stable Factor [*Medicine*] (DMAA)
SF............... Stack Full (MHDI)
SF............... Stainless Steel Fastenings
SF............... Standard Form
SF............... Standard Frequency
SF............... Stanton Foundation [*Later, KCSF*] (EA)
SF............... Star Field (MCD)
SF............... Starlight Foundation (EA)
SF............... Startled Falcon [*Book written by Thomas Dunn English (1844)*]
SF............... State Forces [*India*] [*Army*]
SF............... Statement of Functions (NATG)
sF............... Statfarad [*Also, statF*] [*Unit of capacitance*]
SF............... Static Firing [*NASA*] (NASA)
S/F............... Statute of Frauds [*Business term*]
SF............... Sterile Females [*Genetics*]
SF............... Stifel Financial [*NYSE symbol*] (TTSB)
SF............... Stifel Financial Corp. [*NYSE symbol*] (SPSG)
SF............... Stock Fund (AFM)
SF............... Stopped-Flow [*Spectroscopy*]
S/F............... Store-and-Forward [*Data communications*]
SF............... Stowage Factor [*Shipping*]
SF............... Streptococcus faecilis [*Microbiology*]
SF............... Stress Formula
SF............... Stripping Film (DGA)
SF............... Structural Foam [*Plastics*] (DICI)
SF............... Structure Function
SF............... Subcontractor Furnished [*NASA*] (NASA)
SF............... Subfile (NITA)
SF............... Sub Finem [*Near the End*] [*Latin*]
SF............... Subframe
SF............... Substitute Fragment (NITA)
SF............... Success Factor
SF............... Successful Flight (MCD)
SF............... Su Favor [*Your Favor*] [*Spanish*]
SF............... Sufficient Funding (MCD)
SF............... Sugar Flotation [*Soil testing*]
SF............... Sugar-Free [*Pharmacy*]
SF............... Sulfation Factor [*of blood serum*]
SF............... Sun Factor (ADA)
SF............... Sunk Face [*Construction*]
SF............... Sunshine Foundation (EA)
SF............... Superfund [*Environmental Protection Agency*] (GFGA)
SF............... Supply Fan (AAG)
SF............... Surface Foot
SF............... Surfrider Foundation (EA)
SF............... Sustained Fire [*Military*] (INF)
SF............... Sustaining Fiber
Sf............... Svedberg Flotation Unit (AAMN)
SF............... Swedenborg Foundation (EA)
SF............... Swiss Franc [*Monetary unit*]
SF............... Symbral Foundation (EA)
SF............... Symptom-Free [*Medicine*] (DAVI)
SF............... Syndicat des Fonctionnaires [*Lao Civil Servants' Union*]
SF............... Synovial Fluid [*Medicine*]
SF1............... Shipfitter, First Class [*Navy*]
SF2............... Shipfitter, Second Class [*Navy*]
Sf3............... SAAB-Fairchild 340 [*Airplane code*]
SF3............... Shipfitter, Third Class [*Navy*]
SF3............... Society for the Furtherance and Study of Fantasy and Science Fiction (EA)
SF-4............... Shipping Fever [*An influenza serotype*]
SF-6............... Sulfur Hexafluoride [*Used in fluid-gas exchange*] [*Ophthalmology*] (DAVI)
SFA............... Aerotransportes Entre Rios SRL [*Argentina ICAO designator*] (FAAC)
SFA............... Sachs/Freeman Associates, Inc. [*Telecommunications service*] (TSSD)
SFA............... Sadr Foujdaree Adalat Reports [*India*] [*A publication*] (DLA)
SFA............... Saks Fifth Avenue [*Retail department store*]
SFA............... Saturated Fatty Acid [*Cardiology*] (DAVI)
SFA............... Scandinavian Fraternity of America (EA)
SFA............... Scientific-Atlanta [*NYSE symbol*] (TTSB)
SFA............... Scientific-Atlanta, Inc. [*NYSE symbol*] (SPSG)
SFA............... Scientific Film Association (IAA)
SFA............... Scottish Football Association (DI)
SFA............... Screw Focusing Adjustment [*Optical*] (ROG)
SFA............... Securities and Futures Authority [*Finance British*] (ECON)
SFA............... Segmented Flow Analysis
SFA............... Segment Frequency Algorithm
SFA............... Selected Financial Assistance [*British*] (DCTA)
SFA............... Semantic Feature Analysis (EDAC)
SFA............... Sempervivum Fanciers Association (EA)
SFA............... Sequential Functional Analysis (IAA)
SFA............... Service-Factor Amperes (MSA)
SFA............... Seven Falls [*Quebec*] [*Seismograph station code, US Geological Survey Closed*] (SEIS)
SFA............... Sfax [*Tunisia*] [*Airport symbol*] (OAG)
SFA............... Short Field Aircraft
SFA............... Show Folks of America (EA)
SFA............... Sigmund Freud Archives (EA)
SFA............... Simulated Flight - Automatic
SFA............... Single Failure Analysis [*Nuclear energy*] (NRCH)
SFA............... Single-Frequency Amplifier [*Electronics*] (ECII)
SFA............... Single Frequency Approach [*FAA*] (TAG)
SFA............... Slide Fastener Association [*Defunct*] (EA)
SFA............... Slow Flying Aircraft
SFA............... Small Farmers Association [*British*] (DBA)
SFA............... Snack Food Association (EA)
SFA............... Societe Francaise d'Acoustique [*French Society of Acoustics - FSA*] (EAIO)
SFA............... Society of Filipino Accountants (EA)
SFA............... Soil-Derived Fulvic Acid
SFA............... Solid Fuels Administration [*Terminated, 1954*]
SFA............... Soroptimist Federation of the Americas [*Later, Soroptimist International of theAmericas*] (EA)
SFA............... Southeastern Fabric Association (EA)
SFA............... Southeastern Fisheries Association (EA)
SFA............... Southern Freight Association
SFA............... Spatial Frequency Analyzer
SFA............... Special Forces Association (EA)
SFA............... Special Forces Auxiliary [*Military*]
SFA............... Special Foreign Activities [*Military*] (AABC)
SFA............... Speech Foundation of America (EA)
SFA............... Standard Fuel Assembly [*Nuclear energy*] (NRCH)
SFA............... Stimulated Fibrinolytic Activity [*Medicine*] (DMAA)
SFA............... Stopped-Flow Analyzer [*Chemical analysis*]
SFA............... Students for America (EA)
SFA............... Subcommittee on Frequency Allocations
SFA............... Sun Finder Assembly [*NASA*]
SFA............... Superficial Femoral Artery [*Anatomy*]
SFA............... Supplementary Failure Analysis [*NASA*] (KSC)

SFA .... Support Facility Annex [*Army*]
SFA .... Surface Fibroblast Antigen [*Cytochemistry*]
SFA .... Surface Force Apparatus [*Physical chemistry*]
SFA .... Surface Forces Apparatus [*For study of bilayers*] [*Physical chemistry*]
SFA .... Symphony Foundation of America (EA)
SFAA .... Society for Applied Anthropology (EA)
SFAA .... Society for French-American Affairs [*Defunct*] (EA)
SFAAP .... Sunflower Army Ammunition Plant (AABC)
SFAAW .... Stove, Furnace, and Allied Appliance Workers International Union of North America [*AFL-CIO*]
SFAC .... Solid Fuel Advisory Council [*British*] (DI)
SFAC .... Statement of Financial Accounting Concepts
SFACA .... Solid Fuel Advisory Council of America [*Defunct*] (EA)
SFACI .... Software Flight Article Configuration Inspection [*NASA*] (NASA)
SFAD .... Society of Federal Artists and Designers [*Later, FDC*] (EA)
SFADCO .... Shannon Free Airport Development Company (ACII)
SFADS .... San Francisco Air Defense Sector [*ADC*]
SFAF .... San Francisco AIDS Foundation (EA)
SFAHD .... Society of the Friends of Ancient and Historical Dubrovnik [*Croatia*] (EAIO)
SFAL .... Samuel Feltman Ammunition Laboratory [*Army*]
SFAL .... Stanley Airport [*Falkland Islands*] [*ICAO location identifier*] (ICLI)
SFAM .... SpeedFam International, Inc. [*NASDAQ symbol*] (SAG)
SFAM .... Speedfam Intl [*NASDAQ symbol*] (TTSB)
SF & FW .... Science Fiction and Fantasy Workshop (EA)
SF & S .... Supporting Facilities and Services
SF & T .... Sawyer, Finn & Thatcher [*Advertising agency*]
SFAOD .... Superficial-Femoral Artery Occlusive Disease [*Medicine*]
SFAP .... Single-Fiber Action Potential (DMAA)
SFAP .... Society for Folk Arts Preservation (EA)
SFA-PP .... Slovenian Farmers' Association - People's Party (EY)
SFAPS .... Space Flight Acceleration Profile Simulator [*NASA*]
SFAR .... Sound Fixing and Ranging
SFAR .... Special Federal Aviation Regulation [*FAA*]
SFAR .... Special Flight Area Rule [*Aviation*]
SFAR .... System Failure Analysis Report (IEEE)
SFAR-38 .... Special Federal Aviation Regulation 38 [*FAA*] (TAG)
SFARG .... SIOP [*Single Integrated Operations Plan*] Force Application Review Group (CINC)
SFARP .... Strike Fighter Advanced Readiness Program [*Navy*] (DOMA)
SFAS .... Safety Features Actuation Signal [*Nuclear energy*] (NRCH)
SFAS .... Self-Feeling Awareness Scale [*Psychology*] (EDAC)
SFAS .... Special Forces Assessment and Selection [*Military*] (INF)
SFAS .... Special Forces Association [*Fraternal group of discharged military personnel who returned to live in Saigon*] (VNW)
SFAS .... Statement of Financial Accounting Standards
SFAT .... Scott, Foresman Achievement Test (EDAC)
S F Austin St U ... Stephen F. Austin State University (GAGS)
SFAV .... Surrogate Fast Attack Vehicle [*Two-passenger wheeled vehicle*] (INF)
SFAW .... Solid Fuel Administration for War [*Terminated, 1947*] [*World War II*]
SFAW .... Stove, Furnace, and Allied Appliance Workers International Union of North America [*AFL-CIO*]
SFB .... Air Sofia [*Bulgaria*] [*ICAO designator*] (FAAC)
SFB .... Sanford, FL [*Location identifier FAA*] (FAAL)
SFB .... San Francisco [*California*] [*Seismograph station code, US Geological Survey Closed*] (SEIS)
SFB .... San Francisco Ballet
SFB .... Segmented Filamentous Bacteria
SFB .... Semiconductor Functional Block (IEEE)
SFB .... Sender Freies Berlin [*Radio network*] [*West Germany*]
SFB .... Sir Francis Bacon
SFB .... Society of Friendly Boilermakers [*A union*] [*British*]
SFB .... Society of Furnace Builders [*British*] (BI)
SFB .... Solid Fiberboard
SFB .... Solid-State Functional Block (IAA)
SFB .... Southwestern Freight Bureau, St. Louis MO [*STAC*]
SFB .... Spinning Form Block (MCD)
SFB .... Standard Federal Bank [*NYSE symbol*] (SPSG)
SFB .... Standard Fedl Bancorp'n [*NYSE symbol*] (TTSB)
SFB .... Structural Feedback
SFBA .... Steamship Freight Brokers Association
SFBARTD .... San Francisco Bay Area Rapid Transit District
SFBCS .... Special Forces Burst Communications Systems [*Army*] (RDA)
SFBF .... Standard Forms Bureau Form [*Insurance*] (IIA)
SFBI .... Self-Filling Blind Loop (DMAA)
SFBI .... Spent Fuel Building Isolation [*Nuclear energy*] (NRCH)
SFBL .... Self-Filling Blind Loop [*Gastroenterology*]
SFBM .... Security Bancorp [*Formerly, Security Federal Savings Bank*] [*NASDAQ symbol*] (NQ)
SFBNS .... San Francisco Bay Naval Shipyard
SFBNSY .... San Francisco Bay Naval Shipyard (DNAB)
SFBP .... Siberian Flood Basalt Province [*Geology*]
SFBRI .... Science Fiction Book Review Index 1923-1973 [*A publication*]
SFC .... Chief Shipfitter [*Navy rating*]
SFC .... Colorado Springs, CO [*Location identifier FAA*] (FAAL)
SFC .... Saint Francis College [*Indiana; Maine; New York; Pennsylvania; Wisconsin*]
SFC .... San Francisco [*California*] [*Seismograph station code, US Geological Survey*] (SEIS)
SFC .... S-Band Frequency Converter
SFC .... School Facilities Council of Architecture, Education, and Industry [*Later, ASBO*] (EA)
SFC .... Scottish Film Council
SFC .... Sculptured Flexible Circuit [*Electronics*]
SFC .... Sectored File Channel (NITA)
SFC .... Sectored File Controller
SFC .... Securities and Futures Commission [*Hong Kong*]
SFC .... Selection Filter Control (MCD)
SFC .... Selector File Channel
SFC .... Sequential Function Chart (ACII)
SFC .... Sergeant First Class
SFC .... Serial Frame Camera (CAAL)
SFC .... Shipborne Fighter Control [*Navy*] (CAAL)
SFC .... Ship Fire Control (AAG)
SFC .... Shoes Fan Club (EA)
SFC .... Short Form Catalog (IAA)
SFC .... Shuswap Flight Centre Ltd. [*Canada ICAO designator*] (FAAC)
SFC .... Sight Fire Control
SFC .... Sioux Falls College [*South Dakota*]
SFC .... Sis Fan Club [*Later, RFC*] (EA)
SFC .... Societe Francaise de Chimie [*French Chemical Society - FCS*] (EAIO)
SFC .... Societe Frederic Chopin [*International Frederic Chopin Foundation*] (EAIO)
SfC .... Society for Calligraphy (EA)
SFC .... Society of Flavor Chemists (EA)
sfc .... Society of the Brothers of Charity (TOCD)
SFC .... Solar Forecast [*Air Force*] (IAA)
SFC .... Solar Forecast Center [*Air Force*] (IEEE)
SFC .... Solid Fat Content [*Food analysis*]
SFC .... Soluble Fibrin-Fibrinogen Complex [*Hematology*]
SFC .... Southern Pacific Funding Corp. [*NYSE symbol*] (SAG)
SFC .... Space Flight Center [*NASA*]
SFC .... Space Forecast Center [*Air Force*] (GFGA)
SFC .... Special Flight Charts [*Air Force*]
SFC .... Special Foreign Currency [*US counterpart funds*]
SFC .... Specific Fuel Consumption
SFC .... Spinal Fluid Count [*Medicine*]
SFC .... Sports Fans Connection [*A publication*]
SFC .... Sports Federation of Canada (EAIO)
SFC .... Star Field Camera [*NASA*]
SFC .... Starfleet Command (EA)
SFC .... State Fund Chairmen [*Red Cross*]
SFC .... St. Francis Center (EA)
SFC .... Subcritical Fluid Chromatography
SFC .... Sub-Functional Code (DNAB)
SFC .... Supercritical Fluid Chromatography
SFC .... Superior Fine Cognac
SFC .... Surefire Fan Club [*Defunct*] (EA)
SFC .... Surface (AFM)
SFC .... Switching Filter Connector
SFC .... Sylvia Fan Club (EA)
SFC .... Synchronized Framing Camera
SFC .... Synthetic Fuels Corp. [*Sponsored by the federal government*]
SFCB .... Services de Formation et de Consultation aux Bandes [*Department of Indian and Inuit Affairs*] [*Canada*]
SFCB .... Shipfitter, Construction Battalion [*Navy*]
SFCBB .... Shipfitter, Construction Battalion, Blacksmith [*Navy*]
SFCBM .... Shipfitter, Construction Battalion, Mechanical Draftsman [*Navy*]
SFCBP .... Shipfitter, Construction Battalion, Pipe Fitter and Plumber [*Navy*]
SFCBR .... Shipfitter, Construction Battalion, Rigger [*Navy*]
SFCBS .... Shipfitter, Construction Battalion, Steelworker [*Navy*]
SFCBW .... Shipfitter, Construction Battalion, Welder [*Navy*]
SFCC .... Sisters for a Christian Community
SFCD .... Stopped-Flow Circular Dichroism [*Spectroscopy*]
SFCE .... Surface
SFCES .... Survivable Flight Control Electronic Set [*Aviation*] (PDAA)
SFCH .... Society of Freight Car Historians (EA)
SF Chr .... Science Fiction Chronicle [*A publication*] (BRI)
SFCI .... Spirit of the Future Creative Institute [*Commercial firm*] (EA)
SFCM .... Master Chief Shipfitter [*Later, HTCM*] [*Navy rating*]
SFCM .... Slurry-Fed Ceramic Matter [*Nuclear energy*] (NUCP)
SFCMP .... Self-Rising Flour and Corn Meal Program [*Later, HBA*] (EA)
SFCO .... Safety Fund [*NASDAQ symbol*] (TTSB)
SFCO .... Special Forces Co. [*Military*] (CINC)
SFCP .... Shore Fire Control Party [*Military*]
SFCP .... Special Foreign Currency Program [*National Institute of Standards and Technology*]
SFCP .... Synthetic Fuels Commercialization Program [*Also, SCP*] [*Energy Resources Council*]
SFCPTNG .... Shore Fire Control Party Training [*Navy*] (NVT)
SFCR .... Storage Facility Control Room [*Nuclear energy*] (NRCH)
SFCRS .... State-Federal Crop Reporting Service
SFCS .... Saint Fidelis College and Seminary [*Pennsylvania*]
SFCS .... Secondary Flow Control System [*Nuclear energy*] (NRCH)
SFCS .... Senior Chief Shipfitter [*Later, HTCS*] [*Navy rating*]
SFCS .... Slats and Flaps Control System [*Aerospace technology*] (EECA)
SFCS .... Spent Fuel Cooling System [*Nuclear energy*] (NRCH)
SFCS .... Surveyor Flight Control Section
SFCS .... Survivable Flight Control System [*Military*]
SFCSI .... Special Foreign Currency Science Information [*Program*] [*National Science Foundation*]
SFCSIP .... Special Foreign Currency Science Information Program [*National Science Foundation*]
SFCSR .... Storage Facility Cable Spreading Room [*Nuclear energy*] (NRCH)
SFCT .... State Fire Commission of Tasmania [*Australia*]
SFCU .... State and Function Control Unit [*Computer science*] (MHDI)
SFCV .... State Film Centre of Victoria [*Australia*]
SFCW .... San Francisco College for Women [*California*]

SFCW........ Search for Critical Weakness [*Aerospace*] (AAG)
SFCW........ Sweep Frequency, Continuous Wave
SFCW(I)........ Swept Frequency Continuous Wave Illumination (MCD)
SFD........ Florence-Darlington Technical College Library, Florence, SC [*OCLC symbol*] (OCLC)
SFD........ San Fernando [*Venezuela*] [*Airport symbol*] (OAG)
SFD........ Severe Fuel Damage (GAAI)
SFD........ Short Food Drape [*Dietetics*] (DAVI)
SFD........ Signal Flow Diagram (MCD)
SFD........ Simple Formattable Document [*Telecommunications*] (OSI)
SFD........ Single Family Detached [*Real estate terminology*] (EMRF)
SFD........ Single Family Dwelling [*Economics*]
SFD........ Skin-Film Distance [*Medicine*] (MAE)
SFD........ Small-for-Dates [*Medicine*] (MEDA)
SFD........ Smith's Food & Drug'B' [*NYSE symbol*] (TTSB)
SFD........ Smith's Food & Drug Centers [*NYSE symbol*] (SPSG)
SFD........ Society of Film Distributors [*British*]
SFD........ Software Functional Description [*Computer science*] (MHDI)
SFD........ Solar Flux Density
SFD........ Source-to-Film Distance [*Radiology*]
SFD........ Springfield [*Diocesan abbreviation*] [*Illinois*] (TOCD)
SFD........ Start Frame Delimiter (TNIG)
SFD........ Sudden Frequency Deviation
SFD........ Suore Francescane di Dillingen [*Sisters of St. Francis of Dillingen - SSFD*] [*Italy*] (EAIO)
SFD........ Supercritical Fluid Desorption [*Chemical engineering*]
SFD........ Sydney Fire District [*Australia*]
SFD........ Symbolic File Directory [*Computer science*] (HGAA)
SFD........ Sympathetic Firing Device [*Military*] (CAAL)
SFD........ System Functional Diagram [*or Drawing*] (KSC)
SFD........ System Function Description (IEEE)
SFD........ Systems Flexowriter Double Case
SFDA........ Sale of Food and Drugs Act [*British*]
SFDA........ Shakey's Franchised Dealers Association (EA)
SFDA........ Special Forces Direct Action [*Army*]
SFDA........ Sulfofluorescein Diacetate [*Biological stain*]
SFDALGOL........ System Function Description Algorithmic Language (IAA)
SFDE........ Staff and Faculty Development Elements
SFDI........ Solar Facility Design Integration (MCD)
SFDip........ Society of Floristry Diploma [*British*] (DI)
SFDLR........ Stock Funding Depot - Level Repairables [*Army*]
SFDP........ Societe Francophone de Primatologie [*Francophone Primatological Society - FPS*] [*France*] (EAIO)
SFDP........ Software/Firmware Development Plan
SFDR........ Single-Feeder
SFDR........ Standard Flight Data Recorder
SFDS........ Shipboard Fire Detection System (DWSG)
SFDS........ Smithfield Foods [*NASDAQ symbol*] (TTSB)
SFDS........ Smithfield Foods, Inc. [*NASDAQ symbol*] (NQ)
SFDS........ Standby Fighter Director Ship [*Navy*]
SFDS........ Strike Force Data System (NVT)
SFDS........ System Functional Design Specification (MCD)
SFDT........ Signal Format Development Team [*France*]
SFDT........ Site Format Dump Tape (MCD)
SFDW........ Special Friends of Dottie West (EA)
SFE........ Safeguard Scientifics [*NYSE symbol*] (TTSB)
SFE........ Safeguard Scientifics, Inc. [*NYSE symbol*] (SPSG)
SFE........ Santa Fe [*Diocesan abbreviation*] [*New Mexico*] (TOCD)
SFE........ Scale Factor Error (KSC)
SFE........ Secondary Feedback Element (IAA)
SFE........ Seismic Feature Extraction (MCD)
SFE........ Seller-Furnished Equipment (MCD)
SFE........ Slipped Femoral Epiphysis [*Medicine*] (DMAA)
SFE........ Smart Front End
SFE........ Societe Financiere Europeenne
SFE........ Society of Financial Examiners (EA)
SFE........ Society of Fire Engineers
SFE........ Solar Flare Effect [*Physics*]
SFE........ Solid Fuel Engine
SFE........ Solution [*or Solvent*] Free Energy [*Physical chemistry*]
SFE........ Soviet Far East (FEA)
SFE........ Space Frequency Equivalence (MCD)
SFE........ Special Furnished Equipment (MCD)
SFE........ Stacking Fault Energy [*Alloy*]
SFE........ Staged Field Experiment [*Gas production*]
SFE........ Student-Faculty Evaluation
SFE........ Students in Free Enterprise (EA)
SFE........ Supercritical Fluid Extraction [*Also, SCFE*] [*Chemical engineering*]
SFE........ Surface-Free Energy
SFE........ Surf Inlet Mines [*Vancouver Stock Exchange symbol*]
SFE........ Synthetic Fermented Egg [*Animal repellent*]
SFEA........ Scottish Further Education Association [*British*]
SFEA........ Space and Flight Equipment Association (IAA)
SFEA........ Squib Fuse Electrical Assembly (KSC)
SFEA........ Survival [*formerly, Space*] and Flight Equipment Association [*Later, SAFE Association*]
SFEC........ Standard Facility Equipment Card [*Electronics*]
SFED........ SFS Bancorp [*NASDAQ symbol*] (TTSB)
SFeEnTr........ Santa Fe Energy Trust [*Associated Press*] (SAG)
SFEF........ Santa Fe Financial [*NASDAQ symbol*] (TTSB)
SFEF........ Santa Fe Financial Corp. [*NASDAQ symbol*] (SAG)
SFeGam........ Santa Fe Gaming Corp. [*Associated Press*] (SAG)
SFEL........ Standard Facility Equipment List [*Electronics*]
SFEM........ Segner's Fortified Edd Meat [*Growth medium for phage*]
SFEM........ Southern Farm Equipment Manufacturers (EA)
SFEMG........ Single Fiber Electromyography [*Neurophysiology*]
SFENA........ Societe Francaise d'Equipements pour la Navigation Aerienne (MCD)
SFePGld........ Santa Fe Pacific Gold Corp. [*Associated Press*] (SAG)
SFePP........ Santa Fe Pacific Pipeline Partners Ltd. [*Associated Press*] (SAG)
SFER........ Santa Fe Energy Resources [*Associated Press*] (SAG)
SFER........ Siata/Fiat 8V Register (EA)
SFERC........ San Francisco Energy Research Center [*Energy Research and Development Administration*]
SFERICS........ Atmospherics [*NWS*] (FAAC)
SFERT........ Spinning Satellite for Electric Rocket Test (IAA)
SFERT........ Systeme Fundamental Europeen de Reference pour la Transmission Telephonique [*European master telephone reference system*]
SFES........ Small Firms Employment Subsidy (MHDB)
SFET........ Surface Field Effect Transistor (IAA)
SFEX........ Solar Flare X-Ray Polarimeter (NASA)
SFF........ Santa Fe Energy Tr 'SPERs' [*NYSE symbol*] (TTSB)
SFF........ Santa Fe Energy Trust Co. [*NYSE symbol*] (SAG)
SF/F........ Science Fiction and Fantasy [*Literary genre*]
SFF........ Science Fiction Foundation (EA)
SFF........ Sea Frontier Force [*Navy*]
SFF........ Self-Forging Fragment [*Warhead*] (MCD)
SFF........ Senior Firefighter [*Australia*]
SFF........ Sheffield [*Tasmania*] [*Seismograph station code, US Geological Survey*] (SEIS)
SFF........ Silicone Rubber-Insulated Fixture Wire, Flexible Stranding (IAA)
SFF........ Site Field Force [*Army*] (AABC)
SFF........ Slocan Forest Products Ltd. [*Toronto Stock Exchange symbol Vancouver Stock Exchange symbol*]
SFF........ Slovene Franciscan Fathers (EA)
SFF........ Small Formation Flyer (SSD)
SFF........ Solar Forecast Facility [*Air Force*] (MCD)
SFF........ Solid Freeform Fabrication [*Metallurgy*]
SFF........ Spiritual Frontiers Fellowship [*Later, SFFI*] (EA)
SFF........ Spokane, WA [*Location identifier FAA*] (FAAL)
SFF........ Standard File Format
SFF........ Step Family Foundation (EA)
SFF........ Supplementary Financing Facility [*International Monetary Fund*]
SFFA........ Fireman Apprentice, Shipfitter [*Navy rating*]
SFFA........ Serum Free Fatty Acid [*Medicine*] (DMAA)
SFFAS........ Superfund Financial Assessment System [*Environmental Protection Agency*] (GFGA)
SFFB........ Southern Financial Bancorp [*NASDAQ symbol*] (SAG)
SFFB........ Southern Financial Federal Savings Bank [*NASDAQ symbol*] (SAG)
SFFB........ Southern Finl Bancorp [*NASDAQ symbol*] (TTSB)
SFFC........ Scottish Federation of Fishermen's Co-Operatives (DBA)
SFFC........ StateFed Financial [*NASDAQ symbol*] (TTSB)
SFFC........ Statefed Financial Corp. [*NASDAQ symbol*] (SAG)
SFFD........ SFFed Corp. [*Formerly, San Francisco Federal Savings & Loan Association*] [*NASDAQ symbol*] (SPSG)
SFFed........ SFFED Corp. [*Associated Press*] (SAG)
SFFF........ Scandinavian Association of Zone-Therapeutists [*Denmark*] (EAIO)
SFFF........ Sedimentation Field Flow Fractionation [*For separation of colloids*]
SFFF........ Summary Format of Family Functioning
SFFI........ Spiritual Frontiers Fellowship International (EA)
SF/FIA........ Stock Fund/Financial Inventory Accounting
SFFMP........ State/Federal Fisheries Management Program [*National Marine Fisheries Service*]
SFFN........ Fireman, Shipfitter, Striker [*Navy rating*]
SFFNC........ Society of the Founders and Friends of Norwich, Connecticut (EA)
SFFS........ Satellite Frost Forecast System [*Department of Agriculture*]
SFFS........ Save the Flags of Fort Sumter [*Defunct*] (EA)
SFFT........ Superconducting Flux-Flow Transistor [*Physics*]
SFFUR........ Safety and Flight Failure/Unsatisfactory Report
SFFV........ Spleen Focus Formation Virus
s-fg--........ French Guiana [*MARC geographic area code Library of Congress*] (LCCP)
SFG........ Screen Format Generator (IAA)
SFG........ Serial Publications of Foreign Governments [*A bibliographic publication*]
SFG........ Signal Flow Graph
SFG........ Signal Frequency Generator [*Telecommunications*] (OA)
SFG........ South Pacific Gold [*Vancouver Stock Exchange symbol*]
SFG........ Special Forces Group [*Military*]
SFG........ Staircase Function Generator
SFG........ St. Maarten [*Netherlands Antilles*] [*Airport symbol*] (OAG)
SFG........ Subglottic Foreign Body [*Medicine*] (DMAA)
SFG........ Sudflug Suddeutsche Fluggesellschaft MbH [*Germany ICAO designator*] (FAAC)
SFG........ Sum Frequency Generation
SFGA........ Single Floating-Gate Amplifier [*Electronics*] (PDAA)
SFGA........ Steel Fork Grinders' Association [*A union*] [*British*]
SFGD........ Safeguard (AABC)
SFGD........ Safeguard Health Enterpr [*NASDAQ symbol*] (TTSB)
SFGD........ Safeguard Health Enterprises, Inc. [*NASDAQ symbol*] (NQ)
SFGD........ Shell Flue Gas Desulfurization [*Air pollution control*]
SfgdSc........ Safeguard Scientifics, Inc. [*Associated Press*] (SAG)
SFGE........ San Francisco Grain Exchange [*Defunct*] (EA)
SFGEP........ Space Flight Ground Environment Panel [*NASA*] (KSC)
SFGF........ Shope Fibroma Growth Factor [*Biochemistry*]
SFGL........ Safety Glass [*Technical drawings*]
SFGS........ Southwestern Federation of Geological Societies
SFH........ Simulated Flight Hour (MCD)
SFH........ Slow Frequency Hopping (MCD)
SFH........ Standard Fading Hour [*National Institute of Standards and Technology*]

SFH Super Flux Harness
SFHA Scottish Federation of Housing Associations (DBA)
SFHA Special Flood Hazard Area [*Information service or system*] (EMRF)
SFHb Stroma-Free Hemoglobin [*Hematology*]
SFHC Society of Folk Harpers and Craftsmen (EA)
SFHEA Scottish Further and Higher Education Association (DBA)
SFHF Society of the Friends of the Holy Father
SF/HGF Scatter Factor Hepatocyte Growth Factor [*Biochemistry*]
SFH-P Stroma-Free Hemoglobin Pyridoxylated [*Clinical chemistry*]
SFHR Society for Film History Research [*British*] (BI)
SFHS Society for French Historical Studies (EA)
SFI Savannah Foods & Ind [*NYSE symbol*] (TTSB)
SFI Savannah Foods & Industries, Inc. [*NYSE symbol*] (SPSG)
SFI Sequential Fuel Injection [*Automotive engineering*]
SFI Sexual Function Index [*Medicine*] (DMAA)
SFI SFI Foundation (EA)
SFI Shop-Fixed Interface (DNAB)
SFI Sindacato Ferrovieri Italiani [*Union of Italian Railroad Workers*]
SFI Sky Freighters NV [*Belgium ICAO designator*] (FAAC)
SFI Small Flow Indicator
SFI Social Function Index [*Medicine*] (DMAA)
SFI Societe Financiere Internationale [*International Finance Society*]
SFI Society of Friends of Icons [*Germany*] (EAIO)
SFI Solid Fat Index [*Food analysis*]
SFI Southern Forest Institute [*Defunct*] (EA)
SFI Space Flight Instrumentation (AAG)
SFI Sport Fishing Institute (EA)
SFI Sports Fishing Initiative [*Marine science*] (OSRA)
SFI Sports Fishing Initiative (USDC)
SFI Starfire Resources Ltd. [*Vancouver Stock Exchange symbol*]
SFI Step Function Input
SFI Strategic Facilities Initiative [*Oak Ridge National Laboratory*]
SFI Support for Industry (NITA)
SFI Synovial Fluid Lymphocyte [*Medicine*] (DMAA)
SFIA School Fees Insurance Agency Ltd. [*British*]
SFIA Sea Fish Industry Authority [*British*]
SFIB Southern Freight Inspection Bureau
SFIC San Francisco Information Center [*Army Air Warning Service*]
SFIC Societe et Federation Internationale de Cardiologie [*International Society and Federation of Cardiology*] [*Switzerland*] (EAIO)
SFICEC State-Federal Information Clearinghouse for Exceptional Children
SFID Section Francaise de l'Internationale Ouvriere [*French Section of the Workers International*]
SFID Self-floating Integrated Deck (PDAA)
SFID Set Format Identifier
SFID Supplementary Flight Information Documentation (IAA)
SFIMR Stock Fund Inventory Management Record [*Military*] (AFIT)
S-FIN Semi-Finished [*Automotive engineering*]
SFIN Statewide Financial [*NASDAQ symbol*] (TTSB)
SFIN Statewide Financial Corp. [*NASDAQ symbol*] (SAG)
SFInstE Senior Fellow of the Institute of Energy [*British*] (DBQ)
SFInstF Senior Fellow of the Institute of Fuel [*British*] (DI)
SFIO Section Francaise de l'Internationale Ouvriere [*French Socialist Party*]
SFIR Specific Force Integrating Receiver [*Air Force*]
SFIREG State FIFRA [*Federal Insecticide, Fungicide, and Rodenticide Act*] Issues Research and Evaluation Group [*Environmental Protection Agency*] (EGAO)
SFIS Selective Fisheries Information Service (IID)
SFIT Simplified Fault Isolation Test (MCD)
SFIT Standard Family Interaction Test [*Psychology*]
SFIT Swiss Federal Institute of Technology (IAA)
SFJ Sondre Stromfjord [*Greenland*] [*Airport symbol*] (OAG)
SFJ Standforward Jamming [*Military*] (LAIN)
SFJ Swept Frequency Jamming
SFK Safia [*Papua*] [*Airport symbol*] (AD)
SFK Special Function Key [*Calculators*]
SFK Stonyfork, PA [*Location identifier FAA*] (FAAL)
SFL Salt Flat, TX [*Location identifier FAA*] (FAAL)
SFL San Felipe [*California*] [*Seismograph station code, US Geological Survey*] (SEIS)
SFL Santa Fe Pacific Pipeline Ltd. [*NYSE symbol*] (SPSG)
SFL Santa Fe Pac Pipeline [*NYSE symbol*] (TTSB)
SFL Sao Filipe [*Cape Verde Islands*] [*Airport symbol*] (OAG)
SFL Scholarships, Fellowships, and Loans [*A publication*]
SFL Scientists for Life (EA)
SFL Scottish Football League (DBA)
SFL Secondary Freon Loop (NASA)
SFL Sequence Flash Lights [*FAA*]
SFL Sexual Freedom League (EA)
SFL Short Flashing Light [*Navigation signal*]
SFL Silver Falls Resources [*Vancouver Stock Exchange symbol*]
SFL Sizing Float Level
SFL Slip Full Load (IAA)
SFL Society of Federal Linguists (EA)
SFL Southflight Aviation Ltd. [*New Zealand*] [*ICAO designator*] (FAAC)
SFL Substrate Fed Logic
SFL Surinam Florin [*Monetary unit in Surinam*]
SFL Symbolic Flowchart Language (IAA)
SFLC San Francisco Laser Center [*Research center*] (RCD)
SFLD Seafield Capital Corp. [*NASDAQ symbol*] (SPSG)
SFLIS Sloga Fraternal Life Insurance Society [*Milwaukee, WI*] (EA)
SFLJ San Francisco Law Journal [*A publication*] (DLA)
SFLOC Synopic Reporting of the Location of Sources of Atmospherics [*Aviation*] (DA)
SFLRP Society of Federal Labor Relations Professionals (EA)
SFLS Semiflush
SFLS Stress Fiber-Like Structure [*Biology*]
SFLX Shoulder Flexion [*Sports medicine*]
SFLX Smartflex Systems [*NASDAQ symbol*] (SAG)
SFM Francis Marion College, Florence, SC [*OCLC symbol*] (OCLC)
SFM Sanford, ME [*Location identifier FAA*] (FAAL)
SFM San Francisco - Josephine D. Randall Junior Museum [*California*] [*Seismograph station code, US Geological Survey*] (SEIS)
SFM San Francisco Movers Tariff Bureau, San Francisco CA [*STAC*]
SFM Scanning Force Microscope
SFM Scanning Force Mode [*Microscopy*]
sfm Scarboro Foreign Missions (TOCD)
SFM Scarboro Foreign Missions (TOCD)
SFM Secure File Manager [*Telecommunications*] (OSI)
SFM Serum Free Medium
SFM SFM Corp. [*Later, EXX, Inc.*] [*AMEX symbol*] (SPSG)
sfm Sfumato (VRA)
SFM Shepherds Fold Ministries (EA)
SFM Shipfitter, Metalsmith [*Navy*]
SFM Signal Flow Matrix (IAA)
SFM Simulated Flight - Manual
SFM Simulated Flow Method
SFM Sinai Field Mission [*US government*]
SFM Sinusoidal Frequency Modulation [*Physics*]
SFM Ski-Free Marine [*Vancouver Stock Exchange symbol*]
SFM Society for Foodservice Management (EA)
SFM Society for the Family of Man (EA)
SFM Spectrophotofluorometer
SFM Split Field Motor (IAA)
SFM Storage Facility Manual (MCD)
SFM Surface Feet per Minute
SFM Swept Frequency Modulation
SFM Switching Mode Frequency Multipliers
SFMA Franciscan Missionary Sisters of Assisi (TOCD)
SFMA School Furniture Manufacturers' Association [*British*] (BI)
SFMA Scottish Furniture Manufacturers Association (DBA)
SFMA Soda Fountain Manufacturers Association
SFMA Southern Furniture Manufacturers Association [*Later, AFMA*] (EA)
SFMA Steel Fork Makers' Association [*A union*] [*British*]
SFMA Subscription Fulfillment Managers Association [*Later, FMA*] (EA)
SFMANSW Stock Feed Manufacturers' Association of New South Wales [*Australia*]
SFMAQ Stock Feed Manufacturers' Association of Queensland [*Australia*]
SFMASA Stock Feed Manufacturers' Association of South Australia
SFMAV Stock Feed Manufacturers' Association of Victoria [*Australia*]
SFMAWA Stock Feed Manufacturers' Association of Western Australia
SFME Storable Fluid Management Experiment (NASA)
SFMF Scottish Fish Merchants Federation (DBA)
SFMF Student Foreign Missions Fellowship [*Later, IVMF*] (EA)
SFMG Franciscan Missionary Sisters of Assisi [*Roman Catholic religious order*]
SFMHS San Francisco Men's Health Study [*Aids study*]
SFMI Soft Fibre Manufacturers' Institute [*Defunct*] (EA)
SFMJF Satoko and Franz M. Joseph Foundation (EA)
SFML Standard Facility Material List [*Electronics*]
SFMN Slow Flexor Motoneuron [*Neurology*]
SFMN Superficial Flexor Motoneuron [*Neurology*]
SFMOMA San Francisco Museum of Modern Art
SFMP Surplus Facilities Management Program [*Department of Energy*]
SFMR Stepped-Frequency Microwave Radiometer [*For measuring rain rate and wind speed*]
SFMS Shipwrecked Fishermen and Mariners Royal Benevolent Society [*British*] (BI)
SFMT Scottish Federation of Merchant Tailors (DBA)
SFMTA Scottish Federation of Meat Traders Associations (DBA)
SF-MX Stopped-Flow Multimixing Spectroflourimeter
SFN Grupo Financiero Serfin [*NYSE symbol*] (SPSG)
SFN Grupo Financiero Serfin ADS [*NYSE symbol*] (TTSB)
SFN Safiran Airlines [*Iran*] [*ICAO designator*] (FAAC)
SFN San Francisco Naval Shipyard
SFN Santa Fe [*Argentina*] [*Airport symbol*] (OAG)
SFN Seattle First National Bank, Seattle, WA [*OCLC symbol*] (OCLC)
SFN See Footnote (ROG)
SFN Ships and Facilities, Navy (NG)
SFN Stefan Resources, Inc. [*Vancouver Stock Exchange symbol*]
SFN Strategic Facsimile Network (IAA)
SFNA Stabilized Fuming Nitric Acid
SFNB Security First Network Bank [*NASDAQ symbol*] (TTSB)
SFNB Security First Network Bank [*NASDAQ symbol*] (SAG)
SFNC Simmons First National Corp. [*Pine Bluff, AK*] [*NASDAQ symbol*] (NQ)
SFNC Society of the Founders of Norwich, Connecticut (EA)
SFNCA Simmons First Natl [*NASDAQ symbol*] (TTSB)
SFNCTU Swiss Federation of National-Christian Trade Unions
SFNFC Sally Field National Fan Club (EA)
SFNG Safety Based Negative (VRA)
SFNS San Francisco Naval Shipyard (DNAB)
SFNSY San Francisco Naval Shipyard
SFO Defense Solid Fuels Order [*United States*] [*A publication*] (DLA)
SFO San Fernando Observatory [*Research center*] (RCD)
SFO San Francisco/Oakland [*California*] [*Airport symbol*] (OAG)
SFO Santa Fe Opera [*New Mexico*]
SFO Satellite Field Office [*Marine science*] (OSRA)
SFO Sector Frequency Only [*Military*] (CAAL)

SFO............. Secular Franciscan Order [*Formerly, TOSF*] [*Roman Catholic religious order*]
SFO............. Senior Flag Officer [*British military*] (DMA)
SFO............. Serious Fraud Office [*Proposed*] [*British government*]
SFO............. Service Fuel Oil
SFO............. SFO [*San Francisco and Oakland*] Helicopter Airlines, Inc. [*Air carrier designation symbol*]
SFO............. Simulated Flame Out [*Aviation*]
SFO............. Single-Frequency Oscillator (IDOE)
SFO............. Single-Frequency Outlet
SFO............. Solicitation for Offers [*A publication*] (AAGC)
SFO............. Space Flight Operations [*NASA*]
SFO............. Spot Face Other Side [*Technical drawings*] (MSA)
SFO............. Standard-Frequency Oscillator (IDOE)
SFO............. Sterling Forest [*New York*] [*Seismograph station code, US Geological Survey*] (SEIS)
SFO............. Strathfield Oil & Gas Ltd. [*Toronto Stock Exchange symbol*]
SFO............. Subfornical Organ [*Brain anatomy*]
SFO............. Submarine Fog Oscillator [*Maps and charts*]
SFO............. Superannuation Funds Office [*Inland Revenue*] [*British*]
SFOB........... Special Forces Operational Base [*Army*]
SFOBB......... San Francisco-Oakland Bay Bridge
SFOC........... Space Flight Operations Complex [*NASA*]
SFOD........... San Francisco Ordnance District [*Military*]
SFOD........... Space Flight Operations Director [*NASA*]
SFOD........... Special Forces Operational Detachment [*Army*] (AABC)
SFOF........... Space Flight Operations Facility [*NASA*]
SFOLDS....... Ship Form Online Design System [*British Ship Research Association*] [*Software package*] (NCC)
SFOM........... Shuttle Flight Operations Manual [*NASA*] (MCD)
SFOM........... Space Flight Operations Memorandum [*NASA*]
SFOM........... Special Furnish Off Machine [*Paper*] (DGA)
SFOM........... Stabilized Flight Operations Manual
SFOMS......... Ships Force Overhaul Management Systems [*Navy*]
SFOO........... San Francisco Operations Office [*Energy Research and Development Administration*]
SFOP........... Safety Operating Procedure [*Kennedy Space Center*] [*NASA*] (NASA)
SFOP........... Space Flight Operations Plan [*NASA*]
Sforz........... Sforzando [*With Additional Accent*] [*Music*]
SFOSRC....... South Florida Oil Spill Research Center [*Marine science*] (OSRA)
SFOSRC....... South Florida Oil Spill Research Center (USDC)
SFP............. Franciscan Sisters of the Poor [*Roman Catholic religious order*]
SFP............. San Felipe [*Mexico*] [*Seismograph station code, US Geological Survey*] (SEIS)
SFP............. Santa Fe Public Library, Santa Fe, NM [*OCLC symbol*] (OCLC)
SFP............. Screen Filtration Pressure [*Clinical chemistry*] (AAMN)
SFP............. Security Filter Processor
SFP............. Sforzato Piano [*Sudden change from forte to piano*] [*Music*] (ROG)
SFP............. Sherbrooke Forest Park [*Victoria, Australia*] [*Airport symbol*] (AD)
SFP............. Shipfitter, Pipefitter [*Navy*]
SFP............. Shungwayah Freedom Party [*Kenya*]
SFP............. Simultaneous Foveal Perception [*Ophthalmology*]
SFP............. Single Failure Point [*NASA*] (MCD)
SFP............. Sintered Ferrous Part
SFP............. Skeleton Flight Plan
SFP............. Slack Frame Program
SFP............. Slow Filling Period [*Cardiology*]
SFP............. Solar Flare Proton
SFP............. Spartan-Furnished Property [*Missiles*] (MCD)
SFP............. Special Film Project
SFP............. Special Furnished Property (MCD)
SFP............. Spent Fuel Pit [*Nuclear energy*] (NRCH)
SFP............. Spent Fuel Pool [*Nuclear energy*] (NRCH)
SFP............. Spinal Fluid Pressure [*Medicine*]
SFP............. Stopped Flow Pressure
SFP............. Straight Fixed Price
SFP............. Strike for Peace [*Later, WDFP*] (EA)
SFP............. Students for Peace (EA)
SFP............. Summary Financial Program
SFP............. Summary Flight Plan (MCD)
SFP............. Super Flat Pack
SFP............. Surface Fixed Priority
SFP............. Sustainer Firing Package
SFP............. Svenska Folkpartiet [*Swedish People's Party*] [*Finland Political party*] (PPE)
SFPA........... Science Fiction Poetry Association (EA)
SFPA........... Single Failure Point Analysis [*NASA*] (KSC)
SFPA........... Southern Forest Products Association (EA)
SFPA........... Structural Fire Protection Association [*British*]
SFP-ANGS... Standardization Field Panel for Artillery and Naval Gunfire Support [*Army*] (AABC)
SFPAVS....... Spent Fuel Pool Area Ventilation System [*Nuclear energy*] (NRCH)
SFPC........... Society of Family Practitioner Committees [*British*] (DBA)
SFPCCS....... Spent Fuel Pool Cooling and Cleanup System [*Nuclear energy*] (NRCH)
SFPCS......... Spent Fuel Pool Cooling System [*Nuclear energy*] (NRCH)
SFPE........... San Francisco Port of Embarkation [*Military*]
SFPE........... Society of Fire Protection Engineers (EA)
SFPF........... Special Federal Project Funds [*Medicaid Program*] (GFGA)
SFPL........... San Francisco Public Library [*California*]
SFPM........... Surface Feet per Minute
SFPO........... Senior Functional Policy Official (AAGC)
SFPOE......... San Francisco Port of Embarkation [*Military*]
SFPOMMPAB... Society for the Prevention of Married Men Posing as Bachelors
SFPP........... Spruce Fall Power & Paper [*AAR code*]
SFPP........... Stored Flight Plan Program [*Aviation*] (FAAC)
SFPPC......... Science Fiction Pen Pal Club (EA)
SFPPL......... Short Form Provisioning Parts List [*NASA*] (NASA)
SFPPS......... Shore Facilities Planning and Programming System [*Navy*]
SFPRF......... Semifireproof (MSA)
SFPRL......... Spartan-Furnished Property Request List [*Missiles*] (MCD)
SFPS........... Secure Fast Packet Switching [*Telecommunications*]
SFPS........... Single Failure Point Summary [*NASA*] (NASA)
SFPT........... Society of Fire Protection Technicians (EA)
SFPT........... Standard Fixation Preference Test [*Laboratory science*] (DAVI)
SFPTU......... Swiss Federation of Protestant Trade Unions
SFQ............. Single Flux Quantum [*Pulse*] [*Physics*]
SFQ............. Suffolk, VA [*Location identifier FAA*] (FAAL)
SFQC........... Special Forces Qualification Course [*Military*] (INF)
SFR............. Safair Freighters (Pty) Ltd. [*South Africa ICAO designator*] (FAAC)
SFR............. Safety of Flight Requirements (AFM)
SFR............. San Fernando, CA [*Location identifier FAA*] (FAAL)
SFR............. San Francisco [*Diocesan abbreviation*] [*California*] (TOCD)
SFR............. San Francisco Review [*A publication*] (BRI)
SFR............. San Francisco - Rincon [*California*] [*Seismograph station code, US Geological Survey*] (SEIS)
SFR............. Santa Fe Energy Res [*NYSE symbol*] (TTSB)
SFR............. Santa Fe Energy Resources [*NYSE symbol*] (SPSG)
SFR............. Santa Fe Regional Library [*Gainsville Public Library*] [*UTLAS symbol*]
SfR............. Scholars' Facsimiles & Reprints, Inc., Delmar, NY [*Library symbol Library of Congress*] (LCLS)
SFR............. Screen Filtration Resistance [*Clinical chemistry*] (AAMN)
SFR............. Selective File Retrieval
SFR............. Semi-Fire-Resistive Construction
SFR............. Sequenced Flashing Lights
SFR............. Sequential Filter Regeneration [*Automotive engineering*]
SFR............. Serial Flechette Rifle (PDAA)
SFR............. Signal Frequency Receiver [*Telecommunications*] (OA)
SFR............. Simon Fraser Resources [*Vancouver Stock Exchange symbol*]
SFR............. Sinking Fund Return [*Finance*] (MHDW)
SFR............. Small Fluidal Round Colonies [*Moko disease of Banana*] [*Plant pathology*]
SFR............. Solar Flare Radiation
SFR............. Space Frame RADOME
SFR............. Special Federal Responsibilities (OICC)
SFR............. Special Forces Reconnaissance [*Army*]
SFR............. Spin Flip Raman [*LASER*]
SFR............. Star Formation Rate [*Astronomy*]
SFR............. Starved Feed Reactor [*for Polymerization*]
SFR............. Stroke with Full Recovery [*Neurology*] (DAVI)
SFR............. Submarine Fleet Reactor
SFR............. Supervisory Field Representative [*Department of Commerce*] (GFGA)
S FR........... Swiss Franc [*Monetary unit*]
SFRA........... Science Fiction Research Association (EA)
SFRA........... System Fielding Readiness Analysis [*Army*]
SFRA........... System Fielding Readiness Assessment [*Army*]
SFRB........... [*The*] Atchison, Topeka & Santa Fe Railway Co. - DF Loaders [*AAR code*]
SFRB........... San Francisco Review of Books [*A publication*] (BRI)
SFRC........... Short Form Research Contract (AAGC)
SFRC........... Soya Food Research Council
SFRCS......... Steam and Feedwater Line Rupture Control System [*Nuclear energy*] (NRCH)
SFRD........... [*The*] Atchison, Topeka & Santa Fe Railway Co. - Refrigerator Cars [*AAR code*]
SFRD........... Safe Functional Requirements Document (MCD)
SFRD........... Secret Formerly Restricted
SFRF........... Sport Fishery Research Foundation [*Later, SFRP*] (EA)
SFRJ........... Solid Fuel Ramjet
SFRL........... Spin-Flip Raman LASER (PDAA)
SFRP........... Sport Fishery Research Program (EA)
SFRPr......... Santa Fe Energy Res 7% Pfd [*NYSE symbol*] (TTSB)
SFRPrA....... Santa Fe Ener Res 8.25%'DECS' [*NYSE symbol*] (TTSB)
SFRS........... Search for Random Success [*Aerospace*] (AAG)
SFRS........... Swept Frequency Radiometer System
SFRT........... Science Fiction and Fantasy RoundTable [*GE Information Services*] [*Information service or system*] (CRD)
SFRY........... Socialist Federal Republic of Yugoslavia
SFS............. Free Software Foundation (EA)
SFS............. Saint Francis Seminary [*Wisconsin*]
SFS............. San Fernando [*Spain*] [*Seismograph station code, US Geological Survey*] (SEIS)
SFs............. Saybolt Furol Seconds [*Oil viscosity*]
SFS............. S-Band Feed System
SFS............. School Focused Secondment (AIE)
SFS............. School of Field Studies [*Beverly, MA*]
SFS............. Science-Fiction Studies [*A publication*] (BRI)
SFS............. Seamen's and Firemen's Society [*A union*] [*British*]
SFS............. Secure File System [*Telecommunications*] (OSI)
SFS............. Sektion fuer Systementwicklung [*GID*] [*Information retrieval*]
SFS............. Senior Flight Surgeon [*Army*] (AABC)
SFS............. Serial Focal Seizures [*Medicine*]
SFS............. Shakespeare for Students [*A publication*]
SFS............. Shared File System [*Telecommunications*]
SFS............. Sharm es-Sheikh [*Israel*] [*Airport symbol*] (AD)
SFS............. Shoot-Fail-Shoot [*Military*]
SFS............. Shuttle Flight Status [*NASA*] (MCD)
SFS............. Simplified Firing System

SFS .... Sine Fraude Sua [*Without Fraud on His Part*] [*Latin*] (DLA)
SFS .... Sioux Falls [*Diocesan abbreviation*] [*South Dakota*] (TOCD)
SFS .... Skin and Facial Stapler [*Surgery*] (DAVI)
SFS .... Small Firms Service [*British*]
SFS .... Smith's Flight System [*Aviation*] (AIA)
SFS .... Society for Foodservice Systems (EA)
SFS .... Society for Freedom in Science
SFS .... Society for French Studies [*British*]
SFS .... Sodium Formaldehyde Sulfoxylate [*Organic chemistry*]
SFS .... Software Facilities and Standards [*Computer science*] (TEL)
SFS .... Solicitors' Financial Services [*British*]
SFS .... Sonic Frequency System
SFS .... Southern Frontier Air Transport Ltd. [*Canada ICAO designator*] (FAAC)
SFS .... South San Francisco, CA [*Location identifier FAA*] (FAAL)
SFS .... Space Flight Systems (SAA)
SFS .... Space Futures Society (EA)
SFS .... Split Function Study (MAE)
SFS .... Star Field Sensor
SFS .... State Fleet Services [*New South Wales, Australia*]
SFS .... Statistical Fine Structure [*Physics*]
SFS .... Steam and Feedwater System [*Nuclear energy*] (NRCH)
SFS .... Suomen Standardisomisliitto [*Finnish Standards Association*] [*Information service or system*] (IID)
SFS .... Super Food Services [*NYSE symbol*] (TTSB)
SFS .... Super Food Services, Inc. [*NYSE symbol*] (SPSG)
SFS .... Surfaced Four Sides [*Technical drawings*]
SFS .... Surface Effect Fast Sea Lift Ship [*MTMC*] (TAG)
SFS .... Symbolic File Support
SFS .... System Failure Summaries [*NASA*] (KSC)
SFSA .... Scottish Federation of Sea Anglers (DBA)
SFSA .... Scottish Field Studies Association [*British*]
SFSA .... Steel Founders' Society of America (EA)
SFSAFBI ...... Society of Former Special Agents of the Federal Bureau of Investigation (EA)
SFSAS .... Standard Fuel Savings Advisor System
SFSB .... Suburbfed Financial Corp. [*NASDAQ symbol*] (SAG)
SFSB .... Suburbfed Finl [*NASDAQ symbol*] (TTSB)
SFS Bcp .... SFS Bancorp, Inc. [*Associated Press*] (SAG)
SFSC .... San Francisco State College [*Later, California State University*]
SFSC .... Southeast Fisheries Science Center [*Marine science*] (OSRA)
SFSCL .... Shunt Feedback Schottky Clamped [*Electronics*]
SFSCPD .... San Francisco Signal Corps Procurement District
SFSCT .... Smooth-Face Structural Clay Tile [*Technical drawings*]
SFSD .... Star Field Scanning Device
SFSE .... San Francisco Stock Exchange
SFSK .... Safeskin Corp. [*NASDAQ symbol*] (SAG)
SFSL .... Security First Corp. [*NASDAQ symbol*] (NQ)
SFSMD .... Studia Fransisci Scholten Memorial Dicata (BJA)
SFSN .... Society of French-Speaking Neurosurgeons (EA)
SFSO .... San Francisco Symphony Orchestra
SFSP .... Spent Fuel Storage Pool [*Nuclear energy*] (NRCH)
SFSP .... Summer Food Service Program [*Department of Agriculture*] (GFGA)
SFSR .... Senior Field Service Representative [*DoD*]
SFSR .... Shipfitter, Ship Repair [*Navy*]
SFSRC .... Shipfitter, Ship Repair, Chipper-Caulker [*Navy*]
SFSRD .... Shipfitter, Ship Repair, Diver [*Navy*]
SFSRF .... Shipfitter, Ship Repair, Steelworker-Anglesmith [*Navy*]
SFSRL .... Shipfitter, Ship Repair, Driller-Reamer [*Navy*]
SFSRP .... Shipfitter, Ship Repair, Pipe Fitter-Plumber [*Navy*]
SFSRR .... Shipfitter, Ship Repair, Riveter [*Navy*]
SFSRS .... Shipfitter, Ship Repair, Shipfitter [*Navy*]
SFSRW .... Shipfitter, Ship Repair, Welder [*Navy*]
SFSS .... Satellite Field Services Stations [*National Weather Service*]
SFSS .... Satellite Field Service Station [*Marine science*] (OSRA)
SFST .... Scherenfernrohrstand [*Emplacement of battery commander's telescope*] [*German military - World War II*]
SFST .... Standardized Field Sobriety Test [*NHTSA*] (TAG)
SFSU .... San Francisco State University
SFSU .... Singapore Federation of Services' Unions
SFSU .... Single Frequency Signaling Unit
SFSU-35 ...... San Francisco State University Videotex Cable Service [*Telecommunications service*] (TSSD)
SFSW .... State Financial Services Corp. [*NASDAQ symbol*] (SAG)
SFSW .... State Financial Svcs'A' [*NASDAQ symbol*] (TTSB)
S-FT .... Second-Foot (WDAA)
SFT .... Shaft (MSA)
SFT .... Shift
SFT .... Simulated Flight Tests
SFT .... Skelleftea [*Sweden*] [*Airport symbol*] (OAG)
SFT .... Skinfold Thickness [*Medicine*]
SFT .... Skyfreight, Inc. [*ICAO designator*] (FAAC)
sft .... Soffit (VRA)
sft .... Soft [*Quality of the bottom*] [*Nautical charts*]
SFT .... Soft Top [*Automotive advertising*]
SFT .... Software [*Computer science*] (RDA)
SFT .... Special Flight Test
SFT .... Specific Financial Transactions
SFT .... Spiral Fin Tubing
SFT .... Squeeze Film Test
SFT .... Stacking Fault Tetrahedra [*Metals*]
SFT .... Stanford [*California*] [*Seismograph station code, US Geological Survey*] (SEIS)
SFT .... Static Firing Test [*NASA*] (NASA)
SFT .... Stockpile Flight Tests
SFT .... Stop for Tea [*British*]
SFT .... Structural Firing Test [*Military*] (CAAL)
SFT .... Submerged Floating Tunnell
SFT .... Sudanese Flight [*Sudan*] [*ICAO designator*] (FAAC)
SFT .... Sufficient Feasibility Test
SFT .... Superfast Train
SFT .... Supplemental Flight Test
SFT .... System Fault Tolerant [*Novell, Inc.*] [*Orem, UT*] [*Telecommunications*]
SFTA .... Society of Film and Television Arts Ltd. [*British*] (BI)
SFTA .... Spent Fuel Transportation Accident [*Nuclear energy*] (NRCH)
SFTA .... Structural Fatigue Test Article [*NASA*] (NASA)
SFTAA .... Short Form Test of Academic Aptitude (EDAC)
SFTab .... Special Forces Tab [*Military*] (GFGA)
SFTAR .... Subsystem Fault Tree Analysis Report
SftArt .... Software Artistry [*Associated Press*] (SAG)
SFTB .... Southern Freight Tariff Bureau
SFTC .... Sherman Fairchild Technology Center (MCD)
SFTC .... Standard Freight Trade Classification [*Council for Mutual Economic Assistance*] (DS)
SFTCD .... Senior Fellow, Trinity College, Dublin (ROG)
SFTE .... Society of Flight Test Engineers (EA)
SFTE .... Space Full Time Equivalent (AIE)
SFTF .... Static Firing Test Facility [*NASA*] (NASA)
SFTFC .... Search for Tomorrow Fan Club [*Defunct*] (EA)
SFTI .... Special Flight Test Instrumentation (MCD)
SFTIP .... Special Flight Test Instrumentation Pool (NG)
SFTK .... Single Fiber Tensile Kinetic [*Method for studying permanent hair waving*]
SFTL .... Sonic Fatigue Test Laboratory (AAG)
SFTO .... San Diego Field Test Operations [*Aerospace*] (AAG)
SFTP .... Science for the People (EA)
SftProf .... Software Professionals, Inc. [*Associated Press*] (SAG)
SftQuad .... SoftQuad International, Inc. [*Associated Press*] (SAG)
SFTR .... Shipfitter (AAG)
SFTR .... Summary Flight Test Report (MCD)
SFTS .... San Francisco Theological Seminary [*San Anselmo, CA*]
SFTS .... Scale Factor Temperature Sensitivity
SFTS .... Service Flying Training School [*British*]
SFTS .... Sickle Forgers' Trade Society [*A union*] [*British*]
SFTS .... Society of Friends of the Touro Synagogue (EA)
SFTS .... Space Flight Test System (MCD)
SFTS .... Standard Frequency and Time Signals (IEEE)
SFTS .... Swept Frequency Topside Sounder (SAA)
SFTS .... Swinburne Film and Television School [*Australia*]
SFTS .... Synthetic Flight Training Simulator
SFTS .... Synthetic Flight Training System [*Army*]
SFTT .... Spent Fuel Transfer Tubes [*Nuclear energy*] (NRCH)
SFTW .... Enlighten Software Solutions [*NASDAQ symbol*] (SAG)
SFTW .... Software Professionals [*NASDAQ symbol*] (TTSB)
SFTW .... Software Professionals, Inc. [*NASDAQ symbol*] (SAG)
SFTW .... Stamps for the Wounded (EA)
SFTWD .... Softwood (WGA)
SFTWE .... Software (NASA)
SftwPb .... Software Publishing Corp. [*Associated Press*] (SAG)
SFTWR .... Software [*Computer science*] (MCD)
SFTWR .... Software
SFTY .... Safety
SFTY .... Safety
Sfty1st .... Safety 1st, Inc. [*Associated Press*] (SAG)
SftyCmp .... Safety Components International, Inc. [*Associated Press*] (SAG)
SFU .... Furman University, Greenville, SC [*OCLC symbol*] (OCLC)
SFU .... Safia [*Papua New Guinea*] [*Airport symbol*] (OAG)
SFU .... Signals Flying Unit [*British*]
SFU .... Simon Fraser University [*Canada*]
SFU .... Simon Fraser University Library [*UTLAS symbol*]
SFU .... Societe de Fluoration de l'Uranium [*An international nuclear fuel company*]
SFU .... Space Flyer Unit (SSD)
SFU .... Special Function Unit
SFU .... Standard Firing Unit [*NASA*] (NASA)
SFU .... Status Fill-In Unit [*Telecommunications*] (TEL)
SFU .... Surfdale [*Waiheke Island, New Zealand*] [*Airport symbol*] (AD)
SFU .... Suriname Freedom Union (EA)
SFU .... Syncytium-Forming Units [*Biochemistry*]
SFU .... Synthetic Fuels Update [*A publication*]
SFUDS .... Simplified Federal Urban Driving Schedule [*Electric vehicle testing*]
SFUGE .... Singapore Federation of Unions of Government Employees
SF/UIS .... Space Frame and Unit Integrating System
SFUN .... Standard Fdg Corp. [*NASDAQ symbol*] (TTSB)
SFUN .... Standard Funding Corp. [*NASDAQ symbol*] (SAG)
SFUS .... Statistical Forecasts of the United States [*A publication*]
SF/USA .... Stopped-Flow/Unsegmented Storage Analyzer [*Chemical analysis*]
SFV .... Saybolt Furol Viscosity (BARN)
SFV .... Schizophrenia Fellowship of Victoria [*Australia*]
SFV .... Semliki Forest Virus
SFV .... Shipping Fever Virus [*Medicine*] (DMAA)
SFV .... Shope Fibroma Virus [*Medicine*] (DMAA)
SFV .... Sight Feed Valve
SFV .... Simian Foamy Virus
SFV .... Sports Federation of Victoria [*Australia*]
SFV .... Squirrel Fibroma Virus [*Medicine*] (DMAA)
SFVC .... State Fund Vice Chairmen [*Red Cross*]
SFVCS .... San Francisco Vocational Competency Scale
SFW .... Sante Fe [*Panama*] [*Airport symbol*] (OAG)

SFW .... Sensor Fuzed Weapon
SFW .... Sexual Function of Women [*Medicine*] (DMAA)
SFW .... Shell Fragment Wound [*Medicine*]
SFW .... Shrapnel Fragment Wound (MAE)
SFW .... Software (NASA)
SFW .... Special Filter Wheel [*Military*] (CAAL)
SFW .... Swept Forward Wing [*Aviation*] (PDAA)
SFW .... Williston, ND [*Location identifier FAA*] (FAAL)
SFWA .... Science Fiction Writers of America (EA)
SFWA .... Sierra Foothill Winery Association (EA)
SFWA .... Soccer Federation of Western Australia
SFWA .... Southern Fleece Washers Association [*British*] (DBA)
SFWB .... Single Fronted Weatherboard (ADA)
SFWC .... Supreme Forest Woodmen Circle [*Later, Woodmen of the World Life Insurance Society*] (EA)
SFWEM .... Static Feed Water Electrolysis Module [*NASA*]
SFWI .... Ship's Force Work Item (DNAB)
SFWLI .... Ship's Force Worklist Instruction
SFWM .... Swiss Federation of Watch Manufacturers (EA)
SFWR .... Software 2000 [*NASDAQ symbol*] (TTSB)
SFWR .... Software 2000, Inc. [*NASDAQ symbol*] (SAG)
SFWR .... Stewardesses for Women's Rights
SFWS .... Stopped-Flow Wavelength Scanning [*Spectrometry*]
SFX .... San Felix [*Venezuela*] [*Airport symbol*] (AD)
SFX .... Sound Effects [*Script code*]
SFX .... St. Francis Xavier University Library [*UTLAS symbol*]
SFXB .... SFX Broadcasting, Inc. [*NASDAQ symbol*] (SAG)
SFXBA .... SFX Broadcasting'A' [*NASDAQ symbol*] (TTSB)
SFX Brd .... SFX Broadcasting, Inc. [*Associated Press*] (SAG)
SFXD .... Semifixed
SFXR .... Super Flash X-Ray (MCD)
SFY .... Gulf Flite Center, Inc. [*ICAO designator*] (FAAC)
SFY .... Savanna, IL [*Location identifier FAA*] (FAAL)
SFY .... Special Fund for Youth [*UNESCO*] (EAIO)
SFY .... Standard Facility Years [*FAA*]
SFY .... Swift Energy [*NYSE symbol*] (TTSB)
SFY .... Swift Energy Co. [*NYSE symbol*] (SPSG)
SFYMHS .... San Francisco Young Mens Health Study [*AIDS study*]
SFZ .... Pawtucket, RI [*Location identifier FAA*] (FAAL)
SFZ .... Pawtucket-Woonsocket [*Rhode Island*] [*Airport symbol*] (AD)
Sfz .... Sforzando [*With Additional Accent*] [*Music*]
SG .... Atlantis [*ICAO designator*] (AD)
SG .... Command Surgeon [*AFSC*]
SG .... Goldwyn [*Samuel*] Co. [*AMEX symbol*] (SPSG)
SG .... Royal South Gloucestershire Light Infantry Militia [*British military*] (DMA)
SG .... Sachs-Georgi [*Test for syphilis*] [*Also, S-GT*] [*Obsolete*]
SG .... Safety Guide (NRCH)
SG .... Sa Grace [*His or Her Grace*] [*French*]
SG .... Sa Grandeur [*His or Her Highness*] [*French*]
SG .... Salisbury Group (EAIO)
SG .... Salutis Gratia [*For the Sake of Safety*] [*Latin*]
SG .... Sample Gas
SG .... Sawtooth Generator
SG .... Scanning Gate
SG .... Schedule Generator
SG .... School for Girls (ADA)
SG .... Schutzgemeinschaft Gegen Meinungsterror [*Guard Society Against Opinion Terror*] [*Germany*]
SG .... Scots Guards [*Military unit*] [*British*]
SG .... Screen Grid [*Electrode or vacuum tube*]
SG .... Sculptors Guild (EA)
SG .... Seabird Group (EAIO)
SG .... Sea Grant
SG .... Seaman Gunner [*British Obsolete*]
SG .... Secretary-General [*United Nations*]
SG .... Security Group [*Military*] (DNAB)
SG .... Security Guard (SAA)
SG .... Segment (IAA)
SG .... Selling [*Exchange rate marking*] [*British*]
sg .... Senegal [*MARC country of publication code Library of Congress*] (LCCP)
SG .... Senior Gleaners (EA)
SG .... Senior Grade
SG .... Sergeant (WGA)
SG .... Serum Globulin [*Medicine*] (MAE)
SG .... Serum Glucose [*Medicine*] (DAVI)
SG .... Service Group (MUGU)
SG .... Set Gate
SG .... Sheller-Globe Corp.
SG .... Shell Gland
SG .... Shell Gun
SG .... Sherrgold, Inc. [*Toronto Stock Exchange symbol*]
SG .... Ship and Goods [*British*] (ROG)
SG .... Shipcraft Guild (EA)
SG .... Siebelwerke ATG GmbH [*Germany ICAO aircraft manufacturer identifier*] (ICAO)
SG .... Sign (MAE)
SG .... Signal Generator
SG .... Signal Ground (BUR)
SG .... Signed (WGA)
SG .... Silica Gel [*Analytical chemistry*]
SG .... Singapore [*ANSI two-letter standard code*] (CNC)
SG .... Singing
SG .... Single Gourmet (EA)
SG .... Single Groove [*Insulators*]
Sg .... Singular (BJA)
SG .... Skin Graft [*Medicine*]
S/G .... Slaved Gyro (MCD)
S/G .... Smith/Greenland [*Advertising agency*]
SG .... Smoke Generator
SG .... Snow Grains [*ICAO*] (FAAC)
SG .... Society of Genealogists (EA)
SG .... Society of Gilders (EA)
SG .... Soft Gelatin [*Pharmacy*]
SG .... Solar Generator (IAA)
SG .... Sol-Gel [*Materials science*]
SG .... Solicitor General
SG .... Soluble Gelatin
SG .... Solution of Glucose (OA)
Sg .... Song of Songs [*Old Testament book*] [*Roman Catholic canon*] (BJA)
SG .... Sort Generator (BUR)
SG .... Sound Generation (MCD)
SG .... South Georgia Railway Co. [*AAR code Terminated*]
SG .... Sozialgericht [*Social Security Court*] [*German*] (ILCA)
SG .... Spark Gap (DEN)
SG .... Special Grade (DNAB)
SG .... Special Group [*NATO*]
SG .... Specific Gravity [*Also, SPG, SPGR*]
SG .... Spheroidal Graphite [*Ductile iron*]
SG .... Spheroidal Graphite [*Metallurgy*]
SG .... Stacking Gel [*Biochemistry*]
SG .... Stained Glass
SG .... Standardization Group [*Air Force*] (AFM)
SG .... Standing Group
SG .... Steam Generator (NRCH)
SG .... Steel Girder [*Bridges*]
SG .... Steering Group (MCD)
SG .... Stellate Ganglion [*Neuroanatomy*]
SG .... Stern-Gerlach [*Experiment for measuring atomic magnetism*]
SG .... Strain Gauge (KSC)
SG .... Strategic Group [*Military*]
SG .... Structural Gene
SG .... Structural Glass
SG .... Student Guide
S-G .... Subgeneric (WDAA)
S-G .... Subgenus (WDAA)
SG .... Substantia Gelatinosa [*Anatomy*]
S/G .... Su Giro [*Your Draft*] [*Spanish Business term*]
SG .... Summation Gallop [*Cardiology*]
SG .... Sun Gate
SG .... Sunkist Growers (EA)
SG .... Sunset Gun [*Military ceremonial*]
SG .... Sunsweet Growers (EA)
SG .... Super Group (NATG)
SG .... Super Guppy (KSC)
Sg .... Supplementing [*New matter added to an existing regulation or order*] [*Used in Shepard's Citations*] [*Legal term*] (DLA)
SG .... Surgeon
SG .... [*The*] Surgeon General [*Army, Air Force*]
SG .... Swamp Glider
SG .... Swan-Ganz [*Catheter*] [*Medicine*] (MEDA)
SG .... Swan-Ganz [*Catheter*] [*Cardiology*] (DAVI)
SG .... Sweep Generator
SG .... Sydney Greens [*Political party Australia*]
SG .... Symbol Generator
SG .... Synchronous Generator (IAA)
SG .... Syringe (DNAB)
SG .... System Gain
SG43 MMG .... Stankovyi Goryunova 1943 Medium Machine Gun [*Soviet made*] (VNW)
SGA .... Air Saigon [*Vietnam*] [*ICAO designator*] (FAAC)
SGA .... Saga Communications [*AMEX symbol*] (SPSG)
SGA .... Saga Communications'A' [*AMEX symbol*] (TTSB)
SGA .... Saga Resources [*Vancouver Stock Exchange symbol*]
SGA .... Savoonga, AK [*Location identifier FAA*] (FAAL)
SGA .... Scientific Glass Apparatus Co., Inc.
SGA .... Scottish Games Association (EAIO)
SGA .... Scottish Glass Association (DBA)
SGA .... Screened Granulated Aluminate [*Inorganic chemistry*]
SGA .... Sea Grant Association (EA)
SGA .... Self-Gating and Shipboard, General Use, Armored (IAA)
SGA .... Shirtsleeve Garment Assembly [*NASA*]
SGA .... Showmen's Guild of Australia
SGA .... Sickle Grinders' Association [*A union*] [*British*]
SGA .... Sigma Security, Inc. [*Vancouver Stock Exchange symbol*]
SGA .... Single-Monitor Graphic Adaptor [*Computer graphics*]
SGA .... Slave Gyro Assembly
SGA .... Slavic Gospel Association (EA)
SGA .... Small for Gestational Age [*Pediatrics*]
SGA .... Societe de Geologie Appliquee aux Gites Mineraux [*Society for Geology Applied to Mineral Deposits*] [*ICSU*] (EAIO)
SGA .... Societe Generale Australia
SGA .... Society of Gastrointestinal Assistants [*Later, SGNA*] (EA)
SGA .... Society of Governmental Appraisers [*Later, Association of Governmental Appraisers*] (EA)
SGA .... Society of Graphic Art [*British*]
SGA .... Society of Graphic Art, Toronto [*1912, founded c.1903 as GAC, CSGA from 1923*] [*Canada*] (NGC)
SGA .... Solar Greenhouse Association (EA)

SGA .... Songwriters Guild of America (EA)
SGA .... Soybean Growers of America (EA)
SGA .... Spectrometric Gas Analysis
SGA .... Split Group Aperture
SGA .... Spouses of Gays Association [*Defunct*] (EA)
SGA .... Standards of Grade Authorization [*Military*]
SGA .... State Guaranteed Agency (GFGA)
SGA .... Stephens Glacier [*Alaska*] [*Seismograph station code, US Geological Survey Closed*] (SEIS)
SGA .... Substantial Gainful Activity [*Social Security Administration*] (OICC)
SGA .... Superior Geniculate Artery [*Anatomy*]
SGA .... Switch Group Assembly
SGAA .... Sporting Goods Agents Association (EA)
SGAA .... Stained Glass Association of America (EA)
SGAC .... Secretariat General for Civil Aviation [*French*]
SGAC .... Silvermine Guild Arts Center (EA)
SGAC .... State Governmental Affairs Council (EA)
SGACC .... Secretariat General de l'Aviation Civile et Commerciale [*France*]
SGAD .... Safeguard Army Depot (AABC)
SGAE .... Studiengesellschaft fuer Atomenergie [*Implements Austria's nuclear program*] (NRCH)
SGAHRS ...... Steam Generator Auxiliary Heat Removal System [*Nuclear energy*] (NRCH)
SGAIG .... Scholars Group Against the Invasion of Grenada (EA)
SG & A .... Selling, General, and Administrative Expenses
SGA of M-A... Sod Growers Association of Mid-America (EA)
SGAS .... Asuncion/Presidente General Stroessner [*Paraguay*] [*ICAO location identifier*] (ICLI)
SGAS .... Society for German-American Studies (EA)
SGAS .... Space Geodesy Altimetry Study [*Raytheon Co.*]
SGAS .... Star Gas Partners L.P. SBI [*NASDAQ symbol*] (SAG)
SGAS .... Steam Generator Available Signal [*Nuclear energy*] (NRCH)
SGASZ .... Star Gas Ptnrs L.P. [*NASDAQ symbol*] (TTSB)
SGAUA........ Scitex Graphic Arts Users Association (EA)
SGAUG........ Scitex Graphic Arts Users Group [*Later, SGAUA*] (EA)
SGAUSA...... St. George Association of the USA (EA)
sGAW.......... Specific Airway Conductance
SGAW .... Subgroup on Assessment of Weapons [*NATO*] (NATG)
SGAY .... Ayolas [*Paraguay*] [*ICAO location identifier*] (ICLI)
SGB .... Santa Fe, NM [*Location identifier FAA*] (FAAL)
SGB .... Schweizerischer Gewerkschaftsbund [*Swiss Federation of Trade Unions*]
SGB .... Societe Generale de Banque [*Bank Society*] [*Information service or system*] (IID)
SGB .... Southern Gas Basin [*British*]
SGB .... Southwest Georgia Financial Corp. [*AMEX symbol*] (SAG)
SGB .... Steam Generator Blowdown [*Nuclear energy*] (NRCH)
SGB .... Steam Generator Building [*Nuclear energy*] (NRCH)
SGB .... Steam Gunboat [*British military*] (DMA)
SGB .... Stellate Ganglion Blockade [*Anesthesiology*]
SGB .... Strain Gauge Bridge
SGB .... Switchgear Block (MSA)
SGBA .... Societe Generale de Banque aux Antilles [*Guadeloupe*] (EY)
SGBD .... Steam Generator Blowdown [*Nuclear energy*] (NRCH)
SGBI .... Santa Gertrudis Breeders International (EA)
SGBI .... Schoolmistresses' and Governesses' Benevolent Institution [*British*] (BI)
SGBIP .... Subject Guide to Books in Print [*A publication*]
SGBPS .... Steam Generator Blowdown Processing System [*Nuclear energy*] (NRCH)
SGBS .... Steam Generator Blowdown System [*Nuclear energy*] (NRCH)
SGBS .... Strathclyde Graduate Business School [*Toulouse, France*] (ECON)
SGBV .... Bella Vista [*Paraguay*] [*ICAO location identifier*] (ICLI)
SGC .... Saint Gregory College [*Oklahoma*]
SGC .... Salivary Gland Choristoma [*Medicine*]
SGC .... Sample Gas Cell [*Instrumentation*]
SGC .... Screen Grid Current
SGC .... Simulated Generation Control
SGC .... Software Generation Center (MCD)
SGC .... Solicitor General Canada
SGC .... Southern Governors Conference
SGC .... South Georgia College [*Douglas*]
SGC .... Space General Corp. (MCD)
SGC .... Spartan Guidance Computer [*Missiles*] (AABC)
SGC .... Specialist in Guidance and Counseling (GAGS)
SGC .... Spermicide-Germicide Compound [*Medicine*] (DMAA)
SGC .... Spherical Gear Coupling
SGC .... Stabilized Ground Cloud [*NASA*] (MCD)
SGC .... Stabilizer Gyro Circuit
SGC .... Standard Geographical Classification [*Canada*]
SGC .... Starburst Giant Cells [*Cytology*]
SGC .... State Grants Commission [*Tasmania, Australia*]
SGC .... Strata Energy Corp. [*Vancouver Stock Exchange symbol*]
SGC .... Students Guide to Childcare [*British*]
SGC .... Supergroup Connector [*Telecommunications*] (TEL)
SGC .... Superior Geocentric Conjunction
SGC .... Superior Surgical [*AMEX symbol*] (TTSB)
SGC .... Superior Surgical Manufacturing Co., Inc. [*AMEX symbol*] (SPSG)
Sg C............ Surgeon-Captain [*British military*] (DMA)
SGC .... Swept Gain Control (DA)
SGC .... Washington, DC [*Location identifier FAA*] (FAAL)
SGCA .... Silvermine Guild Center for the Arts [*Later, SGAC*] (EA)
SGCA .... Spacecraft Ground Controlled Approach (IAA)
SGCA .... Subependymal Giant Cell Astrocytoma [*Medicine*] (DMAA)
SGCC .... Safety Glazing Certification Council (EA)
SGCD .... Society of Glass and Ceramic Decorators (EA)
SGCE .... Ship Gyrocompass Equipment [*Navy*] (CAAL)
SGCEC .... Standing Group Communications-Electronics Committee [*Later, MCEWG*] [*NATO*] (NATG)
SGCF .... SNAP [*Systems for Nuclear Auxiliary Power*] Generalized Critical Facility
SGCMG........ Single Gimbal Control Moment Gyro [*Navigation*]
SGCO .... Concepcion [*Paraguay*] [*ICAO location identifier*] (ICLI)
SGCP .... Shipboard Gauge Calibration Program (DNAB)
Sg Cr .... Surgeon-Commander [*British military*] (DMA)
SGCS .... Silicon Gate-Controlled Switch
SGCS .... Slave Gyro Control System
SGD .... Napa, CA [*Location identifier FAA*] (FAAL)
SGD .... Scott's Liquid Gold [*NYSE symbol*] (TTSB)
SGD .... Scotts Liquid Gold Co. [*NYSE symbol*] (SAG)
SGD .... Seafloor Geosciences Division (EA)
SGD .... Self-Generating Dictionary
SGD .... Senior Grand Deacon [*Freemasonry*]
SGD .... Shogun Developments Corp. [*Vancouver Stock Exchange symbol*]
SGD .... Signaling Ground [*Telecommunications*] (TEL)
SGD .... Signed
sgd............. Signed (ODBW)
sgd............. Signed (WDMC)
SGD .... Silicon Grown Diffused (IAA)
SGD .... Sliding Glass Door (ADA)
SGD .... Society of Geniuses of Distinction [*Defunct*] (EA)
SGD .... Society of Glass Decorators [*Later, SGCD*] (EA)
SGD .... Sonderborg [*Denmark*] [*Airport symbol*] (OAG)
SGD .... Sparks-Goosen-Drake Engine [*Auto racing*]
SGD .... Special Government Design (DNAB)
SGD .... Specific Granule Deficiency [*Physiology*]
SGD .... Sperry Gyroscope Division [*Sperry Rand Corp.*] (MCD)
SGD .... Straight Gravity Drainage [*Surgery*] (DAVI)
SGD .... Sui Generis Degree
SGDE .... Steering Gear Dual Emergency (MSA)
SGDE .... System Ground Data Equipment [*RADAR*]
SGDF .... Supergroup Distribution Frame [*Telecommunications*] (TEL)
SGDHF......... Sodium Glycodihydrofusidate [*Hemolytic*]
SGDI .... Swaging Die [*Tool*]
SGDI .... Switched Ground Discrete Input (MCD)
SGDO .... Switched Ground Discrete Output (MCD)
SGDPS......... Second Generation Data Processing System (MCD)
SGDS .... Supergroup Distribution Frame [*Telecommunications*] (OSI)
Sge .... Sagitta [*Constellation*]
SGE............. Secondary Grid Emission
SGE............. Severable Government Equipment
SGE............. Sigma Gamma Epsilon [*Society*]
SGE............. Significant Glandular Enlargement [*Endocrinology*] (DAVI)
SGE............. Slow Glass Etch (IAA)
SGE............. Society of Government Economists (EA)
SGE............. Solutions Generation Environment [*Computer science*] (BTTJ)
SGE............. Starch Gel Electrophoresis (OA)
SGE............. Subscriber Group Equipment [*Telecommunications*]
SGE............. Super-Critical Gas Extraction [*Chemical engineering*]
SGE............. Support Group Europe [*Military*]
SGEM........... Study Group on Environmental Monitoring [*National Research Council*]
SGEMP .... System-Generated Electromagnetic Pulse [*Army*]
SGEN .... Encarnacion [*Paraguay*] [*ICAO location identifier*] (ICLI)
SGEP .... Socialist Group in the European Parliament [*See also GSPE*] (EAIO)
SGES .... Society of Grain Elevator Superintendents [*Later, GEAPS*]
SGET........... Spacecraft Ground Elapsed Time
SGEU .... Singapore General Employees' Union
SGF............. Sample Gas Flow
SGF............. Sarcoma Growth Factor
SGF............. Singapore Fund [*NYSE symbol*] (SPSG)
SGF............. Skeletal Growth Factor [*Genetics*]
SGF............. Small Gene Fragment [*Genetics*]
SGF............. Smoke Generating Fuel (IAA)
SGF............. Southern Group of Forces [*Former USSR*] (NATG)
SGF............. Spermiogenesis Growth Factor [*Biochemistry*]
SGF............. Springfield [*Missouri*] [*Airport symbol*] (OAG)
SGF............. Springfield, MO [*Location identifier FAA*] (FAAL)
SGF............. Steam Generator Feedwater (DNAB)
SGF............. Sydney Garden Festival [*Australia*]
SGFA .... Asuncion [*Paraguay*] [*ICAO location identifier*] (ICLI)
SGFA .... Society of Graphic Fine Art [*British*] (DBA)
SGFC .... Sharon Gless Fan Club (EA)
SGFI............ Filadelfia [*Paraguay*] [*ICAO location identifier*] (ICLI)
SGFID.......... Seventh Generation Fund for Indian Development (EA)
SGFNT......... Significant (FAAC)
SGFP .... Steam Generator Feed Pump (IEEE)
SGFR .... Single-Nephron Glomerular Filtration Rate [*Medicine*] (MAE)
SGG .... Saint George Island, AK [*Location identifier FAA*] (FAAL)
SGG .... Signatures (WGA)
SGG .... Simanggang [*Malaysia*] [*Airport symbol*] (AD)
SGG .... South Georgia [*United Kingdom*] [*Geomagnetic observatory code*]
SGG .... St. George Minerals [*Vancouver Stock Exchange symbol*]
SGG .... Sustainer Gas Generator
SGGP .... Seller's Guide to Government Purchasing [*A publication*]
SGGR........... Guaira [*Paraguay*] [*ICAO location identifier*] (ICLI)
SGH .... Serum Growth Hormone [*Endocrinology*]
SGH .... Servisair Ltd. [*British ICAO designator*] (FAAC)
SGH .... Seth G. Huntington [*Designer's mark on US bicentennial half dollar*]
SGH .... Signal Hill Energy Corp. [*Vancouver Stock Exchange symbol*]

SGH .... Springfield [*Ohio*] [*Airport symbol*] (AD)
SGH .... Springfield, OH [*Location identifier FAA*] (FAAL)
SGH .... Sterling House [*AMEX symbol*] (TTSB)
SGH .... Sterling House Corp. [*AMEX symbol*] (SAG)
SGH .... Sud-Ghoubbet [*Djibouti*] [*Seismograph station code, US Geological Survey*] (SEIS)
SGH .... Surgical Hospital [*Medicine*]
SGHT .... StarSight Telecast [*NASDAQ symbol*] (TTSB)
SGHT .... StarSight Telecast, Inc. [*NASDAQ symbol*] (SAG)
SGHW .... Steam-Generating, Heavy-Water [*Reactor*] [*British Nuclear energy*] (NRCH)
SGHWR .... Steam-Generating, Heavy-Water Reactor [*British Nuclear energy*] (NRCH)
SGI .... Sea Grant Institute [*University of Wisconsin*] [*Research center*] (RCD)
SGI .... Search Group, Inc. [*An association*] (EA)
SGI .... Servicio Geodesico Interamericano [*Inter-American Geodetic Survey - IAGS*] [*United States*]
SGI .... Sheriff Guards International [*Nigeria*] (EAIO)
SGI .... Silicon Graphics [*NYSE symbol*] (SPSG)
SGI .... Silicon Graphics Incorporated [*Computer science*]
SGI .... Small Group Instructor [*or Instruction*] [*Army*] (INF)
SGI .... Society for Gynecologic Investigation (EA)
SGI .... Soka Gakkai International [*An association*]
SGI .... Specific Gravity Indicator
SGI .... Spring Garden Institute
SGI .... Standard Graphic Interface [*XOR Systems*]
SGI .... Systems Group, Inc. [*Telecommunications service*] (TSSD)
SGIA .... Sun Glass Institute of America [*Defunct*] (EA)
SGIB .... Itaipu [*Paraguay*] [*ICAO location identifier*] (ICLI)
SGIC .... Silicon Graphics (MHDW)
SGIG .... Sovereign Grand Inspector-General [*Freemasonry*] (ROG)
SGIH .... Scientific Games Hldgs [*NASDAQ symbol*] (TTSB)
SGIH .... Scientific Games Holding Corp. [*NASDAQ symbol*] (SAG)
SGIM .... Society of General Internal Medicine (EA)
SGINDEX .... System Generation Cross-Reference Index [*NASA*]
SGIS .... Safeguards Initiation Signal [*Nuclear energy*] (NRCH)
SGIS .... Steam Generator Isolation Signal (IEEE)
SGIS .... Student Government Information Service (EA)
SGIT .... Special Group Inclusive Tour [*Airline fare*]
SGITS .... Spacecraft Ground Operational Support System Interface Test System (IAA)
SGJ .... Sagarai [*Papua New Guinea*] [*Airport symbol*] (OAG)
SGJ .... St. Augustine, FL [*Location identifier FAA*] (FAAL)
SGJ .... Supersonic Gas Jet
SGJA .... Sporting Goods Jobbers Association [*Later, NASGW*]
SGJKT .... Society of Goldsmiths, Jewellers, and Kindred Trades [*A union*] [*British*]
SGJN .... San Juan Nepomuceno [*Paraguay*] [*ICAO location identifier*] (ICLI)
SGJP .... Satellite Graphic Job Processor [*Computer science*]
SGK .... Hsinkong [*Republic of China*] [*Also, HSI*] [*Seismograph station code, US Geological Survey*] (SEIS)
SGK .... Knoxville, TN [*Location identifier FAA*] (FAAL)
SGK .... Schawk, Inc. [*Formerly, Filtertek Inc.*] [*NYSE symbol*] (SAG)
SGK .... Schawk Inc.'A' [*NYSE symbol*] (TTSB)
SGK .... Skyward Aviation Ltd. [*Canada ICAO designator*] (FAAC)
SGKA .... Studien zur Geschichte und Kultur des Alterums [*A publication*] (BJA)
SGKB .... Societe Generale-Komercni Banka [*Former Czechoslovakia*] (EY)
SGKF .... Susan G. Komen Foundation (EA)
SGL .... Mount Signal [*California*] [*Seismograph station code, US Geological Survey*] (SEIS)
s gl .... Sans Correction [*Without correction*] [*Ophthalmology*] (DAVI)
SGL .... Senegalair [*Senegal*] [*ICAO designator*] (FAAC)
SGL .... Signal
SGL .... Single (MSA)
SGL .... Sleeping Gold Ltd. [*Vancouver Stock Exchange symbol*]
SGL .... Slightly-Grounded Lightplane (PDAA)
SGL .... Society of Gas Lighting (EA)
SGL .... South State Cooperative Library System, Los Angeles, CA [*OCLC symbol*] (OCLC)
SGL .... Space-Ground Link (MCD)
SGL .... Strategic Global Income Fd [*NYSE symbol*] (TTSB)
SGL .... Strategic Global Income Fund [*NYSE symbol*] (SPSG)
SGL .... Sumerisches Glossar [*A publication*] (BJA)
SGL .... Sunglasses
SGL .... Superannuation Guarantee Levy
SGL .... System Generation Language (IAA)
S GLAM .... South Glamorgan [*County in Wales*]
SGLC .... Strain Gauge Load Cell
Sg L Cr .... Surgeon Lieutenant-Commander [*British military*] (DMA)
SGLE .... Single (AAG)
SGLF .... Scottish Grand Lodge of Freemasons
SGLI .... Service Government Life Insurance (DOMA)
SGLI .... Servicemen's Group Life Insurance [*Military*]
SGLI .... Slave Gyro Leveling Integrator
SGLIC .... Steam Generator Level Instrumentation Cabinet [*Nuclear energy*] (NRCH)
SGLLI .... Section on Gay and Lesbian Legal Issues [*Association of American Law Schools*] (EA)
SGLO .... Lobrego, Fortin [*Paraguay*] [*ICAO location identifier*] (ICLI)
SGLO .... Standing Group Liaison Officer to the North Atlantic Council
SGLP .... Standing Group Representative Liaison Paper to the International Staff [*Obsolete NATO*] (NATG)
SGLS .... Satellite Grand Link System (NATG)
SGLS .... Space-Ground Link Station [*NASA*] (NASA)
SGLS .... Space-Ground Link System (IAA)
SGLS .... Space-to-Ground Link Subsystem [*NASA*]
SGLV .... La Victoria (Ex Casado) [*Paraguay*] [*ICAO location identifier*] (ICLI)
SGLWCH .... Study Group on Labor and Working Class History (EA)
SGM .... College Mathieu, Gravelbourg, Saskatchewan [*Library symbol National Library of Canada*] (NLC)
SGM .... Sahara Gaming [*AMEX symbol*] (SPSG)
SGM .... Santa Fe Gaming [*AMEX symbol*] (TTSB)
SGM .... Santa Fe Gaming Corp. [*AMEX symbol*] (SAG)
SGM .... Screen Grid Modulation
SGM .... Sea Gallantry Medal [*Navy British*]
SGM .... Sergeant Major (AABC)
SGM .... Silver Gate [*Montana*] [*Seismograph station code, US Geological Survey*] (SEIS)
SGM .... Single Geometric Model [*Computer-assisted design*]
SGM .... Sisters of Charity of Montreal (Grey Nuns) (TOCD)
SGM .... Society for General Microbiology [*British*]
SGM .... Society for General Music (EA)
SGM .... Soeurs Grises de Montreal [*Sisters of Charity, Grey Nuns of Montreal*] [*Roman Catholic religious order*]
SGM .... Spark Gap Modulation
SGM .... Standing Group Memorandum [*Obsolete NATO*] (NATG)
SGM .... Stationary Gaussian Markov [*Telecommunications*] (IAA)
SGM .... Strategic Guidance Memo [*Navy*]
SGM .... Strict Good Middling (IAA)
SGMA .... Sigmatron International [*NASDAQ symbol*] (SAG)
SGMA .... Soup and Gravy Manufacturers Association [*British*] (DBA)
SGMA .... Sporting Goods Manufacturers Association [*North Palm Beach, FL*] (EA)
SGMAA .... Sporting Goods Manufacturers Agents Association [*Later, SGRA*]
SGMC .... Standing Group Meteorological Committee [*Obsolete NATO*] (NATG)
SGMCI .... Sporting Goods Manufacturers' Credit Interchange [*Defunct*] (EA)
SGMD .... Swaging Mandel
SGME .... Mariscal Estigarribia [*Paraguay*] [*ICAO location identifier*] (ICLI)
SGME .... Service Generale des Moyens de l'Enseignement [*Canada*]
SGML .... Standard Generalized Markup Language [*Also, GSML*] [*International Standards Organization*]
SGML .... Study Group for Mathematical Learning (EA)
SGMN .... Signalman [*Military British*]
SGMP .... Society of Government Meeting Planners (EA)
SGMPr .... Santa Fe Gaming 8% Ex Pfd [*AMEX symbol*] (TTSB)
SGMS .... Shipboard Gravity Measuring System
SGMSR .... Steam Generator Maximum Steam Rate [*Nuclear energy*] (NRCH)
SGMT .... Simulated Greenwich Mean Time (MCD)
SGMT .... Subgroup Modern Terminal
SGM/USA .... Scripture Gift Mission/USA (EA)
SGN .... Ho Chi Minh [*Vietnam*] [*Airport symbol*] (OAG)
SGN .... Saigon [*Vietnam*]
SGN .... Saigon [*South Vietnam*] [*Airport symbol*] (AD)
SGN .... Sartigan Granite [*Vancouver Stock Exchange symbol*]
SGN .... Scan Gate Number
SGN .... Seamless Garment Network (EA)
SGN .... Self-Generated Noise [*Oceanography*]
SGN .... Service Geologique National [*National Geological Survey*] [*Bureau of Geological and Mining Research*] [*Information service or system*] (IID)
sgn .... Signer [*MARC relator code*] [*Library of Congress*] (LCCP)
SGN .... Standing Group, North Atlantic Treaty Organization
SGN .... Surgeon [*Military British*]
SGN .... Surgeon General of the Navy
SGNA .... Nueva Asuncion [*Paraguay*] [*ICAO location identifier*] (ICLI)
SGNA .... Society of Gastroenterology Nurses and Associates (EA)
SGNET .... Sea Grant Network [*National Oceanic and Atmospheric Administration Information service or system*] (IID)
SgnlApl .... Signal Apparel Co., Inc. [*Associated Press*] (SAG)
SGNLD .... Signalled (ROG)
SGNLS .... Sequential Generalized Nonlinear Least Squares [*Statistics*]
SgnlTech .... Signal Technology Corp. [*Associated Press*] (SAG)
SGNMOS .... Screen-Grid N-Channel Metal Oxide Semiconductor
SGNR .... Signature (AABC)
SGNS .... Signature Inns, Inc. [*NASDAQ symbol*] (SAG)
SGO .... Saint George [*Australia Airport symbol*] (OAG)
SGO .... Sea Gold Oil Corp. [*Vancouver Stock Exchange symbol*]
SGO .... Seagull Energy [*NYSE symbol*] (TTSB)
SGO .... Seagull Energy Corp. [*NYSE symbol*] (SPSG)
SGO .... Society of Geriatric Ophthalmology (EA)
SGO .... Society of Gynecologic Oncologists (EA)
SGO .... Solicitor-General's Office [*Australia*]
SGO .... Squadron Gunnery Officer
SGO .... Stained Glass Overlay [*Commercial firm British*]
SGO .... Strict Good Ordinary (IAA)
SGO .... Subgenual Organ [*Entomology*]
SGO .... Surgeon General's Office
SGO .... Surgery, Gynecology, and Obstetrics (MAE)
SGO .... Sydney Godolphin Osborne [*Literary signature of 19th-century British writer*]
SGOG .... Steam Generators Owners Group [*Nuclear energy*] (NRCH)
SGOG .... Suppressor Grid Orbitron Gauge
SGOL .... Olimpo [*Paraguay*] [*ICAO location identifier*] (ICLI)
SGOL .... Saint Helena Gold Mines [*NASDAQ symbol*] (SAG)
SGOL .... St. Helena Gold Mines Ltd. [*NASDAQ symbol*] (NQ)
SGOLY .... St. Helena Gold Mines ADR [*NASDAQ symbol*] (TTSB)
SGOMSEC .... Scientific Group on Methodologies for the Safety Evaluation of Chemicals [*International Council of Scientific Unions*]
SGOR .... Solution Gas-Oil Ratio

SGOS .... Shuttle Ground Operations Simulator [*NASA*] (NASA)
SGOT .... Serum Glutamic Oxaloacetic Transaminase [*An enzyme*]
SGP .... San Gregorio [*Peru*] [*Seismograph station code, US Geological Survey Closed*] (SEIS)
SGP .... Schering-Plough [*NYSE symbol*] (TTSB)
SGP .... School Guarantee Program (DNAB)
SGP .... Secondary Gun Pointer [*Navy*]
SGP .... Seminiferous Growth Factor [*Biochemistry*]
SGP .... Serine Glycerophosphatide [*Biochemistry*] (MAE)
SGP .... Simulated Ground Plane [*Automotive engineering*]
SGP .... Singapore [*ANSI three-letter standard code*] (CNC)
SGP .... Single Ground Point [*NASA*] (MCD)
SGP .... Society of General Physiologists (EA)
SGP .... Society of Ghana Philatelists [*Defunct*] (EA)
SGP .... Solicitor General, Prairies [*UTLAS symbol*]
SGP .... Soluble Glycoprotein [*Medicine*] (MAE)
SGP .... Southern Galactic Pole
SGP .... Southern Great Plains [*Marine science*] (OSRA)
SGP .... Southern Great Plains (USDC)
SGP .... South Galactic Pole
SGP .... Specialty Glass Products, Inc.
SGP .... Staatkundig Gereformeerde Partij [*Netherlands Political party Benelux*]
SGP .... Stabilized Gyro Platform
SGP .... Standard Guidance Package
SGP .... Stephen Greene Press
SGP .... Subscriber Group Plant (IAA)
SGP .... Sudeten German Party
SGP .... Sulfated Glycoprotein [*Biochemistry*]
SGPA .... Stained Glass Professionals Association [*Inactive*] (EA)
SGPB .... Southern Growth Policies Board
SGPC .... Soviet Government Purchasing Commission [*World War II*]
SGPF .... Spencer Gulf Prawn Fishery [*Australia*]
SGPI .... Pilar [*Paraguay*] [*ICAO location identifier*] (ICLI)
SGPI .... Superintendent of Government Printing, India (ROG)
SGPM .... Saint-Gobain-Pont-A-Mousson [*French industrial giant*]
SgpNL .... National Library, Singapore, Singapore [*Library symbol Library of Congress*] (LCLS)
SgpNU .... Nangang University, Singapore, Singapore [*Library symbol Library of Congress*] (LCLS)
SGPO .... Puerto Pinasco [*Paraguay*] [*ICAO location identifier*] (ICLI)
SGPO .... Speed-Gate-Pull-Off (PDAA)
SGPO .... Standing Group Representative Communication to the Private Office of the NATO Secretary General [*Obsolete*] (NATG)
SGPS .... Ciudad Presidente Stroessner [*Paraguay*] [*ICAO location identifier*] (ICLI)
SGPT .... Gelatin Silver Print (VRA)
SGPT .... Serum Glutamic-Pyruvic Transaminase [*An enzyme*]
SGPT .... Silver Gelatin Print (VRA)
SgpU .... University of Singapore, Singapore, Singapore [*Library symbol Library of Congress*] (LCLS)
SGR .... Greenville County Library, Greenville, SC [*OCLC symbol*] (OCLC)
SGR .... Houston, TX [*Location identifier FAA*] (FAAL)
SGR .... Sachs-Georgi Reaction [*On test for syphilis*] [*Infectious diseases*] (DAVI)
Sgr .... Sagittarius [*Constellation*]
SGR .... Saturn Energy & Resources Ltd. [*Vancouver Stock Exchange symbol*]
SGR .... School of General Reconnaissance [*Air Force British*]
SGR .... Seismic Group Recorder [*Geophysics*]
SGR .... Self-Generation Reactor [*Nuclear energy*] (NRCH)
SGR .... Seminal Groove
SGR .... Set Graphics Rendition [*Computer science*] (PCM)
SGR .... Short Growth Rate (OA)
SGR .... Singer [*Music*]
SGR .... Sodium Graphite Reactor [*Nuclear energy*]
SGR .... Soft Gamma-Ray Repeater [*Astrophysics*]
SGR .... Stack Gas Reheat [*Air pollution control*]
SGR .... Steam Gas Recycle [*Shale oil process*]
S/GR .... Steering Gear [*Automotive engineering*]
SGR .... Submandibular Gland Renin [*Endocrinology*]
SGR .... Substantia Gelatinosa Rolandi [*Medicine*] (DMAA)
SGR .... Sugar Land [*Texas*] [*Airport symbol*] (OAG)
SGRA .... Sporting Goods Representatives Association [*of SIRA*] [*Later, SGAA*] (EA)
Sg RA .... Surgeon Rear-Admiral [*British military*] (DMA)
SGRAC .... Supreme Grand Royal Arch Chapter [*Freemasonry*] (ROG)
SGRAE .... Scientists' Group for Reform of Animal Experimentation (EA)
SGRAM .... Synchronous Graphics RAM [*Random Access Memory*] (PCM)
SGRCA .... Sodium Graphite Reactor Critical Assembly (IEEE)
SGRD .... Signal Ground (AAG)
SGRD .... State Government Research Directory [*A publication*]
SGREP .... Standing Group Representative [*NASA*]
sgrf .... Sgraffito (VRA)
S-GRN .... Surfaced Green [*Lumber*]
SGRO .... Rosario [*Paraguay*] [*ICAO location identifier*] (ICLI)
SGRP .... Seating Reference Point [*49CFR571*] (TAG)
SGRS .... Stockton Geriatric Rating Scale [*Psychology*]
SGRU .... Sawyers' General Representative Union [*British*]
SGS .... Hermanas del Buen Pastor (TOCD)
SGS .... Sage Resources Ltd. [*Vancouver Stock Exchange symbol*]
SGS .... Salem Generating Station [*Nuclear energy*] (GFGA)
SGS .... Scottish Guild of Servers [*Episcopalian*]
SGS .... Secondary Grammar School (ADA)
SGS .... Secretary of the General Staff [*Army*]
SGS .... Segmented Gamma Scanner [*Nuclear energy*] (NRCH)
SGS .... Signal Generating Station (CET)
SGS .... Single Green Silk-Covered [*Wire insulation*]
SGS .... Sisters of the Good Samaritan (ADA)
SGS .... Society of the Golden Section [*Defunct*] (EA)
SGS .... Society of the Good Shepherd [*Anglican religious community*]
SGS .... Software Generation System
SGS .... Solution Gas Drive [*Petroleum engineering*]
SGS .... Song of Songs [*Old Testament book*] [*Roman Catholic canon*]
SGS .... Stactic Gel Strength [*Well drilling technology*]
SGS .... Stage Golfing Society [*British*] (BI)
SGS .... Statistics Gathering System [*NASA*]
SGS .... Steam Generator System [*Nuclear energy*] (NRCH)
SGS .... Steep Glide Slope (NASA)
SGS .... St. George [*South Carolina*] [*Seismograph station code, US Geological Survey*] (SEIS)
SGS .... Strategy Gaming Society (EA)
SGS .... Stream Generation Statement [*Computer science*]
SGS .... Stretch Glass Society (EA)
SGS .... Swiveling Gunner's Station
SGS .... Symbol Generation and Storage [*Computer science*]
SGSC .... Samuel Gompers Stamp Club (EA)
SGSC .... Standing Group Security Committee [*Obsolete NATO*] (NATG)
SGSC .... Strain Gauge Signal Conditioner [*NASA*] (MCD)
SGSE .... Standard Ground Support Equipment
SGSFU .... Salt-Glazed Structural Facing Units [*Technical drawings*]
SGSG .... Scandinavian Glioma Study Group [*Medicine*] (DMAA)
SGSI .... Stabilized Glide Slope Indicator (NVT)
SGSN .... Skylab Ground Support Network [*NASA*]
SGSNY .... St. George's Society of New York (EA)
SGSO .... Space Ground Support Operations [*NASA*] (KSC)
SGSP .... Salt Gradient Solar Ponds [*Energy source*]
SGSP .... Single Groove, Single Petticoat [*Insulators*]
SGSP .... Society for Glass Science and Practices (EA)
SGSR .... Society for General Systems Research (EA)
SGSS .... Study Group on Social Security [*Defunct*] (EA)
SGS TM .... SGS Thomson Microelectronics, NV [*Associated Press*] (SAG)
SGSUB .... Salt-Glazed Structural Unit Base [*Technical drawings*]
SGSVDV .... Steam Generator Stop Valve Dump Valve (IEEE)
S-GT .... Sachs-Georgi Test [*for syphilis*] [*Also, SG*] [*Obsolete*]
SGT .... Satellite Ground Terminal
SGT .... Seagram's Gin and Tonic
SGT .... Section Gunnery Trainer [*Army*]
SGT .... Segment Table [*Computer science*] (IBMDP)
SGT .... Sergeant (AABC)
Sgt .... Sergeant (ODBW)
SGT .... Sergeant
SGT .... Silicon Gate Transistor (IAA)
SGT .... Small Gas Turbine
SGT .... Small Group Therapy
SGT .... Small Group Trial
SGT .... Societa' Aerotaxi SUD [*Italy ICAO designator*] (FAAC)
SGT .... Society of Glass Technology (EAIO)
SGT .... Soligen Technologies, Inc. [*AMEX symbol*] (SAG)
SGT .... Special Gas Taper [*Thread*]
SGT .... Speculative Gains Tax
SGT .... Starter or Ground, Thermoplastic [*Automotive engineering*]
SGT .... Stuttgart, AR [*Location identifier FAA*] (FAAL)
SGT .... Subsystem Ground Test (MCD)
SGTA .... Servo Gear Train Assembly
Sgte .... Sagitta [*Constellation*]
SGT EC .... Soligen Technologies [*ECM Symbol*] (TTSB)
SGTF .... Steam Generator Test Facility [*Nuclear energy*] (NRCH)
SGTI .... SATCOM [*Satellite Communications*] Ground Terminal Interoperability
SGTI .... Surgical Technologies [*NASDAQ symbol*] (TTSB)
SGTI .... Surgical Technologies, Inc. [*NASDAQ symbol*] (SAG)
SGTIA .... Standing Group Technical Intelligence Agency [*NATO*] (NATG)
SGTM .... Strain Gauge Thrust Meter
SGTM .... Titanium Dioxide Manufacturers Sector Group (EAIO)
SGTMAJ .... Sergeant Major
SGTPS .... Saw Grinders' Trade Protective Society [*A union*] [*British*]
Sgtr .... Sagittarius [*Constellation*]
SGTR .... Standard Government Travel Request
SGTR .... Standardized Government Travel Regulations
SGTR .... Steam Generator Test Rig [*Nuclear energy*] (NRCH)
SGTR .... Steam Generator Tube Rupture [*Nuclear energy*] (NRCH)
SGTS .... Satellite Ground Terminal System
SGTS .... Scottish Gaelic Texts Society (DBA)
SGTS .... Second Genration Tank Sight [*Army*]
SGTS .... Standby Gas Treatment System [*Nuclear energy*] (NRCH)
SGTS .... Swing Grip Thermal Stripper
SGTT .... Standard Glucose Tolerance Test [*Medicine*] (DMAA)
SGU .... Saint George [*Utah*] [*Airport symbol*] (OAG)
SGU .... Saint George, UT [*Location identifier FAA*] (FAAL)
SGU .... Sammelbuch Griechischer Urkunden aus Aegypten [*A publication*] (BJA)
SGU .... Scottish Gliding Union (DBA)
SGU .... Scottish Golf Union (DBA)
SGU .... Sidewinder Generator Unit (NG)
SGU .... Single Gun Unit [*British military*] (DMA)
SGU .... Standard Geographical Unit (WDMC)
SGU .... Sveriges Geologiska Undersokning [*Geological Survey of Sweden*] [*Uppsala*] [*Information service or system*] (IID)
S-G(UN) .... Secretary-General of the United Nations

SGUS Slovak Gymnastic Union Sokol of the USA (EA)
SGV Saint Genevieve Resources Ltd. [*Toronto Stock Exchange symbol*]
SGV Salivary Gland Virus
SGV Screen Grid Voltage (IAA)
SGV Selective Gastric Vagotomy [*Medicine*] (DMAA)
SGV Self-Guided Vehicle
SGV Sierra Grande [*Argentina*] [*Airport symbol*] (OAG)
SGV Small Granular Vesicle [*Cytology*]
Sg VA Surgeon Vice-Admiral [*British military*] (DMA)
SGV & P Selective Gastric Vagotomy and Pyloroplasty [*Medicine*] (CPH)
SGVB SGV Bancorp [*NASDAQ symbol*] (TTSB)
SGVB SGV Bancorp, Inc. [*NASDAQ symbol*] (SAG)
SGV BC SGV Bancorp, Inc. [*Associated Press*] (SAG)
SGVHD Syngeneic Graft-Versus-Host Disease [*Medicine*] (DMAA)
SGW Salt-Glazed Ware
SGW Security Guard Window (AAG)
SGW Senior Grand Warden [*Freemasonry*]
SGW Simulated Ground Water [*Analytical chemistry*]
SGW South Carolina State College, Orangeburg, SC [*OCLC symbol*] (OCLC)
SGW Stone Groundwood [*Pulp and paper technology*]
SGW Stratospheric Gravity Waves [*Planetary science*]
SGWD Submarine Ground Water Discharge [*Geophysics*]
SGWLC Steam Generator Water Level Control [*Nuclear energy*] (NRCH)
SGWM Standing Group Working Memorandum [*NATO*] (NATG)
SGWS Shared Graphics Work Space
SGWS Stove Grate Workers' Society [*A union*] [*British*]
SGX Selector Group Matrix [*Telecommunications*] (TEL)
SGX Songea [*Tanzania*] [*Airport symbol*] (OAG)
SGX Synergistics Industries Ltd. [*Toronto Stock Exchange symbol*]
s-gy-- Guyana [*MARC geographic area code Library of Congress*] (LCCP)
SGY Skagway [*Alaska*] [*Airport symbol*] (OAG)
SGY Skagway Air Service, Inc. [*ICAO designator*] (FAAC)
SGY Skagway, AK [*Location identifier FAA*] (FAAL)
SGY Sooner Energy Corp. [*Vancouver Stock Exchange symbol*]
SGY Stone Energy [*NYSE symbol*] (TTSB)
SGY Stone Energy Corp. [*NYSE symbol*] (SPSG)
SGYR Yasyreta [*Paraguay*] [*ICAO location identifier*] (ICLI)
SGZ Green Bay, WI [*Location identifier FAA*] (FAAL)
SGZ Signet Resources, Inc. [*Vancouver Stock Exchange symbol*]
SGZ Singora [*Thailand*] [*Airport symbol*] (AD)
SGZ Surface Ground Zero
SH Air-Cushion Vehicle built by Sealand Hovercraft [*England*] [*Usually used in combination with numerals*]
SH Sacred Heart (ROG)
SH Sacrifice Hit [*Baseball*]
Sh Safe Hit [*Baseball*]
SH Sa Hautesse [*His, or Her, Highness*] [*French*]
SH Samaritan Free Hospital [*British*] (ROG)
S/H Sample and Hold (IEEE)
SH Sash (WGA)
SH Schering AG [*Germany*] [*Research code symbol*]
SH Schistosoma Hematobium [*A parasitic fluke*]
SH Schonlein-Henoch Purpura [*Medicine*] (DMAA)
SH Schoolhouse
SH Scinde Horse [*British military*] (DMA)
SH Scleroscope Hardness
SH Scottish Horse [*British military*] (DMA)
SH Scratch Hardness [*Aerospace*]
SH Scripophila Helvetica (EA)
SH Scripta Hierosolymitana (BJA)
SH Scrum Half [*Rugby*] (WGA)
SH Secondhand (ADA)
SH Second Harmonic (PDAA)
SH Second Harvest, the National Food Bank Network (EA)
SH Section Heading (NITA)
SH Section Heading Code [*Online database field identifier*]
SH Sefer ha-Shanah (BJA)
SH Sekira Hodshit [*Tel Aviv*] (BJA)
SH Semester Hour
SH Send Hub [*Telegraphy*] (TEL)
SH Senior Hunter [*Purebred canine award*]
SH Sephardic House [*An association*] (EA)
SH Sequence History
SH Serum Hepatitis [*Medicine*]
SH Service Hours [*Electronics*] (IEEE)
SH Session Handler
SH Severely Handicapped
SH Severn House [*Publisher*] [*British*]
SH Sex Hormone (MAE)
SH Sexual Harassment
SH Shackle (AAG)
SH Shale [*Lithology*]
SH Shall
Sh Shallow
SH Shandong Huaneng Power Development ADR [*NYSE symbol*] (SAG)
SH Shandong Huaneng Pwr ADS [*NYSE symbol*] (TTSB)
Sh Shand's Reports [*11-41 South Carolina*] [*A publication*] (DLA)
SH Shanghai
SH Share
Sh Shauri (BJA)
Sh Shaw's Scotch Appeal Cases [*A publication*] (DLA)
Sh Shaw's Scotch Justiciary Cases [*A publication*] (DLA)
Sh Shaw's Scotch Session Cases [*A publication*] (DLA)
Sh Shaw's Scotch Teind [*Tithe*] Court Reports [*A publication*] (DLA)
SH Sheathing [*Technical drawings*]
SH Sheep (ROG)
SH Sheep Skin [*Bookbinding*] (ROG)
SH Sheet (AAG)
Sh Sheldon's Superior Court Reports [*Buffalo, New York*] [*A publication*] (DLA)
SH Shelf [*Technical drawings*]
sh Shell [*Computer science*] (CDE)
SH Shell Development Co. [*Research code symbol*]
sh Shells [*Quality of the bottom*] [*Nautical charts*]
Sh Shepherd's Alabama Reports [*A publication*] (DLA)
Sh Shepley's Reports [*13-18, 21-30 Maine*] [*A publication*] (DLA)
Sh Sheriff (DLA)
Sh Sherwood Number
SH Shield (MSA)
Sh Shiel's Cape Times Law Reports [*South Africa*] [*A publication*] (DLA)
Sh Shigella [*Bacteriology*] (AAMN)
SH Shilling [*Monetary unit in Britain*] [*Obsolete*]
SH Ship
S/H Shipping/Handling (WGA)
Sh Shipp's Reports [*66-67 North Carolina*] [*A publication*] (DLA)
SH Ship's Head [*Heading*] [*Navigation*]
SH Ship's Serviceman [*Navy rating*]
SH Shipwright
Sh Shire
Sh Shirley's Reports [*49-55 New Hampshire*] [*A publication*] (DLA)
SH Shoal (ROG)
SH Shock (WGA)
SH Shooting [*FBI standardized term*]
SH Shop (WGA)
SH Short (ROG)
SH Short Brothers & Harland Ltd. [*ICAO aircraft manufacturer identifier*] (ICAO)
S/H Shorthand
sh Shoulder
SH Show (WGA)
SH Showers (AAG)
Sh Shower's English King's Bench Reports [*A publication*] (DLA)
Sh Shower's English Parliamentary Cases [*A publication*] (DLA)
SH Shunt [*Electricity*]
SH Shuttle (MCD)
SH Sick in Hospital
SH Single Heterostructure (MCD)
SH Single-Hung (DAC)
SH Sinus Histiocytosis [*Medicine*]
SH Small Heavy Seeds [*Botany*]
SH Social History
S/H Socialization and Handling [*Pet-adoption terminolgy*]
SH Socially Housed [*Experimental animals*]
SH Society for HematoPathology (EA)
SH Society for the Humanities (EA)
S/H Software/Hardware [*Cost*]
SH Soldiers' Home [*Later, US Soldiers' and Airmen's Home*] [*Government agency*]
SH Somatotrophic [*Growth*] Hormone [*Also, GH, STH*] [*Endocrinology*]
SH Source Handshake
SH Southern Hemisphere
SH Southland Hussars [*British military*] (DMA)
SH Spanish Heritage (EA)
sh Spanish Territories in Northern Morocco [*Spanish North Africa*] [*MARC country of publication code Library of Congress*] (LCCP)
SH Special Hazards
SH Special Honor
SH Specified Hours
SH Spontaneously Hypertensive [*Medicine*]
SH State Hospital (MAE)
sH Stathenry [*Also, statH*] [*Unit of inductance*]
SH Stationary High-Power [*Reactor*] (NRCH)
SH Station Hospital [*Military*]
SH Station House
SH Steel Heads
SH Steelton & Highspire Railroad Co. [*AAR code*]
SH St. Helena [*ANSI two-letter standard code*] (CNC)
SH Stockholder
SH Stored Heading (MCD)
SH Stoy Hayward [*Venture capital group*] [*British*]
SH Student Handout [*Military training document*] (INF)
SH Student Health (MAE)
SH Subharmonic (IAA)
SH Subject Heading (NITA)
S/H Suicidal/Homicidal [*Ideation*] [*Psychiatry*] (DAVI)
SH Sulfhydryl [*Chemistry*]
SH Super-High-Frequency [*Radio wave*] (NG)
SH Superstructure Heater (DS)
SH Surgical Hernia [*Medicine*] (WDAA)
SH Surgical History [*Medicine*]
SH Switch Handler [*Telecommunications*] (TEL)
SH Switch Hook (HGAA)
SH1 Ship's Serviceman, First Class [*Navy rating*]
SH2 Ship's Serviceman, Second Class [*Navy rating*]
sh_2 Shrunken-2 Gene [*In sweet corn*]
SH_2 Supercritical Hydrogen [*NASA*] (NASA)
SH3 Ship's Serviceman, Third Class [*Navy rating*]
Sh3 Shorts 330 [*Airplane code*]
Sh6 Shorts 360 [*Airplane code*]

SHA .... Ozark, AL [*Location identifier FAA*] (FAAL)
SHA .... Safety Hazard Analysis (MCD)
SHA .... Sailplane Homebuilders Association (EA)
SHA .... Sample and Hold Amplifier
SHA .... Scottish Hockey Association (DBA)
SHA .... Scriptores Historiae Augustae [*Classical studies*] (OCD)
SHA .... Secondary Heads Association [*British*] (DBA)
SHA .... Secretariat for Hispanic Affairs (National Conference of Catholic Bishops) (EA)
SHA .... Servicio Aereo de Honduras SA [*ICAO designator*] (FAAC)
SHA .... Shakwak Exploration Co. [*Vancouver Stock Exchange symbol*]
SHA .... Shanghai [*China*] [*Airport symbol*] (OAG)
ShA .... Shulhan 'Arukh (BJA)
SHA .... Sidereal Hour Angle
SHA .... Smith-Hughes Act (MHDW)
SHA .... Smith-Hurd's Illinois Annotated Statutes [*A publication*] (DLA)
SHA .... Socialist Health Association [*British*] (DBA)
SHA .... Societe Historique Acadienne [*Acadian Historical Society*] (EA)
SHA .... Society for Historical Archaeology (EA)
SHA .... Society for Humane Abortion (EA)
SHA .... Society for Humanistic Anthropology (EA)
SHA .... Sodium Hydroxide Addition [*Nuclear energy*] (NRCH)
SHA .... Software Hazard Analysis [*Military*]
SHA .... Software Houses Association (IAA)
SHA .... Solid Homogeneous Assembly [*Nuclear energy*]
SHA .... Southern Historical Association (EA)
SHA .... Special Handling Area (EECA)
SHA .... Special Health Authority [*Government body*] [*British*]
SHA .... Spherical Harmonic Analysis [*Geophysics*]
SHA .... Spring Hill [*Alabama*] [*Seismograph station code, US Geological Survey*] (SEIS)
SHA .... Staphylococcal Hemagglutinating Antibody [*Medicine*] (DMAA)
SHA .... State Highway Agency [*MOCD*] (TAG)
SHA .... Station Housing Allowance [*Military*] (MCD)
sHa .... Suckling Hamster [*Medicine*] (DMAA)
SHa .... Sulgi Hymn A (BJA)
SHA .... Superheated Aerosol (DAVI)
SHA .... Support Harness Assembly
SHA .... System Hazard Analyses [*NASA*] (NASA)
SHAA .... Sealed Head Access Area [*Nuclear energy*] (NRCH)
SHAA .... Serum Hepatitis Associated Antigen [*Hematology*]
SHAA .... Society of Hearing Aid Audiologists [*Later, NHAS*] (EA)
SHAA-Ab ...... Serum Hepatitis Associated Antigen-Antibody [*Hematology*]
SHA-Ab .... Serum Hepatitis Associated Antibody [*Hematology*]
Shab .... Shabbath (BJA)
SHAB .... Soft and Hard Acid and Base (PDAA)
SHABS .... Shock Absorber
SHAC .... School Heads Advisory Committee [*National Association of Independent Schools*] (EDAC)
SHAC .... Small Hydrofoil Aircraft Carrier (DNAB)
SHAC .... Society for the History of Alchemy and Chemistry (EA)
SHAC .... Solar Heating and Air Conditioning
Sh Acc .... Hale's Sheriff's Account [*A publication*] (DLA)
SHACC .... Servicing Hotels and the Caribbean Community
SHACO .... Shorthand Coding
SHACOB .... Solar Heating and Cooling of Buildings [*Energy Research and Development Administration*]
SHACV .... Second Harmonic AC [*Alternating Current*] Voltammetry [*Instrumentation*]
SHAD .... Shallow Habitat Air Dive [*Navy*]
SHAD .... Sharpe Army Depot [*California*]
SHAD .... Shipboard Hazards Appraisal and Defense (CINC)
SHADCOM ... Shipping Advisory Committee [*NATO*]
SHADE .... Shielded Hot-Air-Drum Evaporator [*Concentrator for hazardous wastes*]
SHADO .... Supreme Headquarters, Alien Defense Organization [*in television program "UFO"*]
SHADRAC .... Shelter Housed Automatic Digital Random Access [*Computer science*]
SHAEF .... Supreme Headquarters, Allied Expeditionary Force [*Europe*] [*World War II*]
SH-AF .... Shelter-Afrique (EAIO)
SHAF .... Staying Healthy after Fifty [*Project*] [*AARP*]
SHAFB .... Sheppard Air Force Base [*Texas*] (AAG)
SHAFFT .... Second Husbands Alliance for Fair Treatment
SHAFR .... Society for Historians of American Foreign Relations (EA)
SHAFT .... Sad, Hostile, Anxious, Frustrating, Tenacious Patient Syndrome [*Medicine*] (DMAA)
SHAFT .... Second Home All-Inclusive First Trust [*Real estate*]
SHAFT .... Shaftsbury [*England*]
SHAG .... Share Holder Action Group [*Australia*]
SHAG .... Simplified High-Accuracy Guidance [*NASA*] (NASA)
SHAK .... Shakespeare
Shakes Q ..... Shakespeare Quarterly [*A publication*] (BRI)
Shaks .... Shakespeare (BARN)
SHAL .... Subject Heading Authority List [*Computer science*]
Shale .... Decrees and Judgments in Federal Anti-Trust Cases [*United States*] [*A publication*] (DLA)
SHALE .... Stand-off, High Altitude, Long Endurance (PDAA)
Shalm .... Shalmaneser (BJA)
SHALOM ...... Synchronous Halo Monitor [*NASA*]
SHALTA .... Skin, Hide, and Leather Trades Association [*British*] (DBA)
SHAM .... Salicylhydroxamic Acid [*Chelating agent*]
Shaman .... Shaman Pharmaceuticals, Inc. [*Associated Press*] (SAG)
SHAME .... Save, Help Animals Man Exploits [*Connecticut organization*]
SHAME .... Society to Humiliate, Aggravate, Mortify, and Embarrass Smokers
SHAME .... Stop Hospital and Medical Errors
SHAMP .... Ship Acquisition Project Manager [*Navy*] (DOMA)
SHAMS .... Smart Howitzer Automated Management System [*US Army Human Engineering Laboratory*] (RDA)
SHAMYR ...... Shomrei Mitzvot Yotzei Russia (BJA)
Shan .... Shannon's Unreported Tennessee Cases [*A publication*] (DLA)
Shan Cas ..... Shannon's Tennessee Cases [*A publication*] (DLA)
Shand .... Shand's Reports [*11-41 South Carolina*] [*A publication*] (DLA)
Sh & Dunl ... Shaw and Dunlop's Scotch Court of Session Reports, First Series [*A publication*] (DLA)
Sh & Macl ... Shaw and Maclean's Scotch Appeal Cases [*A publication*] (DLA)
Shand Pr ..... Shand's Practice, Scotch Court of Sessions [*A publication*] (DLA)
Sh & R Neg ... Shearman and Redfield on the Law of Negligence [*A publication*] (DLA)
SH & T .... Shower and Toilet (AAG)
SHANE .... Steerable Hydrophone Array, Nonlinear Element
ShangPt .... Shanghai Petrochemical Co. [*Associated Press*] (SAG)
ShanHua ...... Shandong Huaneng Power Development ADR [*Associated Press*] (SAG)
SHANICLE .... Short-Range Navigation Vehicle [*System*] [*Air Force*]
Shankland's St ... Shankland's Tennessee Public Statutes [*A publication*] (DLA)
Shannon Cas (Tenn) ... Shannon's Unreported Tennessee Cases [*A publication*] (DLA)
Shannon's Code ... Shannon's Tennessee Annotated Code [*A publication*] (DLA)
SHANT .... Shantung [*Province in China*] (ROG)
SHAOB .... Strategic High-Altitude Orbital Bomber (IAA)
SHAP .... Ship Acquisition Plan [*Navy*] (CAAL)
SHAPA .... Solids Handling and Processing Association (EAIO)
SHAPE .... SAGE [*Semiautomatic Ground Environment*] High Altitude Prototype Environment [*Military*] (IAA)
SHAPE .... Simulated Hospital Administration and Planning Exercise
SHAPE .... Supersonic High-Altitude Parachute Experiment [*NASA*]
SHAPE .... Supreme Headquarters, Allied Powers Europe [*NATO*]
SHAPES .... Spatial, High-Accuracy Position Encoding Sensor (SSD)
SHAPEX .... SHAPE [*Supreme Headquarters Allied Powers Europe*] Annual Command Exercise [*NATO*] (NATG)
SHAPM .... Shear Horizontal Acoustic Plate Model [*Instrumentation*]
SHAPM .... Ship Acquisition Project Manager [*Navy*]
Sh App .... Shaw's Scotch Appeal Cases, House of Lords [*A publication*] (DLA)
ShAr .... Shulhan 'Arukh (BJA)
SHAR .... Simplified Hourly Absence Reporting (MCD)
SHAR .... Sriharikota Island Launch Complex [*India*]
SHARC .... Super Harvard Architecture Computer
SHARE .... Schoolboys Harness Aid for the Relief of the Elderly (AIE)
SHARE .... Shared Area Resources Exchange [*Library network*]
SHaRE .... Shared Research Equipment Collaborative Research Program [*Oak Ridge, TN*] [*Oak Ridge National Laboratory*] [*Department of Energy*] (GRD)
SHARE .... SHARE Foundation (EA)
SHARE .... Share Happily and Reap Endlessly [*Hollywood women's charity organization*]
SHARE .... Siblings Helping Persons with Autism through Resources and Energy (MEDA)
SHARE .... Society to Help Avoid Redundant Effort [*in data processing*]
SHARE .... Software Help in Applications, Research and Education [*International program to develop meteorological analysis and display software for developing countries*] [*Marine science*] (OSRA)
SHARE .... Software Help in Applications, Research and Education [*International program to develop meteorological analysis and display software for developing countries*] (USDC)
SHARE .... So Handicapped All Read Easily
SHARE .... Soldier Housing and Retirement Equity
SHARE .... Systems for Heat and Radiation Energy [*Nuclear energy*]
SHAREM ...... Ship ASW [*Antisubmarine Warfare*] Readiness Effectiveness Measuring Program
SHARES .... Shared Acquisitions and Retention System
Shark Elec ... Sharkey's Practice of Election Committees [*2nd ed.*] [*1866*] [*A publication*] (DLA)
SHARNB ...... Sharnbrook [*England*]
SHARP .... School Health Additional Referral Program [*Public Health Service*]
SHARP .... Senior High Assessment of Reading Performance [*Educational test*]
SHARP .... Ships Analysis and Retrieval Program [*Navy*]
SHARP .... Ships and Analysis and Retrieval Project (NITA)
SHARP .... Society for the History of Authorship, Reading and Publishing (EA)
SHARP .... Sperry Heading and Attitude Reference Platform (SAA)
SHARP .... Stationary [*or Strategic*] High-Altitude Relay Platform [*Microwave airplane*] [*Canada*]
SHARP .... Strategic High Altitude Relay Platform [*Aviation*]
Sharp Cong Ct ... Sharp on Congregational Courts [*A publication*] (DLA)
Sharpe .... Calendar of Coroners Rolls of the City of London [*A publication*] (DLA)
SHARPE .... Symbolic Hierarchical Automated Reliability and Performance Evaluator
Sharp Ins Dig ... Sharpstein's Insurance Digest [*A publication*] (DLA)
SHARPS .... Ship/Helicopter Acoustic Range-Prediction System [*Navy*] (NVT)
SHARPS .... Sonic High-Accuracy Ranging and Positioning System
Shars & B Lead Cas Real Prop ... Sharswood and Budd's Leading Cases on Real Property [*A publication*] (DLA)
Shars Black ... Sharswood's Edition of Blackstone's Commentaries [*A publication*] (DLA)
Shars Bl Comm ... Sharswood's Edition of Blackstone's Commentaries [*A publication*] (DLA)
Shars Comm L ... Sharswood's Commercial Law [*A publication*] (DLA)

Shars Law Lec... Sharswood's Lectures on the Profession of the Law [*A publication*] (DLA)
Shars Leg Eth... Sharswood's Legal Ethics [*A publication*] (DLA)
Shars Tab Ca... Sharswood's Table of Cases, Connecticut [*A publication*] (DLA)
SHAS .... Self Help Association for Stammerers [*British*] (DI)
SHAS .... Shared Hospital Accounting System [*Computer science*]
SHaS .... Shishah Sedarim (BJA)
SHATC .... SHAPE [*Supreme Headquarters Allied Powers Europe*] Technical Center [*Formerly, SADTC*] [*NATO*] (NATG)
SHATCPS..... St. Helena, Ascension, and Tristan da Cunha Philatelic Society (EA)
SHAU......... Subject Heading Authority Unit (NITA)
SHAVE......... Sugar Hotel Alpha Victor Echo [*Apollo 10 astronauts' code for shaving operation*]
SHAVIB......... Shaft Alignment and Vibration (DNAB)
SHAW......... Shaw Group [*NASDAQ symbol*] (NQ)
Shaw .... Shaw Industries, Inc. [*Associated Press*] (SAG)
Shaw .... Shaw's Scotch Appeal Cases [*A publication*] (DLA)
Shaw .... Shaw's Scotch Court of Session Cases, First Series [*A publication*] (DLA)
Shaw .... Shaw's Scotch Justiciary Cases [*A publication*] (DLA)
Shaw .... Shaw's Scotch Teind [*Tithe*] Court Reports [*A publication*] (DLA)
Shaw & D...... Shaw and Dunlop's Scotch Court of Session Reports, First Series [*A publication*] (DLA)
Shaw & Dunl... Shaw and Dunlop's Scotch Court of Session Reports, First Series [*A publication*] (DLA)
Shaw & M... Shaw and Maclean's Scotch Appeal Cases [*A publication*] (DLA)
Shaw & Macl... Shaw and Maclean's Scotch Appeal Cases [*A publication*] (DLA)
Shaw & M Sc App Cas... Shaw and Maclean's Scotch Appeal Cases [*1835-38*] [*A publication*] (DLA)
Shaw App.... Shaw's Scotch Appeal Cases, English House of Lords [*A publication*] (DLA)
SHAWCO...... Students' Health and Welfare Centers Organization
Shaw Crim Cas... Shaw's Criminal Cases, Scotch Justiciary Court [*A publication*] (DLA)
Shaw D & B... Shaw, Dunlop, and Bell's Scotch Court of Session Reports, First Series [*A publication*] (DLA)
Shaw D & B Supp... Shaw, Dunlop, and Bell's Supplement, Containing House of Lords Decisions [*Scotland*] [*A publication*] (DLA)
Shaw Dec.... Shaw's Decisions in Scotch Court of Sessions, First Series [*A publication*] (DLA)
Shaw Dig..... Shaw's Digest of Decisions [*Scotland*] [*A publication*] (DLA)
Shaw Dunl & B... Shaw, Dunlop, and Bell's Scotch Court of Session Cases, First Series [*1821-38*] [*A publication*] (DLA)
ShawGp....... Shaw Group [*Associated Press*] (SAG)
Shaw HL...... Shaw's Scotch Appeal Cases, House of Lords [*1821-24*] [*A publication*] (DLA)
Shaw J........ John Shaw's Justiciary Cases [*1848-52*] [*Scotland*] [*A publication*] (DLA)
SHAWL........ Special Hard-Target Assault Weapon LAW (RDA)
ShawN........ Shawmut National Corp. [*Associated Press*] (SAG)
ShawNt....... Shawmut National Corp. [*Associated Press*] (SAG)
Shaw P........ Patrick Shaw's Justiciary Cases [*1819-31*] [*Scotland*] [*A publication*] (DLA)
Shaw PL...... Shaw's Parish Law [*A publication*] (DLA)
Shaw Sc App Cas... Shaw's Scotch Appeal Cases, House of Lords [*1821-24*] [*A publication*] (DLA)
Shaw TC...... Shaw's Scotch Teind [*Tithe*] Cases [*1821-31*] [*A publication*] (DLA)
Shaw T Cas... Shaw's Scotch Teind [*Tithe*] Court Reports [*A publication*] (DLA)
Shaw Teind... Shaw's Scotch Teind [*Tithe*] Court Decisions [*1821-31*] [*A publication*] (DLA)
Shaw W & C... Shaw, Wilson, and Courtenay's Scotch Appeals Reports, House of Lords [*A publication*] (DLA)
SHAZ.......... Spirohydantoin Aziridine [*Biochemistry*]
SHB.......... Nakashibetsu [*Japan*] [*Airport symbol*] (OAG)
SHB.......... Second-Harmonic Band
SHB.......... Sequential Hemibody [*Irradiation*] [*Medicine*] (DMAA)
SHB.......... Shabair [*Zaire*] [*ICAO designator*] (FAAC)
SHB.......... Shark Bay [*Western Australia*] [*Airport symbol*] (AD)
SHB.......... Shelbyville, IN [*Location identifier FAA*] (FAAL)
SHb.......... Sickle Hemoglobin [*Screen*] [*Hematology*] (DAVI)
SHB.......... Silhouette Harness Board (MCD)
SHB.......... Sodium Hydroxybutyrate [*Organic chemistry*]
SHB.......... Subacute Hepatitis with Bridging [*Medicine*]
S Hb.......... Sulfhemoglobin [*Medicine*] (MAE)
SHB.......... Super Highband [*Radio frequency*] (NTCM)
SHBD.......... Serum Hydroxybutyrate Dehydrogenase [*An enzyme*]
SHBD INT.... Shipboard Intelligence (DOMA)
SHBE.......... Southern Hemisphere Balloon Experiment (SAA)
SHBG.......... Sex-Hormone-Binding Globulin [*Endocrinology*]
SHBLDR....... Shipbuilder (MSA)
SHBTh......... Society of Health and Beauty Therapists [*British*] (DBA)
SHBZ.......... ShowBiz Pizza Time [*NASDAQ symbol*] (TTSB)
SHBZ.......... ShowBiz Pizza Time, Inc. [*NASDAQ symbol*] (CTT)
SHC.......... Chief Ship's Serviceman [*Navy rating*]
SHC.......... Mount St. Helena [*California*] [*Seismograph station code, US Geological Survey*] (SEIS)
SHC.......... Sacred Heart College [*Cullman, AL*]
SHC.......... Schult Homes Corp. [*AMEX symbol*] (SPSG)
SHC.......... Self-Help Crafts [*An association*] (EA)
SHC.......... Sensitized Human Cell (PDAA)
SHC.......... SENTRY [*Survey Entry*] Hazard Control
SHC.......... Seton Hill College [*Greensburg, PA*]
SHC.......... Shape and Hamiltonian Consistent [*Physics*]
SHC.......... Shell Canada'A'vtg [*TS Symbol*] (TTSB)
SHC.......... Shell Canada Ltd. [*Toronto Stock Exchange symbol Vancouver Stock Exchange symbol*]
SHC.......... Shipping Coordinating Committee [*Coast Guard*]
SHC.......... Shire Indaselassie [*Ethiopia*] [*Airport symbol*] (OAG)
SHC.......... Siena Heights College [*Adrian, MI*]
SHC.......... Silicones Health Council (EA)
SHC.......... Sky Harbor Air Service, Inc. [*ICAO designator*] (FAAC)
SHC.......... Societe Heraldique du Canada [*Heraldry Society of Canada*] (EAIO)
SHC.......... Societe Historique du Canada [*Canadian Historical Association - CHA*]
SHC.......... Sodium Hypochlorite [*Inorganic chemistry*]
SHC.......... Southern Hemisphere Cap [*on Triton*]
SHC.......... Southern Humanities Conference (EA)
SHC.......... Special Handling Code
SHC.......... Spherical Harmonic Coefficient [*Geophysics*]
SHC.......... Spontaneous Human Combustion
SHC.......... Spring Hill College [*Mobile, AL*]
SHC.......... Stanford Humanities Center [*Stanford University*] [*Research center*] (RCD)
SHC.......... Superheat Control [*Boilers*]
SHC.......... Superhybrid Composite [*Laminate*]
SHC.......... Superior Heliocentric Conjunction
SHC.......... Surveillance Helicopter Co. [*Army*] (AABC)
SHC.......... Synthesized Hydrocarbon (PDAA)
SHC.......... Synthetic Hydrocarbons [*Lubricants*]
SHCA.......... Safety Helmet Council of America (EA)
SHCA.......... Siberian Husky Club of America (EA)
SHCA.......... Solid Homogeneous Critical Assembly [*Nuclear reactor*] [*Japan*]
Sh/Cat.......... Sheaf Catalogue [*Library term*] (DGA)
SHC-BRC..... Small Homes Council-Building Research Council [*University of Illinois*] [*Research center*] (RCD)
SHCC.......... Statewide Health Coordinating Council
SHCC.......... Susan Hayward Collectors Club (EA)
SHCG.......... Social History Curators Group [*British*] (DBA)
SHCGSAS.... Shrimp Harvesters Coalition of the Gulf and South Atlantic States (EA)
SHCI.......... Salick Health Care, Inc. [*Beverly Hills, CA*] [*NASDAQ symbol*] (NQ)
SHCID.......... Salick Health Care(New) [*NASDAQ symbol*] (TTSB)
SHCJ.......... Society for the History of Czechoslovak Jews (EA)
SHCJ.......... Society of the Holy Child Jesus [*Roman Catholic women's religious order*]
SHCM.......... Master Chief Ship's Serviceman [*Navy rating*]
SHCO.......... Schult Homes Corp. (MHDW)
SHCO.......... Sulfated Hydrogenated Castor Oil (MAE)
SHCON.......... Shore Connection (IAA)
SHCOS.......... Supreme Headquarters, Chief of Staff [*World War II*]
SHCPP.......... Sanitation Handbook of Consumer Protection Programs
SHCR.......... Sheridan Healthcare [*NASDAQ symbol*] (TTSB)
SHCR.......... Sheridan Healthcare, Inc. [*NASDAQ symbol*] (SAG)
SHCR.......... Sheridian Healtcare, Inc. [*NASDAQ symbol*] (SAG)
SHCR.......... Shipping Container
SHCR.......... Skyline Hikers of the Canadian Rockies (EA)
Sh Crim Cas... Shaw's Justiciary Court, Criminal Cases [*Scotland*] [*A publication*] (DLA)
SHCRT.......... Short Circuit (AAG)
SHCS.......... Senior Chief Ship's Serviceman [*Navy rating*]
SHCS USAF... School of Health Care Sciences, United States Air Force (AFM)
SHCT.......... Sheriff Court [*Legal*] [*British*]
SHCT.......... Studies in the History of Christian Thought [*A publication*] (BJA)
Sh Ct of Sess... Shaw's Scotch Court of Session Cases [*A publication*] (DLA)
Sh Ct Rep.... Sheriff Court Reports [*Scotland*] [*A publication*] (DLA)
SHCW.......... Scottish History from Contemporary Writers [*A publication*]
SHD.......... Sandhill Decline [*Citrus blight*]
SHD.......... Scottish Home Department (ILCA)
SHD.......... Second Harmonic Distortion (IAA)
SHD.......... Shade
SHD.......... Shade
SHD.......... Shahrud [*Iran*] [*Seismograph station code, US Geological Survey*] (SEIS)
SHD.......... Sherwood Group [*NYSE symbol*] (SAG)
SHD.......... Shield Development [*Vancouver Stock Exchange symbol*]
SHD.......... Ship's Diver [*Navy British*]
SHD.......... Shode
SHD.......... Should (ROG)
SHD.......... Shroud (AAG)
SHD.......... Silo Hardsite Defense
SHD.......... Slant Hole Distance [*Nuclear energy*] (OA)
SHD.......... Society for the History of Discoveries (EA)
SHD.......... Special Handling Designator (MCD)
SHD.......... State Highway Departments [*A publication*] (AAGC)
SHD.......... Staunton [*Virginia*] [*Airport symbol*] (OAG)
SHD.......... Staunton/Waynesboro/Harrisonburg, VA [*Location identifier FAA*] (FAAL)
SHD.......... Sudden Heart Death [*Medicine*] (DMAA)
SHd.......... Sulgi Hymn D (BJA)
SHDA.......... Selenaheptadecanoic Acid [*Organic chemistry*]
SHDC.......... Sacred Heart Dominican College [*Texas*]
SHDC.......... Subject Headings Used in the Dictionary Catalog [*Later, LCSH*] [*A publication*]
SHDCD.......... Shore Duty Commencemnt Date [*Navy*] (DNAB)
SHDI.......... Supraoptic-Hypophyseal Diabetes Insipidus [*Endocrinology*]
Sh Dig.......... Shaw's Digest of Decisions [*Scotland*] [*A publication*] (DLA)
SHDN.......... Shutdown (NASA)
SHDP.......... Supportive Housing Demonstration Program [*Department of Housing and Urban Development*] (GFGA)

SHDPS .... St. Helena and Dependencies Philatelic Society (EA)
SHDR .... Service and Hardware Difficulty Reports (MCD)
SHDS .... Safety and Health Data Sheet [*Army*]
SHDS .... Second-Harmonic Discrimination System (MCD)
ShdTech ...... Shared Technologies, Inc. [*Associated Press*] (SAG)
SHE .... Safety, Health and Environment (ACII)
SHE .... Scheffield Explorations [*AMEX symbol*] (SAG)
SHE .... Securities Hazards Expert [*In film title*]
SHE .... Self-Help Enterprises (EA)
SHE .... Semihomogeneous Experiment [*Nuclear energy*]
SHE .... Sheba Copper Mines [*Vancouver Stock Exchange symbol*]
SHE .... Shell Aircraft Ltd. [*British ICAO designator*] (FAAC)
SHE .... Shemkha [*Former USSR Seismograph station code, US Geological Survey*] (SEIS)
SHE .... Shenyang [*China*] [*Airport symbol*] (OAG)
SHE .... Siderphile Superheavy Element [*Physics*]
SHE .... Signal Handling Equipment (AAG)
SHE .... Society for History Education (EA)
SHE .... Society for Human Ecology (EA)
SHE .... Society for the Health Education [*British*]
SHE .... Sodium Heat Engine
SHE .... Spares Handling Expense
SHE .... Special Handling Equipment
SHE .... Standard Hydrogen Electrode [*Electrochemistry*]
SHE .... Subject Headings for Engineering [*A publication*]
SHE .... Substrate Hot Electron (IAA)
S/HE .... Sundays and Holidays Excepted
SHE .... Supercritical Helium (KSC)
SHE .... Superheavy Element [*Nuclear physics*]
SHE .... Support, Help, and Empowerment
SHE .... Syrian Hamster Embryonic [*Cells*]
SHEA .... Society for Hospital Epidemiology of America
SHEAL .... Shuttle High-Energy Astrophysics Laboratory [*NASA*] (SSD)
SHEAR .... Society for Historians of the Early American Republic (EA)
Shear & R Neg... Shearman and Redfield on the Law of Negligence [*A publication*] (DLA)
Shear Bar Ex... Shearwood's Bar Examinations [*A publication*] (DLA)
Shear Cont... Shearwood on Contract [*1897*] [*A publication*] (DLA)
Shearm & Red Neg... Shearman and Redfield on the Law of Negligence [*A publication*] (DLA)
Shear Pers Pr... Shearwood on Personal Property [*1882*] [*A publication*] (DLA)
Shear R Pr... Shearwood on Real Property [*3rd ed.*] [*1885*] [*A publication*] (DLA)
SHEB .... Shebear [*England*]
Sheb .... Shebi'it (BJA)
SHEBA .... Surface Heat Budget of the Arctic [*Marine science*] (OSRA)
SHEBA .... Surface Heat Budget of the Arctic (USDC)
Shebi .... Shebi'it (BJA)
Shebu .... Shebu'oth (BJA)
SHED .... Sealed Housing for Evaporative Determinations [*EPA engine test*]
SHED .... Settlement Houses Employment Development [*Large group of settlement houses*]
SHED .... SMT Health Services, Inc. [*NASDAQ symbol*] (SAG)
SHED .... SMT Health Svcs [*NASDAQ symbol*] (TTSB)
SHED .... Solar Heat Exchanger Drive (IAA)
SHEDA .... Storage and Handling Equipment Distributors Association [*British*] (DBA)
SHEDS .... Ship Helicopter Extended Delivery System [*Navy*] (NVT)
SHEDW .... SMT Health Svcs Wrrt [*NASDAQ symbol*] (TTSB)
SHEE .... Safe High-Energy Explosive
SHE EC .... Sheffield Exploration [*ECM Symbol*] (TTSB)
SHEENT .... Skin, Head, Eyes, Ears, Nose, and Throat [*Medicine*] (DMAA)
SHEEO .... State Higher Education Executive Officers Association (EA)
Shef .... Sheffield [*England*] (BARN)
SHEF .... Sheffield, IL [*Commercial waste site*] (GAAI)
SHEFD .... Sheffield [*England*]
SHEFF .... Shefford [*England*]
SheldMd ...... Sheffield Medical Technologies [*Associated Press*] (SAG)
SHEG .... Scottish Health Education Group (DI)
SHEG .... Superfluid-Helium Gyroscope
SHEIA .... Steric Hindrance Enzyme Immunoassay [*Clinical chemistry*]
Sheil Ir Bar... Sheil's Sketches of the Irish Bar [*A publication*] (DLA)
SHEK .... Schweizer Hilfswerk fuer Emigrationskinder (BJA)
Shek .... Shekalim (BJA)
SHEL .... Sheldahl, Inc. [*NASDAQ symbol*] (NQ)
SHEL .... Shore ELINT [*Electromagnetic Intelligence*] System [*Navy*] (NG)
Shel Bank.... Shelford's Bankrupt and Insolvency Law [*3rd ed.*] [*1862*] [*A publication*] (DLA)
Shelby .... Shelby Williams Industries, Inc. [*Associated Press*] (SAG)
Shel Ca .... Shelley's Cases in Vol. 1 of Coke's Reports [*A publication*] (DLA)
Sheld .... Sheldon's Superior Court Reports [*Buffalo, New York*] [*A publication*] (DLA)
Sheldl .... Sheldahl Co. [*Associated Press*] (SAG)
Sheldon .... Sheldon's Superior Court Reports [*Buffalo, New York*] [*A publication*] (DLA)
Sheld Subr... Sheldon on Subrogation [*A publication*] (DLA)
SHELF .... Super-Hard Extremely-Low Frequency (MCD)
Shelf J St Cos... Shelford on Joint-Stock Companies [*A publication*] (DLA)
Shelf Lun.... Shelford on Lunacy [*A publication*] (DLA)
Shelf Mar & Div... Shelford on Marriage and Divorce [*A publication*] (DLA)
Shel High .... Shelford on Highways [*4th ed.*] [*1869*] [*A publication*] (DLA)
Shel J St Com... Shelford on Joint Stock Companies [*2nd ed.*] [*1870*] [*A publication*] (DLA)
SHELLREP ... Shelling Report [*Military*] (NATG)
ShellTr .... Shell Transport & Trading Co. Ltd. [*Associated Press*] (SAG)
Shel Lun ...... Shelford on Lunacy [*2nd ed.*] [*1847*] [*A publication*] (DLA)
Shel M & D... Shelford on Marriage and Divorce [*1841*] [*A publication*] (DLA)
Shel Mort .... Shelford on Mortmain and Charitable Uses [*1836*] [*A publication*] (DLA)
Shel Prob .... Shelford on Probate, Legacy, Etc. [*2nd ed.*] [*1861*] [*A publication*] (DLA)
SHELREP ..... Shelling Report [*Military*]
SHELREPT ... Shelling Report [*Military*] (MUGU)
Shel R Pr St... Sheldon's Real Property Statutes [*9th ed.*] [*1893*] [*A publication*] (DLA)
Shel Ry .... Shelford on Railways [*4th ed.*] [*1869*] [*A publication*] (DLA)
SheltCm .... Shelter Components Corp. [*Associated Press*] (SAG)
Shel Will ..... Shelford on Wills [*1838*] [*A publication*] (DLA)
Shel Wills ... Shelford on Wills [*A publication*] (DLA)
SHEM .... Hemolyzed - Unable to Do Test [*laboratory science*] (DAVI)
SHEMA .... Steam Heating Equipment Manufacturers Association [*Defunct*] (EA)
S-HEMP .... System - Hydraulic, Electrical, Mechanical, Pneumatic
SHEN .... First Shenango Bancorp [*NASDAQ symbol*] (TTSB)
SHEN .... First Shenango Bancorp, Inc. [*NASDAQ symbol*] (SAG)
Shen .... Shenandoah [*A publication*] (BRI)
SHEN .... Shenandoah National Park
Shep .... Select Cases [*37-39 Alabama*] [*A publication*] (DLA)
Shep .... Shepard's Citations [*A publication*] (AAGC)
Shep .... Shepherd's Alabama Reports [*A publication*] (DLA)
Shep .... Shepley's Reports [*13-18, 21-30 Maine*] [*A publication*] (DLA)
SHEP .... Shock Hydrodynamic Elastic Plastic (MCD)
SHEP .... Solar High-Energy Particles
SHEP .... Systolic Hypertension in the Elderly Program [*Medicine*]
Shep Abr ..... Sheppard's Abridgment [*A publication*] (DLA)
Shep Act ..... Sheppard's Action on the Case [*A publication*] (DLA)
Shep Cas ..... Sheppard's Cases of Slander, Etc. [*A publication*] (DLA)
Shepherd ..... Shepherd's Reports [*19-21, 24-41, 60, 63, 64 Alabama*] [*A publication*] (DLA)
Sheph Sel Cas... Shepherd's Select Cases [*Alabama*] [*A publication*] (DLA)
Shepley .... Shepley's Reports [*13-18, 21-30 Maine*] [*A publication*] (DLA)
Shep Prec.... Sheppard's Precedent of Precedents [*9th ed.*] [*1825*] [*A publication*] (DLA)
Shep Sel Cas... Shepherd's Select Cases [*Alabama*] [*A publication*] (DLA)
SHER .... Sheriff
SHERB .... Sandia Human Error Rate Bank [*NASA*] (NASA)
SHERB .... Sherborne [*Urban district in England*]
SHERCI .... Safety, Health, and Environmental Resource Center International (EA)
Sher Ct Rep... Sheriff Court Reports [*Scotland*] [*A publication*] (DLA)
Sheridan ...... Sheridan Healthcare, Inc. [*Associated Press*] (SAG)
SHERK .... [*The*] New Schaff-Herzog Encyclopaedia of Religious Knowledge [*A publication*] (BJA)
SHERLOC ..... Something to Help Everyone Reduce Load on Computers [*Army*]
Sher Mar Ins... Sherman's Marine Insurance [*A publication*] (DLA)
Sher Pr .... Sheridan's Practice, King's Bench [*A publication*] (DLA)
SHERVICK .... Sherman Tanks Converted into Tractors by Vickers Armstrong
Sherwin .... Sherwin-Williams Co. [*Associated Press*] (SAG)
Shet .... Shetland (WGA)
Shev .... Shevi'it (BJA)
SHEVE .... Southern Hemisphere VLBI [*Very-Long-Baseline Interferometry*] Experiment [*For observing intergalactic radio components*]
Shevu .... Shevu'ot (BJA)
SHEX .... Sundays and Holidays Excepted [*Business term*]
SHF .... Schiffner Oilfield & Technology Corp. [*Vancouver Stock Exchange symbol*]
SHF .... Schroder Asian Growth [*NYSE symbol*] (SAG)
SHF .... Schroder Asian Growth Fd [*NYSE symbol*] (TTSB)
SHF .... Sea Heritage Foundation (EA)
SHF .... Self Help Foundation (EA)
SHF .... Sensible Heat Factor (IAA)
SHF .... Shawinigan Falls [*Quebec*] [*Seismograph station code, US Geological Survey Closed*] (SEIS)
SHF .... Shift (MSA)
SHF .... Simian Hemorrhagic Fever [*Medicine*] (DMAA)
SHF .... Sisters of the Holy Faith [*Roman Catholic religious order*]
SHF .... Sisters of the Holy Family [*Roman Catholic religious order*]
SHF .... Soil and Health Foundation [*Later, RI*] (EA)
SHF .... Storage-Handling Facility [*Nuclear energy*] (NRCH)
SHF .... Structures Heating Facility
SHF .... Super High Frequency [*Radio wave*]
SHF .... Super High Frequency (DOMA)
shf .... Superhigh Frequency (WDMC)
SHF .... Support Helicopter Flight NI [*British ICAO designator*] (FAAC)
SHF .... Supra-High Frequency [*Radio wavelength*] (IAA)
SHF .... Synthesized Hydrocarbon Fluid [*Petroleum engineering*]
SHF .... University of Sheffield, Postgraduate School of Librarianship, Sheffield, England [*OCLC symbol*] (OCLC)
SHFA .... Single Conductor, Heat and Flame Resistant, Armor [*Cable*]
SHFC .... Seven Hills Financial Corp. [*NASDAQ symbol*] (SAG)
SHFC .... Seven Hills Finl [*NASDAQ symbol*] (TTSB)
SHFCC .... Shriners Hospitals for Crippled Children (EA)
SHFD .... Split Hand/Foot Deformity [*Medicine*] (DMAA)
SHF/EHF ...... Super-High Frequency/Extremely-High Frequency (MCD)
SHFF .... Societe Historique et Folklorique Francaise [*Defunct*] (EA)
SHFG .... Society for History in the Federal Government (EA)
SHF-GMFSC... Super-High-Frequency - Ground Mobile Forces Satellite Communications (MCD)
SHFL .... Shoulder Horizontal Flexion [*Sports medicine*]
SHFL .... Shuffle Master [*NASDAQ symbol*] (TTSB)
SHFL .... Shuffle Master, Inc. [*NASDAQ symbol*] (SAG)
SHFS .... Superhyperfine Structure

SHFT........ Shift
SHF-TDMA-MODEM... Super-High-Frequency - Time Division Multiple Access - MODEM (MCD)
SHFTG........ Shafting [*Freight*]
SHFTGR........ Shaft Gear
SHFTR........ Shift Register (NITA)
SHFV........ Simian Haemorrhagic Fever Virus
SHG........ Sauerbruch, Herrmannsdorfer, Gerson Diet [*Medicine*] (BABM)
SHG........ Sauerbruch, Herrmannsdorfer, Gerson Diet [*For tuberculosis*] (DAVI)
SHG........ Second-Harmonic Generation [*LASER*]
SHG........ Selected Honor Guards (MCD)
SHG........ Sexual Harassment Guidelines
SHG........ Sharpe Energy and Resources Ltd. [*Vancouver Stock Exchange symbol*]
SHG........ Shipping (WGA)
SHG........ Shirttail Gulch [*California*] [*Seismograph station code, US Geological Survey*] (SEIS)
SHG........ Shoprite Group Ltd. [*British ICAO designator*] (FAAC)
SHG........ Short-Handed Goal [*Hockey*]
SHG........ Shorthand Typist (Higher Grade) [*British military*] (DMA)
SHG........ Shungnak [*Alaska*] [*Airport symbol*] (OAG)
SHG........ Shungnak, AK [*Location identifier FAA*] (FAAL)
SHG........ Sister Servants of the Holy Ghost and Mary Immaculate [*Roman Catholic religious order*]
SHG........ Special High Grade [*Zinc metal*]
SHG........ Sun Healthcare Group [*NYSE symbol*] (SPSG)
SHG........ Synthetic Human Gastrin [*Medicine*] (MAE)
SHGF........ Scottish Hang Gliding Federation (DBA)
SHGM........ Society for the History of the Germans in Maryland (EA)
SHGR........ Self-Heating Group Ration [*Military*] (INF)
SHH........ Shenandoah Resources Ltd. [*Vancouver Stock Exchange symbol*]
SHH........ Shishmaref [*Alaska*] [*Airport symbol*] (OAG)
SHH........ Shishmaref, AK [*Location identifier FAA*] (FAAL)
SHH........ Sociedad Honoraria Hispanica (EA)
SHHD........ Scottish Home and Health Department (ILCA)
SHHH........ Self-Help for Hard of Hearing People (EA)
SHHP........ Semihorizontal Heart Position (MAE)
SHHV........ Society for Health and Human Values (EA)
SHI........ Scenic Hudson (EA)
SHI........ Shanghai Petrochemical [*NYSE symbol*] (SPSG)
SHI........ Shanghai Petrochemical ADS [*NYSE symbol*] (TTSB)
SHI........ Sheet Iron
SHI........ Shimojishima [*Japan*] [*Airport symbol*] (OAG)
SHI........ Shiraz [*Iran*] [*Seismograph station code, US Geological Survey*] (SEIS)
SHI........ Substance Hazard Index [*Environmental science*]
S-HI........ System-Human Interaction
SHID........ Spartan Hardware Inspection Discrepancy [*Missiles*] (MCD)
SHIEF........ Shared Information Elicitation Facility [*Computer science*]
Shiel........ Cape Times Law Reports, Edited by Shiel [*A publication*] (DLA)
Shiel........ Shiel's Cape Colony Reports [*A publication*] (DLA)
SHIELD........ Supreme Headquarters, International Espionage Law-Enforcement Division [*Organization in comic book "Nick Fury, Agent of SHIELD"*]
SHIELD........ Sylvania High-Intelligence Electronic Defense (MCD)
Shig........ Shigella [*Bacteriology*]
SHIIP........ Senior Health Insurance Information Program
SHIL........ Shillelagh [*Army surface-to-surface missile*] (AABC)
SHIL........ Shiloh National Military Park
Shill WC...... Shillman's Workmen's Compensation Cases [*Ireland*] [*A publication*] (DLA)
Shiloh........ Shiloh Industries, Inc. [*Associated Press*] (SAG)
SHIM........ Self-Heating Individual Meal [*Military*] (INF)
SHIMM........ Self-Heating Individual Meal Module [*Army*] (RDA)
SHIMMS........ Shipboard Integrated Man-Machine System (SAA)
SHIN BET..... Israel General Security Service [*Acronym represents Hebrew phrase*]
SHINC........ Sundays and Holidays Included [*Business term*]
SHINCOM.... Ship Integrated Communications System [*Canadian Navy*]
SHINE........ Self-Help is Necessary Everywhere [*Navy*] (DNAB)
Shingle........ [*The*] Shingle. Philadelphia Bar Association [*A publication*] (DLA)
SHINMACS... Shipborne Integrated Machinery Control System [*Canadian Navy*]
Shinn Repl... Shinn's Treatise on American Law of Replevin [*A publication*] (DLA)
SHIN PADS... Shipboard Integrated Processing Display System [*Military*]
SHIOER........ Statistical Historical Input/Output Error Rate Utility [*Sperry UNIVAC*]
SHIP........ Search-Height Integration Program (SAA)
SHIP........ Self-Help Improvement Program
SHIP........ Self-Help Issue Point [*Army*]
SHIP........ Separator for Heavy Ion Reaction Products
SHIP........ Shipment
SHIP........ Slater Hall Information Products [*Database producer*] (IID)
SHIP........ Special Handling Inventory Procedure (MCD)
SHIP........ Standard Hardware Interface Program
SHIPACS........ Ship Acquisition Study [*Navy*]
SHIPALT........ Ship Alteration [*Navy*]
SHIPBLDG........ Shipbuilding
SHIPCON........ Shipping Control [*NATO*] (NATG)
SHIPDA........ Shipping Data [*Military*]
SHIPDAFOL... Shipping Data Follows
SHIPDAT........ Shipping Date
SHIPDES........ Ship Descriptions (NITA)
SHIPDTO........ Ship on Depot Transfer Order [*Military*]
SHIPG........ Shipping
Ship Gaz........ Shipping Gazette [*London*] [*A publication*] (DLA)
SHIPGO........ Shipping Order [*Military*]
SHIPIM........ Ship Immediately [*Military*]
SHIPMT........ Shipment (DNAB)
SHIPOPS........ Ship(board) Operations [*Navy*] (DNAB)
SHIPOSI........ Ship Operational Support Inventory [*Navy*] (DNAB)
Shipp........ Shipp's Reports [*66-67 North Carolina*] [*A publication*] (DLA)
Shippensburg U... Shippensburg University of Pennsylvania (GAGS)
SHIPREPTECH... Ship Repair Technician [*Navy*] (DNAB)
SHIPREQ........ Ship to Apply on Requisition [*Military*]
SHIPS........ Shipment Planning System [*Military*]
SHIPS........ Statistical Hurricane Intensity Prediction Scheme (USDC)
SHIPS........ Statistical Hurricane Intensity Prediction Scheme [*Marine science*] (OSRA)
SHIPSTO........ Ship Store Office [*Navy*] (DNAB)
SHIPSUM........ Shipping Summary
SHIPSYSCOM... Ship Systems Command [*Navy*]
SHIPT........ Shipment
SHIR........ Self-Heating Individual Ration [*Army*] (RDA)
SHIR........ Ship History and Inventory Record [*Navy*] (NG)
SHIRAN........ S-Band High-Accuracy Ranging and Navigation
SHIRAN........ S-Band High Presicion Short Range Navigation (IAA)
Shir Cr L........ Shirley's Sketch of the Criminal Law [*2nd ed.*] [*1889*] [*A publication*] (DLA)
Shir DC Ca... Shirley's Dartmouth College Case [*A publication*] (DLA)
Shirl........ Shirley's Reports [*49-55 New Hampshire*] [*A publication*] (DLA)
Shirley........ Shirley's Reports [*49-55 New Hampshire*] [*A publication*] (DLA)
Shirl LC........ Shirley's Leading Crown Cases [*England*] [*A publication*] (DLA)
Shir Mag L... Shirley on Magisterial Law [*2nd ed.*] [*1896*] [*A publication*] (DLA)
SHIRTDIF........ Storage, Handling, and Retrieval of Technical Data in Image Formation [*Computer science*] (IEEE)
SHIRTS........ Smith-Houghton Infrared Temperature Sounder (NOAA)
SHIRW........ Shirwell [*England*]
SHIU........ Steering Hover Indicator Unit (MCD)
Shiva........ Shiva Corp. [*Associated Press*] (SAG)
SHIVA........ Super-High-Intensity Vulnerability Assessor
SHJ........ Shamrock Resources, Inc. [*Vancouver Stock Exchange symbol*]
SHJ........ Sharjah [*United Arab Emirates*] [*Airport symbol*] (OAG)
SHJ........ Sharjah Ruler's Flight [*United Arab Emirates*] [*ICAO designator*] (FAAC)
SHJ........ Shionomisaki [*Japan*] [*Seismograph station code, US Geological Survey*] (SEIS)
SHJ........ Society for Humanistic Judaism (EA)
SHJC........ Sacred Heart Junior College [*North Carolina; Pennsylvania*]
SHJM........ Sisters of the Sacred Hearts of Jesus and Mary [*Roman Catholic religious order*]
SHJM........ Sisters of the Sacred Hearts of Jesus and Mary (TOCD)
SHJP........ [*A*] History of the Jewish People in the Time of Jesus Christ [*Emil Schurer*] [*A publication*] (BJA)
SHJR........ Senate-House Joint Reports [*A publication*] (DLA)
Sh Jus........ Shaw's Scotch Justiciary Cases [*A publication*] (DLA)
SHK........ Sehonghong [*Lesotho*] [*Airport symbol*] (OAG)
SHK........ Shank (AAG)
Shk........ Shikimic Acid [*Biochemistry*]
SHK........ Shiraki [*Japan*] [*Seismograph station code, US Geological Survey*] (SEIS)
SHK........ SHL Systemhouse, Inc. [*Toronto Stock Exchange symbol*]
SHK........ Shock (MSA)
SHK........ Shorouk Air [*Egypt*] [*ICAO designator*] (FAAC)
SHK........ Speaker of the House of Keys [*British*] (ROG)
SHK........ Systems Housekeeping
SHKDN........ Shakedown (AABC)
SHKDNCRU... Shakedown Cruise [*Navy*] (ANA)
SHL........ Sacred Heart League (EA)
SHL........ Samson Aviation Services [*British ICAO designator*] (FAAC)
SHL........ Sensorineural Hearing Loss [*Medicine*]
SHL........ Shaw Industries Ltd. [*Toronto Stock Exchange symbol*]
SHL........ Sheldon, IA [*Location identifier FAA*] (FAAL)
SHL........ Shell (AAG)
SHL........ Shell
shl........ Shell (VRA)
SHL........ Shellac (MSA)
SHL........ Shell Canada Ltd. [*UTLAS symbol*]
SHL........ Shillong [*India*] [*Seismograph station code, US Geological Survey*] (SEIS)
Sh L........ Shipwright Lieutenant [*British military*] (DMA)
SHL........ Shoal
SHL........ Shoal
SHL........ Southall [*British depot code*]
SHL........ Southern Hockey League
SHL........ Student Homophile League [*Superseded by Gay People at Columbia*] (EA)
SHL........ Studio-to-Headend Link [*Transmitter site relay*] (NTCM)
SHL........ Subject Heading Language [*Classification and indexing*] [*Association for Library Collections and Technical Services*]
SHLB........ Simulation Hardware Load Boxes (NASA)
SHLD........ Sheild
SHLD........ Shield (AAG)
SHLD........ Shift Left Double [*Computer science*] (PCM)
SHLD........ Shoulder (AAG)
SHLDR........ Shoulder (MSA)
ShLH........ Shne Luhot Ha-Berit (BJA)
Sh Lit........ Shortt on Works of Literature [*2nd ed.*] [*1884*] [*A publication*] (DLA)
Sh Litt........ Shortt on Works of Literature [*2nd ed.*] [*1884*] [*A publication*] (DLA)
SHLL........ Shells Seafood Restaurants [*NASDAQ symbol*] (TTSB)
SHLL........ Shells Seafood Restaurants, Inc. [*NASDAQ symbol*] (SAG)
ShllsS........ Shells Seafood Restaurants, Inc. [*Associated Press*] (SAG)
ShllsSea...... Shells Seafood Restaurants, Inc. [*Associated Press*] (SAG)

SHLLW Shells Seafood Rest Wrrt [*NASDAQ symbol*] (TTSB)
SHLM Schulman (A.) [*NASDAQ symbol*] (TTSB)
SHLM Schulman [*A.*], Inc. [*NASDAQ symbol*] (NQ)
SHLM Society of Hospital Laundry Managers [*British*] (BI)
SHLMA Southern Hardwood Lumber Manufacturers Association [*Later, HMA*] (EA)
SHLN Shoreline (MSA)
SHLO Shiloh Industries [*NASDAQ symbol*] (TTSB)
SHLO Shiloh Industries, Inc. [*NASDAQ symbol*] (SAG)
SHLP Shiplap (WGA)
SHLR Schuler Homes [*NASDAQ symbol*] (TTSB)
SHLR Schuler Homes, Inc. [*NASDAQ symbol*] (SAG)
SHLRC Speech and Hearing Language Research Centre [*Macquarie University, Australia*]
SHLS Shawnee Library System [*Library network*]
SHLS Shoals (MCD)
SHLS Shoals
SHLTA Skin, Hide, and Leather Traders Association [*British*] (EAIO)
SHLTR Shelter (WGA)
SHLW Simulated High-Level Waste [*Nuclear engineering*]
SHM Nanki Shirahama [*Japan*] [*Airport symbol*] (OAG)
SHM Security Home Mortgage Investment Corp. [*Toronto Stock Exchange symbol*]
SHM Sheffield Medical Technologies, Inc. [*AMEX symbol*] (SPSG)
SHM Sheffield Medl Tech [*AMEX symbol*] (TTSB)
SHM Shimizu [*Japan*] [*Seismograph station code, US Geological Survey*] (SEIS)
SHM Ship Heading Marker [*Navigation*]
SHM Simple Harmonic Motion
SHM Sinusoidal Hydrodynamic Modulation [*Electrochemistry*]
SHM Society for Hybrid Microelectronics (IAA)
SHM Stage Handling Manual [*NASA*] (KSC)
SHMD Safety and Health Management Division [*Department of Agriculture*] (GFGA)
SHMD Shore Manning Document [*Navy*] (NVT)
SHMED State Hazardous Materials Enforcement Development [*Nuclear energy*] (NRCH)
SHMI Saddlery Hardware Manufacturers Institute [*Defunct*] (EA)
SHMIS Society of Headmasters of Independent Schools [*British*]
SHMKR Shoemaker (MSA)
SHMN Shaman Pharmaceuticals [*NASDAQ symbol*] (TTSB)
SHMN Shaman Pharmaceuticals, Inc. [*NASDAQ symbol*] (SAG)
SHMN Subacute Hepatitis with Multilobular Necrosis [*Medicine*]
SHMO Senior Hospital Medical Officer [*British*]
SHMO Shadow Mountain National Recreation Area
SHMO Social/Health Maintenance Organization [*Department of Health and Human Services*]
SHMP Sodium Hexametaphosphate [*Inorganic chemistry*]
SHMV Sunn-Hemp Mosaic Virus [*Plant pathology*]
SHN Sclerosing Hyaline Necrosis [*Medicine*]
SHN Scripps-Howard News Service [*Washington, DC*] (WDMC)
SHN Shaheen Airport Services [*Pakistan*] [*ICAO designator*] (FAAC)
shn Shan [*MARC language code Library of Congress*] (LCCP)
SHN Shandon Resources, Inc. [*Vancouver Stock Exchange symbol*]
SHN Shelton, WA [*Location identifier FAA*] (FAAL)
SHN Shimonoseki [*Japan*] [*Seismograph station code, US Geological Survey*] (SEIS)
SHN Shoney's, Inc. [*NYSE symbol*] (SPSG)
SHN Shorthand Note
SHN Shown (AAG)
SHN Sisterhood of the Holy Nativity [*Episcopalian religious order*]
SHN Spontaneous Hemorrhagic Necrosis [*Medicine*]
SHN St. Helena [*ANSI three-letter standard code*] (CNC)
SHN Subacute Hepatic Necrosis [*Medicine*] (DMAA)
SHNA SHARAF Name Authority [*UTLAS symbol*]
SHNC Scottish Higher National Certificate
SHND Scottish Higher National Diploma
SHNFZ Southern Hemisphere Nuclear Free Zone [*Australia*]
SHNG Shingle
SHNH Society for the History of Natural History [*British*] (EAIO)
S/HNP Skagit/Hanford Nuclear Project (NRCH)
SHNP Sydney Harbour National Park [*Australia*]
SHNPP Shearon Harris Nuclear Power Plant (GFGA)
SHNS Society of Head and Neck Surgeons (EA)
SHO North Shore Aero Club, Inc. [*New Zealand*] [*ICAO designator*] (FAAC)
SHO Schedule Order (MCD)
SHO Secondary Hypertrophic Osteoarthropathy [*Medicine*]
SHO Senate Historical Office
SHO Senior House Officer [*British*]
SHO Serious Habitual Offender [*Criminology*]
SHO Shikotan [*Former USSR Seismograph station code, US Geological Survey*] (SEIS)
sho Shona [*MARC language code Library of Congress*] (LCCP)
SHO Shore
SHO Show [*Automotive advertising*]
SHO Showing [*Technical drawings*]
SHO Shutout [*Sports*]
SHO Starrett Corp. [*AMEX symbol*] (TTSB)
SHO Starrett Housing Corp. [*AMEX symbol*] (SPSG)
SHO Student Health Organizations [*Defunct*]
SHO Super High Output [*Model of Ford automobile*]
SHOA Superannuation, Home, and Overseas Allowances [*Civil Service*] [*British*]
SHOAL Shoal [*Commonly used*] (OPSA)
SHOALS Shoals [*Commonly used*] (OPSA)
SHOAP Symbolic Horribly Optimizing Assembly Program (IAA)
SHOAR Shore [*Commonly used*] (OPSA)
SHOARS Shores [*Commonly used*] (OPSA)
SHOB Shore-Based (CINC)
SHOBOM Shore Bombardment [*Navy*] (NVT)
SHOBOMTNG Shore Bombardment Training [*Navy*] (NVT)
SHOC Self-Help Opportunity Center [*Department of Labor*] [*Washington, DC*] (AEBS)
SHOC SHAPE [*Supreme Headquarters Allied Powers Europe*] Operations Center [*NATO*] (NATG)
SHOC Software/Hardware Operational Control
SHOCK Students Hot on Conserving Kilowatts [*Student legal action organization*]
SHODOP Short-Range Doppler
ShoeCarn Shoe Carnival, Inc. [*Associated Press*] (SAG)
SHOF Shipboard Cable, Heat and Oil Resistant, Flexible (IAA)
SholodgE Sholodge, Inc. [*Associated Press*] (SAG)
SHOLS Single-Hoist Ordnance Loading System [*Navy*] (DNAB)
SHOMADS Short-to-Medium-Range Air Defense System [*Army*] (RDA)
Sho-Me Sho-Me Financial Corp. [*Associated Press*] (SAG)
Shome LR Shome's Law Reporter [*India*] [*A publication*] (DLA)
Shoney Shoney's, Inc. [*Associated Press*] (SAG)
S'HONG Souchong [*Tea trade*] (ROG)
SHOO Madden Steven Ltd. [*NASDAQ symbol*] (SAG)
SHOO Madden (Steven) Ltd [*NASDAQ symbol*] (TTSB)
SHOO Stephen Madden Ltd. [*NASDAQ symbol*] (SAG)
SHOOZ Madden (Steven) Wrrt'B' [*NASDAQ symbol*] (TTSB)
SHOP Shell Higher Olefin Process [*Petrochemistry*]
SHOPA School and Home Office Products Association (EA)
SHOPAIR Short Path Infrared (MCD)
SHOPAT Shore Patrol [*Navy*] (NVT)
Shopco Shopco Laurel Centre Ltd. [*Associated Press*] (SAG)
ShopHm Shop at Home, Inc. [*Associated Press*] (SAG)
Shopko Shopko Stores [*Associated Press*] (SAG)
ShopTV Shopping by Television [*British Telecom*]
SHOR Shore
SHOR Shorewood Packaging [*NASDAQ symbol*] (TTSB)
SHOR Shorewood Packaging Corp. [*NASDAQ symbol*] (NQ)
SHORAD Short-Range Air Defense [*Army*] (NATG)
SHORAD C^2 Short-Range Air Defense Command and Control
SHORADS Short-Range Air Defense System [*Army*] (RDA)
SHORAN Short-Range Aid to Navigation (IAA)
SHORAN Short-Range Navigation
SHORD Short-Range Air Defense
SHORDU Shore Duty [*Navy*]
SHORE Shore [*Commonly used*] (OPSA)
SHOREALT Shore Alteration
SHORES Shores [*Commonly used*] (OPSA)
ShorlnFn Shoreline Financial [*Associated Press*] (SAG)
SHORN Short-Range Navigation System (FAAC)
SHOROC Shore-Required Operational Capability [*Navy*]
SHOROUTPUBINST Shore Duty Beyond the Seas Is Required by the Public Interest [*Navy*]
SHORPUBINT Shore Duty Is Required by the Public Interest [*Navy*]
SHORSTAMPS Shore Requirements, Standards, and Manpower Planning System [*Navy*]
SHORSTAS Short-Range Surveillance and Target Acquisition System (PDAA)
SHORSTRAMPS Shore Requirements Strength and Manpower Planning System [*Navy*] (ANA)
SHORT Shard Hospital Online Real-Time Time-Sharing (PDAA)
SHORT Short Stature, Hyperextensibility of Joints or Hernia or Both, Ocular Depression, Rieger Anomaly, Teething Delayed [*Medicine*] (DMAA)
SHORTD Shortened (ROG)
SHORTIE Short Range Thermal Imaging Equipment (PDAA)
Shortt Inf Shortt on Informations, Criminal, Quo Warranto, Mandamus, and Prohibition [*1887*] [*A publication*] (DLA)
Shortt Inform Shortt on Informations, Criminal, Quo Warranto, Mandamus, and Prohibition [*A publication*] (DLA)
Shortt Lit Shortt on Literature and Art [*2nd ed.*] [*1884*] [*A publication*] (DLA)
SHORVEY Shore Duty Survey
Shorwd Shorewood Packaging Corp. [*Associated Press*] (SAG)
SHOSJ Sovereign Hospitaller Order of St. John (EA)
SHOT Shooting, Hunting, Outdoor Trade Show
SHOT Society for the History of Technology (EA)
Show Shower's English King's Bench Reports [*A publication*] (DLA)
Show Shower's English Parliamentary Cases [*A publication*] (DLA)
SHOW Showscan Entertainment [*NASDAQ symbol*] (TTSB)
SHOW Showscan Entertainment, Inc. [*NASDAQ symbol*] (SAG)
SHOW Showtime [*Cable television channel*]
Showbiz ShowBiz Pizza Time, Inc. [*Associated Press*] (SAG)
Showbt Showboat, Inc. [*Associated Press*] (SAG)
Shower KB Shower's English King's Bench Reports [*89 English Reprint*] [*1678-95*] [*A publication*] (DLA)
Shower KB (Eng) Shower's English King's Bench Reports [*89 English Reprint*] [*A publication*] (DLA)
Shower PC (Eng) Shower's English Parliamentary Cases [*1 English Reprint*] [*A publication*] (DLA)
Show KB Shower's English King's Bench Reports [*A publication*] (DLA)
Show Parl Cas Shower's English Parliamentary Cases [*1 English Reprint*] [*A publication*] (DLA)
Show PC Shower's English Parliamentary Cases [*1 English Reprint*] [*A publication*] (DLA)

SHP .... Santa Helena [*Peru*] [*Seismograph station code, US Geological Survey Closed*] (SEIS)
SHP .... Schonlein-Henoch Purpura [*Medicine*] (MEDA)
SHP .... Schools History Project (AIE)
SHP .... Securities Shipped as Instructed
SHP .... Seeker Head Position
SHP .... Service Aerien Francais [*France ICAO designator*] (FAAC)
SHP .... Shaft Horsepower
SHP .... Shaker Heights Public Library, Shaker Heights, OH [*OCLC symbol*] (OCLC)
SHP .... Shape (MSA)
SHP .... Shearon Harris Plant [*Nuclear energy*] (NRCH)
SHP .... Shoal Petroleum [*Vancouver Stock Exchange symbol*]
SHP .... Shoppe
SHP .... Shreveport [*Diocesan abbreviation*] [*Louisiana*] (TOCD)
SHP .... Single Highest Peak [*Aerospace*]
SHP .... Society for Hospital Planning of the American Hospital Association [*Later, SHPM*] (EA)
SHP .... Society for Hungarian Philately (EA)
SHP .... Sosyal Demokrasi Halkci Partisi [*Social Democratic Populist Party*] [*Turkey Political party*] (EAIO)
SHP .... Southern Hardwood Producers [*Later, HMA*]
ShP .... Southern Historical Press, Easley, SC [*Library symbol Library of Congress*] (LCLS)
SHP .... Standard Hardware Program [*Military*]
SHP .... Standard Holding Pattern [*Aviation*]
SHP .... Standard Holding Procedure [*Aviation*]
SHP .... State Health Plan [*Generic term*] (DHSM)
SHP .... [*The*] Stop & Shop Companies, Inc. [*NYSE symbol*] (SPSG)
SHP .... Stop & Shop Cos. [*NYSE symbol*] (TTSB)
SHP .... Surgical Hypoparathyroidism [*Medicine*] (MAE)
SHP .... Wichita Falls, TX [*Location identifier FAA*] (FAAL)
SHPA .... Prairie Agricultural Machinery Institute, Humboldt, Saskatchewan [*Library symbol National Library of Canada*] (NLC)
SHPBD .... Shipboard (MSA)
SHPC .... Scenic Hudson Preservation Conference [*Later, SHI*] (EA)
SHPCL .... Ship Class
SHPD .... Seeker Head Position Display [*Military*] (CAAL)
SHPD .... Super High-Performance Diesel [*Fuel*]
SHPDA .... State Health Planning and Development Agency
SHPE .... Society of Hispanic Professional Engineers (EA)
SHPG .... Shipping
shpg .... Shipping (ODBW)
SHPHG .... Shipment of Household Goods (NOAA)
SHPI .... Specialized Health Prods Intl [*NASDAQ symbol*] (TTSB)
SHPI .... Specialized Health Products International, Inc. [*NASDAQ symbol*] (SAG)
SHPM .... Society for Hospital Planning and Marketing of the American Hospital Association (EA)
SHPMT .... Shipment (AABC)
SHPNG .... Shipping
SHPO .... State Historic Preservation Office
SHPO .... State Historic Preservation Officer
SHPO .... Subharmonic Parametric Oscillator (IAA)
SHPOL .... Supplemental Health Manpower Shortage Area Placement Opportunity List [*Department of Health and Human Services*] (GFGA)
SHPR .... Shipper
SHPRF .... Shakeproof (MSA)
SHPS .... Seahead Pressure Simulator
SHPS .... Sodium Hydroxide Purge System (IEEE)
SHPSD .... Shipside (AABC)
SHPT .... Shipment (AAG)
shpt .... Shipment (ODBW)
SHPTARBY ... Ship to Arrive By ____ [*Military*]
SHQ .... Shasper Industries Ltd. [*Toronto Stock Exchange symbol*]
SHQ .... Squadron Headquarters [*British military*] (DMA)
SHQ .... Station Headquarters
SHQ .... Supreme Headquarters
SHR .... Scherer [*R.P.*] Corp. [*NYSE symbol*] (SPSG)
SHR .... Scherer (R.P.) [*NYSE symbol*] (TTSB)
SHR .... Semi-Homogeneous Fuel Reactor (IAA)
SHR .... Share [*Stock exchange term*]
shr .... Share (ODBW)
SHR .... Shear
SHR .... Shepard Insurance Group [*Vancouver Stock Exchange symbol*]
SHR .... Sheridan [*Wyoming*] [*Airport symbol*] (OAG)
SHR .... Sheridan, WY [*Location identifier FAA*] (FAAL)
SHR .... Shift Register [*Computer science*] (IAA)
SHR .... Shirakawa [*Japan*] [*Seismograph station code, US Geological Survey*] (SEIS)
SHR .... Shooter Air Courier Corp. [*Canada ICAO designator*] (FAAC)
SHR .... Shore (MCD)
SHR .... Shower
SHR .... Single High-Resolution File [*Computer science*]
SHR .... Sisters of the Holy Redeemer [*Roman Catholic religious order*]
SHR .... Society for Historical Research (EA)
SHR .... Solar Heat Reflecting (KSC)
SHR .... Spontaneously Hypertensive Rats
SHR .... Standard Hourly Rate
SHR .... Step-Height Ratio [*Crystallography*]
SHR .... Student Homelessness Rate [*Australia*]
SHR .... Supervisory Human Relations Test
SHR .... Synchronous Hubbing Regeneration (MHDI)
Shr .... [*The*] Taming of the Shrew [*Shakespearean work*]
SHRA .... Rain Showers [*ICAO*] (FAAC)
SHRAM .... Short-Range Air-to-Surface Missile
SHRAP .... Shrapnel
SHRC .... Safety and Health Regulations for Construction [*Bureau of Reclamation*]
SHRC .... Shared Housing Resource Center [*Later, NSHRC*] (EA)
SHRC .... Shopping Hours Reform Council [*British*] (DBA)
SHRD .... Shift Right Double [*Computer science*] (PCM)
SHRD .... Shredded [*Freight*]
SHRD .... Shroud [*Engineering*]
SHRD .... Supplemental Heat Rejection Devices (NASA)
SHRDF .... Shroud Fin [*Engineering*]
SHRDR .... Shredder (MSA)
ShrdTch .... Shared Technologies Cellular, Inc. [*Associated Press*] (SAG)
SHREAD .... Share Registration and Dividend Warrants (MHDB)
SHREWD .... System for Holding and Retrieving Wanted Data (IAA)
SHRF .... Ship Regular Freight [*Military*] (AABC)
SHRG .... Scottish Homosexual Rights Group (DBA)
SHRI .... Sciences and Humanities Research Institute [*Iowa State University*] [*Research center*] (RCD)
SHRIMP .... Sensitive High Mass Resolution Ion Microprobe
SHRIMP .... Super-High Resolution Ion Microprobe [*Analytical chemistry*]
SHRIV .... Shrivenham [*England*]
SHRM .... Society for Human Resource Management (EA)
ShrMed .... Shared Medical Systems Corp. [*Associated Press*] (SAG)
SHRNG .... Shearing (MSA)
SHROC .... Shore-Required Operational Capability [*Navy*] (DNAB)
SHROPS .... Shropshire [*County in England*]
SHRP .... Sharpener (MSA)
SHRP .... Sharper Image [*NASDAQ symbol*] (TTSB)
SHRP .... Sharper Image Corp. [*NASDAQ symbol*] (NQ)
SHRP .... Society for History, Research, and Preservation (EA)
SHRP .... Strategic Highway Research Program [*National Research Council*]
SHRP .... Strategic Highway Research Program
Shrplm .... Sharper Image Corp. [*Associated Press*] (SAG)
SHRS .... Shores (MCD)
SHRS .... Shores
SHRS .... Shutdown Heat Removal System [*Nuclear energy*] (NRCH)
SHRS .... Supplementary Heat Removal System (IEEE)
SHRSDV .... Scottish Historic and Research Society of Delaware Valley (EA)
Shr Sui .... Shrady on Suicide and Intemperance in Life Insurance [*A publication*] (DLA)
SHRTG .... Shortage (AABC)
SHRTWV .... Shortwave (FAAC)
SHS .... Galveston, TX [*Location identifier FAA*] (FAAL)
SHS .... Sacred Heart Seminary [*Detroit, MI*]
SHS .... Sample Handling System [*Chemistry*]
SHS .... Sayer Head Sling [*Medicine*]
SHS .... Scandinavian Herpetological Society [*Denmark*] (EAIO)
SHS .... Scottish History Society (EA)
SHS .... Self-Propagating High-Temperature Synthesis [*Ceramic technolgy*]
SHS .... Senior High School
SHS .... Shares [*Stock exchange term*]
SHS .... Shashi [*China*] [*Airport symbol*] (OAG)
SHS .... Shasta Dam [*California*] [*Seismograph station code, US Geological Survey Closed*] (SEIS)
SHS .... Sheep Hemolyzate Supernatant
SHS .... Sheet Steel (IAA)
SHS .... Shipley-Hartford Scale [*Psychology*] (DAVI)
SHS .... Ship's Heading Servo
SHS .... Shire Horse Society [*British*] (DI)
SHS .... Shop Television Network [*Vancouver Stock Exchange symbol*]
SHS .... Simulation Hardware System [*NASA*] (MCD)
SHS .... Sisters of the Holy Spirit (TOCD)
SHS .... Small Hydro Society [*Defunct*] (EA)
SHS .... Smoothing Heading Spot (SAA)
SHS .... Social History Society of the United Kingdom
SHS .... Societatis Historiae Socius [*Fellow of the Historical Society*] [*Latin*]
SHS .... Sod House Society (EA)
SHS .... Sodium Hexadecyl Sulfate [*Organic chemistry*]
SHS .... Soil and Health Society [*Later, RI*] (EA)
SHS .... Soviet Hydrometeorological Service
SHS .... Spartan Homing Sensor [*Missiles*]
SHS .... Spherical Harmonic Series (SAA)
SHS .... Sports Hall of Shame [*Defunct*] (EA)
SHS .... Square Hollow Section [*Metal industry*]
SHS .... Standard Heavy Spanwire [*Military*] (CAAL)
SHS .... Student Health Service (DAVI)
SHS .... Sunshine Aviation SA [*Switzerland ICAO designator*] (FAAC)
SHS .... Superheated Steam
SHS .... Surveyors Historical Society (EA)
SHS .... Systemhouse Ltd. [*Toronto Stock Exchange symbol*]
SHS .... University of Sheffield, Postgraduate Librarianship, Sheffield, England [*OCLC symbol*] (OCLC)
SHSA .... Saint Hubert Society of America (EA)
SHSA .... Scottish Harp Society of America (EA)
SHSA .... Seaman Apprentice, Ship's Serviceman, Striker [*Navy rating*]
SHSA .... Southern Hardwood Square Association (EA)
SHSA .... State Highway Safety Agencies [*NHTSA*] (TAG)
SHSAC .... Supreme Headquarters, Supreme Allied Commander [*World War II*]
SHSC .... Sierra Home Services [*NASDAQ symbol*] (SAG)
SHSC .... Sierra Home Svc Cos. [*NASDAQ symbol*] (TTSB)
Sh Sc App .... Shaw's Scotch Appeal Cases, House of Lords [*A publication*] (DLA)
SHS/DC .... Social and Human Sciences Documentation Centre [*UNESCO*] (DUND)

SHSGS Supreme Headquarters, Secretary General Staff [*World War II*]
ShSh Shomer Shabbat (BJA)
SHSLB Street and Highway Safety Lighting Bureau [*Defunct*] (EA)
SHSLC Siouxland Health Sciences Consortium [*Library network*]
SHSMB Safety and Health Standards Management Board (IAA)
SHSN Seaman, Ship's Serviceman, Striker [*Navy rating*]
SHSN Snow Showers [*ICAO*] (FAAC)
SHSN Sod House Society of Nebraska [*Later, SHS*] (EA)
SHSO Southshore Corp. [*NASDAQ symbol*] (SAG)
SHSp Sisters of the Holy Spirit and Mary Immaculate (TOCD)
SHSP Spontaneously Hypertensive Stroke-Prone Rat [*Medicine*] (DMAA)
SHSR Society for Humanity and Social Reform [*British*]
SHSS Stanford Hypnotic Susceptibility Scale [*Psychology*]
SHSS Superhigh Speed Steel (IAA)
SHSTF Scout Helicopter Special Task Force (MCD)
SHSTS Ship Status
SHSV Superstructure Heater Safety Valve (DS)
SHSWD Society for Hospital Social Work Directors (EA)
SHT British Airways Shuttle [*ICAO designator*] (FAAC)
SHT Salvo Honoris Titulo [*Latin*]
SHT Scottish Heritable Trust
SHT Sheet (AAG)
SHT Sheet
sht Sheet (VRA)
SHT Sholia Resources Ltd. [*Vancouver Stock Exchange symbol*]
SHT Short (MSA)
SHT Sidi Hakoma Tuff [*Geology*]
SHT Simple Hypocalcemic Tetany [*Medicine*]
SHT Society for the History of Technology (EA)
SHT Society of the Most Holy Trinity [*Anglican religious community*]
SHT Space Hand Tool [*NASA*]
SHT Subcutaneous Histamine Test [*Medicine*] (MAE)
SHT Swansea Harbour Trust [*Wales*]
SHTC Short Time Constant (MSA)
Sh Teind Ct Shaw's Scotch Teind [*Tithe*] Court Decisions [*A publication*] (DLA)
SHTG Sheeting [*Freight*]
SHTG Shortage (AFM)
SHTH Sheath (IAA)
SHTHG Sheathing (MSA)
SHT IRN Sheet Iron [*Freight*]
SHT IRN STL Sheet Iron or Steel [*Freight*]
SHTL Shuttle (MSA)
SHTL Small Heat-Transfer Loop [*Nuclear energy*] (NRCH)
SHT MTL Sheet Metal [*Freight*]
SHTN Short Ton [*2000 lbs.*]
SHTPB Saturated Hydroxy-Terminated Polybutadiene
SHTR Shutter (AAG)
SHTSD Short Side
SHT STL WRE Sheet Steel Ware [*Freight*]
SHTT Sequential Headturn Test
S-HTTP Secure Hypertext Transport Protocol [*Computer science*]
SHU Sacred Heart University, Library, Bridgeport, CT [*OCLC symbol*] (OCLC)
SHU Sakhalinskie Aviatrassy [*Former USSR*] [*FAA designator*] (FAAC)
SHU Seton Hall University [*South Orange, NJ*]
SHU Shurgard Storage Centers [*NYSE symbol*] (SAG)
SHU Shute Harbour [*Queensland*] [*Airport symbol*] (AD)
SHU Shuyak Island [*Alaska*] [*Seismograph station code, US Geological Survey*] (SEIS)
SHU Skyhigh Resources Ltd. [*Vancouver Stock Exchange symbol*]
ShufMst Shuffle Master, Inc. [*Associated Press*] (SAG)
SHUR Selected History Update and Reporting (MCD)
SHUR System for Hospital Uniform Reporting
Shurgard Shrugard Storage Centers [*Associated Press*] (SAG)
SHUSA Scottish Heritage USA (EA)
SHUT Shuttle (SSD)
SHUTDN Shutdown (NASA)
SHV Series Hybrid Vehicle
SHV Shavano Air, Inc. [*ICAO designator*] (FAAC)
SHV Sheave (MSA)
SHV Shreveport [*Louisiana*] [*Airport symbol*] (OAG)
SHV Shreveport, LA [*Location identifier FAA*] (FAAL)
SHV Solenoid Hydraulic Valve
SHV Sub Hoc Voce [*or Sub Hoc Verbo*] [*Under This Word*] [*Latin*]
SHVA Scottish Health Visitors Association (DBA)
SHVA Shiva Corp. [*NASDAQ symbol*] (SAG)
SHVG Shaving [*Freight*]
SHVHS Sandy Hook Veterans Historical Society (EA)
SHVSCE Shuttle Versus Current Expendable Launch Vehicle [*NASA*] (KSC)
SHVSNE Shuttle Versus New Expendable Launch Vehicle [*NASA*] (KSC)
SHW Air South, Inc. [*ICAO designator*] (FAAC)
SHW Mount St. Helens [*Washington*] [*Seismograph station code, US Geological Survey*] (SEIS)
SHW Sharurah [*Saudi Arabia*] [*Airport symbol*] (OAG)
SHW Sherwin-Williams [*NYSE symbol*] (TTSB)
SHW Sherwin-Williams Co. [*NYSE symbol*] (SPSG)
SHW Short Wave (IAA)
Sh W & C Shaw, Wilson, and Courtenay's Scotch Appeals Reports [*Wilson and Shaw's Reports*] [*A publication*] (DLA)
SHWCS Showcase
ShwdGp Sherwood Group [*Associated Press*] (SAG)
SHWL Seasonal High Water Level (GNE)
SHWL Solidified High Waste Level [*Nuclear energy*] (NUCP)
SHWR Saturated Hydrocarbon Weathering Ratio [*Ecology*] (DAVI)
SHWRM Showroom [*Automotive advertising*]
Shwscn Showscan Entrtainment, Inc. [*Associated Press*] (SAG)
shwy Showy [*Horticulture*]
SHWY Super Highway (TEL)
SHX Shageluk [*Alaska*] (OAG)
SHX Shageluk, AK [*Location identifier FAA*] (FAAL)
SHX Shaw Indus [*NYSE symbol*] (TTSB)
SHX Shaw Industries, Inc. [*NYSE symbol*] (SPSG)
SHx Social History (DAVI)
SHY Kaiser, MO [*Location identifier FAA*] (FAAL)
SHY Sharon Energy Ltd. [*Vancouver Stock Exchange symbol*]
SHY Shinyanga [*Tanzania*] [*Airport symbol*] (OAG)
SHY Syllable Hyphen Character [*Computer science*]
SHZ Seshute's [*Lesotho*] [*Airport symbol*] (OAG)
SHZ Shizuoka [*Japan*] [*Seismograph station code, US Geological Survey*] (SEIS)
SHZ Steelhead Resources Ltd. [*Vancouver Stock Exchange symbol*]
SI ACM Government Spectrum Fund [*NYSE symbol*] (SPSG)
SI ACM Gvt Spectrum Fund [*NYSE symbol*] (TTSB)
SI Air Sierra [*ICAO designator*] (AD)
SI International System [*FHWA*] (TAG)
SI International System of Units (ACII)
SI Sacroiliac [*Medicine*]
SI Safety Injection [*Nuclear energy*] (NRCH)
SI Safety Inspection (IEEE)
SI Sailmakers Institute (EA)
SI Saintpaulia International (EA)
SI Saline Injection [*Abortion technique*]
SI Salinity Indicator
SI Salmon Institute [*Formerly, CSI*] (EA)
SI Salt Institute (EA)
SI Sample Interval
SI Sandwich Islands
SI Sanitary Inspector [*British*] (ROG)
SI Saturation Index [*Chemistry*]
SI Saturday Inspection [*Slang*]
SI Save It [*Energy-saving campaign*] [*British*]
SI School Inventory [*Psychology*]
SI Scientific Instrument (NASA)
SI Screen Grid Input
SI Seal In (IAA)
SI Seasonal Industry (MHDW)
SI Secondary Injection
SI Secondary Item [*Army*]
SI Security Identity
SI Seine Island [*Island off the coast of France*] (ROG)
SI Selected Item (MCD)
SI Selective Identification
SI Self Incompatible
SI Self-Induction (IAA)
SI Self Inflicted (MAE)
si Self Inking (DGA)
SI Semi-Insulating
S-I Sensation-Intuition [*Jungian psychology*]
SI Sense Indicator (IAA)
SI Sensitive Information (MCD)
SI Sensory Integration
SI Septic Inflammation [*Medicine*]
SI Sergeant Instructor [*Military British*]
SI Serial Input [*Computer science*] (EECA)
SI Seriously Ill [*Military*] (AABC)
SI Serra International (EA)
SI Sertoma International (EA)
SI Serum Iron [*Serology*]
SI Servas International (EA)
SI Service Indicator [*Telecommunications*] (TEL)
SI Service Instruction
SI Service Interruption
SI Sex Inventory [*Psychology*]
SI Sexual Intercourse (ADA)
SI Shared Information (PCM)
SI Shetland Isles
SI Shift In [*Transistor*] (IAA)
SI Shift-In Character [*Keyboard*] [*Computer science*]
SI Ship Item (MCD)
SI Shipping Instructions (AFM)
SI Ship's Installation [*Navy*]
SI Short Interest [*Brokerage*]
SI Signal Intelligence (MCD)
SI Signal Interface
S/I Signal-to-Interference
SI Signal-to-Intermodulation [*Ratio*]
S/I Signal-to-Intermodulation Ratio (IDOE)
SI Sign Code (IAA)
SI Signed Integer [*Computer science*]
SI Silence [*Navigation*]
Si Silicon [*Chemical element*]
SI Silicon (IDOE)
Si Silicone [*Organic chemistry*]
Si Silty Soil [*Agronomy*]
si Silver (VRA)
SI Silver Institute (EA)
SI Similarity Index
Si Simon de Bisignano [*Flourished, 1174-79*] [*Authority cited in pre-1607 legal work*] (DSA)
SI Simple Interest [*Banking*]

SI ... Simulation Routine (IAA)
SI ... Simulator Initiation (MCD)
SI ... Sinai (BJA)
si ... Singapore [*MARC country of publication code Library of Congress*] (LCCP)
SI ... Single Instruction
SI ... Single Silk [*Wire insulation*] (AAG)
SI ... Sinus Iridum [*Bay of Rainbows*] [*Lunar area*]
SI ... Sirach [*Ecclesiasticus*] [*Old Testament book*]
SI ... Site, Inc. (EA)
SI ... Site Investigation
SI ... Skill Identifier [*Career development*] [*Army*] (RDA)
SI ... Slaved Illuminator [*Military*] (CAAL)
SI ... Small Inclusions [*Diamond clarity grade*]
SI ... Small Intestine [*Anatomy*]
S/I ... Smectite-Illite [*Clay mineral*]
SI ... Smithsonian Institution
SI ... Social Independiente [*Netherlands Antilles*] [*Political party*] (EY)
SI ... Socialist International [*Political party*] (EAIO)
SI ... Society of Illustrators (EA)
SI ... Society of Indexers (EAIO)
SI ... Software Implementation
SI ... Solar Inertial (MCD)
SI ... Solidarity International (EA)
SI ... Solomon Islands (BARN)
SI ... Solubility Index [*Water*]
SI ... Soluble Insulin
SI ... Soroptimist International [*Cambridge, England*] (EAIO)
SI ... Sound Investment (MHDW)
SI ... Source Impedance
SI ... Southeast Institute for Group and Family Therapy (EA)
SI ... South Island [*New Zealand*] (BARN)
SI ... Southpaw's International [*Defunct*] (EA)
SI ... Space Institute [*University of Tennessee*] [*Research center*] (RCD)
SI ... Space Intelligence [*Parapsychology*]
SI ... Spark Ignition
SI ... Speaker Intercom
SI ... Special Inquiry [*Classification system used by doctors on Ellis Island to detain, re-examine, and possibly deny entry to certain immigrants*]
SI ... Special Inspection (MCD)
SI ... Special Instruction
SI ... Special Intelligence [*Army*] (AABC)
SI ... Special Intervention [*Medicine*]
SI ... Specialist Insectivore
SI ... Specific Impulse (IAA)
SI ... Specific Inventory (OA)
SI ... Spectrum Index
SI ... Speech Intelligibility (RDA)
SI ... Speech Interpolation [*Telecommunications*] (TEL)
SI ... Speed Indicator (IAA)
SI ... Spokane International Railroad Co. [*AAR code*]
SI ... Sponsor Identification [*Television*]
SI ... Spot Inspection [*Military*] (AFM)
SI ... Spot Inventory
SI ... Spratly Islands [*ANSI two-letter standard code*] (CNC)
SI ... Square Inch (MCD)
SI ... Staff Inspector
SI ... Standard International Unit (IAA)
SI ... Standardization and Interoperability
SI ... Standards Institution [*Telecommunications*]
SI ... Standing Instruction (MSA)
SI ... Star of India
SI ... Staten Island
SI ... Station Identification
SI ... Status Indicator (IAA)
SI ... Steer, Inc. [*An association*] (EA)
SI ... Steering Intelligence (MCD)
SI ... Step Index [*Nuclear energy*] (NUCP)
SI ... Step Index (NITA)
SI ... Stereo Imaging (SSD)
SI ... Stimulation Index [*Cytochemistry*]
SI ... Storage Immediate
SI ... Straight-In Approach [*Aviation*]
SI ... Straight, Inc. (EA)
SI ... Strathclyde Institute [*Glasgow, Scotland*]
SI ... Stress Incontinence [*Urology*] (DAVI)
SI ... Stretch-Inactivated Ion Channel
SI ... Stretch Inhibitor
S/I ... Strike/Interdiction (MCD)
SI ... Stroke Index
SI ... Structure-of-Intellect [*Model*]
SI ... Student Investigator (KSC)
S/I ... Subject Issue
SI ... Subscription Item
SI ... Suicidal Ideation [*Psychiatry*] (DAVI)
SI ... Suitability Index [*Fishery science*]
SI ... Sulphur Institute (EA)
si ... Sum Insured (ODBW)
SI ... Sundance Institute (EA)
SI ... Superimpose (MDG)
SI ... Superintendent of Document/Item (NITA)
SI ... Supply Instruction [*Marine Corps*]
SI ... Support Installation (MCD)
SI ... Surface Impoundment (EG)
SI ... Surface Integrity
SI ... Surface Ionization [*Physics*]
SI ... Surveillance Inspection [*Nuclear energy*] (NRCH)
SI ... Survival International [*British*] (EAIO)
SI ... Suspect Index [*British*]
SI ... Swap-In [*Computer science*]
SI ... Switch Interpretation (IAA)
SI ... Symbolic Input [*Computer science*]
SI ... Syncytium Inducing [*Cytology*]
SI ... Systeme International (NITA)
SI ... Systeme International d'Unites [*International System of Units*] [*Also, SIU*]
SI ... System Information [*Computer science*] (PCM)
SI ... System Integration
SI ... System International (IAA)
SI ... System Inventory [*or Review of Systems*] (DAVI)
SIA ... Sailing Industry Association (EA)
SIA ... San Francisco, CA [*Location identifier FAA*] (FAAL)
SIA ... Sanitary Institute of America [*Later, IAWCM*]
SIA ... Sasquatch Investigations of Mid-America (EA)
SIA ... Scaffold Industry Association (EA)
SIA ... Science Information Association
SIA ... Scottish Island Area [*Council*]
SIA ... Securities Industry Association (EA)
SIA ... Self-Insurers Association
SIA ... Self-Interstitial Atom
SIA ... Semiconductor Industry Association (EA)
SIA ... Sensor Interface Assembly
SIA ... Serial Input Adapter
SIA ... Service Industry Accounting [*Sybiz International, Inc.*] [*Computer program*] (PCM)
SIA ... Service in Information and Analysis [*Host*] [*British*] (BUR)
SIA ... Shelter Oil & Gas Ltd. [*Toronto Stock Exchange symbol*]
SIA ... Shuttle Induced Atmosphere (NASA)
SIA ... Sialic Acid [*Biochemistry*]
SIA ... Sian [*Republic of China*] [*Seismograph station code, US Geological Survey Closed*] (SEIS)
SIA ... Sian [*China*] [*Airport symbol*] (AD)
SIA ... Sigma Immunoassay [*Test for rubella*]
SIA ... Signal Apparel [*NYSE symbol*] (TTSB)
SIA ... Signal Apparel Co., Inc. [*NYSE symbol*] (SPSG)
SIA ... Singapore Airlines
SIA ... Singapore Airlines Ltd. [*ICAO designator*] (FAAC)
SIA ... Singles in Agriculture [*An association*] (EA)
SIA ... Ski Industries America (EA)
SIA ... Societa Italiana di Agopuntura [*Italy*]
SIA ... Societe Internationale Arthurienne, [*International Arthurian Society*] North American Branch (EA)
SIA ... Societe Internationale d'Acupuncture [*International Society of Acupuncture*]
SIA ... Society for Industrial Archeology (EA)
SIA ... Society of Industrial Accountants of Canada
SIA ... Society of Insurance Accountants [*Crozet, VA*] (EA)
SIA ... Software Impact Assessment [*NASA*] (NASA)
SIA ... Software Industry Association (IAA)
SIA ... Software Institute of America [*Andover, MA*] [*Telecommunications*] (TSSD)
SIA ... Solar Inertial Attitude (NASA)
SIA ... Solvents Industry Association [*British*] (DBA)
SIA ... Soroptimist International of the Americas (EA)
SIA ... Speaker Intercom Assembly [*NASA*]
SIA ... Special Interest Automobiles [*A publication*]
SIA ... Special Investor Account [*Stock purchasing*]
SIA ... Spinal Injuries Association [*British*]
SIA ... Sprinkler Irrigation Association [*Later, IA*] (EA)
SIA ... Standard Instrument Approach [*RADAR*] [*Aviation*]
SIA ... Standard Interface Adapter
SIA ... Station Interface Adapter (SSD)
SIA ... Station of Initial Assignment
SIA ... Stereo-Image Alternator (PDAA)
SIA ... Storage Instantaneous Audimeter [*Measures television viewing*]
SIA ... Strategic Industries Association (EA)
SIA ... Stress-Induced Analgesia [*Medicine*]
SIA ... Strip Immunoblot Assay [*Immunology*]
SIA ... Structural Inventory and Appraisal [*Of roads and bridges*]
SIA ... Subacute Infectious Arthritis [*Medicine*] (DMAA)
SIA ... Subaru-Isuzu Automotive
SIA ... Subminiature Integrated Antenna
SIA ... Survivors of Incest Anonymous (EA)
SIA ... Swiss Society of Engineers and Architects (IAA)
SIA ... Synalbumin-Insulin Antagonism [*Medicine*]
SIA ... System Integration Area (MCD)
SIA ... Xian [*China*] [*Airport symbol*] (OAG)
SIAA ... Seed Industry Association of Australia
SIAAP ... Sugar Industry Adjustment Assistance Program [*Australia*]
SIABA ... Sindacato Italiano Artisti Belle Arti [*Italian Union of Fine Arts*]
SIABC ... Sociedad Iberoamericana de Biologia Celular [*Ibero-American Society for Cell Biology - IASCB*] (EAIO)
SIAC ... Secretariat International des Artistes Catholiques
SIAC ... Securities Industry Automation Corp. [*NYSE/ASE*] [*New York, NY*]
SIAC ... Shock Isolator Air Compressor (DWSG)
SIAC ... Societe Internationale des Artistes Chretiens [*International Society for Christian Artists*] [*Lydiate, Merseyside, England*] (EAIO)
SIAC ... Southeastern Intercollegiate Athletic Association (MCD)
SIAC ... Special Interest Auto Club [*Defunct*] (EA)

SIAC State Industry Advisory Committee [*Civil Defense*]
SIAC Submarine Integrated Attack Center (MCD)
SIAC Support List Allowance Card
SIACE Scottish Institute of Adult and Continuing Education (DBA)
SIACI Societe Intercontinental d'Assurances pour le Commerce et l'Industrie [*Intercontinental Assurance Company of Commerce and Industry*] [*France*]
SIAD Sierra Army Depot [*California*] (AABC)
SIAD Society of Industrial Artists and Designers [*British*] (DI)
SIADH Syndrome of Inappropriate Antidiuretic Hormone [*Endocrinology*]
SIADS Sensor Integration and Display Sharing [*Military*] (CAAL)
SIAE Scottish Institute of Adult Education (DI)
SIAE Scottish Institute of Agricultural Engineering [*Research center*] (IRC)
SIAF Service Indicator Associated Field [*Telecommunications*] (TEL)
SIAF Small Independent Action Force [*Military*]
SIAGL Survey Instrument, Azimuth Gyroscope, Lightweight (MCD)
SIAL Salon International de l'Alimentation [*World Food Fair*]
SIAL Sialagogue [*Promoting Flow of Saliva*] [*Medicine*] (ROG)
SIAL Sigma-Aldrich [*NASDAQ symbol*] (TTSB)
SIAL Sigma-Aldrich Corp. [*NASDAQ symbol*] (NQ)
SIAL Southeast Iowa Academic Libraries [*Library network*]
SIALON Silicon, Aluminum, Oxygen, and Nitrogen [*A ceramic*]
SIAM Scanning Interferometric Apertureless Microscope
SIAM Self-Initiating Antiaircraft Munition [*ARPA*]
SIAM Separate Index Access Method [*Computer science*] (BUR)
SIAM Signal Information and Monitoring Service [*American radio monitoring service*]
SIAM Society for Industrial and Applied Mathematics (EA)
SIAM Strategic Impact and Assumptions Identification Method
SIAM System for Improved Acquisition of Material (MCD)
SIAM System Integrated Access Method (IAA)
SIAMA Society for Interests of Active Missionaries in Asia, Africa, and America (EAIO)
SIAM Rev SIAM Review [*A publication*] (BRI)
SIAMS Secondary Ion Acclerator Mass Spectrometry
SIAN Societe Industrielle et Agriculturelle du Niari [*Industrial and Agricultural Society of Niari*]
SI & CTF Scottish Industry and Commerce Trade Fair (ITD)
SI & F Spinal Instrumentation and Fusion [*Neurology*] (DAVI)
Si & So Sight and Sound [*A publication*] (BRI)
SIANM Special Inspection, Army Nuclear Matters (MCD)
SI/AO Smithsonian Institution/Astrophysical Observatory (KSC)
SIAON Silicon-Aluminum Oxynitride
SIAP Sociedad Interamericana de Planeficacion [*Inter-American Planning Society*] [*Mexico*]
SIAP Standard Instrument Approach Procedure [*Aviation*]
SIAP Standard-Italo Americana Petroli
SIAP Statistical Institute for Asia and the Pacific [*United Nations*] (ECON)
SIAP Straight-In Approach [*Aviation*]
SIAP System for Improved Acoustic Performance
SIAR Small, Irregular, Agglutinated Rooms [*Architecture*]
SIAS Safety Injection Actuation Signal [*Nuclear energy*] (NRCH)
SIAS Scandinavian Institute of Asian Studies [*See also CINA*] [*Later, NIAS*] (EAIO)
SIAS Signals Intelligence Analysis System (MCD)
SIAS Submarine Integrated Antenna System (MCD)
SIASP Society for Italian-American Scientists and Physicians (EA)
SIAT Single Integrated Attack Team
SIAT Synthesis of Impact Acceleration Technology (MCD)
SIATE-MTS Simulated Intermediate Automatic Test Equipment-Maintenance Training System [*Air Force*]
SIAU Seminario Internacional de Administracao Universitaria
SIAWS Satellite-Interrogated Automatic Weather Station (NOAA)
SIB Satellite Integrated Buoy
SIB Satellite Ionospheric Beacons [*Military*]
SIB Saudi International Bank
SIB Scale plus Index plus Base
SIB Scales of Independent Behavior [*Occupational therapy*]
SIB Screen Image Buffer [*Computer science*]
SIB Securities and Investments Board [*British*]
SIB Selection Interview Blueprint [*LIMRA*]
SIB Self-Injurious Behavior [*Abnormal psychology*]
SIB Serial Interface Board
SIB Severe Impairment Battery [*Neuropsychological test*]
SIB Shipbuilding Industry Board [*British*]
SIB Ship Information Booklet [*Navy*]
SIB Siberia
Sib Siberia (VRA)
SIB Sibiti [*Congo*] [*Airport symbol*] (OAG)
Sib Sibling
sib Sibling (DOG)
SIB Sibola Mines Ltd. [*Vancouver Stock Exchange symbol*]
Sib Sibyllines (BJA)
SIB SIDPERS [*Standard Installation/Division Personnel System*] Interface Branch [*Military*] (INF)
SIB Simulation Interface Buffer (SSD)
SIB Sistema de Informacion Bursatil [*Stock Exchange Information System*] [*Madrid Stock Exchange*] [*Information service or system*] (IID)
SIB Situation Intelligence Brief (DNAB)
SIB Snake in the Box (IAA)
SIB Societa' Siba Aviation [*Italy ICAO designator*] (FAAC)
SIB Societe Internationale de Biometeorologie [*International Society of Biometeorology*] (EAIO)
SIB Special Intelligence Brief (MCD)
SIB Special Investigation Branch [*Army British*]
SIB Standard Index Base (DNAB)
SIB Standard Iron Bar (MSA)
SIB Subject Interface Box (KSC)
SIB System Integration Board (SSD)
SIB System Interconnect Bus [*Computer science*]
SIB Systems Information Bulletin [*Computer science*]
SIBA Scottish Indoor Bowling Association (DBA)
SIBA Small Independent Brewers' Association [*British*] (ECON)
SIBC Saudi Investment Banking Corp.
SIBC Societe Internationale de Biologie Clinique [*World Association of Anatomic and Clinical Pathology Societies*]
SIBD Soviet Independent Business Directory [*A publication*]
SIBE Sustainable Business Entity
SIBEX Second International BIOMASS Experiment
SIBEX Singapore International Building Exhibition
SIBH Salicylideniminobenzohydroxamic Acid [*Biochemistry*]
SIBH Society of Interpretation of Britain's Heritage (DBA)
SIBI SIBIA Neurosciences [*NASDAQ symbol*] (TTSB)
SIBI SIBIA Neurosciences, Inc. [*NASDAQ symbol*] (SAG)
SIBI Survivor Income Benefit Insurance (DICI)
SIBIA SIBIA Neurosciences, Inc. [*Associated Press*] (SAG)
SIBIL Systeme Integre pour les Bibliotheques Universitaires de Lausanne [*Integrated System for the University of Lausanne Libraries*] [*Switzerland*] (IID)
SIBIL System Informatise pour Biblitheques [*Information System for Libraries*] (EAIO)
SIBIS Self-Injurious Behavior Inhibiting System [*Psychology*]
SIBIS Smithsonian Institution Bibliographic Information System
SIBL Science, Industry, and Business Library [*New York, NY*]
SIBL Separate Infantry Brigade Light (INF)
SIBM Societe Internationale de Biologie Mathematique [*International Society of Mathematical Biology*] (EAIO)
SIBMAS Societe Internationale des Bibliotheques et Musees des Arts du Spectacle [*International Association of Libraries and Museums of the Performing Arts*] (EAIO)
SIB-MIBOC Securities and Investments Board and the Marketing of Investments Board Organisation Commission [*British*]
SIBOL Sweden Integrated Banking On-Line (IAA)
SibOr Sibylline Oracles (BJA)
SIBOR Singapore Interbank Offered Rate
SIBP Self-Insured Benefits Plan [*Human resources*] (WYGK)
SIBR Styrene-Isoprene-Butadiene Rubber [*Materials science*]
SI/BRC Strategic Intelligence/Business Research Corp.
SIBS Salk Institute for Biological Studies
SIBS Semiconductor Industry & Business Survey [*Database*] [*HTE Management Resources*] [*Information service or system*] (CRD)
SIBS Specially Important Brothers and Sisters (of Our Patients) [*Medicine*]
SIBS Stellar Inertial Bombing System
sib-ship Sibling Relationship (DAVI)
SIBTN Something Is Better than Nothing
SIC Air Sicilia, SRL [*Italy*] [*FAA designator*] (FAAC)
SIC Covington/Cincinnati, OH [*Location identifier FAA*] (FAAL)
SIC High School Student Information Center (EA)
SIC Safety Information Center [*National Safety Council*] (IID)
SIC Sakharov International Committee (EA)
SIC San Antonio do Ica [*Brazil*] [*Airport symbol*] (AD)
SIC Science Information Council [*National Science Foundation*]
SIC Scientific Information Center
SIC Security Intelligence Centre [*British World War II*]
SIC Security Intelligence Corps
SIC Semiconductor (IAA)
SIC Semiconductor Integrated Circuit
SIC Senior Intelligence Committee (DOMA)
SIC Sept-Iles [*Quebec*] [*Seismograph station code, US Geological Survey*] (SEIS)
SIC Serial Interface Chip
SIC Serum Insulin Concentration [*Medicine*] (DMAA)
SIC Service, Inc., Omaha NE [*STAC*]
SIC Servicio Informativo Continental [*Press agency*] [*Argentina*]
SIC Siccus [*Dry*] [*Latin*] (ADA)
SIC Sicily
Sic Sicily (VRA)
SIC Sico, Inc. [*Toronto Stock Exchange symbol*]
SiC Silicon Carbide (IDOE)
SIC Silicon Coated (IAA)
SIC Silicon-Insulating Compound
SIC Silicon Integrated Circuit
SIC Simulated Interface Calibration
SIC Skills Inventory Coordinator
SIC Social Implications of Computers (IAA)
SIC Social Interaction Code
SIC Societe Internationale de Cardiologie [*International Society of Cardiology*]
SIC Societe Internationale de Chirurgie [*International Society of Surgery - ISS*] [*Basel, Switzerland*] (EA)
SIC Societe Internationale de Criminologie [*International Society of Criminology*] (EA)
SIC Society of Inkwell Collectors (EA)
SIC SONAR Information Center (NVT)
SIC Sorties per Inspection Cycle [*Air Force*] (AFIT)
SIC Special Information Center (MCD)
SIC Special Interest Committee
SIC Specific Inductive Capacitance
SIC Specific Inductive Capacity (IDOE)

SIC Split Investment Company [*Generic term*]
SIC Sports Industries Commission [*New South Wales, Australia*]
SIC Standard Industrial Classification [*File indexing code*] [*Also, an information service or system*]
SIC Standard Industry Code (PCM)
SIC Standard Inspection Criteria
SIC Standard Interface Connector (SSD)
SIC States Information Center [*Council of State Governments*] (IID)
SIC Status of Implementation Chart
SIC Stock Item Catalog (MCD)
SIC Structural Influence Coefficient
SIC Subscriber Interface Control (DOMA)
SIC Sudbury Igneous Complex [*Geology*]
SIC Supervisory Inventory on Communication [*Test*]
SIC Support Identification Code (SSD)
SIC Survey Information Center [*Military*]
SIC Systeme Informatique pour la Conjoncture [*Information System for the Economy*] [*INSEE*] [*France*] [*Information service or system*] (IID)
SIC System Integration Computer (MCD)
SIC Systems Integration Contractor
SIC 72 Standard Industrial Classification 72 (NITA)
SICA Secondary Inventory Control Activity (MCD)
SICA Securities Industry Committee on Arbitration (DFIT)
SICA Soccer Industry Council of America (EA)
SICA Society of Industrial and Cost Accountants of Canada
SICA Subud International Cultural Association (EA)
SICAC Society of Inter-Celtic Arts and Culture (EA)
SICAM Sex Information Council of America [*Later, CSIE*] (EA)
SIC & DH Scientific Instrument Computer and Data Handling (SSD)
SICB Senior Interservice Control Board (DNAB)
SICBM Single-Warhead Intercontinental Ballistic Missile (MCD)
SICBM Small Intercontinental Ballistic Missile (MCD)
SICBM Super Intercontinental Ballistic Missile (IAA)
SICC Safeguard Inventory Control Center [*Army*] (AABC)
SICC Secondary Item Control Center
SICC Secours International de Caritas Catholica [*Belgium*] (EAIO)
SICC Service Inventory Control Center [*DoD*]
SICC Standards Information Center of China [*Library*]
SICC State Interagency Coordinating Council
SICCI Schools Information Centre on the Chemical Industry (AIE)
SICCM Supervisor Information on Civilian Career Management [*Navy*] (DNAB)
SICCS Social Interaction and Creativity in Communication System [*Educational test*]
SICD Sequenced Inventory of Communication Development (EDAC)
SICD Sequenced Inventory of Communicative Development [*Speech and language therapy*] (DAVI)
SICD Serum Isocitric Dehydrogenase (MAE)
SICD Supplier Interface Control Drawing (MCD)
SICDO Society of Industrial Civil Defence Officers [*British*] (BI)
SICDOC Special Interest Committee on Program Documentation [*Association for Computing Machinery*]
SICE Standard Interface Control Electronics (ECII)
SICEA Steel Industry Compliance Extension Act of 1981
SICEJ Society of Instrument and Control Engineers of Japan (IAA)
SICF Societe des Ingenieurs Civils de France
SICF Societe Ivoirienne des Chemins de Fer [*Railway system*] [*The Ivory Coast*] (EY)
SICIS Strategic Issue Competitive Information System (PDAA)
SIC/JIC Secondary Injection Control/Jet Interaction Control
Sick Sickels' Reports [*46-85 New York*] [*A publication*] (DLA)
SICK Sickle Cells [*Hematology*] (DAVI)
Sick Single Income, Couple of Kids [*Lifestyle classification*]
Sick Min Dec Sickels' United States Mining Laws and Decisions [*A publication*] (DLA)
Sick Op Sickels' Opinions of the New York Attorneys-General [*A publication*] (DLA)
SICL Sampling Inspection Checklist
SICL Selected Item Configuration Log
SICL Self-Interview Checklist [*Navy*] (NVT)
SICL Supplier Item Control List (MCD)
SICLOPS Simplified Interpretive COBOL Operating System (PDAA)
SICM Scanning Ion-Conductance Microscope
SICM Scheduled Input Control Method (MCD)
SICM Small Intercontinental Ballistic Missile (MCD)
SICM Soybean Integrated Crop Management Model
SICMA Special Initial Clothing Monetary Allowance [*Military*] (DNAB)
SICMA-CIV Special Initial Clothing Monetary Allowance - Civilian [*Military*] (DNAB)
SICMA-NAOC Special Initial Clothing Monetary Allowance - Naval Aviation Officer Candidate [*Navy*] (DNAB)
SICMA-NAVCAD Special Initial Clothing Monetary Allowance - Naval Aviation Cadet [*Navy*] (DNAB)
SICN Statewide Instructional Computing Network [*New York*] (EDAC)
SICN Syndicate for Fabrication of Fuel Elements [*French Acronym is based on foreign phrase*]
SICO Signal Control (DEN)
SICO Switched in for Checkout [*NASA*] (KSC)
SICO Systems Integration and Checkout
SICOB Salon International de l'Informatique, de la Communication, et de l'Organisationdu Bureau [*Business equipment exhibition*]
SICOM Securities Industry Communication [*Western Union Corp.*] [*Information service or system*]
SI COMMS Special Intelligence Communications (MCD)
SICOMP Siemens Computer (NITA)
SICOT Societe Internationale de Chirurgie Orthopedique et de Traumatologie [*International Society of Orthopaedic Surgery and Traumatology*] [*Brussels, Belgium*] (EAIO)
SICOVAM Societe Interprofessionnelle pour la Compensation des Valeurs Mobilieres [*French depository body*]
SICP Selected Ion Current Profile [*Spectrometry*]
SICP Shut-in Casing Pressure [*Well drilling technology*]
SICP Society of Indochina Philatelists (EA)
SICPS Standardized Integrated Command Post System [*Army*] (INF)
SICR Selected Item Configuration Record (MCD)
SICR Specific Intelligence Collection Requirements [*Military*] (AFM)
SICR Supply Item Change Record
SICRI Substances Immunologically Cross-Reactive with Insulin
SICRYS Sydney Indochinese Refugee Youth Support Group [*Australia*]
SICS Safety Injection Control System [*Nuclear energy*] (NRCH)
SICS Secondary Infrared Calibration System
SICS Ships Integrated Communications System (MCD)
SICS Source Information Control System (NITA)
SICS-PACK Screw Integrated Control System - Pontoon Air Cushion Kit [*Army*] (RDA)
SICSVA Sequential Impaction Cascade Sieve Volumetric Air (MAE)
SICT Scientific Inventory Control Technique (IAA)
SICT Selective Intracoronary Thrombolysis [*Cardiology*] (DAVI)
SICTLM Solomon Islands Cultural Traditional Leaders Movement
SICU Surgical Intensive Care Unit [*Medicine*]
Sicu Ab Abbas Siculus [*Deceased, 1445*] [*Authority cited in pre-1607 legal work*] (DSA)
SID Doctor of Industrial Science
SID ICP [*International Computer Programs, Inc.*] Software Information Database [*Information service or system*] (CRD)
SID Ilha do Sal [*Cape Verde Islands*] [*Airport symbol*] (AD)
SID Sal Island [*Cape Verde Islands*] [*Airport symbol*] (OAG)
SID Scale of Institutional Differentiation (AEBS)
SID Scheduled Issue Date [*Telecommunications*] (TEL)
SID Seal-In Device (MSA)
SID Security and Intelligence Service [*Army*]
SID Seismic Intrusion Detector [*or Device*] [*Army*]
SID Selected Item Drawing (MCD)
sid Semel in Die [*Once a Day*] [*Pharmacy*]
SID Sequence Information Data
SID Serial Input Data [*Computer science*]
SID Servizio Informazioni Difesa [*Defense Intelligence Service*] [*Italy*]
SID Shuttle Integration Device [*NASA*] (NASA)
SID Sida [*Iceland*] [*Seismograph station code, US Geological Survey*] (SEIS)
sid Sidamo [*MARC language code Library of Congress*] (LCCP)
SID Side-Impact Dummy [*Collision testing device*]
Sid Siderfin's King's Bench Reports [*82 English Reprint*] [*A publication*] (DLA)
SID Sidfin Air Ltd. [*Zambia*] [*ICAO designator*] (FAAC)
SID Signal Identification (NITA)
SID Silicon Imaging Device (IEEE)
SID Silver Iodine Generator
SID Simulator Interface Device (MCD)
SID Situation Display
SID Situation Information Display
SID Sketch-in-Depth [*Parthorn*] [*Software package*] (NCC)
SID Skin Inserted Detonator (MCD)
SID Slew-Induced Distortion
SID Society for Information Display (EA)
SID Society for International Development (EA)
SID Society for Investigative Dermatology (EA)
SID Sodium Ionization Detector [*Nuclear energy*] (NRCH)
SID Software Interface Document (MCD)
SID Solid Ink Density (DGA)
SID Solubilization by Incipient Development (OA)
SID Sound Ideas, Inc. [*Vancouver Stock Exchange symbol*]
SID Sound Interface Device [*Computer chip*]
SID Sound Interference Device
SID Source Image Distortion
SID Space and Information Systems Division [*NASA*]
SID Space Intruder Detector [*Burglar alarm*]
SID Special Intelligence Detachment [*Military*] (CINC)
SID Specification Interpretation Documentation (MCD)
SID Specific Infrared Detector
SID Speech Input Device (IAA)
SID Spiritus in Deo [*Spirit Rests in God*] [*Latin*]
SID Sports Information Director
SID Standard Instrument Departure [*RADAR*] [*Aviation*]
SID Standard Interface Document (NASA)
SID Strategic Intelligence Digests [*Military*] (AABC)
SID Structure Isolation Dynamics [*Vehicle development*] [*Automotive engineering*]
SID Subcontract Item Definition
SID Subject Identification Module [*NASA*]
SID Subscriber Identification (CAAL)
SID Subsystem Identification [*Electronics*]
SID Sudden Infant Death [*Syndrome*] [*Medicine*]
SID Sudden Ionospheric Disturbance [*Geophysics*]
SID Suprathermal Ion Detector (PDAA)
SID Surface-Induced Dissociation [*Physics*]
SID Surface Ionization Detector [*Instrumentation*]
SID SWIFT [*Society for Worldwide Interbank Financial Telecommunications*] Interface Device

SID............ Synchronous Identification System (DNAB)
SID............ Syntax Improving Device (IEEE)
SID............ System Integrational Diagnostic (IAA)
SID............ System Interface Document [*NASA*] (NASA)
SID............ Systems Integration and Deployment [*Program*] [*Department of Transportation*]
SID............ Systems Integration Demonstrator [*Aircraft*]
SIDA............ SIOP [*Single Integrated Operations Plan*] Integrated Data Base (MCD)
SIDA............ Societe Internationale Fernand de Vischer pour l'Histoire des Droits de l'Antiquite (EA)
SIDA............ Stable Isotope Dilution Assay [*Analytical chemistry*]
SIDA............ Swedish International Development Agency
SIDAAC............ Snow and Ice Distributed Active Archive Center (USDC)
SIDAAC............ Snow and Ice Distributed Active Archive Center [*Marine science*] (OSRA)
SIDAC............ Single Integrated Damage Anaysis Capability (MCD)
Sid Apoll............ Sidonius Apollinaris [*Fifth century AD*] [*Classical studies*] (OCD)
SIDAR............ Selective Information Dissemination and Retrieval [*Computer science*] (DIT)
SIDAR............ Symposium on Image Display and Recording
SIDASE............ Significant Data Selection
SIDC............ Slaved Illuminator Data Converter [*Military*] (CAAL)
SIDC............ Supply Item Design Change [*Navy*] (NG)
SIDC............ Support Issue Development Committee [*Military*] (CAAL)
SIDC............ Systems Identification Data Cost
SIDD............ Scientific Information and Documentation Division [*Later, ESIC*]
SIDD............ Standard Inside Diameter Dimension Ratio (DAC)
SIDE............ Siding
SIDE............ Suprathermal-Ion-Detector Experiment [*Apollo*] [*NASA*]
SIDEC............ Stanford International Development Education Center [*Stanford University*]
SIDEFCOOP... Sociedad Interamericana de Desarrollo de Financiamiento Cooperativo [*Inter-American Society for the Development of Cooperative Financing*] [*Buenos Aires, Argentina*] (EAIO)
Sid (Eng)............ Siderfin's King's Bench Reports [*82 English Reprint*] [*A publication*] (DLA)
SIDER............ Siderocytes [*In Differential*] [*Hematology*] (DAVI)
SIDES............ Source Input Data Edit System
SIDF............ Sinusoidal Input Describing Function [*Computer science*]
SIDF............ Standard Independent Data Format Association
SIDF............ Standard Interchange Data Form [*Computer science*] (MHDI)
SIDF............ System Independent Data Format [*Computer science*] (PCM)
SIDFA............ Senior Industrial Development Field Adviser [*United Nations*]
Sid Gov............ Sidney on Government [*A publication*] (DLA)
SI Diam............ SI Diamond Technology [*Commercial firm Associated Press*] (SAG)
SIDL............ System Identification Data List [*Navy*] (NG)
SIDLOB............ Side Lobe [*Entomology*]
SIDM............ Shipboard Identification Demolition Model [*Navy*]
SIDM............ Solar Internal Dynamics Mission (SSD)
SIDM............ Syndicat International des Debardeurs et Magasiniers [*International Longshoremen's and Warehousemen's Union ILWU*] [*Canada*]
SIDMS............ Status Inventory Data Management System (MCD)
SIDN............ Small Industry Development Network [*Georgia Institute of Technology*]
SIDO............ Societe Internationale pour le Developpement des Organisations [*International Society for the Development of Organizations*] (EAIO)
SIDOR............ Siderurgica del Orinoco [*Government steel company*] [*Venezuela*]
SIDOS............ Site Document Order Section (SAA)
SIDP............ Seed Industry Development Program [*UN Food and Agriculture Organization*]
SIDP............ Sheep Industry Development Program (EA)
SIDPE............ Sensing, Identitying, Deciding, Predicting, and Executing
SIDPERS............ Standard Installation/Division Personnel System [*Military*] (AABC)
SIDS............ Satellite Imagery Dissemination System (MCD)
SIDS............ Screening Information Data Set [*Environmental science*]
SIDS............ Secondary Imagery Dissemination System (DOMA)
SIDS............ Sensor Interface Data System [*Military*] (CAAL)
SIDS............ Ships Integrated Defense System
SIDS............ Shrike Improved Display System [*Military*] (NVT)
SIDS............ Societe Internationale de Defense Sociale [*International Society for Social Defence - ISSD*] [*Paris, France*] (EAIO)
SIDS............ Societe Internationale de Droit Sociale
SIDS............ Space Investigations Documentation System [*NASA*]
SIDS............ Spares Integrated Data System (MCD)
SIDS............ Specification Interpretation Documents (MCD)
SIDS............ Speech Identification System (IAA)
SIDS............ Standard Information Display System [*Military*] (CAAL)
SIDS............ Stellar Inertial Doppler System
SIDS............ Strike Improved Display System (MCD)
SIDS............ Sudden Infant Death Syndrome [*Medicine*]
SIDS............ Sulfo-Iduronate Sulfatase (DMAA)
SIDS............ Support Integrated Data System (MCD)
SIDSA............ Sudden Infant Death Syndrome Act of 1974
SIDS Alliance... Sudden Infant Death Syndrome Alliance (PAZ)
SIDT............ SI Diamond Technology [*Commercial firm NASDAQ symbol*] (SAG)
SIDT............ Silicon Integrated Device Technology (IAA)
SIDTC............ Single Integrated Development Test Cycle
SIDTEC............ Single Integrated Development Test Cycle (MCD)
SIDTS............ Single Integrated Development Test System
SIDY............ Science Dynamics [*NASDAQ symbol*] (TTSB)
SIDY............ Science Dynamics Corp. [*NASDAQ symbol*] (NQ)
SIE............ Science Information Exchange [*Later, SSIE*] [*Smithsonian Institution*]
SIE............ Sea Isle, NJ [*Location identifier FAA*] (FAAL)
SIE............ Selected Inertial Equipment
SIE............ Selected Item Exchange (MCD)
SIE............ Select Information Exchange [*Information service or system*] (IID)
SIE............ Sensory Isolation Experiment (SAA)
SIE............ Serum Immunoreative Erythropoietin [*Immunochemistry*]
SIE............ Servizio Informazioni Esercito [*Italy*] [*Forces Intelligence Service*]
SIE............ Shanell International Energy Corp. [*Vancouver Stock Exchange symbol*]
SIE............ Shuttle Interface Equipment [*NASA*] (NASA)
Sie............ Siemens [*Unit of electric conductance*]
SIE............ Siena [*Italy*] [*Seismograph station code, US Geological Survey*] (SEIS)
SIE............ Sierra Express, Inc. [*ICAO designator*] (FAAC)
SIE............ Sierra Health Services [*NYSE symbol*] (TTSB)
SIE............ Sierra Health Services, Inc. [*NYSE symbol*] (SAG)
SIE............ Single Instruction Execute
SIE............ Societe Internationale d'Electrochimie [*International Society of Electrochemistry*]
SIE............ Society of Industrial Engineers [*Later, SAM*]
SIE............ Soroptimist International d'Europe [*Soroptimist International of Europe*] (EAIO)
SIE............ Special Inspection Equipment
SIE............ Start Interpretive Execution (HGAA)
SIE............ Stroke in Evolution [*Medicine*] (MEDA)
SIE............ Suicide Information and Education [*Suicide Information and Education Center*] [*Canada Information service or system*] (CRD)
SIE............ Surface Ionization Engine
SIE............ System Integration Equipment (KSC)
SIE............ System Investigation Equipment (KSC)
SIEA............ Sensor Interface Electronics Assembly (MCD)
SIEB............ Satellite-Interrogated Environmental Buoy
SIEB............ Siebert Financial Corp. [*NASDAQ symbol*] (SAG)
SiebelS............ Siebel Systems, Inc. [*Associated Press*] (SAG)
Siebert............ Siebert Financial Corp. [*Associated Press*] (SAG)
SIEC............ Societe Internationale pour l'Enseignement Commercial [*International Society for Business Education*] [*Lausanne, Switzerland*] (EAIO)
SIEC............ Suicide Information and Education Centre [*Canadian Mental Health Association*] [*Information service or system*] (IID)
SIECCAN............ Sex Information and Education Council of Canada
SIECD............ Societe Internationale d'Education Continue en Dentisterie [*International Society of Continuing Education in Dentistry - ISCED*] [*Brussels, Belgium*] (EAIO)
SIECOP............ Scientific Information and Education Council of Physicians (EA)
SIECUS............ Sex Information and Education Council of the US (EA)
SIED............ Supplier Item Engineering Order (MCD)
SIEDS............ Societe Internationale d'Etude du Dix-Huitieme Siecle [*International Society for Eighteenth-Century Studies - ISECS*] (EAIO)
SIEF............ Societe Internationale d'Ethnographie et de Folklore [*International Society for Ethnology and Folklore*]
SIEFA............ Source Inventory and Emission Factor Analysis [*Environmental Protection Agency*]
SIEGE............ Simulated EMP [*Electromagnetic Pulse*] Ground Environment [*Air Force*]
Siego............ Single, Intelligent, and Educated and Growing Old [*Lifestyle classification*]
SIEL............ Superficial Image Emphasis Lithography (NITA)
sien............ Sienna [*Philately*]
Siena Heights C... Siena Heights College (GAGS)
SIEP............ Screening Inspection for Electronic Parts [*NASA*]
SIEP............ State Implementation and Enforcement Program [*Environmental Protection Agency*]
SIEPM............ Societe Internationale pour l'Etude de la Philosophie Medievale [*International Society for the Study of Medieval Philosophy*] (EAIO)
SIER............ Sierra On-Line [*NASDAQ symbol*] (TTSB)
SIER............ Sierra On-Line, Inc. [*NASDAQ symbol*] (CTT)
SieraHm............ Sierra Home Services [*Commercial firm Associated Press*] (SAG)
SierH............ Sierra Home Services [*Commercial firm Associated Press*] (SAG)
SierHS............ Sierra Health Services, Inc. [*Associated Press*] (SAG)
SIERNEV............ Sierra Nevada (FAAC)
SierOn............ Sierra On-Line, Inc. [*Associated Press*] (SAG)
SierPac............ Sierra Pacific Resources [*Associated Press*] (SAG)
Sierra Leone LR... Law Reports, Sierra Leone Series [*A publication*] (ILCA)
Sierra Leone L Rec... Law Recorder (Sierra Leone) [*A publication*] (ILCA)
SierraP............ Sierra Pac Pw [*Associated Press*] (SAG)
SierraSem............ Sierra Semiconductor Corp. [*Associated Press*] (SAG)
SierSm............ Sierra Semiconductor Corp. [*Associated Press*] (SAG)
SierTah............ Sierra Tahoe Bancorp [*Associated Press*] (SAG)
SierWst............ SierraWest Bancorp [*Associated Press*] (SAG)
SIES............ Ship Integrated Electronic System
SIES............ Sobek's International Explorer's Society [*Commercial firm*] (EA)
SIES............ Society of the Incarnation of the Eternal Son [*Anglican religious community*]
SIES............ Supervision, Inspection, Engineering, and Services (NASA)
SIESC............ Secretariat International des Enseignants Secondaires Catholiques [*International Secretariat of Catholic Secondary School Teachers*] [*Acronym used in association name, SIESC Pax Romana Nijmegen, Netherlands*] (EAIO)
SIESO............ Society of Industrial Emergency Services Officers [*British*] (DBA)
SIESTA............ Silent Energy Sources for Tactical Applications (MCD)
SIETAR/INTL... International Society for Intercultural Education, Training, and Research (EA)
SIEUSE............ Secretariat International de l'Enseignement Universitaire des Sciences de l'Education
SI/EW............ Special Intelligence/Electronic Warfare (MCD)

SIF ..... Reidsville, NC [*Location identifier FAA*] (FAAL)
SIF ..... Salvo in Flight [*Military*] (CAAL)
SIF ..... Science Information Facility [*FDA*]
SIF ..... Scleroderma International Foundation (EA)
SIF ..... Scotch-Irish Foundation (EA)
SIF ..... Scott Industrial Foam
SIF ..... Secure Identification Feature
SIF ..... Security and Intelligence Foundation [*Later, CIS*] (EA)
SIF ..... Selective Identification Feature [*Military decoder modification*]
SIF ..... Selective Interrogation Feature (MCD)
SIF ..... Serum-Inhibition Factor [*Medicine*] (DMAA)
SIF ..... Service Incroyance et Foi [*Canadian Catholic Conference*]
SIF ..... Short-Intrusion Fuze (RDA)
SIF ..... SIFCO Indus [*AMEX symbol*] (TTSB)
SIF ..... SIFCO Industries, Inc. [*AMEX symbol*] (SPSG)
SIF ..... Signaling Information Field [*Telecommunications*] (TEL)
SIF ..... Simra [*Nepal*] [*Airport symbol*] (OAG)
SIF ..... Single Face
SIF ..... Skycy Freighters International Ltd. [*Kenya*] [*ICAO designator*] (FAAC)
SIF ..... Small Intensely Fluorescent [*Cytology*]
SIF ..... Social Investment Forum (EA)
SIF ..... Sociedad Iberoamericana de Filosofia [*Spain*] (EAIO)
SIF ..... Society of International Friendship (EA)
SIF ..... Solvent-Induced Force [*Physical chemistry*]
SIF ..... Sound Intermediate Frequency
SIF ..... Source Image Format (DOM)
SIF ..... Source Input Format [*Computer science*]
SIF ..... Standard Image Format [*Computer science*]
SIF ..... Standard Interchange Format
SIF ..... Standard Interface (IAA)
SIF ..... Storage Interface Facility
SIF ..... Stress Intensity Factor (MCD)
SIF ..... Suncorp Insurance and Finance [*Commercial firm Australia*]
SIF ..... Switched In-Flight (KSC)
SIF ..... Synthetic Interstitial Fluid [*Biochemistry*]
SIFA ..... Society of Independent Financial Advisors [*Englewood, CO*] (EA)
SIFAD ..... Separate Ion Formation and Drift
SIFAR ..... Surveillance Imagery Fast Access Recording (MCD)
SIFAT ..... Servants in Faith and Technology (EA)
SIFC ..... Saskatchewan Indian Federated College [*University of Regina*]
SIFC ..... Sparks International Official Fan Club (EAIO)
SIFCC ..... Senate Interstate and Foreign Commerce Committee
Sifco ..... SIFCO Industries, Inc. [*Associated Press*] (SAG)
SIFCON ..... Slurry-Infiltrated Fiber-Concrete (BARN)
SIFCS ..... Sideband Intermediate Frequency Communications System (AAG)
SifDeut ..... Sifrei Deuteronomy (BJA)
SIFE ..... Sanitation Inspection Fish Establishment [*National Marine Fisheries Service*] (NOAA)
SIFE ..... Students in Free Enterprise [*Bolivar, MO*] (EA)
SIFEM ..... Side-Impact Finite Element Model [*Automotive safety*] [*Computer-assisted design*]
SIFF ..... Stock Index Futures Fund
SIFI ..... Starlog Franchise [*NASDAQ symbol*] (TTSB)
SIF/IFF ..... Selective Identification Feature/Identification Friend or Foe [*Military*] (AFM)
SifNum ..... Sifrei Numbers (BJA)
SIFO ..... Societa Italiana di Farmacia Ospedaliera [*Italy*]
SIFO ..... Svenska Institutet foer Opinionsundersoekningar
Si-Fo-An-Di ..... Silica-Forsterite-Anorthite-Diopside [*Lunar geology*]
Si-Fo-Di ..... Silica-Forsterite-Diopside [*Lunar geology*]
SIFPPS ..... Shore Installations and Facilities Planning and Programming System [*Navy*] (MCD)
SIFR ..... Serious Injury Frequency Rate
SIFR ..... Simulated Instrument Flight Rules (AAG)
SIFR ..... Sun-Improved Frequency Response
SIFT ..... Selected-Ion Flow Tube [*Instrumentation*]
SIFT ..... Share Internal FORTRAN Translator [*Computer science*] (IEEE)
SIFT ..... Simplified Input for TIROS Operational Satellite System (IAA)
SIFT ..... Simplified Input for Toss [*Computer science*]
SIFT ..... Software Implemented Fault Tolerance [*NASA*]
SIFT ..... Summary of Information on Film and Television [*British*]
SIFT ..... System Identification from Tracking (MCD)
SIFTER ..... ScIntillating Fiber Telescope for Energetic Radiation [*Proposed, 1996*]
SIFTOR ..... Sifting of Information for Technology of Reactors [*MIT-AEC study*]
SIFX ..... Simulated Installation Fixture (AAG)
SifZut ..... Sifrei Zuta (BJA)
SIG ..... San Juan/Isla Grande [*Puerto Rico*] [*Airport symbol*] (OAG)
SIG ..... San Juan, PR [*Location identifier FAA*] (FAAL)
SIg ..... Secretory Immunoglobin [*Immunology*]
SIG ..... Self-Insurance Group (WYGK)
SIG ..... Senior Interagency Group [*Federal government*]
SIG ..... Senior Interdepartmental Group [*Department of State*]
SIG ..... Serum Immune Globulin [*Immunochemistry*]
SIG ..... Ship Improvement Guide
SIG ..... SIGCORP, Inc. [*NYSE symbol*] (TTSB)
SIG ..... Sigmoidoscope [*or Sigmoidoscopy*] [*Medicine*] (AAMN)
SIG ..... Signa [*Write*] [*Pharmacy*]
SIG ..... Signal
sig ..... Signal (WDMC)
SIG ..... Signalman [*Navy rating British*]
SIG ..... Signature (AFM)
sig ..... Signature (WDMC)
SIG ..... Signetur [*Let It Be Labelled*] [*Pharmacy*]
sig ..... Significant
SIG ..... Significant Testing (IAA)
SIG ..... Signifying (ROG)
SIG ..... Signore [*or Signora*] (EY)
SIG ..... Silicon-Insulated Gate
SIG ..... Silver-Intensified Gold [*Biological stain*]
SIG ..... Silver Ridge Resources, Inc. [*Vancouver Stock Exchange symbol*]
SIG ..... Simplicity Is Greatness [*See also GIS*]
SIG ..... Simplified Inertial Guidance
SIG ..... Society for Integrative Graphology [*Defunct*] (EA)
SIG ..... Southern Indiana Gas & Electric Co. [*NYSE symbol*] (SPSG)
SIG ..... South Ingalls [*Colorado*] [*Seismograph station code, US Geological Survey Closed*] (SEIS)
SIG ..... Special Interest Group
SIG ..... Special Investigative Group [*DoD*]
SIG ..... Starfield Image Generator
SIG ..... State Implementation Grant
SIG ..... Stellar Inertial Guidance Signal
SIG ..... Strapdown Inertial Guidance
SIG ..... Sub-Interface Generator (NITA)
sIg ..... Surface Immunoglobulin [*Immunochemistry*]
SIG ..... Three Sigma Market Newspaper Audiences [*Three Sigma Research Center, Inc.*] [*Information service or system*] (CRD)
S-IgA ..... Secretory Immunoglobulin A [*Immunology*]
SIGA ..... Sigma Circuits [*NASDAQ symbol*] (TTSB)
SIGA ..... Sigma Circuits, Inc. [*NASDAQ symbol*] (SAG)
Siga ..... Signora [*Madam*] [*Italian*]
SIGACT ..... Special Interest Group on Automata and Computability Theory (EA)
SIGADA ..... Special Interest Group on Ada (EA)
SIGAGCY ..... Signal Agency (IAA)
SIG/AH ..... Special Interest Group/Arts and Humanities [*of the American Society for Information Science*]
SIGAIRDEFENGRAGCY ... Signal Air Defense Engineering Agency (IAA)
SIG/ALP ..... Special Interest Group/Automated Language Processing [*American Society for Information Science*]
SIGAP ..... Surrey Investigation Group into Aerial Phenomena [*British*]
SIGAPL ..... Special Interest Group on APL Programming Language (EA)
SIGARCH ..... Special Interest Group for Architecture of Computer Systems (EA)
SIGART ..... Special Interest Group on Artificial Intelligence (EA)
SIGAVNCO ... Signal Aviation Company (IAA)
SIGBAT ..... Signal Battalion [*Army*]
SIG/BC ..... Special Interest Group/Biological and Chemical Information Systems [*of the American Society for Information Science*]
SIGBDP ..... Special Interest Group for Business Data Processing and Management (EA)
SIGBI ..... Soroptimist International of Great Britain and Ireland (EAIO)
SIGBIO ..... Special Interest Group on Biomedical Computing (EA)
SIGBN ..... Signal Battalion (IAA)
SIG/BSS ..... Special Interest Group/Behavioral and Social Sciences [*of the American Society for Information Science*]
SIGC ..... Signal Corps [*Later, Communications and Electronics Command*] [*Army*]
SIGC ..... Signal Corps Engineering Laboratories [*Fort Monmouth, NJ*]
SIGCAPH ..... Special Interest Group for Computers and the Physically Handicapped (EA)
SIGCAS ..... Special Interest Group for Computers and Society (EA)
SIGCAT ..... Special Interest Group on CD-ROM Applications and Technology (AAGC)
SIG/CBE ..... Special Interest Group/Costs, Budgeting, and Economics [*of the American Society for Information Science*]
Sig CD ..... Signature Card [*Banking*] (MHDW)
SIGCEN ..... Signal Center [*Military*] (AABC)
SIGCHI ..... Special Interest Group on Computer and Human Interaction (EA)
SIGCO ..... Signal Company (IAA)
SIGCOA ..... Signal Company, Airline (IAA)
SIGCOC ..... Signal Company, Cable (IAA)
SIGCOM ..... Signal Communication (IAA)
SIGCOMM ..... Special Interest Group on Data Communication (EA)
SIGCOMMAGCY ... Signal Communication Agency (IAA)
SIGCOMMSECAGCY ... Signal Communication Security Agency (IAA)
SIGCONDNET ... Signal Conditioning Network (IAA)
SIGCONDR ... Signal Conditioner (MCD)
SIGCONSBN ... Signal Construction Battalion (IAA)
SIGCOR ..... Signal Corps [*Later, Communications and Electronics Command*] [*Army*]
SIGCOSIM ..... Special Interest Group on Computer Systems, Installation Management [*Association for Computing Machinery*]
SIGCOW ..... Signal Company, Wireless (IAA)
SIGCOWG ..... Signal Company, Wing (IAA)
SIGCOY ..... Signal Company (IAA)
SIGCPR ..... Special Interest Group for Computer Personnel Research (EA)
SIG/CR ..... Special Interest Group/Classification Research [*of the American Society for Information Science*]
SIGCS ..... Special Interest Group for Computers and Society [*Association for Computing Machinery*] (EA)
SIG CSE ..... Special Interest Group for Computer Science Education (EA)
SIGCUE ..... Special Interest Group for Computer Uses in Education (EA)
SIG-D ..... Simplified Inertial Guidance-Demonstration [*Army*] (RDA)
SIGDA ..... Special Interest Group for Design Automation (EA)
SIG/DAT ..... Signal/Data (MHDI)
SIGDEP ..... Signal Depot (IAA)
SIGDEPCO ..... Signal Depot Company [*Military*] (IAA)
SIGDIV ..... Signal Division [*SHAPE*] (NATG)
SIGDOC ..... Special Interest Group for Systems Documentation (EA)
SIGE ..... Silicon Germanium
SiGe ..... Silicon Germanium [*Computer science*]

SIGE............ Societe Internationale de Gastro-Enterologie
SIGEFT........ Special Interest Group on Electronic Funds Transfer (MHDI)
SIGENGRAGCY... Signal Engineering Agency (IAA)
SIGEQUIP.... Signal Equipment (IAA)
SIG/ES........ Special Interest Group/Education for Information Science [*of the American Society for Information Science*]
SIGEX.......... Signal Exercise (NATG)
SIGFET......... Silicon Gate Field Effect Transistor (IAA)
SIGFIDET..... Special Interest Group on File Description and Translation [*Association for Computing Machinery*] [*Later, Special Interest Group on the Management of Data*]
sig fig......... Significant Figures [*Mathematics*] (BARN)
SIG/FIS........ Special Interest Group/Foundations of Information Science [*of the American Society for Information Science*]
SIGG............ Signatures (WGA)
SIGGEN........ Signal Generator (IEEE)
SIGGND........ Signal Ground (IAA)
SIGGRAPH... Special Interest Group on Computer Graphics (EA)
SIGGRAPH... Special Interest Group on Graphics (NITA)
SIGGY.......... Signet Group [*NASDAQ symbol*] (SPSG)
SIGGY.......... Signet Group ADR [*NASDAQ symbol*] (TTSB)
SIGGZ.......... Signet Grp $1.06 Cv Pfd [*NASDAQ symbol*] (TTSB)
SightRes...... Sight Resources Corp. [*Associated Press*] (SAG)
SIGHVCONSTBN... Signal Heavy Construction Battalion (IAA)
SIGI............ Selective Insurance Gr [*NASDAQ symbol*] (TTSB)
SIGI............ Selective Insurance Group, Inc. [*Branchville, NJ*] [*NASDAQ symbol*] (NQ)
SIGI............ System for Interactive Guidance and Information [*Computerized career-counseling service offered by the Educational Testing Service*] [*Princeton, NJ*]
SIG/IAC........ Special Interest Group/Information Analysis Centers [*of the American Society for Information Science*]
SIGILL......... Sigillum [*Seal*] [*Latin*] (WGA)
SIGINT......... Signal Intelligence [*Military*] (AABC)
SIGINTELAGCY... Signal Intelligence Agency (IAA)
SIGINT/EW... Signal Intelligence/Electronic Warfare (MCD)
SIGIPS......... Signals Information Processing System [*Navy*] (DOMA)
SIGIR........... Special Interest Group on Information Retrieval (EA)
SIGIRD......... Systeme Integre de Gestion Informatise des Ressources Documentaires [*Integrated System for the Management of Documentary Resources*] [*University of Quebec, Montreal*] [*Information service or system*] (IID)
SIG/IRG........ Senior Interdepartmental Group / Interdepartmental Regional Group (DNAB)
SIG/ISE........ Special Interest Group/Information Services to Education [*of the American Society for Information Science*]
Sig L............ Signal Lieutenant [*British military*] (DMA)
SIG/LA......... Special Interest Group/Library Automation and Networks [*of the American Society for Information Science*]
SIGLASH....... Special Interest Group on Language Analysis and Studies in the Humanities [*Association for Computing Machinery*]
SIGLE........... System for Information on Grey Literature in Europe [*European Association for Grey Literature Exploitation*] [*Commission of the European Communities*] [*Information service or system*] (IID)
SIGLEX......... Special Interest Group on Lexicography [*National Security Agency*]
SIGLINT....... Signal Intelligence [*US surveillance satellite*]
SIGM........... Sigma Designs [*NASDAQ symbol*] (TTSB)
SIGM........... Sigma Designs, Inc. [*Fremont, CA*] [*NASDAQ symbol*] (NQ)
SIGM........... Syndicat International des Gens de Mer du Canada
SIGMA......... Science in General Management [*British*] (DI)
SIGMA......... Sealed Insulating Glass Manufacturers Association (EA)
SIGMA......... Shielded Inert Gas Metal Arc (IAA)
SIGMA......... Site Information Generation and Material Accountability Plan [*Army*] (AABC)
SIGMA......... Society of Independent Gasoline Marketers of America [*Washington, DC*] (EA)
SIGMA......... Society of In-Plant Graphics Management Associations
SIGMA......... Society of Inventors of Games and Mathematical Attractions [*British*]
SIGMA......... Standardized Inertial Guidance Multiple Application
SigmaC........ Sigma Circuits, Inc. [*Associated Press*] (SAG)
SigmAl......... Sigma-Aldrich Corp. [*Associated Press*] (SAG)
SIGMALOG... Simulation and Gaming Method for Analysis of Logistics [*Army*]
SIGMAP....... Special Interest Group for Mathematical Programming [*Defunct*] (EA)
SIGMAS........ Signal Measurement and Analysis System
Sigmatr........ Sigmatron International [*Associated Press*] (SAG)
SigmDg......... Sigma Designs, Inc. [*Associated Press*] (SAG)
SIGMET........ Significant Meteorological Information [*FAA*] (TAG)
SIGMET........ Significant Meteorological Information (GAVI)
SIGMETRICS... Special Interest Group on Measurement and Evaluation (EA)
SIGMICRO... Special Interest Group on Microprogramming and Microarchitecture (EA)
SIGMINI....... Special Interest Group on Minicomputers [*Later, SIGSMALL*] [*Association for Computing Machinery*] (CSR)
Sig Mis........ Signature Missing
SIGMN......... Signalman
sigmo.......... Sigmoidoscopy [*Medicine*]
SIGMOD....... Special Interest Group on Management of Data (EA)
sigmoid....... Sigmoidoscopy [*Medicine*] (DAVI)
SIGMR......... Signal Master (IAA)
SIGMS......... Signal Material Support (DNAB)
SIGMSGCEN... Signal Message Center (IAA)
SIGMSLSPTAGCY... Signal Missile Support Agency (IAA)
SIGN........... Plasti-Line [*NASDAQ symbol*] (TTSB)
SIGN........... Plasti-Line, Inc. [*NASDAQ symbol*] (NQ)
SIGN........... Signa [*Label*] [*Pharmacy*] (ROG)
SIGN........... Signal (IAA)
sign............ Signature (DAVI)
SIGN........... Strapdown Inertial Guidance and Navigation (MCD)
SIGNA......... Signora [*Madam*] [*Italian*] (ROG)
Signa.......... Signorina [*Miss*] [*Italian*]
SIGNA......... Species Iris Group of North America (EA)
SIGNCE....... Significance (ROG)
SIGNE......... Signature
SIGNET....... Signal Network
SIGNET....... Supplies Invoice Generation Network (PDAA)
SignetB....... Signet Banking Corp. [*Associated Press*] (SAG)
SignetGp..... Signet Group [*Associated Press*] (SAG)
SIGNF......... Signify (ROG)
SignInns..... Signature Inns, Inc. [*Associated Press*] (SAG)
SIGN N P.... Signetur Nomine Proprio [*Let It Be Written Upon with the Proper Name*] [*Pharmacy*] (ROG)
SIGNO......... Signal Officer (IAA)
Signor de Homod... Signorolus de Homodeis de Mediolano [*Flourished, 14th-15th century*] [*Authority cited in pre-1607 legal work*] (DSA)
SIG/NPM...... Special Interest Group/Nonprint Media [*of the American Society for Information Science*]
Sig N Pro..... Signa Nomine Proprio [*Label with the Proper Name*] [*Pharmacy*]
SIG N PRO... Signa Nomine Proprio [*Label with the Proper Name*] [*Latin*] [*Pharmacy*] (DAVI)
SIGNRE....... Signature (ROG)
Signs.......... Signs: Journal of Women in Culture and Society [*A publication*] (BRI)
SigntG......... Signet Group [*Associated Press*] (SAG)
SIGNUM....... Special Interest Group on Numerical Control [*Military*]
SIGNUM....... Special Interest Group on Numerical Mathematics (EA)
SIGO........... Signal Officer
Sigo............ Signorolus de Homodeis de Mediolano [*Flourished, 14th-15th century*] [*Authority cited in pre-1607 legal work*] (DSA)
SIGOA......... Special Interest Group on Office Automation [*Later, SIGOIS*]
SIGOFFR...... Signal Officer (IAA)
SIGOIS........ Special Interest Group on Office Information Systems (EA)
SIGOP......... Signal Optimization Program [*Federal Highway Administration*]
SIGOPNBN... Signal Operation Battalion (IAA)
SIGOPS........ Special Interest Group on Operating Systems (EA)
SIGOUT....... Signal Output (MHDI)
SIGPC......... Special Interest Group on Personal Computing [*Association for Computing Machinery*]
SIGPLAN...... Special Interest Group on Programming Languages (EA)
SIGPRAD..... Special Interest Group on Phobias and Related Anxiety Disorders (EA)
SIGPROCOFC... Signal Procurement Office (IAA)
SIGR........... Signature Resorts, Inc. [*NASDAQ symbol*] (SAG)
SIGRAM....... Sound Intensity Diagram (MCD)
SIGREAL...... Special Interest Group on Real Time Processing [*Association for Computing Machinery*]
SIGREPCO... Signal Repair Company [*Military*] (IAA)
SIGRES........ Signal Corps Reserve [*Military*] (IAA)
SigRsrts...... Signature Resorts, Inc. [*Associated Press*] (SAG)
SIG/RT........ Special Interest Group/Reprographic Technology [*of the American Society for Information Science*]
SIGRTN........ Signal Return [*Electronics*]
SIGS........... Sandia Interactive Graphics System
SIGS........... Simplified Inertial Guidance System (MCD)
SIGS........... Stellar Inertial Guidance System [*Air Force*] (AAG)
SIGSAC........ Special Interest Group on Security, Audit, and Control (EA)
SIGSAM........ Special Interest Group for Symbolic and Algebraic Manipulation (EA)
SIGSCH........ Signal School (IAA)
SIGSCSA...... Special Interest Group on Small Computing Systems and Applications [*Later, SIGSMALL*] [*Association for Computing Machinery*] (EA)
SIG/SDI........ Special Interest Group/Selective Dissemination of Information [*American Society for Information Science*]
SIGSEC........ Signal Section (IAA)
SIGSEC........ Signal Security [*Military*] (AABC)
SIG SEL....... Signal Selector (DNAB)
SIGSERVCO... Signal Service Company [*Military*] (IAA)
SIGSIM........ Special Interest Group on Simulation (EA)
SIGSMALL... Special Interest Group on Small Computing Systems and Applications [*Formerly, SIGSCSA*] [*Association for Computing Machinery*] (EA)
SIGSMALL/PC... [*A*] Special Interest Group on Small and Personal Computing Systems and Applications [*An association for Computing Machinery*] (HGAA)
SIGSOC........ Special Interest Group on Social and Behavioral Science Computing [*Association for Computing Machinery*]
SIGSOFT...... Special Interest Group on Software Engineering (EA)
SIGSOP........ Signals Operator (ADA)
SIGSPAC...... Special Interest Group on Urban Data Systems, Planning, Architecture, and Civil Engineering [*Association for Computing Machinery*]
SIGSPACE.... Senior Interagency Group (Space)
SIGSPCSA.... Special Interest Group on Small and Personal Computing Systems Applications (EA)
SIGSPTBN.... Signal Support Battalion [*Military*] (IAA)
Sig Sta......... Signal Station [*Nautical charts*]
SIGSTN........ Signal Station [*Navigation*]
SIGSTR........ Signal Strength (IAA)
SIGSUPAGNCY... Signal Supply Agency (IAA)
SIGSUPBN... Signal Supply Battalion [*Military*] (IAA)
SIGSVCBN... Signal Service Battalion [*Military*] (IAA)
SIGTC.......... Signal Training Center (IAA)

SIGTNG........ Signal Training (IAA)
SIGTNGCEN... Signal Training Center (IAA)
SIGTNGDET... Signal Training Detachment (IAA)
SIGTRAN...... Special Interest Group on Translation [*National Security Agency*]
SIGTTO....... Society of International Gas Tanker and Terminal Operators (EAIO)
SIGUCC........ Special Interest Group on University Computing Centers (IAA)
SIGUCCS...... Special Interest Group for University and College Computing Services (EA)
Sig Unk........ Signature Unknown
SIG/UOI........ [*A*] Special Interest Group on User Online Interaction [*An association for Computing Machinery*] (HGAA)
SIGVOICE..... Special Interest Group on Voice [*National Security Agency*]
SIG-WEB...... Special Interest Group on the WWW
SIGWX.......... Significant Weather [*Aviation*] (FAAC)
SIG/ZBB/ADP... Special Interest Group on Zero-Based Budgeting and Automated Data Processing (MHDI)
SIH.............. Schweizerisches Institut fuer Hauswirtschaft
SIH.............. Scinde Irregular Horse [*British military*] (DMA)
SIH.............. Seafarers and International House (EA)
SIH.............. Silgarhi Doti [*Nepal*] [*Airport symbol*] (OAG)
SIH.............. Societe Internationale d'Hematologie [*International Society of Hematology - ISH*] [*Buenos Aires, Argentina*] (EA)
SIH.............. Society for Italic Handwriting (EA)
SIH.............. South Irish Horse [*British military*] (DMA)
SIH.............. Stimulation-Induced Hypalgesia [*Medicine*] (DMAA)
SIH.............. Sun Ice Ltd. [*Toronto Stock Exchange symbol*]
SIH.............. Sun International Hotels
SIH.............. Sun Intl Hotels Ord [*NYSE symbol*] (TTSB)
SIH.............. Superstar Ice Hockey [*Computer game*]
SIHAG.......... Experimental Farm, Agriculture Canada [*Ferme Experimentale, Agriculture Canada*], Indian Head, Saskatchewan [*Library symbol National Library of Canada*] (BIB)
SI Hand....... SI Handling Systems [*Associated Press*] (SAG)
SIHBF.......... Sun International [*NASDAQ symbol*] (SAG)
SIHGO.......... Sour, Imported Heavy Gas Oil [*Petroleum chemistry*]
SIHL............ Sun International [*NASDAQ symbol*] (SAG)
SIhPTH........ Serum Immunoreactive Human Parathormone [*Immunology*] (DAVI)
SIHR........... Supervisory Inventory on Human Relations [*Test*]
SIHS........... Scottish Industrial Heritage Scoeity (DBA)
SIHS........... S.I. Handling Sys [*NASDAQ symbol*] (TTSB)
SIHS........... SI Handling Systems, Inc. [*NASDAQ symbol*] (NQ)
SIHS........... Society for Italian Historical Studies (EA)
SIHT........... Space Impact Hand Tool [*NASA*]
SIHW.......... Society for Italic Handwriting (EA)
SII.............. School Interest Inventory [*Psychology*]
SII.............. Security-Insecurity Inventory [*Psychology*]
SII.............. Self-Inflicted Injury [*Medicine*] (DMAA)
SII.............. Self-Interview Inventory [*Psychology*]
SII.............. Severity of Illness Index [*Health insurance*] (GHCT)
SII.............. Short Interval Identification
SII.............. Sidi Ifni [*Morocco*] [*Airport symbol*] (AD)
SII.............. Siimes Aviation AB [*Finland ICAO designator*] (FAAC)
SII.............. Sitkinak Island [*Alaska*] [*Seismograph station code, US Geological Survey*] (SEIS)
SII.............. Smith International, Inc. [*NYSE symbol*] (SPSG)
SII.............. Smith Intl [*NYSE symbol*] (TTSB)
SII.............. Soldier-Information Interface (RDA)
SII.............. Space Industries, Inc.
SII.............. Special Instruction Indicator (AAGC)
SII.............. Special Interest Items (MCD)
SII.............. Sponsor Identification Index [*Advertising*] (NTCM)
SII.............. Standard Identification for Individuals [*Social security*] [*American National Standards Institute*]
SII.............. Statement of Intelligence Interest [*Army*] (RDA)
SII.............. Strategic Impediments Initiative (MHDW)
SII.............. Structural Impediments Initiative [*US-Japan trade negotiations*]
SII.............. Sugar Information, Inc. [*Defunct*] (EA)
SII.............. Supervisory Immigrant Inspector [*Immigration and Naturalization Service*]
SIIA............ Self-Insurance Institute of America (EA)
SIIAEC......... Secretariat International des Ingenieurs, des Agronomes, et des Cadres Economiques Catholiques [*International Secretariat of Catholic Technologists, Agriculturists, and Economists*] [*Paris, France*] (EAIO)
SIIC............ Secretariat International des Groupements Professionnels des Industries Chimiques des Pays de la CEE
SIIC............ Special Interest Item Code [*Military*] (AABC)
SIIFT........... Sociedad Internacional de Ingenieros Forestales Tropicales [*International Society of Tropical Foresters*] (EAIO)
SIII.............. S3, Inc. [*NASDAQ symbol*] (SAG)
SIIL............. Schottky Integrated Injection Logic (IAA)
SIINC.......... Scientific Instrumentation Information Network and Curricula [*National Science Foundation*]
SIIR............ Spares Item Inventory Record (MCD)
SIIRS.......... Smithsonian Institution Information Retrieval System (DIT)
SIITO.......... Standard Installation Instruction Technical Order (SAA)
SIJ.............. Minneapolis, MN [*Location identifier FAA*] (FAAL)
SIJ.............. Sacroiliac Joint
SIJ.............. Siglufjordur [*Iceland*] [*Airport symbol*] (OAG)
SIJADEP....... International Secretariat of Jurists for an Amnesty and Democracy in Paraguay [*Paris, France*] (EAIO)
SIJAU.......... Secretariat International des Juristes pour l'Amnistie en Uruguay [*France*]
SI/JI............ Secondary Injection/Jet Interaction
SIJIC........... Senior International Joint Intelligence Course (MCD)
SIjt............. Sacroiliac Joint [*Anatomy*] (DAVI)
SIK.............. Sikeston, MO [*Location identifier FAA*] (FAAL)
SIK.............. Silknit Ltd. [*Toronto Stock Exchange symbol*]
Sik.............. Single Income, Kids [*Lifestyle classification*]
SIL.............. Ile a la Crosse Public Library, Saskatchewan [*Library symbol National Library of Canada*] (NLC)
SIL.............. Safety Information Letter (IEEE)
SIL.............. Safety Integrity Level (ACII)
SIL.............. Sao Hill [*Tanzania*] [*Airport symbol*] (AD)
SIL.............. Scanner Input Language
SIL.............. Schedule Interface Log
SIL.............. SCN [*Stock Control Number*] Index and Log
SIL.............. Sea Island Air Ltd. [*Canada ICAO designator*] (FAAC)
SIL.............. Selected Item List
SIL.............. Semiconductor Injector LASER
SIL.............. Seriously Ill List [*Military*]
SIL.............. Service Information Letter
SIL.............. Set Indicators of the Left Half (SAA)
SIL.............. Shift Indicator Light [*Automotive engineering*]
SIL.............. Silcorp Ltd. [*Toronto Stock Exchange symbol*]
SIL.............. Silence (MSA)
SIL.............. Silent (NTCM)
SIL.............. Silicate
Sil.............. Silius Italicus [*First century AD*] [*Classical studies*] (OCD)
SIL.............. Sillimanite [*Mineralogy*]
SIL.............. Silurian [*Period, era, or system*] [*Geology*]
SIL.............. Silver (AAG)
Sil.............. Silver Tax Division (Internal Revenue Bulletin) [*A publication*] (DLA)
Sil.............. Silvester Godinho [*Deceased, 1244*] [*Authority cited in pre-1607 legal work*] (DSA)
SIL.............. Single in Line [*Electronics*] (EECA)
SIL.............. Slidel, LA [*Location identifier FAA*] (FAAL)
SIL.............. Smart Integral Linearizer [*Instrumentation*]
SIL.............. Smithsonian Institution Information Leaflets
SIL.............. Smithsonian Institution Libraries
SIL.............. SNOBOL Implementation Language Reimplemented [*1974*] [*Computer science*] (CSR)
SIL.............. Societas Internationalis Limnologiae Theoreticae et Applicae [*International Association of Theoretical and Applied Limnology*]
SIL.............. Societe Internationale de la Lepre [*International Leprosy Association*]
SIL.............. Society for Individual Liberty (EA)
SIL.............. Solid Immersion Lens [*Computer science*] (PCM)
SIL.............. Sound Intensity Level
SIL.............. Sound Interference Level [*NASA*] (NASA)
SIL.............. Special Interest Launch [*Military*] (AFIT)
SIL.............. Specific Individual Licence [*Importing*] [*British*] (DS)
SIL.............. Speech Interference Level
SIL.............. Squamous Intraepithelial Lesion [*Medicine*]
SIL.............. Steam Isolation Line (IEEE)
SIL.............. Store Interface Link
SIL.............. Summer Institute of Linguistics
SIL.............. Supply Information Letter (MCD)
SIL.............. Support Items List (MCD)
SIL.............. Surge Impedance Loading
SIL.............. System Implementation Language [*Computer science*]
SIL.............. Systems Integration Laboratory [*NASA*] (MCD)
SILAF........... Sindacato Italiano Lavoratori Appalti Ferroviari [*Italian Union of Railroad Contract Workers*]
SILAP.......... Sindacato Nazionale Dipendenti Ministero del Lavori Pubblici [*National Union of Employees in the Ministry of Public Welfare*] [*Italy*]
SILAT.......... Society for Iberian and Latin American Thought (EA)
SILAT.......... Subionospheric Latitude
SILC............ Sheep Industry Liaison Committee [*New South Wales, Australia*]
SILC............ Silicon Ltd. [*NASDAQ symbol*] (SAG)
SILCA.......... Sindacato Italiano Lavoratori Cappellai ed Affini [*Italian Federation of Hat and Allied Workers*]
SILCF........... Silicon Ltd [*NASDAQ symbol*] (TTSB)
SilcLtd......... Silicon Ltd. [*Associated Press*] (SAG)
SILCLV........ Silicon Liquid Crystal Light Valve [*NASA*]
SilcnGph....... Silicon Graphics [*Associated Press*] (SAG)
Sil (Ct of Ap)... Silvernail's New York Court of Appeals Reports [*A publication*] (DLA)
SILF............ Societe Internationale de Linguistique Fonctionelle [*International Society of Functional Linguistics*] (EAIO)
SILG........... Silencing (MSA)
SILI............ Siliconix, Inc. [*NASDAQ symbol*] (NQ)
SILI............ Sindacato Nazionale Lavoratori Italcable [*National Union of Cable Workers*] [*Italy*]
SILI............ Standard Item Location Index
SILICA......... System for International Literature Information on Ceramics and Glass [*Fachinformationszentrum Werkstoffe*] [*Database*]
SilicnVl........ Silicon Valley Group, Inc. [*Associated Press*] (SAG)
Silicnx.......... Siliconix, Inc. [*Associated Press*] (SAG)
SiliconS........ Silicon Storage Technology, Inc. [*Associated Press*] (SAG)
SilicVly......... Silicon Valley Bancshares [*Associated Press*] (SAG)
SiliValR........ Silicon Valley Research, Inc. [*Associated Press*] (SAG)
SILJ............ Survey of Inmates of Local Jails [*Department of Justice*] (GFGA)
SILK........... Single Income, Lots of Kids
Sill Comp..... Sill on Composition in Bankruptcy [*A publication*] (DLA)
SilLtd.......... Silicon Ltd. [*Associated Press*] (SAG)
SILM........... Single In-Line Module [*Computer science*]
SILMOD....... Silhouette Model [*Military*] (INF)
SILO........... Schools Industry Liaison Officer (AIE)

SILO............ Security Intelligence Liaison Office [*Central Mediterranean Forces*] [*Navy*]
SILON.......... Subionospheric Longitude
SILP............ Saskatchewan International Labour Program [*Canada*] (CROSS)
SILP............ Section of International Law and Practice (EA)
SILP............ Sindacato Italiano Lavoratori del Petrolio [*Italian Union of Oil Workers*]
SILP............ Sindacato Italiano Lavoratori Postelegrafonici [*Italian Union of Postal and Telegraph Workers*]
SILP............ Solomon Islands Liberal Party [*Political party*] (EY)
SILPT.......... Silhouette Print (VRA)
SILPTG........ Silverplating
SILPWS....... Sheet Iron and Light Plate Workers' Society [*A union*] [*British*]
SILS............ Shipboard Impact Locator System
SILS............ Shipley-Institute of Living Scale for Measuring Intellectual Impairment [*Psychology*]
SILS............ Silver Solder
SILSP.......... Safeguard Integrated Logistics Support Plan [*Army*] (AABC)
Sil (Sup Ct)... Silvernail's New York Supreme Court Reports [*A publication*] (DLA)
SILT............ Stored Information Loss Tree
SILTF........... System Integration Laboratory and Test Facility
SILTS........... Shuttle Infrared Leeside Temperature Sensing [*NASA*] (NASA)
Silv............. Silvae [*of Statius*] [*Classical studies*] (OCD)
SILV............ Silver (ROG)
Silv............. Silvernail's New York Criminal Reports [*9-14 New York*] [*A publication*] (DLA)
Silv............. Silvernail's New York Reports [*1886-92*] [*A publication*] (DLA)
Silv............. Silvernail's New York Supreme Court Reports [*1889-90*] [*A publication*] (DLA)
SILV............ Sunshine Mining & Refining Co. [*NASDAQ symbol*] (SAG)
Silv A.......... Silvernail's New York Court of Appeals Reports [*A publication*] (DLA)
Silv App....... Silvernail's New York Court of Appeals Reports [*A publication*] (DLA)
Silv Cit........ Silvernail's New York Citations [*A publication*] (DLA)
Silv Ct App... Silvernail's New York Court of Appeals Reports [*A publication*] (DLA)
Silv Ct App (NY)... Silvernail's New York Court of Appeals Reports [*A publication*] (DLA)
Silve........... Silvester Godinho [*Deceased, 1244*] [*Authority cited in pre-1607 legal work*] (DSA)
SilverFds..... Silverado Foods, Inc. [*Associated Press*] (SAG)
Silvernail's NY Rep... Silvernail's New York Court of Appeals Reports [*A publication*] (DLA)
SILVIC......... Silviculture
Silvr............ Silvester Godinho [*Deceased, 1244*] [*Authority cited in pre-1607 legal work*] (DSA)
Silv Sup....... Silvernail's New York Supreme Court Reports [*A publication*] (DLA)
Silv (Sup Ct)... Silvernail's New York Supreme Court Reports [*A publication*] (DLA)
SILVTR........ Silent Videotape Recording (DOAD)
Silv Unrep... Silvernail's New York Unreported Cases [*A publication*] (DLA)
SILVW......... Sunshine Mng & Refining Wrrt [*NASDAQ symbol*] (TTSB)
SILWR......... Silverware
SILZ............ Silicon Ltd. [*NASDAQ symbol*] (SAG)
SILZF........... Silicon Ltd Wrrt [*NASDAQ symbol*] (TTSB)
SIM.............. Grupo Simec [*AMEX symbol*] (SPSG)
SIM.............. Grupo Simec ADS [*AMEX symbol*] (TTSB)
SIM.............. Missionaries of the Kingship of Christ (TOCD)
SIM.............. SACLANT [*Supreme Allied Commander, Atlantic*] Staff Instruction Manual (NATG)
SIM.............. SAM [*Surface-to-Air Missile*] Intercept Missile (DNAB)
SIM.............. Scanning Ion Microscope
SIM.............. Schedule of Implementation Procedures [*FAA*] (TAG)
SIM.............. School of Industrial Management [*MIT*] (MCD)
SIM.............. Scientific Instrument Module [*NASA*]
SIM.............. Sclerite-Inducing Membrane [*Entomology*]
SIM.............. Selected Inventory Management [*Military*] (CAAL)
SIM.............. Selected Ion Monitoring [*Chromatography*]
SIM.............. Selected Item Management
SIM.............. Sequential Inference Machine [*Computer science*]
SIM.............. Sergeant Instructor of Musketry
SIM.............. Service Instructions Message [*Telecommunications*] (TEL)
SIM.............. Service International de Microfilm, Paris, France [*Library symbol Library of Congress*] (LCLS)
SIM.............. Servicio Intelligencia Militar [*Military Intelligence Service*] [*Dominican Republic*]
SIM.............. Servizio Informazioni Militare [*Military Intelligence Service*] [*Italy*]
SIM.............. Set Interrupt Mask [*Computer science*]
SIM.............. Shima Resources [*Vancouver Stock Exchange symbol*]
SIM.............. Ship Instrumentation Manager (KSC)
SIM.............. Simbai [*Papua New Guinea*] [*Airport symbol*] (OAG)
SIM.............. Simferopol [*Former USSR Seismograph station code, US Geological Survey*] (SEIS)
SIM.............. Similar (AAG)
SIM.............. Simile [*In a Similar Manner*] [*Music*]
sim............... Simile (WDMC)
Sim............... Simmons' Reports [*95-97, 99 Wisconsin*] [*A publication*] (DLA)
Sim............... Simons' English Chancery Reports [*57-60 English Reprint*] [*1826-50*] [*A publication*] (DLA)
SIM.............. Simplex
SIM.............. Simposio Internacional de Macromoleculas [*International Symposium on Macromolecules*]
SIM.............. Simulated [*or Simulation*] (AABC)
sim............... Simulated (VRA)
SIM.............. Simulated Approach [*Aviation*] (FAAC)
SIM.............. Simulated Flight Training Ltd. [*British ICAO designator*] (FAAC)
SIM.............. Simulation (IAA)
SIM.............. Simulator [*Computer science*]
SIM.............. Single Rotation Machine (IAA)
SIM.............. Small Intestine Metaplasia [*Medicine*]
SIM.............. Societa di Intermediazione Mobiliare [*Finance Italy*] (ECON)
SIM.............. Societa Italiana di Metapsichica [*Italy*]
SIM.............. Societe Internationale de la Moselle [*International Moselle Co.*]
SIM.............. Societe Internationale de Musicologie [*International Musicological Society*]
SIM.............. Society for Industrial Microbiology (EA)
SIM.............. Society for Information Management [*Chicago, IL*] (EA)
SIM.............. Solar Interplanetary Model
SIM.............. Somali Islamic Movement [*Political party*]
SIM.............. Space Interceptor Missile (MCD)
SIM.............. Spatial Information Management
SIM.............. Stage Inert Mass
SIM.............. Standard Injection Method [*Laboratory science*]
SIM.............. Steatite Insulation Material
SIM.............. Stellar Image Monitor
SIM.............. Structural Integrity Monitoring (MCD)
SIM.............. Student Interracial Ministry [*Defunct*]
SIM.............. Submarine Intended Movement (NVT)
SIM.............. Subsystem Interface Module
SIM.............. Subtotal Integration Mode
SIM.............. Sucrose-Isomaltose Deficiency [*Medicine*]
SIM.............. Sudan Interior Mission
SIM.............. Sulfide Production, Indole Production, and Motility [*Growth medium*]
SIM.............. Surveillance Intelligence and Reconnaissance Mission [*Military*] (CAAL)
SIM.............. Symbolic Integrated Maintenance (IAA)
SIM.............. Synchronous Interface Module
SIM.............. Systems Integration Model (MCD)
SIMA............ Salon International de la Machine Agricole
SIMA............ Scientific Instrument Manufacturers' Association [*British*]
SIMA............ Ships Intermediate Maintenance Activity (DOMA)
SIMA............ Shore Intermediate Maintenance Activity [*Navy*] (NVT)
SIMA............ Single Internal Mammary Artery [*Medicine*] (DMAA)
SIMA............ Sonics & Materials [*NASDAQ symbol*] (TTSB)
SIMA............ Sonics & Materials, Inc. [*NASDAQ symbol*] (SAG)
SIMA............ Stanford Integrated Manufacturing Association [*Stanford University*] [*Research center*] (RCD)
SIMA............ Steel Industry Management Association [*Trade union*] [*British*]
SIMAC.......... Sonic Instrument Measurement and Control (AAG)
SIMAJ.......... Scientific Instrument Manufacturers' Association of Japan
SIMAL.......... Simplified Accountancy Language (PDAA)
SIMAL.......... Simulated All-Purpose Language (PDAA)
Sim & C....... Simmons and Conover's Reports [*99-100 Wisconsin*] [*A publication*] (DLA)
Sim & S....... Simons and Stuart's English Chancery Reports [*57 English Reprint*] [*A publication*] (DLA)
Sim & St...... Simons and Stuart's English Chancery Reports [*57 English Reprint*] [*A publication*] (DLA)
Sim & Stu.... Simons and Stuart's English Vice-Chancery Reports [*57 English Reprint*] [*A publication*] (DLA)
Sim & Stu (Eng)... Simons and Stuart's English Chancery Reports [*57 English Reprint*] [*A publication*] (DLA)
SIMANNE..... Simulation of Analogical Network (IAA)
SIMAP......... Satellite Image Mapping
SIMAS......... Shuttle Information Management Accountability System [*NASA*] (NASA)
SIMAS......... SONAR In-Situ Mode Assessment System (MSC)
SIMATS....... Supplementary Interim Medium Antitank System [*Army*] (INF)
SIMAW........ Sonics & Materials Wrrt [*NASDAQ symbol*] (TTSB)
SIMBAD....... Simulation as a Basis for Social Agents' Decisions [*Computer science*]
SIMBAY....... Scientific Instrumentation Module Bay [*NASA*] (KSC)
SIMBOL....... Simulated Boolean-Oriented Language (IAA)
SIMC........... Silicon Integrated Monolithic Circuit
SIMC........... Societe Internationale de Medecine Cybernetique [*International Society of Cybernetic Medicine*]
SIMC........... Societe Internationale de Medecine de Catastrophe [*International Society for Disaster Medicine - ISDM*] [*Switzerland*] (EA)
SIMC........... Societe Internationale pour la Musique Contemporaine [*International Society for Contemporary Music*]
SIMC........... Spacetec IMC [*NASDAQ symbol*] (TTSB)
SIMC........... Spacetec IMC Corp. [*NASDAQ symbol*] (SAG)
SIMC........... Syndicat International des Marins Canadiens [*Seafarers' International Union of Canada - SIU*]
SIMCA......... Simple Modelling of Class Analogy [*Data analysis*] [*Computer science*]
SIMCA......... Societe Industrielle de Mecanique et de Carrosserie Automobile [*French automobile manufacturer; acronym used as name of its cars*]
SIMCA......... Soft Independent Modeling of Class Analogy [*Analytical chemistry technique*]
SIMCA......... Statistical Isolinear MultiCategory Analysis [*Data analysis*] [*Computer science*]
SIMCANSOC... Simulated Canadian Society [*Simulation game*]
SIMCAP....... Simulation, Corps Automated Procedures (MCD)
SIMCE.......... Simulation Communications Electronics [*Group of computer programs*] [*Army*]
SIMCEN....... Simulation Center [*Deep Space Network, NASA*]
SIMCERT..... Simulator Certification
SIMCHE....... Simulation and Checkout Equipment [*NASA*] (KSC)
SIMCO......... Sea Ice Microbial Colony
SIMCOM...... Simulation and Computer [*Computer science*]
SIMCOM...... Simulation Complex (NASA)

SIMCOM Simulator Compiler [*Computer*]
SIMCON Scientific Inventory Management and Control
SIMCON Simplified Control
SIMCON Simulation Controller
Sim Ct M Simmons on Courts-Martial [*A publication*] (DLA)
SIMD Single Input Multiple Data Stream (IAA)
SIMD Single Instruction, Multiple Data (IEEE)
SIMD Single Instruction Multiple Data Stream (NITA)
SIMDEP Simulation Development Program [*DASA*]
Sim Des Pat Simonds' Law of Design Patents [*A publication*] (DLA)
Sim Dig Simmons' Wisconsin Digest [*A publication*] (DLA)
Sim Dig Pat Dec Simonds' Digest of Patent Office Decisions [*United States*] [*A publication*] (DLA)
SIMDS Single Instruction Multiple Data Stream (IAA)
SIME Security Intelligence, Middle East [*Navy*]
Sim Elect Simeon on Elections [*A publication*] (DLA)
Sim (Eng) Simons' English Chancery Reports [*57-60 English Reprint*] [*A publication*] (DLA)
Simes & S Future Interests Simes and Smith on the Law of Future Interests [*A publication*] (DLA)
SIMEX Secondary Item Materiel Excess [*DoD*]
SIMEX Singapore Monetary Exchange (ECON)
SIMFAC Simulation Facility [*NASA*]
SIMFAR Simulated Frequency Analysis and Recording (MCD)
SIMFIRE Simulated Fire
SIMFIRE Simulated Mission Firing
SIMG Societas Internationalis Medicinae Generalis [*International Society of General Practice*] [*Klagenfurt, Austria*] (EAIO)
SIMGCA Similarity Graft Clustering Analysis [*Plant phylogeny*]
SIMGEN Simulation Generating System (MHDI)
SIMHA Societe Internationale de Mycologie Humaine et Animale [*International Society for Human and Animal Mycology - ISHAM*] [*British*] (EA)
SIMI Sea Ice Mechanics Initiative [*Marine science*] (OSRA)
SIMICOR Simultaneous Multiple Image Correlation
SIMILE Simulator of Immediate Memory in Learning Experiments
Sim Int Simons' Law of Interpleader [*A publication*] (DLA)
SIMIS SAIC [*Science Applications International Corp.*] Integrated Management Information System (MCD)
Simkin Simulation Kinetics [*Analysis*] [*Toxicology*] (DAVI)
SIML Similar (AAG)
SIML Simulation Language [*Computer science*] (MHDI)
Simla All India Reporter, Simla [*1951*] [*A publication*] (DLA)
SIMLR Similar (ROG)
SIMM Simmons Outdoor Corp. [*Chicago, IL NASDAQ symbol*] (NQ)
SIMM Single In-Line Memory Module [*Computer science*]
SIMM Symbolic Integrated Maintenance Manual (MCD)
SIMMOD Airport and Airspace Simulation Model [*FAA*] (TAG)
Simmons C Simmons College (GAGS)
SIM M-R Simulation Monitor-Recorder (SAA)
SIMN Simon Transportation Services, Inc. [*NASDAQ symbol*] (SAG)
SIMN Simon Transportation Svcs'A' [*NASDAQ symbol*] (TTSB)
SimnD Simon DeBartolo Group, Inc. [*Associated Press*] (SAG)
SIMNET Simulation Network
SIMNEX Simulation Net Executor (NITA)
SimnFt Simmons First National Corp. [*Associated Press*] (SAG)
SimnOut Simmons Outdoor Corp. [*Associated Press*] (SAG)
Sim NS Simons' English Vice-Chancery Reports, New Series [*61 English Reprint*] [*A publication*] (DLA)
SIMNS Simulated Navigation Systems
Sim NS (Eng) Simons' English Vice-Chancery Reports, New Series [*61 English Reprint*] [*A publication*] (DLA)
SIMO Simultaneously (NASA)
SIMO Special Items Management Office
SIMOBS Simultaneous Observations [*RADAR and optical*]
SIMOC Simulated Occupant [*People Machine*] [*Office of Civil Defense*]
Simon Simonides [*Fifth century BC*] [*Classical studies*] (OCD)
SIMON Software Implementation Monitor [*Computer science*] (MHDI)
SimonDeB Simon DeBartolo Group, Inc. [*Associated Press*] (SAG)
SimonPr Simon Property [*Associated Press*] (SAG)
Simon's TC Simon's Tax Cases [*United Kingdom*] [*A publication*] (DLA)
SimonT Simon Transportation Services, Inc. [*Associated Press*] (SAG)
SIMOP Simultaneous Operation
SIMOS Space Imbalanced Military Occupational Specialty
SIMOS Stacked Gate Injection Metal-Oxide Semiconductor [*Computer science*] (IAA)
SIMOX Separation by Implantation of Oxygen [*Semiconductor technology*]
SIMP Satellite Information Message Protocol
SIMP Satellite Interface Message Processor (IAA)
SIMP Schmele Instrument to Measure the Process of Nursing Care [*Medicine*] (DMAA)
SIMP Shipboard Integrated Maintenance Program [*Navy*] (NG)
simp Simple (DAVI)
SIMP Simpleton (DSUE)
simp Simplex (MAE)
SIMP Simulation Program (IAA)
Simp Single Income, Money Problems [*Lifestyle classification*]
SIMP Societa Italiana di Medicina Psicosomatica [*Italy*]
SIMP Specific Impulse (MSA)
SIMPAC Simplified Programming for Acquisition and Control (IEEE)
SIMPAC Simulation Package [*Computer science*]
SIMPARAG Simultaneous Parallel Array Grammers (MHDI)
Sim Pat L Simond's Patent Law [*A publication*] (DLA)
SimpInd Simpson Industries, Inc. [*Associated Press*] (SAG)
Simp Inf Simpson on Infants [*4th ed.*] [*1926*] [*A publication*] (DLA)
SIMPL Simulation Implementation Machine Programming Languages (KSC)
SIMPL/1 Simulation Language Based on Programming Language, Version One
SIMPLAN Simple Modeling and Planning [*SIMPLAN Users Group*] [*New York, NY*] (CSR)
SIMPLAN Simplified Modeling and Planning [*Programming language*] [*1973*] (CSR)
SIMPLE Savings Incentive Match Plan for Employees [*Business term*]
SIMPLE Semi-Implicit Pressure-Linked Equation [*Algorithm*]
SIMPLE Simulation of Industrial Management Problems [*Program*] [*1958*] [*Computer science*] (CSR)
SIMPLE Solver for Implicit Equations [*Computer language*]
SIMPLE System for Integrated Maintenance and Program Language Extension
SIMPLER System for Information Management and Program Logic for Education and Research (IAA)
SIMPO Simulation of Personnel Operations [*Army Research Institute for the Behavioral and Social Sciences*] (RDA)
SIMPP Simple Image-Processing Package (BYTE)
SIMPP Society of Independent Motion Picture Producers
SimpsnMf Simpson Manufacturing Co., Inc. [*Associated Press*] (SAG)
SIMPU Simulation Punch
SIMR Schenley Instant Market Reports
SIMR Simulator (AAG)
SIMR Societe Internationale de Mecanique des Roches [*International Society for Rock Mechanics - ISRM*] (EAIO)
SIMR Systems Integration Management Review [*NASA*] (MCD)
SIMRAND Simulation of Research and Development
Sim Ry Acc Simon's Law Relating to Railway Accidents [*1862*] [*A publication*] (DLA)
SIMS Schools Information Management System (AIE)
SIMS Secondary Ion Mass Spectrometry [*or Spectroscopy*]
SIMS Second International Mathematics Study
SIMS Sedna Information Management System [*Sedna Corp.*] [*Information service or system*] (IID)
SIMS Selected Item Management System [*Military*] (AABC)
SIMS Selective Interference Modulation Spectrometer
SIMS Services Information Management System [*DoD*] (GFGA)
SIMS Shuttle Imaging Microwave System [*NASA*] (NASA)
SIMS Shuttle Inventory Management System [*NASA*] (NASA)
SIMS SIAM [*Society for Industrial and Applied Mathematics*] Institute for Mathematics and Society
SIMS SIMS Communications [*NASDAQ symbol*] (TTSB)
SIMS Sims Communications, Inc. [*NASDAQ symbol*] (SAG)
SIMS Single Item, Multisource (IEEE)
SIMS Skandinaviska Simuleringssaellskapet [*Scandinavian Simulation Society*] [*Also, SSS*] (EA)
SIMS Societal Institute of the Mathematical Sciences [*Research center*] (RCD)
SIMS Socio-Economic Information Management System (NITA)
SIMS Stable Isotope Mass Spectrometer
SIMS Station Infomation Management System [*Navy*] (DOMA)
SIMS Stellar Inertial Measurement System [*NASA*]
SIMS Strategic Integrated Management System [*American Occupational Therapy Association*]
SIMS Students' International Meditation Society
SIMS Supply Information Management System [*Air Force*] (GFGA)
SIMS Symbolic Integrated Maintenance System
SIMSA Savings Institutions Marketing Society of America
SimsC Sims Communications, Inc. [*Associated Press*] (SAG)
SimsCm Sims Communications, Inc. [*Associated Press*] (SAG)
SIMSCRIPT Simulation High-Level Programming Language [*Computer science*] (BARN)
SIMSEP Simulation of Solar Electric Propulsion [*NASA*]
SIMSER Simple Serial (MHDI)
SIMSGA Sugar Industry Manufacturers and Service Group of Australia
SIMSHO Simulation Scheduled Order (SSD)
SIMSI Selective Inventory Management of Secondary Items [*Navy*]
SIMSIN Simulated Strapdown Inertial Navigation (MCD)
SIMSLIN Safety in Mines Scattered Light Instrument (ADA)
SIMSOC Simulated Society
SIMSTF Societe Internationale de Mecanique des Sols et de Travaux de Fondations [*International Society for Soil Mechanics and Foundation Engineering - ISSMFE*]
SIMSU SIMS Communications Unit [*NASDAQ symbol*] (TTSB)
SIMSUP Simulation Supervisor
SIMSW Sims Communications Wrrt'A' [*NASDAQ symbol*] (TTSB)
SIMS-X Selected Items Management System - Expanded (MCD)
SIMSYS Simulated System (CAAL)
SIMSZ Sims Communications Wrrt'B' [*NASDAQ symbol*] (TTSB)
SIMTC Southwest Center for Manufacturing Technology [*University of New Mexico*] [*Research center*] (RCD)
SIMTOP Silicon Nitride-Masked Thermally-Oxidized Post-Diffused Mesa Process (PDAA)
SIMTOS Simulated Tactical Operations Systems [*Army*] (RDA)
SIMTRACC Simulator Trainer Command and Control
SIMTS Scientific Instrument Makers Trade Society [*A union*] [*British*]
SIMU Simulated Inertial Measurement Unit (NASA)
SIMU Stellar Inertial Measuring Unit (IAA)
SIMU Suspended from Issue, Movement, and Use [*Army*] (ADDR)
SIMUL Simultaneous (AABC)
Simula Simula, Inc. [*Associated Press*] (SAG)
SIMULA Simulation Language [*1964*] [*Computer science*]
SIMUPOL Simulative Procedure Oriented Language (MCD)
SIMV Synchronized Intermittent Mandatory Ventilation [*Medicine*] (DAVI)

SIMWF........ Simware, Inc. [*NASDAQ symbol*] (SAG)
SIN........ Salpingitis Isthmica Nodosum
SIN........ Security Information Network
SIN........ Sensitive Information Network
SIN........ Simultaneous Interpenetrating Networks [*Organic chemistry*]
SIN........ Sinagawa [*Japan*] [*Seismograph station code, US Geological Survey Closed*] (SEIS)
SIN........ Sinair [*France ICAO designator*] (FAAC)
SIN........ Sinclair Community College, Dayton, OH [*OCLC symbol*] (OCLC)
SIN........ Sine [*Mathematics*]
SIN........ Sine [*Without*] [*Latin*]
sin........ Sine (IDOE)
SIN........ Sinecure (ROG)
Sin........ Sinemurian [*Geology*]
SIN........ Singapore [*Airport symbol*] (OAG)
SIN........ Single Identifying Number
SIN........ Sinistra [*Left Hand*] [*Music*]
Sin........ Sinter [*Record label*] [*Brazil*]
SIN........ Social Insurance Number [*Canada*]
SIN........ Society for International Numismatics (EA)
SIN........ Sonically-Induced Narrowing [*Physics*]
SIN........ [*The*] Spanish Information Network [*Later, Spanish International Network*] [*Cable- television system*] (WDMC)
SIN........ Spanish International Network [*Cable-television system*]
SIN........ Special Item Number (AAGC)
SIN........ Squamous Intraepithelial Neoplastic [*Oncology*]
SIN........ Stop Inflation Now [*Variation on the anti-inflation WIN slogan of President Gerald Ford*]
SIN........ Study Item Number [*Army*] (AABC)
S IN........ Sub Initio [*At the Beginning*] [*Latin*] (ROG)
SIN........ Subject Indication Number
SIN........ Support Information Network
SIN........ Swedish Ionosonde Network
SIN........ Symbolic Integrator
SIN........ Syngold Exploration, Inc. [*Toronto Stock Exchange symbol*]
SINA........ Scheduling Information Not Available (KSC)
SINA........ Shellfish Institute of North America [*Also known as Oyster Growers and Dealers Association of North America*] (EA)
SINA........ Society for Indecency to Naked Animals [*A hoax association*]
SINA........ Sports Injury Nurses Association [*Australia*]
SINACMA........ Sindacato Nazionale Dipendenti Corte dei Conti e Magistrature Amministrative [*National Union of General Accounting Office Employees*] [*Italy*]
SINAD........ Signal Plus Noise and Distortion
SINAD........ Signal-to-Noise Ratio and Distortion (IAA)
SINADIMID... Sindacato Nazionale Dipendenti Ministero Difesa [*National Union of Ministry of Defense Employees*] [*Italy*]
SINAF........ Sindacato Nazionale Dipendenti Ministero Agricoltura e Foreste [*National Union of Ministry of Agriculture and Forestry Employees*] [*Italy*]
SINAMAI........ Sindacato Nazionale e Dipendenti Ministero Africa Italiana [*National Union of Former Italian Employees of African Ministry*] [*Italy*]
SINAMIL........ Sindacato Nazionale Dipendenti Ministero del Lavoro e Previdenza Sociale [*National Union of Ministry of Labor and Social Security Employees*] [*Italy*]
SINAMN........ Sindacato Nazionale Dipendenti Marina Mercantile [*National Union of Merchant Marine Workers*] [*Italy*]
SINAP........ Satellite Input to Numerical Analysis and Prediction [*National Weather Service*]
SINAP........ Sinapis [*Mustard*] [*Pharmacology*] (ROG)
SINAPI........ Sindacato Nazionale Ministero Pubblica Istruzione [*National Union of Ministry of Public Instructors*] [*Italy*]
SINASCEL........ Sindacato Nazionale Scuola Elementare [*National Union of Elementary School Teachers*] [*Italy*]
SINB........ Southern Interstate Nuclear Board
SINC........ Nicaraguan International Rescue from Communism (PD)
SinC........ Sisters in Crime [*An association*]
S in C........ Surgeon-in-Chief (WDAA)
SINCGARS... Single-Channel Ground and Airborne Radio System [*or Subsystem*] (MCD)
SINCGARS-V... Single-Channel Ground and Airborne Radio System, Very High Frequency
Sinclair........ Sinclair Broadcast Group, Inc. [*Associated Press*] (SAG)
Sinclair........ Sinclair's Manuscript Decisions, Scotch Session Cases [*A publication*] (DLA)
SINCOE........ Sindacato Nazionale Dipendenti Ministero Industria e Commercio Estero [*National Union of Ministry of Industry and Foreign Commerce Employees*] [*Italy*]
SINCTRAC.... Single Channel Tactical Radio Communications [*Army*] (RDA)
Sind........ All India Reporter, Sind [*1914-50*] [*A publication*] (DLA)
Sind........ Indian Rulings, Sind Series [*A publication*] (DLA)
SIND........ Satellite Inertial Navigation Determination (MCD)
SIND........ Southern Indiana Railway, Inc. [*AAR code*]
SIND........ Strobe Intersection Deghoster
SINDA........ Systems Improved Numerical Differencing Analyses [*Database*]
SINDAF........ Sindacato Nazionale Dipendenti Amministrazioni Finanziarie [*National Union of Financial Administration Employees*] [*Italy*]
SINE........ Short Interspersed Nucleotide Element [*Genetics*]
sine........ Sinusoidal [*Otorhinolaryngology*] (DAVI)
SINES........ Short Interspaced Repeated Segments [*of Deoxyribonucleic Acid*] [*Genetics*] (DAVI)
SINES........ Short Interspaced Repeated Segments [*Of DNA*] [*Medicine*] (BABM)
SIN-ETH........ Swiss Institute of Nuclear Research - Eidgenoessische Technische Hochschule
SINEWS........ Ship Integrated Electronic Warfare System
SINF........ Sinfonia [*Symphony*] [*Music*]
SINFDOK........ Statens Rad for Vetenskaplig Information och Dokumentation [*Swedish Council for Scientific Information and Documentation*] (IID)
SING........ Singapore
SING........ Singing Machine Company, Inc. [*NASDAQ symbol*] (SAG)
SING........ Singular
sing........ Singular (WDMC)
SING........ Singulorum [*Of Each*] [*Pharmacy*]
SINGAN........ Singularity Analyzer [*Computer science*]
Singap........ Singapore Fund [*Associated Press*] (SAG)
Singer........ Singer Co. NV [*Associated Press*] (SAG)
Singer Prob Cas (PA)... Singer's Probate Cases [*Pennsylvania*] [*A publication*] (DLA)
Singers........ Singer's Probate Court [*Pennsylvania*] [*A publication*] (DLA)
Singing........ Singing Machine Co., Inc. [*Associated Press*] (SAG)
SingM........ Singing Machine Co., Inc. [*Associated Press*] (SAG)
SINGR........ Singular
SINH........ Sine, Hyperbolic
Sinh........ Sinhalese [*Language*] (BARN)
SINIE........ Sistema Nacional de Informacion Documental en Educacion [*National System of Documentary Information on Education*] [*Information service or system*] (IID)
SINIST........ Sinister [*Left*] [*Latin*]
Sink........ Single Income, No Kids [*Lifestyle classification*]
SIno........ Thioinosine [*Also, Sno, M*] [*A nucleoside*]
Si Non Val... Si Non Valeat [*If It Is Not Effective*] [*Pharmacy*]
SINPO........ Strength, Interference, Noise, Propagation, and Overall Merit Code [*Signal reception quality rating*] (NTCM)
SINR........ Shoulder Internal Rotation [*Sports medicine*]
SINR........ Signal to Interference plus Noise Ratio (MCD)
SINR........ Swiss Institute for Nuclear Research
SINS........ Satellite Interceptor Navigation System [*Navy*] (CAAL)
SINS........ Ship Inertial Navigational System
SINS........ Ship's Inertial Marine Navigational System (IAA)
SINS........ Ship's Inertial Navigation System
SINS........ Sindacato Scuola non Statale [*Union of Private Schools' Employees*] [*Italy*]
SINS........ Stellar Inertial Navigation System (IAA)
SINS........ Submarine Inertial Navigation System (IAA)
SInstBB........ Student of the Institute of British Bakers (DBQ)
SInstPet........ Student of the Institute of Petroleum [*British*] (DBQ)
SINSW........ Security Institute of New South Wales [*Australia*]
S INT........ Senza Interruzione [*Without Interruption or Pause*] [*Music*]
S INTER........ Senza Interruzione [*Without Interruption or Pause*] [*Music*] (ROG)
SinterMtl........ Sinter Metals Co. [*Associated Press*] (SAG)
SINTO........ Sheffield Interchange Organization (NITA)
SI N VAL........ Si Non Valeat [*If It Is Not Effective*] [*Pharmacy*] (ROG)
SIO........ Sacroiliac Orthosis [*Medicine*]
SIO........ Satellite in Orbit (WDAA)
SIO........ Scripps Institution of Oceanography [*La Jolla, CA*] [*Research center*]
SIO........ Senior Information Officer (DCTA)
SIO........ Senior Instructor Operator [*Military*] (INF)
SIO........ Senior Intelligence Officer (MCD)
SIO........ Serial Input/Output (MCD)
SIO........ Ship's Information Officer [*Navy*]
SIO........ Simultaneous Interface Operation [*Printer technology*] [*Computer science*] (PCM)
SIO........ Sindacato Italiano Ostetriche [*Italian Union of Midwives*]
sio........ Siouan [*MARC language code Library of Congress*] (LCCP)
SIO........ Skidway Institute of Oceanography [*Georgia*] (NOAA)
SIO........ Smithton [*Australia Airport symbol*] (OAG)
SIO........ Smithtown [*Tasmania*] [*Airport symbol*] (AD)
SIO........ Sorting It Out [*An association Defunct*] (EA)
SIO........ Southern Union Resources [*Vancouver Stock Exchange symbol*]
SIO........ Special Inquiry Officer
SIO........ Special Intelligence Officer [*Military*] (NVT)
SIO........ Staged in Orbit
SIO........ Standard Input/Output (MCD)
SIO........ Start Input/Output
SIO........ Step Input/Output (NITA)
SIO........ Systems Integration Office [*NASA*] (NASA)
SIOA........ System Input/Output Adapter (CAAL)
SIOATH........ Source Identification and Ordering Authorization [*DoD*]
SIOC........ Serial Input/Output Channel
SIOD........ Sindacato Italiano Odonototecnici Diplomati [*Italian Union of Odontotechnicians*]
SIOE........ Special Issue of Equipment
SIO/EIA........ Ship Intelligence Officer/Enlisted Intel Assistant (DOMA)
SIOFC........ Sparks International Official Fan Club (EA)
SIOG........ Societe Internationale d'Ophtalmologie Geographique [*International Society of Geographic Opthalmology*] (EAIO)
SIOH........ Supervision, Inspection, and Overhead (AFM)
SIOMS........ Surface Ionization Organic Mass Spectrometry
SIOP........ Secure Identification Operating Procedure
SIOP........ Selector Input/Output Processor [*Computer science*] (IEEE)
SIOP........ Single Integrated Operational [*or Operations*] Plan [*Military*] (AFM)
SIOP........ Societe Internationale d'Oncologie Pediatrique [*International Society of Pediatric Oncology*] [*Leeds, England*] (EAIO)
SIOP........ Strategic Integrated Operational Plan [*Nuclear warfare*]
SIOP-ESI........ Single Integrated Operational Plan - Extremely Sensitive Information [*Security level above Top Secret*]
SI OP SIT........ Si Opus Sit [*If There Be Occasion*] [*Pharmacy*] (ROG)
SIOR........ Society of Industrial and Office Realtors (EA)
SIOS........ Spectrophotometer Input-Output System

SIOSA .... Sicula Oceanicas SA [*Shipping line*] [*Italy*] (EY)
SIOUX .... Sequential and Iterative Operation Unit X (IEEE)
SIOV .... Siemens Metal Oxide Varistor (IAA)
SIP .... Air Spirit, Inc. [*ICAO designator*] (FAAC)
SIP .... Safety Injection Pump (IEEE)
SIP .... Safety Instrumentation Package (MCD)
SIP .... SAGE [*Semiautomatic Ground Environment*] Improvement Program (IAA)
SIP .... Sample Item Portion
SIP .... Sampling Inspection Procedures
SIP .... Saskatchewan Institute of Pedology [*University of Saskatchewan*] [*Research center*] (RCD)
SIP .... Satellite Information Processor
SIP .... Satellite Inspector Program (AAG)
SIP .... Satellite Interceptor Program (IAA)
SIP .... SCANS [*Scheduling and Control by Automated Network Systems*] ImplementationPlan (SAA)
SIP .... Schedule-Induced Polydipsia [*Psychology*]
SIP .... Schedule of Investment Projects
SIP .... Scientific Information [*or Instruction*] Processor [*Honeywell, Inc.*]
SIP .... Scientific Instrument Package [*NASA*] (KSC)
SIP .... Sea Ice Penetrometer (PDAA)
SIP .... Seat Index Point [*Automotive design*]
SIP .... Securities Investor Protection Corp.
SIP .... Selma [*Alabama*] Interreligious Project (EA)
SIP .... Senior Intensified Program [*Education*]
SIP .... Separation Instrument Package [*NASA*] (MCD)
SIP .... Sharebuilder Investment Plan [*Banking*]
SIP .... Sheet Metal Insert Process
SIP .... Shinkiari [*Pakistan*] [*Seismograph station code, US Geological Survey*] (SEIS)
SIP .... Ship Improvement Program
SIP .... Ship in Production
SIP .... Short Interval Plan [*Management principles*]
SIP .... Short Irregular Pulses
SIP .... Sickness Impact Profile [*National Institutes of Health*]
SIP .... Side Impact Protection [*Automotive safety system*] (PS)
SIP .... Silicon-on-Insulator and Polysilicon (PDAA)
SIP .... Simferopol [*Former USSR Airport symbol*] (OAG)
SIP .... Simple Internet Protocol (TNIG)
SIP .... Simulated Input Processor [*Computer science*]
SIP .... Sindacato Italiano Pescatori [*Italian Union of Fishermen*]
SIP .... Single In-Line Package [*Computer science*]
SIP .... Single In-Line PIN [*Computer science*] (PCM)
SIP .... Single In-Line Plastic (IAA)
SIP .... Sipald Resources [*Vancouver Stock Exchange symbol*]
SIP .... Skill Improvement Program [*Bureau of Apprenticeship and Training*] [*Department of Labor*]
SIP .... Slow Inhibitory Potential [*Electrophysiology*]
SIP .... Small Interplanetary Probes (SAA)
SIP .... Smithsonian Institution Press [*Publisher*]
SIP .... Sociedad Interamericana de Prensa [*Inter-American Press Association*]
SIP .... Sociedad Interamericana de Psicologia [*Interamerican Society of Psychology*] (EAIO)
SIP .... Societa Italiana per l'Esercizio Telefonico [*Italian Society for Telephone Use*] [*Information service or system*] (IID)
SIP .... Society for Invertebrate Pathology (EA)
SIP .... Society of Independent Producers (NTCM)
SIP .... Society of Indiana Pioneers (EA)
SIP .... Society of Israel Philatelists (EA)
SIP .... Sodium Iron Pyrophosphate
SIP .... Software in Print [*Technique Learning*] [*Information service or system*] (IID)
SIP .... Software Instrumentation Package [*Sperry UNIVAC*] [*Computer science*]
SIP .... Solar and Interplanetary Programme [*International Council of Scientific Unions*]
SIP .... Solar Instrument Probe (MUGU)
SIP .... SONAR Instrumentation Probe (IAA)
SIP .... SPALT [*Special Projects Alterations*] Improvement Program
SIP .... Special Impact Program (OICC)
SIP .... Standard Initial Provisioning System (MCD)
SIP .... Standard Inspection Procedure [*Military*]
SIP .... Standard Interest Profile
SIP .... Standardization Instructor Pilot [*Military*] (AABC)
SIP .... State Implementation Plan [*Environmental Protection Agency*]
SIP .... Station Independence Program [*Public television project*] (NTCM)
SIP .... Steam-In-Place [*Sterilization process*]
SIP .... Step in Place
SIP .... Stewardship Incentive Program [*Forestry*]
SIP .... Strain Isolator Pad [*Aerospace*]
SIP .... Strategic Information Plan (SSD)
SIP .... Strongly Implicit Procedure
SIP .... Structural Insulated Panel
SIP .... Student Insurance Producers Association (EA)
SIP .... Studies in Process [*Jet Propulsion Laboratory, NASA*]
SIP .... Submerged Injection Process [*Steelmaking*]
SIP .... Supermolecular Information Processor
SIP .... Supersonic Infantry Projectile
SIP .... Supplemental Income Plan
SIP .... Supply Improvement Program
SIP .... Support for Innovation Project (AIE)
SIP .... Surface Impulsion Propulsion (PDAA)
SIP .... Svensk-Internationella Pressbyran [*Swedish-International Press Bureau*] (EY)
SIP .... Symbolic Input Program [*Computer science*] (BUR)
SIP .... System Improvement Plan (INF)
SIP .... System Initialize Program (IAA)
SIP .... Systems Implementation Plan [*Military*]
SIPA .... Secondary Item Procurement Appropriation [*Army*]
SIPA .... Securities Investor Protection Act [*1970*]
SIPA .... Systems Information Processing Analysis (EDAC)
SIPAMA .... Servico de Inspecao dos Produtos Agropecuarios e Materiais Agricolas [*Brazil*]
SIPB .... Safety Injection Permissive Block (IEEE)
SIPC .... Securities Investor Protection Corp. [*Government insurance agency for brok erage accounts*] [*Pronounced "sipic"*]
SIPC .... Simply Interactive PC (PCM)
SIPC .... Stationing and Installations Planning Committee [*Military*]
SIPCO .... Signal Processor Checkout (CAAL)
SIPD .... Supply Item Provisioning Document [*Navy*] (NG)
SIPDE .... Sensing, Identifying, Predicting, Deciding, and Executing
SIPE .... Scientific Information Program on Eutrophication [*University of Wisconsin*]
SIPE .... Societe Internationale de Psychopathologie de l'Expression [*International Society of Art and Psychopathology*]
SIPE .... Soldier-Integrated Protective Ensemble [*Army*] (INF)
SIPE .... System Internal Performance Evaluator (IAA)
SIPES .... Society of Independent Professional Earth Scientists (EA)
SipexCp .... Sipex Corp. [*Associated Press*] (SAG)
SIPG .... Societe Internationale de Pathologie Geographique [*International Society of Geographical Pathology*] [*Australia*] (EAIO)
SIPG .... Special Intercept Priorities Group [*Armed Forces Security Agency*]
SIPI .... Scientists' Institute for Public Information (EA)
SIPI .... Short Imaginal Process Inventory [*Personality development test*] [*Psychology*]
SIPI .... Sisterhood Is Powerful Institute (EA)
SIPI .... Southwestern Indian Polytechnic Institute [*New Mexico*]
SIPI .... Supervisory Immigration Patrol Inspector [*Immigration and Naturalization Service*]
SIPL .... Seeley's Illustrated Pocket Library [*A publication*]
SIPLA .... Student Intellectual Property Law Association (AAGC)
SIPM .... Star Identification Program, Mariner [*NASA*]
SIPN .... Semi-Interpenetrating Polymer Network [*Organic chemistry*]
SIPO .... Serial-In, Parallel-Out [*Telecommunications*] (TEL)
SIPO .... Sicherheitspolizei [*Security Police*] [*NAZI*] (BJA)
SIPO .... Spacecraft Integration Project Office
SIPO .... Swiss Intellectual Property Office [*Bern*] [*Information service or system*] (IID)
SIPOA .... Servico de Inspecao de Produtos de Origem Animal [*Brazil*]
SIPOP .... Satellite Information Processor Operational Program (AFM)
SIPOS .... Semi-Insulating Polycrystalline Silicon [*Photovoltaic energy systems*]
SIPP .... Sodium Iron Pyrophosphate
SIPP .... Standard Interline Passenger Procedures Manual [*Air Traffic Conference of America*] [*IATA*] (DS)
SIPP .... Survey on Income and Program Participation [*Census Bureau, Department of Health and Human Services*]
SIPP .... System Information Processing Program (MCD)
SIPPAP .... Survey of Income and Program Participation Awareness Program [*Bureau of the Census*] (GFGA)
SIPPS .... System of Information Processing for Professional Societies
Sippy .... Senior Independent Pioneer [*Lifestyle classification*]
SIPR .... Special In-Process Review (MCD)
SIPRA .... Societa Italiana Pubblicita Per Azioni [*Italian radio and television advertising company*]
SIPRE .... Snow, Ice, and Permafrost Research Establishment
SIPRI .... Stockholm International Peace Research Institute [*Solna, Sweden*] (EAIO)
SIPRO .... Servicios Informativos Procesados [*Processed Information Services*] [*Mexico*] (CROSS)
SIPROS .... Simultaneous Processing Operation System [*Control Data Corp.*] [*Computer science*]
SIPS .... SAC [*Strategic Air Command*] Intelligence Data Processing System (IAA)
SIPS .... Science Innovation Program [*Australia*]
SIPS .... Shipbuilding Industries Pension Scheme [*British*]
SIPS .... Side-Impact Protection System [*Automotive safety*]
SIPS .... Simulated Input Preparation System (IEEE)
SIPS .... Simulated Interpersonal Problem Situation (EDAC)
SIPS .... Small Instrument Pointing System (MCD)
SIPS .... Societa Internazionale de Psicologia della Scrittura [*International Society of Psychology of Handwriting - ISPH*] (EAIO)
SIPS .... Societe Internationale de Psychologie des Sports [*International Society of Sports Psychology*] (EAIO)
SIPS .... Spartan Improved Performance Study [*Missiles*] (AABC)
SIPS .... Sputter-Induced Photon Spectroscopy (MCD)
SIPS .... State Implementation Plan System [*Environmental Protection Agency*]
SIPS .... Statistical Interactive Programming System
sIPSC .... Spontaneous Inhibitory Postsynaptic Current [*Neurophysiology*]
SIPSDE .... Society of Independent and Private School Data Education [*Later, SDE*] (EA)
SIPSF .... Space Invariant Point Spread Function (PDAA)
SIPT .... Sensory Integration and Praxis Test [*Occupational therapy*]
sipt .... Silverpoint (VRA)
SIPT .... Simulating Part (AAG)
SIPTH .... Serum Immunoreactive Parathyroid Hormone [*Endocrinology*]
SIPTU .... Services Industrial Professional Technical Union [*Ireland*] (EAIO)

SIPU .... Selective Inactivation Photodynamic Unit
SIPX .... SIPEX Corp. [*NASDAQ symbol*] (TTSB)
SIPX .... Sipex Corp. [*NASDAQ symbol*] (SAG)
SIQ .... Sick in Quarters
SIQ .... Singkep Island [*Indonesia*] [*Airport symbol*] (AD)
SIQ .... Social Intelligence Quotient [*In book title*]
SIQ .... Student Interests Quarterly [*A publication*]
SIQ .... Superior Internal Quality (WDAA)
SIQ .... Symptom Interpretation Questionnaire [*Medicine*] (DMAA)
SIQR .... Semi-Interquartile Range [*Medicine*] (DMAA)
SIR .... Safari International Resources [*Vancouver Stock Exchange symbol*]
SIR .... Safeguards Implementation Report [*Nuclear energy*] (NRCH)
SIR .... Safe Integral Reactor [*Nuclear energy*]
SIR .... Salair, Inc. [*ICAO designator*] (FAAC)
SIR .... Scientific Information Retrieval (NITA)
SIR .... Scientific Information Retrieval, Inc. [*Database management system*] [*Information service or system*] (IID)
SIR .... Search, Inspection, and Recovery (NVT)
SIR .... Secondary-Image-Registration [*Photography*]
SIR .... Segment Identification Register
SIR .... Selected Item Reporting
SIR .... Selected Item Review (MCD)
SIR .... Selective Information Retrieval [*Computer science*]
SIR .... Selective Ion Recording [*Spectrometry*]
SIR .... Self-Indication Ratio
SIR .... Self-Insured Retention [*Insurance*]
SIR .... Semantic Information Retrieval [*Massachusetts Institute of Technology*] [*Computer science*] (DIT)
SIR .... Semiannual Inventory Report [*Navy*] (NVT)
SIR .... Serial Infrared Communications Interface [*Hewlett Packard Co.*] (PCM)
SIR .... Serial Infrared Specification [*Computer science*] (PCM)
SIR .... Serious Incident Report [*Military*] (AFM)
SIR .... Serum Inducible Repeat [*Genetics*]
SIR .... Service International de Recherches [*International Tracing Service*] [*Red Cross*]
SIR .... Set Indicators of the Right Half (SAA)
SIR .... Shipboard Intercept Receiver [*Navy*]
SIR .... Shuttle Imaging RADAR [*of earth's surface*] [*NASA*]
SIR .... Signal-to-Interference Ratio
SIR .... Silo Installation Refurbish (SAA)
SIR .... Simulated Robot (NITA)
SIR .... Simultaneous Impact Rate (AFM)
SIR .... Sinclair, WY [*Location identifier FAA*] (FAAL)
SIR .... Single Imaging RADAR
SIR .... Single Isomorphous Replacement [*Crystallography*]
SIR .... Single Item Release
SIR .... Single Item Removal [*Maintenance*]
SIR .... Sion [*Switzerland*] [*Airport symbol*]
Sir .... Sirach [*Old Testament book*] [*Roman Catholic canon*]
SIR .... Siria [*Venezuela*] [*Seismograph station code, US Geological Survey*] (SEIS)
Sir .... Sirius [*Record label*] [*Sweden*]
SIR .... Size Up, Interview, Rate [*Mnemonic used by Responsible Beverage Service in its bartender training program*]
SIR .... Small Intestine Rinse [*Physiology*]
SIR .... Snow and Ice on Runway [*NWS*] (FAAC)
SIR .... Societa Italiana Resine [*Italy*]
SIR .... Societe Rorschach Internationale [*International Rorschach Society*] [*Originally, Societe Internationale du Test de Rorschach et Autres Methodes Projectives*]
SIR .... Society for Individual Responsibility [*Defunct*] (EA)
SIR .... Society of Industrial Realtors [*Association name and designation awarded by this group*] [*Washington, DC*] (EA)
SIR .... Society of Insurance Research [*Appleton, WI*] (EA)
SIR .... Software Incident Report (MCD)
SIR .... Software Initiated Restart (NASA)
SIR .... Sound Isolation Room
SIR .... Spaceborne Imaging RADAR
SIR .... Speaker Independent Recognition (IAA)
SIR .... Special Information Retrieval
SIR .... Special Inspection Requirement
SIR .... Special Investigative Requirement (AFM)
SIR .... Specification Information Retrieval System [*Computer science*] (MCD)
SIR .... Specific Information Requirement [*Military*] (INF)
SIR .... Specific Insulation Resistance
SIR .... Stable Isotopes Resource
SIR .... Standarization, Interoperability, and Readiness [*NATO*] (MCD)
SIR .... Staten Island Rapid Transit Railway Co. [*Later, SIRC*] [*AAR code*]
SIR .... Statistical Information Retrieval
SIR .... Statutory Invention Registration [*Patents*]
SIR .... Strategic Information Review (NITA)
SIR .... Stratified Indexing and Retrieval [*Japan Computer science*]
SIR .... Struthers Industries [*AMEX symbol*] (SPSG)
SIR .... Student Instructional Report [*Test of teacher performance*]
SIR .... Styrene-Isoprene Rubber
SIR .... Subcontractor Information Request
SIR .... Submarine Intermediate Reactor [*Nuclear energy*]
SIR .... Subsurface Interface RADAR [*A trademark*]
SIR .... Supersonic Infantry Rocket
SIR .... Suppliers Information Request
SIR .... Symbolic Input Routine [*Computer science*] (DIT)
SIR .... Synthetic-Aperture Imaging RADAR [*System*]
SIR .... System Initialization Routine
SIR .... System Integration Receiver [*System*]
SIR .... System Interface Requirements (NASA)
SIR .... Systems Integration Review [*NASA*] (NASA)
SIRA .... Safety Investigation Regulations (IEEE)
SIRA .... Scientific Instrument Research Association [*British*]
SIRA .... Social Issues Research Associates (EA)
SIRA .... Sports Industries Representatives Association (EA)
SIRA .... Stable Isotope Ratio Analysis
SIRA .... Strapdown Inertial Reference Assembly (MCD)
SIRA .... Strategic Intelligence Research and Analysis
SIRA .... System for Instructional Response Analysis
SIRAP .... System of Information Retrieval and Analysis, Planning [*Army Information service or system*] (IID)
SIRAS .... Single Isomorphous Replacement, Anomalous Scattering [*Crystallography*]
SIRB .... Sintered Iron Rotating Band
SIRC .... Science Information Resource Center [*Harper & Row*] [*Information service or system*]
SIRC .... Sirco International Corp. [*NASDAQ symbol*] (NQ)
SIRC .... Sirco Intl [*NASDAQ symbol*] (TTSB)
SIRC .... Socialist International Research Council [*British*]
SIRC .... Spares Integrated Reporting and Control [*System*]
SIRC .... Sport Information Resource Centre [*Coaching Association of Canada*] [*Database*] (IID)
SIRC .... [*The*] Staten Island Railroad Corp. [*AAR code*]
SIRC .... Styrene Information and Research Center (EA)
SIRCH .... Scientific Instrumentation & Research Division (ACII)
SIR(CICR) .... Service International de Recherches (du Comite International de la Croix-Rouge) [*International Tracing Service of the International Committee of the Red Cross*]
Sirco .... Sirco International Corp. [*Associated Press*] (SAG)
SIRCS .... Shipboard Intermediate Range Combat System [*Navy*]
SIRCULS ...... San Bernardino-Inyo-Riverside Counties United Library Services [*Library network*]
SIRCUS .... Standard Information Retrieval Capability for Users [*Army*]
SIRD .... Shore-Based Interfare Requirement Date
SIRD .... Support Instrumentation Requirements Document [*NASA*]
SIRE .... Satellite Infrared Experiment (MCD)
SIRE .... Society for the Investigation of Recurring Events (EA)
SIRE .... Symbolic Information Retrieval (IAA)
SIRE .... Syracuse Information Retrieval Experiments (NITA)
SIREF .... Specific Immune Response Enhancing Factor [*Medicine*] (DMAA)
SIREN .... Sanders Intact Reentry Encapsulation (MCD)
SIREN .... SIGSEC Resources and Equipment Needs (MCD)
SirenaA .... [*The*] Sirena Apparel Group [*Associated Press*] (SAG)
SIREWS .... Shipboard Infrared Electronic Warfare System
SIRF .... Severely Impaired Renal Function [*Medicine*] (DMAA)
SIRF .... System Information Reports Formatting (MCD)
SIRI .... Societe Internationale pour la Readaptation des Invalides
SIRIC .... Soybean Insect Research Information Center [*University of Illinois*] [*Champaign, IL*]
SIRIN .... Single Readiness Information System [*NORRS*]
SIRIS .... Sputter-Initiated Resonance Ionization Spectrometry
SIRIS .... Sylloge Inscriptionum Religionis Isiacae et Sarapiacae [*A publication*] (BJA)
SIRIVS .... Spaceborne Intensified Radiometer for Imaging Vetroviolet Spectroscopy (MCD)
SIRL .... Site Installation Requirements List (AAG)
SIRL .... Support Item Requirement List (MCD)
SIRLEJ .... Societe Internationale de Recherche en Litterature d'Enfance et de Jeunesse [*International Research Society for Children's Literature - IRSCL*] (EA)
Sir L Jenk .... Wynne's Life of Sir Leoline Jenkins [*1724*] [*A publication*] (DLA)
SIRLS .... Information Retrieval System for the Sociology of Leisure and Sport [*University of Waterloo*] [*Information service or system*] (IID)
SIRLS .... Southwest Idaho Regional Library System [*Library network*]
SIRLS .... Specialized Information Retrieval and Library Services (IID)
SIRM .... Saturation Isothermal Remanent Magnetization [*Paleomagnetics*]
SIRM .... Sterile Insect Release Method
SIRMA .... Small Independent Record Manufacturers Association [*Stanford, CT*] (EA)
SIRMCE .... Societe Internationale pour la Recherche sur les Maladies de Civilisation et l'Environment [*International Society for Research on Civilization Diseases and Environment*] [*Brussels, Belgium*] (EAIO)
SIRMS .... Stable Isotope Ratio Mass Spectrometer [*or Spectrometry*]
SIRN .... [*The*] Sirena Apparel Group [*NASDAQ symbol*] (SAG)
SIRO .... Service in Random Order (IAA)
SIROF .... Sputtered Iridium Oxide Film (PDAA)
SIROS .... Specialized Operating System (DNAB)
SIROW .... Southwest Institute for Research on Women [*University of Arizona*] [*Research center*] (RCD)
SIRR .... Section on Individual Rights and Responsibilities (EA)
SIRR .... Small Integral Rocket/Ramjet (MCD)
SIRR .... Software Integration Readiness Review [*NASA*] (NASA)
SIRR .... Southern Industrial Railroad, Inc. [*AAR code*]
SIRRA .... Sleep-Induction/Rapid Reawakening System [*Military*] (RDA)
Sirrom .... Sirrom Capital Corp. [*Associated Press*] (SAG)
SIRS .... Salary Information Retrieval System (IEEE)
SIRS .... Satellite Infrared Spectrometer [*NASA*]
SIRS .... Scheduled Issue Release System
SIRS .... School Information and Research Service (EDAC)
SIRS .... Ship Installed RADIAC [*Radiation Detection, Indication, and Computation*] System (NATG)
SIRS .... Skills Inventory Retrieval System (MCD)

SIRS Small Independent Radio Stations [*An association British*]
SIRS Social Issues Resources Series [*A publication*]
SIRS Soils Information Retrieval Systems [*Database*] [*Army Corps of Engineers*]
SIRS Soluble Immune Response Suppressor [*Immunology*]
SIRS Special Issue Rating System [*Veterans Administration*]
SIRS Specification, Instrumentation, and Range Safety
SIRS Statewide Individual Referral System (OICC)
SIRS Structure of Instruction Rating Scale (EDAC)
SIRS Student Information Record System (AEBS)
SIRS Supplemental Inflatable Restraint System [*Automotive engineering*]
SIRS Systemic Inflammatory Response Syndrome [*Medicine*]
SIRS System Integration Receiver System (MCD)
SIRSA Special Industrial Radio Service Association (EA)
SIRT Signaling Information Receiver/Transmitter (MCD)
SIRT Staten Island Rapid Transit Railway Co. [*Later, SIRC*]
SIRTF Space [*formerly, Shuttle*] Infrared Telescope Facility [*NASA*]
Sir T Ray Sir T. Raymond's English King's Bench Reports [*A publication*] (DLA)
SIRU Strapdown Inertial Reference Unit [*Navigation*]
SIRVES SIGINT [*Signal Intelligence*] Requirements Validation and Evaluation Subcommittee
SIRW Safety Injection and Refueling Water [*Nuclear energy*] (NRCH)
SIRW Stuffed Indirect Reference Word [*Computer science*] (MHDI)
SIRWT Safety Injection and Refueling Water Tank [*Nuclear energy*] (NRCH)
SIRWT Safety Injection Reserve Water Tank (IEEE)
SIS Canadian Security and Intelligence Service [*UTLAS symbol*]
SIS Naval Intelligence Service [*Italy*]
SIS Paine Webber Gp Stk Index Sec [*AMEX symbol*] (TTSB)
SIS Paine Webber Group [*AMEX symbol*] (SAG)
SIS Safety Information System [*Department of Transportation*]
SIS Safety Injection Signal [*Nuclear energy*] (IAA)
SIS Safety Injection System [*Nuclear energy*] (NRCH)
SIS Safety Instrumented System (ACII)
SIS SAGE [*Semiautomatic Ground Environment*] Interceptor Simulator
SIS SAIL [*Shuttle Avionics Integration Laboratory*] Interface System [*NASA*] (NASA)
SIS Saline Infusion Sonohysterography [*Gynecological procedure*]
SIS Sample Inlet System [*Automotive exhaust emission testing*]
SIS Satellite Infrared Spectrometer [*NASA*]
SIS Satellite Interceptor System [*Military*] (AFM)
SIS Savage Information Services (IID)
SIS Scale for the Identification of School Phobia [*Test*]
SIS Scanning Image Spectrometer
SIS Science Information Service (EA)
SIS Science Information Services [*Franklin Institute*]
SIS Scientific Instruction Set
SIS Scientific Instrument Society (EA)
SIS Scotch-Irish Society of the United States of America (EA)
SIS Screening/Inspection System (DNAB)
SIS Secondary Injection System
SIS Secretarial Information System (EPA)
SIS Secret Intelligence Service [*British*]
SIS Selected Inventor Service (NITA)
SIS Selected Ion Storage [*For spectometry*]
SIS Semiautomatic Imagery Screening Subsystem (MCD)
SIS Semiconductor-Insulator-Semiconductor
SIS Seminar Information Service Database [*Seminar Information Service, Inc.*] [*Information service or system*] (CRD)
SIS Senior Intelligence Service [*CIA personnel*]
SIS Sensor Image Simulator (MCD)
SIS Sensor Integration System (DWSG)
SIS Serial Input System (MCD)
SIS Serving the Indigent Sick
SIS Settlement Information Strategy [*Australia*]
SIS Seychelles International Safari Air Ltd. [*ICAO designator*] (FAAC)
SIS Shared Information Service (CMD)
SIS Share Information Service [*British*] (DCTA)
SIS Shipping Instruction Sheet
SIS Shock-Isolation Support
SIS Shock-Isolation System
SIS Shorter Interval Scheduling [*Quality control*] (IAA)
SIS Short Interval Scheduling [*Quality control*]
SIS Shut-In Society
SIS Shuttle Information System [*NASA*] (MCD)
SIS Shuttle Interface Simulator [*NASA*] (NASA)
SIS Signaling Interworking Subsystem [*Telecommunications*] (TEL)
SIS Signal Intelligence Service [*Later, Army Security Agency*]
SIS Significant Indications Summary
SIS Silicon of Insulating Substrate (MCD)
SIS Silkridge Resources [*Vancouver Stock Exchange symbol*]
SIS Simian Sarcoma Virus [*Oncology*]
SIS Simulation Interface Subsystem (KSC)
SIS Single Item Squawk Sheet
SIS Singles in Service (EA)
SIS Sion [*Switzerland*] [*Seismograph station code, US Geological Survey Closed*] (SEIS)
SIS Sishen [*South Africa*] [*Airport symbol*] (OAG)
SIS Sister
SIS Sister
SIS Social Information System [*Medicine*] (DMAA)
SIS Societa Internazionale Scotista [*International Scotist Society - ISS*] (EAIO)
SIS Society for Iranian Studies (EA)
SIS Society for Italian Studies (AIE)
SIS Society of International Secretaries
SIS Software Implementation Specifications [*NASA*] (NASA)
SIS Software Integrated Schedule [*NASA*] (NASA)
SIS Solid-State Imaging Spectrometer
SIS Somatic Inkblot Series [*Personality development test*] [*Psychology*]
SIS Sound in Sync (IAA)
SIS Soviet Intelligence Services
SIS Space and Information System
SIS SPALT [*Special Projects Alterations*] Information Shut
SIS SPALT [*Special Projects Alterations*] Information System
SIS Spark Ignition System
SIS Speaker Intercom System (KSC)
SIS Special Industrial Services [*United Nations Industrial Development Organization*]
SIS Special Information System (MCD)
SIS Special Intelligence Service
SIS Special Interest Sessions
SIS Special Isotope Separation [*Physics*]
SIS Specification Information System
SIS Spectral Imaging Sensor
SIS Spectral Index of Sample [*Experimentation*]
SIS Spontaneous Interictal Spike [*Medicine*] (DMAA)
SIS Spuria Iris Society (EA)
SIS Stage Interface Simulator (IAA)
SIS Stage Interface Substitute
SIS Stall Inhibitor System [*Aviation*] (GFGA)
SIS Stand-Alone Information System [*National Library of Medicine*]
SIS Standard Indexing System [*DoD*]
SIS Standard Instruction Set (MSA)
SIS Standard Interface Specification [*NASA*] (GFGA)
SIS Standards Information Service [*Standards Council of Canada*] [*Information service or system*] (IID)
SIS Standards Information Service [*National Institute of Standards and Technology*] (IID)
SIS State Information Service [*Australia*]
SIS Station Identification Store [*Bell Laboratories*]
SIS Stator Interstage Seal
SIS STEP [*Scientific and Technical Exploitation Program*] Information Subsystem
SIS Sterile Injectable Suspension
SIS Stored Information System (IAA)
SIS Strategic Intelligence School [*Military*]
SIS Strategic Intelligence Summary [*Military*] (NATG)
SIS Strategic Intelligence Systems, Inc. [*Also, an information service or system*] (IID)
SIS Streamlined Inspection System [*USDA meat standards*]
SIS Student Instruction Sheet [*Military*]
SIS Student International Service [*Foundation*]
SIS Styrene-Isoprene-Styrene [*Organic chemistry*]
SIS Submarine Integrated SONAR
SIS Successor Instruction Set (IAA)
SIS Superconductivity Information System [*Department of Energy*] [*Information service or system*] (IID)
SIS Superconductor-Insulator-Superconductor [*Transistor technology*]
SIS Supervisory Inventory on Safety [*Test*]
SIS Supplier Identification System [*London Enterprise Agency*] [*Information service or system*] (IID)
SIS Supplies Information System (NITA)
SIS Supply Item Status
SIS Surgical Infection Society (EA)
SIS Sveriges Standardiseringskommission [*Swedish Standards Institution*] [*Also, an information service or system*] (IID)
SIS Swedish Inteplanetary Society (IAA)
SIS Swedish Standards Institution (IID)
SIS Synchronous Identification System (MCD)
SIS Synopsis Information System (AAGC)
SIS System Integration Schedule [*NASA*] (NASA)
SIS System Integration Support
SIS System Interrupt Supervisor
SIsabel Santa Isabel SA [*Associated Press*] (SAG)
SISAC Serials Industry Systems Advisory Committee [*Book Industry Study Group*] [*Information service or system*] (IID)
SISAM Spectrometer with Interference Selective Amplitude Modulation [*Physics*]
SI/SAO Special Intelligence/Special Activities Office (MCD)
SISB SIS Bancorp, Inc. [*NASDAQ symbol*] (SAG)
SISB Springfield Instit'n for Svgs [*NASDAQ symbol*] (TTSB)
SISB Springfield Institution for Savings [*NASDAQ symbol*] (SAG)
SIS Bncp SIS Bancorp, Inc. [*Associated Press*] (SAG)
SISC Sentry Interceptor Subsystem Contractor [*DoD*]
SISC Single Screw
SISC Statewide Information Steering Committee [*California*]
SISCIS Subject Index to Sources of Comparative International Statistics [*A publication*]
SISCO Singer Information Services Co. (IAA)
SISCO Special Inter-Departmental Selection Committee [*UN Food and Agriculture Organization*]
SISCON Science in Social Context
SISD Scientific Information Systems Department [*Information service or system*] (IID)
SISD Single Instruction, Single Data (IEEE)
SISD Single Instruction Single Data Stream (IAA)
SISD Standards and Interface Specification Document
SISDATA Single Instruction Single Data Stream (NITA)
SISDATA Statistical Information System Data (NITA)

SISDG........ Shipboard Information System Development Group [*Maritime Transportation ResearchBoard*] (PDAA)
SISEX........ Satellite Imaging Spectrometer Experiment (USDC)
SISEX........ Shuttle Imaging Spectrometer Experiment [*NASA*]
SISG........ ISG International Software Group [*NASDAQ symbol*] (SAG)
SISGF........ ISG Intl Software Group [*NASDAQ symbol*] (TTSB)
SISH........ Societe Internationale de la Science Horticole [*International Society for Horticultural Science - ISHS*] (EAIO)
SISI........ Short Increment Sensitivity Index [*Medicine*]
SISI........ S I Technologies [*NASDAQ symbol*] (TTSB)
SISI........ SI Technologies, Inc. [*NASDAQ symbol*] (SAG)
SISI........ Structural Instrumentation, Inc. [*NASDAQ symbol*] (SAG)
SISI........ Surveillance and In-Service Inspection [*Nuclear energy*] (NRCH)
SI-SIC........ Siliconized Silicon Carbide (SAA)
SISIR........ Singapore Institute of Standards and Industrial Research
SISK........ Siskon Gold 'A' [*NASDAQ symbol*] (TTSB)
SISK........ Siskon Gold Corp. [*NASDAQ symbol*] (SAG)
Siskon........ Siskon Gold Corp. [*Associated Press*] (SAG)
S Isl........ Sandwich Islands
SISL........ Sons of Italy Supreme Lodge (EA)
SIS-MDS........ Single Instruction Stream, Multiple Data Stream [*Computer science*] (MHDI)
SISMP........ Site Integrated Stabilization Plan
SISMS........ Standard Integrated Support Management System [*Joint Chiefs of Staff*]
SISO........ Science Information Services Organization [*Franklin Institute*] (IID)
SISO........ Shift In, Shift Out (IEEE)
SISO........ Single-Input, Single-Output [*Process engineering*]
SISOR........ Supply Item Status Order Reporting [*Army*]
SISORS........ Supply Item Status and Order Reporting System
SISP........ Sudden Increase of Solar Particles
SISP........ Surface Imaging and Sounding Package
SISPA........ Sequence-Independent Single Primer Amplification [*Genetics*]
SISR........ Selected Items Status Report [*Army*] (AABC)
SISS........ Second International Science Study [*International Association for the Evaluation of Educational Achievement*]
SISS........ Semiconductor-Insulator-Semiconductor System
SISS........ Sensory Integration Special Interest Section [*American Occupational Therapy Association*]
SIS-S........ SENTRY [*Survey Entry*] Interceptor System Simulator
SISS........ Single Item, Single Source (IEEE)
SISS........ Societe Internationale de la Science du Sol
SISS........ Sources of Information on Social Security [*British*]
SISS........ Standoff Imaging Sensor System (MCD)
SISS........ Submarine Integrated SONAR System
SISS........ Synchronous Identification System Study
SISS........ System Integration Support Service
SISSC........ Special Interest Sections Steering Committee [*American Occupational Therapy Association*]
SIS-SDS........ Single Instruction Stream, Single Data Stream [*Computer science*] (MHDI)
SIST........ Self-Inflating Surface Target
SIST........ Sentence Imitation Screening Test [*Speech and language test*]
SIST........ Sister
SISTER........ Special Institution for Scientific and Technological Education and Research [*In proposal stage, 1964, in Great Britain*]
SISTM........ Simulation by Incremental Stochastic Transition Matrices (MCD)
SISTMS........ Standard Integrated Supply/Transportation Manifest System [*Military*] (AABC)
SISTRAN........ System for Information Storage and Retrieval and Analysis
SISU........ Schools In-Service Unit [*University of Birmingham*] [*British*] (AIE)
SISUL........ Serials in Swaziland University Libraries [*A publication*]
SISUSA........ Scotch-Irish Society of the United States of America (EA)
SISV........ Simian Sarcoma Virus [*Also, SSV*]
SISWG........ STS [*Shuttle Test Station*] Integrated Schedule Working Group [*NASA*] (GFGA)
SISWP........ Soroptimist International of the South West Pacific [*Sydney, NSW, Australia*] (EAIO)
SIT........ Safety Injection Tank [*Nuclear energy*] (NRCH)
SIT........ Safety Injection Transmitter [*Nuclear energy*] (NRCH)
SIT........ Satellite Inspector Target (MCD)
SIT........ Self-Ignition Temperature
SIT........ Self-Induced Transparency (IAA)
SIT........ Sensory Integration Training
SIT........ Separation-Initiated Timer
SIT........ Sequential Interval Timer
SIT........ Serum Inhibitory Titer [*Clinical chemistry*]
SIT........ Shorr Imagery Test [*Personality development test*] [*Psychology*]
SIT........ Shuttle Integrated Test [*NASA*] (NASA)
SIT........ Shuttle Interface Test [*NASA*] (NASA)
SIT........ Silicon Intensified Target (NITA)
SIT........ Silicon Intensifier Target
SIT........ Silicon Intensifier Tube
SIT........ Simulation Input Tape
sit........ Sino-Tibetan [*MARC language code Library of Congress*] (LCCP)
SIT........ Sitka [*Alaska*] [*Airport symbol*] (OAG)
SIT........ Sitka, AK [*Location identifier FAA*] (FAAL)
SIT........ Situation (AFM)
SIT........ Slosson Intelligence Test
SIT........ Social Intelligence Test [*Psychology*]
SIT........ Societe International de Telecommunications Aeronautiques [*Belgium ICAO designator*] (FAAC)
SIT........ Society of Industrial Tutors [*British*]
SIT........ Society of Instrument Technology [*British*]
SIT........ Society of International Treasurers (EAIO)
SIT........ Software Integrated Test [*NASA*] (KSC)
SIT........ Software Integration Test (IAA)
SIT........ Spaceborne Infrared Tracker
SIT........ Space Impact Tool [*NASA*]
SIT........ Special Information Tones [*Telecommunications*]
SIT........ Sperm Immobilization Test [*Clinical chemistry*]
SIT........ Spontaneous Ignition Temperature
SIT........ SSV [*Space Shuttle Vehicle*] Integrated Test [*NASA*] (NASA)
SIT........ Stand-Alone Intelligent Terminal (MHDI)
SIT........ State Income Tax (AAGC)
SIT........ State Information Technology [*Western Australia*]
SIT........ Statement of Inventory Transaction [*Military*]
SIT........ Static Induction Transistor [*Telecommunications*] (TEL)
SIT........ Stepped Impedance Transformer (IAA)
SIT........ Sterile Insect Technology
SIT........ Stevens Institute of Technology [*Hoboken, NJ*]
SIT........ Stop Immorality on Television [*An association*]
SIT........ Stopping in Transit
SIT........ Storage Inspection Test [*Navy*] (NG)
SIT........ Storage in Transit
SIT........ Structurally Integrated Thruster (MCD)
SIT........ Sugar Industry Technologists (EA)
SIT........ Swinburne Institute of Technology [*Australia*]
SIT........ System Integration Test
SIT........ Systems Interface Test (NVT)
SITA........ Sociedade Internacional de Trilogia Analitica [*International Society of Analytical Trilogy - ISAT*] [*Sao Paulo, Brazil*] (EAIO)
SITA........ Societe Internationale des Telecommunications Aeronautiques [*International Society of Aeronautical Telecommunications*] [*London, England*]
SITA........ Students' International Travel Association
SITA........ System International Tinplate Area
SITAP........ Simulator for Transportation Analysis and Planning (DNAB)
SITAR........ Societa Incremento Turismo Aereo [*Italy*]
SITAR........ System for Interactive Test Editing, Analysis, and Retrieval (IAA)
SITB........ Shipbuilding Industrial Training Board [*British*]
SITC........ Salford Information Technology Centre (NITA)
SITC........ Satellite International Television Center [*Telecommunications*] (TEL)
SITC........ Single Integrated Test Cycle [*Army*]
SITC........ Standard Industrial Trade Classification [*United Nations*]
SITC........ Standard International Trade Classification
SITCA........ Secretaria de Integracion Turistica Centroamericana
SITCEN........ Situation Center [*NATO*] (NATG)
SITCOM........ Situation Comedy [*Television*]
Sit-Comm........ Situation Commercial [*Advertisement imitating a TV sitcom*]
SITE........ Sample Instruction Test Exercise (MCD)
SITE........ Satellite Instructional Television Experiment [*NASA/Indian Space Research Organization, 1974*]
SITE........ Sculpture in the Environment [*In Best by SITE, Inc.*]
SITE........ Search Information Tape Equipment
SITE........ Securities-Investment Trust Enterprise
SITE........ Shipboard Information, Training, and Education [*System*] [*Navy*] (NVT)
SITE........ Site Holdings, Inc. [*NASDAQ symbol*] (SAG)
SITE........ Situate (ROG)
SITE........ Snow and Ice Traversing Equipment [*Army*]
SITE........ Society of Incentive Travel Executives [*New York, NY*] (EA)
SITE........ Society of Insurance Trainers and Educators (EA)
SITE........ Spacecraft Instrumentation Test Equipment
SITE........ Space Influences on the Terrestrial Environment [*Marine science*] (OSRA)
SITE........ Space Influences on the Terrestrial Environment [*Space Enviromental Laboratory*] (USDC)
SITE........ Suction Infusion Tissue Extractor [*Ophthalmology*]
SITE........ Superfund Innovative Technologies Evaluation Program [*Environmental Protection Agency*]
SI Tech........ SI Technologies, Inc. [*Associated Press*] (SAG)
S-ITED........ Superimposed Integrated Trajectory Error [*Aviation*]
SiteHld........ Site Holdings, Inc. [*Associated Press*] (SAG)
Sitel........ Sitel Corp. [*Associated Press*] (SAG)
SITEL........ Societe des Ingenieurs do Telecommunication [*Belgium*]
SITES........ Smithsonian Institution Traveling Exhibition Service
Sithe........ Sithe Energies, Inc. [*Associated Press*] (SAG)
SITI........ Swiss Institute for Technical Information [*Information service or system*] (IID)
SITIM........ Societe Internationale des Techniques d'Imagerie Mentals [*International Society for Mental Imagery Techniques in Psychotherapy and Psychology*] [*Paris, France*] (EAIO)
SITIP........ School Improvement Through Instructional Process [*Maryland*] (EDAC)
SITK........ Sitka National Monument
SITL........ Sitel Corp. [*NASDAQ symbol*] (SAG)
SITL........ Southwestern Industrial Traffic League (EA)
SITL........ Static Induction Transistor Logic (NITA)
SITLILM........ Subcontractor Interceptor Transporter/Loader Intermediate Level Maintenance Course
SITMAP........ Situation Map (MCD)
SITN........ Situation (ROG)
SITO........ Senior Information Technology Officer
SITOR........ Simplex TELEX over Radio
SITP........ Scheduled into Production
SITP........ Shipyard Installation Test Procedure [*or Program*]
SITP........ Site Inspection and Test Procedure [*Nuclear energy*] (NRCH)
SITP........ System Integration Test Program
SITP........ Systems Integrated Test Plan [*Military*] (CAAL)

SITPB.......... System Integration Test Program Board
SITPRO........ Simplification of International Trade Procedures [*Committee or Board*] [*British*]
SITRAM....... Societe Ivoirienne de Transport Maritime [*The Ivorian national shipping industry*]
SITREP........ Situation Report
SITS............ IEEE Social Implications of Technology Society (EA)
SITS............ SAGE [*Semiautomatic Ground Environment*] Intercept Target Simulation
SITS............ Scientists in the Sea Program [*National Oceanic and Atmospheric Administration*] (MSC)
SITS............ Secondary Influent Treatment System
SITS............ Secure Imagery Transmission System [*Military*] (CAAL)
SITS............ Societe Internationale de Transfusion Sanguine [*International Society of Blood Transfusion - ISBT*] [*Paris, France*] (EA)
SITS............ Still in the Seventies [*Lifestyle classification*]
SITS............ Student Interactive Training System
SITS............ System Integration Test Service
SITS............ System Integration Test Site [*Military*] (CAAL)
SITSUM....... Situation Summary [*Military*] (NVT)
SITT............ System Integration of Triad Technology (IAA)
SITTS.......... Small-Inventory Top-Tier Site [*Industrial hazard designation*] [*British*]
SITU............ Society for the Investigation of the Unexplained (EA)
SITU............ South India Teachers' Union
SITU............ Surgical Intensive Therapy Unit
SITV............ System Integration Test Vehicle
SITVC.......... Secondary Injection Thrust Vector Control
SITW........... State Income Tax Withheld
SITYS.......... See, I Told You So [*Rush Limbaugh's mantra and book title*] (ECON)
Sitz............ Sitzungsberichte [*Proceedings*] [*German*] (OCD)
Sitz Wien..... Sitzungsberichte der Akademie der Wissenschaften in Wien [*A publication*] (OCD)
SIU............. Saturn Instrumentation [*NASA*]
SIU............. Seafarers' International Union of North America [*AFL-CIO*]
SIU............. Sequence Initiate Update
SIU............. Sets in Use [*Television rating*] (WDMC)
SIU............. Shiloh Resources Ltd. [*Vancouver Stock Exchange symbol*]
SIU............. Signal Interface Unit (MCD)
SIU............. Significant Industrial Use
SIU............. Simushir [*Former USSR Seismograph station code, US Geological Survey*] (SEIS)
SIU............. Slide-In Unit [*Telecommunications*] (TEL)
SIU............. Societe Internationale d'Urologie [*International Society of Urology - ISU*] [*Paris, France*] (EAIO)
SIU............. Sonobuoy Interface Unit [*Navy*] (CAAL)
SIU............. Southern Illinois University
SIU............. Station Interface Unit [*Computer science*] (ECII)
SIU............. Systeme International d'Unites [*International System of Units*] [*Also, SI*]
SIU............. System Integration Unit (IAA)
SIU............. System [*or Subsystem*] Interface Unit
SIU-AGLI...... Seafarers' International Union of North America [*AFL-CIO*]; Atlantic, Gulf,Lakes, and Inland Waters District
SIU-AGLIW... Seafarers' International Union of North America [*AFL-CIO*]; Atlantic, Gulf,Lakes, and Inland Waters District
SIUC........... Southern Illinois University, Carbondale
SIUCB......... Societa Italiana della Union Chimique Belge [*Italy*]
SIUFL.......... Suspend Issue and Use of Following Lots
SIU-IUP....... Seafarers' International Union of North America [*AFL-CIO*]; Inlandboatmen'sUnion of the Pacific
SIU-IUPW.... Seafarers' International Union of North America [*AFL-CIO*]; International Union of Petroleum Workers
SIU-MCS...... Seafarers' International Union of North America [*AFL-CIO*]; Marine Cooks and Stewards' Union
SIU-MFOW... Seafarers' International Union of North America [*AFL-CIO*]; Pacific Coast Marine Firemen, Oilers, Watertenders, and Wipers Association
SIUNA......... Seafarers' International Union of North America (EA)
SIUP........... Southern Illinois University Press
SIUPA......... Solomon Islands United Party [*Political party*] (PPW)
SIUSA......... Survival International, USA [*Defunct*] (EA)
SIUSM......... Suspend from Issue and Use as Suspect Material
SIU-SUP...... Seafarers' International Union of North America [*AFL-CIO*]; Sailors' Union of the Pacific
SIU-TSAW.... Seafarers' International Union of North America [*AFL-CIO*]; Transporation Services and Allied Workers
SIV............. Sieve (NASA)
SIV............. Silicon Videcon [*TV system*]
SIV............. Silver Cloud Mines [*Vancouver Stock Exchange symbol*]
SIV............. Simian Immunodeficiency Virus
SIV............. Solar and Interplanetary Variability [*Meteorology*]
SIV............. Special Interest Vessel [*Navy*]
SIV............. Spectrum Identification Voltage [*Military*] (CAAL)
SIV............. Sprague-Dawley-Ivanovas Rat [*Medicine*] (DMAA)
SIV............. Sullivan, IN [*Location identifier FAA*] (FAAL)
SIV............. Survey of Interpersonal Values [*Psychology*]
SIVAN......... Sistema de Vigilancia de Amazonia [*Amazon Surveillance System*] [*Brazil*]
SIVB........... Silicon Valley Bancshares [*NASDAQ symbol*] (NQ)
SIVB........... Silicon Valley Bancshrs [*NASDAQ symbol*] (TTSB)
SIVD........... Spacecraft Information Viewing Device
SIVE........... Shuttle Interface Verification Equipment [*NASA*] (NASA)
SI VIR PERM... Si Vires Permittant [*If the Strength Will Bear It*] [*Pharmacy*] (ROG)
SIVOMAR..... Societe Ivoirenne de Navigation Maritime [*Ivory Coast*] (EY)
SIVZV.......... Sunshine Mining & Refining Wrrt [*NASDAQ symbol*] (TTSB)
SIW............. Congregation of the Incarnate Word and the Blessed Sacrament [*Roman Catholic women's religious order*]
SIW............. Samaria [*Papua*] [*Airport symbol*] (AD)
SIW............. Schmitt Industries, Inc. [*Vancouver Stock Exchange symbol*]
SIW............. Self-Inflicted Wound [*Military*]
SIW............. Serum Samples from Infertile Women [*Immunochemistry*]
SIW............. Socialist International Women (EA)
SIW............. Strassburger Israelitisch Wochenschrift [*A publication*] (BJA)
SIW............. Strategic Intelligence Wing (MCD)
SIW............. Subpolar Intermediate Water [*Oceanography*]
SIWA........... Scottish Inland Waterways Association (DBA)
SIWDR......... Sidewinder [*Naval ordnance*]
SIWIP.......... Self-Induced Water Intoxication and Psychosis [*Medicine*] (DMAA)
SIWL........... Single Isolated Whell Load [*ICAO*] (FAAC)
SIX............. Singleton [*Australia Airport symbol*] (OAG)
SIXATAF..... Sixth Allied Tactical Air Force, Southeastern Europe [*NATO*] (NATG)
Six Circ........ Cases on the Six Circuits [*1841-43*] [*Ireland*] [*A publication*] (DLA)
Six Ct J........ Sixteenth Century Journal [*A publication*] (BRI)
SIXEP.......... Site Ion Exchange Effluent Plant [*Nuclear energy*]
SIXES.......... Selectively-Induced X-Ray Emission Spectroscopy
SIXFLT........ Sixth Fleet [*Atlantic*] [*Navy*]
SIXP........... Sixpenny [*England*]
SIXPAC....... System for Inertial Experiment Priority and Attitude Control (MCD)
SIXT........... Sixth-Plate (VRA)
SIXTHFLT.... Sixth Fleet [*Atlantic*] [*Navy*]
SIXX........... Sixx Hldgs [*NASDAQ symbol*] (TTSB)
Sixx............ Sixx Holdings, Inc. [*Associated Press*] (SAG)
SIXX........... Sixx Holdings, Inc. [*NASDAQ symbol*] (SAG)
SIY............. Aerosiyusa, SA [*Mexico*] [*FAA designator*] (FAAC)
SIY............. Montague, CA [*Location identifier FAA*] (FAAL)
SIY............. Shropshire Imperial Yeomanry [*British military*] (DMA)
SIY............. South of Ireland Yeomanry [*British military*] (DMA)
SIY............. Staffordshire Imperial Yeomanry [*British military*] (DMA)
SIY............. Sussex Imperial Yeomanry [*British military*] (DMA)
SIZ............. Security Identification Zone
SIZ............. Sizeler Property Investors, Inc. [*NYSE symbol*] (SPSG)
SIZ............. Sizeler Property Inv operty Inv [*NYSE symbol*] (TTSB)
SizelerP....... Sizeler Property Investors, Inc. [*Associated Press*] (SAG)
Sizzler......... Sizzler International, Inc. [*Associated Press*] (SAG)
SJ............... Jesuit Fathers and Brothers (TOCD)
sj............... Jesuit Fathers and Brothers, Society of Jesus (TOCD)
SJ............... Sales Journal [*Accounting*]
SJ............... Samuel Johnson [*Initials used as pseudonym*]
SJ............... San Jose [*Diocesan abbreviation*] [*California*] (TOCD)
SJ............... San Juan [*Puerto Rico*]
SJ............... Schistosoma Japonicum [*Parasitic fluke*]
SJ............... Scottish Jurist [*1829-73*] [*A publication*] (DLA)
SJ............... Servants of Jesus (TOCD)
SJ............... Service Junior
SJ............... Show Jumper [*or Jumping*] [*Horsemanship*] [*British*] (DI)
SJ............... Side Judge [*Football*]
SJ............... Single Jewish [*Classified advertising*]
SJ............... SJ Huvudkontor [*Swedish State Railways*] (DCTA)
SJ............... Slip Joint [*Technical drawings*]
SJ............... Sloppy Joe [*Sandwich*]
SJ............... Societas Jesu [*Society of Jesus*] [*Jesuits*] [*Roman Catholic men's religious order*]
SJ............... Solicitors' Journal [*A publication A publication*] (DLA)
SJ............... Source Jamming
SJ............... Statens Jaernvaegar [*Sweden*]
S-J.............. Stevens-Johnson Syndrome [*Medicine*] (AAMN)
SJ............... Stewart Island [*ICAO designator*] (AD)
SJ............... Sub Judice [*Under Consideration*] [*Latin*]
sj............... Sudan [*MARC country of publication code Library of Congress*] (LCCP)
SJ............... Supersonic Jet [*Gas stream*]
SJ............... Support Jamming [*Military*] (LAIN)
SJ............... Svalbard and Jan Mayen Islands [*ANSI two-letter standard code*] (CNC)
SJ............... Swirl Jet
SJ24NACA... San Juan 24 North American Class Association (EA)
SJA............. San Juan de Arama [*Colombia*] [*Airport symbol*] (AD)
SJA............. Service Job Analysis [*A publication*]
SJA............. Servicios Aereos Especiales de Jalisco SA de CV [*Mexico ICAO designator*] (FAAC)
SJA............. Sisters of Ste. Jeanne D'Arc (TOCD)
SJA............. Staff Judge Advocate [*Military*]
SJAA........... Swedish Journalists Association of America (EA)
SJAE........... Steam Jet Air Ejector [*Nuclear energy*] (NRCH)
SJAL........... School Journal Association of London [*British*] (AIE)
SJAOI......... Staff Judge Advocate Office Institute (SAA)
SJART......... San Jacinto Army Terminal
SJB............. San Joaquin [*Bolivia*] [*Airport symbol*] (AD)
SJB............. Sisters of St. John Bosco (Taylor, TX) (TOCD)
SJB............. Society of Jewish Bibliophiles (EA)
SJB............. Society of Journeymen Brushmakers [*A union*] [*British*]
SJB............. St. Joseph Belt Railway Co. [*AAR code*]
SJB............. Westfield, MA [*Location identifier FAA*] (FAAL)
SJBA........... Sephardic Jewish Brotherhood of America (EA)
SJBC........... Saint John the Baptist, Clewer
SJC............. Saint John's College [*California; Kansas; Maryland*]
SJC............. Saint Joseph College [*West Hartford, CT*]
SJC............. Saint Joseph's College [*California; Indiana; Maine; New Jersey; New York, Pennsylvania*]

SJC............ San Javier [*Chile*] [*Seismograph station code, US Geological Survey Closed*] (SEIS)
SJC............ San Jose [*California*] [*Airport symbol*] (OAG)
SJC............ San Jose, CA [*Location identifier FAA*] (FAAL)
SJC............ Sayre Junior College [*Oklahoma*]
SJC............ Sisters of St. Joseph of Cluny (TOCD)
SJC............ Snead Junior College [*Boaz, AL*]
SJC............ Society of Jews and Christians
SJC............ Southend Jet Centre Ltd. [*British ICAO designator*] (FAAC)
SJC............ Southerland, J. C., Dearborn, MI [*STAC*]
SJC............ Standing Joint Committee
SJC............ Supreme Judicial Court
SJC............ Sydney Journalists' Club [*Australia*]
SJCC.......... Cayey [*Puerto Rico*] [*Seismograph station code, US Geological Survey*] (SEIS)
SJCC.......... Saint John College of Cleveland [*Ohio*]
SJCC.......... San Jose City College [*California*]
SJCC.......... Scott Joplin Commemorative Committee (EA)
SJCC.......... Social Justice Consultative Council [*Victoria, Australia*]
SJCC.......... Spring Joint Computer Conference [*American Federation of Information Processing Societies*]
SJCC.......... Sydney Junior Chamber of Commerce [*Australia*]
SJCL.......... Standardized Job Control Language (PDAA)
SJCPS........ Society of Jewish Composers, Publishers, and Songwriters [*Defunct*] (EA)
SJCS.......... Secretary Joint Chiefs of Staff (MCD)
SJCW.......... Saint Joseph's College for Women [*Later, SJC*] [*New York*]
SJD............ Doctor of Judicial Science (GAGS)
SJD............ Doctor of Juridical Science [*or Doctor of the Science of Jurisprudence or Doctor of the Science of Law*]
SJD............ Los Cabos [*Mexico*] [*Airport symbol*] (OAG)
SJD............ Silicon Junction Diode (IDOE)
SJD............ St. Joseph's College, Philadelphia, PA [*OCLC symbol*] (OCLC)
SJD............ Supervisory Job Discipline Test
SJDAOIIA..... Saint John of Damascus Association of Orthodox Iconographers, Iconologists, and Architects (EA)
SJDFC.......... Spirit, John Denver Fan Club (EA)
SJE............ San Jose Del Guaviaro [*Colombia*] [*Airport symbol*] (OAG)
SJE............ Standard Jewish Encyclopedia [*A publication*]
SJE............ St. Jude Express [*An association*] (EA)
SJE............ Swiveling Jet Engine
SJF............ Saint John [*Virgin Islands*] [*Airport symbol*] (OAG)
SJF............ Shortest Job First [*Computer science*]
SJF............ Single Jewish Female [*Classified advertising*]
SJF............ Sonny James and Friends [*An association Defunct*] (EA)
SJF............ Supersonic Jet Flow
SJFC.......... Saint John Fisher College [*Rochester, NY*]
SJFC.......... Skidrow Joe Fan Club (EA)
SJFZ.......... San Jacinto Fault Zone [*Geology*]
SJG............ San Juan [*Puerto Rico*] [*Seismograph station code, US Geological Survey*] (SEIS)
SJGE.......... St. Joseph Grain Exchange (EA)
SJH............ San Juan Del Cesar [*Colombia*] [*Airport symbol*] (OAG)
SJH............ St. Johns [*Antigua, Leeward Islands, West Indies*] [*Airport symbol*] (AD)
SJH............ St. Joseph Seminary [*California*] [*Seismograph station code, US Geological Survey*] (SEIS)
SJI............ Mobile, AL [*Location identifier FAA*] (FAAL)
SJI............ San Jose [*Philippines*] [*Airport symbol*] (OAG)
SJI............ Society for Japanese Irises (EA)
SJI............ South Jersey Industries, Inc. [*NYSE symbol*] (SPSG)
SJI............ Steel Joist Institute (EA)
SJI............ Sun Jet International Airlines, Inc. [*ICAO designator*] (FAAC)
SJI............ Supervisory Job Instruction Test
SJIA.......... Saint Joan's International Alliance [*See also AIJA*] (EAIO)
SJIFC.......... Spike Jones International Fan Club (EA)
SJIS.......... State Judicial Information System (OICC)
SJJ............ Sarajevo [*Former Yugoslavia*] [*Airport symbol*] (OAG)
SJJC.......... Sheldon Jackson Junior College [*Sitka, AK*] [*Later, Sheldon Jackson College*]
SJJR.......... Societe Jean-Jacques Rousseau [*Switzerland*] (EAIO)
SJJR.......... Standard Jack and Jennet Registry of America (EA)
SJK............ Saint John Knits, Inc. [*NYSE symbol*] (SAG)
SJK............ Sao Jose Dos Campos [*Brazil*] [*Airport symbol*] (OAG)
SJK............ Steam-Jacketed Kettle
SJK............ St. John Knits [*NYSE symbol*] (TTSB)
SJK............ St. John Knits, Inc. [*NYSE symbol*] (SPSG)
SJL............ San Joaquin Valley Library System, Fresno, CA [*OCLC symbol*] (OCLC)
SJL............ South Jersey Indus [*NYSE symbol*] (TTSB)
SJL............ St. Jude League (EA)
SJLAC.......... Soviet Jewry Legal Advocacy Center (EA)
SJLB.......... Selected Judgments, Lower Burma [*A publication*] (DLA)
SJLC.......... Single Junction Latching Circulator
SJLC.......... St. Johnsbury & Lamoille County R. R. [*AAR code*]
SJM............ San Jose De Maipo [*Chile*] [*Seismograph station code, US Geological Survey Closed*] (SEIS)
SJM............ Single Jewish Male [*Classified advertising*]
SJM............ Smucker [*J. M.*] Co. [*NYSE symbol*] (SPSG)
SJM............ Southern Air Transport, Inc. [*ICAO designator*] (FAAC)
SJM............ Special Joint Meeting
SJM............ Svalbard and Jan Mayen Islands [*ANSI three-letter standard code*] (CNC)
SJM............ System Junction Module [*Deep Space Instrumentation Facility, NASA*]
SJM.A.......... Smucker (J.M.) Cl'A' [*NYSE symbol*] (TTSB)
SJM.B.......... Smucker (J.M.) Cl'B' [*NYSE symbol*] (TTSB)
SJMC.......... Signed Judgments of the Military Courts in the Administered Territories [*Israel*] (BJA)
SJMJ.......... Societe de Jesus, Marie et Joseph [*Society of Jesus, Mary and Joseph*] [*Netherlands*] (EAIO)
SJMO.......... Smithosonian Jazz Masterworks Orchestra
SJN............ Chartair, Inc. [*ICAO designator*] (FAAC)
SJN............ San Juan [*Peru*] [*Seismograph station code, US Geological Survey Closed*] (SEIS)
SJN............ San Juan [*Diocesan abbreviation*] [*Puerto Rico*] (TOCD)
S/J + N........ Signal-to-Jamming - plus Noise Ratio
SJN............ St. Johns, AZ [*Location identifier FAA*] (FAAL)
SJN............ Supersonic Jet Noise
SJNB.......... SJNB Financial Corp. [*Associated Press*] (SAG)
SJNB.......... SJNB Financial Corp. [*NASDAQ symbol*] (NQ)
SJNB.......... SJNB Finl [*NASDAQ symbol*] (TTSB)
SJO............ San Jose [*Costa Rica*] [*Airport symbol*] (OAG)
SJO............ Service Junior - Oil-Resistant
SJOJ.......... Savez Jevrejskih Opstina Jugoslavije (BJA)
SJP............ Saint Joe Corp. [*NYSE symbol*] (SAG)
SJP............ San Jose Public Library, San Jose, CA [*OCLC symbol*] (OCLC)
SJP............ San Juan [*Puerto Rico*] [*Seismograph station code, US Geological Survey Closed*] (SEIS)
SJP............ San Juan [*Peru*] [*Airport symbol*] (AD)
SJP............ Sao Jose Do Rio Preto [*Brazil*] [*Airport symbol*] (OAG)
SJP............ Serialized Job Processor
SJP............ Singapore Justice Party [*Political party*] (PPW)
SJP............ Socialist Janata Party [*India*] [*Political party*] (ECON)
SJP............ Special Job Procedure [*Navy*] (NG)
SJP............ Stacked Job Processing (IAA)
SJP............ Standard Jet Penetration [*Aviation*]
SJP............ St. James Press [*Publisher*]
SJP............ St. Joe Paper [*NYSE symbol*] (TTSB)
SJP............ St. Joe Paper Co. [*NYSE symbol*] (SPSG)
SJP............ St. Josaphat in Parma [*Diocesan abbrevation*] [*Ohio*] (TOCD)
SJP............ Sun-Jupiter-Probe [*Angle*]
SJPC.......... Standing Joint Pacifist Committee [*Defunct*] (EAIO)
SJPS.......... Saint John's Provincial Seminary [*Plymouth, MI*]
SJQ............ San Joaquin Reservoir [*California*] [*Seismograph station code, US Geological Survey Closed*] (SEIS)
SJQ............ Selected Job Queue (IAA)
SJQ............ Sesheke [*Zambia*] [*Airport symbol*] (AD)
SJR............ San Jose [*Costa Rica*] [*Seismograph station code, US Geological Survey Closed*] (SEIS)
SJR............ San Juan de Uraba [*Colombia*] [*Airport symbol*] (AD)
SJR............ Senate Joint Resolution
SJR............ Shinowara-Jones-Reinhard Unit [*Medicine*] (MAE)
SJRB.......... Soviet Jewry Research Bureau (EA)
SJRES.......... Senate Joint Resolution (AFIT)
SJRF.......... Scott Joplin Ragtime Festival (EA)
SJRMF.......... Senator Joseph R. McCarthy Foundation (EA)
SJRT.......... St. Johns River Terminal [*AAR code*]
SJS............ Saint John's Seminary [*Brighton, MA*]
SJS............ Saint Joseph's Seminary [*Illinois; New York*]
SJS............ San Jose [*Costa Rica*] [*Seismograph station code, US Geological Survey*] (SEIS)
SJS............ San Jose [*Bolivia*] [*Airport symbol*] (AD)
SJS............ Search Jam System
SJS............ Secretary, Joint Staff [*Military*] (CINC)
SJS............ Servants of the Blessed Sacrament (TOCD)
SjS............ Sjogren Syndrome [*Medicine*] (DMAA)
SJS............ Society of Jewish Science (EA)
SJS............ Stevens-Johnson Syndrome [*Medicine*] (DMAA)
SJS............ St. Johns Tracking Station [*Newfoundland*]
SJS............ Supervisory Job Safety Test
SJSB.......... SJS Bancorp [*NASDAQ symbol*] (TTSB)
SJSB.......... SJS Bancorp, Inc. [*NASDAQ symbol*] (SAG)
SJS Bcp........ SJS Bancorp, Inc. [*Associated Press*] (SAG)
SJSC.......... San Jose State College [*California*] [*Later, San Jose State University*]
SJSD.......... Soviet Jewry Solidarity Day (BJA)
SJSM.......... Sisters of St. Joseph of St. Mark (TOCD)
SJSS.......... Saint Joseph's Seraphic Seminary [*New York*]
SJSU.......... San Jose State University [*California*]
SJT............ San Angelo [*Texas*] [*Airport symbol*] (OAG)
SJT............ San Angelo, TX [*Location identifier FAA*] (FAAL)
SJT............ San Juan Basin Royalty Trust [*NYSE symbol*] (SPSG)
SJT............ San Juan Basin Rty Tr [*NYSE symbol*] (TTSB)
Sjt............ Serjeant [*Military British*] (DMA)
SJT............ Service Junior - Thermoplastic
SJT............ St. Joseph Terminal Railroad Co. [*AAR code*]
SJT............ Subsonic [*or Supersonic*] Jet Transport
SJT............ Yorkshire European Airways Ltd. [*British ICAO designator*] (FAAC)
SJTCA.......... San Juan 21 Class Association (EA)
SJTCC.......... State Job Training Coordinating Council (OICC)
SJTh.......... Scottish Journal of Theology [*A publication*] (BJA)
SJU............ Luiz Munoz Marin International Airport [*FAA*] (TAG)
SJU............ San Juan [*Puerto Rico*] [*Airport symbol*] (OAG)
SJU............ St. John's University [*Minnesota; New York*]
SJU............ St. John's University, Division of Library and Information Science, Jamaica, NY [*OCLC symbol*] (OCLC)
SJuanB.......... San Juan Basin Royalty Trust [*Associated Press*] (SAG)
SJUF.......... Skandinavisk Jodisk Ungdomsforbund (BJA)
SJUMPS........ Shipboard Joint Uniform Military Pay System [*Navy*] (DNAB)

S Jur .... Sirey. Jurisprudence [*France*] [*A publication*] (DLA)
S Just .... Shaw's Scotch Justiciary Cases [*A publication*] (DLA)
SJV .... San Javier [*Bolivia*] [*Airport symbol*] (AD)
SJV .... Sharing Joint Venture
SJV .... Societe Jules Verne [*France*] (EAIO)
SJV .... St. John [*Virgin Islands*] [*Seismograph station code, US Geological Survey*] (SEIS)
SJVLS .... San Joaquin Valley Library System [*Library network*]
SJVWGA .... San Joaquin Valley Wine Growers Association (EA)
SJW .... Single Jewish Woman [*Classified advertising*]
SJW .... Sisters of St. Joseph the Worker (TOCD)
SJW .... SJW Corp. [*AMEX symbol*] (SPSG)
SJW .... St. Louis, MO [*Location identifier FAA*] (FAAL)
SJWCP .... Skid Jacket Water Cooling Pump [*Nuclear energy*] (NRCH)
SJWVUSA .... Sons of Jewish War Veterans of the United States of America (EA)
SJX .... Sartaneja [*Belize*] [*Airport symbol*] (OAG)
SJX .... St. James, MI [*Location identifier FAA*] (FAAL)
SJY .... San Jacinto, CA [*Location identifier FAA*] (FAAL)
SJZ .... Angola, IN [*Location identifier FAA*] (FAAL)
SJZ .... Sao Jorge Island [*Azores*] [*Airport symbol*] (OAG)
SJZ .... Selected Judgments, Zambia [*A publication*] (DLA)
SJZ .... Sueddeutsche Juristenzeitung [*German*] (ILCA)
SK .... Sack
SK .... Safekeeping
SK .... Safety-Kleen [*NYSE symbol*] (TTSB)
SK .... Safety-Kleen Corp. [*NYSE symbol*] (SPSG)
S-K .... Saltonstall-Kennedy [*Promote and Develop American Fisheries*] (USDC)
S-K .... Saltonstall-Kennedy Promote and Develop American Fisheries [*Marine science*] (OSRA)
S K .... S & K Famous Brands, Inc. [*Associated Press*] (SAG)
SK .... Sanitaetskompanie [*Medical company*] [*German military - World War II*]
SK .... Santa Klaus (ROG)
SK .... Saskatchewan [*Canadian province, postal code*]
SK .... Scandinavian Airlines System [*Sweden*] [*ICAO designator*] (OAG)
SK .... Sealed Knot [*An association*] (EAIO)
SK .... Seek Command (IAA)
SK .... Senile Keratosis [*Dermatology*] (DAVI)
SK .... Service Kit
SK .... Sick
sk .... Sikkim [*ii (India) used in records cataloged after January 1978*] [*MARC country of publication code Library of Congress*] (LCCP)
SK .... Sikorsky Aircraft Division [*United Aircraft Corp.*] [*ICAO aircraft manufacturer identifier*] (ICAO)
SK .... Sinclair-Koppers Co. [*Later, Arco Polymers, Inc.*]
SK .... Sink (AAG)
SK .... Skein
sk .... Skeletal [*Orthopedics*] (DAVI)
SK .... Skeletals (DCTA)
SK .... Sketch (AAG)
sk .... Sketch (VRA)
sk .... Skewbald [*Color of a horse*] (BARN)
Sk .... Skewness (WGA)
SK .... Skimmed
SK .... Skin (DAVI)
SK .... Skinned (MSA)
SK .... Skip
Sk .... Skiver [*Leather bookbinding*] (DGA)
sk .... Skot [*Unit of luminance*]
SK .... Sky Condition [*Aviation*] (FAAC)
SK .... Sloan-Kettering [*Cancer-treatment compound*] (MAE)
SK .... Smack (ROG)
SK .... Smith Kline Diagnostics (DAVI)
SK .... Socket (DEN)
SK .... Solar Keratosis [*Dermatology*] (DAVI)
SK .... Sonic Key (MCD)
SK .... South Kensington [*District of London*] (ROG)
SK .... South Korea
SK .... Sovetskyaya Kolonia [*Soviet Colony*]
SK .... Spontaneous Killer [*Cells*] [*Immunology*] (DAVI)
SK .... Station-Keeping
SK .... Stockport [*Postcode*] (ODBW)
SK .... Storekeeper [*Navy rating*]
SK .... Streptokinase [*An enzyme*]
SK .... Striae Keratopathy [*Ophthalmology*] (DAVI)
Sk .... Strike [*or Stroke*]
SK .... Substance K [*Biochemistry*]
SK .... Sumerische Kultlieder aus Altbabylonischer Zeit [*A publication*] (BJA)
SK1 .... Storekeeper, First Class [*Navy rating*]
SK2 .... Storekeeper, Second Class [*Navy rating*]
SK3 .... Storekeeper, Third Class [*Navy rating*]
SKA .... Aupracondylar Knee-Ankle[*Orthosis*] [*Orthopedics*] (DAVI)
SKA .... Rio Air Express, SA [*Brazil*] [*FAA designator*] (FAAC)
SKA .... Scottish Knitwear Association (DBA)
SKA .... Skalstugan [*Sweden*] [*Seismograph station code, US Geological Survey*] (SEIS)
SKA .... Skegair [*British ICAO designator*] (FAAC)
SKA .... Skill, Knowledge, and Ability [*or Attitude*] [*Employment*]
SKA .... Spokane, WA [*Location identifier FAA*] (FAAL)
SKA .... Station-Keeping Assistance (DS)
S/KA .... Submarine Kit Allowance [*British military*] (DMA)
SKA .... Switchblade Knife Act
SKAD .... Survival Kit Air-Droppable [*Military Canada*]
SKAMP .... Station-Keeping and Mobile Platform [*Robot sailboat*]
SKAN .... Solidariteits Komitee Argentiniee [*Netherlands*]
SKAND SF .... Skandinaviska Seglarforbundet [*Scandinavian Yachting Association - SYA*] (EAIO)
SKAP .... Armedia/El Elden [*Colorado ICAO location identifier*] (ICLI)
SKAP .... Skills, Knowledge, Abilities, and Personnel [*Attributes*] (MCD)
SKAS .... Puerto Asis [*Colorado ICAO location identifier*] (ICLI)
SKAT .... Kommentar zum Alten Testament [*A publication*] (BJA)
SKAT .... Sex Knowledge and Aptitude [*Test*]
SKAT .... Skysat Communications Network Corp. [*NASDAQ symbol*] (SAG)
SKATA .... Skysat Commun Network'A' [*NASDAQ symbol*] (TTSB)
SKATI .... Skills, Knowledges, Aptitudes, Temperaments, Interests (OICC)
SKATW .... Skysat Communicns Ntwk Wrrt'A' [*NASDAQ symbol*] (TTSB)
SKATZ .... Skysat Communicns Ntwk Wrrt'B' [*NASDAQ symbol*] (TTSB)
SKB .... Saint Kitts [*Leeward Islands*] [*Airport symbol*] (OAG)
SKB .... Skew Buffer
SKB .... Skybridge International, Inc. [*Vancouver Stock Exchange symbol*]
SKB .... Skyfreighters Corp. [*ICAO designator*] (FAAC)
SKB .... Wichita Falls, TX [*Location identifier FAA*] (FAAL)
SKBC .... El Banco/Los Flores [*Colorado ICAO location identifier*] (ICLI)
SKBF .... Schweizerische Koordinationsstelle fuer Bildungsforschung [*Swiss Coordination Center for Research in Education*] [*Information service or system*] (IID)
SKBG .... Bucaramanga/Palo Negro Sur [*Colorado ICAO location identifier*] (ICLI)
SKBO .... Bogota/Eldorado [*Colorado ICAO location identifier*] (ICLI)
SKBQ .... Barranquilla/Ernesto Cortissoz [*Colorado ICAO location identifier*] (ICLI)
SKBS .... Bahia Solano/Jose Celestino Mutis [*Colorado ICAO location identifier*] (ICLI)
SKBU .... Buenaventura [*Colorado ICAO location identifier*] (ICLI)
SKC .... Scottish Kennel Club (BARN)
SKC .... Services Kinema Corp. [*British military*] (DMA)
SKC .... Skycare Management Services Ltd. [*British ICAO designator*] (FAAC)
SKC .... Sky Clear [*ICAO*] (FAAC)
SKC .... Suki [*Papua New Guinea*] [*Airport symbol*] (OAG)
SKC .... Waukesha, WI [*Location identifier FAA*] (FAAL)
SKCATL .... South Korea Conventional Air Target List (MCD)
SKCB .... Skylands Cmnty Bk NJ [*NASDAQ symbol*] (TTSB)
SKCB .... Skylands Community Bank [*NASDAQ symbol*] (SAG)
SKCB .... Storekeeper, Construction Battalion, Stevedore [*Navy rating*]
SKCC .... Cucuta/Camilo Daza [*Colorado ICAO location identifier*] (ICLI)
SKCD .... Condoto/Mandinga [*Colorado ICAO location identifier*] (ICLI)
SKCG .... Cartagena/Rafael Nunez [*Colorado ICAO location identifier*] (ICLI)
SKCH .... Skyline Chili [*NASDAQ symbol*] (TTSB)
SKCH .... Skyline Chili, Inc. [*Cincinnati, OH*] [*NASDAQ symbol*] (NQ)
SKCL .... Cali/Alfonso Bonilla Aragon [*Colorado ICAO location identifier*] (ICLI)
SKCM .... Master Chief Storekeeper [*Navy rating*]
SKCM .... Society of King Charles the Martyr (EA)
SKCMA .... Steel Kitchen Cabinet Manufacturers Association (EA)
SKCO .... Tumaco/La Florida [*Colorado ICAO location identifier*] (ICLI)
SKCS .... Senior Chief Storekeeper [*Navy rating*]
SKCZ .... Corozal/Las Brujas [*Colorado ICAO location identifier*] (ICLI)
SKD .... Samarkand [*Former USSR Airport symbol*] (OAG)
SKD .... Selve-Kornbegel-Dornheim [*Name of a German small arms ammunition factory*] [*World War II*]
SKD .... Semi Knocked Down [*Shipping*] (DS)
SKD .... Sitkalidak Island [*Alaska*] [*Seismograph station code, US Geological Survey*] (SEIS)
SKD .... Skid
SKD .... Skilled (MSA)
SKD .... Skirted
SKD .... Skyguard Ltd. [*British ICAO designator*] (FAAC)
SKD .... Skyworld Resources & Development Ltd. [*Vancouver Stock Exchange symbol*]
SKD .... Smith Kline Diagnostics (DAVI)
SKD .... Station-Keeping Distance [*British military*] (DMA)
SKD .... St. Katherine's Dock [*Shipping*] [*British*] (ROG)
SKD .... Storekeeper, Disbursing [*Navy rating*]
SKDH .... Shikimate Dehydrogenase [*An enzyme*]
SKDL .... Suomen Kansan Demokraattinen Liitto [*Finnish People's Democratic League*] [*Political party*] (PPW)
SKDN .... Shakedown [*Navy*] (NVT)
SKDNC .... Shakedown Cruise [*Navy*]
SKDNCRU .... Shakedown Cruise [*Navy*] (NVT)
SKDP .... Sambungan Komunikasi Data Packet [*Indonesia*] [*Telecommunications service*] (TSSD)
SKDR .... Skydoor Media & Entmt [*NASDAQ symbol*] (TTSB)
SKDU .... Ship's Keyboard Display Unit
SKE .... Belleville, IL [*Location identifier FAA*] (FAAL)
SKE .... Skeena Resources Ltd. [*Vancouver Stock Exchange symbol*]
SKE .... Skien [*Norway*] [*Airport symbol*] (OAG)
SKE .... Sky Tours, Inc. [*ICAO designator*] (FAAC)
SKE .... Station-Keeping Equipment
SKEC .... Barranquilla [*Colorado ICAO location identifier*] (ICLI)
SKED .... Bogota [*Colorado ICAO location identifier*] (ICLI)
SKED .... Schedule (NG)
SKED .... Sort Key Edit [*Library of Congress*]
SKEDCON .... Schedule Conference [*Military*] (NVT)
SKEEC .... Southern Central Kansas Environmental Education Center (EDAC)
SKEJ .... Barrancabermeja/Yariguis [*Colorado ICAO location identifier*] (ICLI)
SKEL .... Skeletal (AAG)
SKET .... Skeleton Key (DSUE)
SKEY .... Softkey International [*NASDAQ symbol*] (TTSB)
SKEY .... Softkey International, Inc. [*NASDAQ symbol*] (SAG)
SKEYW .... Softkey Intl Wrrt [*NASDAQ symbol*] (TTSB)

SKF............ San Antonio, TX [*Location identifier FAA*] (FAAL)
SKF............ SKF AB [*Associated Press*] (SAG)
SKF............ Skycraft, Inc. [*ICAO designator*] (FAAC)
SKF............ SmithKline Corp. [*Formerly, Smith, Kline & French Co.*] [*Research code symbol*]
SKF............ Svenska Kullagerfabriken AB [*Swedish manufacturer, especially of ball bearings; active in many countries*]
SKF............ Svenska Kullager Frabikon [*Swedish Ball Bearing Manufacturing*]
SKFA............ Scottish Keep Fit Association (DBA)
SKFB............ S & K Famous Brands [*NASDAQ symbol*] (TTSB)
SKFB............ S & K Famous Brands, Inc. [*NASDAQ symbol*] (NQ)
SKFL............ Florencia/Capitolio [*Colorado ICAO location identifier*] (ICLI)
SKFR............ SKF AB [*Goteborg, Sweden*] [*NASDAQ symbol*] (NQ)
SKFRY............ SKF AB ADR [*NASDAQ symbol*] (TTSB)
SkFx............ Skull Fracture [*Medicine*]
Skg............ Safekeeping
SKG............ Salonika [*Greece*] [*Airport symbol*] (AD)
SKG............ Sikaman Gold Resources Ltd. [*Toronto Stock Exchange symbol*]
SKG............ Skycraft Air Transport, Inc. [*Canada ICAO designator*] (FAAC)
SKG............ Thessaloniki [*Greece*] [*Airport symbol*] (OAG)
SKGI............ Girardot/Santiago Vila [*Colorado ICAO location identifier*] (ICLI)
SKGP............ Guapi [*Colorado ICAO location identifier*] (ICLI)
SKH............ Selkirk Communications Ltd. [*Toronto Stock Exchange symbol*]
SKH............ Skywatch Ltd. [*British ICAO designator*] (FAAC)
SKH............ Surkhet [*Nepal*] [*Airport symbol*] (OAG)
SKHS............ Sri Kapila Humanitarian Society (EAIO)
SKI............ Sac City, IA [*Location identifier FAA*] (FAAL)
SKI............ Sex Knowledge Inventory [*Premarital and marital relations test*]
SKI............ Sister Kenny Institute (EA)
SKI............ Skiff, Ice [*Coast Guard*] (DNAB)
SKI............ Skilda [*Algeria*] [*Airport symbol*] (AD)
SKI............ SKI Ltd. [*Associated Press*] (SAG)
SKI............ Skin (DAVI)
SKI............ Skylink Airlines [*Canada ICAO designator*] (FAAC)
SKI............ Sloan-Kettering Institute for Cancer Research
SKI............ Spinal Kinematic Instrument [*Medicine*]
SKI............ St. Kitts [*St. Kitts*] [*Seismograph station code, US Geological Survey*] (SEIS)
SKIA............ Secure Key-Issuing Authority [*Computer science*]
SKIB............ Ibague/Perales [*Colorado ICAO location identifier*] (ICLI)
Skid Min...... Skidmore's Mining Statutes [*A publication*] (DLA)
SKIF............ Social Security Number Key Index File [*IRS*]
SKIF............ Sotsyalistisher Kinder Farband (BJA)
SKII............ S-K-I Ltd. [*Killington, VT*] [*NASDAQ symbol*] (NQ)
SKII............ S-K-I Ltd [*NASDAQ symbol*] (TTSB)
SKIL............ Scanner Keyed Input Language
SKILA............ Southern Korean Interim Legislative Assembly
SKILL............ Satellite Kill
Skill Pol Rep... Skillman's New York Police Reports [*A publication*] (DLA)
Skin............ Skinner's English King's Bench Reports [*A publication*] (DLA)
Skinker........ Skinker's Reports [*65-79 Missouri*] [*A publication*] (DLA)
Skinner........ Skinner's English King's Bench Reports [*90 English Reprint*] [*1681-98*] [*A publication*] (DLA)
Skinner (Eng)... Skinner's English King's Bench Reports [*90 English Reprint*] [*A publication*] (DLA)
SKINS............ Supplemental Knowledge Incentive Notes [*Scrip offered to students for good performance*] [*Experimental learning program*]
SKINY............ Pharma Patch plc [*NASDAQ symbol*] (TTSB)
SKIP............ Ipiales/San Luis [*Colorado ICAO location identifier*] (ICLI)
SKIP............ Sick Kids Need Involved People (EA)
SKIP............ Skill/Knowledge Improvement Program [*Navy*] (DNAB)
SKIP............ Skinner Investigation Platform
SKIPI............ Super Knowledge Information Processing Intelligence [*Computer science*]
Skippies...... School Kids with Income, Purchasing Power [*Lifestyle Classification*]
SKJ............ Sitkinak Island, AK [*Location identifier FAA*] (FAAL)
SKJ............ Skyjet, Inc. [*Antigua and Barbuda*] [*ICAO designator*] (FAAC)
SKK............ Shaktoolik [*Alaska*] [*Airport symbol*] (OAG)
SKK............ Shaktoolik, AK [*Location identifier FAA*] (FAAL)
SKK............ Sikka [*Former USSR Seismograph station code, US Geological Survey Closed*] (SEIS)
SKK............ Skylane Air Charter [*British ICAO designator*] (FAAC)
SKK............ Sowjetische Kontrollkommission
SKKCA............ Supreme Knight of the Knights of Columbus of America
SKL............ Isle Of Skye [*Scotland*] [*Airport symbol*] (OAG)
SKL............ Serum-Killing Level [*Pharmacology*] (DAVI)
SKL............ Skiff, Light [*Coast Guard*] (DNAB)
SKL............ Skilak [*Cooper Landing*] [*Alaska*] [*Seismograph station code, US Geological Survey*] (SEIS)
SKL............ Skill Level
SKL............ Skycharter (Malton) Ltd. [*Canada ICAO designator*] (FAAC)
SKL............ Skylight [*Technical drawings*]
SKL............ Smith, Kline & French Laboratories [*Canada*] (IIA)
SKL............ Stackpool Resources Ltd. [*Vancouver Stock Exchange symbol*]
SKL............ Suomen Kristillinen Liitto [*Finnish Christian League*] [*Political party*] (PPE)
SKLC............ Los Cedros/Uraba [*Colorado ICAO location identifier*] (ICLI)
SKLL............ Skill
SKLM............ La Mina/Riohacha [*Colorado ICAO location identifier*] (ICLI)
SKLT............ Leticia/Alfredo Vasquez Cobo [*Colorado ICAO location identifier*] (ICLI)
SKLT............ Station Keeping Light (NFPA)
SKM............ Fayetteville Flying Service & Scheduled Skyways System [*ICAO designator*] (FAAC)
SKM............ Korea Mobile Telecommunications [*NYSE symbol*] (SAG)
SKM............ Schuster-Kubelka-Munk [*Optics*]
SKM............ Sine-Kosine Multiplier
SKM............ Skiff, Medium [*Coast Guard*] (DNAB)
SKMC............ Sickness due to Misconduct [*Military*] (DNAB)
SKMG............ Magangue/Baracoa [*Colorado ICAO location identifier*] (ICLI)
SkMg............ Sulfate of Potash Magnesia Export Association (EA)
SKMQ............ Mariquita/Mariquita [*Colorado ICAO location identifier*] (ICLI)
SKMR............ Monteria/Los Garzones [*Colorado ICAO location identifier*] (ICLI)
SKMU............ Mitu/Mitu [*Colorado ICAO location identifier*] (ICLI)
SKMZ............ Manizales/La Nubia [*Colorado ICAO location identifier*] (ICLI)
SKN............ Skaneateles [*New York*] [*Seismograph station code, US Geological Survey*] (SEIS)
SKN............ Skein (ROG)
SKN............ Skyline Aviation Services, Inc. [*ICAO designator*] (FAAC)
SKN............ Smithville, TN [*Location identifier FAA*] (FAAL)
SKN............ Stokmarknes [*Norway*] [*Airport symbol*] (OAG)
SKNTO............ St. Kitts-Nevis Tourist Office (EA)
S/KNU............ Steering Knuckle [*Automotive engineering*]
SKNV............ Neiva/La Manguila [*Colorado ICAO location identifier*] (ICLI)
SKO............ Deadhorse, AK [*Location identifier FAA*] (FAAL)
SKO............ Saskatchewan Oil & Gas Corp. [*Toronto Stock Exchange symbol*]
SKO............ Scottish Airways Flyers Ltd. [*ICAO designator*] (FAAC)
SKO............ Sets, Kits, and Outfits (MCD)
SKO............ Shopko Stores [*NYSE symbol*] (SPSG)
SKO............ Skopje [*Yugoslavia*] [*Seismograph station code, US Geological Survey*] (SEIS)
SKO............ Society of Kastorians "Omonoia" (EA)
SKO............ Sokoto [*Nigeria*] [*Airport symbol*] (OAG)
SKOC............ Ocana/Aguas Claras [*Colorado ICAO location identifier*] (ICLI)
SKOI............ Suomen Konsulttitoimistojen Liitto [*Finnish Association of Consulting Firms*] (EY)
SKOL............ Suomen Konsulttitoimistojen Liitto [*Finnish Association of Consulting Firms*] (EY)
SKOLD............ Screening Kit of Language Development [*Child development test*]
SKOR............ Sperry Kalman Optical Reset [*Ship's Inertial Navigation System*] [*Navy*] (DNAB)
SKOT............ Otu/Otu [*Colorado ICAO location identifier*] (ICLI)
Skoteys........ Spoiled Kids of the Eighties [*Offspring of the Yuppies*] [*Lifestyle classification*]
SKP............ Aero North Aviation Services [*Canada ICAO designator*] (FAAC)
SKP............ Skip (BUR)
SKP............ Skip Line Printer [*Computer science*] (ECII)
SKP............ Skopje [*Former Yugoslavia*] [*Airport symbol*] (OAG)
SKP............ Station-Keeping Position
SKP............ Suomen Kommunistinen Puolue [*Communist Party of Finland*] [*Political party*] (PPW)
SKP............ Sveriges Kommunistiska Partiet [*Communist Party of Sweden*] [*Political party*] (PPE)
SKPB............ Puerto Bolivar/Riohacha [*Colorado ICAO location identifier*] (ICLI)
SKPC............ Puerto Carreno [*Colorado ICAO location identifier*] (ICLI)
SKPE............ Pereira/Matecana [*Colorado ICAO location identifier*] (ICLI)
SKPI............ Pitalito [*Colorado ICAO location identifier*] (ICLI)
SKPI............ Super Knowledge, Processing Interaction [*Concept advanced by Timothy Leary*]
SK-PJ............ Savez Komunista - Pokret za Jugoslaviju [*League of Communists - Movement for Yugoslavia*] [*Political party*]
SKPL............ Sketch Pad Layout (MCD)
skpo............ Slip One, Knit One, Pass Slipped Stitch Over [*Knitting*] (BARN)
SKPP............ Popayan/Guillermo Leon Valencia [*Colorado ICAO location identifier*] (ICLI)
S-K-P's........ Escapees, Inc. (EA)
SKPS............ Pasto/Antonio Narino [*Colorado ICAO location identifier*] (ICLI)
skpsso............ Slip One, Knit One, Pass Slipped Stitch Over [*Knitting*] (BARN)
SKPV............ Providencia/Providencia [*Colorado ICAO location identifier*] (ICLI)
SKQ............ Sekakes [*Lesotho*] [*Airport symbol*] (OAG)
SKQ............ Sexual Knowledge Questionnaire
SKR............ Bedford, MA [*Location identifier FAA*] (FAAL)
SKR............ Sanskrit [*Language, etc.*]
SKR............ Saskatchewan Regional Libraries [*UTLAS symbol*]
SKR............ Saturn Kilometer-Wave Radiation [*Planetary science*]
SKR............ Sea King Replacement [*Naval aircraft*] [*British*]
SKR............ Seeker
SKR............ Separator-Key Generator-Recombiner (MCD)
SKR............ Severo-Kurilsk [*Former USSR Seismograph station code, US Geological Survey*] (SEIS)
SKR............ Shaker Heights City School District, Shaker Heights, OH [*OCLC symbol*] (OCLC)
Skr............ Skipper [*Navy British*]
SKR............ Skogar [*Iceland*] [*Airport symbol*] (AD)
SKR............ Skylark Resources Ltd. [*Vancouver Stock Exchange symbol*]
SKR............ Skyrover Ltd. [*British ICAO designator*] (FAAC)
SKR............ South Korea Republic
SKR............ Station-Keeping RADAR
SKR............ Substance-K Receptor [*Biochemistry*]
S KR............ Swedish Krona [*Monetary unit*]
Skr............ Swedish Krona [*Monetary unit*] (ODBW)
SKRG............ Rio Negro/Jose Maria Cordova [*Colorado ICAO location identifier*] (ICLI)
SKRH............ Rio Hacha, Guajira [*Colorado ICAO location identifier*] (ICLI)
SKRI............ Striker Industries [*NASDAQ symbol*] (SAG)
SKRSU............ Sikouras Pictures Unit [*NASDAQ symbol*] (TTSB)
Skrt............ Sanskrit [*Language*] (BARN)
SKS............ Career Development Center, Shaker Heights, OH [*OCLC symbol*] (OCLC)
SKS............ Saks Holdings [*NYSE symbol*] (TTSB)

SKS Samozaryadnyi Karabin Simonova Carbine [*Soviet made semiautomatic rifle*] (VNW)
SKS Savezna Komisija za Standardizacija [*Federal Commission for Standardization*] [*Yugoslavia*]
SKS Scanning Kinetic Spectroscopy
SKS Schichtlade Kammer System [*Stratified Combustion Chamber System*] [*Automotive engineering German*]
SKS Skrydstrup [*Denmark*] [*Airport symbol*] (OAG)
SKS Sky Service [*Belgium ICAO designator*] (FAAC)
SKS Soren Kierkegaard Society [*Copenhagen, Denmark*] (EA)
SKS Specialist Knowledge Services [*British organization for occult research*]
SKS Station-Keeping Ship
SKS Svetoveho Kongresu Slovakov [*Canada*] (EAIO)
SKSA Saravena/Saravena El Eden [*Colorado ICAO location identifier*] (ICLI)
SKSA Seaman Apprentice, Storekeeper, Striker [*Navy rating*]
SKSD Streptokinase Streptodornase [*An enzyme mixture*] [*Medicine*]
SKSG Santagueda/Santagueda [*Colorado ICAO location identifier*] (ICLI)
SKSJ San Jose Del Guaviare/S. J. Del Guaviore [*Colorado ICAO location identifier*] (ICLI)
SKSL Skaneateles Short Line Railroad Corp. [*Later, SSL*] [*AAR code*]
SKSM Santa Marta/Simon Bolivar [*Colorado ICAO location identifier*] (ICLI)
SKSN Seaman, Storekeeper, Striker [*Navy rating*]
SKSP San Andres/Sesquicentenario, San Andres [*Colorado ICAO location identifier*] (ICLI)
SKSS Stoleczny Komitet Samopomocy Spolecznej [*Warsaw*] (BJA)
SKSV San Vicente Del Caguan [*Colorado ICAO location identifier*] (ICLI)
SKT Dyad Services Ltd. [*British ICAO designator*] (FAAC)
SKT Sanskrit [*Afrikaans*]
SKT Saskatchewan Trust Co. [*Toronto Stock Exchange symbol*]
SKT Skill Knowledge Tests
SKT Skiptrace (LAIN)
SKT Skirt (MSA)
SKT Skwentna [*Alaska*] [*Seismograph station code, US Geological Survey*] (SEIS)
SKT Socket (MSA)
SKT Specialty Knowledge Test [*Military*] (AFM)
SKT Storekeeper, Technical [*Navy rating*]
SKT Tanger Factory Outlet Centers, Inc. [*NYSE symbol*] (SPSG)
SKT Tanger Factory Outlet Ctrs [*NYSE symbol*] (TTSB)
SKTA Shetland Knitwear Trades Association [*British*] (DBA)
SKTD Trinidad [*Colorado ICAO location identifier*] (ICLI)
SKTF Spring Knife Trade Federation [*A union*] [*British*]
SKTM Tame [*Colorado ICAO location identifier*] (ICLI)
SKTPrA Tanger Fac Outlt Cv Dep Pfd [*NYSE symbol*] (TTSB)
sk tr Skeletal Traction [*Orthopedics*] (DAVI)
SKTU Turbo, Gonzalo Mejia [*Colorado ICAO location identifier*] (ICLI)
SKTV Silver King Communic [*NASDAQ symbol*] (TTSB)
SKTV Silver King Communications [*NASDAQ symbol*] (SAG)
sk tx Skeletal Traction [*Orthopedics*] (DAVI)
SKU Newburgh, NY [*Location identifier FAA*] (FAAL)
SKU Sakura [*Japan*] [*Seismograph station code, US Geological Survey Closed*] (SEIS)
SKU Stock Keeping Unit [*Merchandising system*]
SKUC Arauca/Santiago Perez [*Colorado ICAO location identifier*] (ICLI)
SKUI Quibdo/El Carano [*Colorado ICAO location identifier*] (ICLI)
SKUL Seeker-Killer-Utility Lasers (DOMA)
SKV Santa Katarina [*Egypt*] [*Airport symbol*] (OAG)
SKV Skewing the Pitch Angle
SKV Skukum Gold [*Vancouver Stock Exchange symbol*]
SKV Storekeeper, Aviation [*Navy rating*]
SKVP Valledupar/Alfonso Lopez [*Colorado ICAO location identifier*] (ICLI)
SKVV Schweizerischer Katholischer Volksverein
SKVV Villavicencio/Vanguardia [*Colorado ICAO location identifier*] (ICLI)
SKW Shichikawa [*Japan*] [*Seismograph station code, US Geological Survey*] (SEIS)
SKW Skwentna, AK [*Location identifier FAA*] (FAAL)
SKW Sky West, Inc. [*ICAO designator*] (FAAC)
SKW Sturge-Kalische-Weber [*Syndrome*] [*or Sturge-Weber Syndrome*] [*Medicine*] (DAVI)
SKW Sueddeutsche Kalkstickstoffwerke [*AG*]
SKW Syndicate of North Germany Electric Utilities [*Germany*] [*Acronym is based on foreign phrase*]
SKWOC Structured Keyword Out of Context (NITA)
SKWY Skyway
SKWY Skyway [*Postal Service standard*] (OPSA)
SKX Skyline Explorations Ltd. [*Vancouver Stock Exchange symbol Toronto Stock Exchange symbol*]
SKX Skyways AB [*Sweden ICAO designator*] (FAAC)
SKX Taos, NM [*Location identifier FAA*] (FAAL)
SKY Cooper Skybird Air Charters Ltd. [*Kenya*] [*ICAO designator*] (FAAC)
SKY Sandusky, OH [*Location identifier FAA*] (FAAL)
SKY Skyline Corp. [*NYSE symbol*] (SPSG)
SKY Skyrocket Exploration [*Vancouver Stock Exchange symbol*]
SKYBET Skylab Best Estimate of Trajectory [*NASA*]
SKYC American Mobile Satellite Corp. [*NASDAQ symbol*] (SAG)
SKYC Amer Mobile Satellite [*NASDAQ symbol*] (TTSB)
SKYCAV Sky Cavalry
SkyChili Skyline Chili, Inc. [*Associated Press*] (SAG)
SKYCOM Skylab Communications Engineer [*NASA*]
SKYFC Sky Games International Ltd. [*NASDAQ symbol*] (SAG)
SKYG Sky Games International Ltd. [*NASDAQ symbol*] (SAG)
SKYGF Sky Games Intl [*NASDAQ symbol*] (TTSB)
SkyGms Sky Games International, Ltd. [*Associated Press*] (SAG)
SKYL Skyline Multimedia Entertainment [*NASDAQ symbol*] (SAG)
SKYL Skyline Multimedia Entmt [*NASDAQ symbol*] (TTSB)
SkylandP Skylands Park Management [*Associated Press*] (SAG)
SkylCBk Skylands Community Bank [*Associated Press*] (SAG)
Skyline Skyline Corp. [*Associated Press*] (SAG)
Skylnd Skylands Park Management [*Associated Press*] (SAG)
SKYLW Skyline Multimeida Entmt Wrrt'A' [*NASDAQ symbol*] (TTSB)
SKYLZ Skyline Multimedia Entmt Wrrt'B' [*NASDAQ symbol*] (TTSB)
SkyM Skyline Multimedia Entertainment [*Associated Press*] (SAG)
SKYM SkyMall, Inc. [*NASDAQ symbol*] (SAG)
SkyMall SkyMall, Inc. [*Associated Press*] (SAG)
SkyMl Skyline Multimedia Entertainment [*Associated Press*] (SAG)
SkyMult Skyline Multimedia Entertainment [*Associated Press*] (SAG)
SKYP Skylands Park Management [*NASDAQ symbol*] (SAG)
SKYP Skylands Park Mgmt [*NASDAQ symbol*] (TTSB)
SKYP Suomen Kansan Yhtenaeisyyden Puolue [*People's Unity Party*] [*Finland Political party*] (PPW)
SKYP Yopal/Yopal [*Colorado ICAO location identifier*] (ICLI)
SKYPW Skylands Pk Mgmt Wrrt [*NASDAQ symbol*] (TTSB)
SKYS Sky Scientific [*NASDAQ symbol*] (TTSB)
Skysat Skysat Communications Network Corp. [*Associated Press*] (SAG)
SkysatC Skysat Communications Network Corp. [*Associated Press*] (SAG)
skyscr Skyscraper (VRA)
Skyst Skysat Communications Network Corp. [*Associated Press*] (SAG)
SKYW SkyWest, Inc. [*St. George, UT*] [*NASDAQ symbol*] (NQ)
SKYWAY Skyway [*Commonly used*] (OPSA)
SkyWest SkyWest, Inc. [*Associated Press*] (SAG)
SKZ Sukkur [*Pakistan*] [*Airport symbol*] (OAG)
SL Large-Scale Disturbance Field
SL Lloydminster Public Library, Saskatchewan [*Library symbol National Library of Canada*] (NLC)
SL Rio-Sul [*ICAO designator*] (AD)
SL Safe Locker (AAG)
SL Safety Level [*Army*]
SL Safety Limit [*Nuclear energy*] (NRCH)
SL Sales Letter
SL Salt Loading
SL Salvage Loss
SL Sample Laboratory (MCD)
SL Sand-Loaded [*Technical drawings*]
SL San Luis Obispo [*Mexican state; city and county in California*]
SL Satellite-Like Virus
SL Saturated Logic (IAA)
SL Save Lebanon (EA)
sl Scale Leaf [*Botany*]
SL Scanning Slit (MCD)
SL School Leavers [*Department of Employment*] [*British*]
SL Schutte Lanz [*World War I German aircraft designation*]
SL Scientists for Life [*An association Defunct*] (EA)
SL Sclerosing Leukoencephalopathy [*Medicine*] (DMAA)
SL Scottish Liturgy [*Episcopalian*]
SL Scout Leader (WDAA)
SL Seal (NASA)
SL Sea Level
SL Searchlight
SL Second Lieutenant
SL Section Leader [*Nuclear energy*] (NRCH)
SL Section List (MCD)
SL Secundum Legem [*According to Law*] [*Latin*]
SL Security List (WDAA)
SL Seditious Libeler
SL Sendero Luminoso [*Shining Path*] [*Peru*] (PD)
SL Send Leg [*Telegraphy*] (TEL)
SL Sensation Level [*Audiometry*]
SL Sensu Lato [*In a Broad Sense*] [*Latin*]
SL Separate Lead [*Cables*]
SL Sergeant-at-Law
SL Serious List [*Hospital administration*] (DAVI)
S-L Serosa to Lumen [*Anatomy*] (DAVI)
SL Service Letter (MCD)
SL Servomechanisms Laboratory [*MIT*] (MCD)
SL Session Laws (DLA)
SL Shear Layer [*or Load*]
SL Shelf Life (NASA)
SL Shelf List [*A card catalog arranged in call number order*]
SL Shift Left
S/L Shiplap (DAC)
SL Ship Library [*Maritime Data Network, Inc.*] [*Information service or system*] (CRD)
SL Ship-of-the-Line
SL Shipowner's Liability [*Business term*]
S/L Shops and Labs [*NASA*] (NASA)
SL Short Landed [*Tea trade*] (ROG)
SL Short Lengths [*Construction*]
SL Short Letter (DCTA)
S-L Short-Long [*as of a signal light's flash cycle*]
SL Sibley-Lehninger [*Unit*] (MAE)
SL Sick Leave (AFM)
S/L Side Lay [*Printing machine*] (DGA)
S/L Sidelever [*Rifles*] (DICI)
SL Side Load (AAG)
SL Sidelobe (CAAL)
sl Sierra Leone [*MARC country of publication code Library of Congress*] (LCCP)
SL Sierra Leone [*ANSI two-letter standard code*] (CNC)

SL Sigillo Locus [*Place for the Seal*] [*Latin*] (ROG)
SL Signal Level
SL Significance Level
SL Silicon Lacquer
SL Silvaire [*ICAO aircraft manufacturer identifier*] (ICAO)
SL Silver Library [*A publication*]
SL Simulation Language [*Computer science*] (BUR)
SL Sinding Larsen [*disease*] [*or Larsen's disease, or Larsen-Johansson disease*] [*An association known as Larsen's Disease, or Larsen-Johansson Disease*] [*Orthopedics*] (DAVI)
SL Sine Loco [*Without Place*] [*Latin*]
SL Single Lead [*Cables*] (IAA)
SL Single Ledger [*Accounting*]
SL Single Line
SL Single-Locus [*Light flashes*]
SL Sisters of Loretto at the Foot of the Cross [*Roman Catholic religious order*]
SL Sjogren-Larsson [*Syndrome*] [*Medicine*] (DAVI)
SL Skilled Labor (MHDW)
SL Skill Level
SL Skylab [*NASA*] (KSC)
SL Slain (ROG)
SL Slate (AAG)
SL Sleeve [*Technical drawings*]
SL Slesvigske Parti [*Schleswig Party*] [*Denmark Political party*] (PPE)
SL Slide (AAG)
SL Slightly
sl Slightly (WDMC)
SL SL Industries [*NYSE symbol*] (TTSB)
SL SL Industries, Inc. [*NYSE symbol*] (SPSG)
SL Slip [*Knitting*]
SL Slit Lamp [*Instrumentation*]
SL Slough [*Postcode*] (ODBW)
SL Slovenia [*International civil aircraft marking*] (ODBW)
SL Slow [*Track condition*] [*Thoroughbred racing*]
SL Small Light Seeds [*Botany*]
SL Small Lymphocytes [*Hematology*]
SL Small Lymphoma [*Oncology*]
SL Societas Liturgica (EA)
SL Society of Limerents (EA)
SL Sockellafette [*Pedestal mount*] [*German military - World War II*]
SL Sodium Lactate (MAE)
SL Soft Landing (MCD)
SL Soft LASER
SL Solar Lobby [*An association*] (EA)
SL Sold
SL Solicitor-at-Law
SL Solidified Liquid (MAE)
SL Solid Logic (IAA)
SL Somatolactin [*Biochemistry*]
SL Sonic Log
SL Sonoluminescence [*Physics*]
SL Sons of Liberty (EA)
SL Sortie Lab [*NASA*]
SL Sound Level (NASA)
SL Sound Locator [*Military*]
SL Source Language [*Computer science*] (BUR)
SL Source Level
SL Source Library (IAA)
SL Southeast Airlines, Inc. [*ICAO designator Obsolete*] (OAG)
SL South Latitude
SL Spacelab [*NASA*] (NASA)
S/L Space Laboratory (KSC)
SL Spartacist League (EA)
SL Special Layout (MCD)
SL Special Libraries [*A publication*] (BRI)
SL Special Linear [*Group theory, mathematics*]
S/L Speedletter
SL Speed Lock [*Computer science*] (PCM)
SL Split Level [*Home*] [*Classified advertising*]
SL Spool
SL Sport Leicht [*Sports Lightweight (Car)*] [*German*]
SL Sprinkler Leakage [*Insurance*]
SL Squadron-Leader [*Military*]
SL Stage Left [*A stage direction*]
SL Stagnation Line
SL Standard Label [*Computer science*]
SL Standard Length
SL Standard Load [*Automotive engineering*]
SL Standard Location [*Civil Defense*]
SL Standard of Living
SL Star Line
SL Start Line
SL Stationary Low-Power [*Reactor*] [*Dismantled*] (NRCH)
SL Statistical List
S/L Statute of Limitations (OICC)
SL Stern Loading
SL Stock Length [*Construction or manufacturing materials*]
SL Stock Level (AFM)
SL Stock List (MCD)
SL Stomodeal Lip [*Endocrinology*]
SL Stoplamp [*Automotive engineering*]
SL Storage Location
SL Straight Line
SL Streamline
SL Streptolysin [*Hematology*]
SL Stronnictwo Ludowe [*Peasant Party*] [*Poland Political party*] (PPE)
SL Structures Laboratory [*Army*] (GRD)
SL Student Load
SL Studio Location
SL Suberin Lamella [*Botany*]
SL Sub-Lieutenant [*British military*]
SL Sublingual [*Medicine*]
SL Submarine Lightwave Cable [*AT & T*] [*Telecommunications*]
SL Submarine Qualification Lapsed [*Navy*]
SL Subscriber's Loop [*Telecommunications*] (TEL)
S:L Sucrase to Lactase Ratio (DAVI)
SL Sue and Labor Charges [*Insurance*]
SL Sumerian Laws (BJA)
SL Summary Language (NITA)
SL Sunday League (EA)
sl Suo Loco [*In Its Place*] [*Latin*] (WGA)
SL Superlattice [*Solid state physics*]
SL Superluminal [*Galaxy*]
SL Supplementary List [*Navy British*]
SL Supplier Letter (MCD)
SL Support Line [*Military*]
SL Surface Launch (MUGU)
SL Surveillance Licence [*Importing*] [*British*] (DS)
SL Sydney & Louisburg Railway Co. [*AAR code*]
SL Symmetrizing Line (IAA)
SL Synchronous Line Medium Speed (BUR)
SL Syria and Lebanon
SL System Language
S-L 9 Shoemaker-Levy 9 [*Comet or asteroid that crashed into Jupiter in 1994*]
SLA American Select Portfolio [*NYSE symbol*] (SPSG)
SLA La Ronge Public Library, Saskatchewan [*Library symbol National Library of Canada*] (NLC)
SLA Left Sacroanterior Position [*of the fetus*] [*Obstetrics*]
SLA Sacrolaeva Anterior [*A fetal position*] (AAMN)
SLA Salta [*Argentina*] [*Airport symbol*] (OAG)
SLA Sandia Laboratories, Albuquerque (AABC)
SLA San Lorenzo [*Argentina*] [*Seismograph station code, US Geological Survey*] (SEIS)
SLA Saturn LM [*Lunar Module*] Adapter [*NASA*]
SLA Scanning LASER Altimeter (SSD)
SLA School Leaving Age (AIE)
SLA School Lecturers' Association [*British*]
SLA School Library Association
SLA Scottish Library Association
SLA Scott Library [*A publication*]
SLA Sealed Lead Acid [*Battery*] [*Automotive engineering*]
SLA Second Language Acquisition
SLA Security Lock Association [*British*] (DBA)
SLA Sequential Launch Adapter [*Missiles*] (RDA)
SLA Shared Line Adapter
SLA Short and Long Arm [*Automotive engineering*]
SLA Showmen's League of America (EA)
SLA Side-Looking LASER Altimeter (RDA)
SLA Sierra Leone Airlines
SLA Sierra National Airlines [*Sierra Leone*] [*ICAO designator*] (FAAC)
SLA Single-Line Approach
sla Slate (VRA)
sla Slavic [*MARC language code Library of Congress*] (LCCP)
SLA Sleep-Learning Association (EA)
SLA Slide Latex Agglutination [*Clinical chemistry*] (AAMN)
SLA Slovak League of America (EA)
SLA Small Landlord's Association [*British*] (DBA)
SLA Society for Linguistic Anthropology (EA)
SLA Soluble Leishmania Antigen [*Immuno chemistry*]
SLA Southeastern Library Association (AEBS)
SLA South Lebanon Army
SLA Southwestern Library Association (AEBS)
SLA Spacecraft LM [*Lunar Module*] Adapter [*NASA*]
SLA Special Libraries Association (EA)
SLA Specific Leaf Area [*Botany*]
SLA Sports Lawyers Association (EA)
SLA Square Loop Antenna
SLA Stable Lads' Association [*British*] (ECON)
SLA Standard Life Association (EA)
SLA Standard Location Area [*Civil Defense*]
SLA State Liquor Authority
SLA Statutory Licensing Authority [*Embryology*] [*British*]
SLA Stereolithography [*Desktop manufacturing*]
SLA Stored Logic Array
SLA Strategic Logistics Agency [*Army*] (RDA)
SLA Stripline
SLA Sulfur-Lead Analyzer
SLA Supplies in Liberated Areas [*British World War II*]
SLA Supply Loading Airfield
SLA Support and Logistics Areas [*NASA*] (MCD)
SLA Switching Linear Amplifier
SLA Symbionese Liberation Army [*Defunct*] (EA)
SLA Synchronous Line Adapter
SLA-212 Cyclophosphamide, Vincristine, Methotrexate, Daunomycin, and Prednisone Consolidation and Maintenance [*Antineoplastic drug regimen*] (DAVI)
SLAA Sex and Love Addicts Anonymous (EA)
SLAA Society for Latin American Anthropology (EA)

SLAA.......... State and Local Assistance Act
SLAAP.......... St. Louis Army Ammunition Plant
SLAAS.......... Supersonic Low-Altitude Attack Aircraft System (MCD)
SLAB.......... Abopo [*Bolivia*] [*ICAO location identifier*] (ICLI)
SLAB.......... Sage Laboratories, Inc. [*NASDAQ symbol*] (NQ)
SLAB.......... Sage Labs [*NASDAQ symbol*] (TTSB)
SLAB.......... Students for Labeling of Alcoholic Beverages [*Student legal action organization*]
SLABCON.......... Slab Construction
SLAC.......... Scapholunate Advanced Collapse [*Wrist*] [*Medicine*] (DMAA)
SLAC.......... Special Committee on Latin American Coordination
SLAC.......... Stanford Linear Accelerator Center [*Stanford, CA*] [*Department of Energy*]
SLAC.......... Stanford Linear Accelerator Computer [*Stanford University*] [*Department of Energy*] (IAA)
SLAC.......... Stowage Launch Adapter Container
SLAC.......... Straight-Line (Linear) Accelerator [*Nuclear energy*]
SLAC.......... Subscriber Line Audio Processing Circuit [*Telecommunications*] (EECA)
SLAC.......... Subscriber Line Audio Processor Circuit (NITA)
SLAC.......... Support List Allowance Card (MCD)
SLAD.......... Salon Litteraire, Artistique, et Diplomatique
SLAD.......... Shipboard Landing Assist Device
SLAD.......... SONAR Locator, Altimeter, and Depthometer
SLAD.......... System Logic and Algorithm Development
Slade.......... Slade's Reports [*15 Vermont*] [*A publication*] (DLA)
SLADE.......... Society of Lithographic Artists, Designers, and Engineers [*British*]
SLAE.......... Standard Lightweight Avionics Equipment [*Army*] (RDA)
SLAE.......... Supplementary Leak Collection and Release System [*Nuclear energy*] (IAA)
SLAET.......... Society of Licensed Aircraft Engineers and Technologists (EAIO)
SLAFRS.......... Southwestern Livestock and Forage Research Station [*Oklahoma State University*] [*Research center*] (RCD)
SLAG.......... Monteagudo [*Bolivia*] [*ICAO location identifier*] (ICLI)
SLAG.......... Safe Launch Angle Gate
SLAG.......... Scottish Legal Action Group (ILCA)
SLAG.......... Side-Looking Air-to-Ground [*RADAR*]
SLAHF.......... Slovak League of America Heritage Foundation (EA)
SLAHTS.......... Stowage List and Hardware Tracking System [*NASA*] (MCD)
SLAIS.......... School of Library, Archival, and Information Studies [*University of British Columbia, Vancouver*] [*Canada*]
SLAIT.......... Study Group on Legal Aspects of Intermodal Transportation [*National Research Council*]
SLAK.......... Spacelab Late Access Kit [*NASA*] (NASA)
SLAKSJ.......... Supreme Ladies Auxiliary Knights of St. John (EA)
SLAL.......... Stowage Launch Adapter, Lower
SLALOM.......... Scalable, Language-Independent, Ames Laboratory, One-Minute Measurement [*Computer technology*]
SLAM.......... Samuel Lyman Atwood Marshall [*American general and author, 1900-1977*]
SLAM.......... Scanning Interferometric Apertureless Microscope
SLAM.......... Scanning LASER Acoustic Microscope
SLAM.......... Sea-Launched Air Missile (NVT)
SLAM.......... Seeking, Locating, Annihilating, Monitoring [*Army project, Vietnam*]
SLAM.......... Semiconductor Transistor (IAA)
SLAM.......... Short LOFAR [*Low-Frequency Acquisition and Ranging*] Alerting Message (NVT)
SLAM.......... Shoulder-Launched Antitank Missile [*Army*]
SLAM.......... Side Load Arresting Mechanism (KSC)
SLAM.......... Sierra Leone Alliance Movement (PD)
SLAM.......... Simulation Language for Alternative Modeling [*Computer science*] (CSR)
SLAM.......... Single Layer Metallization (IAA)
SLAM.......... Society's League Against Molestation (EA)
SLAM.......... Space-Launched Air Missile (MCD)
SLAM.......... Spares Level Activity Model (MCD)
SLAM.......... Standoff Land Attack Missile [*Military*]
SLAM.......... Stored Logic Adaptable Metal Oxide (IAA)
SLAM.......... Stowage Launch Adapter, Middle
SLAM.......... Strategic Low Attitude Missile
SLAM.......... Stress Wave in Layered Arbitrary Media (SAA)
SLAM.......... Submarine-Launched Air Missile
SLAM.......... Suburban Lodges America [*NASDAQ symbol*] (TTSB)
SLAM.......... Suburban Lodges of America, Inc. [*NASDAQ symbol*] (SAG)
SLAM.......... Supersonic Low-Altitude Missile [*Later, LASV*] [*NATO*] (NATG)
SLAM.......... Support List Allowance Master
SLAM.......... Surface-Launched Air Missile
SLAM.......... Surface Look-Alike Mine
SLAM.......... Symbolic Language Adapted for Microcomputers
SLAM.......... Systemic Lupus Erythematosus Activity Measure [*Medicine*] (DMAA)
SLAMEX.......... Submarine-Launched Assault Missile Exercise (NVT)
SLAMMR.......... Side Looking Modular Multi-Mission RADAR (PDAA)
SLAMMR.......... Sideways-Looking Airborne Multi-Mode Radar (DOMA)
SLAMS.......... Simplified Language for Abstract Mathematical Structures [*Computer science*] (IEEE)
SLAMS.......... State and Local Air Monitoring Stations [*Environmental Protection Agency*]
SLAMS.......... Successive Linear Approximation at Minimum Step (SAA)
SLAMS.......... Surface Look-Alike Mine System (MCD)
SLAN.......... Angora [*Bolivia*] [*ICAO location identifier*] (ICLI)
SLAN.......... Shock Landing Analysis (MCD)
SLAN.......... Sine Loco, Anno, vel Nomine [*Without Place, Year, or Name*] [*Latin*]
SLAN.......... Slander [*or Slanderous*] [*FBI standardized term*]
SL & A.......... Sine Loco et Anno [*Without Place and Year*] [*Latin*]
SL & C.......... Shipper's Load and Count [*Bills of lading*]
SL & I.......... System Load and Initialization [*NASA*] (NASA)
SL & R.......... Shop Order Load Analysis and Reporting [*IBM Corp.*]
SL & T.......... Shipper's Load and Tally [*Bills of lading*]
SLANG.......... Selected Letter and Abbreviated Name Guide [*Environmental Protection Agency A publication*] (GFGA)
SLANG.......... Systems Language
SLANT.......... Simulator Landing Attachment for Night Landing Training
SLAO.......... Committee on Supply Questions in Liberated Areas (Official) [*World War II*]
SLAP.......... Apolo [*Bolivia*] [*ICAO location identifier*] (ICLI)
SLAP.......... Office of State and Local Assistance Programs [*Department of Energy*]
SLAP.......... Saboted Light Armor Penetrator [*Weaponry*] (MCD)
SLAP.......... Sandia-Livermore Aeroheating Program
SLAP.......... Serum Leucine Aminopeptidase [*An enzyme*] (MAE)
SLAP.......... Service Life Assessment Program [*Military*]
S/LAP.......... Shiplap (DAC)
SLAP.......... Simplified Labor and Performance (MCD)
SLAP.......... Slot Allocation Procedure [*Aviation*] (DA)
SLAP.......... Subscriber Line Access Protocol (IAA)
SLAP.......... Symbolic Language Assembly Program [*Computer science*] (KSC)
SLAPN.......... Succinyl-L-alanyl-L-alanyl-L-alanine-p-nitroanilide [*Biochemistry*]
SLAPP.......... Strategic Lawsuit Against Public Participation [*Term coined by George Pring and Penelope Canan*]
SLAPS.......... Serious Literary, Artistic, Political, or Scientific Value [*Obscenity law*] (NTCM)
SLAPS.......... Subscriber Loop Analysis Program System [*Bell System*]
SLAQ.......... Aiquile [*Bolivia*] [*ICAO location identifier*] (ICLI)
SLAR.......... Select ADC [*Analog-to-Digital Converter*] Register [*Computer science*] (MDG)
SLAR.......... Senior Logistics Aviation Representative (MCD)
SLAR.......... Side-Looking Aerial [*or Airborne*] RADAR [*Military*]
SLAR.......... Side-Looking Airborne Radar [*Marine science*] (OSRA)
SLAR.......... Slant Range
SLAR.......... Slargando [*Slackening*] [*Music*] (ROG)
SLAR.......... Steerable LASER Radiometer (MCD)
SLARF.......... Slant Range Fuze (NG)
SLARG.......... Slargando [*Slackening*] [*Music*]
SLA/RP.......... Stereolithography / Rapid Prototyping [*Design*] (RDA)
SLAS.......... Ascencion De Guarayos [*Bolivia*] [*ICAO location identifier*] (ICLI)
SLAS.......... Society for Latin American Studies [*British*]
SLAS.......... State Library Agency Section [*Association of Specialized and Cooperative Library Agencies*]
SLASC.......... St. Louis Area Support Center [*Military*] (MCD)
SLASER.......... Space LASER (SSD)
SLASH.......... Second Edition List of Australian Subject Headings [*A publication*]
SLASH.......... Seiler Laboratory ALGOL Simulated Hybrid [*Computer science*]
SLASH.......... Small Light Antisubmarine Helicopter
SLAST.......... Submarine-Launched Antiship Torpedo
SLAT.......... Sample Lot Acceptance Testing
s lat.......... Sensu Lato [*In a Wide Sense*] [*Latin*]
SLAT.......... Ship-Launched Air Targeting (MCD)
SLAT.......... Simultaneous Laryngoscopy and Abdominal Thrusts [*Medicine*] (DMAA)
SLAT.......... Sindacato Lavoratori Amministrativi e Technichi [*Union of Administration and Technical Workers*] [*Somalia*]
SLAT.......... South Latitude
SLAT.......... Special Logistics Actions, Thailand (AABC)
SLAT.......... Strike Leader Attack Training [*Navy*] (DOMA)
SLAT.......... Supersonic Low Activities Target (MCD)
SLAT.......... Supersonic Low-Altitude Target [*Navy*]
SLAT.......... Support List Allowance Tape (MCD)
SLAT.......... Surface Launcher Air-Targeted [*Weapon*] (MCD)
SLATE.......... Ship-Launched ASW [*Antisubmarine Warfare*] Two-Way Expendable [*Buoy*] [*Navy*] (CAAL)
SLATE.......... Small, Lightweight Altitude-Transmission Equipment [*FAA*]
SLATE.......... Stimulated Learning by Automated Typewriter Environment
SLATO.......... Secretariado Latinamericano de Trotskismo Orthodoxo [*Peru*]
SLATS.......... Strike Leader Attack Training School [*Navy*] (DOMA)
SLAU.......... San Aurelio [*Bolivia*] [*ICAO location identifier*] (ICLI)
SLAU.......... Stowage Launch Adapter, Upper
SLAUGH.......... Slaughter [*England*]
SLAV.......... Avicaya [*Bolivia*] [*ICAO location identifier*] (ICLI)
SLAV.......... Slavonic [*Language, etc.*]
SLAV.......... Special Logistics Actions, South Vietnam (CINC)
SLAVCA.......... Sindacato Nazionale Lavoratori Vetro e Ceramica [*National Union of Glass and Ceramics' Workers*] [*Italy*]
SlavEnoch.......... Slavic Book of Enoch (BJA)
Slav R.......... Slavic Review [*A publication*] (BRI)
SLAW.......... Conference on the Sociology of the Languages of American Women [*1976*]
SLAW.......... St. Lawrence Railroad [*Division of National Railway Utilization Corp.*] [*AAR code*]
SLAX.......... Ay-Luri [*Bolivia*] [*ICAO location identifier*] (ICLI)
SLB.......... Schlumberger Ltd. [*NYSE symbol*] (SPSG)
SLB.......... Self-Lubricating Bearing
SLB.......... Short Leg Brace [*Medicine*]
SLB.......... Side-Lobe Blanking [*RADAR*]
SLB.......... Signal Light Bare (MSA)
SLB.......... Sintered Lead Bronze
SLB.......... Solomon Islands [*ANSI three-letter standard code*] (CNC)
SLB.......... Steam Line Break (NRCH)
SLB.......... St. Louis Blueliners (EA)
SLB.......... Storm Lake, IA [*Location identifier FAA*] (FAAL)
SLB.......... Superannuation Law Bulletin [*A publication*]

SLBC........ Boca Chapare [*Bolivia*] [*ICAO location identifier*] (ICLI)
SLBD........ Sea Lite Beam Director [*Navy*] (DOMA)
SLBF........ Blanca Flor [*Bolivia*] [*ICAO location identifier*] (ICLI)
SLBH........ Buena Hora [*Bolivia*] [*ICAO location identifier*] (ICLI)
SLBI........ Sidelobe Blanking Indicator
SLBJ........ Bermejo [*Bolivia*] [*ICAO location identifier*] (ICLI)
SLBL........ Soluble (MSA)
SLBM........ Sea [*or Submarine or Surface*]-Launched Ballistic Missile [*Navy*] (CAAL)
SLBM........ Space-Launched Ballistic Missile (IAA)
SLBMD & W... Sea-Launched Ballistic Missile Detection and Warning
SLBMDWS... Submarine-Launched Ballistic Missile Detection and Warning System (IEEE)
SLBMW........ Submarine-Launched Ballistic Missile Warning (IAA)
SLBN........ Bella Union [*Bolivia*] [*ICAO location identifier*] (ICLI)
SLBP........ Spring-Loaded Ball Plunger
SLBS........ Sierra Leone Broadcasting Service
SLBtry........ Searchlight Battery [*Army*]
SLBU........ Baures [*Bolivia*] [*ICAO location identifier*] (ICLI)
SLBV........ Villa Vista [*Bolivia*] [*ICAO location identifier*] (ICLI)
SLBW........ Buena Vista [*Bolivia*] [*ICAO location identifier*] (ICLI)
SLBY........ Boyuibe [*Bolivia*] [*ICAO location identifier*] (ICLI)
SLC........ Salt Lake City [*Utah*] [*Seismograph station code, US Geological Survey*] (SEIS)
SLC........ Salt Lake City [*Utah*] [*Airport symbol*] (OAG)
SLC........ Salt Lake City, UT [*Location identifier FAA*] (FAAL)
SLC........ [*The*] San Luis Central Railroad Co. [*AAR code*]
SLC........ Sarah Lawrence College [*Bronxville, NY*]
SLC........ Satellite LASER Communication [*Military*]
SLC........ Schoool Leaving Certificate [*British*] (BARN)
SLC........ Scottish Land Court Reports [*A publication*] (DLA)
SLC........ Scottish Leaving Certificate
SLC........ Sea-Level Canal Study (IID)
SLC........ Searchlight Control [*Military*]
SLC........ Secretarial Language Certificate [*British*] (DI)
SLC........ Selector (NITA)
SLC........ Selector Channel
SLC........ Set Location Counter (CMD)
SLC........ Shelf Life Code (MCD)
SLC........ Shift Left and Count Instructions [*Computer science*] (MDG)
SLC........ Short Leg Cast [*Medicine*] (MEDA)
SLC........ Short-Leg Cast [*Orthopedics*] (DAVI)
SLC........ Shuttle Launch Center [*Vandenberg Air Force Base, CA*] [*NASA*]
SLC........ Side-Lobe Cancellation [*RADAR*]
SLC........ Side-Lobe Clutter
SLC........ Signal Level Converter (DWSG)
SLC........ Simulataneous-Lobe Comparison [*RADAR*] (IAA)
SLC........ Simulated Linguistic Computer
SLC........ Single Launch Contractor (KSC)
SLC........ Single Lead Covered (IAA)
SLC........ Single Line Control (BUR)
SLC........ Single-Loop Controller (ACII)
SLC........ Slice (MSA)
SLC........ Slicer (IAA)
SLC........ Small Library Computing, Inc. [*Information service or system*] (IID)
SLC........ Smith's Leading Cases [*A publication*] (DLA)
SLC........ Society of Antique Label Collectors (EA)
SLC........ Songwriters and Lyricists Club (EA)
SLC........ Sonobuoy Launch Container (NVT)
SLC........ South London College [*London, England*]
SLC........ Southwestern Life Corp. [*Formerly, ICH Corp.*] [*AMEX symbol*] (SAG)
SLC........ Space Launch Complex [*NASA*]
SLC........ Spanish Literature Committee (EA)
SLC........ Special Libraries Cataloguing, Inc. [*Information service or system*] (IID)
SLC........ Specific-Line Capacitance [*or Capacity*] (IAA)
SLC........ Sport Leicht Coupe [*Sports Lightweight Coupe*] [*German*]
SLC........ Standard Launch Complex (KSC)
SLC........ Standard Location Codes
SLC........ Standby Liquid Control [*Nuclear energy*] (NRCH)
SLC........ Standing Liaison Committee
SLC........ Stanford Linear Collider [*High-energy physics*]
SLC........ State Legislative Committee
SLC........ State Library of Ohio, Catalog Center, Columbus, OH [*OCLC symbol*] (OCLC)
SLC........ Stockage List Code [*Military*] (AABC)
SLC........ Stock Ledger Control
SLC........ Straight-Line Capacitance [*or Capacity*]
SLC........ Straight-Line Capacitor (IAA)
SLC........ Strategic LASER Communications [*Military*] (CAAL)
SLC........ Stuart's Lower Canada Appeal Cases [*1810-35*] [*A publication*] (DLA)
SLC........ Sublingual Cleft [*Medicine*]
SLC........ Submarine LASER Communications
SLC........ Subscriber Line Circuit [*Telecommunications*] (IAA)
SLC........ Subscriber Loop Carrier [*Telecommunications*] (TEL)
SLC........ Sue and Labor Clause [*Business term*]
SLC........ Surgeon Lieutenant-Commander [*British military*]
SLC........ Susquehanna Library Cooperative [*Library network*]
SLC........ Sustained Load Crack [*Titanium alloy*]
SLC........ Swiftlines Ltd. [*Kenya*] [*ICAO designator*] (FAAC)
SLC........ Synchro Loop Closure
SLC........ Synchronous Line Medium Speed with Clock (BUR)
SLC........ Synchronous Link Control [*Computer science*]
SLC........ System Life Cycle
SLCA........ Camiri [*Bolivia*] [*ICAO location identifier*] (ICLI)
SLC App...... Stuart's Lower Canada Appeal Cases [*A publication*] (DLA)
SLCB........ Cochabamba/Jorge Wilsterman [*Bolivia*] [*ICAO location identifier*] (ICLI)
SLCB........ Single-Line Color Bar (IEEE)
SLCBMA...... Solid Leather Case and Bag Makers' Association [*A union*] [*British*]
SLCC........ Copacabana [*Bolivia*] [*ICAO location identifier*] (ICLI)
SLCC........ Lincoln Cent Collectors Society (EA)
SLCC........ Saturn Launch Control Computer [*NASA*] (KSC)
SLCC........ Saturn Launcher Computer Complex (IAA)
SLCC........ Society of Local Council Clerks [*British*]
SLCC........ Soft Launch Control Center (IAA)
SLCC........ Store Level Communications Controller (MHDI)
SLCD........ Surplus Land for Community Development
SLCG........ Charagua [*Bolivia*] [*ICAO location identifier*] (ICLI)
SLCH........ Chapacura [*Bolivia*] [*ICAO location identifier*] (ICLI)
SLCI........ Clara Rios [*Bolivia*] [*ICAO location identifier*] (ICLI)
SLCJ........ Cavinas [*Bolivia*] [*ICAO location identifier*] (ICLI)
SLCL........ Collpani [*Bolivia*] [*ICAO location identifier*] (ICLI)
SLCL........ Shop/Lab Configuration Layout [*NASA*] (MCD)
SLCL........ Sierra Leone Council of Labour
SLCL........ Small Lymphocyte Cell Lymphoma [*Oncology*]
SLCM........ Camiare [*Bolivia*] [*ICAO location identifier*] (ICLI)
SLCM........ Sea-Launched Cruise Missile [*Pronounced "slick-em"*] (AABC)
SLCM........ Ship Life-Cycle Management
SLCM........ Software Life Cycle Management
SLCM........ [*The*] Southland Corp. [*NASDAQ symbol*] (NQ)
SLCM........ Southland Corp. [*NASDAQ symbol*] (TTSB)
SLCM........ Structural Liquid Composite Molding [*Plastics technology*]
SLCM........ Submarine-Launched Cruise Missile (IEEE)
SLCM........ Surface Launch Cruise Missile
SLCMP........ Software Life Cycle Management Plan (DNAB)
SLCN........ Charana [*Bolivia*] [*ICAO location identifier*] (ICLI)
SL Co........ Appendices of Proceedings of the Scottish Land Court [*A publication*] (DLA)
SLCO........ Cobija [*Bolivia*] [*ICAO location identifier*] (ICLI)
SL Co R........ Appendices of Proceedings of the Scottish Land Court [*A publication*] (DLA)
SLCP........ Concepcion [*Bolivia*] [*ICAO location identifier*] (ICLI)
SLCP........ Saturn Launch Computer Program (OA)
SLCP........ Ship's Loading Characteristics Pamphlet [*Navy*] (NVT)
SLCP........ Standing Liaison Committee of Physiotherapists within the EEC [*European Economic Community*] [*See also CPLK*] [*Copenhagen, Denmark*] (EAIO)
SLCQ........ Copaquilla [*Bolivia*] [*ICAO location identifier*] (ICLI)
SLCR........ Comarapa [*Bolivia*] [*ICAO location identifier*] (ICLI)
SLCR........ Scottish Land Court Reports [*A publication*] (DLA)
SLCRM........ Ship Life-Cycle Reference Matrix [*Navy*]
SLCRS........ Supplementary Leak Collection and Release System [*Nuclear energy*] (NRCH)
SLCS........ Cerdas [*Bolivia*] [*ICAO location identifier*] (ICLI)
SLCS........ Standby Liquid Control System [*Nuclear energy*] (NRCH)
SLCSAT........ Submarine LASER Communications Satellite (MCD)
SLCT........ Choreti [*Bolivia*] [*ICAO location identifier*] (ICLI)
SLCT........ Select Software Tools [*NASDAQ symbol*] (SAG)
Slct ADR...... Select Software Tools [*Associated Press*] (SAG)
SlctApp........ Select Appointments Holdings [*Associated Press*] (SAG)
SLCTTS........ Soft-Load Closed Transition Transfer Switch
SLCU........ Standard Landing Craft Unit [*Military*]
SLCU........ Synchronous Line Control Unit
SLCV........ Cavinas [*Bolivia*] [*ICAO location identifier*] (ICLI)
SLCV........ Squash Leaf Curl Virus
SLCY........ Collpa [*Bolivia*] [*ICAO location identifier*] (ICLI)
SLCZ........ Santa Cruz/El Trompillo [*Bolivia*] [*ICAO location identifier*] (ICLI)
SLD........ Sailed
SLD........ San Luis Dam [*California*] [*Seismograph station code, US Geological Survey*] (SEIS)
SLD........ Sea Landing Division [*NATO*]
SLD........ Sealed
SLD........ Secretarial Language Diploma [*British*] (DI)
SLD........ Serum Lactate Dehydrogenase [*Also, SLDH*] [*An enzyme*]
SLD........ Severe Learning Difficulties (AIE)
SLD........ Shelf Life Data [*Army*]
SLD........ Shutdown Logic Diagram [*Nuclear energy*] (NRCH)
SLD........ Simplified Logic Diagram (IAA)
SLD........ Simulated Launch Demonstration [*NASA*] (KSC)
SLD........ Sliac [*Former Czechoslovakia*] [*Airport symbol*] (OAG)
SLD........ Slide
SLD........ Sliding Door (AAG)
SLD........ Slim Line Diffuser (OA)
SLD........ Slowdown (AAG)
SLD........ Slumber Lodge Development Corp. Ltd. [*Vancouver Stock Exchange symbol*]
SLD........ Social and Liberal Democrats [*British Political party*] (ECON)
SLD........ Society of Loyalist Descendants (EA)
SLD........ Sold
SLD........ Solder
SLD........ Solid
SLD........ Solid Logic Dense (BUR)
SLD........ Sonic Layer Depth (NVT)
SLD........ Source Language Debug [*Computer science*] (IEEE)
SLD........ Source-Level Debugger [*Motorola, Inc.*]
SLD........ Special Litigation Division [*Environmental Protection Agency*] (GFGA)
SLD........ Special Low-Dispersion [*Optics*]

SLD............ Specific Language [*or Learning*] Disability [*Education*]
SLD............ Square Law Detection
SLD............ Stiff-Leg Derrick (NASA)
SLD............ Straight Line Depreciation [*Telecommunications*] (TEL)
SLD............ Superluminescent Diode [*Tomography*]
SLD............ Symmetrized Logarithmic Derivative (IAA)
SLD............ Synchronous Line Driver
SLDA............ Solid Logic Design Automation (IAA)
SLDAA............ SACLANT [*Supreme Allied Commander, Atlantic*] Distributing and Accounting Agency (NATG)
SLD CARB DI... Solidified Carbon Dioxide [*Freight*]
SLDD............ Scientific Library and Documentation Division [*National Science and Technology Authority*] [*Philippines*] [*Information service or system*] (IID)
SLDG............ Sliding
SLDH............ Serum Lactate Dehydrogenase [*Also, SLD*] [*An enzyme*]
SLDI............ Sector List Drop Interval [*FAA*] (TAG)
SLDN............ El Desengano [*Bolivia*] [*ICAO location identifier*] (ICLI)
SLDP............ Loma Del Porvenir [*Bolivia*] [*ICAO location identifier*] (ICLI)
SLDP............ Sierra Leone Democratic Party [*Political party*] (EY)
SLDPF............ Spacelab Data Processing Facility (MCD)
SLDR............ Solder (MSA)
SLDR............ Soldier
S/Ldr............ Squadron Leader [*British military*] (DMA)
SLDR............ Sublethal Damage Repair [*Medicine*] (DMAA)
SLDR............ System Loader [*Computer science*]
SLDRAM............ Sync-link DRAM [*Display Random Access Memory*] [*Computer science*]
SLDS............ Scanning LASER Doppler System [*NASA*]
SLDS............ Single-Level Dynamic Scan [*Radiology*] (DAVI)
SLDS............ Skylab Launch Data System [*NASA*] (KSC)
SLDTF............ State and Local Documents Task Force [*Government Documents Round Table*] [*American Library Association*]
SLDTSS............ Single Language Dedicated Time-Sharing System
SLDVS............ Scanning LASER Doppler Vortex System [*NASA*]
SLE............ Salem [*Oregon*] [*Airport symbol*] (OAG)
SLE............ Salem, OR [*Location identifier FAA*] (FAAL)
SLE............ Sara Lee Corp. [*NYSE symbol*] (SPSG)
SLE............ Segment Limits End (NITA)
SLE............ Service Life Evaluation
SLE............ Sierra Leone [*ANSI three-letter standard code*] (CNC)
SLE............ Slit Lamp Examination [*Medicine*] (DMAA)
SLE............ Small Lattice Experiment
SLE............ Small Local Exchange [*Telecommunications*] (TEL)
SLE............ Smith, Leland C., Oakland CA [*STAC*]
SLE............ Snap Lock Environmental [*Electrical engineering*]
SLE............ Societas Linguistica Europaea [*Linguistic Society of Europe*] [*Austria*] (EAIO)
SLE............ Society of Land Economists [*Australia*]
SLE............ Society of Logistics Engineers (MCD)
SLE............ Spacelab Engineering [*European Research National Organization*] (MCD)
SLE............ Sport Luxury Edition [*Automobile classification*]
SLE............ Station Liaison Engineer [*NASA*]
SLE............ St. Louis Encephalitis [*Medicine*]
SLE............ Stochastic Liouville Equation [*Statistical mechanics*]
SLE............ Student Letter Exchange (EA)
SLE............ Studio Lighting Equipment
SLE............ Sulphurets Gold [*Vancouver Stock Exchange symbol*]
SLE............ Superheat Limit Explosion
SLE............ Systemic Lupus Erythematosus [*Medicine*]
SLEA............ Sheep Erythrocyte Antibody [*Medicine*] (DMAA)
SLEAT............ Society of Laundry Engineers and Allied Trades (IAA)
SLEAT............ Society of Licensed Aircraft Engineers and Technologists (DA)
SLEC............ El Cairo [*Bolivia*] [*ICAO location identifier*] (ICLI)
SLED............ El Dorado [*Bolivia*] [*ICAO location identifier*] (ICLI)
SLED............ Single Large Expensive Disk [*Computer science*] (PCM)
SLED............ State Level Electricity Demand [*Model*] [*Nuclear Regulatory Commission*]
SLED............ Surface Light Emitting Diode [*Electronics*]
SLED............ System-Level Engineering Document (SSD)
SledDogs.... Sled Dogs Co. [*Associated Press*] (SAG)
SLEDGE............ Simulating Large Explosive Detonable Gas Experiments
SLEEC............ Shingle Lap Extendable Exit Cone (MCD)
SLEEP............ Scanning Low-Energy Electron Probe (IEEE)
SLEEP............ Silent, Lightweight, Electric Energy Plant (RDA)
SLEEP............ Swedish Low-Energy Experimental Pile [*Nuclear energy*]
SLEF............ El Triunfo [*Bolivia*] [*ICAO location identifier*] (ICLI)
SLEF............ Short-Lived Large Energy Fluctuation [*Physics*]
SLEH............ Stage Loose Equipment Hardware (SAA)
SLEICC............ Statue of Liberty - Ellis Island Centennial Commission (EA)
SLEIF............ Statue of Liberty - Ellis Island Foundation (EA)
SLEJ............ El Jovi [*Bolivia*] [*ICAO location identifier*] (ICLI)
SLEKE............ Sabot-Launched Electric Gun Kinetic Energy [*DoD*]
SLEL............ El Roseda [*Bolivia*] [*ICAO location identifier*] (ICLI)
SLEM............ Solution of Linearized Equations of Motion
SLEMA............ Schiffli Lace and Embroidery Manufacturers Association (EA)
SLEMU............ Spacelab Engineering Model Unit [*NASA*] (MCD)
SLENT............ Slentando [*Slackening*] [*Music*] (ROG)
SLEO............ El Paraiso [*Bolivia*] [*ICAO location identifier*] (ICLI)
SLEP............ El Peru [*Bolivia*] [*ICAO location identifier*] (ICLI)
SLEP............ Secondary Level English Proficiency Test
SLEP............ Second Large ESRO [*European Space Research Organization*] Project
SLEP............ Service Life Extension Program [*Military*] (MCD)
SLEP............ Short Latent Evoked Potential [*Medicine*] (DMAA)
SLEP............ State Line End Point (DNAB)
SLES............ Espiritu [*Bolivia*] [*ICAO location identifier*] (ICLI)
SLES............ Semilinear Erection System (SAA)
sleta............ Sine Loco et Anno [*Without Place and Year*] [*Latin*] (DGA)
SLEU............ Eucaliptos [*Bolivia*] [*ICAO location identifier*] (ICLI)
SLEUTH............ System for Locating Eruptive Underwater Turbidity and Hydrography [*Marine science*] (OSRA)
SLEUTH............ System for Locating Eruptive Underwater Turbidity and Hydrography (USDC)
SLEV............ El Salvador [*Bolivia*] [*ICAO location identifier*] (ICLI)
SLEV............ Salaried Legal Expense Voucher
SLEV............ St. Louis Encephalitis Virus
SLEW............ Standby Local Early Warning and Control Center (PDAA)
SLEW............ Static Load Error Washout
SLEZ............ La Esperanza [*Bolivia*] [*ICAO location identifier*] (ICLI)
SLF............ Saturn Launch Facility [*NASA*]
SLF............ Savings and Loan Foundation [*Later, FSI*] (EA)
SLF............ Scientific Laboratory Facility
SLF............ Scottish Landowners Federation (DBA)
SLF............ Selfcare, Inc. [*AMEX symbol*] (SAG)
SLF............ Shuttle Landing Facility [*NASA*] (MCD)
SLF............ Skandinaviska Lackteknikers Forbund [*Federation of Scandinavian Paint and Varnish Technologists*] [*Sweden*] (EAIO)
SLF............ Society of the Little Flower (EA)
SLF............ South Luzon Force [*Army World War II*]
SLF............ Southwestern Legal Foundation (DLA)
SLF............ Special Landing Forces [*Marine Corps*]
SLF............ Steel Locus Factor [*Genetics*]
SLF............ Straight-Line Frequency
SLF............ Stress Loading Facility [*Fort Huachuca, AZ*] [*United States Army Electronic Proving Ground*] (GRD)
SLF............ Suction Line Filter
SLF............ Sulayel [*Saudi Arabia*] [*Airport symbol*] (AD)
SLF............ Super-Low-Frequency (MCD)
SLF............ System Library File [*Computer science*] (BUR)
SLFA............ Fatima [*Bolivia*] [*ICAO location identifier*] (ICLI)
SLFB............ Solid-Liquid Fluidized Bed [*Chemical engineering*]
SLFC............ Shoreline Financial [*NASDAQ symbol*] (TTSB)
SLFC............ Shoreline Financial Corp. [*NASDAQ symbol*] (NQ)
SLFC............ Sierra Leone Full Court Reports [*A publication*] (DLA)
SLFC............ Steve Long Fan Club [*Defunct*] (EA)
SLFC............ Supervisor of Loan Fund Companies [*New South Wales, Australia*]
SLFC............ Survivable Low-Frequency Communications [*Air Force*]
SLFCLN............ Self-Cleaning [*Engineering*]
SLFCS............ Survivable Low-Frequency Communications System [*Air Force*]
SLFD............ Steam Lava Flow Deflector (MCD)
SLFGEN............ Self-Generating
SLFIA............ Substrate-Labeled Fluorescent Immunoassay
SLFIND............ Self-Indicating
S-LFL............ Short-Long Flashing Light [*Navigation signal*]
SLFLKG............ Self-Locking [*Engineering*]
SLFOEAMTMTS... St. Louis Field Office, Eastern Area, Military Traffic Management and Terminal Service [*Army*] (AABC)
SLFP............ Sri Lanka Freedom Party [*Political party*] (PPW)
SLFSE............ Self-Sealing [*Engineering*]
SLFTPG............ Self-Tapping [*Screw*] [*Design engineering*]
SLFX............ Selfix, Inc. [*NASDAQ symbol*] (CTT)
SLG............ Community of the Sisters of the Love of God [*Anglican religious community*]
SLG............ Lander College, Larry A. Jackson Library, Greenwood, SC [*OCLC symbol*] (OCLC)
SLG............ Sailing (WGA)
SLG............ Saskatchewan Government Air Ambulance Service [*Canada*] [*FAA designator*] (FAAC)
SLG............ Satellite Landing Ground [*British military*] (DMA)
SLG............ Self-Launching Glider
SLG............ Shorthand Typist (Lower Grade) [*British military*] (DMA)
SLG............ Siloam Springs, AK [*Location identifier FAA*] (FAAL)
SLG............ Single Line to Ground (IAA)
SLG............ Sludge (MSA)
SLG............ Slugger [*Percentage*] [*Baseball*]
SLG............ Soda Lime Glass
SLG............ Solid-Liquid-Gas [*Phase diagram line*]
SLG............ Southern Lights [*Vancouver Stock Exchange symbol*]
SLG............ State or Local Government
SLG............ Synchronous Line Group (BUR)
SLGA............ Scottish Ladies Golfing Association (DBA)
SLGB............ Society of Local Government Barristers [*British*] (DLA)
SLGJ............ Guadalajara [*Bolivia*] [*ICAO location identifier*] (ICLI)
SLGM............ Surface-Launched Guided Missile
SLGP............ Student Loan Guaranty Program
SLGR............ Slinger
SLGR............ Small Lightweight GPS [*Global Positioning System*] Receivers [*Army*] (RDA)
SLGRU............ State Local Government Relations Unit [*South Australia*]
SLGW............ Salt Lake, Garfield & Western Railway Co. [*AAR code*]
SLGXT............ Symptom-Limited Graded Exercise Test [*Cardiology*] (DAVI)
SLGY............ Guayaramerin [*Bolivia*] [*ICAO location identifier*] (ICLI)
SLH............ Sociedade Latinoamericana de Hepatologia [*Latin American Society of Hepatology - LASH*] (EAIO)
SLH............ Sola [*Vanuatu*] [*Airport symbol*] (OAG)
SLHA............ Small Luxury Hotel Association (EA)
SLHJ............ Huacaraje [*Bolivia*] [*ICAO location identifier*] (ICLI)
SLHN............ Chane Bedoya [*Bolivia*] [*ICAO location identifier*] (ICLI)

SLHN .... Stearns & Lehman, Inc. [*NASDAQ symbol*] (SAG)
SLHR .... Society for Life History Research (EA)
SLHRP .... Society for Life History Research in Psychopathology [*Later, SLHR*] (EA)
SLHT .... Colquechaca [*Bolivia*] [*ICAO location identifier*] (ICLI)
SLHT .... Spatialight, Inc. [*NASDAQ symbol*] (SAG)
SLHU .... Huachi [*Bolivia*] [*ICAO location identifier*] (ICLI)
SLHY .... Caquiaviri [*Bolivia*] [*ICAO location identifier*] (ICLI)
SLI .... Los Alamitos, CA [*Location identifier FAA*] (FAAL)
SLI .... Seal and Label Institute
SLI .... Sea-Level Indicator (KSC)
SLI .... Servicios Aeroes Litoral SA de CV [*Mexico ICAO designator*] (FAAC)
SLI .... Shelf Life Item [*Military*] (AABC)
SLI .... Shropshire Light Infantry [*British military*] (DMA)
SLI .... Signal Line Isolator
SLI .... Sikh Local Infantry [*British military*] (DMA)
SLI .... Silver Hill Mines [*Vancouver Stock Exchange symbol*]
SLI .... Slick Airways, Inc.
SLI .... Slide Lobe Indicator
SLI .... Society for Louisiana Irises (EA)
SLI .... Somatostatin-Like Immunoreactivity
SLI .... Somerset Light Infantry [*Military unit*] [*British*]
SLI .... Sound Level Indicator
SLI .... Spacelab Integration (MCD)
SLI .... Specific Language Impairment
SLI .... Splenic Localization Index [*Medicine*] (MAE)
SLI .... Starting, Lighting, and Ignition [*Automobile system*]
SLI .... Stations Legers d'Infrastructures [*Light infrastructures*] [*French*]
SLI .... Steam Line Isolation [*Nuclear energy*] (NRCH)
SLI .... St. Lucia [*Seismograph station code, US Geological Survey Closed*] (SEIS)
SLI .... Suppress Length Indication (BUR)
SLI .... Synchronous Line Interface
SLIA .... Spiritual Life Institute of America (EA)
SLIAG .... State Legalization Impact Assistance Grant [*Department of Health and Human Services*]
SLIB .... Source Library [*Computer science*]
SLIB .... Subsystem Library [*Computer science*] (IBMDP)
SLIC .... Coroico [*Bolivia*] [*ICAO location identifier*] (ICLI)
SLIC .... Search of the Library Information Collection [*Search system*]
SLIC .... Selected Listing in Combination (NITA)
SLIC .... Selective Letters [*or Listing*] in Combination
SLIC .... Semiconductor Laser International Corp. [*NASDAQ symbol*] (SAG)
SLIC .... Semiconductor Laser Intl [*NASDAQ symbol*] (TTSB)
SLIC .... Signature Library Intelligence Catalogue
SLIC .... Silent Liquid Integral Cooler (MHDI)
SLIC .... Silicon Language for Integrated Circuit (NITA)
SLIC .... Simulation Linear Integrated Circuit [*Electronics*] (OA)
SLIC .... Subscriber Loop Interface Circuit (NITA)
SLIC .... Subscriber's Line Interface Circuit [*Telecommunications*] (TEL)
SLIC .... System Line Image Composer
SLICB .... Sea-Launched Intercontinental Ballistic Missile (MUGU)
SLICBM .... Sea-Launched Intercontinental Ballistic Missile (SAA)
SLICE .... Source Label Indicating and Coding Equipment
SLICE .... Southwestern Library Interstate Cooperative Endeavor
SLICE .... Students Litigating Against Injurious Can Edges [*Student legal action organization*]
SLICE .... Surrey Library Interactive Circulation Experiment (NITA)
SLICE .... System Life Cycle Estimation
SLICW .... Semiconductor Laser Wrrt [*NASDAQ symbol*] (TTSB)
SLID .... Scanning Light Intensity Device
SLID .... Solid-Liquid Interdiffusion (IAA)
SLID .... Students League for Industrial Democracy [*Later, Students for a Democratic Society*]
SLIDE .... Source Library Image Delivery Expeditor [*Computer science*] (MHDI)
SLIF .... Student Loan Insurance Fund [*Department of Health and Human Services*] (GFGA)
SLIG .... Inglaterra [*Bolivia*] [*ICAO location identifier*] (ICLI)
SLIG .... Sucker, Low-Brow, Idiot, Goodwill-Buster [*Acronym used as word meaning "act of discourtesy or stupid criticism"*] [*World War II*]
SLIGO .... Sand Lake Irish Gatherings Organization
SLIH .... Samaihuate [*Bolivia*] [*ICAO location identifier*] (ICLI)
SLIH .... Second Level Interrupt Handler (CMD)
SLIJ .... Iniguazu [*Bolivia*] [*ICAO location identifier*] (ICLI)
SLIM .... Saint Louis Institute of Music
SLIM .... Side Line Indexing Method [*Spectrometry*]
SLIM .... Simplified Logistics and Improved Maintenance (MCD)
SLIM .... Slewed-Launch Interceptor Missile
SLIM .... Special Language Interpreting Matrix (IAA)
SLIM .... Standards Laboratory Information Manual (NG)
SLIM .... Stock Line Inventory Management (MHDW)
SLIM .... Store Labor and Inventory Management (MHDW)
SLIM .... Submarine-Launched Inertial Missile
SLIMS .... Supply Line Inventory Management System [*Bell System*]
SLIN .... Standard Library Identification Number
SLIN .... Standard Line Item Number [*Army*] (AABC)
SLIN .... Sub-Line Item Number (MCD)
SLIN .... System Line Item Number (MCD)
SL Ind .... SL Industries, Inc. [*Associated Press*] (SAG)
Slink .... Single, Lots of Income, No Kids [*Lifestyle classification*]
SLIP .... Self Leisure Interest Profile
SLIP .... Serial Line Interface Protocol (DMAA)
SLIP .... Serial Line Intermit Protocol
SLIP .... Serial Line Internet Protocol [*Telecommunications*] (PCM)
SLIP .... Single Line Internet Protocol [*Telecommunications*] (DOM)
SLIP .... Skills Level Improvement Program
SLIP .... Symbolic List Processor
SLIP .... Symmetric List Interpretive Program [*Computer science*]
SLIP .... Symmetric List Processor [*FORTRAN extension*]
Slip op .... Slip Opinion (AAGC)
SLIPP .... Second Language Learning in the Primary Classroom (AIE)
Slippery Rock U ... Slippery Rock University of Pennsylvania (GAGS)
SLIPR .... Source Language Input Program
SLIQ .... Special Libraries in Queensland [*Australia A publication*]
SLIR .... Ibori [*Bolivia*] [*ICAO location identifier*] (ICLI)
SLIR .... School of Labor and Industrial Relations [*Michigan State University*] [*Research center*] (RCD)
SLIRBM .... Sea-Launched Intermediate-Range Ballistic Missile (MUGU)
SLIS .... Shared Laboratory Information System
SLIS .... Social Legislation Information Service (EA)
SLISP .... Symbolic List Processing (NITA)
SLIT .... Itaguazurenda [*Bolivia*] [*ICAO location identifier*] (ICLI)
SLIT .... Little S Positive [*Laboratory science*] (DAVI)
SLIT .... Serial/Lot Item Tracking (DNAB)
SLIV .... Isla Verde [*Bolivia*] [*ICAO location identifier*] (ICLI)
S Liv .... Southern Living [*A publication*] (BRI)
SLIV .... Steam Line Isolation Valve [*Nuclear energy*] (NRCH)
SLIX .... Ixiamas [*Bolivia*] [*ICAO location identifier*] (ICLI)
SLIZ .... Izozog [*Bolivia*] [*ICAO location identifier*] (ICLI)
SLJ .... Hattiesburg, MS [*Location identifier FAA*] (FAAL)
SLJ .... School Library Journal [*A publication*] (BRI)
SLJ .... Scottish Law Journal [*Edinburgh*] [*A publication*] (DLA)
S/LJ .... Semiconductor/Liquid Junction
SLJ .... Silly Little Job (DSUE)
SLJ .... Straits Law Journal [*1888-92*] [*Malasia*] [*A publication*] (DLA)
SLJD .... El Jordan [*Bolivia*] [*ICAO location identifier*] (ICLI)
SLJE .... San Jose [*Bolivia*] [*ICAO location identifier*] (ICLI)
SLJM .... San Juan De Fribal [*Bolivia*] [*ICAO location identifier*] (ICLI)
SLJN .... San Juan (Estancias) [*Bolivia*] [*ICAO location identifier*] (ICLI)
SLJO .... San Joaquin [*Bolivia*] [*ICAO location identifier*] (ICLI)
SLJR .... Sudan Law Journal and Reports [*A publication*] (DLA)
SLJT .... Santa Juanita [*Bolivia*] [*ICAO location identifier*] (ICLI)
SLJV .... San Javier [*Bolivia*] [*ICAO location identifier*] (ICLI)
SLK .... Kitsaki School/Public Library, La Ronge, Saskatchewan [*Library symbol National Library of Canada*] (BIB)
SLK .... Lake Placid-Saranac Lake [*New York*] [*Airport symbol*] (AD)
SLK .... Saranac Lake [*New York*] [*Airport symbol*] (OAG)
SLK .... Saranac Lake, NY [*Location identifier FAA*] (FAAL)
slk .... Silk (VRA)
SLK .... Silkair (Singapore) Pte Ltd. [*ICAO designator*] (FAAC)
SLK .... Slick (MCD)
SLK .... Superior Limbic Keratoconjunctivitis [*Ophthalmology*]
SLk .... Surface Linking Number [*Genetics*]
SLKC .... Superior Limbic Keratoconjunctivitis [*Ophthalmology*] (MAE)
SLKP .... Supreme Lodge Knights of Pythias (EA)
SLKPEN .... Slack and Penalty
SLKQ .... San Miguel [*Bolivia*] [*ICAO location identifier*] (ICLI)
slksc .... Silkscreen (VRA)
SLKT .... Survivability, Lethality, and Key Technologies (SDI)
SLKY .... Puerto Yuca [*Bolivia*] [*ICAO location identifier*] (ICLI)
SLL .... La Loche Public Library, Saskatchewan [*Library symbol National Library of Canada*] (NLC)
SLL .... Saarland Airlines AG [*Germany ICAO designator*] (FAAC)
SLL .... Salalah [*Oman*] [*Airport symbol*] (OAG)
SLL .... Sandia Laboratories, Livermore (AABC)
SLL .... Sandwell Swan Wooster, Inc. [*Toronto Stock Exchange symbol*]
SLL .... Shelf Life Limit (MCD)
SLL .... Signal Long Lines
SLL .... Small Lymphocytic Lymphoma [*Medicine*] (DMAA)
SLL .... Society for Libertarian Life [*Defunct*] (EA)
SLL .... Station List Publishing Co., St. Louis MO [*STAC*]
SLL .... Sterling Lord Literistic, Inc. [*Literary agency*] [*British*]
SLL .... Stollet [*Sweden*] [*Seismograph station code, US Geological Survey*] (SEIS)
SLL .... Suffolk University, Law Library, Boston, MA [*OCLC symbol*] (OCLC)
SLLA .... La Asunta [*Bolivia*] [*ICAO location identifier*] (ICLI)
SLLC .... La China [*Bolivia*] [*ICAO location identifier*] (ICLI)
SLLE .... La Ele [*Bolivia*] [*ICAO location identifier*] (ICLI)
SLLI .... La India [*Bolivia*] [*ICAO location identifier*] (ICLI)
SLLJ .... Laja [*Bolivia*] [*ICAO location identifier*] (ICLI)
SLLL .... Laguna Loa [*Bolivia*] [*ICAO location identifier*] (ICLI)
SLLL .... Synchronous Line, Low, Load (BUR)
SLLP .... La Paz/Kennedy Internacional [*Bolivia*] [*ICAO location identifier*] (ICLI)
SLLR .... Sierra Leone Law Recorder [*A publication*] (DLA)
SLLS .... Snap Lock Limit Switch
SLLS .... Solid-State LASER Light Source
SLLT .... Los Tajibos [*Bolivia*] [*ICAO location identifier*] (ICLI)
SLLU .... San Lorenzo [*Cordillera*] [*ICAO location identifier*] (ICLI)
SLLV .... La Selva [*Bolivia*] [*ICAO location identifier*] (ICLI)
SLLZ .... San Lorenzo [*Bolivia*] [*ICAO location identifier*] (ICLI)
SLM .... Samaritan Lay Missioners [*An association*] (EA)
SLM .... School for Latin America [*Military*]
SLM .... Sea-Launched Missile
SLM .... Senior Level Management
SLM .... Ship Launched Missile (IAA)
SLM .... Signal Level Meter (NTCM)
SLM .... Silver Life-Saving Medal [*Military decoration*] (GFGA)
SLM .... Simulated Laboratory Module
SLM .... Single Longitudinal Mode

SLM .... Snow Lake Mines Ltd. [*Vancouver Stock Exchange symbol*]
SLM .... Sound Level Meter
SLM .... Space Laboratory Module (IAA)
SLM .... Spatial Light Modulator [*Optical computing*]
SLM .... Spatial Light Modulator [*Computer imaging*]
SLM .... Standard Laboratory Module
SLM .... Statistical Learning Model (IEEE)
SLM .... St. Louis [*Missouri*] [*Seismograph station code, US Geological Survey*] (SEIS)
SLM .... Student Loan Marketing Association [*NYSE symbol*] (SPSG)
SLM .... Student Loan Mktg [*NYSE symbol*] (TTSB)
SLM .... Submarine-Launched Missile
SLM .... Subscriber Loop Multiplex [*Bell System*]
SLM .... Supported Liquid Membrane [*Separation science and technology*]
SLM .... Surface-Launched Missile [*Navy*] (CAAL)
SLM .... Surinaamse Luchtvaart Maatschappij NV [*Surinam*] [*ICAO designator*] (FAAC)
SLM .... Surrey Local Militia [*British military*] (DMA)
SLM .... Synchronous Line Module
SLMA .... Shoe Lace Manufacturers Association [*Defunct*] (EA)
SLMA .... Southeastern Lumber Manufacturers Association (EA)
SLMA .... Steel Lintel Manufacturers Association [*British*] (DBA)
SLMA .... Student Loan Marketing Association [*Government-chartered private corporation*] [*Nickname: "Sallie Mae"*]
SLMAB .... Single-Line Missile Assembly Building
SLMD .... Madidi [*Bolivia*] [*ICAO location identifier*] (ICLI)
SLMD .... SpaceLabs Medical [*NASDAQ symbol*] (TTSB)
SLMD .... SpaceLabs Medical, Inc. [*NASDAQ symbol*] (SAG)
SLMD(RA) ... Searchlight Militia Depot (Royal Artillery) [*British military*] (DMA)
SLME .... Select Manual Entry Switch
SLMG .... Magdalena [*Bolivia*] [*ICAO location identifier*] (ICLI)
SLMG .... Self-Launching Motor Glider [*Aviation*] (DA)
SL-MICRO .... Statistical Language for Microcomputers (IID)
SLML .... La Madre [*Bolivia*] [*ICAO location identifier*] (ICLI)
SLMM .... Simultaneous Compass Locator at Middle Marker [*Aviation*] (FAAC)
SLMM .... Submarine-Launched Mobile Mine (MCD)
SLMP .... Mapiri [*Bolivia*] [*ICAO location identifier*] (ICLI)
SLMP .... School Library Manpower Project [*American Association of School Librarians*] (EA)
SLMP .... Self-Loading Memory Print (IAA)
SLMPrA .... Student Ln Mktg Adj Rt A Pfd [*NYSE symbol*] (TTSB)
SLMQ .... School Library Media Quarterly [*American Library Association*]
SLMR .... Memore [*Bolivia*] [*ICAO location identifier*] (ICLI)
SLMR .... Sailmaker [*Navy British*]
SLMS .... Saturn-Launched Meteoroid Satellite (IAA)
SLMS .... Scanning LASER Mass Spectrometry
SLMS .... Ship-Based Long-Range Missile System (DNAB)
SLMS .... Ship-Launched Missile System (IAA)
SLMS .... Sound Level Measuring Set
SLMS .... Surface-Launched Missile System
SLMSC .... South London (Volunteers) Medical Staff Corps [*British military*] (DMA)
SLMV .... Monte Verde [*Bolivia*] [*ICAO location identifier*] (ICLI)
SLMW .... Mategua [*Bolivia*] [*ICAO location identifier*] (ICLI)
SLMX .... Monos Arana [*Bolivia*] [*ICAO location identifier*] (ICLI)
SLN .... Salena Research Corp. [*Vancouver Stock Exchange symbol*]
SLN .... Salina [*Kansas*] [*Airport symbol*] (OAG)
SLN .... Salina, KS [*Location identifier FAA*] (FAAL)
SLN .... Salinas [*Chile*] [*Seismograph station code, US Geological Survey*] (SEIS)
SLN .... Salon
SLN .... Santiago Library System, Orange, CA [*OCLC symbol*] (OCLC)
SLN .... Secretariat Linguistiques Nordiques [*Nordic Language Secretariat - NLS*] [*Oslo, Norway*] (EAIO)
SLN .... Section List Number (MCD)
SLN .... Selena Research [*Vancouver Stock Exchange symbol*]
SLN .... Sense Lights On (SAA)
SLN .... Sequence Line Number [*Army*]
SLN .... Service Link Network [*Bell Laboratories*]
SLN .... Sloane Aviation Ltd. [*British ICAO designator*] (FAAC)
SLN .... Solution
SLN .... Southeastern Library Network [*Library network*]
SLN .... Sri Lanka Navy
SLN .... Statement of Logistical Needs [*Air Force*]
SLN .... Sublentiform Nucleus (DMAA)
SLN .... Subsidiary Learning Net (IAA)
SLN .... Superior Laryngeal Nerve [*Neuroanatomy*]
SLNC .... Service Life Not Completed (DNAB)
SLND .... Sine Loco Nec Data [*Without Place or Date of Printing*] [*Latin*]
SLNE .... Nueva Era [*Bolivia*] [*ICAO location identifier*] (ICLI)
SLNK .... SpectraLink Corp. [*NASDAQ symbol*] (SAG)
SLNK .... SpectraLink Corp. [*NASDAQ symbol*] (TTSB)
SLNO .... Nuevo Mundo [*Bolivia*] [*ICAO location identifier*] (ICLI)
SLNP .... Nueva Esperanza [*Bolivia*] [*ICAO location identifier*] (ICLI)
SLNQ .... Nueva Esperanza (Marban) [*Bolivia*] [*ICAO location identifier*] (ICLI)
SLNS .... Department of Northern Saskatchewan, La Ronge, Saskatchewan [*Library symbol National Library of Canada*] (NLC)
SLNV .... Nieve [*Bolivia*] [*ICAO location identifier*] (ICLI)
SLNWC .... Short-Leg Nonwalking Cast [*Medicine*] (DMAA)
SLO .... Edgartown Air, Inc. [*ICAO designator*] (FAAC)
SLO .... Salem, IL [*Location identifier FAA*] (FAAL)
SLO .... Santa Ana [*Columbia*] [*Airport symbol*] (AD)
SLO .... Scanning LASER Ophthalmoscope
SLO .... Searchlight Operator [*British military*] (DMA)
SLO .... Segment Limits Origin
SLO .... Shark Liver Oil
SLO .... Ship Liaison Officer [*Navy*] (CAAL)
SLO .... Single Loop Operation [*Nuclear energy*] (NRCH)
SLO .... Sligo [*County in Ireland*] (ROG)
SLO .... Sloan's Supermarkets [*AMEX symbol*] (TTSB)
SLO .... Sloan's Supermarkets, Inc. [*Formerly, Designcraft Industries, Inc.*] [*AMEX symbol*] (SPSG)
SLO .... Slocan Development [*Vancouver Stock Exchange symbol*]
SLO .... Slough [*British depot code*]
slo .... Slovak [*MARC language code Library of Congress*] (LCCP)
SLO .... Slow [*Aviation*] (DA)
SLO .... Slow Lift-Off (MCD)
SLO .... Space Laboratory Operations
SLO .... Staff Legal Officer [*Navy*] (DNAB)
SLO .... State Liaison Officer
SLO .... State Library of Ohio
SLO .... Stop-Limit Order [*Business term*]
SLO .... Stop-Loss Order [*Business term*]
SLO .... Streptolysin O [*Hematology*]
SLO .... Submarine Liaison Officer [*Navy*] (NVT)
SLO .... Swept Local Oscillator (IEEE)
Sloan L & T... Sloan on Landlord and Tenant [*New York*] [*A publication*] (DLA)
Sloan Leg Reg... Sloan's New York Legal Register [*A publication*] (DLA)
SloanSup ..... Sloans Supermarkets [*Associated Press*] (SAG)
SLOB .... Satellite Low-Orbit Bombardment
SLOB .... Strategic Low-Orbit Bomber (AAG)
SLOB .... Supplemental Layoff Benefits (MCD)
SLOB .... Supply Left of Baseline (MCD)
SLOC .... Sea Lines of Communication [*NATO*] (NATG)
SLOC .... Source Lines of Code (SSD)
SLOCOP ...... Specific Linear Optimal Control Program [*Hydrofoil*] [*Grumman Aerospace Corp.*]
SLOE .... Save Life on Earth (EA)
SLOE .... Special List of Equipment [*Air Force*]
SLOH .... Skylab Operations Handbook [*NASA*] (MCD)
SLOI .... Orialsa [*Bolivia*] [*ICAO location identifier*] (ICLI)
SLOM .... Simultaneous Compass Locator at Outer Marker [*Aviation*] (FAAC)
SLOMAR ...... Space Logistics Maintenance and Repair (IAA)
SLOMAR ...... Space Logistics, Maintenance, and Rescue
SLO MO ...... Slow Motion (NTCM)
SLON .... Saloon
SLOP .... Small Lot Optimum Procurement (PDAA)
SLOP .... Standard Listen Output Program (IAA)
SLOPE .... Study of Lunar Orbiter Photographic Evaluation (MCD)
SLOR .... Oruro [*Bolivia*] [*ICAO location identifier*] (ICLI)
SLOR .... Simultaneous Line Over-Relaxation [*Nuclear energy*]
SLOR .... Successive Line Overrelaxation (IAA)
SLOR .... Swept Local Oscillator Receiver (NG)
SLORC .... State Law and Order Restoration Council [*Myanmar*]
SLORV .... Structural Loads on Reentry Vehicles (MCD)
SLOS .... Scanning Line of Sight (KSC)
SLOS .... Secondary Line of Sight [*Sextants*]
SLOS .... Sierra Leone Organization Society
SLOS .... Star Line-of-Sight (MCD)
SLOS .... Sun Line-of-Sight
SLOS .... Swept Local Oscillator
SLOSH .... Sea, Lake, and Overland Surge Hurricane
SLOSH .... Sea Lake and Overland Surges from Hurricanes [*Model*] (USDC)
SLOSH .... Sea Level and Overland Surge from Hurricanes [*National Oceanic and Atmospheric Administration*]
SLOSJ .... State and Local Officials for Soviet Jews (EA)
SLO/SRI ...... Shift Left Out/Shift Right In
SLOSYN ...... Slow Synchronization (IAA)
SLOT .... Anchor Gaming [*NASDAQ symbol*] (SAG)
SLOT .... Sinaota [*Bolivia*] [*ICAO location identifier*] (ICLI)
SLOT .... Slotted (IAA)
SLOT .... Stabilized Line-of-Sight Tracker
SLOT .... Submarine-Launched One-Way Tactical [*Buoy*] (NVT)
SLOT .... Submarine Launched One-Way Transmitter [*AN/BRT-1*] (DOMA)
SLOTH .... Suppressing Line Operands and Translating to Hexadecimal [*Telecommunications*] (TEL)
Slov .... Slovenia
SLOWPOKE... Safe Low-Power Critical Experiment [*Nuclear energy*]
SLP .... Left Sacroposterior Position [*of the fetus*] [*Obstetrics*]
SLP .... Sacrolaeva Posterior [*A fetal position*] (AAMN)
SLP .... Safe Leeward Position
SLP .... Salpa Aviation Co. Ltd. [*Sudan*] [*ICAO designator*] (FAAC)
SLP .... San Luis Potosi [*Mexico*] [*Airport symbol*] (AD)
SLP .... School Lunch Program
SLP .... Scintilore Explorations Ltd. [*Toronto Stock Exchange symbol*]
SLP .... Scottish Labour Party [*Political party*] (PPW)
SLP .... Scottish Liberal Party [*Political party*]
SLP .... Scouting Landplane
SLP .... Sea-Level Pressure
SLP .... Secretary for Logistics Planning [*Air Force*]
SLP .... Sectional Linear Programming [*Computer science*]
SLP .... Segmental Limb Systolic Pressure [*Medicine*] (DMAA)
SLP .... Segmented Level Programming [*Computer science*] (IEEE)
SLP .... Selective Line Printing (IAA)
SLP .... Service Location Protocol [*Computer science*]
SLP .... Sex-Limited Protein [*Immunology*]
Slp .... Sex-Limited Protein [*Genetics*] (DOG)
SLP .... Shelby, NC [*Location identifier FAA*] (FAAL)
SLP .... Short Luteal Phase [*Medicine*] (DMAA)
SLP .... Silicon Light Pulser

SLP............ Sine Legitima Prole [*Without Lawful Issue*] [*Latin*]
SLP............ Single Langmuir Probe (IAA)
SLP............ Single Layer Polysilicon (IAA)
SLP............ Single Linear Polarization
SLP............ Single Link Procedures (TNIG)
SLP............ Sleep
SLP............ Slip (ADA)
SLP............ Sloop
SLP............ Slope (MSA)
SLP............ Socialist Labor Party [*Egypt*] [*Political party*] (PPW)
SLP............ Socialist Labor Party of America [*Political party*] (EA)
SLP............ Soft Lander Probe [*Aerospace*]
SLP............ Sound Level Plot [*Military*] (CAAL)
SLP............ Source Language Processor [*Computer science*] (BUR)
SLP............ Spacelab Program Office [*European Research National Organization*] (MCD)
SLP............ Specific Line of Precipitin [*Immunology*]
SLP............ Speech Language Pathologist
SLP............ Speed Limiting Point [*Aviation*] (FAAC)
SLP............ Spring-Loaded Pulley
SLP............ Standard Long Play [*VHS recorder playing time mode*] (NTCM)
SLP............ St. Lucie Plant [*Nuclear energy*] (NRCH)
SLP............ Stock List Price [*Military*] (AFIT)
S/LP............ Stop Lamp [*Automotive engineering*]
SLP............ Strategic Locations Planning [*Information service or system*] (IID)
SLP............ Strategic Logistic Program [*Army*] (RDA)
SLP............ Street Legal Performance [*Auto model designation*]
SLP............ Sun Energy Partners LP [*NYSE symbol*] (SPSG)
SLP............ Sun Energy Ptnrs L.P. [*NYSE symbol*] (TTSB)
SLP............ Super Long Play [*Video technology*]
SLP............ Supersonic Local Pressure
SLP............ Supplier Loaned Property (MCD)
SLP............ Surface Launch Platform (NVT)
SLP............ Symbol Location Point (NITA)
SLP............ Systematic Layout Planning [*Industrial engineering*]
SLPA........... Selected Legally Protected Animals [*Marine science*] (MSC)
SLPA........... Silicon Light Pulser Array
SLPA........... Solid Logic Process Automation (IAA)
SLPA........... State Lamb Producers' Association [*Queensland, Australia*]
SLPB........... Spacelab Program Board [*NASA*] (NASA)
SLPC........... Signal Lines Pair Combination (IAA)
SLPC........... Single Loop Programmable Indicating Controller (NITA)
SLPC........... Socialist Labour Party of Canada
SLPC........... St. Louis Production Center
SLPC........... Supported Liquid Phase Catalyst [*Chemical engineering*]
SLPD........... Skylab Program Directive [*NASA*] (KSC)
SLPD........... State and Local Planning Division [*Environmental Protection Agency*] (GFGA)
SLPH........... Seat Lock Pin Handle
SLPHR.......... Sulphur
SLPI........... Secretory Leukoprotease Inhibitor [*Biochemistry*]
SLPL........... Sea Loading Pipe Line [*Technical drawings*]
SLPL........... St. Louis Public Library [*Missouri*]
SLPM........... Palmira [*Bolivia*] [*ICAO location identifier*] (ICLI)
SLPM........... Scanned-LASER Photoluminescence Microscope (PDAA)
SLPM........... Selected List of Published Material [*Her Majesty's Stationery Office*] [*British*]
SLPM........... Silicon Light Pulser Matrix
SLPMS.......... Short Leg Posterior Molded Splint [*Medicine*] (MEDA)
SLPMS.......... Single Level Power Management System
SLPO........... Potosi [*Bolivia*] [*ICAO location identifier*] (ICLI)
SLPO........... Skylab Program Office [*NASA*] (KSC)
SLPP........... Paraparau [*Bolivia*] [*ICAO location identifier*] (ICLI)
SLPP........... Serum Lipophosphoprotein [*Serology*]
SLPP........... Sierra Leone People's Party [*Political party*] (PD)
SLPP........... Sri Lanka People's Party [*Political party*] (PPW)
SLPR........... Puerto Rico [*Bolivia*] [*ICAO location identifier*] (ICLI)
SLPR........... Sidelobe Pulse Rejection [*Military*] (CAAL)
SLPR........... Supplier Loaned Property Request (MCD)
SLPRF.......... Northern Teacher Education Program, Inc., La Ronge, Saskatchewan [*Library symbol National Library of Canada*] (NLC)
SLPS........... Puerto Suarez [*Bolivia*] [*ICAO location identifier*] (ICLI)
SLPS........... Sonobuoy Launcher Pneumatic System
SLPS........... State and Local Program Support [*Nuclear energy*] (NRCH)
SLPT........... Peta [*Bolivia*] [*ICAO location identifier*] (ICLI)
SLPT........... Salted Paper Print (VRA)
SLPT........... Socialist Labor Party of Turkey [*Turkiye Sosyalist Isci Partisi*] [*Political party*] (PPW)
SLPTC.......... Solid-Liquid Phase-Transfer Catalysis
SLPU........... Puchuni [*Bolivia*] [*ICAO location identifier*] (ICLI)
SLPV........... Puerto Villa-Roel [*Bolivia*] [*ICAO location identifier*] (ICLI)
SLPW........... Sloop-of-War
SLQ............ Sleetmute [*Alaska*] [*Airport symbol*] (OAG)
SLQ............ Sleetmute, AK [*Location identifier FAA*] (FAAL)
SLQ............ Surface Layer Quality
SLQY........... Curichi [*Bolivia*] [*ICAO location identifier*] (ICLI)
SLR............ Radcliffe College, Schlesinger Library, Cambridge, MA [*OCLC symbol*] (OCLC)
SLR............ Sales Letter Report
SLR............ Saskatchewan Law Reports [*A publication*] (DLA)
SLR............ Satellite LASER Ranging [*for geodetic and geophysical measurements*]
SLR............ Satellite Laser Ranging
SLR............ Scanning Laser Rangefinder
SLR............ Scottish Land Court Reports [*A publication*] (DLA)
SLR............ Scottish Law Reporter [*Edinburgh*] [*A publication*] (DLA)
SLR............ Scottish Law Review and Sheriff Court Reports [*1885-1963*] [*A publication*] (DLA)
SLR............ Sealer
SLR............ Sea-Level Rise [*Climatology*]
SLR............ Self-Loading Rifle (MCD)
SLR............ Sense Line Register
SLR............ Service Level Reporter [*IBM Corp.*]
SLR............ Seychelles Law Reports [*1921-23*] [*A publication*] (DLA)
SLR............ Short Latency Response [*Neurology*]
SLR............ Side-Looking RADAR (AFM)
SLR............ Sierra Leone Railway (MHDB)
SLR............ Simple Left to Right [*Computer science*]
SLR............ Simple Linear Regression [*Statistics*]
SLR............ Sind Law Reporter [*India*] [*A publication*] (DLA)
SLR............ Singapore Law Reports [*1946-49, 1953-56*] [*A publication*] (DLA)
SLR............ Single-Lens Reflex [*Camera*]
SLR............ Skylab Rescue [*NASA*] (KSC)
SLR............ Slush on Runway [*NWS*] (FAAC)
SLR............ SOBELAIR [*Societe Belge de Transport Aeriens*] [*Belgium ICAO designator*] (FAAC)
SLR............ Solar (AAG)
SLR............ Solar
SLR............ Solectron Corp. [*NYSE symbol*] (SPSG)
SLR............ Sound Level Recorder
SLR............ Southern Law Review [*St. Louis, MO*] [*A publication*] (DLA)
SLR............ South Lancashire Regiment [*British*]
SLR............ Special Leave Refused
SLR............ Special Light Rifle (NATG)
SLR............ Specific Lung Resistance
SLR............ Spin Lattice Relaxation
SLR............ Sport Leicht Renn [*Sports Lightweight Racing (Car)*] [*German*]
SLR............ Stabell Resources [*Vancouver Stock Exchange symbol*]
SLR............ Static Line Regulation
SLR............ Static Loaded Radius [*Automotive engineering*]
SLR............ Statute Law Revision [*A publication*] (DLA)
SLR............ Storage Limits Register
SLR............ Straight Leg Raising [*Medicine*]
SLR............ Streptococcus Lactis, Resistant [*Immunology*] (DAVI)
SLR............ Streptococcus lactis R Factor [*Biochemistry*]
SLR............ Sulphur Springs, TX [*Location identifier FAA*] (FAAL)
SLR............ Surface Layout Release
SLR............ System Level Requirement [*Military*] (CAAL)
SLRA........... San Ramon [*Bolivia*] [*ICAO location identifier*] (ICLI)
SLRA........... Sierra Leone Royal Artillery [*British military*] (DMA)
SLRA........... Soviet Long-Range Air (MCD)
SLRA........... Suede and Leather Refinishers of America [*Defunct*] (EA)
SLRAP.......... Standard Low-Frequency Range Approach
SLRB........... Robore [*Bolivia*] [*ICAO location identifier*] (ICLI)
SLRB........... State Labor Relations Board
SLRB........... Steel Labor Relations Board [*New Deal*]
SLRC........... San Luis Rey College [*California*]
SLRC........... Short Length Record (IAA)
SLRC/MILO... State Library Resource Center - Maryland Interlibrary Organization [*Library network*]
SLRD........... Searchlight RADAR
SLRE........... El Remate [*Bolivia*] [*ICAO location identifier*] (ICLI)
SLRE........... Self-Loading Random Access Edit (IAA)
SLREG.......... Stepwise Linear Regression (IAA)
SL Rev......... Scottish Law Review and Sheriff Court Reports [*A publication*] (DLA)
SLRH........... Rancho Alegre [*Bolivia*] [*ICAO location identifier*] (ICLI)
SLRI........... Riberalta [*Bolivia*] [*ICAO location identifier*] (ICLI)
SLRI........... Shipboard Long-Range Input
SLR Leic...... Leicester's Straits Law Reports [*Malaya*] [*A publication*] (DLA)
SLR Leicester... Leicester's Straits Law Reports [*Malaya*] [*A publication*] (DLA)
SLRN........... Select Read Numerically
SL RNG......... Slope Range
SLRNS.......... Straits Law Reports, New Series [*Malasia*] [*A publication*] (DLA)
SLRP........... Rosapata [*Bolivia*] [*ICAO location identifier*] (ICLI)
SLRP........... Society for Strategic and Long Range Planning [*Later, Strategic Planning Society - SP*] (EAIO)
SLRP........... State Loan Repayment Program [*Department of Health and Human Services*] (GFGA)
SLRP........... Survey, Liaison, and Reconnaissance Party [*Navy*] (ANA)
SLRQ........... Rurrenabaque [*Bolivia*] [*ICAO location identifier*] (ICLI)
SLRR........... Retiro [*Bolivia*] [*ICAO location identifier*] (ICLI)
SLRRB.......... Senior Logistics Readiness Review Board [*Fort Lewis*] (MCD)
SLRS........... Rio Seco [*Bolivia*] [*ICAO location identifier*] (ICLI)
SLRS........... Satellite LASER Ranging System
SLRS........... Sexual Law Reform Society [*British*]
SLRT........... Santa Rita [*Bolivia*] [*ICAO location identifier*] (ICLI)
SLRT........... Straight Leg Raising Test [*or Tenderness*] [*Medicine*]
SLRTB.......... Saskatchewan Department of Tourism and Small Business, La Ronge, Saskatchewan [*Library symbol National Library of Canada*] (NLC)
SLRUM.......... Simple Least Recently Used Stack Model (MHDI)
SLRV........... Shuttle Launched Research Vehicle [*NASA*] (NASA)
SLRV........... South London Regiment of Volunteers [*British military*] (DMA)
SLRV........... Standard Light Rail Vehicle [*Mass transit*]
SLRV........... Strawberry Latent Ringspot Virus [*Plant pathology*]
SLRV........... Surveyor Lunar Roving Vehicle [*Aerospace*] (MCD)
SLRY........... Reyes [*Bolivia*] [*ICAO location identifier*] (ICLI)
SLS............ Aeroservicios Ejecutivos Sinaloenses SA [*Mexico ICAO designator*] (FAAC)

SLS............ Saint Lawrence Seaway Development Corp. [*Department of Transportation*]
SLS............ Saint Lawrence Seminary [*Wisconsin*]
SLS............ Sales
SLS............ Santiago Library System [*Library network*]
SLS............ Sassafras Loamy Sand [*Type of soil*]
SLS............ Saturn Longitude System [*Planetary science*]
SLS............ Scanning LASER System
SLS............ School of Library Service [*Columbia University*] [*Defunct*]
SLS............ School of Logistics Science [*Army*]
SLS............ Scots Language Society [*British*] (DBA)
SLS............ Sea-Land Service, Inc. [*AAR code*]
SLS............ Sea Level, Standard Day
SLS............ Sea-Level Static
SLS............ Secondary Landing Site [*NASA*] (NASA)
SLS............ Securities Lending Service [*Australian Stock Exchange*]
SLS............ Segment Long-Spacing Collagen Fiber
SLS............ Selas Corp. of Amer [*AMEX symbol*] (TTSB)
SLS............ Selas Corp. of America [*AMEX symbol*] (SPSG)
SLS............ Selective LASER [*Light Amplification by Stimulated Emission of Radiation*] Sintering [*Desktop manufacturing*]
SLS............ Serra Cooperative Library System, San Diego, CA [*OCLC symbol*] (OCLC)
SLS............ Shore Labourers Society [*A union*] [*British*]
SLS............ Short-Leg Splint [*Orthopedics*] (DAVI)
SLS............ Side-Lobe Suppression RADAR
SLS............ Side-Looking SONAR
SLS............ Signaling Link Selection [*Telecommunications*] (TEL)
SLS............ Silicon Light Source
SLS............ Silistra [*Bulgaria*] [*Airport symbol*] (OAG)
SLS............ Sindacato Lavoratori della Somalia [*Workers Union of Somalia*]
SLS............ Skylab Simulator [*NASA*] (KSC)
SLS............ Slightly Soluble
SLS............ Slovenska Ljudska Stranka [*Slovene People's Party*] [*Former Yugoslavia*] [*Political party*] (PPE)
SL'S............ Slovenska L'Udova Strana [*Slovak People's Party*] [*Also, HSL'S*] [*Political party*] (PPE)
SLS............ Society for Libyan Studies (EAIO)
SLS............ Society for Literature and Science
SLS............ Society of Landscape Studies [*British*] (DBA)
SLS............ Sodium Lauryl Sulfate [*Also, SDS*] [*Organic chemistry*]
SLS............ Soengei Langka [*Sumatra*] [*Seismograph station code, US Geological Survey Closed*] (SEIS)
SLS............ Software Loadable System [*Computer science*] (PCM)
SLS............ So-Luminaire Systems [*Vancouver Stock Exchange symbol*]
SLS............ Solution-Liquid-Solid [*Chemistry*]
SLS............ Sonobuoy Localization System (NVT)
SLS............ Sortie Lab Simulator [*NASA*] (NASA)
SLS............ Sound Learning Society [*British*]
SLS............ Source Library System [*Computer science*]
SLS............ Spacecraft Landing Strut
SLS............ Space Laboratory Simulator [*NASA*]
SLS............ Space Launch System
SLS............ Specialist in Library Science (PGP)
SLS............ Specific Living Space (AAG)
SLS............ Spoken Language Services, Inc.
SLS............ Standard Light Spanwire [*Military*] (CAAL)
SLS............ Start Launch Sequence [*Military*]
SLS............ Statement Level Simulator [*NASA*] (NASA)
SLS............ Stein-Leventhal Syndrome [*Medicine*] (DMAA)
SLS............ Stephenson Locomotive Society [*British*] (BI)
SLS............ Stores Locator System (MCD)
SLS............ Strained-Layer Superlattices [*Crystalline materials*]
SLS............ Strategic Lunar System (IAA)
SLS............ Student Lesson Sheets
SLS............ Students for a Libertarian Society (EA)
SLS............ Styles of Leadership Survey [*Test*]
SLS............ Suburban Library System [*Library network*]
SLS............ Sun-Load Sensor [*Automotive engineering*]
SLS............ Supplemental Loans for Students [*Department of Education*]
SLS............ Surface Laboratory System [*NASA*] (KSC)
SLS............ SWALCAP Library Services Ltd. [*Information service or system*] (IID)
SLS............ Symbolic Layout System (MCD)
SLSA............ Santa Ana De Yacuma [*Bolivia*] [*ICAO location identifier*] (ICLI)
SLSA............ Seamen's Loyal Standard Association [*A union*] [*British*]
SLSA............ Secondary Lead Smelters Association (EA)
SLSA............ Shuttle Logistics Support Aircraft [*NASA*] (MCD)
SLSA............ Slotting Saw
SLSA............ St. Lawrence Seaway Authority [*See also AVMS*] [*Canada*]
SLSAC............ Saint Lawrence Seaway Authority of Canada
SLSADJ............ Stores Locator System Adjustment (MCD)
SLSB............ San Borja [*Bolivia*] [*ICAO location identifier*] (ICLI)
SLSC............ Santa Clara (Moxos) [*Bolivia*] [*ICAO location identifier*] (ICLI)
SLSD............ San Carlos Gutierrez [*Bolivia*] [*ICAO location identifier*] (ICLI)
SLSDC............ Saint Lawrence Seaway Development Corp. [*Department of Transportation*]
SLSF............ San Francisco (Moxos) [*Bolivia*] [*ICAO location identifier*] (ICLI)
SLSF............ Sodium Loop Safety Facility [*Nuclear energy*]
SLSF............ St. Louis-San Francisco Railway Co. [*AAR code*]
SLSG............ Sipuati [*Bolivia*] [*ICAO location identifier*] (ICLI)
SLSG............ S-Locus-Specific Glycoprotein [*Botany*]
SLSH............ Santa Ana De Huachi [*Bolivia*] [*ICAO location identifier*] (ICLI)
SLSH............ Short Length Super HIPPO [*High Internal Pressure Producing Orifice*] (MCD)
SLSI............ San Ignacio De Velasco [*Bolivia*] [*ICAO location identifier*] (ICLI)
SLSI............ Super Large-Scale Integration
SLSJ............ Salinas [*Bolivia*] [*ICAO location identifier*] (ICLI)
SLSK............ Sauces [*Bolivia*] [*ICAO location identifier*] (ICLI)
SLSL............ Santa Lucia (Cliza) [*Bolivia*] [*ICAO location identifier*] (ICLI)
SLSL............ Statutory Long Service Leave (ADA)
SLSM............ San Ignacio De Moxos [*Bolivia*] [*ICAO location identifier*] (ICLI)
SLSM............ Silver Life-Saving Medal [*Military decoration*]
SLSM............ Simple Line Source Model [*Environmental Protection Agency*] (GFGA)
SLSMGR............ Sales Manager (WGA)
SLSMN............ Salesman (WGA)
SLSMN............ Salesman
SLSMS............ Spacelab Support Module Simulator [*NASA*] (MCD)
SLSN............ Sanandita [*Bolivia*] [*ICAO location identifier*] (ICLI)
SLSO............ Santa Barbara De Parra [*Bolivia*] [*ICAO location identifier*] (ICLI)
SLSO............ Shipyard Labour Supply Officer [*British*]
SLSP............ SACLANT Scheduled Program (MCD)
SLSP............ Slow Speed
SLSQ............ Saahaqui [*Bolivia*] [*ICAO location identifier*] (ICLI)
SLSR............ Santa Rosa De Yacuma [*Bolivia*] [*ICAO location identifier*] (ICLI)
SLSS............ Sasasama [*Bolivia*] [*ICAO location identifier*] (ICLI)
SLSS............ Secondary Life Support System [*NASA*]
SLSS............ Shuttle Launch Support System (MCD)
SL-SS............ Spacelab Subsystem [*NASA*] (NASA)
SLSS............ Swimmer Life Support System [*Navy*] (CAAL)
SLSS............ Systems Library Subscription Service [*Computer science*] (IBMDP)
SLSSM............ Submerged Launched Surface-to-Surface Missile (MCD)
SL-SSS............ Spacelab Subsystem Segment [*NASA*] (NASA)
SLST............ San Antonio [*Bolivia*] [*ICAO location identifier*] (ICLI)
Sl St............ Slade's Compilation of the Statutes of Vermont [*A publication*] (DLA)
SLST............ Slightly Staining
SLST............ Slip Stitch [*Knitting*]
SLST............ St. Louis, San Francisco & Texas Railway Co. [*AAR code*]
SLSU............ Sucre [*Bolivia*] [*ICAO location identifier*] (ICLI)
SLSW............ Santa Barbara (Versalles) [*Bolivia*] [*ICAO location identifier*] (ICLI)
SLSW............ St. Louis Southwestern Railway Co. (IIA)
SLSX............ San Ramon De Senac [*Bolivia*] [*ICAO location identifier*] (ICLI)
SLT............ Pious Society of Our Lady of the Most Holy Trinity (TOCD)
SLT............ Sacrolaeva Transversa [*A fetal position*] (AAMN)
SLT............ Salant Corp. [*AMEX symbol*] (SAG)
SLT............ Salant Corp. [*NYSE symbol*] (SPSG)
SLT............ Salta [*Argentina*] [*Seismograph station code, US Geological Survey Closed*] (SEIS)
SLT............ Saltair Ltd. [*British ICAO designator*] (FAAC)
SLT............ Searchlight
SLT............ Second Law of Thermodynamics
SLT............ Self-Loading Tape (AFM)
SLT............ Sellectek Industries, Inc. [*Vancouver Stock Exchange symbol*]
SLT............ Sense Light Test (SAA)
slt............ Servants of Our Lady of the Most Holy Trinity (TOCD)
SLT............ Shiga-Like Toxin [*Biochemistry*]
SLT............ Ship Letter Telegram
SLT............ Shuttle Loop Transit [*NASA*]
SLT............ Signaling Link Termination [*Telecommunications*]
SLT............ Simulated LASER Target
SLT............ Simulated Launch Test [*NASA*] (KSC)
SLT............ Skylight (AAG)
SLT............ Slate (MSA)
SLT............ Slate Run, PA [*Location identifier FAA*] (FAAL)
SLT............ Slight (DAVI)
SLT............ Slit
SLT............ Solid Logic Technique [*Computer science*] (IEEE)
SLT............ Solid Logic Technology
SLT............ Soluble Lytic Transglycosylase [*An enzyme*]
SLT............ Sonobuoy Launch Tube [*Navy*] (CAAL)
SLT............ Special [*or Specific*] Launch Trajectory (AFM)
SLT............ Speech Language Therapist
SLT............ Spontaneous Lymphocyte Transportation (PDAA)
SLT............ Spotlight (MSA)
SLT............ Squadron Landing Team [*Marine Corps*] (DOMA)
SLT............ Standard Light Source (IAA)
SLT............ Stockpile Laboratory Tests
SLT............ Stress Limit Tests
SLT............ Structured Learning Therapy
S Lt............ Sub-Lieutenant [*British military*] (DMA)
SLT............ Swing [*Parachute*] Landing Trainer [*Military*] (INF)
SLT............ Switchman's Local Test [*Telecommunications*] (TEL)
SLTA............ Scottish Lawn Tennis Association (DBA)
SLTA............ Scottish Licensed Trade Association (DBA)
SLT & SDL... Searchlight and Sound Locator [*Navy*]
SLTB............ Society for Low Temperature Biology (EA)
SLTB............ St. Lucia Tourist Board (EA)
SLTBR............ Society for Light Treatment and Biological Rhythms
SLTC............ Society of Leather Technologists and Chemists [*British*]
SLTD............ Salted
SLTD............ Slotted (MSA)
SLTDP............ Special LASER Technology Development Program
SLTE............ Self-Loading Tape Edit (IAA)
SLTE............ Teoponte [*Bolivia*] [*ICAO location identifier*] (ICLI)
SLTEA............ Sheffield Lighter Trades Employers' Association [*British*] (DCTA)
SLTF............ San Telmo (Cordillera) [*Bolivia*] [*ICAO location identifier*] (ICLI)
SLTF............ Shortest Latency Time First
SLTF............ Silo-Launch Test Facility
SLTG............ Santiago [*Bolivia*] [*ICAO location identifier*] (ICLI)
sltgz............ Saltglaze (VRA)

SLTH .... Tumichucua [*Bolivia*] [*ICAO location identifier*] (ICLI)
SLTI .... San Matias [*Bolivia*] [*ICAO location identifier*] (ICLI)
SLTI .... Surgical Laser Tech [*NASDAQ symbol*] (TTSB)
SLTI .... Surgical Laser Technologies, Inc. [*NASDAQ symbol*] (NQ)
SLTJ .... Tarija [*Bolivia*] [*ICAO location identifier*] (ICLI)
SLT (Lyon Ct)... Scots Law Times (Lyon Court Reports) [*A publication*] (DLA)
SLTM .... Short Lead Time Material (DNAB)
SLTM .... Standard Lap Turn Method (NVT)
SLTM .... Structural Lander Test Model
SLTN .... Solution
SLT (Notes)... Scots Law Times (Notes of Recent Decisions) [*A publication*] (DLA)
SLTO .... Sea-Level Takeoff
SLTP .... Tipuani [*Bolivia*] [*ICAO location identifier*] (ICLI)
SLTR .... Service Life Test Report (AAG)
SlTr .... Silent Treatment [*Psychology*] (DAVI)
Sl Tr .... Slight Trace (CPH)
SLTR .... Trinidad [*Bolivia*] [*ICAO location identifier*] (ICLI)
SLTS .... Todos Santos [*Bolivia*] [*ICAO location identifier*] (ICLI)
SLT (Sh Ct)... Scots Law Times Sheriff Court Reports [*A publication*] (DLA)
sLTSV .... Satellite Lucerne Transient Streak Virus
SLTT .... Total Bolivia [*Bolivia*] [*ICAO location identifier*] (ICLI)
SLTU .... Tucavaca [*Bolivia*] [*ICAO location identifier*] (ICLI)
SLTUF .... Sri Lanka Trade Union Federation [*Sri Lanka Vurthiya Samithi Sammelanaya*]
SLTV .... St. Lucia Television Service
SLT.WS .... Salant Corp. Wrrt [*AMEX symbol*] (TTSB)
SLTX .... Sales Tax
SLTY .... Tiguipa [*Bolivia*] [*ICAO location identifier*] (ICLI)
SLTZ .... Tupiza [*Bolivia*] [*ICAO location identifier*] (ICLI)
SLU .... Pavlovsk [*Later, LNN*] [*Former USSR Geomagnetic observatory code*]
SLU .... Saint Lawrence University [*Canton, NY*]
SLU .... Secondary Logic Unit
SLU .... Serial Line Unit
Slu .... Slough [*Maps and charts*]
SLU .... Slutsk [*Later, LNN*] [*Former USSR Geomagnetic observatory code*]
SLU .... Source Library Update [*Computer science*]
SLU .... Southern Labor Union
SLU .... Special Liaison Unit [*Military intelligence*] [*World War II*]
SLU .... Special Line Unit (NITA)
SLU .... St. Louis University [*Missouri*]
SLU .... St. Louis University, Law Library, St. Louis, MO [*OCLC symbol*] (OCLC)
SLU .... St. Lucia [*West Indies*] [*Airport symbol*] (OAG)
SLU .... Subscriber Line Unit [*Telecommunications*] (IAA)
SLU .... Subscriber Line Use [*Telecommunications*]
SLU .... Switching Logic Unit (CAAL)
SLUC .... Standard Level User Charge
SLUC .... Uncia [*Bolivia*] [*ICAO location identifier*] (ICLI)
SLUD .... Salivation, Lacrimation, Urination, Defecation [*Medicine*] (DMAA)
SLUDGE .... Salivation, Lacrimation, Urination, Defecation, Gastrointestinal Upset, Emesis [*Medicine*] (DMAA)
SLUF .... Short Little Ugly Feller [*Nickname for A-7 aircraft*] (MCD)
SLUFAE .... Surface-Launched Unit, Fire Area Equipment (MCD)
SLUFAE .... Surface-Launched Unit, Fuel-Air Explosive Mine Neutralizer [*Army*] (RDA)
SLUG .... Superconducting Low-Inductance Undulatory Galvanometer
SLUMINE .... Surface-Launched Unit, Mine Layer (MCD)
SLUMT .... Slacked Unconstrained Minimization Technique (PDAA)
SLUR .... Share Library User Report [*Computer science*] (OA)
SLURB .... Slovenly Suburb
SLURP .... Self Leveling Unit for Removing Pollution [*Marine science*] (MSC)
SLURP .... Spiny Lobster Undersea Research Project
SLURREX .... Slurry Reactor Experiment
SLUS .... Subscriber's Line Use System [*AT & T*] [*Telecommunications*] (TEL)
SLUV .... Uvas Verdes [*Bolivia*] [*ICAO location identifier*] (ICLI)
SLUY .... Uyuni [*Bolivia*] [*ICAO location identifier*] (ICLI)
SLV .... El Salvador [*ANSI three-letter standard code*] (CNC)
SLV .... Salivate (KSC)
SLV .... San Jose, CA [*Location identifier FAA*] (FAAL)
SLV .... Sao Paulo de Olivenca [*Brazil*] [*Airport symbol*] (AD)
SLV .... Satellite Launching Vehicle [*Air Force*]
SLV .... Satellite-Like Virus
SLV .... Saturn Launch Vehicle [*NASA*] (KSC)
SLV .... Seldovia [*Alaska*] [*Seismograph station code, US Geological Survey*] (SEIS)
SLV .... Shallot Latent Virus [*Plant pathology*]
SLv .... Sifra on Leviticus [*A publication*] (BJA)
SLV .... Silverado Foods [*AMEX symbol*] (TTSB)
SLV .... Silverado Foods, Inc. [*AMEX symbol*] (SAG)
SLV .... Silver Lady Resources [*Vancouver Stock Exchange symbol*]
SLV .... Simulated Launch Vehicle (MCD)
SLV .... Sleeve (AAG)
slv .... Slovenian [*MARC language code Library of Congress*] (LCCP)
SLV .... Small Launch Vehicle [*Air Force*] (DOMA)
SLV .... Soft Landing Vehicle [*NASA*]
SLV .... Solvent (WGA)
SLV .... Southern Launch Vehicle [*Australia*]
SLV .... Space Launch Vehicle [*NASA*]
SLV .... Space-Like Vector
SLV .... Sport-Luxury Vehicle
SLV .... Standardized Launcher Vehicle (IAA)
SLV .... Standard Launch Vehicle
SLVA .... Villa Aroma [*Bolivia*] [*ICAO location identifier*] (ICLI)
SLVC .... Selvac Corp. [*NASDAQ symbol*] (NQ)
SLVC .... Super Linear Variable Capacitor (PDAA)
SLVD .... Covendo [*Bolivia*] [*ICAO location identifier*] (ICLI)
SLVE .... Venecia [*Bolivia*] [*ICAO location identifier*] (ICLI)
SLVG .... Salvage
SLVG .... Sleeving [*Electricity*]
SLVG .... Special Launch Vehicle Group [*NASA*] (KSC)
SLVG .... Valle Grande [*Bolivia*] [*ICAO location identifier*] (ICLI)
SLVI .... Caranavi [*Bolivia*] [*ICAO location identifier*] (ICLI)
SlvKing .... Silver King Communications [*Associated Press*] (SAG)
SLVM .... Villa Montes [*Bolivia*] [*ICAO location identifier*] (ICLI)
SlvMin .... Silverado Mines Ltd. [*Associated Press*] (SAG)
SLVN .... Sylvan Learning Systems [*Montgomery, AL*] [*NASDAQ symbol*] (NQ)
SLVN .... Valencia [*Bolivia*] [*ICAO location identifier*] (ICLI)
SLVR .... Silver [*Automotive advertising*]
SLVR .... Silver
SLVR .... Silver Diner Dvlpmt [*NASDAQ symbol*] (TTSB)
SLVR .... Viru Viru [*Bolivia*] [*ICAO location identifier*] (ICLI)
SLVRJ .... Surface-Launched Low-Volume Ramjet
SLVS .... San Luis Valley Southern Railroad (IIA)
SLVT .... Solvent (MSA)
SLVTN .... Salvation
SLW .... Saltillo [*Mexico*] [*Airport symbol*] (AD)
SLW .... Silversword Corp. [*Vancouver Stock Exchange symbol*]
SLW .... Single Line Working [*Railway engineering term*] (DCTA)
SLW .... Sisters of the Living Word [*Roman Catholic religious order*]
SLW .... Slow
SLW .... Space-Based LASER Weapon (MCD)
SLW .... Specific Leaf Weight [*Botany*]
SLW .... Spectral Line Width
SLW .... Store Logical Word
SLW .... Straight-Line Wavelength
SLW .... Supercooled Liquid Water (USDC)
SLW .... Supercooled Liquid Water [*Marine science*] (OSRA)
SLW .... Wooster, OH [*Location identifier FAA*] (FAAL)
SLWA .... Santa Rosa De Abuna [*Bolivia*] [*ICAO location identifier*] (ICLI)
SLWC .... Short Leg Walking Cast [*Medicine*] (MEDA)
SLWC .... Short-Leg Walking Cast [*Medicine*] (DMAA)
SLWC .... Short-Leg Walking Cast [*Orthopedics*] (DAVI)
SLWD .... Seis De Agosto [*Bolivia*] [*ICAO location identifier*] (ICLI)
SLWL .... Straight-Line Wavelength (MSA)
SLWMS .... Secondary Liquid Waste Management System [*Nuclear energy*] (NRCH)
SL-Wola Ludu... Stronnictwo Ludowe-Wola Ludu [*Peasant Party-People's Will*] [*Poland Political party*] (PPE)
SLWOP .... Special Leave Without Pay
SLWT .... Side Loadable Warping Tug [*Navy*] (CAAL)
SLX .... Salt Cay [*British West Indies*] [*Airport symbol*] (OAG)
SLX .... Self-Lubricating Exterior (IAA)
SLX .... Siltronics Ltd. [*Toronto Stock Exchange symbol*]
SLX .... Slate Creek, AK [*Location identifier FAA*] (FAAL)
SLY .... Hayward, WI [*Location identifier FAA*] (FAAL)
SLY .... Safety, Liquidity, Yield
SLY .... Skelly Resources Ltd. [*Vancouver Stock Exchange symbol*]
SLY .... Sky Line for Air Services Ltd. [*Sudan*] [*ICAO designator*] (FAAC)
SLY .... Sloppy [*Horse racing*]
SLY .... Southerly
SLYA .... Yacuiba [*Bolivia*] [*ICAO location identifier*] (ICLI)
SLYB .... El Bato [*Bolivia*] [*ICAO location identifier*] (ICLI)
SLYI .... Yapacani [*Bolivia*] [*ICAO location identifier*] (ICLI)
SLYP .... Muyupampa [*Bolivia*] [*ICAO location identifier*] (ICLI)
SLYP .... Short Leaf Yellow Pine [*Lumber*]
SLYY .... San Yo Yo [*Bolivia*] [*ICAO location identifier*] (ICLI)
SLZ .... Sao Luiz [*Brazil*] [*Airport symbol*] (OAG)
SLZ .... Solidor Resources, Inc. [*Vancouver Stock Exchange symbol*]
SLZ .... Suppress Leading Zero [*Computer science*]
SLZA .... Scandinavian Lead Zinc Association [*Stockholm, Sweden*] (EAIO)
SLZB .... San Pedro [*Bolivia*] [*ICAO location identifier*] (ICLI)
SLZF .... San Francisco (Naciff) [*Bolivia*] [*ICAO location identifier*] (ICLI)
SLZG .... San Agustin [*Bolivia*] [*ICAO location identifier*] (ICLI)
SLZJ .... San Pedro (Richard) [*Bolivia*] [*ICAO location identifier*] (ICLI)
SLZK .... San Lucas [*Bolivia*] [*ICAO location identifier*] (ICLI)
SLZR .... San Rafael (Isidoro) [*Bolivia*] [*ICAO location identifier*] (ICLI)
SLZX .... San Pedro (Salvatierra) [*Bolivia*] [*ICAO location identifier*] (ICLI)
SM .... Aberdeen Airways [*Airline flight code*] (ODBW)
SM .... Dr. Schwarz Arzneimittelfabrik GmbH [*Germany*] [*Research code symbol*]
SM .... Geographic Information System-Mobile
sm .... Marist Fathers (TOCD)
SM .... Marist Sisters Congregation of Mary (TOCD)
SM .... Master of Science
SM .... Medal of Service of the Order of Canada
SM .... Meteorological Aids Station [*ITU designation*]
SM .... Misericorde Sisters [*Roman Catholic religious order*]
SM .... Sacred to the Memory of -- [*Epitaphs*] (ROG)
SM .... Sales Manager
SM .... Salvage Mechanic [*Navy*]
Sm .... Samarium [*See Sa*] [*Chemical element*]
Sm .... Samuel [*Old Testament book*]
SM .... Sanctae Memoriae [*Of Holy Memory*] [*Latin*]
SM .... San Marco [*Satellite*] [*NASA/Italy*]
SM .... San Marino [*ANSI two-letter standard code*] (CNC)
sm .... San Marino [*IYRU nationality code*] [*MARC country of publication code Library of Congress*] (LCCP)
SM .... Scheduled Maintenance (MCD)
SM .... Scheuthauer-Marie [*Syndrome*] (DAVI)

SM .... Schistosoma Mansoni [*A parasitic fluke*]
S-M .... Schuetzenmine [*Antipersonnel mine*] [*German military - World War II*]
SM .... Schwarz/Mann [*Supply company in biochemistry and chemistry*]
SM .... Scientific Memorandum
Sm .... Sclerotinia minor [*A fungus*]
SM .... Screw Motorship (IAA)
SM .... Seamen [*British military*] (DMA)
SM .... Search Month (NITA)
SM .... Seat Mile
SM .... Secondary Market [*Investment term*]
SM .... Secondary Memory [*Computer science*] (BUR)
SM .... Second Mortgage [*Banking*]
SM .... Secretary's Memorandum [*Military*]
SM .... Security Manual (AAG)
SM .... Security Monitor (AAG)
SM .... Seed Mass [*Botany*]
SM .... Segment Mark (IAA)
SM .... Self-Monitoring (DAVI)
Sm .... Semahot (BJA)
SM .... Semiconductor Memory
SM .... Semimat (IAA)
SM .... Semimembranous [*Anatomy*] (DAVI)
SM .... Semimonthly
SM .... Senior Magistrate
SM .... Senior Manager
S/M .... Sensory-to-Motor [*Ratio*]
SM .... Sentence Modifier [*Linguistics*]
SM .... Sequence Monitor
SM .... Sergeant Major
SM .... Serious Music [*Canadian Broadcasting Corp. record series prefix*]
SM .... Serratia Marcescens [*Bacterium*]
S/M .... Service/Maintenance (NASA)
SM .... Service Manual
SM .... Service Mark [*Trademarks*]
SM .... Service Member [*Military*] (AABC)
SM .... Service Module [*NASA*]
SM .... Service Monitoring [*Telecommunications*] (TEL)
SM .... Servomotor (IAA)
SM .... Set Mode (BUR)
SM .... Sewage Microparticulates [*Oceanography*]
SM .... Sewing Machine
SM .... Sexual Myths [*Scale*]
SM .... Shape Memory [*Metallurgy*]
SM .... Shared Memory [*Computer science*] (BUR)
SM .... Share of Market (NITA)
SM .... Sheet Metal
SM .... Shell Model
SM .... Shelter Management [*Civil Defense*]
SM .... Shigella Mutant [*A bacterium*] (DAVI)
SM .... Shipment Memorandum [*Navy*]
SM .... Ship Movement Library [*Maritime Data Network, Inc.*] [*Information service or system*] (CRD)
SM .... Shipping Monthly Data [*Department of Commerce*] (GFGA)
SM .... Ship's Manifest (ADA)
SM .... Shock Mount
SM .... Shop Manual [*Air Force*] (AAG)
SM .... Short Meter [*Music*]
SM .... Short Module [*NASA*] (NASA)
SM .... Shuttle Management [*Kennedy Space Center*] [*NASA*] (NASA)
SM .... SIAI-Marchetti SpA [*Italy ICAO aircraft manufacturer identifier*] (ICAO)
SM .... Siam
S/M .... Siemens per Meter
SM .... Signaling Module [*Telecommunications*] (TEL)
SM .... Signalman [*Navy rating*]
SM .... Silver Medalist
SM .... Silver Methenamine [*Biological stain*]
SM .... Silver Mica [*Capacitor*]
SM .... Simple Maintenance
SM .... Simple Mastectomy [*Medicine*]
SM .... Simpson's Multipliers [*Naval architecture*]
SM .... Simulated Missile (AAG)
SM .... Simulators [*JETDS nomenclature*] [*Military*] (CET)
SM .... Single Manager [*Military*]
SM .... Single Mode
SM .... Sinistra Mano [*Left Hand*]
SM .... Sinus Medii [*Central Bay*] [*Lunar area*]
SM .... Sisters of Mercy [*Roman Catholic religious order*]
SM .... Sisters of Mercy (Cork and Ross) (TOCD)
SM .... Sisters of Mercy of Tralee (TOCD)
SM .... Sisters Servants of Mary (TOCD)
SM .... Skim Milk (MAE)
SM .... Slime Mold [*Biochemistry*] (DAVI)
SM .... Slow Moving
SM .... Small (AAG)
SM .... Small
sm .... Small (VRA)
SM .... Small Pica
SM .... Smectic Phase [*Physical chemistry*]
Sm .... Smectite [*Agronomy*]
Sm .... Smith Antigen [*Immunology*]
Sm .... Smith Collection. British Museum [*London*] (BJA)
SM .... SMM Enterprises Ltd. [*Vancouver Stock Exchange symbol*]
SM .... Smoker (DAVI)
SM .... Smooth (MSA)
SM .... Smooth Muscle [*Medicine*] (DMAA)
SM .... Snell Motorcycle
SM .... Socially Maladjusted
SM .... Societa Altair [*Italy ICAO designator*] (ICDA)
SM .... Societas Mariae [*Congregation of Mary*] [*Marists*] [*Roman Catholic religious order*]
SM .... Society of Mary (Marianists) (TOCD)
SM .... Society of Medalists
SM .... Society of Miniaturists (EA)
sm .... Socity of Mary, Marianists (TOCD)
SM .... Soft Manual (NASA)
SM .... Soil Mechanics
SM .... Solar Magnetic [*System*] [*NASA*]
SM .... Solar Magnetospheric
SM .... Soldier's Manual
SM .... Soldier's Medal [*Military decoration*]
SM .... Solicitor's Memorandum [*IRS*] (AAGC)
SM .... Solicitor's Memorandum, United States Internal Revenue Bureau [*A publication*] (DLA)
SM .... Solid Measure (ROG)
SM .... Somatomedin [*Biochemistry*]
SM .... Song of Moses (BJA)
SM .... Sons of Malta
S/M .... Sort/Message (NITA)
SM .... Sound Management [*Radio Advertising Bureau*] [*A publication*]
SM .... Southern Minnesota Railroad
SM .... Space Medicine (SAA)
SM .... Spanish Moss
SM .... Spawning Mark
SM .... Special Memorandum
SM .... Specification Memo (AAG)
SM .... Spectrum Management (NTCM)
SM .... Speculative Masonry [*Freemasonry*]
SM .... SpenderMenders [*An association*] (EA)
SM .... Sphingomyelin [*Also, Sph*] [*Biochemistry*]
SM .... Square Meter
SM .... Stability Margin
SM .... Stabilized Member [*NASA*] (KSC)
SM .... Stack Mark (IAA)
SM .... Staff Manager [*Insurance*]
SM .... Staff Memorandum
SM .... Stage Manager
SM .... Standard Matched
SM .... Standard Memoranda (AAG)
SM .... Standard Methods
SM .... Standard Missile
SM .... Standards Manual
SM .... Stapedius Muscle [*Anatomy*] (DAVI)
SM .... Staphylococcus Medium [*Microbiology*]
SM .... State Militia [*e.g., NJSM - New Jersey State Militia*]
SM .... Static Margin
SM .... Stationary Media (GAAI)
SM .... Stationary Medium-Power [*Reactor*] [*Nuclear energy*]
SM .... Station Manager [*Broadcasting*] (NTCM)
SM .... Station Manager [*Deep Space Instrumentation Facility, NASA*]
SM .... Station Master (WDAA)
SM .... Statistical Multiplexer (MCD)
SM .... Statistiske Meddelelser [*Denmark*]
SM .... Status Monitor
SM .... Statute Mile
SM .... Stipendiary Magistrate
SM .... St. Marys Railroad Co. [*AAR code*]
SM .... Stock Market
SM .... Stock Material (SAA)
SM .... Storage Mark [*Computer science*] (OA)
SM .... Strategic Missile (NATG)
SM .... Streptomycin [*An antibiotic*]
SM .... Stria Medullaris [*Neuroanatomy*]
SM .... Strict Middling (IAA)
SM .... Strip Mine
SM .... Structural Mechanical (MCD)
SM .... Structure Memory
SM .... Structures Memorandum
SM .... Strumpell-Marie [*Disease*] [*Also, Rheumatoid Spondylitis*] [*Medicine*] (DAVI)
SM .... Student Manual [*Civil Defense*]
SM .... Studio SM [*Record label*] [*France*]
SM .... Submandibular [*Anatomy*] (DAVI)
S/M .... Submarine [*British*]
SM .... Submarine Flag [*Navy British*]
SM .... Submarine, Minelaying [*Obsolete*]
S/M .... Submarine Pay
sm .... Submetacentric [*Botany*]
SM .... Subminiature (IAA)
SM .... Submucosal [*Anatomy*] (DAVI)
SM .... Submucous [*Medicine*] (MAE)
SM .... Substituted Metabolites [*Biochemistry*] (DAVI)
SM .... Substitute for Morphine [*Pharmacology*] (DAVI)
SM .... Substitute Materials [*British*]
SM .... Suckling Mice
SM .... Sucrose Medium [*Microbiology*] (DAVI)
SM .... Suction Method [*Medicine*] (MAE)
SM .... Sulphurized Mineral Oil (IAA)
SM .... Sumerian Mythology [*S. N. Kramer*] [*A publication*] (BJA)

SM .... Summary Memorandum
SM .... Superimpose (IAA)
SM .... Superior Mesenteric [*Anatomy*] (DAVI)
SM .... Super Maneuverable Aircraft
S/M .... Super Mare [*On Sea*] [*In place names*] [*Latin*] (ROG)
SM .... Supermarket (WDMC)
SM .... Supply Manual [*Military*]
SM .... Supply Module (SSD)
SM .... Support Module [*NASA*] (NASA)
SM .... Supramamillary [*Neurology*] (DAVI)
SM .... Surface Measure
SM .... Surface Missile (AAG)
SM .... Surface Mount [*Electronics*] (EECA)
SM .... Surgeon Major
SM .... Suspended Matter [*Chemistry*]
SM .... Sustained Medication [*Pharmacology*]
SM .... Sutton [*Postcode*] (ODBW)
SM .... Symbolic Manipulation [*Computer science*]
SM .... Symptom [*Medicine*] (MAE)
SM .... Synaptic Membrane [*Medicine*] (DMAA)
SM .... Synchronous MODEM
SM .... Synovial Membrane [*Anatomy*] (DAVI)
SM .... Synthetic Medium [*Microbiology*]
SM .... Systema Malykh [*Small System*] [*Russian Computer science*]
SM .... Systemic Mastocytosis [*Medicine*]
SM .... System Manager [*Military*] (AFM)
SM .... System Manual (IAA)
SM .... System Mechanics
SM .... System Monitor
SM .... Systems Management [*NASA*] (MCD)
SM .... Systems Memory [*Computer science*] (BUR)
SM .... Systolic Mean [*Cardiology*]
SM .... Systolic Murmur [*Cardiology*]
SM .... Syzygy Mathematics (WDAA)
SM1 .... Signalman, First Class [*Navy rating*]
SM-1 .... Singh's Mosquito [*Tissue culture medium*] [*Microbiology*] (DAVI)
SM2 .... Signalman, Second Class [*Navy rating*]
SM3 .... Signalman, Third Class [*Navy rating*]
SMA .... Andreafsky/St. Marys, AK [*Location identifier FAA*] (FAAL)
SMA .... Atlas Aviation Simera (Pty) Ltd. [*South Africa*] [*FAA designator*] (FAAC)
SMA .... Safe Manufacturers' Association
SMA .... Saigon Mission Association (EA)
SMA .... Salad Manufacturers Association (EA)
SMA .... Salt Manufacturing Association [*British*]
SMA .... Sa Majeste Aulique [*His, or Her, Austrian Majesty*] [*French*] (ROG)
SMA .... San Manuel Arizona Railroad Co. [*AAR code*]
SMA .... Santa Maria [*Azores*] [*Airport symbol*] (OAG)
SMA .... Saw Manufacturers' Association [*British*] (BI)
SMA .... Scale Manufacturers Association (EA)
SMA .... Scheduled Maintenance Action
SMA .... Schools Music Association [*British*] (BI)
SMA .... Science Masters Association (IAA)
SMA .... Screen Manufacturers Association (EA)
SMA .... Scythe Makers' Association [*A union*] [*British*]
SMA .... Search Mode Acquisition [*Telecommunications*] (LAIN)
SMA .... Seasoning Manufacturers Association [*British*] (DBA)
SMA .... Self-Managed Account (WYGK)
SMA .... Semimajor Axis
SMA .... Senior Marine Advisor
SMA .... Senior Military Attache
SMA .... Sequential Multiple Analysis [*or Analyzer*] [*Clinical chemistry*]
SMA .... Sergeant Major Academy [*Army*]
SMA .... Sergeant Major of the Army (AABC)
SMA .... Service Merchandisers of America [*Later, NASM*] (EA)
SMA .... Shape Memory Alloy (RDA)
SMA .... Shelving Manufacturers Association (EA)
SMA .... Shielded Metal Arc [*Nickel and alloy welding*]
SMA .... Ship's Material Account
SMA .... Simulated Machine Analysis (IAA)
SMA .... Simultaneous Multichannel Autoanalyzer [*Laboratory science*] (DAVI)
SMA .... Simultaneous Multiphasic Analysis [*Medicine*]
SMA .... Single Manager Approach
SMA .... Single Manager for Ammunition [*DoD*] (MCD)
SMA .... Site Maintenance Area (AAG)
SMA .... Slave Manipulator Arm [*Astronautics*]
SMA .... Small Arms (NATG)
SMA .... Smooth Muscle Antibody (AAMN)
SMA .... Socialist Medical Association [*British*]
SMA .... Social Maturity Age
SMA .... Societe des Missionnaires d'Afrique [*Society of Missionaries of Africa*] (EA)
SMA .... Society for Medical Anthropology (EA)
SMA .... Society for Medieval Archaeology (EA)
SMA .... Society of African Missions [*Roman Catholic men's religious order*]
sma .... Society of African Missions (TOCD)
SMA .... Society of Make-up Artists (NTCM)
SMA .... Society of Management Accountants
SMA .... Society of Manufacturer's Agents [*Later, SMR*] (EA)
SMA .... Society of Marine Artists [*British*]
SMA .... Society of Maritime Arbitrators (EA)
SMA .... Society of Medical Administrators (EA)
SMA .... Society of Mineral Analysts (EA)
SMA .... Society of Municipal Arborists (EA)
SMA .... Society of Museum Archaeologists [*British*] (DBA)
SMA .... Software Maintenance Association (EA)
SMA .... Solar Maximum Analysis [*Meteorology*]
SMA .... Solder Makers' Association [*British*] (BI)
SMA .... Somatomedin A [*Biochemistry*]
SMA .... Soviet Military Administration
SMA .... Special Market Area (NTCM)
SMA .... Special Miscellaneous Account
SMA .... Special Mission Aircraft (DOMA)
SMA .... Special Mission Alteration
SMA .... Spectral Map Analysis
SMA .... Spinal Muscular Atrophy [*Medicine*]
SMA .... Spiritual Ministry for Adults (EA)
SMA .... Spontaneous Motor Activity [*Neurophysiology*]
SMA .... Squadron Maintenance Area
SMA .... Stabilized Member Assembly [*NASA*]
SMA .... Stage Management Association [*British*]
SMA .... Standard Maintenance Allowance
SMA .... Standard Methods Agar [*Microbiology*]
SMA .... State Meteorology Administration [*China*] [*Marine science*] (OSRA)
SMA .... State Mutual Life Assurance Co. of America
SMA .... Statutory Marketing Authority
SMA .... Steatite Manufacturers Association [*Later, DPCSMA*] (EA)
SMA .... Steel Manufacturers Association (EA)
SMA .... Stichting Mondiaal Alternatief [*Foundation for Ecological Development Alternatives*] [*Netherlands*] (EAIO)
SMA .... Stoker Manufacturers Association (EA)
SMA .... Strategic Management Accounting (ADA)
SMA .... Strategic Mobility Analysis [*Military*]
SMA .... Structured Markov Algorithm (MHDI)
SMA .... Stucco Manufacturers Association (EA)
SMA .... Stylomastoid Artery [*Anatomy*]
SMA .... Styrene-Maleic Anhydride [*Organic chemistry*]
SMA .... Subject Matter Area (AFM)
SMA .... Submerged Metal Arc Welding
SMA .... Submillimeter Array [*Telescope*]
SMA .... Subsequent Maintenance Assessment
SMA .... Suggested for Mature Audiences [*Motion pictures*]
SMA .... Sukuma Exploration [*Vancouver Stock Exchange symbol*]
SMA .... Summerton [*South Carolina*] [*Seismograph station code, US Geological Survey Closed*] (SEIS)
SMA .... Superior Mesenteric Artery [*Anatomy*]
SMA .... Superphosphate Manufacturers' Association [*British*] (BI)
SMA .... Superplastic Metal Alloy
SMA .... Supplemental Maintenance Appraisal
SMA .... Supplementary Motor Area [*Anatomy*]
SMA .... Support Management Area [*Mission Control Center*] [*NASA*]
SMA .... Surface Modulating Assembly [*Cytology*]
SMA .... Surface Mounting Applicator (NITA)
SMA .... Surplus Marketing Administration [*New Deal*]
SMA .... Switch, Modular, Attenuator (IAA)
SMA .... Sydney Metropolitan Area [*Australia*]
SMAA .... Secretaries and Managers' Association of Australia
SMAA .... Submarine Movement Advisory Authority (NVT)
Sma & Giff ... Smale and Giffard's English Vice-Chancellors' Reports [*A publication*] (DLA)
SMAB .... Solid Motor Assembly Building [*for Missiles*]
SMAB .... Spartan Management Action Board [*Missiles*] (MCD)
SMABF .... Superior Mesenteric Artery Blood Flow [*Medicine*] (DMAA)
SMAC .... Scene Matching Area Correlator [*Navy*] (MCD)
SMAC .... Science and Mathematics Analysis Center [*ERIC*]
SMAC .... Scientific Machine Automation Corp.
SMAC .... Senate Military Affairs Committee [*British*] (DAS)
SMAC .... Sequential Multiple Analysis Plus Computer (PDAA)
SMAC .... Sequential Multiple Analyzer Computerized [*Laboratory science*] (DAVI)
SMAC .... Serial Memory Address Counter [*Computer*]
SMAC .... Shielded Metal Arc Cutting [*Welding*]
SMAC .... Simulation, Manual and Computerized
SMAC .... Simulation Model of Automobile Collisions (IAA)
SMAC .... Single Manager for Ammunition, Conventional [*DoD*]
SMAC .... Society of Management Accountants of Canada
SMAC .... Space Maintenance Analysis Center (IAA)
SMAC .... Spartan Material Availability Control [*Army*]
SMAC .... Special Mission Attack Computer
SMAC .... State Minerals Advisory Council [*Australia*]
SMAC .... Store Multiple Access Control (MHDI)
SMAC .... Striated Microtubule-Associated Components [*Botanical cytology*]
SMAC .... Submicron Aerosol Collector
SMAC .... System Management and Control
SMACC .... Scheduling, Manpower Allocation, and Cost Control (MHDB)
SMAC/CRC ... Surface Modification and Characterization Collaborative Research Center [*Oak Ridge, TN*] [*Oak Ridge National Laboratory*] [*Department of Energy*] (GRD)
SMACH .... Sounding Machine [*Engineering*]
SMACK .... Society of Males Who Appreciate Cute Knees [*Group opposing below-the-knee fashions introduced in 1970*]
SMACNA .... Sheet Metal and Air Conditioning Contractors' National Association (EA)
SMACRATRACEN ... Small Craft Training Center
SMACS .... Serialized Missile Accounting and Control System
SMACS .... Simulated Message Analysis and Conversion Subsystem
SMACS .... Small Missions to Asteroids/Comets [*NASA, proposed*]
Sm Act .... Smith's Action at Law [*12th ed.*] [*1876*] [*A publication*] (DLA)
SMACTRACEN ... Small Craft Training Center [*Navy*] (DNAB)
SMAD .... Scaled Median Absolute Deviation [*Mathematics*]

SMAD .... Solvated Metal Atom Dispersion [*Chemistry*]
SMAD .... Sowjetische Militaeradministration
Sm Adm Pr... Smith's Admiralty Practice [*4th ed.*] [*1892*] [*A publication*] (DLA)
SMADS .... Sault Sainte Marie Air Defense Sector (SAA)
SMAE........... Sbornik Muzeia Antropologii i Etnografii [*A publication*] (BJA)
SMAE........... Society of Model Aeronautical Engineers [*British*]
SMAE........... Superior Mesenteric Artery Embolus [*Medicine*]
SMAE........... System Management Application Entity
SMAF........... Afobaka [*Surinam*] [*ICAO location identifier*] (ICLI)
SMAF........... Shipboard Maintenance Action Form (DNAB)
SMAF........... Smooth Muscle Activating Factor
SMAF........... Special Mission Aircraft Flights (NATG)
SMAF........... Specific Macrophage Arming Factor [*Hematology*]
SMAF........... Superior Mesenteric Artery Flow
SMAG .... Simulator Missile Airborne and Ground (MCD)
SMAG .... Special Medical Advisory Group (DMAA)
SMAG .... Star Magnitude (NASA)
SMAG .... Systems Management Analysis Group (MCD)
SMAGOL...... Small Computer Algorithmic Language (DNAB)
SMAI........... Solvated Metal Atom Impregnation [*Chemistry*]
SMAIL.......... Source Mail [*Electronic mail*]
SMAJ .... Sergeant Major
SMAL........... Serum Methyl Alcohol Level [*Medicine*] (DMAA)
SMAL........... Single Mode Alignment (CAAL)
SMAL........... Society for Musteline Arts and Literature (EA)
SMAL........... Storage Multiple Access Control (NITA)
SMAL........... Structural Macroassembly Language
SMAL........... System Material Analysis List
SMALC......... Sacramento Air Logistics Center (MCD)
Smale & G... Smale and Giffard's English Vice-Chancellors' Reports [*A publication*] (DLA)
SMALGOL.... Small Computer Algorithmic Language
SMALL.......... Selenium Diode Matrix Alloy Logic (IAA)
Smallww....... Smallworldwide PLC [*Associated Press*] (SAG)
SMAM.......... Amotopo [*Surinam*] [*ICAO location identifier*] (ICLI)
SMAM.......... Single Mission Air Medal (DNAB)
SMAMA........ Sacramento Air Materiel Area (KSC)
SMAME........ Society of Marine Architects and Marine Engineers (EA)
Sm Amt .... Small Amount (CPH)
sm an .... Small Animal (DAVI)
SMAN .... Standard Management [*NASDAQ symbol*] (TTSB)
SMAN .... Standard Management Corp. [*NASDAQ symbol*] (SAG)
SMAN .... Standard Medium-Accuracy Navigator
SMANCS...... Styrene Maleic Acid Neocarzinostatin [*Antineoplastic drug*]
Sm & Bat..... Smith and Batty's Irish King's Bench Reports [*A publication*] (DLA)
Sm & BRR Cas... Smith and Bates' American Railway Cases [*A publication*] (DLA)
SM & DSL ... Sector Management and Direct Support Logistics Center [*Navy*] (DNAB)
Sm & G .... Smale and Giffard's English Vice-Chancery Reports [*A publication*] (DLA)
Sm & G .... Smith and Guthrie's Missouri Appeal Reports [*81-101 Missouri*] [*A publication*] (DLA)
Sm & M....... Smedes and Marshall's Mississippi Reports [*9-22 Mississippi*] [*A publication*] (DLA)
Sm & M Ch... Smedes and Marshall's Mississippi Reports [*9-22 Mississippi*] [*A publication*] (DLA)
Sm & S........ Smith and Sager's Drainage Cases [*Canada*] [*A publication*] (DLA)
SM & S........ Systems Management and Sequencing (NASA)
Sm & Sod L & T... Smith and Soden on Landlord and Tenant [*2nd ed.*] [*1878*] [*A publication*] (DLA)
SMANP .... Standard Mgmt 11% Cv 'S' Pfd [*NASDAQ symbol*] (TTSB)
SMAO .... Society of Management Accountants of Ontario [*Canada*] (DD)
SMAO .... Superior Mesenteric Artery Occlusion [*Medicine*] (DMAA)
Smap........... Surprised Middle-Aged Person [*Lifestyle classification*]
SMAP........... System Management Application Process [*or Protocol*] [*Telecommunications*]
SMAP........... Systems Management Analysis Project (MCD)
SMAQ .... Stipendiary Magistrates Association, Queensland [*Australia*]
SMAR .... Sheet Metal Assembler Riveter (MCD)
SMAR .... Summary of Monthly Aerological Reports [*Navy*] (DNAB)
SMARC .... Survivable-MOS [*Metal-Oxide Semiconductor*] Array Computer [*Air Force*]
SM Arch S... Master of Science in Architectural Studies (PGP)
SMART .... Salton's Magical Automatic Retriever of Texts [*Computer science*]
SMART .... Satellite Maintenance and Repair Techniques [*Air Force*]
SMART .... Satellite Monitoring and Remote Tracking
SMART .... Scheduled Maintenance and Reliability Team (MCD)
SMART .... Science, Mathematics, and Related Technologies
SMART .... Selected Methods for Attracting the Right Targets [*Bombing system*] (AFM)
SMART .... Self-Monitoring, Analysis and Reporting Technology [*Computer science*]
SMART .... Sensitive-Membrane-Antigen-Rapid-Test
SMART .... Sequential Mechanism for Automatic Recording and Testing
SMART .... Shuttle Meeting Action - Item Review Tracking [*NASA*] (NASA)
SMART .... Simplified Method to Achieve Regulated Training
SMART .... Simultaneous Multiple Angle Reconstruction Technique [*Medicine*] (DMAA)
SMART .... Small Firms Merit Award for Research and Technology [*British*]
SMART .... Socony Mobil Automatic Real Time (DIT)
SMART .... Software Metering and Resource Tracking [*Computer science*]
SMART .... Sort Merge and Reduction Tapes (CAAL)
SMART .... Source Management of Resources and Time (DNAB)
SMART .... Space Maintenance and Repair Techniques
SMART .... Space Management and Retail Tracking System [*Information Resources, Inc.*]
SMART .... Spacesaver Material Accounting Resource Terminal [*Spacesaver Corp.*]
SMART .... Specific, Measurable, Agreed-To, Reachable, Time-Specific [*Management technique*]
SMART .... State and Metropolitan Analyses of Regional Transportation [*BTS*] (TAG)
SMART .... Stop Merchandising Alcohol on Radio and Television
SMART .... Structural Maintenance and Repair Team (MCD)
SMART .... Supermarket Allocation and Recorder Technique (IAA)
SMART .... Supersonic Military Air Research Track
SMART .... Supersonic Missile and Rocket Track
SMART .... Supply and Maintenance Assessment and Review Team [*Army*]
SMART .... System for Management and Allocation of Resources Technique [*Computer science*]
SMART .... System for Manipulation and Retrieval of Text
SMART .... System for the Mechanical Analysis and Retrieval of Text
SMART .... System Malfunction Analysis Reinforcement Trainer
SMART .... System Management and Review Technique (HGAA)
SMART .... System Monitoring and Reporting Tool (HGAA)
SMART .... Systems Management Analysis, Research, and Testing (MCD)
SMART .... Systems Managers Administrative Rating Test [*Simulation game*]
SMART .... University of Saskatchewan Libraries Machine-Assisted Reference Teleservices [*University of Saskatchewan Library*] [*Information service or system*] (IID)
SMARTee .... Smart End-Effector [*Robotics*] (ECON)
Smartel........ Smartel Communications Corp. [*Associated Press*] (SAG)
SMARTIE ..... Simple-Minded Artificial Intelligence (PDAA)
SMARTIE ..... Submarine Automatic Remote Television Inspection Equipment (PDAA)
SMARTII ...... Simple-Minded Artificial Intelligence (IAA)
SmarTlk........ SmarTalk TeleServices, Inc. [*Associated Press*] (SAG)
SMARTS ...... Selective Multiple Addresses Radio and Television Service [*A program delivery service introduced by RCA*]
SMARTS ...... Sport Management Art and Science Society [*Defunct*] (EA)
SMARTS ...... Status Memory and Real Time System [*AT & T*]
SMARTS ...... Submarine Advanced Reactive Tactical Training System
SMART-T ..... Secure Mobile, Anti-Jam, Reliable Tactical Trainer [*Army*]
SMAS........... Society for the Maintenance of the Apostolic See (DICI)
SMAS........... Subcontract Material Availability Schedule
SMAS........... Submuscular Aponeurotic System [*Medicine*]
SMAS........... Superficial Musculoaponeurotic System [*Plastic surgery*]
SMAS........... Switched Maintenance Access System [*Bell System*]
SMASE......... Systems Management Application Service Element [*Telecommunications*] (OSI)
SMASF......... Servicemen's Mutual Aid and Savings Fund [*South Vietnam*]
SMASH......... Small Manned Anti-Submarine Helicopter (SAA)
SMASH......... Southeast Asia Multisensor Armed Surveillance Helicopter
SMASH......... Step-by-Step Monitor and Selector Hold [*Telecommunications*] (TEL)
SMASH......... Students Mobilizing on Auto Safety Hazards [*Student legal action organization*] (EA)
SMASHEX.... Search for Simulated Submarine Casualty Exercise [*Navy*] (NVT)
SMASHT....... Simple-Minded Approach to Squeezed Hollerith Text (SAA)
SMASS .... Small Main-Belt Asteroid Spectroscopic Survey
SMAST......... Short Michigan Alcoholism Screening Test (EDAC)
SMAT........... School Motivation Analysis Test [*Personality development test*] [*Psychology*]
SMAT........... Superior Mesenteric Artery Thrombosis [*Medicine*]
SMATH .... Satellite Materials Hardening (MCD)
SMATS......... Speed-Modulated Augmented Thrust System (NG)
SMATV......... Satellite Master Antenna Television
SMATV......... Satellite Master Antenna Television Systems (NITA)
SMAW .... Second Marine Aircraft Wing
SMAW .... Shielded Metal Arc Welding
SMAW .... Shoulder-Launched Multipurpose Assault Weapon (MCD)
SMAW .... Shoulder-Mounted Assault Weapon (DWSG)
SMAW .... Submerged Metal Arc Weld [*Nuclear energy*] (NRCH)
SMAWT........ Short-Range Man-Portable Antitank Weapons Technology
SMB............. Bachelor of Sacred Music
SMB............. Cerro Sombrero [*Chile*] [*Airport symbol*] (AD)
SMB............. Samaipata [*Bolivia*] [*Seismograph station code, US Geological Survey Closed*] (SEIS)
SMB............. Sa Majeste Britannique [*His or Her Britannic Majesty*] [*French*]
SMB............. Selected Mucosal Biopsy [*Medicine*] (DMAA)
SMB............. Server Message Blocks (PCM)
SMB............. Simba Resources, Inc. [*Vancouver Stock Exchange symbol*]
SMB............. Simulated Moving Bed [*Chemical engineering*]
SMB............. Small and Medium-Sized Businesses
SMB............. Space Meteorology Branch [*NASA*]
SMB............. Standard Merchants Bank [*British*]
SMB............. Standard Mineral Base [*Medium*] [*Medicine*]
SMB............. Static Memory Board [*Computer science*] (BYTE)
SMB............. Steve Miller Band [*Pop music group*]
SMB............. Stock Medicines Board [*Australia*]
sMb............. Suckling Mouse Brain [*Microbiology*] (DMAA)
SMB............. System Message Block [*Telecommunications*] (PCM)
SMB............. System Monitor Board
SMB............. Systems Management Branch [*Space Environmental Laboratory*] (USDC)
SMB............. Systems Management Branch [*Marine science*] (OSRA)
SMBA........... Scottish Marine Biological Association [*British*] (IRUK)
SMBA........... Slovenian Mutual Benefit Association [*Later, AMLA*] (EA)
SMBC........... Santuario Madre del Buon Consiglio [*Pious Union of Our Mother of Good Counsel - PUMGC*] [*Genazzano, Italy*] (EAIO)

SMBC.......... SouMOBc [*NASDAQ symbol*] (SAG)
SMBC.......... Southern Missouri Bancorp [*NASDAQ symbol*] (TTSB)
SMBDB........ Structural Margin Beyond Design Basis [*Nuclear energy*] (NRCH)
SMBF.......... Superior Mesenteric Blood Flow [*Physiology*]
SMBFT......... Small Bowel Follow-Through [*Medicine*]
SMBG.......... Bakhuys [*Surinam*] [*ICAO location identifier*] (ICLI)
SMBG.......... Self-Monitoring of Blood Glucose [*Medicine*]
SMBJ.......... Style Manual for Biological Journals
SMBL.......... Semimobile
SMBL.......... Stratocumulus-Topped Boundary Layer (USDC)
SMBL.......... Stratocumulus-Topped Boundary Layer [*Marine science*] (OSRA)
SMBN.......... Albina [*Surinam*] [*ICAO location identifier*] (ICLI)
SMBO.......... Botopasie [*Surinam*] [*ICAO location identifier*] (ICLI)
SMBS.......... Safeguard Material Balance Simulator
SMBSA........ Stock Medicines Board of South Australia
SMBT.......... Master of Science in Building Technology (PGP)
Sm Bus Rep... Small Business Reports [*A publication*] (BRI)
SMBW.......... Bronsweg [*Surinam*] [*ICAO location identifier*] (ICLI)
SMC............ Chief Signalman [*Navy rating*]
SMC............ Medical University of South Carolina Library, Charleston, SC [*OCLC symbol*] (OCLC)
SMC............ Sabang Merauke Raya Air Charter PT [*Indonesia*] [*ICAO designator*] (FAAC)
SMC............ SAGE [*Semiautomatic Ground Environment*] Maintenance Control
SMC............ Saint Martin's College [*Washington*]
SMC............ Saint Mary's College [*Indiana; Kansas; Michigan; Minnesota*]
SMC............ Saint Michael's College [*Vermont*]
SMC............ Sa Majeste Catholique [*His or Her Catholic Majesty*] [*of Spain*] [*French*]
SMC............ Save the Manatee Club (EA)
SMC............ Scientific Manpower Commission (EA)
SMC............ Scottish Mountaineering Club (BARN)
SMC............ Sealant Manufacturers Conference [*Federation of British Rubber and Allied Manufacturers*] (BI)
SMC............ Secondary Mesenchyme Cell [*Cytology*]
SMC............ Segmented Maintenance Cask [*Nuclear energy*] (NRCH)
SMC............ Selective Market Coverage [*Advertising*] (WDMC)
SMC............ Senior Management Committee (AIE)
SMC............ Senior Medical Consultant
SMC............ Senior Mission Controller (MCD)
SMC............ Sensory Mother Cell [*Genetics*]
SMC............ Sensory Organ Mother Cell [*Genetics*]
SMC............ Sequential Machine Controller [*Programming language*] [*1977-78*] (CSR)
SMC............ Service Men's Center [*World War II*]
SMC............ Sheet Molding Compound [*Plastics technology*]
SMC............ Short-Run Marginal Cost Curve [*Economics*]
SMC............ Shunt Mounted Chip (IAA)
SMC............ Silicon Monolithic Circuit
SMC............ Silva Mind Control [*Psychic system*]
SMC............ Single Mothers by Choice (EA)
smc............ Small Capitals [*Typography*] (BARN)
SMC............ Small Magellanic Cloud [*Astronomy*]
SMC............ Smith [*A. O.*] Corp. [*AMEX symbol*] (SPSG)
SMC............ Smooth Muscle Cell [*Cytology*]
SMC............ Societe Mediterraneenne de Chimiotherapie [*Mediterranean Society of Chemotherapy - MSC*] [*Italy*] (EAIO)
SMC............ Society of Marine Consultants (EA)
SMC............ Soil and Moisture Conservation
SMC............ Solar Monitor Constant (SSD)
SMC............ Somatomedin C [*Biochemistry*]
SMC............ Somerset [*Colorado*] [*Seismograph station code, US Geological Survey*] (SEIS)
SmC............ Southern Microfilm Corporation, Houston, TX [*Library symbol Library of Congress*] (LCLS)
SMC............ Southern Missionary College [*Tennessee*]
SMC............ Southern Motor Carriers Rate Conference, Atlanta GA [*STAC*]
SMC............ Space and Missile Systems Center [*Air Force*] (AAGC)
SMC............ Spanish Music Center [*Commercial firm*] (EA)
SMC............ Special Monthly Compensation (MAE)
SMC............ Special Mouth Care [*Medicine*]
S-M-C.......... Sperm [*or Spore*] Mother-Cell
SMC............ Spin Muon Collaboration [*Nuclear research*]
SMC............ Squared Multiple Correlation [*Psychology*]
SMC............ Squawk Mode Code [*Aviation*] (FAAC)
SMC............ Staff Message Control [*Military*]
SMC............ Standard Mean Chord [*Aviation*] (AIA)
SMC............ Standard-Modern Technologies Corp. [*Toronto Stock Exchange symbol*]
SMC............ Standard Molding Corp.
SMC............ Standard Motorists Centre [*Automotive sales and service chain*] [*British*]
SMC............ Station-Control and Monitor Console Subsystem [*Deep Space Instrumentation Facility, NASA*]
SMC............ Steady Magnetospheric Convection
SMC............ Stepper Motor Control
SMC............ Storage Module Controller
SMC............ Structural Maintenance of Chromosome [*Cytology*]
SMC............ Student Mobilization Committee [*to End the War in Vietnam*] [*Defunct*] (EA)
SMC............ Sub-Machine Carbine [*British military*] (DMA)
SMC............ Succinylmonocholine [*Biochemistry*] (MAE)
SMC............ Sunnybrook Medical Centre, Toronto [*UTLAS symbol*]
SMC............ Super-Multi-Coating [*Camera lenses*]
SMC............ Supply and Maintenance Command [*Army*]
SMC............ Surface Mount Component [*Environmental science*]
SMC............ Surface Movement Control [*Aviation*]
SMC............ Switch Maintenance Center [*Telecommunications*] (TEL)
SMC............ Synchronized Maneuver Countermeasures Model (MCD)
SMC............ System Monitor Console (CAAL)
SMC............ System Monitor Controller (NITA)
SMC............ Systems, Man, and Cybernetics (MCD)
SMCA.......... Cayana [*Surinam*] [*ICAO location identifier*] (ICLI)
SMCA.......... Single Manager for Conventional Ammunition [*DoD*]
SMC.A......... Smith (A.O.) Cl'A' [*AMEX symbol*] (TTSB)
SMCA.......... Sodium Monochloroacetate [*Organic chemistry*]
SMCA.......... Suckling Mouse Cataract Agent [*Microbiology*]
SMCAA........ Sheet Molding Compound Automotive Alliance [*An association*]
SMCAF........ Society of Medical Consultants to the Armed Forces (EA)
sm cap........ Small Capitals [*Typography*] (WGA)
SMCC.......... Saint Mary's College of California
SMCC.......... Santa Monica City College [*California*]
SMCC.......... Shuttle Mission Control Center [*NASA*] (NASA)
SMCC.......... Simulation Monitor and Control Console (KSC)
SMCC.......... SMC Corp. [*NASDAQ symbol*] (SAG)
SMCC.......... Society of Memorial Cancer Center
SMCC.......... Sport Medicine Council of Canada
SMCC.......... Standard Machinery Control Console [*Canadian Navy*]
SMCC.......... State Manpower Coordinating Committee [*Department of Labor*]
SMCC.......... Succinimidyl (Maleimidomethyl)cyclohexanecarboxylate [*Organic chemistry*]
SMCC.......... System Monitoring and Coordinating Center [*National Weather Service*] (USDC)
SMCC.......... System Monitoring and Coordinating Center [*Marine science*] (OSRA)
SMC-CF....... Smooth Muscle Cell-Chemotactic Factor [*Oncology*]
Sm CCM....... Smith's Circuit Courts-Martial Reports [*Maine*] [*A publication*] (DLA)
SMC Cp....... SMC Corp. [*Associated Press*] (SAG)
SMC(Disp)... Spectacle Makers Co. (Dispenser) [*British*] (DI)
SMCE.......... Master of Science in Civil Engineering
SMCE.......... Sociedad Mexicana de Computacion Electronica [*Mexico*]
SMCH.......... Standard Mixed Cargo Harness (NASA)
SMchG......... Southeastern Michigan Gas Enterprises, Inc. [*Associated Press*] (SAG)
SMCHMA..... Supreme Master Ching Hai Meditation Association (EA)
Sm Ch Pr..... Smith's Chancery Practice [*7th ed.*] [*1862*] [*A publication*] (DLA)
SMCI.......... Coeroeni [*Surinam*] [*ICAO location identifier*] (ICLI)
Smckr......... Smucker [*J.M.*] Co. [*Associated Press*] (SAG)
SMCL.......... Secondary Maximum Contaminant Level (EG)
SMCL.......... Southeastern Massachusetts Cooperating Libraries [*Library network*]
SMCLN........ Semicolon (AABC)
SMCM.......... Master Chief Signalman [*Navy rating*]
SMCM.......... Surface Mine Countermeasures [*Navy*] (DOMA)
SMCN.......... Selective Myocardial Cell Necrosis [*Cardiology*]
SMCO.......... Coronie [*Surinam*] [*ICAO location identifier*] (ICLI)
SMCO.......... SAGE [*Semiautomatic Ground Environment*] Maintenance Control Office
SMCO.......... Simpson Manufacturing [*NASDAQ symbol*] (TTSB)
SMCO.......... Simpson Manufacturing Company, Inc. [*NASDAQ symbol*] (SAG)
Sm Com L.... Smith's Manual of Common Law [*12th ed.*] [*1905*] [*A publication*] (DLA)
Sm Con........ Smith on Contracts [*8th ed.*] [*1885*] [*A publication*] (DLA)
Sm Cond Ala... Smith's Condensed Alabama Reports [*A publication*] (DLA)
Sm Const Cons... Smith on Constitutional and Statutory Construction [*A publication*] (DLA)
Sm Conv....... Smith on Conveyancing [*A publication*] (DLA)
SMCP.......... San Marino Communist Party
SMCP.......... Supply and Maintenance Career Program
SMCP.......... Supply and Maintenance Control Point
SMCPA........ System of Multi-Cultural Pluralistic Assessment [*Psychiatry*] (DAVI)
SMCPCF...... Fort Walsh National Historic Park, Parks Canada [*Parc Historique National Fort Walsh, Parcs Canada*] Maple Creek, Saskatchewan [*Library symbol National Library of Canada*] (NLC)
SMCPSTC.... Supply and Maintenance Command Packaging Storage and Transportability Center [*Army*]
SMCR.......... Selected Marine Corps Reserve
SMCR.......... Smith-Magenis Chromosome Region [*Medicine*] (DMAA)
SMCR.......... Society for Menstrual Cycle Research (EA)
SMCRA........ Surface Mining Control and Reclamation Act [*1977*]
SMCRC........ Southern Motor Carriers Rate Conference
SMCS.......... IEEE Systems, Man, and Cybernetics Society (EA)
SMCS.......... Senior Chief Signalman [*Navy rating*]
SMCS.......... Separation Monitor and Control System [*NASA*] (MCD)
SMCS.......... Simulation Monitor and Control System (CAAL)
SMCS.......... Star Multi Care Services, Inc. [*NASDAQ symbol*] (SAG)
SMCS.......... Star Multi Care Svcs [*NASDAQ symbol*] (TTSB)
SMCS.......... Structural Mode Control System (MCD)
SMCSG........ Special Military Construction Study Group (AABC)
SMCT.......... Cottica [*Surinam*] [*ICAO location identifier*] (ICLI)
SMCT.......... Soldier's Manual of Common Tasks [*A publication*] (ADDR)
SMCTG........ Standard Missile Correlation Task Group [*Military*]
SMCTG........ Surface Missile Compatibility Test Group [*Military*]
SMCU.......... Separation Monitoring Control Unit [*NASA*] (MCD)
SMD............ Doctor of Sacred Music
SMD............ Fort Wayne, IN [*Location identifier FAA*] (FAAL)
SMD............ Saint Michael's College, Library, Winooski, VT [*OCLC symbol*] (OCLC)
SMD............ Sauter Mean Diameter (KSC)
SMD............ Sauter Mean Droplet [*Diesel engine fuel injection*]
SMD............ Scheduling Management Display
SMD............ Scottish Malt Distillers [*British*]

SMD............ Semiconductor Magnetic Field Detector (IAA)
SMD............ Senile Macular Degeneration [*Medicine*]
SMD............ Serum Malic Dehydrogenase [*An enzyme*]
SMD............ Service and Methods Demonstration [*Program*] [*TRB*] (TAG)
SMD............ Ship Manning Document [*Navy*]
SMD............ Short Meter Double [*Music*]
SMD............ Silicon Multiplier Detector
SMD............ Single Molecule Detection [*Analytical chemistry*]
SMD............ Singular Multinomial Distribution [*Statistics*]
SMD............ Society of Medical-Dental Management Consultants (EA)
SMD............ Soil Moisture Deficit (PDAA)
SMD............ Spacelab Mission Development [*NASA*] (MCD)
SMD............ Special Measuring Device (NASA)
SMD............ Speed Measuring Device (PDAA)
SMD............ Spondylometaphyseal Dysplasias [*Medicine*]
SMD............ Standardized Military Drawing Program (AAGC)
SMD............ Standardized Military Drawings [*Army*]
SMD............ Statistical Methods Division [*Bureau of the Census*] (OICC)
SMD............ Stop Motion Detector
SMD............ Storage Module Device [*Computer science*]
SMD............ Storage Module Drive
SMD............ Structures and Mechanics Division [*NASA*]
SMD............ Submanubrial Dullness [*Medicine*]
SMD............ Submarine Mine Depot
SMD............ Submersible Mining Device
SMD............ Sunrise Medical [*NYSE symbol*] (TTSB)
SMD............ Sunrise Medical, Inc. [*NYSE symbol*] (SPSG)
SMD............ Superintendent of Mine Design (WDAA)
SMD............ Surface Mountable Device (NITA)
SMD............ Surface Mounted Device [*Microelectronics*]
SMD............ Surplus Materials Division (AAGC)
SMD............ Susceptor Meus Dominus [*God Is My Protector*] [*Motto of Jacob, Margrave of Baden-Hochberg (1562-90); Georg Friedrich, Margrave of Baden-Hochberg (1573-1638)*] [*Latin*]
SMD............ Symptom Medication Diary [*Medicine*]
SMD............ Synchronous Modulator-Demodulator (MCD)
SMD............ System Management Directive (AFM)
SMD............ Systems Display [*Vancouver Stock Exchange symbol*]
SMD............ Systems Manufacturing Division [*IBM Corp.*]
SMD............ Systems Measuring Device (KSC)
SMD............ Systems Monitor Display
SMDA.......... Drietabbetje [*Surinam*] [*ICAO location identifier*] (ICLI)
SMDA.......... Second Marine Division Association (EA)
SMDA.......... Sewing Machine Dealers Association Ltd. [*British*] (BI)
SMDA.......... Sixth Marine Division Association [*Later, 6th MAR DIV*] (EA)
SMDA.......... State Medicaid Directors Association (EA)
SMDC.......... Saint Mary's Dominican College [*Louisiana*]
SMDC.......... Shielded Mild Detonating Cord
SMDC.......... Sisters of Mercy, Daughters of Christian Charity of St. Vincent de Paul [*Roman Catholic religious order*]
SMDC.......... Sisters of Mercy of Christian Charity of St. Vincent de Paul of Hungary (TOCD)
SMDC.......... Sodium Methyldithiocarbamate [*Fungicide*]
SMDC.......... Superconductive Materials Data Center (KSC)
SMDE.......... Static Mercury Drop Electrode [*Electrochemistry*]
SMD-E.......... Storage Module Drive - Enhanced [*Computer science*] (BTTJ)
SM Dendrol... Master of Science in Dendrology
SMDF.......... SCATS [*Simulation, Checkout, and Training System*] Main Distributing Frame
SMDG.......... Standoff Mine Detection Ground [*Army*] (DOMA)
SMDI.......... Surface Miss Distance Indicator [*Navy*] (CAAL)
SMDJ.......... Djoemoe [*Surinam*] [*ICAO location identifier*] (ICLI)
SMDK.......... Donderskamp [*Surinam*] [*ICAO location identifier*] (ICLI)
SMDL.......... Spares Master Data Log (IAA)
SMDL.......... Standard Music Description Language [*Computer science*]
SMDL.......... Subminiature Microwave Delay Line
SMDMC........ Society of Medical-Dental Management Consultants (EA)
SMDO.......... Ladoeanie [*Surinam*] [*ICAO location identifier*] (ICLI)
SMDO.......... Special Microwave Devices Operation [*Raytheon Co.*]
SMD, OCOFS... Staff Management Division, Office, Chief of Staff [*Army*]
SMD OC of SA... Staff Management Division, Office, Chief of Staff, Army (AABC)
SMD OCSA... Staff Management Division, Office, Chief of Staff, Army (AABC)
SMDP.......... Scottish Microelectronics Development Programme (NITA)
SMDP.......... Stock Management Description Pattern
SMDPL........ Supply Management Date and Price List [*Navy*]
SMDPS........ Service Module Deluge Purge System [*NASA*] (KSC)
SMDPS........ Strategic Mission Data Preparation System [*Air Force*] (DOMA)
SMDR.......... Selected Management Data Report [*DoD*]
SMDR.......... Station Message Detail Recorder (NITA)
SMDR.......... Station Message Detail Recording [*Formerly, MDR*] [*Telecommunications*]
SMDR.......... Structure Manning Decision Review
SMDR.......... Summary Management Data Report [*DoD*]
SMDS.......... Switched Multimegabit Data Service [*Telecommunications*] (PCM)
SMDT.......... Shore Mode Data Transmitter (MCD)
SME............ Sales and Marketing Executives-International (EA)
SME............ Sancta Mater Ecclesia [*Holy Mother Church*] [*Latin*]
SME............ Scale Model Engineering [*Initialism is brand name of tone arm*]
SME............ School of Military Engineering
SME............ Science, Mathematics, and Engineering (RDA)
SME............ Semiconductor Manufacturing Equipment [*Sumitomo Metals*]
SME............ Service Merchandise [*NYSE symbol*] (TTSB)
SME............ Service Merchandise Co., Inc. [*NYSE symbol*] (SPSG)
SME............ Shape Memory Effect [*Metal alloy property*]
SME............ Sheet Metal Enclosure
SME............ Shell Metal Extractant
SME............ Shipbuilding and Marine Engineering [*Department of Employment*] [*British*]
SME............ SHOWME [*VERALEX, Inc.*] [*Information service or system*] (CRD)
SME............ Singleton Materials Engineering Laboratories [*Tennessee Valley Authority*] (GRD)
SME............ Small and Medium-Size Enterprises
SME............ Small-to-Medium Enterprise
SME............ SM Exports Ltd. [*British ICAO designator*] (FAAC)
SME............ Society for Mining, Metallurgy, and Exploration, Inc. [*In association name, SME , Inc.*] (EA)
SME............ Society of Manufacturing Engineers (EA)
SME............ Society of Military Engineers (KSC)
SME............ Soil Mechanics Experiment [*NASA*]
SME............ Solar Mesosphere Explorer (MCD)
SME............ Somerset, KY [*Location identifier FAA*] (FAAL)
SME............ Sony Music Entertainment (ECON)
SME............ Spartan Missile Equipment [*Missiles*] (MCD)
SME............ Squadron Medical Element
SME............ Stalk Median Eminence [*Anatomy*]
SME............ Standard Medical Examination [*Military*]
SME............ Static Mission Equivalent (IAA)
SME............ Stellar Mass Ejection
SME............ Subject Matter Expert (NVT)
SME............ Surface Measuring Equipment
SME............ Surface Movement Element (AFIT)
SME............ Suriname [*International vehicle registration*] (ODBW)
SMEA.......... Sun Marine Employees Association (EA)
SMEAC........ Science, Mathematics, and Environmental Education Information Analysis Center
SMEADO...... Selected Major Exploratory Advanced Development Objective (MCD)
SMEAG........ Research Station, Agriculture Canada [*Station de Recherches, Agriculture Canada*], Melfort, Saskatchewan [*Library symbol National Library of Canada*] (BIB)
SMEAR........ SPAN [*Spacecraft Analysis*] Mission Evaluation Action Request [*NASA*] (GFGA)
SMEAT........ Skylab Medical Experiments Altitude Test [*NASA*]
SMEC.......... Single Module Engine Control [*Automotive engineering*]
SMEC.......... Strategic Missile Evaluation Committee [*Air Force*]
Sm Ecc Cts... Smith on Ecclesiastical Courts [*7th ed.*] [*1920*] [*A publication*] (DLA)
SMECTYMNUS... Steven Marshall, Edward Calamy, Thomas Young, Matthew Newcomen, William Spurstow [*Collective author of 17th-century antiepiscopal tract*]
SMED.......... Shared Medical Sys [*NASDAQ symbol*] (TTSB)
SMED.......... Shared Medical Systems Corp. [*NASDAQ symbol*] (NQ)
SMED.......... Single Minute Exchange of Die [*Manufacturing*]
Sm Ed.......... Smith's Education for the English Bar [*A publication*] (DLA)
Smed & M... Smedes and Marshall's Mississippi Reports [*A publication*] (DLA)
Smed & M Ch... Smedes and Marshall's Mississippi Chancery Reports [*A publication*] (DLA)
Smedes and Marshall's Chy Repts... Smedes and Marshall's Mississippi Chancery Reports [*A publication*] (DLA)
Smedes & M Ch... Smedes and Marshall's Mississippi Chancery Reports [*A publication*] (DLA)
Smedes & M (Miss)... Smedes and Marshall's Mississippi Reports [*A publication*] (DLA)
SMEDI.......... Stillbirth-Mummification, Embryonic-Death, Infertility Syndrome [*Medicine*] (DMAA)
SmedvA....... Smedvig Asa [*Associated Press*] (SAG)
SmedvB....... Smedvig Asa [*Associated Press*] (SAG)
Smee........... Collection of Abstracts of Acts of Parliament [*A publication*] (DLA)
SMEE........... Master of Science in Electrical Engineering
SMEE........... Society of Model and Experimental Engineers [*British*] (BI)
SMEF........... Smooth Muscle-Derived Elastogenic Factor [*Biochemistry*]
SME-I.......... Sales and Marketing Executives-International [*Cleveland, OH*] (EA)
SMEI........... Sales and Marketing Executives International [*An association*] [*Cleveland, OH*] (WDMC)
SMEI........... Severe Myoclonic Epilepsy of Infancy [*Medicine*] (DMAA)
SMEK.......... Summary Message Enable Keyboard
Sm El.......... Smith's Elements of Law [*A publication*] (DLA)
SMELT......... Smelting
SMEM.......... Serial Memory (NITA)
SMEM.......... Supplemented Eagle's Minimum Essential Medium [*Medicine*] (DMAA)
SMEMA........ Surface Mount Equipment Manufacturers Association (EA)
Sm Eng........ Smith's English King's Bench Reports [*A publication*] (DLA)
SME of AIME... Society of Mining Engineers of American Institute of Mining, Metallurgical, and Petroleum Engineers [*Later, SME, Inc.*] (EA)
SMEP.......... Society of Multivariate Experimental Psychology (EA)
Sm Eq.......... Smith's Principles of Equity [*A publication*] (DLA)
SMER.......... Skylab Mission Evaluation Report [*NASA*] (MCD)
SM-ER.......... Surface Missile, Extended Range
SMERC........ San Mateo Educational Resources Center [*San Mateo County Office of Education*] [*Information service or system*] (IID)
SMERE........ SPRINT Missile Electromagnetic Radiation Evaluation [*Army*] (AABC)
SMERF........ Social, Military, Ethnic, Religious, and Fraternal Groups [*Market segment*]
SMERFS...... Statistical Modeling and Estimation Review of Functioning Software [*Science Applications International Corp.*]
SMERP........ Supplemental Medical Expense Reimbursement Plan
SMERSH...... Smert' Shpionam [*Death to the Spies*] [*Former Soviet Union state security organization, often referred to in the popular James Bond espionage stories*]
SMES.......... Shuttle Mission Engineering Simulator [*NASA*] (NASA)
SMES.......... Shuttle Mission Evaluation Simulation [*NASA*] (NASA)

SMES .... Strategic Missile Evaluation Squadron
SMES .... Superconducting Magnetic Energy Storage (NASA)
SMESA .... Special Middle East Sealift Agreement (DOMA)
SME/SC .... SPRINT Missile Engineering/Service Course [*Army*] (AABC)
SMET .... Science Mathematics Engineering and Technology
SMET .... Simulated Mission Endurance Test (MCD)
SMET .... Spacecraft Maneuver Engine Transients [*Apollo program*] [*NASA*]
SMETC .... Swiss Mouse Embryo Tissue Culture
SMETDS .... Standard Message Trunk Design System [*Telecommunications*] (TEL)
Smeth LS .... Smethurst on Locus Standi [*1867*] [*A publication*] (DLA)
SMETO .... Staff Meteorological Officer [*NATO*] (NATG)
SMEX .... Singapore International Monetary Exchange
Sm Ex Int .... Smith on Executory Interest [*A publication*] (DLA)
SMF .... Sacramento [*California*] [*Airport symbol*] (OAG)
SMF .... Sacramento, CA [*Location identifier FAA*] (FAAL)
SMF .... Sales Manpower Foundation (EA)
SMF .... Sample Management Facility
SMF .... S & M Photolabels, Inc. [*Toronto Stock Exchange symbol*]
SMF .... Saticon Mixed-Field [*Video technology*]
SMF .... Saw Machine Fixture (MCD)
SMF .... S-Band Multifrequency
SMF .... Schumann Memorial Foundation [*Defunct*] (EA)
SMF .... Scientific Marriage Foundation (EA)
SMF .... Screw Machine Feeder
SMF .... Senior Management Forum [*Information Industry Association*]
SMF .... Service to Military Families [*Red Cross*]
SMF .... Shaker Museum Foundation (EA)
SMF .... Signal De Mont [*France*] [*Seismograph station code, US Geological Survey*] (SEIS)
SMF .... Single-Mode Fiber [*Optics*] (CDE)
SMF .... Site Modification Facility
SMF .... Smart & Final, Inc. [*NYSE symbol*] (SPSG)
SMF .... Snell Memorial Foundation, Inc.
SMF .... Society for the Maintenance of the Faith [*British*]
SMF .... Software Maintenance Function [*Computer science*] (TEL)
SMF .... Solar Magnetic Field
SMF .... Space Manufacturing Facility
SMF .... Spar Material Factor [*Yacht racing regulation*]
SMF .... Special Modifying Factor (DEN)
SMF .... Spectral Multilayer Filter
SMF .... Stable Matrix Form
SMF .... Standard Messaging Format [*Computer science*] (CDE)
SMF .... Standard MIDI [*Musical Instrument Digital Interface*] File
SMF .... Static Magnetic Field
SMF .... Streptozocin, Mitomycin C, Fluorouracil [*Antineoplastic drug regimen*]
SMF .... Student Missions Fellowship [*Later, IVMF*] (EA)
SMF .... Swift Museum Foundation (EA)
SMF .... Switchable Matched Filter
SMF .... Synthetic Mineral Fiber
SMF .... System Management Facility [*IBM Corp.*]
SMF .... System Measurement Facility [*Computer science*] (IEEE)
SMFA .... Simplified Modular Frame Assignment System [*Telecommunications*] (TEL)
SMFA .... Specific Management Functional Area [*Telecommunications*] (OSI)
SMFAS .... Simplified Mainframe Administration System (MCD)
SMFAS .... Simplified Modular Frame Assignment System [*Bell System*]
SMFC .... Shellee Morris Fan Club (EA)
SMFC .... Sho-Me Financial [*NASDAQ symbol*] (TTSB)
SMFC .... Sho-Me Financial Corp. [*NASDAQ symbol*] (SAG)
sm-FeSV .... McDonough Feline Sarcoma Virus [*Veterinary medicine*] (MEDA)
SMFF .... Script Mathematical Formula Formatter [*IBM Corp.*]
SMFL .... Science, Mathematics, Foreign Languages
SmFlts .... Small Faults [*Philately*]
SMFMA .... Sprayed Mineral Fiber Manufacturers Association (EA)
Sm For Med .... Smith on Forensic Medicine [*10th ed.*] [*1955*] [*A publication*] (DLA)
Sm Forms .... Smith's Forms of Procedure [*A publication*] (DLA)
SMFP .... State Medical Facilities Plan [*Generic term*] (DHSM)
SMFR .... Service to Military Families Representative [*Red Cross*]
SMFR .... Summit Family Restaurants [*NASDAQ symbol*] (TTSB)
SMFR .... Summit Family Restaurants, Inc. [*NASDAQ symbol*] (SAG)
SMFT .... Semitrailer-Mounted Fabric Tank [*for water distribution*] [*Army*]
SMFUA .... Silk and Man-Made Fibre Users' Association [*British*] (BI)
SMFW .... Society of Medical Friends of Wine (EA)
SMG .... Megilot Genuzot [*E. L. Sukenik*] [*A publication*] (BJA)
SMG .... San Miguel [*Portugal*] [*Geomagnetic observatory code*]
SMG .... School of Military Government [*World War II*]
SMG .... Science Management Corp. [*AMEX symbol*] (SPSG)
SMG .... Scotts Co.'A' [*NYSE symbol*] (TTSB)
SMG .... Seismocardiogram
SMG .... Senior Master Sergeant (MCD)
SMG .... Sisters Poor Servants of the Mother of God [*Roman Catholic religious order*]
SMG .... Software Message Generator [*Computer science*] (TEL)
SMG .... Solids Moisture Gauge
SMG .... Sort Merge Generator (IAA)
SMG .... Spacecraft Meteorology Group (KSC)
SMG .... Spaceflight Meteorology Group [*NASA*] (NASA)
SMG .... Space Missions Group [*Ford Aerospace & Communications Corp.*] [*Detroit, MI*] [*Telecommunications service*] (TSSD)
SMG .... Specialty Medical Group (DMAA)
SMG .... Speed Made Good [*Navy*] (NVT)
SMG .... Submachine Gun
SMG .... Submandibular Gland [*Anatomy*]
SMGC .... Sun-Maid Growers of California (EA)
SMGC .... Surface Movement Guidance and Control [*FAA*] (TAG)
SMGD .... Supply Management Grouping Designator [*Navy*] (NG)
SM Geol .... Master of Science in Geology
SMGO .... Senior Military Government Officer [*World War II*]
SMGP .... Strategic Missile Group [*Air Force*]
SMGPC .... Small Molecule Gel Permeation Chromatography
SMGS .... Southeastern Mich Gas Ent [*NASDAQ symbol*] (TTSB)
SMGS .... Southeastern Michigan Gas Enterprises, Inc. [*NASDAQ symbol*] (NQ)
SMH .... Scheduled Man-Hours (MCD)
SMH .... Section for Metropolitan Hospitals (EA)
SMH .... Semtech Corp. [*AMEX symbol*] (SPSG)
SMH .... Simple Harmonic Motion (IAA)
SMH .... Smith Air, Inc. [*ICAO designator*] (FAAC)
SMH .... Societe Suisse de Microelectronique et d'Horlogerie [*Commercial firm*] (ECON)
SMH .... Standard Mirror Hybrid (MCD)
SMH .... St. Michael's Hospital, Toronto [*UTLAS symbol*]
SMH .... Strongyloidiasis with Massive Hyperinfection [*Medicine*] (DMAA)
SMH .... Sydney Morning Herald [*Database*]
SMHA .... Southern Mutual Help Association (EA)
SMHA .... State Mental Health Agency (DMAA)
SMHC .... Sarcomeric Myosin Heavy Chain [*Muscle physiology*]
SMHE .... Selected Material Handling Equipment [*Army*] (RDA)
SMHMO .... Staff Model Health Maintenance Organization [*Insurance*] (WYGK)
Sm Homest .... Smyth on the Law of Homesteads and Exemptions [*A publication*] (DLA)
SMHS .... Superstition Mountain Historical Society (EA)
SMI .... Aero Sami SA de CV [*Mexico ICAO designator*] (FAAC)
SMI .... Sales Method Index [*LIMRA*]
SMI .... Sa Majeste Imperiale [*His or Her Imperial Majesty*] [*French*]
SMI .... Samos Island [*Greece*] [*Airport symbol*] (OAG)
SMI .... Scanning Microscopy International (EA)
SMI .... Secondary Metal Institute (EA)
SMI .... Self-Metering Instrumentation
SMI .... Senior Medical Investigator
SMI .... Sergeant-Major Instructor [*British military*] (DMA)
SMI .... Service at Military Installations [*Red Cross*]
SMI .... Severely Mentally Ill (GFGA)
SMI .... Shelter Management Instructor [*Civil Defense*]
SMI .... Ship Missile Interface
SMI .... Simla [*India*] [*Seismograph station code, US Geological Survey Closed*] (SEIS)
SMI .... Simple Mail Interface [*Computer science*] (CDE)
SMI .... Simulation of Machine Indexing
SMI .... Sisters of Mary Immaculate (TOCD)
SMI .... Slipped Mutagenic Intermediate [*Biochemistry*]
SMI .... Small Volume Infusion [*Pharmacology*] (DAVI)
SMI .... Smithsonian Institution, Washington, DC [*OCLC symbol*] (OCLC)
SMI .... Society for Machine Intelligence [*Defunct*] (EA)
SMI .... Soldier-Machine Interface [*Army*] (RDA)
SMI .... Sorptive Minerals Institute (EA)
SMI .... Special Manufacturing Instruction
SMI .... Special Multiperil Insurance
SMI .... Spectrametrics, Inc.
SMI .... SpenderMenders International [*Defunct*] (EA)
SMI .... Spring Manufacturers Institute (EA)
SMI .... Springs Industries'A' [*NYSE symbol*] (TTSB)
SMI .... Springs Industries, Inc. [*Formerly, Springs Mills, Incorporated*] [*NYSE symbol*] (SPSG)
SMI .... Standardized Incidence Ratio
SMI .... Standard Measuring Instrument
SMI .... Start Manual Input (IAA)
SMI .... Static Memory Interface [*Computer science*] (MDG)
SMI .... Statute Miles
SMI .... Structure of Management Information
SMI .... Style of Mind Inventory [*Psychology*]
SMI .... Styles of Management Inventory [*Test*]
SMI .... Success Motivation Institute
SMI .... Super Market Institute [*Later, FMI*] (EA)
SMI .... Supplementary Medical Insurance
SMI .... Supply Management Inspection (NVT)
SMI .... Sustained Maximal Inspiration [*Physiology*]
SMI .... Swiss Market Index (ECON)
SMI .... Synthetic Multiple-Interaction [*For chiral separation*]
SMI .... System Management Interrupt [*Computer science*] (PCM)
SMI .... System Memory Interface [*Computer science*]
SMI .... Systems Measurement Instrument [*Computer science*]
SMI²LE .... Space Migration, Intelligence Increase, Life Extension [*Idea advanced by Timothy Leary, 1960's counterculture figure*]
SMIA .... Serial Multiplexer Interface Adapter (NASA)
SMIA .... Sheet Metal Industries Association [*British*] (BI)
SMIA .... Social Marketing International Association [*Queretaro, Mexico*] [*Defunct*] (EAIO)
SMIA .... Steel Management in Action [*Bethlehem Steel Co.*]
SMIAC .... Soil Mechanics Information Analysis Center [*Army Corps of Engineers*] (IID)
SMIAL .... Software Manufacturing Industry in Australia [*Database*]
Smi & Bat .... Smith and Batty's Irish King's Bench Reports [*A publication*] (DLA)
SMIAT .... Special Military Intelligence Activities Team (CINC)
SMIC .... Missionary Sisters of the Immaculate Conception of the Mother of God [*Roman Catholic religious order*]
SMIC .... Sorghum and Millets Information Center [*ICRISAT*] [*India*]
SMIC .... Special Material Identification Code
SMIC .... Study of Man's Impact on Climate

SMIC........... Submarine Material Identification and Control [*Navy*] (DNAB)
SMIC........... Supply Management Information Center [*Military*] (CAAL)
SMIC........... Surveying and Mapping Industry Council (EERA)
SMICBM...... Semimobile Intercontinental Ballistic Missile
SMID.......... Semiconductor Memory Integrated Device (MCD)
SMID.......... Smith-Midland [*NASDAQ symbol*] (TTSB)
SMID.......... Smith-Midland Corp. [*NASDAQ symbol*] (SAG)
SMIDA........ Small Business Innovation Development Act [*1982*]
SMIDW....... Smith-Midland Wrrt [*NASDAQ symbol*] (TTSB)
SMIEEE....... Senior Member of Institute of Electrical and Electronic Engineers
SMIER......... Societe Medicale Internationale d'Endoscopie et de Radiocinematographie [*International Medical Society for Endoscopy and Radiocinematography*]
SMIF........... Standard Mechanical Interface (NITA)
SMIG........... Sergeant-Major Instructor of Gunnery [*British military*] (DMA)
SmIg........... Surface Membrane Immunoglobulin [*Immunochemistry*]
SMIIS.......... Solar Microwave Interferometer Imaging System
SMIL........... Solidaritet med Israel
SMIL........... Statistics and Market Intelligence Library [*Department of Trade*] [*British*] (DCTA)
SMIL........... Synchronized Multimedia Integration Language [*Computer science*]
SMILAC........ Society for Music in the Liberal Arts College (AEBS)
SMILE......... Safe Military Infrared LASER Equipment
SMILE......... Ship's Master Index Listing of Equipment (MCD)
SMILE......... Significant Milestone Integration Lateral Evaluation [*Computer science*]
SMILE......... Society for Microcomputers in Life and Education (EDAC)
SMILE......... South Central Minnesota Interlibrary Exchange [*Library network*]
SMILE......... Spherical Micro Integrated Lens
SMILE......... Surface Mixed Layer Experiment (NOAA)
SMILES....... Simplified Molecular Input Line Editor [*or Entry*] System [*Computer science*]
SMILI........... Synthetic Model Interferometric LASER Imaging (PDAA)
SMILS.......... Sonobuoy Missile Impact Location System [*Navy*] (CAAL)
SM/IM.......... System Manager or Item Manager (AFIT)
SMIMD........ Switched Multiple Instruction, Multiple Data Stream [*Computer science*] (MHDI)
SMIN........... Southern Mineral [*NASDAQ symbol*] (TTSB)
SMIN........... Southern Mineral Corp. [*NASDAQ symbol*] (NQ)
Sm Ind......... Smith's Reports [*1-4 Indiana*] [*A publication*] (DLA)
SM in Hyg... Master of Science in Hygiene
SMIO........... Spares Multiple Item Order (AAG)
SMIP........... Ship's 3-M Improvement Plan [*Navy*] (NVT)
SMIP........... Spares Management Improvement Program (DOMA)
SMIP........... Specific Management Information Protocol [*Telecommunications*] (OSI)
SMIP........... Structure Memory Information Processor
SMIPE......... Small Interplanetary Probe Experiment (DNAB)
SMIPP......... Sheet Metal Industry Promotion Plan (EA)
SMIPS......... Small Interactive Image Processing System [*NASA*]
SMIR........... Shuttle Multispectral Infrared Radiometer [*NASA*] (GFGA)
SMIRE......... Senior Member of the Institution of Radio Engineers
SMIRR......... Shuttle Multispectral Infrared Radiometer [*NASA*]
SMIRS......... School Management Information Retrieval Service [*University of Oregon*] [*Eugene, OR*]
SMIS........... Safeguard Management Information System [*Army*] (AABC)
SMIS........... School of Management Information Systems [*Army*]
SMIS........... Section of Medical Information Science (IAA)
SMIS........... Ship Management Information System (MCD)
SMIS........... Society for Management Information Systems (EA)
SMIS........... Specific Management Information Service [*Telecommunications*] (OSI)
SMIS........... Supply Management Information System
SMIS........... Survey Methodology Information System [*Inter-University Consortium for Political & Social Research*] [*Database*]
SMIS........... Symbolic Matrix Interpretation System
SMIS INC..... Societe de Microelectronique Industrielle de Sherbrooke, Inc. [*University of Sherbrooke*] [*Canada Research center*] (RCD)
SMISOP....... Safeguard Management Information System Operating Program [*Army*] (AABC)
SMIT........... Schmit Industries, Inc. [*NASDAQ symbol*] (SAG)
SMIT........... Schmitt Industries [*NASDAQ symbol*] (TTSB)
SMIT........... Sherman Mental Impairment Test [*Psychology*]
SMIT........... Simulated Midcourse Interaction Test [*NASA*]
SMIT........... Spin Motor Interruption Technique
SMIT........... Submit (ROG)
SMIT........... System Management Interface Tool [*IBM Corp.*]
SMITE......... Simulated Mechanical Impact Test Equipment (MCD)
SMITE......... Simulation Model of Interceptor Terminal Effectiveness
SMITES....... State-Municipal Income Tax Evaluation System (PDAA)
Smith.......... Smith on English Registration [*A publication*] (DLA)
Smith.......... Smith, Reporter (7, 12 Heiskell's Tennessee Reports) [*A publication*] (DLA)
Smith.......... Smith's Indiana Reports [*A publication*] (DLA)
Smith.......... Smith's New Hampshire Reports [*A publication*] (DLA)
Smith.......... Smithsonian [*A publication*] (BRI)
Smith.......... Smith's Reports [*81-83 Missouri Appeals*] [*A publication*] (DLA)
Smith.......... Smith's Reports [*2-4 South Dakota*] [*A publication*] (DLA)
Smith.......... Smith's Reports [*1-11 Wisconsin*] [*A publication*] (DLA)
Smith.......... Smith's Reports [*54-62 California*] [*A publication*] (DLA)
Smith.......... Smith's Reports [*61-84 Maine*] [*A publication*] (DLA)
Smith Act..... Smith's Actions at Law [*A publication*] (DLA)
Smith & B... Smith and Bates' American Railway Cases [*A publication*] (DLA)
Smith & B... Smith and Batty's Irish King's Bench Reports [*A publication*] (DLA)
Smith & Bat... Smith and Batty's Irish King's Bench Reports [*A publication*] (DLA)
Smith & BRRC... Smith and Bates' American Railway Cases [*A publication*] (DLA)
Smith & G... Smith and Guthrie's Missouri Appeal Reports [*81-101 Missouri*] [*A publication*] (DLA)
Smith & H... Smith and Heiskell [*Tennessee*] [*A publication*] (DLA)
SmithAO...... Smith AO Corp. [*Associated Press*] (SAG)
Smith C....... Smith College (GAGS)
Smith CCM... Smith's Circuit Courts-Martial Reports [*Maine*] [*A publication*] (DLA)
Smith Ch Pr... Smith's Chancery Practice [*A publication*] (DLA)
Smith Com Law... Smith's Manual of Common Law [*A publication*] (DLA)
Smith Cond... Smith's Condensed Alabama Reports [*A publication*] (DLA)
Smith Cond Rep... Smith's Condensed Alabama Reports [*A publication*] (DLA)
Smith Cong Election Cases... Smith's Election Cases [*United States*] [*A publication*] (DLA)
Smith Cont... Smith on Contracts [*A publication*] (DLA)
Smith Dict Antiq... Smith's Dictionary of Greek and Roman Antiquities [*A publication*] (DLA)
SmithEnv..... Smith Environmental Technologies Corp. [*Associated Press*] (SAG)
Smith Ext Int... Smith on Executory Interest [*A publication*] (DLA)
Smith-Hurd... Smith-Hurd's Illinois Annotated Statutes [*A publication*] (DLA)
Smith-Hurd Ann St... Smith-Hurd's Illinois Annotated Statutes [*A publication*] (DLA)
SmithIn........ Smith International, Inc. [*Associated Press*] (SAG)
Smith Ind..... Smith's Indiana Reports [*A publication*] (DLA)
Smith Inst..... Smithsonian Institution (BARN)
Smith KB..... Smith's English King's Bench Reports [*A publication*] (DLA)
Smith Laws PA... Smith's Laws of Pennsylvania [*A publication*] (DLA)
Smith LC..... Smith's Leading Cases [*A publication*] (DLA)
Smith Lead Cas... Smith's Leading Cases [*A publication*] (DLA)
Smith LJ..... Smith's Law Journal [*A publication*] (DLA)
SmithM........ Smith-Midland Corp. [*Associated Press*] (SAG)
Smith Man Eq Jur... Smith's Manual of Equity Jurisprudence [*A publication*] (DLA)
Smith ME..... Smith's Reports [*61-84 Maine*] [*A publication*] (DLA)
Smith Merc Law... Smith on Mercantile Law [*A publication*] (DLA)
SmithMic..... Smith Micro Software, Inc. [*Associated Press*] (SAG)
SmithMid..... Smith-Midland Corp. [*Associated Press*] (SAG)
SmithMo...... Smithway Motor Xpress Corp. [*Associated Press*] (SAG)
Smith NH..... Smith's New Hampshire Reports [*A publication*] (DLA)
Smith NY..... Smith's Court of Appeals Reports [*15-27, 147-162 New York*] [*A publication*] (DLA)
Smith Rec... Smith's Law of Receivers [*A publication*] (DLA)
Smith Repar... Smith's Law of Reparation [*A publication*] (DLA)
SmithRR...... Smith [*Charles E.*] Residential Realty, Inc. [*Associated Press*] (SAG)
Smith Rules... Smith's Chancery Rules [*A publication*] (DLA)
Smith's (Ind) R... Smith's Indiana Reports [*A publication*] (DLA)
Smith's Laws... Smith's Laws of Pennsylvania [*A publication*] (DLA)
Smith's Lead Cas... Smith's Leading Cases [*A publication*] (DLA)
Smith's R.... Smith's Indiana Reports [*A publication*] (DLA)
Smith Wealth Nat... Smith's Inquiry into the Nature and Causes of the Wealth of Nations [*A publication*] (DLA)
Smith Wis.... Smith's Reports [*1-11 Wisconsin*] [*A publication*] (DLA)
SMIU.......... Stove Mounters International Union of North America [*Later, Stove, Furnace, Allied Appliance Workers International Union of North America*]
SMJ............ Moose Jaw Public Library, Saskatchewan [*Library symbol National Library of Canada*] (NLC)
SMJ............ Santa Margherita [*Italy*] [*Airport symbol*] (AD)
SMJ............ Santa Marina Gold [*Vancouver Stock Exchange symbol*]
SMJ............ Services Missionnaires des Jeunes [*Canada*]
SMJ............ Sim [*Papua New Guinea*] [*Airport symbol*] (OAG)
SMJ............ Society of Malawi. Journal [*A publication*]
SMJ............ Society of Medical Jurisprudence (EA)
SMJAB........ State Medical Journal Advertising Bureau (DAVI)
SMJAEM...... Saskatchewan Department of Advanced Education and Manpower, Moose Jaw, Saskatchewan [*Library symbol National Library of Canada*] (NLC)
SMJC.......... Saint Mary's Junior College [*Minnesota; Missouri; North Carolina*]
SMJC.......... Service Module Jettison Controller [*NASA*] (MCD)
SM-JDCC..... Sunshine Music - Jan and Dean Collectors Club (EA)
SMJK.......... Njoeng Jakob Kondre [*Surinam*] [*ICAO location identifier*] (ICLI)
SMJP.......... Palliser Regional Library, Moose Jaw, Saskatchewan [*Library symbol National Library of Canada*] (NLC)
Sm J St Comp... Smith on Joint-Stock Companies [*A publication*] (DLA)
SMJT.......... Saskatchewan Technical Institute, Moose Jaw, Saskatchewan [*Library symbol National Library of Canada*] (NLC)
SMK........... Smack [*Ship*]
SMK........... Smoke (AAG)
SMK........... Software Migration Kit [*Microsoft, Inc.*] [*Computer science*] (PCM)
SMK........... St. Michael [*Alaska*] [*Airport symbol*] (OAG)
SMK........... St. Michael, AK [*Location identifier FAA*] (FAAL)
SMK........... System Monitor Kernal (MHDI)
SMKA......... Kabalebo [*Surinam*] [*ICAO location identifier*] (ICLI)
Sm KB........ Smith's English King's Bench Reports [*A publication*] (DLA)
SMKD......... Smoked (WGA)
SMKE......... Kayser [*Surinam*] [*ICAO location identifier*] (ICLI)
SMKLS........ Smokeless (AAG)
SMKSTK..... Smokestack [*s*] [*Freight*]
SMKW......... Paramaribo/Kwatta [*Surinam*] [*ICAO location identifier*] (ICLI)
SML........... CV Sportsmark International, Inc. [*Vancouver Stock Exchange symbol*]
SML........... Montreal Lake Library, Saskatchewan [*Library symbol National Library of Canada*] (NLC)
SML........... Saluda Motor Lines [*AAR code*]
SML........... Sawmill [*Alaska*] [*Seismograph station code, US Geological Survey*] (SEIS)
SML........... Search Mode Logic
SML........... Security Market Line

SML Semantic-Meta-Language
SML Serials Master List
SML Silent Mating Loci [*Genetics*]
SML Simulate [*or Simulation*] (WDAA)
SML Simulator Load
SM-L Singh's Mosquito [*Tissue culture medium*] (BABM)
SML Single Macro Language [*Computer science*]
SML Skylab Mobile Laboratory [*NASA*] (KSC)
SML Smith Air (1976) Ltd. [*Canada ICAO designator*] (FAAC)
SML Smouldering Leukemia [*Medicine*] (DMAA)
SML Software Master Library [*Computer science*] (TEL)
SML Solicitation Mailing List (AAGC)
SML Southern Maine Library District, Portland, ME [*OCLC symbol*] (OCLC)
SML Spartan Material List [*Missiles*] (MCD)
SML Spectrum Management Licence [*Telecommunications British*]
SML Spool Multileaving [*Computer science*] (IBMDP)
SML Standard Markup Language [*Computer science*]
SML States Marine Lines
SML Stella Maris [*Bahamas*] [*Airport symbol*] (OAG)
SML Structure Mold Line (MCD)
SML Subacute Myeloid Leukemia [*Oncology*]
SML Support Material List
SML Symbolic Machine Language [*Computer science*]
SMLA Kamala Soela [*Surinam*] [*ICAO location identifier*] (ICLI)
Sm L & T Smith's Landlord and Tenant [*A publication*] (DLA)
Sm Lawy Smith's Lawyer and His Profession [*A publication*] (DLA)
SMLC Scottish Mountain Leadership Certificate (DI)
Sm LC Smith's Leading Cases [*A publication*] (DLA)
SMLC Southwest Michigan Library Cooperative [*Library network*]
Sm L Cas Com L Smith's Leading Cases on Commercial Law [*A publication*] (DLA)
SMLCC Synchronous Multiline Communications Coupler (NITA)
SMLD Suckling Mouse Mean Lethal Dose [*Microbiology*]
SMLE Short Magazine Lee-Enfield Rifle
SMLE Small-Medium Local Exchange [*Telecommunications*] (TEL)
Sm LJ Law Journal (Smith) [*England*] [*A publication*] (DLA)
SMLM Simple-Minded Learning Machine (IEEE)
SMLM Soviet Military Liaison Mission [*Army*]
SMLO Senior Military Liaison Officer
SmlOil Smalls Oilfield Services [*Associated Press*] (SAG)
SMLR Stepwise Multiple Linear Regression [*Mathematics*]
SMLS Saint Mary of the Lake Seminary [*Mundelein, IL*]
SMLS Sea-Based Mobile Logistics Supply [*Navy*] (CAAL)
SMLS Seamless (AAG)
SMLS Small and Medium-Sized Libraries Section [*Public Library Association*]
SMLT Langatabbetje [*Surinam*] [*ICAO location identifier*] (ICLI)
SMLV Standard Memory Loader Verifier (DWSG)
SMM Master of Sacred Music (BJA)
smm Montfort Missionaries (TOCD)
SMM Montfort Missionaries (TOCD)
SMM Safeguards and Materials Management [*AEC*]
SMM Saigon Military Mission [*Vietnam*]
SMM Sancta Mater Maria [*Holy Mother Mary*] [*Latin*]
SMM Scanning Multichannel Microwave
SMM Scattering Matrix Method [*Materials research*]
SMM Secondary Mortgage Market (ADA)
SMM Semiconductor Memory Module
SMM Semporna [*Malaysia*] [*Airport symbol*] (OAG)
SMM Shared Main Memory (NITA)
SMM Shared Multiport Memory
SMM Ship, Machinery, Marine Technology International Exhibition
SMM Smoldering Multiple Myeloma [*Medicine*] (DMAA)
SMM Smooth-Muscle Myosin [*Biology*]
SMM Societas Mariae Montfortana [*Missionaries of the Company of Mary*] [*Montfort Fathers*] [*Roman Catholic religious order*]
SMM Solar Maximum Mission [*NASA*] (MCD)
SMM Sooty Mangabey Monkey
SMM Specially Meritorious Medal
SMM Spectral Matrix Method (KSC)
SMM Standard Method of Measurement (IEEE)
SMM Start of Manual Message (BUR)
SMM Stress Memo Manual
SMM Study of Media & Markets [*Simmons Market Research Bureau, Inc.*] [*Information service or system*] (CRD)
SMM Submarine Miners [*British military*] (DMA)
SMM Subsystem Measurement Management [*NASA*] (NASA)
SMM Summit Airlines [*ICAO designator*] (FAAC)
SMM Supervisory Middle Management
SMM Supplemental Minimal Medium [*Microbiology*]
SMM System Maintenance Manual
SMM System Maintenance Monitor [*Telecommunications*] (IAA)
SMM System Management Mode [*Computer science*] (PCM)
SMM Systems Maintenance Management [*Computer science*]
SMMA Small Motor Manufacturers Association [*Libertyville, IL*] (EA)
SMMA Social Mapping Matrix Assessment (EDAC)
Sm M & S Smith on Master and Servant [*8th ed.*] [*1931*] [*A publication*] (DLA)
SMMAS Shipboard Maintenance Manpower Analysis System [*Navy*] (DNAB)
SMMB Scottish Milk Marketing Board (DI)
SMMB Stores Management Multiplex Bus [*Computer science*] (MCD)
SMMC Standard Monthly Maintenance Charge (NITA)
SMMC System Maintenance Monitor Console [*FAA*]
SMMCEQ Standard Method of Measurement for Civil Engineering Quantities (PDAA)
SMMD Specimen Mass Measurement Device [*NASA*] (KSC)
SMMDA Smaller Manufacturers Medical Device Association [*Inactive*] (EA)
Sm ME Smith's Reports [*61-84 Maine*] [*A publication*] (DLA)
SMME Society for Mining, Metallurgy, and Exploration [*In association name, SMME, Inc.*] (EA)
Sm Merc L Smith on Mercantile Law [*13th ed.*] [*1931*] [*A publication*] (DLA)
SMMG Sisters of Mary, Mother of God (TOCD)
SMMH Scheduled Maintenance Man-Hours (MCD)
SMMHC Smooth Muscle Myosin Heavy Chain [*Biochemistry*]
SMMI El Senoussi Multiphasic Marital Inventory [*Psychology*]
SMMI Salesian Missionaries of Mary Immaculate [*See also SSMMI*] [*Gentilly, France*] (EAIO)
SMMI Sisters Minor of the Mary Immaculate (TOCD)
SMMIP Strategic Material Management Information Program (PDAA)
SM MLCK Smooth Muscle Form of Myosin Light Chain Kinase [*An enzyme*]
SMMO Moengo [*Surinam*] [*ICAO location identifier*] (ICLI)
SMMO Soluble Methane Monooxygenase [*Biochemistry*]
SMMP Screw Machine Metal Part
SMMP Standard Methods of Measuring Performance (IEEE)
SMMP System MANPRINT [*Manpower and Personnel Integration*] Management Plan [*Army*]
SMMR Scanning Multichannel [*or Multifrequency or Multispectral*] Microwave Radiometer
SMMR Simmons Major Market Research, Inc. [*New York, NY Information service or system*] (IID)
SMMR Specific Mobilization Material Requirement [*Military*] (AFIT)
SMMR Standard Missile Medium-Range (SAA)
SM-MR Surface Missile, Medium Range
SMMS Shipbuilding Material Management Systems [*Navy*] (NG)
SMMS Society of Mary Missionary Sisters (TOCD)
SMMS Standard Maintenance Management System [*Military*] (CAAL)
SMMS Support Maintenance Management System [*Army*]
SMMT Society of Motor Manufacturers and Traders [*Defunct*] (EA)
SMMT Strategic Missiles Materials Technology (MCD)
SMMT Summit Design, Inc. [*NASDAQ symbol*] (SAG)
SMMW Submillimeter Wave (MCD)
SMN Nazi Texts in the Semitic Museum [*Harvard*] (BJA)
SMN Salmon, ID [*Location identifier FAA*] (FAAL)
SMN Satellite Music Network (NTCM)
SMN Seaman [*Military British*]
SMN Seaman
SMN Second Malignant Neoplasm [*Medicine*] (DMAA)
SMN Single Wire Multiplex Network [*Automotive engineering*]
SMN Sleeping Mountain [*Nevada*] [*Seismograph station code, US Geological Survey Closed*] (SEIS)
SMN Spain-Morocco Network [*Armed Forces Radio-Television*] (DNAB)
SMN Survival Motor Neuron [*Genetics*]
SMNA Safe Manufacturers' National Association (EA)
SMNC Self-Monitoring Negative Checklist (EDAC)
SMNC Splenic Mononuclear Cell [*Cytology*]
Sm Neg Smith on Negligence [*2nd ed.*] [*1884*] [*A publication*] (DLA)
SMNI New Nickerie/Nickerie [*Surinam*] [*ICAO location identifier*] (ICLI)
SMNK Smooth Neck
SMNO Singapore Malays National Organization [*Pertubohan Kebangsaan Melayu Singapore*] [*Political party*] (PPW)
SMNRY Seminary
SMO Medical Officer of Schools (DAVI)
SMO Santa Maria Resources Ltd. [*Toronto Stock Exchange symbol*]
SMO Santa Monica [*California*] [*Airport symbol*] (AD)
SMO Santa Monica Bank [*AMEX symbol*] (SAG)
SMO Santa Monica, CA [*Location identifier FAA*] (FAAL)
SMO Science Management Office [*Marine science*] (OSRA)
SMO Science Management Office (USDC)
SMO Secondary Market Operation
SMO Senior Medical Officer [*Military*]
SMO Service Module Oxidizer [*NASA*]
SMO Slip Made Out (MAE)
SMO Slowly Moving Object [*Astronomy*]
SMO Small Machine Organizer (IAA)
SMO Small Magnetospheric Observatory [*Satellite*] [*NASA*]
SMO Smoke
SMO Society of Military Ophthalmologists (EA)
SMO Society of Military Otolaryngologists [*Later, SMO-HNS*] (EA)
SMO So Much Of
SMO Sovereign Military Order [*British*]
SMO Special Military Operation
SMO Squadron Medical Officer
SMO Stabilized Master Oscillator
SMo Stainless Steel with Molybdenum [*Devices*] [*Orthopedics*] (DAVI)
SMO State Maintenance Office [*or Officer*] [*Military*]
SMO Statistical Model of Overlap
SMO Stock Material Order (SAA)
SMO Supermassive Object [*Cosmology*]
SMO Supplemtary Meteorological Office (BARN)
SMO Supply Management Office [*Air Force*] (AFM)
SMO Surface Mining Office [*Department of the Interior*] (OICC)
SMO Survivability Management Office [*Adelphi, MD*] [*Army*]
SMO Survivability Management Operation
SMO System Management Office (AFIT)
SMO Systems Methodology Office
SMOA Ships Material Office, Atlantic
SMOA Single-Manager Operating Agency [*Military*]
SMOA Superfund Memorandum of Agreement [*Environmental Protection Agency*]
SMOBC Solder Mask Over Bare Copper [*Electronics*]

SMOBE .... Surveys of Minority-Owned Business Enterprises [*Bureau of the Census*] (GFGA)
SMOBSMOD... Strategic Mobility Simulation Model
SMOC .... Simulation Mission Operation Computer [*NASA*] (MCD)
SMOC .... Submodule and Operator Controller [*For sequence of telephonic operations*]
SMOCTA ...... Service Members Occupational Conversions and Training Acts
SMOD .... SMART Modular Tech [*NASDAQ symbol*] (TTSB)
SMOD .... SMART Modular Technologies, Inc. [*NASDAQ symbol*] (SAG)
SMODOS...... Self-Modulating Derivative Optical Spectrometer (IAA)
SMOG .... Sales Management Organization Game
SMOG .... Save Me, Oh God
SMOG .... Smoke and Fog
SMOG .... Special Monitor Output Generator (IEEE)
SMOG .... Sprite-Midget Owners Group (EA)
SMOG .... Structural Modeling Oriented Graphics [*Module*]
SMOH .... Senior Medical Officer of Health [*British*] (DAVI)
SMOH .... Since Major Overhaul (DA)
SMOH .... Society of Medical Officers of Health [*British*]
SMOHI .... Sheet Metal Occupational Health Institute (EA)
SMO-HNS .... Society of Military Otolaryngologists - Head and Neck Surgeons (EA)
SmOi .... Smalls Oilfield Services [*Associated Press*] (SAG)
SMOKE .... Surface Magnetooptic Kerr Effect [*Surface analysis*]
SMOL........... Oelemari [*Surinam*] [*ICAO location identifier*] (ICLI)
SMOLANT .... Ships Material Office, Atlantic (MCD)
SMOM .... Sovereign Military Order of Malta (EA)
SMON .... Subacute Myelo-Optic Neuropathy [*Medicine*]
SMonBk .... Santa Monica Bank [*Associated Press*] (SAG)
SMOOTH...... Spectra Mode of Operation through Hardware (IAA)
SMOP .... Ships Material Office, Pacific
SMOP .... Simple [*or Small*] Matter of Programming (NHD)
SMOP .... So Much of Paragraph
SMOPAC ...... Ships Material Office, Pacific (MCD)
SMOPS .... School of Maritime Operations [*British*]
SMORE .... Self-Heating Meal, Ordered Ready-to-Eat [*Army*] (RDA)
SMORG........ Senior Marketing Officers Research Group [*LIMRA*]
SMORZ .... Smorzando [*Slower and Softer*] [*Music*]
SMOS .... Secondary Military Occupational Specialty
SMOS .... Senior Marketing Officers Seminar [*LIMRA*]
SMOS .... Society of Military Orthopaedic Surgeons (EA)
SMOS .... Submicrometer Metal-Oxide Semiconductor (IAA)
SMOSC .... Secondary Military Occupational Specialty Code (AABC)
SMOTE......... Simulation of Turbofan Engine [*Air Force*]
SMOTEC ...... Special Missions Operational Test and Evaluation Center [*Hurlburt Field, FL*]
Smoult......... Notes of Cases in Smoult's Collection of Orders [*Calcutta, India*] [*A publication*] (DLA)
SMOW .... Standard Mean Ocean Water
SMOWOG .... Simulation Model Object Working Group
SMP............. Daughters of Our Mother of Peace (TOCD)
SMP............. Sacred Music Press (BJA)
SMP............. Saint Mary's Press [*Record label*] [*New York*]
SMP............. Salinity Management Plan [*Australia*]
SMP............. Sampler (DEN)
SMP............. Santa Monica Public Library, Santa Monica, CA [*OCLC symbol*] (OCLC)
SMP............. Scanning and Measuring Projector
SMP............. Scanning Microscope Photometer (OA)
SMP............. Scheduled Maintenance Program (MCD)
SMP............. School Mathematics Project [*British*]
SMP............. See Me Please
SMP............. Self-Maintenance Period [*British military*] (DMA)
SMP............. Self-Management Program (DAVI)
SMP............. Sempati Air Transport PT [*Indonesia*] [*ICAO designator*] (FAAC)
SMP............. Sensitized Material Print (MSA)
SMP............. Servo Meter Panel (AAG)
SMP............. Shipboard Microfilm Program [*Navy*] (DNAB)
SMP............. Ship's Mission Profile [*Navy*] (CAAL)
SMP............. Silicon-Modified Polyether [*Organic chemistry*]
SMP............. Simple Management Protocol [*Computer science*] (DOM)
SMP............. Simplon Resources Ltd. [*Vancouver Stock Exchange symbol*]
SMP............. Simulation Management Plan
SMP............. Simultaneous Macular Perception [*Ophthalmology*]
SMP............. Simultaneous Membership Program [*Military*]
SMP............. Sine Mascula Prole [*Without Male Issue*] [*Latin*]
SMP............. Sisters of St. Mary of the Presentation [*Roman Catholic religious order*]
SMP............. Skimmed Milk Powder (ADA)
SMP............. Slow-Moving Protease
SMP............. Smith, Miller, and Patch [*Commercial firm*] (DAVI)
SMP............. Smudge Pot
SMP............. Social Marginal Productivity
SMP............. Society of Miniature Painters [*British*] (ROG)
SMP............. Society of Our Mother of Peace (TOCD)
smp............. Society of Our Mother of Peace (TOCD)
SMP............. Sodium Mercaptopyruvate [*Organic chemistry*]
SMP............. Software Management Plan [*NASA*] (MCD)
SMP............. Soil Management Program [*of Tasmania*] [*State*] (EERA)
SMP............. Soldier Modernization Plan [*Army*] (INF)
SMP............. Somplago [*Italy*] [*Seismograph station code, US Geological Survey Closed*] (SEIS)
SMP............. Sound Motion Picture Technician [*Navy*]
SMP............. Soviet Military Power [*A publication 1981-1991; changed in 1992 to Forces in Transition*] (DOMA)
SMP............. Special Maintenance Project [*FAA*]
SMP............. Special Manufacturing Procedure
SMP............. Special Marketing Program [*Business*]
SMP............. Special Monthly Pension (DAVI)
SMP............. Special Multiperil [*Insurance*]
SMP............. Stampede Pass, WA [*Location identifier FAA*] (FAAL)
SMP............. Standard Maintenance Procedure
SMP............. Standard Motor Prod [*NYSE symbol*] (TTSB)
SMP............. Standard Motor Products, Inc. [*NYSE symbol*] (SPSG)
SMP............. Standard Motor Pump
SMP............. Standards, Methods, and Planning
SMP............. Statutory Maternity Pay [*British*]
SMP............. St. Martin's Press
SMP............. Stores Management Process (MCD)
SMP............. Submitochondrial Particle [*Cytology*]
SMP............. Sulfamethoxypyridazine [*Antimicrobial compound*]
SMP............. Summary Maneuver Plan
SMP............. Suomen Maaseudun Puolue [*Finnish Rural Party*] [*Political party*] (PPW)
SMP............. Supply Master Plan
SMP............. Symbolic Mathematics Program
SMP............. Symmetric Multiprocessing
SMP............. Symmetric Multiprocessing (PCM)
SMP............. Symmetric Multiprocessor [*Computer science*]
SMP............. Synthesis Measurement Plan (IAA)
SMP............. Syrtis Major Plantia [*A filamentary mark on Mars*]
SMP............. System Maintenance Program (IAA)
SMP............. System Management Plan
SMP............. System Mechanical Performance
SMP............. System Memory Pool (PCM)
SMP............. System Modification Program [*Computer science*]
SMP............. Systems and Management Panel (ACII)
SMP............. Systems Maintenance Procedure (MCD)
SMP............. Systems Management Processor (IAA)
SMP............. Systems Modernization Plan [*Social Security Administration*]
SMP............. Systems Monitoring Panel (NVT)
SMPA........... Paloemeu/Vincent Fajks [*Surinam*] [*ICAO location identifier*] (ICLI)
SMPA........... Saskatchewan Motion Pictures Association [*Canada*] (WWLA)
SMPA........... Scottish Master Plasterers Association (DBA)
SMPA........... Solid Motor Processing Area [*NASA*] (KSC)
SMPA........... Switch Mode Power Amplifier (DWSG)
SMPAD .... Society of Motion Picture Art Directors [*Later, SMPTAD*] (EA)
Sm Pat .... Smith on Patents [*2nd ed.*] [*1854*] [*A publication*] (DLA)
SMPB........... Paramaribo [*Surinam*] [*ICAO location identifier*] (ICLI)
SMPB........... Succinimidyl (Maleimidophenyl)butyrate [*Organic chemistry*]
SMPC........... Saint Mary of the Plains College [*Dodge City, KS*]
SMPC........... Simplified Model Predictive Control [*Chemical engineering*] [*Computer science*]
SMPC........... Sum of Magnitudes of Pitch Matrix - Correlator
SMPD .... Ship Maintenance Planning Data (MCD)
SMPD .... Surface Missile Processing Description (MCD)
SMPDU .... Service Message Protocol Data Unit [*Telecommunications*] (OSI)
SMPE........... Society of Marine Port Engineers (EA)
SMPE........... Society of Motion Picture Engineers [*Later, SMPTE*] (NTCM)
SMPF........... Scientific & Medical Publications of France, Inc.
SMPG .... Poesoegroenoe [*Surinam*] [*ICAO location identifier*] (ICLI)
SMPG .... Seat Miles per Gallon [*BTS*] (TAG)
SMPG .... Small Magazine Publishers Group (EA)
SMPG .... Standardization Management Policy Group
SMPG .... Successful Magazine Publishers Group [*Defunct*] (EA)
SMPI............ Sequential Multipoint Injection [*Automotive engineering*]
SMPI............ Surface Missile Proficiency Inspection (MCD)
SMPL........... Sample
Sm Pl .... Somersetshire Pleas (Civil and Criminal), Edited by Chadwyck-Healey and Landon [*Somerset Record Society Publications, Vols. 11, 36, 41, 44*] [*A publication*] (DLA)
SMPLG .... Sampling (MSA)
SMPM........... Paramaribo [*Surinam*] [*ICAO location identifier*] (ICLI)
SMPM........... Structural Materials Property Manual [*NASA*] (NASA)
SM/PM......... System Management/Performance Monitor [*NASA*] (NASA)
SMPMA........ Sausage and Meat Pie Manufacturers Association [*British*] (BI)
SMPO .... SEATO [*Southeast Asia Treaty Organization*] Military Planning Office (CINC)
SMPO .... Sound Motion Picture Operator [*Navy*]
Sm Poor L... Smith's Scotch Poor Law [*A publication*] (DLA)
SMPP........... Sintered Metal Powder Process (MCD)
S-MPR .... Semimonthly Progress Reports [*Navy*]
Sm Pr .... Small Press [*A publication*] (BRI)
SMPR .... Supply and Maintenance Plan and Report [*Army*] (AABC)
Sm Pr Eq..... Smith's Principles of Equity [*A publication*] (DLA)
Sm Prob L... Smith's Probate Law and Practice [*A publication*] (DLA)
Sm Pr R ...... Small Press Review [*A publication*] (BRI)
SMPS........... Simplified Message Processing Simulation (IEEE)
SMPS........... Simpson Indus [*NASDAQ symbol*] (TTSB)
SMPS........... Simpson Industries, Inc. [*NASDAQ symbol*] (NQ)
SMPS........... Simultaneous Multiple Peptide Synthesis [*Biochemistry*]
SMPS........... Society for Marketing Professional Services [*Alexandria, VA*] (EA)
SMPS........... Society of Master Printers Scotland (DBA)
SMPS........... Special Mobile Provost Section [*British military*] (DMA)
SMPS........... Sum of Magnitudes of Pitch Matrix - Skin
SMPS........... Switched-Mode Power Supply (PDAA)
SMPS........... Switch Mode Power Supply (EECA)
SMPSA .... Solid Motor Processing and Storage Car
SMPT .... Apentina [*Surinam*] [*ICAO location identifier*] (ICLI)
SMPT........... Shuttle Main Propulsion Test (SSD)
SMPT........... Sound Movie Projector Technician [*Navy*] (DNAB)

SMPTAD ...... Society of Motion Picture and Television Art Directors (EA)
SMPTE .... Society of Motion Picture and Television Engineers (EA)
SMPTRB ...... Shuttle Main Propulsion Test Requirement Board [*NASA*] (MCD)
SMPVS .... Central Resource Centre, Prairie View School Division No. 74, Milestone, Saskatchewan [*Library symbol National Library of Canada*] (NLC)
SMPY .... Study of Mathematically Precocious Youth (EDAC)
SMQ .... Silvermaque Mining Ltd. [*Toronto Stock Exchange symbol*]
SMQ .... Social Maturity Quotient
SMQ .... Source One Mortgage Services [*NYSE symbol*] (SAG)
SMQ .... Source One Mtg 9.375%'QUICS' [*NYSE symbol*] (TTSB)
SMQ .... Structure Module Qualification Test (MCD)
SMQ .... Surface Metastable Quenching [*Surface analysis*]
SMQC .... Sunport Medical Corp. [*NASDAQ symbol*] (SAG)
SMQCF .... Sunport Med [*NASDAQ symbol*] (TTSB)
SMR .... Great Falls, MT [*Location identifier FAA*] (FAAL)
SMR .... Midrash Rabbah [*H. Freedman and Maurice Simon*] [*A publication*] (BJA)
SMR .... Sa Majeste Royale [*His, or Her, Royal Majesty*] [*French*]
SMR .... Samaritan Health Services [*ICAO designator*] (FAAC)
SMR .... San Marino [*ANSI three-letter standard code*] (CNC)
SMR .... Santa Marta [*Colombia*] [*Airport symbol*] (OAG)
SMR .... Saskatchewan Mounted Rifles (DMA)
SMR .... Scheduled Maintenance Replacement
SMR .... School of Materiel Readiness [*Formerly, SAM*] [*Army*] (RDA)
SMR .... Secret Marriage Rite (BJA)
SMR .... Semeru [*Java*] [*Seismograph station code, US Geological Survey Closed*] (SEIS)
SMR .... Seminarians for Ministerial Renewal [*Later, NFCS*] (EA)
SMR .... Senior Maintenance Rating [*British military*] (DMA)
SMR .... Senior Medical Resident (DAVI)
SMR .... Sensorimotor Rhythm [*Neurophysiology*]
SMR .... Series Mode Rejection
SMR .... Severely Mentally Retarded
SMR .... Shared Mobile Radio [*Telecommunications*]
SMR .... Sheffield and Midland Railway [*British*] (ROG)
SMR .... Shield Mock-Up Reactor
SMR .... Shiftout Modular Redundancy (MHDI)
SMR .... Side-Looking Mapping RADAR
SMR .... Signal Master (IAA)
SMR .... Signal Memory Recorder (NITA)
SMR .... Skeletal Muscle Relaxant [*Drug*]
SMR .... Small Missile Range (MCD)
SMR .... Society of Manufacturers' Representatives (EA)
SMR .... Society of Mary Reparatrix [*Roman Catholic women's religious order*]
SMR .... Solid Moderated Reactor [*Nuclear energy*]
SMR .... Somnolent Metabolic Rate [*Medicine*]
SMR .... Source, Maintenance, and Recoverability (MCD)
SMR .... Spanish Mustang Registry (EA)
SMR .... Specialized Mobile Radio
SMR .... Special Money Requisition [*Military*]
SMR .... Standardised Minimum Rules [*For the treatment of prisoners*] [*Australia*]
SMR .... Standardized Mortality Ratio
SMR .... Standardized Mortality Ratio
SMR .... Standard Malaysian Rubber [*Grade of natural rubber*]
SMR .... Standard Morbidity Ratio (MAE)
SMR .... Standard Mortality Rate
SMR .... Stanmar Resources Ltd. [*Vancouver Stock Exchange symbol*]
SMR .... Statement of Material Requirements
SMR .... Status Monitoring Routine
SMR .... Statutory Minimum Remuneration [*British*] (DI)
SMR .... Steam-Methane Reforming [*Chemical engineering*]
SMR .... St Mark's Review [*A publication*] (APTA)
SMR .... Stock Management Report [*Military*]
Smr .... Streptomycin Resistance [*Genetics*]
SMR .... Stroke with Minimum Residuum [*Medicine*] (DMAA)
SMR .... Structure-Metabolism Relationship [*For drug design prediction*]
SMR .... Submucous Resection [*Medicine*]
SMR .... Super-Metal Rich [*Astronomy*]
SMR .... Supplemental Medical Report
SMR .... Supply, Maintenance, and Recoverability Code [*Army*]
SMR .... Supply Management Report
SMR .... Supportability, Maintainability, and Repairability (SSD)
SMR .... Surface Movement RADAR
SMR .... Switching Mode Regulator
SMR .... System Malfunction Report
SMR .... Systems Management Responsibility (SAA)
SMRA .... Raleighvallen [*Surinam*] [*ICAO location identifier*] (ICLI)
SMRA .... Scottish Milk Records Association (DBA)
SMRA .... Simultaneous Multicomponent Rank Annihilation [*Mathematics*]
SMRA .... Spare Module Replacement Analysis
Sm R & P Prop... Smith on the Law of Real and Personal Property [*A publication*] (DLA)
SMRAS .... Safeguard Maintenance and Reporting Analysis System [*Army*] (AABC)
SMRB .... Simmons Market Research Bureau, Inc. [*Database producer*] [*New York, NY*]
SMRC .... Scottish Motor Racing Club (DBA)
SMRC .... Silver Marten Rabbit Club (EA)
SMRC .... Society of Miniature Rifle Clubs [*British*] (ROG)
SMRCS .... Service Module Reaction Control System [*NASA*] (KSC)
SMRD .... Spin Motor Rate Detector (IAA)
SMRD .... Spin Motor Rotation [*or Running*] Detector (MCD)
SMRD .... Spin Motor Run Discrete (NASA)
SMRD .... Stress-Related Mucosal Damage [*Medicine*] (DMAA)
SMRE .... Safety in Mines Research Establishment [*British*]
SMRE .... Societe de Marie Reine d'Ecosse [*Mary Queen of Scots Society*] (EAIO)
SMRE .... Submerged Repeater Monitoring Equipment [*RADAR*]
SMRF .... Salvadoran Medical Relief Fund (EA)
SMRF .... Series Mode Rejection Factor (IAA)
SMRF .... Small Materials Recovery Facility [*for recycling of glass, plastics, etc.*]
SMRGC .... Sun-Maid Raisin Growers of California (EA)
SMRI .... Society for Magnetic Resonance Imaging (EA)
SMRI .... Solution Mining Research Institute (EA)
SMRIS .... Soviet Missile Range Instrumented Ship (CINC)
SMRL .... Stanford Magnetic Resonance Laboratory [*Stanford University*] [*Research center*] (RCD)
SMRL .... Submarine Medical Research Laboratory
SMRLA .... Southern Maryland Regional Library Resource Center [*Library network*]
SMRLH .... Soldier's Mail, Rush Like Hell [*On correspondence*]
SMRM .... Solar Maximum Repair Mission [*NASA*] (NASA)
SMR/MIS ..... Supply, Maintenance and Readiness Management Information System [*Logistics Management Information System*] [*Military*] (AABC)
SMRP .... Society for Medieval and Renaissance Philosophy (EA)
SMRP .... Strategic Mobilization Requirements and Program (MCD)
SMRR .... Submucous Resection and Rhinoplasty [*Medicine*] (MAE)
SMRR .... Supplier Material Review Record (MCD)
SMRRF .... Strategic Metals Recovery Research Facility [*University of Arizona*] (RCD)
SMRS .... Specialized Mobile Radio System
SMRS .... Specific Mobilization Reserve Stock [*Military*] (AFIT)
SM/RSF .... Ammunition Stores Management and Remote Set Fuzing (MCD)
SMRT .... Scheduled Maintenance Replacement Time
SMRT .... Single Message Rate Timing
SMRT .... Stein Mart [*NASDAQ symbol*] (TTSB)
SMRT .... Stein Mart, Inc. [*NASDAQ symbol*] (SAG)
SMRTB .... Ship and Marine Requirements Technology Board [*British*] (ODBW)
Smrtflx .... Smartflex Systems [*Associated Press*] (SAG)
SmrtFn .... Smart & Final, Inc. [*Associated Press*] (SAG)
SmrtSr .... SmartServ Online, Inc. [*Associated Press*] (SAG)
SmrtSrv .... SmartServ Online, Inc. [*Associated Press*] (SAG)
SMRU .... Sea Mammal Research Unit [*British*] (ARC)
SMRV .... South Middlesex Rifle Volunteers [*British military*] (DMA)
SMRV .... Squirrel Monkey Retravirus
SMRVS .... Small Modular Recovery Vehicle System [*Nuclear energy*]
SMRY .... Seminary
SMRY .... Summary (FAAC)
SMS .... Marine Service Squadron
SMS .... Safety Management System [*NHTSA*] (TAG)
SMS .... Safety Manual Supplement
SMS .... Saint Marie [*Madagascar*] [*Airport symbol*] (OAG)
SMS .... Saint Mary's Seminary [*Connecticut; Missouri; Ohio; Vermont*]
SMS .... Sales Motivation Survey [*Test*]
SMS .... Sa Majeste Suedoise [*His, or Her, Swedish Majesty*] [*French*] (ROG)
SMS .... Samos [*Greece*] [*Seismograph station code, US Geological Survey Closed*] (SEIS)
SMS .... Sample Management System [*Laboratory science*]
SMS .... Satellite Motion Simulator
SMS .... Satellite Multiservice System (NITA)
SMS .... Scandinavian Migraine Society (EA)
SMS .... School of Mathematical Sciences (EERA)
SMS .... Scientific Microsystems Inc. (NITA)
SMS .... Scientific Mission Support
SMS .... Screen Management System [*Computer technology*]
SMS .... Security Management System [*Computer science*]
SMS .... Semiconductor-Metal-Semiconductor
SMS .... Senior Medical Student (DAVI)
SMS .... Sensor Monitoring Set (MCD)
SMS .... Separation Mechanism Subsystem [*NASA*] (NASA)
SMS .... Sequence Milestone System
SMS .... Serial Motor Seizures [*Medicine*]
SMS .... Service Management System [*Telecommunications*]
SMS .... Service Manipulator System (SSD)
SMS .... Service Module Simulator (IAA)
SMS .... Servicios Aereolineas Mexicanas SA de CV [*Mexico ICAO designator*] (FAAC)
SMS .... Shared Mass Storage
SMS .... Sheet-Metal Screw (DAC)
SMS .... Ship Motion Simulator
SMS .... Ship's Missile System (MCD)
SMS .... Shoreline Modeling System [*US Army Corps of Engineers*]
SMS .... Short Message Service
SMS .... Shuttle Mission Simulator [*NASA*] (NASA)
SMS .... Signal Messenger Service (NATG)
SMS .... Signal Missile Support [*Air Force*] (MUGU)
SMS .... Silane to Molten Silane [*Photovoltaic energy systems*]
SMS .... Silico-Manganese Steel
SMS .... Simulation Modeling System [*FAA*] (TAG)
SMS .... Sinatra Music Society (EAIO)
SMS .... Single Molecule Spectroscopy
SMS .... Skandinavisk Migraeneselskab [*Scandinavian Migraine Society*] (EAIO)
SMS .... Small Magnetospheric Satellite [*NASA*]
SMS .... Small Mass Store (IAA)
SMS .... Smithsonian Institution's Marine Station

SMS............ Snowy Mountains Scheme [*Australia*]
SMS............ Socioeconomic Monitoring Survey (DAVI)
SMS............ Solar Maximum Satellite [*NASA*] (MCD)
SMS............ Sonics & Materials, Inc. [*AMEX symbol*] (SAG)
SMS............ Spanish Market Selection [*Cigars*]
SMS............ Spares Management System
SMS............ Special Mint Set [*Numismatics*]
SMS............ Spectronics Micro Sytems [*Computer science*]
SMS............ Spin Motor Supply
SMS............ SPRINT [*Solid-Propellant Rocket Intercept*] Missile Subsystem [*Army*]
SMS............ Standard Material Specification (MCD)
SMS............ Standard Meteorological Station (SAA)
SMS............ Standard Modular System
SMS............ Standard Molecular System
SMS............ State Medical Society (MAE)
SMS............ State Medical Society (DAVI)
SMS............ Stationary Meteorological Satellite [*NASA*]
SMS............ Status Monitor Software
SMS............ Stiff-Man Syndrome [*Medicine*]
SMS............ Storage Management Service [*Telecommunications*] (PCM)
SMS............ Storage Management System (IAA)
SMS............ Stores Management Sea [*Navy*]
SMS............ Stores Management System (MCD)
SMS............ Strategic Management Society [*British*]
SMS............ Strategic Missile Squadron [*Air Force*]
SMS............ Structures and Mechanical System [*Skylab*] [*NASA*]
SMS............ Student Monitoring System [*Vocational guidance*]
SMS............ Styrene Methylstyrene [*Organic chemistry*]
SMS............ Subject Matter Specialist
SMS............ Success Management System
SMS............ Sumter, SC [*Location identifier FAA*] (FAAL)
SMS............ Surface Missile Ship (MUGU)
SMS............ Surface Missile System [*NASA*]
SMS............ Surface-Water Modeling System
SMS............ SURTASS Measurement System [*Navy*] (CAAL)
SMS............ Suspended Maneuvering System [*McDonnell Douglas Corp.*] (MCD)
SMS............ Switching and Maintenance Set
SMS............ Synchronous Altitude Meteorological Satellite (IAA)
SMS............ Synchronous Meteorological Satellite [*NASA*]
SMS............ Synoptic Meteorological Sounding
SMS............ Syro-Mesopotamian Studies [*Malibu, CA*] [*A publication*] (BJA)
SMS............ System Measurement Software (IAA)
SMS............ System Migration Section [*Social Security Administration*]
SMS............ Systems Maintenance Service (MCD)
SMS............ Systems Management Server [*Microsoft Corp.*] (PCM)
SMS/360PPE... Software Management System/360 Problem Program Efficiency
SMSA.......... Seaman Apprentice, Signalman, Striker [*Navy rating*]
SMSA.......... Selected Metropolitan Statistical Area [*FHWA*] (TAG)
SMSA.......... Shop Missile Assembly and Maintenance
SMSA.......... Signal Missile Support Agency [*Air Force*] (AAG)
SMSA.......... Standard Metropolitan Statistical Area [*Later, MSA*] [*Census Bureau*]
SMSA.......... Super-Cooled Infrared Multispectral Survey and Analysis [*Traces mineral deposits*]
SMSAE........ Surface Missile System Availability Evaluation [*NASA*] (KSC)
SMSanE....... Master of Science in Sanitary Engineering
SMSB.......... Strategic Missile Support Base [*Air Force*] (AFM)
SMSC.......... Service Module Sequence Controller [*NASA*]
SMSC.......... Southeastern Missouri State College
SMSC.......... Standard Microsystems [*NASDAQ symbol*] (TTSB)
SMSC.......... Standard Microsystems Corp. [*NASDAQ symbol*] (NQ)
SMSC.......... Standard Modular System Card [*Computer science*] (BUR)
SMSC.......... State Manpower Service Council [*Department of Labor*]
SMSC.......... Sum of Magnitudes of Sum [*Channel Matrix*] Correlator
SMSCC........ Shuttle Mission Simulator Computer Complex [*NASA*] (MCD)
SMSD.......... Ship Magnetic Submarine Detector
SMSF.......... Special Maintenance Support Facility (MCD)
SMSF.......... Special Mission Support Force [*Navy*] (DOMA)
SMSG.......... School Management Study Group (EA)
SMSG.......... School Mathematics Study Group (IIA)
SMSG.......... Self-Mutilators Support Group (EA)
SMSG.......... Survivability Management Steering Group [*DoD*]
SMSGT........ Senior Master Sergeant
SMSH.......... Sisters of Sainte Marthe [*of St. Hyacinthe*] [*Roman Catholic religious order*]
SMSI........... Sipaliwini [*Surinam*] [*ICAO location identifier*] (ICLI)
SMSI........... Smith Micro Software [*NASDAQ symbol*] (TTSB)
SMSI........... Smith Micro Software, Inc. [*NASDAQ symbol*] (SAG)
SMSI........... Standard Manned Space Flight Initiator [*Later, NSI-I*] [*NASA*] (NASA)
SMSI........... State Microscopical Society of Illinois (EA)
SMSI........... Strong Metal-Support Interaction [*Catalysis*]
SMSIP......... Space Mission Survivability Implementation Plan
SMSIP......... Surface Missile Ship Improvement Program (MCD)
SMSJ........... Scott's Monthly Stamp Journal [*A publication*]
SMSLP........ Smithsonian Marine Station at Link Port
SMSM......... Kwamalasoemoetoe [*Surinam*] [*ICAO location identifier*] (ICLI)
SMSM......... Marist Missionary Sisters (TOCD)
SMSM......... Soeurs Missionnaires de la Societe de Marie [*Missionary Sisters of the Society of Mary*] (EAIO)
SMSMS....... Strategic Missile Squadron Munitions Section [*Air Force*] (AAG)
SMSN.......... Seaman, Signalman, Striker [*Navy rating*]
SMSO.......... Subcontract Material Sales Order
SMSP.......... Security Military Space Program (MUGU)
SMSP.......... Soil Moisture Strength Prediction [*Army*]
SMSP.......... St. Peter's Abbey and College, Muenster, Saskatchewan [*Library symbol National Library of Canada*] (NLC)
SMSq.......... Strategic Missile Squadron [*Air Force*]
SMSR.......... Society of Master Shoe Repairers [*British*] (DBA)
SMSRL........ Sarah Mellon Scaife Radiation Laboratory [*University of Pittsburgh*] (MCD)
SMSRS........ Shipboard Meteorological Satellite Readout Station
SMSS.......... School of Management and Strategic Studies [*Founded 1982 by Richard Farson, offers a two-year management program through GTE Telenet*]
SMSS.......... Strategic Mission Support Study [*DoD*]
SMSS.......... Sum of Magnitudes of Sum [*Channel Matrix*] Skin
SMST.......... Stoelmanseiland [*Surinam*] [*ICAO location identifier*] (ICLI)
Sm Stat Law... Smith's Statute Law [*A publication*] (DLA)
SMSTR........ Signal Master (IAA)
SMSTRS...... Seamstress (WGA)
SMSU.......... Southwest Missouri State University (PDAA)
SMSV.......... San Miguel Sea Lion Virus
SMT............ Sacred Marriage Texts (BJA)
SMT............ Sample Mix Table [*Musical instrument digital interface*]
SMT............ Samuel Manu-Tech, Inc. [*Toronto Stock Exchange symbol*]
SMT............ Satellite Media Tour [*Journalism*] (WDMC)
SMT............ Saturn Missile Test [*NASA*]
SMT............ S-Band Megawatt Transmit
SMT............ Scheduled Maintenance Time [*Automotive engineering*]
SMT............ Segmented Mirror Telescope [*Astronomy*]
SMT............ Selective Message Transaction (NASA)
SMT............ Senior Management Team (AIE)
SMT............ Senior Medical Technician
SMT............ Service Module Technician [*NASA*] (KSC)
SMT............ Sexual Medicine Today [*A publication*]
SMT............ Shelter Management Training [*Civil Defense*]
SMT............ Shipboard Marriage Test
SMT............ Ship Maintenance Test
SMT............ Ship Mean Time (IAA)
SMT............ Ship's Mean Time [*Navigation*]
SMT............ Shop Mechanic's Test
SMT............ Small Missile Telecamera
SMT............ SMT Health Services [*Associated Press*] (SAG)
SMT............ Snow Monitoring Tire [*Automotive engineering*]
SMT............ Societe de Micro-informatique et de Telecommunications (NITA)
SMT............ Society of Metropolitan Treasurers [*British*]
SMT............ South Dakota School of Mines and Technology, Rapid City, SD [*OCLC symbol*] (OCLC)
SMT............ Square Mesh Tracking [*Air Force*]
SMT............ Stabilized March Technique
SMT............ Standard Measurement Technique [*Navy*]
SMT............ Station Management
SMT............ Steiner Minimum Tree [*Mathematics*] (BARN)
SMT............ Student Medical Technologist (MEDA)
SMT............ Subject Matter Trainer (SAA)
SMT............ Sultan-Mazar [*Former USSR Seismograph station code, US Geological Survey Closed*] (SEIS)
SMT............ Summit (MCD)
SMT............ Summit
SMT............ Summit Properties [*NYSE symbol*] (TTSB)
SMT............ Summit Properties, Inc. [*NYSE symbol*] (SAG)
SMT............ Supermedial Thigh [*Flap for plastic surgery*]
SMT............ Supplementary Monophonic Transmission (ADA)
SMT............ Supply, Maintenance, and Transportation [*Directorate*] [*Army*] (RDA)
SMT............ Surface Missile Test [*Navy*] (CAAL)
SMT............ Surface Mounted Technology (NITA)
SMT............ Surface-Mount Technology [*Electronics*]
SMT............ System Maintenance Test
SMT............ System Maintenance Trainer (MCD)
SMT............ System Master Tape (IAA)
SMT............ System Modulation Transfer [*Acutance*] [*Photography*]
SMT............ Systems Manufacturing Technology [*San Marcos, CA*]
SMTA.......... Scottish Motor Trade Association (DBA)
SMTA.......... Sewing Machine Trade Association (EA)
SMTA.......... Surface Mount Technology Association (EA)
SMTA.......... Tabiki [*Surinam*] [*ICAO location identifier*] (ICLI)
SMTAS........ Shuttle Model Test and Analysis System [*NASA*] (NASA)
SMTB.......... Tafelberg/Rudi Kappel [*Surinam*] [*ICAO location identifier*] (ICLI)
SmtBc.......... Smithkline Beecham Ltd. [*Associated Press*] (SAG)
SmtBGA....... Summit Bank Corp. (GA) [*Associated Press*] (SAG)
SmtBIn......... Smith Barney Intermediate Quality Municipal Fund [*Associated Press*] (SAG)
SmtBrnM..... Smith Barney Municipal Fund [*Associated Press*] (SAG)
SmtBTX....... Summit Bancshares Texas [*Associated Press*] (SAG)
SMTC.......... Sa Majeste Tres Chretienne [*His, or Her, Most Christian Majesty*] [*French*]
SMTC.......... Semtech Corp. [*NASDAQ symbol*] (SAG)
SMTD.......... Short Take-Off and Landing and Maneuvering Technology Demonstrator [*Air Force*]
SMTE.......... Segment Map Table Entry (IAA)
SMTE.......... Society for Music Teacher Education (EA)
SMTES........ Small Firms Technical Enquiry Service [*British*]
SMTF.......... Sa Majeste Tres Fidele [*His, or Her, Most Faithful Majesty*] [*French*]
SMTF.......... Spacecraft Magnetic Test Facility [*Goddard Space Flight Center*] [*NASA*]
SMTF.......... Spectrum Management Task Force [*Electromagnetic spectrum regulation*] (NTCM)
SmtFD......... Smith's Food & Drug Centers, Inc. [*Associated Press*] (SAG)
SMTG.......... Solid-State and Molecular Theory Group [*MIT*] (MCD)

SMTG.......... Somatogen, Inc. [*NASDAQ symbol*] (SPSG)
Smth.......... Smith [*A.O.*] Corp. [*Associated Press*] (SAG)
SMTH.......... Smith Environmental Tech [*NASDAQ symbol*] (TTSB)
SMTH.......... Smith Environmental Technologies Corp. [*NASDAQ symbol*] (SAG)
SMTH.......... Smooth [*NWS*] (FAAC)
SmthAO....... Smith [*A.O.*] Corp. [*Associated Press*] (SAG)
SmthAOA..... Smith AO Corp. [*Associated Press*] (SAG)
SmthBc........ SmithKline Beecham Ltd. [*Associated Press*] (SAG)
SmthF.......... Smithfield Foods, Inc. [*Associated Press*] (SAG)
Smthfld......... Smithfield Co., Inc. [*Associated Press*] (SAG)
SMT Hlt....... SMT Health Services, Inc. [*Associated Press*] (SAG)
SMTI.......... Selective Moving Target Indicator (IEEE)
SMTI.......... Sodium Mechanisms Test Installation [*Nuclear energy*] (NRCH)
SMTI.......... Southeastern Massachusetts Technological Institute [*Later, Southeastern Massachusetts University*]
SMTI.......... Tibiti [*Surinam*] [*ICAO location identifier*] (ICLI)
SMTK.......... SmarTalk TeleServices, Inc. [*NASDAQ symbol*] (SAG)
SMTK.......... Sump Tank
SMTL.......... Semitool, Inc. [*NASDAQ symbol*] (SAG)
SmtMod....... SMART Modular Technologies, Inc. [*Associated Press*] (SAG)
SMTN.......... Smoky Mountain R. R. [*AAR code*]
SMTO.......... Senior Mechanical Transport Officer [*British military*] (DMA)
SMTO.......... St. Maarten Tourist Office (EA)
SMTOE........ Sets My Teeth on Edge
SMTP.......... Simple Mail Transfer Protocol [*Computer science*] (PCM)
SMTP.......... Tepoe [*Surinam*] [*ICAO location identifier*] (ICLI)
SMTR.......... Scheduled Maintenance Time Ratio [*Automotive service*]
SMTRB........ Ship and Marine Technology Requirements Board [*British*]
SMTS.......... Simulated Maintenance Training System [*Air Force*]
SMTS.......... Somanetics Corp. [*NASDAQ symbol*] (SAG)
SMTS.......... Southern Manufacturing Technology Show and Conference (ITD)
SMTS.......... Special Machine Tool Standard (IAA)
SMTS.......... Synchronous Meteorological Test Satellite [*NASA*]
SMTSZ........ Somanetics Corp. Wrrt'B' [*NASDAQ symbol*] (TTSB)
SMTT.......... Small Bowel Transit Time [*Gastroenterology*]
SMU........... Scottish Mothers' Union [*Episcopalian*]
SMU........... Secondary Multiplexing Unit
SMU........... Self-Maneuvering Unit [*Air Force*]
SMU........... Sheep Mountain, AK [*Location identifier FAA*] (FAAL)
SMU........... Simula, Inc. [*AMEX symbol*] (SPSG)
SMU........... Single Motor Unit
SMU........... Soft Mock-Up [*NASA*] (MCD)
SMU........... Southeastern Massachusetts University [*North Dartmouth*]
SMU........... Southeastern Massachusetts University, North Dartmouth, MA [*OCLC symbol*] (OCLC)
SMU........... Southern Methodist University [*Texas*]
SMU........... Spectrum Monitoring Unit
SMU........... Statement Match Unit (IAA)
SMU........... St. Mary's University Library [*UTLAS symbol*]
SMU........... Store Monitor Unit
SMU........... Sunnyside Mine [*Utah*] [*Seismograph station code, US Geological Survey Closed*] (SEIS)
SMU........... Super-Module Unit [*Telecommunications*] (TEL)
SMU........... System Maintenance Unit [*Computer science*]
SMU........... System Monitoring Unit
SMUAP........ Simple Motor Unit Action Potential [*Medicine*]
SMUC.......... Societe de Musique des Universites Canadiennes [*Canadian University Music Society - CUMS*]
SMUD.......... Sacramento Municipal Utility District [*Photovoltaic energy systems*]
SMUD.......... Smudge Cell [*hematology*] (DAVI)
SMUD.......... Standoff Munitions Disrupter System (MCD)
SMUG.......... Smuggling [*FBI standardized term*]
SMUN.......... Soviet Mission to the United Nations (LAIN)
SMUS.......... Soviet Mission to the United States (WDAA)
S Mus D....... Doctor of Sacred Music
SMUSE........ Socialist Movement for the United States of Europe
SMUT.......... Shrink Mock-Up Template (MSA)
SMUT.......... Special Mission Utility Transport [*Aviation*]
SMV........... Samovar Hills, AK [*Location identifier FAA*] (FAAL)
SMV........... Samsville [*Illinois*] [*Seismograph station code, US Geological Survey*] (SEIS)
SMV........... Santa Maria Valley Railroad Co. [*AAR code*]
SMV........... Satellite Mutual Visibility
SMV........... Science Museum of Victoria [*State*] (EERA)
SMV........... Short Market Value [*Investment term*]
SMV........... Sinusoidal Membrane Vesicle [*Anatomy*]
SMV........... Skeletal Muscle Ventricle [*Medicine*]
SMV........... Slow Moving Vehicle [*Emblem to prevent rear-end collisions*]
SMV........... Smedvig Asa [*NYSE symbol*] (SAG)
SMV........... Soybean Mosaic Virus [*Plant pathology*]
SMV........... Special Mobility Vehicle
SM/V.......... Squared-Mean to Variance
SMV........... Submento-Vertex [*View*] [*Radiology*] (DAVI)
SMV........... Superior Mesenteric Vein [*Anatomy*]
SMV........... Surveying and Mapping Victoria [*Australia*]
SMVH.......... Service in Military and Veterans Hospitals [*Red Cross*]
SM Vis S..... Master of Science in Visual Studies (PGP)
SMVLF......... Shipboard Mobile Very Low Frequency [*Navy*] (DNAB)
SMVO.......... Avanavero [*Surinam*] [*ICAO location identifier*] (ICLI)
SMVP.......... Shuttle Master Verification Plan [*NASA*] (NASA)
SMVRD........ Shuttle Master Verification Requirements Document [*NASA*] (NASA)
SMVT.......... Sustained Monomorphic Ventricular Tachycardia [*Cardiology*] (DAVI)
SMVU.......... Survey of Motor Vehicle Use (EERA)
SMW........... Second Main Watch
SMW........... Sheet Metal Workers' International Association (EA)
SMW........... Simpatico Wines [*Vancouver Stock Exchange symbol*]
SMW........... Slotted Metal Window
SMW........... Smara [*Morocco*] [*Airport symbol*] (OAG)
SMW........... Society of Magazine Writers [*Later, ASJA*] (EA)
SMW........... Society of Military Widows (EA)
SMW........... South Mountain [*Washington*] [*Seismograph station code, US Geological Survey*] (SEIS)
SMW........... Standard Materials Worksheet [*NASA*] (NASA)
SMW........... Standard Metal Window (WDAA)
SMW........... Strategic Missile Wing [*Air Force*]
SMWA.......... Wageningen [*Surinam*] [*ICAO location identifier*] (ICLI)
Smware....... Simware, Inc. [*Associated Press*] (SAG)
SMWBA........ Scottish Master Wrights and Builders Association (DBA)
SMWC.......... Saint Mary-Of-The-Woods College [*Indiana*]
SMWC.......... Society for the Ministry of Women in the Church [*British*] (BI)
SMWDSEP... Single, Married, Widowed, Divorced, Separated
SMWG.......... Space Shuttle Structures and Materials Working Group [*NASA*] (PDAA)
SMWG.......... Strategic Missile Wing [*Air Force*]
SMWG.......... Synthesis and Modeling Working Group [*Marine science*] (OSRA)
SMWG.......... System Management Work Group
SMWHT........ Somewhat (DNAB)
SMWIA........ Sheet Metal Workers' International Association (EA)
SMWO.......... Society of Mental Welfare Officers [*British*] (BI)
SMWP.......... Strategic Mobility Work Project [*Army*] (AABC)
SMWS.......... Scotch Malt Whisky Society (DBA)
SMWS.......... Washabo [*Surinam*] [*ICAO location identifier*] (ICLI)
SMX........... Santa Maria [*California*] [*Airport symbol*] (OAG)
SMX........... Santa Maria, CA [*Location identifier FAA*] (FAAL)
SMX........... Semi-Micro Xerography
SMX........... Server Macro Expansion [*Computer science*]
SMX........... Server Macro Expansion [*Computer science*]
SMX........... Submultiplex (IAA)
SMX........... Submultiplexer Unit
SMX........... Sulfamethoxazole [*Also, S, SMZ*] [*Antibacterial compound*]
SMX........... Sulfamethoxazole [*or Sulphamethoxazole*] [*An antibacterial*] (DAVI)
SMXC.......... Smithway Motor Xpress Corp. [*NASDAQ symbol*] (SAG)
SMY........... Marianna, FL [*Location identifier FAA*] (FAAL)
SMY........... Scientist-Man Year
SMY........... Shemya [*Alaska*] [*Seismograph station code, US Geological Survey*] (SEIS)
SMY........... Simenti [*Senegal*] [*Airport symbol*] (OAG)
SMY........... Smyrna Public Library, Smyrna, DE [*OCLC symbol*] (OCLC)
Smy........... Smythe's Irish Common Pleas Reports [*1839-40*] [*A publication*] (DLA)
SMY........... Solar Maximum Year [*August, 1979-February, 1981*]
SMY........... Summary (MSA)
Smy & B...... Smythe and Bourke's Irish Marriage Cases [*1842*] [*A publication*] (DLA)
Smy Home... Smyth on the Law of Homestead and Exemptions [*A publication*] (DLA)
SMYS.......... Specified Minimum Yield Strength
Smythe........ Smythe's Irish Common Pleas Reports [*1839-40*] [*A publication*] (DLA)
SMZ........... Sonmez Airlines [*Turkey*] [*ICAO designator*] (FAAC)
SMZ........... Southern Maritime Zone (DNAB)
SMZ........... Stoelmanseiland [*Surinam*] [*Airport symbol*] (OAG)
SMZ........... Sulfamethazine [*Antibacterial*] [*Veterinary medicine*]
SMZ........... Sulfamethoxazole [*Also, S, SMX*] [*Antibacterial compound*]
SMZO.......... Paramaribo/Zorg en Hoop [*Surinam*] [*ICAO location identifier*] (ICLI)
SMZTMP...... Sulamethoxazole and Trimethoprim [*Antibiotics*] (DAVI)
SMZY.......... Paramaribo/Zandery [*Surinam*] [*ICAO location identifier*] (ICLI)
sn----.......... Andean Area [*MARC geographic area code Library of Congress*] (LCCP)
SN............ Parke, Davis & Co. [*Research code symbol*]
SN............ Sacramento Northern Railway [*AAR code*]
SN............ Safety Notice (MCD)
SN............ Sample Name
SN............ SAN [*Societe Aeronautique Normande*] [*France ICAO aircraft manufacturer identifier*] (ICAO)
Sn............ Sanitary
SN............ Santa [*Saint*] [*Italian*]
SN............ Santo
SN............ Saponification Number [*Analytical chemistry*]
SN............ Saturday Night [*A publication*] (BRI)
SN............ Saturn Nuclear [*NASA*] (IAA)
SN............ School of Nursing (AAMN)
SN............ Scientific Note
SN............ Seaman [*Navy rating*]
SN............ Season
SN............ Secretary of the Navy
SN............ Sector Number (MUGU)
SN............ Secundum Naturam [*According to Nature*] [*Latin*]
SN............ See Note (ROG)
SN............ Semiconductor Network (IEEE)
SN............ Senegal [*ANSI two-letter standard code*] (CNC)
SN............ Senior Navigator [*Air Force*]
SN............ Sensory Neuron [*Anatomy*] (DAVI)
S/N........... Sequence Number
SN............ Sergeant Navigator [*British*]
SN............ Serial Number
SN............ Serum Neutralization Test
SN............ Service Note (MSA)
SN............ Service Number [*Military*]
SN............ Session Notes [*Scotland*] [*A publication*] (DLA)

SN .... Shalom Network (EA)
SN .... Shaping Network (MCD)
Sn .... Shingle [*Quality of the bottom*] [*Nautical charts*]
SN .... Shipping Note [*Business term*]
S/N .... Shipping Number
SN .... Side Note
SN .... Sigma Nu [*A national fraternity*]
SN .... Sign (BUR)
SN .... Signal Node
S/N .... Signal to Noise Ratio [*Unweighted*] (CMD)
SN .... Silicon Nitrate
SN .... Sine [*Without*] [*Latin*]
sn .... Sine Nomine [*Without Name*] [*Latin*] (WGA)
sn .... Sine Numero [*Without Number*] [*Latin*]
SN .... Sine of the Amplitude (IEEE)
SN .... Sinoatrial Node [*Medicine*]
SN .... Sinus [*or Sinoatrial*] Nerve [*Anatomy*] (DAVI)
SN .... Siren
sn .... Small Nuclear
SN .... Small-Probe Nephelometer [*NASA*]
SN .... Smoke Number [*Emissions measurement*] (EG)
SN .... Snellen [*Test types*] [*Ophthalmology*]
SN .... Society for Neuroscience (EA)
SN .... Solid Neutral
S/N .... Sons of Norway (EA)
SN .... Sound Negative (IAA)
SN .... Source Name (NITA)
SN .... Special Nuclear [*Material*]
S/N .... Speech/Noise [*Ratio*] [*Electronics*]
SN .... Sponsoring Agency [*Online database field identifier*]
SN .... SSIE Number (NITA)
SN .... Staff Nurse (MEDA)
SN .... Staff Nurse (DAVI)
SN .... Standard Nomenclature
Sn .... Stannum [*Tin*] [*Chemical element*]
SN .... Stationing Flag [*Navy British*]
SN .... Statutes of Newfoundland [*A publication*] (ILCA)
SN .... Steam Navigation
sn .... Stereospecifically Numbered [*Biochemistry*]
SN .... Sterling Nuclear Plant (NRCH)
SN .... Sternal Notch [*Anatomy*] (DAVI)
sn .... Sthene [*Absolute unit of force*]
SN .... Stock Number (MCD)
SN .... Story of the Nations [*A publication*]
SN .... Streptonigrin [*Antineoplastic drug*] (DAVI)
S-N .... Stress Number (NASA)
SN .... Stronnictwo Narodowe [*Nationalist Party*] [*Poland Political party*] (PPE)
SN .... Strouhal Number [*Sound*]
SN .... Student Nurse
SN .... Subject Name (NITA)
SN .... Sub Nanosecond (IAA)
SN .... Subnetwork (IAA)
SN .... Subnormal
SN .... Substantia Nigra [*Brain anatomy*]
SN .... Sun Coast Indus [*NYSE symbol*] (TTSB)
SN .... Sun Coast Industries [*Formerly, Sun Coast Plastics*] [*NYSE symbol*] (SPSG)
SN .... Sunday Nation [*A publication*]
SN .... Supernatant [*Chemistry*]
SN .... Supernova
SN .... Suprasternal Notch [*Anatomy*]
SN .... Survey Number
SN .... Syllable Number [*Entomology*]
SN .... Synchronizers [*JETDS nomenclature*] [*Military*] (CET)
Sn .... Tin [*Chemical element*] (DOG)
Sn .... Tin [*Chemical*] (EERA)
SNA .... Laguna Beach-Santa Ana [*California*] [*Airport symbol*] (AD)
SNA .... Orange County [*California*] [*Airport symbol*] (OAG)
SNA .... Sadr Nizamut Adalat Reports [*India*] [*A publication*] (DLA)
SNA .... Sanae [*Antarctica*] [*Seismograph station code, US Geological Survey*] (SEIS)
SNA .... Santa Ana, CA [*Location identifier FAA*] (FAAL)
SNA .... Santana Petroleum [*Vancouver Stock Exchange symbol*]
SNA .... Satellite Networking Associates, Inc. [*New York, NY*] [*Telecommunications*] (TSSD)
SNA .... Schlaraffia Nordamerika (EA)
SNA .... Scottish Netball Association (DBA)
SNA .... Sella, Nasion, A [*Anthropometric landmark*]
SNA .... Senator Aviation Charter GmbH, Koln [*Germany*] [*FAA designator*] (FAAC)
S_{Na} .... Serum Sodium [*Organic chemistry*] (DAVI)
SNA .... Shaping Network Assembly (SSD)
SNA .... Snap-On Tools Corp. [*NYSE symbol*] (SPSG)
SNA .... Sodium Naphthalene Acetate (IIA)
SNA .... Soil Nutrient Availability
SNA .... Somalia National Alliance
SNA .... Soviet Naval Aviation
SNA .... Specimen Not Available [*Medicine*] (DMAA)
SNA .... Standard National Account [*Economics*]
SNA .... Steel Nail Association [*British*] (BI)
SNA .... Stern Air, Inc. [*ICAO designator*] (FAAC)
SNA .... Student Naval Aviator
SNA .... Student Nurses' Association (DAVI)
SNA .... Suburban Newspapers of America (EA)
SNA .... Sudan News Agency (BJA)
SNA .... Surface Navy Association (DOMA)
SNA .... Surinaams Nieuws Agentschap [*Surinam News Agency*] (EY)
SNA .... Syrian News Agency (BJA)
SNA .... System Numerical Attributes (IAA)
SNA .... System of National Accounts [*United Nations*]
SNA .... System of National Accounts (EERA)
SNA .... Systems Network Architecture [*IBM Corp.*] [*Computer science*]
SNAA .... Syndicat National des Travailleurs de l'Amiante d'Asbestos [*Canada*]
SNAAQS .... Secondary National Ambient Air Quality Standards [*Environmental Protection Agency*] (GFGA)
SNAB .... Staff Nurse Advisory Board (MEDA)
SNAB .... Stock Number Action Bulletin
SNA Beng .... Sadr Nizamut Adalat Reports [*India*] [*A publication*] (DLA)
SNA Beng (NS) ... Sadr Nizamut Adalat Reports, New Series [*1851-59*] [*Bengal, India*] [*A publication*] (DLA)
SNAC .... S-Nitroso-N-Acetylcysteine [*Biochemistry*]
SNAC .... SONAR Automatic Controller (IAA)
SNACC .... Society of Neurosurgical Anesthesia and Critical Care (EA)
SNACMA .... Snack, Nut, and Crisp Manufacturers' Association [*British*]
SNACP .... Subnetwork Access Protocol [*Telecommunications*] (OSI)
SNACS .... Share News on Automatic Coding Systems [*Computer science*]
SNACS .... Single Nuclear Attack Case Study [*DoD*]
SNACS .... Stock Number Assignment Control System [*Air Force*] (AFM)
SNADIGC .... Sindacato Nazionale Dipendenti Ministero Grazia e Giustizia [*National Union of Ministry of Justice Employees*] [*Italy*]
SNAE .... Society of Norwegian American Engineers (IAA)
SNAF .... Soviet Naval Air Force
SNAFU .... Situation Normal, All Fouled Up [*Military slang*] [*Bowdlerized version*]
SNAG .... Sensitive New-Age Guy
SNAG .... Sensitive New Age Guy
SNAG .... Society of North American Goldsmiths (EA)
SNagg .... Serum Normal Agglutinator [*Hematology*]
SNAI .... Standard Nomenclature of Athletic Injuries [*Medicine*] (MAE)
SNAIAS .... Ship's Navigation and Aircraft Inertial Alignment System [*Navy*] (NG)
SNAICC .... Secretariat of National Aboriginal and Islander Child Care [*Australia*]
SNAKE .... Stochastic Network Adaptive Kinematics Evaluator
SNAKE .... Super-Normal Attitude Kinetic Enhancement [*Later, Enhanced Fighter Maneuverability*] [*X-31 experimental aircraft under development by Rockwell International Corp. and Messerschmitt-Boelkow-Blohm GmbH*]
SNAL .... Site Number Assignment List (SAA)
SNA/LEN .... Systems Network Architecture/Local Entry Networking (NITA)
SNAME .... Society of Naval Architects and Marine Engineers (EA)
SNaN .... Signaling Not a Number [*Computer programming*] (BYTE)
Sn & W Ch ... Snow and Winstanley's Chancery Practice [*A publication*] (DLA)
SNANSC .... Society of Neurosurgical Anesthesia and Neurological Supportive Care [*Later, SNACC*] (EA)
SNAO/CWC ... Sustained Naval Aviation Operations in Chemical, Biological, and Radiological Warfare Conditions [*Military*]
SNAP .... Sarawak National Party [*Malaysia*] [*Political party*] (PPW)
SNAP .... Satellite Navigation Alert Plotter (PDAA)
SNAP .... Satellite Nuclear Auxiliary Power [*Military*] (CAAL)
SNAP .... Selective Niobium Anodization Process [*Semiconductor technology*]
SNAP .... Senior Naval Aviator Present
SNAP .... Sensory Nerve Action Potential [*Neurophysiology*]
SNAP .... Sharp National Account Program [*Sharp Electronics Corp.*]
SNAP .... Sharp Numeric Assembler Program [*Sharp Electronics Corp.*] (IAA)
SNAP .... Shelter Neighborhood Action Project
SNAP .... Shielded Neutron Assay Probe [*Nuclear energy*] (NRCH)
SNAP .... Shipboard Nontactical ADP [*Automatic Data Processing*] Program [*Navy*] (CAAL)
SNAP .... Short Notice Annual Practice [*Military*]
SNAP .... Significant New Alternatives Policy [*Environmental science*]
SNAP .... Significant Noncompliance Action Program [*Environmental Protection Agency*] (GFGA)
SNAP .... Simplified Needs Assessment Profile System [*Developed by Texas Instruments, Inc.*]
SNAP .... Simplified Numerical Automatic Programmer [*Computer science*]
SNAP .... Simulated Network Analysis Program (SAA)
SNAP .... Single Number Access Plan [*Telecommunications*] (TEL)
SNAP .... Six Node Averaging Program [*Computer science*]
SNAP .... Small Nuclear Adapted Power Source
SNAP .... Small Nuclear Auxiliary Power
snap .... Snapdragon [*Horticulture*]
SNAP .... S-Nitroso-N-Acetylpenicilamine [*Biochemistry*]
SNAP .... Society of National Association Publications (EA)
SNAP .... Soluble N-Ethylmaleimide-Sensitive Fusion Attachment Proteins [*Biochemistry*]
SNAP .... Soviet Nuclear Artillery Projectile (MCD)
SNAP .... Space Nuclear Auxiliary Power
SNAP .... Special Needs Action Programme [*Education*] (AIE)
SNAP .... Special Night Answer Position [*Telecommunications*]
SNAP .... Specifications for Non-Heat-Set Advertising Printing
SNAP .... Staffing Needs Assessment Process
SNAP .... Standard Navy Accounting Procedures
SNAP .... Standard Network Access Protocol [*Computer science*]
SNAP .... Static Nibble Access Path [*Computer science*]
SNAP .... Steerable Null Antenna Processor (RDA)
SNAP .... Stereonet Analysis Program (PDAA)
SNAP .... Sterile Nitrogen Atmosphere Processing
SNAP .... Strong No-Trump After Passing [*Bridge card games*] (BARN)
SNAP .... Structural Network Analysis Program
SNAP .... Student Naval Aviation Pilot
SNAP .... Student Nursing Assistant Program

SNAP .... Subnetwork Access Point (TNIG)
SNAP .... Summary of Navy Approved Programs
SNAP .... Supersonic Nonequilibrium Analysis Program (MCD)
SNAP .... Survivors Network of Those Abused by Priests [*An association*]
SNAP .... Switching Network Analysis Program [*Bell System*]
SNAP .... Synaptic Pharmaceutical [*NASDAQ symbol*] (TTSB)
SNAP .... Synaptic Pharmaceutical Corp. [*NASDAQ symbol*] (SAG)
SNAP .... Synaptosomal-Associated Protein [*Biochemistry*]
SNAP .... Systematic National Acquisitions Programme [*Public Archives of Canada*]
SNAP .... System for Nuclear Auxiliary Power (IAA)
SNAP .... System Net Activity Program (NITA)
SNAP .... System Network Activity Program [*Sperry UNIVAC*]
SNAP .... Systems for Nuclear Auxiliary Power
SNAP .... Systems Network Analysis Process [*Computer science*] (AEBS)
SNAP(G) ...... Student Naval Aviation Pilot (Glider)
SnapOn .... Snap-On Tools Corp. [*Associated Press*] (SAG)
SNAPPS .... Short-Term Nuclear Annual Power Production Simulation Model [*Department of Energy*] (GFGA)
SNAPS .... Standard Notes and Parts Selection (TEL)
SNAPS .... State and National Apprenticeship Program Statistics [*Bureau of Apprenticeship and Training*] [*Department of Labor*]
SNAPS .... Switching Node and Processing Sites [*ITT*] (TEL)
SNAPTRAN... Systems for Nuclear Auxiliary Power Transient
SNARC .... Short Nickel Line Accumulating Register Calculator (PDAA)
SNARD .... Special Notification Anticipating Receipt of Direction
SNARE .... Sandia Nuclear Assembly for Reactor Experiments
SNARE .... SNAP [*Soluble NAF Attachment Protein*] Receptor [*Medicine*]
SNARE .... Soluble NSF [*N-Ethylmaleimide-Sensitive Fusion Protein*] Receptors [*Biochemistry*]
SNARK .... Snake-Shark (SAA)
SNARL .... Suggested No Adverse Risk Levels [*Environmental Protection Agency*]
SNAS .... Student Need Analysis System
SNase .... Staphylococcal Nuclease [*An enzyme*]
SNASOR ...... Static Nonlinear Analysis of Shells of Revolution [*Computer program*]
SNAT .... Serotonin N-Acetyltransferase [*An enzyme*]
SNATCH ...... Systems Network Architecture and Transdata Coupling of Hosts [*IBM Corp.*] (IAA)
SNAU .... Society for North American Union (EA)
SNAV .... Sindacato Nazionale Attrazionisti Viaggianti [*National Union of Traveling Entertainers*] [*Italy*]
SNAX .... Lincoln Snacks [*NASDAQ symbol*] (TTSB)
SNAX .... Lincoln Snacks Co. [*NASDAQ symbol*] (SAG)
SNB .... Lakeland Library Region, North Battleford, Saskatchewan [*Library symbol National Library of Canada*] (NLC)
SNB .... Scalene Node Biopsy [*Medicine*]
SNB .... Sella, Nasion, B [*Anthropometric landmark*]
SNB .... Sierra Nevada Batholith [*Geology*]
SNB .... Silverman Needle Biopsy [*Pathology*] (DAVI)
SNB .... Small Navigation Buoy (DNAB)
SNB .... Snake Bay [*Australia Airport symbol*] (OAG)
SNB .... Southern National [*NYSE symbol*] (TTSB)
SNB .... Southern National Corp. [*NYSE symbol*] (SAG)
SNB .... Soviet News Bureau
SNB .... Spinal Nucleus of the Bulbocavernosus [*Neuroanatomy*]
SNB .... Statutes of New Brunswick [*Database*] [*Department of Justice*] [*Information service or system*] (CRD)
SNB .... Swiss National Bank
SNBA .... Societe Nationale des Beaux-Arts, Paris [*1890*] [*French*] (NGC)
SNBH .... Battleford Union Hospital Memorial Library, North Battleford, Saskatchewan [*Library symbol National Library of Canada*] (BIB)
SNBL .... Sioux City & New Orleans Barge Line [*AAR code*]
SNBNK .... Snowbank [*NWS*] (FAAC)
SNBR .... Snubber [*Mechanical engineering*]
SNBRTU ...... Screw, Nut, Bolt, and Rivet Trade Union [*British*]
SNBS .... Slovene National Benefit Society (EA)
SNBS .... Sodium Nitrobenzene Sulfonate [*Organic chemistry*]
SNBU .... Switched Network Backup [*Computer science*] (IBMDP)
SNC .... Air Cargo Carriers, Inc. [*ICAO designator*] (FAAC)
SNC .... , and Chassigny [*Egypt*] [*Pronounced "snick" Classification for a group of meteorites recovered from these sites*] [*French*]
SNC .... Saint Norbert College [*Wisconsin*]
SNC .... San Antonio College, San Antonio, TX [*OCLC symbol*] (OCLC)
SNC .... Sanitary Corps [*Army*]
SNC .... San Nicolas Island [*California*] [*Seismograph station code, US Geological Survey Closed*] (SEIS)
snc............. Saskatchewan [*MARC country of publication code Library of Congress*] (LCCP)
SNC .... Satellite News Channel [*Cable-television system*] [*Went off the air October, 1983*]
S/NC .... Satisfactory/No Credit [*University grading system*]
SNC .... School of Naval Co-Operation [*Air Force British*]
SNC .... Scottish National Certificate
SNC .... Servo Nozzle Control (MCD)
SNC .... Shawmut National Corp. [*NYSE symbol*] (SPSG)
SNC .... Shipped Not Credited [*Military*] (AFIT)
SNC .... Significant Noncomplier [*Environmental Protection Agency*] (GFGA)
SNC .... Skilled Nursing Care
SNC .... Snyder Communications
SNC .... Snyder Communications, Inc. [*NYSE symbol*] (SAG)
SNC .... Standard Navigation Computer
SNC .... Stored Program Numeric Control [*Computer science*] (IAA)
SNC .... Submarine Net Controller (MCD)
SNC .... Substantia Nigra [*pars*] Compacta [*Brain anatomy*]
SNC .... Sunatco Development Corp. [*Vancouver Stock Exchange symbol*]
SNC .... Supreme National Council [*Cambodia*]
SNC .... Swiss Nonvaleurs Club [*Later, Scripophila Helvetica - SH*] (EAIO)
SNC .... Syndicat National du Cinema [*National Syndicate of Motion Pictures*]
SNCA .... Scottish National Camps Association (DBA)
SNCC .... Selected Non-Communist Countries
SNCC .... Student National Coordinating Committee [*Pronounced "snick"*] (EA)
SNCC .... System Network Computer Center [*Louisiana State University*] [*Research center*] (RCD)
SNCCDIPP ... Selected Non-Communist Countries Defense Intelligence Projection for Planning (MCD)
SNCF .... SECOMO [*Software Engineering Cost Model*] Non-COCOMO Factor [*Constructive Cost Model*]
SNCF .... Societe Nationale des Chemins de Fer Francais [*French National Railways*]
SNCFA .... Societe Nationale des Chemins de Fer Algeriens [*Algerian Railways*]
SN-CIE .... Statement of Need - Clothing and Individual Equipment [*Military*]
SNCL .... Serial Number Configuration List (MCD)
SNCL .... Serial Number Conversion List
SNCLAR ...... University of Santa Clara School of Law (DLA)
SNCLF .... Societe de Neuro-Chirurgie de Langue Francaise [*Society of French-Speaking Neurosurgeons - SFSN*] (EA)
SNCM .... Second Nicaraguan Campaign Medal
SNCO .... Seaport Navigation Co. [*AAR code*]
SNCO .... Senior Noncommissioned Officer
SNCO .... Staff Noncommissioned Officer [*Military*]
SNCOC .... Senior Noncommissioned Officer Course
SNCP .... Special Navy Control Program (MCD)
SNCR .... Selective Noncatalytic Reduction [*Combustion technology*]
SNCUNESCO... Swedish National Commission for UNESCO (EAIO)
SNCV .... Sensory Nerve Conduction Velocity [*Neurology*] (DAVI)
SND .... San Diego - College [*California*] [*Seismograph station code, US Geological Survey*] (SEIS)
SND .... Sanford, FL [*Location identifier FAA*] (FAAL)
SND .... Sanfred Resources [*Vancouver Stock Exchange symbol*]
SND .... Sap No Defect
SND .... Scottish National Dictionary [*A publication*]
SND .... Scottish National Diploma
SND .... Second Class Passengers [*Shipping*] [*British*]
SND .... Selected Natural Diamond
SND .... Self-Powered Neutron Detector
SND .... Semiconductor Neutron Dosimeter
SND .... Seno [*Laos*] [*Airport symbol*] (AD)
snd............. Sindhi [*MARC language code Library of Congress*] (LCCP)
SND .... Sinus Node Disease [*Cardiology*] (CPH)
SND .... Sinus [*or Sinoatrial*] Node Dysfunction [*Cardiology*] (DAVI)
SND .... Sisters of Notre Dame [*Roman Catholic religious order*]
SND .... Sisters of Notre Dame de Namur [*Roman Catholic religious order*]
SND .... Society of Newspaper Design (EA)
SND .... Sound (AAG)
SND .... Sound
SND .... Standardized Normal Distribution
SND .... Standard Normal Distribution [*Mathematics*]
SND .... Static No Delivery
SNDA .... Scottish National Dancing Association [*Australia*]
SNDA .... Scottish National Dictionary Association
SNDA .... Student National Dental Association (EA)
SNDA .... Sunday Newspaper Distibutors' Association (DGA)
SNDC .... Sand Technology Systems International, Inc. [*NASDAQ symbol*] (NQ)
SNDC .... Serbian National Defense Council (EA)
SNDCF .... Sand Technology Sys'A' [*NASDAQ symbol*] (TTSB)
SNDCF .... Subnetwork Dependent Convergence Function [*Telecommunications*] (OSI)
SNDCP .... Subnetwork Dependent Convergence Protocol [*Telecommunications*] (OSI)
SNDdeN .... Sisters of Notre Dame de Namur (TOCD)
SNDG .... Sending (MSA)
SNDG .... Sounding (MSA)
SNDK .... SanDisk Corp. [*NASDAQ symbol*] (SAG)
SNDL .... Sandale R. R. [*AAR code*]
SNDL .... Special Navy Distribution List (DOMA)
SNDL .... Standard Navy Distribution List
SNDL .... Standard Nomenclature List [*Military*]
SNDLF .... Societe de Nutrition et de Dietetique de Langue Francaise [*French-Language Society of Nutrition and Dietetics - FLSND*] [*France*] (EAIO)
sndlwd .... Sandalwood (VRA)
SNDM .... Secretary of Navy Decision Memorandum
SND-MB ...... Selected Natural Diamond - Metal Bond
SNDN .... Sisters of Notre Dame de Namur [*Roman Catholic religious order Rome, Italy*] (EAIO)
SNDO .... Standard Nomenclature of Diseases and Operations [*Medicine*]
SNDP .... Sustainable National Domestic Product (EERA)
SNDPLG ...... Sandwich Plug (IAA)
SNDPRF ...... Soundproof (MSA)
SNDRY .... Sundry
SNDS .... [*The*] Sands Regent [*Reno, NV*] [*NASDAQ symbol*] (NQ)
SNDS .... Stillbirth and Neonatal Death Society [*British*] (EAIO)
SNDS .... Stock Number Data Section (MCD)
SndSrce .... Sound Source Interactive, Inc. [*Associated Press*] (SAG)
SNDT .... Shreemati Nathibai Domodar Thackersey Women's University [*India*]
SNDT .... Society for Nondestructive Testing [*Later, ASNT*] (KSC)
SNDT .... Sundata Corp. [*NASDAQ symbol*] (SAG)
SNDT .... SunGard Data Systems [*NASDAQ symbol*] (TTSB)

SNDV .... Strategic Nuclear Delivery Vehicle [*Army*] (AABC)
SNDWCH ..... Sandwich
SndySpr .... Sandy Spring Bancorp, Inc. [*Associated Press*] (SAG)
SNE .... Santa Elena, TX [*Location identifier FAA*] (FAAL)
SNE .... Sao Nicolau [*Cape Verde Islands*] [*Airport symbol*] (OAG)
SNE .... Servicios Aereos Norte Sur SA de CV [*Mexico ICAO designator*] (FAAC)
SNE .... Severe Noise Environment
SNE .... Single Nylon Enamelled (IAA)
SNE .... Sinus Node Electrogram [*Medicine*] (DMAA)
SNE .... Society for Nutrition Education (EA)
SNE .... Sony Corp. ADR [*NYSE symbol*] (TTSB)
SNE .... Sony Corp. America [*NYSE symbol Toronto Stock Exchange symbol Vancouver Stock Exchange symbol*] (SPSG)
SNE .... Spatial Nonemotional (Stimuli)
SNE .... Strategic Network Environment (NITA)
SNE .... Subacute Necrotizing Encephalomyelopathy [*Medicine*]
SNE .... Suppress Normal End (IAA)
SNE .... Syndicat National de l'Edition [*French publishers' association*]
SNEA .... Student National Education Association (EA)
SNEC .... Saxton Nuclear Engineering Corp.
SNEC .... Secondary Navy Enlisted Classification (DNAB)
SNEC .... Staff Nurse Executive Committee (MEDA)
SNEC .... Subgroup on Nuclear Export Coordination [*Nuclear Regulatory Commission*] (GFGA)
SNECI .... Sindicato Nacional dos Empregados do Comercio e da Industria da Provincia de Mocambique [*National Union of Commercial and Industrial Workers of Mozambique*]
Sneed .... Sneed's Kentucky Decisions [*2 Kentucky*] [*A publication*] (DLA)
Sneed .... Sneed's Tennessee Reports [*33-37 Tennessee*] [*A publication*] (DLA)
Sneed Dec... Sneed's Kentucky Decisions [*2 Kentucky*] [*A publication*] (DLA)
Sneed Tenn... Sneed's Tennessee Reports [*A publication*] (DLA)
Sneed (Tenn) Rep... Sneed's Tennessee Reports [*A publication*] (DLA)
SN(EF) .... Seaman (Electronics Field) [*Navy rating*] (DNAB)
SNEF .... Skilled Nursing Extended Care Facility (DAVI)
SNEFU .... Situation Normal - Everything Fouled Up [*Bowdlerized version Obsolete*] (DSUE)
SNEG .... Syndicat National des Enseignants de Guinee [*National Union of Guinean Teachers*]
SNEI .... Societe Nouvelle d'Editions pour l'Industrie [*Industrial News Publishing Company*] (IID)
SNEIL .... Secretariat for the Nordic Energy Information Libraries (IID)
SNEL .... Societe Nationale d'Electricite
SNEL .... Special Nuclear Effects Laboratory
Snell Eq .... Snell's Principles in Equity [*A publication*] (DLA)
SNELPIF ...... Sindacato Nazionale Esperti Laureati Propagandisti Industrie Farmaceutiche [*National Union of University Graduated Experts for Propaganda in Pharmaceutical Industries*] [*Italy*]
SNEMSA ...... Southern New England Marine Sciences Association
SNEP .... Saudi Naval Expansion Program (MCD)
SNEP FIT ..... Saudi Naval Expansion Program, Fleet Introduction Team (DNAB)
SNEP PMT ... Saudi Naval Expansion Program, Project Management Team (DNAB)
SNEP PROJMGR... Saudi Naval Expansion Program, Project Manager (DNAB)
SNEP PROJMGRT AFT... Saudi Naval Expansion Program, Project Manager, Technical Assistance Field Team (DNAB)
SNEPT .... Space Nuclear Electric Propulsion Test
SNES .... Super Ninendo Entertainment System
SNES .... Syndicat National de l'Enseignement Secondaire [*National Union of Secondary Schoolteachers*] [*France*]
SNET .... Southern New England Telecommunications Corp. [*New Haven, CT*] (TSSD)
SNET .... Syndicat National de l'Enseignement Technique [*National Union of Technical School Teachers*] [*France*]
SNETel .... Southern New England Telecommunications Corp. [*Associated Press*] (SAG)
SNF .... Sampled N-Path Filter (PDAA)
SNF .... San Felipe [*Venezuela*] [*Airport symbol*] (AD)
SNF .... Secret - No Foreigners [*Security classification*]
SNF .... Serb National Federation (EA)
SNF .... Short-Range Nuclear Forces
SNF .... Sierra Nevada Fault [*Geology*]
SNF .... Silicon Nitride Film
SNF .... Skilled Nursing Facility
SNF .... Solids Not Fat
SNF .... Somali National Front [*Political party*] (EY)
SNF .... Spain Fund [*NYSE symbol*] (SPSG)
SNF .... Spent Nuclear Fuel
SNF .... Spot Noise Figure
SNF .... Sudanese National Front [*Political party*] (PD)
SNF .... System Noise Figure
SNFC .... Security National Financial Corp. [*NASDAQ symbol*] (SAG)
SNFCA .... Security Natl Finl 'A' [*NASDAQ symbol*] (TTSB)
SNFCC .... Shippers National Freight Claim Council [*Later, TCPC*] (EA)
SNFL .... Standing Naval Force, Atlantic (MCD)
SNFLD .... Secret - Limited Distribution - Not Releasable to Foreigners [*Security classification*]
SNFLK .... Snowflake [*NWS*] (FAAC)
SNFO .... Student Naval Flight Officer
SNFPP .... Syndicat National de la Fonction Publique Provinciale [*National Union of Provincial Government Employees - NUPGE*] [*Canada*]
SNFR .... Small-Probe Net Flux Radiometer [*NASA*]
SNFRC .... Seattle National Fisheries Research Center [*Seattle, WA*] [*Department of the Interior*] (GRD)
SNFS .... Student Naval Flight Surgeon
SNFU .... Scottish National Farmers' Union
SNG .... San Ignacio De Velasco [*Bolivia*] [*Airport symbol*] (OAG)
SNG .... Sans Notre Garantie [*Without Our Guarantee*] [*French Business term*]
SNG .... Satellite News Gathering [*Trademark*] (NTCM)
SNG .... Scottish Neuroscience Group (DBA)
SNG .... Sending [*Electronics*] (ECII)
SNG .... Singapore (WDAA)
SNG .... Solidified Nitroglycerol [*or Nitroglycerin*] [*Explosive*]
SNG .... Songkhla [*Thailand*] [*Seismograph station code, US Geological Survey*] (SEIS)
SNG .... Southern New England Telecommunications Corp. [*NYSE symbol*] (SPSG)
SNG .... Southern New Eng Telecom [*NYSE symbol*] (TTSB)
SNG .... Stabilization Network Group
SNG .... Sterling Energy Corp. [*Vancouver Stock Exchange symbol*]
SNG .... Substitute [*or Synthetic*] Natural Gas
Sng .... Synagogue (BJA)
SNG .... Synthetic Natural Gas (IEEE)
SNGA .... Sodium N-Glycoloylarsanilic [*or N-Glycolylarsanilic*] Acid [*Pharmacology*]
SNGFR .... Single Nephron Glomerular Filtration Rate
sngl .... Senegal (VRA)
SNGL .... Single
SNGN .... Segmental Necrotizing Glomerulonephritis [*Medicine*]
SNGOD .... Special NGO [*Nongovernmental Organization*] Committee on Disarmament (EA)
SNGS .... Salem Nuclear Generating Station (NRCH)
SNH .... Savannah, TN [*Location identifier FAA*] (FAAL)
SNH .... Signtech, Inc. [*Toronto Stock Exchange symbol*]
snh .... Sinhalese [*MARC language code Library of Congress*] (LCCP)
SNH .... Skilled Nursing Home
SNH .... Snatch [*Block*] [*Design engineering*]
SNH .... Society for Nursing History [*Defunct*] (EA)
SNH .... South Nottinghamshire Hussars [*British military*] (DMA)
SNH .... Sunshine Point [*Alaska*] [*Seismograph station code, US Geological Survey*] (SEIS)
SNHA .... Shenandoah Natural History Association (EA)
SNHL .... Sensorineural Hearing Loss [*Medicine*] (MAE)
SNHY .... Sun Hydraulics Corp. [*NASDAQ symbol*] (SAG)
SNI .... National Intelligence Service [*Zaire*] (PD)
SNI .... San Nicolas Island
SNI .... Selective Notification of Information
SNI .... Seneca Nation of Indians (DOGT)
SNI .... Seneca Nation of Indians
SNI .... Sequence Number Indicator
SNI .... Serial Network Interface (PDAA)
SNI .... Signal-to-Noise Improvement [*Data transmission*] (IEEE)
S/N + I .... Signal-to-Noise plus Interference Ratio
SNI .... Sinoe [*Liberia*] [*Airport symbol*] (OAG)
SNI .... Sistema Nacional de Informacion [*National Information System*] [*Colorado*] (IID)
SNI .... Societe Nigerienne de Transports Aeriens [*Niger*] [*ICAO designator*] (FAAC)
SNI .... Sonor Investments Ltd. [*Toronto Stock Exchange symbol*]
SNI .... Soviet Naval Infantry (DOMA)
SNI .... Sports Network, Inc. [*Later, HSN*]
SNI .... Standard Network Interconnection [*Telecommunications*]
SNI .... Subscriber Network Interface [*Computer science*] (CDE)
SNI .... Sun City Indus [*AMEX symbol*] (TTSB)
SNI .... Sun City Industries, Inc. [*AMEX symbol*] (SPSG)
SNI .... Syndicat National des Instituteurs [*National Union of Teachers*] [*France*]
SNIC .... Singapore National Institute of Chemistry
SNIC .... Sonic Solutions [*NASDAQ symbol*] (SAG)
SNICP .... Subnetwork Independent Convergence Protocol [*Telecommunications*] (OSI)
SNIE .... Sindacato Nazionale Insegnanti Elementari [*National Union of Elementary Teachers*] [*Italy*]
SNIE's .... Special National Intelligence Estimates [*Summaries of foreign policy information and advice prepared for the president*] [*Known informally as "sneeze"*]
SNIF .... American Sensors, Inc. [*NASDAQ symbol*] (SAG)
SNIF .... Short-Term Note-Issuance Facility [*Banking*]
SNIF .... Signal-to-Noise Improvement Factor (IAA)
SNIF .... Site-Specific Natural Isotope Fractionation [*Analytical chemistry*]
SNIF .... Standby Note Issuance Facility [*Finance*]
SNIF .... Syndicated Note-Issuance Facility [*Banking*] (ADA)
SNIFF .... Amer Sensors [*NASDAQ symbol*] (TTSB)
SNIFFEX ..... Sniffer [*Exhaust trail indicator*] Exercise [*Military*] (NVT)
SNIFTIRS ..... Subtractively Normalized Interfacial FTIR [*Fourier Transform Infrared*] Spectroscopy
SNIG .... Sustainable Non-Inflationary Growth (ODBW)
SNIMOG ...... Sustained Noninflationary Market-Oriented Growth
SNIOS .... Special Needs in the Ordinary School (AIE)
SNIP .... Single Net Information and Position [*Reporting procedures*] [*Navy*] (NVT)
SNIP .... Single Net Integrated Procedure [*Military*] (CAAL)
SNIPA .... Seronegative Inflammatory Polyarthritis [*Medicine*] (DMAA)
SNIPE .... SDI [*Strategic Defense Initiative*] Network Interface Processor Engine (SDI)
SNIPE .... Simple Network Interacting Program Executive (PDAA)
SNIPE .... Soviet Naval Interdiction Possibilities, Europe
SNIPS .... Skillshare National Information Processing System [*Australia*]
SNIR .... Signal-to-Noise Plus Interference Ratio

SNIRD .... Supposedly Noiseless Infrared Detector
SNIT .... Stock Number Identification Table
SNIVT .... Society of Non-Invasive Vascular Technology (EA)
SNJ .... Everett, WA [*Location identifier FAA*] (FAAL)
SNJ .... Sinj [*Yugoslavia*] [*Seismograph station code, US Geological Survey Closed*] (SEIS)
SNJ .... Switching Network Junction [*Telecommunications*] (OA)
SN(JC) .... Seaman (Junior College) [*Navy rating*] (DNAB)
SN(JCE) .... Seaman (Junior College Technical Electrician) [*Navy rating*] (DNAB)
SN(JCNE) .... Seaman (Junior College Nuclear Field Electronics) [*Navy rating*] (DNAB)
SN(JCNSET) ... Seaman (Junior College Nuclear Submarine Engineering Technician) [*Navy rating*] (DNAB)
SN(JCPE) .... Seaman (Junior College Polaris Field Electronics) [*Navy rating*] (DNAB)
SN(JCPL) .... Seaman (Junior College Polaris Field Launcher) [*Navy rating*] (DNAB)
SN(JCT) .... Seaman (Junior College Technical) [*Navy rating*] (DNAB)
SNJM .... Sisters of the Holy Names of Jesus and Mary [*Roman Catholic religious order*]
SNK .... Shannock Corp. [*Vancouver Stock Exchange symbol*]
SNK .... Snyder [*Texas*] [*Airport symbol*] (AD)
SNK .... Snyder, TX [*Location identifier FAA*] (FAAL)
SNK .... Soviet Narodnykh Komissarov [*Council of People's Commissars*] [*Former USSR*] (LAIN)
SNK .... Student-Newman-Keuls [*Statistical procedure*]
SNK .... Survey of Next of Kin [*Department of Health and Human Services*] (GFGA)
SNKE .... Golf Technology Holding, Inc. [*NASDAQ symbol*] (SAG)
SNKI .... Swank, Inc. [*NASDAQ symbol*] (NQ)
SNKIE .... Swank Inc. [*NASDAQ symbol*] (TTSB)
SNKL .... Snorkel (MSA)
SNKORL .... Subject to No Known or Reported Losses [*Insurance*] (AIA)
SNL .... Department of State. Newsletter [*A publication*]
SNL .... Sample Noise Level
SNL .... Sand Creek [*Guyana*] [*Airport symbol*] (AD)
SNL .... Sandia National Laboratories [*Department of Energy*] [*Albuquerque, NM*] (GRD)
SNL .... Saturday Night Live [*Television program*]
SNL .... Selected Nodes List [*Telecommunications*] (TEL)
SNL .... Seminole Resources, Inc. [*Vancouver Stock Exchange symbol*]
SNL .... Sevenhill [*Australia Seismograph station code, US Geological Survey Closed*] (SEIS)
SNL .... Shawnee, OK [*Location identifier FAA*] (FAAL)
SNL .... Snout Length [*Pisciculture*]
SNL .... Somali National League
SNL .... Soonair Lines, Inc. [*ICAO designator*] (FAAC)
SNL .... Spore Newsletter [*A publication*]
SNL .... Springfields Nuclear Laboratories [*British*] (NUCP)
SNL .... Standard Name Line [*Military*]
SNL .... Standard Nomenclature List [*Military*]
SNL .... State Narcotic Law
SNL .... Stock Not Listed (AAG)
SNLA .... Sandia National Laboratory (Albuquerque)
SNLC .... Senior NATO Logistician Conference (NATG)
SNLC .... Service National des Liberations Conditionnelles [*Canada*]
SNL/CA .... Sandia National Laboratories/California (GAAI)
SNL/CA .... Sandia National Laboratory/California (DOGT)
SNL/CA .... Sandia National Laboratory/California
SNLG .... Signaling (MSA)
SNL/NM .... Sandia National Laboratories/New Mexico (GAAI)
SNL/NM .... Sandia National Laboratory/New Mexico (DOGT)
SNL/NM .... Sandia National Laboratory/New Mexico
SNLR .... Services No Longer Required
SNLS .... Society for New Language Study (EA)
SNLV .... Strategic Nuclear Launch Vehicle
SNM .... Saint Mary's University, San Antonio, TX [*OCLC symbol*] (OCLC)
SNM .... San Ignacio de Moxos [*Bolivia*] [*Airport symbol*] (AD)
SNM .... Satellite Navigation Map
SNM .... Senior Naval Member
SNM .... Sensitive Nuclear Material (NUCP)
SNM .... Signal-to-Noise Merit
SNM .... Sinter Metals 'A' [*NYSE symbol*] (TTSB)
SNM .... Sinter Metals Co. [*NYSE symbol*] (SAG)
SNM .... SNAM SpA [*Italy ICAO designator*] (FAAC)
SNM .... Society of Nuclear Medicine (EA)
SNM .... Socorro [*New Mexico*] [*Seismograph station code, US Geological Survey*] (SEIS)
SNM .... Somali National Movement [*Political party*] (PD)
SNM .... Special Nuclear Material
SNM .... Spent Nuclear Material (IEEE)
SNM .... Square Nautical Mile (NVT)
SNM .... Subject Named Member (NVT)
SNM .... Sulfanilamide [*Antimicrobial compound*]
SNM .... Sunmask Petroleum [*Vancouver Stock Exchange symbol*]
SNMA .... Student National Medical Association (EA)
SNMC .... Service Provider's Network Management Center
SNMCB .... Scheduled Not Mission Capable Both [*Maintenance and supply*] (MCD)
SNMCM .... Scheduled Not Mission Capable Maintenance (MCD)
SNMDCS .... Standard Navy Maintenance Data Collection System
SNMMMIS ... Standard Navy Maintenance and Material Management Information System
SNMMMS .... Standard Navy Maintenance and Material Management System
SNMP .... Simple Network Management Protocol [*Computer science*]
SNMP .... Small Network Management Packet [*Marine science*] (OSRA)
SNMP .... Small Network Management Packet (USDC)
SNMP .... Spent Nuclear Material Pool (IEEE)
SNMS .... Secondary Neutrals Mass Spectrometry
SNMS .... Sputtered Neutral Mass Spectrometry [*Surface analysis*]
SNMT .... Society of Nuclear Medical Technologists [*Defunct*] (EA)
SNM-TS .... Society of Nuclear Medicine - Technology Section (DAVI)
SNMV .... Solanum Nodiflorum Mottle Virus [*Plant pathology*]
SNN .... Sha Na Na [*An association Defunct*] (EA)
SNN .... Shannon [*Ireland*] [*Airport symbol*] (OAG)
SNN .... Shared Nearest Neighbor (MCD)
SNN .... Sienna Resources Ltd. [*Toronto Stock Exchange symbol*]
SNN .... Signal Plus Noise-to-Noise (IAA)
SNN .... Sining [*Republic of China*] [*Seismograph station code, US Geological Survey*] (SEIS)
SNN .... Smith College, Northampton, MA [*OCLC symbol*] (OCLC)
SNN .... Structure-Nomenclature Notation [*Chemistry*]
SNNE .... Sustainable Net National Expenditure (EERA)
SNNEB .... Scottish Nursery Nurses Examination Board (DI)
SNO .... Delta Air Charter Ltd. [*Canada ICAO designator*] (FAAC)
SNO .... Seasonal Net Outgassing [*Oceanography*]
SNO .... Semiempirical Natural Orbital [*Physical chemistry*]
SNO .... Senior Naval Officer
SNO .... Senior Navigation Officer [*Air Force British*]
SNO .... Senior Nursing Officer [*British*]
SNO .... Serial Number (MDG)
SNO .... Special Naval Operations (NVT)
SNO .... Stock Number (MSA)
SNO .... Sudbury Neutrino Observatory [*Proposed joint US-Canadian project*]
Sno .... Thioinosine [*Also, SIno, M*] [*A nucleoside*]
SNOAD .... Senior Naval Officer Adriatic [*British*]
SNOB .... Senior Naval Officer on Board
S Nob .... Sine Nobilitate [*Without Nobility*] [*Notation used at Oxford University to indicate that a student was untitled*] [*Latin*]
SNOBOL .... String-Oriented Symbolic Language [*1963*] [*Computer science*]
SNOBS .... Sodium Nonanoyloxybenzene Sulfonate [*Detergent formulation*]
SNODO .... Standard Nomenclature of Diseases and Operations [*Medicine*] (DHSM)
SNOE .... Smart Noise Equipment [*RADAR jammer*] [*Air Force*]
SNOINCR .... Snow Depth Increase in Past Hour [*NWS*] (FAAC)
SNOK .... Secondary Next of Kin [*Army*] (AABC)
SNOL .... Senior Naval Officer, Landings [*British*]
SNOM .... Scanning Near-Field Optical Microscope (ECON)
SNOM .... Scanning Near-Fried Optical Microscope
SNOMed .... Systematized Nomenclature of Medicine
SNOO .... Small Nonoverlapping Offset [*Oceanography*]
SNOOP .... Students Naturally Opposed to Outrageous Prying [*Student legal action organization*] (EA)
SNOOPE .... System for Nuclear Observation of Possible Explosives [*Science Applications International Corp.*] [*Aviation*]
SNOOPI .... System Network Online Operations Information [*Suggested name for the Library of Congress computer system*]
SNOP .... Senior Naval Officer Present
SNOP .... Standard Nomenclature of Pathology [*College of American Pathologists*]
SNOP .... Systematized Nomenclature of Pathology [*NCI*]
SNOPG .... Senior Naval Officer, Persian Gulf [*British military*] (DMA)
SNORE .... Self-Noise Reduction
SNORE .... Signal-to-Noise Ratio Estimator
SNORKEX ... Snorkel Detection Exercise [*Military*] (NVT)
SNORT .... Supersonic Naval Ordnance Research Track [*China Lake, CA*]
SNOS .... Scottish National Orchestra Society
SNOS .... Silicon Nitride Oxide Silicon (IAA)
SNOTEL .... Snow Survey Telemetry Network [*Department of Agriculture*]
SNOW .... Sled Dogs Co. [*NASDAQ symbol*] (SAG)
Snow .... Snow's Reports [*3 Utah*] [*A publication*] (DLA)
SNOW .... Standard Normal Ocean Water
SNOWCAT .... Support of Nuclear Operations with Conventional Air Tactics (NATG)
SNOWFLEX ... Field Exercise under Snow Conditions [*Military*] (NVT)
SNOWI .... Senior Naval Officer, West Indies [*British*]
SNOW TIME ... SAC-NORAD [*Strategic Air Command - North American Air Defense*] OperationalWeapons Test Involving Military Electronics
S-N-P .... Salt and Pepa [*Rap recording group*]
SNP .... Samnordisk Planteforedling [*Internordic plant breeding*] [*An association Sweden*] (EAIO)
SNP .... School Nurse Practitioner
SNP .... Scottish National Party [*Political party*] (PPW)
SNP .... Single Nucleotide Polymorphism [*Genetics*]
SNP .... Single Nucleotide Polymorphism [*Genetics*]
SNP .... Skagit Nuclear Project (NRCH)
SNP .... Slovak National Party [*Former Czechoslovakia*] [*Political party*] (EY)
SNP .... Society for Natural Philosophy (EA)
SNP .... Sodium Nitroprusside [*A vasodilator*]
SNP .... Soluble Nonreactive Phosphorus [*Marine science*]
SNP .... Soluble Nucleoprotein
SNP .... Sonepat [*India*] [*Seismograph station code, US Geological Survey Closed*] (SEIS)
SNP .... Space Nuclear Propulsion
SNP .... Statistical Network Processor
SNP .... St. Paul Island [*Alaska*] [*Airport symbol*] (OAG)
SNP .... St. Paul Island, AK [*Location identifier FAA*] (FAAL)
SNP .... Sudanese National Party [*Political party*] (EY)
SNP .... Suspected, Not Proved
SNP .... Synchronous Network Processor
SNP .... Synchro Null Pulse

SNP System Network Processor
SNPA Scottish Newspaper Publishers' Association (DBA)
snpa Sinopia (VRA)
SNPA Southern Newspaper Publishers Association
SNPA Subnetwork Point of Attachment [*Telecommunications*] (OSI)
SNPDL Springfields Nuclear Power Development Laboratories [*British*] (NUCP)
SN(PFE) Seaman (Polaris Field Electronics) [*Navy rating*] (DNAB)
SN(PFL) Seaman (Polaris Field Launcher) [*Navy rating*] (DNAB)
SNPJ Slovene National Benefit Society (EA)
S-N (Plane) Sella Turcica-Nasion [*Plane that passes through these points*] [*Cephalometrics*]
SNPM Standard and Nuclear Propulsion Module
SNPMA Student National Podiatric Medical Association (EA)
SNPO Society for Nonprofit Organizations (EA)
SNPO Space Nuclear Propulsion Office [*Later, Division of Space Nuclear Systems, of Energy Research and Development Administration*] [*AEC-NASA*]
SNPOA Space Nuclear Propulsion Office, Albuquerque [*See SNPO*]
SNPOC Space Nuclear Propulsion Office, Cleveland [*See SNPO*]
SNPON Space Nuclear Propulsion Office, Nevada [*See SNPO*]
SNPP Sequoyah Nuclear Power Plant (NRCH)
SNPR Screen Print (AAG)
SNPRI Selected Nonpriority List Item [*Military*]
SNPRM Supplemental Notice of Proposed Rulemaking
SNPS Satellite Nuclear Power Station (OA)
SNPS Shoreham Nuclear Power Station (NRCH)
SNPS Synopsys, Inc. [*NASDAQ symbol*] (SAG)
SNQ Sea-1 Aquafarms Ltd. [*Vancouver Stock Exchange symbol*]
SNQ Shared Enqueue (MHDI)
SNR Aero Sonora SA de CV [*Mexico ICAO designator*] (FAAC)
SNR Saint Nazaire [*France*] [*Airport symbol*] (OAG)
SNR Schaffner Ranch [*California*] [*Seismograph station code, US Geological Survey*] (SEIS)
SNR Schenectady Naval Reactors Office [*Energy Research and Development Administration*]
SNR Selective Nitrogen Oxide Reduction [*Combustion technology*]
SNR Selective Noncatalytic Reduction [*Combustion technology*]
SNR Senior
Snr Senior (ODBW)
SNR Senior National Representatives SONAR [*Four Power Army*] (MCD)
SNR Senor [*Mister*] [*Spanish*]
SNR Service Not Required
SNR Signal-to-Noise Ratio
SNR Slow Neutron Reactor [*Nuclear energy*] (NRCH)
SNR Society for Nautical Research [*British*] (EAIO)
SNR SONAR
SNR Subject to Non-Renewal [*Advertising*] (DOAD)
SNr Substantia Nigra Pars Reticulata [*Brain anatomy*]
SNR Sudan Notes and Records [*A publication*]
SNR Sunair Electronics [*AMEX symbol*] (TTSB)
SNR Sunair Electronics, Inc. [*AMEX symbol*] (SPSG)
SNR Supernova Remnant [*Astronomy*]
SNR Supplier Nonconformance Report [*Nuclear energy*] (NRCH)
SNRA Sawtooth National Recreation Area [*Idaho*]
SNRA Senora [*Mrs.*] [*Spanish*]
SNRAFU Situation Normal, Really All Fouled Up [*Military slang*] [*Bowdlerized version*]
SNRC Sudanese National Research Council
SNRCN Signal-to-Noise Ratio Due to Channel Noise (IAA)
SNRE Small Nuclear Rocket Engine
SNRLTCS Skilled Nursing and Related Long Term Care Services (EA)
SNRM Set Normal Response Mode [*Telecommunications*] (OSI)
SNRME Set Normal Response Mode Extended [*Telecommunications*] (OSI)
snRNA Ribonucleic Acid, Small Nuclear [*Biochemistry, genetics*]
snRNP Ribonucleoprotein, Small Nuclear [*Biochemistry*]
SNRO Schenectady Naval Reactors Office [*Department of Energy*] [*Schenectady, NY*] (GAAI)
SNRS Sunrise
SNRT Sinus Node Recovery Time [*Cardiology*]
SNRTC Sinus Node Recovery Time Corrected [*Cardiology*]
SNRTi Sinus Node Recovery Time, Indirect Measuring [*Medicine*] (DMAA)
SNRZ Sunrise Assisted Living [*NASDAQ symbol*] (TTSB)
SNRZ Sunrise Assisted Living, Inc. [*NASDAQ symbol*] (SAG)
SNS Salinas [*California*] [*Airport symbol*] (AD)
SNS Salinas, CA [*Location identifier FAA*] (FAAL)
SNS Samarbeidsnemden for Nordisk Skogforskning [*Nordic Forest Research Cooperation Committee - NFRCC*] [*Finland*] (EAIO)
SNS San Onofre [*California*] [*Seismograph station code, US Geological Survey*] (SEIS)
SNS Scandinavian Neurosurgical Society (EA)
SNS Seabrook Nuclear Station (NRCH)
SNS Selected Numeric Service (NITA)
SNS Senior Nursing Sister [*Navy British*]
SNS Sensorstat System [*Vancouver Stock Exchange symbol*]
SNS Service National des Sauveteurs [*Canada*]
SNS Simulated Network Simulations (KSC)
SNS Skyline Network Service [*Satellite Business Systems*] [*McLean, VA*] [*Telecommunications*] (TSSD)
SNS Slovak National Party [*Political party*] (ECON)
SNS Small Nuclear Stage (KSC)
SNS Societe Centrafricaine de Transport Aerien [*Central African Republic*] [*ICAO designator*] (FAAC)
SNS Society of Neurological Surgeons (EA)
SNS Software Notification Service (NITA)
SNS Somatic Nervous System
SNS Space Navigation System (OA)
SNS Space Nuclear System
SNS Spallation Neutron Source
SNS Special Night Squads [*Palestine*] (BJA)
SNS Stabilized Night Sight
SNS Sundstrand Corp. [*NYSE symbol*] (SPSG)
SNS Sundstrand Corp. [*NYSE symbol*] (TTSB)
SNS Superconductor/Normal Metal/Superconductor [*Physics*]
SNS Switched Network Server [*Tylink Corp.*]
SNS Sympathetic Nervous System [*Physiology*]
SN/SC Stock Number Source Code (MCD)
SNSCNY St. Nicholas Society of the City of New York (EA)
SNSE Society of Nuclear Scientists and Engineers [*Defunct*]
SNSH Snow Showers [*Meteorology*]
SNSHN Sunshine
SNSL Standard Navy Stock List
SNSL Stock Number Sequence Listing (MSA)
SNSM Sindacato Nazionale Scuola Media [*National Union of Intermediate School Teachers*] [*Italy*]
SNSN Standard Navy Stock Number
SNSO Space Nuclear Systems Office [*AEC/NASA*]
SNSO Superintending Naval Stores Officer [*British military*] (DMA)
SNSR Control Devices, Inc. [*NASDAQ symbol*] (SAG)
SNSR Sensor (AAG)
SNSRY Sensory
SNSS School Natural Science Society [*British*]
SNST Sonesta International Hotels Corp. [*NASDAQ symbol*] (NQ)
SNST Special Needs Support Team [*Education*] (AIE)
SNST Sunset
SNSTA Sonesta Intl Hotels [*NASDAQ symbol*] (TTSB)
SNT Saint
SNT [*The*] Scrolls and the New Testament [*K. Stendahl*] [*A publication*] (BJA)
SNT Sealant [*Technical drawings*]
SNT Sears Point [*California*] [*Seismograph station code, US Geological Survey*] (SEIS)
SNT Secretaria Nacional de Transportes [*Brazil*] (EY)
SNT Selective Nuclear Transfer
SNT Serial Number Tracking
SNT Sign on Table (IAA)
SNT Silicon Needle Transducer
SNT Sindacato Nazionale Tabacchine [*National Union of Women Tobacco Workers*] [*Italy*]
SNT Single Negotiating Text [*UN Law of the Sea Conference*]
SNT Sinuses, Nose, and Throat [*Anatomy*] (DAVI)
SNT Society for Nondestructive Testing [*Later, ASNT*] (EA)
SNT Sonat, Inc. [*NYSE symbol*] (SPSG)
SNT Suncoast Aviation, Inc. [*ICAO designator*] (FAAC)
SNT Synthetic Navigation Trainer
SNT System Noise Temperature
SNTA Sodium Nitrilotriacetate
SNTC Syndicat National des Transporteurs de Cameroun [*National Union of Cameroonese Transportation Workers*]
SNTC Syndicat National des Travailleurs Congolais [*National Union of Congolese Workers*] [*Leopoldville*]
SNTC Synetic, Inc. [*NASDAQ symbol*] (NQ)
SNTCC Simplified Neutron Transport Computer Code
SNTF Special Navy Task Force (MUGU)
SNTFC Special Navy Task Force Commander
SNTF(SMS) Special Navy Task Force for Surface Missile Systems (MUGU)
SNTK Senetek Ltd. [*NASDAQ symbol*] (NQ)
Sntk Senetek PLC [*Associated Press*] (SAG)
SNTKY Senetek Plc ADS [*NASDAQ symbol*] (TTSB)
SNTL Superior National Insurance Group, Inc. [*NASDAQ symbol*] (SAG)
SNTL Superior Natl Insurance Grp [*NASDAQ symbol*] (TTSB)
SntO Santander Overseas Bank, Inc. [*Associated Press*] (SAG)
SNTO Sento Technical Innovations Corp. [*NASDAQ symbol*] (SAG)
SNTO Swiss National Tourist Office (EA)
SntOv Santander Overseas Bank, Inc. [*Associated Press*] (SAG)
SNTPC Scottish National Town Planning Council (DAS)
SNTR Sinter [*Metallurgy*]
SNTS Short-Length, Nonbuoyant Torpedo System
SNTS Society for New Testament Study [*Exeter, Devonshire, England*] (EA)
SNTV Sun Television & Appliances [*NASDAQ symbol*] (SAG)
SNTW Senetek Ltd. [*NASDAQ symbol*] (SAG)
SNTWF Senetek Plc Wrrt'A' [*NASDAQ symbol*] (TTSB)
SNTZ Senetek Ltd. [*NASDAQ symbol*] (SAG)
SNTZD Sensitized (MSA)
SNTZF Senetek Plc Wrrt'B' [*NASDAQ symbol*] (TTSB)
SNTZG Sensitizing (MSA)
SNU Santa Clara [*Cuba*] [*Airport symbol*] (AD)
SNU Seoul National University [*Korea*]
SNu Sifre on Numbers (BJA)
SNU SNC Group, Inc. [*Toronto Stock Exchange symbol*]
SNU Snunit Aviation [*Israel*] [*ICAO designator*] (FAAC)
SNU Solar Neutrino Unit [*Astrophysics*]
SNU Somali National Union
SNU Spiritualists National Union [*British*] (DBA)
SNU Street Narcotics Unit [*Criminology*] (LAIN)
SNUB Show Nothing Unless Bad
SNUD Stock Number User Directory [*Air Force*] (AFM)
SNUJ Singapore National Union of Journalists
SNUM Special Nuclear Material

SNUN Significant New Use Notice [*Government emissions regulations*]

SNUPPS Standardized Nuclear Unit Power Plant System [*Nuclear reactor combine*]

SNUR Significant New Use Rule [*Government emissions regulations*]

SNUR Significant New Use Rules [*Environmental Protection Agency*]

SNURP Small Nuclear Ribonucleoprotein Particle [*Genetics*]

SNUS SONUS Pharmaceuticals [*NASDAQ symbol*] (TTSB)

SNUS Sonus Pharmaceuticals, Inc. [*NASDAQ symbol*] (SAG)

SNV Aero Servicio del Norte SA de CV [*Mexico ICAO designator*] (FAAC)

SNV Santa Elena [*Venezuela*] [*Airport symbol*] (OAG)

SNV Satellite Newsgathering Vehicle (WDMC)

SNV Satellite News Vehicle (NTCM)

SNV Spleen Necrosis Virus

SNV Suneva Resources [*Vancouver Stock Exchange symbol*]

SNV Synovus Financial [*NYSE symbol*] (TTSB)

SNV Synovus Financial Corp. [*NYSE symbol*] (SPSG)

SNV Systema Nervosum Vegetativo [*Obsolete term for the autonomic nervous system*] [*Medicine*]

SNV Systemic Necrotizing Vasculitis [*Medicine*] (CPH)

SNVB Society for Northwestern Vertebrate Biology (EA)

SNVPP Simulated Night Vertical Pinpoint

SNVT Short No-Voltage Tester [*Ground surveillance RADAR system*] (MCD)

SNW Sandoway [*Myanmar*] [*Airport symbol*] (OAG)

SNW Scottsdale Charter, Inc. [*ICAO designator*] (FAAC)

S/Nw Signal-to-Noise, Weighted

SNW Slow Negative Wave [*Medicine*] (DMAA)

SNW Snowwater Resources Ltd. [*Vancouver Stock Exchange symbol*]

SNW Strategic Nuclear Weapon

SNWFL Snowfall [*NWS*] (FAAC)

SNWS Shipboard Nuclear Weapon Security [*Navy*] (CAAL)

SNWT Steel Non-Watertight [*Shipfitting*]

SNX Sun Air Aviation Services [*Canada ICAO designator*] (FAAC)

SNX Sunburst Exploration Ltd. [*Toronto Stock Exchange symbol*]

SNY Air Sandy, Inc. [*Canada ICAO designator*] (FAAC)

SNY Sidney [*Nebraska*] [*Airport symbol*] (OAG)

SNY Snyder Oil Corp. [*NYSE symbol*] (SPSG)

SNY Southern New York Railway [*AAR code*]

SNY Spanish Navy

SNY Sunny (MSA)

SNYC South Nottinghamshire Yeomanry Cavalry [*British military*] (DMA)

Snyder Snyder Oil Corp. [*Associated Press*] (SAG)

SnyderC Snyder Communications, Inc. [*Associated Press*] (SAG)

Snyder Mines Snyder on Mines and Mining [*A publication*] (DLA)

SnyderOil Snyder Oil Corp. [*Associated Press*] (SAG)

Snydr Snyder Oil Corp. [*Associated Press*] (SAG)

Sny Not Man Snyder's Notaries' and Commissioners' Manual [*A publication*] (DLA)

SNYPO Sold, Not Yet Paid Out

SNYPrA Snyder Oil cm Dep Ex Pfd [*NYSE symbol*] (TTSB)

Sny Rel Corp Snyder on Religious Corporations [*A publication*] (DLA)

SNZ Senzan [*Japan*] [*Seismograph station code, US Geological Survey*] (SEIS)

SNZ Shipping Corp. of New Zealand (CDA) [*Toronto Stock Exchange symbol*]

SNZO South Karori [*New Zealand*] [*Seismograph station code, US Geological Survey*] (SEIS)

SO Austrian Air [*ICAO designator*] (AD)

SO Austrian Air Services [*Austria ICAO designator*] (ICDA)

SO SAI Ambrosini SpA [*Italy ICAO aircraft manufacturer identifier*] (ICAO)

SO Sail Only (CINC)

SO Sales Office (MHDW)

SO Sales Order

SO Salpingo-Oophorectomy [*Medicine*]

SO Salvis Omissis [*Omissions Excepted*] [*Latin*]

SO Saturdays Only [*British railroad term*]

SO Saturn Orbiter [*NASA*]

SO Schenectady Operation [*Energy Research and Development Administration*] (MCD)

SO Scientific Officer [*Ministry of Agriculture, Fisheries, and Food*] [*Also, ScO*] [*British*]

SO Scottish [*Communion*] Office [*Episcopalian*]

SO Scouting-Observation Plane [*When prefixed to Navy aircraft designation*]

S(O) Seaman (Operator) [*British military*] (DMA)

SO Second Class Open [*Train ticket*] (DCTA)

SO Second Opinion [*An association Defunct*] (EA)

SO Second Opinion (DAVI)

SO Secretary's Office [*Navy*]

SO Secretary's Order

SO Section Officer [*British military*] (DMA)

SO Secure Operations (MCD)

SO Security Office

SO Seder 'Olam (BJA)

SO Select Order (IAA)

SO Seller's Option [*Stock exchange term*]

so Seller's Option (ODBW)

SO Sell-Off (AAG)

SO Send Only

SO Senior Officer [*Military, police*]

SO Sensory Organ [*Anatomy*]

SO Serial Output

SO Serviceability Objective

SO Service Order

SO Sex Offender

SO Sheriff's Office [*or Officer*] (ROG)

SO Shift-Out [*Computer science*] (IAA)

SO Shift-Out Character [*Keyboard*] [*Computer science*]

SO Shipment [*or Shipping*] Order

SO Shipping Order (WGA)

so Shipping Order (ODBW)

SO Ships-on-Order Library [*Maritime Data Network, Inc.*] [*Information service or system*] (CRD)

SO Ship's Option

SO Shop Order

SO Shot

S-O Shut-Off (AAG)

SO Shutout [*Sports*]

SO Signal Officer

SO Signal Oscillator (OA)

SO Significant Other [*Term for members of unmarried couples*]

S/O Sign Off

SO Silvered Optics

SO Sleepout (ADA)

SO Slope Occurrence

SO Slow Operate [*Relay*]

SO Slow Oxidative [*Fibers*] [*Neuroanatomy*]

SO Small Oocyte

SO Small Outline (NITA)

SO Social Studies/Social Science Education [*Educational Resources Information Center (ERIC) Clearinghouse*] [*Indiana University*] (PAZ)

SO Society (ROG)

SO Socket (IAA)

SO Sold Out (ADA)

SO Solicitor's Opinion [*Legal term*] (DLA)

SO Somalia [*ANSI two-letter standard code*] (CNC)

so Somalia [*MARC country of publication code Library of Congress*] (LCCP)

SO SONARman [*Navy*]

S/O Son Of [*Genealogy*]

SO Sorrel Resources Ltd. [*Toronto Stock Exchange symbol*]

SO Sorting Office [*British*] (ROG)

S/O Sound Off

SO Source [*Online database field identifier*]

SO South [*or Southern*]

SO Southern Airways [*ICAO designator*]

SO Southern Co. [*NYSE symbol*] (SPSG)

SO Southern Oscillation [*Meteorology*]

So Southern Reporter [*National Reporter System*] [*A publication*] (DLA)

S/O South Of [*In outdoor advertising*] (WDMC)

SO Special Olympics [*Later, SOI*] (EA)

SO Special Operations

SO Special Orders [*Military*]

SO Spheno-Occipital [*Synchondrosis*] [*Medicine*]

SO Spin-Orbital (IAA)

SO Spiracular Organ [*Fish anatomy*]

SO Spring Opening

SO Staff Office [*Marine science*] (OSRA)

SO Staff Officer

SO Stamp Office [*British*] (ROG)

SO Standing Order

SO State Officer

SO Stationary Orbit (IAA)

SO Stationery Office [*British*]

SO Station Officer [*British police*]

SO Statutes of Ontario [*QL Systems Ltd.*] [*Information service or system*] (CRD)

SO Stay Out [*Official leave from Eton College*] [*British*]

SO Stockage Objectives [*Military*]

SO Stock Option [*Investment term*]

SO Stock Order (AAG)

SO Stock Outboard [*Powerboat*]

SO Stop Order (MCD)

SO Stopover [*Slang*]

SO Stores Officer [*British military*] (DMA)

SO Strategic Outline Chart [*Air Force*]

SO Strikeouts [*Baseball*]

SO Submarine Oscillator (DEN)

SO Suboffice

S/O Substance Of

SO Substitution Oscillator (IAA)

SO Superior Oblique [*Muscle*] [*Anatomy*]

SO Superior Old [*Spirits*]

SO Supply Officer

SO Support Operations

SO Supraoptic [*Nucleus*] [*Ophtalmology*] (DAVI)

SO Surface Operations [*Navy*] (CAAL)

SO Surveillance Officer

SO Switching Oscilloscope

SO Switchover

SO Symbolic Output [*Computer science*]

SO Sympathetic Ophthalmia [*Medicine*]

SO Symphony Orchestra

SO System Override (AAG)

SO Systems Orientation

SO1 SONARman First Class [*Navy*]

SO_2 Arterial Oxygen Saturation [*Medicine*] (DAVI)

SO2 SONARman Second Class [*Navy*]

SO2 Sulfur Dioxide
SO_2 Sulfur Dioxide [*Organic chemistry*] (DAVI)
So 2d Southern Reporter, Second Series [*West*] [*A publication*] (AAGC)
So 2d Southern Reporter, Second Series [*A publication*] (DLA)
SO3 SONARman Third Class [*Navy*]
SO4 Science on 4 [*Radio program*] [*British*]
SO_4 Sulfate (GNE)
SOA Aupraorbita Artery [*Anatomy*] (DAVI)
SOA Safe Operating Area (IEEE)
SOA Sales Order Authority (AAG)
SOA Scandinavian Orthopaedic Association (EA)
SOA School of the Air [*Army*] (TSSD)
SOA Self-Optimizing and Adaptive
SOA Senate Operating Agency (MCD)
SOA Separate Operating Agency [*Air Force*] (AFM)
SOA Serial Output Adapter
SOA Shelby Owners of America (EA)
SOA Ship Operating Automation
SOA Shipyard Overhaul Availability
SOA Shuttle Orbital Application [*NASA*]
SOA Skoda Air [*Czechoslovakia*] [*ICAO designator*] (FAAC)
SOA Smithsonian Office of Anthropology
SOA Society of Actuaries (EA)
SOA Society of Authors [*British*] (EAIO)
SOA Soc Trang [*South Vietnam*] [*Airport symbol*] (AD)
SOA Sonora, TX [*Location identifier FAA*] (FAAL)
SOA Sorata Development, Inc. [*Vancouver Stock Exchange symbol*]
SOA Soundness of Approach (MCD)
SOA Source of Assignment (MCD)
SOA Southern Africa Fund [*NYSE symbol*] (SAG)
SOA Southern Airways (MCD)
SOA Specially-Oriented Advertisements [*Consumer Protection Packet - US Post Office*]
SOA Special Olympics Australia
SOA Special Open Allotment [*Military*] (AABC)
SOA Special Operating Agency [*Military*] (AABC)
SOA Special Operations Aircraft
SOA Speed of Advance [*Military*]
SOA Speed of Approach
SOA Spirit of Adventure (EA)
SOA Staff Officer, Administration [*British military*] (DMA)
SOA Standardbred Owners Association (EA)
SOA Start of Address
SOA Statement of Assurance
SOA State Oceanic Administration [*China*] [*Marine science*] (OSRA)
SOA State of Alert
SOA State of the Art
SOA Stimulus Onset Asynchrony [*Psychology*]
SOA Student Orientation Assistant
SOA Superoxide Anion [*Chemistry*]
SOA Supplement on Aging [*to the 1984 National Health Interview Survey*] [*Department of Health and Human Services*] (GFGA)
SOA Supraorbital Artery Test [*Neurological evaluation*] (CPH)
SOA Swelling of Ankles [*Medicine*] (DMAA)
SOA Switch Off Assembly (MCD)
SOAA Signed Out Against Advice [*Medicine*]
SOAA Staff Officers Association of America (EA)
SOAC State-of-the-Art Car [*Transit*] [*Department of Transportation*]
SOAC Submarine Officer Advanced Course [*Navy*] (DNAB)
SOACMS Special Operations Aviation Combat Mission Simulator [*Military*]
SOAD Spectrometric Oil Analysis Device
SOAD Staff Officer, Air Defence [*British military*] (DMA)
SoAF Soviet Air Force
SOAF Sultanate of Oman Air Force
So Afr South Africa
So Afr LT South African Law Times [*A publication*] (DLA)
So Afr Prize Cas South African Prize Cases (Juta) [*A publication*] (DLA)
SOAI Service des Organisations Aviation Aeronautiques Internationales [*France*]
SOAL Search Optical Augmentation LASER (MCD)
SOALM Scanned Optically Addressed Light Modulators (IAA)
SOA-MCA Superficial Occipital Artery to Middle Cerebral Artery [*Medicine*] (MAE)
SOAMUS Study of One-Atmosphere Manned Underwater Structures
SO & S Scouting, Observation, and Sniping [*British military*] (DMA)
SOAP Sarnia Olefins and Aromatics Project [*Canadian ethylene project*]
SOAP Self-Optimizing Automatic Pilot
SOAP Shaft Optimum Alignment Procedure (DNAB)
SOAP Ship Overhaul Assistance Program (MCD)
SOAP Silicate-Oxy-Apatite (PDAA)
SOAP Simplify Obscure ALGOL [*Algorithmic Language*] Programs (MCD)
SOAP Society for Obstetric Anesthesia and Perinatology (EA)
SOAP Society of Airway Pioneers (EA)
SOAP Society of Office Automation Professionals [*Later, AMS*] [*Telecommunications service Willow Grove, PA*] (TSSD)
SOAP Spectrochemical [*or Spectrographic, Spectrometric, or Spectroscopic*] Oil Analysis Program [*Air Force*]
SOAP Standing Order Advance Payment
SOAP Students Opposed to Advertised Pollutants [*Student legal action organization*]
SOAP Subjective, Objective, Assessment, and Plan [*Medicine*]
SOAP Submarine Overhaul Allowance Parts [*Navy*] (DNAB)
SOAP Sunflower Seed Oil Assistance Program [*Department of Agriculture*]
SOAP Supply Operations Assistance Program [*Military*]
SOAP Symbolic Optimum Assembly Programming [*IBM Corp.*] [*Computer science*]
SOAP Symptoms, Observations, Assessment, Plan
SOAP Systems Operational Analysis Plan
SOAPD Southern Air Procurement District
SOAPIE Subjective, Objective, Assessment, Plan, Implementation, and Evaluation [*Medicine*] (DMAA)
SOAPS Suction, Oxygen, Apparatus, Pharmaceuticals, Saline [*Mnemonic device for anesthetists*] (AAMN)
soapst Soapstone (VRA)
SOAR Safe Operating Area
SOAR Satellite Ocean Analysis for Recruitment [*Marine science*] (OSRA)
SOAR Save Our American Resources [*Boy Scout project*]
SOAR Seminars on Aeroanxiety Relief
SOAR Shuttle Orbital Applications and Requirements [*NASA*]
SOAR Simulation of Airlift Resources [*Air Force*]
SOAR Simulation of Apollo Reliability [*NASA*] (KSC)
SOAR Smalltalk on a RISC (NITA)
SOAR Special Operations Aviation Regiment [*Military*]
SOAR Staff Organization and Regulation
SOAR State-of-the-Art Report [*Navy*]
SOAR State Operator and Result [*Computer program*]
SOAR Stress on Analytical Reasoning
SOAR Support Our Aging Religious, Inc.
SOARS Satellite On-Board Attack Reporting System (MCD)
SOARS Second Order Attitude Reference Set (MCD)
SOARS Shuttle Operations Automated Reporting System [*NASA*] (NASA)
SOAS School of Oriental and African Studies [*University of London*]
SOAS Special Operations ADP [*Automatic Data Processing*] System (DOMA)
SOASC(I) Senior Officer Assault Ships and Craft (India) [*British*]
SOase Sulfite Oxidase [*An enzyme*]
SOATS Support Operations Automated Training System [*NASA*] (NASA)
SOAV Solenoid-Operated Air Valve (IAA)
Sob De Sobrietate [*of Philo*] (BJA)
SOB Second Overtone Band
SOB See Order Blank [*Laboratory science*] (DAVI)
SOB Senate Office Building
SOB Service Observance Bureau [*A telephone-monitoring section of the Bell System*]
SOB Shipped on Board a Specified Vessel (DS)
SOB Shortness of Breath [*Cardiology*]
SOB Silly Old Bugger [*Officer over the age of 39*] [*British*] (DSUE)
SOB Sobral [*Brazil*] [*Airport symbol*] (AD)
SOB Society of Bookmen (DGA)
SOB Son of a Bitch
SOB Souls on Board (BARN)
SOB Soviet Order of Battle (DOMA)
SOB Space Orbital Bomber (AAG)
SOB Start of Block
SOB Sub-Occipito Bregma [*Medicine*] (ROG)
SOB Sudost-Bahn [*Swiss Southeastern Railway*]
SOB Sulfur Oxidizing Bacteria
SOB Superior Official Bureaucrat [*Satirical bureaucracy term*]
SOBA System of Operational Buoys in the North Atlantic [*Marine science*] (OSRA)
SOBASSPIFTAGE Society of Beer and Sordid Sex Professional Invitational Fishing Tournament and Gastronomical Extravaganza
SOBC Save Our Barns Committee (EA)
SOBC Submarine Officer Basic Course [*Navy*] (DOMA)
SOBECOV Societe de Stockage et de Commercialisation des Produits Vivriers [*Development organization*] [*Burundi*] (EY)
SOBELAIR Societe Belge de Transports Pan Air [*Airline*] [*Belgium*]
SOBEP Scale of Beliefs in Extraordinary Phenomena [*Research test*] [*Psychology*]
SOBI Sobieski Bancorp [*NASDAQ symbol*] (TTSB)
SOBI Sobieski Bancorp, Inc. [*NASDAQ symbol*] (SAG)
Sobieski Sobieski Bancorp, Inc. [*Associated Press*] (SAG)
SOBIGM Sign Off Brother, I've Got Mine [*Remark used by seamen who avoided risky assignments during World War II*] [*Also used as hoax by National Maritime Union for name of organization issuing pamphlet about low state of merchant marine service*]
SOBLIN Self-Organizing Binary Logical Network [*OTS*]
SOBND Southbound (WGA)
SOBP Sentral Organisasi Buruh Pantjasila [*Central Organization of Pantjasila Labor*] [*Indonesia*]
SOBS Scanning Ocean Bottom SONAR
SOBS Society for Office-Based Surgery [*Later, ASOS*] (EA)
SOB's Sons of Bosses International [*Later, NFBC*] [*An association*] (EA)
SOB's South of Broad Street [*Reference is to residents of the historic and aristocratic section of Charleston, South Carolina*]
SOBU Student Organization for Black Unity
SOC Chief SONARman [*Navy rating Obsolete*]
SOC Saint Olaf College [*Northfield, MN*]
SOC Satellite Operations Center [*Cape Kennedy*]
SOC Satellite Operations Complex
SOC Satellite Orbit Control
SOC Save Our Constitution [*An association*] (EA)
SOC Scene of Crime
SOC Schedule of Organizational Change [*Air Force*] (AFM)
SOC Scottish Ornithologists' Club [*British*]
SOC Sector Operations Center [*Air Force*]
SOC Sedimentary Organic Carbon [*Marine science*]
SOC Self-Organized Criticality [*Physics*]
SOC Self-Organizing Control
SOC Separated Orbit Cyclotron (IEEE)
SOC Sequence of Controls

SOC .... Sequential Oral Contraceptive (HGAA)
SOC .... Service and Overhaul Change (MSA)
SOC .... Servicemen's Opportunity College [*DoD*]
SOC .... Set Overrides Clear (IEEE)
SOC .... Severity of Ozone Cracking (PDAA)
SOC .... Sexual Over-Seriousness [*Attitude disorder*]
SOC .... Shop Order Control
SOC .... Signal Officer (IAA)
SOC .... Silicon on Ceramic [*Technique for producing solar cells*]
SOC .... Simulated Operational Computer (KSC)
SOC .... Simulation Operation Computer (IAA)
SOC .... Simulation Operations Center [*NASA*] (KSC)
SOC .... Singer Owners Club (EA)
SOC .... Single Orbit Computation
SOC .... Sochi [*Former USSR Seismograph station code, US Geological Survey*] (SEIS)
SOC .... Social
SOC .... Socialist (EY)
Soc .... Socialist (ODBW)
SOC .... Socialist Objectives Committee [*Australian Labor Party*]
SOC .... Society
Soc .... Society (ODBW)
Soc .... Society [*A publication*] (BRI)
SOC .... Society of Cinematologists [*Later, SCS*] (EA)
SOC .... Sociology
Soc .... Sociology (DD)
SOC .... Socket (AAG)
SOC .... Socrates [*Greek philosopher, 470-399BC*] (ROG)
SOC .... Soil Organic Carbon
SOC .... Solo [*Indonesia*] [*Airport symbol*] (OAG)
SOC .... Somerset County College, Somerville, NJ [*OCLC symbol*] (OCLC)
SOC .... Southampton Oceanography Centre [*British*]
So C .... South Carolina Reports [*A publication*] (DLA)
SOC .... Southern Oregon College
SOC .... Spacecraft-Orientation-Control [*NASA*] (IAA)
SOC .... Space Operations Center
SOC .... Space Operations Controller
SOC .... Specialised Oceanographic Centre (EERA)
SOC .... Specialized Oceanographic Center [*National Oceanic and Atmospheric Administration*] (MSC)
SOC .... Special Operations Capability [*Marine Corps*] (DOMA)
SOC .... Special Operations Command [*Military*] (AABC)
SOC .... Specific Optimal Control
SOC .... Spin-Orbit Coupling [*Physical chemistry*]
SOC .... Spouse Observation Checklist
SOC .... Squadron Operations Center [*Air Force*]
SOC .... Standard Occupational Classifications (OICC)
SOC .... Standard Oil Co.
SOC .... Standards of Official Conduct [*A publication*] (DLA)
SOC .... Standing Order Confirmation [*Publishing*]
SOC .... Standing Orders Committee [*British*] (DCTA)
SOC .... Start of Climb [*Aviation*] (DA)
SOC .... Start of Construction [*Military*] (AFIT)
SOC .... Start of Conversion [*Navy*]
SOC .... Start-of-Cycle [*Engineering*]
SOC .... Statement of Capability (MCD)
SOC .... Statement of Charges
SOC .... Statement of Conditions
SOC .... State of Charge
SOC .... State of Charge
SoC .... State of Consciousness
SOC .... State-Operated Contracts
SOC .... State-Owned Corporation
SOC .... Statewide Operations Center
SOC .... Station Operations Console (MCD)
SOC .... Strike Operations Coordinator [*Navy*] (NVT)
SOC .... Strike Options Comparison (MCD)
SOC .... Struck off Charge [*British military*] (DMA)
SOC .... Sunbeam Corp. [*NYSE symbol*] (SAG)
SOC .... Superposition of Configuration [*Atomic physics*]
SOC .... Supply Overhaul Coordinator (MCD)
SOC .... Support Operations Center
SOC .... Suspended Organic Carbon [*Chemistry*]
SOC .... Synthetic Organic Chemical
SOC .... System Operational Complex
SOC .... System Operational Concept
SOC .... System Operations Control [*Canadian Airlines International*]
SOC .... System Option Controller [*NASA*] (NASA)
SOC .... Systems Operation Center
SOCA .... Cayenne/Rochambeau [*French Guiana*] [*ICAO location identifier*] (ICLI)
SOCA .... Soul and Calypso [*Music*]
SOCA .... Staff Officer for Civil Affairs [*British World War II*]
SOCABU .... Societe du Caoutchouc Butyl [*France*]
Soc Action & L... Social Action and the Law [*A publication*] (DLA)
SOCAD .... Serviceman's Opportunity for College Associate Degree [*Military*] (MCD)
SOCAL .... Southern California [*Military*] (NVT)
SOCAL .... Standard Oil Co. of California
So Cal C Optometry... Southern California College of Optometry (GAGS)
So Calif Tax Inst... University of Southern California School of Law Tax Institute (DLA)
SOCALSEC ... Southern California Sector, Western Sea Frontier
Soc Alt .... Social Alternatives [*A publication*]
SOCAN .... Society of Composers, Authors and Music Publishers of Canada [*Canada*] (WWLA)
SOCAP .... Society of Consumer Affairs Professionals in Business [*Alexandria, VA*] (EA)
SOCAR .... Shuttle Operational Capability Assessment Report [*NASA*] (MCD)
So Car .... South Carolina Reports [*A publication*] (DLA)
SOCAR .... Statement of Condition and Recommendation [*Military*] (AABC)
SOCAR .... Systems Operational Compatibility Assessment Review [*NASA*]
So Car BA Rep... South Carolina Bar Association Reports [*A publication*] (DLA)
So Car Const... South Carolina Constitutional Reports (Treadway, Mill, or Harper) [*A publication*] (DLA)
So Car LJ .... South Carolina Law Journal [*Columbia*] [*A publication*] (DLA)
So Car R ...... South Carolina Law Reports [*A publication*] (DLA)
So Car St U... South Carolina State University (GAGS)
SOCAS .... Subcommittee on Chemical Abstracts Service [*American Chemical Society*]
SOCAT .... Student Occupational Competency Achievement Testing [*Educational test*]
SOCATOUR... Societe Camerounaise de Tourisme (EY)
SOCATS .... Scenario Oriented Corps Area Training System (MCD)
SOCB .... Shop Order Control Board
SOCBRO .... Society of Chief Building Regulation Officers [*British*] (DBA)
SOCC .... Salvage Operational Control Center [*On submarine rescue ship during salvage operation*]
SOCC .... Satellite Oceanic Control Center
SOCC .... Satellite Operations Control Center [*NASA*] (NASA)
SOCC .... Sector Operations Control Center [*NORAD*] (FAAC)
SOCC .... Self-Orthogonal Convolutional Code (PDAA)
SOCC .... Spacecraft Operations Control Center
SOCC .... Special Opportunities Counties and Cities Program [*Tennessee Valley Authority*]
SOCC .... Submarine Operations Control Center [*Navy*] (CAAL)
SOCC .... Subordinate Operations Control Center
SOCCE .... Special Operations Command and Control Element
SOCCENT ..... Special Operations Command, Central Command [*Military*]
SOCCER .... SMART's Own Concordance Constructor, Extremely Rapid [*Cornell University*] [*Computer science*]
SoCCS .... Study of Cataloguing Computer Software (AIE)
SOCCS .... Study of Computer Cataloging Software (NITA)
SOCCS .... Summary of Component Control Status [*Nuclear energy*] (NRCH)
SOCCT .... Special Operations Combat Control Team (DOMA)
SOCD .... Source Control Document (MCD)
SOCD .... Source Control Drawing
SOCDS .... Source Codes (MCD)
SOCE .... Staff Officer Construction Engineering
Soc Econ Wetgeving... Social Economisch Wetgeving. Tijdschrift voor Europees en Economisch Recht [*A publication*] (DLA)
SOCELEX ..... Society Against Elephant Exploitation (EA)
SOCEUR .... Special Operations Command, Europe [*Military*] (DOMA)
SOCEX .... Southern Ocean Cloud Experiment (EERA)
SOCEX .... Special Operations Capable Exercise (DOMA)
SOCF .... Spacecraft Operations and Checkout Facility (AAG)
SOCGPA .... Seed, Oil, Cake, and General Produce Association [*British*] (BI)
SOCH .... Spacelab Orbiter Common Hardware [*NASA*] (MCD)
SOCHINAFOR.. South China Force [*World War II*]
SOCIAL SCISEARCH... Social Science Citation Index Search [*Database*]
SOCIM .... Society of Connoisseurs in Murder (EA)
Socin Sen .... Marianus Socinus, the Elder [*Deceased, 1467*] [*Authority cited in pre-1607 legal work*] (DSA)
SOCIOL .... Sociology
Socio R .... Sociological Review [*A publication*] (BRI)
Soc Is .... Society Islands (BARN)
Soc Isl .... Society Islands
socist .... Cistercian Monks of the Strict Observance (TOCD)
SOCist .... Cistercian Monks of the Strict Observance (TOCD)
SO Cist .... Sacer Ordo Cisterciensis [*Order of Cistercians*] [*Roman Catholic men's religious order*]
Socket .... Socket Communications, Inc. [*Associated Press*] (SAG)
SocketC .... Socket Communications, Inc. [*Associated Press*] (SAG)
SOCL .... Social
Soc Lab Bull... Social and Labour Bulletin [*A publication*] (ILCA)
Soc Labour Bull... Social and Labour Bulletin [*A publication*]
SOCLGY .... Sociology
SOCM .... Master Chief SONARman [*Navy rating*]
SOCM .... Standoff Cluster Munitions
SOCMA .... Scottish Operative Coach Makers' Association [*A union*]
SOCMA .... Second Order Coherent Multiple Access (PDAA)
SOCMA .... Synthetic Organic Chemical Manufacturers Association (EA)
SOCMAC ...... Socially-Oriented Comprehensive Memory-Assist Computer (IIA)
SOCMC .... Special Order of the Commandant of the Marine Corps
Soc Mean Leg Con... Social Meaning of Legal Concepts [*A publication*] (ILCA)
SOCMI .... Synthetic Organic Chemical Manufacturing Industry [*Environmental Protection Agency*]
SOCN .... Source Control Number
SOCO .... Scenes-of-the-Crime Officer [*Scotland Yard*]
SOCO .... Source Code (NITA)
SOCO .... Standard Oil Co. of California
SOCO .... Standards of Conduct Office (AAGC)
SOCO .... Switched out for Checkout [*NASA*] (KSC)
SOCOCO ...... Symposium of Software for Computer Control (MHDI)
SOCOM .... Society and Commerce Publications
SOCOM .... Solar Communications
SOCOM .... Solar Optical Communications System (IAA)
SOCOM .... Solar-Orbital Communications (IAA)
SOCOM .... Southern Command (MCD)

SOCOM........ Special Operations Command [*Military*]
So Conn St U... Southern Connecticut State University (GAGS)
SOCONY...... Standard Oil Co. of New York [*Socony Mobil is now official name of firm*]
SOCOORD.... Special Operations Coordination [*DoD*]
So C Optometry... Southern College of Optometry (GAGS)
SOCORICO... Society of Costa Rica Collectors (EA)
SOCP........... Satellite Orbit Control Program (IAA)
SOCPAC....... Special Operations Center, Pacific Command (CINC)
SOCPO......... Society of Chief Personnel Officers [*British*]
SOCQ........... Stages of Concern Questionnaire [*Educational test*]
SocQuim...... Sociedad Quimica [*Associated Press*] (SAG)
SOCR........... Scan-Optics [*NASDAQ symbol*] (TTSB)
SOCR........... Scan-Optics, Inc. [*NASDAQ symbol*] (NQ)
SOCR........... Special Operational Contract Requirements (AAG)
SOCR........... Sustained Operations Control (IAA)
SOCR........... Sustained Operations Control Room [*NASA*] (KSC)
SOCR........... Synchronous Orbit Communication Relay (MCD)
SOCRATES... Service Order, Customer Records, and Terminal Entry System
SOCRATES... Simulation of Closure and Rendezvous Approach Techniques for Early Spacecraft (IAA)
SOCRATES... Simulator or Creative Reasoning Applied to Education Systems (IAA)
SOCRATES... Special Operations Command Research, Analysis, and Threat Evaluation System (DOMA)
SOCRATES... System for Organizing Content to Review and Teach Educational Subjects
SOCRATES... System for Organizing Current Reports to Aid Technologists and Scientists (NITA)
SOCRATES... System for Organizing Current Reports to Aid Technology and Science
SOCRATES... System of Cellular Radio for Traffic Efficiency and Safety [*FHWA*] (TAG)
SOCRED....... Social Credit Party [*British*]
SOCREDO.... Societe pour le Credit et le Developpement en Oceanie [*Commercial bank*] [*French Polynesia*] (EY)
SOC ROS..... Societas Rosicruciana [*Freemasonry*]
SOCS........... Satellite Operations Control System
SOCS........... School of Corresponding Studies [*Military*] (INF)
SOCS........... Senior Chief SONARman [*Navy rating*]
SOCS........... Ship Operational Characteristics Study (DOMA)
SOCS........... Society of County Secretaries [*British*] (DBA)
SOCS........... Spacecraft-Orientation-Control System
SOCS........... Space Operation Command System [*NASA*] (IAA)
SOCS........... Subsystem Operating and Checkout System [*NASA*] (MCD)
SOCS........... Survey of Clerical Skills (AEBS)
SocSc.......... Social Science (DD)
SocSciComR... Social Science Computer Review [*A publication*] (BRI)
SOCSE......... Special Operations Communications Elements [*Military*] (GFGA)
SocSec......... Social Security (DAVI)
Soc Sec J..... Social Security Journal [*A publication*]
Soc Sec Q..... Social Security Quarterly [*A publication*]
Soc Ser R..... Social Service Review [*A publication*] (BRI)
Soc Services Rev... Social Services Review [*A publication*]
S-OCT.......... Serum Ornithine Carbamyltransferase [*Medicine*] (DMAA)
SOCTAP........ Sulfur Oxide Control Technology Assessment Panel [*Federal interagency committee*]
Soc W........... Social Work [*A publication*] (BRI)
SOCY........... Society (ROG)
SOCY........... Sociology (ROG)
SOD............. Secretary of Defense [*DoD*] (VNW)
SOD............. Sediment Oxygen Demand [*of water bodies*]
SOD............. Seller's Option to Double [*Stock exchange term*]
SOD............. Sell-Off Date (AAG)
SOD............. Septo-Optic Dysplasia [*Medicine*] (DMAA)
SOD............. Serial Output Data [*Computer science*]
SOD............. Shorter Oxford Dictionary [*A publication*]
SOD............. Shuttle Operational Data (MCD)
SOD............. Small Object Detector
SOD............. Small Oriented Diode (IAA)
SOD............. Society of Dismas (EA)
SOD............. Sodalite [*A zeolite*]
SOD............. Sodankyla [*Finland*] [*Seismograph station code, US Geological Survey*] (SEIS)
SOD............. Sodium (DHSM)
SOD............. Sodomy [*FBI standardized term*]
SOD............. Soldier Orientation and Development (MCD)
SOD............. Sons of the Desert (EA)
SOD............. Sound-on-Disk (DEN)
SOD............. Space Operation Directorate (SSD)
SOD............. Special Operations Detachment [*Military*] (AABC)
SOD............. Special Operations Division [*Office of Preparedness, General Services Administration*]
SOD............. Special Order Discharge
SOD............. Staff Operations Division [*NASA*] (MCD)
SOD............. Start-Over Dad
SOD............. Statute of Distribution [*Legal shorthand*] (LWAP)
SOD............. Student Organization Development (EDAC)
SOD............. Sudden-Dosage Onset [*Pharmacology*] (DAVI)
SOD............. Sum-of-the-Years Digit [*Statistics*] (IAA)
SOD............. Superintendent of Documents [*US Government Printing Office*]
SOD............. Superoxide Dismutase [*Also, SODI*] [*An enzyme*]
SOD............. Surface-Oriented Diode (IAA)
SOD............. Surgical Officer of the Day (DAVI)
SOD............. Surgical Operations Database [*Medicine*]
SOD............. Sustained Operational Date (AFM)
SOD............. Systems Operational Description [*or Design*]
SODA........... Salmonella Outbreak Detection Algorithm [*Medicine*]
SODA........... Source Oriented Data Acquisition
SODA........... Sportsplex Owners and Directors of America
SODA........... Stamp Out Drug Addiction
SODA........... System Optimization and Design Algorithm (HGAA)
SODAC......... Source Data Collection
sod acid phos... Sodium Acid Phosphatase [*or Sodium Biphosphate*] [*Pharmacology*] (DAVI)
Sodak.......... Sodak Gaming, Inc. [*Associated Press*] (SAG)
So Dak B Jo... South Dakota Bar Journal [*A publication*] (DLA)
So Dak Sch M&T... South Dakota School of Mines and Technology (GAGS)
So Dak St U... South Dakota State University (GAGS)
SODAR......... Sound Detecting and Ranging
SODAS......... Sandia Optical Disk Archival System [*Online map database*] [*Developed by Sandia National Laboratories for the USGS*]
SODAS......... Spheroidal Oral Drug Absorption System [*Medicine*] (DMAA)
SODAS......... Structure-Oriented Description and Simulation (IEEE)
SODAS......... Synoptic Oceanographic Data Acquisition System [*Marine science*] (MSC)
SODB........... Science Organization Development Board [*National Academy of Sciences*]
SODB........... Shuttle [*or Spacecraft*] Operational Data Book [*NASA*]
SODB........... Sodbury [*England*]
SODB........... Start of Data Block (MCD)
sod bicarb... Sodium Bicarbonate [*Inorganic chemistry*] (MAE)
SODC........... Siblings of Disabled Children (EA)
SODC........... Sporting Owner Drivers' Club Ltd. [*British*] (BI)
SODDS......... Submarine Oceanographic Digital Data System [*Navy*] (DNAB)
Sodep.......... Social Democratic Party [*Turkey Political party*] (PPW)
SODEPALM... Societe pour le Developpement et l'Exploitation du Palmier a Huile [*Ivory Coast*]
SODEPAX..... Committee on Society, Development, and Peace [*of the Roman Catholic Church and the World Council of Churches*] [*Defunct*] (EA)
SODEX......... Social Data Exchange Association [*Council for Community Services*] [*Information service or system*] (IID)
SODF........... Sperm Outer Defense Fiber [*Medicine*] (DMAA)
SODH........... Sorbitol Dehydrogenase (DMAA)
SODI............ Superoxide Dismutase [*SOD*] [*Absorbed by An enzyme*]
SODITAL...... Societe de Developpement de l'Industrie Touristique en Algerie (EY)
SODK........... Sodak Gaming [*NASDAQ symbol*] (TTSB)
SODK........... Sodak Gaming, Inc. [*NASDAQ symbol*] (SAG)
SODPAL....... Social Democrat Party and Liberal [*British*]
SODRE......... Servicio Oficial de Difusion Radio Electrica [*Radio and television network*] [*Uruguay*]
SODRS......... Synchronous Orbit Data Relay Satellite
SODS........... Saturn Operational Display System [*NASA*]
SODS........... Shuttle Operational Data System [*NASA*] (MCD)
SODS........... Skylab Orbit-Deorbit System [*NASA*] (MCD)
SODS........... Strategic Offensive Delivery Systems (DOMA)
SODS........... Subordinate Operations Data System (NVT)
SODT........... Scope Octal Debugging Tape
SODTICIOAP... Special Ordnance Depot Tool Identification, Classification, Inventory, and Obsolescence Analysis Program [*Popularly called "Soda Cap"*]
SODU........... Screen Oriented Disk Utility [*Computer science*]
SODW.......... Simulation Object Domain Working Group
SOE............. Senior Officer Escort [*British military*] (DMA)
SOE............. Sequence of Events
SOE............. Short of Exchange [*Economics*]
SOE............. Significant Operating Experience (IEEE)
SOE............. Silicon Overlay Epitaxial (IAA)
SOE............. Silver Oxide Electrode
SOE............. Skylab Operational Environment [*NASA*]
SOE............. Slater Orbital Exponents [*Atomic physics*]
SOE............. Society of Editors (DGA)
SOE............. Souanke [*Congo*] [*Airport symbol*] (OAG)
SOE............. Special Operations Executive [*British research unit corresponding to OSS*] [*World War II*]
SOE............. Specific Optimal Estimation (PDAA)
SOE............. Stage Operations Engineer
SOE............. Standard Option Equipment (DOMA)
SOE............. Start of Entry [*Computer science*]
SOE............. State of Environment [*Australia*]
SOE............. State of the Environment (EERA)
SOE............. State-Owned Enterprise
SOE............. Status of Equipment [*Army*] (AABC)
SOE............. Stripline Opposed Emitter (IAA)
SOE............. Summary of Engagements (MCD)
SOE............. Super Orbit Entry
SOEAP......... Summary of Effective Allowance Parts List [*Navy*]
SOEAPL....... Summary of Effective Allowance Parts List [*Navy*] (DNAB)
SOEASTPAC... Southeast Pacific Command [*Navy*]
So East Rep... Southeastern Reporter [*A publication*] (DLA)
SOEBT......... Stationery and Office Equipment Board of Trade (EA)
SOEC........... Statistical Office of the European Communities (DCTA)
SOED........... Scottish Office Education Department (AIE)
SOED........... Shorter Oxford English Dictionary [*A publication*]
SOEH........... Society for Occupational and Environmental Health (EA)
SoElec......... Southern Electronics Corp. [*Associated Press*] (SAG)
SOEMC......... Senior Officer Executive Management Course [*Naval War College*]
SOEP........... Solar-Oriented Experimental Package [*NASA*]
SOER........... Significant Operating Event Report (IEEE)
SOER........... State of the Environment Report (EERA)

SOERO........ Small Orbiting Earth Resources Observatory (IEEE)
SOES.......... Small Order Execution System [*Business term*]
SOES.......... Special Operations Evaluation System (DNAB)
SOES.......... Station Operations and Engineering Squadron [*Marine Corps*]
SOE/SO....... Special Operations Executive, Special Operations [*British World War II*]
SOF............ Safety of Flight [*NASA*] (NASA)
SOF............ Satisfactory Operation Factor [*Telecommunications*] (TEL)
SOF............ Secretary's Open Forum (EA)
SOF............ Shortest Operation First
SOF............ Signal Officer (IAA)
SOF............ Single Oriental Female [*Classified advertising*]
SoF............ Society of Floristry [*British*] (DBA)
Sof............ Soferim (BJA)
SOF............ Sofia [*Bulgaria*] [*Airport symbol*] (OAG)
SOF............ Sofia [*Bulgaria*] [*Seismograph station code, US Geological Survey*] (SEIS)
SOF............ Softnet Systems [*Formerly, Vader Group, Inc.*] [*AMEX symbol*] (SPSG)
SOF............ Soluble Organic Fraction [*Environmental chemistry*]
SOF............ Soluble Organic Fractions
SOF............ Sound on Film
SOF............ Special Operations Force [*Military*]
SOF............ Spillover Factor
SOF............ Spreading Ocean Floor
SOF............ Start-of-Format Control [*Computer science*]
SOF............ Start of Frame
SOF............ Status of Forces
SOF............ Statute of Fraud [*Legal shorthand*] (LWAP)
SOF............ Storage Oscilloscope Fragments
SOF............ Strategic Offensive Forces [*Army*] (AABC)
SOF............ Sub-Occipito Frontal [*Medicine*] (ROG)
SOF............ Superior Orbital Fissure [*Eye anatomy*]
SOF............ Supervisor of Flying (MCD)
SOFA.......... Krause's Furniture [*NASDAQ symbol*] (TTSB)
SOFA.......... Krauses Furniture, Inc. [*NASDAQ symbol*] (SAG)
S of A......... School of Artillery [*British military*] (DMA)
SOFA.......... Status of Forces Agreement [*International treaty*]
SOFA.......... Student Overseas Flights for Americans
SOFAA........ Society of Fine Art Auctioneers [*British*] (DBA)
Sofamor....... Sofamor Danek Group [*Associated Press*] (SAG)
SOFAR........ Sound Fixing and Ranging [*Navy underground sound system*]
SOFAR........ Sound Fusing and Ranging
SOFAR/BF.... Sound Fixing and Ranging/Bomb Fuze [*Navy underground sound system*] (SAA)
SOFAS........ Suitable Occupation for a Sloane [*British Slang*]
SOFAS........ Survivable Optical Forward Acquisition Sensor
SOFAS........ Survivable Optical Forward Acquisition System (MCD)
SOF ATS...... Special Operations Force Aircrew Training System [*Military*]
SOFC.......... Saturn Operational Flight Control [*NASA*]
SOFC.......... Solid Electrolyte Fuel Cell [*Chemistry*]
SOFC.......... Solid Oxide Fuel Cell [*Energy source*]
S of C......... Statutes of Canada [*A publication*] (DLA)
SOFCS........ Self-Organizing Flight Control System
SofD.......... Sons of David (BJA)
SOFE.......... Society of Financial Examiners (EA)
SOFEX........ Southern Ocean Float Experiment [*Marine science*] (MSC)
S/OFF......... Sign Off [*Computer science*] (MDG)
SOFFEX....... Swiss Options and Financial Futures Exchange
S of G......... School of Gunnery [*British military*] (DMA)
S of I.......... School of Infantry [*British military*] (DMA)
SOFI........... Software Information (IAA)
SOFI........... Spray-On Foam Insulation (NASA)
S of I.......... Superintendent of Instruction [*British military*] (DMA)
SOFI........... Supersearch-Online Friendly Interface [*Computer science*]
SOFIA......... Stratospheric Observatory for Infrared Astronomy [*NASA*]
SOFIE......... Sources de Financement des Entreprises [*CCMC Informatique de Gestion*] [*Database*]
SOFIS......... Sophicated Optimized Fuel Injection System
SOFIS......... Sophisticated Optimized Fuel Injection System [*Automotive engineering*]
SOFIX......... Software Fix [*NASA*]
S-of-L......... Ship-of-the-Line
SOFLAM...... Special Operations Force LASER Marker [*Military*] (RDA)
S of M......... School of Musketry [*Military British*] (ROG)
S of M......... Society of Metaphysicians (EA)
SOFNET....... Solar Observing and Forecasting Network [*Air Force*]
S of P.......... Sons of Phoenix [*Freemasonry*] (ROG)
SOFPAC....... Special Operating Forces, Pacific [*Military*]
SOFR.......... State of the Forests Report (EERA)
SOFRES....... Societe Francaise d'Enquetes par Sondages [*French opinion-polling organization*]
S of S.......... Secretary of State
S of S.......... Secretary of State for Defence [*British*] (RDA)
S of S.......... Song of Solomon [*Old Testament book*]
S of Sol....... Song of Solomon [*Old Testament book*] (ROG)
SOFT.......... Signature of Fragmented Tanks
SOFT.......... Simple Output Format Translator (IEEE)
SOFT.......... Society of Forensic Toxicologists (EA)
SOFT.......... SofTech, Inc. [*NASDAQ symbol*] (NQ)
SOFT.......... Software [*Computer science*]
S of T......... Sons of Temperance
SOFT.......... Space Operations and Flight Techniques [*NASA*] (NASA)
SOFT.......... Special Operational Forces Taiwan (CINC)
SOFT.......... Status of Forces Treaty
S of T......... Superintendent of Transportation
SOFT.......... Support Organization for Trisomy 18, 13 and Related Disorders (PAZ)
SOFT 18/13... Support Organization for Trisomy 18/13 (EA)
SOFTA........ Shippers Oil Field Traffic Association (EA)
SOFTCON..... Software Conference [*Trademark*]
Softdesk...... Softdesk, Inc. [*Associated Press*] (SAG)
Softech........ SofTec, Inc. [*Associated Press*] (SAG)
Softkey........ Softkey International, Inc. [*Associated Press*] (SAG)
SOFTMARK... Software Marketing (IAA)
Softnet........ Softnet Systems [*Associated Press*] (SAG)
SoftSpc........ Software Spectrum, Inc. [*Associated Press*] (SAG)
Software...... Software 2000, Inc. [*Associated Press*] (SAG)
SoftwrDv..... Software Developers [*Commercial firm Associated Press*] (SAG)
SOFTY......... Southern Federation of Temple Youth
SOG........... Same Output Gate [*Computer science*] (AAG)
SOG........... Satellite Operations Group [*Military*]
SOG........... Seat of Government [*Washington, DC*]
SOG........... Second-Order Gradient
SOG........... Senior Officials Group on Telecommunications (OSI)
SOG........... Small Outline Gullwing [*Electronics*] (CDE)
sog............ Sogdian [*MARC language code Library of Congress*] (LCCP)
SOG........... Sogenannt [*So-Called*] [*German*]
SOG........... Sogndal [*Norway*] [*Airport symbol*] (OAG)
SOG........... Special Operations Group [*Navy*]
SOG........... Speed Made Good Over the Ground (NATG)
SOG........... Spin On Glass [*Microlithography*]
SOG........... Statement of Guidance
SOG........... Straits Oil & Gas [*Vancouver Stock Exchange symbol*]
SOG........... Studies and Observations Group [*Military*]
SOG........... Supraoesophageal Ganglion [*Invertebrate nuerology*]
SOGA......... Spouses of Gays Association (EA)
SOGAT........ Society of Graphical and Allied Trades [*British*]
SOGEAC...... Societe de Gestion et d'Exploitation de l'Aeroport de Conakry [*Guinea*] (EY)
SOGEKO...... Korean-French Banking Corp. [*Acronym is based on foreign phrase*] (EY)
SOGITS....... Senior Officials Group on IT [*Information Technologies*] Standardisation [*British*]
SOGp.......... Special Operations Group [*Air Force*] (AFM)
SOGS.......... Saudi-Oriented Guide Specifications (NITA)
SOGS.......... Science Operations Ground System [*Space telescope software*]
SOGWPIP.... Silly Old Grandmother with Pictures in Purse
SOH........... Skylab Operations Handbook [*NASA*]
SOH........... SONARman Harbor Defense [*Navy*] (IAA)
SOH........... Southern Ohio Aviation Sales Co. [*ICAO designator*] (FAAC)
SOH........... Start of Header [*or Heading*] [*Transmission control character*] [*Computer science*]
SOH........... Stichting Oecumenische Hulp aan Kerken en Vluchtelingen [*Netherlands*]
SOH........... Supply Overhaul (MCD)
SOH........... Sympathetic Orthostatic Hypotension [*Medicine*] (DMAA)
SOHAH....... Society in Opposition to Human-Animal Hybridization
SOHAM....... Southampton [*City in England*] (ROG)
SOHC......... Single Overhead Camshaft [*Automotive engineering*]
SOHF.......... Sense of Humor Failure [*British Slang*]
SOHI........... Sponsors of Open Housing Investment [*Later, Fund for an Open Society*] (EA)
SOHIC........ Stress-Oriented Hydrogen-Induced Cracking [*Metallurgy*]
SOHIO........ Standard Oil Co. (Ohio)
SOHN......... Supraoptic Hypothalamic Nucleus [*Medicine*] (DMAA)
SOHO......... Small Office, Home Office (PCM)
SOHO......... Solar and Heliospheric Observatory [*European Space Agency*]
SOHO......... Solar Heliospheric Observatory
SoHo.......... South of Houston Street [*See also NoHo, SoSo, TriBeCa*] [*Artists' colony in New York City*]
SOHR......... Solar Hydrogen Rocket Engine
SOI............ Scientific and Optical Instruments
SOI............ Security and Operational Inspection [*Army*]
SOI............ Severity of Illness [*Medicine*] (DMAA)
SOI............ Shoshoni Gold [*Vancouver Stock Exchange symbol*]
SOI............ Signal Operation [*or Operating*] Instructions
SOI............ Silicon-on-Insulator
SOI............ Simulating Oriented Language
SOI............ SOI Industries, Inc. [*AMEX symbol*] (SPSG)
SOI............ S.O.I Industries(New) [*AMEX symbol*] (TTSB)
SOI............ Solar Oscillations Imager [*Instrumentation*]
SOI............ Southern Illinois University at Carbondale, Carbondale, IL [*OCLC symbol*] (OCLC)
SOI............ Southern Indiana Railway, Inc. [*Later, SIND*] [*AAR code*]
SOI............ Southern Oscillation Index
SOI............ South Molle Island [*Australia Airport symbol*] (OAG)
SOI............ Space Object Identification (AFM)
SOI............ Special Olympics International (EA)
SOI............ Special Olympics Ireland (EAIO)
SOI............ Specific Operating Instruction (AFM)
SOI............ SPEEDEX [*Systemwide Project for Electronic Equipment at Depots Extended*] Operating Instructions
SOI............ Sphere of Influence
SOI............ Standard Operating Instruction (KSC)
SOI............ Start of Injection [*Fuel systems*] [*Automotive engineering*]
SOI............ Statement of Intent
SOI............ State of Stimulus Overinclusion [*Schizophrenia*]
SOI............ Statistics of Income [*IRS*]
SOI............ Stimulus Onset Interval

SOI.............. Structure of Intellect [*Education*] (AEE)
SOI.............. Surety and Operational Inspection [*Military*] (AFIT)
SOI.............. Survey of India [*India*] (EERA)
SOIC............ Small Outline Integrated Circuit [*Computer science*]
SOIC............ Supply Officer-in-Command [*Military*]
SOICAS........ Space Object Identification Central Analysis System
SOICC.......... State Occupational Information Coordinating Committee
SOICS.......... Special Operations Improved Crypto System [*Military*] (RDA)
SOICS.......... Summary of Installation Control Status [*Nuclear energy*] (NRCH)
SOID............ Shipboard Ordnance Infrared Decoy (MCD)
SOIG............ Special Operations Industry Group [*Army*]
SOI Ind........ SOI Industries, Inc. [*Associated Press*] (SAG)
SOI-LA......... Structure of Intellect-Learning Abilities Test (EDAC)
So Ill U......... Southern Illinois University (GAGS)
So Ill U (Edwardsville)... Southern Illinois University at Edwardsville (GAGS)
SO-in-C........ Signal Officer-in-Chief [*British military*] (DMA)
SOINC.......... Supply Officer-in-Charge [*Navy*]
SoIndGs....... Southern Indiana Gas & Electric Co. [*Associated Press*] (SAG)
SOIP............ Sell-Off Impact Prognosticator [*Aerospace*] (AAG)
SOIP............ Ship Overhaul Improvement Program [*Navy*]
SOIP............ Sphere of Influence People
SOIR............ Simultaneous Operations on Intersecting Runways [*FAA*] (TAG)
SOIS............ Shipping Operations Information System (OA)
SOIS............ Silicon on Insulating Substrate (PDAA)
SOIS............ Spacelab/Orbiter Interface Simulator [*NASA*] (NASA)
SOIS............ Space Object Identification System
SOISCUM..... Space Object Identification Summary (MCD)
SOITLM........ Subcontractor Organizational Intermediate Level Maintenance
SOIWR......... Simultaneous Operations on Intersecting Wet Runways [*FAA*] (TAG)
SOJ.............. Sea of Japan (NVT)
SOJ.............. Small Outline J Leaded (NITA)
SOJ.............. Sorkjosen [*Norway*] [*Airport symbol*] (OAG)
SOJ.............. Standoff Jammer (NVT)
SoJerIn......... South Jersey Industries, Inc. [*Associated Press*] (SAG)
So Jersey LS Dictum... South Jersey Law School Dictum [*A publication*] (DLA)
SOJIM........... Standoff Jammer Interceptor Missile (MCD)
SOJS............ Standoff Jammer Suppression (MCD)
SOJS............ Standoff Jammer System (MCD)
SOJSM.......... Standoff Jammer Suppression Missile (MCD)
SOJT............ Structured On-the-Job Training (MCD)
SOJT............ Supervised On-the-Job Training
SOJTA.......... State On-the-Job Training Agencies [*Department of Labor*]
SOK.............. American Sokol Educational and Physical Culture Organization
SOK.............. Semongkong [*Lesotho*] [*Airport symbol Obsolete*] (OAG)
SOK.............. Slovo o Knige [*A publication*]
SOK.............. South Kauai, HI [*Location identifier FAA*] (FAAL)
SOK.............. Supply OK [*i.e., Authorized*]
SOKS............ Sport of Kings Society (EA)
SOKSI........... Sentral Organisasi Karyawan Sosialis Indonesia [*Central Organization of Indonesian Socialist Workers*]
SOL.............. Safe Operating Limit
SOL.............. Sasko Oil & Gas Ltd. [*Toronto Stock Exchange symbol Vancouver Stock Exchange symbol*]
SOL.............. Saturation Output Level [*Recording tapes*]
SOL.............. School of Living (EA)
SOL.............. Second Order Logic
SOL.............. Secretary of Labor (OICC)
SOL.............. Senior Operator License [*Nuclear energy*] (NRCH)
SOL.............. Sequence Operated Lock (IAA)
SOL.............. Shipowner's Liability [*Business term*]
SOL.............. Short Octal Load (IAA)
SOL.............. Short of Luck (DSUE)
SOL.............. Shut-Off Lights (SAA)
SOL.............. Simulation Oriented Language [*Computer science*]
SOL.............. Sisters of Our Lady [*Roman Catholic religious order*]
SOL.............. Social Organisation Limited
SOL.............. Sola International [*NYSE symbol*] (TTSB)
SOL.............. Solar (AAG)
SOL.............. Solder
sol............... Soldier
SOL.............. Soldier out of Luck [*Military slang*]
SOL.............. Solenoid (AAG)
SOL.............. Soleus Muscle [*Anatomy*]
SOL.............. Soliciting [*FBI standardized term*]
SOL.............. Solicitor
SOL.............. Solicitor of Labor [*Department of Labor*]
SOL.............. Solid (MSA)
SOL.............. Soliloquy [*Theater term*]
SOL.............. Solitaire [*Jewelry*] (ROG)
Sol............... Soloman's Court of Request Appeals [*Ceylon*] [*A publication*] (DLA)
SOL.............. Solomon [*Biblical king*] (ROG)
SOL.............. Solomon Airlines Ltd. [*Solomon Islands*] [*ICAO designator*] (FAAC)
SOL.............. Solomon, AK [*Location identifier FAA*] (FAAL)
Sol............... Solon [*of Plutarch*] [*Classical studies*] (OCD)
SOL.............. Solubilis [*Soluble*] [*Pharmacy*]
SOL.............. Soluble
sol............... Soluble (IDOE)
SOL.............. Solutio [*Solution*] [*Pharmacy*]
SOL.............. Solution
sol............... Solution (IDOE)
SOL.............. Solve [*or Solutus*] [*Dissolve or Dissolved*] [*Pharmacy*] (ROG)
SOL.............. Sons of Light [*An association*]
SOL.............. Source/Object Library (NITA)
SOL.............. Southern Illinois University, School of Law Library, Carbondale, IL [*OCLC symbol*] (OCLC)
SOL.............. Space-Occupying Lesion [*Medicine*]
SOL.............. Standard of Living
SOL.............. Statute of Limitations [*Legal shorthand*] (LWAP)
Sol............... Still Out of Luck [*Army Slang*]
SOL.............. Strictly Out of Luck (IIA)
SOL.............. Substitute Optical Landing System (NG)
SOL.............. Sure out of Luck [*Bowdlerized version*]
SOL.............. System Oriented Language
SOLA............ Selected Objects for Living Actively [*Commercial firm specializing in home furnishings for the elderly*]
Sola............. Sola International, Inc. [*Associated Press*] (SAG)
SOLA............ Student Organization for Latin America [*University of Notre Dame*] [*Research center*] (RCD)
SOLACE....... School of Librarianship Automatic Cataloguing Experiment (NITA)
SOLACE....... Society of Local Authority Chief Executives [*British*] (DBA)
SOLAGRAL... Solidarites Agricoles et Alimentaires [*France*] (EERA)
SOLAIR........ Solomon Islands Airways Ltd. (FEA)
SOLAN......... Solid Angles
SOLANT....... South Atlantic Force [*Later, Command*] [*Navy World War II*]
SOLANTFOR... South Atlantic Force [*Later, Command*] [*Navy World War II*]
SOLAR......... Sandel On-Line Automated Reference [*Information service or system*]
SOLAR......... Semantically Oriented Lexical Archive
SOLAR......... Serialized On-Line Automatic Recording [*Computer science*] (IEEE)
SOLAR......... Shared On-Line Airline Reservations (IAA)
SOLAR......... Shop Operations Load Analysis Reporting
SOLAR......... Sociedad Latinoamericana de Estudios sobre America Latina y el Caribe [*Mexico*] (EAIO)
SOLAR......... Society of Loose Actors Revolving [*SOLAR Theater, Inc.*]
SOLAR......... Storage Online Automatic Retrieval (NITA)
SOLARIS...... Submerged Object Locating and Retrieving Identification System
SOLAR MAX... Solar Maximum Mission Satellite
SolarMt........ Solar-Mates, Inc. [*Associated Press*] (SAG)
SOLAS......... International Convention for the Safety of Life at Sea (EERA)
SOLAS......... Safety of Life at Sea [*An international agreement requiring operators of cruise ships to meet certain standards of construction and fire safety*]
SOLAS......... Safety of Life at Sea
SOLAS......... Safety of Life at Sea Conference [*Intergovernmental Maritime Consultative Organization*] (MSC)
SOLAS......... Safety of Life at Sea Convention (BARN)
SOLAT......... Style of Learning and Thinking [*Occupational therapy*]
So Law......... Southern Lawyer [*A publication*] (DLA)
So Law T..... Southern Law Times [*A publication*] (DLA)
SOLB........... Start of Line Block (CET)
SOLCGS...... Sisters of Our Lady of Charity of the Good Shepherd [*Roman Catholic religious order Rome, Italy*] (EAIO)
SOLCHEM.... Solar-Chemical [*Energy conversion process*]
Sol Cl Gaz... Solicitors' Clerks' Gazette [*1921-40*] [*A publication*] (DLA)
SOLCR......... Solicitor
SOLCR......... Solicitor
SOLD........... Simulation of Logic Design
SOLD........... Soldering
SOLD........... Symbolic Debugger [*Also, sdb, SYMDEB*] [*Computer science*]
SOLDIER...... Solution of Ordinary Differential Equations Routine (IAA)
SOLE........... Society of Logistics Engineers (EA)
SOLEC......... Stand on Leg, Eyes Closed [*Equilibrium test*]
Solectron..... Solectron Corp. [*Associated Press*] (SAG)
SOLERS22... Solar Electromagnetic Radiation Study for Solar Cycle 22 (USDC)
SOLERS22... Solar Electromagnetic Radiation Study for Solar Cycle 22 [*Marine science*] (OSRA)
SOLF........... Southern Oregon Library Federation [*Library network*]
SOLFEAS..... Solar Energy System Economic Feasibility Program [*Army*] (RDA)
Sol G........... Solicitor General [*Legal term*] (DLA)
Sol-Gel........ Solution-Gelatin (SDI)
Sol Gen....... Solicitor General [*Legal term*] (DLA)
SOLI............ Symphony Orchestra Library Information [*Sinfonia Software*] [*Piedmont, CA*]
SOLIC.......... Solicitation
SOLIC.......... Special Operations/Low Intensity Conflict [*Army*]
SOLICO........ Sorenson Lighted Controls, Inc.
SOLIC PREP... Solicitation Preparation
SOLID.......... Self-Organizing Large Information Dissemination System (IEEE)
SOLID.......... Simulation of Life Insurance Decisions [*Game*]
solidif.......... Solidification (BARN)
Soligen........ Soligen Technologies, Inc. [*Associated Press*] (SAG)
SOLIMPEX... Societe Lao Import-Export (EY)
SOLINET...... Southeastern Library Network [*Atlanta, GA*] [*Library network*]
SOLINET...... South-Eastern Library Network (NITA)
SOLION........ Solution of Ions [*Office of Naval Research*]
Sol Is........... Solomon Islands
SOLIS.......... Sozialwissenschaftliches LiteraturInformationssystem [*Database*] [*Informationszentrum Sozialwissenschaften Social Sciences Literature Information System*] [*German*] [*Information service or system*] (CRD)
SOLIS.......... Symbionics On-Line Information System [*Computer science*]
SOLISTRON... Solid-State Klystron
So LJ........... Southern Law Journal and Reporter [*A publication*] (DLA)
Sol J & R.... Solicitors' Journal and Reporter [*A publication*] (DLA)
SOLL............ Special Operations, Low Level (MCD)
Sol Labor Op... Opinion of the Solicitor of Labor (AAGC)
SOLLAR....... Soft Lunar Landing and Return (SAA)
SOLM........... Sisters of Our Lady of Mercy [*Mercedarians*] [*Roman Catholic religious order*]
SOLM........... Soldier's Medal [*Military decoration*]

Sol Man Cl Gaz... Solicitor's Managing Clerks' Gazette [*1941-62*] [*A publication*] (DLA)
SOLMC .... Senior Officer Logistics Management Course [*Military*] (INF)
SOLMIS .... Supply Online Management Information System [*Computer science*] (PDAA)
SOLN .... Solution
SOLO .... SAMI Online Operations (NITA)
SOLO .... Selective Optical Lock-On [*Sighting device*]
SOLO .... Senior Officer Legal Orientation (MCD)
SOLO .... Southeastern Ohio Library Organization [*Library network*]
SOLO .... Status of Logistics Offensive [*Military*] (AABC)
SOLO .... Super Oak Leaf Online [*Santa Rosa Junior College online conference*]
SOLO .... Supply On-Line Option [*IMS America Ltd.*] [*Database*]
SOLO .... System for Online Optimization [*Computer science*] (PDAA)
SOLO .... System for Ordinary Life Operations [*Insurance*]
SOLOC .... Southern Line of Communications [*World War II*]
SOLOG .... Standardization of Certain Aspects of Operations and Logistics [*Military*]
SOLOMON ... Simultaneous Operation Limited Ordinal Modular Network (NITA)
SOLOMON ... Simultaneous Operation Linked Ordinal Modular Network
Sol Op .... Solicitor's Opinion [*Especially of Internal Revenue Bureau*] [*United States*] (DLA)
SOLOQ .... Solo Serve Corp. [*NASDAQ symbol*] (SAG)
SOLP .... Salomon Page Group Ltd. [*NASDAQ symbol*] (SAG)
SOLP .... Solomon Page Group Ltd. [*NASDAQ symbol*] (SAG)
SolPage .... Solomon Page Group Ltd. [*Associated Press*] (SAG)
SOLPH .... Sisters of Our Lady of Perpetual Help (TOCD)
SOLPW .... Solomon-Page Grp Wrrt [*NASDAQ symbol*] (TTSB)
Sol Q .... Solicitor Quarterly [*1962-65*] [*A publication*] (DLA)
So LQ .... Southern Law Quarterly [*A publication*] (DLA)
SOLR .... Sidetone Objective Loudness Rating [*of telephone connections*] (IEEE)
SOLR .... Solar-Mates [*NASDAQ symbol*] (TTSB)
SOLR .... Solar-Mates, Inc. [*NASDAQ symbol*] (SAG)
SOLR .... Solicitor
So LR .... Southern Law Review [*Nashville, TN*] [*A publication*] (DLA)
SOLRAD .... Solar Radiation [*Satellite system*] [*Navy*]
SOLRAD-HI... Solar Radiation - High-Altitude [*Satellite system*] [*Navy*]
SOL Rev .... School of Law. Review [*Canada*] [*A publication*] (DLA)
So L Rev ...... Southern Law Review [*A publication*] (DLA)
So L Rev NS... Southern Law Review, New Series [*St. Louis, MO*] [*A publication*] (DLA)
SolrMt .... Solar-Mates, Inc. [*Associated Press*] (SAG)
So LRNS .... Southern Law Review, New Series [*St. Louis, MO*] [*A publication*] (DLA)
SOLRU .... Solar-Mates Inc. Unit [*NASDAQ symbol*] (TTSB)
SOLRW .... Solar-Mates Wrrt [*NASDAQ symbol*] (TTSB)
SOLS .... Substitute Optical Landing System (MCD)
SOL-SAL ...... Solar Scientific Airlock
SOLT .... Our Lady of the Most Holy Trinity Convent (TOCD)
SOLT .... Society of Our Lady of the Most Holy Trinity (TOCD)
solt .... Society of Our Lady of the Most Holy Trinity (TOCD)
So LT .... Southern Law Times [*A publication*] (DLA)
SOLTIP .... Solar Connections to Transient Interplanetary Processes [*Program*] (USDC)
SOLTIP .... Solar Connections to Transient Interplanetary Processes [*Program*] [*Marine science*] (OSRA)
Soltr .... Solutrean (VRA)
SOLTRAN ..... Solar Spectrum and Transmittance [*Solar energy research*]
SOLU .... Solute (AAMN)
SOLUB .... Aqueous Solubility Database [*Chemical Information Systems, Inc.*] [*Information service or system*] (CRD)
SOLUG .... San Antonio On Line User Group (NITA)
SOL U/T .... Solicitor's Undertaking (DCTA)
SOLUT .... Solutus [*Dissolved*] [*Pharmacy*] (ROG)
SOLV .... Solenoid Valve [*Mechanical engineering*]
SOLV .... Solve [*Dissolve*] [*Pharmacy*]
SOLV .... Solvent
SOLV .... Solv-Ex Corp. [*NASDAQ symbol*] (NQ)
SOLV .... Super-Open-Frame Low Voltage (IEEE)
SOLVD .... Studies of Left Ventricular Dysfunction [*National Heart, Lung, and Blood Institute*]
SOLVE C CAL... Solve Cum Calore [*Dissolve by Heating*] [*Pharmacy*]
SolvEx .... Solv-Ex Corp. [*Associated Press*] (SAG)
SOLW .... Society of Our Lady of the Way (EA)
SOLY .... Solubility
Som .... De Somniis [*of Philo*] (BJA)
SOM .... SACLANT [*Supreme Allied Commander, Atlantic*] Staff Organization Manual (NATG)
SOM .... San Tome [*Venezuela*] [*Airport symbol*] (OAG)
SOM .... Scanning Optical Microscope
SOM .... Secretory Otitis Media [*Medicine*] (MAE)
SOM .... Securities Order Matching [*Computer science*]
SOM .... See Our Message
SOM .... Self-Organizing Machine
SOM .... Self-Organizing Map [*Computer science*] (CDE)
SOM .... Send-Only-Multipoint (DNAB)
SOM .... Sensitivity-of-Method [*FDA*]
SOM .... Serous Otitis Media [*Ear inflammation*]
SOM .... Share of Market [*Advertising*]
SOM .... Share of Market [*Lundberg Survey, Inc.*] [*Information service or system*] (CRD)
SOM .... Shift Operations Manager (NRCH)
SOM .... Ship Operations Manager [*NASA*] (KSC)
SOM .... Simulator Operation and Maintenance Program (MCD)
SOM .... Single Oriental Male [*Classified advertising*]
SOM .... Skidmore, Owings & Merrill [*Architectural firm*]
SOM .... Small Office Microfilm
SOM .... Small Office Microfilm Systems (NITA)
SOM .... Society of Medalists [*Defunct*] (EA)
SOM .... Society of Metaphysicians [*British*] (DBA)
SOM .... Society of Occupational Medicine [*British*]
SOM .... Soil Organic Matter
som .... Somalia [*MARC language code Library of Congress*] (LCCP)
SOM .... Somalia [*ANSI three-letter standard code*] (CNC)
SOM .... Somali Airlines [*Somalia*] [*ICAO designator*] (FAAC)
SOM .... Somatostatin [*Biochemistry*]
SOM .... Somatotrophin [*Endocrinology*]
SOM .... Sombrero [*Chile*] [*Seismograph station code, US Geological Survey*] (SEIS)
SOM .... Somerset [*County in England*]
SOM .... Somerset County Library, Bridgewater, NJ [*OCLC symbol*] (OCLC)
Som .... Somerset Legal Journal [*Pennsylvania*] [*A publication*] (DLA)
SOM .... Somersetshire [*County in England*]
SOM .... Somnolent [*A metabolic test*] (DAVI)
SOM .... Somnus [*Sleep*] [*Latin*] (ROG)
SOM .... SONARman [*Navy*]
SOM .... Soundman (IAA)
SOM .... Sound of Music [*Dolls by Alexander*] [*Doll collecting*]
SOM .... Source One Mortgage Services [*NYSE symbol*] (SAG)
SOM .... Spacecraft Operations Manual
SOM .... Spares Optimization Model [*NASA*] (NASA)
SOM .... Stage Operating Manual [*NASA*] (KSC)
SOM .... Standard Online Module (NITA)
SOM .... Standard Operating Manual [*NASA*] (NASA)
SOM .... Standoff Missile (MCD)
SOM .... Start of Message [*Telecommunications*]
SOM .... Start of Message (NITA)
SOM .... State Operations Manual [*Home Health Agency Program*] [*Department of Health and Human Services*] (GFGA)
SOM .... Steward of Meeting [*Auto racing*]
SOM .... Storage Operations Module [*SAILS*] (MCD)
SOM .... Strap-On Motor
SOM .... Suborbital Mission [*NASA*] (SAA)
SOM .... Sulfomethoxine [*Medicine*] (MAE)
SOM .... Superior Oblique Muscle [*Eye anatomy*]
SOM .... Superior Old Marsala
SOM .... Survivability Optimization Model (MCD)
SOM .... Sustained Operations Manual
SOM .... Sustained Operations Model
SOM .... System Object Model [*Computer science*] (PCM)
SOM .... System Operator Manual [*Military*] (CAAL)
SOMA .... Services to Ongoing Mature Aging [*Counseling group*]
SOMA .... Sharing of Missionaries Abroad [*Church of England*]
SOMA .... Signed Out Against Medical Advice
Soma .... Somanetics Corp. [*Associated Press*] (SAG)
SOMA .... Somatix Therapy [*NASDAQ symbol*] (TTSB)
SOMA .... Somatix Therapy Corp. [*NASDAQ symbol*] (SAG)
SoMa .... South of Market [*District of San Francisco*]
SOMA .... Student Osteopathic Medical Association (EA)
SOMA .... Survey of Market Absorption [*Department of Housing and Urban Development*] (GFGA)
SOMADA .... Self-Organizing Multiple-Access Discrete Address [*Computer science*] (IEEE)
Somanetc .... Somanetics Corp. [*Associated Press*] (SAG)
SOMART .... Conseil des Metiers d'Art du Quebec (AC)
somat .... Somatic [*Pertaining to the body or the body wall*] (DAVI)
Somatgn .... Somatogen, Inc. [*Associated Press*] (SAG)
SOMC .... Shadow Open Market Committee
SOM/DSOM... System Object Model/Distributed System Object Model [*Computer science*]
SOME .... Secretary's Office, Management Engineer [*Navy*]
SOME .... Senior Ordnance Mechanical Engineer [*British military*] (DMA)
SOMEG to ADV... Something to Advantage [*Advertising*] [*Legal term*]
SOMER .... State of the Marine Environment Reporting [*Commonwealth*] (EERA)
Somerset LJ... Somerset Legal Journal [*A publication*] (DLA)
SOMET .... Sometimes
So Meth U... Southern Methodist University (GAGS)
SOMF .... SIDPERS [*Standard Installation/Division Personnel System*] Organization Master File [*Military*] (AABC)
SOMF .... Start of Minor Frame (MCD)
SOMH .... SONARman Harbor Defense [*Navy*]
SOM-H .... Start-of-Message - High Precedence (CET)
SOMI .... Skull Occipital Mandibular Immobilization [*Orthosis*] [*Dentistry*] (DAVI)
SOMI .... Sternal-Occipital-Mandibular Immobilization [*Medicine*]
SOMIEX .... Societe Malienne d'Importation et d'Exportation [*Malian Import Export Co.*]
SoMinrl .... Southern Mineral Corp. [*Associated Press*] (SAG)
SOMISA .... Sociedad Mixta Siderurgia Argentina [*Steel producer in Argentina*]
SOMISS .... Study of Management Information Systems Support [*Army*]
SOM-L .... Start-of-Message - Low Precedence (CET)
Som Leg J (PA)... Somerset Legal Journal [*Pennsylvania*] [*A publication*] (DLA)
SOM-LI .... Somatostatin-Like Immunoreactivity
Som LJ .... Somerset Legal Journal [*Pennsylvania*] [*A publication*] (DLA)
Som LR .... Somalia Law Reports [*A publication*] (DLA)
SOMM .... Commission
SOMM .... Shift Operations Maintenance Manager (SSD)
SOMM .... Stand-Off Modular Missile (PDAA)

Somn on Gav... Somner on Gavelkind [*A publication*] (DLA)
SOMO.......... Semioccupied Molecular Orbital [*Physical chemistry*]
SOMO.......... Senior Officer Management Office [*Army*] (INF)
SOMOS......... Society of Military Orthopedics Surgeons (DAVI)
SOM-P......... Start-of-Message - Priority
SOMP.......... Sydney Ocean Meeting Point [*Navy*]
SOMPA......... System of Multicultural Pluralistic Assessment [*Psychological and educational testing*]
Som Pl........ Somersetshire Pleas (Civil and Criminal), Edited by Chadwyck-Healey and Landon [*Somerset Record Society Publications, Vols. 11, 36, 41, 44*] [*A publication*] (DLA)
SOMPrA........ Source One Mtg 8.42%'A'Pfd [*NYSE symbol*] (TTSB)
SOMPRSS....... Compress
SOMR.......... Somerset Group [*NASDAQ symbol*] (TTSB)
SOMR.......... [*The*] Somerset Group, Inc. [*Indianapolis, IN*] [*NASDAQ symbol*] (NQ)
SOMRB......... Senior Officers Materiel Review Board [*Army*] (AABC)
SomrGp........ Somerset Group, Inc. [*Associated Press*] (SAG)
SOMS.......... Senior Officer, Minesweepers [*British military*] (DMA)
SOMS.......... Service Order Mechanization [*or Mechanized*] System [*AT & T*]
SOMS.......... Shuttle Orbiter Medical System [*NASA*] (MCD)
Soms.......... Somerset County [*England*] (BARN)
SOMS.......... Space Operations Management System (PDAA)
SOMS.......... Standard Operations and Maintenance Squadron (DNAB)
SOMS.......... Synchronous, Operational Meteorological Satellite
SOMS.......... Systems Optimization and Monitoring Services (MHDI)
SOMSG......... See Our Message [*Aviation*] (FAAC)
SOMSS......... Submarine Off-Board Mine Search System (DOMA)
SOMST......... Somersetshire [*County in England*] (ROG)
SomstSv....... Somerset Savings Bank [*Associated Press*] (SAG)
SOMT.......... Soldier Operator Maintainer Testing (MCD)
SOMTE......... Soldier-Operator-Maintainer-Tester-Evaluator [*Military*] (PDAA)
Somtix........ Somatix Therapy Corp. [*Associated Press*] (SAG)
SOMTO......... Subversive Operations, Mediterranean Theatre of Operations [*World War II*]
SOMTS......... Division of Ship Operations and Marine Technical Support [*Research center*] (RCD)
SoMV.......... Sowbane Mosaic Virus
SON........... Espiritu Santo [*Vanuatu*] [*Airport symbol*] (OAG)
SON........... Linea Aerea Aerosanta [*Chile*] [*ICAO designator*] (FAAC)
S/ON.......... Sign On [*Computer science*] (MDG)
SON........... Snijders-Oomen Non-Verbal Intelligence Scale (AEBS)
SON........... Society of Nematologists (EA)
SON........... Sonata [*Music*] (WGA)
son........... Songhai [*MARC language code Library of Congress*] (LCCP)
SON........... Sonneberg [*Federal Republic of Germany*] [*Seismograph station code, US Geological Survey Closed*] (SEIS)
Son........... Sonnets [*Shakespearean work*]
SON........... Sonoco Products [*NYSE symbol*] (TTSB)
SON........... Sonoco Products Corp. [*NYSE symbol*] (SAG)
Son........... Sonora [*Record label*] [*Sweden*]
SON........... Sonora Gold Corp. [*Toronto Stock Exchange symbol Vancouver Stock Exchange symbol*]
SON........... Southern (WGA)
SON........... Statement of Operational Need
SON........... Submitting Office Number [*Navy*] (DNAB)
SON........... Support of Other Nations [*Military support furnished certain nations and funded by the Air Force*]
SON........... Supraoptic Nucleus [*Brain anatomy*]
SONA.......... School of Naval Administration, Leland Stanford University
SONA.......... Sonic Environmental Systems, Inc. [*NASDAQ symbol*] (SAG)
SonA.......... Stratford-on-Avon [*British*]
S on A........ Stratford-On-Avon, England
SONAC......... SONAR Nacelle [*Sonacelle*]
SONAD......... Sonic Azimuth Detector (MCD)
SONAD......... Sound-Operated Noise Attenuation Device (IAA)
SONAD......... Speech-Operated Noise Adjusting Device [*Telecommunications*] (TEL)
SONAR......... Sonic Azimuth and Ranging [*British military*] (DMA)
SONAR......... Sound Navigation and Ranging
SONARRAY...... SONAR Array [*Sounding system*] [*Navy*]
Sonat.......... Sonat, Inc. [*Associated Press*] (SAG)
SoNat.......... Southern National Corp. [*Associated Press*] (SAG)
SoNatCp........ Southern National Corp. [*Associated Press*] (SAG)
SonatOff....... Sonat Offshore Drilling, Inc. [*Associated Press*] (SAG)
SONATRACH..... Societe Nationale de Transport et de Commercialisation des Hydrocarbures
So Nazarene U... Southern Nazarene University (GAGS)
SONB.......... Sonobuoy
Sonc.......... Soncino (BJA)
SONC.......... Sonic Corp. [*NASDAQ symbol*] (SPSG)
SoncinoB....... [*The*] Soncino Books of the Bible (Bornemouth) [*A publication*] (BJA)
SONCM......... SONAR Countermeasures and Deception [*Military*]
SONCR......... SONAR Control Room (MSA)
SOND.......... Secretary's Office, Navy Department
Sonesta........ Sonesta International Hotels Corp. [*Associated Press*] (SAG)
SONET......... Synchronous Optical Network [*Computer science*]
SONG.......... Satellite for Orientation, Navigation, and Geodesy (IAA)
SONG.......... Seeking of Noetic Goals Test [*Personality development test*] [*Psychology*]
Song.......... Song of Songs [*Old Testament book*] [*Roman Catholic canon*]
Song 3 Childr... Song of the Three Children [*Old Testament book*] [*Apocrypha*]
SongCh........ Song of the Three Children [*Old Testament book*] [*Apocrypha*] (BJA)
Song of Three Childr... [*The*] Song of the Three Holy Children [*Apocrypha*]
SongR.......... Song of Songs Rabbah (BJA)
SONGS......... San Onofre Nuclear Generating Station (NRCH)
Song Sol...... Song of Solomon [*Old Testament book*]
SONI.......... Staff Officer Navigation Instructor (IAA)
SONIBANQUE... Societe Nigerienne de Banque (EY)
Sonic.......... Sonic Corp. [*Associated Press*] (SAG)
Sonic.......... Sonic Environmental Systems, Inc. [*Associated Press*] (SAG)
SONIC.......... SPAN [*Space Physics Analysis Network*] Ocean Network Information Center [*Database*]
SONIC.......... System-Wide On-Line Network for Information Control [*Computer science*]
SonicEnv....... Sonic Environmental Systems, Inc. [*Associated Press*] (SAG)
SonicM......... Sonics & Materials, Inc. [*Associated Press*] (SAG)
SonicSol....... Sonic Solutions Co. [*Associated Press*] (SAG)
SONITA......... Societe Nigerienne de Transports Aeriens [*Niger*] [*ICAO designator*] (FAAC)
SONK.......... Spontaneous Osteonecrosis of the Knee [*Orthopedics*] (DAVI)
SONN.......... Sonning [*England*]
SONNA......... Somali National News Agency
SONNF......... Sonora Gold Corp. (MHDW)
SONO.......... Satellite Object Number (MUGU)
SONO.......... Sonobuoy
SONO.......... Sonogram [*Medicine*] (DHSM)
SONOAN........ Sonic Noise Analyzer
Sonoco........ Sonoco Products Corp. [*Associated Press*] (SAG)
SonocoP........ Sonoco Products Corp. [*Associated Press*] (SAG)
SONOSW........ Sonoswitch
SONP.......... Solid Organs Not Palpable [*Medicine*]
SONPrA........ Sonoco Prd $2.25 Sr'A'Cv Pfd [*NYSE symbol*] (TTSB)
SONRD......... Secretary's Office, Office of Research and Development [*Navy*]
SONRES........ Saturated Optical Nonresonant Emission Spectroscopy
SONS.......... Seek Out New Suppliers
SONS.......... Society of Non-Smokers (EA)
SONS.......... Statistics of Naval Shipyards
SonusP........ Sonus Pharmaceuticals, Inc. [*Associated Press*] (SAG)
SONV.......... Sonchus Virus [*Plant pathology*]
SonyCp........ Sony Corp. America [*Associated Press*] (SAG)
SOO........... Sault Meadows Energy [*Vancouver Stock Exchange symbol*]
SOO........... Schenectady Operations Office [*Energy Research and Development Administration*]
SOO........... Songo [*Mozambique*] [*Airport symbol*] (OAG)
SOO........... Soo Line Corp. [*NYSE symbol and AAR code*] (SPSG)
SOO........... Specialty Occupational Outlook [*A publication*]
SOO........... Staff Officer Operations [*British*]
SOO........... Statement of Objectives (AAGC)
SOO........... State of Origin [*Soccer*]
SOOA.......... Solus Outdoor Advertising Association [*British*] (BI)
SOOG.......... Saint-Georges-De-L'Oyapock [*French Guiana*] [*ICAO location identifier*] (ICLI)
SOOM.......... Saigon Officers Open Mess [*Vietnam*]
SOOM.......... Saint-Laurent du Maroni [*French Guiana*] [*ICAO location identifier*] (ICLI)
SOON.......... Sequence for Opportunities and Negatives [*Rand Corp.*]
SOON.......... Solar Observing Optical Network [*Air Force*]
SOONS......... Scientific Opportunities Offered by a Nuclear Submarine [*A publication*]
SOONSPOT... SOON's [*Solar Observing Optical Network*] Solar Patrol on Tape (USDC)
SOONSPOT... SOON's [*Solar Observing Optical Network*] Solar Patrol on Tape [*Marine science*] (OSRA)
SOOP.......... Ship of Opportunity Program [*National Oceanic and Atmospheric Administration*] (GFGA)
SOOP.......... Special Old Oil Price
SOOP.......... Submarine Oceanographic Observation Program
SOOR.......... Regina [*French Guiana*] [*ICAO location identifier*] (ICLI)
So Ore St C... Southern Oregon State College (GAGS)
SOOS.......... Saul [*French Guiana*] [*ICAO location identifier*] (ICLI)
SOOSE......... Suborbital Offense Systems Group [*NASA*] (SAA)
SOOY.......... Sinnamary [*French Guiana*] [*ICAO location identifier*] (ICLI)
SOP........... Pinehurst [*North Carolina*] [*Airport symbol*] (OAG)
SOP........... Safety Operating Plan
SOP........... Sales Order Processing [*Manufacturing management*]
SOP........... Saturn Orbiter Probe [*NASA*]
SOP........... Scavenging, Oil Pump (MSA)
SOP........... Scented Orange Pekoe [*Tea trade*] (ROG)
SOP........... Sea of Peace (IAA)
SOP........... Seat of the Pants
SOP........... Secondary Operation
SOP........... Secondary Oxygen Pack [*NASA*]
SOP........... Second Opinion Program [*Later, NSOP*] (EA)
SOP........... Selective Oxidation Process (PDAA)
SOP........... Semiopen Position [*Dancing*]
SOP........... Semiorganic Polymer
SOP........... Senior Officer Present
SOP........... Sensory Organ Precursor [*Biochemistry*]
SOP........... Sensory Organ Precursor [*Cytology*]
SOP........... Ship-of-Opportunity Program [*Marine science*] (OSRA)
SOP........... Ship's Operational Program [*Navy*] (NVT)
SOP........... Shop Overload Parts (AAG)
SOP........... Signal Operating Procedure (IAA)
SOP........... Simulated Output Program [*Computer science*]
SOP........... Simulation Operations Plan [*NASA*] (KSC)
SOP........... Sleeping-Out Pass [*British armed forces*]
SOP........... Solution Output Processor (PDAA)
SOP........... Soprano

SOP .... Sopron [*Hungary*] [*Seismograph station code, US Geological Survey*] (SEIS)
SOP .... Southern Pines [*North Carolina*] [*Airport symbol*] (AD)
SOP .... Southern Pines, NC [*Location identifier FAA*] (FAAL)
SOP .... Spacelab Opportunity Payload [*NASA*] (MCD)
SOP .... Spares Order Processing (MCD)
SOP .... Special Operating Procedure (IEEE)
SOP .... Special Order Price
SOP .... Sphere of Positon (SAA)
SOP .... Staff Officer of Pensioners [*Army British*] (ROG)
SOP .... Standard Operating Plan (OICC)
SOP .... Standard [*or Standing*] Operating Procedure
SOP .... Statement of Policy [*SEC*]
SOP .... Statement of Position (TDOB)
SOP .... State of Polarization
SOP .... State-Operated Program [*Department of Education*] (GFGA)
SOP .... Statewide Operating Plan
SOP .... Station Operating Plan (AAG)
SOP .... Stock Option Plan
SOP .... Strategic Objectives Plan
SOP .... Strategic Orbit Point (KSC)
SOP .... Study Organization Plan (BUR)
SOP .... Subsystem Operating Program (NASA)
SOP .... Subsystems Operating Procedure [*NASA*] (NASA)
SOP .... Successive Organization of Perception [*Pilot behavior*]
SOP .... Sulfate of Potash [*Fertilizer*]
SOP .... Sum-of-Products [*Computer science*] (OA)
SOP .... Supplemental Oxygen Package (MCD)
SOP .... Supplier Operating Procedure (MCD)
SOP .... Supplier-Outside-Price [*Automobile content legislation*]
SOP .... Surface Oil Pickup
SOP .... Surgical Outpatient [*Medicine*]
SOP .... Survey of Use Permits [*Bureau of the Census*] (GFGA)
SOP .... Symbolic Optimum Program
SOP .... System Operations Panel (SSD)
SOP .... Systems Operation Plan [*NASA*] (KSC)
SOPA .... Senior Officer Present Afloat [*Navy*]
SOP(A) .... Senior Officer Present (Ashore) [*Navy*]
SOPA .... Society of Professional Archeologists (EA)
SOPA .... Standard Operating Procedure Amplified (GAVI)
SOPA .... Standoff Precision Attack [*Military*] (CAAL)
SOPA .... Syndrome of Primary Aldosteronism [*Medicine*] (DMAA)
SOPAC .... Joint CCOP/IOC Program of Research on the South Pacific [*Marine science*] (MSC)
SOPAC .... Southern Pacific Railroad Co.
SOPAC .... South Pacific Applied Geoscience Commission (EERA)
SOPAC .... South Pacific Command [*Navy*]
SOPAC .... South Pacific Countries (EERA)
SOPACBACOM ... South Pacific Base Command [*Navy World War II*]
SOPACCOMS ... South Pacific Communications [*Navy*]
SoPacPet .... Southern Pacific Petroleum [*Associated Press*] (SAG)
SOPAD .... SOPA [*Senior Officer Present Afloat*] Administrative Duties [*Military*] (NVT)
SOPAD .... Summary of Proceedings and Debate [*of House of Representatives*]
SOPAG .... Societe des Participations Gardinier [*French fertilizer firm*]
SOPAT .... South China Patrol [*Navy World War II*]
SOPC .... Sales Operations Planning and Control [*Management*]
SOPC .... Selected Outpatient Psychiatric Clinic [*Health insurance*] (GHCT)
SOPC .... Shuttle Operations and Planning Center [*NASA*] (MCD)
SOPC .... Shuttle Operations Planning Complex (NASA)
SOPCA .... Sporadic Olivopontocerebellar Ataxia [*Medicine*] (DMAA)
SoPcPt .... Southern Pacific Petroleum [*Associated Press*] (SAG)
SOPDOSS .... Submersible Oriented Platform for Deep Ocean Sediment Studies [*Marine science*] (MSC)
SOPE .... Simulated Off-the-Pad Ejection [*NASA*]
SO-PE .... Sodium Pentathol [*Nickname*]
Soph .... Sopherim (BJA)
Soph .... Sophista [*of Plato*] [*A publication*] (OCD)
SOPH .... Sophister [*British*] (ROG)
SOPH .... Sophocles [*Greek poet, 496-406BC*] [*Classical studies*] (ROG)
SOPH .... Sophomore
Soph .... Sophonias [*Old Testament book*] [*Douay version*]
SOPH .... Starboard Out, Port Home [*Variation of POSH*]
SOPHE .... Society for Public Health Education (EA)
Soph El .... Sophistici Elenchi [*of Aristotle*] [*Classical studies*] (OCD)
SOPI .... Service Object Pair Instance (DMAA)
SOPI .... Superintendent of Public Instruction (OICC)
SOPLASCO ... Southern Plastics Co.
SOPLC .... Senior Officer Preventive Logistics Course (MCD)
SOPM .... Standard Orbital Parameter Message [*NASA*] (KSC)
SOPMET .... Standing Operating Procedure - Meteorological Plan (NATG)
SOP/MR .... Standard Operating Procedure/Maintenance Requirement (MCD)
SOPN .... First Savings Bancorp [*NASDAQ symbol*] (TTSB)
SOPN .... First Savings Bank of Moore County [*NASDAQ symbol*] (SAG)
SOPO .... Society of Oral Physiology and Occlusion
SOPODA .... Social Planning, Policy & Development Abstracts [*Sociological Abstracts, Inc.*] [*Database*]
SOPP .... Sodium Ortho-Phenylphenoxide [*Organic chemistry*]
SOPP .... Special Order Perfect Price [*for undamaged merchandise*]
SOPP .... Statement of Provisioning Policy [*Military*] (AFIT)
SOPP .... State Operating Permit Program [*Environmental Protection Agency*]
SOPPC .... Special Operations Photo Processing Cell (MCD)
SOPR .... South Pierce Railroad [*AAR code*]
SOPR .... Spanish Open Pool Reactor
SOPR .... Special Officer Personnel Requirements [*Military*]
SOPR .... Standing Operating Procedure Regulation [*Navy*] (MCD)
SOPS .... Select Committee on Ocean Policy [*Interagency Committee on Marine Science and Engineering*] (USDC)
SOPS .... Shot Noise Optical Optimization Communication System with Stops [*NASA*]
S Op S .... Si Opus Sit [*If Needed*] [*Pharmacy*]
SOPS .... Spacecraft Operations Planning Section
SOPS .... Special Operations Power Source [*Military*] (RDA)
SOPSA .... Shuttle Orbit-Injection Propulsion System Analysis [*NASA*]
SOPT .... Science Operations Planning Team
SOPUS .... Senior Officer Present, United States Navy
SOPUSN .... Senior Officer Present, United States Navy (SAA)
SOPWA .... Survivors of a Person with AIDS [*An association*] (CPH)
SOPY .... Support of Positive Youth [*Australia*]
SOQ .... Senior Officers' Quarters
SOQ .... Sick Officer Quarters
Soq .... Soqotri (BJA)
SOQ .... Sorong [*Indonesia*] [*Airport symbol*] (OAG)
SOQ .... Star One Resources, Inc. [*Vancouver Stock Exchange symbol*]
SOQ .... System Optical Quality (MCD)
SOQAS .... Statement of Quality and Support (MCD)
SOQE .... Society for Optical and Quantum Electronics
SOQUEM .... Societe Quebecoise d'Exploration Miniere [*Quebec Mining Exploration Co.*]
SOQUIJ .... Societe Quebecoise d'Information Juridique [*Quebec Society for Legal Information*] [*Information service or system*] (IID)
SOR .... Air Stord AS [*Norway ICAO designator*] (FAAC)
SOR .... Sale or Return [*Business term*] (ADA)
SOR .... Sampling Oscilloscope Recorder
SOR .... Saxon Owners Registry (EA)
SOR .... Schedule Outlook Report (SAA)
SOR .... Seder 'Olam Rabbah (BJA)
SOR .... Sensor Operation Room (AFM)
SOR .... Service Operational Requirement
sor .... Short Open Reading [*Frame*] [*Genetics*] (DAVI)
SOR .... Single Operation Responsibility (IAA)
SOR .... Single Order Release (MCD)
SOR .... Slow Operate Relay (IAA)
SOR .... Society of Rheology (EA)
SoR .... Society of Roadcraft [*British*] (DBA)
SOR .... Sonor Petroleum Corp. [*Toronto Stock Exchange symbol*]
Sor .... Soria [*Record label*]
SOR .... Soroa [*Cuba*] [*Seismograph station code, US Geological Survey*] (SEIS)
SOR .... Source Capital [*NYSE symbol*] (TTSB)
SOR .... Source Capital, Inc. [*NYSE symbol*] (SPSG)
SOR .... Source of Repair (MCD)
SOR .... Specific Operational Requirement [*Military*]
SOR .... Spilled Oil Research Team [*National Oceanic and Atmospheric Administration*] (MSC)
SOR .... Squadron Operational Report
SOR .... Stable-Orbit Rendezvous [*NASA*]
SOR .... Standard Operating Report
SOR .... Standard Operating Rules
SOR .... Standoff Range (MCD)
sor .... Starboard (DS)
SOR .... Starfire Optical Range [*Air Force*]
SOR .... Start of Record (MUGU)
SOR .... Start-of-Run [*Engineering*]
SOR .... Statement of Requirement [*Military*] (AFIT)
SOR .... State of Readiness (MCD)
SOR .... Status or Operating Resources (MCD)
SOR .... Statutory Orders and Regulations (NITA)
SOR .... Statutory Orders and Regulations of Canada [*Canada Department of Justice*] [*Information service or system*]
SOR .... Stearic/Oleic Acid Ratio [*Clinical chemistry*]
SOR .... Stephens Owners Registry [*Defunct*] (EA)
S-O-R .... Stimulus-Organism-Response
SOR .... Stockholder of Record
SOR .... Strategy and Options Review (DOMA)
SOR .... Students for Origins Research (EA)
SOR .... Subcarrier Oscillator Rack
SOR .... Successive Overrelaxation
SOR .... Synchrotron Orbital Radiation [*High-energy physics*]
SOR .... Systems Operational Requirement
SOR .... Winfield/Arkansas City, KS [*Location identifier FAA*] (FAAL)
SORA .... Secretary's Office, Records Administration [*Navy*]
SORA .... Sodium-Cooled Research Reactor [*Nuclear energy*] (NUCP)
SORA .... Sorgento Rapido [*Reactor*] (NRCH)
SORAD .... Sonic Ranging and Detection (KSC)
SORAFOM .... Societe de Radiodiffusion de la France d'Outre-Mer [*Society for Radio Broadcasting of Overseas France*]
SORAK .... Special Operation Radio Antenna Kit [*Military*] (RDA)
SORAP .... Signature Overlap Range Prediction
SORAP .... Standard Omnirange Approach
SORAT .... Submarine Operational Readiness Assessment and Training
Sorb .... Soritol [*Biochemistry*] (DAVI)
SORB .... Submarine Overhaul and Refueling Building [*Navy*] (DNAB)
SORB .... Subsistence Operations Review Board [*Military*] (AABC)
Sorb D .... Sorbitol Dehydrogenase [*Also, SDH*] [*An enzyme*]
SORC .... Serious Offenders Review Council [*New South Wales, Australia*]
SORC .... Signal Officers' Reserve Corps
SORC .... Simultaneous Oxidation-Reduction Catalyst [*Automotive engineering*]
SORC .... Sound Ranging Control
SORC .... Source Co. [*NASDAQ symbol*] (TTSB)

SORC .... Southern Ocean Racing Conference
SORC .... Station Operations Review Committee [*Nuclear energy*] (NRCH)
SORCS .... Shipboard Ordnance Requirement Computer System [*Navy*]
SORD .... Society of Record Dealers of America
SORD .... Southwestern Order Retrieval and Distribution [*Southwest Bell Telephone Co.*]
SORD .... Special Operations and Research Division [*Air Resources Laboratory*] (USDC)
SORD .... Special Operations and Research Division [*Marine science*] (OSRA)
SORD .... Statement of Operational Requirements Document (AAGC)
SORD .... Submerged Object Recovery Device
SORD .... Submerged Ordnance Recovery Device [*Navy*]
SORD .... Systematic Organizational Design
SORD .... System of Operational Requirements Document [*Air Force*] (DOMA)
SORDAC .... Special Operations Research, Development, and Acquisition Center [*Military*]
SORDC .... Southwest Ohio Regional Data Center [*University of Cincinnati*] [*Research center*] (RCD)
SORDID .... Summary of Reported Defects, Incidents and Delays (MHDB)
SORE .... Stamp Out Regulatory Excesses [*An association*] (EA)
SOREL .... Sun-Orbiting Relativity Experiment Satellite
SOREM .... Sleep-Onset REM [*Rapid Eye Movement*]
So Rep .... Southern Reporter [*A publication*] (DLA)
So Repr .... Southern Reporter [*A publication*] (DLA)
SORFO .... Society of Rural Financial Officers [*British*] (BI)
SORG .... Stratospheric Ozone Review Group [*British*] (DBA)
SORG .... Submarine Operations Research Group [*Navy*]
SORI .... Southern Research Institute (AAG)
SORI .... Staff Officer Radio Instructor (IAA)
SORIN .... Societa Ricerche Impianti Nucleari [*Italy*]
SORIS .... Specialised Organics Information Service [*British*] (DBA)
SORM .... Set-Oriented Retrieval Module
SORM .... Ships Organization Manual (DOMA)
SORNE(I) .... Senior Officer, Royal Naval Establishment (India) [*British World War II*]
SORNG .... Sound Ranging
SORO .... Scan on Receive Only (MCD)
SORO .... Sort Program, Sort Routine [*Computer science*] (IAA)
SORO .... Special Operations Research Office
SORP .... Signature Overlay Range Prediction (MCD)
SORP .... Statement of Recommended Practice [*Accounting*] [*British*]
SORPr .... Source Capital $2.40 Pfd [*NYSE symbol*] (TTSB)
SORPTR .... South Repeater [*NASA*] (MCD)
SORR .... SIGINT [*Signal Intelligence*] Operations Readiness Review [*Military*] (AABC)
SORR .... Submarine Operations Research Report [*Navy*]
SORRAT .... Society for Research on Rapport and Telekinesis [*Defunct*] (EA)
SORS .... Shipboard Operational Readiness System [*Navy*] (CAAL)
SORS .... Spacecraft Oscillograph Recording System
SORSA .... Spatially Orientated Referencing Systems Association (EERA)
SORSI .... Sacro Occipital Research Society International (EA)
SORT .... Gunther International, Ltd. [*NASDAQ symbol*] (SAG)
SORT .... Self-Observation and Report Technique
SORT .... Senior Officer Refresher Training
SORT .... Shippers of Recycled Textiles [*An association*] (EA)
SORT .... Ship's Operational Readiness Test
SORT .... Simulated Optical Range Target (MCD)
SORT .... Slosson Oral Reading Tests
SORT .... Spanish Oral Reading Text (EDAC)
SORT .... Special Operations Response Team [*Prison management*]
SORT .... Spilled Oil Response Team [*Marine science*] (MSC)
SORT .... Staff Organizations Round Table [*American Library Association*]
SORT .... Structured-Objective Rorschach Test [*Psychology*]
SORT .... Structures for Orbiting Radio Telescope (MCD)
SORT .... Supply Corps Officer Refresher Training [*Navy*] (DNAB)
SORT .... System Operational Readiness Test (MCD)
SORTE .... Summary of Radiation Tolerant Electronics
SORTEC .... Synchrotron Orbital Radiation Technology [*High-energy physics*]
SORTI .... Satellite Orbital Track and Intercept [*ARPA*]
SORTI .... Star-Oriented Real-Time Teaching Instrument (AAG)
SORTI .... Star-Oriented Real-Time Tracking Instrument [*Aerospace*] (IAA)
SORTIE .... Simulation of Reentry Target Interceptor Endgame (MCD)
SORTIE .... Suborbital Reentry Test Integrated Environment [*NASA*] (IAA)
SORTIE .... Supercircular Orbital Reentry Test Integrated Environment [*NASA*] (IAA)
SORTIE .... Super-Orbital Reentry Test Integrated Environment (MUGU)
SORTRAN .... Syntax-Oriented Translator (PDAA)
SORTS .... Shipboard Organizational Troubleshooting System (MCD)
SORTS .... Status Of Readiness and Training System (DOMA)
SORTS .... Status of Resources and Training System Report [*Military*]
SORWUC .... Service, Office, and Retail Workers Union of Canada
SOS .... Coalition to Protect Social Security (EA)
SOS .... Congress of Scientists on Survival [*Inactive*]
SOS .... Safety Observation Station
SOS .... Safety on the Streets [*Project of National Safety Council*]
SOS .... Same Old Sludge [*Slang phrase used to describe television programming*]
SOS .... Same Old Stew [*Military slang*] [*Bowdlerized version*]
SOS .... Same Old Stuff [*Reference to the weather*]
SOS .... Same Only Softer [*Band leader's signal*] [*Slang*]
SOS .... Sanity on Sex [*Group opposing sex education in schools*]
SOS .... Satellite Observation System
SOS .... Satellite Observing System [*Marine science*] (OSRA)
SOS .... Save Our Schools (EA)
SOS .... Save Our Security (EA)
SOS .... Save Our Ship [*or Souls*] [*Popular explanation of Morse code letters used as a signal for extreme distress*]
SOS .... Save Our Shires [*British*] [*An association*] (DBA)
SOS .... Save Our Shores (EA)
SOS .... Save Our Snails [*An association*]
SOS .... Save Our Sons [*Cancer information service*] [*British*]
SOS .... Save Our Souls
SOS .... Save Our Strays (EA)
SOS .... Save Outdoor Sculpture [*Database producer*] (IID)
SOS .... Scheduled Oil Sampling [*Automotive engineering*]
SOS .... Science of Survival
SOS .... Scientists for Sakharov, Orlov, and Shcharansky (EA)
SOS .... Secretary of State
SOS .... Secular Organizations for Sobriety (EA)
SOS .... Self-Obtained Smear [*Medicine*] (DMAA)
SOS .... Self-Opening Sack [*Paper bag*]
SOS .... Self-Organizing System
SOS .... Send Out Succor
SOS .... Senior Officer Service
SOS .... Senior Officer Structure
SOS .... Senior Opportunities and Services [*OEO*]
SOS .... Sentinel on Station
SOS .... Serial Output Special (MCD)
SOS .... Service off the Shelf (IAA)
SOS .... Service of Supply [*Later, ASF*] [*Army*]
SOS .... Service on Sight [*Computer warranty program offered by Hyundai Electronics*] (PCM)
SOS .... Service Order System [*Telecommunications*] (TEL)
SOS .... Shakespeare Oxford Society (EA)
SOS .... Share Operating System [*Computer science*]
SOS .... Share Our Strength (EA)
SOS .... Ship Our Ships Program [*Navy*] (DNAB)
SOS .... Ships Operational Safety [*A publication*]
SOS .... Ships Ordnance Summary
SOS .... Shock-on-Shock
SOS .... Shop Order Shop (SAA)
SOS .... Shop Out of Stock (SAA)
SOS .... Signed-Off Sick
SOS .... Silicon-on-Sapphire [*Integrated circuit*]
SOS .... Silicon-on-Spinel (IAA)
SOS .... Simulator Operating System (IAA)
SOS .... Simultaneous Oral Spelling [*Gillingham method*] [*Education*]
SOS .... Si Opus Sit [*If Needed*] [*Pharmacy*]
SOS .... Sisters of Service [*Roman Catholic religious order*]
SOS .... Slip on Show [*Indicates a woman's slip is showing*] (DSUE)
SOS .... Slum on a Shingle [*Army breakfast dish*] [*Bowdlerized version*]
SOS .... Sniping, Observation, and Scouting [*Course*] [*World War I*] [*Military British*]
SOS .... Society for Occlusal Studies (EA)
SOS .... Society of Operative Stonemasons [*A union*] [*British*]
SOS .... Society of Scribes (EA)
SOS .... Society of Separationists (EA)
SOS .... Society of Shuttlemakers [*A union*] [*British*]
SOS .... Society of Signalmen (EA)
SoS .... Song of Songs [*Old Testament book*] [*Roman Catholic canon*] (BJA)
SOS .... Sophisticated Operating System [*Apple III microcomputer*] [*Computer science*]
SOS .... Sostenuto [*Sustained*] [*Music*]
SOS .... Sound on Sound (NTCM)
SOS .... Sound on Sync (IAA)
SOS .... Source of Supply
SOS .... Southern Oxidant Study [*Marine science*] (OSRA)
SOS .... Southern Oxidant Study (USDC)
SOS .... Soviet Oceanographic Surveillance (MCD)
SOS .... Space Ordnance Systems, Inc. (MCD)
SOS .... Spare Operation Support
SOS .... Special Operations Squadron [*Air Force*]
SOS .... Special Organizational Services [*An association*] (EA)
SOS .... Speed of Service [*Telecommunications*] (TEL)
SOS .... Speed of Sound
SOS .... SPRINT Operations Shelter [*Army*]
SOS .... Squadron Officers School [*Air Force*]
SOS .... Squadron Operational Support [*Military*] (AFIT)
SOS .... Stabilized Optical Sight
SOS .... Stamp Out Stupidity [*Student group opposing drug abuse*]
SOS .... Stars Organisation for Spastics [*British television awards program*]
SOS .... Start of Significance [*Computer science*] (BUR)
SOS .... Statement of Service [*Military*]
SOS .... Statement of Supply
SOS .... Station Operating Supervisor (IEEE)
SOS .... Stock Order Shipment
SOS .... Storage Computer [*AMEX symbol*] (TTSB)
SOS .... Storage Computer Corp. [*AMEX symbol*] (SAG)
SOS .... Storage-on-Site [*Grolier Electronic Publishing, Inc.*]
SOS .... Store Overstocked [*Inventory*]
SOS .... Strategic Orbital System (AAG)
SOS .... Strongpoint Obstacle System [*Military*] (VNW)
SOS .... Struck off Strength [*British military*] (DMA)
SOS .... Student Orientations Survey [*Student attitudes test*]
SOS .... Student-Originated Studies [*National Science Foundation*]
SOS .... Studies on Smoking, Inc. [*Research center*] (RCD)
SOS .... Suborbital Sequence [*NASA*]
SOS .... Sum-of-the-Squares
SOS .... Sum over States [*Physics*]
SOS .... Supervisor of Shipbuilding [*Navy*]

SOS .... Supplemental Oxygen System (MCD)
SOS .... Supplementary Ophthalmic Service [*Medicine*]
SOS .... Supporters of Silkwood [*Defunct*] (EA)
SOS .... Support on Site [*Computer science*]
SOS .... Support Our Soldiers [*Network of antiwar-oriented coffee houses located near military bases*] (EA)
SOS .... Survivors of Sacrifice [*Defunct*] (EA)
SOS .... Survivors of Stalking
SOS .... Survivors of Suicide
SOS .... Suspend Other Service [*Business term*]
SOS .... Suspension of Service [*Pilots' strike*]
SOS .... Sustain Our Schools
SOS .... Symbolic Operating System [*Computer science*]
SOS .... Symmetry, Orbitals, and Spectra [*Atomic physics*]
SOS .... Synchronous Orbit Satellite (AAG)
SOS .... System Operational Specification [*Military*] (CAAL)
SOSA .... Sell Overseas America, the Association of American Export [*Redondo Beach, CA*] (EA)
SOSA .... Somerset Savings Bank [*NASDAQ symbol*] (SAG)
SOSA .... Starfleet Operations [*An association*] (EA)
SOSA .... State Opera of South Australia
SOSA .... Sustained Operations Support Area [*NASA*] (KSC)
SOSAL .... School of Systems and Logistics [*Military*]
SOSAT .... Submarine One-Way Satellite [*Navy*] (CAAL)
SOSB .... Special Operations Signal Battalion (DOMA)
SOSB .... Special Operations Support Battalion (DOMA)
SOSC .... Safety Observation Station Display Console
SOSC .... Smithsonian Oceanographic Sorting Center
SOSC .... Source of Supply Code
SOSC .... Suburban Ostomy Supply Co., Inc. [*NASDAQ symbol*] (SAG)
SOSCAR .... Supervisor of Shipbuilding, Conversion, and Repair [*Navy*] (DNAB)
SoScLfe .... Southern Security Life Insurance Co. [*Associated Press*] (SAG)
SOSCMOS.... Silicon-on-Sapphire Complementary Metal Oxide Semiconductor (IAA)
SOSCU......... Stamps on Stamps - Centenary Unit (EA)
SOSD .... Spatial Operational Sequence Diagram
SOSD .... System Ordnance Safing Device [*Military*]
SOSE .... Science Operations Support Equipment
SOSE .... Silicon-on-Something-Else [*Telecommunications*] (TEL)
SOSE .... Special Operations Support Element [*Military*] (GFGA)
SOSEC .... Satellite Ocean Surveillance Evaluation Center
SOSED .... Secretary's Office, Shore Establishments Division [*Incorporated into SECP, 1944*] [*Navy*]
SOSF .... Single Organ System Failure [*Medicine*] (DMAA)
SOSFET....... Silicon-on-Sapphire Field Effect Transistor (IAA)
SOSH .... Search for the Odd Shape [*Neuropsychology test*]
SO SH......... Somali Shilling [*Monetary unit*]
SOS:HRG ..... SOS: Human Rights for Guyana (EA)
SOS Intl .... Society of Saunterers, International (EA)
SOSIS .... Status of Support Information System
SOSK .... Squadron Operational Support Kit (MCD)
SO/SL .... Saturn Orbiter Satellite Lander [*NASA*]
SOSM .... Ship Overhaul Schedule Milestone [*Navy*]
SOSM .... Source of Supply Modifier
SOSO .... Safety and Operating Systems Office [*NASA*]
SoSo .... South of SoHo [*See also NoHo, SoHo, TriBeCa*] [*Artists' colony in New York City*]
SOSO .... Synchronous Orbiting Solar Observatory
SOSP .... Squadron Operational Support Package [*Military*] (AFIT)
SOSQ .... Special Operations Squadron
SOSR .... Spin on Straight Rail
SOSR .... Suppress, Obscure, Secure, and Reduce [*Military*] (INF)
SOSRAM...... Silicon-on-Sapphire Random Access Memory (IAA)
SOSS .... Satellite Ocean Surveillance System
SOSS .... Satellite Optical Surveillance Station (MCD)
SOSS .... Shipboard Oceanographic Survey System
SOSS .... SONAR Schoolship [*Navy*] (NVT)
SOSS .... SOS Staffing Services, Inc. [*NASDAQ symbol*] (SAG)
SOSS .... SOS Staffing Svcs [*NASDAQ symbol*] (TTSB)
SOSS .... Sound Search Station
SOSS .... Soviet Ocean Surveillance System (MCD)
SOSS .... Strategic Orbital System Study (AAG)
SOSS .... Structurally Oriented Simulation System [*NASA*]
SOSSI .... Scouts on Stamps Society International (EA)
SOSSI .... SOS Sahel International (EAIO)
SOSSPA....... Service of Supply, South Pacific Area [*Navy World War II*]
SOS Stf........ SOS Staffing Services, Inc. [*Associated Press*] (SAG)
SOSSUS....... Sound Surveillance System [*Navy*]
SOSSUS....... Study on Surgical Services in the United States [*Medicine*]
SOST .... Sostenuto [*Sustained*] [*Music*]
SOST .... Special Operator Service Traffic [*Telecommunications*] (TEL)
SOSTEL....... Solid-State Electric Logic (NG)
SOSTEN .... Sostenuto [*Sustained*] [*Music*]
SOSU .... Scout Observation Service Unit [*Navy*]
SOSU .... Seattle Ocean Services Unit [*National Oceanic and Atmospheric Administration*] (GFGA)
SOSU .... Ships on Stamps Unit (EA)
SOSUS......... SONAR Surveillance System [*Military*]
SOSUS......... Sound Surveillance System (MSA)
SOSUS......... Sound Surveillance Undersea (MCD)
SOSUS......... Sound Surveillance Underwater System [*Navy*]
SOSVS......... Sound Surveillance System
SOT .... Same Old Thing [*Slang*]
SOT............. Scanning Oscillator Technique (IAA)
SOT............. Secretary of Transportation (NATG)
SOT............. Sensation of Transcendence
SOT............. Shower over Tub [*Real estate*]
SOT............. Simulated Operational Training [*Navy*] (DNAB)
SOT............. Sky Wave Observation Timer (IAA)
SOT............. Snowbird, TN [*Location identifier FAA*] (FAAL)
SOT............. Society of Ornamental Turners (EA)
SOT............. Society of Toxicology (EA)
SOT............. Solar Optical Telescope
SOT............. Son of Temperance [*A heavy drinker*] [*Slang*]
Sot.............. Sotah (BJA)
SOT............. Sound on Tape [*Videotape*]
SOT............. Sounds of Our Times, Cook Studio [*Record label*]
SOT............. Southeast Correct Craft, Inc. [*ICAO designator*] (FAAC)
SOT............. South Omaha Terminal Railway Co. [*AAR code*]
SOT............. Soviet Orientation Team (MCD)
SOT............. Spatial Orientation Trainer [*Air Force*]
SOT............. Special Operations Team (ADA)
SOT............. Specified Organ Transplant [*Health insurance*] (GHCT)
SOT............. SRO Entertainment [*Vancouver Stock Exchange symbol*]
SOT............. Start of Tape
SOT............. Start of Text
SOT............. State of Termination [*Telecommunications*] (TEL)
S-O-T.......... Stoke-On-Trent [*City in England*]
SOT............. Strap-On Tank [*NASA*] (NASA)
SOT............. Stream of Thought
SOT............. Structural Operations Technology Group (SSD)
SOT............. Subscriber Originating Trunk [*Telecommunications*] (TEL)
SOT............. Syntax-Oriented Translator (IEEE)
SOT............. Systems Operating Test
SOTA .... SIGINT [*Signal Intelligence*] Operational Tasking Authority [*Military*]
SOTA .... State of the Art
SOTA .... State of the Art, Inc. [*NASDAQ symbol*] (SPSG)
SOTA .... Students Older than Average
SOTAC .... State-of-the-Art Car [*Transit*] [*Department of Transportation*]
SOTACA .... State-of-the-Art Contingency Analysis System [*Science Applications International Corp.*] (MCD)
SOTAP .... Sophisticated Training Program
SOTARSS..... Standoff Target Acquisition Reconnaissance Surveillance System (MCD)
SOTAS .... Standoff Target Acquisition/Attack System
SOTASS....... Standoff Target Acquisition and Surveillance System [*Army*]
SOTB .... Secretary's Office, Transportation Branch [*Navy*]
SOTD .... Stabilized Optical Tracking Device (SAA)
SOTDAT....... Source Test Data System [*Environmental Protection Agency*]
SOTE........... Standard Optical Test Equipment
SOTE........... System Operational Test Evaluation (SAA)
SOTEAG....... Shetland Oil Terminal Environmental Advisory Group
SOTER .... Soil and Terrain Database [*USA*] (EERA)
So Tex C Law... South Texas College of Law (GAGS)
So Tex LJ..... Southern Texas Law Journal [*A publication*] (DLA)
SOTF........... Special Operations Task Force [*Military*] (GFGA)
SOTFE......... Special Operations Task Force, Europe [*Military*]
SOTG .... Sales Other than Gasoline [*Business term*]
SOTG .... Special Operations Training Group [*Marine Corps*] (DOMA)
Sothbys........ Sotheby's Holdings, Inc. [*Associated Press*] (SAG)
SOTI............ [*A*] Survey of Old Testament Introductions [*Gleason L. Archer*] [*A publication*] (BJA)
SOTIM .... Sonic Observation of the Trajectory and Impact of Missiles
SOTP .... Saturn Orbiter/Titan Probe (MCD)
SOTP .... Ship Overhaul Test Program
SOTP .... Shipyard Overhaul Test Program
SOTP .... System Overhaul Test Program
SOTR .... Single Object Tracking RADAR (MCD)
SOTR .... SouthTrust Corp. [*NASDAQ symbol*] (NQ)
SOTS .... Society of Old Testament Study [*British*] (DBA)
SOTS .... Suborbital Tank Separation [*NASA*] (MCD)
SOTS .... Synchronous Orbiting Tracking Stations (MCD)
SOTT........... Second-Order Transition Temperature
SOTT........... Synthetic Medium Old Tuberculin Trichloroacetic Acid Precipitated [*Later, PPD, Purified Protein Derivative*] [*Immunology*]
SOTUS .... Sequentially Operated Teletypewriter Universal Selector
SOU .... Flight Line, Inc. [*ICAO designator*] (FAAC)
SOU .... Scandinavian Ornithological Union [*Lund, Sweden*] (EAIO)
SOU .... Souchong [*Tea trade*] (ROG)
SOU .... Sources Public Library [*UTLAS symbol*]
SOU .... South (ROG)
SOU .... Southampton [*England*] [*Airport symbol*] (OAG)
SOU .... Southern Airways [*Air carrier designation symbol*]
SOU .... Southern Petroleum Corp. [*Vancouver Stock Exchange symbol*]
SOU .... Southern Railway System [*AAR code*]
SOU .... Statens Offentliga Utredningar [*Sweden*]
SOU .... Statute of Uses [*Legal shorthand*] (LWAP)
SouAfrica..... Southern Africa Fund [*Associated Press*] (SAG)
SouAla......... South Alabama Bancorp [*Associated Press*] (SAG)
So U & A&M C... Southern University and Agricultural and Mechanical College (GAGS)
SouBnc......... Southside Bancshares [*Associated Press*] (SAG)
SouUCo........ Southern Union Co. [*Associated Press*] (SAG)
Soudw .... Southdown, Inc. [*Associated Press*] (SAG)
Soudwn........ Southdown, Inc. [*Associated Press*] (SAG)
SouFncl .... Southern Financial Bancorp [*Associated Press*] (SAG)
SouFncl .... Southern Financial Federal Savings Bank [*Associated Press*] (SAG)
SOUL .... Studies of Ocean Upper Layers (MSC)
Soule Syn.... Soule's Dictionary of English Synonymes [*A publication*] (DLA)
SouMoBc...... SouMOBc Co. [*Associated Press*] (SAG)

SoUnCo........ Southern Union Co. [*Associated Press*] (SAG)
SoundA........ Sound Advice, Inc. [*Associated Press*] (SAG)
SoUnF.......... Southern Union Financing [*Associated Press*] (SAG)
So Univ........ Southern University (GAGS)
SOUP........... Software Utility Package (NITA)
SOUP........... Solar Optical Universal Polarimeter
SOUP........... Solid Uncured Propellant (MCD)
SOUP........... Students Opposed to Unfair Practices [*in advertising*] [*Student legal action organization*]
SOUP........... Submarine Operational Update Program [*Canadian Navy*]
SouPacR....... Southern Pacific Rail Corp. [*Associated Press*] (SAG)
SouPoint...... South Pointe Enterprises [*Associated Press*] (SAG)
SOUPr.......... South'n Cal Gas cm6%PfdA vtg [*PC symbol*] (TTSB)
SOUQAR...... Section d'Oceanographie d'Universite de Quebec a Rimouski [*Canada*] (MSC)
SOUR........... Specific Oxygen Uptake Rate [*In wastewater*]
SourcC......... Source Capital, Inc. [*Associated Press*] (SAG)
SOURCE....... Simulation of Utilization, Resources, Cost, and Efficiency
SOURS......... Subcommittee on Use of Radioactivity Standards [*National Research Council*]
SOUSAFE..... Status of United States Air Force Equipment
SOUSSA....... Steady, Oscillatory, and Unsteady, Subsonic, and Supersonic Aerodynamics [*NASA*]
SOUT........... Swap-Out [*Computer science*]
SOUTC......... Satellite Operators and Users Technical Committee [*Defunct*] (EA)
South........... Southern Reporter [*National Reporter System*] [*A publication*] (DLA)
Southard...... Southard's New Jersey Law Reports [*4-5 New Jersey*] [*A publication*] (DLA)
South Car.... South Carolina Reports [*A publication*] (DLA)
SOUTHCOM... Southern Command [*Military*] (AFM)
SouthCp....... Southshore Corp. [*Associated Press*] (SAG)
South CR..... South Carolina Review [*A publication*] (BRI)
South Cul..... Southern Cultures [*A publication*] (BRI)
Southeastern La U... Southeastern Louisiana University (GAGS)
Southeastern Okla St U... Southeastern Oklahoma State University (GAGS)
Southeastern Rep... South Eastern Reporter [*A publication*] (DLA)
Southeast Mo St U... Southeast Missouri State University (GAGS)
Southern...... Southern Reporter [*A publication*] (DLA)
Southern Rep... Southern Reporter [*A publication*] (DLA)
SOUTHFORNET... Southern Forestry Information Network [*Forest Service*] (IID)
South HR..... Southern Humanities Review [*A publication*] (BRI)
South Law J... Southern Law Journal [*Tuscaloosa, AL*] [*A publication*] (DLA)
South Law J & Rep... Southern Law Journal and Reporter [*A publication*] (DLA)
South Law Rev... Southern Law Review [*A publication*] (DLA)
South Law Rev NS... Southern Law Review, New Series [*A publication*] (DLA)
SouthldCp.... Southland Corp. [*Associated Press*] (SAG)
South LJ...... Southern Law Journal [*A publication*] (DLA)
South LJ & Rep... Southern Law Journal and Reporter [*A publication*] (DLA)
South L Rev... Southern Law Review [*A publication*] (DLA)
South L Rev NS... Southern Law Review, New Series [*A publication*] (DLA)
SOUTHN...... Southampton [*City in England*] (ROG)
SouthnCo..... Southern Co. [*Associated Press*] (SAG)
South R....... Southern Review [*A publication*] (BRI)
Southtrst...... Southtrust Corp. [*Associated Press*] (SAG)
SOUTHW...... Southwell [*City in England*] (ROG)
Southwestern Okla St U... Southwestern Oklahoma State University (GAGS)
Southwestern U Law... Southwestern University School of Law (GAGS)
Southwest Mo St U... Southwest Missouri State University (GAGS)
Southwest Tex St U... Southwest Texas State University (GAGS)
Southw LJ... Southwestern Law Journal and Reporter [*A publication*] (DLA)
SouUnCo...... Southern Union Co. [*Associated Press*] (SAG)
Souwal........ Southwall Technologies, Inc. [*Associated Press*] (SAG)
SOV............ Sammons' Opuntia Virus [*Plant pathology*]
SOV............ Saratov Aviation Division [*Former USSR*] [*FAA designator*] (FAAC)
SOV............ Seldovia, AK [*Location identifier FAA*] (FAAL)
SOV............ Sham Ovariectomy [*Endocrinology*]
SOV............ Share of Voice [*Advertising*]
SOV............ Shut-Off Valve
SOV............ Simulated Operational Vehicle (MCD)
SOV............ Single-Occupancy Vehicle (ECON)
SOV............ Solenoid-Operated Valve
SOV............ Somerset County Vocational and Technical School, Bridgewater, NJ [*OCLC symbol*] (OCLC)
SOV............ Sound on Vision (IAA)
SOV............ Sovereign
SOV............ Soviet
SOV............ Study of Values
SOV............ Styles on Video [*AMEX symbol*] (TTSB)
SOV............ Styles on Video, Inc. [*AMEX symbol*] (SPSG)
SOV............ Subjective Optical Vertical
SOVA.......... Society of Voluntary Associates [*British*] (DBA)
SOVAC......... Software Validation and Control System (MCD)
SovAE.......... Soviet Antarctic Expedition [*1955-*]
Sov & E Eur For Tr... American Review of Soviet and Eastern European Foreign Trade [*A publication*] (DLA)
SOVAS......... Scanning Optical Vibration Analysis System (IAA)
SovBcp......... Sovereign Bancorp, Inc. [*Associated Press*] (SAG)
SOVD........... Stabilized Optical Viewing Device
Soviet Jewry L Rev... Soviet Jewry Law Review [*A publication*] (DLA)
Soviet Stat & Dec... Soviet Statutes and Decisions [*A publication*] (DLA)
Soviet YB Int'l L... Soviet Year-Book of International Law [*A publication*] (DLA)
SOVIII.......... Third Survey of Veterans [*Veterans Administration*] (GFGA)
SOVIN.......... Samenwerkingsverband voor Opleiding en Vorming op het Terrein van de Informatieverzorging via Netwerken [*Collective for Training and Education in Connection with Information Provision via Networks*] [*Ceased operation*] [*Netherlands Information service or system*] (IID)
SOVMEDRON... Soviet Mediterranean Squadron [*NATO*] (NATG)
SOVNARKOM... Soviet Narodnykh Komissarov [*Council of People's Commissars*] [*Former USSR*] (LAIN)
SOVNROF.... State of Vietnam Ribbon of Friendship [*Presidential unit commendation*]
SOVOG......... Sozialistiche Volksorganisation [*Socialist National Community*] [*Lithuania*] [*Political party*] (PPE)
SovranSS..... Sovran Self Storage, Inc. [*Associated Press*] (SAG)
SoVrnSS...... Sovran Self Storage, Inc. [*Associated Press*] (SAG)
SOVS........... Sovereigns [*Monetary unit*] [*Obsolete British*]
SOVX........... Sham Ovariectomized [*Endocrinology*]
SOW............ Scope of Work (MCD)
SOW............ Scramble-on-Warning
SOW............ Show Low [*Arizona*] [*Airport symbol Obsolete*] (OAG)
SOW............ Skylab Orbital Workshop [*NASA*]
SOW............ Sowind Air Ltd. [*Canada ICAO designator*] (FAAC)
SOW............ Special Operations Wing [*Military*] (MCD)
SOW............ Standoff Weapons (MCD)
SOW............ Start of Word
SOW............ Start of Work
SOW............ Statement of Work (MCD)
SOW............ Subdivision of Work [*NASA*] (NASA)
SOW............ Sunflower Ordnance Works [*Military*]
SOW............ Synthetic Ocean Water
SOWA.......... Stock Option Writers Association [*Defunct*] (EA)
SOWC.......... Senior Officers' War Course [*British*]
SOWESPAC... Southwest Pacific Command [*Navy*]
SOWESSEAFRON... Southwest Sea Frontier [*Navy*]
SOWESTDIVDOCKS... Southwest Division, Bureau of Yards and Docks [*Navy*] (MUGU)
SOWESTPACCOM... Southwest Pacific Command [*Navy*] (DNAB)
So West Rep... South Western Reporter [*A publication*] (DLA)
SOWETO...... Southwestern Townships [*South Africa*]
SOWEX......... Southern Ocean Waves Experiment [*Marine science*] (OSRA)
SOWEX......... Southern Ocean Waves Experiment (USDC)
SOWg.......... Special Operations Wing [*Air Force*] (AFM)
SOWIDOK.... Sozialwissenschaftliche Dokumentation [*Social Sciences Documentation Center*] [*Vienna Chamber of Labor*] [*Information service or system*] (IID)
SOWM......... Special Ocean Wave Model
SOWN.......... Supportive Older Women's Network [*An association*]
SOWP.......... Society of Wireless Pioneers (EA)
SOWR.......... Submarine Overhaul Work Requirement [*Navy*] (DNAB)
SOWRA........ Submarine Overhaul Work Requirement Authorization [*Navy*] (DNAB)
SOWRBALL... Southwest RADAR Balloon [*for illegal drug interdiction*]
SOW/S & D... Statement of Work/Specifications and Design
SOX............ Sentry Resources Corp. [*Formerly, Sentry Oil & Gas*] [*Vancouver Stock Exchange symbol*]
SOX............ Solid Oxygen
SOX............ Sound Exchange [*A sound conversion program*] (PCM)
SOX............ Sulfur Oxide
SOx............ Sulphur Oxides [*Chemical*] (EERA)
SOX............ Supercritical Oxygen [*NASA*] (KSC)
SOY............ Sioux Center, IA [*Location identifier FAA*] (FAAL)
SOY............ SO Resources [*Vancouver Stock Exchange symbol*]
SOY............ Stronsay [*Scotland*] [*Airport symbol*] (OAG)
SOYD.......... Sum of the Years' Digits Method [*Finance*]
SOYDV........ Soybean Dwarf Virus [*Plant pathology*]
SOYMV........ Soybean Mosaic Virus [*Plant pathology*]
SOYO.......... Society of Orthodox Youth Organizations (EA)
SOZ............ Seder 'Olam Zuta (BJA)
SOZ............ Solo International Resources Ltd. [*Vancouver Stock Exchange symbol*]
SOZ............ Somerset, PA [*Location identifier FAA*] (FAAL)
SOZ............ Soviet Occupied Zone (NATG)
Sp............... Biblioteca Nacional, Madrid, Spain [*Library symbol Library of Congress*] (LCLS)
SP............... Error in Spelling [*Used in correcting manuscripts, etc.*]
SP............... International Society of Philology
sp----.......... La Plata River and Basin [*MARC geographic area code Library of Congress*] (LCCP)
SP............... Motor Patrol Boat [*Navy symbol Obsolete*]
Sp............... [*The*] New Testament of Our Lord and Saviour Jesus Christ (1937) (Francis Aloysius Spencer) [*A publication*] (BJA)
SP............... Office of State Programs [*Nuclear energy*] (NRCH)
SP............... Poland [*International civil aircraft marking*] (ODBW)
SP............... Sacra Pagina [*Paris-Gembloux*] [*A publication*] (BJA)
Sp............... Sacropubic [*Anatomy*] (AAMN)
SP............... Sacrum Posterior [*A fetal position*] (DAVI)
SP............... Sacrum to Pubis [*Medicine*] (DMAA)
SP............... Safety Panel
SP............... Sailing Plan Report
SP............... Salisbury [*Postcode*] (ODBW)
SP............... Salivary Progesterone [*Medicine*] (DMAA)
SP............... Samajwadi Party [*Italy Political party*] (ECON)
SP............... Same Point (ILCA)
SP............... Same Principle (ILCA)
SP............... Sample Part
SP............... Sampling Point (NRCH)
SP............... Sanctissime Pater [*Most Holy Father*] [*Latin*]

SP .... San Pedro [*California*]
SP .... Satellite Processor [*Data transmission*]
SP .... Scalable Processing [*Northgate*] [*Computer science*]
SP .... Scan Programmer (DGA)
SP .... Schering-Plough Corp. [*Commercial firm*]
SP .... Schizotypal Personality [*Medicine*] (DMAA)
SP .... Schools of Philosophy [*A publication*]
SP .... Schwangerschaftsprotein (BABM)
SP .... Schwangerschaftsprotein [*Biochemistry*] (DAVI)
SP .... Science Pilot
SP .... Science Press [*Information service or system*] (IID)
SP .... Scientific Paper
SP .... Scientific Processor (BUR)
S/P .... Scientific Products
SP .... Scottish Peer (ROG)
SP .... Scratch Pad [*Computer science*]
S/P .... Seaplane
SP .... Sea Platform (MCD)
SP .... Secretory Piece [*Superseded by SC, Secretory Component*] [*Immunology*]
SP .... Secretory Protein [*Endocrinology*]
SP .... Section Patrol [*Navy*]
SP .... Security Police [*Air Force*] (AFM)
SP .... Security Procedure (NRCH)
SP .... Security Publication [*Navy*]
SP .... Seed Production [*Agriculture*]
SP .... Seeing Problems [*Research test*] [*Psychology*]
SP .... Selective Purchases
SP .... Self Potential [*Log*]
SP .... Self-Powered [*Gun*] (MCD)
SP .... Self-Propelled [*Military*]
SP .... Selling Price
SP .... Seminar Press
SP .... Semipostal
S/P .... Semiprivate [*Room*]
SP .... Semipublic [*Telecommunications*] (TEL)
SP .... Send Processor
sP .... Senile Parkinsonism [*Medicine*] (DMAA)
SP .... Senile Plaque [*Neurology*]
SP .... Senior Partner
SP .... Senior Pilot [*Air Force*]
SP .... Sensor Processor (BUR)
Sp .... Senterpartiet [*Center Party*] [*Norway Political party*] (PPE)
SP .... Senza Pedale [*Without Pedals*] [*Music*]
SP .... Separate Element Pricing (IAA)
SP .... Septum Pellucidum [*Brain anatomy*]
SP .... Sequence Programmer [*Computer science*] (AAG)
S-P .... Sequential-Phase (CET)
SP .... Sequential Processor
SP .... Sequential Pulse [*Medicine*] (DAVI)
S/P .... Serial to Parallel (KSC)
SP .... Series-Parallel [*Computer science*] (IAA)
SP .... Servants of the Holy Paraclete [*Roman Catholic men's religious order*]
sp .... Servants of the Paraclete (TOCD)
sP .... Servants of the Paraclete (TOCD)
SP .... Service Package (OA)
SP .... Service Panel
SP .... Service Phase (MCD)
SP .... Service Police [*British military*] (DMA)
SP .... Service Processor (IEEE)
SP .... Service Publications (AAG)
SP .... Serving Point [*Telecommunications*]
SP .... Session of Peace [*Legal*] [*British*] (ROG)
SP .... Set Pattern (IAA)
SP .... Set Point
SP .... Severely, Profoundly Handicapped (OICC)
SP .... Sewer Pipe [*Telecommunications*] (TEL)
SP .... Shanti Project (EA)
SP .... Shear Plate [*Technical drawings*]
SP .... Shift Pulses
SP .... Shipping Port
SP .... Shoreline Protection [*Type of water project*]
SP .... Shore Party [*Navy*]
SP .... Shore Patrol [*Navy*]
SP .... Shore Police [*Navy*]
SP .... Shortest Path
SP .... Short Page
SP .... Short Perforation [*Philately*]
SP .... Short Period
SP .... Short Persistence
SP .... Short Position [*Investment term*]
SP .... Short Pulse
SP .... Shoulder Pitch (MCD)
SP .... Shunt Procedure [*Medicine*] (MAE)
SP .... Shuttle Projects Office [*Kennedy Space Center*] [*NASA*] (NASA)
SP .... Sic Porro [*So Forth*] [*Latin*]
SP .... Sidepull [*Bicycle*] (DICI)
SP .... Sieve Pore [*Botany*]
SP .... Signaling Projector [*British*]
S/P .... Signal Processor (NASA)
SP .... Signal Publication [*British*]
SP .... Signed Photograph
SP .... Sign Post
SP .... Sikkim Parishad [*India*] [*Political party*] (PPW)
SP .... Silver Plate
SP .... SilverPlatter Information, Inc. [*Commercial firm*]
SP .... Silver Protein [*An antiseptic*]
SP .... Simple Printing
SP .... Sine Prole [*Died Without Issue*] [*Latin*]
SP .... Singing Point [*Telecommunications*] (TEL)
SP .... Single Particle
SP .... Single Payment (ILCA)
SP .... Single-Peaked (IAA)
SP .... Single-Phase
SP .... Single-Pole [*Switch*]
sp .... Single-Pole (IDOE)
SP .... Single Precision (NASA)
SP .... Single Programmer
SP .... Single Purpose
SP .... Sisters of Providence [*Roman Catholic religious order*]
SP .... Sisters of Providence of Saint Mary-of-the-Woods, IN (TOCD)
SP .... Sisters of the Presentation of Mary [*Roman Catholic religious order*]
SP .... Skin Painting [*Method of administering experimental chemicals*]
SP .... Skin Potential (MAE)
SP .... Skin Prick [*Immunology*]
SP .... Sloop (ROG)
SP .... Slugging Percentage [*Baseball*]
SP .... Small Packet
SP .... Small Paper [*Printing*]
SP .... Small Pica
SP .... Small Plaque
SP .... Small Premises [*Hairdressers, doctors, dentists, etc.*] [*Public-performance tariff class*] [*British*]
SP .... Smith Predictor [*Process control*]
SP .... Smoke Control and Pressurization Panel [*NFPA pre-fire planning symbol*] (NFPA)
SP .... Smokeless Powder
SP .... Smokeless Propellant (NATG)
SP .... Smoki People [*An association*] (EA)
SP .... Sniper's Post [*British military*] (DMA)
SP .... Socialistische Partij [*Socialist Party*] [*Belgium Political party*] (PPW)
SP .... Socialist Party
SP .... Society of Philaticians [*Defunct*] (EA)
SP .... Society of Protozoologists (EA)
SP .... Sociolinguistics Program (EA)
SP .... Softening Point (MCD)
SP .... Soil Pipe
SP .... Soil Pit
SP .... Soil Psychrometer
SP .... Solar Panel
SP .... Solar Physics (NASA)
SP .... Soldiers for Peace (EA)
SP .... Sole Proprietor (MHDW)
SP .... Solid Propellant
SP .... Soluble Powder (GNE)
SP .... Solution Provider [*Microsoft workgroup*] (PCM)
SP .... Sort Program [*Computer science*] (IAA)
SP .... Sosyalist Parti [*Socialist Party*] [*Turkey Political party*] (EY)
S/P .... Sotto Protesto [*Under Protest*] [*Italian*]
SP .... Sound Positive (IAA)
SP .... Sound Powered (CAAL)
SP .... Soundproof [*Technical drawings*]
SP .... Source Program [*Computer science*] (IAA)
SP .... Southern Pacific Transportation Co. [*AAR code*]
SP .... Southern Pine [*Utility pole*] [*Telecommunications*] (TEL)
SP .... South Pacific
SP .... South Pole [*Also, PS*]
SP .... South Proceeding [*Astronomy*]
sp .... Space [*Crocheting*]
SP .... Space (ECII)
SP .... Space
SP .... Space and Power
SP .... Space Character [*Keyboard*] (AAG)
SP .... Space Patrol (AAG)
SP .... Space Platform (SSD)
SP .... Space Probe (IAA)
Sp .... Spacers [*Electron transfer*]
SP .... Spain
sp .... Spain [*MARC country of publication code Library of Congress*] (LCCP)
SP .... Spanish (ROG)
SP .... Spare (AAG)
SP .... Spare Part
SP .... Spares Planning (AAG)
SP .... Spark (AAG)
SP .... Spark Plug (IAA)
SP .... Spartan Program [*Missiles*] (MCD)
SP .... Spasmolytic Polypeptide [*Biochemistry*]
Sp .... Spears' South Carolina Law Reports [*1842-44*] [*A publication*] (DLA)
SP .... Special (AFM)
sp .... Special (IDOE)
Sp .... Special Branch [*Navy British*]
SP .... Speciale Prototipo [*Special Prototype*] [*Italy*]
SP .... Specialist (ADA)
sp .... Specialist (WDMC)
SP .... Specialist Degree (PGP)
SP .... Special Paper
SP .... Special Performance
SP .... Special Planning (AAG)

SP.......... Special Product (MCD)
SP.......... Special Proficiency [*British military*] (DMA)
SP.......... Special Program
SP.......... Special Progress [*Program*] [*Education*]
SP.......... Special Projects
SP.......... Special Propellants
SP.......... Special Provisions (AAGC)
SP.......... Special Publication
SP.......... Special Purchase (ADA)
SP.......... Special Purpose
SP.......... Species [*Also, sp*]
Sp.......... Species (EERA)
SP.......... Specific (AAG)
SP.......... Specific Performance [*Legal shorthand*] (LWAP)
SP.......... Specific Power
SP.......... Specimen
SP.......... Speck (WGA)
SP.......... Spectral Pitch [*Neurophysiology*]
SP.......... Speech (WGA)
SP.......... Speech Pathologist
SP.......... Speed (MSA)
SP.......... Spelling
sp.......... Spelling (WDMC)
SP.......... Spelling Entertainment Group [*Formerly, Charter Co.*] [*NYSE symbol*] (SPSG)
SP.......... Spelling Entertainment Grp [*NYSE symbol*] (TTSB)
sp.......... Spell Out [*Proofreading*] (WDMC)
SP.......... Spherical [*Buoy*]
SP.......... Spherical Polar
sp.......... Spherical Tank [*Liquid gas carriers*]
SP.......... Sphingomyelin [*Also, SM, Sph*] [*Biochemistry*] (DAVI)
S/P.......... Spikes Plant [*Wheat*]
SP.......... Spine [*or Spinal*]
sp.......... Spinel [*CIPW classification*] [*Geology*]
SP.......... Spine Point Bullet
Sp.......... Spinks' English Admiralty Prize Cases [*164 English Reprint*] [*1854-56*] [*A publication*] (DLA)
Sp.......... Spinks' English Ecclesiastical and Admiralty Reports [*A publication*] (DLA)
SP.......... Spin Polarized [*Physics*]
Sp.......... Spirillum (MAE)
SP.......... Spirit
SP.......... Spiritus [*Spirit*] [*Latin*] [*Pharmacy*] (DAVI)
SP.......... Spirometry
SP.......... Spitze [*Point*] [*Music*]
SP.......... Splash Plate
SP.......... Splashproof (MSA)
SP.......... Splinting [*Dentistry*]
SP.......... Splitting [*Electronics*]
SP.......... Sponge (WGA)
SP.......... Sponsor (NITA)
SP.......... Sponsoring Program (NITA)
Sp.......... Spontaneous
SP.......... Spontaneous Potential [*Log*]
SP.......... Spool (MSA)
SP.......... Spoon (WGA)
SP.......... Spore Plasma [*Botany*]
SP.......... Sport
SP.......... Sportavia Puetzer GmbH & Co. KG [*Germany ICAO aircraft manufacturer identifier*] (ICAO)
SP.......... Sports for the People [*Defunct*] (EA)
SP.......... Spot Price [*Investment term*]
SP.......... Spouse
SP.......... Sprague-Dawley [*Rat variety*]
SP.......... Spray Pressure [*Agriculture*]
Sp.......... Spring Tide
SP.......... Square Planar [*Organic chemistry*]
SP.......... Square Punch
SP.......... Stable Platform
SP.......... Stack and Play Hub [*Intellicom, Inc.*] [*Telecommunication switching device*] (PCM)
SP.......... Stack Pointer [*Computer science*]
SP.......... Stack Pool [*Computer memory*] (PCM)
SP.......... Staff Paymaster [*Navy British*] (ROG)
SP.......... Staff Planner [*DoD*]
SP.......... Stained Pollen [*Botany*]
SP.......... Standard Holding Pattern [*Aviation*]
SP.......... Standard or Peculiar (NASA)
SP.......... Standard Peripherals (IAA)
SP.......... Standard Pile [*Nuclear reactor*]
SP.......... Standard Play [*Video technology*]
SP.......... Standard Practice [*or Procedure*]
SP.......... Standard Pressure (IAA)
SP.......... Standard Price
SP.......... Standard Program [*Computer science*] (BUR)
SP.......... Standby Power
SP.......... Standing Procedure (NATG)
SP.......... Standpipe (MSA)
SP.......... Staphylococcal Protease [*Medicine*] (DMAA)
SP.......... Staphylococcal Protein A [*Biochemistry*] (DAVI)
SP.......... Starting Point
SP.......... Starting Price
SP.......... Start Permission (KSC)
SP.......... State Park [*State*] (EERA)
SP.......... State Plan (OICC)
SP.......... Static Pointer [*Computer science*]
SP.......... Static Pressure
SP.......... Station Police [*British military*] (DMA)
SP.......... Status Panel (CAAL)
SP.......... Status Positive [*Medicine*] (CPH)
S/P.......... Status Post [*Medicine*]
SP.......... Steady Potential (MAE)
SP.......... Stern Post
SP.......... Stipule [*Botany*]
SP.......... Stirrup Pump
SP.......... Stool Preservative [*Medicine*]
SP.......... Stop Payment [*Banking*]
SP.......... Stop Press (ADA)
SP.......... Storage Protection (IAA)
SP.......... Storage Protein [*Food industry*]
SP.......... St. Petersburg [*Diocesan abbreviation*] [*Florida*] (TOCD)
SP.......... Straight Partners [*Defunct*] (EA)
SP.......... Strategic Planning Chart [*Air Force*]
SP.......... Strategic Planning Society [*See also SPS*] [*London, England*] (EAIO)
SP.......... Street Price (ROG)
SP.......... Stretcher Party
SP.......... Stronnictwo Pracy [*Labour Party*] [*Poland Political party*] (EY)
SP.......... Structured Programming [*Computer science*] (BUR)
S-P.......... Studebaker-Packard [*Automobile manufacturer*]
SP.......... Study Plan
SP.......... Subject-Predicate
SP.......... Subliminal Perception
SP.......... Submarine Patrol [*Navy*]
S/P.......... Submarine Pay [*British military*] (DMA)
SP.......... Subplate [*Neurology*]
SP.......... Subprofessional [*Civil Service employees designation*]
SP.......... Subprogram (IAA)
SP.......... Substance P [*A peptide*] [*Biochemistry*]
SP.......... Successive Planometric [*A discrimination task*]
SP.......... Sugar Phosphate [*Biochemistry*]
SP.......... Suicide Precaution (MAE)
SP.......... Sulfopropyl [*Organic chemistry*]
SP.......... Sumerian Proverbs (BJA)
SP.......... Summary Plotter [*RADAR*]
SP.......... Summary Punch [*Computer science*] (OA)
SP.......... Summating Potential [*Hearing*]
SP.......... Summus Pontifex [*Supreme Pontiff, Pope*] [*Latin*]
SP.......... Sundries Pack [*Field troops military issue*] (VNW)
SP.......... Sunlit Period
SP.......... Sun's Parallax [*Astronomy*] (ROG)
SP.......... Superficial Pineal Organ [*Neuroanatomy*]
SP.......... Superparamagnetic [*Fraction in rock*] [*Geophysics*]
SP.......... Superseded in Part [*New matter substituted for part of an existing regulation or order*] [*Used in Shepard's Citations*] [*Legal term*] (DLA)
SP.......... Supervisory Package (OA)
SP.......... Supervisory Printer [*Computer science*] (OA)
SP.......... Supervisory Process [*Telecommunications*] (TEL)
SP.......... Supplement
SP.......... Supplemental Pack [*Field troops military issue*] (VNW)
SP.......... Supply Point [*Military*] (NATG)
SP.......... Support
SP.......... Support Plan (MCD)
SP.......... Support Publications (AAG)
SP.......... Supraprotest
SP.......... Suprapubic [*Medicine*]
SP.......... Surveillance Procedure (NRCH)
SP.......... Surviving Propagules [*Botany*]
SP.......... Suspicious Person
SP.......... Sustainer Pitch (AAG)
SP.......... Swelling Power [*Food technology*]
SP.......... Switch Panel
SP.......... Switch Port [*Telecommunications*]
SP.......... Syllable Period [*Entomology*]
SP.......... Symbol Programmer (MUGU)
SP.......... Symphonic Popular [*Armed Forces Radio-Televsion*] (DNAB)
SP.......... Symphysis Pubica [*Anatomy*]
SP.......... Synperiplanar [*Chemistry*]
SP.......... System Parameter (KSC)
SP.......... System Processor (IEEE)
S-P.......... Systems and Procedures
SP.......... Systolic Pressure [*Cardiology*]
SP.......... Teaching and Teacher Education [*Educational Resources Information Center (ERIC) Clearinghouse*] [*American Association of Colleges for Teacher Education*] (PAZ)
Sp3c.......... Specialist, Third Class (GFGA)
SP3T.......... Single-Pole, Triple-Throw [*Switch*] (IEEE)
SP4.......... Specialist 4 [*Army*]
SP4T.......... Single-Pole, Quadruple-Throw [*Switch*] (IEEE)
SP5.......... Specialist 5 [*Obsolete Army*]
SP6.......... Specialist 6 [*Obsolete Army*]
SP7.......... Specialist 7 [*Army*]
SP8.......... Specialist 8 [*Obsolete Army*]
SP9.......... Specialist 9 [*Obsolete Army*]
SPA.......... Greenville/Spartanburg [*South Carolina*] Downtown [*Airport symbol*] (OAG)
SPA.......... Sacrum Palatium Apostolicum [*Sacred Apostolic Palace, Vatican, Quirinal*] [*Latin*]
SPA.......... Salaried Pharmacists' Association [*Australia*]
SPA.......... Salt-Poor Albumin [*Medicine*]

SPA............. Salt Producers Association [*Later, SI*] (EA)
SPA............. Sample Preparation Accessory [*Laboratory analysis*]
SPA............. Satellite Personnel Activity [*Military*]
SPA............. Saudi Press Agency
SPA............. S-Band Power Amplifier
SPA............. Scalable Processing Architecture [*Computer hardware*] [*Northgate*] (PCM)
SPA............. Scatter Propagation Antenna
SPA............. Schedules Planning and Analysis [*Aviation*] (DA)
SPA............. Science and Public Affairs [*A publication*]
SPA............. Scintillation Proximity Assay [*Analytical biochemistry*]
SPA............. Scottish Paraplegic (Spinal Injury) Association [*British*]
SPA............. Scottish Pistol Association (DBA)
SPA............. Scottish Publishers Association (DBA)
SPA............. Screen Producers' Association [*Australia*]
SPA............. Sea Photo Analysis [*Navy*]
SPA............. Seaplane Pilots Association (EA)
SPA............. Self-Phasing Array
SPA............. Self Publishing Association [*British*] (DBA)
SPA............. Semipermanently Associated [*Telecommunications*] (TEL)
SPA............. Service Pay and Allowances [*Military British*]
SPA............. Servo Power Amplifier (NASA)
SPA............. Servo Power Assembly (MCD)
SPA............. Servo Preamplifier
SPA............. Shared Peripheral Area (NASA)
SPA............. Sheep Pulmonary Adenomatosis [*Medicine*] (DMAA)
SPA............. Sierra Pacific Airlines [*ICAO designator*] (FAAC)
SPA............. Signal Processor Assembly [*NASA*]
SPA............. Silicon Pulser Array
SPA............. Singapore People's Alliance
SPA............. Single Parameter Analysis
SPA............. Single Photon Absorptiometry [*Analytical chemistry*]
SPA............. Single Position Automatic [*Tester*]
SPA............. Singles Press Association (EA)
SPA............. Skill Performance Aid [*Army*] (RDA)
SPA............. Small-Particle Aerosol
SPA............. Socialist Party of Albania [*Political party*] (EY)
SPA............. Socialist Party of Australia [*Political party*]
SPA............. Society for Personality Assessment (EA)
SPA............. Society for Personnel Administration [*Later, IPMA*] (EA)
SPA............. Society for Psychological Anthropology (EA)
SPA............. Society for Public Administration
SPA............. Society of Participating Artists [*Record label*]
SPA............. Society of Philatelic Americans [*Defunct*] (EA)
SPA............. Society of Philosophers in America (EA)
SPA............. Society of Professional Assessors [*Address unknown*]
SPA............. Sociological Practice Association (EA)
SPA............. Sodium Polyacrylate [*Organic chemistry*]
SPA............. Software Producers' Association (NITA)
SPA............. Software Product Assurance (SSD)
SPA............. Software Publishers Association (EA)
SPA............. Solar Power Array
SPA............. Songwriters Protective Association [*Later, AGAC*]
SPA............. SOSUS Probability Area (NVT)
SPA............. Southeastern Peanut Association (EA)
SPA............. Southern Pine Association [*Later, SFPA*] (EA)
SPA............. South Pacific Area [*World War II*]
SPA............. South Pole [*Antarctica*] [*Seismograph station code, US Geological Survey*] (SEIS)
SPA............. Southwestern Power Administration [*Department of Energy*]
SPA............. Southwestern Psychological Association (IAA)
SPA............. Southwest Placement Association (AEBS)
SPA............. Space Processing Applications [*Program*] [*NASA*]
SPA............. Spade [*Freight*]
Spa............. Spain (VRA)
SPA............. Spanish
spa............. Spanish [*MARC language code Library of Congress*] (LCCP)
SPA............. Spartanburg, SC [*Location identifier FAA*] (FAAL)
SPA............. Sparton Corp. [*NYSE symbol*] (SPSG)
SpA............. Specialist in Art (GAGS)
SPA............. Specialist in Public Administration (GAGS)
SPA............. Specialist, Physical Training Instructor [*Navy rating*]
SPA............. Specially Protected Area [*Australia*]
SPA............. Specially Protected Area (EERA)
SPA............. Special Project Activities (MCD)
SPA............. Special Public Assistance
SPA............. Special Purchase Allowance (DOAD)
SPA............. Special-Purpose Aircraft [*Drone vehicle*] [*Military*]
SPA............. Special Purpose Alteration (MCD)
SPA............. Specification Preparing Activity (AAGC)
SPA............. Spectair Industry [*Vancouver Stock Exchange symbol*]
SPA............. Spectrum Analyzer
SPA............. Spinal Progressive Amyotrophy [*Medicine*] (DMAA)
SPA............. Splice Plug Assembly
SPA............. Spondyloarthropathy [*Medicine*] (MEDA)
SPA............. Sportsman Pilots Association
SPA............. Standard Plate Agar [*Microbiology*] (OA)
SPA............. Standard Practice Amendment (AAG)
SPA............. Staphylococcal Protein A [*Immunochemistry*]
SPA............. State Planning Agency [*Department of Justice*]
SPA............. State Power Authority (IAA)
SPA............. State Property Agency [*Hungary*] (ECON)
SPA............. Sterile Preparation Area (MCD)
SPA............. Stimulation-Produced Analgesia
SPA............. St. Maarten Patriotic Alliance [*Netherlands Antilles*] [*Political party*] (EY)
SPA............. Strategic Posture Analysis [*Army*] (AABC)
SPA............. Subject to Particular Average [*Insurance*]
SPA............. Submarine Patrol Area [*Navy*] (NVT)
SPA............. Subpoena [*Legal term*]
SPA............. Substance P Antagonist [*Biochemistry*]
SPA............. Substitute Part Authorization (AAG)
SPA............. Sudden Phase Anomaly [*Radio engineering*]
SPA............. Suicide Prevention Association [*Australia*]
SPA............. Sundry Persons' Account [*Banking*]
SPA............. Superphosphoric Acid [*Fertilizer*]
SPA............. Supervisory Performance Appraisal [*Civil Service*]
SPA............. Supplemental Preclaims Assistance [*Department of Education*] (GFGA)
SPA............. Suprapubic Aspiration [*Medicine*]
SPA............. Supreme People's Assembly [*Political party North Korea*] (FEA)
SPA............. Surface Vehicle Power Adapter
SPA............. Surinaamse Partij van de Arvid [*Suriname Labour Party*] [*Political party*] (EY)
SPA............. SURTASS Probability Area [*Navy*] (CAAL)
SPA............. Survey of Personal Attitude [*Psychology*]
SPA............. Symbolic Processing Array [*Computer science*]
SPA............. Syndicated Program Analysis (NTCM)
SPA............. System Performance Analyzer [*Motorola, Inc.*]
SPA............. System Problem Area (SAA)
SPA............. Systems and Procedures Association [*Later, ASM*] (EA)
SPAA........... Caraz [*Peru*] [*ICAO location identifier*] (ICLI)
SPAA........... Scottish Passenger Agents Associaiton (DBA)
SPAA........... Spacecraft Performance Analysis Area
SPAA........... Systems and Procedures Association of America (IAA)
SPAAC......... Syndicat du Personnel Africain de l'Aeronautique Civile [*African Union for Civil Aviation Employees*]
SPA ad TEST... Subpoena ad Testificandum [*Subpoena to Testify*] [*Latin*] (ROG)
SPAAG......... Self-Propelled Anti-Aircraft Gun [*Former Soviet Union*]
SPAALAL..... Society for the Promotion of African, Asian, and Latin American Literature [*See also GFLAAL*] [*Germany*] (EAIO)
SPAAMFAA... Society for the Preservation and Appreciation of Antique Motor Fire Apparatus inAmerica (EA)
SPAAMFAA... Society for the Preservation and Appreciation of Antique Motor Fire Apparatus inAmerica
SPAAN......... Societe Protectrice des Animaux en Afrique du Nord [*Society for the Protection of Animals in North Africa - SPANA*] (EAIO)
SPAASS....... Synod Office, Diocese of Saskatchewan, Angelican Church of Canada, Prince Albert, Saskatchewan [*Library symbol National Library of Canada*] (NLC)
SPAB........... Huancabamba [*Peru*] [*ICAO location identifier*] (ICLI)
SPAB........... Security Pacific Asian Bank
SPAB........... Society for the Protection of Ancient Buildings (EA)
SPAB........... Society of Psychologists in Addictive Behaviors [*Later, PAB*] (EA)
SPAB........... SPACEHAB Inc. [*NASDAQ symbol*] (TTSB)
SPAB........... Supply, Priorities, and Allocations Board [*World War II*]
SPABH......... Society for the Preservation of American Business History (EA)
SPAC........... Ciro Alegria [*Peru*] [*ICAO location identifier*] (ICLI)
SPAC........... Salinity Program Advisory Council (EERA)
SPAC........... Saratoga Performing Arts Center [*Summer home of NYCB*] [*Saratoga Springs, NY*]
SPAC........... Secretary's Pesticide Advisory Committee [*HEW*]
SPAC........... Signal Programmer and Conditioner [*Air Force Eastern Test Range*]
SPAC........... Spacecraft Performance Analysis and Command [*NASA*]
SPAC........... Space Program Advisory Council [*Terminated, 1977*] [*NASA*]
SPAC........... Spacious (ADA)
SPAC........... Spatial Computer
SPACC......... Space Control Center (DOMA)
SPACCS....... Space Command and Control System
SPACE......... Council of AFL-CIO Unions for Scientific, Professional, and Cultural Employees [*Later, Department for Professional Employees, AFL-CIO*]
SPACE......... Sales Profitability and Contribution Evaluator [*Computer science*]
SPACE......... Satellite Precipitation and Cloud Experiment [*National Oceanic and Atmospheric Administration*]
SPACE......... Satellite Project for Adult and Continuing Education (AIE)
SPACE......... Self-Programming Automatic Circuit Evaluator
SPACE......... Sequential Position and Covariance Estimation (IEEE)
SPACE......... Settlement, Payment, Accounting, Credit Extension (MHDB)
SPACE......... Shuttle/Payload Contamination Evaluation Program (MCD)
SPACE......... Sidereal Polar Axis Celestial Equipment
SPACE......... Single Potential Analysis of Cavernous Electrical Activity [*Medicine*] (DMAA)
SPACE......... Society for Private and Commercial Earth Stations [*Telecommunications Information service or system*] (EA)
SPACE......... Spacecraft Prelaunch Automatic Checkout Equipment [*NASA*]
SPACE......... Space Program American Citizens' Effort
SPACE......... Special Political Agricultural Community Education [*Milk cooperative trust fund*]
SPACE......... Speech Analog Compression and Editing [*Loop*] (IAA)
SPACE......... Sperry Program for Advancing Careers through Education
SPACE......... Support Package for Aerospace Computer Emulation (MCD)
SPACE......... Symbolic Programming Anyone Can Enjoy
SPACECOM... Space Command [*Military*]
SPACECOM... Space Communications
SPACECOMPS... Spacecraft Components (NITA)
SpaceLb....... SpaceLabs Medical, Inc. [*Associated Press*] (SAG)
SPACES....... Saving and Preserving Arts and Cultural Environments (EA)

SPACES .... Solving Problems of Access to Careers in Engineering and Science (EDAC)
SPACETAC ... Space and Tactical System Corp. (MCD)
Spacetec...... Spacetec IMC Corp. [*Associated Press*] (SAG)
SPACETRACK... Space Tracking System [*Air Force*] (MCD)
SPacFd .... Southern Pacific Funding Corp. [*Associated Press*] (SAG)
SPacFdg ...... Southern Pacific Funding Corp. [*Associated Press*] (SAG)
SPACG .... Syndicat du Personnel de l'Aeronautique Civile du Gabon [*Union of Civil Aviation Employees of Gabon*]
SPACHEE ..... South Pacific Action Committee for Human Ecology and Environment (EERA)
SPACLALS ... South Pacific Association for Commonwealth Literature and Language Studies (EAIO)
SPACON....... Space Control
SPACS .... Sodium Purification and Characterization System [*Nuclear energy*] (NRCH)
SPAD .... Satellite Position Prediction and Display
SPAD .... Satellite Protection for Area Defense [*ARPA*]
SPAD .... Scratch Pad Memory [*Computer science*]
SPAD .... Seaway Port Authority of Duluth
SPAD .... Shuttle Payload Accommodation Document [*NASA*] (MCD)
SPAD .... Simplified Procedures for Analysis of Data (OA)
SPAD .... Societe pour Aviation et ses Derives [*France*] [*World War I airplane*]
SPAD .... Space Patrol Active Defense
SPAD .... Space Patrol for Air Defense
SPAD .... Space Principles, Applications, and Doctrine [*Air Force Systems Command*]
SPAD .... Special Programs and Analysis Division [*Environmental Protection Agency*] (GFGA)
SPAD .... SPRINT Air-Directed Defense [*Army*]
SPAD .... Stenosing Peripheral Arterial Disease [*Medicine*] (DMAA)
SPAD .... Subcutaneous Peritoneal Access Device [*Nephrology*] (DAVI)
SPAD .... Submarine Patrol Area Definition (MCD)
SPAD .... Subsystem Positioning Aid Device (NASA)
SPADATS..... Space Detection and Tracking System [*Military*]
SPADATSC... Space Detection and Tracking System Center [*Air Force*]
SPADATSIMP... Space Detection and Tracking System Improved [*Air Force*] (IAA)
SPADATSS... Space Detection and Tracking System Sensors [*Air Force*]
SPADCCS..... Space Defense Command and Control System (MCD)
SPADE .... Signal Processing and Display Equipment
SPADE .... Single Channel Per Carrier Multiple Access Demand Assignment Equipment (NITA)
SPADE .... Single-Channel-per-Carrier, Pulse-Code-Modulation, Multiple-Access, Demand-Assignment Equipment [*Telecommunications*]
SPADE .... Small Portable Analysis and Diagnostic Equipment [*Aircraft maintenance*]
SPADE .... Spare Parts Analysis, Documentation, and Evaluation
SPADE .... Sparta Acquisition Digital Equipment (MCD)
SPADE .... Sperry Air Data Equipment
SPADE .... Stratospheric Photochemistry Aerosols, and Dynamics Expedition [*Meteorology*]
SPADE .... Strike Planning and Damage Estimator [*Military*]
SPADES .... Solar Perturbation and Atmospheric Density Measurement Satellite
SPADETS ..... Space Detection Network [*Military*]
SPADL .... Spare Parts Application Data List
SPADNS....... (Sulfophenylazo)dihydroxynaphthalene-disulfonate [*Organic chemistry*]
SPADOC....... Space Defense Operations Center [*DoD*]
SPADS .... Satellite Position and Display System
SPADS .... Shuttle Problem Action [*or Analysis*] Data System [*NASA*] (NASA)
SPADS .... SPRINT Air-Directed Defense System [*Army*] (AABC)
SPADS .... STRATCOM Program Automated Data System [*Army*]
SPA DT .... Subpoena Duces Tecum [*Legal*] [*Latin*] (ROG)
SPAE........... Societe Planetaire pour l'Assainissement de l'Energie [*Planetary Association for Clean Energy*] (EAIO)
SPAEF.......... Societe des Petroles d'Afrique Equatoriale Francaise [*French Equatorial African Petroleum Co.*]
SPAEF.......... Southern Public Administration Education Foundation (EA)
SPAEI.......... South Pacific Association of Environmental Institutions
SPAF............ Forestry Branch, Saskatchewan Department of Natural Resources, Prince Albert, Saskatchewan [*Library symbol National Library of Canada*] (NLC)
SP-AF .... Shuttle Projects - Air Force Liaison Office [*Kennedy Space Center*] [*NASA*] (NASA)
SPAF............ Simulation Processor and Formatter (MCD)
SPAF............ Spontaneous Paroxysmal Atrial Fibrillation [*Medicine*] (DMAA)
SPAF............ Stroke in Patients with Atrial Fibrillation
SPAF............ Student Product Assessment Form (EDAC)
SPAG .... Small-Particle Aerosol Generator (DAVI)
SPAG .... South Plains Association of Governments
SPAG .... Space Radiation Analysis Group [*NASA*]
SPAG .... Spaghetti (DSUE)
SPAG .... Special Program/Analysis Guidance [*DoD*]
SPAG .... Sphenopalatine Ganglion [*Neurology*] (DAVI)
SPAG .... Standards Promotion Application Group [*Telecommunications*]
SPAH .... Society for the Preservation and Advancement of the Harmonica (EA)
SPAH .... Spacelab Payload Accommodations Handbook [*NASA*] (MCD)
SPAI............ Screen Printing Association International (EA)
SPAI............ Steroid Protein Activity Index [*Medicine*] (MAE)
SPAID .... Sheffield Package Analysis and Identification of Data [*Commercial & Industrial Development Bureau*] [*Software package*] (NCC)
SPAID .... Society for the Prevention of Asbestosis and Industrial Diseases [*British*] (DI)
SPAIN.......... Indian and Northern Affairs Canada [*Affaires Indiennes et du Nord Canada*] Prince Albert, Saskatchewan [*Library symbol National Library of Canada*] (NLC)
Spain........... Spain Fund [*Associated Press*] (SAG)
SPAL............ Simulator, Projectile, Airburst, Liquid [*Chemical defense device*] [*Military*] (RDA)
SPAL............ Stabilized Platform Airborne LASER (RDA)
SPAL............ Succinyl-poly-DL-alanine Poly-L-lysine [*Biochemical analysis*]
SPALDA........ Scottish Peat and Land Development Association (DBA)
Spald Cop.... Spalding on Copyright [*A publication*] (DLA)
Spalding C... Spalding College (GAGS)
SPALT.......... Single-Point Articulated Loading Tower [*Engineering*]
SPALT.......... Special Projects Alterations [*Navy*]
SPALTRA..... Special Projects Alterations, Training [*Navy*]
SPAM........... Camana [*Peru*] [*ICAO location identifier*] (ICLI)
SPAM........... Satellite Processor Access Method
SPAM........... Scanning Photoacoustic Microscopy
SPAM........... Scratch Pad Memory Address [*Computer science*] (IAA)
SPAM........... Search Pattern Assessment Model [*Military*] (CAAL)
SPAM........... Shipment Planning and Movement [*Army*]
SPAM........... Ship Position and Attitude Measurement (IEEE)
SPAM........... Shop Portable Aircraft Maintenance [*Army*]
SPAM........... Society for the Publication of American Music [*Record label*]
SPAM........... Soil-Plant-Atmosphere [*Computer simulation model*]
SPAM........... Sonobuoy Placement Assortment Model (MCD)
SPAM........... S-Parameter Acquisition and Manipulation [*Computer software program*] [*General Motors Corp.*]
SPAM........... Special Aeronautical Material [*Navy*] (NG)
SPAM........... Special Personal Attack Message [*Internet-delivered direct mail*] [*Computer science*]
SPAM........... Spiced Ham [*Hormel (George A.) & Co.*]
SPAMA .... Spanish Air Materiel Area
SPAMAG ...... Space Medicine Advisory Group (MCD)
SpamEx....... Spam Exterminator [*Unisyn*] [*Computer science*]
SPAMF......... Seychelles Popular Anti-Marxist Front [*Political party*] (PD)
SPAMM......... Spatial Modulation of Magnetization [*Medicine*] (DMAA)
SPAMMER ... Space Hammer
SPAMS .... Ship Position and Altitude Measurement System (MCD)
SPAN .... Single Payer Across the Nation [*Health insurance*]
SPAN .... Social Planning Around Neighbourhoods [*Australia*]
SPAN .... Social Policy and Administration Network [*A publication*]
SPAN .... Social Studies Priorities, Practices, and Needs (EDAC)
SPAN .... Society of Philatelists and Numismatists (EA)
SPAN .... Solar Particle Alert Network [*National Oceanic and Atmospheric Administration*]
SPAN .... Solar Proton Alert Network
SPAN .... Solid Phase Alloy Nucleation (PDAA)
SPAN .... South Pacific Action Network
SPAN .... Space Communications Network
SPAN .... Spacecraft Analysis (KSC)
SPAN .... Space Navigation
SPAN .... Space Physics Aeronautics Network (USDC)
SPAN .... Space Physics Analysis Network [*Database*]
SPAN .... Space Plasma Analysis Network [*NASA*]
SPAN .... Span-America Medical Systems, Inc. [*NASDAQ symbol*] (NQ)
SPAN .... Span-America Med Sys [*NASDAQ symbol*] (TTSB)
SPAN .... Span Analysis (NITA)
SPAN .... Spaniard (ROG)
SPAN .... Spanish
Span .... Spansule [*Pharmacology*] (DAVI)
SPAN .... Statistical Processing and Analysis [*Computer science*]
SPAN .... Storage Planning and Allocation [*Computer science*]
SPAN .... Stored Program Alphanumerics [*FAA*]
SPAN .... Submarine Piloting and Navigation [*Navy*]
SPAN .... Successive, Proportionate, Additive Numeration [*Decision making*]
SPAN .... Sullana [*Peru*] [*ICAO location identifier*] (ICLI)
SPAN .... System for Projection and Analysis
SPANA .... Society for the Protection of Animals Abroad [*British*] (EAIO)
SPANA .... Society for the Protection of Animals in North Africa [*See also SPAAN*] (EAIO)
SpanAm .... Span-America Medical Systems, Inc. [*Associated Press*] (SAG)
SPANAT .... Systems Planning Approach - North Atlantic [*FAA*]
SPANC .... Wapiti Regional Library, Prince Albert, Saskatchewan [*Library symbol National Library of Canada*] (NLC)
SPAND......... Solar Proton Albedo Neutron Decay
SPANDAR .... Space and Range RADAR [*NASA*]
SP & O .... Special Plans and Operation [*Military*]
SP & S .... Special Processes and Sequencing (NASA)
Sp & Sel Cas... Special and Selected Law Cases [*1648*] [*England*] [*A publication*] (DLA)
Spanet......... Secure Prioritized ATM [*Asynchronous Transfer Mode*] Network [*Telecommunications*]
SPANGLISH... Spanish and English
SPANI .... Northern Institute of Technology, Prince Albert, Saskatchewan [*Library symbol National Library of Canada*] (NLC)
Spanlink ...... Spanlink Communications, Inc. [*Associated Press*] (SAG)
SPANNER .... Special Analysis of Net Radio [*Study*]
SPANNET..... Space Navigation Network (IAA)
SPANPAC..... Sales, Purchases and Nominal Package (MHDB)
SPANRAD .... Superimposed Panoramic RADAR Display
SPANRAD .... Superposed Panoramic RADAR Display (IAA)
SPANS .... Sealift Procurement and National Security [*Study*]
SPANS .... Small Passive Navigation System (DNAB)
spans........... Spansules [*Pharmacology*] (CPH)
SPANS .... Spectral Processing Analysis System (PDAA)

SPANSULE... Space Plus Capsule (WDAA)
SPAO ... San Juan Aposento [*Peru*] [*ICAO location identifier*] (ICLI)
SPAOPSUP... Space Operations Support (NVT)
SPAP ... Picota [*Peru*] [*ICAO location identifier*] (ICLI)
SPAP ... Serum Prostatic Acid Phosphatase [*An enzyme*]
SPAP ... Special Package Auto Policy [*Insurance*]
SpAppBiol... Specialist in Applied Biology (GAGS)
SPAQUA... Sealed Package Quality Assurance (IEEE)
SPAR ... Alerta [*Peru*] [*ICAO location identifier*] (ICLI)
SPAR ... SAC [*Strategic Air Command*] Peacetime Airborne Reconnaissance
SPAR ... Satellite Position Adjusting Rocket (SAA)
SPAR ... Seagoing Platform for Acoustic Research [*NOL*]
SPAR ... Semper Paratus [*Always Ready*] [*Coast Guard motto*]
SPAR ... Sensitivity Prediction from the Acoustic Reflex [*Audiometry*]
SPAR ... Society of Photographers and Artist Representatives (EA)
SPAR ... Soil-Plant-Atmosphere-Research [*Agriculture*]
SPAR ... Space Precision Altitude Reference System (MCD)
SPAR ... Space Processing Applications Rocket [*NASA*]
SPAR ... SPALT [*Special Projects Alterations*] Planning and Authorization Report
Spar... Spartan
SPAR ... Spartan Motors [*NASDAQ symbol*] (TTSB)
SPAR ... Spartan Motors, Inc. [*Charlotte, MI*] [*NASDAQ symbol*] (NQ)
SPAR ... Special Prelaunch Analysis Request [*NASA*] (KSC)
SPAR ... Special Progressive Aircraft Rework
SPAR ... Spelling and Reading Tests
SPAR ... Staff Payroll Allocation and Record (OA)
SPAR ... Staff Procurement Activity Requirement [*Military*]
SPAR ... Stock Point ADP [*Automatic Data Processing*] Replacement Program [*Navy*] (GFGA)
SPAR ... Store Port Allocation Register (PDAA)
SPAR ... Student Profile and Assessment Record [*Student attitudes test*]
SPAR ... Submersible Pipe Alignment Rig [*Deep-sea diving*]
SPAR ... Super-Precision Approach RADAR
SPAR ... Surveillance and Precision Approach RADAR (NATG)
SPAR ... Symbolic Program Assembly Routine [*Computer science*]
SPAR ... Synchronous Position Altitude Recorder
SPAR ... System Program Assessment Review [*Air Force*]
SPARC ... Scalar Processor Architecture Reduced-Instruction-Set Computer (DOM)
SPARC ... Scaleable Processor Architecture [*Computer science*]
SPARC ... Scholarly Publishing & Academic Resources Coalition
SPARC ... Secreted Protein Acidic and Rich in Cysteine [*Biochemistry*]
SPARC ... Shore-Establishment Planning Analysis and Review Cooperation [*or Coordination*] [*Navy*] (NG)
SPARC ... Short Planning Analysis and Review Cooperation
SPARC ... Slab Penetration and Reflection Calculation
SPARC ... Space Air Relay Communications (MCD)
SpARC ... Space Automation and Robotics Center [*University of Michigan*] [*Research center*] (RCD)
SPARC ... Space Program Analysis and Review Council [*Air Force*]
SPARC ... Space Research Capsule [*or Conic*] [*NASA*]
SPARC ... Spare Parts Provisioning for Combat
SPARC ... Spectral Analysis and Recognition Computer [*NASA*]
SPARC ... Standards Planning and Requirements Committee [*ANSI*]
SPARC ... Steam Plant Automation and Results Computer
SPARC ... Stratospheric Processes and their Role in Climate [*Marine science*] (OSRA)
SPARC ... Stratospheric Processes and their Role in Climate (EERA)
SPARC ... Support Planning Analysis Reporting and Control [*Navy*] (NG)
SPARC ... Sustainability Predictions for Army Spare Component Requirements for Combat (RDA)
SPARC ... System Parametric Allocation of Resources and Cost (MCD)
SPARCS... Solar Pointing Aerobee Rocket Control System
SPARCS... Statewide Planning and Research Cooperative System [*New York State Department of Health*] [*Albany*] [*Information service or system*] (IID)
SPARE ... Save Pound Animals from Research Experiments (EA)
SPARE ... System for Projecting Ammunition Repairable End Items [*Military*]
SPAREM ... Spares Provisioning and Requirements Effectiveness Model (PDAA)
SPARES ... Space Radiation Evaluation System [*NASA*] (KSC)
SPAREX ... Canada Regional Industrial Expansion [*Expansion Industrielle Regionale*], Prince Albert, Saskatchewan [*Library symbol National Library of Canada*] (BIB)
SPARK ... Saboteurs for a Philistine America Redeemed from Kultur [*From book, "Bringing Down the House," by Richard P. Brickner*]
SPARK ... Screen Pattern Analyzer and Rescreening Key [*Printing process*]
SPARK ... Seminars on Practical Applications of Research Knowledge [*Advertising Research Foundation*]
SPARK ... Solid Propellant Advanced Ramjet Kinetic Energy (MCD)
SPARK ... Systematic Pulmono/Cardiac Anaphylaxis Resusitation Kit (MCD)
Sparks ... Sparks' Reports [*British Burma*] [*A publication*] (DLA)
SPARM ... Solid-Propellant Augmented Rocket Motor [*Navy*]
SPARM ... Sparrow Antiradiation Missile (MCD)
SPARMIS... Standard Police Automated Resource Management Information System
SPARMO... Solar Particles and Radiations Monitoring Organization
SPARPS... Spares and Repair Parts Support [*Navy*] (NG)
SPARR ... Self-Contained Perspective Approach Rotor Blade RADAR (IAA)
SPARR ... Steerable Paraboloid Azimuth Radio Reflector (IAA)
SPARS ... Semper Paratus [*US Coast Guard Women's Auxiliary; name taken from Coast Guard motto*]
SPARS ... Site Production and Reduction System
SPARS ... Society of Professional Audio Recording Services (EA)
SPARS ... Space Precision Altitude [*or Attitude*] Reference System
SPARSA... Sferics, Position [*or Pulse*], Azimuth, Rate, and Spectrum Analyzer
SPARSIM... Spartan Simulation [*Missile system evaluation*] (RDA)
SPART ... Space Research and Technology [*Report*] [*NASA*] (KSC)
SPART ... Sunny Point Army Terminal
SPARTA ... Sequential Programmed Automatic Recording Transistor Analyzer
SPARTA ... Spatial Antimissile Research Test in Australia (IAA)
SPARTA ... Special Antimissile Research Tests in Australia
SPARTA ... System for Private Access for Reservations and Travel Agents [*British*] (DI)
SpartaFd... Sparta Foods [*Commercial firm Associated Press*] (SAG)
SPARTAN... Shuttle-Pointed Autonomous Research Tool for Astronomy [*NASA*]
SPARTAN... Special Proficiency at Rugged Training and Nation Building [*Training program for Green Berets*] [*Army*]
SPARTAN... System for Personnel Automated Reports, Transactions, and Notices [*Census Bureau, NASA*]
SpartaPh... Sparta Pharmaceutical, Inc. [*Associated Press*] (SAG)
Spartch ... Spartech Corp. [*Associated Press*] (SAG)
SpartMot... Spartan Motors, Inc. [*Associated Press*] (SAG)
Sparton ... Sparton Corp. [*Associated Press*] (SAG)
SPAS ... Safety Performance Analysis System [*FAA*] (TAG)
SPAS ... Security Police Automated System [*Air Force*] (GFGA)
SPAS ... Serial Poll Active State (IAA)
SPAS ... Shipboard Pollution Abatement System [*Navy*] (CAAL)
SPAS ... Shuttle Pallet Satellite [*NASA*]
SPAS ... Skill Performance Aids
SPAS ... Social Service Department, Prince Albert, Saskatchewan [*Library symbol National Library of Canada*] (NLC)
SPA-S ... Societa Prodotti Antibiotici [*Italy*] [*Research code symbol*]
SPAS ... Societatis Philosophicae Americanae Socius [*Member of the American Philosophical Society*] [*Latin*]
SPAS ... Solar Proton Alpha Spectrometer
SPAS ... Student's Perception of Ability Scale (EDAC)
SPASA ... Servicios Politecnicos Aereos SA [*Spain ICAO designator*] (FAAC)
SPASE ... South Pole Air Shower Experiment [*Astronomy*]
SPASEC ... Space Track Sensor Computer (IAA)
SPASEP ... Secretaria Permanente del Acuerdo Sudamericano de Estupefacientes y Psicotropicos [*Permanent Secretariat of the South American Agreement on Narcotic Drugs and Psychotropic Substances - PSSAANDPS*] [*Argentina*] (EAIO)
SPASM ... Self-Propelled Air-to-Surface Missile (MCD)
SPASM ... Smithsonian Package for Algebra and Symbolic Mathematics (MCD)
SPASM ... Space Propulsion Automated Synthesis Modeling [*Program*]
SPASM ... System Performance and Activity Software Monitor [*Computer science*] (IEEE)
SPAST ... Special Assistant [*Navy*]
SPASUR... Space Surveillance System [*Navy*]
SPASYN... Space-Syncromesh
SPAT ... Aguas Calientes [*Peru*] [*ICAO location identifier*] (ICLI)
SPAT ... Self-Propelled Antitank Gun (MCD)
SPAT ... Silicon Precision Alloy Transistor
SPAT ... Slow Paroxysmal Atrial Tachycardia [*Medicine*] (DMAA)
SPAT ... Spleen Antigen [*Complement Fixation*] Test [*Immunology*]
SPAT ... Supplementary Pay Appeals Tribunal [*British*] (DI)
SPAT ... Systems Programming Aptitude Test
SPATA ... Society of Polish-American Travel Agents (EA)
SPATA ... Swimming Pool and Allied Trades Association [*British*] (DBA)
SPATE ... Sergeant Production Automatic Test Equipment
SPATE ... South Pacific Association for Teacher Education [*Later, ATEA*] (EA)
SPATE ... Student Personnel Association for Teacher Education [*Later, AHEAD*] (EA)
Spatialght... Spatialight, Inc. [*Associated Press*] (SAG)
SpatialT ... Spatial Technology, Inc. [*Associated Press*] (SAG)
Spatlzr ... Spatializer Audio Labs, Inc. [*Associated Press*] (SAG)
SPATS ... South Pacific Air Transportation Service [*Navy*]
SPAU ... Signal Processing [*or Processor*] Arithmetic Unit [*Navy*]
SPAU ... Stable Platform Alignment Unit
Spaulding... Spaulding's Reports [*71-73 Maine*] [*A publication*] (DLA)
SPAW ... Learning Resource Centre, Woodland Campus, Saskatchewan Institute of Applied Science and Technology, Prince Albert, Saskatchewan [*Library symbol National Library of Canada*] (BIB)
SPAWAR... Space and Naval Warfare Systems Command [*Washington, DC Navy*] (GRD)
SPAWG ... Special Activity Wing (MUGU)
SPAWN ... Salmon Protection Association of Western Newfoundland [*Canada*] (ASF)
SPAYZ ... Spatial Property Analyzer
SPAZ ... Spatializer Audio Labs [*NASDAQ symbol*] (TTSB)
SPAZ ... Spatializer Audio Labs, Inc. [*NASDAQ symbol*] (SAG)
SPB ... ASA [*Former USSR ICAO designator*] (FAAC)
SPB ... Scottish Prayer Book [*Episcopalian*]
SPB ... Seaplane Base
SPB ... Shergottite Parent Body [*Planetary science*]
SPB ... Ship's Plotting Board
SPB ... Silver-Plated Bronze
SPB ... Society of the Precious Blood [*Anglican religious community*]
SPB ... Solar Particle Beams
SPB ... Sotheby Parke Bernet [*Formerly, PB*] [*Manhattan art auction house*]
SPB ... Special Pathogens Branch [*Centers for Disease Control*]
SPB ... Spindle Pole Body [*Cell biology*]
SPB ... Springboard Resources Ltd. [*Vancouver Stock Exchange symbol*]
SPB ... Standardized Performance Battery [*Acoustics*]
SPB ... Standard Practice Bulletin (MCD)
SPB ... Stored Program Buffer
SPB ... St. Thomas [*Virgin Islands*] Seaplane Base [*Airport symbol*] (OAG)
SPB ... Summary Plot Board (SAA)

SPB .... Surplus Property Board
SPB .... Systems Personnel Branch (SAA)
SPBA .... Society of Professional Benefit Administrators [*Washington, DC*] (EA)
SPBA .... Specialty Paper and Board Affiliates [*Later, API*] (EA)
SpBaU .... Universidad de Barcèlona, Biblioteca Universitaria y Provincal, Barcelona, Spain [*Library symbol Library of Congress*] (LCLS)
SpBaU-SQ .... Universidad de Barcelona, Facultad de Quimica y Fisica, Barcelona, Spain [*Library symbol*] [*Library of Congress*] (LCLS)
SPBB .... Moyobamba [*Peru*] [*ICAO location identifier*] (ICLI)
SPBC .... Caballococha [*Peru*] [*ICAO location identifier*] (ICLI)
SPBC .... Saint Paul Bible College [*Saint Bonifacius, MN*]
SPBC .... Society of Professional Business Consultants [*Chicago, IL*] (EA)
SPBC .... South Pacific Base Command [*Navy World War II*]
SPBC .... St. Paul Bancorp [*NASDAQ symbol*] (TTSB)
SPBC .... St. Paul Bancorp, Inc. [*NASDAQ symbol*] (NQ)
SPBD .... Springboard (NVT)
SPBE .... Service de Presse Baptiste Europeen [*European Baptist Press Service - EBPS*] (EAIO)
SPBE .... Society of Parrot Breeders and Exhibitors (EA)
SPBEC .... South Pacific Bureau for Economic Cooperation in Developing Uniform Maritime Standards for the Pacific Area [*Suva, Fiji*] (EAIO)
SPBI .... Serikat Buruh Pertjetakan Indonesia [*Printing Workers' Union of Indonesia*]
SPBI .... Serum Protein-Bound Iodine [*Clinical chemistry*] (AAMN)
SPBI .... Society for Proclaiming Britain in Israel
SPBI .... Speciality Paperboard, Inc. [*NASDAQ symbol*] (SAG)
SPBI .... Specialty Paperboard [*NASDAQ symbol*] (TTSB)
SPBI .... Specialty Paperboard, Inc. [*NASDAQ symbol*] (SAG)
SPBK .... Speed Brake (NASA)
SPBL .... Bellavista/Huallaga [*Peru*] [*ICAO location identifier*] (ICLI)
SPBM .... Single Point Buoy Mooring [*Oil platform*]
SPBOT .... Stationers and Publishers Board of Trade [*Later, Stationery and Office Equipment Board of Trade*]
SPBP .... Society for the Preservation of Birds of Prey (EA)
SPBR .... Iberia [*Peru*] [*ICAO location identifier*] (ICLI)
SPBR .... Speed Brake (MCD)
SPBS .... Jeberos/Bellavista [*Peru*] [*ICAO location identifier*] (ICLI)
SPBS .... Schweizerische Partei der Behinderten und Sozialbenachteiligten [*Swiss Party of the Handicapped and Socially Disadvantaged*] [*Political party*] (PPW)
SPBS .... Standard Property Book System [*Army*]
SPBS-R .... Standard Property Book System - Redesign [*or Redesigned*] [*Army*]
SPBT .... Obenteni [*Peru*] [*ICAO location identifier*] (ICLI)
SPBT .... Suprapubic Bladder Tap [*Medicine*] (MEDA)
SPBT .... Suprapubic Bladder Tap [*Urology*] (DAVI)
SPBU .... Vista Breau [*Peru*] [*ICAO location identifier*] (ICLI)
SPBW .... Society for the Preservation of Beers from the Wood [*British*] (EAIO)
SPC .... Institute for Studies of Destructive Behaviors and the Suicide Prevention Centerof Los Angeles [*California*] (EA)
SPC .... Political Committee at Senior Level [*NATO*] (NATG)
SPC .... Saint Paul Companies, Inc. [*NYSE symbol*] (SAG)
SPC .... Saint Paul's College [*Missouri; Virginia; Washington, DC*]
SPC .... Saint Paul's College, Lawrenceville, VA [*OCLC symbol*] (OCLC)
SPC .... Saint Peter College [*Maryland; New Jersey*]
SPC .... Saint Procopius College [*Illinois*]
SPC .... Salicylamide, Phenacetin [*Acetophenetidin*], and Caffeine [*Pharmacy*]
SPC .... Salkowski Positive Compound (OA)
SPC .... Santa Cruz La Palma [*Canary Islands*] [*Airport symbol*] (OAG)
SPC .... Saratoga Processing Co. Ltd. [*Vancouver Stock Exchange symbol*]
SPC .... Satellite Processing Center [*Military*]
SPC .... School Psychology Certificate (PGP)
SPC .... Seattle Pacific College [*Washington*]
SPC .... Self-Polishing Copolymer [*Anti-fouling paint*] (DS)
SPC .... Self-Programming Compiler [*Software*] [*Computer science*]
SPC .... Sequence Parameter Checking (SAA)
SPC .... Set Point Control [*Computer science*] (ECII)
SPC .... Set Point Controller
SPC .... Shanghai Petrochemical Co. [*Commercial firm*] [*China*]
SPC .... Shipping and Packing Cost (NASA)
SPC .... Shop Process Card [*Navy*] (DNAB)
SPC .... Shuttle Pin Clutch
SPC .... Shuttle Processing Contractor [*NASA*]
spc .... Silicon Point-Contact (IDOE)
spc .... Silver-Plated Copper (IDOE)
SPC .... Silver-Plated Copper
SPC .... Simple Prose Coefficient [*Publishing*]
SPC .... Simultaneous Prism and Cover (Test) [*Ophthalmology*]
SPC .... Single Palmar Crease [*Medicine*] (DMAA)
SPC .... Single Paper Covered [*Wire insulation*] (IAA)
SPC .... Single Prime Contractor [*Weapon system procurement*] [*Air Force*] (AAG)
SPC .... Sisters of St. Paul of Chartres (TOCD)
SPC .... Site Programmer Course
SPC .... Size-Press Coated [*Publishing*]
SPC .... Skalnate-Pleso [*Czechoslovakia*] [*Seismograph station code, US Geological Survey*] (SEIS)
SPC .... Skyworld Airlines, Inc. [*ICAO designator*] (FAAC)
SPC .... Small Peripheral Controller
SPC .... Soap Perfumery and Cosmetics [*A publication*]
SPC .... Socialist Party of Canada [*Political party*]
SPC .... Socialist Party of Chile
SPC .... Socialist Party of Croatia [*Political party*] (EY)
SPC .... Socialist Party of Cyprus [*Political party*] (EAIO)
SPC .... Society for Philosophy of Creativity (EA)
SPC .... Society for the Prevention of Crime [*Defunct*] (EA)
SPC .... Software Productivity Consortium (MCD)
SPC .... Software Publishing Corp.
SPC .... Solar Pointing Control
SPC .... Solid-Propellant Combustion
SPC .... Solid-Propellant Conference
S/P/C .... Sotto Protesto per Mettere in Conto [*Under Protest to Place to Account*] [*Italian*]
SPC .... Southern Pacific Communications (NITA)
SPC .... Southern Pacific Communications Corp.
SPC .... Southern Ports Foreign Committee, Chicago IL [*STAC*]
SPC .... South Pacific Commission [*See also CPS*] (EAIO)
SPC .... South Polar Cap [*A filamentary mark on Mars*]
SPC .... Soy Protein Council (EA)
SPC .... Space
SPC .... Space Development Conference
SPC .... Space Polymer Chemistry (SSD)
SPC .... Space Projects Center [*NASA*]
SPC .... Spacer [*Technical drawings*]
SpC .... Spanish Columbia, San Sebastian [*Record label*] [*Spain*]
SPC .... Spare Parts Catalog
SPC .... Special Code
Sp C .... Special Commissioner (DLA)
SPC .... Special Common [*Projectile*]
SPC .... Specialist, Classification Interviewer [*Navy rating*]
Sp C .... Specialist in Counseling (PGP)
SPC .... Special Political Committee [*Australia*]
SPC .... Special Premiers Conference (EERA)
SPC .... Special Program Code [*Navy*]
SPC .... Special Project Code [*IRS*]
SPC .... Special Purpose Chaff [*Navy*] (CAAL)
SPC .... Special Purpose Computer
SPC .... Specification
SPC .... Specific Propellant Consumption
SPC .... Speech Processing Chip (NITA)
SPC .... Springfield-Cape Girardeau [*Diocesan abbreviation*] [*Missouri*] (TOCD)
SPC .... Standard Plate Count [*Microbiology*]
SPC .... Standard Products Committee [*Navy*]
SPC .... Standby Pressure Control [*Nuclear energy*] (NRCH)
SPC .... Starting Point Code (NASA)
SPC .... Starting Point Counter [*NASA*] (IAA)
SPC .... Static Power Conservers (MCD)
SPC .... Static Power Converter (IAA)
SPC .... Static Pressure Compensation
SPC .... Station Program Cooperative [*Public television*]
SPC .... Statistical Process Control
SPC .... Sterilizable Potting Compound
SPC .... Stigmastanyl(phosphorylcholine) [*Biochemistry*]
SPC .... Still-Picture Camera (DNAB)
SPC .... Stockage Priority Code [*Military*] (AFIT)
SPC .... Storage Planning Centre [*Shipping*]
SPC .... Storage Program Computer (IAA)
SPC .... Stored Program Command [*or Control*] [*Computer science*]
SPC .... Stored Program Control [*Telecommunications*] (IAA)
SPC .... Storm Prediction Center [*Marine science*] (OSRA)
SPC .... Storms Prediction Center (USDC)
SPC .... St. Paul Cos. [*NYSE symbol*] (TTSB)
SPC .... St. Paul's Cathedral [*London, England*]
SPC .... Strategy and Planning Committee [*Military*]
SPC .... Subcontract Plans Committee
SPC .... Sucrose-Phosphate-Citrate [*A culture medium*]
SPC .... Sugar Packet Club (EA)
SPC .... Suicide Prevention Center (IIA)
SPC .... Summary Punch Control [*Computer science*] (IAA)
SPC .... Supplemental Planning Card (AAG)
SPC .... Supplementary Patent Certificate [*European Community*]
SPC .... Supplementary Protection Certificates [*For European patents*]
SPC .... Suspended Plaster Ceiling [*Technical drawings*]
SPC .... Switching and Processing Center [*EFTS*] [*Banking*]
SPC .... Syndicat des Postiers du Canada [*Canadian Union of Postal Workers - CUPW*]
SPC .... Synoptic Properties Code (MCD)
SPC .... System Professional Computer (HGAA)
SPC .... Systemwide Program Committee [*Individually-guided education*] (AEE)
SPCA .... Barraca [*Peru*] [*ICAO location identifier*] (ICLI)
SPCA .... School Projectionist Club of America [*Defunct*] (EA)
SPCA .... Serum Prothrombin Conversion Accelerator [*Factor VII*] [*Also, PPCA Hematology*]
SPCA .... Society for the Prevention of Cruelty to Animals
SPCA .... Southern Pulpwood Conservation Association [*Later, SFI*] (EA)
SPCA .... Spark Plug Collectors of America (EA)
SPCA .... Special-Purpose Cable Assembly
SPCAP .... Society of Professors of Child and Adolescent Psychiatry (EA)
SPCAT .... Special Category (MSA)
SPCB .... Aguas Blancas [*Peru*] [*ICAO location identifier*] (ICLI)
SPCB .... Single-Pole Circuit Breaker (IAA)
SPCC .... Sample Polarity Coincidence Correlator (IAA)
SPCC .... Servo Pressure Control Console
SPCC .... Ship's Parts Control Center
SPCC .... Society for the Prevention of Cruelty to Children
SPCC .... Southern Pacific Communications Corp.
SPCC .... Space Parts Control Center (MUGU)
SPCC .... Spill Prevention Control and Countermeasure [*Petroleum industry*]

SPCC .... Staggered Phase Carrier Cancellation
SPCC .... Standardization, Policy, and Coordination Committee [*NATO*] (NATG)
SPCC .... State Pollution Control Commission [*of New South Wales*] [*State*] (EERA)
SPCC .... Stored Program CAMAC [*Computer-Aided Measurement and Control*] Channel [*Computer science*]
SPCC .... Strength Power and Communications Cable
SPCC .... STS [*Shuttle Test Station*] Processing Control Center [*NASA*] (GFGA)
SPCC .... Study Planning and Coordinating Committee [*Army*]
SPCC .... Sugar Packet Collectors Club (EA)
SPCC .... Super-Packed Capillary Column [*Spectroscopy*]
SPCC .... System Performance Check Compound
SpcChm .... Specialty Chemical Resources, Inc. [*Associated Press*] (SAG)
SPCD .... Space Communications Division [*Military*]
SPCD .... Specification Control Drawing (MCD)
sp cd .... Spinal Cord [*Medicine*] (MAE)
SPCD .... Syndrome of Primary Ciliary Dyskinesia [*Medicine*] (DMAA)
SPCDS .... Small Permanent Communications and Display Segment (MCD)
SPCEC .... Stereo Photographers, Collectors, and Enthusiasts Club (EA)
SPCF .... Special Project Control File [*IRS*]
SPCFCTN ..... Specification
Sp Ch .... Spears' South Carolina Chancery Reports [*A publication*] (DLA)
SPCH .... Speech
SPCH .... Sport Chalet [*NASDAQ symbol*] (TTSB)
SPCH .... Sport Chalet, Inc. [*NASDAQ symbol*] (SAG)
SPCH .... Tocache [*Peru*] [*ICAO location identifier*] (ICLI)
SPCHG .... Supercharge
SPCHGR ...... Supercharger (AAG)
SPCHR .... Supercharger (IAA)
SPCK .... Society for Promoting Christian Knowledge [*Publisher*] [*British*]
SPCL .... Pucallpa [*Peru*] [*ICAO location identifier*] (ICLI)
SPCL .... Single Product Cost Leadership (MHDB)
SPCL .... Special (MSA)
SPCLASGN ... Special Assignment [*Military*] (NVT)
SpclDv .... Special Devices, Inc. [*Associated Press*] (SAG)
SpclEqp .... Speciality Equipment [*Associated Press*] (SAG)
SpclEqp .... Specialty Equipment [*Commercial firm Associated Press*] (SAG)
SPCLN .... Special Cleaning
SpclPap .... Speciality Paperboard, Inc. [*Associated Press*] (SAG)
SpclPap .... Specialty Paperboard, Inc. [*Associated Press*] (SAG)
SPCLST .... Specialist
SPCLTY .... Specialty
SPCLY .... Especially (FAAC)
SPCM .... Contamana [*Peru*] [*ICAO location identifier*] (ICLI)
SPCM .... Master Chief Steam Propulsionman [*Navy rating*]
SPCM .... Spanish Campaign Medal
SPCM .... Special Court-Martial
SPCMO .... Special Court-Martial Order
SPCMWOMJ ... Special Court-Martial without a Military Judge (AFM)
SPCN .... Silver-Plated Copperweld Conductor (IAA)
SPCN .... Specially Constructed Vehicle [*Automotive engineering*]
SPCN .... Stored Program Controlled Network [*Telecommunications*]
SPCNI .... Society for Pacific Coast Native Irises (EA)
SPCO .... Allegro New Media, Inc. [*NASDAQ symbol*] (SAG)
SPCO .... Software Publishing [*NASDAQ symbol*] (TTSB)
SPCO .... Software Publishing Corp. [*Mountain View, CA*] [*NASDAQ symbol*] (NQ)
SPCO .... Southern Pacific Co.
SPCOA .... Spark Plug Collectors of America (EA)
SPCONV ...... Speed Converter
SPCP .... Pucacaca [*Peru*] [*ICAO location identifier*] (ICLI)
SPCP .... Single Prime Contractor Policy [*Air Force*] (AAG)
SPCP .... Society of Professors of Child Psychiatry [*Later, SPCAP*] (EA)
SPCP .... Standardization and Parts Control Program
SPCP .... Steam Propulsion Control Panel (DNAB)
SPCPrM .... St. Paul Cos. LLC 6%Cv'MIPS' [*NYSE symbol*] (TTSB)
SPCR .... Scratch Pad Control Register [*Computer science*] (IAA)
SPCR .... Silicon Planar Controlled Rectifier (IAA)
SPCR .... Spacer
SPCR .... Spare Parts Change Request
Spcr .... Spectinomycin Resistance
Sp Cr Ct ...... Special Criminal Court (DLA)
SPCS .... Schedule Planning and Control System (MCD)
SPCS .... Selective Paging Communications System
SPCS .... Ship Production Control System (PDAA)
SPCS .... Standard and Poor's Compustat Services (NITA)
SPCS .... Standard & Poor's COMPUSTAT Services, Inc. [*Also, an information service or system*] (IID)
SPCS .... State Plane Coordinate System [*National Geodetic Survey Division*] [*National Oceanic and Atmospheric Administration*]
SPCS .... Static Power Conversion System
SPCS .... Statistical Process Control Society (EA)
SPCS .... Storage and Processing Control System
SPCS .... Surgical Postcaval Shunt [*Medicine*]
SPC/SQC ...... Statistical Process/Statistical Quality Control
SPCT .... Chota [*Peru*] [*ICAO location identifier*] (ICLI)
SPCT .... Science Process Competency Test (EDAC)
SPCT .... Spectrian Corp. [*NASDAQ symbol*] (SAG)
SPCT .... Statistical Process Control Toolbox (RDA)
SPCTG .... Spherical Cartridge
Spctran .... SpecTran Corp. [*Associated Press*] (SAG)
Sp Ct RRRA ... Special Court Regional Railroad Reorganization Act [*A publication*] (DLA)
SpctSig .... Spectrum Signal Processing [*Commercial firm Associated Press*] (SAG)
SPCTYS .... Society for the Prevention of Cruelty to Young Singers
SPCU .... Simulation Process Control Unit (MCD)
SPCU .... Skylab Process Control Unit [*NASA*]
SPCUS .... Sweet Potato Council of the United States (EA)
SPCW .... Specialist, Chemical Warfare [*Navy rating*]
SPCW .... Stored Program Command Word [*Computer science*] (NASA)
SPCZ .... South Pacific Convergence Zone (MCD)
SPD .... Airspeed Aviation, Inc. [*Canada ICAO designator*] (FAAC)
SPD .... Doctor of Political Science
SPD .... Safety Program Directive [*NASA*]
SPD .... Saidpur [*Bangladesh*] [*Airport symbol*] (OAG)
SPD .... Salmon Poisoning Disease [*Medicine*] (AAMN)
SPD .... Salutem Plurimam Dicit [*He Wishes Much Health*] [*Latin*]
SPD .... Sampled [*Tea trade*] (ROG)
SPD .... Sample Preparation and DNA [*Deoxyribonucleic Acid*] Probe
SPD .... S-Band Polarization Diversity
SPD .... Scientific Passenger Pod (MCD)
SPD .... Seaplane Depot Ship
SPD .... Sedona Industries Ltd. [*Toronto Stock Exchange symbol*]
SPD .... Semipermeable Dressing [*Medicine*]
SPD .... Separation Program Designator [*Military*] (AABC)
SPD .... Serial Poll Disable (IAA)
SPD .... Service Project Drawing
SPD .... Shearing, Piling, and Disking [*Forest management*]
SPD .... Ship Performance Department [*David W. Taylor Naval Ship Research and Development Center*]
SPD .... Ship Planning Document (DNAB)
SPD .... Ship Project Directive [*Navy*]
SPD .... Sigma Phi Delta (EA)
SPD .... Silicon Photodiode
SPD .... Single Path Doppler [*RADAR*] (AAG)
SPD .... Situation Projected Display
SPD .... Skylab Program Directive [*NASA*] (KSC)
SPD .... Smokeless Powder, Diphenylamine (DNAB)
SPD .... Social Democratic Party [*Germany*] [*Political party*]
SPD .... Society for Pediatric Dermatology (EA)
SPD .... Society of Professional Drivers (EA)
SPD .... Society of Publication Designers (EA)
SPD .... Sociopathic Personality Disorder [*Psychiatry*] (DAVI)
SPD .... Software Product Description [*Computer science*] (MHDI)
SPD .... Southern Procurement Division [*Navy*]
SPD .... South Pacific Division [*Army World War II*]
SPD .... South Polar Distance
SPD .... Sozialdemokratische Partei Deutschlands [*Social Democratic Party of Germany*] [*West Germany*]
SpD .... Spanish Decca, San Sebastian [*Record label*] [*Spain*]
SPD .... Spectral Power Density [*Electronics*]
SPD .... Spectral Power Distribution (MCD)
SPD .... Speech Processing Device
SPD .... Speed (AABC)
Spd .... Speed
Spd .... Spermidine [*Biochemistry*]
SPD .... Sprayed (WGA)
SPD .... Standard Design Platform
SPD .... Standard Periodical Database [*Oxbridge Communications, Inc.*] [*Information service or system*] (CRD)
SPD .... Standard Periodical Directory [*A publication*]
SPD .... Standard Practice Directive [*NASA*] (NASA)
SPD .... Standard Products [*NYSE symbol*] (TTSB)
SPD .... Standard Products Co. [*NYSE symbol*] (SPSG)
SPD .... Standard Program Device (NITA)
SPD .... State Programs Division [*Environmental Protection Agency*] (GFGA)
SPD .... Static Pressure Distribution
SPD .... Statistical Policy Division [*Office of Management and Budget*]
SPD .... Steamer Pays Dues [*Shipping*]
SPD .... Stick Positioning Device (MCD)
SPD .... Storage Pool Disease
SPD .... Stored Program Decoder [*or Decommutation*]
SPD .... St. Peter's Dome Lookout [*New Mexico*] [*Seismograph station code, US Geological Survey*] (SEIS)
SPD .... Strategic Posture Display (MCD)
SPD .... Student Pilot Disposition (DNAB)
SPD .... Subcorneal Pustular Dermatosis [*Sneddon-Wilkinson disease*] [*Dermatology*]
SPD .... Subjective Probability Distribution
SPD .... Subject to Permission to Deal [*Finance*] (WDAA)
SPD .... Summary Plan Description
SPD .... Superheater Protection Device (DNAB)
SPD .... Supplemental Program Directive (AFIT)
SPD .... Supplementary Petroleum Duty [*Tax*] [*British*]
SPD .... Surge Protective Device (MCD)
SPD .... Suspended-Particle Display [*Glazing technology*]
SPD .... Synchronized Parallel Displacement [*Automotive engineering*]
SPD .... Synchronizer for Peripheral Devices
SPD .... Synchronous Phase Demodulator
SPD .... Synpolydactyly [*Medicine*]
SPD .... System Performance Demonstration
SPD .... System Program Directive (AFIT)
SPD .... System Program Director [*Air Force*] (MCD)
SPD .... Systems Parameters Document (AAG)
SPD .... Systems Program Documentation
SPDA .... Sea Photo Diffraction Analysis (PDAA)
SPDA .... Single-Premium Deferred Annuity [*Insurance*]

SPDAC Societe de Perception de Droit d'Auteur du Canada (AC)
SPDB Subsystem Power Distribution Box (MCD)
SPDBK Speed Brake (MCD)
SPDC Spare Parts Distributing Center [*Navy*]
SPDC Stored Program Data Compressor [*Computer science*] (IAA)
SPDC Strio-Pallido-Dentate Calcinosis [*Medicine*] (DMAA)
SPDCI Standard Payload Display and Control Interface (NASA)
SPDCU Subsurface Probe Data and Control Unit
SP DEL Special Delivery (WDAA)
SPDF Smokeless Powder, Diphenylamine, Flashless (DNAB)
SPDF Special Projects Data Facility
SPDF Swedish Post Defense Forces
SpdFam SpeedFam International, Inc. [*Associated Press*] (SAG)
SPDG Spiral Point Drill Geometry
SPDHF Special Pay for Duty Subject to Hostile Fire [*Military*]
SPDI Special Discriminant (CAAL)
SPDL Spin-Dependent Luminescence [*Physics*]
SPDL Spindle (MSA)
SPDL Standard Page Description Language [*ISO/IEC*] [*Computer science*]
SPDLTR Speedletter
SPDM Special Purpose Dexterous Manipulator
SPDM Subprocessor with Dynamic Microprogramming
SPDMS Shuttle Program Data Management System [*NASA*] (SSD)
SPDMTR Speedometer
SPDN Screen Printing and Display News [*A publication*] (DGA)
SPDN Smokeless Powder, Diphenylamine, Nonvolatile (DNAB)
SPD NAV Speed Navigation (MCD)
SPDO Mollendo [*Peru*] [*ICAO location identifier*] (ICLI)
SPDOM Speedometer (MSA)
SPDP Society of Professional Data Processors (IAA)
SPDP Stored Program Data Processor (KSC)
SPDP Succinimidyl(pyridyldithio)propionate [*Organic chemistry*]
SPDR Software Preliminary Design Review [*NASA*] (NASA)
SPDR Special Drill [*Tool*] (AAG)
SPDR Spider [*Engineering acoustics*]
SPDR Standard & Poors Depositary Receipts [*Associated Press*] (SAG)
SP/DR Systems Performance/Design Requirements
SPDRAB Society for the Prevention of Disparaging Remarks about Brooklyn
SPDS Safe-Practice Data Sheet (MSA)
SPDS Safety Parameter Display System [*Instrumentation*]
SPDS Self-Power Density Spectrum (IAA)
SPDS Sequential Payload Delivery System (MCD)
SPDS Strategic Platform Defense Study [*DoD*]
SPDS Suggestion Program Data System [*Military*]
SPDT Single-Pole, Double-Throw [*Switch*]
SPDTDB Single-Pole, Double-Throw, Double-Break [*Switch*]
SPDTNCDB Single-Pole, Double-Throw, Normally-Closed, Double-Break [*Switch*]
SPDTNO Single-Pole, Double-Throw, Normally-Open [*Switch*]
SPDTNODB Single-Pole, Double-Throw, Normally-Open, Double-Break [*Switch*]
SPDTSW Single-Pole, Double-Throw Switch
SPDU Session Protocol Data Unit [*Telecommunications*] (OSI)
SPDW Smokeless Powder, Diphenylamine, Reworked (DNAB)
SPDW South Pacific Deep Water
SPDWY Speedway
SPDY Speedy
Spe Durandi. Speculum Judiciale [*A publication*] (DSA)
s-pe-- Peru [*MARC geographic area code Library of Congress*] (LCCP)
SPE Secondary Particulate Emissions [*Environmental Protection Agency*] (GFGA)
SPE Senior Project Engineer
SPE Sepulot [*Malaysia*] [*Airport symbol*] (AD)
SPE Serial Poll Enable (IAA)
SPE Serum Protein Electrolytes [*Biochemistry*] (DAVI)
SPE Serum Protein Electrophoresis
SPE Service Propulation Engine (IAA)
SPE Shaft Position Encoder
SPE Sian [*Republic of China*] [*Seismograph station code, US Geological Survey*] (SEIS)
SPE Signal Processing Element [*Navy*]
SPE Silicon Planar Epitaxial (IAA)
SPE Simultaneous Purging Extraction [*Chemistry*]
SPE Sliding Padeye (MCD)
SPE Small Processing Element [*Computer science*]
SPE Society for Photographic Education (EA)
SPE Society for Pure English
SPE Society of Petroleum Engineers (EA)
SPE Society of Plastics Engineers (EA)
SPE Society of Professors of Education (EA)
SPE Solar Proton Event [*Geophysics*]
SPE Solid Phase Epitaxy
SPE Solid-Phase Extraction
SPE Solid Polymer Electrolyte
SPE Sony Pictures Entertainment [*Commercial firm*] (ECON)
SPE Space Processing Equipment [*Astronautics*]
SPE Special Purpose Electronics (MCD)
SPE Special-Purpose Equipment
SPE Sperry UNIVAC Information Center, Blue Bell, PA [*OCLC symbol*] (OCLC)
SPE Spherical Probable Error
SPE Sprague Electric Co. [*ICAO designator*] (FAAC)
SPE Standard Polishing Index
SPE Static Phase Error [*NASA*]
SPE Station Project Engineer [*NASA*]
SPE Stepped Potential Electrode [*Electrode chemistry*]
SPE Stop Project ELF [*Extremely Low Frequency system*] [*Defunct*] (EA)
SPE Stored Program Element
SPE Streptococcal Enterotoxin [*Medicine*]
SPE Studies in Philosophy and Education [*A publication*] (AEBS)
SPE Subport of Embarkation
SPE Sucrose Polyester [*Pharmacology*]
SPE Sun-Planet-Earth [*Astronomy*]
SPE Superficial Punctate Erosions [*Ophthalmology*] (DAVI)
SPE Switch Processing Element (NITA)
SPE System Performance Evaluation (KSC)
SPE Systems Performance Effectiveness
SPE Unilabo [*France*] [*Research code symbol*]
SPEA Panamanian Society of Engineers and Architects (IAA)
SPEA Sales Promotion Executives Association [*Later, MCEI*] (EA)
SPEA Scottish Physical Education Association [*British*]
SPEA Southeastern Poultry and Egg Association (EA)
SPEA Streptococcal Pyrogenic Exotoxin A [*Immunochemistry*]
SPEAC Selma Project Education Alternatives Center [*Alabama*] (EA)
SPEAC Solar Photovoltaic Energy Advisory Committee [*Terminated, 1986*] (EGAO)
SPEAC Special Purpose Electronic Area Correlator (MHDI)
SPEAHR Society for the Protection of East Asians' Human Rights/USA (EA)
SPEAK Society for Promoting and Encouraging the Arts and Knowledge of the Church (EA)
SPEAL Special-Purpose Engineering Analysis Language (MCD)
SPEAR Selective Parenteral and Enteral Anti-Sepsis Regimen [*Medicine*] (DMAA)
SPEAR Signal Processing, Evaluation, Alert, and Report [*Navy*] (NVT)
SPEAR SLAC Positron-Electron Asymmetric Ring
SPEAR Small Payload Ejection and Recovery for the Space Shuttle [*NASA*] (MCD)
SPEAR Source Performance Evaluation and Reporting
SPEAR Spaceborne Earth Applications Ranging System (MCD)
Spear Spears' South Carolina Law Reports [*1842-44*] [*A publication*] (DLA)
SPEAR Special Project Evaluation and Anti-War Warfare Research (DOMA)
SPEAR Squadron Performance Effectiveness Analysis Representation (MCD)
SPEAR Stanford Positron-Electron Axisymmetric Ring
SPEAR Statistical Property Estimation and Regeneration (MCD)
SPEAR Strike Projection Evaluation and Anti-War Warfare Research (DOMA)
SPEAR Supplier Performance Evaluation and Reporting [*or Review*] [*General Motors quality award*]
Spear Ch Spears' South Carolina Chancery Reports [*A publication*] (DLA)
Spear Eq Spears' South Carolina Equity Reports [*A publication*] (DLA)
Spear Ext Spear's Law of Extradition [*A publication*] (DLA)
Spear High Spearman on Highways [*1881*] [*A publication*] (DLA)
SPEARS Satellite Photoelectric Analog Rectification System
SPEARS Satellite Photo Electronic Analog Rectification System (IAA)
SPEARS Screener Proficiency Evaluation and Report System [*FAA*] (TAG)
SPEARS Spaceborne Earth Applications Ranging System [*NASA*]
Spears Spears' South Carolina Equity Reports [*1842-44*] [*A publication*] (DLA)
Spears Spears' South Carolina Law Reports [*A publication*] (DLA)
SPEARS Spill Planning Exercise and Response System [*USCG*] (TAG)
Spears Eq Spears' South Carolina Equity Reports [*A publication*] (DLA)
SPEB Pebas [*Peru*] [*ICAO location identifier*] (ICLI)
SPEB Streptococcal Pyrogenic Exotoxin B [*Immunochemistry*]
SPEBSQSA Society for the Preservation and Encouragement of Barber Shop Quartet Singing inAmerica (EA)
Spec De Specialibus Legibus [*of Philo*] (BJA)
SPEC Scientific Pollution and Environmental Control Society
SPEC Simulation of Propulsion Engine Cycle [*NASA*]
SPEC Society of Professional Engineering Checkers
SPEC South Pacific Bureau for Economic Cooperation (EERA)
SPEC Special [*or Specialist*] (KSC)
SPEC Special
SPEC Species (WGA)
SPEC Specific
SPEC Specification (AFM)
spec Specification (IDOE)
Spec Specification (AAGC)
SPEC Specificity (DMAA)
SPEC Specimen (AAG)
Spec Spectacle [*or Spectacular*] (WGA)
Spec Spectator [*A publication*] (BRI)
SPEC Spectrum
spec Spectrum (IDOE)
SPEC Spectrum Control [*NASDAQ symbol*] (TTSB)
SPEC Spectrum Control, Inc. [*NASDAQ symbol*] (NQ)
SPEC Speculation (WGA)
Spec Speculator [*Guillelmus Durandi*] [*Deceased, 1296*] [*Authority cited in pre-1607 legal work*] (DSA)
spec Speculum [*Obstetrics*] (DAVI)
SPEC Speech Predictive Encoded Communications [*Telephone channels*]
SPEC Speech Predictive Encoding System [*Telephone channels*] (IAA)
SPEC Staff of the Production Executive Committee [*of the WPB*] [*Obsolete*]
SPEC Stored Program Educational Computer
SPEC Streptococcal Pyrogenic Exotoxin C [*Immunochemistry*]
SPEC Studies in the Political Economy of Canada [*Society*]
SPEC Systems and Procedures Exchange Center [*Association of Research Libraries*]
SPECA Society for the Preservation and Enjoyment of Carriages in America [*Defunct*] (EA)
SPECA Supplier Performance Evaluation and Corrective Action (PDAA)
SPECAN Spectral Analysis
spec an Spectrum Analyzer (IDOE)
SPECASTSECNAV Special Assistant to the Secretary of the Navy (DNAB)

SPECAT........ Special Category (AABC)
Sp Ecc & Ad... Spinks' English Ecclesiastical and Admiralty Reports [*164 English Reprint*] [*1853-55*] [*A publication*] (DLA)
SpecCata..... Specialty Catalog Corp. [*Associated Press*] (SAG)
SpecCtl...... Spectrum Controls, Inc. [*Associated Press*] (SAG)
SPECD......... Specification Data Base
SPECDEVCEN... Special Devices Center [*Navy*]
Spec Ed....... Special Education (DAVI)
SPECFORCOM... Special Forces Command [*Navy*] (DNAB)
spec grav..... Specific Gravity (DAVI)
SpecHlth...... Specialized Health Products International, Inc. [*Associated Press*] (SAG)
SPECHNDLG... Special Handling (MCD)
SpecHol....... Spectrum HoloByte, Inc. [*Associated Press*] (SAG)
SPECI.......... Selected Special Weather Report [*Aviation*] (FAAC)
SPECI.......... Special Weather Report [*Aviation*] (DA)
SPECI.......... Specimen (DSUE)
SPECIF........ Specific (WGA)
specif.......... Specification (DAVI)
SPECIFD...... Specified (ROG)
SPECIFN...... Specification (ROG)
SPECINVESDIST... Special Investigations District [*Air Force*]
SPECK......... Safety, Pride, Efficiency, Compatibility, Knowledge (DNAB)
SPECL.......... Special (ROG)
SPECL.......... Specialize
SPECLE........ Specification Language [*Computer science*] (MHDI)
SpecLink..... SpectraLink Corp. [*Associated Press*] (SAG)
SPECLST...... Specialist
SPECMAP.... Spectral Mapping
SpecMu....... Spec's Music, Inc. [*Associated Press*] (SAG)
SPECO......... Steel Products Engineering Co.
SPECOL....... Special Customer-Oriented Language
SPECOM....... Special Command
SPECOMALT... Special Communications Alteration
SPECOMDIV... Special Communications Division [*Navy*] (DNAB)
SPECOMME... Specified Command Middle East [*Military*]
SPECON....... Systems Performance Effectiveness Conference
SPECOPNSSq... Special Operations Squadron [*Air Force*]
SPECOPS...... Special Operations [*Navy*] (NVT)
SPECOR....... Spectral Correlation RADAR (MCD)
SPECPROJOUK... Special Projects Liaison Offices, United Kingdom [*Navy*] (DNAB)
SpecRetl...... Specialty Retail Group [*Commercial firm Associated Press*] (SAG)
specs.......... Specifications (IDOE)
SPECS......... Spectacles (ROG)
SPECS......... Switched Proton Electron Challeltron Spectrometer (BARN)
SpecSci....... SpectraScience, Inc. [*Associated Press*] (SAG)
SPECT.......... Single Photon Emission Computed Tomography
Spect........... Spectacula [*of Martial*] [*Classical studies*] (OCD)
SPECT.......... Spectrograph
SPECT.......... Spectrometer (NASA)
SPECT.......... Spectrum
SPECTA........ Structure-Preserved Error-Correcting Tree Automata (MHDI)
SpecTelec.... Specialty Teleconstructioners [*Associated Press*] (SAG)
SPECTNG..... Specialist Training [*Navy*] (NVT)
SPECTOR..... Single Path Error Correcting Teleprinter over Radio [*Telecommunications*] (IAA)
Spectra........ [*The*] Spectranetics Corp. [*Associated Press*] (SAG)
Spectral...... Spectral Diagnostics, Inc. [*Associated Press*] (SAG)
SPECTRE..... Special Executive for Counterintelligence, Terrorism, Revenge, and Extortion [*Fictitious organization whose agents were characters in the late Ian Fleming's "James Bond" mysteries*]
SPECTRE..... Special Radiation Experiment [*Marine science*] (OSRA)
SPECTRE..... Spectral Radiation Experiment (USDC)
Spectrian..... Spectrian Corp. [*Associated Press*] (SAG)
SPECTROL... Scheduling, Planning, Evaluation, and Cost Control [*Air Force*]
SpectV......... Spectra Vision, Inc. [*Formerly, SPI Holdings, Inc.*] [*Associated Press*] (SAG)
SpectVis...... Spectra Vision, Inc. [*Formerly, SPI Holdings, Inc.*] [*Associated Press*] (SAG)
Specu.......... Speculator [*Guillelmus Durandi*] [*Deceased, 1296*] [*Authority cited in pre-1607 legal work*] (DSA)
Specu.......... Speculum [*A publication*] (BRI)
Specula........ Speculator [*Guillelmus Durandi*] [*Deceased, 1296*] [*Authority cited in pre-1607 legal work*] (DSA)
SPECVER..... Specification Verification [*Computer science*] (IEEE)
SPECWAR.... Special Warfare (DOMA)
SPED........... Special Education
SPED........... Special Education Director
Sp Ed.......... Specialist in Education [*Academic degree*]
SPED........... Sulfur, Phosphorus, Emission Detector [*Chromatograph accessory*]
SPED........... Supersonic Planetary Entry Decelerator (KSC)
SPEDAC....... Solid-State, Parallel, Expandable, Differential Analyzer Computer
SPEDCO....... Southeastern Pennsylvania Development Corp.
SPEDE......... System for Processing Educational Data Electronically
SPEDIAT...... Special Diary Transcript [*Military*]
Sp Ed S....... Special Education Specialist (PGP)
SPEDTAC..... Stored Program Educational Transistorized Automatic Computer
SPEDY......... Summer Program for Economically Disadvantaged Youth [*Department of Labor*]
SPEE........... Society for the Promotion of Engineering Education [*Later, ASEE*]
SPEE........... Society of Petroleum Evaluation Engineers (IAA)
SPEE........... Special Purpose End Effector (MCD)
SPEECS....... Speech Parameter Extraction Experimental Comparison System (IAA)
SPEED......... Scheduled Procurement of Essential Equipment Deliveries [*US Postal Service*]
SPEED......... Self-Programmed Electronic Equation Delineator
SPEED......... Signal Processing in Evacuated Electronic Devices
SPEED......... Single-Point Emergency Equipment Divestment
SPEED......... Special Procedures for Expediting Equipment Development (MCD)
SPEED......... Study and Performance Efficiency in Entry Design
SPEED......... Subsistence Preparation by Electronic Energy Diffusion
SPEED......... Systematic Plotting and Evaluation of Enumerated Data [*National Institute of Standards and Technology Computer science*]
SPEED......... Systems Planning and Effectiveness Evaluation Device (MCD)
SPEED......... Systemwide Project for Electronic Equipment at Depots [*Military*] (AABC)
SPEEDEX..... Systemwide Project for Electronic Equipment at Depots Extended [*Military*] (AABC)
SpeedM....... Speedway Motorsports, Inc. [*Associated Press*] (SAG)
SPEEDO....... Speedometer [*Automotive engineering*]
SPEEDS....... System for Pinpointed, Exhaustive and Expeditious Dissemination of Subjects (PDAA)
SPEEDX....... Society to Preserve the Engrossing Enjoyment of DXing (EA)
SPEEL.......... Shore Plant Electronic Equipment List (MUGU)
SPEER......... Scientists and Professional Engineers Employment Registry [*Career Technologies Corp. - CTC*] [*Andover, MA*] [*Information service or system*] (IID)
SPEERA....... Secretarial Panel For the Evaluation of Epidemiologic Research Activities for the Department of Energy (EGAO)
SPEEREBRA... Speech Research Branch [*Navy*] (DNAB)
Speers......... Speers' [*or Spears'*] South Carolina Law Reports [*A publication*] (DLA)
Speers Eq.... Speers' [*or Spears'*] South Carolina Equity Reports [*A publication*] (DLA)
Speers Eq (SC)... Speers' [*or Spears'*] South Carolina Equity Reports [*A publication*] (DLA)
Speers L (SC)... Speers' [*or Spears'*] South Carolina Law Reports [*A publication*] (DLA)
SPEF........... Single Program Element Funding [*Military*] (AABC)
SPEF........... Student Performance Evaluation Form
SPEG........... Serum Protein Electrophoretogram [*Clinical chemistry*]
SPEG........... Spencerville & Elgin Railroad Co. [*AAR code*]
SPEG........... Staff Planning Evaluation Group (AAG)
SPEH........... May & Speh Inc. [*NASDAQ symbol*] (TTSB)
SPEI............ Savoy Pictures Entertainment [*NASDAQ symbol*] (TTSB)
SPEI............ Savoy Pictures Entertainment, Inc. [*NASDAQ symbol*] (SAG)
Speizmn...... Speizman Industries, Inc. [*Associated Press*] (SAG)
SPEK........... Spec's Music [*NASDAQ symbol*] (TTSB)
SPEK........... Spec's Music, Inc. [*Miami, FL*] [*NASDAQ symbol*] (NQ)
SPELD......... Specific Learning Disability (ADA)
SPELEOL...... Speleological
Spel Feuds... Spelman on Feuds [*A publication*] (DLA)
Spel Gl........ Spelman's Glossarium Archaiologicum [*A publication*] (DLA)
SPELL.......... Society for the Preservation of English Language and Literature (EA)
SpellEnt....... Spelling Entertainment, Inc. [*Associated Press*] (SAG)
Spell Extr Rel... Spelling on Extraordinary Relief in Equity and in Law [*A publication*] (DLA)
Spell Extr Rem... Spelling's Treatise on Injunctions and Other Extraordinary Remedies [*A publication*] (DLA)
Spel LT........ Spelman's Law Tracts [*A publication*] (DLA)
Spelm.......... Spelman's Glossarium Archaiologicum [*3 eds.*] [*1626-87*] [*A publication*] (DLA)
Spelman...... Spelman's Glossarium Archaiologicum [*3 eds.*] [*1626-87*] [*A publication*] (DLA)
SPELPAT...... Spelling Patterns
Spel Rep..... Spelman's Reports, Manuscript, English King's Bench [*A publication*] (DLA)
SPEM........... Semispectral Primitive Equation Model (USDC)
SPEM........... Semispectral Primitive Equation Model [*Marine science*] (OSRA)
SPEM........... Sindacato Petrolieri e Methanieri [*Union of Oil and Methane Gas Workers*] [*Italy*]
SPEMS......... Self-Propelled Elevated Maintenance Stand (MCD)
SPEMU......... Stable-Price Economic and Monetary Union [*Europe*]
SPEN........... Iscozacin [*Peru*] [*ICAO location identifier*] (ICLI)
SPENAVO..... Special Naval Observer
Spenc.......... Spencer's Law Reports [*20 New Jersey*] [*A publication*] (DLA)
Spenc.......... Spencer's Reports [*10-20 Minnesota*] [*A publication*] (DLA)
Spence Ch... Spence's Equitable Jurisdiction of the Court of Chancery [*A publication*] (DLA)
Spence Cop... Spence on Copyright of Designs [*A publication*] (DLA)
Spence Eq Jur... Spence's Equitable Jurisdiction of the Court of Chancery [*A publication*] (DLA)
Spence Or L... Spence's Origin of Laws [*A publication*] (DLA)
Spence Pat Inv... Spence on Patentable Inventions [*1851*] [*A publication*] (DLA)
Spencer....... Spencer's Law Reports [*20 New Jersey*] [*A publication*] (DLA)
Spencer....... Spencer's Reports [*10-20 Minnesota*] [*A publication*] (DLA)
Spencer-M... Spencer-Mead [*Commercial firm*] (DAVI)
Spen (NJ).... Spencer's Law Reports [*20 New Jersey*] [*A publication*] (DLA)
Spens Sel Cas... Spens' Select Cases [*Bombay, India*] [*A publication*] (DLA)
SPEO........... Chimbote [*Peru*] [*ICAO location identifier*] (ICLI)
SPE of AIME... Society of Petroleum Engineers of American Institute of Mining, Metallurgical, and Petroleum Engineers (EA)
SPEOPT....... Special Optical Tracking System [*NASA*]
SPEP........... Puerto Esperanza [*Peru*] [*ICAO location identifier*] (ICLI)
SPEP........... Serum Protein Electrophoresis [*Clinical chemistry*]
SPEP........... Society for Phenomenology and Existential Philosophy (EA)
SPEPD......... Space Power and Electric Propulsion Division [*Formerly, Nuclear Systems and Space Power Division*] [*NASA*]

SPEPOS....... Society of Petroleum Engineers Production Operations Symposium and Exhibition (ITD)
SPEPS......... Specialist, Motion Picture Service - Booker [*Navy rating*]
SPEQ......... Moquegua [*Peru*] [*ICAO location identifier*] (ICLI)
Sp Eq......... Spears' South Carolina Equity Reports [*A publication*] (DLA)
SPEQ......... Special Equipment (AAG)
SPEQ......... Speciality Equipment [*NASDAQ symbol*] (SAG)
SPEQ......... Specialty Equipment [*NASDAQ symbol*] (SAG)
SPERDVAC... Society to Preserve and Encourage Radio Drama, Variety, and Comedy (EA)
SPERM........ Secret Paper Reconstitution Mechanism [*Device to reclaim documents that have been inadvertently shredded*]
sperm......... Spermatozoa (DOG)
sperm......... Spermatozoan (DOG)
SPERMFLOW... Society for the Preservation and Enhancement of the Recognition of Millard Fillmore, Last of the Whigs (EA)
SPERT......... Schedule Performance Evaluation and Review Technique
SPERT......... Schedule Program Evaluation and Review Technique (IAA)
SPERT......... Short Pulse Experimental RADAR Techniques (MCD)
SPERT......... Simplified Program Evaluation and Review Technique [*Trademark*]
SPERT......... Special Power Excursion Reactor Test [*US reactor facilities*]
SPERTTT...... Society for Promotion of Educational Reform through Teacher Training [*British*]
SPeruC........ Southern Peru Copper Corp. [*Associated Press*] (SAG)
SPERW......... Specialist, Recreation and Welfare Assistant [*Navy rating*]
SPES........... Servico de Propaganda e Educacao Sanitaria [*Brazil*]
SPES........... Short Psychiatric Evaluation Scale (CPH)
SPES........... South Place Ethical Society [*British*]
SpES........... Special Education Specialist (GAGS)
SPES........... Stored Program Element System [*Computer science*] (IEEE)
SPESS......... Stored Program Electronic Switching System [*Telecommunications*] (TEL)
SPET........... Single Photon Emission Tomography
SPET........... Solid-Propellant Electric Thruster [*Aerospace*]
SPET........... Super Power Electron Tube
SPETE......... Special Purpose Electronic Test Equipment [*Military*] (CAAL)
SPETERL...... Ship Portable Electrical/Electronic Test Equipment Requirement List [*Navy*] (CAAL)
SPEX........... Small and Specialists Publishers Exhibition
SPEX........... Sozialwissenschaftliche Experten und Gutachter [*Social Science Experts*] [*NOMOS Datapool Database*] (IID)
SPEX........... Space Plasma Experiment [*NASA*] (SSD)
SPEX........... Special Exercise [*Navy*] (NVT)
spex........... Specifications (WDMC)
SPEZ........... Puerto Bermudez [*Peru*] [*ICAO location identifier*] (ICLI)
SPF............ Science Policy Foundation [*Later, ISPF*] [*British*]
SPF............ Scottish Pharmaceutical Federation [*British*]
SPF............ Security Police Flight [*Air Force*]
SPF............ Service Publication Form (AAG)
SPF............ Shortest Path First (TNIG)
SPF............ SIDPERS [*Standard Installation/Division Personnel System*] Personnel File [*Military*] (AABC)
SPF............ Single Point Failure (NASA)
SPF............ Single Project Funding (MCD)
SPF............ Site Population Factor [*Nuclear energy*] (NRCH)
SPF............ Skin Protection Factor [*Medicine*]
SPF............ Society for the Propagation of the Faith (EA)
SPF............ Society of Phantom Friends (EA)
SPF............ Software Production Facility [*NASA*] (NASA)
SPF............ Somali Patriotic Front [*Political party*] (EY)
SPF............ South Pacific Airline SA [*Chile*] [*ICAO designator*] (FAAC)
SPF............ South Pacific Forum [*Australia*]
SPF............ Soy Protein Flour [*Food technology*]
SPF............ Spacelab Processing Facility [*NASA*] (NASA)
SPF............ Space Power Facility
SPF............ Spaero JSP [*Ukraine*] [*FAA designator*] (FAAC)
SPF............ Spearfish [*South Dakota*] [*Airport symbol*] (AD)
SPF............ Spearfish, SD [*Location identifier FAA*] (FAAL)
SPF............ Specialist, Firefighter [*Navy rating*]
SPF............ Special Production Fund [*Australian Film Commission*]
SPF............ Special Purpose Force (MCD)
SPF............ Specific-Pathogen Free [*Medicine*]
SPF............ Spectrophotofluorometer
S-PF........... S Phase Fraction
SPF............ Spinning Form (MCD)
SPF............ Split Product of Fibrin (MAE)
SPF............ Springfield Resources [*Vancouver Stock Exchange symbol*]
SPF............ Standard Pacific [*NYSE symbol*] (TTSB)
SPF............ Standard-Pacific Corp. [*NYSE symbol*] (SPSG)
SPF............ Standard Perfusion Fluid [*Medicine*] (DMAA)
SPF............ Standard Pesticide File [*Derwent Publications Ltd.*] [*Database*]
SPF............ Standard Program Facility (NITA)
SPF............ Standard Project Flood [*Nuclear energy*] (NRCH)
SPF............ Start-Promoting Factor [*Cytology*]
SPF............ St. Paul-En-Foret [*France*] [*Seismograph station code, US Geological Survey*] (SEIS)
SPF............ St. Photios Foundation (EA)
SPF............ Strategic Protection Force
SPF............ Stressed Panel Fasteners
SPF............ Structured Programming Facility [*Computer science*]
SPF............ Studded Panel Fastener (DNAB)
SPF............ Subscriber Plant Factor [*Telecommunications*]
SPF............ Sun-Protection Factor [*Cosmetics industry*]
SPF............ Super Plastic Formed [*Metal fabrication*]
SPF............ Superplastic Forming [*Materials science*]
SPF............ Surrogate Parent Foundation (EA)
SPF............ Survival Probability Function
SPF............ Synthesis-Phase Fraction [*Medicine*] (CDI)
SPF............ Synthetic Phenolic Foam
SPF............ System Performance Factor [*Telecommunications*] (TEL)
SPF............ System Productivity Facility [*Computer science*]
SPFA........... Scottish Pelagic Fishermen's Association (DBA)
SPFA........... Single-Point Failure Analysis (KSC)
SPFA........... Societe des Professeurs Francais et Francophones en Amerique (EA)
SPFA........... Steel Plate Fabricators Association (EA)
SPFC........... Site Peculiar Facility Change (AAG)
SPFC........... Society for the Parents of Fugitive Children [*Fictional organization in film "Taking Off"*]
SPFC........... Solid Polymer Fuel Cell [*Energy source*]
SPFD........... Superplastic Forming/Diffusion Bonding — *see next*; Solid-Particle Filter Dye [*Color film technology*]
SPF/DB........ Superplastic Forming/Diffusion Bonding [*Materials science*]
SpFest......... Spanish Festival [*Record label*]
SPFFA......... South Pacific Forum Fisheries Agency [*Honiara, Solomon Islands*] (EAIO)
SPFFC......... Southern Ports Foreign Freight Committee
SP-FGS........ Shuttle Projects - Flight and Ground Systems Office [*Kennedy Space Center*] [*NASA*] (NASA)
SPFI............ Solid-Phase Fluorescent Immunoassay [*Oncology*] (DAVI)
SPFL........... Southern Philippines Federation of Labor
sp fl........... Spinal Fluid [*Medicine*] (MAE)
SPFM.......... Society for the Preservation of Film Music (EA)
SPFM.......... Society of Priests for a Free Ministry (EA)
SPFM.......... Spinning Form [*Tool*] (AAG)
SPFMV......... Sweet Potato Feather Mottle Virus
SPFO.......... Sparta Foods [*Commercial firm NASDAQ symbol*] (SAG)
SPFP........... Single Pass Fit Program (MCD)
SPFP........... Single-Point Failure Potential (KSC)
SPFP........... Single-Precision Floating Point [*Computer science*]
SPFP........... Sudanese People's Federal Party [*Sudan*] [*Political party*] (MENA)
SPFPAD....... Spacecraft Performance and Flight Path Analysis Directorate [*NASA*]
SPFS........... Soldier Physical Fitness School [*Army*] (INF)
SPFT........... Single-Pedestal Flat-Top [*Desk*]
SPFT........... Sixteen Personality Factors Test [*Psychology*] (DAVI)
SPFW.......... Single-Phase Full Wave
SPFWBR...... Single-Phase Full-Wave Bridge (DWSG)
SPFX........... Special Effects [*Filmmaking*]
SPG............ Saint Paul Guild (EA)
SPG............ Salicyl Phenolic Glucuronide [*Organic chemistry*]
SPG............ Saxifrage Publications Group (EA)
SPG............ Scan Pattern Generator
SPG............ Screen Producers Guild [*Later, PGA*] (EA)
SPG............ Security Police Group [*Air Force*]
SPG............ Seed Pea Group [*Defunct*] (EA)
SPG............ Self-Propelled Gun [*British military*] (DMA)
SPG............ Shift Pattern Generator [*Automotive engineering*]
SPG............ Short Pulse Generator
SPG............ Signal Point Ground (NASA)
SPG............ Signal Processor Group
SPG............ Silver Spring Mining [*Vancouver Stock Exchange symbol*]
SPG............ Simon DeBartolo Group, Inc. [*NYSE symbol*] (SAG)
SPG............ Simon Property Group [*NYSE symbol*] (SPSG)
SPG............ Simple Phrase Grammar
SPG............ Single-Point Ground (MCD)
SPG............ Sinusoidal Pressure Generator
SPG............ Society for the Propagation of the Gospel [*Later, USPG*] [*British*]
SPG............ Sort Program Generator [*Computer science*] (BUR)
SPG............ Source Power Gain
SPG............ Specialist, Gunnery [*Navy rating*]
SPG............ Special Patrol Group [*of the London Metropolitan Police, providing protection for public figures*]
SPG............ Special Performance Group [*In automobile name SAAB 900 Turbo SPG*]
SPG............ Special Planning Group [*Special Operations Force*] (DOMA)
SPG............ Special Project Group [*DoD*]
SPG............ Special Purpose Grant
SPG............ Specific Gravity [*Also, SP, SPGR*]
SPG............ Spiroglycol [*Organic chemistry*]
Spg............ Sponge [*Quality of the bottom*] [*Nautical charts*]
SPG............ Spooling (MSA)
SPG............ Spring (AAG)
SPG............ Spring
SPG............ Springdale Air Services, Inc. [*ICAO designator*] (FAAC)
SPG............ Stereophotogrammetry [*Medicine*]
SPG............ St. Petersburg, FL [*Location identifier FAA*] (FAAL)
SPG............ Study Planning Guide (MCD)
SPG............ Sucrose, Phosphate, Glutamate [*A culture medium*]
SPG............ Synchronization Pulse Generator (IAA)
SPG............ System Phasing Group (MCD)
SPGA.......... Scottish Professional Golfers Association (BARN)
SPGA.......... Southeastern Pecan Growers Association
SPGA.......... Southwestern Peanut Growers Association (EA)
SPGB.......... Socialist Party of Great Britain (PPW)
SPGCPS....... Senior Policy Group for Canadian Production Sharing
SPGD.......... Self-Powered Gamma Detector [*Nuclear energy*] (NRCH)
SPGE.......... Steam Plant Gauge (DNAB)
SPGFP......... Society for the Propagation of the Gospel in Foreign Parts [*British*] (DAS)
SPGG.......... Solid-Propellant Gas Generator (AAG)
SPGH.......... Society for the Preservation of the Greek Heritage (EA)

SPGJ........ Society for the Propagation of the Gospel among the Jews [*British*]
SPGJ........ Stomach-Partitioning Gastrojejunostomy [*Surgery*]
SPGL........ Spiegel, Inc. [*NASDAQ symbol*] (NQ)
SPGLA........ Spiegel Cl'A' [*NASDAQ symbol*] (TTSB)
Sp Glos........ Spelman's Glossarium Archaiologicum [*A publication*] (DLA)
SPGM........ Specialist, Gunnery, Aviation Free Gunnery Instructor [*Navy rating*]
SPGM........ Tingo Maria [*Peru*] [*ICAO location identifier*] (ICLI)
SPGN........ Specialist, Gunnery, Antiaircraft Gunnery Instructor [*Navy rating*]
SPGN........ Sympathetic Post-Ganglionic Neurone [*Neurology*]
SPGNA........ Sepragen Cop. [*NASDAQ symbol*] (SAG)
SPGNA........ Sepragen Corp. 'A' [*NASDAQ symbol*] (TTSB)
SPGNU........ Sepragen Corp. Unit [*NASDAQ symbol*] (TTSB)
SPGNW........ Sepragen Corp. Wrrt'A' [*NASDAQ symbol*] (TTSB)
SPGNZ........ Sepragen Corp. Wrrt'B' [*NASDAQ symbol*] (TTSB)
SPGPM........ Shots per Gun per Minute [*Military*] (NVT)
SPGR........ Specialist Personal GPS Receiver
SPGR........ Specific Gravity [*Also, SG, SPG*]
sp gr........ Specific Gravity (IDOE)
SP GRV........ Specific Gravity [*Also, SP, SPGR, SPG*] (DAVI)
SPGS........ Lagunas [*Peru*] [*ICAO location identifier*] (ICLI)
SPGS........ Secondary Power-Generating Subsystem (IAA)
SPGS........ Spare Guidance System
SPGS........ Springs (MCD)
SPGS........ Springs
SPGT........ Puerto Victoria [*Peru*] [*ICAO location identifier*] (ICLI)
SPGT........ Springfield Terminal Railway Co. [*Later, ST*] [*AAR code*]
SPGTA........ Signal Processor Group Test Assembly
SPGU........ Bagua [*Peru*] [*ICAO location identifier*] (ICLI)
SpgWre........ Spaghetti Warehouse, Inc. [*Associated Press*] (SAG)
SPGX........ Spastic Paraplegia, X-Linked [*Medicine*] (DMAA)
SPH........ San Pedro Hill [*California*] [*Seismograph station code, US Geological Survey Closed*] (SEIS)
SPH........ Scans per Hour [*Photocopying, Microfilming*]
SPH........ Secondary Pulmonary Hemosiderosis [*Medicine*] (MAE)
SPH........ Self-Propelled Howitzer (MCD)
SPH........ Severely and Profoundly Handicapped
SPH........ Sheets per Hour (WDMC)
SPH........ Singapore Press Holdings (ECON)
S-Ph........ Single-Phase
SPH........ Smoothed-Particle Hydrodynamics [*Statistical mechanics*]
SPH........ Smooth Particle Hydrodynamic
SPH........ Sociedade Portuguesa de Helicopteros Lda. [*Portugal*] [*FAA designator*] (FAAC)
SPH........ Society of Public Health (EAIO)
SPH........ Sound Protective Helmet [*Military*]
SPH........ Soy Protein Hydrolyzate
SPH........ Space Heater (KSC)
SPH........ Special Psychiatric Hospital [*Former USSR*]
SPH........ Spherical (ROG)
SPH........ Spherical Lens [*Ophthalmology*]
Sph........ Sphingomyelin [*Also, SM, SP*] [*Biochemistry*] (DAVI)
Sph........ Sphingosine [*Also, SM*] [*Biochemistry*]
SPH........ Springhill, LA [*Location identifier FAA*] (FAAL)
SPH........ Stable Platform Housing
SPH........ Statement of Personal History [*Military*]
SPH........ Suburban Propane Ptnrs L.P. [*NYSE symbol*] (TTSB)
SPH........ Superphantom (IAA)
SPHA........ Chincha [*Peru*] [*ICAO location identifier*] (ICLI)
SPHC........ Chala [*Peru*] [*ICAO location identifier*] (ICLI)
SPHCT........ Simplified Perturbed Hard Chain Theory [*Equation of state*]
SPHD........ Special Pay for Hostile Duty [*Military*] (AFM)
SP/Hd........ Spool Piece Head [*Nuclear energy*] (NRCH)
SPHE........ Society of Packaging and Handling Engineers [*Later, IoPP*] (EA)
SPHE........ Society of Public Health Educators (DAVI)
SPHE........ Spherocytes [*Also, SPHER*] [*Hematology*] (DAVI)
SPHER........ Small-Particle Heat-Exchange Receiver [*Solar energy technology*]
SPHER........ Spherical
SPHER........ Spherocytes [*Also, SPHE*] [*Hematology*] (DAVI)
SPHERE........ Scientific Parameters for Health and the Environment, Retrieval and Estimation [*Database*] [*Environmental Protection Agency Washington, DC*]
SPHF........ Spin-Polarized Hartree-Fock [*Atomic wave-function*]
SPHF........ Spontaneous Hole Filling [*Spectrometry*]
SPHG........ Speed and Heading [*Navy Navigation and Satellite System*] (DNAB)
SPHI........ Chiclayo/Cap. Jose Abelardo Quinones Gonzalez [*Peru*] [*ICAO location identifier*] (ICLI)
SPHI........ Studio Plus Hotels [*NASDAQ symbol*] (TTSB)
SPHI........ Studio Plus Hotels, Inc. [*NASDAQ symbol*] (SAG)
SPHINX........ Space Plasma High-Voltage Interaction Experiment [*Spacecraft*] [*NASA*]
SPHINX........ Survival Probability Hazard in a Nuclear Exchange
SPHL........ Self-Propelled Hyperbaric Lifeboat (DS)
SP-HL........ Sun Present - Horizon Lost
SPHN........ Siphon (MSA)
SPHO........ Ayacucho/Coronel FAP Alfredo Mendivil Duarte [*Peru*] [*ICAO location identifier*] (ICLI)
SPHQ........ Shore Patrol Headquarters
SphrDrk........ Sphere Drake Holdings [*Associated Press*] (SAG)
SPHS........ Society for the Promotion of Hellenic Studies (EA)
SPHS........ Swedish Pioneer Historical Society (EA)
SP/HT........ Specific Heat
SPHT........ Super Pressure - High Temperature
SPHU........ Huancayo [*Peru*] [*ICAO location identifier*] (ICLI)
SPHV........ Huanuco Viejo [*Peru*] [*ICAO location identifier*] (ICLI)
SPHW........ Single-Phase Half Wave
SPHY........ Andahuaylas [*Peru*] [*ICAO location identifier*] (ICLI)
SPHZ........ Anta/Comdte. FAP German Arias Grazziani [*Peru*] [*ICAO location identifier*] (ICLI)
SPI........ Die Sprache der Palmyrenischen Inschriften [*Leipzig*] [*A publication*] (BJA)
SPI........ Illinois State Library, Springfield, IL [*OCLC symbol*] (OCLC)
SPI........ Scanning Pulse Immobilization
SPI........ Schedule Performance Index (MCD)
SPI........ Scottish Provident Institution [*Commercial firm*]
SPI........ Secondary Protocol Identifier (TNIG)
SPI........ Secretariats Professionnels Internationaux
SPI........ Selected Period Investment [*Finance*] (WDAA)
SPI........ Selective Population Inversion [*Physics*]
SPI........ Self-Paced Instruction (IEEE)
SPI........ Self-Perception Inventory [*Personality development test*] [*Psychology*]
SPI........ Semi Process Inc. (NITA)
SPI........ Senior Patrol Inspection [*Immigration and Naturalization Service*]
SPI........ Septum-Equipped Programmable Injector [*Gas chromatography*]
SPI........ Sequence of Pulse Intervals
SPI........ Serial Peripheral Interface [*Electronics*]
SPI........ Series-Parallel Interface [*Computer science*]
SPI........ Serum Precipitable Iodine [*Serology*]
SPI........ Service Pedalogique Interafricain
SPI........ Service Provider Interface [*Computer science*]
SPI........ Service Publication Instruction (AAG)
SPI........ Severely and Profoundly Impaired
SPI........ Shared Peripheral Interface
SPI........ Share Price Index (ADA)
SPI........ Shipley Personal Inventory [*Medicine*] (DMAA)
SPI........ Ship's Plan Index
SPI........ Signal Point Identification (IAA)
SPI........ Signal Presence Indicator (CAAL)
SPI........ Single Point Injection [*Automotive engineering*]
SPI........ Single Processor Interface
SPI........ Single Program Initiated [*Computer science*] (IAA)
SPI........ Single Program Initiation [*Computer science*]
SPI........ Single Program Initiator [*Computer science*] (ECII)
SPI........ Site Peculiar Interference (AAG)
SPI........ Site Population Index [*Nuclear energy*] (NRCH)
SPI........ Smoke Point Improvement [*Petroleum refining*]
SPI........ Smoking Policy Institute (EA)
SPI........ Societe pour l'Informatique [*Company for Informatics*] [*Information service or system Defunct*] (IID)
SPI........ Society of Photographic Illustrators (EA)
SPI........ Society of Professional Investigators (EA)
SPI........ Society of the Plastics Industry (EA)
SPI........ Solid Propellant Information
SPI........ South Pacific Island Airways, Inc. [*ICAO designator*] (FAAC)
SPI........ Soy Protein Isolate [*Food technology*]
SPI........ Spanish Paprika Institute (EA)
SPI........ Specialist, Punched Card Accounting Machine Operator [*Navy rating*]
SPI........ Special Position Identification
SPI........ Specific Productivity Index (IEEE)
SPI........ Spectrophotometric Process Ink (DGA)
Spi........ Spicules [*Quality of the bottom*] [*Nautical charts*]
SPI........ SPI Holdings, Inc. [*Later, SpectraVision, Inc.*] [*AMEX symbol*] (SPSG)
SPI........ Sports Philatelists International (EA)
SPI........ Springfield [*Illinois*] [*Airport symbol*] (OAG)
SPI........ Standard Performance Indicator [*Army*]
SPI........ Standard Practice Instructions (MCD)
SPI........ Standard Protective Item
SPI........ Statement of Policy or Interpretation [*Food and Drug Administration*]
SPI........ Station Program Identification [*Telecommunications*] (TEL)
SPI........ Storage Protein Isolate [*Food industry*]
SPI........ St. Paul Island [*Alaska*] [*Seismograph station code, US Geological Survey Closed*] (SEIS)
SPI........ Strategic Planning Initiative [*Environmental Protection Agency*] (GFGA)
SPI........ Strategic Planning Institute [*Cambridge, MA*]
SPI........ Stuttering Prediction Instruction [*Speech and language therapy*] (DAVI)
SPI........ Sun Position Indicator (IAA)
SPI........ Superintendent of Public Instruction (DNAB)
SPI........ Supervisory Practices Inventory [*Test*]
SPI........ Surface Position Indicator (NASA)
SPI........ Symbolic Pictorial Indicator (MCD)
SPI........ Synergy Power Institute [*Defunct*] (EA)
SPI........ Synthetic Phase Isolation [*Telemetry*]
SPI........ System Performance Indicator
SPI........ System Programming Interface [*Computer science*]
SPIA........ Ica [*Peru*] [*ICAO location identifier*] (ICLI)
SPIA........ Single Premium Immediate Annuities [*Insurance*]
SPIA........ Solid-Phase Immunoabsorption [*Medicine*] (DMAA)
SPIA........ Solid Propellant Information Agency [*Air Force*]
SPIAM........ Sodium Purity In-Line Analytical Module [*Nuclear energy*] (NRCH)
SPIAP........ Shuttle/Payload Integration Activities Plan (NASA)
SPIB........ Scripta Pontificii Instituti Biblici [*A publication*] (BJA)
SPIB........ Shetland Pony Identification Bureau
SPIB........ Social and Prevocational Information Battery
SPIB........ Society of Power Industry Biologists (EA)
SPIB........ Southern Pine Inspection Bureau (EA)
SPIBS........ Satellite Positive-Ion-Beam System [*Air Force*] (MCD)
SPIC........ Ship Position Interpolation Computer

SPIC............ Sisters of Providence and of the Immaculate Conception [*Roman Catholic religious order*]
SPIC............ Society of the Plastics Industry of Canada
SPIC............ Spare Parts Inventory Control (MHDB)
SPIC............ Standard and Poor's Index - Composite [*Stock market*]
SPIC............ Students for Promotion of Identity on Campus [*New York group promoting ethnic pride among Latin American students*]
SPIC............ Summary Punch IBM [*International Business Machines*] Collector
SPICBM....... Solid Propellant Intercontinental Ballistic Missile (IAA)
SPICE.......... Sales-Point Information Computing Equipment [*Merchandising*]
SPICE.......... Self-Paced Instruction for Competency Education (EDAC)
SPICE.......... Simplified Procurement in a Competitive Environment (AAGC)
SPICE.......... Simulation Program with Integrated Circuit Emphasis (MCD)
SPICE.......... Solar Particle Intensity Composition Experiment [*NASA*]
SPICE.......... Space Integrated Controls Experiment (DOMA)
SPICE.......... Spacelab Payload Integration and Coordination in Europe [*NASA*] (NASA)
SPICE.......... Space Power Internal Combustion Engine (MCD)
SPICE.......... Special Programs Incorporating Custom Elective
SPICE.......... Special Programs Increasing Counseling Effectiveness [*Pennsylvania State Department of Public Instruction*]
SPICE.......... Stanford Program on International and Cross Cultural Education [*Stanford University*] [*Research center*] (RCD)
SpiceEnt...... Spice Entertainment Companies, Inc. [*Associated Press*] (SAG)
SPICI........... SPI [*Society of the Plastics Industry*] Composites Institute (EA)
SPID............ Seismic Personnel Intrusion Detector (PDAA)
SPID............ Service Profile Identifier [*Computer science*]
SPID............ Service Provider ID (PCM)
SPID............ SIS [*Superconductivity Information System*] Published Information Database [*Office of Scientific and Technical Information*] [*Department of Energy*]
SPID............ Standard Performance Indicator Dictionary [*Army*]
SPID............ Submersible Portable Inflatable Dwelling
SPID............ Summed Pain Intensity Difference [*Medicine*] (DMAA)
SPID............ Sum of Pain Intensity Differences
SPIDAC........ Specimen Input to Digital Automatic Computer
SPIDE.......... Short Planning Identification File
SPIDER........ Smokeless Propellant in Demonstration Experimental Rocket (KSC)
SPIDER........ Sonic Pulse-Echo Instrument Designed for Extreme Resolution (IEEE)
SPIDER........ Systematic Planning for the Integration of Defense Engineering and Research [*Program*]
SPIDF.......... Support Planning Identification File [*NASA*] (MCD)
SPIDO.......... Shuttle Payload Integration and Development Program Office [*NASA*]
SPIDOT........ Self-Propelled Immersible Drive-Off Trolley [*British*] (DI)
SPIDPO........ Shuttle Payload Integration and Development Program Office [*Johnson Space Center*] (NASA)
SPIDR.......... Society of Professionals in Dispute Resolution (EA)
SPIE............ Scavenging-Precipitation-Ion Exchange (IEEE)
SPIE............ Secretariat Professionnel International de l'Enseignement [*International Federation of Free Teachers' Unions - IFFTU*] [*Amsterdam, Netherlands*] (EAIO)
SPIE............ Self-Programmed Individualized Education (IEEE)
SPIE............ Ships Precise Identification Emitter (MCD)
SPIE............ Simulated Problem Input Evaluation
SPIE............ Society of Photo-Optical Instrumentation Engineers [*International Society for Optical Engineering*]
SPIE............ Society of Political Item Enthusiasts (EA)
SPIE............ Special Patrol Insertion/Extraction (MCD)
SPIE............ SPIE - the International Society for Optical Engineering (EA)
Spiegel........ Spiegel, Inc. [*Associated Press*] (SAG)
SpiekerP...... Spieker Properties [*Associated Press*] (SAG)
Spiekr.......... Spieker Properties [*Associated Press*] (SAG)
SPIES........... Stanford Preschool Internality-Externality Scale (EDAC)
SPIF............ School Practices Information File [*BRS Information Technologies*] [*Information service or system Defunct*]
SPIF............ Sequential Prime Implicant Form
SPIF............ Shuttle Payload Integration Facility [*NASA*] (MCD)
SPIF............ Standard Payload Interface Facility [*NASA*] (MCD)
SPIFC.......... Southern Pacific International Fan Club (EA)
SPIFDA........ South Pacific Islands Fisheries Development Agency [*Noumea, New Caledonia*] (EAIO)
SPIFR.......... Single Pilot Instrument Flight Rules [*Program*]
SPIH............ Superimposed Pregnancy-Induced Hypertension [*Obstetrics*] (DMAA)
SPII............. Shuttle Program Implementation Instruction [*NASA*] (NASA)
SPII............. Standard and Poor's Index - Industrials [*Stock market*]
SPIIC........... Societe de Protection des Infirmieres et Infirmiers du Canada (AC)
SPIIN........... Supplemental Procurement Instrument Identification Number [*DoD*]
SPIKE.......... Specially Prepared Individuals for Key Events [*Paramilitary training*] (ECON)
Spike M & S... Spike on Master and Servant [*3rd ed.*] [*1872*] [*A publication*] (DLA)
SPIL............ Quincemil [*Peru*] [*ICAO location identifier*] (ICLI)
SPIL............ Self-Rating Psychiatric Inventory List [*Personality development test*] [*Psychology*]
SPIL............ Sensitive Projects and Installation List (MCD)
SPIL............ Ship's Parts Integration List
SP-ILS......... Shuttle Projects - Integrated Logistics Support [*Kennedy Space Center*] [*NASA*] (NASA)
SPIM............ Lima-Callao/Internacional Jorge Chavez [*Peru*] [*ICAO location identifier*] (ICLI)
SPIM............ Service de Previsions Ionospherique Militaire
SPIMS.......... Shuttle Program Information Management System [*NASA*]
SPIN............ School Practices Information Network [*Bibliographic Retrieval Services*] [*Information service or system*] (IID)
SPIN............ Science Procurement Information Network [*Canada*]
SPIN............ Searchable Physics Information Notes (NITA)
SPIN............ Searchable Physics Information Notices [*American Institute of Physics*] [*New York, NY Bibliographic database*]
SPIN............ Separation Program Number [*DoD*] (VNW)
SPIN............ Service Parts Information Notice
SPIN............ Space Inspection
SPIN............ Space Intercept (SAA)
SPIN............ Special Inquiry [*FBI term*]
SPIN............ Spinster (ADA)
SPIN............ Standard & Poor's 500 Index Subordinated Notes
SPIN............ Standard and Poor's Indexed Note (TDOB)
SPIN............ Standard Procedure Instructions (KSC)
SPIN............ Strategies and Policies for Informatics [*Intergovernmental Bureau for Informatics*]
SPIN............ Submarine Program Information Notebook
SPIN............ Superconductive Precision Inertial Navigation
Spinakr........ Spinnaker Industries [*Associated Press*] (SAG)
SPINAL........ Stimulator, Planetary Instrument Alignment
SPINAR........ Spinning Star [*Astronomy*]
sp indet....... Species Indeterminata [*Species Indeterminate*] [*Latin*] (MAE)
SPINDEX...... Selective Permutation Indexing [*Library of Congress*]
SPINDEX...... Subject Profile Index [*Computer-based*]
SPINE.......... Simulated Program for Investigation of Nuclear Effects
SPINE.......... Space Informatics Network Experiment [*European Space Agency*]
SPINES........ Science and Technology Policies Information Exchange System [*UNESCO*] [*Bibliographic database*] (IID)
SpineT......... Spine-Tech, Inc. [*Associated Press*] (SAG)
SpineTch..... Spine-Tech, Inc. [*Associated Press*] (SAG)
Spinks......... Spinks' English Ecclesiastical and Admiralty Reports [*164 English Reprint*] [*A publication*] (DLA)
Spinks Eccl & Adm (Eng)... Spinks' English Ecclesiastical and Admiralty Reports [*164 English Reprint*] [*A publication*] (DLA)
Spinks PC.... Spinks' English Admiralty Prize Cases [*A publication*] (DLA)
Spinks Prize Cas... Spinks' English Admiralty Prize Cases [*164 English Reprint*] [*A publication*] (DLA)
Spinks Prize Cas (Eng)... Spinks' English Admiralty Prize Cases [*164 English Reprint*] [*A publication*] (DLA)
SPINOE........ Spin Polarization Induced Nuclear Overhauser Effect [*Physics*]
SPINOE........ Spin Polarization-Induced Nuclear Overhauser Effect [*Physics*]
sp inquir...... Species Inquirendae [*Species of Doubtful Status*] [*Latin*] (MAE)
SPINS.......... Ship Passive Integrated Navigation System (DNAB)
SPINS.......... South Pacific Information Network System [*Australia*]
SPINS.......... Special Instruction (DOMA)
SPINSTRE.... Spencer Information Storage and Retrieval System (DIT)
SPINT.......... Special Intelligence (MCD)
SPINTAC...... Special Interest Aircraft (NVT)
SPINTCOM... Special Intelligence Communications [*Later, DIN/DSSCS*]
SPINTCOMM... Special Intelligence Communications [*Later, DIN/DSSCS*] (CET)
SPINVESWG... Special Investigation Wing (MUGU)
SPIO............ Systems Planning and Integration Office [*NASA*]
SPIP............ Satipo [*Peru*] [*ICAO location identifier*] (ICLI)
SPIP............ Software Process Improvement Plan (AAGC)
SPIP............ Special Position Identification Pulse (CET)
SPIPE.......... Spin-Polarized Inverse Photoemission [*Physics*]
S'PIPE.......... Standpipe
SPIPES........ Spin-Polarized Inverse Photoemission Spectroscopy
SPIR............ Patria [*Peru*] [*ICAO location identifier*] (ICLI)
SPIR............ School Performance Information Regulations (AIE)
SPIR............ Search Program for Infrared Spectra [*Canada Institute for Scientific and Technical Information*] [*Information service or system*]
SPIR............ Sears Point International Raceway [*California*]
SPIR............ Single Pilot Instrument Rating [*Aviation*] (DA)
SPIR............ Spiral
SPIR............ Spire Corp. [*NASDAQ symbol*] (NQ)
SPIR............ Spiritoso [*With Animation*] [*Music*]
SPIR............ Spiritual (DAVI)
SPIR............ Spiritus [*Spirit*] [*Pharmacy*]
SPIR............ Standard and Poor's Index - Rails [*Stock market*]
SPIR............ Standardized Proportional Incidence Ratio [*Epidemiology*]
SPIR............ Student Project for International Responsibility
SPIRAL........ Sperry Inertial RADAR Altimeter
SPIRAS........ Setpoint Precision Infrared Angular Scanner (PDAA)
SPIRAT........ Strategic Program for Innovative Research on AIDS Treatment [*The National Institute of Allergy and Infectious Diseases*]
SPIRBM........ Solid-Propellant Intermediate Range Ballistic Missile (AAG)
SPIRE.......... Spatial Inertial Reference Equipment
SPIRE.......... Spatial Paradigm for Information Retrieval and Exploration [*Computer science*]
Spire............ Spire Corp. [*Associated Press*] (SAG)
SPIREP........ Spot Intelligence Report [*Air Force*]
SPIRES........ Single-Photon Infrared Emission Spectroscopy
SPIRES........ Standard Personnel Information Retrieval System [*Military*]
SPIRES........ Stanford Public Information Retrieval System [*Stanford University Libraries*] [*Stanford, CA Bibliographic database management system*] [*Information service or system*]
SPIREX........ South Pole Infrared Explorer [*University of Chicago*] [*Research center*] (RCD)
SPIRIT......... Sales Processing Interactive Real-Time Inventory Technique [*NCR Corp. trademark*]
SPIRIT......... School for Postgraduate Interdisciplinary Research on Interculturalism and Transnationality [*Aalborg University, Denmark*]
SPIRIT......... Sensible Policy in Information Resources and Information Technology [*Defunct*] (EA)
SPIRIT......... Spiritoso [*With Animation*] [*Music*]
SPIRIT......... Spiritus [*Spirit*] [*Latin*] (ROG)

SPIRIT .... Systmatic Productivity Improvement Review In TRADOC [*Training and Doctrine Command*] [*Army*]
SPIRO .... Students Protesting Illegal Real Estate Operators [*Student legal action organization*] (EA)
SPIRS .... Silver-Platter Information Retrieval System [*Computer science*]
SPIRT .... Short Path Infrared Tester (KSC)
SPIRT .... Stock Point Interrogation/Requirements Technique
SPIS .... Pias [*Peru*] [*ICAO location identifier*] (ICLI)
SPIS .... Senate Permanent Investigating Subcommittee (AAG)
SPIS .... Serial Poll Idle State (IAA)
SPIS .... Space Philatelists International Society (EA)
SPIS .... Standard Production Information Systems (NITA)
SPIS .... State Plantations Impact Study [*Victoria, Australia*]
SPISE .... Special Projects in Science Education
SPISS .... Spissus [*Dried*] [*Pharmacy*]
SPIT .... Paita [*Peru*] [*ICAO location identifier*] (ICLI)
SPIT .... Secondary Power Integration Test (MCD)
SPIT .... Selective Printing of Items from Tape [*Computer science*]
SPITS .... Scan Platform Inertial Thermal Simulator
SPIU .... Ship Position Interpolation Unit
SPIU .... Standard and Poor's Index - Utilities [*Stock market*]
SPIW .... ESCAP [*Economic and Social Commssion for the Asia and Pacific*] Division for Shipping, Ports, and Inland Waterways (EAIO)
SPIW .... Special-Purpose Individual Weapon [*A rifle that fires flechettes or darts*] [*Pronounced "spew"*]
SPIY .... Yauri [*Peru*] [*ICAO location identifier*] (ICLI)
SPIZ .... Uchiza [*Peru*] [*ICAO location identifier*] (ICLI)
SPJ .... Austria (Republic) SIGNs [*NYSE symbol*] (TTSB)
SPJ .... Austria [*Republic of*] Stock Index Growth Notes [*NYSE symbol*] (SPSG)
SPJ .... Saphenopopliteal Junction [*Medicine*] (DMAA)
SPJ .... Senior Puisne Judge [*British*] (ILCA)
SPJ .... Socialist Party of Japan [*Nikon Shakaito*] [*Political party*] (PPW)
SPJ .... Society of Professional Journalists [*Also, SDX*] (NTCM)
SPJ .... Socijalisticka Partija Jugoslavije [*Socialist Party of Yugoslavia*] [*Political party*] (PPE)
SPJ .... Sparta [*Greece*] [*Airport symbol Obsolete*] (OAG)
SPJ .... Special Purpose Jammer [*Military*] (CAAL)
SPJA .... Rioja [*Peru*] [*ICAO location identifier*] (ICLI)
SPJB .... Cajabamba/Pampa Grande [*Peru*] [*ICAO location identifier*] (ICLI)
SPJC .... St. Petersburg Junior College [*Clearwater, FL*]
SP-JFI .... School Principal Job Functions Inventory [*Test*]
SPJI .... Juanjui [*Peru*] [*ICAO location identifier*] (ICLI)
SPJJ .... Jauja [*Peru*] [*ICAO location identifier*] (ICLI)
SPJL .... Juliaca [*Peru*] [*ICAO location identifier*] (ICLI)
SPJN .... San Juan [*Peru*] [*ICAO location identifier*] (ICLI)
SPJR .... Cajamarca/Mayor General FAP Armando Revoredo Iglesias [*Peru*] [*ICAO location identifier*] (ICLI)
SPJ SDX .... Society of Professional Journalists, Sigma Delta Chi (EA)
SPJTG .... Secondary Plant Joint Test Group (DNAB)
SPK .... Diamond Aviation, Inc. [*ICAO designator*] (FAAC)
SPK .... Reno, NV [*Location identifier FAA*] (FAAL)
SPK .... Saporamean Kampuchea News Agency [*Cambodia*]
SPK .... Sapporo [*Japan*] [*Airport symbol*] (OAG)
SPK .... Scotts Peak [*Tasmania*] [*Seismograph station code, US Geological Survey*] (SEIS)
SPK .... Silver Tusk Mines [*Vancouver Stock Exchange symbol*]
SPK .... Socialist Party of Kurdistan [*Iraq*] [*Political party*] (MENA)
SPK .... Spare Parts Kit
SPK .... Spark (MSA)
spk .... Speckled [*Quality of the bottom*] [*Nautical charts*]
SPK .... Spieker Properties [*NYSE symbol*] (SPSG)
SPK .... Spike (MSA)
SPK .... Spinnbarkheit [*With reference to cervical mucus*] [*Medicine*]
SPK .... Spokane [*Diocesan abbreviation*] [*Washington*] (TOCD)
SPK .... Storage Protection Key [*Computer science*] (IAA)
SPK .... Superficial Punctate Keratitis [*Ophthalmology*]
SPKC .... Small Pig Keepers' Council [*British*] (BI)
SPKL .... Spreckels Industries, Inc. [*NASDAQ symbol*] (SAG)
SPKL .... Sprinkle [*NWS*] (FAAC)
SPKP .... Suomen Perustuslaillinen Kansanpuolue [*Finnish Constitutional People's Party*] [*Political party*] (PPW)
SPKPrB .... Spieker Prop 9.45%'B' Pfd [*NYSE symbol*] (TTSB)
SPKPRF .... Spark Proof (IAA)
SPKR .... Speaker (AAG)
spkr .... Speaker (IDOE)
SPKR .... Sprinkler (WGA)
SPKT .... Sprocket
SPL .... San Pedro de Jagua [*Colombia*] [*Airport symbol*] (AD)
SPL .... Saskatoon Public Library [*UTLAS symbol*]
SPL .... Scan-Pol Ltd. [*Poland ICAO designator*] (FAAC)
SPL .... Scott Paper Ltd. [*Toronto Stock Exchange symbol Vancouver Stock Exchange symbol*]
SPL .... Scratch Pad Line [*NASA*] (MCD)
SPL .... Self-Propelled Launcher [*British military*] (DMA)
SPL .... Separate Parts List (MSA)
SPL .... Serialized Parts List [*NASA*] (MCD)
SPL .... Service Priority List (BUR)
SPL .... Set Priority Level [*Computer science*] (NHD)
SPL .... Short-Pulse LASER
SPL .... Signal Processing Language [*Computer science*] (CSR)
SPL .... Signature and Propagation Laboratory [*Army*] (RDA)
SPL .... Simple Phrase Language [*Computer science*]
SPL .... Simple Programming Language [*Computer science*]
SPL .... Simulation Programming Language [*Computer science*]
SPL .... Sine Prole Legitima [*Without Legitimate Issue*] [*Latin*]
SPL .... Single Pet Lover
SPL .... Single-Premium Life [*Insurance*]
SPL .... Single-Premium Whole Life [*Insurance*]
SPL .... Single Propellant Loading (AFM)
SPL .... Skin Potential Level
SPL .... Sloane Physics Laboratory [*Yale*] (MCD)
SPL .... Smoke Puff Limiter [*Automotive engineering*]
SPL .... Software Parts List [*Computer science*] (TEL)
SPL .... Software Programming Language [*Computer science*] (IEEE)
SPL .... Solar Pumped LASER (SSD)
SPL .... Sound Power Level [*Acoustics*]
SPL .... Sound Pressure Level [*Acoustics*]
SPL .... Source Program Library
SPL .... Spaceborne Programming Language [*Computer science*] (IAA)
SPL .... Space Physics Laboratory [*Aerospace corporation*]
SPL .... Space Programming Language [*Computer science*]
SPL .... Space Programs Laboratory [*Fort Belvoir, VA*] [*United States Army Engineer Topographic Laboratories*] (GRD)
SPL .... Spare Parts List
SPL .... Spartanburg County Public Library, Spartanburg, SC [*OCLC symbol*] (OCLC)
SPL .... Special (AAG)
SPL .... Special-Purpose Language [*Computer science*]
SPL .... Speed Phase Lock
SPL .... Spermatophore Length
SPL .... Spiral (MSA)
SPL .... Spiridon Lake [*Alaska*] [*Seismograph station code, US Geological Survey*] (SEIS)
SPL .... Splice [*Telecommunications*] (TEL)
SPL .... Splice Junction Mutation [*Genetics*]
SPL .... Spontaneous Lesion [*Medicine*] (MAE)
SPL .... Sporulation per Lesion [*Plant pathology*]
SPL .... Spritsail [*Ship's rigging*] (ROG)
SPL .... Standard Programming Logic [*Computer science*] (IAA)
SPL .... Standard Pulse LASER
SPL .... Standards Parts Listing (MCD)
SPL .... Staphylococcal Phage Lysate [*Biochemistry*]
SPL .... Student Pilot's Licence (AIA)
SPL .... Succinyl-Poly-L-Lysine [*Biochemical analysis*]
SPL .... Summary Parts List
SPL .... Sun Pumped LASER (MCD)
SPL .... Superior Parietal Lobule [*Neuroanatomy*]
Spl .... Supplement (BJA)
SPL .... Supplementary Flight Plan Message [*Aviation code*]
SPL .... Support Platoon Leader [*Military*] (INF)
SPL .... Swiss Party of Labour
SPL .... Symbolic Programming Language [*Computer science*] (IAA)
SPL .... System Program Loader
SPL .... System Programming Language [*Computer science*] (NASA)
SPL .... Systems Programming Ltd. (IAA)
SPLA .... Louisiana [*Peru*] [*ICAO location identifier*] (ICLI)
SPLA .... Scottish Poetry Library Association (DBA)
SPLA .... Special-Purpose Lead Azide (MCD)
SPLA .... Sudan People's Liberation Army
SPLAASH .... Spacecraft Protective Landing Area for the Advancement of Science and Humanities [*Landing zone for flying saucers near Mt. Rainier, WA*]
Splaj .... Socialist People's Libyan Arab Jamahiriya [*Gathering of the masses*] [*Muammar Qaddafi's name for his country*]
SPLAN .... Support Plan (MCD)
SPLANCH .... Split-Level Ranch [*House*]
SPLASH .... Shipboard Platforms for Landing and Servicing Helicopters
SPLASH .... Special Program to List Amplitudes of Surges from Hurricanes
SplashT .... Splash Technology Holdings, Inc. [*Associated Press*] (SAG)
SPLAT .... Simplified Programming Language for Artists [*1978*] [*Computer science*] (CSR)
SPLAT .... Student Potential Life Achievement Test [*Parody of Scholastic Aptitude Test preparation books*]
SPLATT .... Single Pedestrians League Against Taxes and Traffic [*British*] (DI)
SPLATT .... Split Anterior Tibial Tendon [*Medicine*] (DMAA)
SPLATT .... Split Anterior Tibial Transfer [*Orthopedics*] (DAVI)
SPLATT TALTFR .... Split Anterior Tibial Transfer, Tendo Achillis Lengthening, and Toe Flexor Release [*Orthopedics*] (DAVI)
Sp Laws .... Spirit of the Laws (Montesquieu) [*A publication*] (DLA)
SPLC .... Ship Program Life Cycle [*Navy*]
SPLC .... Short Product Life Cycle [*Business term*] (MHDB)
SPLC .... Simulated Planetary Landing Capsule (DNAB)
SPLC .... Southern Poverty Law Center (EA)
SPLC .... Spare Parts List for Codification
SPLC .... Splice
SPLC .... Standard Point Location Code [*American Trucking Association and Association of American Railroads*]
SPLC .... Student Press Law Center (EA)
SPLCF .... Sustained Peak Low-Cycle Fatigue (PDAA)
SPLD .... Celendin [*Peru*] [*ICAO location identifier*] (ICLI)
SPLEEM .... Spin-Polarized Low-Energy Electron Microscopy
S/PLF .... Station/Platform LIDAR Facility (SSD)
SPLH .... Splash Technology Holdings, Inc. [*NASDAQ symbol*] (SAG)
SPLHC .... Sgt. Pepper's Lonely Hearts Club [*Defunct*] (EA)
SPLI .... Lima [*Peru*] [*ICAO location identifier*] (ICLI)
SPLI .... Single-Premium Life Insurance (MHDW)
SPLI .... Spermatophore Length Index
SPLI .... Substance P-Like Immunoreactivity

SPLICE......... Shorthand Programming Language in COBOL [*Common Business-Oriented Language*] Environment [*Computer science*] (MHDI)
SPLICE......... Stock Point Logistics Integrated Communications Environment Project [*Navy*]
SPLIT.......... Space Program Language Implementation Tool (KSC)
SPLIT.......... Spent Pot Lining Insolubilisation Technology [*Metallurgy*]
SPLIT.......... Sundstrand Processing Language Internally Translated
SPLK.......... Spanlink Communications [*NASDAQ symbol*] (TTSB)
SPLK.......... Spanlink Communications, Inc. [*NASDAQ symbol*] (SAG)
SPLL.......... Self-Propelled Launcher Loader (MCD)
SPLL.......... Standard Phase-Locked Loop
SPLLG......... Stable Production Low Leach Glass [*For nuclear wastes*]
SPLM.......... Space Programming Language Machine
SPLMD......... Soil-Pore Liquid Monitoring Device (GNE)
SP-LMO....... Shuttle Projects - Logistics Management Office [*NASA*] (GFGA)
SPLN.......... Rodriguez de Mendoz/San Nicolas [*Peru*] [*ICAO location identifier*] (ICLI)
SPLN.......... Spline [*Engineering*]
SPLNS......... South Plains (FAAC)
SPLO.......... Ilo [*Peru*] [*ICAO location identifier*] (ICLI)
SPLP.......... Las Palmas [*Peru*] [*ICAO location identifier*] (ICLI)
SPLS.......... Staples, Inc. [*NASDAQ symbol*] (NQ)
SPLS.......... Zorrillos [*Peru*] [*ICAO location identifier*] (ICLI)
SPLT.......... Lobitos [*Peru*] [*ICAO location identifier*] (ICLI)
SPLT.......... Specialist, Link Trainer Instructor [*Navy rating*]
SPLTR......... Splitter
SPLTRK....... Special Tracker [*Military*] (CAAL)
SPLTY......... Specialty (WGA)
S-Plus......... Statistical Software Package [*Computer science*] (EERA)
SPLV.......... Lago Verde [*Peru*] [*ICAO location identifier*] (ICLI)
SPLV.......... Serum Parvovirus-Like Virus [*Medicine*] (DMAA)
SPLV.......... Spinach Latent Virus [*Plant pathology*]
SPLV.......... Stable Plurilamellar Vesicle [*Pharmacology*]
SPLX.......... Simplex [*Mathematics*]
SPLY.......... Supply (MSA)
SPM.......... Air Saint-Pierre SA [*France ICAO designator*] (FAAC)
SPM.......... Saga Petroleum AS [*NYSE symbol*] (SAG)
SPM.......... Scanned Probe Microscopy
SPM.......... Scanning Photoemission Microscope
SPM.......... Scanning Probe Microscopy
SPM.......... Scratch Pad Memory [*Computer science*] (BUR)
SPM.......... Scratch Pad Module [*Computer science*] (IAA)
SPM.......... Scripture Press Ministries (EA)
SPM.......... Security Program Manager [*Military*] (GFGA)
SPM.......... Sedimentary Phosphate Method
SPM.......... Self-Propelled Mount [*Military*]
SPM.......... Semipermeable Membrane
SPM.......... Senior Project Manager
SPM.......... Sequential Processing Machine (DIT)
SPM.......... Serial Parallel Multiplier (IAA)
SPM.......... Session Protocol Machine [*Telecommunications*] (OSI)
SPM.......... Shore Protection Manual [*Army*]
SPM.......... Short Particular Metre [*Music*]
SPM.......... Shots per Minute [*Military*] (RDA)
SPM.......... Significant Probability Mapping
SPM.......... Sine Prole Mascula [*Without Male Issue*] [*Latin*]
SPM.......... Single-Point Management
SPM.......... Single-Point Mooring [*Oil platform*]
SPM.......... Single Program Manager [*Air Force*]
SPM.......... Six Point Mooring [*Oil platform*]
SPM.......... Smaller Profit Margin
SPM.......... Societas Patrum Misericordiae [*Fathers of Mercy*] [*Roman Catholic religious order*]
SPM.......... Society for Policy Modeling (EA)
SPM.......... Society of Pragmatic Mysticism (EA)
SPM.......... Society of Prospective Medicine (EA)
SPM.......... Software Programmer's Manual
SPM.......... Solar Polar Mission (MCD)
SPM.......... Solar Power Module
SPM.......... Solar Proton Monitor
SPM.......... Somali Patriotic Movement [*Political party*] (EY)
SPM.......... Sound-Powered Microphone
SPM.......... Source Program Maintenance [*IBM Corp.*]
SPM.......... Specialist, Mail Clerk [*Navy rating*]
SPM.......... Special-Purpose Materials (MCD)
SPM.......... Spectrophosphorimeter
SPM.......... Spectrum Industrial Resources [*Vancouver Stock Exchange symbol*]
SpM.......... Spiriformis Medialis Nucleus [*Brain anatomy*]
SPM.......... Split Phase Motor
SPM.......... Standard Payload Module (MCD)
SPM.......... Standard Practice Memo (MCD)
SPM.......... Standard Preparation Method
SPM.......... Standard Procedure Manual (AAG)
SPM.......... Standard Process Manual
SPM.......... Standard Progressive Matrices [*Also, Raven's Coloured Progressive Matrices*] [*A type of intelligence test*] (PAZ)
SPM.......... Standard Prototype Microcomputer (NITA)
SPM.......... Static Presentation Mode
SPM.......... Stationary Plasma Motor
SPM.......... Statistical Parametric Mapping [*Data treatment*]
SPM.......... St. Philips Marsh [*Bristol*] [*British depot code*]
SPM.......... St. Pierre and Miquelon [*ANSI three-letter standard code*] (CNC)
SPM.......... Strokes per Minute
SPM.......... Subhuman Primate Model [*Medicine*] (DMAA)
SPM.......... Subscriber's Private Meter [*Telecommunications*] (TEL)
SPM.......... Subsystem Project Manager [*NASA*] (NASA)
SPM.......... Sun Probe-Mars [*NASA*]
SPM.......... Superparamagnetic [*Fraction in rock*] [*Geophysics*]
SPM.......... Support Program Management
SPM.......... Surface Plasmon Microscopy [*Physics*]
SPM.......... Suspended Particulate Matter
SPM.......... Symbol Processing Machine (IEEE)
SPM.......... Synaptic Plasma Membrane [*Neurophysiology*]
SPM.......... Synaptosomal Plasma Membrane [*Neurobiology*]
SPM.......... Synthetic Plasma Membrane [*Biochemistry*]
SPM.......... System Performance Model
S/PM.......... System/Project Management
SPM.......... Systems Program Manager
SPMA.......... Rio Maranon [*Peru*] [*ICAO location identifier*] (ICLI)
SPM.A......... Saga Petroleum ADS'A' [*NYSE symbol*] (TTSB)
SPMA.......... Sewage Plant Manufacturers' Association [*British*] (BI)
SPMA.......... Shoe Pattern Manufacturers Association [*Defunct*] (EA)
SPMA.......... Society for Post-Medieval Archaeology [*British*]
SPMA.......... Soda Pulp Manufacturers Association [*Defunct*] (EA)
SPMA.......... Southwest Parks and Monuments Association (EA)
SPMA.......... Spinal Progressive Muscular Atrophy [*Medicine*] (AAMN)
SPMA.......... String Polling Multiple Access (PDAA)
SPMA.......... Sump Pump Manufacturers Association [*Later, SSPMA*] (EA)
SPMAGTF.... Special Purpose Marine Air Ground Task Force (DOMA)
SPMAR......... Scratch Pad Memory Address Register [*Computer science*] (MHDI)
SPM.B......... Saga Petroleum ADS'B' [*NYSE symbol*] (TTSB)
SPMB.......... Strong Partial Maternal Behavior [*Psychology*]
SPMC.......... Shannon Park Marine Center [*West Washington University*] [*Anacortes, WA*]
SPMC.......... Society of Paper Money Collectors (EA)
SPMC.......... Society of Professional Management Consultants [*Association name and designation awarded by this group*] [*Englewood, NJ*] (EA)
SPMC.......... Special Machine [*Tool*] (AAG)
SPMC.......... Standard Procedure Monitor Chart (PDAA)
SPMD.......... Silicon Planar Multiple Diode (IAA)
SPME.......... Solar Proton-Monitoring Experiment (PDAA)
SPME.......... Solid Phase Microextraction [*Chemistry*]
SPME.......... Solid-Phase Microextraction [*Chemistry*]
SPME.......... Spectroscopic Phase-Modulated Ellipsometry
SPME.......... Tumbes/Pedro Canga [*Peru*] [*ICAO location identifier*] (ICLI)
SPMEA......... Sulfate of Potash Magnesia Export Association (EA)
SPMG.......... Scottish Primary Mathematics Group (AIE)
SPMG.......... Societe pour le Patrimoine Musical Canadien (AC)
SPMI.......... Status Post Myocardial Infarction [*Cardiology*] (DAVI)
SPMid......... Standard & Poor's MidCap 400 Depository Receipts [*Associated Press*] (SAG)
SPML.......... Special Meal [*Diabetic, low-cholesterol, low-calorie, hypoglycemic, or gluten-free*] [*Airline notation*] (ADA)
SPMLF......... Societe de la Psychologie Medicale de Langue Francaise [*French-Language Society of Medical Psychology - FLSMP*] (EA)
SPMM.......... Society for the Promotion of Mohammedan Missions [*Defunct*] (EA)
SPMMV......... Sweet Potato Mild Mottle Virus [*Plant pathology*]
SPMO.......... SAMMS [*Standard Automated Materiel Management System*] Program Management Office [*DoD*]
SPMO.......... Senior Principal Medical Officer [*British*] (DI)
SPMOL......... Source Program Maintenance Online
SPMP.......... Special-Purpose Multiprocessor [*Computer science*]
SP-MPC....... Shuttle Projects - Management Planning and Control Office [*Kennedy Space Center*] [*NASA*] (NASA)
SPMR.......... Southern Provinces Mounted Rifles [*British military*] (DMA)
SPMR.......... Standard Proportionate Mortality Ratio [*Medicine*] (DMAA)
SPMR.......... Sub Postmaster [*British*] (DCTA)
SPMRL......... Sulphite Pulp Manufacturers' Research League (EA)
SPMS.......... Serial Poll Mode State (IAA)
SPMS.......... Sine Prole Mascula Superstite [*Without Surviving Male Issue*] [*Latin*] (ADA)
SPMS.......... Solar Particle Monitoring System [*NASA*] (KSC)
SPMS.......... Special-Purpose Manipulator System [*NASA*] (NASA)
SPMS.......... Special-Purpose Monitoring Station [*Environmental Protection Agency*]
SPMS.......... Strategic Planning and Management System [*Environmental Protection Agency*] (GFGA)
SPMS.......... Suppression Pool Makeup System [*Nuclear energy*] (NRCH)
SPMS.......... Surveyor Payload Mechanism Section
SPMS.......... System Program Management Surveys [*Air Force*]
SPMS.......... Yurimaguas [*Peru*] [*ICAO location identifier*] (ICLI)
Sp Msgr....... Special Messenger [*Army*]
SPMSQ......... Short Portable Mental Status Questionnaire (EDAC)
SPMT.......... Sportmart, Inc. [*NASDAQ symbol*] (SAG)
SPMTA......... Sportmart Inc.'A' [*NASDAQ symbol*] (TTSB)
SPMTS......... Simplified Predetermined Motion Time System (MHDB)
SPMV.......... Satellite Panicum Mosaic Virus
SPMW.......... Subpolar Mode Water [*Marine science*] (OSRA)
SPMY.......... Dos De Mayo [*Peru*] [*ICAO location identifier*] (ICLI)
SPN.......... Cape Shipunski [*Former USSR Seismograph station code, US Geological Survey*] (SEIS)
SPN.......... Pelican Narrows Public Library, Saskatchewan [*Library symbol National Library of Canada*] (NLC)
SPN.......... Saipan [*Mariana Islands*] [*Airport symbol*] (OAG)
SPN.......... Satellite Programming Network [*Cable-television system*]
SPN.......... Satellite Program Network (NITA)
SPN.......... Savanna Pastoral Neolithic [*Archeology*]
SPN.......... Secretariado da Propaganda Nacional [*Portugal*]
SPN.......... Semiconductor Productivity Network (NITA)
SPN.......... Senior Plan Network [*Information service or system*] (HCT)

SPN .... Separation Program Number [*Military*]
SPN .... Series Parallel Network (IAA)
SPN .... Service Part Number
SPN .... Service Protection Network (NITA)
SPN .... Shared Processing Network (USDC)
SPN .... Shared Processing Network [*Marine science*] (OSRA)
SPN .... Shipment/Performance Notification [*DoD*]
SPN .... Shuttle Project Notice [*Kennedy Space Center*] [*NASA*] (NASA)
SPN .... Skorpion Air [*Bulgaria*] [*ICAO designator*] (FAAC)
SPN .... Solitary Pulmonary Nodule [*Medicine*] (DAVI)
SPN .... Sparton Resources, Inc. [*Toronto Stock Exchange symbol*]
SPN .... Special Program Number (MUGU)
sp n .... Species Novum [*New Species*] [*Also, sp nov*] [*Biology*] (DAVI)
SPN .... Specimen (WGA)
SPN .... Sponsor Program Number [*Military*]
SPN .... Standard Precision Navigator
SPN .... Student Practical Nurse (AAMN)
SPN .... Subscriber Premises Network [*Telecommunications*]
SPN .... Switched Public Network [*Telecommunications*] (IAA)
SPN .... Sympathetic Preganglionic Neuron [*Anatomy*]
SPNA .... Punta De Lomas [*Peru*] [*ICAO location identifier*] (ICLI)
SPNB .... Security Pacific National Bank (NITA)
SPNC .... Huanuco/Alferez FAP David Figuerao Fernandini [*Peru*] [*ICAO location identifier*] (ICLI)
SPNC .... [*The*] Spectranetics Corp. [*NASDAQ symbol*] (SPSG)
SPND .... Self-Powered Neutron Detector [*Nuclear energy*] (NRCH)
SPND .... Suspend (NASA)
SPNEA .... Society for the Preservation of New England Antiquities (EA)
SPNF .... Shot Peening Fixture (MCD)
SPNFT .... South Pacific Nuclear Free Treaty
SPNFZ .... South Pacific Nuclear Free Zone (EERA)
SPNFZT .... South Pacific Nuclear Free Zone Treaty
SPNG .... Society for Provincial Notaries General [*British*]
SPNG .... Sponge
SPNG .... Spring [*Commonly used*] (OPSA)
SPN/GEANS ... Standard Precision Navigator/Gimbaled Electrostatic-Gyro Aircraft Navigation System (MCD)
SPN/GEANS ... Standard Precision Navigator/Gimballed Electrostatic Aircraft Navigation System
SPNGS .... Springs [*Commonly used*] (OPSA)
SPNH .... Laguna Choclococha [*Peru*] [*ICAO location identifier*] (ICLI)
SPNH .... Special Purpose Nursing Home [*Australia*]
SPNHC .... Society for the Preservation of Natural History Collections (EA)
SPNI .... Societe pour la Protection de la Nature en Israel [*Society for the Protection of Nature in Israel*] [*Tel Aviv*] (EAIO)
SPNI .... Spinnaker Inds [*NASDAQ symbol*] (SAG)
SPNI .... Spinnaker Industries [*NASDAQ symbol*] (TTSB)
S/PNL .... Side Panel [*Automotive engineering*]
SPNM .... Society for the Promotion of New Music [*British*]
SPNO .... Ancon [*Peru*] [*ICAO location identifier*] (ICLI)
sp nov .... Species Nova [*New Species*] [*Biology*]
SPNP .... Puno [*Peru*] [*ICAO location identifier*] (ICLI)
SPNR .... Ricran [*Peru*] [*ICAO location identifier*] (ICLI)
SPNR .... Society for the Promotion of Nature Reserves [*British*] (BI)
SPNR .... Spanner (AAG)
SPNR .... System Peculiar Non-Repairable
SPNS .... Sapiens International Corp. [*NASDAQ symbol*] (SAG)
SPNS .... Spoons (ROG)
SPNS .... Standard Product Numbering System (PDAA)
SPNS .... Standards of Performance for New Sources [*Power*] (DICI)
SPNS .... Switched Private Network Service [*ITT service mark*]
SPNSF .... Sapiens Intl N.V. [*NASDAQ symbol*] (TTSB)
SPNSN .... Suspension (MSA)
SPNT .... Intuto [*Peru*] [*ICAO location identifier*] (ICLI)
SPNU .... Manu [*Peru*] [*ICAO location identifier*] (ICLI)
SPNZ .... Santa Cruz [*Peru*] [*ICAO location identifier*] (ICLI)
SPNZ .... Socialist Party of New Zealand [*Political party*] (PPW)
SPO .... Aeroservicios Ejecutivos del Pacifico SA [*Mexico ICAO designator*] (FAAC)
SPO .... Denver, CO [*Location identifier FAA*] (FAAL)
SPO .... Sacramento Peak Observatory
SPO .... Sandia Pulse Reactor
SPO .... Saturn Program Office [*NASA*] (KSC)
SPO .... Saturn Project Office [*NASA*] (IAA)
SPO .... Sausages, Potatoes, and Onions [*Meaning a cheap restaurant that specializes in these*] [*British slang*]
SPO .... Sea Post Office
SPO .... Senate Post Office
SPO .... SENTRY [*Survey Entry*] Project Office
SPO .... Separate Partition Option
SPO .... Shore Patrol Officer [*Navy*]
SPO .... Short Period Oscillation
SPO .... Shuttle Project Office [*NASA*] (KSC)
SPO .... Signal Property Office [*Military*]
SPO .... Single Pickle Ordinary [*Metal industry*]
SPO .... Slaving Pick-Off
SPO .... Society of Perinatal Obstetricians (EA)
SPO .... Society of Planning Officials
SPO .... Sozialdemokratische Partei Oesterreichs [*Social Democratic Party of Austria*] [*Political party*]
SPO .... Spacelab Program Office [*NASA*]
SPO .... Spare Parts Order [*NASA*] (NASA)
SPO .... Specialist, Inspector of Naval Material [*Navy rating*]
SPO .... Special Placement Officer (ADA)
SPO .... Special Projects Office [*Navy*]
SPO .... Spokane [*Washington*] [*Seismograph station code, US Geological Survey Closed*] (SEIS)
SPO .... Sponsoring Organization (NITA)
SPO .... Spooner Mines & Oils Ltd. [*Toronto Stock Exchange symbol*]
SPO .... Srpski Pokret Obnove [*Serbian Renaissance Movement*] [*Political party*] (EY)
SPO .... Status Postoperative [*Surgery*] (DAVI)
SPO .... Stoker Petty Officer [*Navy British*] (DSUE)
SPO .... Subpurchase Order (AAG)
SPO .... Supplemental Production Order (AAG)
SPO .... Surplus Property Office [*Transferred to War Assets Administration, 1947*]
SPO .... Synchronized Power On (MHDI)
SPO .... System Program [*or Project*] Office [*Military*]
SPOA .... Les Sagesses du Proche-Orient Ancien. Colloque de Strasbourg [*1962*]. Travaux du Centre d'Etudes Superieurs Specialise d'Histoire des Religions de Strassbourg [*Paris*] [*A publication*] (BJA)
SPOA .... Saposoa [*Peru*] [*ICAO location identifier*] (ICLI)
SPOA .... Scottish Plant Owners Association (DBA)
SPOAV .... Specialist, Inspector of Aviation Material [*Navy rating*]
SPOBS .... Special Observer [*US Army group in London*] [*World War II*]
SPOC .... Shuttle Payload Operations Contractor (NASA)
SPOC .... Shuttle Payload Opportunity Carrier
SPOC .... Shuttle Portable Onboard Computer [*NASA*]
SPOC .... Single Point of Contact (GFGA)
SPOC .... Single-Point Orbit Calculator
SPOC .... Solid Phase Organic Chemistry
SPOC .... Solid-Propulsion Optimization Code (MCD)
SPOC .... Spacecraft Oceanography Project [*Navy*]
SPOC .... Special Projects Operations Center [*Allied Force Headquarters*] [*World War II*]
SPOC .... Splicing of Cross Correlation Function (IAA)
SPOC .... Sydney Paralympic Organising Committee [*Australia*]
SPOC .... Systems Program Office Cadre (MCD)
SPOCC .... South Pacific Organizations Coordinating Committee (EERA)
SPOCK .... Simulated Procedure for Obtaining Common Knowledge
SPOCK .... Special Purpose Operational Computing Kernel [*Pilot training device developed at Georgia Institute of Technology*]
SPOCM .... Society for the Preservation of Old Mills (EA)
SPOCN .... Subpurchase Order Change Notice (AAG)
SPOD .... Seaports of Debarkation (MCD)
SPOD .... Sexual and Personal Relationships of the Disabled (AIE)
SPOD .... Ship's Plan of the Day [*Navy*] (DNAB)
SpOd .... Spanish Odeon, Barcelona [*Record label*] [*Spain*]
SPODA .... Society for the Prevention of Drug Addiction
SPODAC .... SITS [*SAGE Intercept Target Simulation*] Probability of Detection and Conversion (MCD)
SPODP .... Single Precision Orbit Determination Program [*NASA*]
SPOE .... Sea Port of Export [*MTMC*] (TAG)
SPOE .... Seaports of Embarkation (MCD)
SPOE .... Society of Post Office Engineers [*Pronounced "spowee"*] [*British*] (DCTA)
SPOE .... Sozialistische Partei Oesterreichs [*Socialist Party of Austria*]
SPOEN .... Specialist, Engineering Inspector [*Navy rating*]
SP OFF .... Special Offering [*Stocks*] (MHDW)
SPOFOR .... Sportwissenschaftliche Forschungsprojekte [*Bundesinstitut fuer Sportwissenschaft*] [*Germany Information service or system*] (CRD)
SPOG .... Sales of Products Other than Gasoline
SPOL .... Collique [*Peru*] [*ICAO location identifier*] (ICLI)
SPOLIT .... Sportliteratur [*Bundesinstitut fuer Sportwissenschaft*] [*Germany Information service or system*] (CRD)
SPOM .... Society of Post Office Managers [*A union*] [*British*]
SPOM .... STS [*Shuttle Test Station*] Planning and Operations Management [*NASA*] (GFGA)
SPOM .... Suspended Particulate Organic Material [*Environmental chemistry*]
SPOMCUS .... Selective Prepositioning of Materiel Configured to Unit Sets [*Army*] (AABC)
S Pomp .... Sextus Pomponius [*Flourished, 2nd century*] [*Authority cited in pre-1607 legal work*] (DSA)
SPON .... Sponsor (AFM)
SPON .... Sponsor
SPON .... Spontaneous (WGA)
SPON .... Statistical Profile of Old Norse
SPONG .... Sponsoring
SPONT .... Spontaneous
Spont Ab .... Spontaneous Abortion [*Medicine*] (MAE)
SPOOF .... Society for the Protection of Old Fishes (EA)
SPOOF .... Structure and Parity Observing Output Function
SPOOFS .... Society for the Promotion of Otherwise Overlooked Football Scores
SPOOK .... Supervisor Program Over Other Kinds [*Computer science*]
SPOOL .... Simultaneous Peripheral Operation Online [*Computer science*] (MCD)
SPOOL .... Simultaneous Processing of Off-Line Item
SPOOL .... Simultaneous Production Operation Online
SPOOL .... Spontaneous Peripheral Operations Online Spooling [*Computer science*] (IAA)
SPOOM .... Society for the Preservation of Old Mills (EA)
Spoon .... Spooner's Reports [*12-15 Wisconsin*] [*A publication*] (DLA)
Spooner .... Spooner's Reports [*12-15 Wisconsin*] [*A publication*] (DLA)
SPOOR .... Specialist, Ordnance Inspector [*Navy rating*]
SPOP .... Poto [*Peru*] [*ICAO location identifier*] (ICLI)
SPOP .... Scan Platform Operations Program
SPOPE .... Specialist, Petroleum Technician [*Navy rating*]

SP-OPI........ Shuttle Projects - Operations Planning and Integration [*NASA*] (GFGA)
SP-OPN........ Shuttle Projects - Operations Planning Office [*Kennedy Space Center*] [*NASA*] (NASA)
SPO-PO........ System Program Office/Project Office [*Air Force*] (AFIT)
SPOPS........ Special Operations
SPOR........ Sport-Haley [*NASDAQ symbol*] (TTSB)
SPOR........ Sport Haley, Inc. [*NASDAQ symbol*] (SAG)
SPORK........ Spoon and Fork
SPORO........ Sporotrichosis [*A fungal infection*] (DAVI)
SPORS........ Slosson Pre-Observational Record Screen [*Educational test*]
SPORT........ Soldier Portable On-System Repair Tool [*Military*]
SPORT........ Space Probe Optical Recording Telescope [*Army*]
SPORT........ Sporting (ROG)
SPORT........ Sporting
SPORT........ St. Petersburg [*Florida*] Olympic Regatta Training
SPORTFOR... Support Force
SportM........ Sports Media, Inc. [*Associated Press*] (SAG)
Spor Tr........ Sporting Traditions [*A publication*]
SportRec...... Sports & Recreation, Inc. [*Associated Press*] (SAG)
SportsClb..... Sports Club Company, Inc. [*Associated Press*] (SAG)
SportSup..... Sport Supply Group [*Associated Press*] (SAG)
SPORTSWR... Sportswear
SPOS........ Strong Point/Obstacle System [*Military*] (NVT)
SPOS........ System Program Offices (IAA)
SPOS........ Zorritos [*Peru*] [*ICAO location identifier*] (ICLI)
SP-OSO........ Shuttle Projects - Off-Site Offices [*NASA*] (GFGA)
SPOSS........ Society for the Promotion of Science and Scholarship (EA)
SPOT........ Earth Observation Satellite [*France*] [*Marine science*] (OSRA)
SPOT........ PanAmSat Corp. [*NASDAQ symbol*] (SAG)
SPOT........ Satellite and Physicians Office Testing
SPOT........ Satellite Positioning and Tracking
SPOT........ Simulated Pave Penny Omnidirectional Target (MCD)
SPOT........ Skill in Personnel through On-Site Training [*Department of Labor*]
SPOT........ Small Portable Operational Terminal (LAIN)
SPOT........ Smithsonian Precision Optical Tracking
SPOT........ Spectral Pattern-Oblique Transillumination (RDA)
SPOT........ Speed Position and Track (MCD)
Spot........ Spotlight [*Record label*] [*Australia*]
SPOT........ Spot Wind [*Meteorology*] (DA)
SPOT........ Steel Plate Ordering Technique (IAA)
SPOT........ Symptom Pattern Observation Technique [*Aviation*]
SPOT........ System Probatoire d'Observation de la Terre [*of France*] [*Instrument*] (EERA)
SPOTR........ Special Projects Officer, Technical Representative [*Navy*] (DNAB)
SPOTREP..... Spot Report [*Military*] (NVT)
SPOTS........ Sikorsky Program Operations Tracking System (MCD)
SPOTS........ Slosson Post-Observational Testing Screen [*Educational test*]
Spott........ Spottiswoode's Equity [*Scotland*] [*A publication*] (DLA)
Spott Eq Rep... Spottiswoode's English Equity Reports [*A publication*] (DLA)
Spottis CL & Eq Rep... Common Law and Equity Reports, Published by Spottiswoode [*A publication*] (DLA)
Spottis Eq..... Spottiswoode's Equity [*Scotland*] [*A publication*] (DLA)
Spottis Pr..... Spottiswoode's Practices [*Scotland*] [*A publication*] (DLA)
Spottis St..... Spottiswoode's Styles [*Scotland*] [*A publication*] (DLA)
Spottisw...... Spottiswoode's Equity [*Scotland*] [*A publication*] (DLA)
Spottisw Eq... Spottiswoode's Equity [*Scotland*] [*A publication*] (DLA)
SPOTY........ Single Parent of the Year
SPOUT........ System Peripheral Output Utility [*Nuclear energy*] (NRCH)
SPOV........ Leon Velarde/Shiringayoc O Hda. Mejia [*Peru*] [*ICAO location identifier*] (ICLI)
SPOY........ Atico [*Peru*] [*ICAO location identifier*] (ICLI)
SPP........ Menongue [*Angola*] [*Airport symbol*] (OAG)
SPP........ New York Society for the Prevention of Pauperism
SPP........ Peace Corps School Partnership Program [*Later, PCPP*] (EA)
SPP........ Safe-Practice Procedure (MCD)
SPP........ Samoa-Pago Pago [*Diocesan abbreviation*] (TOCD)
SPP........ Scalable Parallel Processor [*Computer science*] (CDE)
SPP........ Scientific Passenger Pod [*NASA*]
SPP........ Sclerosing Papillomatous Pattern [*Medicine*]
SPP........ Scott Paper Co. [*NYSE symbol*] (SPSG)
SPP........ Secular Periodic Perturbation
SPP........ Sensor-Pointing Platform (SSD)
SPP........ Sequenced Packet Protocol [*Computer science*] (PCM)
SPP........ Serpa [*Portugal*] [*Airport symbol*] (AD)
SPP........ Severe Parental Punishment
SPP........ Sexuality Preference Profile
SPP........ Signal Processing Peripheral
SPP........ Signal Processing Program [*BV Engineering*] [*Computer science*]
SPP........ Simulation Planning Panel [*NASA*] (NASA)
SPP........ Skin Perfusin Pressure [*Medicine*] (DMAA)
SPP........ Society for Pediatric Psychology (EA)
SPP........ Society of Private Printers [*Middlesex, England*]
SPP........ Society of Professional Pilots (EA)
SPP........ Sodium Pentachlorophenoxide [*Insecticide*]
SPP........ Soeurs de la Providence de Portieux (EAIO)
SPP........ Solar Photometry Probe (AAG)
SPP........ Solar Physics Payload [*NASA*] (MCD)
SPP........ Solar Pumped Plasma (SSD)
SPP........ Sole Parent's Pension
SPP........ Soluble Protein Preparation [*Biochemistry*]
SPP........ Song Position Pointer [*Computer science*] (PCM)
SPP........ Sound Powered Phone (IAA)
SPP........ Southwest Power Pool [*Regional power council*]
SPP........ Spainair [*Spain ICAO designator*] (FAAC)
SPP........ Spare Parts Provisioning
SPP........ Specialist, Photographic Specialist [*Navy rating*]
SPP........ Specially Promoted Programme [*British*]
SPP........ Special Proficiency Pay [*British military*] (DMA)
SPP........ Special Purpose Processor
SPP........ Species [*Plural form*] [*Also, spp*]
SPP........ Species Plantarum Project (EERA)
SPP........ Specific Purpose Payment
SPP........ Speed Power Product (IAA)
SPP........ Sponsor Program Proposal (MCD)
SPP........ Spot Product Prices [*Database*] [*Petroleum Intelligence Weekly*] [*Information service or system*] (CRD)
SPP........ Standard Parallel Port [*Computer science*] (CDE)
SPP........ Standard Practice Procedures (MCD)
SPP........ Standards Policy Panel (ACII)
SPP........ Still Picture Projector (MSA)
SPP........ Stock Purchase Plan [*Offered by a company to its employees*]
SPP........ St. Paul [*Alaska*] [*Seismograph station code, US Geological Survey Closed*] (SEIS)
SPP........ St. Paul Public Library, St. Paul, MN [*OCLC symbol*] (OCLC)
SPP........ St. Philips Resources [*Vancouver Stock Exchange symbol*]
SPP........ Straight Path Penetration
SPP........ Structured Programming Processor [*Computer science*] (IAA)
SPP........ Suprapubic Prostatectomy [*Medicine*]
SPP........ Surplus Personal Property
SPP........ Swaziland Progressive Party
SPP........ System Package Plan [*or Program*] [*Military*]
SPPA........ Puerto Ocopa [*Peru*] [*ICAO location identifier*] (ICLI)
SPPA........ Scottish Pre-School Play Association (DBA)
SPPA........ Screen Process Printing Association [*Later, SPAI*] (EA)
SPPA........ Social Development Program for Poor Areas [*UNICEF*] (ECON)
SPPA........ Society for Philosophy and Public Affairs (EA)
SPPA........ Society for the Preservation of Poultry Antiquities (EA)
SPPAC........ Salinity Pilot Program Advisory Council (EERA)
SP-PAI........ Shuttle Projects - Project Assessment and Integration Staff [*NASA*] (GFGA)
Sp Path........ Speech Pathology (DAVI)
SPPAY........ Semipost-Pay, Pay-Station [*Telecommunications*] (TEL)
SP-PAY........ Shuttle Projects - Payload Integration Office [*Kennedy Space Center*] [*NASA*] (NASA)
SPPB........ Sodium Pyrophosphate Buffer [*Analytical chemistry*]
SPPB........ Statens Psykologisk-Pedagogiska Bibliotek [*National Library for Psychology and Education*] [*Sweden*] [*Information service or system*] (IID)
SPPC........ Self-Pumped Phase Conjugator [*Optics*]
SPPC........ Spare Parts Provisioning Card
SP-PCO........ Shuttle Projects - Program Control Office [*NASA*] (GFGA)
SPPD........ Space Propulsion and Power Division [*NASA*]
SPPD........ Spin-Polarized Photoelectron Diffraction [*Physics*]
SPPE........ State per Pupil Expenditure [*Education*] (GFGA)
SPPED........ System for Pupil and Program Evaluation and Development (EDAC)
SPPES........ Spin-Polarized Photoemission Spectroscopy
SPPF........ Seychelles People's Progressive Front (PPW)
SPPF........ Solid-Phase Pressure Forming [*Shell Chemical Co.*]
SPPG........ Paramonga [*Peru*] [*ICAO location identifier*] (ICLI)
SPPG........ Space Plasma Physics Payload Group [*NASA*] (SSD)
SP-PG........ Sulfated Polysaccharide-Peptoglycan [*Biochemistry*]
SPPH........ Split Phase [*Electronics*] (IAA)
SPPI........ Southern Production Program, Inc.
SPPI........ Structured Pediatric Psychosocial Interview (EDAC)
SPPI........ Symposium on the Preventability of Perinatal Injury
SPPIL........ Shuttle Preferred Pyrotechnic Items List [*NASA*] (NASA)
SPPK........ Studien zur Palaeographie und Papyruskunde [*C. Wessely*] [*A publication*] (BJA)
SPPL........ Spare Parts Provisioning List [*NASA*] (NASA)
SPPL........ Spark Plug
SPPL........ Statewide Public Library Interlibrary Loan and Reference Network [*Library network*]
SPPLB........ Specialist, Photographer, Laboratory [*Navy rating*]
SPPLITT....... Southern Pacific Pipelines and International Tank Terminals [*Two companies jointly building deepwater port to accommodate outsize oil carriers*]
SpPm........ Biblioteca Publica, Palma De Mallorca, Spain [*Library symbol Library of Congress*] (LCLS)
SPPM........ Pomacocha [*Peru*] [*ICAO location identifier*] (ICLI)
SPPM........ Safe Passage Path Map (SAA)
SPPM........ Serial Parallel Pipeline Multiplier (IAA)
SPPMP........ Specialist, Motion Picture Production [*Navy rating*]
SP-PMS........ Shuttle Projects - Performance Management Systems Office [*NASA*] (GFGA)
SPPN........ Society of Private and Pioneer Numismatics (EA)
SPPO........ Scheduled Program Printout (NATG)
SPPO........ Spacelab Payload Project Office [*NASA*]
SPPO........ Special Projects Program Order (AAG)
SPPP........ Huanacopampa [*Peru*] [*ICAO location identifier*] (ICLI)
SPPP........ Spacelab Payloads Processing Project (NASA)
SPPP........ Superior Performance Proficiency Pay (MCD)
SPPPA........ Spartan Potential Production Problem Analysis [*Missiles*] (MCD)
SPPPA........ Spartan Production Program Producibility Analysis [*Missiles*] (MCD)
SPPPG........ Specialist, Photogrammetry [*Navy rating*]
SPPPM........ Surveyor Project Policy and Procedure Manual [*NASA*]
SPPR........ Specialist, Public Relations [*Coast Guard*]
SPPR........ Special Peacetime Program Requirements [*DoD*]
SPPR........ Supertel Hospitality [*NASDAQ symbol*] (TTSB)
SPPR........ Supertel Hospitality, Inc. [*NASDAQ symbol*] (SAG)

Sp Pr Cas.... Spinks' English Admiralty Prize Cases [*1854-56*] [*A publication*] (DLA)
SPPRT......... Support
SPPS.......... Semipost-Pay, Pay-Station [*Telecommunications*] (TEL)
SPPS.......... Solid-Phase Peptide Synthesis [*Biochemistry*]
SPPS.......... Specialist, Port Security [*Coast Guard*]
SPPS.......... Special Products and Program Support
SPPS.......... Stable Plasma Protein Solution [*Medicine*]
SPPS.......... Subsystem Program Preparation Support [*Programming language*] [*Computer science*]
SPPT.......... Southern Pacific Petroleum NL [*NASDAQ symbol*] (NQ)
SPPT.......... Superprecipitation Response [*Medicine*] (DMAA)
SPPTY......... Southern Pac Petrol NL [*NASDAQ symbol*] (TTSB)
SPPVM......... Specialist, V-Mail [*Navy rating*]
SPPY.......... Chachapoyas [*Peru*] [*ICAO location identifier*] (ICLI)
SPQ........... Memphis, TN [*Location identifier FAA*] (FAAL)
SPQ........... Sandpiper Oil & Gas [*Vancouver Stock Exchange symbol*]
SPQ........... San Pedro [*California*] [*Airport symbol Obsolete*] (OAG)
SPQ........... Special Product Quotation (IAA)
SPQ........... Stanford Parent Questionnaire [*Psychology*]
SPQ........... Student Progress Questionnaire (AIE)
SPQCR......... Specialist, Communications Specialist, Cryptographer [*Navy rating*]
SPQE.......... Subpool Queue Element (MHDI)
SPQIN......... Specialist, Communications Specialist, Radio Intelligence [*Navy rating*]
SPQJ.......... Jaqui [*Peru*] [*ICAO location identifier*] (ICLI)
SPQN.......... Requena [*Peru*] [*ICAO location identifier*] (ICLI)
SPQR.......... Selected Product Quality Review [*DoD*]
SPQR.......... Senatus Populusque Romanus [*The Senate and People of Rome*] [*Latin*]
SPQR.......... Small Profits, Quick Returns
SPQR.......... Speed, Power, Quietness, and Reliability [*Automotive engineering*]
SPQRP......... Specialist, Communications Specialist, Registered Publication Clerk [*Navy rating*]
SPQS.......... Self Profile Q-Sort [*Child development test*]
SPQT.......... Iquitos/Coronel FAP Francisco Secada Vignetta [*Peru*] [*ICAO location identifier*] (ICLI)
SPQTE......... Specialist, Communications Specialist, Technician [*Navy rating*]
SPQU.......... Arequipa/Rodriguez Ballon [*Peru*] [*ICAO location identifier*] (ICLI)
SPR........... Eastern Flying Service Ltd. [*Canada ICAO designator*] (FAAC)
SPR........... Puerto Rico Reports, Spanish Edition [*A publication*] (DLA)
SPR........... Sampling with Partial Replacement
SPR........... Sandia Pulsed Reactor [*Nuclear energy*]
SPR........... San Pedro [*Belize*] [*Airport symbol*] (OAG)
SPR........... Sapper [*Military*]
SPR........... Satellite Parametric Reduction
SPR........... S-Band Planetary RADAR
SPR........... Scientific Process & Research, Inc. [*Information service or system*] (IID)
SPR........... Seal Pressure Ratio
SPR........... Seconds per Revolution [*or Rotation*] (NVT)
SPR........... Secretarial Performance Review [*DoD*] (DOMA)
SPR........... Secretary of the Air Force Program Review (MCD)
SPR........... Selective Parallel Running (NITA)
SPR........... Semipermanent Repellent (ADA)
SPR........... Send Priority and Route Digit [*Telecommunications*] (TEL)
SPR........... Sense Printer
SPR........... Sequential Probability Ratio [*Statistics*]
SPR........... Serial Printer (IAA)
SPR........... Serial Probe Recognition [*Psychometrics*]
SPR........... Shock Position Ratio
SPR........... Shortest Possible Route (MCD)
SPR........... Short Pulse RADAR (IAA)
SPR........... Silicon Power Rectifier
SPR........... Simplified Practice Recommendation
SPR........... Single-Ply Roofing
SPR........... Single-Point Refueling (MCD)
SPR........... Skin Potential Response [*Physiology*]
SPR........... Society for Pediatric Radiology (EA)
SPR........... Society for Pediatric Research (EA)
SPR........... Society for Philosophy of Religion (EA)
SPR........... Society for Physical Research [*British*] (BI)
SPR........... Society for Psychical Research [*British*]
SPR........... Society for Psychophysiological Research (EA)
SPR........... Society for Psychosomatic Research (EAIO)
SPR........... Society of Patient Representatives [*Later, NSPR*] (EA)
SPR........... Software Problem Report [*NASA*] (NASA)
SPR........... Solid-Phase Reactor
SPR........... Solid Phase Receptacle [*Laboratory testing*]
SPR........... Solid-Propellant Rocket
SPR........... South Polar Region
SPR........... Spacer (AAG)
SPR........... Spare [*Telecommunications*] (TEL)
SPR........... Specialist, Recruiter [*Navy rating*]
SPR........... Special Program Requirement (AFM)
SPR........... Special Program Review [*Army*] (RDA)
SPR........... Special Project Report
SPR........... Special-Purpose RADAR
SPR........... Special-Purpose Requirements [*Army*]
SPR........... Specific Price Reduction
SPR........... Specific Resistance (IAA)
SPR........... Spinster
SPR........... Sponsor
SPR........... Sponsor's Program Review [*Navy*] (DOMA)
Spr........... Sprague's United States District Court (Admiralty) Decisions [*A publication*] (DLA)
SPR........... Spratly Islands [*ANSI three-letter standard code*] (CNC)
SPR........... Spring (MSA)
SPR........... Springer Resources [*Vancouver Stock Exchange symbol*]
SPR........... Springfield [*Diocesan abbreviation*] [*Massachusetts*] (TOCD)
Spr........... Sprinkled [*Bookbinding*] (DGA)
SPR........... Sprinkler (AAG)
spr........... Spruce (VRA)
SPR........... Statement of Procedural Rules [*A publication*] (DLA)
SPR........... Statisitcal Pattern Recognition [*Computer science*]
SPR........... Sterling Capital [*AMEX symbol*] (TTSB)
SPR........... Sterling Capital Corp. [*AMEX symbol*] (SPSG)
SPR........... Storage Protection Register
SPR........... St. Pierre [*Quebec*] [*Seismograph station code, US Geological Survey Closed*] (SEIS)
SPR........... Strategic Petroleum Reserve [*Department of Energy*]
SPR........... Strategic Planning Review (SSD)
SPR........... Stroposcopic Pulse Radiolysis [*Physical chemistry*]
SPR........... Structure-Property Relationship [*Chemistry*]
SPR........... Subcontractor Performance Review [*NASA*] (NASA)
SPR........... Sub Petito Remissionis [*With Request for Return*] [*Latin*]
SPR........... Substance P Receptor [*Biochemistry*]
SPR........... Sudden Pressure Relay
SPR........... Sun Protection Required [*Identification system for heat-sensitive cargo*] [*Shipping*] (DCTA)
SPR........... Super
SPR........... Supervisory Printer Read [*Computer science*] (OA)
SPR........... Supplementary Progress Report
SPR........... Supply Performance Report (CINC)
SPR........... Support Period Requirement
SPR........... Support Plans and Requirements
SPR........... Surface Plasmon Resonance [*Physics*]
SPR........... System Parameter Record [*Computer science*] (IBMDP)
SPR........... System Performance Rating
SPR........... System Problem Report (MCD)
SPR........... System Program Review [*Military*] (AABC)
SPrA.......... Sears, Roebuck 8.88% Dep Pfd [*NYSE symbol*] (TTSB)
SPRA.......... Semi-Permanet Release Agent
SPRA.......... Space Probe RADAR Altimeter (KSC)
SPRA.......... Special-Purpose Reconnaissance Aircraft [*Navy*]
SPRA.......... Sponsor's Profit and Risk Allowance [*Department of Housing and Urban Development*] (GFGA)
SPRAA......... Strategic Plans and Resource Analysis Agency (DOMA)
SPRACAY....... Society for Prevention of Rock and Roll and Corruption of American Youth [*Organization in 1956 movie "Shake, Rattle and Roll"*]
SPRAG......... Spray Arrester Gear (MCD)
SPRAG......... STS Payload Requirements and Analysis Group [*NASA*] (NASA)
Sprague....... Sprague's United States District Court (Admiralty) Decisions [*A publication*] (DLA)
SPRANS........ Special Projects of Regional and National Significance [*HHS*]
SPRAT......... Small Portable RADAR Torch
SPRB.......... Senior Performance Review Board (MHDB)
SPR BOG....... Springender Bogen [*Bouncing Bow*] [*Music*]
SPRC.......... Seafood Products Research Center [*Public Health Service*] (GRD)
SPRC.......... Self-Propelled Robot Craft (IEEE)
SPRC.......... Society of Public Relations Counsellors
SPRC.......... Star Petroleum Refinery Complex [*Thailand*]
SPRCHTB....... Senior Parachutist Badge [*Military decoration*] (GFGA)
SPRCS......... Safe Passage Route Creation Sheet (SAA)
SPRD.......... Science Policy Research Division [*of Congressional Research Service, Library of Congress*]
SPRD.......... Survey of Primary Reading Development (AEBS)
SPRDA......... Solid Pipeline Research and Development Association (HGAA)
SPRDNG........ Spreading [*Freight*]
SPRDR......... Spreader (MSA)
SPRDS......... Steam Pipe Rupture Detector System (IEEE)
SPRE.......... Society of Park and Recreation Educators (EA)
SPRE.......... Solid-Propellant Rocket Engine
SPRE.......... Special Prefix Code [*Northern Telecom*] [*Telecommunications*]
SPREAD........ Spring Evaluation Analysis and Design (MCD)
SPREAD........ Supercomputer Project Research Experiment in Advanced Development [*Lawrence Livermore Laboratory, Los Alamos National Laboratory, and SRI*]
SPREAD........ Support Program for Remote Entry of Alphanumeric Displays (NITA)
SPREC......... Specular Reflection Computer Program (MCD)
Spreckel...... Spreckels Industries, Inc. [*Associated Press*] (SAG)
SPREd......... Society of Picture Researchers and Editors [*British*] (DBA)
SPREE......... Solid-Propellant Exhaust Effects (MCD)
SPREE......... Structure Preserving Estimation (ADA)
SPREG......... Speed Regulator
SPREP......... South Pacific Environment Protection Convention (EERA)
SPREP......... South Pacific Regional Environment Program (EERA)
SPREP......... South Pacific Regional Environment Programme [*of the South Pacific Commission*] [*New Caledonia*]
SPRES......... Star Present (NASA)
SPRF.......... Sandia Pulsed Reactor Facility [*Nuclear energy*]
SPRF.......... Space Propulsion Research Facility (AAG)
SPRF.......... Special-Purpose Receiving Facility
SprfldSv...... Springfield Institution for Savings [*Associated Press*] (SAG)
SPRG.......... San Regis [*Peru*] [*ICAO location identifier*] (ICLI)
SPRG.......... Social Policy Research Group, Inc. [*Information service or system*] (IID)
SPRG.......... Spring
SPRG.......... Sprinkling (MSA)

Sprgn.......... Sepragen Corp. [*Associated Press*] (SAG)
SPRI.......... Scott Polar Research Institute [*Cambridge, England*]
SPRI.......... Single Ply Roofing Institute (EA)
SPRI.......... Social Problems Research Institute [*University of South Carolina at Columbia*] [*Research center*] (RCD)
SPRI.......... Social Process Research Institute [*Research center*] (RCD)
SPRI.......... Social Psychiatry Research Institute (EA)
SPRI.......... Sperm Reservoir Length Index
SPRI.......... Sugar Processing Research, Inc.
SPRIA.......... Solid-Phase Radioimmunoassay [*or Radioimmunoprecipitation Assay*] [*Clinical medicine*]
SPRING.......... Spring [*Commonly used*] (OPSA)
Springfield C... Springfield College (GAGS)
Springs.......... Spring Industries, Inc. [*Associated Press*] (SAG)
SPRINGS.......... Springs [*Commonly used*] (OPSA)
SPRINT.......... Selective Printing [*Computer science*]
SPRINT.......... Solid-Propellant Rocket Intercept Missile [*ARPA/AMC*]
SPRINT.......... Southern Pacific Communications' Switched Long Distance Service [*Telecommunications*] (TEL)
SPRINT.......... Spare Parts Review Initiatives [*Army*] (RDA)
SPRINT.......... Special Police Radio Inquiry Network [*New York City*]
Sprint.......... Sprint Corp. [*Associated Press*] (SAG)
SPRINT.......... Strategic Programme for Innovation and Technology Transfer [*European Commission*]
SPRINTER.......... Specification of Profits with Interaction under Trial and Error Response
Spr Int L.......... Sprague on International Law [*A publication*] (DLA)
Sprint00.......... Sprint Corp. [*Associated Press*] (SAG)
SPRITE.......... Sequential Polling and Review of Interacting Teams of Experts (PDAA)
SPRITE.......... Sheffield People's Resource for Information Technology [*British*] (AIE)
SPRITE.......... Signal Processing in the Element (MCD)
SPRITE.......... Solid-Propellant Rocket Ignition Test and Evaluation (KSC)
SPRITE.......... Surveillance, Patrol, Reconnaissance, Intelligence Gathering, Target Designation, and Electronic Warfare [*Unmanned aircraft*] [*Military*]
SPRJ.......... Self-Powered Reference Junction
SPRKLG.......... Sprinkling [*Freight*]
SPRKT.......... Sprocket (MSA)
SPRL.......... Space Physics Research Laboratory [*University of Michigan*] [*Research center*] (RCD)
SPRM.......... San Ramon/Capitan Alvarino [*Peru*] [*ICAO location identifier*] (ICLI)
SPRM.......... Special Reamer [*Tool*] (AAG)
SPRM.......... Spermatozoa (DAVI)
SPRM.......... Supreme
SPRMRKT.......... Supermarket
SPRNG.......... Spring [*Commonly used*] (OPSA)
SPRNGS.......... Springs [*Commonly used*] (OPSA)
SPRO.......... Services Public Relations Officer [*British military*] (DMA)
S-P/ROM.......... Slave Programmable Read-Only Memory
SPROM.......... Slave Programmable ROM (NITA)
SPROM.......... Spontaneous Premature Rupture of Membrane [*Medicine*] (DMAA)
SPROM.......... Spontaneous Rupture of Membranes [*Obstetrics*] (DAVI)
SPROM.......... Switched Programmable Read-Only Memory
SPROM NIL... Spontaneous Rupture of Membranes, Not In Labor [*Obstetrics*] (DAVI)
SPROPS.......... Section Properties [*Camutek*] [*Software package*] (NCC)
SPROSS.......... Simulation Program for Sequential System (PDAA)
SPRP.......... Signalling Preprocessing Program (PDAA)
SPRR.......... Selective Paramagnetic Relaxation Reagent [*Chemistry*]
SPRR.......... Self-Propelled Recoilless Rifle [*British military*] (DMA)
SPRRS.......... Southern Plains Range Research Station [*Oklahoma State University*] [*Research center*] (RCD)
SPRS.......... Single Passenger Reservation System [*DoD*]
SPR's.......... Small Parcels and Rolls [*Postal Service*]
SPRS.......... Society for the Promotion of Roman Studies (EAIO)
SPRS.......... Special-Purpose RADAR Set
SPRS.......... Student Proficiency Rating Scale
SPRS.......... Sublime Power of the Royal Secret [*Freemasonry*] (ROG)
SPRT.......... Rio Tigre [*Peru*] [*ICAO location identifier*] (ICLI)
SPRT.......... Sequential Probability Ratio Test [*Statistics*]
SPRT.......... Sport
SPRT.......... Standard Platinum Resistance Thermometer
SPRT.......... Support (MSA)
SPRT.......... System Performance and Repeatability Test [*Military*] (CAAL)
SprtaP.......... Sparta Pharmaceutical, Inc. [*Associated Press*] (SAG)
SPRTAP.......... Specially Prepared Tape Program (SAA)
SprtaSur.......... Sparta Surgical Corp. [*Associated Press*] (SAG)
SprtHaley.......... Sport Haley, Inc. [*Associated Press*] (SAG)
Sprtmrt.......... Sportmart, Inc. [*Associated Press*] (SAG)
SprtP.......... Sparta Pharmaceutical, Inc. [*Associated Press*] (SAG)
SprtS.......... Sparta Surgical Corp. [*Associated Press*] (SAG)
SprtS.......... Sports Sciences, Inc. [*Associated Press*] (SAG)
SprtS96.......... Sparta Surgical Corp. [*Associated Press*] (SAG)
SprtSci.......... Sports Sciences, Inc. [*Associated Press*] (SAG)
SPRU.......... Science Policy Research Unit [*Research center British*] (IRC)
SPRU.......... Trujillo/Capitan Carlos Martinez de Pinillos - Huanchaco [*Peru*] [*ICAO location identifier*] (ICLI)
SPRUCE.......... Special Programs and Rehabilitation under Unemployment Compensation [*Department of Labor*]
SPS.......... Saint Patrick's Seminary [*Menlo Park, CA*]
SPS.......... Samples per Second
SPS.......... San Pedro De Poas [*Costa Rica*] [*Seismograph station code, US Geological Survey*] (SEIS)
SPS.......... Satellite and Production Services [*Tallahassee, FL*] [*Telecommunications*] (TSSD)
SPS.......... Satellite Power System (MCD)
SPS.......... Saturn Parts Sales [*NASA*]
SPS.......... Saturn Propulsion System [*NASA*]
SPS.......... Scene per Second (MCD)
SPS.......... Scheduled Passenger Service (IIA)
SPS.......... Schedule Promulgated Separately [*Navy*] (NVT)
SPS.......... School of Practical Science
SPS.......... School Psychology Specialist (PGP)
SPS.......... Scientific Power Switching
SPS.......... Seamen's Protection Society [*A union*] [*British*]
SPS.......... Secondary Plant System [*Nuclear energy*] (NRCH)
SPS.......... Secondary Power Source
SPS.......... Secondary Power System [*or Subsystem*] (MCD)
SPS.......... Secondary Propulsion System [*NASA*]
SPS.......... Second Preferred Stock [*Investment term*]
SPS.......... Security Police Squadron [*Air Force*]
SPS.......... Sekcja Pracy Spolecznej [*A publication*] (BJA)
SPS.......... Self Protection System (MCD)
SPS.......... Senior Private Secretary
SPS.......... Sensor Processing Subsystem (GAVI)
SPS.......... Sequential Partition System (IAA)
SPS.......... Serial Parallel Serial (NITA)
SPS.......... Serial-Parallel-Serial Structure (IAA)
SPS.......... Series-Parallel-Serial Configuration [*Electronics*] (MDG)
SPS.......... Service Propulsion System [*or Subsystem*] [*NASA*]
SPS.......... Servo Parameter Shift
SPS.......... Set Point Station
SpS.......... Sharpshooter [*Military decoration*] (AABC)
SPS.......... Sheltered Placement Scheme (AIE)
SPS.......... Shipping/Production Scheduling
SPS.......... Ship Planning System
SPS.......... Ship Program Schedule
SPS.......... Shuttle Procedures Simulator [*NASA*] (NASA)
SPS.......... Signal Pre-emption System
SPS.......... Signal Processing System (KSC)
SPS.......... Silent Propulsion System (MCD)
SPS.......... Simple Phrase System
SPS.......... Simplified Processing Station (MCD)
SPS.......... Simulated Parts Sketch (MCD)
SPS.......... Simulator Panel Set (MCD)
SPS.......... Sine Prole Superstite [*Without Surviving Issue*] [*Latin*]
SPS.......... Single-Pole Switch
SPS.......... Socialistische Partij Suriname [*Surinam Socialist Party*] [*Political party*] (PPW)
SPS.......... Socialist Party of Slovenia [*Political party*] (EY)
SPS.......... Social Problems Series [*A publication*]
SPS.......... Society for Pentecostal Studies (EA)
SPS.......... Society of Pelvic Surgeons (EA)
SPS.......... Society of Physics Students (EA)
SPS.......... Society of Portrait Sculptors [*British*] (BI)
SPS.......... Socijalisticka Partija Srbije [*Socialist Party of Serbia*] [*Political party*] (EY)
SPS.......... Sodium Polyanetholesulfonate [*Analytical biochemistry*]
SPS.......... Sodium Polystyrene Sulfonate [*Organic chemistry*]
SPS.......... Soft Particle Spectrometer [*Geophysics*]
SPS.......... Software Procurement Specification
SPS.......... Software Product Specification
SPS.......... Software Products Scheme [*Computer science*] (DCTA)
SPS.......... Solar Panel Substrate
SPS.......... Solar Power Satellite [*NASA*]
SPS.......... Solar Power System (MCD)
SPS.......... Solar Probe Spacecraft [*Pioneer satellite*]
SPS.......... Solar Proton Stream [*Geophysics*] (SAA)
SPS.......... Solid Phase Synthesis [*Chemistry*]
SPS.......... Soluble Polysaccharide of Soybean [*Food technology*]
SPS.......... SONAR Phase Shifter
SPS.......... Sound Production Sample [*Medicine*] (DMAA)
SPS.......... South Pole Station [*National Weather Service*]
SPS.......... Southwestern Public Service Co. [*NYSE symbol*] (SPSG)
SPS.......... Southwestern PubSv [*NYSE symbol*] (TTSB)
SPS.......... Sozialdemokratische Partei der Schweiz [*Social Democratic Party of Switzerland*] [*Political party*] (PPE)
SPS.......... Sozialdemokratische Partei Suedtirols [*Social Democratic Party of South Tirol*] [*Political party*] (PPE)
SPS.......... Spacecraft Propulsion System (AAG)
SPS.......... Space Planning System [*Applied Research of Cambridge Ltd.*] [*Software package*] (NCC)
SPS.......... Space Power System (CET)
SPS.......... SPASA Servicios Politecnicos Aereos SA [*Spain ICAO designator*] (FAAC)
SPS.......... Special Education Specialist (PGP)
SpS.......... Specialist in Science (GAGS)
SPS.......... Specialist, Personnel Supervisor [*Women's Reserve*] [*Navy rating*]
SPS.......... Specialist, Shore Patrol and Security [*Navy rating*]
SPS.......... Special-Purpose SONAR (MCD)
SPS.......... Special Services [*Military*]
SPS.......... Specific Pavement Studies [*FHWA*] (TAG)
SPS.......... Spectrum Planning Subcommittee [*FCC*]
SPS.......... Speed Switch (IEEE)
SPS.......... Spokane, Portland & Seattle Railway System [*AAR code*]
SPS.......... SPS Technologies, Inc. [*Formerly, Standard Pressed Steel Co.*] (MCD)
SPS.......... Stabilized Platform Subsystem (KSC)

SPS............ Standard Pipe Size
SPS............ Standard Port System (MCD)
SPS............ Standard Positioning Service
SPS............ Standard Positioning Service
SPS............ Standard Process Specification (MCD)
SPS............ Standard Procurement System (AAGC)
SPS............ Standard Project Storm [*Nuclear energy*] (NRCH)
SPS............ Standby Power Source [*Electronics*]
SPS............ Standby Power Supply (PCM)
SPS............ Statement of Prior Submission (NASA)
SPS............ State Permit System [*Environmental Protection Agency*] (GFGA)
SPS............ Static Power System
SPS............ Static Pressure System
SPS............ Statistical Performance Standards [*Navy*] (NG)
SPS............ Stator Pivot Seal
SPS............ Status Projection System
SPS............ Steady Potential Shift
SPS............ Steampipe Survey
SPS............ Steering Pressure Sensor [*Automotive engineering*]
SPS............ Stereo Photographic System
SPS............ Stichting Plurale Samenlevingen [*Foundation for the Study of Plural Societies - FSPS*] (EAIO)
SPS............ Stimulated Protein Synthesis [*Medicine*] (DMAA)
SPS............ Stored Program Simulator
SPS............ St. Patrick's Missionary Society [*Roman Catholic men's religious order*]
sps............ St. Patrick's Missionary Society (TOCD)
SPS............ Strategical Planning Section [*Joint Planning Staff*] [*World War II*]
SPS............ Strategic Planning Society [*Formerly, Society for Strategic and Long Range Planning*] (EA)
SPS............ Strategic Planning Staff [*Social Security Administration*]
SPS............ String Processing System [*Word processing software*]
SPS............ String Process System (NITA)
SPS............ Student Profile Section [*of the American College Testing Test Battery*]
SPS............ Submarine Piping System
SPS............ Submerged Production System [*Deepwater platform*] [*Humble Oil*]
SPS............ Subsea Production System [*Petroleum technology*]
SPS............ Sucrose-Phosphate Synthase [*An enzyme*]
SPS............ Suicide Probability Scale [*Personality development test*] [*Psychology*]
SPS............ Sulfadiazine [*Microbiology*] (DAVI)
SPS............ Sulfite-Polymyxin-Sulfadiazine [*Agar*] [*Microbiology*]
SPS............ Summit Power Station [*Nuclear energy*] (NRCH)
SPS............ Super Proton Synchrotron [*Particle physics*]
SPS............ Supplementary Power Supply (IAA)
SPS............ Supplementary Protection System [*Nuclear energy*] (NRCH)
SPS............ Supply Point Simulation (MCD)
SPS............ Symbolic Programming System [*Computer science*]
SPS............ Symbolic Program System (NITA)
SPS............ Symbols per Second [*Computer science*]
SPS............ Synchronous Program Supervisor (IAA)
SPS............ Syndiotactic Polystyrene [*Organic chemistry*]
SPS............ Syndiotactic Polystyrene
SPS............ Systemic Progressive Sclerosis [*Medicine*] (AAMN)
SPS............ System Performance Score [*Telecommunications*] (TEL)
SPS............ System Performance Simulation
SPS............ Wichita Falls [*Texas*] [*Airport symbol*] (OAG)
SPSA.......... Casma [*Peru*] [*ICAO location identifier*] (ICLI)
SPSA.......... Senate Press Secretaries Association (EA)
SPSA.......... Society of Philippine Surgeons in America (EA)
SPSA.......... Special Projects School for Air
SPSA.......... Standard Page Specification Association (BTTJ)
SPSAA........ Swimming Pool and Spa Association of Australia
SpSAG........ Archivo General de Indias [*Archives of the Indies*], Seville, Spain [*Library symbol Library of Congress*] (LCLS)
SPSBS........ Shetland Pony Study Book Society [*British*] (DBA)
SPSC.......... Saharan People's Support Committee (EA)
SPSC.......... Seventy Plus Ski Club (EA)
SP/SC.......... Shield Plug/Support Cylinder [*Nuclear energy*] (NRCH)
SPSC.......... Signal Processing and Spectral Control
SPSC.......... Space Power Systems Conference
SPSC.......... Standard Performance Summary Charts (AAG)
SPSCR........ Special Screw
SPSD.......... Shipboard Passive Surveillance and Detection System (PDAA)
SPSD.......... Space Power Systems Division [*NASA*]
SPSD.......... State Purchasing and Sales Division [*Tasmania, Australia*]
SP-SDF........ Socialist Party - Social Democratic Federation [*Later, Socialist Party of the United States of America*] (EA)
SPSDM........ Society for the Philosophical Study of Dialectical Materialism (EA)
SPSDS........ Ship's Passive Surveillance and Detection System [*Navy*] (CAAL)
SPSE.......... Society of Photographic Scientists and Engineers (EA)
SPSE.......... Special Purpose Support Equipment
SPSF.......... Self-Propagating-Star Formation [*Galactic science*]
SPSF.......... Society of the President Street Fellows (EA)
SPSF.......... Spent Fuel Storage Pool [*Nuclear energy*] (NUCP)
SPSFM........ St. Patrick's Society for the Foreign Missions [*See also SSPME*] [*Kiltegan, County Wicklow, Republic of Ireland*] (EAIO)
SPSFV........ State Public Services Federation Victoria [*Australia*]
SPSG.......... Sparta Surgical [*NASDAQ symbol*] (TTSB)
SPSG.......... Sparta Surgical Corp. [*NASDAQ symbol*] (SAG)
SPSGU........ Sparta Surgical Unit [*NASDAQ symbol*] (TTSB)
SPSGW........ Sparta Surgical Wrrt [*NASDAQ symbol*] (TTSB)
SP/SHLD...... Splash Shield [*Automotive engineering*]
SPSHP........ Special Shaped
SPSHS........ Stanford Profile Scales of Hypnotic Susceptibility [*Psychology*]
SPSI............ Serikat Pelajaran Seluruh Indonesia [*Sailors' Union of Indonesia*]
SPSI............ Society for the Promotion of Scientific Industry [*British*]
SPSI............ SpectraScience Inc. [*NASDAQ symbol*] (TTSB)
SPSI............ SpectraScience, Inc. [*NASDAQ symbol*] (SAG)
SPSJ............ San Jose De Sisa [*Peru*] [*ICAO location identifier*] (ICLI)
SPSL............ Lamas [*Peru*] [*ICAO location identifier*] (ICLI)
SPSL............ Socialist Party of Sri Lanka
SPSL............ Society for the Philosophy of Sex and Love (EA)
SPSL............ Society for the Protection of Science and Learning [*British*]
SPSL............ Spare Parts Selection List
SPSLGI........ Society for the Psychological Study of Lesbian and Gay Issues (EA)
SPSM.......... Socialist Party of San Marino [*Political party*] (EAIO)
SPSM.......... Society for the Philosophical Study of Marxism (EA)
SPSM.......... Supply Point Simulation Model (MCD)
SPSME........ Spacelab Payload Standard Modular Electronics (MCD)
SP-SMO...... Shuttle Projects - Site Management Office [*NASA*] (GFGA)
SPSN.......... Submitted Package Sequence Number (MCD)
SPSO.......... Pisco [*Peru*] [*ICAO location identifier*] (ICLI)
SPSO.......... Senior Personnel Staff Officer [*Air Force British*]
SPSO.......... Senior Principal Scientific Officer [*Ministry of Agriculture, Fisheries, and Food*] [*British*]
SPSP.......... Small Power System Program (IAA)
SPSP.......... Solid-Propellant Surveillance Panel [*Military*]
SPSP.......... Spare Parts Support Package
SPSP.......... St. Peter and St. Paul [*The Papal seal*]
SPSP-AGE.... Spare Parts Support Package for Aerospace Ground Equipment (MCD)
SPSPS........ Specialist, Personnel Supervisor, V-10 [*Navy rating*]
SPSQ.......... Satisfaction with Performance Scaled Questionnaire
SpsQualBad... Sharpshooter Qualification Badge [*Military decoration*] (AABC)
SPSS.......... Masisea [*Peru*] [*ICAO location identifier*] (ICLI)
SPSS.......... Shield Plug Storage Station [*Nuclear energy*] (NRCH)
SPSS.......... Single-Pole Snap Switch (IAA)
SPSS.......... Single Pulse Selection System
SPSS.......... Society of the Priests of St. Sulpice [*See also CPSS*] [*Paris, France*] (EAIO)
SPSS.......... SPSS, Inc. [*NASDAQ symbol*] (SAG)
SPSS.......... Statistical Package for the Social Sciences [*Programming language*] [*1970*]
SPSS.......... Supplementary Power Supply Set (IAA)
SPS-SCWG... Spanish Philatelic Society Spanish Civil War Study Group [*Defunct*] (EA)
SPSSI.......... Society for the Psychological Study of Social Issues (EA)
Sp St.......... Private and Special Laws [*A publication*] (DLA)
SPST............ Single-Pole, Single-Throw [*Switch*]
SPST............ Social Problem-Solving Test (EDAC)
SPST............ Spent Resin Storage Tank [*Nuclear energy*] (IAA)
SPST............ Symonds Picture-Story Test [*Psychology*]
SPST............ Tarapoto [*Peru*] [*ICAO location identifier*] (ICLI)
SPSTec........ SPS Technologies, Inc. [*Associated Press*] (SAG)
SPSTNC...... Single-Pole, Single-Throw, Normally-Closed [*Switch*]
SPSTNO...... Single-Pole, Single-Throw, Normally-Open [*Switch*]
SPSTNODM... Single-Pole, Single-Throw, Normally-Open, Double-Make [*Switch*]
SPSTP.......... Solid-Propellant Rocket Static Test Panel [*Military*]
SPS Trns..... SPS Transaction Services, Inc. [*Associated Press*] (SAG)
SPSTSW...... Single-Pole, Single-Throw Switch
SP SURF...... Specific Surface (WDAA)
SPSW.......... Single-Pole Switch
S/PSWO...... Service/Parts Sales Work Order (MCD)
SPSWO........ Spare Parts Sales Work Order
S Psy S........ Specialist in Psychological Services (PGP)
SPT.............. Albuquerque, NM [*Location identifier FAA*] (FAAL)
SPT.............. Bengis Aviation (Pty) Ltd. [*South Africa*] [*FAA designator*] (FAAC)
SPT.............. Piedmont Technical College, Greenwood, SC [*OCLC symbol*] (OCLC)
SPT.............. Scaled-Particle Theory
SPT.............. School of Physical Training [*British*]
SPT.............. Scientist-Pilot [*NASA*] (KSC)
SPT.............. Seaport
SPT.............. Sectors per Track
SPT.............. Selective Population Transfer [*Physics*]
SPT.............. Sense Printer Test (SAA)
Spt.............. September (CDAI)
SPT.............. Septic [*Classified advertising*] (ADA)
SPT.............. Septuple (MSA)
SPT.............. Shaft Position Transducer
SPT.............. Shared Page Table [*Computer science*] (OA)
SPT.............. Shipper Pays Taxes
SPT.............. Ship Position Transmitter
SPT.............. Short-Period Tremors [*Volcanology*]
SPT.............. Silicon Planar Transistor
SPT.............. Silicon-Powered Transistor
SPT.............. Skin Prick Test [*Immunology*]
SPT.............. Slowest Processing Time
SPT.............. Small Perturbation Theory
SPT.............. Socialist Party of Thailand [*Political party*] (FEA)
SPT.............. Society for Philosophy and Technology (EA)
SPT.............. Society of Painters in Tempera (EA)
SPT.............. Society of Photo-Technologists (EA)
SPT.............. Society of Projective Techniques [*Later, SPA*] (EA)
SPT.............. Sodium Pyridinethione [*Organic chemistry*]
SPT.............. Sogepet Ltd. [*Toronto Stock Exchange symbol*]
SPT.............. Solar Panel Technology (SSD)
SPT.............. Sound-Powered Telephone

SPT .... South Point [*Hawaii*] [*Seismograph station code, US Geological Survey*] (SEIS)
SPT .... Space Power Tool
SpT .... Spanish Telefunken [*Record label*]
SPT .... Spare Parts Transfer
Spt .... Specialist Degree (PGP)
SPT .... Specialist, Teacher [*Navy rating*]
SPT .... Special Perishable Tool (MCD)
SPT .... Special Purpose Test [*Nuclear energy*] (NRCH)
SP T .... Special Term [*Legal term*] (DLA)
SPT .... Spirit
spt .... Spiritus [*Spirit*] [*Latin Pharmacy*] (MAE)
SPT .... Split (MSA)
SPT .... Spraytight
Spt .... Spritsail [*Ship's rigging*] (DS)
SPT .... Sputum
SPT .... Standard Penetration Test [*Nuclear energy*] (NRCH)
SPT .... Star Point Transfer [*Photography*] (OA)
SPT .... Static Pressure Transducer
SPT .... Streptomycin Phosphotransferase [*An enzyme*]
SPT .... Structural Programming Technique
SPT .... Supervisory Potential Test
SPT .... Support (AFM)
SPT .... Symbolic Play Test [*Child development test*]
SPT .... Symbolic Program Tape [*Computer science*] (IEEE)
SPT .... Symbolic Program Translator [*Computer science*] (IEEE)
SPT .... System Page Table [*Telecommunications*] (TEL)
SPT .... System Parameter Table [*Computer science*] (IBMDP)
SPT .... System Planning Team [*Military*] (AFIT)
SPTA .... Nauta [*Peru*] [*ICAO location identifier*] (ICLI)
SPTA .... Scottish Provision Trade Association (DBA)
SPTA .... Southern Paper Trade Association [*Defunct*] (EA)
SPTA .... Southern Pressure Treaters Association (EA)
SPTA .... Sparta Pharmaceutical, Inc. [*NASDAQ symbol*] (SAG)
SPTA .... Sparta Pharmaceuticals [*NASDAQ symbol*] (TTSB)
SPTA .... Spectrin Alpha (DMAA)
SPTAN .... Spectrin Alpha, Nonerythroid (DMAA)
SPT & PA .... Society for Projective Techniques and Personality Assessment [*Later, SPA*]
SptaP .... Sparta Pharmaceutical, Inc. [*Associated Press*] (SAG)
SptAuth .... [*The*] Sports Authority, Inc. [*Associated Press*] (SAG)
SPTAW .... Sparta Pharmaceuticals Wrrt'A' [*NASDAQ symbol*] (TTSB)
Sp Tax Rul .... Special Tax Ruling [*Internal Revenue Service*] [*United States*] [*A publication*] (DLA)
SPTAZ .... Sparta Pharmaceuticals Wrrt'B' [*NASDAQ symbol*] (TTSB)
SPTC .... Septic
SPTC .... Share-Purchase Tax Credit [*Canada*]
SPTC .... South Pacific Trade Commission [*Australia*]
SPTC .... Specified Period of Time Contract
SPTCEN .... Support Center [*Army*]
SptChalt .... Sport Chalet, Inc. [*Associated Press*] (SAG)
SPTCS .... South Pacific Trade Commissioner Service [*Australia*]
SPTD .... Signal Processor Techniques Department
SPTD .... Supplemental Provisioning Technical Documentation [*NASA*] (NASA)
SPTE .... Special Purpose Test Equipment (MCD)
SPTE .... Teresita [*Peru*] [*ICAO location identifier*] (ICLI)
SPTEA .... Single Persons for Tax Equality Association (EAIO)
SpTelc .... Specialty Teleconstructioners [*Associated Press*] (SAG)
SPTF .... Screen Printing Technical Foundation (EA)
SPTF .... Shortest Processing Time First [*Computer science*] (MHDI)
SPTF .... Shortest Programming Time First (NITA)
SPTF .... Signal Processing Test Facility
SPTF .... Social Progress Trust Fund [*Inter-American Development Bank*]
SPTF .... Sodium Pump Test Facility [*Energy Research and Development Administration*]
SPTF .... Support Flight [*Military*]
SPTG .... Sporting (WDAA)
SPTG .... Support Group [*Military*]
SPTH .... Systolic Threshold Pressure [*Cardiology*]
SPT-HP .... Scholastic Proficiency Test - Higher Primary Level [*Educational test*] [*South Africa*]
SPTI .... Puerto Inca [*Peru*] [*ICAO location identifier*] (ICLI)
SPTI .... Senior Physical Training Instructor [*British military*] (DMA)
SPTI .... Systolic Pressure Time Index [*Cardiology*] (DAVI)
SPTL .... Society of Public Teachers of Law [*British*] (DLA)
SPTL .... Superconducting Power Transmission Line (PDAA)
SPTL .... Support Line [*Military*]
SptM .... Sports Media, Inc. [*Associated Press*] (SAG)
SPTN .... Tacna [*Peru*] [*ICAO location identifier*] (ICLI)
SPTP .... Special-Purpose Test Program (MCD)
SPTP .... Talara/El Pato [*Peru*] [*ICAO location identifier*] (ICLI)
SP(TR) .... Specialist (Transportation) [*Coast Guard*]
SPTR .... SpecTran Corp. [*NASDAQ symbol*] (NQ)
SPTR .... Tournavista [*Peru*] [*ICAO location identifier*] (ICLI)
SPTRJ .... Self-Powered Thermocouple Reference Junction
Sp Trs .... Special Troops [*Army*]
SPTS .... Spirits
SPTS .... Sports Media [*NASDAQ symbol*] (TTSB)
SPTS .... Sports Media, Inc. [*NASDAQ symbol*] (SAG)
SPTS .... Stock Positioning and Transportation Study [*DoD*]
SPTS .... Subjective Posttraumatic Syndrome [*Medicine*] (DMAA)
SPTS .... Support Squadron [*Air Force*]
SPTSL .... Sports Media Wrrt'C' [*NASDAQ symbol*] (TTSB)
SPTSq .... Support Squadron [*Air Force*]
SptSu .... Sparta Surgical Corp. [*Associated Press*] (SAG)
SptSup .... Sport Supply Group [*Associated Press*] (SAG)
SPTSZ .... Sports Media Wrrt'B' [*NASDAQ symbol*] (TTSB)
SPTT .... Single-Pole, Triple-Throw [*Switch*] (CET)
SPTU .... Puerto Maldonado/Padre Aldamiz [*Peru*] [*ICAO location identifier*] (ICLI)
SPTUF .... South Pacific Trade Union Forum [*14-nation group opposed to nuclear testing and dumping in the Pacific*]
SPTURP .... Status Post Transurethral Resection of the Prostate [*Medicine*] (DAVI)
SPTV .... Supersonic Parachute Test Vehicle (IAA)
SPTW .... Single-Pedestal Typewriter [*Desk*]
SPTW .... Society Promoting Training Women [*British*] (DBA)
SPTWC .... Salle Palasz and Tri-Weapon Club (EA)
SPU .... Mount Spur [*Alaska*] [*Seismograph station code, US Geological Survey*] (SEIS)
SPU .... Salinas Public Library, Salinas, CA [*OCLC symbol*] (OCLC)
SPU .... S-Band Polar Ultra
SPU .... School Personnel Utilization
SPU .... Scientific Programs Unit [*Commonwealth*] (EERA)
SPU .... Sekretno-Politicheskoye Upravleniye [*Secret Political Directorate*] [*Former USSR*] (LAIN)
SPU .... Self-Propelled Underwater Missile (IAA)
SPU .... Sense Punch [*Computer science*] (IAA)
SPU .... Service Propulsion Unit
SPU .... Short Procedure Unit [*Medicine*] (CPH)
SPU .... Signal Processing Unit
SPU .... Slave Processing Unit
SPU .... Smallest Publishable Unit
SPU .... Small Peripheral Unit (IAA)
SPU .... Society for Pediatric Urology (EA)
SPU .... Southeast Airmotive Corp. [*ICAO designator*] (FAAC)
SPU .... Specialist, Utility [*Women's Reserve*] [*Navy rating*]
SPU .... Special Power Unit (NTCM)
SPU .... Split [*Former Yugoslavia*] [*Airport symbol*] (OAG)
SPU .... Standard Propulsion Unit (IAA)
SPU .... Student Peace Union [*Defunct*] (EA)
SPU .... Subsurface Propulsion Unit
SPU .... Supertech Industries [*Vancouver Stock Exchange symbol*]
SPU .... System Partitioning Unit [*Computer science*]
SPU .... System Power Unit
SPU .... System Power Up
SPUC .... Huamachuco [*Peru*] [*ICAO location identifier*] (ICLI)
SPUC .... Society for the Protection of Unborn Children (EA)
SPUD .... Sniff, Paw, Urinate, and Defecate [*Ungulate territorial marking procedure*]
SPUD .... Society for Prevention of Unwholesome Diet [*National Potato Council*]
SPUD .... Solar Power Unit Demonstrator
SPUD .... Soon to be Pushing Up Daisies [*Lifestyle classification*] (ECON)
SPUD .... Stored Program Universal Demonstrator
SPUD .... St. Paul Union Depot Co. [*AAR code*]
SpU/In .... Supertrust Trust Index Trust [*Associated Press*] (SAG)
SPUK .... Special Projects, United Kingdom
SpU/MM .... Supertrust Trust Money Market Trust [*Associated Press*] (SAG)
SPUN .... Society for the Protection of the Unborn through Nutrition (EA)
SPUP .... School of Public and Urban Policy [*Pennsylvania University*] (PDAA)
SPUP .... Seychelles People's United Party [*Political party*] (PPW)
SPUR .... Piura/Capitan Concha [*Peru*] [*ICAO location identifier*] (ICLI)
SPUR .... San Francisco Planning and Urban Research Association [*California*] [*Information service or system*] (IID)
SPUR .... Single Precision Unpacked Rounded [*floating-point package*] [*Computer program system Sperry Rand Corp.*]
SPUR .... Software Package for Unique Reports (GFGA)
SPUR .... Source Program Utility Routine
SPUR .... Space Power Unit Reactor [*Air Force*]
SPUR .... Special Purchase Office [*DoD*]
SPUR .... Spur [*Postal Service standard*] (OPSA)
SPUR .... Support for Projects Under Research [*British*]
SPUR .... Support for Promoting the Utilization of Resources [*Esso Education Foundation*]
SPUR .... Symbolic Processing Using RISC [*Reduced Instruction Set Computer*]
SPURM .... Special Purpose Unilateral Repetitive Modulation (IEEE)
SPURS .... Spurs [*Commonly used*] (OPSA)
SPURT .... Simulation Package for University Research and Teaching (PDAA)
SPURT .... Small Primate Unrestrained Test
SPURT .... Spinning Unguided Rocket Trajectory
SPURV .... Self-Propelled Underwater Research Vehicle
SP-USA .... Socialist Party of the United States of America (EA)
SP-USA .... Student Pugwash USA [*An association*] (EA)
SPUT .... Sputum [*Medicine*] (DAVI)
SPUTNIC .... Synchronously Programmed User Terminal and Network Interface Control [*Computer science*] (MHDI)
SPV .... Sa-Pa [*Vietnam*] [*Seismograph station code, US Geological Survey*] (SEIS)
SPV .... Selective Proximal Vagotomy [*Medicine*] (DMAA)
SPV .... Sensor Payload Vehicle
SPV .... Shope Papilloma Virus
SPV .... Slow-Phase Velocity [*Ophthalmology*]
SPV .... Space Position Value [*Outdoor advertising*] (NTCM)
SpV .... Spanish RCA Victor [*Record label*]
SPV .... Spark Port Vacuum [*Automotive engineering*]
SPV .... Specialist, Transport Airman [*Navy rating*]
SPV .... Special-Purpose Vehicle [*Military*]
SPV .... Specification Performance Validation [*Military*] (CAAL)

SPV .... Split-Product Vaccine [*Immunology*]
SPV .... STN Shop Television Network Ltd. [*Vancouver Stock Exchange symbol*]
SPV .... Storage Process Vent [*Nuclear energy*] (NRCH)
SPV .... Storage Protect Violation (CMD)
SPV .... Sulfophosphovanillin (Reaction) [*Clinical chemistry*]
SPV .... Sun Probe near Limb of Venus [*Angle*]
SPV .... Supervisor (ECII)
SPV .... Surface Photovoltage [*Photovoltaic energy systems*]
SPV .... Survey of Personal Values [*Psychology*]
SPVA .... Society for the Preservation of Variety Arts (EA)
SPVEA .... Superintendencia do Plano de Valorizacao Economica da Amazonia [*Brazil*]
SPVL .... Caraveli [*Peru*] [*ICAO location identifier*] (ICLI)
SPVLI .... Single Premium Variable Life Investment [*Insurance*]
SPVN .... Society of Peripheral Vascular Nursing (EA)
SPVN .... Supervision (MSA)
SPVOL .... Specific Volume (DEN)
SPVPF .... Shuttle Payload Vertical Processing Facility [*NASA*] (MCD)
SPVR .... Storage Process Vent Room [*Nuclear energy*] (NRCH)
SPVR .... Systemic Peripheral Vascular Resistance [*Cardiology*] (DAVI)
SPVR .... Vitor/San Isidro [*Peru*] [*ICAO location identifier*] (ICLI)
SPVS .... Supervisors Section [*American Association of School Librarians*]
Spvsr .... Supervisor
SPW .... Self-Protection Weapon
SPW .... Seward Park [*Washington*] [*Seismograph station code, US Geological Survey*] (SEIS)
SPW .... Shipment Planning Worksheet
SPW .... Spare Parts Withdrawal (MCD)
SPW .... Specialist, Chaplain's Assistant [*Navy rating*]
SPW .... Special Warfare (NVT)
SPW .... Speedwings SA [*Switzerland ICAO designator*] (FAAC)
SPW .... Spencer [*Iowa*] [*Airport symbol*] (OAG)
SPW .... SPX Corp. [*Formerly, Sealed Power Corp.*] [*NYSE symbol*] (SPSG)
SPW .... Stock Purchase Warrant (MHDW)
SPW .... Subxiphoid Pericardial Window [*Medicine*] (DMAA)
SPW .... Surface Plasma Wave
SPW .... Wofford College, Spartanburg, SC [*OCLC symbol*] (OCLC)
SPWA .... Southern Peanut Warehousemen's Association (EA)
SPWA .... Steel Products Warehouse Association
SPWAO .... Small Press Writers and Artists Organization (EA)
SPWAR .... Special Warfare
SPWC .... Society for the Punishment of War Criminals (EA)
SPWG .... Space Parts Working Group
SPWL .... Single Premium Whole Life Insurance Policy
SPWLA .... Society of Professional Well Log Analysts (EA)
SPWM .... Single-Sided Pulse Width Modulation [*Telecommunications*]
SPWP .... Society of Prayer for World Peace (EAIO)
SPWR .... Small Pressurized Water Reactor
SPWS .... Self-Protection Weapon System
SPWS .... Shipment Planning Worksheet (MCD)
SPWSM .... Spanish War Service Medal
SPWT .... SSM/I Land Products Working Team (USDC)
SPWT .... SSM/I [*Special Sensor Microwave/Imager*] Land Products Working Team [*Marine science*] (OSRA)
SPWWIII .... Society for the Prevention of World War III [*Defunct*]
SPWY .... Penske Motorsports [*NASDAQ symbol*] (TTSB)
SPWY .... Penske Motorsports, Inc. [*NASDAQ symbol*] (SAG)
SPX .... League City, TX [*Location identifier FAA*] (FAAL)
SPX .... San Pedro [*Colombia*] [*Airport symbol*] (AD)
SPX .... Sequenced Packet Exchange [*Telecommunications*] (PCM)
SPX .... Simplex Circuit
SPX .... Simplex Instrument [*Telegraphy*]
Spx .... Spirex [*Wire binding*] (DGA)
SPX .... Spirit Petroleum [*Vancouver Stock Exchange symbol*]
SPX .... Stepped Piston Crossover (PDAA)
SPX .... Superheat Power Experiment [*Nuclear energy*]
SPXAC .... Specialist, Archivist [*Navy rating*]
SPXAR .... Specialist, Artist [*Navy rating*]
SPXBL .... Specialist, Ballistics [*Navy rating*]
SPXCC .... Specialist, Cable Censor [*Navy rating*]
SPXCG .... Specialist, Crystal Grinder [*Navy rating*]
SPX Cp .... SPX Corp. [*Formerly, Sealed Power Corp.*] [*Associated Press*] (SAG)
SPXCT .... Specialist, Cartographer [*Navy rating*]
SPXDI .... Specialist, Discharge Interviewer [*Navy rating*]
SPXED .... Specialist, Engineering Draftsman [*Navy rating*]
SPXFP .... Specialist, Fingerprint Expert [*Navy rating*]
SPXGU .... Specialist, Gauge Specialist [*Navy rating*]
SPXID .... Specialist, Intelligence Duties [*Navy rating*]
SPXIR .... Specialist, Interpreter [*Navy rating*]
SPXJO .... Specialist, Journalist [*Navy rating*]
SPXKP .... Specialist, Key Punch Operator and Supervisor [*Navy rating*]
SPXNC .... Specialist, Naval Correspondent [*Navy rating*]
SPXOP .... Specialist, Special Project [*Navy rating*]
SPXPC .... Specialist, Position Classifier [*Navy rating*]
SPXPI .... Specialist, Pigeon Trainer [*Navy rating*]
SPXPL .... Specialist, Plastic Expert [*Navy rating*]
SPXPR .... Specialist, Public Information [*Navy rating*]
SPXQM .... Specialist, Operations - Plotting and Chart Work [*Navy rating*]
SPXRL .... Specialist, Research Laboratory [*Navy rating*]
SPXRS .... Specialist, Armed Forces Radio Service and Special Naval Radio Units [*Navy rating*]
SPXSB .... Specialist, Telephone Switchboard Operator and Supervisor [*Navy rating*]
SPXST .... Specialist, Strategic Services [*Navy rating*]
SPXTD .... Specialist, Topographic Draftsman [*Navy rating*]
SPXTS .... Specialist, Air Stations Operations Desk - Time Shack [*Navy rating*]
SPXVA .... Specialist, Visual Training Aids [*Navy rating*]
s-py-- .... Paraguay [*MARC geographic area code Library of Congress*] (LCCP)
SPY .... Saint Paul Island, AK [*Location identifier FAA*] (FAAL)
SPY .... San Pedro [*Ivory Coast*] [*Airport symbol*] (OAG)
spy .... Spray (VRA)
SPY .... Square Pyramidal [*Organic chemistry*]
SPY .... Standard & Poor's Deposit Receipts [*AMEX symbol*] (SPSG)
SPY .... Standard & Poor's Dep Receipts [*AMEX symbol*] (TTSB)
SPYA .... Luya [*Peru*] [*ICAO location identifier*] (ICLI)
SPYC .... Yarinacocha [*Peru*] [*ICAO location identifier*] (ICLI)
SPYG .... Spyglass, Inc. [*NASDAQ symbol*] (SAG)
Spyglss .... Spyglass, Inc. [*Associated Press*] (SAG)
SPYL .... Talara/Capitan Montes [*Peru*] [*ICAO location identifier*] (ICLI)
SPYN .... Spine-Tech, Inc. [*NASDAQ symbol*] (SAG)
SPYO .... Pacasmayo [*Peru*] [*ICAO location identifier*] (ICLI)
SPYR .... Sprayer (MSA)
SPYU .... Yauca [*Peru*] [*ICAO location identifier*] (ICLI)
SPZ .... Spar Aerospace Ltd. [*Toronto Stock Exchange symbol*]
SPZ .... Springdale [*Arkansas*] [*Airport symbol*] (OAG)
SPZ .... Submarine Patrol Zone [*Navy*] (NVT)
SPZ .... Sulfinpyrazone [*Uricosuric compound*]
SPZA .... Nazca [*Peru*] [*ICAO location identifier*] (ICLI)
SPZE .... Spice Entertainment Companies, Inc. [*NASDAQ symbol*] (SAG)
SPZH .... Pachiza [*Peru*] [*ICAO location identifier*] (ICLI)
SPZK .... Sotziki [*Peru*] [*ICAO location identifier*] (ICLI)
SPZN .... Speizman Ind [*NASDAQ symbol*] (TTSB)
SPZN .... Speizman Industries, Inc. [*NASDAQ symbol*] (SAG)
SPZO .... Cuzco/Velazco Astete [*Peru*] [*ICAO location identifier*] (ICLI)
SPZT .... Chazuta [*Peru*] [*ICAO location identifier*] (ICLI)
SQ .... E. R. Squibb & Sons [*Research code symbol*]
SQ .... Safety Quotient
SQ .... Sequens [*Following*] [*Latin*]
SQ .... Sick Quarters [*Navy British*]
SQ .... Singapore Airlines [*ICAO designator*] (AD)
SQ .... Singapore Airlines [*Airline flight code*] (ODBW)
SQ .... Situation Questionnaire
SQ .... Social Quotient [*Psychology*]
SQ .... Specialist Qualifications [*British military*] (DMA)
SQ .... Squadron
SQ .... Squall [*Meteorology*]
SQ .... Squamous [*Cell*] [*Oncology*]
SQ .... Square (EY)
sq .... Square (IDOE)
sq .... Square (ODBW)
SQ .... Square
sq .... Square (VRA)
Sq .... Square (DD)
sq .... Square Tank [*Liquid gas carriers*]
SQ .... Squawk (DA)
SQ .... Squeezed Files [*Computer science*]
SQ .... Squint Quoin [*Construction*] (IAA)
Sq .... Squire (WGA)
SQ .... Staff Qualified [*Military British*]
SQ .... Stereoquadraphonic [*Record playing system*] [*CBS*]
S-Q .... Stock Quality [*Pisciculture*]
SQ .... Subcutaneous [*Beneath the Skin*] [*Medicine*]
SQ .... Superquick [*Fuse*]
SQ .... Survival Quotient (ADA)
sq .... Swaziland [*MARC country of publication code Library of Congress*] (LCCP)
SQ3R .... Survey, Question, Read, Review, Recite [*Psychology*]
SQA .... Sequa Corp. [*NYSE symbol*] (SPSG)
SQA .... Simple, Quick & Affordable [*Office furniture*]
SQA .... Society for Quality Assurance
SQA .... Software Quality Assurance [*Computer science*] (IEEE)
SQA .... South Queensland Airways [*Australia*]
SQA .... Sparrevohn, AK [*Location identifier FAA*] (FAAL)
SQA .... SQA, Inc. [*Associated Press*] (SAG)
SQA .... Squaring Amplifier
SQA .... Stina Resources Ltd. [*Vancouver Stock Exchange symbol*]
SQA .... Supplier Quality Assurance
SQA .... Surveyor Quality Assurance
SQA .... System Queue Area [*Computer science*] (BUR)
SQA.A .... Sequa Corp. Cl'A' [*NYSE symbol*] (TTSB)
SQAA .... Supplier Quality Assurance Assistance
SQA.B .... Sequa Corp. 'B' [*NYSE symbol*] (TTSB)
SQAD .... Surveyor Quality Assurance Directive
SQAI .... Square Industries [*NASDAQ symbol*] (TTSB)
SQAI .... Square Industries, Inc. [*NASDAQ symbol*] (NQ)
SQAP .... Supplemental Quality Assurance Provision [*Military*]
SQAP .... Swedish Question Answering Project (NITA)
SQAPP .... Software Quality Assurance Program Plan [*Computer science*]
SQAPr .... Sequa $5cm Cv Pfd [*NYSE symbol*] (TTSB)
SQAR .... Supplier Quality Assurance Representative
SQAT .... Ship's Qualification Assistance Team [*Navy*]
SQAX .... SQA Inc. [*NASDAQ symbol*] (TTSB)
SQAX .... SQA, Inc [*NASDAQ symbol*] (SAG)
SQB .... Space Qualified Booster
SQBC .... Space Qualified Booster Charger
SQBE .... Small Quantity Burner Exemption [*Environmental Protection Agency*] (EPA)
Sq Bk .... Square Back [*Bookbinding*] (DGA)

SQBLA Scotch Quality Beef and Lamb Association [*British*] (DBA)
SQC Self-Quenching Control
SQC Sierra Madre Resources [*Vancouver Stock Exchange symbol*]
SQC Southern Cross [*Australia Airport symbol*] (OAG)
Sq C Square Corners [*Bookbinding*] (DGA)
SQC Station Quality Control [*RADAR*]
SQC Statistical Quality Control
Sq Ca Squamous Cell Carcinoma [*Endocrinology*] (CPH)
SqCCA Squamous-Cell Carcinoma [*Medicine*] (MEDA)
Sq CCa Squamous-Cell Carcinoma [*Oncology*] (DAVI)
sq cell ca Squamous Cell Carcinoma [*Medicine*] (MAE)
SQCG Squirrel Cage [*Electricity*]
sq ch Square Chain (BARN)
SQCM Square Centimeter (MSA)
SQCP Statistical Quality Control Procedure
SQCS Statements on Quality Control Standards (TDOB)
SQD Self-Quenching Detector
SQD Signal Quality Detector
SQD Silicone Quadrant Detector (MCD)
SQD Social Questions of Today [*A publication*]
SQD Squad (AABC)
SQD Squadron (NVT)
SQDC Special Quick Disconnect Coupling
SQ-DEL Superquick and Delay [*Fuse*] (SAA)
SQDN Squadron (AAG)
Sqdn Ldr Squadron-Leader [*British military*] (DMA)
SQE Signal Quality Error [*Computer science*] (PCM)
SQE Software Quality Evaluation (MCD)
SQE Startec Marketing [*Vancouver Stock Exchange symbol*]
SQE Supplier Quality Engineering (MCD)
SQE Supplier Quality Engineering
SqE & S Square-Edge and Sound (DAC)
SQEP Software [*Firmware*] Quality Evaluation Plan
Sq Epith Squamous Epithelium [*Medicine*] (CPH)
SQF Cleveland, OH [*Location identifier FAA*] (FAAL)
SQF Seligman Quality Municipal Fund [*NYSE symbol*] (SPSG)
SQF Seligman Quality Muni Fd [*NYSE symbol*] (TTSB)
SQF Semiquantitative Fibrinogen [*Hematology*]
SQF Slovak Air Force [*FAA designator*] (FAAC)
SQF Subjective Quality Factor (OA)
SQFT Square Foot (MSA)
SQG Small Quantity Generator [*Automotive engineering Environmental Protection Agency*]
SQH Square Head [*Bolt*]
SQ/H Square of the Hatch [*Stowage*] (DNAB)
SQHA Standard Quarter Horse Association (EA)
SQI Skill Qualification Identifier [*Army*] (INF)
SQI Special Qualifications Identifiers [*Army*] (AABC)
SQI Sterling/Rock Falls [*Illinois*] [*Airport symbol*] (OAG)
SQI Supplier Quality Improvement
SQIC Suppliers Quality Identification Classification
SQIN Sequential Quadrature Inband [*Television system*] (IAA)
SQIN Square Inch (MSA)
SQK Squawk [*Aviation*] (FAAC)
SQKM Square Kilometer (MSA)
SQL San Carlos, CA [*Location identifier FAA*] (FAAL)
SQL School Quota Letter
SQL Servicious de Alquiler Aereo SA de CV [*Mexico ICAO designator*] (FAAC)
SQL Space Qualified LASER
SQL Squelch
SQL Standard High-Level Query Language
SQL Standard Quantum Limit [*Physics*]
SQL Standard Query Language [*Computer science*]
SQL Strand Resources [*Vancouver Stock Exchange symbol*]
SQL Structured Query Language [*IBM Corp.*]
SQL Structured Query Language (GAVI)
SQL/DS Structured Query Language/Data System [*IBM Corp.*]
SQM Level Island, AK [*Location identifier FAA*] (FAAL)
SQM Sao Miguel Do Araguaia [*Brazil*] [*Airport symbol*] (OAG)
SQM Sociedad Quimica y Minera [*NYSE symbol*] (SPSG)
SQM Sociedad Quimica Y Minera ADS [*NYSE symbol*] (TTSB)
SQM Square Meter
SQM Strategic Quality Management (AIE)
SQMC Squadron Quartermaster-Corporal [*British military*] (DMA)
SQMD Squadron Manning Document (NVT)
sq mi Square Mile (CDAI)
sq mm Square Millimeter (MAE)
SQMS Squadron Quartermaster-Serjeant [*Military British*] (ROG)
SQMS Staff Quartermaster Sergeant
SQMV Squash Mosaic Virus
SQN Sanana [*Indonesia*] [*Airport symbol*] (OAG)
SQN School Quota Number
SQN Spin Quantum Number [*Atomic physics*]
SQN Squadron (NATG)
SQNA Sequana Therapeutics [*NASDAQ symbol*] (TTSB)
SQNA Sequana Therapeutics, Inc. [*NASDAQ symbol*] (SAG)
SQNA Squadron Airfield (NATG)
Sqn Ldr Squadron-Leader [*British military*] (DMA)
Sqn Obs Squadron Observer [*British military*] (DMA)
Sqn Offr Squadron-Officer [*British military*] (DMA)
SQNT Sequent Computer Sys [*NASDAQ symbol*] (TTSB)
SQNT Sequent Computer Systems, Inc. [*NASDAQ symbol*] (NQ)
SQO Senior Quarters Officer [*British military*] (DMA)
SQO Squadron Officer
SQORD Separation, Quality Analysis of RADAR Data (SAA)
SQP Secret Pass Mine [*Vancouver Stock Exchange symbol*]
SQP Shippensburg State College, Shippensburg, PA [*OCLC symbol*] (OCLC)
SQP Successive Quadratic Programming [*Algorithm*] [*Computer science*]
SQPCM Slope Quantized Pulse Code Modulation [*Telecommunications*] (IAA)
SQPD Super Quick Point Detonating
SQPN Staggered Quadriphase Pseudorandom Noise (MCD)
SQPP Software Quality Program Plan
SQPSK Staggered Quadraphase Phase Shift Key Modulation [*Computer science*] (PDAA)
SQQ San Quentin Quail [*A minor female*] [*Slang*]
SQQ Sequentibus [*In the Following Places*] [*Latin*]
SQR Sequence Relay (KSC)
SQR Sequoia Resources Ltd. [*Vancouver Stock Exchange symbol*]
SQR Soroako [*Indonesia*] [*Airport symbol*] (OAG)
SQR Square
SQR Square Root [*Computer science*]
SQR Square Rooter (IDOE)
SQR Square-Root Function (IDOE)
SQR Supplier Quality Rating
SQR Supplier Quality Representative [*Nuclear energy*] (NRCH)
sq rd Square Rod (CDAI)
SQRE Square [*Commonly used*] (OPSA)
SQRS Squares [*Commonly used*] (OPSA)
SQRT Seismic Qualification Review Team [*Nuclear energy*] (NRCH)
SQRT Square Root
SQS Skill Qualification Score [*Military*] (AABC)
SQS Squares
SQS Squares [*Postal Service standard*] (OPSA)
SQS Statistische Quellenwerke der Schweiz [*Switzerland*]
SQS Stochastic Queuing System
SQS Stratford American Corp. [*Vancouver Stock Exchange symbol*]
SQS Superquick Sensor (MCD)
SQ/SD Special Qualifications/Special Designation (NVT)
SQSPM Software Quality Standards and Procedures Manual
SQSSE Supplier Quality System Survey Evaluations (MCD)
SQT Melbourne, FL [*Location identifier FAA*] (FAAL)
SQT Queensland State Reports [*A publication*] (DLA)
SQT Ship Qualification Test [*or Trial*] [*Navy*]
SQT Silverquest Resources [*Vancouver Stock Exchange symbol*]
SQT Skill Qualification Test [*Army*]
SQT Soldier Qualification Test (MCD)
SQT Sterilization Qualification Tests
SQT System Qualification Tests
SQTIPT Ship Qualification Trials in Port [*Navy*] (NVT)
SQTNG Squadron Training (NVT)
SQTP System Qualification Test Phase
SQTT Ship Qualification Trial Team [*Navy*] (NG)
SQT(WC) Skill Qualification Test (Written Component) [*Army*] (INF)
SQU E. R. Squibb & Sons, Princeton, NJ [*OCLC symbol*] (OCLC)
SQU Squamous [*Cell*] [*Oncology*] (DAVI)
Squ Square (BJA)
SQU Squaw Peak [*Utah*] [*Seismograph station code, US Geological Survey*] (SEIS)
SQUAD Squadron
SQUADEX Squadron Exercises [*Canadian Navy*]
SQUAF Sonobuoy Qualification Facility [*Navy*] (CAAL)
SQUALL Salary Quotient at Lower Limits [*Business term*]
SQUAM Squamous [*Cell*] [*Oncology*] (DAVI)
SQUANK Simpson Quadrature Used Adaptively - Noise Killed (PDAA)
SQUAP Supplementary Quality Assurance Provisions
SQUAPP Software Quality Assurance Program Plan
SQUARE Specifying Queries as Relational Expressions [*Programming language*] [*1973*] [*Computer science*] (CSR)
SQUARE Square [*Commonly used*] (OPSA)
SQUARE Statistical Quality Analysis Report (MHDB)
SquareI Square Industries, Inc. [*Associated Press*] (SAG)
SQUARES Squares [*Commonly used*] (OPSA)
Squibb Auc Squibb on Auctioneers [*2nd ed.*] [*1891*] [*A publication*] (DLA)
SQUID Semiconducting Quantum Interference Device (MCD)
SQUID Sperry Quick Updating of Internal Documentation (IEEE)
SQUID Submerged Quick Intervention Device [*Human-powered submarine*]
SQUID Superconducting Quantum Interference Detector [*or Device*] [*For study of magnetic fields*]
SQUID Superconducting Quantum Interference Device [*Physics*]
SQUIRE Submarine Quickened Response
SQUIRE System for Quick Ultra-Fiche-Based Information Retrieval [*Computer science*] (PDAA)
SQUO Squadron-Officer [*British military*] (DSUE)
SQUOD Selected Quantile Output Device [*Electronics*]
SQUOFF Squadron-Officer [*British military*] (DSUE)
SQUP Software Quality Assurance Plan [*Computer science*] (IAA)
SQW Single Quantum Well [*Physics*]
SQW Squarewave (MSA)
SQWV Squarewave
SQX Sulfaquinoxaline [*or (Sulfanilamido)quinoxaline*] [*Animal antibiotic*]
sq yd Square Yard (CDAI)
SQZE Stark Quadratic Zeeman Effect [*Physics*]
SQZGR Squeeze Grip
SR Air-Cushion Vehicle built by Saunders Roe [*England*] [*Usually used in combination with numerals*]
SR Air Search RADAR Receiver [*Shipborne*]
SR General Society, Sons of the Revolution (EA)
SR New York State Reporter [*A publication*] (DLA)

SR............... Partiia Sotsialistov Revolyutsionerov [*Socialist Revolutionary Party*] [*Russian Political party*] (PPE)
SR............... Regina Public Library, Saskatchewan [*Library symbol National Library of Canada*] (NLC)
SR............... Saarlandischer Rundfunk [*Radio network*] [*West Germany*]
SR............... Safety Recommendation (AAG)
SR............... Safety Release [*Army*]
S/R............... Safety Relief Valve [*Nuclear energy*] (NRCH)
S/R............... Safety Representative [*Insurance*]
SR............... Safety Rod [*Nuclear energy*] (NRCH)
SR............... Salva Ratificatione [*On Condition of Ratification*] [*Latin*]
SR............... Sample Rate
SR............... Sanctioned Ritual [*British Slang*]
SR............... Santa Rosa [*Diocesan abbreviation*] [*California*] (TOCD)
SR............... Sarcoplasmic Reticulum [*Anatomy*]
SR............... Saturable Reactor
SR............... Saturation Recovery [*NMR imaging*]
SR............... Saudi Riyal [*Monetary unit*] (BJA)
SR............... Savannah River Operations Office (DOGT)
SR............... Savannah River Test Pile [*Nuclear energy*] (NRCH)
SR............... Sawyer Rifle
SR............... Scanning Radiometer
SR............... Scan Radius
SR............... Scan Rate
SR............... Scan Ratio (MCD)
SR............... Schooner [*Shipping*] (ROG)
SR............... Schumann Runge [*Spectral region*]
SR............... Scientific Report
SR............... Scientific Research
SR............... Scoring Reliability (MCD)
SR............... Scottish Regional [*Council*]
SR............... Scottish Rifles [*Military unit*] [*British*]
SR............... Screen (DAVI)
SR............... Scripture Reader (ROG)
SR............... Seaman Recruit [*Navy*]
SR............... Seaplane Reconnaissance Aircraft
SR............... Search and Reconnaissance [*Air Force*]
SR............... Search and Recovery [*Military*]
SR............... Search and Rescue
SR............... Search RADAR
SR............... Secondary RADAR (IAA)
SR............... Second-Harmonic Resonance (MCD)
SR............... Second Routing (MCD)
SR............... Secretion Rate [*Endocrinology*]
SR............... Section Report
SR............... Sedimentation Rate
SR............... Seer (WGA)
SR............... Segment Root (IAA)
SR............... Seizure Resistant [*Neurology*] (DAVI)
SR............... Selective Ringing
SR............... Selenium Rectifier [*Electronics*]
SR............... Self Raising (WDAA)
SR............... Self-Rectifying
SR............... Semantic Reaction
SR............... Senate Recedes
SR............... Senate Report
SR............... Senate Resolution
SR............... Send and Receive
S-R............... Send-Receive (IDOE)
SR............... Send Receive (NITA)
SR............... Senior
Sr............... Senior (ODBW)
SR............... Senior
sr............... Senior (DD)
Sr............... Senior (DFIT)
SR............... Senior Registrar
SR............... Senior Reviewer
SR............... Senor [*Mister*] [*Spanish*]
SR............... Sensibility Reciprocal (WGA)
SR............... Sensitivity Ratio
SR............... Sensitivity Response [*Cell*] [*Radiology*]
SR............... Sensitization Response
SR............... Sensory Rhodopsin [*Biochemistry*]
SR............... Separate Rations [*Military*]
SR............... Series Number [*Online database field identifier*]
SR............... Series Relay [*Electronics*] (IAA)
SR............... Service Record [*Military*]
SR............... Service Report
SR............... Service Rifle [*British military*] (DMA)
S-R............... Set-Reset [*Flip-Flop*] [*Computer science*]
SR............... Settlement Register [*Computer science*]
SR............... Severe, Right-Moving [*Thunderstorm*]
SR............... Sex Ratio [*Biology*]
SR............... Shaft Rate (NVT)
SR............... Sharpened Romberg [*Equilibrium*]
SR............... Shift Register
SR............... Shift Reverse
SR............... Shift Right
SR............... Shipment [*or Shipping*] Request
S/R............... Shipper/Receiver [*Difference*]
SR............... Shipping Receipt [*Business term*]
SR............... Ship Repair Ratings
SR............... Ships Records (MCD)
SR............... Ship-to-Shore RADAR [*or Radio*] (DEN)
SR............... Shock Related
SR............... Shock Resistance
SR............... Shorthair Guinea Pig [*Medicine*] (DMAA)
SR............... Short Range
SR............... Short Rate
SR............... Short Run [*Economics*]
SR............... Shunt Reactor [*Electricity*] (IAA)
SR............... Shutdown Request [*NASA*] (KSC)
SR............... Side Rails [*On a bed*] [*Medicine*]
SR............... Sierra Railroad Co. (IIA)
SR............... Sigma Reaction
SR............... Signal Regulation (IAA)
S/R............... Signal-to-Noise Ratio [*Radio*] (WDMC)
SR............... Signor [*Mister*] [*Italian*]
SR............... Silicon Rectifier
SR............... Silicon Rubber
SR............... Simian Rotavirus [*Pathology*]
SR............... Simla Rifles [*British military*] (DMA)
SR............... Simulation Report
SR............... Single Reduction
SR............... Sinus Rhythm [*Medicine*]
SR............... Sinus Roris [*Bay of Dew*] [*Lunar area*]
SR............... Sir
SR............... Sister
SR............... Sisters of Reparation of the Sacred Wounds of Jesus (TOCD)
SR............... Skagit River Railroad (IIA)
SR............... Skeleton Records [*Army*]
SR............... Skin Resistance [*Physiology*] (MAE)
SR............... Skywave Synchronization (DEN)
SR............... Slant Range
SR............... Slew Rate
SR............... Sling Ring
SR............... Slip Ring [*Electricity*]
SR............... Sloane Ranger [*Member of a British social set satirized in "The Official Sloane Ranger Handbook, The First Guide to What Really Matters in Life"*] [*Name is derived from Sloane Square in Chelsea*]
SR............... Slow Release [*Electronics*]
SR............... Slow Release Relay [*Electronics*] (IAA)
SR............... Slow Running (IAA)
SR............... Small Ring
S-R............... Smooth-Rough Variation [*Medicine*] (MAE)
SR............... Socialist Revolutionary [*Former USSR*]
SR............... Social Register
SR............... Society of Radiographers (EAIO)
SR............... Society of Rheology [*Later, SoR*] (EA)
SR............... Society of Rosicrucians (EA)
SR............... Soft Radiation (IAA)
SR............... Solar Radiation
SR............... Solar Reference
SR............... Solicitor's Recommendation [*Internal Revenue Bureau*] [*United States*] [*A publication*] (DLA)
SR............... Solid Rocket
SR............... Soluble, Repository [*With reference to penicillin*]
SR............... Soror [*Sister*]
SR............... Sorter Reader
SR............... Sortie Rate (MCD)
SR............... Sound Ranging
SR............... Sound Rating (IEEE)
SR............... Sound Recordings [*US Copyright Office class*]
SR............... Sound Reinforcement (NTCM)
SR............... Sound Report
SR............... Source Range [*Nuclear energy*] (NRCH)
SR............... Southern Rhodesia [*Later, Zimbabwe*]
SR............... Southern Rhodesia High Court Reports [*A publication*] (DLA)
SR............... Sparebanken Rogaland [*Rogaland Savings Bank*] [*Norway*]
SR............... Spares Requirement
SR............... Special Reconnaissance [*Special Operations Force*] (DOMA)
SR............... Special Register
SR............... Special Regulations [*Military*]
SR............... Special Report
SR............... Special Reserve
SR............... Specification Requirement
SR............... Specific Range
SR............... Specific Reactivity [*Exhaust emissions*] [*Automotive engineering*]
SR............... Specific Resistance (IAA)
SR............... Spec Racer [*Automotive classification*]
SR............... Spectral Recording [*Trademark of Dolby Laboratories Licensing Corp.*]
SR............... Speculative Resource [*Minerals*]
SR............... Speech Recognition
SR............... Speed Recorder (IEEE)
SR............... Speed Regulator
SR............... Spelling Reform (ADA)
SR............... Spin-Rotation [*Physics*]
SR............... Split Ring [*Technical drawings*]
SR............... Spontaneous Discharge Rate [*Audiology*]
SR............... Sports Racer [*Automotive classification*]
S/R............... Spotter Reconnaissance [*Air Force British*]
S-R............... Spring Inflow-River Inflow [*Geology*]
SR............... Square [*Ship's rigging*] (ROG)
SR............... Stable Recipient [*Medicine*]
SR............... Staff Report
SR............... Stage of Resistance [*in General-Adaptation Syndrome*]
SR............... Stage Right [*A stage direction*]
SR............... Standardization Report

SR............... Standard Range Approach [*Aviation*]
SR............... Standard Register [*NYSE symbol*] (TTSB)
SR............... Standard Repair (AAG)
SR............... Standard Requirement
SR............... Standard Resistor (IAA)
SR............... Standard Speed Radial [*Automobile tires*]
SR............... Star Route [*A type of rural postal delivery route*]
SR............... Starting Relay (DEN)
SR............... Starting Resistor (IAA)
SR............... Statement of Requirements [*NASA*] (MCD)
SR............... State Register
SR............... Stateroom (MSA)
SR............... Stationery Request (MCD)
SR............... Station Radio [*British*]
SR............... Station Regulation
SR............... Statstjanstemannens Riksforbund [*National Association of Salaried Employees in Government Service*] [*Sweden*]
SR............... Status Register [*Computer science*]
SR............... Status Report
SR............... Status Review [*NASA*] (NASA)
SR............... Statutes Revised [*A publication*] (DLA)
SR............... Statutory Rule (ADA)
SR............... Steep Rock Resources, Inc. [*Toronto Stock Exchange symbol*]
sr............... Steradian [*Symbol*] [*SI unit of solid angle*]
SR............... Steroid Receptor [*Endocrinology*]
S-R............... Stimulus-Response
SR............... Stirred-Tank Reactor (IAA)
SR............... Stochastic Resonance [*Dynamical systems*]
SR............... Stock Replacement (AAG)
SR............... Stock Report
SR............... Stoichiometric Ratio [*Chemistry*]
SR............... Stomach Rumble [*Medicine*] (AAMN)
SR............... Storage and Repair (MCD)
SR............... Storage Rack
SR............... Storage Register
SR............... Storage Room
SR............... Stove or Range
SR............... Strategic Reconnaissance [*Military*]
SR............... Strategic Reconnaissance (DOMA)
SR............... Strategic Research (MCD)
SR............... Street Rod [*Automobile modification*]
SR............... Stress-Rupture (MCD)
SR............... Stretch Reflex (MAE)
SR............... Strike Rate (ADA)
SR............... Stripe Rot [*Plant pathology*]
SR............... Strong Reactive [*Laboratory science*] (DAVI)
Sr............... Strontium [*Chemical element*]
Sr............... Strouhal Number [*IUPAC*]
SR............... Study Regulation (MCD)
SR............... Study Requirement [*Air Force*]
SR............... Styrene Rubber
SR............... Subject Ratio
SR............... Submarine Recorder [*British military*] (DMA)
SR............... Subroutine [*Computer science*] (AAG)
SR............... Subscriber Register
SR............... Sugar Requirements and Quotas
SR............... Sulfonamide-Resistant [*Microbiology*]
SR............... Summary Report
SR............... Superficial Reflex [*Neurology*] (DAVI)
SR............... Superior Rectus [*Ophthalmology*] (MAE)
SR............... Supervisor (TEL)
SR............... Supplemental Report
SR............... Supplementary Regulation
SR............... Supplementary Reserve [*British military*] (DMA)
SR............... Supply Room
SR............... Supporting Research [*Military*]
SR............... Support Reaction Load (NRCH)
SR............... Support Request [*or Requirement*] (KSC)
SR............... Support Room (MCD)
SR............... Suppressor Receptor [*Embryology*]
SR............... Supreme Court of Quebec, Reports [*A publication*] (DLA)
SR............... Su Remesa [*Your Remittance*] [*Spanish Business term*]
SR............... Surface Roughness
SR............... Surgical Removal (DAVI)
sr............... Surinam [*MARC country of publication code Library of Congress*] (LCCP)
SR............... Surinam [*ANSI two-letter standard code*] (CNC)
SR............... Surtax Rate (MHDW)
SR............... Surveillance RADAR [*Air Force*]
SR............... Surveillance Requirement [*Nuclear Regulatory Commission*] (GFGA)
SR............... Surveying Recorder [*Navy rating British*]
SR............... Surveyor [*British military*] (DMA)
SR............... Sustained Release [*Pharmacy*]
SR............... Suture Removal [*Surgery*] (DAVI)
SR............... Sveriges Radio
SR............... Swissair [*Airline*] [*ICAO designator*]
SR............... Switched Reluctance
SR............... Switch Register
SR............... Synchrotron Radiation [*High-energy physics*]
SR............... Systemic Resistance [*Medicine*] (MAE)
SR............... System Requirement (SSD)
SR............... Systems Research (DAVI)
SR............... Systems Review [*Medicine*]
SR............... Union of Soviet Socialist Republics [*IYRU nationality code*] (IYR)
SR-11.......... Sapporo Rat (Virus)
SRA............ Sair Aviation [*Canada ICAO designator*] (FAAC)
SRA............ San Ramon [*Costa Rica*] [*Seismograph station code, US Geological Survey*] (SEIS)
SRA............ Santo Rosa [*Brazil*] [*Airport symbol*] (AD)
SRA............ Saskatchewan Archives, Regina, Saskatchewan [*Library symbol National Library of Canada*] (NLC)
SRA............ Satanic Ritual Abuse
SRA............ Satellite RADAR Altimetry [*Instrumentation*]
SRA............ Scanning Radar Altimeter (USDC)
SRA............ Scanning Radar Altimeter [*Marine science*] (OSRA)
SRA............ Science Research Associates (AEBS)
SRA............ Scottish Records Association (DBA)
SRA............ Scottish Rifle Association (DI)
SRA............ Screw Research Association (EA)
SRA............ Scuba Retailers Association (EA)
SRA............ Sea Rangers' Association [*British*] (DI)
SRA............ Selected Reserve Augmentee (DOMA)
SRA............ Selective Restricted Availability (MCD)
SRA............ Self-Regulatory Agency [*Securities*] [*British*]
SrA............ Senior Airman
SRA............ Senior Residential Appraiser [*Society of Real Estate Appraisers*] [*Designation awarded by*]
SRA............ Separate Reporting Activities [*Army*]
SRA............ Service and Regulatory Announcement, Department of Agriculture [*A publication*] (DLA)
SRA............ Servicemen's Readjustment Act
SRA............ Shift Register Available
SRA............ Ship Radio Authorization [*Army*] (AABC)
SRA............ Ship Repair Agreement [*MARAD*] (TAG)
SRA............ Ship Replaceable Assembly (MCD)
SRA............ Shipyard Restricted Availability [*Navy*] (CAAL)
SRA............ Shooters' Rights Association [*British*] (DBA)
SRA............ Shop-Replaceable Assembly [*NASA*]
SRA............ Short-Range Acquisition (MCD)
SRA............ Short Range Aids [*USCG*] (TAG)
SRA............ Short Reflex Arc
SRA............ Significant Regulatory Action [*Office of Management and Budget*] (GFGA)
SRA............ Simultaneous Range Adcock Antenna [*Military RADAR*]
SRA............ Small, Replaceable Assembly (RDA)
SRA............ Smoker's Rights Alliance (EA)
SRA............ Social Research and Applications [*Research center*] (RCD)
SRA............ Social Research Association [*British*]
SRA............ Social Responsibility Auditing (ADA)
SRA............ Society for Risk Analysis (EA)
SRA............ Society of Research Administrators (EA)
SRA............ Society of Residential Appraisers [*Later, AI*]
SRA............ Sociological Research Association (EA)
SRA............ Software Requirements Analysis
SRA............ Southern Rhodesia Artillery [*British military*] (DMA)
SRA............ Southern Rural Action, Inc.
SRA............ Spanish Refugee Aid (EA)
SRA............ Specialized Repair Activity
SRA............ Specially Reserved Area [*Australia*]
SRA............ Special Refractories Association [*Defunct*] (EA)
SRA............ Special Repair Activity (MCD)
SRA............ Special Rules Area
SRA............ Specular Reflectance Accessory [*Spectrophotometry*]
SRA............ Speedway Riders Association [*British*] (DBA)
SRA............ Spherical Radiation Absorber (MCD)
SRA............ Spin Reference Axis (KSC)
SRA............ Spleen Repopulating Activity [*Medicine*] (DMAA)
SRA............ Squash Rackets Association [*British*]
SRA............ Stabilization Reserve Account [*Health insurance*] (GHCT)
SRA............ Standard Reference Aerosol (PDAA)
SRA............ Standards of Readiness and Availability (NATG)
SRA............ State and Regional Associations of the United States [*A publication*]
SRA............ State Recreation Area [*State*] (EERA)
SRA............ Station Representatives Association (EA)
SRA............ Stearman Restorers Association (EA)
SRA............ Stock Record Account (AFM)
SRA............ Strategic Resource Area (PDAA)
SRA............ Stratus Computer [*NYSE symbol*] (TTSB)
SRA............ Stratus Computer, Inc. [*NYSE symbol*] (SPSG)
SRA............ Stress Relieved Annealed [*Metallurgical engineering*]
SRA............ Structures Research Associates
SRA............ Subminiature Rotary Actuator
SRA............ Sugar Rationing Administration [*Department of Agriculture*] [*Ceased functions, 1948*]
SRA............ Sulforicinoleic Acid [*Organic chemistry*]
SRA............ Sun's Right Ascension [*Astrology*] (ROG)
SRA............ Supplemental Retirement Annuities
SRA............ Support Requirements Analysis [*NASA*] (NASA)
SRA............ Surgeon Rear-Admiral [*British military*]
SRA............ Surveillance RADAR Approach
SRA............ System Reaction Analysis [*Bell System*]
SRA............ System Reliability Analysis
SRA............ System Requirements Analysis
SRA............ Systems Research and Applications Corp. [*Arlington, VA*] (TSSD)
SRAA.......... Scholastic Rowing Association of America (EA)
SRAA.......... Senior Army Advisor (AABC)
SRAA.......... Statistical Record of Asian Americans [*A publication*]
SRAAG........ Senior Army Advisor, Army National Guard (AABC)
SRAAM........ Short-Range Air-to-Air Missile (MCD)
SRAAR........ Senior Army Advisor, Army Reserve (AABC)

SRAB .... Allan Blair Memorial Clinic, Regina, Saskatchewan [*Library symbol National Library of Canada*] (NLC)
SRAC .... Alcoholism Commission of Saskatchewan, Regina, Saskatchewan [*Library symbol National Library of Canada*] (NLC)
SRAC .... Safe Return Amnesty Committee (EA)
SRAC .... Sears Roebuck Acceptance Corp.
SRAC .... Second Regional Assistance Command [*US advisory command*] [*Vietnam*] (VNW)
SRAC .... Short Run Average Costs
SRAC .... Societe Royale d'Astronomie du Canada
SRACCMB.... Senior Aircraft Crewman Badge [*Military decoration*] (GFGA)
SrAcftCrmnBad... Senior Aircraft Crewman Badge [*Military decoration*] (AABC)
SR-ACK........ Service Request Acknowledgment [*Air Force*] (CET)
SRACR.......... Southern Rhodesia Armoured Car Regiment [*British military*] (DMA)
SRAD .... Ship's Restricted Availability Date [*Navy*] (DNAB)
SRAD .... Solar Radiation (NOAA)
SRAD .... Steerable Right-Angle Drive (DNAB)
SR/AD.......... Supporting Research and Advanced Development
SRAD .... Surveillance RADAR (MCD)
SRAE .... Solar Radio Astronomy Experiment
SRAEL .... Labour Market Planning and Information Resource Centre, Saskatchewan Department of Advanced Education and Manpower, Regina, Saskatchewan [*Library symbol National Library of Canada*] (NLC)
SRAEN .... Systeme de Reference pour la Determination de l'Affaiblissement Equivalent pour la Nettete [*Master telephone transmission reference system*]
SRAEW .... Women's Services Branch, Saskatchewan Department of Advanced Education and Manpower, Regina, Saskatchewan [*Library symbol National Library of Canada*] (NLC)
SRAF .... Archibald Foundation, Regina, Saskatchewan [*Library symbol National Library of Canada*] (NLC)
SRAF .... Social Revolutionary Anarchist Federation (EA)
SRAF .... Standby Reserve of the Armed Forces
SRAFO .... Senior Royal Air Force Officer [*British military*] (DMA)
SRAG .... Saskatchewan Department of Agriculture, Regina, Saskatchewan [*Library symbol National Library of Canada*] (NLC)
SRAG .... Semiactive RADAR Antiair Guidance System
SRAG .... Space Radiation Analysis Group [*NASA*] (NASA)
SRAG .... Sydney Rainforest Action Group (EERA)
SRAGE .... Shared Services, Agriculture Canada [*Services en Commun, Agriculture Canada*], Regina, Saskatchewan [*Library symbol National Library of Canada*] (NLC)
SRAGR......... Research Station, Agriculture Canada [*Station de Recherches, Agriculture Canada*] Regina, Saskatchewan [*Library symbol National Library of Canada*] (NLC)
SRAI .... Soybean Research Advisory Institute [*Terminated, 1984*] (EGAO)
SRAI .... Supercat Race Association International (EA)
SRAIS .... Statewide Resource Information and Accounting System [*State*] (EERA)
SRAM .... Semirandom Access Memory
SRAM .... Short-Range Attack Missile [*Military*]
SRAM .... Skill Qualification Test Requirements Alert Message
SRAM .... Some Remarks on Abstract Machines [*Computer science*]
SRAM .... Sort Re-Entrant Access Method [*Computer science*] (MHDI)
SRAM .... SQT [*Ship's Qualification Trial*] Requirements Alert Message
SRAM .... Static Random Access Memory [*Computer science*]
SRAM .... System Rehabilitation and Modernization (MCD)
SRAMA......... Spring Research and Manufacturers' Association (EAIO)
SRAMS......... Short-Range Attack Missile System (IAA)
SRAM(T)...... Short-Range Attack Missile (Tactical) [*Military*]
SRAN .... Short-Range Aids to Navigation [*Navy*]
SRAN .... Skill Qualification Test Requirements Alert Notice
SRAN .... Stock Record Account Number (AFM)
SRAN .... Surgical Resident's Admission Note (DAVI)
SRANA......... Shrine Recorders Association of North America (EA)
SRANC......... Southern Rhodesia African National Congress
SR & A........ Strategy, Research & Action [*Commercial firm British*]
SR & F........ Selection, Referral, and Followup
SR & O........ Statutory Rules and Orders [*England*] [*A publication*] (DLA)
SR & O and SI Rev... Statutory Rules and Orders and Statutory Instruments Revised [*England*] [*A publication*] (DLA)
SR & P........ Station Resources and Planning [*Navy*] (DNAB)
SR & PO....... Station Resources and Planning Office [*Navy*] (DNAB)
SR & Q........ Safety, Reliability, and Quality (NASA)
SR & QA....... Safety, Reliability, and Quality Assurance (NASA)
SR&T.......... Supporting Research and Technology (AAGC)
SRAO .... Supplemental Recreational Activities Overseas [*Red Cross*]
SRAP .... Service Record and Allied Papers [*Military*]
SRAP .... Slow Response Action Potentials [*Neurophysiology*]
SRAP .... Standard Range Approach [*Aviation*]
SRAPI .... Speech Recognition API [*All-Purpose Interface*] (PCM)
SRAPI .... Speech Recognition Application Programming Interface Committee [*Microsoft Corp.*]
SRAPMA...... Science Research Associates Primary Mental Abilities [*Psychology*] (AEBS)
SRARAV....... Senior Army Aviator (AABC)
SRARAVB .... Senior Army Aviator Badge [*Military decoration*] (GFGA)
SrArAvBad ... Senior Army Aviator Badge [*Military decoration*]
SRARM......... Short-Range Antiradiation Missile
SRAS .... Albert South Library, Regina, Saskatchewan [*Library symbol National Library of Canada*] (NLC)
SRAS .... Southern Riverina Advisory Service [*Australia*]
SRAS .... State Rural Assistance Scheme [*New South Wales*] [*State*] (EERA)
SRASA......... Small Retailers Association of South Australia
SRASM........ Short-Range Air-to-Surface Missile (MCD)
SRAT .... Search RADAR Alignment Test [*Military*] (CAAL)
SRAT .... Short-Range Applied Technology
SRAT-B........ Self-Report Assertiveness Test for Boys
SRATC .... Short-Run Average Total Cost [*Economics*]
SRATS .... Solar Radiation and Thermospheric Structure [*Japanese satellite*]
SRATUC....... Southern Rhodesian African Trade Union Congress
SRAVC......... Short-Run Average Variable Cost [*Economics*]
SRAW .... Short-Range Antitank Weapon
SRaw .... Specific Resistance, Airway [*Medicine*]
SRAX .... Southern Air Transport, Inc. [*Air carrier designation symbol*]
SRB .... Safety Review Board [*Nuclear energy*] (NRCH)
SRB .... Schilpp, Reed B., Los Angeles CA [*STAC*]
SRB .... Scientific Review Board [*Intergovernmental Oceanographic Commission*] (GFGA)
SRB .... Seaplane Repair Base
SRB .... Selective Reenlistment Bonus [*Military*] (AABC)
SRB .... Self-Retaining Bolt
SRB .... Send Receive Bomb (IAA)
SRB .... Senior Review Board
SRB .... Service Record Book [*Military*]
SRB .... Service Request Block [*Computer science*] (BUR)
SRB .... Sex Ratio at Birth [*Demographics*]
SRB .... Sheftall Record Book [*A publication*] (BJA)
SRB .... Sky Ranch for Boys (EA)
SRB .... Solar Reflectory Beacon
SRB .... Solid-Rocket Booster [*NASA*]
SRB .... Sorter Reader Buffer
SRB .... Sorter Reader Buffered (NITA)
SRB .... Source-Route Bridge [*Computer science*] (PCM)
SRB .... Sparta, TN [*Location identifier FAA*] (FAAL)
SRB .... Special Research Bureau [*Department of External Affairs*] [*Canada*]
SRB .... Special Review Board [*Military*] (INF)
SRB .... Specification Review Board [*Navy*] (DNAB)
SRB .... Spherical Roller Bearing
SRB .... State Research Bureau [*Secret police*] [*Uganda*]
SRB .... State Revenue Board [*Victoria, Australia*]
SRB .... Styrene Rubber Butadiene (NG)
SRB .... Subspecialty Requirements Board [*Navy*] (DNAB)
SRB .... Suburban Air Freight, Inc. [*ICAO designator*] (FAAC)
SRB .... Sulfate Reducing Bacteria
SRB .... Sulfur Reducing Bacteria [*Diesel fuels*]
SRB .... Support Research Branch [*Springfield Armory*]
SRB .... Surface Radiation Budget [*Marine science*] (OSRA)
SRB .... Survey and Reports Branch [*Division of Biometry and Applied Sciences, National Institute of Mental Health*] (GFGA)
SRB .... System Review Board (MCD)
SRBA .... Statistical Record of Black America [*A publication*]
SRBA .... Students for the Right to Bear Arms (EA)
SRBAB......... Solid-Rocket Booster Assembly Building [*NASA*] (NASA)
SRBC .... Serum-Treated Red Blood Cell [*Clinical chemistry*]
SRBC .... Sheep Red Blood Cell [*s*] [*Also, SRC*]
SRBC .... Sickle Red Blood Cells [*Hematology*] (DAVI)
SRBC .... Sunrise Bancorp [*NASDAQ symbol*] (NQ)
SRBC .... Susquehanna River Basin Commission [*Federal government*] (EGAO)
SRBC .... Susquehanna River Basin Compact [*Maryland, Pennsylvania, New York*]
SRBCP .... Satellite Radiation Budget Climatology Project [*Marine science*] (OSRA)
SRBCSS .... Scales for Rating the Behavioral Characteristics of Superior Students [*Educational test*]
SRBD .... Sleep-Related Breathing Disorder [*Medicine*] (DMAA)
SRBDF .... Solid-Rocket Booster Disassembly Facility [*NASA*] (NASA)
SRBDM......... Short-Range Bomber Defense Missile
SRBM .... Short-Range Ballistic Missile
SRBMI .... BMI Finance, Regina, Saskatchewan [*Library symbol National Library of Canada*] (NLC)
SRBOC......... Super Rapid Bloom Off Board Chaff [*Navy*] (NVT)
SRBOW........ Spontaneous Rupture of Bag of Water [*Obstetrics*] (DAVI)
SRBOW........ Spontaneous Rupture of Bag of Waters [*Medicine*] (MEDA)
SRBP .... Synthetic Resin Bonded Paper (IAA)
SRBPF .... Solid-Rocket Booster Processing Facility [*NASA*] (NASA)
SRBR .... Storage and Retrieval of Bibliographic References Program (EDAC)
SRBR .... Surface Reflected Bottom Reflected (IAA)
SRBT .... Single-Rod Burst Test [*Nuclear energy*] (NRCH)
SRBTRY....... Sound Ranging Battery (IAA)
SRBUC......... Scientific Research in British Universities and Colleges [*Later, RBUPC*] [*British Library*]
SRC .... AMF Sunfish Racing Class Association (EA)
SRC .... Richland County Library, Columbia, SC [*OCLC symbol*] (OCLC)
SRC .... Sacra Rituum Congregatio [*Sacred Congregation of Rites*] [*Latin*]
SRC .... Safety Research Center [*Bureau of Mines*]
SRC .... Salinas Road [*California*] [*Seismograph station code, US Geological Survey*] (SEIS)
SRC .... Sample Recovery Container [*NASA*] (KSC)
SRC .... Sample Return Container [*NASA*] (NASA)
SRC .... Sample Rock Container [*NASA*]
SRC .... Sarcoma
SRC .... Saskatchewan Research Council [*University of Saskatchewan*] [*Research center*] (RCD)
SRC .... Saturable Reactor Coil
SRC .... Scheduled Removal Component (MCD)
SRC .... Schedule Request Confirmation (SSD)
SRC .... Science Research Council [*Later, SERC*] [*British*]
SRC .... Scientific Research Committee [*Australia*]

SRC .... Scleroderma Renal Crisis [*Medicine*]
SRC .... Scott's Hospitality, Inc. [*Toronto Stock Exchange symbol*]
SRC .... Searcy, AR [*Location identifier FAA*] (FAAL)
SRC .... Secured Returns Code [*IRS*]
SRC .... Securities Research Co.
SRC .... Security Connecticut Corp. [*NYSE symbol*] (SAG)
SRC .... Sedimented Red Cell [*Hematology*] (MAE)
SRC .... Selective Ride Control [*Suspension systems*] [*Automotive engineering*]
SRC .... Semiconductor Research Cooperative
SRC .... Senate Rail Caucus (EA)
SRC .... Send Register Control [*Computer science*]
SRC .... Se Ruega Contestacion [*The Favor of a Reply Is Requested*] [*Spanish*]
SRC .... Servants of Our Lady Queen of the Clergy [*Roman Catholic women's religious order*]
SRC .... Sheep Red Cell [*s*] [*Also, SRBC*]
SRC .... Shop Resident Control (SAA)
SRC .... Shutdown Reactor Cooling [*Nuclear energy*] (NRCH)
SRC .... Signal Reserve Corps
SRC .... Silicon Readout Cell
SRC .... Silicon Rectifier Column
SRC .... Single Round Container [*for toxic chemicals*] [*Army*]
SRC .... Ski Retailers Council [*Inactive*] (EA)
SRC .... Slow-Recovery Capsules [*Pharmacy*]
SRC .... Snyder Research Co. [*Information service or system*] (IID)
SRC .... Social Rehabilitation Center [*Psychology*] (DAVI)
SRC .... Social Rehabilitation Clinic (EA)
SRC .... Societe Royale du Canada [*Royal Society of Canada - RSC*]
SRC .... Society of Friends Community Relations Committee [*British*]
SRC .... Solvent-Refined Coal
SRC .... Sound Ranging Central (IAA)
SRC .... Sound Ranging Control
SRC .... Sound Recording Co. [*Record label*]
SRC .... Source
SRC .... Source
SRC .... Source Range Channel (IEEE)
SRC .... Southeast Asia Resource Center (EA)
SRC .... Southern Regional Council (EA)
SRC .... Southwest Radio Church [*An association*]
SRC .... Southwest Research Corp.
SRC .... Space Research Council [*British*]
SRC .... Spares Receiving Checklist (NRCH)
SRC .... Special Regular Commissions [*Army British*]
SRC .... Special Release Card (IAA)
SRC .... Special Research Contract (AAGC)
SRC .... Specific Reactant Consumption [*Engine*]
SRC .... Specimen Research Centrifuge (SSD)
SRC .... Specimen Return Container (SAA)
SRC .... Specimen Return Control (SAA)
SRC .... Speech Recognition Computer
SRC .... Standard Requirements Code [*Military*]
SRC .... Standards Review Committee [*American Occupational Therapy Association*]
SRC .... Station Reliability Coordinator
SRC .... Statistical Record of Children [*A publication*]
SRC .... Statuts Revises du Canada [*Revised Statutes of Canada*] [*Database Federal Department of Justice*] [*Information service or system*] (CRD)
SRC .... Stereo Radio Cassette
SRC .... Sterility Research Center [*Public Health Service*] (GRD)
SRC .... Steroid Receptor Coactivator [*Endocrenalogy*]
SRC .... Stock Record Card [*Military*]
SRC .... Stored Response Chain [*Computer science*] (BARN)
SRC .... Strasburg Railroad Co. [*AAR code*]
SRC .... Strategic Reconnaissance Center [*Air Force*] (DOMA)
SRC .... Stray Radiation Chamber
SRC .... Stuart's Lower Canada Reports [*A publication*] (DLA)
SRC .... Student Reaction to College [*Student attitudes test*]
SRC .... Students' Representative Council [*British*]
SRC .... Subject-Field Reference Code (ADA)
SRC .... Submarine Rescue Chamber (MCD)
SRC .... Support Review Code (MCD)
SRC .... Survey Research Center [*Oregon State University*] [*Research center*] (RCD)
SRC .... Survey Research Center [*University of Kentucky*] [*Research center*] (RCD)
SRC .... Sustained-Release Capsule [*Pharmacology*]
SRC .... Swiss Red Cross
SRC .... Synchronous Remote Control
SRC .... Synchrotron Radiation Center [*University of Wisconsin - Madison*] [*Research center*] (RCD)
SRC .... Syracuse Research Corp. [*New York*] [*Information service or system*] (IID)
SRC .... Systems Release Certification [*Social Security Administration*]
SRC .... Systems Research Configuration
SRCA .... Saskatchewan Department of Consumer Affairs, Regina, Saskatchewan [*Library symbol National Library of Canada*] (NLC)
SRCA .... Slovenian Research Center of America (EA)
SRCA .... Specific Red Cell Adherence [*Test*] [*Clinical chemistry*]
SRCAS .... Safety-Related Control Air System [*Nuclear energy*] (NRCH)
SRCB .... Canadian Bible College, Regina, Saskatchewan [*Library symbol National Library of Canada*] (NLC)
SRCB .... Software Requirements Change Board [*NASA*] (NASA)
SRCB .... Software Requirements Control Board [*NASA*] (NASA)
SRCBC .... Serum Reserve Cholesterol Binding Capacity [*Medicine*] (DMAA)
SRCBD .... Software Requirements Change Board Directive [*NASA*] (NASA)
SRCBD .... Software Requirements Control Board Directive [*NASA*] (NASA)
SRCC .... Senior Control Center [*Air Force*]
SRCC .... Sensor Referenced and Computer Controlled [*For remote manipulators*]
SRCC .... Shift, Rotate, Check, Control (IAA)
SRCC .... Simplex Remote Communications Central
SRCC .... Solar Rating and Certification Corp. (EA)
SRCC .... Strikes, Riots, and Civil Commotions [*Insurance*]
SrcCp .... Source Capital, Inc. [*Associated Press*] (SAG)
SRCD .... Set-Reset Clocked Data [*Computer science*]
SRCD .... Society for Research in Child Development (EA)
SRCD .... Society of Richmond County Descendants (EA)
SRCE .... First Source Corp. [*NASDAQ symbol*] (NQ)
SrceCap .... Source Capital Corp. [*Associated Press*] (SAG)
SR-CEF .... Schmidt-Ruppin Chick Embryo Fibroblast [*s*]
SrceMed ...... Source Media, Inc. [*Associated Press*] (SAG)
SrceOne25 ... Source One Mortgage Services [*Associated Press*] (SAG)
SrceSrv .... Source Services Corp. [*Associated Press*] (SAG)
SRCG .... Safety Razor Collectors Guild (EA)
SRCH .... Search (AAG)
SRCI .... Safety-Related Controls and Instrumentation [*Nuclear energy*] (NRCH)
SRCI .... Survey Research Consultants International, Inc. [*Information service or system*] (IID)
SRCL .... Security Requirements Check List (MCD)
SRCL .... Stericycle, Inc. [*NASDAQ symbol*] (SAG)
SRCM .... Savonius Rotor Current Meter
SRCM .... Sisters of Reparation of the Congregation of Mary [*Roman Catholic religious order*]
SRCM .... Source Media [*NASDAQ symbol*] (TTSB)
SRCM .... Source Media, Inc. [*NASDAQ symbol*] (SAG)
SRCMA .... Steel Radiator and Convector Manufacturers' Association [*British*] (BI)
SRCMLT .... Standing Representative Committee for Medical Laboratory Technology in the EEC [*European Econommic Community*] [*England*] (EAIO)
SRCMP .... Southern Rhodesia Corps of Military Police [*British military*] (DMA)
SRCNET .... Science and Engineering Research Council Network [*Later, SERCNET*]
SRCNET .... SRC Network (NITA)
SRCO .... Sealright Co. [*NASDAQ symbol*] (TTSB)
SRCO .... Sealright Co., Inc. [*Kansas City, MO*] [*NASDAQ symbol*] (NQ)
SRCO .... Selected Regardless of Race, Color, Creed, or National Orgin (SAA)
SrcOne .... Source One Mortgage Services [*Associated Press*] (SAG)
SRCP .... Short Range Construction Program [*Military*]
SRCP .... Society of Retired Catholic Persons (EA)
SRCP .... Special Reserve Components Program [*Military*]
SRCR .... Saskatchewan Culture and Recreation, Regina, Saskatchewan [*Library symbol National Library of Canada*] (NLC)
SRCR .... SONAR Control Room
SRCR .... Stability Regulated Controlled Rectifier
SRCR .... System Run Control Record
SRCRA .... Shipowners Refrigerated Cargo Research Association [*Research center British*] (IRUK)
SRCRC .... Snake River Conservation Research Center [*University of Idaho*] [*Research center*] (RCD)
SRCS .... Service (IAA)
SRCS .... Special Reverse Charge (IAA)
SRCT .... Standard Recovery Completion Time
SRCTG .... Sales Representatives and Commercial Travellers Guild [*Australia*]
SRCU .... Credit Union Central, Regina, Saskatchewan [*Library symbol National Library of Canada*] (NLC)
SRCU .... Secretary's Records Correspondence Unit [*Department of Labor*]
SRD .... Safety and Reliability Directorate [*England*] (IID)
SRD .... San Andres [*Colombia*] [*Seismograph station code, US Geological Survey*] (SEIS)
SRD .... Satellite Racing Development [*British*]
SRD .... Scheduled Release Date (MCD)
SRD .... Search & Rescue 22 [*British ICAO designator*] (FAAC)
SRD .... Secret - Restricted Data [*Security classification*]
SRD .... Seldom Reaches Destination
SRD .... Selective Radiation Detector
SRD .... Self-Reading Dosimeter (IEEE)
SRD .... Self-Reported Delinquency (EDAC)
SRD .... Serous Retinal Detachment [*Ophthalmology*]
SRD .... Service Revealed Deficiency [*or Difficulty*]
SRD .... Service Rum Diluted [*British military*] (DMA)
SRD .... Shift Register Drive
S-RD .... Shipper-Receiver Difference (NRCH)
SRD .... Shuttle Requirements Definition [*NASA*] (NASA)
SRD .... Shuttle Requirements Document [*NASA*] (NASA)
SRD .... Silver Drake Resources [*Vancouver Stock Exchange symbol*]
SRD .... Single Radial Diffusion [*or Immunodiffusion*] [*Analytical biochemistry*]
SRD .... Small Rigid Dome
SRD .... Society for the Relief of Distress [*British*]
SRD .... Society for the Right to Die (EA)
SRD .... Sodium Restricted Diet [*Medicine*] (DMAA)
SRD .... Software Requirements Document [*Computer science*]
SRD .... Soluble, Repository, Plus Dihydrostreptomycin [*Referring to penicillin*] [*Pharmacology*] (DAVI)
SRD .... Special Research Detachment [*Army*]
SR-D .... Spectral Recording-Digital [*Sound Technology*] (PS)
SRD .... Stafford Road [*Wolverhampton*] [*British depot code*]

SRD .... Standard Rate and Data (IAA)
SRD .... Standard Reference Data
SRD .... Standard Repair Design [*Navy*] (MCD)
SRD .... Standard Reporting Designator (MCD)
SRD .... State Registered Dietitian
SRD .... Statistical Research Division [*Census*] (OICC)
SRD .... Step Recovery Diode
SRD .... Studio Reference Disc [*Prosonus*] [*Electronic music*]
SRD .... Super-Radiant Diode
SRD .... Surplus Release Date (AAGC)
SRD .... Sutherland Resources [*Vancouver Stock Exchange symbol*]
SRD .... Swing Rate Discriminator (IAA)
SRD .... Systems Requirements Document [*NASA*]
Srd .... Thiouridine [*Also, S, SU*] [*A nucleoside*]
SRDA .... Dunlop Art Gallery, Regina, Saskatchewan [*Library symbol National Library of Canada*] (NLC)
SRDA .... Search RADAR Designation Alignment (MCD)
SRDA .... Sodium Removal Development Apparatus [*Nuclear energy*] (NRCH)
SRDAS .... School Retrofit Design Analysis System (EDAC)
SRDAS .... Service Recording and Data Analysis System (IEEE)
SRDB .... Scientific Research and Development Branch [*Home Office*] [*British*] (IRUK)
SRDC .... Shopfitting Research and Development Council [*British*] (BI)
SRDC .... Standard Reference Data Center
SRDC .... State Rural Development Councils (USGC)
SRDC .... Sugar Research and Development Corp. (EERA)
SRDCS .... Simulation Reconfiguration Data Collection Subsystem (SSD)
SRDE .... Signals Research and Development Establishment [*British*]
SRDE .... Smallest Replaceable Defective Element
SRDG .... Software Research and Development Group [*University of Calgary*] [*Research center*] (RCD)
SRDH .... Subsystems Requirements Definition Handbook [*NASA*] (NASA)
SRDI .... Safety-Related Display Instrumentation [*Nuclear energy*] (NRCH)
SRDL .... Saskatchewan Department of Labour, Regina, Saskatchewan [*Library symbol National Library of Canada*] (NLC)
SRDL .... Semiconductor Research and Development Laboratory (IAA)
SRDL .... Signals Research and Development Laboratory [*Army British*]
SRDM .... Subrate Data Multiplexer [*Telecommunications*] (TEL)
SRDP .... Sulawesi Regional Development Project [*Coordinated by Indonesian and Canadian governments*] (ECON)
SRDS .... Shop Repair Data Sheets
SRDS .... Single Requirements Determination System
SRDS .... Standard Rate and Data Service, Inc. [*Information service or system*] (MCD)
SRDS .... Standard Reference Data System (DIT)
SRDS .... Systems Research and Development Service [*FAA*] (MCD)
SRDT .... Single Radial Diffusion Test [*Medicine*] (DMAA)
SRDT .... Single Rotating Directional Transmission [*Military*] (CAAL)
SRE .... Sanctae Romanae Ecclesiae [*Of the Most Holy Roman Church*] [*Latin*]
SRE .... Sancta Romana Ecclesia [*Most Holy Roman Church*] [*Latin*]
SRE .... Saskatchewan Department of the Environment, Regina, Saskatchewan [*Library symbol National Library of Canada*] (NLC)
SRE .... Scanning Reference Electrode (MCD)
SRE .... Schedule of Recent Experience [*Psychometrics*]
SRE .... Search RADAR Element (IAA)
SRE .... Seminole, OK [*Location identifier FAA*] (FAAL)
SRE .... Sending Reference Equivalent (NITA)
SRE .... Send Reference Equivalent, Search RADAR [*Telecommunications*] (TEL)
SRE .... Senior-Reliability Engineer (IAA)
SRE .... Series Relay [*Electronics*]
SRE .... Serum Response Element [*Genetics*]
SRE .... Serum Response Element [*Biochemistry*]
SRE .... Serum-Response Enhancer [*Genetics*]
SRE .... Shelby's Rabbit Eater [*In model name Omni SRE, proposed for Dodge car designed by Carroll Shelby*]
SRE .... Signaling Range Extender [*Telecommunications*] (TEL)
SRE .... Single Region Execution
SRE .... Single Rotation Engine (IAA)
SRE .... Single Round Effectiveness (NATG)
SRE .... Single Rural Eligible [*Classified advertising*]
SRE .... Site Resident Engineer [*Telecommunications*] (TEL)
SRE .... Society for Reproductive Surgeons (EA)
SRE .... Society of Recreation Executives (EA)
SRE .... Society of Relay Engineers [*British*]
SRE .... Society of Reliability Engineers (EA)
SRE .... Society of Reproduction Engineers [*Later, IAVCM*] (EA)
SRE .... Society of Reproductive Endocrinologists (EA)
SRE .... Sodium Reactor Experiment [*Nuclear energy*]
SRE .... Sound Reproduction Equipment (DEN)
SRE .... Special Re-Education
SRE .... Srednekan [*Later, MGD*] [*Former USSR Geomagnetic observatory code*]
SRE .... Standard RADAR Environment
SRE .... Statistical Record of the Environment [*A publication*]
SRE .... STDN [*Space Tracking and Data Network*] Ranging Equipment [*NASA*] (GFGA)
SRE .... Sterol Regulatory Element [*Genetics*]
SRE .... Stray Radiant Energy
SRE .... Sucre [*Bolivia*] [*Airport symbol*] (OAG)
SRE .... Surveillance RADAR Element
SRE .... Surveillance RADAR Equipment
SREA .... Senior Real Estate Analyst [*Society of Real Estate Appraisers*] [*Designation awarded by*]
SREA .... Society of Real Estate Appraisers [*Later, AI*] (EA)
SREA .... Street Rod Equipment Association (EA)
SREA .... Supplier Request for Engineering Approval
SREAE .... AES Regina Weather Office, Environment Canada [*Bureau Meteorologique du SEA de Regina, Environnement Canada*] Saskatchewan [*Library symbol National Library of Canada*] (NLC)
SREB .... Southern Regional Educational Board
SREB .... Southern Regional Examinations Board [*Education*] (AIE)
SREBP .... Sterol Regulatory Element Binding Protein [*Biochemistry*]
SREC .... Executive Council, Regina, Saskatchewan [*Library symbol National Library of Canada*] (NLC)
SREC .... Southern Rice Export Corp. (EA)
SRED .... Saskatchewan Department of Education, Regina, Saskatchewan [*Library symbol National Library of Canada*] (NLC)
SREEP .... Environmental Protection Service, Environment Canada [*Service de la Protection de l'Environnement, Environnement Canada*] Regina, Saskatchewan [*Library symbol National Library of Canada*] (NLC)
SR(EF) .... Seaman Recruit (Electronics Field) [*Navy rating*] (DNAB)
SREG .... [*The*] Standard Register Co. [*NASDAQ symbol*] (NQ)
SREG .... Standing Register [*Civil Service*]
SREH .... Storm-Relative Environmental Helicity [*Marine science*] (OSRA)
SREH .... Storm-Relative Environmental Helicity (USDC)
SREHP .... Serine-Rich Entamoeba Histolytica Protein [*Biochemistry*]
SREI .... Student Role Expectation Inventory
SREIW .... Inland Waters Directorate, Environment Canada [*Direction Generale des Eaux Interieures, Environnement Canada*] Regina, Saskatchewan [*Library symbol National Library of Canada*] (NLC)
SREJ .... Selective Reject [*Computer science*] (MHDI)
SREL .... Savannah River Ecology Laboratory [*Department of Energy*] [*Aiken, SC*]
SREL .... Southwest Regional Educational Laboratory (AEBS)
SREL .... Space Radiation Effects Laboratory [*Langley, VA*] [*NASA*]
SREM .... Scanning Reflection Electron Microscopy
SREM .... School of Resource and Environmental Management (EERA)
S-REM .... Sleep with Rapid Eye Movement
SREM .... Software Requirements Engineering Methodology
SREM .... Sound Ranging Evaluation Model (MCD)
SREMP .... Source Region Electromagnetic Pulse
SREODB .... Senior Explosive Ordnance Disposal Badge [*Military decoration*] (GFGA)
S Rep .... Senate Reports [*A publication*] (DLA)
S Rep .... Southern Reporter [*A publication*] (DLA)
SREP .... State Rivers and Estuaries Policy [*New South Wales*] (EERA)
SREP .... Sydney Regional Environmental Plan [*Australia*]
SREPT .... Senate Committee Report (AFIT)
SRES .... School for Resource and Environmental Studies [*Dalhousie University*] [*Canada*] (IRC)
SRES .... Senate Resolution (AFIT)
S Res .... Senate Resolution (AAGC)
SRES .... Senores [*Sirs, Gentlemen*] [*Spanish*]
SRES .... Southern Railway Employees' Sangh [*India*]
S Res .... United States Senate Resolution [*A publication*] (DLA)
SRET .... Satellite de Recherches et d'Environment Technique [*Satellite for Environmental and Technical Research*] [*France*]
SRET .... Scanning Reference Electrode [*Corrosion testing*]
SRET .... Subroutine Recipe Entry Pointer Table
SRETL .... Screened Resistor Evaporated Transistor Logic (IAA)
SRE(V) .... Singapore Royal Engineers (Volunteers) [*British military*] (DMA)
SRF .... Salmonellosis-Resistance Factor
SRF .... Sam Rayburn Foundation
SRF .... San Rafael, CA [*Location identifier FAA*] (FAAL)
SRF .... S-Band Receiver Filter
SRF .... Scleroderma Research Foundation (EA)
SRF .... Seal Rescue Fund (EA)
SRF .... Secondary Refrigerant Freezing (PDAA)
SRF .... Secure Reserve Forces [*Military*] (MCD)
SRF .... Selected Reserve Force [*Units*] [*of Army National Guard Discontinued, 1969*]
SRF .... Self-Realization Fellowship (EA)
SRF .... Self-Referenced Fringe (MCD)
SRF .... Self-Resonant Frequency
SRF .... Semireinforcing Furnace [*Carbon black manufacture*]
SRF .... Serum Response Factor [*Biochemistry*]
SRF .... Ship Repair Facility [*Navy*] (NVT)
SRF .... Short Rotary Furnace [*Metallurgy*]
SRF .... Shuttle Refurbish Facility [*NASA*] (NASA)
SRF .... Sido, Robert F., Edwardsville IL [*STAC*]
SRF .... Signal Strength Radio Frequency (IAA)
SRF .... Skin Reactive Factor [*Immunochemistry*]
SRF .... Skin Respiratory Factor [*Physiology*]
SRF .... Sliding Roof [*Automotive advertising*]
SRF .... Slovak Relief Fund (EA)
SRF .... Smithsonian Research Foundation (BARN)
SRF .... Snake Ranch Flats [*New Mexico*] [*Seismograph station code, US Geological Survey Closed*] (SEIS)
SRF .... Software Recording Facility
SRF .... Software Recovery Facility [*Computer science*] (IBMDP)
SRF .... Solar Radiation Flux
SRF .... Somatotrophin-Releasing Factor [*Endocrinology*]
SRF .... Sorter Reader Flow
SRF .... Spacecraft Research Foundation [*Defunct*] (EA)
SRF .... Space Requirement Forms (AAG)
SRF .... Special Reporting Facility [*Department of State*]
SRF .... Spectral Redistribution Function (IAA)

SRF............ Sperm-Release Pheromone [*Biology*]
SRF............ Split Renal Function [*Medicine*] (MAE)
SRF............ Stable Radio Frequency
SRF............ State Revolving Fund [*Environmental Protection Agency*] (GFGA)
SRF............ Strategic Reserve Forces (MCD)
SRF............ Strategic Retaliatory Forces (AAG)
SRF............ Strategic Rocket Forces (MCD)
SRF............ Strength of Radio Frequency (IAA)
SRF............ Submarine Range-Finder
SRF............ Submarine Repair Facility
SRF............ Subretinal Fluid [*Ophthalmology*] (MAE)
SRF............ Summary Reference File (DOMA)
SRF............ Sun River Gold Corp. [*Vancouver Stock Exchange symbol*]
SRF............ Supported Ring Frame
SRF............ Surface Roughness Factor [*Telecommunications*] (TEL)
SRF............ Survival Research Foundation (EA)
SRF............ System Recovery Factor
SRF-A.......... Slow-Reacting Factor of Anaphylaxis [*Medicine*] (MEDA)
SRF-A.......... Slow Releasing Factor of Anaphylaxis [*Immunology*] (DAVI)
SRFB........... Space Research Facilities Branch [*National Research Council of Canada*]
SRFC........... Sheep Red Cell Rosette Forming Cells (AAMN)
SRFC........... Shotgun Red Fan Club (EA)
SRFCS.......... Self-Repairing Flight Control System
SRFD........... Society for the Rehabilitation of the Facially Disfigured [*Later, National Foundation for Facial Reconstruction*] (EA)
SRFF........... Set-Reset Flip-Flop [*Computer science*]
SRFI........... Self-Rising Flour Institute [*Later, HBA*]
SRFI........... Sugar Research Foundation, Inc. [*Later, ISRF*] (EA)
SRFLANT........ Ships Repair Facility, Atlantic (DNAB)
SRFLSBAD....... Senior Flight Surgeon Badge [*Military decoration*] (GFGA)
SrFltSurgBad... Senior Flight Surgeon Badge [*Military decoration*] (AABC)
SRFM........... Source Range Flux Monitoring [*Nuclear energy*] (NRCH)
SRFO........... Society of Rural Financial Officers [*British*] (BI)
SRFPAC......... Ships Repair Facility, Pacific (DNAB)
SRFS........... Split Renal Function Study [*Medicine*] (MAE)
SRFT........... Shortest Remaining First Time (HGAA)
SRFTL.......... Secure Resource Force Target List (MCD)
SRFU........... Seal Research and Fisheries Unit [*British*]
SRG............ Regina General Hospital, Saskatchewan [*Library symbol National Library of Canada*] (NLC)
SRG............ Santa Sarita Mining [*Vancouver Stock Exchange symbol*]
SRG............ Schering-Plough Corp. [*Research code symbol*]
SRG............ Search & Rescue 202 [*British ICAO designator*] (FAAC)
SRG............ Semarang [*Indonesia*] [*Airport symbol*] (OAG)
SRG............ Servomotor Rate Generator
SRG............ Shift Register Generator [*Computer science*] (IAA)
SRG............ Sine-Random Generator
SRG............ Social Research Group [*George Washington University*] [*Research center*] (RCD)
SRG............ Society of Remedial Gymnasts (EA)
SRG............ Sound Ranging
SRG............ Specialty Review Group [*Medicine*] (DMAA)
SRG............ Spectrum Roentgen-Gamma [*Proposed international space observatory*]
SRG............ Statistical Research Group [*Princeton University*] (MCD)
SRG............ Stimulated Raman Gain [*Spectroscopy*]
SRG............ Stock Removal Grinding (MCD)
SRG............ Surge (MSA)
SRG............ System Routing Guide [*Military*] (CAAL)
SRG............ Systems Research Group (CINC)
SRGA........... Stable Reactor, General, Atomic
SRGC........... Specialty Retail Group [*NASDAQ symbol*] (SAG)
SRGD........... Gabriel Dumont Institute, Regina, Saskatchewan [*Library symbol National Library of Canada*] (NLC)
SRGE........... Saskatchewan Government Employees Association, Regina, Saskatchewan [*Library symbol National Library of Canada*] (NLC)
SRGE........... Surge Components, Inc. [*NASDAQ symbol*] (SAG)
SRGH........... Pasqua Hospital, Regina, Saskatchewan [*Library symbol National Library of Canada*] (NLC)
SRGI........... Saskatchewan Government Insurance, Regina, Saskatchewan [*Library symbol National Library of Canada*] (NLC)
SRGM........... Super Rapid Gun Mounting [*Military*]
SRGN........... Seragen, Inc. [*NASDAQ symbol*] (SAG)
SRGN........... Surgeon
SRGR........... Short-Range Guided Rocket
SRGR........... Sound Ranging Group (IAA)
SRGS........... Saskatchewan Genealogical Society, Regina, Saskatchewan [*Library symbol National Library of Canada*] (NLC)
SRGS........... Scottish Rock Garden Club (DBA)
SRGS........... Stimulated Raman Gain Spectroscopy (PDAA)
SRGS........... St. Rosalie Generating Station [*Nuclear energy*] (NRCH)
SRGS........... Survivable Radio Guidance System [*Military*]
SRGSC.......... Southern Rhodesia General Service Corps [*British military*] (DMA)
SRH............ Saskatchewan Housing Corp., Regina, Saskatchewan [*Library symbol National Library of Canada*] (BIB)
SRH............ Secretaria de Recursos Hidraulicos [*Mexico*]
SRH............ Sequential Rough Handling (MCD)
SRH............ Single Radial Hemolysis [*Immunochemistry*]
SRH............ Single Radical Hemolysis [*Hematology*] (DAVI)
SRH............ Smith, R. H., Minneapolis MN [*STAC*]
SRH............ [*A*] Social and Religious History of the Jews [*S. W. Baron*] [*A publication*] (BJA)
SRH............ Somatotropin-Releasing Hormone [*Endocrinology*] (MAE)
SRH............ Spontaneously Responding Hyperthyroidism [*Endocrinology*]
SRH............ Stigmata of Recent Hemorrhage [*Medicine*]
SRH............ Strathcona Resources Industries Ltd. [*Toronto Stock Exchange symbol*]
SRH............ Structural Repair Handbook (DNAB)
SRH............ Subsystems Requirements Handbook [*NASA*] (NASA)
SRH............ Supply Railhead
SRH............ Switchyard Relay House [*Nuclear energy*] (NRCH)
SRHA........... Statistical Record of Hispanic Americans [*A publication*]
SRHB........... Society for Research into Hydrocephalus and Spina Bifida (EA)
SRHC........... Shutdown Reactor Head Cooling [*Nuclear energy*] (NRCH)
SR HCR......... Southern Rhodesia High Court Reports [*1911-55*] [*A publication*] (DLA)
SRHE........... Society for Religion in Higher Education [*Later, SVHE*] (EA)
SRHE........... Society for Research into Higher Education [*Guildford, Surrey, England*] (EAIO)
SRHIT.......... Small RADAR-Homing Interceptor Technology
SRHJ........... [*A*] Social and Religious History of the Jews [*S. W. Baron*] [*A publication*] (BJA)
SRHL........... Small RADAR Homing Interceptor
SRHL........... Southwestern Radiological Health Laboratory [*HEW*]
SRHM........... Statistical Record of Health and Medicine [*A publication*]
SRHP........... Planning Branch, Saskatchewan Department of Highways and Transportation, Regina,Saskatchewan [*Library symbol National Library of Canada*] (NLC)
SRHP........... Section for Rehabilitation Hospitals and Programs [*American Hospital Association*] (EA)
SRHQ........... Subregional Headquarters [*Military British*]
SRHS........... Health Sciences Library, Plains Health Centre, Regina, Saskatchewan [*Library symbol National Library of Canada*] (NLC)
SR(HS)......... Seaman Recruit (High School) [*Navy rating*] (DNAB)
SRHSB.......... Society for Research into Hydrocephalus and Spina Bifida (EA)
SRI............ Air Safaris & Services (NZ) Ltd. [*New Zealand*] [*ICAO designator*] (FAAC)
SRI............ Sacrum Romanum Imperium [*The Holy Roman Empire*] [*Latin*]
SRI............ Samarinda [*Indonesia*] [*Airport symbol*] (OAG)
SRI............ Satellite RADAR Interferometry
SRI............ Scholarly Resources, Incorporated, Wilmington, DE [*Library symbol Library of Congress*] (LCLS)
SRI............ Sefid-Roud [*Iran*] [*Seismograph station code, US Geological Survey*] (SEIS)
SRI............ Selective Retention Indicators (NVT)
SRI............ Senior Resident Inspector [*Nuclear energy*] (NRCH)
SRI............ Serenpet, Inc. [*AMEX symbol*] (SPSG)
SRI............ Serotin Reuptake Inhibitor [*Pharmacology*]
SRI............ Servo Repeater Indicator
SRI............ Severe Renal Insufficiency [*Medicine*]
SRI............ Signal Routing and Interface (MCD)
SRI............ Silicon Rubber Insulation
SRI............ Ski Retailers International (EA)
SRI............ Social Research Institute [*University of Utah*] [*Research center*] (RCD)
SRI............ Society for Rational Individualism [*Later, SIL*] (EA)
SRI............ Sorry [*Communications operator's procedural remark*]
SRI............ Southeastern Reservoir Investigation [*Department of the Interior*] (GRD)
SRI............ Southern Research Institute
SRI............ Southwest Research Institute
SRI............ Space Research Institute [*Defunct*] (EA)
SRI............ Spalling Resistance Index (IEEE)
SRI............ Special Recreation, Inc. (EA)
SRI............ Spectrum Resolver Integrator
SRI............ Spectrum Resources, Inc. [*St. Charles, MO*] [*Telecommunications*] (TSSD)
SRI............ Speech Rehabilitation Institute (EA)
SRI............ Spring Research Institute (EA)
SRI............ Standard Research Institute (MCD)
SRI............ Standby Request for Information [*Military*] (AABC)
SRI............ Standing Request for Information (MCD)
SRI............ Stanford Research Institute [*Later, SRI International*] [*Databank originator*]
SRI............ Statistical Reference Index [*A publication*]
SRI............ Stick to Rudder Interconnect (MCD)
SRI............ Storeroom Item (DNAB)
SRI............ Sugar Research Institute [*Australia*]
SRI............ Sulfate Reduction Index [*Environmental chemistry*]
SRI............ Supply Requisition Inquiry
SRI............ Surface Roughness Indicator
SRI............ Surveillance, Reconnaissance, and Intelligence [*Marine Corps*] (DOMA)
SRI............ Swiss Radio International
SRI............ Syllable Repetition Interval [*Entomology*]
SRI............ System of Reinforcement-Inhibition (PDAA)
SRIA........... Saskatchewan Intergovernmental Affairs, Regina, Saskatchewan [*Library symbol National Library of Canada*] (NLC)
SRIA........... State and Regional Indicators Archive [*University of New Hampshire*] [*Information service or system*] (IID)
SRIAER......... Scientific Research Institute for Atomic Energy Reactors [*Former USSR*]
SRIB........... Strike Route Information Book [*Strategic Air Command*] (AABC)
SRIC........... Short-Run Incremental Cost (ADA)
SRIC........... Southwest Research and Information Center (EA)
SRID........... Search RADAR Input Device (MCD)
SRID........... Single Radial Immunodiffusion [*Medicine*] (DMAA)
SRIF........... Somatotrophin-Releasing Inhibiting Factor [*Also, GH-RIF, GH-RIH, GRIF, SS*] [*Endocrinology*]

SRIF .... Special Risk Insurance Fund [*Federal Housing Administration*]
SRIFC .... Saskatchewan Indian Federated College, Regina, Saskatchewan [*Library symbol National Library of Canada*] (NLC)
SRIG .... Surveillance, Reconnaissance, and Intelligence Group [*Marine Corps*] (DOMA)
SRIH .... Somatostatin [*Biochemistry*]
SRIH .... Somatotropin Release Inhibiting Hormone [*Biochemistry*]
SRILTA .... Stanford Research Institute Lead Time Analysis
SR-IM .... Office of Strategic Research, Intelligence Memoranda [*CIA*]
SRIM .... Short-Range Intercept Missile (MCD)
SRIM .... Standing Order Microfiche Service
SRIM .... Structural Reaction Injection Molding [*Plastics*]
SRIMO .... Senior Radio Installation and Manufacture Officer (IAA)
SRIN .... Indian and Northern Affairs Canada [*Affaires Indiennes et du Nord Canada*],Regina, Saskatchewan [*Library symbol National Library of Canada*] (BIB)
SRINF .... Shorter Range Intermediate-Range Nuclear Forces (DOMA)
SRIO .... Systems Research Integration Office [*Army Air Mobility Research and Development Laboratory*] [*St. Louis, MO*]
SRIP .... Selected Reserve Incentive Program [*Army*]
SRIP .... Ship Readiness Improvement Plan [*Navy*] (NG)
SRIP .... Short-Range Impact Point (MUGU)
SRIP .... Soldier/Robot Interface Program Vehicle [*Military*] (RDA)
SRIP .... Specification Review and Improvement Program [*Navy*] (NG)
SRIP .... Supplier Rating Incentive Program
SRIS .... Safety Recommendation Information System [*Database*]
SRIS .... Safety Research Information Service [*National Safety Council*] (IID)
SRIS .... Science Reference and Information Service (IID)
SRIS .... Surplus Record Information Services (IID)
SRISP .... Interprovincial Steel & Pipe Corp. Ltd., (IPSCO), Regina, Saskatchewan [*Library symbol National Library of Canada*] (NLC)
SRIT .... Service and Repair Identification Tag (MCD)
Srita .... Senorita [*Miss*] [*Spanish*]
SRIY .... Sherwood Rangers Imperial Yeomanry [*British military*] (DMA)
SRJ .... San Borja [*Bolivia*] [*Airport symbol*] (OAG)
SRJ .... Scorcorp Industries, Inc. [*Vancouver Stock Exchange symbol*]
SRJ .... Self-Restraint Joint
SRJ .... Short Run Job (MCD)
SRJ .... Standard-Range Juno [*Survey meter for radiation*]
SRJ .... Static Round Jet
SRJC .... Communications Policy Branch, Saskatchewan Department of Justice, Regina, Saskatchewan [*Library symbol National Library of Canada*] (NLC)
SRJC .... Santa Rosa Junior College [*California*]
SRK .... Skywork SA [*Switzerland ICAO designator*] (FAAC)
SRK .... Soave-Redlich-Kwong [*Equation of state*]
SRK .... Spirit Lake, IA [*Location identifier FAA*] (FAAL)
SRK .... S-Receptor Kinase [*An enzyme*]
SRK .... Sredniy Kalar [*Former USSR Seismograph station code, US Geological Survey*] (SEIS)
SRK .... Stralak Resources [*Vancouver Stock Exchange symbol*]
SRKN .... Single Rotating Knife
SRL .... HRIN [*Human Resource Information Network*] Special Reports Library [*Executive Telecom System, Inc.*] [*Information service or system*] (CRD)
SRL .... Legislative Library of Saskatchewan, Regina, Saskatchewan [*Library symbol National Library of Canada*] (NLC)
SRL .... Santa Rosalia [*Mexico*] [*Seismograph station code, US Geological Survey Closed*] (SEIS)
SRL .... Savannah River Laboratory [*Department of Energy*] [*Aiken, SC*]
SRL .... Save-the-Redwoods League (EA)
SRL .... Sceptre Resources [*AMEX symbol*] (TTSB)
SRL .... Sceptre Resources Ltd. [*AMEX symbol Toronto Stock Exchange symbol*] (SPSG)
SRL .... Schema Representation Language (NITA)
SRL .... Scheme Representation Language [*Artificial intelligence*]
SRL .... Science Reference Library (NITA)
SRL .... Scientific Research Laboratory (AAG)
SRL .... Screwworm Research Laboratory [*Department of Agriculture*] (GRD)
SRL .... Seiler Research Laboratory [*Air Force*] (MCD)
SRL .... Send-Receive Logic (ECII)
SRL .... Service Rights Layer [*Computer science*]
SRL .... Shift Register Label (NITA)
SRL .... Singing Return Loss [*Telecommunications*] (TEL)
SRL .... Skin Resistance Level [*Physiology*]
SRL .... Society of Romance Linguistics [*Nancy, France*] (EAIO)
SRL .... Sonobuoy Receiver Logic [*Navy*] (CAAL)
SRL .... Sound Reference Laboratory [*Orlando, FL*] [*Navy*]
SRL .... Sound Research Laboratories Ltd. [*Research center British*] (IRUK)
SRL .... Space Radar Laboratory [*NASA*]
SRL .... Spares Recommendation List (MCD)
SRL .... Stability Return Loss [*Telecommunications*] (TEL)
SRL .... Standard Reference Library
SRL .... Strangeways Research Laboratory [*British*] (IRUK)
SRL .... Stress Relieving Liner (KSC)
SRL .... Structural Return Loss [*Telecommunications*] (TEL)
SRL .... Student Religious Liberals [*Later, SRL, A Free Religious Fellowship*] [*Defunct*]
SRL .... Study Reference List (AFM)
SRL .... Summary Requirements List (MCD)
SRL .... Support Requirements Letter (CET)
SRL .... Survey Research Laboratory [*University of Illinois*] [*Information service or system*] (IID)
SRL .... System Reference Library (HGAA)
SRL .... Systems Research Laboratory
SRL .... Varmlandsflyg AB [*Sweden ICAO designator*] (FAAC)
SRLA .... Scottish Recreational Land Association (DBA)
SRLC .... Luther College, Regina, Saskatchewan [*Library symbol National Library of Canada*] (NLC)
SRLD .... Small Rocket Lift Device
SRLP .... Leader-Post Ltd., Regina, Saskatchewan [*Library symbol National Library of Canada*] (NLC)
SRLP .... Socialist and Revolutionary Labour Party [*Gambia*] [*Political party*] (PD)
SRLS .... Law Society of Saskatchewan Libraries, Regina [*Library symbol National Library of Canada*] (BIB)
Sr LS .... Senior Life Saving [*Red Cross*]
SRLS .... Starved Rock Library System [*Library network*]
SRLY .... Series Relay (IEEE)
SRLZ .... Southern Rock Lobster Zone [*Australia*]
SRLZ .... Southern Rock Lobster Zone (EERA)
SRM .... Flying Swiss Ambulance Maldives (Pvt) Ltd. [*ICAO designator*] (FAAC)
SRM .... Safety, Reliability, and Maintainability (SSD)
SRM .... Schedule Request Message (MCD)
SRM .... Scrim-Reinforced Material [*Nonwoven sheets*]
SRM .... Seatbelt Retractor Module [*Automotive engineering*]
SRM .... Secretory Rate Maximum [*Physiology*]
SRM .... Selected-Reaction Monitoring [*Spectrometry*]
SRM .... Sensomatic Elect [*NYSE symbol*] (TTSB)
SRM .... Sensor Response Model
SRM .... Serbian Renaissance Movement [*Political party*] (EY)
SRM .... Server Requewst Manager [*Computer science*]
SRM .... Service Repair Manual
SRM .... Shared Resource Management [*Computer science*]
SRM .... Shift Register Memory
SRM .... Ship Repair and Maintenance [*National Shipping Authority*]
SRM .... Shock Remanent Magnetization (OA)
SRM .... Short-Range Missile [*Projected; not to be confused with SRAM*]
SRM .... Short-Range MODEM
SRM .... Single Register Machine
SRM .... Smokeless Rocket Motor (MCD)
SRM .... Snowmelt-Runoff Model [*Hydrology*]
SRM .... Society for Range Management (EA)
SRM .... Sociomoral Reflection Measures (EDAC)
SRM .... Socorro - La Joya [*New Mexico*] [*Seismograph station code, US Geological Survey Closed*] (SEIS)
SRM .... Solid-Rocket Motor
SRM .... Source Range Monitor [*Nuclear energy*] (NRCH)
SRM .... Specification Requirements Manual [*NASA*] (NASA)
SRM .... Specific Repair Methods [*Boeing*]
SRM .... Speed of Relative Movement
SRM .... Spiritual Regeneration Movement [*Foundation of America*] (EA)
SRM .... Square Root Mode [*Computer science*]
SRM .... Standard Reference Material [*National Institute of Standards and Technology*]
SRM .... Standard Reference Module
SRM .... Standard Repair Manual (MCD)
SRM .... Strategic Reconnaissance Missile
SRM .... Structural Repair Manual
SRM .... Subarea Routing Manager (IAA)
SRM .... Subsystem Response Message [*Military*]
SRM .... Superior Rectus Muscle [*Eye anatomy*]
SRM .... Switched Reluctance Motor (ECON)
SRM .... System for Resources Management [*Jet Propulsion Laboratory, NASA*]
SRM .... System Resource Manager [*IBM Corp.*] (BUR)
SRMA .... Silk and Rayon Manufacturers Association [*Defunct*] (EA)
SRMA .... Ski Resort Marketing Association [*Defunct*] (EA)
SRMA .... Split-Channel Reservation Multiple Access (PDAA)
SRM & QA ... Safety, Reliability, Maintainability, and Quality Assurance [*NASA*] (SSD)
SRMBR .... Senior Member (DNAB)
SRMC .... Short Run Marginal Cost (MHDB)
SRMC .... Society of Risk Management Consultants [*Baton Rouge, LA*] (EA)
SRMC .... Specification Requirements Manual (MCD)
SRMC .... Stimulus/Response Measurements Catalog (NASA)
SRMCASE .... Symmetry-Restricted-Multiconfiguration Annihilation of Single Excitations [*Physics*]
SRMD .... Slow Release Matrix Device [*US Army Corps of Engineers*]
SRMD .... Stress-Related Mucosal Damage [*Medicine*]
SRMF .... Short-Run Manufacturing Facility (MCD)
SRMH .... Single Role Mine-Hunter [*Military*] (PDAA)
SRMI .... Swissray International, Inc. [*NASDAQ symbol*] (SAG)
SRMI .... SWISSRAY Intl [*NASDAQ symbol*] (TTSB)
SR-MIR .... Specific Reactivity - Maximum Incremental Reactivity [*Exhaust emissions*] [*Automotive engineering*]
SRML .... Short-Range Missile Launcher
SRMP .... Supply Readiness Milestone Plan [*Military*] (CAAL)
SRMR .... Saskatchewan Department of Mineral Resources, Regina, Saskatchewan [*Library symbol National Library of Canada*] (NLC)
SRMS .... Scheduling and Resource Management System [*Tymshare UK*] [*Software package*] (NCC)
SRMS .... Ships Records Management System (MCD)
SRMS .... Shuttle Remote Manipulator System (SSD)
SRMS .... Sociomoral Reflection Maturity Score (EDAC)
SRMS .... Strategic Research and Management Service
SRMS .... Structure Resonance Modulation Spectroscopy
SRMT .... Southern Rock Mountain Trench [*Geology*]
SRMU .... Signal RADAR Maintenance Unit (IAA)

SRMU .... Solid Rocket Motor Upgrade [*Air Force*]
SRN .... Sabine River & Northern Railroad Co. [*AAR code*]
SRN .... Saskatchewan Registered Nurses Association, Regina, Saskatchewan [*Library symbol National Library of Canada*] (NLC)
SRN .... Satellite Radio Navigation (DNAB)
SRN .... Serial Reference Number
SRN .... Simulation Reference Number
SRN .... Slurry Response Number [*Well drilling technology*]
SRN .... Software Release Notice [*NASA*] (NASA)
SRN .... Southern
SRN .... Southern Air Transport, Inc.
SRN .... Southern Banc(AL) [*AMEX symbol*] (TTSB)
SRN .... Southern Banc Co., Inc. [*AMEX symbol*] (SAG)
SRN .... Specification Revision Notice (MCD)
SRN .... State Registered Nurse [*British*]
SRN .... Strathearn House Group Ltd. [*Toronto Stock Exchange symbol*]
SRN .... Stretch Receptor Neuron
SRN .... Student Registered Nurse (MAE)
SRN .... Subretinal Neovascularization [*Ophthalmology*] (DAVI)
sRNA .... Ribonucleic Acid, Soluble [*Replaced by tRNA*] [*Biochemistry, genetics*]
SRNA .... Shipbuilders and Repairers' National Association [*British*] (BI)
SRNC .... Severn River Naval Command
SR/NE .... Sinus Rhythm, No Ectopy [*Medicine*] (MEDA)
SR/NE .... Sinus Rhythm, No Ectopy [*Cardiology*] (DAVI)
SRNFC .... Source Range Neutron Flux Channel (IEEE)
SR(NFE) .... Seaman Recruit (Nuclear Field Electronics) [*Navy rating*] (DNAB)
SRNG .... Sustained Release Nitroglycerin (DMAA)
SRNG .... Syringe
SRNH .... Service Request Not Honored (IAA)
SRNLS .... Northern Library Services, Saskatchewan Library, Regina, Saskatchewan [*Library symbol National Library of Canada*] (NLC)
SRNNA .... Statistical Record of Native North Americans [*A publication*]
SRNR .... Stock Request Number
SRNS .... Steroid-Responsive Nephrotic Syndrome [*Medicine*]
SRNS .... Surveyor Retro Nozzle Structure
SR(NSET) .... Seaman Recruit (Nuclear Submarine Engineering Technician) [*Navy rating*] (DNAB)
SRNV .... Subretinal Neovascularization [*Ophthalmology*]
SRO .... Safety Recall Order (MCD)
SRO .... Sales Release Order
SRO .... Saskatchewan Oil Co., Regina, Saskatchewan [*Library symbol National Library of Canada*] (NLC)
SRO .... Savannah River Operation [*Office*] [*Energy Research and Development Administration*]
SRO .... S-Band RADAR Operational
SRO .... Scarboro Resources Ltd. [*Toronto Stock Exchange symbol*]
SRO .... Scottish Record Office
SRO .... Seismological Research Observatory [*Australia*]
SRO .... Self-Regulatory Organisation [*Financial Services Act of 1986*] [*British*]
SRO .... Senior Range Officer
SRO .... Senior Ranking Officer [*Army*] (ADDR)
SRO .... Senior Reactor Operator [*Nuclear energy*] (NRCH)
SRO .... Senior Research Officer [*Ministry of Agriculture, Fisheries, and Food*] [*British*]
SRO .... Servicios Aereos Rutas Oriente SA de CV [*Mexico ICAO designator*] (FAAC)
SRO .... Sex-Ratio Organism [*Entomology*]
SRO .... Sharable and Read Only [*Computer science*] (PCM)
SRO .... Shop Readiness Objective
SRO .... Shop Repair Order
SRO .... Short-Range Order [*Solid state physics*]
SRO .... Shrobarova [*Czechoslovakia*] [*Seismograph station code, US Geological Survey*] (SEIS)
SRO .... Single-Room Occupancy [*Housing*]
SRO .... Singly Resonant Oscillator (IEEE)
SRO .... Society of Radio Operators
SRO .... Society of Registration Officers - Births, Deaths, and Marriages [*British*] (DBA)
SRO .... Solar Radio Observatory
SRO .... Spares Requirement Order
SRO .... Special Rate Order [*Business term*]
SRO .... Special Regional Operations (NATG)
SRO .... Specification Release Order [*Nuclear energy*] (NRCH)
SRO .... Squadron Recreation Officer [*Navy British*]
SRO .... Standing Room Only [*Theater*]
SRO .... Standing Route Order [*Army*] (AABC)
SRO .... State Recycling Organizations [*Environment*] (GNE)
SRO .... Station Routine Order (IAA)
SRO .... Statutory Rules and Orders
SRO .... Steele-Richardson-Olszewski Syndrome [*Medicine*]
SRO .... Stock Record Officer
SRo .... Studia Rosenthaliana [*A publication*] (BJA)
SRO .... Superintendent [*or Supervisor*] of Range Operations [*NASA*]
SRO .... Supervisor Range Operations (MCD)
SRO .... Supplementary Reserve of Officers [*Military British*]
SRO .... System Readiness Objective
SRO .... Systems Reproduction Order (MCD)
SROA .... Safety-Related Operator Action [*Nuclear energy*] (NRCH)
SROA .... Society for Radiation Oncology Administrators (EA)
SROA .... Statistical Record of Older Americans [*A publication*]
SROB .... Short-Range Omnidirectional Beacon [*Aerospace*]
SROD .... Stove Rod
SROE .... Statistical Record of the Environment [*A publication*]
SROEQ .... Selected References on Environmental Quality as It Relates to Health [*A publication*]
SROF .... Self-Renewal Occupational Field
SROF .... Sustained Rate of Fire [*Military*] (INF)
SROH .... Societe de Recherche en Orientation Humaine [*Canada*]
SROKA .... Second Republic of Korea Army
SROM .... Sirrom Capital [*NASDAQ symbol*] (TTSB)
SROM .... Sirrom Capital Corp. [*NASDAQ symbol*] (SAG)
SROM .... Sociomoral Reflection Objective Measure (EDAC)
SROM .... Spontaneous Rupture of Membrane [*Medicine*] (DMAA)
SRON .... Space Research Organization Netherlands
SROP .... Senior Registered Options Principal [*Investment term*]
SROS .... Seybold Report on Office Systems (HGAA)
SROS .... Special Run Operations Sheet (IAA)
SROTC .... Senior Reserve Officers' Training Corps [*Military*] (AABC)
SROTS .... Superficial Rays of the Sun [*In reference to suntanning, supposedly occuring before 10am and after 2pm*] [*See also BROTS*]
SROWW .... Statistical Record of Women Worldwide [*A publication*]
SRP .... Safeguard Readiness Posture [*Army*] (AABC)
SRP .... Salary Reduction Plan [*Business term*]
SRP .... Saskatchewan Library and Union Catalogue, Regina, Saskatchewan [*Library symbol National Library of Canada*] (NLC)
SRP .... Saskatchewan Provincial Library [*UTLAS symbol*]
SRP .... Savannah River Plant [*Department of Energy*]
SRP .... Savings and Retirement Plan
SRP .... Scientific Research Proposal (AAG)
SRP .... Sealift Readiness Program [*Military*]
SRP .... Seat Reference Point
SRP .... Seismic Reflection Profile [*Marine science*] (MSC)
SRP .... Selected Reference Point (GAVI)
SRP .... Selective Reenlistment Program [*Air Force*]
SRP .... Self-Recording Penetrometer
SRP .... Sensor Reporting Post
SRP .... Sequential Range Policy (PDAA)
SRP .... Serbian Radical Party [*Political party*]
SRP .... Shags Rocks Passage [*Oceanography*]
SRP .... Shared Resources Programmming (NITA)
SRP .... Shark Research Panel [*Navy*] (DNAB)
SRP .... Shift Register Partition (IAA)
SRP .... Ship's Repair Party [*Navy British*]
SRP .... Short Ragweed Pollen [*Immunology*]
SRP .... Sierra Pacific Resources [*NYSE symbol*] (SPSG)
SRP .... Sierra Pac Pw [*NYSE symbol*] (SAG)
SRP .... Signal Recognition Particle [*Biochemistry*]
SRP .... Sink Resistant Plastic (PDAA)
SRP .... SIOP Reconnaissance Plan (MCD)
SRP .... Slot Reference Point (DA)
SRP .... Small Rotating Plug [*Nuclear energy*] (NRCH)
SRP .... Socialisticka Radnicka Partija Jugoslavije [*Socialist Workers' Party of Yugoslavia*] [*Political party*] (PPE)
SRP .... Socialist Revolutionary Party [*India*] [*Political party*] (PPW)
SRP .... Socialist Revolutionary Party [*Former USSR Political party*]
SRP .... Socialist Revolution Party [*Turkey Political party*] (PPW)
SRP .... Society for Radiological Protection [*British*] (DEN)
SRP .... Society of Recorder Players [*British*] (DBA)
SRP .... Software Renewal Program [*Food and Nutrition Service*] [*Department of Agriculture*] (GFGA)
SRP .... Solar Radiation Pressure
SRP .... Solicitation Review Panel [*Air Force*]
SRP .... Soluble Reactive Phosphorus [*Marine science*] (OSRA)
SRP .... Soluble Reactive Phosphorus (USDC)
SRP .... Sonobuoy Referenced Position [*Navy*] (NG)
SRP .... Source Record Punch
SRP .... Sozialistische Reichspartei [*Socialist Reich Party*] [*Germany Political party*] (PPE)
SRP .... Space Requirement Program (MCD)
SRP .... Spin Recovery Parachute
SRP .... Stabilization Reference Package (MCD)
SRP .... Standard Relative Power
SRP .... Standard Repair Procedures
SRP .... Standard Review Plan [*Nuclear energy*] (NRCH)
SRP .... Start Rendezvous Point (MCD)
SRP .... State Registered Physiotherapist [*British*]
SRP .... Status Report Panels (SAA)
SRP .... Stern Reference Point [*Navy*] (DNAB)
SRP .... Stratospheric Research Program
SRP .... Stray Radiant Power
SRP .... Suggested Retail Price
SRP .... Suggested Retail Price (WDMC)
SRP .... Supply and Repair Parts (DNAB)
SRP .... Supply Readiness Program [*Air Force*]
SRP .... Supply Refuelling Point [*Air Force British*]
SRP .... Traverse City, MI [*Location identifier FAA*] (FAAL)
SRPA .... Senior Real Property Appraiser [*Society of Real Estate Appraisers*] [*Designation awarded by*]
SRPA .... Spherical Retarding Potential Analyzer (MCD)
SRPA .... Squash Rackets Professionals Association [*British*] (DBA)
SRPA .... Sydney Regional Planning Authority [*Proposed*] [*Australia*]
SRPARABAD... Senior Parachutist Badge [*Military decoration*]
SRPB .... Scottish River Purification Board
SRPBA .... Scottish River Purification Boards Association
SRPC .... SaskPower, Regina, Saskatchewan [*Library symbol National Library of Canada*] (NLC)
SRPC .... Sulphate Resisting Portland Cement
SRPC .... Supplier Request for Product Change

SRPCRD ...... Research and Development Center Library, SaskPower, Regina, Saskatchewan [*Library symbol National Library of Canada*] (NLC)
SRPD .... System Research and Planning Division [*NASA*] (KSC)
SRPDAA .... Silk and Rayon Printers and Dyers Association of America (EA)
SRPE .... Senior Rater Potential Evaluation [*Army*]
SR(PFE) .... Seaman Recruit (Polaris Field Electronics) [*Navy rating*] (DNAB)
SR(PFL) .... Seaman Recruit (Polaris Field Launcher) [*Navy rating*] (DNAB)
SRPG .... Scraping
SRPH .... Saskatchewan Department of Health, Regina, Saskatchewan [*Library symbol National Library of Canada*] (NLC)
srph .... Seraph (VRA)
SRPI .... Scrap Rubber and Plastics Institute (EA)
SRPI .... Server Requester Programming Interface [*Computer science*] (CDE)
SRPI .... Silk and Rayon Print Institute [*Defunct*] (EA)
SRPIS .... Southern Regional Plant Introduction Station [*University of Georgia*] [*Research center*] (RCD)
SRPJ .... Self-Restraining Pipe Joint
SRPM .... Shaft Revolutions per Minute (DNAB)
SRPM .... Single Reversal Permanent Magnet (IAA)
SRPM .... Standard Raven's Progressive Matrix [*Psychiatry*] (DAVI)
SRPM .... Stated Redemption Price at Maturity [*of debt instruments*]
SRPMME ..... Society for Research in the Psychology of Music and Music Education [*British*]
SRPN .... Special Requisition Priority Number
SRPNSE .... State Required Public Notification of Standards Exceedances [*Environmental Protection Agency*]
SRPO .... Science Resources Planning Office [*National Science Foundation*]
SRPP .... Public Participation Library, Regina, Saskatchewan [*Library symbol National Library of Canada*] (BIB)
SRPP .... Skeletal Rod of Palp
SRP/PDS ...... Stabilization Reference Package / Position Determination System [*Military*]
SRPR .... Saskatchewan Parks and Renewable Resources, Regina, Saskatchewan [*Library symbol National Library of Canada*] (NLC)
SRPR .... Scraper
SRPR .... Signal Recognition Particle Receptor (DMAA)
SRPR .... Stray Radiant Power Ratio
SrPrchtBad ... Senior Parachutist Badge [*Military decoration*]
SRPS .... Saskatchewan Public Service Commission, Regina, Saskatchewan [*Library symbol National Library of Canada*] (NLC)
SRPS .... Scientific Research Project Support [*National Science Foundation*]
SRPS .... Scottish Railway Preservation Society (DBA)
SRPS .... Secure Record and Playback System (MCD)
SRPS .... Sensor-Referenced Positioning System
SR/PS .... Shipping Request/Packing Sheet (MCD)
SRPS .... Short Rib-Polydactyly Syndrome [*Medicine*] (DMAA)
SRPS .... Supply and Repair Parts Specification (DNAB)
SRPT .... Shortest Remaining Processing Time (PDAA)
SRPT .... Small Repair Parts Transporter
SRPT .... Statements of Responsibilites in Tax Practice (TDOB)
SRPT .... Stress Relaxation Processability Tester (PDAA)
SRPV .... Stationary Remotely Piloted Vehicle (MCD)
SRPW .... Savannah River Plant - Well DRB-10 [*South Carolina*] [*Seismograph station code, US Geological Survey*] (SEIS)
SRQ .... Sarasota/Bradenton [*Florida*] [*Airport symbol*]
SRQ .... Self-Reporting Questionnaire [*Medicine*] (DMAA)
SRQ .... Self-Righteousness Questionnaire [*Psychology*] (EDAC)
SRQ .... Service Request
SRQ .... Status Request Field [*Computer science*] (IAA)
SRQS .... Service Request State (IAA)
SRR .... Central New York Library Resources Council, Syracuse, NY [*OCLC symbol*] (OCLC)
SRR .... Scots Revised Reports [*A publication*] (DLA)
SRR .... Search and Range RADAR
SRR .... Seastar Resource Corp. [*Vancouver Stock Exchange symbol*]
SRR .... Security Rules and Regulations
srr .... Serer [*MARC language code Library of Congress*] (LCCP)
SRR .... Serially Reusable Resource [*Computer science*]
SRR .... Service Representative Report (MCD)
SRR .... Shift Register Recognizer (IEEE)
SRR .... Short-Range RADAR
SRR .... Short-Range Recovery (IEEE)
SRR .... Shuttle Requirements Review [*NASA*] (MCD)
SRR .... Site Readiness Review [*NASA*] (NASA)
SRR .... Skin Resistance Response [*Physiology*]
SRR .... Slow Rotation Room [*NASA*]
SRR .... Socialist Republic of Romania
SRR .... Society for Reformation Research (EA)
SRR .... Software Requirements Review [*NASA*] (NASA)
SRR .... Sorreisa [*Norway*] [*Airport symbol*] (AD)
SRR .... Sound Recorder-Reproducer (MSA)
SRR .... Source-Receptor Relation [*Environmental chemistry*]
SRR .... Special Reimbursement Rate (AFM)
SRR .... Special Report Writer [*NASA*]
SRR .... Spot Radio Report (WDMC)
SRR .... Spurious Response Rejection
SRR .... Stain Release Rating [*Textile technology*]
SRR .... Standardized Rate Ratio (DMAA)
SRR .... Star Air IS [*Denmark ICAO designator*] (FAAC)
SRR .... State Regulation Report: Toxics [*Business Publishers, Inc.*] [*Information service or system*] (CRD)
SRR .... Steering Reversal Rate
SRR .... Strategic Ready Reserve [*Military*]
SRR .... Stride Rite [*NYSE symbol*] (TTSB)
SRR .... Stride Rite Corp. [*NYSE symbol*] (SPSG)
SRR .... Subsystem Requirements Review
SRR .... Supplementary Reserve Regulations [*Army British*]
SRR .... Supplier Rating Report (SAA)
SRR .... Support Requirements Records [*Navy*] (NG)
SRR .... Surgery Recovery Room [*Medicine*] (DMAA)
SRR .... Surplus Review Record (SAA)
SRR .... Survival, Recovery, and Reconstitution [*Military*] (AFM)
SRR .... System Readiness Review (MCD)
SRR .... System Requirements Review [*NASA*]
SRRA .... Statistical Record of Religion in America [*A publication*]
SRRB .... Search and Rescue Radio Beacon
SRRB .... Solar Radiation Research Branch [*Marine science*] (OSRA)
SRRB .... Solar Radiation Research Branch [*Air Resources Laboratory*] (USDC)
SRRC .... Resource Centre, RCMP [*Royal Canadian Mounted Police*] Academy, Regina, Saskatchewan [*Library symbol National Library of Canada*] (NLC)
SRRC .... Scottish Reactor Research Centre (DEN)
SRRC .... Southern Regional Research Center [*Department of Agriculture*] [*New Orleans, LA*] (GRD)
SRRC .... Sperry Rand Research Center (MCD)
SRRC .... Standing Results Review Committee [*Nuclear energy*] (NRCH)
SRRC .... Star Resources Corp. [*NASDAQ symbol*] (SAG)
SRRCP .... Petroleum Division, Saskatchewan Research Council, Regina [*Library symbol National Library of Canada*] (BIB)
SRRCS .... Surface Raid Reporting Control Ship [*Navy*] (NVT)
SRRE .... Prairie Farm Rehabilitation Administration, Agriculture Canada [*Administration du Retablissement Agricole des Prairies, Agriculture Canada*] Regina, Saskatchewan [*Library symbol National Library of Canada*] (NLC)
SRRI .... School Related Resources Index [*Australia*]
SRRI .... Wascana Campus, Saskatchewan Institute of Applied Science and Technology, R egina, Saskatchewan [*Library symbol National Library of Canada*] (NLC)
SRRP .... Source Reduction Review Program [*Environmental science*]
SRRS .... Social Readjustment Rating Scale [*Psychometrics*]
SR-RSV .... Rous Sarcoma Virus, Schmidt-Ruppin Strain
SRRT .... Simultaneous Rotating and Reciprocating Technique (DNAB)
SRRT .... Social Responsibilities Round Table [*American Library Association*] (EA)
SRS .... Sales Relations Survey [*Test*]
SRS .... San Marcos [*Colombia*] [*Airport symbol*] (AD)
SRS .... Saskoil, Regina, Saskatchewan [*Library symbol National Library of Canada*] (NLC)
SRS .... Satellite RADAR Station (NATG)
SRS .... Satellite Readout Station (MCD)
SRS .... Satellite Receiving Station
SRS .... Savannah River Site [*Department of Energy*] [*Aiken, SC*] (GAAI)
SRS .... Savannah River Site
SRS .... Savannah River Site (DOGT)
SRS .... Saved Registers Stack (ECII)
SRS .... Scandinavian Radiological Society (EA)
SRS .... Science Requirements Strategy [*Viking lander mission*] [*NASA*]
SRS .... Scientific Reference Service [*HEW*]
SRS .... Scientific Research Society of America [*Later, Sigma XI, The Scientific Research Society of America*] (AAG)
SRS .... Scottish Record Society [*Glasgow*] (EA)
SRS .... Scottish Reformation Society (DBA)
SRS .... Search and Rescue Ship (KSC)
SRS .... Seat Reservation System (IAA)
SRS .... Secondary RADAR System
SRS .... Secondary Recovery Ships [*NASA*] (KSC)
SRS .... Second Readiness State (AAG)
SRS .... Secure Range Safety [*NASA*] (KSC)
SRS .... Segment Ready Storage
SRS .... Seismic Recording System
SRS .... Selective Record Service (NITA)
SRS .... Selenium Rectifier Stack
SRS .... Self-Rating Scale [*Psychology*]
SRS .... Selkirk Remote Sensing Ltd. [*Canada ICAO designator*] (FAAC)
SRS .... Senate Recording Studio
SRS .... Send Receive Switch [*Telecommunications*] (IAA)
SRS .... Series [*Deltiology*]
SRS .... Shakespeare Reading Society [*British*] (DBA)
SRS .... Shakespeare Recording Society [*Commercial firm*] (EA)
SRS .... Shared Registry System [*Computer science*]
SRS .... Shipboard RADAR System
SRS .... Shorter Range Scheduling
SRS .... Short-Range Search (MCD)
SRS .... Side-Looking RADAR System
SRS .... Sight Restoration Society (EA)
SRS .... Silent Running Society (EA)
SRS .... Silver-Russell Syndrome [*Medicine*]
SRS .... Simple Random Sample [*Statistics*]
SRS .... Simulated Raman Scattering
SRS .... Simulated Remote Sites [*NASA*] (KSC)
SRS .... Simulated Remote Station [*NASA*]
SRS .... Skeletal Repair System [*Medicine*]
SRS .... Slave Register Set
SRS .... Sleep Research Society (EA)
SRS .... Slippery Rock State College, Slippery Rock, PA [*OCLC symbol*] (OCLC)
SRS .... Slow-Reacting Substance [*of anaphylaxis*] [*Leukotriene C Immunology*]
SRS .... Small Research Satellite (KSC)
SRS .... Small Ring Sparger [*Engineering*]

SRS .... Social and Rehabilitation Service [*Abolished, 1977*] [*HEW*]
SRS .... Societatis Regiae Socius [*or Sodalis*] [*Fellow of the Royal Society*] [*Latin*] (GPO)
SRS .... Society for Romanian Studies (EA)
SRS .... Sodium Removal Station [*Nuclear energy*] (NRCH)
SRS .... Software Requirements Specification [*NASA*] (NASA)
SRS .... Solar Radiation Satellite (IAA)
SRS .... Solar Radiation Simulator
SRS .... Solid RADWASTE [*Radioactive Waste*] System [*Nuclear energy*] (NRCH)
SRS .... Songwriters Resources and Services [*Later, NAS*] (EA)
SRS .... Sonobuoy Reference System [*Navy*] (CAAL)
SRS .... Sounding Rocket System
SRS .... Sound Ranging Section (IAA)
SRS .... Sound Ranging Set
SRS .... Sound Recordings Specialists [*Record label*]
SRS .... Sound Retrieval System [*Hughes Aircraft Co.*]
SRS .... Southern Railway System (MCD)
SRS .... Space and Reentry System (IAA)
SRS .... Spaceborne Reconnaissance System
SRS .... Space Recovery Systems (KSC)
SRS .... Spares Recommendation Sheet (MCD)
SRS .... Spares Requirement Schedule (MCD)
SRS .... Spatial Reference System [*Mapping*] (EERA)
SRS .... Special Revenue Sharing (OICC)
SRS .... Specification Requirement Sheet (RDA)
SRS .... Specification Revision Sheet [*NASA*] (NASA)
SRS .... Speech Reinforcement System
SRS .... Splenorenal Shunt [*Medicine*]
SRS .... Spontaneous Reporting System [*Food and Drug Administration*]
SRS .... Squad Radio Set
SRS .... Srpska Radikalna Stranka [*Serbian Radical Party*] [*Former Yugoslavia*] [*Political party*] (PPE)
S/RS .... Staff Returns [*Marine Corps*]
SRS .... Standard Random Sample
SRS .... Standard Reference Section
SRS .... Standard Repair Specification (MCD)
SRS .... State Revenue Society (EA)
SRS .... Statistical Reporting Service [*Later, ESCS*] [*Department of Agriculture*]
SRS .... Stimulated Raman Scattering [*Spectrometry*]
SRS .... Stimulated Rayleigh Scattering (IAA)
SRS .... Strategic Reconnaissance Squadron (MCD)
SRS .... Strike Reporting System
SRS .... Structural Research Series
SRS .... Student Record System [*Australia*]
SRS .... Student Response System [*Automated group instruction*]
SRS .... Submarine Reactor Small
SRS .... Subscriber-Response System [*Study of cable television*] [*Hughes Aircraft Co.*]
SRS .... Substitute Route Structure
SRS .... Sum of All Repairable Subassemblies
SRS .... Sunrise Metals [*Vancouver Stock Exchange symbol*]
SRS .... Supplemental Restraint System [*Automotive engineering*]
SRS .... Supply Response Section [*Navy*]
SRS .... Support Requirement System [*NASA*] (NASA)
SRS .... Surgical Research Society [*British*]
SRS .... Surveillance RADAR Station
SRS .... Survey Research Service [*National Opinion Research Center, University of Chicago*] [*Research center*]
SRS .... Survey Research Singapore (Pte) Ltd. [*Information service or system*] (IID)
SRS .... Swiss Railways Society [*British*] (DBA)
SRS .... Synchronous Node Relay Satellite [*Telecommunications*] (TEL)
SRS .... Synchrotron Radiation Source [*High-energy physics*]
SRS .... System Requirements Specification (MCD)
SRS .... Systems Reliability Service (NUCP)
SRSA .... Saskatchewan Arts Board, Regina, Saskatchewan [*Library symbol National Library of Canada*] (NLC)
SRSA .... Scientific Research Society of America [*Later, Sigma XI, The Scientific Research Society of America*]
SRS-A .... Slow-Reacting Substance of Anaphylaxis [*Immunology*]
SRSAGM .... Short-Range Surface-to-Air Guided Weapon (IAA)
SR SATSIM .... Search RADAR Satellite Simulation [*Military*] (CAAL)
SRSC .... Slippery Rock State College [*Pennsylvania*]
SRSC .... Space Remote Sensing Center
SRSC .... Sul Ross State College [*Later, SRSU*] [*Texas*]
SRSC .... System Centre, Saskatchewan Revenue Supply and Services, Regina, Saskatchewan [*Library symbol National Library of Canada*] (NLC)
SRSCC .... Simulated Remote Station Control Center
SRSCC .... Simulated Remote Station Control Console [*NASA*] (IAA)
SRSCCD .... Saskatchewan Co-Operation and Co-Operative Development, Regina, Saskatchewan [*Library symbol National Library of Canada*] (NLC)
SRSCU .... Saskatchewan Computer Utility Corp. [*SaskComp*], Regina, Saskatchewan [*Library symbol National Library of Canada*] (NLC)
SRSEM .... Saskatchewan Department of Energy and Mines, Regina, Saskatchewan [*Library symbol National Library of Canada*] (NLC)
SRSEMG .... Geological Laboratory, Saskatchewan Department of Energy and Mines, Regina, Saskatchewan [*Library symbol National Library of Canada*] (NLC)
SRSF .... and Subassembly Facility [*or Refurbishment*] [*NASA*] (NASA)
SRSF .... Saskatchewan Finance, Regina, Saskatchewan [*Library symbol National Library of Canada*] (NLC)
SRSG .... Search RADAR Simulation Group [*Military*] (CAAL)
SRSG .... Special Representatives of the Secretary General [*United Nations*]
SRSG .... Subsurface Geological Laboratory, Regina, Saskatchewan [*Library symbol National Library of Canada*] (NLC)
SRSH .... Wascana Hospital, Regina, Saskatchewan [*Library symbol National Library of Canada*] (NLC)
SRSK .... Short-Range Station Keeping (NG)
SRSL .... SRS Labs, Inc. [*NASDAQ symbol*] (SAG)
SRS Lbs .... SRS Labs, Inc. [*Associated Press*] (SAG)
SRSM .... Special Research Study Memorandum
SRSNY .... Stockholder Relations Society of New York (EA)
SRSO .... Scoliosis Research Society (EA)
SRSO .... Silicon-Rich Silicon Oxide [*Inorganic Chemistry*]
SRSP .... Stockpile Reliability/Survivability Program
SRSPMC .... Saskatchewan Property Management Corp., Regina, Saskatchewan [*Library symbol National Library of Canada*] (NLC)
SR Sq .... Strategic Reconnaissance Squadron
SRSR .... Schedule and Resources Status Report [*NASA*] (NASA)
SRS-RSV .... Schmidt-Ruppin Strain Rous Sarcoma Virus [*Oncology*] (DAVI)
SRSS .... Resource Centre, Saskatchewan Department of Social Services, Regina, Saskatchewan [*Library symbol National Library of Canada*] (NLC)
SRSS .... Shuttle Range Safety System [*NASA*] (NASA)
SRSS .... Simulated Remote Sites Subsystem [*NASA*] (KSC)
SRSS .... Sociological Resources for Secondary Schools (AEBS)
SRSS .... Sociological Resources for Social Studies [*Project of American Sociological Association*]
SRSS .... Solar Radiation Simulator System
SRSS .... Square Root of the Sum of the Squares (NRCH)
SR-SS .... Sunrise-Sunset (DA)
SRST .... SASK TEL Corporate Library, Regina, Saskatchewan [*Library symbol National Library of Canada*] (NLC)
SRST .... Speed Reading Self-Taught [*Learning International*]
SRST .... System Resource and Status Table [*Computer science*] (IAA)
SRSTA .... Society of Roller Skating Teachers of America (EA)
SRSU .... Satellite Readout Station Upgrade (DWSG)
SRSU .... Sul Ross State University [*Texas*]
SRSV .... Small Round-Structured Virus [*Medicine*]
SRSV .... Source Services Corp. [*NASDAQ symbol*] (SAG)
SRT .... Sagittal Ray Trace
SRT .... Sarafotoxin [*Biochemistry*]
SRT .... Sarutani [*Japan*] [*Seismograph station code, US Geological Survey*] (SEIS)
SRT .... S-Band Radio Transmitter
SRT .... Scarlet Energy, Inc. [*Vancouver Stock Exchange symbol*]
SRT .... School Readiness Test [*Child development test*]
SRT .... School Response Team
SRT .... Science Recommendation Team
SRT .... Science, Research, and Technology
SRT .... Search RADAR Terminal
SRT .... Security Response Team [*Military*]
SRT .... Sedimentation Rate Test
SRT .... Self-Repair Technique
SRT .... Serials Round Table [*Later, RTSD*] [*American Library Association*]
SRT .... Set Reset Trigger [*Flipflop*] [*Computer science*] (IAA)
SRT .... Shift-Register Transfer [*Computer science*]
SRT .... Short-Range Transport [*Aircraft*] (NATG)
SRT .... Short Residence Time [*Chemical engineering*]
SRT .... Shuttle Requirements Traceability [*NASA*] (MCD)
SRT .... Silica RADOME Technique
SRT .... Simple Reaction Time [*Psychometry*]
SRT .... Single Requesting Terminal [*Computer science*] (IBMDP)
SRT .... Single Run Time (IAA)
SRT .... Sinus Node Recovery Time [*Medicine*] (DMAA)
SRT .... Slow-Run-Through Trials [*Navy*] (NG)
SRT .... Sludge Retention Time [*Wastewater treatment*]
SRT .... Smoke Removal tube [*Used in laser therapy*] [*Gynecology*] (DAVI)
SRT .... Social Relations Test [*Psychology*]
SRT .... Society of Romanian Air Transports [*ICAO designator*] (FAAC)
SRT .... Solar Radiation Test
SRT .... Solar Radio Telescope
SRT .... Solids Retention Time [*Water pollution*]
SRT .... Soroti [*Uganda*] [*Airport symbol*] (OAG)
SRT .... Source Routing Transparent [*Telecommunications*]
SRT .... Special Rated Thrust [*Aerospace*] (MCD)
SRT .... Special Real-Time Command (MCD)
SRT .... Special Review Team [*Nuclear energy*] (NRCH)
SRT .... Specification Requirements Table [*NASA*] (NASA)
SRT .... Speech Reception Test [*Audiometry*] (MAE)
SRT .... Speech Reception Thresholds [*Audiometry*]
SRT .... Speech Recognition Technology [*Computer science*] (CDE)
SRT .... Spent Resin Tank [*Nuclear energy*] (NRCH)
SRT .... Spousal Remainder Trust [*Banking*]
SRT .... Standard Radio & Telefon (NITA)
SRT .... Standard Rate Turn (NVT)
SRT .... Standard Remote Terminal
SRT .... Station Readiness Test
SRT .... Step Recovery Transistor
SRT .... Strategic Relocatable Target [*DoD*]
SRT .... Strategic Rocket Troops (NATG)
SRT .... Stress Relief Tool
SRT .... Stroke Rehabilitation Technician (MAE)
SRT .... Subcaliber Rocket Trainer [*Army*] (INF)
SRT .... Supply Response Time
SRT .... Supporting Research and Technology (MCD)

SRT .... Surface Recording Terminal (MCD)
SRT .... Sustained Release Theophylline [*Medicine*]
SRT .... Synchro and Resolver Transmission
SRT .... System Reaction Time (KSC)
SRT .... System Reliability Test
SRT .... Systems Readiness Test (KSC)
SRTA .... Senorita [*Miss*] [*Spanish*]
SRTA .... Single Relaxation Time Approximation [*Physics*]
SRTA .... Stationary Reflector/Tracking Absorber [*Solar power*] (DICI)
SRTBM .... Short-Range Tactical Ballistic Missile
SRTC .... Scientific Research Tax Credit [*Canada*]
SRTC .... Search RADAR Terrain Clearance (NG)
SRTC .... Search Radar Terrain Clearance (DOMA)
SRTC .... Signal Replacement Training Center (IAA)
SRTC .... Society of Ration Token Collectors (EA)
SRTC .... Southern Rhodesia Transport Corps [*British military*] (DMA)
SRTC .... Special Real-Time Command (KSC)
SRTC .... Stored Program Real-Time Commands (MCD)
SRTCA .... Senate Radio-Television Correspondents Association (NTCM)
SRTD .... Sorted (MCD)
SRTE .... Sound Receiving/Transmitting Equipment
SRTF .... Shortest Remaining Time First [*Computer science*]
SRTF .... Short-Range Task Force
SRTM .... Shuttle Radar Topography Mission [*NASA*]
SRTM .... Simplified Real-Time Monitor [*Computer science*] (MHDI)
SRTN .... Sensor Return [*Automotive engineering*]
SRTN .... Solar Radio Telescope Network
SRTN .... Special Representative for Trade Negotiations [*Later, USTR*] [*Executive Office of the President*]
SRTOS .... Special Real-Time Operating System (PDAA)
SRTP .... Sensitized Room Temperature Phosphorescence
SRTR .... Senior Tour Players Development [*NASDAQ symbol*] (SAG)
SRTR .... Senior Tour Players Dvlmt [*NASDAQ symbol*] (TTSB)
SRTR .... Short-Range Training Round [*Army*] (INF)
SRTRW .... Senior Tour Players Dev Wrrt [*NASDAQ symbol*] (TTSB)
SRTS .... Scaled Range Target System (MCD)
SRTS .... Science Research Temperament Scale [*Psychology*]
SRTS .... Short-Range Thermal Sight [*Army*] (INF)
SRTS .... Steam Railway Traction Society [*British*] (BI)
SRTS .... Strategic Reconnaissance Training Squadron
SRTS .... Surveillance RADAR Test Set
SRTSB .... Business Library, Saskatchewan Department of Tourism and Small Business, Regina,Saskatchewan [*Library symbol National Library of Canada*] (NLC)
SRTT .... Serial Reaction Time Task [*Physiology*]
SRTU .... Ship Repair Training Unit
SRTUC .... Southern Rhodesian Trade Unions Congress
SRTV .... Soldiers Radio and Television [*Information service or system Military*]
SRTVM .... Short-Range Track via Missile [*Military*] (CAAL)
SRU .... Santa Cruz, CA [*Location identifier FAA*] (FAAL)
SRU .... Scottish Rugby Union (DAS)
SRU .... Seaplane Reconnaissance Unit
SRU .... Secondary Replaceable Unit
SRU .... Selective Reserve Unit [*Navy*] (NVT)
SRU .... Self-Recording Unit (IAA)
SRU .... Self-Representing Unit (GFGA)
SRU .... Sensor Readout Unit (MCD)
SRU .... Servo Repeater Unit
SRU .... Ship Repair Unit
SRU .... Shop-Replaceable Unit [*NASA*] (NASA)
SRU .... Side Rails Up [*On a bed*] (DAVI)
SRU .... Signal Responder Unit (AAG)
SRU .... Silver Recovery Unit
SRU .... Smallest Replaceable Unit (MCD)
SRU .... Societe de Raffinage d'Uranium [*France*]
SRU .... Solitary Rectal Ulcer [*Medicine*] (DMAA)
SRU .... Space Replaceable Unit (MCD)
SRU .... Structural Repeating Unit [*Polymer nomenclature system*]
SRU .... Student Response Unit
SRU .... Subassembly Repairable Unit (MCD)
SRU .... Submarine Repair Unit
SRU .... Subscriber-Response Unit (IAA)
SRU .... Sulfur Recovery Unit [*Chemical engineering*]
SRU .... Support Resource Unit (MCD)
SRU .... Suspension and Release Units (AFM)
SRU .... System Replaceable Unit
SRU .... System Resource Unit [*Environmental Protection Agency*] (GFGA)
SRU .... University of Regina, Saskatchewan [*Library symbol National Library of Canada*] (NLC)
SRU .... University of Scranton, Scranton, PA [*OCLC symbol*] (OCLC)
SRUA .... Saskatchewan Urban Affairs, Regina, Saskatchewan [*Library symbol National Library of Canada*] (NLC)
SRUC .... Regina Campus, Campion College, University of Saskatchewan, Saskatchewan [*Library symbol National Library of Canada*] (NLC)
SRUE .... Education Library, University of Regina, Saskatchewan [*Library symbol National Library of Canada*] (BIB)
SRUFA .... Faculty of Fine Arts, University of Regina, Saskatchewan [*Library symbol National Library of Canada*] (NLC)
SRUG .... Department of Geography, University of Regina, Saskatchewan [*Library symbol National Library of Canada*] (NLC)
SRUNM .... Norman MacKenzie Art Gallery, University of Regina, Saskatchewan [*Library symbol National Library of Canada*] (NLC)
SRV .... Safety Relief Valve [*Nuclear energy*] (NRCH)
SRV .... Saline Retention Value
SRV .... Satellite Reentry Vehicle
SRV .... Service Corp. International [*NYSE symbol*] (SPSG)
SRV .... Service Corp. Intl [*NYSE symbol*] (TTSB)
SRV .... Short-Range Viewer
SRV .... Simulated Reentry Vehicle
SRV .... Sirius Resources [*Vancouver Stock Exchange symbol*]
SRV .... Socialist Republic of Vietnam
SRV .... Society of Russian Veterans of the World War (EA)
SRV .... Space Recovery [*or Rescue*] Vehicle
SRV .... Step Recovery Varactor
SRV .... Stony River [*Alaska*] [*Airport symbol*] (OAG)
SRV .... Styling Research Vehicle [*Automotive engineering*]
SRV .... Submerged Research Vehicle
SRV .... Surface Recombination Velocity (DEN)
SRV .... Surface Roving Vehicle [*NASA*] (KSC)
SRV .... Surrogate Research Vehicle [*Army Tank-Automotive Command*]
SRV .... Surveillance (DA)
SRV .... System Readiness Verification
SRVAMPL .... Servo Amplifier (IAA)
Srvc .... Service
SRVC .... Sine-Random Vibration Control
SRVC .... SunRiver Corp. [*NASDAQ symbol*] (SAG)
SRVC .... SunRiver Corp. [*NASDAQ symbol*] (TTSB)
SRVCD .... Serviced [*Automotive advertising*]
SRVCLG ...... Service Ceiling [*Aerospace engineering*]
SRVCW .... SunRiver Corp. Wrrt [*NASDAQ symbol*] (TTSB)
SRVDL .... Safety/Relief Valve Discharge Line [*Nuclear energy*] (NRCH)
Srve .... Service
SRVEILOPS ... Surveillance Operations [*Military*] (NVT)
SRVIN .... Servo Inlet (IAA)
SRVL .... Survival (MSA)
SRVLSCH ..... Survival School [*Air Force*]
SRVPrT .... SCI Fin $3.125'TECONS' [*NYSE symbol*] (TTSB)
SRVRET .... Servo Return (IAA)
SRVT .... Sustained Re-Entrant Ventricular Tachyarrhythmia [*Cardiology*] (DMAA)
SrvTch .... Serv-Tech, Inc. [*Associated Press*] (SAG)
SRVY .... Survey
SRW .... Salisbury, NC [*Location identifier FAA*] (FAAL)
SRW .... Saskatchewan Wheat Pool, Regina, Saskatchewan [*Library symbol National Library of Canada*] (NLC)
SRW .... Search & Rescue HQ [*British ICAO designator*] (FAAC)
SRW .... Short Ragweed [*Immunology*]
SRW .... Silenced Reconnaissance Weapon (MCD)
SRW .... Smith(Charles E.)Res Rlty [*NYSE symbol*] (TTSB)
SRW .... Smith [*Charles E.*] Residential Realty, Inc. [*NYSE symbol*] (SAG)
SRW .... Strategic Reconnaissance Wing [*Air Force*] (MCD)
SRWA .... Swiss Review of World Affairs [*A publication*]
SRWBR .... Short-Range Wideband Radio (MCD)
SRWD .... South Saskatchewan Committee for World Development, Regina, Saskatchewan [*Library symbol National Library of Canada*] (NLC)
SRWG .... Software Review Working Group [*Computer science*] (MHDI)
SRWg .... Strategic Reconnaissance Wing [*Air Force*] (AFM)
SRWL .... Speeded Reading of Word List [*Neuropsychology test*]
SRWR .... Saskatchewan Water Resources Commission, Regina, Saskatchewan [*Library symbol National Library of Canada*] (NLC)
SRWS .... Simplified and Regularized Writing System
SRWS .... Solid Radioactive Waste System [*Nuclear energy*] (NRCH)
SRWS .... Standard Reference Water Sample [*US Geological Survey*]
SRX .... Sert [*Libya*] [*Airport symbol Obsolete*] (OAG)
SRX .... SR Telecom, Inc. [*Toronto Stock Exchange symbol*]
SRY .... Secondary [*ICAO designator*] (FAAC)
SRY .... Sherwood Rangers Yeomanry [*Military unit*] [*British*]
SRY .... Ship Repair Yard (CINC)
SRY .... Shiroyama [*Japan*] [*Seismograph station code, US Geological Survey*] (SEIS)
SRY .... Stryker Resources Ltd. [*Vancouver Stock Exchange symbol*]
SRY .... Surety Capital [*AMEX symbol*] (TTSB)
SRY .... Surety Capital Corp. [*AMEX symbol*] (SAG)
SRZ .... San Marcos, TX [*Location identifier FAA*] (FAAL)
SRZ .... Santa Cruz [*Bolivia*] [*Airport symbol*] (OAG)
SRZ .... Satz Rechen Zentrum [*Computer Composition Center*] [*Hartmann & Heenemann*] [*Information service or system*] (IID)
SRZ .... Special Rules Zone
SRZ .... Stratas Corp. [*Vancouver Stock Exchange symbol*]
SRZ .... Surveillance RADAR Zone (DA)
SRZF .... Synchro Resolver Zeroing Fixture
SRZLO .... Supreme Royal Zuanna, Ladies of the Orient [*Defunct*] (EA)
SS .... Faulty Sentence Structure [*Used in correcting manuscripts, etc.*]
SS .... Passing Stop Sign [*Traffic offense charge*]
SS .... Royal Statistical Society [*British*]
SS .... Saccharin Sodium [*Sweetening agent*]
SS .... Sacred Scripture
SS .... Safer Sex
SS .... Safe Shutdown [*Nuclear energy*] (NRCH)
SS .... Safety Services [*Red Cross*]
SS .... Safety Supervisor (MUGU)
SS .... Safety Supplements [*Air Force*]
SS .... Sagittal Sinus [*Anatomy*]
SS .... Saints [*as in "SS Peter and Paul"*]
SS .... Saint-Sacrement [*Blessed Sacrament*] [*French*]
SS .... Saline Soak
SS .... Saline Solution [*Pharmacology*] (DAVI)
SS .... Saliva Sample (MAE)
SS .... Salmonella-Shigella [*Microbiology*]
SS .... Salt-Sensitive

SS.......... Salt Substitute (DAVI)
SS.......... Same Size [*Photography, publishing*]
S/S.......... Same Size [*Photography*] [*Printing*] (WDMC)
SS.......... Sampled Servo [*Formatting scheme*] [*Computer science*] (PCM)
SS.......... Sample Sink [*Nuclear energy*] (NRCH)
SS.......... Sample Size (EDAC)
S/S.......... Samples per Second (KSC)
SS.......... Sample Station [*Nuclear energy*] (NRCH)
SS.......... Sampling System (NRCH)
SS.......... Sanarelli-Schwartzman [*Reaction*] [*Medicine*] (DAVI)
SS.......... Sancti [*Saints*] [*Latin*]
SS.......... Sanctissimus [*Most Holy*] [*Latin*]
SS.......... Sanctum Sanctorum [*Holy of Holies*] [*Freemasonry*] [*Latin*]
SS.......... Sand Springs Railway Co. [*AAR code*]
SS.......... Sandstone [*Lithology*]
ss.......... Sans [*Without*] [*Latin*] (DAVI)
SS.......... Sans Serif [*Typeface*] [*Printing*] (NTCM)
SS.......... Sartre Society (EA)
SS.......... Sa Saintete [*His Holiness*] [*The Pope*] [*French*]
SS.......... Sa Seigneurie [*His Lordship*] [*French*]
SS.......... Saskatoon Public Library, Saskatchewan [*Library symbol National Library of Canada*] (NLC)
SS.......... Satellite Space System (IAA)
SS.......... Satellite-Switched
SS.......... Satellite System
SS.......... Saturated Solution [*Pharmacy*]
SS.......... Sawin Society [*Defunct*] (EA)
SS.......... Scandinavian Seminar (EA)
SS.......... Scanning Slit
SS.......... Schempp-Hirth KG [*Germany ICAO aircraft manufacturer identifier*] (ICAO)
SS.......... Schizophrenia Spectrum [*Psychiatry*] (DAVI)
SS.......... Schutzstaffel [*Elite Guard*] [*NAZI Germany*]
SS.......... Science Service
SS.......... Scilicet [*Namely*] [*Legal term Latin*]
SS.......... Scintiscanning [*Medicine*]
SS.......... Sclerotinia sclerlatiorum (Causative Agent of Peanut Blight)
SS.......... Screw Steamer
SS.......... Sculptors' Society [*Australia*]
SS.......... Sea Scout - Nonrigid Airship [*Royal Naval Air Service*] [*British*]
SS.......... Sea Service [*British military*] (DMA)
SS.......... Sea State
SS.......... Secondary School
SS.......... Secondary Sources
SS.......... Secondary Surveillance
SS.......... Second Stage
SS.......... Secretary for Scotland
SS.......... Secretary of State
SS.......... Secretary of State Department [*Canada*]
SS.......... Secret Service
SS.......... Sections (ADA)
SS.......... Security Service
SS.......... Security Systems, Inc. [*In TV series "Max Headroom"*]
SS.......... See a Solicitor [*British*]
S/S.......... See Safe [*Bookselling*] (DGA)
SS.......... Seingalt Society (EA)
SS.......... Seizure Sensitive [*Neurology*] (DAVI)
SS.......... Selden Society (EA)
SS.......... Selective Service
SS.......... Selective Signaling
SS.......... Selector Switch (IEEE)
SS.......... Select Standby
S/S.......... Self Shank (WDAA)
SS.......... Self Simulation
SS.......... Selling Short [*or Short Sale*] [*Investment term*]
SS.......... Semifinal Splice [*Telecommunications*] (TEL)
SS.......... Semis [*One-Half*] [*Pharmacy*]
SS.......... Semisteel
SS.......... Semisubmersible [*Drilling unit*]
SS.......... Sempervivium Society [*Burgess Hill, West Sussex, England*] (EAIO)
SS.......... Senior Scholars (EA)
SS.......... Senior Security [*Investment term*]
SS.......... Sensor [*Genetics*]
SS.......... Sensor Supervisor [*Military*] (CAAL)
SS.......... Sensu Stricto [*In a Narrow Sense*] [*Latin*]
SS.......... Sentence Suspended
SS.......... Senza Sordini [*Without Mutes*] [*Music*]
SS.......... Sequentia [*What Follows*] [*Latin*] (ROG)
SS.......... Sequential Switch
SS.......... Serials Section [*Resources and Technical Services Division*] [*American Library Association*]
SS.......... Series Separate
Ss.......... Serum Serologic [*Immunochemistry*]
SS.......... Serum Sickness [*Medicine*]
SS.......... Service Sink (MSA)
SS.......... Service Squadron (AAG)
SS.......... Service Structure (KSC)
SS.......... Sessions
SS.......... Session Service [*Telecommunications*] (OSI)
SS.......... Set Screw [*Technical drawings*]
SS.......... Set Steering
SS.......... Sezary Syndrome [*Dermatology*]
SS.......... Shackamaxon Society (EA)
SS.......... Sharpshooter [*Marine Corps*]
SS.......... Shear Strength (AAG)
SS.......... Shelf Stock
SS.......... Shell Shock
SS.......... Shift Supervisor (IEEE)
SS.......... Shigella Sonnei [*A bacterium*] (DAVI)
SS.......... Shimmy Showing [*From one girl to another, in reference to dress disarrangement*]
SS.......... Shiplovers' Society [*Australia*]
SS.......... Shipmasters' Society [*A union*] [*British*]
SS.......... Shipping Situation [*British*]
SS.......... Ship Service
SS.......... Shipside
SS.......... Ship Station
SS.......... Ship System
S/S.......... Ship-to-Shore (MUGU)
SS.......... Shomrim Society (EA)
SS.......... Shoot Tip Abscission Scar [*Botany*]
SS.......... Shop Steward
SS.......... Short Sight (ADA)
SS.......... Short Sleeves
SS.......... Short Stay (DAVI)
SS.......... Shortstop
SS.......... Shosin Society (EA)
SS.......... Showroom Stock [*Automotive classification*]
SS.......... Shrinking Stock [*Corporate investment*]
SS.......... Shuttle System [*NASA*] (MCD)
SS.......... Siblings (DAVI)
SS.......... Side by Side (AAG)
SS.......... Side Scatter
SS.......... Side Seam
SS.......... Side Slip (MCD)
SS.......... Sidestream Smoke [*from cigarettes*]
SS.......... Side to Side
SS.......... Side-to-Side [*Anastomosis*] [*Cardiology*] (DAVI)
SS.......... Signaling System [*Telecommunications*] (TEL)
SS.......... Signal Selector (DEN)
SS.......... Signal Strength [*Broadcasting*] (KSC)
SS.......... Signed and Sealed
S/S.......... Sign Signature (AAG)
S/S.......... Silk Screen (ADA)
SS.......... Silvernail's New York Supreme Court Reports [*A publication*] (DLA)
SS.......... Silver Spur Resources [*Vancouver Stock Exchange symbol*]
SS.......... Silver Standard [*Vancouver Stock Exchange symbol*]
SS.......... Silver Star [*Military decoration*]
SS.......... Simple Spike
SS.......... Simplified Spelling
SS.......... Simulated Strike (SAA)
SS.......... Simulation Supervisor (SAA)
SS.......... Single Scan
SS.......... Single Scattering [*Photonics*]
SS.......... Single Seated
SS.......... Single Shot
SS.......... Single Sideband
SS.......... Single Signal
SS.......... Single Silk [*Wire insulation*] (IAA)
SS.......... Single Stout [*Beer*] (ROG)
SS.......... Single-Stranded [*or ss*] [*Genetics*]
SS.......... Single Strength [*Citrus juices*]
SS.......... Single String (MCD)
SS.......... Sinistral Sig (EA)
SS.......... Sinner Saved [*Pseudonym used by William Huntington*]
SS.......... Site Safety [*Nuclear energy*] (NRCH)
SS.......... Site Suitability [*Nuclear energy*] (NRCH)
SS.......... Sjoegren's Syndrome [*Medicine*]
SS.......... Skid Strip (KSC)
SS.......... Skinners' Society [*A union*] [*British*]
SS.......... Skull Series [*Radiology*] (DAVI)
SS.......... Slaters' Society [*A union*] [*British*]
SS.......... Sliding Scale (AAG)
SS.......... Slip Sent [*Laboratory science*] (DAVI)
SS.......... Slocum Society (EA)
SS.......... Slop Sink
SS.......... Slowdown Strike (MHDB)
SS.......... Slow Setting [*Asphalt grade*]
SS.......... Slow (Wave) Sleep [*Neurology*] (DAVI)
SS.......... Smallest Subunit [*Genetics*]
SS.......... Small Signal
SS.......... Small Subcompact [*Car size*]
SS.......... Smoke Stand (MSA)
SS.......... Soap Solution
SS.......... Soapsuds
SS.......... Social Science
SS.......... Social Security
SS.......... Social Security Number [*Followed by numerals*] (DAVI)
SS.......... Social Service
SS.......... Social Shopper
SS.......... Social Studies [*A publication*] (BRI)
SS.......... Social Surveys
SS.......... Society for Strings (EA)
SS.......... Society of Separationists (EA)
SS.......... Society of Shuttlemakers [*A union*] [*British*]
SS.......... Society of Signalmen (EA)
SS.......... Society of St. Sulpice [*Sulpicians*] [*Roman Catholic men's religious order*]
ss.......... Society of the Priest of Saint Sulpice, Sulpician Fathers (TOCD)
SS.......... Society of the Silurians (EA)

SS Socket Service [*Computer science*] (PCM)

SS Sodium Salicylate [*Organic chemistry*] (OA)

SS Sodium Sulfite [*Inorganic chemistry*]

SS Soft Sarcoma [*Oncology*]

SS SoftSearch, Inc. [*Information service or system*] (IID)

SS Soft Sized [*Paper*] (DGA)

SS Software Systems

SS Solar Simulator (MCD)

SS Solar System (IAA)

SS Sole Source (SAA)

SS Solid Shield (MCD)

SS Solid Solution (OA)

SS Solid State

SS Soluble Solids [*Chemistry*]

SS Solution Space

SS Somatics Society [*Commercial firm*] (EA)

SS Somatostatin [*Also, GH-RIF, GH-RIH, GRIF, SRIF*] [*Endocrinology*]

SS Songsmith Society (EA)

SS Song Sparrow [*Ornithology*]

SS Sonneck Society (EA)

SS Soprano Saxophone

SS Sound System

SS Source and Special [*Material*] [*Nuclear energy*]

SS Source of Supply (AFM)

SS Source Selection (MCD)

S/S Source/Sink [*Computer science*] (IBMDP)

SS Source/Source [*Inspection/Acceptance point*] (MCD)

SS South Coast Airlines [*ICAO designator*] (AD)

SS South Saxon (ROG)

S/S South Side [*In outdoor advertising*] (WDMC)

SS Souvenir Sheet [*Philately*]

SS Space Sciences (IAA)

SS Space Segment (SSD)

SS Space Shuttle [*NASA*] (KSC)

SS Space Simulator (IEEE)

SS Space Station (AAG)

SS Space Switch [*Telecommunications*] (TEL)

SS Space System (IAA)

ss Spanish Sahara [*Western Sahara*] [*MARC country of publication code Library of Congress*] (LCCP)

SS Sparingly Soluble

SS Special Senses [*Medicine*] (DAVI)

SS Special Series

SS Special Service [*Vessel load line mark*]

SS Special Services [*Military*] (DAVI)

SS Special Session

SS Special Settlement [*Business term*]

SS Special Source Materials [*Nuclear energy*] (NRCH)

SS Special Staff

SS Special Strike (NATG)

SS Special Study

SS Special Subjects

SS Special Survey [*Lloyd's Register of Shipping*] (DS)

SS Specification for Structure

S/S Spectrum Signature (NG)

SS Speed Sensor (NRCH)

SS Spenser Society (EA)

SS Spherical Symmetry

SS Spin-Stabilized [*Rockets*]

SS Spiral to Spiral

SS Spore Surface [*Immunology*]

SS Spread Spectrum (CET)

SS Squawk Sheet (KSC)

S/S Stabilization/Solidification (FFDE)

SS Stabilization System (AAG)

SS Stabilized Screen (IAA)

SS Stable Sarcoidosis [*Medicine*] (DAVI)

SS Staccato Syndrome [*Medicine*] (DAVI)

SS Stack Segment [*Computer science*]

SS Staff Sergeant [*Military British*] (ROG)

SS Staff Specialist [*Military*]

SS Staff Surgeon

SS Stainless Steel

ss Stainless Steel (VRA)

SS Standard Frequency Station [*ITU designation*]

SS Standardized Solution [*Pharmacy*]

SS Standard Score [*Psychology*]

SS Standard Size (ADA)

SS Starlight Scope

S/S Start/Stop

S/S Statement of Service [*Military*]

SS State School (ADA)

SS Statesman Series [*A publication*]

SS State Supervisor

SS Static Stretching [*Medicine*]

SS Stationary Satellite (IAA)

SS Stationary Source [*Environmental Protection Agency*]

SS Station Set [*NASA*] (NASA)

SS Station Supervision

SS Statistically Significant (MAE)

SS Statistical Standards

SS Statistics Sources [*A publication*]

sS Statsiemens [*Also, statS*] [*Unit of electric conductance, admittance, and susceptance*]

SS Steady State

SS Steamship

SS Steel Sash

SS Steering Safety

SS Steering System

SS Step Size (IAA)

SS Stereoscopic Society [*Chessington, Surrey, England*] (EAIO)

SS Stereoscopic Society - American Branch (EA)

SS Sterile Solution

SS Steroid Score [*Immunology*]

SS Steroid Sulfurylation (AAMN)

SS Stickler Syndrome [*Medicine*] (DMAA)

SS Stimulator Substance [*Liver regeneration*]

SS Stock Shot (NTCM)

SS Stopped Stock (MHDB)

SS Stop Scan (IAA)

SS Storage to Storage (MCD)

SS Strachan-Scott [*Syndrome*] [*Medicine*] (DAVI)

SS Straight Shank [*Screw*]

SS Straight Sided

SS Straits Settlements [*in Malaya*]

SS Strategic Squadron

SS Strategic Study [*Military*]

SS Striped Shiner [*Ichthyology*]

SS Strong Safety [*Football*]

SS Structure-Superstructure [*Economics*]

SS Student at Staff College [*Army British*] (ROG)

SS Stumpwork Society (EA)

SS Style Sac

SS Subaortic Stenosis [*Medicine*] (MAE)

SS Subject-Subject [*Education of the hearing-impaired*]

SS Subliminal Self [*Psychical research*]

SS Submarine [*Navy symbol*]

SS Submarine Qualification [*Navy*]

SS Submarine Scout

SS Submarine Studies [*SORG*]

SS Subsagittal [*Medicine*]

SS Subscale

SS Subscapularis [*Muscle*] [*Anatomy*] (DAVI)

SS Subscriber Switching [*Telecommunications*] (TEL)

SS Subsegmental [*Medicine*] (DAVI)

SS Subsequent Sibling (DAVI)

SS Subsolar [*NASA*] (KSC)

SS Substernal [*Anatomy*] (DAVI)

SS Substitutes [*Sports*]

ss Substructure [*Computer science*]

SS Subsystem (AAG)

SS Suburban Service (DD)

SS Successive Stereometric [*A discrimination task*]

SS Suction Socket (AAMN)

SS Sugar Snap [*Peas*] (DICI)

SS Sulfasalazine (MEDA)

SS Summary Sheet

SS Summation Sound

SS Summing Selector (MSA)

SS Summons (ROG)

SS Sum-of-the-Squares

SS Sunday School

SS Sunday Sport [*A publication*]

SS Sun Seeker (AAG)

SS Sun Sensor

SS Sun Simulator (MCD)

SS Superfund Surcharge [*Environmental Protection Agency*] (GFGA)

SS Superintending Scientist [*British*] (ADA)

SS Superintending Sister [*Navy British*]

SS Supersaturated (MAE)

SS Super Search (MCD)

SS Supersensitive (AAG)

SS Supersonic

SS Super Speed

SS Super Sport [*In automobile model name*]

SS Super Stock [*Automotive classification*]

SS Super Symmetric [*Particle physics*]

SS Supervisors Section [*American Association of School Librarians*]

SS Supply Ship (MCD)

SS Supportive Service (OICC)

SS Support System [*Air Force*]

SS Supra Scriptum [*Written Above*] [*Latin*]

SS Surface Ship

SS Surface-Sized [*Paper*]

SS Surface-to-Surface (NATG)

SS Surging Sine [*Mathematics*] (DAVI)

SS Surratt Society (EA)

SS Surveillance Station [*RADAR*]

SS Survivability System [*Military*]

SS Suspended Sentence

SS Suspended Solids [*Wastewater treatment*]

SS Swallow Sidecar [*Automobile manufacturer*] [*Forerunner to Jaguar*]

SS Swedish Society, Discofil [*Record label*] [*Sweden*]

SS Sweet Syndrome [*Medicine*] (DMAA)

SS Switch Selector (KSC)

SS Sworn Statement

SS Symmetrical Strength [*Neurology*] (DAVI)

SS Sympathetically Stimulated [*Physiology*]

SS Synchro Standard

SS Synergetic Society (EA)

SS .... Synopsis Series of the United States Treasury Decisions [*A publication*] (DLA)
SS .... System Sclerosis [*or Scleroderma*] [*Rheumatology*] (DAVI)
SS .... System Segment (MCD)
SS .... System Sensitivity
SS .... System Software [*NASA*] (MCD)
SS .... Systems Specifications [*NASA*] (NG)
SS .... System Summary [*NASA*] (MCD)
SS .... System Supervisor
SSA .... Associate in Secretarial Science
SSA .... Cargo Submarine [*Navy symbol Obsolete*]
SSA .... First Soprano, Second Soprano, and Alto [*in all-women choral groups*]
SSA .... Safe Sector Altitude [*Aviation*] (DA)
SSA .... Salicylaslicylic Acid [*Later, salsalate*] (DAVI)
SSA .... Salicylsalicylic Acid [*Organic chemistry*] (MAE)
SSA .... Salisbury Sound Association (EA)
SSA .... Salsalate [*Anti-inflammatory drug*]
SSA .... Salvador [*Brazil*] [*Airport symbol*] (OAG)
SSA .... Saskatchewan Archives Office, Saskatoon, Saskatchewan [*Library symbol National Library of Canada*] (NLC)
SSA .... SATCOM [*Satellite Command*] Signal Analyser (DWSG)
SSA .... Sauna Society of America (EA)
SSA .... S-Band Single Access (MCD)
SSA .... Scandinavian Society of Anaesthesiologists (EA)
SSA .... Scandinavian Sociological Association (EA)
SSA .... School Secretaries Association (DBA)
SSA .... Schools Sailing Association [*British*]
SSA .... Scottish Schoolmasters Association [*British*]
SSA .... Scottish Shipmasters' Association [*A union*]
SSA .... Secretary of State for Air [*British*]
SSA .... Security Support Activity
SSA .... Security Supporting Assistance [*US government program for promoting economic and political stability in areas of strategic interest*]
SSA .... Segment Search Argument [*Computer science*] (BUR)
SSA .... Seismological Society of America (EA)
SSA .... Selective Service Act
SSA .... Semiconductor Safety Association (EA)
SSA .... Semiotic Society of America (EA)
SSA .... Senior Scientific Assistant [*Ministry of Agriculture, Fisheries, and Food*] [*British*]
SSA .... Sensat Technologies Ltd. [*Vancouver Stock Exchange symbol*]
SSA .... Sequential Spectrometer Accessory [*Instrumentation*]
SSA .... Serial Storage Architecture [*Computer science*] (CDE)
SSA .... Series of Standard Additions
SSA .... Service Support Arrangement
SSA .... Shakespeare Society of America (EA)
SSA .... Shan State Army [*Myanmar*] [*Political party*] (EY)
SSA .... Shaw Society of America [*Defunct*] (EA)
SSA .... Sheath of Skeletal Axis
SSA .... Ship's Stores Ashore [*Navy*]
SSA .... Shuttle Simulation Aircraft [*NASA*] (NASA)
SSA .... Side-Saddle Association [*British*] (DBA)
SSA .... Side-to-Side Anastamosis [*Medicine*] (CPH)
SSA .... Signal Security Agency [*Later, Army Security Agency*]
SSA .... Signal Supply Agency
SSA .... Silo Subassembly (SAA)
SSA .... Simian Society of America (EA)
SSA .... Simpler Spelling Association [*Later, PSC*] (EA)
SSA .... Sinatra Society of America (EA)
SSA .... Single Line Synchronous Adapter (MCD)
SSA .... Single-Strand Annealing [*Genetics*]
SSA .... Singular-Spectrum Analysis [*Meteorology*]
SSA .... Sisters of St. Ann (TOCD)
SSA .... Sisters of St. Anne (TOCD)
SSA .... Sisters of St. Ann of Providence [*Roman Catholic religious order*]
SS-A .... Sjogren's Syndrome A [*Medicine*]
SSA .... Skin Sensitizing Antibody (AAMN)
SSA .... Skin Sympathetic Activity [*Medicine*] (DMAA)
SSA .... Slave Service Area [*Telecommunications*] (IAA)
SSA .... Slaving Signal Amplifier
SSA .... Sleeve Stub Antenna
SSA .... Slovak Studies Association (EA)
SSA .... Small Search Area (SAA)
SSA .... Smith Surface Antigen [*Medicine*] (DMAA)
SSA .... Soaring Society of America (EA)
SSA .... Social Security Act [*1935*] [*Also, SSACT*]
SSA .... Social Security Administration [*Department of Health and Human Services*]
SSA .... Society for the Study of Addiction to Alcohol and Other Drugs (EAIO)
SSA .... Society of Scottish Artists (DBA)
SSA .... Society of Security Analysts
SSA .... Society of Study Addiction [*British*] (DBA)
SSA .... Software Support Activity (SSD)
SSA .... Sole-Source Aquifer (GNE)
SSA .... Solid-State Abstracts
SSA .... Solid-State Amorphization [*Metallurgy*]
SSA .... Solid State Amplifier (NTCM)
SSA .... Sommelier Society of America (EA)
SSA .... Source Selection Activity [*or Authority*] [*Military*]
SSA .... Space Structure Assembly (SSD)
SSA .... Space Suit Assembly (KSC)
SSA .... Spanish-Surnamed American
SSA .... Spatial Sound Around [*Acoustics*]
SSA .... Specialist in School Administration (GAGS)
SSA .... Special Service Agreement [*UN Food and Agriculture Organization*]
SSA .... Special Service Authorization [*FCC*] (NTCM)
SSA .... Special Support Activity [*National Security Agency*] (DOMA)
SSA .... Special Survey Automated Controls [*Lloyd's Register of Shipping*] (DS)
SSA .... Sportswear Salesmen's Association (EA)
SSA .... Staff Supply Assistant [*Military*] (AABC)
SSA .... Staff Support Agencies [*Military*]
SSA .... Staging and Support Area [*NASA*] (KSC)
SSA .... Standard Single Account (INF)
SSA .... Standard Spending Assessment [*Department of the Environment*] [*British*]
SSA .... Standard System Applications [*Military*]
SSA .... Star of Asia [*Kyrgyzstan*] [*FAA designator*] (FAAC)
SSA .... Stars of the Stage [*A publication*]
SSA .... Steel Sleeper Association [*British*] (BI)
SSA .... Steuben Society of America (EA)
SSA .... Stick Sensor Assembly (MCD)
SSA .... Stratford Public Library, Stratford, CT [*OCLC symbol*] (OCLC)
SSA .... Stratosphere Sulfate Aerosol [*Meteorology*]
SSA .... Streptococcal Superantigen [*Immunochemistry*]
SSA .... Structured Systems Analysis (NITA)
SSA .... Student Ski Association (EA)
SSA .... Studio Suppliers Association (EA)
SSA .... Style Sac Artery
ssa .... Sub-Saharan African [*MARC language code Library of Congress*] (LCCP)
SSA .... Sub-Saharan African Country
SSA .... Subterranean Sociological Association (EA)
SSA .... Sulfite Sensitive Asthmatic
SSA .... Sulfosalicylic Acid [*Organic chemistry*]
SSA .... Sumi-E Society of America (EA)
SSA .... Supply Support Activity [*Military*] (AABC)
SSA .... Supply Support Arrangements [*A bilateral agreement between the United States and a friendly foreign government*]
SSA .... Support Services Alliance [*Schoharie, NY*] (EA)
SSA .... Survey of School Attitudes [*Student attitudes test*]
SSA .... Survival Surface-to-Air (MCD)
SSA .... Suspension Specialists Association (EA)
SSA .... Symbol Synchronizer Assembly [*NASA*]
SSA .... Synchro Signal Amplifier
SSA .... System Safety Assessment [*Army*]
SSAA .... Saskatchewan Institute of Applied Arts, Saskatoon, Saskatchewan [*Library symbol National Library of Canada*] (NLC)
SSAA .... Self Storage Association of Australia
SSAA .... Shoe Suppliers Association of America (EA)
SSAA .... Skate Sailing Association of America (EA)
SSAA .... Social Security Acts Amendments [*A publication*] (DLA)
SSAA .... Space Science Analysis Area [*Space Flight Operations Facility, NASA*]
SSAII .... Ses Altesses Imperiales [*Their Imperial Highnesses*] [*French*] (ROG)
SSAANSW .... Stock and Station Agents' Association of New South Wales [*Australia*]
SSAAT .... Sun Sensor Attitude Angle Transducer
SS-Ab .... Sjogren's Syndrome Antibody [*Immunology*] (DAVI)
SSAB .... Source Selection Advisory Board [*Marine science*] (OSRA)
SSAB .... Source Selection Advisory Board (USDC)
SSAB .... Special Surveys and Analysis Branch [*National Center for Education Statistics*] [*Department of Education*] (GFGA)
SSAC .... Armak Chemicals, Saskatoon, Saskatchewan [*Library symbol National Library of Canada*] (NLC)
SSAC .... Auxiliary Submarine [*Navy symbol*]
SSAC .... Scottish Society of Autistic Children (DBA)
SSAC .... Scottish Sub-Aqua Club (DBA)
SSAC .... Secondary School Admissions Center [*Defunct*] (EA)
SSAC .... Signalling System Alternating Current (NITA)
SSAC .... Social Security Advisory Committee [*British*]
SSAC .... Social Security Advisory Council [*Australia*]
SSAC .... Society for the Study of Architecture in Canada [*Established 1974*]
SSAC .... Solid-State Audio Clock (DWSG)
SSAC .... Source Selection Advisory Council [*Military*] (AFM)
SSAC .... Space Science Advisory Committee [*European Space Agency*]
SSAC .... Space Science Analysis and Command [*Team*] [*NASA*]
SSAC .... Sponsors' Standards Advisory Committee [*American National Standards Institute*]
SSAC .... Standing State Advisory Committee [*Terminated, 1977*] [*of Water Resources Council*] (EGAO)
SSAC .... Suprasellar Arachnoid Cyst [*Medicine*]
SSAC .... Suspended Sprayed Acoustical Ceiling [*Technical drawings*]
SSACT .... Social Security Act [*1935*] [*Also, SSA*]
SSADARS ..... Social Security Administration Data Acquisition and Response System
SSADC .... Solid-State Air Data Computer (MCD)
SSADH .... Succinate-Semialdehyde Dehydrogenase [*An enzyme*]
SSADM .... Structured Systems Analysis and Design Method [*British*]
SSADP .... Soldier's, Sailor's, and Airmen's Deposit Program (DNAB)
SSADP .... Support Site Activation Data Package (MCD)
SSAE .... Society of Senior Aerospace Executives (EA)
SSAE .... Stamped Self-Addressed Envelope (WDMC)
SSAEC .... Society for the Study of Alchemy and Early Chemistry [*British*]
SSAEPL .... Space Station Approved EEE [*Electrical, Electronic, and Electromechanical*]Parts List (SSD)
SSAF .... S-Band, Single Access Forward (SSD)
SSAF .... Standard Single Account File [*Number*] (MCD)

SSAFA .... Soldiers, Sailors, and Airmen's Family Association [*British*]
SSAG .... Single-Step Acidulation Granulation [*Fertilizer technology*]
SSAG .... Strategic Studies Advisory Group [*Army*] (AABC)
SSAGA .... Animal Pathology Laboratory, Food Production and Inspection Branch, Agriculture Canada [*Laboratoire de Pathologie Veterinaire, Direction Generale de la Production et de l'Inspection des Aliments, Agriculture Canada*], Saskatoon, Saskatchewan [*Library symbol National Library of Canada*] (BIB)
SSAGR .... Research Station, Agriculture Canada [*Station de Recherches, Agriculture Canada*] Saskatoon, Saskatchewan [*Library symbol National Library of Canada*] (NLC)
SSAIS .... Senior South African Individual Scale [*Intelligence test*]
SSAJ .... Sweep Stop Alarm Jam (MCD)
SSAL .... Sequenced Flashing Lights [*Aviation*] (DA)
SSAL .... Simplified Short Approach Light [*Aviation*]
S-SAL .... Solar Scientific Airlock (MCD)
SSALF .... Simplified Short ALS [*Approach Light System*] with Sequenced Flashers [*Aviation*]
SSALR .... Simplified Short ALS [*Approach Light System*] with Runway Alignment Indicator Lights [*Aviation*]
SSALR .... Simplified Short Approach Light System with Rail [*FAA*] (TAG)
SSALS .... Simplified Short Approach Light System [*Aviation*]
SSALSR .... Simplified Short Approach Light System with Runway Alignment Indicator Lights [*Aviation*]
SSAM .... Seismic Spectral Amplitude Measurement
SSAMA .... Sailors, Soldiers and Airmen's Mothers' Association of Australia
SSAMR .... John Dolan Resource Library, Saskatoon Association for the Mentally Retarded,Saskatoon, Saskatchewan [*Library symbol National Library of Canada*] (NLC)
SSAN .... Social Security Account Number
SS & A .... Space Systems and Applications [*NASA*] (NASA)
SS & C .... Same Sea and Country [*or Coast*] [*Shipping*] (DS)
SS & C .... Supersized and Calendered [*Paper*]
SS & CS ...... Ship's Stores and Commissary Stores [*Navy*]
SS & D .... Synchronization Separator and Digitizer
SS & FO .... Specialized Safety and Flight Operations
SS & P .... Service, Supply, and Procurement [*Military*]
SSAO .... Semicarbazide-Sensitive Amine Oxidase [*Biochemistry*]
SSAO .... Solid-State Audio Oscillator
SSAP .... Source Service Access Point
SSAP .... Statement of Standard Accounting Practice
SSAP .... Survival Stabilator Actuator Package [*Hydraulic power*]
SSAPEA .... Swedish Society Against Painful Experiments on Animals (EAIO)
SSAR .... S-Band, Single Access Return (SSD)
S-SAR .... Secret - Special Access Required [*Security classification*] (MCD)
SSAR .... Site Safety Analysis Report [*Nuclear energy*] (NRCH)
SSAR .... Social Security Acquisition Regulation [*A publication*] (AAGC)
SSAR .... Society for the Study of Amphibians and Reptiles (EA)
SSAR .... Special Save Register [*Computer science*] (IAA)
SSAR .... Spin-Stabilized Aircraft Rocket
SSAR .... Standard Safety Analysis Report [*Nuclear energy*] (NRCH)
SSAR .... Steady State Adiabatic Reactor [*Chemical engineering*]
SSAR .... Stereo Synthetic Aperture RADAR (SSD)
SSARR .... Streamflow Synthesis and Reservoir Regulation [*Computer science*]
SSARS .... Statement on Standards for Accounting and Review Services (TDOB)
SSAS .... Salzburg Seminar in American Studies (EA)
SSAS .... Searchless Self-Adjusting System
SSAS .... Self-Scoring Answer Sheet (DNAB)
SSAS .... Signal Security Assessment System [*Military*] (CAAL)
SSAS .... Small Sample Assay System [*Nuclear energy*] (NRCH)
SSAS .... Small Self-Administered Scheme [*Pensions*] [*British*]
SSAS .... Society for South Asian Studies (EAIO)
SSAS .... Special Signal Analysis System [*Electronic countermeasures system*]
SSAS .... Stable Super-Active Scavenger [*Color film technology*]
SSAS .... Static Stability Augmentation System [*Aviation*]
SSAS .... Station Signaling and Announcement Subsystem [*Telecommunications*] (TEL)
SSAS .... Surface Ship Advance Sonar [*Navy*] (LAIN)
SSAS .... Synthetic Sodium Aluminosilicate [*Inorganic chemistry*]
SSAT .... Screening Speech Articulation Test [*Educational test*]
SSAT .... Secondary School Admission Test Board (EA)
SSAT .... Shuttle Service and Access Tower [*NASA*] (NASA)
SSAT .... Society for Surgery of the Alimentary Tract (EA)
SSAT .... Space Shuttle Access Tower [*NASA*] (MCD)
SSAT .... Space Station Assembly Technology (SSD)
SSAT .... State Student Assessment Test [*Florida*] (EDAC)
SSAT .... Steady-State Advanced TOKAMAK [*Toroidal Kamera Magnetic*] [*Plasma physics*]
SSAT .... Sweep Stop Alarm Target [*Military*] (CAAL)
SSATB .... Secondary School Admission Test Board (EA)
SSAU .... Submarine Search Attack Unit (NVT)
SSAV .... Self-Sealing Aerospace Vehicle (IAA)
SSAV .... Simian Sarcoma Associated Virus
SSAVE .... Special Student Access to Vocational Education Project (EDAC)
SSAW .... Saatchi & Saatchi Advertising Worldwide (ECON)
SSAW .... Sea-Salt Aerosol Water [*Oceanography*]
SSAWS .... Single Seat Attack Weapon System [*Military*]
SSAWS .... Spring, Summer, Autumn, Winter, and Snow [*Pronounced "zausu"*] [*Another name for Skidome, an indoor ski center*] (ECON)
SSAWV .... Sons of Spanish American War Veterans (EA)
SSAX .... System Software [*NASDAQ symbol*] (TTSB)
SSAX .... System Software Associates, Inc. [*NASDAQ symbol*] (NQ)
SSB .... Ballistic Missile Submarine [*Navy symbol*]
SSB .... Cave Junction, OR [*Location identifier FAA*] (FAAL)
SSB .... Fleet Ballistic Submarine [*Navy symbol*]
SSB .... Salvo Squeezebore (PDAA)
SSB .... Scotland Bancorp [*AMEX symbol*] (TTSB)
SSB .... Scotland Bancorp, Inc. [*AMEX symbol*] (SAG)
SSB .... Scots Styles Book [*A publication*] (ILCA)
SSB .... Scottish Society of Boilermakers [*A union*]
SSB .... Security Screening Board [*Army*]
SSB .... Selective Service Board
SSB .... Short Spike Burst [*Medicine*] (DMAA)
SSB .... Signal Sight Back (SAA)
SSB .... Single Sideband
SSB .... Single-Strand Break [*Genetics*]
SSB .... Single-Stranded DNA [*Deoxyribonucleic Acid*] Binding Protein [*Biochemistry*]
SSB .... Sino-Soviet Bloc
SSB .... Size of Spawning Stock [*Fishery management*]
SS-B .... Sjogren's Syndrome B [*Medicine*]
SSB .... Social Security Bank [*Ghana*] (EY)
SSB .... Social Security Board [*Abolished, 1946*]
SSB .... Society for the Study of Blood (EA)
SSB .... Soft Service Building (SAA)
SSB .... Source Selection Board [*NASA*]
SSB .... Space Science Board [*National Research Council*]
SSB .... Special Separation Benefit [*DoD*]
SSB .... Special Service Battalion [*British military*] (DMA)
SSB .... Special Studies Branch [*Supreme Headquarters Allied Powers Europe*] (NATG)
SSB .... Spontaneous Symmetry Breaking [*Physics*]
SSB .... Standard Software Base (MCD)
SSB .... State Seismological Bureau [*China*]
SSB .... State Seismological Bureau [*China*]
SSB .... State Supply Board [*South Australia*]
SSB .... St. Croix [*Virgin Islands*] Seaplane Base [*Airport symbol*] (OAG)
SSB .... Strategic Standardization Board
SSB .... St. Sauveur Badole [*France*] [*Seismograph station code, US Geological Survey*] (SEIS)
SSB .... Submarine, Ballistic Missile [*Diesel*] [*NATO*]
SSB .... Subscriber Busy [*Telecommunications*] (TEL)
SSB .... Subsystem Status Block (MCD)
SSB .... Supersonic Balloon (IAA)
SSB .... Swimmer Support Boat
SSBA .... Scottish Spina Bifida Association (DBA)
SSBA .... Shropshire Sheep Breeders Association and Flock Book Society [*British*] (DBA)
SSBA .... Sons of Scotland Benevolent Association (EA)
SSBA .... Surface Supplied Breathing Apparatus
SSBAM .... Single Sideband Amplitude Modulation (KSC)
SSBARA .... Single Sideband Amateur Radio Association (IAA)
SSBC .... Solar System Barycenter [*Astronomy*]
SSBC .... Stock Status Balance Card (NG)
SSBC .... Summary Sheet Bar Chart [*NASA*] (NASA)
SSBD .... Single-Sideboard (IEEE)
SSBD .... Society for the Study of Breast Disease (EA)
SSB/DPUT .... Serikat Sekerdja Biro/Dinas Pembangunan Usaha Tani [*Agricultural Development Service Workers' Union*] [*Indonesia*]
SSBE .... Saskatoon Board of Education, Saskatchewan [*Library symbol National Library of Canada*] (NLC)
SSBF .... Single Sideband Filter
SSBF .... Solid Surface Burning Facility (SSD)
SSBFH .... Star-Spangled Banner Flag House Association (EA)
SSBFM .... Single Sideband Frequency Modulation (IEEE)
SSBG .... Sex Steroid Binding Globulin [*Endocrinology*]
SSBG .... Single Sideband Generator
SSBG .... Social Services Block Grant [*Department of Health and Human Services*]
SSB/GP .... Source Selection Board/General Procurement (MCD)
SSBH .... Self-Aligned Strip Buried Heterostructure (NITA)
SSBIC .... Specialized Small Business Investment Company
SSBK .... Strongsville Savings Bank [*NASDAQ symbol*] (SAG)
SSBK .... Strongsville Svgs Bk Ohio [*NASDAQ symbol*] (TTSB)
SSBKD .... Serikat Sekerdja/Buruh Ketapradja Djakarta Raja [*General Union of Government Officials of Greater Djakarta*] [*Indonesia*]
SSBKTN .... Serikat Sekerdja Bank Koporasi, Tani dan Nelajan Disingkat [*Cooperative, Farmers and Fishers Bank Employees' Union*] [*Indonesia*]
SSB/L .... Steamship Bill of Lading [*Shipping*]
SSBM .... Single Sideband Amplitude Modulation [*Telecommunications*] (IAA)
SSBM .... Single Sideband Angle Modulation [*Telecommunications*] (IAA)
SSBM .... Single Sideband Modulation
SSBMA .... Students to Save Baltic and Mediterranean Avenues [*Defunct*] (EA)
SSBN .... Fleet Ballistic Missile Submarine (Nuclear powered) [*Navy symbol*]
SSBN .... Ships Submersible Ballistic Nuclear [*British military*] (DMA)
SSBO .... Single Swing Blocking Oscillator (MSA)
SSBPI .... Serikat Sekerdja Bank Pembangunan Indonesia [*Indonesian Development Bank Employees' Union*]
SSBPS .... Social Security Benefit Protection Service (EA)
SSBPT .... Serikat Sekerdja Balai Penelitian Tekstil [*Textile Research Institute Workers' Union*] [*Indonesia*]
SSBR .... See Separate Bacteriology Report (DAVI)
SSBR .... Smooth-Surface Built-Up Roof [*Technical drawings*]
SSBR .... Solid Strand Burning Rate (KSC)
SSBR .... Solution-Based Styrene-Butadiene Rubber [*Materials science*]
SSBS .... Sisters Servants of the Blessed Sacrament [*Roman Catholic religious order*]
SSBS .... Surface-to-Surface Strategic Ballistic Missile System (IAA)
SSBSC .... Single Sideband Suppressed Carrier [*Telecommunications*]

SSBSC .... Single Switched Suppressed Carrier [*Telecommunications*] (IAA)
SSB-SC/AM... Single Sideband Suppressed Carrier Amplitude Modulation (NITA)
SSBSCAM.... Single Sideband with Suppressed Carrier, Amplitude Modulated [*Telecommunications*] (IAA)
SSBSCOM.... Single Sideband Suppressed Carrier Optical Modulator
SSBUS......... South Slavic Benevolent Union Sloga [*Later, Sloga Fraternal Life Insurance Society*] (EA)
SSBUV......... Shuttle SBUV [*Solar Backscatter Ultraviolet*] [*Marine science*] (OSRA)
SSBUV......... Shuttle SBUV [*Solar Backscatter Ultraviolet*] (USDC)
SSBUV......... Shuttle Solar Backscatter Ultraviolet Instrument (MCD)
SSBWC......... Single Sideband with Carrier [*Telecommunications*] (IAA)
SSBWM........ Society of Scale Beam and Weighing Machinists [*A union*] [*British*]
SSC............ Coastal Submarine [*Navy symbol*]
SSC............ Co-Operative College of Canada, Saskatoon, Saskatchewan [*Library symbol National Library of Canada*] (NLC)
SSC............ Cruiser Submarine [*Navy symbol Obsolete*]
SSC............ Missionary Sisters of St. Columban [*Roman Catholic religious order*]
SSC............ Naval Service School Command
SSC............ Safeguard System Command [*Obsolete Army*] (MCD)
SSC............ Saline Sodium Citrate [*Clinical chemistry*]
SSC............ Salisbury State College, Salisbury, MD [*OCLC symbol*] (OCLC)
SSC............ Sandford's New York Superior Court Reports [*A publication*] (DLA)
SSC............ Sarawak Supreme Court Reports [*A publication*] (DLA)
SSC............ Satellite Situation Center
SSC............ Satellite Systems Corp. [*Virginia Beach, VA*] [*Telecommunications*] (TSSD)
SSC............ Savannah State College [*Georgia*]
SSC............ SCANNET Service Centre (NITA)
SSC............ Scan-to-Scan Correlation
SSC............ School of the Salt Creek [*Ballet*]
SSC............ Scientific Support Coordinator (FFDE)
SSC............ Scotch Session Cases [*A publication*] (DLA)
SSC............ Scottish Ski Club (DBA)
SSC............ Sculptors Society of Canada
SSC............ Sea-State Correction [*Doppler navigation*] (DEN)
SSC............ Sea Surveillance and Coordination [*Navy*] (DOMA)
SSC............ Sea Systems Command [*Also, NSSC*] [*Navy*]
SSC............ Second Search Character [*Computer science*] (IAA)
SSC............ Second-Stage Conduit
SSC............ Secretarial Studies Certificate (AIE)
SSC............ Sector Switching Center [*Telecommunications*] (TEL)
SSC............ Secure Systems Corp. [*Manassas, VA*] [*Telecommunications Defunct*] (TSSD)
SSC............ Security Classification Code (MCD)
SSC............ Selector Subchannels
SSC............ Senate Staff Club (EA)
SSC............ Senate Steel Caucus (EA)
SSC............ Senior Service College [*Army*] (AABC)
SSC............ Sensor Signal Conditioner
SSC............ Sequential Subsystem Controllers (MCD)
SSC............ Serendipitous Survey Catalog [*Infrared Astronomical Satellite*] [*Astronomy*]
SSC............ Serial Shift Counter [*Computer science*]
SSC............ Service Schools Command (MCD)
SSC............ Servicing Support Center (SSD)
SSC............ Seton Shrine Center (EA)
SSC............ Seven Springs Center [*An association*] (EA)
SSC............ Shape Selective Cracking (PDAA)
SSC............ Shipbuilding Stabilization Committee [*World War II*]
SSC............ Shipment Status Correlation
SSC............ Ship's Speed Converter (MCD)
SSC............ Ship Structure Committee (EA)
SSC............ Ship Systems Command [*Navy*]
SSC............ Short Segmented Cask [*Nuclear energy*] (NRCH)
SSC............ Short Service Commissions [*Army British*]
SSC............ Short Story Criticism [*A publication*]
SSC............ Shuttle System Contractor [*NASA*] (NASA)
SSC............ Siblings for Significant Change (EA)
SSC............ Side-Stick Controller
SSC............ Signaling and Supervisory Control
SSC............ Silver Star Citation [*Military award*]
SSC............ Simulated Spacecraft [*NASA*]
SSC............ Single Silk-Covered [*Wire insulation*]
ssc............ Single Silk Covered (IDOE)
ssc............ Single Silk Enameled (IDOE)
SSC............ Single-Site Catalyst [*Chemistry*]
SSC............ Single-Stage Command (NASA)
SSC............ Sintered Silicon Carbide (MCD)
SSC............ Sisters of St. Casimir [*Roman Catholic religious order*]
SSC............ Site Selection Criteria (AAG)
SSC............ Skill Specialty Code (MCD)
SSC............ Small Saver Certificate [*Banking*]
SSC............ Small Scientific Computer (IAA)
SSC............ Socialist Scholars Conference (EA)
SSC............ Social Sciences Center [*University of Nevada*] [*Research center*] (RCD)
SSC............ Societas Sanctae Crucis [*Society of the Holy Cross*] [*Latin*]
SSC............ Society for the Study of Caucasia (EA)
SSC............ Society of Silver Collectors (EA)
SSC............ Society of St. Columban (TOCD)
ssc............ Society of St. Columban, St. Columban's Foreign Mission Society (TOCD)
SSC............ Society of the Sacred Cross [*Anglican religious community*]
SSC............ Society of the Sisters of the Church (TOCD)
SSC............ Sodium Chloride-Sodium Citrate [*Analytical chemistry*]
SSC............ Software Steering Committee (LAIN)
SSC............ Software Support Center [*Army*] (RDA)
SSC............ Software System Change (MCD)
SSC............ Solar Stabilization Computer
SSC............ Soldier Support Center
SSC............ Solicitor, Supreme Court
SSC............ Solid-Solution CERMET [*NASA*] (NASA)
SSC............ Solid-State Circuit
SSC............ Solid-State Computer
SSC............ Solid-State Culture [*Biology*]
SSC............ Solid State Frequency Converter (DA)
SSC............ Soluble Solids Content [*Analytical chemistry*]
SSC............ Southeastern Simulation Council
SSC............ Southeastern State College [*Later, Southeastern Oklahoma State University*]
SSC............ Southern Seaplane, Inc. [*ICAO designator*] (FAAC)
SSC............ Southern State College [*Arkansas; South Dakota*]
SSC............ Space Communications Corp. [*Japan*] (ECON)
SSC............ Spacecraft System Console
SSC............ Space Science Committee [*Formerly, Provisional Space Science Advisory Board for Europe*] [*of the European Science Foundation*] (EA)
SSC............ Space Suit Communicator [*Apollo*] [*NASA*]
SSC............ Space Systems Center
SSC............ Speciality Shopping Centre [*British*]
SSC............ Special Service Center [*Bell System*]
SSC............ Special Service Clergyman [*Church of England*]
SSC............ Species Survival Commission (EERA)
SSC............ Spectroscopy Society of Canada [*Societe de Spectroscopie du Canada*]
SSC............ Spin Synchronous Clock
SSC............ Spontaneous Synaptic Current [*Neuroscience*]
SSC............ Squadron Supervisory Console [*Air Force*]
SSC............ Squadron Support Center (AAG)
SSC............ Squib Simulator Console
SSC............ Staff Selection Committee [*UN Food and Agriculture Organization*]
SSC............ Staff Service Center (MCD)
SSC............ Stainless Steel Crown [*Dentistry*] (DAVI)
SSC............ Standardization Status Code [*DoD*]
SSC............ Standard Saline Citrate
SSC............ Standards Steering Committee [*ANSI*]
SSC............ Standard Systems Center [*Military*]
SSC............ Standard Systems Command (AAGC)
SSC............ State Sports Council [*Victoria, Australia*]
SSC............ State Superfund Contract [*Environmental Protection Agency*]
SSC............ State Supply Commission [*Western Australia*]
SSC............ Static Standby Computer [*Mission Control Center*] [*NASA*]
SSC............ Station Selection Code [*Western Union*] (BUR)
SSC............ Statistical Society of Canada [*Societe Statistique du Canada*]
SSC............ Stellar Simulation Complex (OA)
SSC............ Stepping Switch Counter (AAG)
SSC............ Stock Shortage Control (SAA)
SSC............ Stores Stock Catalog
SSC............ Strategic Systems Committee [*DoD*] (DOMA)
SSC............ Strategic Systems Committee (AAGC)
SSC............ Structures, Systems, and Components [*Nuclear energy*] (NRCH)
SSC............ St. Sauveur De Carouges [*Seismograph station code, US Geological Survey*] (SEIS)
SSC............ Submarine Supply Center
SSC............ Subspecialty Codes (DOMA)
SSC............ Subsystem Computer (MCD)
SSC............ Subsystem Sequence Controller [*NASA*] (NASA)
SSC............ Sudden Storm Commencement [*Physics*]
SSC............ Sumter, SC [*Location identifier FAA*] (FAAL)
SSC............ Sunshine Mining & Refining [*Formerly, Sunshine Mining*] Co. [*NYSE symbol*] (SPSG)
SSC............ Superconducting Super Collider [*Particle accelerator*]
SSC............ Superconducting Supercollider (AAGC)
SSC............ Super Serial Card [*Apple Computer, Inc.*]
SSC............ Super Star Cluster [*Astronomy*]
SSC............ Super System Code (NRCH)
SSC............ Supply and Services Canada
SSC............ Supply Status Code [*Army*] (AABC)
SSC............ Supply Support Center [*Navy*]
SSC............ Supply System Command [*Navy*] (MCD)
SSC............ Support Software Center
SSC............ Survey Science Centre [*A consortium of European oranizations*]
SSC............ Synchrotron Self-Compton [*X-ray emission*]
SSC............ System Simulation Center
SSC............ System/Site Control (DOMA)
SSC............ Systems Science and Cybernetics (MCD)
SSC............ Systems Support Center (BUR)
SSC............ System Support Controller (NITA)
SSCA.......... Scottish Ship Chandlers Association (DBA)
SSCA.......... Scottish Stone Cutters' Association [*A union*]
SSCA.......... Seven Seas Cruising Association (EA)
SSCA.......... Single Shoulder Contrast Arthrography [*Radiology*] (DAVI)
SSCA.......... Single-Strand Conformational Analysis [*Analytical biochemistry*]
SSCA.......... Southern Speech Communication Association (EA)
SSCA.......... Spontaneous Suppressor Cell Activity [*Medicine*] (DMAA)
SSCA.......... Spray System Compressed Air [*Nuclear energy*] (NRCH)
SSCA.......... Standard Schnauzer Club of America (EA)
SSCA.......... Strobed Single Channel Analyzer [*Electronics*] (OA)
SSCA.......... Super Sunfish Class Association [*Defunct*] (EA)

SSCA .... Surface Sampler Control Assembly [*NASA*] (NASA)
SSCAEU .... Social Service Commission of the American Ethical Union (EA)
SSCAG .... Research Station, Agriculture Canada [*Station de Recherches, Agriculture Canada*] Swift Current, Saskatchewan [*Library symbol National Library of Canada*] (NLC)
SSCATS .... Skylab Simulation, Checkout, and Training System [*NASA*]
SSCAVC .... Senate Select Committee on Agricultural and Veterinary Chemicals [*Australia*]
SSCB .... Space Station Control Board (SSD)
SSCB .... Super Small-Scale Cook-Off Bomb (MCD)
SSCB(B) .... Submarine Safety Certification Boundary (Book) [*Navy*] (DNAB)
SSCBD .... Space Station Control Board Directive (SSD)
SSCBM .... Shipping and Storage Container Ballistic Missile (IAA)
SSCC .... Common Channel Signaling System [*Telecommunications*] (TEL)
SSCC .... Congregation of the Sacred Hearts and of Perpetual Adoration (TOCD)
sscc .... Congregation of the Sacred Hearts of Jesus and Mary (TOCD)
SSCC .... Congregation of the Sacred Hearts of Jesus and Mary [*Rome, Italy*] (EAIO)
SSCC .... Salt Shaker Collectors Club [*Later, AAGSSCS*] (EA)
SSCC .... SATCOM System Control Center (KSC)
SSCC .... Scottish Sporting Car Club (DBA)
SSCC .... Sea Surface Chlorophyll Concentration
SSCC .... Second-Stage Conduit Container
SSCC .... Solid-State Circuits Council [*IEEE*] (EA)
SSCC .... Sound Surveillance System Control Center (MCD)
SSCC .... Space Surveillance Control Center
SSCC .... Spin-Scan Cloud Camera [*NASA*]
SSCC .... Sulfide Stress Corrosion Cracking (MCD)
SSCC .... Support Services Control Center [*NASA*] (MCD)
SSCCB .... Safeguard System Configuration Control Board [*Army*] (AABC)
SSCCS .... Slow Spinal Cord Compression Syndrome [*Medicine*] (DMAA)
SSCCS .... Solid State Component Control System [*Nuclear energy*] (NRCH)
S SC D .... Doctor of Social Science (WDAA)
SSCD .... Society of Small Craft Designers (EA)
SSCD .... Start Sample Command Delayed
SSCD .... Stationary Source Compliance Division [*Environmental Protection Agency*] (GFGA)
SSCD .... Superheated Superconducting Colloid Detector [*Particle physics*]
SSCD .... Support System Concept Document
SSCDR .... Subsystem Critical Design Review
SSCDS .... Small Ship Combat Data System
SSCE .... Silver/Silver Chloride Electrode
SSCE .... Sodium Chloride Calomel Electrode
SSCE .... Squadron Supervisory and Control Equipment (SAA)
SSCE .... Study Skills Counseling Evaluation Reading (AEBS)
SSCERA .... Senate Standing Committee on the Environment, Recreation, and the Arts [*Australia*]
SS/CF .... Signal Strength, Center Frequency [*Broadcasting*]
SSCF .... Sleep Stage Change Frequency [*Medicine*] (DMAA)
SSCF .... Space Subsystem Control Facility (NATG)
SSCF .... Stress/Strain Controlled Fatigue (MCD)
SSCFADT .... Senate Standing Committee on Foreign Affairs, Defence, and Trade [*Australia*]
SSCFP .... Senior Service College Fellowship Program [*Army*] (RDA)
SSCH .... Sisters of Ste. Chretienne [*Roman Catholic religious order*]
SSCHS .... Space Shuttle Cargo Handling System [*NASA*] (NASA)
SSCI .... Sanitation Suppliers and Contractors Institute [*Defunct*] (EA)
SSCI .... Saskatoon Collegiate Institute, Saskatchewan [*Library symbol National Library of Canada*] (NLC)
SSCI .... Senate Select Committee on Intelligence (MCD)
SSCI .... Sports Sciences [*NASDAQ symbol*] (TTSB)
SSCI .... Sports Sciences, Inc. [*NASDAQ symbol*] (SAG)
SSCI .... Steel Service Center Institute (EA)
SSCI .... Steel Shipping Container Institute (EA)
SSCIA .... Scottish Spinal Cord Injury Association (DBA)
SSCIST .... Senate Standing Committee on Industry, Science, and Technology [*Australia*]
SSCIW .... Sports Sciences Wrrt [*NASDAQ symbol*] (TTSB)
SSCJ .... Sisters of the Sacred Heart of Jesus of Saint Jacut (TOCD)
SSCJ .... Sorores a Sacro Corde Jesus [*Sisters of the Sacred Heart of Jesus*] [*Roman Catholic religious order*]
SSCK .... Sister Servants of Christ the King [*Roman Catholic religious order*]
SSCL .... Shuttle System Commodity List [*NASA*]
SSCL .... Shuttle System Commonality List [*NASA*] (NASA)
SSCL .... Social Science Computing Laboratory [*University of Western Ontario*] [*Information service or system*] (IID)
SSCM .... Scattering Structural Contour Map [*Surface analysis*]
SSCM .... Servants of the Holy Heart of Mary [*Roman Catholic women's religious order*]
SSCM .... Sisters of Saints Cyril and Methodius [*Roman Catholic religious order*]
SSCMA .... Special Supplementary Clothing Monetary Allowance [*Military*]
SSCN .... Nuclear Cruise Missile Submarine (MCD)
SSC-NCR .... Soldier Support Center - National Capitol Region [*Army*]
SSCND .... Senate Special Committee on National Defence [*Canada*]
SSCNS .... Ship's Self-Contained Navigation System
SSCO .... Shipper Service Control Office [*Military*] (AABC)
SSCO .... System Security Control Officer [*Military*] (GFGA)
SSCOM .... Soldier Systems Command [*Army*] (INF)
SSCP .... School Science Curriculum Project
SSCP .... Single-Strand Conformation Polymorphism [*Genetics*]
SSCP .... Small Self-Contained Payload (NASA)
SSCP .... Standard Saline Citrate Phosphate [*A buffer*]
SSCP .... State Service Center Program (OICC)
SSCP .... System Services Control Point [*Computer science*]
SSCPE .... Single-Strand Conformational Polymorphism Electrophoresis [*Analytical biochemistry*]
SSCQT .... Selective Service College Qualifying Test
SSCR .... Scottish Society of Crop Research (DBA)
SSCR .... Set Screw
SSCR .... Sind Sadr Court Reports [*India*] [*A publication*] (DLA)
SSCR .... Space Station Change Request (SSD)
SSCR .... Spectral Shift Control Reactor [*Nuclear energy*]
SSCr .... Stainless Steel Crown [*Dentistry*]
SSCRA .... Soldiers' and Sailors' Civil Relief Act [*1940*]
SSCRI .... Social Science Computer Research Institute [*University of Pittsburgh*] [*Pennsylvania*] [*Information service or system*] (IID)
SSCRN .... Silkscreen (MSA)
SSCS .... Sea Shepherd Conservation Society (EA)
SSCS .... Shipboard Satellite Communications System
SSCS .... Side-Stick Control System
SSCS .... Single Sideband Communications System
SSCS .... Southern Signal Corps School
SSCS .... Space Station Communication System (SSD)
SSCS .... Space Suit Communications System (MCD)
SSCS .... Spatial Spectrum Center Shifting (PDAA)
SSCS .... Standards and Security Compliance Section [*Social Security Administration*]
SSCS .... Steep-Spectrum Compact Sources [*of galactic radio waves*]
SSCS .... Submarine SONAR Calibration Set
SSCS .... Synchronous Satellite Communications System
SSCSP .... Space Shuttle Crew Safety Panel [*NASA*] (NASA)
SSCT .... Sacks Sentence Completion Test [*Psychology*] (DAVI)
SSCT .... Shipboard Communications Terminal
SSCT .... Solid-State Celestial Tracker
SSCT .... Solid State Circuit (IAA)
SSCT .... Solid-State Control Transformer
SSCT .... Stereotactic Subcaudate Tractotomy [*Medicine*] (DMAA)
SSCTC .... Senate Standing Committee on Trade and Commerce [*Australia*]
SSCTS .... Space Station Communication and Tracking System (SSD)
SSCU .... Soil Sampler Control Unit
SSCU .... Spacecraft Systems Controller Unit [*NASA*] (KSC)
SSCU .... Special Signal Conditioning Unit
SSCU .... Store Station Control Unit (MCD)
SSCV .... Semisubmersible Crane Vessel
SSCVYO .... Scottish Standing Conference of Voluntary Youth Organisations (AIE)
SSCW .... Single Silk-Covered Wire [*Insulation*] (IAA)
SSCW .... Slow Space Charge Wave (IAA)
SSCX .... Solid-State Control Transformer
SSD .... Doctor of Sacred Scripture
SSD .... Institute of the Sisters of St. Dorothy [*Roman Catholic religious order*]
SSD .... Safe Separation Device
SSD .... Sanctissimus Dominus [*Most Holy Lord*] [*Latin*]
SSD .... Satellite System Development (IAA)
SSD .... Saturted Surface Dry (DICI)
SSD .... Scientific Support Division [*Marine science*] (OSRA)
SSD .... Scientific Support Division [*National Severe Storms Laboratory*] (USDC)
SSD .... Scrap Salvage Division [*Navy*]
SSD .... SDC Sydney Development Corp. [*Toronto Stock Exchange symbol Vancouver Stock Exchange symbol*]
SSD .... Second-Degree Stochastic Dominance [*Statistics*]
SSD .... Security Support Detachment (MCD)
SSD .... Seize Signal Detector
SSD .... Semiconductor Silicon Detector
SSD .... Separation Systems Division [*Energy Research and Development Administration*]
SSD .... Sequence Switch Driver
SSD .... Short Sequence Deinking [*Recycling*]
SSD .... Signal Seeking Device
SSD .... Silicon Single Diffused (IAA)
SSD .... Silver Sulfadiazine [*An anti-infective used in burn therapy*] (DAVI)
SSD .... Single Station Doppler (IAA)
SSD .... Single-Station DOVAP [*Doppler, Velocity, and Position*]
SSD .... Smoothing by Spectral Dispersion [*LASER technology*]
SSD .... Social Security Disability
SSD .... Social-Services Department [*British*]
SSD .... Software System Design [*Computer science*]
SSD .... Soldiers Service Dress [*British military*] (DMA)
SSD .... Soldier Support Division [*US Army Training and Doctrine Command*] (INF)
SSD .... Solid-State Detector
SSD .... Solid State Devices (IAA)
SSD .... Solid-State Disk [*Computer science*]
SSD .... Solid-State Dosimeter
SSD .... Solid-State Storage Device [*Computer science*]
SSD .... Source-to-Skin [*or -Surface*] Distance [*Radiology*]
SSD .... Spacecraft Software Division [*NASA*] (NASA)
SSD .... Space Sciences Division [*Jet Propulsion Laboratory*]
SSD .... Space Shuttle Display [*NASA*]
SSD .... Space Systems Division [*Air Force*]
SSD .... Specialized Storage Depot
SSD .... Specialized Support Department [*Air Force*] (AFM)
SSD .... Specialized Support Depot [*Army*] (AABC)
SSD .... Special Service Division [*Army Services Forces*] [*World War II*]
SSD .... Specific Surface Diameter
SSD .... Split-Screen Display
SSD .... Split Stage Demonstrator (MCD)
SSD .... Squared Successive Differences [*Computer science*]

SSD Staatssicherheitsdienst [*State Security Service*] [*Germany*]
SSD Stabilized Ship Detector [*Navy*]
SSD Standards Support Document [*Environmental Protection Agency*] (GFGA)
SSD Star Service International [*France ICAO designator*] (FAAC)
SSD Static Sensitive Device [*Electronics*] (EECA)
SSD Station Selected Display [*Electronics*] (ECII)
SSD Statistical Subdivision (EERA)
SSD Steady State Distribution (IAA)
SSD Stock Split-Down [*Investment term*]
SSD Structured Systems Design (NITA)
SSD Subsoil Drain [*Technical drawings*]
SSD Sudden Sniffing Death (DAVI)
SSD Sum of Square Deviation (MAE)
SSD Sum-of-the-Squares of the Differences [*Mathematics*]
SSD Sun Shadow Device
SSD Supplementary Special Deposit [*British*]
SSD Support Software Documentation (MCD)
SSD Surface Sampler Device [*NASA*]
SSD Surveillance Situation Display
SSD Survival Support Device (NVT)
SSD Sydney Statistical Division [*Australia*]
SSD Systems Support Division [*Air Force*]
SSD System Status Display
SSD System Summary Display [*NASA*] (MCD)
SSDA Sequential Similarity Detection Algorithm
SSDA Service Station Dealers of America (EA)
SSDA Social Science Data Archive [*University of Iowa*] [*Iowa City*] [*Information service or system*] (IID)
SSDA Social Science Data Archive [*Carleton University*] [*Canada Information service or system*] (IID)
SSDA Stainless Steel Development Association [*British*] (BI)
SSDA Synchronous Serial Data Adapter
SSDB Shore Station Development Board
SSDC Sclerosing Sweat Duct Carcinoma [*Oncology*]
SSDC Signalling System-Direct Current (NITA)
SSDC Signal Source Distribution Center (AAG)
SSDC Social Science Data Center [*University of Connecticut*] [*Research center*] (IID)
SSDC Social Science Data Center [*University of Pennsylvania*] [*Philadelphia*] [*Information service or system*] (IID)
SSDC Social Science Documentation Centre [*UNESCO*] (IID)
SSDC Social Science Documentation Centre [*Indian Council of Social Science Research*] [*Information service or system*] (IID)
SSDC Society of Stage Directors and Choreographers (EA)
SSDC Space and Strategic Defense Command [*Army*] (RDA)
SSDC Space Science Data Center [*NASA*] (MCD)
SSDC Synoptic-Scale Subprogramme Data Centre [*Marine science*] (MSC)
SSDC System Safety Development Center (IAA)
SSDD Single-Sided Double Density (NITA)
SSDD Single-Sided, Double-Density Disk [*Magnetic disk*] [*Computer science*]
SSDD Software System Design Document (MCD)
SSDD Steroid Sulfatase Deficiency Disease [*Medicine*] (DMAA)
SSDD System Segment Design Document
SSDF Space Science Development Facility (SAA)
SSD(F) Submarine Support Division (Fleet Support) [*Navy*] (DNAB)
SSDF-NAA Space Science Development Facility-North American Aviation (SAA)
SSDG Ship Service Diesel Generator [*Navy*] (CAAL)
SSDG Society for the Study of Development and Growth [*Later, SDB*] (EA)
SSDH Subsystem Data Handbook [*NASA*] (NASA)
SSDHPER Society of State Directors of Health, Physical Education, and Recreation (EA)
SSDI Social Security Disability Income (DAVI)
SSDI Social Security Disability Insurance
SSDI Support System Design Integration (AAG)
SSDK Savannah State Docks Railroad Co. [*AAR code*]
SSDL Secondary Standard Dosimetry Laboratory
SSDL Social Science Data Library [*University of North Carolina*] [*Chapel Hill*] [*Information service or system*] (IID)
SSDL Society for the Study of Dictionaries and Lexicography [*Later, DSNA*] (EA)
SSDM Shielding Standard Design Method (MCD)
SSDM Systematic Software Development and Maintenance [*Computer science*] (MHDI)
SSDMIC Secretariat State-Defense Military Information Control Committee
SSDMS Space Station Data Management System [*NASA*] (SSD)
SSDN Sanctissimus Dominus Noster [*Our Most Holy Lord, Jesus Christ*] [*Latin*]
SSD/N Sun Synchronous Day/Night (SSD)
ssDNA Deoxyribonucleic Acid, Single-Stranded [*Biochemistry, genetics*]
SSDP Standard Source Data Package (AFIT)
SSDP Suomen Sosialidemokraattinen Puolue [*Finnish Social Democratic Party*] [*Political party*] (PPW)
SSDPA Soft-Serv Dairy Products Association [*Later, NSSFFA*] (EA)
SSDPE Society for the Systematic Documentation of Paranormal Experiments (EA)
SSDPS Solar System Data Processing System
SSDR Satellite Situation Display Room
SSDR SIGINT/SIGSEC Facilities Data Reporting System (MCD)
SSDR Species Specific Defense Reaction
SSDR Steady State Determining Routine
SSDR Subsystem Design Review
SSDR Subsystem Development Requirement (AFM)
SSDR Supermarket Subsystem Definition Record [*Computer science*] (IBMDP)
SSDRS Safeguard System Design Release Schedule [*Army*] (AABC)
SSDS Ship Self Defense System
SSDS Single Ship Deep Sweep (DOMA)
SSDS Small Ship Data System (MUGU)
SSDS Space Shuttle Display and Simulation [*NASA*]
SSDS Space Station Data System (NASA)
SSD(S) Submarine Support Division (Shore Facilities) [*Navy*] (DNAB)
SSDS Surface-Supported Diving System (CAAL)
SSDS System of Social and Demographic Statistics (EERA)
SSDSA Solomon Schecter Day School Association (EA)
SSDSG Special State Defense Study Group [*Military*]
SSD(ST) Submarine Support Division (Staff Support) [*Navy*] (DNAB)
SSDT Society of Soft Drink Technologists (EA)
SSDU Session Service Data Unit [*Telecommunications*] (OSI)
SSDVOR Single Sideband Doppler Very-High-Frequency Omnidirectional Range [*FAA*]
SSE Safe Shutdown Earthquake [*Nuclear energy*] (NRCH)
SSE Safety System Engineering (MCD)
SSE Saline Solution Enema [*Medicine*]
SSE Salvador Society of Engineers
SSE Satellite Systems Engineering, Inc. [*Bethesda, MD*] [*Information service or system*] (TSSD)
SSE Scale of Socio-Egocentrism [*Psychology*]
SSE Schick Shaving Experience [*Advertising slogan*]
SSE Scuola de Sviluppo Economico [*Italy*]
SSE Sector Scan Engagement [*Military*] (CAAL)
SSE Security and Safety Equipment (IMH)
SSE Seed Savers Exchange (EA)
SSE Self-Sustained Emission
SSE Separated Statistical Ensemble [*Physical chemistry*]
SSE Servicios Aereos Sunset, SA de CV [*Mexico*] [*FAA designator*] (FAAC)
SSE SIGINT Support Element (MCD)
SSE Signal Security Element [*Military*] (AABC)
SSE Single Sideband Exciter
SSE Single Silk Covering over Enamel Insulation [*Telecommunications*] (TEL)
SSE Sisters of St. Elizabeth [*Roman Catholic religious order*]
SSE Site Server [*Microsoft Corp.*] [*Computer science*]
SSE Skin Self Examination [*Medicine*]
SSE Soap Suds Enema [*Medicine*]
SSE Society for Scientific Exploration (EA)
SSE Society for the Study of Evolution (EA)
sse Society of Saint Edmund (TOCD)
SSE Society of Shipping Executives [*British*] (BI)
SSE Society of St. Edmund [*Roman Catholic men's religious order*]
SSE Software Support Environment (SSD)
SSE Solid-State Electrolyte (IAA)
SSE Solid-State Electronics
SSE South by South East (EERA)
SSE Southeastern Stock Exchange
SSE South-Southeast
SSE Southwest Semiconductor and Electronics Exposition (TSPED)
SSE Space Shuttle Engines [*NASA*] (MCD)
SSE Special Support Equipment
SSE Spokane Stock Exchange [*Washington*]
SSE Squared Sum of Errors [*Statistics*]
SSE Stage Systems Engineer
SSE Stateside Energy Corp. [*Vancouver Stock Exchange symbol*]
SSE Stockholm Stock Exchange
SSE Straight to Services Economy
SSE Submarine Scout Experimental [*British military*] (DMA)
SSE Subsystem Element [*NASA*] (NASA)
SSE Subsystem Support Equipment [*NASA*] (MCD)
SSE Summary Status Entry (SAA)
SSE Sum of Squared Errors [*Statistics*]
SSE Supplemental Support Evaluation
SSE Support System Evaluation
SSE Support Systems Engineering [*Boeing*]
SSE Surface Support Equipment
SSE Switching System Engineer (IAA)
SSE Sydney Stock Exchange [*Australia*] (ADA)
SSE Systemic Side Effects [*Pharmacology*] (DAVI)
SSE System Safety Engineering (AFM)
SSE System Status Evaluation [*Army*] (AABC)
SSE System Support Engineering
SSE System Support Equipment
SSEA Sentinel System Evaluation Agency [*DoD*]
SSEA Separate Sampling and Excitation Analysis [*Spectroscopy*]
SSEA Stage-Specific Embryonic Antigen [*Immunology*]
SSEA System Safety Engineering Analysis (MCD)
SSEAM Ship Systems Equipment Acquisition Manual (MCD)
SSEAT Surveyor Scientific Evaluation Advisory Team [*NASA*]
SSEB Source Selection Evaluation Board [*Military*] (AFM)
SSEB South of Scotland Electricity Board (ECON)
SSEC Secondary School Examinations Council [*British*] (BI)
SSEC Selective Sequence Electronic Calculator [*Computer science*]
SSEC Social Science Education Consortium (EA)
SSEC Society for the Study of Early China (EA)
SSEC Solar System Exploration Committee [*NASA*]
SSEC Solid-State Electronic Chronograph
SSEC Sound Surveillance Evaluation Center [*Navy*] (NVT)

SSEC.......... Space Science and Engineering Center [*University of Wisconsin - Madison*] [*Research center*] (RCD)
SSEC.......... Static Source Error Correction
SSEC.......... Subsystem Executive Control Program (IAA)
SSECO.......... Second-Stage Engine Cutoff
SSECS.......... Space Station Environmental Control System
SSECW.......... Prairie Migratory Bird Research Centre, Canadian Wildlife Service, Environment Canada [*Centre de Recherches sur les Oiseaux Migrateurs des Prairies, Service Canadien de la Faune, Environnement Canada*] Saskatoon, Saskatchewan [*Library symbol National Library of Canada*] (NLC)
SSEDF.......... Software Support Environment Development Facility (SSD)
SSEE.......... Standing-Shock Equilibrium Expansion
S-SEED.......... Symmetric Self Electrooptic Effect Device [*Optical Computing*]
SSE/EWE.......... SIGINT [*Signal Intelligence*] Support Element/Electronic Warfare Element [*Military*] (AABC)
SSEF.......... Solid-State Electro-Optic Filter
SSEF.......... Support Squadron Eastern Flank [*British military*] (DMA)
SSEG.......... Scottish Solar Energy Group (DBA)
SSEG.......... Ship System Engineering Group [*British*]
SSEG.......... System-Segment [*Computer science*]
SSEH.......... National Hydrology Research Centre, Environment Canada [*Centre National de Recherche en Hydrologie, Environnement Canada*] Saskatoon, Saskatchewan [*Library symbol National Library of Canada*] (NLC)
SSEIF.......... Software Support Environment Integration Facility (SSD)
SSEIP.......... Special Stockpile Engineering Investigation Program (MCD)
SSEIS.......... Standard Support and Environmental Impact Statement [*Environmental Protection Agency*] (GFGA)
SSEIS.......... Stationary Source Emissions and Inventory System [*Environmental Protection Agency*] (GFGA)
SSEKP.......... Single Shot Engagement Kill Probability (MCD)
SSEL.......... Solid-State Electronics Laboratory [*Stanford University*] (MCD)
SSEL.......... Space Science and Engineering Laboratory [*Pennsylvania State University*]
SSEL.......... Standard Statistical Establishment List [*Bureau of thé Census*]
SSELA.......... Standing Committee on Social Sciences, Economic, and Legal Aspects [*Great Lakes Research Advisory Board*]
SSEM.......... Serial-Section Electron Microscopy
SSEM.......... Solid State Extended Memory (MCD)
SSEM.......... Space System Effectiveness Model
SSEM.......... Supply Support Element Manager
SSEO.......... SEABEE Support and Equipment Office [*Navy*]
SSEOF.......... Software Support Environment Operation Facility (SSD)
SSEOS.......... Space Shuttle Engineering and Operations Support [*NASA*] (MCD)
SSEP.......... Somatosensory Evoked Potential [*Neurophysiology*]
SSEP.......... Source Selection Evaluation Plan
SSEP.......... Steady State Evoked Potential [*Neurophysiology*]
SSEP.......... Submarine Surveillance Equipment Program (NVT)
SSEP.......... System Safety Engineering Plan (AFM)
SSEPA.......... Society of Spanish Engineers, Planners, and Architects (EA)
SSEPF.......... Software Support Environment Production Facility (SSD)
SSER.......... Site Safety Evaluation Report [*Nuclear energy*] (NRCH)
SSER.......... Somatosensory Evoked Response [*Neurophysiology*]
SSER.......... Supplement to Safety Evaluation Report [*Nuclear energy*] (NRCH)
SSES.......... Sexual Self-Efficacy Scale [*Medicine*] (DMAA)
SSES.......... Shipboard Signal Exploration System (MCD)
SSES.......... Ship Signals Exploitation Space [*Navy*] (CAAL)
SSES.......... Single Strip Engine System
SSES.......... Special Signal Exploitation Spaces (NVT)
SSES.......... Susquehanna Steam Electric Station [*Nuclear energy*] (NRCH)
SSESC.......... College of Emmanuel and St. Chad, Saskatoon, Saskatchewan [*Library symbol National Library of Canada*] (NLC)
SSESI.......... Statistical and Social Enqiry Society of Ireland
SSESM.......... Spent Stage Experimental Support Module (KSC)
SSESPF.......... Software Support Environment Software Production Facility (SSD)
SSESS.......... Soviet Space Event Support Ships (CINC)
SSET.......... Source Selection Evaluation Team (AAGC)
SSET.......... Source Selection Evaluation Test
SSET.......... SSE Telecom [*NASDAQ symbol*] (TTSB)
SSET.......... SSE Telecom, Inc. [*NASDAQ symbol*] (SAG)
SSET.......... State Science, Engineering, and Technology Program [*National Science Foundation*]
SSE TI.......... SSE Telecom, Inc. [*Associated Press*] (SAG)
SSEU.......... System Selector Extension Unit
SS EVAL.......... Skill Specialty Evaluation Code [*Army*]
SSF.......... Congregation of the Sisters of the Family [*Roman Catholic religious order*]
SSF.......... Congregation of the Sisters of the Holy Family (TOCD)
SSF.......... Safe Shutdown Facility [*Nuclear energy*] (NRCH)
SSF.......... Saint Saulge [*France*] [*Seismograph station code, US Geological Survey*] (SEIS)
SSF.......... Samantha Smith Foundation (EA)
SSF.......... San Antonio, TX [*Location identifier FAA*] (FAAL)
SSF.......... Saybolt Seconds Furol [*Oil viscosity*]
SSF.......... S-Band Shuttle Forward (SSD)
SSF.......... Scottish Spring Fair (ITD)
SSF.......... Scottish Surfing Federation (DBA)
SSF.......... Seconds Saybolt Furol [*Oil viscosity*] (IAA)
SSF.......... Semi-Lagrangian and Semi-Geostrophic Finite Element [*Model*] [*Marine science*] (OSRA)
SSF.......... Semi-Lagrangian and Semi-Geostrophic Finite Element [*Model*] (USDC)
SSF.......... Service Storage Facility [*Military*]
SSF.......... Service Support Force [*Military*]
SSF.......... Ship's Service Force [*Navy*]
SSF.......... Simulated Spinal Fluid [*Medicine*]
SSF.......... Simultaneous Saccharification and Fermentation [*Chemical engineering*]
SSF.......... Simultaneous Saccharification and Fermentation [*Biochemistry*]
SSF.......... Single-Seated Fighter
SSF.......... Single Sideband Filter
SSF.......... Single Sided Frame [*Telecommunications*] (TEL)
SSF.......... Single Solar Flare
SSF.......... Single-Stage Fan
SSF.......... Single Stock Fund [*DoD*]
SSF.......... Sjogren's Syndrome Foundation (EA)
SSF.......... Smallest Serving Factor (PDAA)
SSF.......... Small, Shelly Fauna [*Paleontology*]
SSF.......... Society for the Study of Fertility [*British*]
SSF.......... Society of St. Francis [*Anglican religious community*]
SSF.......... Sodium Silicofluoride [*Inorganic chemistry*]
SSF.......... Software Support Facility (MCD)
SSF.......... Solid-State Fermentation
SSF.......... Solid Substrate Fermentation
SSF.......... Soluble Suppressor Factor [*Immunology*]
SSF.......... Somali Salvation Front (PD)
SSF.......... Sona Systems Ltd. (Canada) [*Vancouver Stock Exchange symbol*]
SSF.......... Southern Shark Fishery [*Australia*]
SSF.......... Space Simulation Facility (AAG)
SSF.......... Special Security Facility
SSF.......... Special Security Force (DOMA)
SSF.......... Special Service Force [*Canadian and US troops under combined command*] [*World War II*]
SSF.......... Spin Stretch Factor [*Textile technology*]
SSF.......... Spun Soy Fiber [*Food technology*]
SSF.......... SRB [*Solid-Rocket Booster*] Storage Facility [*NASA*] (NASA)
SSF.......... Stainless Steel Fiber
SSF.......... Standard Saybolt Furol [*Oil viscosity*]
SSF.......... Standby Shutdown Facility [*Nuclear energy*] (NRCH)
SS/F.......... Starboard Side/Forward [*Stowage*] (DNAB)
SSF.......... Straight Filament [*Biochemistry*]
SSF.......... Structured Surfactant Formulation [*Solvent technology*]
SSF.......... Studies in Short Fiction [*A publication*] (BRI)
SSF.......... Style Sac Flap
SSF.......... Supersonic Frequency (IAA)
SSF.......... Supply Status File (MCD)
SSF.......... Symmetrical Switching Function
SSF.......... System Support Facility
SSFA.......... Stainless Steel Fabricators' Association of Great Britain (BI)
SSFC.......... Sequential Single Frequency Code System [*Telecommunications*] (TEL)
SSFC.......... Severe Storm Forecast Center [*U.S. Weather Service*] (BARN)
SSFC.......... Social Science Federation of Canada [*Research center*] (IRC)
SSFC.......... Solid State Frequency Changer [*Military*] (CAAL)
SSFC.......... South Street Financial Center [*NASDAQ symbol*] (SAG)
SSFC.......... Susanne Severeid Fan Club (EA)
SSFD.......... Sisters of St. Francis of Dillingen [*See also SFD*] [*Rome, Italy*] (EAIO)
SSF-DC.......... Solid State Floppy Disk Card (PCM)
SSFDR.......... Solid-State Flight Data Recorder (GAVI)
SSFE.......... Scandinavian Society of Forest Economics (EAIO)
SSFF.......... Scholastic Science Fiction Federation [*Defunct*] (EA)
SSFF.......... Solid Smokeless Fuels Federation [*British*] (BI)
SSFF.......... Space Shuttle Furnace Facility [*NASA*] (SSD)
SSFGSS.......... Space Shuttle Flight and Ground System Specification [*NASA*] (NASA)
SSFI.......... Scaffolding, Shoring, and Forming Institute (EA)
SSFL.......... Santa Susana Field Laboratory [*NASA*] (NASA)
SSFL.......... Steady-State Fermi Level
SSFLC.......... Surface Stabilized Ferroelectric Liquid Crystal [*Physical chemistry*]
SSFM.......... Single Sideband Frequency Modulation
SSFMAC.......... Southern Shark Fishery Management Advisory Committee (EERA)
SSFMP.......... Southern Shark Fishery Management Plan [*Australia*]
SSFN.......... Solidarity: A Socialist-Feminist Network [*Defunct*] (EA)
SSFnTA.......... Stet Societa Finaziaria Telefonica PA [*Associated Press*] (SAG)
SSFnTel.......... Stet Societa Finaziaria Telefonica PA [*Associated Press*] (SAG)
SSFO.......... Scandinavian Society of Forensic Odontology (EA)
SSFO.......... Simultaneous Single Frequency Outlet
SSFP.......... Steady-State Free Precession [*Magnetic resonance imaging*] [*Radiology*] (DAVI)
SSFR.......... Safety Services Field Representative [*Red Cross*]
SSFS.......... Space Shuttle Functional Simulator [*NASA*] (KSC)
SSFS.......... Special Services Forecasting System [*Telecommunications*] (TEL)
SSFS.......... Steven Spielberg Film Society (EA)
SSFT.......... Self-Sealing Fuel Tank
SSFT.......... Self-Service Financial Terminal [*Computer science*] (MHDI)
SSFU.......... Scottish Sea Fishers' Union
SSFVT.......... Subsystems Functional Verification Test [*NASA*]
SSG.......... Guided Missile Submarine [*Navy symbol*]
SSG.......... Malabo [*Equatorial Guinea*] [*Airport symbol*] (OAG)
SSG.......... Safety Study Group (MCD)
SSG.......... Santa Isabel [*Spanish Guinea*] [*Airport symbol*] (AD)
SSG.......... Science Steering Group [*NASA*]
SSG.......... Scientific Software Group
SSG.......... Scientific Software Group
SSG.......... Scientific Steering Group [*Tropical Ocean-Global Atmosphere*] (USDC)
SSG.......... Scientific Steering Group [*Marine science*] (OSRA)
SSG.......... Scleroderma Support Group (EA)

SSG .... Search Signal Generator
SSG .... Security Service Guide (SAA)
SSG .... Senior Savers Guide Publishing, Inc. [*Vancouver Stock Exchange symbol*]
SSG .... Ships Service Generator (DOMA)
SSG .... Shuttle Support Group (MCD)
SSG .... Single Sideband Generator
SSG .... Slovak Government Flying Service [*FAA designator*] (FAAC)
SSG .... Small Signal Gain (IEEE)
SSG .... Society of Saint Gregory [*British*] (DBA)
SSG .... Software Support Group (NITA)
SSG .... Solution-Sol-Gel [*Materials science*]
SSG .... Southern Society of Genealogists (EA)
SSG .... South Sydney Greens [*Political party Australia*]
SSG .... Special Security Group (MCD)
SSG .... Special Studies Group [*Joint Chiefs of Staff*] [*Military*]
SSG .... Special Support Group [*FBI*] (CINC)
SSG .... Staff Sergeant [*Army*] (AABC)
SSG .... Standard Signal Generator (IAA)
SSG .... State Services Group [*Information service or system*] (IID)
SSG .... Stonehenge Study Group (EA)
SSG .... Strategic Studies Group [*Naval War College*] (DOMA)
SSG .... Subscriber Switching Grid (IAA)
SSG .... Subsystem Software Group
SSG .... Supply Spectrum Generator
SSG .... Surface Discharge Spark Gap (IAA)
SSG .... Sweep Signal Generator
SSG .... Symbolic Stream Generator [*Computer science*]
SSG .... System Safety Group [*Air Force*]
SSGA .... Scottish Salmon Growers' Association
SSGA .... Single Conductor, Shipboard General Use, Armored (IAA)
SSGA .... Society of St. Gregory of America [*Later, CMAA*] (EA)
SSGA .... Sterling Silversmiths Guild of America (EA)
SSGA .... Swordsmen and Sorcerers' Guild of America (EA)
SSGB .... Suore di San Giovanni Baptista [*Sisters of St. John the Baptist - SSJB*] [*Rome, Italy*] (EAIO)
SSGC .... Saskatoon Gallery and Conservatory, Saskatchewan [*Library symbol National Library of Canada*] (NLC)
SSGC .... Short System Ground Check
SSGD .... Smoke Screen Generative Device
SSGJ .... Single Strength Grapefruit Juice
SSGJ .... Supersonic Gas Jet
SSGM .... Service Station & Garage Management [*Canada A publication*]
SSGN .... Guided Missile Submarine (Nuclear Propulsion) [*Navy symbol*]
SSGP .... Spin Stabilized Guided Projectile (MCD)
SSGp .... System Safety Group [*Air Force*] (AFM)
SSGS .... Solid-State Gamma Switch
SSGS .... Standard Space Guidance System
SSGT .... Ship Service Gas Turbine [*Navy*] (CAAL)
SSGT .... Small-Scale Gap Test [*Explosive*]
SSGT .... Staff Sergeant [*Military*]
SSGT .... Subsystem Ground Test (MCD)
SSGTG .... Ship's Service Gas Turbine Generator [*Navy*] (NVT)
SSGW .... Surface-to-Surface Guided Weapon (NATG)
SSH .... S-Band Shuttle (SSD)
SSH .... Schwartz-Slawsky-Herzfeld [*Theory*] [*Chemical kinetics*]
SSH .... Sea Surface Height [*Oceanography*]
SSH .... Second-Stage Hydraulics
SSH .... Sharm E Sheikh [*Israel*] [*Airport symbol*] (OAG)
SSH .... Sisters Servants of the Most Sacred Heart (TOCD)
SSH .... Small-Scale Hydroelectric Project
SSH .... Snowshoe Hare
SSH .... Social Sciences and Humanities Research Council of Canada [*UTLAS symbol*]
SSH .... Social Service Handbooks [*A publication*]
SSH .... South Shore [*AAR code*]
SSH .... Special Survey of the Hull [*Lloyd's Register of Shipping*] (DS)
SSH .... Stationary-State Hypothesis [*Chemistry*]
SSH .... Student Semester Hours (EDAC)
SSH .... Substantial Stockholder
SSH .... Sunshine [*Alaska*] [*Seismograph station code, US Geological Survey*] (SEIS)
SSHA .... Subsystem Hazard Analysis
SSHA .... Survey of Study Habits and Attitudes [*Education*]
SSHA .... System Safety Hazard Analysis [*Military*]
SSHACS .... Small Ships Accounting System (DNAB)
SSHB .... Society for the Study of Human Biology (EA)
SSHB .... Stainless Steel Helium Bottle
SSHB .... Station Set Handbook [*NASA*] (NASA)
SSHC .... Single-Stage Hydrocracker [*Chemical engineering*]
SSHC .... Society to Support Home Confinement [*British*] (DBA)
SSHCG .... Students' Series of Historical and Comparative Grammars [*A publication*]
SSHD .... Single-Silo Hardsite Defense
SSHE .... Scraped-Surface Heat Exchanger [*Process engineering*]
SSHI .... Sunstone Hotel Investors [*NASDAQ symbol*] (TTSB)
SSHI .... Sunstone Hotel Investors, Inc. [*NASDAQ symbol*] (SAG)
SSHJM .... Sisters of the Sacred Hearts of Jesus and Mary [*Roman Catholic religious order*]
SSHJP .... Servants of the Sacred Heart of Jesus and of the Poor [*Roman Catholic women's religious order*]
S/SHLD .... Side Shield [*Automotive engineering*]
SSHM .... Scottish Society of History Medicine (DBA)
SSHM .... Society for the Social History of Medicine [*Oxford, England*] (EAIO)
SSHMA .... Senior Secondary Headmasters' Association [*British*]
SSHP .... Single-Shot Hit Probability
SSHPF .... Space Station Hazardous Processing Facility (SSD)
SSHR .... Social Systems and Human Resources [*National Science Foundation*] (MCD)
SSHR .... Spartan Safety Hazard Report [*Missiles*] (MCD)
SSHRC .... Social Sciences and Humanities Research Council of Canada
SSHRCC .... Social Sciences and Humanities Research Council of Canada [*Pronounced "sherk"*] [*See also CRSHC*]
SSHS .... Stainless Steel Helium Sphere
SSHSA .... Steamship Historical Society of America (EA)
S/Shtg .... Slipsheeting (DGA)
SSI .... Brunswick [*Georgia*] [*Airport symbol*] (AD)
SSI .... Brunswick, GA [*Location identifier FAA*] (FAAL)
SSI .... Safe Shutdown Impoundment [*Nuclear energy*] (NRCH)
SSI .... Safeway Stores, Inc.
SSI .... Sale Satisfaction Index [*Business term*]
SSI .... Satellite Sequential Imaging
SSI .... Satellite Services, Inc. [*Houston, TX*] [*Telecommunications*] (TSSD)
SSI .... Scaffolding and Shoring Institute [*Later, SSFI*] (EA)
SSI .... Scientific Systems, Inc.
SSI .... Second-Stage Ignition
SSI .... Sector Scan Indicator
SSI .... Security Systems, Inc. [*In TV series "Max Headroom"*]
SSI .... Security Systems Inspectorate [*Established in 1987*] [*British*]
SSI .... Segmental Sequential Irradiation (AAMN)
SSI .... Seismic Survival Indicator [*Earthquake analysis program*] [*Computer science*]
SSI .... Semiconductor Specialists, Inc. (IAA)
SSI .... Semisopochnoi Island [*Alaska*] [*Seismograph station code, US Geological Survey Closed*] (SEIS)
SSI .... Service Social International [*International Social Service - ISS*] [*Geneva, Switzerland*] (EAIO)
SSI .... Shaft Speed Indicator
SSI .... Ship and Shore Installation (MCD)
SSI .... Shoulder Sleeve Insignia [*Military*] (AABC)
SSI .... Signed Short Integer [*Computer science*]
SSI .... Significant Structural Item (NASA)
SSI .... Single Scale Integration (IAA)
SSI .... Single Service Institute [*Later, FPI*] (EA)
SSI .... Single System Image
SSI .... Site of Special Scientific Interest [*Great Britain*]
SSI .... Size Selective Inlet [*Environmental Protection Agency*] (GFGA)
SSI .... Skill Speciality Identifier (MCD)
SSI .... Sky Survey Instrument
SSI .... Slater Industries, Inc. [*Toronto Stock Exchange symbol*]
SSI .... Slater Steels Corp. [*Formerly, Slater Steel Industries*] [*Toronto Stock Exchange symbol*]
SSI .... Small-Scale Integration
SSI .... Smart Set International [*Program to discourage drug abuse*] [*Defunct*] (EA)
SSI .... Social Science Institute [*Washington University*] [*Research center*] (RCD)
SSI .... Social Security Income (DAVI)
SSI .... Social Security Information
SSI .... Society for Siberian Irises (EA)
SSI .... Society for the Study of Internationalism (EA)
SSI .... Society of Saunterers, International (EA)
SSI .... Society of Scribes and Illuminators (EA)
SSI .... Society of Strip Illustration [*British*] (DBA)
SSI .... Software Sciences Institute (NITA)
SSI .... Solid-State Imaging [*Physics*]
SSI .... Solid-State Inverter
SSI .... Spacecraft System Integration
SSI .... Space Studies Institute (EA)
SSI .... Spares Status Inquiry (AAG)
SSI .... Special Secretariat for Informatics (NITA)
SSI .... Special Subject for Inspection [*DoD*]
SSI .... Special Surveillance Inspection (MCD)
SSI .... Specialty Skill Identifier [*Military*] (AABC)
SSI .... Specific Searching Image [*Tendency of birds to select prey of the color to which they have been accustomed*]
SSI .... Staff Sergeant Instructor [*Military British*]
SSI .... Standards Starts Index [*Horse racing*] (DICI)
SSI .... Standing Signal Instructions [*Military*]
SSI .... Start Signal Indicator [*Telecommunications*] (TEL)
SSI .... Steady-State Irradiation [*Nuclear energy*] (NRCH)
SSI .... Stockpile Surveillance Inspection
SSI .... Storage-to-Storage Instruction (IEEE)
SSI .... Strategic Studies Institute (MCD)
SSI .... Structural Significant Item (MCD)
SSI .... Student/Supervisor Instructions [*Army Training Extension Course*] (INF)
SSI .... Stuttering Severity Index [*Speech and language therapy*] (DAVI)
SSI .... Subshock Insulin [*Pharmacology*] (DAVI)
SSI .... Subsod Injection [*Waste treatment*] (DICI)
SSI .... Sucro-Sac-Ologists Society International [*Defunct*] (EA)
SSI .... Sunstone Hotel Investors, Inc. [*NYSE symbol*] (SAG)
SSI .... Supplemental Security Income [*Social Security Administration*]
SSI .... Supplemental Security Income Program (USGC)
SSI .... Supplemental Security Insurance [*Program*]
SSI .... Supply Support Index (CAAL)
SSI .... Surprise Security Inspection [*Navy*] (NVT)
SSI .... Survey Sampling, Inc. [*Information service or system*] (IID)
SSI .... Sustaining Support Increment [*Military*]
SSI .... Symptom Sign Inventory [*Psychology*]

SSI............ Synchronous Systems Interface
SSI............ Synthetic Sentence Indentification [*Speech and language Therapy*] (DAVI)
SSI............ System Science Institute [*IBM Corp.*]
SSI............ System Sign Inventory (DAVI)
SSI............ System Status Index (IAA)
SSI............ System Status Indicator [*Bell System*]
SSIA............ Scottish Society for Industrial Archaeology (EA)
SSIA............ Shiprepairers and Shipbuilders Independent Association [*British*] (DS)
SSIA............ Shoe Service Institute of America (EA)
SSIA............ Specification Serial of Individual Assigned
SSIAM............ Structured and Scaled Interview to Assess Maladjustment [*Psychometrics*]
SSIB............ Shop Stock Items Bin (MCD)
SSIBD............ Shuttle System Interface Block Diagram [*NASA*] (NASA)
SSIC............ Saskatchewan Indian Cultural College, Saskatoon, Saskatchewan [*Library symbol National Library of Canada*] (NLC)
SSIC............ Small-Scale Integrated Circuit
SSIC............ Southern States Industrial Council [*Later, USIC*] (EA)
SSIC............ Standard Subject Identification Code (NVT)
SSIC............ Stressed-Skin Insulated-Core Panels [*Construction technology*] (PS)
SSICM............ Spin-Stabilized Impulsively Controlled Missile (MCD)
SSID............ Ship Systems Integration Data (MCD)
SSID............ Shuttle Stowage Installation Drawing (NASA)
SSIDA............ Steel Sheet Information and Developement Association [*British*] (BI)
SSIDS............ Siblings of Sudden Infant Death Syndrome Victims [*Medicine*]
SSIE............ Skylab Systems Integration Equipment [*NASA*] (MCD)
SSIE............ Smithsonian Science Information Exchange [*National Technical Information Service*] [*Later, FEDRIP*]
SSIE............ Solid Surface Interaction Experiment
SSIEM............ Society for the Study of Inborn Errors of Metabolism [*Middleway, England*] (EAIO)
SSIFC............ Saskatoon Campus, Saskatchewan Indian Federated College, Saskatchewan [*Library symbol National Library of Canada*] (BIB)
SSIFC............ Sharon Smith International Fan Club (EA)
SSIG............ Single Signal (IEEE)
SSIG............ State Student Incentive Grant [*Department of Education*]
SSIGS............ Special Survey of Inert Gas System [*Lloyd's Register of Shipping*] (DS)
S Sig Sta..... Storm Signal Station [*Nautical charts*]
SSII............ Solid-State Image Intensifier
SSII............ Sound Source Interactive, Inc. [*NASDAQ symbol*] (SAG)
SSIK............ Shipboard SONAR Bouy Interface Kit (DWSG)
SSIL............ Supply Significant Items List (MCD)
SSILA............ Society for the Study of Indigenous Languages of the Americas (EA)
SSILS............ Solid State Instrument Landing System (MCD)
S-SIM............ S-Band Simulator (SSD)
SSIM............ Static Secondary Ion Mass Spectroscopy
SSIM............ Statistical, Sampling Inventory Method [*Military*] (AABC)
SSIMS............ Static Secondary Ion Mass Spectroscopy
SSINI............ System Input Unit I [*Computer science*] (AEBS)
SSIO............ Southern Subtropical Indian Ocean
SSIP............ Ship Support Improvement Program [*DoD*]
SSIP............ Shuttle Student Involvement Project [*NASA*]
SSIP............ Solvent-Separated Ion-Pair [*Physical chemistry*]
SSIP............ Specific, Sincere, Immediate, Private, and Personal [*Management technique*]
SSIP............ Standard Systems Improvement Program
SSIP............ Subsystem Integration Plan (IAA)
SSIP............ Subsystems Integration Program [*or Project*] [*NATO*] (NATG)
SSIP............ System Setup Indicator Panel
SSIP............ Systems Software Interface Processing [*NASA*] (MCD)
SSIPL............ Support and Sustaining Implications of Increased POMCUS Levels [*Military*]
SSIR............ Soil Survey Investigations Report
SSIR............ Special Security Investigation Requirement (AFM)
SSIRT............ Support Staff Interests Round Table [*American Library Association*]
SSIS............ Social Security Information System [*ILO*] [*United Nations*] (DUND)
SSIS............ Society for South India Studies (EA)
SSIS............ Spacecraft System Integration Support
SSIS............ Space Station Information System (NASA)
SSISI............ Statistical and Social Inquiry Society of Ireland (DBA)
SSISS............ Spacecraft System Integration Support Service
SSI/SSP...... Supplemental Security Income/State Supplemental Payment (DAVI)
SSIT............ Semi-Submarine Ice-Breaking Tanker (PDAA)
SSITF............ Standard Shipboard Inspection and Testing Form [*Navy*] (DNAB)
SSITKA............ Steady-State Isotopic Transient Kinetic Analysis [*Chemical physics*]
SSITP............ Shuttle System Integrated Test Plan [*NASA*] (NASA)
SSIU............ Subsystem Interface Unit (MCD)
SSIUL............ Social Sciences Information Utilization Laboratory
SSIUS............ Specialty Steel Industry of the United States (EA)
SSIWA............ Shipwrights' and Shipwrights Iron Workers' Association [*A union*] [*British*]
SSIX............ Submarine Satellite Information Exchange [*Geosynchronous communications satellite*]
SSIXS............ Submarine Satellite Information Exchange System (MCD)
SSJ............ Sandnessjoen [*Norway*] [*Airport symbol*] (OAG)
SSJ............ Savez Sindikata Jugoslavije [*Yugoslavia Federation of Trade Unions*]
SSJ............ Self-Aligning Swivel Joint
SSJ............ Self-Screening Jammer (MCD)
SSJ............ Sequential Spot Jamming [*Military*] (CAAL)
SSJ............ Servants of St. Joseph (TOCD)
SSJ............ Servo Summing Junction
SSJ............ Shinshu-Shinmachi [*Japan*] [*Seismograph station code, US Geological Survey*] (SEIS)
SSJ............ Side-Support Jack
SSJ............ Sinatra Society of Japan [*Tokyo*] (EAIO)
SSJ............ Single Subsonic Jet
SSJ............ Sisters of Saint Joseph of Chestnut Hill, Philadelphia (TOCD)
SSJ............ Sisters of St. Joseph [*Roman Catholic religious order*]
SSJ............ Sisters of St. Joseph (Buffalo) (TOCD)
SSJ............ Sisters of St. Joseph (Burlington) (TOCD)
SSJ............ Sisters of St. Joseph (Erie) (TOCD)
SSJ............ Sisters of St. Joseph (Kalamazoo, Nazareth) (TOCD)
SSJ............ Sisters of St. Joseph of St. Augustine, Florida (TOCD)
SSJ............ Sisters of St. Joseph of the Third Order of St. Francis [*Roman Catholic religious order*]
SSJ............ Sisters of St. Joseph (Ogdensburg) (TOCD)
SSJ............ Sisters of St. Joseph (Rochester) (TOCD)
SSJ............ Sisters of St. Joseph (Springfield, MA) (TOCD)
SSJ............ Sisters of St. Joseph (Wheeling) (TOCD)
SSJ............ Societas Sancti Joseph Sanctissimi Cordis [*St. Joseph's Society of the Sacred Heart*] [*Josephites*] [*Roman Catholic men's religious order*]
SSJ............ Socijalisticka Stranka Jugoslavije [*Yugoslav Socialist Party*] [*Political party*] (EAIO)
SSJ............ Solid-State Jammer
ssj............ St. Joseph's Society of the Sacred Heart, Jospehite Fathers (TOCD)
SSJB............ Sisters of St. John the Baptist [*See also SSGB*] [*Roman Catholic religious order Rome, Italy*] (EAIO)
SSJC............ Sisters of St. Joseph Benedict Cottolengo (TOCD)
SSJC............ Southern Seminary and Junior College [*Virginia*]
SSJD............ Society of St. John the Divine [*Anglican religious community*]
SSJE............ Society of St. John the Evangelist [*Anglican religious community*]
SS-JFI............ School Superintendent Job Functions Inventory [*Test*]
SSJG............ Sisters of St. John of God [*Wexford, Republic of Ireland*] (EAIO)
SSJSM............ Sisters of St. Joseph of St. Mark [*Roman Catholic religious order*]
SSJ-TOSF.... Sisters of St. Joseph of the Third Order of St. Francis (TOCD)
SSK............ Antisubmarine Submarine [*Navy symbol*]
SSK............ Keethanou School/Public Library, Stanley Mission, Saskatchewan [*Library symbol National Library of Canada*] (BIB)
SSK............ Service Sink [*Technical drawings*]
SSK............ Skystar International [*ICAO designator*] (FAAC)
SSK............ Slip, Slip, Knit [*Knitting*] (BARN)
SSK............ Softkey Software Products, Inc. [*Toronto Stock Exchange symbol*]
SSK............ Soil Stack
SSK............ Super Sport Kurz [*Super, Sport, Short chassis*] [*Mercedes-Benz automotive model designation*]
SSKAT............ Socio-Sexual Knowledge and Attitudes Test [*Psychology*]
SSKDN............ Serikat Sekerdja Kementerian Dalam Negeri [*Union of Workers in the Department of Interior*] [*Indonesia*]
SSKI............ Saturated Solution of Potassium Iodide [*Medicine*]
SSKIL............ Library Technician Program, Kelsey Institute of Applied Arts & Sciences, Saskatoon, Saskatchewan [*Library symbol National Library of Canada*] (NLC)
SSKP............ Serikat Sekerdja Kementerian Pertaganan [*Ministry of Defense Workers' Unions*] [*Indonesia*]
SSKP............ Single-Shot Kill Probability
SSKPS............ Solid-State Klystron Power Supply
SSKTP............ Society for Spreading the Knowledge of True Prayer [*British*] (BI)
SSL............ Congregation of the Sisters of St. Louis, Juilly-Monaghan (TOCD)
SSL............ Licentiate of Sacred Scripture
SSL............ Safety Systems Laboratory [*Formerly, Office of Vehicle Systems Research*] [*Department of Transportation*]
SSL............ School of Systems and Logistics [*Military*]
SSL............ Scientific Subroutine Library
SSL............ Scientific Support Laboratory [*CDEC*] (MCD)
SSL............ Seattle, WA [*Location identifier FAA*] (FAAL)
SSL............ Secure Sockets Layer [*Computer science*] (PCM)
SSL............ Seismograph Service Ltd. [*British*]
SSL............ Selected Source List (AAG)
SSL............ Self-Aligned Superintegration Logic (IAA)
SSL............ Self Serve Laundry [*Military*] (INF)
SSL............ Serpentine Superlattice [*Physics*]
SSL............ Service Security Layer [*Computer science*]
SSL............ Shift and Select [*Computer science*] (MDG)
SSL............ Ship Shortage Log (AAG)
SSL............ Shop Stock List (MCD)
SSL............ Signal Selectro Logic (ECII)
SSL............ Skaneateles Short Line Railroad Corp. [*AAR code*]
SSL............ Skin Surface Lipid [*Physiology*]
SSL............ Social Security Administration Library, Baltimore, MD [*OCLC symbol*] (OCLC)
SSL............ Sociosystem Laboratory
SSL............ Sodium Stearoyl Lactylate
SSL............ Soeurs de Saint Louis [*Sisters of Saint Louis*] (EAIO)
SSL............ Software Sciences Ltd. [*British*]
SSL............ Software Slave Library [*Computer science*] (TEL)
SSL............ Software Specification Language
SSL............ Solid State Lamp (MCD)
SSL............ Solid-State LASER
SSL............ Solid Statement Library (HGAA)
SSL............ Source Statement Library [*Computer science*]
SSL............ Southern Star Resources Ltd. [*Vancouver Stock Exchange symbol*]
SSL............ Space Sciences Laboratory [*University of California, Berkeley*] [*Research center NASA*] (MCD)
SSL............ Space Simulation Laboratory
SSL............ Special Sensor-Lightning

SSL.......... Spent Sulfite Liquor [*Papermaking*]
SSL.......... Storage Structure Language
SSL.......... Sunset Lake [*Pennsylvania*] [*Seismograph station code, US Geological Survey Closed*] (SEIS)
SSL.......... Super Speed Logic [*Computer science*] (IAA)
SSL.......... Support Status List (MCD)
SSL.......... Support System Language [*Computer science*] (IAA)
SSL.......... System Software Loader (NASA)
SSL.......... System Specification Language
SSL.......... System Stock List (NATG)
SSLC.......... Ship System Life Cycle [*Navy*]
SSLC.......... Society of Savings and Loan Controllers [*Later, Financial Managers Society*] (EA)
SSLC.......... Synchronous Single-Line Controller
SSLE.......... Subacute Sclerosing Leukoencephalitis [*Medicine*]
SSLF.......... Southern Sudan Liberation Front (BJA)
SSLH.......... Society for the Study of Labour History [*Sheffield, England*] (EA)
SSLI.......... Serum Sickness-Like Illness [*Medicine*]
SSLI.......... Society of School Librarians International (EA)
SSLI.......... Southern Sec Life Ins [*NASDAQ symbol*] (TTSB)
SSLI.......... Southern Security Life Insurance Co. [*NASDAQ symbol*] (NQ)
SSLM.......... Solid-Supported Liquid Membrane [*Chemical engineering*]
SSLO.......... Solid-State Local Oscillator
SSLOG.......... Seton Sisters of Our Lady of Guadalupe, Tucson (TOCD)
SSLORAN.... Skywave Synchronized Long-Range Aid to Navigation
SSLP.......... Simple-Sequence Length Polymorphism [*Genetics*]
SSLP.......... Transport Submarine (MCD)
SSL-POW/MIA... Seaside Support League - POW/MIA [*Prisoner of War/Missing in Action*] (EA)
SSLPS.......... Solid-State Logic Protection System [*Nuclear energy*] (NRCH)
SSLR.......... Straits Settlements Law Reports [*A publication*] (DLA)
SSLR Supp... Straits Settlements Law Reports, Supplement [*1897-99*] [*Malasia*] [*A publication*] (DLA)
SSLS.......... Solid-State LASER System
SSLS.......... Standard Space Launch System [*BSD*]
SSLSM.......... Single Service Logistics Support Manager (MCD)
SSLT.......... Solid-State Logic Timer
SSLT.......... Starboard Side Light (MCD)
SSLT.......... Stock Status Lag Time (AABC)
SSLV.......... Southern San Luis Valley Railroad Co. [*AAR code*]
SSLV.......... Standard Small Launch Vehicle (DOMA)
SSLV.......... Standard Space Launch Vehicle
SSM.......... Aero 1 Prop-Jet, Inc. [*Canada ICAO designator*] (FAAC)
SSM.......... Midget Submarine [*Navy symbol*]
SSM.......... Satellite Stratospheric Monitor (NOAA)
SSM.......... Sault Ste. Marie [*Michigan*] [*Airport symbol*] (OAG)
SSM.......... Scanning SQUID [*SuperConducting Quantum Interference Device*] Microscope [*Physics*]
SSM.......... School in Sales Management [*LIMRA*]
SSM.......... Scientific Survey Module (IAA)
SSM.......... Second-Stage Motor
SSM.......... Second Surface Mirror
SSM.......... Second-Tier Securities Market [*Investment term*]
SSM.......... Self-Sterilizing-Material [*Pharmacology*]
SSM.......... Semiconductor Storage Model (NITA)
SSM.......... Semiconductor Storage Module
SSM.......... Seminaire St. Martial [*Haiti*] [*Seismograph station code, US Geological Survey Closed*] (SEIS)
SSM.......... Semisolid Material [*Metallurgy*]
SSM.......... Serum-Supplemented Medium [*Microbiology*]
SSM.......... Sesquiterpenoid Stress Metabolite [*Plant physiology*]
SSM.......... Set Sign Minus (SAA)
SSM.......... Set System Mask (HGAA)
SSM.......... Ship Simulation Model [*Navy*]
SSM.......... Signal Strength Monitor [*Broadcasting*]
SSM.......... Sign Status Matrix (GAVI)
SSM.......... Silver Star Medal [*Military decoration*]
SSM.......... Simplified Storage Management [*Computer science*]
SSM.......... Simulation Support Module
SSM.......... Single Sideband Modulation
SSM.......... Single Sideband Signal Multiplier [*Telecommunications*]
SSM.......... Sisters of St. Mary of the Third Order of St. Francis [*Roman Catholic religious order*]
SSM.......... Sisters of the Sorrowful Mother [*Third Order of St. Francis*] [*Roman Catholic religious order*]
SSM.......... Small Semiconductor Memory
SSM.......... Society of St. Margaret [*Anglican religious community*]
SSM.......... Society of St. Monica (EA)
SSM.......... Society of the Sacred Mission [*Anglican religious community*]
SSM.......... Society of the Servants of Mary [*Anglican religious community*]
SSM.......... Solar Simulation Module
SSM.......... Solar Stereoscopic Mission [*NASA*]
SSM.......... Solid-State Materials (CET)
SSM.......... Southlands Mining [*Vancouver Stock Exchange symbol*]
SSM.......... Spacecraft Systems Monitor [*NASA*] (MCD)
SSM.......... Space Station Module [*NASA*] (KSC)
SSM.......... Spark Source Mass Spectroscopy
SSM.......... Special Safeguarding Measures [*Telecommunications*] (TEL)
SSM.......... Special Survey of the Machinery [*Lloyd's Register of Shipping*] (DS)
SSM.......... Spread Spectrum Modulation (NATG)
SSM.......... Squadron Sergeant Major
SSM.......... Staff Sergeant Major [*Military*]
SSM.......... Staff Squadron Major [*Military British*]
SSM.......... Stage Scanning Microscope
SSM.......... Standard Schedule Message (DA)
SSM.......... Standard Surfacing Mat [*Fiberglass*]
SSM.......... Stochastic Sequential Machine (IAA)
SSM.......... Stone Street Bancorp [*AMEX symbol*] (TTSB)
SSM.......... Stone Street Bancorp, Inc. [*AMEX symbol*] (SAG)
SSM.......... St. Thomas More College, Saskatoon, Saskatchewan [*Library symbol National Library of Canada*] (NLC)
SSM.......... Subsynaptic Membrane [*Anatomy*]
SSM.......... Subsystem Manager [*NASA*] (NASA)
SSM.......... Superficial Spreading Melanoma [*Oncology*]
SSM.......... Supply Support Management
SSM.......... Support Subsystem Manager
SSM.......... Support Systems Module [*NASA*]
SSM.......... Surface-to-Surface Missile
SSM.......... Sync-Stream Manager (PCM)
SSM.......... System Security Manager [*Military*] (GFGA)
SSM.......... System Software Message [*Computer science*] (IAA)
SSM.......... Systems Support Module [*NASA*] (MCD)
SSM.......... System Supply Manager
SSM.......... System Support Machine [*Telecommunications*]
SSM.......... System Support Management [*or Manager*] [*Military*] (AFM)
SSMA.......... School Science and Mathematics Association (EA)
SSMA.......... Soldiers, Sailors, Marines, and Airmen's Club [*Washington, DC*]
SSMA.......... Solid-State Microwave Amplifier
SSMA.......... Southwest Spanish Mustang Association (EA)
SSMA.......... Spread-Spectrum Multiple Access [*Satellite communications*]
SSMA.......... State Servants and Allied Motoring Association [*British*] (DBA)
SSMA.......... Sterilised Suture Manufacturers Association [*British*] (DBA)
SSMAS.......... Standards for Management Advisory Services (TDOB)
SSMB.......... Ship's Serviceman, Barber [*Navy rating*]
SSMB.......... Space Shuttle Maintenance Baseline [*NASA*] (MCD)
SSMB.......... Special Services Management Bureau [*Telecommunications*] (TEL)
SSMC.......... Second-Stage Motor Container
SSMC.......... Ship's Serviceman, Cobbler [*Navy rating*]
SSMC.......... Silver Spring Metro Complex (USDC)
SSMC.......... Silver Spring Metropolitan Complex [*Marine science*] (OSRA)
SSMCC.......... Space Shuttle Mission Control Center [*NASA*] (SSD)
SSMCIS.......... Secondary School Mathematics Curriculum Improvement Study [*National Science Foundation*]
SSMCNP.......... Safeguard System Management Communications Network Program [*Army*] (AABC)
SSMCO.......... SPARTAN Santa Monica Checkout [*NASA*]
SSMCS.......... Synchronous Satellite Military Communication System
SSMD.......... Saskatchewan Mining Development Corp., Saskatoon, Saskatchewan [*Library symbol National Library of Canada*] (NLC)
SSMD.......... Silicon Stud-Mounted Diode
SSME.......... Satellite System Monitoring Equipment
SSME.......... Society for the Study of Medical Ethics [*British*]
SSME.......... Space Shuttle Main Engine [*NASA*]
SSME.......... Spread Spectrum Modulation Equipment [*NATO*] (MCD)
SSMEC.......... Space Shuttle Main Engine Controller [*NASA*] (MCD)
SSMECA.......... Space Shuttle Main Engine Controller Assembly [*NASA*] (NASA)
SSMES.......... Systems Support Module Equipment Section [*NASA*] (SSD)
SSMF.......... Signalling System Multi-Frequency (NITA)
SSMF.......... Symbol Sink - Matched Filter
SSMG.......... Satellite Systems Monitoring Group [*INTELSAT*]
SSMG.......... Ship's Service Motor Generator [*Navy*] (NVT)
SSMH.......... Scottish Society for the Mentally Handicapped (EAIO)
SSMH.......... Scottish Society of Mentally Handicapped (DBA)
SSMHRC.......... Spanish Speaking Mental Health Research Center [*Public Health Service*] [*Research center*] (RCD)
SSM/I.......... Sensor System Microwave/Imager
SSMI.......... Sister Servants of Mary Immaculate [*Roman Catholic religious order*]
SSMI.......... Special Sensor Microwave Imager [*Marine science*] (OSRA)
SSM/I.......... Special Sensor Microwave/Imager (USDC)
SSMIF & G... Squadron Sergeant-Major Instructor in Fencing and Gymnastics [*Military British*] (ROG)
SSMI/I.......... Special Sensor Microwave/Imager [*Marine science*] (OSRA)
SSM/IM.......... System Support Manager/Inventory Manager (MCD)
SSMIMA.......... Scissor, Shear, and Manicure Implement Manufacturers Association [*Later, National Association of Scissors and Shears Manufacturers*] (EA)
SSMIS.......... Support Services Management Information System [*Army*]
SSML.......... Shaped Substrata Meanderline (MCD)
SSML.......... Ship's Serviceman, Laundryman [*Navy rating*]
SSML.......... Society for the Study of Midwestern Literature (EA)
SSMLL.......... Society for the Study of Medieval Languages and Literature [*British*]
SSMM.......... Space Station Mathematical Model
SSMMA.......... Staple and Stapling Machine Manufacturers Association [*Defunct*]
SSMMI.......... Soeurs Salesiennes Missionnaires de Marie Immaculee [*Salesian Missionaries of Mary Immaculate - SMMI*] [*Gentilly, France*] (EAIO)
SSMN.......... Sisters of St. Mary of Namur [*Roman Catholic religious order*]
SSMO.......... Sisters of St. Mary of Oregon [*Roman Catholic religious order*]
SSMO.......... Summary of Synoptic Meteorological Observations [*National Oceanic and Atmospheric Administration*] (MSC)
SSMOB.......... Surface-to-Surface Missile Order of Battle (MCD)
SSMP.......... Safeguard System Master Plan [*Army*] (AABC)
SSMP.......... Supply Support Management Plan [*Military*] (CAAL)
SSM PEIS.... Stockpile Stewardship and Management Programmatic Environmental Impact Statement
SSMPP.......... Society for the Study of Male Psychology and Physiology (EA)
SSMRP.......... Seismic Safety Margins Research Program [*Nuclear Regulatory Commission*]
SSMS.......... Solid-State Mass Spectrometer
SSMS.......... Sons of Sherman's March to the Sea (EA)

SSMS........... Spark Source Mass Spectroscopy
SSMS........... Submarine Safety Monitoring System
SSMSN........ Surface-to-Surface Mission [*Military*] (AABC)
S SMS N CLSD... Side Seams Not Closed [*Freight*]
SSMT........... Salvage Sales Material Transfer
SSM/T.......... Sensor System Microwave/Temperature
SSMT........... Ship's Serviceman, Tailor [*Navy rating*]
SSMT........... Site Security Maintenance Team
SSMT........... Society for the Study of Myth and Tradition (EA)
SSMT........... Stress Survival Matrix Test (PDAA)
SSMTG........ Solid-State and Molecular Theory Group [*MIT*] (MCD)
SSMTS........ Spade and Shovel Makers' Trade Society [*A union*] [*British*]
SSMUX........ Spread-Spectrum Multiplexing [*Telecommunications*] (IAA)
SSMV........... Single-Shot Multivibrator
SSMVP........ Space Station Master Verification Plan [*NASA*] (SSD)
SSMVR........ Space Station Master Verification Requirement [*NASA*] (SSD)
SSN............. Auburn [*New York*] [*Airport symbol*] (AD)
SSN............. Romulus, NY [*Location identifier FAA*] (FAAL)
SSN............. Samson Gold Corp. [*Vancouver Stock Exchange symbol*]
SSN............. San Juan Del Sur [*Nicaragua*] [*Seismograph station code, US Geological Survey*] (SEIS)
SSN............. Season and Sunspot Number (DNAB)
SSN............. Segment Stack Number
SSN............. Senior Security Network (EA)
SSN............. Senior Strategic Income Fund [*NYSE symbol*] (SAG)
SSN............. Severely Subnormal
SSN............. Ship, Submersible (Nuclear-Powered)
SSN............. Social Security Number (AABC)
SSN............. Soviet Sciences in the News [*A publication*]
SSN............. Space Surveillance Network
SSN............. Specification Serial Number [*Military*]
SSN............. Standard Serial Numbers (DIT)
SSN............. Standard Study Number [*Military*]
SSN............. Station Serial Number (CET)
SSN............. Stock Segregation Notice [*DoD*]
SSN............. Submarine (Nuclear-Powered) [*Navy symbol*] (NVT)
SSN............. Switched Service Network [*Telecommunications*]
SSN............. Sykepleiernes Samarbeid i Norden [*Northern Nurses Federation - NNF*] (EAIO)
SSNAP........ Single Seat Night Attack Program (MCD)
SSNCHK....... Social Security Number Check
SSND........... School Sisters of Notre Dame (IIA)
SSND........... Solid-State Neutral Dosimeter
SSN(DS)...... Submarine (Nuclear-Powered) in Direct Support [*Navy symbol*] (NVT)
SSNDT......... Scottish School of Non-Destructive Testing [*Research center*] (IRUK)
SSNF........... Source Spot Noise Figure
SSNJ........... Self-Screening Noise Jammer (MCD)
SSNLO......... Shan State Nationalities Liberation Organization [*Myanmar*] (PD)
SSNM........... Strategic Special Nuclear Materials
SSNMH........ Scipio Society of Naval and Military History (EA)
SSNNP........ Sustainable Social Net National Product (EERA)
SSNPP......... Small-Size Nuclear Power Plant
SSNS........... Scottish Society for Northern Studies
SSNS........... Standard Study Numbering System [*Military*] (AABC)
SSNS........... Steroid-Sensitive Nephrotic Syndrome [*Medicine*] (DMAA)
SSNTD......... Solid-State Nuclear Track Detection (PDAA)
SSNW........... Social Scientists Against Nuclear War (EA)
SSNY........... Swiss Society of New York (EA)
SSO............. Safety/Security Officer [*Military*] (AABC)
SSO............. Safety Significant Operation [*Aerospace*]
SSO............. Sanitary Sewer Overflow [*Environmental Protection Agency*]
SSO............. Sanitary Sewer Overflow [*Environmental Protection Agency*]
SSO............. San Simon, AZ [*Location identifier FAA*] (FAAL)
SSO............. Saturn Systems Office [*NASA*] (SAA)
SSO............. Second Surgical Opinion [*Insurance*] (WYGK)
SSO............. Security System Organization
SSO............. Senior Safety Officer [*Navy*] (CAAL)
SSO............. Senior Scientific Officer [*Ministry of Agriculture, Fisheries, and Food*] [*British*]
SSO............. Senior Staff Officer [*Military British*]
SSO............. Senior Supply Officer [*Military British*]
SSO............. Sequence-Specific Oligonucleotide [*Probe*] [*Medicine*] (DMAA)
SSO............. Ship Safety Officer
SSO............. Simosato [*Japan*] [*Later, HTY*] [*Geomagnetic observatory code*]
SSO............. Single Sweep Operation
SSO............. Single System Operator (WDMC)
SSO............. Society of Surgical Oncology (EA)
SSO............. Solid-State Oscillator
SSO............. Source Selection Official (NASA)
sso.............. Southern Sotho [*MARC language code Library of Congress*] (LCCP)
SSO............. Spacecraft Systems Officer (SAA)
SSO............. Space Sciences Office (IAA)
SSO............. Space Shuttle Orbiter [*NASA*] (RDA)
SSO............. Space Station Office [*NASA*] (SSD)
SSO............. Spares Shipping Order
SSO............. Special Security Office [*or Officer*] [*Military*] (CINC)
SSO............. Special Sense Organ [*Medicine*] (DMAA)
SSO............. Special Service Officer [*Military*]
SSO............. Spindle Speed Override (IAA)
SSO............. Squadron Signals Officer [*Navy British*]
SSO............. Staff Security Officer (AAG)
SSO............. Staff Signals Officer [*British military*] (DMA)
SSO............. Station Staff Officer [*British military*] (DMA)
SSO............. Statistical Service Office [*Military*]
SSO............. Steady-State Oscillation
SSO............. Submarine Oiler [*Navy ship symbol*]
SSO............. Submarine Supply Office
SSO............. Subsystem Operation [*in Spacelab*] [*NASA*] (MCD)
SSO............. Sunflower Seed Oil
SSO............. Support Services Office [*Environmental Protection Agency*] (GFGA)
SSO............. Support System for OEX [*Orbiter Experiments*] (NASA)
SSO............. System Security Officer
SSO............. System Service Order [*Bell System*]
SSO............. System Staff Office
SSOA........... Submarine Operating Area [*Navy*]
SSOA........... Subsurface Ocean Area (NVT)
SSOB........... Senior Scientist on Board [*Navy*]
SSOC........... Southern Student Organizing Committee [*Defunct*]
SSOC........... Space Station Operations Center [*NASA*] (SSD)
SSOC........... Space Surveillance Operations Center (SAA)
SSOC........... Switching Service Operations Center [*Telecommunications*]
SSOCA......... Senior Staff Officer for Civil Affairs [*British World War II*]
SSOCC......... Space Station Operations and Control Center [*NASA*] (SSD)
SSOD........... Solid-State Optical Detector
SSOD........... Special Session on Disarmament [*A special session of the UN General Assembly held from May 23 to June 28, 1978*]
SSODCM...... Space Systems Operational Design Criteria Manual [*NASA*]
SSODIA....... Special Security Office, Defense Intelligence Agency (CINC)
SSOE........... Special Subject Operational Evaluation
SSOEC......... Ship Suppliers' Organization of the European Community [*Hague, Netherlands*] (EAIO)
SS of A........ Secular Society of America [*Defunct*]
SSOFS......... Smiling Sons of the Friendly Shillelaghs
SSOG........... Satellite Systems Operations Guide [*INTELSAT*]
SSOG........... Scandinavian Association of Obstetricians and Gynaecologists (EA)
SSOG........... Spur Stepover Gear
SSOJ........... Savez Socialisticke Omladine Jugoslavije [*League of Socialist Youth of Yugoslavia*] [*Political party*] (PPE)
SSOJ........... Single Strength Orange Juice
SSOL........... SmartServ Online [*NASDAQ symbol*] (TTSB)
SSOL........... SmartServ Online, Inc. [*NASDAQ symbol*] (SAG)
SSOL........... Space Station Operations Language [*NASA*] (SSD)
SSOLW......... SmartServ Online Wrrt [*NASDAQ symbol*] (TTSB)
SSOM........... Solid-State Optical MASER
SSOM........... [*The*] Space Shuttle Operator's Manual
SSOO........... Satellite Supply Operations Officer [*Military*] (AFIT)
SSOP........... Satellite Systems Operations Plan [*INTELSAT*]
SSOP........... Second Surgical Opinion Program (MEDA)
SSOP........... Second Surgical Opinion Program (DAVI)
SSOP........... Space Systems Operating Procedures [*NASA*] (MCD)
SSOP........... Standard Security Operating Procedure (SSD)
SSOR........... Ship Systems Operational Requirements
SSOR........... Slice Successive Overrelaxation
S SORD......... Senza Sordini [*Without Mutes*] [*Music*]
SSORM........ Standard Ship's Organization and Regulations Manual [*Navy*] (NVT)
SSORM........ Standard Submarine Operations and Regulations Manual (DOMA)
SSORM........ Standing Submarine Operations and Repair Manual [*Navy*] (DNAB)
SSORT......... Ship's Systems Operational Readiness Test (MCD)
SSORT......... Ships Systems Operational Requirements
SSOS........... One Sky, the Saskatchewan Cross Cultural Centre, Saskatoon, Saskatchewan [*Library symbol National Library of Canada*] (NLC)
SSOS........... Single Source of Supply (MCD)
SSOSMFC.... Simply Simon - The Official Simon MacCorkindale Fan Club (EA)
SSOT........... Special Session of Oyer and Terminer [*Legal*] [*British*] (ROG)
SSOTC......... Skinner's School Officers Training Corps [*British military*] (DMA)
SSOU1......... System Output Unit 1 [*IBM Corp.*] (MDG)
SSOW........... Subcontractor Statement of Work (MCD)
SSOWSJ...... Supreme Shrine of the Order of the White Shrine of Jerusalem (EA)
SSP............. Association of the Sons of Poland (EA)
SSP............. Pauline Fathers and Brothers (TOCD)
ssp.............. Pauline Fathers and Brothers, Society of St. Paul for the Apostolate of Communications (TOCD)
SSP............. Plant Biotechnology Institute, National Research Council Canada [*Institut de Biotechologie des Plantes, Conseil National de Recherches Canada*], Saskatoon,Saskatchewan [*Library symbol Obsolete National Library of Canada*] (NLC)
SSP............. SACEUR [*Supreme Allied Commander, Europe*] Schedule Program [*Army*] (AABC)
SSP............. Sagittal Sinus Pressure [*Medicine*]
SSP............. Salt Soluble Protein [*Food industry*]
SSP............. Sanarelli-Shwartzman Phenomenon [*Medical research*] (DAVI)
SSP............. Schwartzman-Sanarelli Phenomenon [*Medicine*] (MAE)
SSP............. Scientific Services Program [*Army Research Office*] (RDA)
SSP............. Scientific Software Products, Inc. [*Information service or system*] (IID)
SSP............. Scientific Subroutine Package [*Computer science*]
SSP............. Scouting Seaplane
SSP............. Scripps EW [*NYSE symbol*] (SAG)
SSP............. Scripps(E.W.)'A' [*NYSE symbol*] (TTSB)
SSP............. Secondary Stock Point (DNAB)
SSP............. Seguro Resources [*Vancouver Stock Exchange symbol*]
SSP............. Seismic Section Profiler
SSP............. Semi-Annual Service Program [*Army*] (INF)
SSP............. Sensor Select Panel (MCD)
SSP............. Sentence Synthesizing Program
SSP............. Serbian Socialist Party [*Political party*]
SSP............. Set Sign Plus (SAA)
SSP............. Ship Speed
SSP............. Ship's Stores Profit [*Navy*]
SSP............. Shortage Specialty Pay [*Navy*] (NVT)

SSP .... Shoshone Peak [*Nevada*] [*Seismograph station code, US Geological Survey*] (SEIS)
SSP .... SIGINT Support Plan (MCD)
SSP .... Signalling and Switching Processor (NITA)
SSP .... Silo Support Plan (SAA)
SSP .... Simulation Support Processor
SSP .... Single-Shot Probability [*Military*]
SSP .... Single Stock Point [*Military*] (AFIT)
SSP .... Site Survey Payload (MCD)
SSP .... Size-Selective Precipitation [*Physics*]
SSP .... Skylab Student Project [*NASA*]
SSP .... Small Sortie Payload [*NASA*] (NASA)
SSP .... Society for Scholarly Publishing (EA)
SSP .... Society of Satellite Professionals [*Later, SSPI*] (EA)
SSP .... Society of St. Paul for the Apostolate of Communications [*Pauline Fathers*] [*Roman Catholic religious order*]
SSP .... Sodium Sampling Package [*Nuclear energy*] (NRCH)
SSP .... Sole Supporting Parent
SSP .... Solid-State Photodiode
SSP .... Solid-State Pneumatic
SSP .... Solid-State Preamplifier
SSP .... Solid-State Products [*Electronics*] (IAA)
SSP .... SONAR Signal Processor
SSP .... Sorghum Soy Pellet (OA)
SSP .... Source Selection Plan
SSP .... South Simpson, AK [*Location identifier FAA*] (FAAL)
SSP .... Space Shuttle Program [*NASA*] (NASA)
SSP .... Space Station Program [*NASA*] (SSD)
SSP .... Specialist in School Psychology (GAGS)
SSP .... Special Services Protection [*Telecommunications*] (TEL)
SSP .... Special Session of Peace [*Legal*] [*British*] (ROG)
SSP .... Special Studies Program [*Australia*]
SSP .... Species Survival Plans [*Program sponsored by the American Association of Zoological Parks and Aquariums to protect certain endangered species*]
SSP .... Sporozoite Surface Protein [*Biochemistry*]
SSP .... Staff Site Position [*Nuclear energy*] (NRCH)
SSP .... Stainless Steel Propeller (DS)
SSP .... Standard Shop Practice (MCD)
SSP .... Standard Stability Prediction (MCD)
SSP .... Standard Subroutine Package
SSP .... Standard Switch Panel (MCD)
SSP .... Standby Status Panel
SSP .... Starspeed Ltd. [*British ICAO designator*] (FAAC)
SSP .... State Supplementary Payment [*Department of Health and Human Services*]
SSP .... Static Sodium Pot [*Nuclear energy*] (NRCH)
SSP .... Static Spontaneous Potential (IAA)
SSP .... Statutory Sick Pay [*British*]
SSP .... Steady-State Pulse [*Telecommunications*] (IAA)
SSP .... Steam Service Pressure
SSP .... Stores Select Panel (SAA)
SSP .... Stores Stressed Platform [*Military British*]
SSP .... St. Philip's College, San Antonio, TX [*OCLC symbol*] (OCLC)
SSP .... Strategic Systems Project [*Office*] [*Navy*]
SSP .... Subacute Sclerosing Panencephalitis [*Medicine*] (DAVI)
SSP .... Submarine Scout Patrol (DMA)
SSP .... Submarine Transport [*Navy symbol Obsolete*]
SSP .... Subsatellite Point [*Telecommunications*] (TEL)
SSP .... Subsolar Point [*Aerospace*]
SSP .... Subspecies [*Also, ssp*]
S/SP .... Subsystem Software Program (MCD)
SSP .... Supersensitivity Perception
SSP .... Supervisory Surveillance Program [*DoD*]
SSP .... Supplemental Standard Practice (AAG)
SSP .... Support Software Package (MCD)
SSP .... Surgical Specialist
SSP .... Sustained Superior Performance [*Military*]
SSP .... System Safety Plan (MCD)
SSP .... System Security Plan
SSP .... System Service Program [*Computer science*] (IAA)
SSP .... System Status Panel
SSP .... System Support Processor (NITA)
SSP .... System Support Program (AFM)
SSPA .... Senescent-Soybean-Pod Agar [*Microbiology*]
SSPA .... Social Security Pensions Act [*1975*] [*British*] (DCTA)
SSPA .... Society of St. Peter Apostle (EA)
SSPA .... Solid State Phased Array (MCD)
SSPA .... Solid State Power Amplifier (DA)
SSPA .... Southern Sudanese Political Association [*Sudan*] [*Political party*] (MENA)
SSPA .... Specialist in Speech Pathology and Audiology (GAGS)
SSPA .... Student Support and Parent Awareness [*Australia*]
SSPANC .... Society of St. Peter the Apostle for Native Clergy [*Later, SSPA*] (EA)
SSPB .... Socket Screw Products Bureau [*Defunct*] (EA)
SSPB .... Swedish State Power Board [*Nuclear energy*]
SSPC .... Missionary Sisters of St. Peter Claver (TOCD)
SSPC .... Seda Speciality Packaging [*NASDAQ symbol*] (SAG)
SSPC .... Solid-State Power Controller [*NASA*]
SSPC .... Spacelab Stored Program Command [*NASA*] (MCD)
SSPC .... Steel Structures Painting Council (EA)
SSPCA .... Scottish Society of Prevention of Cruelty to Animals (DBA)
SSPCL .... System Software Package Component List (MCD)
SSPCL .... System Support Package Component List (MCD)
SSPCP .... Service-Specific Practice Cost Percentage [*Medicine*] (DMAA)
SSPCP .... Shipboard Signal Processing Control Program [*Navy*] (CAAL)
SSPCT .... Technical Library, Potash Corp. of Saskatchewan, Saskatoon, Saskatchewan [*Library symbol National Library of Canada*] (NLC)
SSPD .... Shuttle System Payload Data [*NASA*] (NASA)
SSPD .... Shuttle System Payload Definition Study [*NASA*] (NASA)
SSPD .... Shuttle System Payload Description [*NASA*] (NASA)
S/SPD .... Single Speed [*Automotive engineering*]
SSPDA .... Space Shuttle Payload Data Activity [*NASA*] (NASA)
SSPDA .... Surface Sampler Processing and Distribution Assembly
SSPDB .... Subsystem Power Distribution Box (MCD)
SSPDR .... Subsystem Preliminary Design Review
SSPDS .... Space Shuttle Payload Data Study [*NASA*] (NASA)
SSPE .... Software Spectrum [*NASDAQ symbol*] (TTSB)
SSPE .... Software Spectrum, Inc. [*NASDAQ symbol*] (SPSG)
SSPE .... Space Station Program Element [*NASA*] (SSD)
SSPE .... Subacute Sclerosing Panencephalitis [*Medicine*]
SSPE .... Support System Project Engineer
SSPF .... Signal Structure Parametric Filter [*Telecommunications*] (OA)
SSPF .... Software Support Production Facility (SSD)
SSPF .... Space Station Processing Facility [*NASA*] (SSD)
SSPF .... Structured Soy Protein Fiber [*Food industry*]
SSPFC .... Stainless Steel Plumbing Fixture Council [*Defunct*] (EA)
SSPG .... Steady State Plasma Glucose [*Medicine*] (DMAA)
SSPGSE .... Space Shuttle Program Ground Support Equipment [*NASA*] (GFGA)
SSPHS .... Society for Spanish and Portuguese Historical Studies (EA)
SSPI .... Sight System Passive Infrared [*Sensor*] [*Army*]
SSPI .... Society of Satellite Professionals International (TSSD)
SSPI .... Spectrum Signal Processing [*NASDAQ symbol*] (SAG)
SSPI .... Steady State Plasma Insulin [*Medicine*] (DMAA)
SSP-ICF .... System Support Program-Interactive Communication Feature [*Computer science*] (MHDI)
SSPIF .... Software Support Production Integration Facility (SSD)
SSPIF .... Spectrum Signal Processing [*NASDAQ symbol*] (TTSB)
SSPK .... Single Shot Probability of Kill [*Military*]
SSPL .... Saturation Sound Pressure Level
SSPL .... Solid-State Pneumatic Logic
SSPL .... Steady-State Power Level (IEEE)
SSPL .... System Support Package List (MCD)
SSPM .... Schedule Statusing and Performance Measurement (SSD)
SSPM .... Single Sideband Phase Modulation [*Telecommunications*] (IAA)
SSPM .... Single Strokes per Minute (MSA)
SSPM .... Software Standards and Procedures Manual (SSD)
SSPM .... Space Shuttle Program Manager [*NASA*] (NASA)
SSPMA .... Sump and Sewage Pump Manufacturers Association (EA)
SSPME .... Societa di San Patrizio per le Missioni Estere [*St. Patrick's Society for the Foreign Missions - SPSFM*] [*Kiltegan, County Wicklow, Republic of Ireland*] (EAIO)
SSPMO .... SONAR Systems Project Management Office
SSPN .... Satellite System for Precise Navigation [*Air Force*]
SSPN .... Ship's Stores and Profit, Navy
SSPN .... System for Precise Navigation [*Later, DNSS*] (MCD)
ssp nov .... Subspecies Nova [*New Subspecies*] [*Biology*]
SSPO .... Space Shuttle Program Office [*NASA*] (KSC)
SSPO .... Strategic Systems Project Office [*Navy*]
SSPO .... Survey of Student Personnel Objectives (EDAC)
SSPOTR .... Strategic Systems Project Office, Technical Representative [*Navy*] (DNAB)
SSPP .... POS Pilot Plant Corp., University of Saskatchewan Campus, Saskatoon, Saskatchewan [*Library symbol National Library of Canada*] (NLC)
SSPP .... Sancti Patres [*Holy Fathers*] [*Latin*]
SSPP .... Schedule Status Preprocessor (MCD)
SSPP .... Serikat Sekerdja Pamong Pradja [*Public Officials' Union*] [*Indonesia*]
SSPP .... Shan State Progressive Party [*Myanmar*] [*Political party*] (EY)
SSPP .... Society for the Study of Process Philosophies (EA)
SSPP .... Solar Sea Power Plant [*NASA*]
SSPP .... Space Station Program Participant [*NASA*] (SSD)
SSPP .... Static Strength Prediction Program [*Ergonmetrics*]
SSPP .... Subspecies [*Plural form*] [*Also, sspp*]
SSPP .... Subsynaptic Plate Perforation [*Neurophysiology*]
SSPP .... System Safety Program Plan [*Navy*]
SSPPSG .... Space Shuttle Payload Planning Steering Group [*NASA*] (NASA)
SSPQ .... Science Studies' Perception Questionnaire (AIE)
SSPR .... Subcontract Schedule and Procurement Request
SSPRO .... Space Shuttle Program Resident Office [*NASA*] (NASA)
SSpS .... Missionary Sisters Servants of the Holy Spirit (TOCD)
SSPS .... Satellite Solar Power Station [*or System*] [*NASA*]
SSPS .... Sheffield Sawmakers' Protection Society [*A union*] [*British*] (DCTA)
SSPS .... Side-to-Side Portacaval Shunt [*Medicine*] (DMAA)
SSPS .... Silver/Somatostatin Positive Structure [*Anatomy*]
SSP-S .... Single Source Processor-SIGINT [*Signal Intelligence*]
SSPS .... Small Solar-Power System [*Energy source*]
SSPS .... Solar-Based Solar Power Satellite
SSPS .... Solar Satellite Power Station
SSPS .... Solid-State Protection System [*Nuclear energy*] (IEEE)
SSPS .... Spacecraft Support Planning Section
SSPS .... Space Shuttle Program Schedule [*NASA*] (NASA)
SSPS .... Sunflower Space Power System (IAA)
SSpSdeAP ... Sister Servants of the Holy Spirit of Perpetual Adoration (TOCD)
SSPSF .... Stochastic Self-Propagating Star Formation
SSPSG .... Science and Public Policy Studies Group [*Newsletter*]
SSPSM .... Serikat Sekerdja Pabrik Sendjata dan Mesiu [*Armaments' Union*] [*Indonesia*]
SSPT .... Speech Sounds Perception Test (EDAC)
SSPTF .... Santa Susana Propulsion Test Facility [*NASA*] (NASA)

SSPTS .... Security Support Squadron
SSPTT......... Serikat Sekerdja Pos, Telegrap dan Telepon [*National Postal, Telegraph and Telephone Employees' Union*] [*Indonesia*]
SSPU .... Ship's Service Power Unit [*Navy*] (CAAL)
SSPV .... Scottish Society of Prevention of Vivisection (DBA)
SSPW .... Sun Sportswear [*NASDAQ symbol*] (TTSB)
SSPW .... Sun Sportswear, Inc. [*NASDAQ symbol*] (NQ)
SSPWB .... Studium Spraw Polskich (Wielka Brytania) [*Information Centre for Polish Affairs*] (EAIO)
SSPWR......... Small-Size Pressurized Water Reactor [*Nuclear energy*]
SSQ .... Noosa Air Sunstate Airlines [*Australia ICAO designator*] (FAAC)
SSQ .... Shell Lake, WI [*Location identifier FAA*] (FAAL)
SSQ .... Simple Sinusoidal Quantity
SSQ .... Social Science Quarterly [*A publication*] (BRI)
SSQ .... Society for Software Quality (EA)
SSQ .... Station Sick Quarters
SSQ .... Sum of the Squares (IAA)
SSR .... RADAR Picket Submarine [*Navy symbol*]
SSR .... SACEUR [*Supreme Allied Commander, Europe*] Strategic Reserve [*Army*] (NATG)
SSR .... Safe Secure Railcar [*Army*]
SSR .... Safety Services Representative [*Red Cross*]
SSR .... Saskatchewan Research Council, Saskatoon, Saskatchewan [*Library symbol National Library of Canada*] (NLC)
SSR .... SATCOM Station Reports (MCD)
SSR .... Satellite Situation Report (AAG)
SSR .... S-Band Shuttle Return (SSD)
SSR .... Schedule Shipment Record (MCD)
SSR .... Scratched Surface Recording (IAA)
SSR .... Seal Steam Regulator [*Nuclear energy*] (NRCH)
SSR .... Secondary Surveillance RADAR
SSR .... Security Services [*Vancouver Stock Exchange symbol*]
SSR .... Security Survey Report [*Nuclear energy*]
SSR .... Seek-Storm RADAR
SSR .... Selective Serotonin Re-ceptake Indicator [*Medicine*]
SSR .... Selenium Stack Rectifier
SSR .... Self-Sufficiency Ratio [*Business term*]
SSR .... Sempati Air PT [*Indonesia*] [*ICAO designator*] (FAAC)
SSR .... Separate Superheater Reactor [*Nuclear energy*]
SSR .... Shipbuilding and Ship Repair [*Department of Employment*] [*British*]
SSR .... Shop Support Request [*NASA*] (NASA)
SSR .... SIA [*Semiconductor Industry Association*] Statistical Review [*A publication*] (EAAP)
SSR .... Signal-Sequence Receptor [*Biochemistry*]
SSR .... Simple Sequence Repeat [*Genetics*]
SSR .... Simple Sequence Repeats [*Genetics*]
SSR .... Single Signal Receiver [*Telecommunications*] (IAA)
SSR .... Sink to Source Relation
SSR .... Sisters Island, AK [*Location identifier FAA*] (FAAL)
SSR .... Site Suitability Report [*Nuclear energy*] (NRCH)
SSR .... Slate-Shingle Roof [*Technical drawings*]
SSR .... Slow Strain Rate [*Tensile test*]
SSR .... Societe Suisse de Radiodiffusion et Television [*Radio and television network*] [*Switzerland*]
SSR .... Society for the Study of Reproduction (EA)
SSR .... Software Specification Review
SSR .... Solid State Relay (IEEE)
SSR .... South Staffordshire Regiment [*Military unit*] [*British*]
SSR .... Soviet Socialist Republic
SSR .... Special Scientific Report
SSR .... Special Services Request [*Travel industry*]
SSR .... Special Survey of Refrigerated Machinery [*Lloyd's Register of Shipping*] (DS)
SSR .... Specification Status Report [*Nuclear Regulatory Commission*] (GFGA)
SSR .... Spin-Stabilized Rockets
SSR .... Spotted Swine Record [*Later, National Spotted Swine Record*] (EA)
SSR .... Staff Support Room [*NASA*]
SSR .... Standby Supply Relay [*Telecommunications*] (IAA)
SSR .... Static Shift Register
SSR .... Static Squelch Range
SSR .... Station Set Requirement [*NASA*] (NASA)
SSR .... Statistical Summary Report (AAG)
SSR .... Steady-State Rate [*of production*] [*Medicine*]
SSR .... Stock Status Report
SSR .... Students for Social Responsibility (EA)
SSR .... Subsynchronous Resonance (IEEE)
SSR .... Summarized Spares Requirement
SSR .... Sum of the Squared Residuals [*Econometrics*]
SSR .... Supplemental Security Record [*Social Security Administration*] (GFGA)
SSR .... Supplementary Statement Required [*Civil Service*]
SSR .... Supply Support Request [*or Requirement*] [*Military*] (AFM)
SSR .... Support Staff Rooms (SAA)
SSR .... Surface Search RADAR (SAA)
SSR .... Surface Slip Resistance
s-sr-- .... Surinam [*MARC geographic area code Library of Congress*] (LCCP)
SSR .... Susara [*Romania*] [*Seismograph station code, US Geological Survey*] (SEIS)
SSR .... Sustained Silent Reading [*Education*] (AEE)
SSR .... Switching Selector Repeater (PDAA)
SSR .... Synchronous Stable Relaying (IEEE)
SSR .... System Status Report
SSR .... System Status Review
SSR .... System Study Requirement (AAG)
SSR .... System Subroutines (SAA)
SSR .... System Support Record
SSRA .... Scottish Squash Rackets Association (EAIO)
SSRA .... Spread Spectrum Random Access System [*Telecommunications*] (TEL)
SSRA .... System Safety Risk Analysis [*Army*]
SSRB .... Sole Source Review Board (MCD)
SSRB .... Supply Systems Redevelopment Branch [*Australian Defence Force*]
SSRBD .... Solid State RADAR Beacon Decoder (DWSG)
SSRC .... Single Sideband Reduced Carrier [*Telecommunications*] (IAA)
SSRC .... Social Science Research Center [*Mississippi State University*] [*Research center*] (RCD)
SSRC .... Social Science Research Council (EA)
SSRC .... Social Systems Research Center [*California State University, Dominguez Hills*] [*Research center*] (RCD)
SSRC .... Society for the Study of Religion and Communism (EA)
SSRC .... Structural Stability Research Council (EA)
SSRC .... Swedish Space Research Committee
SSRCA .... Super Sunfish Racing Class Association (EA)
SSRCC .... Social Sciences Research Council of Canada [*See also CCRSS*] [*Later, SSHRCC*]
SSRCR .... Suggested State Regulations for the Control of Radiation [*Nuclear Regulatory Commission*] (NRCH)
SSRD .... Secondary Surveillance RADAR Digitizer (IAA)
SSRD .... Station Set Requirements Document [*NASA*] (NASA)
SSRE .... Shear-Stress Responsive Element [*Biochemistry*]
SSRE .... Society for Social Responsibility in Engineering (EERA)
SSREIU .... Shipbuilding, Ship Repairing, and Engineering Industrial Union [*British*]
SSREX .... Canada Department of Regional Industrial Expansion [*Ministere de l'Expansion Industrielle Regionale*] Saskatoon, Saskatchewan [*Library symbol National Library of Canada*] (NLC)
SSRF .... Shell-Supported Ring Frame
SSRF .... Small-Scale Raiding Force [*Military*]
SSR-F .... Special Scientific Report - Fisheries
SSRFC .... Social Science Research Facilities Center [*University of Minnesota*] [*Research center*] (RCD)
SSRG .... Selective Service Regulations
SSRG .... Simple Shift Register Generator
SSRH .... General Constituency Section for Small or Rural Hospitals (EA)
SSRI .... Selective Serotonin Re-uptake Inhibitor [*Antidepressant*]
SSRI .... Social Science Research Institute [*University of Maine at Orono*] [*Research center*] (RCD)
SSRI .... Social Science Research Institute [*of CRESS*] [*University of Hawaii at Manoa*] [*Research center*] (RDA)
SSRI .... Social Systems Research Institute [*University of Wisconsin - Madison*] [*Research center*] (RCD)
SSRI .... Specific Serotonin Reuptake Inhibitor [*Antidepressant*]
SSRL .... Stanford Synchrotron Radiation Laboratory [*Stanford, CA*] [*Department of Energy*]
SSRL .... Systems Simulation Research Laboratory
SSRM .... Sealectro Small Reliable Miniature (IAA)
SSRM .... Second-Stage Rocket Motor
SSRMS .... Space Station Remote Manipulator System [*NASA*] (SSD)
SSRN .... RADAR Picket Submarine (Nuclear Powered) [*Navy symbol Obsolete*]
SSRN .... Service Shop Requirement Notice
SSRN .... System Software Reference Number [*NASA*] (NASA)
SSRNJ .... Socijalisticka Savez Radnog Naroda Jugoslavije [*Socialist Alliance of Working People of Yugoslavia - SAWPY*] [*Political party*] (PPE)
SSRO .... Sector Scan Receive Only [*Military*] (LAIN)
SSRP .... Single Shot Kill Probability (MCD)
SSRP .... Somali Socialist Revolutionary Party
SSRP .... Stanford Synchrotron Radiation Project
SSRP .... Structure-Specific Recognition Protein [*Biochemistry*]
SSRPOS .... Space Station Rendezvous and Proximity Operations Simulator [*NASA*] (SSD)
SSRQ .... Steep-Spectrum Radio Quasar [*Galaxy*]
SSRR .... Social Service Reporting Requirements [*HEW*]
SSRR .... Station Set Requirements Review [*NASA*] (NASA)
SSRR .... System Software Requirement Review (MCD)
SSRS .... SIGINT Surveillance and Reporting System (MCD)
SSRS .... Society for Social Responsibility in Science (EA)
SSRS .... Source Storage and Retrieval System [*Computer science*] (MHDI)
SSRS .... Start-Stop-Restart System [*NASA*] (KSC)
SSRS .... Submarine Sand Recovery System
SSRSB .... Safety and Special Radio Services Bureau [*of FCC*]
SSRSJC .... Saudi-Sudanese Red Sea Joint Commission [*Commercial firm Jeddah, Saudi Arabia*] (EAIO)
SSRT .... Slow Strain Rate Technique [*Nuclear energy*] (NUCP)
SSRT .... Subsystem Readiness Test (KSC)
SSRTP .... Solid Substrate Room Temperature Phosphorescence
SS-RTP .... Solid-Surface, Room-Temperature Phosphorescence [*Physics*]
SSRU .... Scottish Schools Rugby Union (AIE)
SSS .... Compania de Servicios Aereos SA [*Spain ICAO designator*] (FAAC)
sss .... Congregation of the Blessed Sacrament (TOCD)
SSS .... Congregation of the Blessed Sacrament (TOCD)
SSS .... Safeguard Spartan System [*Aerospace*] (MCD)
SSS .... San Salvador [*El Salvador*] [*Seismograph station code, US Geological Survey*] (SEIS)
SSS .... Satellite Surveillance System (MCD)
SSS .... Satellite Syndicated Systems [*Douglasville, GA*] [*Cable TV programming service*] [*Telecommunications*]
SSS .... Sauna - Swimming Pool - Storage Area [*Key fitting those locks in apartment complex*]

SSS .... Scalded Skin Syndrome [*Medicine*] (MAE)
SSS .... Scaled Skin Syndrome [*Dermatology*] (DAVI)
SSS .... Scandinavian Surgical Society (EAIO)
SSS .... Scene Storage System (MCD)
SSS .... School of Social Studies [*British*]
SSS .... Scientific Subroutine System [*Computer science*] (BUR)
SSS .... Sea Surface Salinity
SSS .... Secondary Sampling System [*Nuclear energy*] (NRCH)
S/SS .... Sector/Subsector
SSS .... Selective Service System
SSS .... Selective Service System (USGC)
SSS .... Self-Service Store
SSS .... Self-Shifting Synchronizing (PDAA)
SSS .... Semitic Study Series [*A publication*] (BJA)
SSS .... Senior Service School [*Military*] (AFM)
SSS .... Sensitized Stainless Steel (NRCH)
SSS .... Sentinel-Spartan System (MCD)
SSS .... Sequential Scheduling System (IAA)
SSS .... Serial Signalling Scheme (PDAA)
SSS .... Servants of the Blessed Sacrament (TOCD)
SSS .... Shevchenko Scientific Society (EA)
SSS .... Shield and Seismic Support [*Nuclear energy*] (NRCH)
SSS .... Shift Ship Superintendent [*Navy*] (DNAB)
SSS .... Ship's Service Stores
SSS .... Ship Stamp Society [*British*] (DBA)
SSS .... Shnat Sherut Scheme (BJA)
SSS .... Shore Signal Service [*British Royal Navy*]
SSS .... Siassi [*Papua New Guinea*] [*Airport symbol*] (OAG)
SSS .... Sick Sinus Syndrome [*Medicine*]
SSS .... Signal Switching System
SSS .... Signature Security Service [*DoD*]
SSS .... Silicon-Symmetrical Switch (CET)
SSS .... Simplified Spelling Society (EA)
SSS .... Simulation Study Series (KSC)
SSS .... Single Screw Ship
SSS .... Single Signal Superhet (IAA)
SSS .... Single Signal Supersonic [*Heterodyne*] (DEN)
SSS .... Sisters of Social Service [*Roman Catholic religious order*]
SSS .... Sisters of Social Service of Los Angeles, Inc. (TOCD)
SSS .... Site Security Supervisor (AFM)
SSS .... Skills Support System [*Education*]
SSS .... Small Scientific Satellite [*NASA*]
SSS .... Small Solar Satellite [*NASA*]
SSS .... Small Starlight Scope [*Light-intensifying device*]
SSS .... Small Structures Survey [*Civil Defense*]
SSS .... Social Science Series [*A publication*]
SSS .... Social Status Study [*Psychology*]
SSS .... Societas Sanctissimi Sacramenti [*Congregation of the Blessed Sacrament*] [*Roman Catholic men's religious order*]
SSS .... Societe Scandinave de Simulation [*Scandinavian Simulation Society*] [*Finland*] (EAIO)
SSS .... Society for Slovene Studies (EA)
SSS .... Society for Socialist Studies [*See also SES*] [*Canada*]
SSS .... Society for the Second Self (EA)
SSS .... Society for the Suppression of Speculative Stamps [*Defunct*]
SSS .... Society of St. Stephen (EA)
SSS .... Sodium Styrenesulfonate [*Organic chemistry*]
SSS .... Software/Segment Specification
SSS .... Software Service System [*Anti-piracy device invented by Ryoichi Mori of the Japan Electronics Industry Development Association*] (BYTE)
SSS .... Software Specification Sheet [*Computer science*] (IAA)
SSS .... Software Staging Section [*Social Security Administration*]
SSS .... Solid-State Scientific (IAA)
SSS .... Solid-State Spectrometer
SSS .... Solid-State Switching (NG)
SSS .... Solid-State System
SSS .... SONAR Signal Simulator
SSS .... Sortie Support System (MCD)
SSS .... Sound Suppression System (NASA)
SSS .... Southern Satellite Systems, Inc. [*Tulsa, OK*] [*Telecommunications*] (TSSD)
SSS .... Sovran Self Storage [*NYSE symbol*] (TTSB)
SSS .... Sovran Self Storage, Inc. [*NYSE symbol*] (SAG)
SSS .... Spacecraft System Support
SSS .... Space Settlers' Society [*Defunct*] (EAIO)
SSS .... Space Shuttle Simulation [*NASA*]
SSS .... Space Shuttle System [*NASA*] (KSC)
SSS .... Space Station Simulator
SSS .... Space Surveillance System [*Navy*] (MCD)
SSS .... Special Safeguards Study [*Nuclear energy*] (NRCH)
SSS .... Special Safety Safeguards (NRCH)
SSS .... Special Security Squadron
SSS .... Special Source Survey (AAGC)
SSS .... Special Support Services
SSS .... Specific Soluble Substance [*Polysaccharide hapten*]
SSS .... Speed-Sensitive Steering [*Automotive engineering*]
SSS .... Spinning Space Station
SSS .... Spin-Stabilized Spacecraft
SSS .... Stability and Safety Screening [*Sailing terminology*]
SSS .... Stabilized Sighting System
SSS .... Staff Summary Sheet (MCD)
SSS .... Stage Separation Subsystem [*NASA*] (NASA)
SSS .... Stainless Steel Sink [*Classified advertising*] (ADA)
SSS .... Standard Scratch Score [*Golf*]
SSS .... Standard Seawater Service [*British*]
SSS .... Standard Supply System [*Army*] (AABC)
SSS .... Stanford Sleepiness Scale
SSS .... Starlight Scope [*Night sighting device*] [*Military*] (VNW)
SSS .... State Supply Service [*Victoria, Australia*]
SSS .... Station Set Specification [*NASA*] (NASA)
SSS .... Stepping Switch Scanner
SSS .... Sterile Saline Soak
SSS .... Stockholders Sovereignty Society [*Later, FFSR*] (EA)
SSS .... STOL Support Ship [*Navy*] (CAAL)
SSS .... Storage Serviceability Standard [*Army*]
SSS .... Strategic Satellite System (MCD)
SSS .... Strategic Studies Staff [*Environmental Protection Agency*] (GFGA)
SSS .... Strategic Support Squadron [*Air Force*]
SSS .... Stratum Super Stratum [*Layer Over Layer*] [*Latin*]
SSS .... Strike Support Ship [*Navy*] (NVT)
SSS .... Strong Soap Solution
SSS .... Structures Subsystem (KSC)
SSS .... Student Support Services Program [*Department of Education*] (GFGA)
SSS .... Study Skills Surveys [*Educational test*]
SSS .... Subjective Stress Scale
SSS .... Subject Specialists Section [*Association of College and Research Libraries*]
SSS .... Subscribers' Switching Subsystem [*Telecommunications*] (TEL)
SSS .... Substructure Search System [*Later, SANSS*] [*NIH/EPA*]
SSS .... Subsystem Segment [*NASA*] (NASA)
SSS .... Subsystem Support Service (BUR)
SSS .... Sunday Shakespeare Society [*British*]
SSS .... Superior Shore Systems [*An association*] (EA)
SSS .... Supply Screening Section [*Navy*]
SSS .... Survivable Satellite System (MCD)
SSS .... Symbolic Shorthand System
SSS .... System Safety Society (EA)
SSS .... System Segment Specification (MCD)
SSS .... Systems, Science, and Software
SSS .... Trois Fois Salut [*Thrice Greeting*] [*Freemasonry*] [*French*] (ROG)
SSSA .... Scottish Salmon Smokers Association (DBA)
SSSA .... Self-Service Storage Association [*Later, SSA*] (EA)
SSSA .... Soil Science Society of America (EA)
SSSA .... Sotos Syndrome Support Association (EA)
SSSA .... St. Andrew's College, Saskatoon, Saskatchewan [*Library symbol National Library of Canada*] (NLC)
SSSA .... Submarine SONAR Subjective Analysis (NVT)
SSSAS .... Society of Spanish and Spanish-American Studies (EA)
SSSAS .... Space Station Systems Analysis Study [*NASA*] (SSD)
SSSB .... Society for the Study of Social Biology (EA)
SSSB .... System Source Selection Board [*Air Force*]
SSSBCR .... Star, Starling, Stuart, and Briton Car Register (EA)
SSSBP .... System Source Selection Board Procedure [*Air Force*]
SSSC .... Self-Service Supply Center [*Military*] (AFIT)
SSSC .... Single Sideband Suppressed Carrier
SSSC .... Soft-Sized Super-Calendered [*Paper*]
SSSC .... Solid-State Sciences Committee [*National Research Council*] [*Physics*]
SSSC .... Space Science Steering Committee
SSSC .... Space Station Support Center [*NASA*] (SSD)
SSSC .... Special Spectrum Study Committee
SSSC .... Stainless Steel Sink Council [*Defunct*] (EA)
SSSC .... Surface/Subsurface Control [*Navy*] (CAAL)
SSSC .... Surface/Subsurface Surveillance Center [*Navy*] (NVT)
SSSC .... Surface/Subsurface Surveillance Coordinator [*Navy*]
SSSCP .... Single Supply Support Control Point (MCD)
SSSD .... Second-Stage Separation Device
SSSD .... Single-Sided, Single-Density Disk [*Magnetic disk*] [*Computer science*]
SSSD .... Solid-State Solenoid Driver
SSSD .... Space Shuttle Simulation Display [*NASA*]
SSSEDA .... Aerospace Products Division, SED Systems Ltd., Saskatoon, Saskatchewan [*Library symbol National Library of Canada*] (NLC)
SSSERC .... Scottish Schools Science Equipment Research Centre (CB)
SSSF .... School Sisters of St. Francis (TOCD)
SSSF .... Stationary Source Simulator Facility [*Environmental science*]
SSSG .... SLCM [*Sea-Launched Cruise Missile*] Survivability Steering Group [*Navy*] (CAAL)
SSSI .... Kelsey Institute of Applied Arts and Sciences, Saskatoon, Saskatchewan [*Library symbol National Library of Canada*] (NLC)
SSSI .... Siegel Scale of Support for Innovation (DMAA)
SSSI .... Site of Special Scientific Interest [*British*]
SSSI .... Society for the Study of Symbolic Interaction (EA)
SSSI .... Special Steel Summary Invoice [*International Trade Administration*]
SSSI .... Steel Scaffolding and Shoring Institute [*Later, SSFI*] (EA)
SSSJ .... Single Subsonic Jet
SSSJ .... Student Struggle for Soviet Jewry (EA)
SSSL .... Society for the Study of Southern Literature (EA)
SSSL .... Supersonic Split Line (KSC)
SSSLF .... South Slavonian Socialist Labor Federation [*Defunct*] (EA)
SSSM .... Site Space Surveillance Monitor (AFM)
SSSM .... South Street Seaport Museum (EA)
SSSM .... Subset-Specified Sequential Machine [*Air Force*]
SSSM .... Systems Support Service Module (SSD)
SSSMC .... Sports Science and Sports Medicine Centre [*Australia*]
SSSMP .... Surface Ship SONAR Moderization Program (MCD)
SSSN .... Secondary Social Security Number
S/S/SN .... System/Subsystem/Subject Number (MCD)
SSSO .... Specialized Satellite Service Operators [*British*]

SSSO .... Specialized Surplus Sales Office [*Military*]
SSSP .... Secondary School Science Project [*Princeton University*] (AEE)
SSSP .... Society for the Study of Social Problems (EA)
SSSP .... Space Settlement Studies Program (EA)
SSSP .... Space Shuttle Synthesis Program [*National Academy of Sciences*]
SSSP .... Station to Station Send Paid [*Telecommunications*] (TEL)
SSSP .... System Source Selection Procedure [*Air Force*]
SSSQ .... McCarron-Dial Street Survival Skills Questionnaire [*Occupational therapy*]
SS/SR .... Safety Standdown/Safety Review (MCD)
SSSR .... SAGE [*Semiautomatic Ground Environment*] System Status Report
SSSR .... Smallest Set of Smallest Rings [*Organic chemistry*]
SSSR .... Social Sciences Services and Resources (EA)
SSSR .... Society for the Scientific Study of Religion (EA)
SSSR .... Soyuz Sovetskikh Sotsialisticheskikh Respublik [*Union of Soviet Socialist Republics*]
SSSR .... Syracuse Scales of Social Relations [*Education*]
SSSS .... Shallow Spherical Sandwich Shell
SSSS .... Society for the Scientific Study of Sex (EA)
SSSS .... Spaceborne Software Systems Study (DNAB)
SSSS .... Space Shuttle System Segment (MCD)
SSSS .... Space Shuttle System Specification [*NASA*] (NASA)
SSSS .... Space Systems Support Squadron
SSSS .... Staphylococcal Scalded Skin Syndrome [*Medicine*]
SSSS .... Stewart & Stevenson [*NASDAQ symbol*] (TTSB)
SSSS .... Stewart & Stevenson Services, Inc. [*NASDAQ symbol*] (NQ)
SSSSC .... Surface/Subsurface Surveillance Coordinator [*Navy*] (CAAL)
SSSSS .... Searched, Silenced, Safeguarded, Segregated, and Sped Out of the Area [*US POW hadling practice*] (VNW)
SSSST .... Subscale Subsonic Targets (MCD)
SSST .... S-Band Spread Spectrum Transponder (MCD)
SSST .... Simulated Social Skills Training (AIE)
SSST .... Site Suitability Source Term [*Nuclear energy*] (NRCH)
SSST .... Solid-State Silicon Target
SSST .... Space Station Simulator Trainee [*or Trainer*] [*NASA*] (SSD)
SSST .... Spectroscopic Survey Telescope [*Proposed*] [*Joint project of the University of Texas and Pennsylvania State University*]
SSStJ .... Serving Sister, Order of St. John of Jerusalem [*British*]
SSSU .... Scottish Speed Skating Union (DBA)
SSSV .... Superior Sagittal Sinus Blood Velocity [*Medicine*] (AAMN)
SSSW .... Surface/Subsurface Warfare [*Navy*] (CAAL)
SST .... Missionary Society of St. Thomas the Apostle (TOCD)
sst .... Missionary Society of St. Thomas the Apostle (TOCD)
SST .... Safe Secure Trailer [*For transporting nuclear materials*]
SST .... Safe Separate/Timing (CINC)
SST .... Sample Sound Technology [*Computer science*]
SST .... Saskatchewan Teachers' Federation Saskatoon, Saskatchewan [*Library symbol National Library of Canada*] (NLC)
SST .... Satellite Servicing Technology (SSD)
SST .... Satellite-to-Satellite Tracking
SST .... Saturated Suction Temperature [*Refrigeration*]
SST .... Saturn Systems Test [*NASA*]
SST .... Scroll Symbolic Tracer (IAA)
SST .... Seaplane Shuttle Transport [*New York-Philadelphia air-link*]
SST .... Sea Surface Temperature [*Oceanography*]
SST .... Secondary Surge Tank [*Nuclear energy*] (NRCH)
SST .... Semi-Submerged Trimaran [*Tri-hull ship design invented by Calvin Gongwer*]
SST .... Serviceability Self-Test (MCD)
SST .... Set Strobe Time [*Computer science*] (OA)
SST .... Shelter Components Corp. [*AMEX symbol*] (SPSG)
SST .... Shipboard [*Weapon*] Suitability Test [*Navy*] (NG)
SST .... Ships Service Turbine (MCD)
SST .... Shore Survey Team (DNAB)
SST .... Sideways-Spinning Tube [*Spectrometry*]
SST .... Sight, Sound, and Touch [*Ways to identify proper belt tension*] [*Automotive engineering*]
SST .... Silicon Storage Technology (PCM)
SST .... Silver Sceptre Resources [*Vancouver Stock Exchange symbol*]
SST .... Simulated Structural Test (KSC)
SST .... Single Sideband Transmission [*Telecommunications*] (TEL)
SST .... Single Step (IAA)
SST .... Single Subscriber Terminal [*Army*] (RDA)
SST .... Single Systems Trainer [*NASA*] (MCD)
SST .... Slide, Script, and Tape
SST .... Social Security Tax Ruling [*Internal Revenue Bulletin*] [*A publication*] (DLA)
SST .... Society for the Study of Theology [*British*]
SST .... Society of Surveying Technicians (EAIO)
SST .... Software Sciences Teleordering (NITA)
SST .... Solid-State Technology (IAA)
SST .... Solid-State Transmitter (MCD)
SST .... SONAR Signaling (NVT)
SST .... Source Selection Team (AAGC)
SST .... Soviet Science and Technology [*IFI/Plenum Data Corp.*] [*Information service or system*] (IID)
SST .... Spacecraft System Test [*NASA*]
SST .... Space Selector Terminal (SAA)
SST .... Space Surveillance Technology
SST .... Special Strike Teletype (NATG)
SST .... Spectroscopic Survey Telescope [*Proposed*] [*Joint project of the University of Texas and Pennsylvania State University*]
SST .... Split Second Timing
SST .... Stainless Steel
SST .... Station Service Transformer [*Nuclear energy*] (NRCH)
SS/T .... Steady-State/Transient Analysis [*Nuclear energy*] (NRCH)
SST .... Step-by-Step Test (IAA)
SST .... Stiffened Super-Tough [*Polymer technology*]
SST .... Stock Size Template (MCD)
SST .... Stream Support Team (MCD)
SST .... Structural Static Test [*NASA*] (NASA)
SST .... Student Science Training [*Program*] [*National Science Foundation*] [*Defunct*]
SST .... Subject Standardized Test
SST .... Submarine Scout Twin-Type [*British military*] (DMA)
SST .... Subscriber Transferred [*Telecommunications*] (TEL)
SST .... Subsystems Test (KSC)
SST .... Subsystem Terminal on Spacelab [*NASA*] (MCD)
SST .... Sunwest Airlines Ltd. [*Canada ICAO designator*] (FAAC)
SST .... Superficial Spreading Type (Melanoma) [*Oncology*]
SST .... SuperSerial Technology [*Equinox Systems, Inc.*] [*Telecommunications*]
SST .... Super Show & Tell [*Ask Me Multimedia Center software*] [*Computer science*] (PCM)
SST .... Super Smoothing Technology [*Apple Computer, Inc.*]
SS/T .... Supersonic Telegraphy [*British military*] (DMA)
SST .... Supersonic Transport
SST .... Super Surface Treatment (IAA)
SST .... Supplementary Service Tariff [*British*] (DCTA)
SST .... Susitna [*Alaska*] [*Seismograph station code, US Geological Survey Closed*] (SEIS)
SST .... Synchronous System Trap
SST .... System Segment Table
SST .... Systems Support Tape
SST .... System Survey Team [*Military*] (AFIT)
SST .... Target and Training Submarine [*Self-propelled*] [*Navy symbol*]
SST .... Training Submarine [*Navy symbol*]
SSTA .... Scottish Secondary Teachers' Association (DI)
SSTA .... Sea-Service Temperature Anomaly [*Marine science*] (OSRA)
SSTA .... Secondary School Theatre Association [*Defunct*] (EA)
SSTA .... Support System Task Analysis (AAG)
SSTADS .... Small Ship Typhoon Air Defense System (MCD)
SSTAR .... Society for Sex Therapy and Research (EA)
SSTC .... Secondary School Theatre Conference [*Later, SSTA*] (EA)
SSTC .... Ship System Test Contractor (MCD)
SSTC .... Single-Sideband Transmitted Carrier (IEEE)
SSTC .... Solid-State Timer-Controller
SSTC .... Spacecraft System Test Console [*NASA*]
SSTC .... Space Shuttle Test Conductor [*NASA*] (NASA)
SSTC .... Specialized System Test Contractor
SSTC .... State Science and Technology Commission [*China*]
SSTC .... Summary of Supplemental Type Certificates
SSTCWN .... Specifications Subject to Change without Notice
SSTD .... Solid State Track Detector [*Instrumentation*]
SSTD .... Surface Ship Torpedo Defense [*Navy*] (CAAL)
SSTDC .... Society of Stage Directors and Choreographers (EA)
SST-DMA .... Satellite Switched Time Division Multiple Access
SSTDMA .... Satellite Switched Time Division Multiple Access (NITA)
SSTDMA .... Spacecraft Switched Time Division Multiple Access [*Telecommunications*]
SS/TDMA .... Spread Spectrum/Time Division Multiple Access (MCD)
SSTDS .... Small Ship Tactical Data System [*Navy*] (CAAL)
SSTEP .... System Support Test Evaluation Program
SSTF .... Saturn Static Test Facility [*NASA*]
SSTF .... Shortest Seek Time First
SSTF .... Space Shuttle Task Force [*NASA*]
SSTF .... Space Simulation Test Facility (AAG)
SSTF .... Space Station Task Force [*NASA*]
SSTF .... Space Station Training Facility [*NASA*] (SSD)
SSTF .... Subject Summary Table File [*US Census Bureau*]
SSTG .... Ship Service Turbo Generator (MSA)
SSTG .... Space Shuttle Task Group [*NASA*] (KSC)
SSTG .... Special Service Training Group [*World War II*]
SSTI .... Serikat Sekerdja Topografi Indonesia [*Indonesian Topography Employees' Union*]
SSTI .... Silicon Storage Tech [*NASDAQ symbol*] (TTSB)
SSTI .... Silicon Storage Technology, Inc. [*NASDAQ symbol*] (SAG)
SSTIR .... Sea Surface Temperature Imaging Radiometer
SSTIXS .... Small Ship Teletype Information Exchange System [*or Subsystem*] (MCD)
SSTL .... Sector System Training Leader (SAA)
SSTL .... Solid State Track Link [*TOW*] (MCD)
SSTLA .... Strip Shunt Transmission Line Antenna [*Aviation*] (AIA)
SSTM .... SAGE [*Semiautomatic Ground Environment*] System Training Mission
SSTM .... Single Service Training Manager (MCD)
SSTM .... Solid-State Target Monoscope (PDAA)
SSTM .... System Support Technical Manager [*Navy*] (NG)
SSTMS .... Standard Supply Transportation Manifest System
SSTN .... Sandostain [*Antineoplastic drug*] (CDI)
SSTO .... Second-Stage Tail Off (IAA)
SSTO .... Single Stage to Orbit [*NASA*]
SSTO .... Superintending Sea Transport Officer [*British military*] (DMA)
SSTP .... Software Support Transition Plan [*Army*]
SSTP .... Student Science Training Program [*National Science Foundation Defunct*]
SSTP .... Subsystems Test Procedure (KSC)
SSTP .... Supersonic Transport Panel [*International Civil Aviation Organization*]
SSTR .... Senior Staff Technical Representative (MCD)
s str .... Sensu Stricto [*In a Narrow Sense*] [*Latin*] (MAE)

SSTR .... Solid-State Track Recorder (PDAA)
SSTRA .... Successive Subtraction with Total Recognition Accuracy [*Algorithm*]
SSTS .... School Student Transport Scheme [*Australia*]
SSTS .... Sight Switch Technology System (PDAA)
SSTS .... Signaling and Supervision Techniques Study
SSTS .... Solid State Transfer Switch
SSTS .... Space Surveillance and Tracking System [*Military*]
SSTS .... Sub-System Technical Specification
SSTT .... Specialized Systems Test Teams (SAA)
SSTT .... Subsea Test Tree (PDAA)
SST-T-T .... Sound, Sense, Today, Tomorrow, Thereafter [*Teacher's Guide, published by Department of Transportation, for promoting supersonic travel*]
SSTU .... SAGE [*Semiautomatic Ground Environment*] System Training Unit
SSTU .... Seamless Steel Tubing
SSTV .... Congregation of Sisters of St. Thomas of Villanova [*Roman Catholic religious order*]
SSTV .... Sea Skimming Test Vehicles
SSTV .... Slow-Scan Television
SSTV .... Submarine Shock Test Vehicle
SStW .... Synoptische Studien fuer A. Wikenhauser [*1953*] [*A publication*] (BJA)
SSU .... Safety Sequence Unit (MCD)
SSU .... Sangamon State University (PDAA)
SSU .... San Pedro Sula [*Honduras*] [*Seismograph station code, US Geological Survey*] (SEIS)
SSU .... Saybolt Seconds Universal [*Oil viscosity*]
SSU .... Self-Service Unit
SSU .... Semiconductor Storage Unit [*Computer science*]
SSU .... Sensor Simulator Unit
SSU .... Sight Survey Unit
SSU .... Signal Summing Unit [*Aviation*]
SSU .... Single Signaling Unit [*Telecommunications*] (TEL)
SSU .... Small Subunit [*Genetics*]
SSU .... Solvent Service Unit
SSU .... Source Resources Ltd. [*Vancouver Stock Exchange symbol*]
SSU .... Spacecraft Support Unit
SSU .... Special Service Unit [*Military*]
SSU .... Species Services Unit [*of the Bureau of Meteorology*] (EERA)
SSU .... Squadron Service Unit [*Aircraft*]
SSU .... Stabilized Sight Unit (MCD)
SSU .... Standard Saybolt Universal [*Oil viscosity*]
SSU .... Statistical Service Unit [*Military*]
SSU .... Sterile Supply Unit (MAE)
SSU .... Strategic Services Unit [*Formerly, OSS*]
SSU .... Stratospheric Sounding Unit [*Telecommunications*] (TEL)
SSU .... Study Skills Unit (AIE)
SSU .... Subscriber Switching Unit [*Telecommunications*] (TEL)
SSU .... Subsequent Signal Unit [*Group of BITS*] [*Telecommunications*] (TEL)
SSU .... Sunday School Union
SSU .... Surface Screen Unit [*Navy*] (NVT)
SSU .... Switch Selector Update
SSU .... System Selector Unit
SSU .... System Support Unification (MCD)
SSU .... University of Saskatchewan, Saskatoon, Saskatchewan [*Library symbol National Library of Canada*] (NLC)
SSU .... White Sulphur Springs, WV [*Location identifier FAA*] (FAAL)
SSUEM .... Uranerz Exploration & Mining Ltd., Saskatoon, Saskatchewan [*Library symbol National Library of Canada*] (NLC)
SSUFT .... Single Station Unit Fielding Training [*Air Force*] [*Navy*] (DOMA)
SSUGP .... Government Publications, University of Saskatchewan, Saskatoon, Saskatchewan [*Library symbol National Library of Canada*] (NLC)
SSUIS .... Space Station User Information System [*NASA*] (SSD)
SSUJD .... [*The*] Right Honourable John G. Diefenbaker Centre, University of Saskatchewan, Saskatoon, Saskatchewan [*Library symbol National Library of Canada*] (NLC)
SSUL .... Law Library, University of Saskatchewan, Saskatoon, Saskatchewan [*Library symbol National Library of Canada*] (NLC)
SSULS .... Lutheran Seminary, University of Saskatchewan, Saskatoon, Saskatchewan [*Library symbol National Library of Canada*] (NLC)
SSUM .... Medical Library, University of Saskatchewan, Saskatoon, Saskatchewan [*Library symbol National Library of Canada*] (NLC)
SSUMC .... Ukrainian Museum of Canada, Saskatoon, Saskatchewan [*Library symbol National Library of Canada*] (NLC)
SSURADS .... Shipboard Surveillance RADAR System (MCD)
SSURO .... Stop Sale, Use and Removal Order [*Environmental Protection Agency*] (GFGA)
SSUS .... Spinning Solid Upper Stage (RDA)
SSUS .... Spin-Stabilized Upper Stage [*NASA*] (NASA)
SSUS .... System Support Unification Subsystem (MCD)
SSUSA .... Special Staff, United States Army
SSUS-A .... Spinning Solid Upper Stage - Atlas Class Spacecraft (MCD)
SSUS-D .... Spinning Solid Upper Stage - Delta Class Spacecraft (MCD)
SSUSN .... Society of Sponsors of the United States Navy (EA)
SSUSP .... Spinning Solid Upper Stage Project (MCD)
SSUTC .... Special Service Unit Training Center [*World War II*]
SSV .... Satellite Servicing Vehicle
SSV .... Schoolman-Schwartz Virus [*Medicine*] (DMAA)
SSV .... Seraphic Society for Vocations [*Defunct*] (EA)
SSV .... Sheep Seminal Vesicle
SSV .... Ship-to-Surface Vessel
SSV .... Simian Sarcoma Virus [*Also, SiSV*]
SSV .... Skyservice FBO, Inc. [*Canada*] [*FAA designator*] (FAAC)
SSV .... Small Synaptic Vesicle [*Neurobiology*]
SSV .... Space Shuttle Vehicle [*NASA*]
SSV .... Spastic Society of Victoria [*Australia*]
SSV .... Special Surveillance Vehicle [*Navy*] (DNAB)
SSV .... Spool Selector Valve
SSV .... SPRINT [*Solid-Propellant Rocket Intercept*] Service Vehicle [*Army*]
SSV .... Static Self-Verification
SSV .... Subjective Scale Value
SSV .... Sub Signo Veneni [*Under a Poison Label*] [*Pharmacy*]
SSV .... Sumac Ventures, Inc. [*Vancouver Stock Exchange symbol*]
SSV .... Supersatellite Vehicle
SSV .... Supersonic Test Vehicles
SSV .... Sydslesvigsk Vaelgerforening [*South Schleswig Voters' Association*] [*Also, SSW*] [*Germany*] [*Political party*] (PPW)
SSVA .... Signal Susceptibility and Vulnerability Assessment [*Military*] (CAAL)
SSVC .... Selective Service [*Military*]
SSVC .... Services Sound and Video Corp. [*British*]
SSVE .... Subacute Spongiform Virus Encephalopathies [*Medicine*]
SSVF .... Straits Settlements Volunteer Force [*British military*] (DMA)
SSV/GC & N... Space Shuttle Vehicle/Guidance, Control, and Navigation [*NASA*]
SSVM .... Self-Scaling Variable Metric [*Algorithms*] [*Computer science*]
SSVN .... Subsystem and Vehicle Number (SAA)
SSVP .... Society of St. Vincent De Paul [*Paris, France*] (EAIO)
SSVP .... Soviet Ship Vulnerability Program
SSVS .... Slow-Scan Video Simulator
SSVS .... Super Smart Vehicle System [*FHWA*] (TAG)
SSV-SSAV .... Simian Sarcoma Virus-Simian Sarcoma Associated Virus [*Complex*]
SSW .... Safety Switch
SSW .... Save the Strippers Wells (EA)
SSW .... Scramble Status and Weather (SAA)
SSW .... Secretary of State for War [*British*]
SSW .... Senior Social Worker (ADA)
SSW .... Sense Switch [*Military*] (AFIT)
SSW .... Shipboard Safety Watch [*Navy*] (DNAB)
SSW .... Siemens-Schuckert Werke [*Germany*]
SSW .... Solid-State Welding
SSW .... South by South West (EERA)
SSW .... South-Southwest
SSW .... Space Support Wing [*Military*]
SSW .... Space Switch [*Telecommunications*] (TEL)
SSW .... Staggered Spondaic Word
SSW .... Staggered Spondiac World Test [*Speech and language therapy*] (DAVI)
SSW .... Standby Service Water [*Nuclear energy*] (NRCH)
SSW .... Sterling Software [*NYSE symbol*] (TTSB)
SSW .... Sterling Software, Inc. [*NYSE symbol*] (SPSG)
SSW .... St. Louis Southwestern Railway Co. [*AAR code*]
SSW .... Sudden Stratospheric Warming (EERA)
SSW .... Suedschleswigscher Waehlerverband [*South Schleswig Voter's League*] [*Also, SSV*] [*Germany*] [*Political party*] (PPE)
SSW .... Support Software (MCD)
SSW .... Surface Science Western [*University of Western Ontario*] [*Research center*] (RCD)
SSW .... Surface Strike Warfare [*Navy*] (CAAL)
SSW .... Swept Square Wave (MCD)
SSW .... Synchro Switch [*Electronics*]
SSW .... Systems West Consultants Ltd. [*Vancouver Stock Exchange symbol*]
SSW .... Wheatland Regional Library, Saskatoon, Saskatchewan [*Library symbol National Library of Canada*] (NLC)
SSWA .... Sanitary Supply Wholesalers Association (EA)
SSWA .... Scottish Society of Women Artists (DBA)
SSWAM .... Single-Sided Wideband Analog Modulation [*Telecommunications*] (IAA)
SSWC .... Surface/Subsurface Warfare Coordinator [*Navy*] (CAAL)
SSWD .... Single, Separated, Widowed, or Divorced
SSWD .... Western Development Museum, Saskatoon, Saskatchewan [*Library symbol National Library of Canada*] (NLC)
SSWF .... Sudden Shortwave Fade
SSWG .... Supplementary Strategies Working Group (EERA)
SSWG .... System Safety Working Group
SSWLH .... Society for the Study of Women in Legal History (EA)
SSWM .... Standing Spin Wave Mode (MCD)
SSWM .... Superimposed Surface Wave Modes
SSWO .... Special Service Work Order [*Telecommunications*] (TEL)
SSWP .... Space Station Work Package [*NASA*] (SSD)
SSWP .... Station Service Water Pump [*Nuclear energy*] (NRCH)
SSWS .... Standby Service Water System [*Nuclear energy*] (NRCH)
SSWU .... Singapore Sawmill Workers' Union
SSWWS .... Seismic Sea-Wave Warning System
SSX .... Samsun [*Turkey*] [*Airport symbol*] (OAG)
SSX .... Small Systems Executive (IAA)
SSX .... Space Ship Experimental
SSX .... SS1 [*Nevada*] [*Seismograph station code, US Geological Survey Closed*] (SEIS)
SSX .... Submarines, Experimental
SSX .... Sulfisoxazole [*An antibiotic*]
SSX .... Supplementary Service Exchange (NITA)
SSXBT .... Submarine Expendable Bathythermograph [*Marine science*] (MSC)
SSY .... M'Banza Congo [*Angola*] [*Airport symbol*] (OAG)
SSY .... Sao Salvador [*Angola*] [*Airport symbol*] (AD)
SSY .... Sharpshooters Yeomanry [*British military*] (DMA)
SSY .... Silver Strike Resources [*Vancouver Stock Exchange symbol*]
SSY .... South Somerset Yeomanry [*British military*] (DMA)
SSYAC .... Selective Service Youth Advisory Committee [*Military*] (VNW)
SSYS .... Stratasys, Inc. [*NASDAQ symbol*] (SAG)
S/SYS .... Subsystem (NASA)
SSZ .... Pocket Submarine (NATG)

SSZ.............. Saigon Special Zone [*Military*]
SSZ.............. Samos Resources, Inc. [*Vancouver Stock Exchange symbol*]
SSZ.............. Santos [*Brazil*] [*Airport symbol*] (AD)
SSZ.............. Sea Scout Zero - Nonrigid Airship [*Royal Naval Air Service*] [*British*]
SSZ.............. Society of Systematic Zoology (EA)
SSZ.............. Specified Strike Zone [*Army*] (AABC)
SSZ.............. Supra-Subduction Zone [*Geology*]
ST.............. Belize Airways [*ICAO designator*] (AD)
St.............. C. H. Boehringer Sohn, Ingelheim [*Germany*] [*Research code symbol*]
St.............. E. Merck AG [*Germany*] [*Research code symbol*]
ST.............. Esotropia [*Ophthalmology*] (MAE)
ST.............. Missionarii Servi Sanctissimae Trinitatis [*Missionary Servants of the Most Holy Trinity*] [*Roman Catholic men's religious order*]
st.............. Missionary Servants of the Most Holy Trinity (TOCD)
ST.............. Saddle Tank [*Trains*] [*British*]
ST.............. Safety Tool (MCD)
ST.............. Saint (EY)
ST.............. Saint
St.............. Saint (ODBW)
St.............. Saint (DD)
ST.............. Sainte
ST.............. Sales Tax
ST.............. Sales Tax Branch, United States Internal Revenue Bureau (DLA)
ST.............. Sales Tax Rulings, United States Internal Revenue Bureau [*A publication*] (DLA)
ST.............. Sample Tube
ST.............. Sanitary Towel [*British*] (DSUE)
ST.............. Sao Tome and Principe [*ANSI two-letter standard code*] (CNC)
ST.............. Save the Theaters [*Defunct*] (EA)
ST.............. Sawtooth [*Architecture*]
ST.............. Scalar Totalizer
ST.............. Scalloped Tinned [*Configuration*] (MCD)
ST.............. Schmidt Telescope
ST.............. Schmitt Trigger [*Electronics*]
ST.............. Schuler Tuning
ST.............. Science Train
ST.............. Sclerotherapy [*Medicine*]
ST.............. Screw Terminal
ST.............. Seaman Torpedoman [*Obsolete Navy*]
S/T.............. Search/Track
ST.............. Seat
ST.............. Secretary/Treasurer [*or Secretary and Treasurer*]
ST.............. Sedimentation Time
ST.............. Segment Table [*Computer science*] (OA)
ST.............. Select Time (WDAA)
ST.............. Self-Test
ST.............. Self-Toning [*Paper*] [*Photography*] (ROG)
ST.............. Semitendinosus [*Muscle*]
ST.............. Senior Teacher (ADA)
ST.............. Sensitivity Training
ST.............. Senza Tempo [*Without Regard to Time*] [*Music*]
ST.............. Sequence Timer
ST.............. Serial Tasking [*Computer science*] (IAA)
ST.............. Service Tabulating (AAG)
ST.............. Service Test [*Military*]
ST.............. Service Tools (AAG)
ST.............. Set Trigger
ST.............. Severance Tax (MHDB)
ST.............. Shares Time With [*Broadcasting term*]
S/T.............. Shelter Taxi [*NASA*] (KSC)
ST.............. Shipping Ticket [*Military*]
ST.............. Ship Trial (MCD)
ST.............. Shock Troops [*Military*] (WDAA)
ST.............. Shock Tube
ST.............. Shock Tunnel
ST.............. Shoot Tip [*Botany*]
ST.............. Shop Telegraph (IAA)
ST.............. Shorthand Writer [*British military*] (DMA)
ST.............. Short-Term Stay [*in hospital*] [*British*]
ST.............. Short Time (IAA)
ST.............. Short Ton [*2000 lbs.*]
ST.............. Short Tour [*Military*]
ST.............. Shrink Template
S-T.............. Sickle-Cell Thalassemia [*Hematology*] (DAVI)
ST.............. Side Tank [*on a ship*] (DS)
ST.............. Sidetone [*Telecommunications*] (TEL)
ST.............. Sigma Tau [*Later, Tau Beta Pi Association*]
ST.............. Silent [*Films, television, etc.*]
ST.............. Silicon Tube
ST.............. Silicotungstate [*Inorganic chemistry*]
ST.............. Simhat Torah (BJA)
ST.............. Simplification Task (MCD)
ST.............. Simulator Training
st.............. Sine Tempore [*At the Time Announced*] [*Latin*]
ST.............. Single Throw [*Switch*]
st.............. Single-Throw (IDOE)
ST.............. Single Tire
ST.............. Single Turn (MSA)
ST.............. Sinus Tachycardia [*Cardiology*]
ST.............. Skill Technical (INF)
ST.............. Skin Temperature (OA)
ST.............. Skin Test
ST.............. Skin Thickness [*Medicine*] (DMAA)
ST.............. Skin Track (MUGU)
ST.............. Sleeping Time
ST.............. Slide and Tape
St.............. Slight (DAVI)
ST.............. Slight Trace
ST.............. Small Tug [*Army*]
ST.............. Societe Theosophique [*Theosophical Society*]
ST.............. Society for Theriogenology (EA)
ST.............. Solar Thermal [*Energy source*]
ST.............. SONAR Technician [*Navy rating*]
S/T.............. Sonic Telegraphy
ST.............. Sons of Temperance
ST.............. Sounding Tube
ST.............. Sound Telegraphy [*Telecommunications*] (IAA)
ST.............. Sound Trap (OA)
ST.............. Source and Time Frame (NITA)
ST.............. Southern Tablelands [*New South Wales*] [*Region*] (EERA)
ST.............. Spaced Triplet (SAA)
ST.............. Spacelab Technology [*NASA*] (NASA)
ST.............. Space Telescope [*NASA*]
ST.............. Space-Time
ST.............. Spasmodic Torticollis [*Medicine*]
ST.............. Special Test
ST.............. Special Text [*Military*]
ST.............. Special Tooling (GFGA)
ST.............. Special Translation
ST.............. Speech Therapist
ST.............. Speech Therapy (DAVI)
ST.............. Speech Threshold [*Speech and language therapy*] (DAVI)
ST.............. Speed Transmitter (NRCH)
ST.............. Sphincter Tone [*Medicine*] (MAE)
ST.............. Spin Transition [*Physics*]
ST.............. Split Thickness [*Skin Graft*] [*Plastic surgery*] (DAVI)
ST.............. Springfield Terminal Railway Co. [*AAR code*]
ST.............. Spring Tide (WDAA)
ST.............. SPS Technologies [*NYSE symbol*] (TTSB)
ST.............. SPS Technologies, Inc. [*Formerly, Standard Pressed Steel Co.*] [*NYSE symbol*] (SPSG)
ST.............. Stable
ST.............. Stage
st.............. Stage [*of Disease*] (DAVI)
ST.............. Stain (WGA)
St.............. Stair's Decisions, Scotch Court of Session [*A publication*] (DLA)
St.............. Stair's Institutes [*5th ed.*] [*1832*] [*A publication*] (DLA)
St.............. Stamen [*Botany*]
ST.............. Stamped [*Stock exchange term*] (SPSG)
ST.............. Stand (WGA)
ST.............. Standard
ST.............. Standardized Test [*Psychology*]
ST.............. Standard Temperature (IAA)
ST.............. Standard Time
ST.............. Standby Time (MCD)
St.............. Stanton Number [*IUPAC*]
ST.............. Stanza
st.............. Stanza (WDMC)
ST.............. Starboard Flag [*Navy British*]
ST.............. Starsky Operupolnomochennyy [*Senior Case Officer*] [*Soviet military rank*]
ST.............. Start
st.............. Start (WDMC)
ST.............. Starter (MCD)
ST.............. Star Tracker [*NASA*] (AAG)
S/T.............. Start Tank (AAG)
ST.............. Start Timing
ST.............. State
st.............. State (WDMC)
ST.............. Statement (WDAA)
ST.............. State Trials [*Legal*] [*British*]
ST.............. Static (KSC)
ST.............. Static Test
ST.............. Static Thrust
ST.............. Statim [*Immediately*] [*Latin*] (ROG)
ST.............. Station [*Medicine*]
ST.............. Statue (WDMC)
st.............. Statue (WDMC)
ST.............. Status
ST.............. Statute
ST.............. Steam (AAG)
ST.............. Steamer (ROG)
ST.............. Steam Tanker
ST.............. Steam Trawler
ST.............. Steam Tug
ST.............. Steam Turbine (MCD)
ST.............. Steel [*Technical drawings*]
ST.............. Steel Truss [*Bridges*]
ST.............. Stem [*Linguistics*] [*Botany*]
ST.............. Stencil
ST.............. Stenographer [*British military*] (DMA)
st.............. Stent [*Let Them Stand*] [*Latin*] (MAE)
st.............. Stere [*Metric measure of volume*]
ST.............. Stereochemical Descriptor (NITA)
ST.............. Stereocilia [*Zoology*]
ST.............. Sternothyroid [*Anatomy*]
ST.............. Sternotomy [*Medicine*]
ST.............. Stern Thruster [*Type of ship*] (DS)
ST.............. Stet [*Let It Stand*] [*Latin*]

ST Stichting Tool [*Tool Foundation - TF*] [*Amsterdam, Netherlands*] (EAIO)

ST Sticky Type [*Bomb*]

ST Stigma [*Botany*]

ST Stimulus [*Medicine*]

ST Stinson [*ICAO aircraft manufacturer identifier*] (ICAO)

ST Stitch

ST St. Lawrence Cement, Inc. [*Toronto Stock Exchange symbol*]

ST Stock Transfer

ST Stoke (IAA)

ST Stoke-on-Trent [*Postcode*] (ODBW)

St Stokes [*Unit of kinematic viscosity*]

St Stomach (MAE)

ST Stone [*Unit of weight*]

st Stone [*Unit of weight*] (ODBW)

st Stone (VRA)

ST Stone Roller [*Ichthyology*]

St Stones [*Quality of the bottom*] [*Nautical charts*]

ST Stony Soil [*Agronomy*]

st Stool [*Gastroenterology*] (DAVI)

ST Stop Tap

ST Stop-Transfer [*Genetics*]

ST Storage Tube

ST Store (AAG)

ST Stored Time

ST Store Transfer (IAA)

ST Story (ROG)

St Story's United States Circuit Court Reports [*A publication*] (DLA)

ST Stotinki [*Monetary unit*] [*Bulgaria*]

st Straight (AAMN)

S/T Straight Time

ST Straight Tip [*Fiber connector for coaxial cable*] [*Telecommunications*] (PCM)

ST Strainer (DAC)

ST Strait

ST Straps [*JETDS nomenclature*] [*Military*] (CET)

ST Strategic Transport [*Aircraft*] [*Military*]

St Stratosphere

ST Stratosphere-Troposphere [*Radar*] (USDC)

ST Stratosphere-Troposphere [*Radar*] [*Marine science*] (OSRA)

ST Stratus [*Meteorology*]

ST Street (EY)

st Street (WDMC)

St Street (ODBW)

st Street (VRA)

St Street (DD)

ST Stress Testing [*Medicine*]

ST Strict [*Medicine*]

S-T Strip-Tin (MSA)

ST Stroma [*Medicine*]

ST Strophe [*Poetry*] (ROG)

ST Structural (NASA)

ST Structure Tee (AAG)

St Stuart, Milne, and Peddie's Scotch Court of Session Cases [*A publication*] (DLA)

ST Student's t-Test [*Statistical mathematics*]

ST Studies in Theology [*A publication*]

ST Studio to Transmitter (IAA)

ST Stumped [*Cricket*]

St Styrene [*Also, Sty*] [*Organic chemistry*]

ST Sublingual Tablet [*Medicine*] (MEDA)

ST Substitution Theorem [*Logic*]

ST Subtalar [*Medicine*] (MAE)

st Subtelocentric [*Botany*]

ST Subtentacular [*Zoology*]

ST Subtotal (MAE)

ST Sub Tuner (IAA)

St Subtype (MAE)

ST Sucrose Tallowate (OA)

ST Sulfotransferase [*An enzyme*]

ST Summer Time [*Daylight saving time*]

ST Superintendent of Transportation

ST Superior Turbinate [*Otorhinolaryngology*] (DAVI)

ST Super Tampella [*Explosive*] (INF)

ST Supplementary Term [*Online database field identifier*]

ST Supporting Technologies [*Military*] (RDA)

ST Surface Target [*Navy*] (CAAL)

ST Surface Tension

ST Surface Tracker [*Navy*] (CAAL)

ST Surgical Technician

ST Surgical Technologist (DAVI)

ST Surtax (WDAA)

ST Surveillance Test (NATG)

ST Survival Time

ST Swept Tone

ST Symbol Table (IAA)

ST Symmetrical TOKAMAK

ST Synchroniztion Table (IAA)

ST Syncopated Time (WDAA)

ST Syndrome of the Trephined [*Medicine*] (DMAA)

ST Synthesis Telescope

ST System Response Time [*Computer order entry*]

ST Systems Technology (IAA)

ST System Table (IAA)

ST System Test

ST Szondi Test [*Psychology*]

St United States Statutes at Large [*A publication*] (DLA)

ST1 SONAR Technician, First Class [*Navy rating*]

ST2 SONAR Technician, Second Class [*Navy rating*]

ST3 SONAR Technician, Third Class [*Navy rating*]

ST 37 Hexylresorcinol [*An antiseptic*] [*Pharmacology*] (DAVI)

STA Japanese Science and Technology Agency (USDC)

STA Sail Training Association (EA)

STA Sales Transaction Audit [*Test*]

STA Santa [*Saint*] [*Italian*]

STA Satara [*India*] [*Seismograph station code, US Geological Survey Closed*] (SEIS)

STA Satellite Test Annex (SAA)

STA Satellite Tracking Annex (MUGU)

STA S-Band Test Antenna

STA Science and Technology Agency

STA Science and Technology Agency [*of Japan*] (EERA)

STA Science and Technology Agent (SDI)

STA Scottish Trampoline Association (DBA)

STA Securities Transfer Association (EA)

STA Security Traders Association (EA)

STA Segment Table Address [*Computer science*] (IAA)

STA Semiconductor Trade Agreement [*US and Japan*] (ECON)

STA Serum Thrombotic Accelerator [*Serology*]

STA Serum Thymic-Like Activity [*Biochemistry*]

STA Servico des Transportes Aereos [*Portuguese West Africa*]

STA Shift Technical Adviser [*Nuclear energy*] (NRCH)

STA Shipboard Transmitting Antenna

STA Shore-Based Transmitting Antenna

STA Short-Term Arrangements [*Department of State*]

STA Short-Term Averaging (CAAL)

STA Short-Terms Abroad

STA Shuttle Training Aircraft [*NASA*]

STA Sialyltransferase Activity [*Medicine*]

STA Single Tape Armored (IAA)

STA Single Target Attack

STA Skills Training Agency [*British*]

STA Slaving Torquer Amplifier

STA Slurry Technology Association [*Later, CSTA*] (EA)

STA Small Tactical Airlifter [*Military British*]

STA Society of Typographic Arts [*Later, ACD*] (EA)

STA Softening Temperature of Ash

STA Solar Trade Association [*British*] (DBA)

STA Solution Treat and Age [*Metals*]

STA Southern Textile Association (EA)

STA Space Technology Applications

STA Space Transportation Association (EA)

STA Spanning Tree Algorithm [*Computer science*] (PCM)

STA Spark Thrust Augmentor (SAA)

STA Special Temporary Allowance

STA Special Temporary Authorization [*FCC*]

STA Spice Trade Association [*British*] (DBA)

STA Stacia Ventures [*Vancouver Stock Exchange symbol*]

STA Staff Training Assistant [*Army*] (AABC)

STA Stagger Tuned Antenna

STA Stamped

STA Stara Dala [*Czechoslovakia*] [*Later, HRB*] [*Geomagnetic observatory code*]

STA Star Aviation [*British ICAO designator*] (FAAC)

STA Starter Corp. [*NYSE symbol*] (SPSG)

STA State Technical Assistance (OICC)

Sta Statham's Abridgment [*A publication*] (DSA)

STA Static Test Article (NASA)

STA Station [*Telecommunications*]

sta Station (IDOE)

STA Station

sta Station (VRA)

sta Stationary (IDOE)

STA Stationary (MSA)

STA Stator (WGA)

STA Status [*Online database field identifier*] (AABC)

STA Statute (WGA)

STA St. Augustine [*Diocesan abbreviation*] [*Florida*] (TOCD)

STA Stauning [*Denmark*] [*Airport symbol*] (OAG)

STA Steel Carriers Tariff Association, Inc., East Riverdale MD [*STAC*]

STA Steel Tape Armored [*Cables*]

STA Stock Transfer Association [*New York, NY*] (EA)

STA Store Accumulator

STA Store Address (SAA)

STA Store Answer (NITA)

STA Straight in Approach [*Aviation*] (DA)

STA Strategic Transportation Analysis [*MTMC*] (TAG)

STA Structural Test Article (NASA)

STA Submarine Tender Availability

STA Subscription Television Association (NTCM)

STA Superficial Temporal Artery [*Anatomy*]

STA Superior Temporal Artery [*Anatomy*]

STA Supersonic Tunnel Association (EA)

STA Surveillance and Target Acquisition [*Marine Corps*] (DOMA)

STA Survival in Target Area (MCD)

STA Swedish Telecommunications Administration [*Telecommunications*]

STA Swimming Teachers' Association [*British*]

STA Systems Test Area

STA University of Santa Clara, Orradre Library, Santa Clara, CA [*OCLC symbol*] (OCLC)

STAA........... Signal Training, All Arms (IAA)
STAA........... Soldiers Total Abstinence Association [*British military*] (DMA)
STAA........... STAAR Surgical [*NASDAQ symbol*] (TTSB)
STAA........... Staar Surgical Co. [*NASDAQ symbol*] (NQ)
STAA........... Surface Transportation Assistance Act [*1978*]
STAA........... Survey Test of Algebraic Aptitude [*Education*] (AEBS)
StAAA.......... Saint Andrew's Ambulance Association [*British*] (DBA)
STAAD.......... Submarine Tender Availability Arrival/Departure [*Obsolete*]
STAAF.......... Study to Align AMC [*Now DAR COM*] Functions (MCD)
STAAG.......... Standard Tachymetric Anti-Aircraft Gun [*British military*] (DMA)
StaarSur...... Staar Surgical Co. [*Associated Press*] (SAG)
STAAS.......... Surveillance and Target Acquisition Aircraft System (AFM)
Staatsverw... Roemische Staatsverwaltung [*A publication*] (OCD)
STAB........... SEAL [*Sea, Air, and Land*] Team Assault Boat [*Navy*] (VNW)
STAB........... Space, Time, and Beyond [*Dance work choreographed by Marie Chouinard*]
STAB........... Squadron Tactical Analysis Board [*Military*] (CAAL)
stab........... Stability (IDOE)
stab........... Stabilization (IDOE)
STAB........... Stabilization [*or Stabilizer*] (IAA)
STAB........... Stabilize [*or Stabilizer*] [*Aviation*] (AAG)
stab........... Stabilizer (IDOE)
Stab........... Stable [*Army*]
STAB........... Standby Advisory Board [*Army*] (INF)
St Ab.......... Statham's Abridgment [*A publication*] (DLA)
STAB........... Strike Assault Boat [*Navy symbol*]
STAB........... Supersonic Tests of Aerodynamic Bombs (MUGU)
STAB........... Supersonic Transport Advisory Board
STABAMP..... Stabilizing Amplifier [*Telecommunications*] (IAA)
STAB AUG... Stability Augmentation [*Aviation*] (MCD)
STABE.......... Second-Time-Around-Beacon-Echo (PDAA)
STABEX........ Stabilization of Export Earnings [*Program of the EEC*]
StAbs.......... Status Absolutus
STABS.......... Suinn Test Anxiety Behavior Scale [*Psychology*]
STABY.......... Stability (MSA)
STAC........... Science and Technology Advisory Committee [*NASA*] (MCD)
STAC........... Software Timing and Control
STAC........... Southern Technology Applications Center [*University of Florida*] [*Gainesville*] [*NASA*] [*Information service or system*] (IID)
STAC........... Staccato [*Detached, Distinct*] [*Music*]
STAC........... Stac Electronics [*NASDAQ symbol*] (SAG)
STAC........... Stac Inc. [*NASDAQ symbol*] (TTSB)
STAC........... Standard Tariff Agents Code
STAC........... Stop the Act Coalition [*An association*]
STAC........... Submarine Tactical Acoustic Communications [*Navy*] (ANA)
STAC........... Submarine-to-Aircraft Communications
STAC........... Surface Target Attack Comparison Model (MCD)
STACAP....... Status and Capability (SAA)
STACC.......... Staccato [*Detached, Distinct*] [*Music*]
STACCS........ Standard Theater Army Command and Control System (RDA)
Staceys........ Staceys Buffet [*Commercial firm Associated Press*] (SAG)
STACK.......... Start Acknowledge [*Computer science*] (MHDI)
STACO.......... Standing Committee for the Study of Scientific Principles of Standardization [*ISO*]
STACOM....... Standard Army Commissary Operating Manual
STACOM....... Standard Computer Output Microform [*Army*]
STACOM....... State Criminal Justice Communications
Sta Com....... Station Complement [*Army*]
STACRES...... Standing Committee on Research and Statistics [*UN Food and Agriculture Organization*]
STACS.......... Subtropical Atlantic Climate Studies [*National Oceanic and Atmospheric Administration*]
STACWV....... Standing Technical Advisory Committee on Water Quality [*Department of the Environment*] [*British*]
Stacys.......... Staceys Buffet [*Commercial firm Associated Press*] (SAG)
STAD........... Start Address [*Telecommunications*] (TEL)
STAD........... Student Teams-Achievement Division (AEE)
STAD........... Student Teams-Achievement Divisions (EDAC)
STAD........... Submarine Tender Availability Document
STADAC....... Station Data Acquisition and Control [*NASA*] (NASA)
STADACOL... Statistical Data Collection Program
STADAD....... Satellite Tracking and Data Acquisition Department
STADAN....... Satellite Tracking and Data Acquisition Network [*Later, STDN*]
STADAN....... Space Tracking and Data Acquisition Network
STADAR....... Servo Tester With Automatic Data Acquisition and Reduction (IAA)
STADB......... Chinese Scientific and Technological Periodical Abstracts [*Information service or system*] (IID)
STADD......... Ship-Towed Acoustic Deception Device (MCD)
STADES....... Standard Army Data Elements Systems (MCD)
STADES....... Standard Data Elements System (MCD)
STADIN........ Standing Administrative Instruction for Army Attaches (AABC)
STADINAIR... Standing Administrative Instruction for Air Attaches (AFM)
St Adm NS... Stuart's Lower Canada Vice-Admiralty Reports, New Series [*A publication*] (DLA)
STADMR....... Station Administrator (FAAC)
STADN......... Space Tracking and Acquisition Data Network
STADSS....... Strategic Transportation Analysis Decision Support System [*MTMC*] (TAG)
STADU......... System Termination and Display Unit (MCD)
STA-DYNULSIMU... Static-Dynamic Ullage Simulation Unit
STAE........... Second Time Around Echo
STAE........... Specify Task Asynchronous Exit [*Computer science*]
Sta Eng........ Stationary Engineer
STAEP......... Scientific and Technical Assessment of Environmental Pollutants [*Marine science*] (MSC)
STAESA....... Society of Turkish Architects, Engineers, and Scientists in America (EA)
STAF........... Science Teachers' Authoring Facility (AIE)
STAF........... Science Team Analysis Facility [*NASA*]
STAF........... Scientific and Technical Application Forecasts
STAF........... Simulation/Test Acceptance Facility [*Army*] (RDA)
STAF........... Staff
STA/F.......... Standard Access and Format [*Reference Technology, Inc. software*]
STAF........... Standard Test and Administrative Form (SAA)
STAF........... Statistical Analysis of Files (IAA)
STAF........... St. Thomas Aquinas Foundation (EA)
StafBld......... Staff Builders, Inc. [*Associated Press*] (SAG)
STAFDA....... Specialty Tools and Fasteners Distributors Association (EA)
STAFEX........ Staff Exercises [*NATO*] (NATG)
STAFF.......... Smart Target-Activated Fire and Forget [*Antitank weapon system*] (RDA)
STAFF.......... Society for Techno-Innovation of Agriculture, Forestry and Fisheries [*Japan*]
STAFF.......... Staffordshire [*County in England*]
STAFF.......... Stellar Acquisition Flight Feasibility
Stafford........ Stafford's Reports [*69-71 Vermont*] [*A publication*] (DLA)
STAFFS........ Staffordshire [*County in England*]
Staffs........... Staffordshire [*County in England*] (ODBW)
STAFS.......... Standard Automated Financial System [*Navy*] (GFGA)
STAFS.......... Sugar, Tobacco, Alcohol, Fat, and Salt
STAFS.......... Supportable Technology for Affordable Fighter Structures [*Air Force*] (DOMA)
STAFT.......... Steerable Antenna Focusing Technique
STAG........... Sharper-than-the-Average-Gook [*American POW slang*] (VNW)
STAG........... Shuttle Turnaround Analysis Group [*NASA*] (NASA)
STAG........... Skills Training Adjustment Group [*Educational project sponsored by The Hartford*]
STAG........... Soils, Trees, and Grass Program (EERA)
STAG........... Special Task Air Group
STAG........... Split Thickness Autogenous Graft [*Plastic surgery*] (DAVI)
STAG........... Standards Technical Advisory Group
STAG........... Steam and Gas [*Turbine*]
STAG........... Straight-Talking American Government [*Comedian Pat Paulsen's political party*]
STAG........... Strategy and Tactics Analysis Group [*Later, Concepts Analysis Agency*] [*Army*] (KSC)
STAG........... Student Agitation [*FBI*]
STAG........... Submarine-Rocket Technical Advisory Group
STAG........... Survivable Tactical Army Generator (RDA)
STAGD......... Syndicat des Travailleurs de l'Administration Generale du Dahomey [*Dahomean Union of General Administration Workers*]
STAGE.......... Simulated Total Atomic Global Exchange [*DoD*]
Stage........... Stage II Apparel Corp. [*Associated Press*] (SAG)
STAGG......... Small-Turbine Advanced Gas Generator
STAGING...... Sturctural Analysis via Generalized Interactive Graphics (PDAA)
STAG-MAG... Stage Manager [*Theater term*] (DSUE)
STAGN......... Stagnation [*NWS*] (FAAC)
STAGS......... Simulated Tank and Antiarmor Gunnery System (INF)
STAGS......... Sterling Transferable Accruing Government Securities (TDOB)
STAGS......... Sterling Transferable Accruing Government Securities (ODBW)
STAGS......... Structural Analysis of General Shells
STAGS......... Swedish Tank Agility/Survivability Test (MCD)
STAGS-D...... Simulated Tank Antiarmor Gunnery System - Dragon [*Army*] (INF)
STAI............ Simulation Tape Alarm Indicator (SAA)
STAI............ Speilberger's Trait-Anxiety Inventory (EDAC)
STAI............ State-Trait Anxiety Inventory [*Psychology*]
STAI............ Subtask ABEND [*Abnormal End*] Intercept [*Computer science*] (BUR)
STAIC.......... State-Trait Anxiety Inventory for Children [*Psychology*]
STAID.......... Station Identification
Stair............ Stair's Decisions of the Lords of Council and Session [*1661-81*] [*Scotland*] [*A publication*] (DLA)
STAIR.......... Structural Analysis Interpretive Routine
Stair I......... Stair's Institutes [*5 eds.*] [*1681-1832*] [*A publication*] (DLA)
Stair Inst..... Stair's Institutes [*5 eds.*] [*1681-1832*] [*A publication*] (DLA)
Stair Prin..... Stair's Principles of the Laws of Scotland [*A publication*] (DLA)
Stair Rep...... Stair's Decisions, Scotch Court of Session [*A publication*] (DLA)
STAIRS........ Standard Advanced Infrared Sensor [*Military*]
STAIRS........ Storage and Information Retrieval System [*IBM Corp.*]
STAIRS........ Storage and Information Retrieval System [*Computer science*] (CDE)
STAIRS/VS... Storage and Information Retrieval System/Virtual Storage [*IBM Corp.*]
STAJ............ Science and Technology Agency of Japan (EERA)
STAJ............ Short-Term Anti-Jam (MCD)
STAK........... Austins Steak & Saloon, Inc. [*NASDAQ symbol*] (SAG)
STAK........... Austins Steaks & Saloon [*NASDAQ symbol*] (TTSB)
StakeTc........ Stake Technology Ltd. [*Associated Press*] (SAG)
STAL........... Screening Test of Adolescent Language [*Educational test*]
STAL........... Stalactite/Stalagmite Formation (DSUE)
STALAG....... Stammlager [*Prisoner-of-war camp*] [*German*]
STALAGLUFT... Stammlagerluft [*Prisoner-of-war camp for airmen*] [*German*]
STALAPCO... State and Local Air Pollution Control Official [*Environmental Protection Agency*] (ERG)
STALAS........ Stationary LASER Site [*NASA*]
Stal Elect..... Stalman on Election and Satisfaction [*1827*] [*A publication*] (DLA)
STALO......... Stabilized Local Oscillator [*RADAR*]
stalo............ Standardized Oscillator (IDOE)
STALOC....... Self-Tracking Automatic Lock-On Circuit (PDAA)
STALOG....... Study of Automation of the Logistic System [*Military*]
STALOS....... Stabilized Tunable Local Oscillator
STALPETH... Steel, Aluminum, Polyethylene [*Components of a type of telecommunications cable*]

STaM .... Sefer Torah. Tefillin. Mezuzah
STAM .... Sequential Thermal Anhysteric Magnetization [*Helical scan videotape duplicating system*] (NTCM)
STAM .... Shared Tape Allocation Manager
STAM .... Statistical Analog Monitor (PDAA)
STAM .... Submarine Tactical Advanced Missile (MCD)
STAM .... Superintendent of Technical Applications of Metals [*Ministry of Supply*] [*British World War II*]
STAM .... Surface Target Acquisition Model (MCD)
STAM .... System Telecommunications Access Method [*NCR Corp.*]
STAMAT .... Schaie-Thurstone Adult Mental Abilities Test [*Intelligence test*] [*Psychology*]
STA-MCA ..... Superficial Temporal Artery to Middle Cerebral Artery [*Anatomy*] (MAE)
StamEx .... Stampeder Exploration Ltd. [*Associated Press*] (SAG)
Sta Mi .... Statute Mile
STAMIC .... Set Theory Analysis and Measure of Information Characteristics
STAMIDS ..... Standoff Minefield Detection System [*Military*] (INF)
STAMINRQ... Status During Minimize Required (MCD)
STAMIS .... Standard Army Management Information System
STAMM .... Systematic Teaching and Measuring Mathematics [*Education*]
STAMMIS .... Standard Army Multicommand Management Information System (MCD)
STAMNI .... Sonic True Airspeed and Mach Number Indicator
STAMO .... Stable Master Oscillator
STAMOCAP... State Monopoly Capitalism
STAMOS ...... Sortie Turn Around Maintenance Operations Simulation [*NASA*] (KSC)
STAMP .... Satellite Telecommunications Analysis and Modeling Program
STAMP .... Small Tactical Aerial Mobility Platform [*Proposed*] [*Marine Corps*]
STAMP .... Space Technology Analysis and Mission Planning (MCD)
STAMP .... Standard Air Munitions Package
STAMP .... Systems Tape Addition and Maintenance Program [*Computer science*] (IEEE)
STAMPED .... Size, Temperature, Application, Material, Pressure, Ends, and Delivery [*To aid selection of industrial hose*]
STAMPEX .... National Stamp Exhibition [*British*] (ITD)
STAMPG ...... Stamping
STAMPS ...... Spectrophotometric Transient Analysis Method for Multiple Positions and Species
STAMPS ...... Stabilized Translation and Maneuvering Propulsion System (IAA)
STAN .... Selectable Two-Area Nozzle (MCD)
STAN .... Stanchion
STAN .... Standard (WGA)
STAN .... Standish Care [*NASDAQ symbol*] (TTSB)
STAN .... Standish Care Co. [*NASDAQ symbol*] (SAG)
STAN .... Stanstead [*England*]
STAN .... Sum Total and Nosegear (MCD)
STANA .... Statistics on the North Atlantic [*Fisheries*] [*UN Food and Agriculture Organization*]
STANAG .... Standardization Agreement [*NATO*]
STANAVFORCHAN... Standing Naval Force, Channel [*NATO*] (NATG)
STANAVFORLANT... Standing Naval Force, Atlantic (ANA)
STANAVFORMED... Standing Naval Force Mediterranean [*NATO*] (DOMA)
STANAVITO... Syndicat des Travailleurs de Transport et de la Navigation du Togo [*Union of Transport and Navigation Workers of Togo*]
STANB .... Stanborough [*England*]
STANCAL ..... Standard Oil Co. of California
STANCHART... Standard Chartered [*International bank*] [*British*]
STANCIB ...... State-Army-Navy Communications Intelligence Board [*Later, USCIB*]
STAND .... Standard
STAND .... Standard
Stand .... Standard (AAGC)
Stand .... Stand Magazine [*A publication*] (BRI)
STANDAN .... Space Tracking and Data Acquisition Network (IAA)
standard ...... Standardization [*or Standardized*] (DAVI)
ST & E .... Security Test and Evaluation [*Military*] (GFGA)
Standex .... Standex International Corp. [*Associated Press*] (SAG)
Stand Ex Prof Tax Rep... Standard Excess Profits Tax Reporter [*Commerce Clearing House*] [*A publication*] (DLA)
Stand Fed Tax Rep... Standard Federal Tax Reporter [*Commerce Clearing House*] [*A publication*] (DLA)
Stand GA Prac... Standard Georgia Practice [*A publication*] (DLA)
St & H Abor... Storer and Heard on Criminal Abortion [*A publication*] (DLA)
Stan Dig .... Stanton's Kentucky Digest [*A publication*] (DLA)
St & Loc Taxes (BNA)... State and Local Taxes (Bureau of National Affairs) [*A publication*] (DLA)
St & Loc Tax Serv (P-H)... State and Local Tax Service (Prentice-Hall, Inc.) [*A publication*] (DLA)
St & P .... Stewart and Porter's Alabama Reports [*A publication*] (DLA)
Stand PA Prac... Standard Pennsylvania Practice [*A publication*] (DLA)
St and Port... Stewart and Porter's Alabama Reports [*A publication*] (DLA)
StAndr .... Saint Andrews Golf Corp. [*Associated Press*] (SAG)
StAndrew ..... Saint Andrews Golf Corp. [*Associated Press*] (SAG)
Standsh .... Standish Care Co. [*Associated Press*] (SAG)
ST & SP ...... Start and Stop
STAN/EVAL... Standardization/Evaluation
STANFINS.... Standard Financial System [*Military*] (AABC)
STANFINS-R... Standard Finance System Redesign [*DoD*] (GFGA)
STANFLT ...... Standardization Flight [*Naval Air Training and Operating Procedures Standardization*] (DNAB)
Stanford .... Stanford's English Pleas of the Crown [*A publication*] (DLA)
Stanford U ... Stanford University (GAGS)
StanfTl .... Stanford Telecommunications, Inc. [*Associated Press*] (SAG)
Stanhm .... Stanhome, Inc. [*Associated Press*] (SAG)
STANINE ...... Standard Nine Score [*Military*]
STANLANCRU... Standard Landing Craft Unit [*Military*]
StanlFrn .... Stanley Furniture Co. [*Associated Press*] (SAG)
StanlWk .... [*The*] Stanley Works [*Associated Press*] (SAG)
STANO .... Surveillance, Target Acquisition, and Night Observation [*DoD*]
STANOC .... Surveillance, Target Acquisition, Night Observation, and Counter - Surveillance [*British*] (MCD)
STANOLIND... Standard Oil Co. (Indiana)
STANORD .... Standardization Order [*Navy*] (NG)
Stan PA Prac... Standard Pennsylvania Practice [*A publication*] (DLA)
StanPsych .... Standard Psychiatric [*Medicine*] (DMAA)
STANS .... Soviet Tactical Nuclear Study (MCD)
STANS .... Standard Aircraft Navigation System
STANS .... Standard Army Nonappropriated System (MCD)
StAns .... Studia Anselmiana [*Rome*] [*A publication*]
STANSM ...... STANO [*Surveillance, Target Acquisition, and Night Observation*] System Manager [*Army*] (RDA)
Stant .... Stant Corp. [*Associated Press*] (SAG)
STANTEC ..... Standard Telephones Electronic Computer (MCD)
Stanton .... Stanton's Reports [*11-13 Ohio*] [*A publication*] (DLA)
Stanton's Rev St... Stanton's Revised Kentucky Statutes [*A publication*] (DLA)
STANVAC ..... Standard Vacuum Oil Co.
STANY .... Security Traders Association of New York
Staody .... Staodyn, Inc. [*Associated Press*] (SAG)
Staodyn .... Staodyn, Inc. [*Associated Press*] (SAG)
STAP .... Science and Technology Advisory Panel
STAP .... Scientific and Technical Analysis and Programs Directorate
STAP .... Screening Test for Auditory Perception
STAP .... Shipbuilding Temporary Assistance Program
STAP .... Ships Towed Acoustic Project (DWSG)
STAP .... Special Technical Assistance Program (EA)
STAP .... Stapleton [*England*]
STAP .... Staploe [*England*]
STAP .... State Transit Authority Plan [*Victoria, Australia*]
STAP .... Survivability Test Advisory Panel [*Military*] (CAAL)
Sta P C .... Staundeforde's Pleas of Crown [*A publication*] (DSA)
STAPFUS ..... Stable Axis Platform Follow-Up System
STAPH .... Staphylococcus [*Medicine*]
Staph Epi ..... Staphylococcus Epidermidis [*A bacterium*] (DAVI)
STAPL .... Ship Tethered Aerial Platform (PDAA)
STAPL .... SIGPLAN Technical Committee on APL [*A Programming Language*] [*Association for Computing Machinery*] (CSR)
STAPLAN ..... Status, Time, Attrition, Planning Methodology
Staples .... Staples, Inc. [*Associated Press*] (SAG)
STAPP .... Short-Term Anxiety-Provoking Psychotherapy (PDAA)
STAPP .... Simulation Tape Print Program
STAPP .... Single-Thread All-Purpose Program
STAPP .... Standard Tape Print Program [*Computer science*] (IAA)
STAPPA .... State and Territorial Air Pollution Program Administrators (EA)
Sta Pr .... Staundeforde's Exposition of the King's Prerogative [*A publication*] (DSA)
STAPRC .... Scientific and Technical Association of the People's Republic of China
STAQ .... Security Traders Automated Quotation [*System*]
STAQ .... Student Teachers' Attitude Questionnaire
STAQC .... Statistical Quality Control System [*Military*]
STAR .... Lone Star Steakhouse & Saloon, Inc. [*NASDAQ symbol*] (SAG)
STAR .... Lone Star Steakhouse/Saloon [*NASDAQ symbol*] (TTSB)
STAR .... Safe Teenage Rocketry
STAR .... San Clemente 3-D Acoustic Range (MCD)
STAR .... Satellites for Telecommunications, Applications, and Research [*Consortium*]
STAR .... Satellite Telecommunications Automatic Routing
STAR .... Satellite Television Asia Region [*Hong Kong*]
STAR .... Satellite Transponder Addressable Receiver
STAR .... Scheduled Theater Airlift Route [*Air Force*] (DOMA)
STAR .... Science and Technology Aerospace Reports (NITA)
STAR .... Science Teaching Achievement Recognition
STAR .... Score, Teach, and Record [*Teaching machine*]
STAR .... Screening Test of Academic Readiness [*Child development test*]
STAR .... Screening Tracking and Retrieval
STAR .... Second Time Around Racers [*Car racing*]
STAR .... Segment Table Address Register [*Computer science*] (IAA)
STAR .... Selective Training and Retention [*Navy*]
STAR .... Self-Steering Array Repeater (IAA)
STAR .... Self-Test Antenna Radiation [*Military*] (CAAL)
STAR .... Self-Test Automatic Readout
STAR .... Self-Testing and Repairing [*Computer self-repair*]
STAR .... Self-Training and Assessment of Readiness
STAR .... Serials Titles Automated Records [*US National Agricultural Library*] [*Beltsville, MD*] [*A publication*]
STAR .... Set-Theoretic Approach to Relations (PDAA)
STAR .... Shell Transient Asymmetric Response
STAR .... Shield Test Air Reactor [*Nuclear energy*]
STAR .... Shipboard Tactical Airborne Remote Piloted Vehicle [*Navy*] (CAAL)
STAR .... Ship-Tended Acoustic Relay [*Military*]
STAR .... Shock Thermodynamics Applied Research [*Department of Energy*]
STAR .... Shuttle Turnaround Analysis Report [*NASA*] (NASA)
STAR .... Simple Test Approach for Readability [*General Electric*]
STAR .... Simulation of Tactical Alternative Responses (MCD)
STAR .... Simultaneous Temperature Alarm Readout
STAR .... Simultaneous Transmission and Reception RADAR [*DoD*] (ECON)
STAR .... Sled Towed Array (MCD)
STAR .... Society for Test Anxiety Research (EA)
STAR .... Society of Romanian Air Transports [*ICAO designator*] (FAAC)

STAR .... Space Technology and Advanced Research
STAR .... Space Technology and Research Center [*Research center*] (RCD)
STAR .... Space Terminal Auxiliary Reactor (IAA)
STAR .... Space Thermionic Auxiliary Reactor [*Nuclear energy*]
STAR .... Space-Time Autoregressive [*Statistics*]
STAR .... Specialized Training and Reassignment [*Military*]
STAR .... Specialized Training for Army Readiness [*Army Reserve*]
STAR .... Special Treatment and Review [*Navy*] (NG)
STAR .... Special Tube Analyzing Recorder
STAR .... Spectral Technology and Applied Research
STAR .... Speed through Aerial Resupply [*Air Force*]
STAR .... Sport, Travel, Art, and Recreation
STAR .... Standard Routine (IAA)
STAR .... Standard Telecommunications Automatic Recognizer [*Computer science*]
STAR .... Standard Tensioned Alongside Receiver [*Navy*] (NVT)
STAR .... Standard Terminal Arrival Route [*Aviation*]
STAR .... Standard Test Authorization and Report System [*Navy*]
Star.......... Starkie's English Nisi Prius Reports [*A publication*] (DLA)
STAR .... State Acid Rain Projects [*Environmental Protection Agency*] (GFGA)
STAR .... Statistical Analysis Routine (IAA)
STAR .... Statistical Table Assembly and Retrieval System [*Proposed for Social Security Administration*]
STAR .... Statistical Treatment of Aircraft Returns (MCD)
STAR .... Status Application Resource (HGAA)
STAR .... Steerable Array RADAR
STAR .... Stellar Attitude Reference
STAR .... Steps to Abstract Reasoning
STAR .... STING [*Swift Target Identification Notification Grid*] Array [*Computer system*]
STAR .... Stock Technical Analysis Reports [*Innovest Systems, Inc.*] [*Database*]
STAR .... Stop the Arms Race [*Women's International League for Peace and Freedom*]
STAR .... Storage Address Register [*Telecommunications*] (IAA)
STAR .... Strategic Technologies for the Army
STAR .... Streamlined Acquisition Requirements System [*DoD*]
STAR .... Stream Tension Actuated Remotely [*Navy*] (DOMA)
STAR .... Strike, Transfers, Acquisitions, or Removals [*Navy*] (NG)
STAR .... String Array [*Computer system*] (MCD)
STAR .... String Array Processor
STAR .... Structural Testing, Analysis, and Reporting
STAR .... Students Taking Action with Recognition [*Kentucky*] (EDAC)
STAR .... Students Taught Awareness and Resistance [*An association*]
STAR .... Submarine Test and Research (MCD)
STAR .... [*The*] Sunday Times Atlantic Riband [*Award offered by a London newspaper to any sailboat beating the 1905 record for a transatlantic crossing*]
STAR .... Supplementary Teaching Assistance in Reading (AEBS)
STAR .... Supplier Transmittal and Approval Request (MCD)
STAR .... Support to Aftermarket Repairs [*Toyota automobile service repair program*]
STAR .... Surface-to-Air Recovery
STAR .... Surveillance, Target Acquisition, and Reconnaissance
STAR .... Swedish Tactical Attack RADAR
STAR .... System for Telephone Administrative Response [*Computer science*]
STAR .... System for Time and Accomplishment Reporting (MCD)
STAR .... Systems Test Bed for Avionics Research
STAR .... System Threat Assessment Report [*Army*]
STAR .... System to Automate Records (NITA)
STAR .... System Training Application Requirements
STARA .... Scientific and Technical Aerospace Reports Administrator (AAGC)
STARAD.......... Starfish Radiation [*Satellite*] [*NASA*]
STARAN.......... Stellar Attitude Reference and Navigation
Starbase.......... Starbase Corp. [*Associated Press*] (SAG)
StarBc.......... Star Banc Corp. [*Associated Press*] (SAG)
Starbcks .... Starbucks Corp. [*Associated Press*] (SAG)
STARC .... Solar Thermal Advanced Research Center [*University of Houston*] [*Research center*] (RCD)
STARC .... State Area Commands (MCD)
Star Ch Ca... Star Chamber Cases [*1477-1648*] [*England*] [*A publication*] (DLA)
Star Ch Cas... Star Chamber Cases [*1477-1648*] [*England*] [*A publication*] (DLA)
STARCIPS.... Standard Army Civilian Pay System
STARCIPS-R... Standard Army Civilian Pay System Redesign (GFGA)
STARCOM.... Strategic Army Command Network
STARCOM.... Strategic Army Communications System
Starcraft .... Starcraft Automotive Corp. [*Associated Press*] (SAG)
STARE .... Scandinavian Twin Auroral RADAR Experiment [*Ionospheric science*]
STARE .... Steerable Telemetry Antenna Receiving Equipment
STARFIARS... Standard Army Financial Inventory Accounting and Reporting System
STARFIRE.... System to Accumulate and Retrieve Financial Information with Random Extraction [*Computer science*]
StarGas.......... Star Gas Partners L.P. SBI [*Associated Press*] (SAG)
STARIMAR... Space-Time Autoregressive Integrated Moving Average [*Statistics*]
Stark.......... Starkie's English Nisi Prius Reports [*1815-22*] [*A publication*] (DLA)
Stark CL .... Starkie's Criminal Law [*A publication*] (DLA)
Stark Cr Pl... Starkie's Criminal Pleading [*A publication*] (DLA)
Stark Ev.... Starkie on Evidence [*A publication*] (DLA)
Starkie.......... Starkie's English Nisi Prius Reports [*A publication*] (DLA)
Starkie (Eng)... Starkie's English Nisi Prius Reports [*171 English Reprint*] [*A publication*] (DLA)
Starkie Ev .... Starkie on Evidence [*A publication*] (DLA)
Starkie's.......... English Nisi Prius Reports [*171 English Reprint*] [*A publication*] (DLA)
Starkie Sland & L... Starkie on Slander and Libel [*A publication*] (DLA)
Stark Jury Tr... Starkie on Trial by Jury [*A publication*] (DLA)
Stark Lib.......... Starkie on Libel [*A publication*] (DLA)
Stark NP.......... Starkie's English Nisi Prius Reports [*A publication*] (DLA)
Stark Sl & L... Starkie on Slander and Libel [*A publication*] (DLA)
STARLAB .... Space Technology Applications and Research Laboratory [*NASA*]
STARLab.......... Space, Telecommunications, and Radioscience Laboratory [*Stanford University*] [*Research center*] (RCD)
Starl I Cr Law... Starling's East India Criminal Law and Procedure [*A publication*] (DLA)
STARLO .... Special Test Army Reserve Limited Objective
StarMC .... Star Multi Care Services, Inc. [*Associated Press*] (SAG)
St Arm Leg Pow... St. Armand on the Legislative Power of England [*A publication*] (DLA)
STARNET.... Sustaining Base Army Network (GFGA)
STARP .... Supplemental Training and Readiness Program
STARPAHC... Space Technology Applied to Rural Papago Advanced Health Care (SSD)
STARPUBS... Standard Army Publications System
STARR .... Schedule, Technical, and Resources Report [*NASA*] (NASA)
STARR .... Staff Assessment of Readiness Report (MCD)
STARR .... Study Techniques for Advanced RADAR Requirements
Starr & C Ann St... Starr and Curtis' Annotated Statutes [*Illinois*] [*A publication*] (DLA)
StarRes.......... Star Resources Corp. [*Associated Press*] (SAG)
Starret .... Starrett [*L.S.*] Co. [*Associated Press*] (SAG)
StarrtCp .... Starrett Corp. [*Associated Press*] (SAG)
STARS .... Satellite Telemetry Automatic Reduction System [*NASA*]
STARS .... Satellite Transmission and Reception Specialists [*Houston, TX*] [*Telecommunications*] (TSSD)
STARS .... Seaborne Tracking and Ranging Station
STARS .... Sealink Ticket and Reservation System [*Sealink UK Ltd.*] [*Information service or system*] (IID)
STARS .... Secondary Training for Alaskan Rural Students (EDAC)
STARS .... Services and Techniques for Advanced Real-Time Systems [*Computer science*] (IAA)
STARS .... Shell Theory Automated for Rotational Structures
STARS .... Ship Tracking and Retrieval System [*MARAD*] (TAG)
STARS .... Short-Term Auction-Rate Stock [*Investment term*]
STARS .... Short-Term Auditory Retrieval and Storage Test
STARS .... Short Track Auto Racing Series [*Car racing*]
STARS .... Short Track Auto Racing Stars [*An association*]
STARS .... Silent Tactical Attack Reconnaissance System
STARS .... Simmons Teen-Age Research Study [*Simmons Market Research Bureau, Inc.*] [*Information service or system*] (CRD)
STARS .... Simplified Three Axes Reference System (IAA)
STARS .... Simulation and Training Advanced Research System [*Air Force*]
STARS .... Software Technology for Adaptable, Reliable Systems [*Military*]
STARS .... Soot Trap and Regeneration System [*Diesel engine exhaust emission controls*]
STARS .... Spaulding Teacher Activity Rating Schedule (EDAC)
STAR(S).......... Specialized Training and Reassignment (Student) [*Military*]
STARS .... Stabilized Twin-Gyro Attitude Reference System
STARS .... Standard Accounting and Reporting Systems (MCD)
STARS .... Standard Terminal Arrival Routes [*Aviation*] (MCD)
STARS .... Standard Terminal Automation Replacement System [*FAA*] (TAG)
STARS .... Standard Time and Rate Setting (MHDB)
STARS .... Standard, TRADOC Automated Retrieval System (MCD)
STARS .... Star Shot (SAA)
STARS .... Stationary Automotive Road Simulator
STARS .... Stellar Tracking Attitude Reference System
STARS .... Strategically Targeted Activities for Results System
STARS .... Strategic Target System [*Rocket*]
STARS .... Study of Tactical Airborne RADAR System
STARS .... Support Tracking Analysis Reporting Systems (MCD)
STARS .... Surface-to-Air Recovery System
STARS .... Surveillance Target Attack RADAR System
STARS .... Synchronized Time, Automated Reporting System
STARS .... System Test and Astronaut Requirement Simulation
STARS .... System Thermal Air Platform Reconnaissance Signature (MCD)
Star SC.......... Star Session Cases [*1824-25*] [*A publication*] (DLA)
STARS II.......... Shell Theory Automated for Rotational Structures - II (MCD)
START .... Safety Technology Applied to Rapid Transit [*Committee*] [*American Public Transit Association*]
START .... Selection to Activate Random Testing [*Module*] [*NASA*]
START .... Service Technician Advancement, Recruitment, and Training
START .... Small Tight Aspect Ratio Tokamak [*Plasma physics*]
START .... Spacecraft Technology and Advanced Reentry Tests [*Air Force*]
START .... Space Test and Reentry Technology
START .... Space Transport and Reentry Tests
START .... Special Treatment and Rehabilitative Training [*Prisons project*]
START .... Spend Today and Retire Tomorrow [*Consumer pension plan*]
START .... Sports Technique and Reaction Trainer [*Computerized training program for baseball and tennis*]
START .... State of the Total Army Report Team
START .... Story-Telling Automatic Reading Tutor
START .... Strategic Arms Reduction Talks (USGC)
START .... Strategic Arms Reduction Talks (AAGC)
START .... Strategic Arms Reduction Treaty
START .... Summary Tape Assistance, Research, and Training
START .... Systematic Tabular Analysis of Requirements Technique (IEEE)
START .... System for Analysis, Research and Training (EERA)
START .... System for Analysis, Research, and Training (USDC)
START .... System of Transportation Applying Rendezvous Technique (MCD)
StarTc.......... Star Technologies, Inc. [*Associated Press*] (SAG)

StarTel... StarSight Telecast, Inc. [*Associated Press*] (SAG)
Starter... Starter Corp. [*Associated Press*] (SAG)
STARTEX... Start of the Exercise (MCD)
STARTLE... Surveillance and Target Acquisition RADAR for Tank Location and Engagement [*Army*] (MCD)
STARTS... Software Tools for Application to Real Time Systems [*British*]
STARUTE... Stable Parachute
Starwd... Starwood Lodging Trust [*Associated Press*] (SAG)
StarwdLT... Starwood Lodging Trust [*Associated Press*] (SAG)
STAS... Safe-to-Arm Signal
STAS... Safe-to-Arm System (MUGU)
STAS... Short Term Analysis Services [*Scientific Services Program*] [*Army*] (RDA)
STAS... Space Transportation Architecture Study [*1985*]
STAS... Sporadic Testicular Agenesis Syndrome [*Medicine*] (DMAA)
STAS... Statutes
STAS... Strategic Transportation Analysis System [*MTMC*] (TAG)
STASH... Student Association for the Study of Hallucinogens [*Defunct*] (EA)
STASHIP... Station Ship [*Navy*] (NVT)
STASS... Special Tactical Air Surveillance System (IAA)
STASS... Submarine Tactical Array SONAR System
STASS... Submarine Towed Array SONAR System [*Navy*]
STASS... Submarine-Towed Array Surveillance System (NVT)
STASS... Surveillance Target Acquisition Support System (IAA)
StaSTBos... State Street Boston, Inc. [*Associated Press*] (SAG)
stat-... Electrostatic (IDOE)
STAT... i-STAT [*NASDAQ symbol*] (TTSB)
STAT... I-Stat Corp. [*NASDAQ symbol*] (SAG)
STAT... Photostat (NTCM)
STAT... SEABEE Technical Assistance Team [*Navy*]
STAT... SEABEE Training Advisory Team [*Navy*]
STAT... Seeing through Arithmetic Tests (AEBS)
STAT... Signal Transducer and Activator of Transcription [*Biochemistry*]
STAT... Signal Transducers and Activators of Transcription [*Biochemistry*]
STAT... Small Transport Aircraft Technology (MCD)
STAT... Society of Teachers of the Alexander Technique (EAIO)
STAT... State
STAT... Static (AAG)
STAT... Statim [*Immediately*] [*Latin*]
STAT... Station
STAT... Stationary [*Chemistry*]
STAT... Stationery Office [*British*]
STAT... Statistic (AFM)
Stat... Statius [*First century AD*] [*Classical studies*] (OCD)
Stat... Stative (BJA)
STAT... Statuary
STAT... Status (MSA)
STAT... Statute
Stat... [*United States*] Statutes at Large (USGC)
STAT... Statutory Tenant (DSUE)
STAT... Stop Teen-Age Addiction to Tobacco (EA)
STAT... Stratospheric Tracers of Atmospheric Transport [*Marine science*] (OSRA)
STAT... Stratospheric Tracers of Atmospheric Transport (USDC)
statA... Statampere [*Also, sA*] [*Unit of electric current*]
STAT AN... Statistical Annals (DLA)
Stat at L... United States Statutes at Large [*A publication*] (DLA)
StatAut... State Auto Financial Corp. [*Associated Press*] (SAG)
statC... Statcoulomb [*Also, sC*] [*Unit of electric charge*]
StatCan... Statistics Canada [*Statistics Canada Library*] [*Information service or system*]
StatCas... Station Casinos, Inc. [*Associated Press*] (SAG)
STATCAT... Statistical Context-Aided Testing [*North-Holland Publishing Co.*] [*Software package*] (NCC)
STATCO... Statistical Passenger Data Collection System [*MTMC*] (TAG)
StatConst... Status Constructus (BJA)
Stat Def... Statutory Definition [*Legal term*] (DLA)
STATDSB... Status Disable [*Computer science*] (MHDI)
STATE... Simplified Tactical Approach and Terminal Equipment
STATE... Simulation for Tank/Antitank Evaluation (NATG)
STATE... Space Transportation Air-Breathing Technology Evaluation [*DoD*]
StateBcp... State Bancorp, Inc. [*Associated Press*] (SAG)
State Dept Bull... United States State Department. Bulletin [*A publication*] (DLA)
StateF... Statewide Financial Corp. [*Associated Press*] (SAG)
StateFn... Statefed Financial Corp. [*Associated Press*] (SAG)
STATEM... Shipment Status System [*Military*] (AABC)
State Mot Carr Guide... State Motor Carrier Guide [*Commerce Clearing House*] [*A publication*] (DLA)
State R... New York State Reporter [*A publication*] (DLA)
State Rep... New York State Reporter [*A publication*] (DLA)
STATES... Simplified Tactical Approach and Terminal Equipment System
states... Statesman [*or Stateswoman*]
State Tax Cas Rep... State Tax Cases Reporter [*Commerce Clearing House*] [*A publication*] (DLA)
State Tr... State Trials (Howell) [*England*] [*A publication*] (DLA)
State Tr NS... State Trials, New Series, Edited by Macdonell [*England*] [*A publication*] (DLA)
StatewdeF... Statewide Financial Corp. [*Associated Press*] (SAG)
statF... Statfarad [*Also, sF*] [*Unit of capacitance*]
Stat Glo... Statute of Gloucester [*First statute to give costs in actions*] [*A publication*] (DLA)
statH... Stathenry [*Also, sH*] [*Unit of inductance*]
STATH... Statherin (DMAA)
Stath Abr... Statham's Abridgment [*A publication*] (DLA)
StatHlt... Stat Healthcare, Inc. [*Associated Press*] (SAG)
StatHlth... Stat Healthcare, Inc. [*Associated Press*] (SAG)
STATIC... Student Taskforce Against Telecommunication Information Concealment [*Student legal action organization*]
Stat ICJ... Statute of the International Court of Justice [*A publication*] (DLA)
STATINDEX... Stationery Industry Exhibition [*British*] (ITD)
STATINF... Statistical Information System [*Bundesamt fuer Statistik*] [*Switzerland Information service or system*] (CRD)
Stat Inst... Statutory Instruments [*A publication*] (DLA)
STATION... Station [*Commonly used*] (OPSA)
STATIS... Statistics
Statl... Statistical [*Army*]
St at Large... Statutes at Large [*A publication*] (DLA)
STATLIB... Statistical Computing Library [*Bell System*]
Stat Local... Governments Statute of Local Governments [*A publication*] (DLA)
Stat Marl... Statute of Marlbridge [*A publication*] (DLA)
Stat Mer... Statute of Merton [*A publication*] (DLA)
Stat Mert... Statute of Merton [*A publication*] (DLA)
STATMUX... Statistical Multiplexer [*Computer science*]
STATN... Station [*Commonly used*] (OPSA)
StatnCas... Station Casinos, Inc. [*Associated Press*] (SAG)
STATNET... Statistical Analysis of Network
STATNR... Stationer
STATNRY... Stationary
Stat NZ... Statutes of New Zealand [*A publication*] (DLA)
Stat O & R... Statutory Orders and Regulations [*Canada*] [*A publication*] (DLA)
statOe... Statoersted (IDOE)
STATPAC... Statistics Package [*Computer program*] (IEEE)
STAT-PACK... Statistical Package (MHDI)
STATRAFO... Standard Transfer Order
Stat R & O... Statutory Rules and Orders [*1890-1947*] [*England*] [*A publication*] (DLA)
Stat R & O & Stat Inst Rev... Statutory Rules and Orders and Statutory Instruments Revised [*England*] [*A publication*] (DLA)
Stat R & ONI... Statutory Rules and Orders of Northern Ireland [*A publication*] (DLA)
Stat Realm... Statutes of the Realm [*England*] [*A publication*] (DLA)
Stat Reg NZ... Statutory Regulations [*New Zealand*] [*A publication*] (DLA)
STATREP... Advise Present Grade, Status, Physical Condition, and Mailing Address of Following Named [*Military*]
STATS... Simulated Tax and Transfer System [*Social Security Administration*] (GFGA)
STATS... Stationary Tank Automatic Target System (MCD)
Stats... Statistics (DD)
statS... Statsiemens [*Also, sS*] [*Unit of electric conductance, admittance, and susceptance*]
STATS... Strategic/Tactical Area Test System (MCD)
STATSBOBP... Scale of Teacher Attitudes toward Selective Behavior of Boy Pupils [*Satirical*]
Stats Can... Statistics Canada
STAT-SEL... Status Select [*Army*]
STATSERVOFF... Statistical Service Office [*Supreme Headquarters Allied Powers Europe*] (NATG)
STATSVS... Statistical Services (MUGU)
STATT... Statement
statT... Stattesla [*Unit of magnetic flux density*]
STATTS... Stationary Automatic Tank Target System (MCD)
statV... Statvolt [*Also, sV*] [*Electrostatic unit of potential difference*]
statWb... Statweber [*Unit of magnetic flux*]
Stat Westm... Statute of Westminster [*A publication*] (DLA)
Stat Winch... Statute of Winchester [*A publication*] (DLA)
STATY... Stationary (WGA)
STATY... Statutory (ROG)
Staundef... Staundeforde's Exposition of the King's Prerogative [*A publication*] (DLA)
Staundf Prerog... Staundeforde's Exposition of the King's Prerogative [*A publication*] (DLA)
Staund Pl... Staundeforde's Pleas of Crown [*A publication*] (DLA)
Staunf Pr... Staundeforde's Exposition of the King's Prerogative [*A publication*] (DLA)
STAVRA... Supreme High Command of the Soviet Armed Forces [*Russian*] (MCD)
STAX... Sludge Tracking Acoustical Experiment [*Marine science*] (MSC)
STAY... Extended Stay Amer [*NASDAQ symbol*] (TTSB)
STAY... Extended Stay America [*NASDAQ symbol*] (SAG)
STB... Bachelor of Sacred Theology (NADA)
STB... Bachelor of the Science of Theology
StB... Kommentar zum Neuen Testament aus Talmud und Midrasch (H. L. Strack - F. Billerbeck) [*A publication*] (BJA)
STB... Sacrae Theologiae Baccalaureus [*Bachelor of Sacred Theology*] [*Latin*] (GPO)
STB... Santa Barbara [*Venezuela*] [*Airport symbol*] (OAG)
STB... Save the Bush Project [*Commonwealth*] (EERA)
STB... Scandinavian Tourist Boards (EA)
STB... Scan True Bearing (NVT)
STB... Scottish Tourist Board (EAIO)
STB... Segment Table Base [*Computer science*] (IAA)
STB... Segment Tag BITS [*Binary Digits*]
STB... September Resources Ltd. [*Vancouver Stock Exchange symbol*]
STB... Shore Terminal Box (MSA)
STB... Signal Training Brigade (MCD)
STB... Snci-Tours Benin Inter Regional [*ICAO designator*] (FAAC)
STB... Soprano, Tenor, Bass
STB... Southern Tourist Board [*British*] (DCTA)
STB... Special Tax Bond
Stb... Staatsblad [*Official Bulletin*] [*Netherlands*] (ILCA)

STB............ Stable (MSA)
STB............ Staged Turbulent Bed Process [*Chevron Corp.*] [*Oil shale pyrolysis*]
STB............ Standard Torsion Bar (MCD)
STB............ Star Banc Corp. [*NYSE symbol*] (SAG)
STB............ State Tender Board [*Victoria, Australia*]
STB............ St. Blazey [*British depot code*]
STB............ Steinbach [*Federal Republic of Germany*] [*Seismograph station code, US Geological Survey*] (SEIS)
STB............ Stillborn [*Medicine*]
STB............ Stock-Tank Barrel [*Petroleum industry*]
STB............ Stop Bar (DA)
STB............ Stourbridge [*British depot code*]
STB............ Strata Titles Board [*New South Wales, Australia*]
STB............ Streaming Tape Backup Unit
STB............ Stretch Block (MCD)
STB............ Subsystems Test Bed (MCD)
STB............ Sun's True Bearing [*Navigation*]
STB............ Supertropical Bleach [*Sanitizing agent*]
STB............ Surface Transportation Board [*Formerly, the ICC - Interstate Commerce Commission, 1996*]
STB............ Surface Transportation Board [*Department of Transportation*]
STB............ Systems Testing Branch [*Social Security Administration*]
STB............ System [*or Subsystem*] Test Bed [*NASA*] (KSC)
STBA........... S & T Bancorp [*NASDAQ symbol*] (SAG)
STBA........... Selective Top-to-Bottom Algorithm (DIT)
St Bar Rev... State Bar Review [*A publication*] (DLA)
STBC........... School Readiness Tests for Blind Children
STBC........... State Bancorp, Inc. [*NASDAQ symbol*] (SAG)
STBC........... State Bancorp NY [*NASDAQ symbol*] (TTSB)
STBD........... Starboard
STBDQ........ Supervising Teacher Behavior Description Questionnaire (EDAC)
STBE........... Society of Teachers in Business Education [*British*] (EAIO)
STBE........... Space Transportation Booster Engine
STBF........... Southeastern Thrift & Bank Fund [*NASDAQ symbol*] (SAG)
sTBG........... Slow Thyroxine-Binding Globulin [*Endocrinology*]
STBI............ STB Systems [*NASDAQ symbol*] (TTSB)
STBI............ STB Systems, Inc. [*NASDAQ symbol*] (SAG)
STBL........... Stable
STBLN......... Stabilization (MSA)
STBLZ......... Stabilize (AABC)
STBM........... Shaft-to-Bore Misalignment
St Bonaventure U... St. Bonaventure University (GAGS)
StBPt........... Standard Brands Paint Co. [*Associated Press*] (SAG)
STBRIAV...... Saint Briavels [*England*]
St Brown...... Stewart-Brown's Cases in the Court of the Star Chamber [*1455-1547*] [*A publication*] (DLA)
STBS........... Sierra Tahoe Bancorp [*NASDAQ symbol*] (SAG)
STBSCP....... Stroboscope [*Engineering*]
STB Sy......... STB Systems, Inc. [*Associated Press*] (SAG)
STBT........... Steamboat (ADA)
STBT........... Subcaliber Tracer Bullet Trainer [*Army*] (INF)
STBU........... Statistical Bulletin
STBY........... Standby (AAG)
STC............ Chief SONAR Technician [*Navy rating*]
STC............ Sacramento Test Center (MCD)
STC............ Said to Contain [*Cargo manifest description*]
STC............ Samuel Taylor Coleridge [*Nineteenth-century British poet*]
STC............ Satellite Television Corp. [*Washington, DC*] [*Telecommunications*] (TSSD)
STC............ Satellite Test Center [*Air Force*]
STC............ Satellite Tracking Center [*Sunnyvale, CA*]
STC............ Satellite Tracking Committee [*Military*]
STC............ Scandinavian Travel Commission [*Later, Scandinavian National Travel Offices*] (EA)
STC............ Science and Technology Center [*National Science Foundation*]
STC............ Science and Technology Corp. (RDA)
STC............ Security Time Control
STC............ Security Training Center
STC............ Senate Tourism Caucus (EA)
STC............ Senior Training Corps [*British*]
STC............ Sensitivity-Time Control [*RADAR*]
STC............ Sequence-Tagged Connector [*Genetics*]
STC............ Serum Theophylline Concentration [*Clinical chemistry*]
STC............ Service Technology Corp. [*of Ling-Temco-Vought, Inc.*]
STC............ Service to Chapters [*Red Cross*]
STC............ Service to Claimants [*Unemployment Insurance Service*] [*Department of Labor*]
STC............ Serving Test Center [*Bell System*]
STC............ Set Carry
STC............ [*The*] Seven Tablets of Creation [*L. W. King*] [*A publication*] (BJA)
STC............ SHAPE [*Supreme Headquarters Allied Powers Europe*] Technical Center [*Formerly, SADTC*] [*The Hague, Netherlands*] [*NATO*]
STC............ Short Time Constant
STC............ Short Title Catalog [*A publication*]
STC............ Short Training Courses (AIE)
STC............ Signal Training Centre [*British military*] (DMA)
STC............ Silicon Transistor Corp. (IAA)
STC............ Simulation Tape Conversion
STC............ Single-Trip Container
STC............ Ski Touring Council [*Defunct*] (EA)
STC............ Slow Time Constant (MCD)
STC............ Smokeless Tobacco Council (EA)
STC............ Societe de Transports et de Tourisme [*Mali*] [*ICAO designator*] (FAAC)
STC............ Society for Technical Communication (EA)
STC............ Society of Telecommunications Consultants (EA)
STC............ Society of Theatrical Carpenters [*A union*] [*British*]
STC............ Society of Town Clerks [*British*] (BI)
STC............ Soft Tissue Calcification [*Medicine*]
STC............ Solar Thermal Commission (PDAA)
STC............ Solidaridad de Trabajadores Cristianos [*Nicaragua*] [*Political party*] (EY)
STC............ Solid Tantalum Capacitor (PDAA)
STC............ Sound Transmission Class [*Followed by number, indicates FHA rating of sound insulating quality of a partition construction*]
STC............ Source Telecomputing Corp. [*McLean, VA*] [*Telecommunications*] (TSSD)
STC............ South Thames College [*London, England*]
STC............ Spacecraft Test Conductor [*NASA*] (KSC)
STC............ Space Technology Center
STC............ Space Test Center [*Air Force*]
STC............ Space-Time Continuum
STC............ Spatiotemporal Chaos [*Physics*]
STC............ Specialists Training Center
STC............ Specific Taste Changes
STC............ Specific Thermal Capacity
STC............ Spectral Transfer Coefficient
STC............ Standard Telephone and Cable [*IT & T affiliate*] [*Research center British*]
STC............ Standard Test Chamber (MCD)
STC............ Standard Test Configuration [*NASA*] (NASA)
STC............ Standard Transmission Code [*Computer science*]
STC............ Standing Technical Committee [*British*] (DCTA)
STC............ State Tax Cases [*Commerce Clearing House*] [*A publication*] (DLA)
STC............ State Teachers College
STC............ State Total Cost [*Bookselling*] (DGA)
STC............ Station Technical Control [*Telecommunications*] (TEL)
STC............ Station Test and Calibration
StC............. Status Constructus (BJA)
STC............ St. Cloud, MN [*Location identifier FAA*] (FAAL)
STC............ Stepchild
St C............ Stephen's Commentaries on the Laws of England [*21st ed.*] [*1950*] [*A publication*] (DLA)
STC............ Step Timing Control [*Truck engineering*]
STC............ Stereo Tape Club of America
STC............ Stern Telecommunications Corp. [*New York, NY*] [*Telecommunications*] (TSSD)
STC............ Stewart Information Services Corp. [*NYSE symbol*] (SPSG)
STC............ Stewart Information Sv [*NYSE symbol*] (TTSB)
STC............ Stewart, Tabori & Chang [*Publisher*]
STC............ Still Traffic Camera
STC............ Stock Trust Certificate [*Investment term*]
STC............ Stone Canyon Observatory [*California*] [*Seismograph station code, US Geological Survey*] (SEIS)
STC............ Storage Container (MCD)
STC............ Storage Technology Corp. (IAA)
STC............ Stored Time Command
STC............ Straight Cactus [*Horticulture*]
STC............ Streamtube Curvature
STC............ Subtropical Convergence [*Oceanography*]
STC............ Summit Technical Center [*Celanese Research Co.*]
STC............ Supplemental Type Certificate
STC............ Surgical Textiles Conference [*British*] (DBA)
STC............ Symbol Table Counter [*Computer science*] (IAA)
STC............ Synaptic Transporter Current [*Neurochemistry*]
STC............ Synthetic Turf Council [*Defunct*] (EA)
STC............ Systems Test Complex [*NASA*]
STC............ System Technical Control
STC............ System Test Complex (IAA)
STC............ System Test Configuration
STC............ System Test Console
STC............ System Transfer Constant
STCA........... Scottish Terrier Club of America (EA)
STCA........... Short Term Conflict Alert System [*Aviation*] (DA)
STCA........... Short Tests of Clerical Ability
STCA........... Silky Terrier Club of America (EA)
STCA........... Skye Terrier Club of America (EA)
STCA........... Sodium Trichloroacetate [*Organic chemistry*]
STCA........... Staffordshire Terrier Club of America (EA)
S/TCAC....... Scientific/Technical Careers Advisory Committee [*Environmental Protection Agency*] (GFGA)
STCAC......... Sydney Transport Coordination Advisory Council [*New South Wales, Australia*]
STCAN/FOM... Services Techniques des Construction et Armes Navales / France Outre Mer [*French river patrol boat used in Vietnam*] (VNW)
St Cas.......... Stillingfleet's English Ecclesiastical Cases [*A publication*] (DLA)
StCath.......... Studia Catholica [*Nijmegen*] [*A publication*] (BJA)
STCB........... Subtask Control Block [*Computer science*] (IBMDP)
STCC........... Spacecraft Technical Control Center (MDG)
STCC........... Springfield Technical Community College [*Massachusetts*]
STCC........... Standards Council of Canada [*See also CCNO*]
STCC........... Standard Transportation Commodity Classification [*or Code*]
STCC........... Syndicat des Travailleurs en Communication du Canada
STCC........... Syndicat des Travailleurs en Communication, Electronique, Electricite, Techniciens, et Salaries du Canada [*Communications, Electronic, Electrical, Technical, and Salaried Workers of Canada - CWC*]
STCCF......... Smartel Communications [*NASDAQ symbol*] (TTSB)
STCCF......... Smartel Communications Corp. [*NASDAQ symbol*] (SAG)
STCDHS....... Spacecraft Telemetry Command Data Handling System

STCDS .... System Test Complex Data System
STCDSS .... Standing Technical Committee on Disposal of Sewage Sludge [*British*] (DCTA)
STCE .... System Test Complex Equipment
STCFEO .... Science and Technology Center, Far East Office [*Army*] (AABC)
STCG .... Super Tension Cables Group [*British*] (DBA)
STCH .... Shared Tech Fairchild [*NASDAQ symbol*] (TTSB)
STCH .... Shared Technologies, Inc. [*NASDAQ symbol*] (NQ)
STCH .... Stitch (MSA)
St Ch Cas .... Star Chamber Cases [*England*] [*A publication*] (DLA)
STCI .... Siebert Telecommunications Consulting, Inc. [*Cincinnati, OH*] [*Telecommunications*] (TSSD)
STCI .... Station Casinos [*NASDAQ symbol*] (TTSB)
STCI .... Station Casinos, Inc. [*NASDAQ symbol*] (SAG)
STCICS .... Strike Command Integrated Communications System [*British*]
STCIP .... Station Casinos $3.50 Cv Pfd [*NASDAQ symbol*] (TTSB)
STCK .... Stock
STCKHLDR... Stockholder
STCL .... Shared Tech Cellular [*NASDAQ symbol*] (TTSB)
STCL .... Shared Technologies Cellular, Inc. [*NASDAQ symbol*] (SAG)
STCL .... Source-Term Control Loop [*Nuclear energy*] (NRCH)
STCLB .... Start Climb [*Aviation*] (FAAC)
St Clem .... St. Clement's Church Case [*Philadelphia, PA*] [*A publication*] (DLA)
St Cloud St U... St. Cloud State University (GAGS)
STCM .... Master Chief SONAR Technician [*Navy rating*]
STCO .... Strata and Tenancy Commissioner's Office [*New South Wales, Australia*]
STCO .... Supervisor Training Conference Outline [*Air Force*] (MCD)
STCOL .... Steel Column [*Camutek*] [*Software package*] (NCC)
STCP .... Short-Term Cost Plan [*NASA*] (NASA)
STCP .... Society of Tympanuchus Cupido Pinnatus (EA)
STCR .... Solar Thermal Central Receiver
STCR .... Starcraft Automotive Corp. [*NASDAQ symbol*] (SAG)
STCR .... Starcraft Corp. [*NASDAQ symbol*] (TTSB)
STCR .... Systems, Test, and Checkout Report (DICI)
STCRS .... Solar Thermal Central Receiver System
STCS .... Science and Technology Center for Superconductivity [*National Science Foundation*]
STCS .... Senior Chief SONAR Technician [*Navy rating*]
STCS .... Society of Technical Civil Servants [*British*] (BI)
STCS .... Surveyor Thermal Control Section
STCST .... Second Telecommunications Carrier Selection Team [*Australia*]
STCT .... Small Transportable Communications Terminal
STCT .... System Technical Coordinator Technician (SAA)
StCu .... Stratocumulus [*Cloud*] [*Meteorology*] (AIA)
STCV .... Strawberry Crinkle Virus [*Plant pathology*]
STCVS .... Society of Thoracic and Cardiovascular Surgeons [*British*] (DBA)
STCW .... Standard of Training, Certification, and Watchkeeping Convention (DS)
STCW .... Stichting Technisch Centrum Waalsteen [*Research center Netherlands*] (IRC)
STCW .... System Time Code Word
STD .... Banco de Santander SA [*NYSE symbol*] (SPSG)
STD .... Banco Santander ADS [*NYSE symbol*] (TTSB)
STD .... Doctor of Sacred Theology (NADA)
STD .... Doctor of the Science of Theology
STD .... Sacrae Theologiae Doctor [*Doctor of Sacred Theology*] [*Latin*]
STD .... Safety Topic Discussion (AAG)
STD .... Salinity, Temperature and Depth [*Probe*] [*Marine science*] (OSRA)
STD .... Salinity/Temperature/Density [*or Depth*] [*Oceanography*]
STD .... Santo Domingo [*Venezuela*] [*Airport symbol*] (AD)
std .... Saturated (MAE)
STD .... Schools of Theology in Dubuque [*Library network*]
STD .... Seated (WGA)
STD .... Sea Transport Department [*British military*] (DMA)
STD .... Seismic Tunnel Detector [*DoD*] (VNW)
STD .... Semiconductor on Thermoplastic on Dielectric [*Technology*] (IAA)
STD .... Servo Tape Display
STD .... Set Driver (SAA)
STD .... Sexually Transmitted Disease [*Medicine*]
STD .... Ship Training Detachment
STD .... Short-Term Debt (MHDW)
STD .... Short-Term Disability
STD .... Short Time Duty (IAA)
STD .... Shuttle Test Director [*NASA*] (MCD)
STD .... Silicon Triple Diffused (IAA)
STD .... Skin Test Dose
STD .... Skin to Tumor Distance [*Medicine*] (MAE)
STD .... Skytrak Aeronautical Systems Ltd. [*British*] [*FAA designator*] (FAAC)
STD .... Sledborne Time Digitizer
STD .... Society for Theological Discussion [*Defunct*] (EA)
STD .... Society of Typographic Designers [*British*] (EAIO)
STD .... Sodium Tetradecyl Sulfate [*Pharmacology*] (DAVI)
STD .... Sodium Thermionic Detector (SAA)
STD .... Software Test Description [*DoD*]
STD .... South Tibetan Detachment [*Geology*]
STD .... South Tropical Disturbance [*of the planet Jupiter*] (BARN)
STD .... Spacecraft Technology Division [*NASA*] (KSC)
STD .... Spectral Theory of Diffraction (IAA)
STD .... Sports Trainers Digest [*A publication*]
STD .... Standard (AFM)
std .... Standard (WDMC)
STD .... Standard Test Dose
STD .... Standard Trustco Ltd. [*Toronto Stock Exchange symbol*]
STD .... Standing (AABC)
STD .... Started (ADA)
STD .... State Taxation Department [*Western Australia*]
STD .... State-Transition Diagram [*Computer science*]
STD .... Stepwise Thermal Desorption [*Surface analysis*]
STD .... Steward [*British*]
ST D .... Stopped Diapason [*Organ stop*] [*Music*]
STD .... Storage Target Date
STD .... Storage Tube Display
STD .... Store Decrement (SAA)
STD .... Strain Gauge Transient Dosimetry
STD .... Strategic Technical Directorate [*South Vietnamese studies and observations group*] (VNW)
STD .... Stream Tree Data (PDAA)
STD .... Stripline Tunnel Diode
STD .... Studio
STD .... Subscriber Toll Dialing [*Telecommunications*] (TSSD)
STD .... Subscriber Trunk Dialing [*Telephone communications*]
STD .... Sunbeam-Talbot-Darracq [*Automobile manufacturer*]
STD .... Superconductive Tunneling Device (IAA)
STD .... Supporting Technology Development (KSC)
STD .... Suspension Technology Demonstrator [*Army*] (RDA)
STD .... Synopsis Series of the United States Treasury Decisions [*A publication*] (DLA)
STD .... System Technology Demonstration Program (RDA)
S-TDA .... Selenium-Tellurium Development Association (EA)
STDA .... Steward's Assistant [*Navy*]
STDA .... StreetTalk Directory Assistance [*VINES*] [*Computer science*] (PCM)
STDA .... Stripline Tunnel Diode Amplifier
STDB .... Steward's Branch [*Marine Corps*]
STDBY .... Standby (NVT)
STDC .... Society of Typographic Designers of Canada (DGA)
STDC .... Southern Travel Directors Council
STDC .... Standards Council of Canada [*See also CCNO*]
STDCF .... Space Telescope Data Capture Facility [*NASA*] (SSD)
StdCm .... Standard Commercial Corp. [*Associated Press*] (SAG)
STD/DEV ..... Standard Deviation (MCD)
STDDS .... Submarine Tactical Data Display Subsystem (MCD)
St Dept .... State Department Reports [*A publication*] (DLA)
STDF .... Sodium Taurodihydrofusidate [*Organic chemistry*]
STDF .... Standoff
StdFdBcp ..... Standard Federal Bancorp [*Associated Press*] (SAG)
StdFincl .... Standard Financial Co. [*Associated Press*] (SAG)
StdFndg .... Standard Funding Corp. [*Associated Press*] (SAG)
STDFT³ .... Standard Cubic Feet (WDAA)
stdgls .... Stained Glass (VRA)
STDH .... Skin Test for Delayed Hypersensitivity [*Medicine*] (DMAA)
ST DIAP .... Stopped Diapason [*Organ stop*] [*Music*]
STDL .... Standard Distribution List [*NASA*] (NASA)
STDL .... Submarine Tactical Data Link (NVT)
StdM .... Standard Matched (DAC)
STDM .... Statistical Time Division Multiplexer [*or Multiplexing*]
STDM .... Synchronous Time-Division Multiplexing [*Computer science*] (MDG)
StdMgt .... Standard Management Corp. [*Associated Press*] (SAG)
StdMic .... Standard Microsystems Corp. [*Associated Press*] (SAG)
STDN .... Set the Date Now [*Association supporting the end of US military involvement in Indochina*] [*Defunct*] (EA)
STDN .... Spacecraft Tracking and Data Network (NITA)
STDN .... Space Flight Tracking and Data Network [*Formerly, STADAN*] [*NASA*]
STDN .... Standardization (AFM)
STDNT .... Student
STDP .... Short-Term Dynamic Psychotherapy
STDP .... Special Training Devices Program (AFM)
StdPac .... Standard-Pacific Corp. [*Associated Press*] (SAG)
StdProd .... Standard Products Co. [*Associated Press*] (SAG)
STDR .... Science and Technology Desk Reference [*A publication*]
STDR .... Space Technology Data Report
STDR .... Standard
StdReg .... Standard Register Co. [*Associated Press*] (SAG)
STDS .... Set Theoretic Data Structure (IAA)
STDS .... Snake Torpedo Destruction System
STDS .... South Tibetan Detachment System [*Geology*]
STDS .... Standards [*Timber measurement*] (EY)
STDS .... Strategic Target Data System (SSD)
STDS .... Submarine Tactical Data System (MCD)
STDS .... Survey of Teacher Demand and Shortage [*Department of Education*] (GFGA)
STDS .... System for Thermal Diagnostic Studies
STDST .... Start Descent [*Aviation*] (FAAC)
STD TF .... Standard Tube Feeding [*Gastroenterology*] (DAVI)
STDV .... Start Tank Discharge Valve (KSC)
STDVG .... Stern Diving
STDW .... Standard Deviation Waveform [*Physics*]
STDWN .... Stand Down (MCD)
STDY .... Saturday
STDY .... Steady (MSA)
STDZN .... Standardization (AABC)
STE .... Sainte [*French*] (EY)
STE .... Scholars for Teaching Excellence (DMAA)
STE .... Segment Table Entry [*Computer science*] (MDG)
STE .... Self-Trapped Exciton [*Physical chemistry*]
STE .... Semitool Europe Ltd. [*British ICAO designator*] (FAAC)
STE .... Service Technique Externe (IAA)
STE .... Shield Test Experiment [*Nuclear energy*] (NRCH)
STE .... Shift Technical Engineer [*Nuclear energy*] (NRCH)

STE .... Signalling Terminal Equipment [*Telecommunications*] (OSI)
STE .... [*The*] Simplified Test Equipment [*Army*] (INF)
STE .... Single Threshold Element [*Computer science*] (IAA)
Ste .... Societe [*Company*] [*French Business term*]
STE .... Society of Telecom Executives [*Trade union*] [*British*]
STE .... Society of Telecommunications Executives (NITA)
STE .... Society of Test Engineers [*British*] (DBA)
STE .... Society of Tractor Engineers [*Later, SAE*]
STE .... Spacecraft Test Engineering [*NASA*] (KSC)
STE .... Span Terminating Equipment [*Telecommunications*] (TEL)
STE .... Special Temporary Enlistment [*Coast Guard*]
STE .... Special Test Equipment
STE .... Special-Type Ellipsometer
STE .... Specific Temperature Excursion
STE .... Standard Terminal Equipment [*Computer science*] (HGAA)
STE .... Star Tracker Electronics [*Apollo*] [*NASA*]
STE .... Station Test Equipment [*Deep Space Instrumentation Facility, NASA*]
STE .... Statute
STE .... Stelco, Inc. [*Toronto Stock Exchange symbol Vancouver Stock Exchange symbol*]
STE .... Stepanavan [*Former USSR Seismograph station code, US Geological Survey Closed*] (SEIS)
Ste .... Stephanus Provincialis [*Flourished, 1290-97*] [*Authority cited in pre-1607 legal work*] (DSA)
Ste .... Stephanus Tornacensis [*Deceased, 1203*] [*Authority cited in pre-1607 legal work*] (DSA)
STE .... Stet Societa Finaziaria Telefonica PA [*NYSE symbol*] (SAG)
STE .... STET-Societa Fin Tel Ord ADS [*NYSE symbol*] (TTSB)
STE .... Stevens Point [*Wisconsin*] [*Airport symbol Obsolete*] (OAG)
STE .... Stockton Terminal & Eastern Railroad [*AAR code*]
STE .... Stop Transfer Effector [*Genetics*]
STE .... Suitability Test Evaluation (AAG)
STE .... Suite
STE .... Supergroup Translation Equipment
STE .... Support Test Equipment (MCD)
STE .... Syrian Telecommunications Establishment [*Syrian Arab Republic*] (TSSD)
STE .... System Test and Evaluation
STE .... System Test Engineer [*NASA*] (NASA)
STE .... System Timing Element (ECII)
STE .... System Training Exercise (SAA)
STEA .... Short-Term Emergency Assistance
STE.A .... Stelco Inc.'A' [*TS symbol*] (TTSB)
STE A .... STET-Societa Fin Tele Svg ADS [*NYSE symbol*] (TTSB)
STEA .... Surveyor Test Equipment Assembly
STEA .... System Test, Evaluation, and Assembly
STEADY .... Simulation Tables - Environment and Dynamic (SAA)
STEAG .... Steinkohlen-Elektrizitaet AG [*West Germany*]
STEAM .... Department of Science, Technology, Energy, and Materials [*Proposed Cabinet department*]
STEAM .... Schema Tuning, Evaluation, and Analytical Model (PDAA)
STEAM .... Sensor Technology as Applied to the Marine Corps
STEAM .... Standard Towing Equipment for Aircraft Maintenance (MCD)
STEAM .... Stimulated Echo Acquisition Mode [*Medicine*] (DMAA)
STEAM .... Stochastic Evolutionary Adoption Model (PDAA)
STEAM .... Streptonigrin, Thioguanine, Endoxan [*Cyclophosphamide*], Actinomycin, Mitomycin C [*Antineoplastic drug regimen*]
STEAP .... Simulated Trajectories Error Analysis Program [*NASA*]
Stearns RA... Stearn's Real Actions [*A publication*] (DLA)
Stearns Real Act... Stearn's Real Actions [*A publication*] (DLA)
SteArt .... State of the Art, Inc. [*Associated Press*] (SAG)
steat .... Steatite (VRA)
STEC .... Serv-Tech, Inc. [*NASDAQ symbol*] (NQ)
STEC .... Solar Thermal Electric Conversation (MCD)
STEC .... Surface Treatment Enhancement Council [*Metallurgy*]
STEC .... Syndicat des Travailleurs de l'Energie et de la Chimie [*Energy and Chemical Workers Union - ECWU*] [*Canada*]
St Eccl Cas... Stillingfleet's English Ecclesiastical Cases [*A publication*] (DLA)
Stecher Agency & Partnership... Stecher's Cases on Agency and Partnership [*A publication*] (DLA)
SteckVn .... Steck-Vaughn Publishing Corp. [*Associated Press*] (SAG)
STECR .... Ships Tactical Environmental Control Receiver
STECS .... Software Technology and Engineering Center Staff [*Social Security Administration*]
STED .... Science, Technology, and Economic Development
STED .... Science Technology and Education Division [*British Council*] (AIE)
STED .... Solar Turboelectric Drive (IAA)
STED .... Standard Technical Equipment Development Division [*National Security Agen cy*] [*Obsolete*]
STEDBAC ..... Stearyldimethylbenzylammonium Chloride [*Organic chemistry*]
STEDI .... Space Thrust Evolution and Disposal Investigation [*Air Force*]
STEDI .... Student Explorer Demonstration Initiative [*NASA*]
STEDMIS ..... Ships Technical Data Management Information System [*Navy*]
STEDMIS ..... Standard Technical Data Management Information System (CAAL)
St Edward's U... St. Edward's University (GAGS)
STEEG .... Scanned Topographic Electroencephalograph
STEEL .... Simulation Test Environment to Evaluate Team Load (SAA)
STEELFACTS... Materials Database Steel and Iron [*German Iron and Steel Engineers Association*] [*Ceased operation*] [*Information service or system*] (IID)
SteelTch ...... Steel Technologies, Inc. [*Associated Press*] (SAG)
Steenth .... Sixteenth [*Stock and commodity price quotes*]
STEEP .... Safety Training for the Execution of Emergency Procedures [*NASA*]
STEEP .... Shock Two-Dimensional Eulerian Elastic Plastic [*Computer code*]
STEEP .... Solution to Environmental and Economic Problems
Steer PL ...... Steer on Parish Law [*6th ed.*] [*1899*] [*A publication*] (DLA)
STEG .... Staatliche Gesellschaft zur Erfassung von Ruestungsgut [*German Public Corporation for the Collection and Distribution of War Materials*]
STEG .... Supersonic Transport Evaluation Group
STEI .... Stewart Enterprises'A' [*NASDAQ symbol*] (TTSB)
STEI .... Stewart Enterprises, Inc. [*NASDAQ symbol*] (SPSG)
STE/ICE .... Simplified Test Equipment for Internal Combustion Engines (RDA)
STE/ICE .... Standard Test Equipment / Internal Combustion Engine
STE/ICEPM... Simplified Test Equipment for Internal Combustion Engine Powered Material (MCD)
STEIN .... System Test Environment Input
S Teind .... Shaw's Scotch Teind [*Tithe*] Cases [*A publication*] (DLA)
SteinMrt ...... Stein Mart, Inc. [*Associated Press*] (SAG)
STEK .... Steck-Vaughn Publishing [*NASDAQ symbol*] (TTSB)
STEK .... Steck-Vaughn Publishing Corp. [*NASDAQ symbol*] (SAG)
STEL .... SA Holdings [*NASDAQ symbol*] (SAG)
STEL .... SA Telecommunications [*NASDAQ symbol*] (TTSB)
STEL .... SA Telecommunications, Inc. [*NASDAQ symbol*] (SAG)
STEL .... Short-Term Exposure Limit [*Environmental chemistry*]
STEL .... Society of Telegraphic Engineers [*British*]
STEL .... Structure Tests, English Language [*Educational test*]
STEL .... Studenta Tutmonda Esperantista Liga [*World League of Esperanto-Speaking Students*]
STELCO .... Steel Co. of Canada
STELLA .... Satellite Transmission Experiment Linking Laboratories [*European Space Agency*]
STELLA .... Structural Thinking Experiential Learning Laboratory with Animation [*Software*]
STELLA .... System Ten European Language Ledger Accounting (PDAA)
STELLAR ...... Star Tracker for Economical Long Life Attitude Reference [*NASA*]
STEM .... Scanning Transmission Electron Microscope
STEM .... Scanning Transmission Electron Microscopy
STEM .... Science and Technology Employment [*Longman Cartermill Ltd.*] [*Scotland*] [*Information service or system*] (CRD)
STEM .... Science, Technology, and Mathematics [*Adult Literacy Project*] [*Australia*]
STEM .... SEABEE Tactical Equipment Management [*Navy*]
STEM .... Searching Together Educational Ministries (EA)
STEM .... Self-Storing Tubular Extensionable Member (IAA)
STEM .... Shaped Tube Electrolytic Machining [*GE*]
STEM .... Shoplifters Take Everybody's Money
STEM .... Short-Term Energy Monitoring [*Colorado State University*]
STEM .... Situated Atop an Extendable Mast (SAA)
STEM .... Society of Teachers of Emergency Medicine (EA)
STEM .... Socio-Technological-Economic-Military [*DoD*]
STEM .... Solar-Terrestrial Environment Model [*to predict the terrestrial effects of solar events*]
STEM .... Special Technical and Economic Mission
STEM .... Special Telemetry Equipped Missile
STEM .... Statistically-Tensioned Extension Mast (DNAB)
STEM .... Stay Time Extension Module [*NASA*]
STEM .... Stellar Tracker Evaluation Missile
STEM .... Storable Tubular Extendable Member
STEM .... Systems for Tools and Equipment Management [*Military*] (AFIT)
STEM .... Systems Training and Exercise Module (MCD)
STEM .... System Test Equipment Mission [*NASA*] (KSC)
STEMBOR .... Supervision Through Educational Management by Objectives and Results (EDAC)
STEMFAB ..... Storable Tubular Extendable Member Fabrication
STEMPRA .... Science, Technology, Engineering, Medicine Public Relations Association [*Great Britain*]
STEMS .... Small Terminal Evasive Missile System (MCD)
STEMS .... Society to Encourage Miniskirts [*New York group opposing below-the-knee fashions introduced in 1970*]
STEMS .... Structural Tracking and Engine Monitoring System (MCD)
STEM-TEM... Scanning Transmission Electron Microscopy - Transmission Electron Microscopy
STEN .... Sheppard-Turpin-England [*Machine carbine codesigned by Sheppard and Turpin*]
STEN .... Stencil
STEN .... Stenographer
Sten .... Submachine Gun [*Named after Sheppard, Turpin and England, its Inventors*] (BARN)
STENCH .... Society to Exterminate Neo-Communist Harbingers
ST-ENDOR ... Special Triple-Electron Nuclear Double Resonance [*Spectroscopy*]
STENO .... Stenographer (MUGU)
STENS .... Standard Terrestrial Navigation System (MCD)
STENS .... STD Terrestrial Navigation System (MCD)
Stenton .... Stenton. Rolls of the Justices in Eyre [*A publication*] (ILCA)
Stenton G .... Rolls of the Justices in Eyre for Gloucestershire, Worcestershire, and Staffordshire [*A publication*] (ILCA)
Stenton Y..... Rolls of the Justices in Eyre in Yorkshire [*A publication*] (ILCA)
STEO .... Special Test Equipment Order (MCD)
STEP .... Safeguard Test and Evaluation Program [*Army*] (AABC)
STEP .... Safety Test Engineering Program [*AEC*]
STEP .... Sales Tax Exemption Processing System [*Software*]
STEP .... School to Employment Program
STEP .... Science and Technology for Environmental Protection Program [*Australia*]
STEP .... Scientific and Technical Exploitation Program (AFM)
STEP .... Selective Traffic Enforcement Program [*Department of Transportation*]
STEP .... Self-Teaching Exportable Package
STEP .... Sensitivity Temperature Error Program (MCD)

STEP........... Sequentially Timed Events Plotting [*In publication title, "Investigating Accidents with STEP"*] [*Marcel Decker, Inc.*]
STEP........... Sequentially Timed Events Process [*Engineering*]
STEP........... Sequential Test of Educational Programs (DMAA)
STEP........... Sequential Tests of Educational Progress [*of ETS; given in 10th and 12th grades*]
STEP........... Service Technician Education Program
STEP........... Service Test and Evaluation Program
STEP........... Service Test and Evaluation Program [*FAA*] (TAG)
STEP........... Shell Technology Enterprise Programme [*British*]
STEP........... Ship Type Electronics Plan [*Navy*] (NG)
STEP........... Short Term Enrichment Program [*of US Information Agency*]
STEP........... Simple Transition to Economical Processing (IEEE)
STEP........... Simple Transition to Electronic Processing
STEP........... Simulated Tracking Evaluation Program (SAA)
STEP........... Software T & E Panel (RDA)
STEP........... Software Test and Evaluation Process [*DoD*]
STEP........... Solar-Terrestrial Energy Program
STEP........... Solutions to Employment Problems [*A program of National Association of Manufacturers*]
STEP........... Space Technology Experiments Platform
STEP........... Space Terminal Evaluation Program
STEP........... Space Thermoelectric Power (IAA)
STEP........... Special Temporary Employment Programme (AIE)
STEP........... Special Training Enlistment Program
STEP........... Special Training Equipment Program Document (AFIT)
STEP........... Specificaiton Technology Evaluation Program (MHDI)
STEP........... Staff Training Extramural Programs [*National Institutes of Health*]
STEP........... Standard Equipment Practice (IAA)
STEP........... Standard for the Exchange of Product Data [*Materials science*]
STEP........... Standard Tape Executive Package [*or Program*] [*NCR Corp.*]
STEP........... Standard Tape Executive System (NITA)
STEP........... Standard Terminal Program [*Computer science*] (IEEE)
STEP........... Standard Test Equipment Procedure (NG)
STEP........... Stand for Exchange of Product Model Data [*Computer-assisted engineering*]
STEP........... State Technology Extension Program [*National Institute of Standards and Technology*]
STEP........... Statistical Trajectory Estimation Program [*NASA*]
STEP........... Strategies for Today's Environmental Partnership
STEP........... Stratosphere-Troposphere Exchange Project [*NASA*]
STEP........... Stripes for Exceptional Performers [*Air Force*] (DOMA)
STEP........... Structures Technology Experiments Platform (MCD)
STEP........... Student Education Program
STEP........... Students toward Environmental Participation [*UNESCO and National Park Service*]
STEP........... Student Transfer Education Plan [*National Urban League*] [*Defunct*]
STEP........... Summer Training Employment Program (MCD)
STEP........... Supervisory Tape Executive Program [*Computer science*]
STEP........... Supplemental Training and Employment Program (OICC)
STEP........... Systematic Training for Effective Parenting
STEP........... System for Testing Evaluation of Potential [*Employee evaluation software*] [*London House, Inc.*]
STEP........... Systems Test Equipment Program (MCD)
Stepan........ Stephan Co. [*Associated Press*] (SAG)
STEPCLB....... StepClimb (GAVI)
Steph.......... Stephanus Pragensis [*Flourished, 14th century*] [*Authority cited in pre-1607 legal work*] (DSA)
Steph.......... Stephanus Tornacensis [*Deceased, 1203*] [*Authority cited in pre-1607 legal work*] (DSA)
Steph.......... Stephens' Supreme Court Decisions [*1774-1923*] [*Jamaica*] [*A publication*] (DLA)
Stepha Bertrand... Stephanus Bertrandus [*Flourished, 16th century*] [*Authority cited in pre-1607 legal work*] (DSA)
Stephan....... Stephan Co. [*Associated Press*] (SAG)
Steph Cl...... Stephens on Clergy [*1848*] [*A publication*] (DLA)
Steph Com... Stephen's Commentaries on the Laws of England [*A publication*] (DLA)
Steph Comm... Stephen's Commentaries on the Laws of England [*A publication*] (DLA)
Steph Const... Stephens on the English Constitution [*A publication*] (DLA)
Steph Cr...... Stephen's Digest of the Criminal Law [*A publication*] (DLA)
Steph Crim Dig... Stephen's Digest of the Criminal Law [*A publication*] (DLA)
Steph Cr L... Stephen's General View of the Criminal Law [*9 eds.*] [*1877-1950*] [*A publication*] (DLA)
Steph Cr Law... Stephen's General View of the Criminal Law [*A publication*] (DLA)
Steph Dig.... Stephen's Digest, New Brunswick Reports [*A publication*] (DLA)
Steph Dig Cr L... Stephen's Digest of the Criminal Law [*A publication*] (DLA)
Steph Dig Cr Law... Stephen's Digest of the Criminal Law [*A publication*] (DLA)
Steph Dig Ev... Stephen's Digest of the Law of Evidence [*A publication*] (DLA)
Steph Elect... Stephens on Elections [*1840*] [*A publication*] (DLA)
Stephen HCL... Stephen's History of Criminal Law [*A publication*] (DLA)
Stephens..... Supreme Court Decisions, by J. E. R. Stephens [*A publication*] (DLA)
Steph Ev..... Stephen's Digest of the Law of Evidence [*A publication*] (DLA)
Steph Gen View... Stephen's General View of the Criminal Law [*2nd ed.*] [*1890*] [*A publication*] (DLA)
Steph J St Comp... Steph's Joint-Stock Companies in Canada [*A publication*] (DLA)
Steph Lect... Stephen's Lectures on the History of France [*A publication*] (DLA)
Steph NP..... Stephen's Law of Nisi Prius [*A publication*] (DLA)
Steph Pl..... Stephen on Pleading [*A publication*] (DLA)
Steph Proc... Stephens on Procurations [*A publication*] (DLA)
Steph Slav... Stephens on Slavery [*A publication*] (DLA)
STEPO......... Self-Contained, Toxic Environment, Protective Outfit [*Army*] (INF)
STEPP......... Society of Teachers in Education of Professional Photography (EA)
STEPPS........ Some Tools for Evaluating Parallel Programs [*Computer science*] (MHDI)
STEPR......... Saturation Transfer Electron Paramagnetic Resonance [*Physics*]
STEPS.......... School-Leavers' Training and Employment Preparation Scheme [*New Zealand Labor Department*] (BARN)
STEPS.......... Science and Technology Evaluation and Prioritization System [*Program*] (RDA)
STEPS.......... Ships Technical Publication System [*Navy*]
STEPS.......... Solar Thermionic Electrical Power System
STEPS.......... Solar Thermionic Electrical Propulsion System (IAA)
STEPS.......... Staff Training Exercise for Programming Supervisor (SAA)
STEPS.......... Stored Thermal Energy Propulsion System
STEPS.......... Strategy Evaluator and Planning-Production System (PDAA)
STEPS.......... Surviving Today's Experiences and Problems Successfully Curriculum [*West Virginia*] (EDAC)
STEP-W....... Sequential Test of Educational Progress-Writing Test (EDAC)
STER........... Seater
STER........... Steradian
ster............ Stereo (VRA)
STER........... Stereo
STER........... Stereotype
STER........... Stereoview (VRA)
STER........... Sterilize (AABC)
STER........... Sterling
ster............ Sterling (ODBW)
STER........... Sterling Healthcare Group [*NASDAQ symbol*] (SAG)
STER........... Successively Truncated Expectation of the Reciprocal [*Statistics*]
STER........... System Training Equipment Requirement
Stereo......... Stereogram [*Radiology*] (DAVI)
STEREO....... Stereophonic (MSA)
Stereo......... Stereo Review [*A publication*] (BRI)
STEREO....... Stereoscope [*or Stereoscopic*]
STEREO....... Stereotype [*Refers to old news*] [*Slang*] (DSUE)
STERF......... Special Test Equipment Repair Facility
SterileC....... Sterile Concepts Holdings, Inc. [*Associated Press*] (SAG)
Steris......... Steris Corp. [*Associated Press*] (SAG)
STERL......... Sterling (ADA)
SterlEl......... Sterling Electronics Corp. [*Associated Press*] (SAG)
SterlHlth...... Sterling Healthcare Group [*Associated Press*] (SAG)
SterlHous.... Sterling House Corp. [*Associated Press*] (SAG)
SterlHs....... Sterling House Corp. [*Associated Press*] (SAG)
SterlSft....... Sterling Software, Inc. [*Associated Press*] (SAG)
STERNUT..... Sternutamentum [*Snuff*] [*Pharmacy*]
SterRecv...... Sterile Recoveries, Inc. [*Associated Press*] (SAG)
STES........... Solar Thermal Energy System
STESD......... Software Tool for Evaluating System Designs [*Computer science*] (MHDI)
STESS......... Subject's Treatment Emergent Symptom Scale [*Medicine*] (DMAA)
S (Test)....... Suitability Test [*Military*] (CAAL)
STESTG....... Space Test Group [*Military*]
STE-T.......... Simplified Test Equipment - Transitional [*Army*]
STET........... Specialized Technique for Efficient Typesetting
STET........... Steward, Technical [*Marine Corps*]
STET........... Submaximal Treadmill Exercise Test (AAMN)
STET........... System Test Experiments Tape
STETF......... Solar Total Energy Test Facility [*Energy Research and Development Administration*]
STETS......... Solar-Terrestrial Energy Transfer Studies [*Meteorology*]
Stetson U.... Stetson University (GAGS)
STEV........... Spinach Temperate Virus [*Plant pathology*]
STEV........... Stevedore
Stev & Ben Ins... Stevens and Benecke on Insurance [*A publication*] (DLA)
Stev & G...... Stevens and Graham's Reports [*98-139 Georgia*] [*A publication*] (DLA)
Stev Arb...... Stevens on Arbitration [*2nd ed.*] [*1835*] [*A publication*] (DLA)
Stev Av....... Stevens on Average [*5th ed.*] [*1835*] [*A publication*] (DLA)
Stev Dig...... Stevens' New Brunswick Digest [*A publication*] (DLA)
STEVE......... Space Tool for Extravehicular Emergencies
Stevens & G... Stevens and Graham's Reports [*98-139 Georgia*] [*A publication*] (DLA)
Stevens Inst Tech... Stevens Institute of Technology (GAGS)
StevInt......... Stevens International, Inc. [*Associated Press*] (SAG)
STEVS......... Spartan Tactical Equipment Verification Site [*Missiles*] (MCD)
STEVS......... Subsystem Tactical Equipment Verification Site
Stew........... Stewart's Alabama Reports [*1827-31*] [*A publication*] (DLA)
Stew........... Stewart's Equity Reports [*28-45 New Jersey*] [*A publication*] (DLA)
Stew........... Stewart's Nova Scotia Admiralty Reports [*A publication*] (DLA)
Stew........... Stewart's Reports [*1-10 South Dakota*] [*A publication*] (DLA)
Stew Adm.... Stewart's Nova Scotia Vice-Admiralty Reports [*1803-13*] [*A publication*] (DLA)
Stew Admr... Stewart's Nova Scotia Admiralty Reports [*A publication*] (DLA)
Stew (Ala)... Stewart's Alabama Reports [*A publication*] (DLA)
Stew & P..... Stewart and Porter's Alabama Supreme Court Reports [*1831-34*] [*A publication*] (DLA)
Stew and Porter... Stewart and Porter's Alabama Reports [*A publication*] (DLA)
Stew & P Rep... Stewart and Porter's Alabama Reports [*A publication*] (DLA)
Stew Ans..... Stewart's Answers to Dirleton's Doubts [*2 eds.*] [*1715, 1762 Scotland*] [*A publication*] (DLA)
Stewart........ Stewart's Alabama Reports [*1827-31*] [*A publication*] (DLA)
Stewart........ Stewart's Equity Reports [*28-45 New Jersey*] [*A publication*] (DLA)
Stewart........ Stewart's Nova Scotia Admiralty Reports [*A publication*] (DLA)
Stewart........ Stewart's Reports [*1-10 South Dakota*] [*A publication*] (DLA)
Stewart (Ala)... Stewart's Alabama Reports [*A publication*] (DLA)
Stewart-Brown... Stewart-Brown's Lancashire and Cheshire Cases in the Court of Star Chamber [*A publication*] (DLA)

Stewart R .... Stewart's Alabama Reports [*A publication*] (DLA)
Stew Dig ...... Stewart's Digest of Decisions of Law and Equity [*New Jersey*] [*A publication*] (ILCA)
Stew Eq .... Stewart's Equity Reports [*28-45 New Jersey*] [*A publication*] (DLA)
StewInfo ...... Stewart Information Services [*Associated Press*] (SAG)
Stew N Sc ... Stewart's Nova Scotia Admiralty Reports [*A publication*] (DLA)
STEWS .... Shipboard Tactical Electronic Warfare System [*Navy*]
STEWS .... Standardized Test of Essential Writing Skills (EDAC)
Stewt Rep .... Stewart's Alabama Reports [*A publication*] (DLA)
Stew VA .... Stewart's Nova Scotia Vice-Admiralty Reports [*A publication*] (DLA)
STE-X .... Simplified Test Equipment-Expandable [*Army*] (RDA)
STEX .... Statute Expired [*IRS*]
STeZ .... South Temperate Zone
STF .... Safety Test Facility [*Nuclear energy*]
STF .... Satellite Tracking Facility [*Air Force*]
STF .... S-Band Temperature Fahrenheit
STF .... S-Band Transmit Filter
STF .... Service Tabulating Form (AAG)
STF .... Setif [*Algeria*] [*Airport symbol*] (AD)
STF .... SFT-Sudanese Flight [*ICAO designator*] (FAAC)
STF .... Shield Test Facility [*Nuclear energy*] (GFGA)
STF .... Shock-Induced Thermal Fragmentation [*Astrophysics*]
STF .... Short Title File (NITA)
STF .... Signal Tracking Filter
STF .... Signal Transducing Factor [*Biochemistry*]
STF .... Snap Shield Test Facility Reactor [*Nuclear energy*] (IAA)
STF .... Sociedad Colombiana de Transporte Ferroviario SA [*Public rail services*] (EY)
STF .... Software Test Facility [*NASA*] (MCD)
STF .... Spacecraft Test Facility
STF .... Space Track Facility
STF .... Specialized Treatment Facility [*Medicine*] (MEDA)
STF .... Special Task Force [*Army*]
STF .... Special Technical Factors (MCD)
STF .... Special Tube Feeding [*Medicine*]
STF .... Spin Test Facility [*NASA*]
STF .... Staff (AFM)
STF .... Stamford Ukrainian [*Diocesan abbreviation*] [*Connecticut*] (TOCD)
STF .... Standardized Test of Fitness [*Canadian Association of Sports Sciences*]
STF .... Stanford Resources Ltd. [*Toronto Stock Exchange symbol*]
St F .... Starch-Free [*Pharmacy*]
STF .... Starkville, MS [*Location identifier FAA*] (FAAL)
STF .... Static Test Facility (KSC)
STF .... Stereochemistry Fragment (NITA)
stf .... Stiff [*Quality of the bottom*] [*Nautical charts*]
STF .... Stirred-Tank Fermentors [*Chemical engineering*]
STF .... Structural Fatigue Test (MCD)
STF .... Subjective Transfer Function (MCD)
STF .... Subject to Finance (ADA)
STF .... Summary Tape File [*Bureau of the Census*] (GFGA)
STF .... Supervisory Time Frame
STF .... Systemic Transformation Facility [*Former USSR*] (ECON)
STF .... Systems Technology Forum [*Fairfax, VA*] [*Telecommunications*] (TSSD)
STF .... System Test Facility
STFA .... Step-Father (DAVI)
STFAS .... Support to Total Force Analysis [*TRADOC*] (MCD)
STFC .... State Auto Financial [*NASDAQ symbol*] (TTSB)
STFC .... State Auto Financial Corp. [*NASDAQ symbol*] (SPSG)
STF DDC ...... System Test Facility Data Display Control (SAA)
ST-FeSv .... Snyder-Thielen Feline Sarcoma Virus [*Veterinary medicine*] (MEDA)
STFF .... Safeguard Tactical Field Force [*Army*] (AABC)
STFF .... Stuff
STFG .... Staffing Guides [*Army*] (AABC)
STFG .... Stuffing (MSA)
STFM .... Society of Teachers of Family Medicine (EA)
STFM .... Stretcher Form [*Tool*] (AAG)
StFncl .... State Financial Services Corp. [*Associated Press*] (SAG)
STFR .... Saint Francis Capital Corp. [*NASDAQ symbol*] (SAG)
STFR .... St. Francis Capital [*NASDAQ symbol*] (TTSB)
StFrancis ..... Saint Francis Capital Corp. [*Associated Press*] (SAG)
St Francis C (Ind)... St. Francis College (Indiana) (GAGS)
St Francis C (Penn)... St. Francis College (Pennsylvania) (GAGS)
STFRM .... Stratiform [*NWS*] (FAAC)
STFSGT .... Staff Sergeant [*Marine Corps*]
STFT .... Short-Time Fourier Transform (DMAA)
STFT .... Stray Field Test (NVT)
STG .... Saint George Island [*Alaska*] [*Airport symbol*] (OAG)
STG .... Santiago [*Brazil*] [*Airport symbol*] (AD)
STG .... Satellite Terminal Guidance
Stg .... Sea-Tangle [*Nautical charts*]
STG .... Seating [*Technical drawings*]
STG .... Sedalia-Marshall-Booville Stage Line, Inc. [*ICAO designator*] (FAAC)
STG .... Short-Term Goal (DAVI)
STG .... SONAR Technician, Ground [*Navy rating*] (DNAB)
STG .... Souther Gold Resources [*Vancouver Stock Exchange symbol*]
STG .... Space Task Group [*Later, Manned Spacecraft Center*] [*NASA*]
STG .... Space Telescope Guidance [*NASA*]
STG .... Special Technology Group [*National Technical Information Service*] (MCD)
STG .... Special Training Group [*Military*]
STG .... Split Thickness Graft [*Medicine*]
STG .... Staging (AABC)
STG .... Standing [*Numismatics*]
STG .... Starting (MSA)
STG .... Steering Task Group
STG .... Sterling
stg .... Sterling (ODBW)
STG .... Stomatogastric Ganglion [*Neuroanatomy*]
STG .... Storage
Stg .... Storage (AAGC)
STG .... Storage Properties, Inc. [*AMEX symbol*] (SAG)
STG .... Storage Triacylglycerol [*Biochemistry*]
STG .... Strathgordon [*Tasmania*] [*Seismograph station code, US Geological Survey*] (SEIS)
STG .... Study Group [*NATO*]
STG .... Sturmgewehr [*Storm Rifle*] [*German military - World War II*]
STGA .... Saratoga Brands [*NASDAQ symbol*] (TTSB)
STGA .... Saratoga Brands, Inc. [*NASDAQ symbol*] (NQ)
STGA .... Scottish Tourist Guides Association (DBA)
STGA .... Shrub and Tree Growers of Australia
STGAA .... Shade Tobacco Growers Agricultural Association (EA)
STGAR .... Staging Area [*Military*]
STGB .... Staging Base [*Military*]
StGB .... Strafgesetzbuch [*Penal Code*] [*German*]
STGC .... Secure Task Group, Common (MCD)
STGE .... Stage
STGE .... Stage Stores, Inc. [*NASDAQ symbol*] (SAG)
STGE .... Storage
STGEN .... Steam Generator
St Ger D & S... St. German's Doctor and Student [*A publication*] (DLA)
StgeStrs ...... Stage Stores, Inc. [*Associated Press*] (SAG)
STGG .... Staging (AAG)
STGHT .... Straight
St Gloc .... Statute of Gloucester [*First statute to give costs in actions*] [*A publication*] (DLA)
STGP .... Subcontract Task Group Procurement
STGR .... Stringer (AAG)
STGSA .... SONAR Technician, Ground, Seaman Apprentice [*Navy rating*] (DNAB)
STGSN .... SONAR Technician, Ground, Seaman [*Navy rating*] (DNAB)
STG/STF ...... Special Task Group/Special Task Force [*Army*] (MCD)
STGT .... Secondary Target [*Military*]
STGT .... Stargardt Disease [*Medicine*]
S Th .... Scholar in Theology [*British*]
STH .... Seton Hall University, South Orange, NJ [*OCLC symbol*] (OCLC)
STH .... Short-Term Holiday (MHDB)
STH .... Soft tissue Hematoma [*Hematology*] (DAVI)
STH .... Somatotrophic [*Growth*] Hormone [*Also, GH, SH*] [*Endocrinology*]
STH .... South
STH .... Southern Airlines Ltd. [*British ICAO designator*] (FAAC)
STH .... Stanhome, Inc. [*NYSE symbol*] (SPSG)
STH .... Stoney Hill [*Jamaica*] [*Seismograph station code, US Geological Survey*] (SEIS)
STH .... Stray Horse Resources, Inc. [*Vancouver Stock Exchange symbol*]
STH .... Student in Theology [*British*]
STh .... Subthalamus [*Anatomy*]
STH .... Subtotal Hysterectomy [*Medicine*]
STH .... Toronto School of Theology Library, University of Toronto [*UTLAS symbol*]
Sth Afr Rep... South African Republic High Court Reports [*A publication*] (DLA)
SThB .... Sacrae Theologiae Baccalaureus [*Bachelor of Sacred Theology*]
SthCoB .... Southern Community Bancshares, Inc. [*Associated Press*] (SAG)
SThD .... Sacrae Theologiae Doctor [*Doctor of Sacred Theology*]
STHE .... Special Tools and Handling Equipment
Sthen .... Stheneboea [*of Euripides*] [*Classical studies*] (OCD)
STHEST .... Southeast
STHESTN ...... Southeastern
Sthfst .... Southfirst Bancshares, Inc. [*Associated Press*] (SAG)
SthfstB .... Southfirst Bancshares, Inc. [*Associated Press*] (SAG)
S ThL .... Sacrae Theologiae Lecentiatus [*Licentiate in Sacred Theology*]
StHlGd .... Saint Helena Gold Mines Ltd. [*Associated Press*] (SAG)
STHLY .... Southerly [*A publication*]
STHMPN ...... Southampton [*England*]
STHN .... Southern
SthnBnc .... Southern Banc Co., Inc. [*Associated Press*] (SAG)
SthnEH .... Southern Energy Homes, Inc. [*Associated Press*] (SAG)
SthnEnH .... Southern Energy Homes, Inc. [*Associated Press*] (SAG)
StHR .... Stress Hypertensive Rats
STHRN .... Southern
STHS .... Scottish Thoracic Society
STHSD .... Southside
SthStrF .... South Street Financial Center [*Associated Press*] (SAG)
SthwestB ...... Southwest Banks, Inc. [*Associated Press*] (SAG)
STHWST .... Southwest
STHWSTN .... Southwestern
STI .... Mountain Home, ID [*Location identifier FAA*] (FAAL)
STI .... Santiago [*Dominican Republic*] [*Airport symbol*] (OAG)
STI .... Saskatoon Technical Institute [*UTLAS symbol*]
STI .... Saxton Industries [*Vancouver Stock Exchange symbol*]
STI .... Scientific and Technical Information [*Facility*] [*NASA*]
STI .... Scientific and Technical Information [*System*] [*Canada*]
STI .... Screw Thread Insert
STI .... Self-Test Input [*Electronics*]
STI .... Serum Trypsin Inhibitor [*Serology*]
STI .... Server Technology, Inc. [*Information service or system*] (IID)
STI .... Service Tools Institute [*Later, HTI*] (EA)
STI .... Sexually-Transmitted Infection [*Medicine*] (DI)
STI .... Shear Thinning Index (PDAA)

STI .... Shielding Technologies Inc.
STI .... Short-Term Integration (CAAL)
STI .... Silicon Target Intensifier
STI .... Single Tooth Indexer
STI .... Skin Test Index [*Chemical medicine*]
STI .... Small Towns Institute (EA)
STI .... Societa Servizi Trasporti [*Italy*] [*FAA designator*] (FAAC)
STI .... Software Tool Information Database [*Air Force Systems Command*] [*Information service or system*] (CRD)
STI .... Soybean Trypsin Inhibition [*Biochemistry*]
STI .... Space Technology, Inc. (MCD)
STI .... Special Test Instructions (SAA)
STI .... Specifications Technology, Inc.
STI .... Speech Transmission Index
STI .... Standard Technical Institute (SSD)
STI .... Star Valley [*Idaho*] [*Seismograph station code, US Geological Survey*] (SEIS)
STI .... State Technical Institute
STI .... Steel Tank Institute (EA)
STI .... Steel Tube Institute
STI .... Stem Tolerance Index [*Botany*]
sti .... Stich (VRA)
STI .... Stilbite [*A zeolite*]
Sti .... Stinson [*Record label*]
STI .... Store Indicators (SAA)
STI .... Straight Times Index [*Singapore Stock Exchange*]
STI .... St. Thomas Institute [*Research center*] (RCD)
STI .... SunTrust Banks [*NYSE symbol*] (TTSB)
STI .... SunTrust Banks, Inc. [*NYSE symbol*] (SPSG)
STI .... Surface Targets of Interest (MCD)
STI .... Survive Tomorrow, Inc. [*Commercial firm*] (EA)
STI .... Systems Technology Inc.
STI .... Systolic Time Interval [*Cardiology*]
STIA .... Satellite Television Industry Association [*Formerly, SPACE*] (NTCM)
STIA .... Scientific, Technological, and International Affairs Directorate [*National Science Foundation*]
STIAC .... Science Technology and Innovation Advisory Council [*Ireland*]
STIAP .... Standard Instrument Approach [*RADAR*] [*Aviation*]
STIB .... Stimulus Train-Induced Bursting [*Neuroscience*]
STIB .... Stratosphere-Troposphere Interactions and the Biosphere (EERA)
STIC .... Scientific and Technical Intelligence Center [*DoD*]
STIC .... SEAL [*Sea, Air, Land*] Tactical Insertion Craft [*Navy*] (DOMA)
STIC .... Security Threat Intelligence Cell (LAIN)
STIC .... Solid-State Transducer Intercompartmental Catheter [*Instrumentation*]
STIC .... Space Technical Information Control (MCD)
STIC .... Space Toy Information Center [*Defunct*] (EA)
STICAP .... Stiff Circuit Analysis Program [*Computer science*]
STICEC .... Special Travel Industry Council on Energy Conservation
ST/ICERD .... Suntory Toyota International Centre for Economics and Related Disciplines [*London School of Economics and Political Science*] [*British*] (CB)
Stich .... Stichus [*of Plautus*] [*Classical studies*] (OCD)
STICO .... Standard Interpretation and Compilation System (IAA)
STICTION .... Static Friction
STID .... Scientific and Technical Information Dissemination [*NASA*]
STID .... Scientific and Technical Information Division [*NASA*] (IEEE)
STID .... Ship's Test and Inspection Department [*Navy*] (DNAB)
STIDAS .... Speech Transmission Index Device [*Using*] Artificial Signals
STIF .... Scientific and Technical Information Facility [*NASA*]
STIF .... Search Track Intermediate Frequency [*Military*]
STIF .... Short-Term Irradiation Facility [*Nuclear energy*] (NRCH)
STIF .... Spectral Transmission Interference Filter
STIF .... Stiffener [*Civil engineering*]
STIFC .... Space Track Interim Fire Control
Stifel .... Stifel Financial Corp. [*Associated Press*] (SAG)
STIFS .... Short-Term Integrated Forecasting System [*Department of Energy*] (GFGA)
STIG .... Steam-Injected Gas Turbine
STII .... Science and Technology Information Institute [*Information service or system*] (IID)
STII .... Stanford Telecommun [*NASDAQ symbol*] (TTSB)
STII .... Stanford Telecommunications, Inc. [*NASDAQ symbol*] (NQ)
STIL .... Short-Term Inhalation Limits [*of air pollutants*]
STIL .... Software Test and Integration Laboratory [*NASA*] (NASA)
STIL .... Statistical Interpretive Language [*Computer science*] (MDG)
Stil .... Stillingfleet's English Ecclesiastical Cases [*1702-04*] [*A publication*] (DLA)
STILE .... Students' and Teachers' Integrated Learning Environment (AIE)
Stiles .... Stiles' Reports [*22-29 Iowa*] [*A publication*] (DLA)
Stiles (IA) .... Stiles' Reports [*22-29 Iowa*] [*A publication*] (DLA)
STILLAT .... Stillatim [*By Drops or In Small Quantities*] [*Pharmacy*]
STILLB .... Stillborn [*Medicine*]
Still Ecc Law ... Stillingfleet's Discourse on Ecclesiastical Law [*A publication*] (DLA)
Still Eccl Cas ... Stillingfleet's English Ecclesiastical Cases [*A publication*] (DLA)
StillwtrM .... Stillwater Mining Co. [*Associated Press*] (SAG)
STILO .... Scientific and Technical Intelligence Liaison Officer (MCD)
STILS .... Stinger Launch Simulator (MCD)
STIM .... Scanning Transmission Ion Microscopy
STIM .... Sensitivity Training Impact Model
STIM .... Stimsonite Corp. [*NASDAQ symbol*] (SAG)
STIM .... Stimulant (DSUE)
STIM .... Stimulating (ROG)
stim .... Stimulus
STIM .... Subsystem: Short-Term Integrating Model [*Department of Energy*] (GFGA)
S Times .... Sunday Times [*A publication*]
Stim Gloss ... Stimson's Law Glossary [*A publication*] (DLA)
Stim Law Gloss ... Stimson's Law Glossary [*A publication*] (DLA)
Stim L Gl .... Stimson's Law Glossary [*A publication*] (DLA)
stimn .... Stimulation (DAVI)
STIMS .... Scientific and Technical Information Modular System [*NASA*] (MCD)
Stimson .... Stimsonite Corp. [*Associated Press*] (SAG)
Stimson .... Stimson's Law Glossary [*A publication*] (DLA)
STIMSUP .... Stimulant to Sustain Performance (RDA)
STIN .... Science Teacher Inventory of Need (EDAC)
STINA .... Steel Tube Institute of North America (EA)
STINCOM .... Scientific and Technical Information and Communication (SAA)
Stiness .... Stiness' Reports [*20-34 Rhode Island*] [*A publication*] (DLA)
STINET .... Scientific and Technical Information Network [*Internet*] (AAGC)
STINFO .... Scientific and Technical Information Office [*Army*]
STINFO .... Scientific and Technical Information Officers (NITA)
STINFO .... Scientific/Technical Information (AAGC)
STING .... Swift Target Identification Notification Grid (MCD)
STINGER .... SEABEE Tactically Installed, Navy Generated, Engineer Resources [*System*] [*Navy*] (NVT)
STINGS .... Stellar Inertial Guidance System [*Air Force*]
St Inst .... Stair's Institutes [*5th ed.*] [*1832*] [*A publication*] (ILCA)
STIO .... Scientific and Technical Information Office [*NASA*]
STIO .... Store Input-Output [*Computer science*] (IAA)
STIP .... Basophilic Stippling [*Biochemistry*] (DAVI)
STIP .... Scientific and Technical Information Program (MCD)
STIP .... Skill Training Improvement Program [*Department of Labor*]
STIP .... Solar Technical Information Program [*Solar Energy Research Institute*] [*Information service or system*] (IID)
STIP .... Statewide Transportation Improvements Program [*MOCD*] (TAG)
STIP .... Stipend [*or Stipendiary*]
Stip .... Stipites [*Stalk*] [*Latin*]
STIP .... Stipulation (DAS)
STIP .... Study of Travelling Interplanetary Phenomena [*Meteorology*]
STIPE .... Stipendiary Magistrate [*British*] (DSUE)
STIPIS .... Scientific, Technical, Intelligence, and Program Information System [*HEW*]
STIQ .... Survival Technology [*NASDAQ symbol*] (TTSB)
STIQ .... Survival Technology, Inc. [*NASDAQ symbol*] (SAG)
STIR .... Scientific and Technical Intelligence Register (AFM)
STIR .... Separate Track and Illumination RADAR [*Military*] (CAAL)
STIR .... Shield Test and Irradiation Reactor [*Nuclear energy*]
STIR .... Short Tau Inversion Recovery [*Medicine*] (DMAA)
STIR .... Signal Track and Illuminating RADAR [*Canadian Navy*]
STIR .... SNAP [*Systems for Nuclear Auxiliary Power*] Shield Test Irradiation Reactor
STIR .... Statistics Indexing and Retrieval Project (NITA)
STIR .... Stirrup (WGA)
STIR .... Surplus to Immediate Requirements (ADA)
STIRD .... SAIL [*Shuttle Avionics Integration Laboratory*] Test Implementation Requirements Document [*NASA*] (NASA)
STIRS .... Self-Training Interpretive Retrieval System
STIS .... Science and Technology Information System [*National Science Foundation*]
STIS .... Scientific & Technical Information Services, Inc. [*Information service or system*] (IID)
STIS .... Silicon Target Image Sensor
STIS .... Space Telescope Imaging Spectrograph
STIS .... Specialized Textile Information Service
STIS .... Sumika Technical Information Service, Inc. [*Information service or system*] (IID)
STISP .... Science and Technology Information Service for Parliament [*British*] (IAA)
STI/SS .... Scientific and Technical Information System and Service (PDAA)
STIT .... Scientific and Technical Information Team [*Army*] (GFGA)
STIT .... Signal Technical Intelligence Team [*Army*] (AABC)
STIT .... Simulated Time in Turn (SAA)
STIT .... Sweet's Technical Information Test [*Vocational guidance test*]
STIT-CONUS ... Scientific and Technical Information Team, Continental United States [*Army*] (AABC)
STIT-EUR .... Scientific and Technical Information Team, Europe [*Army*] (AABC)
STIT-FE .... Scientific and Technical Information Team, Far East [*Army*] (AABC)
STIV .... Silicon Target Intensifier Vidicon
StIves .... Saint Ives Laboratories, Inc. [*Associated Press*] (SAG)
STIZ .... Scientific Technologies [*NASDAQ symbol*] (TTSB)
STIZ .... Scientific Technology, Inc. [*NASDAQ symbol*] (NQ)
StiZ .... Stimmen der Zeit [*A publication*] (BJA)
STIZ .... Submarine Transit Identification Zones (NVT)
STJ .... Saint Joseph College, West Hartford, CT [*OCLC symbol*] (OCLC)
STJ .... Saint Jude Medical, Inc. [*NYSE symbol*] (SAG)
STJ .... Series Tee Junction
STJ .... Severn Tunnel Junction [*British depot code*]
STJ .... Society of St. Teresa of Jesus (TOCD)
STJ .... Special Trial Judge [*US Tax Court*]
STJ .... St. John's [*Newfoundland*] [*Seismograph station code, US Geological Survey*] (SEIS)
STJ .... St. Joseph [*Missouri*] [*Airport symbol*] (AD)
STJ .... St. Joseph, MO [*Location identifier FAA*] (FAAL)
StJ .... St. Joseph Railway
STJ .... Subtalar Joint [*Anatomy*] (DAVI)
STJ .... Subtropical Jet Stream (ADA)
STJ .... Superconducting Tunnel Junction [*Physics*]
STJ .... Superconducting Tunnel Junction [*Physics*]
STJA(NC) .... St. John Ambulance (Nursing Cadets) [*British*]
STJM .... St. Jude Medical [*NASDAQ symbol*] (TTSB)

STJM .... St. Jude Medical, Inc. [*NASDAQ symbol*] (NQ)
St J MO PUC... St. Joseph, Missouri, Public Utilities Commission Reports [*A publication*] (DLA)
StJoe .... Saint Joe Corp. [*Associated Press*] (SAG)
StJoe .... St. Joe Paper Co. [*Associated Press*] (SAG)
StJohn .... Saint John Knits, Inc. [*Associated Press*] (SAG)
StJohn .... St. John Knits, Inc. [*Associated Press*] (SAG)
St John's C... St. John's College (Sante Fe) (GAGS)
St John's U (Minn)... St. John's University (Minnesota) (GAGS)
St John's U (NY)... St. John's University (New York) (GAGS)
StJoLP .... Saint Joseph Light & Power [*Associated Press*] (SAG)
StJoLP .... St. Joseph Light & Power Co. [*Associated Press*] (SAG)
St Joseph C (Conn)... St. Joseph College (Connecticut) (GAGS)
St Joseph's U (Penn)... St. Joseph's University (Pennsylvania) (GAGS)
STJU .... St. John's University [*Minnesota; New York*]
StJude .... Saint Jude Medical, Inc. [*Associated Press*] (SAG)
STJW .... Stretcher Jaws [*Tool*] (AAG)
STK .... Satellite Tool Kit
stk .... Scotland [*MARC country of publication code Library of Congress*] (LCCP)
STK .... Serine-Threonine Kinase [*An enzyme*]
STK .... Single Tone Keying
STK .... Situation Track Display
STK .... Soiuz Trudovogo Krest'ianstva [*Union of Working Peasantry*] [*Russian*]
STK .... Stack (MSA)
STK .... Stakes Race [*Horse racing*]
STK .... Standard Test Key [*Computer science*]
STK .... Steak
STK .... Stephens Creek [*Australia Seismograph station code, US Geological Survey*] (SEIS)
STK .... Sterling, CO [*Location identifier FAA*] (FAAL)
STK .... Stick Shift [*Automotive advertising*]
stk .... Sticky [*Quality of the bottom*] [*Nautical charts*]
STK .... Stock (AAG)
stk .... Stock (VRA)
STK .... Storage Technology [*NYSE symbol*] (TTSB)
STK .... Storage Technology Corp. [*NYSE symbol*] (SPSG)
STK .... Strake [*Mining engineering*]
STK .... Streptokinase [*An enzyme*] (AAMN)
STK .... Strike [*Navy*] (DOMA)
STK .... Sturmkanone [*Self-propelled assault gun*] [*German military - World War II*]
STKD .... Stockade (AABC)
STK EX .... Stock Exchange
STKF .... Stock Fund [*Military*]
STKFA .... Stock Fund Accounting [*Military*]
STKFS .... Stock Fund Statement [*Military*]
STKG .... Sturzkampfgeschwader [*Dive-bomber wing*] [*German military - World War II*]
STKL .... Stake Technology Ltd. [*Oakville, ON*] [*NASDAQ symbol*] (NQ)
STKLF .... Stake Technology Ltd [*NASDAQ symbol*] (TTSB)
STK NO .... Stock Number
STKR .... Stocker & Yale [*NASDAQ symbol*] (TTSB)
STKR .... Stockroom (AABC)
STKR .... Stoker [*Navy British*]
STKS .... Stakes (ROG)
StkVC .... Stokely-Van Camp, Inc. [*Associated Press*] (SAG)
StkVC .... Stokley Van Camp [*Associated Press*] (SAG)
STKY .... Stokely USA [*NASDAQ symbol*] (TTSB)
STKY .... Stokely USA, Inc. [*Oconomowoc, WI*] [*NASDAQ symbol*] (NQ)
STKYD .... Stockyard
STL .... Bibliotheque Municipale de Saint-Laurent [*UTLAS symbol*]
STl .... Esotropia, Left [*Ophthalmology*] (DAVI)
STL .... Licentiate in Sacred Theology (GAGS)
STL .... Sacrae Theologiae Lector [*Reader in Sacred Theology*] [*Latin*]
STL .... Sacrae Theologiae Licentiatus [*Licentiate in Sacred Theology*] [*Latin*]
STL .... Safe Tow Length
STL .... Santa Lucia [*Chile*] [*Seismograph station code, US Geological Survey Closed*] (SEIS)
STL .... Satellite
STL .... Schottky Transistor Logic (IEEE)
STL .... Seatrain Lines, Inc. [*AAR code*]
STL .... Secondary Target Line [*Army*]
STL .... Selective Tape Listing [*Computer science*] (IAA)
STL .... Self-Test Logic [*Navy Navigation Satellite System*] (DNAB)
STL .... Sequential Table Lookup
STL .... Short Term Leaflet. Ministry of Agriculture, Fisheries, and Food [*A publication*]
STL .... Short-Term Loan (ADA)
STL .... Simulated Tape Load
STL .... Site Team Leader [*Nuclear energy*] (NRCH)
STL .... Southern Traffic League
STL .... Southern Transportation League (EA)
STL .... Space Technology Laboratories [*of TRW Group*]
STL .... Special Tool List
STL .... Stall (WGA)
STL .... Standard Telecommunications Laboratory (IAA)
STL .... Standard Telegraph Level [*Telecommunications*] (TEL)
STL .... Stapleford Flight Center [*British ICAO designator*] (FAAC)
STL .... Station Transmission Link [*Telecommunications*] (IAA)
STL .... Status and Telling (SAA)
STL .... Steel (KSC)
stl .... Steel (VRA)
STL .... Steel
STL .... Step-Through Latencies
STL .... Stereo Lithography
STL .... Sterling Bancorp [*NYSE symbol*] (SPSG)
STL .... Stile (WGA)
STL .... St. Louis [*Missouri*] [*Airport symbol*]
STL .... St. Louis [*Diocesan abbreviation*] [*Missouri*] (TOCD)
STL .... Stockage List [*Military*]
STL .... Stock, Time Limitation (DNAB)
STL .... Storage Time Limit (DNAB)
STL .... Strategic Technology Leveraging
STL .... Studio-Transmitter Link
STL .... Supersonic Transition Locus [*Galactic winds*]
STL .... Support Table Load
STL .... Suppressor T Lymphocyte [*Immunology*]
STL .... Swelling, Tenderness, Limitation of Movement [*Medicine*]
STL .... Symmetrizing and Transformation Line (IAA)
STL .... Synchronous Transistor Logic (MDG)
STL .... Systems Techniques Laboratory [*Stanford University*] (MCD)
STL .... System Test Loop (IEEE)
STLA .... Strip Transmission Line Adapter [*or Assembly*]
StL & OR .... St. Louis & Ohio River Railroad
StL & SW .... St. Louis & South Western Railway
StLAR .... St. Lawrence & Atlantic Railway
St Law .... Loughborough's Digest of Statute Law [*Kentucky*] [*A publication*] (DLA)
St Lawrence U... St. Lawrence University (GAGS)
STLB & M.... St. Louis, Brownsville & Mexico [*Railway*]
STLBY .... Stolt-Nielsen S.A. ADS [*NASDAQ symbol*] (TTSB)
STLC .... Sequence Thin-Layer Chromatography
STLC .... Short-Term Lethal Concentration [*of air pollutants*]
STLC .... Soluble Threshold Limit Concentration [*Environmental chemistry*]
STLC .... StreamLogic Corp. [*NASDAQ symbol*] (SAG)
STLC .... StreamLogic Corp. [*NASDAQ symbol*] (TTSB)
STLD .... Support Teacher Learning Difficulties
STLD .... Surface Transport Loading Data [*MTMC*] (TAG)
STLDD .... Software Top Level Design Document [*Army*]
STLE .... Senior Test Laboratory Engineer (IAA)
STLE .... Society of Tribologists and Lubrication Engineers (EAIO)
STLF .... Southern Troops and Landing Force
STLG .... Sterling (WGA)
STLI .... Statue of Liberty National Monument
STLI .... Stockage List Item [*Military*]
STLI .... Subtotal Lymphoid Irradiation [*Medicine*] (DMAA)
St Lim .... Statute of Limitations [*A publication*] (DLA)
StLIM & S .... St. Louis, Iron Mountain & Southern Railway
STLL .... Submarine Tender Load List
STLM .... Safeguard Tactical Logistics Management
STLO .... Scientific and Technical Liaison Office [*AFSC*]
STLOS .... Star Line-of-Sight (KSC)
St Louis L Rev... St. Louis Law Review [*A publication*] (DLA)
St Louis U... Saint Louis University (GAGS)
STLR .... Semitrailer
STLS .... Ship's Transducer Location System (DNAB)
STLS .... Southern Tier Library System [*Library network*]
STLS .... South Texas Library System [*Library network*]
STLS .... Stinger Training Launch Simulator (MCD)
STL-SF .... St. Louis-San Francisco Railway Co.
STL-SF & T... St. Louis, San Francisco & Texas Railway Co.
STL STL and WD... Steel or Steel and Wood [*Freight*]
STLSW of T... St. Louis Southwestern Railway Co. of Texas
STLT .... Small Transportable Link Terminal
STLT .... Stellite [*Metallurgy*]
STLT .... Studio-Transmitter Link-Television
STLTF .... Stolt Nielson SA [*NASDAQ symbol*] (SAG)
STLTF .... Stolt Tankers & Terminals SA (MHDW)
STLU .... St. Louis University [*Missouri*]
St LU Intra L Rev... St. Louis University. Intramural Law Review [*A publication*] (DLA)
STLV .... Simian T-Cell Lymphotropic Virus
STL WD .... Steel or Wood [*Freight*]
STL WI .... Steel or Wire [*Freight*]
StlWVa .... Steel West Virginia, Inc. [*Associated Press*] (SAG)
STLY .... Stanley Furniture [*NASDAQ symbol*] (TTSB)
STLY .... Stanley Furniture Co. [*NASDAQ symbol*] (SAG)
STM .... Groupement International d'Editeurs Scientifiques, Techniques, et Medicaux [*International Group of Scientific, Technical, and Medical Publishers*] (EAIO)
STM .... International Group of Scientific, Technical, and Medical Publishers (EAIO)
STM .... Master of Arts in Theology
STM .... Master of Sacred Theology (NADA)
STM .... Master of the Science of Theology
STM .... Sacrae Theologiae Magister [*Master of Sacred Theology*]
STM .... Safety Test Missile (MCD)
STM .... Santarem [*Brazil*] [*Airport symbol*] (OAG)
STM .... Satellite Technology Management, Inc. [*Torrance, CA*] [*Telecommunications*] (TSSD)
STM .... Save the Manatee Club (EA)
STM .... Scanning Tunneling Microscope
STM .... Scientific, Technical, and Medical
STM .... Screened through Matching [*Parapsychology*]
STM .... Section Technical Manual [*Jet Propulsion Laboratory, NASA*]
STM .... Self-Test Mode
STM .... Send Test Message (AAG)
STM .... Service Technique Militaire [*Switzerland*]

STM .... Service Test Model (NG)
STM .... SGS Thomson Microelectronics, NV [*NYSE symbol*] (SAG)
STM .... SGS-THOMSON N.V. [*NYSE symbol*] (TTSB)
STM .... Shielded Tunable Magnetron
STM .... Short-Term Memory
STM .... Signal Termination Module [*NASA*] (NASA)
STM .... Signature-Tagged Transposon Method [*Genetics*]
STM .... Significant Technical Milestone (SDI)
STM .... Simply Transformed Manufacture
STM .... Simulated Test Markets [*Market research*] (WDMC)
STM .... Slate Mountain [*Nevada*] [*Seismograph station code, US Geological Survey Closed*] (SEIS)
STM .... Society for Traditional Music (EA)
STM .... Sonet Transmission Manager [*Adaptive Corp.*]
STM .... Southam, Inc. [*Toronto Stock Exchange symbol Vancouver Stock Exchange symbol*]
STM .... Specialized Trade Mission [*Department of Commerce*]
STM .... Special Test Missile
STM .... Specification Test Material (MCD)
STM .... Spin Tuned Magnetron
STM .... Spore Tip Mucilage [*Mycology*]
STM .... Standards Tool Master (MCD)
STM .... Standard Test Methods Bulletins [*A publication*] (EAAP)
STM .... Standard Type Material (MCD)
STM .... Statement (ECII)
STM .... State Transition Matrix
STM .... Static Test Model (MCD)
STM .... Statistical Multiplexing [*Telecommunications*]
STM .... Statute Mile
STM .... Steam
STM .... Steam
STM .... Steward's Mate [*Navy rating*]
STM .... St. Martin Hospitals Group [*British*]
STM .... STM Publishers (NITA)
STM .... Store Multiple [*Computer command*] (PCM)
STM .... Straddle the Market [*Investment term*] (MHDW)
STM .... Stream [*Board on Geographic Names*]
STM .... Streamline Aviation [*British ICAO designator*] (FAAC)
STM .... Streptomycin [*An antibiotic*] (AAMN)
STM .... Structural Test Model
STM .... Subject to Mortgage (ADA)
STM .... Supersonic Tactical Missile (MCD)
STM .... Supplementary Technical Manual [*Military*]
STM .... Support Test Manager (NASA)
STM .... Surface-to-Target-to-Missile
STM .... Synthetic Timing Mode
STM .... System Training Mission (AFM)
STMA .... Space-Time Moving Average [*Statistics*]
STMA .... Sports Turf Managers Association [*Defunct*] (EA)
STMA .... Stuffed Toy Manufacturers Association
St Mark .... St. Mark's Church Case [*Philadelphia, PA*] [*A publication*] (DLA)
St Marlb ...... Statute of Marlbridge [*A publication*] (DLA)
StMary .... Saint Mary Land & Exploration [*Associated Press*] (SAG)
St Mary's C... St. Mary's College of Minnesota (GAGS)
St Mary's U... St. Mary's University (GAGS)
STMCGMW... Subcommission for Tectonic Maps of the Commission for the Geological Map of the World (EAIO)
STMD .... Stormedia 'A' [*NASDAQ symbol*] (TTSB)
STMD .... Stormedia, Inc. [*NASDAQ symbol*] (SAG)
STME .... Space Transportation Main Engine
STME .... Stellar Television Monitor Equipment
St Mert .... Statute of Merton [*A publication*] (DLA)
STMEV .... Storm Evasion [*Navy*] (NVT)
STMFR .... Steamfitter (WGA)
STMG .... Steaming (MSA)
STMGR .... Station Manager (FAAC)
STMI .... Satellite Technology Management [*NASDAQ symbol*] (SAG)
St Mi .... Statute Mile [*Nautical charts*]
STMI .... STM Wireless [*NASDAQ symbol*] (TTSB)
STMI .... STM Wireless, Inc. [*NASDAQ symbol*] (SAG)
St Michael's C... St. Michael's College (GAGS)
STMIS .... System Test Manufacturing Information System (IEEE)
STML .... Separate Transporter and Mobile Launcher
STML .... Sindicato de Trabajadores Mineros de Llallagua
STML .... Stimulate (MSA)
STMM .... Short-Term Money Market
STMNT .... Statement (IAA)
STMO .... Step-Mother (DAVI)
St Mot Carr Guide (CCH)... State Motor Carrier Guide (Commerce Clearing House) [*A publication*] (DLA)
StMotr .... Standard Motor Products, Inc. [*Associated Press*] (SAG)
STMP .... Ship Test Management Plan [*Navy*] (CAAL)
STMP .... Single Track Master Operational Recording Tape Processing (IAA)
STMP .... Stamp
STMP .... System Training Management Plan (MCD)
STMR .... Steamer
S/T-MR .... Surplus Termination Material Requisition (MCD)
STMS .... Scientific and Technical Modular System
STMS .... Scottish Tramway Museum Society (DCTA)
STMS .... Short-Term Monetary Support [*Finance*]
STMS .... Spring Trap Makers' Society [*A union*] [*British*]
STMS .... State Tax Management System [*Price Waterhouse & Co.*] (PCM)
STMS .... St. Thomas More Society (EA)
STMT .... Statement (AFM)
STMT of SVC... Statement of Service [*Military*]
STMU .... Special Test and Maintenance Unit
STMV .... Satellite Tobacco Mosaic Virus [*Immunology*]
STMV .... Stump-Tailed Macaque Virus (PDAA)
STMW .... Subtropical Mode Water [*Oceanography*]
STMWire ..... STM Wireless, Inc. [*Associated Press*] (SAG)
STMX .... SyStemix, Inc. [*NASDAQ symbol*] (SPSG)
STN .... SAC [*Strategic Air Command*] Telephone Net
STN .... Satellite Television Network [*Telecommunications Defunct*] (TSSD)
STN .... Satellite Theater Network [*Falls Church, VA*] (TSSD)
STN .... Satellite Tracking Network (MCD)
STN .... Saturn Airways, Inc. (MCD)
STN .... Scientific and Technical Information Network
STN .... Seatoun [*New Zealand*] [*Seismograph station code, US Geological Survey Closed*] (SEIS)
STN .... Society of Trauma Nurses
STN .... Software Trouble Note [*NASA*] (NASA)
STN .... Solar Telescope Network
STN .... Solitary Tract Nucleus [*Also, NST*] [*Anatomy*]
STN .... Special Traffic Notice [*British*] (DCTA)
STN .... Specification Transmittal Notice (MCD)
STN .... Stain [*Deltiology*]
STN .... Stainless
STN .... Stansted [*England*] [*Airport symbol*] (OAG)
STN .... Statement of Technology Needs [*Air Force*]
STN .... St. Athan MU [*British ICAO designator*] (FAAC)
STN .... Station
Stn .... Station (DD)
stn .... Station (IDOE)
STN .... Station Casinos, Inc. [*NYSE symbol*] (SAG)
STN .... St. Nicholas in Chicago Ukrainian [*Diocesan abbreviation*] [*Illinois*] (TOCD)
STN .... Stomatogastric Nerve [*Neuroanatomy*]
STN .... Stone
STN .... Stone [*Unit of weight*] (AAG)
STN .... Strategic Air Command Telephone Network (IAA)
STN .... Subthalamic Nucleus [*Neurobiology*]
STN .... SuperTwisted Nematic [*Electronics*] (CDE)
STN .... Switched Telecommunications Network
STNA .... Scottish Teachers Nursing Association (DBA)
STNA .... Sons of Temperance of North America [*Defunct*] (EA)
STNAG .... Standardization Agreement [*NATO*]
STnC .... Skeletal Troponin C [*Biochemistry*]
stncl .... Stencil (VRA)
STND .... Stained (WGA)
STND .... Standard [*Legal shorthand*] (LWAP)
STND .... Standard Financial [*NASDAQ symbol*] (SAG)
StneWb .... Stone & Webster, Inc. [*Associated Press*] (SAG)
STNG .... Sustaining
STNI .... Subtotal Nodal Irradiation [*Oncology*]
STNLS .... Stainless (MSA)
STNLS .... Stainless
sTNM .... Surgical-Evaluative Staging of Cancer [*Classification of malignant tumors*] [*T refers to the size of the tumor, N refers to the status of the nodes, and M refers to metastases*] (DAVI)
STNR .... Stationary
STNR .... Symmetric Tonic Neck Reflex [*Medicine*] (DMAA)
STNT .... Stant Corp. [*NASDAQ symbol*] (SAG)
STNV .... Satellite Tobacco Necrosis Virus
STNWRE ...... Stoneware [*Freight*]
STO .... Aero Santos SA de CV [*Mexico ICAO designator*] (FAAC)
STO .... Science and Technology Objectives (MCD)
STO .... Sea Transport Officer
STO .... Segment Table Origin
STO .... Self-Test Output [*Automotive engineering*]
STO .... Senior Technical Officer (WDAA)
STO .... Senior Training Officer
STO .... Service du Travail Obligatoire [*French labor force*] [*World War II*]
STO .... Ship Test Organization (DNAB)
STO .... Short Takeoff (MCD)
STO .... Short-Term Objective
STO .... Slater-Type Orbital [*Atomic structure*]
STO .... Small-Time Operator [*Slang*]
STO .... Soft Target of Opportunity [*Terrorism*] (DI)
STO .... Sojourner Truth Organization (EA)
STO .... Solar Terrestrial Observatory (SSD)
STO .... Source Translation and Optimization [*Computer science*]
STO .... Standard Transfer Order
STO .... Standing Order [*Business term*] (DCTA)
STO .... Standing Orders (NITA)
STO .... Standing Tool Order (KSC)
STO .... State Taxation Office [*Australia*]
StO .... Steuerordnung [*Tax Law*] [*German*] (ILCA)
STO .... Stockholm [*Sweden*] [*Airport symbol*] (OAG)
STO .... Stockton [*Diocesan abbreviation*] [*California*] (TOCD)
STO .... Stoker [*Navy British*]
StO .... St. Olaf [*Record label*]
STO .... Stone Container [*NYSE symbol*] (TTSB)
STO .... Stone Container Corp. [*NYSE symbol*] (SPSG)
STO .... Stonehill College, North Easton, MA [*OCLC symbol*] (OCLC)
STO .... Stonyhurst [*Blackburn*] [*England*] [*Seismograph station code, US Geological Survey*] [*Closed*] (SEIS)
STO .... Storage (IDOE)
STO .... Storage Processor
STO .... Store (IDOE)
STO .... Storekeeper [*Coast Guard*]

Sto .... Storey's Delaware Reports [*A publication*] (DLA)
STO .... Story (WGA)
Sto .... Story's United States Circuit Court Reports [*A publication*] (DLA)
STO .... Stow (NASA)
STO .... Strategic Technology Office [*Arlington, VA*] [*DoD*] (GRD)
STO .... Swedish Trade Office (EA)
STO .... System Test Objective (IAA)
STO .... System Test Objectives
STO .... System Test Operator (IAA)
STOA .... Shock Time-of-Arrival [*Marine science*] (OSRA)
STOA .... Shock Time-of-Arrival (USDC)
Sto Abr Const... Story's Abridgment of the Constitution [*A publication*] (DLA)
STOAD .... Scientific and Technical Organizations and Agencies Directory [*A publication*]
Sto Ag .... Story on Agency [*A publication*] (DLA)
STOAL .... Short Takeoff Arrested Landing (MCD)
Sto & G .... Stone and Graham's Private Bills Decisions [*1865*] [*A publication*] (DLA)
Sto & H Cr Ab... Storer and Heard on Criminal Abortion [*A publication*] (DLA)
Sto Att Lien... Stokes on Lien of Attorneys and Solicitors [*1860*] [*A publication*] (DLA)
Sto Bailm .... Story on Bailments [*A publication*] (DLA)
Sto Bills ...... Story on Bills [*A publication*] (DLA)
STobRV........ Satellite Tobacco Ringspot Virus
STOC .... Spontaneous Transient Outward Current [*Physiology*]
STOC .... Standard Tactical Operating Condition
STOC .... Systems for Test Output Consolidation [*Computer science*]
STOCC .... Space Telescope Operations Control Center [*NASA*] (NASA)
Sto CC .... Story's United States Circuit Court Reports [*A publication*] (DLA)
Stock .... Stockton's New Brunswick Vice-Admiralty Reports [*1879-91*] [*A publication*] (DLA)
Stock .... Stockton's New Jersey Equity Reports [*A publication*] (DLA)
Stock Adm ... Stockton's New Brunswick Vice-Admiralty Reports [*A publication*] (DLA)
Stockett .... Stockett's Reports [*27-53 Maryland*] [*A publication*] (DLA)
STOCKH....... Stockholmia [*Stockholm*] [*Imprint*] (ROG)
Stock Non Com... Stock on Non Compotes Mentis [*A publication*] (DLA)
Stockt .... Stockton's New Jersey Equity Reports [*9-11 New Jersey*] [*A publication*] (DLA)
Stockt Ch..... Stockton's New Jersey Equity Reports [*9-11 New Jersey*] [*A publication*] (DLA)
Stockton ...... Stockton's New Brunswick Vice-Admiralty Reports [*A publication*] (DLA)
Stockton Adm (New Br)... Stockton's New Brunswick Vice-Admiralty Reports [*A publication*] (DLA)
Stockt Vice-Adm... Stockton's New Brunswick Vice-Admiralty Reports [*A publication*] (DLA)
Sto Comm ... Story's Commentaries on the Constitution of the United States [*A publication*] (DLA)
Sto Con........ Story on Contracts [*A publication*] (DLA)
Sto Conf Law... Story on Conflict of Laws [*A publication*] (DLA)
Sto Const..... Story's Commentaries on the Constitution of the United States [*A publication*] (DLA)
Sto Const Cl B... Story's Constitutional Class Book [*A publication*] (DLA)
Sto Cont ...... Story on Contracts [*A publication*] (DLA)
STOCS .... Small Terminal-Oriented Computer System (IAA)
STOCS .... South Texas Outer Continental Shelf
STOC-TV...... Satellite Technical and Operational Committee - Television (NTCM)
STOD .... Stodden [*England*]
Sto Eq Jur ... Story on Equity Jurisprudence [*A publication*] (DLA)
Sto Eq Pl .... Story on Equity Pleadings [*A publication*] (DLA)
STOG .... Science and Technology Objectives Guide (MCD)
STOG .... State/Territorial Operational Guidelines [*Australia*]
STOGW .... Short Takeoff Gross Weight [*Aviation*]
STOIAC .... Static Technology Office Information Analysis Center (NITA)
STOIAC .... Strategic Technology Office Information Analysis Center [*Battelle Memorial Institute*] (MCD)
STOIC .... Stack-Oriented Interactive Compiler [*Computer science*] (MHDI)
STOIIP .... Stock Tank Oil Initially in Place [*Petroleum technology*]
Stokely .... Stokely USA, Inc. [*Associated Press*] (SAG)
Stokes L of Att... Stokes on Liens of Attorneys [*A publication*] (DLA)
STOKPAC..... Stock Control Package (IAA)
STOL............ Saturn Test Oriented Language [*NASA*]
STOL............ Short Takeoff and Landing [*Aviation*]
STOL............ Slow Takeoff and Landing (IAA)
STOL............ Standing Operating and Landing
STOL............ Systems Test and Operation Language
STOLAND.... STOL Navigation and Landing System (MCD)
Sto Laws ..... Story's Laws of the United States [*A publication*] (DLA)
Stolport........ Short Takeoff and Landing Airport [*London, England*]
Stolt............ Stolt Nielsen SA [*Associated Press*] (SAG)
StoltCmx...... Stolt Comex Seaway SA [*Associated Press*] (SAG)
StoltNiel ...... Stolt-Nielsen, SA [*Associated Press*] (SAG)
STOM............ Safe Transport of Munitions (MCD)
STOM............ Shot through Obscuration MILES [*Multiple Integrated LASER Engagement System*] [*Army*]
STOM............ Stomachic [*To Strengthen the Stomach*] [*Medicine*] (ROG)
STOM............ Stomatocytes [*Hematology*] (DAVI)
STOM............ System Test and Operations Manual
Sto Miscel Writ... Story's Miscellaneous Writings [*A publication*] (DLA)
STOMPER .... Soil Test Ordnance Multipurpose Exploration Rocket (SAA)
STON .... GreenStone Indus [*NASDAQ symbol*] (TTSB)
STON .... GreenStone Industries, Inc. [*NASDAQ symbol*] (SAG)
STON .... Short Ton [*2000 lbs.*] (AABC)
StonC............ Stone Container Corp. [*Associated Press*] (SAG)
Stone .... Stone's Justices' Manual (Annual) [*A publication*] (DLA)
Stone Ben Bdg Soc... Stone's Benefit Building Societies [*1851*] [*A publication*] (DLA)
StoneC......... Stone Container Corp. [*Associated Press*] (SAG)
StoneEn....... Stone Energy Corp. [*Associated Press*] (SAG)
STONEH....... Stonehouse [*England*]
Stone Just Man... Stone's Justices' Manual (Annual) [*A publication*] (DLA)
StoneStB...... Stone Street Bancorp, Inc. [*Associated Press*] (SAG)
STONW .... GreenStone Inds Wrrt [*NASDAQ symbol*] (TTSB)
STOP .... Safe Tables Our Priority [*Protest organization compreised of parents and friends of E. coli victims*] (ECON)
STOP .... Safe Tables Our Priority
STOP .... Save the Oppressed People Committee [*Defunct*] (EA)
STOP .... Security Trading of Office Property
STOP .... Selected Test Optimization Program (MCD)
S/TOP .... Selective Tubal Occlusion Procedure [*Medicine*]
STOP .... Ship's Toxicological Protective System
STOP .... Single Title Order Plan [*Formerly, SCOP*] [*ABA*]
STOP .... Society that Opposes Pornography
STOP .... Software Theft Opposition Project [*Project STOP*] [*Information service or system*] (CRD)
STOP .... Stable Ocean Platform
STOP .... Stable Tubule Only Polypeptide [*Biochemistry*]
STOP .... Start Tromping on Pedal [*Facetious interpretation of the traffic sign*]
STOP .... Stop forced busing; Teach children, not bus them; Operate neighborhood schools for those in the neighborhood wishing to attend them; Put an end to government interference in the parent-child relationship [*An association*] (EA)
STOP .... Stopped Bonds [*Stock exchange term*] (MHDB)
STOP .... Stop the Oil Profiteers [*Antioil price slogan*]
STOP .... Stop the Olympic Prison [*Lake Placid Olympics, 1980*] [*Opposed possible later use of an Olympic building as a prison*] [*Defunct*]
STOP .... Stop This Outrageous Purge [*Group opposed to extremist measures used by segregationists in Arkansas; opposed by CROSS*]
STOP .... Storage Protector [*Computer science*] (IAA)
STOP .... Strategic Orbit Point (AFM)
STOP .... Strategic Talks on Prevention [*of accidental atomic war and nuclear weapons proliferation*] [*Proposed by Sen. Gary Hart, 1982*]
STOP .... Students Tackle Ocean Plastics
STOP .... Student/Teacher Organization to Prevent Nuclear War [*Defunct*] (EA)
STOP .... Sudden Tetanus of Prey [*Biology*]
STOP .... Supersonic Transport Optimization Program [*NASA*]
STOP ABC.... Stop Abuse by Counselors (EA)
Sto Part .... Story on Partnership [*A publication*] (DLA)
STOP-H........ Swedish Trial in Old Patients with Hypertension
Sto Pl .... Story's Civil Pleading [*A publication*] (DLA)
STOP-NSA ... Students to Oppose Participation in the National Student Association (EA)
STOPP .... Society of Teachers of Professional Photography [*Later, STEPP*] (EA)
STOPP .... Society of Teachers Opposed to Physical Punishment
STOPP .... Stop Planned Parenthood [*An association*] (EA)
STOPPS....... Standard Transportation Operations Personnel Property (MCD)
Sto Pr .... Story on Prize Courts [*A publication*] (DLA)
STOPrE......... Stone Container Cv Ex Pfd [*NYSE symbol*] (TTSB)
Sto Pr Notes... Story on Promissory Notes [*A publication*] (DLA)
STOPS .... Shipboard Toxicological Operational Protective System [*Navy*]
STOPS .... Stability Operations
STOPS .... Stabilized Terrain Optical Position Sensor [*Army*]
STOPS .... Standard Transportation Operations Property System (MCD)
STOPS .... Supreme Temple Order Pythian Sisters (EA)
StopSh......... [*The*] Stop & Shop Companies, Inc. [*Associated Press*] (SAG)
STOQ .... Storage Queue
STOR .... Scripps Tuna Oceanographic Research
STOR .... Segment Table Origin Register [*Computer science*] (BUR)
STOR .... Segment Table Origin Register (ECII)
STOR .... Storage (AFM)
STOR .... Summary Tape Operations Rental [*Bureau of the Census*]
STOR .... System Test and Operations Report
STORAD....... Stored Address [*Computer science*]
STORADS .... Site Tactical Optimized Range Air Defense System
Stor & H Abor... Storer and Heard on Criminal Abortion [*A publication*] (DLA)
STORC .... Self-Ferrying Trans-Ocean Rotary-Wing Crane [*Helicopter*]
STORCH....... Syphilis, Toxoplasmosis, Other Agents Rubella, Cytomegalovirus, and Herpes [*Medicine*] (DAVI)
STORCH....... Syphilis, Toxoplasmosis, Rubella, Cytomegalovirus, and Herpesvirus [*Medicine*] (DMAA)
Stor Dict....... Stormouth's Dictionary of the English Language [*A publication*] (DLA)
STORE .... Storage Technology for Operational Readiness
STORE .... Student's Own Record of Education (AIE)
STORE .... Students to Observe Retail Establishments [*Student legal action organization*] (EA)
STORES .... Syntactic Tracer Organized Retrospective Enquiry System [*Instituut voor Wiskunde, Informatiewerk, en Statistiek*] [*Computer science Netherlands*]
STORET .... Storage and Retrieval [*Computer science*]
STORET .... Storage and Retrieval for Water Quality Data [*Databank*] [*Environmental Protection Agency*] (MSC)
STORLAB..... Space Technology Operations and Research Laboratory (IEEE)
STORM .... Safe Transport of Munitions Project (MCD)
STORM .... Sensor, Tank, Off-Route Mine (MCD)
STORM .... Somali, Tigray, and Ormo Resistance Monitor [*British*]
STORM .... Statistically Oriented Matrix Program (IEEE)
STORM .... Stormscale Operational and Research Meteorology [*National Oceanic and Atmospheric Administration*]

Stormda........ Stormedia, Inc. [*Associated Press*] (SAG)
STORM-FEST... STORM [*Stormscal Operational and Research Meteorology*] Fronts Experiment Systems Test (USDC)
STORM-FEST... STORM [*Stormscale Operational and Research Meteorology*] Fronts Experiment Systems Test [*Marine science*] (OSRA)
STORMS...... Standardized Operation Research Management System (MCD)
STORMSAT... Storm Satellite (MCD)
StorPr.......... Storage Properties, Inc. [*Associated Press*] (SAG)
STORS......... Sludge to Oil Reactor System [*Battelle Memorial Institute*]
StorTc......... Storage Technology Corp. [*Associated Press*] (SAG)
StorTch........ Storage Technology Corp. [*Associated Press*] (SAG)
StorTRlt....... Storage Trust Realty [*Associated Press*] (SAG)
Story........... Story on Equity Jurisprudence [*1836-1920*] [*A publication*] (DLA)
Story........... Story's United States Circuit Court Reports [*A publication*] (DLA)
Story Ag...... Story on Agency [*A publication*] (DLA)
Story Bailm... Story on Bailments [*A publication*] (DLA)
Story Comm Const... Story's Commentaries on the Constitution of the United States [*A publication*] (DLA)
Story Confl Laws... Story on Conflict of Laws [*A publication*] (DLA)
Story Const... Story's Commentaries on the Constitution of the United States [*A publication*] (DLA)
Story Cont... Story on Contracts [*A publication*] (DLA)
Story Eq Jur... Story on Equity Jurisprudence [*A publication*] (DLA)
Story Eq Pl... Story's Equity Planning [*A publication*] (DLA)
Story Laws... Story's Laws of the United States [*A publication*] (DLA)
Story Merchants... Abbott's Merchant Ships and Seamen, by Story [*A publication*] (DLA)
Story Partn... Story on Partnership [*A publication*] (DLA)
Story Prom Notes... Story on Promissory Notes [*A publication*] (DLA)
Story R......... Story's United States Circuit Court Reports [*First Circuit*] [*A publication*] (DLA)
Story Sales... Story on Sales of Personal Property [*A publication*] (DLA)
Story's Circuit CR... Story's United States Circuit Court Reports [*First Circuit*] [*A publication*] (DLA)
Story's Laws... Story's United States Laws [*A publication*] (DLA)
Story's Rep... Story's United States Circuit Court Reports [*A publication*] (DLA)
Story US Laws... Story's Laws of the United States [*A publication*] (DLA)
STOS.......... Santos Ltd. [*NASDAQ symbol*] (NQ)
STOS.......... Space Test Operations Section
S to S.......... Station to Station
Sto Sales..... Story on Sales of Personal Property [*A publication*] (DLA)
STOSY......... Santos Ltd ADR [*NASDAQ symbol*] (TTSB)
STOT........... Scheduled Time over Target (AFM)
STOT........... Stockpile-to-Target (AFM)
STOTINS...... Standoff Techniques for Parachute Insertion (MCD)
StOTPr......... Studies in Old Testament Prophecy Presented to T. H. Robinson [*A publication*] (BJA)
StOU........... Stimmen Orient und Uebersee [*A publication*] (BJA)
STOU........... Super Tractor Oil-Universal [*Lubricants*]
Sto US Laws... Story's Laws of the United States [*A publication*] (DLA)
STOV........... State Theatre of Victoria [*Australia*]
Stov Hors..... Stovins' Law Respecting Horses [*A publication*] (DLA)
STOVL......... Short Takeoff and Vertical Landing (MCD)
STOW.......... Side Transfer Optimum Warehousing
STOW.......... Stowage (AAG)
STOW.......... Swim the Ontario Waterways [*Personal incentive program for fitness swimmers*] [*Ontario Masters Swimming Club*]
STOW.......... Synthetic Theater of War [*Army*]
STOW.......... System for Takeoff Weight
STOW-SKID... Synthetic Theater of War-Systems Engineering, Integration, and Demonstration [*Military*] (RDA)
STP............. 2,5-Dimethoxy-4-Methylamphetamine [*Also, Methyldimethoxy-Amphetamine and DOM*] [*An illicit hallucinogenic drug*] (DAVI)
STP............. Holidair Airways [*Canada ICAO designator*] (FAAC)
STP............. Sacrae [*or Sacrosanctae*] Theologiae Professor [*Professor of Sacred Theology*]
STP............. SAGE [*Semiautomatic Ground Environment*] System Training Program
STP............. Saint Peter's College, Jersey City, NJ [*OCLC symbol*] (OCLC)
STP............. Sao Tome and Principe [*ANSI three-letter standard code*] (CNC)
STP............. Satellite Ticket Printer [*Travel industry*]
STP............. Satellite Tracking Program [*of the Smithsonian Institution's Astrophysical Observatory*]
STP............. Save the Tallgrass Prairie [*An association*] (EA)
STP............. Science and Technology Policy (USDC)
STP............. Science and Technology Policy [*Marine science*] (OSRA)
STP............. Scientifically Treated Petroleum [*A motor fuel oil additive*] [*Initials reported, by extension of meaning, also to stand for a hallucinogenic drug, DOM*]
STP............. Scientifically Treated Petroleum [*Trade-name for a gasoline additive*] (BARN)
STP............. Seal to Parents [*Genealogy*] (PCM)
STP............. Sea Test Phase [*Navy*] (CAAL)
STP............. Secure Transfer Protocol [*Computer science*] (DOM)
STP............. Selective Tape Print
STP............. Self-Test Program (MCD)
STP............. Sent to Printer [*Publishing*]
STP............. Separation Transfer Point [*Army*] (ADDR)
STP............. Serenity, Tranquility, Peace [*Experimental hallucinogen developed by DOW Chemical Co.*] (IIA)
STP............. Sewage Treatment Plant
STP............. Shielded Twisted-Pair [*Computer science*] (PCM)
STP............. Short-Term Potentiation [*Neurology*]
STP............. Short-Term Program [*Nuclear energy*] (NRCH)
STP............. Short Term Projections [*Townsend, Greenspan & Co., Inc.*] [*No longer available online*] [*Information service or system*]
STP............. Shuttle Technology Panel [*NASA*] (NASA)
STP............. Signal Transfer Point [*Telecommunications*] (TEL)
STP............. Simultaneous Test Procedure [*Statistics*]
STP............. Simultaneous Track Processor
STP............. Singing Tree Press [*Publisher's imprint*]
STP............. Site Treatment Plan (DOGT)
STP............. Skills Training Program
ST-P............ Small Transmitter Coated with Paraffin
STP............. Socialism: Theory and Practice [*A publication*]
STP............. Society for Thai Philately (EA)
STP............. Society of Telecommunications Professionals (TSSD)
STP............. Society of Television Pioneers (EA)
STP............. Society of Toxicologic Pathologists (EA)
STP............. Sodium Thiopental [*A general anesthetic*] (DAVI)
STP............. Sodium Triphosphate [*or Sodium Tripolyphosphate*] [*Also, STPP Inorganic chemistry*]
STP............. Software Test Plan [*DoD*]
STP............. Solar-Terrestrial Physics (IID)
STP............. Solar-Terrestrial Probe [*NASA*]
STP............. Soldier Training Publications [*Military*] (INF)
STP............. South Texas Project [*Nuclear energy*] (NRCH)
STP............. Space Technology Payload [*NASA*] (MCD)
STP............. Space Technology Products [*NASA*] (IAA)
STP............. Space Test Program [*Air Force*]
STP............. Special Technical Publication (MCD)
STP............. Special Tool Production
STP............. Special Trade Passenger Ship (PDAA)
STP............. Spectrum of Time Project [*Astronomy*]
STP............. Stamp (MSA)
STP............. Standardized Test Program
STP............. Standard Program [*Computer science*] (IAA)
STP............. Standard Temperature and Pressure
STP............. Standard [*Normal*] Temperature and Pulse [*Medicine*]
STP............. Standard Test Procedure
STP............. Standard Thermal Profile
STP............. Standard Type Process (MCD)
St P............. State Papers [*A publication*] (DLA)
STP............. Stepping (WGA)
STP............. Sterilization Test Program
STP............. Steroidogenesis-Stimulating Protein [*Physiology*]
STP............. Stop Character [*Computer science*]
STP............. Stoppage (AABC)
STP............. Stop the Pentagon/Serve the People (EA)
STP............. Storage Tube Processor
STP............. Storm Track Prediction (MCD)
STP............. St. Paul and Minneapolis [*Diocesan abbreviation*] [*Minnesota*] (TOCD)
STP............. St. Paul, MN [*Location identifier FAA*] (FAAL)
STP............. Strength, Toughness, Pride
STP............. Strip
STP............. Structural Test Plan (ACII)
STP............. Submarine Technology Program [*Defense Advanced Research Projects Agency*] (DOMA)
STP............. Subsystem Test Plan [*NASA*] (NASA)
STP............. Supracondylar Tibial Prosthesis [*Medicine*]
STP............. Surface Transportation Program [*MOCD*] (TAG)
STP............. Sustainment Training Program [*Army*] (INF)
STP............. Sycamore Test Procedure [*Aerospace*] (AAG)
STP............. Systems Technology Program (MCD)
STP............. Systems Training Program [*RADAR*]
STP............. System Test Plan
STP............. System Test Procedure [*Nuclear energy*] (GFGA)
STP............. System Test Program [*Navy*] (CAAL)
STPA........... Statistical Training Programme for Africa [*United Nations*] (EY)
StP & D....... St. Paul & Duluth Railroad
StP & P....... St. Paul & Pacific Railroad
StP & SC...... St. Paul & Sioux City Railroad
StPaul.......... Saint Paul Companies, Inc. [*Associated Press*] (SAG)
StPaul.......... [*The*] St. Paul Companies, Inc. [*Associated Press*] (SAG)
StPaulBc...... Saint Paul Bancorp, Inc. [*Associated Press*] (SAG)
StPaulC....... Saint Paul Capital LLC [*Associated Press*] (SAG)
StPaulC....... St. Paul Capital LLC [*Associated Press*] (SAG)
StPCyRy...... St. Paul City Railway
STPD.......... Stamped (ROG)
STPD.......... Standard Temperature and Pressure, Dry
STPD.......... Stripped (MSA)
STPD.......... Stumped (WGA)
STPD.......... System Training Production Department (SAA)
STPDN........ Stepdown
STPDS........ Scientific and Technical Personnel Data System [*National Science Foundation*] (GFGA)
STPF........... Shield Test Pool Facility [*Nuclear energy*]
STPF........... Stabilized Temperature Platform Furnace
STPFM........ Subsystem: Short-Term Price Forecasting Model [*Department of Energy*] (GFGA)
STPG.......... Sequential Test Plan Generator (PDAA)
STPG.......... Spare-Time Production for Gain [*FAO*]
STPG.......... Stamping (ROG)
STPG.......... Stepping (MSA)
STPH.......... Static Phase Error [*NASA*] (NASA)
STPI........... Science and Technology Policy Implementation [*Project*]
STPI........... Static Power Inverter (DWSG)
STPL.......... Short-Term Public Exposure Limit (MCD)

STPL........... Sidetone Path Loss [*Telecommunications*] (TEL)
STPL........... Standard Test Processing Language (NITA)
STPL........... Steeple (DS)
STPL........... Stern Plane
St Pl Cr....... Staundeforde's Pleas of Crown [*A publication*] (DLA)
STP-M......... Solar-Terrestrial Physics - Meteorology
STPM........... Syndicat Togolais du Personnel de la Meteorologie [*Togolese Union of Meteorological Personnel*]
StPM & M... St. Paul, Minneapolis & Manitoba Railway
STP-MET...... Solar-Terrestrial Physics - Meteorology [*International Council of Scientific Unions*]
STPN........... South Pointe Enterprises [*NASDAQ symbol*] (SAG)
STPNG......... Stopping (MSA)
STPO........... Science and Technology Policy Office [*Supersedes OST*] [*National Science Foundation*]
STPO........... Strategic Targets Product Office [*Army*] (RDA)
STPO........... Systems Technology Project Office
STPP........... Sodium Tripolyphosphate [*Also, STP*] [*Inorganic chemistry*]
STPP........... Student Teacher Performance Profile
STPP........... Surface Transportation Policy Project [*Military*]
STPR........... Semiannual Technical Progress Report
STPR........... Software Test Procedure
St Pr........... Staundeforde's Exposition of the King's Prerogative [*A publication*] (DLA)
STPR........... Stepper [*Motor*] [*Electronics*]
STPR........... Stripper
STPR........... Stumper [*Freight*]
St Pr Reg..... Style's Practical Register [*England*] [*A publication*] (DLA)
STPS........... S-Band Tracking Processor System
STPS........... Series-Tuned Parallel-Stabilized [*Computer science*] (IAA)
STPS........... Solar Thermal Power System
STPS........... Specific Thalamic Projection System [*Medicine*] (DMAA)
STPS........... Stern Teacher Preference Schedule
STPS........... Summary Task Planning Sheet
STPS........... Systems Test Planning Section (SAA)
STPST......... Stop-Start [*Telecommunications*] (TEL)
STPT........... Society of Town Planning Technicians [*British*]
STPTC......... Standardization of Tar Products Test Committee
STPUB......... Stem Pubescence [*Botany*]
StPUD......... St. Paul Union Depot
StPUSY....... St. Paul Union Stock Yards Co.
STPV........... Semitrailer Petroleum Van (DWSG)
STPX........... Systems Training Program Exercise (AABC)
STQ............. Society of Translators of Quebec [*Canada*]
STQ............. Streator, IL [*Location identifier FAA*] (FAAL)
STQ............. Superior Temporal Quadrant [*Medicine*] (DMAA)
STr.............. Esotropia, Right [*Ophthalmology*] (DAVI)
STR............. Questar Corp. [*NYSE symbol*] (SPSG)
STR............. Scientific and Technological Research (DEN)
STR............. Scientific Technical Report
STR............. Search and Track RADAR
STR............. Seater (ADA)
STR............. Sea Test Range (MUGU)
STR............. Segment Table Register
STR............. Senior Technical Representative
STR............. Service Test Review
STR............. Service Trouble Report
STR............. Short Term Reinitialization [*Army*]
STR............. Short-Term Returns
STR............. Sidetone Reduction [*Telecommunications*] (TEL)
STR............. Single Token Ring [*Telecommunications*] (OSI)
STR............. Society for Theatre Research (EA)
STR............. Society of Thoracic Radiology (EA)
STR............. Software Test Report
STR............. Software Trouble Report (MCD)
STR............. Software Trouble Reporting Service (NITA)
STR............. Solar Transition Region [*Solar physics*]
STR............. Spacecraft Telemetry Regenerator (MCD)
STR............. Special Theory of Relativity
STR............. Special Trade Representative
STR............. Special Treatment Room [*Medicine*] (DAVI)
STR............. Speed Tolerant Recording [*Electronic Processors, Inc.*]
STR............. Staff Technical Representative
STR............. Standard Broadcasting Corp. Ltd. [*Toronto Stock Exchange symbol*]
STR............. Standard Taxiway Routing
STR............. Standard Telephon und Radio [*Switzerland*] (NITA)
STR............. Standard Tool Request
STR............. Standard Training Requirements [*Navy*] (NVT)
STR............. Start Address Register [*Telecommunications*] (IAA)
STR............. Status Register [*Computer science*]
STR............. Steamer
STR............. Stellair [*France ICAO designator*] (FAAC)
STR............. Stirred-Tank Reactor [*Chemical engineering*]
STR............. Storage Rack (MCD)
STR............. Store
STR............. Store
STR............. Straight (AAG)
STR............. Strainer (AAG)
STR............. Strait [*Maps and charts*]
Str.............. Strange's Cases of Evidence [*1698-1732*] [*England*] [*A publication*] (DLA)
Str.............. Strange's English King's Bench Reports [*1716-49*] [*A publication*] (DLA)
STR............. Strasbourg [*France*] [*Seismograph station code, US Geological Survey*] (SEIS)
STR............. Strasse [*Street*] [*German*]
Str.............. Strategemata [*of Frontinus*] [*Classical studies*] (OCD)
STR............. Strategic Training Range (MCD)
STR............. Streak
str.............. Streaky [*Quality of the bottom*] [*Nautical charts*]
STR............. Stream [*Maps and charts*]
STR............. Stream Routing [*Computer science*]
STR............. Street
STR............. Streichinstrumente [*Stringed Instruments*] [*Music*]
STR............. Strength (AFM)
STR............. Streptococcus [*Medicine*]
STR............. Stretch [*Horse racing*]
Str.............. Striatum [*Brain anatomy*] [*Also, ST*]
STR............. Striking (WGA)
STR............. String
STR............. Stringendo [*Hastening*] [*Music*]
STR............. Strings [*of an orchestra*]
STR............. Strip (AAG)
STR............. Strobe [*NASA*] (IAA)
STR............. Stroke
STR............. Strophe [*Classical studies*] (OCD)
STR............. Structural [*Lumber*]
St R............. Stuart's Lower Canada Appeal Cases [*Quebec*] [*A publication*] (DLA)
STR............. Stuttgart [*Germany Airport symbol*] (OAG)
STR............. Submarine Test Reactor
STR............. Submarine Thermal Reactor [*Nuclear energy*]
STR............. Submersible Test Rack
STR............. Summary Technical Report
STR............. Super Transportable RADAR
STR............. Surplus to Requirements (ADA)
STR............. Symbol Time Recovery (NITA)
STR............. Synchronous Transmit Receive (NITA)
STR............. Synchronous Transmitter Receiver [*Computer science*]
STR............. Systems Technology RADAR (MCD)
STR............. Systems Technology Report (MCD)
STR............. System Test Report [*Military*]
STR............. System Test Review [*NASA*] (NASA)
STRA........... Stravenue
STRA........... Stravenue [*Postal Service standard*] (OPSA)
STRA........... Strayer Education, Inc. [*NASDAQ symbol*] (SAG)
STRA........... Supply and Training Mission [*Military*] (CINC)
STRAAD....... Special Techniques Repair Analysis Aircraft Damage [*Navy*] (NVT)
STRAB......... Strabismus [*Medicine*]
Strab........... Strabo [*First century BC*] [*Classical studies*] (OCD)
STRABAD..... Strategic Base Air Defense [*Military*] (AABC)
STRAC......... Standards in Training Commission [*Army*] (INF)
STRAC......... Strategic Army Corps [*Acronym has come to mean "ordered" or "neat"*]
STRACNET... Strategic Rail Corridor Network [*MTMC*] (TAG)
STRACOS..... Strategic Air Combat Operations Staff
STRACS....... Small Transportable Communications Stations
STRACS....... Surface Traffic Control System (MCD)
STRAD......... Signal Transmission Reception and Distribution (IEEE)
Strad........... Stradivari [*Record label*]
STRAD......... Stradivarius Violin [*Music*] (DSUE)
STRAD......... Strategic Aerospace Division [*Air Force*] (AFM)
STRAD......... Switching, Transmitting, Receiving, and Distribution
STRADAP..... Storm RADAR Data Processor [*ESD*]
STRADIS...... Structured Analysis, Design and Implementation of Information Systems (MHDI)
STRAF......... Special Therapeutic and Rehabilitation Activities Fund [*Department of Veterans Affairs*]
STRAF......... Strategic Army Forces
STRAFE........ Students Resisting Aerosol Flurocarbon Emissions [*Student legal action organization*] (EA)
Strafford...... Smith's New Hampshire Reports [*A publication*] (DLA)
STRAFIP...... Strategic Army Forces Readiness Improvement Program (AABC)
STRAFLO...... Straight-Flow [*Water turbine*]
STRAFPOA... Strategic Air Force, Pacific Ocean Area
STRAG......... Straggler
STRAGL....... Straggler Line [*Military*]
Strahan........ Strahan's Reports [*19 Oregon*] [*A publication*] (DLA)
Strah Domat... Strahan's Domat's Civil Law [*A publication*] (DLA)
STRAHNET... Strategic Highway Corridor Network [*BTS*] [*MTMC*] (TAG)
STRAIN........ Structural Analytical Interpreter
STRAIRPOA... Strategic Air Force, Pacific Ocean Area
Straits LJ & Rep... Straits Law Journal and Reporter [*A publication*] (DLA)
STRAM......... Synchronous Transmit Receive Access Method (CMD)
Str & HC....... Streets and Highways Code [*A publication*] (DLA)
STRANGE..... SAGE [*Semiautomatic Ground Environment*] Tracking and Guidance Evaluation System
Strange........ Strange's English Court Reports [*A publication*] (DLA)
Strange (Eng)... Strange's English Courts Reports [*93 English Reprint*] [*A publication*] (DLA)
Strange Madras... Strange's Notes of Cases, Madras [*A publication*] (DLA)
STRAP......... SCAR Team Report Analysis Program (MCD)
STRAP......... Simplified Transient Radiation Analysis Program (MCD)
STRAP......... Simultaneous Transmission and Recovery of Alternating Pictures [*TV system*]
STRAP......... Sonobuoy Thinned Random Array Program [*Navy*] (CAAL)
STRAP......... Star [*or Stellar*] Tracking Rocket Attitude Positioning [*System*] [*NASA*]
STRAP......... Stretch Assembly Program [*IBM Corp.*]
STRAP......... Structural Analysis Package
STRAP......... System Training Plan

STRAPP .... Standard Tanks, Racks, Adapter, and Pylon Packages (MCD)
STRASB .... Strasbourg [*Imprint*] (ROG)
STRAT .... Strategic (AFM)
STRAT .... Stratigraphic
STRAT .... Stratton [*England*]
STRATA .... Short-Term Reconaissance and Target Acquisition Team [*US Special Forces*] (VNW)
STRATAD ...... Strategic Aerospace Division [*Air Force*]
STRATANALSUPPGRU... Strategic Analysis Support Group [*Navy*] (DNAB)
Stratasys ..... Stratasys, Inc. [*Associated Press*] (SAG)
Stratcm .... Stratacom, Inc. [*Associated Press*] (SAG)
STRATCOM... Strategic Air Command [*Air Force*]
STRATCOM... Strategic Communications [*Army*] (IAA)
STRATCOM... Strategic Communications Command [*Army*] (RDA)
STRATCOM... Stratospheric Composition (MCD)
STRATCOMMEX... Strategic Communications Military Exchange [*Army*] (IAA)
StratCp .... Stratosphere Corp. [*Associated Press*] (SAG)
STRATF .... Stratford [*England*]
STRATMAS... Strategic Mobility [*Planning and*] Analysis System [*Military*] (NVT)
STRATMID ... Strategic Military Intelligence Detachment [*Army*] (MCD)
STRATO .... Stratosphere (AFM)
STRATOSCOPE... Stratosphere Telescope (IAA)
STRATSAT ... Strategic Satellite System [*Air Force Telecommunications*] (TEL)
Strattec .... Strattec Security Corp. [*Associated Press*] (SAG)
Stratton .... Stratton's Reports [*12-14 Oregon*] [*A publication*] (DLA)
Stratus .... Stratus Computer, Inc. [*Associated Press*] (SAG)
STRATWARM... Stratospheric Warming
STRAV .... Stravenue [*Commonly used*] (OPSA)
STRAVE .... Stravenue [*Commonly used*] (OPSA)
STRAVEN ..... Stravenue [*Commonly used*] (OPSA)
STRAVENUE... Stravenue [*Commonly used*] (OPSA)
STRAVN ...... Stravenue [*Commonly used*] (OPSA)
STRAW .... Simultaneous Tape Read and Write
Strayer .... Strayer Education, Inc. [*Associated Press*] (SAG)
STRB .... Strobe (NASA)
STRB .... Strober Organization [*NASDAQ symbol*] (TTSB)
STRB .... [*The*] Strober Organization, Inc. [*Brooklyn, NY*] [*NASDAQ symbol*] (NQ)
STRBK .... Strongback
STRb M .... Grupo Situr'B' [*ME symbol*] (TTSB)
STRC .... Science and Technology Research Center [*North Carolina*] (MCD)
STRC .... Scientific, Technical, and Research Commission (EY)
STRC .... Society of Traditional Roman Catholics (EA)
STRC .... Sterile Recoveries, Inc. [*NASDAQ symbol*] (SAG)
STRC .... Switch Tail Ring Counter
Str Cas Ev ... Strange's Cases of Evidence ("Octavo Strange") [*A publication*] (DLA)
STRCH .... Stretch (AAG)
StrchMb .... Streicher Mobile Fueling, Inc. [*Associated Press*] (SAG)
STRC-IVS ..... STRC [*Science and Technology Research Center*] Inverted File Search System [*Search system*]
StrCmp .... Storage Computer Corp. [*Associated Press*] (SAG)
Strctlns .... Structural Instrumentation, Inc. [*Associated Press*] (SAG)
STRCTRD ..... Structured
STRD .... Short Tour Return Date [*Military*]
STRD .... Stored
STRD .... Strand [*Engineering*]
STRD .... Strategic Distribution [*NASDAQ symbol*] (SAG)
STRE .... Specialist Teams Royal Engineers [*Military British*]
STREAM ...... Standard Tensioned Replenishment Alongside Method [*Military*] (NVT)
STREAM ...... Stream [*Commonly used*] (OPSA)
S Treaty Doc... Senate Treaty Documents [*A publication*] (DLA)
STREET .... Street [*Commonly used*] (OPSA)
Street Ry Rep... Street Railway Reports [*A publication*] (DLA)
STREETS ...... Streets [*Commonly used*] (OPSA)
STREME .... Stream [*Commonly used*] (OPSA)
STRENGTHD... Strengthened (ROG)
STREP .... Ship's Test and Readiness Evaluation Procedure
STREP .... Space Trajectory Radiation Exposure Procedure
St Rep .... State Reporter [*A publication*] (DLA)
St Rep .... State Reports [*A publication*] (DLA)
STREP .... Status Report [*IRS*]
Strep .... Strepsiptera [*Entomology*]
STREP .... Streptococcus [*Medicine*]
STREP .... Systems Technology Reentry Experiment Program [*Military*]
strept .... Streptococcus [*A bacterium*] [*Medicine*] (DAVI)
STREPTO ..... Streptomycin [*An antibiotic*] (DSUE)
StRes .... Sight Resources Corp. [*Associated Press*] (SAG)
STRES .... Store Release Evaluation System (MCD)
STRESS .... Satellite Transmission Effects Simulation (MCD)
STRESS .... Stop the Robberies, Enjoy Safe Streets [*Detroit police unit*] [*Disbanded*]
STRESS .... Structural Engineering Systems Solver [*Programming language*] [*1962*]
STRET .... Street
stret .... Stretcher (VRA)
STRETCH ..... Space Technology Requirements Engineering Test of Component Hardware [*NASA*] (KSC)
Str Ev .... Strange's Cases of Evidence [*1698-1732*] [*England*] [*A publication*] (DLA)
STRF .... Sea Turtle Rescue Fund (EA)
STRFLD .... Star Field (MCD)
STRG .... Steering (AAG)
STRG .... String (NASA)
strg .... String (VRA)
STRG .... Strong (MSA)
StrgCmp ...... Storage Computer Corp. [*Associated Press*] (SAG)
strgcr .... Stringcourse (VRA)
StrGlob .... Strategic Global Income Fund [*Associated Press*] (SAG)
STRG WND... String or Wind [*Freight*]
Str HL .... Strange's Hindoo Law [*A publication*] (DLA)
STRI .... Smithsonian Tropical Research Institute [*Miami, FL*]
STRI .... Sports Turf Research Institute [*British*] (IRUK)
STRI .... Stones River National Battlefield
Strick Ev ...... Strickland on Evidence [*1830*] [*A publication*] (DLA)
STRICOM ..... Simulation, Training, and Instrumentation Command [*Army*] (RDA)
STRICOM ..... Strike Command [*Military*]
Stricycle .... Stericycle, Inc. [*Associated Press*] (SAG)
STRIDE .... Science and Technology for Regional Innovation and Development in Europe [*EC*] (ECED)
STRIDE .... Standard Reactor Island Design [*Nuclear energy*] (NRCH)
STRIDE .... System to Retrieve Information from Drug Evidence [*Drug Enforcement Administration*]
StrideRt .... Stride Rite Corp. [*Associated Press*] (SAG)
STRIKEOPS... Strike Operations [*Military*] (NVT)
Striker .... Striker Industries [*Associated Press*] (SAG)
STRIKEX ...... Strike Exercise [*Navy NATO*] (NATG)
STRIKFLTLANT... Striking Fleet Atlantic [*Military*]
STRIKFORSOUTH... Striking and Support Forces Southern Europe [*Navy*]
STRIKFTLANTREPEUR... Striking Fleet Atlantic Representative in Europe [*NATO*] (NATG)
STRIKWARN... Strike Warning Message [*Army*] (ADDR)
STRING .... Stringendo [*Hastening*] [*Music*]
Stringf .... Stringfellow's Reports [*9-11 Missouri*] [*A publication*] (DLA)
Stringfellow... Stringfellow's Reports [*9-11 Missouri*] [*A publication*] (DLA)
STRINGS ...... Stellar Inertial Guidance System (DNAB)
STRINO .... Stringendo [*Hastening*] [*Music*] (ROG)
STRIP .... Select Technical Requirements Information Program
STRIP .... Specification Technical Review and Improvement Program [*Navy*] (NG)
STRIP .... Standard Requisition and Issue Procedures [*Military*] (CINC)
STRIP .... Standard Taped Routines for Image Processing [*National Institute of Standards and Technology*]
STRIP .... Stock Turn-In and Replenishment Invoicing Procedures
STRIP .... Strategic Intermediate Planner (PDAA)
STRIP .... String Processing Language [*Computer science*] (DIT)
STRIPE .... Stress-Induced Pseudoelasticity (PDAA)
STRIPE .... Swap Transferring Risk with Participating Element [*Finance*]
STRIPS .... Separate Trading of Registered Interest and Principal of Securities [*Investment term*]
STRIPS .... Separate Trading of Registered Interest and Principal of Securities (TDOB)
STRIPS .... Stanford Research Institute Problem Solver [*Computer system*]
STRIVE .... Society for the Preservation of Rural Industries and Village Enterprises [*British*] (ODBW)
STRIVE .... Standard Techniques for Reporting Information on Value Engineering
STRJ .... Self-Powered Thermocouple Reference Junction
STRK .... Star Tracker (NASA)
STRK .... Stroke (MSA)
STRKP .... Storekeeper
STRKR .... Striker [*Automotive engineering*]
STRL .... Schottky Transistor Resistor Logic [*Electronics*] (IAA)
STRL .... Sea Trials [*Navy*] (NVT)
STRL .... Steris Corp. [*NASDAQ symbol*] (SAG)
STR L .... Straight Line [*Freight*]
STRL .... Structural
STRL .... Structural
StrlBcp .... Sterling Bancorp [*Associated Press*] (SAG)
StrlBnc .... Sterling Bancshares, Inc. [*Associated Press*] (SAG)
StrlCap .... Sterling Capital Corp. [*Associated Press*] (SAG)
StrlCh .... Sterling Chemicals, Inc. [*Associated Press*] (SAG)
STRLEN .... String Length [*Computer science*] (PCM)
StrlF .... Sterling Financial Corp. [*Associated Press*] (SAG)
StrlFnWA ..... Sterling Financial Corp. [*Associated Press*] (SAG)
STR LGTHS... Straight Lengths [*Freight*]
StrLhmn .... Stearns & Lehman, Inc. [*Associated Press*] (SAG)
STRLN .... Streamline (MSA)
STRLNG ...... Sterling
strl si .... Sterling Silver (VRA)
StrlVis .... Sterling Vision, Inc. [*Associated Press*] (SAG)
StrlWst .... Sterling West Bancorp [*Associated Press*] (SAG)
STRM .... Storeroom (MSA)
strm .... Store Room (VRA)
STRM .... Stratacom, Inc. [*NASDAQ symbol*] (SAG)
STRM .... Stream
STRM .... Stream
StrMb .... Streicher Mobile Fueling, Inc. [*Associated Press*] (SAG)
STRMD .... Strategic Missile Division [*Military*]
StrmLog .... StreamLogic Corp. [*Associated Press*] (SAG)
STRN .... Standard Technical Report Number
STRN .... Strength (AAG)
STRNG .... Steering
STRNR .... Strainer (AAG)
STRO .... Scandinavian Tire and Rim Organization (EA)
STRO .... Stereo Routes [*Aviation*] (FAAC)
STRO .... Strouds, Inc. [*NASDAQ symbol*] (SAG)
Strob .... Strobhart's South Carolina Law Reports [*1846-50*] [*A publication*] (DLA)
Strob Ch ...... Strobhart's South Carolina Equity Reports [*A publication*] (DLA)

STROBE....... Satellite Tracking of Balloons and Emergencies
STROBE....... Stroboscopic (MSA)
Strob Eq...... Strobhart's South Carolina Equity Reports [1846-50] [A publication] (DLA)
Strober........ Strober Organization, Inc. [Associated Press] (SAG)
STROBES..... Shared-Time Repair of Big Electronic Systems [Computer science]
Strobh Eq (SC)... Strobhart's South Carolina Equity Reports [A publication] (DLA)
Strobh L (SC)... Strobhart's South Carolina Law Reports [A publication] (DLA)
STROFAC..... Stabilized Routing for Afloat Commands (MCD)
STR OFF FIXT... Store or Office Fixture [s] [Freight]
STROG......... Strait of Gibraltar (DOMA)
Strom........... Stromateis [of Clemens Alexandrinus] [Classical studies] (OCD)
STROM........ Stromberg [Automotive engineering]
StrongSv...... Strongsville Savings Bank [Associated Press] (SAG)
STROP......... Stock Ratio Optimizing (MHDB)
Strouds........ Strouds, Inc. [Associated Press] (SAG)
Stroud Sl..... Stroud on Slavery [A publication] (DLA)
StroUSA....... Storage USA, Inc. [Associated Press] (SAG)
STRP........... Short Tandem Repeat Polymorphisms [Genetics]
STRP........... Strap
STRR........... Star Technologies [NASDAQ symbol] (TTSB)
STRR........... Star Technologies, Inc. [Sterling, VA] [NASDAQ symbol] (NQ)
STRS........... SAGE [Semi-Automatic Ground Equipment] Training Requirements Section (SAA)
STRS........... Stimulated Thermal Rayleigh Scattering (PDAA)
STRS........... Strategic Transportation Research Study [FHWA] (TAG)
STRS........... Submarine Technical Repair Standard [Navy] (DNAB)
STRSPH....... Stratosphere (WGA)
STRT........... Skin Temperature Recovery Time [Medicine] (DMAA)
STRT........... Start
STRT........... [The] Stewartstown Railroad Co. [AAR code]
STRT........... Strait [Board on Geographic Names]
STRT........... Strattec Security [NASDAQ symbol] (TTSB)
STRT........... Strattec Security Corp. [NASDAQ symbol] (SAG)
STRT........... Street [Commonly used] (OPSA)
StrtCp......... Stratosphere Corp. [Associated Press] (SAG)
StrtDiag....... Strategic Diagnostics, Inc. [Associated Press] (SAG)
STRTGC....... Strategic
StrtgDist...... Strategic Distribution [Associated Press] (SAG)
STRTL......... Structural
STRTR......... Starter [Automotive engineering]
STRU........... Styrelserepresentationsutredningen [Sweden]
STRUBAL..... Structured Basic Language [Computer science] (CSR)
STRUC......... Structure (AABC)
StrucD......... Structural Dynamics Research Corp. [Associated Press] (SAG)
STRUCT....... Structure (AAG)
STRUDL....... Structural Design Language [Computer science] (MCD)
STRUDLDYNAL... Structural Design Language Dynamic Analysis [Computer science]
STRUDLPLOTS... Structural Design Language Output Plots
STRUDLTOWER... Structural Design Language for Transmission Tower
STRUFO....... Structural Formula [Chemistry] [Computer science]
ST Rulings... Sales Tax Rulings [Australia A publication]
Struther....... Struthers Industries [Associated Press] (SAG)
Struve.......... Struve's Washington Territory Reports [1854-88] [A publication] (DLA)
STRV........... Short Tons Raw Value
STRVN......... Stravenue [Commonly used] (OPSA)
STRVNUE..... Stravenue [Commonly used] (OPSA)
STRW........... Straw [Colored] [Laboratory science] (DAVI)
STRW........... Strawbridge & Clothier [NASDAQ symbol] (NQ)
STRWA......... Strawbridge/Clothier'A' [NASDAQ symbol] (TTSB)
StrwbCl....... Strawbridge Clothier [Associated Press] (SAG)
STRY........... Stryker Corp. [NASDAQ symbol] (NQ)
STRYCH....... Strychnina [Strychnine] [Pharmacy] (ROG)
Stryker........ Stryker Corp. [Associated Press] (SAG)
St Ry Rep.... Street Railway Reports [United States] [A publication] (DLA)
STrZ............ South Tropical Zone [Planet Jupiter]
STS............. Office of State Technical Services [Also, OSTS] [Abolished, 1970 Department of Commerce]
STS............. SAGE [Semi-Automatic Ground Equipment] Training Specialist (SAA)
Sts............. Saints (ODBW)
STS............. Saint Thomas Seminary [Colorado; Connecticut; Kentucky]
STS............. Santa Rosa [California] [Airport symbol] (OAG)
STS............. Santiago [Spain] [Seismograph station code, US Geological Survey] (SEIS)
STS............. Satellite-to-Satellite (CET)
STS............. Satellite Tracking Station
STS............. Satellite Transmission Systems, Inc. [Hauppauge, NY] [Telecommunications] (TSSD)
STS............. S-Band Transmitter System
STS............. Scanning Tunneling Spectroscopy
STS............. Scheduled Truck Service [Army]
STS............. School Television Service
STS............. School-to-School [Red Cross Youth]
STS............. Science and Technology Section [Association of College and Research Libraries]
STS............. Science of To-Day Series [A publication]
STS............. Science Talent Search (EA)
STS............. Science, Technology, and Society
STS............. Scientific Terminal System (IAA)
STS............. Scottish Tartans Society (EA)
STS............. Sea Training Staff [Canadian Navy]
STS............. Security Termination Statement [Military] (AFM)
STS............. Self-Test Select
STS............. Seminex [Concordia Seminary in Exile] Library, St. Louis, MO [OCLC symbol] (OCLC)
STS............. Sequence-Tagged Site [Genetics]
STS............. Serological Test for Syphilis [Medicine]
STS............. Servicios Auxiliares de Transportes Aereos [Brazil] [ICAO designator] (FAAC)
STS............. Servocylinder Test Set (MCD)
STS............. Servo Test System
STS............. Seville Touring Sedan [General Motors Corp.]
STS............. Sewage Treatment System [Navy] (CAAL)
STS............. Shared Tenant Services [Telecommunications] (TSSD)
STS............. Ship-to-Shore
STS............. Shuttle Test Station (NASA)
STS............. Shuttle Transportation System (MCD)
STS............. Siltstone [Lithology]
STS............. Simulator Test Set (CAAL)
STS............. Single Thread System
STS............. Skaggs Telecommunications Service [Salt Lake City, UT] [Telecommunications] (TSSD)
STS............. Skylab Terminal System [NASA]
STS............. Society for Textual Scholarship (EA)
STS............. Society of Thoracic Surgeons (EA)
STS............. Socio-Technical Systems [Management technique]
STS............. Sodium Tetradecyl Sulfate [Organic chemistry]
STS............. Sodium Thiosulfate [Inorganic chemistry, biochemistry]
STS............. Soft Tissue Sarcoma [Oncology]
STS............. Soft-Tissue Swelling [Radiology] (DAVI)
STS............. Solar Tracking System
STS............. SONAR Technician, Submarine [Navy rating] (DNAB)
STS............. SONAR Test System
STS............. Sonic Telex System [Sonicair] [Phoenix, AZ] [Telecommunications] (TSSD)
STS............. Spacecraft Telecommunications System
STS............. Spacecraft Tracking Station [NASA] (KSC)
STS............. Space Technology Satellite (IAA)
STS............. Space-Time-Space [Digital switching structure] [Telecommunications] (TEL)
STS............. Space Transportation System
STS............. Special Task Stores [Military British]
STS............. Special Test System [Air Force] (AFM)
STS............. Special Training Standard [Air Force] (AFM)
STS............. Special Treatment Steel
STS............. Specialty Training System
STS............. Specific Tensile Strength
STS............. Spring Trapmakers' Society [British] (DCTA)
STS............. Stabilized Telescope System
StS............. Stamp Seal (BJA)
STS............. Standard (Galilean) Telescopes [Instrumentation]
STS............. Standard Technical Specifications [Nuclear energy] (NRCH)
STS............. Standard Test for Syphilis [Medicine]
STS............. Standard Threshold Shift
STS............. State Technical Services [Abolished, 1970]
STS............. Static Test Stand
STS............. Stationary Time Series
STS............. Station to Station
STS............. Status [ICAO designator] (FAAC)
STS............. Sterol-sulphatase [An enzyme]
STS............. Stimulated Thermal Scattering [Photonics]
STS............. Stockpile-to-Target Sequence [Military]
STS............. Stock Trading System
STS............. Stomatogastric Nervous System [Neuroanatomy]
STS............. Strategic Technical Service (CINC)
STS............. Strategic Training Squadron (MCD)
STS............. Streets
STS............. Streets [Postal Service standard] (OPSA)
STS............. Structural Transition Section [NASA] (MCD)
STS............. Student Travel School
STS............. Sugar-Tong Splint [Medicine] (MEDA)
STS............. Superior Temporal Sulcus [Brain anatomy]
STS............. Supernatant Treatment System [Nuclear energy] (NUCP)
STS............. Supersonic Target System
STS............. Supplementary Test Site [Nuclear energy] (IID)
STS............. Suprasonic Transport [Aviation] (DAVI)
STS............. Supreme Industries [Formerly, ESI Industries Corp.] [AMEX symbol] (SPSG)
STS............. Supreme Industries'A' [AMEX symbol] (TTSB)
STS............. Surface Target Simulator [Navy] (DNAB)
STS............. Surveillance Test Set (MCD)
STS............. Survey Tabulation Services, Inc. [Information service or system] (IID)
STS............. Synchronous Transport Signal [Computer science]
STS............. Synchrony Service and Transport System [Ascom Timeplex, Inc.]
STS............. System Technical Services
STS............. System Test Set
STS............. System Test Software (CAAL)
STS............. System Test Station (SAA)
STS............. System Training Section (SAA)
STS............. System Training Specialist (SAA)
STS............. System Trouble Shooting
STS............. System Trouble Survey (CET)
STSA........... Seaman Apprentice, SONAR Technician, Striker [Navy rating]
STSA........... Southern Thoracic Surgical Association (EA)
STSA........... State Technical Services Act
STSA........... Sterling Financial Corp. [NASDAQ symbol] (SAG)
STSA........... Sterling Finl (WA) [NASDAQ symbol] (TTSB)
STSA........... Sub-tropical Seedgrowers' Association [Australia]

STSALV........ Standby Salvage Ship [*Navy*] (NVT)
STSAP......... Sterling Finl $1.8125 Cv Pfd [*NASDAQ symbol*] (TTSB)
ST-SAS........ Septic Tank-Subsurface Absorption System
STSC........... Scientific Time Sharing Corp. [*Host*] [*Information service or system*] (IID)
STSC........... Scottish Teachers Salaries Committee [*British*]
STSC........... Shipboard Tactical Satellite Communications (DNAB)
ST SCI......... Space Telescope Science Institute [*Johns Hopkins University*] [*Research center*] (RCD)
STScI........... Space Telescope Science Institute
STSCM......... Space Transportation System Cost Model [*NASA*] (KSC)
STSD........... Society of Teachers of Speech and Drama [*British*]
STSE........... Split-Thickness Skin Excision [*Medicine*] (DMAA)
STSF........... Spatial Transformation of Sound Fields
STSFCTN...... Satisfaction
STSFSC........ Scarf Trailers Science Fiction Social Club [*Defunct*] (EA)
STSG........... Screening Test of Spanish Grammar (EDAC)
STSG........... Shuttle Test Group [*NASA*] (NASA)
STSG........... Space Topics Study Group (EA)
STSG........... Split Thickness Skin Graft
STSH........... Stabilized Shunt [*Electricity*]
STSI............ Scientific Technical and Societal Information (NITA)
STSI............ Space Telescope Science Institute [*NASA*]
STSJHA........ St. Thomas - St. John Hotel Association [*Virgin Islands*] (EAIO)
STSK........... Scandinavian Committee for Satellite Communications [*Telecommunications*] (TEL)
STSM........... Statesman (WGA)
STSM........... Surface-to-Target-to-Surface-to-Missile
STSN........... Seaman, SONAR Technician, Striker [*Navy rating*]
STSN........... Set-and-Test-Sequence-Number [*Computer science*] (IBMDP)
STSO........... Senior Technical Staff Officer [*British*]
STSOC......... Space Transportation System Operations Contact [*NASA*] (SSD)
STSOPO....... Shuttle Transportation Systems Operations Program Office [*Johnson Space Center*] (NASA)
STS-QN........ Serological Test for Syphilis-Quantitation [*Medicine*] (DAVI)
ST-SR.......... Small Transmitter Coated with Silicon Rubber
STSR........... Stepped-Temperature Stress-Rupture [*Ceramics*] (DICI)
STSR........... System Test Summary Report [*NASA*] (NASA)
STSS........... Sensitive Thrust Stand System
STSS........... Series-Tuned Series-Stabilized [*Computer science*] (IAA)
STSS........... Society for Traumatic Stress Studies (EA)
STSS........... Staphylococcal Toxic Shock Syndrome [*Medicine*] (DMAA)
STSSA......... SONAR Technician, Submarine, Seaman Apprentice [*Navy rating*] (DNAB)
STSSN......... SONAR Technician, Submarine, Seaman [*Navy rating*] (DNAB)
STSSPF........ Space Transportation System Spacelab Processing Facility [*NASA*] (SSD)
STSTA......... Small Aerial Surveillance and Target Acquisition (PDAA)
STSTB......... Status Strobe (MHDI)
ST/STE........ Special Tooling / Special Test Equipment [*Navy*] (DNAB)
Sts Tog........ Saints Together [*Library cataloging*] (DGA)
STSV........... Satellite-to-Space Vehicle (SAA)
STS.WS........ Supreme Indus Wrrt [*AMEX symbol*] (TTSB)
STT............. Air St. Thomas [*ICAO designator*] (FAAC)
STT............. Charlotte Amalie, VI [*Location identifier FAA*] (FAAL)
STT............. Cyril E. King Airport [*FAA*] (TAG)
STT............. Saigon Transportation Terminal Command [*Republic of Vietnam Armed Forces*]
STT............. Save the Theatres (EA)
STT............. Scaphotrapeziotrapezoid [*Joint*] [*Anatomy*] (DAVI)
STT............. School of Tank Technology [*British military*] (DMA)
STT............. School of Technical Training [*British military*] (DMA)
STT............. SEAL [*Sea, Air, Land*] Tactical Training (DOMA)
STT............. Seattle - Marshall [*Washington*] [*Seismograph station code, US Geological Survey Closed*] (SEIS)
STT............. Secure Transaction Technology [*Telecommunications*]
STT............. Secure Transaction Technology
STT............. Seek Time per Track
STT............. Semitendinosus Tendon [*Anatomy*]
STT............. Sensitization Test
STT............. Sent to Typesetter [*Publishing*]
STT............. Serial Thrombin Time [*Medicine*] (MAE)
STT............. Ship Turn Transmitter
STT............. Shock Tube Test
STT............. Shore Targeting Terminal [*Navy*] (CAAL)
STT............. Short-Term Test [*Toxicology*]
STT............. Short Time Test (IAA)
STT............. Signal Tracing Tester
STT............. Single Target Track [*Navy*] (NG)
STT............. Single Transition Time (IAA)
STT............. Single Transmission Time (NITA)
STT............. Skid-to-Turn
STT............. Skin Temperature Test [*Physiology*]
STT............. Small Tactical Terminal (USDC)
STT............. Small Tactical Terminal [*Marine science*] (OSRA)
STT............. Spacecraft Terminal Thrust
STT............. Spacelab Transfer Tunnel (NASA)
STT............. Spade Tongue Terminal
STT............. Spinothalamic Tract [*Brain anatomy*]
STT............. Standard Triple Therapy [*For hypertension*]
STT............. Start Time (IAA)
STT............. State Str Boston [*NYSE symbol*] (TTSB)
STT............. State Street Boston, Inc. [*NYSE symbol*] (SAG)
STT............. Stenographer, Medical [*Navy*]
STT............. Store Tag (SAA)
STT............. Strain-Transport-Time [*Geology*]
STT............. St. Thomas [*Virgin Islands*] [*Airport symbol*]
STT............. Sutton Resources Ltd. [*Vancouver Stock Exchange symbol*]
STT............. Syndicat des Travailleurs en Telecommunications [*Telecommunications Workers Union - TWU*] [*Canada*]
STTA........... Scottish Table Tennis Association (DBA)
STTA........... Scottish Timber Trade Association (DBA)
St Tax Cas Rep (CCH)... State Tax Cases Reporter (Commerce Clearing House) [*A publication*] (DLA)
St Tax Rep (CCH)... State Tax Reporter (Commerce Clearing House) [*A publication*] (DLA)
STTC........... Schottky Transistor-Transistor Logic (NITA)
STTC........... Scottish Textile and Technical Centre Ltd. [*British*] (IRUK)
STTC........... Sheppard Technical Training Center (AFM)
StTDJ........... Studies on the Texts of the Desert of Judah [*J. Van Der Ploeg*] [*Leiden*] [*A publication*] (BJA)
STTE........... Society of Travel and Tourism Educators (EA)
STTE........... Special Tools and Test Equipment
STTF........... Service to the Fleet [*A publication*] (DNAB)
STTF........... SONAR Test Tower Facility
STTF........... Special Tank Task Force (MCD)
STTF........... System Technology Test Facility (MCD)
STT-FNB....... Suomen Tietotoimisto-Finska Notisbyran [*Press agency*] [*Finland*]
STTL........... Schottky Clamped Transistor-Transistor Logic [*Electronics*] (IAA)
S/TTL.......... Schottky Transistor-Transistor Logic
STTL........... Sit Tibi Terra Levis [*May the Earth Lie Light on Thee*] [*Letters found on Roman tombs*] [*Latin*]
STTM........... Stabilized Tracking Tripod Module (RDA)
STTMA......... Screw Thread Tool Manufacturers Association [*British*] (DBA)
STTNG......... Star Trek, the Next Generation [*Television program*]
STTO........... Sawtooth Timing Oscillator (DEN)
STTO........... Staking Tool (AAG)
STTOT......... Single Target Track on Target [*Navy*]
STTP........... Space Test and Transportation Program (DOMA)
St Tr........... Howell's English State Trials [*1163-1820*] [*A publication*] (DLA)
STTR........... Small Business Technology Transfer Resources (GAVI)
STTR........... Stator
St Tri.......... State Trials [*A publication*] (DLA)
St Tr NS...... Macdonell's State Trials [*1820-58*] [*A publication*] (DLA)
STTS........... S-Band Transponder Test Set (MCD)
STTS........... Scottish Tramway and Transport Society (DBA)
STTS........... Shipboard Target Tracking System
STTSRA....... Scoot-Tours Touring Scooter Riders Association (EA)
STTT........... Space Telescope Task Team [*NASA*]
STTX........... Steel Technologies [*NASDAQ symbol*] (TTSB)
STTX........... Steel Technologies, Inc. [*Louisville, KY*] [*NASDAQ symbol*] (NQ)
STTZ........... Sutton Resource Ltd. [*NASDAQ symbol*] (SAG)
STTZF......... Sutton Resources [*NASDAQ symbol*] (TTSB)
STU............. Secure Telephone Unit [*Computer science*]
STU............. Seeker Test Unit (MCD)
STU............. Service Trials Unit
STU............. Servo Test Unit
STU............. Shock Trauma Unit [*Emergency medicine*] (DAVI)
STU............. Short Ton Unit
STU............. Signal Transfer Unit
STU............. Skin Test Unit
STU............. Space-Time Unit [*Computer*]
STU............. Special Test Unit (CET)
STU............. Special Training Unit
STU............. Star Tracker Unit [*NASA*] (MCD)
STU............. Static Test Unit (KSC)
STU............. Step Up
STU............. Steubenville [*Diocesan abbreviation*] [*Ohio*] (TOCD)
STU............. Stuart (ROG)
STU............. Stuart [*D. A.*] Ltd. [*Toronto Stock Exchange symbol*]
stu............. Stucco (VRA)
STU............. Student (AFM)
STU............. Student Loan Corp. [*NYSE symbol*] (SPSG)
STU............. Stuttgart [*Federal Republic of Germany*] [*Seismograph station code, US Geological Survey*] (SEIS)
STU............. Styrelsen foer Teknisk Utveckling [*Swedish Board for Technical Development*]
STU............. Submarine Test Unit
STU............. Submersible Test Unit [*Navy*]
STU............. Subscribers' Trunk Unit [*Telecommunications*] (TEL)
STU............. Systems Test Unit (KSC)
STU............. System Time Unit (NITA)
STU............. System Timing Unit
STU............. System Transition Unit [*Computer science*]
STU............. System Transmission Unit (NITA)
STU............. Transportes Aereos Fueguino [*Argentina ICAO designator*] (FAAC)
STU............. University of Steubenville, Steubenville, OH [*OCLC symbol*] (OCLC)
STUA........... Stuart Entertainment [*NASDAQ symbol*] (SPSG)
Stu Adm....... Stuart's Lower Canada Vice-Admiralty Reports [*A publication*] (DLA)
Stu Adm NS... Stuart's Lower Canada Vice-Admiralty Reports, New Series [*A publication*] (DLA)
Stu Ap......... Stuart's Lower Canada King's Bench Reports, Appeal Cases [*A publication*] (DLA)
Stuart.......... Stuart, Milne, and Peddie's Scotch Court of Session Cases [*A publication*] (DLA)
Stuart.......... Stuart's Lower Canada Reports [*A publication*] (DLA)
Stuart.......... Stuart's Lower Canada Vice-Admiralty Reports [*A publication*] (DLA)
Stuart Adm NS... Stuart's Lower Canada Vice-Admiralty Reports, New Series [*A publication*] (DLA)

Stuart & Por... Stuart [*or Stewart*] and Porter's Alabama Reports [*A publication*] (DLA)

Stuart & Porter... Stuart [*or Stewart*] and Porter's Alabama Reports [*A publication*] (DLA)

Stuart Beng... Stuart's Select Cases [*1860*] [*Bengal, India*] [*A publication*] (DLA)

Stuart KB..... Stuart's Lower Canada King's Bench Reports [*1810-25*] [*Quebec*] [*A publication*] (DLA)

Stuart KB (Quebec)... Stuart's Lower Canada King's Bench Reports [*Quebec*] [*A publication*] (DLA)

Stuart LCKB... Stuart's Lower Canada King's Bench Reports [*A publication*] (DLA)

Stuart LCVA... Stuart's Lower Canada Vice-Admiralty Reports [*A publication*] (DLA)

Stuart M & P... Stuart, Milne, and Peddie's Scotch Court of Session Cases [*1851-53*] [*A publication*] (DLA)

Stuart's Adm... Stuart's Lower Canada Vice-Admiralty Reports [*A publication*] (DLA)

Stuart's R.... Stuart's Lower Canada King's Bench Reports, Appeal Cases [*Quebec*] [*A publication*] (DLA)

Stuart Vice-Adm... Stuart's Lower Canada Vice-Admiralty Reports [*A publication*] (DLA)

STUB........... Stadt- und Universitaetsbibliothek Frankfurt [*Database producer*]

Stubbs CH... Stubb's Constitutional History [*A publication*] (DLA)

Stubbs Sel Ch... Stubb's Select Charters [*A publication*] (DLA)

STUC........... Sarawak Trade Union Congress

STUC........... Scottish Trades Union Congress

STUC........... Singapore Trade Union Congress

STUCENFL... Student Census-Date Report File (EDAC)

STUD........... Standard Tractor, Universal with Dozer [*Army*]

STUD........... Student

STUD........... Studies

STUD........... Study

Stud Anc Technol... Studies in Ancient Technology [*A publication*] (OCD)

Stud Cont Ed... Studies in Continuing Education [*A publication*]

Stud Doc Hist Iur... Studia et Documenta Historiae et Iuris [*Rome*] [*A publication*] (OCD)

STUDE......... Studebaker [*Automotive engineering*]

StudentIElecIE... Student of the Institution of Electrical and Electronic Incorporated Engineers [*British*] (DBQ)

StudentIWHTE... Student of the Institution of Works and Highways Technician Engineers [*British*] (DBQ)

Student Law J... Student Lawyer Journal [*A publication*] (DLA)

Student L Rev... Student Law Review [*A publication*] (DLA)

Stud Etr....... Studi Etruschi [*Firenze*] [*A publication*] (OCD)

Stud Gesch Kult Alt... Studien zur Geschichte und Kultur des Altertums [*A publication*] (OCD)

Stud Gr Rom Hist... Studies in Greek and Roman History [*A publication*] (OCD)

Stud Hist..... Studies in History, Economics, and Public Law [*A publication*] (DLA)

Studies Crim L... Studies in Criminal Law and Procedure [*A publication*] (DLA)

StudIManf.... Student Member of the Institute of Manufacturing [*British*] (DBQ)

StudIMS....... Student of the Institute of Management Specialists [*British*] (DBQ)

StudInstBTM... Student Member of the Institute of Business and Technical Management [*British*] (DBQ)

Stud Int'l Fiscal L... Studies on International Fiscal Law [*A publication*] (DLA)

StudioP........ Studio Plus Hotels, Inc. [*Associated Press*] (SAG)

StudioPH..... Studio Plus Hotels, Inc. [*Associated Press*] (SAG)

Studi Stor.... Studi Storici per l'Antichita Classica [*A publication*] (OCD)

Stud Ital....... Studi Italiani di Filologia Classica [*A publication*] (OCD)

Stud L & Econ Dev... Studies in Law and Economic Development [*A publication*] (DLA)

Stud Law Lex... Students' Pocket Law Lexicon [*A publication*] (DLA)

StudSCP...... Student of the Society of Certified Professionals [*British*] (DBQ)

StudSE......... Student of the Society of Engineers [*British*] (DBQ)

StudSLAET... Student of the Society of Licensed Aircraft Engineers and Technologists [*British*] (DBQ)

Stud Urb...... Studi di Urbanistica Antica [*A publication*] (OCD)

Stud W Aust Hist... Studies in Western Australian History [*A publication*]

StudWeldI.... Student of the Welding Institute [*British*] (DBQ)

STUF............ Student Flight [*Military*]

STUFF.......... System to Uncover Facts Fast

STUFT.......... Ships Taken Up from Trade

STUG........... Student Group [*Military*]

STUG........... Sturmgeschuetz [*Self-propelled assault gun*] [*German military - World War II*]

STU-IIM........ Secure Terminal Unit-II Militarized

STUK........... Sturmkanone [*Self-propelled assault gun*] [*German military - World War II*]

STUKA......... Sturzkampfflugzeug [*Dive bomber*] [*German military - World War II*]

Stu KB......... Stuart's Lower Canada King's Bench Reports [*1810-35*] [*A publication*] (DLA)

Stu LC......... Stuart's Lower Canada King's Bench Reports [*1810-35*] [*A publication*] (DLA)

StuLnCp....... Student Loan Corp. [*Associated Press*] (SAG)

Stu M & P... Stuart, Milne, and Peddie's Scotch Court of Sessions Reports [*A publication*] (DLA)

Stu Mil & Ped... Stuart, Milne, and Peddie's Scotch Court of Sessions Reports [*A publication*] (DLA)

STUMP......... Submersible, Transportable Utility, Marine Pump (PDAA)

Stun............. Serial Tunneling [*Computer science*]

STUP........... Spinning Tubular Projectile (MCD)

STUPID........ Simulation of the Underlying Processes in Decisions (MCD)

STURAA....... Surface Transportation and Uniform Relocation Assistance Act [*1987*]

Stur & Porter... Stuart [*or Stewart*] and Porter's Alabama Reports [*A publication*] (DLA)

S Turb.......... Steam Turbine (DS)

Sturg BL....... Sturgeon. Bankrupt Acts [*A publication*] (ILCA)

Sturg Ins D... Sturgeon's Insolvent Debtors Act [*1842*] [*A publication*] (DLA)

STURM......... Sturminster [*England*]

SturmR........ Sturm Ruger & Co. [*Associated Press*] (SAG)

STURP......... Shroud of Turin Research Project (EA)

SturtEn......... Stuart Entertainment, Inc. [*Associated Press*] (SAG)

STUS........... Student Squadron

STUTIS........ Secondary, Technical, and University Teachers' Insurance Society [*British*] (BI)

STUTNG....... Student Training [*Navy*] (DNAB)

Stu VA......... Stuart's Lower Canada Vice-Admiralty Reports [*A publication*] (ILCA)

STUW........... Subtropical Underwater [*Marine science*] (OSRA)

STV............. Santa Anna Di Valdieri [*Italy*] [*Seismograph station code, US Geological Survey*] (SEIS)

STV............. Satellite Test Vehicle (IAA)

STV............. Scottish Television (DI)

STV............. Separation Test Vehicle

STV............. Short-Tube Vertical [*Evaporator*]

STV............. Single Transferable Vote

STV............. Small Test Vessel [*Nuclear energy*] (NRCH)

STV............. Soft-Tissue View [*Radiology*] (DAVI)

STV............. Solar Thermal Vacuum

STV............. Solidaridad de Trabajadores Vascos [*Solidarity of Basque Workers*] [*In exile Spain*]

STV............. Southern Aviation Ltd. [*Ghana*] [*ICAO designator*] (FAAC)

STV............. Southern Television [*British*] (DI)

STV............. Space Test Vehicle [*NASA*] (KSC)

STV............. Special Test Vehicle

STV............. Standard Test Vehicle

STV............. Staverton [*England*] [*Airport symbol*] (AD)

STV............. Steam Tank Vessel (DNAB)

STV............. Steerable Low-Light-Level Television (PDAA)

STV............. Stikine Silver [*Vancouver Stock Exchange symbol*]

STV............. Stonewall, TX [*Location identifier FAA*] (FAAL)

STV............. Stove [*Classified advertising*] (ADA)

STV............. Structural Test Vehicle [*NASA*] (KSC)

STV............. St. Thomas [*Diocesan abbreviation*] [*Virgin Islands*] (TOCD)

STV............. STV Group, Inc. [*Associated Press*] (SAG)

STV............. Submarine Target Vessel (NVT)

STV............. Subscription Television

STV............. Subscription Television Authority [*FCC*] (NTCM)

STV............. Subscription TV, Inc. (NTCM)

STV............. Superior Temporal Vein [*Medicine*] (DMAA)

STV............. Supersonic Test Vehicle (AAG)

STV............. Surveillance Television (AFM)

STVA........... Self-Tuning Vibration Absorber [*Navy*] (CAAL)

STVA........... Subscription Television Association [*Defunct*] (EA)

STVA........... Subtotal Villose Atrophy [*Medicine*] (MAE)

STVC........... Space Thermal Vacuum Chamber (SAA)

STVC........... Sumerian Texts of Varied Context [*E. Chiera*] [*A publication*]

STVD........... Spacecraft Television Video Data

stvdr............ Stevedore (DS)

STVI............ STV Group [*NASDAQ symbol*] (TTSB)

STVI............ STV Group, Inc. [*NASDAQ symbol*] (SAG)

STVM........... Semitrailer Van Mount

STVP........... Salinity, Temperature, Sound-Velocity and Pressure-Sensing System (PDAA)

STVP........... Short-Term Vehicle Park (DS)

STVS........... Short-Term Visual Storage [*or Store*] [*Psychophysiology*]

STVS........... Surinaamse Televisie Sichtung [*Television network*] [*Surinam*]

STVS........... Surinaamse Televisie Stichtig (EY)

STW............ Save the Whales (EA)

STW............ Sewage Treatment Works

STW............ Short-Term Waviness [*Surface finish*]

STW............ Southwest Tech [*Vancouver Stock Exchange symbol*]

STW............ Speed Made Good Through the Water (NATG)

STW............ Standard Commercial [*NYSE symbol*] (TTSB)

STW............ Standard Commercial Corp. [*NYSE symbol*] (SPSG)

STW............ Star Trek Welcommittee (EA)

STW............ Starways SA [*Switzerland ICAO designator*] (FAAC)

STW............ Stern Wheel [*of a ship*] (DS)

STW............ Stillwater, NJ [*Location identifier FAA*] (FAAL)

STW............ Stillwater Public Library, Stillwater, OK [*OCLC symbol*] (OCLC)

STW............ Store Word [*Computer science*] (IAA)

STW............ Storm Water

STW............ Striped Peak [*Washington*] [*Seismograph station code, US Geological Survey*] (SEIS)

STW............ Subtropical Water

STW............ System Tape Writer [*Computer science*] (IAA)

ST. WAPNIACL... State, Treasury, War, Attorney General, Postmaster General, Navy, Interior, Agriculture, Commerce, Labor [*Pre-1947 mnemonic guide to names of the departments in the President's Cabinet, in order of creation*] [*Obsolete*]

STWBRD...... Strawboard [*Shipping*]

STWE.......... Society of Technical Writers and Editors [*Later, STWP, STC*]

St Westm.... Statute of Westminster [*A publication*] (DLA)

STWG.......... Stowage (MSA)

STWL.......... Stopway Light [*Aviation*] (FAAC)

STWO.......... Staff Tactical Watch Officer (DOMA)

STWP.......... Society of Technical Writers and Publishers [*Formerly, STWE*] [*Later, STC*] (EA)

STWP.......... Steam Working Pressure (MSA)

stwr............. Stoneware (VRA)

StwStv......... Stewart & Stevenson Services, Inc. [*Associated Press*] (SAG)

STWY.......... Stairway (AAG)

STX............. Aerocharter [*Czechoslovakia*] [*ICAO designator*] (FAAC)

STX............. Christiansted, St. Croix, VI [*Location identifier FAA*] (FAAL)

STX .... Saxitoxin [*A neurotoxin*]
STX .... Situational Training Exercise [*Army*] (INF)
STX .... Spherical Torus Experiment [*Oak Ridge National Laboratory*]
STX .... Starrex Mining Corp. Ltd. [*Toronto Stock Exchange symbol*]
STX .... Start of Text [*Telecommunications*] (OSI)
STX .... Start of Text Character [*Keyboard*] [*Computer science*]
STX .... Station 2 [*Nevada*] [*Seismograph station code, US Geological Survey Closed*] (SEIS)
STX .... St. Croix [*Virgin Islands*] [*Airport symbol*]
STX .... Sterling Chemicals [*NYSE symbol*] (TTSB)
STX .... Sterling Chemicals, Inc. [*NYSE symbol*] (CTT)
St Xavier U ... St. Xavier University (GAGS)
STXM .... Scanning Transmission X-Ray Microscopy (MCD)
STXRF .... Source-Tuned X-Ray Fluorescence [*Spectroscopy*]
STY .... Salto [*Uruguay*] [*Airport symbol*] (OAG)
STY .... Space-Time Yield [*Chemical engineering*]
STY .... Spatial Technology, Inc. [*AMEX symbol*] (SAG)
StY .... Standard Yiddish (BJA)
STY .... Stony River [*Alaska*] [*Seismograph station code, US Geological Survey*] (SEIS)
Sty .... Story [*Journalism*]
Sty .... Style's English King's Bench Reports [*1646-55*] [*A publication*] (DLA)
sty .... Stylus (VRA)
Sty .... Styrene [*Also, St*] [*Organic chemistry*]
STYCAR .... Screening Tests for Young Children and Retardates (MAH)
STYL .... Style
Style .... Style's English King's Bench Reports [*A publication*] (DLA)
Style Pr Reg ... Style's Practical Register [*A publication*] (DLA)
StyleVid .... Styles On Video, Inc. [*Associated Press*] (SAG)
STYLG .... Styling
STYLST .... Stylist
STYP .... Styptic [*Stopping Bleeding*] [*Medicine*] (ROG)
Sty Pr Reg ... Style's Practical Register [*1657-1710*] [*A publication*] (DLA)
STZ .... Santa Terezinha [*Brazil*] [*Airport symbol*] (OAG)
STZ .... Schweizerische Theologische Zeitschrift [*Zurich*] [*A publication*] (BJA)
STZ .... Serum-Treated Zymosan [*Clinical chemistry*]
STZ .... Signal Technology [*AMEX symbol*] (TTSB)
STZ .... Signal Technology Corp. [*AMEX symbol*] (SAG)
STZ .... Southern Transgressive Zone [*Geology*]
STZ .... Stallion Resources Ltd. [*Vancouver Stock Exchange symbol*]
STZ .... Store Zero [*Computer science*] (IAA)
STZ .... Stratford [*New Zealand*] [*Seismograph station code, US Geological Survey Closed*] (SEIS)
STZ .... Streptozocin [*Antineoplastic drug*]
Su .... Ciba-Geigy Corp. [*Research code symbol*]
SU .... Egypt [*International civil aircraft marking*] (ODBW)
SU .... Optical Device [*JETDS nomenclature*] [*Military*] (CET)
SU .... Salicyluric Acid [*Also, SUA*] [*Biochemistry*]
SU .... Salmon Unlimited (EA)
su .... Saudi Arabia [*MARC country of publication code Library of Congress*] (LCCP)
SU .... Savings Unit
SU .... Scorable Unit
SU .... Scripture Union [*British*]
SU .... Seamen's Union [*British*]
SU .... Seasonal Unemployment (MHDW)
SU .... Secular Unemployment [*Business term*] (MHDW)
SU .... Selectable Unit (BUR)
SU .... Sensation Units
SU .... Sensory Urgency [*Neurology*] (DAVI)
SU .... Separation Ullage
SU .... Service Unit [*Military*]
SU .... Set Up [*Freight*]
SU .... Shipment Unit [*Army*]
SU .... Siemens Unit
SU .... Sigma Units
SU .... Signaling Unit
SU .... Single Uptake [*Boilers*]
SU .... Single User [*The military activity that has the sole interest in an item of supply*] [*DoD*]
SU .... Society of St. Ursula (TOCD)
SU .... Society of the Sisters of St. Ursula of the Blessed Virgin [*Roman Catholic religious order*]
SU .... Somogyi Unit [*of amylase*] [*Clinical chemistry*]
SU .... Sonics and Ultrasonics (MCD)
SU .... Sosialistisk Ungdom [*Norway*]
SU .... Soviet Union [*The USSR*]
SU .... Space Unit (EA)
SU .... Special Unitary [*Algebra*]
S/U .... Squared Up [*Typography*] (DGA)
SU .... Standard Upkeep
SU .... Stanford University [*California*]
S/U .... Startup [*Nuclear energy*] (NRCH)
SU .... Start Up [*of a relay, power switchgear*] (IEEE)
SU .... Station Unit [*Telecommunications*] (OA)
SU .... Statistical Unit [*UNRISD*] [*United Nations*] (DUND)
SU .... Storage Unit [*Computer science*]
SU .... Stripers Unlimited (EA)
SU .... Strontium Units [*Nuclear energy*]
SU .... Structural Unemployed [*Business term*] (MHDW)
SU .... Student Union
SU .... Stunts Unlimited (EA)
SU .... Subject [*Online database field identifier*]
SU .... Submarine School Graduate [*Navy*] (DNAB)
SU .... Subscriber Unit [*RADA*] [*Army*] (RDA)
SU .... Sub-Unit (DNAB)
Su .... Sufentanil [*or Sulfentanyl*] [*An analgesic*]
su .... Sugary [*A gene in sweet corn*]
SU .... Suit (DNAB)
Su .... Suite
SU .... Sukhoy [*Aircraft*]
Su .... Sulcus [*Brain anatomy*]
SU .... Sulfonamide [*An antibiotic*] (DAVI)
Su .... Sumet [*Let Him, or Her, Take*] [*Pharmacy*]
SU .... Suncor, Inc. [*Toronto Stock Exchange symbol AMEX symbol*]
SU .... Sunday
Su .... Superb [*Philately*]
SU .... Supercommutation (SAA)
Su .... Superior Court (DLA)
SU .... Super Unleaded (Gasoline)
SU .... Supply [*Business term*]
SU .... Support (IAA)
SU .... Support Unit [*NASA*] (NASA)
SU .... Suppressor [*Electronics*] (MDG)
SU .... Surface to Underwater (IAA)
SU .... Surgery (DAVI)
SU .... Switching Unit
SU .... Sydney University [*State*] (EERA)
SU .... Symbolic Unit (IAA)
SU .... Syne Unit [*Telecommunications*] (OA)
SU .... Syracuse University [*New York*]
SU .... Thiouridine [*Two-letter symbol; see Srd*]
SU .... Union of Soviet Socialist Republics [*ANSI two-letter standard code*] (CNC)
SUA .... Aviation Associates, Inc. [*St. Croix*] [*ICAO designator*] (FAAC)
SUA .... Salicyluric Acid [*Also, SU*] [*Biochemistry*]
SUA .... Satellite Unfurlable Antenna
SUA .... Sedative Urinary Antibiotic (DAVI)
SUA .... Serum Uric Acid [*Clinical chemistry*]
SUA .... Shipped Unassembled (MHDW)
SUA .... Silver Users Association (EA)
SUA .... Single Umbilical Artery [*Medicine*] (MAE)
SUA .... Small Unit Action [*Military*] (CINC)
SUA .... Society for Urban Anthropology (EA)
SUA .... Special Use Airspace (GAVI)
SUA .... Special Use Airspace [*FAA*] (TAG)
SUA .... Standard Unit of Accounting [*Computer science*]
SUA .... State Universities Association [*Later, NASULGC*]
SUA .... Stuart [*Florida*] [*Airport symbol*] (OAG)
SUA .... Stuart, FL [*Location identifier FAA*] (FAAL)
SUA .... Summit Tax Exempt Bond [*AMEX symbol*] (TTSB)
SUA .... Summit Tax Exempt Bond Fund Ltd. [*AMEX symbol*] (SPSG)
SUA .... Superior Acceptance Corp. Ltd. [*Toronto Stock Exchange symbol*]
SUA .... Supplemental Unemployment Assistance
SUA .... Supply/Utilization Accounts [*FAO*] [*Information service or system United Nations*] (DUND)
SUA .... Susitna [*Alaska*] [*Seismograph station code, US Geological Survey*] (SEIS)
SUA .... Sweetener Users Association (EA)
SUAA .... Montevideo/Angel S. Adami [*Uruguay*] [*ICAO location identifier*] (ICLI)
SUAB .... Svenska Utvecklingsaktiebolaget [*Swedish Corporation for Development*]
SUAC .... Scottish Universities Accommodation Consortium (AIE)
SUADPS .... Shipboard Uniform Automatic Data Processing System [*Navy*]
SUAEWICS .... Soviet Union Airborne Early Warning and Interceptor Control System (MCD)
SUAG .... Artigas/Aeropuerto Deptal [*Uruguay*] [*ICAO location identifier*] (ICLI)
SUALM .... Submerged Anchor Leg Mooring [*Engineering*]
SUAR .... Start Unload Address Register
Suas .... Suasoriae [*of Seneca the Elder*] [*Classical studies*] (OCD)
SUAS .... System for Upper Atmosphere Sounding (MCD)
SUAVE .... Submersible System Used to Assess Vented Emissions (USDC)
SUAVE .... Submersible [*System*] Used to Assess Vented Emissions [*Marine science*] (OSRA)
SUAWACS .... Soviet Union Airborne Warning and Control System (MCD)
SUB .... Skene's, Urethral, and Bartholin's [*Glands*] [*Anatomy*] (DAVI)
SUB .... Student Union Building [*Canada*]
SUB .... Subaddressing [*Telecommunications*] (DOM)
SUB .... Subaltern
SUB .... Subaud [*Understand*] [*Latin*]
Sub .... Subcommittee (DLA)
SUB .... Subcontractor (WGA)
SUB .... Subdrift (IAA)
SUB .... Subeditor
sub .... Subfloor (BARN)
SUB .... Subject
SUB .... Subjunctive [*Grammar*]
SUB .... Sublevel (IAA)
SUB .... Submarine (AFM)
SUB .... Submerged
SUB .... Subordinate (DSUE)
SUB .... Subroutine
Sub .... Subscriber [*Finance*]
SUB .... Subscription [*Finance*]
SUB .... Subsidiary [*Business term*]
SUB .... Subsistence (WDAA)
SUB .... Substantive (WDAA)
SUB .... Substation (IAA)

SUB .... Substitute
SUB .... Substitute
SUB .... Substitute Character [*Keyboard*] (AFM)
SUB .... Substitution (IAA)
SUB .... Substratum
SUB .... Subtract
SUB .... Subtract Binary Number [*Computer science*]
SUB .... Suburban
SUB .... Subway (AAG)
SUB .... Summit Bancorp [*NYSE symbol*] (TTSB)
SUB .... Supplemental Unemployment Benefits
SUB .... Surabaya [*Indonesia*] [*Airport symbol*] (OAG)
Subac .... Subacute [*Medicine*] (DMAA)
SUBACLANT... Submarine Allied Command, Atlantic [*NATO*] (NATG)
SUBACS .... Submarine Advanced [*or Active*] Combat System
SUBAD .... Submarine Air Defense
SUBAD .... Submarine Force, Pacific Fleet Administration
SUBADMI..... Submarine Force, Pacific Fleet Administration, Mare Island
SUBASE .... Submarine Base [*Navy*]
SUBASELANT... Submarine Bases, Atlantic [*Navy*]
SUBASEPAC... Submarine Bases, Pacific [*Navy*]
SUBASSY..... Subassembly
SUBASWEX.... Submarine-Antisubmarine Warfare Exercise (NVT)
SUB-BELL .... Submarine Fog Bell [*Mechanical*]
Sub Bk.... Subscription Book (DGA)
SubBn......... Suburban Bancshares, Inc. [*Associated Press*] (SAG)
SubBnc........ Suburban Bancshares, Inc. [*Associated Press*] (SAG)
SubBncp ...... Suburban Bancorp [*Associated Press*] (SAG)
SubBncsh .... Suburban Bancshares, Inc. [*Associated Press*] (SAG)
SUBC .... Subler, Carl, Agent, Versailles OH [*STAC*]
SUBCAL .... Subcaliber
SUBCERT.... Submarine Safety Certification [*Navy*] (DNAB)
SUBCH......... Subchapter (DNAB)
SUBCOM...... Subcommittee
SUBCOM...... Subordinate Command, Service Force, Pacific Fleet
SUBCOMNELM... Subordinate Command, [*US*] Naval Forces, Eastern Atlantic and Mediterranean
subconj........ Subconjunctival [*Ophthalmology*] (DAVI)
SUBCOR ...... Subject to Correction (DNAB)
subcrep........ Subcrepitant [*Medicine*]
SUBCU.......... Subcutaneous [*Beneath the Skin*] [*Medicine*]
subcu........... Subcuticular [*Medicine*] (DAVI)
subcut.......... Subcutaneous [*Beneath the Skin*] [*Medicine*]
Subd .... Subdivision (DLA)
SUBDEVGRUONE... Submarine Development Group One [*San Diego*]
SUBDEVGRUTWO... Submarine Development Group Two [*New York*]
SUBDIV......... Submarine Division [*Navy*]
SUBDIZ......... Submarine Defense Identification Zone
SUBEASTLANT... Submarine Force, Eastern Atlantic [*NATO*]
SUBED .... Submarine Electromagnetic Deception System
SUBEX .... Submarine Exercise (NATG)
SUBFIN COCT... Sub Finem Coctionis [*When the Boiling Is Nearly Finished*] (ROG)
SUBFLOT..... Submarine Flotilla [*Navy*]
subg............ Subgenus
SUBGEN....... Subgenus
SUBGRU ...... Submarine Group
SUBH .... Scripta Universitatis atque Bibliotecae Hierosolymitanarum Jerusalem [*A publication*] (BJA)
Sub Hdg ...... Subsidiary Heading (DGA)
SUBI .... Sun Bancorp [*NASDAQ symbol*] (TTSB)
SUBI .... Sun Bancorp, Inc. [*NASDAQ symbol*] (SAG)
SUBIC .... Submarine Integrated Control Systems
Sub Init........ Sub Initio [*At the Beginning*] [*Latin*]
SUBINSURV... Inspection and Survey Board Sub Board [*Navy*]
SUBINSURV (LANT) (PAC)... Sub Board of Inspection and Survey of Atlantic and Pacific [*Navy*] (ANA)
SUBJ............ Subject (AFM)
SUBJ............ Subjective (ROG)
SUBJ............ Subject To [*ICAO designator*] (FAAC)
SUBJ............ Subjunctive [*Grammar*]
SUBJV .... Subjunctive [*Grammar*] (WGA)
SUBK .... Suffolk Bancorp [*Riverhead, NY*] [*NASDAQ symbol*] (NQ)
SUBL .... Sublimation Point (IAA)
SUBL .... Sublime [*or Subliming*]
SUBLANT...... Submarine Force, Atlantic Fleet
SubLdgs ...... Suburban Lodges of America, Inc. [*Associated Press*] (SAG)
subling .... Sublingual [*Medicine*]
Sub-Lt.......... Sub-Lieutenant [*British military*] (DMA)
SUBM .... Submarine (WGA)
SUBM .... Submerged
SUBM .... SubMicron Systems [*NASDAQ symbol*] (TTSB)
SUBM .... SubMicron Systems Corp. [*NASDAQ symbol*] (SAG)
SUBM .... Submission [*or Submit*] (AFM)
SUBMACOM... Major Army Subcommand (AABC)
submand...... Submandibular [*Medicine*]
SUBMED ...... Submarines Mediterranean [*NATO*] (NATG)
SUBMEDCEN... Submarine Medical Center [*Navy*]
SUBMEDNOREAST... Submarines Northeast Mediterranean [*NATO*] (NATG)
SUBMG .... Submerged (MSA)
SubMicr....... SubMicron Systems Corp. [*Associated Press*] (SAG)
SUBMIN....... Subminiature
SUBMISS..... Submarine Missing [*Navy*] (NVT)
SUBMIS/SUBSUNK... Submarine Missing/Presumed Sunk [*Navy*]
SUBMON...... Submission (ROG)
Subm W ...... Submerged Well [*Nautical charts*]
SUBN........... Suburban
SUBN........... [*The*] Summit Bancorporation [*NASDAQ symbol*] (NQ)
SUBNAVPERS... Submit to Naval Personnel (DNAB)
SUBNEWSTA... Submit New Duty Station [*Navy*] (DNAB)
SUBNO........ Substitutes Not Desired [*Military*]
sub nom........ Sub Nomine [*Under the Name*] [*Latin*] (DLA)
SUBNOT....... Submarine Notice (MCD)
SUBNOTE..... Submarine Notice [*Navy*] (NVT)
SUBOK......... Substitution Acceptable [*Military*]
SUBOPAUTH... Submarine Operating Authority [*Navy*] (NVT)
sub opn .... Subsequent Opinion (HGAA)
SUBOR......... Subordinate (AFM)
SUBORCOM... Subordinate Command
SUBORCOMDSERVLANT... Subordinate Command, Service Force, Atlantic Fleet
SUBORCOMDSERVPAC... Subordinate Command, Service Force, Pacific Fleet
SUBORD ...... Subordinate [*Linguistics*]
SUB-OSC ..... Submarine Oscillator
SubOstm...... Suburban Ostomy Supply Co., Inc. [*Associated Press*] (SAG)
SUBP .... Subpoena [*Legal shorthand*] (LWAP)
SUBPA.......... Antisubmarine Warfare Barrier Submarine Patrol Area [*Navy*] (NVT)
SUBPAC........ Submarine Force, Pacific Fleet
SUBPACAD... Submarine Force, Pacific Fleet, Administrative Command
SUBPACSUBORDCOM... Submarine Force, Pacific Fleet, Subordinate Command
Subpar .... Subparagraph (DLA)
SUBPARA .... Subparagraph
SUBPrB........ Summit Bcp Adj B Pfd [*NYSE symbol*] (TTSB)
SUBPT .... Subpart (WDAA)
SUBPZ .... Antisubmarine Warfare Barrier Submarine Patrol Zone [*Navy*] (NVT)
SUB Q.......... Subcutaneous [*Beneath the Skin*] [*Medicine*]
Sub-Q .... Subcuticular [*Medicine*] (DAVI)
SUBQ........... Subsequent (AABC)
SUBRAP....... Submarine Range Prediction System [*Navy*] (NVT)
Subrfed........ Suburbfed Financial Corp. [*Associated Press*] (SAG)
SUBRO......... Subrogation
SUBROC ...... Submarine Rocket
SUBROCK .... Submarine Rocket (IAA)
SUBRON ...... Submarine Squadron [*Navy*]
SUBRPIO ..... Sub-Registered Publications Issuing Office
SUBRQMT.... Subrequirement
SUBRU......... Submarine Repair Unit
SUBS .... Miami Subs [*NASDAQ symbol*] (TTSB)
SUBS .... Miami Subs Corp. [*NASDAQ symbol*] (SAG)
SUBS .... Salford University Business Services [*British*]
SUBS .... Subscription (WGA)
SUBS .... Subsidiary [*Business term*]
SUBS .... Subsistence (AABC)
SUBS .... Substantive [*Grammar*]
SUBS .... Substitute
SUBSAFE ..... Submarine Safety [*Program*]
SUBSAFECEN... Submarine Safety Center [*Navy*]
SUBSALVEX... Submarine Salvage Exercise [*Navy*] (DNAB)
SUBSAM....... Submarine Surface-to-Air Missile [*Military*] (LAIN)
Subsc........... Subscription (DLA)
SUBSCD....... Subscribed (ROG)
SUBSCOFOR... Submarines Scouting Force [*Pacific Fleet*]
SUBSCR........ Subscription [*Finance*] (ROG)
SUBSCR........ Subscription
SUBSCRON... Subscription [*Finance*] (ROG)
SUBSEC .... Subsection
SUBSECT ..... Subsection [*Legal shorthand*] (LWAP)
SUBSELS ..... Subsisting Elsewhere
SUBSEQ ...... Subsequent (ROG)
SUBSET .... Subscriber Set (CET)
SUBSID........ Subsidiary [*Business term*] (ROG)
SUBSIS......... Subsistence (AFM)
SUBSLANT... Submarines, Atlantic Fleet
SUBSLY .... Subsequently (ROG)
SUBSP .... Subspecies
SUBSPAC..... Submarines, Pacific Fleet
subspp........ Subspecies [*Plural form*]
SUBSQ......... Subsequently (ADA)
SUB-SRA ..... Sub-Shop Replaceable Assembly
SUBSS .... Submarine Schoolship [*Navy*] (NVT)
SUBSSOWESPAC... Submarines, Southwest Pacific Force
SUBST .... Substance (ROG)
SUBST .... Substantive (ROG)
SUBST .... Substitute (AAG)
SUBSTA........ Substation
SubstAb....... Substance Abuse Technology, Inc. [*Associated Press*] (SAG)
SubstAbus.... Substance Abuse Technology, Inc. [*Associated Press*] (SAG)
Substand ..... Substandard (WGA)
substd.......... Substandard (DAVI)
SUBSTD....... Substituted (ROG)
SUB-STD...... Substitute Standard [*Army*]
SUBSTG........ Substituting (AAG)
SUBSTN........ Substitution
SUBSTR........ Substructure (AAG)
SUBSTTD..... Substituted
SUBSUNK.... Submarine Sunk [*Navy*] (NVT)
SUBSYS....... Subsystem (AAG)
SUBTACGRU... Submarine Tactical Group [*NATO*] (NATG)
SUBTAG........ Submarine Tactics Analysis Group
SUBTEL........ Submarine Telegraph [*Military*] (IAA)
SUBTEL........ Submarine Telephone [*Military*] (IAA)
SUBTIL .... Synthesized User-Based Terminology Index Language (NITA)

SUBTR .... Subtraction (MSA)
SUBTRAFAC... Submarine Training Facility
SUBTRAP..... Submersible Training Platform [*Marine science*] (MSC)
subtrop .... Subtropical
SUBV .... Subversion (AABC)
Sub Vol........ Submarine Volcano [*Nautical charts*]
SUBWESTLANT... Submarine Force, Western Atlantic Area [*NATO*] (NATG)
Suby .... Subsidiary [*Business term*]
SUBY .... Subsidiary
SUC .... Society of University Cartographers [*British*]
SUC .... Southern Union College [*Wadley, AL*]
SUC .... Start-Up Costs [*Business term*] (MHDB)
SUC .... Succeeding (MSA)
SUC .... Successor (ADA)
Suc .... Succinoyl [*Biochemistry*]
SUC .... Succus [*Juice*] [*Pharmacy*]
SUC .... Sucre [*Bolivia*] [*Seismograph station code, US Geological Survey Closed*] (SEIS)
SUC .... Sucrose [*Organic chemistry*]
SUC .... Suction (ADA)
SUC .... Suncoast Petroleum [*Vancouver Stock Exchange symbol*]
SUC .... Sundance, WY [*Location identifier FAA*] (FAAL)
SUC .... University of South Carolina, Columbia, SC [*OCLC symbol*] (OCLC)
SUCA .... Colonia/Aeropuerto Deptal. [*Uruguay*] [*ICAO location identifier*] (ICLI)
SUCAP .... Surface Combat Air Patrol (DOMA)
SUCC .... State University Computation Center [*Iowa State University*] [*Research center*] (RCD)
SUCC .... Succentor [*Ecclesiastical*] (ROG)
SUCC .... Successor (ROG)
SUCC .... Succinate
SUCC .... Succinum [*Amber*] [*Latin*] (ROG)
succ .... Succursale (DD)
SUCCESS..... Sources to Upgrade the Career Counseling and Employment of Special Students [*Florida*] (EDAC)
Success .... Successories, Inc. [*Associated Press*] (SAG)
SUCCESS..... Sulfonium Compounds Containing Expellable Sophisticated Sidegroups [*Photoresists*]
SUCCN .... Succession (ROG)
SUCCON ...... Succession
SUCCR .... Successor
SUCE .... South Universal Commodity Exchange [*Ukraine*] (EY)
SUCEE .... Socialist Union of Central and Eastern Europe (PD)
SUCHTRANS... Such Transportation as Command Indicated Designates
SUCHTRANSAVAIL... Such Transportation as Available
SUCI .... Socialist Unity Center of India [*Political party*] (PPW)
SUCKER....... Society for Understanding Cats, Kangaroos, Elks, and Reptiles [*Slang*]
SUCL .... Set Up in Carloads [*Freight*]
SUCL .... Stetson University College of Law (DLA)
SUCO .... Service Universitaire Canadien Outre-Mer [*Canadian University Service Overseas - CUSO*]
SUCR .... Successor (WGA)
SUCR .... Sunset Crater National Monument
SUCT .... Suction (AAG)
Su Ct Rev.... Supreme Court Review [*A publication*] (ILCA)
SUD .... Skin Unit Dose [*Medicine*] (DMAA)
SUD .... Stretched Upper Deck (AIA)
SUD .... Stroud, OK [*Location identifier FAA*] (FAAL)
SUD .... Sudan Airways [*ICAO designator*] (FAAC)
SUD .... Sudbury [*Ontario*] [*Seismograph station code, US Geological Survey*] (SEIS)
SUD .... Sudbury Board of Education [*UTLAS symbol*]
SUD .... Sudbury Contact Mines Ltd. [*Toronto Stock Exchange symbol*]
SUD .... Sudden Unexpected [*or Unexplained*] Death [*Medicine*]
SUD .... Sudorific [*Causing Sweat*] [*Pharmacy*] (ROG)
SUDAAN .... Survey Data Analysis [*Computer science*]
SUDAER....... Stanford University, Department of Aeronautics and Astronautics (MCD)
SUDAM .... Sunk or Damaged [*Navy*]
Sudan LJ & Rep... Sudan Law Journal and Reports [*Khartoum*] [*A publication*] (DLA)
SUDAP .... Superintendencia da Agricultura e Producao [*Brazil*]
Sudbury .... Sudbury, Inc. [*Associated Press*] (SAG)
Sud Dew Ad... Sudder Dewanny Adawlut [*or Sadr Diwani Adalat*] Reports [*India*] [*A publication*] (DLA)
Sud Dew Rep... Sudder Dewanny [*or Sadr Diwani*] Reports, Northwest Province [*India*] [*A publication*] (DLA)
SUDEC .... Superintendencia do Desenvolvimento Economico e Cultural [*Brazil*]
SUDEL .... Groupe Regional pour la Coordination de la Production et du Transport de l'Energie Electrique entre l'Autriche, la Grece, l'Italie et la Yougoslavie (EA)
SUDENE....... Superintendencia do Desenvolvimento do Nordeste [*Brazil*]
SUDEP .... Sudden Unexplained Death in Epilepsy [*Medicine*]
SUDH .... Succinyldehydrogenase (DMAA)
SUDI .... State Unemployment Disability Insurance (AAG)
SUDI .... Sudden Unexpected Death in Infancy [*Medicine*] (DMAA)
SUDIC .... Sulfur Development Institute of Canada
SUDIC .... Sulphur Development Institute of Canada
SUDM .... Single User Drive Module [*Computer science*] (MHDI)
Su Doc......... Superintendent of Documents, Government Printing Office (DLA)
SUDOSAT .... Sudanian Satellite
SUDS .... Satellite Undetected Duds
SUDS .... Silhouetting Underwater Detecting System
SUDS .... Single-Use Diagnostic System [*Trademark of the Murex Corp.*]
SUDS .... Small Unit Delivery System (MCD)
SUDS .... Software Update Distribution System [*Computer software*] [*Frye Computer Systems, Inc.*] (PCM)
SUDS .... State's Urban Development Something-or-Other [*Slang for Urban Development Corporation, New York*]
SUDS .... Steps Up Developmental Screening Program [*Child development test*] [*Psychology*]
SUDS .... Subjective Units of Disturbance
SUDS .... Submarine Detecting System
SUDS .... Sudbury, Inc. [*NASDAQ symbol*] (NQ)
SUDT .... Silicon Unilateral Diffused Transistor
SUDU .... Durazno/Santa Bernardina Internacional de Alternativa [*Uruguay*] [*ICAO location identifier*] (ICLI)
SUE.............. Aerolineas del Sureste SA [*Mexico ICAO designator*] (FAAC)
SUE.............. Sahara Upwelling Experiment [*US, Spain*] (MSC)
SUE.............. Seismic Underwater Explorer
SUE.............. Servants' United Effort [*Lemonade*] [*Slang British*] (DSUE)
SUE.............. Shuttle Unique Equipment (MCD)
SUE.............. Signal Underwater Exploding [*British military*] (DMA)
SUE.............. Significantly Underutilized Employee Program [*DoD*]
SUE.............. Skylab Upwelling Experiment [*Marine science*] (MSC)
SUE.............. Strontium Unit Equivalent
SUE.............. Sturgeon Bay, WI [*Location identifier FAA*] (FAAL)
SUE.............. Sub-Unit Evaluation (MCD)
SUE.............. Sudden Expansion
SUE.............. Suzie Mining Exploration [*Vancouver Stock Exchange symbol*]
SUE.............. System User Engineered (IAA)
SUEDE .... Surface Evaluation and Definition
SUEL .... Sperry Utah Engineering Laboratory (MCD)
SUEM.......... Syndicat Unique des Enseignants de Mauritanie [*Unitary Union of Mauritanian Teachers*]
SUEO .... Montevideo [*Uruguay*] [*ICAO location identifier*] (ICLI)
SUEOTU .... Supreme Unsurpassable Engineers of the Universe [*Rank in Junior Woodchucks organization mentioned in Donald Duck comic by Carl Barks*]
SUERF .... Societe Universitaire Europeenne de Recherches Financieres (EAIO)
SUET .... Small Unit Evaluation and Training (MCD)
Suet .... Suetonius [*First century AD*] [*Classical studies*] (OCD)
SUF.............. Lametia-Terme [*Italy*] [*Airport symbol*] (OAG)
SUF.............. Scottish Union of Fishermen
SUF.............. Sequential Ultrafiltration [*Nephrology*] (DAVI)
SUF.............. Socialist Unity Front [*Romania*] [*Political party*] (PPW)
SUF.............. Southernera Resources Ltd. [*Toronto Stock Exchange symbol*]
SUF.............. Sufficient (AFM)
SUF.............. Suffolk University, Boston, MA [*OCLC symbol*] (OCLC)
SUF.............. Sunflower Airlines Ltd. [*Fiji*] [*ICAO designator*] (FAAC)
SUF.............. Swaziland United Front
SUFF............ Sufficient
SUFF............ Sufficit [*Suffices*] [*Latin*]
SUFF............ Suffix (AAG)
SUFF............ Suffolk [*County in England*]
SUFF............ Suffragan [*Ecclesiastical*] (ROG)
SuffBnc .... Suffolk Bancorp [*Associated Press*] (SAG)
SUFFER .... Save Us from Formaldehyde Environmental Repercussions [*Later, CURE FormaldehydePoisoning Association*] (EA)
SUFFER .... System Utility Facility for Easy Recovery [*NASA*]
Suffolk U ..... Suffolk University (GAGS)
SUFFR.......... Suffragan [*Ecclesiastical*] (WGA)
SUFFT.......... Sufficient
SUFFTY........ Sufficiently (ROG)
SUFPAC .... Surface Force Pacific (MCD)
SUFSW .... Small Unit Fire Support Weapon (MCD)
SUG .... Asheville, NC [*Location identifier FAA*] (FAAL)
SUG .... Sell Under the Guise of Market Research [*Marketing*] [*British*]
SUG .... Smartmac User Group (EA)
SUG .... Southern Union [*NYSE symbol*] (TTSB)
SUG .... Southern Union Co. [*NYSE symbol*] (SAG)
SUG .... Southern Union Financing [*NYSE symbol*] (SAG)
SUG .... Sugar
SUG .... Sugar
SUG .... Sugar Island [*Michigan*] [*Seismograph station code, US Geological Survey Closed*] (SEIS)
SUG .... Suggest (AFM)
SUG .... Sun User Group [*An association*]
SUG .... Surigao [*Philippines*] [*Airport symbol*] (OAG)
SUGAR......... Software Users Guide to Available Resources [*Australia A publication*]
Sugd Powers... Sugden on Powers [*A publication*] (DLA)
Sugd Vend... Sugden on Vendors and Purchasers [*A publication*] (DLA)
SUGEN .... SUGEN, Inc. [*Associated Press*] (SAG)
SUGEND ...... Sugendus [*To Be Sucked*] [*Pharmacy*]
Sug Est........ Sugden on the Law of Estates [*A publication*] (DLA)
SUGG........... Suggestion (ROG)
Sug Hd Bk ... Sugden's Hand-Book of Property Law [*A publication*] (DLA)
SUGI............ SAS [*Statistical Analysis System*] Users Group International (EA)
SUGN........... SUGEN, Inc. [*NASDAQ symbol*] (SAG)
Sug Pow....... Sugden on Powers [*8 eds.*] [*1808-61*] [*A publication*] (DLA)
Sug Pr .... Sugden on the Law of Property [*A publication*] (DLA)
SUGPrA........ So Union Financing 9.48%'TOPrS' [*NYSE symbol*] (TTSB)
Sug Prop ...... Sugden on the Law of Property as Administered by the House of Lords [*A publication*] (DLA)
Sug Pr St..... Sugden on Property Statutes [*A publication*] (DLA)
SUGR........... Summagraphics [*NASDAQ symbol*] (TTSB)
SUGR........... Summagraphics Corp. [*NASDAQ symbol*] (NQ)
Sug V & P ... Sugden on Vendors and Purchasers [*14 eds.*] [*1805-62*] [*A publication*] (DLA)

Sug Vend Sugden on Vendors and Purchasers [*A publication*] (DLA)
SUH Rockland, ME [*Location identifier FAA*] (FAAL)
SUHL Sylvania Ultrahigh-Level Logic (IEEE)
SUHL Sylvania Universal High-Level Logic (IAA)
SUHT Squared Up Halftone [*Typography*] (DGA)
SUI Bundesamt fur Militarflugplatze [*Switzerland ICAO designator*] (FAAC)
SUI Safe Use Instructions [*General Motors Corp.*]
SUI Speleological Union of Ireland (EAIO)
SUI Standard Universal Identifier (NITA)
SUI Standard Universal Identifying Number
SUI Stanford University Institute for Plasma Research
SUI State University of Iowa [*Later, University of Iowa*]
SUI Stress Urinary Incontinence [*Medicine*] (DMAA)
SUI Suihwa [*Republic of China*] [*Seismograph station code, US Geological Survey*] (SEIS)
SUI Sukhumi [*USSR*] [*Airport symbol*] (AD)
SUI Summit Resources Ltd. [*Toronto Stock Exchange symbol*]
SUI Sun Communities [*NYSE symbol*] (SPSG)
SUIAP Simplified Unit Invoice Accounting Plan
SUIC Salford University Industrial Centre Ltd. [*British*] (IRUK)
SUID Sudden Unexpected Infant Death [*Medicine*]
SUID Sudden Unexplained Infant Death [*Neonatology*] (DAVI)
SUIH State University of Iowa Hospitals (DAVI)
SUIP Support Unit Improvement Program (MCD)
SUIS Ship Upkeep Information System [*Ministry of Defense*] [*British*] (PDAA)
SUIS Smoloskyp, Ukrainian Information Service (EA)
SUIT Mens Warehouse [*NASDAQ symbol*] (SAG)
SUIT Sight Unit Infantry Trilux [*British*]
SUIT Simple User Interface Toolkit [*University of Virginia*]
SUITS Scottish and Universal Investments
SUIV Suivant [*Following*] [*French*]
SuizaF Suiza Foods Corp. [*Associated Press*] (SAG)
SUJ Satu Mare [*Romania*] [*Airport symbol*] (OAG)
SUJ Side Upset Jaw (MSA)
SUJ Suntac Minerals [*Vancouver Stock Exchange symbol*]
SUJB Southern Universities Joint Board [*for school examinations*] [*British*] (DCTA)
SUK Suckling Hill [*Alaska*] [*Seismograph station code, US Geological Survey*] (SEIS)
Suk Sukkah (BJA)
suk Sukuma [*MARC language code Library of Congress*] (LCCP)
SUKLO Senior United Kingdom Liaison Officer [*Later, BJSM*] [*British*]
SUL Simplified User Logistics [*Military*] (AABC)
SUL Small University Libraries
SUL Sophia University [*UTLAS symbol*]
SUL Standard User Labels [*Computer science*]
SUL State University of New York, Union List of Serials, Albany, NY [*OCLC symbol*] (OCLC)
SUL Sui [*Pakistan*] [*Airport symbol*] (OAG)
SUL Sulcus Computer [*AMEX symbol*] (TTSB)
SUL Sulcus Computer Corp. [*AMEX symbol*] (SPSG)
SUL Sulpetro Ltd. [*Toronto Stock Exchange symbol*]
SUL Sulphur Creek [*New Britain*] [*Seismograph station code, US Geological Survey*] (SEIS)
SULCL Set Up in Less than Carloads [*Freight*]
Sulcus Sulcus Computer Corp. [*Associated Press*] (SAG)
SuLEXCo Sulphur Export Corp. [*An association*] (EA)
SULF Speedball Up-Range Launch Facility [*Army*] (AABC)
sulf Sulfate [*or Sulphate*] [*Chemistry*] (DAVI)
SULF Sulfur [*Chemical element*] (DAVI)
SULFHB Sulfhemoglobin [*Also, Sulfmethemoglobin*] [*Biochemistry*] (DAVI)
SULF-PRIM Sulfamethoxazole and Trimethoprim [*Medicine*] (DMAA)
SULINAC Super Linear Accelerator [*Space flight simulator*]
SULIRS Syracuse University Libraries' Information Retrieval System (NITA)
SULIS Syracuse University Libraries Information System [*Syracuse University Libraries*] [*New York*] [*Information service or system*] (IID)
Sull Pro Sulla [*of Cicero*] [*Classical studies*] (OCD)
Sull Sulla [*of Plutarch*] [*Classical studies*] (OCD)
SULL Sullivan Dental Products [*NASDAQ symbol*] (SAG)
Sull Dnt Sullivan Dental Products [*Associated Press*] (SAG)
Sullivan Smith's New Hampshire Reports [*A publication*] (DLA)
Sull Ld Tit Sullivan's Land Titles in Massachusetts [*A publication*] (DLA)
Sull Lect Sullivan's Lectures on Constitution and Laws of England [*A publication*] (DLA)
sulph Sulphate [*or Sulfate*] [*Chemistry*] (DAVI)
sulpha Sulphonamide [*or Sulfonamide*] [*An antibacterial*] (DAVI)
Sul Ross St U Sul Ross State University (GAGS)
SULS Maldonado/Base Aeronaval C/C Carlos A. Curbelo [*Uruguay*] [*ICAO location identifier*] (ICLI)
SULT Sultan
Sum Hale's Summary of the Pleas of the Crown [*England*] [*A publication*] (DLA)
SUM San Juan de Cesar [*Colombia*] [*Airport symbol*] (AD)
SUM Saturn Umbilical Maintenance [*NASA*]
SUM Save Uganda Movement
SUM Servicio Universitario Mundial [*World University Service*]
SUM Set-Up [*Control*] Module [*Telecommunications*] (TEL)
SUM Shallow Underwater Missile
SUM Shallow Underwater Mobile (IAA)
SUM Socialist Unionist Movement [*Al Haraka at Tawhidiyya al Ishtirakiyya*] [*Syria*] [*Political party*] (PPW)
SUM Software User's Manual [*Army*]
SUM Solar Ultraviolet Monitor (MCD)
SUM Sullivan Mines, Inc. [*Toronto Stock Exchange symbol*]
SUM Sumantur [*Let It Be Taken*] [*Latin*] [*Pharmacy*] (DAVI)
SUM Sumat [*Let Him Take, Let the Person Take*] [*Latin*] [*Pharmacy*] (DAVI)
Sum Sumatra
SUM Sume [*Take*] [*Pharmacy*]
SUM Sumendum [*To Be Taken*] [*Latin*] [*Pharmacy*] (DAVI)
Sum Sumerian (BJA)
SUM Summary (AABC)
SUM Summation (AAMN)
SUM Summator (IAA)
SUM Summer
SUM Summing
Sum Summit: Journal of the Liturgical Commission [*of the Archdiocese of Melbourne*] [*A publication*] (APTA)
SUM Summoned
Sum Sumner's United States Circuit Court Reports [*A publication*] (DLA)
SUM Sumoto [*Japan*] [*Seismograph station code, US Geological Survey*] (SEIS)
SUM Sumter [*South Carolina*] [*Airport symbol*] (OAG)
SUM Surface-to-Underwater Missile
SUM Symantec Utilities for Macintosh [*Computer software*] (CDE)
SUM System Check and Utility Master (MCD)
SUM Systems Unit Method [*Medical transcription*]
SUM System Utilization Monitor [*Computer science*]
SUM University of South Carolina, School of Medicine, Columbia, SC [*OCLC symbol*] (OCLC)
SUMA Sporadic Ulcerating and Mutilating Acropathy [*Medicine*] (DMAA)
SUMA Suma Four [*NASDAQ symbol*] (TTSB)
SUMA Summa Four, Inc. [*NASDAQ symbol*] (SAG)
SUMAC Sheffield University Metals Advisory Centre [*British*] (IRUK)
SUMARPI Supplemental Maintenance and Repair Parts Instruction
Sumat Sumatra (VRA)
SUMC Space Ultrareliable Modular Computer
SUMC Stanford University Medical Center
SUMC Summit Care [*NASDAQ symbol*] (TTSB)
SUMC Summit Care Corp. [*NASDAQ symbol*] (SAG)
SUMCM Summary Court-Martial
SUMCMO Summary Court-Martial Order
Sum Dec Summary Decisions [*Bengal, India*] [*A publication*] (DLA)
SUME Mercedes/Ricardo de Tomasi [*Uruguay*] [*ICAO location identifier*] (ICLI)
SUMED Suez-Mediterranean [*Pipeline*]
SUMER Solar Ultraviolet Measurements of Emitted Radiation [*Instrumentation*]
SUMEX Stanford University Medical Experimental Computer Project [*Stanford University*] [*Research center*] (RCD)
SUMEXAIM Stanford University Medical Experiment-Applications of Artificial Intelligence to Medical Research (NITA)
Sumgph Summagraphics Corp. [*Associated Press*] (SAG)
SUMI Sumitomo Bank (CA) [*NASDAQ symbol*] (TTSB)
SUMI Sumitomo Bank of California [*NASDAQ symbol*] (NQ)
SUMIT Single-Concept User-Adaptable Microcomputer-Based Instructional Technique (EDAC)
SUMIT Standard Utility Means for Information Transformation [*Computer science*]
SUMIT Summit [*Commonly used*] (OPSA)
SumitB Summit Bancorp New Jersey [*Associated Press*] (SAG)
SumitFR Summit Family Restaurants, Inc. [*Associated Press*] (SAG)
Sumito SumitomoBank of California [*Associated Press*] (SAG)
Sumito Sumitomo Bank of California [*Associated Press*] (SAG)
SUMITT Summit [*Commonly used*] (OPSA)
SumitTc Summit Technology, Inc. [*Associated Press*] (SAG)
SUMIZ Sumitomo Bank CA Dep'A'Pfd [*NASDAQ symbol*] (TTSB)
SUMM Summarize (IAA)
SUMM Summary
SUMM Summer
SUMM Summitatis [*Summits or Tops*] [*Pharmacy*] (ROG)
SUMM Summit Financial [*NASDAQ symbol*] (SAG)
SUMM Summons [*Legal shorthand*] (LWAP)
Summa Summa Industries [*Associated Press*] (SAG)
SUMMA Superconducting Magnetic Mirror Apparatus
SUMMAC Stanford University Modified Markers and Cell Method
SummaF Summa Four, Inc. [*Associated Press*] (SAG)
SUMMCO Summary Court-Martial Order
Summ Dec Summary Decisions [*Bengal, India*] [*A publication*] (ILCA)
Summerfield Summerfield's Reports [*21 Nevada*] [*A publication*] (DLA)
Summerfield S S. Summerfield's Reports [*21 Nevada*] [*A publication*] (DLA)
SUMMIT Sperry UNIVAC Minicomputer Management of Interactive Terminals
SUMMIT Summit [*Commonly used*] (OPSA)
SUMMIT Supervisor of Multiprogramming, Multiprocessing, Interactive Time Sharing [*Computer science*] (IEEE)
Summ NP Summary of the Law of Nisi Prius [*A publication*] (DLA)
Sumn Sumner's United States Circuit Court Reports [*A publication*] (DLA)
Sumner Sumner's United States Circuit Court Reports [*A publication*] (DLA)
SUMNS Summons (ROG)
Sumn Ves Sumner's Edition of Vesey's Reports [*A publication*] (DLA)
SUMO Melo/Aeropuerto Deptal de Cerro Largo [*Uruguay*] [*ICAO location identifier*] (ICLI)
SUMPAC Southampton University Man-Powered Aircraft [*British*]
SUMPM Summary Performance Measure (MCD)
sumpt Sumptuary (VRA)
Sum Rep Sumner's United States Circuit Court Reports [*A publication*] (DLA)
SUMS Shuttle Upper-Atmosphere Mass Spectrometer [*NASA*] (MCD)

SUMS .... Southern Universities' Management Services (AIE)
SUMS .... Specialized Unit Maintenance Support (MCD)
SUMS .... Sperry UNIVAC Material System
SUMS .... Standard USAREUR Munitions System
SUMS .... Summons (ROG)
SUMSTAT .... Summary Statistical Data [*Federal government*]
SUMT .... Sequential Unconstrained Minimization Technique
SUMT .... Summit Medical System [*NASDAQ symbol*] (TTSB)
SUMT .... Summit Medical Systems, Inc. [*NASDAQ symbol*] (SAG)
SUM TAL ..... Sumat Talem [*Take One Like This*] [*Pharmacy*]
SumtBTX ...... Summit Bancshares TX [*Associated Press*] (SAG)
SumtCre ...... Summit Care Corp. [*Associated Press*] (SAG)
SumtDsg ...... Summit Design, Inc. [*Associated Press*] (SAG)
SumtFn .... Summit Financial [*Associated Press*] (SAG)
SumtMd .... Summit Medical Systems, Inc. [*Associated Press*] (SAG)
SumtPrp ...... Summit Properties, Inc. [*Associated Press*] (SAG)
SumtTx .... Summit Tax Exempt Bond Fund Ltd. [*Associated Press*] (SAG)
SUMU .... Montevideo/Carrasco Internacional [*Uruguay*] [*ICAO location identifier*] (ICLI)
Sum UCCR ... Sumner's United States Circuit Court Reports [*A publication*] (DLA)
Sum Ves ...... Sumner's Edition of Vesey's Reports [*A publication*] (DLA)
SUMX .... Suma Industries [*NASDAQ symbol*] (SAG)
SUMX .... Summa Industries [*NASDAQ symbol*] (SAG)
SUMX .... Summa Industries [*NASDAQ symbol*] (TTSB)
SUN .... Antillana de Nevegacion Aerea SA [*Dominican Republic*] [*ICAO designator*] (FAAC)
SUN .... Hailey, ID [*Location identifier FAA*] (FAAL)
SUN .... OPTEVFOR [*Operational Test and Evaluation Force*] Detachment, Sunnyvale, CA [*Navy*] (CAAL)
SUN .... Serum Urea Nitrogen [*Clinical medicine*]
SUN .... Spanish Universal Network [*Cable-television system*]
SUN .... SPINDEX Users' Network (NITA)
SUN .... Spiritual Unity of Nations [*An association*]
SUN .... Standard Units and Nomenclature (MCD)
SUN .... State University of Nebraska
SUN .... Sun Co. [*NYSE symbol*] (TTSB)
SUN .... Sun Co., Inc. [*NYSE symbol*] (SPSG)
sun .... Sundanese [*MARC language code Library of Congress*] (LCCP)
SUN .... Sunday (AFM)
Sun .... Sunday (ODBW)
SUN .... Sundstrand-Turbo Division (AAG)
SUN .... Sun Life Assurance Co. of Canada [*UTLAS symbol*]
SUN .... Sunnyside [*Utah*] [*Seismograph station code, US Geological Survey Closed*] (SEIS)
SUN .... Sunset Railway Co. [*AAR code*]
SUN .... Suntech Library and Information Center, Marcus Hook, PA [*OCLC symbol*] (OCLC)
SUN .... Suntec Ventures Ltd. [*Vancouver Stock Exchange symbol*]
SUN .... Sun Valley [*Idaho*] [*Airport symbol*] (OAG)
SUN .... Switching Unit
SUN .... Symbolic Unit Number [*Computer science*] (WDAA)
SUN .... Symbols, Units, and Nomenclature [*Commission*] [*IUPAC*]
SUN .... Symphony for United Nations (EA)
SUN .... Union of Soviet Socialist Republics [*ANSI three-letter standard code*] (CNC)
SUNA .... Seafarers' International Union of North America [*AFL-CIO*] (EA)
SUNA .... Sudan News Agency
Suna .... Sunamerica, Inc. [*Associated Press*] (SAG)
SUNA .... Switchmen's Union of North America [*Later, United Transportation Union*]
SunaC .... Sunamerica Capital Trust [*Associated Press*] (SAG)
SunaC .... Sunamerica Capital Trust II [*Associated Press*] (SAG)
SunaC .... Sunamerica Capital Trust III [*Associated Press*] (SAG)
Sunair .... Sunair Electronics, Inc. [*Associated Press*] (SAG)
Sunamer ...... Sunamerica, Inc. [*Associated Press*] (SAG)
SUNAT .... Scandinavian Union for Non-Alcoholic Traffic (EA)
SunBanc ...... Sun Bancorp, Inc. [*Associated Press*] (SAG)
SunBCA .... Sunrise Bancorp [*Associated Press*] (SAG)
SunBcNY ..... Sunrise Bancorp, Inc. NY [*Associated Press*] (SAG)
SunBcp .... Sun Bancorp, Inc. [*Associated Press*] (SAG)
Sunbeam ..... Sunbeam Corp. [*Associated Press*] (SAG)
Sunbelt .... Sunbelt Companies [*Associated Press*] (SAG)
SUnBH .... Scripta Universitatis atque Bibliotecae Hierosolymitanarum Jerusalem [*A publication*] (BJA)
SunCmts ...... Sun Communities [*Associated Press*] (SAG)
SunCo .... Sun Co., Inc. [*Associated Press*] (SAG)
SunCoast ..... Sun Coast Industries, Inc. [*Associated Press*] (SAG)
Suncor .... Suncor, Inc. [*Associated Press*] (SAG)
SUNCOR ...... Sun Oil Co. of Radnor [*Pennsylvania*]
SunCty .... Sun City Industries, Inc. [*Associated Press*] (SAG)
SUND .... Sound Advice [*NASDAQ symbol*] (TTSB)
SUND .... Sound Advice, Inc. [*NASDAQ symbol*] (NQ)
SUND .... Sunday
SUND .... Sundries
SUNDAE .... Stanford University Division of Aero Engineering (AAG)
Sunday Rev ... Sunday Review [*A publication*]
Sund H .... Sunday Herald [*Melbourne*] [*A publication*]
SundHme ...... Sundance Homes, Inc. [*Associated Press*] (SAG)
SunDis .... Sun Distributors Ltd. [*Associated Press*] (SAG)
SunDist .... Sun Distributors Ltd. [*Associated Press*] (SAG)
SUNDS .... Sudden Unexpected Nocturnal Death Syndrome [*Medicine*] (ECON)
SUNDS .... Sundries (ROG)
SUNEC .... Seaborne Supply of the Northeast Command (DNAB)
SunEng .... Sun Energy Partners Ltd. [*Associated Press*] (SAG)
SUNET .... [*The*] Swedish University Network (TNIG)
SUNF .... Sunstar Foods, Inc. (MHDW)
SUNFED .... Special United Nations Fund for Economic Development
Sunglss .... Sunglass Hut International, Inc. [*Associated Press*] (SAG)
SunGrd .... Sundata Corp. [*Associated Press*] (SAG)
SUNH .... Sundance Homes [*NASDAQ symbol*] (TTSB)
SUNH .... Sundance Homes, Inc. [*NASDAQ symbol*] (SAG)
SunHltcr ...... Sun Healthcare Group, Inc. [*Associated Press*] (SAG)
SunHydr .... Sun Hydraulics Corp. [*Associated Press*] (SAG)
SUNI .... Southern Universities Nuclear Institute
SUN III .... Sydney UNIX Network (TNIG)
SunInt .... Sun International [*Associated Press*] (SAG)
SunIntl .... Sun International [*Associated Press*] (SAG)
SUNIST .... Serveur Universitaire National de l'Information Scientifique et Technique [*Online service*]
Sunk .... Single, Unemployed, No Kids [*Lifestyle classification*]
SUNL .... Sunrise Resources [*NASDAQ symbol*] (TTSB)
SUNL .... Sunrise Resources, Inc. [*NASDAQ symbol*] (SAG)
SunM .... Sunshine Mining & Refining Co. [*Associated Press*] (SAG)
SunMed .... Sunrise Medical, Inc. [*Associated Press*] (SAG)
SunMic .... Sun Microsystems, Inc. [*Associated Press*] (SAG)
SunMn .... Sunshine Mining & Refining Co. [*Associated Press*] (SAG)
SunNur .... Sunbelt Nursery Group, Inc. [*Associated Press*] (SAG)
SUNO .... Southern University in New Orleans
SUNOCO ...... Sun Oil Co. [*Later, Sun Co., Inc.*]
SUNP .... SunPharm Corp. [*NASDAQ symbol*] (SAG)
SunPh .... SunPharm Corp. [*Associated Press*] (SAG)
SunPhm .... SunPharm Corp. [*Associated Press*] (SAG)
Sunport .... Sunport Medical Corp. [*Associated Press*] (SAG)
SUNPrD .... Sun Co.'A'Dep'TARGETS' [*NYSE symbol*] (TTSB)
SUNPW .... Sunpharm Corp. Wrrt [*NASDAQ symbol*] (TTSB)
SUNQ .... Sunquest Information Sys [*NASDAQ symbol*] (TTSB)
SUNQ .... Sunquest Information Systems, Inc. [*NASDAQ symbol*] (SAG)
Sunquest ..... Sunquest Information Systems, Inc. [*Associated Press*] (SAG)
SUNR .... Sunrise Preschools [*NASDAQ symbol*] (TTSB)
SUNR .... Sunrise Preschools, Inc. [*NASDAQ symbol*] (SAG)
SunrAss .... Sunrise Assisted Living, Inc. [*Associated Press*] (SAG)
SunResc ...... Sunrise Resources, Inc. [*Associated Press*] (SAG)
Sunrise .... Sunrise Preschools, Inc. [*Associated Press*] (SAG)
SunRiver ...... SunRiver Corp. [*Associated Press*] (SAG)
SUNRP .... Sunrise Preschools Cv'C' Pfd [*NASDAQ symbol*] (TTSB)
Sunrst .... Sunresorts Ltd. NV [*Associated Press*] (SAG)
SUNS .... New Day Beverage, Inc. [*NASDAQ symbol*] (SAG)
SUNS .... Small Unit Navigation System
SUNS .... Sonic Underwater Navigation System (WDAA)
SUNS .... SunStar Healthcare [*NASDAQ symbol*] (TTSB)
SUNS .... SunStar Healthcare, Inc. [*NASDAQ symbol*] (SAG)
SUNSAT .... Sun-Energy Collecting Satellite
SunSav .... Suncoast Savings & Loan Association [*Associated Press*] (SAG)
SunshJr .... Sunshine-Jr Stores, Inc. [*Associated Press*] (SAG)
SunsMn .... Sunshine Mining & Refining Co. [*Associated Press*] (SAG)
Sunsource ... Sunsource LP [*Associated Press*] (SAG)
SUNSPOT .... Study of Utilization Systems, Policies, and Techniques (MCD)
SunSpt .... Sun Sportswear, Inc. [*Associated Press*] (SAG)
SunsrceB ..... Sunsource LP [*Associated Press*] (SAG)
SUNSTAR .... Stanford University Network for Space Telescience Applications Research [*Research center*] (RCD)
SunStar .... SunStar Healthcare, Inc. [*Associated Press*] (SAG)
Sunstat .... Sunstates Corp. [*Associated Press*] (SAG)
Sunstate ...... Sunstates Corp. [*Associated Press*] (SAG)
SunstH .... Sunstone Hotel Investors, Inc. [*Associated Press*] (SAG)
SunstoneH ... Sunstone Hotel Investors, Inc. [*Associated Press*] (SAG)
Sunstrnd ...... Sundstrand Corp. [*Associated Press*] (SAG)
SunSv .... Suncoast Savings & Loan Association [*Associated Press*] (SAG)
SunTrst .... SunTrust Banks, Inc. [*Associated Press*] (SAG)
SunTV .... Sun Television & Applicances, Inc. [*Associated Press*] (SAG)
SUNW .... Sun Microsystems [*NASDAQ symbol*] (TTSB)
SUNW .... Sun Microsystems, Inc. [*Mountain View, CA*] [*NASDAQ symbol*] (NQ)
SUNWACD ... Swaleureniddwharfeairecalderdon [*British town*]
SUNY .... State University of New York [*Computer retrieval and control projects*] [*Albany, NY*]
SUNY .... Sunrise Bancorp, Inc. New York [*NASDAQ symbol*] (SAG)
SUNYA .... State University of New York at Albany
SUNYAB ...... State University of New York at Buffalo
SUNY (Albany) ... State University of New York at Albany (GAGS)
SUNY BCN ... State University of New York Biomedical Communication Network (EA)
SUNY (Binghampton) ... State University of New York at Binghampton (GAGS)
SUNY (Buffalo) ... State University of New York at Buffalo (GAGS)
SUNYC (Brockport) ... State University of New York College at Brockport (GAGS)
SUNYC (Buffalo) ... State University of New York College at Buffalo (GAGS)
SUNYC (Cortland) ... State University of New York College at Cortland (GAGS)
SUNYC Environ Sci & For (Syracuse) ... State University of New York College of Environmental Science and Forestry at Syracuse (GAGS)
SUNYC (Fredonia) ... State University of New York College at Fredonia (GAGS)
SUNYC (Geneseo) ... State University of New York College at Geneseo (GAGS)
SUNYC (New Paltz) ... State University of New York College at New Paltz (GAGS)
SUNYC (Oneonta) ... State University of New York College at Oneonta (GAGS)
SUNYC (Oswego) ... State University of New York College at Oswego (GAGS)
SUNYC (Plattsburg) ... State University of New York College at Plattsburg (GAGS)
SUNYC (Potsdam) ... State University of New York College at Potsdam (GAGS)
SUNY H Sci Cent ... State University of New York Health Science Center at Brooklyn (GAGS)
SUNY H Sci Cent ... State University of New York Health Science Center at Syracuse (GAGS)

SUNY/OCLC... State University of New York Online Computer Library Center [*Library network*]
SunyP .... State University of New York Press, Albany, NY [*Library symbol Library of Congress*] (LCLS)
SUNY (Stony Brook)... State University of New York at Stony Brook (GAGS)
SUO .... Senior Under-Officer [*Royal Military Academy*] [*British*] (ROG)
SUO .... Shell Oil Co. [*Toronto Stock Exchange symbol*] (SPSG)
SUO .... Society of University Otolaryngologists [*Later, SOU-HNS*] (EA)
SUO .... Sun River [*Oregon*] [*Airport symbol Obsolete*] (OAG)
SUO-HNS..... Society of University Otolaryngologists - Head and Neck Surgeons (EA)
SUOT .... Spacelab Ultraviolet Telescope
SUP .... Aerosuper AS de CV [*Mexico ICAO designator*] (FAAC)
SUP .... Sabah United Party [*Malaysia*] [*Political party*]
SUP .... Sailors' Union of the Pacific (EA)
SUP .... Single Unit Pack [*for vehicles*]
SUP .... Single Unit Package [*Pharmacy*]
SUP .... Single Unit Parameter
SUP .... Southern University Press (DGA)
SUP .... Special Utility Program [*NASA*] (KSC)
SUP .... Standard Unit of Processing [*Computer science*]
SUP .... Stanford University Press (DGA)
SUP .... Statistical Utility Program
SUP .... Super
sup............. Super (WDMC)
SUP .... Superannuation
SUP .... Superficial (AAMN)
SUP .... Superfine
SUP .... Superior (AFM)
sup............. Superior (WDMC)
SUP .... Superior Indus Intl [*NYSE symbol*] (TTSB)
SUP .... Superior Industries International, Inc. [*NYSE symbol*] (SPSG)
SUP .... Superior Oil Co., Exploration Library, Houston, TX [*OCLC symbol*] (OCLC)
SUP .... Superlative
SUP .... Supersede (WGA)
SUP .... Supervisor (IAA)
sup............. Supervisor (WDMC)
SUP .... Supination [*or Supinator*] [*Medicine*] (DAVI)
SUP .... Supine
SUP .... Supplement (AFM)
sup............. Supplement (WDMC)
SUP .... Supply [*Business term*] (AFM)
SUP .... Supply Contract (AAGC)
SUP .... Support
SUP .... Suppresor [*Electronics*] (ECII)
SUP .... Suppress (DEN)
sup............. Suppression (IDOE)
sup............. Suppressor (IDOE)
SUP .... Supra [*Above*] [*Latin*]
Sup .... Supraphon [*Record label*] [*Former Czechoslovakia*]
SUP .... Supreme
SUP .... Supreme Resources, Inc. [*Vancouver Stock Exchange symbol*]
SUP .... Sydney University Press [*Australia*] (ADA)
SUP .... Syracuse University Press (DGA)
SUP .... System Utilization Procedure
sup............. What's Up? [*Internet language*] [*Computer science*]
SUPA .... Society of University Patent Administrators (EA)
SUPAC .... Scale-Up and Post Approval Changes [*FDA*]
SUPAC .... Scale-Up and Post Approval Changes [*Food and Drug Administration*]
SUPAD......... Supplementary Address (MCD)
SUPADS....... Suppression of Air Defense System (MCD)
SUPANX....... Supply Annex
SUPARCO .... Space and Upper Atmospheric Research Committee [*Pakistan*]
SUPARS....... Supply Acquisition Regulation Supplement [*Navy*]
SUPARS....... Syracuse University Psychological Abstracts Retrieval Service (NITA)
SUPC .... Superior Consultant Holdings Corp. [*NASDAQ symbol*] (SAG)
Sup C.......... Superior Court (BARN)
Sup C.......... Supreme Court (BARN)
Sup C.......... Supreme Court Reporter (BARN)
SUPCE .... Syracuse University Publications in Continuing Education (EA)
SUPCEN....... Supply Center
SUPCHG ...... Supercharge (FAAC)
SUPCOM ...... Support Command [*Army*]
SUPCOM ...... Supreme Command
SUPCON ...... Superintending Constructor
SupConsl ..... Superior Consultant Holdings Corp. [*Associated Press*] (SAG)
SUPCOSTINS... Supervisory Cost Inspector [*Navy*]
Sup Court Rep... Supreme Court Reporter [*A publication*] (DLA)
SUPCRIT...... Super Critical (MCD)
Sup Ct .... Supreme Court (DLA)
Sup Ct .... Supreme Court Reporter [*National Reporter System*] [*A publication*] (DLA)
Sup Ct App... Supreme Court Appeals [*India*] [*A publication*] (DLA)
Sup Ct J ...... Supreme Court Journal [*India*] [*A publication*] (DLA)
Sup Ct MR... Supreme Court Monthly Review [*India*] [*A publication*] (DLA)
Sup Ct Pr.... Supreme Court Practice [*A publication*] (DLA)
Sup Ct R...... Supreme Court Reports [*India*] [*A publication*] (DLA)
Sup Ct R...... United States Supreme Court Rule [*A publication*] (DLA)
Sup Ct Rep... Supreme Court Reporter [*A publication*] (DLA)
Sup Ct Repr... Supreme Court Reporter [*A publication*] (DLA)
Sup Ct R (NY)... New York Supreme Court Reports [*A publication*] (DLA)
SUPCUR ...... Superimposed Current
SUPDEP....... Supply Depot
SUPDIV........ Supervisor of Diving [*Navy*]
SUPDIVE...... Supervisor of Diving [*Navy*]
SUPDOC ...... Superintendent of Documents-Government Printing Office (TAG)
SUPDT......... Superintendent (ADA)
SUPE .... Punta Del Este/Aeropuerto Deptal de Maldonado [*Uruguay*] [*ICAO location identifier*] (ICLI)
SUPE .... Super Eight [*Motion picture*] (VRA)
SupE .... Superior Energy Services, Inc. [*Associated Press*] (SAG)
SupEnrgy..... Superior Energy Services, Inc. [*Associated Press*] (SAG)
SUPER......... Superannuation
SUPER......... Supercalendered (NTCM)
SUPER......... Superficial
SUPER......... Superfine
SUPER......... Superimpose
SUPER......... Superimposition (NTCM)
SUPER......... Superintendent
SUPER......... Superior
SUPER......... Superior
Super.......... Superior Court (DLA)
Super.......... Superior Court Reports [*A publication*] (DLA)
SUPER......... Supernumerary
SUPER......... Supersede (MUGU)
SUPER......... Supervisor (DSUE)
SUPER......... System Used for Prediction and Evaluation of Reliability [*Computer science*] (MHDI)
Super Ct ...... Superior Court (DLA)
Super Ct App Div... Superior Court, Appellate Division (DLA)
Super Ct Ch Div... Superior Court, Chancery Division (DLA)
Super Ct Law Div... Superior Court, Law Division (DLA)
Super Ct Rep... Superior Court Reports [*New York, Pennsylvania, etc.*] [*A publication*] (DLA)
Super Ct (RI)... Rhode Island Superior Court (DLA)
Supercut ...... Supercuts, Inc. [*Associated Press*] (SAG)
SUPERFL...... Superficial (ROG)
SuperG .... SuperGen, Inc. [*Associated Press*] (SAG)
SuperGn ...... SuperGen, Inc. [*Associated Press*] (SAG)
SUPERHET.... Superheterodyne
SuperInd..... Superior Industries International, Inc. [*Associated Press*] (SAG)
SuperJANET... Super Joint Academic Network [*UK*] (EERA)
SUPERL....... Superlative
SUPERMAG... Superconducting Magnet (SSD)
SUPERSTR... Superstructure
Supertel...... Supertel Hospitality, Inc. [*Associated Press*] (SAG)
SUPG .... SuperGen, Inc. [*NASDAQ symbol*] (SAG)
SUPG .... SuperGen Inc. [*NASDAQ symbol*] (TTSB)
SUPG .... System Utilization Procedural Guide
SUP GOSSYP... Super Gossypium [*On Cotton Wool*] [*Pharmacy*]
SUPGW........ SuperGen Inc. Wrrt [*NASDAQ symbol*] (TTSB)
SUPHTD....... Superheated (AAG)
SUPHTR....... Superheater (AAG)
SUPI .... Supreme International [*NASDAQ symbol*] (TTSB)
SUPI .... Supreme International Corp. [*NASDAQ symbol*] (SAG)
SUPIER........ Supply Pier [*Navy*]
supin .... Supination [*Medicine*] (DMAA)
SupIn........... Supreme Industries [*Associated Press*] (SAG)
SUPINSMAT... Supervising Inspector of Naval Material
SUPINSP...... Supply Inspection [*Navy*] (NVT)
SupIntl........ Supreme International Corp. [*Associated Press*] (SAG)
SUPINTREP... Supplementary Intelligence Report [*Military*] (AABC)
SUPIR.......... Supplementary Photographic Interpretation Report [*Military*]
Sup Jud Ct... Supreme Judicial Court [*Massachusetts*] (DLA)
SUPL .... Supply
SUP LINT..... Super Linteum [*On Lint*] [*Pharmacy*]
SUPLO .... Scottish Union of Power Loom Overlookers
SUPLS .... Supplies (WGA)
SUPMG........ Southern University Press Marketing Group [*Acronym is pronounced "soupmug"*]
SUPMTL ...... Supplemental
SupNatl....... Superior National Insurance Group, Inc. [*Associated Press*] (SAG)
SUPNZ......... Socialist Unity Party of New Zealand
SUPO .... Super Power [*Water boiler*] [*Nuclear reactor*]
SUPO .... Supply Officer
SUPOH DI.... Supply on Hand or Due In
SUPOHDU.... Supply from Stock on Hand or Due In
SUPOPS....... Supply Operations [*DoD*]
Supp .... New York Supplement Reports [*A publication*] (DLA)
SUPP .... Sarawak United People's Party [*Malaysia*] [*Political party*] (PPW)
SUPP .... Supplement (KSC)
Supp .... Supplement (AAGC)
Supp .... Supplices [*of Euripides*] [*Classical studies*] (OCD)
Supp .... Supplices Contra Thebas [*of Aeschylus*] [*Classical studies*] (OCD)
SUPP .... Supply
SUPP .... Support (AAG)
SUPP .... Suppositorium [*Suppository*] [*Pharmacy*]
supp............ Suppurative [*Medicine*]
SUPPACT...... Support Activity
Supp Aesch... Supplementum Aeschyleum [*A publication*] (OCD)
SUPP BAS ... Supplemental Basic Allowance for Subsistence [*Military*] (DNAB)
SUPPL .... Supplement (AABC)
Suppl .... Supplementary (DLA)
SUPPLOT...... Supplemental Plot (MCD)
SUPPLT .... Supply Platoon [*Military*] (DNAB)
SUPPORT .... Study to Understand Prognoses and Preferences for Outcomes and Risks of Treatments
SUPPOS....... Suppository [*Pharmacy*]

SUPPR......... Suppression (MSA)
SUPPREP..... Supplemental Reporting Code
Supp Rev..... Supplement to the Revision [*A publication*] (DLA)
Supp Rev St... Supplement to the Revised Statutes [*A publication*] (DLA)
Supp Rev Stat... Supplement to the Revised Statutes [*A publication*] (GFGA)
SUPPS......... Regional Supplementary Procedures [*Aviation code*]
SUPPT......... Supply Point [*Military*]
Supp Ves Jun... Supplement to Vesey, Junior's, Reports [*A publication*] (DLA)
SUPR.......... Superintendent (ROG)
SUPR.......... Superior (AABC)
SUPR.......... Superior Services [*NASDAQ symbol*] (TTSB)
SUPR.......... Superior Services, Inc. [*NASDAQ symbol*] (SAG)
SUPR.......... Supervisor
SUPR.......... Suppress
SUPR.......... Supreme
SUPRA......... Suppression Pool Retention Analysis [*Nuclear energy*]
supra cit...... Supra Citato [*Cited Above*] [*Latin*] (DAVI)
SUPRAD...... Supplementary Radio (NG)
Supr Ct........ Pennsylvania Superior Court Reports [*A publication*] (DLA)
Supr Ct Rep... Supreme Court Reporter [*A publication*] (DLA)
SuprFd......... Super Food Services, Inc. [*Associated Press*] (SAG)
Suprmlnd..... Supreme Industries [*Associated Press*] (SAG)
SUPRN......... Suppression
SUPROX...... Successive Approximation (IEEE)
SuprSrg...... Superior Surgical Manufacturing Co., Inc. [*Associated Press*] (SAG)
SUPRSTR.... Superstructure (AAG)
Suprtex....... Supertex, Inc. [*Associated Press*] (SAG)
SUPRVRADSTA... Supervisory Radio Station (IAA)
SUPRVSN.... Supervision
SUPS........... Seamen's United Protection Society [*A union*] [*British*]
SUPS........... Services to User Populations Section [*Disbanded by the Board at the Midwinter meeting*]
SUPS........... Supply Squadron
SUPSAL....... Supervisor of Salvage [*Navy*]
SUPSALREPWCOAST... Supervisor of Salvage Representative, West Coast [*Navy*] (DNAB)
SUPSALV..... Supervisor of Salvage [*Navy*]
SUPSD........ Supersede (AFM)
SUPSENS..... Supersensitive
SupServ....... Superior Services, Inc. [*Associated Press*] (SAG)
SUPSGT....... Supply Sergeant [*Marine Corps*]
SUPSHIP...... Supervisor of Shipbuilding [*Navy*]
SUPSHIPS... Superintendent of Shipbuilding [*Navy*] (AAGC)
SupSpcl....... Suprema Specialities, Inc. [*Associated Press*] (SAG)
SUPSTARS... Supply Selective Treatment and Review System
SUPSYSCOM... Supply System Command [*Navy*]
SUPSYSECGRU... Supply System, Security Group [*Navy*] (DNAB)
SUPT........... Specialized Undergraduate Pilot Training [*Air Force*]
SUPT........... Superintendent (EY)
supt............ Superintendent (DD)
SUPT........... Superintendent
SUPT........... Support (CINC)
SupTech...... Superconductor Technologies [*Commercial firm Associated Press*] (SAG)
SUPTG......... Supporting (AAG)
SUPTNAVOBSY... Superintendent, Naval Observatory
SUPU........... Paysandu/Aeropuerto Deptal [*Uruguay*] [*ICAO location identifier*] (ICLI)
SUPV........... Super Vision International [*NASDAQ symbol*] (SAG)
SUPV........... Supervisor (AAG)
SUPVA......... Super Vision Intl'A' [*NASDAQ symbol*] (TTSB)
Supval......... Supervalu, Inc. [*Associated Press*] (SAG)
SUPVG......... Supervising
SUPVR......... Supervisor (AFM)
supvr.......... Supervisor (DD)
supvry......... Supervisory (MHDW)
SUPVRY...... Supervisory
SupVs......... Super Vision International [*Associated Press*] (SAG)
SUPVSN...... Supervision
SupVsn....... Super Vision International [*Associated Press*] (SAG)
SUPVSR...... Supervisor
SUPVW....... Super Vision Intl Wrrt'A' [*NASDAQ symbol*] (TTSB)
SUPVZ......... Super Vision Intl Wrrt'B' [*NASDAQ symbol*] (TTSB)
SUPWB........ Socialist Unity Party of West Berlin [*Germany*]
SUP X.......... Super Extra [*Bookbinding*] (DGA)
SUPX........... Supertex, Inc. [*NASDAQ symbol*] (NQ)
SUPY........... Supervisory (DEN)
SUR............. SCOR US Corp. [*NYSE symbol*] (SPSG)
SUR............. Seemingly Unrelated Regression [*Statistics*]
SUR............. Small Unit Radio [*Military*] (INF)
SUR............. Speech Understanding Research
SUR............. Starcke [*Queensland*] [*Airport symbol*] (AD)
SUR............. Start-Up Rate (NRCH)
SUR............. State University Railroad Co. [*AAR code*]
SUR............. Sufonylurea Receptor [*Biochemistry*]
SUR............. Sul Ross State University, Library, Alpine, TX [*OCLC symbol*] (OCLC)
SUR............. Supervisory Union Relations Test
Sur.............. Sural Nerve
SUR............. Suramin [*Antineoplastic drug*] (CDI)
SUR............. Surcharge [*Business term*] (ROG)
Sur.............. Surety (DLA)
SUR............. Surface (AABC)
sur.............. Surface (VRA)
sur.............. Surface (WDMC)
SUR............. Surgery
SUR............. Surinam [*ANSI three-letter standard code*] (CNC)
SUR............. Surlari [*Romania*] [*Geomagnetic observatory code*]
SUR............. Surplus [*Business term*]
SUR............. Surrender (DNAB)
SUR............. Surrendered (WGA)
SUR............. Surround
SUR............. Survivor (DNAB)
SUR............. Sutherland [*South Africa*] [*Seismograph station code, US Geological Survey*] (SEIS)
Sur.............. Thiouracil [*Also, SUra*] [*Biochemistry*]
SURA........... Shan United Revolutionary Army [*Myanmar*] (PD)
SUra........... Thiouracil [*Also, Sur*] [*Biochemistry*]
SURAnet....... [*The*] Southeastern Universities Research Association Network (TNIG)
SURANO....... Surface RADAR and Navigation Operation
SURBAT....... Simultaneous Unlimited Rigorous Block Analytical Triangulation [*Apollo program*] [*NASA*]
SURC........... Syracuse University Research Corp.
SURCAL....... Surveillance Calibration Satellite
SURCAP....... Surviving Capability Plan [*Military*]
SURCO......... State University Research Center at Oswego [*State University College at Oswego*] [*Research center*] (RCD)
Sur Ct.......... Surrogate's Court (DLA)
SURE........... Safeguards Upgrade Rule Evaluation (PDAA)
SURE........... Sensor Upgrade and Refurbishment Effort [*Marine Corps*] (MCD)
SURE........... Shuttle Users Review and Evaluation [*NASA*] (NASA)
SURE........... Simplicity, Useability, Reliability, Economy
SURE........... Space Ultraviolet Radiation Environment (MCD)
SURE........... Subsystem Replacement
SURE........... Sulphate Regional Experiment [*Electric Power Research Institute*]
SURE........... Symbolic Utilities Revenue Environment [*IBM Corp.*]
SUREA......... Syracuse University Resources for Educators of Adults (EDAC)
SUREJ......... Surface Ship Electromagnetic Jammer
SUREPI....... Surface Ship Electromagnetic Passive Intercept System
SUREQ......... Submit Requisition (NOAA)
SureSh........ Sure Shot International, Inc. [*Associated Press*] (SAG)
SuretyC....... Surety Capital Corp. [*Associated Press*] (SAG)
SURF........... Antisubmarine Warfare Barrier Surface Patrol Ship [*Navy*] (NVT)
SURF........... Single Unit Retrieval Format
SURF........... Space Ultravacuum Research Facility (LAIN)
SURF........... Standard UNREP [*Underway Replenishment*] Receiving Fixture [*Navy*] (NVT)
SURF........... Support of User Records and Files [*Computer science*]
SURF........... Surface
surf............ Surfactant
SURF........... Synchrotron Ultraviolet Radiation Facility [*National Institute of Standards and Technology*]
SURF........... Synthetic Unrandomization of Randomized Fragments [*Chemistry*]
SURF........... System Utilization Reporting Facility (HGAA)
SURFAC....... Surveillance Facility [*Navy*]
Surface DJ... Surface Design Journal [*A publication*] (BRI)
SURFC......... Surface
SURFCO....... Surf Code (DNAB)
SURF DET TRKR... Surface Detector/Tracker [*Navy*] (CAAL)
SURF EWO... Surface Electronic Warfare Officer [*Course*] (DOMA)
SUR/FIN....... American Electroplaters' and Surface Finishers Society Exposition (ITD)
SURFPA....... Antisubmarine Warfare Barrier Surface Patrol Area [*Navy*] (NVT)
SURFPZ....... Antisubmarine Warfare Barrier Surface Patrol Zone [*Navy*] (NVT)
SURFRAD.... Surface Radiation [*Marine science*] (OSRA)
SURFRAD.... Surface Radiation (USDC)
SURFSIDE.... Small Unified Reactor Facility Systems for Isotopes, Desalting, and Electricity [*Nuclear energy*]
SURFWARDEVGRU... Surface Warfare Development Group [*Also, SWDG*] [*Navy*]
SURG........... Surgeon [*or Surgery or Surgical*] (AFM)
SURG........... Surgery
SurgAf......... Surgical Care Affiliates, Inc. [*Nashville, TN*] [*Associated Press*] (SAG)
Surg Cdr...... Surgeon-Commander [*British military*]
SURGCL....... Surgical
SURGE......... SEASAT Users Group of Europe (MSC)
SURGE......... Sorting, Updating, Report Generating, Etc. [*IBM Corp.*] [*Computer science*]
SurgeC........ Surge Components, Inc. [*Associated Press*] (SAG)
SurgeCm...... Surge Components, Inc. [*Associated Press*] (SAG)
SURGEN....... [*The*] Surgeon General [*Army, Air Force*]
Surg Gen..... Surgeon General (GFGA)
SurgLsr....... Surgical Laser Technologies, Inc. [*Associated Press*] (SAG)
Surg Lt........ Surgeon Lieutenant [*British military*]
SURGN......... Surgeon
SurgTc......... Surgical Technologies, Inc. [*Associated Press*] (SAG)
SURI........... Syracuse University Research Institute (MCD)
SURIC......... Surface Integrated Control (MCD)
SURIC......... Surface Ship Integrated Control System [*Obsolete Navy*]
SURISS....... Sheffield Urban and Regional Instructional Simulation System [*British*]
surj............ Surjet [*Knitting*] [*French*] (BARN)
SURM.......... Standard Usage Rate Modifier
SURMAC...... Surface Magnetic Confinement (MCD)
SUROB........ Surf Observation Report [*Navy*] (NVT)
SURORDTECH... Surface Ordnance Technician [*Navy*] (DNAB)
SURP........... Submerged Unmanned Recovery Platform (NVT)
SURPIC........ Surface Picture [*AMVER*] [*Coast Guard*]
SURPL......... Surplus

SURPO Survey of Pupil Opinion (EDAC)
Surps Surplus
SURR Surrender (AABC)
SURR Surrey [*County in England*]
SURR Surrogate
SURRC Scottish Universities Research and Reactor Centre [*Research center*] (IRC)
Surr Ct Proc Act Surrogate's Court Procedure Act [*A publication*] (DLA)
SURRD Surrendered (ROG)
SURRO Surrogate (ADA)
SURS Solitary Ulcer of Rectum Syndrome [*Medicine*] (DMAA)
SURS Standard Umbilical Retraction System (NASA)
SURS Surface Export Cargo System [*Military*] (AABC)
SURS Surveillance Squadron
SURSAN Superintendencia de Urbanizacao e Saneamento [*Brazil*]
SURSAT Satellite Surveillance Program [*Canada*] (MSC)
SURSAT Survey Satellite [*NASA*]
SUR/SATCOM Survivable Satellite Communications
SURSHIP Suretyship [*Legal shorthand*] (LWAP)
SurShot Sure Shot International, Inc. [*Associated Press*] (SAG)
SURT Sarcoidosis of Upper Respiratory Tract [*Medicine*] (CPH)
SURTAC NORAD Surveillance and Tactical Network (MCD)
SURTAC Surveillance Tactical (MCD)
SURTASS Surveillance Towed Array Sensor System [*Marine science*] (OSRA)
SURTASS Surveillance Towed Array Sensor System (USDC)
SURTASS Surveillance Towed Array SONAR System
SURTEMS Surface Temperature Measuring System
SURTOPS Surveillance Training and Operating Procedures Standardization [*Military*] (CAAL)
SURV Rivera/Aeropuerto Deptal [*Uruguay*] [*ICAO location identifier*] (ICLI)
SURV Standard Underwater Research Vehicle
SURV Surveillance (AAG)
SURV Surveillance Aircraft Company [*Army*] (VNW)
SURV Survey (AABC)
SURV Surveyor
SURV Survival (AFM)
SURV Surviving
Surv Survivor
SURVAL Simulator Universal Radio Variability Library
Survey Calif L Survey of California Law [*A publication*] (DLA)
SURVFOR Surveillance Force (DNAB)
SURVI Surveillance
SURVIAC Survivability/Vulnerability Information Analysis Center [*Wright-Patterson Air Force Base, OH*] [*DoD*] (MCD)
SURVL Surveillance (AFM)
SURVM Surveillance and Maintenance [*Army*] (AABC)
SURVOPS Survey Operations [*Navy*] (NVT)
SURVOR Survivor
SURVR Surveyor
SURVR Survivor (AAG)
SURVRAP Surveillance Range Acoustics Prediction System (MCD)
SURVSA Survivable Satellite Communications System (MCD)
SURVSAT Survivable Satellite
SURVSATCOM Survivable Satellite Communications System
SURVSUM Surveillance Summary Reports (NVT)
SurvTc Survival Technology, Inc. [*Associated Press*] (SAG)
SURVYR Surveyor
SURWAC Surface Water Automatic Computer (AAG)
SUS Samband Ungra Sjalfstaedismanna [*National Youth Organization of the Independence Party*] [*Iceland*] [*Political party*] (EAIO)
SUS Saybolt Universal Seconds [*Oil viscosity*]
SUS Scottish Union of Students (AEBS)
SUS Second User Systems Ltd. (NITA)
SUS Semiconductor Unilateral Switch (MSA)
SUS Signal Underwater Sound
SUS Silicon Unidirectional Switch (IAA)
SUS Silicon Unilateral Switch
SUS Single Underwater Sound (MCD)
SUS Small Ultimate Size [*Telecommunications*] (TEL)
SUS Society for Utopian Studies (EA)
SUS Society of University Surgeons (EA)
SUS Solitary Ulcer Syndrome [*Medicine*] (DMAA)
SUS Sound Underwater Source [*Navy*] (CAAL)
SUS Special Urban Survey 1987 [*Bureau of the Census*] (GFGA)
SUS Speech Understanding System
SUS Stained Urinary Sediment [*Medicine*] (MAE)
SUS Startup System [*Nuclear energy*] (NRCH)
SUS Steel User Service [*British*] (BI)
SUS St. Louis [*Missouri*] Spirit of St. Louis Airport [*Airport symbol Obsolete*] (OAG)
SUS Stop Unnecessary Spending
SUS Storage USA [*NYSE symbol*] (TTSB)
SUS Storage USA, Inc. [*NYSE symbol*] (SAG)
SUS Suit Umbilical System (MCD)
SUS Sun-Air of Scandinavia AS [*Denmark ICAO designator*] (FAAC)
SUS Sunshine Columbia [*Vancouver Stock Exchange symbol*]
SUS Suppressor Sensitive [*Laboratory scienc*] (DAVI)
SUS Surkhet [*Nepal*] [*Airport symbol*] (AD)
SUS Susaki [*Mitsui*] [*Japan*] [*Seismograph station code, US Geological Survey*] [*Closed*] (SEIS)
Sus Susanna [*Apocryphya*] (BJA)
SUS Suspect
SUS Suspended [*Technical drawings*]
SUS Suspicion Law [*Statute permitting policemen to detain individuals suspected of criminal activity*] [*British*]
SUS Susquehanna University, Selinsgrove, PA [*OCLC symbol*] (OCLC)
SUS Sustainer (AAG)
sus Susu [*MARC language code Library of Congress*] (LCCP)
SUSA Service Industries USA [*A publication*]
SUSA Seventh United States Army
SUSAFFS Society of United States Air Force Flight Surgeons
SUSAI SIAMA [*Society for Interest of Active Missionaries Abroad*] USA, Inc. [*Defunct*] (EA)
SUSAN System Utilizing Signal-Processing for Automatic Navigation (MCD)
SUSAT Sight Unit Small Arms Trilux [*British*]
SUSC Religieuses de la Sainte-Union des Sacres-Coeurs de Jesus et Marie [*Religious of the Holy Union of the Sacred Hearts*] [*Roman Catholic women's religious order*]
SUSC Sisters of the Holy Union (TOCD)
SUSD State University of South Dakota
SUSDP Standard for the Uniform Scheduling of Drugs and Poisons (EERA)
SUS DUP Suspected Duplicate
SUSEME Superintendencia de Servicos Medicos [*Brazil*]
SUSF Scottish Universities Sports Federation (AIE)
SUSF State University System of Florida (NOAA)
SUSFU Situation Unchanged, Still Fouled Up [*Military slang*] [*Bowdlerized version*]
SUSGR Southwestern Union for the Study of Great Religions (EA)
SUSH Set-Up Sheet (AAG)
SUSIE Sequential Unmanned Scanning and Indicating Equipment (IAA)
SUSIE Stock Updating Sales Invoicing Electronically (IEEE)
SUSIE Surface/Underwater Ship Intercept Equipment (DNAB)
SUSIM Solar Ultraviolet Spectral Irradiance Monitor (MCD)
SUSIO State University System of Florida Institute of Oceanography (NOAA)
SUSIS Sport und Sportwissenschaftliche Informationssystem [*Sport and Sports-Scientific Information System*] [*West Germany*] (IID)
Sus Leg Chron Susquehanna Legal Chronicle [*Pennsylvania*] [*A publication*] (DLA)
SUSLO Senior United States Liaison Officer [*National Security Agency*]
SUSM Scottish United Services Museum [*British military*] (DMA)
SUSMOP Senior United States Military Observer Palestine
SUSNO Senior United States Naval Officer
SUSO Salto/Aeropuerto Deptal [*Uruguay*] [*ICAO location identifier*] (ICLI)
SUSOPS Sustained Operations [*Study of soldier performance in extended combat situation*] [*Army*]
SUSP Suspected [*Passage or line of a work*] [*Literary criticism*] (ROG)
SUSP Suspend [*or Suspension*] (AFM)
SUSP Suspicion [*FBI standardized term*]
SUSPD Suspended
SUSPDNG Suspending [*Freight*]
Sus Per Col Suspensio per Collum [*Execution by Hanging*] [*Latin*]
Sus Per Coll Suspendatur per Collum [*Let Him Be Hanged by the Neck*] [*Latin*]
SUS per COLL Suspensio per Collum [*Hanged by the Neck*] [*Latin*]
SUSP L Suspecta Lectio [*Double Reading*] [*Latin*] (ROG)
SUSPNSN Suspension
SUSQ Susquehanna Bancshares, Inc. [*Lititz, PA*] [*NASDAQ symbol*] (NQ)
SusqBnc Susquehanna Bancshares, Inc. [*Associated Press*] (SAG)
Susq LC Susquehanna Leading Chronicle [*Pennsylvania*] [*A publication*] (DLA)
Susq L Chron Susquehanna Legal Chronicle [*Pennsylvania*] [*A publication*] (DLA)
Susq Legal Chron Susquehanna Legal Chronicle [*Pennsylvania*] [*A publication*] (DLA)
Susq Leg Chron Susquehanna Legal Chronicle [*Pennsylvania*] [*A publication*] (DLA)
SUSQU Susquehanna Bancshares [*NASDAQ symbol*] (TTSB)
Susquehanna Leg Chron (PA) Susquehanna Legal Chronicle [*Pennsylvania*] [*A publication*] (DLA)
SUSREP Senior United States Representative to Defense Production Board [*NATO*] (NATG)
SUSS Shuttle Upper-Stage System (SSD)
SUSS Signalmen's United and Sick Society [*A union*] [*British*]
SUSS Sound Underwater Signal Source (MCD)
SUSS Submarine Schoolship [*Navy*] (NVT)
SUSS Sussex [*County in England*]
SUST Sunstates Corp. [*NASDAQ symbol*] (SAG)
SUST Sustainer
SUSTD Sustained [*Legal*] (ROG)
SUSTE Sunstates Corp. [*NASDAQ symbol*] (TTSB)
SUSTN Sustain [*Legal*] (ROG)
SUSTN Sustentation [*Ecclesiastical*] (ROG)
SUSTP Sunstates $3.75 cm Pfd [*NASDAQ symbol*] (TTSB)
SUSV Small Unit Support Vehicle [*Military*] (RDA)
SUSY Subsystem (IAA)
SUSY Such Systems (NITA)
SUSY Survey System (IAA)
SUSY's Supersymmetric Theories [*Particle physics*]
SUT Satellite under Test
SUT Set-Up Time
SUT Small Unit Transceiver [*Military*] (INF)
SUT Society for Underwater Technology (EA)
SUT Southport, NC [*Location identifier FAA*] (FAAL)
SUT Start-Up Transformer (NRCH)
SUT State Unemployment Tax (MCD)
SUT Subunit Test
SUT Surface and Underwater Target (MCD)
SUT Suttsu [*Japan*] [*Seismograph station code, US Geological Survey*] (SEIS)
SUT Swinburne University of Technology [*Australia*]

SUT.......... Syndicat Uni du Transport [*United Transportation Union - UTU*] [*Canada*]
SUT.......... System under Test (AAG)
SUTAGS.......... Shuttle Uplink Text and Graphics Scanner (NASA)
SUTARS.......... Search Unit Tracing and Recording System
SUTB.......... Tacuarembo [*Uruguay*] [*ICAO location identifier*] (ICLI)
SUTEC.......... Seneca Underwater Test and Evaluation Center
SUTH.......... Sutherland [*County in Scotland*]
Suth.......... Sutherland's Calcutta Reports [*India*] [*A publication*] (DLA)
Suth App.......... Sutherland's Appeal Reports, Small Causes Court [*1861-65*] [*Bengal, India*] [*A publication*] (DLA)
Suth Bengal.......... Sutherland's Bengal High Court Reports [*India*] [*A publication*] (DLA)
Suth Dam.......... Sutherland on the Law of Damages [*A publication*] (DLA)
Suth FBR.......... Sutherland's Bengal Full Bench Reports [*India*] [*A publication*] (DLA)
Suth Mis.......... India Weekly Reporter, Miscellaneous Appeals [*A publication*] (DLA)
Suth PCA.......... Sutherland's Privy Council Appeals [*A publication*] (DLA)
Suth PCJ.......... Sutherland's Privy Council Judgments [*A publication*] (DLA)
Suth Sp N.......... Full Bench Rulings [*Calcutta*] [*A publication*] (DLA)
Suth Sp N.......... Sutherland's Special Number of Weekly Reporter [*A publication*] (DLA)
Suth Stat Const.......... Sutherland on Statutes and Statutory Construction [*A publication*] (DLA)
Suth St Const.......... Sutherland on Statutes and Statutory Construction [*A publication*] (DLA)
Suth WR.......... Sutherland's Weekly Reporter, Calcutta [*1864-76*] [*A publication*] (DLA)
Suth WR Mis.......... Sutherland's Weekly Reports, Miscellaneous Appeals [*India*] [*A publication*] (DLA)
SUTI.......... Symptomatic Urinary Tract Infection [*Medicine*] (DMAA)
SUTR.......... Treinta Y Tres [*Uruguay*] [*ICAO location identifier*] (ICLI)
SUTRA.......... Saturated-Unsaturated Transport [*Ground-water modeling*]
SUTRASFCO.......... Sindicato Unificado de Trabajadores de la Standard Fruit Co. [*Honduras*]
SUTT.......... Small Unit Training Team [*Military*]
Sutton.......... Sutton on Personal Actions at Common Law [*A publication*] (DLA)
SuttRsc.......... Sutton Resource Ltd. [*Associated Press*] (SAG)
SUU.......... Fairfield, CA [*Location identifier FAA*] (FAAL)
SUU.......... Santaquin Canyon [*Utah*] [*Seismograph station code, US Geological Survey*] (SEIS)
SUU.......... Society of University Urologists (EA)
SUU.......... Suspension Unit (AFM)
SUU.......... Suspension Unit Universal [*Weaponry*] [*Air Force*] (INF)
SUUD.......... Sudden, Unexpected, Unexplained Death (DAVI)
SUV.......... Saybolt Universal Viscosity (IAA)
SUV.......... Small Unilamellar Vesicle [*Pharmacy Biochemistry*]
SUV.......... Small Unilamellar Vessel [*Medicine*] (DMAA)
SUV.......... Socicated Unilamellar Vesicles
SUV.......... Souvenir
SUV.......... Sport-Utility Vehicle [*Type of truck*]
SUV.......... Sumpter Valley Railway [*AAR code*]
SUV.......... Suva [*Fiji*] [*Airport symbol*] (OAG)
SUV.......... Suva [*Fiji*] [*Seismograph station code, US Geological Survey*] (SEIS)
SUVAT.......... Support Unit Vehicle Automatic Tester
SUVCW.......... Sons of Union Veterans of the Civil War (EA)
SUVI.......... Strong Ultraviolet Index
SUW.......... Superior, WI [*Location identifier FAA*] (FAAL)
SUW.......... Surface Warfare (NVT)
SUWC.......... Surface Warfare Coordinator [*Also, SWC*] (NVT)
SUWU.......... Skilled and Unskilled Workers' Union - Somali Republic
SUX.......... Sioux City [*Iowa*] [*Airport symbol*] (OAG)
SUX.......... Succinylcholine [*A muscle relaxant*] (DAVI)
sux.......... Sumerian [*MARC language code Library of Congress*] (LCCP)
SUY.......... Aerial Surveys (1980) Ltd. [*New Zealand*] [*ICAO designator*] (FAAC)
SUY.......... State University Railroad Co. [*Later, SUR*] [*AAR code*]
SUY.......... Sudureyri [*Iceland*] [*Airport symbol*] (OAG)
s-uy--.......... Uruguay [*MARC geographic area code Library of Congress*] (LCCP)
SUYR.......... Southampton University Yacht Research Group [*British*]
SUZ.......... Suez Petroleum Corp. [*Vancouver Stock Exchange symbol*]
SUZ.......... Suria [*Papua New Guinea*] [*Airport symbol*] (OAG)
SV.......... El Salvador [*ANSI two-letter standard code*] (CNC)
SV.......... Safety Valve (AAG)
SV.......... Sailing Vessel
SV.......... Sales Voucher [*Business term*] (DCTA)
SV.......... Sampling Visit (GNE)
SV.......... Sancta Virgo [*Holy Virgin*] [*Latin*]
SV.......... Sanctitas Vestra [*Your Holiness*] [*Latin*]
SV.......... Saponification Value [*Organic analytical chemistry*]
SV.......... Sapper Vehicle [*Military*]
SV.......... Sarcoma Virus [*Medicine*] (MAE)
SV.......... Satellite Vehicle [*Instrument*] (EERA)
SV.......... Satellite Virus
SV.......... Saudi Arabian Airlines [*ICAO designator*] (AD)
SV.......... Saudia-Saudi Arabia Airlines [*Airline flight code*] (ODBW)
SV.......... Saves [*Baseball*]
SV.......... Savings Transfer [*Banking*]
SV.......... Scalp Vein [*Medicine*]
SV.......... Schedule Variance (MCD)
SV.......... Schweizerische Volkspartei [*Swiss People's Party*] [*Political party*]
SV.......... Scientific Visualization (CDE)
SV.......... Secondary Valve
SV.......... Secular Variation [*Geophysics*]
SV.......... Security Violation (AAG)
SV.......... Selecta Vision [*RCA brand name for tape cartridges of TV programs*]
SV.......... Selective Volunteer [*Navy*]
SV.......... Selenoid Valve (MCD)
SV.......... Self-Ventilated (MSA)
SV.......... Self Verification
SV.......... Seminal Vesicle [*Anatomy*]
SV.......... Service
SV.......... Service Vehicle
S/V.......... Servovalve
SV.......... Set Value
SV.......... Severe (MAE)
SV.......... Shutter Value [*Photography*]
SV.......... Shuttle Vehicle [*NASA*] (NASA)
SV.......... Side Valve [*Automotive engineering*]
SV.......... Side View (MSA)
SV.......... Sieve
Sv.......... Sievert [*SI unit for radioactive dose equivalent*]
SV.......... Sigmoid Volvulus [*Gastroenterology*] (DAVI)
SV.......... Silicone Varnish
SV.......... Silvercraft SpA [*Italy ICAO aircraft manufacturer identifier*] (ICAO)
SV.......... Simian Virus
SV.......... Simulated Video (MCD)
SV.......... Single Silk Varnish [*Wire insulation*] (AAG)
SV.......... Single Value
SV.......... Single Valve [*Automobile model, Stutz Motors*]
SV.......... Single Ventricle [*Cardiology*] (DAVI)
SV.......... Single Vibrations [*Half cycles*]
SV.......... Sinus Venosus [*Anatomy*]
SV.......... Siste, Viator [*Stop, Traveller*] [*Latin*] (ROG)
SV.......... Slide Valve
SV.......... Slowed-Down Video [*RADAR*] (CET)
SV.......... Sluice [*or Stop*] Valve
SV.......... Snake Venom [*Medicine*]
SV.......... Sodium Vapor
SV.......... Soft Valve
SV.......... Solenoid Valve (KSC)
SV.......... Solicited Volunteer [*In drug studies*]
SV.......... Sons of Veterans
SV.......... Sophisticated Vocabulary (AAG)
SV.......... Sosialistisk Valgforbund [*Socialist Electoral Alliance*] [*Norway Political party*] (PPE)
SV.......... Sosialistisk Venstreparti [*Socialist Left Party*] [*Norway Political party*] (PPE)
SV.......... Sotto Voce [*In an Undertone*] [*Music*]
SV.......... Space Vehicle
SV.......... Space Velocity [*Chemical engineering*]
SV.......... Space Visualization [*Visual perception*]
SV.......... Specified Value (MCD)
sv.......... Spiritus Vini [*Alcoholic Spirit*] [*Latin*]
SV.......... Spiritus Vinosus [*Ardent Spirit*] [*Pharmacy*] (ROG)
SV.......... Spoken Voice (MEDA)
SV.......... Spoken Voice (DAVI)
SV.......... Spontaneous Ventilation [*Medicine*] (MEDA)
SV.......... Star of Valour [*British*] (ADA)
SV.......... State Vector (KSC)
SV.......... Status Valid
sV.......... Statvolt [*Also, statV*] [*Electrostatic unit of potential difference*]
SV.......... Steam Valve
SV.......... Stimulation Value [*Psychology*]
SV.......... Stimulus Valve [*Medicine*] (BABM)
SV.......... Stimulus Valve [*Medicine*] (DAVI)
SV.......... Stock Volume (DAVI)
SV.......... Stop Valve (IAA)
SV.......... Storm Vulcan
SV.......... Stripping Voltammetry [*Electroanalytical chemistry*]
SV.......... Stroke Volume [*Physiology*]
SV.......... Study of Values [*Psychology*]
SV.......... Subclavian Vein [*Cardiology*]
SV.......... Subdivision Flag [*Navy British*]
SV.......... Subjective Vertical [*Neurology*]
SV.......... Subject-Verb [*Education of the hearing-impaired*]
SV.......... Sub Verbo [*or Sub Voce*] [*Under the Word*] [*Latin*]
sv.......... Sub Vi [*Under Compulsion*] [*Latin*]
SV.......... Supervisor (IAA)
SV.......... Super Volkswagen [*Auto racing*]
S/V.......... Supply Valve (MCD)
SV.......... Support Vehicle [*British military*] (DMA)
SV.......... Supraventricular [*Cardiology*]
SV.......... Supravital [*Medicine*] (MAE)
SV.......... Surface Vessel
S/V.......... Surface/Volume [*Ratio*]
S/V.......... Surrender Value [*Insurance*]
sv.......... Surrender Value (ODBW)
S/V.......... Survivability/Vulnerability [*Applied to ability of weapon systems to survive attacks*] [*Military*]
sv.......... Swan Islands [*used in records cataloged after January 1978*] [*MARC country of publication code Library of Congress*] (LCCP)
SV.......... Swept Volume
SV.......... Symptomatic Volunteer [*In drug studies*]
SV.......... Synaptic Vesicle [*Neurobiology*]
SV.......... Synchronous Voltage (OA)
SV 40.......... Simian Virus 40 [*A DNA virus in non-human primates*] (DOG)
SVA.......... Sample Valve Assembly
SVA.......... Saudi Arabian Airlines [*ICAO designator*] (FAAC)
SVA.......... Savoonga [*Alaska*] [*Airport symbol*] (OAG)
SVA.......... School of Visual Arts [*New York, NY*]
SVA.......... Scottish Volleyball Association (DBA)

SVA............ SEABEE Veterans of America (EA)
SVA............ Sectionalized Vertical Antenna
SVA............ Security and Vulnerability Analysis (MCD)
SVA............ Selective Visceral Angiography [*Medicine*] (AAMN)
SVA............ Shared Virtual Area [*Computer science*]
SVA............ Shareholder Valuation Analysis
SVA............ Singapore Volunteer Artillery [*British military*] (DMA)
SVA............ Single-Valve First-Actuation [*Nuclear energy*] (NRCH)
SVA............ Single Vehicle Accident [*Automotive safety*]
SVA............ Singular-Value Analysis [*Industrial control*]
SVA............ Society for Visual Anthropology (EA)
SVA............ Solar Vane Actuators
SVA............ Statistical Vibration Analysis
SVA............ Stock Valuation Adjustment [*Business term*] (ADA)
SVA............ Suva [*Fiji*] [*Seismograph station code, US Geological Survey*] (SEIS)
SVAA.......... Super Vernier Auto Alert [*Military*] (CAAL)
SVAB.......... Shuttle Vehicle Assembly Building [*NASA*] (NASA)
SVAC.......... Acarigua, Portuguesa [*Venezuela ICAO location identifier*] (ICLI)
SVAC.......... Senate Veterans Affairs Committee
SVAC.......... Shuttle Vehicle Assembly and Checkout [*NASA*] (GFGA)
SVAC.......... Singapore Volunteer Artillery Corps [*British military*] (DMA)
SVAD.......... Savanna Army Depot [*Illinois*] (AABC)
SVADA........ Savanna Army Depot Activity (AABC)
SVAF.......... South Vietnamese Armed Forces (VNW)
SVAFB........ South Vandenberg Air Force Base [*California*] (NASA)
SVALC........ Sangamon Valley Academic Library Consortium [*Library network*]
SV-AMC....... Suspect-Variant Anomalous Mental Condition
SVAN.......... Anaco, Anzoategui [*Venezuela ICAO location identifier*] (ICLI)
SVAO.......... Service at Veterans Administration Offices [*Red Cross*]
SVAR.......... Sequential Variance
SVAR.......... Stuart's Lower Canada Vice-Admiralty Reports [*A publication*] (DLA)
SVAS.......... Supravalvular Aortic Stenosis [*Cardiology*] (MAE)
SVAS.......... Supraventricular Aortic Stenosis [*Medicine*] (DMAA)
SVAT.......... San Fernando De Atabapo, T. F. Amazonas [*Venezuela ICAO location identifier*] (ICLI)
SVAT.......... Soil Vegetation Atmosphere Transfer (EERA)
SVAT.......... Standard Version Acceptance Test (MCD)
SVAT.......... Synaptic Vesicle Amine Transporter [*Biochemistry*]
SVB............ Sambava [*Madagascar*] [*Airport symbol*] (OAG)
SVB............ Saphenous Vein Bypass [*Cardiology*] (DMAA)
SVB............ Shuttle Vehicle Booster [*NASA*] (NASA)
SVB............ Space Vehicle Booster [*NASA*] (MCD)
SVB............ Sterivet Laboratories Ltd. [*Toronto Stock Exchange symbol*]
SV:B.......... Study of Values: British Edition [*Psychology*]
SVBC.......... Barcelona/Gral. Jose Antonio Anzoategui Internacional Anzoategui [*Venezuela ICAO location identifier*] (ICLI)
SVBEEQV..... Si Vales, Bene Est; Ego Quoque Valeo [*I Hope You're Well; I Am*] [*Latin*]
SVBI.......... Barinas, Barinas [*Venezuela ICAO location identifier*] (ICLI)
SVBL.......... Maracay/El Libertador, Base Aerea Aragua [*Venezuela ICAO location identifier*] (ICLI)
SVBM.......... Barquisimeto/Internacional, Lara [*Venezuela ICAO location identifier*] (ICLI)
SVBP.......... Single-Variable Bypass Program [*DoD*]
SVBPG........ Saphenous Vein Bypass Graft [*Cardiology*] (DAVI)
SVBS.......... Maracay/Mariscal Sucre, Base Aerea Aragua [*Venezuela ICAO location identifier*] (ICLI)
SVBT.......... Space Vehicle Booster Test (AAG)
SVBV.......... Strawberry Vein Banding Virus [*Plant pathology*]
SVBZ.......... Bruzual, Apure [*Venezuela ICAO location identifier*] (ICLI)
SVC............ Saint Vincent College [*Latrobe, PA*]
SVC............ Selective Venous Catheterization [*Cardiology*]
SVC............ Service (AFM)
SVC............ Service
SVC............ Service Command [*Army*]
SVC............ Service Message [*Aviation code*]
SVC............ Silver City [*New Mexico*] [*Airport symbol*] (OAG)
SVC............ Silver Creek [*California*] [*Seismograph station code, US Geological Survey*] (SEIS)
SVC............ Sine Vibration Control
SVC............ Singapore Volunteer Corps [*British military*] (DMA)
SVC............ Single Variable Control
SVC............ Slow Vital Capacity [*Medicine*] (MAE)
SVC............ Society of Vacuum Coaters (EA)
SVC............ Space Vehicle Code
SVC............ Special Verification Commission (DOMA)
SVC............ Spiroplasmavirus citri [*Bacteriology*]
SVC............ Spring Viremia of Carp
SVC............ Still Video Camera
SVC............ Stokely-Van Camp, Inc. [*NYSE symbol*] (SPSG)
SVC............ Stokley Van Camp [*NYSE symbol*] (SAG)
SVC............ Superior Vena Cava [*Anatomy*]
SVC............ Supervisor Call (NASA)
SVC............ Suprahepatic Vena Cava [*Medicine*] (AAMN)
SVC............ Switched Virtual Call [*Telecommunications*] (NITA)
SVC............ Switched Virtual Circuit
SVCA.......... Caracas Maiquetia Distrito Federal [*Venezuela ICAO location identifier*] (ICLI)
SVCAB........ Saphenous Vein Coronary Artery Bypass [*Cardiology*]
SVCB.......... Ciudad Bolivar, Bolivar [*Venezuela ICAO location identifier*] (ICLI)
SVCBL........ Serviceable
SVCBV........ Solenoid Valve-Carburetor Bowl Vent [*Automotive engineering*]
SVCC.......... Caracas Ciudad Distrito Federal [*Venezuela ICAO location identifier*] (ICLI)
SVCD.......... Caicara De Orinoco, Bolivar [*Venezuela ICAO location identifier*] (ICLI)
SVCE.......... Service
SvceCp........ Service Corp. International [*Associated Press*] (SAG)
SVCG.......... Servicing (IAA)
SVCG.......... Spatial Vectorcardiogram [*Cardiology*]
SVCH.......... Achaguas, Apure [*Venezuela ICAO location identifier*] (ICLI)
SVCI.......... Cachipo, Monagas [*Venezuela ICAO location identifier*] (ICLI)
SVCJ.......... San Carlos, Cojedes [*Venezuela ICAO location identifier*] (ICLI)
SVCL.......... Calabozo, Guarico [*Venezuela ICAO location identifier*] (ICLI)
SvcMer........ Service Merchandise Co., Inc. [*Associated Press*] (SAG)
SVCMN........ Service Man (NVT)
Svcmst........ Servicemaster Ltd. Partnership [*Associated Press*] (SAG)
Svcmstr....... ServiceMaster Ltd. [*Associated Press*] (SAG)
SVCN.......... Canaima, Bolivar [*Venezuela ICAO location identifier*] (ICLI)
SVCO.......... Carora, Lara [*Venezuela ICAO location identifier*] (ICLI)
SVCO.......... Superior Vena Cava Obstruction [*Cardiology*] (DAVI)
SVCP.......... Carupano/Gral. en Jefe Jose Francisco Bermudez, Sucre [*Venezuela ICAO location identifier*] (ICLI)
SVCP.......... Special Virus Cancer Program [*National Cancer Institute*]
SVCPr........ Stokely-Van Camp 5% Pref [*NYSE symbol*] (TTSB)
SVCR.......... Coro/Internacional, Falcon [*Venezuela ICAO location identifier*] (ICLI)
SVC-RPA...... Superior Vena Cava - Right Pulmonary Artery Shunt [*Anatomy*] (MAE)
SVCS.......... Caracas/Internacional del Centro Miranda [*Venezuela ICAO location identifier*] (ICLI)
SVCS.......... Star Vector Calibration Sensor [*Aviation*] (OA)
SVCS.......... Superior Vena Caval Syndrome [*Medicine*]
SvcStrs....... Service Stars [*Military decoration*]
SVCT.......... Supervisor Call Address Table (IAA)
SVCU.......... Cumana, Sucre [*Venezuela ICAO location identifier*] (ICLI)
SVCU.......... Space Visualization Contralateral Use [*Occupational therapy*]
SVD............ Seismic Velocity Discontinuity [*Geology*]
SVD............ Share Valuation Division [*Inland Revenue*] [*British*]
SVD............ Silver Talon Mines Ltd. [*Vancouver Stock Exchange symbol*]
SVD............ Simple Vertex Delivery [*Medicine*]
SVD............ Simplified Vapor Detector
SVD............ Simultaneous Voice/Data
SVD............ Singular Value Decomposition [*Mathematics*]
SVD............ Societas Verbi Divini [*Society of the Divine Word*] [*Roman Catholic men's religious order*]
svd............ Society of the Divine Word (TOCD)
SVD............ Society of the Divine Word (TOCD)
SVD............ Space Vehicles Division [*NASA*] (MCD)
SVD............ Spontaneous Vaginal Delivery [*Gynecology*]
SVD............ Spontaneous Vetex Delivery [*Obstetrics*] (DAVI)
SVD............ St. Vincent [*Windward Islands*] [*Airport symbol*] (OAG)
SVD............ Surveyor Vehicle Department
SVD............ Sverdlovsk [*Former USSR Geomagnetic observatory code*]
SVD............ Swine Vesicular Disease [*Medicine*] (DMAA)
SVDA.......... Savanna Depot Activity [*Army*]
SVDF.......... Segmented Virtual Display File
SVDP.......... La Divina Pastora, Bolivar [*Venezuela ICAO location identifier*] (ICLI)
SVDP.......... Saint Vincent de Paul (ADA)
SVDP.......... Skylab Video Documentation Project [*NASA*] (KSC)
SVDS.......... Space Vehicle Dynamic Simulator [*NASA*] (NASA)
SVE............ Aero Servicios Especializados SA de CV [*Mexico ICAO designator*] (FAAC)
SVE............ Secure Voice Equipment (NATG)
SVE............ Seminal Vesicle Epithelium [*Anatomy*]
SVE............ Severide Resources, Inc. [*Vancouver Stock Exchange symbol*]
SVE............ Society for Vector Ecology (EA)
SVE............ Society for Veterinary Ethology [*See also SEV*] [*Edinburgh, Scotland*] (EAIO)
SVE............ Society for Visual Education, Inc. (AEBS)
SVE............ Soil Vacuum Extraction [*Computer science*]
SVE............ Soil Vapor Extraction [*Environmental science*]
SVE............ Space Vehicle Electronics (SAA)
SVE............ Special Vehicle Engineering [*Ford Motor Co.*]
SVE............ Sterile Vaginal Examination [*Obstetrics*] (DAVI)
SVE............ Sum of Vector Elements (IAA)
SVE............ Supraventricular Ectopic [*Beat*] [*Cardiology*]
SVE............ Susanville, CA [*Location identifier FAA*] (FAAL)
SVE............ Sverdlovsk [*Ekaterinburg*] [*Former USSR Seismograph station code, US Geological Survey*] (SEIS)
SVE............ Swept Volume Efficiency [*Air Force*]
SVE............ System Valve Engineering
s-ve--.......... Venezuela [*MARC geographic area code Library of Congress*] (LCCP)
SVEA.......... Schweizerischer Verband Evangaelischer Arbeitnehmer [*A union*] [*Switzerland*] (DCTA)
SVEA.......... Slowly Varying Envelope Approximation [*Computer science*] (IAA)
SVEA.......... Supplemental Vocational Education Assistance (OICC)
SVEAA........ Schweizerischer Verband Evangelischer Arbeiter und Angestellter [*Swiss Federation of Protestant Trade Unions*]
SVEAD........ State Variable Estimation and Accuracy Determination
SVECF........ ScanVec Co. [*NASDAQ symbol*] (TTSB)
SVECF........ ScanVec Co. Ltd. [*NASDAQ symbol*] (SAG)
SVED.......... El Dorado, Bolivar [*Venezuela ICAO location identifier*] (ICLI)
SVEN.......... Shipboard Voice-Enhanced Navigation System [*for blind sailors*]
SVER.......... Spatial Visual Evoked Response (OA)
SVER.......... State Veterans Employment Representative [*Department of Labor*]
SVERT........ Subvert (ROG)
SVES.......... Satellite Video Exchange Society [*Canada*] (EAIO)
SVEZ.......... Elorza, Apure [*Venezuela ICAO location identifier*] (ICLI)

SVF .... Save [*Benin*] [*Airport symbol*] (OAG)
SVF .... Services Flight [*Military*]
SVF .... Set Vertical Format (IAA)
SVF .... Silverleaf Resources Ltd. [*Vancouver Stock Exchange symbol*]
SVF .... Simple Vector Format [*Proposed Standard*] (EERA)
SVF .... Standard Vented Furnace
SVF .... Standard Volume Flow (IAA)
SVF .... State Variable Filter
SVF .... Stoicorum Veterum Fragmenta [*A publication*] (OCD)
SVFM .... Caracas/Generelisimo Francisco De Miranda Base Aerea La Carlota, Miranda [*Venezuela ICAO location identifier*] (ICLI)
SVFR .... Special Visual Flight Rules [*Aviation*]
SVG .... Saphenous Vein Graft [*Cardiology*]
SVG .... Sauvagine [*A polypeptide*]
SVG .... Saving (WDAA)
SVG .... Servicing
SVG .... Serving (FAAC)
SVG .... Spiritus Vini Gallici [*Brandy*] [*Pharmacy*] (ROG)
SVG .... Stavanger [*Norway*] [*Airport symbol*] (OAG)
SVG .... Stevens International, Inc. [*AMEX symbol*] (SPSG)
SVG .... Sun Valley Gold Mines Ltd. [*Vancouver Stock Exchange symbol*]
SVG.A .... Stevens Intl Cl'A' [*AMEX symbol*] (TTSB)
SVGA .... Super Video Graphics Array [*Computer science*]
SVG.B .... Stevens Intl Cl'B' [*AMEX symbol*] (TTSB)
SVGC .... Secure Voice and Graphic Conferencing (MCD)
SVGD .... Guasdualito, Apure [*Venezuela ICAO location identifier*] (ICLI)
SVGI .... Guiria, Sucre [*Venezuela ICAO location identifier*] (ICLI)
SVGI .... Silicon Valley Group [*NASDAQ symbol*] (TTSB)
SVGI .... Silicon Valley Group, Inc. [*NASDAQ symbol*] (NQ)
SVGL .... Silicon Valley Group Lithography (ECON)
SVGS .... Savings
SVGT .... Guasipati, Bolivar [*Venezuela ICAO location identifier*] (ICLI)
SVGU .... Guanare, Portuguesa [*Venezuela ICAO location identifier*] (ICLI)
SVH .... Seven Mile High Resources, Inc. [*Vancouver Stock Exchange symbol*]
SVH .... Severely Handicapped
SVH .... Solar Vacuum Head [*Astronomy*] (OA)
SVH .... Statesville, NC [*Location identifier FAA*] (FAAL)
SVHE .... Society for Values in Higher Education (EA)
SVHG .... Higuerote, Miranda [*Venezuela ICAO location identifier*] (ICLI)
SVHS .... Super Video Home System [*Japan Victor Co.*]
SVI .... San Vincente Del Caguan [*Colombia*] [*Airport symbol*] (OAG)
SVI .... Service Interception [*Telecommunications*] (TEL)
SVI .... Servicios de Transporte Aereo, SA de CV [*Mexico*] [*FAA designator*] (FAAC)
SVI .... Singapore Volunteer Infantry [*British military*] (DMA)
SVI .... Single Vendor Integrity (MCD)
SVI .... Single Vibrational Level [*Physics*]
SVI .... Sludge Volume Index [*Wastewater treatment*]
SVI .... Sound Velocity Indicator
SVI .... Spiritus Vini Industrialis [*Industrial Alcohol*] [*Pharmacy*]
SVI .... Stroke Volume Index [*Medicine*]
SVI .... St. Vincent [*St. Vincent*] [*Seismograph station code, US Geological Survey Closed*] (SEIS)
SVI .... System Verification Installation
SVIA .... Specialty Vehicles Institute of America (EA)
SVIB .... Strong Vocational Interest Blank [*Psychology*]
SVIC .... Icabaru, Bolivar [*Venezuela ICAO location identifier*] (ICLI)
SVIC .... Shock and Vibration Information Center [*Terminated Navy*] (MCD)
SVIC .... Silicon Valley Information Center [*Database producer*] (IID)
SVICLC .... Shenandoah Valley Independent College Library Cooperative [*Library network*]
SVID .... System V Interface Definition (NITA)
SVIE .... Isla De Coche, Nueva Esparta [*Venezuela ICAO location identifier*] (ICLI)
SVIF .... Svenski Indianska Foerbundet [*Sweden*]
SVIMR .... St. Vincent's Institute of Medical Research [*Australia*]
SVIMS .... Short Vehicle Integrated Management System
SVIO .... Superintending Veterinary Investigation Officer [*Ministry of Agriculture, Fisheries, and Food*] [*British*]
SVIP .... Secure Voice Improvement Program [*DoD*]
SVIPA .... Swiss Videotex Industry Association [*Information service or system*] (IID)
SVIPA .... Swiss Viewdata Information Providers Association [*Zurich*] [*Telecommunications*]
SVJ .... Lompoc, CA [*Location identifier FAA*] (FAAL)
SVJ .... Steed Ventures Corp. [*Formerly, Poney Explorations Ltd.*] [*Vancouver Stock Exchange symbol*]
SVJ .... Svolvaer [*Norway*] [*Airport symbol*] (OAG)
SVJC .... Paraguana/Josefa Camejo Internacional, Falcon [*Venezuela ICAO location identifier*] (ICLI)
SVK .... Air Slovakia BWJ Ltd. [*FAA designator*] (FAAC)
SVK .... Secure Voice Kit (DWSG)
SVKA .... Kavanayen, Bolivar [*Venezuela ICAO location identifier*] (ICLI)
SVKM .... Kamarata, Bolivar [*Venezuela ICAO location identifier*] (ICLI)
SVL .... Saak [*Russian Federation*] [*ICAO designator*] (FAAC)
SVL .... Sapphire Vacuum Lens
SVL .... Savonlinna [*Finland*] [*Airport symbol*] (OAG)
SVL .... Scripps Visibility Laboratory
SVL .... Set-Valued Logic [*Computer science*]
SVL .... Silver Lake Resources, Inc. [*Toronto Stock Exchange symbol*]
SVL .... Snout-to-Vent Length [*Biometry*]
SVL .... Star Valley Resources [*Vancouver Stock Exchange symbol*]
SVL .... Support Validation Laboratory [*Army*]
SVLA .... Steered Vertical Line Array [*Military*] (CAAL)
SVLB .... Sapphire Vacuum Lens Blank
SVLF .... La Fria, Tachira [*Venezuela ICAO location identifier*] (ICLI)
SVLF .... Shipboard Very Low Frequency [*Navy*] (NG)
SVLH .... Surma Valley Light Horse [*British military*] (DMA)
SVLL .... Short Vertical Lower Left
SVLO .... La Orchila - Dependencia Federal [*Venezuela ICAO location identifier*] (ICLI)
SVLOG .... Servicing Log [*Telecommunications*] (TEL)
SVLP .... Special Virus Leukemia Program [*National Cancer Institute*]
SVLR .... Short Vertical Lower Right
SVLTE .... Services Valve Life Test Establishment [*British*] (MCD)
SVLW .... Sectoraal Verband Landbouwwetenschappen [*Committee on International Education in Agricultural Sciences*] [*Netherlands*] (EAIO)
SVM .... Aeroservicios Monterrey SA de CV [*Mexico ICAO designator*] (FAAC)
SVM .... Salem, MI [*Location identifier FAA*] (FAAL)
SVM .... Seminal Vesicle Mesenchyme [*Anatomy*]
SVM .... Seminal Vesicle Microsome [*Anatomy*]
SVM .... Semitrailer Van Mount
SVM .... ServiceMaster L.P. [*NYSE symbol*] (TTSB)
SVM .... ServiceMaster Ltd. [*NYSE symbol*] (SPSG)
SVM .... Service Volontaire Mennonite [*Mennonite Voluntary Service*]
SVM .... Ship's Value Manual (DNAB)
SVM .... Ship Vulnerability Model (MCD)
SVM .... Silicon Video Memory
SVM .... Silver City [*New Mexico*] [*Seismograph station code, US Geological Survey*] (SEIS)
SVM .... Silver Hart Mines Ltd. [*Vancouver Stock Exchange symbol*]
SVM .... Sisters of the Visitation of the Congregation of the Immaculate Heart of Mary [*Roman Catholic religious order*]
SVM .... Special Vehicle Management [*Automotive engineering*]
SVM .... Spiritus Vini Methylatus [*Methylated Spirit*] [*Pharmacy*]
SVM .... Stamp Vending Machine (DCTA)
SVM .... Syncytiovascular Membrane [*Medicine*] (MAE)
SVM .... System Validation Model (NVT)
SVMA .... Space Vehicle Mission Analysis
SVMC .... Maracaibo/La Chinita Internacional, Zulia [*Venezuela ICAO location identifier*] (ICLI)
SVMD .... Merida/Alberto Carnevalli, Merida [*Venezuela ICAO location identifier*] (ICLI)
SVMG .... Margarita/Internacional del Caribe Gral Santiago Marino, Neuva Esparta [*Venezuela ICAO location identifier*] (ICLI)
SVMI .... Caracas/Simon Bolivar Internacional Maiquetia Distrito Federal [*Venezuela ICAO location identifier*] (ICLI)
SVML .... Standard Vehicle Mounted Launcher [*Army*]
SVMP .... Caracas/Metropolitano Internacional, Miranda [*Venezuela ICAO location identifier*] (ICLI)
SVMPCG .... Grasslands National Park, Parks Canada [*Parc National Grasslands, Parcs Canada*] Val Marie, Saskatchewan [*Library symbol National Library of Canada*] (NLC)
SVMR .... Maracay/Centro Nacional de Comunicaciones/Meteorologicos, Aragua [*Venezuela ICAO location identifier*] (ICLI)
SVMT .... Maturin/Internacional, Monagas [*Venezuela ICAO location identifier*] (ICLI)
SVMTR .... Servomotor [*Control systems*]
SVN .... Saravena [*Colombia*] [*Airport symbol*] (AD)
SVN .... Savanair (Angola) Lda. [*FAA designator*] (FAAC)
SVN .... Savannah, GA [*Location identifier FAA*] (FAAL)
SVN .... Small Volume Nebulizer [*Pharmacology*] (DAVI)
SVN .... South Vietnam (CINC)
SVN .... Space Vehicle Number [*Aviation*] (FAAC)
SVN .... Spectra Vision, Inc. [*Formerly, SPI Holdings, Inc.*] [*AMEX symbol*] (SAG)
SVN .... SpectraVision Inc. 'B' [*AMEX symbol*] (TTSB)
SVNAF .... South Vietnamese Air Force (VNW)
SVNESE .... South Vietnamese
SVNG .... Seventh Generation [*NASDAQ symbol*] (TTSB)
SVNGS .... Savings
SVNLA .... South Vietnamese Liberation Army (VNW)
SVNM .... St. Vincent National Movement [*Political party*] (PPW)
SVNMC .... South Vietnamese Marine Corps (VNW)
SVNN .... South Vietnamese Navy (VNW)
SVNNP .... South Vietnamese National Police Force (VNW)
SVNRF .... State of Vietnam Ribbon of Friendship [*Military decoration*] (AABC)
SVNSF .... South Vietnamese Special Forces (VNW)
SVNVAC .... Sunny Von Bulow National Victim Advocacy Center [*Later, NVC*] (EA)
SVO .... Moscow Sheremetyevo Airport [*Former USSR Airport symbol*] (OAG)
SVO .... Scottish Variety Orchestra (DI)
SVO .... Senior Veterinary Officer [*British military*] (DMA)
SVO .... Servo (KSC)
SVO .... Space Vehicle Operations (MCD)
SVO .... Special Vehicle Operation [*Ford Motor Co.*]
SVO .... Special Vehicle Option [*Automobile production*]
SVO .... Subject-Verb-Object [*Education of the hearing-impaired*]
SVOIR .... Specification Verification Open Item Report
SVP .... Bie [*Angola*] [*Airport symbol*] (OAG)
SVP .... Saturated Vapor Pressure (IAA)
SVP .... Security Vehicle Patrol [*Air Force*] (AFM)
SVP .... Seminal Vesicle Protein [*Biochemistry*]
SVP .... Senior Vice President
SVP .... Service Processor (BUR)
SVP .... Services Vegetable Production [*British military*] (DMA)
SVP .... Sewer Vent Pipe
SVP .... Silver Princess Resources [*Vancouver Stock Exchange symbol*]

SVP............ S'il Vous Plait [*If You Please*] [*French*]
SVP............ Single-Voyage Permit
SVP............ Small Volume Parenteral [*Pharmacy*]
SVP............ Snake Venom Phosphodiesterase [*Also, SVPD, SVPDE*] [*An enzyme*]
SVP............ Societe pour Vaincre la Pollution [*Canada*]
SVP............ Society of St. Vincent de Paul
SVP............ Society of Vertebrate Paleontology (EA)
SVP............ Software Verification Plan [*Computer science*] (IAA)
SVP............ Sound Velocity Profile
SVP............ Special Visitors Program [*Australia*]
SVP............ Specific Vocational Preparation [*US Employment Service*] [*Department of Labor*]
SVP............ Star-Vaporizing Millisecond Pulsar [*Cosmology*]
SVP............ Steam Vacuum Pulse
SVP............ St. Louis Public Library, St. Louis, MO [*OCLC symbol*] (OCLC)
SVP............ Sudtiroler Volkspartei [*South Tyrolean People's Party*] [*Italy Political party*] (EAIO)
SVP............ Supplemental Vacation Plan
SVP............ Surface Velocity Program [*Marine science*] (OSRA)
SVP............ Surface Velocity Programme (USDC)
SVP............ Surge Voltage Protection (IAA)
S/VP............ Surveillance/Vantage Point [*Military*] (INF)
SVPA............ Puerto Ayacucho, T. F. Amazonas [*Venezuela ICAO location identifier*] (ICLI)
SVPB............ Supraventricular Premature Beats [*Cardiology*]
SVPC............ Puerto Cabello/Gral. Bartolome Salom Internacional, Carabobo [*Venezuela ICAO location identifier*] (ICLI)
SVPD............ Snake Venom Phosphodiesterase [*Also, SVP, SVPDE*] [*An enzyme*]
SVPDE............ Snake Venom Phosphodiesterase [*Also, SVP, SVPD*] [*An enzyme*]
SVPM............ San Cristobal/Paramillo, Tachira [*Venezuela ICAO location identifier*] (ICLI)
SVPM............ Small Vehicles, Program Manager
SVPP............ Schweizerische Vereinigung fuer Parapsychologie
SVPR............ Guayana/Puerto Ordaz Internacional, Bolivar [*Venezuela ICAO location identifier*] (ICLI)
SVPT............ Palmarito, Apure [*Venezuela ICAO location identifier*] (ICLI)
SVPT............ Supraventricular Paroxysmal Tachycardia [*Cardiology*] (DAVI)
SVQ............ Scottish Vocational Qualification (AIE)
SVQ............ Seville [*Spain*] [*Airport symbol*] (OAG)
SVR............ Shop Visit Rate (DOMA)
SVR............ Singapore Volunteer Rifles [*British military*] (DMA)
SVR............ Slant Visual Range
SVR............ Society of Vietnamese Rangers (EA)
SVR............ Software Verification Report [*Computer science*] (IAA)
SVR............ Spiritus Vini Rectificatus [*Rectified Spirit of Wine*] [*Pharmacy*]
SVR............ Spirit Varnish Resistance Ink (DGA)
SVR............ Super Video Recorder
SVR............ Supply-Voltage Rejection (IEEE)
SVR............ Surface/Volume Ratio
SVR............ Sverdlovsk Airline [*Russian Federation*] [*ICAO designator*] (FAAC)
SVR............ Systemic Vascular Resistance [*Medicine*]
SVR............ Ural Airlines [*Former USSR*] [*FAA designator*] (FAAC)
SVRA............ Sportscar Vintage Racing Association (EA)
SVRA............ State Vehicular Recreation Area
SVRB............ Supervisor Request Block [*Computer science*] (BUR)
SVRC............ Short-Range Vehicle to Roadside Communication [*FHWA*] (TAG)
SVRD............ Silicon Voltage Reference Diode
SVREP............ Southwest Voter Registration Education Project (EA)
SVRI............ Silicon Valley Research [*NASDAQ symbol*] (TTSB)
SVRI............ Silicon Valley Research, Inc. [*NASDAQ symbol*] (SAG)
SVRI............ Southwest Voter Research Institute [*San Antonio, TX*] (CROSS)
SVRI............ Systemic Vascular Resistance Index
SVRN............ Sovereign Bancorp [*NASDAQ symbol*] (TTSB)
SVRN............ Sovereign Bancorp, Inc. [*NASDAQ symbol*] (NQ)
SVRNP............ Sovereign Bancorp 6.25% Cv Pfd [*NASDAQ symbol*] (TTSB)
SVRR............ Software Verification Readiness Review [*NASA*] (NASA)
SVRS............ Los Roques, Dependencia Federal [*Venezuela ICAO location identifier*] (ICLI)
SVS............ Schedule Visibility System (AAG)
SVS............ Secure Voice Switch
SVS............ Secure Voice System [*Telecommunications*]
SVS............ Service School [*Military*]
SVS............ Services Squadron
SVS............ Silverside Resources, Inc. [*Toronto Stock Exchange symbol*]
SVS............ Single Virtual Storage [*IBM Corp.*] [*Computer science*]
SVS............ Slandsville [*South Carolina*] [*Seismograph station code, US Geological Survey*] (SEIS)
SVS............ Society for Vascular Surgery (EA)
SVS............ Society for Visiting Scientists Ltd. [*British*] (BI)
SVS............ Soil Vapor Survey [*Environmental chemistry*]
SVS............ Sound Velocity Structure
SVS............ Space Vehicle Simulator (AAG)
SVS............ Space Vehicle System (IAA)
SVS............ Spectroradiometer Visible System
SVS............ Spinning Vehicle Simulator
SVS............ Stabilized Viewing System
SVS............ Stamp Ventures [*Printer of U.S. postage stamps*] (BARN)
SVS............ Stationary Control Variable Speed (IAA)
SVS............ Stevens Village [*Alaska*] [*Airport symbol*] (OAG)
SVS............ Still-Camera Video System [*Canon, Inc.*]
SVS............ Suit Ventilation System [*Aerospace*] (MCD)
SVS............ Supervisory Signal (IAA)
SVS............ Synthetic Vision Systems, Inc.
SVSA............ San Antonio, Tachira [*Venezuela ICAO location identifier*] (ICLI)
SVSB............ Santa Barbara De Barinas, Barinas [*Venezuela ICAO location identifier*] (ICLI)
SVSC............ San Carlos De Rio Negro, T. F. Amazonas [*Venezuela ICAO location identifier*] (ICLI)
SVSC............ Space Vehicle Sectoring Code
SVSE............ Santa Elena de Uairen, Bolivar [*Venezuela ICAO location identifier*] (ICLI)
SVSO............ Santo Domingo/Mayor Buenaventura Vivas A. B., Tachira [*Venezuela ICAO location identifier*] (ICLI)
SVSO............ Superintending Victualling Stores Officer [*British*]
SVSP............ San Felipe/Subteniente Nestor Arias, Yaracuy [*Venezuela ICAO location identifier*] (ICLI)
SVSP............ School Volunteer Services Program
SV-SP............ Spray Volume - Spray Pressure
SVSR............ San Fernando De Apure, Apure [*Venezuela ICAO location identifier*] (ICLI)
SVSS............ Sprague Voltage-Sensitive Switch
SVST............ San Tome, Anzoategui [*Venezuela ICAO location identifier*] (ICLI)
SVSZ............ Santa Barbara Del Zulia, Zulia [*Venezuela ICAO location identifier*] (ICLI)
SVT............ Sakhaviatrans [*Former USSR*] [*FAA designator*] (FAAC)
SVT............ Secure Voice Terminal (MCD)
SVT............ Self Valuation Test [*Psychology*]
SVT............ Servotronics, Inc. [*AMEX symbol*] (SPSG)
SVT............ Silicon Vidicon Target
SVT............ Silverton Resources Ltd. [*Toronto Stock Exchange symbol*]
SVT............ Solar Vacuum Telescope
SVT............ Space Vehicle Test
SVT............ Space Visualization Test
SVT............ Special Vehicle Team [*Automotive engineering*]
SVT............ Spiritus Vini Tenuis [*Proof Spirit of Wine*] [*Pharmacy*]
SVT............ Stray Voltage Tester
SVT............ St. Vincent [*St. Vincent*] [*Seismograph station code, US Geological Survey*] (SEIS)
SVT............ Subclavian Vein Thrombosis [*Medicine*] (DMAA)
SVT............ Supralaryngeal Vocal Tract [*Anatomy*]
SVT............ Supraventricular Tachyarrhythmia [*Cardiology*] (DAVI)
SVT............ Supraventricular Tachycardia [*Cardiology*]
SVT............ System Validation Testing
SVT............ System Verification Test [*Automotive engineering*]
SVTC............ Surrey Volunteer Training Corps [*British military*] (DMA)
SVTC............ Tucupita, T. F. Delta Amacuro [*Venezuela ICAO location identifier*] (ICLI)
SVTL............ Semivital
SVTL............ Services Valve Test Laboratory [*British*] (NATG)
SVTM............ Shielded Voltage Tunable Magnetron
SVTM............ Tumeremo, Bolivar [*Venezuela ICAO location identifier*] (ICLI)
S/VTOL............ Short/Vertical Takeoff and Landing [*Aviation*] (NATG)
SVTP............ Sound, Velocity, Temperature, Pressure
SVT(S)............ Space Vehicle Test (Supervisor)
SVTSV............ Space-Vehicle-to-Space-Vehicle (SAA)
SVTT............ Surface Vessel Torpedo Tube (NVT)
SVU............ Savusavu [*Fiji*] [*Airport symbol*] (OAG)
S/VU............ Sound/Video Unlimited
SVU............ Spur Ventures [*Vancouver Stock Exchange symbol*]
SVU............ Supervalu Inc. [*NYSE symbol*] (TTSB)
SVU............ Surface Vehicular Unit
SVU............ System Verification Unit
SVUL............ Short Vertical Upper Left
SVUL............ Suomen Valtakunnan Uhreiluliitto [*Finnish Central Sports Federation*]
SVUM............ Uriman, Bolivar [*Venezuela ICAO location identifier*] (ICLI)
SVUQ............ Uonquen, Bolivar [*Venezuela ICAO location identifier*] (ICLI)
SVUR............ Short Vertical Upper Right
SVV............ Empresa Servicicious Avensa SA [*Venezuela*] [*ICAO designator*] (FAAC)
SVV............ Sit Venia Verbo [*Forgive the Expression*] [*Latin*]
SVV............ Solenoid Vent Valve [*Automotive engineering*]
svv............ Sub Vocibus [*Latin*]
SVVA............ Valencia/Internacional, Carabobo [*Venezuela ICAO location identifier*] (ICLI)
SVVL............ Valera/Dr. Antonio Nicolas Briceno, Trujillo [*Venezuela ICAO location identifier*] (ICLI)
SVVP............ Valle De La Pascua, Guarico [*Venezuela ICAO location identifier*] (ICLI)
SVW............ Silverhawk Resources [*Vancouver Stock Exchange symbol*]
SVW............ Sparrevohn [*Alaska*] [*Seismograph station code, US Geological Survey*] (SEIS)
SVW............ Sparrevohn, AK [*Location identifier FAA*] (FAAL)
SVX............ Socanav, Inc. [*Toronto Stock Exchange symbol*]
SVY............ Cooper Aerial Surveys Ltd. [*British*] [*FAA designator*] (FAAC)
SVY............ GCA Surveys [*British ICAO designator*] (FAAC)
SVY............ Survey
SVZ............ San Antonio [*Venezuela*] [*Airport symbol*] (OAG)
SVZ............ Sisters of Charity of St. Vincent de Paul [*Roman Catholic religious order*]
SVZ............ Subventricular Zone [*Anatomy*]
SVZM............ Maiquetia [*Venezuela ICAO location identifier*] (ICLI)
SVZZ............ Maiquetia [*Venezuela ICAO location identifier*] (ICLI)
SW............ Methylphosphonous Dichloride [*Toxic compound*] [*Army symbol*]
SW............ Namib Air [*ICAO designator*] (AD)
Sw............ Royal Swedish Library (Kungl. Biblioteket), Stockholm, Sweden [*Library symbol Library of Congress*] (LCLS)
SW............ Sadler's Wells Theatre [*London*]
SW............ Salt Water
SW............ Sandwich-Wound (DEN)

SW Sapwood [*Botany*]
SW Satan Worship
SW Schwartz-Watson Test [*Medicine*] (MAE)
SW Seaboard World Airlines, Inc.
SW Seawater
S/W Seaworthy (ADA)
SW Secretary of War [*Obsolete*]
SW Secret Writing [*Espionage*]
SW Security Watch
SW Semiweekly
SW Senior Warden [*Freemasonry*]
SW Senior Wolf [*An accomplished philanderer*] [*Slang*]
SW Senior Woodward [*Ancient Order of Foresters*]
SW Sent Wrong [*i.e., misdirected*]
SW Series Winding [*Wiring*] (DNAB)
SW Seriously Wounded (DAVI)
SW Service Water [*Nuclear energy*] (NRCH)
SW Sewing Machine Repair Program [*Association of Independent Colleges and Schools specialization code*]
SW Shallow Water (DOMA)
SW Shallow Water Attack Craft [*Navy symbol*]
SW Shallow Water Diver [*British military*] (DMA)
SW Shelter Warden [*British Home Defence*] [*World War II*]
SW Shipper's Weights [*Bills of lading*]
SW Ship's Warrant [*Marine Corps*]
SW Shirl J. Winter [*Designer's mark when appearing on US coins*]
SW Shock Wave (IAA)
SW Shorter Workweek [*Business term*] (MHDB)
SW Shortwave [*Electronics*]
SW Short Weight
SW Shotgun Wedding [*Forced marriage*] [*Slang*]
SW Side Wheel
SW Sidewinder
SW Simple Wear
SW Single Wall (AAG)
SW Single Weight
SW Single Wheel [*Landing gear*] [*Aviation*] (DA)
SW Slow Wave [*Electroencephalograph*]
SW Smith's Weekly [*A publication*]
SW Snow [*Ship's rigging*] (ROG)
SW Snow Shower [*Meteorology*] (BARN)
SW Social Work [*or Worker*]
SW Socket Weld
SW Software [*Computer science*]
S/W Software (EERA)
SW Softwood
SW Solar Wind [*Astronomy*]
SW Solar Wing (MCD)
SW Solid Waste
SW Son of a Witch (EA)
SW Sound Whistle [*British railroad term*]
SW South Wales
SW Southwest
SW Southwest Africa (MCD)
S-W South-Western Educational Publishing [*International Thomson Publishing Co.*]
SW South Western Reporter [*National Reporter System*] [*A publication*] (DLA)
SW Special Warfare
SW Special Weapon
SW Specification of Wiring (IAA)
SW Specific Weight
SW Sperm Whale
SW Spike Wave [*Medicine*] (DMAA)
SW Spiral Wound [*Medicine*] (MAE)
SW Spontaneous Swallows [*Gastroenterology*]
SW Spores Injected into Wounded Kernels [*Plant pathology*]
SW Spore Wall [*Botany*]
SW Spotweld [*Technical drawings*]
SW Stab Wound [*Medicine*] (MAE)
SW Stall Warning System (MCD)
SW Standard Winter
SW Standby Service Water [*Nuclear energy*] (NRCH)
SW Standing Wave (IAA)
SW Stationary Wave (IAA)
SW Station Wagon [*Car*]
SW Status of Women [*Canada*]
SW Status Word
SW Steam Wagon [*British*]
SW Steel Wire (IAA)
SW Steelworker [*Navy rating*]
SW Stenciled Weight
SW Sterile Water
SW Stewart-Warner Corp.
SW Stock Width [*Construction or manufacturing materials*]
SW Stone & Webster [*NYSE symbol*] (TTSB)
SW Stone & Webster, Inc. [*NYSE symbol*] (SPSG)
SW Strategic Warning (MCD)
SW Strategic Wing [*Military*]
SW Stroke Work [*Cardiology*]
SW Struthers Wells Corp. (IAA)
SW Stud-Arc Welding
SW Subjective Weakness [*Medicine*]
SW Subject Word (NITA)
SW Surface Warfare (MCD)
S/W Surface Wind [*Meteorology*] (DA)
Sw Swabey's English Admiralty Reports [*A publication*] (DLA)
Sw Swabey's English Ecclesiastical Reports [*1855-59*] [*A publication*] (DLA)
sw Swamp [*Maps and charts*]
Sw Swann [*Blood group*]
Sw Swan's Tennessee Reports [*31, 32 Tennessee*] [*A publication*] (DLA)
Sw Swanston's English Chancery Reports [*A publication*] (DLA)
SW Swash
SW Swatch (WGA)
SW Swear
SW Swearingen Aircraft [*ICAO aircraft manufacturer identifier*] (ICAO)
sw Sweden [*MARC country of publication code Library of Congress*] (LCCP)
Sw Sweden (ODBW)
Sw Swedish (ODBW)
Sw Sweeney's New York Superior Court Reports [*A publication*] (DLA)
SW Swell Organ
Sw Swine [*Veterinary medicine*] (DAVI)
Sw Swinton's Scotch Justiciary Cases [*A publication*] (DLA)
SW Swiss
SW Swiss Webster Mouse [*Medicine*] (DMAA)
SW Switch (AAG)
sw Switch (IDOE)
SW Switchband Wound [*Relay*]
SW Switcher [*Broadcasting*] (WDMC)
SW Switzerland
SW1 Steelworker, First Class [*Navy rating*]
SW2 Steelworker, Second Class [*Navy rating*]
SW 2d South Western Reporter, Second Series [*A publication*] (DLA)
SW2d South Western Reporter, Second Series [*West*] [*A publication*] (AAGC)
SW3 Steelworker, Third Class [*Navy rating*]
SWA Namibia [*International vehicle registration*] (ODBW)
SWA Reports of the High Court of South-West Africa [*1920-46*] [*A publication*] (DLA)
SWA Scheduler Work Area [*Computer science*] (IBMDP)
SWA Scope of Word Addendum (MCD)
SWA Scotch Whisky Association [*British*] (DBA)
SWA Seaboard World Airlines (MHDW)
SWA Seriously Wounded in Action [*Military*]
SWA Shallow Water Acoustics
SWA Shantou [*China*] [*Airport symbol*] (OAG)
SWA Shayna International Industry [*Vancouver Stock Exchange symbol*]
SWA Single Wire Armored [*Cables*]
SWA SLow-Wave Activity [*Medicine*] (DMAA)
SWA Society of Women Artists [*British*] (DBA)
SWA Solo Wargamers Association (EAIO)
SWA Southern Water Authority [*British*] (DCTA)
SWA Southern Wholesalers Association [*Atlanta, GA*] (EA)
SWA Southern Woodwork Association [*Defunct*] (EA)
SWA Southwest Africa
SWA Southwest Airlines Co. [*ICAO designator*] (FAAC)
SWA Southwest Approach (DNAB)
SWA Southwest Asia
SWA Specialty Wire Association [*Later, AWPA*]
SWA Sports Writers' Association [*British*] (BI)
SWA Standing Wave Apparatus
SWA State Welfare Agency [*Social Security Administration*] (OICC)
SWA Steel Window Association [*British*] (DBA)
SWA Straight Wire Antenna
SWA Stunt Women of America [*Later, SAMP*] (EA)
SWA Superwomen's Anonymous (EA)
SWA Support Work Authorization [*NASA*] (MCD)
swa Swahili [*MARC language code Library of Congress*] (LCCP)
SWA Swan Island [*Seismograph station code, US Geological Survey Closed*] (SEIS)
SWA Swedish Warmblood Association (EA)
SWA Swissair [*Airline*] (MCD)
SWA System Work Area
SWAA Slovak Writers and Artists Association (EA)
SWAA Spacelab Window Adapter Assembly (NASA)
SWAAA Scottish Women's Amateur Athletic Association (DBA)
Swaacs Small Waterplane Air Cushion Ship
SWAAG Solidarity with Aboriginal Australians Group
SWAAT Sea-Water Acetic Acid Test (PDAA)
Swab Swabey's English Ecclesiastical Reports [*1855-59*] [*A publication*] (DLA)
SWAB Swap Byte [*Computer science*] (NHD)
Swab Admr Swabey's English Admiralty Reports [*166 English Reprint*] [*A publication*] (DLA)
Swab & T Swabey and Tristram's Probate and Divorce Reports [*164 English Reprint*] [*A publication*] (DLA)
Swab & Tr Swabey and Tristram's Probate and Divorce Reports [*164 English Reprint*] [*A publication*] (DLA)
Swab Div Swabey on Divorce and Matrimonial Causes [*3rd ed.*] [*1859*] [*A publication*] (DLA)
Swabey Adm Swabey's English Admiralty Reports [*166 English Reprint*] [*1855-59*] [*A publication*] (DLA)
Swabey Adm (Eng) Swabey's English Admiralty Reports [*166 English Reprint*] [*A publication*] (DLA)
Swabey & T (Eng) Swabey and Tristram's Probate and Divorce Reports [*164 English Reports*] [*A publication*] (DLA)
SWAC Shallow Water Attack Craft, Light (MCD)
SWAC Special Warhead Arming Control (AFM)

SWAC .... Specification Writers Association of Canada
SWAC .... Spotweld Accessory [*Tool*] (AAG)
SWAC .... Standards Western Automatic Computer [*National Institute of Standards and Technology*]
SWACHA ...... Southwestern Automated Clearing House Association
SWACS .... Space Warning and Control System [*NORAD*]
SWAD .... Special Warfare Aviation Detachment [*Army*]
SWAD .... Subdivision of Work Authorization Document [*NASA*] (NASA)
SWADE .... Second Wives of America Demanding Equality
SWADS .... Scheduler Work Area Data Set [*IBM Corp.*] (MCD)
SW Af .... South-West Africa
SWAFAC ...... Southwest Atlantic Fisheries Advisory Commission [*FAO*]
SWAG .... Scientific Wild Aim Guess [*Bowdlerized version*]
SWAG .... Standard Written Agreement [*Military*]
SWAG .... Systems Work Assignment Group (SAA)
SWAGS .... Scientific Wild-Aim Guess System [*Bowdlerized version*] (MCD)
SWAH .... Studies in Western Australian History [*A publication*]
SWAJB .... South and Western Australia Judgements Bulletin [*A publication*]
SWAK .... Sealed with a Kiss [*Correspondence*]
SWAK .... Spinners and Weavers Association of Korea [*Defunct*] (EA)
SWAL .... Shallow Water Attack Craft, Light [*Navy symbol*] (NVT)
SWALC .... Southwest Academic Library Consortium [*Library network*] (IID)
SWALCAKWS... Sealed with a Lick 'Cause a Kiss Won't Stick [*Correspondence*] (DSUE)
SWALCAP .... South West Academic Libraries Cooperative Automation Project (NITA)
SWALK .... Sealed with a Loving Kiss [*Correspondence*]
SWALM .... Switch Alarm (AAG)
SWAM .... Shallow Water Attack Craft, Medium [*Navy symbol*] (NVT)
SWAM .... Sine Wave Amplitude Modulation
SWAMI .... Software-Aided Multiform Input [*Software*] [*Computer science*]
SWAMI .... Speech with Alternating Masking Index [*Discrimination test*]
SWAMI .... Stall Warning and Margin Indicator
SWAMI .... Standing Wave Area Monitor Indicator (MUGU)
SWAMI .... Stanford Worldwide Acquisition of Meteorological Information [*Weather prediction system*]
SWAMP .... Southwest Area Monsoon Project (USDC)
SWAN .... School of Women Artists Network [*Australia*]
SWAN .... Second Wives Association of North America (EA)
SWAN .... Severe Weather Avoidance Nationwide [*National Oceanic and Atmospheric Administration*]
SWAN .... Society of Wildlife Art Nations [*British*] (DBA)
Swan .... Swan's Tennessee Supreme Court Reports [*1851-53*] [*A publication*] (DLA)
Swan .... Swanston's English Chancery Reports [*A publication*] (DLA)
Swan & CR St... Swan and Critchfield's Revised Statutes [*Ohio*] [*A publication*] (DLA)
Swan & S St... Swan and Sayler's Supplement to the Revised Statutes [*Ohio*] [*A publication*] (DLA)
Swan Ch ...... Swanston's English Chancery Reports [*A publication*] (DLA)
Sw & Tr .... Swabey and Tristram's Probate and Divorce Reports [*164 English Reprint*] [*A publication*] (DLA)
Swan Eccl C... Swan's Ecclesiastical Courts [*1830*] [*A publication*] (DLA)
Swan Just.... Swan's Justice [*Ohio*] [*A publication*] (DLA)
SWANK .... Sealed with a Nice Kiss [*Correspondence*]
Swank .... Single Woman and No Kids [*Lifestyle classification*]
Swank .... Swank, Inc. [*Associated Press*] (SAG)
Swan Pl & Pr... Swan on Pleading and Practice [*Ohio*] [*A publication*] (DLA)
Swan Pr .... Swan on Practice [*Ohio*] [*A publication*] (DLA)
Swan's .... Swan's Tennessee Reports [*A publication*] (DLA)
Swans .... Swanston's English Chancery Reports [*A publication*] (DLA)
Swan's R ...... Swan's Tennessee Reports [*A publication*] (DLA)
Swan's St .... Swan's Ohio Statutes [*A publication*] (DLA)
Swanst .... Swanston's English Chancery Reports [*36 English Reprint*] [*A publication*] (DLA)
Swanst (Eng)... Swanston's English Chancery Reports [*36 English Reprint*] [*A publication*] (DLA)
Swan Tr .... Swan's Ohio Treatise [*A publication*] (DLA)
SWANU .... South West Africa National Union [*Namibia*] [*Political party*] (PPW)
SWAP .... Section on Women and Psychology [*Canadian Psychology Association*]
SWAP .... Severe Weather Avoidance Plan (FAAC)
SWAP .... Severe Weather Avoidance Program (GAVI)
SWAP .... Smith-Winnick-Abrams-Prausnitz [*Vapor pressure correlation equation*]
SWAP .... Society for Wang Applications and Programs (CSR)
SWAP .... Standard Wafer Array Programming
SWAP .... Stewart-Warner Array Program [*Electronics*] (EECA)
SWAP .... Stress Wave Analyzing Program
SWAP .... Student Woodlawn Area Project [*Chicago, IL*]
SWAP .... Surface Water Acidification Project [*Joint venture involving Norway, Sweden, and Great Britain*]
SWAP .... SWAP [*Salesmen with a Purpose*] Club International [*Arvada, CO*] (EA)
SWAP .... Sydney Wastewater Action Program [*Australia*]
SWAP .... Systems Worthiness Analysis Program [*FAA*]
SWAPDOP ... Southwest Asia Petroleum Distribution Operation Project [*Army*]
SWAPO .... South West African People's Organisation (EERA)
SWAPO .... South West Africa People's Organization [*Namibia*] (PD)
SWAPS .... Ship Workload and Priority Systems [*Navy*]
SWAPS .... Special Wire Assembly Planning System (MCD)
SWAPS .... Standing-Wave Acoustic Parametric Source (PDAA)
SWARK .... Southwark [*Borough of London*] (ROG)
SWARM .... Southwestern and Rocky Mountain Division [*AAAS division*]
SWARMS ..... Small Warhead and Reentry Multiple System
SWAS .... Slim Whitman Appreciation Society of the United States (EA)
SWAS .... Submillimeter Wave Astronomy Satellite [*Military*]
SWASG .... Submarine Sensor to Weapon Alignment Steering Group
SWASGB ...... Slim Whitman Appreciation Society of Great Britain (EAIO)
Swash .... Small Waterplane Area Single Hull Ship
SWASS .... Screwworm Adult Suppression System [*Medicine*]
SWASS .... Slim Whitman Appreciation Society of Scotland (EAIO)
SWAT .... Secure Wire Access Terminal (MCD)
SWAT .... Service Weapons Acceptability Tests
SWAT .... Sidewinder Acquisition Track (IEEE)
SWAT .... Sidewinder Angle Tracking [*Missiles*] (NG)
SWAT .... Simultaneous Wide Area Telecommunications Service (TSSD)
SWAT .... Sipay Word Analysis Test [*Educational test*]
SWAT .... Sodium-Water Reaction Test [*Nuclear energy*] (NUCP)
SWAT .... Solid Waste Assessment Test
SWAT .... Special Warfare Armored Transporter [*A vehicle*]
SWAT .... Special Weapons and Tactics [*Police*]
SWAT .... Special Wrenches and Techniques [*Automotive repair*]
SWAT .... Squad Weapon Analytical Trainer (MCD)
SWAT .... Steering Wheel Anti-Theft [*Device*] [*Auto Alarm*]
SWAT .... Strengths, Weaknesses, Alternatives, Threats [*Analysis*] (ADA)
SWAT .... Stress Wave Analysis Technique
SWAT .... Study With a Teacher Program [*Ohio*] (EDAC)
SWATCH ...... Swiss Watch
SWATH .... Small Waterplane Area Twin Hull [*Ship*] [*Navy*]
SWATH .... Small Waterplane Area Twin Hull
SWATH .... Space Weather and Terrestrial Hazards [*Proposed satellite*]
SWATM .... Shallow Water Antitraffic Mine [*Military*]
SWATS .... Sea-Based Weapons and Advance Tactics School (DOMA)
SWATS .... Shallow Water Acoustic Tracking System [*Navy*] (CAAL)
SWATT .... Simulator for Antitank Tactical Training [*Army*] (INF)
SWAX .... Southwest Airlines Co. [*Air carrier designation symbol*]
SWAZ .... Swaziland (WDAA)
Swazil .... Swaziland
SWB .... Sandia Wind Balloon (MUGU)
SWB .... Short Wheelbase
SWB .... Single Weight Baryta [*Photography*] (OA)
SWB .... Single with Bath [*Hotel room*]
SWB .... South Wales Borderers [*Military unit*] [*British*]
SWB .... Southwestbound [*ICAO designator*] (FAAC)
SWB .... South Westchester BOCES [*Boards of Cooperative Educational Services*] [*UTLAS symbol*]
SWB .... Southwestern Motor Freight Bureau, Dallas TX [*STAC*]
SWB .... Subjective Well-Being [*Psychology*]
SWB .... Summary of World Broadcasts [*British Broadcasting Corporation*]
SWB .... Sweden Airways [*ICAO designator*] (FAAC)
SWB .... Switchboard (NATG)
SWBA .... Southwest Banks [*NASDAQ symbol*] (TTSB)
SWBA .... Southwest Banks, Inc. [*NASDAQ symbol*] (SAG)
SWB & IE .... South West Business and Industry Exhibition [*British*] (ITD)
SWBC .... Sterling West Bancorp [*NASDAQ symbol*] (SAG)
SwBcsh .... Southwest Bancshares, Inc. [*Associated Press*] (SAG)
SWBD .... Switchboard (AAG)
SWBDOP ...... Switchboard Operator (IAA)
SWBHD .... Swash Bulkhead
SWBI .... Southwest Bancshares [*NASDAQ symbol*] (TTSB)
SWBI .... Southwest Bancshares, Inc. [*NASDAQ symbol*] (SAG)
SWBM .... Still-Water Bending Moment (PDAA)
SWBP .... Service Water Booster Pump [*Nuclear energy*] (IEEE)
SWBS .... Ship Work Breakdown Structure [*Navy*] (CAAL)
SWBS .... SierraWest Bancorp [*NASDAQ symbol*] (SAG)
SWBS .... Software Work Breakdown Structure (MCD)
SWBS .... Solid Waste Barrel Storage [*Nuclear energy*] (NRCH)
SWbS .... Southwest by South
SWBS .... Subcontract Work Breakdown Structure (MCD)
SWbW .... Southwest by West
SWC .... Chief Steelworker [*Navy rating*]
SWC .... Omaha, NE [*Location identifier FAA*] (FAAL)
SWC .... Safe Water Coalition (EA)
SWC .... Saline Water Conversion (MCD)
SWC .... Scanning with Compensation
SWC .... Scan-with-Composition (MCD)
SWC .... Second Wives Coalition (EA)
SWC .... Semi-Wadcutter [*Ammunition*]
SWC .... Senate Wine Caucus (EA)
SWC .... Settlement with Conditions [*Environmental Protection Agency*] (GFGA)
SWC .... Share the Work Coalition [*Defunct*] (EA)
SWC .... Ship Weapon Coordinator (NVT)
SWC .... Shock Wave Control
SWC .... Shortwave Converter
SWC .... Signals Warfare Center [*Warrenton, VA*] [*Army*]
SWC .... Simon Wiesenthal Center (EA)
SWC .... Single Wire Connector
SWC .... Skywave Correction [*Aircraft navigation*]
SWC .... Slovak World Congress (EAIO)
SWC .... Soft Wired Control (IAA)
SWC .... Soil and Water Conservation Research Division [*of ARS, Department of Agriculture*]
SWC .... Solar Wind Compensator [*or Composition*] [*Apollo 11*] [*NASA*]
SWC .... Solid Wastes Cask [*Nuclear energy*] (NRCH)
SWC .... South West Air Ltd. [*Canada ICAO designator*] (FAAC)
SWC .... Southwest Conference [*College sports*]
SWC .... Southwestern Connecticut Library Council, Bridgeport, CT [*OCLC symbol*] (OCLC)

SWC............ Special Warfare Center [*Later, J. F. Kennedy Center for Special Warfare*] [*Army*]
SWC............ Special Warfare Craft [*Navy*] (CAAL)
SWC............ Special Weapons Center [*or Command*]
SWC............ Sportscar World Championship [*Auto racing*]
SWC............ Stall Warning Computer (MCD)
SWC............ Stawell [*Australia Airport symbol*] (OAG)
SWC............ Step-Wise Cracking (MCD)
SWC............ Stormwater Channel
SWC............ Submaximal Working Capacity (DMAA)
SWC............ Submersible Work Chamber
SWC............ Superior White Crystal [*Sugar*]
SWC............ Supreme War Council [*World War II*]
SWC............ Surewin Resources Corp. [*Vancouver Stock Exchange symbol*]
SWC............ Surface Warfare Coordinator [*Also, SUWC*] (NVT)
SWC............ Surface Weapons Control
SWC............ Surface Weapons Coordinator [*Navy*] (CAAL)
SWC............ Surge Withstand Capability (IEEE)
SWC............ Switching Control [*Telecommunications*] (IAA)
SWC............ System Weapons Coordinator [*Navy*] (CAAL)
SWCA.......... Constructionman Apprentice, Steelworker, Striker [*Navy rating*]
SWCA.......... Silver Wyandotte Club of America (EA)
SWCAA........ Soil and Water Conservation Association of Australia (EERA)
SWCB.......... [*The*] Sandwich Co-Operative Bank [*Sandwich, MA*] [*NASDAQ symbol*] (NQ)
SWCC.......... Second World Climate Conference (EERA)
SWCD.......... Solar Wind Composition Detector (PDAA)
SWCE.......... Solar Wind Composition Experiment (PDAA)
SWCEL........ Southwestern Cooperative Educational Laboratory
SWCENT...... Switching Central [*Telecommunications*] (AABC)
SWCH.......... Switch (MCD)
SWCHMN..... Switchman (WGA)
SWCL.......... Seawater Conversion Laboratory (KSC)
SWCL.......... Special Warfare Craft, Light [*Navy symbol*]
SWCL.......... State Worker's Compensation Law (OICC)
SWCLR........ Southwest Council of La Raza [*Mexican-American organization*] (EA)
SWCM.......... Master Chief Steelworker [*Navy rating*]
SWCM.......... Social Work Case Manager (DMAA)
SW/CM........ Software Configuration Management (MCD)
SWCM.......... Special Warfare Craft, Medium [*Navy symbol*]
SWCN.......... Constructionman, Steelworker, Striker [*Navy rating*]
SWCP.......... Saline Water Conversion Program [*Department of the Interior*]
SWCP.......... Salt-Water Circulating Pump (MSA)
SWCP.......... Society of the War of 1812 in the Commonwealth of Pennsylvania (EA)
SWCPI........ Solid Waste Council of the Paper Industry [*Defunct*] (EA)
SWCS.......... SAC Warning and Control System (MCD)
SWCS.......... Salt-Water Cooling System [*Nuclear energy*] (NRCH)
SWCS.......... Senior Chief Steelworker [*Navy rating*]
SWCS.......... Space Warning and Control System [*NORAD*] (IAA)
SWCST........ Saturn Workshop Cockpit Simulation Trainer [*NASA*]
SWD............ Self-Wiring Data [*Telecommunications*] (TEL)
SWD............ Senior Weapon Director [*Air Force*]
SWD............ Seward, AK [*Location identifier FAA*] (FAAL)
SWD............ Sewed
SWD............ Short-Wave Diathermy [*Medicine*]
SWD............ Sideward (WGA)
SWD............ Side Water Depth
SWD............ Single Word Dump
SWD............ Sliding Watertight Door
SWD............ Smaller Word
SWD............ Softwood
SWD............ Soil Water Deficit [*Soil science*]
SWD............ Southwestern Division [*Army Corps of Engineers*]
SWD............ Special Water Dispenser [*British military*] (DMA)
SWD............ Standing Wave Detector
SWD............ Stormwater Drain
SwD............ Students with Disabilities
SWD............ Submarine Wire Dispenser
SWD............ Sun, Wind, Dust [*Goggles*] (MCD)
SWD............ Surface Wave Dielectrometer
SWD............ Swaziland [*Swaziland*] [*Seismograph station code, US Geological Survey*] (SEIS)
SWD............ Swinderby FTU [*British ICAO designator*] (FAAC)
SWD............ Synchronous Wave Device
SWDA.......... Scottish Wholesale Druggist Association (DBA)
SWDA.......... Solid Waste Disposal Act [*1965*]
SWDA.......... South West Development Authority [*Western Australia*]
SWDA.......... Step-Wise Discriminant Analysis
SWDB.......... Special Weapons Development Board
SWDC.......... Shock Wave Data Center [*Lawrence Radiation Laboratory*]
SwdEC.......... Swedish Export Credit Corp. [*Associated Press*] (SAG)
SWDG.......... Sun, Wind, Dust Goggles [*Military*] (INF)
SWDG.......... Surface Warfare Development Group [*Also, SURFWARDEVGRU*] [*Navy*]
SWDL.......... Safe Winter Driving League [*Defunct*] (EA)
SWDL.......... Surface Wave Delay Line
SwdMtch...... Swedish Match [*Associated Press*] (SAG)
SWDS.......... Scrolls from the Wilderness of the Dead Sea. Smithsonian Institution Exhibit Catalogue [*Washington, DC*] (BJA)
SWDS.......... Software Development System (MCD)
SWDVS........ Software Development and Verification System [*NASA*]
SWDYN........ Single-Wheel Dynamometer
SWE............ Scalar Wave Equation
SWE............ Shift Word, Extracting
SWE............ Simulated Work Experience
SWE............ Single Wafer Etching (NITA)
SWE............ Slow-Wave Encephalography [*Neurology*] (DAVI)
SWE............ Society of Wine Educators (EA)
SWE............ Society of Women Engineers (EA)
SWE............ Solar Wind Experiment [*NASA*] (KSC)
SWE............ Spherical Wave Expansion [*Telecommunications*] (TEL)
SWE............ Status Word Enable
SWE............ Steelworker Erector [*Navy rating*]
SWE............ Stress Wave Emission
SWE............ Swedair AB [*Sweden ICAO designator*] (FAAC)
SWE............ Sweden [*ANSI three-letter standard code*] (CNC)
Swe............ Sweden (VRA)
swe............ Swedish [*MARC language code Library of Congress*] (LCCP)
SWE............ Swensen's, Inc. [*Vancouver Stock Exchange symbol*]
SWEA.......... Swedish Women's Educational Association, International (EA)
SWEB.......... SoftQuad International, Inc. [*NASDAQ symbol*] (SAG)
SWEBF........ SoftQuad Intl [*NASDAQ symbol*] (TTSB)
SWECS........ Small Wind Energy Conversion Systems
SWED.......... Sweden [*or Swedish*]
SwedAE........ Swedish Antarctic Expedition [*1901-04*]
SWEDIS....... Swedish Drug Information System [*Swedish National Board of Health and Welfare*] [*Databank*] (IID)
SWEDL........ Southwest Educational Development Laboratory
SWEDTEL..... Swedish Telecoms International AB [*Telecommunications*]
SWEE.......... Southwest Electronic Exhibit
Sween.......... Sweeney's New York Superior Court Reports [*31-32 New York*] [*1869-70*] [*A publication*] (DLA)
Sweeney (NY)... Sweeney's New York Superior Court Reports [*31-32 New York*] [*A publication*] (DLA)
Sweeny........ Sweeney's New York Superior Court Reports [*31-32 New York*] [*A publication*] (DLA)
SWEEP........ Structures with Error Expurgation Program
SWEET........ Stay at Work, Earn Extra Time [*United Auto Workers*]
Sweet.......... Sweet on the Limited Liability Act [*A publication*] (DLA)
Sweet.......... Sweet on Wills [*A publication*] (DLA)
Sweet.......... Sweet's Law Dictionary [*A publication*] (DLA)
Sweet.......... Sweet's Marriage Settlement Cases [*A publication*] (DLA)
Sweet.......... Sweet's Precedents in Conveyancing [*A publication*] (DLA)
Sweet LD..... Sweet's Dictionary of English Law [*1882*] [*A publication*] (DLA)
Sweet LL...... Sweet on the Limited Liability Act [*A publication*] (DLA)
Sweet M Sett Cas... Sweet's Marriage Settlement Cases [*England*] [*A publication*] (DLA)
Sweet Pr Conv... Sweet's Precedents in Conveyancing [*4th ed.*] [*1886*] [*A publication*] (DLA)
SweetW........ SweetWater, Inc. [*Associated Press*] (SAG)
SWEFCO...... Special Weapons Ferry Control Office [*or Officer*]
SWEHAC...... Statewide Ear Health Advisory Committee [*Australia*]
SWEJDFC.... Sing with the Earth John Denver Fan Club (EA)
SWEL.......... Special Weapons Equipment List
Swell.......... Single Woman Earning Lots in London [*Lifestyle classification*]
SWELSTRA... Special Weapons Equipment List Single Theater Requisitioning Agency
SWEMED..... Swedish Medical Literature [*Database*] [*Karolinska Institute Library and Information Center/Medical Information Center*] [*Information service or system*] (CRD)
SWEMS....... Soil, Water, Estuarine Monitoring [*Environmental Protection Agency*] (GFGA)
Swen.......... Sweeney's New York Superior Court Reports [*31-32 New York*] [*A publication*] (DLA)
SWEPS........ Safety Weather Probability Study
SWERD........ Solid Waste and Emergency Response [*Environmental Protection Agency*] (GFGA)
SWESS........ Special Weapons Emergency Separation System (AFM)
SWESSAR.... Stone and Webster Standard Safety Analysis Report [*Nuclear energy*] (NRCH)
SWET.......... Simulated Water Entry Test [*Nuclear energy*]
SWET.......... Society of West End Theatre [*British*] (DBA)
SWET.......... Special Weapon Equipment Test (SAA)
SWETS........ Solid Waste Engineering Transfer System
SWETTU...... Special Weapons Experimental Tactical Test Unit
SWExB........ South Western Examinations Board [*Education*] (AIE)
SWF............ Air Swift [*British ICAO designator*] (FAAC)
SWF............ Newburgh [*New York*] [*Airport symbol*] (OAG)
SWF............ Screw Worm Fly
SWF............ Seawater Feed
SWF............ Shortwave Fadeouts
SWF............ Silver Wings Fraternity (EA)
SWF............ Single White Female [*Classified advertising*]
SWF............ Small Winemakers' Forum [*Australia*]
SWF............ Special Warning Function (MCD)
SWF............ Special Weapons Facility [*Navy*]
SWF............ Steelworker Fabricator [*Navy rating*]
SWF............ Stelway Food [*Vancouver Stock Exchange symbol*]
SWF............ Still Waters Foundation (EA)
SWF............ Sturge-Weber Foundation (EA)
SWF............ Sudden Wave Fade Out (IAA)
SWF............ Suedwestfunk [*Radio network*] [*West Germany*]
SWFB.......... Southwestern Freight Bureau
SWFC.......... Southwest Fisheries Center [*La Jolla, CA*] [*Department of Commerce*]
SWFC.......... Surface Weapons Fire Control
SWFG.......... Secondary Waveform Generator [*Telecommunications*] (TEL)
SWFI........... Sterile Water for Injection [*Pharmacology*] (DAVI)
SWFI........... Stratified Fuel-Water Injection [*Automotive engineering*]

SWFM .... Standing-Wave Fluorescence Microscopy
SWFPA .... Scottish White Fish Producers Association (DBA)
SWFPA .... Structural Wood Fiber Products Association [*Later, SCFPA*] (EA)
SWFR .... Slow Write, Fast Read [*Computer science*] (IEEE)
SWFSC .... Southwest Fisheries Science Center [*San Diego, CA*]
SWFT .... Swift Transportation [*NASDAQ symbol*] (TTSB)
SWFT .... Swift Transportation Co. [*NASDAQ symbol*] (SAG)
SwftEng .... Swift Energy Co. [*Associated Press*] (SAG)
SWFX .... Spotweld Fixture [*Tool*]
SWG .... Ground Air Transfer, Inc. [*ICAO designator*] (FAAC)
SWG .... Salam-Weinberg-Glashow [*One unified field theory in physics*]
SWG .... Science Working Group (EERA)
SWG .... Scientific Working Group [*EXAMETNET*]
SWG .... Screen Writers Guild (WDMC)
SWG .... Seabed Working Group [*Nuclear energy*] (NUCP)
SWG .... Shock Wave Generator
SWG .... Shuttle Working Group [*NASA*] (MCD)
SWG .... Sine Wave Generator
SWG .... Slotted Waveguide
SWG .... Society of Woman Geographers (EA)
SWG .... Software Working Group [*NASA*] (NASA)
SWG .... Songwriters Guild of Great Britain
SWG .... South-West Gold Corp. [*Vancouver Stock Exchange symbol*]
SWG .... Space Wing [*Military*]
SWG .... Special Wireless Group [*World War II British*]
SWG .... Special Working Group
SWG .... Spirit Airlines, Inc. [*FAA designator*] (FAAC)
SWG .... Squarewave Generator
SWG .... Staff Working Group
SWG .... Standard Wire Gauge [*Telecommunications*]
SWG .... Standard/Working Group (MCD)
SWG .... Strictly Wild Guess (SAA)
SWG .... Stubs Wire Gauge
SWG .... Sub-Working Group
SWG .... Swing (MSA)
SWG .... Swing-N-Slide Corp. [*AMEX symbol*] (SAG)
SWG .... Switching (WGA)
SwGAFn .... Southwest Georgia Financial Corp. [*Associated Press*] (SAG)
SwGas .... Southwest Gas Capital I [*Associated Press*] (SAG)
SWGD .... Swinging Door
SWGM .... Spanish World Gospel Mission (EA)
SWGR .... Switchgear
SWGS .... Surface Wire Grounding System [*Electronics*] (RDA)
SwGU .... Goteborgs Universititsbibliotek, Goteborg, Sweden [*Library symbol Library of Congress*] (LCLS)
SWH .... Scottish Women's Hospital [*British military*] (DMA)
SWH .... Seaway Multi-Corp Ltd. [*Toronto Stock Exchange symbol*]
SWH .... Significant Wave Height [*Oceanography*]
SWH .... Solar Water Heating
SWH .... Spaghetti Warehouse [*NYSE symbol*] (TTSB)
SWH .... Spaghetti Warehouse, Inc. [*NYSE symbol*] (SPSG)
SWH .... Standard Working Home [*Pet-adoption terminology*]
SWH .... Swan Hill [*Victoria, Australia*] [*Airport symbol*] (AD)
SWHA .... Social Welfare History Archives Center [*University of Minnesota*] [*Research center*] (RCD)
SwHelv .... Swiss Helvetia Fund, Inc. [*Associated Press*] (SAG)
SWHG .... Social Welfare History Group [*Western Michigan University*] [*Kalamazoo*] (EA)
SWHS .... Scissor Workboard Hands' Society [*A union*] [*British*]
SWI .... Salt-Water Igniter
SWI .... Scottish Woollen Industry
SWI .... Scudder World Income Opportunities Ltd. [*NYSE symbol*] (SAG)
SWI .... Scudder World Inc. Oppt Fd [*NYSE symbol*] (TTSB)
SWI .... Sealant and Waterproofers Institute (EA)
SWI .... Seawind Resources, Inc. [*Vancouver Stock Exchange symbol*]
SWI .... Seaworthiness Impairment (NVT)
SWI .... Sherman [*Texas*] [*Airport symbol*] (OAG)
SWI .... Shock Wave Interaction
SWI .... Short-Wave Interference [*Telecommunications*] (IAA)
SWI .... Sidewall Indentation [*Tire manufacturing*]
SWI .... Sine Wave Inverter
SWI .... Software Interrupt [*Computer science*]
SWI .... Special Weather Intelligence (MCD)
SWI .... Special World Intervals
SWI .... Stall Warning Indicator
SWI .... Standing Wave Indicator
SWI .... Steel Window Institute (EA)
SWI .... Sterile Water for Injection [*Pharmacology*] (DAVI)
SWI .... Stroke Work Index [*Neurology*]
SWI .... Sunworld International Airways, Inc. [*ICAO designator*] (FAAC)
SWIA .... Southwest Association of Indian Arts (BARN)
SWIBA .... Scottish Women's Indoor Bowling Association (DBA)
SWICA .... Self Winding Clock Association (EA)
SWICS .... Solar Wind Ion Composition Spectrometer (MCD)
SWIDOC .... Sociaal-Wetenschappelijk Informatie- en Documentatiecentrum [*Social Science Information and Documentation Center*] [*Netherlands Information service or system*] (IID)
SWIE .... Southern Waste Information Exchange (GNE)
SWIFT .... Selected Words in Full Title (NITA)
SWIFT .... Sequential Weight Increasing Factor Technique (IAA)
SWIFT .... Significant Word in the Full Title [*Computer science*] (DIT)
SWIFT .... Society for Worldwide Interbank Financial Telecommunication [*Banking netw ork*] [*Belgium*]
SWIFT .... Society for Worldwide Interbank Financial Transactions (NITA)
SWIFT .... Software Implemented Friden Translator [*Computer science*]
SWIFT .... Stored Wave Inverse Fourier Transform [*Spectrometry*]
SWIFT .... Strength of Wings Including Flutter
SWIFT .... Swept Wing with Inboard Flap for Trim [*Hang glider*] (PS)
SWIFT .... System Workshops in Forecasting Techniques [*Bell System*]
SWIFT-ANSWER... Special Word Indexed Full Text Alpha Numeric Storage with Easy Retrieval [*Software*]
Swift Dig ..... Swift's Connecticut Digest [*A publication*] (DLA)
Swift Ev .... Swift on Evidence, and Bills and Notes [*A publication*] (DLA)
SWIFT LASS... Signal Word Index of Field and Title - Literature Abstract Specialized Search (DIT)
SWIFT SIR... Signal Word Index of Field and Title - Scientific Information Retrieval (DIT)
Swift Sys ..... Swift's System of the Laws of Connecticut [*A publication*] (DLA)
SwiftT .... Swift Transportation Co. [*Associated Press*] (SAG)
SWIG .... Southwestern Irrigated Cotton Growers Association
SWIM .... Sea Warfare Interim Model (CINC)
SWIM .... Ship Weapons Installation Manual (MCD)
SWIM .... Soil-Water Infiltration & Movement
SWIM .... Sperm-Washing Insemination Method
SWIM .... Standard Wozniak Integrated Machine [*Computer science*]
SWIM .... Super Wozniak Integrated Machine [*Computer science*]
SWIM .... Surface Water Improvement and Management (MCD)
SWIM .... Switch Tail Interceptor Missile (MCD)
SWIMCRIT... Swim Criteria
SWIMS .... Serialized Weapons Information Management System [*Navy*]
SWIMS .... Skills for Working in a Multicultural Society [*Australia*]
SWIMS .... Solid Waste Information Management System (GAAI)
Swin .... Swinburne on Wills [*10 eds.*] [*1590-1803*] [*A publication*] (DLA)
SWIN .... Swinehead [*England*]
Swin .... Swinton's Scotch Justiciary Reports [*1835-41*] [*A publication*] (DLA)
Swinb Desc... Swinburne on Descents [*1825*] [*A publication*] (DLA)
Swinb Mar... Swinburne on Married Women [*1846*] [*A publication*] (DLA)
Swinb Spo... Swinburne on Spousals [*A publication*] (DLA)
Swinb Wills... Swinburne on Wills [*A publication*] (DLA)
SWINC .... Soft Wired Integrated Numerical Controller (IAA)
SWINE .... Students Wildly Indignant about Nearly Everything [*Group in "L'il Abner" comic strip*]
SWING .... Sterling Warrant into Gilt-Edged Stock [*British*]
SwingNSI .... Swing-N-Slide [*Associated Press*] (SAG)
SWINGR .... Sweep Integrator (AAG)
SwingSl .... Swing-N-Slide Corp. [*Associated Press*] (SAG)
Swin Jus Cas... Swinton's Scotch Justiciary Cases [*A publication*] (DLA)
Swin Reg App... Swinton's Scotch Registration Appeal Cases [*1835-41*] [*A publication*] (DLA)
Swint .... Swinton's Scotch Justiciary Cases [*A publication*] (DLA)
SWINTER .... Service Women in Non-Traditional Environmental Roles [*Canadian armed forces*]
SWIO .... SACLANT [*Supreme Allied Commander, Atlantic*] War Intelligence Organization (NATG)
SWIP .... Secret Work in Process (MCD)
SWIP .... Shared Whois Project
SWIP .... Society for Women in Philosophy (EA)
SWIP .... Soil-Wheel Interaction Performance
SWIP .... Standing Wave Impedance Probe [*Geophysical instrument*]
SWIP .... Stichting Werkgroep Indianen Projekt [*Netherlands*]
SWIP .... Super-Weight Improvement Program [*Navy*] (NG)
SWIP .... Systems Weapon Improvement Program [*A-6 Intruder*] (DOMA)
SWIPMD .... Society for Women in Philosophy, Midwest Division (EA)
SWIPS .... Soil Water Information Processing System
SWIR .... Shortwave Infrared
SWIR .... Special Weapons Inspection Report
SWIRL .... South Western Industrial Research Ltd. [*British*] (ARC)
SWIRLS .... Southwest Regional Library System [*Library network*]
SWIRS .... Solid Waste Information Retrieval System [*Environmental Protection Agency*]
SWIS .... Satellite Weather Information System [*National Oceanic and Atmospheric Administration*]
SWIS .... Satellite Weather Information System [*Marine science*] (OSRA)
SWIS .... Sensitive Wildlife Information System [*Army*] (IID)
SWIS .... Special Weapons Integration Subcommittee (SAA)
SWIS .... St. Ives Laboratories, Inc. [*NASDAQ symbol*] (NQ)
SWIS .... Swiss Wildlife Information Service [*Zurich*] [*Information service or system*] (IID)
Swish .... Swisher International [*Commercial firm Associated Press*] (SAG)
Swisher .... Swisher International [*Commercial firm Associated Press*] (SAG)
Swissray .... Swissray International, Inc. [*Associated Press*] (SAG)
SWIT .... Switzerland
SWITL .... Southwestern Industrial Traffic League (EA)
SWITT .... Surface Wave Independent Tap Transducer (IEEE)
SWITZ .... Switzerland
Switz .... Switzerland (VRA)
SWJ .... Single Wire Junction
SWJ .... Society of Women Journalists (DGA)
SWJ .... Socket Wrench Joint
SWJ .... StatesWest Airlines, Inc. [*ICAO designator*] (FAAC)
SWK .... General Aerospace, Inc. [*Canada ICAO designator*] (FAAC)
SWK .... Southwark [*England*]
SWK .... [*The*] Stanley Works [*NYSE symbol*] (SPSG)
SWK .... Stewart Lake Resources, Inc. [*Toronto Stock Exchange symbol*]
SWKO .... Sawako Corp. [*NASDAQ symbol*] (SAG)
SWKOY .... Sawako Corp. ADR [*NASDAQ symbol*] (TTSB)
SW KR .... Swedish Krona [*Monetary unit*]
SWL .... Safe Working Load [*Shipping*]
SWL .... Short Wavelength LASER
SWL .... Short Wavelength Limit

SWL............ Shortwave Listener [*Radio*]
SWL............ Signals Warfare Laboratory [*Army*] (RDA)
SWL............ Single-Wheel Loading [*Aviation*]
SWL............ Snow Hill, MD [*Location identifier FAA*] (FAAL)
SWL............ Solid Waste Litter
SWL............ Southwest Realty Ltd. [*Later, Southwestern Property Trade*] AM (SPSG)
SWL............ Spanish Wells [*Bahamas*] [*Airport symbol*] (AD)
SWL............ Special Weapons Loading (SAA)
SWL............ Still Water Level
SWL............ Strategic Weapons Loader (DWSG)
SWL............ Sulfite Waste Liquor
SWL............ Surface Wave Line
SWLA.......... Southwestern Library Association
SWLC.......... Southwestern Connecticut Library Council [*Library network*]
SWLC.......... South West London College [*London, England*]
SWLD.......... Smallworldwide PLC [*NASDAQ symbol*] (SAG)
SWLDG........ Socket Welding
SWLF.......... Southwestern Legal Foundation (EA)
SWLG.......... Scottish Wild Land Group (DBA)
SWLIN......... System Work List Item Number (DNAB)
SWL Rev..... Southwestern Law Review [*A publication*] (DLA)
SwLU.......... Lunds Universitet [*University of Lund*], Lund, Sweden [*Library symbol Library of Congress*] (LCLS)
SwLuH......... Hogskolan i Lulea [*Lulea University*], Lulea, Sweden [*Library symbol*] [*Library of Congress*] (LCLS)
Swm............ Metro Prop-Jet [*Airplane code*]
SWM............ Sawmill [*California*] [*Seismograph station code, US Geological Survey Closed*] (SEIS)
SWM............ Schweitzer Mauduit International Inc. [*NYSE symbol*] (SAG)
SWM............ Schweitzer-Mauduit Intl [*NYSE symbol*] (TTSB)
SWM............ Segmental Wall Motion [*Medicine*] (DMAA)
SWM............ Serber-Wilson Method [*Nuclear energy*] (NRCH)
SWM............ Shipboard Wave Meter
SWM............ Single White Male [*Classified advertising*]
SWM............ Society of Women Musicians, Inc. [*British*] (BI)
SwM............ Southwest Microfilm, Inc., El Paso, TX [*Library symbol Library of Congress*] (LCLS)
SWM............ Special Warfare Mission (AABC)
SWM............ Spotweld Machine [*Tool*]
SWM............ Stan West Mining Corp. [*Toronto Stock Exchange symbol*]
SWM............ Stewart Warner Microcircuits (IAA)
SWM............ Suia-Missu [*Brazil*] [*Airport symbol*] (OAG)
SWM............ Surface Wave Mode
SWMA.......... Scottish Wirework Manufacturers Association (DBA)
SWMA.......... Society of Women in Military Aviation (EA)
SWMA.......... Solid Waste Management Association
SWMA.......... Southwestern Monuments Association [*Later, SPMA*] (EA)
SWMA.......... Steel Wool Manufacturers' Association [*British*] (BI)
SWMA.......... Swedish Match [*NASDAQ symbol*] (SAG)
SWMAT........ Switch Matrix (MCD)
SWMAY........ Swedish Match AB ADR [*NASDAQ symbol*] (TTSB)
SWMC.......... Sanctuary Wood Multimedia [*NASDAQ symbol*] (SAG)
SWMCCS...... Standard Weather Messages Command and Control System (MCD)
SWMCF........ Sanctuary Woods Multimedia [*NASDAQ symbol*] (TTSB)
SWMCM........ Shallow-Water Mine Countermeasures (DOMA)
SWMF.......... South Wales Miners' Federation (DAS)
SWMFB........ Southwestern Motor Freight Bureau
SWMO.......... Solid Waste Management Office [*Later, Office of Solid Waste Management Programs*] [*Environmental Protection Agency*]
SWMS.......... Solid Waste Management System [*Nuclear energy*] (NRCH)
SWMTEP...... System-Wide Medium-Term Environment Programme (GNE)
SWMU.......... Solid Waste Management Unit (GNE)
SWMU.......... Solid Waste Management Unit [*Environmental science*]
SWN............ Leadville, CO [*Location identifier FAA*] (FAAL)
SWN............ Notre Dame College, Wilcox, Saskatchewan [*Library symbol National Library of Canada*] (NLC)
SWN............ Southwestern Energy [*NYSE symbol*] (TTSB)
SWN............ Southwestern Energy Co. [*NYSE symbol*] (SPSG)
SWN............ Sworn (ROG)
SWNCC........ State, War, Navy Coordinating Committee [*Later, SANAAC*]
SWND.......... Social Workers for Nuclear Disarmament (EA)
SwnEnrg...... Southwestern Energy Co. [*Associated Press*] (SAG)
SWNJ.......... Southwest New Jersey Consortium for Health Information Services [*Library network*]
SwnLfe........ Southwestern Life Corp. [*Formerly, ICH Corp.*] [*Associated Press*] (SAG)
SwnLife....... Southwestern Life Corp. [*Formerly, ICH Corp.*] [*Associated Press*] (SAG)
SWNT.......... Single-Wall Nanotube [*Materials science*]
SWNT.......... Single Wall [*Carbon*] Nanotube
SWO............ Senior Watch Officer [*Navy*] (NVT)
SWO............ Shallow Resources, Inc. [*Vancouver Stock Exchange symbol*]
SWO............ Signal Wireless Officer (IAA)
SWO............ Solid Waste Office [*Later, Office of Solid Waste Management Programs*] [*Environmental Protection Agency*]
SWO............ Southwestern Oregon Community College, Coos Bay, OR [*OCLC symbol*] (OCLC)
SWO............ Squadron Wireless Officer [*Navy British*]
SWO............ Squarewave Oscillator
SWO............ Staff Watch Officer (NVT)
SWO............ Staff Weather Officer [*Military*]
SWO............ Station Warrant Officer [*Air Force British*]
SWO............ Stillwater [*Oklahoma*] [*Airport symbol*] (OAG)
SWO............ Stop Work Order
SWO............ Stud Welding Outfit
SWO............ Support Work Order (AAG)
SWO............ Surface Warfare Officer [*Navy*] (NVT)
SW/O.......... Switchover
SWOAPQS... Surface Warfare Officer, Personnel Qualification Standards [*Navy*] (DNAB)
SWOB.......... Salaries, Wages, Overhead, and Benefits (NASA)
SWOB.......... Ship Waste Off-Loading Barge [*Navy*] (CAAL)
SWOC.......... Special Weapons Operation Center [*Army*] (AABC)
SWOC.......... Steel Workers Organizing Committee [*Became United Steelworkers of America*]
SWOC.......... Subject Word out of Context [*Computer science*] (DIT)
SWOD.......... Special Weapons Ordnance Devices
SWOE.......... Smart Weapons Operability Enhancement (RDA)
SWOG.......... Special Weapons Overflight Guide (AFM)
SWOP.......... Service Weapons Operational Procedures (MCD)
SWOP.......... Special Leave Without Pay
SWOP.......... Special Weapons Ordnance Publication [*Navy*] (NVT)
SWOP.......... Specifications for Web Offset Publications [*Printing technology*]
SWOP.......... Standard Web Offset Press [*Computer science*] (PCM)
SWOP.......... Stereo Wave Observation Project (IAA)
SWOP.......... Stop without Pay
SWOP.......... Structural Weight Optimization Program [*NASA*] (KSC)
SWOP.......... Switchboard Operator [*British military*] (DMA)
SWOP AMP... Switchable-Input Operational Amplifier [*Electronics*] (EECA)
SWOPS........ Single Well Oil Production Ship [*British*]
SWOPSI...... Stanford Workshop on Political and Social Issues [*Stanford University*]
SWORD........ Separated, Widowed, or Divorced [*New York City association*]
SWORD........ Shallow Water Oceanographic Research Data [*System*] [*Naval Ordnance Laboratory and Naval Oceanographic Office*]
SWORD........ Small Wars Operational Research Division [*Military*] (INF)
SWORD........ Software Optimization for the Retrieval of Data [*Computer science*] (MHDI)
SWORD........ Submarine Warfare Operations Research Department (DOMA)
SWORDS...... Standard Work Ordering and Reporting Data System [*Army*]
SWORL........ Southwestern Ohio Rural Libraries [*Library network*]
SwOrM........ Regionsjukhuset, Medicinska Biblioteket [*Regional Hospital, Medical Library*], Orebro, Sweden [*Library symbol Library of Congress*] (LCLS)
SWOS.......... Surface Warfare Officer's School [*Navy*] (NVT)
SWOSCOLCOM... Surface Warfare Officer's School Command [*Navy*] (NVT)
SWOSCOLCOMDET... Surface Warfare Officer's School Command Detachment [*Navy*] (DNAB)
SWOSU........ Southwestern Oklahoma State University
SWOT.......... Strengths, Weaknesses, Opportunities, Threats [*Analysis for organizations*]
SWOV.......... Switchover (MSA)
SWP............ Safe Working Pressure
SWP............ Salt-Water Pump (MSA)
SWP............ Science Working Panel [*NASA*]
SWP............ Scientific Word Processor [*Computer science*]
SWP............ Sector Working Party [*British*] (DCTA)
SWP............ Semi-Tech Microelectronics, Inc. [*Toronto Stock Exchange symbol*]
SWP............ Service Water Pump [*Nuclear energy*] (NRCH)
SWP............ Shock Wave Profile
SWP............ Short Wavelength Prime [*Camera for spectra*]
SWP............ Socialist Workers' Party [*British Political party*] (PPW)
SWP............ Society for Women in Plastics (EA)
SWP............ Society of Wedding Photographers [*British*] (DBA)
SWP............ Society of Wireless Pioneers
SWP............ Soil-Test Water Probe
SWP............ Solid Waste Packaging [*Nuclear energy*] (NRCH)
SWP............ Solid Waste Processing [*Nuclear energy*] (NRCH)
SWP............ Southwestern Property Trust, Inc. [*Later, South West Property Trust*] [*NYSE symbol*] (SPSG)
SWP............ Southwest Pacific
SWP............ South West Prop Tr [*NYSE symbol*] (TTSB)
SWP............ Space, Weight, and Power
SWP............ Special Weapons Project [*Military*]
SWP............ Special Working Party [*Military*]
SWP............ Standard Work Procedure (SAA)
SWP............ Standby Warning Panel (MCD)
SWP............ State Water Project [*California*] (ECON)
SWP............ Stichting Waakzaamheid Persoonregistratie [*Netherlands*]
SWP............ Stiftung Wissenschaft und Politik [*Foundation for Science and Politics*] [*Information service or system*] (IID)
SWP............ Submersible Water Pump
SWP............ Summer Work Program
SWP............ Supply Working Party of Official Committee on Armistice Terms and Civil Administration [*World War II*]
SWP............ Surface Warfare Plan [*Navy*] (CAAL)
SWP............ Surface Wave Phenomena
SWP............ Survey of Western Palestine [*C. R. Conder et al*] [*A publication*] (BJA)
SWP............ Swakopmund [*South-West Africa*] [*Airport symbol*] (AD)
SWP............ Swamp (ADA)
SWP............ Swamp Creek [*Montana*] [*Seismograph station code, US Geological Survey Closed*] (SEIS)
SWP............ Sweep
SWP............ Sweep
SWPA.......... Section for Women in Public Administration (EA)
SWPA.......... Southwestern Power Administration [*Department of Energy*]
SWPA.......... Southwestern Psychological Association (MCD)
SWPA.......... Southwest National [*NASDAQ symbol*] (TTSB)

SWPA Southwest National Corp. [*Greensburg, PA*] [*NASDAQ symbol*] (NQ)
SWPA Southwest Pacific Area [*World War II*]
SWPA Southwest Placement Association (AEBS)
SWPA Spotweld Pattern [*Tool*] (AAG)
SWPA Steel Works Plant Association [*British*] (BI)
SWPA Submersible Wastewater Pump Association (EA)
SWPA Surplus War Property Administration [*Terminated, 1944*]
SWPAN Special Weapons Project Analysis (SAA)
SWPB Surplus War Property Board [*Terminated, 1945*]
SWPC Short Wing Piper Club (EA)
SWPC Smaller War Plants Corp. [*World War II*]
SWPC Southwest Pacific Command [*Navy*]
SWPCP Prince Albert National Park, Parks Canada [*Parc National Prince Albert, ParcsCanada*] Waskesiu Lakes, Saskatchewan [*Library symbol National Library of Canada*] (NLC)
SWPF Southwest Pacific Force [*Later, Southwest Pacific Command*] [*Navy*]
SWPIA Southwest Pacific Island Arc [*Oceanography*]
SWPJ Study of Western Palestine: Jerusalem [*C. Warren and C. R. Conder*] [*A publication*] (BJA)
SWPlan Solid Waste Management Planning Software
SWPM Survey of Western Palestine: Memoirs [*C. R. Conder*] [*A publication*] (BJA)
SW/PM System Management/Performance Monitor
SW Pol Sci Q Southwestern Political Science Quarterly [*A publication*] (DLA)
SWPP Service Water Pressurization Pump [*Nuclear energy*] (IEEE)
SWPP Southwest Power Pool [*Regional power council*] (NRCH)
SWPPD Society for Women in Philosophy, Pacific Division (EA)
SWPPP Storm Water Pollution Prevention Plan [*Environmental science*]
SwPropT Southwestern Property Trust, Inc. [*Associated Press*] (SAG)
SWP(S) Solid Waste Processing System [*Nuclear energy*] (NRCH)
SWPS Strategic War Planning System [*Air Force*]
SWPSA Southwestern Peanut Shellers Association (EA)
SWPSD Society for Women in Philosophy, Southwest Division (EA)
SWPSP Survey of Western Palestine: Special Papers [*A publication*] (BJA)
SWPT Service Weapons Test (NVT)
SWQ Sumbawa [*Indonesia*] [*Airport symbol*] (AD)
SWQI South West Queensland Initiative (EERA)
SWR Serum Wassermann Reaction [*Clinical chemistry*]
SWR Service Water Reservoir [*Nuclear energy*] (NRCH)
SWR Sewer
SWR Short Wavelength Radiation (KSC)
SWR Shortwave Ratio (DEN)
SWR Sine Wave Response
SWR Siphon Withdrawal Response
SWR Sodium-Water Reaction [*Nuclear energy*] (NRCH)
SWR Sons of the Whiskey Rebellion (EA)
SWR Southwestern Railway [*British*] (ROG)
SWR South Western Reporter [*A publication*] (DLA)
SWR Southwest Review [*A publication*] (BRI)
SWR Special Warning Receiver (MCD)
SWR Sperm Wassermann Reaction [*Urology*] (DAVI)
SWR Standing Wave Ratio [*Voltage*] [*Electronics*]
SWR State Wildlife Reserve [*State*] (EERA)
SWR Steel Wire Rope
SWR Stepwise Refinement (IAA)
SWR Stonewall Resources [*Vancouver Stock Exchange symbol*]
SWR Stress Wave Riveter [*Metal forming*]
SWR Submarine Water Reactor [*Nuclear energy*] (NRCH)
SWR Swisher International Group
SWR Swissair (Societe Anonyme Switzerland pour la Navigation Aerienne) [*ICAO designator*] (FAAC)
SWR Switch Rails
SWR2 Scaled Weapons Radius Squared (SAA)
SWRA Selected Water Resources Abstracts [*US Geological Survey*] [*Information service or system*] (CRD)
SWRA Stepwise Regression Analysis (PDAA)
SWRB Sadler's Wells Royal Ballet [*British*]
SWRB Standing Wave Ratio Bridge [*Electronics*]
SWRCB State Water Resources Control Board (DOGT)
SW Rep South Western Reporter [*A publication*] (DLA)
SW Repr South Western Reporter [*A publication*] (DLA)
SWRF Sine Wave Response Filter [*Program*]
SWRHL Southwestern Radiological Health Laboratory [*HEW*]
SWRI Scottish Women's Rural Institutes (DI)
SWRI Sea World Research Institute [*Marine science*] (GNE)
SWRI Southwestern Research Institute [*San Antonio, TX*] [*Research center*]
SWRJ Split Wing Ramjet
SWRL Southwest Regional Laboratory [*Research center*] (RCD)
SWRL Southwest Regional Laboratory for Educational Research and Development
SWRLSS Southwest Regional Library Service System [*Library network*]
SWRM Standing Wave Ratio Meter [*Electronics*]
SWRMPAC Southwestern Regional Manpower Advisory Committee [*Terminated, 1974*] [*Department of Labor*] (EGAO)
SWROM Standing Wave Read-Only Memory [*Computer science*]
SWROSS Southwest Regional Office for Spanish Speaking (EA)
SWRP Satellite Wildlife Research Project
SWRP Sectionalized Work Requirements Package (MCD)
SWRPRS Sodium-Water Reaction Pressure Relief Subsystem [*Nuclear energy*] (NRCH)
SWRSIC Southern Water Resources Scientific Information Center [*Raleigh, NC*]
SWRT Software Artistry [*NASDAQ symbol*] (SAG)
SWS Lindquist Investment Co., Inc. [*ICAO designator*] (FAAC)
SWS Saturn Workshop [*NASA*]
SWS Seam Welding System
SWS Service Water System [*Nuclear energy*] (NRCH)
SWS Service-Wide Supply
SWS Shallow Water SONAR
SWS Shift Word, Substituting
SWS Shock Wave Sensor (RDA)
SWS Shore Wireless Service [*British military*] (DMA)
SWS Short-Wave Sleep (OA)
SWS Single White Silk-Covered [*Wire insulation*]
SWS Slow-Wave Sleep
SWS Slow Wave Structure [*Satellite delay tube*] (NTCM)
SWS Smart Weapons Systems [*Army*] (RDA)
SWS Sniper Weapon Sight (INF)
SWS Sniper Weapon System (INF)
SWS Sniper Weapon System [*Army*]
SWS Social World Service (DAVI)
SWS Sociologists for Women in Society (EA)
SWS Solar Wind Spectrometer
SwS Solidarity with Solidarity [*See also SzS*] [*Defunct*] (EAIO)
SWS Solid Waste System [*Nuclear energy*] (NRCH)
SWS Space Weapon Systems [*Air Force*]
SWS Special Weapon Systems [*Military*]
SWS Spike-Wave Stupor [*Medicine*] (DMAA)
SWS Standard Weapon Station [*Nuclear arms control*]
SWS Static Water Supply (ADA)
SWS Still Water Surface
SWS Strategic Warning Staff
SWS Strategic Weapon System [*Military*] (CAAL)
SWS Stripline with Stud (IAA)
SWS Student Ward Secretary [*Hospital administration*] (DAVI)
SWS Sturge-Weber Syndrome [*Medicine*] (DAVI)
SWS Swansea [*Wales*] [*Airport symbol*] (OAG)
SWS Swift Minerals Ltd. [*Vancouver Stock Exchange symbol*]
SWS Switch Scan (MCD)
SWS Switch Stand
SWS Systolic Wall Stress [*Cardiology*]
SWSA Scottish Water Ski Associaton (DBA)
SWSA Southern Wood Seasoning Association
SWSD Special Weapons Supply Depot
SWSE Southeast Regional Library, Weyburn, Saskatchewan [*Library symbol National Library of Canada*] (NLC)
SWSF Society for a World Service Federation [*Defunct*] (EA)
SWSG Security Window Screen and Guard
SWSH Swisher International [*NASDAQ symbol*] (SAG)
SWSHW Swisher Intl Wrrt [*NASDAQ symbol*] (TTSB)
SWSI Single Width, Single Inlet (OA)
SWSI Surface Water Supply Index [*to measure drought*]
SWSIR Ship Weapons System Integration Requirements [*Navy*]
SwSK Kungliga Tekniska Hoegskolan [*Royal Institute of Technology*], Stockholm, Sweden [*Library symbol Library of Congress*] (LCLS)
SwSKB Kungliga Biblioteket, Bibliotheca Regia Holmiensis, Stockholm, Sweden [*Library symbol Library of Congress*] (LCLS)
SwSKM Kungliga Karolinska Mediko-Kirurgiska Institutes, Stockholm, Sweden [*Library symbol Library of Congress*] (LCLS)
SwSL Latinamerika-Institutet, Stockholm, Sweden [*Library symbol Library of Congress*] (LCLS)
SWSL Supplemental Weather Service Location [*Aviation*] (FAAC)
SWSM Special Weapons Supply Memorandum [*Army*] (AABC)
SWSR Solid Waste Shipping Room [*Nuclear energy*] (NRCH)
SWSR Standing Wave Signal Ratio (IAA)
SWS/SUM PTS Selection Work Sheets/Summary Parts
SWST Service Water Storage Tank [*Nuclear energy*] (IEEE)
SWST Society of Wood Science and Technology (EA)
SWST Southwest Securities Group [*NASDAQ symbol*] (SPSG)
SWST Southwest Securities Grp [*NASDAQ symbol*] (TTSB)
SwstAirl Southwest Airlines Co. [*Associated Press*] (SAG)
SwstBc Southwest Bancorp [*Associated Press*] (SAG)
SwstBcp Southwest Bancorp [*Associated Press*] (SAG)
SwstNat Southwest National Corp. [*Associated Press*] (SAG)
SwstSec Southwest Securities Group [*Associated Press*] (SAG)
SwSU Stockholms Universitetsbibliotheket, Stockholm, Sweden [*Library symbol Library of Congress*] (LCLS)
SwSU-T University of Stockholm, Department of Physical Geography, Trafala Glaciological Station, Stockholm, Sweden [*Library symbol*] [*Library of Congress*] (LCLS)
SWSVC Souris Valley Regional Care Center, Weyburn, Saskatchewan [*Library symbol National Library of Canada*] (NLC)
SW-SWIP Society for Women in Philosophy, Southwestern Division (EA)
SWSWTU Sheffield Wool Shear Workers' Trade Union [*British*] (DCTA)
SWT Safe Women's Transport [*British*]
SWT Scottish Wildlife Trust [*British*]
SWT Scout Weapons Team [*Army*] (DOMA)
SWT Search-while-Track (CAAL)
SWT Seward, NE [*Location identifier FAA*] (FAAL)
SWT Shortwave Transmitter
SWT Silent Witness [*Vancouver Stock Exchange symbol*]
SWT Single-Weight [*Paper*]
SWT Special Weapons Test
SWT Spiral Wrap Tubing
SWT Spotweld Template (MCD)
SWT Stab Wound of the Throat (DAVI)
SWT Steel Watertight [*Shipfitting*]
SWT Supersonic Wind Tunnel (MCD)
SWT Sweat

SWT .... Sweet
SWT .... Swept Frequency Transform (CAAL)
SWT .... Swiftair SA [*Spain ICAO designator*] (FAAC)
SWT .... Switch Ties
SWT .... System Work Team (MCD)
SWTA .... Special Weapons Training Allowance
SWTC .... Special Weapon Technical Command [*Navy*] (MCD)
SWTC .... Stop War Toys Campaign (EA)
SWTG .... Switching (WGA)
SwtGas .... Southwest Gas Corp. [*Associated Press*] (SAG)
SWTI .... Special Weapons Technical Instructions [*Army*] (AABC)
SWTL .... Surface Wave Transmission Line
SWTMA .... Scottish Woollen Trade Mark Association (DBA)
SwtPS .... Southwestern Public Service Co. [*Associated Press*] (SAG)
SWTR .... Surface Water Treatment Rule [*Environmental Protection Agency*]
SWTS .... Secondary Waste Treatment System [*Nuclear energy*] (NRCH)
SWTT .... Single-Well Tracer Test [*Petroleum technology*]
SWTTEU .... Special Weapons Test and Tactical Evaluation Unit
SWTX .... Southwall Technologies [*NASDAQ symbol*] (TTSB)
SWTX .... Southwall Technologies, Inc. [*NASDAQ symbol*] (NQ)
SWTZ .... Switzerland
SWU .... Idaho Falls, ID [*Location identifier FAA*] (FAAL)
SWU .... Sagami Women's University [*UTLAS symbol*]
SWU .... Separative Work Unit [*Measure of uranium enrichment capability*]
SWU .... Septic Workup [*Bacteriology*] (DAVI)
SWU .... Slovenian Women's Union (EA)
SWU .... Special Wash Up [*Printing*] (DGA)
SWU .... Standard Work Unit (EG)
SWU .... Steelhawk Resources Ltd. [*Vancouver Stock Exchange symbol*]
SWUCNET .... Southwest Universities Computer Network (NITA)
SWULANT .... Special Weapons Unit, Atlantic [*Navy*] (DNAB)
SWULSCP .... Southwest University Libraries Systems Cooperative Project (NITA)
SwUmU .... Umea Universitetsbibliotek, Umea, Sweden [*Library symbol Library of Congress*] (LCLS)
SWUPAC .... Special Weapons Unit, Pacific [*Navy*] (DNAB)
SWUS .... Southwest United States
SWUSL .... Southwestern University School of Law (DLA)
SwUU .... Universitet i Uppsala [*University of Uppsala*], Uppsala, Sweden [*Library symbol Library of Congress*] (LCLS)
SWV .... Squarewave Voltammetry [*Electrochemistry*]
SWV .... Swan View [*Australia Seismograph station code, US Geological Survey*] (SEIS)
SWV .... Swivel (AAG)
SWVA .... Scottish War Veterans of America (EA)
SWVA .... Shemya WWII Veterans Association (EA)
SWVA .... Steel of West Virgina [*NASDAQ symbol*] (TTSB)
SWVA .... Steel of West Virginia, Inc. [*NASDAQ symbol*] (NQ)
SWVA .... Steel West Virginia [*NASDAQ symbol*] (SAG)
SWVB .... Social Work Vocational Bureau (EA)
SWVL .... Swivel (MSA)
SWVR .... Standing Wave Voltage Ratio [*Electronics*] (IAA)
SWW .... Intersun Havacilik Anonim Sirketi [*Turkey*] [*FAA designator*] (FAAC)
SWW .... Severe Weather Warning (KSC)
SWW .... Society of Women Writers (DGA)
SWW .... Soft White Winter [*Wheat*] (OA)
SWW .... Stow Resources [*Vancouver Stock Exchange symbol*]
SWW .... Sweetwater [*Texas*] [*Airport symbol*] (AD)
SWW .... Sweetwater, TX [*Location identifier FAA*] (FAAL)
SWW .... Winthrop College, Rock Hill, SC [*OCLC symbol*] (OCLC)
SWWA .... South-West Water Authority [*British*] (DCTA)
SwWatr .... Southwest Water Co. [*Associated Press*] (SAG)
SWWBDS .... Software Work Breakdown Structure (MCD)
SWWBS .... Software Work Breakdown Structure
SWWC .... Southwest Water Co. [*La Puente, CA*] [*NASDAQ symbol*] (NQ)
SWWF .... Speed-Welding Wire Feeder
SWWJ .... Society of Women Writers and Journalists (DGA)
SWWOAH .... Society of World War One Aero Historians [*Defunct*] (EA)
SWWT .... Sweetwater Inc. [*NASDAQ symbol*] (TTSB)
SWWT .... SweetWater, Inc. [*NASDAQ symbol*] (SAG)
SWWU .... Singapore Wood Workers' Union
SWX .... Southwest Gas [*NYSE symbol*] (TTSB)
SWX .... Southwest Gas Corp. [*NYSE symbol*] (SPSG)
SWXO .... Staff Weather Officer [*NASA*] (KSC)
SWXPrA .... So West Gas Cap 1 9.125%'TOPrS' [*NYSE symbol*] (TTSB)
SWY .... Albemarle, NC [*Location identifier FAA*] (FAAL)
SWY .... Safeway, Inc. [*NYSE symbol*] (SPSG)
SWY .... Skyway Business Travel Ltd. [*British ICAO designator*] (FAAC)
SWY .... Stopway
SWY .... Stornaway Resources Corp. [*Vancouver Stock Exchange symbol*]
SWY .... Swiss Yiddish (BJA)
SWY.WS .... Safeway Inc. Wrrts [*NYSE symbol*] (TTSB)
SWZ .... Smyrna, TN [*Location identifier FAA*] (FAAL)
SWZ .... Special Watch Zone [*Navy*] (NVT)
SWZ .... Swaziland [*ANSI three-letter standard code*] (CNC)
SWZ .... Swiss Helvetia Fund [*NYSE symbol*] (SPSG)
SWZA .... Suiza Foods [*NASDAQ symbol*] (TTSB)
SWZA .... Suiza Foods Corp. [*NASDAQ symbol*] (SAG)
Swzld .... Swaziland (VRA)
SX .... Christman Air System [*ICAO designator*] (AD)
SX .... Pia Societas Sancti Francisci Xaverii pro Exteris Missionibus [*St. Francis Xavier Foreign Mission Society*] [*Xaverian Missionary Fathers*] [*Roman Catholic religious order*]
SX .... Sacks
SX .... Sigma Xi [*Society*]
Sx .... Signs (DAVI)
SX .... Simplex [*Transmission direction*] (CET)
SX .... Simplex Signaling (IAA)
SX .... Society of St. Francis Xavier for the Foreign Missions [*Also known as Xaverian Missionaries*] (EAIO)
SX .... Solvent Extraction (DEN)
sx .... South West Africa [*Namibia*] [*MARC country of publication code Library of Congress*] (LCCP)
sx .... Suction [*Surgery*] (DAVI)
SX .... Surgeries (DAVI)
SX .... Sussex [*County in England*]
SX .... SXT Resources Ltd. [*Vancouver Stock Exchange symbol*]
Sx .... Symptoms [*Medicine*] (WGA)
SX .... Union of Soviet Socialist Republics [*Later, FC*] [*License plate code assigned to foreign diplomats in the US*]
SX .... Xaverian Missionary Fathers (TOCD)
sx .... Xaverian Missionary Fathers, St. Francis Xavier Mission Society (TOCD)
SX70 .... SX-70 (VRA)
SXA .... Shannon Executive Aviation Ireland Ltd. [*ICAO designator*] (FAAC)
SXA .... Stored Index to Address
SXAD .... Sioux Army Depot
SXAP .... Soft X-Ray Appearance Potential (IAA)
SXAPS .... Soft X-Ray Appearance Potential Spectrometer [*or Spectroscopy*]
SXB .... Strasbourg [*France*] [*Airport symbol*] (OAG)
SXBT .... Shipboard Expendable Bathythermograph [*System*] [*Naval Oceanographic Office*]
SXC .... Saint Xavier College [*Chicago, IL*]
SXC .... Santa Catalina, CA [*Location identifier FAA*] (FAAL)
SXC .... Santa Catalina Island [*California*] [*Airport symbol*] (AD)
SXCT .... Spiral X-Ray Computed Tomography [*Medicine*] (DMAA)
SXD .... Springfield, VT [*Location identifier FAA*] (FAAL)
SXD .... Store Index in Decrement (SAA)
SXE .... Sale [*Australia Airport symbol*] (OAG)
SXE .... Soft X-Ray Experiment [*Also, SXX*]
SXE .... Spencar Explorations Ltd. [*Vancouver Stock Exchange symbol*]
SXEW .... Solvent Extraction and Electrowinning [*Metallurgy*]
SXF .... Berlin [*Germany Airport symbol*] (OAG)
SXF .... Solvent Extraction Feed [*Nuclear energy*] (NRCH)
SXG .... Senanga [*Zambia*] [*Airport symbol*] (OAG)
SXH .... Sehulea [*Papua New Guinea*] [*Airport symbol*] (OAG)
SXI .... Software Extraordinaire, Inc. [*Telecommunications service*] (TSSD)
SXI .... Solar X-Ray Imager [*Marine science*] (OSRA)
SXI .... Solar X-Ray Imager (USDC)
SXI .... Standex International Corp. [*NYSE symbol*] (SPSG)
SXI .... Standex Intl [*NYSE symbol*] (TTSB)
SXI .... Synex International, Inc. [*Toronto Stock Exchange symbol*]
SXIS .... Scattered X-Ray Internal Standard [*for surface analysis*]
SXL .... Sexless [*Connector*]
SXL .... Short-Arc Xenon Lamp
SXL .... Soft X-Ray LASER
SXL .... Summersville, WV [*Location identifier FAA*] (FAAL)
SXM .... Scanning X-Ray Microscopy (MCD)
SXM .... Sint Maarten [*Netherlands Antilles*] [*Airport symbol*] (AD)
SXM .... Sphinx Mining Inc. [*Vancouver Stock Exchange symbol*]
SXM .... St. Maarten [*Netherlands Antilles*] [*Airport symbol*]
SXML .... San Xavier Mining Laboratory [*University of Arizona*] [*Research center*] (RCD)
SXN .... Sal Luftverkehrs GmbH, Flughafen Leipzig-Halle [*Germany*] [*FAA designator*] (FAAC)
SXN .... Sao Jose Do Xingu [*Brazil*] [*Airport symbol*] (OAG)
SXN .... Section (MDG)
SXO .... Senior Experimental Officer [*Also, SEO, SExO*] [*Ministry of Agriculture, Fisheries, and Food*] [*British*]
SXP .... Sheldon Point [*Alaska*] [*Airport symbol*] (OAG)
SXP .... Sunnyvale Public Library, Sunnyvale, CA [*OCLC symbol*] (OCLC)
SXPL .... Soft X-Ray Projection Lithography
SXQ .... Soldotna, AK [*Location identifier FAA*] (FAAL)
SXR .... Soft X-Ray Region
SXR .... Srinagar [*India*] [*Airport symbol*] (OAG)
SXRB .... Soft X-Ray Background [*Astronomy*]
SXRF .... Synchrotron X-Ray Fluorescence [*Spectrometry*]
SXRT .... Soft X-Ray Telescope (SSD)
SXS .... Gunes Ekspres Havacilik AS (Sunexpress) [*Turkey*] [*ICAO designator*] (FAAC)
SXS .... Sigma Xi Society
SXS .... Stellar X-Ray Spectra
SXS .... Step by Step Switch (NITA)
SxS .... Step-by-Step Switching System [*Telecommunications*]
SXS .... Surface X-Ray Scattering [*Physics*]
SXT .... Lehman Br G1 Tele'SUNS'2000 [*AMEX symbol*] (TTSB)
SXT .... Lehman Brothers, Inc. [*AMEX symbol*] (SAG)
SXT .... Sextant (NASA)
SXT .... Sexton Summit, OR [*Location identifier FAA*] (FAAL)
SXT .... Sextuple (MSA)
SXT .... Soft X-Ray Telescope [*Astronomy*] (PS)
SXT .... Stable X-Ray Transmitter
SXT .... Sulfamethoxazole [*An antibacterial*] (DAVI)
SXTF .... Satellite X-Ray Test Facility
SXTN .... Sextant (MSA)
SXU .... Soddu [*Ethiopia*] [*Airport symbol*] (AD)
SXX .... Satellite Aero, Inc. [*ICAO designator*] (FAAC)
SXX .... Soft X-Ray Experiment [*Also, SXE*]
SXY .... Sidney [*New York*] [*Airport symbol*] (OAG)
SY .... Air Alsace [*ICAO designator*] (AD)
SY .... School Year (AABC)

SY Search Year (NITA)
SY Security
SY Sefer Yezirah (BJA)
SY Seychelles
SY Shelby Williams Ind [*NYSE symbol*] (TTSB)
SY Shelby Williams Industries, Inc. [*NYSE symbol*] (SPSG)
SY Shipyard
SY Shoulder Yaw (MCD)
SY Shropshire Yeomanry [*British military*] (DMA)
SY Sloppy [*Track condition*] [*Thoroughbred racing*]
SY Southern Yiddish (BJA)
SY Spectroscopy [*Medicine*] (DMAA)
SY Spring Yearling
SY Square Yard
SY Staff Years (OICC)
SY Steam Yacht (ROG)
SY Sticky (WGA)
SY Stripping Yield [*Agriculture*] (OA)
SY Supply [*Business term*]
SY Surrey [*County in England*]
SY Survey
SY Sussex Yeomanry [*British military*] (DMA)
SY Sustainer Yaw (AAG)
SY Symbol (IAA)
Sy Symmachus (BJA)
SY Symmetry [*or Symmetrical*] (DAVI)
Sy Symptoms [*Medicine*]
SY Synchronized (MDG)
SY Synchronoscope (IAA)
Sy Synchronous System [*on a ship*] (DS)
SY Synonyms (NITA)
SY Syphilis [*Medicine*]
SY Syphilitic [*Medicine*] (DMAA)
SY Syracuse [*Diocesan abbreviation*] [*New York*] (TOCD)
SY Syria [*or Syrian Arab Republic*] [*ANSI two-letter standard code*] (CNC)
sy Syria [*MARC country of publication code Library of Congress*] (LCCP)
SY Syrup (WGA)
SY System
SYA Save Your Afterdeck [*Bowdlerized version*]
SYA Scandinavian Yachting Association [*See also SKAN SF*] (EAIO)
SYA Shemya Island [*Alaska*] [*Airport symbol*] (OAG)
SYA Subud Youth Association (EA)
SYADS Syracuse Air Defense Sector (SAA)
SYAH Aishalton [*Guyana*] [*ICAO location identifier*] (ICLI)
SYAN Annai [*Guyana*] [*ICAO location identifier*] (ICLI)
SY & LI Sherwood Yeomanry and Light Infantry [*British military*] (DMA)
SYAP Apoteri [*Guyana*] [*ICAO location identifier*] (ICLI)
SYAW Awaruwaunawa [*Guyana*] [*ICAO location identifier*] (ICLI)
SYB Seal Bay [*Alaska*] [*Airport symbol*] (OAG)
SYB Statesman's Yearbook [*A publication*]
SYB Sybron International Co. [*Formerly, Sybron Corp.*] [*NYSE symbol*] (SAG)
SYB Sybron Intl [*NYSE symbol*] (TTSB)
SYB Symbol [*Spain ICAO designator*] (FAAC)
SYB Syracuse University, Syracuse, NY [*OCLC symbol*] (OCLC)
SYBA S.Y. Bancorp [*NASDAQ symbol*] (SAG)
Sybase Sybase, Inc. [*Associated Press*] (SAG)
SY Bcp S.Y. Bancorp [*Associated Press*] (SAG)
SYBF Share Your Birthday Foundation [*Defunct*] (EA)
SyblTc Symbol Technologies, Inc. [*Associated Press*] (SAG)
SYBR Baramita [*Guyana*] [*ICAO location identifier*] (ICLI)
Sybron Sybron Chemical Industries [*Associated Press*] (SAG)
SybronInt Sybron International Co. [*Formerly, Sybron Corp.*] [*Associated Press*] (SAG)
SYBS Sybase, Inc. [*NASDAQ symbol*] (SPSG)
SYBT Bartica [*Guyana*] [*ICAO location identifier*] (ICLI)
SYC Sanday [*Scotland*] [*Airport symbol*] (AD)
SYC Seychelles [*ANSI three-letter standard code*] (CNC)
SYC Small, Yellow, Constipated [*Stool*] [*Gastroenterology*] (DAVI)
SYC Swedish Export Credit Corp. [*AMEX symbol*] (SAG)
SYC Sycamore (AAG)
SYC Symbol Correspondence Element [*Computer science*] (PCM)
SYC Symbolic Corrector (SAA)
SYC Synco Development [*Vancouver Stock Exchange symbol*]
SYCATE Symptom-Cause-Test
SYCLOPS SYFA Concurrent Logic Operating System
SYCLOPS SYFA Current Logic Operating System (NITA)
SYCM Sybron Chemicals [*NASDAQ symbol*] (TTSB)
SYCM Sybron Chemicals, Inc. [*NASDAQ symbol*] (SPSG)
SYCOM Sydney Computerised Overnight Market [*Australia*]
SYCOM Synchronous Communications [*Satellite*] [*GSFC*]
SYCOM Systems Command
SYCOSPARE Shipyard Checkout Spare
SYCOT Shipyard Checkout Test
SYCR Sychronize (IAA)
SYD Air Yendis Ltd. [*Zambia*] [*FAA designator*] (FAAC)
SYD Casper, WY [*Location identifier FAA*] (FAAL)
SYD Scheer Energy Development Corp. [*Vancouver Stock Exchange symbol*]
SYD Scotland Yard
SYD Shipyard
SYD South Yemen Dinar (BJA)
SYD Sum of the Year's Digits [*Statistics*]
SYD Sydney [*Australia Airport symbol*] (OAG)
SYD Sydney [*Australia Seismograph station code, US Geological Survey Closed*] (SEIS)
SYDAS System Data Acquisition System
SYDEC Selective Yield Delayed Coking [*Foster Wheeler USA Corp. process*]
SYDIA System Developer Interface Activity [*Computer science*]
Syd Inst Crim Proc University of Sydney Faculty of Law. Proceedings of the Institute of Criminology [*A publication*]
Sydney Univ Gaz Sydney University. Gazette [*A publication*]
Sydney Univ Rev Sydney University. Review [*A publication*]
SYDP Six-Year Defense Plan [*Used briefly from the late 1980s to 1991*] (DOMA)
Syd R Sydney Review [*A publication*]
SYE Sa'Dah [*Yemen Arab Republic*] [*Airport symbol*] (OAG)
SYE Sheba Aviation [*Yemen*] [*FAA designator*] (FAAC)
SYE Square Yards Equivalent (DICI)
SYE Symbol Element [*Computer science*] (PCM)
SYEB Ebini [*Guyana*] [*ICAO location identifier*] (ICLI)
SYEP Summer Youth Employment Program [*Department of Labor*]
SYEP Symmetrical Disubstituted Ethoxy Propane [*Organic chemistry*] (MCD)
SYERS Senior Year Electro-optical Reconnaissance System [*Air Force*] (DOMA)
SYF Sky One Express Airlines, Inc. [*ICAO designator*] (FAAC)
SYF Spiritualist Yoga Fellowship (EAIO)
SYF St. Francis, KS [*Location identifier FAA*] (FAAL)
SYFA System for Access [*Computer science*] (IAA)
SYFA System for Application [*Computer science*]
SYFANET System for Access Network [*Wespac*] (TSSD)
SYG Arcola, TX [*Location identifier FAA*] (FAAL)
SYG Secretary-General (NATG)
SYG Symbol Graph [*Computer science*] (PCM)
SYG Synergy International [*Vancouver Stock Exchange symbol*]
SYGA Systems Gauge [*Tool*] (AAG)
SYGC Georgetown [*Guyana*] [*ICAO location identifier*] (ICLI)
SYGH Good Hope [*Guyana*] [*ICAO location identifier*] (ICLI)
SYGO Ogle [*Guyana*] [*ICAO location identifier*] (ICLI)
SYGR Synagro Technologies, Inc. [*NASDAQ symbol*] (SAG)
SYGRU Synagro Tech Unit [*NASDAQ symbol*] (TTSB)
SYGRW Synagro Technologies Wrrt [*NASDAQ symbol*] (TTSB)
SYGT Georgetown [*Guyana*] [*ICAO location identifier*] (ICLI)
SYH Scottish & York Holdings Ltd. [*Toronto Stock Exchange symbol*]
SYH See You Home [*Teen slang*]
Syh Syrohexapla (BJA)
SYHA Scottish Youth Hostels Association
SYI Shelbyville [*Tennessee*] [*Airport symbol*] (AD)
SYI Shelbyville, TN [*Location identifier FAA*] (FAAL)
SYI Symes Resources [*Vancouver Stock Exchange symbol*]
SYIB Imbaimadai [*Guyana*] [*ICAO location identifier*] (ICLI)
SYJ Slate Falls Airways Ltd. [*Canada ICAO designator*] (FAAC)
SYK Skyhawk Resources, Inc. [*Vancouver Stock Exchange symbol*]
SYK Stykkisholmur [*Iceland*] [*Airport symbol*] (OAG)
SYKA Kaieteur [*Guyana*] [*ICAO location identifier*] (ICLI)
SYKE Sukes Enterprises [*NASDAQ symbol*] (TTSB)
SYKE Sykes Enterprises Inc. [*NASDAQ symbol*] (SAG)
SykesEn Sykes Enterprises Inc. [*Associated Press*] (SAG)
SYKI Kaow Island [*Guyana*] [*ICAO location identifier*] (ICLI)
SYKK Kurukabaru [*Guyana*] [*ICAO location identifier*] (ICLI)
SYKM Kamarang [*Guyana*] [*ICAO location identifier*] (ICLI)
SYKR Karanambo [*Guyana*] [*ICAO location identifier*] (ICLI)
SYKS Karasabai [*Guyana*] [*ICAO location identifier*] (ICLI)
SYKT Kato (Karto) [*Guyana*] [*ICAO location identifier*] (ICLI)
SYKW Kwakwani [*Guyana*] [*ICAO location identifier*] (ICLI)
SYL Salvation Army Youth Line [*Australia*]
SYL San Miguel, CA [*Location identifier FAA*] (FAAL)
SYL Somali Youth League [*Political party*] (AF)
SYL Spartacus Youth League (EA)
Syl [*The*] Syllabi [*A publication*] (DLA)
SYL Syllable (ADA)
SYL Syllabus (WDAA)
SYLCU Synchronous Line Control Unit [*Computer science*] (MHDI)
SYLD Linden [*Guyana*] [*ICAO location identifier*] (ICLI)
SYLK Symbolic Link [*Data format*]
SYLL Syllable
SYLN Sylvan, Inc. [*NASDAQ symbol*] (SAG)
SYLP Lumid Pau [*Guyana*] [*ICAO location identifier*] (ICLI)
SYLP Support Your Local Police
SYLT Lethem [*Guyana*] [*ICAO location identifier*] (ICLI)
Sylvan Sylvan Foods Holdings, Inc. [*Associated Press*] (SAG)
SylvnLrn Sylvan Learning Systems [*Commercial firm Associated Press*] (SAG)
SYM Salesian Youth Movement (EA)
SYM Secondary Yield Measurement
SYM Seymour Resources [*Vancouver Stock Exchange symbol*]
SYM Simao [*China*] [*Airport symbol*] (OAG)
SYM Symbiont
SYM Symbol [*or Symbolic*] (AAG)
sym Symbol (IDOE)
Sym Symmachus' Greek Translation of the Bible [*A publication*] (BJA)
sym Symmetrical [*Also, s*] [*Chemistry*]
SYM Symmetry
sym Symmetry (IDOE)
SYM Symphony
Sym Symphony Recording Co. [*Record label*]
sym Symptom [*Medicine*] (CPH)
SYM Syms Corp. [*NYSE symbol*] (SPSG)

SYM........ System (MDG)
SYMAN........ Symbol Manipulation [*Computer science*]
SYM/ANNOT... Symbology Annotation (MCD)
SYMAP........ Synagraphic Mapping System [*Computer-made maps*]
SYMB........ Mabaruma [*Guyana*] [*ICAO location identifier*] (ICLI)
SYMB........ Symbol
Symb........ Symbollon Corp. [*Associated Press*] (SAG)
SYMBA........ Symbollon Corp. [*NASDAQ symbol*] (TTSB)
SYMBAL........ Symbolic Algebraic Language [*Computer science*]
SYMBAS........ Symbolization All Series (ADA)
Symbl........ Symbollon Corp. [*Associated Press*] (SAG)
SYMBOL........ System for Mass Balancing in Off-line (IAA)
SYMBOLANG... Symbolic Manipulation Language [*Computer science*] (CSR)
Symboln........ Symbollon Corp. [*Associated Press*] (SAG)
Symb Philol Danielsson... Symbolae Philologicae [*O. A.*] Danielsson Octogenario Dicatae [*Uppsala*] [*A publication*] (OCD)
SYMBUG........ Symbolic Debugger [*Computer science*] (MHDI)
SYMBW........ Symbollon Corp. Wrrt'A' [*NASDAQ symbol*] (TTSB)
SYMBZ........ Symbollon Corp. Wrrt'B' [*NASDAQ symbol*] (TTSB)
SYMC........ Symantec Corp. [*NASDAQ symbol*] (NQ)
SyMC........ Syracuse Microfilm Co., Syracuse, NY [*Library symbol*] [*Library of Congress*] (LCLS)
Sym Code.... Syms' Code of English Law [*1870*] [*A publication*] (DLA)
SYMD........ Mahdia [*Guyana*] [*ICAO location identifier*] (ICLI)
SYMDEB........ Symbolic Debugger [*Also, sdb, SOLD*] [*Computer science*]
Syme........ Syme's Scotch Justiciary Reports [*1826-30*] [*A publication*] (DLA)
SYMES........ Systematic Machinery and Equipment Selection (PDAA)
Symetr........ Symetrics Industries, Inc. [*Associated Press*] (SAG)
Symetric........ Symmetricom, Inc. [*Associated Press*] (SAG)
SYMEVETOPHARSA... Syndicat des Medecins, Veterinaires, Pharmaciens, et Sages Femmes Africains du Mali [*Union of African Doctors, Pharmacists, Midwives, and Veterinarians of the Mali Federation*]
Symf........ Symfoni & Artist [*Record label*] [*Sweden*]
SYMGR........ Sympalmograph (VRA)
Symix........ Symix Systems [*Associated Press*] (SAG)
SYMM........ Monkey Mountain [*Guyana*] [*ICAO location identifier*] (ICLI)
SYMM........ Symmetrical (MSA)
SYMM........ Symmetricom, Inc. [*NASDAQ symbol*] (SAG)
SYMMOD........ Symbolic Modeling [*Computer science*]
SYMMTRAC... Sylvania Multimode Tracking [*Aerospace*] (MCD)
SYMN........ Manari [*Guyana*] [*ICAO location identifier*] (ICLI)
Symntc........ Symantec Corp. [*Associated Press*] (SAG)
SYMP........ Mountain Point [*Guyana*] [*ICAO location identifier*] (ICLI)
Symp........ Symposium [*of Plato*] [*Classical studies*] (OCD)
SYMP........ Symposium (MSA)
SYMP........ Symptom [*Medicine*] (AAMN)
SYMPAC........ Symbolic Program for Automatic Control
sympat........ Sympathetic [*Neurology*]
sympath........ Sympathetic [*Neurology*] (DAVI)
SYMPH........ Symphony (ADA)
SYMPLE........ Syntax Macro Preprocessor for Language Evaluation [*Computer science*] (PDAA)
Symposum Jun Bar... Symposium. Association de Jeune Barreau de Montreal [*A publication*] (DLA)
sympt........ Symptom [*Medicine*]
SYMR........ Matthews Ridge [*Guyana*] [*ICAO location identifier*] (ICLI)
SYMRO........ System Management Research Operation (DIT)
SYMS........ Secondary Yield Measurement System
SymsCp........ Syms Corp. [*Associated Press*] (SAG)
SYMT........ Symetrics Industries [*NASDAQ symbol*] (TTSB)
SYMT........ Symetrics Industries, Inc. [*NASDAQ symbol*] (NQ)
SYMW........ Maruranawa [*Guyana*] [*ICAO location identifier*] (ICLI)
SYMWAR........ System for Estimating Wartime Attrition and Replacement Requirements (AABC)
SYMX........ Symix Systems [*NASDAQ symbol*] (SPSG)
SYN........ Stanton, MN [*Location identifier FAA*] (FAAL)
SYN........ Synagogue
SYN........ Synaptec, a Knowledge Engineering Corp. [*Vancouver Stock Exchange symbol*]
Syn........ Synbiotics Corp.
SYN........ Synchronize (IAA)
SYN........ Synchronous (AAG)
SYN........ Synchronous Idle [*Transmission control character*] [*Computer science*]
SYN........ Syncrude Canada Ltd. [*ICAO designator*] (FAAC)
SYN........ Syndicate (ROG)
SYN........ Synergist (WGA)
SYN........ Synod
SYN........ Synonym
Syn........ Synopsis (DLA)
syn........ Synovial [*Fluid*] [*Medicine*]
syn........ Synovitis [*Medicine*]
SYN........ Syntex Corp., Palo Alto, CA [*OCLC symbol*] (OCLC)
SYN........ Synthesizer
SYN........ Synthetic (AAG)
SYN........ Syntype
SYNA........ New Amsterdam [*Guyana*] [*ICAO location identifier*] (ICLI)
SYNAC........ Synthesis of Aircraft (MCD)
Synagro........ Synagro Technologies, Inc. [*Associated Press*] (SAG)
Synaloy........ Synalloy Corp. [*Associated Press*] (SAG)
SynapPhm.... Synaptic Pharmaceutical Corp. [*Associated Press*] (SAG)
SYNAPSE........ CUEA Synthesis and Publication Segment [*Marine science*] (MSC)
SYNBAPS........ Synthetic Bathymetric Profiling System [*Naval Oceanographic Office*]
Synbio........ Synbiotics Corp. [*Associated Press*] (SAG)
SYNC........ Synalloy Corp. [*NASDAQ symbol*] (SAG)
SYNC........ Synchromechanism
sync........ Synchronism (IDOE)
sync........ Synchronization (IDOE)
SYNC........ Synchronize (AAG)
SYNC........ Synchronizing Character [*Computer science*] (IAA)
sync........ Synchrony
SYNCCODE... Synchronization Code (IAA)
SYNCD........ Synchronized (AAG)
SYNCELL........ Synthetic Cell [*Biological research*]
SYNCG........ Synchronizing (AAG)
SYNCH........ Synchronize
SYNCH........ Synchronous Transmission [*Computer science*] (TSSD)
SYNCIN........ Synchronization Input [*Computer science*] (IAA)
SYNCOM........ Synchronous Communications [*Hughes Aircraft Co.*]
SYNCOM........ Synchronous Communication Satellite [*Telecommunications*] (IAA)
SYNCOM........ Synchronous-Orbiting Communications Satellite [*GSFC*]
Syncor........ Syncor International Corp. [*Associated Press*] (SAG)
SYNCOUT.... Synchronization Output (IAA)
SYNCR........ Synchronizer (AAG)
SyncRes........ Sync Research, Inc. [*Associated Press*] (SAG)
SYNCRO........ Synchromesh [*Automotive engineering*]
SYNCRUDE... Synthetic Crude
SYNCS........ Synchronous (AAG)
SYNCSCP........ Synchronoscope (IAA)
SYND........ Syndicate
synd........ Syndicate (WDMC)
synd........ Syndrome [*Medicine*]
SYNDARC.... Standard Format for Exchange of MAPMOPP Data among Data Centers (MSC)
syndet........ Synthetic Detergent (BARN)
SYNDETS........ Synthetic Detergents
SYNDEX........ Syndicated Exclusivity [*FCC*]
SYNEC........ Synecdoche (WDAA)
SYNEP........ Syntech International, Inc. (MHDW)
SYNESCI........ Syndicat National des Enseignants du Second Degre de Cote d'Ivoire
Synetic........ Synetic, Inc. [*Associated Press*] (SAG)
syn fl........ Synovial Fluid [*Medicine*] (MAE)
SYNFRQ........ Synthesizer Frequency
synfuel........ Synthetic Fuel (BARN)
SYNFUELS... Synthetic Fuels
syngas........ Synthetic Gas (BARN)
SYNGLISH... Synthetic English (MHDI)
Syngro........ Synagro Technologies, Inc. [*Associated Press*] (SAG)
SYNH........ Synergistic Hldg [*NASDAQ symbol*] (TTSB)
SYNH........ Synergistic Holding Corp. [*NASDAQ symbol*] (SAG)
SynHld........ Synergistic Holding Corp. [*Associated Press*] (SAG)
SynHold........ Synergistic Holding Corp. [*Associated Press*] (SAG)
SYNHW........ Synergistic Hldg Wrrt [*NASDAQ symbol*] (TTSB)
SYNL........ Syntellect, Inc. [*NASDAQ symbol*] (SAG)
SYNMAS........ Synchronous Missile Alarm System
SYNON........ Synonym (ROG)
SYNOP........ Synopsis (AABC)
Synopsy........ Synopsys, Inc. [*Associated Press*] (SAG)
Synovus........ Synovus Financial Corp. [*Associated Press*] (SAG)
Synpt........ Synoptic [*or Synoptist*] (BJA)
SYNRAMS........ Synoptic Random Access Measurement System (NOAA)
SYNROC........ Synthetic Rock [*For storage of nuclear waste*]
SYNS........ Synopsis (MSA)
SYNSCP........ Synchroscope (KSC)
SYNSEM........ Syntax and Semantics (IEEE)
Syn Ser........ Synopsis Series of the United States Treasury Decisions [*A publication*] (DLA)
SYNSPADE... Symposium on the Numerical Solution of Partial Differential Equations [*Book title, Academic Press*]
synt........ Synthetic (VRA)
SYNT........ Synthetic
SYNTAC........ Synthetic Tactics
SYNTEEDISETO... Syndicat des Travailleurs de l'Energie Electrique et de Distribution d'Eau du Togo [*Union of Electrical and Water Distribution Workers of Togo*]
SYNTH........ Synthesizer
SYNTH........ Synthetic
Synthe........ Synthetech, Inc. [*Associated Press*] (SAG)
SYNTI........ Synchro Tie
SYNTIRT........ Syndicat des Travailleurs des Industries Reunies du Togo [*Union of Workers of United Industries of Togo*]
Syntlct........ Syntellect, Inc. [*Associated Press*] (SAG)
SYNTOL........ Syntagmatic Organization Language [*Computer science*]
SYNTRAN.... Syntax Translation [*Computer science*] (DIT)
SYNV........ Sonchus Yellow Net Virus [*Plant pathology*]
SYNX........ Sync Research [*NASDAQ symbol*] (TTSB)
SYNX........ Sync Research, Inc. [*NASDAQ symbol*] (SAG)
SYNZYMES... Synthetic Enzymes
SYO........ Sayre, OK [*Location identifier FAA*] (FAAL)
SYO........ Skygold Resources [*Vancouver Stock Exchange symbol*]
SYO........ Syowa [*Ongul*] [*Antarctica*] [*Seismograph station code, US Geological Survey*] (SEIS)
SYO........ Syowa Base [*Antarctica*] [*Geomagnetic observatory code*]
SYOR........ Orinduik [*Guyana*] [*ICAO location identifier*] (ICLI)
SYP........ Parkland Regional Library, Yorkton, Saskatchewan [*Library symbol National Library of Canada*] (NLC)
SYP........ Santa Ynez Peak [*California*] [*Seismograph station code, US Geological Survey*] (SEIS)
SYP........ Society of Young Publishers (DGA)
SYP........ Southern Yellow Pine

SYP .... Suomen Yksityisyrittaejaein Puoluejaerjesto [*Finnish Private Entrepreneurs' Party*] [*Political party*] (PPE)
SYP .... Swedish Export Credit Corp. [*AMEX symbol*] (SAG)
Syp .... Syropalaestinum (BJA)
SYPH .... Syphilis (DSUE)
Syph .... Syphilology [*or Syphilologist*] [*Medicine*] (DAVI)
Sy PO .... Supply Petty Officer [*British military*] (DMA)
SYPR .... Paruima [*Guyana*] [*ICAO location identifier*] (ICLI)
SyQstTc .... SyQuest Technology, Inc. [*Associated Press*] (SAG)
SYQT .... SyQuest Technology, Inc. [*NASDAQ symbol*] (TTSB)
SYQT .... SyQuest Technology, Inc. [*NASDAQ symbol*] (SPSG)
syr .... Sirop [*Syrup*] [*Pharmacy*]
SYR .... Smyrna [*Washington*] [*Seismograph station code, US Geological Survey*] (SEIS)
SYR .... South Yorkshire Railway [*British*] (ROG)
SYR .... Syracuse [*New York*] [*Airport symbol*]
SYR .... Syratech Corp. [*NYSE symbol*] (SPSG)
SYR .... Syria [*or Syrian Arab Republic*] [*ANSI three-letter standard code*] (CNC)
Syr .... Syria (VRA)
syr .... Syriac [*MARC language code Library of Congress*] (LCCP)
SYR .... Syrian [*Language, etc.*] (ROG)
SYR .... Syrian Arab Airlines [*ICAO designator*] (FAAC)
SYR .... Syrian Hamster [*Medicine*] (DMAA)
SYR .... Syringe [*Medicine*]
SYR .... Syrupus [*Syrup*] [*Pharmacy*]
SYRACUSE ... System of Radio Communications Using a Satellite [*Telecommunications*] (TSSD)
Syracuse J Int'l L ... Syracuse Journal of International Law [*A publication*] (DLA)
Syracuse U ... Syracuse University (GAGS)
Syratch .... Syratech Corp. [*Associated Press*] (SAG)
Syr D .... De Syria Dea [*of Lucian*] [*Classical studies*] (OCD)
SyrH .... Hexaplaric Syriac (BJA)
SYRIUS .... Symbolic Representations for Image Understanding System (MHDI)
SYRP .... Summer Youth Recreation Program
SYRUCL .... Syracuse University College of Law (DLA)
SyrW .... Syriac Version in Walton's Polyglot (BJA)
SYS .... See Your Service (FAAC)
SYS .... Shawbury FTU [*British ICAO designator*] (FAAC)
SYS .... Sobeys Stores Ltd. [*Toronto Stock Exchange symbol*]
SYS .... Somerset, PA [*Location identifier FAA*] (FAAL)
SYS .... Sterile Concepts [*NYSE symbol*] (TTSB)
SYS .... Sterile Concepts Holdings, Inc. [*NYSE symbol*] (SAG)
SYS .... Stretching-Yawning Syndrome [*Medicine*] (DMAA)
SYS .... Sweet Yet Simple [*Computer science*]
SYS .... Synthesewerk Schwarzheide [*Former East German chemical company*] (ECON)
SYS .... System (AFM)
sys .... Systemic [*Medicine*] (DAVI)
SYSAD .... Systems Adviser
SYSADMIN ... System Administrator [*Computer science*]
SYSCAP .... System of Circuit Analysis Program
SYSCMA .... System Core Image Library Maintenance Program [*Computer science*] (IAA)
Sysco .... Sysco Corp. [*Associated Press*] (SAG)
SYSCOM .... System Communications
SYSCOM .... Systems Command [*Navy*]
SYSCON .... Systems Control [*Military*] (AABC)
SYSCTLG .... System Catalog [*Computer science*] (ECII)
SYSDEV .... Systems Development (NOAA)
SYSEC .... System Synthesizer and Evaluation Center
SYSEX .... System Executive (MHDB)
SYSF .... Systemsoft Corp. [*NASDAQ symbol*] (SAG)
SYSGEN .... System Generator Program (NITA)
SYSGEN .... Systems Generator [*or Generation*] [*Computer science*]
SYSIN .... System Input [*Computer science*] (MDG)
SYSIPT .... System Input Stream [*or Unit*] [*Computer science*] (MHDI)
SYSLIB .... System Library [*Computer science*] (MDG)
SYSLOG .... System Log [*Computer science*]
SYSM .... Systemed [*NASDAQ symbol*] (SAG)
SYSM .... SysteMed Inc. [*NASDAQ symbol*] (TTSB)
SYSMIN .... System for Mineral Products [*European Community*] (MHDB)
SYSMIN .... System for Safeguarding and Developing Mineral Production [*EC*] (ECED)
SYSOP .... System Operator [*Computer networking*]
SYSOP .... Systems Operator (EERA)
SYSOPO .... System Programmed Operator [*Computer science*] (MHDB)
SYSOUT .... System Output [*Computer science*] (IBMDP)
SYSP .... Sixth-Year Specialist Program [*Library science*]
SYSPCH .... System Punch [*Computer science*] (MHDI)
SYSPLLTM ... System Purchase of Long Lead Time Material
SYSPM .... System Performance Measure (MCD)
SYSPOP .... System Programmed Operators [*Computer science*] (MDG)
SYSRDR .... System Reader [*Computer science*] (MHDI)
SysReg .... System Request [*Computer science*] (CDE)
SYSRES .... System Residence [*Computer science*]
SYST .... System
SYST .... System
syst .... Systemic [*Medicine*]
syst .... Systolic [*Cardiology*]
SystCpt .... Systems & Computer Technology Corp. [*Associated Press*] (SAG)
Systemix .... Systemix, Inc. [*Associated Press*] (SAG)
SYSTEP .... Systems Test and Evaluation Plan [*Military*] (AABC)
SYSTID .... System Time-Domain Simulation Program [*Computer science*] (PDAA)
SYSTIM .... Systematic Interaction Model (PDAA)
SYST M .... Systolic Murmur [*Cardiology*] (BABM)
syst m .... Systolic Murmur [*Cardiology*] (DAVI)
Systmd .... Systemed, Inc. [*Associated Press*] (SAG)
SystmSft .... Systemsoft Corp. [*Associated Press*] (SAG)
SYSTO .... System Staff Office [*or Officer*]
SYSTRAN .... Systems Analysis Translator [*Computer science*]
SYSTRAN .... System Transatlantic [*Foreign language translator*] (EECA)
SystSft .... System Software Associates [*Associated Press*] (SAG)
SystSftw .... System Software Associates, Inc. [*Associated Press*] (SAG)
SYSTSW .... System Software [*Computer science*] (IAA)
SYSVER .... System Specification Verification (IEEE)
SYSX .... Systems Exchange [*Computer science*] (IAA)
SYT .... Sithe Energies USA, Inc. [*NYSE symbol*] (SPSG)
SYT .... Sweet Young Thing [*An attractive girl*] [*Slang*]
SYT .... Synaptotagmin [*Neurochemistry*]
SYTA .... Sustained-Yield Tropical Agroecosystem
SYTM .... Georgetown/Timehri Internacional [*Guyana*] [*ICAO location identifier*] (ICLI)
SYU .... Sudanese Youth Union
SYU .... Synchronization Signal Unit [*Telecommunications*]
SYU .... Syuhurei [*South Korea*] [*Seismograph station code, US Geological Survey Closed*] (SEIS)
SYUS .... Specialized Youth Units [*Canada*]
SYV .... Saynor Varah, Inc. [*Toronto Stock Exchange symbol*]
SYV .... Society for Young Victims [*Later, SYV/MCC*] (EA)
SYV .... Solanum Yellows Virus [*Plant pathology*]
SYV .... Sylvester, GA [*Location identifier FAA*] (FAAL)
SYV .... Symbol Value [*Computer science*] (PCM)
SYV .... Syva Research Library, Palo Alto, CA [*OCLC symbol*] (OCLC)
SYV/MCC .... Society for Young Victims, Missing Children Center (EA)
SYVV .... Sowthistle Yellow Vein Virus
SYW .... Skyway Resources Ltd. [*Vancouver Stock Exchange symbol*]
SYWI .... Wichabai [*Guyana*] [*ICAO location identifier*] (ICLI)
SYX .... Astral Aviation, Inc. d/b/a Skyway Airlines [*FAA designator*] (FAAC)
SYY .... Stornoway [*Scotland*] [*Airport symbol*] (OAG)
SYY .... Sysco Corp. [*NYSE symbol*] (SPSG)
SYZ .... Shelbyville, IL [*Location identifier FAA*] (FAAL)
SYZ .... Shiraz [*Iran*] [*Airport symbol*] (OAG)
SZ .... China Southwest Airlines [*ICAO designator*] (AD)
SZ .... ProAir Services [*ICAO designator*] (AD)
SZ .... Sceptre Investment Counsel Ltd. [*Toronto Stock Exchange symbol*]
sz .... Schizophrenia [*Psychology*]
Sz .... Schweizerische Landesbibliothek [*Swiss National Library*], Bern, Switzerland [*Library symbol Library of Congress*] (LCLS)
SZ .... Secondary Zone
SZ .... Seizure [*Telecommunications*] (TEL)
sz .... Seizure [*Medicine*]
SZ .... Sha'arei Zedek (BJA)
SZ .... Size (IAA)
sz .... Size (VRA)
SZ .... Sizzler International [*NYSE symbol*] (SPSG)
Sz .... Skin Impedance [*Neurology*] (DAVI)
SZ .... Splash Zone
SZ .... Sponsoring Organization Zip Code (NITA)
SZ .... Streptozocin [*Antineoplastic drug*]
SZ .... Subduction Zone [*Geology*]
SZ .... Suction [*Surgery*] (DAVI)
SZ .... Surface Zero [*Navy*] (NVT)
SZ .... Surf Zone (DOMA)
SZ .... Swaziland [*ANSI two-letter standard code*] (CNC)
sz .... Switzerland [*MARC country of publication code Library of Congress*] (LCCP)
SZA .... Aerolineas de El Salvador SA [*ICAO designator*] (FAAC)
SZA .... Santo Antonio do Zaire [*Angola*] [*Airport symbol*] (AD)
SZA .... Solar Zenith Angle [*Geophysics*]
SZA .... Soyo [*Angola*] [*Airport symbol*] (OAG)
SZB .... Santa Barbara [*Honduras*] [*Airport symbol*] (AD)
SZB .... Silver-Zinc Battery
SZB .... Sintered Zinc Battery
SZB .... SouthFirst Bancshares [*AMEX symbol*] (TTSB)
SZB .... Southfirst Bancshares, Inc. [*AMEX symbol*] (SAG)
SzBaL .... Lonza Aktiengesellschaft, Zentralbibliothek, Basel, Switzerland [*Library symbol Library of Congress*] (LCLS)
SzBaM .... Museum fur Volkerkunde und Schweizerisches Museum fur Volkskunde, Basel, Switzerland [*Library symbol Library of Congress*] (LCLS)
SzBaU .... Universitat Basel, Basel, Switzerland [*Library symbol Library of Congress*] (LCLS)
SzBaU-IO .... Institut fur Organische Chemie der Universitat Basel, Basel, Switzerland [*Library symbol Library of Congress*] (LCLS)
SZC .... Silver-Zinc Cell
SZD .... Sovetski Zhelezno-Dorozhni [*Soviet railways*] [*Former USSR*]
SZD .... St. George, SC [*Location identifier FAA*] (FAAL)
SzDP .... Magyarorszagi Szocialdemokrata Part [*Hungarian Social-Democratic Party*] [*Political party*] (EY)
SZDSZ .... Alliance of Free Democrats [*Hungary Political party*]
SzDSz .... Szabad Demokratak Szovetsege [*Alliance of Free Democrats*] [*Hungary Political party*] (EY)
SZE .... Szeged [*Hungary*] [*Seismograph station code, US Geological Survey Closed*] (SEIS)
SZEC .... Silver-Zinc Electrochemical Cell
SZECC .... Silver-Zinc Electrochemical Cell
SZG .... Salzburg [*Austria*] [*Airport symbol*] (OAG)
SZG .... Soviet Zone Germany (NATG)

SzGB .... Bibliotheque Battelle, Centre de Recherche, Geneve, Switzerland [*Library symbol Library of Congress*] (LCLS)
SzGBNU .... Bibliotheque des Nations Unies, Geneve, Switzerland [*Library symbol Library of Congress*] (LCLS)
SzGE .... Ecole de Chimie, Geneva, Switzerland [*Library symbol Library of Congress*] (LCLS)
SzGPAr .... Archives Jean Piaget, Geneve, Switzerland [*Library symbol Library of Congress*] (LCLS)
SzGSI .... Societe Generale pour l'Industrie, Geneve, Switzerland [*Library symbol Library of Congress*] (LCLS)
SZI .... Seattle, WA [*Location identifier FAA*] (FAAL)
SZI .... Service Zone Indication [*Computer science*] (IAA)
SZI .... Soroti [*Uganda*] [*Airport symbol*] (AD)
SZI .... Subzonal Sperm Insertion [*In-vitro fertilization*] (PAZ)
SZJ .... Atlanta, GA [*Location identifier FAA*] (FAAL)
SZK .... Roanoke, VA [*Location identifier FAA*] (FAAL)
SZK .... Skukuza [*South Africa*] [*Airport symbol*] (OAG)
SZL .... Knob Noster, MO [*Location identifier FAA*] (FAAL)
SZL .... SZL Sportsight [*Vancouver Stock Exchange symbol*]
SzLaCU .... Bibliotheque Cantonal et Universitaire de Lausanne, Lausanne, Switzerland [*Library symbol Library of Congress*] (LCLS)
SzLaS .... Station Federale d'Essais Agricoles, Lausanne, Switzerland [*Library symbol Library of Congress*] (LCLS)
SZM .... Stereo Zoom Microscope
SZM .... Synthetic Zeolite Molecule
SZN .... Santa Barbara, CA [*Location identifier FAA*] (FAAL)
SZN .... Streptozocin [*Antineoplastic drug*]
SZO .... Student Zionist Organization [*Defunct*] (EA)
SZOG .... Soviet Zone of Occupation of Germany (NATG)
SZOR .... Sintered Zinc Oxide Resistor
SZOT .... Szakszervezetek Orszagos Tanacsa [*National Trade Union Council*] [*Hungary*]
SZP .... Santa Paula, CA [*Location identifier FAA*] (FAAL)
SZP .... Surf Zone Process
SZP .... Synchro Zeroing Procedure
SZR .... Sintered Zinc Resistor
SZR .... Stargazer Resources Ltd. [*Vancouver Stock Exchange symbol*]
SZR .... University of South Carolina, Regional Campus Processing Center, Columbia, SC [*OCLC symbol*] (OCLC)
SzS .... Solidarnosc z Solidarnoscia [*Solidarity with Solidarity - SwS*] [*Defunct*] (EAIO)
SZS .... Srpska Zemljoradnicka Stranka [*Serbian Agrarian Party*] [*Former Yugoslavia*] [*Political party*] (PPE)
SZS .... Staatliche Zentrale fuer Strahlenschutz Berlin [*East Germany*]
SZS .... Stewart Island [*New Zealand*] [*Airport symbol*] (OAG)
SZSB .... Silver-Zinc Secondary [*or Storage*] Battery
SzStg .... Stadtbibliothek Vadiana, St. Gallen, Switzerland [*Library symbol Library of Congress*] (LCLS)
SZT .... Sandpoint, ID [*Location identifier FAA*] (FAAL)
SZU .... Segou [*Mali*] [*Airport symbol*] (AD)
SZutNu .... Sifre Zuta on Numbers (BJA)
SZVR .... Silicon Zener Voltage Regulator
SZY .... Selmer, TN [*Location identifier FAA*] (FAAL)
SZZ .... Szczecin [*Poland*] [*Airport symbol*] (OAG)
SzZ .... Zentralbibliothek Zurich, Zurich, Switzerland [*Library symbol Library of Congress*] (LCLS)
SzZE .... Eidgenoessische Technische Hochschule, Zurich, Switzerland [*Library symbol Library of Congress*] (LCLS)
SzZU .... Universitat Zurich, Universitatsspital-Bibliothek, Kantonsspital, Zurich, Switzerland [*Library symbol Library of Congress*] (LCLS)

T
By Acronym

T .... Absolute Temperature [*Symbol*] [*IUPAC*]

T .... Aerotec [*Sociedade Aerotec Ltda.*] [*Brazil ICAO aircraft manufacturer identifier*] (ICAO)

T .... Air Temperature Correction

T .... American Telephone & Telegraph Co. [*Wall Street slang name: "Telephone"*] [*NYSE symbol*] (SPSG)

t----- .... Antarctic [*MARC geographic area code Library of Congress*] (LCCP)

T .... AT&T Corp. [*NYSE symbol*] (TTSB)

T .... Backhoe Trench [*Archaeology*]

t .... Celsius Temperature [*Symbol*] [*IUPAC*]

T .... Half-Life of a Radioactive Substance (BARN)

T .... Internal Transmittance [*Symbol*] [*IUPAC*]

T .... Kinetic Energy [*Symbol*] [*IUPAC*]

t .... Marginal Propensity to Tax [*Economics*]

T .... Meridian Angle

t .... Metric Ton

T .... Military Sealift Command Ship [*When precedes vessel classification*] [*Navy symbol*]

T .... Octodecimo [*Book from 12-1/2 to 15 centimeters in height*] [*Bibliography*]

T .... Ribothymidine [*One-letter symbol; see Thd*]

T .... Shape Descriptor [*T-bar and T-square, for example. The shape resembles the letter for which it is named*]

T .... Surface Tension [*Physics*] (WDAA)

T .... Table

T .... Tablespoon [*Measure*]

T .... Tablet (WGA)

T .... Tablet-Shaped [*As in "T-grains"*] [*Photography*]

t .... Tabula [*Plate*] [*Latin*]

T .... Tabulated [*or Charted*] LORAN Reading [*Long-Range Aid to Navigation*]

T .... Tace [*Be Silent*]

T .... Tackle [*Football*]

T .... Tactical Organization

T .... Tactual

T .... Taenia [*Medicine*] (MAE)

t .... Tag [*Computer science*] [*Telecommunications*]

T .... Taken

T .... Tala [*Monetary unit in Western Samoa*]

T .... Talc

T .... Talk/Monitor (NASA)

T .... Talon [*Heel of the Bow*] [*Music*]

T .... Tamoxifen [*Antineoplastic drug*]

T .... Tamper (NFPA)

T .... Tango [*Phonetic alphabet*] [*International*] (DSUE)

T .... Tanhuma (BJA)

T .... Tank [*Trains*] [*British*]

T .... Tanna (BJA)

T .... Taped Commentary [*On a bus tour*] [*British*]

T .... Taper

T .... Tapered Hatchway [*on a ship*] (DS)

T .... Tappan's Ohio Common Pleas Reports [*A publication*] (DLA)

T .... Tare [*Phonetic alphabet*] [*World War II*] (DSUE)

T .... Target

T .... Tasmania [*State*] (EERA)

T .... Tasto [*Touch, Key, Fingerboard*] [*Music*]

T .... Tau [*Nineteenth letter of the Greek alphabet*] (DAVI)

T .... Taxation [*Economics*]

T .... Taxes (DLA)

T .... Teacher

T .... Tear [*Phonetic alphabet*] [*World War II*]

t .... Teaspoon [*Measure*]

T .... Technical [*or Technician*]

T .... Technical College [*British*]

T .... Technological Service [*Queen's Award*] [*British*]

T .... Tee [*Piping joint, etc.*] [*Technical drawings*]

T .... Teeth [*Technical drawings*]

T .... Teich [*Pond*] [*German military*]

T .... Telefunken [*Record label*] [*Germany, etc.*]

T .... Telegram (BJA)

T .... Telegraph (ROG)

T .... Telegrapher [*Navy*]

T .... Telemeter [*or Telemetry*] [*Telecommunications*] (IAA)

T .... Telephone

T .... Telephone Trunk Call [*British*] (ROG)

T .... Teletype

T .... Television [*FCC*] (NTCM)

T .... Telnet [*Internet*]

t .... Telocentric

T .... Temperance [*i.e., entitled to a daily rum ration but voluntarily not drawing it and receiving money instead*] [*See also G, UA*] [*Navy*] [*British*]

T .... Temperature

T .... Tempo

T .... Temporal

T .... Temporary

T .... Tempore [*In the Time of*] [*Latin*]

T .... Tenant [*Legal shorthand*] (LWAP)

T .... Tender [*Horticulture*]

T .... Tendre [*Tender*] [*Music*]

T .... Tenero [*Tender*]

T .... Tennessee State Library and Archives, Nashville, TN [*Library symbol Library of Congress*] (LCLS)

T .... Tenor

T .... Tenor [*Genotype of Phlox paniculata*]

T .... Tense

T .... Tension

T .... Tension [*Intraocular*] [*Opthalmology*] (DAVI)

T .... Tensor

T .... Tentative Target

T .... Ter [*Three Times*] [*Pharmacy*]

T .... Tera [*A prefix meaning multiplied by 10^{12}*] [*SI symbol*]

T .... Teracycle (BUR)

T .... Term [*Medicine*]

T .... Term [*Mathematics*] (WDAA)

T .... Terminal

T .... Terminal Area Chart [*Followed by identification*] [*Aviation*]

T .... Termination

T .... Terminator [*Genetics*]

T .... Terminus [*Biochemistry*]

T .... Terrain

T .... Terrain Clearance Altitude [*Aviation*] (DA)

T .... Territory

t .... Tertiary [*Also, tert*] [*Chemistry*]

T .... Tesla [*Symbol*] [*SI unit of flux density*]

T .... Test (MSA)

T .... Testament (ROG)

T .... Testamentum [*Will*] [*Latin*]

T .... Testator [*Legal term*]

T .... Test Equipment (NG)

t .... Test of Significance [*Medicine*] (MAE)

T .... Test Reactor

T .... Test Set

T .... Tetra [*Prefix meaning four*] (DAVI)

T .... Tetracycline [*Antibiotic compound*]

T .... Thaler [*or Talari*] [*Monetary unit Ethiopia*]

T .... Than

T .... That

T .... Theatres [*Public-performance tariff class*] [*British*]

T .... Theft

T .... Theophylline [*Pharmacology*]

T .... Thermodynamic Temperature [*Symbol*] [*IUPAC*]

T .... Thermometer

T .... Thermoplastic [*Also, TP*] [*Plastics technology*] (MSA)

T .... Thermostabilized (NASA)

T .... Thickness

T .... Thief

T .... Thioguanine [*Also, TG*] [*Antineoplastic drug*]

T .... Thiopental [*An anesthetic*]

T .... Third Word Designator [*Computer science*]

T .... Thomas Mieres [*Flourished, 1429-39*] [*Authority cited in pre-1607 legal work*] (DSA)

T .... Thoracic [*Anatomy*]

T .... Thorax [*Anatomy*] (MAE)

T .... Thread

T .... Threonine [*One-letter symbol; see Thr*] [*An amino acid*]

T .... Threshold Lighting [*Aviation*] (DA)

T .... Thrill [*Cardiology*] (DAVI)

T .... Thromboxane [*Also, TA, Tx, TX*] [*Biochemistry*]

T .... Throttle Command (NASA)

T .... Thrust (IAA)

T .... Thruster [*of a ship*] (DS)

T .... Thrust of Propeller [*Naval engineering*] (DAS)
T .... Thunderstorm [*Meteorology*]
T .... Thursday (WGA)
T .... Thymidine [*Medicine*] (MAE)
T .... Thymine [*Also, Thy*] [*Biochemistry*]
T .... Thymus [*Medicine*]
T .... Thymus Derived [*Hematology*]
T .... Thyroid [*Medicine*]
T .... Tidal Gas [*Respiration*] [*Medicine*]
T .... Tide Rips [*Navigation*]
T .... Tie [*Sports*]
T .... Tier [*Psychology*]
T .... Tiler [*Freemasonry*]
T .... Tilic Subgroup [*Ilmenite, titanite, perofskite, rutile*] [*CIPW classification Geology*]
T .... Time
t .... Time [*Symbol*] [*IUPAC*]
T .... Time Constant (IAA)
T .... Time Consumed in Playing Game [*Baseball*]
t .... Time in Seconds [*Aerospace*]
T .... Timekeeper [*Sports*]
T+ .... Time Postintegration (NASA)
T .... Time Prior to Launch [*Usually followed by a number*] [*NASA*] (KSC)
T .... Timer (IAA)
T .... Time-Reversal [*Atomic physics*]
T .... Time Trial
T .... Tip [*Switchboard plug*] [*Telecommunications*] (TEL)
T .... Tipper [*Shipping*] (DS)
T .... Tithing [*Geographical division*] [*British*]
T .... Title [*Bibliography*]
T .... Toarcian [*Geology*]
T .... Tobacco Tax Ruling, Internal Revenue Bureau [*United States*] [*A publication*] (DLA)
T .... Toc [*Phonetic alphabet*] [*Pre-World War II*] (DSUE)
T .... Tocopherol [*Biochemistry*]
T .... Toe
T .... Toggle [*Telecommunications*] (IAA)
T .... Toilet (MSA)
T .... Toll
T .... Tommy [*Phonetic alphabet*] [*Royal Navy World War I*] (DSUE)
T .... Tomo [*Volume*] [*Italian*] (ILCA)
T .... Tomus [*Volume*]
T .... Ton
T .... Tone (IAA)
T .... Tonnage [*Shipping*]
t .... Tonne [*Metric*]
T .... Tonometer Reading [*Medicine*] (MEDA)
T .... Tooth
T .... Top
T .... Topical (ADA)
t .... Top [*or Truth*] (Quark) [*Atomic physics*]
T .... Top Secret
T .... Toronto Stock Exchange
T .... Torpedo [*Obsolete Navy British*] (ROG)
T .... Torpedoman [*Navy British*]
T .... Torque
T .... Tosefta (BJA)
T .... Total
T .... Tourist [*Rate*] [*Value of the English pound*]
T .... Toward [*Altitude difference*]
T .... Town
T .... Township
T .... Toxicity (MAE)
T .... Trace (DAVI)
T .... Trace of Precipitation [*Less than 0.005 inch of rain or 0.05 inch of snow*]
T .... Tracer [*Ammunition*] (NATG)
T .... Trachea [*Anatomy*]
T .... Tracheotomy Set (CPH)
T .... Track
T .... Tracker [*British military*] (DMA)
T .... Traded
T .... Tradesman [*British military*] (DMA)
T .... Traditional (BJA)
T .... Trafalgar [*On army list*] [*British*] (ROG)
T .... Traffic Cases [*A publication*] (DLA)
T .... Traffic Headquarters
T .... Trainer [*Designation for all US military aircraft*]
T .... Trainer Aircraft Designation [*MTMC*] (TAG)
t .... Trans [*Chemical conformation*]
T .... Transaction
T .... Transcription
T .... Transducer
t .... Transfer [*Genetics*]
T .... Transferred [*Navy*]
T .... Transferrin [*Also, TF, TRF*] [*Biochemistry*]
T .... Transformation Rule [*Linguistics*]
T .... Transformer
T .... Transfusion [*Medicine*]
T .... Transient [*Bureau of the Census*]
T .... Transistor [*Electronics*] (IAA)
T .... Transit
T .... Transition
T .... Transition point (DAVI)
T .... Transitive
T .... Translated (ROG)
T .... Translation
T .... Translocation
T .... Transmission [*Telecommunications*] (IAA)
T .... Transmission Stop (NTCM)
T .... Transmissivity (FFDE)
T .... Transmit [*or Transmitting*]
T .... Transmittance [*A symbol used in spectrophotometry*] (DAVI)
T .... Transmitter
T .... Transpiration [*Botany*]
T .... Transponder (IAA)
T .... Transport (NATG)
t .... Transport Number [*Symbol*] [*Electrochemistry*]
T .... Transport Number [*Chemistry*] (BARN)
T .... Transvaal Provincial Division Reports [*South Africa*] [*A publication*] (DLA)
T .... Transverse (AAMN)
T .... Transverse Tubule [*Muscle neurobiology*]
T .... Travel News [*Wire service code*] (NTCM)
T .... Trawling
T .... Tread [*Stair details*] [*Technical drawings*]
T .... Treasurer
T .... Treasury [*As in T-Bill, T-Bond, T-Note*]
T .... Treated
T .... Treatment
T .... Treaty [*Legal shorthand*] (LWAP)
T .... Treble [*Music*] (ROG)
t .... Trend Landing Forecast [*Aviation*] (DA)
T .... Treponema [*Microbiology*] (AAMN)
T .... Triangle
T .... Trichome [*Botany*]
T .... Trichomonas [*A parasite*] (DAVI)
T .... Trichophyton [*Medicine*] (MAE)
T .... Trigger (IAA)
T .... Triggered [*Cardiology*]
T .... Trillion [10^{12}]
T .... Trillo [*Trill*] [*Music*]
T .... Trimethoprim [*Also, TMP*] [*Antibacterial compound*]
T .... Trimmer (IAA)
T .... Trinitas [*The Trinity*]
T .... Triode
T .... Triple
T .... Tritium [*Also, H_3*] [*Radioisotope of hydrogen*]
t .... Triton [*A nuclear particle*]
T .... Triton Industries, Inc. [*Toronto Stock Exchange symbol*]
T .... Tropical [*Load line mark, or air mass*]
T .... Trotter
T .... Troy [*A system of weights for precious metals*]
T .... Truce
T .... True [*Direction*]
T .... Trunk (IAA)
T .... Truss (AAG)
T .... Trypanosoma [*Medicine*] (MAE)
T .... Tube (IAA)
T .... Tubular (IAA)
T .... Tubulin [*A protein*]
T .... Tuesday
T .... Tufa [*Quality of the bottom*] [*Nautical charts*]
T .... Tug [*Navy*]
T .... Tumor [*Oncology*]
T .... Tun [*Unit of liquid capacity*]
T .... Turbocharged [*Automotive engineering*]
T .... Turkish
t .... Turn [*or Turning*]
T .... Turner [*Navy rating British*]
T .... Turnkey [*Medicine*] (DMAA)
T .... Turnover Index [*Botany*]
T .... Tutti [*Sing or Play Together*] [*Music*]
T .... Twentyfourmo [*Book up to 15 centimeters in height*]
T .... Twin Screw [*Shipping*] (DS)
T .... Type
T .... Typed [*Manuscript descriptions*]
T .... Typhlosole [*Biology*]
T .... Typhoid
T .... Wrong Tense of Verb [*Used in correcting manuscripts, etc.*]
T-0 .... Time Zero (MCD)
T1 .... First Thoracic Nerve [*T2 Second Thoracic Nerve, etc., through T12*] [*Anatomy*] (DAVI)
T1 .... First Thoracic Vertebra [*T2 Second thoracic vertebra, etc., through T12*] [*Anatomy*] (DAVI)
T1 .... First Transcript [*Genetics*]
T1 .... Longitudinal Relaxation Time Constant [*Radiology*] (DAVI)
T_1 .... Tricuspid First Heart Sound [*Cardiology*]
T_1 .... Tricuspid First Sound [*Cardiology*] (DAVI)
T_2 .... Diiodothyronine [*Endocrinology*]
T-2 .... Protocol [*A chemotherapy regimen including dactinomycin, doxorubicin, vincristine, cyclophosphamide, and radiation therapy*] (DAVI)
T2 .... Second Transcript [*Genetics*]
T2 .... Terminator 2 [*Motion picture*]
T2 .... Time of Flight to Intercept [*Military*] (CAAL)
T2 .... Transverse Relaxation Time Constant [*On magnetic resonance imaging (MRI) scans*] [*Also called spin-spin relaxation time constant*] [*Radiology*] (DAVI)
T_2 .... Tricuspid Second Heart Sound [*Cardiology*]

T2 ... Tuvalu [*International civil aircraft marking*] (ODBW)
T2G ... Technician, Second Grade [*Military*]
T^2L ... Transistor-Transistor Logic [*Also, TTL*]
T^2L ... Transistor-Transistor Logic (IDOE)
T2S ... Technology Transfer Society (EA)
T2S2 ... Total Tank System Study [*Army*]
T3 ... Kiribati [*International civil aircraft marking*] (ODBW)
T3 ... Tank Track Test [*Army*]
T-3 ... Tocotrienol [*Biochemistry*]
T_3 ... Train-the-Trainer [*Army*]
T_3 ... Triiodothyronine [*Also, TITh*] [*Endocrinology*]
T_3(RIA) ... Serum Triiodothyronine Radioimmunoassay [*Endocrinology*] (DAVI)
T_3RIA ... Triiodothyronine Radioimmunoassay [*Endocrinology*] (DAVI)
T_3RU ... Triiodothyronine Resin Uptake [*Endocrinology*] (MAE)
T_3SU ... Triiodothyronine Serum Uptake [*Endocrinolgy*] (CPH)
T_3U ... Triiodothyronine Uptake [*Endocrinology*]
T_3UP ... Tri-Iodothyronine Uptake [*Endocrinology*] (DAVI)
T_3UR ... Triiodothyronine Uptake Radio [*Endocrinology*] (DAVI)
T4 ... Thyroxine [*Also, Thx, Ty*] [*An amino acid Endocrinology*]
T_4(c) ... Serum Thyroxine [*Measured by column chromatographic technique*] [*Endocrinology*] (DAVI)
T4C ... Technology for Children [*Vocational program*]
T4C ... Termination for Convenience (AAGC)
T_4(D) ... Serum Thyroxine [*Measured by displacement analysis*] [*Endocrinology*] (DAVI)
T_4I ... Total Serum Thyroxine Iodine Also, called tri-iodothyronine [*Endocrinology*] (DAVI)
T_4(RIA) ... Serum Thyroxine Radioisotope Assay [*Endocrinology*] (DAVI)
T_4RIA ... Thyroxine Radioisotope Assay [*Endocrinology*] (DAVI)
T_4SA ... Thyroxine-Specific Activity [*Medicine*] (MAE)
T/5 ... Technician Fifth Grade [*Army*]
T7 ... San Marino [*International civil aircraft marking*] (ODBW)
T-1824 ... Evans Blue Dye [*Radiology*] (DAVI)
T2000I ... Transport 2000 International [*British*] (EAIO)
TA ... Chinese Taipei [*IYRU nationality code*] (IYR)
Ta ... Ta'anith (BJA)
TA ... Tabled Agreement [*in labor relations*]
TA ... Table of Allowances (MCD)
TA ... Table of Allowances (DOMA)
TA ... Table of Authorization
TA ... Tablet (ADA)
TA ... TACA International Airlines SA [*El Salvador*] [*ICAO designator*] (ICDA)
TA ... Tactical Aircraft
T/A ... Tactical Airlift [*Tactical Air Command*]
TA ... Tactical Air Missile
TA ... Tactile Afferent [*Medicine*] (DMAA)
TA ... Tailhook Association (EA)
TA ... Talanta [*A publication*]
TA ... Talmudical Academy (BJA)
TA ... Talmudische Archaeologie [*A publication*] (BJA)
TA ... Tanabe Seiyaku Co. Ltd. [*Japan*] [*Research code symbol*]
TA ... Tangible Asset
TA ... Tank Army (MCD)
TA ... Tanker [*Shipping*] (DCTA)
TA ... Tank Tainers [*Shipping*] (DCTA)
TA ... Tannic Acid [*Urology*] (DAVI)
Ta ... Tantalum [*Chemical element*]
TA ... Tape (IAA)
TA ... Tape Adapter
TA ... Tape Advance (AAG)
TA ... Tape Armored [*Telecommunications*] (TEL)
TA ... Target (DEN)
TA ... Target Acquisition (MCD)
TA ... Target Aircraft (MUGU)
TA ... Target Area [*Military*] (AFM)
TA ... Targeting Agent [*Medicine*]
TA ... Tariff Act [*1930*]
TA ... Tartana [*Ship's rigging*] (ROG)
TA ... Task Analysis
TA ... Task Assignment (AAG)
TA ... Tax Abatement
TA ... Tax Agent
TA ... Tax Amortization [*Plan*]
TA ... Tea Association of the USA [*Defunct*] (EA)
TA ... Teacher Assessment (AIE)
TA ... Teaching Assistant [*in a university*]
TA ... Technical Advisor (MCD)
TA ... Technical Analysis (NG)
TA ... Technical Applications [*Branch*] [*Marine science*] (OSRA)
TA ... Technical Applications [*Branch*] [*Forecast Systems Laboratory*] (USDC)
TA ... Technical Architecture [*Computer science*] (RDA)
TA ... Technical Assessor
TA ... Technical Assistance [*or Assistant*]
TA ... Technology Assessment Database [*Fachinformationszentrum Karlsruhe GmbH*] [*Germany Information service or system*] (CRD)
TA ... Technonet Asia (EA)
TA ... Teichoic Acids [*Biochemistry*]
TA ... Tel Aviv [*Israel*] (BJA)
TA ... Teleflora Australia
TA ... Telegraphic Address
TA ... Teleoperator Assembler (SSD)
TA ... Telephone Apparatus [*JETDS nomenclature*] [*Military*] (CET)
TA ... Telescope Assembly (KSC)
TA ... Television Associates [*Mountain View, CA*] (TSSD)
TA ... Telex Network Adapter (MHDB)
TA ... Tell-Amarna [*Egypt*] (BJA)
TA ... Tell Asmar [*Iraq*] (BJA)
TA ... Telluride Association (EA)
TA ... Temperature Alarm [*Engineering*]
TA ... Temperature, Axillary
TA ... Temple Autobiographies [*A publication*]
TA ... Temporal Arteritis [*Medicine*]
T/A ... Temporary Assistant (WDAA)
TA ... Tendo Achilis Reflex [*Neurology*] (DAVI)
TA ... Tennis Australia
TA ... Tension Arterielle [*Blood Pressure*] [*Medicine*]
TA ... Tension by Applanation [*Ophthalmology*]
TA ... Tenuazonic Acid [*Biochemistry*]
TA ... Teologinen Aikakauskirja [*Helsinki*] [*A publication*] (BJA)
TA ... Terephthalic Acid [*Also, TPA*] [*Organic chemistry*]
TA ... Terminal Adapter [*Telecommunications*]
TA ... Terminal Address (IAA)
TA ... Terrain Avoidance [*Helicopter*]
TA ... Terrarium Association (EA)
TA ... Territorial Army
TA ... Test Access [*Telecommunications*] (TEL)
TA ... Test Accessory (AAG)
TA ... Test Announcer (IAA)
TA ... Testantibus Actis [*As the Records Show*] [*Latin*]
TA ... Test Article (NASA)
TA ... Theater Army
TA ... Theatre Authority (EA)
TA ... Therapeutic Abortion [*Medicine*]
TA ... Thermal Activation [*Physics*]
TA ... Thermal Analysis
TA ... Thermophilic Actinomyces [*Microbiology*]
TA ... Third Attack [*Men's lacrosse position, until 1933*]
TA ... Thoracoabdominal Stapler [*Surgery*] (DAVI)
TA ... Threat Analysis (MCD)
TA ... Threat Axis [*Military*] (NVT)
TA ... Thromboxane [*Also, T, Tx, TX*] [*Biochemistry*]
TA ... Thromboxane A [*Also, TxA, TXA*] [*Biochemistry*]
TA ... Throw Away
TA ... Thunderbirds of America (EA)
TA ... Thyroglobulin Auto-Precipitation [*Endocrinology*] (AAMN)
TA ... Thyroid Autoantibody [*Endocrinology*] (DAVI)
TA ... Tibialis Anterior [*A muscle*]
TA ... Time Actual (NASA)
T/A ... Time and Amount (DMAA)
TA ... Time and Attendance
TA ... Tippers Anonymous (EA)
TA ... Tithe Annuity
TA ... [*Journal*] Title Abbreviation (NITA)
TA ... Title Annotation (NITA)
TA ... Titratable Acid [*Clinical chemistry*]
TA ... Titration Alkalinity [*Oceanography*]
TA ... Tnu'at 'Aliyah (BJA)
TA ... Tobacco Associates (EA)
TA ... Tool Available
TA ... Top Assembly
TA ... Torah Atmosphere (BJA)
TA ... Total Aboard (FAAC)
TA ... Total Adenine [*Nucleotide pool*] [*Medicine*]
TA ... Total Alkaloids [*Medicine*]
TA ... Total Audience [*Television ratings*]
TA ... Toward
TA ... Toxin-Antitoxin [*Also, TAT*] [*Immunology*]
T-A ... Toxin-Antitoxin [*Medicine*] (DMAA)
TA ... Tracers Association [*A union*] [*British*]
TA ... Track Accelerator [*Missile simulator*]
TA ... Track Address (IAA)
TA ... Traction Assist [*Automotive engineering*]
T/A ... Trade Acceptance [*Business term*]
TA ... Trade Acceptance [*Investment term*] (DFIT)
TA ... Trade Agreements Act
TA ... Trade Association (DCTA)
TA ... Trading As
ta ... Trading As (AAGC)
TA ... Traffic Accident (DAVI)
TA ... Traffic Agent [*or Auditor*]
T/A ... Traffic Analysis [*National Security Agency*]
TA ... Trained Aide [*Medicine*]
TA ... Training Advisor (WDAA)
TA ... Training Agency (EERA)
TA ... Training Allowance [*British military*] (DMA)
TA ... Training Analyst (HGAA)
T/A ... Training As
TA ... Transactional Analysis [*System of psychotherapy developed by Eric Berne, MD*]
TA ... Transaldolase [*An enzyme*] (AAMN)
TA ... Transalta Corp. [*TS symbol*] (TTSB)
TA ... Transalta Resources Corp. [*Toronto Stock Exchange symbol*]
TA ... Trans Am [*Model of automobile*]
TA ... Transamerica Corp. [*NYSE symbol*] (SPSG)
TA ... Transamerica Delaware Ltd. [*NYSE symbol*] (SAG)
TA ... Transantral [*Medicine*] (AAMN)
TA ... Transfer Agent [*Business term*]

TA Transfer Aisle (NRCH)
T/A Transfer of Accountability
TA Transfusion Associated
TA Transient Alert (MCD)
TA Transit Authority
TA Transition Agreement
TA Transition Altitude
TA Transition Area [*For chart use only*] [*Aviation*]
TA Transmission Authenticator [*Telecommunications*] (TEL)
TA Transplantation Antigen [*Medicine*]
TA Transportability Approval [*Army*]
TA Transport Association [*British*] (DBA)
TA Transportation Act of 1989 (WYGK)
TA Transportation Agent
TA Transportation Alternatives (EA)
TA Transportation Authorization (AAG)
TA Transverse Acoustic
TA Travel Allowance
TA Travel [*or Trip*] Authorization (MCD)
TA Traveler's Advisory [*Weather information*]
TA Triacetin [*Antifungal compound*] [*Organic chemistry*]
TA Triamcinolone Acetonide [*Also, TAA*] [*Synthetic steroidal drug*]
TA Tribunal Administratif [*Administrative Court*] [*French*] (ILCA)
TA Tricuspid Atresia [*Cardiology*]
TA Tricycle Association [*British*] (DBA)
TA Trinidad Artillery [*British military*] (DMA)
TA Trip Authorization
TA Triple Antigen [*Medicine*]
TA Triplex Annealed
TA Triumph Adler Computer Series (NITA)
TA Trophoblast Antigen [*Immunochemistry*]
TA Truck Assembly
TA True Altitude [*Height*] [*Navigation*]
TA True Anomaly
TA Truncus Arteriosus [*Medicine*] (DMAA)
TA Trunk Amplifier (IAA)
TA Trunnion Angle (KSC)
TA Trustee under Agreement [*Legal term*] (DLA)
TA Truth in Advertising [*An association Defunct*] (EA)
TA Tryptophane Acid (AAMN)
TA Tryptose Agar [*Medicine*] (DMAA)
TA Tube Agglutination [*Medicine*] (MAE)
TA Tuberculin, Alkaline [*Medicine*]
TA Tubular Atrophy [*Nephrology*]
TA Tumor Associated [*Medicine*] (DMAA)
T/A Turboalternator
TA Turbulence Amplifier
TA Turkish Army (NATG)
T/A Turnaround (NASA)
TA Turning Angle [*Automotive engineering*]
Ta T-wave Atrial [*Found on electrocardiograms*] (DAVI)
TA Type Americain [*World War I troop train in France made according to US specifications*]
TA Type Approval
TA Type Availability
TA Typographic Adviser (DGA)
TA VEB Fahlberg-List [*East Germany*] [*Research code symbol*]
TA1 Trophoblast Antigen One [*Immunochemistry*]
TA3DPT Twitchell-Allen Three-Dimensional Personality Test [*Psychology*]
TA_4 Tetraiodothyroacetic Acid [*Medicine*] (MAE)
TAA Aerotamatan SA de CV [*Mexico ICAO designator*] (FAAC)
TAA Tactical Air Army (NATG)
TAA Tactical Army Automation (MCD)
TAA Tactical Assembly Area [*Army*] (INF)
TAA Tactical Assembly Area [*Army*] (DOMA)
TAA Tactical Automation Appraisal (MCD)
TAA Taiwanese Association of America (EA)
TAA Tamburitza Association of America (EA)
TAA Tannic Acid Agar [*Culture media*]
TAA Taxpayers' Association of Australia
TAA Technical Assistance Administration [*United Nations*]
TAA Technical Assistance Agreement [*NASA*] (NASA)
TAA Technology Assessment Annex (MCD)
TAA Telephone Artifacts Association (EA)
TAA Television Appliance Association
TAA Temporary Access Authorization (NASA)
TAA Terre Adelie [*Antarctica*] [*Seismograph station code, US Geological Survey Closed*] (SEIS)
TAA Territorial Army Association [*British*]
TAA Tertiary-Amyl Alcohol [*Organic chemistry*]
TAA Texas Armadillo Association [*Commercial firm*] (EA)
TAA Textbook Authors Association (EA)
TAA Thioacetamide [*Organic chemistry*]
TAA Thoracic Aortic Aneurysm [*Cardiology*]
TAA Three-Axis Accelerometer
TAA Ticket Agents' Association [*British*]
TAA Timber Arbitrators Association [*British*] (DBA)
TAA Time and Attendance (IAA)
TAA Tobacconists' Association of America (EA)
TAA Total Aerospace Vehicle [*or Aircraft*] Authorization
TAA Total Aircraft Authorized (MCD)
TAA Total Ankle Arthroplasty [*Medicine*] (DMAA)
TAA Total Antioxidant Activity [*Chemistry*]
TAA Total Army Analysis (AABC)
TAA Total Army Authorization
TAA Trade Adjustment Act
TAA Trade Adjustment Assistance [*Department of Commerce*]
TAA Trade Agreements Act
TAA Trade Agreements Act of 1979 (AAGC)
TAA Trans-American Airline
TAA Trans-Antarctic Association [*British*]
TAA Trans-Australia Airlines (ADA)
TAA Transcript of Absentee's Account
TAA Transferable Account Area [*Business term*] (DCTA)
TAA Transfer and Accountability (IAA)
TAA Transient Absorption Anisotropy [*Physics*]
TAA Transit Advertising Association [*Washington, DC*] (EA)
TAA Transportation Association of America (EA)
TAA Triamcinolone Acetonide [*Also, TA*] [*Synthetic steroidal drug*]
TAA Triticale Association of Australia
TAA Tumor-Associated Antibody [*Medicine*] (DAVI)
TAA Tumor-Associated Antigen [*Immunology*]
TAA Turbine Alternator Assembly
TAA Turfgrass Association of Australia
TAA Turkish-American Associations (EA)
TAA Typical Address Access (NITA)
TAAA Teen-Age Assembly of America (EA)
TAAA Thoracoabdominal Aortic Aneurysm [*Cardiology*]
TAAA Total Active Aircraft Authorized (MCD)
TAAA Travelers Aid Association of America [*Defunct*] (EA)
TAAB Tasmanian Arts Advisory Board [*Australia*]
TAABS [*The*] Army Automated Budget System
TAAC [*The*] Association of American Cultures (EA)
TAAC Target Area Advisory Council (OICC)
TAAC Technology Assessment Advisory Council [*Washington, DC*] (EGAO)
TAAC Trade Adjustment Assistance Center [*Department of Commerce*]
TAAC Training Ammunition Authorization Committee (MCD)
TAAC Troubles d'Apprentissage - Association Canadienne [*Learning Disabilities Association of Canada*] (EAIO)
TAACOM Theater Army Area Command (AABC)
TAAD Task Assignment and Directive (MCD)
TAAD Terrain Avoidance Accessory Device
TAADC Theater Army Air Defense Command (AABC)
TAADCOM Theater Army Air Defense Command (AABC)
TAADS TOE [*Table of Organization and Equipment*] Army Authorization Document System
TAAF Test, Analyze, and Fix (AAGC)
TAAF Test, Analyze, and Fix Program [*Navy*] (MCD)
TAAF Thromboplastic Activity of Amniotic Fluid [*Medicine*]
TAAFA Territorial Army and Air Force Association [*British military*] (DMA)
TAAFFEE Tactical Air Against First and Following Enemy Echelons (MCD)
TAAG Technical Analysis and Advisory Group [*Navy*] (MCD)
TAAG Tropical Africa Advisory Group [*British Overseas Trade Board*] (DS)
TAAI Total Active Aircraft Inventory (MCD)
TAALODS [*The*] Army Automated Logistic Data System
TAALS [*The*] American Association of Language Specialists (EA)
TAALS [*The*] Judge Advocate General Automated Army Legal System
TAALS Tactical Army Aircraft Landing Systems
TAAM Terminal Area Altitude Monitoring (PDAA)
TAAM Theoretical and Applied Mechanics (IAA)
TAAM Tomahawk Air Field Attack Missile (MCD)
TAAM Transportation Army Aviation Maintenance
Ta'an Ta'anith (BJA)
TAAN Transporte Aereo Andino SA [*Venezuela*] [*ICAO designator*] (FAAC)
TAAN Transworld Advertising Agency Network [*Englewood, CO*] (EA)
TAANA [*The*] American Association of Nurse Attorneys (EA)
TAAP Three-Axis Antenna Positioner
TAAP Trade Adjustment Assistance Program [*Department of Commerce*]
TAAP Transient Analysis Array Program
TAAR Target Area Analysis-RADAR
TAAR Target Area Analysis-Repair (MCD)
TAARS [*The*] Army Ammunition Reporting System (AABC)
TAAS Tactical Air Armament Study (MCD)
TAAS Terminal Advanced Automation System [*Aviation*]
TAAS Texas Assessment of Academic Skills
TAAS Thorotrast-Associated Angiosarcoma [*Oncology*]
TAAS Three-Axis Attitude Sensor (IEEE)
TAAS Traffic Account Analysis System [*Military British*]
TAASC [*The*] Association of American Sword Collectors (EA)
TAASP [*The*] Association for the Anthropological Study of Play (EA)
TAB Airborne Tanker, Boom (NVT)
TAB Tab-automated Bonded [*Computer science*] (PCM)
TAB Tabella [*Tablet*] [*Pharmacy*]
TAB Table
TAB Tablet (WDAA)
TAB Tabloid (NTCM)
TAB Tabloncillo [*Race of maize*]
TAB Tabriz [*Iran*] [*Seismograph station code, US Geological Survey*] (SEIS)
TAB Tabular Language [*Computer science*] (IEEE)
TAB Tabulate (AAG)
TAB Tabulating Machine (IAA)
TAB Tabulation (NITA)
TAB Tactical Air Base (AFM)
TAB Tactical Analysis Branch [*Military*] (DNAB)
TAB Tamper Attempt Board
TAB Tape Automated Bonding [*Integrated circuit technology*]
TAB Target Acquisition Battalion [*Military*]
TAB Target Acquisition Battery (MCD)
TAB Tax Anticipation Bill [*Obligation*] [*Department of the Treasury*]

TAB Technical Abstract Bulletin [*ASTIA*] [*A publication*]
TAB Technical Activities Board (MCD)
TAB Technical Advisory Board (IAA)
TAB Technical Assistance Board [*United Nations*]
TAB Technical Assistance Bureau [*ICAO*] (DA)
TAB Technology Assessment Board [*Washington, DC*] (EGAO)
TAB Telecommunications Advisory Board
TAB Temporarily Able-Bodied
TAB Testing, Adjusting, and Balancing [*Heating and cooling technology*]
TAB Tetraaminobiphenyl [*Organic chemistry*]
T-AB Thai-American Business [*A publication*] (IMH)
TAB Therapeutic Abortion [*Medicine*] (MEDA)
TAB Thermactor Air Bypass [*Automotive engineering*]
TAB Thiolacetoxybenzanilide [*Organic chemistry*]
TAB Title Abstract Bulletin (IAA)
TAB Title Announcement Bulletin
TAB Tobago [*Trinidad and Tobago*] [*Airport symbol*] (OAG)
TAB Tone Answer Back [*Telecommunications*] (IAA)
TAB Top and Bottom (IAA)
TAB Total Abstinence Brotherhood
TAB Total Annual Benzene-in-Waste [*Environmental Protection Agency*]
TAB Total Autonomic Blockage [*Medicine*] (DMAA)
TAB Totalizer Agency Board (IAA)
TAB Towed Assault Bridge [*Army*]
TAB Traffic Audit Bureau [*Later, TABMM*] (EA)
TAB Training Aid Bulletins [*Navy*]
TAB Transatlantic Broadcasting Co. [*In TV series "W.E.B."*]
TAB Transportes Aereos Boliviands [*Bolivia*] [*ICAO designator*] (FAAC)
TAB Transportes Aereos da Bacia Amazonica SA [*Brazil*] [*ICAO designator*] (FAAC)
TAB Transports Aeriens du Benin [*Benin*] (EY)
TAB Triple Antibiotic [*Bacitracin, neomycin, and polymyxin*] [*Pharmacology*] (DAVI)
TAB Truck, Airplane, Boat (SAA)
TAB Turned and Bored (IAA)
TAB Typhoid, Paratyphoid A and B [*Vaccine*]
TABA [*The*] American Book Award [*Later, ABA*]
TABA Transcaribe [*Airline*] [*Colorado*]
TABA Transportes Aereos da Bacia Amazonica [*Airline*] [*Brazil*]
TABAMLN Tampa Bay Medical Library Network [*Library network*]
TABBSS Tactical Bare Base Support Study [*Air Force*]
TABC Tabulator Character (IAA)
TABC Total Aerobic Bacteria Counts
TABC Typhoid-Paratyphoid A, B and C [*Vaccine*] [*Medicine*] (BABM)
TABCASS Tactical Air Beacon Command and Surveillance System (MCD)
TAB-CD Tabulating Card
TABE Tests of Adult Basic Education [*Achievement test*]
TABE Texas Association for Bilingual Education (EDAC)
TABEL Tabella [*Tablet*] [*Pharmacy*] (ROG)
TABKO All Brit Karate Organisation (DBA)
TABL Tropical Atlantic Biological Laboratory
TABLASER Trace Element Analyzer Based on LASER Ablation and Selectivity (MCD)
TABMM Traffic Audit Bureau for Media Measurement (EA)
TABNSW Totalisator Agency Board of New South Wales [*Australia*]
TABP Tetraaminobenzophenone [*Organic chemistry*]
TABP Type A Behavior Pattern [*Medicine*] (DMAA)
TABPM Transportation Authorized in Accordance with BUPERS Manual, Article ____
TabPrd Tab Products Co. [*Associated Press*] (SAG)
TABS Tabulator Stops (AAG)
TABS Tactical Airborne Beacon System (AFM)
TABS Tailored Abstracts (NITA)
TABS Tangential Bomb Suspension (MCD)
TABS Team Approach to Better Schools [*National Education Association program*]
TABS Technical and Business Service
TABS Telephone Area Billing System
TABS Telephone Automated Briefing Service (DA)
TABS Terminal Access to Batch Service [*Computer science*] (BUR)
TABS Tests of Achievement in Basic Skills [*Educational test*]
TABS Texas Assessment of Basic Skills (EDAC)
TABS Theater Air Base Survivability [*Air Force*]
TABS Time Analysis and Billing System (BUR)
TABS Total Army Basing Study (DOMA)
TABS Total Automatic Banking System [*Trademark of Diebold, Inc.*]
TABS Transatlantic Book Service [*British*]
TABS TRIS-Acetate-Buffered Saline [*Clinical chemistry*]
TABSIM Table Simulation [*or Simulator*] (IAA)
TABSIM Tabulating Simulator (NITA)
TABSIM Tabulator Simulator
TABSOL Tabular Systems-Oriented Language [*General Electric Co.*] [*British*]
TABSTONE Target and Background Signal-to-Noise Evaluation (MUGU)
TABSTONE Target and Background Signal-to-Noise Experiment (IAA)
TABT Typhoid, Paratyphoid A, and Paratyphoid B, and Tetanus Toxoid Combined [*A vaccine*] (DAVI)
TABTD Typhoid, Paratyphoid A, and Paratyphoid B, Tetanus Toxoid, and Diptheria Toxoid Combined [*A vaccine*] (DAVI)
TABU Typical Army Ball-Up [*Slang for a military muddle*]
TABV Theater Air Base Vulnerability [*Air Force*] (AFM)
TAB VEE Theater Air Base Vulnerability [*Air Force*]
TABWAG Tank Battle War Game
TABWDS Tactical Air Base Weather Dissemination System [*Air Force*]
TABWE Tactical Air Base Weather Element [*Air Force*]
TABWS Tactical Airborne Weather Stations (MCD)
TABWX Tactical Air Base Weather
TAC [*The*] Aeroplane Collection [*British*]
TAC [*The*] Architects Collaborative [*Design firm*]
TAC [*The*] Athletics Congress [*Track*] [*An association*]
TAC Austin Community College, Austin, TX [*OCLC symbol*] (OCLC)
Tac Tacitus [*First century AD*] [*Classical studies*] (OCD)
TAC Tacloban [*Philippines*] [*Airport symbol*] (OAG)
TAC Tacon [*Flamenco dance term*]
TAC Tactical (AAG)
TAC Tactical Air Command [*Air Force*]
TAC Tactical Air Controller (NVT)
TAC Tactical Air Coordinator (SAA)
TAC Tactical Air Cover
TAC Tactical Assignment Console
TAC Tactical Command Post [*Army*] (INF)
TAC Tactical Coordinator (NATG)
TAC Tacubaya [*Mexico*] [*Seismograph station code, US Geological Survey*] (SEIS)
TAC Taiwan Aerospace Corp. (ECON)
TAC Tamoxifen, Adriamycin, Cyclophosphamide [*Antineoplastic drug regimen*]
TAC Tandycrafts, Inc. [*NYSE symbol*] (SPSG)
TAC Tape Adapter Cabinet (IAA)
TAC Target Acquisition Center [*Army*]
TAC Target Acquisition Console [*Military*] (CAAL)
TAC Targeted Amortization-Class Bond [*Investment term*]
TAC Targeting and Control (IAA)
TAC Tasmanian AIDS [*Acquired Immune Deficiency Syndrome*] Council [*Australia*]
TAC Taxable Adjustment Column (AAGC)
TAC Tax Court of the United States Reports [*A publication*]
TAC Team Activity Chart
TAC Technical Activities Committee (SAA)
TAC Technical Advisory Center [*National Bureau of Standards*]
TAC Technical Advisory Committee
TAC Technical Advisory Group (EERA)
TAC Technical and Agricultural College (AIE)
TAC Technical Applications Center [*Air Force*]
TAC Technical Area Coordinator
TAC Technical Assignment Control [*Nuclear energy*] (NRCH)
TAC Technical Assistance Center [*Telecommunications*]
TAC Technical Assistance Center [*State University College at Plattsburgh*] [*Research center*] (RCD)
TAC Technical Assistance Center [*Operated by the Helen Keller National Center for Deaf-Blind Youths and Adults (HKNC)*] (PAZ)
TAC Technical Assistance Committee [*of the Economic and Social Council of the United Nations*]
TAC Technical Assistance Contract [*Nuclear energy*] (NRCH)
TAC Technology Application Center [*University of New Mexico*] [*Albuquerque, NM*]
TAC Teleconference Association of Canada [*Toronto, ON*] [*Information service or system*] (TSSD)
TAC Telemetry and Command (MCD)
TAC TELENET Access Controller
TAC Television Advertising Council [*Australia*]
TAC Television Advisory Committee [*British*] (DEN)
TAC Temperature Altitude Chamber
TAC Terminal Access Controller [*Advanced Research Projects Agency Network*] [*DoD*]
TAC Terminal Atrial Contraction [*Cardiology*] (DAVI)
TAC Terrain Analysis Center [*Army*] (RDA)
TAC Test Access Control [*Telecommunications*] (TEL)
TAC Test Advisory Committee (MUGU)
TAC Test of Auditory Comprehension
TAC [*Official*] Texas Administrative Code (AAGC)
TAC Thai Airways Co. Ltd. [*Later, Thai Airways International*] [*ICAO designator*] (FAAC)
TAC Theatres Advisory Committee [*British*]
TAC Theoretical Astrophysics Centre
TAC Thermostatic Air Cleaner [*Automotive engineering*]
TAC Time Action Calendar [*Management*]
TAC Time and Charges [*Telecommunications*] (IAA)
TAC Time at Completion (MCD)
TAC Time-to-Amplitude Converter
TAC Tobacco Advisory Council [*British*]
TAC Tokyo Automatic Computer (IAA)
TAC Total Alkaloids of Cinchona [*Medicine*]
TAC Total Allowable Catch [*Fishing regulation proposed by EEC*]
TAC Total Annualized Cost
TAC Total Automatic Color (IAA)
TAC Total Average Cost (KSC)
TAC Totally Accurate Clock
TAC Toxic Air Contaminant
TAC Toyota Atlantic Championship [*Auto racing*]
TAC Tracking Accuracy Control
TAC Trade Agreements Committee [*An interagency committee of the executive branch of US government*] [*Terminated, 1963*]
TAC Traders and Contacts
TAC Trades Advisory Council [*British*]
TAC Training Alarm Controller
TAC TRANSAC [*Transistorized Automatic Computer*] Assembler Compiler
TAC Trans-Aminocrotonic Acid [*Also, TACA*] [*Organic chemistry*]
TAC Transformer Analog Computer
TAC Transistor-Assisted Circuit (ADA)
TAC Transistorized Automatic Computer (IAA)

TAC .... Transistorized Automatic Control
TAC .... Translations Activities Committee [*Special Libraries Association*]
TAC .... Translator, Assembler, Compiler
TAC .... Transmitter Assembler Compiler [*Telecommunications*] (IAA)
TAC .... Transonic Aerodynamic Characteristics
TAC .... Transportation Account Code [*Military*] (AFM)
TAC .... Transportation Acquisition Circular (AAGC)
TAC .... Transportation Association of Canada (EAIO)
TAC .... Transportes, Aduanas, y Consignaciones SA [*Shipping company*] [*Spain*] (EY)
TAC .... Transportes Aereos Coyhaique [*Chile*] [*ICAO designator*] (FAAC)
TAC .... Trapped Air Cushion
TAC .... Traskei Airways Corp. [*South Africa*] (EY)
TAC .... Travel Air Club (EA)
TAC .... Travelcraft Ambassadors Club [*Defunct*] (EA)
TAC .... Trialkoxycitrate [*Organic chemistry*]
TAC .... Triallyl Cyanurate [*Organic chemistry*]
TAC .... Triamcinolone Cream [*Anti-inflammatory steroid*]
TAC .... Trouble Analysis Chart
TAC .... True Airspeed Computer
TAC .... Turboalternator Compressor
TAC .... Type Address Code
TAC .... Type of Activity Code [*Military*]
TAC .... Types of Assistance Code [*Army*]
TACA .... [*The*] Association of Comedy Artists (EA)
TACA .... Tactical Airborne Controller Aircraft [*Military*] (CAAL)
TAC(A) .... Tactical Air Coordinator [*or Controller*] (Airborne) [*Military*] (NVT)
TACA .... TELECOMS Authorities Cryptographic Algorithm [*Bell Telephone encryption chip*]
TACA .... Test of Adult College Aptitude
TACA .... Trans-Aminocrotonic Acid [*Also, TAC*] [*Organic chemistry*]
TACA .... Tucker Automobile Club of America (EA)
TACAC .... Theater Army Civil Affairs Command (AABC)
TACAD .... Tactical Advisory [*Military*] (CAAL)
TACAD .... Traffic Alert and Collision Avoidance Detection [*Aviation*]
TACADE .... Teachers' Advisory Council on Alcohol and Drug Education [*British*]
TACADS .... Tactical Automated Data Processing System
TAC/AFSC .... Tactical Air Command/Air Force Systems Command
TACAID .... Tactical Airborne Information Document (NVT)
TACAIR .... Tactical Air [*Military*] (AABC)
TACAIRLIFTSq... Tactical Airlift Squadron [*Air Force*]
TACAIRLIFTTNGSq... Tactical Airlift Training Squadron [*Air Force*]
TACAIR TED... Tactical Air Threat Environment Description (MCD)
TACALS .... Tactical Air Control and Landing System [*Military*] (IAA)
TACAMO ...... Take Charge and Move Out Aircraft [*Military*]
TACAN .... Tactical Air Navigation [*System*]
TACAN .... Tactical Air Navigation
TACANCEN... Tactical Air Navigation Control Center (DNAB)
TACAN-DME... Tactical Air Navigation Distance Measuring Equipment
TACAP .... Tactical Air Command Aircraft Profiler Capability [*Air Force*]
TACAV .... Linea Aerea TACA de Venezuela
TACAV .... Tactical Aviation Model
TACAWS ...... [*The*] Army Combined Arms Weapons System
TACAWS ...... [*The*] Army Counter-Air Weapons System
TACBOMBSq... Tactical Bomb Squadron [*Air Force*]
TACC .... Tactical Air Command and Control [*Air Force*]
TACC .... Tactical Air Command Center [*Air Force*] (NVT)
TACC .... Tactical Air Command, Central
TACC .... Tactical Air Control Center [*Air Force*]
TACC .... Tactical Air Coordination Center [*Military*] (CAAL)
TACC .... Temporary Augmentation for Command and Control [*Navy*] (ANA)
TACC .... Thorotrast-Associated Cholangiocarcinoma [*Oncology*]
TACC .... Time Averaged Clutter Coherent (MCD)
TACC .... Total Army Career Counselor [*Inservice recruiter*] (INF)
TACCAR .... Time Averaged Clutter Coherent Airborne RADAR
TACCIMS ..... Theater Automated Command and Control Information Management System (MCD)
TACCO .... Tactical Air Control Coordinator
TACCO .... Tactical Control Officer [*Army*] (AABC)
TACCOM ...... Tactical Communications (MCD)
TACCOMSIM... Tactical Communications Simulator
TACCONSq... Tactical Control Squadron [*Air Force*]
TACCOPS ..... Tactical Air Control Center Operations (NVT)
TAC COUNT... Tactical Countermeasure
TACCP .... Tactical Command Post [*Army*]
TACCS .... Tactical Airborne Command, Control, and Surveillance
TACCS .... Tactical Air Command Control System (MCD)
TACCS .... Tactical Air Control Center Squadron
TACCS .... Tactical Army Combat Service Support Computer System
TACCSF .... Theater Air Command and Control Simulator Facility [*Air Force*]
TACCS-K ...... Theater Automated Command and Control System - Korea
TACCTA .... Tactical Commander's Terrain Analysis [*Military*] (AABC)
TAC-D .... Tactical Deception (MCD)
TACD .... Transport and Communications Division, United Nations ESCAP [*Economic and Social Commission for Asia and the Pacific*] [*Thailand*] (EAIO)
TACDA .... [*The*] American Civil Defense Association (EA)
TACDACS ..... Target Acquisition and Data Collection System
TAC D & E... Tactical Development and Evaluation [*Military*] (CAAL)
TACDAS .... Target Acquisition and Data Collection System
TACDEN .... Tactical Data Entry [*Army*] (IAA)
TACDEN .... Tactical Data Entry Unit [*Army*]
TACDEP .... (One-Day) Tactical Deception [*Orientation*] (DOMA)
TACDEW .... Tactical Advanced Combat Direction and Electronic Warfare (MCD)
TACDEW/EGCS... Tactical Advanced Combat Direction and Electronic Warfare Environmental Generation Control System [*Navy*]
TACDIFINSPRO... Temporary Active Duty under Instruction in a Flying Status Involving ProficiencyFlying [*Navy*] (DNAB)
TACDIFPRO... Temporary Active Duty in a Flying Status Involving Proficiency Flying [*Navy*] (DNAB)
TACE .... Tactical Air Coordination Element
TAC-E .... Tactical Emergency [*Army*]
TACE .... Talos Conversion Equipment (MCD)
TACE .... Teichoic Acid Crude Extract [*Medicine*] (DMAA)
TACE .... Tri-para-anisylchloroethylene [*Estrogen*]
TACE .... Turbine Automatic Control Equipment (IAA)
TACED .... Tank Appended Crew Evaluation Device (MCD)
TACELECRON... Tactical Electronic Warfare Squadron [*Air Force*] (DNAB)
TACELECRONDET... Tactical Electronic Warfare Squadron Detachment [*Air Force*] (DNAB)
TACELINT .... Tactical Electronic Intelligence [*Navy*] (ANA)
TACELIS .... Tactical Communications Emitter Location and Identification System [*Army*] (MCD)
TACELRON... Tactical Electronic Warfare Squadron [*Navy*] (ANA)
TACES .... Tactical Electronics Squadron
TACESS .... Tactical Communications-Electronics Simulation and Support System
TACEST .... Tactical Test [*Military*] (NVT)
TACET .... Television Advisory Committee for Educational Television (NTCM)
TACEVAL .... Tactical Evaluation (MCD)
TACEXEC ...... Tactical Executive
TACF .... Temporary Alteration Control Form (IAA)
TACFAX .... Tactical Digital Facsimile Equipment (MCD)
TACFDC .... Tactical Fire Direction Center [*Army*] (AABC)
TACFIRE ...... Tactical Fire [*Military*]
TACFO .... TASAMS [*The Army Supply and Maintenance System*] Coordination Field Office (AABC)
TACFTRRSq... Tactical Fighter Replacement Squadron [*Air Force*]
TACG .... Tactical Air Control Group [*Military*]
TACG .... Tactical Group [*Military*]
TACGP .... Tactical Air Control Group [*Military*]
TACGRU .... Tactical Air Control Group [*Military*] (NVT)
TACH .... Athens Community Hospital, Athens, TN [*Library symbol Library of Congress*] (LCLS)
TACH .... Tachometer (AAG)
tach .... Tachometer (IDOE)
TACH .... Tachometer Generator (IAA)
tach .... Tachycardia [*Cardiology*] (DAVI)
TACHA .... Tennessee Automated Clearing House Association
TACHO .... Tachometer (DSUE)
TACHY .... Tachycardia [*Cardiology*] (AAMN)
TACI .... Tactical Initialization [*Computer software*] [*Military*]
TACI .... Test Access Control Interface [*Telecommunications*] (TEL)
TACI .... Transport Accident Commission Insurance [*Victoria, Australia*]
TACIMPS ..... Tactical Integrated Mission Planning Station (MCD)
TACINTEL .... Tactical Intelligence Information Exchange System (NVT)
TACIS .... Technical Assistance to Commonwealth of Independent States
TACIT .... Technical Advisory Committee on Inland Transport
TACIT .... Time-Authenticated Cryptographic Identity Transmission [*Military*]
TACJAM .... Tactical Jamming
TACL .... Tactical Air Command Letter [*Air Force*]
TACL .... Tactical Loader [*Preparation software*] [*Army*]
TACL .... Tank-Automotive Concepts Laboratory [*Army*] (RDA)
TACL .... Test for Auditory Comprehension of Language [*Speech and language therapy*] (DAVI)
TACL .... Theater Authorized Consumption List [*Army*] (AABC)
TACL .... Time and Cycle Log [*NASA*] (KSC)
TACLAND ..... Tactical Instrument Landing (MCD)
TACLET .... Tactical Law Enforcement Teams [*Coast Guard*]
TACLINC ...... Tactical Communications Location Identification Navigation and Control System [*Military*] (ECON)
TACLO .... Tactical Air Command Liaison Officer (FAAC)
TACLOG .... Tactical-Logistical [*Army*] (AABC)
TACLOG GP... Tactical-Logistics Control Group [*Military*]
TACM .... Tactical Air Command Manual [*Air Force*]
TACM .... Transit Air Cargo Manifest
TACMAN ...... Tactical Manuals [*Aircraft*] (MCD)
TACMAR ...... Tactical Memory Address Register [*Computer science*] (IAA)
TACMAR ...... Tactical Multifunction Array RADAR [*Air Force*]
TACMAS ...... Tactical Computer Modeling Analysis and Simulation (SSD)
TACMEMO ... Tactical Memorandum [*Navy*] (ANA)
TACMIS .... Tactical Management Information System [*Army*] (RDA)
TACMOD ...... Tactical Modular Display [*Army*] (PDAA)
TACMS .... Tactical Missile System [*Provisional*] [*Army*] (RDA)
TACN .... Triazacyclononane [*Organic chemistry*]
TACNAV ...... Tactical Navigation System
TACNAVMOD... Tactical/Navigational Modernization [*Navy*]
TACNOTE ..... Tactical Notice (NVT)
TACO .... Taco Cabana'A' [*NASDAQ symbol*] (TTSB)
TACO .... Taco Cabana, Inc. [*NASDAQ symbol*] (SAG)
TACO .... Tactical Coordinator (NG)
TACO .... Tamoxifen, Adriamycin, Cyclophosphamide, Oncovin [*Vincristine*] [*Antineoplastic drug regimen*]
TACO .... Technical Appliance Corp. (IAA)
TACO .... Test and Checkout Operations [*NASA*] (NASA)
TAC-OA .... Tactical Air Command Office of Operations Analysis [*Langley Air Force Base, VA*]
TACOC .... Tactical Air Control Operation Center
TacoCab ...... Taco Cabana, Inc. [*Associated Press*] (SAG)
TACODA ...... Target Coordinate Data (IEEE)

TACOL .... Thinned Aperture Computed Lens (IEEE)
TACOM .... Tactical Area Communications System (MCD)
TACOM .... Tactical Communications (AFM)
TACOM .... Tank-Automotive Command [*Warren, MI*] [*Army*] (MCD)
TACOMA .... Television Advisory Committee of Mexican Americans (NTCM)
TACOMM ..... Tactical Communications [*Military*] (AABC)
TACOMPLAN... Tactical Communications Plan [*NATO*]
TACOMSAT... Tactical Communications Satellite [*Also, TACSAT*] [*DoD*]
TACON .... Tactical Control [*Military*] (CAAL)
TACOPNSSq... Tactical Operations Squadron [*Air Force*]
TACOPS .... Tactical Air Combat Operations Staff (MCD)
TACOPS .... Tactical Organization Paperless System [*Army*]
TACOR .... Threat Assessment and Control Receiver [*Air Force*]
TACOS .... Tactical Airborne Countermeasures or Strike [*Air Force*]
TACOS .... Tactical Air Combat Operations Staff
TACOS .... Tactical Air Combat Simulation (NATG)
TACOS .... Tactical Communications System
TACOS .... Talos Adaptable Computer System [*Navy*]
TACOS .... Tool for Automatic Conversion of Operational Software
TACOS .... Travel Agents Computer Society [*Defunct*] (EA)
TACOSS .... Tactical Container Shelter System [*Rockwell International Corp.*]
TACP........... Tactical Air Command Pamphlet [*Air Force*]
TACP........... Tactical Air Command Post [*Air Force*] (MCD)
TACP........... Tactical Air Control Party [*Air Force*]
TACP........... Tactical Air Control Point
TACP........... Technical Analysis of Cost Proposals [*DoD*]
TACPACS ..... Tactical Packet Switching System [*Army*] (RDA)
TACPOL .... Tactical Procedure Oriented Language [*Computer science*] (CSR)
TACPOL .... Tactile Procedure-Oriented Language (CSR)
TACR .... Tachykinin Receptor [*Medicine*] (DMAA)
TACR .... Tactical Air Command Regulation [*Air Force*]
TAC/R .... Tactical Reconnaissance
TACR .... Time and Cycle Record [*NASA*] (KSC)
TAC/RA .... TACAN [*Tactical Air Navigation*] RADAR Altimeter (NASA)
TACRAC .... Tactical Warfare Research Advisory Committee [*Military*] (RDA)
TACRAC .... Technical and Cost Reduction Assistance Contract
TACRAPS ...... Tactical Range Prediction System
TACREACT ... Tactical Reconnaissance Reaction Aircraft (MCD)
TACREDD ..... Tactical Readiness Drill [*Military*] (DNAB)
TACREP .... Tactical Report (DOMA)
TAC RISE ..... Tactical Reconnaissance Intelligence System Enhancement [*Air Force*]
TACRON .... Tactical Air Control Squadron [*Military*]
TACRON .... Tactical Air Squadron (DOMA)
TACRV .... Tracked Air-Cushion Research Vehicle [*DoD*]
TACS .... Auxiliary Crane Ship [*Navy symbol*]
TACS .... Tactical Air Control System [*Air Force*]
TACS .... Talker Active State [*Telecommunications*] (IAA)
TACS .... Tasmanian Association of Children's Services [*Australia*]
TACS .... Technical Assignment Control System [*Nuclear energy*] (NRCH)
TACS .... Telemetry and Command System (MCD)
TACS .... Test Assembly Conditioning Station [*Nuclear energy*] (NRCH)
TACS .... Theater Area Communications Systems [*Military*]
TACS .... Theater Army Communications System (MCD)
TACS .... Thruster Attitude Control System [*NASA*]
TACS .... Total Access Communications System [*Commercial firm British*]
TACSAT .... Tactical Communications Satellite [*Also, TACOMSAT*] [*DoD*]
TACSAT .... Tactical Satellite [*Military*] (IAA)
TACSATCOM... Tactical Satellite Communications [*Military*]
TACSCE .... Texas Association for Community Service and Continuing Education (EDAC)
TACSI .... Tactical Air Communications [*or Control*] System Improvements [*Air Force*] (MCD)
TACSIM .... Tactical Simulation
TACSOP .... Tactical Standing Operating Procedure [*Army*] (INF)
TACSQ .... Tactical Air Control Squadron [*Air Force*]
TACSS .... Tactical Army Combat Service Support (DOMA)
TACSS .... Tactical Schoolship [*Navy*] (NVT)
TACSS .... Takenaka Aqua-Reactive Chemical Soil-Stabilisation System [*Nuclear energy*] (NUCP)
TACS/TADS... Tactical Air Control System/Tactical Air Defense System
TACSYR .... Tactical Communications Systems Requirements (MCD)
TACT .... [*The*] Association of Corporate Trustees [*British*] (EAIO)
Tact .... Tactica [*of Arrian*] [*Classical studies*] (OCD)
TACT .... Tactical
TACT .... Tactical Air Control Training
TACT .... Tactical Transport [*Aircraft*]
TACT .... Technological Aid to Creative Thought (PDAA)
TACT .... Television Action Committee for Today and Tomorrow [*Later, American Council forBetter Broadcasts*] (AEBS)
TACT .... Terminal Activated Channel Test
TACT .... Tories Against Cruise and Trident [*Missiles*] [*British*] (DI)
TACT .... Total Audit Concept Technique (PDAA)
TACT .... Transactional Analysis Control Technique [*Training program*] [*American Airlines*]
TACT .... TransAct Technologies
TACT .... TransAct Technologies Inc. [*NASDAQ symbol*] (SAG)
TACT .... Transistor and Component Tester
TACT .... Transonic Aircraft Technology [*Program*] [*NASA and Air Force*]
TACT .... Truth about Civil Turmoil [*An association Defunct*] (EA)
TAC/TADS .... Tactical Air Control/Tactical Air Defense System [*Military*] (CAAL)
TACTAN .... Tactical Air Control and Navigation
TACTAS .... Tactical Towed Array Sensor [*Formerly, ETAS*] [*Navy*]
TACTAS .... Tactical Towed Array SONAR [*Navy*]
TACTASS ..... Tactical Tone and Acoustic Surveillance System [*Military*] (CAAL)
TACTASS ..... Tactical Towed-Array Surveillance System (DOMA)
TACTEC .... Tactical Technology Information Analysis Center [*Columbus, OH*] [*DoD*] (GRD)
TACTEC .... Totally Advanced Communications Technology
TACTECS ...... Tables and Charts through Extended Character Sets [*Computer science*]
TACTIC .... Technical Advisory Committee to Influence Congress [*Federation of American Scientists*]
TACTICS ...... Technical Assistance Consortium to Improve College Services [*Defunct*] (EA)
TACTL .... Tactical (AAG)
TACTLASS ... Tactical Towed Array Surveillance System [*Military*] (MCD)
TAC T MR .... Tactical Transport Medium Range [*Aircraft*]
TACTOOL ..... Tactical [*Software*] Tools
TACTRAGRULANT... Tactical Training Group, Atlantic [*Military*] (DNAB)
TACTRAGRUPAC... Tactical Training Group, Pacific [*Military*] (DNAB)
TACTRUST ... [*The*] Athletics Congress/USA Trust Fund
TACTS .... Tactical Aircrew Combat Training System (NVT)
TACTS/ACMI... Tactical Aircrew Combat Training System/Air Combat Maneuvering Instrumentation (MCD)
TAC T SR ..... Tactical Transport Short Range [*Aircraft*]
TAC/USA ...... [*The*] Athletics Congress/USA (EA)
TACV .... Tracked Air-Cushion Vehicle [*High-speed ground transportation*]
TACV .... Transportes Aereos de Cabo Verde [*Cape Verde*] [*ICAO designator*] (FAAC)
TACVA .... Tactical Vulnerability Assessment [*Military*] (MCD)
TACVA/CEWIS... Tactical Communications Vulnerability Assessment of Combat Electronics Warfare Intelligence System (MCD)
TACV/LIM .... Tracked Air Cushion Vehicle Powered by Linear Induction Motor (PDAA)
TACWAR ...... Tactical Warfare (Model) [*Army*]
TACWE .... Tactical Weather System (MCD)
TAD .... Airborne Tanker, Drogue (NVT)
TAD .... Tactical Action Display [*SAGE*]
TAD .... Tactical Air Defense (MCD)
TAD .... Tactical Air Direction [*Military*]
TAD .... Tactical Atomic Demolition [*Munitions*] [*Obsolete Military*] (NG)
TAD .... Tadiran Limited [*NYSE symbol*] (SPSG)
TAD .... Tadiran Limited ADS [*NYSE symbol*] (TTSB)
TAD .... Tadotu [*Japan*] [*Seismograph station code, US Geological Survey Closed*] (SEIS)
TAD .... Target Acquisition Data
TAD .... Target Activation Date (AAG)
TAD .... Target Area Designator [*Air Force*]
TAD .... Target Audience Description [*Army*]
TAD .... Task Assignment Directive (KSC)
TAD .... Task Assignment Drawing (MCD)
TAD .... Technical Acceptance Date (AAG)
TAD .... Technical Acceptance Demonstration (IAA)
TAD .... Technical Analysis Division [*National Bureau of Standards*]
TAD .... Technical Approach Demonstration
TAD .... Technical Approval Demonstration (AAG)
TAD .... Technology Area Description (MCD)
TAD .... Technology Availability Date (MCD)
TAD .... Telecommunications Automation Directorate [*Army*] (RDA)
TAD .... Telemetry Analog to Digital [*Information converter*]
TAD .... Telemetry and Data [*Telecommunications*] (IAA)
TAD .... Telephone Answering Device
TAD .... Television Advertising Duty
TAD .... Temperature and Dew Point (NASA)
TAD .... Temporary Additional Duty [*Military*]
TAD .... Temporary Assigned Duty [*Military*] (VNW)
TAD .... Temporary Attached Duty
TAD .... Terminal Address Designator
TAD .... Test Acceptance Document [*Computer science*] (IAA)
TAD .... Test and Development (MCD)
TAD .... Theater Air Defense [*Military*]
TAD .... Thermactor Air Diverter [*Automotive engineering*]
TAD .... Thermal Analysis Data
TAD .... Thioguanine, ara-C, Daunomycin [*Daunorubicin*] [*Antineoplastic drug regimen*]
TAD .... Thomas Aloysius Dorgan [*Satirical cartoonist*]
TAD .... Thoracic Asphyxiant Dystrophy [*Medicine*] (MAE)
TAD .... Throw Away Detector [*Space shuttle*] [*NASA*]
TAD .... Thrust-Augmented Delta [*NASA*]
TAD .... Time Available for Delivery (CET)
TAD .... Tobyhanna Army Depot, Library, Tobyhanna, PA [*OCLC symbol*] (OCLC)
TAD .... Tooele Army Depot [*Utah*]
TAD .... Top Assembly Drawing
TAD .... Toward Affective Development [*Educational tool*]
TAD .... Traffic Accident Data [*Project*] [*National Safety Council*]
TAD .... Trailing-Arm-Drive
TAD .... Training Aid and Device [*Military*]
TAD .... Training Aids Division [*Navy*]
TAD .... Traitement Automatique des Donnees [*Automatic Data Processing*] [*French*]
TAD .... Transaction Application Drive [*Computer Technology, Inc.*]
TAD .... Transmission and Distribution (IAA)
TAD .... Transporte Aereo Dominicano SA [*Dominican Republic*] [*ICAO designator*] (FAAC)
TAD .... Transverse Abdominal Diameter (DAVI)
TAD .... Traveling Around Drunk
TAD .... Trinidad [*Colorado*] [*Airport symbol Obsolete*] (OAG)
TAD .... Trio Archean Developments [*Vancouver Stock Exchange symbol*]

TAD .... Twin and Add (SAA)
TADA .... Tasmanian Amateur Diving Association [*Australia*]
TADA .... Terrorist and Disruptive Activities Act [*India*] (ECON)
TADA .... Tracking and Data Acquisition (IAA)
TADAAS .... TEMPEST Automated Data Acquisition and Analysis System
TADAC .... Therapeutic Abortion, Dilation, Aspiration, Curettage [*Medicine*] (MAE)
TADAR .... Tactical Area Defense Alerting RADAR (MCD)
TADARS .... Target Acquisition/Designation Aerial Reconnaissance System (MCD)
TADAS .... Tactical Air Defense Alerting System [*Army*]
TADC .... Tactical Air Direction Center [*Military*]
TADC .... Training and Distribution Center [*Navy*]
TADD .... Tangential Abrasive Dehulling Device [*for grains*]
TADD .... Target Alert Data Display Set (MCD)
TADD .... Termite and Ant Detection Dog [*In TADD Services Corp.*]
TADD .... Truckers Against Drunk Drivers [*Defunct*] (EA)
TADDS .... Target Alert Data Display Set (RDA)
TADE .... Tetraaminodiphenylether [*Organic chemistry*]
TADF .... Thermally Activated Delayed Fluorescence [*Analytical chemistry*]
TADF .... Thomas A. Dooley Foundation [*Later, Dooley Foundation/Intermed-USA*]
TADGC .... Tactical Air Designation Grid System [*Tactical Air Command*]
TADI .... Time Assigned Data Interpolation (HGAA)
TADIC .... Telemetry Analog-Digital Information Converter
TADIL .... Tactical Data Information Link [*DoD*]
TADIL .... Tactical Digital Information Link
TADIL-J .... Tactical Data Information Link-JTIDS [*Joint Tactical Information Distribution System*] [*DoD*]
TADIL-J .... Tactical Digital Information Link - Joint
TADILS .... Tactical Automatic Data Information Links (MCD)
Tadiran .... Tadiran Ltd. [*Associated Press*] (SAG)
TADIX .... Tactical Data Information Exchange Subsystem [*Navy*] (ANA)
TADIXS .... Tactical Data Information Exchange Subsystem
TADJET .... Transport Air Drop and Jettison Test [*Air Force, Army*]
TADLR .... Tooling Automated Direct Labor Reporting (MCD)
TADM .... Tactical Atomic Demolition Munitions [*Obsolete Military*] (AABC)
TADO .... Tactical Airlift Duty Officer (AFM)
TADOR .... Table Data Organization and Reductions
TADP .... Tactical Air Direction Post [*Military*]
TAD/P .... Terminal Area Distribution Processing
TADP .... Toronto Anti-Draft Programme [*Defunct*] (EA)
TADR .... Tabulated Drawing (MSA)
TADR .... Test Answer Document Reader
TADREPS ..... Tactical Data Replay System (NVT)
TADRS .... Target Acquisition/Designation Reconnaissance System (MCD)
TADS .... Tactical Air Defense Systems (RDA)
TADS .... Tactical Automatic Digital Switch [*Military*]
TADS .... Target Acquisition and Data System [*Army*] (DOMA)
TADS .... Target Acquisition and Designation System (MCD)
TADS .... Target Acquisition Designation Sight [*Army*]
TADS .... Target and Activity Display System [*Military*]
TADS .... Target Designation System [*Navy*]
TADS .... Technical Assistance Data
TADS .... Teletypewriter Automatic Dispatch System
TADS .... Test and Debug System (HGAA)
TADS .... Thermal Analysis Data Station
TADS .... Throw Away Detector (PDAA)
TADS .... Tracking and Display System
TADS .... Transportable Automatic Digital Switch (PDAA)
TADS .... Type [*Command*] Automated Data System [*Navy*]
TADSIXS-B ... Tactical Data Information Exchange System-B (DOMA)
TADSO .... Tactical Digital Systems Office [*Navy*] (MCD)
TADS/PNVS ... Target Acquisition Designation System/Pilot Night Vision System [*Army*] (RDA)
TADSS .... Tactical Automatic Digital Switching System
TADSS .... Training Aid, Device, Simulation and Simulator [*Military*]
TADSYS .... Turbine Automated Design System
TADYL .... Tom Dooley Youth League [*Defunct*]
TadzhSSR .... Tadzhik Soviet Socialist Republic
TAE .... Tactical Aeromed Evacuation (CINC)
TAE .... Taegu [*South Korea*] [*Seismograph station code, US Geological Survey Closed*] (SEIS)
TAE .... Taligent Application Environment [*Taligent, Inc.*] [*Computer science*]
TAE .... Tallow Amine Ethoxylate
TAE .... Tannic Acid Equivalent [*Analytical chemistry*]
TAE .... Technician Aeronautical Engineering (IAA)
TAE .... Test and Evaluation (MCD)
TAE .... Textes Arameens d'Egypte [*A publication*] (BJA)
TAE .... Time and Event (IAA)
TAE .... Transantarctic Expedition (ADA)
TAE .... Transcatheter Arterial Embolization [*Medicine*]
TAE .... Transferable Atom Equivalent [*Chemical modeling*]
TAE .... Transoceanic Airborne Environment
TAE .... Transportes Aereos Militares Ecatorianos CA [*Ecuador*] [*ICAO designator*] (FAAC)
TAE .... Tris-Acetate-EDTA [*Ethylenediaminetetraacetate*] [*Buffer*]
TAEA .... Tangipahoa & Eastern [*AAR code*]
TAEAS .... Tactical ASW [*Antisubmarine Warfare*] Environmental Acoustic Support [*Navy*] (CAAL)
TAEC .... Thailand Atomic Energy Commission for Peace
TAEC .... Turkish Atomic Energy Commission
TAED .... Tetraacetylethylenediamine [*Laundry bleaching agent*]
TAEDP .... Total Army Equipment Distribution Program (AABC)
TAEDS .... Texas Association for Educational Data Systems (EDAC)
TAEDS .... Total Army Equipment Distribution System (MCD)
TAEE .... Tertiary Amyl Ethyl Ether [*Gasoline*] [*Organic chemistry*]
TAEG .... Training Analysis and Evaluation Group [*Navy*]
TAEG .... Training and Evaluation Group [*Navy*] (MCD)
TAEM .... Terminal Area Energy Management [*NASA*] (NASA)
TAEMS .... Transportable Automated Electromagnetic Measurement System (MCD)
TAEO .... Test Article Engineering Order (MCD)
TAER .... Time, Azimuth, Elevation, and Range [*Aerospace*]
TAEREC .... Time and Event Recorder (IAA)
TAERS .... [*The*] Army Equipment Record System [*Later, TAMMS*]
TAES .... Tactical Aeromedical Evacuation System
TAES .... Techicas Aereas de Estudios y Servicios SA [*Spain ICAO designator*] (FAAC)
TAES .... Texas Agricultural Experiment Station [*Texas A & M University*] [*Research center*] (RCD)
TAES .... Transportes Aereos de El Salvador SA de CV [*ICAO designator*] (FAAC)
TAETGM .... Test and Evaluation Task Group Manager (MCD)
TAF .... Arnold Engineering Development Center, Arnold Air Force Station, TN [*OCLC symbol*] (OCLC)
TAF .... [*The*] Asia Foundation (EA)
TAF .... Oran-Tafaraoui [*Algeria*] [*Airport symbol*] (OAG)
TAF .... Stores Ship [*Military Sea Transportation Service*] (CINC)
TAF .... Tactical Air Force
TAF .... Tactical Area Files [*Military*] (CAAL)
TAF .... Taforalt [*Morocco*] [*Seismograph station code, US Geological Survey*] (SEIS)
TAF .... Task Analysis Form
TAF .... Taxpayers Against Fraud [*Washington, DC*] (AAGC)
TAF .... Technology Access Fund [*Chrysler Corp.*]
TAF .... Terminal Aerodrome Forecast [*Also, TAFOR*]
TAF .... Test, Analyze, Fix (MCD)
TAF .... Third Air Force
TAF .... Thousand Acre-Feet [*Measurement*]
TAF .... Time Air Ltd. [*Canada ICAO designator*] (FAAC)
TAF .... Time and Frequency (MHDB)
TAF .... Tissue Angiogenesis Factor [*Medicine*] (DMAA)
TAF .... Top of Active Fuel [*Nuclear energy*] (NRCH)
TAF .... Toxoid-Antitoxin Floccules [*Immunology*]
TAF .... Traditional Acupuncture Foundation (EA)
TAF .... Training Analysis and Feedback (MCD)
TAF .... Transaction Facility
TAF .... Transaxel Fluid (IAA)
TAF .... Transcription Activation Function [*Genetics*]
TAF .... Trend Asignment File [*Computer science*] (ECII)
TAF .... Trim after Forming (MSA)
TAF .... Trypsin-Aldehyde-Fuchsin [*Medicine*] (MAE)
TAF .... Tuberculin Albumose-Frei [*Albumose-Free Tuberculin*] [*German Medicine*]
TAF .... Tumor-Angiogenesis Factor [*Medicine*]
TAF .... Turkish Air Force (NATG)
TAFA .... Territorial and Auxiliary Forces Association [*British military*] (DMA)
TAFAD .... Task Force Air Defense (MUGU)
TAFB .... Travis Air Force Base [*California*]
TAFB .... Tyndall Air Force Base [*Florida*]
TAFCSD .... Total Active Federal Commissioned Service to Date [*Military*]
TAFCV .... Tobacco and Associated Farmers' Cooperative of Victoria [*Australia*]
TAFD .... Test for Auditory Figure-Ground Discrimination
TAFDS .... Tactical Airfield Fuel Dispensing System (NG)
TAFE .... Technical and Further Education (ODBW)
TAFE .... Telemetry Auto Following Equipment
TAFE .... Transverse Alternating Field Electrophoresis
TAFECNSW ... Technical and Further Education Commission New South Wales [*Australia*]
TAFEDAB ..... Technical and Further Education Discipline Appeals Board [*Victoria, Australia*]
TAFEESC ...... Technical and Further Education External Studies College [*Western Australia*]
TAFENCRD ... Technical and Further Education National Centre for Research and Development [*Australia*]
TAFERS .... Technical and Further Education Rural Studies [*South Australia*]
TAFETANSW ... Technical and Further Education Teachers' Association of New South Wales [*Australia*]
TAFETSAB .... Technical and Further Education Teaching Service Appeals Board [*Victoria, Australia*]
TAFF .... Thermally Activated Flux Flow [*Physics*]
TAFF .... Timer, Actuator, Fin, Fuze (DWSG)
TAFFE .... Tactical Air Against First and Follow-On Eschelon (MCD)
Taffie .... Technologically Advanced Family [*Lifestyle classification*]
TAFFS .... [*The*] Army Functional Files System
TAFFTS .... [*The*] Army Functional Files Test System (MCD)
TAFG .... Two-Axis Free Gyro (AAG)
TAFHQ .... Tactical Air Force Headquarters
TAFI .... Technical Association of the Fur Industry
TAFI .... Turnaround Fault Isolation [*Aviation*]
TAFIC .... Tasmanian Fishing Industry Council (EERA)
TAFIES .... Tactical Air Forces Intelligence Exploitation System
TAFIG .... Tactical Air Forces Interoperability Group [*Air Force*]
TAFIIS .... Tactical Air Force Integrated Information Systems (MCD)
TAFIM .... Technical Architecture Framework for Information Management [*Army*] (RDA)
TAFIM .... Technical Architecture Framework for Information Management [*Army*]
TAFIM .... Turnaround Fault Isolation Manual
TAFIN .... Tactical Air Force Initiative (MCD)

TAFIS........ TCATA [*TRADOC Combined Arms Test Activity*] Automated Field InstrumentationSystem (MCD)
TAFIS........ TEXCOM [*Test and Experimentation Command*] Automated Field Instrumentation System [*Army*]
TAFLE........ Thornton Aviation Fuel Lubricity Evaluator [*Fuels and lubricants testing*]
TAFMM........ Tactical Air Force Maintenance Management (MCD)
TAFMS........ Total Active Federal Military Service (DNAB)
TAFMSD........ Total Active Federal Military Service to Date
TAFNORNOR... Allied Tactical Air Force, Northern Norway [*NATO*]
TAFO........ Theater Accounting and Finance Office [*Military*] (AFM)
TAFOR........ Terminal Aerodrome Forecast [*Also, TAF*]
TAFPD........ Technical Assessment and Fraud Prevention Division [*Environmental Protection Agency*] (GFGA)
TAF QR........ Taxpayers Against Fraud Quarterly Review (AAGC)
TAFR........ Total Age-Specific Fertility Rate [*Population studies*]
TAFR........ Trouble and Failure Report [*Army*]
TAFROC........ Tactical Air Force Required Operational Capability (MCD)
TAFS........ Stores Ship
TAFS........ Training Aid Feasibility Studies (AAG)
TAFSEA........ Technical Applications for Southeast Asia [*Air Force*]
TAFSEG........ Tactical Air Force Systems Engineering Group (MCD)
TAFSONOR... Allied Tactical Air Force, South Norway [*NATO*] (NATG)
TAFSUS........ Turkish American Friendship Society of the United States (EA)
TAFT........ Technical Assistance Field Team (MCD)
TAFUBAR........ Things Are Fouled Up Beyond All Recognition [*Military slang*] [*Bowdlerized version*]
TAFVER........ Terminal Aerodrome Forecast Verification
TAFX........ Tapping Fixture
TAFY........ American Theatre Arts for Youth (EA)
TAFY........ Technically Advanced Family (PS)
TAG........ [*The*] Acronym Generator [*An RCA computer program*]
TAG........ [*The*] Acrylonitrile Group (EA)
TAG........ [*The*] Adjutant General [*Army*]
TAG........ Airborne Tanker, General (NVT)
TAG........ American Group of CPA Firms [*Lombard, IL*] (EA)
TAG........ [*The*] Association for the Gifted (EA)
TAG........ [*The*] Attorneys Group (EA)
TAG........ [*The*] Audiotex Group [*Princeton, NJ*] [*Telecommunications service*] (TSSD)
TAG........ Orion Air, Inc. [*ICAO designator*] (FAAC)
TAG........ Tactical Air Group [*MTMC*] (TAG)
TAG........ Tactical Airlift Group (MCD)
TAG........ Tactical Analysis Group [*Military*] (CAAL)
tag........ Tagalog [*MARC language code Library of Congress*] (LCCP)
TAG........ Tagbilaran [*Philippines*] [*Army*] (OAG)
TAG........ Talented and Gifted (EDAC)
TAG........ Target Attaching Globulin [*Medicine*] (AAMN)
TAG........ Target Attitude Group [*Advertising*]
TAG........ Tavern and Guild Association [*Division of Homophile Effort for Legal Protection*] (EA)
TAG........ Taxi Air Group, Inc.
TAG........ Technical Advisory Group (IAA)
TAG........ Technical Advisory Group (EERA)
TAG........ Technical Air-to-Ground (NASA)
TAG........ Technical Art Group
TAG........ Technical Assessment Group [*Navy*]
TAG........ Technical Assistance Grant
TAG........ Technical Assistance Group [*NASA*] (KSC)
TAG........ Technical Assistance Guides (OICC)
TAG........ Technician Affiliate Group [*of American Chemical Society*]
TAG........ Technology Applications Group [*Commercial firm*] (IID)
TAG........ Telecomputer Applications Group
TAG........ Telegraphist Air Gunner [*British military*] (DMA)
TAG........ Telemetry System Analysis Group
TAG........ Tennessee, Alabama & Georgia Railway Co. [*AAR code*]
TAG........ Terminal Applications Group, Inc.
TAG........ Terminating Amber Codon [*Genetics*]
TAG........ Terminating and Grounding
TAG........ Test Analysis Guide
TAG........ Test Assembly Grapple [*Nuclear energy*] (NRCH)
TAG........ Test Automation Growth
TAG........ Texas A & M University at Galveston, Galveston, TX [*OCLC symbol*] (OCLC)
TAG........ Thalassemia Action Group [*Organization concerned with Cooley's anemia*] (PAZ)
TAG........ Theatre about Glasgow [*Acting company*] (ECON)
TAG........ Thymine, Adenine, Guanine [*Laboratory science*] (DAVI)
TAG........ Time Arrive Guarantee (AAG)
TAG........ Time Automated Grid
TAG........ Tongue and Groove [*Lumber*] (IAA)
TAG........ Training Aids Guide [*Navy*]
TAG........ Trans-Atlantic Geotraverse [*Project*] [*National Oceanic and Atmospheric Administration*]
TAG........ Transatlantic Geotraverse [*Geology*]
TAG........ Transfer Agent [*Business term*] (MHDB)
TAG........ Transient Analysis Generator
TAG........ Transport Air Group [*Joint Army, Navy, and Marine Corps*]
TAG........ Transportation Acronym Guide [*BTS*] (TAG)
TAG........ Transportation Alternatives Group [*Transportation 2000*] [*MTMC*] (TAG)
TAG........ Trauma Action Group [*Defunct*] (EA)
TAG........ Treatment Action Group [*for AIDS medication*] [*FDA*]
TAG........ Tree-Adjoining Grammar [*Artificial intelligence*]
TAG........ Triacylglycerol [*Food technology*]
TAG........ Turmor-Associated Glycoprotein [*Biochemistry*]
TAGA........ Tasmanian Amateur Gymnastics Association [*Australia*]
TAGA........ Technical Association of the Graphic Arts (EA)
TAGA........ Telegraphist Air Gunner's Association [*Navy British*]
TAGA........ Trace Atmospheric Gas Analyser [*Instrument*]
TAGA........ Travel Agents Guild of America (EA)
TAGAMET.... Antagonist Cimetidine [*Ulcer medicine manufactured by SmithKline Beckman Corp.*]
TAGBDUSA... [*The*] Adjutant General's Board, United States Army
TAGC........ Tripped Automatic Gain Control
TAGCEN........ [*The*] Adjutant General Center [*Army*] (AABC)
TAGER........ [*The*] Association for Graduate Education and Research
TAGH........ Triiodothyronine, Amino Acids, Glucagon, and Heparin [*Medicine*] (DMAA)
TagHeur........ Tag Heuer International SA [*Associated Press*] (SAG)
TAGIS........ Tracking and Ground Instrumentation System (DNAB)
TAGIU........ Tracking and Ground Instrumentation Unit [*NASA*]
TAGM........ Range Instrumentation Ship
TAGM........ Table and Art Glassware Manufacturers [*Defunct*] (EA)
TAGN........ Triaminoguanidine Nitrate [*Propellant ingredient*]
TAGO........ [*The*] Adjutant General's Office [*Army*]
TAGOTA........ TACFIRE [*Tactical Fire*] Ad Hoc Group on Testing and Analysis (MCD)
TAGRDCUSA... [*The*] Adjutant General's Research and Development Command, United States Army
TAGRET........ Thermal Advanced Gas-Cooled Reactor Exploiting Thorium [*Nuclear energy*] (IAA)
TAGS........ FBM [*Fleet Ballistic Missile*] Support Ship
TAGS........ Tactical Aircraft Guidance System [*Air Force*]
TAGS........ Tarrant Apparel Group [*NASDAQ symbol*] (SAG)
TAGS........ Technology for the Automated Generation of Systems (NITA)
TAGS........ Teledyne Airborne Geophysical Services
TAGS........ Text and Graphics System [*or Subsystem*] (NASA)
TAGS........ Theater Air-Ground Warfare Simulation (MCD)
TAGS........ Total Associates Guest Satisfaction
TAGS........ Tower Automated Ground Surveillance System (MCD)
TAGSRWC.... [*The*] Andy Griffith Show Rerun Watchers Club (EA)
TAGSUSA.... [*The*] Adjutant General's School [*United States*], Army
TAH........ Air Moorea [*France ICAO designator*] (FAAC)
TAH........ Hospital Ship
Tah........ Taehti [*Record label*] [*Finland*]
TAH........ Tahiti [*Society Islands*] [*Seismograph station code, US Geological Survey Closed*] (SEIS)
TAH........ Tanna Island [*Vanuata*] [*Airport symbol*] (OAG)
TAH........ Tell Abu Huwam (BJA)
TAH........ Total Abdominal Hysterectomy [*Medicine*]
TAH........ Total Artificial Heart
TAH........ Total Artificial Heart [*Cardiology*] (DMAA)
TAH........ Transabdominal Hysterectomy [*Medicine*] (MAE)
TA/H........ Turn Altitude/Height [*Aviation*] (DA)
TAHA........ Tapered Aperture Horn Antenna
TAHBSO........ Total Abdominal Hysterectomy Bilateral Salpingo-Oophorectomy [*Medicine*] (MAH)
TAHE........ Thin Line Array Handling Equipment (DWSG)
TAHOE........ TOW Against Helicopter Operational Equipment (RDA)
TAHOP........ Tank/Attack Helicopter Operational Performance (MCD)
TAHQ........ Theater Army Headquarters
TAI........ National Organization for Travelers Aid Societies [*Also known as Travelers Aid International*] (EA)
TAI........ TACA International Airlines SA [*El Salvador*] [*ICAO designator*] (FAAC)
TAI........ Tactical Area of Interest [*Military*] (INF)
TAI........ Tainan [*Republic of China*] [*Seismograph station code, US Geological Survey*] (SEIS)
Tai........ Taiwan
TAI........ Taiz [*Yemen Arab Republic*] [*Airport symbol*] (OAG)
TAI........ Target Area of Interest [*Army intelligence matrix*] (INF)
TAI........ Teacher Attitude Inventory [*Teacher evaluation test*]
TAI........ Team-Assisted Individualization (EDAC)
TAI........ Temps Atomique International [*International Atomic Time*] [*Telecommunications*]
TAI........ Test Anxiety Inventory [*Educational test*]
TAI........ Thai Airways International (MCD)
TAI........ Therapy Attitude Inventory [*Test*] [*Psychology*]
TAI........ Thermal Anti-Ice (GAVI)
TAI........ Time-to-Autoignition [*NASA*] (KSC)
TAI........ Total Active Inventory (MCD)
TAI........ Total Aircraft Inventory
TAI........ Traditionally Administered Instruction (BUR)
TAI........ Transamerica Income Shares, Inc. [*NYSE symbol*] (SPSG)
TAI........ TransAmerica Inc. Shrs [*NYSE symbol*] (TTSB)
TAI........ Transports Aeriens Intercontinentaux [*Privately owned French airline*]
TAI........ Turnaround Index [*Computer science*]
TAI........ Tuskegee Airmen, Inc. (EA)
TAIB........ Trans-Arabian Investment Bank (MENA)
TAIC........ Technical Air Intelligence Center [*Navy*]
TAIC........ Tokyo Atomic Industrial Consortium
TAIC........ Triallylisocyanurate [*Organic chemistry*]
TAICH........ Technical Assistance Information Clearing House [*of ACVAFS*] [*Information service or system*] (EA)
TAID........ Thrust-Augmented Improved Delta [*Launch vehicle*] [*NASA*]
TAID........ Thunderbird American Indian Dancers (EA)
TAIDB........ Tank-Automotive Integrated Database (MCD)
TAIDET........ Triple Axis Inertial Drift Erection Test
TAIDHS........ Tactical Air Intelligence Data Handling System (NATG)

TAIDSC........ Tasmanian AIDS [*Acquired Immune Deficiency Syndrome*] Council [*Australia*]
TAIF............ [*The*] Australasian Institute of Fundraising
TAILRATS.... Tail RADAR Acquisition and Tracking System (MCD)
TAILS.......... Tactical Automatic Landing System [*Aviation*] (NG)
TAIM........... Technical Area Integration Manager (SSD)
TAIM........... Total Army Inventory Management [*Army*]
TAIM........... Trial of Antihypertensive Interventions and Management [*Medicine*]
TAINS.......... TERCOM [*Terrain Contour Mapping*]-Assisted Inertial Navigation System (MCD)
TAIP............ Terminal Area Impact Point (MUGU)
TAIR............ Terminal Area Instrumentation RADAR (MCD)
TAIR............ Test Assembly Inspection Record [*NASA*] (NASA)
TAIRCF........ Tactical Air Control Flight [*Military*]
TAIRCG........ Tactical Air Control Group [*Military*] (AFIT)
TAIRCS........ Tactical Air Control Squadron [*Air Force*]
TAIRCW....... Tactical Air Control Wing [*Air Force*]
TAIS............ Tactical Air Intelligence System [*Military*] (MCD)
TAIS............ Technology Applications Information System
TAIS............ Time Assessment Interview Schedule (DMAA)
TAISEL......... Taiwan International Standard Electronics Ltd. (NITA)
TAISSA........ Travelers Aid - International Social Service of America [*Later, ISS/AB*]
TAIT............ Taitron Components'A' [*NASDAQ symbol*] (TTSB)
TAIT............ Taitron Components, Inc. Class A [*NASDAQ symbol*] (SAG)
Tait............. Tait's Index to Morison's Dictionary [*Scotland*] [*A publication*] (DLA)
Tait............. Tait's Index to Scotch Session Cases [*1823*] [*A publication*] (DLA)
Tait............. Tait's Manuscript Decisions, Scotch Session Cases [*A publication*] (DLA)
Tait Ev........ Tait on Evidence [*A publication*] (DLA)
Tait Ind....... Tait's Index to Scotch Session Cases [*1823*] [*A publication*] (DLA)
Tait JP........ Tait's Justice of the Peace [*A publication*] (DLA)
Taitron........ Taitron Components, Inc. Class A [*Associated Press*] (SAG)
TAIU............ Technical Aircraft Instrument Unit [*Navy*]
TAIU............ Training Agency Intelligence Unit (AIE)
Taiw............ Taiwan (VRA)
Taiwan........ Taiwan Fund, Inc. [*Associated Press*] (SAG)
TaiwanE....... Taiwan Equity Fund, Inc. [*Associated Press*] (SAG)
TAJ............. Tadji [*Papua New Guinea*] [*Airport symbol*] (OAG)
taj............... Tajik [*MARC language code Library of Congress*] (LCCP)
TAJ............. Tanegashima [*Ryukyu Islands*] [*Seismograph station code, US Geological Survey*] (SEIS)
TAJ............. Taracua [*Brazil*] [*Airport symbol*] (AD)
TAJ............. Thermal Arc Jet
TAJ............. Tunisavia - Societe de Transport, Services et Travaux Aeriens [*Tunisia*] [*ICAO designator*] (FAAC)
TAJ............. Turbulent Air Jet
TAJA........... [*The*] Abibi Jazz Artists [*British*]
TAJA........... [*The*] Australian Journal of Anthropology [*A publication*]
TAJAG......... [*The*] Assistant Judge Advocate General [*Army*] (AABC)
TAK............. Cargo Ship [*Military Sea Transportation Service*] (CINC)
TAK............. Takaka [*New Zealand*] [*Seismograph station code, US Geological Survey Closed*] (SEIS)
TAK............. Takamatsu [*Japan*] [*Airport symbol*] (OAG)
TAK............. Taken
TAK............. Trainer Appraisal Kit
TAK............. Transkei Airways [*South Africa ICAO designator*] (FAAC)
TAK............. Transparent Armor Kit
TAKC........... Theological Associate, King's College [*London*]
TAKCAL........ Tachometer Calibration (DNAB)
TAKIS.......... Tutmonda Asocio pri Kibernetiko, Informatiko, kaj Sistemiko [*World Association of Cybernetics, Computer Science, and System Theory*] (EAIO)
TAKIT.......... Teaching Aids Kit [*Red Cross Youth*]
TAKR........... Vehicle Cargo Ship
TAKRX......... Fast Sealift Ship
TAKV........... Cargo Ship and Aircraft Ferry [*Military Sea Transportation Service*] (CINC)
TAKX........... Maritime Prepositioning Ship
TAL............. [*The*] Apocryphal Literature: A Brief Introduction [*1945*] [*A publication*] (BJA)
Tal.............. Cases Tempore Talbot, English Chancery [*1734-38*] [*A publication*] (DLA)
TAL............. Tailor (MSA)
TAL............. Talair Pty Ltd. [*New Guinea*] [*ICAO designator*] (FAAC)
TAL............. Talara [*Peru*] [*Seismograph station code, US Geological Survey*] (SEIS)
Tal.............. Talbot's Cases in Equity [*1734-38*] [*A publication*] (DLA)
TAL............. Talcorp Ltd. [*Toronto Stock Exchange symbol*]
TAL............. Talis [*Such*] [*Pharmacy*]
TAL............. Talladega College, Talladega, AL [*OCLC symbol*] (OCLC)
TAL............. Talley Indus [*NYSE symbol*] (TTSB)
TAL............. Talley Industries, Inc. [*NYSE symbol*] (SPSG)
TAL............. Talmud
TAL............. Tanana [*Alaska*] [*Airport symbol*] (OAG)
TAL............. Target Acquisition Laboratory
TAL............. Teacher Assessment of Leverage (EDAC)
TAL............. Technische Akademie der Luftwaffe [*Germany*] (MCD)
TAL............. Telecommunications Access Language
TAL............. Tendo Achillis Lengthening [*Orthopedics*] (DAVI)
TAL............. TEPI [*Technical Equipment Planning Information*] Approved Letter
TAL............. Terminal Application Language
TAL............. Territory Airlines [*Australia*]
TAL............. Tetraalkyllead [*Organic chemistry*]
TAL............. Thymic Alymphoplasia [*Medicine*] (MAE)
TAL............. Timeslips III Accounting Link [*Computer science*]
TAL............. Track Adjusting Link [*Army*] (RDA)
TAL............. Training Aids Library [*Navy*]
TAL............. Transaction Application Language [*Computer science*] (MHDB)
TAL............. TransAlpine [*Pipeline*] [*Western Europe*]
TAL............. Transatlantic (SSD)
TAL............. Transatlantic Landing
TAL............. Transocean Air Lines
TAL............. Transoceanic Abort Landing (NASA)
TAL............. Transporter Air Lock [*Nuclear energy*] (NRCH)
TALA........... Teacher Author League of America [*Formerly, TALNY*] (EA)
TALA........... Textile Association of Los Angeles (EA)
TALA........... Travel Agents' Licensing Authority [*Victoria, Australia*]
TALAFIT....... Tank, Laying, Aiming, and Firing Trainer (MCD)
TALANT........ Thiokol Nuclear Development Center; Allison Division, General Motors; Linde Division, Union Carbide; and Nuclear Development Corp. Team (SAA)
TALAR......... Tactical Approach and Landing RADAR [*NASA*]
TALAR......... Talos Activity Report (MCD)
Talb............ Cases Tempore Talbot, English Chancery [*1734-38*] [*A publication*] (DLA)
Talb............ Talbot's Cases in Equity [*1734-38*] [*A publication*] (DLA)
TALB........... Travel Agents' Licensing Board [*Australia*]
TALBE......... Talk and Listen Beacon [*Radio*]
Talbots........ Talbots, Inc. [*Associated Press*] (SAG)
TALC........... Tactical Airborne Laser Communication (DOMA)
TALC........... Tactical Airborne Laser Communications [*Military*] (LAIN)
TALC........... Tactical Airlift Center (AFM)
TALC........... Take-a-Look-See (MCD)
TALC........... Tank-Automotive Logistics Command [*Army*]
TALC........... Territory Anti-Litter Committee [*Northern Territory, Australia*]
TALC........... Tutoring Adults through Literacy Councils (EDAC)
TALCM........ Tactical Air-Launched Cruise Missile (MCD)
TALC-OA...... Tactical Airlift Center Office of Operations Analysis [*Pope Air Force Base, NC*]
TALCOR....... Transponder Array Location by Co-Planar Ranges [*Oceanography*] (DICI)
TALD........... Tactical Air Launched Decoy (DOMA)
TALDT......... Total Administrative and Logistics Downtime (MCD)
TALF........... Take a Look Foundation (EA)
TALF........... Trial Attorney's Litigation File (AAGC)
TALFF......... Total Allowable Level of Foreign Fishing
TALFF......... Total Allowance Level of Foreign Fishing [*Marine science*] (OSRA)
TALH........... Thick Ascending Limb of Henle's Loop [*Medicine*] (DMAA)
TALIS.......... Topics in Australasian Library and Information Studies [*A publication*]
TALISMAN... Transfer Accounting, Lodging for Investments, and Stock Management for Jobbers [*Stock exchange term British*]
TALISSI....... Tactical Light Shot Simulation (MCD)
TALK........... Tel-Save Holdings [*NASDAQ symbol*] (TTSB)
TALK........... Tel-Save Holdings, Inc. [*NASDAQ symbol*] (SAG)
TALK........... Titles Alphabetically Listed by Keyword (KSC)
Talk............ Total Alkalinity [*Marine science*] (OSRA)
T-ALL.......... T-Cell Acute Lymphoblastic Leukemia [*Oncology*]
Talley.......... Talley Industries, Inc. [*Associated Press*] (SAG)
TALM........... Tactical Air-Launched Missile (MCD)
TALMIS........ Technology-Assisted Learning Market Information Services [*Educational Programming Systems, Inc.*]
TALMS......... Tangier American Legation Museum Society (EA)
TALMS......... Tunable Atomic Line Molecular Spectroscopy
TALNY......... Teacher Author League of New York [*Later, TALA*] (EA)
TALO........... Tactical Air Liaison Officer [*Air Force*]
TALO........... Time after Lift-Off
TALO........... Total Audience Listening Output [*Television ratings*] (WDMC)
TALOG......... Theater Army Logistical Command
TALON......... South Central Regional Medical Library Program [*Library network*]
TALON......... Tactical Air-Land Operations (MCD)
TALON......... Testing and Analysis of Local Area Optical Networks (NITA)
TALON......... Texas Arkansas Louisiana Oklahoma, New Mexico (NITA)
TALONS....... Tactical Airborne LORAN Navigation System [*Model*] (MCD)
TALOP......... Terminology, Administrative, Logistical, and Operational Procedures [*Military*]
TALPrB........ Talley Indus,$1.00 Cv B Pfd [*NYSE symbol*] (TTSB)
TALPS......... Transactional Analysis Life Position Survey [*Psychology*]
TAL QUAL.... Talis Qualis [*Such As It Is*] [*Latin*] (ROG)
TALR........... Law Reports of the District Court of Tel Aviv [*A publication*] (BJA)
TALS........... [*The*] American Lupus Society (EA)
TALS........... [*The*] Army Language School
TALS........... Barge Cargo Ship
TALS........... Transport Approach and Landing Simulator
TALT........... Tracking Altitude (MCD)
TALTC......... Test Access Line Termination Circuit [*Telecommunications*] (TEL)
TALTER....... Teno [*or Tendo*] Achillis Lengthening and Toe Flexor Release [*Orthopedics*] (DAVI)
TALTT.......... Thrust Augmented Long Tank Thor (MCD)
TALUS......... Transportation and Land Use Study [*Michigan*]
TALX........... Talx Corp. [*NASDAQ symbol*] (SAG)
TalxCp......... Talx Corp [*Associated Press*] (SAG)
TAM............ [*The*] Access Method (IAA)
TAM............ [*The*] Associated Missions (EA)
TAM............ Tactical Airlift Modernization
TAM............ Tactical Air Missile
TAM............ Tactical Air Mission [*Air Force*]
TAM............ Tamanrasset [*Algeria*] [*Seismograph station code, US Geological Survey*] (SEIS)
TAM............ Tamara Resources, Inc. [*Vancouver Stock Exchange symbol*]

TAM .... Tamerton [*England*]
Tam .... Tamid (BJA)
TAM .... Tamil [*Language, etc.*] (ROG)
tam .... Tamil [*MARC language code Library of Congress*] (LCCP)
Tam .... Tamlyn's English Rolls Court Reports [*48 English Reprint*] [*A publication*] (DLA)
TAM .... Tamoxifen [*Antineoplastic drug*]
TAM .... Tampico [*Mexico*] [*Airport symbol*] (OAG)
TAM .... Tangent Approximating Manifold
TAM .... Target Acquisition Model [*Military*]
TAM .... Target Activated Munition [*Air-delivered land mines*]
TAM .... Technical Acknowledgment Message [*Aviation*]
TAM .... Technical Advice Memorandum
TAM .... Technical Ammunition
TAM .... Technical Area Manager
TAM .... Techniques of Alcohol Management [*Campaign, sponsored in part by the National Licensed Beverage Association, to prevent drunk driving*]
TAM .... Telecommunications Access Method
TAM .... Telephone Answering Machine (IEEE)
TAM .... Teleprocessing Access Method [*Telecommunications*] (IAA)
TAM .... Television Audience Measurement
TAM .... Teresian Apostolic Movement [*See also MTA*] [*Italy*] (EAIO)
TAM .... Terminal Access Method
TAM .... Test Access Multiplexer [*Telecommunications*] (TEL)
TAM .... Texas A & M University [*College Station, TX*]
TAM .... Thermal Analytical Model [*Apollo*] [*NASA*]
TAM .... Thermoaciduranss Agar Modified [*Microbiology*] (DAVI)
TAM .... Throw Away Maintenance
TAM .... Time and Materials (MCD)
TAM .... Tituli Asiae Minoris [*Vienna*] [*A publication*] (OCD)
TAM .... Total Active Motion [*Orthopedics*]
TAM .... Towed Acoustic Monitor (PDAA)
TAM .... Toxoid-Antitoxin Mixture [*Immunology*]
TAM .... Traction Asynchronous Motor (PDAA)
TAM .... Trajectory Application Method (MCD)
TAM .... Transantarctic Mountains
TAM .... Transistor-Amplifier-Multiplier (IIA)
TAM .... Transparent Anatomical Manikin [*An exhibit at the Chicago Museum of Science and Industry*]
TAM .... Transportacion Aerea Mexicana [*Mexico ICAO designator*] (FAAC)
TAM .... Transportation Acquisition Manual [*A publication*] (AAGC)
TAM .... Transportes Aereos Regionais SA [*Brazil*] [*ICAO designator*] (FAAC)
TAM .... Trialkylamine [*Organic chemistry*]
TAM .... Triangle Amplitude Modulation
TAM .... Tubos de Acero de Mexico [*AMEX symbol*] (SPSG)
TAM .... TubosDeAceroMex ADR [*AMEX symbol*] (TTSB)
TAM .... Tumor-Associated Macrophages [*Immunology*]
TAM .... Twentieth Anniversary Mobilization (EA)
TAM .... Type-Approval Model
TAM .... Tyrosine Activation Motif [*Biochemistry*]
TAMA .... Technical Assistance and Manufacturing Agreement
TAMA .... Threat to Army Mission Areas
TAMA .... Training Aids Management Agency [*Army*] (AABC)
TAMAC .... Three-Axis Manual Attitude Controller
TAMALAN .... Table Manipulation Language (MHDB)
Tamb .... Tambyah's Reports [*Ceylon*] [*A publication*] (DLA)
TAMBA .... Twins and Multiple Births Association [*British*] (DBA)
Tambd .... Tambrands, Inc. [*Associated Press*] (SAG)
TAMC .... Tactical Aviation Maintenance Co. [*Army*]
TAMC .... Transportation Aircraft Maintenance Company [*Army*]
TAMC .... Tripler Army Medical Center (AABC)
TAMCO .... Training Aid for MOBIDIC Console Operations
TAME .... Tactical Air-to-Air Mission Evaluation (MCD)
TAME .... Tactical Missile Encounter [*Air Force*] (KSC)
TAME .... Tertiary-Amyl Methyl Ether [*Gasoline additive*]
TAME .... Toluene-Sulfo-Trypsin Arginine Methyl Ester [*Organic chemistry*] (MAE)
TAME .... Tosyl-L-arginine Methyl Ester [*Also, TosArgOMe*] [*Biochemical analysis*]
TAMED .... Totally Automated Method Development [*High-performance liquid chromatography*]
TAMF .... Tactical Automated Maintenance Facility
TAMI .... Tanks and Mechanized Infantry Experiment (MCD)
TAMI .... Television Accessory Manufacturers Institute (NTCM)
TAMI .... Thrombolysis and Angioplasty in Myocardial Infarction [*Cardiology study*]
TAMI .... Tip Air Mass Injection [*Helicopter*]
TAMICSS .... TAFIES [*Tactical Air Force Intelligence Exploitation System*] Microfilm Subsystem (MCD)
TAMIRAD .... Tactical Mid-Range Air Defense Program [*Army*] (AABC)
TAMIS .... Telemetric Automated Microbial Identification System
TAMIS .... Training Ammunition Management Information System (MCD)
Taml .... Tamlyn's English Rolls Court Reports [*48 English Reprint*] [*A publication*] (DLA)
TAML .... Taunton Municipal Lighting Plant [*Nuclear energy*] (NRCH)
TAMLA .... Technical Assistance and Manufacturing License Agreement
Taml Ev .... Tamlyn's Evidence in Chancery [*2nd ed.*] [*1846*] [*A publication*] (DLA)
Taml TY .... Tamlyn's Terms of Years [*1825*] [*A publication*] (DLA)
Tamlyn .... Tamlyn's English Rolls Court Reports [*48 English Reprint*] [*A publication*] (DLA)
Tamlyn Ch ... Tamlyn's English Rolls Court Reports [*48 English Reprint*] [*A publication*] (DLA)
Tamlyn (Eng) ... Tamlyn's English Rolls Court Reports [*A publication*] (DLA)
TAMM .... Tetrakis(acetoxymercuri)methane [*Organic chemistry*]
TAMMC .... Theater Army Materiel Management Center
TAMMIS .... Theater Army Medical Management Information System (GFGA)
TAMMIS-D ... Theater Army Medical Management Information System - Division
TAMMS .... [*The*] Army Maintenance Management System [*Formerly, TAERS*] (AABC)
TAMO .... Tooling Advance Material Order (MCD)
TAMO .... Training Aids Management Office [*Army*] (AABC)
TAMOS .... Terminal Automatic Monitoring System
TAMOS .... Terminal Auto-Operator and Monitor System (NITA)
TAMP .... Tactical Antimissile Measurement Program [*Military*] (IAA)
TAMP .... Tactical Armament Master Plan (MCD)
TAMP .... Tampering [*FBI standardized term*]
TAMP .... Terminally (Guided) Anti-Armor Mortar Projectile [*Navy*] (DOMA)
TAMP .... Tertiary-Amylphenol [*Disinfectant*]
TAMP .... Thailand Ammunition Manufacturing Plant (CINC)
TAMP .... Theater Aviation Maintenance Program [*Army*] (DOMA)
TAMP .... Transition Assistance Management Program [*Army*]
TAMP .... Tufts Assessment of Motor Performance [*Occupational therapy*]
TAMPA .... Tender Assist Minimum Platform Arrangement (PDAA)
Tampa .... Transportes Aereos Mercantiles Panamericanos [*National airlines*] [*Colorado*] (EY)
TAMPER .... Tables for Approximation of Midpoints for Exponential Regression (MCD)
TAMPNL ...... Trigger and Monitor Panel (IAA)
TAMPS .... Tactical Aircraft Mission Planning System (DOMA)
TAMPS .... Teaming Analysis Model Personnel Selector (MCD)
TAMR .... Teen Association of Model Railroading (EA)
TAMRA .... Technical and Miscellaneous Revenue Act of 1988
TAMS .... Defender Tank Antimissile System [*British*] [*Military*] (INF)
TAMS .... Intime Systems International, Inc. [*NASDAQ symbol*] (SAG)
TAMS .... Tactical Avionics Maintenance Simulation (KSC)
TAMS .... Tandem Accelerator Mass Spectrometry
TAMS .... Target Activated Munitions System
TAMS .... Technical Assistance and Management Services [*General Services Administration*] (GFGA)
TAMS .... Test and Monitoring System (MCD)
TAMS .... Texas Assesment Modeling Systems (EDAC)
TA-MS .... Thermal Analysis Mass Spectrometry
TAMS .... Thruster-Assisted Mooring System [*of a ship*] (DS)
TAMS .... Token and Medal Society (EA)
TAMS .... Total Active Military Service (AFM)
TAMS .... Total Automotive Management Service
TAMS .... Toxic Air Monitoring System [*Environmental Protection Agency*] (GFGA)
TAMS .... Trade Action Monitoring System [*Office of the United States Trade Representative*] (GFGA)
TAMS .... Training Ammunition Management Study [*Army*] (MCD)
TAMSA .... Intime Systems Intl'A' [*NASDAQ symbol*] (TTSB)
TAMSA .... Transportes Aereos Mexicano, Sociedad Anonima
Tam Shr ...... [*The*] Taming of the Shrew [*Shakespearean work*] (BARN)
TAMSU .... Intime Systems Intl Unit [*NASDAQ symbol*] (TTSB)
TAMSW .... Intime Sys Intl Wrrt [*NASDAQ symbol*] (TTSB)
TAMT .... [*The*] American Mime Theatre (EA)
TAMTAC .... Toxic Air Monitoring Technical Advisory Committee [*Environmental Protection Agency*] (GFGA)
TAMU .... Texas A & M University
TAMU .... Texas A&M University, College Station (USDC)
TAMV .... Tulare Apple Mosaic Virus [*Plant pathology*]
TAMVEC .... Texas A & M University Variable Energy Cyclotron
TAN .... Tananarive [*Madagascar*] [*Seismograph station code, US Geological Survey*] (SEIS)
Tan .... Tancredus [*Deceased circa 1236*] [*Authority cited in pre-1607 legal work*] (DSA)
TAN .... Tandem (AAG)
TAN .... Tandy Corp. [*NYSE symbol*] (SPSG)
Tan .... Taney's United States Circuit Court Reports [*A publication*] (DLA)
TAN .... Tangent [*Mathematics*]
tan .... Tangent [*Mathematics*] (ODBW)
tan .... Tangent (IDOE)
TAN .... Tangential Cell [*Neurology*]
TAN .... Tanglewood Consolidated Resources, Inc. [*Toronto Stock Exchange symbol*]
Tan .... Tanhuma (BJA)
TAN .... Tanned (MSA)
TAN .... Tanning
TAN .... Tanzania (WDAA)
TAN .... Task Authorization Notice
TAN .... Tasman Air Services [*New Zealand*] [*FAA designator*] (FAAC)
TAN .... Taunton, MA [*Location identifier FAA*] (FAAL)
TAN .... Tax Administrators News [*Federation of Tax Administrators*] [*A publication*]
TAN .... Tax Anticipation Note [*Obligation*] [*State or local government*]
TAN .... Taxation Assessment Notice
TAN .... Technische Arbeitsnorm
TAN .... Technology Alert Network (GNE)
TAN .... Telephone Answering Service (NITA)
TAN .... Teletype Alert Network (NVT)
TAN .... Test Area North [*AEC*]
TAN .... Thiazolylazonaphthol [*An indicator*] [*Chemistry*]
TAN .... Title Analytic [*Bibliography*]
TAN .... Tonically Active Neurons [*Neurobiology*]
TAN .... Total Acid Number [*Oil analysis*]
TAN .... Total Adenine Nucleotide [*Medicine*]
TAN .... Total Ammonia Nitrogen

TAN.............. Trainable Adaptive Network
TAN.............. Transall-Normen (MCD)
TAN.............. Transonic Aerodynamic Nozzle
TAN.............. Transportes Aereos Nacionales, SA [*TAN Airlines*]
TAN.............. Transportes Aeros Nacionales [*National Air Line*] [*Honduras*] (PDAA)
TAN.............. Twilight All Night
TAN ALT...... Tangent Altitude [*Photography*]
TANB............ Trailerable Aids to Navigation Boat [*USCG*] (TAG)
Tanc.............. Tancredus [*Deceased circa 1236*] [*Authority cited in pre-1607 legal work*] (DSA)
TANC............ Through-Axis Navigational Control
TANC............ Total Absorption Nuclear Cascade
TANCAV....... Tactical Navigation and Collision Avoidance [*Military*] (CAAL)
Tanc QW...... Tancred. Quo Warranto [*A publication*] (ILCA)
Tancre.......... Tancredus [*Deceased circa 1236*] [*Authority cited in pre-1607 legal work*] (DSA)
Tancred........ Tancredus [*Deceased circa 1236*] [*Authority cited in pre-1607 legal work*] (DSA)
T & A........... Test and Adjust (SSD)
T & A........... Time and Allowance
T&A.............. Time and Attendance (USDC)
T & A........... Tonsillectomy and Adenoidectomy [*or Tonsils and Adenoids*] [*Medicine*]
T & A........... Tops and Accessories [*Show business slang*] [*Bowdlerized version*]
T & A........... Turnbull & Asser [*Men's fashions*]
T & AT......... Tank and Antitank [*Artillery and ammunition*] (NATG)
T & AVR...... Territorial and Army Volunteer Reserve [*British*]
T & B........... Taylor and Bell's Calcutta Supreme Court Reports [*India*] [*A publication*] (DLA)
T & B........... Top and Bottom [*Technical drawings*]
T & B........... Truck and Bus
T & B........... Turn-and-Bank Indicators
T and B........ Turned and Bored
T & BB......... Top and Bottom Bolt [*Technical drawings*]
T&C.............. Technology and Culture [*A publication*] (BRI)
T & C........... Telemetry and Command (SSD)
T & C........... Terms and Conditions
T & C........... Test and Crossmatch [*Medicine*] (MAH)
T & C........... Thompson and Cook's New York Supreme Court Reports [*A publication*] (DLA)
T & C........... Time and Charges [*Telecommunications*] (TEL)
T & C........... Touch and Concern [*Legal shorthand*] (LWAP)
T & C........... Town & Country [*A publication*]
T & C........... Turn and Cough [*Medicine*]
T & CCA...... Turks and Caicos Canadian Association
T & CCP...... Telecommunications and Command and Control Program [*Air Force*] (AFIT)
T & CD........ Timing and Countdown [*NASA*] (NASA)
T & CTB...... Thames and Chilterns Tourist Board [*British*] (DCTA)
T & D........... Taps and Dies (WDAA)
T & D........... Training and Detention (ADA)
T & D........... Transmission and Distribution
T & D........... Transposition and Docking [*NASA*] (KSC)
T & DC........ Training and Distribution Center [*Navy*]
T & E........... Test and Evaluation [*Navy*] (NG)
T & E........... Time and Events (AAG)
T & E........... Training and Education
T & E........... Travel and Entertainment [*IRS*]
T & E........... Traverse and Elevation [*Weapons*] [*Army*] (INF)
T & EC........ Test and Evaluation Command [*Army*]
T & EC........ Trauma and Emergency Center [*Medicine*]
TANDEL....... Temperature Autostabilizing Nonlinear Dielectric Element (IAA)
Tandem....... Tandem Computers, Inc. [*Associated Press*] (SAG)
TANDEM...... Tibi Aderit Numen Divinum, Expecta Modo [*God Will Help Thee - Only Wait*] [*Motto of Elisabeth Ernestine Antonie, Duchess of Saxony (1681-1766)*] [*Latin*]
T & EO......... Training and Evaluation Outline
T & ETGM.... Test and Evaluation Task Group Manager
T & F........... Ticknor & Fields [*Publisher*]
T & G........... Tongue and Groove [*Lumber*]
T & G........... Tonopah & Goldfield Railroad (IIA)
T & G........... Touch and Go [*Landings*] [*Aviation*] (MCD)
T & G........... Tremont & Gulf Railroad (IIA)
T & G........... Tyrwhitt and Granger's English Exchequer Reports [*1835-36*] [*A publication*] (DLA)
T & H........... Test and Handling [*Equipment*] (NG)
T & H........... Thames & Hudson [*Publisher*]
T & HCA...... Towboat and Harbor Carriers Association of New York and New Jersey (EA)
T & HP......... Transportation and Handling Procedure
T & H Prac... Troubat and Haly's Pennsylvania Practice [*A publication*] (DLA)
T & I............ Tax and Insurance Payment [*Banking*]
T and I......... Trade and Industrial Education (AEE)
T & L........... Thrift & Loans [*Industrial loan company*]
T & M........... Temple and Mew's English Criminal Appeal Cases [*A publication*] (DLA)
T & M........... Temple and Mew's English Crown Cases [*1848-51*] [*A publication*] (DLA)
T & M........... Test and Maintenance (WDAA)
T & M........... Test and Measurement [*Quality control*]
T & M........... Test and Monitor (CAAL)
T & M........... Time and Materials
T & M........... Trichomonas and Monilia [*cultures*] (DAVI)
T & NC......... Tennessee & North Carolina [*Railroad*] (MHDB)
T & NC......... Tennessee & North Carolina Railroad (IIA)
T & O........... Taken and Offered [*Sporting*] [*British*]
T & O........... Test and Operation [*NASA*] (KSC)
T & O........... Training and Operations [*Military*]
TANDOC....... Tanzania National Documentation Centre [*National Central Library*] [*Information service or system*] (IID)
T & OE......... Tentage and Organizational Equipment B ranch [*US Army Natick Research, Development, and Engineering Center*]
T & OHI....... Truck & Off-Highway Industries [*A publication*]
T & P........... Tank and Pump Unit [*Mechanized infantry battalion*] (DWSG)
T and P........ [*The*] Texas & Pacific Railway Co. [*Absorbed into Missouri Pacific System*]
T and P........ Theft and Pilferage
T & P........... Turner and Phillips' English Chancery Reports [*A publication*] (DLA)
T & PI.......... Totally and Permanently Incapacitated [*Insurance*] (ADA)
T & R........... Testing and Regulating Department [*Especially, in a wire communications maintenance division*]
T & R........... Training and Readiness [*Marine Corps*] (DOMA)
T & R........... Turner and Russell's English Chancery Reports [*1822-25*] [*A publication*] (DLA)
T and RA..... Tennis and Rackets Association [*British*] (DBA)
T & RNP...... Transportation and Recruiting Naval Personnel [*Budget appropriation title*]
T and S........ Technical and Scientific Information [*United Nations Development Program*]
T & S........... Thomson and Steger's Tennessee Statutes [*A publication*] (ILCA)
T and S........ Touch and Stay
T & S........... Type and Screen
T & SA......... Task and Skill Analysis (AAG)
T & SER...... Tilbury & Southend Railway [*British*] (ROG)
T & S Pr...... Tillinghast and Shearman's New York Practice [*A publication*] (DLA)
T & SW........ Temperance and Social Welfare [*Free Church*] [*British*]
T & T........... Tanqueray [*Gin*] and Tonic
T & T........... Targets and Timetables
T & T........... Tax and Tip
T & T........... Technicals and Turnovers [*Basketball*]
T & T........... Tijuana & Tecate Railway Co. (IIA)
T & T........... Time and Temperature
T & T........... Touch and Tone [*Neurology*] (DAVI)
T & T........... Transportation and Transportability
T&T.............. Travel and Tourism (EERA)
T & T........... Tympanostomy with Tube Placement [*Otorhinolaryngology*] (DAVI)
T & TA......... Training and Technical Assistance (OICC)
T & TEC....... Trinidad & Tobago Electricity Commission
T & TP......... Terry and the Pirates [*Pop music group*]
T & T Sup.... Trinidad and Tobago Supreme Court Judgments [*A publication*] (ILCA)
T & V........... Test and Verify Programs [*Computer science*] (MDG)
T & X........... Type and Crossmatch [*Clinical chemistry*]
Tandy........... Tandy Corp. [*Associated Press*] (SAG)
TandyBr....... Tandy Brands Accessories, Inc. [*Associated Press*] (SAG)
TANE............ Transportes Aereos Nacionales Ecuatorianas [*Airline*] [*Ecuador*]
TANESCO..... Tanzania Electric Supply Co.
Taney........... Taney's United States Circuit Court Reports [*A publication*] (DLA)
TANEYCOMO... Taney County, MO [*A lake at Branson, MO*]
Taney's CC Dec... Taney's United States Circuit Court Reports [*A publication*] (DLA)
Taney's Dec (USCC)... Taney's United States Circuit Court Reports [*A publication*] (DLA)
TANF............ Temporary Assistance for Needy Families
TANF............ Temporary Assistance to Needy Families [*An association*]
TANF............ Transition Assistance for Needy Families [*Welfare program*]
TANG............ Tangential (AAG)
TangEnt....... Tangram Enterprise Solutions, Inc. [*Associated Press*] (SAG)
Tanger.......... Tanger Factory Outlet Centers [*Associated Press*] (SAG)
TANGLE....... Angle at Tip of Leaf [*Botany*]
Tangr........... Tanger Factory Outlet Centers [*Associated Press*] (SAG)
tanh............. Hyperbolic Tangent (IDOE)
TANH............ Tangent, Hyperbolic
Tanh............. Tanhuma (BJA)
TANI............. Total Axial Lymph Node Irradiation [*Medicine*]
TANJUG....... Telegrafska Agencija Nove Jugoslavije [*Press agency*] [*Yugoslavia*]
TANK............ Floatation Tank Association (EA)
TANK............ Tanknology Environmental [*NASDAQ symbol*] (SPSG)
TANKBAT..... Tank Battalion [*Army*]
TANKEX....... Tank Field Exercise (NVT)
Tanklgy........ Tankology Environmental, Inc. [*Associated Press*] (SAG)
TANKOPINS... Tanker Operating Instructions (DNAB)
Tan LR......... Tanganyika Territory Law Reports [*A publication*] (DLA)
Tann............. Tanner's Reports [*8-14 Indiana*] [*A publication*] (DLA)
Tann............. Tanner's Reports [*13-17 Utah*] [*A publication*] (DLA)
Tanner......... Tanner's Reports [*13-17 Utah*] [*A publication*] (DLA)
Tanner......... Tanner's Reports [*8-14 Indiana*] [*A publication*] (DLA)
TANO............ Triacetoneamine Nitroxide [*Organic chemistry*]
TANREM...... Tactical Nuclear Weapons Requirements Methodology
TANS............ Tactical Air Navigation System [*Helicopter*]
TANS............ Tax Anticipation Notes
TANS............ Terminal Area Navigation System
TANS............ Territorial Army Nursing Service [*British*]
TA-NS.......... Total Abstinence - No Smoking [*On social invitations*]
TANSE.......... Transportes Aereos Neuquinos Sociedad de Estado [*Argentina ICAO designator*] (FAAC)
TANSTAAFL... There Ain't No Such Thing As a Free Lunch [*Principle of economics indicating that one cannot get something for nothing*] [*See also TINSTAAFL*]
TANSW........ Taxpayers' Association of New South Wales [*Australia*]

TANT .... Tennant Co. [*NASDAQ symbol*] (NQ)
TANU .... Tanganyika African National Union [*Political party*]
TANWERE .... Tactical Nuclear Weapons Requirements (CINC)
TANY .... Typographers Association of New York (EA)
Tanz .... Tanzania
TAN-ZAM ..... Tanzania-Zambia [*Railway*]
TAO .... Auxiliary Oiler [*Military Sea Transportation Service*]
TAO .... Hammond, LA [*Location identifier FAA*] (FAAL)
TAO .... Qingdao [*China*] [*Airport symbol*] (OAG)
TAO .... Tactical Action Observer [*Military*] (CAAL)
TAO .... Tactical Action Officer [*Navy*] (NVT)
TAO .... Tactical Air Observation [*or Observer*] (NATG)
TAO .... Tactical Air Officer (NVT)
TAO .... Tactical Air Operations
TAO .... Technical Analysis Office (MCD)
TAO .... Technical Analysis Order
TAO .... Technical Assistance Office
TAO .... Technical Assistance Operations [*United Nations*]
TAO .... Technical Assistance Order (KSC)
TAO .... Technology Applications Office [*NASA*]
TAO .... Technology Assistance Officer [*Small Business Administration*]
TAO .... Telephone Area Office [*British*]
TAO .... Terrain Avoidance Override (MCD)
TAO .... Test Analysis Outline
TAO .... Test and Operation (IAA)
TAO .... Thermal Array for the Ocean (USDC)
TAO .... Thromboangitis Obliterans [*Cardiology*]
TAO .... Time and Altitude Over [*Aviation*] (FAAC)
TAO .... Tokyo Astronomical Observatory
TAO .... Total Acid Output [*Clinical chemistry*]
TAO .... Transition Assistance Office [*Army*] (INF)
TAO .... Transportation Applications Office [*Jet Propulsion Laboratory, NASA*]
TAO .... Transportes Aeromar [*Mexico ICAO designator*] (FAAC)
TAO .... Triacetylole-Andomycin [*Medicine*] (DMAA)
TAO .... Troleandomycin [*Formerly, Triacetyloleandomycin*] [*Antibacterial compound*]
TAO .... Tropical Array Ocean
TAO .... Tropical Atmosphere-Ocean [*Marine science*] (OSRA)
TAO .... Tropical Atmosphere/Ocean [*Array*] (USDC)
TAO .... TSCA [*Toxic Substances Control Act*] Assistance Office [*Environmental Protection Agency*] (GFGA)
TAOBBATED ... [*The*] Adventures of Buckaroo Banzai across the Eighth Dimension [*1984 movie title*]
TAOC .... [*The*] Army Operations Center
TAOC .... Tactical Air Operations Center
TAOC .... Train Axis Optical Cube
TAOCC .... Tactical Air Operations Control Center (NATG)
TAOG .... Gasoline Tanker [*Military Sea Transportation Service*] (CINC)
TAOI .... Tactical Area of Interest [*Military*]
TAOM/MCE .... Tactical Air Operations Module/Modular Control Equipment [*Military*] (RDA)
TAOO .... Tactical Air Operations Officer [*Tactical Air Command*]
TAOR .... Tactical Area of Responsibility [*Military*] (AFM)
TAOS .... Thrust-Assisted Orbiter Shuttle [*NASA*]
TAOS .... Travel Allowance on Separation [*Military*]
TA/OSD ...... Task Analysis/Operational Sequence Diagram
TAOT .... Transport Oiler Ship
TAP .... [*The*] Ada Project [*World Wide Web*]
TAP .... Amarillo Public Library, Amarillo, TX [*OCLC symbol*] (OCLC)
TAP .... [*The*] Angel Planes (EA)
TAP .... [*The*] Antarctica Project [*An association*] (EAIO)
TAP .... [*The*] Army Plan
TAP .... Onitap Resources, Inc. [*Toronto Stock Exchange symbol*]
TAP .... Table of Authorized Personnel (NATG)
TAP .... Tackled Attempting to Pass [*Football*]
TAP .... Tactical Action Programs
TAP .... Tactical Armament Plan (MCD)
TAP .... Taipei [*Taihoku*] [*Taiwan*] [*Seismograph station code, US Geological Survey*] (SEIS)
TAP .... Tapachula [*Mexico*] [*Airport symbol*] (OAG)
TAP .... Tapestry (ADA)
tap .... Tapestry (VRA)
Tap .... Tappan's Ohio Common Pleas Reports [*A publication*] (DLA)
TAP .... Tapping Achievement Potential Project (EDAC)
TAP .... Target Aim Points
TAP .... Target Analysis and Planning [*Computer system*] [*Military*]
TAP .... Target and Penetration (IAA)
TAP .... Target Angular Position [*Photonics*]
TAP .... Target Assignment Panel
TAP .... Task Area Plan
TAP .... T-Cell-Activating Protein [*Biochemistry*]
TAP .... Teacher's Aide Program
TAP .... Technical Achievement Plan [*NASA*] (NASA)
TAP .... Technical Action Panel [*Department of Agriculture*]
TAP .... Technical Action Program (OICC)
TAP .... Technical Advisory Panel [*United Nations*]
TAP .... Technical Area Plan [*Navy*] (MCD)
TAP .... Technical Assistance Program [*Environmental Protection Agency*] (GFGA)
TAP .... Technical Assistance Project (EA)
TAP .... Technological Adjustment Pay
TAP .... Technological American Party (EA)
TAP .... Technology Adaptation Program [*Massachusetts Institute of Technology*] [*Research center*] (RCD)
TAP .... Technology Applications Program [*University of Kentucky*] [*Lexington, KY*] [*NASA*]
TAP .... Technology Assistance Program [*Army*]
TAP .... Telemetry Acceptance Pattern (KSC)
TAP .... Telemetry Antenna Pedestal
TAP .... Temporal Analysis of Products [*System developed by Monsanto Chemical Co.*]
TAP .... Tension by Applanation [*Ophthalmology*]
TAP .... Term Availability Plan (IAA)
TAP .... Terminal Access Point [*Telecommunications*] (OSI)
TAP .... Terminal Access Processor
TAP .... Terminal Applications Package (IEEE)
TAP .... Terminal Area Productivity (GAVI)
TAP .... Terrain Analysis Program [*Military*]
TAP .... Terrestrial Auxiliary Power
TAP .... Test Administration Plan (NASA)
TAP .... Test Anxiety Profile [*Educational test*]
TAP .... Test Assistance Program [*Sperry UNIVAC*]
TAP .... Test of Auditory-Perceptual Skills
TAP .... Tests of Achievement and Proficiency [*Educational test*]
TAP .... Theater of All Possibilities [*International touring company of actor-authors*]
TAP .... Thermal Analysis Program [*Nuclear energy*]
TAP .... Thermodynamics and Physical Properties Package (NITA)
TAP .... Thermosiphoning Air Pan
TAP .... Thermoviscoelastic Analysis Program (MCD)
TAP .... Thesaurus at Play [*Acronym is trademark for word game*]
TAP .... Thiol Alkaline Phosphatase [*An enzyme*]
TAP .... Three-Axis Package
TAP .... Tibetan Aid Project (EA)
TAP .... Time-Sharing Accounting Package (MHDB)
TAP .... Time-Sharing Assembly Program [*Computer science*] (DIT)
TAP .... Total Action Against Poverty [*A federal government program*]
TAP .... Total Air Pressure (NASA)
TAP .... Total Annualized Profit
TAP .... Total Audience Plan [*Radio advertising*] (NTCM)
TAP .... Toxic Air Pollutant
TAP .... Toxicological Agent Protective Item [*or Suit*] (MCD)
TAp .... Tracheal Antimicrobial Peptide [*Biochemistry*]
TAP .... Tracking Alarms Processor [*Space Flight Operations Facility, NASA*]
TAP .... Training Access Point (AIE)
TAP .... Trajectory Analysis Program (MCD)
TAP .... Transaction Application Program [*Computer science*]
TAP .... Trans-Alaska Pipeline
TAP .... Transcription Activating Protein [*Biochemistry*]
TAP .... Transferable Assets Program
TAP .... Transformation-Associated Protein [*Biochemistry*]
TAP .... Transition Assistance Program [*Military*]
TAP .... Transmission Access Processor [*Newbridge Networks, Inc.*]
TAP .... Transponder Access Program [*Satellite Business Systems*] [*McLean, VA*] [*Telecommunications*] (TSSD)
TAP .... Transporter Associated with Antigen Processing [*Biochemistry*]
TAP .... Transportes Aereos Portugueses EP [*Portugal ICAO designator*] (FAAC)
TAP .... Transportes Aereos Portugueses, SARL [*Portuguese Air Transport*]
TAP .... Transport Ship [*Military Sea Transportation Service*] (CINC)
TAP .... Travelers/Aetna Prop Casual'A' [*NYSE symbol*] (TTSB)
TAP .... Travelers Aetna Property Casualty Corp. [*NYSE symbol*] (SAG)
TAP .... Travelers Corp. P & C Capital I [*NYSE symbol*] (SAG)
TAP .... Travelers Corp. P & C Capital II [*NYSE symbol*] (SAG)
TAP .... Trend Analysis Program [*American Council of Life Insurance*] [*Washington, DC Information service or system*] (IID)
TAP .... Triaminopyrimidine [*Organic chemistry*]
TAP .... Trickle Ammonia Process [*for drying grain feedstuffs*]
TAP .... Trimethylaminoethylpiperazine [*Organic chemistry*]
TAP .... Truck Assembly Plants
TAP .... Trustee, Administration, and Physician's Institute [*Seminar*]
TAP .... Tuition Assistance Program [*New York*] (EDAC)
TAP .... Tunis-Afrique Presse [*Press agency*] [*Tunisia*]
TAPA .... St. Johns/V. C. Bird [*Antigua Island*] [*ICAO location identifier*] (ICLI)
TAPA .... (Tetranitrofluorylideneaminooxy)propionic Acid
TAPA .... Three-Dimensional Antenna Pattern Analyzer [*Air Force*]
TAPA .... Total Army Personnel Agency (INF)
TAPA .... Trade Assistance and Planning Office (AAGC)
TAPA .... Trans-Alaska Pipeline Authorization Act
TAPA .... Turkish American Physicians Association (EA)
TAPAC .... Tape Automatic Positioning and Control
TAPAC .... Transportation Allocations, Priorities, and Controls Committee [*Military*]
TAPAK .... Tape-Pack
TAPAT .... Tape Programmed Automatic Tester
TAPATS .... Threat Artillery Preparation Against Thermal Sights (MCD)
TAPC .... Total Army Personnel Command (DOMA)
TAPCC .... Technology and Pollution Control Committee [*Environmental Protection Agency*]
TAPCHAN ...... Tapered Channel [*Wave power technology*]
TAPCIS .... [*The*] Access Program for the CompuServe Information Service (PCM)
Tap CM .... Tapping's Copyholder's Manual [*A publication*] (DLA)
TAPCO .... Thompson Products, Inc. [*Later, Thompson Ramo Woolridge, Inc.*]
TAP-D .... Test of Articulation Performance - Diagnostic
TAPDB .... Total Army Personnel Database (GFGA)
TAPDS .... Toxic Air Pollutant Data System [*Environmental Protection Agency*] (GFGA)
TAPE .... Tactical Air Power Evaluation [*Air Force*]

TAPE........ Tape Automatic Preparation Equipment
TAPE........ Target Profile Examination Technique [*RADAR analysis concept*] [*Air Force*]
TAPE........ Technical Advisory Panel for Electronics [*Air Force*]
TAPE........ Television Audience Program Evaluation
TAPE........ Tentative Annual Planning Estimate (NVT)
TAPE........ Timed Access to Pertinent Excerpts
TAPE........ Total Application of Prerecorded Evidence
TAPE........ Totally Automated Programming Equipment
TAPE........ Transactional Analysis of Personality and Environment [*Psychology*] (AEBS)
TAPER........ [*The*] Army Plan for Equipment Records
TAPER........ Tailored Performance Test Vehicle (SAA)
TAPER........ Temporary Appointment Pending Establishment of a Register [*Civil Service*]
TAPER........ Theater Army Personnel (MCD)
TAPER........ Turbulent Air Pilot Environment Research [*NASA-FAA project*]
TAPES........ Total Army Personnel Evaluation System
TAPES........ Transformer Analog Polynomial Equation Solver (PDAA)
TAPEX........ Tape Executive Program (SAA)
TAPFOR........ [*The*] Army Portion of Force Status and Identify Report [*Force Status Report*] (AABC)
TAPGA........ Tasmanian Apple and Pear Growers' Association [*Australia*]
TAPGEN........ Terminal Applications Program Generator [*Computer science*] (MHDI)
TAPH........ Codrington [*Barbuda Island*] [*ICAO location identifier*] (ICLI)
TAPH........ Toluic Acid Phenylhydrazide [*Organic chemistry*]
TAPI........ Tapistron International, Inc. [*NASDAQ symbol*] (SAG)
TAPI........ Tapistron Intl [*NASDAQ symbol*] (TTSB)
TAPI........ Telephony Application Programming Interface [*Microsoft Corp.*] (PCM)
TAPIO........ Tape Input and Output [*Computer science*] (DNAB)
Tapist........ Tapistron International, Inc. [*Associated Press*] (SAG)
Tapistrn........ Tapistron International, Inc. [*Associated Press*] (SAG)
TAPIT........ Tactical Photographic Image Transmission
TAPITS........ Tactical Airborne Processing, Interpretation, and Transmission System [*Military*]
TAPITS........ Tactical Photographic Image Transmission System
TAPIW........ Tapistron Intl Wrrt [*NASDAQ symbol*] (TTSB)
TAPLF........ Trans-Alaska Pipeline Liability Fund
TAPLINE........ Trans-Alaska Pipeline
TAPLINE........ Trans-Arabian Pipeline
TAPM........ Technology Application Program Management [*Air Force*]
Tap Man........ Tapping on the Writ of Mandamus [*1848*] [*A publication*] (DLA)
TAPO........ Termination Accountable Property Officer
TAPO........ Tris(l-aziridinyl) Phosphine Oxide [*Organic chemistry*]
TAPOC........ Theater Army Personnel Operations Center
TAPOL........ Comite de Defense des Prisonniers en Indonesie [*France*]
Tapp........ Tappan's Ohio Common Pleas Reports [*A publication*] (DLA)
TAPP........ Technical Assistance for Parents Program [*Established under the EHC (Education for all Handicapped Children act)*] (PAZ)
TAPP........ Time and Attendance, Payroll, and Personnel (GFGA)
TAPP........ Trade Association of Proprietary Plants (EA)
TAPP........ Tumor Acquisition, Processing, and Preservation [*Oncology*]
TAPP........ Two-Axis Pneumatic Pickup (IEEE)
Tappan........ Tappan's Ohio Common Pleas Reports [*A publication*] (DLA)
Tappan (Ohio)... Tappan's Ohio Common Pleas Reports [*A publication*] (DLA)
Tappan's Ohio Rep... Tappan's Ohio Common Pleas Reports [*A publication*] (DLA)
Tappan's R... Tappan's Ohio Common Pleas Reports [*A publication*] (DLA)
TAPPI........ Technical Association of the Pulp and Paper Industry (EA)
Tapping........ Tapping on the Writ of Mandamus [*A publication*] (DLA)
Tapp M & Ch... Tapp on Maintenance and Champerty [*1861*] [*A publication*] (ILCA)
TAPPrA........ Travelers P&C Cap 1 8.08% Pfd [*NYSE symbol*] (TTSB)
TAPPrB........ Travelers P&C Cap II 8.00% Pfd [*NYS*] (TTSB)
TAPPS........ [*The*] Automated Procurement Planning System
TAPR........ Tactical Automation Program Review [*Military*]
TAPR........ Toxic Altitude Propulsion Research (MCD)
TAPR........ [*Department of*] Transportation Acquisition Procurement Regulation [*A publication*] (AAGC)
TAPR........ Treasury Acquisition/Procurement Regulation (AAGC)
TAPrA........ Transamerica Del L.P.'MIPS' [*NYSE symbol*] (TTSB)
TAPrD........ Transamerica 8.50% Dep Pfd [*NYSE symbol*] (TTSB)
TAPRE........ Tracking in an Active and Passive RADAR Environment
TAPS........ Tactical Area Positioning System [*Military*]
TAPS........ Tactical Protective Structures (MCD)
TAPS........ Tarapur Atomic Power Station [*India*]
TAPS........ Teachers Audio Placement System
TAPS........ Technical Analysis Positions System
TAPS........ Teenage Attitudes and Practices Survey [*Centers for Disease Control*]
TAPS........ Telemetry Antenna Positions System [*Military*] (CAAL)
TAPS........ TERCOM [*Terrain Contour Mapping*] Aircraft Positioning Systems [*Air Force*]
TAPS........ Terminal Application Processing System
TAPS........ Terminal Application Program System [*Computer science*]
TAPS........ Terminal Area Positive Separation [*FAA*]
TAP-S........ Test of Articulation Performance - Screen
TAPS........ Time Analysis of Program Status
TAPS........ Total Atoll Production System (NOAA)
TAPS........ Training for Aboriginals Program Scheme [*Australia*]
TAPS........ Trajectory Accuracy Prediction System [*Air Force*]
TAPS........ Trans-Alaskan Pipeline [*Marine science*] (OSRA)
TAPS........ Trans-Alaskan Pipeline (USDC)
TAPS........ Trans-Alaska Pipeline System [*Department of Energy*]
TAPS........ Trial Assessment Procedure Scale [*Medicine*] (DMAA)
TAPS........ Tris(hydroxymethyl)methylamino Propanesulfonic Acid
TAPS........ Tropical Assimilation and Prognosis System (EERA)
TAPS........ Turboalternator Power System (IEEE)
TAPS........ Turret-Anchored Production System [*Petroleum engineering*]
TAPSC........ Trans-Atlantic Passenger Steamship Conference [*Later, IPSA*] (EA)
TAPSHA........ Technology and Physical Science History Associates (IID)
TAPSYS........ Total Army Personnel System
TAPU........ Tanganyika African Postal Union
TAPVC........ Total Anomalous Pulmonary Venous Connection [*Cardiology*]
TAPVD........ Total Anomalous Pulmonary Venous Drainage [*Cardiology*] (AAMN)
TAPVR........ Total Anomalous Pulmonary Venous Return [*Cardiology*]
TapZee........ Tappen Zee Financial, Inc. [*Associated Press*] (SAG)
TAQ........ Task Attribution Questionnaire (EDAC)
Taq........ Thermus Aquaticus [*Bacteria*]
TAQ........ Trans Asian Resources [*Vancouver Stock Exchange symbol*]
TAQ........ Transient Airman Quarters [*Air Force*] (AFM)
TAQA........ Test and Quality Assurance (IAA)
TAQT........ Task Assignment Queue Table (MCD)
TAQTD........ Task Assignment Queue Table Display (MCD)
TAQTU........ Task Assignment Queue Table Update (MCD)
TAQW........ Transient Abnormal Q Wave [*Medicine*] (DMAA)
TAQW........ Transient Abnormal Q Waves [*Medicine*] (AAMN)
TAR........ Tactical Aircraft Recovery (CINC)
TAR........ Tactical Air Reconnaissance (AFM)
TAR........ Tactical Air Request (NVT)
tar........ Tadzhik Soviet Socialist Republic [*MARC country of publication code Library of Congress*] (LCCP)
TAR........ Tansy Resources, Inc. [*Vancouver Stock Exchange symbol*]
TAR........ Tape Address Register [*Demography*]
TAR........ Tape Address Register File [*Bureau of the Census*] (GFGA)
TAR........ Tape Archive [*Computer science*] (DOM)
TAR........ Tara Exploration & Development Co. Ltd. [*Toronto Stock Exchange symbol*]
TAR........ Taranto [*Italy*] [*Seismograph station code, US Geological Survey*] (SEIS)
TAR........ Taranto [*Italy*] [*Airport symbol*] (AD)
TAR........ Target
tar........ Tatar [*MARC language code Library of Congress*] (LCCP)
TAR........ Tax Advance Rulings [*Database*] [*Taxation Canada*] [*Information service or system*] (CRD)
TAR........ Team Acceptance Review (SAA)
TAR........ Technical Action Request [*Army*] (AABC)
TAR........ Technical Amendment Regulation [*Federal government*] (EG)
TAR........ Technical Analysis Request [*NASA*] (KSC)
TAR........ Technical Assistance Request [*Nuclear energy*] (NRCH)
TAR........ Teen Age Republican [*Lifestyle classification*]
TAR........ Telefonica De Argentina ADS [*NYSE symbol*] (TTSB)
TAR........ Telefonica de Argentina SA [*NYSE symbol*] (SAG)
TAR........ Temporary Accumulator (IAA)
TAR........ Temporary Accumulator Register (IAA)
TAR........ Temporary Active Reserve (DNAB)
TAR........ Tennessee Administrative Register [*A publication*] (AAGC)
TAR........ Terminal Address Register
TAR........ Terminal Area Surveillance RADAR
TAR........ Terrain Avoidance RADAR
TAR........ Terrier Advanced RADAR (DNAB)
TAR........ Territorial Army Regulations [*British military*] (DMA)
TAR........ Test Action Requirement (NASA)
TAR........ Test Agency Report (NASA)
TAR........ Test Analysis Report
TAR........ Test and Return (IAA)
TAR........ Therm Advanced Research (SAA)
TAR........ Threat Avoidance Receiver (MCD)
TAR........ Thrombocytopenia with Absent Radii [*Medicine*]
TAR........ Thrust-Augmented Rocket [*NASA*]
TAR........ Total Accomplishment Requirement (DNAB)
TAR........ Total Ankle Replacement [*Orthopedics*] (DAVI)
TAR........ Total Assets Reporting (MCD)
TAR........ Towed Array RADAR
TAR........ Track Address Register
TAR........ Training and Administration of the Reserve
TAR........ Trajectory Analysis Room [*NASA*] (KSC)
TAR........ Trans-Acting Responsive Sequence [*Genetics*]
TAR........ Transaction Area (IAA)
TAR........ Trans-Activator Response Element [*Genetics*]
TAR........ Transactivator-Responsive Region [*Genetics*]
TAR........ Transformation-Associated Recombination [*Genetics*]
TAR........ Transmit and Receive (IAA)
TAR........ [*Department of*] Transportation Acquisition Regulation [*A publication*] (AAGC)
TAR........ Transportes Aereos Regionais [*Airline*] [*Brazil*]
TAR........ Treatment-Authorization Request [*Medicine*] (MEDA)
TAR........ Triannual Review (NATG)
TAR........ Truck and Rail
TAR........ Tunis Air-Societe Tunisienne de l'Air [*Tunisia*] [*ICAO designator*] (FAAC)
TAR........ Turnaround Ratio
TAR........ Two-Axis Rate (SAA)
TARA........ Technical Assistant, Royal Artillery [*British military*] (DMA)
TA/RA........ Technical Availability/Restricted Availability [*Navy*] (NVT)
TARA........ Terrain Avoidance RADAR (IAA)
TARA........ Territorial Army Rifle Association [*British military*] (DMA)
TARA........ Total Articular Replacement Arthroplasty [*Orthopedics*]
TARA........ Truck-Frame and Axle Repair Association (EA)
TARA........ Tumor-Associated Rejection Antigen [*Immunology*] (MAE)

TARA .... Turmor-Associated Rejection Antigen [*Immunology*]
TARABS .... Tactical Air Reconnaissance and Aerial Battlefield Surveillance System [*Military*]
TARAC .... Terminology, Aids, References, Applications, and Coordination (IAA)
TARAD .... Tracking Asynchronous RADAR Data (DA)
TARADCOM... Tank-Automotive Research and Development Command [*Army*]
TARAN .... Tactical Attack RADAR and Navigation
TARAN .... Test and Repair [*or Replace*] as Necessary
Tarb .... Tarbiz. Jerusalem (BJA)
TARBIT .... Three-Axis Rout Byro Inertial Tracker (IAA)
TARC .... [*The*] Army Research Council
TARC .... Tactical Air Reconnaissance Center [*Shaw Air Force Base*]
TARC .... Television Allocation Research Committee [*or Council*]
TARC .... Theater Army Replacement Command
TARC .... Through Axis Rotational Control [*Aerospace*] (MCD)
TARC .... Thru-Axis Rotational Control
TARC .... Total Available Residual Chlorine [*Water quality*]
TARC .... Toxics Testing and Assessment Research Committee [*Terminated, 1984*] [*Environmental Protection Agency*] (EGAO)
TARC .... Trace Analysis Research Centre [*Dalhousie University*] [*Canada*] (IRC)
TARC .... Transport Airworthiness Reports Committee [*AIA*] (MCD)
TARCAP .... Target Combat Air Patrol [*Navy*]
TARC-OA...... Tactical Air Reconnaissance Center Office of Operations Analysis [*Shaw Air Force Base, SC*]
TARCOG....... Top of Alabama Regional Council of Governments
TARCOM .... Tank-Automotive Materiel Readiness Command [*Army*]
TARCOMSA... Tank-Automotive Materiel Readiness Command, Selfridge Activity (MCD)
TArDC .... Arlington Development Center, Arlington, TN [*Library symbol Library of Congress*] (LCLS)
TARDEC .... Tank-Automotive Research, Development, and Engineering Center [*Army*] (RDA)
TARDIS .... Time and Relative Dimensions in Space [*Acronym is name of spaceship in British TV series "Dr. Who"*]
TARDIS .... Titles Automated Register and Document Information System [*Australian*] (EERA)
TARDIS .... Tropical Analysis and Real-Time Display [*National Oceanic and Atmospheric Administration*]
TARE........... Telegraphic Automatic Relay [*or Routing*] Equipment (NG)
TARE........... Telemetry Automatic Reduction Equipment
TARE........... Transistor Analysis Recording Equipment
TAREA .... Terminal Leaf Area [*Botany*]
TAREF......... [*The*] Acronym Generator Reference [*RCA computer program*] (IAA)
TAREWS ...... Tactical Air Reconnaissance and Electronic Warfare Support (MCD)
TAREX .... Target Exploitation [*Military*] (AABC)
TARF........... [*The*] Acid Rain Foundation (EA)
TARF........... Tracking and Reporting Format [*Military*] (CAAL)
TARFS .... Three Axis Rotational Flight Simulator [*Military*] (RDA)
TARFU .... Things Are Really Fouled Up [*Military slang*] [*Bowdlerized version*]
TARFX .... Tracking and Reporting Format Extended [*Military*] (CAAL)
Targ............ Targum (BJA)
TARGA......... Truevision Advanced Raster Graphics Adapter [*AT & T*]
TARGET .... Team to Advance Research for Gas Energy Transformation [*Group of US gas and gas-electric companies*]
TARGET .... Thames Action and Resources Group for Education and Training [*British*] (AIE)
TARGET .... Thermal Advanced Reactor, Gas-Cooled, Exploiting Thorium [*Nuclear energy*]
TARGET .... Trans-European Automated Real-Time Gross-Settlement Express Transfer [*Banking*]
TARGET .... Transportability Analysis Reports Generator [*Military*] (MCD)
TARGET .... Transportation Accident Research Graduate Education and Training
TargetT........ Target Therapeutics, Inc. [*Associated Press*] (SAG)
TargGene..... Targeted Genetics Corp. [*Associated Press*] (SAG)
TargJer........ [*The*] Jerusalem Targum of the Pentateuch (BJA)
TargJon........ Targum Jonathan (BJA)
TargOnk....... Targum Onkelos (BJA)
TargTch .... Target Technologies, Inc. [*Associated Press*] (SAG)
TargYer........ Targum Yerusahlmi (BJA)
TARIF........... Telegraphic Automatic Routing in the Field (MCD)
TARIT........... Telegraph Automatic Routing in the Field (IAA)
TARL............ Training Aids Research Laboratory [*Air Force*] (MCD)
Tarleton St U... Tarleton State University (GAGS)
TARLOCS..... Target Locating System [*Military*] (MCD)
TARM........... Telephone Answering and Recording Machine (NITA)
TARMAC ...... Tar Macadam
TARMAC ...... Terminal Area RADAR/Moving Aircraft (KSC)
TARMOCS.... [*The*] Army Operations Center System
TARN .... Tactical Air Request Net [*Army*] (DOMA)
TARN .... Team Acceptance Review Notice (SAA)
TArnA........... ARO, Inc., AEDC Library, Arnold Air Force Station, TN [*Library symbol Library of Congress*] (LCLS)
TARND......... Turn Around [*Aviation*] (FAAC)
TARO .... Taro Pharmaceutical Industries [*NASDAQ symbol*] (SAG)
TARO .... Territorial Army Reserve of Officers [*British*]
TAROF .... Taro Pharmaceutical Ind [*NASDAQ symbol*] (TTSB)
TAROM .... Transporturi Aeriene Romane [*Romanian Air Transport*]
TaroPh......... Taro Pharmaceutical Industries [*Associated Press*] (SAG)
TAROT .... [*The*] Associated Readers of Tarot International (EA)
TARP .... Tactical Airborne Reconnaissance Pod
TARP .... Tactical Airborne Recording Package
TARP .... Tarpaulin (AAG)
tarp .... Tarpaulin (VRA)
TARP .... Test and Repair Processor [*Computer science*]
TARP .... Theater Army Repair Program
TARP .... Total Army Requirements Program
TARP .... Tour Advisory Review Panel [*Army National Guard*] (INF)
TARP .... Transient Acoustic Radiation Program
TARP .... Transportation Accounts Receivable and Payment System [*GSA*] (TAG)
TARP .... Typical Airland Resupply Profile (MCD)
TARPAC .... Television and Radio Political Action Committee [*National Association of Broadcasters*]
TARPS .... Tactical Aerial Reconnaissance Pod System (MCD)
TARPS .... True and Relative Motion Plotting System (IAA)
TARPTOLA... Theologiae Apud Remonstrantes Professorem, Tyrannidis Osorem, Limburgium Amstelodamensem [*Pseudonym used by John Locke*]
TARR .... Time-Adjusted Rate of Return
Tarrant......... Tarrant Apparel Group [*Associated Press*] (SAG)
TARS .... [*The*] Arthur Ransome Society [*British*] (EAIO)
TARS .... Tactical Air Reconnaissance School [*Air Force*]
TARS .... Tactical Air Research and Survey Office [*Air Force*]
TARS .... Target Acquisition Reconnaissance and Surveillance System (SAA)
TARS .... Technical Aircraft Reliability Statistics (IAA)
TARS .... Technical Assistance Recruitment Service [*United Nations*]
TARS .... Teen Age Republicans
TARS .... Terminal Automated RADAR Services [*Aviation*] (FAAC)
TARS .... Terrain Analog RADAR Simulator
TARS .... Terrain and RADAR Simulator (IAA)
TARS .... Terrain Avoidance RADAR System (MCD)
TARS .... Test and Repair Station
TARS .... Tethered Aerostat RADAR System [*Aviation*] (FAAC)
TARS .... Theater Army Replacement System (AABC)
TARS .... Three-Axis Reference System [*Used in reference to Titan missile*]
TARS .... Training and Administrative Reserves [*on permanent active duty*]
TARS .... Transportation Aircraft Rebuild Shops [*National Guard*] (MCD)
TARS .... Turnaround Ranging Station [*Telecommunications*] (TEL)
TARS-75 .... Tactical Reconnaissance and Surveillance - 1975 [*Army*]
TARSA .... Transportes Aereos Ranquetes, Sociedad Anonima [*Argentina*]
TARSCC .... Three-Axis Reference System Checkout Console [*Used in reference to Titan missile*]
TARSLL........ Tender and Repair Ship Load List [*Navy*] (NG)
TARS OCUL... Tarsis Oculorum [*To the Eyelids*] [*Pharmacy*]
TARS/SEA.... Theater Army Replacement System / Southeast Asia (SAA)
TART .... Tactical Antiradiation Tracker [*Military*] (CAAL)
TART .... Tartarum [*Tartar*] [*Pharmacy*] (ROG)
TART........... Tartrate
TART........... Task Analysis Reduction Technique [*Navy*]
TART........... Theodore Army Terminal
TART........... Transonic Armament Technology (MCD)
TART........... Twin Accelerator Ring Transfer (IEEE)
TARTA .... Tactical RADAR Target Analysis [*Military*] (CAAL)
TARTC .... Theater Army Replacement and Training Command
TARVAN....... Truck and Rail Van
TARWI .... Target Weather Information
TAS............. [*The*] Air Surgeon [*Army*]
TAS............. [*The*] Army Staff
TAS............. TACAN [*Tactical Air Navigation*] Antenna System (DWSG)
TAS............. Tactical Advisory Service [*Department of Commerce*]
TAS............. Tactical Airlift Squadron [*Air Force*]
TAS............. Tactical Air Support [*Tactical Air Command*]
TAS............. Tactical Area Switching
TAS............. Tactical Automated System (MCD)
TAS............. Tactical Automatic Switch [*Military*] (AABC)
TAS............. Taiwanese-American Society (EA)
TAS............. Tallow Alkyl Sulfate [*Surfactant*]
TAS............. Tampa Southern Railroad [*AAR code*]
TAS............. Taos, NM [*Location identifier FAA*] (FAAL)
TAS............. Tape Alteration Subroutine
TAS............. Target Acquisition System
TAS............. Tashkent [*Former USSR Seismograph station code, US Geological Survey*] (SEIS)
TAS............. Tashkent [*Former USSR Airport symbol*] (OAG)
TAS............. Tasmania
Tas.............. Tasmania (ODBW)
TAS............. Tasmanian Ambulance Service [*Australia*]
TAS............. Tasu Resources Ltd. [*Vancouver Stock Exchange symbol*]
TAS............. Tax Administration System [*Internal Revenue Service*]
TAS............. Teacher Authoring System (EDAC)
TAS............. Team Apache Systems [*Army*]
TAS............. Technical Advisory Services [*Army*] (RDA)
TAS............. Technological and Applied Studies
TAS............. Telecom Analysis Systems, Inc.
TAS............. Telecommunications Authority Singapore
TAS............. Telegraphy with Automatic Switching [*Telecommunications*] (IAA)
TAS............. Telemetry Antenna Subsystem (NASA)
TAS............. Telephone Answering Service [*or System*]
TAS............. Telephone Area Staff [*British*]
TAS............. Teleprogrammer Assembly System [*Computer science*] (IAA)
TAS............. Tempelhof Automatic System (DWSG)
TAS............. Temperature-Actuated Switch (IEEE)
TAS............. Tenancy Advice Service [*Australia*]
TAS............. Tenure Administration System [*Queensland*] [*State*] (EERA)
TAS............. Terminal Access System (MCD)
TAS............. Terminal Address Selector
TAS............. Test Access Selector [*Telecommunications*] (TEL)
TAS............. Test Analyzer System [*Electronics*]
TAS............. Test and Set [*Computer science*]

TAS............ Test Answer Sheets
TAS............ Test Article Specification (NASA)
TAS............ Texture Analysis System [*Image analysis for biochemistry*]
TAS............ Theatre Arts Society [*British*]
TAS............ Therapeutic Activities Specialist [*Physical therapy*] (DAVI)
TAS............ Three-Axis Stabilization (AAG)
TAS............ Time Air Speed (NATG)
TAS............ Torpedo and Antisubmarine [*Obsolete Navy British*]
TAS............ Towed Array SONAR
TAS............ Tracking Adjunct System [*I-HAWK*] (MCD)
TAS............ Tracking Antenna System
TAS............ Traditional Acupuncture Society [*Stratford-Upon-Avon, Warwickshire, England*] (EAIO)
TAS............ Traffic Analysis Survey (MCD)
TAS............ Training Aids Section [*Navy*]
TAS............ Transalsace [*France*] [*FAA designator*] (FAAC)
TAS............ Transfer Alignment Set (DNAB)
TAS............ Transportes Aereos Salvador [*Brazil*]
TAS............ Transverse Air Spring
TAS............ Tribunal Arbitral du Sport [*Court of Arbitration of Sport - CAS*] [*Switzerland*] (EAIO)
TAS............ Triple Axis Spectrometer [*Biochemistry*]
TAS............ Troop Airlift Squadron (CINC)
TAS............ True Airspeed
TAS............ TRW Advanced Steering [*Automotive components*]
TAS............ Tychon's Assembler (MCD)
TAS3............ Transportation Aviation Supply Support System
TASA............ [*The*] Aircraft Service Association
TASA............ [*The*] Antique Stove Association (EA)
TASA............ [*The*] Assistant Secretary of the Army
TASA............ Tactical Air Support Aircraft
TASA............ Task and Skill Analysis [*Military*] (AABC)
TASA............ Tasmanian Association for Sustainable Agriculture [*Australia*]
TASA............ Taxpayers' Association of South Australia [*Australia*]
TASA............ Technical Advisory Service for Attorneys [*Technical Advisory Service, Inc.*] [*Information service or system*]
TASA............ Telecommunicacoes Aeronauticas SA [*Brazil*] [*ICAO designator*] (FAAC)
TASA............ Television Audio Support Activity [*Army*]
TASA............ Test Area Support Assembly
TASA............ Touchstone Applied Science [*NASDAQ symbol*] (TTSB)
TASA............ Touchstone Applied Sciences [*NASDAQ symbol*] (SAG)
TASA............ Tumor-Associated Surface Antigen [*Immunology*]
TASAE............ Training and Audio-Visual Support Activity - Europe (MCD)
TASAG............ TACOM [*Tank Automotive Command*] Scientific Advisory Group [*DoD*] (EGAO)
TASAMS............ [*The*] Army Supply and Maintenance System (AABC)
TASAP............ [*The*] Army Scientific Advisory Panel
TASAPS............ [*The*] Army Security Assistance Program Study Group
Tas Build............ Tasmanian Builder [*A publication*]
Tas Build J............ Tasmanian Building Journal [*A publication*]
TASC............ [*The*] Analytic Sciences Corp.
TASC............ Centre for Technology and Social Change (EERA)
TASC............ Tabular Sequence Control
TASC............ Tactical Air Support Center (CINC)
TASC............ Tactical Articulated Swimmable Carrier (OA)
TASC............ Target Area Sequential Correlator (MCD)
TASC............ Teaching as a Career [*British*]
TASC............ Technical Activity Steering Committee [*Nuclear energy*] (NRCH)
TASC............ Technology and Social Change [*Australia*]
TASC............ Tehran Area Support Center [*Military*] (MCD)
TASC............ Telecommunication Alarm Surveillance and Control [*AT & T*]
TASC............ Terminal Area Sequencing and Control
TASC............ Test Anxiety Scale for Children [*Psychology*]
TASC............ Total Absorption Shower Cascade
TASC............ Total Avionic Support Capability
TASC............ Training Aids Support Center [*Army*]
TASC............ Training and Audiovisual Support Center [*Army*]
TASC............ Treatment Alternatives to Street Crime [*Antidrug program*]
TASC............ True Airspeed Computer
TASCC............ Tactical Air Support Coordination Center (MCD)
TASCC............ Tandem Accelerator Superconducting Cyclotron Facility [*Canadian nuclear physics facility*]
TASCC............ Test Access Signaling Conversion Circuit [*Telecommunications*] (TEL)
TASCFORM............ Technique for Assessing Comparative Force Modernization [*Army*]
Tasch Cr Acts............ Taschereau's Criminal Law Acts [*Canada A publication*] (DLA)
TASCO............ Tactical Automatic Switch Control Office
TASCOM............ Theater Army Support Command [*Terminated, 1975*] [*West Germany*] (AABC)
TASCOM(S)............ Theater Army Support Command (Supply)
TASCON............ Television Automatic Sequence Control
TASCORP............ Tasmanian Public Finance Corp. [*Commercial firm Australia*]
TASCS............ Tactical Air Support Control System [*Military*] (PDAA)
TASC/SC............ Training and Audiovisual Support Center/Subcommunity [*Army*]
TASD............ Tactical Action Situation Display
TASD............ Technical and Administrative Support Division [*Marine science*] (OSRA)
TASD............ Technical and Adminstrative Support Division [*Pacific Marine Environmental Laboratory*] (USDC)
TASD............ Terminal Railway, Alabama State Docks [*AAR code*]
TASDA............ [*The*] American Safe Deposit Association (EA)
TASDA............ Tactical Airborne SONAR Decision Aid
TASDAC............ Tactical Secure Data Communication [*Air Force*] (DOMA)
TASDC............ Tank-Automotive Systems Development Center [*Army*]
TASE............ Tactical Air Support Element [*Military*] (AABC)
TASE............ Tactical Support Equipment
TASE............ Tel Aviv Stock Exchange [*Israel*] (IMH)
T'ASE............ Tryptophane Synthetase [*An enzyme*] (DAVI)
Taseko............ Taseko Mines Ltd. [*Associated Press*] (SAG)
TASER............ Teleactive Shock Electronic Repulsion [*Nonlethal weapon*]
TASER............ Tom Swift and His Electric Rifle [*Electronic "stun gun"*] [*A trademark*]
TASES............ Tactical Airborne Signal Exploitation System (MCD)
TASF............ Tactical Air Strike Force [*Air Force*]
TASF............ Tactical Air Support Force [*Air Force*]
TASFMA............ Target Acquisition Systems Force Mix Analysis [*Military*]
TASFMEA............ Target Acquisition Systems Force Mix Evaluation Analysis
TASFUIRA............ Things Are So Fouled Up It's Really Amazing [*Military slang*] [*Bowdlerized version*]
TASG............ Tactical Air Support Group [*Air Force*] (AFIT)
TASH............ The Association for Persons with Severe Handicaps (PAZ)
TASH............ The Association for the Severely Handicapped [*Later, TASH: the Association for Persons with Severe Handicaps*] (EA)
TAS/I............ Target Acquisition System / Integrated [*Military*] (DNAB)
TASI............ Time Assignment Speech Interpolation [*Timesharing technique*] [*Telecommunications*]
TASI............ Torpedo and Anti-Submarine Instructor [*British military*] (DMA)
TASI............ Transactional Analysis Systems Institute
TASIC............ Thermal Analysis of Substrates and Intergrated Circuits (PDAA)
TAS/IRAS............ Target Acquisition System / Infrared Automatic System [*Military*] (DNAB)
Tas Irreg Notes............ Tasmanian Irregular Notes [*A publication*]
TASIS............ [*The*] American School in Switzerland
TASK............ Team of Advocates for Special Kids
TASK............ Temporary Assembled Skeleton [*Computer science*] (IAA)
TASK............ Temporary Assigned Skeleton [*Computer science*]
TASK............ Test of Academic Skills [*Sanford University*] (EDAC)
TASK............ Training and Skills Program
TASKFLOT............ Task Flotilla
TASKFORNON............ Allied Task Force, North Norway [*NATO*] (NATG)
TASL............ Theater Authorized Stockage List [*Military*] (AABC)
TASL............ Toronto Art Students' League [*1886-1903*] [*Canada*] (NGC)
TASLAP............ Tasmanian Labour Adjustment Package [*Australia*]
Tas LN............ Tasmanian Law Newsletter [*A publication*]
TASM............ Tactical Air-to-Surface Missile (NATG)
TASM............ Tactical Antiship Missile (MCD)
TASM............ Tasmania (ROG)
TASM............ Tomahawk Antiship Missile (MCD)
TASM............ Trialkylstannylmaleate [*Organic chemistry*]
TASM............ Turbo Assembler [*Computer science*]
Tasm Acts............ Tasmania Acts of Parliament [*A publication*] (DLA)
Tasmania LR............ University of Tasmania. Law Review [*A publication*] (DLA)
Tasmanian J............ Tasmanian Journal of Natural Science [*A publication*]
TASME............ Tosyl-L-arginyl Sarcosine Methyl Ester [*Biochemistry*]
TASMGS............ Tomahawk Antiship Missile Guidance Set (MCD)
TASMO............ Tactical Air Support for Maritime Operations [*Navy*] (NVT)
TASMOL............ Tactical Aircraft Support Model (MCD)
TASNSW............ Travellers' Aid Society of New South Wales [*Australia*]
TASO............ Television Allocations Study Organization [*Defunct*]
TASO............ Terminal Area Security Officer [*Military*] (AABC)
TASO............ Training Aids Service Office [*Army*] (AABC)
TASO............ Training and Audiovisual Support Officer [*Military*]
TASOS............ Towed Array SONAR System
TASOSC............ Theater Army Special Operations Support Command
TASP............ [*The*] Army Studies Program (AABC)
TASP............ Target Antisubmarine Patrol (NVT)
TASP............ Telemetry Analysis and Simulation Program [*Spacecraft*] [*NASA*]
TASP............ Template-Assisted Synthetic Protein [*Biochemistry*]
TASP............ Tentative Acceptance Sampling Procedure [*Army*]
TASP............ Texas Academic Skills Program
TASP............ Toll Alternatives Studies Program [*Telecommunications*] (TEL)
TAS-PAC............ Total Analysis System for Production, Accounting, and Control [*Computer science*]
TASPAWS............ Tasmanian Parks and Wildlife Service [*State*] (EERA)
TASPR............ Technical and Schedule Performance Report [*NASA*] (NASA)
TASQ............ Tactical Airlift Squadron [*Air Force*]
TASQUE............ University of Tasmania Consultative Unit [*State*] (EERA)
TASR............ Tactical Automated Situation Receiver [*Military*]
TASR............ Temperature Auto Stabilizing Regime (IAA)
TASR............ Terminal Area Surveillance RADAR
TASR............ Torque Arm Speed Reducer
TASRA............ Tabular System Reliability Analysis
TASRA............ Thermal Activation-Strain Rate Analysis
TAS/RAS............ Target Acquisition System / RADAR Automatic System [*Military*] (DNAB)
TAS/RMS............ Target Acquisition Sytem / RADAR Manual System [*Military*] (DNAB)
TASROCO............ Tactical Aerial Surveillance and Reconnaissance Operational Capability Objectives [*1995*] (MCD)
TASS............ [*The*] Army Study System
TASS............ Tactical Air Support Section [*Military*]
TASS............ Tactical Air Support Squadron [*Military*]
TASS............ Tactical Avionics System Simulator [*Army*] (MCD)
TASS............ Tactical Signal Simulator [*Canadian Astronautics Ltd. RADAR threat simulation system*]
TASS............ Technical, Administrative, and Supervisory Section [*Amalgamated Union of Engineering Workers - Engineering Section*] [*British*]
TASS............ Technical Assembly System
TASS............ Telegraphnoye Agentstvo Sovyetskovo Soyuza [*Telegraph Agency of the Soviet Union*] [*News agency*]
TASS............ Teleprinter Automatic Switching System (NITA)

TASS .... Terminal Air Surveillance System [*FAA*] (TAG)
TASS .... Terminal Application Support System (MCD)
TASS .... Terrain Analyst's Synthesizer Station [*Army*] (RDA)
TASS .... Theater Army Signal System (IAA)
TASS .... Total Army School System (INF)
TASS .... Towed Acoustic Surveillance System [*Marine science*] (MSC)
TASS .... Towed Array SONAR System
TASS .... Towed Array Surveillance System [*Navy*] (CAAL)
TASS .... Trouble Analysis System or Subsystem [*Telecommunications*] (TEL)
TASSA .... [*The*] Army Signal Supply Agency
TASSC .... [*The*] American Specialty Surety Council [*Later, ASA*] (EA)
TASSEL .... Three-Astronaut Space System Experimental Laboratory (MCD)
TASSI .... Tactical Airborne SIGINT Support Improvement Acquisition Plan (MCD)
TASSO .... Tactical Special Security Office [*Army*] (AABC)
TASSO .... Transatlantic Air Safety Service Organization
TASSO .... Two-Arm Spectrometer Solenoid (MCD)
TASSq .... Tactical Air Support Squadron [*Military*] (AFM)
TASSRAP .... Towed Array Surveillance Range Prediction (MCD)
TASST .... Tentative Airworthiness Standards for Supersonic Transports
TAST .... Tactical Assault Supply Transport (MCD)
TAST .... Test Article Signal Translator (MCD)
TAST .... Thermoacoustic Sensing Technique (IEEE)
TAST .... Tracking Adjunct Systems Trainer
TASTA .... [*The*] Administrative Support Theaters Army
TASTE .... Thermal Accelerated Short Time Evaporator [*Facetious term used in orange juice industry*]
TASTG .... Tactical Air Support Training Group [*Air Force*]
TASTNGSq .... Tactical Air Support Training Squadron [*Air Force*]
TASTS .... Tactical Air Support Training Squadron [*Air Force*]
Tasty .... Tasty Baking Co. [*Associated Press*] (SAG)
TASV .... Travellers' Aid Society of Victoria [*Australia*]
TASWD .... Torpedo, Anti-Submarine, and Mine Warfare Division [*British military*] (DMA)
Tasw Lang Hist .... Taswell-Langmead's English Constitutional History [*10th ed.*] [*1946*] [*A publication*] (DLA)
TASWM .... Test ASW [*Antisubmarine Warfare*] Missile [*Navy*] (CAAL)
TAT .... [*The*] Absolute Truth [*In Julian Barnes' novel "Staring at the Sun"*]
TAT .... [*The*] Associated Turtles [*Defunct*] (EA)
TAT .... European Airlines [*France ICAO designator*] (FAAC)
TAT .... Tactical Analysis Team [*Military drug interdiction program*]
TAT .... Tactical Armament Turret (NG)
TAT .... Target Abilities Test [*Psychometrics*]
TAT .... Target Aircraft Transmitter
TAT .... Task Assignment Table (MCD)
TAT .... Tateyama [*Japan*] [*Seismograph station code, US Geological Survey*] (SEIS)
TAT .... Tatry/Poprad [*Former Czechoslovakia*] [*Airport symbol*] (OAG)
TAT .... Taxpayers' Association of Tasmania [*Australia*]
TAT .... Technical Acceptance Team [*NASA*] (AAG)
TAT .... Technical Approval Team
TAT .... Technical Assistance and Training
TAT .... Technical Assistance Team [*Air Force*] (AFM)
TAT .... Technology Application Team [*NASA*]
TAT .... Telephone and Telegraph (IAA)
TAT .... Television Awareness Training
TAT .... Temporary Ambulance Train [*British military*] (DMA)
TAT .... Tensile Adhesion Test [*for coatings*]
TAT .... Terrorist Action Team [*Military*] (MCD)
TAT .... Tetanus Antitoxin [*Medicine*]
TAT .... Thematic Apperception Test [*Psychology*]
TAT .... Thinned Aperture Telescope
TAT .... Thromboplastin Activation Test [*Clinical chemistry*]
TAT .... Thromboplastin Activation Time [*Clinical chemistry*] (DAVI)
TAT .... Thrust-Augmented Thor [*NASA*]
TAT .... Till All Taken [*Pharmacy*] (DAVI)
TAT .... Time and Attendance Terminal (MHDI)
TAT .... To Accompany Troops
TAT .... Tochas Affen Tish [*In television production company name "TAT Productions." Words are Yiddish and translate figuratively as "Let's Be Honest"*]
TAT .... Torpedo Attack Teacher [*Navy*]
TAT .... Total Aircraft Time (MCD)
TAT .... Total Air Temperature (NASA)
TAT .... Total Alert Time
TAT .... Total Antitryptic Activity [*Medicine*] (MAE)
TAT .... Touraine Air Transport [*Private airline*] [*French*] (EY)
TAT .... Tourist Authority of Thailand (ECON)
TAT .... Toxin-Antitoxin [*Also, TA*] [*Immunology*]
TAT .... Trace Acceptance Tester
TAT .... Training and Technology
TAT .... Trans-Activator [*Genetics*]
TAT .... Trans Atlantic Resources, Inc. [*Vancouver Stock Exchange symbol*]
TAT .... Transatlantic Telephone [*Cable*]
TAT .... Transcontinental Air Transport
TAT .... Transportes Aeroside Timor [*Portuguese Timor*]
TAT .... Triaminotrinitrobenzene [*Organic chemistry*]
TAT .... Triamterene [*Diuretic*]
TAT .... True Air Temperature (AFM)
TAT .... Tumor Activity Test [*Medicine*] (DMAA)
TAT .... Tuned Aperiodic Tuned (IAA)
TAT .... Turbine Trip and Throttle Valve [*Nuclear energy*] (IAA)
TAT .... Turnaround Time
TAT .... Two-Axis Tracking
TAT .... Type-Approval Test
TAT .... Tyrosine Aminotransferase [*An enzyme*]
TAT 8 .... Transatlantic Telecommunications 8 (NITA)
TATA .... Tumor-Associated Transplantation Antigen [*Medicine*] (DMAA)
TATAC .... Temporary Air Transport Advisory Committee [*NATO*] (NATG)
TATAWS .... Tank, Antitank, and Assault Weapons Study [*or System*] [*Army*]
TATB .... Theater Air Transportation Board
TATB .... Triaminotrinitrobenzene [*Organic chemistry*]
TATC .... Tactical Air Traffic Control (NVT)
TATC .... Terminal Air Traffic Control
TATC .... Transatlantic Telephone Cable (IEEE)
TATCA .... Terminal Air Traffic Control Automation [*FAA*] (TAG)
TATCA .... Terminal Air Traffic Control Automation (GAVI)
TATCA .... Trialkoxytricarballylate [*Organic chemistry*]
TATCE .... Terminal Air Traffic Control Element
TATCF .... Terminal Air Traffic Control Facility
TATCO .... Tactical Automatic Telephone Central Office [*Military*]
TATCS .... Terminal Air Traffic Control System
TATD .... Task Assignment Table Display (MCD)
TATDL .... Tabulated Assembly Technical Data List
TATE .... Tank Arrangement Thermal Efficiency [*Computer program*] (KSC)
TATE .... Traditional Aboriginal Teacher Education [*Australia*]
TATER .... Talos-Terrier-Recruit [*Flight-test vehicle*]
Tate's Dig .... Tate's Digest of Laws [*Virginia*] [*A publication*] (DLA)
TATG .... Tactical Airlift Training Group [*Air Force*]
TATG .... Tuned Anode Tuned Grid (DEN)
Tatham .... Tatham Offshore, Inc. [*Associated Press*] (SAG)
TATHS .... Tool and Trades History Society (EAIO)
TATI .... Total Air Temperature Indicator
TATI .... Tumor-Associated Trypsin Inhibitor [*Medicine*]
TATO .... Taipei [*Taiwan*] [*Seismograph station code, US Geological Survey*] (SEIS)
TATP .... TACFIRE [*Tactical Fire*] Advanced Training Program [*Army*]
TATP .... Two-Axis Tracking Pedestal
TATR .... Tactical Air Target Recommender
TATr .... Tyrosine Aminotransferase Regulator
TATRC .... Type-Approval Test Review Committee
TATS .... Tactical Aerial Targets Squadron (MCD)
TATS .... Tactical Airlift Training Squadron [*Air Force*]
TATS .... Tactical Armament Turret System
TATS .... Tactical Transmission System Summary (KSC)
TATS .... Target Acquisition and Track System (MUGU)
TATS .... Technical Assistance and Training Survey [*Department of Labor*] (OICC)
TATS .... Test and Training Satellite [*Also, TETR, TTS*] [*NASA*]
TATSA .... Transportation Aircraft Test and Support Activity [*Military*]
TATSC .... Total Army Training System Course (INF)
TATST .... Tetanus Antitoxin Skin Test [*Medicine*] (MAE)
TATSU .... Transportation Aviation Test and Support
TATT .... Technical Assistance and Technology Transfer (NOAA)
TAT Tch .... TAT Technologies [*Associated Press*] (SAG)
TATTE .... Talos [*Missile*] Tactical Test Equipment
TATTF .... TAT Technologies [*NASDAQ symbol*] (SAG)
TATTF .... TAT Technologies Ltd [*NASDAQ symbol*] (TTSB)
TATU .... Technical Advanced Training for Units (MCD)
TAU .... Fort Meade, MD [*Location identifier FAA*] (FAAL)
TAU .... Tape Adapter Unit [*Computer science*] (IAA)
TAU .... Tasmania University [*Tasmania*] [*Seismograph station code, US Geological Survey*] (SEIS)
TAU .... Tauramena [*Colombia*] [*Airport symbol*] (AD)
Tau .... Taurus [*Constellation*]
TAU .... Technical Advisory Unit (OICC)
TAU .... Tel Aviv University [*Israel*]
TAU .... Temporary Authorization [*Personnel*] (OICC)
TAU .... Test Access Unit [*Telecommunications*] (TEL)
TAU .... Thesaurus Alphabetical Up to Date (NITA)
TAU .... Thousand Astronomical Units
TAU .... Toros Airlines [*Turkey*] [*ICAO designator*] (FAAC)
TAU .... Transalta Utilities Corp. [*Toronto Stock Exchange symbol*]
TAU .... Triton Acid Urea
TAU .... Trunk Access Unit
TAU .... Twin Agent Unit [*Fire fighting*] (NVT)
Taubmn .... Taubman Centers Co., Inc. [*Associated Press*] (SAG)
TauCA .... Taurus Municipal California Holdings [*Associated Press*] (SAG)
TAUCH .... Tauchnitz [*Bibliography*] (ROG)
TAUF .... Test Assembly Unloading Fixture [*Nuclear energy*] (NRCH)
TAUM .... Groupe de Recherches pour la Traduction Automatique [*Universite de Montreal*] [*Canada Research center*]
Taun .... Taunton's English Common Pleas Reports [*A publication*] (DLA)
TAUN .... Technical Assistance of the United Nations
Taunt (Eng) .... Taunton's English Common Pleas Reports [*127, 129 English Reprint*] [*A publication*] (DLA)
TauNY .... Taurus Municipal New York Holdings [*Associated Press*] (SAG)
Taur .... Taurus [*Constellation*]
TAURUS .... Transfer and Automated Registration of Uncertificated Stock [*London Stock Exchange computer project*] (ECON)
TAUS .... Tobacco Association of United States (EA)
TAUSA .... Trans-Atlantic Universities Speech Association
Taut .... Taunton's English Common Pleas Reports [*A publication*] (DLA)
TAUT .... Tautology (ADA)
TAUVEX .... Tel Aviv University Ultra-Violet Explorer [*Israel*]
TAV .... Compania de Servicios Aereos, TAVISA [*Spain ICAO designator*] (FAAC)
TAV .... Tau [*American Samoa*] [*Airport symbol*] (OAG)
TAV .... Tavern (ROG)
TAV .... Tavistock [*England*]

TAV .... Tavurvur [*New Britain*] [*Seismograph station code, US Geological Survey*] (SEIS)
TAV .... Taxpayers' Association of Victoria [*Australia*]
TAV .... Technical Assistance Visit (MCD)
TAV .... Technical Availability [*Navy*] (NG)
TAV .... Temperature-Activated Vacuum [*Automotive engineering*]
TAV .... Tender Availability [*Navy*]
TAV .... Test and Validation (KSC)
TAV .... Tomato Aspermy Virus
TAV .... Total Asset Visibility [*Army*]
TAV .... Toward, Away, versus Selection System [*Psychology*] (AEBS)
TAV .... Transatmospheric Vehicle [*Proposed futuristic plane capable of flying at hypersonic speeds*]
TAV .... Trapped Air Volume [*Medicine*] (DMAA)
TAV .... Triathlon Association of Victoria [*Australia*]
TAVC .... Total Active Vitamin C [*Nutrition*]
TAVE .... Average Temperature (NRCH)
TAVE .... Thor-Agena Vibration Experiment [*NASA*]
TAVERNS ..... Test and Verification Environment for Remote Network Systems (SSD)
TAVET .... Temperature Acceleration Vibration Environmental Tester
TAVG .... Temperature Average (IAA)
TAVI .... Thorn Apple Valley [*NASDAQ symbol*] (TTSB)
TAVI .... Thorn Apple Valley, Inc. [*Southfield, MI*] [*NASDAQ symbol*] (NQ)
TAVIP .... Tahun Vivere Pericoloso [*The Year of Living Dangerously*] [*President Sukarno's national policy in 1964 Indonesia*]
TAVRA .... Territorial Auxiliary and Volunteer Reserve Association [*British Armed Forces*]
TAVS .... Turbine Area Ventilation System [*Nuclear energy*] (NRCH)
TAVSC .... Training and Audiovisual Support Center [*Army*]
TAVT .... Terminal Airspace Visualization Tool [*FAA*] (TAG)
TAW .... Tactical Air [*or Airlift*] Wing
TAW .... Tactical Assault Weapon
TAW .... Tawu [*Republic of China*] [*Seismograph station code, US Geological Survey*] (SEIS)
TAW .... Tennessee Wesleyan College, Athens, TN [*Library symbol Library of Congress*] (LCLS)
TAW .... Terrawest [*Vancouver Stock Exchange symbol*]
TAW .... Thrust-Augmented Wing [*NASA*] (MCD)
TAW .... [*The*] Toledo, Angola & Western Railway Co. [*AAR code*]
TAW .... Train America's Workforce [*An association*] (WYGK)
TAW .... Transway Air Services, Inc. [*Liberia*] [*ICAO designator*] (FAAC)
TAW .... Troop Airlift Wing (CINC)
TAW .... Twice a Week [*Advertising frequency*]
TAWACS ...... Tactical Airborne Warning and Control System (AFM)
TAWAR .... Tactical All Weather Attack Requirements [*Air Force*] (MCD)
TAWB .... Through Air Waybill [*Shipping*] (DS)
TAWC .... Tactical Air Warfare Center [*Air Force*]
TAWC .... Tactical Armored Weapons Carrier (MCD)
TAWC .... Tasmanian Amateur Walking Club [*Australia*]
TAWCS .... Tactical Air Weapons Control System
TAWDS .... Target Acquisition Weapon Delivery System [*Air Force*] (MCD)
TAWDS .... Terminal Area Weapon Delivery Simulator (MCD)
TAWG .... Tactical Air Warfare Group
TAWG .... Target Acquisition Working Group [*Air Force*]
TAWOG .... Travel Arrangements Without Government Expense (FAAC)
TAWRS .... Tower Aviation Weather Reporting Station (NOAA)
TAWS .... Tactical Area Weather Sensor (MCD)
TAWS .... Tactical Automatic Weather Station [*Buoy*] (MSC)
TAWS .... Tactical Warfare Center [*Army*] (AABC)
TAWS .... Technical Analysis Work Sheet (AAG)
TAWS .... Terrain Analyst Work Station [*Army*] (RDA)
TAWS .... Thomasville Aircraft and Warning Station (IAA)
TAWS .... Total Airborne Weapon Systems (MUGU)
TAWS .... Total Armament Weapons System (MUGU)
TAWS .... Transonabuoy Automatic Weather System (SAA)
TA Wst .... TransAmerican Waste Industries, Inc. [*Associated Press*] (SAG)
TAWT .... Tawton [*England*]
TAX .... Madison, WI [*Location identifier FAA*] (FAAL)
TAX .... Tactical Air Exercise (CINC)
TAX .... Tarxien International, Inc. [*Toronto Stock Exchange symbol*]
tax .... Taxation (DD)
TAX .... Taxiing [*Aviation*]
TAX .... Taxol (DMAA)
TAX .... Training Assessment Exercise
TAX .... Travelair GmbH [*Germany ICAO designator*] (FAAC)
Tax ABC .... Canada Tax Appeal Board Cases [*A publication*] (DLA)
Tax Acct ...... Taxation for Accountants [*A publication*] (DLA)
Tax Adm'rs News... Tax Administrators News [*A publication*] (DLA)
Tax & Rev ... Taxation and Revenue (DLA)
Tax Aust ...... Taxation in Australia [*A publication*]
Tax Cas .... Tax Cases [*A publication*] (DLA)
Tax Ct Mem Dec... Tax Court Memorandum Decisions [*Commerce Clearing House*] [*A publication*] (DLA)
Tax Ct Rep... Tax Court Reporter [*Commerce Clearing House*] [*A publication*] (DLA)
Tax Ct Rep & Mem Dec (P-H)... Tax Court Reported and Memorandum Decisions (Prentice-Hall, Inc.) [*A publication*] (DLA)
Tax Ct Rep Dec... Tax Court Reported Decisions [*Prentice-Hall, Inc.*] [*A publication*] (DLA)
Taxes .... Tax Magazine [*A publication*] (DLA)
TAXI .... Medallion Financial [*NASDAQ symbol*] (TTSB)
taxi .... Taximeter Cabriolet
TAXI .... Transparent Asynchronous Transceiver Interface
TAXIR .... Taxonomic Information Retrieval [*Computer science*] (DIT)
Tax Law Rep... Tax Law Reporter [*A publication*] (DLA)
TAXLE .... Tandem Cantilevered Axle
Tax LR .... Tax Law Reporter [*A publication*] (DLA)
Tax L Rep.... Tax Law Reporter [*A publication*] (DLA)
Tax Mag ...... Tax Magazine [*A publication*] (DLA)
Tax Man ...... Tax Management [*A publication*] (DLA)
Tax Mgmt (BNA)... Tax Management (Bureau of National Affairs) [*A publication*] (DLA)
Tax Mgmt Int'l J... Tax Management International Journal [*A publication*] (DLA)
Tax Mngm't... Tax Management [*Bureau of National Affairs*] [*A publication*] (DLA)
TAXN .... Taxation (ROG)
TAXON .... Taxonomy
Tax Pl Int..... Tax Planning International [*A publication*] (DLA)
Tax Pl Rev... Tax Planning Review [*A publication*] (DLA)
Tax Pract Forum... Tax Practitioners Forum [*A publication*] (DLA)
Tax R .... Taxation Reports [*England*] [*A publication*] (DLA)
t-ay-- .... Antarctica [*MARC geographic area code Library of Congress*] (LCCP)
TAY .... Talia Airlines [*Turkey*] [*ICAO designator*] (FAAC)
TAY .... Taylor, FL [*Location identifier FAA*] (FAAL)
Tay .... Taylor's North Carolina Reports [*1 North Carolina*] [*1798-1802*] [*A publication*] (DLA)
Tay .... Taylor's Supreme Court Reports [*1847-48*] [*Bengal, India*] [*A publication*] (DLA)
Tay .... Taylor's Upper Canada King's Bench Reports [*1823-1827*] [*A publication*] (DLA)
Tay .... Tayside [*Scotland*] (WGA)
TAY .... Tule Lake Aster Yellows [*Plant pathology*]
Tay & B .... Taylor and Bell's Bengal Reports [*India*] [*A publication*] (DLA)
Tay Bank L... Taylor on the Bankruptcy Law [*A publication*] (DLA)
Tay Bk R...... Taylor's Book of Rights [*1833*] [*A publication*] (DLA)
Tay Civ L ..... Taylor's Elements of Civil Law [*A publication*] (DLA)
TAYD .... Taylor Devices [*NASDAQ symbol*] (TTSB)
TAYD .... Taylor Devices, Inc. [*NASDAQ symbol*] (NQ)
Tay Eq Jur... Taylor on Equity Jurisprudence [*A publication*] (DLA)
Tay Ev .... Taylor on Evidence [*12th ed.*] [*1931*] [*A publication*] (DLA)
Tay Glos ...... Taylor's Law Glossary [*2nd ed.*] [*1823*] [*A publication*] (DLA)
Tay Gov ...... Taylor on Government [*A publication*] (DLA)
Tay L & T.... Taylor's Landlord and Tenant [*A publication*] (DLA)
Tayl Civil Law... Taylor on Civil Law [*A publication*] (DLA)
Tayl Corp..... Taylor on Private Corporations [*A publication*] (DLA)
Tayl Ev .... Taylor on Evidence [*A publication*] (DLA)
Tay L Gl ...... Taylor's Law Glossary [*A publication*] (DLA)
Tayl Gloss ... Taylor's Law Glossary [*A publication*] (DLA)
Tayl Landl & Ten... Taylor's Landlord and Tenant [*A publication*] (DLA)
Tayl Med Jur... Taylor's Medical Jurisprudence [*A publication*] (DLA)
Tayl NC .... Taylor's North Carolina Reports [*1 North Carolina*] [*A publication*] (DLA)
Taylor .... Taylor's Customary Laws of Rembau [*1903-28*] [*Malaya*] [*A publication*] (DLA)
Taylor .... Taylor's North Carolina Reports [*1 North Carolina*] [*A publication*] (DLA)
Taylor .... Taylor's North Carolina Term Reports [*4 North Carolina*] [*A publication*] (DLA)
Taylor .... Taylor's Reports [*Bengal, India*] [*A publication*] (DLA)
Taylor .... Taylor's Upper Canada King's Bench Reports [*A publication*] (DLA)
Taylor KB (Can)... Taylor's Upper Canada King's Bench Reports [*A publication*] (DLA)
Taylor (Malaya)... Taylor's Customary Laws of Rembau [*1903-28*] [*Malaya*] [*A publication*] (DLA)
Taylor UC .... Taylor's Upper Canada King's Bench Reports [*A publication*] (DLA)
Tayl Priv Corp... Taylor on Private Corporations [*A publication*] (DLA)
TaylrDv .... Taylor Devices, Inc. [*Associated Press*] (SAG)
Tayl St .... Taylor's Revised Statutes [*Wisconsin*] [*A publication*] (DLA)
Tay Med Jur... Taylor's Medical Jurisprudence [*12th ed.*] [*1966*] [*A publication*] (DLA)
TAYMEL .... Taylor Woodrow Management & Engineering Ltd. [*British*] (IRUK)
Tay NC .... Taylor's North Carolina Reports [*1 North Carolina*] [*A publication*] (DLA)
Tay Poi .... Taylor on Poisons [*3rd ed.*] [*1875*] [*A publication*] (DLA)
Tay Rep .... Taylor's North Carolina Reports [*1 North Carolina*] [*A publication*] (DLA)
Tay Tit .... Taylor on Tithe Commutation [*1876*] [*A publication*] (DLA)
Tay UC .... Taylor's Upper Canada King's Bench Reports [*1 vol.*] [*1823-27*] [*A publication*] (DLA)
Tay Wills..... Taylor's Precedents of Wills [*A publication*] (DLA)
Tay Wis Stat... Taylor's Wisconsin Statutes [*A publication*] (DLA)
TAZ .... Tactical Alert Zone (NATG)
TAZ .... Taylorville, IL [*Location identifier FAA*] (FAAL)
TAZ .... Theater Administrative Zone [*Military*]
TAZ .... Traffic Analysis Zone [*Bureau of the Census*] (GFGA)
TAZ .... Transportation Analysis Zone [*MM*] (TAG)
TAZ .... Transporte Aereo de la Amazonia [*Colombia*] [*ICAO designator*] (FAAC)
TAZ .... Triazolam [*Tranquilizer*]
TAZARA .... Tanzania-Zambia Railway
TB .... Aerospatiale (SOCATA) Stark KG [*Germany ICAO aircraft manufacturer identifier*] (ICAO)
TB .... Automotive Engine Rebuilders Association. Technical Bulletin [*A publication*] (EAAP)
Tb .... Body Temperature [*Medicine*]
TB .... Mycobacterium Tuberculosis [*A bacterium*] [*Medicine*] (DAVI)
tb .... Tablespoon [*Measure*] (WGA)
TB .... Tabulation Block (MSA)
TB .... Tail Back [*Football*]
TB .... Talk Back [*NASA*] (KSC)

TB .... Talmud Bavli (BJA)
TB .... Tangential Bracket
TB .... Tank Battalion [*Army*]
TB .... Tape Backup Unit
TB .... Tapes for the Blind [*Defunct*] (EA)
TB .... Tariff Bureau
TB .... Tasmanian Bank [*Australia Commercial firm*]
TB .... Techbyte, Inc. [*Vancouver Stock Exchange symbol*]
TB .... Technical Bulletin [*Military*]
TB .... Tejas Airlines [*ICAO designator*] (AD)
TB .... Telegraph Bureau
TB .... Temple Biographies [*A publication*]
TB .... Temporary Buoy [*Nautical charts*]
TB .... Tenor, Bass (CDAI)
Tb .... TeraBIT [*Binary Digit*] [10^{12} *BITs*]
TB .... Terabyte [10^{12} *bytes*]
Tb .... Terabyte [*Computer science*] (EERA)
Tb .... Terbium [*Chemical element*]
TB .... Terminal Base (MCD)
TB .... Terminal Block
TB .... Terminal Board
TB .... Terminal Bronchiole [*Medicine*] (MAE)
TB .... Test Bed (MCD)
TB .... Test Bulletin
TB .... Thermobarometer
TB .... Thexylborane [*Organic chemistry*]
T-B .... Thomas-Binetti [*Test*] [*Laboratory science*] (DAVI)
TB .... Thoroughbred
TB .... Thromboxane B [*Also, TxB, TXB*] [*Biochemistry*]
TB .... Throttle Body [*Automotive engineering*]
TB .... Through Bolt (DAC)
T/B .... Thunderbird [*Automobile*]
TB .... Thymol Blue [*An indicator*]
TB .... Ticket Board (DGA)
TB .... Tile Base [*Technical drawings*]
T/B .... Tile Block [*Technical drawings*]
TB .... Time-Bandwidth
TB .... Time Base
TB .... Time between Points [*Experimentation*]
TB .... Time Duration of Burn (MCD)
TB .... Times at Bat [*Baseball*]
T/B .... Title Block (SAA)
Tb .... Tobit [*Old Testament book*] [*Roman Catholic canon*]
TB .... Toggle Buffer (MCD)
TB .... Toluidine Blue [*Organic chemistry*]
tb .... Tomb (VRA)
TB .... Tone Burst
TB .... Top Boy [*British*] (DSUE)
T/B .... Top to Bottom
TB .... Torch Bible Commentaries [*A publication*] (BJA)
TB .... Torch Brazing
TB .... Torpedo Boat [*Navy symbol Obsolete*]
TB .... Torpedo Bomber [*or Bombing*]
TB .... Torsion Bar [*Automotive engineering*]
TB .... Total Bases
TB .... Total Bilirubin [*Clinical chemistry*]
TB .... Total Blank [*Entertainment slang for poor show town*]
TB .... Total Body [*Nuclear energy*] (NRCH)
TB .... Total Body [*Medicine*] (DAVI)
TB .... Total Bouts [*Boxing*]
TB .... Total Burn
TB .... Tourism Brisbane [*Australia*]
TB .... Towel Bar [*Technical drawings*]
TB .... Tracer Bullet
TB .... Tracheal-Bronchiolar [*Region*] [*Medicine*]
TB .... Tracheobronchitis [*Medicine*]
TB .... Tractor Biplane
TB .... Trading Bank
TB .... Trafalgar Brookmount [*British*]
TB .... Traffic Bureau
TB .... Training Back [*Main parachute*]
TB .... Training Battalion [*British military*] (DMA)
TB .... Tranquility Base [*Moon landing site*]
TB .... Transfer Building
TB .... Transmitter-Blocker (DEN)
TB .... Transmitter Buffer [*Telecommunications*] (IAA)
TB .... Trapezoid Body [*Audiometry*]
TB .... Treasury Bill
TB .... Treasury Board Secretariat [*Canada*]
TB .... Trial Balance [*Bookkeeping*]
tb .... Trial Balance [*Bookkeeping*] (ODBW)
TB .... Trial Balloon
TB .... Triple-Braided (CET)
TB .... Troop Basis [*Military*]
TB .... True Bearing [*Navigation*]
TB .... True Blue [*A fluorescent dye*]
TB .... Trump Shuttle [*ICAO designator*] (AD)
TB .... Trunk Barrier [*Telecommunications*] (IAA)
TB .... Tryptone Broth [*Culture medium*]
TB .... Tubercle Bacillus [*Bacteriology*]
TB .... Tuberculin [*or Tuberculosis*] (AABC)
TB .... Tumor-Bearing [*Animal*]
TB .... Tundra Biome [*Ecological biogeographic study*]
TB .... Turbine Building [*Nuclear energy*] (NRCH)
TB .... Turbulence [*Aviation*] (FAAC)
TB .... Twin Branch Railroad Co. [*AAR code*]
TB .... Twirly Birds (EA)
TBA .... [*The*] Bettmann Archive [*A publication*]
TBA .... [*The*] Black Agenda [*An association*]
TBA .... Tabibuga [*Papua New Guinea*] [*Airport symbol*] (OAG)
TBA .... Tables of Basic Allowances [*Previously, Basic Tables of Commissioning Allowances*] [*Navy*]
TBA .... Task Budget Allocation (MCD)
TBA .... Tasmanian Badminton Association [*Australia*]
TBA .... Tasmanian Bar Association [*Australia*]
TBA .... Tasmanian Basketball Association [*Australia*]
TBA .... Tasmanian Beekeepers' Association [*Australia*]
TBA .... Tasmanian Bookmakers' Association [*Australia*]
TBA .... Tasmanian Bridge Association [*Australia*]
TBA .... Taurine Bibliophiles of America (EA)
TBA .... Tea Brokers' Association [*British*] (DBA)
TBA .... Tea Buyers' Association [*British*] (EAIO)
TBA .... Television Bureau of Advertising
TBA .... Terminal Board Assembly (MSA)
TBA .... Tertiary Butyl Acetate [*Organic chemistry*]
TBA .... Tertiary Butyl Alcohol [*Gasoline additive*]
TBA .... Tertiary-Butylamine [*Organic chemistry*]
TBA .... Tertiary-Butylarsine [*Organic chemistry*]
TBA .... Test Bed Aircraft
TBA .... Test Boring Association (EA)
TBA .... Test of Basic Assumptions [*Psychology*]
TBA .... Testosterone-Binding Affinity [*Endocrinology*] (MAE)
TBA .... Thermo Bioanalysis Corp. [*AMEX symbol*] (SAG)
TBA .... Thiobarbituric Acid [*Organic chemistry*]
TBA .... Thoroughbred Breeders' Association [*British*] (BI)
TBA .... Thyroxine-Binding Albumin [*Biochemistry*] (MAE)
TBA .... Tires, Batteries, and Accessories
TBA .... To Be Absorbed [*Pharmacology*] (DAVI)
TBA .... To Be Activated [*Military*]
TBA .... To Be Added (AAG)
TBA .... To Be Admitted [*Medicine*] (DAVI)
TBA .... To Be Agreed (AIA)
TBA .... To Be Announced
TBA .... To Be Assigned
TBA .... To Be Avoided [*Slang*]
TBA .... Torsional Braid Analysis [*Instrumentation*]
TBA .... Towed Buoy Antenna
TBA .... Traditional Birth Attendant
TBA .... Transbrasil SA Linhas Aereas [*Brazil*] [*ICAO designator*] (FAAC)
TBA .... Tributylamine [*Organic chemistry*]
TBA .... Trichlorobenzoic Acid [*Herbicide*] [*Organic chemistry*]
TBA .... Tuba [*Music*]
TBA .... Tumor-Bearing Animal (AAMN)
TBA .... Twin Bonanza Association (EA)
TBAB .... Tetrabutylammonium Bromide [*Organic chemistry*]
TBAB .... Theosophical Book Association for the Blind (EA)
TBAB .... Tryptose Blood Agar Base [*Medicine*] (DMAA)
TBAC .... Tandy Brands Accessories [*NASDAQ symbol*] (TTSB)
TBAC .... Tandy Brands Accessories, Inc. [*NASDAQ symbol*] (SAG)
TBAC .... Tertiary-Butylacetyl Chloride [*Organic chemistry*]
TBACC .... Tetrabutylammonium Chlorochromate [*Organic chemistry*]
TBAC/FLM .... Treasury Board Advisory Committee on Federal Land Management [*Canada*]
TBAD .... To Be Advised (AIA)
TBAF .... Tetrabutylammonium Fluoride [*Organic chemistry*]
TBAF .... Tetrabutylammonium Fluoroborate [*Organic chemistry*]
TBAG .... To Be Agreed (AIA)
TBAH .... Tetrabutylammonium Hydroxide [*Organic chemistry*]
TBAHS .... Tetrabutylammonium Hydrogen Sulfate [*Organic chemistry*]
TBAI .... Temporary Base Activation Instruction (AAG)
TBAM .... Tone Burst Amplitude Modulation
TBAN .... To Be Announced [*Army*] (AABC)
TBAN .... Transbronchial Aspiration Needle [*Medicine*] (DMAA)
TB & B .... Tuberculosis and Brucellosis [*Medicine*] (ADA)
TB & M .... Tracewell, Bowers, and Mitchell's United States Comptroller's Decisions [*A publication*] (DLA)
TB & S .... Top, Bottom, and Sides [*Lumber*]
TBAP .... Tetrabutylammoniumperchlorate [*Photovoltaic energy systems*]
TBARA .... Trakehner Breed Association and Registry of America [*Defunct*] (EA)
TBARS .... Thiobarbituric Acid Reactive Substance [*Analytical chemistry*]
TBAS .... [*The*] Band Appreciation Society (EAIO)
TBAT .... Tow/Bushmaster Armored Turret [*Military*]
TBAV .... Tenpin Bowling Association of Victoria [*Australia*]
TBAV .... ThunderBYTE Anti-Virus [*Computer software*] (PCM)
TBAVF .... Translocated Basilic Vein Arteriovenous Fistula [*Surgery*]
TBAWRBA .... Travel by Military Aircraft, Military and/or Naval Water Carrier, Commercial Rail and/or Bus Is Authorized [*Army*] (AABC)
TBAX .... Tube Axial
TBAZFCA .... Toledo Bird Association, Zebra Finch Club of America (EA)
TBB .... Columbus, MS [*Location identifier FAA*] (FAAL)
TBB .... Die Tempel von Babylon und Borsippa [*A publication*] (BJA)
TBB .... Temporal Bone Banks [*Otology*] (EA)
TBB .... Tenor, Baritone, Bass
TBB .... Tobex Resources Ltd. [*Vancouver Stock Exchange symbol*]
TBB .... Transbronchial Biopsy [*Medicine*]
TBB .... Trolleybus Bulletin [*A publication*] (EAAP)
TBB .... Tuy Hoa [*South Vietnam*] [*Airport symbol*] (AD)
TBBA .... Tea Buying Brokers' Association [*British*] (DBA)
TBBA .... Terephthalyl Bis(butylaniline) [*Organic chemistry*]
TBBF .... Top Baseband Frequency

TBBM Total Body Bone Mineral
TBBPA Tetrabromobisphenol-A [*Organic chemistry*]
TBBS [*The*] Bread Board System [*eSoft, Inc.*] [*Computer science*] (PCM)
TBC Belmont College, Nashville, TN [*OCLC symbol*] (OCLC)
TBC Confederation College of Applied Arts and Technology [*UTLAS symbol*]
TBC Taiwan Base Command (CINC)
TBC Tanker and Bulk Carrier
TBC Tasmanian Bowls Council [*Australia*]
TBC Tasty Baking [*AMEX symbol*] (TTSB)
TBC Tasty Baking Co. [*AMEX symbol*] (SPSG)
TBC TBC Corp. [*Associated Press*] (SAG)
TBC Technology & Business Communications, Inc. [*Information service or system*] (IID)
TBC Television Briefing Console
TBC Tembec Inc. [*Toronto Stock Exchange symbol*]
TBC Terminal Buffer Controller (NASA)
TBC Tertiary-Butylcatechol [*Organic chemistry*]
TBC Theatre Ballet of Canada
TBC Thermal Barrier Coating (RDA)
TBC Thyroxine-Binding Capacity [*Biochemistry*]
TBC Thyroxine-Binding Coagulin [*Biochemistry*] (MAE)
TBC Tie Line Bias Control [*Telecommunications*] (IAA)
TBC Time Base Corrector [*Videotape recording element*] [*Early processing device*]
TBC Time Base Corrector (NITA)
TBC Time-Based Competition [*Business term*]
TBC To Be Cooked [*Food*]
TBC Token Bus Controller [*Motorola, Inc.*]
TBC Torch Bible Commentaries [*New York/London*] [*A publication*] (BJA)
TBC Torrey Botanical Club (EA)
TBC Toss Bomb Computer
TBC Total Body Calcium
TBC Total Body Carbon
TBC Trinidad Base Command [*World War II*]
TBC Trunk Block Connector
TBC Tuba City, AZ [*Location identifier FAA*] (FAAL)
TBC Tube Bending Chart
TBC Tubercle Bacillus [*Bacteriology*]
TBC Tuberculosis
TBC Turbulent Bed Contactor [*Chemical engineering*]
TBCA Test Boring Contractors Association [*Later, TBA*] (EA)
TBCA Transportation Brokers Conference of America (EA)
TBCC TBC Corp. [*NASDAQ symbol*] (NQ)
TBCC Tom Baker Cancer Centre [*University of Calgary*] [*Formerly, Southern Alberta Cancer Centre*] [*Research center*] (RCD)
TBCCW Turbine-Building Closed Cooling Water [*Nuclear energy*] (NRCH)
TBCE Time Buffered Coarse Fine (IAA)
TBCITC Tasmanian Building and Construction Industry Training Committee [*Australia*]
TBCOA Triathalon Broadcasting Co. [*NASDAQ symbol*] (SAG)
TBCOA Triathlon Broadcasting 'A' [*NASDAQ symbol*] (TTSB)
TBCOL Triathlon Brdcst 9% Pfd [*NASDAQ symbol*] (TTSB)
TBCR Times British Colonies Review [*London*] [*A publication*]
TBD Tactical Battle Drill [*Army*] (INF)
TBD Target Bearing Designator [*Navy*]
TBD Terminal Bomber Defense [*Army*] (AABC)
TBD Thibodaux, LA [*Location identifier FAA*] (FAAL)
TBD Thousand Barrels per Day [*Also, KBD*]
TBD Thunderbird Tours [*Canada*] [*FAA designator*] (FAAC)
TBD To Be Declassified (AAG)
TBD To Be Defined
TBD To Be Designated (MCD)
TBD To Be Determined (AFM)
TBD To Be Developed (NASA)
TBD To Be Disbanded
TBD To Be Done (AAG)
TBD Too Badly Decomposed
TBD Torpedo-Boat Destroyer [*Obsolete*]
TBD Total Body Density [*Medicine*] (MAE)
TBD Trans Border Energy [*Vancouver Stock Exchange symbol*]
TBD Triazabicydo-decene [*Organic chemistry*]
TBD Troubleshooting Block Diagram
TBD Tube Bending Data (MCD)
TBD Twin Boundary Diffusion
TBDA Thexylborane-N, N-Diethylaniline [*Organic chemistry*]
TBDD Tetrabromodibenzo-p-dioxin [*Organic chemistry*]
TBDF Transborder Data Flows [*Also, TDF*] [*Telecommunications*]
TBDI TMBR/Sharp Drilling [*NASDAQ symbol*] (TTSB)
TBDI TMBR Sharp Drilling, Inc. [*NASDAQ symbol*] (SAG)
TBDL To Be Designated Later (CINC)
TBDL Total Bile-Duct Ligation [*Medicine*]
TBDMIM Tertiary-Butyldimethylsilylimidazole [*Organic chemistry*]
TBDMS Tertiary-Butyldimethylsilyl [*Organic chemistry*]
TBDMSCI Tertiary-Butyldimethylsilyl Chloride [*Also, TBSCI*] [*Organic chemistry*]
TBDPS Tertiary-Butyldiphenysilyl [*Also, TBDMS, TBS*] [*Organic chemistry*]
TBDS Test Base Dispatch Service (AAG)
TBD/TDA Too Badly Decomposed/Technician Destroyed Animal [*Laboratory testing*]
TBE Federation Europeenne des Fabricants de Tuiles et de Briques [*European Association of Brick and Tile Manufacturers*] (EAIO)
TBE Tenant by the Entirety [*Legal shorthand*] (LWAP)
TBE Tetrabromoethane [*Microscopy*]
TBE Thread Both Ends (MSA)
TBE Tiber Energy Corp. [*Toronto Stock Exchange symbol*]
TBE Tick-Borne Encephalitis
TBE Time Base Error
TBE Tobe, CO [*Location identifier FAA*] (FAAL)
TBE To Be Evaluated (NASA)
TBE To Be Expended (AAG)
TBE Toronto Board of Education, Professional Library [*UTLAS symbol*]
TBE Total Binding Energy (IAA)
TBE Total Body Ergometer
TBE Total Breech Extraction [*Gynecology*]
TBE Transmitter Buffer Empty [*Computer science*]
TBE Tris-Borate Buffer Electrophoresis
TBE Tris-Borate-EDTA [*Ethylenediaminetetraacetate*] [*Buffer*]
TBE Tuberculin Bacillen Emulsion [*Medicine*]
TBEA Tennessee Business Education Association (EDAC)
TBEA Truck Body and Equipment Association [*Defunct*] (EA)
TBED Time Base Error Difference [*Computer science*] (IAA)
TBEM Terminal-Based Electronic Mail
TBeP Polk County High School, Benton, TN [*Library symbol Library of Congress*] (LCLS)
TBEP Technology Base Enhancement Project
TBEP Tri(butoxyethyl) Phosphate [*Organic chemistry*]
TBESC Tech Base Executive Steering Committee [*Army*] (RDA)
TBESC Technology Base Executive Steering Commitee [*Army*] (RDA)
TBESI Turbine-Building Exhaust System Isolation [*Nuclear energy*] (NRCH)
TBEX Tube Expander
TBF Tabiteuea North [*Kiribati*] [*Airport symbol*] (OAG)
TBF Tail Bomb Fuse (KSC)
TBF Teachers' Benevolent Fund (AIE)
TBF Test de Bon Fonctionnement [*Spacelab*] (MCD)
TBF Testicular Blood Flow [*Physiology*]
TBF Tie Bus Fault
TBF Time between Failures [*Quality control*] (AFIT)
TBF To Be Funded [*Contracting*] [*Military*]
TBF Torpedo Bomber Fighter (NATG)
TBF Total Body Fat
TBF Tour Basing Fare [*Air travel term*]
TBF Tributyl Phosphate [*Organic chemistry*]
TBF Two-Body Force
TBFC Teresa Brewer Fan Club (EA)
TBFC Tom Burford Fan Club (EA)
TBFC Tony Booth Fan Club (EA)
TBFFU Twin-Ball Fire Fighting Unit [*Military*] (PDAA)
TBFG Tom Baker Friendship Group (EAIO)
TBFI Throttle Body Fuel Injection [*Fuel systems*] [*Automotive engineering*]
TBFU Twin-Ball Fire Fighting Unit [*Navy*] (DNAB)
TBFX Tube Fixture [*Tool*] (AAG)
TBG Tabubil [*Papua New Guinea*] [*Airport symbol*] (OAG)
TBG Testosterone-Binding Globulin [*Endocrinology*]
TBG Teubners Bibliotheca Scriptorum Graecorum et Romanorum (BJA)
TBG Thyroglobulin [*Endocrinology*] (DAVI)
TBG Thyroxine-Binding Globulin [*Biochemistry*]
TBG Thyssen-Bornemisza Group NV [*Netherlands*]
TBG Tidy Britain Group [*An association*] (EAIO)
TBG Tipping Bucket Gauge (NOAA)
TBG Tubing (MSA)
TBGAA Travel by Government Automobile Authorized
TBG cap Thyroxine-Binding Capacity of Thyroxine-Binding Globulin Assays [*Endrocrinology*] (DAVI)
TBGP Tactical Bomb Group [*Air Force*]
TBGP Total Blood Granulocyte Pool [*Hematology*]
TBGR Tropical Botanical Garden and Research Institute [*India*]
TBGTA Travel by Government Transportation Authorized [*Military*] (AABC)
TBH Tablas [*Philippines*] [*Airport symbol*] (OAG)
TBH Technical Benzene Hexachloride [*Organic chemistry*]
TBH Test Bed Harness (MCD)
TBH Test Bench Harness (NG)
TBH Total Body Hematocrit [*Medicine*] (MAE)
TBH TourBase Hotel-/Unterkunftsdaten [*Jaeger-Verlag GmbH*] [*Germany Information service or system*] (CRD)
TBH Trinidad [*Brigand Hill*] [*Trinidad-Tobago*] [*Seismograph station code, US Geological Survey*] (SEIS)
TBH Trinity Air Bahamas [*ICAO designator*] (FAAC)
TBHB Trisbicyclo Thexabenzene [*Organic chemistry*]
TBHBA Tribromo(hydroxy)benzoic Acid [*Organic chemistry*]
TBHP Tertiary-Butylhydroperioxide [*Organic chemistry*]
TBHP Tertiary-Butyl Hydroperoxide [*Organic chemistry*]
TBHP Trihydroxybutyrophenone [*Antioxidant*] [*Organic chemistry*]
TBHQ Tertiary-Butylhydroquinone [*Also, MTBHQ*] [*Organic chemistry*]
TBI Target Bearing Indicator [*Military*]
TBI Teacher-Based Instruction (EDAC)
TBI Telecom Broadcasting, Inc. [*Oceanside, CA*] [*Telecommunications service*] (TSSD)
TBI Test Bed Installation (MCD)
TBI Test Bench Installation (NG)
TBI Thomson Business Information [*The Thomson Corp.*] [*Publishing*]
TBI Threaded Blind Insert
TBI Throttle Body Fuel Injection [*Automotive engineering*]
TBI Through-Bulkhead Initiator [*Military*] (MCD)
TBI Thyroxine-Binding Index [*Biochemistry*] (MAE)
TBI Time between Inspections [*Quality control*]
TBI Time, Bulb, Instantaneous [*Initials on certain Kodak cameras*]
TBI Tissue Banks International [*An association*] (EA)
TBI To Be Inactivated
TBI To Be Indicated (AIA)
TBI To Be Initiated (IAA)

TBI............. Toothbrushing Instruction [*Dentistry*] (DMAA)
TBI............. Total Body Irradiation [*Medicine*]
TBI............. Traditionally Black Institutions (EDAC)
TBI............. Traumatic Brain Injury [*Medicine*]
TBI............. Trinity Bible Institute, Ellendale, ND [*OCLC symbol*] (OCLC)
TBI............. Tromboni [*Trombones*]
TBI............. Tubuai [*Tubuai Islands*] [*Seismograph station code, US Geological Survey*] (SEIS)
TBIFC.......... Thom Bierdz International Fan Club (EA)
TbIG............ Terbium Iron Garnet (IEEE)
TBII............ [*TSH*] Thyroid-stimulating hormone Binding Inhibitory Immunoglobulin [*Endocrinology*] (DAVI)
TBII............ Thyrotropin-Binding Inhibitor Immunoglobulin
TBIL............ Total Bilirubin [*Clinical chemistry*]
T Bili.......... Total Bilirubin [*Clinical chemistry*] (MAE)
T-bill.......... Treasury Bill (TDOB)
TBIP............ Tomahawk Baseline Improvement Program (DOMA)
TBIRD.......... Terrestrial Background Infrared Detection (SAA)
T-BIRD......... Terrestrial Ballistic Infrared Development (SAA)
T (Bird)....... Thunderbird [*Automobile*] (DSUE)
TBIS............ Technology Base Investment Strategy [*Army*]
TBIT............ Telebit Corp. [*NASDAQ symbol*] (SAG)
TBJ............. Turbulent Bounded Jet
TBK............. TEFLON Bonding Kit
TBK............. Tolland Bank [*AMEX symbol*] (SPSG)
TBK............. ToolBook [*Computer format*] (PCM)
TBK............. Total Body Potassium [*Clinical chemistry*]
T/BKL.......... Turn Buckle [*Automotive engineering*]
TBL............. [*The*] Berline, Berlin-Brandenburgisches Luftfahrtunternehmen GmbH [*Germany ICAO designator*] (FAAC)
TBL............. Tabele [*Papua New Guinea*] [*Seismograph station code, US Geological Survey*] (SEIS)
TBL............. Table
TBL............. Table
TBL............. Tableland [*Western Australia*] [*Airport symbol*] (AD)
tbl.............. Tablespoon [*Measurement*] (DAVI)
TBL............. Tactical Bomb Line (NVT)
TBL............. [*The*] Tamarind Book of Lithography
TBL............. Tasmanian Baseball League [*Australia*]
TBL............. Terminal Ballistics Laboratory [*Army*]
TBL............. Thin Base Laminate
TBL............. Thomas Branigan Memorial Library, Las Cruces, NM [*OCLC symbol*] (OCLC)
TBL............. Through Back of Loop [*Knitting*]
TBL............. Through Bill of Lading [*Shipping*]
TBL............. Timberland Co. [*NYSE symbol*] (SPSG)
TBL............. Timberland Co. Cl'A' [*NYSE symbol*] (TTSB)
TBL............. Tombill Mines Ltd. [*Toronto Stock Exchange symbol*]
TBL............. Tootal Broadhurst Lee [*Textile testing*] [*Obsolete*]
TBL............. Trouble [*Telecommunications*] (TEL)
TBL............. True Blood Loss
TBL............. Turbulent Boundary Layer
TBLB........... Transbronchial Lung Biopsy [*Medicine*] (DMAA)
TBLB........... Transbronchial Lung Brush [*Medicine*] (DAVI)
TBLC........... Term Birth, Living Child [*Medicine*]
TBLE........... Top Blacks in Law Enforcement [*Later, BLE*] (EA)
TBLE........... Trouble (IAA)
TBLI............ Term Birth, Living Infant [*Obstetrics*] (DAVI)
T/BLK.......... Terminal Block [*Automotive engineering*]
TBLN........... Tracheobronchial Lymph Node [*Anatomy*]
TBLR........... Tumbler (MSA)
TBLS........... Trail Blazer Library System [*Library network*]
TBLSP......... Tablespoon
TBM............ Morgan StanGp 6% Telebras'PERQS' [*AMEX symbol*] (TTSB)
TBM............ School of Aerospace Medicine, Brooks AFB, TX [*OCLC symbol*] (OCLC)
TBM............ Tactical Ballistic Missile [*Military*] (CAAL)
TBM............ Tax Board Memorandum [*Internal Revenue Bulletin*] [*United States*] [*A publication*] (DLA)
TBM............ TBM NT Corp. [*Toronto Stock Exchange symbol*]
TBM............ Tell Beit Mirsim (BJA)
TBM............ Temporary Bench Mark
TBM............ TeraBIT [*Binary Digit*] Memory [*Computer science*]
TBM............ Terrestrial Biogeochemical Model [*for climate effects*]
TBM............ Tertiary Butyl Mercaptan [*Organic chemistry*]
TBM............ Theater Ballistic Missile
TBM............ Theater Battle Model (MCD)
TBM............ Tone Burst Modulation
TBM............ Trailokya Bauddha Mahasangha [*Friends of the Western Buddhist Order*] [*British*] (EAIO)
TBM............ Treasury Board Manual [*Canada*] (AAGC)
TBM............ Trophoblastic Basement Membrane (PDAA)
TBM............ Tuberculous Meningitis [*Medicine*]
TBM............ Tubular Basement Membrane
TBM............ Tunnel Boring Machine
TBMA.......... Textile Bag Manufacturers Association (EA)
TBMA.......... Timber and Building Materials Association [*New South Wales, Australia*]
TBMAA........ Travel by Military Aircraft Authorized
TBMAC........ Tributylmethylammonium Chloride [*Organic chemistry*]
TBMC.......... Test Bed Mode Control
TBMD.......... Tactical Ballistic Missile Defense (DOMA)
TBMD.......... Terminal Ballistic Missile Defense [*Army*] (AABC)
TBMD.......... Theater Ballistic Missile Defense (DOMA)
TBMN.......... Thin Basement Membrane Nephropathy [*Medicine*] (DMAA)
TBMO.......... Test Base Material Operation (AAG)
T B Mon....... T. B. Monroe's Kentucky Supreme Court Reports [*17-23 Kentucky*] [*1824-28*] [*A publication*] (DLA)
T B Mon (KY)... T. B. Monroe's Kentucky Reports [*17-23 Kentucky*] [*A publication*] (DLA)
TBMOS........ TeraBIT Memory Operating System (NOAA)
TBMS.......... Text-Based Management Systems [*Computer science*]
TBMSG........ Trailokya Bauddha Mahasangha Sahayaka Gana [*Friends of the Western Buddhist Order*] [*British*] (EAIO)
TBMT.......... Transmitter Buffer Empty [*Computer science*]
TBMU.......... Transitional Butterworth Modified Ultraspherical Filter (PDAA)
TBMX.......... Tactical Ballistic Missile Experiment
TBN............ Bacillus Emulsion [*Medicine*] (DAVI)
TBN............ Banker's Note [*AMEX symbol*] (SAG)
TBN............ Fort Leonard Wood [*Missouri*] [*Airport symbol*] (OAG)
TBN............ Tertiary-Butylnaphthalene [*Organic chemistry*]
TBN............ Tetrabenzonaphthalene [*Organic chemistry*]
TBN............ The Baseball Network
TBN............ Titratable Base Number [*Analytical chemistry*]
TBN............ To Be Negotiated (NASA)
TBN............ To Be Nominated
TBN............ Total Base Number [*Automotive engineering*]
TBN............ Total Body Nitrogen [*Medicine*] (DMAA)
TBN............ Traveling Businesswomen's Network (EA)
TBN............ Trinity Broadcasting Network [*Cable-television system*]
TBN............ Turbine Helicopters Ltd. [*British*] [*FAA designator*] (FAAC)
TBNA.......... Total Body Neutron Activation (AAMN)
TBNA.......... Transbronchial Needle Aspiration [*Medicine*] (DMAA)
TBNA.......... Treated but Not Admitted [*Medicine*]
TBNAA........ Total Body Neutron Activation Analysis
TBN.EC....... Banker's Note [*ECM Symbol*] (TTSB)
TBNHL........ Tippecanoe Battleground National Historical Landmark (EA)
Tbnl............ Tribunal
tbnle........... Tabernacle (VRA)
TBO............ Tabora [*Tanzania*] [*Airport symbol*] (OAG)
TBO............ Thermal Bakeout
TBO............ Time Between Oil Changes [*Automotive servicing*]
TBO............ Time between Overhauls [*of engine, or other equipment*]
TBO............ Total Blackout (IIA)
TBO............ Total Blood Out [*Medicine*] (DMAA)
TBO............ TourBase Ortsdaten [*Jaeger-Verlag GmbH*] [*Germany Information service or system*] (CRD)
TBO............ Transactions by Others [*Military*]
TBO............ Tropical Biennial Oscillation [*Climatology*]
TBOA.......... T-18 Builders and Owners Association (EA)
TBOA.......... Tuna Boat Owners' Association [*Defunct*] (EA)
TBOAA........ Tuna Boat Owners' Association of Australia
TBOASA...... Tuna Boat Owners' Association of South Australia
t-Boc........... Butoxycarbonyl [*or t-BOC*] [*Biochemistry*]
t-BOC.......... tert-Butyloxycarbonyl [*Also, t-Boc*] [*Organic chemistry*]
TBOI........... Tentative Basis of Issue [*Army*] (AABC)
TBOIP......... Tentative Basis of Issue Plan [*Army*] (AABC)
TBOIPFD..... Tentative Basis of Issue Plan Feedback Data [*Army*]
TBoIMH....... Western Mental Health Institute, Boliver, TN [*Library symbol Library of Congress*] (LCLS)
TBON.......... [*The*] Bank of Nashville [*NASDAQ symbol*] (NQ)
TBOS.......... Tracer Burst Obscuration System [*Weaponry simulation*] [*Military*] (INF)
TBP............ Bithionol [*A Bacteriostatic*] [*Pharmacology*] (DAVI)
TBP............ Tab Products [*AMEX symbol*] (TTSB)
TBP............ Tab Products Co. [*AMEX symbol*] (SPSG)
TbP............ Tampa Blue Print Co., Tampa, FL [*Library symbol Library of Congress*] (LCLS)
TBP............ Target Benefit Plan [*Human resources*] (WYGK)
TBP............ TATA Box-Binding Protein (DOG)
TBP............ Tat-Binding Protein [*Genetics*]
TBP............ Tau Beta Pi Association
TBP............ Tertiary Butyl Phosphine [*Organic chemistry*]
TBP............ Testosterone-Binding Protein [*Endocrinology*] (MAE)
TBP............ Tethered Buoyed Platform [*Petroleum engineering*]
TBP............ Tetraphenylboron [*Analytical chemistry*]
TBP............ Thiobisdichlorophenol [*Pharmacology*]
TBP............ Thyroxine-Binding Protein [*Biochemistry*]
TBP............ Timing Belt Pulley
TBP............ To Be Planned (MCD)
TBP............ To Be Provided (NASA)
TBP............ To be Published
TBP............ Trainable Bow Propeller
TBP............ Tributyl Phosphate [*Organic chemistry*]
TBP............ Tributyl Phosphine [*Organic chemistry*]
TBP............ Trigonal Bipyramidal [*Geometry of molecular structure*]
TBP............ True Boiling Point
TBP............ Tuberculous Peritonitis [*Medicine*] (DAVI)
TBP............ Tumbes [*Peru*] [*Airport symbol*] (OAG)
TBP............ Twisted Bonded Pair
TBP............ Two-Body Problem
TBPA.......... Tetrabromophthalic Anhydride [*Flame retardant*] [*Organic chemistry*]
TBPA.......... Textile Bag and Packaging Association (EA)
TBPA.......... Thyroxine-Binding Prealbumin [*Biochemistry*]
TBPA.......... Torso Back Protective Armor (PDAA)
TBPA.......... Transatlantic Brides and Parents Association (EA)
TBPB.......... Bridgetown/Grantley Adams Internacional [*Barbados*] [*ICAO location identifier*] (ICLI)
TBPB.......... Tertiary-Butyl Perbenzoate [*Organic chemistry*]
TBPC.......... Tertbutyl-P-Cresol (DICI)

TBPC Text-Books of Physical Chemistry [*A publication*]
TBPH Tetrabutylperoxyhydroxide [*Organic chemistry*]
TBPI Thigh Brachial Pressure Index
TBPO Bridgetown [*Barbados*] [*ICAO location identifier*] (ICLI)
TBPS Terabits per Second (EECA)
TBPS Tert-Butylbicyclophosphorothionate [*Biochemistry*]
TBPT Total Body Protein Turnover [*Medicine*] (DMAA)
TBPU To Be Picked Up [*Postal service marking*] [*British*]
TBQ Addison, TX [*Location identifier FAA*] (FAAL)
TBR Advisory Tax Board Recommendation [*Internal Revenue Bureau*] [*United States*] [*A publication*] (DLA)
TBR Statesboro, GA [*Location identifier FAA*] (FAAL)
TBR Table Base Register
TBR Table Rock [*New York*] [*Seismograph station code, US Geological Survey*] (SEIS)
TBR Telecommunicacoes Brasileiras SA Telebras [*NYSE symbol*] (SAG)
TBR Telecomun Brasil-Telbras ADS [*NYSE symbol*] (TTSB)
TBR Temporary Base Register [*Computer science*] (IAA)
TBR Test of Behavioral Rigidity [*Psychology*]
TBR Tilt Board Reach [*Test*] [*Occupational therapy*]
TBR To be Released (SAA)
TBR To be Resolved (SSD)
TBR Torpedo Bomber Reconnaissance Aircraft [*Navy*]
TBR Total Bed Rest [*Medicine*] (MEDA)
TBR Total Bilirubin [*Gastroenterology*] (DAVI)
TBR Training Base Review (MCD)
TBR Treasury Bill Rate (MHDW)
TBR Trickle Bed Reactor [*Chemical engineering*]
TBR Tubelair [*Tunisia*] [*FAA designator*] (FAAC)
TBR Tumor-Bearing Rabbit Serum [*Immunology*]
TBR Turbo Resources Ltd. [*Toronto Stock Exchange symbol*]
TBRC Time-Based Recurring Cost
TBRC Top-Blown Rotary Converter [*Nonferrous metallurgy*]
TB-RD Tuberculosis - Respiratory Disease (MAE)
TBRG Thomson Book/Reference Group [*The Thomson Corp.*] [*Publishing*]
TBRI Technical Book Review Index
TBriH Bristol Memorial Hospital, Bristol, TN [*Library symbol Library of Congress*] (LCLS)
TBriK King College, Bristol, TN [*Library symbol Library of Congress*] (LCLS)
TBRL Timber Lodge Steakhouse [*NASDAQ symbol*] (TTSB)
TBRL Timber Lodge Steakhouse, Inc. [*NASDAQ symbol*] (SAG)
TBroH Haywood Park General Hospital, Brownsville, TN [*Library symbol Library of Congress*] (LCLS)
TBRV Tomato Black Ring Virus [*Plant pathology*]
TBS [*The*] Buddhist Society [*British*] (EAIO)
TBS Sir Thomas Beecham Society (EA)
TBS Tablespoon
TBS Tactical Bomb Squadron [*Air Force*]
TBS Talk-between-Ships [*which are tactically maneuvering; also, the VHF radio equipment used for this purpose*]
TBS Tall Building Syndrome
TBS Tape and Buffer System [*Computer science*]
TBS Tapered Bearing Simulator [*Lubricant testing*]
TBS Task Breakdown Structure (NASA)
TBS Taut Band Suspension (IAA)
TBS Tbilisi [*Former USSR Airport symbol*] (OAG)
TBS Temple, Barker & Sloane, Inc. [*Lexington, MA*] [*Telecommunications service*] (TSSD)
TBS Tensile Bond Strength [*Materials science*]
TBS Terminal Business System [*Computer science*] (IAA)
TBS Tertiary-Butyldimethylsilyl [*Also, TBDMS, TBDPS*] [*Organic chemistry*]
TBS Tertiary Butylphenyl Salicylate [*Food packaging*]
TBS Tertiary-Butylstyrene [*Organic chemistry*]
TBS Test Bench Set (MCD)
TBS Tetrapropylene Alkylbenesulfonate [*Surfactant*] [*Organic chemistry*]
TBS Text-Books of Science [*A publication*]
TBS #The Basic School [*Marine Corps*] (DOMA)
TBS Theta-Burst Stimulation [*Neurophysiology*]
TBS Tight Building Syndrome [*Air quality*]
TBS Tired Bureaucrat Syndrome
TBS Tobacco Black-Shank Nematode [*Plant pathology*]
TBS To Be Selected (KSC)
TBS To Be Specified (NASA)
TBS To Be Superseded (NASA)
TBS To Be Supplied (KSC)
TBS Tokyo Broadcasting System
TBS Toronto Baptist Seminary
TBS Toronto Board of Education, Secondary Schools [*UTLAS symbol*]
TBS Torsion Bar Spring [*Automotive engineering*]
TBS Total Body Solute [*Biochemistry*]
TBS Total Body Surface [*Medicine*]
TBS Total Burn Size [*Medicine*] (DMAA)
TBS Training and Battle Simulation [*SAGE*]
TBS Translator Bail Switch
TBS Treasury Board Secretariat [*Canada*]
TBS Tribromosalicylanilide [*or Tribromsalan*] [*Organic chemistry*]
TBS Triethanolamine-Buffered Saline [*Organic chemistry*] (MAE)
TBS Trinitarian Bible Society [*British*]
TBS TRIS-Buffered Saline [*Solution*]
TBS Tubeshaft (DS)
TBS Turbine Bypass System [*Nuclear energy*] (NRCH)
TBS Turner Broadcasting System, Inc. [*AMEX symbol*] (SPSG)
TBS Turner Broadcasting Systems (NITA)
TBSA Total Body Surface Area [*Medicine*]
TBSA Total Burn Surface Area (DAVI)
TBSA Total Serum Bile Acid [*Clinical chemistry*]
TBSA TRIS-Buffered Saline Azide [*Culture media*]
TBS.A Turner Broadcast'A' [*AMEX symbol*] (TTSB)
TBS.B Turner Broadcast'B' [*AMEX symbol*] (TTSB)
TBSCCW Turbine Building Secondary Closed Cooling Water [*Nuclear energy*] (NRCH)
TBSCl Tertiary-Butyldimethylsilyl Chloride [*Also, TBDMSCl*] [*Organic chemistry*]
TBSG Test Base Support Group (AAG)
TBSM Tributylstannylmaleate [*Organic chemistry*]
TBSP Tablespoon
tbsp Tablespoonful (ODBW)
TBSR Total Business System Review (AAGC)
TBST'G Troubleshooting
TBSV Time between Scheduled Visits (MCD)
TBSV Tomato Bushy Stunt Virus
TBT Mid American Baptist Theological Seminary, Memphis, TN [*OCLC symbol*] (OCLC)
TBT Tabatinga [*Brazil*] [*Airport symbol*] (OAG)
TBT Taburiente [*Canary Islands*] [*Seismograph station code, US Geological Survey*] (SEIS)
TBT Target Bearing Transmitter
TBT Tax-Benefit Transfer (WGA)
TBT Terminal Ballistic Track
TBT Tetrabutyl Titanate [*Organic chemistry*]
TBT Thallium Beam Tube
TBT Tilt Board Tip [*Test*] [*Occupational therapy*]
TBT Tolbutamide - Tolerance Test [*Clinical chemistry*] (MAE)
TBT Tracheobronchial Toilet [*Medicine*] (MAE)
TBT Transitional Butterworth Thomson (IAA)
TBT Tributyltin [*Antimicrobial agent*]
TBT Tributyl Tin [*Chemical*] (EERA)
TBT Tulsa Ballet Theatre
TBTA Thames Boating Trades' Association [*British*] (BI)
TBTC Transportable Blood Transfusion Shipment Center (DWSG)
TBTD Tetrabutylthiuram Disulfide [*Organic chemistry*]
TBTF Tributyltin Fluoride [*Antimicrobial agent*]
TBTH Tributyltin Hydride [*Organic chemistry*]
TBTNR Toronto Biculture Test of Nonverbal Reasoning [*Speech and language therapy*] (DAVI)
TBTO Tributyltin Oxide [*Organic chemistry*]
TBTP Tributyl Trithiophosphate [*Defoliant*] [*Organic chemistry*]
TBTS Tributyltin Sulfide [*Organic chemistry*]
TBTT Tuberculin Time Test [*Medicine*] (DMAA)
TBTU Tributylthiourea [*Organic chemistry*]
TBU Telemetry Buffer Unit (SSD)
TBU Terminal Buffer Unit [*Telecommunications*] (TEL)
TBU Test Before Using (MCD)
TBU Time Base Unit
TBU Tongatapu [*Tonga Island*] [*Airport symbol*] (OAG)
TBU Transitional Butterworth Ultraspherical Filter (PDAA)
TBUD Team Rental Group [*NASDAQ symbol*] (SAG)
TBUD Team Rental Group'A' [*NQS*] (TTSB)
TBUP Tributylphosphine [*Organic chemistry*]
TBUS Digital Recorders [*NASDAQ symbol*] (TTSB)
TBUS Digital Recorders, Inc. [*NASDAQ symbol*] (SAG)
TBUSW Digital Recorders Wrrt [*NASDAQ symbol*] (TTSB)
TBV Thermal Bypass Valve
TBV Total Blood Volume [*Physiology*]
TBV Trabecular Bone Volume
TBV Transluminal Balloon Valvuloplasty [*Cardiology*] (DAVI)
TBV Tubercle Bacillus Vaccine [*Medicine*]
TBV Tulip Breaking Virus [*Plant pathology*]
TBV Turbine Building Ventilation [*Nuclear energy*] (NRCH)
TBVD Torsional-Bending Vibration Damper [*Mechanical engineering*]
TBVE Two-Point Boundary Value Equation [*Mathematics*]
TB-Vis Isoniazid [*An Antibacterial*] [*Pharmacology*] (DAVI)
TBV$_P$ Total Blood Volume Predicted from Body Surface [*Physiology*] (MAH)
TBW [*The*] Business World [*A publication*]
TBW Tampa Bay-Ruskin, FL [*Location identifier FAA*] (FAAL)
TBW T B Wood's [*NYSE symbol*] (TTSB)
TBW TB Woods Corp. [*NYSE symbol*] (SAG)
TBW That Bloody Woman [*Nickname given to British Prime Minister Margaret Thatcher*]
TBW Time Band-Width (IAA)
TBW Titanium Butt Weld
TBW Tobacco Bud Worm [*Agronomy*]
TBW To Be Withheld
TBW Total Bandwidth
TBW Total Body Water [*Man*]
TBW Total Body Weight [*Medicine*]
TBW Tracking Band Width (MCD)
TBWCA Texas Barbed Wire Collectors Association (EA)
TBWEP Trial Boll Weevil Eradication Program [*Department of Agriculture*]
TBWG Tactical Bomb Wing [*Air Force*]
TBWO Tuned Backward Wave Oscillator
TB Wood TB Woods Corp. [*Associated Press*] (SAG)
TBWP Triple-Braid Weatherproof (IAA)
TBX Tactical Ballistic Missile, Experimental
TBX Tactical Range Ballistic Missile [*Military*] (IAA)
TBX Total Body Irradiation [*Radiation therapy*] (DAVI)
TBX$_2$ Thromboxane B_2 [*Hematology*] (DAVI)
TBY Oxford, CT [*Location identifier FAA*] (FAAL)
TBY TCBY Enterprises [*NYSE symbol*] (TTSB)

TBY TCBY Enterprises, Inc. [*NYSE symbol*] (CTT)
TBY Terrace Bay Resources [*Vancouver Stock Exchange symbol*]
Tbyte Terabyte [*Computer science*] (EERA)
TBZ Istanbul [*Trabzon*] [*Turkey*] [*Seismograph station code, US Geological Survey*] (SEIS)
TBZ Tabriz [*Iran*] [*Airport symbol*] (OAG)
TBZ Tetrabenazine [*Tranquilizer*]
TBZ Thiabendazole [*or Thiazolyl*] Benzimidazole [*Pesticide*]
TBZ Toy Biz'A' [*NYSE symbol*] (TTSB)
TBZ Toy Biz, Inc. [*NYSE symbol*] (SAG)
TC Air Tanzania [*ICAO designator*] (AD)
TC All India Reporter, Travancore-Cochin [*1950-57*] [*A publication*] (DLA)
TC Chattanooga-Hamilton County Bicentennial Library, Chattanooga, TN [*Library symbol Library of Congress*] (LCLS)
TC Cold Leg Temperature [*Nuclear energy*] (NRCH)
Tc Core Temperature [*Medicine*]
TC [*The*] Courier [*Code name for Robert W. Owen, participant in the Iran-Contra affair during the Reagan Administration*]
Tc Generation Time [*Laboratory Science*] (DAVI)
TC Neurotrauma Center [*Medicine*] (DAVI)
TC Order of the Trinity Cross [*Trinidad and Tobago*]
TC Table of Contents (IT)
TC Tablettes Cappadociennes [*Paris*] [*A publication*] (BJA)
TC Tabulating Card (AAG)
TC Tactical Command (NATG)
TC Tactical Communications [*Military*] (DWSG)
TC Tactical Computer (IEEE)
T/C Tactical Coordinator (NVT)
TC Tactile Communicator [*Device which aids the deaf by translating certain sounds into coded vibrations*]
TC Tag Code (NITA)
TC Tail Clamp
TC Talk[*ing*] Club
TC Tall Copy [*Publishing*] (DGA)
TC Tank Car
TC Tank Circuit (IAA)
TC Tank Commander (RDA)
TC Tank Company [*Military*] (MCD)
TC Tank Corps
TC Tantalum Capacitor (IEEE)
TC Tape Command
TC Tape Core
TC Target Cell [*Immunology*]
TC Target Concentration [*or Toxic*] (GNE)
TC Target Control (MCD)
TC Tariff Circular
TC Tariff Commission [*Later, International Trade Commission*]
TC Taurocholate [*Microbiology*] (MAE)
TC Tax Cases [*Legal*] [*British*]
TC Tax Certificate
TC Tax Code [*A publication*] (AAGC)
TC Tax Council (EA)
TC Tax Court [*of the United States*] [*Also, TCUS Later, United States Tax Court*]
TC Taxiway Centerline Lighting [*Aviation*] (DA)
TC Taxonomic Code (NITA)
TC Taxpayers' Committee [*Defunct*] (EA)
TC Taylorcraft [*ICAO aircraft manufacturer identifier*] (ICAO)
TC Tayu Center (EA)
TC T-Carrier [*Telecommunications*] (TEL)
TC Teachers' Centre (AIE)
TC Teacher's Certificate [*British*]
TC Teachers College
TC Tea Council of the United States of America (EA)
TC Teardown Compliance
Tc Technetium [*Chemical element*]
TC Technical Center [*Environmental Protection Agency*] (GFGA)
TC Technical Characteristics [*Military*] (AABC)
TC Technical Circular
TC Technical College
TC Technical Committee
TC Technical Communication
TC Technical Control (MSA)
TC Technical Cooperation
TC Technical Corrigendum [*Correction*] (OSI)
TC Technically Classified (BARN)
TC Technician's Certificate [*British*] (DI)
TC Technicolor (KSC)
TC Tekakwitha Conference National Center [*Later, TCNC*] (EA)
T/C Telecine
TC Telecommunications
TC Telecommunications Counselor [*Voice & Data Resources, Inc.*] [*Information service or system Defunct*] (IID)
TC TeleCommuting Report [*Electronic Services Unlimited*] [*Information service or system*] (CRD)
TC Telecomputing Corp. (IAA)
TC Telefunken Computer AG (IAA)
TC Telephone Center (IAA)
TC Telephone Central Office (IAA)
TC Telescoping Collar (OA)
TC Temperament Comparator [*Psychology*]
TC Temperature Capability
TC Temperature Change [*Refrigeration*]
TC Temperature Coefficient
TC Temperature Compensating (MSA)
TC Temperature Control
TC Temperature Controller [*Nuclear energy*] (NRCH)
TC Temperature in Degrees Centigrade (IAA)
TC Temple Classics [*A publication*]
TC Temporary Chaplain [*British military*] (DMA)
TC Temporary Constable
TC Temporary Correction
TC Tennessee Central Railway Co. [*AAR code*]
TC Tennis Club
TC Teracycle
TC Terciarios Capuchinos de Nostra Signora de los Dolores [*Tertiary Capuchins of Our Lady of Sorrows*] [*Italy*] (EAIO)
TC Term Coordination (NITA)
TC Terminal Computer (BUR)
TC Terminal Concentrator
TC Terminal Congestion [*Telecommunications*] (TEL)
TC Terminal Control (NITA)
TC Terminal Controller
TC Terminating Contracting Officer (AAGC)
T/C Termination Check [*NASA*] (NASA)
T/C Termination for Convenience [*DoD*]
TC Terra Cotta [*Technical drawings*]
TC Terrain Clearance [*Military*] (NG)
TC Terrain Correlation (MCD)
TC Test Case Specification (IAA)
TC Test Chief
TC Test Collection [*Educational Testing Service*] [*Information service or system*] (IID)
TC Test Conductor (AAG)
TC Test Console
TC Test Controller
TC Test Coordinator
TC Testing Complete (CAAL)
TC Tetracycline [*Antibiotic compound*]
TC Tetrahedral Cubic [*Metallography*]
TC Texas Central Railroad Co.
TC Thai Capital Fund [*NYSE symbol*] (TTSB)
TC Thai Capital Fund, Inc. [*NYSE symbol*] (SPSG)
TC Thames Conservancy [*British*] (BI)
TC Therapeutic Concentration [*Pharmacology*]
TC Thermal Conductivity
TC Thermal Control (KSC)
TC Thermal Cracker [*Chemical engineering*]
TC Thermal Cutting [*Welding*]
TC Thermocouple
TC Thermocurrent (IEEE)
TC Thickness Chord Wing [*Aviation*] (AIA)
TC Thinking Cap [*Layman's term for neocortex*]
TC Thomas C. Calvin [*Character in TV series "Magnum, P.I."*]
TC Thoracic Cage [*Medicine*]
TC Thread Cutting (MSA)
TC Threshold Circuit [*Telecommunications*] (OA)
TC Throat Culture [*Clinical chemistry*]
TC Thrust Chamber [*Air Force, NASA*]
TC Thyrocalcitonin [*Endocrinology*] (MAE)
TC Tical [*Monetary unit in Thailand*]
TC Tidal Constants [*Marine science*] (MSC)
TC Tie Connector (MCD)
TC Tierce [*Unit of measurement*]
TC Till Cancelled [*Press advertisements*] (DGA)
T/C Till Counterbalanced
TC Till Countermanded
TC Tilt Covered [*Truck*] (DCTA)
Tc Time Called [*Baseball*]
TC Time Certificate of Deposit [*Banking*]
T/C Time Charter [*Shipping*]
TC Time Check
TC Time Clock
TC Time Closing (MSA)
TC Time Code (NTCM)
TC Time Compensation
TC Time Compression [*Computer science*] (IAA)
TC Time Constant (MSA)
TC Time-Constrained [*Computer science*]
TC Time Controlled [*Computer science*] (IAA)
TC Time to Circular (MCD)
TC Time to Computation
TC Timing Channel
TC Timing Cover Gasket [*Automotive engineering*]
TC Tinned Copper
TC Tissue Culture [*Microbiology*]
TC Title Card (NTCM)
TC Tobramycin-Clindamycin [*Antibiotic compound*]
T/C To Consider (DAVI)
TC To Contain [*Pipet calibration*]
TC Today's Computers [*A publication*]
TC Togoland Congress [*Ghana*] [*Political party*]
TC Toilet Case (MSA)
TC Toll Center [*Telecommunications*]
TC Toll Completing [*Telecommunications*]
TC Toluene-Cellosolve [*Scintillation solvent*]
TC Tone Control [*Telecommunications*] (IAA)
TC Top Cap (IAA)
TC Top Carnivore

TC .... Top Cat [*Cartoon character*]
TC .... Top Center [*Valve position*]
TC .... Top Chord
TC .... Top Contact [*Valve*] (DEN)
T/C .... Top-of-Climb (GAVI)
TC .... Top of Column
TC .... Topographic Center [*Defense Mapping Agency*]
TC .... Torpedo Control [*British military*] (DMA)
TC .... Torpedo Coxswain [*British military*] (DMA)
TC .... Total Capacity [*Lung*]
TC .... Total Carbon
TC .... Total Chances
TC .... Total Cholesterol [*Medicine*]
TC .... Total Colonoscopy [*Proctoscopy*]
TC .... Total Control (PCM)
TC .... Total Cost
TC .... Touring Club
TC .... Towed Cable [*Telecommunications*] (IAA)
Tc .... Towing Chock [*Shipfitting*]
TC .... Town Clerk [*or Councillor*]
TC .... Toxicity Characteristic [*Environmental Protection Agency*]
TC .... Traceability Code (NASA)
TC .... Track Circuit (DCTA)
TC .... Track Commander [*Army*] (INF)
TC .... Tracking Camera
TC .... Tracking Console
TC .... Trade Cases [*Commerce Clearing House*] [*A publication*] (DLA)
TC .... Traffic Collision
TC .... Traffic Commissioner [*or Consultant*]
TC .... Traffic Consultant (WGA)
TC .... Traffic Controller (CAAL)
TC .... Training Center [*Military*]
TC .... Training Chest [*Emergency parachute*]
TC .... Training Circular [*Military*]
TC .... Training Command (AAG)
TC .... Training Corps [*British military*] (DMA)
TC .... Transaction Code [*Military*]
TC .... Transceiver Code [*Navy*]
TC .... Transcobalamin [*Biochemistry*]
TC .... Transcontinental (DOAD)
TC .... Transcutaneous
TC .... Transfer Canal [*Nuclear energy*] (NRCH)
TC .... Transfer Clerk
TC .... Transfer Control [*or Controller*] (HGAA)
TC .... Transfer Count (MHDB)
TC .... Transistorized Carrier
TC .... Transit Canal (NVT)
TC .... Transitional Control (IAA)
TC .... Translation Controller
TC .... Transmission Control [*Telecommunications*] (IAA)
TC .... Transmission Controller
TC .... Transmitter Controller [*Electronics*] (ECII)
TC .... Transmitter Tuning Circuit [*Telecommunications*] (IAA)
TC .... Transmitting Circuit [*Telecommunications*] (OA)
TC .... Transpersonal Consciousness [*Parapsychology*]
TC .... Transponder Component (MCD)
TC .... Transport and Communications [*Department of Employment*] [*British*]
TC .... Transportation Corps [*Military*]
TC .... Transport Canada [*Government regulatory agency*]
TC .... Transport Cargo (NATG)
TC .... Transport Combine [*Combined Transport*] [*French Business term*]
TC .... Transport Command [*British military*] (DMA)
TC .... Transporte Combinado [*Combined Transport*] [*Spanish Business term*]
TC .... Transporto Combinato [*Combined Transport*] [*Italian Business term*]
TC .... Transvaal Cadets [*British military*] (DMA)
TC .... Travellers Cheque [*British*] (ADA)
TC .... Treacher Collins Syndrome [*Medicine*] (DMAA)
TC .... Treasury Circular
T/C .... Treated Versus Cured [*Medicine*]
T/C .... Treatment Charge [*Metallurgy*]
TC .... Treatment Code (NITA)
TC .... Treatment Completed [*Medicine*] (MEDA)
TC .... Tre Corde [*With Three Strings, or Release the Soft Pedal*] [*Music*]
TC .... Trial Counsel [*Military*]
TC .... Tribology Centre [*British*]
TC .... Tribunal des Conflits [*Tribunal of Conflicts*] [*French*] (ILCA)
TC .... Tricuspid Closure [*Cardiology*]
TC .... Tricycle Club [*British*]
TC .... Triennial Cycle (BJA)
TC .... Trilateral Commission (EA)
TC .... Trim Coil (AAG)
TC .... Trip Cell (IAA)
TC .... Trip Coil
TC .... Triplet Connection (EA)
TC .... Triton Corp. (EA)
TC .... Troop Carrier [*Air Force*]
TC .... Tropical Continental [*American air mass*]
TC .... Tropical Cyclone (ADA)
TC .... Tropocollagen [*Genetics*] (DAVI)
TC .... Truck Commander [*Military*] (INF)
TC .... True Color (CDE)
T/C .... True Complement
TC .... True Conjugate [*Ophthalmology*] (DAVI)
TC .... True Course
TC .... Truncated Cone [*Golf balls*]
TC .... Trunk Control
TC .... Trusteeship Council [*of the United Nations*]
T/C .... Trust or Complement (MHDI)
TC .... Tuberculosis, Contagious [*Medicine*] (AAMN)
TC .... Tubing Connector [*Instrumentation*]
TC .... Tubocurarine [*Muscle relaxant*]
TC .... Tuned Circuit [*Telecommunications*] (IAA)
TC .... Tungsten Carbide (IAA)
TC .... Turbocharger [*Automotive engineering*]
TC .... Turf Course [*Horse racing*]
TC .... Turkey Coryza [*Pathology*]
tc .... Turks and Caicos Islands [*MARC country of publication code Library of Congress*] (LCCP)
TC .... Turks and Caicos Islands [*ANSI two-letter standard code*] (CNC)
TC .... Turn-Cock (ROG)
TC .... Turning Circle [*Automotive engineering*]
TC .... Turnip Crinkle Virus
TC .... Turret Captain [*Navy*]
TC .... [*The*] Twentieth Century New Testament [*A publication*] (BJA)
TC .... Twin Camshaft [*Automotive engineering*]
TC .... Twin Carburetor [*Automotive engineering*]
TC .... Two Cycle [*Mechanics*]
TC .... Type and Crossmatch [*of blood*]
TC .... Type Certificate
TC .... Type Classification
TC .... United States Tax Court Cases [*A publication*] (DLA)
TC .... United States Tax Court Reporters [*A publication*] (AAGC)
TC3 .... Telecommunications, Command, Control, and Computer System
Tc-99 .... Technetium-99
TCA .... Adventist Network of Georgia, Cumberland Elementary Library, Collegedale, TN [*OCLC symbol*] (OCLC)
TCA .... Tactical Combat Aircraft (IEEE)
TCA .... Tactical Communications Area
TCA .... Tahiti Conquest Airlines [*France ICAO designator*] (FAAC)
TCA .... Tandem Club of America (EA)
TCA .... Tanner's Council of America [*Later, LIA*] (EA)
TCA .... Tanzer 22 Class Association (EA)
TCA .... Target Class Assignment
TCA .... Task Control Area (IAA)
TCA .... Tasmanian Canoe Association [*Australia*]
TCA .... Tasmanian Council on the Ageing [*Australia*]
TCA .... Tasmanian Croquet Association [*Australia*]
TCA .... Tattoo Club of America (EA)
TCA .... TCA Cable TV, Inc. [*Associated Press*] (SAG)
TCA .... Teach Cable Assembly [*Robot technology*]
TCA .... Teaching Curriculum Association [*A generic term; not the name of a specific organization*]
TCA .... Technical Change Analysis (MCD)
TCA .... Technical Contract Administrator
TCA .... Technical Cooperation Administration [*Transferred to Foreign Operations Administration, 1953*]
TCA .... Technician in Costing and Accounting [*British*] (DBQ)
TCA .... Tele-Communications Association (EA)
TCA .... Telecomputing Corporation of America (NITA)
TCA .... Telemarketing Corp. of America [*Phoenix, AZ*] (TSSD)
TCA .... Telemetering Control Assembly (AAG)
TCA .... Telephone Consultants of America [*Bergenfield, NJ*] [*Telecommunications*] (TSSD)
TCA .... Television Critics Association (EA)
TCA .... Tempelhof Central Airport [*West Berlin*]
TCA .... Temperance Collegiate Association [*British*] (AEBS)
TCA .... Temperature Control Amplifier (IAA)
TCA .... Temperature Control Assembly (KSC)
TCA .... Temperature-Controlled Animal
TCA .... Temporary Care Arrangement
TCA .... Ten Class Association (EA)
TCA .... Tennant Creek [*Australia Airport symbol*] (OAG)
TCA .... Tennessee Code Annotated [*A publication*]
TCA .... Terminal Cancer [*Medicine*]
TCA .... Terminal Carcinoma [*Oncology*] (DAVI)
TCA .... Terminal Communication Adapter
TCA .... Terminal Control Area [*Aviation*] (AFM)
TCA .... Tertiary Colleges Association [*British*] (DBA)
TCA .... Tetracyanoanthracene [*Organic chemistry*]
TCA .... Textile Converters Association (EA)
TCA .... Thalamocortical Axon [*Neurophysiology*]
TCA .... Theater Commander's Approval [*Military*]
TCA .... Therapeutic Communities of America (EA)
TCA .... Thermal Critical Assembly [*Nuclear energy*]
TCA .... Thermo Cardiosystems [*AMEX symbol*] (TTSB)
TCA .... Thermo Cardio Systems, Inc. [*AMEX symbol*] (SAG)
TCA .... Thermocentrifugometric Analysis [*Analytical chemistry*]
TCA .... Thiocarbanilide [*Organic chemistry*]
TCA .... Thistle Class Association (EA)
TCA .... Thoroughbred Club of America (EA)
TCA .... Thrust Chamber Assembly [*Missile technology*]
TCA .... Thyrocalcitonin [*Also, CT, TCT*] [*Endocrinology*]
TCA .... Tiger Cat Association [*Defunct*] (EA)
TCA .... Tile Council of America (EA)
TCA .... Tilt-Up Concrete Association (EA)
TCA .... Time of Closest Approach [*Aerospace*]
TCA .... Tissue Culture Association (EA)
TCA .... Tithe Commutation Act [*British*]
TCA .... To Come Again [*in a given number of days*] [*Medicine*]

TCA............ TOKAMAK [*Toroidal Kamera Magnetic*] Chauffage Alfven [*Plasma physics instrumentation*]
TCa............ Total Calcium [*Clinical chemistry*]
TCA............ Total Circulating Albumin [*Medicine*] (DMAA)
TCA............ Trace Contamination Analysis
TCA............ Track Continuity Area (NATG)
TCA............ Track Crossing Altitude [*or Attitude*]
TCA............ Track Crossing Angle
TCA............ Traffic Control Area [*Aviation*]
TCA............ Trailer Coach Association [*Later, Manufactured Housing Institute*] (EA)
TCA............ Train Collectors Association (EA)
TCA............ Trans-Canada Airlines [*Facetious translation: "Two Crashes Apiece"*]
TCA............ Trans-Caribbean Airways (IIA)
TCA............ Transcontinental Control Area [*Aviation*] (DA)
TCA............ Transfer Control A Register (SAA)
TCA............ Translation Controller Assembly (NASA)
TCA............ Transluminal Coronary Angioplasty [*Cardiology*]
TCA............ Transportation Corridor Agencies
TCA............ Travellers Cheque Association Ltd. [*British*]
TCA............ Tricalcium Aluminate [*Inorganic chemistry*] (MAE)
TCA............ Tricarboxylic Acid [*Cycle*] [*Biochemistry*]
TCA............ Trichloroacetate [*Organic chemistry*]
TCA............ Trichloroacetic Acid [*Also, TCAA*] [*Organic chemistry*]
TCA............ Trichloroanisole [*Organic chemistry*]
TCA............ Trichosanic Acid [*Biochemistry*]
TCA............ Tricuspid Atresia [*Cardiology*] (DAVI)
TCA............ Tricyclic Antidepressant [*Medicine*]
TCA............ Turbulent Contacting Absorber
TCA............ Turks and Caicos Islands [*ANSI three-letter standard code*] (CNC)
TCA............ Two Hundred Contemporary Authors [*A publication*]
TCA............ Typographic Communications Association (EA)
TCAA............ Tile Contractors' Association of America (EA)
TCAA............ Trichloroacetic Acid [*Also, TCA*] [*Organic chemistry*]
TCAA............ Trustee Companies' Association of Australia
TCAAP........ Twin Cities Army Ammunition Plant (AABC)
TCAB............ Temperature of Cabin [*Aerospace*] (MCD)
TCAB............ Tetrachloroazobenzene [*Organic chemistry*]
TCABG........ Triple Coronary Artery Bypass Graft [*Cardiology*]
TCAC............ Technical Committee on Agricultural Chemicals (EERA)
TCAC............ Technical Control and Analysis Center
TCAC............ Tone-Count Audiometric Computer (PDAA)
TC ACCIS..... Transportation Coordination [*or Coordinator*] Automated Command and ControlInformation System [*Military*]
TCAC-D........ Technical Control and Analysis Center - Division
TCAD............ Technology Computer-Aided Design [*Computer science*]
TCAD............ Traffic Alert and Collision Avoidance Device [*Aviation*] (DA)
TCAD............ Tricyclic Antidepressant [*Pharmacology*] (DAVI)
TCADS......... Truck Crash Analysis Data System [*FHWA*] (TAG)
TCAE............ Technical Control and Analysis Element (INF)
TCAF............ TEFLON-Coated Aluminum Foil
TCAI............ Tutorial Computer-Assisted Instruction (IEEE)
TC-AIMS...... Transportation Coordinator's Automated Information for Movement System (DOMA)
TCAL............ Tasmanian Council for Adult Literacy [*Australia*]
T-cal............ Thermal calibration (CDE)
TCAL............ Total Calorimeter (KSC)
T-Cal............ Triconix Control Application Language (NITA)
TCA LM........ Tele-Communications Class A [*Associated Press*] (SAG)
TCAM............ Telecommunications Access Method [*IBM Corp.*] [*Computer science*]
TCAM............ Telegraph Construction and Maintenance (IAA)
TCAM............ Thinking Creatively in Action and Movement [*Test*]
TCAM............ Transport Corp. Amer [*NASDAQ symbol*] (TTSB)
TCAM............ Transport Corp. of America, Inc. [*NASDAQ symbol*] (SAG)
TCaMH......... Smith County Memorial Hospital, Carthage, TN [*Library symbol Library of Congress*] (LCLS)
TCAM-IMS/VS... TCAM-Information Management System/Virtual Storage (NITA)
TC & DB........ Turn, Cough, and Deep Breathe [*Medicine*]
TC & M.......... Telemetry Control and Monitoring
TCAOB.......... Tetrachloroazoxybenzene [*Organic chemistry*]
T-CAP............ Baker's Antifol, Cyclophosphamide, Adriamycin, and Cisplatin [*Antineoplastic drug regimen*] (DAVI)
TCAP............ Tactical Channel Assignment Panel [*Military radio*]
T/CAP............ Thermal Capacitor (MCD)
TCAP............ Tricyanoaminopropene [*Organic chemistry*]
TCAP............ Trimethylcetylammonium Pentachlorphenate [*Organic chemistry*]
TCAPE.......... Truck Computer Analysis of Performance and Economy
TCAR............ T-Cell Antigen Receptor [*Medicine*] (DMAA)
TCARC.......... Tropical Cyclone Aircraft Reconnaissance Coordinator [*Navy*] (DNAB)
T-carrier system... Telecommunications Carrier System (NITA)
TCARS.......... Test Call Answer Relay Set (PDAA)
TCaS............ Smith County High School Library, Carthage, TN [*Library symbol Library of Congress*] (LCLS)
TCAS............ T-Carrier Administration System [*Minicomputer*] [*Bell System*]
TCAS............ Technical Control and Analysis System (MCD)
T/CAS............ Threat Alert Collision Avoidance System
TCAS............ Three Counties Agricultural Society [*British*]
TCAS............ Traffic Alert and Collision Avoidance System [*Aviation*]
TCASNY....... Turkish Cypriot Aid Society of New York (EA)
TCAT............ Tape-Controlled Automatic Testing
TCAT............ TCA Cable TV, Inc. [*NASDAQ symbol*] (NQ)
TCAT............ Test Coverage Analysis Tool (IEEE)
TCAT............ Thermal Catalyst Aging Tester [*Chemical engineering*]
TCAT............ Transmission Computer-Assisted Tomography [*Medicine*] (DAVI)
TCAT............ Type Commander Amphibious Training (DOMA)
TCATA.......... Textile Care Allied Trades Association (EA)
TCATA.......... TRADOC Combined Arms Test Activity [*Army*] (MCD)
TCATA.......... TRADOC [*Training and Doctrine Command*] Combined Arms Test Agency [*Army*]
TCAV............ Tennis Coaches' Association of Victoria [*Australia*]
TCAWA........ Tennis Coaches' Association of Western Australia
TCAX............ Trans Continental Air Transport [*Air carrier designation symbol*]
TCB............ [*The*] College Board (EA)
TCB............ [*The*] Computer Bulletin (IAA)
TCB............ [*The*] Conference Board (EA)
TCB............ Fort Worth, TX [*Location identifier FAA*] (FAAL)
TCB............ Take Care of Business [*Slang*]
TCB............ Taking Care of Business [*Brand name of Alberto-Culver Co.*]
TCB............ Tantalum Carbon Bond
TCB............ Tape Control Block [*Computer science*] (IAA)
TCB............ Target Control Box [*Army*]
TCB............ Task Control Block [*Computer science*]
TCB............ Task Force for Community Broadcasting (EA)
TCB............ Tasmanian Convention Bureau [*Australia*]
TCB............ Taylor-Carlisle Bookseller [*ACCORD*] [*UTLAS symbol*]
TCB............ TCF Financial [*NYSE symbol*] (TTSB)
TCB............ TCF Financial Corp. [*NYSE symbol*] (SAG)
TCB............ Teachers' Certification Board [*Australia*]
TCB............ Technical Coordinator Bulletin [*NASA*] (KSC)
TCB............ TEN Private Cable Systems, Inc. [*Vancouver Stock Exchange symbol*]
TCB............ Tent City Bravo [*Area near Tan Son Nhut Air Base, formerly site of USAR headquarters*]
TCB............ Terminal Control Block [*Computer science*] (OA)
TCB............ Tetrachlorobiphenyl [*Organic chemistry*]
TCB............ Themes Concerning Blacks [*Personality development test*] [*Psychology*]
TCB............ Thermal Compression Bond
TCB............ Time Correlation Buffer (MCD)
TCB............ Title Certificate Book [*A publication*] (DLA)
TCB............ TMIS [*Technical and Management Information System*] Control Board [*NASA*] (SSD)
TCB............ Total Cardiopulmonary Bypass [*Medicine*] (MAE)
TCB............ TOW [*Tube-Launched, Optically-Tracked, Wire-Guided Weapon*] Control Box (INF)
TCB............ Trans-Continental Freight Bureau, Chicago IL [*STAC*]
TCB............ Transfer Control Block
TCB............ Transporte del Caribe [*Colombia*] [*ICAO designator*] (FAAC)
TCB............ Treasure Cay [*Bahamas*] [*Airport symbol*] (OAG)
TCB............ Trichlorobenzene [*Organic chemistry*]
TCB............ Tropical Chocolate Bar [*Military issue*] (VNW)
TCB............ Trouble Came Back [*Computer hacker terminology*] (NHD)
TCB............ Truss Connector Bulletin [*Department of Housing and Urban Development*] [*A publication*] (GFGA)
TCB............ Trusted Computing Base
TCB............ Tulare County Free Library System, Visalia, CA [*OCLC symbol*] (OCLC)
TCB............ Tumor Cell Burden [*Oncology*]
TCBA............ Tesla Coil Builders Association (EA)
T-CBA............ Transfluxor, Constant Board Assembly (AAG)
TCBC............ Trichlorobenzyl Chloride [*Organic chemistry*]
TCBC............ Twin Cities Biomedical Consortium [*Library network*]
TCBCO.......... Thallium Calcium Barium Copper Oxide [*Inorganic chemistry*]
TCBCS.......... Blue Cross and Blue Shield of Tennessee, Chattanooga, TN [*Library symbol Library of Congress*] (LCLS)
TCBE............ Thermocompression Bonding Equipment
TCBEFC........ TCB [*Taking Care of Business*] for Elvis Fan Club (EA)
TCBG............ Training Centre Brigade of Gurkhas [*British military*] (DMA)
TCBH............ Time Consistent Busy Hour (NITA)
TCBHHA....... The Church of the Brethren Homes and Hospitals Association [*Later, BHOAM*] (EA)
TCBI............ Television Center for Business and Industry
TCBK............ Trico Bancshares [*NASDAQ symbol*] (SAG)
TCB LM........ Tele-Communications Class A [*Associated Press*] (SAG)
TCBM............ Time-Consistent Busy Hour [*Telecommunications*] (EECA)
TCBM............ Transcontinental Ballistic Missile [*Air Force*]
TCBO............ Trichlorobutylene Oxide [*Organic chemistry*]
TCBS............ Thiosulfate-Citrate-Bile Salt Sucrose [*Growth medium*]
TCBT............ [*The*] Circuit Board Thermometer [*Computer science*]
TCBV............ Temperature Coefficient of Breakdown Voltage
TCBY............ [*The*] Country's Best Yogurt [*Store franchise*]
TCBY............ TCBY Enterprises, Inc. [*Associated Press*] (SAG)
TCC............ AT&T Capital [*NYSE symbol*] (TTSB)
TCC............ AT & T Capital Corp. (SPSG)
TCC............ Capita Preferred Trust [*NYSE symbol*] (SAG)
TCC............ [*The*] Cesarean Connection (EA)
TCC............ [*The*] Coin Coalition (EA)
TCC............ [*The*] Cola Clan [*Later, Coca-Cola Collectors Club International*] (EA)
TCC............ [*The*] Comedy Channel
TCC............ [*The*] Computer Co. [*Information service or system*] (IID)
TcC............ [*The*] Computer Co., Richmond, VA [*Library symbol*] [*Library of Congress*] (LCLS)
TCC............ [*The*] Conservative Caucus (EA)
TCC............ [*The*] Creative Coalition
TCC............ [*The*] Curwood Collector [*A publication*] (EA)
TCC............ New Mexico Institute of Mining and Technology Computer Center [*Research center*] (RCD)
TCC............ Tactical Command Center (DOMA)
TCC............ Tactical Command Control (MCD)
TCC............ Tactical Communications Center

TCC............ Tactical Control Center [*Military*]

TCC............ Tactical Control Computer (AAG)

TCC............ Tactical Control Console (NATG)

TCC............ Tactics Certification Course [*Army*] (INF)

TCC............ Tag Closed Cup [*Flash point test*]

TCC............ Tagliabue Closed Cup [*Analytical chemistry*]

TCC............ Tank Car Committee [*RSPA*] (TAG)

TCC............ Tara Collectors Club (EA)

TCC............ Target Coordination Center

TCC............ Task Control Character (CMD)

TCC............ Tasmanian Cancer Committee [*Australia*]

TCC............ Tasmanian Chamber of Commerce [*Australia*]

TCC............ T-Cell Clone [*Cytology*]

TCC............ Teachers College of Connecticut

TCC............ Technical Change Centre [*British*] (CB)

TCC............ Technical Computing Center (IEEE)

TCC............ Technical Control Center

TCC............ Technological Change Committee (EERA)

TCC............ Technology Commercialization Center [*Minority Business Development Administration*]

TCC............ Telecommunications Center (CET)

TCC............ Telecommunications Consumer Coalition [*Defunct*] (EA)

TCC............ Telecommunications Coordinating Committee [*Department of State*]

TCC............ Teleconcepts in Communications, Inc. [*New York, NY*] [*Telecommunications*] (TSSD)

TCC............ Telegraph Condenser Co. (IAA)

TCC............ Telemetry Standards Coordination Committee (HGAA)

TCC............ Television Control Center

TCC............ Temperature Coefficient of Capacitance

TCC............ Temperature Control Circuit

TCC............ Temporary Council Committee [*NATO*]

TCC............ Terminal Control Corridor [*Aviation*]

TCC............ Test Conductor Console (AAG)

TCC............ Test Control Center [*NASA*]

TCC............ Test Control Commission [*NATO*]

TCC............ Test Controller Computer (MCD)

TCC............ Test Controller Console (KSC)

TCC............ Test Coordinating Center [*Army*]

TCC............ Test Coordinator Console (CAAL)

TCC............ Tethys Circumglobal Current [*Paleooceanography*]

TCC............ Tetrachlorocatechol [*Organic chemistry*]

TCC............ Theater Communications Center (MCD)

TCC............ Theater Communications Command (MCD)

TCC............ Thermal Control Coating

TCC............ Therofor Catalytic Cracking

TCC............ Thiamine Cobalt Chlorophyllin [*Antiulcer*]

TCC............ Thiokol Chemical Corp. [*Later, Thiokol Corp.*] (AAG)

TCC............ Third Continental Congress (EA)

TCC............ Thromboplastic Cell Component [*Hematology*]

TCC............ Through-Connected Circuit [*Telecommunications*] (TEL)

TCC............ Time Compression Coding

TCC............ Tocix Chemicals Committee (EERA)

TCC............ Toll Centre Code (NITA)

TCC............ Toroidal Combustion Chamber

TCC............ Torque Converter Clutch [*Automotive engineering*]

TCC............ TOS [*TIROS Operational Satellite*] Checkout Center [*Goddard Space Flight Center*] (NOAA)

TCC............ Total Car Coefficient [*Formula*] [*Automobile analysis*]

TCC............ Total COBOL [*Common Business-Oriented Language*] Capability [*Computer science*] (IAA)

TCC............ Total Comparative Costs [*Army*]

TCC............ Tracking and Communication Component

TCC............ Tracking and Control Center

TCC............ Tracking Computer Controls (MCD)

TCC............ Tractor Computing Corp. (IAA)

TCC............ Traffic Control Center

TCC............ Traffic Control Complex (SAA)

TCC............ TRANS-CIS Commodities [*Monte Carlo*] (ECON)

TCC............ Transcontinental Corps [*Amateur radio*]

TCC............ Transfer Channel Control (IEEE)

TCC............ Transient Combustion Chamber [*Analysis*] (MCD)

TCC............ Transit Control Center (SAA)

TCC............ Transitional Cell Carcinoma

TCC............ Transmission Control Character [*Telecommunications*] (TEL)

TCC............ Transmit Carry and Clear

TCC............ Transparent Conductive Coating [*Organic chemistry*]

TCC............ Transportable Cassette Converter (IAA)

TCC............ Transport and Communications Commission [*United Nations*] (WDAA)

TCC............ Transportation Commodity Classification Code

TCC............ Transportation Component Command (DOMA)

TCC............ Transportation Control Card [*Military*]

TCC............ Transportation Control Center

TCC............ Transportation Control Committee [*Navy*]

TCC............ Transport Control Center [*Air Force*]

TCC............ Travel Classification Code

TCC............ Travel Correction Calculator (MSA)

TCC............ Travelers' Century Club (EA)

TCC............ Triactor Resources Corp. [*Vancouver Stock Exchange symbol*]

TCC............ Trichlorocarbanilide [*Organic chemistry*]

TCC............ Triclocarban [*Pharmacology*]

TCC............ Trilobita-Crustacea-Chelicerata [*Evolution history*]

TCC............ Triple Cotton-Covered [*Wire insulation*]

TCC............ Troop Carrier Command [*World War II*]

TCC............ Tucumcari, NM [*Location identifier FAA*] (FAAL)

TCC............ Turbine Close Coupled (MSA)

TCC............ Turnbull Canyon [*California*] [*Seismograph station code, US Geological Survey Closed*] (SEIS)

TCC............ Type of Changed Code [*Army*]

TCCA........... Teachers' Committee on Central America (EA)

TCCA........... Textile and Clothing Contractors' Association [*British*] (BI)

TCCA........... Textile Color Card Association of the US [*Later, CAUS*]

TCCA........... Thermometer Collectors Club of America (EA)

TCCA........... Tin Container Collectors Association (EA)

TCCA........... Trichloroisocyanuric Acid [*Organic chemistry*]

TCCB........... Test and County Cricket Board [*British*]

TCCB........... Transitional-Cell Carcinoma of Bladder [*Oncology*] (DAVI)

TCCBL.......... Tons of Cubic Capacity Bale Space [*Shipping*]

TCCC........... 3CI Complete Compliance [*NASDAQ symbol*] (TTSB)

TCCC........... Three CI Complete Compliance Corp. [*NASDAQ symbol*] (SAG)

TCCC........... Tower Control Computer Complex [*Aviation*]

TCCCS.......... Tactical Command, Control, and Communications System [*Canada*]

TCC/CT......... Telecommunications/Communications Terminal (MCD)

TCCD........... Transcranial Color-Coded Doppler [*Medicine*] (DMAA)

TCCDC.......... Chattem Drug and Chemical Co., Chattanooga, TN [*Library symbol Library of Congress*] (LCLS)

TCCF........... Tactical Communications Control Facility [*Air Force*] (MCD)

TCCFU.......... Typical Coastal Command Foul Up [*RAF slang*] [*World War II*]

TCCH........... Tracer Control Chassis

TCC Inds....... TCC Industries, Inc. [*Formerly, Telecom Corp.*] [*Associated Press*] (SAG)

TCCKA.......... Tai Chi and Chi Kung Academy [*Australia*]

TCCL........... T-Cell Chronic Lymphoblastic Leukemia [*Medicine*] (DMAA)

TCCM........... Thermal Control Coating Material

TCCN........... TransCanada Computer Communications Network (IAA)

TCCO........... Technical Communications [*NASDAQ symbol*] (TTSB)

TCCO........... Technical Communications Corp. [*NASDAQ symbol*] (NQ)

TCCO........... Temperature-Compensated Crystal Oscillator (MCD)

TCCO........... Temperature-Controlled Crystal Oscillator (IAA)

TC CO_2........ Transcutaneous Carbon Dioxide [*Monitor*] [*Medicine*] (DAVI)

TC-CON......... Type Classification - Contingency

TCCP........... Tissue Culture for Crops Project [*Colorado State University*] [*Research center*] (RCD)

TCCPSWG........ Tactical Command and Control Procedures Standardization Working Group [*Army*] (AABC)

TCCRAEF........ [*The*] Conservative Caucus Research, Analysis, and Education Foundation (EA)

TCCS........... Technical Committee on Communications Satellites

TCCS........... Tide Communication Control Ship (NATG)

TCCS........... Toyota's Computer-Controlled System (ADA)

TCCS........... Trace Contaminant Control System

TCCS........... Transcranial Color-Coded Sonography [*Medicine*] (DMAA)

TCC/SCA........ Tai Chi Chuan/Shaolin Chuan Association (EA)

TCCT........... Tactical Communications Control Terminal (MCD)

TCCT........... Tooling Contour Check Tool (MCD)

TCCT........... Type Commander Core Training (DOMA)

TCCU........... Tribally Controlled Colleges and Universities

TCCWCA......... Tasmanian Council of Churches World Christian Action [*Australia*]

TCD............ Chad [*ANSI three-letter standard code*] (CNC)

TCD............ Department of Technical Cooperation for Development [*United Nations*]

TCD............ Tactical Communications Division [*Military*]

TCD............ Tapetochoroidal Dystrophy [*Ophthalmology*]

TCD............ Target Center Display

TCD............ Task Completion Date (AAG)

TCD............ Technical Contracts Department

TCD............ Telemetry and Command Data (KSC)

TCD............ Teletype Conversion Device (DWSG)

TCD............ Temperature Control Device for Crystal Units (IAA)

TCD............ Tentative Classification of Damage

TCD............ Tentative Classification of Defects (NG)

TCD............ Tentative Classification of Documents

TCD............ Terminal Countdown Demonstration

TCD............ Test Communications Division (SAA)

TCD............ Test Completion Date (NASA)

TCD............ Test Control Document [*NASA*] (MCD)

TCD............ Test Control Drawings (MCD)

TCD............ Thermal Conductivity Detector [*Analytical instrumentation*]

TCD............ Thermochemical Deposition

TCD............ Three-Channel Decoder

TCD............ Thyratron Core Driver

TCD............ Time Compliance Directive [*Air Force*] (MCD)

TCD............ Time Correlation Data

TCD............ Tissue Culture Dose (AAMN)

TCD............ Tor-Cal Resources Ltd. [*Toronto Stock Exchange symbol*]

TCD............ Total Cost Approach to Distribution

TCD............ Tour Completion Date

TCD............ TOXLINE Chemical Dictionary [*A publication*]

TCD............ Traffic Control Devices [*MOCD*] (TAG)

TCD............ Transistor Chopper Driver

TCD............ Transistor-Controlled Delay (MCD)

TCD............ Transportability Clearance Diagram (MCD)

TCD............ Trinity College, Dublin [*Ireland*]

TCD............ Tumor Cell Detection [*Medicine*]

TCD............ Tumor Control Dose [*Oncology*]

TCD............ Type Classification Date [*Army*]

TCD_{50}........... Tissue Culture Dose, 50% Infectivity

TCDA........... Touring Car Drivers Association [*Automobile racing*]

TCdaC.......... TransCanada Pipeline Ltd. Capital [*Associated Press*] (SAG)

TCDB........... Turn, Cough, Deep Breathe [*Medicine*] (DMAA)

TCDC .... Taurochenodeoxycholate [*Biochemistry*]
TCDC .... Technical Cooperation among Developing Countries [*United Nations*]
TCDC/INRES... Information Referral System for Technical Co-operation among Developing Countries [*United Nations Development Programme*] [*Information service or system*] (IID)
TCDD .... Tetrachlorodibenzodioxin [*Organic chemistry*]
TCDD .... Tower Cab Digital Display (PDAA)
TCDF.......... File [*Document Locator Number*] [*IRS*]
TCDF.......... Temporary Container Discharge Facility
TCDF.......... Tetrachlorodibenzofuran [*Organic chemistry*]
TCDL.......... Tasmanian Canine Defence League [*Australia*]
TCDMS .... Telecommunication/Data Management System
TCDN .... Techdyne, Inc. [*NASDAQ symbol*] (SAG)
TCDP .... Transmitter Control and Display Panel
TCDS .... Tryptamine Chemical Delivery System [*Pharmacology*]
TCDU .... Transport Command Development Unit [*British military*] (DMA)
TCE.......... [*The*] Chemical Engineer [*A publication*]
TCE.......... Taking Care of Elvis [*Motto of Elvis Presley fans*]
TCE.......... Talker Commission Error (MUGU)
TCE.......... Talker Communication Error (IAA)
TCE.......... Tax Counseling for the Elderly [*Internal Revenue Service*]
TCE.......... Teachers' Centers Exchange (EA)
TCE.......... Telemetry Checkout Equipment (KSC)
TCE.......... Telephone Co. Engineered [*Telecommunications*] (TEL)
TCE.......... Temperature Coefficient of Expansion
TCE.......... Terminal Control Element (CAAL)
TCE.......... Terminal Cretaceous Event [*Geology*]
TCE.......... Terrace (ROG)
TCE.......... Test Connection Equipment (IAA)
TCE.......... Tetrachloro-Diphenyl- Ethane [*An insecticide*] (DAVI)
TCE.......... Tetrachloroethylene [*Also, P*] [*Organic chemistry*]
TCE.......... Thermal Canister Experiment [*Space shuttle*] [*NASA*]
TCE.......... Thermal Coefficient of Expansion
TCE.......... Thomson's Loss-Making Consumer-Electronics [*France*] (ECON)
TCE.......... Tons of Coal Equivalent
TCE.......... Top Computer Executive (MHDB)
TCE.......... Total Composite Error
TCE.......... Total Concept Engineering
TCE.......... TOW [*Tube-Launched, Optically Tracked, Wire-Guided (Weapon)*] Crew Evaluator [*Military*] (INF)
TCE.......... Transaction Cost Estimator (MHDI)
TCE.......... Trans-Colorado Airlines, Inc. [*ICAO designator*] (FAAC)
TCE.......... Transportation-Communication Employees Union [*Later, TCIU*]
TCE.......... Trichloroethanol [*Organic chemistry*]
TCE.......... Trichloroethanol [*An anesthetic and hypnotic*] [*Pharmacology*] (DAVI)
TCE.......... Trichloroethylene [*Also, TRI*] [*Organic chemistry*]
TCE.......... Tubular Carbon Electrode
TCE.......... Tulcea [*Romania*] [*Airport symbol*] (OAG)
TCE.......... Tyumen Commodity Exchange [*Russian Federation*] (EY)
TCEA.......... Texas Computer Education Association (EDAC)
TCEA.......... Training Center for Experimental Aerodynamics [*NATO*]
TCEA.......... Trichloroethane [*Organic chemistry*]
TCEC.......... Erlanger Medical Center, Medical Library, Chattanooga, TN [*Library symbol Library of Congress*] (LCLS)
TCEC-N .... Erlanger Medical Center, Nursing School, Chattanooga, TN [*Library symbol Library of Congress*] (LCLS)
TCEC-P .... Erlanger Medical Center, I. C., Thompson's Children's Pediatric Library, Chattanooga, TN [*Library symbol Library of Congress*] (LCLS)
TCED.......... Thrust Control Exploratory Development (KSC)
TCEEA.......... Tasmanian Catholic Education Employees' Association [*Australia*]
TCEL.......... T Cell Sciences [*NASDAQ symbol*] (TTSB)
TCEL.......... T Cell Sciences, Inc. [*Cambridge, MA*] [*NASDAQ symbol*] (NQ)
T Cell.......... T Cell Sciences, Inc. [*Associated Press*] (SAG)
TCEO.......... Theatre Committee for Eugene O'Neill (EA)
TCEP.......... Tris(chloroethyl)phosphite [*Organic chemistry*]
TCEP.......... Tris(cyanoethoxy)propane [*Organic chemistry*]
TCEPA.......... Tasmanian Commercial Egg Producers' Association [*Australia*]
TCert.......... Teacher's Certificate [*British*] (DBQ)
TCES.......... Transcutaneous Cranial Electrical Stimulation [*Medicine*]
TCESOM ...... Trichlorethylene-Extracted Soybean Oil Meal
TCET.......... Transcerebral Electrotherapy
TCEU.......... Transportation-Communication Employees Union (MHDB)
TCF.......... [*The*] Charity Forum [*British*] (EAIO)
TCF.......... [*The*] Children's Foundation (EA)
TCF.......... [*The*] Compassionate Friends (EA)
TCF.......... Tactical Control Flight
TCF.......... Tank Checkout Facility [*NASA*] (NASA)
TCF.......... Tasmanian Cycling Federation [*Australia*]
TCF.......... TCF Financial Corp. [*Associated Press*] (SAG)
TCF.......... Technical Control Facility [*or Function*]
TCF.......... Technical Cooperation Fund (EERA)
TCF.......... Temporary Chaplain to the Forces [*British*]
TCF.......... Terminal Communication Facility [*Telecommunications*] (TSSD)
TCF.......... Terminal Configuration Facility [*Computer science*]
TCF.......... Territorial Cadet Force [*British military*] (DMA)
TCF.......... Test Control Fixture (MCD)
TCF.......... Time Correction Factor (ADA)
TCF.......... Tissue Coding Factor [*Medicine*] (DMAA)
TCF.......... T-Lymphocyte Chemotactic Factor
TCF.......... To Be Called For [*British Rail parcel service*] [*Obsolete*] (DI)
TCF.......... Total Coronary Flow [*Medicine*] (MAE)
TCF.......... Totally Chlorine-Free [*Pulp and paper processing*]
TCF.......... Toulx Ste. Croix [*France*] [*Seismograph station code, US Geological Survey*] (SEIS)
TCF.......... Training Check Frame [*Computer science*]
TCF.......... Transparent Computing Facility
TCF.......... Treacher Collins Foundation (EA)
TCF.......... Trillion Cubic Feet
TCF.......... Troop Carrier Forces [*Military*]
TCF.......... Tunable Control Frequency
TCF.......... Twentieth Century Fund (EA)
TCFB.......... Trans-Continental Freight Bureau
TCFC.......... [*The*] Cars Fan Club (EA)
TCFC.......... Thom Christopher Fan Club (EA)
TCFC.......... Tom Cruise Fan Club (EA)
TCFC.......... Tommy Cash Fan Club [*Defunct*] (EA)
TCFC.......... Turkish Children Foster Care (EA)
TCFCA.......... Textile Clothing and Footwear Council of Australia
TCFD.......... Technical Committee on Fish Diseases [*Australia*]
TCF Fn.......... TCF Financial Corp. [*Associated Press*] (SAG)
TCFIC.......... Textile, Clothing, and Footwear Industries Committee [*British*] (DCTA)
TCFlt.......... Tactical Control Flight
TCFM.......... Teilhard Centre for the Future of Man (EAIO)
TCFM.......... Temperature Control Flux Monitor [*NASA*]
TCFNO .... [*The*] Common Fund for Nonprofit Organizations [*Ford Foundation*]
TCFNSW .... Teachers' Christian Fellowship of New South Wales [*Australia*]
TCFP.......... Thrust Chamber Fuel Purge (SAA)
TCFS.......... Turkish Cypriot Federated State
TCFU.......... Tumor Colony-Forming Unit [*Oncology*]
TCG.......... [*The*] Crimson Group [*Cambridge, MA*] [*Telecommunications*] (TSSD)
TCG.......... Tactical Control Group [*Air Force*]
TCG.......... Technical Coordination Group (MCD)
TCG.......... Telecommunications Consulting Group, Inc. [*Washington, DC*] (TSSD)
TCG.......... Telecommunications Group [*Range Commanders Council*] [*NASA*]
TCG.......... Territorial College of Guam
TCG.......... Test Call Generator [*Telecommunications*] (TEL)
TCG.......... Test Control Group [*NASA*] (NASA)
TCG.......... Theatre Communications Group (EA)
TCG.......... Threat Coordinating Group [*DoD*]
TCG.......... Time Code Generator
TCG.......... Time-Compensated Gain [*Cardiology*]
TCG.......... Time Controlled Gain (AAG)
TCG.......... Tooling Coordination Group (AAG)
TC/G.......... Total Fielding Chances per Game [*Baseball*]
TCG.......... Trans Canada Glass Ltd. [*Toronto Stock Exchange symbol Vancouver Stock Exchange symbol*]
TCG.......... Transponder Control Group
TCG.......... Tritocerebral Commissure, Giant [*Zoology*]
TCG.......... Tucson, Cornelia & Gila Bend Railroad Co. [*AAR code*]
TCG.......... Tune-Controlled Gain
TCGA.......... Tasmanian Chicken Growers' Association [*Australia*]
TCGE.......... Tool and Cutter Grinding Equipment (MCD)
TCGF.......... T-Cell Growth Factor [*See also IL-2*] [*Biochemistry*]
TCGF.......... Thymus Cell Growth Factor [*Cytology*]
TCGH .... Downtown General Hospital, Chattanooga, TN [*Library symbol Library of Congress*] (LCLS)
TCGI.......... Teleport Communications Group, Inc. [*NASDAQ symbol*] (SAG)
TCGP .... Girls' Prepatory School, Chattanooga, TN [*Library symbol*] [*Library of Congress*] (LCLS)
TCGp.......... Tactical Control Group [*Air Force*] (AFM)
TCGT.......... Georgia-Tennessee Regional Health Commission, Chattanooga, TN [*Library symbol Library of Congress*] (LCLS)
TCGT .... Tool and Cutter Grinding Tool (MCD)
TCGU .... Texaco Continuous Grease Unit
TCH.......... Chattanooga-Hamilton County Bicentennial Library, Chattanooga, TX [*OCLC symbol*] (OCLC)
TCH.......... Tasmanian College of Hospitality [*Australia*]
TCH.......... Tchibanga [*Gabon*] [*Airport symbol*] (OAG)
TCH.......... Tchimkent [*Former USSR Seismograph station code, US Geological Survey Closed*] (SEIS)
TCH.......... Tchoupitoulas [*Virus*]
TCH.......... Tea Clearing House [*British*] (DBA)
TCH.......... Technologie-Centrum Hannover GmbH [*Database producer*] (IID)
TCH.......... Tec Tech [*Vancouver Stock Exchange symbol*]
TCH.......... Templeton China World Fd [*NYSE symbol*] (TTSB)
TCH.......... Templeton China World Fund [*NYSE symbol*] (SPSG)
TCH.......... Temporary Construction Hole [*Technical drawings*]
TCH.......... Tetrachlorohydroquinone [*Organic chemistry*]
TCH.......... Thiocarbohydrazide [*Organic chemistry*]
TCH.......... Threshold Crossing Height [*FAA*] (TAG)
TCH.......... Threshold Crossing Height [*Aviation*] (FAAC)
TCH.......... Total Circulating Hemoglobin [*Medicine*] (MAE)
TCH.......... Touch
TCH.......... Trans-Canada Highway
TCH.......... Trans-Charter [*Former USSR*] [*FAA designator*] (FAAC)
TCH.......... Transfer in Channel
TCH.......... Trust Chamber [*NASA*] (KSC)
TCH.......... Turn, Cough, Hyperventilate [*Medicine*]
TCHA .... Tasmanian Community Health Association [*Australia*]
TchA .... Touchstone Applied Sciences [*Associated Press*] (SAG)
TchApld .... Touchstone Applied Sciences [*Associated Press*] (SAG)
TCHCB .... Chattanooga-Hamilton County Bicentennial Library, Chattanooga, TN [*Library symbol Library of Congress*] (LCLS)
TchCom .... Technical Communications Corp. [*Associated Press*] (SAG)
TCHD .... Threshold Crossing Height Downwind [*Aviation*] (FAAC)
Tchdyn.......... Techdyne, Inc. [*Associated Press*] (SAG)
Tchdyne....... Techdyne, Inc. [*Associated Press*] (SAG)

TchElec Tech Electro Industries, Inc. [*Associated Press*] (SAG)
TCHEP Technical Committee on High Energy Physics [*of the Federal Council for Science and Technology*]
TCHG Teaching
TCHHNLGCL Technological
TCHHW Tropic Higher High Water [*Tides*]
TCHHWI Tropic Higher High-Water Interval [*Tides*]
TcHIDA Technetium Hepatoiminodiacetic Acid [*Scan*] [*Radiology*] (DAVI)
TCHIP Town Campers' Housing and Infrastructure Program [*Australia*]
TCHK Text Check [*Computer science*]
TCHLW Tropic Higher Low Water [*Tides*]
Tchnal Technalysis Corp. [*Associated Press*] (SAG)
TCHNG Teaching
TChO Olin Corp., D. B. Beene Technical Information Center, Charleston, TN [*Library symbol Library of Congress*] (LCLS)
TCHOG Technical Operations Group [*Air Force*]
TCHOS Technical Operations Squadron [*Air Force*]
TCHP Telechips Corp. [*NASDAQ symbol*] (SAG)
TCHPW Telechips Corp. Wrrt [*NASDAQ symbol*] (TTSB)
TCHR Teacher
TchRsh Technology Research Corp. [*Associated Press*] (SAG)
TchSym Tech-Sym Corp. [*Associated Press*] (SAG)
TCHT Tanned-Cell Hemagglutination Test [*Immunology*]
TCHTS Technical Training Squadron [*Air Force*]
TCHTW Technical Training Wing [*Air Force*]
TCHU Threshold Crossing Height Upwind [*Aviation*] (FAAC)
TCI Santa Cruz de Tenerife [*Canary Islands*] [*Airport symbol*] (AD)
TCI Tall Clubs International (EA)
TCI Tasmanian Confederation of Industries [*Australia*]
TCI TCI: The Business of Entertainment Technology and Design [*A publication*] (BRI)
TCI TDRS Command Interface (MCD)
TCI Technical Component Industries [*Aerospace British*]
TCI Technical Critical Item (NASA)
TCI Technology Catalysts, Inc. [*Information service or system*] (IID)
TCI Technology Communications, Inc.
TCI Technology Concepts, Inc. [*Sudbury, MA*] [*Telecommunications*] (TSSD)
TCI Technology for Communications International
TCI Technology for Communications International, Inc. (AAGC)
TCI Tele-Communications, Inc. [*Brookpark, OH*] (TSSD)
TCI Teleconferencing Systems International, Inc. [*Elk Grove Village, IL*] [*Telecommunications*] (TSSD)
TCI Telemetry Components Information (KSC)
TCI Telephone Collectors International (EA)
TCI Temperature Control Instrument
TCI Temporary Customs Impost [*British*]
TCI Tenerife [*Canary Islands*] [*Airport symbol*] (OAG)
TCI Terminal Communications Interface
TCI Terrain Clearance Indicator
TCI Test Control Instruction (KSC)
TCI Theoretical Chemistry Institute [*University of Wisconsin - Madison*] [*Research center*] (RCD)
TCI Thermo Cardiosystems, Inc. (PS)
TCI Thimble Collectors International (EA)
TCI Thomson CEA Industries [*France*] (ECON)
TCI Time Change Item (MCD)
TCI To Come In [*to hospital*] [*Medicine*]
TCI Torque Control Isolation [*Automotive engineering*]
TCI Total Cerebral Ischemia
TCI Traffic Clubs International (EA)
TCI Transcontinental Realty Investors [*NYSE symbol*] (SPSG)
TCI Transcontinental Rlty [*NYSE symbol*] (TTSB)
TCI Transient Cerebral Ischemia [*Medicine*]
TCI Transportation Clubs International (EA)
TCI Travel Consultants, Inc.
TCI Tricuspid Insufficiency [*Medicine*] (MEDA)
TCI Trunk Cut-In
TCI Turbocharged Generation One [*Automotive engine identification*]
TCI Turks & Caicos National Airlines [*ICAO designator*] (FAAC)
TCIA Truck Cap Industry Association (EA)
TCIAS Texas Council of Industrial Arts Supervisors (EDAC)
TCIATE Texas Council on Industrial Arts Teacher Education (EDAC)
TCIC Technical Committee on Industrial Classification [*Office of Management and Budget*] [*Washington, DC*] (EGAO)
TCI Cm TCI Communications Financing I [*Associated Press*] (SAG)
TCICm TCI Communications Financing II [*Associated Press*] (SAG)
TCID Terminal Computer Identification (KSC)
TCID Test Configuration Identifier (NASA)
TCID Tissue Culture Infectious [*or Infective*] Dose
TCID$_{50}$ Median Tissue Culture Infective Dose [*Laboratory science*] (DAVI)
Tc-IDA Technetium Iminodiacetic Acid [*Clinical chemistry*]
TCIE Transient Cerebral Ischemic Episode [*Medicine*] (MAE)
TCIF Telecommunications Industry Forum (EA)
TCII TCI International, Inc. [*NASDAQ symbol*] (NQ)
TCII TCI Intl [*NASDAQ symbol*] (TTSB)
TCI Int TCI International, Inc. [*Associated Press*] (SAG)
TCI Pac TCI Pacific Communications [*Associated Press*] (SAG)
TCIR Technical Command Informal Reports [*Army*] (MCD)
TCIS TELEX Computer Inquiry Service
TCI Sat TCI Satellite Entertainment, Inc. [*Associated Press*] (SAG)
TCITP Terminal Communications Interface Test Program (MCD)
TCIU Transportation Communications International Union (EA)
TCIV Turbocharged Generation 4 [*Automotive engine identification*]
TCIX Total Containment [*NASDAQ symbol*] (SAG)
TCJ Tactical Communications Jamming [*Military*] (CAAL)
TCJ Tarrant County Junior College, Hurst, TX [*OCLC symbol*] (OCLC)
TCJ Thermocouple Junction
TCJ Turbulent Confined Jet
TCJCC Trades Councils' Joint Consultative Committee [*British*] (DCTA)
TCK Thermochemical-Kinetic
TCK Thermo Ecotek [*AMEX symbol*] (TTSB)
TCK Thermo Ecotek Corp. [*AMEX symbol*] (SAG)
TCK Tilletia controversa Kuehn [*Wheat fungus*]
TCK TOW [*Tube-Launched, Optically-Tracked, Wire-Guided Weapon*] Cooler Kit (DWSG)
TCK Track [*or Tracking*] (AAG)
TCK Two-Cavity Klystron
TCKL Tackle
TCL [*The*] Command Language [*Computer science*] (PCM)
TCL Escape Aviation [*ICAO designator*] (FAAC)
TCL Takeoff Cruise Landing [*Aviation*]
TCL Target Cleanup Level [*Environmental science*] (ERG)
TCL Telecommunication Laboratories [*Taiwan*]
TCL Telephone Cables Ltd. [*British*]
TCL Terminal Command Language [*Applied Digital Data Systems*]
TCL Terminal Control Language
TCL Textes Cuneiformes. Departement des Antiquites Orientales. Musee du Louvre [*A publication*] (BJA)
TCL Thin Charcoal Layer
TCL Through-Camera-Lens
TCL Time and Cycle Log [*NASA*] (KSC)
TCL Toll Circuit Layout [*Telecommunications*] (TEL)
TCL Tool Command Language [*Computer science*]
TCL Tool Control List [*Military*] (AFIT)
TCL Total Capacity of the Lung [*Medicine*] (DMAA)
TCL Traction Control [*Mitsubishi*] [*Transmission systems*]
TCL Transatlantic Carriers Ltd. [*Steamship line*] (MHDW)
TCL TransCanada Pipeline Ltd. Capital [*NYSE symbol*] (SAG)
TCL Transfer Chemical LASER (IEEE)
TCL Transistor Contact Land
TCL Transistor Coupled Logic
TCL Transmit Clock (IAA)
TCL Transportable Calibration Laboratory
TCL Transport Canada Library, Ottawa [*UTLAS symbol*]
TCL Trap Control Line
TCL Trinity College, London
TCL Troposcatter Communications Link
TCL Tulane Computer Laboratory [*Tulane University*] [*Research center*] (RCD)
TCL Tuscaloosa [*Alabama*] [*Airport symbol*] (OAG)
TCL Tusculum College, Greenville, TN [*Inactive*] [*OCLC symbol*] (OCLC)
TCIA Austin Peay State University, Clarksville, TN [*Library symbol Library of Congress*] (LCLS)
TCLA T-Cell Line Adapted [*Cytology*]
TCLAS Type Classification [*Military*] (AABC)
TCLBRP Tank Cannon Launched Beam Rider Projectile (MCD)
TCLBS Tropical Constant-Level Balloon System [*Meteorology*]
TCLC Tri-State College Library Cooperative [*Rosemont College Library*] [*Rosemont, PA*] [*Library network*]
TCLC Twentieth-Century Literary Criticism [*A publication*]
TC/LD Thermocouple/Lead Detector [*Nuclear energy*] (NRCH)
TCle Cleveland Public Library, Cleveland, TN [*Library symbol Library of Congress*] (LCLS)
TCLE Thermal Coefficient of Linear Expansion [*Rocket motor stress*]
TCleB Bradley Memorial Hospital, Cleveland, TN [*Library symbol Library of Congress*] (LCLS)
TCleC Cleveland State Community College, Cleveland, TN [*Library symbol Library of Congress*] (LCLS)
TCleL Lee College, Cleveland, TN [*Library symbol Library of Congress*] (LCLS)
TCIH Clarksville Memorial Hospital, Clarksville, TN [*Library symbol Library of Congress*] (LCLS)
TCIH Clarksville Memorial Hospital, Clarksville, TN [*Library symbol*] [*Library of Congress*] (LCLS)
TCLHW Tropic Lower High Water [*Tides*]
TCLL T-Cell Chronic Lymphocytic Leukemia [*Oncology*]
TCLLW Tropic Lower Low Water [*Tides*]
TCLLWI Tropic Lower Low-Water Interval [*Tides*]
TCLN Techniclone International Corp. [*NASDAQ symbol*] (SAG)
TCLN Techniclone Intl [*NASDAQ symbol*] (TTSB)
TCLNA Tall Cedars of Lebanon of North America (EA)
TC^{Lo} Toxic Concentration Low (ERG)
TCLP Toxic Characteristic Leaching Procedure
TCLP Toxic Characteristics Leaching Procedure [*Environmental Protection Agency*]
TCLP Toxicity Characteristic Leaching Procedure [*Environmental Protection Agency*]
TCLP Toxicity Characteristic Leading Procedure [*Hazardous materials control*]
TCLP Type Classification, Limited Procurement
TC-LP Type Classification - Limited Production
TC-LPT Type Classified - Limited Producation Test
TC-LPU Type Classification - Limited Production Urgent
TCLR Toll Circuit Layout Record [*Telecommunications*] (TEL)
TCLSC Theater COMSEC [*Communications Security*] Logistic Support Center [*Army*] (AABC)
TCLSC-E Theater COMSEC Logistics Support Center - Europe (MCD)
TCLT Tentative Calculated Landing Time [*FAA*] (TAG)
TCM Tacoma, WA [*Location identifier FAA*] (FAAL)

TCM .... Tactical Cruise Missile (MCD)
TCM .... Tasmanian Chamber of Mines [*Australia*]
TCM .... Tax Court Memorandum Decisions [*Commerce Clearing House or Prentice-Hall, Inc.*] [*A publication*] (DLA)
TCM .... Teaching Career Month
TCM .... Technical Committee Minutes [*Military*] (AFIT)
TCM .... Technical Coordination Meeting (MCD)
TCM .... Telecommunications Manager (MHDB)
TCM .... Telecommunications Monitor
TCM .... Teledyne Continental Motors [*ICAO designator*] (FAAC)
TCM .... Telemetry Code Modulation
TCM .... Telephone Channel Monitor
TCM .... Temperature-Compensated Mask (IAA)
TCM .... Temperature-Compensation (IAA)
TCM .... Temperature Control Model
TCM .... Terminal Capacity Matrix (OA)
TCM .... Terminal-to-Computer Multiplexer
TCM .... Termination of Centralized Management (MCD)
TCM .... Terrain Clearance Measurement
TCM .... Terrestrial Carbon Model [*Earth science*]
TCM .... Test Call Module [*Telecommunications*] (TEL)
TCM .... Tetrachloromercurate [*Inorganic chemistry*]
TCM .... Texas Climatological Model [*Environmental Protection Agency*] (GFGA)
TCM .... Theater Combat Model (NATG)
TCM .... Thermal Conduction Module [*IBM Corp.*]
TCM .... Thermocouple Meter (IDOE)
TCM .... Thermoplastic Cellular Molding [*Plastics technology*]
TCM .... Time Compression Multiplex (IAA)
TCM .... Tissue Culture Medium
TCM .... Tone Code Modulation (IAA)
TCM .... Toroidal Carbohydrate Module [*i.e., doughnut*] [*Slang*]
TCM .... Torpedo Countermeasures (NVT)
TCM .... Total Catchment Management (EERA)
TCM .... Total Downtime for Corrective Unscheduled Maintenance [*Quality control*] (MCD)
TCM .... Toxic Chemical Munitions [*Army*]
TCM .... Traditional Chinese Medicine
TCM .... Trajectory Correction Maneuver
TCM .... Transcutaneous [*Oxygen*] Monitoring [*Medicine*]
TCM .... Transfluxor Constants Matrix (AAG)
TCM .... Translator CAM [*Computer-Aided Manufacturing*] Magnet (IAA)
TCM .... Translator Command Module [*Fluorescence technique*]
TCM .... Transportation Control Measure [*Environmental Protection Agency*] (GFGA)
TCM .... Travel Cost Method
TCM .... Trellis-Coded Modulation [*Data transmission*] (BYTE)
TCM .... Troop Corporal-Major [*British military*] (DMA)
TCM .... Truck Components Marketing [*Eaton Corp.*]
TCM .... T/SF Communications [*AMEX symbol*] (TTSB)
TCM .... T/SF Communications Corp. [*AMEX symbol*] (SPSG)
TCM .... Tubing Connector Manifold [*Instrumentation*]
TCM .... Tucuman [*Argentina*] [*Seismograph station code, US Geological Survey Closed*] (SEIS)
TCM .... Turner Classic Movies [*Television*]
TCM .... Twin-Cartridge Machine
TCMA .... Tabulating Card Manufacturers Association [*Later, IOSA*] (EA)
TCMA .... Telephone Cable Makers' Association [*British*] (BI)
TCMA .... Textile Chemical Manufacturers Association [*Later, IOSA*] (EA)
TCMA .... Theater Container Management Agency
TCMA .... Third Class Mail Association (EA)
TCMA .... Tooling Component Manufacturers Association (EA)
TCM/A .... Toxic Chemical Munitions/Agents (MCD)
TCMA .... Tufted Carpet Manufacturers' Association [*British*] (BI)
TCMB .... Turkiye Cumhuriyet Merkez Bankasi [*The Central Bank of the Republic of Turkey*]
TCM (CCH) ... Tax Court Memorandum Decisions (Commerce Clearing House) [*A publication*] (DLA)
TCMD .... Transportation Cargo Manifest Document
TCMD .... Transportation Control and Movement Document [*Military*]
TC Memo ..... Memorandum Opinion of the United States Tax Court (AAGC)
TC Memo ..... Tax Court Memorandum Decisions [*Commerce Clearing House or Prentice-Hall, Inc.*] [*A publication*] (DLA)
TCMF .... Touch Calling Multifrequency (IEEE)
TCMH .... Memorial Hospital, Chattanooga, TN [*Library symbol Library of Congress*] (LCLS)
TCMH .... Tumor-Direct Cell-Mediated Hypersensitivity [*Oncology*] (DAVI)
TCMI .... Moccasin Bend Mental Health Institute, Chattanooga, TN [*Library symbol Library of Congress*] (LCLS)
TCMIS .... Trade Control Measures Information System [*UNCTAD*] [*United Nations*] (DUND)
TCMIS .... TRADOC [*Training and Doctrine Command*] Command Management Information System [*Military*]
T C MITS ..... [*The*] Common Man in the Street [*The average man*] [*See also MITS*]
TCMJA .... Tasmanian Country Music Jamboree Association [*Australia*]
TCML .... Target Coordinate Map Locator [*Military*] (PDAA)
TCMP .... Taxpayer Compliance Measurement Program [*IRS*]
TCMP .... Thematic Content Modification Program (DMAA)
TCM (P-H) ... Tax Court Memorandum Decisions (Prentice-Hall, Inc.) [*A publication*] (DLA)
TCMS .... Technical Control and Management Subsystem (MCD)
TCMS .... Telecommunications Management System (MHDI)
TC-MS .... Thermal Chromatography/Mass Spectrometry
TCMS .... Toll Centering and Metropolitan Sectoring [*AT & T*] [*Telecommunications*] (TEL)
TCMS .... Track Combat Status (SAA)
TCMS .... Training Certification Management System [*NASA*]
TCMS .... Turbocharger Management System [*Automotive electronics*]
TCMTB .... (Thiocyanomethylthio)benzothiazole [*Fungicide*] [*Organic chemistry*]
TCMZ .... Trichloromethiazide [*Diuretic*]
TCN .... Carson-Newman College, Jefferson City, TN [*OCLC symbol*] (OCLC)
TCN .... Telecommunications Cooperative Network (EA)
TCN .... Teleconference Network [*University of Nebraska Medical Center*] [*Omaha, NE*] [*Telecommunications*] (TSSD)
TCN .... Territorial Command Net
TCN .... Test Change Notice [*NASA*] (MCD)
TCN .... Tetracycline [*Antibiotic*]
TCN .... Texcan Technology Corp. [*Vancouver Stock Exchange symbol*]
TCN .... Tobacco Cyst Nematode [*Plant pathology*]
TCN .... Toconce [*Chile*] [*Seismograph station code, US Geological Survey*] (SEIS)
TCN .... Tracing Change Notice
TCN .... Track Channel Number (SAA)
TCN .... Trade Commission of Norway (EA)
TCN .... Trans Continental Airlines [*ICAO designator*] (FAAC)
TCN .... Transfer on Channel Not in Operation (SAA)
TCN .... Transportation Control Number [*Air Force*] (AFM)
TCN .... Trolley Coach News [*A publication*] (EAAP)
TCNA .... Tube Council of North America (EA)
TCNB .... Tetracyanobenzene [*Organic chemistry*]
TC-NBT .... Thiocarbamyl-nitro-blue Tetrazolium [*Organic chemistry*]
TCNC .... Tekakwitha Conference National Center (EA)
TCNCO .... Test Control Noncommissioned Officer (AFM)
TCNE .... Tetracyanoethylene [*Organic chemistry*]
TCNEO .... Tetracyanoethylene Oxide [*Organic chemistry*]
TCNJ .... Trust Co. of New Jersey [*NASDAQ symbol*] (NQ)
TCNL .... Tecnol Medical Products [*NASDAQ symbol*] (SPSG)
TCNM .... Trimethylcyclopropenyl(nitrophenyl)malononitrile [*Organic chemistry*]
TCNO .... Tecnomatix Technologies Ltd. [*NASDAQ symbol*] (SAG)
TCNOF .... Tecnomatix Technologies Ltd [*NASDAQ symbol*] (TTSB)
TCNQ .... Tetracyanoquinodimethane [*Organic chemistry*]
TCNS .... Transcutaneous Nerve Stimulation [*Medicine*] (MAE)
TCNSW .... Travel Centre of New South Wales [*Australia*]
TCNT .... Transpiration-Cooled Nose Tip
TCO .... Aerotranscolombiana de Carga Ltda. [*Columbia*] [*FAA designator*] (FAAC)
TCO .... Tactical Combat Operations
TCO .... Tactical Control Officer [*Army*]
TCO .... Taken Care Of (MCD)
TCO .... Taubman Centers [*NYSE symbol*] (TTSB)
TCO .... Taubman Centers, Inc. [*NYSE symbol*] (SPSG)
TCO .... Technical Checkout [*Nuclear*] (MCD)
TCO .... Technical Contracting Office [*Navy*]
TCO .... Technical Cooperation Officer [*British*]
TCO .... Telecommunications Certifying Officer [*Air Force*] (AFIT)
TCO .... Telemetry and Command Subsystem [*Deep Space Instrumentation Facility, NASA*]
TCO .... Temperature Coefficient of Offset (IAA)
TCO .... Terminal Control Office [*or Officer*]
TCO .... Termination Contracting Officer [*Military*]
TCO .... Test and Checkout [*NASA*] (GFGA)
TCO .... Test Control Officer [*Military*]
TCO .... Thrust Cutoff (NVT)
TCO .... Tillamook County Library, Tillamook, OR [*OCLC symbol*] (OCLC)
TCO .... Time and Charges, Operate
TCO .... Tjaenstemaennens Centralorganisation [*Central Organization of Salaried Employees*] [*Sweden*]
TCO .... Tool Change Order (MCD)
TCO .... Torpedo Control Officer [*British military*] (DMA)
TCO .... Total Cost of Ownership (PCM)
TCO .... Traffic Camera Office [*Victoria, Australia*]
TCO .... Train Conducting Officer [*British military*] (DMA)
TCO .... Trans Canada Options [*Stock exchange network of VSE, TSE, and MSE*]
TCO .... Trans-Canada Resources Ltd. [*Toronto Stock Exchange symbol*]
TCO .... Transfer on Channel in Operation (IAA)
TCO .... Translational Control (SAA)
TCO .... Translocation Crossover [*Geology*]
TCO .... Transparent Conductive Oxide [*Photovoltaic energy systems*]
TCO .... Transportation Co. [*Army*]
TCO .... Transportation Control Officer [*Air Force*] (AFM)
TCO .... Trinity College, Oxford [*British*] (DAS)
TCO .... Triode Cavity Oscillator
TCO .... Trunk Cutoff
TCO .... Tumaco [*Colombia*] [*Airport symbol*] (OAG)
TCOA .... Telephone Contract Officers' Association [*A union*] [*British*]
TCOA .... Trustee Companies Officers' Association [*Australia*]
T-COAP .... Vincristine, Prednisone, Cytosine Arabinoside, Cyclophosphamide, and 6-Thioguanine [*Antineoplastic drug regimen*] (DAVI)
TCOBS .... Type Classification - Obsolete (MCD)
TCoC .... Columbia State Community College, Columbia, TN [*Library symbol*] [*Library of Congress*] (LCLS)
TCOC .... Transverse Cylindrical Orthomorphic Chart
TCOCD .... Thermocouple Open Circuit Detection (IAA)
T (Colds) .... Toxic Colds [*Medicine*]
TColISM .... Southern Missionary College, Collegedale, TN [*Library symbol Library of Congress*] (LCLS)
TCOM .... Tele-Communications Class A [*NASDAQ symbol*] (SAG)

TCOM.......... Tele-Communications, Inc. [*NASDAQ symbol*] (NQ)
TCOM.......... Terminal or Computer Originated Mail Systems, Inc. [*Washington, DC*] (TSSD)
TCOM.......... Tethered Communications, Inc. [*Westinghouse subsidiary*]
TCOM.......... Texas College of Osteopathic Medicine
TCOM.......... Transcutaneous Oxygen Monitor [*Laboratory Science*] (DAVI)
TCOMA......... Tele-Communic'ATCI Group [*NASDAQ symbol*] (TTSB)
TCOMB......... Tele-Communic'B'TCI Group [*NASDAQ symbol*] (TTSB)
T-Comm........ Terret Communications [*Whitehouse Station, NJ*] (TSSD)
TCOMP......... Tape Compare Processor [*Computer science*]
TCOMP......... TeleComm TCI Grp 6% Exch Pfd [*NASDAQ symbol*] (TTSB)
T/COMP........ Trimmed Complete [*Automotive engineering*]
TCON.......... Naval Telecommunications Command (AAGC)
TCON.......... Trailer Container [*MTMC*] (TAG)
TCON.......... Transportation Constructor [*MTMC*] (TAG)
T/CONT........ Throttle Control [*Automotive engineering*]
T/CONV........ Torque Converter [*Automotive engineering*]
TCoo.......... Putnam County Public Library, Cookeville, TN [*Library symbol Library of Congress*] (LCLS)
TCooH......... Cookeville General Hospital, Stephen Farr Health Sciences Library, Cookeville, TN [*Library symbol Library of Congress*] (LCLS)
TCooP......... Tennessee Technological University, Cookeville, TN [*Library symbol Library of Congress*] (LCLS)
TCOP.......... Test and Checkout Plan [*NASA*] (KSC)
TCOP.......... Thrust Chamber Oxidizer Purge (SAA)
TCOR.......... Chrysler Town and Country Owners Registry (EA)
TCOS.......... The Canadian Orthoptic Society (AC)
TCOS.......... Trunk Class of Service [*Telecommunications*] (TEL)
TCOSS......... Tasmanian Council of Social Service [*Australia*]
TCOT.......... Tension Control Optimisation Theory [*Tire manufacturing*]
T-COUNT....... Terminal Count [*Flight readiness count*] (MCD)
TCovH......... Tipton County Hospital, Covington, TN [*Library symbol Library of Congress*] (LCLS)
TCP........... [*The*] Acronym Generator Converter Program [*RCA computer program*] (IAA)
TCP........... Tactical Computer Processor
TCP........... Tactical Control Panel (MCD)
TCP........... Tactical Cryptologic Program [*DoD*]
TCP........... Tape Carrier Package (PCM)
TCP........... Tape Carrier Packaging [*Computer science*]
TCP........... Tape Conversion Program [*Computer science*] (MDG)
TCP........... Task Change Proposal (AAG)
TCP........... Task Control Packet (NASA)
TCP........... Task Control Program
TCP........... Teachers College Press
TCP........... Technical Change Proposal
TCP........... Technical Coordination Program [*Military*] (AFIT)
TCP........... Technical Cost Proposal (AAG)
TCP........... Technological Capabilities Panel (LAIN)
TCP........... Technology Coordinating Paper
TCP........... Telecommunications Processor (IAA)
TCP........... Telemetry and Command Processor Assembly [*Deep Space Instrumentation Facility, NASA*]
TCP........... Temple Cyclopaedic Primers [*A publication*]
TCP........... Temporary Change Procedure (AAG)
TCP........... Terminal Control Program
TCP........... Test and Checkout Procedure [*NASA*] (KSC)
TCP........... Test Change Proposal (CAAL)
TCP........... Test Checkout Panel
TCP........... Test Control Package (NASA)
TCP........... Test of Creative Potential
TCP........... Tetrachlorobiphenyl [*Organic chemistry*]
TCP........... Tetrachlorophenol [*Organic chemistry*]
TCP........... Tetracyanoplatinate [*Inorganic chemistry*]
TCP........... Tetracyanopyrazine [*Organic chemistry*]
TCP........... Texaco Combustion Process [*Automotive engineering*]
TCP........... Therapeutic Continuous Penicillin [*Medicine*] (MAE)
TCP........... Thermoform Continuous Percolation (IAA)
TCP........... Thienyl(cyclohexyl)piperidine [*Biochemistry*]
TCP........... Thrust Chamber Pressure [*Aerospace*] (IEEE)
TCP........... Time, Cost, and Performance
TCP........... Time Limited Correlation Processing
TCP........... Timing and Control Panel
TCP........... Tocopilla [*Chile*] [*Seismograph station code, US Geological Survey Closed*] (SEIS)
TCP........... Tool Center Point [*Robotics*]
TCP........... Torpedo Certification Program [*Military*] (CAAL)
TCP........... Total Cell Protein [*Biochemistry*]
TCP........... Total Circulating Protein [*Medicine*] (DMAA)
TCP........... Total Clottable Protein [*Clinical chemistry*]
TC + P........ Total Colonoscopy plus Polypectomy [*Proctoscopy*]
TCP........... Town and Country Planning Act [*British*]
TCP........... Toxin-Coregulated Pili [*Biochemistry*]
TCP........... Traffic Control Point [*or Post*] [*Military*]
TCP........... Trainer Change Proposal [*Military*] (AFIT)
TCP........... Training Controller Panel
TCP........... Transcorp Airways [*British ICAO designator*] (FAAC)
TCP........... Transfer of Control Point [*Aviation*] (FAAC)
TCP........... Transmission Control Program [*Telecommunications*] (OSI)
TCP........... Transmission Control Protocol [*Telecommunications*] (PCM)
TCP........... Transmission Control Protocol [*Advanced Research Projects Agency Network*] [*DoD*]
TCP........... Transmitter Control Pulse (NITA)
TCP........... Transparent Conducting Polymers [*Photovoltaic energy systems*]
TCP........... Transportation Control Plan [*Environmental Protection Agency*] (GFGA)
TCP........... Transport Command Police [*British military*] (DMA)
TCP........... Transport Control Protocol [*Telecommunications*]
TCP........... Tranylcypromine [*Organic chemistry*]
TCP........... Tricalcium Phosphate [*Inorganic chemistry*]
TCP........... Trichlorophenol [*Organic chemistry*]
TCP........... (Trichlorophenoxy)acetic Acid [*Also known as 2,4,5-T*] [*Herbicide*]
TCP........... Trichloropropane [*Organic chemistry*]
TCP........... Tricresyl Phosphate [*Organic chemistry*]
TCP........... Tropical Canine Pancytopenia (RDA)
TCP........... Tropical Conservation Program (GNE)
TCP........... True Conservative Party [*British*] (ECON)
TCP........... Trust Chamber Pressure [*Missile technology*] (KSC)
TCPA.......... Tantawangalo Catchment Protection Association (EERA)
TCPA.......... Tetrachlorophthalic Anhydride [*Flame retardant*] [*Organic chemistry*]
TCPA.......... Time to Closest Point of Approach [*Navigation*]
TCPA.......... Town and Country Planning Association [*British*]
TCPA.......... Trichlorophenylacetic Acid [*Herbicide*] [*Organic chemistry*]
TCPAM......... Tentative CNO [*Chief of Naval Operations*] Program Analysis Memorandum (NVT)
TCPC.......... Tab Card Punch Control
TCPC.......... Telephone Cable Process Controller (MHDB)
TCPC.......... Time-Correlated Photon Counting [*Spectrometry*]
TCPC.......... Town and Country Planning Commission [*Tasmania, Australia*]
TCPC.......... Transportation Claims and Prevention Council (EA)
TCP(CC)R...... Town and Country Planning (Compensation and Certificates) Regulations [*British*]
TCP(CPRW)R.... Town and Country Planning (Churches, Places of Religious Worship, and Burial Grounds) Regulations [*British*]
TCP-E......... Thermal Case Penetrator - External (MCD)
TCPGR......... Town and Country Planning General Regulations [*British*]
TCPH.......... Toluoyl Chloride Phenylhydrazine [*Drug for sheep*]
TCPI.......... Technical Chemicals & Products [*NASDAQ symbol*] (SAG)
TCP-I......... Thermal Case Penetrator - Internal (MCD)
TCPI.......... "To Complete" Performance Index (MCD)
TCPI.......... Transportation Club of the Petroleum Industry (EA)
TCP/IP........ Transmission Control Protocol [*or Program*] and Internet Protocol (PCM)
TCP/IP........ Transmission Control Protocol/Internet Protocol [*Computer science*] (EERA)
TCP/IP........ Transmission Control Protocol/Internet Protocol [*Computer science*] (DOM)
Tc-PIPIDA..... Technetium Pertechnetate/N-Paraisoproplyacetanilide-Iminodiacetic Acid Scan [*Radiology*] (DAVI)
TCPL.......... TransCanada Pipelines Ltd. [*Commercial firm*]
TCPLD......... Tunable Compound Phase-Locked Demodulator (IAA)
TCP(M)R....... Town and Country Planning (Minerals) Regulations [*British*]
TCPO.......... bis(Trichlorophenyl) Oxalate [*Organic chemistry*]
TCPO.......... Third-Class Post Office
TC pO_2..... Transcutaneous Partial Pressure of Oxygen [*Monitor*] [*Medicine*] (DAVI)
TCPP.......... (Tetrachlorophenyl)pyrrole [*Organic chemistry*]
TCPPA......... (Trichlorophenoxy)propionic Acid [*Plant hormone*] [*Herbicide*]
TCPS.......... Texas Center for Policy Studies (CROSS)
TCPS.......... Total Cavopulmonary Shunt [*Medicine*] (DMAA)
TCPS.......... Trailerless Collective Protection Station [*Military*]
TCPS.......... Transportable Collective Protection System (DWSG)
TCPTF......... Target Cost plus Target Fee
TC Pub........ Tariff Commission Publications [*A publication*] (DLA)
TCpY.......... Transcarpathian Yiddish (BJA)
TCQ........... Tacna [*Peru*] [*Airport symbol*] (OAG)
TCQ........... Teacher Concerns Questionnaire (EDAC)
TCQ........... Trichlorobenzoquinoneimine [*Reagent*]
TCQC.......... Tank Crew Qualification Course [*Army*]
TCQM.......... [*The*] Chief Quartermaster [*Military*]
TCQM.......... Tetracyanoquionodimethane [*Organic chemistry*] (SAA)
TCR........... Laneas Aeraes Trans Costa Rica SA [*ICAO designator*] (FAAC)
TCR........... Tab Card Reader
TCR........... Tactical Control RADAR (IAA)
TCR........... Tantalum-Controlled Rectifier
TCR........... Tape Cassette Recorder
TCR........... Task Change Request [*Army*]
TCR........... T-Cell Reactivity
TCR........... T-Cell Receptor [*Immunology*]
TCR........... T-Cell Recovery Column [*Chromatography*]
TCR........... T-Cell Rosette [*Medicine*] (DMAA)
TCR........... Teacher Contact Ratio (AIE)
TCR........... Teachers' Central Register [*Australia*]
TCR........... Teachers College Record [*A publication*] (BRI)
TCR........... Technical Change Request
TCR........... Technical Characteristics Review
TCR........... Technical Compliance Record
TCR........... Technical Cost Review (SSD)
TCR........... Telemetry Compression Routine
TCR........... Television Cathode Ray (IAA)
TCR........... Temperature Coefficient of Resistance
TCR........... Temperature Control Reference
TCR........... Tentative Cancellation Request
TCR........... Terrain Clearance RADAR
TCR........... Test Compare Results (MCD)
TCR........... Test Condition Requirements [*Army*]
TCR........... Test Conductor (MCD)
TCR........... Test Constraints Review [*NASA*] (MCD)
TCR........... Tetrachlororesourcinol [*Organic chemistry*]

TCR............ Thalamocortical Relay [*Neurology*]
TCR............ Thermal Coefficient of Resistance (IAA)
TCR............ Thermal Concept Review (NASA)
TCR............ Thermochemical Recuperator [*Proposed heat recovery system*]
TCR............ Thitec Recovery [*Vancouver Stock Exchange symbol*]
TCR............ Tie Control Relay (MCD)
TCR............ Time Code Reader
TCR............ Time Critical Requirements (MCD)
TCR............ Tonecraft Realty, Inc. [*Toronto Stock Exchange symbol*]
TCR............ Tool Completion Report
TCR............ Tooling Change Request
TCR............ Total Contractual Requirements (MCD)
TCR............ Total Controlled Return (WDAA)
TCR............ Total Control Racing [*Road-racing game*] [*Ideal Toy Corp.*]
TCR............ Total Core Recovery [*Nuclear energy*] (NUCP)
TCr............ Total Creatine [*Pool*]
TCR............ Tracer (AAG)
TCR............ Traffic Control RADAR
TCR............ Trainer Change Request [*Military*]
TCR............ Training/Conversion/Replacement (MCD)
TCR............ Transceiver (AABC)
TCR............ Transcription-Coupled Repair [*Genetics*]
TCR............ Transfer Control Register
TCR............ Transistorized Car Radio (IAA)
TCR............ Transit Commission Reports [*New York*] [*A publication*] (DLA)
TCR............ Transmittal Control Record [*Computer science*]
TCR............ Transportable Cassette Recorder (IAA)
TCR............ Transportation Corps Release [*Military*]
TCR............ Travaux. Centre de Recherche sur le Proche-Orient et la Grece Antiques. Universite de Sciences Humaines de Strasbourg [*A publication*] (BJA)
TCR............ Tubing Connector Reducer [*Instrumentation*]
TCR............ Two-Color Radiometer
TCrA............ Art Circle Public Library, Crossville, TN [*Library symbol Library of Congress*] (LCLS)
TCRA............ T-Cell Receptor Alpha (DMAA)
TCRA............ Telegraphy Channel Reliability Analyzer [*Telecommunications*] (OA)
TCRB............ T-Cell Receptor Beta (DMAA)
TCRC............ Time and Cycle Record Card [*NASA*] (KSC)
TCRD............ T-Cell Receptor Delta (DMAA)
TCRD............ Test and Checkout Requirements Document [*NASA*] (KSC)
TCRE............ Temperature-Compensated Reference Element
TCRE............ Transcervical Endometrial Resection [*Medicine*]
TCREC............ Transportation Research Command [*Army*] (MCD)
TCRF............ Toxic Chemical Release Form
TCRI............ Toxic Chemical Release Inventory (GNE)
TCRJ............ Thermocouple Reference Junction
TCRM............ Thermochemical Remanent Magnetization
TCRMG............ Tripartite Commission for the Restitution of Monetary Gold [*Belgium*] (EAIO)
TCRN............ Temporary Chaplain to the Royal Navy [*British*]
tcRNA............ Translation Control Ribonucleic Acid (MAE)
TCRP............ Tactical Command Readiness Program [*Army*]
TCRP............ Total Cellular Receptor Pool (DMAA)
TCRP............ Transit Cooperative Research Program [*FTA*] (TAG)
TCRPA............ Trans-Continental Railroad Passenger Association [*Defunct*] (EA)
TCRPC............ Tri-County Regional Planning Commission [*Information service or system*] (IID)
TCRSD............ Test and Checkout Requirements Specification Documentation [*NASA*] (NASA)
TCRTA............ Terracotta Roofing Tile Association [*Australia*]
TCRV............ Total Red Cell Volume [*Medicine*] (DMAA)
TCRZ............ T-Cell Receptor Z (DMAA)
TCS............ [*The*] Classification Society (EA)
TCS............ [*The*] Coastal Society (EA)
TCS............ [*The*] Constant Society (EA)
TCS............ [*The*] Cousteau Society (EA)
TCS............ [*The*] Crustacean Society (EA)
TCS............ [*The*] Cybele Society (EA)
TCS............ Tactical Call Sign (IAA)
TCS............ Tactical Computer System [*Army*] (MCD)
TCS............ Tactical Control Squadron
TCS............ Tanking Control System (AAG)
TCS............ Target Control System
TCS............ Target Cost System
TCS............ Tasmanian Caledonian Society [*Australia*]
TCS............ Teacher Characteristics Schedule
TCS............ Teaching Company Scheme [*British*]
TCS............ Teaching Company Scheme (AIE)
TCS............ Technical Change Summary [*NASA*] (MCD)
TCS............ Technical Classification of Soils [*For pine plantations*] [*Australia*]
TCS............ Technical Concurrence Sheets [*NASA*] (NASA)
TCS............ Technical Countdown Sequences (KSC)
TCS............ Telecommunications Consulting Services [*Richard A. Eisner & Co.*] [*New York, NY*] (TSSD)
TCS............ Telecommunications Control System [*Toshiba Corp.*] [*Computer science*]
TCS............ Telecommunications System
TCS............ Teleconference System [*Memorial University of Newfoundland*] [*St. John's, NF*] [*Telecommunications*] (TSSD)
TCS............ Telemetry and Command Station [*Aerospace*] (MCD)
TCS............ Telephone Conference Summary (NRCH)
TCS............ Television Camera System
TCS............ Television Control Set
TCS............ Telex Communications Service (NITA)
TCS............ Temperature Coefficient of Sensitivity (IAA)
TCS............ Temperature Control Subsystem (KSC)
TCS............ Temporary Change of Station [*Military*]
TCS............ Temporary Conditioning Station [*Nuclear energy*] (NRCH)
TCS............ Temporary Correction Sheet (MCD)
TCS............ Terminal Communications Subsystem
TCS............ Terminal Computer System (BUR)
TCS............ Terminal Control System [*Hewlett-Packard Co.*]
TCS............ Terminal Countdown Sequencer [*or Sequences*] [*NASA*] (KSC)
TCS............ Terminal Count Sequence (IAA)
TCS............ Ternary Compound Semiconductor
TCS............ Test Call Sender (NITA)
TCS............ Test Control Supervisor (NASA)
TCS............ Test Control System (NASA)
TCS............ Test of Cognitive Skills [*Achievement test*]
TCS............ Texas Centennial Society (EA)
TCS............ Texts from Cuneiform Sources [*A publication*] (BJA)
TCS............ Theater Communications System (MCD)
TCS............ Thermal Conditioning Service (IAA)
TCS............ Thermal Conditioning System (KSC)
TCS............ Thermal Control System [*or Subsystem*]
TCS............ Thermally Stimulated Charge [*Analytical chemistry*]
TCS............ Timing Cover and Seal Set [*Automotive engineering*]
TCS............ Tin Can Sailors (EA)
TCS............ Tire Control System [*Automotive engineering*]
TCS............ Token Corresponding Society [*British*] (DBA)
TCS............ Tone Call Squelch [*Telecommunications*] (IAA)
TCS............ Tool Clearance Slip (AAG)
TCS............ Tool Coordinate System
TCS............ Total Commissioned Service (DOMA)
TCS............ Total Communication Systems [*Pittsburgh, PA*] [*Telecommunications service*] (TSSD)
TCS............ Total Current Spectroscopy
TCS............ Tracheal Cellular Score [*Medicine*]
TCS............ Trac Industries, Inc. [*Toronto Stock Exchange symbol Vancouver Stock Exchange symbol*]
TCS............ Traction Control System [*Alfred Teves GmbH*] [*Automotive engineering*]
TCS............ Trade Commission of Spain (EA)
TCS............ Traffic Control Satellite
TCS............ Traffic Control Station
TCS............ Traffic Control System [*Army*]
TCS............ Transaction Control System [*Hitachi Ltd.*]
TCS............ TransCanada Telephone System [*Later, Telecom Canada*] (TSSD)
TCS............ Transcutaneous Stimulation
TCS............ Transducer Calibration System
TCS............ Transfer Carry Subtract
TCS............ Transmission Controlled Spark (MCD)
TCS............ Transmission-Controlled Speed (IIA)
TCS............ Transmission Control System (IAA)
TCS............ Transportable Communications System
TCS............ Transportation and Communications Service [*of GSA*] [*Abolished, 1972*]
TCS............ Transportation Consulting & Service Corp., Chicago IL [*STAC*]
TCS............ Transportation Costing Service [*Database*] [*A. T. Kearney, Inc.*] [*Information service or system*] (CRD)
TCS............ Transportes de Carga Aerea Especializada y Servicios Aeronauticos [*Mexico ICAO designator*] (FAAC)
TCS............ Trichlorosilane [*Inorganic chemistry*]
TCS............ Trichosanthin [*Botany*]
TCS............ Trim Control System
TCS............ Tripanel, Convoluted, Y-Strap [*A knee immobilizer*] [*Orthopedics*] (DAVI)
TCS............ Troop Carrier Squadron [*Military*] (CINC)
TCS............ Troposcatter Communications System
TCS............ Truth Or Consequences, NM [*Location identifier FAA*] (FAAL)
TCS............ Tube Cooling Supply
TCS............ Turbine Control System [*Nuclear energy*] (NRCH)
TCS............ Two-Photon Coherent States (MCD)
TCSA............ Tetrachlorosalicylanilide [*Organic chemistry*]
TCSA............ Trunk Cross Sectional Area [*of a tree*]
TCSAA............ Twentieth Century Spanish Association of America (EA)
TCS-AF............ Telecommunications Control System-Advanced Function (MHDI)
TCS & D............ Temperature Controlled Storage and Distribution Exhibition [*British*] (ITD)
TCSC............ Time-Critical Shipment Committee [*Defunct*] (EA)
TCSC............ Toyota Celica Supra Club (EA)
TCSC............ Trainer Control and Simulation Computer
TCSC............ Two-Channel Scan Camera (NOAA)
TCSCLC............ Two-Carrier Space-Charge-Limited Current
TCSD............ Telemetry and Communications Systems Division [*Apollo*] [*NASA*]
TCSEC............ Trusted Computer System Evaluation Criteria (MCD)
TCSEV............ Twin-Cushion Surface Effect Vehicle (PDAA)
TCSF............ T-Colony-Stimulating Factor (DMAA)
TCSF............ Thomson-CSF [*France NASDAQ symbol*]
TCSF............ Total Counts of Successive Fractions [*Chromatography*]
TCSFY............ Thomson-CSF ADS [*NASDAQ symbol*] (TTSB)
TCSG............ [*The*] Center for Social Gerontology (EA)
TCSI............ TCSI Corp. [*NASDAQ symbol*] (TTSB)
TCSI............ TCSI Corp. [*NASDAQ symbol*] (SAG)
TCSI............ Teknekron Communications Systems [*NASDAQ symbol*] (SPSG)
TCSI Cp............ TCSI Corp. [*Associated Press*] (SAG)
TCSL............ Transistor Current Switching Logic [*Electronics*] (IAA)
TCSM............ Test of Cognitive Style in Mathematics [*Educational test*]
TCSM............ Tropospheric Chemistry Systems Model (MCD)

TCSM........ Twin Channel Substrate Mesa (NITA)
TCSMC........ Transportation Corps Supply Maintenance Command [*Army*]
TCSnet........ Thai Computer Science Network (TNIG)
TCSP........ Tactical Communications Satellite Program [*DoD*] (MCD)
TCSP........ Tandem Cross-Section Program [*Bell System*]
TCSP........ Test Checkout Support Plan (KSC)
TCSP........ Tourism Council of the South Pacific (EERA)
TCSPC........ Time-Correlated Single Photon Counting [*Analytical chemistry*]
TCSPr........ Second Presbyterian Church Library, Chattanooga, TN [*Library symbol Library of Congress*] (LCLS)
TCSq........ Troop Carrier Squadron [*Air Force*] (AFM)
TCSR........ Typographic Council for Spelling Reform (EA)
TCSS........ Tactical Control Surveillance System
TCSS........ Tasmanian Council of Social Service [*Australia*]
TCSS........ Tri-Cone Support Structure [*NASA*]
TCSSS........ Thermal Control Subsystem Segment [*NASA*] (NASA)
TCST........ Chattanooga State Technical Community College, Chattanooga, TN [*Library symbol Library of Congress*] (LCLS)
TC STD........ Type Classification - Standard (MCD)
TCSTE........ Triangle Coalition for Science and Technology Education (EA)
TCSUH........ Texas Center for Superconductivity, University of Houston [*Research center*] (RCD)
TCSW........ Thinking Creatively with Sounds and Words [*Educational test*]
TCT........ Tactical Communications Terminal
TCT........ Tactical Computer Terminal [*Army*] (MCD)
TCT........ Takotna [*Alaska*] [*Airport symbol*] (OAG)
TCT........ Takotna, AK [*Location identifier FAA*] (FAAL)
TCT........ Tasmanian Conservation Trust [*State*] (EERA)
T Ct........ Tax Court of the United States, Reports [*A publication*] (DLA)
TCT........ Telemetry-Computer Translator [*Bell Laboratories*]
TCT........ Tennessee Temple Schools, Chattanooga, TN [*Library symbol Library of Congress*] (LCLS)
TCT........ Tennessee Temple University, Chattanooga, TN [*OCLC symbol*] (OCLC)
TCT........ Terminal Control Table [*Computer science*] (IAA)
TCT........ Terracotta Tile [*Classified advertising*] (ADA)
TCT........ Texas City Terminal Railway Co. [*AAR code*]
TCT........ Thrombin Clotting Time [*Clinical chemistry*]
TCT........ Thyrocalcitonin [*Also, CT, TCA*] [*Endocrinology*]
TCT........ Time Code Translator
TCT........ Tin Can Tourists of the World (EA)
Tct........ Tinctura [*Tincture*] [*Latin*]
TCT........ Toll Connecting Trunk [*Telecommunications*] (TEL)
TCT........ Tool Change Time
TCT........ Tool Cost Transportation [*MTMC*] (TAG)
TCT........ Total Composite Tolerance
TCT........ Total Controlled Tabulation (WDAA)
TCT........ Town & Country Corporate Trust [*NYSE symbol*] (SPSG)
TCT........ Town & Country Trust [*NYSE symbol*] (TTSB)
TCT........ Traffic Control Transponder
TCT........ Translator and Code Treatment Frame (IEEE)
TCT........ Trial Court [*Legal shorthand*] (LWAP)
TCT........ Trichloromethyltriazine
TCT........ True Centerline Tested
TCT........ Trunk Coin Telephone (OA)
TCT........ Tur Avrupa Havayollari AS [*Turkey*] [*ICAO designator*] (FAAC)
TCT........ Turbid Creamy Layer on Top [*Laboratory science*] (DAVI)
TCT........ Two-Component TOKAMAK
TcT........ Tympanostomy with Tube Placement [*Otorhinolaryngology*] (DAVI)
TCTA........ Teaching Certificate for Teachers of Art [*British*]
TCTC........ Temperature-Controlled Test Chamber [*EPA engine test*]
TCTC........ Tompkins City Trustco [*NASDAQ symbol*] (TTSB)
TCTC........ Tompkins County Trust Co. [*Ithaca, NY*] [*NASDAQ symbol*] (NQ)
TCTC........ Transportation Corps Technical Committee [*Army*]
TCTFE........ Trichlorotrifluoroethane [*Organic chemistry*]
TCTI........ Time Compliance Technical Instruction (NASA)
TCTL........ Tactical (AAG)
TCTM........ Aircraft Time Compliance Technical Manuals
T Ct Mem.... Tax Court of the United States, Memorandum [*A publication*] (DLA)
TCTNB........ Trichlorotrinitrobenzene [*Organic chemistry*]
TCTO........ Technical Changes to Technical Orders
TCTO........ Time Compliance Technical Order [*NASA*] (AAG)
TCTP........ Tetrachlorothiophene [*Organic chemistry*]
TCTP........ Tricapped Triangular Prism
TCTS........ Tactical Combat Training System [*Navy*]
TCTS........ Tactical Communications Systems Technical Standards [*Military*]
TCTS........ Tank Crew Turret Simulator (MCD)
TCTS........ Trans-Canada Telephone System (MCD)
TCTU........ Turkish Confederation of Trade Unions
TCTV........ Tel-Com Wireless Cable TV [*NASDAQ symbol*] (TTSB)
TCTV........ Tel-Com Wireless Cable TV Corp. [*NASDAQ symbol*] (SAG)
TCTV........ Telemedia Communication Television [*Cable-television system*]
TCTV........ Today's Child, Tomorrow's Victim [*Book title*]
TCTVA........ Tennessee Valley Authority, Technical Library, Chattanooga, TN [*Library symbol Library of Congress*] (LCLS)
TCTVW........ Tel-Com Wireless CATV Wrrt [*NASDAQ symbol*] (TTSB)
TCu........ Copper T [*An intrauterine contraceptive device*] (DAVI)
TCU........ Tactical Control Unit (MCD)
TCU........ Taichung [*Taityu*] [*Republic of China*] [*Seismograph station code, US Geological Survey*] (SEIS)
TCU........ Tape Control Unit
TCU........ Target Control Unit (IAA)
TCU........ Tecumseh, MI [*Location identifier FAA*] (FAAL)
TCU........ Telecommunications Control Unit (NITA)
TCU........ Teletype Communications Unit (NVT)
TCU........ Teletypewriter Control Unit (CET)
TCU........ Temperature Control Unit
TCU........ Tentative Clean Up (MCD)
TCU........ Terminal Cluster Unit
TCU........ Terminal Control Unit (MCD)
TCU........ Test Computer Unit
TCU........ Test Control Unit
TCU........ Test of Concept Utilization [*Psychometrics*]
TCU........ Texas Christian University [*Fort Worth, TX*]
TCU........ Thermal Control Unit
TCU........ Threshold Control Unit (CET)
TCU........ Thrust Control Unit
TCU........ Tight Close-Up [*Cinematography*] (NTCM)
TCU........ Time Change Unit (MCD)
TCU........ Timing Control Unit
TCU........ Topping Control Unit (AAG)
TCU........ Torpedo Control Unit
TCU........ Towering Cumulus [*Meteorology*]
TCU........ Transmission Control Unit
TCU........ Transmission Control Unit
TCU........ Transportable Computer Unit
TCU........ Transportation-Communication Employees Union [*Later, TCIU*]
TCU........ Transportation, Communications, and Utilities
TCU........ Transportation Control Unit [*MTMC*] (TAG)
TCU........ Transport Conversion Unit [*British military*] (DMA)
TCU........ Trauma Care Unit [*Medicine*] (DMAA)
TCU........ Treatment Control Unit [*Medicine*] (DMAA)
TCU........ Tri-College University Library Consortium [*Library network*]
TCU........ Turbine Control Unit
TCU........ University of Tennessee at Chattanooga, Chattanooga, TN [*Library symbol Library of Congress*] (LCLS)
TCUA........ [*The*] Committee to Unite America [*Defunct*] (EA)
TCUA........ Time-Critical, Unspecified Area
TCUCC........ Texas Christian University Computer Center [*Research center*] (RCD)
TCUL........ Tap Changing Under Load (MSA)
TC(UN)........ Trusteeship Council of the United Nations
TCUS........ Tax Court of the United States [*Also, TC*] [*Later, United States Tax Court*]
TCUSA........ Trans Am Club USA (EA)
TCV........ Tank Cleaning Vessel (ADA)
TCV........ Temperature Coefficient of Voltage
TCV........ Temperature Control Valve (AAG)
TCV........ Terminal-Configured Vehicle [*NASA*]
TCV........ Thoracic Cage Volume [*Medicine*]
TCV........ Three Concept View [*Medicine*] (DMAA)
TCV........ Throttle Control Valve
TCV........ Thrust Chamber Valve (MCD)
TCV........ Thrust Control Valve
TCV........ TOKAMAK [*Toroidal Kamera Magnetic*] Chauffage Variable [*Plasma physics instrumentation*]
TCV........ Total Containment Vessel (CAAL)
TCV........ Tracked Combat Vehicle (MCD)
TCV........ Transportes Aereos de Cabo Verde [*Cape Verde*] [*ICAO designator*] (FAAC)
TCV........ Travelling Convection Vortices
TCV........ Treasury Corp. Victoria [*Australia*]
TCV........ Troop Carrying Vehicle
TCV........ Turbine Control Valve [*Nuclear energy*] (NRCH)
TCV........ Turnip Crinkle Virus
TCVA........ Terminal-Configured Vehicles and Avionics [*Program*] [*NASA*]
TCVA........ Thromboembolic Cerebrovascular Accident [*Cardiology*] (DAVI)
TCVC........ Tape Control via Console
TCVD........ Technical Committee on Veterinary Drugs (EERA)
TCVR........ Transceiver (CET)
TCW........ Tactical Control Wing [*Air Force*]
TCW........ TCW Convertible Security Fund [*Associated Press*] (SAG)
TCW........ Time Code Word
TCW........ Tinned Copper Weld
TCW........ Tocumwal [*Australia Airport symbol*] (OAG)
TCW........ Track Confirmation Word [*Computer science*]
TCW........ Triple-Crown Resources [*Vancouver Stock Exchange symbol*]
TCW........ Troop Carrier Wing [*Military*] (CINC)
TCW 00........ TCW/DW Term Trust 2000 [*Associated Press*] (SAG)
TCW 02........ TCW/DW Term Trust 2002 [*Associated Press*] (SAG)
TCW 03........ TCW/DW Term Trust 2003 [*Associated Press*] (SAG)
T-CW & IB... Trans-Continental Weighing and Inspection Bureau
TCWC........ Texas Cooperative Wildlife Collections [*Texas A & M University*] [*Research center*] (RCD)
TCWEM........ TCW/DW Emerging Markets Opportunities Trust [*Associated Press*] (SAG)
TCWG........ Tasmanian Carpet Wool Growers' Ltd. [*Commercial firm Australia*]
TCWG........ Telecommunication Working Group
TCWg........ Troop Carrier Wing [*Air Force*] (AFM)
TCX........ Transfer of Control Cancellation Message [*Aviation*]
TCXO........ Temperature-Compensated Crystal Oscillator
TCXO........ Temperature-Controlled Crystal Oscillator
TCXW........ Tracer Petroleum Corp. [*NASDAQ symbol*] (SAG)
TCXWF........ Tracer Pete Wrrt [*NASDAQ symbol*] (TTSB)
TCXXF........ Tracer Petroleum [*NASDAQ symbol*] (TTSB)
TCXXF........ Tracer Petroleum Corp. [*NASDAQ symbol*] (SAG)
TCYAW........ Twentieth Century Young Adult Writers [*A publication*]
TCZD........ Temperature-Compensated Zener Diode
TD........ Area Training Director [*Red Cross*]
TD........ Chad [*ANSI two-letter standard code*] (CNC)

Td .... Dorsal Touch Neurons [*of a leech*]
TD .... Table of Distribution [*Military*]
TD .... Tabular Data (BUR)
TD .... Tactical Director [*Military*] (GFGA)
TD .... Tactical Division [*Air Force*]
TD .... Takayasu's Disease (DAVI)
TD .... Tank Destroyer [*Military*]
TD .... Tank Division (MCD)
TD .... Tansavio [*ICAO designator*] (AD)
TD .... Tape Degausser
TD .... Tape Distributor [*Computer science*] (IAA)
TD .... Tape Drive
TD .... Tardive Dyskinesia [*Medicine*]
TD .... Target Designator (MCD)
TD .... Target Discrimination
TD .... Target Drone
TD .... Task Description (AAG)
TD .... Task Directive (AAG)
Td .... T-Cell, Delayed Type [*Immunology*]
TD .... T-Dependent [*Immunology*]
TD .... Teacher's Diploma [*British*]
TD .... Teachta Dala [*Member of Parliament*] [*Ireland*]
TD .... Tealto Dail [*Member of the Dail*] [*Irish*] (ILCA)
TD .... Technical Data
TD .... Technical Demonstration (AAG)
TD .... Technical Design (AAG)
TD .... Technical Development (WDAA)
TD .... Technical Direction [*or Directive*]
TD .... Technical Director [*Television*]
TD .... Technical Discussion
TD .... Technical Division
TD .... Technical Drawing
TD .... Technician's Diploma [*British*] (DI)
TD .... Technological Dependence
TD .... Technology Demonstration [*NASA*] (RDA)
TD .... Technology Document (KSC)
TD .... Telegraph Department
TD .... Telegraphist Detector [*British military*] (DMA)
TD .... Telemetry Data
TD .... Telephone Department
TD .... Telephone Depot (IAA)
TD .... Telephone Directory
T/D .... Temperature Datum (NG)
TD .... Temperature Differential (MSA)
TD .... Temporarily Discontinued [*Fog signal*]
TD .... Temporary Disability
TD .... Temporary Duty
TD .... Ter in Die [*Three Times a Day*] [*Pharmacy*]
TD .... Terminal Device [*of a prosthesis*]
TD .... Terminal Digit [*Telecommunications*] (TEL)
TD .... Terminal Display (BUR)
TD .... Terminal Distributor (KSC)
TD .... Termination Date (NITA)
TD .... Territorial Decoration [*Military British*]
TD .... Test and Diagnostics (IAA)
TD .... Test Data
TD .... Test Design Specification (IEEE)
TD .... Test Directive (AAG)
TD .... Test Director
TD .... Test Distributor [*Telecommunications*] (TEL)
TD .... Test Drawing (MCD)
TD .... Testing and Development Division [*Coast Guard*]
TD .... Testing Device (MSA)
TD .... Tetanus and Diphtheria [*Toxoids*] [*Medicine*]
Td .... Tetrahedral [*Molecular geometry*]
TD .... Thanatophoric Dysplasia [*Lethal dwarfism*]
TD .... Theoretical Density [*Nuclear energy*] (NRCH)
TD .... Therapy [*or Treatment*] Discontinued [*Medicine*]
TD .... Thermal Desorption [*from surfaces*]
TD .... Thermodilution
TD .... Thiamine Deficient (OA)
TD .... Thioredoxin [*Also, TR, Trx*] [*Biochemistry*]
TD .... Third Defense [*Men's lacrosse position, until 1933*]
TD .... Thoracic Duct [*Anatomy*]
TD .... Thor-Delta [*Satellite*]
TD .... Thoria Dispersed [*Nickel*]
TD .... Threat Determination (MCD)
TD .... Threshold Decoding [*Computer science*] (IAA)
TD .... Threshold Detection
TD .... Threshold Dose [*Medicine*]
TD .... Threshold of Discomfort [*Medicine*] (MAE)
TD .... Thymus Dependent [*Cells*] [*Hematology*]
TD .... Tibial Dyschondroplasia [*Medicine*]
TD .... Tidal [*Volume*] [*Laboratory science*] (DAVI)
TD .... Tidal Disruption [*Astronomy*]
TD .... Tied
TD .... Tilbury Docks (ROG)
TD .... Tile Drain [*Technical drawings*]
TD .... Timed Disintegration [*Pharmacy*]
TD .... Time Delay
TD .... Time Deposit [*Banking*]
TD .... Time Difference [*or Differential*]
TD .... Time Disintegration (MEDA)
TD .... Time Division (SAA)
TD .... Time Docket (DGA)
TD .... Time of Departure
TD .... Timing Device
TD .... Tinned
TD .... Tod [*Unit of weight*]
TD .... To Deliver [*Pipet calibration*]
TD .... Tolerance Detector
TD .... Tone Decay [*Audiometry*] (MAE)
TD .... Tons per Day
TD .... Tool Design
TD .... Tool Disposition
TD .... Tool Drawing (MCD)
TD .... Top Down
T/D .... Top-of-Descent (GAVI)
TD .... Topographic Draftsman [*Navy*]
TD .... Toronto Dominion Bank [*Toronto Stock Exchange symbol Vancouver Stock Exchange symbol*]
TD .... Toronto-Dominion Bk [*TS symbol*] (TTSB)
TD .... Torpedo Dive Bomber Aircraft
TD .... Torsion Dystonia [*Medicine*] (AAMN)
TD .... Total Damage [*Meteorology*]
TD .... Total Denier [*Textile technology*]
TD .... Total Depth
TD .... Total Dictatorship
TD .... Total Disability [*Medicine*]
TD .... Total Discectomy [*Medicine*]
TD .... Total Dose [*of radiation*]
TD .... Touchdown [*Football*]
T/D .... Touchdown [*NASA*] (NASA)
TD .... Touring Diesel [*Automobile model, Mercedes-Benz Motors*]
TD .... Toxic Dose (EG)
TD .... Toyota Diffusion/Deposition
TD .... Tracing Dye (OA)
TD .... Track Data
TD .... Track Display
TD .... Track Dog [*Dog show term*]
TD .... Tracking Dog
TD .... Tractor-Drawn
TD .... Trade Development (AAGC)
TD .... Trade Dispute (OICC)
TD .... Trade Division [*British military*] (DMA)
TD .... Tradesman [*British military*]
TD .... TRADEVMAN [*Training Devices Man*] [*Navy rating*]
TD .... Traffic Decisions [*Interstate Commerce Commission*]
TD .... Traffic Department [*Scotland Yard*]
TD .... Traffic Director
TD .... Training Detachment
TD .... Training Developments
TD .... Training Device (MCD)
TD .... Training of Documentalists
TD .... Trajectory Diagram [*Army*] (MCD)
TD .... Transaction Diaries [*Bureau of the Census*] (GFGA)
TD .... Transaction Driven (IAA)
TD .... Transdermal (DAVI)
TD .... Transducer [*Electronics*] (IAA)
TD .... Transfer Dolly [*Bottom-loading transfer cask*] [*Nuclear energy*] (NRCH)
TD .... Transform Domain
TD .... Transient Detector
TD .... Transmission Distributor (NITA)
TD .... Transmit Data (IEEE)
T-D .... Transmitter-Distributor
TD .... Transportation and Docking (MCD)
TD .... Transportation Department
TD .... Transportation Disadvantaged [*MOCD*] (TAG)
TD .... Transport Driver (NOAA)
TD .... Transverse Diameter [*Of heart*] [*Anatomy*]
TD .... Transverse Direction
TD .... Transverse Division [*Cytology*]
TD .... Trapped Domain (IAA)
TD .... Traveler's Diarrhea [*Medicine*] (DMAA)
TD .... Treasury Decision [*In references to rulings*]
TD .... Treasury Department
TD .... Treatment Day
T/D .... Treatment Discontinued [*Medicine*]
TD .... Trinidad and Tobago
TD .... Tropical Depression [*Meteorology*]
TD .... Tropical Deterioration Committee Reports [*of NDRC*] [*World War II*]
TD .... Truck Driving Program [*Association of Independent Colleges and Schools specialization code*]
TD .... True Depth [*Diamond drilling*]
TD .... Trust Deed
TD .... Tuberoinfundibular Dopaminergic [*Neurons*] [*Neurology*]
TD .... Tumor Dose [*Radiation therapy*] (DAVI)
TD .... Tunnel Diode
TD .... Turbine Direct
TD .... Turbine Drive [*or Driven*]
TD .... Turbodiesel [*Automotive engineering*]
TD .... Turning Diameter [*Automotive engineering*]
TD .... Turntable Desk (DEN)
TD .... Tyne Division [*British military*] (DMA)
TD .... Typhoid Dysentery (AAMN)
TD .... Typographic Draftsman [*Navy*]
TD1 .... TRADEVMAN [*Training Devices Man*], First Class [*Navy rating*]
TD2 .... TRADEVMAN [*Training Devices Man*], Second Class [*Navy rating*]
TD3 .... TRADEVMAN [*Training Devices Man*], Third Class [*Navy rating*]

TD_{50} Median Toxic Dose [*Pharmacology*] [*Radiation therapy*] (DAVI)
TDA American Train Dispatchers Association
TDA [*The*] Disposables Association
TDA Table of Distribution and Allowances [*Military*] (AABC)
TDA Table of Distribution-Augmentation [*Military*]
TDA Tactical Decision Aid
TDA Tactical Development Agent [*Military*] (CAAL)
TDA Taking and Driving Away [*Motoring offense*] [*British*] (DI)
TDA Target Docking Adapter [*NASA*] (KSC)
TDA Tax Deferred Annuity [*Insurance*]
TDA Tax Deposit Account [*Banking*] (MHDW)
TDA Taxi Drivers' Association [*Australia*]
TDA Taxpayer Delinquent Account [*IRS*]
TDA Technical Directing Agency
TDA Telecommunications Dealers Association (EA)
TDA Telemetric Data Analyzer
TDA Temporary Danger Area (DA)
TDA Test Development Activity [*Army*]
TDA Test Development Agent (CAAL)
TDA Tetradecenyl Acetate [*Organic chemistry*]
TDA Textile Distributors Association (EA)
TDA Thermal Depolarization Analysis
TDA Thermodifferential Analysis
TDA Thyroid-Stimulating Hormone-Displacing Antibody [*Medicine*] (DMAA)
TDA Timber Drying Association [*British*] (DBA)
TDA Time Delay Amplifier
TDA Timeshare Developers Association [*British*] (DBA)
TDA Titanium Development Association (EA)
TDA Today (FAAC)
TDA Toll Dial Assistance [*Telecommunications*] (TEL)
TDA Toluenediamine [*Organic chemistry*]
TDA Tornado Detection Algorithm [*Marine science*] (OSRA)
TDA Torpedo Danger Area (NVT)
TDA Total Dissolved Arsenic
TDA Town Development Act [*Town planning*] [*British*]
TDA Tracking and Data Acquisition
TDA Tracking Data Analysis
TDA Trade and Development Agency (USGC)
TDA Training and Development Alert [*Advanced Personnel Systems*] [*Information service or system*] (CRD)
TDA Training Development Advisors (MCD)
TDA Transcarga SA [*Costa Rica*] [*ICAO designator*] (FAAC)
TDA Transportation Development Agency [*British*]
TDA Transport Distribution Analysis (DCTA)
TDA Treatment Development and Assessment Committee [*National Institutes of Health*] (EGAO)
TDA Trinidad [*Colombia*] [*Airport symbol*] (AD)
TDA Trunnion Drive Axis (SAA)
TDA Tundra Gold Mines [*Vancouver Stock Exchange symbol*]
TDA Tuning Device Assembly
TDA Tunnel-Diode Amplifier
TDA Tyrosine-D-Arginine [*Biochemistry*]
TDAA Airman Apprentice, TRADEVMAN [*Training Devices Man*], Striker [*Navy rating*]
TDA/AE Tracking and Data Acquisition/Advanced Engineering
TDaB William Jennings Bryan University, Dayton, TN [*Library symbol Library of Congress*] (LCLS)
TDAC Training Data and Analysis Center
TDAC Tropical Deterioration Administrative Committee [*of NDRC*] [*World War II*]
TDAC Tumor-Derived Activated Cell [*Oncology*]
TDAD Trade Development Assistance Division [*Bureau of East-West Trade*] [*Former USSR*] (IMH)
TDAE Tactics Development and Evaluation [*Military*] (MCD)
TDAE Test Design and Evaluation (MCD)
TDAE Tetrakis(dimethylamino)ethylene [*Also, TKDE, TMAE*] [*Organic chemistry*]
TDAE Tetrakis Dimethylamino Ethylene [*Organic chemistry*]
TDAFP Turbine-Driven Auxiliary Feed Pump [*Nuclear energy*] (NRCH)
TDAFWP Turbine-Driven Auxiliary Feedwater Pump [*Nuclear energy*] (NRCH)
TDAG Technology Development Advocacy Group [*NASA*] (SSD)
TDAIR Taxpayer Delinquent Account Information Record [*IRS*]
TDAL Tetradecenal [*Biochemistry*]
TDAMM Training Device Acquisition Management Model (MCD)
TDAMTB Tables of Distribution and Allowances Mobilization Troop Basis [*Army*] (AABC)
TDAN Airman, TRADEVMAN [*Training Devices Man*], Striker [*Navy rating*]
TDANA Time-Domain Automatic Network Analyzer [*National Institute of Standards and Technology*]
TD & E Test Design and Evaluation
TD & E Transposition, Docking, and Ejection [*NASA*] (KSC)
TD & G Tall, Dark, and Gruesome [*Slang*]
TD & GS Technical Documentation and Graphic Services
TD & H Tall, Dark, and Handsome [*Slang*]
TD & I Technology Development and Integration
TD & RA Threat Determination and Resource Allocation
TD & RA Twist Drill and Reamer Association [*British*] (DBA)
TD & SA Telephone, Data, and Special Audio (NASA)
TDANSW Timber Development Association (New South Wales) [*Australia*]
TDAP Total Distribution Action Plan
TDAP Training Development Action Plan (DOMA)
TDAR Tactical Defense Alerting RADAR
TDARA Threat Determination and Resource Allocation (MCD)
TDARDS Truth Data Acquisition, Recording, and Display System
TDaRI Tropical Development and Research Institute (PDAA)
TDAS Tactical Data Automation System (IAA)
TDAS Thermal Decomposition Analytical System [*For study of incineration*]
TDAS Thermocouple Data Acquisition System
TDAS Thickness Data Acquisition System [*Southwest Research Institute*]
TDAS Tracking and Data Acquisition Satellite (SSD)
TDAS Tracking and Data Acquisition System
TDAS Traffic Data Administration System [*Bell System*]
TDAS Training Device Acquisition Strategy
TDAS Tunnel-Diode Amplifier System
TDASA Timber Development Association of South Australia
TDASS Tracking and Data Acquisition Satellite System (SSD)
TDAT Technical Directorate Assistance Team [*South Vietnamese studies and observation group team*] (VNW)
TDATD Total Distribution Advanced Technology Demonstration [*Army*]
TDAY Today's Bancorp [*NASDAQ symbol*] (TTSB)
TDAY Todays Bancorp, Inc. [*NASDAQ symbol*] (SAG)
T (Day) Transition Day [*Based on the expected transition from a two-front to a one-front war*] [*World War II*]
T (Day) Truce Day
TDB Task Database [*Computer science*] (PCM)
TDB Technical Directive Bulletin (MCD)
TDB Temporary Disability Benefits [*Insurance*]
TDB Temps Dynamique Barycentrique [*Barycentric Dynamical Time*] [*French*]
TDB Terminological Data Bank
TDB Terminology Database (NITA)
TDB Terrain Data Base [*Army*] (RDA)
TDB Terrestrial Dust Belt
TDB Test Documentation Booklet [*Navy*] (CAAL)
TDB Tetebedi [*Papua New Guinea*] [*Airport symbol*] (OAG)
TDB Top Drawing Breakdown (AAG)
TDB Total Disability Benefit (DLA)
TDB Toxicology Data Bank [*National Library of Medicine*] [*Information service or system*] (IID)
TDB Track Database (MCD)
TDB Trade and Development Board [*United Nations Conference on Trade and Development*]
TDB Trade Development Bank [*Subsidiary of American Express Bank*]
TDB Transportable Database [*Telecommunications*]
TDB Turbine-Driven Blower
TDB Welch Aviation, Inc. [*ICAO designator*] (FAAC)
TdbE Tanna di-be Eliahu (BJA)
TDBG Training Depot Brigade of Gurkhas [*British military*] (DMA)
TDBI Training Directory for Business and Industry [*A publication*]
TDBM Tactical Data Base Manager (DOMA)
TDBMS Tactical Database Management System
TDBP Tris(dibromopropyl) Phosphate [*Also, TDBPP, Tris, T ris-BP*] [*Flame retardant, mutagen*]
TDBPP Tris(dibromopropyl) Phosphate [*Also, TDBP, Tris, Tris-BP*] [*Flame retardant, mutagen*]
TDBS Texas Data Base System (EDAC)
TDC Chief TRADEVMAN [*Training Devices Man*] [*Navy rating*]
TDC Dallas Christian College, Dallas, TX [*OCLC symbol*] (OCLC)
TDC [*The*] Discovery Channel [*Television*]
TDC Tactical Data Converter
TDC Tactical Digital Computer (MCD)
TDC Tactical Document Copier (MCD)
TDC Tadair SA [*Spain ICAO designator*] (FAAC)
TDC Taiwan Defense Command (MCD)
TDC Tank Destroyer Center [*Army*]
TDC Target Data Collection
TDC Target Data Communicator (DWSG)
TDC Target Designator Control (MCD)
TDC Tarif Douanier Commun [*Common Customs Tariff*]
TDC Taurodeoxycholate [*or Taurodeoxycholic*] Acid [*Biochemistry*]
TDC Technical Data Center [*Department of Labor*] [*Information service or system*] (IID)
TDC Technical Development Capital (IAA)
TDC Technical Development Center
TDC Technical Development Contractor
TDC Technical Directive Compliance (MCD)
TDC Technical Document Center
TDC Technical Document Change (MCD)
TDC Technology Development Corp.
TDC TEFLON Dielectric Capacitor
TDC Tektronix Development Co. (NITA)
TDC Teledyne Canada Ltd. [*Toronto Stock Exchange symbol*]
TDC Temperature Density Computer
TDC Temporary Detective Constable [*Scotland Yard*]
TDC Terminal Data Corp. [*Information service or system*] (IID)
TDC Termination Design Change
TDC Test Director Console
TDC Thermal Diffusion Chamber
TDC Thermal Diffusion Coefficient [*Nuclear energy*] (NRCH)
TDC Through Deck Cruisers [*British*]
TDC Time Data Card (AAG)
TDC Time Delay Closing
TDC Time Distribution Card (AAG)
TDC Time-Domain Coding
TDC Time of Day Clock (IAA)
TDC Time-to-Digital Converter [*Instrumentation*]
TDC Tone Digital Command (IAA)
TDC Tooling Design Change
TDC Top Dead Center
TDC Top Desk Computer (IAA)

TDC............ Torpedo Data Computer [*Navy*] (NVT)
TDC............ Total Design Concept [*Sarcastic reference to a completely coordinated wardrobe, decorating scheme, etc.*] [*Slang*]
TDC............ Total Dietary Calories [*Dietetics*] (DAVI)
TDC............ Total Distributed Control [*Computer science*]
TDC............ Totally Decentralized Control (IAA)
TDC............ Tourist Development Corp. of Malaysia
TDC............ Track Data Center
TDC............ Track Data Central
TDC............ Track Data Corp. [*Software firm*] [*Information service or system*] (IID)
TDC............ Track Detection Circuit [*Electronics*] (OA)
TDC............ Trade Development Corp. [*South Australia*] [*Commercial firm*]
TDC............ Trade Development Council (EERA)
TDC............ Training Device Center
TDC............ Transferable Development Credit
TDC............ Transistor Digital Circuit (IAA)
TDC............ Transistor Digital Control (IAA)
TDC............ Transmission Distribution Center (IAA)
TDC............ Transportation Development Center [*Cambridge, MA*] [*Department of Transportation Formerly, NASA Electronic Research Center*]
TDC............ Transportation Development Centre [*Transport Canada*] [*Research center*] (RCD)
TDC............ Transportation Development Centre Library [*UTLAS symbol*]
TDC............ Transport Code for Computer (IAA)
TDC............ [*US*] Travel Data Center [*BTS*] (TAG)
TDC............ Treasury Department Circular [*A publication*] (DLA)
TDC............ Tridecylcyclohexane [*Organic chemistry*]
TDC............ Trinidad [*Colorado*] [*Seismograph station code, US Geological Survey Closed*] (SEIS)
TDC............ Tristate Data Consultants, Inc. [*Database producer*] (IID)
TDC............ Tube Deflection Coil
TDC............ Two-Dimensional Finite Cylinder (IAA)
TDC............ Type Directors Club (EA)
TDC............ Tyrosine Decarboxylase [*An enzyme*]
TDCA.......... Therapeutic Discovery Corp. [*NASDAQ symbol*] (SAG)
TDCB.......... Tapered Double Cantilever Beam (MCD)
TDCC.......... Tactical Data Communications Center
TDCC.......... Transportation Data Coordinating Committee [*Later, EDIA*]
TDCC/EDIA... TDCC [*Transportation Data Coordinating Committee*]: the Electronic Data Interchange Association [*Telecommunications service*] (TSSD)
TDCE.......... Technical Direction Contract Effort
TDCF.......... Technical Directive Compliance Form (NVT)
TDCH.......... Tridecylcyclohexane [*Organic chemistry*]
TDCK.......... Technisch Documentatie Centrum voor der Krijgsmacht [*Netherland Armed Services Technical Documentation and Information Center*] (MCD)
TDCM.......... Master Chief TRADEVMAN [*Training Devices Man*] [*Navy rating*]
TDCM.......... Transistor Driver Core Memory
TD/CMS....... Technical Data/Configuration Management System (MCD)
TDCN.......... Technical Data Change Notice (MCD)
TDCN.......... Time Delay Compression Network
TDCO.......... Test Director Console Operator [*Navy*] (CAAL)
TDCO.......... Thermal Dilution Cardiac Output
TDCO.......... Torpedo Data Computer Operator [*Navy*]
TDCR.......... Teacher's Diploma of the College of Radiographers [*British*] (DBQ)
TDCR.......... Technical Data Change Request [*NASA*] (KSC)
TDCR.......... Technical Data Contract Requirement (MCD)
TDCR.......... Test Deficiency Change Request [*Nuclear energy*] (NRCH)
TDCS.......... Senior Chief TRADEVMAN [*Training Devices Man*] [*Navy rating*]
TDCS.......... Tactical Deployment Control Squadron
TDCS.......... Tape Data Control Sheet [*Computer science*]
TDCS.......... Target Detection-Conversion Sensor
TDCS.......... Time-Division Circuit Switching [*Telecommunications*]
TDCS.......... Traffic Data Collection System (MCD)
TDCSP........ Tactical Defense Communications Satellite Program (MCD)
TDCT.......... Time-Domain Coding Technique
TDCT.......... Track Data Central Tables (SAA)
TDCT.......... Tunnel-Diode Charge Transformer
TDCTL........ Tunnel-Diode Charge-Transformer Logic
TDCU.......... Target Data Control Unit (AAG)
TDCU.......... Target Designator Control Unit (MCD)
TDCU.......... Threat Display Control Unit (MCD)
TDCU.......... Tinned Copper
TDD........... Tactical Data Display
TDD........... Target Detecting Device
TDD........... Task Description Document (NASA)
TDD........... Teardown Deficiency (MCD)
TDD........... Technical Data Digest [*Air Force*]
TDD........... Technical Documents Division [*Naval Air Systems Command*]
TDD........... Telecommunications Device for the Deaf
TDD........... Telecommunications for the Deaf and Disabled
TDD........... Telemetry Data Digitizer
TDD........... Telephone Device for the Deaf
TDD........... Test Data Division (SAA)
TDD........... Test Definition Document
TDD........... Test Design Description [*Nuclear energy*] (NRCH)
TDD........... Test Development Director
TDD........... Tetradecadiene [*Organic chemistry*]
TDD........... Thedford, NE [*Location identifier FAA*] (FAAL)
TDD........... Thoracic Duct Drainage [*Medicine*]
TDD........... Three D Departments, Inc. [*AMEX symbol*] (SPSG)
TDD........... Timing Data Distributor (IAA)
TDD........... Timing Defense Depot (SAA)
TDD........... Top Down Development (MHDB)
TDD........... Total Digitalizing Dose [*Medicine*] (MEDA)
TDD........... Tracy Defense Depot (SAA)
TDD........... Transdermal Drug Delivery [*Medicine*]
TDD........... Treasury Department Decision (AFIT)
TDD........... Trinidad [*Bolivia*] [*Airport symbol*] (OAG)
TDD........... Tuberculous Diseases Diploma [*British*]
TDDA.......... Tetradecadienyl Acetate [*Biochemistry*]
TDDA.......... Three Depts Cl'A' [*AMEX symbol*] (TTSB)
TDD.B......... Three D Depts Cv Cl'B' [*AMEX symbol*] (TTSB)
TDDD.......... ThreeD Labs, Inc. Ltd. [*NASDAQ symbol*] (SAG)
TDDL.......... Time-Division Data Link [*Radio*]
TDDLPO....... Time-Division Data Link Print-Out [*Telecommunications*] (IAA)
TDDM.......... Time-Division Digital Multiplexer (MCD)
TDDM.......... Training Device Development Management [*Model*] (MCD)
TDDn.......... Tank Destroyers Division [*Army*]
TDDO.......... Time Delay Dropout [*Relay*] (AAG)
TDDR.......... Technical Data Department Report [*NASA*] (KSC)
TDDR.......... Transdermal Drug Delivery Research
TDDRS........ Total Dose/Dose Rate Simulator
TDDS.......... Tactical Data Display System (MCD)
TDDS.......... Talking Directory Display System [*FTA*] (TAG)
TDDS.......... Teacher Development in Desegregating Schools [*Office of Education*]
TDDS.......... Television Data Display System (KSC)
TDDS.......... Two-Dimensional Deflection System (IAA)
TDE........... Tactical Deception Element (NVT)
TDE........... Tactics Development Evaluation (MCD)
TDE........... Technical Data Engineer (MCD)
TDE........... Technical Data Evaluation
TDE........... Testing Difficulty Estimator
TDE........... Tetrachlorodiphenylethane [*Also, DDD*] [*Insecticide*]
TDE........... Three Day Event [*Horseriding*] [*British*] (DI)
TDE........... Time Displacement Error (IAA)
TDE........... Toluene-Dioxane-Ethanol [*Scintillation solvent*]
TDE........... Total Daily Energy [*Requirement*] [*Dietary*] (DAVI)
TDE........... Total Data Entry
TDE........... Total Differential Equation
TDE........... Total Digestible Energy [*Nutrition*]
TDE........... Transdermal Estradiol [*Pharmacology*]
TDE........... Trans-Dominion Energy Corp. [*Toronto Stock Exchange symbol*]
TDE........... Triethylene Glycol Diglycidyl Ether [*Medicine*]
TDE........... Two-Dimensional Equilibrium
TDEC.......... Technical Development Evaluation Center
TDEC.......... Technical Division and Engineering Center [*FAA*] (MCD)
TDEC.......... Telephone Line Digital Error Checking
TDEC.......... Tennessee Department of Environmental Conservation (DOGT)
TDEC.......... Tennessee Department of Environmental Conservation
TDEC.......... Tennessee Department of Environmental Conservation
TDEC.......... Therapeutic Device Evaluation Committee [*Australia*]
TDECC........ Tactical Display Engagement Control Console [*Military*] (RDA)
TDED.......... Trade Data Elements Directory (DS)
TDEFWP...... Turbine-Driven Emergency Feedwater Pump [*Nuclear energy*] (NRCH)
TDEL.......... Time Delay (FAAC)
TDEM.......... Time-Domain Electromagnetics [*Technique for searching for underground water*]
TDEN.......... Total Density [*Ecology*]
TDEP.......... Tracking Data Editing Program [*NASA*]
TDES.......... [*The*] Duke Ellington Society (EA)
TDF........... Tactical Digital Facsimile (MCD)
TDF........... Tape Data Family
TDF........... Target Development Facility [*Proposed, 1986, for fusion research*]
TDF........... Task Deletion Form [*Nuclear energy*] (NRCH)
TDF........... Telediffusion de France [*Broadcasting agency*] [*French*]
TDF........... Templeton Dragon Fd [*NYSE symbol*] (TTSB)
TDF........... Templeton Dragon Fund [*NYSE symbol*] (SAG)
TDF........... Temporary Detention Facility
TDF........... Testis-Determining Factor [*Genetics*]
TDF........... Theatre Development Fund (EA)
TDF........... Thin Dielectric Film
TDF........... Thoracic Duct Fistula [*Medicine*] (MAE)
TDF........... Thoracic Duct Flow [*Medicine*] (MAE)
TDF........... Time-Dependence Fluorescence [*Chemistry*]
TDF........... Time-Domain Filter
TDF........... Time Dose Fractionation Factor [*Roentgenology*]
TDF........... Tonga Defence Force [*British military*] (DMA)
TDF........... Training Directors' Forum [*An association*] (EA)
TDF........... Transborder Data Flows [*Also, TBDF*] [*Telecommunications*]
TDF........... Transformer Differential (IAA)
TDF........... Transkei Defence Force [*South Africa*]
TDF........... Trial-Dependent-Forgetting [*Process*] [*Psychology*]
TDF........... Trim and Drill Fixture (MCD)
TDF........... Trunk Distribution Frame (DEN)
TDF........... Tumor Dose Fractionation [*Oncology*] [*Radiation therapy*] (DAVI)
TDF........... Two Degrees of Freedom
TDFC.......... Thomas Dolby Fan Club (EA)
TDFCHB....... Telemetry Data Format Control Handbook (KSC)
TDFL.......... Tunnel-Diode FET [*Field-Effect Transistor*] Logic (IAA)
TDFR.......... Total Duration-Specific Fertility Rate [*Population studies*]
TDFS.......... Terminal Digit Fitting System [*Military*] (AABC)
TDG........... Tactical Decision Game [*Marine Corps*] (DOMA)
TDG........... Tactical Development Group [*Military*] (CAAL)
TDG........... Tactical Drone Group (MCD)
TDG........... Talladega, AL [*Location identifier FAA*] (FAAL)
TDG........... Tandag [*Philippines*] [*Airport symbol*] (OAG)

TDG .... Technical Design Guide
TDG .... Technical Developing Group [*of the Publishers' Association*] [*British*]
TDG .... Telemetry Data Generation
TDG .... Test Data Generator (BUR)
TDG .... Test Display Generator
TDG .... Test Documentation Group
TDG .... Tetradecanylglutarate [*Biochemistry*]
TDG .... Textile Designers Guild (EA)
TDG .... Thio(deaza)guanine [*Antineoplastic drug*]
TDG .... Thiodigalactoside [*Organic chemistry*]
TDG .... Thiodiglycol [*Organic chemistry*]
TDG .... Time Delay Generator
TDG .... Timesharer Developers' Group [*British*]
TDG .... Toodoggone Gold [*Vancouver Stock Exchange symbol*]
TDG .... Top-Down Greedy
TDG .... TOTAL Energold Corp. [*Toronto Stock Exchange symbol*]
TDG .... Trading (DCTA)
TDG .... Transportation of Dangerous Goods [*International symposium*]
TDG .... Transport Development Group Ltd. [*British*]
TDG .... Twist Drill Gauge
TDGL .... Test Data Generating Language (MHDB)
TDGO .... 3-D Geophysical [*NASDAQ symbol*] (TTSB)
TDGO .... Three D Geophysical, Inc. [*NASDAQ symbol*] (SAG)
TDGS .... Test Data Generation Section [*Social Security Administration*]
TDH .... Terre des Hommes [*An international organization*]
TDH .... Total Dynamic Head (AAG)
TDH .... Toxic Dose High (OA)
TDH .... Tracking Data Handling
TDH .... Transport Disengaging Height [*Fluidized beds of particles*]
TDHC .... Thermadyne Holdings [*NASDAQ symbol*] (TTSB)
TDHC .... Thermadyne Holdings Corp. [*NASDAQ symbol*] (SAG)
TDHGA .... Travel of Dependents and Household Goods Authorized [*Military*] (AABC)
TDHL .... Transdihydrolisuride [*Biochemistry*]
TDHS .... Tape Data Handling System
TDHS .... Time Domain Harmonic Scaling [*Telecommunications*] (LAIN)
TDI .... [*The*] Democracy International (EA)
TDI .... TACAN [*Tactical Air Navigation*] Distance Indicator
TDI .... Target Data Inventory [*Military*] (AFM)
TDI .... Target Doppler Indicator [*RADAR*]
TDI .... Task Description Item (MCD)
TDI .... Taxpayer Delinquent Investigation [*IRS*]
TDI .... Teardown Inspection
TDI .... Technical Data International [*Information service or system*] (IID)
TDI .... Technology Dynamics Institute [*Telecommunications service*] (TSSD)
TDI .... Telecommunications Data Interface
TDI .... Telecommunications for the Deaf, Inc. (EA)
TDI .... Telegraphist Detector Instructor [*British military*] (DMA)
TDI .... Teletec Development, Inc. [*Vancouver Stock Exchange symbol*]
TDI .... Temporary Disability Insurance [*Unemployment*]
TDI .... Test Data Interpolation
TDI .... Textile Dye Institute [*Later, American Dye Manufacturers Institute*]
TDI .... Therapeutic Donor Insemination [*Obstetrics*]
TDI .... Therapy Dogs International (EA)
TDI .... Time Delay and Integration (MCD)
TDI .... Tolerable Daily Intake [*Toxicology*]
TDI .... Toluene [*or Tolylene*] Diisocyanate [*Organic chemistry*]
TDI .... Tool and Die Institute (KSC)
TDI .... Total Domestic Incomes [*Department of Employment*] [*British*]
TDI .... Total Dose Infusion [*Medicine*] (MAE)
TDI .... Trade Data Interchange (DS)
TDI .... Training Development and Improvement Program [*Department of Education*]
TDI .... Training Developments Institute [*Army*]
TDI .... Transportation Displays, Inc. [*A company*] [*Advertising*] [*New York, NY*] (WDMC)
TDI .... Trasport Device Interface [*Computer science*]
TDI .... TSH [*Thyroid-Stimulating Hormone*] Displacing Immunoglobulin [*Endocrinology*]
TDI .... Turbine Disk Integrity [*Nuclear energy*] (NRCH)
TDI .... Twin Disc [*NYSE symbol*] (TTSB)
TDI .... Twin Disc, Inc. [*NYSE symbol*] (SPSG)
TDI .... Two-Wire Direct Interface (MHDB)
TDI .... Tymnet DTS, Inc. [*San Jose, CA*] [*Telecommunications*] (TSSD)
TDIA .... Tasmanian Dairy Industry Authority [*Australia*]
TDIA .... Transient Data Input Area [*Computer science*] (IAA)
TDIC .... Target Data Input Computer
TDIC .... Total Dissolved Inorganic Carbon [*Environmental chemistry*]
TDIL .... Target Detection, Identification, and Location
TDINF .... Taxpayer Delinquency Investigation Notice File [*IRS*]
TDIO .... Timing Data Input-Output
TDIP .... Total Disability Income Provisions [*Military*] (AABC)
TDIPR .... Test Design In-Process Review (MCD)
TDIPRE .... Target Data Inventory Master Tape Preparation [*Military*] (IAA)
TDIS .... Technical Data Impact Summary (MCD)
TDIS .... Terminal Data Input System (MCD)
TDIS .... Terminal Defense Interceptor Subsystem [*DoD*]
TDIS .... Thai Development Information Service (EAIO)
TDIS .... Time Distance [*Military*] (AABC)
TDIS .... Time Distance Terminal Data Input System (MCD)
TDIS .... Training Development Information System [*Army*]
TDIS .... Travel Document and Issuance System [*US passport*] [*Department of State*]
TDISTR .... Tape Distributor (MSA)
TDIU .... Target Data Input Unit
TDJ .... Dallas County Community College District, Dallas, TX [*OCLC symbol*] (OCLC)
TDJ .... Tadjoura [*Djibouti*] [*Seismograph station code, US Geological Survey*] (SEIS)
TDJ .... Tadjoura [*Djibouti*] [*Airport symbol*] (OAG)
TDJC .... Technical Data Justification Code [*Army*]
TDK .... Tardive Dyskinesia [*Neurology*] (DAVI)
TDK .... TDK Corp. [*NYSE symbol*] (SPSG)
TDK .... TDK Corp. ADS [*NYSE symbol*] (TTSB)
TDK .... Test of Diabetes Knowledge
TDK .... Tokyo Denki Kagaku [*Tokyo Electronics and Chemical Co.*] [*Initialism is now name of recording tape manufacturer and brand name of its products*]
TDKF .... Fahrzeugtestdatenbank [*Dokumentation Kraftfahwesen eV*] [*Germany Information service or system*] (CRD)
TDKP .... Turkish Revolutionary Communist Party [*Political party*] (PD)
TDL .... David Lipscomb College, Nashville, TN [*OCLC symbol*] (OCLC)
TDL .... Tactical Data Link
TDL .... Tandil [*Argentina*] [*Airport symbol*] (OAG)
TDL .... Tapped Delay Line
TDL .... Target Development Laboratory [*Eglin AFB*] (AAG)
TDL .... Task-Directed Learning
TDL .... Technical Data Laboratory [*National Weather Service*]
TDL .... Technical Document List
TDL .... Telemetry Data Link [*Telecommunications*] (IAA)
TDL .... Test and Diagnostic Language (MCD)
TDL .... Test Description Log (MCD)
TDL .... Thoracic Duct Lymphocyte [*Immunochemistry*]
TDL .... Threshold Damage Level
TDL .... Threshold Detection Level
TDL .... Thymus-Dependent Lymphocyte [*Hematology*]
TDL .... Topographic Developments Laboratory [*Fort Belvoir, VA*] [*United States Army Engineer Topographic Laboratories*] (GRD)
TDL .... Toxic Dose Low (OA)
TDL .... Transaction Definition Language
TDL .... Transformation Definition Language [*Computer science*] (IBMDP)
TDL .... Translation Definition Language
TDL .... Transparent Data Link (SSD)
TDL .... Tunable Diode LASER [*Also, SDL*]
TDL .... Tunnel-Diode Logic
TDLAS .... Tunable Diode LASER Absorption Spectrometry
TDLB .... Training and Development Lead Body (AIE)
TDLCA .... Thoracic Duct Lining Cells Antigen [*Immunology*]
TD^{Lo} .... Toxic Dose Low (ERG)
TDLOA .... Training Device Letter of Agreement
TDLR .... Terminal Descent and Landing RADAR
TDLR .... Training Device Letter Requirement [*Military*]
TDLS .... Topographic Data Library System
TDLS .... Tower Data-Link Services [*FAA*] (TAG)
TDLU .... Terminal Duct Lobular Unit [*Of mammary gland*]
TDM .... Mount Alvernia Friary, Wappingers Falls, NY [*Inactive*] [*OCLC symbol*] (OCLC)
TDM .... Palmyra [*Syria*] [*Airport symbol*] (AD)
TDM .... Tandem (AAG)
TDM .... Tandem Computers [*NYSE symbol*] (TTSB)
TDM .... Tandem Computers, Inc. [*NYSE symbol*] (SPSG)
TDM .... Tandem Resources [*Vancouver Stock Exchange symbol*]
TDM .... Tank Destroyer Armed with Missiles (INF)
TDM .... Task Description Memo (MCD)
TDM .... Technical Division Manager
TDM .... Technology Development Mission [*NASA*] (SSD)
TDM .... Telecommunications Data-Link Monitor (CET)
TDM .... Teledifusao de Macau [*Radio and television broadcasting company*] [*Macau*] (FEA)
TDM .... Telemetric Data Monitor
TDM .... Template Descriptor Memory
TDM .... Ternary Delta Modulation
TDM .... Tertiary Dodecyl Mercaplan (OA)
TDM .... Test Data Memorandum (AAG)
TDM .... Test Development Manager [*Military*] (CAAL)
TDM .... Text and Date Messaging (HGAA)
TDM .... Therapeutic Drug Monitoring
TDM .... Thermal Development Model
TDM .... Thermal Diffusion Method
TDM .... Thermodynamic Molding
TDM .... Time Division Multiplex [*Electronics*]
TDM .... Time Division Multiplexing [*Telecommunications*]
TDM .... Time-Division Multiplexor [*Computer science*] (DOM)
TDM .... Time Driven Monitor (MHDI)
TDM .... Time Duration Modulation (DEN)
TDM .... Tire Degradation Monitor (MCD)
TDM .... Tool Design Manual (MCD)
TDM .... Torpedo Detection Modification [*SONAR*]
TDM .... Total Dissolvable Manganese [*Chemistry*]
TDM .... Tracking Data Message (SSD)
TDM .... Transportation Demand Management [*MOCD*] (TAG)
TDM .... Trehalose Dimycolate [*Biochemistry*]
TDM .... Trouble Detection and Monitoring
TDM .... True Dipole Moment [*Geodesy*]
TDM .... Tunnel-Diode Mixer
TDMA .... Tape Direct Memory Access
TDMA .... Tape Direct Memory Address (NITA)
TDMA .... Time Distributed Multiple Access (IAA)
TDMA .... Time-Division [*or Time-Domain*] Multiple Access [*Computer control system*]

TDMA.......... Time Division Multiple Access
TDMA.......... Trophy Dealers and Manufacturers Association (EA)
TDMAC........ Tridodecylmethylammonium Chloride [*Organic chemistry*]
TDMC.......... Technical Data Management Center [*Department of Energy*] [*Information service or system Defunct*] (IID)
TDMD.......... Time-Division Multiplex Device [*Radio*]
TDME.......... Test, Diagnostic, and Measurement Equipment (MCD)
TDMG.......... Telegraph and Data Message Generator (MCD)
TDMM.......... International Union of Tool, Die, and Mold Makers
TDMO.......... Technical Data Management Office [*Navy*]
TDMP.......... Technical Data Management Program [*Navy*]
TDMP.......... Technology Development Mission Polar [*Canada*] (SSD)
TDMR.......... Technical Division Memo Report [*Army World War II*]
TDMRA........ Texas Delaine-Merino Record Association [*Later, TDSA*] (EA)
TDMS.......... Telegraph Distortion Measuring System
TDMS.......... Telegraphic Distortion Measuring Set (IAA)
TDMS.......... Telemetry Data Monitor Set
TDMS.......... Thermal Desorption Mass Spectroscopy
TDMS.......... Time-Division Multiplex System [*Radio*] (MCD)
TDMS.......... Time-Shared/Data Management System
TDMS.......... Toxicology Data Management System [*Department of Health and Human Services*] (GFGA)
TDMS.......... Transmission Distortion Measuring Set
TDMTB........ Tables of Distribution Mobilization Troop Basis [*Army*] (AABC)
TDM-VDMA... Time-Division Multiplex - Variable Destination Multiple Access [*Telecommunications*] (TEL)
TDMWG....... Technology Development Missions Working Group [*NASA*] (SSD)
TDN............ Target Doppler Nullifier [*RADAR*]
TDN............ Total Digestible Nutrients
TDN............ Travel as Directed Is Necessary in the Military Service (MUGU)
TDN............ Trimethyldihydronapthalene [*Organic chemistry*]
T-DNA......... Transfer-Deoxyribonucleic Acid
TDNCA......... Texas Date Nail Collectors Association (EA)
TDNN.......... Time Delay Neural Network [*Computer science*]
TDNS.......... Total Data Network System (TEL)
TDNS.......... Training Device Needs Statement [*Army*]
TDNT.......... Theological Dictionary of the New Testament [*A publication*] (BJA)
TDO............ Task Direction Order [*Military*]
TDO............ Technical Development Objective
TDO............ Technical Direction Order
TDO............ Technical Directives Ordnance (NG)
TDO............ Technical Divisions Office [*Jet Propulsion Laboratory, NASA*]
TDO............ Telegraph Delivery Order
TDO............ Time Delay Opening
TDO............ Toledo, WA [*Location identifier FAA*] (FAAL)
TDO............ Tornado
TDO............ Training Development Office [*Army*]
TDO............ Training Development Officer [*British*]
TDO............ Transistor Dip Oscillator (IAA)
TDO............ Transporte Aereco Dominicano [*Dominican Republic*] [*ICAO designator*] (FAAC)
TDO............ Treasury Department Order [*A publication*] (DLA)
TDO............ Tuesday Downtown Operators and Observers [*An association*] (EA)
TDOA.......... Time Delay of Arrival (MCD)
TDOA.......... Time Deposit, Open Account [*Banking*]
TDOA.......... Time Difference of Arrrival
TDOA/DD..... Time Difference of Arrival and Differential Doppler (MCD)
TDOA/DME... Time Difference of Arrival / Distance Measuring Equipment (PDAA)
TDOC.......... Technical Document (DNAB)
TDOL.......... Tetradecanol [*Organic chemistry*]
TDOP.......... Time Dilution of Precision
TDOP.......... Truck Design Optimization Project [*Railroads*]
TDOS.......... Tape Disk Operating System [*Computer science*]
TDOT.......... Thorndike Dimensions of Temperament [*Psychology*]
TDP............ Tactical Data Processor (DOMA)
TDP............ Tag Distribution Protocol [*Computer science*]
TDP............ Tank Development Program [*Military*]
TDP............ Target Data Processor (NVT)
TDP............ Target Director Post [*RADAR*] [*Military*]
TDP............ Technical Data Package [*Military*]
TDP............ Technical Development Plan
TDP............ Technical Documentation for Provisioning [*Military*] (AFIT)
TDP............ Teledata Processing
TDP............ Telefonica del Peru SA [*NYSE symbol*] (SAG)
TDP............ Telegu Desam Party [*India*] [*Political party*]
TDP............ Temperature and Dew Point (KSC)
TDP............ Temperature Density Plotter
TDP............ Temporary Detention of Pay
TDP............ Terminal Defense Program [*Military*]
TDP............ Test Design Plan [*Army*]
TDP............ Thermal Death-Point
TDP............ Thermistor Detector Package
TDP............ Thiamine Diphosphate [*Also, DPT, TPP*] [*Biochemistry*]
TDP............ Thiodiphenol [*Organic chemistry*]
TDP............ Thoracic Duct Pressure [*Medicine*] (MAE)
TDP............ Thymidine Diphosphate [*Biochemistry*]
TDP............ Toluene Disproportionation Process [*Organic chemistry*]
TdP............ Torsade de Pointes [*Fringe of Pointed Tips*] [*Found on electrocardiograms*] [*Cardiology*] (DAVI)
TDP............ Total Development Plan
TDP............ Touchdown Protection [*Military*] (MCD)
TDP............ Tracking and Display Processor (CAAL)
TDP............ Tracking Data Processor
TDP............ Trade and Development Program [*US International Development Cooperation Agency*]
TDP............ Traffic Data Processing
TDP............ Traffic Demand Predictor [*Aviation*]
TDP............ Trainee Discharge Program [*Army*]
TDP............ Transit Development Program [*TRB*] (TAG)
TDP............ Trim and Drain Pump [*Navy*] (CAAL)
TDPA.......... Textile Data Processing Association [*Later, ATMI*] (EA)
TDPA.......... Thiodipropionic Acid [*Organic chemistry*]
TDPAC........ Time Differential Perturbed Angular Correlation [*Physics*]
TDPB.......... Tactical Display Plotting Board
TDPD.......... Dominica/Melville Hall [*Dominica*] [*ICAO location identifier*] (ICLI)
TDPD.......... Technical Data Package Depository [*Army*]
TDPF.......... Tail Damping Power Factor [*Aviation*]
TDPF.......... Target Data Planning File (SAA)
TDPFO........ Temporary Duty Pending Further Orders [*Military*]
TDPI........... Tasmanian Department of Primary Industry [*State*] (EERA)
TDPI........... Two-Dimensional Probabilistic Image (PDAA)
TDPJ.......... Truck Discharge Point Jet (NATG)
TDPL.......... Technical Data Package List [*Military*] (AABC)
TDPL.......... Top-Down Parsing Language
TDPM.......... Time-Domain Prony Method (IAA)
TDPM.......... Truck Discharge Point Mogas (NATG)
TDPMP........ Technical Data Package Management Plan [*Army*]
TDPOB........ Thrift Depositor Protection Oversight Board (BARN)
TDPP.......... Traffic Data Processing Program (MCD)
TDPR.......... Roseau [*Dominica*] [*ICAO location identifier*] (ICLI)
TDPRha....... Thymidine Diphosphorhamnose [*Biochemistry*]
TDPS.......... Tracking Data Processor System (MCD)
TDPSA........ Association for Totally Dependent Persons of South Australia
TDPSK........ Time Differential Phase-Shift Keying
TDPU.......... Telemetry Data Processing Unit (CAAL)
TDQP.......... Trimethyldihydroquinoline Polymer [*Organic chemistry*]
TDR............ Canair Cargo [*Canada ICAO designator*] (FAAC)
TDR............ Short Tour Return Date [*Military*]
TDR............ Tail Damping Ratio [*Aviation*]
TDR............ Talos Discrepancy Report (MCD)
TDR............ Tape Data Register
TDR............ Target Detection and Recognition (MCD)
TDR............ Target Discrimination RADAR (IEEE)
TDR............ TDR: The Drama Review [*A publication*] (BRI)
TDR............ Teacher Demonstration Rating (OA)
TDR............ Teardown Deficiency Report
TDR............ Technical Data Relay (IEEE)
TDR............ Technical Data Report
TDR............ Technical Data Requests
TDR............ Technical Deficiency Report
TDR............ Technical Design Review (NASA)
TDR............ Technical Development Requirement
TDR............ Technical Directive Records (NG)
TDR............ Technical Documentary Report
TDR............ Temperature-Dependent Resistor (BYTE)
TDR............ Temperature Depth Recorder
TDR............ Temporarily Disconnected at Subscriber's Request [*Telecommunications*] (TEL)
TDR............ Tender [*Navy*] (NVT)
TDR............ Terminal Digit Requested [*Telecommunications*] (TEL)
TDR............ Test Data Recorder
TDR............ Test Data Report (AAG)
TDR............ Test Deficiency Report [*Nuclear energy*] (NRCH)
TD/R........... Test Disable/Reset (AAG)
TDR............ Test Discount Rate
TDR............ Test Discrepancy Report (MCD)
TDR............ Threat Detection RADAR [*Military*] (CAAL)
TdR............ Thymidine [*Genetics*] (DAVI)
TDR............ Time Delay Receiver (NITA)
TDR............ Time Delay Relay
TDR............ Time Domain Reflectometer (NITA)
TDR............ Time Domain Reflectometry [*or Reflectometer*]
TDR............ Todoroki [*Japan*] [*Seismograph station code, US Geological Survey Closed*] (SEIS)
TDR............ Tone Dial Receiver
TDR............ Tool Design Request (KSC)
TDR............ Torque-Differential Receiver (MUGU)
TDR............ Total Defect Rate
TDR............ Track Data Request (CAAL)
TDR............ Tracking and Data Relay [*NASA*]
TDR............ Traffic Data Record (DA)
TDR............ Training Device Requirement [*Army*] (AABC)
TDR............ Transactional Document Recorder (NITA)
TDR............ Transferable Development Rights [*Community planning*]
TDR............ Transistorized Digital Readout
TDR............ Transmit Data Register [*Computer science*] (MDG)
TDR............ Transnational Data and Communicative Report [*A publication*] (TSSD)
TDR............ Transportation Discrepancy Report [*MTMC*] (TAG)
TDR............ Trap Designator Register
TDR............ Treasury Deposit Receipt
TDR............ Triplet-Doublet Resonance [*Physics*]
TDR............ Tropical Disease Research [*WHO*]
TDR............ Tudor Corp. Ltd. [*Toronto Stock Exchange symbol*]
TDR............ Turndown Ratio
TdR-^{3}H........ Tritiated Thymidine [*Genetics*] (DAVI)
TDRC.......... Total Diet Research Center [*Public Health Service*] (GRD)
TDRE.......... Tracking and Data Relay Experiment [*Telecommunications*] (TEL)
TDRF.......... Target Doppler Reference Frequency

TDRI .... Tropical Development and Research Institute [*Research center British*] (IRC)
TDRL .... Temporary Disability Retired List [*Military*]
T/DRLY .... Time Delay Relay
TDRM .... Time-Domain Reflectometry Microcomputer
TDRP .... TearDrop Golf Co. [*NASDAQ symbol*] (SAG)
TDRR .... Test Data Recording and Retrieval (NASA)
TDRRB .... Technical Data Requirement Review Board
TDRRC .... Training Device Requirements Review Committee [*Army*]
TDRS .... Technical Data Requirements Sheet
TDRS .... Telemetering Data Recording Set (CAAL)
TDRS .... Telemetry Downlist Receiving Site (NASA)
TDRS .... Text Data Retrieval System (NITA)
TDRS .... Tracking and Data Relay Satellite [*NASA*]
TDRS .... Traffic Data Recording System [*Bell System*]
TDRS .... Transnational Data Reporting Service, Inc. [*Springfield, VA*] [*Telecommunications service*] (TSSD)
TDRS .... Travelers, Defect Route Sheet (DNAB)
TDRSS .... Tracking and Data Relay Satellite Services [*or System*] [*NASA*]
TDRSS .... Tracking and Data Relay Satellite System [*Instrument*] (EERA)
TDRTC .... Tank Destroyer Replacement Training Center
TDS............. Tactical Data System
TDS............. Tactical Deployment Support
TDS............. Tactical Display System (CAAL)
TDS............. Tactical Drone Squadron
TDS............. Tape Data Selector
TDS............. Tape Decal System
TDS............. Target Data Sheet (MCD)
TDS............. Target Designation System [*Navy*]
TDS............. Tasmanian Deaf Society [*Australia*]
TDS............. Teacher Demand and Shortage Survey [*Department of Education*] (GFGA)
TDS............. Technical Database Services, Inc. [*Information service or system*] (IID)
TDS............. Technical Data Specialist
TDS............. Technical Data System (KSC)
TDS............. Technical Description Sheet
TDS............. Technical Directive System (MCD)
TDS............. Technology Delivery System (NUCP)
TDS............. Technology Demonstration Satellite [*NASA*] (NASA)
TDS............. Teleflora Delivery Service (EA)
TDS............. Telemetry Decommutation System
TDS............. Telephone & Data Sys [*AMEX symbol*] (TTSB)
TDS............. Telephone & Data Systems, Inc. [*AMEX symbol*] (SPSG)
TDS............. Teleprocessing Design Center [*Army*] (PDAA)
TDS............. Temperature-Depth-Salinity [*Oceanography*]
TDS............. Temperature-Determined Sex [*Laboratory science*] (DAVI)
TDS............. Temporary Duty Station [*Air Force*] (AFM)
TDS............. Ter in Die Sumendum [*To Be Taken Three Times a Day*] [*Pharmacy*]
TDS............. Tertiary Data Set [*Computer science*] (OA)
TDS............. Test Data Sheet (KSC)
TDS............. Test Data Specification (IAA)
TDS............. Test Data System (NASA)
TDS............. Thermal Degradation Sample [*Apollo*]
TDS............. Thermal Desorption Spectroscopy
TDS............. Time Delay Switch
TDS............. Time, Distance, Speed
TDS............. Time Distribution System (MCD)
TDS............. Time-Division Switching [*Telecommunications*]
TDS............. Time-Domain Spectroscopy (IEEE)
TDS............. Tool Data Sheet (MCD)
TDS............. Tool Design Service (MCD)
TDS............. Tool Design Study (MCD)
TDS............. Torpedo Deflection Sight
TDS............. Torpedo Destruction System
TDS............. Total Dissolved Solids
TDS............. Total Dissolved Solids
TDS............. Track Data Simulator
TDS............. Track Data Storage
TDS............. Tracking and Data System [*NASA*]
TDS............. Training Depot Station [*British military*] (DMA)
TDS............. Training Developments Study
TDS............. Training Directors Seminar [*LIMRA*]
TDS............. Transaction Distribution System
TDS............. Transaction Driven System [*Honeywell, Inc.*]
TDS............. Transistor Display and Data-Handling System [*Computer science*] (MDG)
TDS............. Translation and Docking Simulator [*Navy*] (KSC)
TDS............. Transportation Data Sampler [*BTS*] (TAG)
TDS............. Trap Designator Set
TDS............. Trash Disposal System
TDS............. Traverse des Sioux Library System, Mankato MN [*OCLC symbol*] (OCLC)
TDS............. Tuned LASER Differential Spectrometry (IAA)
TDS............. Tunnel Destruct System
TDSA .... Technical Data Status Accounting (MCD)
TDSA .... Technical Directive Status Accounting
TDSA .... Telegraph and Data Signals Analyzer (MCD)
TDSA .... Texas Delaine Sheep Association (EA)
TDSA .... TRADEVMAN [*Training Devices Man*], Seaman Apprentice [*Navy rating*]
TDSC .... 3-D Systems Corp. [*NASDAQ symbol*] (TTSB)
TDSC .... Three D Systems [*NASDAQ symbol*] (SAG)
TDSC .... Training Device Support Center [*Army*]
TDSCC .... Tidbinbilla Deep Space Communications Complex
TDSDT .... Tactical Data System Development Testbed
TDSF .... Tasmanian Department of Sea Fisheries [*Australia*]
TDSF .... Technical Data Support Facility
TDSIC .... Theatre/Drama, and Speech Information Center (IID)
TDSMO .... Tactical Data Systems Management Office [*Fort Leavenworth*] [*Army*] (MCD)
TDSN .... TRADEVMAN [*Training Devices Man*], Seaman [*Navy rating*]
TDSO .... Training Device Supply Office [*Navy*] (DNAB)
TDSP .... Technical Data Support Package [*Navy*]
TDSP .... Top Down Structured Programming (MHDB)
TDSQB .... Time Delay Squib [*Navy*]
TDSS .... Telemetry Data Signal Simulator (MCD)
TDSS .... Time-Dependent Stokes Shift [*Physical chemistry*]
TDSS .... Time Dividing Spectrum Stabilization [*Electronics*] (OA)
TDSS .... Turret Drive Subsystem (DWSG)
TDSSC .... Tone Dial Switching System Control (IAA)
TDST .... Track Data Storage (MSA)
TDSTP .... Trainer Digital Self-Test Program
TDT............. Tactical Data Terminal (MCD)
TDT............. Tank Driver Trainer [*Army*]
TDT............. Target Designation Transmitter
TDT............. Target Docking Trainer [*NASA*] (KSC)
TDT............. Task Dispatch Table [*Computer science*] (OA)
TDT............. Tavil-Dara [*Former USSR Seismograph station code, US Geological Survey Closed*] (SEIS)
TDT............. TCW/DW Term Trust 2000 [*NYSE symbol*] (SPSG)
TDT............. Tentative Drainage Tomorrow [*Surgery*] (DAVI)
TDT............. Terminal Death Time (OA)
TDT............. Terminal Deoxynucleotidyl Transferase [*An enzyme*]
TDT............. Terminal Deoxytransferase [*An enzyme*] (DAVI)
TDT............. Terrestrial Dynamic Time (WGA)
TDT............. Test Direction Team
TDT............. Test Dwell Time
TDT............. Thermal Death Time [*Bacteriological testing*]
TDT............. Thiodiethanethiol [*Organic chemistry*]
TDT............. This Day Tonight (ADA)
TDT............. Tidioute, PA [*Location identifier FAA*] (FAAL)
TDT............. Tone Decay Test [*Audiometry*]
TDT............. Toronto Dance Theatre
TDT............. Total Delay Time
TDT............. Total Downtime
TDT............. Tower Disconnect Technician (SAA)
TDT............. Translation and Docking Trainer
TDT............. Transmission Disequilibrium Test [*Genetics*]
TDT............. Transonic Dynamic Tunnel [*NASA*]
TDT............. Tumor Doubling Time [*Cytology*]
TDT............. Tunnel-Diode Transducer
TDT............. Turret Director Trainer [*British military*] (DMA)
TDTA............ Templin Darley Test of Articulation [*Speech and language therapy*] (DAVI)
TDT and CU.... Target Designation Transmitter and Control Unit
TD/TDNA...... Tardive Dyskinesia/Tardive Dystonia National Association (EA)
TDT/FC......... Tank Destroyer Tactical and Firing Center
TDTG .... True Date-Time Group [*Military*]
TDTL .... Tunnel-Diode Transistor Logic
TDTL............ Tunnel Diode Tunnel Logic (NITA)
TDTO .... Transmission and Drive Train Oil
TDTS............ Tactical Data Transfer System (NATG)
TDTTEABL.... Tax Detectable to the Extent Allowed by Law
TDU .... Tactical Deception Unit (NVT)
TDU .... Tactical Display Unit (NVT)
TDU .... Talos Defense Unit (SAA)
TDU .... Target Detection Unit
TDU .... Teamsters for a Democratic Union (EA)
TDU .... Threat Display Unit (MCD)
TDU .... Time Display Unit (NASA)
TDU .... Tondu [*British depot code*]
TDU .... Torpedo Development Unit [*Ministry of Technology*] [*British*]
TDU .... Towed Unit [*Aerial Target*] (CAAL)
TDU .... Tracking Display Unit
TDU .... Trash Disposal Unit (DNAB)
TDU .... Traverse Displacement Unit (DNAB)
TDU .... Trigger Delay Unit
TDU .... Tropendienstunfaehig [*Unfit for service in tropics*] [*German military - World War II*]
TDUM .... Tape Dump and Utility Monitor [*Computer science*]
TDUP .... Technical Data Usage Program
TDUR .... Therapeutic Drug Utilization Review [*Insurance*] (WYGK)
TDV............. Technology Development Vehicle (IEEE)
TDV............. Terminal Delivered Vehicle [*Army*]
TDV............. Test Data Van (NASA)
TDV............. Test Data Variation
TDV............. Touchdown Velocity [*Aviation*]
TDV............. Tumbleweed Diagnostic Vehicle
TDW............ Amarillo, TX [*Location identifier FAA*] (FAAL)
TDW............ Tidewater, Inc. [*NYSE symbol*] (SPSG)
TDW............ Tons Deadweight (DS)
TDW............ Trunk Destination Words (CET)
TDW............ Turbo Debugger for Windows [*Computer science*] (PCM)
TDWB .... Touch-Down Weight-Bearing [*Orthopedics and rehabilitation*] (DAVI)
TDWG .... Taxonomic Databases Working Group for Plant Sciences (EERA)
TDWO .... Test and Development Work Order
TDWR .... Terminal Doppler Weather RADAR (DWSG)
TDWT........... Transonic Dynamic Wind Tunnel [*NASA*] (KSC)
TDWU .... Transport and Dock Workers' Union [*India*]

TDX............ Thermal Demand Transmitter (MSA)
TDX............ Time-Division Exchange
TDX............ Torque-Differential Transmitter (MUGU)
TDX............ Tracking Dog Excellent
TDX............ Transportation Data Xchange, Inc. (IID)
TDX............ Tridex Corp. [*AMEX symbol*] (SPSG)
TDX............ Wrangler Aviation, Inc. [*FAA designator*] (FAAC)
TDXT............ ThreeDX Technologies, Inc. [*NASDAQ symbol*] (SAG)
TDY............ Air Today, Inc. [*ICAO designator*] (FAAC)
TDY............ Teledyne, Inc. [*NYSE symbol*] (SPSG)
TDY............ Temporary Duty
TDY............ Trading Bay, AK [*Location identifier FAA*] (FAAL)
TDYPrE........ Teledyne Inc. Sr'E' Pfd [*NYSE symbol*] (TTSB)
TDZ............ Thioridazine [*Tranquilizer*]
TDZ............ Thymus-Dependent Zone [*Hematology*] (MAE)
TDZ............ Toledo, OH [*Location identifier FAA*] (FAAL)
TDZ............ Torpedo Danger Zone (NVT)
TDZ............ Trade Development Zone (ADA)
TDZ............ Transcontinental Dislocation Zone [*Geology*]
TDZ............ Tridel Enterprises, Inc. [*Toronto Stock Exchange symbol*]
TDZA............ Trade Development Zone Authority [*Northern Territory, Australia*]
TDZ/CL......... Touchdown Zone/Centerline [*Aviation*] (DNAB)
TDZE............ Touchdown Zone Elevation [*Aviation*] (DA)
TDZL............ Touchdown Zone Light System [*Aviation*] (FAAC)
TE............ Electron Temperature [*Plasma physics*] (OA)
TE............ [*The*] Engelettes [*An association Defunct*] (EA)
T-e............ Erythrocyte Tri-Iodothyronine [*Endocrinology*] (DAVI)
TE............ Light Temporarily Extinguished [*Navigation*]
TE............ Ling-Temco-Vought [*LTV*] [*ICAO aircraft manufacturer identifier*] (ICAO)
TE............ Table of Equipment [*Army*]
T/E............ Tactical Emergency [*Army*]
TE............ Tageseinfluesse [*Weather factors, a gunnery term*] [*German military - World War II*]
TE............ Talmudic Encyclopedia [*A publication*] (BJA)
TE............ Tamper Evident
TE............ Tangent Elevation (MSA)
TE............ Tape Error [*Computer science*] (IAA)
TE............ Task Element
TE............ Tatin Experimental [*British military*] (DMA)
TE............ Tax-Equivalent (TDOB)
TE............ Taxiway Edge Lighting [*Aviation*] (DA)
TE............ Teacher of Electrotherapy [*British*]
TE............ Technical Engineer
TE............ Technical Evaluation [*Army*]
TE............ Technical Exchange
TE............ Technician [*Communications*] [*Navy rating*]
TE............ Technological Engineer [*A publication*]
TE............ TECO Energy [*NYSE symbol*] (TTSB)
TE............ TECO Energy, Inc. [*NYSE symbol*] (SPSG)
TE............ Telecom Eireann [*Dublin, Ireland*] [*Telecommunications service*] (TSSD)
TE............ Telecommunications Engineering (WDAA)
TE............ Tele-Engineering Corp. [*Telecommunications service*] (TSSD)
TE............ Telegram
TE............ Telegraph Editor [*Journalism*] (WDMC)
TE............ Teleman [*Navy rating British*]
TE............ Telemetry Event [*Telecommunications*] (IAA)
TE............ Telephone Equipment Room [*NFPA pre-fire planning symbol*] (NFPA)
TE............ Teller of the Exchequer [*British*] (ROG)
Te............ Tellurium [*Chemical element*]
TE............ Temperature Element [*Nuclear energy*] (NRCH)
TE............ Temporary Employee [*Business term*] (MHDB)
TE............ Tenants by the Entirety [*Legal term*]
TE............ Tennis Elbow [*Medicine*] (DMAA)
TE............ Tension Equalizer [*Electrical*] Wave
TE............ Terminal [*Computer science*] (IAA)
TE............ Terminal Equipment
TE............ Terminal Exchange (MCD)
TE............ Test and Engineering (MCD)
TE............ Test Ear [*Otorhinolaryngology*] (DAVI)
TE............ Test Equipment
TE............ Test Exception [*Nuclear energy*] (NRCH)
TE............ Test Explicit
Te............ Tetanus [*Medicine*] (WGA)
TE............ Tetracycline [*Antibiotic compound*]
TE............ Text Editor [*Computer science*]
TE............ Theatre in Education (EA)
TE............ Theistic Evolutionist
TE............ Theological Educator [*A publication*]
TE............ Theological Examination
TE............ Thermactor Emission [*Automotive engineering*]
TE............ Thermal Efficiency
TE............ Thermal Element (KSC)
TE............ Thermal Expansion Load [*Nuclear energy*] (NRCH)
TE............ Thermoelectric
TE............ Thioesterase [*An enzyme*]
TE............ Threat Evaluation (NVT)
TE............ Threshold Element (IAA)
TE............ Threshold Energy [*Medicine*] (MAE)
TE............ Threshold Exceeded
TE............ Thromboembolic [*Medicine*]
TE............ Throughput Efficiency (CAAL)
TE............ Thunder Engines Corp. [*Vancouver Stock Exchange symbol*]
TE............ Thymus Epithelial [*Cell*] [*Immunology*] (DAVI)
TE............ Tight End [*Football*]
Te............ Tigre (BJA)
TE............ Time Earliest/Expected (NASA)
TE............ Time Electronics (GFGA)
TE............ Time Equipment (IAA)
TE............ Time Error in Psychophysical Judgments [*Psychology*]
TE............ Time Estimation (DAVI)
T/E............ Time Expired (ADA)
TE............ Time to Echo [*Medicine*]
TE............ Timing Electronics (KSC)
TE............ Tissue-Equivalent [*Medicine*] (MAE)
TE............ Tocopherol Equivalent [*Nutrition*]
TE............ Toluene-Ethanol [*Scintillation solvent*]
TE............ Tonsillectomy [*Medicine*] (DAVI)
TE............ Tonsils Excised [*Medicine*] (DAVI)
TE............ Tooth Extracted (MAE)
TE............ Top Eliminator [*Automobile racing*] (DICI)
TE............ Topographical Engineer
TE............ Tornisterempfaenger [*Pack-type portable receiver*] [*German military - World War II*]
TE............ Total Earnings (MHDB)
TE............ Total Estrogen [*Medicine*] (MAE)
TE............ Total Expenditure
TE............ Totally Embedded (DAVI)
TE............ Totally Enclosed (MSA)
TE............ Toxoplasma Encephalitis [*Neurology*] (DAVI)
TE............ Trace Elements [*Chemistry*] (DAVI)
TE............ Tracheary Element [*Botany*]
TE............ Tracheoesophageal [*Also, TOE*] [*Medicine*]
TE............ Tracking Enhancement (MCD)
TE............ Traction Engine [*British*]
TE............ Trade Expenses [*Business term*]
TE............ Trading Expert
TE............ Trailing Edge [*Aviation*]
TE............ Training and Evaluation (OICC)
TE............ Training Equipment
TE............ Training Establishment [*British military*] (DMA)
TE............ Trajectory Engineer
TE............ Transearth (SAA)
TE............ Transequatorial [*Scatter*]
TE............ Transient Eddy
TE............ Transient Event [*Nuclear energy*] (NRCH)
TE............ Transistor Equivalent [*Electronics*] (IAA)
TE............ Transitional Engineering (MCD)
TE............ Transmission Error [*Automotive engineering*]
TE............ Transportation Engineer Magazine [*A publication*] (EAAP)
TE............ Transport Empty
T/E............ Transporter-Erector [*NASA*] (KSC)
TE............ Transposable Element [*Genetics*]
TE............ Transverse Electric [*or Electrostatic*] [*Wave propagation mode*]
TE............ Transverse Electrostatic (IAA)
TE............ Treadmill Exercise (DAVI)
TE............ Trial and Error
TE............ Triple Expansion (DS)
TE............ Trunk Equalizer [*Telecommunications*] (OA)
TE............ Tuning Eye
TE............ Turbine Electric Drive
TE............ Turbine Engine (WDAA)
TE............ Twin Engine
TE............ Type Equipment (MCD)
TE2............ That's Entertainment, Part 2 [*Initialism is shortened form of movie title*]
TEA............ Targeted Export Assistance Program [*Later, MAP*] [*Department of Agriculture*]
TEA............ Task Equipment Analysis
TEA............ T Early Alpha [*Genetics*]
TEA............ Technical Engineers Association (EA)
TEA............ Technical Exchange Agreement
TEA............ Tegra Enterprises, Inc. [*Vancouver Stock Exchange symbol*]
TEA............ Tela [*Honduras*] [*Airport symbol*] (AD)
TEA............ Templeton Emerging Market Appreciation Fund [*NYSE symbol*] (SAG)
TEA............ Templeton Energ Mkts Apprec [*NYSE symbol*] (TTSB)
TEA............ Temporary Employment Assistance
TEA............ Tensile Energy Absorption [*Physics*]
TEA............ Test and Evaluation Agency
TEA............ Test Engineer's Assistant [*Computer-aided design tool*]
TEA............ Test Equipment Accessory (MCD)
TEA............ Test Equipment Analysis
TEA............ Tetraethylammonium [*Organic chemistry*]
TEA............ Textile Educators' Association [*Australia*]
TEA............ Textile Export Association of the US (EA)
TEA............ Thai Exiles Association (CINC)
TEA............ Theatre Equipment Association (EA)
TEA............ The Easy Animator [*Computer software*]
TEA............ Thermal Energy Analysis [*or Analyzer*]
TEA............ Thiazoylethylamine [*Organic chemistry*]
TEA............ Thromboendarterectomy [*Medicine*] (DMAA)
TEA............ Tiselius Electrophoresis Apparatus
TEA............ Titanic Enthusiasts of America [*Later, THS*] (EA)
TEA............ Torque Equilibrium Attitude (SSD)
TEA............ Total Elbow Arthroplasty [*Medicine*] (DMAA)
TEA............ Total Endarterectomy [*Cardiology*] (DAVI)
TEA............ Trade Expansion Act [*1962*]
TEA............ Training Effectiveness Analysis

TEA Trans European Airways [*Belgium ICAO designator*] (FAAC)
TEA Transferred Electron Amplifier
TEA Transportability Engineering Analysis [*Army*]
TEA Transversely Excited Atmospheric [*LASER*] (RDA)
TEA Treasury Enforcement Agent
TEA Triethanolamine [*Organic chemistry*]
TEA Triethylaluminum [*Organic chemistry*]
TEA Triethylamine [*Organic chemistry*]
TEA Triethylammonium [*Organic chemistry*]
TEA Tunnel-Emission Amplifier (IEEE)
TEAA Triethylammonium Acetate [*Organic chemistry*]
TEAAC Trade Expansion Act Advisory Committee [*Terminated, 1975*] (EGAO)
TEAB Tetraethylammonium Bromide [*Organic chemistry*]
TEAC Test and Evaluation Advisory Council [*Military*] (CAAL)
TEAC Tetraethylammonium Chloride [*Organic chemistry*]
TEAC Tokyo Electro Acoustical Co. [*Acronym is now name of electronics company and brand name of its products*]
TEAC Transition Education Advisory Committee (AIE)
TEAC Turbine Engine Analysis Check (AABC)
TEACH [*The*] Equity and Choice Act
TEACH Teacher
TEACH Teacher Equity and Choice Act [*Proposed*]
TEACH Teaching Each Other about Conquering Handicaps (EA)
TEACH Training and Education Activities Clearing House [*Military*]
TEACHCERT Teaching Certificate
Teach Mus Teaching Music [*A publication*] (BRI)
TEAD Tooele Army Depot [*Utah*] (AABC)
TEADDA Teledyne Electrically-Alterable Digital Differential Analyzer (IAA)
TE/AE Tigers East/Alpines East (EA)
TEAE Triethylaminoethyl [*Organic chemistry*]
TEA-ER Traffic Executives Association, Eastern Railroads [*Later, ERA*]
TEAF Total Environmental Action Foundation [*Defunct*] (EA)
TEAF Triethylammonium Formate [*Organic chemistry*]
TEAHA Trans-East African Highway Authority (EA)
TEAHAT Thrombolysis Early in Acute Heart Attack Trial [*Cardiology study*]
TEAL Tactics, Equipment, and Logistics Conference [*between US, Great Britain, Australia, and Canada*] [*Developed "duck" designations for Mallard and Gander military communications systems*]
TEAL Tasman Empire Airways Ltd. [*Australia*] (ADA)
TEAL Teeside Automated Library (NITA)
TEAL Transversely Excited Atmospheric LASER (RDA)
TEAL TriTeal Corp. [*NASDAQ symbol*] (SAG)
TEALS Triethanolamine Lauryl Sulfate [*Organic chemistry*]
TEAM [*The*] European-Atlantic Movement [*British*]
TEAM [*The*] Evangelical Alliance Mission (EA)
TEAM National TechTeam, Inc. [*NASDAQ symbol*] (NQ)
TEAM Natl TechTeam Inc. [*NASDAQ symbol*] (TTSB)
TEAM Teacher Education and Mathematics Project (EDAC)
TEAM Teacher Education and Media [*Project*]
Team Team, Inc. [*Associated Press*] (SAG)
TEAM Teamster Economic Action Mobilization
TEAM Tech-Base Enhancement for Autonomous Machines [*Military*] (RDA)
TEAM Technical Engineer-Architect Management (MCD)
TEAM Technical Engineering and Maintenance
TEAM Technique for Evaluation and Analysis of Maintainability
TEAM Techniques for Effective Alcohol Management [*NHTSA*] (TAG)
TEAM Technology Evaluation and Acquisition Method
TEAM Teleterminals Expandable Added Memory
TEAM Terminology Evaluation and Acquisition Method
TEAM Test and Evaluation of Air Mobility
TEAM Test, Evaluation, Analysis, and Modeling [*Army*] (RDA)
TEAM Together Everyone Achieves More
TEAM Top European Advertising Media
TEAM Torpedo Evasive Maneuvering (MCD)
TEAM Total Environment Analysis and Management (EERA)
TEAM Total Exposure Assessment Methodology [*or Monitoring*] [*Environmental chemistry*]
TEAM Training and Education in Adoption Methods [*Conference sponsored by the North American Council on Adoptable Children*]
TEAM Training/Employment of Automotive Mechanics [*Project*]
TEAM Training Equipment and Maintenance [*Aviation*] (DA)
TEAM Training in Expanded Auxiliary Management
TEAM Trend Evaluation and Monitoring [*Congressional Clearinghouse on the Future*] (EA)
TEAM Trimmed Element Analysis Method [*Computer modeling*]
TEAM Truck Expense Analysis and Management [*Computer science*]
TEAM Truth, Esteem, Attitude, and Motivation [*Name of actor Chuck Norris' anti-gang project*]
TEAM Tube Earphone and Microphone (DNAB)
TEAM A Theological Education Association of Mid-America, Library Section [*Library network*]
TEAMA Top End Aboriginal Music Association [*Australia*]
TEAME Teacher Educators and Advisers in Media Education (AIE)
TEAMMATE Total Electronic Advanced Microprocessing Maneuvers and Tactics Equipment [*A game*]
TeamRn Team Rental Group [*Associated Press*] (SAG)
TEAMS Technical Evaluation and Acquisition Management Support [*Air Force*]
TEAMS Test Evaluation and Monitoring System
TEAMS Tests of Engineering Aptitude, Mathematics, and Science
TEAMS Texas Educational Assessment of Minimum Skills
TEAMS Trend and Error Analysis Methodology System (MCD)
TEAM-UP Test, Evaluation, Analysis, and Management Uniformity Plan [*or Procedure*] [*Army*]

TE & I Technology Evaluation and Integration (MCD)
TE & R Tactical Engagement and Range [*Army*]
TEAP Tetraethylammonium Perchlorate [*Organic chemistry*]
TEAP Trajectory Error Analysis Program [*NASA*]
TEAP Transversely Excited Atmospheric Pressure
TEAP Triethylammonium Phosphate [*Organic chemistry*]
TEAPA Triethanolamine Phosphoric Acid [*Organic chemistry*]
TEAR [*The*] Evangelical Alliance Relief [*of The TEAR Fund*] (EA)
TEAR Time, Elevation, Azimuth, Range (MCD)
TEARR Times, Elevations, Azimuths, Ranges, and Range Rates [*Aerospace*]
TEARS [*The*] Exeter Abstract Reference System [*Exeter University*] [*Information service or system*] (IID)
TEARS Traffic Engineering for Automatic Route Selection (PDAA)
TEAS Technical and Engineering Acquisition Support [*Air Force*]
TEAS Test and Evaluation, Aircraft Survivability
TEAS Threat Evaluation and Action Selection [*Civilian defense program*]
TEAS Time Elapsed After Study (MHDI)
TEASE Tracking Errors and Simulation Evaluation [*RADAR*]
TEASER Tunable Electron Amplifier for Stimulated Emission of Radiation (MCD)
TEASOL Teaching of English to Adult Speakers of Other Languages [*Australia*]
teasp Teaspoonful
TEAT Obras de Teatro Estrenadas en Espana [*Ministerio de Cultura*] [*Spain Information service or system*] (CRD)
TEA-TOW Training Effectiveness Analysis - Tube-Launched Optically Tracked Wire-Guided (MCD)
TEAV Totalisator Employees' Association of Victoria [*Australia*]
TEAWC Totally-Enclosed Air Water-Cooled Reactor [*Nuclear energy*] (IAA)
TEB Tape Error Block [*Computer science*] (IAA)
TEB Tax-Exempt Bond [*Investment term*]
TEB Teterboro [*New Jersey*] [*Airport symbol*] (AD)
TEB Teterboro, NJ [*Location identifier FAA*] (FAAL)
TEB Textile Economics Bureau
TEB Tone Encoded Burst
TEB Transcutaneous Endomyocardial Biopsy [*Cardiology*] (CPH)
TEB Transient Electric Birefringence [*Physics*]
TEB Triethylbenzene [*Organic chemistry*]
TEB Triethylborane [*Organic chemistry*]
TEB Tris-Ethylenediaminetetra-Acetate Borate [*Organic chemistry*] (MAH)
TEB Tropical Experiment Board [*of World Meteorological Organization and International Council on Scientific Unions*]
TEBA Tutmonda Esperantista Biblioteka Asocio [*International Association for Esperanto in Libraries - IAEL*] (EAIO)
TEBAC Triethylbenylammonium Chloride [*Organic chemistry*]
TEBBS The Ethics Bulletin Board System (AAGC)
TEBDA Truck Equipment and Body Distributor Association [*Later, NTEA*] (EA)
TeBG Testosterone Binding Globulin [*Endocrinology*] (AAMN)
TeBG Testosterone-Estradiol Binding Globulin [*Endocrinology*]
TEBOL Terminal Business-Oriented Language
TEBPP Theoretical and Experimental Beam-Plasma Physics
TEBUTATE Tertiary Butyl Acetate [*USAN*] [*Organic chemistry*]
TEC Blacksburg, VA [*Location identifier FAA*] (FAAL)
TEC Commercial Intertech [*NYSE symbol*] (SAG)
TEC [*The*] Electrification Council (EA)
TEC [*The*] Elongated Collectors [*An association*] (EA)
TEC [*The*] Entertainment Channel [*Pay-television network*] [*Obsolete*]
TEC [*The*] Executive President's Council [*New Deal*]
TEC Tactical Electromagnetic Coordinator (IEEE)
TEC Tactical Exercise Controller [*Marine Corps*] (MCD)
TEC Target Engagement Console
TEC Target Entry Console
TEC Tarif Exterieur Commun [*Common External Tariff*] [*for EEC countries*]
TEC Tasmanian Environment Centre [*State*] (EERA)
TEC Teacher Education Center (EDAC)
TEC Tea Cyprus Ltd. [*ICAO designator*] (FAAC)
TEC Technical
TEC Technical Education Center
TEC Technical Escort Center [*Army*] (RDA)
TEC Technical Evaluation Committee [*Environmental Protection Agency*] (GFGA)
TEC Technician Education Council [*British*] (DI)
Tec Technischord [*Record label*]
TEC Technological Excellence Commission
TEC Technology for Energy Corporation (NRCH)
TEC Tele-Engineering Corp. [*Framingham, MA*] [*Telecommunications*] (TSSD)
TEC Telemetry and Command
TEC Telephone Engineering Center [*Telecommunications*] (TEL)
TEC Temporary Engineering Change (AAG)
TEC Temporary Extended Compensation [*Labor*]
TEC Ternary Eutectic Chloride [*Fire extinguishing agent*]
TEC Test and Evaluation Committee [*DoD*] (RDA)
TEC Test Equipment Center [*NASA*] (NASA)
TEC Test Equipment Committee (AAG)
TEC Test Evaluation and Control (IAA)
TEC Test of Ecology Comprehension (EDAC)
TEC Thermal End Cover
TEC Thermal Expansion Coefficient
TEC Thermal Unit End Cover (MCD)
TEC Thermionic Energy Converter (RDA)
TEC Thermoelectric Cooler (IAA)
TEC Thymic Epithelial Cell [*Cytology*]

TEC .... Tlemcen [*Algeria*] [*Seismograph station code, US Geological Survey*] (SEIS)
TEC .... Tokyo Electronics Corp.
TEC .... Ton Equivalent of Coal
TEC .... Topographic Engineering Center [*Ft. Belvoir, VA*] [*Army*] (RDA)
TEC .... TOS [*TIROS Operational Satellite*] Test Evaluation Center [*Goddard Space Flight Center*] (NOAA)
TEC .... Total Electron Content (MCD)
TEC .... Total Environment Centre (EERA)
TEC .... Total Eosinophil Count [*Hematology*]
TEC .... Total Estimated Cost
TEC .... Tower en Route Control [*Aviation*] (FAAC)
TEC .... Track Entry Console (MCD)
TEC .... Tract Evaluation Computer (NATG)
TEC .... Training and Enterprise Council [*British*]
TEC .... Training Evaluation and Control
TEC .... Training Exercise Coordinator [*Military*] (NVT)
TEC .... Training Extension Course [*Army*]
TEC .... Transearth Coast [*AEC*]
TEC .... Transient Early Curvature [*Orthopedics*]
TEC .... Transient Erythroblastopenia of Childhood [*Hematology*]
TEC .... Transitional Executive Council [*Implemented in 1993 to work with the Cabinet and ensure fair political campaigning*] [*South Africa*] (ECON)
TEC .... Transmission Electronic Control [*Bradley Fighting Vehicle*] [*Army*] (DWSG)
TEC .... Tripartite Engineering Committee [*Allied German Occupation Forces*]
TEC .... Triple Erasure Correction
TEC .... Tropical Experiment Council [*of World Meteorological Organization and International Council on Scientific Unions*]
TEC .... Truck Electrical Center [*Volvo White Truck Corp.*]
TEC .... Turtle Excluder Device [*Fishing*]
TEC .... Type Equipment Code (MCD)
TECA .... Tartan Educational and Cultural Association (EA)
TECA .... Technetium Albumin Study [*Radiology*] (DAVI)
TECA .... Technical Evaluation and Countermeasures Assignment
TECA .... Temporary Emergency Court of Appeals
TECA .... Totally Enclosed - Closed-Air Circuit
TECA .... Tower en Route Control Area [*Aviation*] (FAAC)
TECAD .... Technical Advisory [*Military*] (CAAL)
TECADS .... Techniques to Counter Air Defense Suppression (MCD)
TECC .... Technology Education for Children Council (EA)
TECC .... Texas Educational Computer Courseware Database [*Texas Education Computer Cooperative*] [*Information service or system Defunct*] (CRD)
TECC .... Texas Education Computer Cooperative [*Houston*] [*Information service or system*] (IID)
TECCE .... Tactical Exploitation Collection and Coordination Element (MCD)
TECCS .... Tactical Engagement Close Combat System [*Army*]
TECD .... Tech Data Corp. [*Clearwater, FL*] [*NASDAQ symbol*] (NQ)
TECD .... Training Equipment Change Directives [*Navy*]
TECDA .... Thai Environmental and Community Development Association (EERA)
TECDOC .... Technical Documentation [*DoD*]
TECE .... Teleprinter Error Correction Equipment
TECEPT .... Training Equipment Cost Effectiveness Prediction Techniques [*Navy*]
TECG .... Test and Evaluation Coordinating Group [*Military*] (CAAL)
TECH .... Teach Each Customer How [*Tire repair training seminar*] [*Technical Rubber Co.*]
TECH .... Techne Corp. [*NASDAQ symbol*] (SAG)
TECH .... Technical (AAG)
TECH .... Technician
TECH .... Technique
TECH .... Technological Education Clearinghouse
TECH .... Technologist
TECH .... Technology (AAG)
tech .... Technology (DD)
TECH .... Texas Instruments, Canon, Hewlett-Packard [*Joint Venture*]
TECH .... Toxic, Explosive, Corrosive, Hazardous Cargo [*Shipping*] (DS)
TECHAD .... Technical Advisor [*Navy*]
Tech Adj .... Technical Adjutant [*British military*] (DMA)
TECHAUTHIND .... Technical Paper / Author Cross-Index System (DNAB)
TECHAV .... Technical Availability [*Navy*] (NVT)
Tech(CEI) .... Technician (Council of Engineering Institutions) [*British*] (DI)
TechCh .... Technical Chemicals & Products Co. [*Associated Press*] (SAG)
TechChm .... Technical Chemicals & Products [*Associated Press*] (SAG)
Techclne .... Techniclone International Corp. [*Associated Press*] (SAG)
TechData .... Tech Data Corp. [*Associated Press*] (SAG)
TECHDATA .... Technical Data [*DoD*]
Teche .... Teche Holding Co. [*Associated Press*] (SAG)
Tech Ed .... Technical Editor (DGA)
TechEl .... Tech Electro Industries, Inc. [*Associated Press*] (SAG)
TECHEVAL .... Technical Evaluation [*Navy*] (NG)
TECH EX .... Technical Exchange (MHDI)
TechFrce .... Tech Force Corp. [*Associated Press*] (SAG)
TechGeol .... Technical Associate of the Geological Society [*British*] (DBQ)
TECHGL .... Technological
Tech Inf Bull .... Technical Information Bulletin. National Information Service on Drug Abuse [*A publication*]
TECHINFO .... Technical Information [*DoD*]
TECHINT .... Technical Intelligence [*Spy satellites, etc.*]
Techknit .... TechKnits, Inc. [*Associated Press*] (SAG)
TECHL .... Technical
TECHL .... Technical
TECHLGY .... Technology
TECHMAN .... Technical Manual (DNAB)
TECH MEMO .... Technical Memorandum (MHDB)
TechMIWPC .... Technician Member of the Institute of Water Pollution Control [*British*] (DI)
TECHMOD .... Technology Modernization (AAGC)
TECHMOD .... Technology Modernization Program [*DoD*]
TECHN .... Technical (EY)
TECHN .... Technician
TECHN .... Technician
TECHN .... Technology
Techn Dict .... Crabb's Technological Dictionary [*A publication*] (DLA)
Techne .... Techne Corp. [*Associated Press*] (SAG)
Technign .... Technigen Corp. [*Associated Press*] (SAG)
Technitrl .... Technitrol, Inc. [*Associated Press*] (SAG)
TECHNOL .... Technologic
Technols .... Technologies
Technop .... Technopaegnion [*of Ausonius*] [*Classical studies*] (OCD)
TECHNOTE .... Technical Note [*or Notice*] (DNAB)
TECHNQ .... Technique
TECHOPEVAL .... Technical Operational Evaluation
TECHREP .... Technical Representative [*Military*]
TECH REPT .... Technical Report (MHDI)
TechRMS .... Technological Qualification in Microscopy, Royal Microscopical Society [*British*] (DBQ)
TECHS .... Technical School [*Air Force*]
TECHSAT .... Technology Satellite (MCD)
TechSol .... Technology Solutions Co. [*Associated Press*] (SAG)
TECHSPECS .... Technical Specifications (IAA)
TechSvc .... Technology Service Group, Inc. [*Associated Press*] (SAG)
TECHSVS .... Technical Services [*Army*]
TECHTAF .... Technical Training Air Force
TECHTNG .... Technical Training (NVT)
TECHTNGSq .... Technical Training Squadron [*Air Force*]
TECHTRA .... Air Technical Training [*Navy*]
TechWeldI .... Technician of the Welding Institute [*British*] (DBQ)
TECL .... Test Equipment Configuration Log [*NASA*] (KSC)
TECL .... Transmission-Engine Communication Link [*Automotive engineering*]
TECM .... Test Equipment Commodity Manager
TECMA .... Technical Ceramics Manufacturers Association (EA)
TECMOD .... Technology Modernization (MCD)
TECN .... Technalysis Corp. [*NASDAQ symbol*] (NQ)
TEC-NACS .... Teachers Educational Council - National Association Cosmetology Schools
TECNET .... Technologies Network [*Database*] [*EC*] (ECED)
Tecnmtx .... Tecnomatix Technologies Ltd. [*Associated Press*] (SAG)
TecnolM .... Tecnol Medical Products, Inc. [*Associated Press*] (SAG)
TECO .... Technical Co-Operation Committee [*OECD*] (DS)
TECO .... TECO Energy, Inc. [*Associated Press*] (SAG)
TECO .... Terra Cotta [*Pronounced "tee-ko"*] [*Type of American art pottery*]
TECO .... Text Editor and Corrector [*Computer science*] (MHDI)
TECO .... Tooling Expenditure Control Order (MCD)
TECO .... Trinity Engineering Co. [*Huxley, IA*] [*Telecommunications service*] (TSSD)
TECO .... Turbine Engine Checkout
TECOM .... Test and Evaluation Command [*Aberdeen Proving Ground, MD*] [*Army*]
TECOMAP .... Technical Conference of the Observation and Measurement of Atmospheric Pollution [*Helsinki, 1973*]
TecOpS .... Tech/Ops Sevcon, Inc. [*Associated Press*] (SAG)
TecOpsSv .... Tech-Ops Sevcon, Inc. [*Associated Press*] (SAG)
TECP .... Training Equipment Checkout Procedure
TECR .... Technical Reason [*Aviation*]
TECR .... Technical Requirement (AABC)
Tec R .... Technology Review [*A publication*] (BRI)
TECR .... Test Equipment Change Requirement (NATG)
TECRAS .... Technical Reconnaissance and Surveillance (MCD)
TECS .... Technical Editing and Composition System [*Computer science*] (DGA)
TECS .... Television Confirming Sensor (MCD)
TECS .... Text Editing and Composition System [*Computer science*] (DGA)
TECS .... Total Energy Control System
TECS .... Total Environmental Control System [*Army*] (RDA)
TECS .... Treasury Enforcement Communications System [*Customs Service*]
TECSTAR .... Technical Missions, Structures and Career Development [*Military*]
TECTRA .... Technology Transfer Data Bank [*California State University*] [*Sacramento*] [*Information service or system*] (IID)
TECU .... Tecumseh Products Co. [*NASDAQ symbol*] (NQ)
TECU .... Thermoelectric Environmental Control Unit
TECU .... Transportation Employees' Canadian Union
TECUA .... Tecumseh Products Cl'A' [*NASDAQ symbol*] (TTSB)
TECUB .... Tecumseh Products Cl'B' [*NASDAQ symbol*] (TTSB)
Tecum .... Tecumseh Products Co. [*Associated Press*] (SAG)
TECV .... Test of Energy Concepts and Values (EDAC)
TECV .... Traumatic Epiphyseal Coxa Vara [*Medicine*] (DMAA)
TED .... Electrical Distributor [*A publication*] (EAAP)
TED .... International Association for Training and Education in Distribution
TED .... Tasks of Emotional Development Test [*Psychology*]
TED .... Tax-Exempt Dividend (MHDW)
TED .... Teacher Education Division [*Council for Exceptional Children*]
TED .... Technology, Entertainment and Design [*Conference*]
TED .... Teddy Air AS [*Norway ICAO designator*] (FAAC)
Ted .... Teddy Boy (ODBW)
TeD .... Te Deum [*Music*]
TeD .... Telefunken-Decca [*Video disk system*]
TED .... Teleprinter Error Detector (IAA)

TED .... Television Disc (NITA)
TED .... Tenders Electronic Daily [*Office for Official Publications of the European Communities*] [*Database Luxembourg*]
TED .... Terminal Editor (ADA)
TED .... Test and Evaluation Division [*National Weather Service*]
TED .... Test Engineering Division [*Navy*]
TED .... Test Engineering Documentation (MCD)
TED .... Test, Evaluation, and Development (MUGU)
TED .... Text Editor [*Computer science*] (MHDI)
TED .... Thermionic Emission Detector [*For gas chromatography*]
TED .... Thermoelectric Device
TED .... Thisted [*Denmark*] [*Airport symbol*] (OAG)
TED .... Thomas Edmund Dewey [*Republican candidate for President, 1948*]
TED .... Threshold Erythema Dose [*Medicine*]
TED .... Threshold Extension Demodulator
TED .... Thromboembolic Disease [*Medicine*]
TED .... Toledo Edison Co. [*AMEX symbol*] (SAG)
TED .... Toledo Edison Co. [*NYSE symbol*] (SPSG)
TED .... Total Energy Detector
TED .... Trace Element Doping
TED .... Tracking Error Detector (MCD)
TED .... Trailing Edge Down [*Aviation*] (MCD)
TED .... Training Equipment Development [*Military*]
TED .... Traitement Electronique des Donnees [*Electronic Data Processing - EDP*] [*French*]
TED .... Transfer Effective Date [*Military*] (AFM)
TED .... Transferred Electron Device [*Air Force*]
TED .... Translation Error Detector (DIT)
TED .... Transmission Electron Diffraction (MCD)
TED .... Trawl Efficiency Device (USDC)
TED .... Trawl Efficiency Device [*Marine science*] (OSRA)
TED .... Troop Exercise Director (CINC)
TED .... True Economic Depreciation
TED .... Trunk Encryption Device [*Telecommunications*] (TEL)
TED .... Turbine Electric Drive
TED .... Turbine Engine Diagnosis [*Army*]
TED .... Turbine Engine Division [*Air Force*]
TED .... Turtle Excluder Device [*Marine science*] (OSRA)
TED .... Turtle Exclusion Device [*Tool attached to shrimp boats in the Gulf of Mexico which allows the endangered Kemp's ridley turtle to escape the shrimp nets*] [*Facetious translations: "Trawler Extinction Device," "Trawling Efficiency Device"*]
TEDA .... Theatre Equipment Dealers Association [*Later, TEA*] (EA)
TEDA .... Triethylenediamine [*Organic chemistry*]
TEDAR .... Telemetered Data Reduction (AAG)
TEDC .... Technical Education Center
TEDC .... Tellurium Diethyldithiocarbamate [*Organic chemistry*]
TEDDS .... Tactical Environmental Dissemination and Display System (MCD)
TEDE .... Temperature-Enhanced Displacement Effect
TEDES .... Telemetry Data Evaluation System
TEDIS .... Trade Data Interchange System [*Telecommunications*] (OSI)
TEDL .... Transferred-Electron-Device Logic (MSA)
TEDMA .... Triethylene Dimethacrylate [*Organic chemistry*]
TEDP .... Tetraethyl Dithionopyrophosphate [*Organic chemistry*]
TEDPAS .... Technical Data Package Automated System
TEDPrA .... Toledo Edison 8.32% Pfd [*AMEX symbol*] (TTSB)
TEDPrC .... Toledo Edison 7.76% Pfd [*AMEX symbol*] (TTSB)
TEDPrD .... Toledo Edison 10% Pfd [*AMEX symbol*] (TTSB)
TEDPrE .... Toledo Ed 8.84%cm Pfd [*NYSE symbol*] (TTSB)
TEDPrF .... Toledo Edison $2.365 Pfd [*NYSE symbol*] (TTSB)
TEDPrK .... Toledo Edison Adj A Pfd [*NYSE symbol*] (TTSB)
TEDPrL .... Toledo Edison Adj Rt B Pfd [*NYSE symbol*] (TTSB)
TEDS .... Tactical Expendable Drone System (MCD)
TEDS .... Target Effluent Detection System (MCD)
TEDS .... Teleteach Expanded Delivery System [*US Air Force*] [*Wright-Patterson AFB, OH*] [*Telecommunications*] (TSSD)
TEDS .... Thromboembolic Disease Stockings [*Cardiology*] (DAVI)
TEDS .... Thromboembolus Deterrant Stocking (MEDA)
TEDS .... Turbine-Electric Drive Submarine (DNAB)
TEDS .... Twin Exchangeable Disc Storage (NITA)
TEDSCO .... Test Equipment Documentation Scheduling Committee
TEE .... [*The*] Entrepreneurial Economy [*Corporation for Enterprise Development*] [*A publication*]
TEE .... National Golf Properties [*NYSE symbol*] (SPSG)
TEE .... Natl Golf Properties [*NYSE symbol*] (TTSB)
TEE .... Tape Editing Equipment
TEE .... Tbessa [*Algeria*] [*Airport symbol*] (OAG)
TEE .... Teeples Ranch [*Montana*] [*Seismograph station code, US Geological Survey Closed*] (SEIS)
TEE .... Teeshin Resources Ltd. [*Vancouver Stock Exchange symbol*]
TEE .... Telecommunications Engineering Establishment [*British*]
TEE .... Terminal Effects and Experimentation (MCD)
TEE .... Test Equipment Engineering (AAG)
TEE .... Text Entry and Edit (DGA)
TEE .... Theological Education by Extension [*Church of England*]
TEE .... Thermal Effect of Exercise (MEDA)
TEE .... Torpedo Experimental Establishment [*British*]
TEE .... Total Effective Exposure [*Advertising*]
TEE .... Training Effectiveness Evaluation
TEE .... Transesophageal Echocardiography
TEE .... Trans-Europ-Express [*Continental high-speed train*]
TEE .... Triaxial Earth Ellipsoid
TEE .... Tubular Extendible Element (PDAA)
TEE .... Tyee [*Alaska*] [*Airport symbol*] (AD)
TEE .... Tyrosine Ethyl Ester [*Organic chemistry*] (MAE)
TEEAR .... Test Equipment Error Analysis Report (IAA)
TEEC .... Transactions Editorial Executive Committee (ACII)
TEECG .... Tactical Exercise Evaluation Control Group [*Marine Corps*] (DOMA)
TeeCm .... Tee Comm Electronics, Inc. [*Associated Press*] (SAG)
TeeCom .... Tee Com Electronics, Inc. [*Associated Press*] (SAG)
TEEF .... Tax-Exempt Equity Fund
Teekay .... Teekay Shipping Corp. [*Associated Press*] (SAG)
TEEL .... Temporary Expedient Equipment List [*Army*] (AABC)
TEEM .... Techno-Economic-Environmental Model (EERA)
TEEM .... Technology through Electricity, Electronics, and Microelectronics (AIE)
TEEM .... Test for Examining Expressive Morphology [*Educational test*]
TEEM .... Trans-Europ-Express-Marchandises [*Continental high-speed train*]
TEES .... Texas Engineering Experiment Station [*Texas A & M University*] [*Research center*]
TEES .... Thermochemical Environmental Energy System [*Service mark*] [*Battelle Development Corp.*]
TEESS .... Tank Engine Exhaust Smoke System (MCD)
TEEZI .... Threat Evaluation Equipment Zone of Interior (SAA)
TEF .... [*The*] Eagle Foundation [*Defunct*] (EA)
TEF .... [*The*] Environmental Fund [*Later, PEB*] (EA)
TEF .... Tear Efficiency Factor [*Textiles*]
Tef .... Tefillin (BJA)
TEF .... Telefonica de Espana ADS [*NYSE symbol*] (TTSB)
TEF .... Telefonica de Espana SA [*NYSE symbol*] (SPSG)
TEF .... Telfer [*Australia Airport symbol*] (OAG)
TEF .... Temperance Education Foundation [*Defunct*] (EA)
TEF .... Test and Evaluation Facility [*Nuclear energy*] (NUCP)
TEF .... Test and Evaluation Flight [*Military*]
TEF .... Tetralogy of Fallot [*Neonatology*] (DAVI)
TEF .... Thermal Effect of Food (MEDA)
TEF .... Thyrotroph Embryonic Factor [*Genetics*]
TEF .... Tilted Electric Field (PDAA)
TEF .... Total Effective Fare (PDAA)
TEF .... Total Energy Feasibility (IAA)
TEF .... Total Environment Facility (SAA)
TEF .... Toxic Equivalency Factor [*Environmental Protection Agency*]
TEF .... Tracheoesophageal Fistula [*Medicine*]
TEF .... Transfer on End of File (SAA)
TEF .... Transverse Electric Field
TEF .... Trunk Extension-Flexion [*Medicine*] (DMAA)
TEF .... Tunable Etalon Filter
TEF .... Turkey Embryo Fibroblast [*Biochemistry*]
TEFA .... Total Essential Fatty Acid [*of foodstuffs*]
TEFA .... Total Esterified Fatty Acid
TEFA .... Tube-Excited X-Ray Fluorescence Analyzer
TEFAP .... Temporary Emergency Food Assistance Program [*Department of Agriculture*]
TEFC .... Totally Enclosed - Fan Cooled
TEFC .... Totally-Enclosed Force-Cooled Reactor [*Nuclear energy*] (IAA)
TEFL .... Teaching English as a Foreign Language
TEFLON .... Tetrafluoroethylene Resin [*Du Pont*]
TEFORS .... Technological Forecasting and Simulation for Program Selection (MCD)
TEFP .... Transportability Engineering Focal Point
TEFRA .... Tax Equity and Fiscal Responsibility Act (AAGC)
TEFRA .... Tax Equity and Fiscal Responsibility Act of 1982
TEFS .... Transmural Electrical Field Stimulation [*Medicine*] (DMAA)
TEG .... Tactical Employment Guide [*Military*] (CAAL)
Teg .... Tegula [*Entomology*]
TEG .... Templar Mining [*Vancouver Stock Exchange symbol*]
TEG .... Tenkodogo [*Upper Volta*] [*Airport symbol*] (AD)
TEG .... Test Element Group
TEG .... Tetraethylene Glycol [*Organic chemistry*]
TEG .... Thermoelectric Generator
TEG .... Thromboelastogram [*or Thromboelastograph*] [*Medicine*]
TEG .... Top Edge Gilt [*Bookbinding*]
teg .... Top-Edge Gilt [*Bookbinding*] (WDMC)
TEG .... Training and Education Group (NITA)
TEG .... Triethylene Glycol [*Organic chemistry*]
TEG .... Triethyl Gallium [*Organic chemistry*]
Tegal .... Tegal Corp. [*Associated Press*] (SAG)
TEGAS .... Test Generation and Simulation
TEGAS .... Time Generation and Simulation [*Telecommunications*] (TEL)
TEGD .... Technical Enforcement Guidance Document [*Environmental Protection Agency*]
TEGDME .... Tetraethylene Glycol Dimethyl Ether [*Organic chemistry*]
TEGDN .... Triethylene Glycol Dinitrate [*An explosive*]
TEGG .... Thermogrip Electric Glue Gun
TEGI .... Train-Elevated Guideway Interaction (PDAA)
TEGMA .... Terminal Elevator Grain Merchants Association (EA)
TEGMA .... Triethylene Glycol Dimethacrylate [*Organic chemistry*] (MCD)
TEGO .... Taylor's Encyclopedia of Government Officials [*A publication*]
TEGWAR .... [*The*] Exciting Game Without Any Rules [*Card game*]
TEH .... Blare Lake, AK [*Location identifier FAA*] (FAAL)
Teh .... Tehillim (BJA)
TEH .... Tehran [*Iran*] [*Seismograph station code, US Geological Survey*] (SEIS)
TEH .... Tehua [*Race of maize*]
TEH .... Tempelhof Airways, Inc. [*Germany ICAO designator*] (FAAC)
TEH .... Twin-Engined Helicopter (MCD)
TEHOS .... Tetrakis(ethylhexoxy)silane [*Organic chemistry*]
TEHP .... Thermoelectric Heat Pump (MCD)
TEI .... [*The*] Entrepreneurship Institute (EA)
TEI .... Societa' Tea Italia [*Italy ICAO designator*] (FAAC)

TEI.............. Tax Executives Institute (EA)
TEI.............. Technical Education Institute (AIE)
TEI.............. Technical Engineering Item (MCD)
TEI.............. Telecommunications Engineering, Inc. [*Dallas, TX*] (TSSD)
TEI.............. Templeton Emerging Markets Income Fund [*NYSE symbol*] (SPSG)
TEI.............. Templeton Emerg Mkts Income [*NYSE symbol*] (TTSB)
TEI.............. Temporary Engineering Instruction [*Navy*] (NG)
TEI.............. Text Encoding Initiative [*Computer science*]
TEI.............. Thorne Ecological Institute (EA)
TEI.............. Time Error Indicated
TEI.............. Trait Evaluation Index [*Psychology*]
TEI.............. Transearth Injection [*AEC*]
TEI.............. Transfer on Error Indication
TEI.............. Trucking Employers, Inc. [*Later, TMI*]
TEIB.............. Triethyleneiminobenzoquinone [*Organic chemistry*] (MAE)
TEIC.............. Tissue Equivalent Ionization Chamber
TEIGN.......... Teignmouth [*Urban district in England*]
TEIGNBR...... Teignbridge [*England*]
Teikyo Marycrest U... Teikyo Marycrest University (GAGS)
TEIM.............. Travel Economic Impact Model [*Department of Commerce*]
TEIP.............. Tax-Exempt Investor Program [*Investment term*]
TEIRDC.......... Tamil Eelam International Research and Documentation Centre [*Canada*]
TEIS.............. Training Equipment Item Specification (MCD)
TEISS............ [*The*] Enhanced Integrated Soldier System [*Army*]
Teiss.............. Teissler's Court of Appeal, Parish of Orleans, Reports [*1903-17*] [*A publication*] (DLA)
Teissler.......... Teissler's Court of Appeal, Parish of Orleans, Reports [*1903-17*] [*A publication*] (DLA)
TEJ.............. Emmanuel School of Religion, Johnson City, TN [*OCLC symbol*] (OCLC)
TEJ.............. Tejas Gas Corp. [*NYSE symbol*] (SPSG)
TEJ.............. Transportes Aeros Ejecutivos SA de CV [*Mexico ICAO designator*] (FAAC)
TEJ.............. Transverse Expansion Joint [*Technical drawings*]
TEJA.............. Tutmonda Esperantista Jurnalista Asocio [*World Association of Esperanto Journalists - WAEJ*] (EAIO)
TEJAC.......... Trade Effluent Joint Advisory Committee [*British*] (DCTA)
Tejas.............. Tejas Gas Corp. [*Associated Press*] (SAG)
TejasGas...... Tejas Gas Corp. [*Associated Press*] (SAG)
TejasGs.......... Tejas Gas Corp. [*Associated Press*] (SAG)
TejasPw.......... Tejas Power [*Associated Press*] (SAG)
TejnR.............. Tejon Ranch Co. [*Associated Press*] (SAG)
TEJO.............. Tutmonda Esperantista Junulara Organizo [*World Organization of Young Esperantists*] (EAIO)
TEJPr.............. Tejas Gas Cp 9.96% Dep Pfd [*NYSE symbol*] (TTSB)
TEJPrA.......... Tejas Gas 5.25% Cv Dep Pfd [*NYSE symbol*] (TTSB)
TEK.............. Teck Corp. [*Toronto Stock Exchange symbol Vancouver Stock Exchange symbol*]
TEK.............. Teekin [*Tonga*] [*Seismograph station code, US Geological Survey*] (SEIS)
TEK.............. Tektronix, Inc. [*NYSE symbol*] (SPSG)
TEK.............. Test Equipment Kit
TEK.............. Truppenentgiftungskompanie [*Personnel decontamination company*] [*German military - World War II*]
TEK.............. Tunnel Exploration Kit [*Army*] (VNW)
TEK A.......... Teck Corp Cl'A' [*TS symbol*] (TTSB)
TEKE.............. Tau Kappa Epsilon [*Fraternity*] (EA)
Tekelec.......... Tekelec, Inc. [*Associated Press*] (SAG)
TEKSIF.......... Turkiye Tekstil ve Orme Sanayii Iscileri Sendikalari Federasyonu [*National Federation of Textile Unions*] [*Turkey*]
Tektrnx.......... Tektronix, Inc. [*Associated Press*] (SAG)
TEL.............. Task Execution Language
TEL.............. Taxpayers Education Lobby (EA)
TEL.............. TCC Industries [*NYSE symbol*] (TTSB)
TEL.............. TCC Industries, Inc. [*Formerly, Telecom Corp.*] [*NYSE symbol*] (SAG)
TEL.............. Telegram
tel.............. Telegram (WDMC)
tel.............. Telegraph (WDMC)
TEL.............. Telegraph
TEL.............. Telegraphic (NTCM)
TEL.............. Telemetry (KSC)
TEL.............. Telephone (AAG)
Tel.............. Telephone (ODBW)
TEL.............. Telephone
TEL.............. Telephone Group (IAA)
TEL.............. Telephone Station (IAA)
TEL.............. Telephonic (NTCM)
TEL.............. Telephony (NTCM)
TEL.............. Telescope (AAG)
Tel.............. Telescopium [*Constellation*]
TEL.............. Teletype (NTCM)
TEL.............. Teletypewriter [*Telecommunications*] (NOAA)
TEL.............. Television (IAA)
TEL.............. Telford Aviation, Inc. [*ICAO designator*] (FAAC)
TEL.............. Tell City, IN [*Location identifier FAA*] (FAAL)
tel.............. Telugu [*MARC language code Library of Congress*] (LCCP)
TEL.............. Terex Equipment Ltd.
TEL.............. Test Log
TEL.............. Test of Economic Literacy [*Educational test*]
TEL.............. Tests for Everyday Living [*Educational test*]
TEL.............. Tetraethyllead [*Organic chemistry*]
TEL.............. Thalner Electronic Laboratories, Inc. [*Ann Arbor, MI*] (TSSD)
TEL.............. Thomas Edward Lawrence [*Lawrence of Arabia*] [*British archaeologist, soldier, and writer, 1888-1935*]
TEL.............. Tokyo Electron Ltd. (IAA)
TEL.............. Total Energy Loss (IAA)
TEL.............. Training Equipment List
TEL.............. Transporter-Erector-Launcher [*Air Force*]
TELACS.......... Tunnel Explorer, Locator and Communications System [*Army*] (VNW)
Tel Add.......... Telegraphic Address (DS)
Telan.............. Telenoticiosa Americana [*Press agency*] [*Argentina*]
TELAR.............. Transporter-Erector-Launcher and RADAR (MCD)
TelArg.............. Telefonica de Argentina SA [*Associated Press*] (SAG)
TELATEL...... Telephone and Telegraph (IAA)
TELATS.......... Tactical Electronic Locating and Targeting System (MCD)
TELAU.............. Teleautograph [*ICAO designator*] (FAAC)
Tel Aviv Univ Stud L... Tel Aviv University Studies in Law [*Tel-Aviv, Israel*] [*A publication*] (DLA)
Tel-Aviv U Stud L... Tel-Aviv University Studies in Law [*Tel-Aviv, Israel*] [*A publication*] (DLA)
TELB.............. Telephone Booth
TelBrasl.......... Telecommunicacoes Brasilerias SA Telebras [*Associated Press*] (SAG)
TELC.............. Telco Systems [*NASDAQ symbol*] (TTSB)
TELC.............. Telco Systems, Inc. [*NASDAQ symbol*] (NQ)
TelC.............. Tele-Communications Class A [*Associated Press*] (SAG)
TELC.............. Teleglobe Canada
TelC.............. Telegraph Communications [*Commercial firm Associated Press*] (SAG)
TELCAM.......... Telecommunication Equipment Low-Cost Acquisition Method [*Navy*]
TelC Int.......... Tele-Communications International, Inc. [*Associated Press*] (SAG)
TelCm.............. Tel-Communications [*Associated Press*] (SAG)
TelcNZ.............. Telecom Corp. of New Zealand [*Associated Press*] (SAG)
TELCO.............. Tata Engineering & Locomotive Co. [*India*]
Telco.............. Telco Systems, Inc. [*Associated Press*] (SAG)
TELCO.............. Telephone Central Office
TELCO.............. Telephone Communications (IAA)
TELCO.............. Telephone Company [*ICAO designator*] (FAAC)
TELCO.............. Telephone Operating Co. [*Also, TELOP*]
TELCOM.......... Telecommunications (NASA)
TELCOM.......... Telemetry & Communications Division (ACII)
TELCON.......... Telephone Conference [*or Conversation*] (AAG)
TelCSm.......... TelCom Semiconductor, Inc. [*Associated Press*] (SAG)
TelCTV.............. Tel-Com Wireless Cable TV Corp. [*Associated Press*] (SAG)
TELD.............. Teledate Equipment [*Military*]
TELD.............. Test of Early Language Development
TELD.............. Transferred Electron Logic Device (IAA)
TELDEC.......... Telefunken-Decca [*Video disk system*] (IAA)
TelDta.............. Telephone & Data Systems, Inc. [*Associated Press*] (SAG)
Teldy.............. Teledyne, Inc. [*Associated Press*] (SAG)
Teldyn.............. Teledyne, Inc. [*Associated Press*] (SAG)
TELE.............. Tech Electro Industries [*NASDAQ symbol*] (TTSB)
TELE.............. Tech Electro Industries, Inc. [*NASDAQ symbol*] (SAG)
TELE.............. Telegram
TELE.............. Telegraph
tele.............. Telemetry [*Cardiology*] (DAVI)
TELE.............. Telephone
TELE.............. Telephoto (NTCM)
Tele.............. Telescopium [*Constellation*]
TELE.............. Television (ADA)
TELE.............. Trilanguage Education Learning Environment Program [*New York City*] (EDAC)
Telebit.............. Telebit Corp. [*Associated Press*] (SAG)
TELEC.............. Telecommunication
TELEC.............. Teleglobe Canada
TELEC.............. Thermoelectronic LASER Energy Converter
TELECAMRA... Television Camera (MDG)
TELECAR.......... Telemetry Carrier Acquisition and Recovery (MCD)
TELECAST.... Television Broadcasting (CET)
TELECC.......... Telecommunication
Telech.............. Telechips Corp. [*Associated Press*] (SAG)
Telechps.......... Telechips Corp. [*Associated Press*] (SAG)
TELECOM...... Telecommunications (AFM)
TELECOM...... Telecommunications
TeleCom.......... Tele-Communications Class A [*Associated Press*] (SAG)
telecommun... Telecommunications (DD)
TELECOMS... Telecommunications Authority of Singapore (TSSD)
TELECON...... Telephone [*or Teletype*] Conference [*or Conversation*] (AFM)
TELECON...... Teletypewriter Conference (IAA)
TELECONV... Telephone Conversation
TELEDAC...... Telemetric Data Converter
TeleDan.......... Tele Danmark Co. [*Associated Press*] (SAG)
TELEDAQ...... Television Data Acquisition System (MCD)
TELEDIS.......... Teletypewriter Distribution (NATG)
TELEDOC...... Telecommunications Documentation (NITA)
Teledta.............. Teledata Communications [*Associated Press*] (SAG)
Telef.............. Telefonica de Espana SA [*Associated Press*] (SAG)
TELEFAC...... Telecommunications Facility
TELEFAC...... Television Facsimile (NTCM)
TelefEsp.......... Telefonica de Espana SA [*Associated Press*] (SAG)
Teleflex.......... Teleflex, Inc. [*Associated Press*] (SAG)
TELEFLORA... Telegraph Florists Delivery Service
TelefMex.......... Telefonos de Mexico [*Associated Press*] (SAG)
TELEG.............. Telegram
TELEG.............. Telegraph
TelegCm.......... Telegraph Communications [*Commercial firm Associated Press*] (SAG)

Telegen .... Telegen Corp. [*Associated Press*] (SAG)
TELEMAN ..... Telephone Management System
Telem Ant .... Telemetry Antenna
TELEMUX ..... Telegraph Multiplexer (MHDB)
TELENET ...... Cooperative Extension Service Telephone Network [*University of Illinois at Champaign-Urbana*] [*Telecommunications service*] (TSSD)
TELENET ...... TELENET Communications Corp. [*GTE*] (TEL)
TELENGR ..... Telephone Engineer [*Telecommunications*] (IAA)
Telepad ...... Telepad Corp. [*Associated Press*] (SAG)
TELEPAK ...... Telemetering Package
Telepanel .... Telepanel Systems, Inc. [*Associated Press*] (SAG)
TELEPH .... Telephone
TeleprtC ...... Teleport Communications Group, Inc. [*Associated Press*] (SAG)
TELEPUTER ... Television and Computer (EECA)
TELER .... Telecommunications Requirements (MCD)
TELERAN ..... Television and RADAR Navigation System (MUGU)
TELESAT ...... Telecommunications Satellite
Telescan ...... Telescan, Inc. [*Associated Press*] (SAG)
Telescription ... Television Transcription (NTCM)
TELESIM ...... Teletypewriter Simulator
Telesoft .... Telesoft Corp. [*Associated Press*] (SAG)
TeleSpec ..... TeleSpectrum Worldwide, Inc. [*Associated Press*] (SAG)
TELESUN ..... Telecommunications Software User's Network [*Telesun Corp.*] [*Englewood, OH*] (TSSD)
Teletch .... Teletouch Communications, Inc. [*Associated Press*] (SAG)
TELETECH .... National Telecommunications & Technology Fund, Inc. [*New York, NY*] (TSSD)
TeleTech ...... TeleTech Holdings, Inc. [*Associated Press*] (SAG)
Teletek .... Teletek, Inc. [*Associated Press*] (SAG)
Teletouch .... Teletouch Communications, Inc. [*Associated Press*] (SAG)
TELETYPE .... Teletypewriter [*Telecommunications*]
TELEU .... Tech Electro Industries Unit [*NASDAQ symbol*] (TTSB)
Televerket ... National Swedish Telecommunications Administration [*Stockholm*] [*Information service or system*] (IID)
TELEW .... Tech Electro Industries Wrrt [*NASDAQ symbol*] (TTSB)
TeleWest ...... TeleWest Communications PLC [*Associated Press*] (SAG)
TELEX .... Automatic Teletypewriter Exchange Service [*of Western Union*]
TELEX .... Telegraph Exchange [*Telecommunications*] (IAA)
TELEX .... Teleprinter Exchange [*Telecommunications*] (IAA)
TELEX .... Teleprocessing Executive [*Telecommunications*] (IAA)
TELEX .... Teletype Exchange (NITA)
TelexChil ..... Telex Chile SA [*Associated Press*] (SAG)
TELF .... Tamil Eelam Liberation Front [*Sri Lanka*] [*Political party*] (PPW)
TELFAD .... Telephone Executive Leader for a Day [*New England Telephone Co. program for high school students*]
TELG .... Telegram
TELG .... Telegraph
TELG .... Telegraph Communications [*NASDAQ symbol*] (SAG)
TELGF .... Telegraph Communic Ltd [*NASDAQ symbol*] (TTSB)
TELID .... Teletypewriter Identification (NOAA)
TELINT .... Telemetry Intelligence
TELIS .... Test Equipment Logistics Information Source [*Army*]
TELISA .... Thermometric Enzyme-Linked Immunosorbent Assay [*Analytical biochemistry*]
TELIST .... Telegraphist (DSUE)
TELL .... [*The*] Excellent Lodge Leader [*Freemasonry*]
TELL .... Teacher-Aiding Electronic Learning Link (PDAA)
TELL .... Teletouch Communications, Inc. [*NASDAQ symbol*] (SAG)
Tellabs .... Tellabs Co. [*Associated Press*] (SAG)
Tellurn .... Tellurian, Inc. [*Associated Press*] (SAG)
Tellus .... Tellus Industries, Inc. [*Associated Press*] (SAG)
TELLW .... Teletouch Communicns Wrrt'A' [*NASDAQ symbol*] (TTSB)
TELM .... Telegram (ROG)
TelMd .... TelMed, Inc. [*Associated Press*] (SAG)
TelMed .... TelMed, Inc. [*Associated Press*] (SAG)
TelMex .... Telefonos de Mexico SA [*Associated Press*]
TELMKTG ..... Telemarketing
Telmn .... Telemundo Group, Inc. [*Associated Press*] (SAG)
TELMTR .... Telemotor
Telmun .... Telemundo Group, Inc. [*Associated Press*] (SAG)
TELN .... Telephone (IAA)
TELNET .... Georgia Telecommunications Network [*Georgia Hospital Association*] [*Atlanta, GA*] [*Telecommunications*] (TSSD)
TELNET .... Telecommunication Network (OSI)
TELNO .... Telephone Number (IAA)
TELO .... Tamil Eelam Liberation Organization [*Sri Lanka*] [*Political party*]
TELO .... Tel Offshore Trust [*NASDAQ symbol*] (NQ)
Tel Off .... Telegraph Office
TEL Off .... TEL Offshore Trust [*Associated Press*] (SAG)
TELOP .... Telephone Operating Co. [*Also, TELCO*]
TELOP .... Television Optical (NTCM)
TELOPS .... Telemetry Online Processing System [*Computer science*]
TELOZ .... TEL Offshore Tr UBI [*NASDAQ symbol*] (TTSB)
TELPAK .... Telephone Package
TelPeru .... Telefonica del Peru SA [*Associated Press*] (SAG)
TELR .... Telor Ophthalmic Pharm [*NASDAQ symbol*] (TTSB)
TELR .... Telor Ophthalmic Pharmaceuticals [*NASDAQ symbol*] (SAG)
TelrOph .... Telor Ophthalmic Pharmaceuticals [*Commercial firm Associated Press*] (SAG)
TELS .... TEL Electronics, Inc. [*American Fork, UT*] [*NASDAQ symbol*] (NQ)
TELS .... TELS Corp. [*Associated Press*] (SAG)
TELS .... TELS Corp. [*NASDAQ symbol*] (SAG)
TELS .... Test of Early Learning Skills [*Child development test*]
TELS .... Turbine Engine Loads Simulator
TELSAM .... Telephone Service Attitude Measurement [*Telephone interviews*] [*AT & T*]
TELSAR .... Tracking and Evolution of Solar Active Regions (USDC)
TELSAR .... Tracking and Evolution of Solar Active Regions [*Marine science*] (OSRA)
TELSAT .... Television Satellite (NTCM)
TelSave .... Tel-Save Holdings, Inc. [*Associated Press*] (SAG)
Telscape ...... Telscape International, Inc. [*Associated Press*] (SAG)
TELSCAR ..... Transmit Electronically Location Shippers' Car Advice Reports
TELSCOM .... Telemetry-Surveillance-Communications
TELSCPD ..... Telescoped
Telscpe .... Telscape International, Inc. [*Associated Press*] (SAG)
TELSIM .... Teletypewriter Simulation [*or Simulator*]
TELSTATS .... Telemetry Station System [*Telecommunications*] (IAA)
TELSUN .... Television Series for United Nations [*A foundation formed to produce, and telecast on a commercial basis, dramatized descriptions of UN activities*]
TEL SUR ...... Telephone Survey (MUGU)
TEL-SYS ...... Telephone System
TELT .... Teltronics, Inc. [*NASDAQ symbol*] (NQ)
TELTA .... Tethered Lighter-than-Air (KSC)
TELTAP .... Telephone Tape (IAA)
TELTIPS .... Technical Effort Locator and Technical Interest Profile System [*Army*] (PDAA)
TELTRAC ...... Telemetry Tracking [*Telecommunications*] (IAA)
Teltrnd .... Teltrend, Inc. [*Associated Press*] (SAG)
Teltron .... Teltronics, Inc. [*Associated Press*] (SAG)
TELU .... Total-Tel USA Communic [*NASDAQ symbol*] (TTSB)
TELU .... Total Tel USA Communications [*NASDAQ symbol*] (SAG)
Telular .... Telular Corp. [*Associated Press*] (SAG)
TELUQ .... Tele-Universite [*University of Quebec*] [*Telecommunications service*] (TSSD)
TELUQ .... Tele-Universite (University of Quebec) [*Quebec, PQ*] [*Telecommunications*] (TSSD)
TELUS .... Telemetric Universal Sensor
TELV .... TeleVideo Systems [*NASDAQ symbol*] (TTSB)
TELV .... TeleVideo Systems, Inc. [*NASDAQ symbol*] (NQ)
Telvid .... Tele Video Systems, Inc. [*Associated Press*] (SAG)
Telxon .... Telxon Corp. [*Associated Press*] (SAG)
TEM .... Memphis University School, Hyde Library, Memphis, TN [*OCLC symbol*] (OCLC)
TEM .... Officers for Temporary Service [*Navy British*] (ROG)
TEM .... Roswell Park Memorial Institute [*Research code symbol*]
TEM .... Target Engagement Message (NVT)
TEM .... Target Evaluation Maintenance (MCD)
TEM .... Technical Error Message [*Aviation*]
TEM .... TELEX Extended Memory (IAA)
TEM .... Temiskaming & Northern Ontario Railway [*AAR code*]
tem .... Temne [*MARC language code Library of Congress*] (LCCP)
TEM .... Temora [*Australia Airport symbol*] (OAG)
TEM .... Temperature (DEN)
TEM .... Tempered (DEN)
Tem .... [*The*] Templar [*1788-79*] [*London*] [*A publication*] (DLA)
TEM .... Template (DEN)
Tem .... Tempo [*Record label*] [*Germany*]
TEM .... Tempo [*Music*]
Tem .... Tempore [*In the Time Of*] [*Latin*] (DLA)
TEM .... Temuco [*Chile*] [*Seismograph station code, US Geological Survey Closed*] (SEIS)
TeM .... Tennessee Microfilms, Nashville, TN [*Library symbol Library of Congress*] (LCLS)
TEM .... Terramar Resources Corp. [*Toronto Stock Exchange symbol Vancouver Stock Exchange symbol*]
TEM .... Terrestrial Ecosystem Model [*for climate effects*]
TEM .... Texas Episodic Model [*Environmental Protection Agency*] (GFGA)
TEM .... Text Excursion Module (IAA)
TEM .... Thermal Expansion Molding (MCD)
TEM .... Thermoelectric Module
TEM .... Tomato Extract Medium (OA)
TEM .... Torpedo Evasive Maneuvering [*Navy*]
TEM .... Transmission Electron Micrograph
TEM .... Transmission Electron Microscope [*or Microscopy*]
TEM .... Transmission Engineering Memorandum (IAA)
TEM .... Transverse Electromagnetic [*Wave*] [*Radio*]
TEM .... Transverse Electromagnetic Mode [*Telecommunications*] (IAA)
TEM .... Transverse Exitation Mode (NITA)
TEM .... Triethylenemelamine [*Organic chemistry*]
tem .... Triethylene Melamine [*An arizidine mutagen*] [*Genetics*] (DOG)
TEM .... Typical Egg Mass
TEMA .... Tank Equipment Manufacturers Association (NUCP)
TEMA .... Telecommunication Engineering and Manufacturing Association [*British*] (IAA)
TEMA .... Test and Evaluation Management Agency [*Army*] (RDA)
TEMA .... Test Macro [*Computer science*] (IAA)
TEMA .... Test of Early Mathematics Ability
TEMA .... Trace Elements in Man and Animals [*An international symposium*]
TEMA .... Training, Education, and Mutual Assistance (USDC)
TEMA .... Training, Education and Mutual Assistance [*Marine science*] (OSRA)
TEMA .... Training, Education, and Mutual Assistance in the Marine Sciences [*IOC working committee*] (MSC)
TEMA .... Tubular Exchanger Manufacturers Association (EA)
TEMAC .... Temporary Active Duty
TEMAC .... Turbine Engine Monitoring and Control [*ASMAP Electronics Ltd.*] [*Software package*] (NCC)

TEMACDIFOT... Temporary Active Duty in a Flying Status Involving Operational or Training Flights [*Navy*]
TEMACDIFOTINS... Temporary Active Duty under Instruction in a Flying Status Involving Operationalor Training Flights [*Navy*]
TEMACDU.... Temporary Active Duty [*Navy*]
TEMACINS... Temporary Active Duty under Instruction [*Navy*]
TEMADD...... Temporary Additional Duty [*Navy*]
TEMADDCON... Temporary Additional Duty in Connection with [*Specified activity*] [*Navy*]
TEMADDINS... Temporary Additional Duty under Instruction [*Navy*]
TEMAF......... Templeton Emerging Market Appreciation Fund [*Associated Press*] (SAG)
TEMANS...... Tactical Effectiveness of Minefields in the Antiarmor Weapons System (PDAA)
TEMARS...... Transportation Environmental Measurement and Recording System (MCD)
TEMAS......... "Tell-Me-A-Story" Thematic Appreciation Test (EDAC)
TEMAW........ Tactical Effectiveness of Minefields in Antiarmor Warfare Systems [*Army*] (INF)
TEMAWS...... Tactical Effectiveness of Minefields in Antiarmor Warfare Systems [*Army*]
TEMC........... Test and Evaluation Management Course (MCD)
TEM-CAS..... Temporary-Casualty Pay Record [*Navy*] (DNAB)
TEMCON...... Temporary Duty Connection [*Navy*] (DNAB)
TEMD........... TelMed, Inc. [*NASDAQ symbol*] (SAG)
TEMDIFOT... Temporary Duty in a Flying Status Involving Operational or Training Flights [*Navy*]
TEMDIFOTINS... Temporary Duty under Instruction in a Flying Status Involving Operational or Training Flights [*Navy*]
TEMDIFPRO... Temporary Duty in a Flying Status Involving Proficiency Flying [*Navy*] (DNAB)
TEMDU........ Temporary Duty [*Navy*]
TEMDUCON... Temporary Duty in Connection With [*Specified activity*] [*Navy*]
TEMDU DIS... Temporary Duty Pending Disciplinary Action [*Navy*] (DNAB)
TEMDU FFA... Temporary Duty for Further Assignment [*Navy*] (DNAB)
TEMDU FFT... Temporary Duty for Further Transfer [*Navy*] (DNAB)
TEMDUINS... Temporary Duty under Instruction [*Navy*]
TEMDU PAT... Temporary Duty as a Patient [*Navy*] (DNAB)
TEMDU PSI... Temporary Duty - Programmed Student Input [*Navy*] (DNAB)
TEMDU SEP... Temporary Duty Pending Separation [*Navy*] (DNAB)
TEMDW........ TelMed Inc. Wrrt [*NASDAQ symbol*] (TTSB)
TEMEC......... Translational Electromagnetic Environment Chamber (MCD)
TEMED......... Tetramethylethylenediamine [*Also, TMED, TMEDA*] [*Organic chemistry*]
TEMFI.......... Templeton Emerging Market Fund, Inc. [*Associated Press*] (SAG)
TEMFLY........ Temporary Duty Involving Flying [*Navy*]
TEMFLYINS... Temporary Duty Involving Flying under Instruction [*Navy*]
TEM-GEN..... Temporary-General [*Navy*] (DNAB)
TEMIC.......... Telecommunications Executive Management Institute of Canada (TSSD)
TEMIC.......... Telefunken Microelectronik
TEMIF.......... Templeton Emerging Markets Income Fund [*Associated Press*] (SAG)
TEMINS........ Temporary Duty under Instruction [*Navy*]
TEMIS.......... TRADOC [*Training and Doctrine Command*] Engineer Management Information System [*Army*]
TEMMA........ Transmission Electron Microscopy and Microprobe Analysis (PDAA)
TEMMF........ Tax-Exempt Money Market Fund [*Investment term*]
TEMO........... Test and Evaluation Management Office [*Army*] (RDA)
TEMOD........ Terminal Environment Module [*Computer science*] (MHDB)
TEMOD........ Test Equipment Modernization [*Army*] (RDA)
TEMOD........ Test, Measurement, and Diagnostic Equipment Modernization [*Military*] (RDA)
temp........... Distemper (VRA)
TEMP........... Electrical Resistance Temperature (MCD)
TEMP........... [*The*] Expanded Memory Print Program (SAA)
TEMP........... Tachyelectromagnetic Pulse
TEMP........... Taxation Employment Number [*Canada*]
TEMP........... Technique for Econometric Modeling Program (BUR)
temp........... [*Egg*] Tempera (VRA)
TEMP........... Temperance (ADA)
TEMP........... Temperate Zone
TEMP........... Temperature (AAG)
TEMP........... Temperature
TEMP........... Tempered (AAG)
Temp........... [*The*] Tempest [*Shakespearean work*] (BARN)
TEMP........... Template (AAG)
TEMP........... Tempo [*Music*]
TEMP........... Temporal
TEMP........... Temporary
Temp........... Temporary Light [*Navigation signal*]
TEMP........... Temporary Worker
temp........... Tempore [*In the Time Of*] [*Latin*] (GPO)
TEMP........... Test and Evaluation Management Plan [*Army*]
TEMP........... Test Evaluation Master Plan (MCD)
TEMP........... Texas Educational Microwave Project
TEMP........... Thermal Energy Management Process (MCD)
T(EMP)........ Time to Emplacement [*Military*]
TEMP........... Total Energy Management Professionals [*Defunct*] (EA)
TEMP........... Triethoxymethoxy Propanes [*Organic chemistry*]
Temp & M... Temple and Mew's English Crown Cases [*1848-51*] [*A publication*] (DLA)
TEMPATT..... Temporarily Attached [*Navy*] (DNAB)
TEMPB......... Temporary Dummy Symbol B [*NASDAQ symbol*] (SAG)
Temp Ctf..... Temporary Certificate (MHDW)
TEMPDETD... Temporary Detached Duty [*Navy*] (DNAB)
TEMP DEXT... Tempus Dextra [*Right Temple*] [*Medicine*]
Temp Emer Ct App... Temporary Emergency Court of Appeals [*United States*] (DLA)
TEMPER....... Technological, Economic, Military, and Political Evaluation Routine [*Computer-based simulation model*]
TEMPER....... Tent, Extendable, Modular, Personnel [*DoD*]
TEMPEST..... Transient Electromagnetic Pulse Emanation Standard (MCD)
Temp Geo II... Cases in Chancery Tempore George II [*England*] [*A publication*] (DLA)
TempGu....... Templeton Global Utilities, Inc. [*Associated Press*] (SAG)
TEMPISTORS... Temperature Compensating Resistors (NATG)
TEMPL......... Template [*Engineering*]
Temple & M... Temple and Mew's English Crown Cases [*A publication*] (DLA)
Temple & M (Eng)... Temple and Mew's English Crown Cases [*A publication*] (DLA)
Temple U...... Temple University (GAGS)
Templl......... Temple-Inland, Inc. [*Associated Press*] (SAG)
TEMPO......... Tactical Electromagnetic Project Office [*Military*] (CAAL)
TEMPO......... Technical Electronic Management Planning Organization
TEMPO......... Technical Military Planning Operation (AAG)
TEMPO......... Technique for Extreme Point Optimization (BUR)
TEMPO......... Temporary (AAG)
TEMPO......... Tetramethylpiperidinol N-oxyl [*Organic chemistry*]
TEMPO......... Time and Effort Measurement through Periodic Observation (MCD)
TEMPO......... Total Evaluation of Management and Production Output
TEMPOS...... Timed Environment Multipartitioned Operating System
TEMP PRIM... Tempo Primo [*Original Tempo*] [*Music*]
TEMPRO...... Template-Assisted Intelligence Report Fusion Process
TEMPROX.... Temporary Duty Will Cover Approximately [*Navy*]
TEMPS......... Transportable Electromagnetic Pulse Simulator (RDA)
TEMPSAL.... Temperature-Salinity Data [*Oceanography*] (MCD)
TEMP SINIST... Tempori Sinistro [*To the Left Temple*] [*Pharmacy*] (ADA)
TempSymbB... Temporary Dummy Symbol B [*Associated Press*] (SAG)
Temp Univ LQ... Temple University. Law Quarterly [*A publication*] (DLA)
TEMPUS...... Trans-European Mobility Scheme for University Students [*EC*] (ECED)
Temp Wood... Manitoba Reports Tempore Wood [*Canada*] [*A publication*] (DLA)
TEMPY......... Temporary
TEMPY......... Temporary
TEM-RET...... Temporary Pay Record for a Retired Member [*Called to Active Duty*] [*Navy*] (DNAB)
TEMS........... Teacher Examiner Mark Sheet (AIE)
TEMS........... Technical Engineering Management Support [*Air Force*]
TEMS........... Test Equipment Maintenance Set
TEMS........... Thermal Elastic Model Study
TEMS........... Tornado Electronic Messaging System [*Computer science*]
TEMS........... Toyota Electronically Modulated Suspension [*Automotive engineering*]
TEMS........... Transport Environment Monitoring System [*NASA*] (MCD)
TEMS........... Turbine Engine Monitoring System
TEMSE......... Technical and Managerial Support Environment (DOMA)
TEMSEPRAD... Temporary Duty Connection, Separation Processing. Upon Completion and When Directed Detach; Proceed Home for Release from Active Duty in Accordance with Instructions [*Navy*]
TEMSS......... Total Emergency Medical Services System
Temtex........ Temtex Industries, Inc. [*Associated Press*] (SAG)
TEMWAIT..... Temporary Duty Awaiting [*Specified event*] [*Navy*]
TEN............. Canarias [*Formerly, Tenerife*] [*Spain*] [*Geomagnetic observatory code*]
Ten............. Littleton's Tenures [*A publication*] (DSA)
TEN............. Tee-Comm Electronics, Inc. [*Toronto Stock Exchange symbol*]
ten.............. Tenacious [*Quality of the bottom*] [*Nautical charts*]
TEN............. Tenant (WDAA)
TEN............. Tenerife [*Canary Islands*] [*Seismograph station code, US Geological Survey*] (SEIS)
TEN............. Tenneco Inc. [*NYSE symbol*] (SAG)
TEN............. Tennessee (ROG)
TEN............. Tennessee Airways, Inc. [*ICAO designator*] (FAAC)
Ten............. Tennessee Reports [*A publication*] (ILCA)
TEN............. Tennis
TEN............. Tenor
TEN............. Tenuto [*Held, Sustained*] [*Music*]
TEN............. The Entertainment Network (NITA)
TEN............. Total Enteral Nutrition
TEN............. Total Entertainment Network [*Online gaming service*]
TEN............. Total Excreted [*or Excretory*] Nitrogen
TEN............. Toxic Epidermal Necrolysis [*Medicine*]
TEN............. Trainee Enrolled Nurse
TEN............. Trans-European Network [*European Union*] (ECON)
tenac.......... Tenaculum [*Medicine*] (MAE)
Tenakh........ Torah, Veni'im, Ketubim (BJA)
Ten App...... Tennessee Appeals Reports [*A publication*] (DLA)
TENCAP...... Tactical Exploitation of National Space Capabilities
Ten Cas....... Shannon's Tennessee Cases [*A publication*] (DLA)
Ten Cas....... Thompson's Unreported Tennessee Cases [*A publication*] (DLA)
TEN COM..... Tenants in Common (MHDB)
Tencor........ Tencor Instruments, Inc. [*Associated Press*] (SAG)
TENCY......... Tenancy (ROG)
TENDR......... Tendring [*England*]
TENEMT...... Tenement (ROG)
Tenera........ Tenera Ltd. [*Associated Press*] (SAG)
TENES......... Teaching English to the Non-English Speaking
TENET......... [*The*] Texas Education Network [*A data communications network*] (TNIG)

TenetHlt....... Tenet Healthcare Corp. [*Associated Press*] (SAG)
TENG........... Technical Engineers Association
TEng........... Technician Engineer [*British*] (DBQ)
TEngAMIN.... Technician Engineer of the Institution of Metallurgists [*British*] (DBQ)
TENN........... Tennessee (AAG)
Tenn........... Tennessee (ODBW)
TENN........... Tennessee Railway Co. [*AAR code*]
Tenn........... Tennessee Supreme Court Reports [*A publication*] (DLA)
Tenn........... Tennyson (BARN)
Tenn Admin Comp... Official Compilation of the Rules and Regulations of the State of Tennessee [*A publication*] (DLA)
Tenn Admin Reg... Tennessee Administrative Register [*A publication*] (DLA)
Tennant....... Tennant Co. [*Associated Press*] (SAG)
Tenn App..... Tennessee Appeals Reports [*A publication*] (DLA)
Tenn App..... Tennessee Appellate Bulletin [*A publication*] (DLA)
Tenn App..... Tennessee Civil Appeals Reports [*A publication*] (DLA)
Tenn App Bull... Tennessee Appellate Bulletin [*A publication*] (DLA)
Tenn Appeals... Tennessee Appeals Reports [*A publication*] (DLA)
Tenn App R... Tennessee Appeals Reports [*A publication*] (DLA)
Tenn Cas..... Shannon's Unreported Tennessee Cases [*1847-1894*] [*A publication*] (DLA)
Tenn Cas (Shannon)... Thompson's Unreported Tennessee Cases [*1847-69*] [*A publication*] (DLA)
Tenn CCA..... Tennessee Court of Civil Appeals (DLA)
Tenn CCA (Higgins)... Higgins' Tennessee Court of Civil Appeals Reports [*A publication*] (DLA)
Tenn Ch....... Cooper's Tennessee Chancery Reports [*A publication*] (DLA)
Tenn Ch A.... Tennessee Chancery Appeals [*A publication*] (DLA)
Tenn Chancery... Tennessee Chancery Reports (Cooper) [*A publication*] (DLA)
Tenn Chancery App... Tennessee Chancery Appeals Reports (Wright) [*A publication*] (DLA)
Tenn Ch App... Tennessee Chancery Appeals (Wright) [*A publication*] (DLA)
Tenn Ch App Dec... Tennessee Chancery Appeals Decisions [*1895-1907*] [*A publication*] (DLA)
Tenn Ch Ap Reps... Wright's Tennessee Chancery Appeals Reports [*A publication*] (DLA)
Tenn Ch R.... Tennessee Chancery Reports (Cooper) [*A publication*] (DLA)
Tenn Civ A... Tennessee Civil Appeals [*A publication*] (DLA)
Tenn Civ App... Tennessee Civil Appeals [*A publication*] (DLA)
Tennco......... Tenneco, Inc. [*Formerly, Tennessee Gas Transmission Co.*] [*Associated Press*] (SAG)
Tenn Code Ann... Tennessee Code, Annotated [*A publication*] (DLA)
Tenn Cr App... Tennessee Criminal Appeals [*A publication*] (DLA)
Tenn Crim App... Tennessee Criminal Appeals Reports [*A publication*] (DLA)
Tennessee R... Tennessee Reports [*A publication*] (DLA)
Tennessee Rep... Tennessee Reports [*A publication*] (DLA)
Tenn Jur...... Tennessee Jurisprudence [*A publication*] (DLA)
Tenn Juris... Tennessee Jurisprudence [*A publication*] (DLA)
Tenn Law..... Tennessee Lawyer [*A publication*] (DLA)
Tenn Leg Rep... Tennessee Legal Reporter [*A publication*] (DLA)
Tenn Priv Acts... Private Acts of the State of Tennessee [*A publication*] (DLA)
Tenn Pub Acts... Public Acts of the State of Tennessee [*A publication*] (DLA)
Tenn R......... Tennessee Reports [*A publication*] (DLA)
Tenn Rep..... Tennessee Reports [*A publication*] (DLA)
Tenn St U.... Tennessee State University (GAGS)
Tenn Tech U... Tennessee Technological University (GAGS)
TENN-TOM.... Tennessee-Tombigbee [*Proposed waterway*]
TENOC......... Ten-Year Oceanographic Program [*Navy*]
TENOR......... Tennessee Open Records [*An association*]
TENPrB....... Tenneco $7.40 cm Pfd [*NYSE symbol*] (TTSB)
TENR........... Technically Enhanced Naturally Radioactive (NRCH)
TENRAP....... Technically Enhanced Naturally Radioactive Product (NRCH)
TENS........... Tensile
TENS........... Tension (AAG)
TENS........... Training Element Need Statement
TENS........... Transcutaneous Electrical Nerve Stimulation [*Also, TES, TNS*] [*A method of pain control*] [*Medicine*]
TENSEGRITY... Tensional Integrity [*Construction principle named by Buckminster Fuller*]
TENT........... Tenant (ROG)
TENT........... Tenement (ROG)
TENT........... Tentative (AAG)
TENV........... Totally Enclosed - Nonventilated
TENWF......... Tee Comm Electronics, Inc. [*NASDAQ symbol*] (SAG)
TENX........... Tee Comm Electronics, Inc. [*NASDAQ symbol*] (SAG)
TENXF......... Tee-Comm Electronics [*NASDAQ symbol*] (TTSB)
TEO............. Teal Industry Ltd. [*Vancouver Stock Exchange symbol*]
TEO............. Technical Electronic Office [*Data General Corp.*]
TEO............. Tel Argentina-France Tel'B'ADS [*NYSE symbol*] (TTSB)
TEO............. Telecom Argentina Stet France Telecom SA [*NYSE symbol*] (SAG)
TEO............. Telephone Equipment Order [*Telecommunications*] (TEL)
TEO............. Teoloyucan [*Mexico*] [*Geomagnetic observatory code*]
TEO............. Terapo [*Papua New Guinea*] [*Airport symbol*] (OAG)
TEO............. Terato Resources Ltd. [*Toronto Stock Exchange symbol*]
TEO............. Test Equipment Operator
TEO............. Third World Education Outreach (EA)
TEO............. To Expiry Only (AIA)
TEO............. Total Extractable Organic [*Analytical chemistry*]
TEO............. Transferred Electron Oscillator
TEO............. Transmittal Engineering Order
TEOA........... Test and Evaluation Objectives Annex (MCD)
TEOA........... Triethanolamine [*Organic chemistry*]
TEOF........... Triethyl Orthoformate [*Organic chemistry*]
TEOM........... Tapered Element Oscillating Microbalance
TEOM........... Transformer Environment Overcurrent Monitor (IEEE)
TEORS......... Transient Electro-Optic Raman Scattering [*Physics*]
TEOS........... Tetraethoxysilane [*Organic radical*]
TEOS........... Tetraethyl Orthosilicate [*Organic chemistry*] (NASA)
TEOS........... Tillotson Equation of State [*Physical chemistry*]
TEOSS......... Tactical Emitter Operational Support System (MCD)
TEOTA......... [*The*] Eyes of the Army (AAG)
TEP............. Table Editing Process
TEP............. Tactical ELINT Processor (MCD)
TEP............. Tape Edit Processor [*Computer science*]
TEP............. Tau Epsilon Phi [*Fraternity*]
TEP............. Technical Education Program (OICC)
TEP............. Technical Evaluation Panel [*In various federal government agencies*] (NASA)
TEP............. Temperature Extreme Pressure (DNAB)
TEP............. Temporary Entry Permit
TEP............. Tepecintle [*Race of maize*]
TEP............. Teptep [*Papua New Guinea*] [*Airport symbol*] (OAG)
TEP............. Terminal Error Program
TEP............. Territory Enterprises Proprietary
TEP............. Test and Evaluation Plan [*Military*] (CAAL)
TEP............. Test Executive Processor (NITA)
TEP............. Tetraethoxypropane [*Organic chemistry*]
TEP............. Tetraethyl Pyrophosphate [*Insecticide*] [*Pharmacology*] (IAA)
TEP............. Thermal Enzyme Probe
TEP............. Thermoelectric Power [*Thermodynamics*]
TEP............. Thromboendophlebectomy [*Medicine*] (MAE)
TEP............. Token Economy Program [*Psychiatry*]
TEP............. Tons Equivalent of Petroleum [*Fuel measure*]
TEP............. Torpedo Ejection Pump (DNAB)
TEP............. Total Extractable Protein [*Food technology*]
TEP............. Toxicant Extraction Procedure
TEP............. Trace Element Pattern (KSC)
TEP............. Tracheo-Esophageal Puncture [*Medicine*]
TEP............. Training Equipment Plan
TEP............. Trans Equatorial Propagation
TEP............. Transmitter Experiment Package
TEP............. Transparent Electrophotographic (NITA)
TEP............. Transparent Electrophotography [*Proposed archival storage medium*]
TEP............. Transportable Equation Program (DNAB)
TEP............. Triethyl-Phosphine [*Organic chemistry*]
TEP............. Tube Evaluation Program
TEP............. Tucson Electric Power Co. [*NYSE symbol*] (SPSG)
TEP............. Tucson Ele Power(New) [*NYSE symbol*] (TTSB)
TEP............. Turbine Extreme Pressure (MCD)
TEP............. Turkiye Emekci Partisi [*Workers' Party of Turkey*] [*Political party*] (PPW)
TEP............. Tyrone Energy Park (NRCH)
TEPA........... Roswell Park Memorial Institute [*Research code symbol*]
TEPA........... Tetraethylenepentamine [*Organic chemistry*]
TEPA........... Triethylenephosphoramide [*Also, APO*] [*Organic chemistry*]
TEPAC......... Tube Engineering Panel Advisory Council [*Defunct*] (EA)
TEPC........... Test and Evaluation Planning Committee [*Military*] (CAAL)
TEPC........... Tissue Equivalent Proportional Counter (PDAA)
Tepco........... Teppco Partners Ltd. [*Associated Press*] (SAG)
TEPCO......... Tokyo Electric Power Co. (ECON)
TEPD........... Trademark Examining Procedure Directives [*A publication*]
TEPE........... Target Engagement Proficiency Exercise [*Military*]
TEPG........... Test Evaluation Planning Group (MCD)
TEPG........... Thermionic Electrical Power Generator (IEEE)
TEPH........... Thromboembolic Pulmonary Hypertension [*Medicine*] (CPH)
TEPI............ Technical Equipment Planning Information
TEPI............ Terminal Endpoint Identifier (TNIG)
TEPI............ Terminal Phase Intercept
TEPI............ Training Equipment Planning Information [*Military*] (AFM)
TEPI............ Triadal Equated Personality Inventory [*Psychology*]
TEPIAC......... Thermophysical and Electronic Properties Information Analysis Center [*Later, HTMIAC*] [*Purdue University*]
TEPIC........... Tris(epoxypropyl)isocyanurate [*Organic chemistry*]
tepid............ Tepidarium (VRA)
TEPID........... Tepidus [*Lukewarm*] [*Pharmacy*] (ROG)
TEPIGEN...... Television Picture Generator (MCD)
TEPOS......... Test Program Operating System
TEPP........... Tetraethyl Pyrophosphate [*Insecticide*] [*Pharmacology*]
TEPP........... Turbine Engine Power Plant (DWSG)
TEPPS......... Technique for Establishing Personnel Performance Standards [*Navy*]
TEPR........... Tomahawk Experimental Reaction [*Navy*]
TEPR........... Training Equipment Progress Report
TEPrB......... Toledo Edison 4 1/4% Pfd [*AMEX symbol*] (TTSB)
TEPRSSC..... Technical Electronic Product Radiation Safety Standards Committee (MCD)
TEPS........... National Commission on Teacher Education and Professional Standards [*Defunct*]
TEPSA......... Trans European Policy Studies Association (EA)
TEQ............. Total Engagement Quality [*Computer science*]
TEQ............. Toxicity Equivalent
TEQ............. Trian Equities Ltd. [*Vancouver Stock Exchange symbol*]
TEQ............. Twenty-Foot Equivalent [*Shipping*]
TEQU........... Test Equivocal, Possible Low Titer [*Laboratory science*] (DAVI)
TER............. Australian Territory (EERA)
TER............. Tape Error Recovery [*Routine*] [*Computer science*] (ECII)
TER............. Tardeable Emmission Rights (EERA)
TER............. Tau Epsilon Rho [*Fraternity*]
TER............. Technical Evaluation Report [*Nuclear energy*] (NRCH)
TER............. Telecommunications Electronic Reviews [*A publication*]
TER............. Teleprinter Retransmitting [*Telecommunications*] (IAA)

TER .... Teradyne, Inc. [*NYSE symbol*] (SPSG)
TER .... Tera Mines Ltd. [*Toronto Stock Exchange symbol*]
TER .... Terceira [*Azores*] [*Airport symbol*] (OAG)
TER .... Tere [*Rub*] [*Pharmacy*]
Ter .... Terence [*Second century BC*] [*Classical studies*] (OCD)
ter .... Tereno [*MARC language code Library of Congress*] (LCCP)
TER .... Terrace
TER .... Terrace
ter .... Terracotta (VRA)
TER .... Terra Mines Ltd. [*Toronto Stock Exchange symbol Vancouver Stock Exchange symbol*]
TER .... Terranova [*Guatemala*] [*Seismograph station code, US Geological Survey*] (SEIS)
TER .... Terrazzo
TER .... Territorial Airlines, Inc. [*ICAO designator*] (FAAC)
TER .... Territory
Ter .... Terry's Delaware Reports [*A publication*] (DLA)
TER .... Tertiary (KSC)
Ter .... Terumot (BJA)
TER .... Test Effectiveness Ratio [*Computer science*]
TER .... Test Equipment Readiness [*NASA*] (NASA)
TER .... Test Evaluation Report [*NASA*] (KSC)
TER .... Thermal Enhancement Ratio
TE-R .... Thermostable E-Rosetting [*Cells*] [*Medicine*]
TER .... Threefold (DAVI)
TER .... Three Times [*Pharmacy*] (DAVI)
TER .... Time and Event Recorder
TER .... Time Estimating Relationship (NASA)
TER .... Total Endoplasmic Reticulum [*Cytology*]
TER .... Total Energy Ratio [*Mechanical engineering*]
TER .... Total External Reflection
TE/R .... Trailing Edge Radius (MSA)
TER .... Training Equipment Requirements Plan
TER .... Transcapillary Escape Rate
TER .... Transcapillary Escape Route [*Medicine*] (DAVI)
TER .... Transepithelial Electrical Resistance [*Cytology*]
TER .... Transfer Effectiveness Ratio
TER .... Transmission Engineering Recommendation [*Telecommunications*] (IAA)
TER .... Transmission Equivalent Resistance (IEEE)
TER .... Travel Expense Report (SAA)
TER .... Triple Ejection [*or Ejector*] Rack (NVT)
TER .... True Height Above Aerodrome Level [*Aviation*] (AIA)
TERA .... Tax Equity and Responsibility Act of 1982 (WYGK)
TERA .... Temporary Early Retirement Authority (DOMA)
TERA .... Tera Computer [*NASDAQ symbol*] (TTSB)
TERA .... Tera Computer Co. [*NASDAQ symbol*] (SAG)
TERA .... Terminal Effects Research and Analysis Group [*New Mexico Institute of Mining and Technology*] [*Research center*] (RCD)
TERA .... Test of Early Reading Ability
TERA .... #The Early Retirement Authority
TERA .... Tradable Emission Reduction Assessments [*Environmental Protection Agency*]
tera- .... Trillion 10^{12} (IDOE)
TERA .... TSCA [*Toxic Substances Control Act*] Experimental Release Application [*Environmental Protection Agency*]
TERAC .... Tactical Electromagnetic Readiness Advisory Council (MCD)
TeraCo .... Tera Computer Co. [*Associated Press*] (SAG)
TERAG .... Transportable Electronic Receiving Antenna Group (DWSG)
TERAS .... Tactical Energy Requirements and Supply System (MCD)
TERAT .... Teratology (ROG)
TERAW .... Tera Computer Wrrt [*NASDAQ symbol*] (TTSB)
TERB .... Terrazzo Base
TERC .... Technical Education Research Centers, Inc. [*Cambridge, MA*] [*Research center*]
TERC .... Tertiary Education Research Centre [*British*] (AIE)
TERC .... Total Environmental Remediation Contracts (AAGC)
TERCO .... Telephone Rationalization by Computer (PDAA)
TERCOM .... Terrain Contour Mapping (MCD)
TERCOM .... Terrain Contour Matching [*Navigation system*] [*Air Force*]
TERCOM .... Terrain Correlation Method
TERD .... Turbine Electric Reduction Drive
Terdyn .... Terradyne, Inc. [*Associated Press*] (SAG)
TEREBINTH... Terebinthinae Oleum [*Oil of Turpentine*] [*Pharmacology*] (ROG)
TEREC .... Tactical Electromagnetic Reconnaissance [*Air Force*] (IAA)
TEREC .... Tactical Electronic Reconnaissance [*Aircraft*]
TERENA .... Trans-European Research and Education Networking Association [*Formed from merger of Reseaux Associes pour le Recherche Europeenne and European Academic and Research Network*] [*Internet*]
Terent .... Terentius Clemens [*Flourished, 2nd century*] [*Authority cited in pre-1607 legal work*] (DSA)
TERENVSVC... Terrestrial Environmental Services [*Army*] (AABC)
Terex .... Terex Corp. [*Associated Press*] (SAG)
TERF .... Trudeau Early Retirement Fund [*Established 1982 by Canadians who hoped t hat the money would persuade their prime minister to retire from office*] [*Defunct*]
TERG .... Training Equipment Requirements Guide (KSC)
TERI .... Table of Equipment Ready Issue [*Navy*] (ANA)
TERI .... Tata Energy Research Institute [*New Delhi, India*] (ECON)
TERI .... Torpedo Effective Range Indicator
TERL .... Test Engineer Readiness List [*NASA*] (NASA)
TERL .... Test Equipment Readiness List [*NASA*] (NASA)
Terleu .... Tertiary Leucine (BABM)
TERLS .... Thumba Equatorial Launching Station [*Indian rocket station*]
TERM .... Tank Extended Range Munition [*Army*]
TERM .... Temporary Equipment Recovery Mission (CINC)
TERM .... Terminal (AAG)
TERM .... Terminate (AFM)
TERM .... Termination (ECII)
TERM .... Terminology
TERM .... Termite (ADA)
Term .... Term Reports [*North Carolina*] [*1816-18*] [*A publication*] (DLA)
Term .... Term Reports, English King's Bench (Durnford and East's Reports) [*A publication*] (DLA)
Termes de la Ley... Terms of the Common Laws and Statutes Expounded and Explained by John Rastell [*1685*] [*A publication*] (DLA)
TERMIA .... Association Internationale de Terminologie [*International Association of Terminology*] [*Quebec, PQ*] (EAIO)
TERMINACTRAORD... Directed to Request Termination of Inactive Duty Training Orders [*Navy*]
TERMINON... Termination (ROG)
TERMINOQ... Banque de Terminologie de Quebec [*Terminology Bank of Quebec*] [*French Language Board*] [*Information service or system*]
TERMN .... Termination
Term NC .... Taylor's North Carolina Term Reports [*A publication*] (DLA)
TERMNET ... International Network for Terminology [*INFOTERM*] [*Vienna, Austria*]
TERM PWR... Terminator Power [*Computer science*]
Term R .... Term Reports, English King's Bench (Durnford and East's Reports) [*A publication*] (DLA)
Term Rep .... Term Reports, English King's Bench (Durnford and East's Reports) [*England*] [*A publication*] (DLA)
Term Rep (NC)... Taylor's North Carolina Term Reports [*4 North Carolina*] [*A publication*] (DLA)
TERMS .... Terminal Management System [*Military*] (AABC)
TERMTRAN... Terminal Translator (KSC)
TERN .... Terminal and Enroute Navigation (PDAA)
TERN .... Transnational European Rural Network [*Belgium*] (EAIO)
TERO .... Tribal Employment Rights Office
TERP .... Terminal Equipment Replacement Program [*Electronic communications system*] [*Department of State*]
TERP .... Terminal Instrument Procedure [*Aviation*]
TERP .... Terrain Elevation Retrieval Program (IEEE)
TERP .... Turbine Engine Reliability Program (PDAA)
TERPACIS .... Trust Territory of the Pacific Islands
TERPE .... Tactical Electronic Reconnaissance Processing and Evaluation [*Air Force*] (MCD)
TERPES .... Tactical Electronic Reconnaissance Processing and Evaluation System (MCD)
TERPROM.... Terrain Profile Matching [*British*]
TERPS .... Tactical Electronic Reconnaissance Processing (and Evaluation) System [*Navy*] (DOMA)
TERPS .... Terminal Enquiry/Response Programming System [*British*]
TERPS .... Terminal Instrument Procedures [*Military*]
TERPS .... Terminal Planning System [*Military*]
TERR .... Terrace
Terr .... Terrace (DD)
terr .... Terrace (VRA)
TERR .... Terraza
Terr .... Terrell's Reports [*38-71 Texas*] [*A publication*] (DLA)
TERR .... Territory (AFM)
Terr .... Terrorist [*Slang term used by whites in Zimbabwe to refer to a black nationalist guerrilla*]
Terra .... Terra Industries, Inc. [*Associated Press*] (SAG)
TERRA .... Terrain Evaluation and Retrieval for Road Alignment (IAA)
TERRA .... Terricide-Escape by Rethinking, Research, Action [*An association*]
TERRACE ..... Terrace [*Commonly used*] (OPSA)
Terrace .... Terrace Holdings, Inc. [*Associated Press*] (SAG)
Terr & Wal... Terrell and Walker's Reports [*38-51 Texas*] [*A publication*] (DLA)
Terr & Walk... Terrell and Walker's Reports [*38-51 Texas*] [*A publication*] (DLA)
TerraNit .... Terra Nitrogen Co. Ltd. [*Formerly, Agricultural Minerals Ltd.*] [*Associated Press*] (SAG)
TERRAP .... TERRAP [*Territorial Apprehensiveness*] Programs [*Commercial firm*] (EA)
TERREL .... Terrain Elevation (SAA)
TERRES .... Territorial Residents
TERRESTAR... Terrestrial Application of Solar Technology and Research (MCD)
TERRHICO ... Territorial Rhine Coordination [*NATO*] (NATG)
TERRIT .... Territory
Terr L .... Territories Law [*Northwest Territories*] [*A publication*] (DLA)
Terr L (Can)... Territories Law Reports [*1885-1907*] [*Canada*] [*A publication*] (DLA)
Terr LR .... Territories Law Reports [*1885-1907*] [*Canada*] [*A publication*] (DLA)
TerrNov .... Terra Nova Bermuda Holdings Ltd. [*Associated Press*] (SAG)
Terrorilla ..... Terrorism and Guerrilla Warfare [*Israel*]
TERS .... Tactical Electronic Reconnaissance System (IEEE)
TERS .... Tactical Event Reporting System (DOMA)
TerS .... Terra Santa [*Jerusalem*] (BJA)
TER SIM .... Tere Simul [*Rub Together*] [*Latin*] (ADA)
TERSS .... Tasmanian Earth Resources Satellite Station [*Commonwealth*] [*State*] (EERA)
TERSSE .... Total Earth Resources System for the Shuttle Era [*NASA*]
tert .... Tertiary [*Also, t*] [*Chemistry*]
TERT .... Tertiary [*Period, era, or system*] [*Geology*]
TERT .... Tertius [*Third*] [*Latin*]
Tert .... Tertullian [*160-240AD*] [*Classical studies*] (OCD)
TERT .... Tracking/Erosion Resistance Tester
TERTM .... Thermal Expansion Resin Transfer Molding
TERTSD .... Tertiary Sand [*Agronomy*]
Tertul .... Tertullianus [*Flourished, 2nd-3rd century*] [*Authority cited in pre-1607 legal work*] (DSA)

Teruv ... Teruvenkatachariar's Railway Cases [*India*] [*A publication*] (DLA)
TES ... [*The*] Engineers School (MCD)
TES ... [*The*] Executive Speaker (IID)
TES ... Tableaux Entrees-Sorties [*Database*] [*EC*] (ECED)
TES ... Tactical Environment Simulator [*Navy*] (MCD)
TES ... Tactical Environment System [*Navy*]
TES ... Target Engagement Simulator [*Military*] (MCD)
TES ... Team Effectiveness Survey [*Test*]
TES ... Technical Enforcement Support [*Environmental Protection Agency*] (GFGA)
TES ... Technical Engagement Simulation
TES ... Technical Enquiry Service [*British*] (DCTA)
TES ... Telemetry Evaluation Station
TES ... Temporary Employment Subsidy [*British*] (DCTA)
TES ... Terminal Encounter System
TeS ... Terre Sainte (BJA)
TES ... Territorial Experiment Stations Division [*of ARS, Department of Agriculture*]
TES ... Tessenei [*Ethiopia*] [*Airport symbol*] (AD)
tes ... Tessera (VRA)
TES ... Test and Evaluation Squadron
TES ... Test and Evaluation Support
TES ... Test Squadron [*Air Force*]
TES ... Tetraethylsulfamide [*Organic chemistry*]
TES ... Text Editing System
TES ... Theatre Education Society (EA)
TES ... Therapeutic Electrical Stimulation
TES ... Thermal Emission Spectrometer
TES ... Thermal Energy Storage
TES ... Thermoset Elastomer Styrene Plastic [*Materials science*]
TES ... Thin Elastic Shell
TES ... Thymic Epithelial Supernatant [*Endocrinology*]
TES ... Tidal Electric Station
TES ... Time Encoded Speech [*Telecommunications*] (TEL)
TES ... Times Educational Supplement [*A publication*] (BRI)
TES ... Training Equipment Summary (MCD)
TES ... Transcutaneous Electrical Stimulation [*Also, TENS, TNS*] [*A method of pain control*] [*Medicine*]
TES ... Transmural Electrical Stimulation
TES ... Transportable Earth Station [*British*]
TES ... Transportes Aereos de El Salvador SA de CV [*ICAO designator*] (FAAC)
TES ... Transthoracic Endoscopic Sympathectomy
TES ... Treatment of Emergent Symptom [*Medicine*] (MEDA)
TES ... Triethylsilyl [*Organic chemistry*]
TES ... Tris(hydroxymethyl)methylaminoethanesulfonic Acid [*A buffer*]
TES ... Tropospheric Emission Sensor
TES ... Tungsten Electron Snatcher
TES ... Twelve English Statesmen [*A publication*]
TESA ... Television and Electronics Service Association
TESAC ... Temperature-Salinity-Currents [*Oceanography*] (IID)
TESAR ... Tactical Endurance Synthetic Aperture RADAR [*Army*] (RDA)
TESAT ... Teaching Sample Table (PDAA)
TESC ... [*The*] Evergreen State College [*Olympia, WA*]
TESC ... Tescorp, Inc. [*NASDAQ symbol*] (SAG)
TESCP ... Tescorp 10% 1990 Cv Pfd [*NASDAQ symbol*] (TTSB)
Tescp ... Tescorp, Inc. [*Associated Press*] (SAG)
Tescrp ... Tescorp, Inc. [*Associated Press*] (SAG)
TESE ... Tactical Exercise Simulator and Evaluator (NVT)
TESEM ... Television Esmeraldena Compania de Economia Mixta [*Ecuador*] (EY)
TE(S)FC ... Totally-Enclosed (Separately) Fan-Cooled [*Reactor*] (DEN)
TESG ... Target Echo Signature Generator [*SONAR*]
TESH ... Technical Shop (NASA)
TESH ... Test Shop
TESI ... Tangram Enterprise Solutions, Inc. [*NASDAQ symbol*] (SAG)
TESI ... Teaching Events Stress Inventory (EDAC)
TESI ... Transfer of Electrostatic Images [*Electrophotography*]
TESICO ... Threshold Electron Secondary Ion Coincidence [*Spectroscopy*]
TESL ... Teaching English as a Second Language
TESLA ... Technical Standards for Library Automation
TESLAC ... Testolactone [*Antineoplastic drug*]
TESM ... Triethylstannylmaleate [*Organic chemistry*]
Tesma ... Tesma International, Inc. [*Associated Press*] (SAG)
TESMA ... Theatre Equipment and Supply Manufacturers Association [*Later, TEA*] (EA)
TESOL ... Teachers of English to Speakers of Other Languages (EA)
Tesor ... Tesoro Petroleum Corp. [*Associated Press*] (SAG)
Tesoro ... Tesoro Petroleum Corp. [*Associated Press*] (SAG)
TESPA ... Triethylenethiophosphoramide [*Antineoplastic drug*] (DAVI)
TESR ... Tactical Environment Satellite Readout (MCD)
TESR ... Test Equipment Status Report
TESR ... Time of Sunrise
TESRP ... Test and Evaluation Support Resource Plan (MCD)
TESS ... [*The*] Educational Software Selector [*Database*] (AEE)
TESS ... Tactical and Environmental Support System [*Military*] (CAAL)
TESS ... Tactical Electromagnetic Systems Study (IEEE)
TESS ... Tactical Engagement Simulation System [*Developed by Sandia National Laboratories for the Defense Nuclear Agency*]
TESS ... Technical Engineering and Spacelift Services [*Air Force*] (AAGC)
TESS ... Temporary Employment Subsidy Scheme [*Department of Employment*] [*British*]
TESS ... TESSCO Technologies [*NASDAQ symbol*] (TTSB)
TESS ... TESSCO Technologies, Inc. [*NASDAQ symbol*] (SAG)
TESS ... The Expert System Shell (NITA)
TESS ... Time of Sunset
TESS ... Times Educational Supplement Scotland (AIE)
TESS ... Top Electronic Security Systems [*Commercial firm British*]
TESS ... Total Energy Systems Service (IAA)
TESS ... Total Engineering Support System (HGAA)
TESS ... TRW Environmental Safety Systems, Inc. (GAAI)
TESSA ... Tax-Exempt Special Savings Account [*British*]
Tessa ... Tax Exempt Special Savings Account [*British*] (ODBW)
TESSA ... Total Energy Suppression Shield Array [*Nuclear structure*]
TESSAC ... Tactical Electromagnetic Systems Study Action Council [*Navy*] (ANA)
TESSAR ... Test Event Sequencing, Simulating, and Recording System (PDAA)
TESSCO ... TESSCO Technologies, Inc. [*Associated Press*] (SAG)
TEST ... Tanner Eclectic Stuttering Therapy Program
TEST ... Teen-Age Employment Skills Training, Inc.
TEST ... Testament
Test ... Testamentary [*Legal term*] (DLA)
TEST ... Testator (ADA)
TEST ... Testatrix (WDAA)
TEST ... Testimonial (ADA)
TEST ... Testing
TEST ... Thesaurus of Engineering and Scientific Terms [*A publication*]
TEST ... Track Evaluation System [*Canadian National Railways*]
TEST ... Transamerica Electronic Scoring Technique [*Credit risk evaluation*]
TEST ... Tubal Embryo Stage Transfer
TEST ... Two Element Synthesis Telescope (ADA)
TestAbr ... Testament of Abraham [*Pseudepigrapha*] (BJA)
TestAsh ... Testament of Asher [*Pseudepigrapha*] (BJA)
TestBen ... Testament of Benjamin [*Pseudepigrapha*] (BJA)
testco ... Terra Sancta Tourist Co. Ltd. [*Jordan*]
TESTCOMDNA ... Test Command Defense Nuclear Agency [*Military*] (AABC)
TESTFAC ... Test Facility
TESTG ... Test Group [*Military*]
TESTICLES ... Teamwork, Enthusiasm, Stamina, Tenacity, Initiative, Courage, Loyalty, Excellence, and a Sense of Humor [*Military slang*] (VNW)
TestIss ... Testament of Issachar [*Pseudepigrapha*] (BJA)
TestJos ... Testament of Joseph [*Pseudepigrapha*] (BJA)
TestJud ... Testament of Judah [*Pseudepigrapha*] (BJA)
TestLevi ... Testament of Levi [*Pseudepigrapha*] (BJA)
TestNaph ... Testament of Naphtali [*Pseudepigrapha*] (BJA)
TESTO ... Testigo [*Witness*] [*Latin*] (ADA)
TESTOR ... Testator (ROG)
TESTOS ... Testosterone [*Endocrinology*] (DAVI)
TESTRAN ... Test Translator [*Computer science*]
TestReub ... Testament of Reuben [*Pseudepigrapha*] (BJA)
TESTRIX ... Testatrix (ROG)
TESTS ... Technical-Engineering-Science Training for Secretaries
TESTS ... Test Squadron (MCD)
TestSim ... Testament of Simeon [*Pseudepigrapha*] (BJA)
TESTT ... Testament
TESTW ... Test Wing [*Military*]
TestXII ... Testaments of the Twelve Patriarchs [*Pseudepigrapha*] (BJA)
TESTY ... Testamentary (ROG)
TestZeb ... Testament of Zebulun [*Pseudepigrapha*] (BJA)
TESV ... Tephrosia Symptomless Virus [*Plant pathology*]
TESY ... Terminal Editing System [*Computer science*] (PDAA)
TET ... East Tennessee State University, Johnson City, TN [*OCLC symbol*] (OCLC)
TET ... Teacher Effectiveness Training [*A course of study*]
TET ... Teacher of Electrotherapy [*British*]
TET ... Technical Evaluation Team (MCD)
TET ... Technical Evaluation Test (MCD)
TET ... Telescope and Electron Telescope
TET ... Test Equipment Team (AAG)
TET ... Test Equipment Tool (AAG)
TET ... Test Evaluation Team [*NASA*] (KSC)
Tet ... Tetanus [*Medicine*]
TET ... Tete [*Mozambique*] [*Seismograph station code, US Geological Survey*] (SEIS)
TET ... Tete [*Mozambique*] [*Airport symbol*] (OAG)
TET ... Tetrachloride [*Chemistry*] (AAG)
Tet ... Tetracycline [*Antibiotic compound*]
Tet ... Tetralogy [*Medicine*]
TET ... Tetralogy of Fallot [*Neonatology*] (DAVI)
TET ... Tetrode [*Electronics*]
TET ... Thermionic Emission Technique
TET ... Thermometric Enthalpy Titration [*Analytical chemistry*]
TET ... Titanium Elevon Track
TET ... Total Elapsed Time (KSC)
TET ... Trailing Edge Tracking [*Aviation*] (LAIN)
TET ... Transistor Evaluation Test
TET ... Transportable Electronic Tower (MCD)
TET ... Traveling-Wave Tube (IAA)
TET ... Treadmill Exercise Test [*Physiology*] (CPH)
TET ... Troop Evaluation Tests [*Army*]
TET ... Tubal Embryo Stage Transfer [*Alternative to traditional in-vitro fertilization (IVF)*] [*Also, TEST*] (PAZ)
TET ... Turbine Entry Temperature [*Aviation*]
TET ... Turbo-Electric Tanker
TETA ... Test Equipment Technical Adviser
TETA ... Test-Estrin Time(d) Action [*Pharmacology*] (DAVI)
TETA ... Travelers Emergency Transportation Association [*Sought to pool transportation of salesmen traveling similar routes*] [*World War II*]
TETA ... Triethylenetetramine [*Organic chemistry*]
TETAM ... Tactical Effectiveness Testing of Antitank Missiles [*DoD*]

TETB .... Tetbury [*England*]
TETC .... Teroson Europe Technical Centre [*Research center Germany*]
TETCYC .... Tetracycline [*An Antibiotic*] [*Pharmacology*] (DAVI)
TETD .... Tetraethylthiuram Disulfide [*Also, TTD*] [*Organic chemistry*]
TETEP .... Test for Entrance into Teacher Education Programs [*Achievement test*]
TETF .... Terminal Equipment Test Facility [*Army*] (RDA)
TETFLEYNE... Tetrafluorethylene [*Organic chemistry*]
TETM .... Tetraethylthiuram Monosulfide [*Organic chemistry*]
TETM .... Thermal Effects Tests Model
TETOC .... Council for Technical Education and Training for Overseas Countries [*British*]
TETR .... Test and Training Satellite [*Also, TATS, TTS*] [*NASA*]
TETR .... Tetragonal
TETRA .... Terminal Tracking Telescope
TETRA .... Terminal Trajectory Telescope (IAA)
tetra .... Tetraploid [*Genetics*]
Tetra .... Tetra Technologies, Inc. [*Associated Press*] (SAG)
TETRAC .... Tension Truss Antenna Concept
TETRAC .... Tetraiodothyroacetic Acid [*Organic chemistry*] (MAH)
TetraTc .... Tetra Tech, Inc. [*Associated Press*] (SAG)
TETROON .... Tethered Meteorological Balloon (IAA)
TETROON .... Tetrahedral Balloon [*Meteorology*]
TETSS .... Test and Evaluation Technical Support Services [*Army*]
TET TOX .... Tetanus Toxin (WDAA)
Tet Tox .... Tetanus Toxoid [*Medicine*] (CPH)
TEtWH .... Woods Memorial Hospital, Etowah, TN [*Library symbol*] [*Library of Congress*] (LCLS)
TEU .... Te Anau [*New Zealand*] [*Airport symbol*] (OAG)
TEU .... Technical Edit Unit [*Navy*] (DNAB)
TEU .... Technical Escort Unit [*Army*] (AABC)
TeU .... Tekst en Uitleg (BJA)
TEU .... Telemetry Equipment Unit
TEU .... Temple University, Philadelphia, PA [*OCLC symbol*] (OCLC)
TEU .... Test of Economic Understanding
TEU .... Tetraethyl Urea [*Organic chemistry*]
TEU .... Trailing Edge Up
TEU .... Transducer Excitation Unit
TEU .... Tropical Experimental Unit [*British military*] (DMA)
TEU .... Turret Electronics Unit [*Military*] (RDA)
TEU .... Twenty-Foot Container Equivalent Unit [*MARAD*] (TAG)
TEU .... Twenty-Foot Equivalent Unit [*Used to compare capacity of containerships*]
TEUC .... TADS [*Target Acquisition Designation Sight*] Electronics Unit Card [*Army*]
TEUC .... Temporary Extended Unemployment Compensation [*Labor*]
TEUN .... Trust for Education on the United Nations (EA)
TEUT .... Teuton
TEV .... Tadpole Edema Virus [*Medicine*] (DMAA)
TEV .... Talipes Equinovarus [*Anatomy*]
T Ev .... Taylor on Evidence [*12th ed.*] [*1931*] [*A publication*] (DLA)
TEV .... Terminal Equipment Vehicle [*British military*] (DMA)
TeV .... Tetra-Electron Volt
TEV .... Thermoelectric Voltage
TEV .... Thermostatic Expansion Valve [*Refrigeration*]
TEV .... Time Expanded Video
TEV .... Tobacco Etch Virus
TEV .... Today's English Version [*of the Bible*]
TEV .... Tomato Etch Virus
TEV .... Total Economic Value
TEV .... Total Evaporative Emissions [*Automotive engineering*]
TEV .... T-Platform Electric Van [*Chrysler*] [*Automotive engineering*]
TeV .... Trillion Electron Volts
TEV .... Turbo-Electric Vessel
TEV .... Victoria College, Victoria, TX [*OCLC symbol*] (OCLC)
Teva .... Teva Pharmaceutical Industries Ltd. [*Associated Press*] (SAG)
TEVA .... Tutmonda Esperantista Vegetara Asocio [*World Esperantist Vegetarian Association - WEVA*] (EAIO)
TEVAL .... Target Engagement Evaluation [*Military*]
TEVI .... Teva Pharmaceutical Industries Ltd. [*NASDAQ symbol*] (NQ)
TEVIY .... Teva Pharm Indus ADR [*NASDAQ symbol*] (TTSB)
TEVROC .... Tailored Exhaust Velocity Rocket
TEVROK .... Tailored Exhaust Velocity Rocket
TEW .... Tactical Early Warning
TEW .... Tactical Electronic Warfare [*Aircraft*] (NATG)
TEW .... Total Equivalent Weight
TE/W .... Tractive Effort to Weight Ratio (MCD)
TEW .... Transort of Equatorial Waters [*Project*] [*Marine science*] (OSRA)
TEWA .... Target Evaluation and Weapon Assignment (MCD)
TEWA .... Threat Evaluation and Weapons Assignment (NVT)
TEWC .... Totally-Enclosed Water-Cooled [*Reactor*] (DEN)
TEWDS .... Tactical Electronic Warfare Deception System (MCD)
TEWG .... Tactical Electronic Warfare Group [*Military*]
TEWG .... Test and Evaluation Work Group [*Military*] (CAAL)
TEWG .... Transitional Environmental Working Group (EERA)
TEWGp .... Tactical Electronic Warfare Group [*Air Force*] (AFM)
TEWI .... Total Environmental Warming Impact
TEWI .... Total Equivalent Warming Impact [*Greenhouse gases*]
TEWK .... Tewkesbury [*Municipal borough in England*]
TEWL .... Transepidermal Water Loss [*Physiology*]
TEWR .... Thrust to Earth Weight Ratio (IAA)
TEWS .... Tactical Effectiveness of Weapons Systems [*Army*] (AABC)
TEWS .... Tactical Electronic Warfare Set
TEWS .... Tactical Electronic Warfare Squadron [*Air Force*]
TEWS .... Tactical Electronic Warfare Support (MCD)
TEWS .... Tactical Electronic Warfare System (DOMA)
TEWS .... Threat Evaluation and Weapon Selection [*Military*] (CAAL)
TEWSq .... Tactical Electronic Warfare Squadron [*Air Force*]
TEWT .... Tactical Exercise without Troops
TEWTS .... Tactical Electronic Warfare Training Squadron
TEX .... Automatic Teleprinter Exchange Service [*of Western Union Corp.*]
TEX .... Catex Compagnie [*France ICAO designator*] (FAAC)
TEX .... Tau Epsilon Xi [*Text Formatter*] [*Computer science*]
TEX .... Teleprinter Exchange Service [*Telecommunications*] (IAA)
TEX .... Teletype Exchange
TEX .... TELEX
TEX .... Temperature Excess (PDAA)
TEX .... Terex Corp. [*NYSE symbol*] (SPSG)
tex .... Tex [*Formerly, den*] [*Linear density*] [*SI unit*]
TEX .... Texas (AAG)
Tex .... Texas (ODBW)
Tex .... Texas Supreme Court Reports [*A publication*] (DLA)
TEX .... Textile (AABC)
TEX .... Transaction Exception Code [*Military*] (AFIT)
TEX .... Tumbling Explorer [*Aerospace*]
TEX .... University of Texas at Tyler, Tyler, TX [*OCLC symbol*] (OCLC)
Tex A&I U .... Texas A&I University (GAGS)
Tex A&M U .... Texas Agricultural and Mechanical University (GAGS)
Tex A Civ .... White and Wilson's [*or Willson's*] Civil Cases, Texas Court of Appeals [*A publication*] (DLA)
Tex A Civ Cas... White and Wilson's [*or Willson's*] Civil Cases, Texas Court of Appeals [*A publication*] (DLA)
Tex A Civ Cas (Wilson)... Texas Court of Appeal Civil Cases (Wilson) [*or Willson*] [*A publication*] (DLA)
Texaco .... Texaco, Inc. [*Associated Press*] (SAG)
TEXACO .... Texas Co.
Tex Admin Code... Texas Administrative Code [*A publication*] (DLA)
Tex App .... Texas Civil Appeals Cases [*A publication*] (DLA)
Tex App .... Texas Court of Appeals Reports (Criminal Cases) [*A publication*] (DLA)
Tex App Civ Cas (Wilson)... White and Wilson's [*or Willson's*] Civil Cases, Texas Court of Appeals [*A publication*] (DLA)
TexarkF .... Texarkana First Financial Corp. [*Associated Press*] (SAG)
TEXAS .... Tactical Exchange Automation System (MCD)
Texas Civ .... Texas Civil Appeals Reports [*A publication*] (DLA)
Texas Civ App... Texas Civil Appeals Reports [*A publication*] (DLA)
Texas Cr App... Texas Court of Appeals Reports [*A publication*] (DLA)
Texas Crim... Texas Criminal Reports [*A publication*] (DLA)
Texas Crim App... Texas Criminal Appeals Reports [*A publication*] (DLA)
Texas Crim Rep... Texas Criminal Reports [*A publication*] (DLA)
Texas Cr Rep... Texas Criminal Reports [*A publication*] (DLA)
Texas Ct App... Texas Court of Appeals Reports [*A publication*] (DLA)
Texas Ct App Civ Cas... Texas Civil Cases [*A publication*] (DLA)
Texas Ct of App... Texas Court of Appeals Reports [*A publication*] (DLA)
Texas Ct Rep... Texas Court Reporter [*1900-1908*] [*A publication*] (DLA)
Texas Dig .... Texas Digest [*A publication*] (DLA)
Texas R .... Texas Reports [*A publication*] (DLA)
Texas Rep .... Texas Reports [*A publication*] (DLA)
TexBi .... Texas Biotechnology Corp. [*Associated Press*] (SAG)
TexBiotch .... Texas Biotechnology Corp. [*Associated Press*] (SAG)
Tex Bus Corp Act Ann... Texas Business Corporation Act, Annotated [*A publication*] (DLA)
TEXC .... Texas Central Railroad Co. [*AAR code*]
Tex Christ U... Texas Christian University (GAGS)
Tex Civ App... Texas Civil Appeals Reports [*A publication*] (DLA)
Tex Civ Cas... Texas Court of Appeals Decisions, Civil Cases (White and Wilson) [*or Willson*] [*1876-92*] [*A publication*] (DLA)
Tex Civ Rep... Texas Civil Appeals Reports [*A publication*] (DLA)
Tex Code Ann... Texas Codes, Annotated [*A publication*] (DLA)
Tex Code Crim Proc Ann... Texas Code of Criminal Procedure, Annotated [*A publication*] (DLA)
TEXCOM .... Test and Experimentation Command [*TRADOC*] [*Fort Hood, TX*]
Tex Cr .... Texas Criminal [*A publication*] (DLA)
Tex Cr App... Texas Criminal Appeals Reports [*A publication*] (DLA)
Tex Crim .... Texas Criminal Reports [*A publication*] (DLA)
Tex Crim Rep... Texas Criminal Reports [*A publication*] (DLA)
Tex Cr R .... Texas Criminal Appeals Reports [*A publication*] (DLA)
Tex Cr Rpts... Texas Criminal Reports [*A publication*] (DLA)
Tex Ct App... Texas Court of Appeals Reports [*A publication*] (DLA)
Tex Ct App Civ... Texas Civil Cases [*A publication*] (DLA)
Tex Ct App Dec Civ... Texas Civil Cases [*A publication*] (DLA)
Tex Ct App R... Texas Court of Appeals Reports [*A publication*] (DLA)
Tex Ct Rep... Texas Court Reporter [*A publication*] (DLA)
TEXDEALAM... Textile Dealers Association of America (EA)
Tex Dec .... Texas Decisions [*A publication*] (DLA)
Tex Dig Op Att'y Gen... Digest of Opinions of the Attorney General of Texas [*A publication*] (DLA)
Tex Elec Code Ann... Texas Election Code, Annotated [*A publication*] (DLA)
Texfi .... Texfi Industries, Inc. [*Associated Press*] (SAG)
Tex Gen Laws... General and Special Laws of the State of Texas [*A publication*] (DLA)
TEXGRP .... Texas Group [*Navy*] (DNAB)
TEXIN .... Texas Intersection Air Quality Model [*Environmental Protection Agency*] (GFGA)
TexInd .... Texas Industries, Inc. [*Associated Press*] (SAG)
Tex Ins Code Ann... Texas Insurance Code, Annotated [*A publication*] (DLA)
TexInst .... Texas Instruments, Inc. [*Associated Press*] (SAG)
Tex Jur .... Texas Jurisprudence [*A publication*] (DLA)
Tex Jur 2d... Texas Jurisprudence [*2nd ed.*] [*A publication*] (DLA)
Tex Law .... Texas Lawman [*A publication*] (DLA)

Tex Law & Leg... Texas Law and Legislation [*A publication*] (DLA)
TexLex........ Texas Lexicon [*Slang*]
Tex LJ........ Texas Law Journal [*A publication*] (DLA)
Tex L Rep.... Texas Law Reporter [*1882-84*] [*A publication*] (DLA)
TexMer........ Texas Meridian Resources Ltd. [*Associated Press*] (SAG)
TexMex........ Texas and Mexico [*Refers to fashion, food, language, or lifestyle that has characteristics of these two regions*]
TEX MEX...... Texas Mexican Railway Co.
Texo........... Texoil, Inc. [*Associated Press*] (SAG)
Texoil......... Texoil, Inc. [*Associated Press*] (SAG)
TEXP........... Time Exposure [*Photography*]
TEXP........... Titan Exploration, Inc. [*NASDAQ symbol*] (SAG)
TEXPLOT...... Texas Instruments Plotter (NITA)
TEXPROCIL... [*The*] Cotton Textiles Export Promotion Council of India (ECON)
TexRegl....... Texas Regional Bancshares, Inc. [*Associated Press*] (SAG)
Tex Rev Civ Stat Ann (Vernon)... Texas Revised Civil Statutes, Annotated (Vernon) [*A publication*] (DLA)
TEXS........... Tactical Explosive System [*Military*] (RDA)
TEXS........... Texas Star Resources Corp. [*NASDAQ symbol*] (SAG)
Tex S........... Texas Supreme Court Reports, Supplement [*A publication*] (DLA)
Tex S Ct...... Texas Supreme Court Reporter [*A publication*] (DLA)
Tex Sess Law Serv... Texas Session Law Service (Vernon) [*A publication*] (DLA)
TEXSF......... Texas Star Resources [*NASDAQ symbol*] (TTSB)
TEXSIM/B..... TEGAS Extended Simulator Behavioral (NITA)
TEXSIS........ Texas Student Information System (EDAC)
Tex So Intra L Rev... Texas Southern Intramural Law Review [*A publication*] (DLA)
Tex So U..... Texas Southern University (GAGS)
TexStar....... Texas Star Resources Corp. [*Associated Press*] (SAG)
Tex Stat Ann... Texas Statutes, Annotated [*A publication*] (DLA)
Tex Supp..... Texas Supplement [*A publication*] (DLA)
Tex Suppl.... Texas Supplement [*A publication*] (DLA)
TEXT........... Texas Experimental TOKAMAK [*Atomic physics*]
TEXT........... Textile
text............ Texture (VRA)
TEXT........... Trans-European Exchange and Transfer Consortium (AIE)
Tex Tax-Gen Ann... Texas Tax-General, Annotated [*A publication*] (DLA)
Tex Tech U... Texas Tech University (GAGS)
TEXTINDY.... Textile Industry (IAA)
TEXTIR........ Text Indexing and Retrieval [*Computer science*]
TEXTLINE..... Text Online (NITA)
TEXTOR....... TOKAMAK [*Toroidal Kamera Magnetic*] Experiment for Technical Oriented Research [*Oak Ridge National Laboratory*]
Textr........... Textron, Inc. [*Associated Press*] (SAG)
TEXT REC.... Textus Receptus [*The Received Text*] [*Latin*]
Textron........ Textron, Inc. [*Associated Press*] (SAG)
Tex Unrep Cas... Posey's Unreported Cases [*Texas*] [*A publication*] (DLA)
TexUtil......... Texas Utilities Co. [*Associated Press*] (SAG)
Tex Woman's U... Texas Woman's University (GAGS)
TEY............. Thingeyri [*Iceland*] [*Airport symbol*] (OAG)
TEY............. Total Electron Yield [*Spectroscopy*]
TEZ............. Tezpur [*India*] [*Airport symbol*] (OAG)
TEZG........... Tribological Experiments in Zero Gravity
TF............... [*The*] FORUM [*Foundation of Research for Understanding Man*] (EA)
TF............... Iceland [*International civil aircraft marking*] (ODBW)
TF............... Tabulating Form (AAG)
TF............... Tactical Fighter (AFM)
TF............... Tactile Fremitus [*Medicine*]
TF............... Taeria Foundation (EA)
Tf............... Tafel (BJA)
TF............... Talker Function [*Telecommunications*] (IAA)
TF............... Tallulah Falls Railway Co. [*AAR code*]
TF............... Tank Farm (NATG)
TF............... Tape Feed
TF............... Target File (MCD)
TF............... Task Force
TF............... Tax Foundation (EA)
TF............... Tax Free (WDAA)
TF............... Tayu Fellowship (EA)
TF............... Teaching Fellow
TF............... Tear Fund [*An association*] (EA)
TF............... Teased Fibers [*Neurology*]
TF............... Technical File (MCD)
TF............... Technological Forecasting
TF............... Telegram for Delivery by Telephone
TF............... Telegraph Form (ROG)
TF............... Telephone (NATG)
TF............... Temperature Factor
TF............... Temporary Fix (AAG)
TF............... Terminal Forecast
TF............... Terminal Frame (NATG)
TF............... Terrain-Following [*Helicopter*]
TF............... Territorial Force [*Military British*]
TF............... Test Facility [*NASA*] (NASA)
TF............... Test Fixture (KSC)
TF............... Test Flight [*Air Force*]
TF............... Test Frame [*Telecommunications*] (TEL)
TF............... Test to Failure (SAA)
TF............... Tetralogy of Fallot [*Cardiology*]
TF............... Text-Fiche
TF............... THEOS [*They Help Each Other Spiritually*] Foundation (EA)
TF............... Thermionic Field (IAA)
TF............... Thin-Film
TF............... Thoreau Fellowship (EA)
TF............... Thread Forming (MSA)
TF............... Threshold Factor (OA)
TF............... Threshold Function (IAA)
TF............... Thymidine Factor [*Endocrinology*]
TF............... Thymol Flocculation [*Clinical chemistry*]
TF............... Tibet Fund (EA)
TF............... Tile Floor [*Technical drawings*]
TF............... Till Forbidden [*i.e., repeat until forbidden to do so*] [*Advertising*]
TF............... Time Factor (CAAL)
TF............... Time Frame
TF............... Time Frequency (IAA)
T/F............. Time of Fail (MSA)
T/F............. Time of Fall (SAA)
TF............... Time of Flight [*Ballistics*]
TF............... Time to Function
TF............... Tissue-Damaging Factor [*Medicine*] (MAE)
TF............... Tissue Factor [*Clinical chemistry*]
TF............... To Fill
TF............... To Follow
TF............... Tolkien Fellowships [*Defunct*] (EA)
TF............... Tolstoy Foundation (EA)
TF............... Tool Fabrication (SAA)
TF............... Tool Foundation [*See also ST*] [*Amsterdam, Netherlands*] (EAIO)
TF............... Toroidal Field (MCD)
TF............... Torpedo Fighter Aircraft [*Navy*]
TF............... Total Float (IAA)
TF............... Total Flow (MAE)
TF............... Total Flowers [*Plant pathology*]
TF............... Total Forfeiture [*of all pay and allowances*] [*Army*] (AABC)
TF............... Toward Freedom (EA)
TF............... Toxicology Forum (EA)
TF............... Tracheal Fistula [*Otorhinolaryngology*] (DAVI)
TF............... Tracking Filter
TF............... Trailfinders [*Travel agency*] [*British*]
TF............... Trainer Fighter
TF............... Training Film [*Military*]
TF............... Training Flight [*British military*] (DMA)
TF............... TransAfrica Forum (EA)
TF............... Transcription Factor [*Genetics*]
TF............... Transfer (IAA)
TF............... Transfer Factor [*Immunochemistry*]
TF............... Transfer Fee [*Banking*]
TF............... Transfer Function (AAG)
T/F............. Transfer of Function [*Military*] (AFM)
TF............... Transferrin [*Also, T, TRF*] [*Biochemistry*]
TF............... Transformers [*JETDS nomenclature*] [*Military*] (CET)
TF............... Transfrontal (AAMN)
TF............... Transmit Filter (MHDB)
TF............... Transmitter Frequency
TF............... Transportation Factor (MCD)
TF............... Transportes Aereos Regionais (TAR) SA [*Brazil ICAO designator*] (ICDA)
TF............... Transversal Filter (IAA)
TF............... Trap Flag [*Computer memory language*] (PCM)
TF............... Travail Force [*Penal Servitude*] [*French*]
TF............... Travellers Fare [*Train catering service*] [*British*]
TF............... Trench Feet [*or Fever*]
TF............... Trench Fighter [*British military*] (DMA)
TF............... Trichloroethylene Finishing
TF............... Triple Frequency
TF............... Triple Fronted [*Classified advertising*] (ADA)
TF............... Tritium Fluoride
TF............... Tropical Fresh Water [*Vessel load line mark*]
T/F............. True/False (CDAI)
Tf............... Trufocus [*Lamp base type*] (NTCM)
TF............... Trunk Frame [*Telecommunications*] (TEL)
TF............... Trust Fund
TF............... Tube Feeding [*Medicine*] (DMAA)
TF............... Tuberculin Filtrate [*Medicine*]
TF............... Tubular Fluid [*Medicine*] (MAE)
TF............... Tuning Fork (AAMN)
TF............... Turbofan [*Engine*]
TF............... Twins Foundation (EA)
TF............... Type of Flight (SAA)
TF............... Type of Foundation [*IRS*]
TF............... Veeneal [*ICAO designator*] (AD)
TF1............. Channel One [*French television station*]
TFA............. [*The*] Ferroalloys Association (EA)
TFA............. Municipal Income Trust [*Formerly, Allstate Municipal Income Trust*] [*NYSE symbol*] (SPSG)
TFA............. Take Five Australia [*An association*]
TFA............. Target Factor Analysis [*Statistical technique*]
TFA............. Task Force A
TFA............. Task Force Alpha [*DoD*]
TFA............. Tasmanian Floricultural Association [*Australia*]
TFA............. Tax Free America (EA)
TFA............. Teach for America
TFA............. Technology Forecasting and Assessment (IAA)
TFA............. TELEX File Adapter (IAA)
TFA............. Tenant Farmers' Association [*British*] (DBA)
TFA............. Textile Finishers Association (DBA)
TFA............. Tie Fabrics Association [*Defunct*] (EA)
TFA............. Timing Filter Analyzer
TFA............. Top Farmers of America Association [*Defunct*] (EA)
TFA............. Total Fatty Acids
TFA............. Transaction Flow Auditing (ADA)
TFA............. Trans Fatty Acids

TFA .... Transfer Function Analyzer
TFA .... Trans-Florida Airlines, Inc. [*ICAO designator*] (FAAC)
TFA .... Transistor Feedback Amplifier
TFA .... Transmit Frame Acquisition [*Telecommunications*] (LAIN)
TFA .... Transverse Fascicular Area [*Neuroanatomy*]
TFA .... Transverse Film Attenuator
TFA .... Triathlon Federation of Australia
TFA .... Trifluoroacetic [*or Trifluoroacetyl*] Acid [*Organic chemistry*]
TFA .... Trifluoroacetic Anhydride [*Organic chemistry*]
TFA .... Trifluoroacetyl [*Organic chemistry*]
TFA .... Tube Failure Alarm
TFA .... Two-Way Finite Automata
TFA .... United States Trout Farmers Association
TFAA .... Track and Field Athletes of America
TFAA .... Trifluoroacetic Anhydride [*Organic chemistry*]
TFAA .... Trout Farmers' Association of Australia
TFAD .... Thin-Film Active Device (IAA)
TFAG .... Tropical Forest Action Group (EA)
TFAI .... Territoire Francaise des Afars et des Issas [*French Territory of the Afars and Issas*]
TFAI .... Trifluoroacetylimidazole [*Organic chemistry*]
TFAIP .... Task Force on Alternatives in Print (EA)
TF & T .... Theatre, Film, and Television Biographies Master Index [*A publication*]
TFANP .... Task Force Against Nuclear Pollution (EA)
TFAP .... Trifluoroacetylprolyl Chloride (BARN)
TFAP .... Tropical Forestry Action Plan [*World Bank, UN, and other groups*]
TFAR .... Tentative Findings and Recommendations
TFA/USA .... Track and Field Association of the United States of America (EA)
TFAW .... Tasmania Fellowship of Australia Writers [*Australia*]
TFB .... Municipal Income Trust [*Formerly, Allstate Municipal Income Trust*] [*NYSE symbol*] (SPSG)
TFB .... Municipal Income Trust II [*NYSE symbol*] (TTSB)
TFB .... Technology for Business (NITA)
TFB .... Testing Facilities Branch [*Social Security Administration*]
TFB .... Thai Farmers' Bank
TFB .... Thin-Film Barrier
TFB .... Towed Flexible Barge (PDAA)
TFB .... Trifascicular Block [*Medicine*] (AAMN)
TFBA .... Textile Fibers and By-Products Association [*Charlotte, NC*]
TFBP .... Transferrin Binding Protein [*Biochemistry*]
TFBPA .... Textile Fibers and By-Products Association (EA)
TFBR .... Technical Feedback Report (DNAB)
TFC .... [*The*] Felician College [*Chicago, IL*]
TFC .... [*The*] Freedom Council [*Defunct*] (EA)
TFC .... Municipal Income Trust [*Formerly, Allstate Municipal Income Trust*] [*NYSE symbol*] (SPSG)
TFC .... Municipal Income Trust III [*NYSE symbol*] (TTSB)
TFC .... Tactical Fire Control (MCD)
TFC .... Tactical Flag Commander (MCD)
TFC .... Tactical Flight Control
TFC .... Tactical Fusion Center (MCD)
TFC .... Tank Fire Control
TFC .... Tantalum Foil Capacitor
TFC .... Task Force Commander [*Navy*] (DNAB)
TFC .... Tasmanian Forestry Commission [*State*] (EERA)
TFC .... Terminal Flight Control (NATG)
TFC .... Territorial Fund Campaign [*Red Cross*]
TFC .... Thin-Film Capacitor
TFC .... Thin-Film Cell
TFC .... Thin-Film Circuit
TFC .... Time from Cutoff [*NASA*] (NASA)
TFC .... Time of First Call [*Navy*]
TFC .... Toccoa Falls College [*Georgia*]
TFC .... Top Flight Club [*Northwest Airlines' club for frequent flyers*] (EA)
TFC .... Torpedo Fire Control
TFC .... Total Final Cost [*Business term*]
TFC .... Total Fixed Cost
TFC .... Total Flow Control [*Automotive engineering*]
TFC .... Total Fuel Consumption (KSC)
TFC .... Traffic
TFC .... Traffic Control (NG)
TFC .... Transfer Function Computer
TFC .... Transfer Function, Cumulative
TFC .... Transferrin, Common Form [*or Siderophilin*] (DAVI)
TFC .... Transistorized Frequency Converter
TFC .... Transmission Fault Control [*Telecommunications*] (TEL)
TFC .... Transparent Ferroelectric Ceramics [*Physics*]
TFC .... Transportation Facilitation Center [*Department of Transportation*]
TFC .... Transport for Christ International (EA)
TFC .... Trifluoromethyldichlorocarbanilide [*Organic chemistry*]
TFC .... Trigonometric Function Computer
TFC .... Trilon Financial Corp. [*Toronto Stock Exchange symbol Vancouver Stock Exchange symbol*]
TFC .... Trustees for Conservation [*Defunct*] (EA)
TFC .... Turret Fire Control
TFC .... United States Overseas Tax Fairness Committee (EA)
TFC .... US-Japan Trade Facilitation Committee (IMH)
TFCA .... Thin-Film Cell Array
TF-CAS .... Time Frequency Collision Avoidance System
TFCB .... Thanks for Coming By [*Exxon slogan*]
TFCC .... Tactical Flag Command Center [*Navy*]
TFCC .... Tank Fire Combat Computer
TFCC .... Task Force Command Center [*Navy*] (DOMA)
TFCC .... Triangular Fibrocartilage Complex [*Anatomy*]
TFCCS .... Tactical Flag Command Center System [*Navy*]
TFCE .... TFC Enterprises [*NASDAQ symbol*] (TTSB)
TFCE .... TFC Enterprises, Inc. [*NASDAQ symbol*] (SAG)
TFC Ent .... TFC Enterprises, Inc. [*Associated Press*] (SAG)
TFCF .... Twenty-First Century Foundation (EA)
TFCG .... Thin-Film Crystal Growth
TFCG .... Tropical Forestry Contact Group [*Australia*]
TFCHS .... Tasmanian Federation of Cooperative Housing Societies [*Australia*]
TFCM .... Three Factor Contribution Method [*Insurance*]
TFCNN .... Task Force Commander, North Norway [*NATO*] (NATG)
TFCO .... Tufco Technologies [*NASDAQ symbol*] (SAG)
TFCOS .... Task Force on Children Out of School (EA)
TFCP .... Technical Facility Change Procedure (AAG)
TFCS .... Tank Fire Control System
TFCS .... Task Force for Child Survival (EA)
TFCS .... Torpedo Fire Control System
TFCS .... Treasury Financial Communication System [*Department of the Treasury*]
TFCS .... Triplex Flight Control System [*or Subsystem*] [*NASA*] (NASA)
TFCSD .... Total Federal Commissioned Service to Date [*Military*]
TFCU .... Transportable Field Calibration Unit
TFCX .... TOKAMAK [*Toroidal Kamera Magnetic*] Fusion Core Experiment [*Plasma physics*]
TFCYC .... Terry Fox Canadian Youth Centre
TFD .... Tactical Fighter Dispenser (MCD)
TFD .... Target-to-Film Distance [*X-Ray machine*] [*Navy*]
TFD .... Television Feasibility Demonstration [*NASA*] (KSC)
TFD .... Terrain-Following Display
TFD .... Test Flow Diagram (MCD)
TFD .... Thin-Film Diode Descriptor Electronics
TFD .... Thin-Film Distillation
TFD .... Time Frequency Digitizer (MCD)
TF/D .... Time-Frequency Dissemination (IEEE)
TFD .... Total Frequency Deviation (AAG)
TFD .... Transcription Factor Database (EERA)
TFD .... Tube Flood and Drain
TFD .... Tube Form Die (MCD)
TFDA .... Textile Fabric Distributors Association [*Later, TDA*] (EA)
TFDD .... Text File Device Driver [*Computer science*] (PCM)
TFDM .... Tactical Fighter Defense Munitions [*Air Force*]
TFDM .... Tactical Fighter Dispensing Munition (AFM)
TFDM .... Technical Feasibility Demonstration Model
TFDOP .... Total Field Detection Only Processor (CAAL)
TFDRL .... Trustees of the Franklin Delano Roosevelt Library [*Abolished, 1958*] [*Library is now operated by the General Services Administration*]
TFDS .... Tactical Ferret Display System
TFDS .... Tactical Fighter Display Systems [*Air Force*]
TFDS .... Tactical Flag Data System (NG)
TFDS .... Troms Fylkes Dampskipsselskap [*Shipping line*] [*Norway*]
TFDTB .... Tactical Fighter Dispenser Test Bed
TFDU .... Thin Film Deposition Unit
TFE .... Orlando, FL [*Location identifier FAA*] (FAAL)
TFE .... Polytetrafluoroethylene (DAVI)
TFE .... Tactical Field Exchange [*Air Force*] (DOMA)
TFE .... Targets for Excellence
TFE .... Television Film Exhibit (NTCM)
TFE .... Terminal Flight Evaluation
TFE .... Terrain-Following Evaluator
TFE .... Tetrafluoroethylene [*Organic chemistry*]
TFE .... Thermal Field Emission (IAA)
TFE .... Thermionic Fuel Element [*Nuclear energy*]
TFE .... Thin-Film Electrode [*Electrochemistry*]
TFE .... Time from Event [*NASA*] (KSC)
TFE .... Total Fly-By Energy
TFE .... Trainer Flight Equipment (MCD)
TFE .... Transform Fault Effect [*Geology*]
TFE .... Transportation Feasibility Estimator
TFE .... Trifluoroethanol [*Organic chemistry*]
TFE .... Turbofan Engine
TFE .... Two-Flow Electronic [*Automotive engineering*]
TFE .... Two-Fraction Fast Exchange [*Biophysics*]
TFECB .... Task Force on Emphysema and Chronic Bronchitis [*Public Health Service and National Lung Association*] (EA)
TFECS .... Theater Force Evaluation by Combat Simulation (MCD)
TFEDRA .... Task Force for European Digital Road-mapping Association
TFEDSA .... Tetrafluoroethanedisulfonic Acid [*Organic chemistry*]
TFEF .... Triangle Fraternity Education Fund
TFEL .... Thin-Film Electroluminescence
TFEO .... Tetrafluoroethylene-Epoxide [*Organic chemistry*]
TFEO .... Tetrafluoroethylene Oxide [*Organic chemistry*]
TFER .... Transfer
TFET .... Thin-layer Field-Effect Transistor (IAA)
TFEV .... Timed Forced Expiratory Volume [*Laboratory science*] (DAVI)
TFEWJ .... Task Force on Equality of Women in Judaism [*Defunct*] (EA)
TFF .... Fletcher School of Law and Diplomacy, Tufts University, Medford, MA [*OCLC symbol*] (OCLC)
TFF .... Tactical Fighter Force (ADA)
TFF .... Tangential Flow Filtration
TFF .... Tefe [*Brazil*] [*Airport symbol*] (OAG)
TFF .... Terrain-Following Flight
TFF .... Thermoplastic Covered Fixture Wire Flexible Stranding (IAA)
TFF .... Thin-Film FET [*Field-Effect Transistor*] (IAA)
TFF .... Time of Free Fall [*NASA*] (KSC)
TFF .... Toggle Flip-Flop [*Computer science*] (IAA)
TFF .... Total Feedwater Flow

TFF Transverse Flow Fan
TFF Tropical Forest Foundation (EA)
TFF Tube-Fed Food [*Medicine*] (DMAA)
TFF Tuning Fork Filter
TFF Turbine Flow Function
TFFA Desirade/Grande-Anse, Guadeloupe [*French Antilles*] [*ICAO location identifier*] (ICLI)
TFFASF Temporaries Food for All Seasons Foundation (EA)
TFFB Basse-Terre/Baillif [*French Antilles*] [*ICAO location identifier*] (ICLI)
TFFC [*The*] Fixx Fan Club (EA)
TFFC Saint-Francois [*French Antilles*] [*ICAO location identifier*] (ICLI)
TFFC Task Force on Families in Crisis (EA)
TFFD Fort-De-France, Martinique [*French Antilles*] [*ICAO location identifier*] (ICLI)
TFFE Terrain-Following Flight Evaluator
Tf-Fe Transferrin-Bound Iron [*Biochemistry*] (MAE)
TFFET Thin-Film Field-Effect Transistor (IAA)
TFFF Fort-De-France/Le Lamentin, Martinique [*French Antilles*] [*ICAO location identifier*] (ICLI)
TFFG Saint-Martin/Grand'Case, Guadeloupe [*French Antilles*] [*ICAO location identifier*] (ICLI)
TF Fincl TF Financial Corp. [*Associated Press*] (SAG)
TFFIS Tasmanian Forests and Forest Industry Strategy [*Australia*]
TFFJ Saint-Barthelemy [*French Antilles*] [*ICAO location identifier*] (ICLI)
TFFLU Trimmers, Firemen, and Foundry Labourers Union [*British*]
TFFM Grand-Bourg/Marie-Galante [*French Antilles*] [*ICAO location identifier*] (ICLI)
TFFR Pointe-A-Pitre/Le Raizet, Guadeloupe [*French Antilles*] [*ICAO location identifier*] (ICLI)
TFFR Task Force Final Report [*DoD*]
TFFS Les Saintes/Terre-De-Haut [*French Antilles*] [*ICAO location identifier*] (ICLI)
TFFS Thermoform, Fill, and Seal [*Pharmaceutical packaging*]
TFFT Truly Fast Fourier Transform (PDAA)
TFG [*The*] Fashion Group (EA)
TFG [*The*] Futures Group [*Commercial firm*] (EA)
TFG Tactical Fighter Group [*Air Force*]
TFG Tentative Fiscal Guidance (MCD)
TFG Tentative Force Guidance (NG)
TFG Terminal Facilities Guide [*DoD*]
TFG Test File Generator [*Computer science*]
TFG Textile Foremen's Guild
TFG Thermo Fibergen, Inc. [*AMEX symbol*] (SAG)
TFG Thrust Floated Gyroscope (PDAA)
TFG Transmit Format Generator
TFG Typefounding (ADA)
TFGA Tasmanian Field and Game Association [*Australia*]
TFGM Tank-Fired Guided Missile (MCD)
TFGM Tentative Fiscal Guidance Memorandum [*Military*] (AFIT)
TFGP Tactical Fighter Group [*Air Force*]
TFH Temporal Fourier Hologram (PDAA)
TFH Thai Flying Helicopter Service Co. Ltd. [*Thailand*] [*ICAO designator*] (FAAC)
TFH Thick-Film Hybrid
TFH Touch for Health Foundation (EA)
TFH Transfer Function Hazard
TFH Transit Financial Holdings, Inc. [*Toronto Stock Exchange symbol*]
TFH Tufts University, Health Sciences Library, Boston, MA [*OCLC symbol*] (OCLC)
TFHC Thick-Film Hybrid Circuit (IAA)
TFHRC Turner-Fairbank Highway Research Center [*FHWA*] (TAG)
TFI Deutsches Teppich-Forschungsinstitut [*German Carpet Research Institute - GCRI*] (EAIO)
TFI [*The*] Fertilizer Institute (EA)
TFI Table Fashion Institute (EA)
TFI Taurus Footwear, Inc. [*Toronto Stock Exchange symbol*]
TFI Tax Foundation, Inc.
TFI Tax-Free Investment [*Finance*]
TFI TCI Communications Financing I [*NYSE symbol*] (SAG)
TFI TCI Communications Financing II [*NYSE symbol*] (SAG)
TFI Textile Foundation, Inc.
TFI Theatre for Ideas [*Defunct*] (EA)
TFI Thick Film Ignition [*System*] [*Ford Motor Co.*] [*Automotive engineering*]
TFI Thick-Film Integrated [*Electronics*]
TFI Time from Ignition [*Apollo*] [*NASA*]
tfi Travel for Industry [*Commercial firm*] [*British*]
TFI Tropical Forest Initiative (EERA)
TFI True Fibrous Involution [*Medicine*]
TFI Tufi [*Papua New Guinea*] [*Airport symbol*] (OAG)
TFIB Thin-Film Interface Barrier
TFIC Tasmanian Fishing Industry Council [*Australia*]
TFIC Thin-Film Integrated Circuit (IAA)
TFIFO Transmit First-In First-Out [*Computer science*]
TFI-I Thin-Film Ignition [*Automotive engineering*]
TFIM Tool Fabrication Instruction Manual (MCD)
TFIO Thin Film Integrated Optics (PDAA)
TFIPr TCI Commun Fin 1 8.72%'TOPrS' [*NYSE symbol*] (TTSB)
TFIS Thai Aquatic Sciences and Fisheries Information System [*Marine science*] (OSRA)
TFIS Theft from Interstate Shipment [*FBI standardized term*]
TFITC Tasmanian Fishing Industry Training Council [*Australia*]
TFITC Tasmanian Food Industry Training Council [*Australia*]
TFITC Tasmanian Forest Industries Training Council [*Australia*]
TFITC Tasmanian Furniture Industry Training Council [*Australia*]
TFL Tail-Flick Latency
TFL Taiwan Federation of Labor [*Nationalist China*]
TFL Tanganyika Federation of Labor
TFL Tasmanian Football League [*Australia*]
TFL Tayflight Ltd. [*British ICAO designator*] (FAAC)
TFL Telemetry Format Load (MCD)
TFL Tensor Fascia Lata [*Anatomy*]
TFL Through Flow Line
TFL Time from Launch [*NASA*]
TFL Time to Failure Location
TFL Training for Life [*Young Men's Christian Association*] [*British*]
TFL Transformerless (IAA)
TFL Transient Fault Locator
TFL Trees for Life [*An association*] (EA)
TFLA Texas Foreign Language Association (EDAC)
TFLAC Fellowship of Reconciliation Task Force on Latin America and Caribbean (EA)
TFLC Tulane Factors of Liberalism-Conservatism [*Psychology*]
TFLWA Torchbearers for Legacy in Western Australia
TFM Tactical Flight Management (MCD)
TFM Tape File Management
TFM Teaching Family Model [*Psychology*]
TFM Telefomin [*Papua New Guinea*] [*Airport symbol*] (OAG)
TFM Tentative Final Monograph [*Food and Drug Administration*]
TFM Terminal Forecast Manual
TFM Testicular Feminization [*Endocrinology*]
TFM TFTR [*Tokamak Fusion Test Reactor*] Flexibility Modification
TFM Thin-Film Microelectronics
TFM Time Quantized Frequency Modulation [*Telecommunications*] (IAA)
TFM Tool Fabrication Manual (MCD)
TFM Toronto International Furniture Market [*Canada*] (ITD)
TFM Traffic Flow Management [*FAA*] (TAG)
TFM Traffic Flow Management (GAVI)
TFM Transmit Frame Memory
TFM Transmitter Frequency Multiplier
TFM Transportation Financial Management [*Army*]
TFM Transverse Field Modulator
TFM Trifluoromethylnitrophenol [*Organic chemistry*]
TFM Turbine Flow Meter (KSC)
TFM Two-Fluid Manometer
TFMA Technical Facility Modification Authorization (AAG)
TFMBA Tasmanian Fine Merino Breeders' Association [*Australia*]
TFME Thin-Film Mercury Electrode [*Electrochemistry*]
TFMG Tank Force Management Group [*Army*]
TFMMS Total Force Manpower Management System [*Navy*] (GFGA)
TFMO Tank Forces Management Office [*Army*]
TFMP Test Facility Master Plan [*DoD*] (RDA)
TFMPP Trifluoromethyl(phenyl)piperazine [*Organic chemistry*]
TFMRA Top Fuel Motorcycle Riders Association (EA)
TFMRC Thermo-Fluid Mechanics Research Centre [*University of Sussex*] [*British*] (CB)
TFMS Tactical Frequency Management System (MCD)
TFMS Text and File Management System
TFMS Traffic Facilities Management System [*Australia*]
TFMS Trunk and Facilities Maintenance System [*Telecommunications*] (TEL)
TFMSA Trifluoromethanesulfonic Acid [*Organic chemistry*]
TFN Till Further Notice
TFN Total Fecal Nitrogen
TFN Total Fixed Nitrogen [*Chemistry*]
TFN Total Fruit Number [*Botany*]
TFN Track File Number (CAAL)
TFNA Tennis Foundation of North America [*Later, ATF*] (EA)
TFNC Tasmanian Field Naturalists' Club [*Australia*]
TFNG Thirty-Five New Guys [*Group of new astronauts*] [*NASA*]
TFNR Taper-Faced Napier Ring [*Automobile engines*]
TFNS Territorial Force Nursing Service
TFO Telemedicine for Ontario [*Toronto, ON*] [*Telecommunications*] (TSSD)
TFO Tiffany Resources, Inc. [*Vancouver Stock Exchange symbol*]
TFO Tonto Forest Array [*Arizona*] [*Seismograph station code, US Geological Survey Closed*] (SEIS)
TFO Transactions for Others [*Military*]
TFO Triplex-Forming Oligonucleotide [*Biochemistry*]
TFO Tuning Fork Oscillator
TFOA Things Falling Off Aircraft (MCD)
TFOCA Tactical Fiber Optic Cable Assembly [*Army*]
TFOE Task Force on the Environment [*American Library Association*]
TFOF Taxi Fleet Operators' Federation [*British*] (BI)
TFOL Tape File Octal Load
TFON Telefonos de Mexico SA de CV [*NASDAQ symbol*] (NQ)
TFONY Telefonos de Mexico'A'ADR [*NASDAQ symbol*] (TTSB)
TFOPS Task Force Operations [*Navy*] (NVT)
T (for) D Termination for Default (MCD)
TFORMR Transformer
TFOS Total Federal Officer Service [*Military*] (AABC)
TFOTB [*The*] Friends of Tom Baker (EA)
TFOUT Thin-Film Oxygen Uptake Test
TFOV Total Field of View (MCD)
TFP American Society for the Defense of Tradition, Family and Property (EA)
TFP [*The*] Feminist Press (EA)
TFP [*The*] Friends Program (EA)
TFP [*The*] Fund for Peace [*An association*] (EA)
TFP Teachers for Peace (EAIO)

TFP .... Teachers Freedom Party (EA)
TFP .... Temporary Forfeiture of Pay
TFP .... Test Facility Program [*NASA*] (KSC)
TFP .... Total Factor Productivity [*Economics*]
TFP .... Total Finish Positions [*Horse racing*]
TFP .... Total Force Policy [*DoD*]
TFP .... Trans-Fiberoptic-Photographic [*Electron microscopy*]
TFP .... Transportability Focal Point [*Army*] (MCD)
TFP .... Travaux. Faculte de Philosophie et Lettres. Universite Catholique de Louvain [*A publication*] (BJA)
TFP .... Trees on Farms Program (EERA)
TFP .... Trifluoperazine [*Also, Trifluoroperazine*] [*Organic chemistry*]
TFP .... Trifluoroperazine [*Also, Trifluoperazine*] [*Organic chemistry*]
TF/P .... Tubular Fluid Plasma [*Medicine*] (MAE)
TF/P .... Tubule Fluid-to-Plasma [*Ratio*] [*Medicine*] (DAVI)
TFPA .... Tall Fashion Promotions of Australia
TFPA .... Tubular Finishers and Processors Association [*Defunct*] (EA)
TFPC .... Thin-Film Photovoltaic Cell
TFPCA .... Thin-Film Photovoltaic Cell Array
TFPCTS .... Thin-Film Personal Communications and Telemetry System (MCD)
TFPECTS .... Thin-Film Personal Communications and Telemetry System (MCD)
TFPG .... Task Force Planning Group [*DoD*]
TFPI .... Tissue Factor Pathway Inhibitor [*Biochemistry*]
TFPIA .... Textile Fiber Products Identification Act [*1960*]
(TF/P)In .... Tubule Fluid-to-Plasma Insulin Ratio [*Medicine*] (DAVI)
TFPL .... Task Force Pro Libra Ltd. (IID)
TFPL .... Texas Forest Products Laboratory
TFPL .... Training Film Production Laboratory [*Military*]
TFR .... Pueblo, CO [*Location identifier FAA*] (FAAL)
TFR .... Taft's Foundation Reporter [*A publication*]
TFR .... Tape-to-File Recorder
TFR .... Tarbes [*France*] [*Airport symbol*] (AD)
TFR .... Teknikvetenskapliga FoskningsRadet [*Swedish Research Council for Engineering Sciences*]
TFR .... Television Film Recorder
TFR .... Terrain-Following RADAR
TFR .... Territorial Force Reserve [*British*]
TFR .... Test Failure Report (CAAL)
TFR .... Theoretical Final Route [*Telecommunications*] (TEL)
TFR .... Thin-Film Resist
TFR .... TOKAMAK [*Toroidal Kamera Magnetic*] at Fontenay-aux-Roses
T/FR .... Top of Frame (AAG)
TFR .... Torus Fontenay AWY-Roses
TFR .... Total Fertility Rate [*Medicine*]
TFR .... Total Final Reports
TFR .... Total Follicular Response (OA)
TFR .... Trafalgar Resources, Inc. [*Vancouver Stock Exchange symbol*]
TFR .... Trainer Facilities Report [*Army*]
TFR .... Transaction Formatting Routines
TFR .... Trans European Airways SA [*France ICAO designator*] (FAAC)
TFR .... Transfer
TFR .... Transfer Function Response
TfR .... Transferrin Receptor [*Immunology*]
TFR .... Traveler/Failure Report [*Deep Space Instrumentation Facility, NASA*]
TFR .... Trouble and Failure Report [*NASA*]
TFR .... Tubular Flow Reactor
TFR .... Tunable Frequency Range
TFRC .... TechForce Corp. [*NASDAQ symbol*] (SAG)
TFRC .... TechForce Corp. [*NASDAQ symbol*] (TTSB)
TFR/CAR .... Trouble and Failure Report/Corrective Action Report
TFRCD .... Traffic Received (FAAC)
TFRD .... Test Facilities Requirements Document
TFS .... Tactical Fighter Squadron [*Air Force*]
TFS .... Tape File Supervisor
TFS .... Tasmanian Fire Service [*Australia*]
TFS .... Tax Free Shopping
TFS .... Tbilisi [*Former USSR Geomagnetic observatory code*]
TFS .... Teacher Follow-Up Survey [*Department of Education*] (GFGA)
TFS .... Telemetry Format Selection (NASA)
TFS .... Tenerife-Reina Sofia [*Canary Islands*] [*Airport symbol*] (OAG)
TFS .... Tennessee Folklore Society (EA)
TFS .... Terrain-Following System
TFS .... Testicular Feminization Syndrome [*Endocrinology*]
TFS .... Thomson Financial Services [*The Thomson Corp.*] [*Publishing*]
TFS .... Three-Five Systems [*NYSE symbol*] (TTSB)
TFS .... Three Five Systems Co. [*NYSE symbol*] (SAG)
TFS .... Thrombus-Free Surface [*Hematology*]
TFS .... Time and Frequency Standard
TFS .... Tin-Free Steel
TFS .... Torpedo Firing System (DNAB)
TFS .... Traffic Flow Security [*Telecommunications*] (TEL)
TFS .... Traffic Forecasting System [*Telecommunications*] (TEL)
TFS .... Transaction Forwarding System [*Computer science*]
TFS .... Transport Ferry Service [*English Channel*]
TFS .... Transverse Feed System
TFS .... Trim Fuel System (MCD)
TFS .... Trunk Forecasting System [*Telecommunications*] (TEL)
TFS .... Tuliptree Flower Spiroplasma [*Plant pathology*]
TFS .... Tunable Frequency Source
TFS .... Turbine First Stage [*Nuclear energy*] (NRCH)
TFS .... Turbine Flow Sensor
TFS .... Type Finish Specification (MCD)
TFSA .... Thin-Film Spreading Agent [*For enhanced oil recovery*]
TFSC .... Turkish Federated State of Cyprus
TFS-CT .... Tin-Free Steel Chromium-Type (PDAA)
TFSF .... Time to First System Failure (MHDI)
TFSK .... Time Frequency Shift Keying [*Computer science*] (IAA)
TFSO .... Tonto Forest Seismological Observatory [*Arizona*]
TFSP .... Task Force on Service to the Public [*Canada*]
TFSQ .... Tactical Fighter Squadron [*Air Force*]
TFSR .... Tools for Self Reliance [*British*] (EAIO)
TFSS .... Technical Facilities Subsystem [*Space Flight Operations Facility, NASA*]
TFSUSS .... Task Force on Scientific Uses of the Space Station [*NASA*]
TFT .... Tabular Firing Table [*Military*] (AABC)
TFT .... Tangential Flow Torch [*For plasma generation*]
TFT .... Technical Feasibility Testing [*Army*]
TFT .... Temporary Facility Tool (SAA)
TFT .... Temporary Full-Time (GFGA)
TFT .... Termo Fibertek, Inc. [*AMEX symbol*] (SPSG)
TFT .... Thermal Fatigue Test
TFT .... Thermo Fibertek [*AMEX symbol*] (TTSB)
TFT .... Thin-Film Field-Effect Transistor
TFT .... Thin-Film Technique
TFT .... Thin-Film Technology
TFT .... Thin-Film Transducer
TFT .... Thin-Film Transistor
TFT .... Threshold Failure Temperatures
TFT .... Thyroid Function Test [*Endocrinology*] (DAVI)
TFT .... Tight Filum Terminale [*Medicine*] (DMAA)
TFT .... Tight Fingertip [*Medicine*]
TFT .... Time-to-Frequency Transformation [*Electronics*] (OA)
TFT .... Tit for Tat [*Slang*]
TFT .... Transfer Factor Test [*Medicine*] (DAVI)
TFT .... Trifluorothymidine [*Pharmacology*]
TFT .... Triple Thin Film [*Electronics*]
TFT^3 .... Trillion Cubic Feet (WDAA)
TF/TA .... Terrain Following/Terrain Avoidance (MCD)
TFTAS .... Tactical Fighter Training Aggressor Squadron [*Air Force*]
TFTASq .... Tactical Fighter Training Aggressor Squadron [*Air Force*]
TFTB .... Taping for the Blind (EA)
TFTC .... Thin-Film Thermocouple (IAA)
TFTE .... Temporary Full-Time Equivalent (GFGA)
TFTG .... Tactical Fighter Training Group [*Military*]
TF/TG .... Task Force/Task Group
TFTNGSq .... Tactical Fighter Training Squadron [*Air Force*]
TFTP .... Task Force on Teaching as a Profession [*Defunct*] (EA)
TFTP .... Television Facility Test Position [*Telecommunications*] (TEL)
TFTP .... Trivial File Transfer Protocol (BYTE)
TFTR .... TOKAMAK [*Toroidal Kamera Magnetic*] Fusion Test Reactor [*Princeton, NJ*]
TFTR .... Toroidal Fusion Test Reactor [*Nuclear energy*] (MCD)
TFTS .... Tactical Fighter Training Squadron [*Air Force*] (MCD)
TFTS .... TOW [*Tube-Launched, Optically Tracked, Wire-Guided (Weapon)*] Field Test Set (MCD)
TFTT .... TOW [*Tube-launched, Optically-tracked, Wire-guided*] Field Tactical Trainer [*Army*] (INF)
TFTW .... Tactical Fighter Training Wing [*Air Force*] (MCD)
TFU .... Tactical Forecast Unit
TFU .... Telecommunications Flying Unit [*British*]
TFU .... Test Facility Utilization [*NASA*] (NASA)
TFU .... Theoretical First Unit [*Economics*]
TFU .... Time and Frequency Unit (ECII)
TFU .... Tool Follow Up
TFUC .... Theoretical First Unit Cost
TFV .... Tangential Force Variation [*Automotive fire testing*]
TFV .... Twin Falls Victory [*Tracking ship*] [*NASA*]
TFVA .... Training Film and Video Association (NITA)
TFVC .... Traffic Flow Visualization and Control
TFVC .... Traffic Flow Visualization and Control [*FHWA*] (TAG)
TFW .... Tactical Fighter Wing [*Air Force*]
TFW .... Tethered Free-Floating Worker
TFW .... Thermoplastic Fan Wheel
TFW .... Tokyo Financial Wire [*COMLINE International Corp.*] [*Japan Information service or system*] (CRD)
TFW .... Tropical Fresh Water
TFW .... Tufts University, Medford, MA [*OCLC symbol*] (OCLC)
TFW .... Turbulent Far Wake
TFWC .... Tactical Fighter Weapons Center [*Air Force*] (AFM)
TFWCRG .... Tactical Fighter Weapons Center Range Group [*Military*]
TFWG .... Tactical Fighter Wing [*Air Force*]
TFWRR .... Task Force on Women's Rights and Responsibilities [*National Council on Family Relations*] (EA)
TFWS .... Tactical Fighter Weapon School [*Air Force*] (MCD)
TFWS .... Task Force on Women in Sports [*of NOW*] (EA)
TFX .... Tactical Fighter Experimental [*Air Force*]
TFX .... Teleflex, Inc. [*NYSE symbol*] (SAG)
TFX .... Thymic Factor X [*Endocrinology*]
TFX .... Tri-Service Fighter, Experimental (MCD)
TFXA .... Time-Focused Crystal Analyzer [*Spectrometer*]
TFX-N .... Tactical Fighter Experimental - Navy
TFX-O .... Tactical Fighter Experimental - Offensive
TFX-R .... Tactical Fighter Experimental - Reconnaissance
TFY .... Tarfaya [*Morocco*] [*Airport symbol*] (AD)
TFY .... Target Fiscal Year (MCD)
TFY .... Tayside Aviation Ltd. [*British ICAO designator*] (FAAC)
TFYAA .... Task Force on Youth Allowance Administration [*Australia*]
TFYAP .... Tobacco Free Young America Project (EA)
TFYQA .... Think for Yourself and Question Authority [*Term coined by Dr. Timothy Leary*]

TFZ .... Tail Fuze (MSA)
TFZ .... Traffic Zone (FAAC)
TFZ .... Trifluroperazine [*Tranquilizer*]
TFZ .... Tropospheric Frontal Zone
Tg .... Generation Time (DAVI)
Tg .... Glass Transition
TG .... Positioning Devices [*JETDS nomenclature*] [*Military*] (CET)
TG .... Tail Gear
TG .... Tangent [*Mathematics*] (IAA)
TG .... Tangent Group (EA)
TG .... Tape Gauge
TG .... Target Gate (CAAL)
TG .... Task Group [*Military*]
TG .... Task Guidance
TG .... Tasmanian Greens [*Australia Political party*]
TG .... Technology Gap
TG .... Telecom Gold (NITA)
TG .... Telegram
TG .... Telegraph
TG .... Teleilaet Ghassul (BJA)
TG .... Temporary Gentleman [*British slang term for officer for duration of the war*] [*World War I*]
TG .... Tendon Graft [*Orthopedics*] (DAVI)
TG .... Terminal Guidance
TG .... Terminator Group
TG .... Testamentsgesetz [*Law on Wills*] [*German*] (ILCA)
TG .... Test Group
TG .... Test Guaranteed
TG .... Testosterone Glucuronide [*Medicine*] (MAE)
TG .... Tetraglycine (DAVI)
TG .... Tetrapyrrole Group [*British*] (EAIO)
TG .... Text Change [*Computer science*] (PCM)
TG .... Thai Airways [*ICAO designator*] (AD)
TG .... Thapsigargin [*Organic chemistry*]
TG .... Theatre Guild (EA)
TG .... Thermogravimetry
TG .... Thioglucose [*Biochemistry*]
TG .... Thioglycolate [*Biochemistry*]
TG .... Thioguanine [*Also, T*] [*Antineoplastic drug*]
TG .... Third Generation (EA)
TG .... Thoracic Ganglion [*Neuroanatomy*]
TG .... Thromboglobulin [*Clinical chemistry*]
TG .... Thyroglobulin [*Also, Thg*] [*Endocrinology*]
TG .... Timing Gage (IAA)
TG .... Timing Gate (AAG)
TG .... Tinted Glass
TG .... Tithing [*Church of England*]
tg .... Togo [*MARC country of publication code Library of Congress*] (LCCP)
TG .... Togo [*ANSI two-letter standard code*] (CNC)
TG .... Tollgate [*Maps and charts*]
TG .... Top Grille (OA)
TG .... Torpedo Group
TG .... Torque Generator (IAA)
TG .... Total Graph (OA)
TG .... Toxic Goiter [*Medicine*] (MAE)
TG .... Track Geometry [*In TG-01, an Austrian built subway inspection car*]
TG .... Tracking and Guidance
TG .... Traders Group Ltd. [*Toronto Stock Exchange symbol Vancouver Stock Exchange symbol*]
TG .... Traffic Guidance [*Aviation*]
TG .... Training Group (WDAA)
TG .... Transfer Gate (IAA)
T-G .... Transformational-Generative [*Linguistics*]
TG .... Transformational Grammar
TG .... Transgenic [*Genetics*]
TG .... Transglutaminase [*An enzyme*]
TG .... Transgranular [*Metallurgy*]
TG .... Translators' Guild (WDAA)
TG .... Transmissible Gastroenteritis [*Virus*]
TG .... Transmission Group (IAA)
TG .... Tredegar Indus [*NYSE symbol*] (TTSB)
TG .... Tredegar Industries, Inc. [*NYSE symbol*] (SPSG)
TG .... Tribune de St. Gervais [*A publication*]
TG .... Trigeminal Ganglion [*Neuroanatomy*]
TG .... Trigger (IAA)
TG .... Trigger Generator
TG .... Triglyceride [*Biochemistry*]
TG .... Tropical Gulf [*American air mass*]
TG .... Tuned Grid (KSC)
TG .... Turbine Generator (NRCH)
TG .... Turbogenerator
TG .... Tying Goals [*Sports*]
TG .... Type Genus
TGA .... Antibody Thyroglobulin [*Immunology*]
TGA .... [*The*] Generation After [*An association*] (EA)
TGA .... [*The*] Glutamate Association - United States (EA)
TGA .... Taurocholate-Gelatin Agar [*Microbiology*]
T/GA .... Temperature Gauge [*Automotive engineering*]
TGA .... Therapeutic Goods Administration [*Australia*]
TGA .... Therapeutic Goods Administration [*Australia*]
TGA .... Therapeutic Goods Administration (EERA)
TGA .... Thermogravimetric [*or Thermogravimetry*] Analysis [*Instrumentation*]
TGA .... Thioglycolic Acid [*Organic chemistry*]
TGA .... Togo Airlines [*ICAO designator*] (FAAC)
TGA .... Toilet Goods Association [*Later, CTFA*] (EA)
TGA .... Tolmetin Glycine Amide [*Biochemistry*]
TGA .... Total Glycoalkaloids [*Analytical biochemistry*]
TGA .... Touristische Gemeinschaft der Alpenlander [*Alpine Tourist Commission - ATC*] [*Zurich, Switzerland*] (EAIO)
TGA .... Trace Gas Analysis
TGA .... Trans Global Airlines [*FAA*] (TAG)
TGA .... Transient Global Amnesia [*Medicine*]
TGA .... Transposition of Great Arteries [*Cardiology*]
TGA .... Treasury General Account [*Department of the Treasury*]
TGA .... Triglycollamic Acid [*Organic chemistry*]
TGA .... Tropical Growers' Association (EAIO)
TGA .... Tumor Glycoprotein Assay [*Medicine*] (DMAA)
TGAb .... Thyroglobulin Antibody
TGAC .... Table Grape Advisory Committee [*Western Australia*]
TGAC .... Technical Grade Active Constituent (EERA)
TGAC .... Therapeutic Goods Advertising Code [*Australia*]
TGAL .... Tegal Corp. [*NASDAQ symbol*] (SAG)
TGAL .... Teledyne Geotech Alexandria Laboratories
T-GAM .... Training - Guided Air Missile (MUGU)
TGAOTU .... [*The*] Great Architect of the Universe [*Freemasonry*]
TGAQ .... Treasury of Great American Quotations [*A publication*]
TGAR .... Total Graft Area Rejected [*Medicine*] (MAE)
TGARQ .... Telegraphic Approval Requested (NOAA)
TGAS .... TACAN [*Tactical Air Navigation*] Guidance Augmentation System [*Military*] (CAAL)
TGAS .... Trace Gas Acquisition System
TG-ATS .... Theatre Guild-American Theatre Society (EA)
TGaV .... Volunteer State Community College, Learning Resources Center, Gallatin, TN [*Library symbol Library of Congress*] (LCLS)
TGB .... Temporary Guidebase [*Oil*] (DICI)
TGB .... Tongued, Grooved, and Beaded [*Lumber*]
TGB .... Torpedo Gunboat (ROG)
TGB .... Triple A and Gvt Ser'97(New) [*AMEX symbol*] (TTSB)
TGB .... Triple A Government Series 1997, Inc. [*AMEX symbol*] (SAG)
TGB .... Turbine Generator Building [*Nuclear energy*] (NRCH)
TGB .... Twist-Grain-Boundary [*Liquid crystal science*]
TGBL .... Through Government Bill of Lading [*Military*] (AABC)
TGBR .... Trans-Global Resources NL [*NASDAQ symbol*] (NQ)
TGBRY .... Trans-Global Resource NL ADR [*NASDAQ symbol*] (TTSB)
TGC .... [*The*] Grantsmanship Center (EA)
TGC .... Tasmanian Gaming Commission [*Australia*]
TGC .... Tasmanian Golf Council [*Australia*]
TGC .... Teleglobe Canada
TGC .... Terminator Group Controller (IAA)
TGC .... TG Aviation Ltd. [*British ICAO designator*] (FAAC)
TGC .... Theater Ground Command [*Military*]
TGC .... Therapeutic Goods Committee [*Australia*]
TGC .... Thermocouple Gauge Control
TGC .... Throttle Governor Control
TGC .... Time Gain Compensation [*Radiology*] (DAVI)
TGC .... Time Gain Control (IAA)
TGC .... Tomato Genetics Cooperative (EA)
TGC .... Total Gas-Phase Carbon [*Environmental chemistry*]
TGC .... Tougaloo College, Tougaloo, MS [*OCLC symbol*] (OCLC)
TGC .... Transfer Gear Case (MCD)
TGC .... Transmit Gain Control (MSA)
TGC .... Travel Group Charter [*Airline fare*]
TGC .... Trenton, TN [*Location identifier FAA*] (FAAL)
TGCA .... Texas Gun Collectors Association
TGCA .... Tobacco Growers' Council of Australia
TGCA .... Transportable Ground Control Approach (IAA)
TGCA .... Transportable Group Control Approach (NG)
TGCI .... TGC Industries [*NASDAQ symbol*] (TTSB)
TGCI .... TGC Industries, Inc. [*NASDAQ symbol*] (SAG)
TGC In .... TGC Industries, Inc. [*Associated Press*] (SAG)
TGC Ind .... TGC Industries, Inc. [*Associated Press*] (SAG)
TGC Inds .... TGC Industries, Inc. [*Associated Press*] (SAG)
TGCR .... Tactical Generic Cable Replacement
TGCS .... Transportable Ground Communications Station
TGD .... Task Group Delta (MCD)
TGD .... Technical Guidance Directions
TGD .... Titograd [*Former Yugoslavia*] [*Airport symbol*] (OAG)
TGD .... Trajectory and Guidance Data
TGDDM .... Tetraglycidyl(diaminodiphenyl)methane [*Organic chemistry*]
TGE .... Trabajos Aereos SA [*Spain ICAO designator*] (FAAC)
TGE .... Transmissible Gastroenteritis [*Virus*]
TGE .... Traverse Gravimeter Experiment (KSC)
TGE .... Trialkoxyglyceryl Ether [*Organic chemistry*]
TGE .... Tryptone Glucose Extract [*Cell growth medium*]
TGE .... Tuskegee, AL [*Location identifier FAA*] (FAAL)
TGEB .... Tasmanian Grain Elevators Board [*Australia*]
TGEEP .... Terminal Guidance Environmental Effects Program (MCD)
TGEN .... Targeted Genetics [*NASDAQ symbol*] (TTSB)
TGEN .... Targeted Genetics Corp. [*NASDAQ symbol*] (SAG)
TGEP .... Turbine Generator Emergency Power [*Nuclear energy*] (NRCH)
TGET .... Target Ground Elapsed Time
TGET .... Target Therapeutics [*NASDAQ symbol*] (TTSB)
TGET .... Target Therapeutics, Inc. [*NASDAQ symbol*] (SAG)
TGEV .... Transmissible Gastroenteritis Virus [*Virology*]
TGF .... Aerotaxis del Golfo, SA de CV [*Mexico*] [*FAA designator*] (FAAC)
TGF .... Emerging Tigers Fund [*NYSE symbol*] (SAG)
TGF .... Therapeutic Gain Factor [*Medicine*]
TGF .... Through Group Filter [*Telecommunications*] (TEL)
TGF .... Top Groove Fill [*Lubricating oil test*]

TGF............ Tragicorum Graecorum Fragmenta [*A publication*] (OCD)
TGF............ Training Guarantee Fund [*Australia*]
TGF............ Transforming Growth Factor
TGF............ Transonic Gasdynamics Facility [*Air Force*]
TGF............ Treasury Guard Force
TGF............ Triglycine Fluoberyllate [*Ferroelectrics*]
TGF............ Tumor Growth Factor [*Oncology*]
TGFA........... Tasmanian Game Fishing Association [*Australia*]
TGF-A.......... Transforming Growth Factor - Alpha
TGFA........... Triglyceride Fatty Acid [*Biochemistry*]
TGFC........... Tammy Graham Fan Club (EA)
TGFC........... Terri Gibbs Fan Club (EA)
TGFM........... Tasmanian Guild of Furniture Manufacturers [*Australia*]
TGG............ Kuala Trengganu [*Malaysia*] [*Airport symbol*] (OAG)
TGG............ Templeton Global Government Income Trust [*NYSE symbol*] (CTT)
TGG............ Templeton Global Gvts [*NYSE symbol*] (TTSB)
TGG............ Temporary Geographic Grid
TGG............ Third Generation Gyro (MCD)
TGG............ Turkey Gamma G [*Immunology*]
TGGE........... Temperature-Gradient Gel Electrophoresis [*Analytical biochemistry*]
TGH............ Tongoa [*Vanuatu*] [*Airport symbol*] (OAG)
TGH............ Tripler General Hospital [*Army*] (GFGA)
TGI............ Tactics Guide Issued (CAAL)
TGI............ Taghi Ghambar [*Iran*] [*Seismograph station code, US Geological Survey*] (SEIS)
TGI............ Tangier, VA [*Location identifier FAA*] (FAAL)
TGI............ Target Group Index [*British Market Research Bureau Ltd.*] [*Information service or system*]
TGI............ Target Intensifier
TGI............ Telco Group, Inc. [*Telecommunications service*] (TSSD)
TGI............ Textbuch zur Geschichte Israels [*A publication*] (BJA)
TGI............ Tingo Maria [*Peru*] [*Airport symbol*] (OAG)
TGI............ Tournament Golf International
TGIA........... Toy and Giftware Importers Association [*British*] (DBA)
TGIC........... Tobacco Growers' Information Committee (EA)
TGIC........... Triad Guaranty [*NASDAQ symbol*] (TTSB)
TGIC........... Triad Guaranty, Inc. [*NASDAQ symbol*] (SAG)
TGIC........... Triglycidyl Isocyanurate [*Organic chemistry*]
TGID........... Transmission Group Identifier [*Telecommunications*] (MHDI)
TGID........... Trunk Group Identification [*Telecommunications*] (TEL)
TGIF........... Tactical Ground Intercept Facility [*Air Force*] (DOMA)
TGIF........... Terminal Guidance Indirect Fire (MCD)
TGIF........... Thank God It's Friday [*Meaning work-week is nearly over*]
TGIF........... Toe Goes in First [*As is "You're so dumb you have TGIF on your shoes"*]
TGIF........... Transportable Ground Intercept Facility
TGIF-OTMWDUM... Thank God It's Friday - Only Two More Work Days Until Monday [*Pentagon saying*]
TGIS........... Thank God It's Summer
TGIS........... Thomas Group [*NASDAQ symbol*] (TTSB)
TGIS........... Thomas Group, Inc. [*NASDAQ symbol*] (SAG)
TGJ............ Tiga [*Loyalty Islands*] [*Airport symbol*] (OAG)
TGL+........... [*The*] Graphics Link Plus [*Printer software*] [*TerraVision*] (PCM)
TGL............ Tagula [*Papua New Guinea*] [*Airport symbol*] (OAG)
TGL............ Tangent Oil & Gas [*Vancouver Stock Exchange symbol*]
TGL............ Task Group Leader
TGL............ Temperature Gradient Lamp [*Spectroscopy*]
TGL............ Thin Glass Laminate
TGL............ Toggle (AAG)
TGL............ Touch and Go Landings [*Aviation*]
TGL............ Trans-Atlantic Airlines Ltd. [*Gambia*] [*ICAO designator*] (FAAC)
TGL............ Treasury Gold License (MCD)
TGL............ Triangular Guide Line
TGL............ Triglyceride [*Biochemistry*] (MAE)
TGL............ Triglyceride Lipase [*Clinical chemistry*]
TGL............ Triglycerides [*Clinical chemistry*]
TGL............ Triton Group Ltd. [*AMEX symbol*] (SPSG)
TGLC........... Total Gate Leakage Current
TGLE........... Transglobe Energy Corp. [*NASDAQ symbol*] (SAG)
TGLEF.......... Transglobe Energy [*NASDAQ symbol*] (TTSB)
TGLM........... Task Group Lung Model [*ICRP*]
TG-LORAN....... Traffic-Guidance Long-Range Aid to Navigation (DEN)
TGLS........... Tongueless
TGLVQ.......... Terminal Guidance for Lunar Vehicles [*Aerospace*] (AAG)
TGL.WS......... Triton Group Ltd Wrrt [*AMEX symbol*] (TTSB)
TGM............ Tactical Generic Multiplex
TGM............ Task Group Manager (CAAL)
TGM............ Telegram (ROG)
TGM............ Tirgu Mures [*Romania*] [*Airport symbol*] (OAG)
TGM............ Torpedo Gunner's Mate [*Obsolete Navy British*]
TGM............ Total Gaseous Mercury [*Environmental chemistry*]
TGM............ Training Guided Missile [*Air Force*]
TGM............ Transportability Guidance Manual
TGM............ Trunk Group Multiplexer [*Telecommunications*] (TEL)
TGM............ Turbine Generator Management
TGMA........... Tone Generator and Master Alarm (KSC)
TGMD........... Test of Gross Motor Development [*Sensorimotor skills test*]
TG-MS.......... Thermogravimetry - Mass Spectrometry
TGMTS.......... Tank Gunnery and Missile Tracking System
TGMV........... Tomato Golden Mosaic Virus
TGN............ Anchorage, AK [*Location identifier FAA*] (FAAL)
TGN............ Tarragona [*Spain*] [*Airport symbol*] (AD)
TGN............ Tournigan Mining Explorations Ltd. [*Vancouver Stock Exchange symbol*]
TGN............ Trans Golgi Network [*Cytology*]
TGN............ Trigeminal Neuralgia [*Medicine*]
TGN............ Trigen Energy [*NYSE symbol*] (TTSB)
TGN............ Trigen Energy Corp. [*NYSE symbol*] (SAG)
TGN............ Trunk Group Number [*Telecommunications*] (TEL)
TGNMO.......... Total Gaseous Non-Methane Organic [*Environmental chemistry*]
TGNR........... Tactics Guide Not Required (CAAL)
TGNSW.......... Teachers' Guild of New South Wales [*Australia*]
TGNU........... Transitional Government of National Unity [*South Africa*]
TGO............ Canada-Transport Canada [*ICAO designator*] (FAAC)
TGO............ Time to Go [*Apollo*] [*NASA*]
TGO............ Togo [*ANSI three-letter standard code*] (CNC)
TGO............ Tongliao [*China*] [*Airport symbol*] (OAG)
TGO............ Total Gross Output (GNE)
TGO............ Tuned Grid Oscillator
TGOPS.......... Task Group Operations [*Navy*] (NVT)
TG or UA....... Temperance, Grog, or Underage [*British military*]
TGOWG.......... Teleoperator Ground Operations Working Group [*NASA*] (NASA)
TGP............ [*The*] Giraffe Project [*An association*] (EA)
TGP............ Technigen Platinum Corp. [*Vancouver Stock Exchange symbol*]
TGP............ Theft of Government Property [*FBI standardized term*]
TGP............ Timothy Grass Pollen [*Immunology*]
TGP............ Tobacco Glycoprotein [*Biochemistry*]
TGP............ Tone Generator Panel
TGP............ Turbulence-Generating Pot [*Automotive engineering*]
TGPA........... Technigen Corp. [*NASDAQ symbol*] (SAG)
TGPAF.......... Technigen Corp. [*NASDAQ symbol*] (TTSB)
TGPG........... St. Georges [*Grenada*] [*ICAO location identifier*] (ICLI)
TGPO........... Tasmanian Government Printing Office [*Australia*]
TGPSG.......... Tactical Global Positioning System Guidance (MCD)
TGPWU.......... Transport, General and Port Workers' Union [*Aden*]
TGPY........... Point Saline [*Grenada*] [*ICAO location identifier*] (ICLI)
TGR............ Tenderness, Guarding, Rigidity [*On abdominal examination*] [*Medicine*] (DAVI)
TGR............ Things Gone Right [*Measure of automobile customer satisfaction*]
TGR............ Touggourt [*Algeria*] [*Airport symbol*] (OAG)
TGRLSS......... Two-Gas Regenerative Lift Support System
TGrT........... Tusculum College, Greeneville, TN [*Library symbol Library of Congress*] (LCLS)
TGS............ [*The*] Galactic Society (EA)
TGS............ Gulf States Utilities Co., Beaumont, TX [*OCLC symbol*] (OCLC)
TGS............ Target Generating System
TGS............ Taxiing Guidance System [*Aviation*]
TGS............ Telemetry Ground Station
TGS............ Telemetry Ground System (NASA)
TGS............ Telemetry Guidance System [*From computer game "Hacker II"*]
TGS............ Template Graphics Software
TGS............ Terminal Guidance Sensor [*or System*]
TGS............ Thermogravimetric [*or Thermogravimetry*] System [*Instrumentation*]
TGS............ Ticket-Granting Server
TGS............ Tide Gauge System
TGS............ Tincture of Green Soap [*Medicine*] (DMAA)
TGS............ Top Gear Switch [*Automotive engineering*]
TGS............ Traite de Grammaire Syriaque [*A publication*] (BJA)
TGS............ Transcontinental Geophysical Survey (NOAA)
TGS............ Transfer Generator System (IAA)
TGS............ Translator Generator System (IEEE)
TGS............ Transportable Ground Station
TGS............ Transportadora De Gas ADS [*NYSE symbol*] (TTSB)
TGS............ Transportadora de Gas Del Sur SA [*NYSE symbol*] (SAG)
TGS............ Triglycine Sulfate [*Ferroelectrics*]
TGS............ True Ground Speed (IAA)
TGS............ Turbine Generator System [*Nuclear energy*] (NRCH)
TGS............ Turkish General Staff (NATG)
TGS............ Turret Gun System [*Army*]
TGS............ Tuxtla Gutierrez [*Mexico*] [*Airport symbol*] (AD)
TGSE........... Tactical Ground Support Equipment
TGSE........... Telemetry Ground Support Equipment [*NASA*] (KSC)
TGSF........... Test Group Support Facility
TGSI........... Concept Tech Group [*NASDAQ symbol*] (SAG)
TGSI........... Trans Global Services, Inc. [*NASDAQ symbol*] (SAG)
TGSI........... Trans Global Svcs [*NASDAQ symbol*] (TTSB)
TGSIFC......... T. G. Sheppard International Fan Club (EA)
TGSIW.......... Trans Global Svcs Wrrt [*NASDAQ symbol*] (TTSB)
TGSM........... Terminally Guided Submissile (MCD)
TGSM........... Terminally Guided Submunitions (MCD)
TGSR........... Triglyceride Secretion Rate [*Physiology*]
TGSS........... Terminal Guidance Sensor System
TGSS........... Transmission Gear Selection Switch [*Automotive engineering*]
TGSS........... Turbine Gland Sealing System [*Nuclear energy*] (NRCH)
TGSSA.......... Transactions. Geological Society of South Africa [*A publication*]
TGSS/UGS....... Tactical Ground Sensor System/Unattended Ground Sensor (MCD)
TGT............ AB Nyge Aero [*Sweden*] [*FAA designator*] (FAAC)
TGT............ Tail Gate
TGT............ Tanga [*Tanzania*] [*Airport symbol*] (OAG)
TGT............ Target (AAG)
TGT............ Teams-Games-Tournaments [*Education*] (AEE)
TGT............ Thermocouple Gauge Tube
TGT............ Thromboplastin Generation Test [*Hematology*]
TGT............ Thromboplastin Generation Time [*Hematology*] (MAE)
TGT............ Ticket-Granting Ticket [*Computer science*]
TGT............ Tissue Glucose Threshold [*Medicine*] (BARN)
TGT............ TOW [*Tube-launched, Optically Tracked, Wire-Guided (weapon)*] Gunnery Trainer [*Army*] (INF)
TGT............ Transformational Grammar Tester (IAA)
TGT............ True Ground Track (MCD)

TGT Turbine Gas Temperature (NATG)
TGTBT Too Good to be True [*Internet language*] [*Computer science*]
TGTM Transportability Guidance Technical Manual
TGTP Tuned Grid Tuned Plate [*Electronic plate*] (IAA)
TGTU Tail-Gas Treating Unit [*Petroleum engineering*]
TGU Technical Guidance Unit (NVT)
TGU Tegucigalpa [*Honduras*] [*Airport symbol*] (OAG)
TGU Templeton Global Utilities, Inc. [*AMEX symbol*] (SPSG)
TGU Triglycidylurazol [*Antineoplastic drug*]
TGU Tri Gold Industry [*Vancouver Stock Exchange symbol*]
TGURG Telegraphic Authority Requested (NOAA)
TGV Targovishte [*Bulgaria*] [*Airport symbol*] (OAG)
TGV Thomson Gold Co. [*Vancouver Stock Exchange symbol*]
TGV Thoracic Gas Volume [*Medicine*] (AAMN)
TGV Tobacco Growers of Victoria [*Australia*]
TGV Train a Grande Vitesse [*High-speed train*]
TGV Transposition of the Great Vessels [*Cardiology*]
TGV Turbine Governor Valve [*Nuclear energy*] (NRCH)
TGV Two Gentlemen of Verona [*Shakespearean work*]
TGVI TGV Software, Inc. [*NASDAQ symbol*] (SAG)
TGV Sft TGV Software, Inc. [*Associated Press*] (SAG)
TGW Terminally Guided Warhead [*or Weapon*]
TGW Things Gone Wrong [*Measure of automobile customer satisfaction*]
TGW Troposheric Gravity Wave [*Planetary science*]
TGWU Transport and General Workers' Union [*British*]
TGX Taguatinga [*Brazil*] [*Airport symbol*] (AD)
TGX Tube-Generated X-Ray
TGY Punta Gorda [*British Honduras*] [*Airport symbol*] (AD)
TGY Tryptone Glucose Yeast [*Cell growth medium*] (MAE)
TGYA Tryptone Glucose Yeast Agar [*Cell growth medium*] [*Medicine*] (DMAA)
TGZ Tuxtla Gutierrez [*Mexico*] [*Airport symbol*] (OAG)
TGZM Temperature-Gradient Zone-Melting [*Chemistry*]
TGZMP Temperature-Gradient Zone-Melting Process [*Chemistry*] (IAA)
Th C. H. Boehringer Sohn, Ingelheim [*Germany*] [*Research code symbol*]
TH Harriman Public Library, Harriman, TN [*Library symbol Library of Congress*] (LCLS)
TH Hot Leg Temperature [*Nuclear energy*] (NRCH)
TH Reports of the Witwatersrand High Court [*Transvaal, South Africa*] [*A publication*] (DLA)
T-H Taft-Hartley [*Act*]
TH Tally Ho [*Air Force*]
TH Tape-Handler [*Computer science*] (IAA)
TH Tax Haven (MHDW)
Th T-Cell, Helper Type [*Immunology*]
TH Teacher of Hydrotherapy [*British*]
TH Teaching Hospital [*British*]
TH Technische Hochschule [*Technical College*] [*German*]
TH Telegraph (IAA)
TH Telegraph Apparatus [*JETDS nomenclature*] [*Military*] (CET)
Th Tell Halaf (BJA)
TH Temporary Hold
TH Terraced Heterostructure (NITA)
TH Terrain Height (MCD)
TH Territory of Hawaii [*to 1959*]
TH Test Header (Fire Pump) [*NFPA pre-fire planning symbol*] (NFPA)
TH Tetrahydrocortisol (MAE)
TH Thai Airways [*ICAO designator*] (AD)
TH Thailand [*IYRU nationality code*] [*ANSI two-letter standard code*] (CNC)
th Thailand [*MARC country of publication code Library of Congress*] (LCCP)
TH Tharsis Region [*A filamentary mark on Mars*]
TH Theatre (ROG)
TH Their Highnesses (ADA)
Th T-Helper [*Immunology*]
Th Thenar [*Anatomy*]
th Thenardite [*CIPW classification*] [*Geology*]
Th Theodotion (BJA)
Th Theogonia [*of Hesiod*] [*Classical studies*] (OCD)
TH Theology
TH Theophylline [*Pharmacology*] (DAVI)
TH Theraplix [*France*] [*Research code symbol*]
TH Therapy [*Medicine*] (DHSM)
TH Thermal
T/H Thermal and Hydraulic [*Nuclear energy*] (NRCH)
TH Thermoid (SAA)
Th Thessalonians [*New Testament book*] (BJA)
TH Thick [*Automotive engineering*]
Th Thin [*Philately*]
TH Thionine [*Organic chemistry*]
TH Thiopental [*An anesthetic*]
Th Thomas de Piperata [*Flourished, 1268-72*] [*Authority cited in pre-1607 legal work*] (DSA)
th Thoracic [*Anatomy*] (MAE)
TH Thoracic Surgery [*Medicine*]
Th Thorax [*Anatomy*] (DAVI)
Th Thorium [*Chemical element*]
TH Thoroughbred (WGA)
TH Thorvald Hansen [*Steamship*] (MHDW)
TH Threat
TH Threshold (WGA)
TH Thrill [*Cardiology*] (DAVI)
TH Through-Hole [*Computer science*]
TH Thunder
TH Thursday
TH Thyrohyoid [*Medicine*] (MAE)
TH Thyroid Hormone [*Thyroxine*] [*Endocrinology*]
TH Thyssen Henschel
TH Titan Holdings [*NYSE symbol*] (TTSB)
TH Titan Holdings, Inc. [*NYSE symbol*] (SAG)
TH Toilet-Paper Holder
TH Toluene-Hyamine [*Scintillation solvent*]
TH Tommy Hilfiger [*Fashion designer*]
TH Total Hysterectomy [*Medicine*]
TH Town Hall (ROG)
TH Townhouse
TH Toy and Hobby Retailer [*A publication*]
TH Tracing-Hold
TH Tracking Head (IAA)
TH Trailer Height [*Automotive engineering*]
T-H Transhydro (AABC)
TH Transient Hyperphosphatasemia [*Medicine*]
TH Transmission Header [*Computer science*] (IBMDP)
TH Transponder-Hopping
T/H Transportation and Handling [*Army*]
TH Trinity House [*British*] (BARN)
TH True Heading
TH Trust House [*British*]
TH Two Hands
TH Tyrosine Hydroxylase [*An enzyme*]
TH Tzivos Hashem (EA)
TH_2O Free Water Reabsorption (DAVI)
TH_2O Titrated Water (DAVI)
ThA Associate in Theology (ADA)
THA Taft-Hartley Act [*1947*]
THA Tasmanian Hockey Association [*Australia*]
T-HA Terminal High Altitude
THA Tetrahydroaminoacridine [*Pharmacology*]
tha Thai [*MARC language code Library of Congress*] (LCCP)
THA Thai Airways International Ltd. [*Thailand*] [*ICAO designator*] (FAAC)
THA Thailand [*ANSI three-letter standard code*] (CNC)
THA Thames Ontario Library Service Board [*UTLAS symbol*]
ThA Thoracic Aorta [*Medicine*]
THA Thorcheron Hunter Association [*Defunct*] (EA)
THA Time Warner Financing Trust PERCS [*NYSE symbol*] (SAG)
THA Time Warner Fin Tr'PERCS' [*NYSE symbol*] (TTSB)
THA Total Hip Arthroplasty [*Orthopedics*]
THA Total Hydrocarbon Analyzer
THA Total Hydroxyapatite [*Clinical chemistry*] (MAE)
THA Tower Hill School, Wilmington, DE [*OCLC symbol*] (OCLC)
THA Transient Hemispheric Attack [*Medicine*] (DAVI)
THA Transvaal Horse Artillery [*British military*] (DMA)
THA Treasury Historical Association (EA)
THA Tullahoma [*Tennessee*] [*Airport symbol*] (AD)
THA Tullahoma, TN [*Location identifier FAA*] (FAAL)
THA Turk Haberler Ajansi [*Press agency*] [*Turkey*]
THAA Total Haloacetic Acid [*Environmental chemistry*]
THAA Tourist House Association of America (EA)
THAAD Theater High-Altitude Area Defense [*Military*]
THAB Tetrahexylammonium Benzoate [*Organic chemistry*]
THABTS Thereabouts [*Legal term British*]
Thac Cr Cas Thacher's Criminal Cases [*1823-42*] [*Massachusetts*] [*A publication*] (DLA)
Thach Cr Thacher's Criminal Cases [*Massachusetts*] [*A publication*] (DLA)
Thacher Cr Thacher's Criminal Cases [*Massachusetts*] [*A publication*] (DLA)
Thacher Cr Cas Thacher's Criminal Cases [*Massachusetts*] [*A publication*] (DLA)
Thacher Crim Cas (Mass) Thacher's Criminal Cases [*Massachusetts*] [*A publication*] (DLA)
Thack Thackeray Corp. [*Associated Press*] (SAG)
THAE Transcatheter Hepatic Artery Embolization [*Medicine*]
THAI Thai Airways International
Thai Thai Fund [*Associated Press*] (SAG)
Thai Thailand
ThaiCF Thai Capital Fund, Inc. [*Associated Press*] (SAG)
Thail Thailand
THAJ Tasmania House of Assembly - Journals [*A publication*]
Thal Thalassemia [*Medicine*]
THAM 2-Amino-2-(Hydroxymethyl)-1,3-Propanediol (DAVI)
THAM Tris(hydroxymethyl)aminomethane [*Also, TRIS*] [*Biochemical analysis*]
THAMA Toxic and Hazardous Materials Agency [*Army*] (RDA)
THAN Transient Hyperammonemia of Newborn [*Neonatology*] (DAVI)
TH & B [*The*] Toronto, Hamilton & Buffalo Railway Co. [*Nickname: To Hell and Back*]
TH & C Terpin Hydrate and Codeine [*Medicine*]
Th & C Thompson and Cook's New York Supreme Court Reports [*1873-75*] [*A publication*] (DLA)
TH & P Terre Haute & Peoria Railroad [*Nickname: Take Hold and Push*]
THANSW Teacher Housing Authority of New South Wales [*Australia*]
THAP Tactical High-Altitude Penetration (MCD)
THAQ Tetrahydroanthraquinone [*Organic chemistry*]
THARIES Total Hip Articular Replacement with Internal Eccentric Shells [*Orthopedics*]
THaroL Lincoln Memorial University, Harrogate, TN [*Library symbol Library of Congress*] (LCLS)
THART Theodore Army Terminal
THAS Tumbleweed High-Altitude Samples (MUGU)
ThAT Theologie des Alten Testaments [*A publication*] (BJA)

THAT........... Twenty-Four-Hour Automatic Teller [*Trademark for self-service banking display panel*]
THav........... Trousdale County Public Library, Hartsville, TN [*Library symbol*] [*Library of Congress*] (LCLS)
THAWS.......... Tactical Homing and Warning System
Thayer......... Thayer's Reports [*18 Oregon*] [*A publication*] (DLA)
Thayer Prelim Treatise Ev... Thayer's Preliminary Treatise on Evidence [*A publication*] (DLA)
THB............ Thaba Tseka [*Lesotho*] [*Airport symbol*] (OAG)
Th B........... Theologiae Baccalaureas [*Bachelor of Theology*]
ThB............ Theologische Buecherei. Neudrucke und Berichte aus dem 20 Jahrhundert [*Munich*] [*A publication*] (BJA)
THB............ Third-Harmonic Band
THB............ [*The*] Toronto, Hamilton & Buffalo Railway Co. [*AAR code*]
THBC........... Troy Hill Bancorp [*NASDAQ symbol*] (TTSB)
THBC........... Troy Hill Bancorp, Inc. [*NASDAQ symbol*] (SAG)
THBF........... Total Hepatic Blood Flow
THBF........... Traditional Hi-Bye Function [*Army*]
THBI........... Thyroid Hormone Binding Inhibitor [*Clinical chemistry*]
ThBNL.......... National Library, Bangkok, Thailand [*Library symbol Library of Congress*] (LCLS)
THBP........... Tetrahydrobenzopyrene [*Organic chemistry*]
Th Br.......... Thesaurus Brevium [*2 eds.*] [*1661, 1687*] [*A publication*] (DLA)
THBR........... Thoroughbred Half-Bred Registry (EA)
THBR........... Thyroid Hormone Binding Ratio [*Clinical chemistry*]
THBY........... Thereby
Th C........... Candidate of Theology
THC............ Houston Community College System, Learning Resource Center, Houston, TX [*OCLC symbol*] (OCLC)
THC............ Target Homing Correlator
THC............ Tar Heel Aviation, Inc. [*ICAO designator*] (FAAC)
THC............ Tchien [*Liberia*] [*Airport symbol*] (OAG)
THC............ Tenet Healthcare [*NYSE symbol*] (TTSB)
THC............ Tenet Healthcare Corp. [*NYSE symbol*] (SAG)
THC............ Tetrahydrocannabinol [*Active principle of marijuana*]
THC............ Tetrahydrocortisol
THC............ THC Homecare, Inc. [*Associated Press*] (SAG)
THC............ Thermal Converter (MSA)
THC............ Thermohaline Circulation [*Oceanography*]
THC............ Thermohaline Circulation [*Marine science*] (OSRA)
THC............ Thiocarbanidin [*Pharmacology*]
THC............ Third-Harmonic Distortion [*Physics*] (IAA)
THC............ Throttled Homogeneous Combustion
THC............ Thrust Hand Controller [*NASA*] (KSC)
THC............ Total Hydrocarbon
THC............ Transhepatic Cholangiogram [*Medicine*]
THC............ Translation Hand Controller [*NASA*]
THC............ Trident Health Care, Inc. [*Toronto Stock Exchange symbol*]
THC............ True Heading Computer (DNAB)
THC............ Tube Humidity Control
T-HCA.......... Trans-Hydroxycrotonic Acid [*Organic chemistry*]
THCA........... Trihydroxycholestanoic Acid [*Biochemistry*]
THCA........... Trihydroxycoprostanic Acid [*Biochemistry*]
Th Ca Const Law... Thomas' Leading Cases in Constitutional Law [*A publication*] (DLA)
ThCar.......... Thermo Cardiosystems, Inc. [*Associated Press*] (SAG)
Th CC.......... Thacher's Criminal Cases [*1823-42*] [*Massachusetts*] [*A publication*] (DLA)
THCC........... Tube Heating and Cooling Control
Th C Const Law... Thomas' Leading Cases on Constitutional Law [*A publication*] (DLA)
THC-CRC........ Tetrahydrocannabinol Cross-Reacting-Cannabinoid [*Active principle of marijuana*] (PDAA)
THCF........... Thompson-Huston Co. of France
THC Hm......... THC Homecare, Inc. [*Associated Press*] (SAG)
THCI........... THC Homecare, Inc. [*NASDAQ symbol*] (SAG)
THCN........... Tetrahydrocorynantheine [*Biochemistry*]
THCOL.......... Thorn Color [*Botany*]
THCS........... Temperature of Hot-Channel Sodium [*Nuclear energy*] (NRCH)
TH-CULT........ Throat Culture [*Medicine*] (DAVI)
THCUR.......... Thorn Curvature [*Botany*]
tHcy........... Total Homocysteine [*Clinical chemistry*]
THD............ 611 897 Alberta Ltd. [*Canada*] [*FAA designator*] (FAAC)
ThD............ Doctor of Thinkology [*Honorary degree awarded the scarecrow by the wizard in 1939 film "The Wizard of Oz"*]
Thd............ Ribothymidine [*Also, T*] [*A nucleoside*]
THD............ Testicular Hypothermia Device [*Medicine*]
Th D........... Theologiae Doctor [*Doctor of Theology*]
THD............ Third Canadian General Investment Trust Ltd. [*Toronto Stock Exchange symbol*]
THD............ Third-Harmonic Distortion [*Physics*] (IAA)
THD............ Thread (AAG)
THD............ Thread
THD............ Total Harmonic Distortion [*Electronics*]
THD............ Tube Heat Dissipator
THD............ University of Houston, Downtown College, Houston, TX [*OCLC symbol*] (OCLC)
THDA........... Telluraheptadecanoic Acid [*Organic chemistry*]
THDA........... Thermal Hydrodealkylation [*Petroleum technology*]
THDA........... Toluene Hydrodealkylation [*Organic chemistry*]
THDC........... Technical Handbook Distribution Code (MCD)
THDG........... True Heading (GAVI)
THDI........... Thread Die
ThDip.......... Diploma in Theology (ADA)
THDNK.......... Threaded Neck
THDO........... 3D0 Company [*NASDAQ symbol*] (TTSB)
THDO........... Three Do Co. [*NASDAQ symbol*] (SAG)
THDOC.......... Tetrahydrodeoxycorticosterone [*Biochemistry*]
ThDP........... Thiamine Diphosphate [*Biochemistry*]
THDPC.......... Threadpiece
THDr........... Doctor of Theology
THDS........... Thermal Helium Desorption Spectrometry (MCD)
THDS........... Time Homogenous Data Set (MCD)
THE............ T & H Resources Ltd. [*Toronto Stock Exchange symbol*]
THE............ Tape-Handling Equipment
THE............ Technical Help to Exporters [*British Standards Institution*]
THE............ Teresina [*Brazil*] [*Airport symbol*] (OAG)
THE............ Tetrahydrocortisone [*Endocrinology*]
ThE............ Theologische Existenz Heute [*Munich*] [*A publication*] (BJA)
THE............ Thomas Hewett Edward Cat [*In TV series "T.H.E. Cat"*]
THE............ Tonic Hind Limb Extension (BABM)
THE............ Total Height Expansion
THE............ Transhepatic Embolization [*Medicine*]
THE............ Transportable Helicopter Enclosure (RDA)
THE............ Tropical Hypereosinophilia [*Medicine*] (DMAA)
THE............ Tube Heat Exchanger
THEA........... Theatrical
THEAT.......... Theatrical
Theat J........ Theatre Journal [*A publication*] (BRI)
Theb........... Thebais [*of Statius*] [*Classical studies*] (OCD)
THEBES......... [*The*] Electronic Banking Economics Society [*New York, NY*] (EA)
THECC.......... Truck and Heavy Equipment Claims Council (EA)
THEED.......... Tetrahydroxyethylethylenediamine [*Organic chemistry*]
THEIC.......... Tris(hydroxyethyl)isocyanurate [*Organic chemistry*]
Thel........... Theloall's Le Digest des Briefs [*2 eds.*] [*1579, 1687*] [*A publication*] (DLA)
THELEP......... Chemotherapy of Leprosy Program [*World Health Organization*] (BABM)
THELEP......... Chemotherapy of Leprosy Program [*of the World Health Organization*] (DAVI)
Them........... American Themis [*A publication*] (DLA)
Them........... La Themis [*A publication*] (DLA)
Them........... Themistocles [*of Plutarch*] [*Classical studies*] (OCD)
THEN........... Those Hags Encourage Neuterism [*Organization opposed to NOW (National Organization for Women)*]
THenF.......... Freed-Hardeman College, Loden-Daniel Library, Henderson, TN [*Library symbol*] [*Library of Congress*] (LCLS)
THEO........... Theology
THEO........... Theophylline [*Pharmacology*]
THEO........... Theoretical
Theo Am A...... Theobald's Act for the Amendment of the Law [*A publication*] (DLA)
Theobald....... Theobald on Wills [*11 eds.*] [*1876-1954*] [*A publication*] (DLA)
Theoc.......... Theocritus [*Third century BC*] [*Classical studies*] (OCD)
Theod.......... Theodotion (BJA)
Theog.......... Theogonia [*of Hesiod*] [*Classical studies*] (OCD)
THEOL.......... Theological
TheolArb....... Theologische Arbeiten [*A publication*] (BJA)
TheolM......... Master of Theology
THEOLOG........ Theology Student (DSUE)
Theol St....... Theological Studies [*A publication*] (BRI)
Theom L........ Theomonistic Licensee
Theoph......... Theophilus [*Sixth century*] [*Early Christian bishop*] (BARN)
Theoph......... Theophrastus [*Third Century BC*] [*Classical studies*] (BARN)
Theophil....... Theophilus [*Flourished, 6th century*] [*Authority cited in pre-1607 legal work*] (DSA)
Theophr........ Theophrastus [*Third century BC*] [*Classical studies*] (OCD)
Theopomp....... Theopompus Historicus [*Fourth century BC*] [*Classical studies*] (OCD)
Theo Pr & S... Theobald's Principal and Surety [*1832*] [*A publication*] (DLA)
Theo Pres Pr... Theory of Presumptive Proof [*A publication*] (DLA)
THEOR.......... Theorem (ROG)
THEOR.......... Theoretical (AAG)
THEOS.......... Theosophy
THEOS.......... They Help Each Other Spiritually [*Motto of THEOS Foundation*]
THEOS R........ Theosophical Review [*A publication*] (ROG)
Theo Wills..... Theobald on Wills [*13th ed.*] [*1971*] [*A publication*] (DLA)
THEP........... TOGA [*Tropical Ocean and Global Atmosphere*] Heat Exchange Program [*Marine science*] (OSRA)
THEP........... Topical Hazard Evaluation Program [*Toxicology*] [*Military*] (RDA)
THer........... Ladies Hermitage Association, Hermitage, TN [*Library symbol Library of Congress*] (LCLS)
THER........... Therapeutic
THER........... Therapeutic [*Range*] [*Laboratory science*] (DAVI)
THER........... Therapy (DAVI)
Ther........... Theriaca [*of Nicander*] [*Classical studies*] (OCD)
THER........... Thermometer (DAVI)
THERAP......... Therapeutic
TheraTx........ TheraTx, Inc. [*Associated Press*] (SAG)
TherD.......... Therapeutic Discovery Corp. [*Associated Press*] (SAG)
TherDiscA...... Therapeutic Discovery Corp. [*Associated Press*] (SAG)
THERE.......... [*The*] Heterogeneous Environment for Remote Execution [*Computer science*]
TherEl......... Thermo Electron Corp. [*Associated Press*] (SAG)
The Rep........ [*The*] Reporter, Phi Alpha Delta [*A publication*] (DLA)
The Rep........ [*The*] Reports, Coke's English King's Bench [*A publication*] (DLA)
Ther Ex........ Therapeutic Exercise [*Physical therapy*] (DAVI)
THERM.......... Thermal (DEN)
THERM.......... Thermometer (AAG)
THERM.......... Thermostat (DEN)
THERMA......... Transfer of Heat Reduced Magnetically

Thermat...... Thermatrix, Inc. [*Associated Press*] (SAG)
Thermed...... Thermedics, Inc. [*Associated Press*] (SAG)
THERMISTOR... Thermal Resistor
THERMO...... Thermal and Hydrodynamic Experiment Research Module in Orbit (MCD)
THERMO...... Thermodynamic Property Values Database [*Chemical Information Systems, Inc.*] [*Information service or system*] (CRD)
THERMO...... Thermostat (AAG)
thermochem... Thermochemistry (BARN)
THERMODYN... Thermodynamics (AAG)
THerP...... [*The*] Papers of Andrew Jackson, Hermitage, TN [*Library symbol Library of Congress*] (LCLS)
THERP...... Technique for Human Error Rate Prediction
TherRe...... Thermo Remediation [*Associated Press*] (SAG)
THES...... Theses of Economics and Business in Finland [*Helsinki School of Economics Library*] [*Information service or system*] (CRD)
Thes...... Theseus [*of Plutarch*] [*Classical studies*] (OCD)
THES...... Thesis (ADA)
Thes...... Thessalonians [*New Testament book*]
THES...... Times Higher Education Supplement (AIE)
THESIS...... [*The*] Honeywell Engineering Status Information System (SAA)
THESLA...... Tennessee Health Science Library Association [*Library network*]
Thesm...... Thesmophoriazusae [*of Aristophanes*] [*Classical studies*] (OCD)
Thess...... Thessalonians [*New Testament book*]
Thess...... Thessaly [*District of both ancient and modern Greece*] (BARN)
THETA...... [*The*] Handicapped and Elderly Travelers Association [*Defunct*] (EA)
THETA...... Teenage Health Education Teaching Assistants [*National Foundation for the Prevention of Oral Disease*]
THETA...... Tunneling Hot-Electron Transfer Amplifier [*Semiconductor technology*]
THEUS...... Theoretical Earth Utilization System (PDAA)
ThExNF...... Theologische Existenz Heute. Neue Folge [*A publication*] (BJA)
THF...... Freelance Research Service, Houston, TX [*OCLC symbol*] (OCLC)
THF...... Target Height Finding (MCD)
THF...... Tetrahydrocortisol [*Endocrinology*] (DAVI)
THF...... Tetrahydro F [*Also, called tetrahydrocortisone*] [*Endocrinology*] (DAVI)
THF...... Tetrahydrofluorenone [*Organic chemistry*]
THF...... Tetrahydrofolate [*Biochemistry*]
THF...... Tetrahydrofolic Acid [*Also, THFA*] [*Organic chemistry*]
THF...... Tetrahydrofuran [*Organic chemistry*]
THF...... Thermal Hysteresis Factor
THF...... Thymic Humoral Factor [*Endocrinology*]
THF...... Thymic Hypocalcemic Factor [*Biochemistry*]
THF...... Tian Hua Fen [*Chinese herbal medicine*]
THF...... Tremendously High Frequency [*Telecommunications*] (TEL)
THF...... Trust Houses Forte Ltd. [*Hotel empire*]
THFA...... Tetrahydrofolic Acid [*Biochemistry*]
THFA...... Tetrahydrofurfuryl Alcohol [*Organic chemistry*]
THFA...... Thermal Hartree-Fock Approximation (PDAA)
THFA...... Three-Conductor, Heat and Flame Resistant, Armor Cable
THFC...... Troy Hess Fan Club (EA)
THFF...... First Financial Corp. [*NASDAQ symbol*] (SAG)
THFF...... First Finl Corp. Ind [*NASDAQ symbol*] (TTSB)
THFM...... Therefrom [*Legal term British*]
THFOR...... Therefor [*Legal term British*] (ROG)
THFR...... Three-Conductor, Heat and Flame Resistant, Radio Cable
THFROM...... Therefrom [*Legal term British*] (ROG)
THG...... Biloela [*Australia Airport symbol*]
THG...... Thangool [*Queensland*] [*Airport symbol*] (AD)
THG...... Third-Harmonic Generation [*Physics*]
THG...... Thomson, GA [*Location identifier FAA*] (FAAL)
THG...... Thurston Aviation Ltd. [*British ICAO designator*] (FAAC)
Thg...... Thyroglobulin [*Also, TG*] [*Endocrinology*]
THGA...... Thread Gauge
THGA...... Trihydroxyglutamic Acid [*Organic chemistry*]
THGA...... Trihydroxyglutaric Acid [*Organic chemistry*]
THGAS...... Tasmanian Hospitality Group Apprenticeship Scheme [*Australia*]
TH GAZ...... Therapeutic Gazette [*Philadelphia*] [*A publication*] (ROG)
THGG...... Transportable Horizontal Gravity Gradiometer
THHF...... Tetrahydrohomofolate [*Organic chemistry*]
ThHK...... Theologischer Hand-Kommentar zum Neuen Testament [*A publication*] (BJA)
THHN...... Thermoplastic, Heat-Resistant, High-Temperature, Nylon-Jacketed [*Electric cable*]
THHP...... Target Health Hazard Program [*Occupational Safety and Health Administration*]
THI...... Telehop, Inc. [*Fresno, CA*] [*Telecommunications*] (TSSD)
THI...... Temperature-Humidity Index
THi...... Tennessee Historical Society, Nashville, TN [*Library symbol Library of Congress*] (LCLS)
THI...... Terre Haute [*Indiana*] [*Seismograph station code, US Geological Survey*] (SEIS)
THI...... Texas Heart Institute [*University of Texas*] [*Research center*] (RCD)
THI...... Theodor Herzl Institute (EA)
THI...... Thermo Instrument Sys [*AMEX symbol*] (TTSB)
THI...... Thermo Instrument Systems, Inc. [*AMEX symbol*] (SPSG)
THI...... Thios Resources, Inc. [*Vancouver Stock Exchange symbol*]
THI...... Time Handed In [*Navy*]
THI...... Total Height Index (OA)
THI...... Transient Hypogammaglobinemia of Infancy [*Immunology*] (DAVI)
THI...... Travelers Health Institute [*Later, ITHI*]
THI...... Trihydroxyindol [*Organic chemistry*]
Thia...... Theologia [*Theology*] [*Latin*] (BARN)
THIA...... Thiamylal [*An anesthetic*] (DAVI)
THIEF...... [*The*] Human-Initiated Equipment Failures
THilfgr...... Tommy Hilfiger Sportwear, Inc. [*Associated Press*] (SAG)
THINGS...... Totally Hilarious Incredibly Neat Games of Skill [*Milton-Bradley product*]
ThinkNw...... Think New Ideas, Inc. [*Associated Press*] (SAG)
THIO...... Thiopental [*An anesthetic*]
Thiokl...... Thiokol Corp. [*Associated Press*] (SAG)
Thio-T...... Triethylenethiophosphoramide [*Also, ThioTepa, TSPA*] [*Antineoplastic drug*] (DAVI)
THioTEPA.... Triethylenethiophosphoramide [*Also, TSPA*] [*Antineoplastic drug*]
THIP...... Tetrahydroisooxazolopyridineol [*Organic chemistry*]
THIQ...... Tetrahydraisoquinolon (DAVI)
THIR...... Temperature-Humidity Infrared Radiometer
THIR...... Third Financial [*NASDAQ symbol*] (TTSB)
THIR...... Third Financial Corp. [*NASDAQ symbol*] (SAG)
TH-IR...... Tyrosine Hydroxylase-Immunoreactivity [*Physiology*]
THIRA...... Thorium High-Temperature Reactor Association
THIS...... [*The*] Hospitality and Information Service [*For diplomatic residents and families in Washington, DC*]
THIS...... Terrace Holdings [*NASDAQ symbol*] (TTSB)
THIS...... Terrace Holdings, Inc. [*NASDAQ symbol*] (SAG)
THIS...... Tobacco and Health Information Services (NITA)
THISW...... Terrace Holdings Wrrt [*NASDAQ symbol*] (TTSB)
THJ...... Laurel, MS [*Location identifier FAA*] (FAAL)
THJ...... Theodore [*Queensland*] [*Airport symbol*] (AD)
THJ...... Thermal Joining
THK...... Taiheiyo Hoso Kyokai [*Pacific Broadcasting Association*] [*Japan*] (EAIO)
THK...... Thackeray Corp. [*NYSE symbol*] (SPSG)
THK...... Thakhek [*Laos*] [*Airport symbol*] (AD)
THK...... Thick [*or Thickness*] (AAG)
THKF...... Thick Film (MSA)
THKNS...... Thickness
THKR...... Thicker (MSA)
ThkTools...... Thinking Tools, Inc. [*Associated Press*] (SAG)
THL...... Air Thanet [*British ICAO designator*] (FAAC)
Th L...... Licentiate in Theology
THL...... Tachilek [*Myanmar*] [*Airport symbol*] (OAG)
THL...... Tally-Ho Explorations Ltd. [*Vancouver Stock Exchange symbol*]
'tHL...... 'T Heiling Land [*Nijmegen*] [*A publication*] (BJA)
THL...... Thermoluminescence [*Also, TL*]
THL...... Thule [*Denmark*] [*Geomagnetic observatory code*]
THL...... Transhybrid Loss [*Telecommunications*] (TEL)
THL...... Tuned Hybrid Lattice
THL...... University of Houston, Law Library, Main, Houston, TX [*OCLC symbol*] (OCLC)
ThlBer...... Theologischer Literaturbericht [*A publication*] (BJA)
THLD...... Threshold
THLEN...... Thorn Length [*Botany*]
THLR...... Thaler [*Numismatics*]
THLRA...... Taft-Hartley Labor Relations Act (OICC)
THLS...... Turret Head Limit Switch
ThM...... Master of Theology (GAGS)
THM...... Tapia House Movement [*Trinidad and Tobago*] [*Political party*] (PPW)
Th M...... Theologiae Magister [*Master of Theology*]
THM...... Therm (MSA)
THM...... Thermwood Corp. [*AMEX symbol*] (SPSG)
THM...... Thompson Falls, MT [*Location identifier FAA*] (FAAL)
THM...... Thomson Newspapers Ltd. [*Toronto Stock Exchange symbol*]
THM...... Total Heme Mass [*Medicine*] (MAE)
THM...... Traveling Heater Method
THM...... Trihalomethane [*Organic chemistry*]
THM...... TRIS, HEPES, Mannitol [*A buffer*]
THM...... Trotting Horse Museum (EA)
THM...... Turbo Hydramatic [*Automotive engineering*]
THM...... University of Tennessee at Martin, Martin, TN [*OCLC symbol*] (OCLC)
THMA...... Trailer Hitch Manufacturers Association (EA)
ThmBet...... Thomas & Betts Corp. [*Associated Press*] (SAG)
ThmFib...... Thermo Fibertek, Inc. [*Associated Press*] (SAG)
THMFP...... Trihalomethane Formation Potential [*Environmental chemistry*]
THMF-TS-TGSE... Teachers Have More Fun - They Should - They Get Stewed Enough [*Slogan*] [*Bowdlerized version*]
ThmoCrd...... Thermo Cardiosystems, Inc. [*Associated Press*] (SAG)
Thmolse...... Thermolase Corp. [*Associated Press*] (SAG)
ThmoM...... Thermo-Mizer Environmental Corp. [*Associated Press*] (SAG)
ThmoMz...... Thermo-Mizer Environmental Corp. [*Associated Press*] (SAG)
ThmoOp...... Thermo Opportunity Fund, Inc. [*Associated Press*] (SAG)
THMOV...... Thistle Mottle Virus [*Plant pathology*]
THMP...... Tetrahydromethanopterin [*Biochemistry*]
THMP...... Thermal Industries [*NASDAQ symbol*] (TTSB)
THMP...... Thermal Industries, Inc. [*NASDAQ symbol*] (NQ)
ThmPBE...... Thompson PBE, Inc. [*Associated Press*] (SAG)
Thmqst...... Thermoquest Corp. [*Associated Press*] (SAG)
THMS...... Thermistor [*Electronics*]
Thmsn...... Thomson CSF SA [*Associated Press*] (SAG)
THMT...... Tactical High-Mobility Terminal (DOMA)
THMTG...... Target Holding Mechanism, Tank Gunnery
THMZ...... Thermo-Mizer Environmental [*NASDAQ symbol*] (TTSB)
THMZ...... Thermo-Mizer Environmental Corp. [*NASDAQ symbol*] (SAG)
THMZ...... Three Hundred Mile Zone
THMZW...... Thermo-Mizer Env Wrrt [*NASDAQ symbol*] (TTSB)
THN...... Athens Air [*Greece*] [*ICAO designator*] (FAAC)
THN...... Thermo Remediation [*AMEX symbol*] (SPSG)

THN .... Trihydroxynaphthalene [*Organic chemistry*]
THN .... Trollhattan [*Sweden*] [*Airport symbol*] (OAG)
THNG .... Thing
THNK .... Think New Ideas, Inc. [*NASDAQ symbol*] (SAG)
THNR .... Thinner [*Freight*]
THNR T .... Thinner Than [*Freight*]
THO .... Thogoto Virus [*Virology*]
Tho .... Thomas Aquinas [*Deceased, 1274*] [*Authority cited in pre-1607 legal work*] (DSA)
Tho .... Thomas de Piperata [*Flourished, 1268-72*] [*Authority cited in pre-1607 legal work*] (DSA)
Tho .... Thomas Mieres [*Flourished, 1429-39*] [*Authority cited in pre-1607 legal work*] (DSA)
THO .... Thomsonite [*A zeolite*]
THO .... Thorco Resources, Inc. [*Toronto Stock Exchange symbol*]
THO .... Thor Industries [*NYSE symbol*] (TTSB)
THO .... Thor Industries, Inc. [*NYSE symbol*] (SPSG)
THO .... Thorshofn [*Iceland*] [*Airport symbol*] (OAG)
THO .... Though
THO .... Thursdays Only [*British railroad term*]
THO .... Titrated Water [*Laboratory science*] (DAVI)
THO .... Tonto Hills Observatory [*Arizona*] [*Seismograph station code, US Geological Survey Closed*] (SEIS)
THO .... Trans-Hudson Orogen [*Geology*]
THO .... Tritium-Labeled Water [*Laboratory Science*] (DAVI)
ThO_2 .... Thorium Dioxide (DAVI)
Tho de For... Thomas de Formaginis [*Flourished, 1331-38*] [*Authority cited in pre-1607 legal work*] (DSA)
Tho de Lya... Thomas de Elya [*Authority cited in pre-1607 legal work*] (DSA)
THOF .... Thereof
THOF .... Triple Conductor, Heat, Oil, and Flame Resistant (IAA)
Tho For .... Thomas de Formaginis [*Flourished, 1331-38*] [*Authority cited in pre-1607 legal work*] (DSA)
Tho Form ..... Thomas de Formaginis [*Flourished, 1331-38*] (DSA)
Tho Foroli.... Thomas Foroliviensis [*Authority cited in pre-1607 legal work*] (DSA)
Tho Grama... Thomas Grammaticus [*Flourished, 16th century*] [*Authority cited in pre-1607 legal work*] (DSA)
THOLD .... Threshold (NASA)
Thom .... Thomas' Reports [*1 Wyoming*] [*A publication*] (DLA)
THOM .... Thompson PBE [*NASDAQ symbol*] (TTSB)
THOM .... Thompson PBE, Inc. [*NASDAQ symbol*] (SAG)
Thom .... Thomson's Nova Scotia Reports [*A publication*] (DLA)
Thom & Fr... Thomas and Franklin's Chancery Reports [*1 Maryland*] [*A publication*] (DLA)
Thomas .... Thomas' Reports [*1 Wyoming*] [*A publication*] (DLA)
ThomasG ..... Thomas Group, Inc. [*Associated Press*] (SAG)
Thomas Mortg... Thomas on Mortgages [*A publication*] (DLA)
Thomas Negl... Thomas on Negligence [*A publication*] (DLA)
Thom B & N... Thomson on Bills and Notes [*A publication*] (DLA)
Thom BBS ... Thompson. Benefit Building Societies [*A publication*] (ILCA)
Thom Bills... Thomson on Bills and Notes [*A publication*] (DLA)
Thom Camp... Thomas Campegius [*Deceased, 1564*] [*Authority cited in pre-1607 legal work*] (DSA)
THOMCAT .... Thomas Register Catalog File [*A publication*]
Thom Co Lit... Thomas' Edition of Coke upon Littleton [*A publication*] (DLA)
Thom Co Litt... Thomas' Edition of Coke upon Littleton [*A publication*] (DLA)
Thom Const L... Thomas' Leading Cases on Constitutional Law [*A publication*] (DLA)
Thom Cooley Law... Thomas M. Cooley Law School (GAGS)
Thom Dec.... Thomson's Nova Scotia Reports [*1834-52*] [*A publication*] (DLA)
ThomIn .... Thomas Industries, Inc. [*Associated Press*] (SAG)
THOMIS .... Total Hospital Operating and Medical Information System
Thom Jefferson U... Thomas Jefferson University (GAGS)
Thom LC ...... Thomas' Leading Cases on Constitutional Law [*A publication*] (DLA)
ThomMA ...... Thomaston Mills Class B [*Associated Press*] (SAG)
ThomMB ...... Thomaston Mills Class B [*Associated Press*] (SAG)
Thom Mort... Thomas on Mortgages [*A publication*] (DLA)
Thom N Sc... Thomson's Nova Scotia Reports [*1834-51, 1856-59*] [*Canada*] [*A publication*] (DLA)
THOMOTROL... Thyratron Motor Control [*Electronics*] (IAA)
Thomp & C... Thompson and Cook's New York Supreme Court Reports [*A publication*] (DLA)
Thomp & Cook... Thompson and Cook's New York Supreme Court Reports [*A publication*] (DLA)
Thomp & M Jur... Thompson and Merriam on Juries [*A publication*] (DLA)
Thomp & St... Thompson and Steger's Code [*Tennessee*] [*A publication*] (DLA)
Thomp & St Code... Thompson and Steger's Code [*Tennessee*] [*A publication*] (DLA)
Thomp Cal... Thompson's Reports [*39, 40 California*] [*A publication*] (DLA)
Thomp Car... Thompson on Carriers [*A publication*] (DLA)
Thomp Cas... Thompson's Cases [*Tennessee*] [*A publication*] (DLA)
Thomp Ch Jur... Thompson on Charging the Jury [*A publication*] (DLA)
Thomp Cit.... Thompson's Ohio Citations [*A publication*] (DLA)
Thomp Corp... Thompson's Commentaries on Law of Private Corporations [*A publication*] (DLA)
Thomp Dig... Thompson's Digest of Laws [*Florida*] [*A publication*] (DLA)
Thomp Ent... Thompson's Entries [*A publication*] (DLA)
Thomp Farm... Thompson's Law of the Farm [*A publication*] (DLA)
Thomp H & Ex... Thompson on Homesteads and Exemptions [*A publication*] (DLA)
Thomp High... Thompson on the Law of Highways [*A publication*] (DLA)
Thomp Liab Off... Thompson on Liability of Officers of Corporations [*A publication*] (DLA)
Thomp Liab St... Thompson on Liability of Stockholders [*A publication*] (DLA)
Thomp Liab Stockh... Thompson on Liability of Stockholders [*A publication*] (DLA)
Thomp NB Cas... Thompson's National Bank Cases [*A publication*] (DLA)
Thomp Neg... Thompson's Cases on Negligence [*A publication*] (DLA)
Thomp Pat... Thompson on Patent Laws of All Countries [*13th ed.*] [*1905*] [*A publication*] (DLA)
Thomp Prov Rem... Thompson's Provisional Remedies [*A publication*] (DLA)
Thomps Cas... Thompson's Tennessee Cases [*A publication*] (DLA)
Thompson... Thompson's Reports [*39, 40 California*] [*A publication*] (DLA)
Thompson & C... Thompson and Cook's New York Supreme Court Reports [*A publication*] (DLA)
Thompson's Fla Dig... Thompson's Digest of Laws [*Florida*] [*A publication*] (DLA)
Thompson Unrep (PA)... Thompson's Unreported Cases (Pennsylvania) [*A publication*] (DLA)
Thomp Tenn Cas... Thompson's Unreported Tennessee Cases [*A publication*] (DLA)
Thomp Trials... Thompson on Trials [*A publication*] (DLA)
Thom Rep.... Thomson's Nova Scotia Reports [*A publication*] (DLA)
Thom Sc Acts... Thomson's Scotch Acts [*A publication*] (DLA)
Thom Sel Dec... Thomson's Nova Scotia Select Decisions [*A publication*] (DLA)
Thoms Jud Fac... Thoms' Judicial Factors [*A publication*] (DLA)
Thom St Sum... Thomas' Leading Statutes Summarized [*A publication*] (DLA)
Thom Un Jur... Thomas' Universal Jurisprudence [*2nd ed.*] [*1829*] [*A publication*] (DLA)
THON .... Thereon [*Legal term British*]
Tho Parpal... Thomas Parpalea [*Flourished, 16th century*] [*Authority cited in pre-1607 legal work*] (DSA)
THOPS .... Tape-Handling Operational System [*Computer science*] (IEEE)
THOR .... Tandy [*Corp.*] High-Performance Optical Recording System [*Dye-polymer technology*] (PCM)
THOR .... Tape-Handling Optional Routines [*Honeywell, Inc.*]
THOR .... Thesaurus-Oriented Retrieval [*Information service or system*]
THOR .... Thoracentesis [*Fluid*] [*Medicine*] (DAVI)
THOR .... Thoratec Labs Corp. [*NASDAQ symbol*] (SAG)
Thor .... Thorax [*Anatomy*] (DAVI)
Thor .... Thorington's Reports [*107 Alabama*] [*A publication*] (DLA)
THOR .... Thought Organizer [*Computer program produced by Fastware, Inc.*]
THOR .... Trace Hierarchy of Requirements [*Science Applications International Corp.*]
THOR .... Transistorized High-Speed Operations Recorder
THOR .... Tsing Hua Open-Pool Reactor [*Formosa*]
THORAC .... Thoraci [*To the Throat*] [*Pharmacy*]
THORAD ...... Thor-Agena D [*Rocket*] [*NASA*]
THORAD ...... Transistorized High-Speed Operations Recorder Advanced (IAA)
Thoratc .... Thoratec Labs Corp. [*Associated Press*] (SAG)
Thor Bank .... Thorborn on Bankers' Law [*A publication*] (DLA)
THOREX .... Thorium Extraction (GAAI)
ThorInd .... Thor Industries, Inc. [*Associated Press*] (SAG)
Thorn .... Thornton's Notes of Ecclesiastical and Maritime Cases [*1841-50*] [*A publication*] (DLA)
THORNB ...... Thornbury [*England*]
Thornbg .... Thornburg Mortgage Asset Corp. [*Associated Press*] (SAG)
Thorn Conv... Thornton's Conveyancing [*A publication*] (DLA)
Thornt & Bl Bldg & Loan Ass'ns... Thornton and Blackledge's Law Relating to Building and Loan Associations [*A publication*] (DLA)
Thornton Gifts... Thornton on Gifts and Advancements [*A publication*] (DLA)
Thoro .... Thoroughfare [*Maps and charts*]
THORP .... Thermal Oxide Reprocessing Plant [*Nuclear energy*]
Thorpe .... Thorpe's Annual Reports [*52 Louisiana*] [*A publication*] (DLA)
Thorpe Anc L... Thorpe's Ancient Laws of England [*A publication*] (DLA)
THORS .... Thermal-Hydraulic Out-of-Reactor Safety Facility [*Department of Energy*]
Thos Co Lit... Thomas' Edition of Coke upon Littleton [*A publication*] (DLA)
THOT .... Thought
THOT .... Transportation Horoscope of Trade Goods (PDAA)
THOU .... Thousand (AFM)
THOUS .... Thousand (NASA)
THP .... [*The*] Hunger Project (EA)
THP .... Take-Home Pay (MHDB)
THP .... Terminal Handling Processor
THP .... Terminal Holding Power [*Advertising*] (IIA)
THP .... Tetrahydropalmatine [*Organic chemistry*]
THP .... Tetrahydropapaveroline [*Biochemistry*]
thp .... Tetrahydropyranyl [*Organic chemistry*]
THP .... Tetrakis(hydroxymethyl)phosphonium [*Organic chemistry*]
THP .... Thermal Hysteresis Proteins [*Biochemistry*]
THP .... Thermopolis, WY [*Location identifier FAA*] (FAAL)
THP .... Thermo Power [*AMEX symbol*] (TTSB)
THP .... Thermo Power Corp. [*Formerly, Tecogen, Inc.*] [*AMEX symbol*] (SPSG)
THP .... Thousands Position (IAA)
THP .... Through Hole Probe
THP .... Through the Hole Plating [*Electronics*] (EECA)
THP .... Thrust Horsepower [*Jet engines*]
THP .... Total Hydroxyproline [*Clinical chemistry*] (MAE)
THP .... Transmitter Holding Register (MHDB)
THP .... Trihexphenidyl Hydrochloride [*An anti-cholinergic*] (DAVI)
THP .... Trihydroxypropane [*Organic chemistry*]
THP .... (Trimethylhydrazinium) Propionate [*Biochemistry*]
THP .... Tris(hydroxymethyl)phosphine [*Organic chemistry*]
THPA .... Tetrahydrophthalic Anhydride [*Organic chemistry*]
THPA .... Tetrahydropteric Acid [*Organic chemistry*] (MAE)
THPC .... Tetrakis(hydroxymethyl)phosphonium Chloride [*Flame retardant*]
Th PC .... Thick Paper Copy (DGA)
THPDX .... Tetrahydropyranyldoxorubicin [*Antineoplastic drug*]
THPF .... Total Hepatic Plasma Flow [*Physiology*]
THPFB .... Treated Hard-Pressed Fiberboard [*Technical drawings*]
THPI .... Tetrahydrophthalimide [*Organic chemistry*]

THPO .... Tris(hydroxymethyl)phosphine Oxide [*Organic chemistry*]
ThPract .... Theologie en Practijk [*Rotterdam*] [*A publication*] (BJA)
ThPrM .... Theologisch-Praktische Monatsschrift [*A publication*] (BJA)
THPS .... Tetrakis(hydroxymethyl)phosphonium Sulfate [*Flame retardant*] [*Organic chemistry*]
THQ .... Telecommunications Headquarters (NITA)
THQ .... Tetrahydroxyquinone [*Chemical indicator*]
THQ .... Theater Headquarters [*Military*]
THQ .... THQ, Inc. [*Associated Press*] (SAG)
THQ .... Troop Headquarters
THR .... Target Heart Rate [*Exercise*] (INF)
THR .... Tehran [*Iran*] [*Airport symbol*] (OAG)
THR .... Their (ROG)
THR .... Their Royal Highnesses [*British*] (ROG)
THR .... There (ROG)
THR .... Three Rivers Financial Corp. [*AMEX symbol*] (SAG)
THR .... Three Rivers Finl [*AMEX symbol*] (TTSB)
Thr .... Threni (BJA)
Thr .... Threonine [*Also, T*] [*An amino acid*]
thr .... Threonine [*An amino acid*] (DOG)
THR .... Threshold
Thr .... Threshold Lights [*Aviation*] (DA)
THR .... Through (ADA)
THR .... Throughput
THR .... Throughput Rate
THR .... Thrust (AAG)
THR .... Total Heat Rejection (IAA)
THR .... Total Hip Replacement [*Medicine*]
THR .... Total Hydrocarbon Reforming [*Hydrogen production*]
THR .... Transmittal Header Record [*Computer science*]
THR .... Transmitter Holding Register
THR .... Turbine Heat Rate (DNAB)
THRABTS .... Thereabouts [*Legal term British*] (ROG)
THRAPP .... Tasmanian Historical Research Association. Papers and Proceedings [*A publication*]
THRAR .... Thereafter [*Legal term British*] (ROG)
THRAT .... Thereat [*Legal term British*] (ROG)
THRB .... Theodore Roosevelt Birthplace National Historic Site
THR-CT .... Thrombin Control [*Hematology*] (DAVI)
THRD .... TF Financial [*NASDAQ symbol*] (TTSB)
THRD .... TF Financial Corp. [*NASDAQ symbol*] (SAG)
THRD .... Thread
thrd .... Thread (VRA)
ThrD .... Three D Departments, Inc. [*Associated Press*] (SAG)
ThrdFn .... Third Financial Corp. [*Associated Press*] (SAG)
THREAD .... Three-Dimensional Reconstruction and Display (MHDB)
ThreeFS .... Three Five Systems Co. [*Associated Press*] (SAG)
THRES .... Threshold (IAA)
THRF .... Thyrotrophic Hormone-Releasing Factor [*Endocrinology*]
ThrFibr .... Thermo Fibergen, Inc. [*Associated Press*] (SAG)
THRFT .... Thrift
THRFTR .... Thereafter (FAAC)
THRFTY .... Thrifty
Thrgen .... Theragenics Corp. [*Associated Press*] (SAG)
Thr Hist Tr ... Thrupp's Historical Law Tracts [*A publication*] (DLA)
THR HOLD ... Throttle Hold (GAVI)
THRIC .... Treasure Hunter Research and Information Center (EA)
THRILLO .... Transfer to Higher Rated Job in Lieu of Layoff (MCD)
THRIN .... Therein
THRINAR .... Thereinafter [*Legal term British*] (ROG)
THRINBEFE ... Thereinbefore [*Legal term British*] (ROG)
Thring J St Com ... Thring on Joint Stock Companies [*5th ed.*] [*1889*] [*A publication*] (DLA)
Thring LD .... Thring on the Land Drainage Act [*1862*] [*A publication*] (DLA)
ThrInst .... Thermo Instrument Systems, Inc. [*Associated Press*] (SAG)
THRIP .... Thriplow [*England*]
THRIVE .... Tower Hamlets Reading Initiative via Exploration [*British*] (AIE)
THRM .... Thermal (AAG)
Thrmady .... Thermadyne Holdings Corp. [*Associated Press*] (SAG)
ThrmBio .... Thermo Bioanalysis Corp. [*Associated Press*] (SAG)
ThrmIn .... Thermal Industries, Inc. [*Associated Press*] (SAG)
Thrmogn .... Thermogenesis Corp. [*Associated Press*] (SAG)
Thrmolse .... Thermolase Corp. [*Associated Press*] (SAG)
Thrmotx .... Thermotrex Corp. [*Associated Press*] (SAG)
ThrmP .... Thermo Process Systems, Inc. [*Associated Press*] (SAG)
ThrmPw .... Thermo Power Corp. [*Associated Press*] (SAG)
ThrmRe .... Thermo Remediation [*Associated Press*] (SAG)
THRMST .... Thermostat
THRMSTC .... Thermostatic (MSA)
ThrmTch .... Thermo Tech Technologies [*Associated Press*] (SAG)
ThrmTer .... Thermo Terratech [*Associated Press*] (SAG)
Thrmtx .... Thermotrex Corp. [*Associated Press*] (SAG)
Thrmwd .... Thermwood Corp. [*Associated Press*] (SAG)
ThrnAV .... Thorn Apple Valley, Inc. [*Associated Press*] (SAG)
THRO .... Theodore Roosevelt National Memorial Park
THRO .... Through
THRO .... Throw the Hypocritical Rascals Out [*An association*]
ThroBL .... Through Bill of Lading [*Shipping*]
THROE .... Tessaral Harmonic Resonance of Orbital Elements (PDAA)
THROF .... Thereof
THROM .... Thrombosis (AAMN)
THROMB .... Thrombin Time Tritium [*Hematology*] (DAVI)
thromb .... Thrombosis (CPH)
thrombo .... Thrombophlebitis [*Medicine*] (DAVI)
thrombo .... Thrombosis [*Medicine*] (BARN)
THRON .... Thereon [*Legal term British*] (ROG)
Throop Pub Off ... Throop's Treatise on Public Officers [*A publication*] (DLA)
ThrOptk .... Thermo Optek Corp. [*Associated Press*] (SAG)
THROT .... Throttle (AAG)
THROUGHWAY ... Throughway [*Commonly used*] (OPSA)
THROUT .... Thereout [*Legal term British*] (ROG)
THRP .... Therapist
THRPST .... Therapist
THRPY .... Therapy
THRPY .... Therapy
ThrRvF .... Three Rivers Financial Corp. [*Associated Press*] (SAG)
ThrSent .... Thermo Sentron, Inc. [*Associated Press*] (SAG)
THRSHL .... Thrust Shell
ThrSpec .... ThermoSpectra Corp. [*Associated Press*] (SAG)
ThrSpect .... Thermo Spectra Corp. [*Associated Press*] (SAG)
THRSUM .... Threat Summary Message (MCD)
THRT .... TheraTech, Inc. [*NASDAQ symbol*] (SAG)
THRT .... Threat [*or Threatening*] [*FBI standardized term*]
THRT .... Throat
ThrTch .... TheraTech, Inc. [*Associated Press*] (SAG)
THRU .... Through (AAG)
THRU .... Toxic Hazards Research Unit [*NASA*] (KSC)
THRUPON .... Thereupon [*Legal term British*] (ROG)
THRUSH .... Technological Hierarchy for the Removal of Undesirables and the Subjugation of Humanity [*Fictitious organization in "The Man from UNCLE" television series*]
Thrust .... Thrustmaster, Inc. [*Associated Press*] (SAG)
THRUST .... Tsunami Hazard Reduction Using Systems Technology [*Marine science*] (OSRA)
THRUST .... Tsunami Hazard Reduction Using System Technology (USDC)
Thr Verb Agr ... Throop on the Validity of Verbal Agreements [*A publication*] (DLA)
ThrVolt .... Thermo Voltek Corp. [*Associated Press*] (SAG)
THRWY .... Thruway
THRX .... Theragenics Corp. [*NASDAQ symbol*] (NQ)
thry .... Theory (VRA)
THS .... [*The*] Hydrographic Society [*Dagenham, Essex, England*] (EAIO)
THS .... St. Thomas, PA [*Location identifier FAA*] (FAAL)
THS .... Tactical Hybrid Switch (LAIN)
THS .... Target Homing System
THS .... Technical High School (ADA)
THS .... Tenement House Smell [*British*] (ROG)
THS .... Territorial Highway System [*FHWA*] (TAG)
THS Tetrahydro-11-Deoxycortisol
THS .... Tetrahydro-Compound S [*Organic chemistry*] (MAE)
THS .... Textile History Society [*Defunct*] (EA)
THS .... Theatre Historical Society (EA)
THS .... Theatre History Studies [*A publication*] (BRI)
THS .... ThermoSpectra Corp. [*AMEX symbol*] (SAG)
THS .... Thermostat Switch
THS .... Thomas Hardy Society (EAIO)
THS .... Three-Stage Least Squares [*Econometrics*]
ThS .... Thymidylate Synthase [*Also, TS*] [*An enzyme*]
THS .... Titanic Historical Society (EA)
THS .... Tourist Hospitality Service [*British*]
THS .... Transmission Hydraulic Switch [*Automotive engineering*]
THS .... Transparent Hull Submersible [*Navy*]
THS .... Transports Aeros Hispanos SA [*Spain ICAO designator*] (FAAC)
THS .... Trimmable Horizontal Stabilizer [*Aviation*]
THS .... Tube Heating Supply
THSA .... Thomas Hardy Society of America [*Defunct*] (EA)
THSA .... Traveling Hat Salesmen's Association [*Defunct*] (EA)
THSAM .... Topographie Historique de la Syrie Antique et Medievale [*A publication*] (BJA)
THSC .... Totipotent Hematopoietic Stem Cell [*Hematology*] (MAE)
THSG .... Transactions. Historical Society of Ghana [*A publication*]
THSP .... Temporary-Help Supplier Personnel
THSP .... Thermal Spray [*Also, TS*] [*Coating technology*]
ThSzemle .... Theologiai Szemle [*Budapest*] [*A publication*] (BJA)
THT .... Papeete [*Orstom*] [*Society Islands*] [*Seismograph station code, US Geological Survey*] (SEIS)
THT .... Teacher of Hydrotherapy [*British*]
THT .... Tetrahydrothiophene [*Organic chemistry*]
Tht .... Theaetetus [*of Plato*] [*Classical studies*] (OCD)
THT .... Thrust Resources, Inc. [*Vancouver Stock Exchange symbol*]
THT .... THT, Inc. [*Associated Press*] (SAG)
THT .... Token-Holding Time [*Computer science*]
THT .... Total Homing Time
THT .... Turk Hava Tasimaciligi [*Turkish Air Transport*] [*ICAO designator*] (FAAC)
THTA .... Thread Tap
THTD .... Too Hard to Do (CAAL)
THTF .... Thermal Hydraulic Test Facility [*Nuclear energy*] (NRCH)
THTH .... Too Hot to Handle
THTMS .... Tetramethylthiuram Monosulfide [*Also, TMTD*] [*Organic chemistry*]
THTO .... Thereto
THTO .... Threading Tool (AAG)
THTR .... Theater (AFM)
THTR .... Theater
thtr .... Theatre (VRA)
THTR .... Thorium High-Temperature Reactor [*Nuclear energy*]
THTRA .... Thorium High Temperature Reactor Association (IAA)
THTX .... TheraTx, Inc. [*NASDAQ symbol*] (SAG)
THU .... Tetrhydrouridine [*Biochemistry*]
THU .... Thule [*Greenland*] [*Seismograph station code, US Geological Survey Closed*] (SEIS)

THU Thunder Explorations [*Vancouver Stock Exchange symbol*]
THU Thursday (AFM)
THU Truck Hub Unit [*Suspension*] [*Automotive engineering*]
Thuc De Thucydide [*of Dionysius Halicarnassensis*] [*Classical studies*] (OCD)
THUC Thucydides [*Greek historian, c. 460-400BC*] [*Classical studies*] (ROG)
THUD Thorium, Uranium, Deuterium
THUDD Thermal Uplink Data Display [*Computer science*]
THUMB Tiny Humans Underground Military Bureau [*Government organization in TV cartoon series "Tom of T.H.U.M.B."*]
THUMS Texaco, Humble, Union, Mobil, and Shell [*Petroleum companies*]
Thur Thursday (WGA)
THURIS [*The*] Human Role in Space [*Study*] (SSD)
Thur Mar L Rev Thurgood Marshall Law Review [*A publication*] (DLA)
THURS Thursday
Thurs Thursday (ODBW)
THURST Thurstable [*England*]
THUT Thyroid Hormone Uptake Test [*Clinical chemistry*]
THV Terminal Homing Vehicle
THV Thoracic Vertebra [*Medicine*]
THV Tool Handling Vehicle (MCD)
THV Total Heart Volume [*Physiology*]
THV York, PA [*Location identifier FAA*] (FAAL)
THW Tag Heuer International SA [*NYSE symbol*] (SAG)
ThW Theologisches Woerterbuch zum Neuen Testament [*A publication*] (BJA)
THW Therewith [*Legal term British*] (ROG)
THW Thermoplastic, Heat-Resistant, Wet-Location [*Electric cable*]
Thw Thwartship (DS)
THW Torsion Head Wattmeter
ThWAT Theologisches Woerterbuch zum Alten Testament [*A publication*] (BJA)
ThWB Theologisches Woerterbuch zum Neuen Testament [*A publication*] (BJA)
ThWBNT Theologisches Woerterbuch zum Neuen Testament [*A publication*] (BJA)
THWITH Therewith [*Legal term British*] (ROG)
THWM Trinity High-Water Mark
THWN Thermoplastic, Heat-Resistant, Wet-Location, Nylon-Jacketed [*Electric cable*]
ThWNT Theologisches Woerterbuch zum Neuen Testament [*A publication*] (BJA)
THWR Thrower
THWT Throwout [*Mechanical engineering*]
Thwy Thruway (BARN)
THX Houston Exploration Co. (The) [*NYSE symbol*] (SAG)
THX Thor Explorations [*Vancouver Stock Exchange symbol*]
THX Three Rivers, TX [*Location identifier FAA*] (FAAL)
THX Thyroxine [*Also, T4, Ty*] [*An amino acid Endocrinology*]
THX Tomlinson-Holman Cross-Over [*Motion picture theater sound system*]
THX Total Hypophysectomy [*Medicine*]
THY Thylungra [*Queensland*] [*Airport symbol*] (AD)
Thy Thymine [*Also, T*] [*Biochemistry*]
THY Thymocyte [*Clinical chemistry*]
THY Thyratron [*Electronics*] (IAA)
thy Thyratron (IDOE)
THY Transitional Hospitals Corp. [*NYSE symbol*] (SAG)
THY Turk Hava Yollari [*Turkish Airlines*] [*ICAO designator*] (FAAC)
THY Turk Hava Yollari AO [*Turkish Airlines, Inc.*]
THYB Tai Hei Yo Bashi [*Bridge over the Great Ocean*] (EA)
THYMOTRO Thyratron Motor Control [*Electronics*] (MCD)
THYMOTROL Thyratron Motor Control [*Electronics*]
Thym Turb Thymol Turbidity [*Clinical chemistry*] (CPH)
THYP Total Hydroxyproline [*Clinical chemistry*]
THYR Thyristor [*Electronics*]
THZ Tahoua [*Niger*] [*Airport symbol*] (OAG)
THz Terahertz
TI Table Indicator [*Computer science*]
TI Tamarind Institute (EA)
TI Tamiment Institute (EA)
TI Tape Indicator [*Computer science*] (IAA)
TI Tape Inverter
TI Target Identification
TI Target Indicator
TI Target Intelligence (MCD)
TI Tariff Item
TI Taxable Income
TI Teardown Inspection
ti Technical Indexes Ltd. [*Information service or system*] (IID)
TI Technical Information (CINC)
TI Technical Inspection [*Military*]
TI Technical Institute
TI Technical Instruction [*or Instructor*]
TI Technical Integration [*NASA*] (NASA)
TI Technical Intelligence [*Military*]
TI Technical Interchange (KSC)
TI Technology Incubator
TI Technology Insertion [*Military*] (RDA)
TI Technoogy Innovation (IAA)
TI Tehrik-i-Istiqlal [*Solidarity Party*] [*See also TIP Pakistan*] [*Political party*] (FEA)
TI Telecommunication Industry
TI Teleos Institute (EA)
TI Television Intercity [*FCC*] (NTCM)
TI Temperature Indicator
Ti Temperature of Injectate
TI Temporary Instruction [*Nuclear energy*] (NRCH)
TI Temporary Intermittent (GNE)
TI Teresian Institute (EA)
TI Terminal Ileum [*Gastroenterology*] (DAVI)
TI Terminal Interface
TI Terminal Island [*San Pedro*] [*Navy base*]
TI Termination Instruction
TI Terminator Interrupt [*Computer science*] (IAA)
TI Terrestrial Interference (WDMC)
TI Test Implicit
TI Test Index (CAAL)
TI Test Instruction (MCD)
TI Test Instrumentation
TI Texas Instruments (NITA)
TI Texas Instruments, Inc.
TI Texas International (GAVI)
TI Texas International Airlines [*ICAO designator*] (AD)
TI Textile Industry (WDAA)
TI Textile Institute [*Manchester, England*] (EAIO)
TI Thalassemia Intermedia [*Hematology*]
TI Therapeutic Index [*Medicine*] (DMAA)
TI Thermal Imaging [*Criminology*] (LAIN)
TI Think Ink [*An association*] (EA)
TI Thoracic Index [*Medicine*] (MAE)
TI Thread Institute [*Defunct*] (EA)
TI Thymidine-Labeling Index [*Biochemical analysis*]
TI Thymus Independent [*Cells*] [*Hematology*]
TI Tie In (MCD)
TI Tiferet Israel (BJA)
Ti Timaeus [*of Plato*] [*Classical studies*] (OCD)
TI Time Index
TI Time Interval (IEEE)
TI Time-to-Intercept
TI Tippers International (EA)
Ti Titanium [*Chemical element*]
TI Title [*Online database field identifier*] [*Computer science*]
TI Title Information [*Publishing*]
TI TI Travel International, Inc. [*Vancouver Stock Exchange symbol*]
Ti Titus [*New Testament book*]
TI Toastmasters International (EA)
TI Tobacco Institute (EA)
TI Together, Inc. (EA)
TI Together International/Anti-Soviet Research Center [*Defunct*] (EA)
TI Tonic Immobility [*Neurophysiology*]
TI Torpedo Instructor [*British military*] (DMA)
T/I Torque/Inertia
TI Total Immersion [*Language study*]
TI Total Inventory (DOMA)
TI Tourismo Internationale [*International Touring*] [*Italian*]
T/I TPFDD Interface
TI Track Identity
TI Track Initiator
TI Trade and Industry Index [*Information Access Corp.*] [*Information service or system*] (IID)
TI Trade International (BARN)
TI Traditional Instruction
TI Traffic Identification
TI Training Instructor
TI Training Integrator [*or Integration*] (MCD)
TI Trajectory Integration (CAAL)
TI Transaction Interpretation (MCD)
TI Transfer Impedance (IEEE)
TI Transfrigoroute International (EA)
TI Transillumination
TI Transmission Identification (NG)
TI Transportation Institute [*Camp Springs, MD*] (EA)
TI Transport Index [*Nuclear energy*] (NUCP)
TI Transverse Inlet [*Medicine*] (MAE)
TI Treasure Island [*San Francisco Bay*] [*Navy base*]
TI Treasury Instruction (ADA)
TI Trial Installation (MCD)
TI Tricuspid Incompetence [*Cardiology*] (MAE)
TI Tricuspid Insufficiency [*Cardiology*]
TI Troop Information
TI Trusteeship Institute (EA)
TI Trypsin Inhibitor [*Food technology*]
TI Tube Investments Ltd. [*British*]
Ti Tumor-inducing [*Plasmids*] [*Plant cytology*]
TI Tungsten Institute [*Defunct*] (EA)
TI Tuning Indicator (DEN)
TI Tuning Inductance (IAA)
ti Tunisia [*MARC country of publication code Library of Congress*] (LCCP)
TI Turing Institute [*British*] (IRUK)
TI Turismo Internationale [*Automobile model designation*]
TI Type Item [*Military*]
TIA [*The*] International Alliance, an Association of Executive and ProfessionalWomen [*Baltimore, MD*] (EA)
TIA [*The*] Internet Adapter [*Intermind Corp.*]
TIA Tactical Identification and Acquisition [*Navy*] (NG)
TIA Taian [*Republic of China*] [*Seismograph station code, US Geological Survey*] (SEIS)
TIA Task Item Authorization (MCD)

TIA .... Taxation Institute of Australia (EERA)
TIA .... Tax Institute of America [*Later, NTA-TIA*] (EA)
TIA .... Teacher Investigator Awards
TIA .... Telecommunications Industry Association (EA)
TIA .... Temperature Indicating Alarm [*Engineering*]
TIA .... Temporary Incapacity Allowance
TIA .... Test Interface Assembly
TIA .... Thallium Acetate
TIA .... Thanks in Advance [*Internet language*] [*Computer science*]
TIA .... Thin-Layer Immunoassay [*Analytical biochemistry*]
TIA .... Tiaprofenic Acid
TIA .... Tilapia International Association (EAIO)
TIA .... Tirana [*Albania*] [*Airport symbol*] (OAG)
TIA .... Tortilla Industry Association (EA)
TIA .... Total Inactive Aerospace Vehicle [*or Aircraft*] Authorization
TIA .... Traffic Improvement Association
TIA .... Transient Ischemic Attack [*Medicine*]
TIA .... Transimpedance Amplifier [*Instrumentation*]
TIA .... Trans International Airlines [*ICAO designator*] (FAAC)
TIA .... Transportation in America [*BTS*] (TAG)
TIA .... Transportation Intelligence Agency (AAG)
TIA .... Travel Industry Association of America (EA)
TIA .... Treaties and Other International Acts
TIA .... Trend Impact Analysis [*The Futures Group, Inc.*] [*Information service or system*] (IID)
TIA .... Trends, Indicators, and Analyses [*on the Southeast Asia war*] [*Classified Air Force document*]
TIA .... Tri-Basin Resources Ltd. [*Vancouver Stock Exchange symbol*]
TIA .... Tricot Institute of America [*Defunct*] (EA)
TIA .... Trouser Institute of America [*Absorbed by NOSA*] (EA)
TIA .... Trypsin Inhibitor Activity [*Food technology*]
TIA .... Tumor-Induced Angiogenesis [*Immunology*]
TIA .... Turbidimetric Immunoassay [*Immunology*]
TIA .... Typographers International Association (EA)
TIAA .... Task Identification and Analysis (MCD)
TIAA .... Teachers Insurance and Annuity Association [*New York, NY*] (EA)
TIAA .... Timber Importers Association of America
TIAA .... Travel Industry Association of America
TIAA-CREF ... Teachers Insurance and Annuity Association-College Retirement Equities Fund (AEE)
TIAC .... Technical Information Advisory Committee [*AEC*]
TIAC .... Technical Information Analysis Centers
TIAC .... Texas Instruments Automatic Computer
TIAC .... Tourism Industry Association of Canada
TIAC .... Travel [*later, Tourism*] Industry Association of Canada
TIACS .... TEWS [*Tactical Electronic Warfare System*] Intermediate Age Commercial System
TIAFT .... [*The*] International Association of Forensic Toxicologists [*Newmarket, Suffolk, England*] (EAIO)
TI Agree ...... Treaties and Other International Agreements of the United States of America [*A publication*] (DLA)
TIAH .... Totally Implantable Artificial Heart
TIA-IR .... Transient Ischemic Attack-Incomplete Recovery [*Cardiology*] (DAVI)
TIALD .... Thermal Imaging, Airborne LASER Designator [*Royal Air Force*] [*British*]
TIAM .... Terminal Interactive Access Method [*Computer science*] (IAA)
TI & A .... Task Identification and Analysis
TI & E .... Troop Information and Education
TIAP .... Theater Intelligence Architecture Program (DOMA)
TIARA .... Tactical Intelligence and Related Activity
TIARA .... Target Illumination and Recovery Aid
TIARA .... Telephone Installation and Requisition Application (MCD)
TIARA .... There Is a Radical Alternative [*Parliamentary slang*] [*British*] (DI)
TIAS .... Target Identification and Acquisition System
TIAS .... Team Integrated Avionic System (MHDI)
TIAS .... True Indicated Airspeed (GAVI)
TIAVSC .... [*The*] International Assets Valuation Standards Committee [*of the American Institute of Real Estate Appraisers*] [*British*] (EAIO)
TIAX .... Trans International Airlines [*Air carrier designation symbol*]
TIB .... Tasmanian Imperial Bushmen [*British military*] (DMA)
TIB .... Tax Interpretation Bulletins [*Canada*] (IID)
TIB .... Technical Information Base (MCD)
TIB .... Technical Information Branch [*US Public Health Service*] [*Information service or system*] (IID)
TIB .... Technical Information Bulletin [*Cincinnati, OH*] (AAG)
TIB .... Technical Information Bureau [*British*]
TIB .... Technical Intelligence Branch [*National Coal Board*] (PDAA)
TIB .... Technische Informationsbibliothek [*Technical Information Library*] [*Germany*]
TIB .... Temporary Importation Bond (MCD)
TIB .... This I Believe Test [*Education*]
Tib .... Tiberius [*of Suetonius*] [*Classical studies*] (OCD)
Tib .... Tibet (VRA)
tib .... Tibetan [*MARC language code Library of Congress*] (LCCP)
Tib .... Tibia [*Anatomy*] (DAVI)
tib .... Tibialis [*Muscle*] (DAVI)
Tib .... Tibullus [*First century BC*] [*Classical studies*] (OCD)
TIB .... Tourist Information Board (WDAA)
TIB .... Toxicology Information Brief [*Environmental*] (GNE)
TIB .... Training Improvement Board [*Military*] (CAAL)
TIB .... Treasury Indexed Bond (ADA)
TIB .... Triisopropylbenzene [*Also, TIPB*] [*Organic chemistry*]
TIB .... Trimmed in Bunkers [*Shipping*] (DS)
TIB .... Tuck in Back [*Sit up straight*] [*Slang British*] (DI)
TIB .... Twin I-Beam [*Ford Motor Co.*] [*Truck front suspension*]
TIBA .... Traffic Information Broadcast by Aircraft (DA)
TIBA .... Triiodobenzoic Acid [*Plant growth regulator*]
TIBA .... Triisobutylaluminum [*Organic chemistry*]
TIBA .... Triisobutylamine [*Organic chemistry*]
TIBALD .... Tibaldstone [*England*]
TIB and FIB ... Tibia and Fibula (DSUE)
TIBC .... Total Iron-Binding Capacity [*Hematology*]
TIBL .... Thermal Internal Boundary Layer (GFGA)
TIBO .... Tetrahydroimidazobenzodiazepin [*Antiviral*]
TIBOE .... Transmitting Information by Optical Electronics (KSC)
TIBS .... Tactical Information Broadcast System [*Air Force*] (DOMA)
TIBS .... Through Ice Bathymetry System (EERA)
TIBTPG .... Texas Instruments Bourdon Tube Pressure Gauge
tic .... Diverticulum [*Gastroenterology*] (DAVI)
TIC .... [*The*] Interchurch Center (EA)
TIC .... Tactical Information Coordinator (DOMA)
TIC .... Tactical Intelligence Concepts (MCD)
TIC .... Tactical Intercom Systems (MCD)
TIC .... Taken into Consideration
TIC .... Tantalum Integrated Circuit [*Electronics*] (PDAA)
TIC .... Tantalum Producers International Study Center [*Later, Tantalum-Niobium International Study Center*] (EAIO)
TIC .... Tape Identification Card
TIC .... Tape Intersystem Connection [*Computer science*]
TIC .... Targeted Industry Categories (AAGC)
TIC .... Target Integration Center (MCD)
TIC .... Target Intercept Computer [*Military*]
TIC .... Tax Information Circular [*Canada*] (IID)
TIC .... Teacher in Charge (ADA)
TIC .... Teacher Information Center (EA)
TIC .... Technical Information Capability
TIC .... Technical Information Center [*Department of Energy*]
TIC .... Technical Information Coordinator [*Environmental Protection Agency*] (GFGA)
TIC .... Technical Institute Council (EA)
TIC .... Technical Instructors Course [*Air Force*] (AFM)
TIC .... Technical Intelligence Center [*Navy*]
TIC .... Technical Interface Concepts (RDA)
TIC .... Technicon Integrator/Calculator
TIC .... Technology and Innovation Council [*Information Industry Association*]
TIC .... Technology Innovation Center [*University of Iowa*] [*Research center*] (RCD)
TIC .... Telecommunications Information Center [*George Washington University*] [*Information service or system*] (IID)
TIC .... Telemetry Instruction Conference (KSC)
TIC .... Telemetry Instrumentation Controller
TIC .... Temperature Indicator Controller
TIC .... Tenancy in Common (MHDB)
TIC .... Tentatively Identified Compounds (GNE)
TIC .... Terminal Identification Code
TIC .... Texas Instruments Co.
TIC .... Thai Information Center (EA)
TIC .... Thermal Image Camera (PDAA)
TIC .... Thermionic Integrated Circuit [*Electronics*]
TIC .... Thermostatic Ignition Control [*Automotive engineering*]
TIC .... Time Interval Counter
TIC .... Tinak [*Marshall Islands*] [*Airport symbol*] (OAG)
TIC .... Token Ring Interface Coupler (PCM)
TIC .... Tool Issue Center [*Military*] (AFIT)
TIC .... Total Inorganic Carbon [*Chemistry*]
TIC .... Total Installed Cost [*Engineering*]
TIC .... Total Ion Chromatography
TIC .... Total Ion Current [*Spectroscopy*]
TIC .... Total Item Change (NASA)
TIC .... Toumodi [*Ivory Coast*] [*Seismograph station code, US Geological Survey*] (SEIS)
TIC .... Trade Information Committee [*Department of State*] (EA)
TIC .... Transaction Identification Code [*Military*] (AFIT)
TIC .... Transducer Information Center (MCD)
TIC .... Transfer-In Channel (CMD)
TIC .... Transport Industries Committee [*Trades Union Congress*] [*British*] (DCTA)
TIC .... Transvaal Indian Congress [*South Africa*] (PD)
TIC .... Travel Information Center [*An association*] (EA)
TIC .... Troops-in-Contact
TIC .... True Interest Cost [*Finance*]
TIC .... Trypsin Inhibitory Capacity [*Biochemistry*]
TIC .... Tuned Integrated Circuit
TICA .... [*The*] International Cat Association (EA)
TICA .... Tactical Intercom Assembly [*Ground Communications Facility, NASA*]
TICA .... Technical Information Center Administration [*Conference*]
TICA .... Thermal Insulation Contractors' Association [*British*] (BI)
TICA .... Timpanogos Cave National Monument
TICACE .... Technical Intelligence Center Allied Command Europe [*NATO*] (NATG)
TICAF .... [*The*] Industrial College of the Armed Forces [*Later, UND*]
TICAS .... Taxonometric Intra-Cellular Analytic System (OA)
TICC .... Technical Industrial Cooperation Contract
TICC .... Technical Intelligence Coordination Center [*NATO*] (NATG)
TICCIH .... [*The*] International Committee for the Conservation of the Industrial Heritage (EA)
TICCIT .... Time-Shared Interactive Computer-Controlled Information Television [*System*] [*Mitre Corp. Brigham Young University 1971*]
TICE .... Time Integral Cost Effectiveness

TICER.......... Temporary International Council for Educational Reconstruction (DLA)
TICF.......... Transient Installation Confinement Facility [*Military*] (AABC)
Tichb Tr.......... Report of the Tichborne Trial [*London*] [*A publication*] (DLA)
TICKS.......... Two Incomes, Kids [*Lifestyle classification*]
Ticktmst.......... Ticketmaster Group, Inc. [*Associated Press*] (SAG)
TICLER.......... Technical Input Checklist/Evaluation Report (MCD)
TICM.......... Test Interface and Control Module (MCD)
TICM.......... Thermal Imaging Common Modules
TICM.......... Trust Investment Committee Memorandum [*A publication*] (DLA)
TICO.......... Technical Information Contact Officer [*Navy*] (DNAB)
TICO.......... Transactions. International Congress of Orientalists [*A publication*] (BJA)
TICODS.......... Time Compression Display System (NVT)
TICOM.......... Texas Institute for Computational Mechanics [*University of Texas at Austin*] [*Research center*] (RCD)
TICOS.......... Truncated Icosahedra [*Crystallography*]
TICP.......... Theater Inventory Control Point [*Military*] (AABC)
TICP.......... Travaux. Institut Catholique de Paris [*A publication*] (BJA)
TICS.......... Teacher Interactive Computer System (IEEE)
TICS.......... Telecommunication Information Control System
TICS.......... Timing and Injection Rate Control System [*Diesel engines*]
TICS.......... Turret Interaction Crew Simulator (MCD)
TICT.......... Tactical Intelligence Collection Team [*Military*] (AFM)
TICT.......... Twisted Intramolecular Charge Transfer [*Biochemistry*]
TICTAC.......... Time Compression Tactical Communications
TIC-TOC.......... Telecommunications Information Centre-Telecommunications Office for Consumers (NITA)
TICU.......... Trauma Intensive Care Unit [*Medicine*]
TICUS.......... Tidal and Current Survey (NOAA)
TICUS.......... Tidal Current Survey System [*National Oceanic and Atmospheric Administration*]
TICWAN.......... Trailerable Intracoastal Waterway Aids to Navigation [*Boat*]
TID.......... Tactical Information Display
TID.......... Tactical Intrusion Detectors (MCD)
TID.......... Target Identification Device [*Military*] (CAAL)
TID.......... Task Initiation Date (WDAA)
TID.......... Tax Installment Deduction
TID.......... Technical Information Division [*Romar Consultants, Inc.*] [*Information service or system*] (IID)
TID.......... Technology Information Division [*Department of Energy, Mines, and Resources*] (IID)
TID.......... Ter in Die [*Three Times a Day*] [*Pharmacy*]
TID.......... Test Identify (CAAL)
TID.......... Thermal Identification Device
TID.......... Thermal Imaging Devices (MCD)
TID.......... Thermionic Ionization Detector [*Instrumentation*]
TID.......... Thread Identifier [*Computer science*]
TID.......... Ticket Information Data
TID.......... Time Interval Distribution
TID.......... Titrated Initial Dose (AAMN)
TID.......... Total Integrated Dose [*Nuclear energy*] (NRCH)
TID.......... Total Ion Detector (OA)
TID.......... Touch Information Display
TID.......... Touch Input Device [*Computer science*] (IAA)
TID.......... Traitement Integre des Donnees [*Integrated Data Processing - IDP*] [*French*]
TID.......... Traveling Ionospheric Disturbance
TID.......... Trifluoromethyl(iodophenyl)deazirine [*Biochemistry*]
TID.......... Turn-In Document [*DoD*]
TID.......... Type Issue/Defuel Codes (AAGC)
TIDA.......... Tuberoinfundibular Dopaminergic System [*Medicine*] (DMAA)
TIDAR.......... Texas Instruments Digital Analog Readout
TIDAR.......... Time Delay Array RADAR
Tidd.......... Tidd's Costs [*A publication*] (DLA)
Tidd.......... Tidd's Practice [*A publication*] (DLA)
TIDDAC.......... Time in Deadband Digital Attitude Control
Tidd App.......... Appendix to Tidd's Practice [*A publication*] (DLA)
Tidd Co.......... Tidd's Costs [*A publication*] (DLA)
Tidd Pr.......... Tidd's Practice [*A publication*] (DLA)
Tidd Prac.......... Tidd's Practice [*A publication*] (DLA)
Tidd's Pract... Tidd's Practice [*A publication*] (DLA)
TIDE.......... Tactical International Data Exchange (NG)
TIDE.......... Technical Intelligence Data Extraction (MCD)
TIDE.......... Tide West Oil [*NASDAQ symbol*] (TTSB)
TIDE.......... Tide West Oil Co. [*NASDAQ symbol*] (NQ)
TIDE.......... Timer Demodulator
TIDE.......... Transponder Interrogation and Decoding Equipment [*Telecommunications*] (IAA)
TIDE.......... Travel Industry and Disabled Exchange (EA)
TideMrk.......... TideMark Bancorp [*Associated Press*] (SAG)
TideR.......... Tidelands Royalty [*Associated Press*] (SAG)
TideR.......... Tidelands Royalty Class B [*Associated Press*] (SAG)
TIDES.......... Time-Division Electronics Switching System (KSC)
TideWst.......... Tide West Oil Co. [*Associated Press*] (SAG)
TIDF.......... Trunk Intermediate Distribution Frame [*Telecommunications*] (TEL)
TIDG.......... TAPER Isolated Dynamic Gain (IAA)
TIDL.......... Test Instrumentation Data Link
TIDMA.......... Tape Interface Direct Memory Access
TIDOC.......... Technical Information Documentation Center [*Advisory Group for Aerospace Research and Development*] (NATG)
TIDOS.......... Table and Item Documentation System
TIDP.......... Technical Interface Design Plans
TIDP-TE.......... Technical Interface Design Plan - Test Edition (RDA)
TIDR.......... Tool Investigation and Disposition Report (SAA)
TIDS.......... Tactical Information Distribution Systems [*Army*] (RDA)
TIDS.......... Talker Idle State [*Telecommunications*] (IAA)
TIDS.......... Technical Information Distribution Service [*Publisher*]
TIDS.......... Tower Integrated Display System [*FAA*] (TAG)
TIDUP.......... Technical Information Directive Update Panel
Tidwtr.......... Tidewater, Inc. [*Associated Press*] (SAG)
TIDY.......... Teletypewriter Integrated Display (NVT)
TIDY.......... Track Identity
TIE.......... [*The*] Information Exchange (EA)
TIE.......... [*The*] Information Exchange on Young Adult Chronic Patients (EA)
TIE.......... [*The*] Institute of Ecology [*Defunct*]
TIE.......... [*The*] Issue Exchange (EA)
TIE.......... Target Identification Equipment (MCD)
TIE.......... Technical Idea Exchange (MCD)
TIE.......... Technical Independent Evaluator [*Army*]
TIE.......... Technical Information Exchange [*National Bureau of Standards*]
TIE.......... Technical Integration and Evaluation [*Apollo*] [*NASA*]
TIE.......... Technology Information Exchange (IID)
TIE.......... Telescopes in Education
TIE.......... Temporary/Intermittent Employee
TIE.......... Terminal Interface Equipment
TIE.......... Texas Information Exchange
TIE.......... Texas Israel Exchange [*A trade and research venture*]
TIE.......... Threshold Ignition Energy (MCD)
TIE.......... TIE Communications, Inc. [*AMEX symbol*] (SPSG)
TIE.......... Tientsin [*Republic of China*] [*Seismograph station code, US Geological Survey*] (SEIS)
TIE.......... Time Interval Error [*Telecommunications*] (TEL)
TIE.......... Tippi [*Ethiopia*] [*Airport symbol*] (OAG)
TIE.......... Toxicity Identification Evaluation
TIE.......... Toyota Industrial Equipment
TIE.......... Training ICON Environment
TIE.......... Training Instrumentation Evaluation (MCD)
TIE.......... Transient Ischemic Episode [*Medicine*]
TIE.......... Transnationals Information Exchange
TIE.......... Travel Industry for the Environment
TIEA.......... Tax Information Exchange Agreement (ECON)
TIED.......... Troop Information and Education Division
Tiedeman Real Prop... Tiedeman on Real Property [*A publication*] (DLA)
Tied Lim Police Power... Tiedeman's Treatise on the Limitations of Police Power in the United States [*A publication*] (DLA)
Tied Mun Corp... Tiedeman's Treatise on Municipal Corporations [*A publication*] (DLA)
TIEG.......... Teen International Entomology Group [*Later, YES*] (EA)
TIE-IN.......... Technology Information Exchange-Innovation Network [*Ohio State Department of Development*] [*Information service or system*] (IID)
TIEO.......... Toyota Industrial Engine Operations [*Torrance, CA*]
TIER.......... Tierce [*Unit of measurement*] (ROG)
TIERS.......... Title I Evaluation and Reporting System [*Department of Education*]
TIES.......... [*The*] Interactive Encyclopedia System [*University of Maryland research project*] (PCM)
TIES.......... Tactical Information Exchange System [*Navy United Nations*] (MCD)
TIES.......... Technological Information Exchange System [*UNIDO*] [*United Nations*]
TIES.......... Textbook Information and Exchange Service [*Regional clearinghouses for used textbooks*]
TIES.......... Theater Information and Engagement System [*Military*] (MCD)
TIES.......... The International English School (AIE)
TIES.......... Time-Independent Escape Sequence [*Computer science*] (CDE)
TIES.......... Torpedo Installation and Exercise System [*Military*] (DWSG)
TIES.......... Total Information for Educational Systems [*Saint Paul, MN*] (BUR)
TIES.......... Total Integrated Engineering System
TIES.......... Translators' and Interpreters' Educational Society (EA)
TIES.......... Transmission and Information Exchange System
TIEYACP.......... [*The*] Information Exchange on Young Adult Chronic Patients (EA)
TIF.......... [*The*] International Foundation (EA)
TIF.......... Tagged Image File [*Computer science*] (PCM)
TIF.......... Taif [*Saudi Arabia*] [*Airport symbol*] (OAG)
TIF.......... Tape Inventory File (IEEE)
TIF.......... Target Intelligence File (CINC)
TIF.......... Task Initiation Force [*Nuclear energy*] (NRCH)
TIF.......... Task Initiation Form [*Nuclear energy*] (NRCH)
TIF.......... Tax Increment Financing
TIF.......... Taxpayer Information File [*IRS*]
TIF.......... Technical Information File
TIF.......... Telecommunication Interference Filter [*Computer science*]
TIF.......... Telephone Influence Factor
TIF.......... Telephone Interference Factor (DEN)
TIF.......... Terminal Independent Format
TIF.......... Testicular Interstitial Fluid [*Physiology*]
TIF.......... Text Interchange Format [*Telecommunications*] (OSI)
TIF.......... Thin Iron Film
TIF.......... Tiffany & Co. [*NYSE symbol*] (SPSG)
TIF.......... Tiflis [*Tbilisi*] [*Former USSR Seismograph station code, US Geological Survey*] (SEIS)
TIF.......... Tilapia International Foundation (EA)
TIF.......... Tomato Intercellular Fluid
TIF.......... Transfer if Indicators Off (SAA)
TIF.......... Transport International par Fer [*International Transport of Goods by Railway*] [*French*]
TIF.......... Treaties in Force [*A publication*] (DLA)
TIF.......... True Involute Form
TIF.......... Tumor-Inducing Factor [*Oncology*]
TIF.......... Tumor-Infiltrating Lymphocyte [*Immunotherapy*]

TIF .... Tumor Inhibitory Factor [*Oncology*]
TIFA .... Tourist Information Facts and Abstracts [*Economic Documentation and Information Ltd.*] [*Ringmer Near Lewes, East Sussex, England*] [*Information service or system*] (IID)
TIFA .... Trucks Involved in Fatal Accidents [*NHTSA*] (TAG)
Tif & Bul Tr... Tiffany and Bullard on Trusts and Trustees [*A publication*] (DLA)
Tif & Sm Pr... Tiffany and Smith's New York Practice [*A publication*] (DLA)
Tifany .... Tiffany & Co. [*Associated Press*] (SAG)
TIFET .... Thin-Layer Field Effect Transistor (IAA)
TIFF .... [*The*] Integrated FORSTAT [*Force Status and Identity Reporting System*] File
TIFF .... Tagged Image File Format [*Computer science*]
tiff .... Tagged Image File Format [*Computer science*]
Tiff .... Tiffany's Reports [*28-39 New York Court of Appeals*] [*A publication*] (DLA)
TIFF .... Tokyo International Film Festival [*Japan*]
Tiffany .... Tiffany's Reports [*28-39 New York Court of Appeals*] [*A publication*] (DLA)
Tiffany Landl & T... Tiffany on Landlord and Tenant [*A publication*] (DLA)
Tiffany Landlord & Ten... Tiffany on Landlord and Tenant [*A publication*] (DLA)
Tiffany Real Prop... Tiffany on Real Property [*A publication*] (DLA)
Tif Gov .... Tiffany on Government and Constitutional Law [*A publication*] (DLA)
TIFO .... Technical Inspection Field Office, Office of the Inspector General
TIFR .... Tata Institute for Fundamental Research [*British*]
TIFR .... Total Improved Frequency Response
TIFR .... Total Investment for Return (MHDW)
TIFS .... Total In-Flight Simulation [*or Simulator*] [*Air Force*]
TIG .... [*The*] Inspector General [*Army*]
TIG .... Tactical Intelligence Group [*Military*]
TIG .... Target Image Generator
TIG .... Taxicab Industry Group (EA)
TIG .... Telegram Identification Group [*Telecommunications*] (TEL)
TIG .... Teletype Input Generator
TIG .... Tetanus Immune Globulin [*Immunology*]
TIG .... TIG Holdings [*NYSE symbol*] (TTSB)
TIG .... TIG Holdings, Inc. [*NYSE symbol*] (SPSG)
tig .... Tigre [*MARC language code Library of Congress*] (LCCP)
TIG .... Tigris Minerals [*Vancouver Stock Exchange symbol*]
TIG .... Time in Grade [*Air Force*]
TIG .... Time of Ignition
TIG .... Transearth Injection Geometry (SAA)
TIG .... Tungsten-Inert-Gas
TIGA .... TI [*Texas Instruments, Inc.*] Graphics Architecture [*Computer science*]
TIGA .... Transport Issues Group Australia (EERA)
TIGEM .... Telethon Institute of Genetics and Medicine [*Italy*]
TIGER .... Terrestrial Initiative in Global Environmental Research [*UK government research program*]
TIGER .... Terrorist Intelligence Gathering Evaluation and Review [*British*]
TIGER .... Topologically Integrated Geographic Encoding and Referencing [*Bureau of the Census*]
TIGER .... Topologically Integrated Geographic Encoding Referencing
TIGER .... Total Information Gathering and Executive Reporting [*International Computers Ltd.*]
TIGER .... Traitement Integral des Galaxies par l'Etude de leurs Raies [*An integral field spectrograph*]
TIGER .... Traveling Industrial Gaseous Emission Research [*Vehicle*] [*Exxon Corp.*]
TIGER .... Treasury Investment Growth Receipt (MHDW)
TIGFFO .... Teenage, Infants, and Girls' Fashion Fair Organisation [*British*] (BI)
TIG(H) .... Tetanus Immune Globulin (Human) [*Immunology*]
TIGHAR .... [*The*] International Group for Historic Aircraft Recovery [*Wilmington, DE*]
TIG Hd .... TIG Holdings,Inc. [*Associated Press*] (SAG)
TIGN .... Time of Ignition
TIGOR .... Time Interval Gage of Relays [*Telecommunications*] (IAA)
TIGR .... [*The*] Institute of Genomic Research
TIGR .... Topographically Integrated Geographic Referencing[*and Coding System*] [*Electronic map used for political demography*]
TIGR .... Transmission Integrated Rotor
TIGR .... Treasury Investment Growth Receipts [*Merrill Lynch & Co.*] [*Finance*]
TIGR .... Turbine-Integrated Geared Rotor
Ti Gracch .... Tiberius Gracchus [*of Plutarch*] [*Classical studies*] (OCD)
TIGRIS .... Televised Images of Gaseous Region in Interplanetary Space
TIGS .... Terminal Independent Graphics System
TIGT .... Turbine Inlet Gas Temperature [*Aviation*]
TIH .... Technical Information Handbook
TIH .... Their Imperial Highnesses
TIH .... Tikehau [*French Polynesia*] [*Airport symbol*] (OAG)
TIH .... Time in Hold (SAA)
TIH .... Toromont Industries Ltd. [*Toronto Stock Exchange symbol*]
TIH .... Total Installed Horsepower
TIH .... Trinity International Holdings [*British*]
TIH .... Trunk Interface Handler
TIHB .... Target Intelligence Handbook (MCD)
TIHBSS .... [*The*] I Hate Barney Secret Society (EA)
TIHP .... Total Installed Horsepower
TII .... European Association for the Transfer of Technologies, Innovation, and Industrial Information [*Information service or system*] (IID)
TII .... [*The*] Independent Institute [*An association*] (EA)
TII .... Table and Item Inventory (SAA)
TII .... Talos Integration Investigation
TII .... Texas Instruments, Inc.
TII .... Texas Instruments, Incorporated, IS & S Library, Dallas, TX [*OCLC symbol*] (OCLC)
TII .... Thomas Indus [*NYSE symbol*] (TTSB)
TII .... Thomas Industries, Inc. [*NYSE symbol*] (SPSG)
TII .... Tiffin, OH [*Location identifier FAA*] (FAAL)
TII .... TII Industries, Inc. [*Associated Press*] (SAG)
TII .... Tooling Inspection Instrumentation (NASA)
TII .... Total Inactive Aerospace Vehicle [*or Aircraft*] Inventory
TII .... Tourismo Internationale Injection [*International Touring-fuel Injection*] [*Italian*]
TII .... Trusteeship Institute, Inc. (EA)
TII .... Turn Indicator Interference
TIIAL .... [*The*] International Institute of Applied Linguistics
TIIAP .... Telecommunications and Information Infrastructure Assistance Program
TIIAP .... Telecommunications and Information Infrastructure Assistance Program [*Department of Commerce*]
TIIC .... Technical Industrial Intelligence Committee [*US Military Government, Germany*]
TIID .... Technical Industrial Intelligence Division [*Allied Board set up to send experts into Germany to ferret out Germany's war-developed scientific secrets*] [*Post-World War II*]
TIIF .... Tactical Imagery Interpretation Facility [*Military*]
TIII .... TII Indus [*NASDAQ symbol*] (TTSB)
TIII .... TII Industries, Inc. [*NASDAQ symbol*] (SAG)
TII Inds .... TII Industries, Inc. [*Associated Press*] (SAG)
TIIP .... Terrain-Intelligence Integration Prototype [*Army*] (RDA)
TIIPS .... Technically Improved Interference Prediction System (IEEE)
TIJ .... Tijuana [*Mexico*] [*Airport symbol*] (OAG)
TIJ .... Tijuana [*Mexico*] [*Airport symbol*] (AD)
TIJI .... Tribune Internationale des Jeunes Interpretes [*International Rostrum of Young Performers - IRP*] (EAIO)
TIK .... Oklahoma City, OK [*Location identifier FAA*] (FAAL)
TIK .... Target Indicator Kit
TIK .... Thermal Imagery Kit (DWSG)
TIK .... Tiara Enterprises Ltd. [*Vancouver Stock Exchange symbol*]
tik .... Ticking (VRA)
TIK .... Tiksi [*Former USSR Seismograph station code, US Geological Survey*] (SEIS)
TIK .... Tixie [*Former USSR Geomagnetic observatory code*]
TIKP .... Turkiye Isci Koylu Partisi [*Worker-Peasant Party of Turkey*] [*Political party*] (PD)
TIL .... Tajikistan International Airlines [*FAA designator*] (FAAC)
TIL .... Technical Indexes Ltd. (NITA)
TIL .... Technical Information and Library Services [*Ministry of Technology*] [*British*]
TIL .... Temperature Indicating Label
TIL .... Temporary Instructor Lieutenant [*Navy British*]
TIL .... Tire Inflation Label [*Automotive engineering*]
TIL .... Tree Island Industries Ltd. [*Toronto Stock Exchange symbol Vancouver Stock Exchange symbol*]
T-i-L .... Truth-in-Lending Act [*1968*]
TIL .... Tumor Infiltrating Lymphocyte [*Oncology*]
TILA .... Telemail International Licensees' Association (TSSD)
TILA .... Truth-in-Lending Act [*1968*]
Til & Sh Pr... Tillinghast and Shearman's New York Practice [*A publication*] (DLA)
TILCAR .... Tactical Infantry Load Carrier Amphibious Remote [*Military*] (PDAA)
TILF .... Tactical Integrity Loss Factor
TILL .... Total Initial Lamp Lumens
Till & Yates App... Tillinghast and Yates on Appeals [*A publication*] (DLA)
Tillman .... Tillman's Reports [*68, 69, 71, 73, 75 Alabama*] [*A publication*] (DLA)
TILLO .... Transfer in Lieu of Layoff (MCD)
TILMC .... Tobacco Industry Labor/Management Committee (EA)
TILO .... Technical Industrial Liaison Office
Til Prec .... Tillinghast's Precedents [*A publication*] (DLA)
TILRA .... Tribal Indian Land Rights Association (EA)
TILS .... Tactical Instrument Landing System
TILS .... Technical Information & Liaison Service [*Information service or system*] (IID)
TILSRA .... Truth-in-Lending Simplification and Reform Act [*1980*]
Tils St L ...... Tilsley on Stamp Laws [*3rd ed.*] [*1871*] [*A publication*] (DLA)
TILT .... Taxpayer Inquiry Lookup Table [*IRS*]
TILT .... Texas Instruments Language Translator [*Computer science*] (IAA)
TILT .... Transmission Intercept and Landing Terminated (MCD)
TIM .... Star Asia [*Philippines*] [*FAA designator*] (FAAC)
TIM .... Table Input to Memory
TIM .... Tactical Instrumental Missile (MCD)
TIM .... Tangential Inlet Manifold
TIM .... Target Intelligence Material (MCD)
TIM .... Technical Information Manager [*Environmental Protection Agency*] (GFGA)
TIM .... Technical Information Manual
TIM .... Technical Information on Microfilm [*British*] (DIT)
TIM .... Technical Interchange Meeting (NASA)
TIM .... TEFLON Insulation Material
TIM .... Tembagapura [*Indonesia*] [*Airport symbol*] (OAG)
TIM .... Temperature Independent Material (IAA)
TIM .... Temperature Indicator Monitor
TIM .... Terminal Interface Monitor (IAA)
TIM .... Test Instrumented Missile [*Army*]
TIM .... Test Interface Module (CAAL)
TIM .... Test Item Malfunction (MCD)
TIM .... Texas Instruments, Inc., Central Library Services, Dallas, TX [*OCLC symbol*] (OCLC)
TIM .... Thailand Independence Movement [*Communist-directed activity outside Thailand*] [*Merged with TPF*]
TIM .... Ticket Issue Machines

TIM............ Time Indicator (IAA)
TIM............ Time Indicator, Miniature (MUGU)
TIM............ Time Initiator Monitor (SAA)
TIM............ Time in Mode (EG)
TIM............ Time Interval Measurement
TIM............ Time Interval Meter
TIM............ Time Interval Monitor (NASA)
Tim............ Timely [*Record label*]
TIM............ Time Meter (AAG)
TIM............ Timisoara [*Romania*] [*Seismograph station code, US Geological Survey*] (SEIS)
TIM............ Timminco Ltd. [*Toronto Stock Exchange symbol*]
Tim............ Timoleon [*of Plutarch*] [*Classical studies*] (OCD)
Tim............ Timon of Athens [*Shakespearean work*]
Tim............ Timothy [*New Testament book*]
TIM............ Titanium Mesh [*Medicine*]
TIM............ Token/Net Interface Module [*Telecommunications*] (TSSD)
TIM............ Topic Indexing Matrix
TIM............ Total Information Management (NITA)
TIM............ Total Ion Scanning Mode [*Spectroscopy*]
TIM............ Track Imitation (MSA)
TIM............ Tracking Information Memorandum
TIM............ Tracking Instruction Manual
TIM............ Tracking Instrument Mount (MUGU)
TIM............ Track Initiator Monitor (CAAL)
TIM............ Transient Intermodulation [*Distortion*]
TIM............ Transistor Information Microfile
TIM............ Transthoracic Intracardiac Monitoring [*Medicine*] (DMAA)
TIM............ Trends in Microbiology [*A publication*]
TIM............ Trigger Inverter Module
TIM............ Triose Phosphate Isomerase [*An enzyme*]
TIMA............ Technical Illustrators Management Association [*Later, IG*]
TIMA............ Truth in Mileage Act of 1986
TIMADS....... Timber Management Decision System (PDAA)
TIMAR......... Near-Term Improvement in Materiel Asset Reporting [*Military*] (AABC)
TIMARC....... Time Multiplexed Analogue Radio Control (PDAA)
TIMASS........ Time Interval Miss Distance Acoustical Scoring System (MCD)
TIMATION.... Time Location System [*Navy*]
TIMB............ Timballes [*Kettle drum*]
TIMB............ Timber (ADA)
TimbCo........ Timberland Co. [*Associated Press*] (SAG)
TimbLdg...... Timber Lodge Steakhouse, Inc. [*Associated Press*] (SAG)
TimbSf........ Timberline Software Corp. [*Associated Press*] (SAG)
TIMC............ Tumor-Induced Cytatocity [*Medicine*] (DAVI)
TIM/DL......... Trunk Interface Module for Data Links [*Telecommunications*]
TIME............ Technique for Information Management and Employment
TIME............ Technology, Immediate-Diagnosis, Mammography Effective Treatment
TIME............ Terminal Instruction (System) for Managed Education
TIME............ Tsunami Inundation Modeling Exchange Project [*Marine science*] (OSRA)
Time A.......... Time Australia [*A publication*] (APTA)
Timeline...... Timeline, Inc. [*Associated Press*] (SAG)
Timeln......... Timeline, Inc. [*Associated Press*] (SAG)
Times L (Eng)... Times Law Reports [*England*] [*A publication*] (DLA)
Times LR..... Times Law Reports [*England*] [*A publication*] (DLA)
Times LR..... Times Law Reports [*Ceylon*] [*A publication*] (DLA)
Times L Rep... Times Law Reports [*England*] [*A publication*] (DLA)
Times L Rep... Times Law Reports [*Ceylon*] [*A publication*] (DLA)
TimeWa........ Time Warner, Inc. [*Associated Press*] (SAG)
TimeWarn..... Time Warner, Inc. Holding Co. [*Associated Press*] (SAG)
TIMI............ Technical Information Maintenance Instruction
TIMI............ Thrombolysis in Myocardial Infarction (Study) [*Medicine*]
TIMIG........... Time in Grade [*Army*]
TIMINT......... Time Interval (AABC)
TIMIX........... [*The*] International Microcomputer Information Exchange (EA)
TIMIX........... Texas Instruments Minicomputer Information Exchange (IAA)
TiMixE.......... TI-MIX [*Texas Instruments Mini/Microcomputer Information Exchange*] Europe (EA)
Timken......... [*The*] Timken Co. [*Associated Press*] (SAG)
TIMM............ The Intelligent Machine Model (NITA)
TIMM............ Thermionic Integrated Micromodule
TimM............ Times Mirror Co. [*Associated Press*] (SAG)
TimM01......... Times Mirror Co. [*Associated Press*] (SAG)
TimMir.......... Times Mirror Co. [*Associated Press*] (SAG)
TIMMS.......... Total Integrated Manpower Management System
TIMNET........ Time Share International Data Communications Network [*Telecommunications*] (IAA)
TIMOT.......... Track, Initiation, Monitoring Overlap Technician (SAA)
TIMP............ Tavistock Institute of Medical Psychology [*British*]
TIMP............ Texas Instructional Media Project [*Education*]
TIMP............ Timpani [*Kettle drum*]
TIMP............ Tissue Inhibitor of Metalloproteinases [*Biochemistry*]
TIMS............ [*The*] Institute of Management Sciences [*Providence, RI*] (EA)
TIMS............ [*The*] International Molinological Society (EA)
TIMS............ Tactical Incapacitating Munitions System (MCD)
TIMS............ Technical Information Management System
TIMS............ Technology Integration of Missile Subsystems (MCD)
TIMS............ Telecommunications Instruction Module System (IAA)
TIMS............ Telephone Information and Management Systems (ADA)
TIMS............ Test Interactive Management System
TIMS............ Text Information and Management System [*Computer science*]
TIMS............ Thaad Information Management System
TIMS............ Thermal Infrared Mapping Spectrometer (SSD)
TIMS............ Thermal Infrared Multispectral Scanner [*Airborne instrument for geological applications*]
TIMS............ Thermal Ionization Mass Spectrometry
TIMS............ Total Ion Measurement Source
TIMS............ Traffic and Incident Management System
TIMS............ Transmission Impairment Measuring Set [*Telecommunications*] (TEL)
TIMS............ Transmission Impairment Measuring System (IAA)
TIMS............ Trust for Investments in Mortgages (MHDW)
TIMSA.......... Thermal Insulation Manufacturers and Suppliers Association (DBA)
TIMSS.......... Third International Mathematics and Science Study
TIMSS.......... Third International Mathematics and Science Study [*Education research*]
TIMT............ Titanium Metals Corp. [*NASDAQ symbol*] (SAG)
TIM/TOM...... Table Input to Memory/Table Output from Memory (NITA)
TIN............ Taino Tours [*Dominican Republic*] [*ICAO designator*] (FAAC)
TIN............ Taro Industries Ltd. [*Toronto Stock Exchange symbol*]
TIN............ Task Implementation Notice
TIN............ Taxpayer Identification Number [*IRS*]
TIN............ Temperature Independent [*Ferrite computer memory core*]
TIN............ Temple-Inland [*NYSE symbol*] (TTSB)
TIN............ Temple-Inland, Inc. [*NYSE symbol*] (SPSG)
TIN............ Temporary Identification Number [*Military*]
TIN............ Temporary Instruction Notice
TIN............ Ter in Nocte [*Three Times a Night*] [*Pharmacy*]
TIN............ Tindouf [*Algeria*] [*Airport symbol*] (OAG)
TIN............ Tinemaha [*California*] [*Seismograph station code, US Geological Survey*] (SEIS)
TIN............ Tooling Impound Notice
TIN............ Transaction Identification Number (AFM)
TIN............ Transmission Identification Number [*Automotive engineering*]
TIN............ Triangulated Irregular Network (EERA)
TIN............ Tubulointerstitial Nephritis [*Nephrology*]
T/In............ Turn In (DGA)
TINA............ [*The*] Integrated Nozzle Assembly (MCD)
TINA............ There Is No Alternative [*Nickname given to British Prime Minister Margaret Thatcher because she so often uses this phrase to defend her government's economic policies*]
TINA............ Truth in Negotiations Act
TINALEA...... This Is Not a Legally Enforceable Agreement [*Legal term*] (NUCP)
tinc............ Tinctura [*tincture*] [*Latin*] [*Pharmacology*] (DAVI)
TINC............ Tincture (ADA)
TINCT.......... Tinctura [*Tincture*] [*Pharmacy*]
TINDECO...... Tin Decorating Co.
TINDX.......... Texas Instruments Index Access Method
TINE............ There Is No Excuse (ECON)
TI-NET......... Transparent Intelligent Network
TINET.......... Travel Industry Network, Inc. [*Winter Springs, FL*] [*Telecommunications*] (TSSD)
TINFO.......... Tieteellisen Informoinnin Neuvosto [*Finnish Council for Scientific Information and Research Libraries*] (EAIO)
TIN/FS......... Taxpayer Identification Number/File Source [*IRS*]
Tink............ Two Incomes, No Kids [*Lifestyle classification*]
TINKER........ Timber Information Keyword Retrieval [*Timber Research and Development Association*] [*Information service or system*] (IID)
TINNER........ Tea and Dinner [*Slang British*] (DSUE)
TINO............ There Is No Opposition [*Parliamentary slang*] [*British*] (DI)
TINOP.......... Transponder Inoperative [*Aviation*] (FAAC)
TINPOT........ There Is No Possible Other Tactic [*Parliamentary slang*] [*British*] (DI)
TINR............ Target Identification Navigation RADAR
TINS............ Tax Identification Number System [*IRS*]
TINS............ Thermal Imaging Navigation Set [*Hughes Aircraft Co.*] [*Navy*] (ECON)
TINS............ Trains Inertial Navigation System (IAA)
Tinsley........ Tinsley Labs, Inc. [*Associated Press*] (SAG)
TINSTAAFL... There Is No Such Thing as a Free Lunch [*Principle of economics indicating that one cannot get something for nothing*] [*See also TANSTAAFL*]
TINSY.......... Treasure Island Naval Shipyard [*San Francisco Bay*]
TINT............ Target Intercept Timer (MCD)
TINT............ Teletype Interpreter (PDAA)
TINTA.......... Tele-Communications International, Inc. [*NASDAQ symbol*] (SAG)
TINTA.......... Tele-Communications Intl [*NASDAQ symbol*] (TTSB)
TINTM.......... Triisononyl Trimellitate [*Organic chemistry*]
TINTS.......... Tactical Intelligence Transfer System
TINTS.......... Turret Integrated Night Thermal Sight
Tinw............ Tinwald's Reports, Scotch Court of Session [*A publication*] (DLA)
TIO............ Target Indication Officer [*Navy*]
TIO............ Target Information Officer [*Marine Corps*] (DOMA)
TIO............ Technical Information Office
TIO............ Technology Innovation Office [*Environmental Protection Agency*]
TIO............ Technology Integration Office [*Army*] (RDA)
TIO............ Television Information Office [*Defunct*] (EA)
TIO............ Terminal Input/Output (NITA)
TIO............ Test Input/Output [*Computer science*]
TIO............ Time Interval Optimization (IEEE)
TIO............ Tiouine [*Morocco*] [*Seismograph station code, US Geological Survey*] (SEIS)
TIO............ Transistorized Image Orthicon
TIO............ Transistorized Image Orthicon Camera (IAA)
TIO............ Troop Information Officer
TIOC............ Terminal Input/Output Controller (NITA)
TIOC............ Terminal Input/Output Coordinator [*Computer science*] (IBMDP)
TIOC............ Triumph International Owners Club (EA)
TIOF............ [*The*] International Osprey Foundation (EA)
TIOH............ [*The*] Institute of Heraldry [*Military*]

TIOL .... Texas Instruments Cassette Operating Language (IAA)
TIOLR .... Texas Instruments Online Reporting System [*Computer science*]
TIOM .... Telegraph Input-Output Multiplexer [*Telecommunications*] (OA)
TIOM .... Terminal Input/Output Module [*Computer science*]
TIOS .... Tactical Integrated Ocean Surveillance [*Military*] (CAAL)
TIOT .... Task Input/Output Table [*Computer science*] (BUR)
TIOTM .... Triisooctyl Trimellitate [*Organic chemistry*]
TIOWQ .... Terminal Input/Output Wait Queue [*Computer science*]
TIP .... C & M Aviation, Inc. [*ICAO designator*] (FAAC)
TIP .... [*The*] Information Partnership [*Information service or system*] (IID)
TIP .... [*The*] Information Place [*Information service or system*] (IID)
TIP .... TACAMO [*Take Charge and Move Out*] Improvement Program
TIP .... Tactical Implementation Time
TIP .... Tactical Improvement Program [*Military*]
TIP .... Tactile Information Presentation [*Biotechnology*]
TIP .... TAO [*Tropical Atmosphere-Ocean*] Implementation Panel [*Marine science*] (OSRA)
TIP .... Target Identification Point (NATG)
TIP .... Target Impact Point
TIP .... Target Industries Program [*Occupational Safety and Health Administration*]
TIP .... Target Input Panel
TIP .... Target Intelligence Package (MCD)
TIP .... Task Initiation and Prediction
TIP .... Tax-Based Incomes Policy
TIP .... Taxpayer Information Processing [*IRS*]
TIP .... Teachers Instructional Plan
TIP .... Technical Improvement Program
TIP .... Technical Information Panel [*Terminated, 1971*] [*AEC*]
TIP .... Technical Information Pilot [*A publication Obsolete*]
TIP .... Technical Information Pilot (DOMA)
TIP .... Technical Information Pool
TIP .... Technical Information Processing (IEEE)
TIP .... Technical Information Program
TIP .... Technical Information Project [*MIT*]
TIP .... Technical Integration Panel [*NASA*] (SSD)
TIP .... Technology in Production (IAA)
TIP .... Technology Internship Program [*Oak Ridge National Laboratory*]
TIP .... Tehrik-i-Istiqlal [*Solidarity Party*] [*See also TI Pakistan*] [*Political party*] (FEA)
TIP .... Telefiche Image Processor (NITA)
TIP .... TELENET Interface Processor
TIP .... Telephone Information Processing (MCD)
TIP .... Teletype Input Processing
TIP .... Temperature-Independent Paramagnetism
TIP .... Terminal Impact Prediction
TIP .... Terminal Interface Package [*Computer science*]
TIP .... Terminal Interface [*Message*] Processor [*Computer science DoD*]
TIP .... Terminal Interface Program (NITA)
TIP .... Thermal Inactivation Point [*Medicine*] (DMAA)
TIP .... Threshold by Identification of Pictures (DAVI)
TIP .... Thrust Inlet Pressure (MCD)
TIP .... Tiburon Petroleum [*Vancouver Stock Exchange symbol*]
TIP .... Tilt Isolation Platform
TIP .... Times of Increased Probability [*Earthquake prediction*]
Tip .... Tipperary [*County in Ireland*] (WGA)
TIP .... TIROS [*Television and Infrared Observation Satellite*] Information Processor [*Telecommunications*]
TIP .... To Insure Promptness
TIP .... Tool Inventors Program [*Automobile tool design*]
TIP .... Total Information Processing (BUR)
TIP .... Total Isomerization Process [*Petroleum refining*]
TIP .... Toxic Integration Program [*Environmental Protection Agency*]
TIP .... Toxicology Information Program [*National Library of Medicine*] [*Bethesda, MD*]
TIP .... Tracking Impact Prediction [*of satellites*]
TIP .... Track Initiation and Prediction [*RADAR*]
TIP .... Training Implementation Plan [*Military*]
TIP .... Transaction Interface Package [*Sperry UNIVAC*] [*Computer science*]
TIP .... Transaction Interface Processor
TIP .... Transient [*or Traveling or Traversing*] In-Core Probe [*Nuclear energy*] (NRCH)
TIP .... Trans-Israel Pipeline
TIP .... Transit Improvement Program [*Satellite*] (MCD)
TIP .... Translation Inhibitory Protein
TIP .... Transponder Interrogator Processor
TIP .... Transportation Improvement Program
TIP .... Transport Individuel Publique [*Also known as PROCOTIP*] [*French auto cooperative*]
TIP .... Traveling in Core Probe (IAA)
TIP .... Traverisng In-Core Probe
TIP .... Tripoli [*Libya*] [*Airport symbol*] (OAG)
TIP .... Troop Information Program
TIP .... Tumor-Inducing Principle [*Plant cytology*]
TIP .... Tumor Inhibitory Principle [*Oncology*]
TIP .... Turbine Inlet Pressure (MSA)
TIP .... Turbine Integral Propellant (MCD)
TIP .... Turn In a Pusher [*Organization combating drug traffic*]
TIPA .... Triisopropanolamine [*Organic chemistry*]
TIPACS .... Texas Instruments Planning and Control System
TIPAT .... Technical Information on Patents [*Swiss Intellectual Property Office*] [*Bern*] [*Information service or system*] (IID)
TIPB .... Triisopropylbenzene [*Also, TIB*] [*Organic chemistry*]
TIPC .... Texas Instruments Pressure Controller
TIPCC .... TI [*Texas Instruments*] Programmable Calculator Club (EA)
TIPE .... Transponder, Interrogator, Pinger, and Echo Sounder
TIPEM .... Toolkit for Interoperable Privacy-Enhanced Messaging [*RSA Data Security, Inc.*]
TIPG .... Thomson Information/Publishing Group [*The Thomson Corp.*]
TIPI .... Tactical Information Processing and Interpretation [*Military*] (AFM)
TIPI .... Transportable Automated Intelligence Processing and Interpretation System (MCD)
TIPIC .... Turkish Investment Promotion and Information Center [*Subdivision of the Union of Chambers of Commerce, Industry, and Commodity Exchanges of Turkey*]
TIPIF .... Instant Publisher [*NASDAQ symbol*] (TTSB)
TIPIF .... [*The*] Instant Publisher, Inc. [*NASDAQ symbol*] (SAG)
TIPISPO .... Tactical Intelligence Processing and Interpretation System Program Office [*Air Force*] (PDAA)
TIPIT .... TDRSS [*Tracking and Data Relay Satellite System*] Interface Prepocessor Into TELOPS [*Telemetry Online Processing System*]
TIPITEF .... Tactical Information Processing and Interpretation Total Environment Facility (MCD)
TIPL .... Tactical Imagery Processing Laboratory [*Army*] (MCD)
TIPL .... Tactical Information Processing Laboratory [*Army*] (MCD)
TIPL .... Teach Information Processing Language
TIPMG .... [*The*] International Project Management Group, Inc. [*Glyndon, MD*] [*Telecommunications*] (TSSD)
TIPP .... Target Intelligence Production Program
TIPP .... Technology and Information Policy Program [*Syracuse University*] [*Research center*] (RCD)
TIPP .... Time Phasing Program [*NASA*] (KSC)
TIPP .... Tipperary [*County in Ireland*]
Tippery .... Tipperary Corp. [*Associated Press*] (SAG)
TIPPS .... Tetraiodophenolphthalein Sodium [*Pharmacology*]
TIPPS .... Total In-House Publication Production System (MCD)
TIPR .... Tactical Inertial Performance Requirements
TIPR .... Tactics Inspection Procedures Report
TIPRE .... Tactical Inertial Performance Requirements (MCD)
TIPRO .... Texas Independent Producers and Royalty Owners Association (EA)
TIPS .... Intrahepatic Portosystemic Shunt [*Medicine*]
TIPS .... [*The*] Italia Philatelic Society (EA)
TIPS .... Tactical Imagery Processing Set
TIPS .... Tactical Information about Perilous Situations [*New York City Fire Department program*]
TIPS .... Tactical Information Processing System [*Military*] (CAAL)
TIPS .... Teaching Improvement Project System [*University of Kentucky*] [*Research center*] (RCD)
TIPS .... Teaching Individual Protective Strategies and Teaching Individual Positive Solutions [*In association name TIPS Program*] (EA)
TIPS .... Teaching Information Processing System
TIPS .... Technical Information and Product Service
TIPS .... Technical Information for Product Safety [*Consumer Product Safety Commission*] (IID)
TIPS .... Technical Information Periodicals Service [*General Electric Co.*]
TIPS .... Technical Information Processing System [*Rockwell International Corp.*] [*Downey, CA*] (AFM)
TIPS .... Technical Interest Profiles (SAA)
TIPS .... Techniques in Product Selection [*National Association of Manufacturers*]
TIPS .... Telemetry Impact Prediction System [*Air Force*]
TIPS .... Telemetry Integrated Processing System [*Air Force*]
TIPS .... Terminal Information Processing [*Aviation*] (FAAC)
TIPS .... Test Information Processing System [*Air Force*]
TIPS .... Test of Integrated Process Skills (EDAC)
TIPS .... Textile Industry Product Safety [*A publication*]
TIPS .... Text Information Processing System
TIPS .... The Internet Product Site
TIPS .... Thermally Induced Phase Separation [*Chemistry*]
TIPS .... Thousands of Instructions Per Second (NITA)
Tips .... Tiny Income, Parents Supporting [*Lifestyle classification*]
TIPS .... Total Information Processing System [*Veterans Administration*]
TIPS .... Total Integrated Pneumatic System (MCD)
TIPS .... Transistorized Inverter Power Supply
TIPS .... Transjugular Intrahepatic Portosystemic Shunt
TIPS .... Transportation Induced Pollution Surveillance [*Marine science*] (MSC)
TIPS .... Treasury's Inflation Protection Securities
TIPS .... Treasury's Inflation Protection Securities
TIPS .... Trends in Pharmacological Sciences [*A publication*]
TIPS .... Triisopropysilyl [*Organic chemistry*]
TIPS .... Truevision Image Processing Software [*AT & T*]
TIPS .... Tunable Infrared Photomission Sensor
TIPSY .... Task Input Parameter Synthesizer
TIP/TAP .... Target Input Panel and Target Assign Panel
TIPTOP .... Tape Input - Tape Output [*Honeywell, Inc.*] [*Computer science*]
TIP TOP .... Tax Information Plan and Total Owed Purchase Accounting
TIQ .... Paris, TN [*Location identifier FAA*] (FAAL)
TIQ .... Task Input Queue [*Computer science*] (IBMDP)
TIQ .... Tetrahydroisoquinoline [*Biochemistry*]
TIQ .... Tinian [*Mariana Islands*] [*Airport symbol*] (OAG)
TI/QC .... Technical Inspection/Quality Control (MCD)
TIQRC .... Toxicology Information Query Response Center [*National Library of Medicine*]
TIR .... Antair, SA de CV [*Mexico*] [*FAA designator*] (FAAC)
TIR .... China Tire Holdings Ltd. [*NYSE symbol*] (SPSG)
TIR .... Target Illuminating RADAR [*Air Force*]
TIR .... Target Indication Room [*Navy*]
TIR .... Target Industries [*Industry segments which have been selected by the US Department of Commerce for special trade promotion emphasis*]

TIR.............. Target Instruction Register
TIR.............. Technical Information Release
TIR.............. Technical Information Report (IEEE)
TIR.............. Technical Intelligence Report
TIR.............. Telecommunications Industry Research [*British*] (ECON)
TIR.............. Temperature Indicator Recorder (ECII)
TIR.............. Terminal Imaging RADAR [*Military*] (RDA)
TIR.............. Terminal Innervation Ratio [*Psychiatry*]
TIR.............. Test Incidence and Reporting System
TIR.............. Test Incident Report (IAA)
TIR.............. Thermal Infrared (PDAA)
tir.............. Tigrina [*MARC language code Library of Congress*] (LCCP)
TIR.............. Time in Rate
TIR.............. Tirana [*Albania*] [*Seismograph station code, US Geological Survey*] (SEIS)
TIR.............. Tiree Island [*Scotland*] [*Airport symbol*] (AD)
TIR.............. Tirupati [*India*] [*Airport symbol*] (OAG)
TIR.............. Tolerance in Radius
TIR.............. Tooling Investigation Report
TIR.............. Total Image Readout
TIR.............. Total Immunoreaction [*Immunochemistry*]
TIR.............. Total Indicated Runout
TIR.............. Total Indicator Reading
TIR.............. Total Internal Reflecting
TIR.............. Total Item Record (MCD)
TIR.............. Transaction Item Report [*Navy*] (NG)
TIR.............. Transmission Infrared [*Spectroscopy*]
TIR.............. Transport International Routier [*International Transport of Goods by Road*] [*French*]
TIR.............. True Indicated Radius (IAA)
TIRA.............. Thrift Industry Recovery Act [*1987*]
TIRA.............. Thrift Institutions Restructuring Act [*1982*]
TIRACS........ Telecommanded Inertially Referenced Attitude Control System (MCD)
TIRAS.......... Technical Information Retrieval and Analysis System (CAAL)
TIRB.............. Transportation Insurance Rating Bureau [*Later, AAIS*] (EA)
TIRC.............. Temperature Indicator Recorder Controller (ECII)
TIRC.............. Tobacco Industry Research Committee (EA)
TIRC.............. Toxicology Information Research Center [*Department of Energy*] [*Oak Ridge National Laboratory Oak Ridge, TN*]
TIRC.............. Toxicology Information Response Center [*Information service or system*] (IID)
TIRC.............. TRADOC [*Training and Doctrine Command*] Instrumentation Review Committee [*Army*]
TIRC.............. Transimpedence Receiver Circuit
TIRC.............. T Tauri Infrared Companion [*Object believed to be first planet sighted that is not in our solar system*]
TIRE.............. EC02, Inc. [*NASDAQ symbol*] (SAG)
TIRE.............. Eco 2 Inc. [*NASDAQ symbol*] (TTSB)
TIRE.............. Tank Infrared Elbow [*Night vision device*] [*Army*] (RDA)
TIRE.............. Tires as Imaginative Recreation Equipment
TIREC.......... TIROS [*Television and Infrared Observation Satellite*] Ice Reconnaissance [*NASA*]
TIREM.......... Terrain Integration Rough Earth Model
TIRES.......... Transient Infrared Emission Spectroscopy
TIRES.......... Transportation Interface and Reporting System [*GSA*] (TAG)
TIREW.......... Eco 2 Inc. Wrrt'A' [*NASDAQ symbol*] (TTSB)
TIRF.............. Total Internal Reflection Fluorescence
TIRF.............. Traffic Injury Research Foundation of Canada [*Research center*] (RCD)
TIRFM.......... Total Internal Reflectiona Fluorescence Microscopy
TIR-FPL....... Total Internal Reflection Face-Pumped LASER
TIRH.............. Theoretical Indoor Relative Humidity
TIRIS.......... Texas Instruments Registration and Identification System [*Auto theft deterrent*]
TIRIS.......... Texas Instruments Registration and Identification System [*Texas Instruments, Inc.*] [*Automobile anti-theft protection*]
TIRIS.......... Traversing Infrared Inspection System (MCD)
TIRKS.......... Trunks Integrated Record Keeping System [*Bell System*]
TIRM.............. Transparent Infrared Material
TIRMMS...... Technical Information Reports for Music-Media Specialists [*Music Library Association publication series*]
TIROD.......... Test Instruction Record of Discussion (MCD)
TIROS.......... Television and Infrared Observation Satellite [*NASA*]
TIROS.......... Television Infrared Observational Satellite [*Marine science*] (OSRA)
TIROS.......... Topographical Infrared Operations Satellite (NASA)
TIROS-M....... Television and Infrared Observation Satellite - Meteorological [*NASA*] (DNAB)
TIROS-N....... Television Infrared-Observation Satellite NOAA [*National Oceanographic and Atmospheric Administration*] [*Navy*] (ANA)
TIRP.............. Textile Information Retrieval Program (NITA)
TIRP.............. Total Internal Reflection Prism
TIRPC.......... Transport-Independendt Remote Procedure Call [*Computer science*]
TIRPF.......... Total Integrated Radial Peaking Factor (IEEE)
TIRR.............. [*The*] Institute for Rehabilitation and Research [*Houston, TX*]
TIRR.............. Tactics Inspection Results Report
TIRR.............. Texas Institute of Rehabilitation and Research (BABM)
TIRR.............. Trainer Installation Requirements Report
TIRS.............. Tactical Information Recording System [*Military*] (CAAL)
TIRS.............. Target Index Reference System [*Army*] (DOMA)
TIRS.............. Terrain Index Reference System [*Army*] (INF)
TIRS.............. Thermal Infrared Scanner (RDA)
TIR/SLIT...... Transaction Item Reporting / Serial Lot Item Tracking [*Navy*] (DNAB)
TIRT.............. Tidelands Royalty Trust "B" [*NASDAQ symbol*] (NQ)
TIRT.............. Total Internal Reflection Technique
TIRTZ.......... Tidelands Rlty Tr B SBI [*NASDAQ symbol*] (TTSB)
TIRU.............. Service du Traitement Industriel des Residus Urbains [*France*]
TIRU.............. Trade Information Research Unit [*ITC*] [*United Nations*] (DUND)
TIS.............. [*The*] Infantry School [*Army*]
TIS.............. Tactical Intelligence Squadron (MCD)
TIS.............. Tactical Interdiction System
TIS.............. Taft Information System [*Provides information on private foundations*] (IID)
TIS.............. Target Identification Software [*Military*] (CAAL)
TIS.............. Target Information Sheet [*Air Force*]
TIS.............. Target Information System
TIS.............. Tate Integrated Systems
TIS.............. Technical Information Section [*Navy*]
TIS.............. Technical Information Series (IAA)
TIS.............. Technical Information Service [*American Institute of Aeronautics and Astronautics*] (IID)
TIS.............. Technical Information Service [*Caribbean Industrial Research Institute*] [*Trinidad and Tobago*]
TIS.............. Technical Information Services [*Acurex Corp.*] (IID)
TIS.............. Technical Information Staff [*Environmental Protection Agency*] (GFGA)
TIS.............. Technical Information Systems [*Department of Agriculture*]
TIS.............. Technical Interface Specification (NATG)
TIS.............. Technical Research Centre of Finland, Espoo, Finland [*OCLC symbol*] (OCLC)
TIS.............. Technology, Information, and Society
TIS.............. Technology Information System [*Lawrence Livermore National Laboratory*] [*University of California*] (IID)
TIS.............. Telemetry Input System
TIS.............. Telephone Information Services [*Commercial firm*] [*British*]
TIS.............. Temperature Indicating Switch
TIS.............. Terminal Interface Subsystem [*Telecommunications*] (TEL)
TIS.............. Termination Inventory Schedule (SAA)
TIS.............. Tern Island Station (SAA)
TIS.............. Terrain Information System
TIS.............. Tesis [*Russian Federation*] [*ICAO designator*] (FAAC)
TIS.............. Test Information Sheet (MCD)
TIS.............. Test Instrumentation System
TIS.............. Test Interface Subsystem (NASA)
TIS.............. Test Interface Summary (MCD)
TIS.............. Test Item Simulator [*Fort Huachuca, AZ*] [*United States Army Electronic Proving Ground*] (GRD)
TIS.............. Tetracycline-Induced Steatosis [*Medicine*]
TIS.............. Tetrahydroisoquinoline Sulfonamide [*A drug*]
TIS.............. Theater Intelligence Section [*Navy*]
TIS.............. The Information System (NITA)
TIS.............. Thermal Imaging Scanner
TIS.............. Thermal Imaging Sight [*Artillery*] [*Army*] (INF)
TIS.............. Thermal Insulation System
TIS.............. Thursday Island [*Australia Airport symbol*] (OAG)
TIS.............. Timber Industry Strategy [*Victoria, Australia*]
TIS.............. Time in Service [*Military*] (DOMA)
TIS.............. Time Resources Corp. [*Vancouver Stock Exchange symbol*]
TIS.............. TIS Mortgage Investment Co. [*NYSE symbol*] (CTT)
TIS.............. TIS Mortgage Investors Co. [*Associated Press*] (SAG)
TIS.............. TIS Mtge Investment [*NYSE symbol*] (TTSB)
tis.............. Tissue (VRA)
TIS.............. Tissue (ADA)
TIS.............. Tobacco Inspection Service [*Philippines*]
TIS.............. Total Information System [*Computer science*]
TIS.............. Tracking and Injection Station
TIS.............. Tracking Instrumentation Subsystem (MCD)
TIS.............. Track Initiation Supervisor (SAA)
TIS.............. Trade Information Service [*ESCAP*] [*United Nations*] (DUND)
TIS.............. Trading Information System [*AutEx Systems*] [*Information service or system*] (CRD)
TIS.............. Traffic Information System
TIS.............. Transaction Information Systems
TIS.............. Transit Injection Station (IAA)
TIS.............. Transponder Interrogation SONAR
TIS.............. Travelers Information Service [*Oracle Corp.*] [*Information service or system*] (IID)
TIS.............. Travel Information Service (EA)
TIS.............. Travel to Interview Scheme (AIE)
TIS.............. Triskaidekaphobia Illuminatus Society (EA)
TIS.............. Trusted Information Systems [*Commercial firm*]
TIS.............. Trypsin-Insoluble Segment [*Cytochemistry*]
TIS.............. Tumor in Situ [*Oncology*]
TIS.............. Two-Impinging-Stream Reactor [*Chemical engineering*]
TISA.............. Technical Information Support Activities [*Army*]
TISA.............. Technique for Interactive Systems Analysis (NVT)
TISA.............. Top Image Systems Ltd. [*NASDAQ symbol*] (SAG)
TISA.............. Troop Issue Subsistence Activity [*Military*] (AABC)
TISA.............. Troop Issue Support Agency (MCD)
TISAB.......... Total Ionic Strength Adjustment Buffer (PDAA)
TISAL.......... Tactical Instrument Steep Approach and Landing System (MCD)
TISAP.......... Technical Information Support Activities Project [*Army*] (DIT)
TISAP.......... Totalized Interface Subroutine and Post Processor [*Computer science*] (BUR)
TISC.............. Technology Integration Steering Committee [*Army*] (RDA)
TISC.............. Textile Industry Support Campaign [*British*] (DBA)
TISC.............. Timed Induction with Supercharge [*Automotive engineering*]
TISC.............. Tire Industry Safety Council (EA)
TISC.............. Treasury Inter-Services Committee [*British military*] (DMA)
TISCA.......... Technical Information System for Carrier Aviation [*Navy*] (MCD)
TISCO.......... Tata Iron and Steel Co. (ECON)

TISE Take It Somewhere Else [*The Solid Waste Syndrome*] (GNE)
TISE Technical Information Service (IAA)
TISE Technical Information Service Extension (SAA)
TISEA Tasmanian Institute of Senior Educational Administrators [*Australia*]
TISEO Target Identification System, Electro-Optical [*Air Force*]
TISK Thailand Informations und Solidaritaetskomitee [*Germany*]
TISL Telecommunications and Information Systems Laboratory [*University of Kansas*] [*Research center*] (RCD)
TISL Thomson Information Services Ltd. [*The Thomson Corp.*] [*Publishing*]
TISN Todai International Science Network
TISO Threat Integrated Staff Officer [*Army*]
TISO TRADOC [*Training and Doctrine Command*] Integration Staff Officer [*Army*]
TISO Troop Issue Subsistence Officer [*Military*] (AABC)
TISP Technical Information Support Personnel [*Department of Labor*]
TISP Thickness-Insensitive Solar Paint [*Coating technology*]
TISPOC Trent Institute for the Study of Popular Culture [*Trent University*] [*Canada Research center*] (RCD)
TISq Tactical Intelligence Squadron [*Air Force*]
TIS-RET Thermal Imaging System - Reticle
TISS Tactical Intermediate Support System [*Military*] (MCD)
TISS Therapeutic Intervention Scoring System (MEDA)
TISS Thermal Imaging Sensor System
TISS Trans-Ionospheric Sensing System (DWSG)
TISS Troop Issue Support System [*Army*]
TISSG Travel Industry Systems Standards Group [*British*]
TIST St. Thomas/Harry S. Truman [*Virgin Islands*] [*ICAO location identifier*] (ICLI)
TISTHR Tool Inspection Small Tools Historical Record (MCD)
TISU Trade Information Supply Unit [*ITC*] [*United Nations*] (DUND)
TISX St. Croix/Alexander Hamilton [*Virgin Islands*] [*ICAO location identifier*] (ICLI)
TISX Trusted Information Systems, Inc. [*NASDAQ symbol*] (SAG)
Tit Divus Titus [*of Suetonius*] [*Classical studies*] (OCD)
TIT Technician-in-Training (ADA)
TIT Technology in Training [*DoD*]
TIT Terminal Interface Table (MCD)
TIT Ternary Digit (IAA)
TIT Test Item Taker
TIT Thermal Inactivation Time
TIT Thermoisolation Technique
Tit Titan [*Record label*]
Tit Tithe (ILCA)
TIT Title [*Bibliography*]
TIT Titular (WDAA)
Tit Titus [*New Testament book*]
Tit Titus Andronicus [*Shakespearean work*]
TIT Total Indication Time (MCD)
TIT Total Insertion Time
TIT Treponema Immobilization Test [*Clinical chemistry*]
TIT Triiodothyronine [*Endocrinology*] (MAE)
TIT Trouble Indicator Trunk [*Telecommunications*] (IAA)
TIT Turbine Inlet Temperature
TIT Turbine Interstage Temperature
TIT Tustin Institute of Technology [*California*]
Tit A Titus Andronicus [*Shakespearean work*] (BARN)
TitalPh Tital Pharmaceuticals, Inc. [*Associated Press*] (SAG)
TITAN Teamster's International Terminal and Accounting Network (IAA)
TitanCp Titan Corp. [*Associated Press*] (SAG)
TitanEx Titan Exploration, Inc. [*Associated Press*] (SAG)
TitanHld Titan Holdings, Inc. [*Associated Press*] (SAG)
TitanMet Titanium Metals Corp. [*Associated Press*] (SAG)
TitanW Titan Wheel International [*Associated Press*] (SAG)
TITC Toxic Substances Control Act Interagency Testing Committee [*Environmental Protection Agency*] (GFGA)
TITC Traction-Immune Track Circuits [*Railway signals system*] [*British*]
TITE Technologies and Innovations in Training Equipment
TITE TEWS [*Tactical Electronic Warfare System*] Intermediate Test Equipment [*Military*]
TITE Tijuana & Tecate Railway Co. [*Later, TTR*] [*AAR code*]
TITF Test Item Transmittal Form (IAA)
TITh Triiodothyronine [*Also, T_3*] [*Endocrinology*]
TITL Title
TitleWve Title Wave Stores, Inc. [*Associated Press*] (SAG)
TITO Troops In, Troops Out
TITOS Telivision Infrared Orbital Satellite [*Instrument*] (EERA)
TITPG Taft Institute for Two-Party Government [*Later, TTI*] (EA)
titr Titrate [*Analytical chemistry*]
TITTI Texas Instruments Transistor Transistor Logic (IAA)
TI/TTR Target Illumination/Target Tracking RADAR (MCD)
TITUS Textile Information Treatment Users' Service [*French Textile Institute*] [*Bibliographic database*] [*Information service or system*] (IID)
TIU Tape Identification Unit
TIU Target Indication Unit [*Navy*]
TIU Telecommunications International Union [*Defunct*] (EA)
TIU Telephone Interface Unit [*Telecommunications*]
TIU Terminal Interface Unit [*Bell System*]
TIU Timaru [*New Zealand*] [*Airport symbol*] (OAG)
TIU Time Isolation Unit
TIU Toxicologically Insignificant Usage
TIU Trigger Inverter Unit
TIU Trustworthy Interface Unit [*Telecommunications*] (OSI)
TIU Trypsin Inhibitory Unit [*Food analysis*]
TIUC Textile Information Users Council (EA)
TI UCL Texas Instruments Universal Command Language (NITA)
TIUS Truck Inventory and Use Survey [*BTS*] (TAG)
TIUV Total Intrauterine Volume [*Gynecology*]
TIV Target Intensifier Vidicon
TIV Thermactor Idle Vacuum [*Automotive engineering*]
TIV Time in View
TIV Tivat [*Former Yugoslavia*] [*Airport symbol*] (OAG)
TIV Tiverton [*Municipal borough in England*]
TIV Tiverton Petroleums Ltd. [*Toronto Stock Exchange symbol*]
TIV Tivoli Music Hall [*London*] (DSUE)
TIV Total Indicator Variation (IAA)
TIVC Thoracic Inferior Vena Cava [*Medicine*] (MAE)
TIVICON Texas Instruments Vidicon (IAA)
Tivoli Tivoli Industries, Inc. [*Associated Press*] (SAG)
TivoliSy Tivoli Systems, Inc. [*Associated Press*] (SAG)
TIVS Thermally Initiated Venting System (MCD)
TIVS Tivoli Systems, Inc. [*NASDAQ symbol*] (SAG)
TIW Tacoma [*Washington*] [*Airport symbol*] (AD)
TIW Tacoma, WA [*Location identifier FAA*] (FAAL)
TIW Tactical Intelligence Wing [*Military*]
TIW Tamarind Institute Workshop [*Graphic arts school*] [*New Mexico*]
TIW TEFLON-Insulated Wire
tiw Three Times a Week [*Pharmacology*]
TIW Today's Insurance Woman [*National Association of Insurance Women (International)*] [*A publication*]
TIW Twice a Week [*Pharmacy*] (DAVI)
TIWE Tropical Instability Wave Experiment (USDC)
TIWE Tropical Instability Wave Experiment [*Marine science*] (OSRA)
TIWG Terrorism Incident Working Group [*Bureau of Diplomatic Security*] [*Department of State*] (EGAO)
TIWG Test Integration Working Group [*Military*] (GFGA)
TIWP Toxicology Information Working Party (PDAA)
TIWSS Theater Integrated Warfare Scenarios Study
TIX Titusville [*Florida*] [*Airport symbol*] (AD)
TIX Titusville, FL [*Location identifier FAA*] (FAAL)
TIX Transfer on Index [*Telecommunications*] (IAA)
TIX Triax Airlines Ltd. [*Nigeria*] [*ICAO designator*] (FAAC)
TIXA Thioxanthone [*Organic chemistry*]
TIXI Turret Integrated Xenon Illuminator
TIY Tidjikja [*Mauritania*] [*Airport symbol*] (OAG)
TIY Tir Systems Ltd. [*Vancouver Stock Exchange symbol*]
TIZ Tari [*Papua New Guinea*] [*Airport symbol*] (OAG)
TIZ Traffic Information Zone (DA)
TIZZY Tinny and Buzzing [*Sounds*]
TJ Cameroon [*Aircraft nationality and registration mark*] (FAAC)
TJ East Germany [*License plate code assigned to foreign diplomats in the US*]
TJ Oceanair [*ICAO designator*] (AD)
TJ Tait's Justice of the Peace [*A publication*] (DLA)
TJ Talk Jockey [*Radio*]
TJ Talmud Jerushalmi (BJA)
TJ Targum Jonathan (BJA)
TJ Technical Journal (MCD)
TJ Telephone Jack (DEN)
TJ Temperature Junction (MCD)
TJ Tendon Jerk [*Neurology*] (DAVI)
TJ Terajoule [*SI unit of energy*]
TJ Test Jack (DEN)
TJ Thermal Junction (KSC)
TJ Thomas Jefferson [*US president, 1743-1826*]
TJ Tijuana [*Mexico*]
TJ Tomato Juice
TJ Tommy John [*Baseball pitcher*]
TJ Trajectory (AABC)
TJ Trans-Jordan (BJA)
TJ Triceps Jerk
TJ Troell-Junet [*Syndrome*] [*Genetics*] (DAVI)
TJ Trunk Junctor [*Telecommunications*] (IAA)
TJ Turbojet
TJA Table Jellies Association (DBA)
TJA Tarija [*Bolivia*] [*Airport symbol*] (OAG)
TJA Trial Judge Advocate [*Army*]
TJA Turbojet Aircraft
TJaC Jackson State Community College, Jackson, TN [*Library symbol*] [*Library of Congress*] (LCLS)
TJADC Theater Joint Air Defense Command [*Military*] (AABC)
TJAETDS Turbine and Jet Aircraft Engine Type Designation System
TJAG [*The*] Judge Advocate General [*Army*]
TJAGC [*The*] Judge Advocate General's Corps [*Army*]
TJaGH Jackson-Madison County General Hospital, Learning Center, Jackson, TN [*Library symbol Library of Congress*] (LCLS)
TJAGSA [*The*] Judge Advocate General's School, Army
TJaL Lane College, Jackson, TN [*Library symbol Library of Congress*] (LCLS)
TJaLam Lambuth College, Jackson, TN [*Library symbol Library of Congress*] (LCLS)
TJaLaw Tennessee State Law Library, Jackson, TN [*Library symbol Library of Congress*] (LCLS)
TJAS Tom Jones Appreciation Society (EAIO)
TJaU Union University, Jackson, TN [*Library symbol Library of Congress*] (LCLS)
TJB Tijuana Brass [*Musical group*]
TJB Tilting Journal Bearing
TJB Time-Sharing Job Control Block [*Computer science*] (IBMDP)
TJB Trench Junction Box

TJBQ .... Aguadilla/Borinquen [*Puerto Rico*] [*ICAO location identifier*] (ICLI)
TJC .... [*The*] Jockey Club (EA)
TJC .... Targeted Jobs Credit [*Tax credit*]
TJC .... Temple Junior College [*Texas*]
TJC .... Thomas Jefferson Center (EA)
TJC .... Thornton Junior College [*Illinois*]
TJC .... Tower Jettison Command (SAA)
TJC .... Trajectory Chart
TJC .... Trinidad [*Colorado*] [*Seismograph station code, US Geological Survey*] (SEIS)
TJC .... Tyler Junior College [*Texas*]
TJC .... Vanderbilt University Library, Nashville, TN [*OCLC symbol*] (OCLC)
TJCDR .... Temporary Joint Committee on Deficit Reduction
TJCG .... Vieques/Camp Garcia Airstrip [*Puerto Rico*] [*ICAO location identifier*] (ICLI)
TJCI .... Paramark Enterprises, Inc. [*NASDAQ symbol*] (SAG)
TJCI .... T.J. Cinnamons [*NASDAQ symbol*] (TTSB)
TJCI .... TJ Cinnamons, Inc. [*NASDAQ symbol*] (SAG)
TJ Cinn .... TJ Cinnamons, Inc. [*Associated Press*] (SAG)
TJCIW .... T J Cinnamons Wrrt'A' [*NASDAQ symbol*] (TTSB)
TJCIZ .... T J Cinnamons Wrrt'B' [*NASDAQ symbol*] (TTSB)
TJ Cn .... TJ Cinnamons, Inc. [*Associated Press*] (SAG)
TJCO .... T J International [*NASDAQ symbol*] (TTSB)
TJCO .... TJ International, Inc. [*NASDAQ symbol*] (NQ)
TJCP .... Culebra [*Puerto Rico*] [*ICAO location identifier*] (ICLI)
TJD .... Trajectory Diagram
TJDP .... Targeted Jobs Demonstration Program (EDAC)
TJE .... Trojan Energy Corp. [*Vancouver Stock Exchange symbol*]
TJE .... Turbojet Engine
TJEDS .... Trainer Jet Exhaust Decontamination System
TJefC .... Carson-Newman College, Jefferson City, TN [*Library symbol Library of Congress*] (LCLS)
TJETS .... Thomas Jefferson Equal Tax Society (EA)
TJF .... Test Jack Field [*Telecommunications*] (IAA)
TJF .... Time-to-Jitter Flag
TJFA .... Fajardo [*Puerto Rico*] [*ICAO location identifier*] (ICLI)
TJFC .... [*The*] Johnsons Fan Club (EA)
TJFC .... Tex Jones Fan Club [*Defunct*] (EA)
TJFC .... Tom Jones Fan Club (EA)
TJFC .... Tomy Jennings Fan Club (EA)
TJFF .... Ramey [*Puerto Rico*] [*ICAO location identifier*] (ICLI)
TJFF .... Trans-Jordan Frontier Force [*British military*] (DMA)
TJFS .... T. J.'s [*Tom Jones'*] Fans of Soul (EA)
TJG .... Tom Jones Gadabouts (EA)
TJG .... Travel Journalists Guild (EA)
TJGTOI .... [*The*] Judge GTO International (EA)
TJI .... Tex Johnston, Inc.
TJI .... Trujillo [*Honduras*] [*Airport symbol*] (AD)
TJI .... Trus-Joist I-Beam
TJID .... Terminal Job Identification (BUR)
TJIG .... San Juan/Isla Grande [*Puerto Rico*] [*ICAO location identifier*] (ICLI)
TJ Intl .... TJ International, Inc. [*Associated Press*] (SAG)
TJISRF .... Thomas Jefferson Institute for the Study of Religious Freedom (EA)
TJK .... Tajikair [*Tajikistan*] [*ICAO designator*] (FAAC)
TJM .... Tower Jettison Motor
TJM .... Vanderbilt Medical Center, Nashville, TN [*OCLC symbol*] (OCLC)
TJMZ .... Mayaguez [*Puerto Rico*] [*ICAO location identifier*] (ICLI)
TJN .... Twin Jet Nebulizer [*Pharmacology*] (DAVI)
TJNR .... Roosevelt Roads Naval Air Station [*Puerto Rico*] [*ICAO location identifier*] (ICLI)
T Jo .... T. Jones' English King's Bench Reports [*84 English Reprint*] [*A publication*] (DLA)
TJOC .... Theater Joint Operations Center [*Military*]
TJoE .... Emmanuel School of Religion, Johnson City, TN [*Library symbol Library of Congress*] (LCLS)
TJoMC .... Johnson City Medical Center Hospital, Learning Resources Center, Johnson City, TN [*Library symbol Library of Congress*] (LCLS)
T Jones .... T. Jones' English King's Bench Reports [*84 English Reprint*] [*A publication*] (DLA)
T Jones (Eng)... T. Jones' English King's Bench Reports [*84 English Reprint*] [*A publication*] (DLA)
TJoS .... East Tennessee State University, Johnson City, TN [*Library symbol Library of Congress*] (LCLS)
TJoS-M .... East Tennessee State University, Medical Library, Johnson City, TN [*Library symbol Library of Congress*] (LCLS)
TJoV .... United States Veterans Administration Center, Johnson City, TN [*Library symbol Library of Congress*] (LCLS)
TJP .... Tactical Jamming Pod [*Military*] (CAAL)
TJP .... Turbojet Propulsion
TJPOI .... Twisted Jute Packing and Oakum Institute [*Defunct*] (EA)
TJPS .... Ponce/Mercedita [*Puerto Rico*] [*ICAO location identifier*] (ICLI)
TJQ .... Tanjung Pandan [*Indonesia*] [*Airport symbol*] (OAG)
TJQ .... Treasury of Jewish Quotations [*A publication*]
TJR .... Tactical Jammer [*Military*] (CAAL)
TJR .... Tajee Resources Ltd. [*Vancouver Stock Exchange symbol*]
TJR .... Total Joint Replacement [*Orthopedics*] (DAVI)
TJR .... Trunk and Junction Routing [*Telecommunications*] (TEL)
TJRC .... Thomas Jefferson Research Center [*Later, TJC*] (EA)
TJS .... Tactical Jamming System
TJS .... Target Jamming System
TJS .... Tenajon Resources Corp. [*Formerly, Tenajon Silver*] [*Vancouver Stock Exchange symbol*]
TJS .... Terminal Junction System
TJS .... Transverse Junction Stripe (MCD)
TJSF .... Temperature Jump-Stopped Flow [*Spectroscopy*]
TJSJ .... San Juan/Puerto Rico International [*Puerto Rico*] [*ICAO location identifier*] (ICLI)
TJ Sys .... TJ Systems Corp. [*Associated Press*] (SAG)
TJT .... Tactical Jamming Transmitter [*Navy*]
TJT .... TJT, Inc. [*Associated Press*] (SAG)
TJT .... Tough Jeans Territory [*Sears, Roebuck & Co. advertising slogan*]
TJT .... Tri-Junction Transistor (IAA)
TJTA .... Taylor-Johnson Temperament Analysis [*Psychology*]
TJTC .... Targeted Jobs Tax Credits [*Federal program*]
TJTCC .... Targeted Jobs Tax Credit Coalition (EA)
TJTTFC .... Tom Jones "Tom Terrific" Fan Club (EA)
Tju .... Tjuringa: an Australasian Benedictine Review [*A publication*] (APTA)
TJVQ .... Vieques [*Puerto Rico*] [*ICAO location identifier*] (ICLI)
TJW .... North Haven, ME [*Location identifier FAA*] (FAAL)
TJX .... TJX Companies [*NYSE symbol*] (SPSG)
TJX .... TJX Companies [*Associated Press*] (SAG)
TJXPrC .... TJX Co's $3.125 cm Cv'C'Pfd [*NYSE symbol*] (TTSB)
TJY .... Tulsa, OK [*Location identifier FAA*] (FAAL)
TJZS .... San Juan [*Puerto Rico*] [*ICAO location identifier*] (ICLI)
Tk .... Milli Kutuphane [*National Library*], Ankara, Turkey [*Library symbol Library of Congress*] (LCLS)
TK .... Taegu [*South Korea*] (ECON)
TK .... Talent-Keyhole [*Satellite photography*] [*Military*] (LAIN)
TK .... Tank (AAG)
TK .... Tanker
Tk .... T-Cell, Killer Type [*Immunology*]
TK .... Teekay Shipping [*NYSE symbol*] (TTSB)
TK .... Teekay Shipping Corp. [*NYSE symbol*] (SAG)
TK .... Thick (ROG)
TK .... Through Knee [*Medicine*]
TK .... Thymidine Kinase [*An enzyme*]
TK .... Tokelau Islands [*ANSI two-letter standard code*] (CNC)
TK .... Tokodynamometer [*Obstetrics*] (DAVI)
TK .... To Kum [*i.e., To Come*] [*Publishing*]
TK .... Tool Kits [*JETDS nomenclature*] [*Military*] (CET)
TK .... Torath Kohanim (BJA)
TK .... Track
TK .... Transducer Kit (MCD)
TK .... Transketolase [*An enzyme*]
TK .... Truck (AAG)
TK .... Trunk (IAA)
TK .... Trunk Equipment [*Telecommunications*] (TEL)
TK .... Turkey [*IYRU nationality code*]
TK .... Turk Hava Yollari [*ICAO designator*] (AD)
TK .... Turkish Airlines [*Airline flight code*] (ODBW)
TK .... Tuskegee R. R. [*AAR code*]
TK .... Tyrosine Kinase Domain [*Genetics*]
TKA .... Air Troika [*Russian Federation*] [*ICAO designator*] (FAAC)
TKA .... Talkeetna, AK [*Location identifier FAA*] (FAAL)
TKA .... Tanaka [*New Britain*] [*Seismograph station code, US Geological Survey*] (SEIS)
TKA .... Terminator Kit Assembly [*Robot*]
TKA .... Thermokinetic Analysis
TKA .... Throttle Kicker Actuator [*Automotive engineering*]
TKA .... Total Knee Arthroplasty [*Medicine*]
TKA .... Toy Knights of America (EA)
TKA .... Transketolase Activity [*Medicine*] (MAE)
TKAM .... Knoxville Academy of Medicine, Knoxville, TN [*Library symbol Library of Congress*] (LCLS)
TKB .... Kingsville, TX [*Location identifier FAA*] (FAAL)
TKB .... Task Builder [*Computer science*] (MHDI)
TKBD .... Tackboard [*Technical drawings*]
TKBN .... Tank Battalion [*Marine Corps*]
TKC .... Thiokol Corp. [*NYSE symbol*] (SPSG)
TKC .... Tiko [*Cameroon*] [*Airport symbol*] (AD)
TKCS .... Knoxville City School, Knoxville, TN [*Library symbol Library of Congress*] (LCLS)
TKD .... Takada [*Japan*] [*Seismograph station code, US Geological Survey*] (SEIS)
TKD .... Takoradi [*Ghana*] [*Airport symbol*] (AD)
TKD .... Thymidine Kinase Deficiency [*Medicine*] (DMAA)
TKD .... Tokodynamometer
TKD .... Top Kit Drawing
TKDE .... Tetrakis(dimethylamino)ethylene [*Organic chemistry*]
TkDtyr .... Tank Destroyer [*Military*]
TKE .... Tau Kappa Epsilon [*Fraternity*] [*Later, TEKE*]
TKE .... Tenakee [*Alaska*] [*Airport symbol*] (OAG)
TKE .... Tenakee Springs, AK [*Location identifier FAA*] (FAAL)
TKE .... Total Kinetic Energy
TKE .... Track Angle Error
TKE .... Trek Airways [*South Africa ICAO designator*] (FAAC)
TKE .... Turbulent Kinetic Energy
TKEBH .... East Tennessee Baptist Hospital, Knoxville, TN [*Library symbol Library of Congress*] (LCLS)
TKECH .... East Tennessee Children's Hospital, Pediatric Library, Knoxville, TN [*Library symbol*] [*Library of Congress*] (LCLS)
TKETHi .... East Tennessee Historical Society, Knoxville, TN [*Library symbol Library of Congress*] (LCLS)
TKF .... Turkish Investment Fund [*NYSE symbol*] (SPSG)
TKFSM .... Fort Sanders Regional Medical Center, Knoxville, TN [*Library symbol Library of Congress*] (LCLS)
TKG .... Bandar Lampung [*Indonesia*] [*Airport symbol*] (OAG)
TKG .... Capsule Technology Group, Inc. [*Toronto Stock Exchange symbol*]
TKG .... Tanking (AAG)
TKG .... Telukbetung [*Sumatra, Indonesia*] [*Airport symbol*] (AD)

TKG Tokodynagraph
TKG Tongkang [*Ship's rigging*] (ROG)
TKGA [*The*] Knitting Guild of America (EA)
TKGS Church of Jesus Christ of Latter-Day Saints, Genealogical Society Library, Knoxville Branch, Knoxville, TN [*Library symbol Library of Congress*] (LCLS)
TKH Thick [*Aviation*] (DA)
TKH Tikhaya Bay [*Later, HIS*] [*Former USSR Geomagnetic observatory code*]
TKi Kingsport Public Library, Kingsport, TN [*Library symbol Library of Congress*] (LCLS)
TKI McKinney, TX [*Location identifier FAA*] (FAAL)
TKI Trial Kit Installation (CAAL)
TKI Turks Islands [*West Indies*] [*Airport symbol*] (AD)
TKIBU Transmission-Keying Indicator Buffer (DNAB)
TKIF Training Name and Address Key Index File [*IRS*]
TKiH Holston Valley Community Hospital, Health Science Library, Kingsport, TN [*Library symbol Library of Congress*] (LCLS)
TKimJ Johnson Bible College, Knoxville, TN [*Library symbol Library of Congress*] (LCLS)
TKIO [*The*] Tokio Marine & Fire Insurance Co. Ltd. [*NASDAQ symbol*] (NQ)
TKIOY [*The*] Tokio Marine & Fire Insurance Co. (MHDW)
TKIOY Tokio Marine/Fire ADR [*NASDAQ symbol*] (TTSB)
TKJ Tok, AK [*Location identifier FAA*] (FAAL)
TKK Token Kenkyu Kai [*Defunct*] (EA)
TKK Toyo Kogyo Co. [*Auto manufacturer*]
TKK Truk [*Caroline Islands*] [*Airport symbol*] (OAG)
TKKTFSLB [*The*] Kandy-Kolored Tangerine-Flake Streamline Baby [*Title of book by Tom Wolfe*]
TKL Knoxville-Knox County Public Library, Knoxville, TN [*OCLC symbol*] (OCLC)
TKL Public Library of Knoxville and Knox County, Knoxville, TN [*Library symbol Library of Congress*] (LCLS)
TKL Tackle [*Mechanical engineering*]
TKL Tak [*Thailand*] [*Airport symbol*] (AD)
TKL Taku Lodge, AK [*Location identifier FAA*] (FAAL)
TKL Tanker Oil & Gas [*Vancouver Stock Exchange symbol*]
TKL Tokelau Islands [*ANSI three-letter standard code*] (CNC)
TKLaw Tennessee State Law Library, Knoxville, TN [*Library symbol Library of Congress*] (LCLS)
TKLC TEKELEC [*Calabasas, CA*] [*NASDAQ symbol*] (NQ)
TKLI Tachykinin-Like Immunoreactivity [*Laboratory science*] (DAVI)
TKLMI Lakeshore Mental Health Institute, Staff Library, Knoxville, TN [*Library symbol Library of Congress*] (LCLS)
TKM Merrill Lynch & Co. [*NYSE symbol*] (SAG)
TKM Takamatsu [*Japan*] [*Seismograph station code, US Geological Survey*] (SEIS)
TKM TRIS, Potassium Chloride, Magnesium Chloride [*A buffer*]
TKMT Municipal Technical Advisory Service, Knoxville, TN [*Library symbol*] [*Library of Congress*] (LCLS)
TKN Tek-Net International Ltd. (Canada) [*Vancouver Stock Exchange symbol*]
TKN Thermotrex Corp. [*AMEX symbol*] (SPSG)
TKN Tokuno Shima [*Japan*] [*Airport symbol*] (OAG)
TKN Total Kjeldahl Nitrogen [*Organic analysis*]
TKN University of Tennessee, Knoxville, TN [*OCLC symbol*] (OCLC)
TKNO To Keep Needle Open [*Pharmacology*] (DAVI)
TKO Mankato, KS [*Location identifier FAA*] (FAAL)
TKO Taseko Mines Ltd. [*Vancouver Stock Exchange symbol*]
TKO Technical Knockout [*Boxing*]
TKO Technische Kontrollorganisation
TKO To Keep Open [*Medicine*]
TKO Trunk Offer [*Telecommunications*] (TEL)
TKO Trunk Offering (NITA)
TKOC Taseko Mines Ltd. [*NASDAQ symbol*] (SAG)
TKOCF Taseko Mines [*NASDAQ symbol*] (TTSB)
TKOF Takeoff [*Aviation*]
TKOS Tokos Medical Corp. [*NASDAQ symbol*] (SAG)
TKP [*The*] Knapp Press [*Book publisher*]
TKP Takapoto Island [*French Polynesia*] [*Airport symbol*] (OAG)
TKP Thermokeratoplasty [*Medicine*] (CPH)
TKP Theta Kappa Phi [*Fraternity*]
TKP Ton-Kilometer Performed
TKP Toplumcu Kurtulus Partisi [*Communal Liberation Party*] [*Cyprus*] [*Political party*] (EY)
TKP Trans Korea Pipeline
TKP Turkiye Komunist Partisi
TKPH Park West Hospital, Knoxville, TN [*Library symbol Library of Congress*] (LCLS)
TKPK Basseterre/Golden Rock [*St. Kitts Island*] [*ICAO location identifier*] (ICLI)
TKP-ML People's Revolutionary Union - Marxist-Leninist [*Turkey*] (PD)
TKPN Charlestown/Newcastle [*Nevis Island*] [*ICAO location identifier*] (ICLI)
TKPP Tetrapotassium Pyrophosphate [*Organic chemistry*] (DICI)
TKPS Tuvalu and Kiribati Philatelic Society (EA)
TKPT Pellissippi Stat Technical Community College, Knoxville, TN [*Library symbol*] [*Library of Congress*] (LCLS)
TKQ Kigoma [*Tanzania*] [*Airport symbol*] (OAG)
TKR Canadian Interagency Forest Fire Centre [*ICAO designator*] (FAAC)
TKR Tanker (AAG)
TKR Terrestrial Kilometric Radiation [*Physics*]
TKR Thakurgaon [*Bangladesh*] [*Airport symbol*] (AD)
TKR [*The*] Timken Co. [*Formerly, TDX*] [*NYSE symbol*] (SPSG)
TKR Total Knee Replacement [*Medicine*]
tkr Turkmen Soviet Socialist Republic [*MARC country of publication code Library of Congress*] (LCCP)
TKS Knoxville City School, Knoxville, TN [*OCLC symbol*] (OCLC)
TKS Tackstrip [*Technical drawings*]
TKS Tamavack Resources, Inc. [*Vancouver Stock Exchange symbol*]
TKS Thanks (ADA)
TKS Throttle Kicker Solenoid [*Automotive engineering*]
TKS Tokushima [*Japan*] [*Airport symbol*] (OAG)
TKS Tokushima [*Japan*] [*Seismograph station code, US Geological Survey*] (SEIS)
TKS Tokyo Kikai Seisakusho [*Japan*]
TKS Tomkins PLC [*NYSE symbol*] (SAG)
TKS Tomkins plc ADS [*NYSE symbol*] (TTSB)
TK-SC Tennessee State Supreme Court Law Library, Knoxville, TN [*Library symbol Library of Congress Obsolete*] (LCLS)
TKSMC Saint Mary's Medical Center, Medical Library, Knoxville, TN [*Library symbol Library of Congress*] (LCLS)
TKSMC-N Saint Mary's Medical Center, Nursing School Library, Knoxville, TN [*Library symbol Library of Congress*] (LCLS)
TK SUP Track Supervisor (CAAL)
TKT Tashkent [*Former USSR Geomagnetic observatory code*]
TKT Ticker Tape Resources Ltd. [*Vancouver Stock Exchange symbol*]
TKT Ticket
TKTF Tanker Task Force
TKTM Ticketmaster Group, Inc. [*NASDAQ symbol*] (SAG)
TKTN Task Termination Notice [*Computer science*] (MHDB)
TKTRANSR Tank Transporter [*Military*] (AABC)
TKTS Thermodynamic Kelvin Temperature Scale
TKTU Thymidine Kinase (Activity) Transforming Unit [*Biochemistry*]
TKTVA Tennessee Valley Authority, Knoxville, TN [*Library symbol Library of Congress*] (LCLS)
TKTX Transkaryotic Therapies, Inc. [*NASDAQ symbol*] (SAG)
TKU Takayasuyama [*Japan*] [*Seismograph station code, US Geological Survey*] (SEIS)
TKU Turku [*Finland*] [*Airport symbol*] (OAG)
TKV Tatakoto [*French Polynesia*] [*Airport symbol*] (OAG)
TKW Thermal Kilowatts
TKWC Whittle Communications Corp., Knoxville, TN [*Library symbol*] [*Library of Congress*] (LCLS)
TKX Kennett, MO [*Location identifier FAA*] (FAAL)
TKY Takayama [*Japan*] [*Seismograph station code, US Geological Survey*] (SEIS)
TKY Turkey Creek [*Western Australia*] [*Airport symbol*] (AD)
TL Central African Republic [*International civil aircraft marking*] (ODBW)
TL Empresas Telex-Chile ADS [*NYSE symbol*] (TTSB)
Tl Lateral Touch Neuron [*of a leech*]
TL Reports of the Witwatersrand High Court [*Transvaal, South Africa*] [*A publication*] (DLA)
TL Skyport [*Airport symbol*]
TL Tackline [*British naval signaling*]
T/L Tactical Landing
TL Tail Lamp [*Automotive engineering*]
TL Tail-Lift [*of trucks and vans*] (DCTA)
T/L Talk/Listen (NASA)
TL Tank Lease (ADA)
TL Tape Library (BUR)
TL Target Language
TL Target Loss (OA)
TL Task Leader (NRCH)
T/L Task List (KSC)
TL Taxilane [*FAA*] (TAG)
TL Team Leader (AABC)
TL Technical Letter
TL Technical Library
TL Technical Limit
TL Telegraphist-Lieutenant [*Navy British*]
TL Telex Chile SA [*NYSE symbol*] (SAG)
T-L Tennessee State Law Library, Nashville, TN [*Library symbol Library of Congress*] (LCLS)
TL Terminal Limen
TL Terminology Library [*Computer science*] (IAA)
TL Terra Lliure [*Free Land*] [*Spanish terrorist group*]
TL Test Laboratory (AFM)
TL Test Link
TL Test Load
TL Test Log (IEEE)
TL Testolactone [*Biochemistry*]
TL Texas League [*Baseball*]
Tl Thallium [*Chemical element*]
TL Therapeutic Level [*Medicine*]
TL Thermal Liquefaction [*Chemical engineering*]
TL Thermoluminescence [*Also, THL*]
TL Thoreau Lyceum (EA)
TL Throws Left-Handed [*Baseball*]
TL Thrust Level (NASA)
TL Thrust Line
TL Thymic Lymphoma [*Medicine*]
T-L Thymus-Dependent Lymphocyte [*Hematology*] (DAVI)
TL Thymus-Derived Lymphocyte [*Hematology*]
TL Thymus Leukemia [*Hematology*]
TL Ticket of Leave (ADA)
TL Tie Line [*Communication channel*]
TL Time Lapse (MAE)
TL Time Latest (NASA)
TL Time Lengths

T-L .... Time-Life Books [*Publisher*]
TL .... Time Limit
TL .... Timeline (MCD)
TL .... Time Line
T/L .... Time Loan [*Banking*]
TL .... Time of Landing
TL .... Time to Launch [*Navy*] (CAAL)
TL .... Title List
tl .... Tokelau Islands [*MARC country of publication code Library of Congress*] (LCCP)
TL .... Ton Load
TL .... Tool Life
TL .... Tool List
TL .... Tools [*JETDS nomenclature*] [*Military*] (CET)
TL .... Torpedo Lieutenant [*Navy British*]
TL .... Torus Longitudinalis [*Anatomy*]
TL .... Total
TL .... Total Body Length [*Of Crustacea*]
TL .... Total Length
TL .... Total Lipids [*Clinical chemistry*]
TL .... Total Load [*Engineering*]
TL .... Total Loss [*Insurance*]
tl .... Total Loss [*Insurance*] (ODBW)
TL .... Total Luminescence [*Spectroscopy*]
TL .... Tower of London
TL .... Tracker Lock [*NASA*] (KSC)
TL .... Trade-Last
TL .... Trade List (IIA)
tl .... Trade List (ODBW)
TL .... Trading Limit
TL .... Trailer Length [*Specifications*] [*Automotive engineering*]
T/L .... Training Literature
TL .... Transaction Language
TL .... Transaction Listing (AFM)
TL .... Transfer Line [*Manufacturing*]
TL .... Transformation Line [*Telecommunications*] (IAA)
T/L .... Transformer Load (NASA)
TL .... Transforming Lens
TL .... Transient Load (MCD)
TL .... Transistor Logic (IAA)
TL .... Transition Level (DA)
TL .... Translocation Defect [*Medicine*]
TL .... Trans Mediterranean [*ICAO designator*] (AD)
TL .... Transmission Level [*or Line*]
TL .... Transmission Line [*Telecommunications*] (IAA)
TL .... Transmission Loss [*Telecommunications*] (IAA)
TL .... Transmittal Letter (AAG)
TL .... Transmitter Location
T/L .... Transporter/Launcher [*NASA*] (KSC)
T/L .... Transporter/Loader (MCD)
TL .... Trial
TL .... Triboluminescence [*Atomic physics*]
TL .... Triple-Layer [*Pharmacy*]
TL .... Triple Lindy [*Dance step*]
TL .... Truckload [*24,000 pounds or more*]
TL .... Truck Lock [*Nuclear energy*] (NRCH)
TL .... Trunk Load [*Telecommunications*] (IAA)
TL .... Tubal Ligation [*Medicine*]
TL .... Turkish Lira (BJA)
TL .... Turntable Ladder
TL .... Twin Lens [*Photography*] (DGA)
TL2 .... Taxonomic Literature, edition 2 [*Index*] (EERA)
TL$_{50}$ .... Median Tolerance Limit (GNE)
TLA .... Talker Listener Adapter (NITA)
TLA .... Tatlar Resources Ltd. [*Vancouver Stock Exchange symbol*]
TLA .... TELEX Line Adapter (IAA)
TLA .... Teller [*Alaska*] [*Airport symbol*] (OAG)
TLA .... Teller, AK [*Location identifier FAA*] (FAAL)
TLA .... Temporary Lodging Allowance [*Military*]
TLA .... Terminal Low Altitude
TLA .... Textile Labor Association [*India*]
TLA .... Theatre Library Association (EA)
TLA .... Thin-Layer Activation [*Engine wear testing*]
TLA .... Three Letter Acronym
TLA .... Three-Letter Acronym [*Computer hacker terminology*] (NHD)
TLA .... Throttle Lever Angle (MCD)
TLA .... Time Line Analysis
TLA .... Toy Libraries Association [*British*]
TLA .... Transaction Log Analysis
TLa .... Transition Layer
TLA .... Translift Airways Ltd. [*British ICAO designator*] (FAAC)
TLA .... Translumbar Aortogram [*Medicine*]
TLA .... Transluminal Angioplasty [*Cardiology*] (DAVI)
TLA .... Transmission Line Adapter [*or Assembly*]
TLA .... Transportation Lawyers Association (EA)
TLA .... Travel and Living Allowance [*Military*] (AABC)
TLA .... Trunk Line Association
TLAA .... T-Lymphocyte-Associated Antigen [*Hematology*] (DAVI)
TLAB .... Tellabs, Inc. [*NASDAQ symbol*] (NQ)
TLAB .... Translation Lookaside Buffer [*Computer science*] (CMD)
TLAC .... Test Listening Accuracy in Children [*Educational test*]
TLAC .... Top Loading Air Cleaner (MCD)
TLACV .... Track-Laying Air-Cushion Vehicle
TLAM .... Tomahawk Land Attack Missile (MCD)
TLAM/C .... Tomahawk Land Attack Missile/Conventional [*Navy*] (ANA)
TLAM-N .... Tomahawk Land Attack Missile - Nuclear (MCD)
T-LAR .... That Looks about Right [*Aviation*]
TLAS .... Tactical Logical and Air Simulation
TLAT .... TOW [*Tube-Launched, Optically Tracked, Wire-Guided (Weapon)*] Light Antitank Battalion (MCD)
T Lawyr .... Tax Lawyer [*A publication*] (ILCA)
TLAY .... Tule Lake Aster Yellows [*Plant pathology*]
TLB .... Table Lookaside Buffer [*Computer science*] (MHDB)
TLB .... Talbots, Inc. [*NYSE symbol*] (SPSG)
TLB .... Temporary Lighted Buoy [*Maps and charts*]
TLB .... Texas-Louisiana Freight Bureau, St. Louis MO [*STAC*]
TLB .... Time-Life Books
TLB .... Tortola [*British Virgin Islands*] [*Airport symbol*] (AD)
TLB .... Tractor/Loader/Backhoe
TLB .... Trailer Launch Bridge (DWSG)
TLB .... Translation Lookaside Buffer [*Computer science*] (BUR)
TLBAA .... Texas Longhorn Breeders Association of America (EA)
TL/BBC .... Tax Limitation/Balanced Budget Coalition [*Defunct*] (EA)
TLBID .... TLB [*Translation - Lookaside - Buffers*] Identifier
TLBR .... Tactical LASER Beam Recorder (MCD)
TLC .... Caribbean Express, Inc. [*ICAO designator*] (FAAC)
TLC .... [*The*] Learning Channel [*Cable-television system*]
TLC .... Lee College, Cleveland, TN [*OCLC symbol*] (OCLC)
TLC .... Maximum Recoil Pressure [*Medicine*] (DAVI)
TLC .... Tactical Leadership Course [*Army*] (INF)
TLC .... Tangent Latitude Computer
TLC .... Tank Landing Craft [*Army British*]
TLC .... Task Level Controller
TLC .... Teachable Language Comprehender (PDAA)
TLC .... Teaching, Learning and Curriculum Model (EDAC)
TLC .... Technology Life Cycle (NITA)
TLC .... Telecommand (NASA)
TLC .... Tele-Link, Inc. [*Miami, FL*] [*Telecommunications service*] (TSSD)
TLC .... Teletype, Line Printer, Card Reader Controller (NOAA)
TLC .... Television Licensing Center [*Defunct*] (EA)
TLC .... Temperature Level Control (IAA)
TLC .... Tender Loving Care
TLC .... Test of Language Competence [*Educational test*]
TLC .... Texaco Lubricants Co. [*Automotive industry supplier*]
TLC .... Texas Lutheran College
TLC .... Textile Laundry Council (EA)
TLC .... The Learning Co.
TLC .... The Library Corp.
TLC .... Thermochromic Liquid Crystal
TLC .... Thin-Layer Chromatography [*Analytical chemistry*]
TLC .... Tillicum Industry [*Vancouver Stock Exchange symbol*]
TLC .... Time-Lapse Cinematography
TLC .... Time Line Controller
TLC .... T-Lymphocyte Clones [*Immunology*]
TLC .... Tom's Love Connection (EA)
TLC .... Total L-Chain Concentration
TLC .... Total Library Computerization
TLC .... Total Light Chain Concentration [*Immunology*] (DAVI)
TLC .... Total Load Control (MCD)
TLC .... Total Lung Capacity [*Physiology*]
TLC .... Total Lung Compliance [*Medicine*]
TLC .... Total Lymphocyte Count [*Clinical chemistry*]
TLC .... Touch and Learn Computer
TLC .... Touch Logic Controlled [*Electronics*]
TLC .... Traditional Life Cycle (PDAA)
TLC .... Transferable Loan Certificate
TLC .... Transient Late Curvature [*Orthopedics*]
TLC .... Translunar Coast [*Aerospace*]
TLC .... Transmit Level Control (PDAA)
TLC .... Tri-County Library Council, Inc. [*Library network*]
TLC .... Trilateral Commission [*International study group*]
TLC .... Troubles/Requests Logging and Coordination [*Staff*] [*Computer science*]
TLC .... Type and Learn Concept [*Minolta Corp. office system*]
TLCA .... Tangent Latitude Computer Amplifier
TLCACT .... Trades and Labour Council of the Australian Capital Territory
TLCC .... Thin-Line Communications Connectivity
TLC(C) .... Trades and Labour Congress of Canada [*1883-1956*]
TLCC .... Training Launch Control Center (IAA)
TLCCP .... Total Life Cycle Competition Plan [*Army*]
TLCCS .... Total Life Cycle Competition Strategy [*Army*]
TLCE .... Transmission Line Conditioning Equipment (MCD)
TLCF .... Tactical Link Control Facility [*Military*] (CAAL)
TLCI .... Tea Leaf Club International (EA)
TLC/IR .... Thin-Layer Chromatography/Infrared [*Analytical chemistry*]
TLCK .... Tosyllysine Chloromethyl Ketone [*Biochemistry*]
T-LCL .... T-Cell Lymphosarcoma Cell Leukemia [*Oncology*]
TlCl .... Thallium Chloride [*A radioactive isotope*] (DAVI)
TLCM .... TelCom Semiconductor, Inc. [*NASDAQ symbol*] (SAG)
TLCM .... TelCom Semiconductor [*NASDAQ symbol*] (TTSB)
TlcmArg .... Telecom Argentina Stet France Telecom SA [*Associated Press*] (SAG)
TLCPC .... Trunk Line-Central Passenger Committee
TLCQ .... Trades and Labour Council of Queensland [*Australia*]
TLCSC .... Top Level Computer Software Component
TLCT .... Total Life Cycle Time
TL-CTR .... Trunk Line-Central Territory Railroad Tariff Bureau
TLCV .... Tobacco Leaf Curl Virus [*Plant pathology*]
TLCWA .... Trades and Labour Council of Western Australia
TLD .... Technical Logistics Data [*Army*] (AABC)

TLD .... Tele Danmark A/S ADS [*NYSE symbol*] (TTSB)
TLD .... Tele Danmark Co. [*NYSE symbol*] (SAG)
TLD .... Telephone Line Doubler (IAA)
TLD .... Thermoluminescent Device
TLD .... Thermoluminescent Dosimeter [*or Dosimetry*]
TLD .... Thoracic Lymph Duct [*Medicine*] (MAE)
TLD .... Tiled [*Classified advertising*] (ADA)
tld .... Tooled (BARN)
TLD .... Top-Level Demonstration [*Military*] (INF)
TLD .... Top-Level Domain [*Internet Name*]
TLD .... Traffic Loading Device (CAAL)
TLD .... Tumor Lethal Dose [*Medicine*] (MAE)
T/LD_{100} .... Minimum Dose Causing Malformation or Death of 100 Percent of Fetuses [*Radiation therapy*] (DAVI)
TLDB .... Transportation Legislative Data Base [*Battelle Memorial Institute*] [*Department of Energy Information service or system*] (IID)
TLDC .... Taiwan Land Development Corp.
TLDC .... Teledata Communications [*NASDAQ symbol*] (SAG)
TLDCF .... Teledata Communication [*NASDAQ symbol*] (TTSB)
TLDF .... Thomas Legal Defense Fund (EA)
TLDI .... Technical Logistics Data and Information [*Army*] (AABC)
TLDIP .... Technical Logistics Data Information Program
TLDP .... Technical Logistics Data Program [*Navy*] (DNAB)
TLE .... Air Toulouse [*France ICAO designator*] (FAAC)
TLE .... [*The*] Learning Exchange [*Defunct*] (EA)
TLE .... Target Location Error [*Military*] (AABC)
TLE .... Technical Liaison Engineer
TLE .... Temperature-Limited Emission
TLE .... Temporal Lobe Epilepsy [*Medicine*]
TLE .... Temporary Living Expenses
TLE .... Temporary Lodging Entitlement (DOMA)
TLE .... Temporary Lodging Expense (DOMA)
TLE .... Temporary Lodging Expense [*DoD*]
TLE .... Test Laboratory Engineer (IAA)
TLE .... Theoretical Line of Escape (WDAA)
TLE .... Thin-Layer Electrophoresis [*Analytical chemistry*]
TLE .... Thin Leading Edge
TLE .... Time-Life Education
TLE .... Total Erickson Resources Ltd. [*Toronto Stock Exchange symbol Vancouver Stock Exchange symbol*]
TLE .... Total Lipid Extract [*Biochemistry*]
TLE .... Toward Liberal Education [*In book title*]
TLE .... Tower Lighting Equipment
TLE .... Tracking Light Electronics (KSC)
TLE .... Traffic Law Enforcement
TLE .... Transferline Heat Exchanger [*Chemical engineering*]
TLE .... Treaty Limited Equipment (DOMA)
TLE .... Tulear [*Madagascar*] [*Airport symbol*] (OAG)
TLebC .... Cumberland College of Tennessee, Lebanon, TN [*Library symbol Library of Congress*] (LCLS)
TLEICS .... Treasury Law Enforcement Information and Communications System
T-lens .... Therapeutic Contact Lens [*Opthalomology*] (DAVI)
Tlepd .... Telepad Corp. [*Associated Press*] (SAG)
TLET .... Transitional Low-Emission Truck
TLEV .... Transitional Low-Emission Vehicle
TLF .... Leather Factory [*AMEX symbol*] (TTSB)
TLF .... Leather Factory, Inc. [*AMEX symbol*] (SPSG)
TLF .... Temporary Loading Facilities (MCD)
TLF .... Temporary Lodging Facility
TLF .... Terminal Launch Facility
TLF .... Thrust Required for Level Flight [*Aviation*] (MCD)
TLF .... Time Line Form
TLF .... Trunk Link Frame [*Telecommunications*] (TEL)
TLF .... Trypanosome Lytic Factor [*Biochemistry*]
TLF .... Two-Level Fluctuation [*Physics*]
TLFB .... Texas-Louisiana Freight Bureau
TLFC .... Terri LaVelle Fan Club (EA)
TLFC .... Traci Lords Fan Club [*Defunct*] (EA)
TLFE .... Tasmanian Licensed Fruit Exporters [*Australia*]
TLFN .... Tunison Laboratory of Fish Nutrition [*Cortland, NY*] [*Department of the Interior*] (GRD)
TLG .... Consolidated Thompson-Lundmark Gold Mines Ltd. [*Toronto Stock Exchange symbol*]
TLG .... Tail Landing Gear
TLG .... Talgar [*Also, AAB*] [*Alma-Ata*] [*Former USSR Seismograph station code, US Geological Survey*] (SEIS)
TLG .... Telegram (IAA)
TLG .... Telegraph (AAG)
TLG .... Tentative Logistics Guidance (MCD)
TLG .... Thin-Layer Gel [*Filtration*] [*Analytical chemistry*]
TLG .... Tilting
TLG .... Timing Level Generator (IAA)
TLG .... Tres Lagoas [*Brazil*] [*Airport symbol*] (AD)
TLGB .... Tube-Launched Guided Projectiles (MCD)
TLGD .... Tollgrade Communications [*NASDAQ symbol*] (TTSB)
TLGN .... Telegen Corp. [*NASDAQ symbol*] (SAG)
TLGZ .... Telegraph Communications [*NASDAQ symbol*] (SAG)
TLGZF .... Telegraph Communications Wrrt [*NASDAQ symbol*] (TTSB)
TLH .... Tallahassee [*Florida*] [*Airport symbol*] (OAG)
TLH .... Tulloch Resources [*Vancouver Stock Exchange symbol*]
TLHS .... Thin Line Handling System (DWSG)
TLI .... Tank Level Indicator (DNAB)
TLI .... Telephone Line Interface (IEEE)
TLI .... Term Life Insurance
TLI .... Theoretical Lethality Index (MCD)
TLI .... Thymidine-Labeling Index [*Oncology*]
TLI .... Time-Life International
tli .... Tlingit [*MARC language code Library of Congress*] (LCCP)
TLI .... T-Logic, Inc. [*Information service or system*] (IID)
TLI .... Tolitoli [*Indonesia*] [*Airport symbol*] (OAG)
TLI .... Total Lymphoid Irradiation
TLI .... Transferable Loan Instrument (MHDW)
TLI .... Translunar Injection [*Aerospace*]
TLI .... Transport Layer Interface [*Computer science*] (PCM)
TLI .... Transport Layer Interface [*Application program interface*] (TNIG)
TLI .... Triangle Resources, Inc. [*Vancouver Stock Exchange symbol*]
TLI .... Trinidad Light Infantry [*British military*] (DMA)
TLI .... True Life Institute (EA)
TLIB .... Tape Library [*National Center for Atmospheric Research*]
TLIB .... Transportation Library [*National Academy of Sciences*] [*Information service or system*] (IID)
TLIC .... Transport Holdings'A' [*NASDAQ symbol*] (TTSB)
TLIC .... Transport Holdings, Inc. [*NASDAQ symbol*] (SAG)
TLIEF .... Thin-Layer Isoelectric Focusing [*Analytical chemistry*]
TLII .... Trans Leasing International, Inc. [*Northbrook, IL*] [*NASDAQ symbol*] (NQ)
TLII .... Trans Leasing Intl. [*NASDAQ symbol*] (TTSB)
TLIR .... Time-Limited Impulse Response [*Telecommunications*] (IAA)
TLJ .... Laredo Junior College, Laredo, TX [*OCLC symbol*] (OCLC)
TLJ .... Tatalina [*Alaska*] [*Airport symbol*] (OAG)
TLJ .... Tatalina, AK [*Location identifier FAA*] (FAAL)
TLJ .... Travancore Law Journal [*India*] [*A publication*] (DLA)
TLJP .... Thermal Liquid Junction Potential (PDAA)
TLK .... Indonesian Telekomunikas [*NYSE symbol*] (SAG)
TLK .... New York, NY [*Location identifier FAA*] (FAAL)
TLK .... P.T. Telekomunikasi ADS [*NYSE symbol*] (TTSB)
TLK .... Talkeetna Mountains [*Alaska*] [*Seismograph station code, US Geological Survey*] (SEIS)
TLK .... Talking [*Telecommunications*] (TEL)
TLK .... Test Link (IEEE)
TLK .... University of Tennessee, Law Library, Knoxville, TN [*OCLC symbol*] (OCLC)
TLL .... Tallinn [*Former USSR Airport symbol*] (OAG)
TLL .... Tank Lighter
T-LL .... T-Cell Lymphoblastic Lymphoma [*Oncology*]
TLL .... Teachers' Labour League [*British*] (AIE)
TLL .... Television LASER Link
TLL .... Tender Load List
TLL .... Threshold Lactose Load [*Clinical chemistry*]
TLL .... Tololo Astronomical Observatory [*Chile*] [*Seismograph station code, US Geological Survey*] (SEIS)
TLL .... Tom's Look of Love (EA)
TLL .... Transporter, Loader, Launcher
TLLD .... Total Load
TLLE .... Twin Linear Loop Exciter (IAA)
TLLM .... Temperature and Liquid Level Monitor [*Nuclear energy*] (NRCH)
TLLS .... Tellus Industries, Inc. [*Sacramento, CA*] [*NASDAQ symbol*] (NQ)
TLLTD .... Tre Lateral Load Transfer Distribution
TLLW .... Tank Lighter (Medium Tank-Well Type)
TLM .... Median Tolerance Limit (GNE)
TLM .... Technical Liaison Memo
TLM .... Telemeter [*or Telemetry*] (AAG)
TLM .... Thin Lipid Membrane (OA)
TLM .... Tilimsen [*Algeria*] [*Airport symbol*] (OAG)
TLM .... Toledo-Lucas County Public Library, Toledo, OH [*OCLC symbol*] (OCLC)
TLM .... Tolmezzo [*Italy*] [*Seismograph station code, US Geological Survey*] (SEIS)
TLM .... Transformer Load Management (IAA)
TLM .... Transmission Line Method [*Photovoltaic energy systems*]
TLM .... Transmitted Light Microscope
TLM .... Trillium Telephone Systems, Inc. [*Toronto Stock Exchange symbol*]
TLM .... Tube-Launched Missile (MCD)
TLMA .... Tag and Label Manufacturers Association (DGA)
TLMA .... Trial Lawyers Marketing Association (EA)
TLMA .... Tunnel Lining Manufacturers Association [*British*] (DBA)
TLMB .... Telemetry Data Buffer
TLMB .... Tobacco Leaf Marketing Board [*Australia*]
TLMCTLPNL .... Telemetry Control Panel (IAA)
TLMD .... Telemundo Group 'A' [*NASDAQ symbol*] (TTSB)
TLMD .... Telemundo Group, Inc. [*NASDAQ symbol*] (SAG)
TLMDW .... Telemundo Group Wrrt [*NASDAQ symbol*] (TTSB)
TLMG .... Telemetering (AAG)
TLMI .... Tag and Label Manufacturers Institute (EA)
TLMS .... Tape Library Management System
TLMY .... Telemetry (MSA)
TLN .... Talang [*Sumatra*] [*Seismograph station code, US Geological Survey Closed*] (SEIS)
TLN .... Tasmanian Law Newsletter [*A publication*]
TLN .... Thermolysin [*An enzyme*]
TLN .... Title plus Last Name
TLN .... Torque-Limiting Nut
TLN .... Toulon/Hyeres [*France*] [*Airport symbol*] (OAG)
TLN .... Transmittal Locator Number [*Computer science*]
TLN .... Trunk Line Network
TLO .... [*The*] Last One [*A microcomputer program manufactured by DJ-AI*]
TLO .... [*The*] Lifestyles Organization (EA)
TLO .... Technical Liaison Office [*Military*]
TLO .... Terminal Learning Objective
TLO .... Tol [*Papua New Guinea*] [*Airport symbol*] (OAG)

TLO............ Toledo [*Spain*] [*Seismograph station code, US Geological Survey*] (SEIS)
TLO............ Total Loss Only
tlo............ Total Loss Only [*Insurance*] (ODBW)
TLO............ Tracking Local Oscillator
TLO............ Training Liaison Officer [*Ministry of Agriculture, Fisheries, and Food*] [*British*]
TLOBS........ Tailored List of Base Spares [*Military*] (AFIT)
TLOF.......... Touchdown Lift-Off Surface [*OST*] (TAG)
TLOS.......... Tailored List of Spares [*Military*] (AFIT)
TLOS.......... Troop List for Operations and Supply
TLO(S)........ Turbine Lube Oil (System) [*Nuclear energy*] (NRCH)
TLOST........ Turbine Lube Oil Storage Tank [*Nuclear energy*] (NRCH)
TLP............ Tabular List of Parts (AAG)
TLP............ Tactical Leadership Program [*Military*]
T/LP........... Tail Lamp [*Automotive engineering*]
TLP............ Talpa [*New Mexico*] [*Airport symbol*] (AD)
TLP............ Tapered Link Pin
TLP............ Target Letter Position [*Psychology*]
TLP............ Telegraph Line Pair (BUR)
TLP............ Telephone Line Patch
TLP............ Tension-Leg Platform [*Oil exploration*]
TLP............ Term Lease Plan (IAA)
TLP............ Term-Limit Pricing [*Agreement*] [*Price Commission*]
TLP............ Therapeutic Learning Program [*Psychology*]
TLP............ Threshold Learning Process (IEEE)
TLP............ Top Load Pad (NRCH)
TLP............ Top Load Plane [*Nuclear energy*] (NRCH)
TLP............ Torpedo Landplane [*Navy*]
TLP............ Total Language Processor [*Computer science*] (IEEE)
TLP............ Total Liquid Product [*Chemical engineering*]
TLP............ Total Loss of Pay [*Court-martial sentence*] [*Military*]
TLP............ Transient Lunar Phenomena
TLP............ Transmission Level Point [*Telecommunications*]
TLP............ Tribal Liaison Program [*Bureau of the Census*] (GFGA)
TLP............ Troop-Leading Procedure [*Military*] (INF)
TLP............ Trouble Location Problem (AAG)
TLP............ Truck Loading Point (NATG)
tlp............ Tulip (VRA)
TLP............ Tulip Air [*Netherlands ICAO designator*] (FAAC)
TLPC.......... Castries/Vigie [*St. Lucia*] [*ICAO location identifier*] (ICLI)
TLPC.......... Tailpiece
TLPJ........... Trial Lawyers for Public Justice (EA)
TLPL........... Vieux-Fort/Hewanorra International [*St. Lucia*] [*ICAO location identifier*] (ICLI)
TLPR.......... Terrestrial Low-Power Reactor
TLPWD....... Tory Legacy Plus World Depression [*British*] (DI)
TLQ............ Temporary Lodging Quarters [*Military*] (DNAB)
TLQ............ Tender Load Quantities (DNAB)
TLQ............ Total Living Quotient (MAE)
TLR............ Northern Airlines [*British ICAO designator*] (FAAC)
TLR............ Tailor
TLR............ Tailor
TLR............ Talgarno [*Western Australia*] [*Airport symbol*] (AD)
TLR............ Tally Resources [*Vancouver Stock Exchange symbol*]
TLR............ Tanganyika Law Reports [*1921-52*] [*A publication*] (DLA)
TLR............ Tanzania Gazette Law Reports [*A publication*] (DLA)
TLR............ Tape Loop Recorder
TLR............ Teller
TLR............ Tiler [*Freemasonry*]
TLR............ Tiller (MSA)
TLR............ Times Law Reports [*1884-1952*] [*England*] [*A publication*] (DLA)
TLR............ Toll Line Release
TLR............ Tool Liaison Request (AAG)
TLR............ Top Level Requirements [*Navy*]
TLR............ Topped Long Resid [*Petroleum technology*]
TLR............ Trailer (AAG)
TLR............ Travancore Law Reports [*India*] [*A publication*] (DLA)
TLR............ Triangulation-Listening-Ranging [*SONAR*]
TLR............ Tulare, CA [*Location identifier FAA*] (FAAL)
TLR............ Twin Lens Reflex [*Camera*] (MCD)
TLRB.......... Textile Labor Relations Board [*Terminated, 1937; functions absorbed by US Conciliation Service, Department of Labor*]
TLRC.......... Canadian Association of Toy Libraries and Parent Resource Centers (EAIO)
TLRC.......... Technology and Livelihood Resource Center [*Philippines*] [*Information service or system*] (IID)
TLRG.......... Tailoring
TLRG.......... Target List Review Group (CINC)
TLRMTD...... Trailer Mounted
TLRN.......... Tellurian, Inc. [*NASDAQ symbol*] (SAG)
TLRNC........ Tolerance (FAAC)
TLRP.......... Trace Last Reference Position (IAA)
TLRP.......... Track Last Reference Position
TLR (R)....... Tanganyika Law Reports (Revised) [*1921-52*] [*A publication*] (DLA)
TLR/S......... Total Logistic Readiness/Sustainability Analysis [*Military*]
TLRS.......... Tramway and Light Railway Society [*British*] (BI)
TLRS.......... Transportable LASER Ranging Station [*for measurement of earth movement*]
TLRV.......... Tracked Levitated Research Vehicle
TLS............ Laredo State University, Laredo, TX [*OCLC symbol*] (OCLC)
TLS............ Tactical Landing System
TLS............ Talasea [*New Britain*] [*Seismograph station code, US Geological Survey*] (SEIS)
TLS............ Tank LASER Sight (MCD)
TLS............ Tape Librarian System
TLS............ Target Level of Safety (DA)
TLS............ Target Location System
TLS............ Teaching and Learning Support (AIE)
TLS............ Technical Library Service (IID)
TLS............ Tekniska Litteratursallskapet (NITA)
TLS............ Telecommunication Liaison Staff (IEEE)
TLS............ Telemetry Listing Submodule
TLS............ Telepanel Systems [*Toronto Stock Exchange symbol*] (SPSG)
TLS............ Telescope (KSC)
TLS............ Terminal Landing System (KSC)
TLS............ Territorial Long Service Medal [*Military British*]
TLS............ Testing the Limits for Sex [*Psychology*]
TLS............ Test Line Signal (IAA)
TLS............ Theater Level Scenario [*Military*]
TLS............ Thin Liquid Stillage [*Fermentation byproduct*]
TLS............ Thoracolumbosacral [*Drain*] [*Surgery*] (DAVI)
TLS............ Throttle Lever Setting (KSC)
TLS............ Tifton Loamy Soil [*Agronomy*]
TLS............ Time-Limited Signal
TLS............ Time Line Sheet [*NASA*]
TLS............ Times Literary Supplement [*A publication*] (BRI)
TLS............ TLC Air, Inc. [*ICAO designator*] (FAAC)
TLS............ Top Left Side (MCD)
TLS............ Top Level Specification [*Military*] (CAAL)
TLS............ Total Library System [*OCLC*]
TLS............ Total Logic Solution
TLS............ Total Luminescence Spectroscopy
TLS............ Toulouse [*France*] [*Airport symbol*] (OAG)
TLS............ Training Launch Station (MCD)
TLS............ Translocated in Liposarcoma [*Genetics*]
TLS............ Transparent LAN [*Local Area Network*] Service (TNIG)
TLS............ Tulsa [*Diocesan abbreviation*] [*Oklahoma*] (TOCD)
TLS............ Two-Level System [*Physics*]
TLS............ Typed Letter Signed
TLSA.......... Torso Limb Suit Assembly (MCD)
TLSA.......... Transparent Line Sharing Adapter
TLSC.......... Target Logistics Support Costs
TLSCP........ Telescope (MSA)
TLSD.......... Torque-Limiting Screwdriver
TLSER........ Theoretical Linear Solvation Energy Relationship [*Physical chemistry*]
TLSFT........ Tailshaft
TLSG.......... Turret Lathe Stop Gauge
TLSGT........ Tactical Landing System Guidance Techniques (MCD)
TLSI........... Telepanel Systems, Inc. [*NASDAQ symbol*] (SAG)
TLSIF.......... Telepanel Systems [*NASDAQ symbol*] (TTSB)
TLSO.......... Thoracolumbosacral Orthosis [*Medicine*]
TLSP.......... TeleSpectrum Worldwide, Inc. [*NASDAQ symbol*] (SAG)
TLSP.......... Transponder Location by Surface Positioning [*RADAR*]
TLSS.......... Tactical Life Support System [*G-suit developed by Boeing Co.*]
TLSS.......... Technical Library Services Section
TLT............ LeTourneau College, Longview, TX [*OCLC symbol*] (OCLC)
TLT............ Telecommunications Translator (IAA)
TLT............ Teleprinter Load Tables (KSC)
TLT............ Telstar Resource Corp. [*Vancouver Stock Exchange symbol*]
TLT............ Terminal List Table (IAA)
TLT............ Toilet
TLT............ Transportable Link Terminal [*AMC*]
TLT............ Travancore Law Times [*India*] [*A publication*] (DLA)
TLT............ Tuluksak [*Alaska*] [*Airport symbol*] (OAG)
TLT............ Tuluksak, AK [*Location identifier FAA*] (FAAL)
TLT............ Turtle Airways Ltd. [*Fiji*] [*ICAO designator*] (FAAC)
TLTA.......... Thin Line Towed Array [*Navy*] (CAAL)
TLTA.......... Two-Loop Test Apparatus [*Nuclear energy*] (NRCH)
TLTB.......... Trunk Line Tariff Bureau
TLTK.......... Teletek, Inc. [*NASDAQ symbol*] (NQ)
TLTK.......... Tool Truck
TLTM.......... Third Level Thermal Margin [*Nuclear energy*] (NRCH)
TLTN.......... Teltrend, Inc. [*NASDAQ symbol*] (SAG)
TL to TL...... Tangent Line to Tangent Line [*Engineering*]
TLTP.......... Teletype (IAA)
TLTP.......... Too Long to Print (FAAC)
TLTP.......... Trunk Line Test Panel [*Telecommunications*] (TEL)
TLTR.......... Translator (AFM)
TLTS.......... Tracking Loop Test Set
TLTV.......... Total Loan-to-Value [*Real estate*] (EMRF)
TLTYP........ Teletype
TLU............ Table Look Up [*Computer science*]
TLU............ Teaching-Learning Unit (AEE)
TLU............ Terminal Logic Unit [*Telecommunications*] (TEL)
TLU............ Threshold Logic Unit
TLU............ Tight Little Unit [*Ski-bum slang*]
TLU............ Time of Last Update
TLU............ Tolu [*Colombia*] [*Airport symbol*] (OAG)
TLU............ Transportable LASER Unit
TLU............ Tropical Livestock Unit [*Ratio of livestock to humans*]
TLV............ Talemon Investments Ltd. [*Vancouver Stock Exchange symbol*]
TLV............ Target Launch Vehicle [*NASA*]
TLV............ Tel Aviv-Yafo [*Israel*] [*Airport symbol*] (OAG)
TLV............ Television (IAA)
TLV............ Test Launch Vehicle (MCD)
TLV............ Threshold Limit Value [*Industrial hygiene*]
TLV............ Total Lung Volume [*Physiology*]
TLV............ Track Levitated Vehicle [*Department of Transportation*]
TLv............ Transition Level

TLV .... Transporter - Loader Vehicle [*NASA*] (NASA)
TLV .... Two-Lung Ventilation [*Medicine*]
TLV .... Type Length and Value (TNIG)
TLV-C .... Threshold Limit Value - Ceiling [*Industrial hygiene*] (PDAA)
TLV-STEL ..... Threshold Limit Value - Short Term Exposure Limit [*Industrial hygiene*] (PDAA)
TLV-TWA ..... Threshold Limit Value - Time-Weighted Average [*Industrial hygiene*] (PDAA)
TLW .... [*The*] Lighted Way [*An association*] (EA)
TLW .... Talasea [*New Britain, New Guinea*] [*Airport symbol*] (AD)
TLW .... Test Load Wire
TLW .... Torpedo Lieutenant's Writer [*British military*] (DMA)
TLW .... Total Lung Water [*Medicine*] (DMAA)
TLWM .... Trinity Low-Water Mark
TLWS .... Terrier Land Weapon System
TLX .... TELEX [*Automated Teletypewriter Exchange Service*] [*Western Union Corp.*]
TLX .... Telex
TLX .... Thin-Layer Explosive (MCD)
TLX .... Transfer-Line Exchanger [*Manufacturing technology*]
TLX .... Trans-Lux [*AMEX symbol*] (TTSB)
TLX .... Trans-Lux Corp. [*AMEX symbol*] (SPSG)
TLX .... Tri-Line Expressways Ltd. [*Toronto Stock Exchange symbol*]
TLX .... Trophoblast/Lymphocyte Cross-Reactive (Antigens) [*Immunochemistry*]
TLXA .... Toolex-Alpha [*NASDAQ symbol*] (SAG)
TLXAF .... Toolex-Alpha N.V. [*NASDAQ symbol*] (TTSB)
TLXN .... Telxon Corp. [*NASDAQ symbol*] (NQ)
TLY .... Tally
tlymn .... Tallyman
TLZ .... Target Launch Zone
TLZ .... Thermolase Corp. [*AMEX symbol*] (SAG)
TLZ .... Titanium-Lead-Zinc
TLZ .... Transfer on Less than Zero
TM .... Assessment and Evaluation [*Educational Resources Information Center (ERIC) Clearinghouse*] [*The Catholic University of America*] (PAZ)
TM .... Institute of Travel Management [*British*] (DBA)
TM .... [*The*] Maccabees [*Southfield, MI*] (EA)
Tm .... Maximal Renal Tubular Excretory Capacity [*Medicine*] (DAVI)
TM .... Memphis-Shelby County Public Library and Information Center, Memphis, TN [*Library symbol Library of Congress*] (LCLS)
TM .... National Income Tax Magazine [*A publication*] (DLA)
TM .... Table Maintenance (NASA)
TM .... Tactical Manager [*Military*] (CAAL)
TM .... Tactical Missile [*Air Force*]
TM .... Tactical Monitor
TM .... Tailor-Made (DSUE)
TM .... Take-Off Mass (SAA)
TM .... Talking Machine
TM .... Tangent Mechanism
TM .... Tape Mark [*Computer science*] (BUR)
TM .... Tape Module (DEN)
TM .... Target Mechanism (MCD)
TM .... Task Memory [*Computer science*] (IAA)
TM .... Taurine Mustard [*Antineoplastic drug*]
TM .... Tax Magazine [*A publication*] (DLA)
TM .... Tax Management [*A publication*] (DLA)
TM .... Tax Memo [*A publication*] (DLA)
TM .... Tax Module [*IRS*]
TM .... T-Cell Marker [*Biochemistry*]
TM .... Team (AABC)
TM .... Team Manager
TM .... Team Member
TM .... Technical Management (AAGC)
TM .... Technical Manager
TM .... Technical Manual
TM .... Technical Memorandum
TM .... Technical Minutes
TM .... Technical Monograph
TM .... Tectorial Membrane [*of the cochlea*] [*Ear anatomy*]
TM .... Telegramme Multiple [*Telegram with Multiple Addresses*] [*French*] (ROG)
TM .... Tele-Metropole, Inc. [*Toronto Stock Exchange symbol*]
TM .... Telemetry
TM .... Telephone Museum (EA)
TM .... Temperature, Mean
TM .... Temperature Meter
TM .... Temperature Monitor (NRCH)
TM .... Temple Magazine [*A publication*] (ROG)
TM .... Temple of Man (EA)
TM .... Temporomandibular [*Anatomy*]
TM .... Tenu'at Ha-Moshavim (BJA)
TM .... Terminal Multiplexer [*Computer science*] (IAA)
TM .... Test Manual
TM .... Test Mode
TM .... Test Model [*NASA*]
TM .... Texas Mexican Railway Co. [*AAR code*]
TM .... Thalassemia Major [*Hematology*]
TM .... Thames Measurement [*Formula for rating yachts*] [*British*]
TM .... Thayer-Martin Medium [*Medicine*] (DMAA)
TM .... Their Majesties
TM .... Thematic Mapper [*Satellite technology*]
TM .... Thermal Mapper
TM .... Third Market [*Securities*]
TM .... Third Mortgage (MHDW)
Tm .... Thulium [*Chemical element*]
TM .... Tight Money (MHDW)
TM .... Time (FAAC)
TM .... Time Management (MCD)
TM .... Time, Mission
TM .... Time Modulation
TM .... Time Monitor
TM .... Time Motion Technique
TM .... Timing of Movements [*Physiology*]
Tm .... Timothy [*New Testament book*]
TM .... Titanium Chloride [*Inorganic chemistry*]
TM .... Toastmaster, Inc. [*NYSE symbol*] (SPSG)
TM .... Tobramycin [*An antibiotic*]
TM .... Tolerant Majority [*An association Defunct*] (EA)
TM .... Tone Modulation
TM .... Ton-Miles
TM .... Tons per Minute
TM .... Top Man
TM .... Top Management
TM .... Torpedoman's Mate [*Navy rating*]
T/M .... Torque Meter (NG)
TM .... Torque Motor
TM .... Tour du Monde [*World Tour*] [*French*] (JA)
TM .... Town Major [*British military*] (DMA)
TM .... Trabecular Meshwork (DAVI)
TM .... Track Monitor (CAAL)
TM .... Tractor Monoplane
TM .... Trademark
TM .... Trade Mission
TM .... Traffic Manager [*or Management*]
TM .... Traffic Model (NASA)
TM .... Trager's Medium [*Chemically defined culture medium*]
TM .... Trained Man [*British military*] (DMA)
TM .... Training Manual [*Military*]
TM .... Training Memorandum (DAS)
TM .... Training Missions [*Air Force*]
TM .... Trainmaster [*Railroading*]
TM .... Transaction Manager [*Computer science*]
TM .... Transaction Mode (IAA)
TM .... Transcendental Meditation
TM .... Transfer Memorandum
TM .... "Transitional" Mucosa [*Oncology*]
TM .... Transition Management
TM .... Transition Metal (MCD)
TM .... Translator Code Magnet (IAA)
TM .... Transmedullary [*Anatomy*]
TM .... Transmembrane Domain [*Genetics*]
TM .... Transmembrane Substitution Mutants [*Genetics*]
TM .... Transmetatarsal [*Anatomy*]
TM .... Transmission Matrix (IEEE)
TM .... Transmittal Memorandum (MCD)
Tm .... Transport Maximum [*Physiology*] (DAVI)
TM .... Transport Mechanism [*Physiology*]
TM .... Transport Medium [*Laboratory science*] (DAVI)
TM .... Transport Messenger [*Laboratory science*] (DAVI)
TM .... Transverse Magnetic
TM .... Travelwriter Marketletter [*Information service or system*] (IID)
TM .... Trench Mortar
TM .... Trial Modification (SAA)
TM .... Trombone, Muted
TM .... Tropical Maritime
TM .... Tropical Medicine
TM .... Tropomyosin [*Biochemistry*]
TM .... True Mean
TM .... True Motion [*RADAR*] (DEN)
TM .... Truncation Mutant
TM .... Trunk Mark [*Telecommunications*] (IAA)
TM .... Tuberal Magnocellular [*Nuclei, neuroanatomy*]
TM .... Tunicamycin [*Biochemistry*]
TM .... Tuning Meter (DEN)
TM .... Turing Machine [*Mathematical model*] [*Computer science*]
TM .... Twisting Moment
TM .... Tympanic Membrane [*Anatomy*]
TM .... Type Metal [*Printing*] (DGA)
TM1 .... Torpedoman's Mate, First Class [*Navy rating*]
T/M^2 .... Metric Tons per Square Meter
TM2 .... Torpedoman's Mate, Second Class [*Navy rating*]
T/M^3 .... Metric Tons per Cubic Meter
TM3 .... Torpedoman's Mate, Third Class [*Navy rating*]
TMA .... Memphis Academy of Arts, Memphis, TN [*Library symbol Library of Congress*] (LCLS)
TMA .... Memphis State University, Memphis, TN [*OCLC symbol*] (OCLC)
TMA .... [*The*] Mosquito Association (EA)
TMA .... Taiwan Maintenance Agency [*Military*] (AABC)
TMA .... Target Motion Analyzer
TMA .... Technical Manual Management Agent
TMA .... Telecommunications Management Association (NITA)
TMA .... Telecommunications Managers Association [*Orpington, England*] (TSSD)
TMA .... TeleManagement Associates [*Telecommunications service*] (TSSD)
TMA .... Telemetry Manufacturers' Association (IAA)
TMA .... Telephone Management and Accounting (HGAA)
TMA .... Temperature Monitoring Apparatus
TMA .... Tennis Manufacturers Association [*Later, ATF*] (EA)

TMA........... Terminal Maneuvering Area [*Aviation*]
TMA........... Tetramethylammonium [*Organic chemistry*]
TMA........... Theatre Managers' Association [*Australia*]
TMA........... Theatrical Management Association [*British*] (DBA)
TMA........... Theatrical Mutual Association (EA)
TMA........... Thermomagnetic Analysis [*Analytical chemistry*]
TMA........... Thermomechanical Analysis [*or Analyzer*]
TMA........... Thienylmalonic Acid [*Organic chemistry*]
TMA........... Thiomalic Acid [*Organic chemistry*]
TMA........... Thomas More Association (EA)
TMA........... Thornburg Mortgage Asset [*NYSE symbol*] (TTSB)
TMA........... Thornburg Mortgage Asset Corp. [*NYSE symbol*] (SPSG)
TMA........... Thrombotic Microangiopathy [*Nephrology*]
TMA........... Thyroid Microsomal Antibody [*Immunology*]
TMA........... Tifton, GA [*Location identifier FAA*] (FAAL)
TMA........... Tile Manufacturers Association (EA)
TMA........... Time-Modulated Antenna
TMA........... Tobacco Mechanics' Association [*A union*] [*British*] (DCTA)
TMA........... Tobacco Merchants Association of United States (EA)
TMA........... Toiletry Merchandising Association [*Later, NASM*] (EA)
TMA........... Tooling and Manufacturing Association (EA)
TMA........... Toronto Musicians Association [*Canada*] (WWLA)
TMA........... Torpedo Main Assembly
TMA........... Total Maintenance Actions (MCD)
TMA........... Total Market Coverage [*Advertising*] (NTCM)
TMA........... Total Materiel Assets [*Military*]
TMA........... Toy Manufacturers of America (EA)
TMA........... Toyota Manufacturing Australia Ltd.
TMA........... Trace Metals Analyzer
TMA........... Traffic Management Advisor [*FAA*] (TAG)
TMA........... Traffic Management Advisor (GAVI)
TMA........... Traffic Management Agency (CINC)
TMA........... Trailer Manufacturers Association [*Later, NAMPS*] (EA)
TMA........... Trainee Mobility Assistance [*Australia*]
TMA........... Training Media Association (EA)
TMA........... Transistor Magnetic-Pulse Amplifier
TMA........... Translater Mixer Amplifier (DWSG)
TMA........... Trans Mediterranean Airlines [*Lebanon*] [*ICAO designator*] (FAAC)
TMA........... Trans-Mediterranean Airways (BJA)
TMA........... Transmetatarsal Amputation [*Medicine*]
TMA........... Transportation Management Association
TMA........... Transport Museum Association (EA)
TMA........... Travelling and Meal Allowance
TMA........... Treasury Management Association
TMA........... Trimac Ltd. [*Toronto Stock Exchange symbol*]
TMA........... Trimellitic Acid [*Organic chemistry*]
TMA........... Trimellitic Anhydride
TMA........... Trimellitic Anhydride [*Chemistry*]
TMA........... Trimethoxyamphetamine [*Organic chemistry*] (MAE)
TMA........... Trimethoxyphenyl Aminopropane [*Organic chemistry*] (MAE)
TMA........... Trimethyladenine [*Biochemistry*]
TMA........... Trimethylaluminum [*Organic chemistry*]
TMA........... Trimethylamine [*Organic chemistry*]
TMA........... Trimethylammonium [*Organic chemistry*]
TMA........... Truck Manufacturers Association
TMA........... Truck Master Association [*Auto enthusiast organization*]
TMAA.......... Tractor and Machinery Association of Australia
TMAA.......... Trimethylamine Alane [*Organic chemistry*]
TMaab......... Thyroid Microsomal Autoantibody [*Immunology*]
TMAB.......... Telecommunications Managers Association - Belgium
TMAB.......... Temporary Missile Assembly Building (AAG)
TMAB.......... Tetramethylammonium Borohydride [*Organic chemistry*]
TMA BITS.... TMA [*Tobacco Merchants Association*] Bibliographic Index to the Tobacco Scene [*Database*]
TMAC.......... Agrico Chemical Co., Memphis, TN [*Library symbol Library of Congress*] (LCLS)
TMAC.......... Telecommunication Management and Control [*AT & T*]
TMAC.......... Temperature-Modulated Air Cleaner [*Automotive engineering*]
T-MAC......... Test of Minimal Articulation Competence [*Speech evaluation test*]
TMAC.......... Time-Division Multiplexed Analogue Components (NITA)
TMAC.......... Treasury Multi-User Acquisition Contract (AAGC)
TMAC.......... Trimellitic Anhydride Chloride [*Organic chemistry*]
TMACA......... Telecommunications Managers Association of the Capital Area (TSSD)
TMACS......... Tone Multiplex Apollo Command System [*NASA*] (KSC)
TMACS......... Training Management Control System [*Army*] (INF)
TM/ACS........ True-Motion, Anti-Collision System (PDAA)
TMAD.......... Tank Main Armament Development (MCD)
TMAD.......... Target Marker Air Droppable (MCD)
TMAD.......... Target Marker and Dispenser (MCD)
TMadH......... Nashville Memorial Hospital, Madison, TN [*Library symbol Library of Congress*] (LCLS)
TMadM......... Madison Academy, Madison College, TN [*Library symbol Library of Congress*] (LCLS)
TMADWG..... Tank Main Armament Development Working Group [*Army*]
TMAE.......... Tetrakis(dimethylamino)ethylene [*Organic chemistry*]
TMAG.......... Tasmanian Museum and Art Gallery [*Australia*]
TMAG.......... Travel More Advantageous to the Government (AAG)
TMAH.......... Tetramethylammonium Hydroxide [*Organic chemistry*]
TMAI........... Tetramethylammonium Iodide [*Organic chemistry*]
TMAIC......... Trimethallyl Isocyanurate [*Organic chemistry*]
TMAM.......... Training and Doctrine Command Mission Area Manager [*Army*]
TMAMA........ Textile Machinery and Accessory Manufacturers Association [*British*] (BI)
TMAN.......... Todays Man, Inc. [*NASDAQ symbol*] (SAG)
TM & B........ Tunnels, Mines, and Booby Trap School [*Army*] (VNW)
TM & DE...... Test, Measuring, and Diagnostic Equipment [*Later, TMDE*] [*Army*] (AABC)
TMANQ........ Today's Man [*NASDAQ symbol*] (TTSB)
TMAO.......... Trimethylamine Oxide [*Organic chemistry*]
TMAO.......... Troop Movement Action Officer
TMAO.......... Troop Movement Assignment Order
TMAP.......... Tactical Multipurpose Automated Platform [*Military*]
TMAP.......... Teleoperated Mobile Antiarmor Platform [*Army*] (INF)
TMAP.......... Temporary Mortgage Assistance Payments Program [*HUD*]
TMAP.......... Thermal Modeling and Analysis Project [*Marine science*] (OSRA)
TMAP.......... Thermal Modeling and Analysis Project (USDC)
TMAR.......... Trico Marine Services, Inc. [*NASDAQ symbol*] (SAG)
TMAR.......... Trico Marine Svcs [*NASDAQ symbol*] (TTSB)
TMARS......... Technical Manual Audit and Requirement Reporting System (MCD)
TMaryB........ Blount Memorial Hospital, Medical Library, Maryville, TN [*Library symbol Library of Congress*] (LCLS)
TMaryC........ Maryville College, Maryville, TN [*Library symbol Library of Congress*] (LCLS)
TMAS.......... Tank Main Armament Systems (RDA)
TMAS.......... Taylor Manifest Anxiety State [*Psychology*]
TMAS.......... Technical and Management Advisory Service [*ADPA*] (MCD)
TMASA........ Timber Merchants' Association of South Australia
TMaU.......... University of Tennessee at Martin, Martin, TN [*Library symbol Library of Congress*] (LCLS)
TMAV.......... Timber Merchants' Association of Victoria [*Australia*]
TMAX.......... Maximum Time [*Telecommunications*] (TEL)
T-MAX......... Temperature Maximum (DAVI)
T_{max}.......... Time of Maximum Concentration [*Laboratory science*] (DAVI)
TMAY.......... Tell Me About Yourself [*Interviewing technique*]
TMB............ David W. Taylor Model Basin [*Also, DATMOBAS, DTMB*] [*Later, DTNSRDC, NSRDC*]
TMB............ Miami, FL [*Location identifier FAA*] (FAAL)
TMB............ Tambrands, Inc. [*NYSE symbol*] (SPSG)
TMB............ Task Maintenance Burden
TMB............ Taylor Model Basin [*Navy*]
TMB............ Tetramethylbenzene [*Organic chemistry*]
TMB............ Tetramethylbenzidine [*Organic chemistry*]
TMB............ Textes Mathematiques Babyloniens [*A publication*] (BJA)
TMB............ Thimble
TMB............ Tide-Measuring Buoy
TMB............ Time Maintenance Began [*Military*] (AFIT)
TMB............ Too Many Birthdays (MEDA)
TMB............ Transient Monocular Blindness [*Medicine*]
TMB............ Transportation Management Bulletin [*NASA*] (NASA)
TMB............ Trench Mortar Battery [*British military*] (DMA)
TMB............ Trimethoxyboroxine [*Organic chemistry*]
TMB............ Trimethylbenzene [*Organic chemistry*]
TMB............ Tumble (MSA)
TMB............ University of Texas, Medical Branch Library, Galveston, TX [*OCLC symbol*] (OCLC)
TMBA.......... Brooks Art Gallery, Memphis, TN [*Library symbol Library of Congress*] (LCLS)
TMBA.......... Tetramethylene-bis-Acetamide [*Biochemistry*]
TMBA.......... Trimethylbenzaldehyde [*Organic chemistry*]
TMBA.......... Trimethylbenzanthracene [*Carcinogen*]
TMBAC........ Trimethylbenzylammonium Chloride [*Also, BTM*] [*Organic chemistry*]
TM/BAC....... True-Motion, Basic Collision Avoidance (PDAA)
TMBC.......... Buckeye Cellulose Corp., Technical Division Library, Memphis, TN [*Library symbol Library of Congress*] (LCLS)
TMBD.......... Tetramethylbutanediamine [*Also, TMBDA*]
TMBDA........ Tetramethylbutanediamine [*Organic chemistry*]
TMBDB........ Thermal Margin beyond Design Basis [*Nuclear energy*] (NRCH)
TMBGIC....... They Might Be Giants Information Club (EA)
TMBH.......... Baptist Memorial Hospital, Memphis, TN [*Library symbol Library of Congress*] (LCLS)
TMBH-N....... Baptist Memorial Hospital, School of Nursing, Memphis, TN [*Library symbol Library of Congress*] (LCLS)
TMBL.......... Buckman Laboratories, Inc., Memphis, TN [*Library symbol Library of Congress*] (LCLS)
TMBL.......... Tacoma Municipal Belt Line Railway [*AAR code*]
TMBO.......... Team Management by Objectives [*Management technique*] (ADA)
TMBP.......... (Tetramethylbutyl)phenol [*Organic chemistry*]
TMBR.......... Brown [*Tom*], Inc. [*NASDAQ symbol*] (SAG)
TMBR.......... Timber (AAG)
TMBR.......... Timber
TMBR.......... Tom Brown [*NASDAQ symbol*] (TTSB)
TMBR Sh..... TMBR Sharp Drilling, Inc. [*Associated Press*] (SAG)
TMBS.......... Timberline Software [*NASDAQ symbol*] (TTSB)
TMBS.......... Timberline Software Corp. [*NASDAQ symbol*] (NQ)
TMBS.......... Torque Motor Beam Steerer (MCD)
TMBU.......... Table Maintenance Block Update (NASA)
TM Bull....... Trade Mark Bulletin, New Series [*A publication*] (DLA)
TMC............ Chief Torpedoman's Mate [*Navy rating*]
TMC............ Houston Academy of Medicine for Texas Medical Center, Houston, TX [*OCLC symbol*] (OCLC)
TMC............ [*The*] Maintenance Council of the American Trucking Associations (EA)
TMC............ [*The*] Mouse Club (EA)
TMC............ [*The*] Movie Channel [*Cable-television system*]
TMC............ Table Mountain [*California*] [*Seismograph station code, US Geological Survey Closed*] (SEIS)
TMC............ Tactical Medical Center
T/MC........... Talker per Megacycle (SAA)
TMC............ Tambolaka [*Indonesia*] [*Airport symbol*] (OAG)

TMC.......... Tape Management Catalog
TMC.......... Target Market Coverage [*Advertising*] (BARN)
TMC.......... Tarmac Plc [*British ICAO designator*] (FAAC)
TMC.......... Telamarketing Communications, Inc. [*Louisville, KY*] [*Telecommunications*] (TSSD)
TMC.......... Telecommunications Management College (NITA)
TMC.......... Telecommunications Management Corp. [*Needham Heights, MA*] (TSSD)
TMC.......... Telecommunications Marketing Corp. [*Bay Shore, NY*] (TSSD)
TMC.......... TeleMonteCarlo [*Private television operation*] [*Italy*]
TMC.......... Telephone Manufacturing Company (IAA)
TMC.......... Temporary Minor Change (MCD)
TMC.......... Terminal Control (DA)
TMC.......... Terramycin Capsule [*Antibacterial, trademark of Pfizer, Inc.*]
TMC.......... Terrestrial Microcosm Chamber [*For environmental studies*]
TMC.......... Test, Monitor, and Control [*Aviation*]
TMC.......... Test Monitoring Center [*ASTM*] [*Engineering standards*]
TMC.......... Test Monitoring Console (NASA)
TMC.......... The Maintenance Council
TMC.......... #The Military Coalition
TMC.......... Thermal Micrometeoroid Cover (MCD)
TMC.......... Thick Molding Compound [*Plastics technology*]
TMC.......... Thick Molding Compound
TM-C.......... Thomas Micro-Catalogs
TMC.......... Three-Mode Control (AAG)
TMC.......... Threshold Management Center [*Environmental Protection Agency*] (GFGA)
TMC.......... Thrust Magnitude Control (KSC)
TMC.......... Thrust Management Computer (GAVI)
TMC.......... Times Mirror 'A' [*NYSE symbol*] (TTSB)
TMC.......... Times Mirror Co. [*NYSE symbol*] (SAG)
TMC.......... Titan Missile Contractor (AAG)
TMC.......... Tool Management Culture
TMC.......... Total Manufacturing Cost (MHDB)
TMC.......... Total Market Coverage [*Advertising*]
TMC.......... Tourism Ministers Council (EERA)
TMC.......... Toyota Motor Corp.
TMC.......... Traffic Management Center [*Highway operations*]
TMC.......... Traffic Management Channel [*Navigation and driver information systems*]
TMC.......... Traffic Message Channel [*FHWA*] (TAG)
TMC.......... Traffic Message Channel
TMC.......... Transmedia Enterprises, Inc. [*Vancouver Stock Exchange symbol*]
TMC.......... Transmission Maintenance Center [*Telecommunications*] (TEL)
TMC.......... Transmural Colitis [*Crohn's disease*] (CPH)
TMC.......... Transportation Management Center
TMC.......... Transportation Materiel Command [*AMC - Mobility*]
TMC.......... Transport Movement Control [*Military*] (AFM)
TMC.......... Travel Management Center [*General Services Administration*] (GFGA)
TMC.......... Triamcinolone [*Synthetic steroidal drug*]
TMC.......... Trimethylcyclohexanol [*Organic chemistry*]
TMC.......... Trinity Ministries Center (EA)
TMC.......... Triple Molecular Collision
TMC.......... Tube Moisture Control
TMC.......... Type Maintenance Code (MCD)
TMCA.......... Thrust Management Control Analysis
TMCA.......... Titanium Metals Corp. of America
TMCA.......... Toxic Materials Control Activity [*General Motors Corp.*]
TMCA.......... Trimethyl Colchicinic Acid [*Organic chemistry*] (MAE)
TMCA.......... Truth Missionaries Chapter of Positive Accord (EA)
TMCBC.......... Christian Brothers College, Memphis, TN [*Library symbol Library of Congress*] (LCLS)
TMCC.......... Chapman Chemical Co., Memphis, TN [*Library symbol Library of Congress*] (LCLS)
TMCC.......... Theater Movement Control Center [*Military*] (AABC)
TMCC.......... Time-Multiplexer Communications Channels
TMCC.......... Traffic Management Computer Complex [*FAA*] (TAG)
TMCDT.......... Trimethylcyclododecatriene [*Organic chemistry*]
TM Cent.......... TM Century, Inc. [*Associated Press*] (SAG)
TMCF.......... Campbell Foundation, Memphis, TN [*Library symbol Library of Congress*] (LCLS)
TMCF.......... Toastmasters and Masters of Ceremonies Federation [*British*] (BI)
TMCH.......... City of Memphis Hospital, Memphis, TN [*Library symbol Library of Congress*] (LCLS)
TM CHG.......... Technical Manual Change Number [*Army*]
TMCI.......... Telemetering Control Indicator
TMCI.......... TM Century [*NASDAQ symbol*] (NQ)
TMCIEI.......... TMCI Electronics, Inc. [*Associated Press*] (SAG)
TMCIOB.......... Technician Member of the Chartered Institute of Building [*British*] (DI)
TMckB.......... Bethel College, McKenzie, TN [*Library symbol Library of Congress*] (LCLS)
TMckB-C.......... Cumberland Presbyterian Theological Seminary, Bethel College, McKenzie, TN [*Library symbol Library of Congress*] (LCLS)
TMCL.......... Target Map Coordinate Locator [*Military*]
TMCM.......... Master Chief Torpedoman's Mate [*Navy rating*]
TMCM.......... Tooling Machine Control Medium (MCD)
TMCN.......... Technical Management Requirements Document Change Notice (MCD)
TMCOMP.......... Telemetry Computation
TMCOT.......... Tetramethylcyclooctatetraene [*Organic chemistry*]
TMCP.......... Technical Manual Control Panel (IAA)
TMCP.......... Thermal Mechanical Controlled Processing (PDAA)
TMCP.......... Trimethylcyclopentanone [*Organic chemistry*]
TMCPrP.......... Times Mirror cm Sr'B'Pfd [*NYSE symbol*] (TTSB)
TMCR.......... Technical Manual Change Request [*or Requirement*]
TMCR.......... Technical Manual Contract Requirement
TMCRL.......... Tailored Master Cross Reference List [*Military*] (AABC)
TMCS.......... Memphis City Schools Professional Library, Memphis, TN [*Library symbol Library of Congress*] (LCLS)
TMCS.......... Senior Chief Torpedoman's Mate [*Navy rating*]
TMCS.......... Tactical Maintenance Control System
TMCS.......... Toshiba Minicomputer Complex System
TMCS.......... Trimethylchlorosilane [*Organic chemistry*]
TMCXD.......... Transverse Magnetic Circular X-Ray Dichroism [*Physics*]
TMD.......... Meharry Medical College, Nashville, TN [*OCLC symbol*] (OCLC)
TMD.......... Tactical Metrology Device (DWSG)
TMD.......... Tactical Missile Defense [*Army*] (DOMA)
TMD.......... Tactical Mission Data [*Military*] (AFM)
TMD.......... Tactical Munitions Dispenser (MCD)
TMD.......... Tagged Material Detector (DWSG)
TMD.......... Technical Manual Designation
TMD.......... Telemedia, Inc. [*Toronto Stock Exchange symbol*]
TMD.......... Telemetered Data (AAG)
TMD.......... Temperature of Maximum Density
TMD.......... Tensor Meson Dominance [*Physics*] (OA)
TMD.......... Test & Measurement Division (ACII)
TMD.......... Tetramethyldioxetane [*Organic chemistry*]
TMD.......... Text Matter Depth [*Typography*] (DGA)
TMD.......... Theater Missile Defense
TMD.......... Theoretical Maximum Density
TMD.......... Thermedics, Inc. [*AMEX symbol*] (SPSG)
TMD.......... Timbedra [*Mauritania*] [*Airport symbol*] (AD)
TMD.......... Timed (MSA)
TMD.......... Toluene-Methanol-Dioxane [*Scintillation solvent*]
TMD.......... Total Mean Downtime [*Computer science*] (IAA)
TMD.......... Toxicology and Microbiology Division [*Cincinnati, OH*] [*Environmental Protection Agency*] (GRD)
TMD.......... Training Media Database [*Access Innovations, Inc.*] [*Information service or system*] (CRD)
TMD.......... Transient Mass Distribution Code [*Nuclear energy*] (NRCH)
TMD.......... Transmed Airlines [*Egypt*] [*ICAO designator*] (FAAC)
TMD.......... Transmembrane Domain [*Genetics*]
TMD.......... Trimethylhexamethylene Diamine [*Organic chemistry*]
TMDA.......... Training Media Distributors Association [*Later, TMA*] (EA)
TMDAG.......... This Mode of Transportation has been Determined to be More Advantageous to the Government
TMDC.......... Technical Manual Data Cards [*DoD*] (MCD)
TMDC.......... Transportation Movement Document Control (MCD)
TMDE.......... Test Management and Diagnostic Equipment [*Army*]
TMDE.......... Test, Measuring [*or Measurement*], and Diagnostic Equipment [*Formerly, TM & DE*] [*Army*] (AABC)
TMDESE.......... Test, Measurement, and Diagnostic Equipment Support Equipment [*Army*]
TMDESG.......... Test, Management, and Diagnostic Equipment Support Group [*Army*] (MCD)
TMDI.......... Tactical Missile Defense Initiative (DOMA)
TMDI.......... Theater Missile Defense Initiative [*Army*] (DOMA)
TMDI.......... Theoretical Maximum Daily Intake [*Toxicology*]
TMDI.......... Transponder Miss Distance Indicator
TMDI.......... Trimethylhexamethylene Diisocyanate [*Organic chemistry*]
TMDI.......... United States Defense Industrial Plant Equipment Center, Memphis, TN [*Library symbol Library of Congress*] (LCLS)
TMDL.......... Technical Manual Data List [*DoD*]
TMDL.......... Total Maximum Daily Load [*Environmental Protection Agency*]
TMDO.......... Training Management Development Office [*Army*]
TMDP.......... Technetium Methylene Diphosphonate [*Organic chemistry*]
TMDR.......... Technical Manual Data Record [*DoD*] (MCD)
TMDS.......... Test, Measurement, and Diagnostic Systems [*Army*] (RDA)
TMDS.......... Tetramethyldisilazane [*Organic chemistry*]
TMDS.......... Trilineage Myelodysplasia Syndrome [*Medicine*]
TMDT.......... Total Mean Downtime
TMDT.......... Trace Metals Detection Technique
TMDT.......... Trimethyldodecatetraene [*Organic chemistry*]
TME.......... Eastwood Hospital, Memphis, TN [*Library symbol Library of Congress*] (LCLS)
TME.......... [*The*] Main Event [*A publication*]
TME.......... Tame [*Colombia*] [*Airport symbol*] (OAG)
TME.......... Teacher of Medical Electricity [*British*]
TME.......... Temperature Measuring Equipment (IAA)
TME.......... Termex Resources, Inc. [*Vancouver Stock Exchange symbol*]
TME.......... Test and Measurement Equipment (MCD)
TME.......... Test Maintenance Equipment [*Computer science*]
TME.......... Test Marketing Exemption [*Environmental Protection Agency*]
TME.......... Tetramethylethylene [*Organic chemistry*]
TME.......... Theatre Mask Ensemble
TME.......... Thermal Marrow Expansion [*Roentgenology*]
TME.......... Thermal/Mechanical Enzyme [*Fermentation*]
TME.......... Thrust Monopropellant Engine
TME.......... Times Mirror 4.25%'PEPS'2001 [*NYSE symbol*] (TTSB)
TME.......... Times Mirror Co. [*NYSE symbol*] (SAG)
TME.......... TME Resources, Inc. [*Vancouver Stock Exchange symbol*]
TME.......... Torpedoman's Mate, Electrical [*Navy rating*]
TME.......... Total Market Estimate (ADA)
TME.......... Total Metabolizable Energy [*Nutrition*]
TME.......... Transmissible Mink Encephalopathy
TME.......... Transmural Enteritis [*Medicine*]
TME.......... Transverse-Mounted Engine
TME.......... Trimethylolethane [*Organic chemistry*]

TME .... True Metabolizable Energy
TMEA .... Typewriter Manufacturers Export Association [*Defunct*]
TMEC .... TRADOC [*Training and Doctrine Command*] Materiel Evaluation Committee [*Army*]
TmEco .... Thermo Ecotek Corp. [*Associated Press*] (SAG)
TMECO .... Time of Main Engine Cutoff [*Aerospace*] (MCD)
TMED .... Tetramethylethylenediamine [*Also, TEMED, TMEDA*] [*Organic chemistry*]
TMED .... Trimedyne, Inc. [*NASDAQ symbol*] (NQ)
TMEDA .... Tetramethylethylenediamine [*Also, TEMED, TMED*] [*Organic chemistry*]
TMEDA .... Trimethylenediamine [*Organic chemistry*]
TME/FH .... Total Maintenance Effort per Flight Hour [*Navy*] (NG)
TMEI .... TMCI Electronics [*NASDAQ symbol*] (TTSB)
TMEI .... TMCI Electronics, Inc. [*NASDAQ symbol*] (SAG)
TMEIW .... TMCI Electronics Wrrt [*NASDAQ symbol*] (TTSB)
TMEL .... Tender Master Equipment List
TMEL .... Trimethylethyllead [*Organic chemistry*]
TMEMC .... Test and Measurement Equipment for Maintenance Calibration
TM-ENG .... Technical Manual - Engineering [*Marine Corps*]
TMEP .... Trademark Manual of Examining Procedure [*A publication*] (DLA)
TMeP .... Trimethylpsoralen [*Photochemotherapeutic compound*]
TMEPS .... Transverse-Mounted Engine Propulsion System
TMER .... Technical Manual Evaluation Record (MCD)
TMES .... Tactical Missile Electrical Simulator [*Obsolete*]
TMESS .... Telemessage (DS)
TMET .... Treadmill Exercise Test [*Medicine*] (DMAA)
TMETN .... Trimethylolethane Trinitrate [*Organic chemistry*]
TMEV .... Theiler's Murine Encephalitis Virus
TMF .... Technical Transmitter Holding Fixture
TMF .... Technical Transmitter Holding Future (MCD)
TMF .... Telemetry Module Facility
TMF .... Test Mode Fail [*Apollo*] [*NASA*]
TMF .... Thermo Opportunity Fund, Inc. [*AMEX symbol*] (SAG)
TMF .... Third Moment of Frequency (PDAA)
TMF .... Thrust Management Function (GAVI)
TMF .... Time Marker Frequency
TMF .... Time Multiplication Factor [*Offshore racing*]
TMF .... Transaction Monitoring Facility [*Tandem Computers*]
TMF .... Transfer Mold Forming (MCD)
TMF .... Transformed Mink Fibroblast [*Cell line*] [*Laboratory science*] (DAVI)
TMF .... Transmission Monitoring Facility (NITA)
TMF .... Transporter Maintenance Facility [*NASA*] (NASA)
TMF .... Trunk Maintenance Files [*Telecommunications*] (TEL)
TMFC .... Ted McGinley Fan Club (EA)
TMFGC .... Technical Manual Functional Group Code
TMFL .... Time of Flight (MSA)
TMG .... Goodwyn Institute, Memphis, TN [*Library symbol Library of Congress*] (LCLS)
TMG .... Tactical Missile Group [*Air Force*]
TMG .... Tactical Multinet Gateway [*Computer science Military*] (RDA)
TMG .... Tape Manufacturers Group [*British*] (DBA)
TMG .... Tetramethylguanidine [*Organic chemistry*]
TMG .... Thermal Meteoroid [*or Micrometeoroid*] Garment [*NASA*] (KSC)
TMG .... Thermomagnetometry [*Analytical chemistry*]
TMG .... Thermometeroid Garnet (IAA)
TMG .... Thiomethylgalactoside [*Organic chemistry*]
TMG .... Time Mark Generator
TMG .... Timing
TMG .... Tomanggong [*Malaysia*] [*Airport symbol*] (OAG)
TMG .... Track Made Good [*Aviation*]
TMG .... Traffic Monitoring Guide [*FHWA*] (TAG)
TMG .... Transmontaigne Oil Co. [*AMEX symbol*] (SAG)
TMG .... Trimethylgallium [*Organic chemistry*]
TMG .... Trimethylguanosine [*Biochemistry*]
TMG .... Tubular Maximum Reabsorption Rate for Glucose [*of Kidney*] [*Nephrology*] (DAVI)
TMGA .... Tetramethyleneglutaric Acid [*Organic chemistry*]
TMGC .... W. R. Grace & Co., Agricultural Chemicals Group, Memphis, TN [*Library symbol Library of Congress*] (LCLS)
TMGD .... Timing Devices (MSA)
TMGE .... Thermomagnetic-Galvanic Effect
TMGFC .... [*The*] Mel Gibson Fan Club [*Defunct*] (EA)
TMGG .... Goldsmith Civic Garden Center, Memphis, TN [*Library symbol Library of Congress*] (LCLS)
TMGRS .... Trace Material Generation Rate Simulator
TMGS .... Church of Jesus Christ of Latter-Day Saints, Genealogical Society Library, Memphis Branch, Memphis, TN [*Library symbol Library of Congress*] (LCLS)
TMGS .... Terrestrial Magnetic Guidance System [*Aerospace*] (AAG)
TMGS .... Transportable Mobile Ground Station (MCD)
TMH .... Harding Graduate School of Religion, Memphis, TN [*Library symbol Library of Congress*] (LCLS)
TMH .... Tanahmerah [*Indonesia*] [*Airport symbol*] (OAG)
TMH .... Tasmania Museum and Art Gallery, Tasmania [*State*] (EERA)
TMH .... Texte und Materialien der Frau Professor Hilprecht Collection of Babylonian Antiquities im Eigentum der Universitaet Jena (BJA)
TMH .... Tomahawk Resources [*Vancouver Stock Exchange symbol*]
TMH .... Tons per Man-Hour
TMH .... Trainable Mentally Handicapped
TMH .... Trimethylhexane [*Organic chemistry*]
TMH .... Trolley-Mounted Hoist (NRCH)
TMHA .... Memphis Housing Authority, Memphis, TN [*Library symbol Library of Congress*] (LCLS)
TMHA .... [*The*] Military Housing Association
TMHB .... Harland Bartholomew & Associates, Memphis, TN [*Library symbol Library of Congress*] (LCLS)
TMHC .... Transcultural Mental Health Centre [*Australia*]
TMHF .... Transit Missile Hold Facility [*Military*] (IAA)
TMHI .... Holiday Inns of America, Memphis, TN [*Library symbol Library of Congress*] (LCLS)
TMHI-U .... Holiday Inn University, Olive Branch, MS [*Library symbol Library of Congress*] (LCLS)
TMHL .... Triplet Metastable Helium Level
TMHR .... Tandem Mirror Hybrid Reactor (PDAA)
TMI .... International Harvester Co., Memphis, TN [*Library symbol Library of Congress*] (LCLS)
TMI .... [*The*] Media Institute (EA)
TMI .... Midwestern State University, George Moffett Library, Wichita Falls, TX [*OCLC symbol*] (OCLC)
TMI .... [*The*] Monroe Institute (EA)
TMI .... [*The*] Mortgage Index, Inc. [*Remote Computing Corp.*] [*Information service or system*] (IID)
TMI .... Taylor Mountain [*Idaho*] [*Seismograph station code, US Geological Survey*] (SEIS)
TMI .... Team, Inc. [*AMEX symbol*] (SPSG)
TMI .... Technical Management Items (NASA)
TMI .... Technical Manual Index [*Navy*]
TMI .... Teen Missions International (EA)
TMI .... Telecommunications Management, Inc. [*Oakbrook, IL*] [*Telecommunications*] (TSSD)
TmI .... Telematica, Inc. [*Telecommunications service*] (TSSD)
TMI .... Telemeter Magnetics, Inc. (IAA)
TMI .... Texas Microelectronics, Inc. (IAA)
TMI .... Thornicroft's Mounted Infantry [*Military British*] (ROG)
TMI .... Threatened Myocardial Infarction [*Cardiology*] (MEDA)
TMI .... Three Mile Island [*Pennsylvania*] [*Site of nuclear reactor accident, 1979*]
TMI .... Time Air Corp. [*Toronto Stock Exchange symbol*]
TMI .... Time Manager International [*Commercial firm British*]
TMI .... Tolyl(mono)isocyanate [*Organic chemistry*]
TMI .... Tool Manufacturing Instruction (AAG)
TMI .... Tracking Merit Interception
TMI .... Transfer on Minus (SAA)
TMI .... Trans-Mars Injection [*Aerospace*]
TMI .... Transmural Myocardial Infarction [*Cardiology*]
TMI .... Travel Managers International (EA)
TMI .... Trimethylindium [*Organic chemistry*]
TMI .... Trucking Management, Inc. (EA)
TMI .... Tumlingtar [*Nepal*] [*Airport symbol*] (OAG)
TMI .... Tune-Up Manufacturers Institute (EA)
TMI .... Tuning Meter Indicator (IAA)
TMIA .... Tasmanian Music Industry Association [*Australia*]
TMIA .... Three Mile Island Alert (EA)
TMIAC .... Tasmanian Meat Industry Advisory Council [*Australia*]
TMIC .... Test Management Information System
TMIC .... Thomas Marketing Information Center [*Thomas Publishing Co.*] [*Information service or system*] (IID)
TMIC .... Toxic Materials Information Center [*Oak Ridge National Laboratory*] (IID)
TMICP .... Topographic Map Inventory Control Point [*Army*] (AABC)
TMIF .... Tumor-Cell Migratory Inhibition Factor [*Immunology*]
TMIFC .... Tom Mix International Fan Club (EA)
TMIG .... Time in Grade [*Navy*]
TMIL .... Traffic Management Information Letter [*MTMC*] (TAG)
TMiIM .... Milligan College, Milligan College, TN [*Library symbol Library of Congress*] (LCLS)
TMIMGTechE ... Technician Member of the Institution of Mechanical and General Technician Engineers [*British*] (DI)
TMIMIS .... Technical Manual Integrated Management Information Systems [*DoD*]
TMIN .... Minimum Time [*Telecommunications*] (TEL)
TMiNA .... United States Naval Air Station Library, Millington, TN [*Library symbol Library of Congress*] (LCLS)
TMINDCD .... Technical Manual Indenture Code [*Army*]
TMiNH .... United States Naval Hospital, Millington, TN [*Library symbol Library of Congress*] (LCLS)
TMINS .... Technical Manual Identification Numbering System (MCD)
TMINS .... Three Mile Island Nuclear Station (NRCH)
TMIP .... Training Management Instruction Packet
TMIP .... Travel Model Improvement Program [*BTS*] (TAG)
TMIS .... Tank Management Information System (MCD)
TMIS .... Technical and Management Information System (SSD)
TMIS .... Technical Medical Information System (DAVI)
TMIS .... Technical Meetings Information Service
TMIS .... Technician Maintenance Information System (MHDB)
TMIS .... Television Management Information System (IAA)
TMIS .... Television Measurement [*or Metering*] Information System (OA)
TMIS .... Theater Medical Information System (DOMA)
TMIS .... Total Management Information System
TMIS .... Transmission Impairment Measuring Set [*Telecommunications*] (IAA)
TMIU .... Teletype Modulator Interface Units (MCD)
TMJ .... Temporomandibular Joint [*Anatomy*]
TMJ .... Temporomandibular Joint [*Dentistry*] (DAVI)
TMJ .... Temporomandibular Joint Disorder [*Medicine*]
TMJS .... Temporomandibular Joint Syndrome [*Medicine*]
TMK .... Kimberly-Clark Corp., Memphis, TN [*Library symbol Library of Congress*] (LCLS)
TMK .... Timiskaming [*Quebec*] [*Seismograph station code, US Geological Survey Closed*] (SEIS)

TMK .... Tiravita Munnerrat Kalam
TMK .... Tomahawk Airways, Inc. [*ICAO designator*] (FAAC)
TMK .... Tomsk [*Former USSR Geomagnetic observatory code*]
TMK .... To My Knowledge [*Computer science*] (DOM)
TMK .... Tonnage Mark [*Found on each side of the ship aft*] (DS)
TMK .... Torchmark Corp. [*NYSE symbol*] (SPSG)
TMK .... Transistor Mounting Kit
TMK .... Trumark Resource Corp. [*Vancouver Stock Exchange symbol*]
TmkCa .... Torchmark Capital LLC, Inc. [*Associated Press*] (SAG)
Tmk Plc .... Tomkins Ltd. [*Associated Press*] (SAG)
Tmk plc .... Tomkins PLC [*Associated Press*] (SAG)
TMKPR .... Timekeeper (WGA)
TMKPrM .... Torchmark Capital 'MIPS' [*NYSE symbol*] (TTSB)
TML .... Lakeside Hospital, Memphis, TN [*Library symbol Library of Congress*] (LCLS)
TML .... Tamale [*Ghana*] [*Airport symbol*] (OAG)
TML .... Tandem Matching Loss [*Telecommunications*] (TEL)
TML .... Technical Manual List (MCD)
TML .... Television Microwave Link [*FAA*] (TAG)
TML .... Terminal (AABC)
TML .... Terrestrial Microwave Link
TML .... Tetramethyl Lead (MCD)
TML .... Texas Tech University, School of Medicine at Lubbock, Library of the Health Science, Lubbock, TX [*OCLC symbol*] (OCLC)
TML .... Thermomechanical Loading
TML .... Three-Mile Limit
TML .... Titanium Metallurgical Laboratory (MCD)
TML .... Traffic Management Laboratory [*FHWA*] (TAG)
TML .... Transmanche-Link [*Eurotunnel*] (ECON)
TML .... Transportable Moisture Limit [*Shipping*] (DS)
TML .... Two Mixed Layer (IAA)
TMLBC .... Le Bonheur Children's Medical Center, Health Sciences Library, Memphis, TN [*Library symbol Library of Congress*] (LCLS)
TMLE .... Transient-Mode Liquid Epitaxy
TMLG .... Memphis Light, Gas, and Water Division Library, Memphis, TN [*Library symbol Library of Congress*] (LCLS)
TMLJ .... Thurgood Marshall Law Journal [*A publication*] (DLA)
TMLN .... Timeline, Inc. [*NASDAQ symbol*] (SAG)
TMLO .... LeMoyne-Owen College, Memphis, TN [*Library symbol Library of Congress*] (LCLS)
TM/LP .... Thermal Margin/Low Pressure [*Nuclear energy*] (NRCH)
TML Rev .... Thurgood Marshall Law Review [*A publication*] (DLA)
TMM .... Memphis State University, Memphis, TN [*Library symbol Library of Congress*] (LCLS)
TMM .... Tamatave [*Madagascar*] [*Airport symbol*] (OAG)
TMM .... Tank Master Mechanic (MCD)
TMM .... Tax Management Memorandum [*Bureau of National Affairs*] [*A publication*] (DLA)
TMM .... Technologico De Monterrey [*Mexico*] [*Seismograph station code, US Geological Survey*] (SEIS)
TMM .... TELEX Main Memories [*Telecommunications*] (IAA)
TMM .... Test Message Monitor
TMM .... Thermal Mathematical Model
TMM .... Times Mirror Magazines [*A publication*]
TMM .... Too Many Metaphors [*Used in correcting manuscripts, etc.*]
TMM .... Transition Metal-Metalloid [*Physical chemistry*]
TMM .... Transportacion Maritima ADS [*NYSE symbol*] (TTSB)
TMM .... Transportacion Maritima Mexicana [*NYSE symbol*] (SPSG)
TMM .... Trimethylenemethane [*Organic chemistry*]
TMM .... Trimethylolmelamine [*Organic chemistry*]
TMM.A .... Transpt'n Marit Part Ctfs ADS [*NYSE symbol*] (TTSB)
TMMAB .... Mid-America Baptist Theological Seminary, Memphis, TN [*Library symbol Library of Congress*] (LCLS)
TMM-B .... Memphis State University, Bureau of Business Research Library, Memphis, TN [*Library symbol Library of Congress*] (LCLS)
TMMB .... Truck Mixer Manufacturers Bureau (EA)
TMMBC .... Mid-South Bible College, Memphis, TN [*Library symbol Library of Congress*] (LCLS)
TMMC .... Tetramethylammonium Manganese Chloride [*Organic chemistry*]
TMMC .... Theater Materiel Management Center [*Military*] (AABC)
TMMD .... Tactical Moving Map Display (MCD)
TMM-E .... Memphis State University, Engineering Library, Memphis, TN [*Library symbol Library of Congress*] (LCLS)
TMME .... Toyota Motor Marketing and Engineering [*Automotive industry, corporate subsidiary*]
TMMEE .... Memphis Eye and Ear Hospital, Memphis, TN [*Library symbol Library of Congress*] (LCLS)
TMMexA .... Transportacion Maritima Mexicana [*Associated Press*] (SAG)
TMMG .... Teacher of Massage and Medical Gymnastics [*British*]
TMMH .... Methodist Hospital, Stratton Medical Library, Memphis, TN [*Library symbol Library of Congress*] (LCLS)
TMMH-P .... Methodist Hospital, Pathology Library, Memphis, TN [*Library symbol Library of Congress*] (LCLS)
TMMIS .... Technical Manual Management Information System [*Navy*] (DNAB)
TMM-L .... Memphis State University, School of Law, Memphis, TN [*Library symbol Library of Congress*] (LCLS)
TMMM .... Textes et Monuments Figures Relatifs aux Mysteres de Mithra [*A publication*] (BJA)
TMMM .... Tomahawk Multi-Mission Missile (DOMA)
TMMNA .... Toyota Motor Manufacturing of North America
TMMP .... Technical Manual Management Program [*Navy*] (NVT)
TMMPS .... Tris(methoxy)mercaptopropylsilane [*Organic chemistry*]
TMMS .... Tactical Missile Maintenance Squadron [*Air Force*]
TMM-SH .... Memphis State University, Speech and Hearing Center, Memphis, TN [*Library symbol Library of Congress*] (LCLS)
TMMT .... Technical Manual Management Team [*DoD*]
TMN .... Charlotte Amalie, St. Thomas, VI [*Location identifier FAA*] (FAAL)
TMN .... Memphis and Shelby County Public Library and Information Center, Memphis, TN [*OCLC symbol*] (OCLC)
TMN .... National Cotton Council of America, Memphis, TN [*Library symbol Library of Congress*] (LCLS)
TMN .... Tamana [*Kiribati*] [*Airport symbol*] (OAG)
TMN .... Tax Matters Newsletter [*Australia A publication*]
TMN .... Technical and Management Note (IEEE)
TMN .... Telecommunications Management Network (MCD)
TMN .... Timber Mountain [*Nevada*] [*Seismograph station code, US Geological Survey*] (SEIS)
TMN .... Tjumenaviatrans [*Russian Federation*] [*ICAO designator*] (FAAC)
TMN .... Transmedia Network [*NYSE symbol*] (TTSB)
TMN .... Transmedia Network, Inc. [*NYSE symbol*] (SAG)
TMN .... Transmission (AFM)
TMN .... Trigeminal Mesencephalic Nucleus [*Neuroanatomy*]
TMN .... True Mach Number
TMNA .... Transmedia Asia Pacific [*NASDAQ symbol*] (TTSB)
TMNA .... Transmedia Asia Pacific, Inc. [*NASDAQ symbol*] (SAG)
TMNE .... Transmedia Europe, Inc. [*NASDAQ symbol*] (SAG)
TMNT .... Teen-Age Mutant Ninja Turtles [*Name of comic book and cartoon characters and line of toys by Playmates Toys*]
TMO .... Table Mountain Observatory [*Marine science*] (OSRA)
TMO .... Table Mountain Observatory (USDC)
TMO .... Targets Management Office [*MIRCOM*] (RDA)
TMO .... Technology Management Office [*Army*]
TMO .... Telegraph Money Order
TMO .... Test Manufacturing Order (NASA)
TMO .... Thermo Electron [*NYSE symbol*] (TTSB)
TMO .... Thermo Electron Corp. [*NYSE symbol*] (SPSG)
TMO .... Thermomagnetic Optical Disk
TMO .... Thermomagneto-Optic (MCD)
TMO .... Time Out
TMO .... Tooling Manufacturing Outline
TMO .... Tool Manufacturing Order [*NASA*] (NASA)
TMO .... Total Materiel Objective [*Military*]
TMO .... Traffic Management Office [*or Officer*] [*Air Force*] (AFM)
TMO .... Transition Metal Oxide (MCD)
TMO .... Transportation Management Officer (AAGC)
TMO .... Transportation Movements Office [*or Officer*] [*Military*]
TMO .... Treminco Resources Ltd. [*Toronto Stock Exchange symbol Vancouver Stock Exchange symbol*]
TMO .... Trimethylamine N-Oxide [*Organic chemistry*]
TMO .... Tumeremo [*Venezuela*] [*Airport symbol*] (OAG)
TMOB .... Trade Marks Opposition Board [*Information service or system*] (IID)
TM(od) .... [*The*] Masons (of detroit) [*Rock music group*]
TMOD .... TMDE [*Test, Measuring, and Diagnostic Equipment*] Modernization [*Army*] (RDA)
TMOE .... Trimethoxyethane [*Organic chemistry*]
TMOF .... Trypsin-Modulating Oostatic Factor [*Biochemistry*]
T-MOP .... Methotrexate, 6-Thioguanine, Oncovin, Prednisone [*Antineoplastic drug regimen*] (DAVI)
TMOP .... Trimethylolpropane [*Organic chemistry*]
TMOPS .... TRADOC [*Training and Doctrine Command*] Mobilization and Operations Planning System [*Military*]
TMOR .... Technical Manual Ordtask Requirement (MCD)
TMorM .... Morristown College, Morristown, TN [*Library symbol Library of Congress*] (LCLS)
TMorNR .... Nolichucky Regional Library Center, Morristown, TN [*Library symbol Library of Congress*] (LCLS)
TMorW .... Walters State Community College, Learning Resources Center, Morristown, TN [*Library symbol*] [*Library of Congress*] (LCLS)
TMOS .... Tetramethoxysilane [*Organic chemistry*]
TMOS .... Thermosetting (MSA)
T-MOS .... Trench-Metal Oxide Silicon [*Transistor*]
TMOS .... Two Main Orbiting Spacecraft (SAA)
TMOT .... Target [*or Total*] Maximum Operating Time
TMOTFSM .... [*The*] Master of the Free School, Margate [*Pseudonym used by Zachariah Cozens*]
TMP .... East Timor [*ISO three-letter standard code*] (CNC)
TMP .... [*The*] Madison Project (EA)
TMP .... [*The*] Management Processor (MCD)
TMP .... Tampere [*Finland*] [*Airport symbol*] (OAG)
TMP .... Target Materials Program [*DoD*]
TMP .... Technical Manual Parts [*Army*] (AABC)
TMP .... Technical Manual Plan [*DoD*]
TMP .... Telecommunications Modernization Project (AAGC)
TMP .... Teleprinter Message Pool
TMP .... Temazepam [*Tranquilizer*]
TMP .... Temperature (BUR)
Tmp .... [*The*] Tempest [*Shakespearean work*]
tmp .... Temporary (BARN)
TMP .... Terminal Monitor Program [*Computer science*] (BUR)
TMP .... Terminal Panel (NASA)
TMP .... Ternary Mobile Phase [*Physical chemistry*]
TMP .... Terrain Mortar Positioning [*Military*] (INF)
TMP .... Test Maintenance Panel [*Computer science*]
TMP .... Test Management Protocol [*Telecommunications*] (OSI)
TMP .... Test Market Plan [*Advertising*] (NTCM)
TMP .... Test Market Profile [*Advertising*] (NTCM)
TMP .... Test Methods and Procedures
TMP .... Tetramesitylporphyrin [*Organic chemistry*]
TMP .... Tetramethoxypropane [*Organic chemistry*]
TMP .... Tetramethylpiperidine [*Organic chemistry*]

TMP........ Thallium Myocardial Perfusion [*Test*] [*Cardiology*] (DAVI)
TMP........ Theodolite Measuring Point (MUGU)
TMP........ Thermal Mass Penalty (KSC)
TMP........ Thermal Modeling Program
TMP........ Thermo Magnetic Printing (HGAA)
TMP........ Thermomechanical Processing
TMP........ Thermo Mechanical Pulp (EERA)
TMP........ Thermomechanical Pulps
TMP........ Thermomicrophotometry
TMP........ Thymidine Monophosphate [*Biochemistry*]
TMP........ Thymine Ribonucleoside-5-Phosphate [*Genetics*] (DAVI)
TMP........ Thymocyte Mitogenic Protein [*Immunology*]
TMP........ Thymolphthalein Monophosphate [*Biochemistry*]
TMP........ Time Management Processor (NASA)
TMP........ Times Mirror Press
TMP........ Top Management Program
TMP........ Total Material Package [*Military*] (DNAB)
TMP........ Total Milk Proteinate [*Trademark of New Zealand Milk Products, Inc.*]
TMP........ Traditional Medical Practice
TMP........ Transistor Mounting Pad
TMP........ Transitional Manpower Program [*Navy*] (DNAB)
TMP........ Transmembrane Potential [*Biochemistry*]
TMP........ Transmembrane Pressure [*Biomedicine*]
TMP........ Transmembrane Protein [*Biochemistry*]
TMP........ Trans Mountain Pipe Line Co. Ltd. [*Toronto Stock Exchange symbol Vancouver Stock Exchange symbol*]
TMP........ Transportable Measurement Package (MCD)
TMP........ Transportation Motor Pool [*Military*] (AABC)
TMP........ Transversely Magnetized Plasma
TMP........ Trimetaphosphate [*Organic chemistry*]
TMP........ Trimethoprim [*Also, T*] [*Antibacterial compound*]
TMP........ Trimethylolpropane [*Organic chemistry*]
TMP........ Trimethylpentane [*Organic chemistry*]
TMP........ Trimethyl Phosphate [*Organic chemistry*]
TMP........ Trimethylphosphine [*Organic chemistry*]
TMP........ Trimethylpsoralen [*Photochemotherapeutic compound*] (AAMN)
TMPA........ Traffic Management Program Alert [*Aviation*] (FAAC)
TMPA........ Transocean Marine Paint Association [*Netherlands*] (EAIO)
TMPA........ Trimethylphosphoramide [*Organic chemistry*]
Tmpah........ Tubular Maximum for Para-Aminohippuric Acid [*Biochemistry*] (MAE)
TMPC........ Memphis Planning Commission, Memphis, TN [*Library symbol Library of Congress*] (LCLS)
TMPC........ Theater Mission Planning Center (AAGC)
TmpChin........ Templeton China World Fund [*Associated Press*] (SAG)
TMPD........ Tempered (MSA)
TMPD........ Tetramethyl-para-phenylenediamine [*Analytical chemistry*]
TMPD........ Trimethylpentanediol [*Organic chemistry*]
TMPDF........ Trade Marks, Patents, and Designs Federation [*British*] (DBA)
TmpDrgn........ Templeton Dragon Fund [*Associated Press*] (SAG)
TMPDS........ Temporomandibular Pain and Dysfunction Syndrome [*Medicine*] (DMAA)
TMPEP........ Timber Management Policy Reform Program (GNE)
TMPG........ Ton-Miles per Gallon [*Automotive fuel*]
TmpGlb........ Templeton Global Income Fund [*Associated Press*] (SAG)
TMPH........ Ton-Mile Per Hour [*Heavy tires*] (DICI)
TMPI........ Plough, Inc., Memphis, TN [*Library symbol Library of Congress*] (LCLS)
TMPI........ Target Material Production Instruction [*Air Force*]
tmpl........ Temple (VRA)
TMPL........ Temple
TMPN........ Tetramethylpiperidinol N-oxyl [*Organic chemistry*]
TMPO........ Total Materiel Procurement Objective [*Military*]
TMPO........ Traffic Management and Proceedings Office [*CONUS*] (MCD)
TMPRG........ Tempering
TMPRLY........ Temporarily (MDG)
TMPROC........ Telemetry Processing
TmpRus........ Templeton Russia Fund [*Associated Press*] (SAG)
TmpRuss........ Templeton Russia Fund [*Associated Press*] (SAG)
TMPRY........ Temporary (AFM)
TMPS........ Temperature Monitoring Power Supply
TMPS........ Test Maintenance Panel Subassembly [*Computer science*]
TMPS........ Theater Mission Planning System [*Military*] (CAAL)
TMPS........ Tracking Modifier Power Supply
TMPS........ Trans-Mississippi Philatelic Society (EA)
TMP/SMX........ Trimethoprim-Sulfamethoxazole [*Antibacterial*] [*Antineoplastic drug*]
TMP-SMZ........ Trimethoprim-Sulfamethoxazole [*Antineoplastic drug*] (MEDA)
TMP-SMZ-DS... Trimethoprim-Sulfamethoxazole-Double-Strength [*Antineoplastic drug*] (MEDA)
TMPSS........ Trailer-Mounted Power Support System (DWSG)
TMPT........ Tactical Marine Petroleum Terminal (MCD)
TMPTA........ Trimethylolpropane Triacrylate [*Organic chemistry*]
TMPTMA........ Trimethylolpropane Trimethacrylate [*Organic chemistry*]
TMPV........ Torque Motor Pilot Valve (NASA)
TmpViet........ Templeton Vietnam Opportunities Fund [*Associated Press*] (SAG)
TMPW........ TMP Worldwide, Inc. [*NASDAQ symbol*] (SAG)
TMP Wr........ TMP Worldwide, Inc. [*Associated Press*] (SAG)
TMPZ........ Tetramethylpyrazine [*Biochemistry*]
TMQ........ Tambao [*Upper Volta*] [*Airport symbol*] (AD)
TMQ........ Thames Air Services & Charter Ltd. [*Nigeria*] [*ICAO designator*] (FAAC)
TMQ........ ThermoQuest Corp. [*AMEX symbol*] (TTSB)
TMQ........ Thermoquest Corp. [*AMEX symbol*] (SAG)
TMQAP........ Technical Manual Quality Assurance Plan [*Navy*] (DNAB)
TMR........ Tactical Microwave Radio
TMR........ Tactical Missile Receiver
TMR........ Tamanrasset [*Algeria*] [*Airport symbol*] (OAG)
TMR........ Tandem Mirror Reactor (MCD)
TMR........ Technical Memorandum Report
TMR........ Technology Management Review [*Military*] (AFIT)
TMR........ Telecommunications Marketing Resource Ltd. [*Telecommunications service*] (TSSD)
TMR........ Teledyne Materials Research (IAA)
TMR........ Telemanagement Resources, Inc. [*Charlotte, NC*] [*Telecommunications*] (TSSD)
TMR........ Temo Resources Ltd. [*Vancouver Stock Exchange symbol*]
TMR........ Terrestrial Myriametric Radiation [*Physics*]
TMR........ Test Malfunction Report
TMR........ Tetramethylrhodamine [*Fluorescent dye*]
TMR........ Texas Meridian Resources [*AMEX symbol*] (TTSB)
TMR........ Texas Meridian Resources Ltd. [*AMEX symbol*] (SPSG)
TMR........ Thermistor Micropower Resistor
TMR........ Timber Management Research [*Department of Agriculture*] (GRD)
TMR........ Time Meter Reading
TMR........ Timer (AAG)
TMR........ Tomakomai [*Japan*] [*Seismograph station code, US Geological Survey*] (SEIS)
TMR........ Topical Magnetic Resonance [*Medical diagnostic technique*]
TMR........ Total Materiel Requirement [*Military*] (AABC)
TMR........ Total Metal Removed
TMR........ Total Mission Recorder [*Navy*]
TMR........ Trainable Mentally Retarded
TMR........ Transmembrane Receptors [*Biochemistry*]
TMR........ Transportation Movements Release [*Military*] (AABC)
TMR........ Transvaal Mounted Rifles [*British military*] (DMA)
Tmr........ Trimmer [*British military*] (DMA)
TMR........ Triple Modular Redundancy [*Computer science*]
TMR........ True Money Rate [*Finance*]
TMR........ True Motion RADAR (IAA)
TMRA........ Technical and Miscellanous Revenue Act (MHDB)
TMRAO........ Table Mountain Radio Astronomy Observatory
TMRBM........ Transportable Medium-Range Ballistic Missile
TMRC........ Technical Maintenance Repair Center (MCD)
TMRC........ Theoretical Maximum Residue Contribution [*to acceptable daily intake*] [*Environmental Protection Agency*]
TMRD........ Technical Management Requirements Document
TMRD........ Transportation Movement Requirements Data (MCD)
TM Rec........ Trade Mark Record [*United States*] [*A publication*] (DLA)
TM/RF........ Telemetry/Radio Frequency
TMRI........ RAMCON, Inc., Environmental Engineering Library, Memphis, TN [*Library symbol Library of Congress*] (LCLS)
TMRI........ Tetramethylrhodamine Isothiocyanate [*Analytical biochemistry*]
TMRK........ Canadian Trade Marks [*Canada Systems Group*] [*Information service or system*] (IID)
TMRK........ Trimark Holdings [*NASDAQ symbol*] (TTSB)
TMRK........ Trimark Holdings, Inc. [*NASDAQ symbol*] (SPSG)
TMRM........ Tetramethylrhodamine-Maleimide [*Organic chemistry*]
TMRP........ Technology Mobilization and Reemployment Program [*Department of Labor*]
TMRP........ Tropical Meteorology Research Programme [*Marine science*] (OSRA)
TMR Prac........ Trademark Rules of Practice [*A publication*] (DLA)
TMRS........ Traffic Measuring and Recording System [*Telecommunications*] (TEL)
TmRSV........ Tomato Ringspot Virus
TMRVDP........ Terminal-Modified RADAR Video Data Processor [*Noise control*]
TMS........ [*The*] Magnolia Society (EA)
TMS........ [*The*] Manufacturing System [*Burroughs Machines Ltd.*] [*Software package*] (NCC)
TMS........ [*The*] Masonry Society (EA)
TMS........ [*The*] Metallurgy Society [*Formerly, MS*] (IAA)
TMS........ Minerals, Metals, and Materials Society (EA)
TMS........ Sao Tome Island [*Sao Tome Islands*] [*Airport symbol*] (OAG)
TMS........ Siena College, Memphis, TN [*Library symbol Library of Congress*] (LCLS)
TMS........ Southern Missionary College, Collegedale, TN [*OCLC symbol*] (OCLC)
TMS........ Tactical Missile Squadron [*Air Force*]
TMS........ Tape Management Software [*Computer science*] (IAA)
TMS........ Tape Management System (MCD)
TMS........ Target Marking System
TMS........ Target Materials Squadron (MCD)
TMS........ Technisonic [*Record label*]
TMS........ Technological Market Segmentation
TMS........ Telecommunications Message Switcher
TMS........ Telegraphy with Manual Switching [*Telecommunications*] (IAA)
TMS........ Telemeter Transmitter (IAA)
TMS........ Telemetry Modulation System
TMS........ Telemetry Multiplex System
TMS........ Teleoperator Maneuvering System (MCD)
TMS........ Telephone Management System (HGAA)
TMS........ Telex Management Systems (NITA)
TMS........ Temperature Management Station
TMS........ Temperature Measurement Society
TMS........ Temporomandibular Syndrome [*Medicine*]
TMS........ Temsco Helicopters, Inc. [*ICAO designator*] (FAAC)
TMS........ Tesla Memorial Society (EA)
TMS........ Test and Monitoring Station
TMS........ Test Monitor System
TMS........ Tetramethoxysilane [*Organic chemistry*]
TMS........ Tetramethylsilane [*Organic chemistry*]
TMS........ Textile Market Studies [*British*]

TMS .... Text Message System (MCD)
TMS .... Thallium Myocardial Scintigraphy [*Cardiology*]
TMS .... Thematic Mapper Simulator [*for aerial photography*]
TMS .... Thermal Management System [*Dell Computer Corp.*] (PCM)
TMS .... Thermal Maneuvering System (SSD)
TMS .... Thermomechanical System [*Instrumentation*]
TMS .... Thread Mate System [*Dentistry*]
TMS .... Thrust Measuring System
TMS .... Tight Model Series (MCD)
TMS .... Time and Motion Study (NG)
TMS .... Time Multiplexed Switching [*Telecommunications*]
TMS .... Time-Shared Monitor System [*Computer science*] (IEEE)
TMS .... Times Square Energy Resource Ltd. [*Vancouver Stock Exchange symbol*]
TMS .... Tissu Musculaire Specifique [*France*] [*Medicine*]
TMS .... Tomisaki [*Mera*] [*Japan*] [*Seismograph station code, US Geological Survey*] [*Closed*] (SEIS)
TMS .... Top Management Simulation [*Game*]
TMS .... TOW [*Tube-Launched, Optically Tracked, Wire-Guided (Weapon)*] Missile System (RDA)
TMS .... Toyota Motor Sales, Inc.
TMS .... Track Monitor Supervisor (IAA)
TMS .... Trademark Section, Official Gazette [*Federal government*]
TMS .... Trademark Society (EA)
TMS .... Traffic Management System [*FAA*] (TAG)
TMS .... Traffic Measurement System
TMS .... Traffic Monitoring System [*FHWA*] (TAG)
TM/S .... Trained in Minesweeping [*British military*] (DMA)
TMS .... Trainee Management System (MCD)
TMS .... Training Material Support
TMS .... Training Media Services
TMS .... [*The*] Tramway Museum Society [*British*] (DCTA)
TMS .... Transaction Management System (BUR)
TMS .... Transcranial Magnetic Stimulation [*Proposed therapy for depression*]
TMS .... Transmatic Money Service
TMS .... Transmission Measuring Set [*Bell Laboratories*]
TMS .... Transportation Management School [*Navy*]
TMS .... Transport Management Survey (MCD)
TMS .... Trascranial Magnetic Stimulation [*Medicine*]
TMS .... Treasury Management Services [*British*]
TMS .... Treasury Market Securities (MHDW)
TMS .... TriMas Corp. [*NYSE symbol*] (SPSG)
TMS .... Trimethoprim and Sulfamethoxazole [*Antibacterials*] (DAVI)
TMS .... Trimethylsilyl [*Organic chemistry*]
TMS .... Truth-Maintenance System [*Artificial intelligence*] (ECON)
TMS .... Turbine Management Station
TMS .... Turbulence Measuring System
TMS .... Type, Model, and Series
TMSA .... Technical Marketing Society of America (EA)
TMSA .... Telecommunications Marketing/Sales Association [*Defunct*] (EA)
TMSA .... Thomas More Society of America (EA)
TMSA .... Trimethylsilyl Azide [*Organic chemistry*]
TMSAN .... Trimethylsilylacetonitrile [*Organic chemistry*]
TMSB .... Memphis and Shelby County Bar Association, Memphis, TN [*Library symbol Library of Congress*] (LCLS)
TMSC .... Southwestern at Memphis, Memphis, TN [*Library symbol Library of Congress*] (LCLS)
TMSC .... Talcott Mountain Science Center for Student Involvement, Inc. [*Avon, CT*] [*Telecommunications service*] (TSSD)
TMSC .... Texas Male Sterility Cytoplasm [*Agriculture*] (OA)
TMSCC .... Shelby County Court House, Memphis, TN [*Library symbol*] [*Library of Congress*] (LCLS)
TMSCH .... Memphis and Shelby County Health Department, Memphis, TN [*Library symbol Library of Congress*] (LCLS)
TMSCJ .... Trade Movement Society of Carpenters and Joiners [*A union*] [*British*]
TMSCI .... Trimethylsilyl Chloride [*Organic chemistry*]
TMSCN .... Trimethylsilylcyanide [*Organic chemistry*]
TMS-CPG .... Trimethylsilylated Controlled-Pore Glass [*Packing for chromatography*]
TMSCS .... Memphis and Shelby County Safety Council, Memphis, TN [*Library symbol Library of Congress*] (LCLS)
TMSD .... Total Military Service to Date
TMSD .... Training Material Support Detachment [*Army*]
TMSDC .... Thermomechanical Model Software Development Center [*Research center*] (RCD)
TMSDEA .... Trimethylsilyldiethylamine [*Organic chemistry*]
TMSIM .... (Trimethylsilyl)imidazole [*Also, TSIM*] [*Organic chemistry*]
TMSM .... Shiloh Military Trail Library, Memphis, TN [*Library symbol Library of Congress*] (LCLS)
TMSM .... Trimethylstannylmaleate [*Organic chemistry*]
TMSMC .... Semmes-Murphey Clinic, Memphis, TN [*Library symbol Library of Congress*] (LCLS)
TMSO .... Southern College of Optometry, Memphis, TN [*Library symbol Library of Congress*] (LCLS)
TMSq .... Tactical Missile Squadron [*Air Force*]
TMSR .... Technical Manual Status Report (MCD)
TMSR .... Thrustmaster, Inc. [*NASDAQ symbol*] (SAG)
TMSS .... Shelby State Community College, Memphis, TN [*Library symbol Library of Congress*] (LCLS)
TMSS .... Technical Manual Specifications and Standards [*Military*] (AFIT)
TMSS .... Technical Munitions Safety Study [*Air Force*]
TMSS .... Tecmar Music Synthesis System
TMSS .... Towanda-Monroeton Shippers Lifeline, Inc. [*AAR code*]
TMSSR .... Technical Manual Status and Schedule Report (MCD)
TMST .... Thomaston Mills, Inc. [*NASDAQ symbol*] (NQ)
TMST .... Treadmill Stress Test [*or Study*] [*Cardiology*] (DAVI)
TMSTA .... Thomaston Mills'A' [*NASDAQ symbol*] (TTSB)
TMSTB .... Thomaston Mills'B' [*NASDAQ symbol*] (TTSB)
TMStF .... Saint Francis Hospital, Medical Library, Memphis, TN [*Library symbol Library of Congress*] (LCLS)
TMStJ .... Saint Jude Children's Research Hospital, Memphis, TN [*Library symbol Library of Congress*] (LCLS)
TMStJo .... Saint Joseph Hospital, Memphis, TN [*Library symbol Library of Congress*] (LCLS)
TMSVCS .... TOW [*Tube-Launched, Optically Tracked, Wire-Guided (Weapon)*] Missile SightVideo Camera System (MCD)
TMT .... Tactical Marine Terminal (MCD)
TMT .... Talcott Mountain [*Connecticut*] [*Seismograph station code, US Geological Survey Closed*] (SEIS)
TMT .... Tarsometatarsal [*Joint*] [*Anatomy*] (DAVI)
TMT .... TCW/DW Term Trust 2003 [*NYSE symbol*] (SPSG)
TMT .... Temora [*New South Wales*] [*Airport symbol*] (AD)
TMT .... Temperature (MDG)
TMT .... Terminal Monitor Program [*Computer science*] (MDG)
TMT .... Testing Methods and Techniques [*Telecommunications*] (TEL)
TMT .... Tetramethylthiourea [*Also, TMTU*] [*Organic chemistry*]
TMT .... Thermal Measurement Treatment
TMT .... Thermomechanical Treatment
TMT .... Thousand Metric Tons (IMH)
TMT .... Tire Management Terminal [*Automotive engineering*]
TMT .... Total Maintenance Time (MCD)
TMT .... Total Mission Time
TMT .... TOW [*Tube-Launched, Optically Tracked, Wire-Guided (Weapon)*] Missile Transporter (MCD)
TMT .... Toxic Materials Transport [*Business Publishers, Inc.*] [*Information service or system*] (CRD)
TMT .... Trail Making Test [*Psychiatry*] (DAVI)
TMT .... Trans Midwest Airlines, Inc. [*ICAO designator*] (FAAC)
TMT .... Transonic Model Tunnel [*NASA*]
TMT .... Transportation Motor Transport [*Military*] (AABC)
TMT .... Treatment [*Medicine*]
TMT .... Troy Mineral & Tech [*Vancouver Stock Exchange symbol*]
TMT .... Turret Maintenance Trainer (MCD)
TMTC .... Thru-Mode [*or Tri-Mode*] Tape Converter
TMTC .... Too Many to Count [*Laboratory science*] (DAVI)
TMTD .... Tetramethylthiuram Disulfide [*Also, THTMS, TMTDS*] [*Organic chemistry*]
TMTDS .... Tetramethylthiuram Disulfide [*Also, TMTD, THTMS*] [*Organic chemistry*]
TMTF .... Tile, Marble, and Terrazzo Finishers and Shopmen International Union
TMTG .... Tactical Missile Training Group [*Military*]
TMTI .... State Technical Institute at Memphis, Memphis, TN [*Library symbol Library of Congress*] (LCLS)
TMTP .... Tennessee Psychiatric Hospital and Institute, Memphis, TN [*Library symbol Library of Congress*] (LCLS)
TMTR .... Thermistor (AAG)
TMTR .... Transmitter
TMTS .... Memphis Theological Seminary of the Cumberland Presbyterian Church, Memphis, TN [*Library symbol Library of Congress*] (LCLS)
TMTS .... Tactical Missile Training Squadron [*Air Force*]
TMTSF .... Tetramethyltetraselenafulvene [*Organic chemistry*]
TMTU .... Tetramethylthiourea [*Also, TMT*] [*Organic chemistry*]
TMTX .... Temtex Indus [*NASDAQ symbol*] (TTSB)
TMTX .... Temtex Industries, Inc. [*NASDAQ symbol*] (NQ)
TMU .... Groton, CT [*Location identifier FAA*] (FAAL)
TMU .... Tactical Mobile Unit [*Police*]
TMU .... Temperature Measurement Unit (NASA)
TMU .... Temuco [*Chile*] [*Seismograph station code, US Geological Survey*] (SEIS)
TMU .... Test Maintenance Unit [*Computer science*]
TMU .... Tetramethylurea [*Organic chemistry*]
TMU .... Thermal-Mechanical Unit
TMU .... Time Measurement Unit [*Industrial engineering*]
TMU .... Time-Multiplexer Unit [*Telecommunications*] (IAA)
TMU .... Traffic Management Unit [*FAA*] (TAG)
TMU .... Traffic Management Unit (GAVI)
TMU .... Transmission Message Unit
TMU .... Turret Mock-Up (MCD)
TMU .... Twin and Multiply (IAA)
TMUP .... Union Planters National Bank, Memphis, TN [*Library symbol Library of Congress*] (LCLS)
TMurH .... Highland Rim Regional Library Center, Murfreesboro, TN [*Library symbol Library of Congress*] (LCLS)
TMurS .... Middle Tennessee State University, Murfreesboro, TN [*Library symbol Library of Congress*] (LCLS)
TMurS-M .... Center for Popular Music, Middle Tennessee State University, Murfreesboro, TN [*Library symbol*] [*Library of Congress*] (LCLS)
TMUS .... Temporarily Mounted User Set [*Computer science*] (ADA)
TMUS .... Toy Manufacturers of the United States
TMUSAE .... United States Army Engineers Library, Memphis, TN [*Library symbol Library of Congress*] (LCLS)
TMUSDC .... United States Department of Commerce, Memphis, TN [*Library symbol Library of Congress*] (LCLS)
TMUX .... Transmultiplexer (LAIN)
TMV .... Tactical Wheeled Vehicle
TMV .... Tanker Motor Vessel [*Shipping*] (DS)
TMV .... Telemetry Van

TMV .... Texas A & M University, Medical Sciences Library, College Station, TX [*OCLC symbol*] (OCLC)
TMV .... Tobacco Mosaic Virus
TMV .... Torpedoman's Mate, Aviation [*Navy rating*]
TMV .... Total Molecular Volume [*Chemistry*]
TMV .... Triplicated Majority Voting (IAA)
TMV .... True Mean Value
TMV .... Turnip Mosaic Virus
TMV .... United States Veterans Administration Hospital, Memphis, TN [*Library symbol Library of Congress*] (LCLS)
TMV-C .... Turnip Mosaic Virus - Common
TMV-L .... Turnip Mosaic Virus - Legume
TMVP .... Tobacco Mosaic Virus Protein
TMVS .... Times Mirror Videotex Services, Inc. [*Information service or system Inactive*] (IID)
TMW .... Tactical Missile Wing [*Air Force*]
TMW .... Tamworth [*Australia Airport symbol*] (OAG)
TMW .... Thermal Megawatt [*Also, Mwt*]
TMW .... Toyota Motor Workers' Union
TMW .... Transverse Magnetic Wave [*Radio*]
TMWC .... Waring Cox Law Firm, Memphis, TN [*Library symbol*] [*Library of Congress*] (LCLS)
TMWR .... Tax Management Weekly Report [*Bureau of National Affairs*] [*Information service or system*] (CRD)
TMWR .... Technical Manual Work Request
TMWR .... Technical Manual Work Requirement (MCD)
TMX .... Tactical Missile Experimental (IAA)
TMX .... Tamoxifen [*Antineoplastic drug*]
TMX .... Tandem Mirror Experiment [*Atomic fusion*]
TMX .... Telefonos de Mexico [*NYSE symbol*] (SAG)
TMX .... Telefonos de Mexico'L'ADS [*NYSE symbol*] (TTSB)
TMX .... Telemeter Transmitter
TMX .... Timimoun [*Algeria*] [*Airport symbol*] (AD)
TMX .... Transportacion Aerea Mexicana [*Mexico ICAO designator*] (FAAC)
TMXDI .... Tetramethylxylene Diisocyanate [*Organic chemistry*]
TMXDI .... Trimethylxylene Diisocyanate [*Organic chemistry*]
TMXI .... Thermatrix, Inc. [*NASDAQ symbol*] (SAG)
TMXO .... Tactical Miniature Crystal Oscillator
TMXRT .... Three-Mirror X-Ray Telescope [*NASA*]
TMZ .... Houston, TX [*Location identifier FAA*] (FAAL)
TMZ .... Termez [*USSR*] [*Airport symbol*] (AD)
TN .... Australian Airlines [*Airline flight code*] (ODBW)
Tn .... Intraocular Tension [*Ophthalmology*] (DAVI)
TN .... [*The*] Navigators (EA)
Tn .... Normal Intraocular Pressure [*Ophthalmology*] (DAVI)
Tn .... Normal Intraocular Tension [*Ophthalmology*] (DAVI)
TN .... Public Library of Nashville and Davidson County, Nashville, TN [*Library symbol Library of Congress*] (LCLS)
TN .... Stewardsman [*Nonrated enlisted man*] [*Navy*]
TN .... Tagesarbeitsnormen [*Workday Standards*] [*German*]
T/N .... Tar and Nicotine [*In cigarettes*]
TN .... Tariff Number
TN .... Tarragon Oil & Gas Ltd. [*Toronto Stock Exchange symbol*]
TN .... Task Number [*Computer science*] (IAA)
TN .... Taunton [*British depot code*]
TN .... TDRSS [*Tracking and Data Relay Satellite System*] Network [*NASA*] (SSD)
TN .... Team Nursing
TN .... Technical Note
TN .... Technology Needs (MCD)
TN .... Telephone (NATG)
TN .... Telephone Number
TN .... Tell en-Nasbeh (BJA)
TN .... Temperature Normal [*Medicine*]
TN .... Temple Name (BJA)
TN .... Tennessee [*Postal code*]
TN .... Tennessee Reports [*A publication*] (DLA)
TN .... Terminal Node
TN .... Test Narrative (CAAL)
TN .... Test Negative [*Clinical chemistry*]
TN .... Test Number (AAG)
TN .... Texas & Northern Railway Co. [*AAR code*]
TN .... Thanks (IAA)
TN .... Thermonuclear
TN .... Tin
tn .... Titanite [*CIPW classification*] [*Geology*]
TN .... Ton
TN .... Tonbridge [*Postcode*] (ODBW)
TN .... Tone (MSA)
tn .... Toned (VRA)
TN .... Total Negative (MAE)
TN .... Total Nitrogen [*Analytical chemistry*]
TN .... Town
TN .... Track Number
TN .... Trade Name (DEN)
TN .... Train (AAG)
TN .... Trans-Australia Airlines [*ICAO designator*] (AD)
TN .... Transferable Notice [*Business term*]
TN .... Transfer on Negative
TN .... Transfield (NSW) Pty. Ltd. [*Transavia Division*] [*Australia ICAO aircraft manufacturer identifier*] (ICAO)
TN .... Translator's Note
TN .... Transport
TN .... Transportation
Tn .... Transposon [*Genetics*] (DOG)
TN .... Transverse Nerve [*Neuroanatomy*]
TN .... Triafol
TN .... Troponin [*Biochemistry*]
T/N .... True Name
TN .... True Negative [*Medicine*]
TN .... True North
Tn .... Tukulti-Ninurta (BJA)
TN .... Tuning (IAA)
TN .... Tuning Unit [*JETDS nomenclature*] [*Military*] (CET)
TN .... Tunisia [*IYRU nationality code*] [*ANSI two-letter standard code*] (CNC)
TN .... Twelfth Night [*Shakespearean work*]
TN .... Twisted Nematic [*Telecommunications*] (TEL)
TN^2 .... [*The*] News Is the News [*Television comedy program*]
TNA .... Jinan [*China*] [*Airport symbol*] (OAG)
TNA .... [*The*] National Archives [*of the United States*]
TNA .... Office of Terrorism and Narcotics Analysis [*Bureau of Intelligence and Research*] [*Department of State*] [*Washington, DC*] (GRD)
TNA .... Tanavco Airways Ltd. [*Tanzania*] [*ICAO designator*] (FAAC)
TNA .... Tasmanian Netball Association [*Australia*]
TNA .... Telecommunications Network Architects [*Telecommunications service*] (TSSD)
TNA .... Telocator Network of America (EA)
TN A .... Tennessee Appeals Reports [*A publication*] (DLA)
TNA .... Terra Nova (Bermuda)Hldg [*NYSE symbol*] (TTSB)
TNA .... Terra Nova Bermuda Holdings Ltd. [*NYSE symbol*] (SAG)
TNA .... Tetranitroadamantane [*Explosive*] [*Organic chemistry*]
TNA .... Tetranitroaniline [*Organic chemistry*]
TNA .... The National Alliance of Professional and Executive Women's Networks [*Later, TIA*] (EA)
TNA .... Thermal Neutron Activation [*FAA*]
TNA .... Thermal Neutron Analysis [*For detection of explosives*]
TNA .... Thermal Nuclear Analyzer
TNA .... Thomas Nelson - Australia [*Publisher*]
Tna .... Tigrinya (BJA)
TNA .... Time of Nearest Approach
TNA .... Tin City [*Alaska*] [*Seismograph station code, US Geological Survey*] (SEIS)
TNA .... Total Nucleic Acid
TNA .... Total Nutrient Admixtures [*Parenteral emulsions*]
TNA .... Training Needs Analysis (AIE)
TNA .... Transient Network Analyzer (IEEE)
TNA .... Transistor Noise Analyzer (IAA)
TNA .... Trigeminal Neuralgia Association (EA)
TNA .... Trinitroaniline [*Organic chemistry*]
TNA .... Tropicana Development Corp. [*Vancouver Stock Exchange symbol*]
TNA .... Turn Altitude [*Aviation*] (FAAC)
TNAC .... Aquinas Junior College, Nashville, TN [*Library symbol*] [*Library of Congress*] (LCLS)
TNAC .... Turkish News Agency of Cyprus (EAIO)
TNAE .... United States Army Engineer District, Nashville, Nashville, TN [*Library symbol Library of Congress*] (LCLS)
TNAF .... Training Name and Address File [*IRS*]
TNAM .... Theater Network Analysis Model [*Europe*] (MCD)
TNAS .... Tuberculosis Nursing Advisory Service (DAVI)
TNAUK .... Talking Newspaper Association, United Kingdom
TNAZ .... Trinitroazetidine [*An explosive*]
TNB .... Tanabu [*Japan*] [*Seismograph station code, US Geological Survey Closed*] (SEIS)
TNB .... Technical News Bulletin [*National Bureau of Standards*]
TNB .... Technion News Bulletin [*Haifa*] [*A publication*] (BJA)
TNB .... Thio(nitro)benzoic Acid [*Analytical biochemistry*]
TNB .... Thomas & Betts [*NYSE symbol*] (TTSB)
TNB .... Thomas & Betts Corp. [*NYSE symbol*] (SPSG)
TNB .... Transnasal Butorphanol [*Analgesic*]
TNB .... Trinitrobenzene [*Explosive*]
TNB .... Tru-Cut Needle Biopsy [*Surgery*] (DAVI)
TNB .... Turnbull Associates [*British ICAO designator*] (FAAC)
TNBA .... Tri-Normal-Butylaluminum [*Organic chemistry*]
TNBA .... Tri-normal-butylamine [*Organic chemistry*]
TNBe .... Belmont College, Nashville, TN [*Library symbol Library of Congress*] (LCLS)
TNBH .... Baptist Hospital, Medical Library, Nashville, TN [*Library symbol Library of Congress*] (LCLS)
TNBP .... Tri-N-Butyl Phosphate [*Organic chemistry*] (AAMN)
TNBS .... Trinitrobenzenesulfonic Acid [*Biochemistry*]
TNBT .... American Baptist Theological Seminary, Nashville, TN [*Library symbol Library of Congress*] (LCLS)
TNBT .... Tetranitro Blue Tetrazolium [*A dye*] [*Organic chemistry*]
TNBT .... The Next Big Thing
TNC .... Country Music Foundation Library and Media Center, Nashville, TN [*Library symbol Library of Congress*] (LCLS)
TNC .... National Aviation Consultants Ltd. [*Canada ICAO designator*] (FAAC)
TNC .... [*The*] National Crossbowmen (EA)
TNC .... [*The*] Nature Conservancy (EA)
TNC .... [*The*] Nature Conservancy (EERA)
TNC .... [*The*] Nerve Center (EA)
TNC .... Tail Number Change [*Air Force*] (AFIT)
TNC .... Tekniska Nomenklaturcentralen [*Swedish Center for Technical Terminology*] [*Information service or system*] (IID)
TNC .... Terminal Network Controller
TNC .... Terminal Node Controller [*Computer science*]
TNC .... Texas Nuclear Corp. (KSC)
TNC .... Theater Naval Commander
TNC .... Theatres National Committee [*British*] (DBA)

TNC Threaded-Neill-Concelman (DOM)
TNC Threaded Nut Connector (IAA)
TNC Threaded-Nut Coupling [*Electronics*] (EECA)
TNC Thymic Nurse Cell [*Cytology*]
TNC Tide Net Controller (NATG)
TNC Tin City [*Alaska*] [*Airport symbol*] (OAG)
TNC Tin City, AK [*Location identifier FAA*] (FAAL)
TNC Too Numerous to Count
TNC Total Nonstructural Carbohydrates
TNC Total Numerical Control (IAA)
TNC Town & Country Cl'A' [*AMEX symbol*] (TTSB)
TNC Town & Country Corp. [*AMEX symbol*] (SPSG)
TNC Track Navigation Computer
TNC Track No Conversion
TNC Track Number Conversion (IAA)
TNC Trade Negotiations Committee [*Australia*]
TNC Trans-National Communications, Inc.
TNC Transnational Corp.
TNC Transnational Operation (EERA)
TNC Transport Network Controller
TNC Trevecca Nazarene College [*Tennessee*]
TNC Trinitrocellulose [*Organic chemistry*]
TNC Trionics Technology Ltd. [*Vancouver Stock Exchange symbol*]
TNC Tripartite Naval Commission [*Allied German Occupation Forces*]
TnC Troponin C [*Biochemistry*]
TNC Turbid No Creamy Layer [*Laboratory science*] (DAVI)
TNC Twisted Nematic Liquid [*Telecommunications*] (IAA)
TNCA Oranjestad/Reina Beatrix, Aruba Island [*Netherlands Antilles*] [*ICAO location identifier*] (ICLI)
TNCA Thionaphthenecarboxylic Acid [*Organic chemistry*]
TNCB Kralendijk/Flamingo, Bonaire Island [*Netherlands Antilles*] [*ICAO location identifier*] (ICLI)
TNCC Tripartite Nuclear Cross-Sections Committee [*British, Canadian, and US*]
TNCC Willemstad/Hato, Curacao Island [*Netherlands Antilles*] [*ICAO location identifier*] (ICLI)
TNCD Ten Nation Committee on Disarmament [*Defunct, 1960*]
TNCE Oranjestad/F. D. Roosevelt, Sint Eustatius Island [*Netherlands Antilles*] [*ICAO location identifier*] (ICLI)
TNCF Curacao [*Netherlands Antilles*] [*ICAO location identifier*] (ICLI)
TNCL Tail Number Configuration List [*Navy*] (NG)
TNCM Philipsburg/Prinses Juliana, Sint Maarten Island [*Netherlands Antilles*] [*ICAO location identifier*] (ICLI)
Tnco Tenneco, Inc [*Formerly, Tennessee Gas Transmission Co.*] [*Associated Press*] (SAG)
TNCR Tencor Instruments [*NASDAQ symbol*] (TTSB)
TNCR Tencor Instruments, Inc. [*NASDAQ symbol*] (SAG)
TN Cr Tennessee Criminal Appeals Reports [*A publication*] (DLA)
TNCS Saba/Yrausquin [*Netherlands Antilles*] [*ICAO location identifier*] (ICLI)
TnCSI Technician of the Construction Surveyor's Institute [*British*] (DBQ)
TNCSS Temporary National Commission on Supplies and Shortages [*Initiated 1974*]
TNCV Televisao Nacional de Cabo Verde [*National Television of Cape Verde*] (EY)
TNCX Network Connection [*NASDAQ symbol*] (TTSB)
TNCX Network Connection, Inc. [*NASDAQ symbol*] (SAG)
TNCXW Network Connection Wrrt [*NASDAQ symbol*] (TTSB)
TND Telecommunications Network for the Deaf
TND Term Normal Delivery [*Obstetrics*] (MAE)
TND Tim Donut Ltd. [*Canada ICAO designator*] (FAAC)
TND Tinned
TND Todwind Development Corp. [*Vancouver Stock Exchange symbol*]
TND Trace Narcotics Detector
TND Trade Names Database [*Information service or system*] (IID)
TND Trade Names Dictionary [*Later, BTC*] [*A publication*]
TND Traditional Neighborhood Development Ordinance
TND Trinidad [*Cuba*] [*Airport symbol*] (AD)
TND Turned (AAG)
TNDC Disciples of Christ Historical Society, Nashville, TN [*Library symbol Library of Congress*] (LCLS)
TNDC Thai National Documentation Center (IID)
TNDC Thai National Documentation Centre (NITA)
TNDC Trade Negotiations among Developing Countries (IMH)
TND:CI Trade Names Dictionary: Company Index [*Later, CTB*] [*A publication*]
TNDCY Tendency (FAAC)
TNDP Tetranitrodiphenyl [*Organic chemistry*]
TNDS Tactical Navigational Display System
TNDS Total Network Data System [*Bell System*]
TNDV Tobacco Necrotic Dwarf Virus [*Plant pathology*]
Tndycft Tandycrafts, Inc. [*Associated Press*] (SAG)
TNDZR Tenderizer
TNE Tanegashima [*Japan*] [*Airport symbol*] (OAG)
TNE Taxis Aereos del Noroeste SA de CV [*Mexico ICAO designator*] (FAAC)
TNE Terra Nova Energy [*Vancouver Stock Exchange symbol*]
TNE TRIS, Sodium Chloride, EDTA [*A buffer*]
TNEC Temporary National Economic Committee [*Congressional committee which studied the American economic system*] [*World War II*]
TNEF Trinitroethyl Formal [*An explosive*]
TNEL Total Noise Exposure Level (DA)
TNEOC Trinitroethyl Orthocarbonate [*An explosive*]
TNEOF Trinitroethyl Orthoformate [*An explosive*]
TNEP Total Noise Equivalent Power [*Electronics*] (EECA)
TNET Terminal and Computer Network (MHDI)
TNetix T-Netix, Inc. [*Associated Press*] (SAG)
TNF Fisk University, Nashville, TN [*Library symbol Library of Congress*] (LCLS)
TNF Tactical Nuclear Force (MCD)
TNF Theater Nuclear Forces
TNF Thin Nickel Film
TNF Third Normal Form [*Databases*]
TNF Timing Negative Film
TNF Trainfire
TNF Transfer on No Overflow
TNF Trinitrofluorenone [*Organic chemistry*]
TNF True North Film [*Vancouver Stock Exchange symbol*]
TNF Tumor Necrosis Factor [*Immunology*] [*Antineoplastic drug*]
TNF Tumor Neurosis Factor [*Biochemistry*]
TNF-A Tumor Necrosis Factor-Alpha
TNFB Free-Will Baptist Bible College, Nashville, TN [*Library symbol Library of Congress*] (LCLS)
TNFE Twisted Nemetic Field Effect [*Telecommunications*] (IAA)
TNFI North Face, Inc. (The) [*NASDAQ symbol*] (SAG)
TNFR Tumor Necrosis Factor Receptor [*Immunology*]
TNF/S Theater Nuclear Forces Security [*DoD*]
TNFS Theater Nuclear Forces Survivability (MCD)
TNFS3 Theater Nuclear Forces, Survivability, Security, and Safety (MCD)
TNFSS Theater Nuclear Forces Survivability and Security (MCD)
TNG G & B Aviation Ltd. [*British ICAO designator*] (FAAC)
TNG [*The*] Newspaper Guild (EA)
TNG Tanger [*Morocco*] [*Airport symbol*] (OAG)
TNG Tangerang [*Java*] [*Seismograph station code, US Geological Survey*] (SEIS)
TNG Tennessee Air National Guard (164th Airlift Group) [*FAA designator*] (FAAC)
TNG The Next Generation
TNG Tongue (MSA)
TNG Touch N' Go [*Computer Interface*] [*Touch N' Go Systems, Inc*] (PCM)
TNG Training (AAG)
TNG Transdermal Nitroglycerine Patch [*Medicine*]
TNG Trinitroglycerin [*Also, TNT*] (DAVI)
TNG Tungco Resources Corp. [*Vancouver Stock Exchange symbol*]
TNGANCH Training Anchorage [*Navy*] (NVT)
TNGE Tonnage [*Shipping*]
TNGLIT Training Literature [*Military*]
TNGS Theory of Neuronal Group Selection [*Neurology*]
TngS Training Subject
TNGSUP Training Support [*Navy*] (NVT)
TNGSVCS Training Services [*Navy*] (NVT)
TNH Tampa-Hillsborough County Public Library, Tampa, FL [*OCLC symbol*] (OCLC)
TNH Tax Notes Highlights [*Tax Analysts*] [*Information service or system*] (CRD)
TNH Terra Nitrogen Co. Ltd.[*Formerly, Agricultural Minerals Ltd.*] [*NYSE symbol*] (SAG)
TNH Terra Nitrogen L.P. [*NYSE symbol*] (TTSB)
TNH Tienshui [*Republic of China*] [*Seismograph station code, US Geological Survey*] (SEIS)
TNH Turn Height [*Aviation*] (FAAC)
TNHCA Hospital Corp. of America, Research/Information Services, Nashville, TN [*Library symbol Library of Congress*] (LCLS)
TNHQ Theater Navy Headquarters
TNI [*The*] Network, Inc. [*An association*] (EA)
TNI [*The*] Networking Institute [*Commercial firm*] (EA)
TNI Peipeinimaru, TT [*Location identifier FAA*] (FAAL)
TNI Thin Nickel Iron
TNI Total Nodal Irradiation [*Oncology*]
TNI Traffic Noise Index [*Department of Transportation*]
TNI Transcisco Indus [*AMEX symbol*] (TTSB)
TNI Transcisco Industries [*AMEX symbol*] (SPSG)
TNI Trans International Gold [*Vancouver Stock Exchange symbol*]
TNI Transnational Institute [*Netherlands*]
TnI Troponin I [*Biochemistry*]
TNIA [*The*] Network Inc. of America [*Information service or system*] (IID)
TNIF Thin Nickel Iron Film
TnIMBM Technician of the Institute of Municipal Building Management [*British*] (DBQ)
TNIP TDRSS/NASCOM [*Tracking and Data Relay Satellite System/NASA Communications Network*] Interface Panel (SSD)
TNIU Trustworthy Network Interface Unit [*Telecommunications*] (OSI)
TNJ Joint University Libraries, Nashville, TN [*Library symbol Library of Congress*] (LCLS)
TNJ Tanjung Pinang [*Indonesia*] [*Airport symbol*] (OAG)
TNJ-L Joint University Libraries, Vanderbilt School of Law, Nashville, TN [*Library symbol Library of Congress*] (LCLS)
TNJ-M Joint University Libraries, Vanderbilt Medical Center, Nashville, TN [*Library symbol Library of Congress*] (LCLS)
TNJ-P Joint University Libraries, George Peabody College for Teachers, Nashville, TN [*Library symbol Library of Congress*] (LCLS)
TNJ-R Joint University Libraries, Vanderbilt School of Religion, Nashville, TN [*Library symbol Library of Congress*] (LCLS)
TNJ-S Joint University Libraries, Scarritt College for Christian Workers, Nashville, TN [*Library symbol Library of Congress*] (LCLS)
TNK Tank (AAG)
TNK Tinkers Knob [*California*] [*Seismograph station code, US Geological Survey*] (SEIS)
TNK Torah Nebi'im Ketubim [*Teaching, prophets, writing*] [*Pronounced Tanakh*] [*The Hebrew Bible*]
TNK Tunkwa Copper Mining [*Vancouver Stock Exchange symbol*]

TNK .... Tununak [*Alaska*] [*Airport symbol*] (OAG)
TNK .... [*The*] Two Noble Kinsmen [*Shakespearean work*]
TNL .... David Lipscomb College, Nashville, TN [*Library symbol Library of Congress*] (LCLS)
TNL .... Technical Newsletter
TNL .... Technitrol, Inc. [*AMEX symbol*] (SPSG)
TNL .... Terminal Net Loss
TNL .... Times Newspapers Ltd. [*British*]
TNL .... Tunnel (MSA)
TnL .... Tunnel Luminescence [*Physics*]
TNLCD .... Twisted Nematic Liquid Crystal Display [*Telecommunications*] (IAA)
TNLDIO .... Tunnel Diode [*Electronics*]
TNLR .... Railroad Tunnel [*Board on Geographic Names*]
TNM .... Meharry Medical College, Nashville, TN [*Library symbol Library of Congress*] (LCLS)
TNM .... Nelson [*Thomas*], Inc. [*NYSE symbol*] (SAG)
TNM .... Tashota-Nipigon Mines [*Vancouver Stock Exchange symbol*]
TNM .... Telecommunications and Network Management
TNM .... Tetranitromethane [*Organic chemistry*]
TNM .... Texas-New Mexico Railway Co. [*AAR code*]
TNM .... Thomas Nelson [*NYSE symbol*] (TTSB)
TNM .... Topical Nitrogen Mustard [*Dermatology*]
TNM .... Tumor, Node, and Metastasis [*Criteria for staging*] [*Pathology*] (DAVI)
TNM .... Tumor, Node, Metastases [*System*] [*Medicine*] (HCT)
TNM .... Twisted Nematic Mode [*Telecommunications*] (IAA)
TNM.B .... Thomas Nelson 'B' [*NYSE symbol*] (TTSB)
TNMCS .... Total Not-Mission Capable, Supply [*Air Force*] (DOMA)
TNMH .... Metro General Hospital, Nashville, TN [*Library symbol Library of Congress*] (LCLS)
TNMPH .... Methodist Publishing House Library, Nashville, TN [*Library symbol Library of Congress*] (LCLS)
TNMR .... Tritium Nuclear Magnetic Resonance [*Spectrometry*]
TNN .... [*The*] Nashville Network [*Cable-television system*]
TNN .... Nashville Public Library, Nashville, TN [*OCLC symbol*] (OCLC)
TNN .... Tainan [*Taiwan*] [*Airport symbol*] (OAG)
TNN .... Tanana [*Alaska*] [*Seismograph station code, US Geological Survey*] (SEIS)
TNN .... The Nurturing Network (PAZ)
TNO .... Nederlandse Centrale Organisatie voor Toegepast Natuurwetenschappelijk Onderzoek [*Netherlands Institute for Applied Scientific Research*]
TNO .... Tamarindo [*Costa Rica*] [*Airport symbol*] (OAG)
TNO .... Tenore Oil & Gas [*Vancouver Stock Exchange symbol*]
TNO .... Texas & New Orleans R. R. [*AAR code*]
TNO .... Torino [*Italy*] [*Seismograph station code, US Geological Survey*] (SEIS)
TNO .... Transfer on No Overflow (SAA)
TNO .... True North Communications, Inc. [*Formerly, Foote, Cone & Belding*] [*NYSE symbol*] (SAG)
TNO .... True North Communicns [*NYSE symbol*] (TTSB)
TNOC .... Threads No Couplings
TNOP .... Total Network Operations Plan [*Telecommunications*] (TEL)
TNOR .... Temiskaming & Northern Ontario Railway
TNOT .... Total Not Operating Time
TNP .... [*The*] National Party [*Grenada*] [*Political party*] (EY)
TNP .... [*The*] New Party [*Australia Political party*]
TNP .... Thailand National Police (CINC)
TNP .... Theatre National Populaire [*France*]
TNP .... TNP Enterprises [*NYSE symbol*] (TTSB)
TNP .... TNP Enterprises, Inc. [*NYSE symbol*] (SPSG)
TNP .... Tonopah [*Nevada*] [*Seismograph station code, US Geological Survey*] (SEIS)
TNP .... Transkei National Party [*Political party*] (EY)
TNP .... Trinitrophenol [*or Trinitrophenyl*] [*Organic chemistry*]
TNP .... Trojan Nuclear Plant (NRCH)
TNP .... Twentynine Palms [*California*] [*Airport symbol*] (OAG)
TNP .... Twentynine Palms, CA [*Location identifier FAA*] (FAAL)
TNPA .... Tri-Normal-Propylaluminum [*Organic chemistry*]
TNPA .... Tri-normal-propylamine [*Organic chemistry*]
TNPC .... Taiwan New PC [*Personal Computer*] Consortium [*Computer science*]
TNPF .... Tidewater Nicaragua Project Foundation (EA)
TNPG .... [*The*] Nuclear Power Group [*British*]
TNPH .... Tennessee Department of Public Health, Nashville, TN [*Library symbol Library of Congress*] (LCLS)
TNPK .... Turnpike
TNP-KLH .... Trinitrophenyl Keyhole Limpet Hemocyanin [*Immunology*]
TNPM .... Transient Neonatal Pustular Melanosis [*Medicine*] (MEDA)
TNPO .... Terminal Navy Post Office (AFM)
TNPP .... Planned Parenthood of Nashville, Nashville, TN [*Library symbol Library of Congress*] (LCLS)
TNPP .... Tris(nonylphenyl) Phosphite [*Organic chemistry*]
TNPZOW .... Towarzystwo Niesienia Pomocy Zydom Ofiarom Wojny [*A publication*] (BJA)
TNQ .... Tongo [*Sierra Leone*] [*Airport symbol*] (AD)
TNR .... Antananarivo [*Madagascar*] [*Airport symbol*] (OAG)
TNR .... [*The*] New Repertory
TNR .... Tanana Air Service [*ICAO designator*] (FAAC)
TNR .... Tananarive [*Malagasy*] [*Airport symbol*] (AD)
TNR .... Tanganyika Notes and Records [*A publication*]
TNR .... Tenera, Inc. [*AMEX symbol*] (SAG)
TNR .... Thinner
TNR .... Titan Resources Ltd. [*Vancouver Stock Exchange symbol*]
TNR .... Tone Not Relevant
TNR .... Tonic Neck Reflex [*Physiology*]
TNR .... Total Network Recall [*Systems Enhancement Corp.*] [*Computer science*] (PCM)
TNR .... Trainer (AAG)
TNR .... Transit Nuclear Radiation
TNR .... Trinucleotide Repeat Sequence [*Genetics*]
TNR .... True Negative Rate [*Medicine*] (DAVI)
TNRCC .... Texas Natural Resource Conservation Commission
TNRCC .... Texas Natural Resources Conservation Council (DOGT)
TNRDA .... Transit Network Route Decision Aid [*FHWA*] (TAG)
TNRE .... Transit Nuclear Radiation Effect
TNRIS .... Texas Natural Resources Information System [*Austin*] [*Information service or system*] (IID)
TNRIS .... Transportation Noise Research Information Service [*Department of Transportation*]
TNRY .... Tannery
TNS .... [*The*] Names Society (EA)
TNS .... [*The*] National Switchboard [*Phoenix, AZ*] [*Telecommunications*] (TSSD)
TNS .... [*The*] New Salesmanship [*Book by Steve Salerno*]
TNS .... [*The*] Next Step [*Physics*]
TNS .... Servicios Aereos do Vale Amazonico SA [*Brazil*] [*ICAO designator*] (FAAC)
TNS .... Tactical Navigation System (DWSG)
TNS .... Tank Nitrogen Supply (AAG)
TNS .... Tanos Petroleum Corp. [*Vancouver Stock Exchange symbol*]
TNS .... Taunus [*Federal Republic of Germany*] [*Seismograph station code, US Geological Survey*] (SEIS)
TNS .... Telecommunications Network Services [*Data Resources*] [*Information service or system*] (CRD)
TNS .... Tennessee State Library and Archives, Nashville, TN [*OCLC symbol*] (OCLC)
TNS .... Thames Navigation Service [*British*] (DS)
TNS .... Thermal Night Site
TNS .... Thomas Nast Society (EA)
TNS .... Times Network for Schools (NITA)
TNS .... Toensberg [*Norway*] [*Airport symbol*] (AD)
TNS .... Toluidinylnaphthalene Sulfonate [*Organic chemistry*]
TNS .... Topical Numismatic Society (EA)
TNS .... Toronto Normal School
TNS .... Track Number Sorted Table (SAA)
TNS .... Transaction Network Service [*AT & T*]
TNS .... Transcutaneous Nerve Stimulation [*Also, TENS, TES*] [*A method of pain control*] [*Medicine*]
TNS .... Triple Nine Society (EA)
TNS .... Tumor Necrosis Serum (PDAA)
TNS .... Tunable Noise Source
TNSA .... [*The*] National Spiritual Alliance of the United States of America
TNSA .... Technical Nuclear Safety (MCD)
TNSB .... Southern Baptist Convention Historical Commission, Nashville, TN [*Library symbol Library of Congress*] (LCLS)
TNSB-S .... Sunday School Board of the Southern Baptist Convention, Nashville, TN [*Library symbol*] [*Library of Congress*] (LCLS)
TNSDUNSPHI ... [*The*] National Society to Discourage Use of the Name Smith for Purposes ofHypothetical Illustration
TNSI .... [*A*] Text-Book of North-Semitic Inscriptions [*A publication*] (BJA)
TNSI .... Transaction Network Services [*NASDAQ symbol*] (SAG)
TNSI .... Transaction Network Svcs [*NASDAQ symbol*] (TTSB)
TNSL .... Tensile
TNSL .... Tinsley Laboratories, Inc. [*NASDAQ symbol*] (NQ)
TNSL .... Tinsley Labs [*NASDAQ symbol*] (TTSB)
TNSN .... Tension (MSA)
TNSP .... Transportation (CINC)
TNSTI .... Nashville State Technical Institute, Educational Resource Center, Nashville, TN [*Library symbol*] [*Library of Congress*] (LCLS)
TNStT .... Saint Thomas Hospital, Health Sciences Library, Nashville, TN [*Library symbol Library of Congress*] (LCLS)
TNT .... Miami, FL [*Location identifier FAA*] (FAAL)
TNT .... [*The*] Next Trend
TNT .... Target Network Television [*Cable television network*] (NTCM)
TNT .... Tax Notes Today [*Database*] [*Tax Analysts*] [*Information service or system*] (CRD)
TNT .... Teleconference Network of Texas [*University of Texas*] [*San Antonio*] [*Telecommunications*] (TSSD)
TNT .... Test for the Necessity of Therapy [*Medicine*]
TNT .... Theater Network Television (IAA)
tnt .... Tint (VRA)
TNT .... Tinto Gold Corp. [*Vancouver Stock Exchange symbol*]
TNT .... Titles Now Troublesome [*School books*] [*American Library Association*]
TNT .... TNT Tariff Agents, Inc., New York NY [*STAC*]
TNT .... Tobramycin-Nafcillin-Ticarcillin [*Antibiotic combination*]
TNT .... Toronto [*Ontario*] [*Seismograph station code, US Geological Survey Closed*] (SEIS)
TNT .... Torque, Nip, and Tension [*Winding technology*]
TNT .... Transient Nuclear Test
TNT .... Transnational Terrorism (ADA)
TNT .... Trans North Turbo Air Ltd. [*Canada ICAO designator*] (FAAC)
TNT .... Transparent Network Transport [*Computer science*] (CDE)
TNT .... Transportation News Ticker [*Knight-Ridder Business Information Services*] [*Information service or system*] (CRD)
TNT .... Treasury Northern Territory [*Australia*]
TNT .... Trim, Neat, and Terrific [*Slang*]
TNT .... Trinitrotoluene [*Explosive*]
TnT .... Troponin T [*Biochemistry*]

TNT Tuned-Not-Tuned (IAA)
TNT Turner Network Television [*Cable-television system*]
TNT Twist and Turn [*Barbie doll collector term*]
TNTA Textron Aero-Structures, Nashville, TN [*Library symbol*] [*Library of Congress*] (LCLS)
TNTBP Trinitrotoluene and Black Powder (SAA)
TNTC Too Numerous to Count [*Microbiology*]
TNTC Tyndale New Testament Commentary [*A publication*] (BJA)
TNTDL Tabulated Numerical Technical Data List
TNTDR Thermonuclear TOKAMAK Demonstration Reactor [*Particle physics*]
TNTF TNT Freightways Corp. [*NASDAQ symbol*] (SAG)
TNT Frt TNT Freightways Corp. [*Associated Press*] (SAG)
TNTHA Tennessee Hospital Association, Nashville, TN [*Library symbol Library of Congress*] (LCLS)
TNTN Trevecca Nazarene College, Nashville, TN [*Library symbol Library of Congress*] (LCLS)
TNT-S Test for The Necessity of Therapy for Seniors [*Medicine*]
TNTU University of Tennessee, Nashville, TN [*Library symbol Library of Congress*] (LCLS)
TNTV Tentative (AFM)
TNTX T-Netix, Inc. [*NASDAQ symbol*] (SAG)
TNU Newton, IA [*Location identifier FAA*] (FAAL)
tnu Tennessee [*MARC country of publication code Library of Congress*] (LCCP)
TNU Upper Room Devotional Library and Museum, Nashville, TN [*Library symbol Library of Congress*] (LCLS)
TNUK Thomas Nelson - United Kingdom [*Publisher*]
TNUM United Methodist Publishing House, Nashville, TN [*Library symbol Library of Congress*] (LCLS)
TNUSA Ted Nugent United Sportsmen of America
TNV Navasota, TX [*Location identifier FAA*] (FAAL)
TNV Tecnavia [*France ICAO designator*] (FAAC)
TNV Tobacco Necrosis Virus
TNV Total Net Value
TNV Total Nonvolatile [*Chemistry*]
TNV Trinova Corp. [*NYSE symbol*] (SPSG)
TNVS Thermal Night Vision System
TNW Tactical Nuclear Warfare (MCD)
TNW Tactical Nuclear Weapon
TNW Talking Newspaper Week [*British*]
TNW Theater Nuclear Weapon
TNW/CW Tactical Nuclear Warfare/Chemical Warfare (MCD)
TN WP Thermonuclear Weapon (WDAA)
TNWRRI Tennessee Water Resources Research Center [*Knoxville, TN*] [*Department of the Interior*] (GRD)
TNX Thanks [*Communications operator's procedural remark*]
TNX Tonopah, NV [*Location identifier FAA*] (FAAL)
TNX Transfer on No Index (SAA)
TNX Trinitroxylene [*Organic chemistry*]
TNY Trinity University, Library, San Antonio, TX [*OCLC symbol*] (OCLC)
TNYT The New York Times Online (NITA)
TNYTI [*The*] New York Times Index
TNZ Rex Aviation (New Zealand) Ltd. [*ICAO designator*] (FAAC)
TNZ Tarata [*New Zealand*] [*Seismograph station code, US Geological Survey*] (SEIS)
TNZ Thermoneutral Zone
TNZ Transfer on Nonzero
TNZ Transfer on No Zero (IAA)
TNZ Tranzonic Cos. [*AMEX symbol*] (SPSG)
TNZ.A Tranzonic Cos 'A' [*AMEX symbol*] (TTSB)
TNZ.B Tranzonic Cos Cl'B' [*AMEX symbol*] (TTSB)
TO Alkan Air Ltd. [*ICAO designator*] (AD)
TO Games Taken Out [*Baseball*]
TO No Evidence of Primary Tumor [*Oncology*] (DAVI)
TO Oak Ridge Public Library, Oak Ridge, TN [*Library symbol Library of Congress*] (LCLS)
TO Table of Organization
TO Tactical Observer
TO Tactical Officer [*Military*] (RDA)
TO Takeoff [*Aviation*]
TO Take-Off (IAA)
T/O Takeoff (GAVI)
T/O Take Over (MCD)
TO Tandem Outlet
T/O Target of Opportunity
TO Target Organ [*Medicine*] (AAMN)
TO Targum Onkelos (BJA)
TO Task Order (MCD)
TO TDRS [*Tracking and Data Relay Satellite*] Operations [*NASA*] (SSD)
TO Technical Objective
TO Technical Observer
TO Technical Officer [*Military British*]
TO Technical Order
TO Tech/Ops Sevcon [*AMEX symbol*] (TTSB)
TO Tech-Ops Sevcon, Inc. [*AMEX symbol*] (SAG)
TO Telegraphic Order (WDAA)
TO Telegraph Office
TO Telemetry Oscillator (IAA)
TO Telephone Office
TO Telephone Order [*Medicine*]
TO Tell el-Obed (BJA)
TO Temperature, Oral [*Medicine*]
TO Terminal Office [*Computer science*] (IAA)
TO Test Operation (AAG)
TO Test Outline (CAAL)
TO Theater of Operations [*Military*]
TO Theatre Ontario [*Canada*] (WWLA)
TO Theiler's Original [*Strain of mouse encephalitis virus*]
TO Thiazole Orange [*Organic chemistry*]
TO Through Ownership [*Shipping*]
TO Ticked Off [*Slang*]
T-0 Time of Launch [*NASA*] (KSC)
TO Time Opening
TO Time-Out
TO Time Over (IAA)
TO Tinctura Opii [*Tincture of Opium*]
TO Tincture of Opium [*Pharmacology*] (DAVI)
to Tonga [*MARC country of publication code Library of Congress*] (LCCP)
TO Tonga [*ANSI two-letter standard code*] (CNC)
TO Tonight Only [*Newspapers*] (DGA)
TO Tonnage Opening (DS)
T/O To Oblige (AIA)
TO Tool Offset (IAA)
TO Tool Order
TO Tops Order (MCD)
TO Toronto
TO Torpedo Officer [*Obsolete Navy British*]
TO Township
TO Tracheo-Oesophageal [*Medicine*] (DAVI)
TO Tracking Officer (IAA)
TO Traded Options Market [*London Stock Exchange*]
TO Traditional Orthography [*Writing system*]
TO Traffic Officer
TO Trained Operator [*British military*] (DMA)
TO Transfer Order
TO Transistor Outline (IEEE)
TO Transmission Only [*Telecommunications*]
TO Transmitter Oscillator
TO Transportation Officer [*Military*]
TO Transverse Optic
TO Travel Order
TO Treasury Obligation [*Finance*]
TO Treasury Order [*British*] (ROG)
TO Tricuspid Valve Opening [*Cardiology*]
TO Troy Ounce
TO Tryptophan Oxygenase [*Also, TP, TPO*] [*An enzyme*]
TO Tuberculin Ober [*Supernatant portion*] [*Medicine*]
TO Tuberculin Old [*or Original*] [*Also, OT*] [*Medicine*]
TO Tubo-Ovarian [*Medicine*] (MAE)
TO Tuesdays Only [*British railroad term*]
T/O Turned Out [*for Examination*] [*Tea trade*] (ROG)
TO Turnout (AAG)
TO Turnover [*Number*] [*With reference to enzyme activity*]
TO Turnover (NTCM)
TO [*A*] Turn Over [*A prospective customer who cannot be sold by one clerk and is turned over to another*] [*Merchandising slang*]
TO Type of Organization Code [*IRS*]
TO Tyrosine Oxidase [*An enzyme*]
TOA Table of Allowances
TOA Table of Organization and Allowance
TOA Telecommunications Officers' Association [*Australia*]
TOA Terms of Agreement [*Army*] (AABC)
TOA Terre Ocean Atmosphere [*Marine science*] (OSRA)
TOA Theatre Owners of America [*Later, NATO*] (EA)
TOA Thermal Optical Analysis
TOA Time of Arrival (AFM)
TOA Time Out of Area (MCD)
TOA Tolsona [*Alaska*] [*Seismograph station code, US Geological Survey*] (SEIS)
TOA Top of the Atmosphere [*Meterology*]
TOA Torrance, CA [*Location identifier FAA*] (FAAL)
TOA Total Obligational Authority [*Military*]
TOA Toyota Owners Association (EA)
TOA Trace Organic Analysis [*Environmental Protection Agency*] (GFGA)
TOA Trade-Off Analysis [*Military*]
TOA Transferred on Assembly (IAA)
TOA Trans Oceanic Airways Ltd. [*British*]
TOA Transportation Operating Agencies (AFM)
TOA Transportation Operations Authority (MCD)
TOA Trim on Assembly (MCD)
TOA Tromsoe [*Norway*] [*Airport symbol*] (AD)
TOA Truck Operation Analysis
TOA Tubemakers of Australia Ltd. [*Commercial firm*]
TOA Tubo-Ovarian Abscess [*Medicine*]
TOA Type of Address (TNIG)
TOA Type of Agent
TOAA Total Overall Aerospace Vehicle [*or Aircraft*] Authorization
TOAA Trawler Owners' Association of Australia
TOAC Tool Accessory (AAG)
TOAD Take Off and Die [*Surfers' slang for a very dangerous wave*]
TOAD Terahertz Optical Asymmetric Demultiplexer [*Optical computing*]
TOAD Tobyhanna Army Depot [*Pennsylvania*] (AABC)
TOAD Towed Optical Assessment Device [*Marine science*] (MSC)
TOADS Take Off and Die Syndrome
TOADS Terminal-Oriented Administrative Data System
TOAI Total Overall Aerospace Vehicle [*or Aircraft*] Inventory
TOAL Test of Adolescent Language
TOAL Total Ordnance Alteration Application List [*Navy*]
TOAMAC [*The*] Optimum Army Materiel Command (RDA)

TOAN .... Tropical Ocean-Atmosphere Newsletter [*Marine science*] (OSRA)
TO-AN .... Tropical Ocean-Atmosphere Newsletter [*Now Tropical Ocean-Global Atmosphere Notes*] (USDC)
TO & E .... Tables of Organization and Equipment [*Military*] (AAG)
TOAP .... Thioguanine, Oncovin [*Vincristine*], ara-C, Prednisone [*Antineoplastic drug regimen*]
Toastmst .... Toastmaster, Inc. [*Associated Press*] (SAG)
TOB .... Takeoff Boost [*Aviation*]
TOB .... Telemetry Output Buffer [*Computer science*]
TOB .... Tender Option Bond [*Finance*]
TOB .... Test One BIT [*Binary Digit*] (SAA)
TOB .... Tobacco (ADA)
TOB .... Tobacco
Tob .... Tobacco Branch, Internal Revenue Bureau [*United States*] (DLA)
TOB .... Tobias [*Old Testament book*] [*Douay version*]
TOB .... Tobit [*Old Testament book*] [*Roman Catholic canon*] (ROG)
TOB .... Toboggan
TOB .... Tobruk [*Libya*] [*Airport symbol*] (OAG)
TOB .... Tow Bar (MCD)
TOB .... Transistor Output Buffer (DNAB)
TOB .... Tube over Bar [*Suspension*] (MCD)
TOB .... Type of Blast
TOBA .... Theater Owners Booking Association [*Vaudeville*] [*Facetious translation: Tough on Black Artists*]
TOBA .... Thoroughbred Owners and Breeders Association (EA)
TOBA .... Tough on Black Actors [*Facetious translation of acronym for Theater Owners Booking Association*]
TOBE .... Test of Basic Experiences [*Child development test*]
Tobey .... Tobey's Reports [*9, 10 Rhode Island*] [*A publication*] (DLA)
TOBI .... Test of Basic Information [*Education*]
TOBI .... Towed Ocean Bottom Instrument [*Oceanography*]
TOBI .... Toxicity Bibliography [*MEDLARS*]
TOBP .... Tobramycin Peak [*An antibiotic*] (DAVI)
TobRV .... Tobacco Ring Spot Virus
TOBS .... Telemetering Ocean Bottom Seismometer [*Marine science*] (MSC)
TOBT .... Tobramycin, Trough [*An antibiotic*] (DAVI)
TOBWE .... Tactical Observing Weather Element [*Air Force*]
TOC .... AT&T Capital Corp. [*NYSE symbol*] (SAG)
TOC .... [*The*] Operations Council of the American Trucking Associations (EA)
TOC .... Table of Coincidences [*Telecommunications*] (TEL)
TOC .... Table of Contents
TOC .... Tactical Operations Center [*Military*]
TOC .... Tagliabue Open Cup [*Analytical chemistry*]
TOC .... Tag Open Cup [*Flash point test*]
TOC .... Tanker Operational Circular
TOC .... Task Order Contract
TOC .... Task-Oriented Costing [*Telecommunications*] (TEL)
TOC .... Tasmanian Olympic Council [*Australia*]
TOC .... Technical Operating Center [*Telecommunications*] (TSSD)
TOC .... Technical Order Compliance [*Military*]
TOC .... Television Operating Center
TOC .... Television Operators Caucus (EA)
TOC .... Test of Cure [*Medicine*]
TOC .... Test Operations Center [*NASA*] (NASA)
TOC .... Test Operations Change [*NASA*] (NASA)
TOC .... Tetradichlorozylene (GNE)
TOC .... Theater of Operations Command [*Military*]
TOC .... Thermo Optek Corp. [*AMEX symbol*] (SAG)
TOC .... Thomson Corp. [*TS symbol*] (TTSB)
TOC .... Tiers Ordre Carmelitaine [*Carmelite Third Order*] [*An association Italy*] (EAIO)
TOC .... Timber Operators Council (EA)
TOC .... Time of Correlation (MCD)
TOC .... Time Optimal Control (MCD)
TOC .... Time Out Circuit (MHDI)
TOC .... Timing Operation Center
TOC .... Tinctura Opii Camphorata [*Paregoric Elixir*] [*Pharmacy*] (ROG)
TOC .... Toccoa, GA [*Location identifier FAA*] (FAAL)
TOC .... Tocklai [*India*] [*Seismograph station code, US Geological Survey*] (SEIS)
TOC .... Tooling Order Change
TOC .... Top of Climb [*Aviation*]
TOC .... TOS [*TIROS Operational Satellite*] Operations Center (NOAA)
TOC .... Total Operational Cost [*Engineering*]
TOC .... Total Optical Color [*Photography*] (OA)
TOC .... Total Organic Carbon
TOC .... Total Organic Compound [*Organic chemistry*] (DAVI)
TOC .... Traditional Organized Crime
TOC .... Traffic Order Change (SAA)
TOC .... Trainer Operator Console (SAA)
TOC .... Training Occupational Classification (AIE)
TOC .... Transfer of Control
TOC .... Transportation Operating Command [*MTMC*] (TAG)
TOC .... Transportation Operations Center
TOC .... Trap Oxidizer-Continuous [*Automotive engineering*]
TOC .... Tubo-Ovarian Complex [*Anatomy*] (DAVI)
TOC .... Turn-On Command (KSC)
TOCA .... [*The*] Order of the Crown in America (EA)
TOCAP .... Terminal-Oriented Control Applications Program
TOCC .... TDRSS [*Tracking and Data Relay Satellite System*] Operations Control Center [*NASA*]
TOCC .... Technical and Operations Control Center [*INTELSAT*]
TOCC .... Test Operations Control Center [*NASA*]
TOCC .... Transfer of Control Card
TOC/CP .... Tactical Operations Center/Command Post [*Military*]
TOCCWE .... Tactical Operations Control Center Weather Element [*Air Force*]
TOC/ECP .... Technical Order Compliance/Engineering Change Proposal [*Military*] (AFIT)
TOCED .... Table of Contents Editor Processor [*Computer science*]
Toch .... Tocharian [*Language group*] (BARN)
TOCI .... Total Organic Chlorine [*Analytical chemistry*]
TOCM .... Trust Officers Committee Minutes [*A publication*] (DLA)
TOCN .... Technical Order Change Notice [*Air Force*] (MCD)
TOCOM .... Tokyo Commodity Exchange for Industry [*Japan*] (ECON)
TOCP .... Tri-ortho-cresyl Phosphate [*Organic chemistry*]
TOCR .... Turn-Off Controlled Rectifier (PDAA)
TOCS .... Technological Aides to Creative Thoughts (IAA)
TOCS .... Terminal Operations Control System
TOCS .... Terminal-Oriented Computer System
TOCS .... Textile Operational Control System [*Computer science*]
TOCS .... Tool Order Control System (MCD)
TOCS .... Tropical Ocean Climate Study [*Marine science*] (OSRA)
TOCSY .... Total Correlation Spectroscopy
TOCTTOU .... Time of Check to Time of Use (MHDI)
TOCU .... Tornado Operational Conversion Unit [*British military*] (DMA)
TOD .... Target-Organ Damage [*Medicine*]
TOD .... Technical Objective Directive [*or Document*] [*Air Force*] (MCD)
TOD .... Technical Operations Department
TOD .... Technical Order Dilemma (SAA)
TOD .... Test Operations Directorate (RDA)
TOD .... Theater-Oriented Depot [*Military*]
TOD .... Theoretical Oxygen Demand [*Analytical biochemistry*]
TOD .... Time of Day
TOD .... Time of Delivery
TOD .... Time of Departure (NVT)
TOD .... Time of Despatch [*British*]
TOD .... Tioman [*Malaysia*] [*Airport symbol*] (OAG)
TOD .... Titanium Optimized Design [*Plate*] [*Orthopedics*] (DAVI)
TOD .... Todd Shipyards [*NYSE symbol*] (TTSB)
TOD .... Todd Shipyards Corp. [*NYSE symbol*] (SAG)
TOD .... Top of Descent (GAVI)
TOD .... Top of Duct (OA)
TOD .... Total Oxygen Demand [*Analytical chemistry*]
TOD .... Tourist-Oriented-Directional [*Traffic sign*]
TOD .... Trade-Off Determination [*Military*] (AABC)
TOD .... Transfer on Death [*Finance*]
TOD .... Turnover Device
TODA .... Takeoff Distance Available [*FAA*] (TAG)
TODA .... Take-Off Distance Available [*ICAO*] (FAAC)
TODA .... Technical Order Distribution Activity
TODA .... Third-Octave Digital Analyzer
TODARS .... Terminal-Oriented Data Analysis and Retrieval System [*National Institute of Standards and Technology*]
TODAS .... Towed Oceanographic Data Acquisition System (MSC)
TODAS .... Typewriter-Oriented Documentation-Aid System
TodayM .... Today's Man, Inc. [*Associated Press*] (SAG)
TodaysBc .... Todays Bancorp, Inc. [*Associated Press*] (SAG)
TODC .... Technical Order Distribution Code [*Air Force*]
TODC .... Theater-Oriented Depot Complex [*Military*] (AABC)
TODC .... Triple Overriding Dual Control (IAA)
TODD .... [*The*] Todd-AO Corp. [*NASDAQ symbol*] (NQ)
TODDA .... Todd-AO Corp.'A' [*NASDAQ symbol*] (TTSB)
TODD-AO .... Todd-American Optical Co. [*Wide-screen system used by producer Michael Todd and the American Optical Co.*]
ToddAO .... Todd AO Corp. [*Associated Press*] (SAG)
ToddShp .... Todd Shipyards Corp. [*Associated Press*] (SAG)
TODE .... Transcript of Data Extraction (DNAB)
To de For .... Thomas de Formaginis [*Flourished, 1331-38*] [*Authority cited in pre-1607 legal work*] (DSA)
TODES .... Transcript of Data Extraction System (MCD)
TODH .... Todhunter International, Inc. [*NASDAQ symbol*] (SAG)
TODH .... Todhunter Intl [*NASDAQ symbol*] (TTSB)
Todhuntr .... Todhunter International, Inc. [*Associated Press*] (SAG)
TODN .... Telephone Order Dispatch Notice
TODO .... Technical Order Distribution Office [*or Officer*]
TODOS .... Tools for Designing Office Information Systems (NITA)
TODR .... Takeoff Distance Required [*Aviation*] (AIA)
TODS .... Technical Oriented Disk System [*Computer science*] (ECII)
TODS .... Test-Oriented Disk System (IEEE)
TODS .... Transactions on Database Systems
TODT .... Tool Detail (AAG)
TOE .... Epidermatophyton
TOE .... Table of Organization Equipment
TOE .... Tables of Organization and Equipment [*Military*]
TOE .... Talker Omission Error (MUGU)
TOE .... Tape Overlap Emulator [*Computer science*] (IAA)
TOE .... Term of Enlistment [*Military*]
TOE .... Texas, Oklahoma & Eastern Railroad Co. [*AAR code*]
TOE .... Theory of Everything [*Cosmology*]
TOE .... Thread One End (MSA)
TOE .... Time of Entry (MCD)
TOE .... Time of Event [*Military*] (CAAL)
TOE .... Ton of Oil Equivalent [*Energy equivalent*]
TOE .... Tons of Oil Equivalent
TOE .... Tony, Oscar, Emmy [*Refers to actors who have won these three major awards, for stage, film, and television work, respectively*]
TOE .... Top of Edge (AAG)
TOE .... Total Operating Expense
TOE .... Tozeur [*Tunisia*] [*Airport symbol*] (OAG)

TOE Tracheoesophageal [*Also, TE*] [*Medicine*]
TOE Trainborne Operational Equipment
TOE Tryout Employment [*Job Training and Partnership Act*] (OICC)
TOE United States Department of Energy, Office of Scientific and Technical Information, Oak Ridge, TN [*Library symbol*] [*Library of Congress*] (LCLS)
TOEFL Teaching of English as a Foreign Language
TOEFL Test of English as a Foreign Language
TOEFL Test of English as a Foreign Language (GAGS)
TOEIC Test of English for International Communication
TOEL Time Only Emitter Location System (MCD)
TOEMTB Tables of Organization and Equipment Mobilization Troop Basis [*Army*] (AABC)
TO EPR Takeoff Engine Pressure Ratio (GAVI)
TOES [*The*] Other Economic Summit [*of North America*] (CROSS)
TOES Telephone Order Entry System (AAGC)
TOES Toxic Oil Epidemic Syndrome [*Medicine*] (DMAA)
TOES Trade-Off Evaluation System
TOESD Test of Early Socioemotional Development [*Child development test*]
TOES-NA [*The*] Other Economic Summit of North America (EA)
TOET Test of Elementary Training (WDAA)
TOEWG Table of Organization and Equipment Working Group [*Army*]
TOF Beverly, MA [*Location identifier FAA*] (FAAL)
TOF [*The*] Obesity Foundation (EA)
TOF Test Operations Facility [*NASA*] (MCD)
TOF Tetralogy of Fallot [*Cardiology*]
TOF Time of Filing
TOF Time of Fire [*Military*] (CAAL)
TOF Time of Flight
TOF Tofutti Brands [*AMEX symbol*] (TTSB)
TOF Tofutti Brands, Inc. [*AMEX symbol*] (SPSG)
TOF Tone Off [*Telecommunications*] (TEL)
TOF To Order From
TOF Topcliffe FTU [*British ICAO designator*] (FAAC)
TOF Top of File
TOF Top of Form [*Computer science*]
TOF Tracheo-Esophageal Fistula [*Medicine*] (DAVI)
TOF Transfer of Function (MCD)
TOF Turnover Frequency [*Chemical engineering*]
TOF Turnover Frequency
TOFA Tall Oil Fatty Acids [*Organic chemistry*]
T of A Terms of Agreement (NATG)
TOFA Time-of-Flight and Absorbance [*Physics*]
T of A Transposition of Aorta [*Cardiology*] (MAE)
TOFABS Time-of-Flight Aerosol Beam Spectrometry
TOFC Tony Orlando Fan Club [*Defunct*] (EA)
T of C Tournament of Champions
TOFC Trailer on Flatcar [*Railroad*]
TOFCN Technical Order Field Change Notice [*Air Force*] (MCD)
TOFD Time of Flight Diffraction [*Nuclear energy*] (NUCP)
TOFD Time of Flight Diffraction [*Ultrasonic imaging*]
TOFDC Total Operational Flying Duty Credit [*Military*] (AABC)
TOFF Tatham Offshore [*NASDAQ symbol*] (TTSB)
TOFF Tatham Offshore, Inc. [*NASDAQ symbol*] (SAG)
TOFI Time-of-Flight Isochronous Spectrometer
TOFL Takeoff Field Length [*Aviation*]
TOFM Tooling Form (AAG)
TOFMS Time-of-Flight Mass Spectrometer
T of OPNS Theater of Operations [*Military*]
To For Thomas de Formaginis [*Flourished, 1331-38*] [*Authority cited in pre-1607 legal work*] (DSA)
TOFRAN Tofranil [*Also, called imipramine hydrochloride*] [*An antidepressant*] [*Geigy Pharmaceuticals*] (DAVI)
TOFS Time-of-Flight Spectrometer [*or Spectroscopy*]
TOFSARS Time-of-Flight Scattering and Recoiling Spectrometry
TOFSIMS Time-of-Flight Secondary Ion Mass Spectrometry
Tofutti Tofutti Brands, Inc. [*Associated Press*] (SAG)
TOG Takeoff Gross [*Weight*] [*Aviation*]
TOG Target-Observer-Gun [*Method*] [*Army*]
TOG Target Opportunity Generator (KSC)
TOG Technical Operations Group [*Air Force*]
TOG Temagami Oil & Gas Ltd. [*Toronto Stock Exchange symbol*]
TOG Togane [*Japan*] [*Seismograph station code, US Geological Survey Closed*] (SEIS)
TOG Together
TOG Toggle
TOG Togiak [*Alaska*] [*Airport symbol*] (OAG)
TOG Togiak Village, AK [*Location identifier FAA*] (FAAL)
TOG Top of Grade (MCD)
TOG Toronto Game [*Simulation game*]
TOG Total Canada Oil & Gas Ltd. [*Later, Rigel Energy*] [*AMEX symbol*] (SPSG)
TOGA Saratoga Beverage Group [*NASDAQ symbol*] (SAG)
TOGA Saratoga Beverage Group'A' [*NASDAQ symbol*] (TTSB)
TOGA Take Off/Go Around (MCD)
TOGA Tests of General Ability [*Education*] (AEBS)
TOGA Tooling Gauge (AAG)
TOGA Tropical Ocean-Global Atmosphere [*Program*] (USDC)
TOGA Tropical Ocean Global Atmosphere Program (EERA)
TOGA Tropical Oceans and Global Atmosphere Project [*World Meteorological Organization*]
TOGA COARE TOGA [*Tropical Ocean Global Atmosphere Program*] Coupled Ocean-Atmosphere Response Experiment (EERA)
TOGA NEG Tropical Ocean Global Atmosphere Program Numerical Experiment Group (EERA)
Tog Cand Oratio in Senatu in Toga Candida [*of Cicero*] [*Classical studies*] (OCD)
TOGI Trans-Oceanic Geophysical Investigations [*Marine science*] (MSC)
TOGLA Tea Operators' and General Labourers' Association [*A union*] [*British*]
TOGMV Tomato Golden Mosaic Virus [*Plant pathology*]
TOGO Time to Go (SAA)
TOGR Together (ROG)
TOGS Thermal Observation and Gunnery Sights [*British*]
TOGS Transmission-Operating Gear Switch [*Automotive engineering*]
TOGV Transposition of the Great Vessels [*Medicine*] (DAVI)
TOGW Takeoff Gross Weight [*Aviation*]
TOH Natchitoches, LA [*Location identifier FAA*] (FAAL)
TOH Oak Ridge Hospital, Oak Ridge, TN [*Library symbol Library of Congress*] (LCLS)
TOH Tesero Oolite Horizon [*Geology*]
TOH Time Overhead (NVT)
Toh Tohoroth [*or Toharoth*] (BJA)
TOH Transient Osteoporosis of Hip [*Medicine*] (DMAA)
TOH Tyrosine Hydroxylase [*An enzyme*]
TOHM Terohmmeter (IEEE)
Toho Tohoroth [*or Toharoth*] (BJA)
TOHP Takeoff Horsepower [*Aviation*]
TOHP Trials of Hypertension Prevention [*Medicine*]
TOI Tactical Operations Initiation
TOI Target of Interest [*Military*] (CAAL)
TOI Technical Operation Instruction (KSC)
TOI Technical Operations, Inc. (MCD)
TOI Term of Induction [*Military*]
TOI Time of Intercept [*Military*] (CAAL)
TOI Transfer Orbital Insertion [*NASA*]
TOI Troy, AL [*Location identifier FAA*] (FAAL)
TOID Technical Order Identification (MCD)
TOIL Time Off in Lieu
TOIL Toilet
TOJ Telecommunications of Jamaica [*Commercial firm*] (ECON)
TOJ Time on Jamming (IAA)
TOJ Track on Jamming
TOJV Track-on-Jam Valid [*Military*]
TOK Thrust Okay [*NASA*] (KSC)
TOK Tokheim Corp. [*NYSE symbol*] (SPSG)
TOK Tokyo [*Japan*] [*Seismograph station code, US Geological Survey*] (SEIS)
TOK Torokina [*Papua New Guinea*] [*Airport symbol*] (OAG)
TOKAMAK Toroidal Kamera Magnetic [*Thermonuclear-fusion system*] [*Acronym formed from the Russian*]
Tokhem Tokheim Corp. [*Associated Press*] (SAG)
TokioF Tokio Marine & Fire Insurance Co. Ltd. [*Associated Press*] (SAG)
TokosMd Tokos Medical Corp. [*Associated Press*] (SAG)
TOKTEN Transfer of Know-How Through Expatriate Nationals [*Council of Scientific and Industrial Research*] [*India*]
TOKTEN Transfer of Know-How through Expatriate Nationals [*British*] (DI)
TOL Tailored Outfitting List (MCD)
TOL Temporary Occupation License (EERA)
TOL Test-Oriented Language [*Computer science*]
TOL Ticket of Leave
TOL Tol-Air Services, Inc. [*ICAO designator*] (FAAC)
TOL Toledo [*Spain*] [*Seismograph station code, US Geological Survey*] (SEIS)
TOL Toledo [*Ohio*] [*Airport symbol*] (OAG)
TOL Tolerance (AAG)
tol Tolerated (DAVI)
TOL Toll Brothers [*NYSE symbol*] (TTSB)
TOL Toll Brothers, Inc. [*NYSE symbol*] (SPSG)
TOL Tower of London
TOL Tree of Life [*Internet phylogeny project originating from the University of Arizona, Tucson*]
TOL Trial of Labor [*Gynecology*]
TOL Trucial Oman Levies [*British military*] (DMA)
TOL University of Toledo, Toledo, OH [*OCLC symbol*] (OCLC)
TOLA Takeoff and Landing Analysis [*Air Force*]
TOLA Theatre of Latin America [*Defunct*] (EA)
TOLAR Terminal On-Line Availability Reporting
TOLCAT Takeoff and Landing Clear Air Turbulence [*Aviation*]
TOLCAT Takeoff and Landing Critical Atmosphere Turbulence [*Aviation*] (MCD)
TOLCCS Trends in Online Computer Control Systems (PDAA)
TOLD TELECOMS On-Line Data System [*Telecommunications*] (TEL)
TOLD Test of Language Development [*Education*]
TolE Toledo Edison Co. [*Associated Press*] (SAG)
TOLED Transparent Organic Light-Emitting Device [*Photonics*]
TOLIP Trajectory Optimization and Linearized Pitch [*Computer program*]
TOLL Tollerford [*England*]
Tolland Tolland Bank [*Associated Press*] (SAG)
TollBro Toll Brothers, Inc. [*Associated Press*] (SAG)
Toller Toller on Executors [*A publication*] (DLA)
Toll Ex Toller on Executors [*A publication*] (ILCA)
TOLO Time of Lockout (SAA)
TOLO Tool and Operation Liaison Order (AAG)
TOLO Tooling Layout (AAG)
TOLO Type of Legal Organization
TOLP Test for Oral Language Production [*Educational test*]
TOLR Toll Restricted [*Telecommunications*] (TEL)
TOLR Transmitting Objective Loudness Rating [*of telephone connections*] (IEEE)

TOLS........ Times On-Line Services [*Information service or system*] (IID)
Tolst Div...... Tolstoy on Divorce and Matrimonial Causes [*A publication*] (DLA)
TOLT........ Test of Logical Thinking (EDAC)
TOLT........ Towing Light (AAG)
TOLTE........ Teleprocessing Online Test (NITA)
TOLTEP........ Teleprocessing On-Line Test Executive Program [*IBM Corp.*]
TOLTS........ Total On-Line Testing System [*Honeywell, Inc.*]
TOM........ GMT [*Greenwich Mean Time*] of Orbital Midnight
TOM........ [*The*] Old Man
TOM........ Table of Organization and Management
TOM........ Technical Operations Manager [*Navy*]
TOM........ Teleprinter on Multiplex [*Telecommunications*] (IAA)
TOM........ Terz'Ordine dei Minimi [*Third Order of Minimi*] [*Italy*] (EAIO)
TOM........ Test Set, Overall Missile (IAA)
TOM........ Texas College of Osteopathic Medicine, Fort Worth, TX [*OCLC symbol*] (OCLC)
TOM........ Text on Microform [*Information Access Co. - IAC*] [*Information service or system*] (IID)
TOM........ The Office Manager (NITA)
TOM........ Third Order of Mary (EA)
TOM........ Thompson-Lundmark Gold Mines Ltd. [*Toronto Stock Exchange symbol*]
TOM........ Time of Maximum [*Particle physics*]
tom........ Tomato (BARN)
TOM........ Tombouctou [*Mali*] [*Airport symbol*] (OAG)
TOM........ Tomie [*Japan*] [*Seismograph station code, US Geological Survey Closed*] (SEIS)
TOM........ Tommy Hilfiger [*NYSE symbol*] (TTSB)
TOM........ Tommy Hilfiger, Inc. [*NYSE symbol*] (SPSG)
Tom........ Tomus [*Volume*] [*Latin*]
TOM........ Toolmanager [*Computer science*] (IAA)
TOM........ Topological Optimization Module [*Computer science*] (OA)
TOM........ Toronto, Ottawa, Montreal [*Derogatory reference to people in these cities; used by other Canadians who think people living in these cities "run things"*]
TOM........ Totem Capital Corp. [*Vancouver Stock Exchange symbol*]
TOM........ Tracking Operation Memorandum [*Obsolete*]
TOM........ Transistor Oscillator Multiplier (IAA)
TOM........ Translator Octal Mnemonic
TOM........ Transmitted Optical Microscopy
TOM........ Transparent Office Manager [*Computer science*] (IAA)
TOM........ Typical Ocean Model [*Oceanography*]
TOMA........ Technical Order Management Agency [*Military*] (AFIT)
TOMA........ Test of Mathematical Abilities
TOMA........ Turn Off My Addiction [*Proposed clinic*]
TOMAC........ Toroidal Magnetic Chamber (DI)
TOMAC........ Trioctylmethylammonium Chloride [*Organic chemistry*]
Tom & J Comp... Tomkins and Jenckens' Compendium of the Modern Roman Law [*A publication*] (DLA)
Tom & Lem Gai... Tomkins and Lemon's Translation of Gaius [*A publication*] (DLA)
TOMARA........ Texas Outlaw Midget Automobile Racing Association [*Car racing*]
TOMB........ Technical Organizational Memory Bank (RDA)
TOMCAT........ Telemetry On-Line Monitoring Compression and Transmission
TOMCAT........ Teleoperator for Operations, Maintenance, and Construction Using Advanced Technology
TOMCAT........ Theater of Operations Missile Continuous-Wave Antitank Weapon
TOMCIS........ Test of Multiple Corridor Identification System (IAA)
TOMH........ Regional Mental Health Center of Oak Ridge, Oak Ridge, TN [*Library symbol Library of Congress*] (LCLS)
TOMHS........ Treatment of Mild Hypertension Study
Tom Inst........ Tomkins' Institutes of Roman Law [*A publication*] (DLA)
Tomkins & J Mod Rom Law... Tomkins and Jencken's Compendium of the Modern Roman Law [*A publication*] (DLA)
Toml........ Tomlins' Election Cases [*1689-1795*] [*A publication*] (DLA)
Toml Cas........ Tomlins' Election Cases [*1689-1795*] [*A publication*] (DLA)
Toml Cr L........ Tomlin's Criminal Law [*A publication*] (DLA)
Tomlins........ Tomlins' Law Dictionary [*A publication*] (DLA)
Toml Law Dict... Tomlins' Law Dictionary [*A publication*] (DLA)
Toml LD........ Tomlins' Law Dictionary [*A publication*] (DLA)
Toml Supp Br... Tomlins' Supplement to Brown's Parliamentary Cases [*A publication*] (DLA)
TOMM........ Time-Oriented Metropolitan Model (MCD)
TOMMI........ Total Online Medical Material Integration [*Computer science*]
TOMMS........ Terminal Operations and Movements Management System (MCD)
TomNDV........ Tomato Necrotic Dwarf Virus
TOMO........ Tomogram [*Radiology*] (DAVI)
TOMO........ Tomography [*Radiology*] (DAVI)
TOMP........ Toxic Organic Management Plan [*Pollution prevention*]
Tompkn........ Tompkins County Trust [*Associated Press*] (SAG)
TOMR........ Tomorrow (ROG)
TomRSV........ Tomato Ringspot Virus
TomRSV-S... Tomato Ringspot Virus - Seed Borne
TOMS........ Torus Oxygen Monitoring System (IEEE)
TOMS........ Total Ozone Mapping Spectrometer (MCD)
TOMS........ Total Ozone Mapping Spectrophotometer [*Marine science*] (OSRA)
TOMS........ Total Ozone Mapping System [*Meteorology*]
TOMS........ Total Ozone Measurement Scanner (SSD)
TOMS........ Transactions on Mathematical Software
TOMSI........ Transfer of Master Scheduled Item
TOMSS........ Theater of Operations Medical Support System [*Military*] (MCD)
TOMT........ Target Organizational Maintenance Trainer (MCD)
TOMUS........ [*The*] On-Line Multi-User System [*Carlyle Systems, Inc.*] [*Information service or system*] (IID)
TOMV........ Tomato Mosaic Virus [*Plant pathology*]
TON........ Aero Tonala [*Mexico ICAO designator*] (FAAC)
TON........ Taiwanese Oscilliation Network [*For solar observation*]
TON........ Talk Only (IAA)
TON........ Threshold Odor Number [*Water analysis*]
TON........ Tone On [*Telecommunications*] (TEL)
TON........ Tonga [*ANSI three-letter standard code*] (CNC)
TON........ Tongariro [*New Zealand*] [*Seismograph station code, US Geological Survey Closed*] (SEIS)
TON........ Tonic [*Permanently Strengthening*] [*Pharmacy*] (ROG)
TON........ Tonopah Resources, Inc. [*Vancouver Stock Exchange symbol*]
TON........ Top of the News [*A publication*]
TON........ Turnover Number
TON........ Tyrone, PA [*Location identifier FAA*] (FAAL)
TONAC........ Technical Order Notification and Completion System (AAG)
TONC........ Transient On-State Characteristics (PDAA)
TONE........ Touch Tone America [*NASDAQ symbol*] (TTSB)
TONE........ Touch Tone America, Inc. [*NASDAQ symbol*] (SAG)
TONEW........ Touch Tone America Wrrt [*NASDAQ symbol*] (TTSB)
TON/FT²........ Tons per Square Foot
TONI........ Test of Nonverbal Intelligence
TONL........ Union Carbide Nuclear Co., Oak Ridge National Laboratories, Oak Ridge, TN [*Library symbol*] [*Library of Congress*] (LCLS)
TONLAR........ Tone-Operated Net Loss Adjuster Receiving
TONL-B........ Union Carbide Nuclear Co., Oak Ridge National Laboratories, Biology Library, OakRidge, TN [*Library symbol Library of Congress*] (LCLS)
TONL-G........ Union Carbide Nuclear Co., Oak Ridge National Laboratories, Gaseous Diffusi, Oak Ridge, TN [*Library symbol*] [*Library of Congress*] (LCLS)
TONL-T........ Union Carbide Nuclear Co., Oak Ridge National Laboratories, Thermal-Nuclear Library, Oak Ridge, TN [*Library symbol Library of Congress*] (LCLS)
TONL-Y........ Union Carbide Nuclear Co., Oak Ridge National Laboratories, Y-12 Technical Library, Oak Ridge, TN [*Library symbol Library of Congress*] (LCLS)
TONN........ Tonnage [*Shipping*]
TONOC........ Tonight (DAVI)
TONS........ Topical Numismatic Society (EA)
TONS........ Transportation Office Network System [*Department of Transportation*] (GFGA)
TONT........ Tonto National Monument
TOO........ Target of Opportunity [*Military*] (CAAL)
TOO........ Test Operations Order [*NASA*]
TOO........ Threshold of Odor (NASA)
TOO........ Time of Origin [*Communications*]
TOO........ Toolangi [*Australia Seismograph station code, US Geological Survey*] (SEIS)
TOO........ To Order Only [*Commerce*] (ODBW)
TOOL........ Teams of Our Lady [*See also END*] (EAIO)
TOOL........ Test-Oriented Operated Language [*Programming language*] [*Computer science*]
ToolAlph........ Toolex-Alpha [*Associated Press*] (SAG)
TOOL CD........ Tool Requirement Code [*Army*]
TOOLS........ Technology for Object-Oriented Linking and Sharing [*Computer science*]
TOOS........ Torque Overload Switch (NRCH)
TOOS........ Transaction-Oriented Operating System (IAA)
TOOTJFC........ [*The*] One and Only Tom Jones Fan Club (EA)
TootsRl........ Tootsie Roll Industries, Inc. [*Associated Press*] (SAG)
TOP........ Aero Top SRL Societa [*Italy ICAO designator*] (FAAC)
TOP........ [*The*] Olympic Programme (ECON)
TOP........ [*The*] Opportunity Prospector [*A publication*]
TOP........ [*The*] Option Process [*HUD*]
TOP........ Table of Output Products
TOP........ Tactical Operations Plot [*Military*] (CAAL)
TOP........ Targeted Outreach Program [*Department of Labor*]
TOP........ Target Occulting Processor (MCD)
TOP........ Tax-Offset Pension [*Account*]
TOP........ Teacher Organizing Project (EA)
TOP........ Technical and Office Protocol [*Data communications standards*]
TOP........ Technical, Office, and Professional Department [*UAW*]
TOP........ Technical Operating Procedure
TOP........ Temple Opportunity Program [*Temple University*] (EA)
TOP........ Temporarily Out of Print
TOP........ Termination of Pregnancy (MAE)
TOP........ Terrestrial Observation Panel (EERA)
TOP........ Tertiary Operation
TOP........ Tertiary Orientation Program [*Australia*]
TOP........ Test and Operations Plan
TOP........ Test Operating Procedure
TOP........ Test Outline Plan [*Army*] (AABC)
TOP........ Tool Package (IAA)
TOP........ Top Air Havacilik Sanayi Ve Ticaret, AS [*Turkey*] [*FAA designator*] (FAAC)
TOP........ Topeka [*Kansas*] [*Airport symbol*] (OAG)
TOP........ Topeka, KS [*Location identifier FAA*] (FAAL)
Top........ Topic [*Record label*] [*Great Britain*]
Top........ Topica [*of Aristotle*] [*Classical studies*] (OCD)
top........ Topical
TOP........ Top of Potentiometer [*Electronics*] (IAA)
TOP........ Topographic
TOP........ Topoisomerase [*An enzyme*]
TOP........ Topology
TOP........ Topolovo [*Former USSR Seismograph station code, US Geological Survey*] (SEIS)

TOP............ Toponymic [*Anatomy*]
TOP............ Torque Oil Pressure [*Air Force*]
TOP............ Total Obscuring Power [*Smoke cloud*]
TOP............ Total Office Products Group [*Commercial firm British*]
TOP............ Trade Opportunities Program [*Departments of State and Commerce*]
TOP............ Training for Opportunities in Programming (IAA)
TOP............ Training Operation Plan [*Military*] (CAAL)
TOP............ Transient Overpower Accident [*Nuclear energy*]
TOP............ Transovarial Passage [*Virology*]
TOP............ Transverse Optical Pumping (MCD)
TOP............ Trap Oxidizer-Periodic [*Automotive engineering*]
TOP............ Trinity Occasional Papers [*A publication*]
TOP............ Turn Out Perfection [*US Air Force Southern Command's acronym for the Zero Defects Program*]
TOP............ Turn Over, Please [*Correspondence*] (ROG)
TOP............ Two-Axis Optical Pickoff (PDAA)
TOPA.......... Tooling Pattern
TopAir......... Top Air Manufacturing, Inc. [*Associated Press*] (SAG)
T-OPAM....... Tentative OMA [*Operations and Maintenance Army*] Program Analysis Memorandum
TOPAZ......... Technique for the Optimum Placement of Activities in Zones (PDAA)
TOPCAP....... Total Objective Plan for Career Airmen Personnel [*Air Force*] (AFM)
TOPCAT....... Texas Onboard Program of Computer Assisted Training (NITA)
TOPCAT....... Trajectory Optimization Program for Comparing Advanced Technology (MCD)
TOPDIE........ Thermally Optimized Die
TOPES......... Telephone Office Planning and Engineering System [*Telecommunications*] (TEL)
TOPEX......... Ocean Topography Experiment [*Marine science*] (OSRA)
TOPEX......... Topographic Experiment [*Proposed oceanographic satellite*]
TOPEX......... Typhoon Operational Experiment [*Meteorology*]
TOPEX......... Typhoon Operation Experiment (EERA)
TOPF.......... Transplant Organ Procurement Foundation (EA)
TOPG.......... Topping (MSA)
TOPHAT....... Terrier Operation Proof High-Altitude Target (MUGU)
TOPI........... Three-Dimensional OPFOR [*Opposing Force*] Plastic Individual Target [*Army*] (INF)
TOPI........... Tons of Paper In [*Computer science*] (IAA)
TOPIC......... [*The*] Objective Personnel Inventory - Civilian [*Air Force*]
TOPIC......... Teletext Output of Price Information by Computer [*London Stock Exchange*]
TOPIC......... Time-Ordered Programmer Integrated Circuit [*NASA*]
TOPICS....... Test of Performance in Computational Skills [*Educational test*]
TOPICS....... Total On-Line Program and Information Control System [*Japan*]
TOPICS....... Traffic Operations to Increase Capacity and Safety [*Department of Transportation*]
TopIm......... Top Image Systems Ltd. [*Associated Press*] (SAG)
TopImge...... Top Image Systems Ltd. [*Associated Press*] (SAG)
TOPIX......... Tokyo Stock Price Index [*Japan*] (ECON)
TOPKAT....... Toxicity Prediction by Komputer Assisted Technology
TOPL.......... Terminal-Operated Production Language (IAA)
TOPLAS....... Transactions on Programming Languages and Systems (MCD)
TOPLINE...... Total Officer Personnel Objective Structure for the Line Officer Force (DNAB)
TOPM.......... Takeoff Performance Monitor [*Aviation*] (DA)
TOPM.......... Top Air Manufacturing, Inc. [*NASDAQ symbol*] (NQ)
TOPM.......... Top Air Mfg [*NASDAQ symbol*] (TTSB)
TOPMIS....... Total Officer Personnel Management [*Army*] (RDA)
TOPMS........ Take off Performance Monitoring System
TOPNS........ Theater of Operations [*Military*]
TOPO.......... Test Operations and Policy Office [*TECOM*] (RDA)
TOPO.......... Tons of Paper Out [*Computer science*] (IAA)
TOPO.......... Topography (AFM)
TOPO.......... Tri-n-Octyl Phosphine Oxide [*Organic chemistry*]
TOPO.......... Trioctylphosphine Oxide [*Organic chemistry*]
TOPOCOM.... Topographic Command [*Army*]
TOPOENGR... Topographical Engineer
TOPOG........ Topography
TOPO-MIBK... Trioctylphosphorine Oxide/Methyl Isobutyl Keton [*Solvent mixture*]
TOPOPLT..... Topographic Platoon (DNAB)
TOPP.......... [*The*] Organization of Plastics Processors [*Defunct*] (EA)
TOPP.......... Task Oriented Plant Practice (MHDI)
TOPP.......... Terminal-Operated Production Program (BUR)
TOPP.......... Threat Orientation Protection Posture [*Military equipment*]
TOPP.......... Topps Co. [*NASDAQ symbol*] (TTSB)
TOPP.......... [*The*] Topps Co., Inc. [*NASDAQ symbol*] (NQ)
TOPP.......... Training Outside Public Practice (PDAA)
TOPPER....... Toy Press Publishers, Editors, and Reporters
Topps......... Topps Co., Inc. [*Associated Press*] (SAG)
TOPR.......... Taiwan Open Pool Reactor
TOPR.......... Thermoplastic Optical Phase Recorder (IAA)
TOPREP....... Total Objective Plan for Reserve Personnel [*Air Force*] (AFM)
Topro.......... Topro, Inc. [*Associated Press*] (SAG)
TOPrS......... Trust Originated Preferred Securities [*Finance*]
TOPS.......... [*The*] Operational PERT System
TOPS.......... [*The*] Optimum Publishing System [*IBM Corp.*]
TOPS.......... Tactical Optical Projection System (NVT)
TOPS.......... Tailored Owner Protection System [*Automotive optional warranty*]
TOPS.......... Take Off Pounds Sensibly (EA)
TOPS.......... Technical Order Page Supplement [*Air Force*]
TOPS.......... Telemetry On-Line Processing System [*Computer science*]
TOPS.......... Telephone Order Personalities and Smiles [*Organization of chief telephone operators*]
TOPS.......... Telephone Order Processing System
TOPS.......... Telephone Order Purchasing System (MCD)
TOPS.......... Teleregister Omni Processing and Switching [*Computer science*]
TOPS.......... Teletype Optical Projection System (IEEE)
TOPS.......... Terminal-Oriented Planning System (MCD)
TOPS.......... Tested Overhead Projection Series [*Education*]
TOPS.......... Testing and Operating System
TOPS.......... Test of Problem Solving [*Intelligence test*]
TOPS.......... Test Operations Procedures [*Army*] (RDA)
TOPS.......... Theatre Organ Preservation Society [*British*]
TOPS.......... The Online Publishing System (NITA)
TOPS.......... Thermal Noise Optical Optimization Communication System [*NASA*]
TOPS.......... Thermodynamic Ocean Prediction System [*Navy*] (GFGA)
TOPS.......... Thermoelectric Outer Planet Spacecraft [*NASA*]
TOPS.......... Time-Sharing Operating System [*Computer science*]
TOPS.......... Top One Percent Society (EA)
TOPS.......... Tops Appliance City [*NASDAQ symbol*] (SAG)
TOPS.......... Total Ocean Profiling System (USDC)
TOPS.......... Total Ocean Profiling System [*Marine science*] (OSRA)
TOPS.......... Total Operations Processing System (NITA)
TOPS.......... Total Operations Processing System [*Computer science*]
TOPS.......... Total Organ Perfusion System
TOPS.......... Total Ozone Portable Spectroradiometer [*Measures ozone layer*] (ECON)
TOPS.......... Total Personnel Service
TOPS.......... Toward Other Planetary Systems [*NASA*]
TOPS.......... Traffic Operator Position System [*Telecommunications*] (TEL)
TOPS.......... Training Operations and Planning Station (MCD)
TOPS.......... Training Opportunities Schemes [*Department of Employment*] [*British*]
TOPS.......... Transcendental Network [*Centram Systems West, Inc.*] [*Berkeley, CA*] [*Telecommunications*] (TSSD)
TOPS.......... Transistorized Operational Phone System (MCD)
TOPS.......... Transparent Operating System [*Computer science*] (CDE)
TOPS.......... Transportation Operational Personal Property System [*Army*]
TOPS.......... Truck Ordering and Pricing System
TOPS.......... United States Travelers' Overseas Personalized Service [*Also known as USTOPS*]
TopsApl....... Tops Appliance City [*Associated Press*] (SAG)
TOPSEC....... Top Secret [*Security classification*]
TOPSEP....... Targeting/Optimization for Solar Electric Propulsion [*NASA*]
TOPSI......... Topside Sounder, Ionosphere [*NASA*]
TopSrce....... Top Source, Inc. [*Associated Press*] (SAG)
TOPSTAR..... [*The*] Officer Personnel System, The Army Reserve (AABC)
TOPSY......... Test Operations Planning System
TOPSY......... Thermally Operated Plasma System
TOPSY......... Time-Sharing Operation of Product Structure Directory System (PDAA)
TOPTS......... Test-Oriented Paper-Tape System [*Computer science*] (IEEE)
TOPV.......... Trivalent Oral Poliomyelitis Vaccine [*Medicine*]
TOQ........... Tocopilla [*Chile*] [*Airport symbol*] (AD)
TOR........... Tactical Operational Requirement [*Military*] (CAAL)
TOR........... Tactical Operations Room [*Air Force*]
TOR........... Tall Oil Rosin [*Organic chemistry*]
TOR........... Technical Operating Report
TOR........... Technical Operations Research (KSC)
TOR........... Technical Override
TOR........... Technical Oversight Representative
TOR........... Technique of Operations Review [*Engineering*]
TOR........... Telegraph on Radio [*Telecommunications*] (TEL)
TOR........... Teleprinter on Radio [*Telecommunications*] (TSSD)
TOR........... Teleprinter Over Radio (NITA)
TOR........... Teletype on Radio [*Telecommunications*] (IAA)
TOR........... Tentative Operational Requirement
TOR........... Terms of Reference [*Army*] (AABC)
TOR........... Test Operation Report (KSC)
TOR........... Thermal Overload Relay (IAA)
tor............ Third Order Regular of Saint Francis (TOCD)
TOR........... Third Order Regular of St. Francis [*Roman Catholic men's religious order*]
TOR........... Threshold of Regulation [*FDA*]
TOR........... Time of Receipt [*Military*] (AABC)
TOR........... Time of Reception [*Communications*]
TOR........... Time on Risk [*Insurance*] (AIA)
TOR........... Tool Order Release (SAA)
TOR........... Torhsen Energy Corp. [*Vancouver Stock Exchange symbol*]
TOR........... Torishima [*Japan*] [*Seismograph station code, US Geological Survey Closed*] (SEIS)
TOR........... Toronto (ROG)
TOR........... Toronto Airways Ltd. [*Canada ICAO designator*] (FAAC)
Tor............ Torpedo [*Army*]
TOR........... Torque (AAG)
TOR........... Torrance [*California*]
Tor............ Torrid Zone (BARN)
TOR........... Torrington, WY [*Location identifier FAA*] (FAAL)
TOR........... Totalizing Relay
TOR........... Tournament of Roses Association (EA)
TOR........... Track-on-Repeater [*Military*]
TOR........... Traffic on Request [*Aviation*] (FAAC)
TOR........... Turn-On Rate (CAAL)
TORA.......... Take-Off Run Available [*FAA*] (TAG)
TORA.......... TRADOC [*Training and Doctrine Command*] Operations Research Activity [*Military*]
TORAC........ Torpedo Acquisition
TORACCS..... Tool Order-Reporting and Cost Control System (SAA)
TORAH........ Tough Orthodox Rabbis and Hassidim [*An association*]
TORC.......... Test of Reading Comprehension

TORC .... Traffic Overload Reroute Control
TORCH .... Toxoplasma, Other [*Viruses*], Rubella, Cytomegaloviruses, Herpes [*Virus*]
TorchEn .... Torch Energy Royalty Trust [*Associated Press*] (SAG)
TORCHS .... Toxoplasmosis, Other Viruses, Rubella, Cytomegalovirus, Herpes Virus, and Syphilis [*Titer*] (DAVI)
TOREADOR ... Torero-Matador [*Said to have been coined by Georges Bizet for opera "Carmen"*]
TORES .... Toxicological Research (SAA)
TORF .... Time of Retrofire [*NASA*] (KSC)
torm .... Tormentor [*Theater*] (WDMC)
TORM .... Torquemeter
TORNL .... Torsional
Toro .... Toro Corp. [*Associated Press*] (SAG)
Toronto U Faculty L Rev ... Toronto University. Faculty Law Review [*Canada*] [*A publication*] (DLA)
TORP .... Test of Orientation for Rehabilitation Patients [*Occupational therapy*]
TORP .... Torpedo (AABC)
TORP .... Total Ossicular Replacement Prosthesis
TORPCM .... Torpedo Countermeasures and Deception
TORPEX .... Torpedo Exercise (NVT)
TORPRON ... Torpedo Squadron
TORQ .... Torquay [*England*]
TORQ .... Torque [*Automotive engineering*]
TORQUE .... Tests of Reasonable Quantitative Understanding of the Environment [*Education*]
TORQUE .... Truck Operators Road Qualifying Exam [*National Highway Traffic Safety Administration*]
TORR .... Takeoff Run Required [*Aviation*] (AIA)
TORR .... Torricelli [*Unit of pressure*]
TORR .... Torrington [*England*]
TorRoy .... Toreador Royalty Corp. [*Associated Press*] (SAG)
TORS .... Time-Ordered Reporting System (MCD)
TORS .... Torsion [*Automotive engineering*]
TORS .... Trade Opportunity Referral Service [*Department of Agriculture*] [*Information service or system*] (IID)
TORSEN .... Torque Sensing Differential [*Audi*] [*Automotive engineering*]
TORSV .... Tomato Ringspot Virus [*Plant pathology*]
TORT .... Tactical Operational Readiness Trainer
tort .... Tortoise (VRA)
TORT .... Truck Operator Road Test [*Part of TORQUE*]
Tortel .... Torotel, Inc. [*Associated Press*] (SAG)
TORTOS .... Terminal Oriental Real-Time Operating System [*Computer science*] (IAA)
TOS .... Tactical Offense Subsystem
TOS .... Tactical Operation Simulator
TOS .... Tactical Operations Squadron [*Air Force*]
TOS .... Tactical Operations System [*ADSAF*]
TOS .... Taken on Strength [*British military*] (DMA)
TOS .... Taken Out of Service [*Telecommunications*] (TEL)
TOS .... Taligent Object Services [*Taligent, Inc.*] [*Computer science*]
TOS .... Tape Operating System [*IBM Corp.*] [*Computer science*]
TOS .... Technical Operational Support
TOS .... Technical Operations Squadron [*Air Force*]
TOS .... Temporarily Out of Service (DEN)
TOS .... Temporarily Out of Stock [*Business term*]
TOS .... Terminal-Oriented Software [*Computer science*] (IEEE)
TOS .... Terminal-Oriented System [*Computer science*] (IEEE)
TOS .... Term of Service [*Military*]
TOS .... Test Operating System (MCD)
TOS .... Thermally and Oxidatively Stable
TOS .... Thoracic Outlet Syndrome [*Medicine*]
TOS .... Time-on-Station [*Military*] (INF)
TOS .... Time-On-Stream [*Theory*] [*Engineering*]
TOS .... Time-Ordered System (MCD)
TOS .... Time-Sharing Operating System [*Computer science*] (IAA)
TOS .... TIROS [*Television and Infrared Observation Satellite*] Operational Satellite [*NASA*]
TOS .... TIROS [*Television and Infrared Observation Satellite*] Operational System (USDC)
TOS .... TIROS [*Television Infrared Observational Satellite*] Operational System [*Marine science*] (OSRA)
TOS .... Top of Stack [*Computer science*]
TOS .... Top of Steel [*Flooring*] (AAG)
TOS .... Torque Overload Switch [*Nuclear energy*] (NRCH)
Tos .... Tosafoth (BJA)
TOS .... Tosco Corp. [*NYSE symbol*] (SPSG)
TOS .... Tosco Corp., Los Angeles, CA [*OCLC symbol*] (OCLC)
Tos .... Tosefta (BJA)
Tos .... Tosyl [*Also, Ts*] [*Organic chemistry*]
TOS .... Toxic Oil Syndrome [*Medicine*]
TOS .... Traffic Orientation Scheme (DA)
TOS .... Tramiel Operating System [*Atari, Inc.*]
TOS .... Transfer Orbit Stage [*Satellite booster*]
TOS .... Tromso [*Norway*] [*Airport symbol*] (OAG)
TOS .... Tropical Air Services [*Belize*] [*ICAO designator*] (FAAC)
TOS .... Trucial Oman Scouts [*British military*] (DMA)
TOS .... Turkiye Ogretmenler Sendikasi
TOS .... Type of Service (TNIG)
TOS .... Type of Shipment
TOS2 .... Tactical Operations System Operable Segment (MCD)
TOSA .... Takeoff Space Available [*Aviation*] (DA)
Tosaf .... Tosafoth (BJA)
TOSAR .... Topological Representation of Synthetic and Analytical Relations of Concepts (PDAA)
TosArgOMe ... Tosylarginine Methyl Ester [*Also, TAME*] [*Biochemistry*]
TOSBAC .... Toshiba Scientific and Business Automatic Computer [*Toshiba Corp.*]
TOSC .... Tactical Ocean Surveillance Coordinator [*Military*] (CAAL)
TOSC .... To Other Service Center [*IRS*]
TOSC .... Touch-Operated Selector Control
TOSCA .... Test of Scholastic Abilities [*Achievement test*]
TOSCA .... Total On-Line Searching and Cataloging Activities [*Information service or system*]
TOSCA .... Toxic Substances Control Act [*1976*]
Tosco .... Tosco Corp. [*Associated Press*] (SAG)
TOSCOM .... TOS [*TIROS Operational Satellite*] Communications System (NOAA)
TOSCW .... Top of Stack Control Word [*Computer science*] (MHDI)
TOSD .... Telephone Operations and Standards Division [*Rural Electrification Administration*] [*Telecommunications*] (TEL)
TOSD .... Third Order of Saint Dominic [*Rome, Italy*] (EAIO)
TOSE .... Tooling Samples
Tosef .... Tosefta (BJA)
Toseph .... Tosephta (BJA)
TOSF .... Tertiary of Third Order of St. Francis [*Later, SFO*] [*Roman Catholic religious order*]
TOSF .... Test of Oral Structures and Functions [*Speech evaluation test*]
TOSFQ .... Teacher Occupational Stress Factor Questionnaire (EDAC)
TOSI .... Technical On-Site Inspection
TOSL .... Terminal-Oriented Service Language
TOSMIC .... Toluenesulfonylmethyl Isocyanide [*or Tosylmethylisocyanide*] [*Organic chemistry*]
TOSMIC .... Tosylmethyl Isocyanide [*Organic chemistry*]
TOS/OITDS ... Tactical Operations System/Operations and Intelligence Tactical Data Systems [*Military*] (RDA)
TOSP .... Top of Stack Pointer (MHDB)
TOSPDR .... Technical Order System Publication Deficiency Report [*Military*] (AFIT)
TosPheCH$_2$Cl ... Tosylphenylalanine Chloromethyl Ketone [*Biochemistry*]
TOSR .... Technical Order Status Report (MCD)
TOSR .... Thermally and Oxidatively Stable Resin
TOSS .... Tactical Operational Scoring System (MCD)
TOSS .... Tactical Operations Support System (MCD)
TOSS .... Technical Operations and Systems Support (AAGC)
TOSS .... Television Ordnance Scoring System. (MCD)
TOSS .... Terminal-Oriented Support System
TOSS .... Test Operation Support Segment
TOSS .... Tethered Orbiting Satellite Simulator
TOSS .... TIROS [*Television and Infrared Observation Satellite*] Operational Satellite System [*NASA*]
TOSS .... Total Office Support System (HGAA)
TOS-S .... Transfer Orbit Stage - Shortened Version [*Space technology*]
TOSS .... Transient and/or Steady State [*Nuclear energy*] (NRCH)
TOSS .... Turbine-Operated Suspension System [*NASA*]
TOSSA .... Transient or Steady-State Analysis [*Computer science*]
TOSSG .... TACS/TADS OED [*Tactical Air Control System/Tactical Air Defense System Operational Effectiveness Demonstration*] Special Study Group [*Military*]
TOST .... Turbine Oil Stability Test [*Lubricant testing*] [*Automotive engineering*]
TOST .... Turbine Oxidation Stability Test (OA)
Tosyl .... Tolylsulfonyl [*Organic chemistry*]
TOT .... Denver, CO [*Location identifier FAA*] (FAAL)
T/OT .... Table of Organization (Tentative)
TOT .... Takeoff Trim [*Aviation*] (MCD)
TOT .... Task Oriented Training (MCD)
TOT .... Telephone Organization of Thailand (NITA)
TOT .... Terms of Trade
TOT .... Texaco Overseas Tankerships
TOT .... Texas Opera Theatre
TOT .... Theatrum Orbis Terrarum [*Dutch firm*]
TOT .... Time of Takeoff [*Air Force*] (AFIT)
TOT .... Time of Transmission [*Communications*]
TOT .... Time of Travel (MCD)
TOT .... Time on Tape [*Military*]
TOT .... Time on Target [*Artillery support*]
TOT .... Time on Track
TOT .... Time over Target [*Air support*]
TOT .... Tincture of Time [*Medical slang for treatment of problems that are better left alone*]
TOT .... Tip-of-Tongue Phenomenon [*Medicine*]
tot .... To Derive a Total (IDOE)
TOT .... Toe-Out-in-Turns [*Automotive engineering*]
TOT .... Total (AAG)
tot .... Total (WDMC)
TOT .... TOTAL 'B' ADS [*NYSE symbol*] (TTSB)
TOT .... Total Corp. [*NYSE symbol*] (SAG)
TOT .... Total Outage Time (IAA)
TOT .... Totem Industries [*Vancouver Stock Exchange symbol*]
Tot .... Tothill's English Chancery Reports [*A publication*] (DLA)
Tot .... Tothill's Transactions in Chancery [*21 English Reprint*] [*A publication*] (DLA)
TOT .... Totnes [*Municipal borough in England*]
TOT .... Tottori [*Japan*] [*Seismograph station code, US Geological Survey*] (SEIS)
TOT .... Tourist Organization of Thailand (DS)
TOT .... Trade-Off and Technology
TOT .... Transfer of Technology [*Telecommunications*] (TEL)
TOT .... Transfer-of-Training
TOT .... Transmission Oil Temperature [*Automotive engineering*]
TOT .... Transovarial Transmission [*Virology*]

TOT Transportation Office Will Furnish the Necessary Transportation [*Military*]
TOT Trioctyltin [*Organic chemistry*]
TOT Tris-ortho-thymotide [*Organic chemistry*]
TOT Turbine Outlet Temperature (NG)
TOT Turn-On Time
TOT Type of Transport [*Shipping*] (DS)
TOTAL Teacher Organized Training for the Acquisition of Language (EDAC)
Total Total [*Associated Press*] (SAG)
TotalRs Total Research Corp. [*Associated Press*] (SAG)
TotCont Total Containment Co. [*Associated Press*] (SAG)
TOTE Autotote Corp. [*NASDAQ symbol*] (NQ)
TOTE Teleprocessing On-Line Test Executive [*Computer science*] (IBMDP)
TOTE Test-Operator-Test-Exit [*Unit*] [*Psychology*]
TOTE Time Out to Enjoy (EA)
TOTE Transportable Operations Tactical Equipment (NITA)
TOTEM Theater Operations and Tactical Evaluation Model
TOTEM Tomahawk Test Missile (MCD)
TOTES Time-Ordered Techniques Experiment System
TOTFORF Total Forfeiture [*of all pay and allowances*] [*Army*] (AABC)
Toth Tothill's English Chancery Reports [*A publication*] (DLA)
Toth Tothill's Transactions in Chancery [*21 English Reprint*] [*A publication*] (DSA)
Tothill (Eng) Tothill's English Chancery Reports [*A publication*] (DLA)
Tothill (Eng) Tothill's Transactions in Chancery [*21 English Reprint*] [*A publication*] (DLA)
TOTJ Training on the Job
TOTL Test Operating Time Log
TOTL Total Research [*NASDAQ symbol*] (TTSB)
TOTL Total Research Corp. [*NASDAQ symbol*] (NQ)
TOTLN Totalization (ECII)
TotlPet Total Petroleum (North America) Ltd. [*Associated Press*] (SAG)
TotlSys Total System Services, Inc. [*Associated Press*] (SAG)
TotlTel Total Tel USA Communications [*Associated Press*] (SAG)
TOTLZ Totalize
TOTM Trioctyl Trimellitate [*Chemistry*]
TOTO Tongue of the Ocean [*Area of the Bahama Islands*] [*Navy*]
TOTO Totable Tornado Observatory [*National Oceanic and Atmospheric Administration*]
TOTP Tooling Template
TOTP Top of the Pops [*Television program*] [*British*]
TOTP Triorthotolylphosphate [*Organic chemistry*]
TOTPAR Total Pain Relief [*Medicine*]
tot prot Total Protein (MAE)
TOTR Test Observation and Training Room [*Military*] (CAAL)
TOTRAD Tape Output Test Rack Autonetics Diode
TotRenl Total Renal Care Holdings, Inc. [*Associated Press*] (SAG)
TOTS Total Operating Traffic System [*Bell System*]
TOTS Tower Operator Training System [*Air traffic control*]
TOTS Turn Off Television Saturday [*of Action for Children's Television organization*]
TottaAc Totta & Acores Financing Ltd. [*Associated Press*] (SAG)
TOU Neah Bay, WA [*Location identifier FAA*] (FAAL)
TOU Oak Ridge Associated Universities, Oak Ridge, TN [*Library symbol Library of Congress*] (LCLS)
TOU Time of Use [*Utility rates*]
TOU Touho [*New Caledonia*] [*Airport symbol*] (OAG)
Tou Toulon [*France*] (BARN)
TOU Touraine [*South Vietnam*] [*Airport symbol*] (AD)
TOU Trace Operate Unit
Touch Sheppard's Touchstone [*A publication*] (DLA)
TouchSt TouchStone Software Corp. [*Associated Press*] (SAG)
Toull Toullier's Droit Civil Francais [*A publication*] (DLA)
TOUR Coach USA [*NASDAQ symbol*] (TTSB)
TOUR Tourist Class Passengers [*British*]
Tourg Dig Tourgee's North Carolina Digest [*A publication*] (DLA)
TOURN Tournament
Touro C Touro College (GAGS)
TOURS Tourist Observation and Underwater Research Submarine (PDAA)
TOUS Test on Understanding Science
TOUS Transmission Oscillator Ultrasonic Spectrometer
TouTne Touch Tone America, Inc. [*Associated Press*] (SAG)
TouTone Touch Tone America, Inc. [*Associated Press*] (SAG)
TOV El Indio, TX [*Location identifier FAA*] (FAAL)
TOV El Tocuyo [*Venezuela*] [*Seismograph station code, US Geological Survey*] (SEIS)
TOV Telemetering Oscillator Voltage
TOV Time out of View
TOV Tooele Valley Railway Co. [*AAR code*]
TOV Transfer on Overflow (IAA)
TOVA [*The*] Other Victims of Alcoholism (EA)
TOVALOP Tanker Owners Voluntary Agreement on Liability for Oil Pollution
TOVD Transistor-Operated Voltage Divider
TOVR Turnover (NVT)
TOVS TIROS [*Television and Infrared Observation Satellite*] Operational VerticalSounder [*NASA*]
TOW Cooperstown, ND [*Location identifier FAA*] (FAAL)
TOW Takeoff Weight [*Aviation*]
TOW Tank and Orbiter Weight [*NASA*] (MCD)
TOW Target on Wire [*British military*] (DMA)
TOW Time of Wait [*Vehicle location systems*]
TOW Time of Week (SSD)
TOW Tororo [*Uganda*] [*Airport symbol*] (AD)
TOW Towards (ROG)
TOW Tower Air, Inc. [*ICAO designator*] (FAAC)
TOW Towing
TOW Tube-Launched, Optically Tracked, Wire-Guided [*Weapon*]
TOWA Terrain and Obstacle Warning and Avoidance
TOW CAP TOW [*Tube-Launched, Optically Tracked, Wire-Guided (Weapon)*] Cover Artillery Protection
towd Toward (VRA)
TOWER Testing Orientation and Work Evaluation for Rehabilitation
TowerS Tower Semiconductor Ltd. [*Associated Press*] (SAG)
TO WHD Two Wheeled [*Freight*]
TOWL Test of Written Language
Towle Const Towle's Analysis of the United States Constitution [*A publication*] (DLA)
Town Co Townshend's Code [*A publication*] (DLA)
Town Com Law Townsend on Commercial Law [*A publication*] (DLA)
TownCty Town & Country Jewelry Corp. [*Associated Press*] (SAG)
town ha Town Hall (VRA)
Town Jud Townsend's Judgment [*A publication*] (DLA)
Town Pl Townshend's Pleading [*A publication*] (DLA)
Town Pr Townshend's Practice [*A publication*] (DLA)
Town Pr Pl Townshend's Precedents of Pleading [*A publication*] (DLA)
Townsh Pl Townshend's Pleading [*A publication*] (DLA)
Townsh Sland & L Townshend on Slander and Libel [*A publication*] (DLA)
Town Sl & Lib Townshend on Slander and Libel [*A publication*] (DLA)
Town St Tr Townsend's Modern State Trials [*1850*] [*A publication*] (DLA)
Town Sum Proc Townshend's Summary Landlord and Tenant Process [*A publication*] (DLA)
TOWPROS TOW [*Tube-Launched, Optically Tracked, Wire-Guided (Weapon)*] Protective Shelters (MCD)
TOWR Tower Air [*NASDAQ symbol*] (TTSB)
TOWR Tower Air, Inc. [*NASDAQ symbol*] (SAG)
TowrAir Tower Air, Inc. [*Associated Press*] (SAG)
TowrTch Tower Tech, Inc. [*Associated Press*] (SAG)
Towson St U Towson State University (GAGS)
TOWT Take Off Weight (IAA)
TOWV Stratosphere Corp. [*NASDAQ symbol*] (SAG)
TOX Time of Expiration (MHDB)
TOX Tocantina [*Goias, Brazil*] [*Airport symbol*] (AD)
TOX Total Organic Halide (ACII)
TOX Total Oxidants
tox Toxemia (BARN)
tox Toxic (CPH)
TOX Toxicology
tox Toxin (CPH)
TOXBACK Toxicology Information Backup (NITA)
TOXBACK TOXLINE Back-File
TOXBIB Toxicity Bibliography [*MEDLARS*]
TOXGR Toxic Granulation-Differential [*Laboratory science*] (DAVI)
TOXI Toxic Granulation [*Laboratory science*] (DAVI)
TOXICOL Toxicology
TOXICON Toxicology Information Conversational On-Line Network [*National Library of Medicine*] [*Later, TOXLINE*]
TOXLINE Toxicology Information On-Line [*National Library of Medicine*] [*Bethesda, MD Bibliographic database*]
TOXLIST Toxic Regulatory Listings [*American Petroleum Institute*] [*Information service or system*] (CRD)
TOXNET Toxicology Data Network [*National Library of Medicine*] [*Information service or system*] (IID)
TOXO Toxoplasmosis [*Medicine*]
TOXREP Toxic Incident Report
TOXREPT Toxic Incident Report (MUGU)
TOXT Toxteth (ROG)
TOXTIPS Toxicology Testing in Progress (NITA)
TOY Toyama [*Japan*] [*Seismograph station code, US Geological Survey*] (SEIS)
TOY Toyota Canada, Inc. [*ICAO designator*] (FAAC)
TOY Toys R Us [*NYSE symbol*] (TTSB)
TOY Toys R Us, Inc. [*NYSE symbol*] (SPSG)
TOY Troy, IL [*Location identifier FAA*] (FAAL)
Toy Biz Toy Biz, Inc. [*Associated Press*] (SAG)
TOYDV Tomato Yellow Dwarf Virus [*Plant pathology*]
TOYH THQ, Inc. [*NASDAQ symbol*] (SAG)
TOYH T-HQ Inc. [*NASDAQ symbol*] (TTSB)
TOYM Ten Outstanding Young Men of America [*Jaycees' program*]
TOYMV Tomato Yellow Mosaic Virus [*Plant pathology*]
TOYO Toyota Motor Corp. [*NASDAQ symbol*] (NQ)
Toyota Toyota Motor Co. [*Associated Press*] (SAG)
TOYOY Toyota Motor Corp. ADR [*NASDAQ symbol*] (TTSB)
ToyRU Toys R Us, Inc. [*Associated Press*] (SAG)
TOZ Harvard University, Tozzer Library, Cambridge, MA [*OCLC symbol*] (OCLC)
TOZ Touba [*Ivory Coast*] [*Airport symbol*] (OAG)
TOZ Towarzystwo Ochrony Zdrowia [*A publication*] (BJA)
TP East Timor [*ISO two-letter standard code*] (CNC)
tp Mean Transit Time [*Radiology*] (DAVI)
TP Palestinian Talmud (BJA)
TP [*The*] Prosperos (EA)
T-P Tabloncillo Perla [*Race of maize*]
TP Tail-Pinch Stress
TP Tangible Property [*Business*] (MHDW)
TP Tank Parliament [*British*]
TP Tank Piercing [*Ammunition*] [*Military*]
TP Tank Pressure (DS)
TP Tape (BUR)
tp Tape (WDMC)
TP Target Point

TP .... Target Population
TP .... Target Practice [*Military*]
TP .... Task Processor [*Telecommunications*] (TSSD)
TP .... Tasmanian Police [*Australia*]
TP .... Taxpayer
TP .... Tax Planning [*A publication*] (DLA)
TP .... Teaching Practice
TP .... Technical Pamphlet
TP .... Technical Paper
TP .... Technical Performance (MCD)
TP .... Technical Problem
TP .... Technical Professional
TP .... Technical Proposal
TP .... Technical Publication
TP .... Technographic Publication
TP .... Technology Parameter
TP .... Technophility Index [*Mining technology*]
TP .... Telecommunications Processor [*FAA*] (TAG)
TP .... Telemetry Processor
TP .... Telephone (CET)
TP .... Teleprensa [*Press agency*] [*Colombia*]
TP .... Teleprinter
TP .... Teleprocessing [*Computer science*] (MCD)
TP .... Television Pickup [*FCC*] (NTCM)
TP .... Temperature and Pressure [*Medicine*]
TP .... Temperature and Pressure [*Temporoparietal*] [*Anatomy*] (DAVI)
T + P .... Temperature and Pulse [*Medicine*]
TP .... Temperature Probe (AAG)
T/P .... Temperature to Precipitation Ratio [*Botany*]
TP .... Tempo Primo [*Original Tempo*] [*Music*]
TP .... Temporary Patient [*British*]
TP .... Tempore Paschale [*At Easter Time*] [*Latin*]
TP .... Tensile Properties (MCD)
TP .... Tentative Pamphlet
TP .... Terminal Phalanx [*Anatomy*]
TP .... Terminal Point (NATG)
TP .... Terminal Pole [*Telecommunications*] (TEL)
TP .... Terminal Portability [*Telecommunications*] (DOM)
TP .... Terminal Processor
TP .... Terminal Protocol (MHDI)
TP .... Term Pass (AAG)
TP .... Terrestrial Plants
TP .... Territorial Party [*Northern Marianas*] (PPW)
TP .... Terza Posizione [*Third Position*] [*Italy*]
TP .... Testosterone Propionate [*Endocrinology*]
T/P .... Test Panel (AAG)
TP .... Test Plan
TP .... Test Point
TP .... Test Port (KSC)
TP .... Test Position
TP .... Test Positive [*Clinical chemistry*]
TP .... Test Pressure [*Nuclear energy*] (NRCH)
TP .... Test Procedure (NATG)
TP .... Test Process
TP .... Test Program
TP .... [*The*] Texas & Pacific Railway Co. [*Absorbed into Missouri Pacific System*] [*AAR code*]
TP .... Text Processing (NITA)
TP .... Text Processor
TP .... Thermoplastic [*Also, T*] [*Plastics technology*]
TP .... Thermosphere Probe
TP .... Thiamphenicol [*Antimicrobial compound*]
TP .... Thiopental [*An anesthetic*]
T/P .... Third Party (ADA)
TP .... Third Party [*Insurance*] (ODBW)
TP .... Thomas Power [*"Tay Pay"*] O'Connor [*Irish journalist and politician, 1848-1929*]
TP .... Thomson Press (India) Ltd. [*Publisher*]
TP .... Threshold Potential (MAE)
TP .... Thrombocytopenic Purpura [*Medicine*]
TP .... Thrombophlebitis [*Medicine*]
TP .... Throttle Positioner [*Automotive engineering*]
TP .... Throttle Potentiometer [*Automotive engineering*]
TP .... Thymic Polypeptide [*Endocrinology*]
TP .... Thymidine Phosphorylase [*An enzyme*]
TP .... Thymolphthalein [*Organic chemistry*]
TP .... Thymopentin [*Biochemistry*]
TP .... Thymopoietin
TP .... Thymus Protein
TP .... Tibialis Posterior [*Anatomy*]
TP .... Tie Plate [*Technical drawings*]
TP .... Tie Point
T-P .... Timbre Poste [*Postage Stamp*] [*French*]
TP .... Time Pulse
tp .... Time-to-Peak Tension (DAVI)
TP .... Time to Perigee (MCD)
TP .... Timing Point (AFM)
TP .... Timpano [*Music*]
TP .... Tin Plate
TP .... Tinted Printing [*Paper*] (DGA)
TP .... Tire Pressure [*Automotive engineering*]
TP .... Title Page [*Bibliography*]
tp .... Title Page (WDMC)
TP .... Toilet Paper [*To be "TP'd" is to have your yard covertly decorated with u nrolled toilet paper*] [*Slang*]
TP .... Toll Point [*Telecommunications*] (TEL)
TP .... Toll Prefix [*Telecommunications*] (TEL)
TP .... Toothpick
TP .... Top
TP .... To Pay (ADA)
TP .... Top Priority
TP .... Torpedo Part of Beam (MSA)
TP .... Totally Positive
TP .... Total Particulate Matter [*BTS*] (TAG)
TP .... Total Parts
TP .... Total Phenolic Levels [*Chemistry*]
TP .... Total Phosphorus [*Analytical chemistry*]
TP .... Total Points
TP .... Total Positives [*Medicine*] (DMAA)
TP .... Total Power
TP .... Total Pressure
TP .... Total Production [*or Product*] [*Ecology*]
TP .... Total Protein
TP .... Touchdowns Passing [*Football*]
TP .... Tower Proof [*Gunpowder*] (DICI)
TP .... Township
TP .... Toxic Pregnancy [*Gynecology*]
TP .... Tracking Program (MUGU)
TP .... Trade Protection Service [*or Society*] [*British*]
TP .... Traffic Post
TP .... Trailer Point [*MTMC*] (TAG)
TP .... Training Period [*Military*] (AFM)
TP .... Training Plan (NASA)
TP .... Training, Practicing [*Ammunition*]
TP .... Train Printer [*Computer science*] (IAA)
TP .... Transaction Processing [*Computer science*]
TP .... Transaction Program [*Computer science*] (BYTE)
TP .... Transaction Provider (WDMC)
TP .... Transannular Patch [*Cardiology*]
TP .... Transfer on Positive
TP .... Transforming Principle [*Bacteriology*]
TP .... Transition Period (NASA)
TP .... Transition Plans (MCD)
TP .... Translucent Paper (ADA)
TP .... Transnational Prospectives [*A publication*]
TP .... Transplant
TP .... Transportation Priority [*Military*] (AFM)
TP .... Transporter (DCTA)
TP .... Transport Pack
TP .... Transport Pilot
TP .... Transport Protein [*Superseded by SC, Secretory Component*] [*Immunology*]
TP .... Transport Protocol [*Computer science*]
TP .... Transvaal Province [*Republic of South Africa*]
TP .... Transvaal Supreme Court Reports [*South Africa*] [*A publication*] (DLA)
TP .... Transverse Process [*Neurosurgery*] (DAVI)
TP .... Travaux Forces a Perpetuite [*Penal Servitude for Life*] [*French*]
TP .... Travaux Publics [*Public Works*] [*French*]
TP .... Travers Pensions [*Formerly, Naval Knights of Windsor*] [*Military British*] (ROG)
TP .... Treaty Port
TP .... TreePeople (EA)
TP .... Tree Project (EA)
TP .... Treponema Pallidum [*A spirochete*] [*Clinical chemistry*]
TP .... Trial Preparation (LAIN)
TP .... Trigger Point [*Medicine*] (DMAA)
TP .... Trigger Pulse [*Telecommunications*] (IAA)
TP .... Trigonometrischer Punkt [*Triangulation Point*] [*German military - World War II*]
TP .... Triphosphate (MAE)
TP .... Triple Play [*Baseball*]
TP .... Triple Pole [*Switch*]
TP .... Troop
TP .... Troop Program [*Military*] (AABC)
TP .... Tropical Pacific [*American air mass*]
TP .... True Position
TP .... True Positive [*Medicine*]
TP .... True Profile [*Technical drawings*]
TP .... Trumpet
TP .... Tryptophan [*An amino acid*] (MAE)
TP .... Tryptophan Pyrrolase [*Also, TPO*] [*An enzyme*]
TP .... Tube Precipitin [*Laboratory science*] (DAVI)
TP .... Tuberculin Precipitation [*Medicine*]
TP .... Tuned Plate (DEN)
TP .... Turboprop (AAG)
TP .... Turbopump (AAG)
TP .... Turning Point
TP .... Tyndale Paper [*A publication*] (APTA)
TP .... Type (NASA)
TPA .... Austin Peay State University, Clarksville, TN [*OCLC symbol*] (OCLC)
TPA .... Taildragger Pilots Association (EA)
TPA .... Tala Pozo [*Argentina*] [*Seismograph station code, US Geological Survey Closed*] (SEIS)
TPA .... Tallgrass Prairie Alliance (EA)
TPA .... Tampa/St. Petersburg/Clearwater [*Florida*] [*Airport symbol*]
TPA .... Tannic Acid, Phosphomolybdic Acid, Amido Acid Black [*A staining technique*]
TPA .... Tantalum Producers Association [*Defunct*] (EA)
TPA .... Tape Pulse Amplifier

TPA .... Target Position Analyzer [*Military*] (CAAL)
TPA .... Target Presentation Area [*Army*] (RDA)
TPA .... Tariff Programs and Appraisals [*Canada Customs*]
TPA .... TASS [*Towed Array SONAR System*] Probability Area (NVT)
TPA .... Technical Performance Audit
TPA .... Technical Practice Aid (ADA)
TPA .... Technical Publications Agent (MCD)
TPA .... Technical Publications Announcement
TPA .... Telemetry Power Amplifier
TPA .... Telepanel, Inc. [*Vancouver Stock Exchange symbol*]
TPA .... Telephone Pioneers of America (EA)
TPA .... Temperature-Programmed Analysis
TPA .... Tennis Professionals Association [*Canada*]
TPa .... Terapascal [*Pressure unit*]
TPA .... Terephthalic Acid [*Also, TA*] [*Organic chemistry*]
TPA .... Test Plans and Analysis
TPA .... Test Point Access (IAA)
TPA .... Test Preparation Area [*NASA*] (KSC)
TPA .... Test Project Agreement (NG)
TPA .... Tetradecanoylphorbolacetate [*Also, PMA, PTA*] [*Organic chemistry*]
TPA .... Tetrapropylammonium [*Chemical radical*]
TPA .... Texture Profile Analysis [*Food technology*]
TPA .... Thermal Polyaspartate [*Organic chemistry*]
TPA .... Theta Phi Alpha [*Sorority*]
TPA .... Third Party Administrator
TPA .... Timber Producers Association of Michigan and Wisconsin (EA)
TPA .... Time-Phased Allocation (MCD)
TPA .... Tissue Plasminogen Activator [*Anticlotting agent*]
TPA .... Tissue Polypeptide Antigen [*Immunochemistry*]
TPA .... Toll Pulse Accepter [*Telecommunications*] (TEL)
TPA .... Tons per Annum (ADA)
TPA .... Top Pumparound [*Chemical engineering*]
TPA .... Total Parenteral Alimentation [*Medicine*] (DMAA)
TPA .... Tournament Players Association (EA)
TPA .... Track Production Area [*Air Force*]
TPA .... Trading Partner Agreement (AAGC)
TPA .... Traffic Pattern Altitude [*Aviation*]
TPA .... Training Problem Analysis (MCD)
TPA .... Transfer of Pay Account [*Military*]
TPA .... Transient Program Area
TPA .... Transistor Power Amplifier (LAIN)
TPA .... Transmission Products Association [*Defunct*] (EA)
TPA .... Trans-Pacific Airlines Ltd.
TPA .... Transportation Payment Act of 1972 (AAGC)
TPA .... Transportes Aereos Mercantiles Panamericanos [*Colombia*] [*ICAO designator*] (FAAC)
TPA .... Travel by Personal Auto Authorized [*Military*]
TPA .... Travelers Protective Association of America [*St. Louis, MO*] (EA)
TPA .... Travel Professionals Association (EA)
TPA .... Treponema Pallidum Agglutination [*Medicine*] (DAVI)
TPA .... Trim Power Assembly
TPA .... Tri-Party Agreement (DOGT)
TPA .... Triphenylamine [*Organic chemistry*]
TPA .... Tripropylamine [*Organic chemistry*]
TPA .... Truck Performance Analysis
TPA .... Tumor Polypeptide Antigen [*Oncology*] (DAVI)
TPA .... Tunable Parametric Amplifier
TPA .... Turboprop Aircraft
TPA .... Turbopump Assembly (KSC)
TPA .... Tutmonda Parolspuro-Asocio [*Universal Association for Speech Tracing - UAST*] (EAIO)
TPA .... Two-Photon Absorption (PDAA)
TPA .... Type of Professional Activity
TPAA .... Timber Preservers' Association of Australia
TPAA .... Travelers Protective Association of America (EA)
TPAC .... TCI Pacific Communications [*NASDAQ symbol*] (SAG)
TPAC .... Technology Policy and Assessment Center [*Georgia Institute of Technology*] [*Research center*] (RCD)
TPAC .... Telescope Precision Angle Counter
TP-AD .... Technical Publications - Administration [*Naval Facilities Engineering Command Publications*]
TPAD .... Telepad Corp. [*NASDAQ symbol*] (SAG)
TPAD .... Teleprocessing Analysis and Design Program [*Computer science*] (IAA)
TPAD .... Trunnion Pin Attachment Device [*NASA*]
TPADA .... TelePad Corp. 'A' [*NASDAQ symbol*] (TTSB)
TPADL .... TelePad Corp. Wrrt 'D' [*NASDAQ symbol*] (TTSB)
TPADM .... TelePad Corp. Wrrt'C' [*NASDAQ symbol*] (TTSB)
TPADU .... TelePad Corp. Unit [*NASDAQ symbol*] (TTSB)
TPADW .... TelePad Corp. Wrrt'A' [*NASDAQ symbol*] (TTSB)
TPADZ .... TelePad Corp. Wrrt'B' [*NASDAQ symbol*] (TTSB)
TP-AGB .... Thermally Pulsing, Asymptotic Giant Branch [*Astronomy*]
TPAI .... Teacher Performance Assessment Instruments (EDAC)
TPAM .... Teleprocessing Access Method
TPAM .... Three-Phase Aquatic Microcosms [*Technique for study of waters*]
TP & C .... Thermal Protection and Control (NASA)
TP & N .... Triple Pole and Neutral [*Switch*]
TP & P .... Time, Place, and Person
TP & W .... Toledo, Peoria & Western Railroad Co.
TPAOH .... Tetrapropylammonium Hydroxide [*Organic chemistry*]
TPAP .... Time-Phased-Action Plan [*DoD*]
TPAP .... Transaction Processing Applications Program (MHDI)
TPAPOABITCOS ... [*The*] Precentor and Prebendary of Alton Borealis in the Church of Sarum [*Pseudonym used by Arthur Ashley Sykes*]
TPAR .... Tactical Penetration Aids Rocket
TPARR .... TRADOC Program Analysis and Resource Review [*Military*] (MCD)
TP-ASE .... Transaction Processing Application Service Element [*Telecommunications*] (OSI)
TPAT .... Test Point Algorithm Technique (MCD)
TPB .... Nebraska Library Commission, Lincoln, NE [*OCLC symbol*] (OCLC)
TPB .... Tape Playback BIT [*Binary Digit*] [*Computer science*]
TPB .... Tarnished Plant Bug [*Entomology*]
TPB .... Tetraphenylbutadiene [*Organic chemistry*]
TPB .... Tetraphenylbutane [*Organic chemistry*]
TPB .... Triphenylbenzene [*Organic chemistry*]
TpB .... Trypan Blue [*Biological stain*]
TPB .... Tryptone Phosphate Broth
TPB .... Twinwire Pulp Board (DGA)
T(PBEIST) .... Transport - Planning Board European Inland Surface Transport (NATG)
TPBF .... Total Pulmonary Blood Flow [*Physiology*]
TPBI .... Third Party Bodily Injury [*Insurance*] (AIA)
TPBK .... Tape Block
T(PBOS) .... Transport - Planning Board Ocean Shipping (NATG)
TPBS .... Tetrapropylenbenzenesulfonate [*Organic chemistry*]
TPBS .... Three-Phase Radionuclide Bone Scanning [*Radiology*] (DAVI)
TPBT .... Technical Papers for the Bible Translator [*A publication*] (BJA)
TPBV .... Two-Point Boundary Value (PDAA)
TPBVP .... Two-Point Boundary Value Problem
TPC .... Air Caledonie [*France ICAO designator*] (FAAC)
TPC .... Nebraska Library Commission, Lincoln, NE [*OCLC symbol*] (OCLC)
TPC .... Tactical Pilotage Chart
TPC .... Tangential Period Correction
TPC .... Technical Performance Criteria (SSD)
TPC .... Technical Prime Contractor
TPC .... Technical Progress Committee [*British*] (DCTA)
TPC .... Technical Protein Colloid
TPC .... Technology Partnerships Canada [*Science and technology strategy*]
TPC .... Tejas Power Corp. [*AMEX symbol*] (SPSG)
TPC .... Telecommunications Planning Committee [*Civil Defense*]
TPC .... Telecommunications Program and Control (IAA)
TPC .... Telemetry Preprocessing Computer (MCD)
TPC .... Telephone Pickup Coil
TPC .... Territorial Production Complex [*Russian*]
TPC .... Test Point Controller
TPC .... Texas Petroleum Corp. [*Vancouver Stock Exchange symbol*]
TPC .... Thermafor Pyrolytic Cracking [*A chemical process developed by Surface Combustion*]
TPC .... Thermally Protected Composite
TPC .... Thick Paper Copy (DGA)
TPC .... Third Party Traffic [*Radio*]
TPC .... Thromboplastic Plasma Component [*Factor VIII*] [*Also, AHF, AHG, PTF Hematology*]
TPC .... Thymolphthalein complexone [*Analytical reagent*]
TPC .... Timber Promotion Council [*Victoria, Australia*]
TPC .... Time Polarity Control
TPC .... Time Projection Chamber [*High-energy physics*]
TPC .... Tire Performance Criteria [*General Motors Corp.*]
TPC .... Tons per Centimeter (DCTA)
TPC .... Topical Pulmonary Chemotherapy [*Medicine*]
TPC .... Topographic Center [*Defense Mapping Agency*]
TPC .... Total Package Contract
TPC .... Total Patient Care [*Nursing*] (DAVI)
TPC .... Total Plasma Catecholamines [*Hematology*] (DMAA)
TPC .... Total Plasma Cholesterol [*Clinical chemistry*]
TPC .... Total Print Control [*Computer science*] (IAA)
TPC .... Total Program Costs (KSC)
TPC .... Total Project Cost (DOMA)
TPC .... Total Protein Concentration
TPC .... Tournament Players Championship
TPC .... TPC Corp. [*AMEX symbol*] (TTSB)
TPC .... Trade Policy Committee [*Advisory to President*] [*Abolished, 1963*]
TPC .... Trade Practices Commission (EERA)
TPC .... Training Plans Conference
TPC .... Transaction Processing Performance Council (EA)
TPC .... Transistor Photo Control
TPC .... Trans-Pacific Freight Conference of Japan/Korea Agent, San Francisco CA [*STAC*]
TPC .... Transport Plane Commander
TPC .... Transvascular Protein Clearance [*Medicine*]
TPC .... Travaux Publics Canada [*Public Works Canada - PWC*]
TPC .... Travel by Privately-Owned Conveyance Permitted for Convenience [*Military*] (AFM)
TPC .... Treated Paper Copier [*Reprography*]
TPC .... Treponema Pallidum Complement [*Clinical chemistry*] (MAE)
TPC .... Tricalcium Phosphate Ceramic [*Inorganic chemistry*]
TPC .... Triple Paper-Covered [*Wire insulation*] (DEN)
TPC .... Triple-Product Convolver [*Acousto-optic technology*] (RDA)
TPC .... Turbopump Control
TPC .... Turns per Centimeter [*Yarn*]
TPC .... Twentynine Palms [*California*] [*Seismograph station code, US Geological Survey*] (SEIS)
TPC .... Twisted-Pair Cable
TPCA .... Test Procedure Change Authorization (NATG)
TPCB .... [*The*] Personal Computer Book
TPCC .... Trade Promotion Coordinating Committee [*Department of Commerce*] (EGAO)
TPCCOA .... Telephone Provincial Clerical and Contract Officers' Association [*A union*] [*British*]
TPCD .... Tetraphenylcyclopentadienone [*Organic chemistry*]

TPCF Treponema Pallidum Complement Fixation [*Clinical chemistry*]

TPCK Tosylaminophenylethyl Chloromethyl Ketone [*Organic chemistry*]

TPCK Tosyl Phenylalanine Chloromethyl Ketone [*Biochemistry*]

TPCN Task Plan Change Notice (MCD)

TPCO Teleprinter Coordinator

TPCOMP Tape Compare [*Computer science*] (IAA)

TPCP Trainer Power Control Panel

TPCP Treponema Pallidum Cryolysis Complement Fixation [*Test for Syphilis*] (DAVI)

TPCR Task Plan Change Request (MCD)

TPCRP Tool and Production Change Planning Record (SAA)

TPCS Torquay Pottery Collectors' Society (EA)

TPCSDS-T Target Practice Cone Stabilized Discarding Sabot with Tracer [*Army*] (DOMA)

TPCU Test Power Control Unit (IAA)

TPCU Thermal Preconditioning Unit

TPCV Total Packed Cell Volume [*Hematology*] (DMAA)

TPCV Turbine Power Control Valve

TPD Five Associated University Libraries, Rochester, NY [*OCLC symbol*] (OCLC)

TPD South African Law Reports, Transvaal Provincial Division [*South Africa*] [*A publication*] (DLA)

T/PD Table of Personnel Distribution (NATG)

TPD TAFE (Technical and Further Education) and People with Disabilities [*Australia*]

TPD Tape Playback Discriminator

TPD Tapped (MSA)

TPD Technical Programs Division [*Environmental Protection Agency*] (GFGA)

TPD Technical Publications Documentation [*Army*]

TPD Temperature-Programmed Desorption [*Catalysis*]

TPD Temporary Partial Disablement [*Insurance*] (AIA)

TPD Terminal Protective Device (MSA)

TPD Terracamp Development [*Vancouver Stock Exchange symbol*]

TPD Test Plasma Produced by Discharge (MCD)

TPD Test Point Data

TPD Test Procedure Deviation [*Nuclear energy*] (NRCH)

TPD Test Procedure Drawing [*NASA*] (KSC)

TPD Theophylline, Proxyphylline, and Dyphylline [*Antineoplastic drug regimen*]

TPD Thermoplastic Photoconductor Device

TPD Thiamine Propyl Disulfide (MAE)

TPD Thrifty Payless Hldg'B' [*NYSE symbol*] (TTSB)

TPD Time Pulse Distributor (MCD)

TPD Toilet Paper Dispenser [*Technical drawings*]

TPD Tons per Day

TPD Torque Proportioning Differential [*Automotive engineering*]

TPD Total Permanent Disability [*or Disablement*] [*Insurance*] (AIA)

TPD Total Program Diagnostic [*Computer science*] (IAA)

TPD Total Purity by Difference [*Gas analysis*]

TPD Tournament Players Division of the Professional Golfers Association of America [*Later, TPA*]

TPD Toxics and Pesticides Division [*Environmental Protection Agency*] (GFGA)

TPD Training Programs Directorate [*Army*]

TPD Transient Photodichroism [*Physics*]

TPD Trivial Problem Discriminator [*Computer science*] (IAA)

TPD Tropical Pancreatic Diabetes [*Endocrinology*] (DAVI)

TPD Tumor-Producing Dose [*Virology*]

TPDB Tape Deblock

TPDC Test Point Data Chart [*Military*]

TPDC Training and Performance Data Center [*Military*]

Tpd I Tipped In (DGA)

TPDLRI Textile Printers and Dyers Labor Relations Institute (EA)

TPDRS Time-Phased Downgrading and Reclassification System [*Military*] (DNAB)

TPDS Tape Playback Discriminator System

TPDS Test Procedures Development System (NASA)

TPDSA Totally and Permanently Disabled Soldiers' Association [*Australia*]

TPDSASR Tooling Project Data Sheet Assembly Sequence Record

TPDS-T Target Practice Discarding Sabot-Tracer [*Projectile*] (MCD)

TPDT Tree-Walking Pushdown Transducer (MHDI)

TPDT Triple-Pole, Double-Throw [*Switch*]

TPDT True Position Dimensioning and Tolerancing (PDAA)

TPDU Transport Protocol Data Unit [*Telecommunications*] (OSI)

TPDUP Tape Duplicate [*Computer science*] (IAA)

TPE Five Associated University Libraries, Rochester, NY [*OCLC symbol*] (OCLC)

TPE Tactical Performance Evaluation

TPE Taipei [*Taiwan*] [*Airport symbol*] (OAG)

TPE Task of Public Education Questionnaire (AEBS)

TPE Teacher Performance Evaluation (EDAC)

TPE Technology, People, Environment [*National Science Foundation project*]

TPE Telomere Position Effect [*Genetics*]

TPE Test Planning and Evaluation

TPE Test Project Engineer (NASA)

TPE Tetraphenylethylene [*Organic chemistry*]

TPE Therapeutic Plasma Exchange [*Hematology*] (CPH)

TPE Thermoplastic Elastomer [*Plastics technology*]

TPE Threshold Photoelectron [*Spectroscopy*]

TPE Total Potential Energy

TPE Total Protective Environment [*Immunology*] (DAVI)

TPE Total Publishing Environment [*Computer science*] (IAA)

TPE T-Pulse Effectiveness [*Neurology*]

TPE Transaction Processing Executive (MCD)

TPE Transmission Parity Error [*Computer science*] (IAA)

TPE Transport Planning and Economics [*British*]

TPE Triple Crown Electronics, Inc. [*Toronto Stock Exchange symbol*]

TPE Turbopropeller Engine

TPE Twisted-Pair Ethernet [*Intel Corp.*]

TPE Two-Photon Excitation [*Fluorescence spectrometry*]

TPE Two Pion Exchange [*Nuclear physics*] (OA)

TPEA Television Program Export Association (EA)

TPED Trade and Professional Exhibits Directory [*Later, TSW*] [*A publication*]

T-PEES Triplane Elevated Evaluation System [*Army*] (RDA)

TPEG Producers Entertainment Group [*NASDAQ symbol*] (SAG)

TPEG Producers Entertainment Grp [*NASDAQ symbol*] (TTSB)

TPEGP Producers Entmt 8.50% Cv'A'Pfd [*NASDAQ symbol*] (TTSB)

TPEM Tactical Peripherals Equipment Monitor [*Military*]

TPEN Tetrakis(pyridylmethyl)ethylenediamine [*Organic chemistry*]

TPEO Trunk Piston Engine Oil [*Automotive lubricants*]

TPER Total Primary Energy Requirement [*BTS*] (TAG)

TPES Threshold Photoelectron Spectroscopy [*Physics*]

TPESP Technical Panel on the Earth Satellite Program

TPEY Tellurite-Polymyxin-Egg Yolk [*Agar*] [*Microbiology*]

TPF [*The*] Pygmy Fund (EA)

TPF Tactical Patrol Force [*Police*]

TPF Tailored Probability Forecast

TPF Tampa, FL [*Location identifier FAA*] (FAAL)

TPF Taxis Aereos del Pacifico, SA de CV [*Mexico*] [*FAA designator*] (FAAC)

TPF Telemetry Processing Facility (MCD)

TPF Temporary Program File [*Computer science*]

TPF Terminal Phase Finalization [*or Finish*] [*NASA*] (KSC)

TPF Terrestrial Planet Finder [*Proposed*]

TPF Tetraphenylfuran [*Organic chemistry*]

TPF Thai Patriotic Front [*Communist-directed activity outside Thailand*] [*Merged with TIM*]

TPF Theoretical Point of Fog (MSA)

TPF Thymus Permeability Factor

TPF Time Prism Filter [*Telecommunications*] (TEL)

TPF Toilet Preparations Federation [*British*] (BI)

TPF Total Package Fielding [*Army*]

TPF Total Peaking Factor [*Nuclear energy*] (NRCH)

TPF Trainer Parts Fabrication (AAG)

TPF Transaction Processing Facility (HGAA)

TPF Transfer Phase Final (MCD)

TPF Tri-Pacific Resources Ltd. [*Vancouver Stock Exchange symbol*]

TPF Tube and Pipe Fabricators Association, International (EA)

TPF Tug Processing Facility [*NASA*] (NASA)

TPF Two-Phase Flow

TPF Two Photon Fluorescence [*Electronics*] (OA)

TPF-A Total Package Fielding - Activation [*Military*]

TPFA Tube and Pipe Fabricators Association, International (EAIO)

TPF & C Towers, Perrin, Forster & Crosby [*Compensation and actuarial consulting company*]

TPFC [*The*] Platters Fan Club (EA)

TPFC Tasmanian Public Finance Corp. [*Australia Commercial firm*]

TPF-C Total Package Fielding-(Unit)Conversion [*Military*]

TPFDD Time-Phased Force Deployment Data [*Military*] (AABC)

TPFDL Time-Phased Force Deployment List [*Military*] (AFM)

TPFDL Troop Program Field Deployment List [*Military*]

TPFI Terminal Pin Fault Insertion

TPFN 2-Spirited of the First Nations (AC)

TPFP Transkei People's Freedom Party [*South Africa*] [*Political party*] (PPW)

TPFR Time to Peak Filling Rate [*Cardiology*]

TPFW Thermoplastic Fan Wheel

TPFW Three-Phase Full Wave

TPG Taiping [*China*] [*Airport symbol*] (AD)

TPG Tapping

TPG Technology Planning Guide [*Military*] (AFIT)

TPG Telecommunication Program Generator

TPG Telecom Publishing Group (IID)

TPG Teletype Preamble Generator

TPG Thermionic Power Generator

TPG Timing Pulse Generator

TPG Total Pressure Gauge

TPG Transmembrane Potential Gradient (DAVI)

TPG Transmission Project Group (IAA)

TPG Transplacental Gradient [*Obstetrics*] (MAE)

TPG Transportes Aereos Pegaso SA de CV [*Mexico ICAO designator*] (FAAC)

TPG Trinity Peninsula Group [*Geology*]

TPG Triphenylguanidine [*Organic chemistry*]

TPG Trypticase, Peptone, Glucose

TPG Tryptophan Peptone Glucose [*Broth*] [*Microbiology*] (DAVI)

TPGC Temperature-Programmed Gas Chromatography

TpGGv Templeton Global Governments Income Trust [*Associated Press*] (SAG)

TPGID Tank Precision Gunnery in Bore Device [*Army*]

TPGS [*The*] Pennsylvania German Society (EA)

TPGS Tocopherol Polyethylene Glycol Succinate [*Organic chemistry*]

TPGY Trypticose-Peptone-Glucose-Yeast Extract-Trypsin [*Medium*] [*Microbiology*] (DAVI)

TPH Central Transport Rental Group Ltd. [*Formerly, Tiphook Ltd. ADS*] [*NYSE symbol*] (SAG)

TPH Central Trans Rental Gp ADS [*NYSE symbol*] (TTSB)

TPH............ Temperature Programmed Hydrogenation [*Chemical engineering*]
TPH............ Theosophical Publishing House
TPH............ Thromboembolic Pulmonary Hypertension [*Medicine*]
TPH............ Through Plated Hole [*Printed circuit board feature*] (IAA)
TPH............ Tonopah [*Nevada*] [*Seismograph station code, US Geological Survey*] (SEIS)
TPH............ Tonopah [*Nevada*] [*Airport symbol*] (AD)
TPH............ Tonopah, NV [*Location identifier FAA*] (FAAL)
TPH............ Tons per Hour
TPH............ Total Petroleum Hydrocarbon [*Analytical chemistry*]
TPH............ Total Possessed Hours (MCD)
TPH............ Transplacental Hemorrhage [*Obstetrics*] (MAE)
TPH............ Triumph Resources Corp. [*Vancouver Stock Exchange symbol*]
TPH............ University of Texas, Health Science Center at Houston, School Public Health, Houston, TX [*OCLC symbol*] (OCLC)
TPHA............ Treponema Pallidum Hemagglutination
TPHA............ Truman Philatelic and Historical Association (EA)
TPHASAP..... Telephone as Soon as Possible (NOAA)
TPHAT......... Telephone at [*Followed by time*] (NOAA)
TPHAYC....... Telephone at Your Convenience (NOAA)
TPHC............ Time-to-Pulse Height Converter
TPhl............ Turfan Pahlavi (BJA)
TPHO............ Telephotograph
TPHR............ Tons per Hour
TPHSG.......... Troop Housing [*Army*] (AABC)
TPHW............ Three-Phase Half Wave
TPI............ [*The*] Progress Interview
TPI............ P.T. Tri Polyta Indonesia ADS [*NYSE symbol*] (TTSB)
TPI............ Tape Phase Inverter
TPI............ Tape-Position Indicator (DEN)
TPI............ Tapini [*Papua New Guinea*] [*Airport symbol*] (OAG)
TPI............ Target Position Indicator
TPI............ Task Parameter Interpretation
TPI............ Tax and Price Index
TPI............ Taxpayer Inquiry [*IRS*]
TPI............ Tax Planning Ideas [*A publication*] (DLA)
TPI............ Teatro Popolare Italiano [*Italian theatrical troupe*]
TPI............ Technical Proficiency Inspection [*Military*]
TPI............ Teeth per Inch [*of cog wheels*]
TPI............ Tennessee Polytechnic Institute
TPI............ Terminal Phase Ignition [*NASA*]
TPI............ Terminal Phase Initiate [*NASA*] (KSC)
TPI............ Terminal Phase Insertion [*NASA*]
TPI............ Test Program Instruction (MCD)
TPI............ Test Program Interaction (MCD)
TPI............ Text Preparation and Interchange [*Telecommunications*]
TPI............ Thai Petro-chemical Industry
TPI............ Thermal Protection Investigation
TPI............ Thermoplastic Imide [*Plastics*]
TPI............ Thermoplastic Polyimide
TPI............ Thermo Process Systems, Inc. [*AMEX symbol*] (SPSG)
TPI............ Threads per Inch
TPI............ Time Perception Inventory [*Test*]
TPI............ Timing Pulse Idler
TPI............ Tire Pressure Indicating System (MCD)
TPI............ Title, Page, and Index
TPI............ Tons per Inch
TPI............ Topair Ltd. [*Czechoslovakia*] [*ICAO designator*] (FAAC)
TPI............ Total Positive Income [*IRS*]
TPI............ Town Planning Institute [*Later, Royal Town Planning Institute*] [*British*] (ILCA)
TPI............ Tracks per Inch [*Magnetic storage devices*] [*Computer science*]
TPI............ TRADOC Procurement Instruction (MCD)
TPI............ Training Place in Industry (AIE)
TPI............ Training Plan Information (MCD)
TPI............ Transmission Performance Index [*Telecommunications*] (TEL)
TPI............ Treponema Immobilization Test [*Clinical chemistry*] (MAE)
TPI............ Treponema Pallidum Immobilization [*or Immobilizing*] [*Clinical chemistry*]
TPI............ Trim Position Indicator
TPI............ Triosephosphate Isomerase [*An enzyme*]
TPI............ Triphosphoinositide [*Biochemistry*]
TPI............ Tropical Products Institute [*Overseas Development Administration*] [*British*] (DS)
TPI............ Truss Plate Institute (EA)
TPI............ Tuned Port Fuel Injection
TPI............ Turns per Inch
TPIA............ Take Pride in America Program [*Forest Service*] (GFGA)
TPIA............ Treponema Pallidum Immune Adherence [*Clinical chemistry*]
TPIB............ Technical Panel for International Broadcast (NTCM)
TPIC............ Thermophysical Properties Information Center [*Purdue University*] (PDAA)
TPIC............ Town Planning Institute of Canada
TPID............ Telecommunications Performance and Interface Document (MCD)
TPIE............ TPI Enterprises [*NASDAQ symbol*] (TTSB)
TPIE............ TPI Enterprises, Inc. [*NASDAQ symbol*] (NQ)
TPI En.......... TPI Enterprises, Inc. [*Associated Press*] (SAG)
TPIF............ Thornton Pacific Investment Fund
TPIFY.......... Tri Polyta Indonesia [*NASDAQ symbol*] (SAG)
TPIM............ Tool Process Instruction Manual (MCD)
TPIN............ True Personal Identification Number [*Banking*]
TPINIT......... Tape Initializer [*Computer science*] (IAA)
TPIS............ Telecommunicatinos Products Information Retrieval and Simulation (MHDI)
TPIS............ Tire Pressure Indicating System (MCD)
TPJ............ Tangkuban-Prahu [*Java*] [*Seismograph station code, US Geological Survey Closed*] (SEIS)
TPK............ Test of Practical Knowledge
TPK............ Tropicair Cargo [*Burundi*] [*FAA designator*] (FAAC)
TPK............ Tulare Free Public Library, Tulare, CA [*OCLC symbol*] (OCLC)
TPK............ Turnpike
TPK............ Turns per Knot [*Navy*] (CAAL)
TPKE............ Turnpike (MCD)
TPKE............ Turnpike
TPKrR.......... Theologicka Priloha (Krestanske Revue) [*A publication*] (BJA)
TPL............ Table Producing Language [*1971*] [*Computer science*] (IID)
TPL............ Tabular Parts List
TPL............ Target Position Location (MCD)
TPL............ Teacher Programming Language [*Computer science*] (PDAA)
TPL............ Technical Publications Library (MCD)
TPL............ Telecommunications Programming Language (IAA)
TPL............ Temple [*Texas*] [*Airport symbol*] (OAG)
TPL............ Temple, TX [*Location identifier FAA*] (FAAL)
TPL............ Terminal per Line [*Telecommunications*]
TPL............ Terminal Processing Language
TPL............ Terminal Programming Language [*Computer science*] (IAA)
TPL............ Test Parts List
TPL............ Test Plan (CAAL)
TPL............ Test Plan Log (MCD)
TPL............ Test Point Logic
TPL............ Texas Pacific Land Trust [*NYSE symbol*] (SPSG)
TPL............ Texas Pac Ld Tr [*NYSE symbol*] (TTSB)
TPL............ Text Processing Language [*Computer science*]
TPL............ THERE Programming Language [*Computer science*]
TPL............ Third Party Liability
TPL............ Tocopilla [*Chile*] [*Seismograph station code, US Geological Survey*] (SEIS)
TPL............ Toll Pole Line [*Telecommunications*] (TEL)
TPL............ Tons Poids Lourd [*Deadweight Tons*] [*French*]
TPL............ Topsail [*Ship's rigging*] (ROG)
TPL............ Toronto Public Library [*UTLAS symbol*]
TPL............ Total Peak Loss (IAA)
TPL............ Track Path Length [*Army*] (RDA)
TPL............ Traditional Products Line (MHDI)
TPL............ Training Parts List (AAG)
TPL............ Transfer on Plus (SAA)
TPL............ Transistorized Portable Laboratory
TPL............ Trap Processing Line
TPL............ Tripartite Leader [*Genetics*]
TPL............ Triple (MSA)
TPL............ Triumph Petroleums Ltd. [*Vancouver Stock Exchange symbol*]
TPL............ Troop Program List [*Army*]
TPL............ Tropicalized (MSA)
TPL............ Trust for Public Land (EA)
TPL............ Tunable Pulsed LASER
TPL............ Turbopool Ltd. [*British ICAO designator*] (FAAC)
TPL............ Turns per Layer
TPL............ Twyford Plant Laboratories Ltd. [*British*] (IRUK)
TPL-6.......... Titanium Proximal Loading-6-Inch Stem [*Total hip system*] [*Orthopedics*] (DAVI)
TPLA............ [*The*] Product Liability Alliance (EA)
TPLA............ Triphenyllead Acetate [*Organic chemistry*]
TPLA............ Turkish People's Liberation Army (PD)
TPLAB.......... Tape Label [*Information*] [*Computer science*]
TPLAF.......... Thai People's Liberation Armed Forces [*Thailand*]
TPLC............ Test Program Logic Computer (DWSG)
TPLD............ Test Planning Liaison Drawing (AAG)
TPLF............ Tigre People's Liberation Front [*Ethiopia*] [*Political party*] (PD)
T-PLL.......... T-Cell Polymphocytic Leukemia [*Oncology*]
TPLP............ Tobacco Products Liability Project (EA)
TPLP............ Turkish People's Liberation Party [*Political party*] (PD)
TPLP/F......... Turkish People's Liberation Party/Front
TPLS............ Technology in Public Libraries Section [*Public Library Association*]
TPLS............ Terminal Position Location System
TPLS............ Texas Panhandle Library System [*Library network*]
TPLS............ Tunable Pulsed LASER System
TPLSM.......... Two Photon Laser Scanning Microscope
TPLSM.......... Two-Photon Laser Scanning Microscopy
T/PLT.......... Tapping Plate [*Automotive engineering*]
TPLW............ Triple Wall
TPM............ Tape Preventive Maintenance
TPM............ Tape Processing Machine
TPM............ Technical Performance Management
TPM............ Technical Performance Measurement (AAGC)
TPM............ Technical Performance Measurement System [*NASA*]
TPM............ Technical Performance Module (MCD)
TPM............ Telemetry Processor Module
TPM............ Teleprocessing Monitor
TPM............ Temporary Pacemaker [*Cardiology*] (MEDA)
TPM............ Tepoztlan [*Mexico*] [*Seismograph station code, US Geological Survey*] (SEIS)
TPM............ Terminal Phase Maneuver [*Aerospace*] (MCD)
TPM............ Terminal Phase Midcourse [*Aerospace*] (MCD)
TPM............ Test Performance Management [*Army*]
TPM............ Test Planning Manager [*NASA*] (KSC)
TPM............ Theoretical Platers per Meter [*Chromatography*]
TPM............ Thermal Power Monitor [*Nuclear energy*] (NRCH)
TPM............ Thermal Protection Material
TPM............ Third-Party Maintenance (BTTJ)
TPM............ Timber Products Manufacturers (EA)

TPM .... Title Page Mutilated
TPM .... Tons per Minute
TPM .... Tons per Month
TPM .... Torpedo Prize Money [*British military*] (DMA)
TPM .... Total Active Preventive Maintenance Time (MCD)
TPM .... Total Downtime for Preventive Scheduled Maintenance [*Quality control*] (MCD)
TPM .... Total Particulate Matter [*The "tar" of cigar and cigarette smoke*]
TPM .... Total Passive Motion
TPM .... Total Polar Material [*Analytical chemistry*]
TPM .... Total Population Management [*Department of Agriculture*]
TPM .... Total Preventative Maintenance [*Manufacturing*]
TPM .... Total Productive Maintenance [*Japanese industrialization theory*]
TPM .... Tours par Minute [*Revolutions per Minute*] [*French*]
TPM .... TP Monitor [*Computer science*]
TPM .... Transfer Phase Midcourse [*Aerospace*] (MCD)
TPM .... Transfiguration Prison Ministries (EA)
TPM .... Transmission and Processing Model
TPM .... Trigger Pricing Mechanism
TPM .... Triphenylmethane [*Class of organic dyes*] [*Organic chemistry*]
TPM .... Triplate Module
TPM .... Tubular Products Manual [*A publication*] (EAAP)
TPMA .... Thermodynamic Properties of Metals and Alloys (KSC)
TPMA .... Timber Products Manufacturers Association [*Later, TPM*]
TP-MAU .... Twisted-Pair Medium Attachment Unit (PCM)
TPMF .... Tax Practitioner Master File [*IRS*]
TPMG .... [*The*] Provost Marshal General [*Army*]
TPMI .... Personnel Management [*NASDAQ symbol*] (TTSB)
TPMI .... Personnel Management, Inc. [*NASDAQ symbol*] (SAG)
TPMM .... Teleprocessing Multiplexer Module
TPMM .... Triphenylmethyl Methacrylate [*Organic chemistry*]
TP-MO .... Technical Publications - Maintenance Operation [*Naval Facilities Engineering Command Publications*]
TPMP .... Tender Production Management Program
TPMP .... Texas Pacific-Missouri Pacific Terminal [*Railroad of New Orleans*] [*AAR code*]
TPMR .... Transfer of Program Management Responsibility
TPMR .... Trunked Private Mobile Radio
TPMS .... Transaction Processing Management System (NITA)
TPMV .... Tomato (Peru) Mosaic Virus
TPN .... Pan American University, Library, Edinburg, TX [*OCLC symbol*] (OCLC)
TPN .... Sandoz Pharmaceuticals [*Research code symbol*]
TPN .... Tapini [*Papua New Guinea*] [*Seismograph station code, US Geological Survey Closed*] (SEIS)
TPN .... Tetrachlorophthalodinitrile [*Organic chemistry*]
TPN .... Thalamic Projection Neurons [*Neurology*]
TPN .... Total Parenteral Nutrition
TPN .... Total Petroleum (North America) Ltd. [*AMEX symbol Toronto Stock Exchange symbol*] (SPSG)
TPN .... Total Petrol'm NA [*AMEX symbol*] (TTSB)
TPN .... Triphosphopyridine Nucleotide [*See NADP*] [*Biochemistry*]
TPN .... Two-Position Nozzle (MCD)
TPND .... Theft, Pilferage, and Nondelivery [*Insurance*]
TPNEG .... Travel Will Be Performed at No Expense to the Government [*Military*]
TPNG .... Territory of Papua and New Guinea
TPNG .... Topping (AAG)
TPNH .... Triphosphopyridine Nucleotide (Reduced) [*See NADPH*] [*Biochemistry*]
TPNL .... Townsend Plan National Lobby (EA)
T/PNL .... Trim Panel [*Automotive engineering*]
TPNS .... Teleprocessing Network Simulator
TPNZ .... Tappan Zee Fin'l [*NASDAQ symbol*] (TTSB)
TPNZ .... Tappan Zee Financial, Inc. [*NASDAQ symbol*] (SAG)
TPO .... Sandoz Pharmaceuticals [*Research code symbol*]
TPO .... Tanalian Point, AK [*Location identifier FAA*] (FAAL)
TPO .... Tank Pressurizing Orifice (KSC)
TPO .... Technical Planning Office
TPO .... Technical Project Officer
TPO .... Technology Planning Objectives (MCD)
TPO .... Telecommunications Program Objective [*Army*] (AABC)
TPO .... Temperature-Programmed Oxidation [*For surface analysis*]
Tpo .... Tempo [*Record label*] [*Germany*]
TPO .... Temporary Printing Officer (DGA)
TPO .... Tentative Program Objectives [*Navy*]
TPO .... Test of Perceptual Organization [*Neuropsychology test*]
TPO .... Test Program Outline [*Military*]
TPO .... Thermoplastic Olefinic [*Elastomer*]
TPO .... Thermoplastic Polyolefin [*Materials science*]
TPO .... Threshold Planning Quantity (ERG)
TPO .... Thrombopoietin [*Hematology*]
TPO .... Thyroid Peroxidase [*An enzyme*]
TPO .... Track Production Officer [*NATO Air Defense Ground Environment*] (NATG)
TPO .... Trade Promotion Organisation
TPO .... Transmitter Power Output (NTCM)
TPO .... Transportation Packaging Order (AFM)
TPO .... Traveling Post Office
TPO .... Tree Preservation Order [*Town planning*] [*British*]
TPO .... Tryptophan Oxygenase [*Also, TO, TP*] [*An enzyme*]
TPO .... Tryptophan Peroxidase [*An enzyme*] (AAMN)
TPO .... Tuned Plate Oscillator
TPOA .... Travel Ports Amer [*NASDAQ symbol*] (TTSB)
TPOA .... Travel Ports of America, Inc. [*NASDAQ symbol*] (SAG)
TPOCP .... Turbopump Oxidizer Cavity Purge (SAA)
TPOD .... Test Plan of the Day
TPOH .... [*The*] Pursuit of Happiness [*Rock music group*]
TPOM .... Tentative Program Objectives Memorandum [*Military*] (CAAL)
TPOM .... Tube Propagation d'Ondes Magnetron
T-POP .... TOGA [*Tropical Ocean-Global Atmosphere*] Program on Prediction (USDC)
T-POP .... TOGA [*Tropical Ocean and Global Atmosphere*] Program on Prediction [*Marine science*] (OSRA)
TPorH .... Highland Hospital, Portland, TN [*Library symbol Library of Congress*] (LCLS)
TPORT .... Transport
T-POS .... Target Position
TPOS .... Track Position
TPP .... Tarapoto [*Peru*] [*Airport symbol*] (OAG)
TPP .... Teacher Participation Project (EDAC)
TPP .... Technical Performance Parameter (MCD)
TPP .... Technology Program Plan [*Military*] (AFIT)
TPP .... Telephony Preprocessor [*Telecommunications*] (TEL)
TPP .... Teletype Page Printer
TPP .... Teppco Partners Ltd. [*NYSE symbol*] (SPSG)
TPP .... Teppco Ptnrs L.P. [*NYSE symbol*] (TTSB)
TPP .... Tertiary-Pentylphenol [*Organic chemistry*]
TPP .... Test Point Pace (KSC)
TPP .... Test Point Prelaunch Automatic Checkout Equipment [*NASA*] (IAA)
TPP .... Test Program Plan (MCD)
TPP .... Tetraphenylporphine [*Organic chemistry*]
TPP .... Tetraphenylporphyrin [*Biochemistry*]
TPP .... Textured Peanut Protein [*Food industry*]
TPP .... Thermally Protected Plastic
TPP .... Thermal Power Plant (CINC)
TPP .... Thermal Protection Panel
TPP .... Thiamine Pyrophosphate [*Also, DPT, TDP*] [*Biochemistry*]
TPP .... Thomson Professional Publishing [*The Thomson Corp.*]
TPP .... Toledo Progressive Party [*Belize*] [*Political party*] (PPW)
TPP .... Tool and Production Planning (SAA)
TPP .... Total Package Procurement [*Government contracting*]
TPP .... Total Program Planning/Procurement
TPP .... Trained Profile Panel [*Sensory testing*]
TPP .... Training Program and Planning
TPP .... Transducer Power Programmer
TPP .... Transients, Patients, and Prisoners [*Military*]
TPP .... Trans-Pluto Probe
TPP .... Transport Policies and Programme [*British*] (DCTA)
TPP .... Transuranium Processing Plant
TPP .... Trinidad [*Pointe-A-Pierre*] [*Trinidad-Tobago*] [*Seismograph station code, US Geological Survey*] (SEIS)
TPP .... Triphenylphosphine [*Organic chemistry*]
TPP .... Triphenyl Phosphite [*Organic chemistry*]
TPP .... Tripolyphosphate [*Food industry*]
TPP .... Tri-Power Petroleum Corp. [*Toronto Stock Exchange symbol*]
TPP .... True Path Party [*Turkey Political party*]
TPP .... Two-Phase Principle
TPPC .... Total Package Procurement Concept [*Government contracting*]
TPPC .... Transaction Processing Performance Council (BTTJ)
TPPC .... Trans-Pacific Passenger Conference [*Later, PCC*] (EA)
TPPCR .... Tool and Production Planning Change Record (SAA)
TPPD .... Technical Program Planning Division [*Air Force*] (MCD)
TPPD .... Technical Program Planning Document [*Air Force*] (IAA)
TPPE .... Thermoplastic Polyester [*Materials science*]
TPPE .... Two-Photon Photoemission Spectroscopy
TPPEP .... Turkey Point Performance Enforcement Program [*Nuclear energy*] (NRCH)
TPPG .... Training Program and Planning Guidance
TPPGM .... Tentative Planning and Programming Guidance Memorandum [*Navy*] (NVT)
TPPIS .... Treasury Payroll/Personnel Information System
TP-PL .... Technical Publications - Planning [*Naval Facilities Engineering Command Publications*]
TP-PMD .... Twisted Pair-Physical Medium Dependent [*Telecommunications*] (CDE)
TPPN .... Total Peripheral Parenteral Nutrition
TPPN .... Trans-Pacific Profiler Network (USDC)
TPPN .... Trans-Pacific Profiler Network [*Marine science*] (OSRA)
TPPP .... Third Party Prescription Program
TPPP .... Triple P [*NASDAQ symbol*] (SAG)
TPPPF .... Triple P N.V. [*NASDAQ symbol*] (TTSB)
TPPR .... Tape-to-Printer [*Computer science*] (IAA)
TPPS .... Tape Post-Processing System
TPPS .... Tetraphenylporphinesulfonate [*Reagent*]
TPPTS .... Triphenylphosphine Trisulphonate [*Organic chemistry*]
TP-PU .... Technical Publications - Public Utilities [*Naval Facilities Engineering Command Publications*]
TPQ .... AMIGOS [*Access Method for Indexed Data Generalized for Operating System*] Bibliographic Council, Dallas, TX [*OCLC symbol*] (OCLC)
TPQ .... Tepic [*Mexico*] [*Airport symbol*]
TPQ .... Threshold Planning Quantity [*Hazardous substances*]
TPQI .... Teacher-Pupil Question Inventory
TPR .... Air Transport Pyrenees [*France ICAO designator*] (FAAC)
TPR .... AMIGOS [*Access Method for Indexed Data Generalized for Operating System*] Bibliographic Council, Dallas, TX [*OCLC symbol*] (OCLC)
TPR .... Tamper-Protected Recording [*3M Co.*]
TPR .... Tape Programmed Row [*Data scanner*]
TPR .... Taper (MSA)

TPR .... Target Practice Round (SAA)
TPR .... Team Power Rating [*Hockey*]
TPR .... Technical Program Review
TPR .... Technical Progress Report
TPR .... Technical Proposal Requirement (MCD)
TPR .... Teleprinter (AAG)
TPR .... Telescopic Photographic Recorder
TPR .... Teletypewriter [*International telex abbreviation*] (WDMC)
TPR .... Temperature (DAVI)
TPR .... Temperature Profile Recorder (AAG)
TPR .... Temperature-Programmed Reaction [*Chemistry*]
TPR .... Temperature-Programmed Reduction [*For analysis of surfaces*]
TPR .... Temperature, Pulse, Respiration [*Medicine*]
TPR .... Temporary Price Reduction
TPR .... Termination of Parental Rights (PAZ)
TPR .... Terrain Profile Recorder
TPR .... Testosterone Production Rate [*Endocrinology*] (MAE)
TPR .... Test Performance Recorder
TPR .... Test Phase Report
TPR .... Test Problem Report [*NASA*] (NASA)
TPR .... Test Procedure Record (NATG)
TPR .... Test Program Report
TPR .... Tetratricopeptide Repeat [*Genetics*]
TPR .... Thermoplastic Recording
TPR .... Thermoplastic Rubber
TPR .... Third Party Reimbursement (HCT)
TPR .... Threepenny Review [*A publication*] (BRI)
TPR .... Tom Price [*Australia Airport symbol*]
TPR .... Tool Performance Report [*Navy*] (DNAB)
TPR .... Total Peripheral Resistance
TPR .... Total Pulmonary Resistance [*Cardiology*]
TPR .... T-Pulse Response [*Telecommunications*] (IAA)
TPR .... Trade Practices Reports [*Australia A publication*]
TPR .... Trained Personnel Requirements [*Air Force*]
TPR .... Transmitter Power Rating
TPR .... Transpro, Inc. [*NYSE symbol*] (SAG)
TPR .... Trapped Pressure Ratio [*Gas analysis*]
TPR .... Trooper
TPR .... True Positive Rate [*Medicine*] (DMAA)
TPRA .... Tape-to-Random Access [*Computer science*] (IAA)
TPRA .... Target Practice Round, Aerobee (SAA)
TPRC .... Thermophysical Properties Research Center [*DoD*]
TPRC .... Trade Policy Research Centre [*British*] (ECON)
TPRC .... Transition Program for Refugee Children [*Department of Education*] (GFGA)
TPRD .... Technology Planning and Research Division [*Central Electricity Generating Board*] [*British*] (IRUK)
TPRG .... Technology Performance Requirements Guideline
TPRI .... Teacher-Pupil Relationship Inventory
TPRI .... Time Problems Inventory [*Test*]
TPRI .... Total Peripheral Resistance Index
TPRI .... Training Priority Requirements Index
TPRL .... Thermophysical Properties Research Laboratory [*Purdue University*] [*Research center*] (RCD)
TPRO .... Topro, Inc. [*NASDAQ symbol*] (SAG)
TPROC .... Test Procedure Specification [*NASA*] (IAA)
TPROW .... Topro Inc. Wrrt [*NASDAQ symbol*] (TTSB)
TPRR .... Test Procedures and Results Report
TPRS .... Temperature-Programmed Reaction Spectroscopy
TPRS .... Temperature-Programmed Reaction System
TPRU .... Technical Processing and Reporting Unit (CAAL)
TPRU .... Tropical Pesticides Research Unit [*Later, Centre for Overseas Pest Research*] [*British*]
TPRV .... Transient Peak Reverse Voltage
TPS .... Bibliographic Center for Research, Denver, CO [*OCLC symbol*] (OCLC)
TPS .... [*The*] Planetary Society
TPS .... Tactical Paint Scheme (MCD)
TPS .... Tactical Probe System (SAA)
TPS .... Tandem Propeller Submarine
TPS .... Tangent Plane System (MUGU)
TPS .... Tank Pressure Sensing (AAG)
TPS .... Tape Plotting System
TPS .... Tape Processing System (CMD)
TPS .... Tape Programming System (NITA)
TPS .... Tape Punch Subassembly
TPS .... Task Parameter Synthesizer
TPS .... Technical Publishing Society [*Later, STC*]
TPS .... Technical Publishing Software [*Interleaf, Inc.*]
TPS .... Technology Policy Statement [*1982*] [*India*]
TPS .... Technopolymer Structure [*Engineering plastics*]
TPS .... Telecommunications Programming System
TPS .... Telemation Program Services
TPS .... Telemetry Processing System [*Space Flight Operations Facility, NASA*]
TPS .... Teleprocessing System [*Computer science*] (IAA)
TPS .... Television Program Standard
TPS .... Terminal Performance Specification
TPS .... Terminal Polling System
TPS .... Terminal Programming System [*Computer science*] (ECII)
TPS .... Terminals per Station [*Telecommunications*]
TPS .... Test Package Set (DOMA)
TPS .... Test Pilot School [*Navy*]
TPS .... Test Plotting System
TPS .... Test Point Selector
TPS .... Test Preparation Sheet [*NASA*] (AAG)
TPS .... Test Procedure Specification [*NASA*] (KSC)
TPS .... Test Program Set [*Aviation*] (MCD)
TPS .... Theater Production Service (AEBS)
TPS .... Thermally Processed Silver (NITA)
TPS .... Thermal Protection System [*or Subsystem*]
TPS .... Thermoplastic Storage
TPS .... Thomas Paine Society [*Nottingham, England*] (EAIO)
TPS .... Threat Platform Simulator [*Military*] (CAAL)
TPS .... Throttle Position Sensor [*Automotive engineering*]
TPS .... Thyristor Power Supply [*Electronics*] (IAA)
TPS .... Tiered Premium System [*Insurance*] (WYGK)
TPS .... Top Source, Inc. [*AMEX symbol*] (SPSG)
TPS .... Top Source Technol [*AMEX symbol*] (TTSB)
TPS .... Total Parameter Space [*Statistics*]
TPS .... Total Product Support
TPS .... Tough Plastic-Sheathed
TPS .... Toyota Production System [*Innovative lean-production manufacturing*] (ECON)
TPS .... Tracking Antenna Pedestal System (IAA)
TPS .... Track Processing Special (SAA)
TPS .... Tracks per Second (WGA)
TPS .... Trade Promotion Services Group [*British*]
TPS .... Trail Pilot Sensor
TPS .... Training Package System Planning (IAA)
TPS .... Tramp Power Supply
TPS .... Transaction Processing System [*Trademark of Software Consulting Service, Inc.*]
TPS .... Transactions per Second
TPS .... Transduodenal Pancreatic Sphincteroplasty
TPS .... Translunar Propulsion Stage [*Aerospace*] (AAG)
TPS .... Trans-Pacific Sections [*Marine science*] (OSRA)
TPS .... Transportation Protective Service [*MTMC*] (TAG)
TPS .... Trans Rampart Industry [*Vancouver Stock Exchange symbol*]
TPS .... Trapani [*Italy*] [*Airport symbol*] (OAG)
TPS .... Tree Pruning System
TPS .... Trigger-Price System [*Department of the Treasury*]
TPS .... Triphenylsulfonium Chloride [*Organic chemistry*]
TPS .... Troops [*Military British*]
TPS .... Trypsin (MAE)
TPS .... Tube Pin Straightener
TPS .... Tumor Polysaccharidal Substance [*Oncology*]
TPS .... Turkey Point Station [*Nuclear energy*] (NRCH)
TPS .... Turner Program Services [*Broadcasting*]
TPS .... Tuvalu Philatelic Society (EA)
TPS .... Twisted-Pair Shielded
TPSB .... Telemetry Processing System Buffer [*Space Flight Operations Facility, NASA*]
TPSC .... Test Planning and Status Checker [*Computer science*]
TPSC .... Trade Policy Staff Committee [*Federal interagency group*]
TPSE .... Thermal Protection Subsystem Experiments (NASA)
TPSE .... Transaction Processing Service Element [*Telecommunications*]
TPSE .... (Tritylphenyl)sulfonylethanol [*Organic chemistry*]
TPSF .... Telephonie sans Fil [*Wireless Telephony*]
TPSF .... Terminal Profile Security File [*IRS*]
TPSFG .... Two-Post Signal Flow Graph (PDAA)
TPSI .... Texas Preschool Screening Inventory (EDAC)
TPSI .... Torque Pressure in Pounds per Square Inch
TPSIS .... Transportation Planning Support Information System [*TRB*] (TAG)
TPSL .... Tyoevaeen ja Pienviljelijaein Sosialidemokraattinen Liitto [*Social Democratic League of Workers and Smallholders*] [*Finland Political party*] (PPE)
TPSMP .... Test Program Set Management Plan
TPSN .... Transposition (AAG)
TPSN .... Troop Program Sequence Number [*Military*]
TPSO .... Triphenylstibine Oxide [*Organic chemistry*]
TPSP .... Tape Punch Subassembly Panel
TPSRS .... Terminal Primary and Secondary RADAR System (DA)
TPSS .... Thermal Protection System Selection
TPSS .... Trespass [*Legal shorthand*] (LWAP)
TPST .... Training and Personnel Systems Technology (MCD)
TPST .... Triple-Pole, Single-Throw [*Switch*]
TPST .... True Positive Stress Test [*Medicine*] (DMAA)
TPSTe .... Triisopropylbenzenesulfonyl Tetrazolide [*Organic chemistry*]
TPSU .... Transaction Processing Service User [*Telecommunications*]
TPSY .... Task Parameter Synthesizer (SAA)
TPT .... Bibliographic Center for Research, Denver, CO [*OCLC symbol*] (OCLC)
TPT .... Tactical Petroleum Terminal
TPT .... Tail Pipe Temperature (NG)
TPT .... Tappet [*Mechanical engineering*]
TPT .... Tappit Resources [*Vancouver Stock Exchange symbol*]
TPT .... Target Practice [*Ammunition*] with Tracer
TPT .... Tasmanian Peace Trust [*Australia*]
TPT .... Telecommunication Products Plus Technology [*Pennwell Publishing Co.*] [*Littleton, MA*] (TSSD)
TPT .... Teleprinter Planning Table
TPT .... Temporary Part Time [*Personnel*] (MCD)
TPT .... Test Pilot Training
TPT .... Test Program Tape (MCD)
TPT .... Tetraisopropyl Titanate [*Organic chemistry*]
TPT .... Tetraphenyl Tetrazolium [*Histochemical stain*] (AAMN)
TPT .... Third-Party Transaction [*Business term*]
TPT .... Time Period Tape [*Database*] [*Arbitron Ratings Co.*] [*Information service or system*] (CRD)

TPT Time Priority Table
TPT Time to Peak Tension
TPT Tiputa [*Tuamotu Archipelago*] [*Seismograph station code, US Geological Survey*] (SEIS)
TPT Total Pressure Transducer
TPT Total Prime Time (WDMC)
TPT Total Protein Tuberculin [*Medicine*] (MAE)
TPT Totul pentru Tara [*"All for the Fatherland"*] [*Romania*] [*Political party*] (PPE)
TPT Toy Preference Test [*Psychology*] (AEBS)
TPT Training Proficiency Test [*Army*] (INF)
TPT Transonic Pressure Tunnel [*NASA*]
TPT Transport
TPT Trenton-Princeton Traction Co. [*Absorbed into Consolidated Rail Corp.*] [*AAR code*]
TPT Troop Proficiency Trainer
TPT Trumpet
TPT Typhoid-Paratyphoid [*Medicine*]
TPTA Thiophosphoryl Triamide [*Fertilizer technology*]
TPTA Tin Triphenyl [*or Triphenyltin*] Acetate [*Organic chemistry*]
TPTB [*The*] Powers That Be [*E-Mail discussion*]
TPTC Teleprocessing Test Center (MHDI)
TPTC Temperature Pressure Test Chamber (IAA)
TPTC Triphenyltin Chloride [*Organic chemistry*]
TPTD Test Pilot Training Division
TPTD Transported
TPTE (Tritylphenyl)thioethanol [*Organic chemistry*]
TPTF Tributyl Phosphate Task Force (EA)
TPTG Terminal Program Testing Guide
TPTG Tuned Plate Tuned Grid [*Electronic tube*]
TPTH Triphenyltin Hydroxide [*Organic chemistry*]
TPTHS Total Parathyroid Hormone Secretion [*Endocrinology*] (MAE)
TPTMS Tropical Pacific Thermal Monitoring System [*Marine science*] (OSRA)
TPTN Toilet Partition [*Technical drawings*]
TPTOL True Position Tolerance (MSA)
TPTP Tape-to-Tape [*Computer science*] (IAA)
TPTR Transporter
TPTR Trumpeter
TPTRL Time-Phased Transportation Requirements List [*Military*] (AABC)
TPTS Two-Phase Thermosyphon [*Heat exchanger*]
TPTX Thyroid-Parathyroidectomy [*Endocrinology*] (DAVI)
TPTX Thyroparathyroidectomized [*Medicine*]
TPTZ Triphenyltetrazolium Chloride [*Also, RT, TTC*] [*Chemical indicator*]
TPTZ Tris(pyridyl)-s-triazine [*Analytical chemistry*]
TPU Capitol Consortium Network, Washington, DC [*OCLC symbol*] (OCLC)
TPU Tactical Patrol Unit [*Military*] (LAIN)
TPU Tank and Pump Unit [*Mechanized infantry battalion*] (INF)
TPU Tank Petroleum Unit [*Army*] (INF)
TPU Tape Preparation Unit
TPU Taputuquara [*Brazil*] [*Airport symbol*] (AD)
TPU Tarn Pure Technology Corp. [*Vancouver Stock Exchange symbol*]
TPU Task Processing Unit
TPU Tax Payers United [*Australia*]
TPU Telecommunications Processing Unit
TPU Terminal Processing Unit [*Computer science*] (IAA)
TPU Text Processing Utility [*Computer science*]
TPU Thermoplastic Urethane [*or Polyurethane*] [*Plastics technology*]
TPU Threatened Plants Unit (EERA)
TPU Time Processing Unit [*Automotive engineering Electronics*]
TPU Transient Personnel Unit [*Navy*] (DNAB)
TPU Transverse Propulsion Unit (PDAA)
TPU Troop Program Unit [*Army*] (AABC)
TPU Trunk Processing Unit [*Bell System*]
TPU Turbo Pascal Unit [*Borland International*] [*Computer science*] (PCM)
TPU Turbopower Unit
TPUC Telephone Pickup Coil
TPUG Toronto PET Users Group [*Canada*]
TPuGH Giles County Hospital, Pulaski, TN [*Library symbol*] [*Library of Congress*] (LCLS)
TP/UMF Total Package/Unit Materiel Fielding [*Army*] (RDA)
TPUN Test Procedure Update Notice (NASA)
TPUR Transperineal Urethral Resection [*Medicine*] (DAVI)
TPUS Transportation and Public Utilities Service [*Later, part of Transportation and Communication Service, GSA*]
TPV Capitol Consortium Network, Washington, DC [*OCLC symbol*] (OCLC)
TPV Thermophotovoltaic
TPV Thermoplastic Vulcanizate [*Plastics technology*]
TPV Time to Peak Flow Velocity [*Cardiology*]
TPV Tonopah [*Nevada*] [*Seismograph station code, US Geological Survey Closed*] (SEIS)
TPV Total Pore Volume [*Geology*]
TPV Transverse Pallial Vein
TPV Triple Polio Vaccine [*Medicine*]
TPVE Two Phase Vacuum Extraction [*Engineering*]
TPVM Teleprocessing Virtual Machine (MHDI)
TPVR Total Pulmonary Vascular Resistance (AAMN)
TPW Target Planning Worksheet (DOMA)
TPW Tenth-Power Width
TPW Title Page Wanting
TPW Toledo, Peoria & Western Railroad Co. [*AAR code*]
TPW Tons per Week
TPW True Polar Wandering [*Geophysics*]
TPW Turbo Pascal for Windows [*Computer science*]
TPWAC Territory Parks and Wildlife Advisory Council [*Northern Territory, Australia*]
TPWBH Tax Paid Wine Bottling House
TPWG Test Planning Working Group [*Military*]
TPWIC Theater Prisoner of War Information Center
TPWU Tanganyika Plantation Workers Union
TPWU Tea Plantation Workers' Union [*Kenya*]
TPX Total Pancreatectomy [*Medicine*]
TPX Transponder (KSC)
TPX Transportes Aereos de Xalapa, SA de CV [*Mexico*] [*FAA designator*] (FAAC)
tpx Triplex [*Paper*] (DGA)
TPY FEDLINK [*Federal Library and Information Network*], Washington, DC [*OCLC symbol*] (OCLC)
TPY Tapestry (ADA)
TPY Tipperary Corp. [*AMEX symbol*] (SAG)
TPY Tocantinopolis [*Brazil*] [*Airport symbol*] (AD)
TPY Tons per Year
TPY Trans-Provincial Airlines Ltd. [*Canada ICAO designator*] (FAAC)
tpyt Triptych (VRA)
TPZ FEDLINK [*Federal Library and Information Network*], Washington, DC [*OCLC symbol*] (OCLC)
TPZ Thioperazine [*or Thioproperazine*] [*Tranquilizer*]
TPZ Transportes La Paz SA de CV [*Mexico ICAO designator*] (FAAC)
TQ Las Vegas Airlines [*ICAO designator*] (AD)
TQ [*The*] Questers (EA)
TQ Tale Quale [*Of Conditions on Arrival*] [*Latin*]
TQ Thought Quality [*Psychology*]
TQ Three-Quarter Midget [*Horse racing*]
TQ Three-Quarter Size [*Car racing*]
TQ Tocopherolquinone [*Vitamin E*] [*Biochemistry*]
TQ Torquay [*Postcode*] (ODBW)
TQ Total Quality
Tq Tourniquet [*Medicine*] (MAE)
TQ Track Quality
TQ Transition Quarter [*Between fiscal years 1976 and 1977*]
TQ Turf Quality (OA)
TQ Tyrolean Airways [*Austria ICAO designator*] (ICDA)
TQ2 Thirst Quencher
TQ-3 Tocotrienolquinone [*Biochemistry*]
TQA Abilene, TX [*Location identifier FAA*] (FAAL)
TQA ILLINET [*Illinois Library Information Network*], Springfield, IL [*OCLC symbol*] (OCLC)
TQA Total Quality Assurance (OA)
TQB ILLINET [*Illinois Library Information Network*], Springfield, IL [*OCLC symbol*] (OCLC)
TQC Indiana Cooperative Library Services Authority, Indianapolis, IN [*OCLC symbol*] (OCLC)
TQC Technical Quality Control [*Telecommunications*] (TEL)
TQC Time, Quality, Cost
TQC Tobacco Quota Committee [*Australia*]
TQC Total Quality Control
TQCA Textile Quality Control Association (EA)
TQCM Thermoelectric Quartz Crystal Microbalance
TQD Indiana Cooperative Library Services Authority, Indianapolis, IN [*OCLC symbol*] (OCLC)
TQD Ter Quaterve in Die [*Three or Four Times a Day*] [*Pharmacy*]
TQD Total Quality Design (RDA)
TQE Michigan Library Consortium, Detroit, MI [*OCLC symbol*] (OCLC)
TQE Technical Quality Evaluation [*Polaris*]
TQE Tekamah, NE [*Location identifier FAA*] (FAAL)
TQE Timer Queue Element
TQF Michigan Library Consortium, Detroit, MI [*OCLC symbol*] (OCLC)
TQF [*The*] Queen's Flight [*British ICAO designator*] (FAAC)
TQF Threshold Quality Factor
TQG MIDLNET [*Midwest Regional Library Network*], St. Louis, MO [*OCLC symbol*] (OCLC)
TQG Tactical Quiet Generator (RDA)
TQH MIDLNET [*Midwest Regional Library Network*], St. Louis, MO [*OCLC symbol*] (OCLC)
TQH Tahlequah, OK [*Location identifier FAA*] (FAAL)
TQI MINITEX [*Minnesota Interlibrary Teletype Exchange*], Minneapolis, MN [*OCLC symbol*] (OCLC)
TQI Training Quality Index [*Military*] (CAAL)
TQJ MINITEX [*Minnesota Interlibrary Teletype Exchange*], Minneapolis, MN [*OCLC symbol*] (OCLC)
TQK NELINET [*New England Library Information Network*], Newton, MA [*OCLC symbol*] (OCLC)
TQL NELINET [*New England Library Information Network*], Newton, MA [*OCLC symbol*] (OCLC)
TQL Total Quality Leadership
TQLR Tune-In, Question, Listen, Review Technique [*Education*] (EDAC)
TQM OCLC [*Online Computer Library Center*] Western Services Center, Claremont, CA [*OCLC symbol*] (OCLC)
TQM Total Quality Management
TQM Transport Quartermaster
TQMG [*The*] Quartermaster General [*Army*]
TQMS Technical Quartermaster Sergeant
TQMS Total Quality Management System (MCD)
TQMS Triple Quadrupole Mass Spectrometer
TQMS Troop Quartermaster-Sergeant [*British military*] (DMA)
TQN OCLC [*Online Computer Library Center*] Western Services Center, Claremont, CA [*OCLC symbol*] (OCLC)
TQNT TriQuint Semiconductor [*NASDAQ symbol*] (TTSB)
TQNT Triquint Semiconductor, Inc. [*NASDAQ symbol*] (SAG)

TQO .... OHIONET, Columbus, OH [*OCLC symbol*] (OCLC)
TQP .... OHIONET, Columbus, OH [*OCLC symbol*] (OCLC)
TQP .... Total Quality and Productivity
TQP .... Transistor Qualification Program
TQPF .... [*The*] Valley/Wall Blake [*Anguilla Island*] [*ICAO location identifier*] (ICLI)
TQPP .... Total Quality Planning and Producibility (MCD)
TQQ .... Pennsylvania Area Library Network, Philadelphia, PA [*OCLC symbol*] (OCLC)
TQQPRI .... Tentative Qualitative Quantitative Personnel Requirements Information [*Army*]
TQR .... Pennsylvania Area Library Network, Philadelphia, PA [*OCLC symbol*] (OCLC)
TQR .... Saginaw, MI [*Location identifier FAA*] (FAAL)
TQR .... Tenquille Resources Ltd. [*Vancouver Stock Exchange symbol*]
TQS .... Pittsburgh Regional Library Center, Pittsburgh, PA [*OCLC symbol*] (OCLC)
TQS .... Total Quality Service
TQS .... Tres Esquinas [*Colombia*] [*Airport symbol*] (OAG)
TQT .... Pittsburgh Regional Library Center, Pittsburgh, PA [*OCLC symbol*] (OCLC)
TQT .... Transistor Qualification Test
TQTMT .... TACJAM [*Tactical Communications Jamming System*] Quickfix, Trail Blazer Maintenance Trainer [*Army*]
TQTP .... Transistor Qualification Test Program
TQTYREC .... Total Quantity Recommended [*Army*]
TQU .... Southeastern Library Network, Atlanta, GA [*OCLC symbol*] (OCLC)
TQV .... Southeastern Library Network, Atlanta, GA [*OCLC symbol*] (OCLC)
TQV .... St. Moritz [*Switzerland*] [*Airport symbol*] (AD)
TQW .... Pittsburgh, PA [*Location identifier FAA*] (FAAL)
TQW .... State University of New York, OCLC [*Online Computer Library Center*], Albany, NY [*OCLC symbol*] (OCLC)
TQX .... State University of New York, OCLC [*Online Computer Library Center*], Albany, NY [*OCLC symbol*] (OCLC)
TQY .... Tanquery Resources Ltd. [*Vancouver Stock Exchange symbol*]
TQY .... Wisconsin Library Consortium, Madison, WI [*OCLC symbol*] (OCLC)
TQZ .... Wisconsin Library Consortium, Madison, WI [*OCLC symbol*] (OCLC)
TR .... Caines' Term Reports [*New York*] [*A publication*] (DLA)
TR .... Compania de Aviacion Trans-Europa [*Spain ICAO designator*] (ICDA)
t_r .... Recovery Time (IDOE)
TR .... Right Triceps [*Anatomy*] (DAVI)
t_r .... Rise Time (IDOE)
TR .... Royal Air [*ICAO designator*] (AD)
TR .... Stewardsman Recruit [*Navy*]
TR .... Tactical RADAR [*Military*] (IAA)
TR .... Tactical Reconnaissance (NATG)
TR .... Talyllyn Railway [*Wales*]
TR .... Tank Regiment (MCD)
TR .... Tape Reader
TR .... Tape Recorder
TR .... Tape Register
TR .... Tape Resident
TR .... Tare (ROG)
TR .... Target Recognition (AFM)
TR .... Target Rifle (WDAA)
TR .... Tariff Reform
TR .... Task Register [*Computer science*] (BYTE)
TR .... Taxa Referencial de Juros [*Brazil*] (ECON)
TR .... Taxation Reports [*England*] [*A publication*] (DLA)
TR .... Tax Rate
TR .... Teaching and Research [*Medicine*]
TR .... Teaching Resources (AEBS)
TR .... Team Recorder [*Sports*]
TR .... Tear [*Deltiology*]
TR .... Technical Readiness
TR .... Technical Regulation
TR .... Technical Report
TR .... Technical Reporter [*World Council of Credit Unions*] [*A publication*]
TR .... Technical Report Program (NITA)
TR .... Technical Representative
TR .... Technical Requirement (MCD)
TR .... Technical Review [*Nuclear energy*] (NRCH)
TR .... Tekniska Rapporter (NITA)
TR .... Telegraphe Restant [*Telegram to Be Called for at a Telegraph Office*] [*French*] (ROG)
TR .... Telegraph Repeater [*Telecommunications*] (IAA)
TR .... Telephone Rentals [*Commercial firm*]
TR .... Tell-Rimah (BJA)
TR .... Temperature Range
TR .... Temperature Recorder
TR .... Temperature, Rectal [*Medicine*]
TR .... Temporary Regulation (AAGC)
TR .... Temporary Resident
TR .... Tempore Regis [*In the Time of the King*] [*Latin*]
TR .... Terbium [*Symbol is Tb*] [*Chemical element*] (ROG)
TR .... Terminalischer Reiz [*Terminal Stimulus*] [*German Psychology*]
TR .... Terminal Ready [*Computer science*]
TR .... Terminal Rendezvous
TR .... Terminal Repeat [*Genetics*]
TR .... Term Reports [*Legal*] [*British*]
TR .... Term Reports, English King's Bench [*Durnford and East's Reports*] [*England*] [*A publication*] (DLA)
TR .... Terms of Reference
TR .... Territorial Reserve [*British military*] (DMA)
TR .... Testa Rossa [*Red engine cylinder head*] [*Ferrari automotive model designation*] [*Italian*]
TR .... Test Regulation (MCD)
TR .... Test Report
TR .... Test Request
TR .... Test-Retest
TR .... Test Routine (AAG)
TR .... Test Run
TR .... Tetrazolium Reduction (MAE)
TR .... Tetrode [*Electronics*] (IAA)
TR .... Textus Receptus (BJA)
TR .... Thalamic Radiation [*Neurology*]
TR .... Theater Reserve [*Army*] (DOMA)
TR .... Theatre Royal (ROG)
TR .... Thematic Resource Nomination [*National Register of Historic Places*]
TR .... Theodore [*Teddy*] Roosevelt [*US president, 1858-1919*]
TR .... Therapeutic Radiology
TR .... Thermal Resistance (IAA)
TR .... Thioredoxin [*Also, TD, Trx*] [*Biochemistry*]
TR .... Thioredoxin Reductase [*An enzyme*]
TR .... Threaded Rod
TR .... Threat Reaction [*Military*] (CAAL)
TR .... Throws Right-Handed [*Baseball*]
TR .... Thrust Reverser (MCD)
TR .... Thyroid Hormone Receptor [*Endocrinology*]
TR .... Time Delay Relay [*Computer science*] (IAA)
TR .... Timed-Release [*Pharmacy*]
T/R .... Time of Rise (MSA)
TR .... Time Rate [*Payment system*]
TR .... Time Record (MCD)
TR .... Time Release (MAE)
TR .... Time Resolved [*Fluoroscopy*]
TR .... Time Routine [*Computer science*] (IAA)
TR .... Times Roman [*Typography*] (DGA)
TR .... Time to Repetition [*Medicine*]
TR .... Time to Retrofire
TR .... Time-to-Retrograde [*NASA*] (KSC)
TR .... Tinctura [*Tincture*] [*Pharmacy*]
TR .... Tincture [*Pharmacy*] (DAVI)
TR .... Tirailleur Regiments [*Military*]
TR .... Tone Relevant
TR .... Tons Registered [*Shipping*]
TR .... Tool Resistant [*Rating for safes*]
TR .... Toothed Ring [*Technical drawings*]
TR .... Tootsie Roll Indus [*NYSE symbol*] (TTSB)
TR .... Tootsie Roll Industries, Inc. [*NYSE symbol*] (SPSG)
TR .... Topical Report [*Nuclear energy*] (NRCH)
TR .... Topotactic Reaction [*Inorganic synthesis*]
TR .... Top Register (OA)
TR .... Torpedo Reconnaissance Aircraft [*Navy*]
TR .... Torque Receiver (IAA)
TR .... Torque Repeater (IAA)
TR .... Torque Synchro Receiver (MUGU)
TR .... Total Reaction (DA)
TR .... Total Regulation
TR .... Total Resistance (MAE)
TR .... Total Response [*Medicine*] (MAE)
TR .... Total Revenue
TR .... Touchdowns Running [*Football*]
TR .... Touche Remnant [*Investment firm*] [*British*]
TR .... Towel Rack (MSA)
TR .... Tower
TR .... Trace
TR .... Tracer
tr .... Traces (VRA)
TR .... Track
TR .... Tracking RADAR
TR .... Tract
tr .... Traction [*Orthopedics*] (DAVI)
TR .... Trade
TR .... Trade Representative (MHDW)
TR .... Traffic Route [*Telecommunications*] (TEL)
TR .... Tragedy
TR .... Trail [*Commonly used*] (OPSA)
TR .... Trailer (AAG)
TR .... Train (ADA)
TR .... Trainee (WDAA)
TR .... Trainer (AAG)
TR .... Training (ROG)
TR .... Training Regulations [*Military*]
TR .... Training Requirements
TR .... Tramway (ROG)
TR .... Transaction
TR .... Transaction Record
TR .... Transbrasil [*ICAO designator*] (AD)
T/R .... Transceiver
TR .... Transcontinental Resources [*Vancouver Stock Exchange symbol*]
Tr .... Transcript (DLA)
TR .... Transducers [*JETDS nomenclature*] [*Military*] (CET)
TR .... Transfer (DEN)
TR .... Transferable Rouble [*International Bank for Economic Co-Operation*] (EY)
TR .... Transfer Register
TR .... Transfer Reset
TR .... Transformation Ratio

TR .... Transformer (DEN)

T-R .... Transformer-Rectifier

TR .... Transfusion Reaction [*Medicine*]

TR .... Transfusion Receptors [*Oncology*]

TR .... Transient Response (IEEE)

TR .... Transilluminator [*Chromatography*]

TR .... Transistor [*Electronics*] (EECA)

TR .... Transitive

TR .... Translate [*or Translation, or Translator*]

TR .... Translation (IAA)

TR .... Translation Register

tr .... Translator

TR .... Transmission Report [*Telecommunications*] (TEL)

T/R .... Transmit and Receive (WDMC)

TR .... Transmit-Receive (IDOE)

T-R .... Transmit-Receive

TR .... Transmitter

TR .... Transmitter Receiver (IAA)

TR .... Transom (MSA)

TR .... Transponder RADAR (IAA)

TR .... Transport

TR .... Transportability Report [*Army*]

TR .... Transportation [*or Travel*] Request [*Military*]

TR .... Transpose

tr .... Transpose [*Proofreading*] (WDMC)

TR .... Transverse (DEN)

TR .... Travel and Relocation

T/R .... Travel Request

TR .... Travel Required [*Civil Service*]

TR .... Trawler

TR .... Tray (WGA)

TR .... Tread (WGA)

TR .... Treasurer

TR .... Treasury Receipt

TR .... Treatise (ROG)

TR .... Treatment [*Medicine*] (AAMN)

TR .... Treaty (ROG)

TR .... Treble [*Knitting*]

TR .... Treble [*Music*]

TR .... Trees [*Ecology*]

TR .... Tremor [*Medicine*] (AAMN)

TR .... Trenton [*Diocesan abbreviation*] [*New Jersey*] (TOCD)

TR .... Trial (ROG)

TR .... Trial Report

TR .... Tributary (ROG)

TR .... Tricuspid Regurgitation [*Cardiology*]

TR .... Trident Aircraft Ltd. [*Canada ICAO aircraft manufacturer identifier*] (ICAO)

TR .... Trigonal [*Molecular geometry*]

TR .... Trillo [*Trill*] [*Music*]

tr .... Trinidad and Tobago [*MARC country of publication code Library of Congress*] (LCCP)

TR .... Triple Reduction (DS)

TR .... Triple Screw [*Shipping*] (DS)

TR .... Trip Report

Tr .... Tristia [*of Ovid*] [*Classical studies*] (OCD)

Tr .... Tristram's Consistory Judgments [*England*] [*A publication*] (DLA)

TR .... Tritium Ratio [*Measure of tritium activity*] [*AEC*]

TR .... Tritium Recovery [*Nuclear energy*] (NRCH)

Tr .... Trityl [*Organic chemistry*]

TR .... Triumph [*Automobile model*]

TR .... Troop

TR .... Trouble Report

TR .... Trough (ADA)

TR .... Troupe (ROG)

TR .... Truck

TR .... Trumpet

TR .... Trunnion [*Pivot*]

TR .... Truro [*British depot code*]

TR .... Truro [*Postcode*] (ODBW)

TR .... Truss (MSA)

TR .... Trust

TR .... Trustee

TR .... Trustee

T/R .... Trust Receipt [*Banking*]

TR .... Tubercular Rueckstand [*Medicine*]

TR .... Tuberculin R [*Also called new tuberculin*] [*Infectious diseases*] (DAVI)

TR .... Tuberculin Residue [*Medicine*]

TR .... Tuberculin Rest [*Infectious diseases*] (DAVI)

TR .... Tubular Reabsorption [*Medicine*] (MAE)

TR .... Tunnel Rectifier

TR .... Turbidity Reducing (AAMN)

TR .... Turbine Rate (NVT)

TR .... Turkey [*ANSI two-letter standard code*] (CNC)

TR .... Turkish Reactor

TR .... Turnaround Requirements (MCD)

TR .... Turning Radius [*Automotive engineering*]

TR .... Turn Rule (WDMC)

TR8CCA .... TR8 Car Club of America (EA)

Tra .... Epistulae ad Traianum [*of Pliny the Younger*] [*Classical studies*] (OCD)

TRA .... La Tuyere a Reverse Aval [*Concorde*]

TRA .... [*The*] Razorback Award (IAA)

TRA .... Tackle Representatives Association (EA)

TRA .... Taiwan Relations Act [*1979*] (DOMA)

TRA .... Tandem Rotary Activator

TRA .... Tape Recorder Amplifier

TRA .... Taramajima [*Japan*] [*Airport symbol*] (OAG)

TRA .... Tasmanian Racing Authority [*Australia*]

TRA .... Tasmanian Rifle Association [*Australia*]

TRA .... Tax Reform Act [*1969, 1976, 1984, 1986*]

TRA .... Tax Reform Australia

TRA .... Technical Requirement Analysis (OA)

TRA .... Technical Review and Analysis

TRA .... Technical Risk Assessment (MCD)

TRA .... Temperature Recording Alarm [*Engineering*]

TRA .... Temporary Rental Allowance

TRA .... Temporary Reserved Airspace [*ICAO designator*] (FAAC)

TRA .... Temporary Restricted Area [*Former USSR*] (NATG)

TRA .... Terminal Repeat Array [*Genetics*]

TRA .... Terra Industries [*NYSE symbol*] (TTSB)

TRA .... Terra Industries, Inc. [*Formerly, Inspiration Resources Corp.*] [*NYSE symbol*] (SPSG)

TRA .... Terrain-Related Accident [*Aviation*]

TRA .... Test Reactor Area

TRA .... Test Requirement Analysis (CAAL)

TRA .... Textile Refinishers Association (EA)

TRA .... Theodore Roosevelt Association (EA)

TRA .... Therapeutic Recreation Associate [*Rehabilitation*] (DAVI)

TRA .... Thoroughbred Racing Associations (EA)

TRA .... Thrace Requirements Analysis [*Military*]

TRA .... Throttle Resolver Angle (MCD)

TRA .... Thrust Reduction Altitude (GAVI)

TRA .... Tinctura [*Tincture*] [*Pharmacy*] (ROG)

TRA .... Tire and Rim Association (EA)

TRA .... Total Renin Activity [*Medicine*] (DMAA)

TRA .... Tournament of Roses Association [*Later, TOR*] (EA)

TRA .... Tracan Oil & Gas [*Vancouver Stock Exchange symbol*]

TRA .... Trade Readjustment Allowance [*or Assistance*]

TRA .... Trade Recovery Act

TRA .... Trade Relations Association (EA)

TRA .... Training

TRA .... Training Readjustment Allowance (OICC)

TRA .... Training Requirements Analysis [*NASA*] (NASA)

TRA .... Transaldolase [*An enzyme*] (MAE)

TRA .... Transavia Holland BV [*Netherlands ICAO designator*] (FAAC)

TRA .... Transfer

TRA .... Transportation Reform Alliance

TRA .... Transracial Adoption

TRA .... Travnik [*Yugoslavia*] [*Seismograph station code, US Geological Survey Closed*] (SEIS)

TrA .... Triangulum Australe [*Constellation*]

TRA .... Triaxial Recording Accelerometer

TRA .... Tripoli Rocketry Association (EA)

TRA .... Triumph Register of America (EA)

TRA .... Tubular Reactor Assembly [*Nuclear energy*] (NRCH)

TRA .... Turkish Reactor Assembly (SAA)

TRA .... Turnaround Requirements Analysis [*NASA*] (NASA)

TRA .... United States Army TRADOC, Institute for Military Assistance, Library, Fort Bragg, NC [*OCLC symbol*] (OCLC)

TRAA .... Towing and Recovery Association of America (EA)

TRAAC .... Transit Research and Attitude Control [*Navy satellite*]

TRAACS .... Transit Research and Attitude Control Satellite [*Navy*] (IEEE)

trab .... Trabeated (VRA)

TRAB .... Triaminobenzene [*Organic chemistry*]

TRABOT .... Terrier RADAR and Beacon Orientation Test (MUGU)

TRAC .... DTIC [*Defense Technical Information Center*] Technical Awareness Circular [*Information service or system*] (CRD)

TRAC .... Tactical Radar Correlator [*Army*] (DOMA)

TRAC .... Tandem Razor and Cartridge [*Gillette Co.*]

TRAC .... Target Research Analysis Center (CINC)

TRAC .... Tax Reform Action Coalition (EA)

TRAC .... Technical Reports Announcement Checklist

TRAC .... Telecommunications Research and Action Center [*Washington, DC*] [*Information service or system Telecommunications*] (TSSD)

TRAC .... Teleprocessing Recording for Analysis by the Customer

TRAC .... Telescoping Rotor Aircraft Concept (MCD)

TRAC .... Test of Reading Affective Cues [*Psychology*]

TRAC .... Texas Reconfigurable Array Computer

TRAC .... Text Reckoning and Compiling [*Computer science*]

TRAC .... Thermally Regenerative Alloy Cell

TRAC .... Total Record Access Control (SAA)

TRAC .... Total Recycling Advisory Committee [*Northern Territory, Australia*]

TRAC .... Tracer (AABC)

trac .... Tracery (VRA)

TRAC .... Track Data Corp. [*NASDAQ symbol*] (TTSB)

TRAC .... Track Data Corp. [*NASDAQ symbol*] (SAG)

TRAC .... Tracking and Communications [*Aviation*] (IAA)

TRAC .... Tractor (AAG)

TRAC .... Trade Reform Action Coalition [*Defunct*] (EA)

TRAC .... TRADOC Analysis Command

TRAC .... TRADOC [*Training and Doctrine Command*] Research and Analysis Center [*Army*]

TRAC .... Train Regulation Advisory Control (PDAA)

TRAC .... Transaction Reporting and Control System (MCD)

TRAC .... Transient Radiation Analysis by Computer (KSC)

TRAC .... Transient Reactor Analysis Code (NRCH)

TRAC .... Transportation Account Code (AFM)

TRAC .... Trials Recording and Analysis Console (PDAA)

TRACAB .... Terminal RADAR Approach Control in Tower Cab [*Aviation*] (FAAC)
TRACAD .... Training for [*US Military Academy*] Cadets (NVT)
TRACAL .... Traffic Control and Landing [*Aviation*] (IAA)
TRACALS ..... Traffic Control and Landing System [*Aviation*] (IAA)
TRACALS ..... Traffic Control Approach and Landing System [*Aviation electronics*]
TRACAP .... Transient Circuit Analysis Program [*Computer science*]
TRACC .... Target Review and Adjustment for Continuous Control (MCD)
TRACDR .... Tractor-Drawn
TRACE .... Tactical Readiness and Checkout Equipment
TRACE .... Tactical Resources and Combat Effectiveness Model (MCD)
TRACE .... Tape-Controlled Reckoning and Checkout Equipment [*Component of automatic pilot*] [*Aviation*] (IAA)
TRACE .... Tape-Controlled Recording Automatic Checkout Equipment [*Component of automatic pilot*] [*Aviation*]
TRACE .... Task Reporting and Current Evaluation
TRACE .... Taxiing and Routing of Aircraft Coordinating Equipment (MCD)
TRACE .... Taxiway Routing and Coordination Equipment [*Aviation*]
TRACE .... Technical Report Analysis, Condensation, Evaluation
TRACE .... Teleprocessing Recording for Analysis by the Customer (IEEE)
TRACE .... Test Equipment for Rapid Automatic Checkout and Evaluation [*Pan American Airways*]
TRACE .... Time Repetitive Analog Contour Equipment (PDAA)
TRACE .... Time-Shared Routines for Analysis, Classification, and Evaluation (DIT)
TRACE .... Tolls Recording and Computing Equipment (IEEE)
TRACE .... Toronto Region Aggregation of Computer Enthusiasts [*Canada*]
TRACE .... Total Remote Access Center (MHDI)
TRACE .... Total Resource Allocation Cost Estimating (RDA)
TRACE .... Total Risk Assessing Cost Estimate [*Army*] (RDA)
TRACE .... Trace [*Commonly used*] (OPSA)
TRACE .... Trace Remote Atmospheric Chemical Evaluation [*National Center for Atmospheric Research*]
TRACE .... Tracking and Communications, Extraterrestrial
TRACE .... Track Retrieve and Account for Configuration of Equipment (MCD)
TRACE .... Traffic Routing and Control Equipment (MCD)
TRACE .... Training and Approaches to Careers Education [*Project*] (AIE)
TRACE .... Trane Air Conditioning Economics [*The Trane Co.*]
TRACE .... Transaction, Accounting, Control, and Endorsing (PDAA)
TRACE .... Transaction Control and Encoding (IAA)
TRACE .... Transistor Radio Automatic Circuit Evaluator
TRACE .... Transition Region and Coronal Explorer [*Satellite*]
TRACE .... Transportable Automated Control Environment
TRACE .... Transport and Atmospheric Chemistry Near the Equator
Trace & M ...... Tracewell and Mitchell's United States Comptroller's Decisions [*A publication*] (DLA)
TRACEN .... Training Center
TRACE-P .... Total Risk Assessing Cost Estimate - Production [*Army*] (RDA)
TRACER .... Technical Reporting of Automated Configuration Electrical Requirements
TRACER .... Turnaround Time, Repair Survival Rate and Cost Evaluation Report [*Navy*] (DNAB)
TRACERS ..... Teleprocessed Record and Card Entry Reporting System (MCD)
TRACES .... Technology in Retrospect and Critical Events in Science [*IITRI*]
TRACES .... Trace [*Commonly used*] (OPSA)
TRACEX .... Amphibious Tractor Exercise [*Navy*] (NVT)
Tracey Evidence... Tracey's Cases on Evidence [*A publication*] (DLA)
TRAC-F .... TRADOC [*Training and Doctrine Command*] Analysis Command - Fort Leavenworth [*Kansas*] [*Army*]
TRACH .... Trachea [*or Tracheotomy*] [*Medicine*]
Trach .... Tracheostomy [*Medicine*] (DAVI)
Trach .... Trachiniae [*of Sophocles*] [*Classical studies*] (OCD)
Trach Asp .... Tracheal Aspiration (CPH)
TRACHY .... Tracheotomy (DSUE)
TRACINFO .... Tracer, Number as Indicated. Furnish Information Immediately or Advise
TRACIR .... Tracking Air with Circularly Polarized Radar (USDC)
TRACIR .... Tracking Air with Circularly Polarized Radar [*Marine science*] (OSRA)
TRACIRS ...... [*The*] Recording and Controlling of In-Transit Requisition System [*Army*]
TRACIS .... Traffic Records Criminal Justice Information System (OICC)
TRACK .... Timing Results and Competition Knowledge [*Auto racing*]
TRACK .... Track [*Commonly used*] (OPSA)
TrackD .... Track Data Corp. [*Associated Press*] (SAG)
TRACKEX ..... Tracking Exercise [*Navy*] (NVT)
TRAC-MTRY... TRADOC [*Training and Doctrine Command*] Analysis Command-Monterey [*California*] [*Army*] (GRD)
TRACOMD.... Training Command [*Navy*] (DNAB)
TRACOMDLANT... Training Command, Atlantic Fleet [*Navy*]
TRACOMDPAC... Training Command, Pacific Fleet [*Navy*]
TRACOMDSUBPAC... Training Command, Submarines, Pacific Fleet [*Navy*]
TRACOMDWESTCOAST... Training Command, West Coast [*Navy*]
TRACOMP.... Tracking Comparison
TRACON .... Terminal RADAR Approach Control [*FAA*]
TRACON .... Terminal RADAR Approach Control Facility [*Aviation*] (FAAC)
TRACON .... Terminal RADAR Control (IAA)
TRACOPS ..... Trailerless Collective Protection System (DWSG)
Tracor .... Tracor, Inc. [*Associated Press*] (SAG)
TracrP .... Tracer Petroleum Corp. [*Associated Press*] (SAG)
TracrPt .... Tracer Petroleum Corp. [*Associated Press*] (SAG)
TRACS .... Teleprocessing Remote Access Control System (HGAA)
TRACS .... Tool Record Accountability System [*NASA*] (NASA)
TRACS .... Traffic Reporting and Control System (IAA)
TRACS .... Transport and Road Abstracting and Cataloguing System (NITA)
TRACS .... Travel Accounting Control System [*Citicorp Diners Club*]
TRACS .... Triangulation Ranging and Crossfix System [*Military*] (CAAL)
TracSup .... Tractor Supply Co. [*Associated Press*] (SAG)
tract .... Traction
TRACT .... Triggered Reconnection Adiabatically Compressed Torus (MCD)
TRACW .... Track Data Corp. Wrrt [*NASDAQ symbol*] (TTSB)
TRAC-WSMR... TRADOC [*Training and Doctrine Command*] Analysis Command - White Sands Missile Range [*New Mexico*] [*Army*]
TRACY .... Technical Reports Automated Cataloging - Yes [*National Oceanic and Atmospheric Administration*]
TRAD .... Terminal RADAR [*Aviation*] (FAAC)
TRAD .... Tradition
TRAD .... Traductrice (IAA)
TRAD .... Training Requirements Analysis Directorate [*Army*]
TRAD .... Training Research and Development (IAA)
TRADA .... Timber Research and Development Association [*Research center British*] (IRC)
TRADAC .... Trajectory Determination and Acquisition Computation
TRADAD .... Trace to Destination and Advise [*Military*]
TRADAR .... Transaction Data Recorder (DNAB)
TRADAT .... Transit Data Transmission System (SAA)
TrADAT .... (Triazolyl-Azo) diaminotoluene [*Organic chemistry*]
TRADCOM .... Transportation Corps Research and Development Command [*Army*]
TRADE .... Tracking RADAR Angle Deception Equipment (NG)
TRADE .... Trading
TRADE .... Training Devices (RDA)
TRADE .... Training Devices and Equipment
TRADEC .... Training Device Computer (DNAB)
Trade Cas .... Trade Cases [*Commerce Clearing House*] [*A publication*] (DLA)
Trademark Bull... Bulletin. United States Trademark Association Series [*A publication*] (DLA)
Trademark Bull (NS)... Trademark Bulletin. United States Trademark Association (New Series) [*New York*] [*A publication*] (DLA)
TRADER .... Training Devices Requirements Office [*TRADOC*] (MCD)
TRADER .... Transient Radiation Effects Recorder (MCD)
Trade Reg Rep... Trade Regulation Reporter [*Commerce Clearing House*] [*A publication*] (DLA)
Trade Reg Rev... Trade Regulation Review [*A publication*] (DLA)
TRADES .... Technology Requirement and Definition Study
TRADES .... TRADOC Data Evaluation Study (MCD)
TRADET .... Training Detachment [*Navy*]
TRADEVCO... Trading & Development Bank Ltd. [*Liberia*]
Tra Devel Aust... Training and Development in Australia [*A publication*]
TRADEVMAN... Training Devices Man [*Navy rating*]
TRADEX .... Target Resolution and Discrimination Experiment [*ARPA*]
TRADEX .... Tracking RADAR Experiment (IAA)
TRADEX .... Trade Data Element Exchange
TRADIC .... Transistor Digital Computer
TRADIC .... Transistorized Airborne Digital Computer [*Air Force*]
TRADIC .... Transistorized Digital Computer [*Air Force*] (IAA)
TRADIS .... Tape Repeating Automatic Data Integration System
TRADIS .... Tropical Resources for Agricultural Development Information System [*Overseas Development Natural Resources Institute*] [*British Information service or system*] (IID)
TRADO .... Transporte Aereo Dominicano [*Dominican Republic*] [*ICAO designator*] (FAAC)
TRADOC .... Training and Doctrine Command [*Army*]
TRADOC-R ... Training and Doctrine Command Regulation [*Army*]
TRADR .... Tactical Radio Analysis, Division Restructuring [*Army*]
TRADSTAT ... World Trade Statistics Database [*Data-Star*] [*British Information service or system*] (IID)
Trad Un Dig... Trades Union Digest [*A publication*]
TRAE .... Transport Airlift Estimator [*Air Force*]
TRAEX .... Training and Experience [*Military*] (AFM)
TRAF .... Traffic
TRAF .... Tumor Neurosis Factor Receptor-Associated Factor [*Biochemistry*]
TRAFAC .... Training Facility [*Navy*] (DNAB)
TRAFCO .... Television, Radio and Film Communications [*of the Methodist Church*]
TRAFF .... Traffic (ROG)
Traff Cas ...... Railway, Canal, and Road Traffic Cases [*A publication*] (DLA)
TRAFFIC ...... Trade Records Analysis of Flora and Fauna in Commerce [*An association*]
TRAFFIC ...... Trade Records Analysis of Flora and Fauna in Commerce (GNE)
TRAFFIC ...... Transaction Routing and Form Formatting in COBOL [*Common Business-Oriented Language*] [*Computer science*] (MHDI)
TRAFFICWAY... Trafficway [*Commonly used*] (OPSA)
TRAFO .... Transformer (IAA)
TRAFOLPERS... Transfer Following Enlisted Personnel
TRAG .... Traffic Responsive Advance Green [*Control strategy*]
TRAG .... Tragedy
Trag .... Tragoedopodagra [*of Lucian*] [*Classical studies*] (OCD)
TRAI .... Tackle Representatives Association International [*Later, TSSAA*] (EA)
TRAIF .... Torso Restraint Assembly with Integrated Flotation
TRAIL .... Trail [*Commonly used*] (OPSA)
TRAILS .... Trail [*Commonly used*] (OPSA)
TRAIN .... Telerail Automated Information Network [*Association of American Railroads*]
TRAIN .... To Restore American Independence Now [*An association*]
TRAIN .... Tourist Railway Association, Inc. (EA)
train .... Training
TRAIN .... Training
TRAINBASEFOR... Training Base Force, Pacific Fleet [*Navy*]
TRAINCON ... Training Conference (MCD)
TRAINDIV .... Training Division [*Canadian Navy*]
TRAINLANT... Training Atlantic Fleet [*Navy*]

TRAINMAN...... Training Management [*Navy*] (DNAB)
TRAINPACHQ... Training Group Pacific Headquarters [*Canadian Navy*]
TRAINRON..... Training Squadron [*Later, SERRON*] [*Navy*]
TRA INT'L..... Tackle Representatives Association International [*Later, TSSAA*] (EA)
TRAIS.......... Transportation Research Activities Information Service [*Department of Transportation*]
TRAJ............ Trajectory (AAG)
TRAJ/PS...... Trajectory/Parametric Study (SAA)
TRAK........... Canterbury Park Holdings [*NASDAQ symbol*] (SAG)
TRAK........... Canterbury Pk Hldg Corp. [*NASDAQ symbol*] (TTSB)
TRAK........... Track [*Postal Service standard*] (OPSA)
TRAK........... Track
TrakAu......... Trak-Auto Corp. [*Associated Press*] (SAG)
TRAK TROL... Trackless Trolley [*Freight*]
TRAKW......... Canterbury Pk Hldg Wrrt [*NASDAQ symbol*] (TTSB)
TRALA.......... Truck Renting and Leasing Association (EA)
TRALANT..... Fleet Training Command, Atlantic [*Navy*]
TRALINET.... TRADOC Library Information Network (MCD)
TRAM........... Target Recognition Attack Multisensor [*DoD*]
TRAM........... Tensioned Replacement Alongside Method (MCD)
TRAM........... Test Reliability and Maintenance Program [*Navy*] (NVT)
TRAM........... Tethered Rover for Atmospheric Measurement [*Ozone measurement*]
TRAM........... Tracking RADAR Automatic Monitoring (AFM)
TRAM........... Tractor, Rubber-Tired, Articulated, Multipurpose (DOMA)
TRAM........... Training Readiness Analysis Monitor (MCD)
TRAM........... Translocating Chain Associating Membrane [*Biochemistry*]
TRAM........... Transputer Module [*Computer science*]
TRAM........... Transverse Rectus Abdominis Myocutaneous [*Breast reconstruction*] (DAVI)
TRAM........... Treatment Rating Assessment Matrix [*Medicine*] (MAE)
TRAM........... Treatment Response Assessment Method [*Medicine*] (MAE)
TRAMAR...... Tropical Rain Mapping Radar [*Instrument*] (EERA)
TRAMEA...... TRADOC [*Training and Doctrine Command*] Management Engineering Activity [*Military*]
TRAMID....... Training for [*US Naval Academy/Naval Reserve Officers Training Corps*] Midshipmen (NVT)
TRAMIS....... TRADOC [*Training and Doctrine Command*] Management Information System [*Army*]
TRAMIT........ Especialidades Farmaceuticas en Tramite de Registro [*Ministerio de Sanidad y Consumo*] [*Spain Information service or system*] (CRD)
TRAMMS..... Transportation Automated Material Movements System [*Army*] (PDAA)
TRAMOD...... Training Requirements Analysis Model (MCD)
TRAMP........ Target Radiation Measurement Program (IAA)
TRAMP........ Temperature Regulation and Monitor Panel
TRAMP........ Test Retrieval and Memory Print [*Computer science*]
TRAMP........ Time-Shared Relational Associative Memory Program [*Computer science*] (IEEE)
TRAMPCO.... Thioguanine, Rubidomycin [*Daunorubicin*], ara-C, Methotrexate, Prednisolone, Cyclophosphamide, Oncovin [*Vincristine*] [*Antineoplastic drug regimen*]
TRAMPCOL... Thioguanine, Rubidomycin [*Daunorubicin*], ara-C, Methotrexate, Prednisolone, Cyclophosphamide, Oncovin , L-Asparaginase [*Vincristine*] [*Antineoplastic drug regimen*]
TRAMPL...... TRADOC Master Priority List (MCD)
TRAMPS...... Temperature Regulator and Missile Power Supply
TRAMPS...... Text Information Retrieval and Management Program System [*Computer science*] (IAA)
TRAMPS...... Traffic Measure and Path Search [*Telecommunications*] (TEL)
TRAMPS...... Transportation Movement Planing System (SAA)
TRAMS........ Traffic Routing and Management System (NITA)
TRAN........... Tax Revenue Anticipation Note [*Finance*]
TRAN........... Transaction
TRAN........... Transformer
TRAN........... Transient (AABC)
TRAN........... Transit
TRAN........... Transit
TRAN........... Transmit
TRAN........... Transport
TRANC......... Transient Center [*Marine Corps*]
TRAND......... Tone Reproduction and Neutral Determination [*Chart*] [*Printing technology*]
Tr & Cr........ Troilus and Cressida [*Shakespearean work*] (BARN)
TR & DL....... Tung Research and Development League [*Defunct*] (EA)
T/R & G........ Transmit, Receive, and Guard (MSA)
Tr & H Pr...... Troubat and Haly's Pennsylvania Practice [*A publication*] (DLA)
Tr & H Prec Ind... Train and Heard's Precedents of Indictment [*A publication*] (DLA)
TRANDIR...... Translation Director (IEEE)
Tr & TT........ Trial and Tort Trends [*A publication*] (DLA)
TRANET....... Tracking [*or Transit*] Network [*Navy*]
TRANET....... Transnational Network for Appropriate/Alternative Technologies
TRANEX....... Transaction Executive (IAA)
TranIn.......... Trans-Industries, Inc. [*Associated Press*] (SAG)
TranInc........ Transamerica Income Shares, Inc. [*Associated Press*] (SAG)
TRAN-PRO... Transaction Processing [*Computer science*]
Tranq........... De Tranquillitate Animi [*of Seneca the Younger*] [*Classical studies*] (OCD)
tranq........... Tranquilize(r) [*Pharmacology*] (DAVI)
TRANQ........ Tranquillo [*Quietly*] [*Music*] (ROG)
TRANS......... Telemetry Redundancy Analyzer System
TRANS......... Transaction
TRANS......... Transcript (ADA)
TRANS......... Transfer (AAG)
trans........... Transfer (ODBW)
TRANS......... Transformer (AFM)
trans........... Transformer (IDOE)
TRANS......... Transient (AFIT)
TRANS......... Transistor (ADA)
trans........... Transit (ODBW)
TRANS......... Transition (ROG)
TRANS......... Transitive
TRANS......... Transitory
TRANS......... Translation
Trans........... Translator (DLA)
TRANS......... Transmission
TRANS......... Transmission
trans........... Transmit (IDOE)
TRANS......... Transmittance (AAG)
trans........... Transmitter (IDOE)
trans........... Transparency (VRA)
TRANS......... Transparent (MSA)
TRANS......... Transport [*or Transportation*] (AAG)
trans........... Transportation (DD)
TRANS......... Transpose [*Proofreading*]
TRANS......... Transverse
trans........... Transverse (IDOE)
TRANSA....... Transaction (MSA)
TRANSAC..... Transistorized Automatic Computer
TransAct...... TransAct Technologies Inc. [*Associated Press*] (SAG)
TRANSAIEE... Transactions of the American Association of Electrical Engineers (IAA)
TRANSALT... Transition Altitude [*Aviation*] (DA)
Trans & Proc Roy Soc SA... Transactions and Proceedings. Royal Society of South Australia [*A publication*]
Trans & Proc Roy Soc Vic... Transactions and Proceedings. Royal Society of Victoria [*Australia A publication*]
Trans & Wit... Transvaal and Witswatersrand Reports [*A publication*] (DLA)
Trans Ap...... Transcript Appeals [*New York*] [*1867-68*] [*A publication*] (DLA)
Trans App.... Transcript Appeals [*New York*] [*A publication*] (DLA)
Trans Appeal R... New York Transcript Appeals Reports [*A publication*] (DLA)
Trans Aust Med Congress... Transactions. Australian Medical Congress [*A publication*]
TRANSC....... Transcribe (IAA)
TRANSC....... Transcription (IAA)
Transc A...... Transcript Appeals [*New York*] [*A publication*] (DLA)
TRANSCAD... Transportation Computer Assisted Design [*MTMC*] (TAG)
TRANSCAER... Transportation Community Awareness and Emergency Response
TRANSCAER... Transportation Community Awareness and Emergency Response
TRANSCEIVER... Transmitter-Receiver (NATG)
Transcis....... Transcisco Industries [*Associated Press*] (SAG)
Transcm....... Transcom International Ltd. [*Associated Press*] (SAG)
Transcnd...... Tanscend Services, Inc. [*Associated Press*] (SAG)
Transcnd...... Transcend Services, Inc. [*Associated Press*] (SAG)
TRANSCOM... Transportable Communications
TRANSCOM... Transportation Command [*Army*]
TRANSCOM... Transportation Operations Coordinating Committee [*FHWA*] (TAG)
TRANSCOM... United States Transportation Command [*MTMC*] (TAG)
TRANSCON... Transcontinental (MCD)
Transcor....... Transcor Waste Services, Inc. [*Associated Press*] (SAG)
TRANSCR..... Transcribed
Transcr A..... Transcript Appeals [*New York*] [*A publication*] (DLA)
TRANSCRON... Transcription (ROG)
Trans D........ Transverse Diameter [*Anatomy*] (CPH)
TRANSDEC... SONAR Transducer Test and Evaluation Center, Naval Electronics Laboratory [*San Diego, CA*] [*Navy*]
TRANSDEF... Transducer Evaluation Facility
TRANS/DEP... Transportation of Dependents [*Navy*] (DNAB)
TRANSDIV... Transport Division [*Navy*]
TRANSDOC... Transport Documentation (NITA)
TRANSEC..... Transmission Security [*Communications*]
TRANSED..... Transition Education
transf........... Transfer (VRA)
TRANSF....... Transferred
TRANSF....... Transformer (AAG)
TRANSFAX... Facsimile Transmission [*Telecommunications*]
TRANSFD..... Transferred (ROG)
TRANSFDESENGR... Transformer Design Engineer (IAA)
TRANSFER... Transportation Simulation for Estimating Requirements (DNAB)
TRANSFIG.... Transfiguration
TRANSFLTNG... Transitional Flight Training (NVT)
TRANSFOR... Translator for Structured FORTRAN [*Formula translation*] [*Computer science*] (MHDI)
TRANSFORM... Trade-Off Analysis - Systems/Force Mix Analysis [*Military*]
TRANSFRMR... Transformer
TRANSGRPPHIBFOR... Transportation Group Amphibious Forces [*Navy*]
TRANSGRPSOPAC... Transport Group, South Pacific Force [*Navy*]
TransH......... Trnasport Holdings, Inc. [*Associated Press*] (SAG)
TransHosp... Transitional Hospitals Corp. [*Associated Press*] (SAG)
Trans ILA..... Transactions. International Law Association [*1873-1924*] [*A publication*] (DLA)
TRANSIM..... Transit Simplified Receiver [*Satellite navigation system*]
TRANSIM..... Transportation Simulator (DNAB)
Trans Instn Eng Aust... Transactions. Institution of Engineers of Australia [*A publication*]
TRANSIS...... Transportation Safety Information System [*Department of Transportation*] (IID)
TRANSISTOR... Transfer Resistor

TRANSITEX.... Transit Exercise (NVT)
TRANSL....... Translation (AAG)
transl.......... Translucent (VRA)
TRANSLANG... Translator Language [*Computer science*]
TRANSLANT... Transit Atlantic [*By ship or aircraft*] (DOMA)
TRANSLANT... Transports, Atlantic Fleet [*Navy*]
TRANSLANTEX... Transatlantic Training Exercise (MCD)
Translat....... Translation (BJA)
TRANSLEV... Transition Level (DA)
TRANSLIT.... Transliteration
TRANSLOC... Trade-Off Analysis Systems/Force Mix (MCD)
TRANSLOC... Transportable LORAN-C (MCD)
TranslRev.... Translation Review [*A publication*] (BRI)
TranslRevS... Translation Review Supplement [*A publication*] (BRI)
Transm........ Transamerica Corp. [*Associated Press*] (SAG)
TRANSM....... Transmission (AFM)
TRANSMAN... Enlisted Transfer Manual [*Military*]
TRANSMGTSCOL... Transportation Management School [*Navy*] (DNAB)
TRANSMO.... Transportation Model [*Military*]
TRANSMON... Transmission (ROG)
TRANSMONUNIT... Transient Monitoring Unit (DNAB)
TRANSMTG... Transmitting
TRANSMUX... Transmission Multiplexer (NITA)
Transn........ Transition [*A publication*]
Transnatl..... Transnational (DLA)
Transnat'l Rep... Transnational Reporter [*A publication*] (DLA)
Transocn...... Transocean Offshore, Inc. [*Associated Press*] (SAG)
TRANSP....... Transparency (AAG)
TRANSP....... Transportation
transp.......... Transportation (VRA)
TRANSPAC... North Pacific Ocean Monitoring for Climate Research [*Japan-USA*] [*Marine science*] (OSRA)
TRANSPAC... Thermal Structure Monitoring Program in the Pacific [*Marine science*] (MSC)
TRANSPAC... Transpacific
TRANSPACMAG... Trans-Pacific Magnetic Anomaly Study [*National Oceanic and Atmospheric Administration*] (NOAA)
TRANSPHIBLANT... Transports, Amphibious Force, Atlantic Fleet [*Navy*]
TRANSPHIBPAC... Transports, Amphibious Force, Pacific Fleet [*Navy*]
Trans Phil Inst Vic... Transactions. Philosophical Institute of Victoria [*Australia A publication*]
Trans Phil Soc NSW... Transactions. Philosophical Society of New South Wales [*Australia A publication*]
TRANSPIRE... Transpiration-Cooled Stacked Platelet Injection (MCD)
transpl......... Transplant
TRANSPLAN... Transaction Network Service Planning Model [*Telecommunications*] (TEL)
TRANSPONDER... Transmitter/Responder [*Telecommunications*] (EECA)
Trans Qld Phil Soc... Transactions. Queensland Philosophical Society [*Australia A publication*]
TRANSRA.... Transistorized RADAR (IAA)
TRANSRON... Transport Squadron [*Navy*]
Trans Roy Soc NSW... Transactions. Royal Society of New South Wales [*Australia A publication*]
Trans Roy Soc SA... Transactions. Royal Society of South Australia [*A publication*]
TransSBA..... Transactions. Society of Biblical Archaeology [*London*] [*A publication*] (BJA)
Trans Sect... Transverse Section [*Medicine*] (AAMN)
transsex....... Transsexual (DAVI)
TransSys...... Transition Systems, Inc. [*Associated Press*] (SAG)
Transtl........ Transitional (DLA)
TranstxGs.... Transtexas Gas Corp. [*Associated Press*] (SAG)
TRANSV....... Transvaal [*South Africa*] (ROG)
TRANSV....... Transverse (AAG)
TRAO.......... Trade Remedy Assistance Office (AAGC)
TRAP........... Tactical Recovery of Aircraft and Personnel
TRAP........... Tandem Recursive Algorithm Process (HGAA)
TRAP........... Tank, Racks, Adapters, Pylons [*Military*]
TRAP........... Tape Recorder Action Plan [*Committee*] [*NASA/Air Force*]
TRAP........... Tartrate Resistant Acid Phosphatase [*An enzyme*]
TRAP........... Telepresent Rapid Aiming Platform [*Remotely operated rifle*]
TRAP........... Telomere Repeat Amplification Protocol [*Analytical biochemistry*]
TRAP........... Telomeric Repeat Amplification Protocol [*Analytical biochemistry*]
TRAP........... Terminal Radiation Airborne Program [*Air Force*]
TRAP........... Tetra-N-Propylammonium Perruthenate [*Organic chemistry*]
TRAP........... Thioguanine, Rubidomycin [*Daunorubicin*], Cytosine arabinoside , Prednisone [*ara-C*] [*Antineoplastic drug regimen*]
TRAP........... Thrombin Receptor Activating Peptide [*Biochemistry*]
TRAP........... Thrombospondin-Related Anonymous Protein [*Biochemistry*]
TRAP........... Time Response Approximation
TRAP........... Tracker Analysis Program (MCD)
TRAP........... Transmission Reliability Analysis Program
trap............ Trapezius [*Muscle*] [*Anatomy*] (DAVI)
TRAP........... Trapezoid (MSA)
trap............ Trapping (VRA)
TRAP........... Treasury Relief Aid Project
TRAP........... Tyrosine-Rich Amelogenin Polypeptide [*Biochemistry of dental enamel*]
TRAPAC....... Fleet Training Command, Pacific [*Navy*]
TRAPATT..... Trapped Plasma Avalanche Transit Time [*Bell Laboratories*] (IAA)
TRAPATT..... Trapped Plasma Avalanche Triggered Transit [*Bell Laboratories*]
TRAPCON.... Transportable RADAR Approach Control [*Army*]
TRAPP........ Training and Retention as Permanent Party [*Army*] (AABC)
Tr App......... Transcript Appeals [*New York*] [*1867-68*] [*A publication*] (DLA)
TRAPS......... Tactical Rapid Access Processing System (KSC)
TRAPS......... Training Requirements and Planning Subsystem [*Military*]
TRAPS......... Transportable Reliable Acoustic Path SONAR (MCD)
TRAPS......... Troop Reaction and Posture Sequence (MCD)
TRAPV......... Trap on Overflow BIT [*Binary Digit*] Set [*Computer science*]
TRAQS......... Trans Tasman Recognition Arrangement for Qualifications and Skills [*Australia*]
TRAR........... Total Radiation Absolute Radiometer [*NASA*]
TRARON....... Training Squadron
TRAS........... Tax Return Avoidance Syndrome
TRAS........... Training Requirements Analysis System [*Army*]
TRASANA..... TRADOC [*Training and Doctrine Command*] Systems Analysis Activity [*White Sands Missile Range, NM*] [*Army*]
TRASANA..... TRADOC [*Training and Doctrine Command*] Systems Analysis Agency [*Army*]
TRASER....... Transformer LASER (IAA)
TRASH......... Trash Remover and Satellite Hauler [*Proposed device to remove orbiting space debris*]
TRASH......... Tsunami Research Advisory System of Hawaii
TRASOP....... Tax Reduction Act Stock Ownership Plan
TRASSO....... TRADOC Systems Staff Officer [*or Office*] [*Army*]
TRASTA....... Training Station [*Navy*]
TRAT............ Torpedo Readiness Assistance Team
TRAT............ Trade Aptitude Test [*Vocational guidance test*]
TRAT............ Triacetylhexahydrotriazine [*Organic chemistry*]
TRATE.......... Trace Test and Evaluation
TRATEL........ Tracking through Telemetry [*Air Force*]
Tratt............ Trattenuto [*Music*]
TRAU........... Tanganyika Railway African Union
trau............ Trauma (DAVI)
trau............ Traumatic (DAVI)
TrAu............ Triangulum Australe [*Constellation*]
TRAV........... Intrav, Inc. [*NASDAQ symbol*] (SAG)
TRAV........... Television, Radio, and Audio-Visuals of the Presbyterian Church in the United States (NTCM)
TRAV........... Training Availability [*Navy*] (NVT)
TRAV........... Travancore [*India*] (ROG)
Trav............ Travel-Holiday [*A publication*] (BRI)
TRAV........... Travels [*or Traveler*]
TRAV........... Traverse (AABC)
TravAet........ Travelers Aetna Property Casualty Corp. [*Associated Press*] (SAG)
Trav & Tw L of N... Travers and Twiss on Law of Nations [*A publication*] (DLA)
TravBt......... Travis Boats & Motors, Inc. [*Associated Press*] (SAG)
TRAVC......... Travail Canada [*Labour Canada - LC*]
TRAVCHAR... Cost Travel Chargeable
Trav-Cochin... Indian Law Reports, Kerala Series [*A publication*] (DLA)
TRAVEL........ Transportable Vertical Erectable Launcher
Travel.......... [*The*] Travelers Group, Inc. [*Associated Press*] (SAG)
Travelrs....... [*The*] Travelers Corp. [*Associated Press*] (SAG)
Travelrs....... Travelers Group, Inc. [*Associated Press*] (SAG)
TRAVINFO.... Travel Information
TRAVIS........ Traffic Retrieval Analysis Validation and Information System [*Telecommunications*] (TEL)
TRAVIS........ Travel Industry School (AIE)
Travl........... [*The*] Travelers Corp. [*Associated Press*] (SAG)
Trav LJ........ Travancore Law Journal [*India*] [*A publication*] (DLA)
Trav LR........ Travancore Law Reports [*India*] [*A publication*] (DLA)
Trav LT........ Travancore Law Times [*India*] [*A publication*] (DLA)
TRAVNEC..... Subject Travel Was Necessary at This Time and Time Consumed in Administrative Channels Prevented Written Orders Being Issued
TravPC......... Travelers Corp. P & C Capital I [*Associated Press*] (SAG)
TravPrt........ Travel Ports of America, Inc. [*Associated Press*] (SAG)
TRAWL......... Tape Read and Write Library
TRAX........... Three-Axis (IAA)
TRAXS......... Total Reflection Angle X-Ray Spectroscopy
Tray Lat Max... Trayner's Latin Maxims and Phrases, Etc. [*A publication*] (DLA)
Tray Leg Max... Trayner's Latin Maxims and Phrases [*A publication*] (ILCA)
TRB............. Tactical Review Board [*Military*] (CAAL)
TRB............. Tapered Roller Bearing
TRB............. Tax Review Board [*Canada*]
TRB............. Technical Reference Branch [*Department of Transportation*] (IID)
TRB............. Technical Review Board [*NASA*] (KSC)
TRB............. Test Requirement Bulletins [*NASA*] (KSC)
TRB............. Test Review Board [*NASA*] (NASA)
TRB............. Tom Robinson Band
TRB............. Topical Reference Books [*A publication*]
TRB............. Torpedo Recovery Boat
TRB............. Toyota Reflex Burn [*Automotive engineering*]
TRB............. Trabaccolo [*Small coasting vessel of the Adriatic*] (DS)
TRB............. Trans Air Bretagne [*France ICAO designator*] (FAAC)
TRB............. Transportation Research Board (EA)
TRB............. Trapped Radiation Belt
TRB............. Treble
TRB............. [*The*] Tribune Co. [*NYSE symbol*] (SPSG)
Trb.............. Tribunus [*Tribune*] [*Latin*]
TRB............. Trombone [*Music*]
TRB............. Troop Basis (MUGU)
TRB............. Turbo [*Colombia*] [*Airport symbol*] (OAG)
TRB............. United States Army TRADOC, Engineering School Library and Learning Resource Center, Fort Belvoir, VA [*OCLC symbol*] (OCLC)
TRBC........... Triangle Bancorp [*NASDAQ symbol*] (SAG)
TRBF........... Total Renal Blood Flow [*Medicine*]
TRBL........... Troubleshooting (NASA)
TRBN........... Trombone [*Music*]
TRBO........... Turbochef, Inc. [*NASDAQ symbol*] (SAG)

TRBP Trainable Retractable Bow Propeller
TRBR Transportation Branch [*Navy*] (DNAB)
TRBS Texas Regional Banc'A' [*NASDAQ symbol*] (TTSB)
TRBS Texas Regional Bancshares, Inc. [*NASDAQ symbol*] (SAG)
TRBU Treasury Bulletin
TRC [*The*] Radiochemical Centre [*British*]
TRC [*The*] Ranchero Club (EA)
TRC [*The*] Revitalization Corps (EA)
TRC Tanned Red Cell [*Clinical chemistry*]
TRC Tape Reader Calibrator
TRC Tape Reader Control
TRC Tape Record Coordinator [*Computer science*]
TRC Tape Relay Center (NATG)
TRC Tasmanian Rowing Council [*Australia*]
TRC Tasmanian Rural Counselling [*Australia*]
TRC Taste Receptor Cell [*Biochemistry*]
TrC Tayloreed Corporation, Rochester, NY [*Library symbol Library of Congress*] (LCLS)
TRC Taylor Ranch [*California*] [*Seismograph station code, US Geological Survey*] (SEIS)
TRC Technical Repair Center [*Air Force*] (AFIT)
TRC Technical Research Center (MCD)
TRC Technical Resources Center [*Syracuse University*] [*Research center*]
TRC Technical Review Committee [*International Atomic Energy Agency*] (NRCH)
TRC Technical Review Committee [*Environmental Protection Agency*] (GFGA)
TRC Technical Review Committee
TRC Technical Review Criteria (ERG)
TRC Technology Reports Centre [*British*]
TRC Technology Resource Center [*Information service or system Phillipines*] (IID)
TRC Tejon Ranch [*AMEX symbol*] (TTSB)
TRC Tejon Ranch Co. [*AMEX symbol*] (SPSG)
TRC Telecommunications Research Center [*University of Louisville*] [*Research center*] (RCD)
TRC Telemetry and Remote Control (IEEE)
TRC Telephone Relay Coupler (HGAA)
TRC Temperature Recording Controller
TRC Teryl Resources Corp. [*Vancouver Stock Exchange symbol*]
TRC Test Readiness Certificate (AAG)
TRC Textile Research Council [*British*]
TRC Thames Rowing Club [*British*] (DI)
TRC Therapeutic Referral Center (DAVI)
TRC Therapeutic Residential Center (DAVI)
TRC Thermal Regenerative Cracking [*Hydrocarbon pyrolysis process*]
TRC Thermodynamics Research Center [*College Station, TX*] [*Department of Commerce*] (GRD)
TRC Thoroughbred Racing Communications [*An association*] (EA)
TRC Thrombosis Research Center [*Temple University*] [*Research center*] (RCD)
TRC Tierce [*Unit of measurement*]
TRC Time Ratio Control (IAA)
TRC Tithe Rent-Charge
TRC Tobacco Research Council [*British*] (BI)
TRC Token Ring Controller
TRC Topic [*Record label*] [*Great Britain*]
TRC Toroidal Propellant Container
TRC Torreon [*Mexico*] [*Airport symbol*] (OAG)
TRC Total Relevant Cost
TRC Total Renin Concentration [*Laboratory science*] (DAVI)
TRC Total Residual Chlorine [*Environmental chemistry*]
TRC Total-Response Chromatogram
TRC Total Ridge Count [*Anthropology*]
TRC Tough Rubber-Sheathed Cable
TRC Toyon Research Corp.
TRC Tracking, RADAR-Input, and Correlation
TRC Trade Relations Council of the United States (EA)
TRC Traffic Count and Listing [*Aviation*] (DA)
TRC Traffic Records Committee (EA)
TRC Training Readiness Condition
TRC Trans Air Charter, Inc. [*ICAO designator*] (FAAC)
TRC Transcaribbean (MCD)
TRC Transmission Release Code (DNAB)
TRC Transmit (NITA)
TRC Transmit/Receive Control Unit
TRC Transmitter Circuit (IAA)
TRC Transportation Research Center [*Ohio*]
TRC Transportation Research Command [*Army*] (IAA)
TRC Transverse Redundancy Check [*Computer science*] (IBMDP)
TRC Travelers Research Center [*Oceanography*]
TRC TRC, Companies [*Associated Press*] (SAG)
trc Treble Crochet
TRC Triumph Roadster Club (EA)
TRC Trona Railway Co. [*AAR code*]
TRC Type Requisition Code [*Military*]
TRC United States Army TRADOC, Fort Leavenworth Post Library, Commander, General Staff, Fort Leavenworth, KS [*OCLC symbol*] (OCLC)
TRCA Tricycle Racing Club of America
TRC-AS Transmit/Receive Control Unit-Asynchronous Start/Stop
TRCC T-Carrier Restoration Control Center [*Bell System*]
TRCC Theodore Roosevelt Centennial Commission [*Government agency*] [*Terminated, 1959*]
TRCC Tripartite Research Coordination Committee (SAA)
TRCCC Tracking RADAR Central Control Console [*BMEWS*]
TRCD Tricord Systems [*NASDAQ symbol*] (TTSB)
TRCD Tricord Systems, Inc. [*NASDAQ symbol*] (SAG)
TrCda TransCanada Pipeline Ltd. [*Associated Press*] (SAG)
TRCE Tactical Radio Communications Equipment
TRCE Terrace [*Classified advertising*] (ADA)
TRCE Thermionic Reactor Critical Experiment [*NASA*]
TRCE Trace
TRCE Trace
TRCF Transcription-Repair Coupling Factor [*Genetics*]
TRCH Tanned Red Cell Hemagglutination [*Immunology*] (MAE)
Tr Ch Transactions of the High Court of Chancery (Tothill's Reports) [*A publication*] (DLA)
TRCHI Tanned Red Cell Hemagglutination Inhibition Test [*Immunology*]
TRCHII Tanned Red Cell Hemagglutination Inhibition Immunoasay [*Immunology*] (PDAA)
Trchmrk Torchmark Corp. [*Associated Press*] (SAG)
TRCI Technology Research [*NASDAQ symbol*] (TTSB)
TRCI Technology Research Corp. [*Clearwater, FL*] [*NASDAQ symbol*] (NQ)
TRCK Truck
TRCKNG Trucking
TRCO Technical Representative of the Contracting Officer (MCD)
TRCO Transportation Research Command [*Army*] (KSC)
Tr Co Trust Company (MHDB)
TRCONS Theater Rate Consolidation Data File [*Military*]
Tr Consist J Tristram's Consistory Judgments [*1872-90*] [*England*] [*A publication*] (DLA)
TRCP Tape Recorder Control Panel (MCD)
TRCR Tracer (MSA)
TRCR Tractor
TRCR Trail Riders of the Canadian Rockies (EA)
TRCR Transcend Services [*NASDAQ symbol*] (TTSB)
TRCR Transcend Services, Inc. [*NASDAQ symbol*] (SAG)
Tr-Cro Trichromatic (DGA)
TRCS Tactical Radio Communications System
TRCS Techniques for Determining RADAR Cross Section [*Air Force*]
TRCS Traffic Reporting and Control System (NITA)
TRC-SC Transmit/Receive Control Unit-Synchronous Character
TRC-SF Transmit/Receive Control Unit-Synchronous Framing
TRCTR Tractor
TRCV Total Red Cell Volume [*Immunology*] (DAVI)
TRCV Tri-color Visual Approach Slope Indicator [*Aviation*] (FAAC)
TRCVR Transceiver (CET)
TRCVR Transceiver Transmitter Receiver (IAA)
TRCW Transcor Waste Services [*NASDAQ symbol*] (TTSB)
TRCW Transcor Waste Services, Inc. [*NASDAQ symbol*] (SAG)
TRD Registry of Tissue Reactions to Drugs [*Later, DETP*] (EA)
TRD Target-Recognizing Domain [*Genetics*]
TRD Taxa Referencial Diaria [*Brazil*] (ECON)
TRD Technical Requirements Document
TRD Technical Resource Document
TRD Technical Review Document (GNE)
TRD Test Requirements Document [*NASA*] (AAG)
TRD Texas Red-Conjugated Dextran [*Analytical biochemistry*]
TRD Thermo-Reactive Deposition [*Metal treating*]
TRD Thread (AAG)
TRD Three-Axis Rotational Control-Direct (SAA)
TRD Tongue-Retaining Device [*Medicine*]
TRD Toyota Racing Development [*Toyota Motor Corp.*]
TRD Traction Retinal Detachment [*Ophthalmology*] (DAVI)
Trd Trade (BARN)
TRD Trade
TRD Transferred (ROG)
TRD Trans Island Air [*Barbados*] [*ICAO designator*] (FAAC)
TRD Transit Routing Domain (TNIG)
TRD Transmission Ratio Distortion [*Genetics*]
TRD Trapped Radiation Detector
TRD Tread
Trd Trinidad (BARN)
TRD Trivandrum [*India*] [*Seismograph station code, US Geological Survey*] (SEIS)
TRD Trondheim [*Norway*] [*Airport symbol*] (OAG)
TRD Trouble Reporting Desk [*NASA*] (KSC)
TRD Troudor Resources, Inc. [*Vancouver Stock Exchange symbol*]
TRD Try Repeating Dose [*Medicine*]
TRD Turbine Reduction Drive
TRD United States Army TRADOC, Fort Dix Post Library, Fort Dix, NJ [*OCLC symbol*] (OCLC)
TRDAC Timber Research and Development Advisory Council [*Australia*]
TRDC Tobacco Research and Development Council [*Australia*]
TRDC Transport Research and Development Command [*Army*] (MCD)
TRDCR Tandem-Rocket Dual-Combustion Ramjet (MCD)
TRDE Transparent Rotating Disk Electrode [*Electrochemistry*]
TRDET Trouble Detection (IAA)
TRDG Trading (DCTA)
TRDI Trim Die (AAG)
TRDJSDOPII [*The*] Reverend Doctor Jonathan Swift, Dean of Patrick's in Ireland [*Pseudonym used by Jonathan Swift*]
TRDL Tactical Reconnaissance Data Link (MCD)
TRDM Tactical Reconnaissance Data Marking
TRDMRK Trademark
TRDO Treasury Regional Disbursing Office (AAGC)
TRDR Test Readiness Design Review
TrDrpG Tear Drop Golf Co. [*Associated Press*] (SAG)

TrDrpGf TearDrop Golf Co. [*Associated Press*] (SAG)
TRDS Towards (ROG)
TRDSMAN Tradesman
TRDT Trident Intl [*NASDAQ symbol*] (TTSB)
TRDT Trim and Drill Template (MCD)
TRDT Triple Rotating Directional Transmission [*Military*] (CAAL)
TRDTO Tracking RADAR Data Takeoff
TRDx Texas Red-Labeled Dextran [*Analytical biochemistry*]
TRDX Tridex Corp. [*NASDAQ symbol*] (SAG)
TRE Tactical Readiness Evaluation [*Submarines*] (DOMA)
TRE Tactical Receive Element (DOMA)
TRE Tactical Receive Equipment (DOMA)
TRE Tax-Response Element [*Genetics*]
TRE Telecommunications Research Establishment [*British military*] (DMA)
TRE Temperature-Resistant Element (DNAB)
TRE Tempore Regis Edwardi [*In the Time of King Edward*] [*Latin*] (DLA)
TRE Terratech Resources, Inc. [*Toronto Stock Exchange symbol*]
TRE Theologische Realenzyklopaedie [*A publication*]
TRE Thyroid Hormone Response Element [*Endocrinology*]
TRE Thyroid-Responsive Element [*Genetics*]
TRE Tidal Regenerator Engine
TRE Timing Read Error
TRE Tiree Island [*Scotland*] [*Airport symbol*] (OAG)
TRE Total Rare Earths (NRCH)
TRE Total Resource Effectiveness Index [*Environmental Protection Agency*]
TRE Toxicity Reduction Evaluation
TRE Training Equipment (KSC)
TRE Training Readiness Evaluation (MCD)
TRE Training-Related Expenses [*Work Incentive Program*]
TRE Trans-Eastern Airlines Ltd. [*Kenya*] [*ICAO designator*] (FAAC)
TRE Transient Radiation Effects
TRE Transmit Reference Equivalent (NITA)
TRE Treasury
TRE Tremont Corp. [*NYSE symbol*] (SPSG)
TRE Trente [*Italy*] [*Seismograph station code, US Geological Survey Closed*] (SEIS)
TRE Trent University [*UTLAS symbol*]
TRE True Radiation Emittance
TRE Type Rating Examiner [*Aviation*] (DA)
TRE United States Army TRADOC, Fort Eustis Post Library and Translation School Library, Fort Eustis, VA [*OCLC symbol*] (OCLC)
TREA [*The*] Retired Enlisted Association (EA)
TREA Triethanolamine [*Medicine*] (DMAA)
TREA & A [*The*] Real Estate Appraiser and Analyst [*Society of Real Estate Appraisers*] [*A publication*]
Tread Treadway's South Carolina Constitutional Reports [*A publication*] (DLA)
Tread Treadway's South Carolina Law Reports [*1812-16*] [*A publication*] (DLA)
TREAD Troop Recognition and Detection (MCD)
Treadco Treadco, Inc. [*Associated Press*] (SAG)
Tread Const Treadway's South Carolina Constitutional Reports [*A publication*] (DLA)
Treadway Const (SC) Treadway's South Carolina Constitutional Reports [*A publication*] (DLA)
TREAS Treasure
TREAS Treasurer (EY)
treas Treasurer (DD)
treas Treasury (VRA)
TREAS Treasury (ROG)
Treas Dec Treasury Decisions under Customs and Other Laws [*United States*] [*A publication*] (DLA)
Treas Dec Int Rev Treasury Decisions under Internal Revenue Laws [*A publication*] (DLA)
TREAS DEPT Department of the Treasury
Treas Dept Cir Treasury Department Circular [*A publication*] (DLA)
Treas Regs United States Treasury Regulations [*A publication*] (DLA)
TREAT Transient Radiation Effects Automated Tabulation
TREAT Transient Reactor Test Facility
TREAT Treatment (AAG)
TrEAT Trial for Early Alcohol Treatment
TREAT Trouble Report Evaluation and Analysis Tool (MCD)
Treat Tro Treatise on Trover and Conversion [*A publication*] (DLA)
TREB Treble (ROG)
TREC Text Retrieval Conference [*Sponsored by National Institute of Standards and Technology*]
TREC Total Rosette-Forming Cell [*Medicine*] (DMAA)
TREC Tracking RADAR Electronic Component (AFM)
TREC Transistor Radiation Effects Compilation [*Program*] (MCD)
TRECOM Transportation Research and Engineering Command (MUGU)
TRECOM Transportation Research Command [*Fort Eustis, VA*] [*Army*]
TRED TDA [*Taxpayer Delinquent Account*] Report Edit Data [*IRS*]
TRED Technology-Based Regional Economic Development
TRED Transmitting and Receiving Equipment Development (MCD)
TRED Treadco, Inc. [*NASDAQ symbol*] (SPSG)
Tred Tredgold's Cape Colony Reports [*A publication*] (DLA)
TREDAT Tree Crops Database
Tredgar Tredegar Industries [*Associated Press*] (SAG)
Tredgar Tredegar Industries, Inc. [*Associated Press*] (SAG)
TREDS TRADOC Educational Data System
TREDS-NRI TRADOC [*Training and Doctrine Command*] Educational Data System - Nonresident Instruction [*Army*]
TREE Doubletree Corp. [*NASDAQ symbol*] (SAG)
TREE Teacher Recruitment for Educational Excellence (EDAC)
TREE Transient Radiation Effects on Electronics [*Military*]
TREE Tropical Rainforest Ecology Experiment (USDC)
TREE Tropical Rainforest Ecology Experiment [*Marine science*] (OSRA)
TREE Trustee
TREELS Time-Resolved Electron Energy-Loss Spectroscopy
TREES Time-Resolved Europium Excitation Spectroscopy
TREES Transient Radiation Effects on Electronic Systems [*Air Force*] (MCD)
TREESHIP Trusteeship [*Legal shorthand*] (LWAP)
TREESS Tactical Reflected and Emitted Energy Suppression System
TREF Temperature Rising Elution Fractionation [*Analytical chemistry*]
Trehern British and Colonial Prize Cases [*A publication*] (DLA)
TREK Touring Riders Emergency Kare [*An association*]
TREKZINE Trek Magazine [*Generic term for a publication of interest to fans of the television program "Star Trek"*]
TREM Tape Reader Emulator Module
TREM TRADOC Research Center [*Monterey, CA*] [*Army*] (GRD)
Trem Tremaine's Pleas of the Crown [*England*] [*A publication*] (DLA)
trem Tremolo [*Tremulous*] [*Music*] (WGA)
TREM Tropical Rainfall Explorer Mission (MCD)
Tremnt Tremont Corp. [*Associated Press*] (SAG)
TREMORS Tsunami Risk Evaluation through Seismic Moment from Real-Time System [*Marine science*] (OSRA)
Trem PC Tremaine's Pleas of the Crown [*England*] [*A publication*] (DLA)
tren Trendelenburg [*Position*] [*Surgery*] (DAVI)
TREN Trenwick Group [*NASDAQ symbol*] (TTSB)
TREN Trenwick Group, Inc. [*NASDAQ symbol*] (NQ)
tren Tris(aminoethyl)amine [*Organic chemistry*]
TREND Trade-Offs for Lifting Reentry Vehicle Evaluation and Nominal Design
Trend Trendelenburg (MEDA)
TREND Tropical Environmental Data
TrendL Trend-Lines, Inc. [*Associated Press*] (SAG)
TR (Eng) Term Reports [*99-101 English Reprint*] [*A publication*] (DLA)
TRENS Transcutaneous Random Electrical Nerve Stimulator [*Medicine*]
Trenton St C Trenton State College (GAGS)
TrentS Trenton Savings Bank [*Associated Press*] (SAG)
Trep Treponema [*Microbiology*]
Tr Eq Fonblanque's Treatise of Equity [*A publication*] (DLA)
TRER Transient Radiation Effect on Radiation (SAA)
TRES Tayside Rehabilitation Engineering Services [*British*] (IRUK)
TRES Terminal Replacement and Enquiry System (NITA)
TRES Terminal Retrieval and Enquiry Services [*Department of Employment*] [*British*]
TRES Thermally Regenerative Electrochemical System [*Power source*]
TRES Time-Resolved Emission Spectra
TRES Treasurer
TRES TresCom International [*NASDAQ symbol*] (TTSB)
TRES TresCom International, Inc. [*NASDAQ symbol*] (SAG)
TRES Trestle (WGA)
TresCom TresCom International, Inc. [*Associated Press*] (SAG)
TRESI Target Resolution Extraction of Statistical Invariances
TRESNET Trent Interlibrary Loan and Communication Network [*Canada Information service or system*] (IID)
TRESNET Trent Resource Sharing Network [*Ontario Library Service Trent*] [*Richmond Hill, ON*] [*Telecommunications*] (TSSD)
TREVI Terrorisme, Radicalisme, Extremisme, Violence Internationale [*International anti-terrorist group*] [*Belgium*]
Trev Tax Suc Trevor's Taxes on Succession [*4th ed.*] [*1881*] [*A publication*] (DLA)
TREX Transnational Re'A' [*NASDAQ symbol*] (TTSB)
TREX Transnational Re Corp. [*NASDAQ symbol*] (SAG)
Trex Tyrannosaurus Rex [*A dinosaur*]
TrexMed Trex Medical Corp. [*Associated Press*] (SAG)
TRF Air Transafrik Ltd. [*Ghana*] [*ICAO designator*] (FAAC)
TRF Tank Range-Finder
TRF Tariff
TRF T-Cell Replacing Factor [*Biochemistry*]
TRF Teacher Rating Form (EDAC)
TRF Technical Reference File
TRF Technical Replacement Factor
TRF Tele-Radio Systems Ltd. [*Toronto Stock Exchange symbol*]
TRF Telomeric Repeat-Binding Factor [*Genetics*]
TRF Templeton Russia Fund [*NYSE symbol*] (SAG)
TRF Terminal Renal Failure [*Medicine*]
TRF Terminal Restriction Fragment [*Genetics*]
TRF Terminal Restriction Fragment [*Cytology*]
TRF Terrestrial Radio Frequency
TRF Test Tube and Ring-Shaped Forms [*AIDS cytology*]
TRF Thermal Radiation at Microwave Frequencies
TRF Thymus Cell Replacing Factor [*Immunology*]
TRF Thymus-Dependent Cell-Replacing Factor [*Hematology*] (DAVI)
TRF Thyrotrophin-Releasing Factor [*Later, TRH*] [*Endocrinology*]
TRF Tissue Respiratory Factors [*Medicine*]
TRF Tragicorum Romanorum Fragmenta [*A publication*] (OCD)
TRF Transducer Repair Facility
TRF Transfer (AABC)
TRF Transferrin [*Also, T, TF*] [*Biochemistry*]
TRF Transportation Research Forum (EA)
TRF Transportation Research Foundation
TRF Tropical Forest Program (EERA)
TRF Tuna Research Foundation (EA)
TRF Tuned Radio Frequency
trf Tuned Radio Frequency (IDOE)
TRF Turf Research Foundation [*Defunct*] (EA)

TRF United States Army TRADOC, Fort McClellan, Fort McClellan, AL [*OCLC symbol*] (OCLC)
TRFA Triple Revolving Fund Account (AABC)
TRFAD Thomas Roderick Fraser and Andrew Dewar [*Pseudonym*]
TRFB Tariff Board [*Canada*]
TRFC Tanya Roberts Fan Club (EA)
TRFC Tex Ritter Fan Club (EA)
TRFC Total Rosette-Forming Cell [*Laboratory science*] (DAVI)
TRFC Traffic (MSA)
TRFC Traffic
TRFC Tristan Rogers Fan Club [*Defunct*] (EA)
TRFCA Tea Research Foundation (Central Africa) [*Malawi*] (EAIO)
TRFCS Temperature Rate Flight Control System
TRFD Tramford International Ltd. [*NASDAQ symbol*] (SAG)
Trfd Transferred [*Army*]
TRFI Trans Financial [*NASDAQ symbol*] (TTSB)
TRFI Trans Financial Bancorp, Inc. [*Bowling Green, KY*] [*NASDAQ symbol*] (NQ)
TR/FLRES Transferred to Fleet Reserve (DNAB)
TR Fnc TR Financial Corp. [*Associated Press*] (SAG)
TRFO Time Resolved Fluorescence Spectroscopy
TRFS Trace Fuselage Station (MCD)
TRFW Tramford International Ltd. [*NASDAQ symbol*] (SAG)
TRFY Trafficway [*Postal Service standard*] (OPSA)
TRFY Trafficway
TRG Atlantic Island Air [*Iceland*] [*ICAO designator*] (FAAC)
TRG [*The*] Record Group [*Funded by N. V. Philips*]
TRG Tactical Reconnaissance Group
TRG Tauranga [*New Zealand*] [*Airport symbol*] (OAG)
TRG T-Cell Rearranging Gene [*Genetics*]
TRG Technical Research Group, Inc. (MCD)
TRG Technical Review Group
TRG Telecommunications Research Group [*Culver City, CA*] [*Telecommunications*] (TSSD)
TRG Tertiary Research Group [*British*]
TRG Tory Reform Group [*British*] (DBA)
TRG Track-Rich Grains [*s*] [*Cosmic-ray path in meteorites*]
TRG Trailing (AAG)
TRG Training
trg Triangle (BARN)
TRG Trilogy Resource Corp. [*Toronto Stock Exchange symbol*]
TRG Triton Research Group (EA)
TRG Trudeau, R. G., Bloomfield Hills MI [*STAC*]
TRG Tuned Rotor Gyro (MCD)
TRG United States Army TRADOC, Fort Benning Post and Infantry School Library, Fort Benning, GA [*OCLC symbol*] (OCLC)
TrGasSur Transportadora de Gas Del Sur SA [*Associated Press*] (SAG)
TRGB Tail Rotor Gearbox [*Aviation*] (DA)
TRGC Theta Rho Girls' Club (EA)
TrgGpRM Training Group, Royal Marines [*British*]
TRGH Trough [*Freight*]
TRGI Trident Rowan Group [*NASDAQ symbol*] (SAG)
TRGI Triglycerides Incalculable [*Laboratory science*] (DAVI)
TRGL Toreador Royalty [*NASDAQ symbol*] (TTSB)
TRGL Toreador Royalty Corp. [*NASDAQ symbol*] (NQ)
TRGP Tactical Reconnaissance Group [*Air Force*]
TRGT Target (AAG)
TRH Airmark Aviation, Inc. [*ICAO designator*] (FAAC)
TRH Technical Reference Handbook
TRH Test Requirements Handbook (MUGU)
TRH Their Royal Highnesses
TRH Thyrotrophin-Releasing Hormone [*Formerly, TRF*] [*Endocrinology*]
TRH Transatlantic Holdings [*NYSE symbol*] (SPSG)
TRH Truss Head [*Engineering*]
TRH United States Army TRADOC, Fort Benjamin Harrison Library System, Fort Benjamin Harrison, IN [*OCLC symbol*] (OCLC)
TRHAZCON Training Hazardous Condition (MCD)
TRHD Twin-Row High-Density [*Trees*] (DICI)
TRH-R Thyrotrophin-Releasing Hormone Receptor [*Endocrinology*]
TRI Bristol, TN [*Location identifier FAA*] (FAAL)
TRI [*The*] Refractories Institute (EA)
TRI Tactical Reconnaissance/Intelligence [*Air Force*] (AFM)
TRI Technical Report Instruction (AAG)
TRI Technical Research Institute [*Japan*]
TRI Telecomputer Research, Inc. [*Bala Cynwyd, PA*] [*Information service or system Telecommunications*] (TSSD)
TRI Telemanagement Resources International, Inc. (TSSD)
TRI Test Requirement Identification (DNAB)
TRI Tetrazolium Reduction Inhibition (MAE)
TRI Textile Research Institute (EA)
TRI Time-Reversal Invariance [*Physics*]
TRI Tin Research Institute (EA)
TRI Tire Retreading Institute (EA)
TRI Torsion Reaction Integrating
TRI Total Response Index [*Psychology*]
TRI Toxic Chemical Release Inventory [*National Library of Medicine*] [*Information service or system*] (CRD)
TRI Toxic Release Inventory [*Environmental Protection Agency*]
TRI Toxics Release Inventory [*Environmental Protection Agency*]
TRI Transaction Routing Index
TRI Translation Research Institute (EA)
TR-I Translations Register - Index (MCD)
TRI Transmission Interface Converter (IAA)
TRI Transpacific Resources, Inc. [*Toronto Stock Exchange symbol*]
TRI Transponder Receiver Isolation
TRI Transportation Research Institute [*Carnegie-Mellon University*]
TRI Transportation Research Institute [*Oregon State University*] [*Research center*] (RCD)
TRI Triangle
Tri Triangulation
Tri Triangulum [*Constellation*]
TRI Triassic [*Period, era, or system*] [*Geology*]
TRI Trichloroethylene [*Anesthesiology*]
TRI Trichloroethylene [*A solvent*] [*Chemistry*] (DAVI)
TRI Tri-City Airport [*Tennessee*] [*Airport symbol*] (OAG)
TRI Triclinic [*Crystallography*] (IAA)
TRI Tri-College Library, Moorhead, MN [*OCLC symbol*] (OCLC)
TRI Tricycle (AAG)
TRI Trieste [*Grotta Gigante*] [*Italy*] [*Seismograph station code, US Geological Survey*] (SEIS)
TRI Trinet Corporate Realty Trust [*NYSE symbol*] (SPSG)
TRI Triode (AAG)
TRI TrNet Corporate Rlty Tr [*NYSE symbol*] (TTSB)
TRI Tropical Research Institute [*Smithsonian Institution*]
TRI Tropical Resources Institute [*Yale University*] [*Research center*] (RCD)
TRI Trucking Research Institute [*Research center*] (RCD)
TRI Tuboreticular Inclusions [*Hematology*]
TRI Tubuloreticular Inclusion [*Medicine*] (DAVI)
TRIA Target Radiant Intensity, Aerobee (SAA)
TRIA Telemetry Range Instrumentation Aircraft
TRIA Temperature Removable Instrument Assembly [*Nuclear energy*] (NRCH)
TRIA Tracking Range Instrumented Aircraft (PDAA)
TRIA Triacontanol [*Plant growth regulator*]
Tria Triangulum [*Constellation*]
TRIAC Test Resources Improvement Advisory Council [*Military*]
TRIAC Triiodothyroacetic Acid [*Endocrinology*]
TRIAC Triode Alternating Current (IAA)
TRIAC Triode Alternating Current Semiconductor Switch
TRIAD Target Resolving Information Augmentation Device (MCD)
TriadGty Triad Guaranty, Inc. [*Associated Press*] (SAG)
TriadSy Triad Systems Corp. [*Associated Press*] (SAG)
TRIAL Technique to Retrieve Information from Abstracts of Literature [*Computer science*]
Trial Advoc Q Trial Advocate Quarterly [*A publication*] (DLA)
Trial Law Forum Trial Lawyers Forum [*A publication*] (DLA)
TrianBc Triangle Bancorp [*Associated Press*] (SAG)
Triarc Triarc Co. [*Associated Press*] (SAG)
TRIASS Triumph Adler Assembler (IAA)
TriathB Triathalon Broadcasting Co. [*Associated Press*] (SAG)
TRIB Tire Retread Information Bureau (EA)
TRIB Transfer Rate of Information BITs [*Binary Digits*] [*Dial telephone network American National Standards Institute*]
TRIB Tribal
TRIB Tribulation (DSUE)
Trib Tribunal
Trib Tribunale [*Ordinary Court of First Instance*] [*Italian*] (DLA)
TRIB Tribunus [*Tribune*] [*Latin*] (OCD)
trib Tribus [*Tribe*] [*Latin*]
TRIB Tributary
TRIB Tribute (ADA)
TRIB Trinity Biotech [*NASDAQ symbol*] (SAG)
Trib Bks Tribune Books [*A publication*] (BRI)
TRIBE Teaching and Research in Bicultural Education [*Indian organization in Maine*]
TriBeCa Triangle Below Canal Street [*Artists' colony in New York City*] [*See also NoHo, SoHo, SoSo*]
Tri Bish Trial of the Seven Bishops [*A publication*] (DLA)
TRIB POT Tribunicia Potestas [*Latin*] (OCD)
Tribune [*The*] Tribune Co. [*Associated Press*] (SAG)
TRIBY Trinity Biotech plc ADS [*NASDAQ symbol*] (TTSB)
TRIC Television and Radio Industry Club [*British*] (DBA)
TRIC Trachoma-Inclusion Conjunctivitis [*Ophthalmology*]
TRIC Tracking RADAR Input and Correlation (MSA)
TRIC Transaction Identification Code [*Military*] (AFIT)
TRIC Transition Radiation and Ionization Calorimeter (SSD)
TRIC Transit Research Information Center [*Department of Transportation*] [*Washington, DC*] (GRD)
TRIC Tri-Camera (IAA)
TRIC Trichloroethylene [*A solvent*] [*Chemistry*] (DAVI)
TRIC Tricks for Research in Cancer
TRIC Triclinic [*Crystallography*]
TRIC Tri County Bancorp [*NASDAQ symbol*] (SAG)
Tric Tricycle [*A publication*]
TRICAP Triple Capability [*Army*]
TRICAP Triple Capacity Division [*Army*] (VNW)
triCB Trichlorobiphenyl [*Chemistry*] (DAVI)
TRICC Tariff Rules of the Interstate Commerce Commission
TRICCSMA Trident Command and Control Systems Maintenance Facility (DNAB)
TRICE Textile Care and Rental Industry Council for Education (AIE)
TRICE Transistorized Real-Time Incremental Computer
TRICE Transistorized Real-Time Incremental Computer Expandable (IAA)
TRICH Trichinosis [*Gastroenterology*] (DAVI)
Trich Trichomonas [*A protozoan*] [*Medicine*]
Trich Trichoptera [*Entomology*]
Tri-Chro Trichromatic (DGA)
Trich V Trichomonas Vaginitis [*A parasite*] (DAVI)
TRICI Trichinopoli Cigar (DSUE)
TRICINE Tris(hydroxymethyl)methylglycine [*Biochemical analysis*]

TRICL Triclinic
tricl Triclinium (VRA)
TriCn Tri-Continental Corp. [*Associated Press*] (SAG)
TriCnty Tri County Bancorp [*Associated Press*] (SAG)
TRICO Tri- [*or Triple*] Coincidence Navigation (IAA)
TriCoBn Trico Bancshares [*Commercial firm Associated Press*] (SAG)
TricoMr Trico Marine Services, Inc. [*Associated Press*] (SAG)
TRICOMS Triad Computer Systems (DOMA)
TriCon Tri-Continental Corp. [*Associated Press*] (SAG)
Tricord Tricord Systems, Inc. [*Associated Press*] (SAG)
TRICS Threat Reactive Integrated Combat System
TRICS Trajectory Incremental Correction System (MCD)
TRID Track Identity
TRID Trident Microsystems [*NASDAQ symbol*] (SAG)
TRID Triduum [*Three Days*] [*Latin*] (ADA)
TRIDAC Three-Dimensional Analog Computer [*British*] (MCD)
TRIDECC Three (TRI) Dimensional Error Correcting Code (NITA)
TRIDENT South Atlantic Cooperative Investigation Phase [*Marine science*] (MSC)
TridentR Trident Rowan Group [*Associated Press*] (SAG)
Tridex Tridex Corp. [*Associated Press*] (SAG)
TridMic Trident Microsystems, Inc. [*Associated Press*] (SAG)
TRIDO Table Ronde Internationale pour le Developpement de l'Orientation [*International Round Table for the Advancement of Counselling - IRTAC*] (EAIO)
TRIDOP Tridoppler
Tri E of Cov Trial of the Earl of Coventry [*A publication*] (DLA)
TRI-FED Triathlon Federation/USA (EA)
TRIFED/USA Triathlon Federation/USA [*Later, TRI-FED*] (EA)
TRIFLATE Trifluoromethanesulfonate [*Organic chemistry*]
TRIFLIC Trifluoromethanesulfonic [*Organic chemistry*]
triFMA Time-Resolved Immunofluorometric Assay [*Clinical chemistry*]
trifr Triforium (VRA)
TRIG Triangulation (AABC)
TRIG Trigger (AAG)
trig Triglycerides [*Clinical chemistry*]
TRIG Trigonal [*Crystallography*]
trig Trigonometric (IDOE)
trig Trigonometry (IDOE)
TRIG Trigonometry
TRIGA Training Reactor, Isotopes General Atomic [*Nuclear energy*]
TRIGA Traitement Industrial des Gadoues [*French company*]
TRIGAT Third Generation Antitank [*Army*]
TrigenE Trigen Energy Corp. [*Associated Press*] (SAG)
TRIGLYME Triethylene Glycol Dimethyl Ether [*Organic chemistry*]
TRIGON Trigonometry (ROG)
TRIGS TR-1 [*Aircraft*] Ground Station [*Air Force*] (DOMA)
TRII Transcrypt International, Inc. [*NASDAQ symbol*] (SAG)
TRIL Tailored Requirements Items List (MCD)
Tri-Lite Tri-Lite, Inc. [*Associated Press*] (SAG)
TRIM Tailored Reliable Integrated Modular
TRIM Tailored Retrieval and Information Management
TRIM Target Radiant Intensity Measurement (MCD)
TRIM Targets, Receivers, Impacts, and Methods
TRIM Task Related Instructional Methodology (PDAA)
TRIM Tax Reform Immediately (EA)
TRIM Tax Reform Information Materials
TRIM Technical Requirements Identification Matrix (MCD)
TRIM Technique for Report and Index Management [*No longer available*] [*Information service or system*] (IID)
TRIM Technique for Responsive Inventory Management (MHDB)
TRIM Tele-Research Item Movement, Inc. [*Commercial firm*] (WDMC)
TRIM Test Rules for Inventory Management
TRIM Thin Region Integral Method
TRIM Throw Away/Repair Implications on Maintenance
TRIM Timely Responsive Integrated Multiuse System (MCD)
TRIM Trails, Roads, and Interdiction Missions [*or Multisensor*] Program [*Navy*]
TRIM Training Relation and Instruction Mission [*Vietnam, France, United States*] [*Military*]
TRIM Training Requirements and Information Management System [*Navy*]
TRIM Transfer Income Model [*Department of Health and Human Services*] (GFGA)
TRIM Transformation of Imagery [*Computer science NASA*]
TRIM Tri-Mask Process (IAA)
TRIM Trimmer [*Mining engineering*]
TRI-M Tri-M Music Honor Society [*Modern Music Masters Society*] [*Acronym is based on former name,*] (EA)
trim arh Triumphal Arch (VRA)
Trimark Trimark Holdings, Inc. [*Associated Press*] (SAG)
Trimas TriMas Corp. [*Associated Press*] (SAG)
Trimble Trimble Navigation Ltd. [*Associated Press*] (SAG)
Trimed Trimedyne, Inc. [*Associated Press*] (SAG)
TRIMET Trimethylolethane [*Organic chemistry*]
TRIMIS Tri-Service Medical Information Systems [*Military*]
TRIMM Triple Missile Mount (MCD)
TRIMMS Telecom Canada Remote Interface Monitoring and Management System
TRIMMS Total Refinement and Integration of Maintenance Management Systems [*Army*]
TRIMS Trade-Related Investment Measures [*International finance*] (ECON)
TRIMS Training Requirements and Information Management System (MCD)
TRIMS Transportation Integrated Management System [*Air Force*]
TRIN Trading Index [*Short term*] (MHDW)
TRIN Trans International Airlines
Trin Trinidad
TRIN Trinity
Trin Trinity Term [*British Legal term*] (DLA)
TRINCO Trincomalee [*Sri Lanka port city*] (DSUE)
TriNet Trinet Corporate Realty Trust [*Associated Press*] (SAG)
Trinidad LR Trinidad Law Reports [*A publication*] (DLA)
Trinitech Trinitech Systems, Inc. [*Associated Press*] (SAG)
Trinity C Trinity College (GAGS)
TrinityIn Trinity Industries, Inc. [*Associated Press*] (SAG)
Trinity U Trinity University (GAGS)
Trinova Trinova Corp. [*Associated Press*] (SAG)
Trint T Trinity Term [*British Legal term*] (DLA)
TRIO Transplant Recipients International Organization (EA)
Trion Trion, Inc. [*Associated Press*] (SAG)
TRIOS Thermionic Reactor for Installed Oceanic Service (KSC)
TrioTch Trio-Tech International [*Associated Press*] (SAG)
Trip All India Reporter, Tripura [*A publication*] (DLA)
TRIP [*The*] Road Information Program (EA)
TRIP Tartar Reliability Improvement Plan [*Military*]
TRIP Technical Reports Indexing Project (KSC)
TRIP Terrier/Tartar Reliability Improvement Program (SAA)
TRIP Test Requirement Implementation Plan (CAAL)
TRIP Thunderstorm Research International Project [*Meteorology*]
TRIP Total Replenishment Inventory Program (PDAA)
TRIP Toxic Release Inventory Program (GNE)
TRIP Trade-Related Aspects of Intellectual Property Right
TRIP Trajectory Integration Program (PDAA)
TRIP Transformation and Identification Program [*Commercial & Industrial Development Bureau*] [*Software package*] (NCC)
TRIP Transformation-Induced Plasticity [*Steel*]
TRIP Translating Research into Practice
TRIP Transport Infrastructure Programme [*EDF*]
TRIP Triangle Pacific [*NASDAQ symbol*] (TTSB)
TRIP Triangle Pacific Corp. [*NASDAQ symbol*] (SAG)
TRIP Triplicate (AABC)
Trip Tripoli
Trip Tripolitania [*Libya*] (BJA)
TRIP Truck Routing Improvement Program (IAA)
TriPacf Triangle Pacific Corp. [*Associated Press*] (SAG)
TRIPER Trident Planned Equipment Replacement (DNAB)
Tri per P Trials per Pais [*A publication*] (DLA)
TRIPI Tactical Reconnaissance Information Processing and Interpretation (SAA)
Tripl Triplicate (WGA)
Triple-A Adult Alternative Album [*Radio stations*]
TripleP Triple P [*Associated Press*] (SAG)
TripleS Triple S Plastics Co. [*Associated Press*] (SAG)
TRipLH Lauderdale County Hospital, Ripley, TN [*Library symbol Library of Congress*] (LCLS)
TRIPLTEE True Temperature Tunnel [*Acronym pronounced, "Triple T"*]
TRIPOD Tactical Reconstruction Information Pod [*Navy*] (ANA)
TRIPOD Transit Injector Polaris Derived (AAG)
TRIPOLD Transit Injector Polaris Derived
TriPolyta Tri Polyta Indonesia [*Associated Press*] (SAG)
Tripos Tripos, Inc. [*Associated Press*] (SAG)
Tripp Tripp's Reports [*5, 6 Dakota*] [*A publication*] (DLA)
TRIPREC Triplet Recall [*Neuropsychology test*]
TRIPS TALON Reporting and Information Processing System (NITA)
TRIPS Trade-Related Intellectual Property (ECON)
TRIPS Transformation-Induced Plasticity (Steel)
TRIPS Transportation Intelligent Planning System [*MTMC*] (TAG)
TRIPS Transportation Planning Suite [*MVA Systematica*] [*Software package*] (NCC)
TRIPS Travel Information Processing System (NITA)
TRIPS Triplets [*Slang*] (DSUE)
Triquint Triquint Semiconductor, Inc. [*Associated Press*] (SAG)
TRIREFFAC Trident Refit Facility (DNAB)
TRIS Target Radiant Spectral Intensity Measurements from a Spin-Stabilized Vehicle (SAA)
TRIS Toxic Release Inventory System [*Environmental Protection Agency*]
TRIS Tracking RADAR Instrumentation Ship (SAA)
TRIS Transmit-Receive Image System (DNAB)
TRIS Transportation Research Information Services [*National Academy of Sciences*] [*Bibliographic database*] [*Washington, DC*]
Tris Tris(2,3-dibromopropyl)phosphate [*Also, TDBP, TDBPP, Tris-BP*] [*Flame retardant, mutagen*]
TRIS Tris(hydroxymethyl)aminomethane [*Also, THAM*] [*Biochemical analysis*]
Tris Trito-Isaiah (BJA)
TRI-SACH Tri-State Automated Clearing House Association (MHDB)
TRISAFE Triple Redundancy Incorporating Self-Adaptive Failure Exclusion (MCD)
TRISAT Target Recognition through Integral Spectrum Analysis Techniques (MCD)
Tris-BP Tris(2,3-dibromopropyl)phosphate [*Also, TDBP, TDBPP, Tris*] [*Flame retardant, mutagen*]
TRISECT Total Reconnaissance Intelligence System Evaluation and Comparison Technique (MCD)
Trism Trism, Inc. [*Associated Press*] (SAG)
TRISNET Transportation Research Information Services Network [*Department of Transportation*] [*Library network*]
Tris Pr Pr Tristram's Probate Practice [*25th ed.*] [*1978*] [*A publication*] (DLA)
TRISS Tactical Reconnaissance Intelligence Support Squadron
Trist Supplement to 4 Swabey and Tristram's Probate and Divorce Reports [*England*] [*A publication*] (DLA)

TRIST.......... Traveling Image Storage Tube (MCD)
Trist.......... Tristram's Consistory Judgments [*England*] [*A publication*] (DLA)
TRISTAN...... Terridic Reactor Isotope Separator To Analze Nuclides [*Brookhaven National Laboratory*]
Tristar.......... Tristar Corp. [*Associated Press*] (SAG)
Tristram....... Tristram's Consistory Judgments [*1872-90*] [*A publication*] (DLA)
Tristram....... Tristram's Probate Practice [*25th ed.*] [*1978*] [*A publication*] (DLA)
Tristram....... Tristram's Supplement to 4 Swabey and Tristram [*A publication*] (DLA)
TRISYLL...... Trisyllable (ROG)
TRIT.......... Triiodothyronine [*Endocrinology*] (MAE)
TRIT.......... Tritura [*Triturate*] [*Pharmacy*]
TRITAC........ DIFAR Triangular Tactic (NVT)
TRITAC........ Tri-Service Tactical Communications System [*DoD*]
TRITAC........ Triservice Tactical Switch
TRITB.......... Tasmanian Retail Industry Training Board [*Australia*]
TRITB.......... Tasmanian Rural Industry Training Board [*Australia*]
TRITC.......... Tetramethyl Rhodamine Isothiocyanate [*Organic chemistry*]
TriTeal........ TriTeal Corp. [*Associated Press*] (SAG)
TritEng........ Triton Energy Corp. [*Associated Press*] (SAG)
TRITET........ Triode-Tetrode (IAA)
Triton.......... Triton Group Ltd. [*Associated Press*] (SAG)
TRITRAFAC... Trident Training Facility (DNAB)
TRIUMF....... Tri-University-Meson Facility [*Nuclear research facility at the University of British Columbia*]
TRIUN.......... Department of Trusteeship and Information from Non-Self-Governing Territories ofthe United Nations
TRIW.......... Trinity Biotech [*NASDAQ symbol*] (SAG)
TRIWF.......... Trinity Biotech plc Wrrt'A' [*NASDAQ symbol*] (TTSB)
TRIX.......... Total Rate Imaging with X-Rays
TRIX.......... Transcom International Ltd. [*NASDAQ symbol*] (SAG)
TRIXIE......... Transistor and Nixie Tube (IAA)
TRIZ.......... Trinity Biotech [*NASDAQ symbol*] (SAG)
TrizecH........ Trizec Hahn Corp. [*Associated Press*] (SAG)
TrizecHhn.... Trizec Hahn Corp. [*Associated Press*] (SAG)
TRIZF.......... Trinity Biotech plc Wrrt'B' [*NASDAQ symbol*] (TTSB)
TRJ.......... AJT Air International [*Russian Federation*] [*ICAO designator*] (FAAC)
TRJ.......... Tarija [*Bolivia*] [*Seismograph station code, US Geological Survey*] (SEIS)
TRJ.......... Thermocouple Reference Junction
TRJ.......... Towards Racial Justice [*British*]
TRJ.......... United States Army TRADOC, Fort Jackson, Fort Jackson, SC [*OCLC symbol*] (OCLC)
Tr Judge J... Trial Judges' Journal [*A publication*] (DLA)
TRK.......... Air Truck [*Spain ICAO designator*] (FAAC)
TRK.......... Roche Products Ltd. [*Great Britain*] [*Research code symbol*]
TRK.......... Speedway Motorsports [*NYSE symbol*] (TTSB)
TRK.......... Speedway Motorsports, Inc. [*NYSE symbol*] (SAG)
TRK.......... Tank Range-Finder Kit
TRK.......... Tarakan [*Indonesia*] [*Airport symbol*] (OAG)
TRK.......... Track (AAG)
TRK.......... Transketolase [*An enzyme*] (MAE)
TRK.......... Truck (AAG)
TRK.......... Truckee, CA [*Location identifier FAA*] (FAAL)
TRK.......... Trunk (AAG)
TRK.......... United States Army TRADOC, Fort Knox, Library Service Center, RSL Section, Fort Knox, KY [*OCLC symbol*] (OCLC)
TRKA.......... Trak Auto [*NASDAQ symbol*] (TTSB)
TRKA.......... Trak-Auto Corp. [*NASDAQ symbol*] (NQ)
TRKD.......... Tracked
TRKDR........ Truck-Drawn
TRKG.......... Tracking (AAG)
TrKH.......... Die Transkriptionen des Hieronymus in Seinem Kommentarwerken [*A publication*] (BJA)
TRKHD........ Truck Head
TRKMTD...... Truck-Mounted (AABC)
TRKR.......... Tracker
TRKS.......... Track [*Commonly used*] (OPSA)
TRKWHL...... Trick Wheel
TRL.......... Tariff Reform League [*British*] (ROG)
TRL.......... Terrell, TX [*Location identifier FAA*] (FAAL)
TRL.......... Test Readiness List [*NASA*] (NASA)
TRL.......... Thermodynamics Research Laboratory [*National Institute of Standards and Technology*] (MCD)
TRL.......... Time Recovery Loop [*Navy Navigation Satellite System*] (DNAB)
TRL.......... Tool Room Lathe
TRL.......... Total Renal Care Hldgs [*NYSE symbol*] (TTSB)
TRL.......... Total Renal Care Holdings, Inc. [*NYSE symbol*] (SAG)
TRL.......... Trading Law [*British*]
TRL.......... Trail (MCD)
TRL.......... Trail
TRL.......... Training Research Laboratory [*Army Research Institute for the Behavioral and Social Sciences*] (RDA)
TRL.......... Transistor Resistor Logic
trl.......... Translator [*MARC relator code*] [*Library of Congress*] (LCCP)
TrL.......... Transmitted Light [*Microscopy*]
TRL.......... Transportation Research Laboratory
TRL.......... Transuranium Research Laboratory [*AEC*]
TRL.......... Trax Petroleums [*Vancouver Stock Exchange symbol*]
TRL.......... Trial (ROG)
TRL.......... Trillo [*Trill*] [*Music*] (ROG)
TRL.......... Trunk Register Link [*Telecommunications*] (TEL)
TRL.......... United States Department of Transportation, Library, Washington, DC [*OCLC symbol*] (OCLC)
TRLA.......... Textile Rental and Laundry Association [*Australia*]
Trla.......... Triola [*Record label*] [*Finland*]
TRLA.......... Truck Renting and Leasing Association (EA)
TRLA(NSW)... Textile Rental and Laundry Association of New South Wales [*Australia*]
TRLA(Q)....... Textile Rental and Laundry Association (Queensland) [*Australia*]
TRLA(V)....... Textile Rental and Laundry Association (Victoria) [*Australia*]
TRLAWA...... Textile Rental and Laundry Association of Western Australia
TRLB.......... Temporarily Replaced by Lighted Buoy Showing Same Characteristic [*Maps and charts*]
TRLFSW...... Tactical Range Landing Force Support Weapon
TRLP.......... Transport Landplane [*Navy*]
TRLR.......... Trailer
TRLR.......... Trailer
Tr LR.......... Trinidad Law Reports [*A publication*] (DLA)
TRLS.......... Trail [*Commonly used*] (OPSA)
TR-LSC........ Time-Resolved Liquid Scintillation Counting [*Instrumentation*]
TRLSC........ Time-Resolved Liquid Scintillation Counting [*Analytical procedure*]
TRLU.......... TISEO RADAR Logic Unit [*Air Force*] (MCD)
TRLVL.......... Transition Level [*Aviation*] (FAAC)
TRLY.......... Trolley
TRM.......... Task Response Module [*Office furniture*]
TRM.......... Tay River Petroleum [*Vancouver Stock Exchange symbol*]
TRM.......... TCW/DW Term Trust 2002 [*NYSE symbol*] (SPSG)
TRM.......... Technical Reference Model [*Army*] (RDA)
TRM.......... Technical Reference Model
TRM.......... Terminal Response Monitor
TRM.......... Test Request Message [*Computer science*]
TRM.......... Test Requirements Manual
TRM.......... Test Responsibility Matrix (MCD)
TRM.......... Theater Rates Model [*Military*]
TRM.......... Thermal, CA [*Location identifier FAA*] (FAAL)
TRM.......... Thermal Remanent Magnetization [*Geophysics*] (IEEE)
TRM.......... Thermal Resistance Measurement
TRM.......... Thermoremanence
TRM.......... Thermoremanent Magnetism [*or Magnetization*]
TRM.......... Thickness Readout Module
TRM.......... Thomason, Richland, and Martens [*Air-charter business*]
TrM.......... Three R Microfilm Service, Record Retention & Retrieval Corp., Lynbrook, NY [*Library symbol*] [*Library of Congress*] (LCLS)
TRM.......... Time Ratio Modulation
TRM.......... Time Release Mechanism [*Martin-Baker seat system*] [*Aviation*] (NG)
TRM.......... Time-Reversal Mirrors [*For acoustic study*]
TRM.......... Totally Reflective Mirror
TrM.......... Track Magnetic [*Aviation*] (DA)
TRM.......... TRADOC Resources Management (MCD)
TRM.......... TRADOC [*Training and Doctrine Command*] Review of Manpower
TRM.......... Transports Aeriens Mediterraneens [*France ICAO designator*] (FAAC)
TRM.......... Trial Run Model (SAA)
TRM.......... Turner [*Maine*] [*Seismograph station code, US Geological Survey*] (SEIS)
TRM.......... United States Army TRADOC, Fort Monroe Post Library and Headquarters Technical Library, Fort Monroe, VA [*OCLC symbol*] (OCLC)
TRMAP........ Theater Rate Mapping Data File [*Military*]
TRMB.......... Trimble Navigation Ltd. [*NASDAQ symbol*] (SAG)
TRMC.......... Tetramethylrhodamino-Isothiocyanate [*Organic chemistry*] (MAH)
TRMC.......... Time-Resolved Microwave Conductivity [*Physical chemistry*]
TRMCpy........ TRM Copy Centers Corp. [*Associated Press*] (SAG)
TRMD.......... Trimmed
TRME.......... Theater Readiness Monitoring Equipment (MCD)
TRMF.......... Test Report Management Forms (MCD)
TRMF.......... Theater Readiness Monitoring Facility [*Missile testing*]
TRMF.......... Theodore Roethke Memorial Foundation (EA)
Trmfrd.......... Tramford International Ltd. [*Associated Press*] (SAG)
TRMG.......... Tread Rubber Manufacturers Group (EA)
TRMG.......... Trimming
TRMI.......... Tubular Rivet and Machine Institute (EA)
TRMK.......... Trustmark Corp. [*NASDAQ symbol*] (SPSG)
TRML.......... Target Reference Material List [*Air Force*]
TRML.......... Terminal (AFM)
TRML.......... Tropical Research Medical Laboratory [*Army*]
TRMM.......... TRM Copy Centers [*NASDAQ symbol*] (TTSB)
TRMM.......... TRM Copy Centers Corp. [*NASDAQ symbol*] (SPSG)
TRMM.......... Tropical Rainfall Measurement Mission [*NASA*] [*Marine science*] (OSRA)
TRMM.......... Tropical Rainfall Measuring Mission [*Proposed satellite*]
TrMMex........ Transportacion Maritima Mexicana [*Associated Press*] (SAG)
TRMNL........ Terminal
TRMPS........ Temperature Regualtor and Missile Power Supply (IAA)
TRMR.......... Trimmer [*Mining engineering*]
TRMS.......... Technical Requirements Management System
TRMS.......... Test Resource Management System [*TECOM*] (RDA)
TRMS.......... Transmission Resource Management System [*Australia*]
TRMS.......... True Root Mean Square [*Statistics*]
TRM-SMX.... Trimethoprim-Sulfamethoxazole [*Medicine*] (DMAA)
TRMT.......... Termite
TRMT.......... Treatment (AFM)
TRN.......... OCLC [*Online Computer Library Center*] Training Symbol, Columbus, OH [*OCLC symbol*] (OCLC)
TR(N).......... Registered Technologist (Nuclear) (DAVI)
TRN.......... Technical Research Note (IEEE)
TRN.......... Tectoreticular Neuron [*Neurology*]
TRN.......... Temporary Record Number
TRN.......... Teriton Resources Ltd. [*Vancouver Stock Exchange symbol*]
TRN.......... Theron Airways [*South Africa ICAO designator*] (FAAC)

TRN .... Thomson Regional Newspapers [*The Thomson Corp.*] [*Publishing*]
TRN .... Three-Axis Rotational Control-Normal (SAA)
TRN .... Track Reference Number (IAA)
TRN .... Trade Name (MSA)
TRN .... Trainee
TRN .... Transfer (DEN)
TRN .... Transformation Research Network [*Canada Research center*] (RCD)
TRN .... Translation (IAA)
TRN .... Transmit (BUR)
TRN .... Trinidad [*Trinidad-Tobago*] [*Seismograph station code, US Geological Survey*] (SEIS)
TRN .... Trinity Indus [*NYSE symbol*] (TTSB)
TRN .... Trinity Industries, Inc. [*NYSE symbol*] (SPSG)
TRN .... Trunnion (NASA)
TRN .... Turin [*Italy*] [*Airport symbol*] (OAG)
tRNA .... Ribonucleic Acid, Transfer [*Replaces sRNA*] [*Biochemistry, genetics*]
TRNA .... Topolino Register of North America (EA)
tRNA .... Transfer Ribonucleic Acid (CPH)
TrnAsia .... Transmedia Asia Pacific, Inc. [*Associated Press*] (SAG)
TrnatH .... Transatlantic Holdings [*Associated Press*] (SAG)
TrnB .... Trinity Biotech [*Associated Press*] (SAG)
TrnBi .... Trinity Biotech [*Associated Press*] (SAG)
TrnBio .... Trinity Biotech [*Associated Press*] (SAG)
TRNBKL .... Turnbuckle [*Aerospace*] (AAG)
TRNC .... Turkish Republic of North Cyprus (BARN)
TRNCAP .... Training Capability [*Military*]
TRN CRD .... Turn Coordination (MSA)
TRND .... Trend-Lines'A'Inc. [*NASDAQ symbol*] (TTSB)
TRND .... Trend-Lines, Inc. [*NASDAQ symbol*] (SAG)
TRND .... Turned (MSA)
TrnDE .... Transamerica Delaware Ltd. [*Associated Press*] (SAG)
TRNE .... Trainee (AABC)
TRNFR .... Transfer (KSC)
TRNG .... Training
TRNGL .... Triangle (MSA)
TrnGlb .... Trans Global Services, Inc. [*Associated Press*] (SAG)
TrnGlbR .... Trans-Global Resources NL [*Associated Press*] (SAG)
TRNGR .... Turning Gear
TRNGRS .... Training Readiness Squadron
TRNI .... Trans-Industries, Inc. [*NASDAQ symbol*] (NQ)
TrnLsg .... Trans Leasing International, Inc. [*Associated Press*] (SAG)
TrnmdEu .... Transmedia Europe, Inc. [*Associated Press*] (SAG)
Trnmedia .... Transmedia Network, Inc. [*Associated Press*] (SAG)
TrnNtw .... Transaction Network Services [*Associated Press*] (SAG)
TRNPK .... Turnpike [*Commonly used*] (OPSA)
TRNPS .... Transpose (MSA)
TRNR .... Touche Remnant Natural Resources [*Investment fund*] [*British*]
TRNR .... Trainer (AAG)
TRNR .... Trainer
TrnReCp .... Transnational Re Corp. [*Associated Press*] (SAG)
TRNS .... Terrain-Referenced Navigation System [*Navy*]
TRNS .... Transition (AABC)
TRNS .... Transmation, Inc. [*NASDAQ symbol*] (NQ)
TrnsEn .... Trans Energy, Inc. [*Associated Press*] (SAG)
TrnsFin .... Trans Financial, Inc. [*Associated Press*] (SAG)
TRNSFR .... Transfer
TrnsglbE .... Transglobe Energy Corp. [*Associated Press*] (SAG)
TrnsGlbl .... Trans Global Services, Inc. [*Associated Press*] (SAG)
Trnskry .... Transkaryotic Therapies, Inc. [*Associated Press*] (SAG)
TrnsLx .... Trans-Lux Corp. [*Associated Press*] (SAG)
Trnsm .... Transamerica Corp. [*Associated Press*] (SAG)
Trnsmt .... Transmation, Inc. [*Associated Press*] (SAG)
TRNSMT .... Transmitter
TRNSN .... Transition (MSA)
Trnsnt .... TransNet Corp. [*Associated Press*] (SAG)
TRNSP .... Transport [*or Transportation*] (AFM)
TrnspAm .... Transport Corp. of America, Inc. [*Associated Press*] (SAG)
TRNSPF .... Transportation Flight [*Military*]
TRNSPLF .... Transportation Liaison Flight [*Military*]
TRNSPN .... Transportation (KSC)
TRNSPOPS .... Transportation Operations Squadron
TRNSPR .... Transporter (KSC)
Trnspro .... Transpro, Inc. [*Associated Press*] (SAG)
TRNSPRT .... Transport
TRNSPRTN .... Transportation
TRNSPS .... Transportation Squadron
TrnsRty .... Transcontinental Realty Investors [*Associated Press*] (SAG)
TrnsTec .... TransTechnology Corp. [*Associated Press*] (SAG)
TrnsWst .... TransAmerican Waste Industries, Inc. [*Associated Press*] (SAG)
TrnsWste .... TransAmerican Waste Industries [*Associated Press*] (SAG)
TrnSwtc .... TranSwitch Corp. [*Associated Press*] (SAG)
TrnSyA .... Transaction System Architects, Inc. [*Associated Press*] (SAG)
TRNT .... TransNet [*NASDAQ symbol*] (TTSB)
TRNT .... TransNet Corp. [*NASDAQ symbol*] (NQ)
TRNTBL .... Turntable (MSA)
TRNTY .... Trinity
Trnwck .... Trenwick Group, Inc. [*Associated Press*] (SAG)
TrnWEnt .... Trans World Entertainment Corp. [*Associated Press*] (SAG)
TR (NY) .... Caines' Term Reports [*New York*] [*A publication*] (DLA)
Trnzn .... Tranzonic Cos. [*Associated Press*] (SAG)
TRO .... Air Molokai-Tropic Airlines [*ICAO designator*] (FAAC)
TRO .... Taree [*Australia Airport symbol*] (OAG)
TRO .... Tarron Industry [*Vancouver Stock Exchange symbol*]
TRO .... Tax Reduction Option
TRO .... Technical Records Office [*or Officer*] [*British*]
TRO .... Technical Reviewing Office (AFM)
TRO .... Temporary Restraining Order
TRO .... Terminal Release Order [*Military*] (AFIT)
TRO .... Test Requirements Outline
TRO .... Transportation Officer
TRO .... Trip Reduction Ordinance [*MOCD*] (TAG)
Tro .... Troades [*of Euripides*] [*Classical studies*] (OCD)
Tro .... Troilus and Cressida [*Shakespearean work*]
TRO .... Tromsoe [*Norway*] [*Seismograph station code, US Geological Survey*] (SEIS)
TRO .... Tropical [*Broadcasting antenna*]
TRO .... Truck Route Order [*Army*] (AABC)
TRO .... United States Army TRADOC, Fort Sill Post Library, Fort Sill, OK [*OCLC symbol*] (OCLC)
TROA .... [*The*] Retired Officers Association (EA)
TROA .... Thoroughbred Racehorse Owners' Association [*Australia*]
TROC .... Tritium Removal with Organic Compound [*Nuclear energy*]
TROC .... Trocadero [*London*] (DSUE)
TROC .... Trochiscus [*Lozenge*] [*Pharmacy*] (ROG)
TROC .... Trouble Reporting Operations Center [*Federal Telecommunications System*] (GFGA)
TROCA .... Tangible Reinforcement Operant Conditioning Audiometry
TROCH .... Troche [*Lozenge*] [*Pharmacy*] (DAVI)
TROCH .... Trochiscus [*Lozenge*] [*Pharmacy*]
TRODI .... Touchdown Rate of Descent Indicator [*Aviation*]
TROFF .... Typesetting Run Off (DGA)
TROL .... Tapeless Rotorless On-Line Cryptographic Equipment (NATG)
Trol .... Troland [*Unit of light intensity at the retina*]
TROLAMINE .... Triethanolamine [*USAN*] [*Organic chemistry*]
TROLL .... Time-Shared Reactive On-Line Laboratory [*Computer science*] (MHDI)
TRO Lrn .... TRO Learning, Inc. [*Associated Press*] (SAG)
TROM .... Trombone
TROMB .... Tromba [*Trumpet*] [*Music*] (ROG)
TROMB .... Trombone
TROMEX .... Tropical Oceanographic and Meteorological Experiment [*National Science Foundation*]
TROMP .... Testable Read Only Memory Programmed [*Computer science*] (DGA)
TROMP .... Trompette [*Trumpets*] [*Music*]
TRON .... [*The*] Real-Time Operating System Nucleus [*Computer science*] (PCM)
TRON .... Trion, Inc. [*NASDAQ symbol*] (NQ)
TROO .... Transponder On-Off
TROP .... Tropical
Trop .... Tropical Agriculture [*A publication*]
TROPAG .... Tropical Agriculture [*Royal Tropical Institute*] [*Bibliographic database*] [*Netherlands*]
TROPARC .... Center for Tropical and Subtropical Architecture Planning and Construction [*University of Florida*] [*Research center*] (RCD)
TROP CAN .... Tropic of Cancer (WDAA)
TROP CAP .... Tropic of Capricorn (WDAA)
TROPEX .... Tropical Experiment [*Proposed by BOMEX*]
Trop F H .... Tropical Fish Hobbyist [*A publication*]
TROPH .... Trophy
TROPIC HEAT .... Tropical Pacific Upper Ocean Heat and Mass Budgets [*USA*] [*Marine science*] (OSRA)
TROPICS .... Tour Operators Integrated Computer System [*Airline ticket system*]
TROPM .... Tropical Man [*Leiden*] [*A publication*]
TROPMED .... Regional Project for Tropical Medicine and Public Health [*SEAMEO*] [*Thailand*] [*Research center*] (IRC)
TropMed .... Tropical Medicine (DAVI)
TROPO .... Tropospheric
TROPRAN .... Tropical Regional Analysis [*National Weather Service*]
TROS .... Tape Resident Operating System [*Computer science*] (IEEE)
TROS .... Time-Sharing Real-Time Operating System (IAA)
TROS .... Transducer Read Only Storage (IAA)
TROS .... Transformer Read Only Storage
TROSCOM .... Troop Support Command [*Formerly, MECOM*] [*St. Louis, MO*] [*Army*]
TROT .... Trail Riders of Today (EA)
TROTTS .... Theater Realignment of Traffic Transportation Support (MCD)
Troub & H Prac .... Troubat and Haly's Pennsylvania Practice [*A publication*] (DLA)
Troub Lim Partn .... Troubat on Limited Partnership [*A publication*] (DLA)
TROV .... Telepresence-Controlled Remotely-Operated Vehicle [*NASA*]
TROV .... Tethered Remotely Operational Vehicle [*Marine science*] (MSC)
TROV .... Turnip Rosette Virus [*Plant pathology*]
TROW .... T.Rowe Price Assoc [*NASDAQ symbol*] (TTSB)
TROW .... T. Rowe Price Associates, Inc. [*Baltimore, MD*] [*NASDAQ symbol*] (NQ)
Trow D & Cr .... Trower's Debtor and Creditor [*1860*] [*A publication*] (DLA)
Trow Eq .... Trower's Manual of the Prevalance of Equity [*1876*] [*A publication*] (DLA)
TroyHill .... Troy Hill Bancorp, Inc. [*Associated Press*] (SAG)
Troy St U .... Troy State University (GAGS)
Troy St U (Dorhan) .... Troy State University at Dorhan (GAGS)
TRP .... Maryland State Police [*FAA designator*] (FAAC)
TRP .... Table of Replaceable Parts
TRP .... Tamper Resistant Packaging [*Food and Drug Administration*]
TRP .... Tangible Research Property [*Business*]
TRP .... Target Rating Point [*Television*] (WDMC)
TRP .... Target Reference Point (AABC)
TRP .... Target Reporting Parameters (MCD)
TRP .... Technical Report
TRP .... Technical Requirements Package (MCD)

TRP .... Technology Reinvestment Project [*for converting military to civilian applications*]
TRP .... Television Remote Pickup
TRP .... Terminal Rendezvous Phase
TRP .... Threat Recognition Processor [*Navy*] (MCD)
TRP .... Threat Recognizer Programmer
TRP .... Thunderstorm Research Project [*Environmental Science Services Administration*]
TRP .... Timber Rights Purchase
TRP .... Time-Resolved Phosphorimetry [*Analytical chemistry*]
TRP .... Time to Repair Part
TRP .... Timing Release Pin
TRP .... Total Refractory Period (MAE)
TRP .... Trade Pattern (MSA)
TRP .... Traffic Regulation Point [*Military*]
TRP .... Trainable Retractable Propeller
TRP .... Training Review Panel (CAAL)
TRP .... TransCanada Pipeline Ltd. [*NYSE symbol Toronto Stock Exchange symbol Vancouver Stock Exchange symbol*] (SPSG)
TRP .... TransCanada P.L. [*NYSE symbol*] (TTSB)
TrP .... Transpatent [*German*] (DLA)
TRP .... Tree Point, AK [*Location identifier FAA*] (FAAL)
TRP .... Trichorhinophalangeal [*Syndrome*] (DAVI)
TRP .... Tricommand Review Panel [*Military*] (AFIT)
TRP .... Tripped
TRP .... Troop (AFM)
TRP .... Tropical (WGA)
TRP .... Trujillo [*Peru*] [*Seismograph station code, US Geological Survey*] (SEIS)
Trp .... Tryptophan [*Also, W*] [*An amino acid*]
trp .... Tryptophan [*An amino acid*] (DOG)
TRP .... Tubular Reabsorption [*or Resorption*] of Phosphate
TRPA .... Tryptophan-Rich Prealbumin [*Biochemistry*]
TrpAG97 .... Triple A Government Series 1997, Inc. [*Associated Press*] (SAG)
TRPB .... Thoroughbred Racing Protective Bureau (EA)
TRPC .... Triple Phosphate (DAVI)
TRPCAR .... Troop Carrier [*Military*] (CINC)
TRPCAR(M) ... Troop Carrier (Medium) (CINC)
TRPCD .... Tropical Continental [*Meteorology*] (FAAC)
TRPCL .... Tropical [*NWS*] (FAAC)
TRPCL .... Tropical
TRPCSq .... Troop Carrier Squadron [*Air Force*]
TRPF .... Tax Resisters' Penalty Fund (EA)
TRPGDA .... Tripropylene Glycol Diacrylate [*Organic chemistry*]
TRPH .... Total Recoverable Petroleum Hydrocarbon
TRPI .... Training Requirement Priority Index
TRPK .... Turnpike [*Commonly used*] (OPSA)
TRPL .... Terneplate [*Materials*]
TRPL .... Triple
trpl .... Triplicate (WDMC)
TRPLYR .... Trapping Layer [*NWS*] (FAAC)
TRPM .... Plymouth/Blackburne [*Montserrat Island*] [*ICAO location identifier*] (ICLI)
Trp-mRNA ... Ribonucleic Acid, Messenger - Tryptophan Constitutive [*Biochemistry, genetics*]
TRPN .... Transportation
TRPO .... Track Reference Printout
TRPO .... Trialkylphosphine Oxide [*Organic chemistry*]
TRPO .... Truck and Recreation Products Office
TRPR .... Trooper
TRPS .... Temperature Regulating Power Supply
TRPS .... Trichorhinophalangeal Syndrome (DAVI)
TRPS .... Tripos, Inc. [*NASDAQ symbol*] (SAG)
TRPS .... Troops
TRPSC .... Triple Screw
TRPSK .... Transmitted Reference Phase Shift Keying [*Computer science*] (IAA)
TRPT .... Theoretical Renal Phosphorus Threshold [*Medicine*] (MAE)
TRPT .... Time to Reach Peak Tension
TRQ .... Tarauaca [*Brazil*] [*Airport symbol*] (AD)
TRQ .... Task Ready Queue
TRQ .... Torque (AAG)
TRQ .... Total Requirements (AAG)
TRQ .... United States Army TRADOC, Fort Ord, CDEC Library, Fort Ord, CA [*OCLC symbol*] (OCLC)
TRR .... [*The*] Research Ranch [*An association*] (EA)
TRR .... Tactical Range Recorder [*Navy*]
TRR .... Tactical Reaction Reconnaissance
TRR .... Take Real Result [*Computer science*] (IAA)
TRR .... Tape Read Register
TRR .... Target Ranging RADAR
TRR .... Tarraleah [*Tasmania*] [*Seismograph station code, US Geological Survey*] (SEIS)
TRR .... Teaching and Research Reactor
TRR .... Technical Report Request
TRR .... Technical Requirements Review (MCD)
TRR .... Technical Risk Reduction [*Military*]
TRR .... Test and Research Reactor [*Nuclear energy*] (NRCH)
TRR .... Test Readiness Review [*NASA*] (NASA)
TRR .... Tethered RADAR Reflector
TRR .... Thailand Research Reactor
TRR .... Theoretical Research Report
TRR .... Thioredoxin Reductase [*An enzyme*]
TRR .... Topical Report Request [*or Review*] [*Nuclear energy*] (NRCH)
TRR .... Trade Regulation Reporter [*A publication*] (DLA)
TRR .... Trade Regulation Rule (MHDW)
TRR .... Trader Resource Corp. [*Toronto Stock Exchange symbol*]
TRR .... Tramson Ltd. [*Sudan*] [*ICAO designator*] (FAAC)
TRR .... Transfer Relay Rack (CAAL)
TRR .... Transmitted-Reflected-Reflected [*Wave mechanics*]
TRR .... TRC Cos. [*NYSE symbol*] (TTSB)
TRR .... TRC Cos., Inc. [*NYSE symbol*] (SPSG)
TRR .... Trincomalee [*Ceylon*] [*Airport symbol*] (AD)
TRR .... Trouble Recorder (IAA)
TRR .... True Rate of Return [*Finance*] (ADA)
TRR .... United States Army TRADOC, Fort Rucker Post Library and Aviation School Library,Fort Rucker, AL [*OCLC symbol*] (OCLC)
TRRA .... Terminal Railroad Association of St. Louis [*AAR code*]
TRRA .... Tilt Rotor Research Aircraft
TRRA H & TS ... Terminal Railroad Association Historical and Technical Society (EA)
TRRAPS .... Transportable Reliable Acoustic Path Sonobuoy (NVT)
TRRB .... Test Readiness Review Board [*NASA*]
TRRC .... Test Resources Review Committee [*DoD*]
TRRC .... Textile Resource and Research Center (EA)
TRRF .... [*The*] Refrigeration Research Foundation (EA)
TRRF .... Training Review File [*IRS*]
TRRG .... Tax Reform Research Group [*Defunct*] (EA)
TRRL .... Tooling Rejection and Rework Laboratory
TRRL .... Transport and Road Research Laboratory [*Departments of the Environment and Transport*] [*Information service or system*] (IID)
TRR of ST L ... Terminal Railroad Association of St. Louis
TRRR .... Trilateral Range and Range Rate System
TRRT .... Test Results Review Team [*Nuclear energy*] (NRCH)
TRRT .... Tooling Rejection and Rework Tag
TRS .... Tactical RADAR System
TRS .... Tactical Radio Set
TRS .... Tactical Reconnaissance Squadron [*Air Force*]
TRS .... Tactical Reconnaissance System
TRS .... Tandy Radio Shack (NITA)
TRS .... Tape Recorder Subsystem
TRS .... Target Range Servo
TRS .... Technical Repair Standards
TRS .... Technical Requirements Specification (MCD)
TRS .... Technical Research Ship
TRS .... Telecommunications Relay Service [*Hearing-impaired technology*]
TRS .... Teleoperator Retrieval System [*NASA*]
TRS .... Telephone Repeater Station (IAA)
TRS .... Terrestrial Radio System
TRS .... Testa Rossa Sport
TRS .... Test Reference System
TRS .... Test Requirement Specification (MCD)
TRS .... Test Requirements Summary (MUGU)
TRS .... Test Research Service [*Defunct*] (EA)
TRS .... Test Research Station
TRS .... Test Response Spectrum (IEEE)
TRS .... Tetrahedral Research Satellite
TRS .... Textes Religieux Sumeriens du Louvre [*A publication*] (BJA)
TRS .... Theatre Recording Society (EA)
TRS .... Thermal Radiation Simulator
TRS .... Thermal Reactor Safety [*Nuclear energy*] (NRCH)
TRS .... Thermal Residue Stress (MCD)
TRS .... Third Readiness State (AAG)
TRS .... Threat Reaction System
TRS .... Ticket Reservation Systems, Inc.
TRS .... Time Reference System (MCD)
TRS .... Time-Resolved Spectrometry
TRS .... Toll Room Switch [*Telecommunications*] (TEL)
TRS .... Top Right Side (MCD)
TRS .... Torry Research Station [*British*]
TRS .... Total Reduced Sulfur [*Environmental chemistry*]
TRS .... Total Reducing Sugars [*Food science*]
TRS .... Tough Rubber-Sheathed [*Cable*] (DEN)
TRS .... Traceability and Reporting System
TRS .... Track and Store [*Computer science*] (IAA)
TRS .... Training Reservation System (MCD)
TRS .... Transfer (ADA)
TRS .... Transmission-Regulated Spark [*Automotive engineering*]
TRS .... Transmit-Receive Switch (IAA)
TRS .... Transmitter (IAA)
TRS .... Transportable Relay Station
TRS .... Transport International Aerien [*Belgium ICAO designator*] (FAAC)
TRS .... Transpose (ROG)
TRS .... Transverse Rupture Strength [*Metallurgy*]
TRS .... Traumatic Surgery [*Medical specialty*] (DHSM)
TRS .... Travel Related Services Co., Inc.
TRS .... Treasure Island Resources [*Vancouver Stock Exchange symbol*]
TRS .... Tree-Ring Society (EA)
TRS .... Trieste [*Italy*] [*Seismograph station code, US Geological Survey Closed*] (SEIS)
TRS .... Trieste [*Italy*] [*Airport symbol*] (OAG)
TRS .... Tropical Rainforest Society [*Australia*]
TRS .... Tropical Revolving Storm [*Meteorology*]
TRS .... Troubleshooting Record Sheet [*NASA*] (NASA)
TRS .... Truss [*Shipping*]
TRS .... Trustees
TRS .... Tuboreticular Structure [*Cytology*]
TRS .... Tug Rotational System [*NASA*] (NASA)
TRS .... Twin Ridge Substrate (NITA)
TRS .... United States Department of Transportation, Transportation System Center, Cambridge, MA [*OCLC symbol*] (OCLC)

TRSA .... Tax Reduction and Simplification Act of 1977
TRSA .... Terminal Radar Service Area [*FAA*] (TAG)
TRSA .... Terminal RADAR Service Area [*Aviation*] (FAAC)
TRSA .... Textile Rental Services Association of America (EA)
TRSA .... Training System Requirements Analysis (DOMA)
TRSB .... Time Reference Scanning Beam [*Aviation*]
TRSBG .... Transcribing (MSA)
TRSBMLS .... Time Reference Scanning Beam Microwave Landing System [*Aviation*] (OA)
TRSBR .... Transcriber (MSA)
TR/SBS .... Teleoperator Retrieval/Skylab Boost System [*Aerospace*] (MCD)
TRSC .... Triad Systems [*NASDAQ symbol*] (TTSB)
TRSC .... Triad Systems Corp. [*NASDAQ symbol*] (NQ)
TRSCB .... Transcribe (MSA)
Trscrypt .... Transcrypt International, Inc. [*Associated Press*] (SAG)
TRSD .... Test Requirements/Specification Document [*NASA*] (MCD)
TRSD .... Total Radiance Spectral Distribution
TRSD .... Total Rated Service Date [*Air Force*] (AFM)
TRSD .... Transferred
TRSD .... Transposed
Tr Ser .... Treaty Series [*A publication*] (DLA)
TRSF .... Torque-Regulated Speed Follower
TRSG .... Third Reich Study Group (EA)
TRSG .... Track RADAR Simulation Group [*Military*] (CAAL)
TRSH .... Trim Shell
TRSI .... Test of Retail Sales Insight
TRSL .... Toms River Signal Laboratory [*Army*] (MCD)
TRSM .... Trism, Inc. [*NASDAQ symbol*] (SAG)
TRSN .... Torsion (MSA)
TRSOC .... Trademark Society, Inc.
TRSP .... Total Radiance Spectral Polarization
trsp .... Transept (VRA)
TRSP .... Transport Seaplane [*Navy*]
TRSq .... Tactical Reconnaissance Squadron [*Air Force*] (AFM)
TRSR .... Taxi and Runway Surveillance RADAR
TRSRY .... Treasury
TRSS .... Tactical Remote Sensor System (DWSG)
TRSS .... Teleoperator and Robotic System Simulation (MCD)
TRSS .... Triple Screw Ship
TRSSCOMM... Technical Research Ship Special Communications [*System*] [*Pronounced "triss-com"*] [*Navy*]
TRSSGM .... Tactical Range Surface-to-Surface Guided Missile
TRSSM .... Tactical Range Ship-to-Shore Missile (IAA)
TRSSM .... Tactical Range Surface-to-Surface Missile
TRST .... Throttle Reset
TRST .... Trust
TRST .... Trustco Bank Corp. New York [*NASDAQ symbol*] (SAG)
TrstNY .... Trustco Bank Corp. New York [*Associated Press*] (SAG)
TRSV .... Tobacco Ring Spot Virus
TRSY .... Treasury (AABC)
TRT .... San Antonio, TX [*Location identifier FAA*] (FAAL)
TRT .... TACFIRE Remote Terminal (MCD)
TRT .... Tanker Recovery Team [*Air Force*] (DOMA)
TRT .... Technical Review Team [*Nuclear energy*] (NRCH)
TRT .... Television Resource Teachers [*Canada*]
TRT .... Tempo di Restituzione Termica [*Thermal Restitution Test*] [*Italian*] [*Medicine*]
TRT .... TEREC [*Tactical Electronic Reconnaissance*] Remote Terminal (DWSG)
TRT .... Text Retrieval Terminal [*Computer science*] (DGA)
TRT .... Thermoradiotherapy [*Radiation therapy*] (DAVI)
TRT .... Tiaret [*Algeria*] [*Airport symbol*] (AD)
TRT .... Torpedo Rocket Thrown
TRT .... Total Relaxation Time [*Cardiology*]
TRT .... Total Repair Time [*Automotive maintenance*]
TRT .... Total Running Time [*Broadcasting*] (WDMC)
TrT .... Track True [*Aviation*] (DA)
TRT .... Trademark Registration Treaty
TRT .... Traffic Route Testing [*Telecommunications*] (TEL)
TRT .... Trans Arabian Air Transport [*Sudan*] [*ICAO designator*] (FAAC)
TRT .... Translate and Test (IAA)
TRT .... Transonic Research Tunnel (MCD)
trt .... Treatment [*Medicine*]
TRT .... Treherbert [*Cardiff*] [*Welsh depot code*]
TRT .... Trent Regional Library System [*UTLAS symbol*]
TRT .... Tretes [*Java*] [*Seismograph station code, US Geological Survey*] (SEIS)
TRT .... Trim Template (MCD)
TRT .... Trinity Resources Ltd. [*Toronto Stock Exchange symbol*]
Trt .... Trityl [*Biochemistry*]
TRT .... Tropical Radio Telegraph [*Telecommunications*] (IAA)
TRT .... Tuned Receiver Tuner
TRT .... Turkish Radio & Television Corp.
TRT .... Turn Round Time (NITA)
TRT .... Turret (AABC)
TRT .... Twisted Racetrack
TRT .... United States Army TRADOC, Fort Bliss, Fort Bliss, TX [*OCLC symbol*] (OCLC)
TrT_3 .... Total Reverse Triiodothyronine
TRTA .... Tasmanian Registered Teachers' Association [*Australia*]
TRTA .... Traders' Road Transport Association [*British*] (BARN)
TRTC .... Tactical Record Traffic Center (MCD)
TRTC .... Trio-Tech International [*NASDAQ symbol*] (SAG)
TRTC .... Trio-Tech Intl [*NASDAQ symbol*] (TTSB)
TRTD .... Treated (MSA)
TR/TEA .... Transportability Report/Transportability Engineering Analysis [*Army*]
TRTF .... Tactical Reconnaissance Task Force (CINC)
TRTF .... Tactical Record Traffic Facsimile (MCD)
TRTF .... Tasking Requirements and Tasking File (MCD)
TRTG .... Tactical RADAR Threat Generator (MCD)
TRTG .... Treating
TRTITC .... Tasmanian Road Transport Industry Training Council [*Australia*]
TRTL .... Transistor-Resistor-Transistor Logic (IEEE)
TRTMNT .... Treatment
TRTMT .... Treatment (MSA)
TRTP .... Toxicology Research and Testing Program [*National Institutes of Health*]
TRTS .... Tactical Reconnaissance Training Squadron
TRTS .... Tactical Record Traffic System (MCD)
TRTS .... Track RADAR Test Set (MCD)
TRTS .... Triple Redundant Timing Systems (MCD)
TRTT .... Tactical Record Traffic Terminal [*Army*] (MCD)
TRU .... Tasmanian Rugby Union [*Australia*]
TRU .... Taurus Resources [*Vancouver Stock Exchange symbol*]
TRU .... Test Replaceable Unit
TRU .... Thermal Receiver Unit [*Army*]
TRU .... Time Release Unit (MCD)
TRU .... Torch Energy Royalty Trust [*NYSE symbol*] (SPSG)
TRU .... Total Recycle Unit (OA)
TRU .... Transformer-Rectifier Unit (MCD)
TRU .... Transmit-Receive Unit
TRU .... Transportable Radio Unit [*Military*]
TRU .... Transuranic [*or Transuranium*] [*Chemistry*]
TRU .... Transuranium Processing Plant (NRCH)
TRU .... Triangle Airline (Uganda) Ltd. [*FAA designator*] (FAAC)
TRU .... Truancy [*FBI standardized term*]
TRU .... True (GAVI)
Tru .... Trueman's New Brunswick Equity Cases [*1876-93*] [*A publication*] (DLA)
TRU .... Trujillo [*Peru*] [*Airport symbol*] (OAG)
TRU .... Truk [*Caroline Islands*] [*Seismograph station code, US Geological Survey Closed*] (SEIS)
TRU .... Truncated Variant [*Genetics*]
TRU .... Trustee (WGA)
TRU .... Turbidity Reducing Unit (AAMN)
TRU .... United States Army TRADOC, Fort Hood, Fort Hood, TX [*OCLC symbol*] (OCLC)
TRU/ARPS ... Theater Reserve Unit/Army Readiness Package, South
TRUB .... Temporarily Replaced by Unlighted Buoy [*Maps and charts*]
TRUD .... Time Remaining until Dive [*Air Force*]
TRUE .... Teacher Resources for Urban Education (AEBS)
TRUE .... Training in Urban Environment [*Navy*] (DOMA)
True .... Trueman's New Brunswick Reports [*A publication*] (DLA)
Trueman Eq Cas... Trueman's New Brunswick Equity Cases [*A publication*] (DLA)
Truem Eq Cas... Trueman's New Brunswick Equity Cases [*A publication*] (DLA)
TrueNrth .... True North Communications, Inc. [*Formerly, Foote, Cone & Belding*] [*Associated Press*] (SAG)
Truevision ... Truevision, Inc. [*Associated Press*] (SAG)
TRUEX .... Transuranium Extraction
TRUF .... Transferable Revolving Underwriting Facility [*Finance*] (ADA)
TRUFOS .... True Unidentified Flying Objects
TRUK .... Builders Transport [*NASDAQ symbol*] (TTSB)
TRUK .... Builders Transport, Inc. [*NASDAQ symbol*] (NQ)
trum .... Trumeau (VRA)
TRUMF .... Total Package Unit Material Fielding [*Army*]
TRUMP .... Target Radiation Ultraviolet Measurement Program (AAG)
TRUMP .... Technical Review Updated Manuals and Publications (MCD)
TRUMP .... Teller Register Unit Monitoring Program (IEEE)
TRUMP .... Threat Reaction Upgrade Modernization (MCD)
TRUMP .... Total Revision and Upgrading of Maintenance Procedures [*Marine Corps*]
TRUMP .... Transportable Understanding Mechanism Package [*Software system*] (IT)
TRUMP .... Tribal Class Update and Modernization Project [*Canadian Navy*]
Trump .... Trump Hotels & Casino Resorts, Inc. [*Associated Press*] (SAG)
TRUN .... Trunnion [*Pivot*] (KSC)
TRUNANG .... Trunnion Angle (MCD)
Truppie .... Trucker with Upscale Living Quarters in His or Her Vehicle [*Lifestyle classification*]
Tru Railw Rep... Truman's American Railway Reports [*A publication*] (DLA)
TRURON .... Truronensis [*Signature of the Bishop of Truro*] [*Latin*] (ROG)
TRUS .... Transrectal Ultrasonography [*Medicine*]
TRUS .... Transrectal Ultra Sounds [*Medicine*]
TRUST .... Tamper-Resistant Unattended Safeguard Technique (PDAA)
TRUST .... Television Relay Using Small Terminals (MCD)
TRUST .... Terminal Repeller Unconstrained Subenergy Tunneling [*An algorithm for global optimization*]
TRUST .... Toluidine Red Unheated Serum Test
TRUST .... Total Reevaluation Under SPRINT Thrust [*Army*]
TRUST .... Transportable Units and Self-Sufficient Teams (MCD)
TRUST .... Trieste United States Troops
Trust Co Mag... Trust Companies Magazine [*1904-38*] [*A publication*] (DLA)
TrustInf .... Trusted Information Systems, Inc. [*Associated Press*] (SAG)
Trust Lett .... Trust Letter. American Bankers Association [*A publication*] (ILCA)
TrUstmk .... Trustmark Corp. [*Associated Press*] (SAG)
TrustNJ .... Trust Co. of New Jersey [*Associated Press*] (SAG)
Trust Terr .... Trust Territory Reports [*A publication*] (DLA)
TRUT .... Time Remaining until Transition [*Air Force*]
TRUV .... Truevision, Inc. [*NASDAQ symbol*] (SAG)
TRUW .... Transuranic Waste (GAAI)

TRUX Deflecta Shield Corp. [*NASDAQ symbol*] (SAG)
TRUX Deflecta-Shield Corp. [*NASDAQ symbol*] (TTSB)
TRV Tank Recovery Vehicle [*Army*] (AABC)
TRV Thrust Reduction Valve
TRV Timing Relay Valve
TRV Tobacco Rattle Virus
TRV Torpedo-Recovery Vessel [*Navy British*]
TRV Transavia (Pty) Ltd. [*South Africa ICAO designator*] (FAAC)
TRV Transient Recovery Voltage (IEEE)
TRV Traveler Group, Inc. Capital I [*NYSE symbol*] (SAG)
TRV Travelers Group [*NYSE symbol*] (TTSB)
TRV [*The*] Travelers, Inc. [*NYSE symbol*] (SAG)
TRV Traverse
TRV Treviso [*Italy*] [*Seismograph station code, US Geological Survey Closed*] (SEIS)
TRV Trivandrum [*India*] [*Airport symbol*] (OAG)
TRV Trove Resources [*Vancouver Stock Exchange symbol*]
TRV United States Army TRADOC, Fort Lee Post, Logistic Center, Logistic, Quartermaster, Fort Lee, VA [*OCLC symbol*] (OCLC)
TRVA Thermally Released Volatile Aromatics [*i.e., odors*] [*Slang*]
TRVB Tables of Redemption Values for US Savings Bonds
TRVEH Tracked Vehicle (AABC)
TRVL Travel
TRVLG Traveling (MSA)
TRVLMT Travel Limit
TRVLR Traveler (MSA)
TRVM Transistorized Voltmeter
TRVN Tavern
TrvPC Travelers Corp. P & C Capital II [*Associated Press*] (SAG)
TRVPrA Travelers Grp 8.125%'A'Dep Pfd [*NYSE symbol*] (TTSB)
TRVPrB TravelersGrp5.5%CV'B'Pfd [*NYSE symbol*] (TTSB)
TRVPrD Travelers Grp 9.25% Dep Pfd [*NYSE symbol*] (TTSB)
TRVS Travis Boats & Motors, Inc. [*NASDAQ symbol*] (SAG)
TRV/SRV Tower Restoral Vehicle and Surveillance Restoral Vehicle [*Air Force*] (DOMA)
trvtn Travertine (VRA)
TRVV Time Radius and Velocity Vector
TRV.WS Travelers Grp Wrrt [*NYSE symbol*] (TTSB)
TRW Tactical Reconnaissance Wing [*Air Force*] (MCD)
TRW Tarawa [*Kiribati*] [*Airport symbol*] (OAG)
TRW Trade Winds Resources [*Vancouver Stock Exchange symbol*]
TRW Trail Riders of the Wilderness [*Later, AFA*] (EA)
TRW Trans Western Airlines of Utah [*ICAO designator*] (FAAC)
TRW TRW, Inc. [*Formerly, Thompson Ramo Wooldridge, Inc.*] [*NYSE symbol*] (SPSG)
TRW United States Army TRADOC, Fort Leonard Wood Post Library, Fort Leonard Wood, MO [*OCLC symbol*] (OCLC)
TRWA Trackway
TRWC Threat Responsive Weapon Control [*Military*] (CAAL)
TRWG Tactical Reconnaissance Wing [*Air Force*]
TRW IND TRW Information Networks Division [*TRW, Inc.*] [*Torrance, CA*] (TSSD)
TrwlBc Transworld Bancorp [*Associated Press*] (SAG)
TRWOV Transit Without Visa
TRWPrB TRW Inc.,$4.40 Cv II Pref [*NYSE symbol*] (TTSB)
TRWPrD TRW Inc.,$4.50 Cv II Pref [*NYSE symbol*] (TTSB)
TRWY Throughway [*Postal Service standard*] (OPSA)
TRWY Throughway
TRX Air Terrex [*Czechoslovakia*] [*ICAO designator*] (FAAC)
Trx Thioredoxin [*Also, TD, TR*] [*Biochemistry*]
TRX Transaction
TRX Transsexual (DAVI)
TRX Trenton, MO [*Location identifier FAA*] (FAAL)
TRX Triplex
TRX Tri-State Resources Ltd. [*Vancouver Stock Exchange symbol*]
TRX Two-Region Physics Critical Experiment (NRCH)
TRX United States Army TRADOC, Ordnance and Chemical School Library, Aberdeen Proving Ground, MD [*OCLC symbol*] (OCLC)
TRXAS Time Resolved X-Ray Absorption Spectroscopy
TRXRD Time-Resolved X-Ray Diffraction
TRY Teens for Retarded Youth [*Program in Fairfax County, Virginia*]
TRY Toronto Railway
TRY Tororo [*Uganda*] [*Airport symbol*] (OAG)
TRY Treviso [*Italy*] [*Airport symbol*] (AD)
TRY Triarc Co., Inc. [*Formerly, DWG Corp.*] [*NYSE symbol*] (SPSG)
TRY Triarc Cos Cl'A' [*NYSE symbol*] (TTSB)
TRY Tri-Arc Energy Ltd. [*Vancouver Stock Exchange symbol*]
TRY Tri Star Airlines, Inc. [*FAA designator*] (FAAC)
TRY Troy [*New York*] [*Seismograph station code, US Geological Survey*] (SEIS)
TRY Truly (ROG)
Try Tryptophan [*An amino acid*] (MAE)
TRY United States Army TRADOC, TRADOC System Analysis [*TRASANA*], White Sands Range, NM [*OCLC symbol*] (OCLC)
Trye Jus Filiz Trye's Jus Filizarii [*A publication*] (ILCA)
Tryp Tryptophan (MEDA)
TRYPSN Trypsin [*An enzyme*] (DAVI)
TRZ Prime Air, Inc. [*FAA designator*] (FAAC)
TRZ Taradale [*New Zealand*] [*Seismograph station code, US Geological Survey*] (SEIS)
TRZ Thioridazine [*Tranquilizer*]
TRZ Tiruchirappalli [*India*] [*Airport symbol*] (OAG)
TRZ Trichinopoly [*India*] [*Airport symbol*] (AD)
TRZ United States Army Intelligence Center and School Library, Fort Huachuca, AZ [*OCLC symbol*] (OCLC)
TRZO Terrazzo [*Classified advertising*] (ADA)
TRZON Three Ton Range and Azimuth Only (IAA)
TS Cleveland [*Postcode*] (ODBW)
TS Iraq [*Later, BZ*] [*License plate code assigned to foreign diplomats in the US*]
TS Samoa Air [*ICAO designator*] (AD)
Ts Skin Temperature [*Medicine*]
TS [*The*] Steamboaters (EA)
TS Taboo Search [*Optimization method*]
TS Tab Set [*Typography*] (WDMC)
ts Tab Set [*Typesetting*] (WDMC)
TS Tailshaft Survey
TS Tall Salicornia Zone [*Ecology*]
TS Tamper Switch [*NFPA pre-fire planning symbol*] (NFPA)
TS Tangent to Spiral
TS Tank Scope (DNAB)
TS Tank Steamer
TS Taoist Sanctuary [*Later, DS*] (EA)
TS Taper Shank [*Screw*]
TS Taper Sided
TS Tape Status [*Computer science*] (OA)
T/S Target Seeker
TS Target Strength
TS Task Statement (MCD)
TS Task-Switched [*Computer science*] (BYTE)
TS Tasmanian Swimming Inc. [*Commercial firm Australia*]
TS Tasto Solo [*Bass without Accompaniment*] [*Music*]
TS Taxpayers' Society [*British*]
TS Tax Shelter
TS Tax Straddle (MHDW)
TS Taylor-Schechter Collection. University Library [*Cambridge, England*] (BJA)
TS Teachers Section [*Library Education Division*] [*American Library Association*]
TS Teacher Survey
TS Team Surtees [*Automobile manufacturer*]
ts Teaspoon [*Measure*] (WGA)
TS Technical School (ADA)
TS Technical Secretariat (NATG)
TS Technical Services Co.
TS Technical Specification (MCD)
TS Technical Support (NASA)
TS Ted Smith Aircraft [*ICAO aircraft manufacturer identifier*] (ICAO)
TS Telecommunications System
TS Telegraph System (MSA)
TS Telephone Set (IAA)
TS Telephone Switchboard (LAIN)
TS Television, Sound Channel
TS Television Studio-Transmitter-Link [*FCC*] (NTCM)
TS Telophase Society [*Commercial firm*] (EA)
T-S Temperature-Salinity [*Oceanography*]
TS Temperature Sensitive
TS Temperature Switch
TS Template Set-Up (MCD)
TS Temporal Stem [*Brain anatomy*]
TS Tenancy Service [*New South Wales, Australia*]
TS Tennyson Society (EA)
TS Tensile Strength
ts Tensile Strength (IDOE)
TS Tensile Stress
TS Ten Silhouettes [*Psychological testing*]
T_s Tension, Schiotz [*Opthalmology*] (DAVI)
TS Tentative Specification
TS Teratology Society (EA)
TS Terminal [*or Greater*] Sensation
TS Terminal Series (IAA)
TS Terminal Service
TS Terminal Station (IAA)
TS Terminal Strip (DEN)
TS Terminal Student (OICC)
TS Terminating System (IAA)
TS Terra Santa [*Jerusalem*] [*A publication*] (BJA)
TS Test
TS Test and Set [*Computer science*] (IAA)
TS Test Items [*JETDS nomenclature*] [*Military*] (CET)
TS Test Set (KSC)
TS Test Site [*NASA*] (NASA)
TS Test Solution [*of a chemical*] [*Medicine*]
TS Test Specification (MSA)
T/S Test Stand (AAG)
TS Test Station [*NASA*] (MCD)
TS Test Stimulus
TS Test Summary
TS Test System
TS Textes Sogdiens. Edites. Traduits et Commentes [*A publication*] (BJA)
TS Texts and Studies [*Cambridge*] [*A publication*] (BJA)
TS Text Setting [*Computer science*] (PCM)
TS Theologische Studien [*Utrecht*] [*A publication*] (BJA)
TS Theosophical Society
TS Thermal Microscope Stage
TS Thermal Spray [*Also, THSP*] [*Coating technology*]
TS Thermal Stethoscope [*Medical instrumentation*]
TS Thermal Synchrotron [*High-energy physics*]
TS Thermosetting [*Plastics technology*]

TS .... Thermospray [*Also, TSP*] [*Ionization Physics*]
T/S .... Third Stage [*Aerospace*] (AAG)
TS .... Thoracic Surgery [*Medicine*]
TS .... Thoreau Society (EA)
TS .... Threaded Stud
TS .... Three-State [*Computer science*] (IAA)
TS .... Three Stooges Club (EA)
TS .... Thymidylate Synthase [*Also, ThS*] [*An enzyme*]
TS .... Thymostimulin [*Endocrinology*]
T/S .... Thyroid:Serum [*Radioiodide ratio*]
TS .... Tibet Society (EA)
TS .... Tide Surveyor [*British*] (ROG)
TS .... Tidewater Southern Railway Co. [*AAR code*]
TS .... Till Sale
TS .... Tilt and Shift [*Camera lens*] (DICI)
TS .... Time Scheduled (NASA)
TS .... Time Service (IAA)
TS .... Time Shack [*NAS operations desk*]
TS .... Time-Sharing [*Computer science*]
TS .... Time Slot [*Telecommunications*] (TEL)
TS .... Time Switch (MSA)
TS .... Timing Selector
TS .... Timing System (MCD)
TS .... Tinting Strength [*Dye chemistry*]
TS .... Tippers [*Shipping*] (DCTA)
TS .... Tip Speed
TS .... Titan Society (EA)
TS .... Titration System Software [*Metter Instruments*]
TS .... Today Show [*Television program*]
TS .... Tolkien Society [*Hove, East Sussex, England*] (EAIO)
TS .... Toll Switching [*Trunk*] [*Telecommunications*] (TEL)
TS .... Tool Sharpness
TS .... Tool Shed (IIA)
TS .... Tool Steel
TS .... Tool Storage
TS .... Tool Strength (ADA)
TS .... Too Short [*Symbol stamped in shoes which are not actually of the size marked*]
TS .... Topic Statement (WGA)
TS .... Top Secret
TS .... Top Spare
TS .... Torch Soldering
TS .... Torpedo Station (MCD)
TS .... Torque Synchro Transmitter (IAA)
TS .... Torque Transmitter (IAA)
TS .... Torstar Corp. [*Toronto Stock Exchange symbol*]
Ts .... Tosyl [*Also, Tos*] [*Organic chemistry*]
TS .... Totally Smutted [*Plant pathology*]
TS .... Total Solids [*Medicine*]
TS .... Tough Situation [*Bowdlerized version*]
TS .... Tough Stuff
TS .... Tourette Syndrome [*Neurology*]
TS .... Touring Sedan [*As in Olds 98 TS*]
TS .... Touring Sport [*Automobile model*]
TS .... Tower Station
TS .... Toxic Substance (MAE)
TS .... Tracheal Sound [*Medicine*] (AAMN)
ts .... Tracheosyringeal [*Neuroanatomy of birds*]
TS .... Tracking Scope
TS .... Tracking Supervisor (SAA)
TS .... Tracking System (AAG)
TS .... Track Store Unit (IAA)
TS .... Trademark Society (EA)
TS .... Trade Study (MCD)
TS .... Traffic Superintendent [*British*] (DCTA)
TS .... Trained Soldier [*British military*] (DMA)
TS .... Training School (DAVI)
TS .... Training Ship
TS .... Training Squadron [*British military*] (DMA)
TS .... Transaction Services (MCD)
TS .... Transfer Set
TS .... Transient Source
TS .... Transient State (AAG)
TS .... Transient Synovitis [*Medicine*]
TS .... Transition State [*Physical chemistry*]
TS .... Transit Storage
TS .... Translation Service
TS .... Translator Synthesizer (DWSG)
TS .... Transmission Service [*Telecommunications*]
TS .... Transmission Set
TS .... Transmit [*or Transmitter*] (IAA)
TS .... Transmittal Sheet [*Military*]
TS .... Transmitted Shock
TS .... Transmitter Station
TS .... Transparent Substrate [*Materials science*]
TS .... Transplantation Society (EA)
TS .... Transport and Supply
TS .... Transport Service (ROG)
TS .... Transport Ship (ROG)
TS .... Transsexual [*Medicine*]
T/S .... Transtage [*Upper stage for Titan III C rocket*]
TS .... Transvaal Supreme Court Reports [*South Africa*] [*A publication*] (DLA)
TS .... Transversale Spyder [*Ferrari automotive model designation*]
TS .... Transverse Section [*Medicine*]
TS .... Transverse Staggering (IAA)
TS .... Transverse System [*Cytology*]
TS .... Transverse Tubular System (DAVI)
TS .... Travelling Showmen [*Public-performance tariff class*] [*British*]
TS .... Travel Supplement [*Publishing*]
TS .... Treadmill Score [*Medicine*] (DMAA)
TS .... Treasury Solicitor [*British*]
TS .... Treasury Stock
TS .... Treatment System [*Nuclear energy*] (NRCH)
TS .... Treaty Series [*A publication*] (ILCA)
TS .... Tree Sparrow [*Ornithology*]
TS .... Tres Sage [*Wisest*] [*Presiding officer in the French rite Freemasonry*]
TS .... Tricuspid Stenosis [*Cardiology*]
T/S .... Trimethoprim Sulfamethoxazole
TS .... Trinidad Sector [*World War II*]
TS .... Triple Strength
TS .... Tristate [*Electronics*] (IAA)
TS .... Tropical Sprue [*Medicine*] (MAE)
TS .... Troubleshoot (MCD)
ts .... Trucial States [*United Arab Emirates*] [*MARC country of publication code Library of Congress*] (LCCP)
TS .... Trumann Southern Railroad (IIA)
TS .... Trust Secretary
TS .... Trypticase Soy [*Plate*] [*Laboratory*] (DAVI)
Ts .... T Suppressor [*Cell*] [*Immunology*]
TS .... Tuberous Sclerosis [*Medicine*]
TS .... Tube Sheet (MSA)
TS .... Tub-Sized [*Paper*]
TS .... Tubular [*Tracheal*] Sound
TS .... Tumor Specific [*Medicine*]
TS .... Tuning Stability
TS .... Turbine Steamship (WDAA)
ts .... Turboshaft Engine (IEEE)
TS .... Turbosynchro Transmitter (IAA)
TS .... Turner Society [*British*] (EAIO)
TS .... Turner Syndrome [*Medicine*] (DMAA)
T/S .... Turn-In Slip [*Military*]
TS .... Turn per Second (IAA)
T-S .... Turonian-Santonian [*Paleontology*]
TS .... Tutto Solo [*All by Itself*] [*Music*]
TS .... Twin Screw (ADA)
TS .... Two-Stage Least Squares [*Statistics*]
TS .... Tyneside Scottish [*British military*] (DMA)
TS .... Type of Shift (IAA)
TS .... Typescript
TS .... Type-Specific [*Antibodies*] [*Microbiology*] (DAVI)
TS .... Type Specification
TS .... United States Treaty Series [*A publication*] (DLA)
TSA .... Aloha Airlines, Inc. [*Air carrier designation symbol*]
TSA .... [*The*] Securities Association [*British*]
TSA .... Sports Authority [*NYSE symbol*] (TTSB)
TSA .... [*The*] Sports Authority, Inc. [*NYSE symbol*] (SAG)
TSA .... Tablettes Sumeriennes Archaiques [*A publication*] (BJA)
TSA .... Taipei-Sung Shan [*Taiwan*] [*Airport symbol*] (OAG)
TSA .... Tamworth Swine Association (EA)
TSA .... Target Service Agent [*Computer science*]
TSA .... Target Service Agents [*Computer science*] (PCM)
TSA .... Target Signature Analysis
TSA .... Target System Alternatives (MCD)
TSA .... Targhee Sheep Association (EA)
TSA .... Tariff Schedules of the United States, Annotated
TSA .... Tasmanian Shippers' Association [*Australia*]
TSA .... Tasmanian Soccer Association [*Australia*]
TSA .... Taxiway Safety Area [*FAA*] (TAG)
TSA .... Tax-Sheltered Annuity
TSA .... Technical Supplemental Allowance [*Military*]
TSA .... Technical Support Activity [*Army*] (RDA)
TSA .... Technical Support Agent (MCD)
TSA .... Technical Support Alliance [*Computer science*] (PCM)
TSA .... Technical Support Asset
TSA .... Technical Surgical Assistance [*Medicine*] (MAE)
TSA .... Technology Student Association (EA)
TSA .... Telegraph System Analyzer
TSA .... Tele-Systems Associates, Inc. [*Bloomington, MN*] [*Telecommunications service*] (TSSD)
TSA .... Temperature Swing Adsorption [*Chemical engineering*]
TSA .... Temporary Substitution Approval
TSA .... Test of Syntactic Abilities [*Speech and language therapy*] (DAVI)
TSA .... Test Signal Analyser (NITA)
TSA .... Test Site Activation [*NASA*] (KSC)
TSA .... Test Start Approval [*NASA*] (NASA)
TSA .... Test Support Agent (MCD)
TSA .... Texas Shrimp Association (EA)
TSA .... Textile Salesmen's Association [*Defunct*] (EA)
TSA .... Textile Services Association [*British*] (DBA)
TSA .... Theater Service Area (MCD)
TSA .... Theater Storage Area [*Military*]
TSA .... Theosophical Society in Australia
TSA .... Thermal Swing Adsorption [*Chemical engineering*]
TSA .... Time Series Analysis
TSA .... Time-Shared Amplifier
TSA .... Time Slot Access
TSA .... Time Study Analysis
TSA .... Tissue-Specific Antigens [*Immunology*] (DAVI)
TSA .... Tolkien Society of America

TSA.............. Toluenesulfonic Acid [*Organic chemistry*]
TSA.............. Tom Skinner Associates (EA)
TSA.............. Total Molecular Surface Area
TSA.............. Total Scan Area (OA)
TSA.............. Total Shoulder Arthroplasty [*Medicine*] (DMAA)
TSA.............. Total Shoulder Arthroplasty [*Orthopedics*] (DAVI)
TSA.............. Total Surface Area [*Chemistry*]
TSA.............. Total Survey Area (WDMC)
TSA.............. Total System Analyzer (IAA)
TSA.............. Tourette Syndrome Association (EA)
TSA.............. Tourism South Australia
TSA.............. Toxic Shock Antigen [*Immunology*] (DAVI)
TSA.............. Toy Safety Act (MHDB)
TSA.............. Track Subsystem Analyst (MUGU)
TSA.............. Track Supply Association
TSA.............. Training Services Agency [*Department of Employment*] [*British*]
TSA.............. Training Situation Analysis [*Navy*]
TSA.............. Training Support Agency [*Army*]
TSA.............. Transair France [*ICAO designator*] (FAAC)
TSA.............. Trans America Industries [*Vancouver Stock Exchange symbol*]
TSA.............. Transition State Analog
TSA.............. Transportation Service, Army
TSA.............. Transportation Standardization Agency [*DoD*]
TSA.............. Transportation Stores Assignment [*British*]
TSA.............. Tree Structured Attribute (IAA)
TSA.............. Tripoli Science Association (EA)
TSA.............. Troop Support Agency [*Army*] (AABC)
TSA.............. Troubleshooting Aid (MCD)
TSA.............. Trypticase Soy Agar [*Cell growth medium*]
TSA.............. Tuberous Sclerosis Association of Great Britain
TSA.............. Tube Support Assembly [*Nuclear energy*] (NRCH)
TSA.............. Tumor-Specific Antibody [*Immunology*] (DAVI)
TSA.............. Tumor-Specific Antigens [*Immunology*]
TSA.............. Turkish Studies Association (EA)
TSA.............. Twilight Sentinel Amplifier [*Automotive engineering*]
TSA.............. Two-Step Antenna
TSA.............. Type-Specific Antibody [*Immunology*]
TSA.............. University of Texas, Health Science Center at San Antonio, San Antonio, TX [*OCLC symbol*] (OCLC)
TSAA.............. Tobacco Salesmen's Association of America (EA)
TSAA.............. Tuberous Sclerosis Association of America [*Also known as American Tuberous Sclerosis Association and Asociacion de Esclerosis Tuberosa de America*] (EA)
TSaab.............. Thyroid-Stimulating Autoantibody [*Endocrinology*]
TSAB.............. Theatre-Screen Advertising Bureau [*Defunct*]
TSAb.............. Thyroid-Stimulating Antibodies [*Endocrinology*]
TSABF.............. Troop Support Agency Bagger Fund (MCD)
TSAC.............. Target Signature Analysis Center (MCD)
TSAC.............. Testing Accessories (AAG)
TSAC.............. Time Slot Assignment Circuit [*Telecommunications*] (TEL)
TSAC.............. Title, Subtitle, and Caption
TSAC.............. Topographic Scientific Advisory Committee [*Terminated, 1973*] [*Army*] (EGAO)
TSAC.............. Tracking System Analytical Calibration
TSAC.............. Trade Standards Advisory Council [*Australia*]
TSAD.............. Test System Analysis Directorate [*Army*] (MCD)
TSAD.............. Trajectory-Sensitive Arming Device (SAA)
TSAD.............. Tub-Sized Air-Dried [*Paper*] (DGA)
TSAE.............. Training Support Activity - Europe (MCD)
TSAF.............. Todos Santos Ambulance Fund [*An association*] (EA)
TSAF.............. Transportation Service for the Army in the Field (MCD)
TSAF.............. Typical System Acquisition Flow
TSAG.............. Tracking System Analysis Group [*NASA*]
TSAG.............. Trivalent Sodium Antimony Gluconate [*Pharmacology*]
TsAGI.............. Tsentralyni Aero-Gidrodinamichescky Institute [*Institute of Aeronautical Research*] [*Former USSR*]
TSAI.............. Transaction Sys Architects'A' [*NYSE symbol*] (TTSB)
TSAI.............. Transaction Systems Architects, Inc. [*NASDAQ symbol*] (SAG)
TSAK.............. Test Stand Adapter Kit
TSAK.............. Training Support Activity - Korea (MCD)
TSAM.............. [*The*] Skill Alignment Module [*Army*] (INF)
TSAM.............. Time Series Analysis and Modeling [*Software*]
TSAM.............. Training Surface-to-Air Missile
TSAM².............. Total System Acquistion Management Methodology [*Army*] (RDA)
TS & POP.............. Testing and Popping (SAA)
TS & SCP.............. Task, Schedule, and Status Control Plan (AAG)
TSANZ.............. Transplantation Society of Australia and New Zealand
TSAP.............. Time Series Analysis Package
TSAP.............. Toxic Shock-Associated Protein [*Biochemistry*] (DAVI)
TSAP.............. Transport Service Access Point [*Telecommunications*]
TSAPG.............. Telecommunications Systems Architecture Planning Group (DNAB)
TSAP GOOS.............. Technical and Scientific Advisory Panel for GOOS (EERA)
TSAPI.............. Telephony Services Application Programming Interface [*Novell, Inc.*] (PCM)
TSAR.............. Telemetry System Application Requirements
TSAR.............. Throttleable Solid Augmented Rocket (MCD)
TSAR.............. Timed Scanned Array RADAR
TSAR.............. Time-Sharing Activity Report System [*Computer science*] (IAA)
TSAR.............. Time Sows and Reaps [*Acronym used in name of Tsar Publishing Co.*]
TSAR.............. TransAmerica Solar Auto Run [*In name of solar-powered car TSAR Phoenix*]
TSAR.............. TRANSCOM [*Transportation Command*] Siting and Readiness [*Model*]
TSAR.............. Transmission Security Analysis Report (AFM)
TSAR.............. Transportation Statistics Annual Report [*BTS*] (TAG)
TSAR.............. Tristar Corp. [*NASDAQ symbol*] (SAG)
TSARC.............. Test Schedule and Review Committee [*Army*] (AABC)
TSARCOM.............. Troop Support and Aviation Materiel Readiness Command [*Army*]
TSAS.............. Total Severity Assessment Score (DAVI)
TSAS.............. Training Standards Advisory Service (AIE)
TSAT.............. TCI Satellite Entertainment, Inc. [*NASDAQ symbol*] (SAG)
TSAT.............. Tube-Slide Agglutination Test [*Clinical chemistry*]
TSATA.............. TCI Satellite Entertainment
TSATLC.............. Trans-Atlantic [*Aviation*] (FAAC)
TSAU.............. Time Slot Access Unit [*Telecommunications*] (TEL)
TSAZ.............. Target Seeker-Azimuth
TSAZ.............. Target Selector Azimuth (IAA)
TSB.............. [*The*] School Brigade [*Army*] (INF)
TSB.............. Technical Service Bulletin
TSB.............. Temporary Stowage Bag [*NASA*] (KSC)
TSB.............. Terminal Status Block [*Computer science*] (IBMDP)
TSB.............. Test Support Building
TSB.............. Textiles Surveillance Body [*Textile trade agreement*]
TSB.............. Thermally Stabilized Burner [*Engineering*]
TSB.............. Thrust Section Blower (AAG)
TSB.............. Towed SONAR Body
TSB.............. Toxic Substances Bulletin [*A publication*]
TSB.............. Trade Show Bureau (EA)
TSB.............. Transportation Services Branch [*Air Force*]
TSB.............. Transports Aeriens du Benin [*ICAO designator*] (FAAC)
TSB.............. Trustee Savings Bank [*British*]
TSB.............. Trypticase Soy Broth [*Cell growth medium*]
TSB.............. Tsumeb [*Namibia*] [*Airport symbol*] (OAG)
TSB.............. Twin Sideband
TSB.............. Typtone Soy Broth [*Cell growth medium*] (DAVI)
TSBA.............. Teeswater Sheep Breeders Association [*British*] (DBA)
TSBA.............. Transactions of the Society of Biblical Archaeology [*London*] [*A publication*] (BJA)
TSBARA.............. Tasmanian Small Bore and Air Rifle Association [*Australia*]
TSBB.............. Transtracheal Selective Bronchial Brushing [*Medicine*] (AAMN)
TSB(CI).............. Trustee Savings Bank (Channel Islands) [*British*]
TSBD.............. Tracking Servobridge Detector (MCD)
TSBFA.............. Traditional Siamese Breeders and Fanciers Association (EA)
TSBP.............. Time-Sharing Business Package [*Computer science*] (IAA)
TSBS.............. Trenton Savings Bank [*NASDAQ symbol*] (SAG)
TSBY.............. Tuscola & Saginaw Bay Railway Co., Inc. [*AAR code*]
TSC.............. Air Transat [*Canada ICAO designator*] (FAAC)
TSC.............. Passed a Territorial Army Course in Staff Duties [*British*]
TSC.............. Stephan Co. [*AMEX symbol*] (SAG)
TSC.............. Tactical Support Center
TSC.............. Tanker Service Committee
TSC.............. Tape Station Conversion (CET)
TSC.............. Targeted Selection Criteria (GFGA)
TSC.............. Target Selection Console (MCD)
TSC.............. Tarleton State College [*Later, TSU*] [*Texas*]
TSC.............. Technetium Sulfur Colloid [*Medicine*] (MAE)
TSC.............. Technical Services Center, Memphis, Tenn (AAGC)
TSC.............. Technical Subcommittee
TSC.............. Technical Support Center [*Nuclear energy*] (NRCH)
TSC.............. Techniscope Development [*Vancouver Stock Exchange symbol*]
TSC.............. Telecommunications Systems Corp. (IAA)
TSC.............. Teleconferencing Systems Canada Ltd. [*Etobicoke, ON*] [*Telecommunications service*] (TSSD)
TSC.............. Teledyne Systems Corp.
TSC.............. Telephone Software Connection, Inc.
TSC.............. Television Scan Converter
TSC.............. Terminal Sterilization Chamber
TSC.............. Terrestrial Science Center (MCD)
tsc.............. Territorial Staff Course [*British military*] (DMA)
TSC.............. Test Acquisition Module Self Check (CAAL)
TSC.............. Test Score Category [*DoD*]
TSC.............. Test Set Computer
TSC.............. Test Set Connection
TSC.............. Test Setup Complete [*NASA*] (NASA)
TSC.............. Test Shipping Cask [*Nuclear energy*] (NRCH)
TSC.............. Test Steering Committee [*Military*]
TSC.............. Test Support Controller [*or Coordinator*] [*NASA*] (KSC)
TSC.............. Texas Southmost College
TSC.............. Thermally Stimulated Conductivity [*or Currents*]
TSC.............. Thermal Shape Control (SSD)
TSC.............. Thermal Stress Crack [*Plastics*]
TSC.............. Thermal Surface Coating
TSC.............. Thiosemicarbazide [*Organic chemistry*]
TSC.............. Three-State Control [*Computer science*]
TSC.............. Time-Sharing Control (NITA)
TSC.............. Time-Sharing Control Task [*Computer science*] (BUR)
TSC.............. Tonic Sol-Fa College [*London*]
TS-C.............. Tooling Supplement to Contract (SAA)
TSC.............. Top Secret Control (MCD)
TSC.............. Totally Self-Checking
TSC.............. Total System Control [*Architecture*]
TSC.............. Total System Cost [*Aviation*]
TSC.............. Towson State University, Towson, MD [*OCLC symbol*] (OCLC)
TSC.............. Toxic Substances Coordinator [*Environmental Protection Agency*] (GFGA)
TSC.............. Training Support Center [*Army*] (MCD)
TSC.............. Transfer System C (SAA)
TSC.............. Transit Switching Center [*Telecommunications*] (TEL)
TSC.............. Transmitter Start Code [*Bell System*]

TSC Transmitting Switch Control (IAA)
TSC Transportation Systems Center [*Department of Transportation*] [*Cambridge, MA*]
TSC Treatment Services Control
TSC Tri-Service Support Center [*Military*] (MCD)
TSC Tristate Control [*Electronics*] (IAA)
TSC Troop Support Center [*Army*]
TSC Troop Support Command [*Formerly, MECOM*] [*Army*]
TSC Trouble-Shooting Checklist [*Test for academic institutions*]
TSC Tryptose-Sulfite Cyclosterone [*Agar*] [*Microbiology*] (DAVI)
TSC Tryptose-Sulphite Cyclosterone [*Agar*] (BABM)
TSC Tuberous Sclerosis Complex [*Medicine*]
TSC Tuscaloosa Oil & Gas [*Vancouver Stock Exchange symbol*]
TSC Two-Stage Command [*NASA*] (GFGA)
TSC Two Subcarrier (IAA)
TSCA Target Satellite Controlled Approach (MUGU)
TSCA Textile Supplies and Credit Association (EA)
TSCA TIGA Sailboard Class Association [*Defunct*] (EA)
TSCA Timing Single-Channel Analyzer
TSCA Tool Subcontract Authorization (AAG)
TSCA Top Secret Control Agency (MCD)
TSCA Toxic Substances Control Act [*1976*]
TSCA Traditional Small Craft Association (EA)
TSCAP Thermally Stimulated Capacitance [*Photovoltaic energy systems*]
TSCAPP Toxic Substances Control Act Plant and Production Data [*Chemical Information Systems, Inc.*] [*Information service or system*]
TSCATS Toxic Substances Control Act Test Submissions [*Database*] [*Environmental Protection Agency*]
TSCC Technology Solutions [*NASDAQ symbol*] (TTSB)
TSCC Technology Solutions Co. [*NASDAQ symbol*] (SPSG)
TSCC Telemetry Standards Coordination Committee
TSCC Test Support Control Center [*NASA*] (KSC)
TSCC Top Secret Control Channels [*Military*]
TSCC Toxic Substances Coordinating Committee [*Environmental Protection Agency*] (GFGA)
TSCD Test Specification and Criteria Document (MCD)
TSCD Tool Specification Control Drawing (MCD)
TSCDP Technical Service Career Development Program [*Military*]
TSCF Task Schedule Change Form [*Nuclear energy*] (NRCH)
TSCF Template Set-Up Check Fixture (MCD)
TSCF Top Secret Cover Folder (AAG)
TSCHLT Test Support Center High-Level Terminal (CAAL)
TSCIXS Tactical Support Center Information Exchange Subsystem
TSCLT Transportable Satellite Communications Link Terminal
TSCM Taylor Series Correction Method
TSCM Technical Surveillance Countermeasures [*Program*] [*Air Force*]
TSCM Test Station Configuration Model (MCD)
TSCN Telescan, Inc. [*NASDAQ symbol*] (SAG)
TSCN Trainer Specification Change Notice (MCD)
TSCO Test Support Coordination Office [*NASA*] (MCD)
TSCO Test Support Coordinator (NASA)
TSCO Top Secret Control Officer [*Military*]
TSCO Tractor Supply [*NASDAQ symbol*] (SAG)
TSCO Tri-Service Contracting Officer (AAGC)
TSCOM TS Communications [*Springfield, IL*] [*Telecommunications*] (TSSD)
t-scope Tachistoscope (WDMC)
TSCP Tactical Satellite Communications Program (SAA)
TSCP Telscape International, Inc. [*NASDAQ symbol*] (SAG)
TSCP Top Secret Control Proceeding [*Navy*]
TSCP Training Simulator Control Panel [*NASA*] (MCD)
TSCPAM Tentative Summary CPAM [*Military*] (CAAL)
TSCR Telecom Securitor Cellular Radio Ltd. [*British*]
TSCRA Texas and Southwestern Cattle Raisers Association (EA)
TSCRS Teacher's Self-Control Rating Scale
TSCS Tactical Satellite Communications System [*Air Force*] (CET)
TSCS Tactical Software Control Site [*Missile system evaluation*] (RDA)
TSCS Tennessee Self-Concept Scale [*Psychology*]
TSCS Top Secret Control Section [*Navy*]
TSCS Transportation System Capability Study [*MTMC*] (TAG)
TSCT Time-Sharing Control Task (NITA)
TSCT Transportable Satellite Communications Terminal
TSCV Transmission Spark Control Valve [*Automotive engineering*]
TSCVT TACSATCOM Single Channel Vehicular Terminal System (MCD)
TSCVT Thomas Self-Concept Values Test [*Psychology*]
TSCW Top Secret Codeword (MCD)
TSD Tactical and Staff Duties [*British military*] (DMA)
TSD Tactical Situation Display
TSD TARAN [*Tactical Attack RADAR and Navigation*] System Data
TSD Target Skin Distance
TSD Tay-Sachs Disease [*Medicine*]
TSD Technical Support Division [*Environmental Protection Agency*] (GFGA)
TSD Technical Support Document
TSD Temperature-Dependent Sex Determination
TSD Temperature-Dependent Sex Determination [*Reptile Embryology*]
TSD Temperature-Salinity-Density-Depth [*Oceanography*]
TSD Tertiary of the Order of St. Dominic [*Roman Catholic religious order*]
TSD Test Sequence Document (SAA)
TSD Test Start Date [*NASA*] (NASA)
TSD Theater Shipping Document [*Military*]
TSD Theory of Signal Detection
TSD Thermally Stimulated Depolarization [*Chemistry*]
TSD Thermionic Specific Detector [*Analytical instrumentation*]
TSD Third-Degree Stochastic Dominance [*Agricultural statistics*]
TSD Time-Span-of-Discretion (PDAA)
TSD Time-Speed-Distance [*Vehicle testing*]
TSD Time Synchronization Device
TSD Torque Screwdriver
TSD Total Spectral Density
TSD Total Squared Distance
TSD Touch Sensitive Digitizer [*Electronics*] (OA)
TSD Toured Sea Duty (DNAB)
TSD Track Situation Display
TSD Traffic Situation [*Status*] Display
TSD Transfer Summary Dictated [*Followed by date*] [*Medical records*] (DAVI)
TSD Transient Signal Detector
TSD Transportation Safeguards Division
TSD Transportation Stores Depot [*British military*] (DMA)
T/S/D Treatment, Storage, and Disposal (GAAI)
TSD Treatment, Storage and Disposal Facilities (AAGC)
TSD Treatment, Storage, or Disposal [*Hazardous waste management*]
TSD Triple-Sequence Diffusion
TSD Tubeless Steel Disc [*Wheel*] [*Automotive engineering*]
TSD United States Army TRADOC, Fort Devens, USAISD, Fort Devens, MA [*OCLC symbol*] (OCLC)
TSDA Tasmanian Soft Drink Association [*Australia*]
TSDA Television Service Dealers' Association (IAA)
TSDA Theory of Signal Detection Analysis
TSDA Thermal Single-Determinant Approximation (PDAA)
TSDB SCB [*Statistika Centralbyran*] Time Series Data Base [*Sweden Information service or system*] (CRD)
TSDC Tennessee State Data Center [*Tennessee State Planning Office*] [*Nashville*] [*Information service or system*] (IID)
TSDC Thermally Stimulated Discharge Current [*Voltage-induced polarization*]
TSDC TOGA [*Tropical Ocean and Global Atmosphere*] Subsurface Data Center [*Marine science*] (OSRA)
TSDD Temperature-Salinity-Density-Depth (IEEE)
TSDF Tactical Software Development Facility
TSDF Target System Data File
TSDF Torres Strait Defence Force [*Australia*]
TSDF Treatment, Storage, and Disposal Facility [*Hazardous waste*]
TSDG Toxic Substances Dialogue Group [*Environmental Protection Agency*] (GFGA)
TS-DHFR Thymidylate Synthetase Dihydrofolate Reductase [*Biochemistry*]
TSDI Tactical Situation Display Indicator
TSDK Torque Screwdriver Kit
TSDM Time-Shared Data Management [*System*] [*Computer science*] (IEEE)
TS/DMS Time-Shared/Data Management System
TSDOS Time-Shared Disk Operating System [*Computer science*] (IEEE)
T/SDPS Tube/Sea Differential Pressure Subsystem
TSDR Treatment, Storage, Disposal, or Recycling [*Hazardous waste management*]
TSDS Technological Services Delivery System [*UNIDO*]
TSDS Two-Speed Destroyer Sweeper [*Military*]
TSDSM Test Site Data Source Matrix
TSDU Target System Data Update
TSDU Transport Service Data Unit [*Telecommunications*]
TS D/W Tons Deadweight (DS)
TSE Memphis, TN [*Location identifier FAA*] (FAAL)
TSE Tactical Support Element (AFM)
TSE Tactical Support Equipment [*Military*] (MCD)
TSE Taipei Stock Exchange [*Taiwan*]
TSE Target State Estimator (MCD)
TSE Target Support Element (MCD)
TSE Technical Support Effort
TSE Technical Support Equipment
TSE Telecommunications Systems Engineering (IAA)
TSE Telemetry Support Equipment (IAA)
TSE Tender Support Equipment
TSE Terminal Source Editor
TSE Testicular Self-Examination
TSE Test of Spoken English
TSE Test Scoring Equipment
TSE Test Set Electrical
TSE Test Support Equipment [*NASA*]
TSE Texas South-Eastern Railroad Co. [*AAR code*]
TSE Thorn Security and Electronics [*A division of Thorn EMI Corp.*] (ECON)
TSE Time Slice End [*Computer science*] (OA)
TSE Tokyo Stock Exchange [*Japan*]
TSE Toronto Stock Exchange [*Toronto, ON*]
TSE Total Shielding Effectiveness (IAA)
TSE Total Skin Examination [*Dermatology*] (DAVI)
TSE Total Subsystem Evaluation
TSE Track Security Element [*Military*] (INF)
TSE Transmile Air Service (M) Sdn, Bhd. [*Malaysia*] [*FAA designator*] (FAAC)
TSE Transmissible Spongiform Encephalothi [*Medicine*]
TSE Transmission Secondary Emission [*Physics*]
TSE Transportation Support Equipment (NASA)
TSE Trisodium Edetate [*Inorganic chemistry*] (MAE)
TSE Turboshaft Engine
TSE1 Tissue-Specific Extinguisher 1 [*Genetics*]
TSEA Training Subsystem Effectiveness Analysis
TSEB Total Skin Electron Beam [*Medicine*] (DMAA)
TSEB Twin Sideband (IAA)
TSEC Taft Sanitary Engineering Center
TSEC Telecommunications Security [*Army*] (AABC)

TSEC .... Terminal Secondary RADAR Beacon [*Aviation*] (FAAC)
TSEC .... Top Secret (MCD)
T-SECT .... Transverse Cross Section [*Medicine*] (CPH)
TSED .... Training Simulators Engineering Department
TSEE .... Test Support Equipment Evaluation (MCD)
TSEE .... Thermally Stimulated Exoelectron Emission [*Dosimetry*]
TSEG .... Tactical Satellite Communications Executive Steering Group
TSEG .... Toronto Stock Exchange - Gold
TS-EI .... Thermospray-Electron Ionization [*Chemistry*]
TSEI .... Toronto Stock Exchange - Industrials
TSEI .... Transportation Safety Equipment Institute (EA)
T/S-EL .... Target Selector-Elevation (SAA)
TSEL .... Tentative Safe Exposure Level [*Toxicology*]
TSEM .... Toronto Stock Exchange - Mines
TSEM .... Tower Semiconductor Ltd. [*NASDAQ symbol*] (SAG)
TSEM .... Transmission Secondary Electron Multiplication [*Physics*] (IAA)
TSEM .... Transmission Secondary Emission Multiplier [*Physics*]
TSEMF .... Tower Semiconductor [*NASDAQ symbol*] (TTSB)
Tseng .... Tseng Labs, Inc. [*Associated Press*] (SAG)
TSEO .... Toronto Stock Exchange - Oils
TSEPP .... Telecom Small Enterprise Policy Panel [*Australia*]
TSEQ .... Time Sequenced [*NASA*] (KSC)
TSERR .... Type of Leaf Serration [*Botany*]
TSES .... Technical Simulation and Evaluation System
TSES .... Transportable Satellite Earth Station
TSESG .... Tactical Satellite Executive Steering Group
TSET .... Transmitter Signal Element Timing (IAA)
T-setting .... Time-Exposure Setting [*Photography*] (WDMC)
TSewU .... University of the South, Sewanee, TN [*Library symbol Library of Congress*] (LCLS)
TSewU-T .... University of the South, School of Theology, Sewanee, TN [*Library symbol Library of Congress*] (LCLS)
TSEXEC .... Time-Shared Executive [*Computer science*] (IAA)
TSF .... Tab Sequence Format
TSF .... Tactical Strike Fighter (MCD)
TSF .... Tasmanian Soccer Federation [*Australia*]
TSF .... Telephone Service Fitting
TSF .... Ten-Statement FORTRAN [*Computer science*] (IEEE)
TSF .... Terminal Sterilization Facility
TSF .... Tetraselenofulvalene [*Organic chemistry*]
TSF .... Textured Soy Flour
TSF .... Thai Support Foundation (EA)
TSF .... Theological Students Fellowship [*Defunct*] (EA)
TSF .... Thermally Stable Fuel (MCD)
TSF .... Thermoplastic Structural Foam (MCD)
TSF .... Thin Solid Films (IEEE)
TSF .... Thrombopoietic Stimulating Factor [*Medicine*]
TSF .... Through Supergroup Filter (IAA)
TSF .... Tissue-Coding Factor [*Clinical chemistry*] (MAE)
TSF .... Tower Shielding Facility [*Nuclear energy*]
TSF .... Track Synthesis Frequency
TSF .... Transverse Shear Force
TSF .... Treasury Security Force [*Department of the Treasury*]
TSF .... Triceps Skinfold [*Medicine*]
TSF .... Truncation Safety Factor [*In biological systems*]
TSF .... T/SF Communications Corp. [*Associated Press*] (SAG)
TSF .... Two-Seater Fighter [*Air Force British*]
TSFA .... Two-Step Formal Advertising (MCD)
TSFC .... Tactical Support Functional Components (NVT)
TSFC .... Thrust Specific Fuel Consumption
TSFC .... Tom Sneva Fan Club (EA)
TSFC .... Twisted Sister Fan Club (EA)
TSFCER .... Technical System for Continued Emissions Reduction [*Environmental Protection Agency*]
TSFET .... Theater Service Forces, European Theater [*World War II*]
TSFGA .... Tasmanian Stone Fruit Growers' Association [*Australia*]
TSFO .... Training Set, Fire Observation (MCD)
TSFO .... Training Set, Forward Observer [*Army*]
TSFO .... Transportation Support Field Office [*Federal disaster planning*]
TSFR .... Transfer (AFM)
TSFS .... Trunk Servicing Forecasting System [*Telecommunications*] (TEL)
TSFSOILITU .... [*The*] Search for Signs of Intelligent Life in the Universe [*Lily Tomlin one-woman show written by Jane Wagner*]
TSFSR .... Transcaucasian Soviet Federation Socialist Republic
TSFT .... Telesoft Corp. [*NASDAQ symbol*] (SAG)
TSG .... Sabre Group Holdings, Inc. (The) [*NYSE symbol*] (SAG)
TSG .... [*The*] Stelle Group (EA)
TSG .... [*The*] Surgeon General [*Army*]
TSG .... Tanacross, AK [*Location identifier FAA*] (FAAL)
TSG .... Technical Service Group (IAA)
TSG .... Technical Specialty Group [*AIAA*]
TSG .... Technical Steering Group (OICC)
TSG .... Technical Subgroup (NATG)
TSG .... Technology Support Group
TSG .... Telecommunications Strategy Group [*Australia*]
TSG .... Tempered Safety Glass [*Automotive engineering*]
TSG .... Territorial Support Group [*Scotland Yard*] [*British*]
TSG .... Test and Switching Gear [*NASA*] (KSC)
TSG .... Test Signal Generator
TSG .... Time Signal Generator
TSG .... Timeslot Generator [*Telecommunications*] (TEL)
TSG .... Timing Systems Group [*NASA*]
TSG .... Tracking Signal Generator
TSG .... Transglobe Resources [*Vancouver Stock Exchange symbol*]
TSG .... Transport Supplement Grant [*British*]
TSG .... Transversely Adjusted Gap (IEEE)
TSG .... Travel Security Guide [*Control Risks Information Services - CRIS*] [*British Information service or system*] (IID)
TSG .... Triggered Spark Gap (IAA)
TSG .... Tri-Service Group [*NATO*]
TSG .... Troubleshooting Guide (MCD)
TSG .... Truebner's Simplified Grammars [*A publication*]
TSG .... Tumor-Specific Glycoprotein [*Biochemistry*] (DAVI)
TSG .... United States Army TRADOC, Fort Gordon, United States Army Signal School and Fort Gordon, Fort Gordon, GA [*OCLC symbol*] (OCLC)
TSGA .... Technical Service Guild of Australia
TSGA .... Three-Conductor, Shipboard, General Use, Armor Cable
TSGAD .... Tri-Service Group on Air Defense [*NATO*] (NATG)
TSGAS .... Time-Shared General Accounting System [*Computer science*] (MHDI)
TSGB .... Tensor Society of Great Britain
TSGCEE .... Tri-Service Group on Communications and Electronic Equipment [*NATO*] (NATG)
TSGF .... T-Suppressor-Cell Growth Factor [*Immunology*]
TSGI .... Technology Service Group, Inc. [*NASDAQ symbol*] (SAG)
TSGI .... Technology Service Grp [*NASDAQ symbol*] (TTSB)
TSGIW .... Technology Service Grp Wrrt [*NASDAQ symbol*] (TTSB)
TSGMS .... Test Set Guided Missile Set [*or System*]
TSGP .... Test Sequence Generator Program [*European Space Research and Technology Center*] (NASA)
TSGR .... Thunderstorm with Hail [*Meteorology*]
TSGS .... Time Series Generation System
TSGT .... Technical Sergeant [*Military*]
TSGT .... Throgmorton Secured Growth Trust [*Commercial firm British*]
TSGT(C) .... Technical Sergeant (Commissary) [*Marine Corps*]
TSh .... Tanzanian Shilling [*Monetary unit*] (ODBW)
TSH .... Teche Holding [*AMEX symbol*] (TTSB)
TSH .... Teche Holding Co. [*AMEX symbol*] (SAG)
TSH .... Temperature Switch, High [*Nuclear energy*] (NRCH)
TSH .... Tendency to Seek Help Questionnaire (EDAC)
TSH .... Tensor Surface Harmonic [*Physics*]
TSH .... Their Serene Highnesses
TSH .... Thermodynamic Suppression Head
TSH .... Through-Surface Hardening [*Metallurgy*]
TSH .... Thyroid-Stimulating Hormone [*Thyrotrophin*] [*Also, TTH Endocrinology*]
TSH .... Toluenesulfonyl Hydrazide [*Organic chemistry*]
TSh .... Torah Shelemah [*A publication*] (BJA)
TSH .... Transfer Scheme Handbook (AIE)
TSH .... TSC Shannock Corp. [*Toronto Stock Exchange symbol Vancouver Stock Exchange symbol*]
TSH .... Tshikapa [*Zaire*] [*Airport symbol*] (OAG)
TSHC .... Two-Stage Hydrocracker [*Chemical engineering*]
TSHIRTS .... TSHIRTS: [*The*] Society Handling the Interchange of Remarkable T-Shirts [*Defunct*] (EA)
TSHR .... Thyrotropin-Stimmulating Hormone Receptor [*Endocrinology*]
TSH-RF .... Thyroid-Stimulating Hormone-Releasing Factor [*Endocrinology*] (MAE)
TSH-RH .... Thyroid-Stimulating Hormone-Releasing Factor [*Endocrinology*] (CPH)
TSI .... Target Signature Investigation
TSI .... Task Status Index [*Computer science*] (OA)
TSI .... Tax Shelter Insider [*Newsletter Management Corp.*] [*Defunct Information service or system*] (CRD)
TSI .... Tayson Systems, Inc. [*Telecommunications service*] (TSSD)
TSI .... Technical Standardization Inspection [*Military*]
TSI .... Technical Systems, Inc. (IAA)
TSI .... Telebase Systems, Inc. [*Information service or system*] (IID)
TSI .... Teleconferencing Systems International, Inc. [*Elk Grove Village, IL*] (TSSD)
TSI .... Teleguard System International [*Vancouver Stock Exchange symbol*]
TSI .... Television Services International [*British*]
TSI .... Tensile Safety Index [*Engineering design*]
TSI .... Test of Social Insight [*Psychology*]
TSI .... Tests of Social Intelligence [*Psychology*]
TSI .... Test Structure Input (NITA)
TSI .... Test Support Instructions [*NASA*] (KSC)
TSI .... Theological School Inventory [*Psychology*]
TSI .... Threshold Signal-to-Interference Ratio (IEEE)
TSI .... Threshold Soot Index
TSI .... Thyroid-Stimulating Immunoglobulin [*Endocrinology*]
TSI .... Timber Stand Improvement (DICI)
TSI .... Time-Significant Item (MCD)
TSI .... Time Slot Input [*Telecommunications*] (IAA)
TSI .... Time Slot Interchange [*Telecommunications*] (TEL)
TSI .... Time Sterile Indicator
TSI .... Tons per Square Inch (MCD)
TSI .... Top Surface Imaging [*Microlithography*]
TSI .... Total Sum Insured (AIA)
TSI .... Transistor Specialities, Inc. (IAA)
TSI .... Transmitting Subscriber Information [*Computer science*]
TSI .... Transmitting Subscriber's Identification (NITA)
TSI .... Transportation Safety Institute [*Department of Transportation*]
TSI .... Transport Studies and Inquiries [*British*]
TSI .... Trans-Service Inc., Bala-Cynwyd PA [*STAC*]
TSI .... Triad Systems Integration Corp.
TSI .... Trinitech Systems [*AMEX symbol*] (TTSB)
TSI .... Trinitech Systems, Inc. [*AMEX symbol*] (SPSG)
TSI .... Triple Sugar-Iron [*Agar*] [*Microbiology*]
TSI .... True Speed Indicator (IAA)

tsi .... Tsimshian [*MARC language code Library of Congress*] (LCCP)
TSI .... Turbo Sport Intercooler [*Automotive engineering*]
TSI .... Turkish Standards Institution
TSIA .... Tasmanian Sawmillers' Industrial Association
TSIA .... Trading Stamp Institute of America (EA)
TSIA .... Triple Sugar-Iron Agar [*Microbiology*]
TSIAB .... Torres Strait Islander Advisory Board [*Australia*]
TSIAJ .... This Scherzo Is a Joke [*Used by American composer Charles Edward Ives*]
TSIC .... Time Slot Interchange Circuit [*Telecommunications*] (IAA)
TSID .... Track Sector Identification
TSIE .... Transformed Special Index of the External Standard [*Scintillation analysis*]
TSIFL .... Trade Society of Iron Foundry Labourers [*A union*] [*British*]
T/SIG .... Turn Signal [*Automotive engineering*]
TSII .... TSI, Inc. [*NASDAQ symbol*] (NQ)
TSI Inc .... TSI, Inc. [*Associated Press*] (SAG)
TSIL .... Time-Significant Item List (AAG)
TSIM .... Thinking Tools, Inc. [*NASDAQ symbol*] (SAG)
TSIM .... (Trimethylsilyl)imidazole [*Also, TMSIM*] [*Organic chemistry*]
TSIMA .... Torres Strait Islander Media Association [*Australia*]
TSIMS .... Telemetry Simulation Submodule
TSIN .... Total Soluble Inorganic Nitrogen [*Analytical chemistry*]
TS in A .... Theosophical Society in America (EA)
TSIO .... Time-Shared Input/Output [*Data processing*]
TSI-OH .... Tube Sheet Inlet and Outlet Head (MSA)
TSIP .... Tank [*Missile*] Sight Improvement Program [*Army*]
TSIP .... Technical Study Implementation Plan (SSD)
TSIR .... Total System Integration Responsibility
TSIS .... Total Specifications Information System
TSIT .... Technical Service Intelligence Team [*Military*]
TSIU .... Telephone System Interface Unit
TSIX .... Transition Systems [*NASDAQ symbol*] (TTSB)
TSIX .... Transition Systems, Inc. [*NASDAQ symbol*] (SAG)
TSJ .... Tsushima [*Japan*] [*Airport symbol*] (OAG)
TSJC .... Trinidad State Junior College [*Colorado*]
TSK .... Computer Task Group [*NYSE symbol*] (TTSB)
TSK .... Computer Task Group, Inc. [*NYSE symbol*] (SPSG)
TSK .... Fort Hamilton Post Library, Morale Support Activities, Brooklyn, NY [*OCLC symbol*] (OCLC)
TSK .... Task
TSK .... Time Shift Keying
TSK .... Torque Screwdriver Kit
TSK .... Tsukuba - Telemeter [*Japan*] [*Seismograph station code, US Geological Survey*] (SEIS)
TSKT .... Test Kit (AAG)
TSL .... Chicago, IL [*Location identifier FAA*] (FAAL)
TSL .... [*The*] Software Link, Inc. [*Software manufacturer*]
TSL .... Temporary Storage Location
TSL .... Test Set Logic
TSL .... Test Source Library
TSL .... Test Stand Level (AAG)
TSL .... Test Support List (CAAL)
TSL .... Texas Short Line Railway [*AAR code*]
TSL .... Thermally-Stimulated Luminescence (PDAA)
TSL .... Thin Shock Layer
TSL .... Three-State Logic [*Computer science*] (IAA)
TSL .... Time Series Language (MHDB)
TSL .... Time Spent Listening (WDMC)
TSL .... Top of Slab [*Technical drawings*]
TSL .... Torsatron/Stellarator Laboratory [*University of Wisconsin - Madison*] [*Research center*] (RCD)
TSL .... Total Service Life [*Telecommunications*] (TEL)
TSL .... Total Signal Lines (IAA)
TSL .... Translator (IAA)
TSL .... Trans Siberian Landbridge (DS)
TSL .... Tree Searching Language [*Computer science*] (PDAA)
TSL .... Triservice LASER
TSL .... Tristate Logic [*Electronics*]
TSL .... Troop Safety Line
TSL .... Troubleshooting Loop
TSL .... Tsaile [*Navajo Community College*] [*Arizona*] [*Seismograph station code, US Geological Survey*] (SEIS)
TSL .... Two-Stage Liquefaction [*Chemical engineering*]
TSL .... Typesetting Lead (MSA)
TSL .... United States Army TRADOC, Defense Language Institute, Presidio of Monterey, CA [*OCLC symbol*] (OCLC)
TSLAET .... Technician of the Society of Licensed Aircraft Engineers and Technologists [*British*] (DBQ)
TSLC .... TOGA [*Tropical Ocean-Atmosphere*] Sea Level Center (USDC)
TSLC .... TOGA [*Tropical Ocean and Global Atmosphere*] Sea Level Center [*Marine science*] (OSRA)
TSLCC-E .... Total System Life Cycle Cost-Effectiveness
TSLCN .... Texas State Library Communication Network [*Library network*]
TSLD .... Troubleshooting Logic Diagram (NASA)
TSLI .... Time Since Last Inspection (MCD)
TSLS .... Toxic Shock-Like Syndrome [*Medicine*]
TSLS .... Triservice LASER Seeker [*DoD*]
TSLS .... Two-Stage Least Squares [*Statistics*]
TSM .... Methodist Theological School in Ohio, Delaware, OH [*OCLC symbol*] (OCLC)
TSM .... Tactical Survey Meter
TSM .... Tail Service Mast [*NASA*] (KSC)
TSM .... Tandem Scanning Microscope
TSM .... Target Signature Model
TSM .... Target-to-Surface-to-Missile Path
TSM .... Tentative Standard Method [*of analysis*]
TSM .... Terminal Support Module
TSM .... Test Site Manager [*Army*]
TSM .... Test Standards Module
TSM .... Test Support Manager [*NASA*] (KSC)
TSM .... Thermal Scale Model (MCD)
TSM .... Thermoplastic Solid Molding [*Materials science*]
TSM .... Thickness-Shear-Mode [*Instrumentation*]
TSM .... Time Scheduled Maintenance
TSM .... Time-Shared Monitor System [*Computer science*] (IEEE)
TSM .... Time-Sharing Multiplex [*Telecommunications*] (IAA)
TSM .... Time, Space, and Matter [*Princeton University course title*] (AEE)
TSM .... Ton Statute Mile (AAG)
TSM .... Total Scheduled Maintenance [*Army*]
TSM .... Total Suspended Matter [*Environmental science*]
TSM .... Total System Management Concept (MCD)
TSM .... Trade Study Management (NASA)
TSM .... TRADOC System Manager [*Army*]
TSM .... Training and Doctrine Command System Manager [*Army*] (MCD)
TSM .... Training Site Manager (MCD)
TSM .... Training System Manager (MCD)
TSM .... Transair Mali SA [*ICAO designator*] (FAAC)
TSM .... Transportability Summary Manual [*MTMC*] (TAG)
TSM .... Transportation Systems Management
TSM .... Troop Sergeant-Major [*British military*] (DMA)
TSM .... Trouble Shooting Manual (IAA)
TSM .... Type, Series, and Model (MCD)
TSM .... Type-Specific M (Protein) [*Immunology*]
TSMA .... Tinplate Stockholders' and Merchants' Association [*British*] (BI)
TSMAF .... Tesma International, Inc. [*NASDAQ symbol*] (SAG)
TSMAF .... Tesma Intl'A' [*NASDAQ symbol*] (TTSB)
TSMC .... Taiwan Semiconductor Manufacturing Co.
TSMC .... Technical Supply Management Code
TSMC .... Transportation Supply and Maintenance Command
TSMDA .... Test-Section Melt-Down Accident [*Nuclear energy*] (NRCH)
TSMFM .... Tunneling Stabilized Magnetic Force Microscopy [*Physics*]
TSMG .... Thompson Submachine Gun
TSMO .... TACSATCOM Management Office
TSMO .... TRADOC Systems Management Office [*Military*] (RDA)
tsm publishing ... Technical, Scientific, and Medical Publishing (WDMC)
TSMS .... Time Series Modeling System (MHDB)
TSMS .... Tobacco Strippers Mutual Society [*A union*] [*British*]
TSMT .... Transmit
TSMT .... Trident SONAR Maintenance Trainer (DWSG)
TSMTR .... Transmitter (DA)
TSMTS .... Tri-State Motor Tariff Service
TSMU .... Time-Sharing Multiplex Unit [*Telecommunications*] (IAA)
ts mutation ... Temperature Sensitive Mutation [*Genetics*] (DOG)
TSN .... [*The*] Sierra Network [*Computer science*]
TSN .... [*The*] Sports Network [*Cable-television system*] [*Information service or system*] (IID)
TSN .... Tailshaft Renewed
TSN .... Tan Son Nhut [*Air base*] [*Vietnam*]
TSN .... Tape Serial Number [*Computer science*]
TSN .... Task Sequence Number (IAA)
TSN .... TecSyn International [*TS Symbol*] (TTSB)
TSN .... Tecsyn International, Inc. [*Toronto Stock Exchange symbol*]
TSN .... Temporary Sort Number [*Computer science*]
TSN .... Test Sequence Network (CAAL)
TSN .... Thymosin [*A thymus hormone*]
TSN .... Tianjin [*China*] [*Airport symbol*] (OAG)
TSN .... Tientsin [*China*] [*Airport symbol*] (AD)
TSN .... Time since New [*Navy*] (NG)
TSN .... Traffic Safety Now [*Defunct*] (EA)
TSN .... Trans-Air Services Ltd. [*Nigeria*] [*ICAO designator*] (FAAC)
TSN .... Trimethoprim, Sulfamethoxazole, Nystatin [*Medicine*]
TSN .... Tryptone Sulfite Neomycin (OA)
TSN .... Tryptophan Peptone Sulfide Neomycin [*Agar*] (MAE)
TSN .... Tsingtau [*Republic of China*] [*Seismograph station code, US Geological Survey*] (SEIS)
TSN .... United States Army TRADOC, Fort Wadsworth, Chaplains Center Library, Fort Wadsworth, NY [*OCLC symbol*] (OCLC)
TSNA .... Tobacco-Specific Nitrosamine [*Biochemistry*]
TSNC .... Time-Sharing and Multiplexing Numerical Control [*Telecommunications*] (IAA)
TSNG .... Tseng Labs [*NASDAQ symbol*] (TTSB)
TSNG .... Tseng Labs, Inc. [*Newtown, PA*] [*NASDAQ symbol*] (NQ)
TSNI .... (Toluenesulfonyl)nitroimidazole [*Organic chemistry*]
TSNT .... (Toluenesulfonyl)nitrotriazole [*Organic chemistry*]
TSO .... Carrollton, OH [*Location identifier FAA*] (FAAL)
TSo .... Fayette County Free Library, Somerville, TN [*Library symbol Library of Congress*] (LCLS)
TSO .... Isles Of Scilly-Tresco [*Airport symbol*] (OAG)
TSO .... Table Structure Overview [*NASA*]
TSO .... Tactical Surveillance Officer (MCD)
TSO .... Target Systems Office [*Army Materiel Command*] (RDA)
TSO .... Technical Service Order [*Aviation*] (DA)
TSO .... Technical Service Organization [*A generic term*]
TSO .... Technical Specification Order
TSO .... Technical Staff Officer
TSO .... Technical Standard Order [*FAA*]
TSO .... Technical Standing Order (KSC)
TSO .... Technical Support Organization [*AEC*]
TSO .... Telecommunications Service Order [*Telecommunications*] (TEL)

TSO .... Telephone Service Observation [*Telecommunications*] (TEL)
TSO .... Terminator Sensor Output
TSO .... Tesoro Petroleum [*NYSE symbol*] (TTSB)
TSO .... Tesoro Petroleum Corp. [*NYSE symbol*] (SPSG)
TSO .... Test Site Office [*NASA*]
TSO .... Test Support Operations [*NASA*] (KSC)
TSO .... Thrust Section Observer (AAG)
TSO .... Time-Sharing Option [*Computer science*]
TSO .... Time Since Overhaul [*of engine, or other equipment*]
TSO .... Time Slot Zero [*Telecommunications*] (IAA)
TSO .... Toronto Symphony Orchestra (CDAI)
TSO .... Town Suboffice
TSO .... Trading Standards Officer (ODBW)
TSO .... Training for Skill Ownership (AIE)
TSO .... Transaero Airlines [*Former USSR ICAO designator*] (FAAC)
TSO .... Transportation Supply Officer [*Military*]
TSO .... Tulsa [*Oklahoma*] [*Seismograph station code, US Geological Survey Closed*] (SEIS)
TSOA .... Technical Standard Order Authorization (MCD)
TSOA .... Triumph Sports Owners Association (EA)
TSOC .... Tape System Output Converter [*Computer science*] (IAA)
TSOC .... Time-Sharing Operating Control System [*Computer science*] (IAA)
TSOC .... Totally Synthetic Organic Chemical [*or Compound*] (GNE)
TSODB .... Time Series Oriented Database
TSO/E .... Time-Sharing Option Extensions (HGAA)
TSOET .... Tests of Elementary Training [*Military British*]
TSOL .... [*The*] Sound of London [*Record label*]
TSOL .... True Sounds of Liberty [*Musical group*]
TSOP .... [*The*] Sound of Philadelphia [*Song*]
TSOP .... Tactical Standing Operating Procedure [*Army*]
TSOP .... Technical Standard Operating Procedure [*NASA*] (KSC)
TSOP .... Thin Small-Outline Package [*Computer science*]
TSOR .... Tentative Specific Operational Requirement [*Military*]
TSORT .... Transmission System Optimum Relief Tool [*Telecommunications*] (TEL)
TSOS .... Time-Sharing Operating System [*Computer science*] (IEEE)
TSOSC .... Test Set Operational Signal Converter (AAG)
TSO/VTAM ... Time-Sharing Option for the Virtual Telecommunications Access Method [*Computer science*] (MHDI)
TSP .... [*The*] Sentencing Project (EA)
TSP .... Tailspike Protein [*Biochemistry*]
TSP .... Teaspoonful (GPO)
tsp .... Teaspoonful (ODBW)
TSP .... Technical Specification
TSP .... Technical Support Package [*NASA*]
TSP .... Tehachapi, CA [*Location identifier FAA*] (FAAL)
TSP .... Telemetry Simulation Program
TSP .... Telephone Switching Planning (ADA)
TSP .... Teleprocessing Services Program [*General Service Administration*]
TSP .... Temperature-Sensitive Period
TSP .... Temporary Standard Practice [*or Procedure*] (AAG)
TSP .... Terminal Support Processor [*Computer science*] (PDAA)
TSP .... Test Site Position [*NASA*] (KSC)
TSP .... Test Software Program [*NASA*] (NASA)
TSP .... Test Status Panel (MCD)
TSP .... Test Support Package
TSP .... Test Support Plan [*Army*]
TSP .... Test Support Position
TSP .... Test Support Program
TSP .... Tesuque Peak [*New Mexico*] [*Seismograph station code, US Geological Survey*] (SEIS)
TSP .... Textured Soy Protein [*Food industry*]
TSP .... Thermospray [*Also, TS*] [*Ionization Physics*]
TSP .... Theta Sigma Phi [*Later, Women in Communications*]
TSP .... Threat Support Package [*DoD*]
TSP .... Threat Support Plan (MCD)
TSP .... Thrift Savings Plan [*Office of Personnel Management*] (GFGA)
TSP .... Thrombospondin [*or Thrombin-Sensitive Protein*] [*Hematology*]
TSP .... Throttle Solenoid Positioner [*Automotive engineering*]
TSP .... Thyroid-Stimulating Hormone of the Prepituitary Gland [*Endocrinology*]
TSP .... Time and Space Processing (MCD)
TSP .... Time Series Processor Software [*Bureau of the Census*] (GFGA)
TSP .... Time-Share Peripherals [*Computer science*] (IAA)
TSP .... Time Sorting Program
TSP .... Titanium Sublimation Pump (OA)
TSP .... Toronto Sun Publishing Corp. [*Toronto Stock Exchange symbol*]
TSP .... Torpedo Seaplane [*Navy*]
TSP .... Torpedo Setting Panel [*Military*] (CAAL)
TSP .... Total Serum Protein [*Medicine*]
TSP .... Total Suspended Particulates
TSP .... Total Systems Performance [*MODCOMP*]
TSP .... Tracking Signal Processor (LAIN)
TSP .... Traffic Service Position [*Telephone*]
TSP .... Transponder
TSP .... Transshipment Point (AFM)
TSP .... Traveling Salesman Problem [*Mathematics*]
TSP .... Traveling Scholar Program (EA)
TSP .... Trial Shot Point
TSP .... Tribal Sovereignty Program [*Later, SGFID*] (EA)
TSP .... Trimethylsilyl Propionate [*Organic chemistry*]
TSP .... Triple-Super Phosphates
TSP .... Triservice Program [*Military*]
TSP .... Trisodium Phosphate [*Inorganic chemistry*]
TSP .... Tropical Spastic Paraparesis [*Neurology*]
TSP .... Tube Support Plate [*Nuclear energy*] (NRCH)
TSP .... Twisted Shielded Pairs [*Cables*] (NASA)
TSP .... United States Army TRADOC, Carlisle Barracks, Carlisle Barracks, PA [*OCLC symbol*] (OCLC)
TSPA .... Triethylenethiophosphoramide [*Also, THioTEPA*] [*Antineoplastic drug*]
TSPAK .... Time Series Package [*Bell System*]
TSPAP .... Total Serum Prostatic Acid Phosphatase [*Medicine*] (MAE)
TSPC .... Thermal Sciences and Propulsion Center [*Purdue University*] [*Research center*] (RCD)
TSPC .... Toxic Substances Priority Committee [*Terminated, 1984*] [*Environmental Protection Agency*] (EGAO)
TSPC .... Tropical Stored Products Centre [*Tropical Products Institute*] [*Overseas Development Administration*] [*British*] (DS)
TSPE .... Thunderstorm with Ice Pellets [*ICAO*] (FAAC)
TSPEC .... Test Specification (MSA)
TSPED .... Trade Shows and Professional Exhibits Directory [*Formerly, TPED*] [*Later, TSW*] [*A publication*]
TSPI .... Time-Space-Position-Information (MCD)
TSPIRS .... Timber Sales Program Information Reporting System [*Department of the Interior*]
TSPL .... Telephone Systems Programming Language [*Computer science*] (MHDB)
TSPLIB .... Traveling Salesman Problem Library [*Electronic mail*]
TSPM .... Total Suspended Particulate Matter
TSpMH .... South Pittsburg Municipal Hospital, South Pittsburg, TN [*Library symbol Library of Congress*] (LCLS)
tspn .... Teaspoon [*Measure*] (WGA)
TSPO .... Threat Simulator Project Office [*Army Intelligence Agency*] (RDA)
TSPP .... Tanker Safety and Pollution Prevention
TSPP .... Technetium Stannous Pyrophosphate [*Radiochemistry*]
TSPP .... Tetrasodium Pyrophosphate [*Inorganic chemistry*]
TSPP .... Training System Procurement Package
TSPR .... Total Systems Performance Reliability [*or Responsibility*] (MCD)
TSPR .... Training System Program Requirements (MCD)
TSPRT .... Truncated Sequential Probability Ratio Test (PDAA)
TSPRTR .... Truncated Sequential Probability Ratio Test for Reliability (PDAA)
TSPS .... Time-Sharing Programming System [*Computer science*] (IEEE)
TSPS .... Traffic Service Position System [*Telecommunications*]
TSPSCAP .... Traffic Service Position System Real-Time Capacity Program [*Telecommunications*] (TEL)
TSPT .... Transport (WGA)
TSPZ .... Torres Strait Protected Zone [*Commonwealth*] (EERA)
TSP-Z .... Trisodium Phosphate - Zephiran [*Clinical chemistry*]
TSPZA .... Torres Strait Protected Zone Authority [*Australia*]
TSQ .... Technical Services Quarterly [*A publication*]
TSQ .... Time and Super Quick
TSQ .... Trade Specialty Qualification (MCD)
TSQ .... Triple Stage Quadrupole [*Instrumentation*]
TSQAP .... Tasmanian Shellfish Quality Assurance Program (EERA)
TSR .... Tactical SONAR Range (NVT)
TSR .... Tactical Strike and Reconnaissance
TSR .... Tactical Studies Rules [*In corporation name TSR, Inc.*]
TSR .... Technically Specified Natural Rubber
TSR .... Technical Sales Representative
TSR .... Technical Services Report [*A publication*] (EAAP)
TSR .... Technical Services Representative (MCD)
TSR .... Technical Status Review [*NASA*] (NASA)
TSR .... Technical Study Report
TSR .... Technical Summary Report
TSR .... Technical Support Review (SSD)
TSR .... Telecommunications Service Request (CET)
TSR .... Telemarketing Sales Representative
TSR .... Telemarketing Service Representative (WDMC)
TSR .... Telephone Sales Representative (WDMC)
TSR .... Telephone Support Request
TSR .... TeleService Resources
TSR .... Temporary Storage Register
TSR .... Tensile Strength Retention [*Textile technology*]
TSR .... Terminate and Stay Resident [*Computer science*]
TSR .... Testosterone Sterilized Rat
TSR .... Test Schedule Request
TSR .... Test Status Report [*NASA*] (NASA)
TSR .... Test Summary Report (IAA)
TSR .... Test Support Requirements (KSC)
TSR .... Thermally Stable Resin
TSR .... Thermal Shock Rig [*Nuclear energy*] (NRCH)
TSR .... Thermal Stress Relief [*Mechanical engineering*]
TSR .... Thermochemical Sulfate Reduction [*Chemistry*]
TSR .... Thermo Sentron [*AMEX symbol*] (TTSB)
TSR .... Thermo Sentron, Inc. [*AMEX symbol*] (SAG)
TSR .... Thyroid Hormone Secretion Rate (OA)
TSR .... Thyroid-to-Serum Ratio [*Medicine*] (MAE)
TSR .... Tile-Shingle Roof [*Technical drawings*]
TSR .... Time Sharing Resources, Inc. [*Information service or system*] (IID)
TSR .... Time Status Register
TSR .... Time to Sustained Respirations [*Obstetrics*]
TSR .... Timisoara [*Romania*] [*Airport symbol*] (OAG)
TSR .... Tokyo Shoko Research Ltd. [*Database producer*] [*Japan*]
TSR .... Torpedo-Spotter Reconnaissance [*Obsolete Military British*]
TSR .... Total Shoulder Replacement [*Medicine*]
TSR .... Total Solar Radiation [*Botany*]
TSR .... Total Stress Range [*Nuclear energy*] (NUCP)
TSR .... Total System Responsibility
TSR .... Towed SONAR Response
TSR .... Tower Shielding Reactor [*Nuclear energy*]

TSR............ Trade Study Report
TSR............ Training Support Requirements [*Military*]
TSR............ Transistor Saturable Reactor
TSR............ Transportable Surveillance RADAR (MCD)
TSR............ Trans Service Airlift [*Zaire*] [*ICAO designator*] (FAAC)
TSR............ Trans-Siberian Railway
TSR............ Traveling Stock Reserve
TSR............ Tri-Star Resources [*Vancouver Stock Exchange symbol*]
TSR............ TSR, Inc. [*Associated Press*] (SAG)
TSR............ Tsuruga [*Japan*] [*Seismograph station code, US Geological Survey*] (SEIS)
TSR............ Turbine Shaft Rate [*Military*] (CAAL)
TSR............ Turnover Summary Report [*Military*]
TSR............ United States Army TRADOC, Redstone Arsenal, USAMMCS [*United States Army Missile and Munitions Center School*] Technical Library, Redstone Arsenal, AL [*OCLC symbol*] (OCLC)
TSRA.......... Thunderstorm with Rain [*ICAO*] (FAAC)
TSRA.......... Torres Strait Regional Authority [*Australia*]
TSRA.......... Total System Requirements Analysis (NASA)
TSRA.......... Training Support Requirements Analysis (MCD)
TSRB.......... Teachers and Schools Registration Board [*Australia*]
TSRB.......... Top Salaries Review Board [*British*]
TSRC.......... Theta-Sensitive Regulatory Cell [*Hypothetical*] [*Hematology*]
TSRC.......... Transmitter-Receiver (IAA)
TSRC.......... Transportation Systems Review Committee [*MTMC*] (TAG)
TSRC.......... Tubular and Split Rivet Council [*Later, TRMI*] (EA)
TSRE.......... Tropospheric Scatter Radio Equipment (AAG)
TSRG.......... Trans Energy [*NASDAQ symbol*] (TTSB)
TSRG.......... Trans Energy, Inc. [*NASDAQ symbol*] (SAG)
TSRI.......... Technical Skill Reenlistment Incentive
TSRI.......... TSR, Inc. [*Hauppauge, NY*] [*NASDAQ symbol*] (NQ)
TSRL.......... [*The*] Special Relief League [*Defunct*] (EA)
TSRL.......... Total Support Requirements List (AAG)
TSRLM........ Tandem Scanning Reflected Light Microscopy
TSRMP........ Training System Resource Management Plan [*Army*]
TSRO.......... Two-Stage Reverse Osmosis [*Chemical engineering*]
TSRP.......... Technical Support Real Property
TSRP.......... Toll Service Results Plan [*Bell System*]
TSR PEIS..... Tritium Supply and Recycling Programmatic Environmental Impact Statement
TSRS.......... Training Site Requirements Study [*DoD*]
TSRT.......... Teacher Situation Reaction Test
TSRTAMAA... Tactical Surveillance, Reconnaissance, and Target Acquisition Mission Area Analysis (MCD)
TSRU.......... Tuberculosis Surveillance Research Unit [*Netherlands*] (EAIO)
TSRV.......... Torpedo Ship Ranging Vessel [*Canadian Navy*]
TSRV.......... Transport Systems Research Facility (GAVI)
TSRV.......... Transport Systems Research Vehicle
TSS............ New York [*New York*] E. 34th Street [*Airport symbol*] (OAG)
TSS............ [*The*] Safety Society (EA)
TSS............ St. Andrews School, St. Andrews, TN [*Library symbol Library of Congress*] (LCLS)
TSS............ [*The*] Super Show (ITD)
TSS............ TACFIRE Software Specialist (MCD)
TSS............ Tactical Shelter System (DOMA)
TSS............ Tactical Strike System
TSS............ Tactical Surveillance Sonobuoy (MCD)
TSS............ Tangential Signal Sensitivity
TSS............ Tank Surveillance Service [*Military Traffic Management Command*]
TSS............ Tape Search System
TSS............ Tape Storage System
TSS............ Target Selection Standard [*Military*] (INF)
TSS............ Target Selector Switch
TSS............ Target Sensing Switch
TSS............ Task-State Segment [*Operating system data structure*] [*Computer science*]
TSS............ Teacher Stress Scale (EDAC)
TSS............ Tebessa [*Algeria*] [*Airport symbol*] (AD)
TSS............ Technical Sales Seminars [*Department of Commerce*]
TSS............ Technical School Squadron [*Army*]
TSS............ Technical Services Staff [*Environmental Protection Agency*] (GFGA)
TSS............ Technical Specification Sheet
TSS............ Technical Staff Surveillance [*Military*] (IAA)
TSS............ Technical Support Services
TSS............ Technical Support Staff [*Environmental Protection Agency*] (GFGA)
TSS............ Telecommunications Security System (MCD)
TSS............ Telecommunications Service System (NITA)
TSS............ Telecommunication Switching System
TS/S........... Telemeter Set/Synthesized (DWSG)
TSS............ Teletype Switching System [*or Subsystem*]
TSS............ Temporary Storage Site [*DoD*]
TSS............ Tensile Shear Specimen [*Plastics technology*]
TSS............ Terminal Security System [*Computer science*]
TSS............ Terminal Send Side
TSS............ Terminal Support Subsystems (NITA)
TSS............ Terminal Support System
TSS............ Test Set Simulator
TSS............ Tethered Satellite System (MCD)
TSS............ Threatened Species Strategy (EERA)
TSS............ Thrust Stand System
TSS............ Time-Shared Supervisory System (IAA)
TSS............ Time-Shared System (NITA)
TSS............ Time-Sharing System [*Computer science*]
TSS............ Toll Switching System [*Telecommunications*] (TEL)
TSS............ Topographic Support System [*Army*] (RDA)
TSS............ Toroidal Space Station
TSS............ Toroidal Support Submarine
TSS............ Total Ship Survivability (DOMA)
TSS............ Total Soluble Sulfur [*Analytical chemistry*]
TSS............ Total Subscriber Satisfaction [*HBO (Home Box Office) rating system*]
TSS............ Total Sum of Squares
TSS............ Total Suspended Solids [*Environmental chemistry*]
TSS............ Total Systems Services, Inc. [*NYSE symbol*] (SPSG)
TSS............ Total System Svcs [*NYSE symbol*] (TTSB)
TSS............ TOW [*Tube-Launched, Optically Tracked, Wire-Guided (Weapon)*] Subsystem [*Army*]
TSS............ Toxic Shock Syndrome [*Medicine*]
TSS............ Track Store Switch (IAA)
TSS............ Track Suspension System [*MTMC*] (TAG)
TSS............ Tradeoff Study Suggestion (SSD)
TSS............ Trade Support System (MHDW)
TSS............ Traffic Separation Scheme
TSS............ Traffic Surveillance System [*Traffic management*]
TSS............ Trainer System Software
TSS............ Training Services [*Job Training and Partnership Act*] (OICC)
TSS............ Training Subsystem (MCD)
TSS............ Training Support Service [*ILO*] [*United Nations*] (DUND)
TSS............ Train Supervisory System (IAA)
TSS............ Transistor Servo Simulator
TSS............ Transition State Spectroscopy [*Physics*]
TSS............ Transmission Surveillance System [*Bell System*]
TSS............ Transparent Semiconductor Shutter
TSS............ Transverse Spinal Sclerosis [*Orthopedics*] (DAVI)
TSS............ Treatment System Support
TSS............ Trend-Set Industry [*Vancouver Stock Exchange symbol*]
TSS............ Tropical Sea Airlines [*Thailand*] [*ICAO designator*] (FAAC)
TSS............ Tropical Splenomegaly Syndrome [*Medicine*] (MAE)
TSS............ Tropospheric Scatter System
TSS............ Trunk Servicing System [*Bell System*]
TSS............ Tsurugisan [*Anabuki*] [*Japan*] [*Seismograph station code, US Geological Survey*] (SEIS)
TSS............ Tug Structural Support [*NASA*] (NASA)
TSS............ Turbine Steam Ship
TSS............ Turbine Supersonic Speed (ERG)
TSS............ Turner's Syndrome Society of the US (EA)
TSS............ Tutor Support Scheme [*Australia*]
TSS............ Twin-Screw Steamer [*Nautical*]
TSS............ Typescripts [*Typography*] (WDAA)
TSS............ Typographic Support System (MCD)
TSS............ United States Army TRADOC, Fort Story, Fort Story, VA [*OCLC symbol*] (OCLC)
TSSA.......... Tackle and Shooting Sports Agents Association (EA)
TSSA.......... Telecommunications Sales Superintendents' Association [*A union*] [*British*]
TSSA.......... Telemetry Subcarrier Spectrum Analyzer
TSSA.......... Test Scorer and Statistical Analyzer [*Computer science*]
TSSA.......... Test Site Support Activity [*NASA*]
TSSA.......... Thunderstorm with Sandstorm [*Meteorology*]
TSSA.......... Trade Show Services Association [*Defunct*] (EA)
TSSA.......... Transport Salaried Staff's Association [*A union*] [*British*] (DCTA)
TSSA.......... Tumor-Specific Surface Antigen [*Immunology*]
TSSAA........ Tackle and Shooting Sports Agents Association (EA)
TSSAM........ Tri-Service Standoff Attack Missile [*Military*]
TSS & TP.... Test Suite Structure and Test Purpose [*Telecommunications*]
TSSB.......... Two-Step Sealed Bidding (AAGC)
TSSC.......... Target Selection and Seeking Console
TSSC.......... Target System Service Charge (NG)
TSSC.......... Toxic Substances Strategy Committee [*Nuclear energy*] (NRCH)
TSS-C......... Transmission Surveillance System - Cable [*Telecommunications*] (TEL)
TSSCC........ Toy Stores Steiff Collectors Club (EA)
TSSCS........ Tactical Synchronous Satellite Communication System
TSSD.......... Torsional Simple Shear Device [*Nuclear energy*] (NUCP)
TSSD.......... Typesetting System for Scientific Document [*Computer science*] (PDAA)
TSSDT........ Thrust Subsystem Design Team [*NASA*]
TSSE.......... Tactical Security Support Equipment [*Military*]
tsse............ Terrasse (DD)
TSSE.......... Toxic Shock Syndrome Exotoxin
T/SSI.......... Technology/Scientific Services, Inc.
TSSIC......... Tool and Stainless Steel Industry Committee (EA)
TSSLS........ Titan Standardized Space Launch System (SAA)
TSSM......... Thruster Subsystem Module [*NASA*]
TSSM......... Total Ship Simulation Model
TSSMCP...... Time-Sharing System Message Control Program (NITA)
TSSMS........ Time Sharing Services Management System (GFGA)
TSSNM........ Technologist Section of the Society of Nuclear Medicine (EA)
TSSP.......... Tactical Satellite Signal Processor (RDA)
TSSP.......... Thickness-Sensitive Solar Paint [*Coating technology*]
TSSP.......... Two Stripper in Series Permeater [*Chemical engineering*]
TS/SPAR..... Time Sharing System Performance Activity Recorder (PDAA)
TSSPS........ Tsentralniya Suvet na Profesionalnite Suyuzi [*Central Council of Trade Unions*] [*Bulgaria*]
TSSR.......... Theater Stock Status Report [*Military*]
TSSS.......... Trainer Software Support System [*Military*]
TSSS.......... Triple S Plastics [*NASDAQ symbol*] (SAG)
TSSSP........ Tennessee Study of State Science Policy [*National Science Foundation*] (EA)
TSSST........ Time-Space-Space-Space-Time [*Telecommunications*] (TEL)
TSST.......... Threat Simulation System Terminal [*Military*]

TSST .... Toxic Shock Syndrome Toxin [*Medicine*]
TSSU .... Test Signal Switching Unit (MCD)
TSSU .... Theater Sterile Supply Unit [*Surgery*] (DAVI)
TSSW .... TouchStone Software [*NASDAQ symbol*] (TTSB)
TSSW .... TouchStone Software Corp. [*NASDAQ symbol*] (SAG)
TST .... Media Logic, Inc. [*AMEX symbol*] (SPSG)
TST .... [*The*] Science Teacher [*A publication*]
TST .... Tail Stop and Turning [*Automotive engineering*]
TST .... Technical and Scholastic Test [*Vocational guidance test*]
TST .... Telemetry Simulation Terminal
TST .... Television Signal Tracer (DEN)
TST .... Temperature Sensing Transducer
TST .... Test (AAG)
TST .... Test Support Table
TSt .... Texts and Studies [*A publication*] (BJA)
TST .... Thermistor Sterilization Test
TST .... Threshold Setting Tracer
TST .... Time-Shared Terminal [*Computer science*] (IAA)
TST .... Time-Sharing Terminals, Inc.
TST .... Time-Space-Time [*Digital switching*] [*Telecommunications*] (TEL)
TST .... Titmus Stereocuity Test [*Medicine*] (DAVI)
TST .... Torres Strait Treaty (EERA)
TST .... Total Story Time [*Broadcasting*] (WDMC)
TST .... Total Surface Tested
TST .... Toxic Shock Toxin [*Biochemistry*]
TST .... Trang [*Thailand*] [*Airport symbol*] (OAG)
TST .... Transaction Step Task
TST .... Transition State Theory [*Physical chemistry*]
TST .... Transmission Scheme Translator (MCD)
TST .... Transmission System Test (MCD)
TST .... Treadmill Stress Testing [*Physiology*]
TST .... Treatment Selection Team (DOGT)
TST .... Triceps Skinfold Thickness [*Medicine*]
TST .... Trilogy Screening Technique
TST .... Troubleshooting Time (SAA)
TST .... Truncated Sequential Test (PDAA)
TST .... Trust
TST .... Tuberculin Skin Test [*Medicine*] (PDAA)
TST .... Tumor Skin Test [*Medicine*] (MAE)
TST .... Twenty Statements Test
TST .... Two-Station Training
TST .... United States Army TRALINET, Systems Center, ATPL-AOT, Fort Monroe, VA [*OCLC symbol*] (OCLC)
TSTA .... Tailored Ship Training Availability [*Navy*] (DOMA)
TSTA .... Technology Security Technical Assessment [*DoD*]
TSTA .... Transmission, Signaling, and Test Access
TSTA .... Tritium Systems Test Assembly (MCD)
TSTA .... Tumor-Specific Tissue Antigen [*Immunology*] (DAVI)
TSTA .... Tumor-Specific Transplantation Antigen [*Immunology*]
TSTC .... Target Selection and Tracking Console
TSTD .... Total Ship Test Director [*Navy*] (CAAL)
TSTE .... Training System Test and Evaluation (MCD)
TSTEE .... Trustee
TSTEQ .... Test Equipment
TSTF .... Two-Step,Two-Frequency
TSTFA .... Tasmania Sashimi Tuna Fisherman's Association (EERA)
TSTFLT .... Test Set Fault (AAG)
TSTG .... Testing (MSA)
TSTI .... TST Impreso, Inc. [*NASDAQ symbol*] (SAG)
TSTI .... TST/Impresso [*NASDAQ symbol*] (TTSB)
TSTICT .... Test Incoming Trunk [*Telecommunications*] (IAA)
TSTImp .... TST Impreso, Inc. [*Associated Press*] (SAG)
TStL & KC .... Toledo, St. Louis & Kansas City Railroad
TSTN .... Triple Supertwist Nematic [*Video technology*] (PCM)
TSTNG .... Testing
TSTO .... Testing Tool (AAG)
TSTO .... Test Site Tool Order [*NASA*] (AAG)
TSTO .... Two-Stage-to-Orbit [*Aerospace technology*] (PS)
TSTP .... Talking Screen Textwriting Program (EDAC)
TSTP .... Test of Selected Topics in Physics
TSTP .... Thermistor Sterilization Test Program
TSTP .... Total Ship Test Program [*Navy*] (CAAL)
TSTP .... Traffic Safety Training Program
TSTPAC .... Transmission and Signaling Test Plan and Analysis Concept [*Telecommunications*] (TEL)
TSTP/AFS .... Total Ship Test Program/Active Fleet Surface Ships [*Navy*] (CAAL)
TSTPI .... Tapered Steel Transmission Pole Institute [*Defunct*] (EA)
TSTP/SP .... Total Ship Test Program/Ship Production [*Navy*] (CAAL)
TSTR .... Tester (MSA)
TSTR .... Transistor (AAG)
TSTRZ .... Transistorized (MSA)
TSTS .... Tail Section Test Stand (AAG)
TSTS .... Thermal Sight Test Set [*Army*]
TSTS .... Third Stage Test Set [*Aerospace*] (MCD)
TSTS .... Thrust Structure Test Stand (AAG)
TSTS .... Tomahawk System Test Set
TSTS .... Tracking System Test Set (AAG)
TSTS .... Tracking System Test Stand (IAA)
TSTWCS .... Temporary Short-Time Working Compensation Scheme (AIE)
TSU .... Contract Air Cargo, Inc. [*FAA designator*] (FAAC)
TSU .... Tabiteuea South [*Kiribati*] [*Airport symbol*] (OAG)
TSU .... Tandem Signal Unit [*Telecommunications*] (TEL)
TSU .... Tape Search Unit (CET)
TSU .... Tariff Selection Unit (OA)
TSU .... Tarleton State University [*Formerly, TSC*] [*Texas*]
TSU .... Task-Specific Utility
TSU .... Technical Service Unit
TSU .... Technical Support Unit (IAA)
TSU .... Telecommunications Study Unit [*American Topical Association*] [*Defunct*] (EA)
TSU .... Telephone Signal Unit [*Telecommunications*] (TEL)
TSU .... Telescope Sight Unit (MCD)
TSU .... Tennessee State University, Nashville, TN [*Library symbol Library of Congress OCLC symbol*] (LCLS)
TSU .... Terminating Signal Unit [*Electronics*] (ECII)
TSU .... Test Signal Unit [*Telecommunications*] (TEL)
TSU .... Texas Southern University
TSU .... Thermal Systems Unit (KSC)
TSU .... This Side Up
TSU .... Time Standard Unit
TSU .... Transfer Switch Unit (AAG)
TSU .... Transportation System Utilization Program [*Department of Energy*]
TSU .... Trans-Species Unlimited [*Later, ARM*] (EA)
TSU .... Triple Sugar-Urea Base [*Agar*] [*Microbiology*]
TSU .... Trunk Switching Unit (NITA)
TSU .... Tsu [*Japan*] [*Seismograph station code, US Geological Survey*] (SEIS)
TSU .... Tsumeb [*South-West Africa*] [*Geomagnetic observatory code*]
TSU .... Tulsa-Sapulpa Union Railway Co. [*AAR code*]
TSU .... Twin and Subtract (SAA)
TSUP .... Trunk Supervisor [*Telecommunications*] (IAA)
TSUR .... Tectonic Surface Uplift Rate [*Biology*]
TSUS .... Tariff Schedules of the United States [*Later, HTSUS*]
TSUSA .... Tariff Schedules of the United States, Annotated
TSV .... Terminal Stage Vehicle
TSV .... Thermal Sensitive Vote [*Automotive interior comfort survey*]
TSV .... Thru-Sight Video [*Army training device*] (INF)
TSV .... Tobacco Streak Virus
TSV .... Townsville [*Australia Airport symbol*] (OAG)
TSV .... Tropair Airservices [*British ICAO designator*] (FAAC)
TSV .... Turbine Stop Valve [*Nuclear energy*] (NRCH)
TSV .... Turnkey Systems Vendor [*Computer science*] (MHDI)
TSV .... Twin Springs [*Nevada*] [*Seismograph station code, US Geological Survey Closed*] (SEIS)
TSVP .... Tournez s'il Vous Plait [*Please Turn Over*] [*See also PTO*] [*French*]
TSVR .... Total Systemic Vascular Resistance
TSVS .... Time-Sharing - Virtual System [*Computer science*] (MCD)
TSW .... Southwestern Baptist Theological Seminary, Fort Worth, TX [*OCLC symbol*] (OCLC)
TSW .... Task Status Word (NITA)
TSW .... Technical Scope of Work
TSW .... Telesoftware (NITA)
TSW .... Temperature Switch (MSA)
TSW .... Test Software (MCD)
TSW .... Test Switch
TSW .... The Searchers Workbench (NITA)
TSW .... Time Switch [*Telecommunications*] (TEL)
TSW .... Trade Shows Worldwide [*Formerly, TSPED*] [*A publication*]
TSW .... Trans European Airways [*Switzerland ICAO designator*] (FAAC)
TSW .... Transfer Switch
TSW .... Transmitting Slide Wire
TSW .... Trau, Schau, Wem [*Trust, but Be Careful Whom*] [*Motto of Christian I, Elector of Saxony (1560-91)*] [*German*]
TSW .... Tropical Summer Winter [*Vessel load line mark*]
tsw .... Tswana [*MARC language code Library of Congress*] (LCCP)
TSW .... T Switch Cell [*Immunology*]
TSW .... Turbine-Building Service Water [*Nuclear energy*] (NRCH)
TSWE .... Test of Standard Written English
TSWG .... Training Support Working Group [*Army*]
TSWL .... Tulsa Studies in Women's Literature [*A publication*] (BRI)
TSWTT .... Test Switch Thrust Termination
TSWV .... Tomato Spotted Wilt Virus
TSX .... Telephone Satellite, Experimental
TSX .... Time-Sharing Execution [*Computer science*] (IAA)
TSX .... Time-Sharing Executive [*Modular Computer Systems*] [*Computer science*]
TSX .... Time-Sharing Executive System [*Computer science*] (IAA)
TSX .... Transfer and Set Index (SAA)
TSX .... True Seed Exchange [*Later, SSE*] (EA)
TSX-4 .... Touring Sport Extra-4WD [*In automotive name Ghia Vignale TSX-4*]
TSX Cp .... TSX Corp. [*Associated Press*] (SAG)
TSXX .... TSX Corp. [*NASDAQ symbol*] (SAG)
TSY .... Tech-Sym [*NYSE symbol*] (TTSB)
TSY .... Tech-Sym Corp. [*NYSE symbol*] (SPSG)
TSY .... Trypticase Soy Yeast [*Cell growth medium*] (MAE)
TT .... Caroline Islands (VRA)
TT .... Chad [*International civil aircraft marking*] (ODBW)
TT .... Marshall Islands (VRA)
TT .... Royal West [*ICAO designator*] (AD)
TT .... Tablet Triturate [*Pharmacy*]
TT .... Tactical Training [*Followed by location*] [*Military*]
TT .... Tactile Tension [*Ophthalmology*]
TT .... Tail-to-Tail [*Polymer structure*]
TT .... Talar Tilt [*Angle of ankle joint*]
TT .... Talith and Tefillin (BJA)
TT .... Talmud Torah (BJA)
TT .... Tanganyika Territory
TT .... Tank Technology (WDAA)
TT .... Tank Top (DS)
TT .... Tank Truck [*Freight*]

TT .... Tantato Resources, Inc. [*Vancouver Stock Exchange symbol*]
TT .... Target Towing Aircraft [*Navy*]
TT .... Teacher Training
TT .... Technical Team
TT .... Technical Test
TT .... Technical Training (OICC)
TT .... Technical Translation [*A publication Obsolete*]
TT .... Technology Transfer (DS)
TT .... Teetotaler [*Slang*]
TT .... Telecommunications Technician [*British military*] (DMA)
TT .... Telegraphic Transfer [*of funds*] [*Banking*]
TT .... Teletype
TT .... Teletypewriter [*Telecommunications*]
TT .... Teletypewriter and Facsimile Apparatus [*JETDS nomenclature*] [*Military*] (CET)
TT .... Teller Terminal (MHDW)
TT .... Tell Taanach (BJA)
TT .... Tempelurkunden aus Tello [*A publication*] (BJA)
TT .... Temperature Transmitter [*Nuclear energy*] (NRCH)
TT .... Temporarily Transferred [*Telecommunications*] (TEL)
TT .... Tendon Transfer [*Surgery*]
T/T .... Terminal Timing (KSC)
tt .... Terminus Technicus (BJA)
TT .... Terms of Trade (MHDW)
TT .... Testamentary Trust [*Legal term*]
TT .... Test Temperature [*Nuclear energy*] (NRCH)
TT .... Test Terminator (IAA)
TT .... Test [*or Testing*] Time (IAA)
TT .... Test Tube (IAA)
TT .... Tetanus Toxoid [*Medicine*]
TT .... Tetrathionate [*Nutrient broth*] [*Microbiology*]
TT .... Tetrazol (MAE)
TT .... Texas Tower (SAA)
TT .... Text Telephone [*Hearing-impaired technology*] [*See also TDD*]
TT .... Text Typewriter (PAZ)
TT .... Theology Today [*A publication*] (BRI)
TT .... Thermally Tuned (IAA)
TT .... Thermal-Tow
TT .... Thermomagnetic Treatment (IAA)
TT .... Thermometric Titrimetry
TT .... Thermostat Switch (IAA)
TT .... Think Time [*Computer order entry*]
TT .... Thomas Thorpe [*Publisher of a 1609 edition of Shakespeare's sonnets*]
TT .... Thrombin Time [*Hematology*]
TT .... Thrust Termination
TT .... Thymol Turbidity [*Clinical chemistry*]
TT .... Tibial Torsion [*Orthopedics*] (DAVI)
TT .... Tibial Tubercle [*Anatomy*]
TT .... Ticarcillin and Tobramycin [*Antibacterial mixture*]
TT .... Tidningarnas Telegrambyra [*Press agency*] [*Sweden*]
TT .... Tight Torso [*Women's fashions*]
TT .... Tile Threshold (MSA)
TT .... Tilt Table [*Orthopedics*] (DAVI)
TT .... Tilt Trailers (DCTA)
TT .... Timetable (DS)
T/T .... Timing and Telemetry
TT .... Title Terms (NITA)
Tt .... Titus [*New Testament book*] (BJA)
TT .... Tobacco Tax Ruling Term (DLA)
TT .... Tobramycin-Ticarcillin [*Antibiotic combination*]
TT .... Token Test (EDAC)
TT .... [*The*] Toledo Terminal Railroad Co. [*AAR code*]
TT .... Tolytriazole [*Organic chemistry*]
TT .... Tooling Tag (SAA)
TT .... Tooling Template (MCD)
TT .... Tooth Treatment [*Dentistry*] (DAVI)
TT .... Topical Time [*A publication*]
TT .... Top-to-Top (IAA)
TT .... Torpedo Tube
TT .... Total Run Time [*Robotic assay*]
TT .... Total Task Chaining [*Psychology*]
TT .... Total Temperature (MCD)
TT .... Total Thyroxine [*Endocrinology*]
TT .... Total Time (MSA)
TT .... Totus Tuus [*All Yours*] [*Latin*]
TT .... Touch-Tone [*Telecommunications*] (IAA)
TT .... Touring Twin Carburetor [*Automobile model*]
TT .... Tourism Tasmania [*Australia*]
TT .... Tourist Trophy [*Motorcycle racing*] [*British*]
TT .... Townsend Thoreson [*Company running English Channel ferries*]
TT .... Tow Truck
T/T .... Trace of/Trace of Referring to findings of traces of different substances on tests (DAVI)
TT .... Tracking Technician (SAA)
TT .... Tracking Telescope
TT .... Traffic Tester [*Telecommunications*] (TEL)
TT .... Training Text
TT .... Transaction Terminal (BUR)
TT .... Transfer Trip [*Telecommunications*] (IAA)
TT .... Transformation Toughened (MCD)
TT .... Transient Tachypnea [*Medicine*] (DMAA)
TT .... Transit Time [*of blood through heart and lungs*]
TT .... Transmitting Tract [*Botany*]
TT .... Transmitting Typewriter [*Telecommunications*] (IAA)
TT .... Transonic Tunnel [*NASA*]
TT .... Transport Trust [*British*] [*An association*] (DBA)
TT .... TransTechnology [*NYSE symbol*] (TTSB)
TT .... TransTechnology Corp. [*NYSE symbol*] (SPSG)
TT .... Trans-Texas Airways
TT .... Transthoracic [*Medicine*]
TT .... Transtracheal [*Medicine*] (DAVI)
TT .... Travel and Tourism Program [*Association of Independent Colleges and Schools specialization code*]
T/T .... Travel/Tourism
TT .... Trees for Tomorrow (EA)
TT .... Tree Test [*Psychology*]
TT .... Tree Tops
TT .... Tributary Team [*Military*]
TT .... Tricycle and Tail Skid [*Aerospace*] (AAG)
T/T .... Trienoic/Tetraenoic [*Ratio of unsaturated chemicals*]
TT .... Trigesimo-Secundo [*Book from 10 to 12-1/2 centimeters in height*] [*Bibliography*]
TT .... Trinidad and Tobago [*ANSI two-letter standard code*] (CNC)
TT .... Trinity Term
TT .... Triple Thermoplastic (SAA)
TT .... Troop Test
TT .... Trunk Test [*Telecommunications*] (IAA)
TT .... Trust Termination
TT .... Trust Territories
TT .... Trust Territory of the Pacific Islands [*Postal code*]
tt .... Trust Territory of the Pacific Islands [*MARC country of publication code Library of Congress*] (LCCP)
TT .... Tuberculin Tested [*Milk*]
TT .... Tufted Titmouse [*Ornithology*]
TT .... Turbine Tanker
TT .... Turbine Trip (IEEE)
TT .... Turntable (ADA)
TT .... Turret Trainer [*British military*] (DMA)
TT .... Twitch Tension [*Neurology*] (DAVI)
TT .... Tyne and Tees [*50th Northumbrian Division*] [*British military*] (DMA)
TT_3 .... Total Triiodothyronine [*Endocrinology*]
TT4 .... Total Thyroxine [*Endocrinology*]
TTA .... Tan Tan [*Morocco*] [*Airport symbol*] (OAG)
TTA .... Tasmanian Touch Association [*Australia*]
TTA .... Tatalina [*Alaska*] [*Seismograph station code, US Geological Survey*] (SEIS)
TTA .... Telecommunications and Telephone Association [*Arlington, VA*] [*Telecommunications service*] (TSSD)
TTA .... Telecommunication Traffic Association [*British*] (BI)
TTA .... Television Technicians' Association (IAA)
TTA .... Test Target Array (AFM)
TTA .... Theatre Television Authority (EA)
TTA .... Theatrical Traders Association Ltd. [*British*] (BI)
TTA .... Thenoyltrifluoroacetone [*Also, TTB*] [*Organic chemistry*]
TTA .... Thermomechanical Test Area [*NASA*] (NASA)
TTA .... Throughput Time Average [*Compression algorithm*] (MCD)
TTA .... Throughput Transmitted Algorithm
TTA .... Thrust Termination Assembly
TTA .... Tilt Table Angle [*Vehicle rollover*] [*Automotive safety*]
TTA .... Time to Apogee [*Aerospace*] (MCD)
TTA .... Tolyltriazole [*Organic chemistry*]
TTA .... Toronto Theatre Alliance [*Canada*] (WWLA)
TTA .... Total Tangible Assets [*Business term*] (ADA)
TTA .... Total Titratable Acidity [*Analytical chemistry*]
TTA .... Total Toe Arthroplasty [*Medicine*] (DMAA)
TTA .... Tourism Training Australia
TTA .... Trade and Tourism Alliance [*Defunct*] (EA)
TTA .... Traffic Trunk Administration [*Telecommunications*] (TEL)
TTA .... Trainer Training Assistance [*Australia*]
TTA .... Transformation Toughened Alumina (MCD)
TTA .... Transit Time Accelerometer
TTA .... Transporte e Trabalho Aero [*Mozambique*] [*ICAO designator*] (FAAC)
TTA .... Trans-Texas Airways
TTA .... Transtracheal Aspiration [*Medicine*]
TTA .... Travel and Tourism Association (EA)
TTA .... Travel Time Authorized
TTA .... Triplet-Triplet Annihilation [*Spectroscopy*]
TTA .... Tritolylamine [*Organic chemistry*]
TTA .... Turbine-Alternator Assembly (MCD)
TTAB .... Tasmanian Totalisator Agency Board [*Australia*]
TTAB .... Tetradecyltrimethylammonium Bromide [*Organic chemistry*]
TTAB .... Trademark Trial and Appeal Board [*of Patent Office*]
TTAC .... Tracking, Telemetry, and Command [*AEC*] (IAA)
TTAD .... Temporary Tour of Active Duty [*Military*]
TTADB .... Tactical Terrain Analysis Database [*Army*]
TTAF .... Technical Training Air Force
TT & E .... Technical Test and Evaluation
TT & L .... Treasury Tax and Loan Account [*Banking*]
TT & P .... Training, Transient and Patient
TTAP .... Telemetry Technical Analysis Position (MCD)
TTAT .... TACFIRE Training Assistance Team (MCD)
TTAT .... Torpedo Tube Acceptance Trials [*Navy*] (NG)
TTAW .... Table Tennis Association of Wales (DBA)
TTAWA .... Typewriter Trade and Allied Workers' Association [*A union*] [*British*]
TTB .... Tanker, Transport, Bomber [*Requirements*] [*Air Force*]
TTB .... Target Triggered Burst
TTB .... Tatuoca [*Brazil*] [*Geomagnetic observatory code*]
TTB .... Technical Test Battery [*Aptitude test*]
TTB .... Teletypewriter Buffer (CET)

TTB .... Test Two Bits (IAA)
TTB .... Tetragonal Tungsten Bronze
TTB .... Time to Blackout
TTB .... Toll Testboard [*Telecommunications*] (TEL)
TTB .... Trifluoro(thienyl)butanedione [*Also, TTA*] [*Organic chemistry*]
TTB .... Twin Traction-Beam [*Ford Motor Co.*] [*Truck four-wheel drive front suspension*]
TTB .... Typing Test for Business
TTBASIC ...... Tattletale Beginner's All-Purpose Symbolic Instruction Code [*Computer science*]
TTBB .... First Tenor, Second Tenor, First Bass, and Second Bass [*in all-male choral groups*]
TTBL .... Task Table (MHDB)
TTBOY .... To the Best of You [*An association*] (EA)
TTBS .... Timber Trades' Benevolent Society [*British*] (BI)
TTBT .... Threshold Test Ban Treaty [*1974*]
TTBWR .... Twisted Tape Boiling Water Reactor (IEEE)
TTC .... Tactical Telephone Central [*Telecommunications*] (IAA)
TTC .... Taltal [*Chile*] [*Airport symbol*] (AD)
TTC .... Tape to Card
TTC .... Tape Transport Cassette
TTC .... Target Track Central
TTC .... Target Tracking Console (MCD)
TTC .... Tatung [*Republic of China*] [*Seismograph station code, US Geological Survey*] (SEIS)
TTC .... Teacher Training College
TTC .... Technical Training Center [*Air Force*]
TTC .... Technical Training Command [*Army Air Forces*] [*World War II*]
TTC .... Technology Training Corporation (AAGC)
TTC .... Telecommunications Techniques Corp.
TTC .... Telecommunication Training Centre [*Fiji*] [*Telecommunications*]
TTC .... Telemetry, Tracking, and Command (NASA)
TTC .... Telemetry Traffic Control (SSD)
TTC .... Telephone Terminal Cables (KSC)
TTC .... Telephone Toll Call (IAA)
TTC .... Teletype Center [*Telecommunications*] (IAA)
TTC .... Teletype Message Converter [*Telecommunications*] (IAA)
TTC .... Teletypewriter Center [*Military*]
TTC .... Television Training Centre Ltd. [*British*] (CB)
TTC .... Temperature Test Chamber
TTC .... Tender to Contract Policy [*Export Credits Guarantee Department*] [*British*]
TTC .... Terminating Toll Center (DEN)
TTC .... Test Transfer Cask [*Nuclear energy*] (NRCH)
TTC .... Textile Technology Centre (AC)
TTC .... [*The*] Thomson Corp.
TTC .... Tight Tape Contact
TTC .... Time to Circularize Orbit (MCD)
TTC .... Time to Control
TTC .... Tin Telluride Crystal
TTC .... Tobacco Tax Council (EA)
TTC .... Tobramycin, Ticarcillin, and Cephalothin
TTC .... Toro Co. [*NYSE symbol*] (TTSB)
TTC .... Toro Corp. [*NYSE symbol*] (SPSG)
TTC .... Toronto Transit Commission [*Canada*] (BARN)
TTC .... Tow Target Cable
TTC .... Tracking, Telemetry, and Command
TTC .... Tracking, Telemetry, and Control [*NASA*] (NASA)
TTC .... Training Technology Centers [*Army*]
TTC .... Transient Temperature Control
TTC .... Translation Thrust Control
TTC .... Translunar Trajectory Characteristics [*AEC*] (IAA)
TTC .... Transportation Test Center [*Department of Transportation*] [*Pueblo, CO*] (GRD)
TTC .... Travel for Tomorrow Council (EA)
TTC .... Travelmaster Travel Club [*Defunct*] (EA)
TTC .... Treasure Trove Club (EA)
TTC .... Triphenyltetrazolium Chloride [*Also, RT, TPTZ*] [*Chemical indicator*]
TTC .... Tropic Test Center [*Army*] (MCD)
TTC .... Tube Temperature Control
TTC .... Tubulinyl Tyrosine Carboxypeptidase
TTC .... Tunnel Thermal Control (NASA)
TTCA .... Thiothiazolidinecarboxylic Acid [*Organic chemistry*]
T/TCA .... Thrust/Translation Control Assembly [*NASA*] (KSC)
TTCA .... Tibetan Terrier Club of America (EA)
TTCA .... T-Ten Class Association (EA)
TTC & M ...... Telemetry, Tracking, Command, and Monitoring
TTCC .... [*The*] Technical Cooperation Committee [*Army*] (AABC)
TTCC .... Tomahawk Tactical Commanders Course (DOMA)
TTCE .... Tooth-to-Tooth Composite Error
TTCE .... Transportation Terminal Command Europe [*MTMC*] (TAG)
TTC/FES ...... Tender to Contract and Forward Exchange Supplement [*Export Credits Guarantee Department*] [*British*] (DS)
TTCI .... Transient Temperature Control Instrument
TTC-L .... Toyota Total Clean-Lean [*Automotive engineering*]
TTCMSC ...... Tonga and Tin Can Mail Study Circle (EA)
TTCN .... Tree and Tabular Combined Notation [*Telecommunications*] (OSI)
TTCP .... Scarborough/Crown Point, Tobago [*Trinidad and Tobago*] [*ICAO location identifier*] (ICLI)
TTCP .... [*The*] Technical Cooperation Program [*US, UK, Canada, Australia*] [*Research*]
TTCP .... Transmitting Typewriter with Card Punch (IAA)
TTCP .... Tripartite Technical Cooperation Program [*Military*] (NG)
TTCQF .... Technology Transfer Component Qualification Facility (SSD)
TTCS .... Tank Turret Camouflage System [*Army*]
TTCS .... Target Tracking and Control System (MCD)
TTCS .... Toy Train Collectors Society (EA)
TTCS .... Truck Transportable Communications Station
TTCT .... Torrance Tests of Creative Thinking [*Educational test*]
TTCU .... Teletypewriter Control Unit (AABC)
TTCV .... Tracking, Telemetry, Command, and Voice [*Aerospace*]
TTD .... Palm Island [*Windward Islands, West Indies*] [*Airport symbol*] (AD)
TTD .... Tactical Terrain Data [*Army*]
TTD .... Tank Training Devices (MCD)
TTD .... Teachers Training Diploma
TTD .... Technical Test Director
TTD .... Technical Training Detachment
TTD .... Temporary Text Delay
TTD .... Temporary Total Disablement [*Insurance*] (AIA)
TTD .... Temporary Travel Document (NATG)
TTD .... Tetraethylthiuram Disulfide [*Also, TETD*] [*Organic chemistry*]
TTD .... Thermal Time Distribution [*Chemical engineering*]
TTD .... Things to Do
TTD .... [*The*] Third Degree [*A publication*] (EAAP)
TTD .... Tissue Tolerance Dose (MAE)
TTD .... Totals to Date (MCD)
TTD .... Total Time to Doctorate
TTD .... Transponder Transmitter Detector
TTD .... Transportation Technical Data [*Army*]
TTD .... Triazolo-Thiadiazine [*Organic chemistry*]
TTD .... Trichothiodystrophy [*Medicine*]
TTD .... Trichothiodystrophy [*Medicine*]
TTD .... Trondhjemite-Tonalite-Dacite [*Geology*]
TTD .... Troutdale, OR [*Location identifier FAA*] (FAAL)
TTDF .... Tariff and Trade Data Files (NITA)
TTDI .... Teacher Training in Developing Institutions
TTD keyterm index... Textile Technology Digest Keyterm Index (NITA)
TTDL .... Terminal Transparent Delay Language (NITA)
TTDL .... Terminal Transparent Display Language [*Computer science*] (MHDI)
TTDR .... Tracking Telemetry Data Receiver (AAG)
TTDT .... Tactical Test Data Translator (MUGU)
TTE .... Autotote Corp. Cl'A' [*AMEX symbol*] (TTSB)
TTE .... Task Training Exercise
TTE .... Technical Training Engineer
TTE .... Technical [*or Tactical*] Training Equipment (MCD)
TTE .... Telephone Terminal Equipment
TTE .... Temporary Test Equipment (AAG)
TTE .... Tentative Tables of Equipment
TTE .... Ternate [*Indonesia*] [*Airport symbol*] (OAG)
TTE .... Thermal Transfer Equipment (IAA)
TTE .... Thermal Transient Equipment [*Nuclear energy*] (NRCH)
TTE .... Time-Tagged Event [*Remote sensing*]
TTE .... Time to End
TTE .... Time to Event [*NASA*] (KSC)
TTE .... Tool and Test Equipment [*DoD*]
TTE .... Total Tax Expenditures [*Economics*]
TTE .... Total Transportation Expenditure [*Department of Transportation*]
TTE .... Trailer Test Equipment (AAG)
TTE .... Trigon Tech, Inc. [*Vancouver Stock Exchange symbol*]
TTE .... Two-dimensional Transthoracic
TTEB .... Transfert de la Technologie de l'Energie dans les Batiments [*Buildings Energy Technology Transfer Program*] [*Canada*]
TTEC .... TeleTech Holdings, Inc. [*NASDAQ symbol*] (SAG)
TTEC .... Teletypewriter Technician
TTEE .... Trustee
TTeF .... Tetratellurafulvalene [*Organic chemistry*]
TTEGDA .... Tetraethylene Glycol Diacrylate [*Organic chemistry*]
TTEL .... Tool and Test Equipment List [*NASA*] (NASA)
TTELF .... Tadiran Telecomm [*NASDAQ symbol*] (TTSB)
TTEM .... Tooling Test Equipment Team (AAG)
T-TEN .... Toyota Technical Education Network
TTEP .... Tactical Torpedo Evaluation Program [*Navy*]
TTEP .... Training and Training Equipment (MCD)
TTET .... Turbine Transport Evaluation Team [*FAA*] (MUGU)
TTF .... Tactical Task Force (AFM)
TTF .... Tactical Training Flight [*Military*]
TTF .... Tanker Task Force (AFM)
TTF .... Target Towing Flight [*British military*] (DMA)
TTF .... Test to Failure (NATG)
TTF .... Tetrathiofulvalene [*Organic chemistry*]
TTF .... Thai Fund [*NYSE symbol*] (SPSG)
TTF .... Thoriated-Tungsten Filament (SAA)
TTF .... Thyroid Transcription Factor [*Genetics*]
TTF .... Timber Trades Federation (DAS)
TTF .... Time to Failure
TTF .... Time to Fire [*Military*] (CAAL)
TTF .... Tone Telegraph Filter
TTF .... Training Task Force
TTF .... Transcription Termination Factor [*Genetics*]
TTF .... Transient Time Flowmeter [*Nuclear energy*] (NRCH)
TTF .... Transistor Test Fixture
TTF .... Trend Type Forecast (ADA)
TTF .... TrueType Font [*Computer science*] (CDE)
TTF .... Two/Ten Foundation (EA)
TTFA .... Target Transformation Factor Analysis [*Environmental Protection Agency*] (GFGA)
TTFA .... Thallium Trifluoroacetate [*Organic chemistry*]
TTFA .... Training Technology Field Activity [*Army*]
TTF & T .... Technology Transfer, Fabrication, and Test (RDA)
TTFB .... Tetrachlorotrifluoromethylbenzimidazole [*Organic chemistry*]

TTFC .... Tactical and Technical Fire Control (MCD)
TTFC .... Tanya Tucker Fan Club (EA)
TTFD .... Thiamine Tetrahydrofurfuryl Disulfide [*Pharmacology*]
TTFE .... Transportation Terminal Command Far East [*MTMC*] (TAG)
TTFF .... Time to First Fix [*Quality control*]
TTFN .... Ta Ta for Now
TTFT .... Tetra(trifluoromethyl)thiophene [*Organic chemistry*]
TTF-TCNQ .... Tetrathiafulvene-Tetracyanoquinodimethane [*Organic chemistry*]
TTFTT .... Terminal Tax Filing Time Trauma
TTFW .... Too Tacky for Words [*Slang*]
TTG .... General Trustco of Canada [*Toronto Stock Exchange symbol*]
TTG .... Gibson General Hospital, Trenton, TN [*Library symbol Library of Congress*] (LCLS)
TTG .... Tactical Training Group [*Military*]
TTG .... Tactical Transport Group [*Military*]
TTG .... Tartagal [*Argentina*] [*Airport symbol*] (AD)
TTG .... Technical Translation Group (IEEE)
TTG .... Tellurite, Taurocholate, and Gelatin [*Microbiology*] (DMAA)
TTG .... Test Target Generator
TTG .... Time to Go [*Air Force*]
TTG .... Titograd [*Yugoslavia*] [*Seismograph station code, US Geological Survey*] (SEIS)
TTG .... Tobacco Tax Guide [*Internal Revenue Service*]
TTG .... Tonalite-Trondhjemite-Granodiorite [*Geology*]
TTG .... Travel with Troops Going
TTG .... Trondhjemite-Tonalite-Granodiorite [*Geology*]
TTGA .... Tellurite-Taurocholate-Gelatin Agar [*Microbiology*]
TTGAC .... Travel and Tourism Government Affairs Council (EA)
TTGD .... Time-to-Go Dial
TTGR .... Time-to-Go Rating [*Air Force*] (IAA)
TTH .... Thyrotrophic Hormone [*Also, TSH*] [*Endocrinology*]
TTH .... Title Tech, Inc. [*Vancouver Stock Exchange symbol*]
TTH .... Tritiated Thymidine (MAE)
TTHA .... Triethylenetetraminehexaacetic Acid [*Organic chemistry*]
TTHE .... Thermal Transient Histogram Equivalent [*Nuclear energy*] (NRCH)
TTHFA .... Twisted-Pair, Telephone, Heat and Flame Resistant, Armored [*Wire technology*] (IAA)
TTHFC .... Tom T. Hall Fan Club [*Defunct*] (EA)
TTHM .... Total Trihalomethane [*Analytical chemistry*]
TTI .... Tactical Target Illustration (AFM)
TTI .... [*The*] Teachers, Inc. (EA)
TTI .... Technology Transfer Institute [*Santa Monica, CA*] [*Telecommunications*] (TSSD)
TTI .... Teletype Input (IAA)
TTI .... Teletype Test Instruction (KSC)
TTI .... Tension Time Index (AAMN)
TTI .... Texas Transportation Institute [*Texas A & M University*] [*Research center*]
TTI .... Thoracic Trauma Index [*Automotive safety research*]
TTI .... TIE/Telecommunications Canada Ltd. [*Toronto Stock Exchange symbol*]
TTI .... Time-Temperature Index
TTI .... Time Temperature Indicator (IEEE)
TTI .... Time Template Indicator
TTI .... Time to Intercept [*Missiles*] (NG)
TTI .... Training-Testing Intervals
TTI .... Transthoracic Impedance [*Medicine*]
TTI .... Traveling Ticket Inspector (DCTA)
TTI .... Travel Trends International [*Commercial firm British*]
TTI .... True Total Ion
TTI .... Tuck Tummy In [*Slang*]
TTI .... Turner Teleport, Inc. [*Atlanta, GA*] [*Telecommunications service*] (TSSD)
TTI .... Tyco Toys [*NYSE symbol*] (TTSB)
TTI .... Tyco Toys, Inc. [*NYSE symbol*] (SPSG)
TTIA .... Timber Trade Industrial Association [*Australia*]
TTIA .... Tube Temperature Indication and Alarm
TTIB .... Tension-Time Index per Beat [*Neurology*] (DAVI)
TTIC .... Test Technology Information Center (MCD)
TTIC .... Tropical Timber Information Center [*College of Environmental Science and Forestry at Syracuse*] [*Research center*] (RCD)
TTIF .... Training Taxpayer Information File [*IRS*]
TTIG .... Training Task Indentification Guide
TT/IOTE .... Technical Testing/Initial Operator Test and Evaluation [*Army*]
TTIPS .... Ticker Tape Information Processing System [*Online stock information service*]
TTIS .... Traveling Trickle Irrigation System
TTITS .... Thrust Termination Initiator Test Set
TTIU .... Trustworthy Terminal Interface Unit [*Telecommunications*] (OSI)
TTJ .... Thermo Technology International [*Vancouver Stock Exchange symbol*]
TTJ .... Tottori [*Japan*] [*Airport symbol*] (OAG)
TTK .... Terminate Task Key
TTK .... Tie Trunk [*Telecommunications*]
TTK .... Tokyo Tsushin Kogyo [*Tokyo Telecommunications Engineering Co.*]
TTK .... Two-Tone Keying
TTL .... Tatalina [*Alaska*] [*Seismograph station code, US Geological Survey Closed*] (SEIS)
TTL .... Teletype Telling
TTL .... Texas Tech University, School of Law Library, Lubbock, TX [*OCLC symbol*] (OCLC)
TTL .... Theological Translation Library [*A publication*]
TTL .... Thomson T-Line [*Commercial firm British*]
TTL .... Through the Lens [*Trademark of Spiratone, Inc.*]
TTL .... Time-to-Live (TNIG)
TTL .... Title [*Online database field identifier*] [*Computer science*]
TTL .... Torotel, Inc. [*AMEX symbol*] (SPSG)
TTL .... Torrent Resources Ltd. [*Vancouver Stock Exchange symbol*]
TTL .... To Take Leave
TTL .... Total
TTL .... Total Time to Launch [*NASA*] (KSC)
TTL .... TRADOC Troop List (MCD)
TTL .... Trail Termination Line (MCD)
TTL .... Training and Test Lung [*Simulator*] [*Medicine*] (DAVI)
TTL .... Transistor-Transistor Logic [*Also, T^2L*]
TTL .... Transit-Time LIDAR (MCD)
TTL .... Tribal Trust Land [*Zimbabwe*]
TTL .... Tribothermoluminescence
TTL .... Tubulinyl Tyrosine Ligase
TTL .... Turtle Island [*Fiji*] [*Airport symbol*] (OAG)
TTL .... Twin Trapezoidal Links [*Mazda*] [*Automotive engineering*]
TTLC .... Themes and Topics of Literature Criticism [*A publication*]
TTLC .... Total Threshold Limit Concentration [*Environmental chemistry*]
TTLM .... Through-the-Lens Light Metering (MCD)
TTLR .... Tanganyika Territory Law Reports [*1921-47*] [*A publication*] (DLA)
TTLS .... Team Training Launch Station (AAG)
TTL-S .... Transistor-Transistor Logic - Schottky
TtlWrld .... Total World Telecommunications, Inc. [*Associated Press*] (SAG)
TTM .... Tablon de Tamara [*Colombia*] [*Airport symbol*] (AD)
TTM .... Tactical Target Materials
TTM .... Tactical Telemetry
TTM .... Temperature Test Model
T/TM .... Test and Training Monitor (AAG)
TTM .... Thermal Test Model
TTM .... Torpedo Tube Missile (MCD)
TTM .... Total Time Management [*Industrial engineering*]
TTM .... Transit Time Modulation (DEN)
TTM .... Turtle Mountains [*California*] [*Seismograph station code, US Geological Survey*] (SEIS)
TTM .... Two-Tone Modulation
TTMA .... TRACON Traffic Management Advisor [*FAA*] (TAG)
TTMA .... Truck Trailer Manufacturers Association (EA)
TTMA .... Tufted Textile Manufacturers Association [*Later, CRI*] (EA)
TTMAD .... Testing-Teaching Module of Auditory Discrimination [*Child development test*]
TTMC .... Tactical Target Materials Catalogue (MCD)
T/TMC .... Traffic/Traffic Management and Control [*British*]
TTMCFC .... Theater-Type Mobilization Corps Force Capabilities [*Military*]
TTMCFO .... Theater-Type Mobilization Corps Force Objective [*Military*]
TTMF .... Touch-Tone Multifrequency (CET)
TTML .... Transistor-Transistor Micrologic (IAA)
TTMM .... Tergotrochanteral Muscle Motoneuron [*Zoology*]
TTMM .... True Tape Motion Monitor
TTMP .... Tactical Targets Materials Program (AFM)
TTMP .... Transit Time Magnetic Pumping
TTMS .... Telephoto Transmission Measuring Set
TTMT .... Tower Tech [*NASDAQ symbol*] (TTSB)
TTMT .... Tower Tech, Inc. [*NASDAQ symbol*] (SAG)
TTN .... Highland Express [*British ICAO designator*] (FAAC)
TTN .... Taitung [*Taito*] [*Republic of China*] [*Seismograph station code, US Geological Survey*] (SEIS)
TTN .... Technology Transfer Network [*Michigan State Department of Commerce*] [*Lansing, MI*] [*Information service or system*] (IID)
TT/N .... Test Tone to Noise Ratio [*Telecommunications*] (TEL)
TTN .... [*The*] Titan Corp. [*NYSE symbol*] (SPSG)
TTN .... Titan Corp. [*NYSE symbol*] (TTSB)
TTN .... Transient Tachypnea of Newborn [*Gynecology*]
TTN .... Trenton [*New Jersey*] [*Airport symbol*] (OAG)
TTN .... Trenton, NJ [*Location identifier FAA*] (FAAL)
TTN .... Trevecca Nazarene College, Nashville, TN [*OCLC symbol*] (OCLC)
TTN .... Triton Canada Resources Ltd. [*Toronto Stock Exchange symbol*]
TTN .... Tumor Site, T-Stage, N-Stage [*Oncology*]
TTNA .... Trinidad and Tobago National Alliance [*Political party*] (PPW)
TTNB .... Transient Tachypnea of the Newborn [*Medicine*] (MEDA)
TTNF .... Two/Ten National Foundation [*Later, TTF*] (EA)
TTNG .... Tightening (MSA)
TTNN .... (Tetrahydrotetramethylnaphthyl) Naphthoic Acid [*Antineoplastic drug*]
TTNN .... [*The*] True Nature Network (EA)
TTNP .... Tactical Telephone Numbering Plan (MCD)
TTNP .... Titan Pharmaceuticals [*NASDAQ symbol*] (TTSB)
TTNP .... Titan Pharmaceuticals, Inc. [*NASDAQ symbol*] (SAG)
TTNPB .... ((Tetrahydrotetramethylnaphthalenyl)propenyl)benzoic Acid [*Antineoplastic drug*]
TTNPr .... Titan Corp., $1.cm Cv Pfd [*NYSE symbol*] (TTSB)
TTNPU .... Titan Pharmaceuticals Unit [*NASDAQ symbol*] (TTSB)
TTNS .... The Times Network for Schools (NITA)
TTNS .... TOW [*Tube-Launched, Optically Tracked, Wire-Guided (Weapon)*] Thermal NightSight [*Night vision device*] [*Army*] (RDA)
TTNV .... Tomato Top Necrosis Virus [*Plant pathology*]
TTO .... Tactical Technology Office [*Arlington, VA*] [*DoD*] (GRD)
TTO .... Tactical Training Officer [*Army*]
TTO .... Telecommunications Technical Officer [*British*]
TTO .... Teletype Output [*Telecommunications*] (IAA)
TTO .... Ten-to-Twelve-Year Oscillation [*Meteorology*]
TTO .... Terminal Training Objective [*Army*] (INF)
TTO .... To Take Out [*Medicine*]
TTO .... Total Toxic Organics [*Environmental chemistry*]
TTO .... Traffic Trunk Order [*Telecommunications*] (TEL)
TTO .... Trailing-Throttle Oversteer [*Automobile driving*]
TTO .... Transit Tracers in the Ocean [*Oceanography*]

TTO .... Transmitter Turn-Off
TTO .... Travel and Transportation Order
TTO .... Trinidad and Tobago [*ANSI three-letter standard code*] (CNC)
TTO .... Truck Technical Operations [*Automobile manufacturer corporate structure*]
TTOE .... Tentative Tables of Organization and Equipment [*Army*]
TTOMT .... Tank Turret Organizational Maintenance Trainer [*Army*]
TTOS .... Toy Train Operating Society (EA)
TT/OTE .... Technical Testing/Operational Testing Evaluation [*Army*]
TTP .... Tabular [*or Tabulator*] Tape Processor [*Computer science*] (IAA)
TTP .... Tactical Targeting Program (AFM)
TTP .... Tactics, Techniques, and Procedures
TTP .... Tape-to-Print
TTP .... Temporary Transmission Permit [*Australia*]
TTP .... Test Transfer Port [*Nuclear energy*] (GFGA)
TTP .... Tetilla Peak [*New Mexico*] [*Seismograph station code, US Geological Survey*] (SEIS)
TTP .... Thermal-Transfer Printing
TTP .... Thermistor Test Program
TTP .... Thrombotic Thrombocytopenic Purpura [*Medicine*]
TTP .... Thymidine Triphosphate [*Biochemistry*]
TTP .... Time-to-Peak [*tension*] [*Neurology*] (DAVI)
TTP .... Time to Perigee (MCD)
TTP .... Total Taxable Pay
TTP .... Total Temperature Probe (MCD)
TTP .... Trailer Transfer Point
TTP .... Trainer Test Procedure [*Army*]
TTP .... Transverse Thrust Propeller
TTP .... Trick-Taking Potential [*Statistics*]
TTP .... Turn toward Peace [*Later, WWWC*] [*An association*] (EA)
TTP .... Tu-Tahl Petroleum, Inc. [*Vancouver Stock Exchange symbol*]
TTPA .... Triethylenethiophosphoramide [*Antineoplastic drug*] (MAE)
TTP & S .... Trainees, Transients, Patients, and Students Program [*Military*]
TTPB .... Tasmanian Timber Promotion Board [*Australia*]
TTPC .... Titanium Toroidal Propellant Container
TTPC .... Tripartite Technical Procedures Committee (SAA)
TTPE .... Total Taxable Pay Earned
TTPES .... Torpedo Tube Pump Ejection System [*Navy*] (CAAL)
TTPFC .... Terry and the Pirates Fan Club (EA)
TTPG .... (Thenoylthio)propionylglycine [*Biochemistry*]
TTPH .... Team Trainer, Pearl Harbor
TTPI .... Trust Territory of the Pacific Islands
TTPQ .... Theater Targets Product Office [*Army*] (RDA)
TTPP .... Port-Of-Spain/Piarco, Trinidad [*Trinidad and Tobago*] [*ICAO location identifier*] (ICLI)
TTPR .... Trainer Test Procedures and Results [*Army*]
TTPRR .... Trainer Test Procedures and Results Report [*DoD*]
TTPS .... Port-Of-Spain/Port-Of-Spain, Trinidad [*Trinidad and Tobago*] [*ICAO location identifier*] (ICLI)
TTQ .... Murphy, NC [*Location identifier FAA*] (FAAL)
TTQ .... Tourism Training Queensland [*Australia*]
TTQ .... Tryptophan Tryptophylquinone [*Biochemistry*]
TTQAP .... Teletherapy Treatment Quality Assurance Program [*Nuclear energy*] (NRCH)
TTR .... 2002 Target Term Trust [*NYSE symbol*] (TTSB)
TTR .... Table Top Rotaprint (DGA)
TTR .... Tab-Tronic Recorder (DIT)
TTR .... Tactical Technical Requirements (RDA)
TTR .... Tall Timbers [*An association*] (EA)
TTR .... Tana Toraja [*Indonesia*] [*Airport symbol*] (OAG)
TTR .... Tape-Reading Tripping Relay
TTR .... Tape Reading Typing Relay (IAA)
TTR .... Target Tracking Receiver [*Military*] (CAAL)
TTR .... Target Track [*or Tracking*] RADAR [*Air Force*]
TTR .... Tarl Town Reports [*New South Wales*] [*A publication*] (DLA)
TTR .... Tatra Air [*Slovakia*] [*ICAO designator*] (FAAC)
TTR .... Teletype Translator [*Telecommunications*] (IAA)
TTR .... Teletypewriter Translator (CET)
TTR .... Terminal Radiation Airborne Program Translator [*Air Force*] (IAA)
TTR .... Thermal Test Reactor [*Nuclear energy*] (AAG)
TTR .... Thermal Timing Relay
TTR .... Thermal Transpiration Ratio
TTR .... Thermotolerance Ratio [*Roentgenology*]
TTR .... Tijuana & Tecate Railway Co. [*AAR code*]
TTR .... Time-Temperature Recorder
TTR .... Time to Repair [*Military*] (CAAL)
TTR .... Tonopah Test Range
TTR .... Toshiba Training Reactor [*Japan*] (NRCH)
TTR .... Total Tank Requirement
TTR .... Touch-Tone Receiver [*Telecommunications*] (IAA)
TTR .... Transient Thermal Radiation
TTR .... Transistor Telegraph Relay [*Telecommunications*] (IAA)
TTR .... Transmission Test Rack (NITA)
TTR .... Transthyretin [*Biochemistry*]
TTR .... Travel with Troops Returning
TTR .... Triplet-Triplet Resonance [*Physics*]
TTR .... Trunk Test Rack (NITA)
TTR .... Trust Territory Reports of Pacific Island [*A publication*] (DLA)
TTR .... Two Thousand Two Target Term Trust, Inc. [*NYSE symbol*] (SAG)
TTR .... Type-Token Ratio [*Education of the hearing-impaired*]
TTRA .... TETRA Technologies [*NASDAQ symbol*] (TTSB)
TTRA .... Tetra Technologies, Inc. [*NASDAQ symbol*] (SAG)
TTRA .... Tongass [*National Forest*] Timber Reform Act
TTRA .... Travel and Tourism Research Association (EA)
TTRB .... Timken Tapered Roller Bearing
TTRC .... Transistorized Thyratron Ring Counter
TTRDC .... Tourism and Travel Research Development Council [*Australia*]
TTRE .... Task Training Remedial Exercise [*Army*]
TTRI .... Thermo Tech Technologies [*NASDAQ symbol*] (SAG)
TTRI .... Time-Temperature Recorder and Integrator (MCD)
TTRIF .... Thermo Tech Technologies Inc. [*NASDAQ symbol*] (TTSB)
TTRR .... Technical Test Readiness Review [*Army*]
TTRR .... Tracor, Inc. [*NASDAQ symbol*] (SAG)
TTRRW .... Tracor Inc.Wrrt'A' [*NASDAQ symbol*] (TTSB)
TTRSA .... Twisted Telephone Radio, Shielded, Armored
TTRT .... Target Token Rotation Time [*Computer science*]
TTS .... TACFIRE Training System (MCD)
TTS .... Tactical Test Set (MCD)
TTS .... Tactical Training Squadron
TTS .... Tank Thermal Site
TTS .... Target Trajectory Sensor
TTS .... Tarleton State University, Dick Smith Library, Stephenville, TX [*OCLC symbol*] (OCLC)
TTS .... TASD (Transporti Aerei Speciali) [*Italy ICAO designator*] (FAAC)
TTS .... Technical Training Squadron (MCD)
TTS .... Telecommunications Terminal Systems
TTS .... Telecom Technology Showcase [*British*]
TTS .... Telemetry Transmission System
TTS .... Tele-Tech Services [*McAfee, NJ*] [*Information service or system Telecommunications*] (TSSD)
TTS .... Teletypesetter
TTS .... Teletypesetting (NITA)
TTS .... Teletypesetting Code (NITA)
TTS .... Teletypewriter System
TTS .... Temperature Test Set
TTS .... Temporary Threshold Shift
TTS .... Terminal Testing Section [*Social Security Administration*]
TTS .... Terrain Trend System (MCD)
TTS .... Test and Training Satellite [*Also, TATS, TETR*] [*NASA*]
TTS .... Text-to-Speech [*Computer science*]
TTS .... Thanks to Scandinavia (EA)
TTS .... [*The*] Theban Tombs Series [*London*] [*A publication*] (BJA)
TTS .... Thermal Transfer Standard
TTS .... Thermo-Time Switch [*Electronics*]
TTS .... Thomas Tallis Society [*British*]
TTS .... Three-State Transceiver [*Computer science*] (IAA)
TTS .... Through the Skin (DAVI)
TTS .... Thule Tracking Station (MCD)
TTS .... Thurstone Temperament Schedule [*Psychology*]
TTS .... Time to Station (DA)
TTS .... Tintina Mines Ltd. [*Toronto Stock Exchange symbol*]
TTS .... Tissue Type Specific [*Antigen*]
TTS .... Total Tectonic Subsidence
TTS .... Touring Twin Carburetor Sport [*Automobile model*]
TTS .... Tracker Test Set [*Dragon*] (MCD)
TTS .... [*The*] Training School at Vineland [*An association*] (EA)
TTS .... Transaction Terminal System (NITA)
TTS .... Transaction Tracking System (PCM)
TTS .... Transdermal Therapeutic System [*Medicine*]
TTS .... Transducer Tubing System
TTS .... Transistor-Transistor Logic Schottky Barrier (IEEE)
TTS .... Transmission Temperature Switch [*Automotive engineering*]
TTS .... Transmission Test Set (IEEE)
TTS .... Transponder Test Set
TTS .... Transportable Telemetry Set
TTS .... Transport Ticket Society [*British*] (DBA)
TTS .... Triple Transit Suppression (IAA)
TT's .... Tripoli Trots [*Term used by entertainers in World War II*]
TTS .... True to Scale
TTS .... Tsaratanana [*Madagascar*] [*Airport symbol*] (OAG)
TTS .... Tuesday, Thursday, Saturday (BARN)
TTSA .... Tactical Traffic and System Analysis (MCD)
TTSA .... Tandem Truck Safety Act [*1984*] (GFGA)
TTSA .... Tank Turret Safety Adapter [*Army*]
TTSA .... Transition Training Squadron, Atlantic [*Navy*]
TTSD .... Technical Test Support Divisions [*Army*] (RDA)
TTSD .... Telephone Tracking System Directory (MCD)
TTSF .... Test and Timesharing Facility [*Social Security Administration*]
TTSF .... Time to Subsequent Fix [*Quality control*]
TTSF .... Tongass [*National Forest*] Timber Supply Fund [*Department of the Interior*]
TTSG .... Twinless Twins Support Group (EA)
TTSL .... Total Time Spent Listening [*Radio*] (WDMC)
TTSM .... Theater Transition and Sustainment Model
TTSOA .... Telecommunications Traffic and Supervisory Officers' Association [*Australia*]
TTSP .... Training Test Support Package [*Army*]
TTSP .... Transition Training Squadron, Pacific [*Navy*]
TTSPN .... Two Terminal Series Parallel Networks
TTSR .... Temporary Threshold Shift Reduction (SAA)
TTSS .... [*The*] Trumpeter Swan Society (EA)
TTSt .... Trierer Theologische Studien [*Trier*] [*A publication*] (BJA)
TTSU .... Tracker Test Set Supplemental Unit (MCD)
TTSW .... Tractor Truck, Six Wheel [*Automotive engineering*]
TTT .... Tactical Training Team [*Military*] (CAAL)
TTT .... Taitung [*Taiwan*] [*Airport symbol*] (OAG)
TTT .... Tallulah, LA [*Location identifier FAA*] (FAAL)
TTT .... Tatiko-Tekhnicheskye-Trebovaniya [*Tactical Technical Requirement*] [*for military materiel*] [*Former USSR*] (RDA)
TTT .... Template Tracing Technique (DA)

TTT .... Tetrathiotetracene [*Organic chemistry*]
TTT .... Texas College, Tyler, TX [*OCLC symbol*] (OCLC)
TTT .... Thermo Terratech [*AMEX symbol*] (TTSB)
TTT .... Thermo Terratech [*AMEX symbol*] (SAG)
TTT .... Thymol Turbidity Test [*Clinical chemistry*]
TTT .... Time Temperature Transformation
TTT .... Time, Temperature, Turbulence [*Fuel technology*]
TTT .... Time to Target (AAG)
TTT .... Time to Turn [*Ship or aircraft*]
TTT .... Tolbutamide Tolerance Test [*Clinical chemistry*]
TTT .... Training of Teacher Trainers
TTT .... Transamerican Trailer Transport
TTT .... Trilateral Tracking Technique
TTT .... Trinidad & Tobago Television Co.
TTT .... True Temperature Tunnel
TTT .... Tyne Tees Television [*British*] (DI)
TTTA .... Teletypewriter Terminal Assembly
TTTA .... Timber Trade Training Association [*British*] (DBA)
TTTA .... Tobacco Trade Travellers' Association [*British*] (BI)
TTTA .... Training Technology Transfer Act of 1984 (WYGK)
TTTAP .... Territorial Teacher Training Assistance Program [*Department of Education*] (GFGA)
TTTE .... Tri-National Tornado Training Establishment [*British military*] (DMA)
TTTL .... Transistor-to-Transistor-to-Transistor Logic (HGAA)
TTTN .... Tandem Tie Trunk Network (PDAA)
TTTP .... Transmitting Typewriter with Tape Punch (IAA)
TTTS .... Tanker-Transport Trailer System (MCD)
TTTS .... Tanker Transport Training System [*Air Force*]
TTTT .... Tartar-Talos-Terrier-Typhon [*Military*] (DNAB)
TTTT .... Test Tube Turbidity Test [*Laboratory science*] (DAVI)
TTU .... Tantalus Resources Ltd. [*Vancouver Stock Exchange symbol*]
TTU .... Target Transfer Unit (MCD)
TTU .... Tartu [*Dorpat, Jurjeio*] [*Former USSR Seismograph station code, US Geological Survey Closed*] (SEIS)
TTU .... Tennessee Technical University, Cookville, TN [*OCLC symbol*] (OCLC)
TTU .... Terminal Timing Unit [*NASA*] (KSC)
TTU .... Terminal Transportation Unit [*Military*] (GFGA)
TTU .... Tetuan [*Morocco*] [*Airport symbol*] (OAG)
TTU .... Texas Technological University (PDAA)
TTU .... Through-Transmission Ultrasound [*Materials testing*] (RDA)
TTU .... Thrust Termination Unit (MSA)
TTU .... Timing Terminal Unit (NASA)
TTU .... Tracer Test Unit (IAA)
TTU .... Transportable Treatment Unit
TTU .... Transportation Terminal Unit [*Army*]
TTUC .... Tasmanian Trades Union Council [*Australia*]
TTuGS .... Church of Jesus Christ of Latter-Day Saints, Genealogical Society Library, Tennessee South District Branch, Tullahoma, TN [*Library symbol Library of Congress*] (LCLS)
TTUL .... Talk to U Later [*Internet language*] [*Computer science*]
TTUSA .... Trireme Trust USA [*An association*] (EA)
TTV .... Cabletel Communications [*AMEX symbol*] (TTSB)
TTV .... Cabletel Communications Corp. [*AMEX symbol*] (SAG)
TTV .... Taiwan Television Enterprise (EY)
TTV .... Teletape Video
TTV .... Tenth Thickness Value [*Nuclear energy*] (NRCH)
TTV .... Termination, Test, and Verification (NASA)
TTV .... Territorial Petroleum [*Vancouver Stock Exchange symbol*]
TTV .... Thermal Test Vehicle
TTV .... Tow Test Vehicle [*Aerospace*]
TTVM .... Thermal Transfer Voltmeter
TTVP .... Temporary Transvenous Pacemaker [*Cardiology*] (DAVI)
TTVP .... Trentiner Tiroler Volkspartei [*Trentino Tirol People's Party*] [*Italy Political party*] (PPE)
TTVW .... Total Towed Vehicle Weight [*Automotive engineering*]
TTW .... Tactical Training Wing [*Air Force*]
TTW .... Teletypewriter [*Telecommunications*]
TTW .... Total Temperature and Weight
TTWA .... Travel to Work Area (AIE)
TTWB .... Turbine Trip with Bypass [*Nuclear energy*] (NRCH)
TTWL .... Twin Tandem Wheel Loading [*Aviation*]
TTWS .... Terminal Threat Warning System
TTX .... Air Team, AS [*Norway*] [*FAA designator*] (FAAC)
TTX .... Den Sivile Flyskole [*Norway ICAO designator*] (FAAC)
TTX .... Teletex [*Telecommunications*]
TTX .... Tetrodotoxin [*A poison*] [*Biochemistry*]
TTX .... Thiothixene [*Tranquilizer*]
TTX .... Tultex Corp. [*NYSE symbol*] (SPSG)
TTX .... Tut Enterprises, Inc. [*Toronto Stock Exchange symbol*]
TTXAU .... Teletex Access Unit [*Telecommunications*] (OSI)
TTXG .... TransTexas Gas [*NASDAQ symbol*] (TTSB)
TTXG .... Transtexas Gas Corp. [*NASDAQ symbol*] (SAG)
TTY .... Teletype (CAAL)
TTY .... Teletypewriter [*Telecommunications*]
TTY .... Teletypewriter Equipment (IAA)
TTY .... TELEX-Type [*Terminal*]
TTY .... Torque-to-Yield [*Automotive engineering*]
TTYA .... Teletypewriter Assembly
TTYC .... TTY Controller (NITA)
TTYD .... Tele-Typewriters for the Deaf [*An association*]
TTYL .... Talk to You Later [*Internet language*] [*Computer science*]
TTYL .... Talk to You Later (EERA)
TTYP .... Tintype (VRA)
TTYPP .... Teletype Point-To-Point Online Communications Driver (NITA)
TTYQ/RSS .... Teletypewriter Query-Reply Subsystem (CET)
TTZ .... Tactical-Technical Assignment [*Army*] (RDA)
TTZ .... Titizima [*Bonin Islands*] [*Seismograph station code, US Geological Survey Closed*] (SEIS)
TTZ .... Tornquist-Teisseyre Zone [*Geology*]
TTZ .... Transformation Toughened Zirconia [*Metallurgy*]
TTZ .... Treats, Inc. [*Toronto Stock Exchange symbol*]
TTZP .... Piarco, Trinidad [*Trinidad and Tobago*] [*ICAO location identifier*] (ICLI)
TU .... Societe Tunisienne de l'Air [*Tunisia*] [*ICAO designator*]
TU .... Take-Up (IAA)
TU .... Tanking Unit (AAG)
TU .... Tanners' Union [*British*]
TU .... Tape Unit
TU .... Task Unit [*Military*]
TU .... Taxicrinic Unit [*Computer science*]
TU .... Technical Service Unit [*Military*]
TU .... Technische Universitat [*Technical University*] [*German*]
TU .... Technology Utilization
TU .... Tenebrio Unit [*Endocrinology*]
TU .... Terminal Unit
TU .... Testo Unico [*Consolidated Statutes*] [*Italian*] (ILCA)
TU .... Test Unit
TU .... Thank You [*Communications operator's procedural remark*]
TU .... Thermal Unit
TU .... Thiouracil [*Biochemistry*] (MAE)
TU .... Thulium [*Symbol is Tm*] [*Chemical element*] (ROG)
TU .... Time-of-Update
TU .... Timing Unit
TU .... Todd Unit [*Medicine*] (MAE)
TU .... Torah Umesorah - National Society for Hebrew Day Schools [*Defunct*] (EA)
TU .... Toxic Unit [*Medicine*]
TU .... Trade Union
TU .... Traffic Unit
TU .... Training Unit [*Army*]
TU .... Transfer Unconditionally
TU .... Transfer Unit (AAG)
TU .... Transmission Unit [*Telecommunications*]
TU .... Transport Unit (MCD)
TU .... Transuranium [*Chemistry*]
TU .... Tritium Unit [*Nuclear energy*]
TU .... Trophic Unit [*Analytical biochemistry*]
TU .... Trout Unlimited (EA)
TU .... Tuba
TU .... Tube
Tu .... Tubercle [*Anatomy*] [*Medicine*]
TU .... Tuberculin Unit
TU .... Tudor (ROG)
TU .... Tuesday
TU .... Tugboatmen's Union [*British*]
TU .... Tuition
TU .... Tulane University [*New Orleans, LA*]
TU .... Tulsa University [*Oklahoma*] (PDAA)
TU .... Tuning Unit [*JETDS nomenclature*] [*Military*] (IAA)
TU .... Tunis Airline (DS)
TU .... Tupolev [*Former USSR ICAO aircraft manufacturer identifier*] (ICAO)
TU .... Turbidity Unit
TU .... Turkey [*NATO*]
tu .... Turkey [*MARC country of publication code Library of Congress*] (LCCP)
TU .... Type Unique [*French standard troop train, World War I*]
TU .... University of Tennessee, Knoxville, TN [*Library symbol Library of Congress*] (LCLS)
TUA .... Syndicat International des Travailleurs Unis de l'Automobile, de l'Aerospatiale,et de l'Outillage Agricole d'Amerique [*International Union, United Automobile, Aerospace, and Agricultural Implement Workers of America - UAW*] [*Canada*]
TUA .... Teichuronic Acid [*Biochemistry*]
TUA .... Telecommunications Users' Association (TSSD)
TUA .... Telephone Users Association (EA)
TUA .... Test Unit Adapter [*Aviation*]
TuA .... Texte und Arbeiten [*Beuron*] [*A publication*] (BJA)
TUA .... Time Use Analysis [*Test*]
TUA .... Tuai [*New Zealand*] [*Seismograph station code, US Geological Survey*] (SEIS)
TUA .... Tulcan [*Ecuador*] [*Airport symbol*] (OAG)
TUA .... Turkmenistan [*ICAO designator*] (FAAC)
TUAC .... Trade Union Advisory Committee [*British*] (DAS)
TUAC .... Trade Union Advisory Committee (EERA)
TUAC .... Union Internationale des Travailleurs Unis de l'Alimentation et du Commerce [*United Food and Commercial Workers Union*] [*Canada*]
TUAC OECD ... Trade Union Advisory Committee to the Organization for Economic Cooperation and Development [*Paris, France*] (EAIO)
TuAF .... Turkish Air Force
T/U/Ag .... Trustee under Agreement [*Legal term*] (DLA)
TUAL .... Tentative Unit Allowance List [*Air Force*] (AFM)
Tu & Rus ..... Turner and Russell's English Chancery Reports [*1822-24*] [*A publication*] (DLA)
TUAR .... Turning Arbor
TUB .... Temporary Unlighted Buoy [*Maps and charts*]
TUB .... Troop Unit Basis [*Military*]
TUB .... Tubarao [*Brazil*] [*Airport symbol*] (AD)
tub .... Tubing (VRA)

TUB............ Tubing (AAG)
TUB............ Tubingen [*Federal Republic of Germany*] [*Seismograph station code, US Geological Survey*] (SEIS)
TUB............ Tubouterine [*Junction*] [*Gynecology*] (DAVI)
TUB............ Tubuai Island [*Austral Islands*] [*Airport symbol*] (OAG)
TUB............ Tubular [*Automotive engineering*]
tub............ Tubular (VRA)
TUB............ [*The*] Unborn Book [*A publication*]
TUBA.......... Tubists Universal Brotherhood Association (EA)
Tubbys........ Tubby's, Inc. [*Associated Press*] (SAG)
TUBCS......... Trade Union Badge Collectors Society [*British*] (DBA)
TUBE.......... Terminating Unfair Broadcasting Excesses [*Student legal action organization*] (EA)
TUBE.......... Trans-Urban Bicentennial Exposition
tuberc........ Tuberculosis [*Medicine*]
TUBITAK...... Scientific and Technical Research Council of Turkey [*Ankara*] [*Information service or system*] (IID)
TUBLR......... Tubular [*Freight*]
TubMex........ Tubos De Acero De Mexico [*Associated Press*] (SAG)
TUBO.......... Tuboscope Vetco International [*NASDAQ symbol*] (SAG)
TUBO.......... Tuboscope Vetco Intl [*NASDAQ symbol*] (TTSB)
TUBS.......... Tubular Tires [*Cyclist term*] [*British*] (DSUE)
Tubscp........ Tuboscope Vetco International Corp. [*Associated Press*] (SAG)
TUBY.......... Tubby's, Inc. [*NASDAQ symbol*] (SAG)
TUC............ Teaching Usefulness Classification [*of a hospital patient*]
TUC............ Technology Utilization Center
TUC............ Telecommunications Users Coalition (EA)
TUC............ Teleordering Users' Council [*British*]
TUC............ Temporary Unemployment Compensation [*Labor*]
TUC............ Terminal Usage Charge [*Computer science*] (HGAA)
TUC............ Time of Useful Consciousness [*Medicine*]
TUC............ Tracer Resources [*Vancouver Stock Exchange symbol*]
TUC............ Trades Union Congress [*British*]
TUC............ Trade [*or Trades*] Union Council
TUC............ Transportation, Utilities, Communications
Tuc............ Tucana [*Constellation*]
TUC............ Tucker Properties [*NYSE symbol*] (SPSG)
TUC............ Tucson [*Arizona*] [*Seismograph station code, US Geological Survey*] (SEIS)
TUC............ Tucuman [*Argentina*] [*Airport symbol*] (OAG)
TUC............ Type Unit Code (CINC)
TUC............ University of Tennessee at Chattanooga, Chattanooga, TN [*OCLC symbol*] (OCLC)
TUCA.......... Tilt-Up Concrete Association (EA)
TUCA.......... Transient Undercooling Accident [*Nuclear energy*]
TUCA.......... Turning Cam [*Tool*] (AAG)
TUCC.......... Transport Users' Consultative Council [*British*] (ILCA)
TUCC.......... Triangle Universities Computation Center [*Durham, NC*]
TUCE.......... Test of Understanding of College Economics
TUCHA........ Type Unit Characteristics
Tu Civ LF..... Tulane Civil Law Forum [*A publication*] (DLA)
Tuck............ Tucker and Clephane's Reports [*21 District of Columbia*] [*1892-93*] [*A publication*] (DLA)
TUCK.......... Tucker Drilling [*NASDAQ symbol*] (TTSB)
TUCK.......... Tucker Drilling Co., Inc. [*NASDAQ symbol*] (NQ)
Tuck............ Tucker's New York Surrogate's Court Reports [*A publication*] (DLA)
Tuck............ Tucker's Reports [*156-175 Massachusetts*] [*A publication*] (DLA)
Tuck............ Tucker's Reports [*District of Columbia*] [*A publication*] (DLA)
Tuck............ Tucker's Select Cases [*Newfoundland*] [*A publication*] (DLA)
Tuck & C..... Tucker and Clephane's Reports [*21 District of Columbia*] [*A publication*] (DLA)
Tuck & Cl.... Tucker and Clephane's Reports [*21 District of Columbia*] [*1892-93*] [*A publication*] (DLA)
Tuck Bl Com... Tucker's Blackstone's Commentaries [*A publication*] (DLA)
Tuck Dist of Col... Tucker's District of Columbia Appeals [*A publication*] (DLA)
TuckDr........ Tucker Drilling Co., Inc. [*Associated Press*] (SAG)
Tucker......... Tucker's New York Surrogate's Court Reports [*A publication*] (DLA)
TuckerPr...... Tucker Properties [*Associated Press*] (SAG)
Tucker's Blackstone... Tucker's Blackstone's Commentaries [*A publication*] (DLA)
Tuck Lect...... Tucker's Lectures [*A publication*] (DLA)
Tuck Pl....... Tucker's Pleadings [*A publication*] (DLA)
Tuck Sel Cas... Tucker's Select Cases [*1817-28*] [*Newfoundland*] [*A publication*] (DLA)
Tuck Sur...... Tucker's Surrogate Reports, City of New York [*A publication*] (DLA)
Tuck Surr..... Tucker's Surrogate Reports, City of New York [*A publication*] (DLA)
TUCN.......... Trades Union Congress of Nigeria
Tucn........... Tucana [*Constellation*]
TUCOPS....... [*The*] Universal Coterie of Pipe Smokers (EA)
TUCOSP....... Tehran Union Catalogue of Scientific Periodicals [*A publication*]
TUCR.......... Troop Unit Change Request
TUCSA......... Trade Union Council of South Africa
TucsEP........ Tucson Electric Power Co. [*Associated Press*] (SAG)
TUD............ Tambacounda [*Senegal*] [*Airport symbol*] (OAG)
TUD............ Technology Utilization Division [*NASA*] (IEEE)
TUD............ Total Underground Distribution (IAA)
TUD............ Total Urethral Discharge [*Medicine*]
TUD............ Tugold Resources, Inc. [*Vancouver Stock Exchange symbol*]
TUDAT......... Tunnel-Diode Arithmetic Tester (IAA)
TUDC.......... Tauroursodeoxycholate [*Biochemistry*]
TUDC.......... Trade Unionists' Defence Committee [*Australia*]
TUDCA......... Tauroursodeoxycholic Acid [*Biochemistry*]
Tud Cas Merc Law... Tudor's Leading Cases on Mercantile Law [*3 eds.*] [*1860-84*] [*A publication*] (DLA)
Tud Cas RP... Tudor's Leading Cases on Real Property [*4 eds.*] [*1856-98*] [*A publication*] (DLA)
Tud Char Tr... Tudor's Charitable Trusts [*2nd ed.*] [*1871*] [*A publication*] (DLA)
Tud Char Trusts... Tudor's Charitable Trusts [*2nd ed.*] [*1871*] [*A publication*] (DLA)
Tudor Lead Cas Real Prop... Tudor's Leading Cases on Real Property [*A publication*] (DLA)
Tudor's LCML... Tudor's Leading Cases on Mercantile Law [*A publication*] (DLA)
Tudor's LCRP... Tudor's Leading Cases on Real Property [*A publication*] (DLA)
TUDRIP........ Tube Plate Drilling Program [*Kongsberg Vaapenfabrikk*] [*Software package*] (NCC)
TUDS.......... Tunnel Detection System (MCD)
TUE............ Texas Utilities Electric Co. [*NYSE symbol*] (SPSG)
TUE............ Tolerance of Unrealistic Experience [*Psychometrics*]
TUE............ Trainer Unique Equipment [*Navy*]
TUE............ TU Electric Capital I [*NYSE symbol*] (SAG)
TUE............ TU Electric Capital II [*NYSE symbol*] (SAG)
TUE............ TU Electric Capital III [*NYSE symbol*] (SAG)
TUE............ Tuesday (AFM)
Tue............ Tuesday (ODBW)
TUE............ Tupile [*Panama*] [*Airport symbol*] (OAG)
TUE............ University of Tokyo (EDUCATSS) [*UTLAS symbol*]
TUEL.......... Trade Union Educational League
TUEPr......... Texas Util Elec Dep Pfd [*NYSE symbol*] (TTSB)
TUEPrA....... Texas Util Elec'A'Dep Pfd [*NYSE symbol*] (TTSB)
TUEPrB....... Texas Util Elec'B'Dep Pfd [*NYSE symbol*] (TTSB)
TUEPrM....... TU Electric Cap 1 8.25%'TOPrS' [*NYSE symbol*] (TTSB)
TUEPrN....... TU Electric Cap II 9.00%'TOPrS' [*NYSE symbol*] (TTSB)
TUEPrO....... TU Elec Cap II 8.00%'QUIPS' [*NYSE symbol*] (TTSB)
TUES.......... Tuesday (EY)
Tues........... Tuesday (ODBW)
TUES.......... Tuesday Morning [*NASDAQ symbol*] (TTSB)
TUES.......... Tuesday Morning Corp. [*NASDAQ symbol*] (NQ)
TuesM......... Tuesday Morning Corp. [*Associated Press*] (SAG)
TUF............ Tactical Undercover Function [*Chicago police operation*]
TUF............ Thermal Utilization Factor (MCD)
TUF............ Time of Useful Function [*Computer science*] (MHDB)
TUF............ Totally User Friendly
TUF............ Tours [*France*] [*Airport symbol*] (OAG)
TUF............ Trade Union Federation [*British*] (EY)
TUF............ Transmitter Underflow
TUFA.......... Total Unsaturated Fatty Acid [*of foodstuffs*]
TUFA.......... Trans Unsaturated Fatty Acids
TUFCDF....... Thorium-Uranium Fuel Cycle Development Facility [*Nuclear energy*]
Tufco.......... Tufco Technologies [*Associated Press*] (SAG)
TUFEC......... Thailand-UNESCO Fundamental Education Centre
TUFF-TUG.... Tape Update of Formatted Files-Format Table Tape Updater and Generator [*Computer science*]
TUFI........... This Umbrella Folds Itself [*Trademark for type of umbrella*]
TUFL.......... Trade Unionists for Labour [*British*]
TU-FM......... University of Tennessee Center for the Health Sciences/Memphis Department of Family Medicine, Memphis, TN [*Library symbol Library of Congress*] (LCLS)
TUFMIS....... Tactical Unit Financial Management Information System
Tufts U........ Tufts University (GAGS)
TUFX.......... Turning Fixture
TUG............ British Columbia Trade Union Group [*Canada*] (CROSS)
TUG............ Maritrans, Inc. [*NYSE symbol*] (SPSG)
TUG............ Tape Unit Group [*Telecommunications*] (TEL)
TUG............ Telecommunications Users Group [*Montclair, NJ*] [*Telecommunications service*] (TSSD)
TUG............ Teleram Users Group (EA)
TUG............ Tire Uniformity Grading [*Automotive engineering*]
TUG............ Total Urinary Gonadotropin [*Clinical chemistry*]
TUG............ Touch and Go Ltd. [*Former USSR*] [*FAA designator*] (FAAC)
TUG............ Towed Universal Glider
TUG............ TRANSAC [*Transistorized Automatic Computer*] Users Group
TUG............ Transistorized Automatic Computer Users' Group (IAA)
TUG............ Transtex Universal Gateway [*Computer science*]
Tug............ Tugrik [*Monetary unit*] [*Mongolia*] (BARN)
TUG............ Tuguegarao [*Philippines*] [*Airport symbol*] (OAG)
TUG............ Tunable Ultraviolet Generation
TUGV.......... Tactical Unmanned Ground Vehicle [*Army*] (PS)
TUH............ Tullahoma, TN [*Location identifier FAA*] (FAAL)
TU-H.......... University of Tennessee Center for the Health Sciences/Knoxville, Preston Medical Library, Knoxville, TN [*Library symbol Library of Congress*] (LCLS)
TUHTKP....... Time Urgent Hard Target Kill Potential (MCD)
TUI............ Green Bay, WI [*Location identifier FAA*] (FAAL)
TUI............ Text User Interface [*Computer science*]
TUI............ Tool Usage Instructions (MCD)
TUI............ Trade Union Immunities [*British*]
TUI............ Trade Union International
TUI............ Trade Unions International of Transport Workers (EAIO)
TUI............ Trypsin Units Inhibited [*Food technology*]
TUI............ Tuition (DSUE)
TUI............ Tuninter [*Tunisia*] [*ICAO designator*] (FAAC)
TUI............ Turaif [*Saudi Arabia*] [*Airport symbol*] (OAG)
TUIAFPW..... Trade Unions International of Agriculture, Forestry, and Plantation Workers [*See also UISTAFP*] [*Prague, Czechoslovakia*] (EAIO)
TUIC........... Trade Unions' Industrial Council [*Australia*]
TUIFU......... [*The*] Ultimate in Foul Ups [*Military slang*] [*Bowdlerized version*]
TUIMWE...... Trade Unions International of Miners and Workers in Energy [*See also UISMTE*] (EAIO)
TUIP........... Transurethral Incision of the Prostate [*Medicine*]
TUIPAE........ Trade Unions International of Public and Allied Employees [*Berlin, Federal Republic of Germany*] (EAIO)
TUIR........... Time until in Range

TUIREC .... Trade Union International Research and Education Group [*England*] (EAIO)
TUITW .... Trade Unions International of Transport Workers (EAIO)
TUIWC .... Trade Unions International of Workers in Commerce [*Prague, Czechoslovakia*] (EAIO)
TUJ .... Tubouterine Junction [*Anatomy*]
TUJ .... Tum [*Ethiopia*] [*Airport symbol*] (OAG)
TUK .... Nantucket, MA [*Location identifier FAA*] (FAAL)
TUK .... TEA (UK) Ltd. [*British ICAO designator*] (FAAC)
TUK .... Tuckahoe Financial Corp. [*Toronto Stock Exchange symbol*]
TUK .... Turbat [*Pakistan*] [*Airport symbol*] (OAG)
tuk .... Turkmen [*MARC language code Library of Congress*] (LCCP)
TUL .... Aero Toluca Internacional, SA de CV [*Mexico*] [*FAA designator*] (FAAC)
TuL .... Tod und Leben nach der Vorstellungen der Babylonier [*A publication*] (BJA)
TUL .... Tula Peak, New Mexico [*Spaceflight Tracking and Data Network*] [*NASA*]
TUL .... Tulsa [*Oklahoma*] [*Airport symbol*] (OAG)
TUL .... Tulsa [*Oklahoma*] [*Seismograph station code, US Geological Survey*] (SEIS)
TUL .... Tulsa City-County Library System, Tulsa, OK [*OCLC symbol*] (OCLC)
TU-L .... University of Tennessee, Law Library, Knoxville, TN [*Library symbol Library of Congress*] (LCLS)
TULACS .... Tactical Unit Location and Communication System (MCD)
Tulane U .... Tulane University (GAGS)
TULAR .... Tularemia [*An infectious, plague-like disease*] (DAVI)
TULC .... Trade Union Leadership Council (EA)
TULCC .... Triangle University Library Cooperative Committee [*Library network*]
Tul Civ LF .... Tulane Civil Law Forum [*A publication*] (DLA)
TULE .... Transistorized Universal Logic Elements
TULF .... Tamil United Liberation Front [*Sri Lanka*] (PD)
TULIP .... Transurethral Ultrasound - Guided LASER-Induced Prostatectomy [*Medicine*]
TULIPS .... Telemetered Ultrasonic Liquid Interface Plotting System (PDAA)
TULRA .... Trade Union and Labour Relations Act [*1974 and 1976*] [*British*] (DCTA)
TULS .... TRON [*The Real-Time Operating System Nucleus*] Universal Language System [*Computer science*]
TU-LS .... University of Tennessee, Graduate School of Library and Information Sciences, Knoxville, TN [*Library symbol*] [*Library of Congress*] (LCLS)
Tultex .... Tultex Corp. [*Associated Press*] (SAG)
TUM .... Aeriantur-M Airlines [*Moldova*] [*FAA designator*] (FAAC)
TUM .... Technical University in Munich [*Germany*]
TUM .... Terminal User's Manual
TuM .... Texte und Materialien der Frau Professor Hilprecht Collection of Babylonian Antiquities im Eigentum der Univerisitaet Jena [*A publication*] (BJA)
TuM .... Torah Umesorah - National Society for Hebrew Day Schools
TUM .... Total Unscheduled Maintenance Time
TUM .... Trades Union Movement
TUM .... Tumut [*Australia Airport symbol*] (OAG)
TUM .... Tumwater [*Washington*] [*Seismograph station code, US Geological Survey*] (SEIS)
TUM .... Tuning Unit Member (IEEE)
TUM .... University of Tennessee, Center for the Health Sciences, Memphis, TN [*OCLC symbol*] (OCLC)
TU-M .... University of Tennessee Medical Units, Memphis, TN [*Library symbol Library of Congress*] (LCLS)
TUM .... [*The*] Unsatisfied Man [*A publication*]
TUMA .... Tumacacori National Monument
TU-MDC .... University of Tennessee, Downtown Memphis Center, Memphis, TN [*Library symbol Library of Congress*] (LCLS)
TUME .... [*The*] Ultimate Musical Experience [*Rock music group*]
TU-MS .... University of Tennessee Center for the Health Sciences Library, Stollerman Library, Memphis, TN [*Library symbol Library of Congress*] (LCLS)
TuMV .... Turnip Mosaic Virus
TUN .... Air Tungaru [*British ICAO designator*] (FAAC)
TUN .... Flint, MI [*Location identifier FAA*] (FAAL)
TUN .... Technical University of Nova Scotia [*UTLAS symbol*]
TUN .... Tennessee State University, Downtown Campus, Nashville, TN [*OCLC symbol*] (OCLC)
TUN .... Transfer Unconditionally
TUN .... Tuning (AAG)
TUN .... Tunis [*Tunisia*] [*Seismograph station code, US Geological Survey Closed*] (SEIS)
TUN .... Tunis [*Tunisia*] [*Airport symbol*] (OAG)
TUN .... Tunisia [*ANSI three-letter standard code*] (CNC)
Tun .... Tunisia (VRA)
TUN .... Turner Energy & Resources [*Vancouver Stock Exchange symbol*]
TUNA .... Tunable Attribute Display Subsystem (CAAL)
TUNE .... DMX, Inc. [*NASDAQ symbol*] (SAG)
TUNEL .... Tunnel [*Commonly used*] (OPSA)
TUNG .... Tungsten (AAG)
TUNICAT .... Tunicatae [*Coated*] [*Pharmacy*]
TUNISAIR .... Societe Tunisienne de l'Air [*Airline*] [*Tunisia*]
TUNL .... Triangle Universities Nuclear Laboratory [*Research center*] (RCD)
TUNL .... Tunnel
TUNL .... Tunnel
TUNLS .... Tunnel [*Commonly used*] (OPSA)
TUNNEL .... Tunnel [*Commonly used*] (OPSA)
TUNNELS .... Tunnel [*Commonly used*] (OPSA)
TUNNET .... Tunnel Transit Time (IAA)
TUNNL .... Tunnel [*Commonly used*] (OPSA)
TUO .... Taupo [*New Zealand*] [*Airport symbol*] (OAG)
TUO .... Technology Utilization Office [*NASA*]
TUO .... Teuton Resources Corp. [*Vancouver Stock Exchange symbol*]
TUO .... Tucson Observatory [*Arizona*] [*Seismograph station code, US Geological Survey*] (SEIS)
TUOC .... Tactical Unit Operations Center (AFM)
TUP .... Technology Utilization Program [*Defunct*]
TUP .... Telephony [*or Telephone*] User Part [*Telecommunications*] (TEL)
TUP .... Temple University Press
TUP .... Torres United Party [*Australia Political party*]
TUP .... Tovarystvo Ukrainskykh Progresystiv [*Ukrainian Progressive Association*] [*Russian Political party*] (PPE)
TUP .... Trickle Up Program (EA)
TUP .... Tupelo [*Mississippi*] [*Airport symbol*] (OAG)
TUP .... Tupik [*Former USSR Seismograph station code, US Geological Survey*] (SEIS)
TUP .... Tupperware Corp. [*NYSE symbol*] (TTSB)
TUP .... Twin Unit Pack [*for vehicles*]
Tup App .... Tupper's Appeal Reports [*Ontario*] [*A publication*] (DLA)
TUPC .... Transfer Underwater Pressure Chamber (DNAB)
TUPC .... T. U. P. Charlton's Georgia Reports [*A publication*] (DLA)
T U P Charlt .... T. U. P. Charlton's Georgia Reports [*A publication*] (DLA)
TUPE .... Tanganyika Union of Public Employees
TUPE .... Tupelo National Battlefield
TUPJ .... Roadtown/Beef Island [*Virgin Islands*] [*ICAO location identifier*] (ICLI)
TUPONA .... [*The*] United Provinces of North America [*See also EFISGA*] [*Suggested early name for Canada*]
Tupp .... Tupper's Appeal Reports [*Ontario*] [*A publication*] (DLA)
Tupp .... Tupper's Upper Canada Practice Reports [*A publication*] (DLA)
Tupp App .... Tupper's Appeal Reports [*Ontario*] [*A publication*] (DLA)
Tupper .... Tupper's Appeal Reports [*Ontario*] [*A publication*] (DLA)
Tupper .... Tupper's Upper Canada Practice Reports [*A publication*] (DLA)
TUPS .... Technical User Performance Specifications [*US Independent Telephone Association*] [*Telecommunications*] (TEL)
TUPW .... Virgin Gorda [*Virgin Islands*] [*ICAO location identifier*] (ICLI)
TUQ .... Tougan [*Upper Volta*] [*Airport symbol*] (AD)
TUR .... Aerotur SA [*Mexico ICAO designator*] (FAAC)
TUR .... American Turners [*An association*]
TUR .... Temporary Unattached Register [*Employment*] [*British*]
TUR .... Total Unemployment Rate
TUR .... Toxics Use Reduction [*Environmental science*]
TUR .... Toxic Use Reduction [*Manufacturing*]
TUR .... Traffic Usage Recorder [*Telecommunications*]
TUR .... Transurethral Resection [*of prostate gland*]
TUR .... Tucurui [*Brazil*] [*Airport symbol*] (OAG)
TUR .... Turbat [*Former USSR Seismograph station code, US Geological Survey Closed*] (SEIS)
TUR .... Turbine
TUR .... Turkey [*ANSI three-letter standard code*] (CNC)
tur .... Turkish [*MARC language code Library of Congress*] (LCCP)
TUR .... Turner Corp. [*AMEX symbol*] (SPSG)
Tur .... Turner's Reports [*99-101 Kentucky*] [*A publication*] (DLA)
Tur .... Turner's Reports [*35-48 Arkansas*] [*A publication*] (DLA)
Tur .... Turner's Select Pleas of the Forest [*Selden Society Publication, Vol. 13*] [*A publication*] (DLA)
TUR .... Turret (MSA)
Tur & R .... Turner and Russell's English Chancery Reports [*37 English Reprint*] [*1822-24*] [*A publication*] (DLA)
Tur & Ru .... Turner and Russell's English Chancery Reports [*37 English Reprint*] [*1822-24*] [*A publication*] (DLA)
Tur & Rus .... Turner and Russell's English Chancery Reports [*37 English Reprint*] [*1822-24*] [*A publication*] (DLA)
TURB .... Transurethral Resection of the Bladder [*Medicine*] (AAMN)
TURB .... Turbidity (AAMN)
TURB .... Turbinate [*Medicine*] (DAVI)
TURB .... Turbine (AAG)
TURB .... Turbulence
TURBN .... Transurethral Resection of Bladder Neck [*Medicine*] (DAVI)
TURBO .... Turbocharger [*Automotive engineering*]
TURBOALT .... Turboalternator (AAG)
TURBOCAT .... Turbine-Powered Catapult
Turbochf .... Turbochef, Inc. [*Associated Press*] (SAG)
TURBOGEN .... Turbogenerator (AAG)
TURBOPROP .... Turbine Propelled (WDAA)
TURBT .... Transurethral Resection of Bladder Tumor [*Medicine*] (MAH)
TURBT .... Turbulent [*NWS*] (FAAC)
TURC .... Trades Union Research Centre (AIE)
TURCO .... Turnaround Control [*Navy*]
TURF .... Thorium-Uranium Recycle Facility [*Oak Ridge National Laboratory*]
TURI .... Toxics Use Reduction Institute [*University of Massachusetts, Lowell*] [*Research center*] (RCD)
TURK .... Turkey
Turk .... Turkey (VRA)
Turkest .... Turkestan
TurkmSSR .... Turkmen Soviet Socialist Republic
Turksh .... Turkish Investment Fund [*Associated Press*] (SAG)
TURN .... Toward Utility Rate Normalization
Turn .... Turner's Reports [*99-101 Kentucky*] [*A publication*] (DLA)
Turn .... Turner's Reports [*35-48 Arkansas*] [*A publication*] (DLA)
Turn .... Turner's Select Pleas of the Forest [*Selden Society Publication, Vol. 13*] [*A publication*] (DLA)
Turn & P .... Turner and Phillips' English Chancery Reports [*A publication*] (DLA)
Turn & Ph .... Turner and Phillips' English Chancery Reports [*A publication*] (DLA)

Turn & R ..... Turner and Russell's English Chancery Reports [*37 English Reprint*] [*A publication*] (DLA)
Turn & R (Eng)... Turner and Russell's English Chancery Reports [*37 English Reprint*] [*A publication*] (DLA)
Turn & Rus... Turner and Russell's English Chancery Reports [*37 English Reprint*] [*A publication*] (DLA)
Turn & Russ... Turner and Russell's English Chancery Reports [*37 English Reprint*] [*A publication*] (DLA)
Turn Anglo Sax... Turner's History of the Anglo Saxon [*A publication*] (DLA)
TurnB.......... Turner Broadcasting System, Inc. [*Associated Press*] (SAG)
TURNBKLE... Turnbuckle [*s*] [*Freight*]
Turn Ch Pr... Turner's Practice of the Court of Chancery [*4th ed.*] [*1821*] [*A publication*] (DLA)
Turn Cop...... Turner on Copyright in Designs [*1849*] [*A publication*] (DLA)
Turn Pat ...... Turner on Patents [*1851*] [*A publication*] (DLA)
TURNPIKE.... Turnpike [*Commonly used*] (OPSA)
TURNPK....... Turnpike [*Commonly used*] (OPSA)
Turn Pr........ Turnbull's Practice [*New York*] [*A publication*] (DLA)
Turn Qui Tit... Turner on Quieting Titles [*A publication*] (DLA)
TurnrC .... Turner Corp. [*Associated Press*] (SAG)
TURP............ Transurethral Resection of the Prostate [*Medicine*]
turp............. Turpentine [*Chemistry*] (DAVI)
TURPS......... Terrestrial Unattended Reactor Power System
turq............. Turqoise (VRA)
TURQ........... Turquoise (ROG)
TURS........... Terminal Usage Reporting System [*Computer science*]
TURV........... Transurethral Resection of Valves [*Urology*] (DAVI)
TUS............. Tailored Upper Stage (MCD)
TUS............. Treasurer of the United States (AFM)
TUS............. Tucson [*Arizona*] [*Airport symbol*] (OAG)
TUS............. Tugboat Underwriting Syndicate [*Defunct*] (EA)
TUS............. Tuscarora [*New York*] [*Seismograph station code, US Geological Survey Closed*] (SEIS)
TUS............. Tushaun Resources, Inc. [*Vancouver Stock Exchange symbol*]
TUS............. Tuskegee Institute, Tuskegee, AL [*OCLC symbol*] (OCLC)
TUS............. Tussis [*Cough*] [*Pharmacy*]
TUSA........... Third United States Army [*Terminated, 1973*]
TUSA........... Trekville USA (EA)
TUSAB......... [*The*] United States Army Band (AABC)
TUSAC......... [*The*] United States Army Chorus (AABC)
TUSAFG....... [*The*] United States Air Force Group, American Mission for Aid to Turkey
TUSC........... Technology Use Studies Center [*Southeastern State College*]
TUSC........... Tuscarora, Inc. [*NASDAQ symbol*] (NQ)
Tusc............ Tusculanae Disputationes [*of Cicero*] [*Classical studies*] (OCD)
Tuscln.......... Tuscarora, Inc. [*Associated Press*] (SAG)
TU-SI........... University of Tennessee, Space Institute Library, Tullahoma, TN [*Library symbol Library of Congress*] (LCLS)
TUSIDBAD... Tomb of the Unknown Soldier Identification Badge [*Military decoration*] (GFGA)
Tuskegee U... Tuskegee University (GAGS)
TUSLOG....... Turkish-United States Logistic Group
TUSLOG....... [*The*] United States Logistics Group [*Military*] (AABC)
TUSLOGDET... Turkish-United States Logistics Group Detachment (DNAB)
tuss............ Tussis [*Cough*] [*Latin*] (CPH)
TUSSI.......... Temple University Short Syntax Inventory [*Educational test*]
TUSSIL........ Tussilago [*Coltsfoot*] [*Pharmacology*] (ROG)
TUSS MOL... Tussi Molesta [*When the Cough Is Troublesome*] [*Pharmacy*]
TUSS URG... Tussi Urgente [*When the Cough Is Troublesome*] [*Pharmacy*]
TUST............ Texarkana Union Station Trust [*AAR code*]
TUT............. GB Air Academy Ltd. [*British ICAO designator*] (FAAC)
TUT............. Tafuna, AS [*Location identifier FAA*] (FAAL)
TUT............. Tenants' Union of Tasmania [*Australia*]
TUT............. Transistor under Test (IEEE)
TUT............. Travailleurs Unis des Transports [*United Transportation Union - UTU*] [*Canada*]
TUT............. Travailleurs Unis du Telegraphe [*United Telegraph Workers - UTW*] [*Canada*]
TUT............. Tube Template (MCD)
TUT............. Tube under Test (MSA)
TUT............. Tucson - Telemeter [*Arizona*] [*Seismograph station code, US Geological Survey Closed*] (SEIS)
tut.............. Turko-Tataric [*MARC language code Library of Congress*] (LCCP)
TUT............. Twente University of Technology (NITA)
TUT............. University of Saint Thomas, Houston, TX [*OCLC symbol*] (OCLC)
TUTase........ Terminal Uridylyl Transferase [*An enzyme*]
TUTR........... TRO Learning [*NASDAQ symbol*] (TTSB)
TUTR........... TRO Learning, Inc. [*NASDAQ symbol*] (SAG)
TUT's.......... Totally Unified Theories [*Cosmology*]
TUTS............ True Ultimate Tensile Strength (MCD)
TUTT............ Tropical Upper Tropospheric Trough [*Meteorology*]
Tutt & C....... Tuttle and Carpenter's Reports [*52 California*] [*A publication*] (DLA)
Tutt & Carp... Tuttle and Carpenter's Reports [*52 California*] [*A publication*] (DLA)
Tuttle........... Tuttle and Carpenter's Reports [*52 California*] [*A publication*] (DLA)
Tuttle & Carpenter... Tuttle and Carpenter's Reports [*52 California*] [*A publication*] (DLA)
TUU............. Compania Aerea de Servicios Tur Air [*Spain ICAO designator*] (FAAC)
TUU............. Huntington, WV [*Location identifier FAA*] (FAAL)
TUU............. Tabuk [*Saudi Arabia*] [*Airport symbol*] (OAG)
TUU............. Transitional Ultraspherical-Ultraspherical Filter (PDAA)
TUUL........... Trade Union Unity League
TUUL........... Transurethral Ultrasonic Uterolithotripsy [*Urology*]
TUV............. Tactical Unmanned Vehicle [*Military*] (INF)
TUV............. Technischer Ueberwachungs-Verein [*Technical Watch-Over Association*] [*European product safety organization*] (CDE)
TUV............. Tucupita [*Venezuela*] [*Airport symbol*] (OAG)
TUV............. Turavia [*Poland ICAO designator*] (FAAC)
TUV............. Tuvalu [*ANSI three-letter standard code*] (CNC)
TUVX........... Tulip Virus X [*Plant pathology*]
TUW............ Trustee under Will [*Legal term*] (DLA)
TUW............ Tubala [*Panama*] [*Airport symbol*] (OAG)
TUWAH........ Trade Union Women of African Heritage (EA)
TUWC.......... Tactical Utilization Working Committee [*Navy*] (MCD)
TUWR.......... Turning Wrench [*Tool*] (AAG)
TUX............. Tuxedo (DSUE)
TUX............. Tuxpan [*Mexico*] [*Airport symbol*] (AD)
TUX............. Tuxpeno [*Race of maize*]
TUY............. Empresa Aerotuy [*Venezuela*] [*ICAO designator*] (FAAC)
TUY............. Tulum [*Mexico*] [*Airport symbol Obsolete*] (OAG)
TUZI............ Tuzigoot National Monument
TV............... Grupo Televisa S.A. [*NYSE symbol*] (SPSG)
TV............... Grupo Televisa S.A.GDS [*NYSE symbol*] (TTSB)
TV............... Haiti Trans Air [*ICAO designator*] (AD)
TV............... Taff Vale Railway [*Wales*]
TV............... Talipes Varus [*Orthopedics*] (DAVI)
TV............... Target Valve (MCD)
T/V............. Target Vehicle [*Air Force*] (AAG)
TV............... Target Velocity
TV............... Target Vulnerability (MCD)
TV............... Telefunken Variable Microgroove [*Record label*] [*Germany*]
TV............... Television
TV............... Television
TV............... Television, Vision Channel
T/V............. Temperature-to-Voltage (IDOE)
TV............... Terminal Velocity [*Navy*]
TV............... Test Vehicle
TV............... Test Voltage (IAA)
TV............... Tetrazolium Violet [*Also, TZV*]
TV............... Thames Valley [*England*]
TV............... Thermal Vacuum
TV............... Threshold Value (NITA)
TV............... Throttle Valve
TV............... Thrust Vector [*Aerospace*] (NASA)
TV............... Thyroid Vein [*Medicine*] (PDAA)
TV............... Tidal Volume [*Amount of air that moves in and out of lungs under given conditions*] [*Physiology*]
TV............... Time Variation of Gain
TV............... Title Verso [*Publishing*] (WDMC)
TV............... Total Value
TV............... Total Volume
TV............... Transamerica [*ICAO designator*] (AD)
TV............... Transfer and Void (MCD)
TV............... Transfer Varnish (DGA)
TV............... Transfer Vector
TV............... Transfer Vector (NITA)
TV............... Transfer Voucher (AFM)
TV............... Transport Vehicle [*Military*]
TV............... Transvenous (DAVI)
TV............... Transversion [*Molecular biology*]
TV............... Transvestite [*Medicine*]
TV............... Travel Voucher (GFGA)
TV............... Traverse (IEEE)
TV............... Trial Visit (AAMN)
TV............... Trichomonas vaginalis [*A protozoan*] [*Medicine*]
TV............... Trichomonas Vaginitis [*A parasitic infection*] (DAVI)
TV............... Tricuspid Valve [*Anatomy*]
TV............... Trinidad Volunteers [*British military*] (DMA)
TV............... Trip Valve [*Railroad term*]
TV............... Truncal Vagotomy [*Medicine*] (DMAA)
TV............... Tuberculin Volutin [*Medicine*] (MAE)
TV............... Tube Tester [*JETDS nomenclature*] [*Military*] (CET)
TV............... Tube Voltmeter (IAA)
TV............... Tunica Vaginalis [*Anatomy*]
TV............... Turbo Vision [*Borland International*] [*Computer science*] (PCM)
TV............... Tuvalu [*ANSI two-letter standard code*] (CNC)
Tv............... Ventral Touch Neurons [*of a leech*]
TV............... [*The*] Voluntaryists (EA)
TV5............. Television Francophone par Satellite [*France*] (EAIO)
TVA............. Morafenobe [*Madagascar*] [*Airport symbol*] (OAG)
TVA............. Target Value Analysis [*Army*] (ADDR)
TVA............. Taxe a la Valeur Ajoutee [*Value-Added Tax*] [*French Business term*]
TVA............. Tax on Value Added [*European manufacturing tax*]
TvA............. Television Associates Network [*Canada*]
TVA............. Television Australia Ltd.
TVA............. Temporary Variance Authority [*or Authorization*] [*NASA*] (AAG)
TVA............. Temporary Volume Allowance
TVA............. Temporary Voluntary Allowance
TVA............. Tennessee Valley Authority [*NYSE symbol*] (SAG)
TVA............. Tennessee Valley Authority [*Also, an information service or system*]
TVA............. Tennessee Valley Authority, Technical Library, Knoxville, TN [*OCLC symbol*] (OCLC)
TVA............. Tenn Val Auth 8.00%'QUIDS' [*NYSE symbol*] (TTSB)
TVA............. Textile Veterans Association (EA)
TVA............. Thrust Vector Actuator
TVA............. Thrust Vector Alignment [*Aerospace*] (MCD)
TVA............. Time Variant Automation (IAA)
TVA............. Torah Va'Avodah (BJA)
TVA............. Trans America Airlines, Inc. [*ICAO designator*] (FAAC)

TVA Tuned Vertical Array (CAAL)
TVA 45 Tennessee Valley Authority [*Associated Press*] (SAG)
TVA 46 Tennessee Valley Authority [*Associated Press*] (SAG)
TVAC Thrust Vector Activation Control [*Aerospace*]
TVAC Time-Varying Adaptive Correlation
TVAHVF Textile Veterans Association Hospitalized Veterans Fund [*Defunct*] (EA)
TVAR Television Advertisers' Report [*A publication*] (DOAD)
TVAR Test Variance (NASA)
TV-ARBS Television Angle Rate Bombing System (MCD)
TVAT Television Air Trainer
TVB Cabool, MO [*Location identifier FAA*] (FAAL)
TVB Television Broadcasts [*Hong Kong television company*] (ECON)
TVB Television Bureau of Advertising (DOAD)
TVB Tennessee Valley Authority [*NYSE symbol*] (SAG)
TVB Tenn Val Auth 7.50%'QUIDS' [*NYSE symbol*] (TTSB)
TVB Total Volatile Bases [*Chemistry*]
TVB Treu und Bestaendig [*Faithful and Steadfast*] [*Motto of Johann Georg, Margrave of Brandenburg (1577-1624)*] [*German*]
TVBN Total Volatile Basic Nitrogen [*Food analysis*]
TVBS Television Broadcast Satellite [*NASA*]
TVC Technical Value Committee (BARN)
TVC Televideo Consultants, Inc. [*Evanston, IL*] [*Telecommunications*] (TSSD)
TVC Television Camera (MHDB)
TVC Temperature Valve Control
TVC Thermal Vacuum Chamber (NASA)
TVC Thermal Voltage Converter
TVC Thoracic Vena Cava [*Medicine*]
TVC Throttle Valve Control
TVC Thrust Vector Control [*Aerospace*]
TVC Tientsin Volunteer Corps [*British military*] (DMA)
TVC Timed Vital Capacity
TVC Time-Varying Coefficient
TVC Torsional Vibration Characteristics
TVC Total Annual Variable Cost
TVC Total Variable Cost Curve [*Economics*]
TVC Total Variable Costs
TVC Total Viable Cells [*Microbiology*]
TVC Total Vital Capacity [*Medicine*] (DAVI)
TVC Total Volume Capacity [*Physiology*]
TVC Transvaginal Cone [*Medicine*] (MAE)
TVC Traverse City [*Michigan*] [*Airport symbol*] (OAG)
TVC Triple Voiding Cystogram [*Medicine*]
TVC True Vocal Cord (MEDA)
TVCA Thrust Vector Control Actuator [*Aerospace*] (NASA)
TVCA Thrust Vector Control Assembly [*Aerospace*]
TVCA Total Vegetative Control Agents [*Agriculture*]
TVCAM Television Camera and Control Equipment
TVCD Thrust Vector Control Driver [*Aerospace*] (NASA)
TVC/JIC Thrust Vector Control/Jet Interaction Control
TVCL Toxic Victims Compensation Legislation
TVCS Television Communications Subsystem
TVCS Thrust Vector Control System [*Aerospace*] (KSC)
TVCS Tyler Vocational Card Sort [*Guidance*]
TVD Teatr Voennykh Deistvii [*Theater of Military Operations*] [*Former USSR*]
TVD Television Display (MCD)
TVD Thermal Voltaic Detection [*Analytical chemistry*]
TVD Total Virus Defense [*Computer Security System*]
TVD Total Virus Defense [*McAfee*] [*Computer science*]
TVD Toxic Vapor Detector
TVD Toxic Vapor Disposal [*NASA*] (KSC)
TVD Transmissable Virus Dementia [*Psychiatry*]
TVD Triple-Vessel Disease [*Cardiology*] (DAVI)
TVD True Vertical Depth [*Diamonds*]
TVD Tuned Viscoelastic Damper
TVDALV Triple Vessel Disease with Abnormal Left Ventricle [*Cardiology*]
TVDC Test Volts, Direct Current
TVDC Tidewater Virginia Development Council
TVDP Terminal Vector Display Unit
TVDR Tag Vector Display Register
TVDS Toxic Vapor Detection System (SAA)
TVDT Tumor Volume Doubling Time [*Cytology*]
TVDY Television Deflection Yoke
TVE Technology Validation Experiment (SDI)
TVE Television Espanola [*Television network*] [*Spain*]
TVE Test Vehicle Engine (AAG)
TVE Thermal Vacuum Environment
TVE Total Vertical Error [*Aviation*] (DA)
TVE Town and Village Enterprise (EERA)
TVE Township and Village Enterprise [*People's Republic of China*] (ECON)
TVE Tricuspid Valve Echophonocardiogram [*Cardiology*]
TVED Tuned Viscoelastic Damper
TVEI Technical and Vocational Education Initiative [*Manpower Services Commission*] [*British*]
TVEI(P) Technical and Vocational Education Initiative: Pilot (AIE)
TVEL Target Velocity
TVEL Track Velocity
TVER Tumor Virus Epidemiology Repository [*National Institutes of Health*]
TVERS Television Evaluation and Renewal Standards [*Student legal action organization*]
TVEXPIS Television Experiment Interconnecting Station [*NASA*] (NASA)
TVF Tactile Vocal Fremitus [*Medicine*]
TVF Tape Velocity Fluctuation
TVF Taylor Vortex Flow [*Fluid mechanics*]
TVF Templeton Vietnam Opport Fd [*NYSE symbol*] (TTSB)
TVF Templeton Vietnam Opportunities Fund [*NYSE symbol*] (SAG)
TVF Thief River Falls [*Minnesota*] [*Airport symbol*] (OAG)
TVF Total Variable Factor Curve [*Economics*]
TVFA Total Volatile Fatty Acid [*of foodstuffs*]
TV Flme TV Filme, Inc. [*Associated Press*] (SAG)
TVFN Television Food Network
TVFS Tactical Vehicle Fleet Simulation (MCD)
TVFT Television Flyback Transformer
TVG Tavares & Gulf R. R. [*AAR code*]
TVG Television Video Generator
TVG Temperature-Voltage-Gases (DNAB)
TVG Test Vector Generator
TVG Threshold Voltage Generator
TVG Time Variation of Gain
TVG Triggered Vacuum Gap
TVG TVG Technologies [*Associated Press*] (SAG)
TVGDHS Television Ground Data Handling System [*NASA*]
TVGEN TV Guide Entertainment Network
TVGLF TVG Technologies [*NASDAQ symbol*] (SAG)
TVGLF T V G Technologies Wrrt'C' [*NASDAQ symbol*] (TTSB)
TVG Tch TVG Technologies [*Associated Press*] (SAG)
TVGTF TVG Technologies [*NASDAQ symbol*] (SAG)
TVGUF TVG Technologies [*NASDAQ symbol*] (SAG)
TVGWF TVG Technologies [*NASDAQ symbol*] (SAG)
TVGWF T V G Technologies Wrrt'A' [*NASDAQ symbol*] (TTSB)
TVGZF TVG Technologies [*NASDAQ symbol*] (SAG)
TVGZF T V G Technologies Wrrt'B' [*NASDAQ symbol*] (TTSB)
TVH Total Vaginal Hysterectomy [*Gynecology*]
TVH Transvaginal Hysterectomy [*Gynecology*] (DAVI)
TVH Turkey Virus Hepatitis [*Medicine*] (DMAA)
TVHH Television Household [*Ratings*] (NTCM)
TVI Television Interface (ECII)
TVI Television Interference [*Communications*]
TVI Temperament and Values Inventory [*Interpersonal skills and attitudes test*]
TVI Temperature-Viscosity Index (DAVI)
TVI Thomasville, GA [*Location identifier FAA*] (FAAL)
TVI Total Vision, Inc. [*Houston, TX*] (TSSD)
TVI Trade Valuers Institute [*British*] (DBA)
TVI Transcript/Video Index [*A publication*]
TVI Transient Voltage Indicator
TVI Turbo Vapor Injector
TVI Tutored Videotape Instruction
TVIC Television Input Converter
TVIC Television Interference Committee
TVID Television Frame Identification Data [*NASA*]
TVID Television Sight Unit Identification (MCD)
TVIG Television and Inertial Guidance
TVIS Television Information Storage (IAA)
TVIS Time Video Information Services, Inc. (IID)
T-VIS Toyota's Variable Induction System [*Automotive engineering*]
TVIS Tropical Vegetable Information Service [*Asian Vegetable Research and Development Center*] [*Information service or system*] (IID)
TVIS Turbine Vibration Indication System (NG)
TVIST Television Information Storage Tube
TVJ Tavaj Transportes Aereos Regulares, SA [*Brazil*] [*FAA designator*] (FAAC)
TVJ Thomas Jefferson University, Philadelphia, PA [*OCLC symbol*] (OCLC)
TV/JI Thrust Vector/Jet Interaction
TVK Target Value Kills (MCD)
TVK Toimihenkilo - ja Virkamiesjarjestojen Keskusliitto [*Confederation of Intellectual and Government Workers*] [*Finland*]
TVKMF Theodore Von Karman Memorial Foundation (EA)
TVL Aviata [*Former USSR*] [*FAA designator*] (FAAC)
TVL Lake Tahoe [*California*] [*Airport symbol*] (OAG)
TVL Television Listener (IDOE)
TVL Television Listening (IDOE)
TVL Tenth Value Layer
TVL Thermo Voltek [*AMEX symbol*] (TTSB)
TVL Thermo Voltek Corp. [*AMEX symbol*] (SAG)
TVL Time Variation of Loss (IAA)
TVL Townsville [*Australia Seismograph station code, US Geological Survey Closed*] (SEIS)
TVL Transmit [*or Transmitting*] Variolosser (IAA)
Tvl Transvaal [*South Africa*]
TVL Transverse Vertical Longitudinal
TVL Travel (AABC)
TVLADVP Travel Advance Payment [*TDY*]
TVLALWADV Travel Allowance Advance [*in PCS*]
TVLALWS Travel Allowance on Separation [*Army*]
TVLF Transportable Very-Low-Frequency [*Transmitter*]
TVLI Tivoli Indus Inc. [*NASDAQ symbol*] (TTSB)
TVLI Tivoli Industries, Inc. [*NASDAQ symbol*] (SAG)
TVLIW Tivoli Inds Wrrt'A' [*NASDAQ symbol*] (TTSB)
TVLIZ Tivoli Inds Wrrt'B' [*NASDAQ symbol*] (TTSB)
TVLRO Television Licensing and Records Office [*Post Office*] [*British*]
TVM Tachometer Voltmeter
TVM Target Via Missile [*Aviation*]
TVM Tavria-Mak [*Ukraine*] [*FAA designator*] (FAAC)
TVM Techno Venture Management [*Germany*]
TVM Television Malta

TVM .... Television Monitor [*Video only*]
TVM .... Thrust Vectoring Motor [*Aerospace*] (MUGU)
TVM .... TOW [*Tube-Launched, Optically Tracked, Wire-Guided (Weapon)*] Visual Module [*Army*]
TVM .... Track-Via-Missile
TVM .... Trailer Van Mount
TVM .... Transistorized Voltmeter
TVM .... TRV Minerals Corp. [*Vancouver Stock Exchange symbol*]
TVMAP .... Track-via-Missile Analog Processor [*Military*]
TVMS .... Test of Visual-Motor Skills [*Sensorimotor skills test*]
TVMV .... Tobacco Vein Mottling Virus
TVN .... Target Velocity, North
TVN .... Television News, Inc.
TVN .... Televisora Nacional [*Television network*] [*Venezuela*]
TVN .... Test Verification Network [*NASA*] (NASA)
TVN .... Total Volatile Nitrogen [*Analytical chemistry*]
TVN .... Transcolombiana de Aviacion SA [*Colombia*] [*ICAO designator*] (FAAC)
TVO .... Ditta Transavio di I. Ballerio [*Italy ICAO designator*] (FAAC)
TVO .... Taravao [*Society Islands*] [*Seismograph station code, US Geological Survey*] (SEIS)
TVO .... Throttle Valve Opening [*Automotive engineering*]
TVO .... Total Value of Ownership
TVO .... Tractor Vaporizing Oil [*Automotive engineering*]
TVO .... Transistor Volt-Ohmmeter (IDOE)
TVOC .... Television Operations Center [*NASA*] (KSC)
TVOM .... Transistorized Volt Ohm Milliammeter (IAA)
TVOM .... Transistor Volt-Ohmmeter (IDOE)
TVOP .... Television Observation Post (CET)
TVOR .... Terminal Very High Frequency Omnirange (IAA)
TVOR .... Terminal VHF [*Very-High Frequency*] Omnidirectional Range
TVOR .... Terminal Visual Omnirange
TVOR .... Translational Vestibulo-Ocular Reflex [*Ophthalmology*]
TVP .... Tamil Vimukhti Peramena [*Sri Lanka*] [*Political party*] (PPW)
TVP .... Test Verification Program [*NASA*] (NASA)
TVP .... Textured Vegetable Protein [*Trademark of Archer Daniels Midland Co. for soybean product*]
TVP .... Thermo-Photo-Voltaic
TVP .... Time Variable Parameter (IAA)
TVP .... Transvenous Pacemaker [*Cardiology*] (DAVI)
TVP .... Transvesical Prostatectomy [*Urology*] (DAVI)
TVP .... Tricuspid Valve Prolapse [*Cardiology*]
TVP .... True Vapor Pressure
TVP .... Victoria Public Library, Victoria, TX [*OCLC symbol*] (OCLC)
TVPC .... TOW [*Tube-Launched, Optically Tracked, Wire-Guided (Weapon)*] Vehicle PowerConditioner (MCD)
TVPPA .... Tennessee Valley Public Power Association (EA)
TVPS .... Test of Visual-Perceptual Skills
TV Q .... Television Quarterly [*A publication*] (BRI)
TVQ .... Top Visual Quality
TVR .... Tadcaster Volunteer Rifles [*British military*] (DMA)
TVR .... Tag Vector Response (NITA)
TVR .... Tavrey, Aircompany [*Ukraine*] [*FAA designator*] (FAAC)
TVR .... Television Rating
TVR .... Television Recording (WDMC)
TVR .... Temperature Variation of Resistance [*Electricity*]
TVR .... Tennessee Valley Region
TVR .... Thermal Vapor Recompressors [*For evaporators*]
TVR .... Time Variable Reflectivity (MCD)
TVR .... Tonic Vibration Reflex [*or Response*] [*Medicine*]
TVR .... Total Vascular Resistance [*Medicine*] (DMAA)
TVR .... Trajectory Velocity RADAR (MCD)
TVR .... Trevor (Wilkinson) [*Sports car named for its designer*] [*British*]
TVR .... Tricuspid Valve Replacement [*Cardiology*]
TVRB .... Tactical Vehicle Review Board [*Army*] (AABC)
TVRCC .... TVR Car Club [*Later, TVRCCNA*] (EA)
TVRE .... Transportable Vehicle Refuelling Equipment (PDAA)
TVRI .... Televisi Republik Indonesia [*Indonesian television network*] (FEA)
TVRM .... Television Receiver/Monitor
TVRN .... Tavern
TVRO .... Television Receive Only [*Telecommunications*]
TVRP .... Television Reading Program
TVRS .... Television and Radio Suppression [*Electronics*]
TVRS .... Television Video Recording System (MCD)
TVS .... Tactical Vocoder System
TVS .... Telemetry Video Spectrum
TVS .... Telephone Video System [*NEC America, Inc.*] [*Wood Dale, IL*] [*Telecommunications*] (TSSD)
TVS .... Television Subsystem [*Spacecraft*]
TVS .... Thermal [*or Thermostatic*] Vacuum Switch [*Automotive engineering*]
TVS .... Thrust Vector System [*Aerospace*]
TVS .... Tornado Vortex Signature (USDC)
TVS .... Tornado Vortex Signature [*Marine science*] (OSRA)
TVS .... Total Volatile Solids [*Analytical chemistry*]
TVS .... Toxic Vapor Suit [*NASA*] (NASA)
TVS .... Transient Voltage Suppressor
TVS .... Tube-Vehicle System (MCD)
TVS .... Volunteer State Community College, Gallatin, TN [*OCLC symbol*] (OCLC)
TVSA .... Thrust Vector Position Servo Amplifier [*Aerospace*]
TV-SAT .... Satellite Television [*Germany*]
TVSC .... Television Videotape Satellite Communications [*Group W Productions*] [*Pittsburgh, PA*] (TSSD)
TVSD .... Time-Varying Spectral Display
TVSG .... Television Signal Generator
TVSM .... Television System Monitor
TVSM .... Time-Varying Sequential Measuring [*Device*]
TVSM .... Time-Varying Signal Measurement (IAA)
TVSO .... Television Space Observatory
TVSP .... Tactical Vehicle Special Program [*Army*] (RDA)
TV SPOTTS ... Tuneful Viewer's Society for the Preservation of Television Theme Songs
TVSS .... Tactile Vision Substitution System (PDAA)
TVSS .... Television and Video Switching Subsystem (MCD)
TVSS .... Television Systems Section
TVSS .... Transient Voltage Surge Suppression
TVSSIS .... Television Subsystem Interconnecting Station [*NASA*] (NASA)
TVSU .... Television Sight Unit
TVSV .... Kingstown/Arnos Vale [*St. Vincent*] [*ICAO location identifier*] (ICLI)
TVSV .... Thermostatic Vacuum Switching Valve [*Automotive engineering*]
TVSYS .... Television System (IAA)
TVT .... Target Verification Test [*Military*] (CAAL)
TVT .... Television of Thailand (FEA)
TVT .... Television Terminal (CMD)
TVT .... Television Trainer/Tapes (MCD)
TVT .... Television Typewriter
TVT .... Thermal Vacuum Test
TVT .... Tiverton, OH [*Location identifier FAA*] (FAAL)
TVT .... Traffic Volume Trends [*BTS*] (TAG)
TVT .... Transaviation, SA [*Spain*] [*FAA designator*] (FAAC)
TVT .... Tunica Vaginalis Testis [*Anatomy*]
TVTA .... Thermal Vacuum Test Article (NASA)
TV TR .... Television Tower [*Mast*]
TVTV .... Thermostatic Vacuum Transmitting Valve [*Automotive engineering*]
TVTV .... Top Value Television [*Group of 26 young people who photographed the 1972 Democratic convention and presented it on TV*]
TVU .... Taveuni [*Fiji*] [*Airport symbol*] (OAG)
TVU .... Total Volume Urine [*in 24 hours*]
TVV .... Thermal Vacuum Valve [*Automotive engineering*]
TVV .... Thermal Vent Valve [*Automotive engineering*]
TVV .... Transmissible Venereal Virus [*Infectious diseases*] (DAVI)
TVW .... Tag Vector Word (NITA)
TVW .... Total Ventricular Weight [*Cardiology*]
TVW .... Towed Vehicle Weight [*Automotive engineering*]
TVX .... Target Vehicle Experimental [*Air Force*]
TVX .... Tulip Virus X
TVX .... TVX Gold [*NYSE symbol*] (TTSB)
TVX .... TVX Gold, Inc. [*NYSE symbol*] (SAG)
TVX .... TVX Mining Corp. [*Formerly, Treasure Valley Explorations Ltd.*] [*Toronto Stock Exchange symbol*]
TVX Gld .... TVX Gold, Inc. [*Associated Press*] (SAG)
TVY .... Tavoy [*Myanmar*] [*Airport symbol*] (OAG)
TVZ .... Taupo Volcanic Zone [*Geology*]
TW .... 20th Century Indus [*NYSE symbol*] (TTSB)
TW .... Tactical Warning (MCD)
TW .... Tail Warning [*RADAR*] (NATG)
TW .... Tailwater
TW .... Tail Wind
TW .... Taiwan [*ANSI two-letter standard code*] (CNC)
TW .... Tankwagon
TW .... Tapes and Recording Wires [*JETDS nomenclature*] [*Military*] (CET)
TW .... Tap Water [*Medicine*]
TW .... Tapwater (DAVI)
TW .... Taxiway [*Aviation*]
TW .... Teamwork (MSA)
TW .... Technical Win [*Boxing*] (DICI)
TW .... Technical Works [*Air Force*] (MCD)
TW .... Temperature Well (MSA)
TW .... Tempered Water
TW .... Temporary Warrant
TW .... Terawatt
TW .... Test Weight
TW .... Textil-Wirtschaft [*Textile Industry*] [*Deutscher Fachverlag GmbH*] [*Information service or system*] (IID)
TW .... Text Word(s) (NITA)
TW .... Thermal Wire (KSC)
TW .... Thermit Welding
TW .... Thermoplastic Wire
T-W .... Three-Wheeler [*Type of motorcycle*]
T/W .... Thrust-to-Weight
TW .... Thumbwheel (MCD)
TW .... Tight Wrapped (MSA)
TW .... Tile Wainscot [*Technical drawings*]
TW .... Time Word
TW .... Top of Wall [*Technical drawings*]
TW .... Torpedo Water
TW .... Total Body Water
TW .... Total Weight
TW .... Total Woman [*Title of a 1973 book by Marabel Morgan and of TV seminars based on this book*]
TW .... Total Work
TW .... Trail Watcher (CINC)
TW .... Transit Working [*Telecommunications*] (TEL)
TW .... Trans World Airlines, Inc. [*ICAO designator*]
TW .... Traveling Wave
TW .... Travel Warrant
TW .... Travel Writer [*A publication*] (EAAP)
TW .... Tropical Worsted Uniform [*Army*] (VNW)
TW .... Trow [*Ship's rigging*] (ROG)
TW .... True Watt (MSA)

TW............ Trustee under Will [*Legal term*] (DLA)
TW............ Tru-Wall Group Ltd. [*Toronto Stock Exchange symbol*]
TW............ Twaddell [*Specific gravity scale*] [*Physics*]
TW............ Twentieth Century Industries [*NYSE symbol*] (SPSG)
TW............ Twickenham [*Postcode*] (ODBW)
TW............ Twin (IAA)
TW............ Twin Screw (DS)
TW............ Twisted (IAA)
TW............ Twister (AAG)
TW............ Typewriter (AAG)
TW3............ That Was The Week That Was [*Also, TWTWTW*] [*Television program of English origin*]
TWA............ Tap Water Agar [*Microbiology*]
TWA............ Textile Waste Association [*Later, Textile Fibers and By-Products Association*] (EA)
TWA............ Thames Water Authority [*British*]
TWA............ Time Weighted Average [*Data sampling*]
TWA............ Tooling Work Authorization
TWA............ Toy Wholesalers Association of America (EA)
TWA............ Trailing Wire Antenna [*on aircraft*]
TWA............ Transaction Work Area
TWA............ Transcontinental & Western Airlines [*Later, Trans World Airlines, Inc.*]
TWA............ Trans World Airlines [*Associated Press*] (SAG)
TWA............ Trans World Airlines, Inc. [*Humorously interpreted as "Try Walking Across" and "Teeny Weeny Airlines"*] [*AMEX symbol*] (SPSG)
TWA............ Trans World Airlines, Inc. [*ICAO designator*] (FAAC)
TWA............ Traveling-Wave Amplifier
TWA............ Trelew [*Argentina*] [*Geomagnetic observatory code*]
TWA............ Two-Way Alternate (IAA)
TWA............ Typewriter Adapter (MHDB)
TWA............ [*The*] Waferboard Association [*Later, SBA*] (EA)
TWA............ [*The*] Woman Activist (EA)
TW/AA............ Tactical Warning/Attack Assessment
TWAB............ Textile Work Assignment Boards [*Terminated, 1935*]
TWAC............ Tactical Weather Analysis Center (MCD)
TWAC............ Time-Weighted Average Concentration [*Toxicology*]
Twad............ Twaddell [*Physics*]
TWADL............ Two-Way Air Data Link [*Tactical Air Command*]
TWAE............ Time-Weighted Average Exposure [*Toxicology*]
TWAES............ Tactical Warfare Analysis and Evaluation System (MCD)
TWAH............ This Week at Headquarters [*Military publication*] (DNAB)
TWAIN............ Technology Without an Interesting Name [*Computer science*]
TWALNDG............ Turnaway Landing [*Navy*] (NVT)
TWAP............ Thin Wire Analysis Program [*Air Force*]
TWAPA............ Teens with a Positive Attitude
TWAR............ Taiwan Acute Respiratory Disease [*Pneumonia-causing chlamydia strain named after the ailment that results from it*]
TWAS............ Third World Academy of Sciences [*Trieste, Italy*] (EAIO)
TWASPIT............ Therapeutic Work Aid Station for Physically Inactive Thinkers (MCD)
TWAT............ Traveling-Wave Amplifier Tube
TWA.WS............ Trans World Airlines Wrrt [*AMEX symbol*] (TTSB)
TWB............ Toowoomba [*Australia Airport symbol*] (OAG)
TWB............ Total Water Burden [*Environmental science*]
TWB............ Towed Vehicle Brake
TWB............ Traveling-Wave Beam [*LASER*]
TWB............ Twin with Bath [*Tourist accommodations*] (WDAA)
TWB............ Typewriter Buffer
TWB............ Wayland Baptist College, Plainview, TX [*OCLC symbol*] (OCLC)
TWBA............ Tasmanian Wool Brokers' Association [*Australia*]
TWBC............ Total White Blood Cells [*Medicine*]
TWBC............ Transworld Bancorp [*NASDAQ symbol*] (NQ)
TWBFA............ Treeing Walker Breeders and Fanciers Association (EA)
TWBNT............ Theologisches Woerterbuch zum Neuen Testament [*A publication*] (BJA)
TWBS............ Traditional Wooden Boat Society [*Defunct*] (EA)
TWC............ Express Airlines II, Inc. [*ICAO designator*] (FAAC)
TWC............ Suao [*Republic of China*] [*Seismograph station code, US Geological Survey*] (SEIS)
TWC............ Teletype Service Without Voice Communication [*Telecommunications*] (IAA)
TWC............ Tennessee Wesleyan College
TWC............ Texas Wesleyan College
TWC............ Texas Wesleyan College, Fort Worth, TX [*OCLC symbol*] (OCLC)
TWC............ Texas Western College [*Later, UTEP*]
TWC............ Theater Weather Central [*Military*]
TWC............ Three-Way Catalyst [*Vehicle exhaust control*]
TWC............ Total Wear Coefficient [*Materials science*]
TWC............ Truncated Whitworth Coarse [*Thread*] (MSA)
TWC............ [*The*] Weather Channel [*Cable TV programming service*]
TWCA............ T. W. Cape and Associates [*Atlanta, GA*] [*Telecommunications service*] (TSSD)
TWCap............ Time Warner Capital I [*Associated Press*] (SAG)
TWCF............ Third World Conference Fund
TWCRT............ Traveling-Wave Cathode-Ray Tube (IEEE)
TWCS............ Test of Work Competency and Stability [*Psychology*]
TWCS............ Through-Water Communications System [*Navy*] (CAAL)
TWCS............ Tomahawk Weapon Control System (DOMA)
TWD............ Hualien [*Republic of China*] [*Seismograph station code, US Geological Survey*] (SEIS)
TWD............ Tactical Weapons Delivery
TWD............ Tail Wags Dog [*Airspace effects*]
TWD............ Thermal Warning Device (MCD)
TWD............ Torpedo Wire Dispenser
TWD............ Total White and Differential Count [*Hematology*]
TWD............ Touch Wire Display (PDAA)
TWD............ Toward
TWD............ Tween Deck [*on a ship*] (DS)
TWD............ Twisted Double Shielded (MCD)
TWDC............ Tyne and Wear Development Corp. [*British*] (ECON)
TWDD............ Two-Way/Delay Dial [*Telecommunications*] (TEL)
TWDM............ Two-Way Data Messaging
TWDR............ Terminal Weather Doppler Radar [*FAA*] (TAG)
TWDS............ Tactical Water Distribution System (MCD)
TWE............ Tap Water Enema [*Medicine*]
TWE............ Test of Written English [*Educational test*]
TWE............ Test of Written English (GAGS)
TWE............ Textile Waste Exchange [*Later, Textile Fibers and By-Products Association*]
TWE............ Thumb Wheel Encoder
TWE............ Time Warner Entertainment (ECON)
TWE............ Transwede [*Sweden ICAO designator*] (FAAC)
TWE............ Trans-Western Exploration, Inc. [*Toronto Stock Exchange symbol*]
TWE............ Trans World Entertainment [*Movie production*]
TWE............ [*The*] Washington Establishment
TWEA............ Trading with the Enemy Act
TWEB............ Transcribed Weather Broadcast
Tweener............ Between Two Outfielders [*Baseball*] [*Also, a lifestyle classification*]
Twel N............ Twelfth Night [*Shakespearean work*] (BARN)
TWEP............ Terminate with Extreme Prejudice [*To kill*] [*Counterintelligence*]
TWER............ Tower Automotive [*NASDAQ symbol*] (TTSB)
TWER............ Tower Automotive, Inc. [*NASDAQ symbol*] (SAG)
TWERL............ Tropical Wind, Energy Conversion, and Reference Level [*National Science Foundation*]
TWERLE............ Tropical Wind, Energy Conversion, and Reference Level Experiment [*National Science Foundation*]
TWERLE............ Tropical Wind, Energy Conversion and Reference Level Experiment [*Marine science*] (OSRA)
TWETC............ Tapwater Enema Till Clear [*Pharmacology*] (DAVI)
TWF............ Third World Forum [*Cairo, Egypt*] (EAIO)
TWF............ Third World Foundation [*British*] (EAIO)
TWF............ Transylvanian World Federation (EAIO)
TWF............ Trasco Wind-Force [*Vancouver Stock Exchange symbol*]
TWF............ Truncated Whitworth Fine [*Thread*] (MSA)
TWF............ Twin Falls [*Idaho*] [*Airport symbol*] (OAG)
TWF............ Yuli [*Republic of China*] [*Seismograph station code, US Geological Survey Closed*] (SEIS)
TWF1............ Yuli [*Republic of China*] [*Seismograph station code, US Geological Survey*] (SEIS)
TWFC............ Tom Wopat Fan Club (EA)
TW Fin............ Time Warner Financing Trust PERCS [*Associated Press*] (SAG)
TWG............ Taitung [*Republic of China*] [*Seismograph station code, US Geological Survey*] (SEIS)
TWG............ Technical Working Group [*of the Conference on the Discontinuance of Nuclear Weapon Tests*]
TWG............ Technical Working Group (EERA)
TWG............ Telemetry Working Group
TWG............ Television Writer's Guild (NTCM)
TWG............ Test Working Group [*in various federal government agencies*] (KSC)
TWG............ Transfer Working Group (MCD)
TWG............ Transition Work Group
TWG............ Transport Working Group [*Australia*]
TWG............ Trans Wings AS [*Norway ICAO designator*] (FAAC)
TW Gam............ Trans World Gaming Corp. [*Associated Press*] (SAG)
TWGC............ Treatment of War Gas Casualties (MCD)
TWGSS............ Tank Weapons Gunnery Simulation System (MCD)
TWH............ Catalina Island [*California*] [*Airport symbol Obsolete*] (OAG)
TWH............ Houston Baptist University, Houston, TX [*OCLC symbol*] (OCLC)
TWh............ Terawatt Hour (ADA)
TWH............ Toronto Western Hospital [*UTLAS symbol*]
TWHA............ Western Tasmanian Wilderness National Parks World Heritage Area (EERA)
TWHBEA............ Tennessee Walking Horse Breeders' and Exhibitors' Association (EA)
TWHBEAA............ Tennessee Walking Horse Breeders' and Exhibitors' Association of America [*Later, TWHBEA*] (EA)
TWHD............ Tons per Workable Hatch per Day [*Shipping*]
TWHF............ Technoserve's World Harvest Fund (EA)
TWHH............ Transworld Home HealthCare, Inc. [*NASDAQ symbol*] (SAG)
TWHH............ Transworld Home Hlthcare [*NASDAQ symbol*] (TTSB)
TWHHW............ Transworld Home Hlthcr Wrrt [*NASDAQ symbol*] (TTSB)
TWHL............ Tail Wheel [*Aviation*]
TWHO............ [*The*] White House Office
TWHTA............ Tennessee Walking Horse Trainers' Association [*Later, Walking Horse Trainers Association*]
TW(I)............ Tail Warning (Indicator) [*RADAR*] (DEN)
TWI............ Threat Warning Information [*Air Force*]
TWI............ Titan Wheel International Co. [*NYSE symbol*] (SAG)
TWI............ Titan Wheel Intl [*NYSE symbol*] (TTSB)
TWI............ Toxic Waste Incinerator
TWI............ Trade-Weighted Index (ADA)
TWI............ Training with Industry Program [*Army*] (RDA)
twi............ Twi [*MARC language code Library of Congress*] (LCCP)
TWI............ [*The*] Way International [*An association*] (EA)
TWI............ [*The*] Welding Institute [*Information service or system*] (IID)
TWI............ Wichita, KS [*Location identifier FAA*] (FAAL)
TWI............ [*The*] Women's Institute (EA)
TWIB............ This Week in Baseball [*Television program*]
TWIC............ Theater Watch Intelligence Condition (NATG)
TWID............ Two-Way/Immediate Dial [*Telecommunications*] (TEL)
TWIDS............ Threat Warning Information Display System (MCD)

TWIF........ Tug-of-War International Federation [*Zevenhuizen, Netherlands*] (EAIO)
TWIFC........ Tammy Wynette International Fan Club (EA)
TWIFT........ Toronto Women in Film and Theatre [*Canada*] (WWLA)
TWIG........ Tandem Wing in Sound Effect (MCD)
TWIMC........ To Whom It May Concern
TWIN........ Test Ware Instrument (PDAA)
TWIN........ Third World Information Network [*British*] (EAIO)
TWIN........ Together Women in Neighborhoods
TWIN........ Twin City Bancorp [*NASDAQ symbol*] (TTSB)
TWIN........ Twin City Bancorp, Inc. [*NASDAQ symbol*] (SAG)
TWI-N........ Twi-Night [*or Twilight-Night*] [*Doubleheader in baseball*]
TwinCtyB........ Twin City Bancorp, Inc. [*Associated Press*] (SAG)
TwinDs........ Twin Disc, Inc. [*Associated Press*] (SAG)
TWIP........ Twentieth of a Point [*Computer science*] (CDE)
TWIRP........ [*The*] Woman Is Requested to Pay [*Some claim that this acronym, originally a designation for certain school dances, evolved into a slang term denoting any male unable to afford a date*]
TWIS........ Technically Workable Ideal System [*Industrial engineering*]
TWIS........ Technical Writing Improvement Society
TWITAS........ Third World Institute of Theatre Arts Studies
TWITW........ [*The*] Wind in the Willows [*Book by Kenneth Grahame*]
TWIU........ Tobacco Workers International Union [*Later, BCTWIU*] (EA)
TWIX........ Teletypewriter Message
TWIZN........ Twilight Zone [*Aviation*]
TWJ........ Tack Welded Joint
TWK........ Hsinying [*Republic of China*] [*Seismograph station code, US Geological Survey*] (SEIS)
TWK........ Tool Welders Kit
TWK........ Too Well Known
TWK........ Traveling-Wave Klystron
TWK........ Typewriter Keyboard
TWL........ Leased Teletypewriter Service
TWL........ Telex World Letter [*MCI International, Inc.*] [*Rye Brook, NY*] (TSSD)
TWL........ Top Water Level
TWL........ Total Weight Loss (MCD)
TWL........ Tradewinds Aviation Ltd. [*Canada ICAO designator*] (FAAC)
TWL........ Transepidermal Water Loss [*Physiology*] (MAE)
TWL........ Transition to Working Life [*Project*] (AIE)
TWL........ Traveling-Wave LASER
TWL........ Tuberculosis Welfare League [*Defunct*] (EA)
TWL........ Twin Lakes [*California*] [*Seismograph station code, US Geological Survey*] (SEIS)
TWL........ Twin Wheel Loading [*Aviation*]
TWLA........ Turkish Women's League of America (EA)
TWLC........ Two Way Logic Circuit (PDAA)
TwldH........ Transworld Home HealthCare, Inc. [*Associated Press*] (SAG)
TwldHH........ Transworld Home HealthCare, Inc. [*Associated Press*] (SAG)
TWLT........ Twilight
TWM........ Kaohsiung [*Republic of China*] [*Seismograph station code, US Geological Survey Closed*] (SEIS)
TWM........ Tape Wrapping Machine
TWM........ Traveling-Wave Magnetron (IAA)
TWM........ Traveling-Wave MASER
TWM........ Two-Way Mirror
TWM1........ Kaohsiung [*Republic of China*] [*Seismograph station code, US Geological Survey*] (SEIS)
TW-MAE-W... Third World Movement Against the Exploitation of Women [*Quezon City, Philippines*] (EAIO)
TWMAS........ Tobacco Workers' Mutual Assistance Society [*A union*] [*British*]
TWMBK........ Traveling-Wave Multiple-Beam Klystron (MSA)
TWMC........ Transport, Wages, Maintenance, and Care
TWMC........ Trans World Entertainment [*NASDAQ symbol*] (TTSB)
TWMC........ Trans World Entertainment Corp. [*NASDAQ symbol*] (NQ)
TWMD........ Toxics and Waste Management Division [*Environmental Protection Agency*] (GFGA)
TWMIP........ Third World Moving Images Project (EA)
TWMP........ Track Width Mine Plow (MCD)
TWMR........ Tungsten Water Moderated Reactor (KSC)
TWN........ Taiwan [*ANSI three-letter standard code*] (CNC)
TWN........ Taiwan Fund [*NYSE symbol*] (TTSB)
TWN........ Taiwan Fund, Inc. [*NYSE symbol*] (SPSG)
TWN........ Third World Network (EERA)
TWN........ Town (MCD)
TWN........ Town
TWN........ Twin Eagles Resources, Inc. [*Vancouver Stock Exchange symbol*]
TWN........ Twin Peaks [*California*] [*Seismograph station code, US Geological Survey*] (SEIS)
TWNA........ Truck Writers of North America [*An association*] (EA)
Tw Nat P..... Twiss. Law of Nations in Time of Peace [*2nd ed.*] [*1884*] [*A publication*] (DLA)
Tw Nat W.... Twiss. Law of Nations in Time of War [*2nd ed.*] [*1875*] [*A publication*] (DLA)
TwnCtry........ Town & Country Trust [*Associated Press*] (SAG)
TWNE........ Towne
TWNG........ Towing
TWNP........ Tape-Wound Nylon Phenolic (SAA)
TWNS........ Trans World News Service (NTCM)
TWNT........ Theologisches Woerterbuch zum Neuen Testament [*A publication*] (BJA)
TWO........ Meishan [*Republic of China*] [*Seismograph station code, US Geological Survey*] (SEIS)
TWO........ Neoucom Processing Center, Rootstown, OH [*OCLC symbol*] (OCLC)
TWO........ Ontario, CA [*Location identifier FAA*] (FAAL)
TWO........ This Week Only (ADA)
TWO........ Tooling Work Order (MCD)
TWO........ Travelling-Wave Oscillator
TWO........ Twente Airlines [*Netherlands*] [*FAA designator*] (FAAC)
TWOATAF.... Second Allied Tactical Air Force Central Europe
TWOC........ Taken Without Owner's Consent
TWODEPEP... Two Dimensional Elliptic, Parabolic and Eigenvalue Problems (MHDI)
TWODS........ [*The*] World of Dark Shadows (EA)
Two Gent..... Two Gentlemen of Verona [*Shakesperean work*] (BARN)
TWOM........ The Well Oiled Machine (NITA)
TWOM........ Traveling-Wave Optical MASER
TWOS........ Total Warrant Officer System [*Army*]
TWOS........ Tropical Wind Observing Ships [*Marine science*] (MSC)
TW/OT........ Travel without Troops
TWOV........ Transit-without-Visa
TWP........ Tactical Work Program
TWP........ Task Work Package (KSC)
TWP........ Technological War Plan
TWP........ Territory Wildlife Park [*Northern Territory, Australia*]
TWP........ Torwood [*Australia Airport symbol Obsolete*] (OAG)
TWP........ Total Wave Pressure
TWP........ Township
TWP........ Township
Twp........ Township (DD)
TWP........ Traveling-Wave Phototube
TWP........ Trawler Petroleum Explorations Ltd. [*Vancouver Stock Exchange symbol*]
TWP........ Trial Work Period [*Social Security Administration*] (OICC)
TWP........ Tropical Western Pacific (USDC)
TWP........ Tropical Western Pacific [*Marine science*] (OSRA)
TWP........ True Whig Party [*Liberia*] (AF)
TWP........ Twisted Wire Pair
TWPA........ Traveling-Wave Parametric Amplifier
TWPB........ Total Work Package Budget (MCD)
TWPL........ Teletypewriter, Private Line
TWPL........ Total Weighted Pollutant Load (ERG)
TWPLA........ Turkish Workers' and Peasants' Liberation Army
TWPP........ Truncated Whitworth, British Standard Pipe (Parallel) [*Thread*]
TWPS........ Traveling-Wave Phase Sifter
TWQ........ Tungshih [*Republic of China*] [*Seismograph station code, US Geological Survey*] (SEIS)
TWQM........ Tailwater Quality Numerical Model [*Army Corps of Engineers*]
TWR........ Tactical Weather RADAR
TWR........ Tape Write Register
TWR........ Test Work Release (MCD)
TWR........ Theater War Reserves [*Army*]
TWR........ Third World Resources [*A publication*] (BRI)
TWR........ Threat Warning RADAR
TWR........ Threat Warning Receiver
TWR........ Tom Walkinshaw Racing [*Auto racing*]
TWR........ Tool Wear Rate
TWR........ Torpedo Weapons Receiver
TWR........ Total Wrist Replacement [*Medicine*]
TWR........ Tower (AAG)
twr........ Tower (VRA)
TWR........ Towet
TWR........ TransWorld Radio (EA)
TWR........ Trans World Radio Pacific [*Guam*] (FEA)
TWR........ Traveling-Wave Resonator
TWR........ Twin Richfield Oils Ltd. [*Toronto Stock Exchange symbol*]
TWRA........ Transpacific Westbound Rate Agreement (DS)
TwrAuto........ Tower Automotive, Inc. [*Associated Press*] (SAG)
TWRI........ Texas Water Resources Institute [*Texas A & M University*] [*Department of the Interior Research center*] (RCD)
TWRL........ Taylor Woodrow Research Laboratories [*Research center British*] (IRUK)
TWRL........ Two-Way Radio Link (LAIN)
TWRS........ Towers
TWS........ Southwestern at Memphis, Memphis, TN [*OCLC symbol*] (OCLC)
TWS........ Tactical Warning System (AAG)
TWS........ Tactical Weapon System (NG)
TWS........ Tactical Weather Station [*Military*]
TWS........ Tail Warning Set [*or System*] [*Aerospace*] (MCD)
TWS........ Tartar Weapons System
TWS........ Tasmanian Wilderness Society (EERA)
TWS........ Teletypewriter Exchange Service
TWS........ Terrier Weapons System
TWS........ Test of Written Spelling [*Education*]
TWS........ Texas World Speedway [*Auto racing*]
TWS........ Thermal Weapon Sight [*Army*] (INF)
TWS........ Thermal Wire Stripper
TWS........ Thomas Wolfe Society (EA)
TWS........ Timed Wire Service (WDAA)
TWS........ Track-while-Scan [*Communications*]
TWS........ Translator Writing System [*Computer science*] (IAA)
TWS........ Trans West African Airlines Ltd. [*Gambia*] [*ICAO designator*] (FAAC)
TWS........ Truncated Whitworth Special [*Thread*] (MSA)
TWS........ Tsunami Warning System [*National Oceanic and Atmospheric Administration*]
TWS........ Twin-Wheel Stripper
TWS........ Two-Way Simultaneous (IAA)
TWS........ [*The*] Wilderness Society (EERA)
TWS........ [*The*] Wildlife Society (EA)
TWSB........ Twin Sideband
TWSb/6........ Antimony Sodium Dimercaptosuccinate [*Stibocaptate*] (BABM)

TWSBA .... Tasmanian Wool Selling Brokers' Association [*Australia*]
TWSC .... Twin Screw
TWSEAS ...... Tactical Warfare Simulation, Evaluation, and Analysis System [*Marine Corps*] (MCD)
TWSO .... Tactical Weapon Systems Operation
TWSP .... Tactical Warfare Simulation Program
TWSR .... Track-while-Scan RADAR
TWSRO .... Track-while-Scan on Receive Only (NG)
TWSRS .... Track-while-Scan RADAR Simulator
TWSST .... Time without Symptoms of Disease and Systemic Treatment [*Medicine*] (CDI)
TWST .... TeleWest Communications Ltd. [*NASDAQ symbol*] (SAG)
TWST .... Torus Water Storage Tank (IEEE)
TWSTY .... TeleWest PLC ADS [*NASDAQ symbol*] (TTSB)
TWT .... Sturgis, KY [*Location identifier FAA*] (FAAL)
TWT .... Tawi-Tawi [*Philippines*] [*Airport symbol*] (OAG)
TWT .... Time Wire Transmission (IAA)
TWT .... Torpedo Water Tube
TWT .... Toy World Test [*Psychology*]
TWT .... Transonic Wind Tunnel [*NASA*] (AAG)
TWT .... Traveling-Wave Tube [*Radio*]
TWT .... Travel with Troops
TWT .... Tritiated Waste Treatment [*Subsystem*] (MCD)
TWT .... Tri-West Resources Ltd. [*Vancouver Stock Exchange symbol*]
TWT .... Two-Way Time [*Seismology*]
TWT .... Two-Way-Traffic-in-Ideas Conference [*of Labor Party*] [*British*]
TWT .... West Texas State University, Canyon, TX [*OCLC symbol*] (OCLC)
TWT .... [*The*] Write Thing [*An association*] (EA)
TWTA .... Traveling-Wave Tube Amplifier [*Radio*]
TWTC .... Taipei World Trade Center
TWTDS .... Treatment Works Treating Domestic Sewage [*Environmental Protection Agency*]
TWTI .... Total World Telecommunications, Inc. [*NASDAQ symbol*] (SAG)
TWTT .... Two-Way Travel Time [*Seismology*]
TWTWTW ..... That Was The Week That Was [*Also, TW3*] [*Television program of English origin*]
TWU .... Tactical Weapons Unit [*British military*] (DMA)
TWU .... Tata Workers' Union [*India*]
TWU .... Tawau [*Malaysia*] [*Airport symbol*] (OAG)
TWU .... Technical Writing Unit [*NASA*]
TWU .... Telecommunications Workers Union [*Canada*]
TWU .... Texas Woman's University
TWU .... Theatre Writers' Union [*British*] (DBA)
TWU .... Tobacco Workers' Union [*British*] (DCTA)
TWU .... Trace Watch Unit (IAA)
TWU .... Transport Workers' Union [*British*]
TWU .... Transport Workers Union of America (EA)
TWU .... University of the South, Sewanee, TN [*OCLC symbol*] (OCLC)
TWUA .... Textile Workers Union of America [*Later, ACTWU*]
TWUA .... Transport Workers' Union of Australia
TWUC .... The Writers Union of Canada [*Canada*] (WWLA)
TWUD .... Tactical Weapons Unit Diagnostics
TWV .... Tactical Wheeled Vehicle (DOMA)
TWV .... Three-Way Valve [*Hydraulics*]
TWV .... Two-Wire Vertical [*Grape culture*]
TWVMP .... Tactical Wheeled Vehicle Modernization Program [*Army*]
TWVRP .... Tactical Wheeled Vehicles Remanufacture Program [*Army*] (RDA)
TWW .... Independent Television for Wales and the West of England
TWW .... Trans Air Welwitchia [*Angola*] [*FAA designator*] (FAAC)
TWWD .... Tapwater Wet Dressing [*Surgery*] (DAVI)
TWWHA .... Tasmanian Wilderness World Heritage Area
TWWP .... Third World Women's Project [*Defunct*] (EA)
TWWS .... Two-Way/Wink Start [*Telecommunications*] (TEL)
TWWT .... Tilting Wind-Water Tunnel [*Environmental technology*]
TWX .... Telegraphic Message (MSA)
TWX .... Teletypewriter Exchange Service [*Western Union*] [*Term also used generically for teletypewriter message*]
TWX .... Teletypewriter Wire Transmission
TWX .... Time Warner Capital I [*NYSE symbol*] (SAG)
TWX .... Time Warner, Inc. [*NYSE symbol*] (SPSG)
TWX .... Time Wire Transmission
TWXIL .... TWX Interlibrary Loan Network [*Library network*]
TWXPrT .... Time War Cp 1 8.78% Pfd Tr Sec [*NYSE symbol*] (TTSB)
TWY .... Taxiway [*Aviation*] (AAG)
TWY .... Twenty (ADA)
TWYL .... Taxiway-Link [*Aviation*]
TWZ .... Neifu [*Republic of China*] [*Seismograph station code, US Geological Survey*] (SEIS)
TWZO .... Trade Wind Zone Oceanography
TX .... Nondramatic Literary Works [*US Copyright Office class*]
TX .... Tax
TX .... Taxonomic Descriptor (NITA)
TX .... Telephone Exchange (NITA)
TX .... TELEX
TX .... Terminal Executive [*Computer science*] (MHDB)
TX .... Terminating Toll Operator [*Telecommunications*] (TEL)
TX .... Tested Extra (MCD)
TX .... Texaco, Inc. [*NYSE symbol*] (SPSG)
TX .... Texas [*Postal code*]
TX .... Texas Reports [*A publication*] (DLA)
Tx .... Texas State Library and Historical Commission, Austin, TX [*Library symbol Library of Congress*] (LCLS)
TX .... Text Editor
Tx .... Therapy [*Medicine*]
TX .... Thromboxane [*Also, T, TA, Tx*] [*Biochemistry*]
Tx .... Thyroidectomy [*Medicine*]
TX .... Time to Equipment Reset [*Computer science*] (MDG)
TX .... Toilet Exhaust (OA)
TX .... Torque Transmitter
TX .... Traction [*Medicine*]
TX .... Transformer
Tx .... Transfusion [*Medicine*] (CPH)
TX .... Translation Hand Controller X-Axis Direction (MCD)
TX .... Transmit (NITA)
TX .... Transmitter
TX .... Transparency [*Photography*] (WDMC)
Tx .... Transplant [*or Transplantation*] [*Medicine*]
TX .... Transportes Aereos Nacionales [*ICAO designator*] (AD)
TX .... Treatment
TX .... Treble Cash Ruling [*Business term*]
TXA .... Task Extension Area [*Computer science*] (IAA)
TXA .... Terminal Exchange Area [*Computer science*] (MHDB)
TXA .... Texair Charter, Inc. [*ICAO designator*] (FAAC)
TXA .... Texas A & M University, College Station, TX [*OCLC symbol*] (OCLC)
TXA .... Texeira [*Portugal*] [*Airport symbol*] (AD)
TXA .... Thromboxane A [*Also, TA, TxA*] [*Biochemistry*]
TxAb .... Abilene Public Library, Abilene, TX [*Library symbol Library of Congress*] (LCLS)
TxAbC .... Abilene Christian University, Abilene, TX [*Library symbol Library of Congress*] (LCLS)
TxAbH .... Hardin-Simmons University, Abilene, TX [*Library symbol Library of Congress*] (LCLS)
TxAbM .... McMurry College, Abilene, TX [*Library symbol Library of Congress*] (LCLS)
TxAdTC .... Trinity Christian Academy, Addison, TX [*Library symbol*] [*Library of Congress*] (LCLS)
TxAl .... Stella Hill Memorial Library, Alto, TX [*Library symbol Library of Congress*] (LCLS)
TxAlpS .... Sul Ross State University, Alpine, TX [*Library symbol Library of Congress*] (LCLS)
TxAlvC .... Alvin Junior College, Alvin, TX [*Library symbol Library of Congress*] (LCLS)
TxAm .... Amarillo Public Library, Amarillo, TX [*Library symbol Library of Congress*] (LCLS)
TxAmC .... Amarillo College, Amarillo, TX [*Library symbol Library of Congress*] (LCLS)
TxAmM .... Mason & Hanger-Silas Mason Co., Inc., Pantex Plant Library, Amarillo, TX [*Library symbol Library of Congress*] (LCLS)
TxAmSP ...... Southwestern Public Service Co., Amarillo, TX [*Library symbol Library of Congress*] (LCLS)
TxAmV .... United States Veterans Administration Hospital, Amarillo, TX [*Library symbol Library of Congress*] (LCLS)
TxAng .... Brazoria County Library, Angleton, TX [*Library symbol Library of Congress*] (LCLS)
TxArB .... Arlington Baptist Junior College, Arlington, TX [*Library symbol Library of Congress*] (LCLS)
TxAr-G .... Arlington Public Library, Genealogy Department, Arlington, TX [*Library symbol Library of Congress*] (LCLS)
TxArJ .... Jet Research Center, Inc., Arlington, TX [*Library symbol Library of Congress*] (LCLS)
TxArU .... University of Texas at Arlington, Arlington, TX [*Library symbol Library of Congress*] (LCLS)
TxAtH .... Henderson County Junior College, Athens, TX [*Library symbol Library of Congress*] (LCLS)
TxAu .... Austin Public Library, Austin, TX [*Library symbol Library of Congress*] (LCLS)
TxAuA .... Charles E. Stevens American Atheist Library and Archives, Inc., Austin, TX [*Library symbol Library of Congress*] (LCLS)
TxAu-AT ...... Austin Public Library, Austin-Travis County Collection, Austin, TX [*Library symbol Library of Congress*] (LCLS)
TxAuC .... Concordia Lutheran College, Austin, TX [*Library symbol Library of Congress*] (LCLS)
TxAuCC .... Austin Community College, Austin, TX [*Library symbol Library of Congress*] (LCLS)
TxAuCH .... Church Historical Society, Austin, TX [*Library symbol Library of Congress*] (LCLS)
TxAuDR .... Daughters of the Republic of Texas Museum, Austin, TX [*Library symbol Library of Congress*] (LCLS)
TxAuE .... Episcopal Theological Seminary of the Southwest, Austin, TX [*Library symbol Library of Congress*] (LCLS)
TxAuEd .... Texas Education Agency, Austin, TX [*Library symbol Library of Congress*] (LCLS)
TxAuGS .... Church of Jesus Christ of Latter-Day Saints, Genealogical Society Library, Austin Branch, Austin, TX [*Library symbol Library of Congress*] (LCLS)
TxAuHi .... Texas State Department of Highways and Public Transportation, Materials and Tests Research Library, Austin, TX [*Library symbol Library of Congress*] (LCLS)
TxAuHT .... Huston-Tillotson College, Austin, TX [*Library symbol Library of Congress*] (LCLS)
TxAuL .... Legislative Library Board, Legislative Reference Library, Austin, TX [*Library symbol Library of Congress*] (LCLS)
TxAuLBJ ...... Lyndon B. Johnson School of Public Affairs, Lyndon Baines Johnson Library, Austin, TX [*Library symbol Library of Congress*] (LCLS)
TxAuM .... Texas Medical Association, Austin, TX [*Library symbol Library of Congress*] (LCLS)
TxAuMH .... Texas Department of Mental Health and Mental Retardation, Austin, TX [*Library symbol Library of Congress*] (LCLS)
TxAuP .... Austin Presbyterian Theological Seminary, Austin, TX [*Library symbol Library of Congress*] (LCLS)

TxAuPW....... Texas Department of Parks and Wildlife, Austin, TX [*Library symbol Library of Congress*] (LCLS)
TxAuR......... Radian Corp., Austin, TX [*Library symbol Library of Congress*] (LCLS)
TxAuSE........ Saint Edward's University, Austin, TX [*Library symbol Library of Congress*] (LCLS)
TxAuSHos.... Austin State Hospital, Austin, TX [*Library symbol Library of Congress*] (LCLS)
TxAuT......... Tracor, Inc., Technical Library, Austin, TX [*Library symbol Library of Congress*] (LCLS)
TxAuTI......... Texas Instruments, Inc., Austin Site Library, Austin, TX [*Library symbol*] [*Library of Congress*] (LCLS)
TxAuTL........ Travis County Law Library, Austin, TX [*Library symbol*] [*Library of Congress*] (LCLS)
TxAuW......... Texas Water Development Board, Austin, TX [*Library symbol Library of Congress*] (LCLS)
TXB............. Abilene Public Library, Abilene, TX [*OCLC symbol*] (OCLC)
TXB............. Bell Helicopter, Textron Canada [*FAA designator*] (FAAC)
TXB............. Texas Biotechnology [*AMEX symbol*] (TTSB)
TXB............. Texas Biotechnology Corp. [*AMEX symbol*] (SAG)
TXB............. Thromboxane B [*Also, TB, TxB*] [*Biochemistry*]
TxBea.......... Tyrrell Public Library, Beaumont, TX [*Library symbol Library of Congress*] (LCLS)
TxBeaAM..... Beaumont Art Museum, Beaumont, TX [*Library symbol Library of Congress*] (LCLS)
TxBeaE........ Beaumont Enterprise & Journal, Beaumont, TX [*Library symbol Library of Congress*] (LCLS)
TxBeaG........ Gulf States Utilities Co., Beaumont, TX [*Library symbol Library of Congress*] (LCLS)
TxBeaL......... Lamar University, Beaumont, TX [*Library symbol Library of Congress*] (LCLS)
TxBeaMC..... Mobil Chemical Co., Research and Development Laboratory, Beaumont, TX [*Library symbol Library of Congress*] (LCLS)
TxBeaSE...... Saint Elizabeth Hospital, Health Science Library, Beaumont, TX [*Library symbol Library of Congress*] (LCLS)
TxBee.......... Bee County Public Library, Beeville, TX [*Library symbol Library of Congress*] (LCLS)
TxBeeC........ Bee County College, Beeville, TX [*Library symbol Library of Congress*] (LCLS)
TxBelM......... Mary Hardin-Baylor College, Belton, TX [*Library symbol Library of Congress*] (LCLS)
TxBHi.......... Brownsville Historical Association, Brownsville, TX [*Library symbol Library of Congress*] (LCLS)
TxBl............. Bellaire City Library, Bellaire, TX [*Library symbol Library of Congress*] (LCLS)
TXBL........... Taxable
TxBlT........... Texaco, Inc., Bellaire, TX [*Library symbol Library of Congress*] (LCLS)
TxBor.......... Hutchinson County Library, Borger, TX [*Library symbol Library of Congress*] (LCLS)
TxBorF......... Frank Phillips College, Borger, TX [*Library symbol Library of Congress*] (LCLS)
Tx-BPH........ Texas Regional Library, Division for the Blind and Physically Handicapped, Austin, TX [*Library symbol Library of Congress*] (LCLS)
TxBrd........... Brownwood Public Library, Brownwood, TX [*Library symbol Library of Congress*] (LCLS)
TxBrdH......... Howard Payne College, Brownwood, TX [*Library symbol Library of Congress*] (LCLS)
TxBreB......... Blinn College, Brenham, TX [*Library symbol Library of Congress*] (LCLS)
TxBry........... Bryan Public Library, Bryan, TX [*Library symbol Library of Congress*] (LCLS)
TxBryA......... Allen Academy, Bryan, TX [*Library symbol Library of Congress*] (LCLS)
TxBs............. Howard County Library, Big Spring, TX [*Library symbol Library of Congress*] (LCLS)
TxBS............ Texas Southmost College, Brownsville, TX [*Library symbol Library of Congress*] (LCLS)
TxBsaA......... Ambassador College, Big Sandy, TX [*Library symbol Library of Congress*] (LCLS)
TxBsC.......... Howard County Library, Big Spring, TX [*Library symbol*] [*Library of Congress*] (LCLS)
TxBsH.......... Howard County Junior College, Big Spring, TX [*Library symbol Library of Congress*] (LCLS)
TxBsV.......... United States Veterans Administration Hospital, Big Spring, TX [*Library symbol Library of Congress*] (LCLS)
TxBUC.......... Union Carbide Corp., Chemicals and Plastics Library, Brownsville, TX [*Library symbol Library of Congress*] (LCLS)
TXB.WS....... Texas Biotechnology Wrrt [*AMEX symbol*] (TTSB)
TxBy............. Sterling Municipal Library, Baytown, TX [*Library symbol Library of Congress*] (LCLS)
TxByH.......... Humble Oil & Refining Co., Technical Library, Baytown, TX [*Library symbol Library of Congress*] (LCLS)
TxByH-E....... Humble Oil & Refining Co., Engineering Division Library, Baytown, TX [*Library symbol Library of Congress*] (LCLS)
TxByL........... Lee College, Baytown, TX [*Library symbol Library of Congress*] (LCLS)
TXC.............. Abilene Christian University, Abilene, TX [*OCLC symbol*] (OCLC)
TXC.............. Texaco Capital LLC [*NYSE symbol*] (SPSG)
TXC.............. Thurman, CO [*Location identifier FAA*] (FAAL)
TXC.............. Transaviaexport [*Belarus*] [*ICAO designator*] (FAAC)
TxCap.......... Texaco Capital [*Associated Press*] (SAG)
TxCarP......... Panola College, Carthage, TX [*Library symbol Library of Congress*] (LCLS)
TxCaW......... West Texas State University, Canyon, TX [*Library symbol Library of Congress*] (LCLS)
TxCc............. La Retama Public Library, Corpus Cristi, TX [*Library symbol Library of Congress*] (LCLS)
TXCC............ TranSwitch Corp. [*NASDAQ symbol*] (SAG)
TxCcD.......... Del Mar College, Corpus Christi, TX [*Library symbol Library of Congress*] (LCLS)
TxCcG.......... United States Geological Survey, Office of Marine Geology, Corpus Cristi, TX [*Library symbol*] [*Library of Congress*] (LCLS)
TxCcGS........ Church of Jesus Christ of Latter-Day Saints, Genealogical Society Library, Corpus Christi Branch, Corpus Christi, TX [*Library symbol Library of Congress*] (LCLS)
TxCcMST..... Art Museum of South Texas, Corpus Christi, TX [*Library symbol Library of Congress*] (LCLS)
TxCcNHi....... Nueces County Historical Society, La Retama Public Library, Corpus Christi, TX [*Library symbol Library of Congress*] (LCLS)
TxCcT........... Texas A & I University at Corpus Christi, Corpus Christi, TX [*Library symbol Library of Congress*] (LCLS)
TxCcU.......... University of Corpus Christi, Corpus Christi, TX [*Library symbol Library of Congress Obsolete*] (LCLS)
TX-CEL......... Throughput X-Cellerator [*Celeritas Technologies*] [*Cellular data transmission*] (PCM)
TxCeN.......... Northwood Institute of Texas, Cedar Hill, TX [*Library symbol Library of Congress*] (LCLS)
TX Ci............ Texas Civil Appeals Reports [*A publication*] (DLA)
TxCiC........... Cisco Junior College, Cisco, TX [*Library symbol Library of Congress*] (LCLS)
TxClaC......... Clarendon College, Clarendon, TX [*Library symbol Library of Congress*] (LCLS)
TxClcU......... University of Houston at Clear Lake City, Houston, TX [*Library symbol Library of Congress*] (LCLS)
TxCle........... Cleburne Public Library, Cleburne, TX [*Library symbol Library of Congress*] (LCLS)
TxCli............ Nellie Pederson Civic Library, Clifton, TX [*Library symbol Library of Congress*] (LCLS)
TxClv........... Cleveland Public [*Charles O. Austin Memorial*] Library, Cleveland, TX [*Library symbol Library of Congress*] (LCLS)
TxClwC......... Celanese Corp., Clarkwood, TX [*Library symbol Library of Congress*] (LCLS)
TxCM............ Texas A & M University, College Station, TX [*Library symbol Library of Congress*] (LCLS)
TxCM-M....... Texas A & M University, Medical Sciences Library, College Station, TX [*Library symbol Library of Congress*] (LCLS)
TXCO........... [*The*] Exploration Co. [*NASDAQ symbol*] (NQ)
TxComf......... Comfort Public Library, Comfort, TX [*Library symbol Library of Congress*] (LCLS)
TxComS....... East Texas State University, Commerce, TX [*Library symbol Library of Congress*] (LCLS)
TxComS-M... East Texas State University, Museum, Commerce, TX [*Library symbol Library of Congress*] (LCLS)
TxCoN.......... Navarro Junior College, Corsicana, TX [*Library symbol Library of Congress*] (LCLS)
TxConM........ Montgomery County Memorial Library, Conroe, TX [*Library symbol Library of Congress*] (LCLS)
TXCPrA........ Texaco Capital LLC 'MIPS' [*NYSE symbol*] (TTSB)
TXCPrB........ Texaco Cap LLC'B'Adj MIPS [*NYSE symbol*] (TTSB)
TxCr............. Crockett Public Library, Crockett, TX [*Library symbol Library of Congress*] (LCLS)
TX Cr........... Texas Criminal Appeals Reports [*A publication*] (DLA)
TxCrMA........ Mary Allen Junior College, Crockett, TX [*Library symbol Library of Congress*] (LCLS)
TxCvS.......... ARCO Chemical Co., Channelview, TX [*Library symbol Library of Congress*] (LCLS)
TxCvT........... Texas Butadine & Chemical Corp., Channelview, TX [*Library symbol Library of Congress*] (LCLS)
TXD.............. McMurry College, Abilene, TX [*OCLC symbol*] (OCLC)
TXD.............. Telephone Exchange (Digital) [*Telecommunications*] (TEL)
TXD.............. Transmit Data [*Computer science*]
TxDa............ Dallas Public Library, Dallas, TX [*Library symbol Library of Congress*] (LCLS)
TxDaABC...... AMIGOS [*Access Method for Indexed Data Generalized for Operating System*] Bibliographic Council, Dallas, TX [*Library symbol Library of Congress*] (LCLS)
TxDaAC........ Anderson, Clayton & Co., Foods Division Technical Library, Dallas, TX [*Library symbol Library of Congress*] (LCLS)
TxDaAR-G.... Atlantic Richfield Co., Geoscience Library, Dallas, TX [*Library symbol Library of Congress*] (LCLS)
TxDaAR-R.... Atlantic Richfield Co., R and D Library, Dallas, TX [*Library symbol Library of Congress*] (LCLS)
TxDaAR-T.... Atlantic Richfield Co., Technical Library, Dallas, TX [*Library symbol Library of Congress*] (LCLS)
TxDaB.......... Dallas Baptist College, Dallas, TX [*Library symbol Library of Congress*] (LCLS)
TxDaBC........ Bishop College, Dallas, TX [*Library symbol Library of Congress*] (LCLS)
TxDaBM........ Burgess-Manning Co., Dallas, TX [*Library symbol Library of Congress*] (LCLS)
TxDaBU........ Baylor University in Dallas, Dallas, TX [*Library symbol Library of Congress*] (LCLS)
TxDaCB........ Criswell Bible College, Dallas, TX [*Library symbol*] [*Library of Congress*] (LCLS)
TxDaCC........ Christian College of the Southwest, Dallas, TX [*Library symbol Library of Congress*] (LCLS)
TxDaCCD..... Callier Center for Communication Disorders, Dallas, TX [*Library symbol Library of Congress*] (LCLS)

TxDaCiA....... Court of Civil Appeals, Dallas, TX [*Library symbol Library of Congress*] (LCLS)
TxDaCL........ Core Laboratories, Inc., Dallas, TX [*Library symbol Library of Congress*] (LCLS)
TxDaCR........ Collins Radio Co., Dallas, TX [*Library symbol Library of Congress*] (LCLS)
TxDaCS........ Dallas County Community College System, Dallas, TX [*Library symbol Library of Congress*] (LCLS)
TxDaDC........ Dallas Christian College, Dallas, TX [*Library symbol Library of Congress*] (LCLS)
TxDaDF........ DeGoyler Foundation, Dallas, TX [*Library symbol Library of Congress*] (LCLS)
TxDaDL........ Dallas County Law Library, Dallas, TX [*Library symbol Library of Congress*] (LCLS)
TxDaDM........ DeGoyler and MacNaughton Library, Dallas, TX [*Library symbol Library of Congress*] (LCLS)
TxDaE.......... El Centro College, Dallas, TX [*Library symbol Library of Congress*] (LCLS)
TxDaET........ East Texas State University, Metroplex Center, Dallas, TX [*Library symbol Library of Congress*] (LCLS)
TxDaFR........ Federal Reserve Bank of Dallas, Dallas, TX [*Library symbol Library of Congress*] (LCLS)
TxDaGI......... Geological Information Library of Dallas, Dallas, TX [*Library symbol*] [*Library of Congress*] (LCLS)
TxDaGS........ Church of Jesus Christ of Latter-Day Saints, Genealogical Society Library, Dallas Branch, Dallas, TX [*Library symbol Library of Congress*] (LCLS)
TxDah.......... Dallam County Free Library, Dalhart, TX [*Library symbol*] [*Library of Congress*] (LCLS)
TxDaHi......... Dallas Historical Society, Dallas, TX [*Library symbol Library of Congress*] (LCLS)
TxDaI........... Informart Resources Center, Dallas, TX [*Library symbol*] [*Library of Congress*] (LCLS)
TxDaJS......... Johnson and Swanson, Law Library, Dallas, TX [*Library symbol Library of Congress*] (LCLS)
TxDaL........... Lone Star Gas Co., Dallas, TX [*Library symbol Library of Congress*] (LCLS)
TxDaM.......... Southern Methodist University, Dallas, TX [*Library symbol Library of Congress*] (LCLS)
TxDaM-B...... Southern Methodist University, Business Information Center, Dallas, TX [*Library symbol*] [*Library of Congress*] (LCLS)
TxDaME........ Mobil Exploration & Producing Services, Inc., Dallas, TX [*Library symbol Library of Congress*] (LCLS)
TxDaMF........ Dallas Museum of Fine Arts, Dallas, TX [*Library symbol Library of Congress*] (LCLS)
TxDaM-L...... Southern Methodist University, Law Library, Dallas, TX [*Library symbol Library of Congress*] (LCLS)
TxDaMN........ Dallas Morning News, Dallas, TX [*Library symbol*] [*Library of Congress*] (LCLS)
TxDaM-P...... Southern Methodist University, Perkins School of Theology, Dallas, TX [*Library symbol Library of Congress*] (LCLS)
TxDaM-SE.... Southern Methodist University, Science/Engineering Library, Dallas, TX [*Library symbol Library of Congress*] (LCLS)
TxDaMV........ Mountain View College, Dallas, TX [*Library symbol Library of Congress*] (LCLS)
TxDaP........... Dallas Power & Light Co., Dallas, TX [*Library symbol Library of Congress*] (LCLS)
TxDaPCC...... Parker College of Chiropractic, Dallas, TX [*Library symbol*] [*Library of Congress*] (LCLS)
TxDaPO........ Placid Oil Co. Exploration Library, Dallas, TX [*Library symbol Library of Congress*] (LCLS)
TxDaPP........ Planned Parenthood of Northeast Texas, Dallas, TX [*Library symbol Library of Congress*] (LCLS)
TxDaR........... Richland College, Dallas, TX [*Library symbol Library of Congress*] (LCLS)
TxDaRI.......... Rockwell International, Collins Radio Group, Technical Information Center, Dallas, TX [*Library symbol Library of Congress*] (LCLS)
TxDaS........... University of Texas, Health Science Center at Dallas, Dallas, TX [*Library symbol Library of Congress*] (LCLS)
TxDaSM........ Mobil Research & Development Corp., Dallas, TX [*Library symbol Library of Congress*] (LCLS)
TxDaSSC...... Super Conducting Super Collider Liability Library, Dallas, TX [*Library symbol*] [*Library of Congress*] (LCLS)
TxDaTI-A...... Texas Instruments, Inc., Apparatus Division Library, Dallas, TX [*Library symbol Library of Congress*] (LCLS)
TxDaTI-C...... Texas Instruments, Inc., Central Research and Engineering Library, Dallas, TX [*Library symbol Library of Congress*] (LCLS)
TxDaTI-F...... Texas Instruments, Inc., Forest Lane Technical Library, Dallas, TX [*Library symbol*] [*Library of Congress*] (LCLS)
TxDaTI-IS .... Texas Instruments, Inc., IS & S Library, Dallas, TX [*Library symbol Library of Congress*] (LCLS)
TxDaTI-N ..... Texas Instruments, Inc., North Building Library, Dallas, TX [*Library symbol*] [*Library of Congress*] (LCLS)
TxDaTI-R ..... Texas Instruments, Inc., Research Building Library, Dallas, TX [*Library symbol*] [*Library of Congress*] (LCLS)
TxDaTI-S...... Texas Instruments, Inc., Semiconductor Division, Dallas, TX [*Library symbol Library of Congress*] (LCLS)
TxDaTI-SS ... Texas Instruments, Inc., Science Services Division, Dallas, TX [*Library symbol Library of Congress*] (LCLS)
TxDaTS......... Dallas Theological Seminary and Graduate School, Dallas, TX [*Library symbol Library of Congress*] (LCLS)
TxDaU........... University of Dallas, Irving, TX [*Library symbol Library of Congress*] (LCLS)
TxDaUSAF ... United States Army and Air Force Exchange Service, Dallas, TX [*Library symbol Library of Congress*] (LCLS)
TxDaUSFD ... United States Food and Drug Administration, Dallas, TX [*Library symbol Library of Congress*] (LCLS)
TxDaVA......... United States Veterans Administration Hospital, Dallas, TX [*Library symbol Library of Congress*] (LCLS)
TXDE............ Toluene-Xylene-Dioxane-Ethanol [*Scintillation solvent*]
TxDeni.......... Denison Public Library, Denison, TX [*Library symbol Library of Congress*] (LCLS)
TxDeniG........ Grayson County College, Denison, TX [*Library symbol Library of Congress*] (LCLS)
TxDib............ T. L. L. Temple Memorial Library, Diboll, TX [*Library symbol Library of Congress*] (LCLS)
TxDN............ North Texas State University, Denton, TX [*Library symbol Library of Congress*] (LCLS)
TxDN-Hi........ North Texas State University, State Historical Collection, Denton, TX [*Library symbol Library of Congress*] (LCLS)
TxDpS.......... Shell Oil Co., Deer Park, TX [*Library symbol Library of Congress*] (LCLS)
TxDpSC........ Shell Chemical Co., Deer Park, TX [*Library symbol Library of Congress*] (LCLS)
TXDRMY...... Taxidermy
TXDS............ TI Diskette Operating System (NITA)
TxDunv......... Duncanville Public Library, Duncanville, TX [*Library symbol Library of Congress*] (LCLS)
TxDW............ Texas Woman's University, Denton, TX [*Library symbol Library of Congress*] (LCLS)
TXE.............. El Paso Community College, El Paso, TX [*OCLC symbol*] (OCLC)
TxE............... El Paso Public Library, El Paso, TX [*Library symbol Library of Congress*] (LCLS)
TXE.............. Telephone Exchange (Electronics) [*Telecommunications*] (IEEE)
TXE.............. Telephone Exchange (Equipment) [*Telecommunications*]
TxEC............ El Paso Community College, El Paso, TX [*Library symbol Library of Congress*] (LCLS)
TxEdP.......... Pan American University, Edinburg, TX [*Library symbol Library of Congress*] (LCLS)
TxEGS.......... Church of Jesus Christ of Latter-Day Saints, Genealogical Society Library, El Paso Branch, El Paso, TX [*Library symbol Library of Congress*] (LCLS)
TxEHD.......... Hotel-Dieu Medical-Nursing Educational Media Center, El Paso, TX [*Library symbol Library of Congress*] (LCLS)
TxENG.......... El Paso Natural Gas Co., Technical Information Center, El Paso, TX [*Library symbol Library of Congress*] (LCLS)
TxEU............ University of Texas at El Paso, El Paso, TX [*Library symbol Library of Congress*] (LCLS)
TxEWB.......... United States Army, William Beaumont General Hospital, Medical and Technical Library, El Paso, TX [*Library symbol Library of Congress*] (LCLS)
TXF.............. Corpus Christi State University, Corpus Christi, TX [*OCLC symbol*] (OCLC)
TxF............... Fort Worth Public Library, Fort Worth, TX [*Library symbol Library of Congress*] (LCLS)
TXF.............. Tax Exchange Format [*Computer science*] (PCM)
TXF.............. Texfi Indus [*NYSE symbol*] (TTSB)
TXF.............. Texfi Industries, Inc. [*NYSE symbol*] (SPSG)
TxFACM........ Amon Carter Museum of Western Art, Fort Worth, TX [*Library symbol Library of Congress*] (LCLS)
TxFAI........... Alcon Laboratories, Inc., Fort Worth, TX [*Library symbol Library of Congress*] (LCLS)
TxFbAD......... United States Army, Air Defense School, Fort Bliss, TX [*Library symbol Library of Congress*] (LCLS)
TxFBH.......... Bell Helicopter Co., Fort Worth, TX [*Library symbol Library of Congress*] (LCLS)
TxFCB........... Carter & Burgess, Inc., Fort Worth, TX [*Library symbol Library of Congress*] (LCLS)
TxFCC........... Fort Worth Christian College, Fort Worth, TX [*Library symbol Library of Congress*] (LCLS)
TxFCO........... Texas College of Osteopathic Medicine, Fort Worth, TX [*Library symbol Library of Congress*] (LCLS)
TxFF............. Fort Worth Art Museum, Fort Worth, TX [*Library symbol Library of Congress*] (LCLS)
TxFFAA......... United States Federal Aviation Administration, Fort Worth, TX [*Library symbol Library of Congress*] (LCLS)
TxFG............. General Dynamics/Convair Aerospace Division, Fort Worth, TX [*Library symbol Library of Congress*] (LCLS)
TxFGS........... Church of Jesus Christ of Latter-Day Saints, Genealogical Society Library, Fort Worth Branch, North Richland Hills, Fort Worth, TX [*Library symbol Library of Congress*] (LCLS)
TxFhH........... Darnell Army Hospital, Medical Library, Fort Hood, TX [*Library symbol Library of Congress*] (LCLS)
TxFJPS......... John Peter Smith Hospital, Fort Worth, TX [*Library symbol Library of Congress*] (LCLS)
TxFK............. Kimbell Art Museum, Fort Worth, TX [*Library symbol Library of Congress*] (LCLS)
TxFM............. Fort Worth Museum of Science and History, Fort Worth, TX [*Library symbol Library of Congress*] (LCLS)
TxFNA........... United States National Archives and Record Center, Fort Worth, TX [*Library symbol Library of Congress*] (LCLS)
TxFNIMH...... National Institute of Mental Health, Clinical Research Center Medical Library, Fort Worth, TX [*Library symbol Library of Congress*] (LCLS)
TxFrB........... Brazosport Junior College, Freeport, TX [*Library symbol Library of Congress*] (LCLS)
TxFrD........... Dow Chemical Co., Texas Division, Freeport, TX [*Library symbol Library of Congress*] (LCLS)
TxFS............. Southwestern Baptist Theological Seminary, Fort Worth, TX [*Library symbol Library of Congress*] (LCLS)

TxFshBH .... Brooke General Hospital, Medical Library, Fort Sam Houston, TX [*Library symbol Library of Congress*] (LCLS)
TxFshM .... Medical Field Service School, Fort Sam Houston, TX [*Library symbol Library of Congress*] (LCLS)
TxFSJ .... Saint Joseph Hospital, Medical and Nursing Library, Fort Worth, TX [*Library symbol Library of Congress*] (LCLS)
TxFT .... Tarrant County Junior College, Fort Worth, TX [*Library symbol Library of Congress*] (LCLS)
TxFTC .... Texas Christian University, Fort Worth, TX [*Library symbol Library of Congress*] (LCLS)
TxFTE .... Texas Electric Service Co., Fort Worth, TX [*Library symbol Library of Congress*] (LCLS)
TxFTM .... Terrell's Laboratories Medical Library, Fort Worth, TX [*Library symbol Library of Congress*] (LCLS)
TxFT-NE .... Tarrant County Junior College, Northeast Campus, Hurst, TX [*Library symbol Library of Congress*] (LCLS)
TxFT-S .... Tarrant County Junior College, South Campus, Fort Worth, TX [*Library symbol Library of Congress*] (LCLS)
TxFTW .... Texas Wesleyan College, Fort Worth, TX [*Library symbol Library of Congress*] (LCLS)
TXG .... Austin Public Library, Austin, TX [*OCLC symbol*] (OCLC)
TXG .... Taichung [*Formosa*] [*Airport symbol*] (AD)
TxGA .... United States Army, Army Engineering District, Office of Administrative Services, Galveston, TX [*Library symbol Library of Congress*] (LCLS)
TxGaiC .... Cooke County Junior College, Gainsville, TX [*Library symbol Library of Congress*] (LCLS)
TxGar .... Nicholson Memorial Library, Garland, TX [*Library symbol Library of Congress*] (LCLS)
TxGarA .... Amber University, Garland, TX [*Library symbol*] [*Library of Congress*] (LCLS)
TxGarD .... Dresser Industries, Inc., Garland, TX [*Library symbol Library of Congress*] (LCLS)
TxGarV .... Varo, Inc., Texas Division, Garland, TX [*Library symbol Library of Congress*] (LCLS)
TxGat .... Gatesville Public Library, Gatesville, TX [*Library symbol Library of Congress*] (LCLS)
TxGC .... Galveston Community College, Galveston, TX [*Library symbol Library of Congress*] (LCLS)
TxGeoS .... Southwestern University, Georgetown, TX [*Library symbol Library of Congress*] (LCLS)
TxGilGS .... Church of Jesus Christ of Latter-Day Saints, Genealogical Society Library, Longview Branch, Gilmer, TX [*Library symbol Library of Congress*] (LCLS)
TxGML .... Texas A & M University, Moody College of Marine Sciences and Maritime Resources,Galveston, TX [*Library symbol Library of Congress*] (LCLS)
TxGoS .... Spanish Texas Microfilm Center, Goliad, TX [*Library symbol Library of Congress*] (LCLS)
TxGR .... Rosenberg Library, Galveston, TX [*Library symbol Library of Congress*] (LCLS)
TxGrp .... Grand Prairie Memorial Library, Grand Prairie, TX [*Library symbol Library of Congress*] (LCLS)
TxGUSFW .... United States National Marine Fisheries Service, Biological Laboratory, Galveston, TX [*Library symbol Library of Congress*] (LCLS)
TxH .... Houston Public Library, Houston, TX [*Library symbol Library of Congress*] (LCLS)
TXH .... Transfer on Index High
TXH .... University of Houston, Houston, TX [*OCLC symbol*] (OCLC)
TxHAE .... Atkinson Elementary School, Houston, TX [*Library symbol*] [*Library of Congress*] (LCLS)
TxHaJ .... Jarvis Christian College, Hawkins, TX [*Library symbol Library of Congress*] (LCLS)
TxHAM .... Houston Academy of Medicine for Texas Medical Center, Houston, TX [*Library symbol Library of Congress*] (LCLS)
TxHAS .... Aramco Services Co., Corporate Information Center, Houston, TX [*Library symbol*] [*Library of Congress*] (LCLS)
TxHAWD ...... Arnold, White & Durkee, Houston, TX [*Library symbol Library of Congress*] (LCLS)
TxHBa .... National Lead Industries, Inc., Baroid Division, Houston, TX [*Library symbol Library of Congress*] (LCLS)
TxHBB .... Baker, Botts, Shepherd & Coates, Houston, TX [*Library symbol Library of Congress*] (LCLS)
TxHBC .... Houston Baptist University, Houston, TX [*Library symbol Library of Congress*] (LCLS)
TxHBE .... Burnett Elementary School, Houston, TX [*Library symbol*] [*Library of Congress*] (LCLS)
TxHBec .... Bechtel Group, Inc., Technical Library, Houston, TX [*Library symbol Library of Congress*] (LCLS)
TxHBhI .... Beverly Hills Intermediate School, Houston, TX [*Library symbol*] [*Library of Congress*] (LCLS)
TxHBJ .... Bernard Johnson, Inc., Houston, TX [*Library symbol*] [*Library of Congress*] (LCLS)
TxHBR .... Brown & Root, Inc., Technical Library, Houston, TX [*Library symbol Library of Congress*] (LCLS)
TxHC .... Houston Community College System, Houston, TX [*Library symbol Library of Congress*] (LCLS)
TxHCC .... Continental Carbon Co., Houston, TX [*Library symbol Library of Congress*] (LCLS)
TxHCC-L ...... Conoco, Inc., Law Library, Houston, TX [*Library symbol*] [*Library of Congress*] (LCLS)
TxHCC-N ...... Conoco, Inc., North American Exploration Headquarters, Houston, TX [*Library symbol*] [*Library of Congress*] (LCLS)
TxHCCo .... Compaq Computer Corp., Component Engineering Library, Houston, TX [*Library symbol*] [*Library of Congress*] (LCLS)
TxHCG .... Columbia Gulf Transmission Co., Houston, TX [*Library symbol Library of Congress*] (LCLS)
TxHCI .... Cameron Iron Works, Inc., Houston, TX [*Library symbol Library of Congress*] (LCLS)
TxHCS .... Community Welfare Planning Association, Social Research Library, Houston, TX [*Library symbol Library of Congress*] (LCLS)
TxHDC .... Dow Chemical Co., E and CS Information Center, Houston, TX [*Library symbol Library of Congress*] (LCLS)
TxHDE .... Dresser Industries, Inc., Lane-Wells Co., Houston, TX [*Library symbol Library of Congress*] (LCLS)
TxHDH .... Dobie High School, Houston, TX [*Library symbol*] [*Library of Congress*] (LCLS)
TxHDom .... Dominican College, Houston, TX [*Library symbol Library of Congress*] (LCLS)
TxHe .... Edwards Public Library, Henrietta, TX [*Library symbol Library of Congress*] (LCLS)
TxHE .... United States Air Force, Base Library, Ellington AFB, Houston, TX [*Library symbol Library of Congress*] (LCLS)
TxHebO .... Our Lady of Guadalupe Parish Library, Hebbronville, TX [*Library symbol Library of Congress*] (LCLS)
TxHeE .... Edwards Public Library, Henrietta, TX [*Library symbol*] [*Library of Congress*] (LCLS)
TxHE-NA ...... United States Air Force, National Aerospace Education Library, Ellington AFB, Houston, TX [*Library symbol Library of Congress*] (LCLS)
TxHF .... Captain Theodore C. Freeman Memorial Library, Houston, TX [*Library symbol Library of Congress*] (LCLS)
TxHFE .... Fluor Engineers & Constructors, Fluor Houston Library, Houston, TX [*Library symbol Library of Congress*] (LCLS)
TxHFO .... Fluor Ocean Services, Engineering Library, Houston, TX [*Library symbol Library of Congress*] (LCLS)
TxHFR .... Freelance Research Service, Houston, TX [*Library symbol Library of Congress*] (LCLS)
TxHFrE .... Freeman Elementary School, Houston, TX [*Library symbol*] [*Library of Congress*] (LCLS)
TxHFzE .... Frazier Elementary School, Houston, TX [*Library symbol*] [*Library of Congress*] (LCLS)
TxHG .... Gulf Coast Bible College, Houston, TX [*Library symbol Library of Congress*] (LCLS)
TxHGE .... Genoa Elementary School, Houston, TX [*Library symbol*] [*Library of Congress*] (LCLS)
TxHGfE .... Garfield Elementary School, Houston, TX [*Library symbol*] [*Library of Congress*] (LCLS)
TxHGO .... Gulf Oil Co.-US, Central Reference Library, Houston, TX [*Library symbol Library of Congress*] (LCLS)
TxHGP .... Gulf Publishing Co., Houston, TX [*Library symbol Library of Congress*] (LCLS)
TxHGS .... Church of Jesus Christ of Latter-Day Saints, Genealogical Society Library, Houston Branch, Houston, TX [*Library symbol Library of Congress*] (LCLS)
TxHGS-E ...... Church of Jesus Christ of Latter-Day Saints, Genealogical Society Library, Houston East Branch, Houston, TX [*Library symbol Library of Congress*] (LCLS)
TxHH .... Black, Syvalls & Bryson, Inc., HOMCO Division, Houston, TX [*Library symbol Library of Congress*] (LCLS)
TxHHC .... Houston Chronicle, Houston, TX [*Library symbol Library of Congress*] (LCLS)
TxHHG .... Houston-Galveston Area Council Library, Houston, TX [*Library symbol Library of Congress*] (LCLS)
TxHHH .... Herman Hospital, Houston, TX [*Library symbol Library of Congress*] (LCLS)
TxHHL .... Houston Lighting & Power Co., Houston, TX [*Library symbol Library of Congress*] (LCLS)
TxHHO .... Humble Oil & Refining Co., General Services Library, Houston, TX [*Library symbol Library of Congress*] (LCLS)
TxHHO-E ..... Humble Oil & Refining Co., Marketing Research Library, Houston, TX [*Library symbol Library of Congress*] (LCLS)
TxHHOM ...... Houston Oil and Mineral Corp., Corporate Library, Houston, TX [*Library symbol Library of Congress*] (LCLS)
TxHHP .... Houston Post, Houston, TX [*Library symbol Library of Congress*] (LCLS)
TxHHT .... Hughes Tool Co., Houston, TX [*Library symbol Library of Congress*] (LCLS)
TxHI .... International Business Machines Corporation, Corporation Library, Houston, TX [*Library symbol Library of Congress*] (LCLS)
TXHI .... THT, Inc. [*Formerly, Texas Hitech, Inc.*] [*NASDAQ symbol*] (NQ)
TxHiC .... Hill Junior College, Hillsboro, TX [*Library symbol Library of Congress*] (LCLS)
TxHIR .... Institute of Religion, Texas Medical Center, Houston, TX [*Library symbol Library of Congress*] (LCLS)
TxHJE .... Jessup Elementary School, Houston, TX [*Library symbol*] [*Library of Congress*] (LCLS)
TxHLD .... City of Houston Legal Department, Houston, TX [*Library symbol Library of Congress*] (LCLS)
TxHLJ .... Memorial Baptist Hospital, Lillie Jolly School of Nursing, Houston, TX [*Library symbol Library of Congress*] (LCLS)
TxHLS .... Lunar Science Institute, Houston, TX [*Library symbol Library of Congress*] (LCLS)
TxHLT .... Layne Texas Co., Houston, TX [*Library symbol Library of Congress*] (LCLS)
TxHM .... Museum of Fine Arts, Houston, TX [*Library symbol Library of Congress*] (LCLS)

TxHMa......... Magcobar Corp., Houston, TX [*Library symbol Library of Congress*] (LCLS)
TxHMC......... Houston Academy of Medicine, Houston, TX [*Library symbol Library of Congress*] (LCLS)
TxHMc......... McClelland Engineers, Inc., Houston, TX [*Library symbol Library of Congress*] (LCLS)
TxHMcE....... McCelland Engineers, Inc., Houston, TX [*Library symbol*] [*Library of Congress*] (LCLS)
TxHME......... Meador Elementary School, Houston, TX [*Library symbol*] [*Library of Congress*] (LCLS)
TxHMM........ Milwhite Co., Houston, TX [*Library symbol Library of Congress*] (LCLS)
TxHMoE....... Moore Elementary School, Houston, TX [*Library symbol*] [*Library of Congress*] (LCLS)
TxHMon....... Monsanto Co., Houston, TX [*Library symbol Library of Congress*] (LCLS)
TxHN........... National Association of Corrosion Engineers, Houston, TX [*Library symbol Library of Congress*] (LCLS)
TxHNASA..... National Aeronautics and Space Administration, Manned Spacecraft Center, Technical Library, Houston, TX [*Library symbol Library of Congress*] (LCLS)
TxHNH......... North Harris County College, Houston, TX [*Library symbol Library of Congress*] (LCLS)
TxHP........... Texas Research Institute of Mental Sciences, Houston, TX [*Library symbol Library of Congress*] (LCLS)
TxHPC......... Pace Co., Houston, TX [*Library symbol Library of Congress*] (LCLS)
TxHPen....... Pennzoil Exploration Library, Houston, TX [*Library symbol Library of Congress*] (LCLS)
TxHPH......... Port of Houston World Trade Center, Houston, TX [*Library symbol Library of Congress*] (LCLS)
TxHPI.......... Prudential Insurance Co. of America, Houston, TX [*Library symbol Library of Congress*] (LCLS)
TxHPT......... Petro-Tex Chemical Corp., Research Library, Houston, TX [*Library symbol Library of Congress*] (LCLS)
TxHR........... Rice University, Houston, TX [*Library symbol Library of Congress*] (LCLS)
TxHRa......... Raymond International, Inc., Houston, TX [*Library symbol Library of Congress*] (LCLS)
TxHRH......... Roy M. Huffington, Inc., Library, Houston, TX [*Library symbol Library of Congress*] (LCLS)
TxHRI.......... Houston Research Institute, Houston, TX [*Library symbol Library of Congress*] (LCLS)
TxHSB......... Southern Bible College, Houston, TX [*Library symbol Library of Congress*] (LCLS)
TxHSD......... Shell Development Co., Bellaire Research Center, Houston, TX [*Library symbol Library of Congress*] (LCLS)
TxHSDW...... Shell Oil Development Co., Westhollow Research Center Library, Houston, TX [*Library symbol Library of Congress*] (LCLS)
TxHSE......... Stuchbery Elementary School, Houston, TX [*Library symbol*] [*Library of Congress*] (LCLS)
TxHSJM....... San Jacinto Museum of History Association, Deer Park, TX [*Library symbol Library of Congress*] (LCLS)
TxHSOC....... Standard Oil Co. of Texas, Houston, TX [*Library symbol Library of Congress*] (LCLS)
TxHSOF....... Shell Oil Co., Information and Library Services Library, Houston, TX [*Library symbol Library of Congress*] (LCLS)
TxHSOIC...... Shell Oil Co., Information and Computing Services Center Library, Houston, TX [*Library symbol Library of Congress*] (LCLS)
TxHSP......... Shell Pipe Line Corp., R and D Library, Houston, TX [*Library symbol Library of Congress Obsolete*] (LCLS)
TxHSR......... Southwestern Research Institute, Houston, TX [*Library symbol Library of Congress*] (LCLS)
TxHST......... University of Saint Thomas, Houston, TX [*Library symbol Library of Congress*] (LCLS)
TxHSTC....... South Texas Junior College, Houston, TX [*Library symbol Library of Congress*] (LCLS)
TxHSTL....... South Texas College of Law, Houston, TX [*Library symbol Library of Congress*] (LCLS)
TxHSU......... Superior Oil Exploration Library, Houston, TX [*Library symbol Library of Congress*] (LCLS)
TxHSW......... Schlumberger Well Services, Houston, TX [*Library symbol Library of Congress*] (LCLS)
TxHSWE....... Shell Western E & P Inc., Woodcreek Library, Houston, TX [*Library symbol*] [*Library of Congress*] (LCLS)
TxHTC......... Transcontinental Gas Pipe Line Corp., Houston, TX [*Library symbol Library of Congress*] (LCLS)
TxHTE......... Texas Eastern Transmission Corp., Houston, TX [*Library symbol Library of Congress*] (LCLS)
TxHTen....... Tennessee Gas Transmission Co., Houston, TX [*Library symbol Library of Congress*] (LCLS)
TxHTexG...... Texas Gas Exploration Co., Houston, TX [*Library symbol Library of Congress*] (LCLS)
TxHTexO...... Texasgulf Oil & Gas Co., Houston, TX [*Library symbol Library of Congress*] (LCLS)
TxHTG......... Trunkline Gas Co., Houston, TX [*Library symbol Library of Congress*] (LCLS)
TxHTGP....... Tennessee Gas Pipeline Co., Houston, TX [*Library symbol Library of Congress*] (LCLS)
TxHTGS....... Texas Gulf Sulphur Co., Inc., Houston, TX [*Library symbol Library of Congress*] (LCLS)
TxHTI.......... Texas Instruments, Inc., Houston, TX [*Library symbol Library of Congress*] (LCLS)
TxHTide....... Getty Oil Co., Houston, TX [*Library symbol Library of Congress*] (LCLS)
TxHTide(Res)... Getty Oil Co., Exploration and Production Research Library, Houston, TX [*Library symbol Library of Congress*] (LCLS)
TxHTI-I........ Texas Instruments, Inc., Industrial Products Division, Houston, TX [*Library symbol Library of Congress*] (LCLS)
TxHTM......... Texas Manufacturers Association, Houston, TX [*Library symbol Library of Congress*] (LCLS)
TxHTO......... Tenneco Oil Co., Exploration Research Library, Houston, TX [*Library symbol Library of Congress*] (LCLS)
TxHTRW...... TRW Systems Group, Houston, TX [*Library symbol Library of Congress*] (LCLS)
TxHTSU....... Texas Southern University, Houston, TX [*Library symbol Library of Congress*] (LCLS)
TxHTSU-L.... Texas Southern University, Law Library, Houston, TX [*Library symbol*] [*Library of Congress*] (LCLS)
TxHTu......... Turner, Collie & Braden, Inc., Houston, TX [*Library symbol Library of Congress*] (LCLS)
TxHU........... University of Houston, Houston, TX [*Library symbol Library of Congress*] (LCLS)
TxHUC......... Union Carbide Corp., Houston, TX [*Library symbol Library of Congress*] (LCLS)
TxHU-D........ University of Houston, Downtown College, Houston, TX [*Library symbol Library of Congress*] (LCLS)
TxHU-L........ University of Houston, Law School, Houston, TX [*Library symbol Library of Congress*] (LCLS)
TxHurT......... Tarrant County Junior College District, Hurst, TX [*Library symbol Library of Congress*] (LCLS)
TxHUSC....... United States Department of Commerce, Houston Field Office Library, Houston, TX [*Library symbol Library of Congress*] (LCLS)
TxHuT......... Sam Houston State University, Huntsville, TX [*Library symbol Library of Congress*] (LCLS)
TxHUTP....... Union Texas Petroleum Co., Houston, TX [*Library symbol Library of Congress*] (LCLS)
TxHVA......... United States Veterans Administration Hospital, Houston, TX [*Library symbol Library of Congress*] (LCLS)
TxHVE......... Vinson, Elkins, Searls, Connally & Smith, Law Library, Houston, TX [*Library symbol Library of Congress*] (LCLS)
TxHW........... Welex Division, Haliburton Co., Houston, TX [*Library symbol Library of Congress*] (LCLS)
TxHWB......... World Book Encyclopaedia Science Service, Inc., Houston, TX [*Library symbol Library of Congress*] (LCLS)
TxHWG........ Western Geophysical Co., Houston, TX [*Library symbol Library of Congress*] (LCLS)
TxHWH........ Westbury Senior High School, Houston, TX [*Library symbol Library of Congress*] (LCLS)
TxHWN........ Western Natural Gas Co., Houston, TX [*Library symbol Library of Congress*] (LCLS)
TXI.............. Aereotaxis SA de CV [*Mexico ICAO designator*] (FAAC)
TXI.............. Southwest Texas State University, San Marcos, TX [*OCLC symbol*] (OCLC)
TXI.............. Texas Indus [*NYSE symbol*] (TTSB)
TXI.............. Texas Industries, Inc. [*NYSE symbol*] (SPSG)
TXI.............. Texas International Airlines, Inc. [*Air carrier designation symbol*]
TXI.............. Torex Minerals Ltd. [*Vancouver Stock Exchange symbol*]
TXI.............. Transfer with Index Incremented
TxIr............. Irving Municipal Library, Irving, TX [*Library symbol Library of Congress*] (LCLS)
TxIrG........... GTE Service Corp., Library, Irving, TX [*Library symbol*] [*Library of Congress*] (LCLS)
TxIrS........... Irving Independent School District, Irving, TX [*Library symbol Library of Congress*] (LCLS)
TXJ.............. University of Texas at San Antonio, San Antonio, TX [*OCLC symbol*] (OCLC)
TxJaB........... Baptist Missionary Association Theological Seminary, Jacksonville, TX [*Library symbol Library of Congress*] (LCLS)
TxJaC........... Jacksonville College, Jacksonville, TX [*Library symbol Library of Congress*] (LCLS)
TxJaL........... Lon Morris College, Jacksonville, TX [*Library symbol Library of Congress*] (LCLS)
TxJoTI.......... Texas Instruments, Inc., Johnson City Technical Library, Johnson City, TX [*Library symbol*] [*Library of Congress*] (LCLS)
TXK.............. Stephen F. Austin University, Nacogdoches, TX [*OCLC symbol*] (OCLC)
TXK.............. Telephone Exchange (Crossbar) [*Telecommunications*] (TEL)
TXK.............. Texarkana [*Arkansas*] [*Airport symbol*] (OAG)
TxKeeS......... Southwestern Union College, Keene, TX [*Library symbol Library of Congress*] (LCLS)
TxKerS.......... Schreiner Institute, Kerrville, TX [*Library symbol Library of Congress*] (LCLS)
TXKF............ Bermuda Naval Air Station [*Bermuda*] [*ICAO location identifier*] (ICLI)
TxKiC........... Central Texas College, Killeen, TX [*Library symbol Library of Congress*] (LCLS)
TxKilC.......... Kilgore College, Kilgore, TX [*Library symbol Library of Congress*] (LCLS)
TxKT............ Texas A & I University, Kingsville, TX [*Library symbol Library of Congress*] (LCLS)
TXL.............. Aereo Taxi de Leon SA de CV [*Mexico ICAO designator*] (FAAC)
TXL.............. Berlin [*Germany Airport symbol*] (OAG)
TxL.............. Lubbock City-County Libraries, Lubbock, TX [*Library symbol Library of Congress*] (LCLS)
TXL.............. Transfer on Index Low (IAA)
TxLaH.......... United States Air Force, Base Library, Lackland Air Force Base, TX [*Library symbol Library of Congress*] (LCLS)
TxLaM.......... United States Air Force, Wilford Hall Medical Center, Lackland AFB, TX [*Library symbol Library of Congress*] (LCLS)

TxLapU .... Upjohn Co., Polymer Chemicals Division Library, La Porte, TX [*Library symbol Library of Congress*] (LCLS)
TxLar .... Laredo Public Library, Laredo, TX [*Library symbol Library of Congress*] (LCLS)
TxLarC .... Laredo Junior College, Laredo, TX [*Library symbol Library of Congress*] (LCLS)
TxLarU .... Laredo State University, Laredo, TX [*Library symbol Library of Congress*] (LCLS)
TxLC .... Lubbock Christian College, Lubbock, TX [*Library symbol Library of Congress*] (LCLS)
TxLcD .... Soil and Water Conservation Districts Foundation, Davis Conservation Library, League City, TX [*Library symbol Library of Congress*] (LCLS)
TxLeaHS ...... Leander High School, Leander, TX [*Library symbol*] [*Library of Congress*] (LCLS)
TxLeS .... South Plains College, Levelland, TX [*Library symbol Library of Congress*] (LCLS)
TXLI .... Texoil, Inc. [*NASDAQ symbol*] (SAG)
TxLib .... Liberty City Library, Liberty, TX [*Library symbol Library of Congress*] (LCLS)
TxLivP .... Polk County Enterprise, Livingston, TX [*Library symbol Library of Congress*] (LCLS)
TXLIW .... Texoil Inc. Wrrt'A' [*NASDAQ symbol*] (TTSB)
TXLIZ .... Texoil Inc. Wrrt'B' [*NASDAQ symbol*] (TTSB)
TX LJ .... Texas Law Journal [*A publication*] (DLA)
TxLjB .... Brazosport College, Lake Jackson, TX [*Library symbol Library of Congress*] (LCLS)
TxLMH .... Methodist Hospital, Lubbock, TX [*Library symbol Library of Congress*] (LCLS)
TxLoL .... LeTourneau College, Longview, TX [*Library symbol Library of Congress*] (LCLS)
TxLT .... Texas Tech University, Lubbock, TX [*Library symbol Library of Congress*] (LCLS)
TxLTM .... Texas Tech University, School of Medicine at Lubbock, Lubbock, TX [*Library symbol Library of Congress*] (LCLS)
TxLTM-E ...... Texas Tech University, Regional Academic Health Center, El Paso, TX [*Library symbol*] [*Library of Congress*] (LCLS)
TxLT-SW ...... Texas Tech University, Southwest Collection, Lubbock, TX [*Library symbol*] [*Library of Congress*] (LCLS)
TxLufA .... Angelina College, Lufkin, TX [*Library symbol Library of Congress*] (LCLS)
TxLufFS .... Texas Forest Service, Forest Products Laboratory Library, Lufkin, TX [*Library symbol Library of Congress*] (LCLS)
TxLufK .... Kurth Memorial Library, Lufkin, TX [*Library symbol Library of Congress*] (LCLS)
TxLvTI .... Texas Instruments, Inc., Lewisville Technical Library, Lewisville, TX [*Library symbol*] [*Library of Congress*] (LCLS)
TXM .... Middle Tennessee State University, Murfreesboro, TN [*OCLC symbol*] (OCLC)
TXM .... Tank Exchange Model
TXM .... Taxi Aereo de Mexico [*ICAO designator*] (FAAC)
TXM .... Teminabuan [*West Irian, Indonesia*] [*Airport symbol*] (AD)
Tx-M .... Texas State Medical Library, Austin, TX [*Library symbol Library of Congress*] (LCLS)
TXM .... Trex Medical Corp. [*AMEX symbol*] (SAG)
TXM .... Trimel Corp. [*Toronto Stock Exchange symbol*]
TxMaEB .... East Texas Baptist University, Marshall, TX [*Library symbol*] [*Library of Congress*] (LCLS)
TxMalC .... ICI America, Inc., Darco Experimental Laboratory Library, Marshall, TX [*Library symbol Library of Congress*] (LCLS)
TxMaW .... Wiley College, Marshall, TX [*Library symbol Library of Congress*] (LCLS)
TxMCa .... McAllen Memorial Library, McAllen, TX [*Library symbol Library of Congress*] (LCLS)
TxMcaH .... Hidelgo County Library System, McAllen, TX [*Library symbol Library of Congress*] (LCLS)
TxMcgR .... North American Rockwell Corp., Solid Rocket Division, McGregor, TX [*Library symbol Library of Congress*] (LCLS)
TxMck .... McKinney Memorial Public Library, McKinney, TX [*Library symbol Library of Congress*] (LCLS)
TxMckC .... Collin County Community College District, McKinney, TX [*Library symbol*] [*Library of Congress*] (LCLS)
TxMckTI .... Texas Instruments, Inc., McKinney Technical Library, McKinney, TX [*Library symbol*] [*Library of Congress*] (LCLS)
TxMe .... Mesquite Public Library, Mesquite, TX [*Library symbol Library of Congress*] (LCLS)
TxMeE .... Eastfield College, Mesquite, TX [*Library symbol Library of Congress*] (LCLS)
TxMM .... Midland County Public Library, Midland, TX [*Library symbol Library of Congress*] (LCLS)
TxMtpN .... Northeast Texas Community College, Mount Pleasant, TX [*Library symbol*] [*Library of Congress*] (LCLS)
TXN .... Houston Public Library, Houston, TX [*OCLC symbol*] (OCLC)
TXN .... Taxation
TXN .... Texas Instruments [*NYSE symbol*] (TTSB)
TXN .... Texas Instruments, Inc. [*NYSE symbol*] (SPSG)
TXN .... Texas National Airlines [*ICAO designator*] (FAAC)
TXN .... Texas Northern Oil & Gas [*Vancouver Stock Exchange symbol*]
TXN .... Texas Satellite Network [*Telecommunications service*] (TSSD)
TXN .... Tunxi [*China*] [*Airport symbol*] (OAG)
TxNacS .... Stephen F. Austin State University, Nacogdoches, TX [*Library symbol Library of Congress*] (LCLS)
TXO .... Texico, NM [*Location identifier FAA*] (FAAL)
TXO .... University of Texas of the Permian Basin, Odessa, TX [*OCLC symbol*] (OCLC)
TxOC .... Odessa College, Odessa, TX [*Library symbol Library of Congress*] (LCLS)
TxOE .... Ector County Public Library, Odessa, TX [*Library symbol Library of Congress*] (LCLS)
TxOEP .... El Paso Products Co., Odessa, TX [*Library symbol Library of Congress*] (LCLS)
TxOGS .... Church of Jesus Christ of Latter-Day Saints, Genealogical Society Library, Odessa Stake Branch, Odessa, TX [*Library symbol Library of Congress*] (LCLS)
TxOr .... Orange Public Library, Orange, TX [*Library symbol Library of Congress*] (LCLS)
TXOrD .... E. I. Du Pont de Nemours & Co., Sabine River Works, Orange, TX [*Library symbol Library of Congress*] (LCLS)
TxOrL .... Lamar University-Orange, Orange, TX [*Library symbol*] [*Library of Congress*] (LCLS)
TXP .... El Paso Public Library, El Paso, TX [*OCLC symbol*] (OCLC)
TXP .... Linea Aerea Taxpa Ltda. [*Chile*] [*ICAO designator*] (FAAC)
TxP .... Pasadena Public Library, Pasadena, TX [*Library symbol Library of Congress*] (LCLS)
TXP .... Taxpayer [*Legal shorthand*] (LWAP)
TxPac .... Texas Pacific Land Trust [*Associated Press*] (SAG)
TxPaIMS ...... Institute of Marine Science, University of Texas, Port Aransas, TX [*Library symbol Library of Congress*] (LCLS)
TxParC .... Paris Junior College, Paris, TX [*Library symbol Library of Congress*] (LCLS)
TxPBE .... Bailey Elementary School, Pasadena, TX [*Library symbol*] [*Library of Congress*] (LCLS)
TxPC .... Champion Papers, Inc., Pasadena, TX [*Library symbol Library of Congress*] (LCLS)
TxPCS .... Challenger School, Pasadena, TX [*Library symbol*] [*Library of Congress*] (LCLS)
TxPE .... Ethyl Corp., Pasadena, TX [*Library symbol Library of Congress*] (LCLS)
TxPFE .... Fisher Elementary School, Pasadena, TX [*Library symbol*] [*Library of Congress*] (LCLS)
TxPGaE .... Golden Acres Elementary School, Pasadena, TX [*Library symbol*] [*Library of Congress*] (LCLS)
TxPGE .... Gardens Elementary School, Pasadena, TX [*Library symbol*] [*Library of Congress*] (LCLS)
TxPISD .... Pasadena Independent School District, Pasadena, TX [*Library symbol*] [*Library of Congress*] (LCLS)
TxPISD-P ..... Pasadena Independent School District, Professional Library, Pasadena, TX [*Library symbol*] [*Library of Congress*] (LCLS)
TxPJE .... Jensen Elementary School, Pasadena, TX [*Library symbol*] [*Library of Congress*] (LCLS)
TxPJI .... Jackson Intermediate School, Pasadena, TX [*Library symbol*] [*Library of Congress*] (LCLS)
TxPKE .... Kruse Elementary School, Pasadena, TX [*Library symbol*] [*Library of Congress*] (LCLS)
TxPlao .... Plano Public Library, Plano, TX [*Library symbol Library of Congress*] (LCLS)
TxPlW .... Wayland Baptist College, Plainview, TX [*Library symbol Library of Congress*] (LCLS)
TxPME .... McMasters Elementary School, Pasadena, TX [*Library symbol*] [*Library of Congress*] (LCLS)
TxPMI .... Miller Intermediate School, Pasadena, TX [*Library symbol*] [*Library of Congress*] (LCLS)
TxPnT .... Texas-United States Chemical Co., Process Engineering Section, R and D Library, Port Neches, TX [*Library symbol Library of Congress*] (LCLS)
TxPo .... Gates Memorial Library, Port Arthur, TX [*Library symbol Library of Congress*] (LCLS)
TxPPE .... Parks Elementary School, Pasadena, TX [*Library symbol*] [*Library of Congress*] (LCLS)
TxPPH .... Pasadena High School, Pasadena, TX [*Library symbol*] [*Library of Congress*] (LCLS)
TxPPoE .... Pomeroy Elementary School, Pasadena, TX [*Library symbol*] [*Library of Congress*] (LCLS)
TxPPvI .... Park View Intermediate School, Pasadena, TX [*Library symbol*] [*Library of Congress*] (LCLS)
TxPQI .... Queens Intermediate School, Pasadena, TX [*Library symbol*] [*Library of Congress*] (LCLS)
TxPRbE .... Red Bluff Elementary School, Pasadena, TX [*Library symbol*] [*Library of Congress*] (LCLS)
TXPRD .... Tax Period
TxPRE .... Richey Elementary School, Pasadena, TX [*Library symbol*] [*Library of Congress*] (LCLS)
TxPRH .... Sam Rayburn High School, Pasadena, TX [*Library symbol*] [*Library of Congress*] (LCLS)
TxPS .... San Jacinto College, Pasadena, TX [*Library symbol Library of Congress*] (LCLS)
TxPSE .... Mae Smythe Elementary School, Pasadena, TX [*Library symbol*] [*Library of Congress*] (LCLS)
TxPSI .... Southmore Elementary School, Pasadena, TX [*Library symbol*] [*Library of Congress*] (LCLS)
TxPSjI .... San Jacinto Intermediate School, Pasadena, TX [*Library symbol*] [*Library of Congress*] (LCLS)
TxPSpE .... Sparks Elementary School, Pasadena, TX [*Library symbol*] [*Library of Congress*] (LCLS)
TxPSSE .... South Shaver Elementary School, Pasadena, TX [*Library symbol*] [*Library of Congress*] (LCLS)
TxPT .... Tenneco Chemicals, Inc., Pasadena, TX [*Library symbol Library of Congress*] (LCLS)
TxPTC .... Texas Chiropractic College, Pasadena, TX [*Library symbol*] [*Library of Congress*] (LCLS)

TxPTE .... Teague Elementary School, Pasadena, TX [*Library symbol*] [*Library of Congress*] (LCLS)
TxPvC .... Prairie View Agricultural and Mechanical College, Prairie View, TX [*Library symbol Library of Congress*] (LCLS)
TxPWE .... Williams Elementary School, Pasadena, TX [*Library symbol*] [*Library of Congress*] (LCLS)
TxPYE .... Young Elementary School, Pasadena, TX [*Library symbol*] [*Library of Congress*] (LCLS)
TXPYR .... Taxpayer
TXQ .... University of Texas, Austin, Law Library, Austin, TX [*OCLC symbol*] (OCLC)
TXR .... Lamar University, Beaumont, TX [*OCLC symbol*] (OCLC)
TXR .... Susitna Valley, AK [*Location identifier FAA*] (FAAL)
TXR .... Tanbar [*Queensland*] [*Airport symbol*] (AD)
TXR .... Tank Exchange Ratio (MCD)
TXR .... Taxirey SA de CV [*Mexico ICAO designator*] (FAAC)
TXR .... Triex Resources Ltd. [*Vancouver Stock Exchange symbol*]
TxRaC .... Ranger Junior College, Ranger, TX [*Library symbol Library of Congress*] (LCLS)
TXRC .... Texas Export [*AAR code*]
TxReTR .... Texas Research Foundation, Renner, TX [*Library symbol Library of Congress*] (LCLS)
TXRF .... Total-Reflection X-Ray Fluorescence [*Analytical chemistry*]
TxRi .... Richardson Public Library, Richardson, TX [*Library symbol Library of Congress*] (LCLS)
TxRiA .... Anderson Clayton Foods [*of Anderson, Clayton & Co.*], Richardson, TX [*Library symbol Library of Congress*] (LCLS)
TxRic .... Fort Bend County Library System, George Memorial Library, Richmond, TX [*Library symbol*] [*Library of Congress*] (LCLS)
TxRiS .... Sun Oil Co., Richardson, TX [*Library symbol Library of Congress*] (LCLS)
TxRr .... Round Rock Public Library, Round Rock, TX [*Library symbol*] [*Library of Congress*] (LCLS)
TXRX .... Transmitter-Receiver
TXS .... Hardin-Simmons University, Abilene, TX [*OCLC symbol*] (OCLC)
TXS .... Taxpayer Service [*IRS*]
TXS .... Telephone Exchange (Strowger) [*Telecommunications*] (TEL)
TXS .... Texas Airlines, Inc. [*ICAO designator*] (FAAC)
TXS .... Texas Star Resources Corp. [*Vancouver Stock Exchange symbol*]
TxSa .... San Antonio Public Library, San Antonio, TX [*Library symbol Library of Congress*] (LCLS)
TxSaBAM .... United States Air Force, School of Aerospace Medicine, Brooks Air Force Base, San Antonio, TX [*Library symbol Library of Congress*] (LCLS)
TxSaBHR .... United States Air Force, Human Resources Laboratory Library, Brooks Air Force Base, San Antonio, TX [*Library symbol Library of Congress*] (LCLS)
TxSaBM .... Bexar County Medical Library Association, San Antonio, TX [*Library symbol Library of Congress*] (LCLS)
TxSaC .... San Antonio College, San Antonio, TX [*Library symbol Library of Congress*] (LCLS)
TxSaGH .... Robert B. Green Memorial Hospital, San Antonio, TX [*Library symbol Library of Congress*] (LCLS)
TxSaGS .... Church of Jesus Christ of Latter-Day Saints, Genealogical Society Library, San Antonio Branch, San Antonio, TX [*Library symbol Library of Congress*] (LCLS)
TxSaI .... Incarnate Word College, San Antonio, TX [*Library symbol Library of Congress*] (LCLS)
TxSal .... Tom Green County Library, San Angelo, TX [*Library symbol Library of Congress*] (LCLS)
TxSalA .... Angelo State University, San Angelo, TX [*Library symbol Library of Congress*] (LCLS)
TxSaO .... Our Lady of the Lake College, San Antonio, TX [*Library symbol Library of Congress*] (LCLS)
TxSaOC .... Oblate College of the Southwest, San Antonio, TX [*Library symbol Library of Congress*] (LCLS)
TxSaPA .... Palo Alto College, San Antonio, TX [*Library symbol*] [*Library of Congress*] (LCLS)
TxSaSFRE .... Southwest Foundation for Research and Education, San Antonio, TX [*Library symbol Library of Congress*] (LCLS)
TxSaSM .... Saint Mary's University, San Antonio, TX [*Library symbol Library of Congress*] (LCLS)
TxSaSM-L .... Saint Mary's University, Law Library, San Antonio, TX [*Library symbol Library of Congress*] (LCLS)
TxSaSP .... St. Philip's College, San Antonio, TX [*Library symbol Library of Congress*] (LCLS)
TxSaSR .... Southwest Research Institute, San Antonio, TX [*Library symbol Library of Congress*] (LCLS)
TxSaStJ .... Saint John's Seminary, San Antonio, TX [*Library symbol Library of Congress*] (LCLS)
TxSaT .... Trinity University, San Antonio, TX [*Library symbol Library of Congress*] (LCLS)
TxSaT-W .... Trinity University, Whitsett Library Museum, San Antonio, TX [*Library symbol Library of Congress*] (LCLS)
TxSaU .... University of Texas at San Antonio, San Antonio, TX [*Library symbol Library of Congress*] (LCLS)
TxSaUS .... United Services Automobile Association, San Antonio, TX [*Library symbol Library of Congress*] (LCLS)
TxSaV .... United States Veterans Administration Hospital, San Antonio, TX [*Library symbol Library of Congress*] (LCLS)
Tx-SC .... Texas State Law Library, Austin, TX [*Library symbol Library of Congress*] (LCLS)
TxSeTL .... Texas Lutheran College, Seguin, TX [*Library symbol Library of Congress*] (LCLS)
TxSh .... Sherman Public Library, Sherman, TX [*Library symbol*] [*Library of Congress*] (LCLS)
TxShA .... Austin College, Sherman, TX [*Library symbol Library of Congress*] (LCLS)
TxShoHH .... South Houston High School, South Houston, TX [*Library symbol*] [*Library of Congress*] (LCLS)
TxShoHI .... South Houston Intermediate School, South Houston, TX [*Library symbol*] [*Library of Congress*] (LCLS)
TxShoPE .... Pearl Hall Elementary School, South Houston, TX [*Library symbol*] [*Library of Congress*] (LCLS)
TxShoSE .... L.F. Smith Elementary School, South Houston, TX [*Library symbol*] [*Library of Congress*] (LCLS)
TxShoShE .... South Houston Elementary School, South Houston, TX [*Library symbol*] [*Library of Congress*] (LCLS)
TxShpM .... United States Air Force, Regional Hospital, Medical Library, Sheppard AFB, TX [*Library symbol Library of Congress*] (LCLS)
TxShTI .... Texas Instruments, Inc., Sherman Technical Library, Sherman, TX [*Library symbol*] [*Library of Congress*] (LCLS)
TxSiW .... Rob and Bessie Welder Wildlife Foundation, Sinton, TX [*Library symbol Library of Congress*] (LCLS)
TxSjM .... San Jacinto Museum of History Association, San Jacinto Monument, TX [*Library symbol Library of Congress*] (LCLS)
TxSmS .... Southwest Texas State University, San Marcos, TX [*Library symbol Library of Congress*] (LCLS)
TxSn .... Scurry County Library, Snyder, TX [*Library symbol Library of Congress*] (LCLS)
TxSvT .... Tarleton State University, Stephenville, TX [*Library symbol Library of Congress*] (LCLS)
TxSw .... Sweetwater City-County Library, Sweetwater, TX [*Library symbol Library of Congress*] (LCLS)
TXT .... Group One, Inc. [*FAA designator*] (FAAC)
TXT .... Texas Southern University, Houston, TX [*OCLC symbol*] (OCLC)
TXT .... Text
txt .... Text or ASCII File [*Computer science*]
TXT .... Textron, Inc. [*NYSE symbol*] (SPSG)
TxTA .... American Oil Co. [*Later, Amoco Oil Co.*], Texas City, TX [*Library symbol Library of Congress*] (LCLS)
TxTCM .... College of the Mainland, Texas City, TX [*Library symbol Library of Congress*] (LCLS)
TxTe .... Texarkana Public Library, Texarkana, TX [*Library symbol Library of Congress*] (LCLS)
TxTeC .... Texarkana College, Texarkana, TX [*Library symbol Library of Congress*] (LCLS)
TxTeET .... East Texas State University, Texarkana, TX [*Library symbol Library of Congress*] (LCLS)
TxTehW .... Westminster College, Tehuacana, TX [*Library symbol Library of Congress*] (LCLS)
TxTemC .... Temple Junior College, Temple, TX [*Library symbol Library of Congress*] (LCLS)
TxTemH .... Scott and White Memorial Hospital, Temple, TX [*Library symbol Library of Congress*] (LCLS)
TxTerS .... Southwestern Christian College, Terrell, TX [*Library symbol Library of Congress*] (LCLS)
TxTeS .... East Texas State University at Texarkana, Texarkana, TX [*Library symbol Library of Congress*] (LCLS)
TXTL .... Textile (MSA)
txtl .... Textile (VRA)
TXTL .... Textile
TXTLE .... Textile
TXTM .... Text Maintenance [*Computer science*] (MHDB)
TxTMC .... Monsanto Co., Texas City, TX [*Library symbol Library of Congress*] (LCLS)
TXTPrA .... Textron, $2.08 Cv A Pfd [*NYSE symbol*] (TTSB)
TXTPrB .... Textron, $1.40 Cv B Pfd [*NYSE symbol*] (TTSB)
TXTPrT .... Textron Cap 1 7.92% Tr Sec [*NYSE symbol*] (TTSB)
TxTUC .... Union Carbide Corp., Chemicals and Plastics Division, Texas City, TX [*Library symbol Library of Congress*] (LCLS)
TxTy .... Tyler Carnegie Public Library, Tyler, TX [*Library symbol Library of Congress*] (LCLS)
TxTyB .... Butler College, Tyler, TX [*Library symbol Library of Congress*] (LCLS)
TxTyC .... Texas Eastern University, Tyler, TX [*Library symbol Library of Congress*] (LCLS)
TxTyT .... Texas College, Tyler, TX [*Library symbol Library of Congress*] (LCLS)
TxTyU .... University of Texas at Tyler, Tyler, TX [*Library symbol*] [*Library of Congress*] (LCLS)
TXU .... Tabou [*Ivory Coast*] [*Airport symbol*] (OAG)
txu .... Texas [*MARC country of publication code Library of Congress*] (LCCP)
TXU .... Texas Utilities [*NYSE symbol*] (TTSB)
TXU .... Texas Utilities Co. [*NYSE symbol*] (SPSG)
TXU .... Texoro Resources Ltd. [*Vancouver Stock Exchange symbol*]
TXU .... University of Texas at El Paso, El Paso, TX [*OCLC symbol*] (OCLC)
TxU .... University of Texas, Austin, TX [*Library symbol Library of Congress*] (LCLS)
TxU-A .... University of Texas, M. D. Anderson Hospital and Tumor Institute, Houston, TX [*Library symbol Library of Congress*] (LCLS)
TxU-B .... University of Texas, Business Administration and Economics Library, Austin, TX [*Library symbol Library of Congress*] (LCLS)
TxU-D .... University of Texas, School of Dentistry, Houston, TX [*Library symbol Library of Congress*] (LCLS)
TxU-Da .... University of Texas at Dallas, Richardson, TX [*Library symbol Library of Congress*] (LCLS)
TxU-GP .... University of Texas, Austin, Institute of Geo-Physics, Austin, TX [*Library symbol*] [*Library of Congress*] (LCLS)

TxU-Hu .... Humanities Research Center, University of Texas, Austin, TX [*Library symbol Library of Congress*] (LCLS)
TxU-J .... University of Texas, Lyndon Baines Johnson Presidential Library, Austin, TX [*Library symbol Library of Congress*] (LCLS)
TxU-L .... University of Texas, Law Library, Austin, TX [*Library symbol Library of Congress*] (LCLS)
TxU-LS .... University of Texas at Austin, Graduate School of Library and Information Science, Austin, TX [*Library symbol*] [*Library of Congress*] (LCLS)
TxU-M .... University of Texas, Medical School, Galveston, TX [*Library symbol Library of Congress*] (LCLS)
TxU-O .... University of Texas of the Permian Basin, Odessa, TX [*Library symbol Library of Congress*] (LCLS)
TxU-PH .... University of Texas, School of Public Health, Houston, TX [*Library symbol Library of Congress*] (LCLS)
TxU-STM .... University of Texas Medical School at San Antonio, San Antonio, TX [*Library symbol Library of Congress*] (LCLS)
TxUtEl .... Texas Utilities Electric [*Associated Press*] (SAG)
TxUtEl .... TU Electric Capital I [*Associated Press*] (SAG)
TxUtEl .... TU Electric Capital II [*Associated Press*] (SAG)
TxUtEl .... TU Electric Capital III [*Associated Press*] (SAG)
TxUvS .... Southwest Texas Junior College, Uvalde, TX [*Library symbol Library of Congress*] (LCLS)
TXV .... Fairfield, CA [*Location identifier FAA*] (FAAL)
TXV .... Puerto Vallarta Taxi Aereo, SA de CV [*Mexico*] [*FAA designator*] (FAAC)
TXV .... Throttling Expansion Valve [*Automotive air conditioning*]
TXV .... University of Houston, Victoria Center, Victoria, TX [*OCLC symbol*] (OCLC)
TxVeC .... Vernon Regional Junior College, Vernon, TX [*Library symbol Library of Congress*] (LCLS)
TxVi .... Victoria Public Library, Victoria, TX [*Library symbol Library of Congress*] (LCLS)
TxViC .... Victoria College, Victoria, TX [*Library symbol Library of Congress*] (LCLS)
TxVidGS .... Church of Jesus Christ of Latter-Day Saints, Genealogical Society Library, Beaumont Branch, Vidor, TX [*Library symbol Library of Congress*] (LCLS)
TxViHU .... University of Houston, Victoria Center, Victoria, TX [*Library symbol Library of Congress*] (LCLS)
TxW .... Waco-McLennan County Library, Waco, TX [*Library symbol Library of Congress*] (LCLS)
TxWaS .... Southwestern Assemblies of God College, Waxahachie, TX [*Library symbol Library of Congress*] (LCLS)
TxWB .... Baylor University, Waco, TX [*Library symbol Library of Congress*] (LCLS)
TxWB-B .... Baylor University, Armstrong Browning Library, Waco, TX [*Library symbol Library of Congress*] (LCLS)
TxWB-L .... Baylor University, Law School Library, Waco, TX [*Library symbol Library of Congress*] (LCLS)
TxWB-Mus .... Baylor University, Museum Collection, Waco, TX [*Library symbol Library of Congress*] (LCLS)
TxWB-N .... Baylor University School of Nursing, Dallas, TX [*Library symbol*] [*Library of Congress*] (LCLS)
TxWeaC .... Weatherford College, Weatherford, TX [*Library symbol Library of Congress*] (LCLS)
TxWeiM .... Weimar Mercury, Weimar, TX [*Library symbol Library of Congress*] (LCLS)
TxWFM .... Masonic Grand Lodge of Texas, Waco, TX [*Library symbol Library of Congress*] (LCLS)
TxWhaC .... Wharton County Junior College, Wharton, TX [*Library symbol Library of Congress*] (LCLS)
TxWhaW .... Wharton County Library, Wharton, TX [*Library symbol Library of Congress*] (LCLS)
TxWic .... Kemp Public Library, Wichita Falls, TX [*Library symbol Library of Congress*] (LCLS)
TxWicM .... Midwestern State University, Wichita Falls, TX [*Library symbol Library of Congress*] (LCLS)
TxWM .... McClennan Community College, Waco, TX [*Library symbol Library of Congress*] (LCLS)
TxWPQ .... Paul Quinn College, Waco, TX [*Library symbol Library of Congress*] (LCLS)
TxWV .... United States Veterans Administration Hospital, Waco, TX [*Library symbol Library of Congress*] (LCLS)
TXX .... Southwestern University, Georgetown, TX [*OCLC symbol*] (OCLC)
TY .... Air Caledonie [*ICAO designator*] (AD)
TY .... Benin [*Aircraft nationality and registration mark*] (FAAC)
TY .... Talmud Yerushalmi (BJA)
TY .... Target Year
TY .... Tax Year
TY .... Tebul [*or Tevul*] Yom (BJA)
TY .... Teletypewriter [*Telecommunications*] (IAA)
Ty .... Temporary
TY .... Territorial Yeomanry [*British military*] (DMA)
TY .... Territory
Ty .... Territory (ODBW)
TY .... Thank You
Ty .... Thyroxine [*Also, T4, Thx*] [*An amino acid Endocrinology*]
TY .... Total Yield (AABC)
TY .... Translation Hand Controller Y-Axis Direction (MCD)
TY .... Transposon Yeast [*Genetics*]
TY .... Tri-Continental [*NYSE symbol*] (TTSB)
TY .... Tri-Continental Corp. [*NYSE symbol*] (SPSG)
TY .... Truly
Ty .... Tyndale New Testament Commentaries [*A publication*] (BJA)
TY .... Type
TY .... Typhoid Fever (DSUE)
TYA .... Tygas Resources Corp. [*Vancouver Stock Exchange symbol*]
TYA .... Yalova [*Turkey*] [*Airport symbol*] (AD)
TYAA .... Textured Yarn Association of America (EA)
TYB .... Tibooburra [*New South Wales*] [*Airport symbol*] (AD)
TYC .... Thames Yacht Club [*Later, RTYC*] [*British*] (DI)
TYC .... Toby Creek Resources Ltd. [*Vancouver Stock Exchange symbol*]
TYC .... Trinity College, Hartford, CT [*OCLC symbol*] (OCLC)
TYC .... Two-Year[*-Old*] Course [*Horse racing*]
TYC .... Tyco International [*NYSE symbol*] (SPSG)
TYC .... Tylerdale Connecting [*AAR code*]
T-YCDT .... Ten-Year Chinese Dong Tang [*Turmoil*] Cycle [*Reference to the Kuomintang's defeat in 1946-48, Mao's Great Leap Forward in 1956, the Cultural Revolution in 1966, the Gang of Four's fall in 1976*] [*Term coined by William Safire*]
TYCO .... Tylenol [*McNeil Consumer Products Co.*] (DAVI)
TYCO .... Tylenol and Codeine [*Pharmacy*]
TycoInt .... Tyco International [*Associated Press*] (SAG)
TYCOM .... Type Commander
TYCOMSLANT... Type Commands, Atlantic (DNAB)
TYCOMSPAC... Type Commands, Pacific (DNAB)
TycoT .... Tyco Toys [*Associated Press*] (SAG)
TycoToy .... Tyco Toys, Inc. [*Associated Press*] (SAG)
TYD .... Temporary Duty (MCD)
tyd .... Type Designer [*MARC relator code*] [*Library of Congress*] (LCCP)
TYDAC .... Typical Digital Automatic Computer
TYDE .... Type Designators (MSA)
TYDV .... Tobacco Yellow Dwarf Virus [*Plant pathology*]
TYE .... Tyee Airways Ltd. [*Canada ICAO designator*] (FAAC)
TYE .... Tye Explorations, Inc. [*Vancouver Stock Exchange symbol*]
TYE .... Tyonek, AK [*Location identifier FAA*] (FAAL)
TYF .... Panama City, FL [*Location identifier FAA*] (FAAL)
TYF .... Tung Yeun Feng [*Republic of China*] [*Seismograph station code, US Geological Survey*] (SEIS)
TYFC .... Tysons Financial [*NASDAQ symbol*] (TTSB)
TYFSOK .... Thank You for Shopping Our K-Mart [*or Kresge's*] [*Slogan of K-Mart Corp.*]
TYG .... Temple Youth Group [*Local groups of National Federation of Temple Youth, sometimes called TYG-ers, pronounced "tigers"*]
TYG .... Trypticase, Yeast-Extract, Glucose [*Cell growth medium*]
tyg .... Typographer [*MARC relator code*] [*Library of Congress*] (LCCP)
TYGN .... Tylan General [*NASDAQ symbol*] (TTSB)
TYGN .... Tylan General, Inc. [*NASDAQ symbol*] (SAG)
TYH .... Tihany [*Hungary*] [*Geomagnetic observatory code*]
TYI .... Rocky Mount, NC [*Location identifier FAA*] (FAAL)
TYJ .... Tyrolean Jet Service [*Austria ICAO designator*] (FAAC)
TYK .... Toyooka [*Japan*] [*Seismograph station code, US Geological Survey*] (SEIS)
TYL .... Talara [*Peru*] [*Airport symbol*] (OAG)
TYL .... TANU [*Tanganyika African National Union*] Youth League [*Tanganyika*]
tyl .... Tylenol [*McNeil Consumer Products Co.*] (DAVI)
TYL .... Tyler [*Diocesan abbreviation*] [*Texas*] (TOCD)
TYL .... Tyler Corp. [*NYSE symbol*] (SPSG)
Tyl .... Tyler's Vermont Supreme Court Reports [*1800-03*] [*A publication*] (DLA)
Tyl .... Tyloma [*Also called a callus*] [*Orthopedics*] (DAVI)
TylanG .... Tylan General, Inc. [*Associated Press*] (SAG)
Tyl Boun .... Tyler on Boundaries, Fences, Etc. [*A publication*] (DLA)
TYLC .... Tomato Yellow Leaf Curl [*Plant pathology*]
TYLCV .... Tomato Yellow Leaf Curl Virus
Tyl Eccl L .... Tyler's American Ecclesiastical Law [*A publication*] (DLA)
Tyl Eject .... Tyler on Ejectment and Adverse Enjoyment [*A publication*] (DLA)
Tyler .... Tyler Corp. [*Associated Press*] (SAG)
Tyler .... Tyler's Vermont Reports [*1800-03*] [*A publication*] (DLA)
Tyler Ej .... Tyler on Ejectment and Adverse Enjoyment [*A publication*] (DLA)
Tyler Steph Pl... Tyler's Edition of Stephen on Principles of Pleading [*A publication*] (DLA)
Tyl Fix .... Tyler on Fixtures [*A publication*] (DLA)
Tyl Inf .... Tyler on Infancy and Coverture [*A publication*] (DLA)
Tyl Part .... Tyler on Partnership [*A publication*] (DLA)
Tyl St Pl .... Tyler's Edition of Stephen on the Principles of Pleading [*A publication*] (DLA)
Tyl Us .... Tyler on Usury, Pawns, and Loans [*A publication*] (DLA)
TYM .... Tyumen Airlines [*Russian Federation*] [*ICAO designator*] (FAAC)
TYME-GRAM... Tymnet Telegram (NITA)
TYMNET .... Timeshare, Inc. Network [*Telecommunications*] (TEL)
Tymp .... Tympanicity [*Referring to auscultation of the chest*] [*Medicine*] (DAVI)
tymp .... Tympanium (VRA)
tymp .... Tympanostomy [*Otorhinolaryngology*] (DAVI)
tymp .... Tympany
Tymp Mem... Tympanic Membrane [*Anatomy*] (CPH)
tymp memb... Tympanic Membrane [*Otorhinolaryngology*] (DAVI)
TYMV .... Turnip Yellow Mosaic Virus
TYN .... Taiyuan [*China*] [*Airport symbol*] (OAG)
TYN .... Taiyuan [*China*] [*Seismograph station code, US Geological Survey*] (SEIS)
TYN .... Taywin Resources Ltd. [*Vancouver Stock Exchange symbol*]
TyndHB .... Tyndale House Bulletin [*Cambridge*] [*A publication*] (BJA)
Tyng .... Tyng's Reports [*2-17 Massachusetts*] [*A publication*] (DLA)
TYO .... Tokyo [*Japan*] [*Airport symbol*] (OAG)
TYO .... Two-Year-Old [*Horse racing*] (ROG)
TYOG .... Take Your Own Gadgets
TYP .... Transitional Year Program [*Brandeis University*] (EA)

TY-P............ Trial Y-Plane
Typ............ Typed (BJA)
TYP............ Typical (AAG)
TYP............ Typography [*or Typographer*] (AAG)
TYP............ [*The*] Youth Project (EA)
typ cons...... Typus Conservandus [*Conserved Type*] [*Latin*]
TYPER......... Typographical Error (AAG)
TYP-H.......... Typhoid H [*Infectious diseases*] (DAVI)
TYPH........... Typhoon
TYPL............ Type-Plate
TYPNO......... Teletypewriter Communications out of Service (FAAC)
Typo............ Typographed [*Philately*]
TYPO........... Typographical
TYPO........... Typographical Error (NTCM)
TYPOE......... Ten Year Plan for Ocean Exploration [*National Council on Marine Resources and Engineering Development*] (MSC)
TYPOG......... Typographer [*or Typography*]
typogr.......... Typography (VRA)
TYPOK......... Teletypewriter Communications Returned to Service (FAAC)
TYPOUT....... Typewriter Output
TYPr............ Tri-Continental, $2.50 Pfd [*NYSE symbol*] (TTSB)
TYPSG......... Typesetting
TYPSTG....... Typesetting (MSA)
TYPW.......... Typewriter (ADA)
TYPWRT...... Typewriter
TYPWRTR.... Typewriter
TYPWRTR.... Typewriter
TYQ............ Indianapolis, IN [*Location identifier FAA*] (FAAL)
TYR............ Tyler [*Texas*] [*Airport symbol*] (OAG)
TYR............ Tyrolean Airways [*Austria ICAO designator*] (FAAC)
TYR............ Tyrone [*County in Ireland*] (ROG)
Tyr............. Tyrone County [*Ireland*] (BARN)
tyr.............. Tyrosine [*An amino acid*] (DOG)
Tyr............. Tyrosine [*Also, Y*] [*An amino acid*]
Tyr............. Tyrwhitt and Granger's English Exchequer Reports [*1830-35*] [*A publication*] (DLA)
Tyr & Gr...... Tyrwhitt and Granger's English Exchequer Reports [*1830-35*] [*A publication*] (DLA)
Tyrex.......... Tyrex Oil Co. [*Associated Press*] (SAG)
TyRIA.......... Thyroid Radioisotope Assay (BABM)
Tyrol........... Tyrolean [*or Tirolean*] [*Reference to a state in western Austria*] [*Reference to an alpine region that is divided between Austria and Italy*] (BARN)
TyrRS.......... Tyrosyl-tRNA [*Transfer Ribonucleic Acid*] Synthetase
Tyr Trig....... Tyranni Triginta [*of Scriptores Historiae Augustae*] [*Classical studies*] (OCD)
Tyrw........... Tyrwhitt and Granger's English Exchequer Reports [*1830-35*] [*A publication*] (DLA)
Tyrw & G..... Tyrwhitt and Granger's English Exchequer Reports [*1835-36*] [*A publication*] (DLA)
Tyrw & G (Eng)... Tyrwhitt and Granger's English Exchequer Reports [*1835-36*] [*A publication*] (DLA)
TYRX........... Tyrex Oil [*NASDAQ symbol*] (TTSB)
TYRX........... Tyrex Oil Co. [*NASDAQ symbol*] (NQ)
TYS............ Knoxville [*Tennessee*] [*Airport symbol*] (OAG)
TYS............ McGhee Tyson Airport [*FAA*] (TAG)
TYS............ Tensile Yield Strength
TYS............ Tyler Resources, Inc. [*Toronto Stock Exchange symbol*]
TYS............ Tyseley [*British depot code*]
TYS............ Tyson Valley [*Missouri*] [*Seismograph station code, US Geological Survey*] (SEIS)
TYSD.......... Total Years Service Date
TYSN.......... Tyson Foods, Inc. [*NASDAQ symbol*] (NQ)
TYSNA........ Tyson Foods Cl'A' [*NASDAQ symbol*] (TTSB)
Tyson.......... Tyson Foods, Inc. [*Associated Press*] (SAG)
TYSP.......... Tibetan Youth Sponsorship Programs (EA)
TYT............ Nantucket, MA [*Location identifier FAA*] (FAAL)
TYT............ Type Training [*Navy*] (NVT)
TYTIPT........ Type Training in Port [*Navy*] (NVT)
Tytler Mil Law... Tytler on Military Law and Courts-Martial [*A publication*] (DLA)
Tyt Mil L...... Tytler on Military Law and Courts-Martial [*3rd ed.*] [*1812*] [*A publication*] (DLA)
TYTV........... Tomato Yellow Top Virus
TYU............ Tyuratam [*Satellite launch complex*] [*Former USSR*]
TYV............ Little Rock, AR [*Location identifier FAA*] (FAAL)
TYV............ Turnip Yellows Virus [*Plant pathology*]
TYVM.......... Thank You Very Much
TYW........... Taiwan Equity Fd [*NYSE symbol*] (TTSB)
TYW........... Taiwan Equity Fund, Inc. [*NYSE symbol*] (SAG)
TYX............ Tylox Resources Corp. [*Vancouver Stock Exchange symbol*]
TYY............ Abilene, TX [*Location identifier FAA*] (FAAL)
TYZ............ Taylor [*Arizona*] [*Airport symbol Obsolete*] (OAG)
TZ.............. American Trans Air [*ICAO designator*] (AD)
TZ.............. Der Treue Zionswaechter [*Altona*] [*A publication*] (BJA)
TZ.............. Mali [*International civil aircraft marking*] (ODBW)
TZ.............. Tactical Zone [*Military*] (AABC)
tz............... Tanzania [*MARC country of publication code Library of Congress*] (LCCP)
TZ.............. Terrazo [*Technical drawings*]
TZ.............. Tidal Zone
TZ.............. Time Zero
TZ.............. Transition Zone [*in plant growth*] [*Botany*]
TZ.............. Translation Hand Controller Z-Axis Direction (NASA)
TZ.............. Transmitter Zone [*Telecommunications*] (TEL)
TZ.............. Transportation Zone [*Department of Transportation*]
TZ.............. Treatment Zone (GNE)
TZ.............. Trennzahl Values [*For carrier gas flow rates*] [*Chromatography*]
TZ.............. Tropical Zodiac
TZ.............. Tuberculin Zymoplastiche [*Medicine*] (MAE)
TZ.............. Tubolare Zagato [*Automotive model designation*] [*Alfa-Romeo*]
TZ.............. [*The*] Twilight Zone [*Television program created by Rod Serling*]
TZ.............. Twilight-Zoner [*Undecided voter*] [*Political slang*]
TZ.............. United Republic of Tanzania [*ANSI two-letter standard code*] (CNC)
TZA............ United Republic of Tanzania [*ANSI three-letter standard code*] (CNC)
TZC............ Tetrazolium Chloride Agar [*Biological stain*]
TZC............ Trizec Corp. Ltd. [*Toronto Stock Exchange symbol*]
TZC.WS....... Trizec Corp. Ltd'A'Wrrt [*NYSE symbol*] (TTSB)
TZD............ True Zenith Distance [*Navigation*]
TZE............ Topaz Exploration Ltd. [*Vancouver Stock Exchange symbol*]
TZE............ Transfer on Zero
TZG............ Thermofit Zap Gun
TZG............ Waha Leaf [*British Honduras*] [*Airport symbol*] (AD)
TZH............ Trizec Hahn Corp. [*NYSE symbol*] (SAG)
TZJ............ Tubular Zippered Jacket
TZK............ Tajikistan [*ICAO designator*] (FAAC)
TZM............ Titanium-Zirconium-Molybdenum [*Alloy*]
TZN............ South Andros [*Bahamas*] [*Airport symbol*] (OAG)
TZN............ Tchaikazan Enterprises, Inc. [*Vancouver Stock Exchange symbol*]
Tzn............ Total Estrogens After Zinc and Hydrochloric Acid [*Zn-HCl Treatment*] [*Laboratory*] (DAVI)
TZO............ Thorne-Zytkow Object [*Astronomy*]
TZP............ Temperate Zone Phase
TZP............ Time Zero Pulse
TZP............ Triazolopyridazine [*Potential antianxiety drug*]
TZR............ Tanzania-Zambia Railway (PDAA)
TZR............ Torrez Resources Ltd. [*Vancouver Stock Exchange symbol*]
TZS............ Technologie Zentrum Steyr [*Steyr Technology Center*] [*German*]
TZT............ Triazinate [*Antineoplastic drug*] (CDI)
TZTh.......... Tuebinger Zeitschrift fuer Theologie [*A publication*] (BJA)
TZV............ Tetrazolium Violet [*Also, TV*]
TZX............ Trabzon [*Turkey*] [*Airport symbol*] (OAG)
TZY............ Warsaw, IN [*Location identifier FAA*] (FAAL)
TZZ............ Tabubil [*Papua New Guinea*] [*Seismograph station code, US Geological Survey*] (SEIS)

U
By Acronym

U .... Asymmetrical [*Chemistry*] (BARN)
U/ .... At the Umbilicus [*Obstetrics*] (DAVI)
U .... Audio and Power Connectors [*JETDS nomenclature*] [*Military*] (CET)
u----- .... Australasia [*MARC geographic area code Library of Congress*] (LCCP)
U .... Benzon [*Denmark*] [*Research code symbol*]
U .... Eased Up [*Horse racing*]
U .... Eaton Laboratories, Inc. [*Research code symbol*]
U .... Electric Tension [*Symbol*] [*IUPAC*]
u .... Group Velocity [*Symbol*] (DEN)
U .... Heat Transfer Coefficient (BARN)
U .... Internal Energy [*Symbol*] [*Thermodynamics*]
U .... International Unit [*of enzyme activity*] (DAVI)
U .... Intrinsic Energy [*Symbol*] [*Physics*]
u .... Micro (IDOE)
u .... Micron (DAVI)
U .... Potential Difference [*in Volts*] (DMAA)
U .... Quartermon Versor [*Symbol of a function*] [*Mathematics*] (ROG)
U .... Shape Descriptor [*U-turn, for example. The shape resembles the letter for which it is named*]
U .... Thermal Transmittance per Unit of Area [*Heat transmission symbol*]
U .... Uafhaengige Parti [*Independent Party*] [*Denmark Political party*] (PPE)
U .... Ubiquinone [*Coenzyme Q*] [*Also, CoQ, Q, UQ*] [*Biochemistry*]
u .... Uebersetzen [*Translate*] [*German*]
U .... Ugly Sky [*Navigation*]
U .... Ugly Threatening Weather [*Meteorology*]
U .... Ugutio [*Huguccio*] [*Deceased, 1210*] [*Authority cited in pre-1607 legal work*] (DSA)
U .... Uhr [*Clock*] [*German*]
U .... Ullage (AAG)
U .... Ultra High Frequency [*Also, UHF*] (DOAD)
U .... Ultralente Insulin [*Pharmacology*] (DAVI)
U .... Ultraphon & Supraphon [*Record label*] [*Former Czechoslovakia*]
U .... Umpire [*Baseball*]
U .... Unbalanced
U .... Unburned [*Ecology*]
U .... Uncirculated
U .... Unclassified
U .... Uncle
U .... Uncle [*Phonetic alphabet*] [*Royal Navy World War I Pre-World War II*] [*World War II*] (DSUE)
U .... Uncommon Species
U .... Und [*And*] [*German*]
U .... Undefined (IAA)
u .... Undelete [*Computer science*] [*Telecommunications*]
U .... Under
U .... Underfloor (NASA)
U .... Underwater [*Missile launch environment symbol*]
U .... Unemployed Parent [*Aid to Families with Dependent Children*] (OICC)
U .... Unemployment
U .... Unerupted (MAE)
U .... Unified
U .... Unified Atomic Mass [*Physics*] (WDAA)
U .... Unified Atomic Mass Unit [*Nuclear energy*] (IAA)
u .... Unified Atomic Mass Unit (IDOE)
U .... Uniform
U .... Uniform [*Phonetic alphabet*] [*International*] (DSUE)
U .... Uniformly Labeled [*Also, UL*] [*Compound, with radioisotope*]
U .... Union [*or Unionist*]
U .... Union Association [*Major league in baseball, 1884*]
U .... Unionist Party [*Northern Ireland*] [*Political party*]
U .... Union of Sets (IDOE)
U .... Unit
U .... United
U .... United States Air Group [*NYSE symbol*] (SAG)
U .... Unit of Measure (IAA)
U .... Universal
U .... Universal Set (IDOE)
U .... Universal/Unrestricted [*Film certificate*] [*British*]
U .... Universe (MHDB)
U .... University
U .... Unknown
U .... Unlicensed (DA)
U .... Unlimited Time [*Broadcasting term*]
U .... Unnumbered Acknowledge [*or Acknowledgement*] [*Telecommunications*] (IAA)
U .... Unoccupied
u .... Unpaved Surface [*Aviation*] (DA)
U .... Unpleasant
U .... Unseated Rider [*Horse racing*]
U .... Unsubscribe [*Computer science*] [*Telecommunications*]
U .... Unsymmetrical
U .... Unter [*Among*] [*German*]
U .... Until (DA)
U .... Untreated [*Medicine*]
U .... Unwatched [*With reference to a light*] [*Maps and charts*]
U .... Up [*or Upper*]
U .... Update [*Computer science*]
U .... Upjohn Co. [*Research code symbol*]
U .... Upper (ROG)
U .... Upper Bow [*Music*] (ROG)
U .... Upper-Class Speech [*"Non-U" designates the opposite*]
U .... Upper School [*British*]
u .... Up (quark) [*Atomic physics*]
U .... Upstage (WDMC)
U .... Uracil [*Biochemistry*] (MAE)
U .... Uranium [*Chemical element*]
U .... Urban [*District Council*] [*British*]
U .... Urban Association [*Baseball*]
U .... Urgent
U .... Uridine [*One-letter symbol; see Urd*]
U .... Urinal (ROG)
U .... Urinate [*or Urine*] [*Medicine*]
U .... Urine (DAVI)
U .... Urological Surgery [*Medical specialty*] (DHSM)
U .... Urologist (DAVI)
U .... Urology (DAVI)
U .... Urology [*Medical Officer designation*] [*British*]
U .... Urschrift [*Original, as of a document*] [*German military*]
U .... Uruguay [*IYRU nationality code*]
U .... USAIR Group [*NYSE symbol*] (SPSG)
U .... Use
U .... Utah
U .... Utah Reports [*A publication*] (DLA)
U .... Utah State Library, Salt Lake City, UT [*Library symbol Library of Congress*] (LCLS)
U .... Utendus [*To Be Used*] [*Pharmacy*]
U .... Utility [*Designation for all US military aircraft*]
U .... UTVA Aircraft Factory [*Former Yugoslavia*] [*ICAO aircraft manufacturer identifier*] (ICAO)
U .... U-Wave [*on electrocardiogram*] [*Cardiology*] (DAVI)
U/1 .... One Finger Breadth below the Umbilicus [*Obstetrics*] (DAVI)
U^2 .... Unclassified, Unlimited [*DoD*]
U/3 .... Upper Third [*Referring to long bones*] [*Medicine*] (DAVI)
U24H .... Twenty-Four-Hour Urine [*Urology*] (DAVI)
U-233 .... Uranium-233
U-234 .... Uranium-234
U-235 .... Uranium-235
U-236 .... Uranium-236
U-238 .... Uranium-238
UA .... Ukrainian Soviet Socialist Republic [*ISO two-letter standard code*] (CNC)
UA .... Ultra-Audible
UA .... Umbilical Artery [*Anatomy*]
UA .... Unable to Approve Arrival for the Time Specified [*Aviation*] (FAAC)
UA .... Unaggregated (MAE)
UA .... Unanesthetized [*Physiology*]
UA .... Unassigned [*Telecommunications*] (IAA)
UA .... Unauthorized Absence (MUGU)
UA .... Unavailable
UA .... Unbleached Arnold [*Paper*] (DGA)
UA .... Unburned plus Ash [*Ecology*]
UA .... Uncertain About (DAVI)
UA .... Und Andere [*And Others*] [*German*]
UA .... Under Age [*i.e., entitled neither to a daily rum ration nor money instead*] [*See also G, T*] [*Obsolete*] [*Navy*] [*British*]
U/A .... Under Agreement [*Legal term*] (DLA)
UA .... Understanding Aging (EA)
UA .... Underwater Actuator

UA............... Underwater Association for Scientific Research [*Margate, Kent, England*] [*Defunct*] (EAIO)
U/A.............. Underwriting Account [*Insurance*]
UA............... Unidad Alavesa [*Spain Political party*] (EY)
UA............... Uniform Allowance [*Military*]
UA............... Unionamerica Hldgs ADS [*NYSE symbol*] (TTSB)
UA............... Unionamerica Holdings PLC [*NYSE symbol*] (SAG)
UA............... Union Association [*Major league in baseball, 1884*]
UA............... Union des Artistes [*Union of Artists*] [*Canada*]
UA............... Unit Assets [*Army*]
UA............... United (GAVI)
UA............... United Air Lines, Inc. [*ICAO designator*]
ua............... United Arab Republic [*Egypt*] [*MARC country of publication code Library of Congress*] (LCCP)
UA............... United Artists Communications, Inc.
UA............... United Association of Journeymen and Apprentices of the Plumbing and Pipe Fitting Industry of the United States and Canada (OICC)
UA............... United Society of Artists [*British*] (BI)
UA............... Unit First Appearance (SAA)
U/A.............. Unit of Account [*European Monetary Agreement*] (EY)
U_a............... Unit of Activity (IDOE)
U/A.............. Units per Application (DNAB)
UA............... University of Akron [*Ohio*] (PDAA)
UA............... University of Alaska [*Anchorage, AK*]
UA............... University of Arizona [*Tucson, AZ*]
UA............... University of Auckland [*New Zealand*]
UA............... Unnumbered Acknowledge [*or Acknowledgment*] [*Telecommunications*] (IEEE)
UA............... Unstable Angina [*Medicine*]
UA............... Until Advised (DA)
UA............... Upper Arm
UA............... Uranyl Ammonium Phosphate [*Inorganic chemistry*] (SAA)
UA............... Urban Area (NTCM)
UA............... Urbanized Area (OICC)
UA............... Uric Acid
UA............... Urinalysis [*Medicine*] (KSC)
UA............... Urinary Basement Membrane Antigen [*Immunology*] (DAVI)
UA............... Urocanic Acid [*Organic chemistry*] (AAMN)
UA............... Urostomy Association [*British*] (DBA)
UA............... User Agency
UA............... User Agent [*Telecommunications*] (PCM)
UA............... User Area [*Information storage*]
UA............... Usque Ad [*As Far As*] [*Latin*] (ADA)
UA............... Uterine Aspiration [*Medicine*]
UAA............. Uas-One [*British ICAO designator*] (FAAC)
UAA............. Undergarment Accessories Association (EA)
UAA............. Uniform Adoption Act [*Proposed state law*]
UAA............. Union des Avocats Arabes [*Arab Lawyers Union - ALU*] (EAIO)
UAA............. United Action for Animals (EA)
UAA............. United African Appeal (EA)
UAA............. United American and Australasian Film Productions
UAA............. United Arab Airlines
UAA............. University Athletic Association (EA)
UAA............. University Aviation Association (EA)
UAA............. University of Alaska, Anchorage
UAA............. Upper Advisory Area [*Aviation*] (DA)
UAA............. Uracil Adenine Adenine [*Genetics*]
UAA............. Urban Affairs Association (EA)
UAA............. User Action Analyzer
UAA............. Utility Arborist Association (EA)
UAAA........... Alma-Ata [*Former USSR ICAO location identifier*] (ICLI)
UAAF........... United Action Armed Forces [*A publication*]
UAAN........... Uzunagach [*Former USSR ICAO location identifier*] (ICLI)
UAAPU......... Under Armor Auxiliary Power Unit [*US Army tanks*] (RDA)
UAAR........... United Activists for Animal Rights (EA)
UAAS........... Ukrainian Academy of Arts and Sciences in the US (EA)
UAAS........... Union Africaine des Artistes de Spectacle [*Union of African Performing Artists - UAPA*] (EAIO)
UAAUSA....... Ukrainian Artists Association in USA (EA)
UAB............. Underwriters Adjustment Bureau
UAB............. Unemployment Assistance Board
UAB............. University Appointments Board [*British*] (DAS)
UAB............. University of Alabama in Birmingham
UAB............. University of Alberta Biotron [*University of Alberta*] [*Research center*] (RCD)
UABS........... Union of American Biological Societies (BARN)
u-ac--........... Ashmore and Cartier Islands [*MARC geographic area code Library of Congress*] (LCCP)
UAC............. Umbilical Artery Catheter [*Neonatology*] (DAVI)
UAC............. Underwriters Adjusting Company
UAC............. Unified Arab Command (BJA)
UAC............. Uniform Annual Cost
UAC............. Uninterrupted Automatic Control
UAC............. Union Army of Commemoration
UAC............. United African Co.
UAC............. United Air Charters [*Zimbabwe*] [*ICAO designator*] (FAAC)
UAC............. United Aircraft Corp. [*Later, United Technologies Corp.*]
UAC............. United American Croats
UAC............. United Association of Coremakers [*A union*] [*British*]
UAC............. Universal Airline Codes
UAC............. Universal Area Code [*Bureau of Census*]
UAC............. Universities Advisory Council
UAC............. University Analytical Center [*University of Arizona*] [*Research center*] (RCD)
UAC............. University of Alberta, Faculty of Library Science, Edmonton, AL, Canada [*OCLC symbol*] (OCLC)
UAC............. Unusual Appearing Child [*Medicine*]
UAC............. Upper Air Control (IAA)
UAC............. Upper Area Control Center [*Aviation*]
UAC............. Uric Acid (DAVI)
UA/C........... Uric Acid-Creatinine Ratio [*Physiology*] (MAH)
UAC............. User Advisory Committee [*Environmental Protection Agency*] (GFGA)
UAC............. Utah Administrative Code [*A publication*] (AAGC)
UAC............. Utility Airplane Company [*Army*] (VNW)
UAC............. Utility Airplane Council [*Defunct*] (EA)
UAC............. Utility Assemble Communication Pool (IAA)
UAC............. Utility Assemble Compool
UACA........... Union Acceptance'A' [*NASDAQ symbol*] (TTSB)
UACA........... Union Acceptance Corp. Class A [*NASDAQ symbol*] (SAG)
UACA........... United American Contractors Association (EA)
UACANT....... Union of Australian College Academics Northern Territory
UACASA....... Union of Australian College Academics South Australia
UACC........... Universal Autograph Collectors Club (EA)
UACC........... Upper Area Control Center [*Aviation*]
UACCDD...... University Affiliated Cincinnati Center for Developmental Disorders [*University of Cincinnati*] [*Research center*] (RCD)
UACCI.......... United Association of Christian Counselors International (EA)
UACES......... University Association for Contemporary European Studies [*British*]
UACL........... United Aircraft of Canada Ltd.
UACMC........ Union Arabe de Ciment et des Materiaux de Construction [*Arab Union for Cement and Building Materials - AUCBM*] (EAIO)
UACN........... Unified Automated Communication Network
UACN........... University of Alaska Computer Network [*Research center*] (RCD)
UACNPM...... United American and Captive Nations Patriotic Movement (EA)
UACRL......... United Aircraft Corp. Research Laboratory (KSC)
UACSC......... United Aircraft Corporate Systems Center (KSC)
UACTA......... United Against Cruelty to Animals [*British*] (DI)
UACTE......... Universal Automatic Control and Test Equipment
UAD............. Salinas, CA [*Location identifier FAA*] (FAAL)
UAD............. Underwater Acoustic Decoupler
UAD............. Undetermined Aerodynamic Disturbance (MCD)
UAD............. Unit Assembly Drawing
UAD............. Univex SRL [*Italy ICAO designator*] (FAAC)
UAD............. Upper Advisory Route [*Aviation*] (DA)
UAD............. Upper-Airway Disease (DAVI)
UAD............. User Attribute Definition [*Computer science*] (IAA)
UADA........... United Abalone Divers' Association [*Australia*]
UADBU......... Unattended Automatic Dial Back Up [*Telecommunications*]
UADC........... Universal Air Data Computer
UADP........... Uniform Automated [*or Automatic*] Data Processing
UADPS......... Uniform Automated [*or Automatic*] Data Processing System
UADPS-ICP... Uniform Automated [*or Automatic*] Data Processing System for Inventory Control Points [*Navy*]
UADPS/INAS... Uniform Automated [*or Automatic*] Data Processing System/ Industrial Naval Air Station
UADPS-SP.... Uniform Automated [*or Automatic*] Data Processing System for Stock Points [*Navy*]
UADS........... User Attribute Data Set [*Computer science*] (MDG)
UADV........... University of Alberta Devonian Botanic Garden [*Canada*]
UADW.......... Universal Alliance of Diamond Workers [*See also AUOD*] [*Antwerp, Belgium*] (EAIO)
UAE............. Unilateral Absence of Excretion [*Medicine*]
UAE............. Uninterruptible Application Error [*Computer science*] (CDE)
UAE............. United Arab Emirates [*ICAO designator*] (FAAC)
UAE............. Unrecoverable Application Error [*Computer science*] (PCM)
UAE............. User Agent Entity [*Telecommunications*] (OSI)
UAEDE......... Union des Associations Europeennes des Distributeurs d'Eau [*Union of European Associations of Water Suppliers*] [*Belgium*] (EAIO)
UAEE........... Union des Associations Europeennes d'Etudiants [*Union of European Student Associations*]
UAEM........... Union of Associations of European Meat Meal Producers [*See also UAPEFV*] [*Later, Eurpoean Renderers Association - EURA*] (EAIO)
UA/EM......... University Association for Emergency Medicine (EA)
UAEM........... University Association for Emergency Medicine
UAES........... Utah Agricultural Experiment Station [*Utah State University*] [*Research center*] (RCD)
UAF............. Uganda Air Force (PDAA)
UAF............. Ultimate Asbestos Fibril
UAF............. Unit Authorization File
UAF............. United Arab Emirates Air Force [*ICAO designator*] (FAAC)
UAF............. Universal Active Filter (IAA)
UAF............. University-Affiliated Facility
UAF............. University of Alaska, Fairbanks
UAF............. Upper Atmospheric Facilities Program [*Washington, DC National Science Foundation*] (GRD)
UAFA........... Union of Arab Football Associations (EAIO)
UAFC........... Universal Air Freight Corp.
UAFF........... Frunze [*Former USSR ICAO location identifier*] (ICLI)
UAFMMEEC... Union of Associations of Fish Meal Manufacturers in the EEC (EAIO)
UAF-MR....... University-Affiliated Facility for the Mentally Retarded
UAFRA......... Uniform Aircraft Financial Responsibility Act [*National Conference of Commissioners on Uniform State Laws*]
UAFSC......... Utilization Air Force Specialty Code
UAFS/T........ Universal Aircraft Flight Simulator/Trainer
UAFUR......... Urgent Amplified Failure of Unsatisfactory Report
UAG............. Uas-Two [*British ICAO designator*] (FAAC)
UAG............. Underwater Acoustic Group [*British*]
UAG............. Union of Anarchist Groups [*British*]

UAG .... United Auto Group [*NYSE symbol*] (SAG)
UAG .... Untersuchungen zur Altorientalischen Geschichte [*H. Winckler*] [*A publication*] (BJA)
UAG .... Upper Atmosphere Geophysics (KSC)
UAG .... Uracil Adenine Guanine [*Genetics*]
UAG .... User Advisory Group (RDA)
UAG .... User Advisory Group (EERA)
UAGA .... Uniform Anatomical Gift Act [*For organ donation*]
UAGSA .... University of Adelaide General Staff Association [*Australia*]
UAH .... Ua Huka [*Marquesas Islands*] [*Airport symbol*] (OAG)
UAH .... Union of Arab Historians (EA)
UAH .... United Amer Healthcare [*NYSE symbol*] (TTSB)
UAH .... United American Healthcare Corp. [*NYSE symbol*] (SPSG)
UAH .... University of Alabama in Huntsville
UAHC .... Union of American Hebrew Congregations (EA)
UAHRI .... University of Alabama in Huntsville Research Institute
UAHS .... Ulster Architectural Heritage Society
UAI .... Uni Air SA [*France ICAO designator*] (FAAC)
UAI .... Union Academique Internationale [*International Academic Union - IAU*] (EAIO)
UAI .... Union Astronomique Internationale [*International Astronomical Union - IAU*]
UAI .... Union des Associations Internationales [*Union of International Associations - UIA*] (EAIO)
UAI .... Universal Azimuth Indicator
UAI .... Urban Affairs Institute (EA)
UAI .... Uterine Activity Interval [*Obstetrics*]
UAICC .... Underwater Acoustic Interference Coordinating Committee [*Military*]
UAIDE .... Users of Automatic Information Display Equipment (EA)
UAII .... Chimkent [*Former USSR ICAO location identifier*] (ICLI)
UAIM .... United Andean Indian Mission [*Superseded by Ecuador Concerns Committee*]
UAIMS .... United Aircraft Information Management System
UAirSp .... United Air Specialists, Inc. [*Associated Press*] (SAG)
UAJ .... Uas-Three [*British ICAO designator*] (FAAC)
UAJ .... Union of Arab Jurists [*Baghdad, Iraq*] (EAIO)
UAJAPPFI .... United Association of Journeymen and Apprentices of the Plumbing and Pipe Fitting Industry of the U.S. and Canada (BARN)
UAJG .... Union d'Action des Jeunes de Guinee [*Guinean Union of Youth Action*]
UAK .... Kiev Aviation Plant [*Ukraine*] [*FAA designator*] (FAAC)
UAK .... Narssarssuaq [*Greenland*] [*Airport symbol*] (OAG)
U Akron .... University of Akron (GAGS)
UAL .... UAL Corp. [*NYSE symbol*] (SPSG)
UAL .... Ukrainian American League (EA)
UAL .... Umbilical Artery Line [*Neonatology*] (DAVI)
UAL .... Unit Allowance List (SAA)
UAL .... Unit Area Loading (AAG)
UAL .... Unit Authorization List
UAL .... Unite, Action, Liberation [*Guadeloupe*] [*Political party*] (EY)
UAL .... Unite Arithmetique et Logique [*Arithmetic and Logic Unit - ALU*] [*French*]
UAL .... United Air Lines, Inc. [*ICAO designator*] (FAAC)
UAL .... Universal Airline Codes (MCD)
UAL .... Universal Assembly Language (IAA)
UAL .... Upper Acceptance Limit
UAL .... Urea-Ammonia Liquor
UAL .... User Adaptive Language
UAL .... User Agent Layer [*Telecommunications*] (OSI)
U Ala .... University of Alabama (GAGS)
U Ala (Birm) ... University of Alabama at Birmingham (GAGS)
U Ala (Huntsville) ... University of Alabama at Huntsville (GAGS)
U Alaska .... University of Alaska (GAGS)
UALE .... Universala Artista Ligo de Esperantistoj [*Universal Artist League of Esperantists*] (EAIO)
UALI .... Unit Authorization List Item
UALI .... Universal Automatic LASER Interferometer (DNAB)
UALPrB .... UAL Corp. 12.25% Dep'B'Pfd [*NYSE symbol*] (TTSB)
UAM .... Ultrasonically Assisted Machining [*Manufacturing term*]
UAM .... Und Anderes Mehr [*And So Forth*] [*German*]
UAM .... Underwater-to-Air Missile [*Air Force*]
UAM .... Union Africaine et Malagache [*African and Malagasy Union*] [*Later, Common Afro-Malagasy Organization*]
UAM .... United American Mechanics (EA)
UAM .... United Asset Management Corp. [*NYSE symbol*] (SPSG)
UAM .... United Asset Mgmt [*NYSE symbol*] (TTSB)
UAM .... United States Medical Intelligence and Information Agency, Frederick, MD [*OCLC symbol*] (OCLC)
UAM .... Universidad Autonoma Metropolitana [*Mexico*] (CROSS)
UAM .... Unnormalized Aid Magnitude (SAA)
UAM .... Urban Airshed Model [*Environmental Protection Agency*] (GFGA)
UAMA .... United Arab Muslim Association [*Australia*]
UAMBD .... Union Africaine de Management de Banques pour le Developpement [*African Union of Development Bank Management*] [*Benin*] (EAIO)
UAMBD .... Union Africaine et Mauricienne de Banques pour le Developpement [*African and Mauritian Union of Banks for Development*] [*Benin*] (AF)
UAMC .... Utility Assemble Master Communication (IAA)
UAMC .... Utility Assemble Master Compool
UAMCMDS .... Uniform Ambulatory Medical Case Minimum Data Set [*Department of Health and Human Services*] (GFGA)
UAMCT .... Union of Automobile, Motorcycle, and Cycle Technology
UAMH .... University of Alberta Microfungus Collection and Herbarium [*Canada*]
UAMR .... United Association of Manufacturers' Representatives (EA)
UAMS .... Ukrainian Academy of Medical Sciences (EA)
UAMS .... Upper Atmosphere Mass Spectrometer
UAN .... Aviaton [*Ukraine*] [*FAA designator*] (FAAC)
UAN .... Unidentified Atmospheric Noise (DNAB)
UAN .... Unified Automatic Network [*Telecommunications*] (OA)
UAN .... United Animal Nations (EAIO)
UAN .... Urea-Ammonium Nitrate [*Fertilizer*]
UAN .... Uric Acid Nitrogen
UANAS .... Urea-Ammonium Nitrate Ammonium Sulfate [*Fertilizer*]
UANC .... United African National Congress
UANC .... United African National Council [*Zimbabwe*] [*Political party*] (PPW)
U & C .... Urethral and Cervical [*Medicine*]
U & C .... Usual and Customary
U & L .... Upper and Lower (MSA)
U & LC .... Uppercase and Lowercase [*i.e., capital and small letters*] [*Typography*]
U & M .... Utilization/Reutilization and Marketing [*DoD*]
U & O .... Use and Occupancy [*Real estate*]
U & P .... Uttering and Publishing [*Legal term*]
U & S .... Unified and Specified [*or Strategic*] Command (MCD)
UANM .... United African Nationalist Movement (EA)
UANM .... Universal African Nationalist Movement (EA)
UAO .... Unconventional Aerial Object
UAO .... Und Andere Orte [*And Elsewhere*] [*German*]
UAO .... Unexplained Aerial Object
UAO .... Unilateral Administrative Order
UAO .... Upper-Air Observation (SAA)
UAO .... Upper Airway Obstruction [*Medicine*] (DMAA)
UAOD .... United Ancient Order of Druids [*Freemasonry*] (ROG)
UAOO .... Kzyl-Orda [*Former USSR ICAO location identifier*] (ICLI)
UAP .... UAP, Inc. [*Toronto Stock Exchange symbol*]
UAP .... Ua Pou [*Marquesas Islands*] [*Airport symbol*] (OAG)
UAP .... Ukraine Airtrack [*FAA designator*] (FAAC)
UAP .... Ulnar Anconeal Process
UAP .... Unabhaengige Arbeiterpartei [*Independent Labor Party*] [*Germany Political party*] (PPE)
UAP .... Unidentified Atmospheric Phenomena
UAP .... Union Africaine de Physique [*African Union of Physics - AUP*] (EAIO)
UAP .... Union of American Physicians [*Later, UAPD*] (EA)
UAP .... Unite Australia Party [*Political party*]
UAP .... United Amateur Press (EA)
UAP .... United Australia Party [*Political party*]
UAP .... Universal Availability of Publications [*International Federation of Library Associations*]
UAP .... Universal Availability of Publications
UAP .... University-Affiliated Program
UAP .... Unmanned Airborne Position (MCD)
UAP .... Upper Air Project
UAP .... Upper Arlington Public Library, Upper Arlington, OH [*OCLC symbol*] (OCLC)
UAP .... Upper Atmosphere Phenomena (IAA)
UAP .... Urea-Ammonium Phosphate [*Organic chemistry*]
UAP .... User Area Profile
UAP .... Utility Amphibian Plane [*Navy*]
UAPA .... Union of African Performing Artists [*See also UAAS*] (EAIO)
UAPA .... United Amateur Press Association [*Later, UAP*] (EA)
UAPA .... United American Progress Association (EA)
UAPD .... Union of American Physicians and Dentists (EA)
UAPDU .... User Agent Protocol Data Unit [*Telecommunications*] (OSI)
UAPEFV .... Union des Associations des Producteurs Europeens de Farine de Viande [*Union of Associations of European Meat Meal Producers UAEM*] [*Later, European Renderers Association - EURA*] (EAIO)
UAPPA .... Union of Air Pollution Prevention Associations (EAIO)
UAPRE .... University Association for Professional Radio Education [*Broadcast Education Association*] (NTCM)
UAPT .... United Association for the Protection of Trade [*British*]
UAQ .... San Juan [*Argentina*] [*Airport symbol*] (OAG)
UAQI .... Uniform Air Quality Index [*Environmental Protection Agency*] (GFGA)
UAR .... Underwater Acoustic Resistance
UAR .... Underwater Angle Receptacle
UAR .... Uni Air [*France ICAO designator*] (FAAC)
UAR .... Uniform Airman Record
UAR .... Unit Address Register
UAR .... United Arab Republic [*Egypt and Syria*] [*Obsolete*]
UAR .... Upper Air Route
UAR .... Upper Atmosphere Research
UAR .... Use as Required (MSA)
UARBC .... United Arab Republic Broadcasting Corp. (IAA)
UARC .... University Affiliated Research Centers (AAGC)
UARCEE .... Union des Associations des Riziers de la CEE [*Union of Rice Associations of the EEC*] (ECED)
UARCO .... UARCO, Inc. [*Formerly, United Autographic Register Co.*]
UARDS .... Unexplained Acute Respiratory Distress Syndrome
UAREP .... Universities Associated for Research and Education in Pathology (EA)
UARG .... Utility Air Regulatory Group [*Environmental Protection Agency*] (GFGA)
UARI .... University of Alabama Research Institute (KSC)
U Ariz .... [*The*] University of Arizona (GAGS)
U Ark .... University of Arkansas (GAGS)
UARL .... United Aircraft Research Laboratories
UARP .... Upper Atmospheric Research Program [*NASA*] (PDAA)
UARP .... Upper Atmospheric Research Program [*NASA*] [*Marine science*] (OSRA)
UARR .... Uralsk [*Former USSR ICAO location identifier*] (ICLI)

UARRSI Universal Aerial Refueling Receptacle Slipaway Installation (MCD)
UARS Underwater Acoustic Receiving System [*Navy*] (MCD)
UARS Unmanned Aerial Reconnaissance System (DOMA)
UARS Unmanned Arctic Research Submersible
UARS Upper Atmosphere Research Satellite (MCD)
UART Universal Asynchronous Receiver/Transmitter
U Arts University of the Arts (GAGS)
UARV Unmanned Air Reconnaissance Vehicle (DOMA)
UARZ University of Arizona (PDAA)
UARZ/COM University of Arizona College of Medicine [*Tucson*]
UAS Uas-Four [*British ICAO designator*] (FAAC)
UAS Ulster Archaeological Society
UAS Uniform Accounting System (OICC)
UAS Union of African States
UAS Unit Approval System [*for approval of aircraft materials, parts, and appliances*] [*FAA*]
UAS Unit Assets by State [*Army*]
UAS United Arab States
UAS University Air Squadrons
UAS Unmanned Aerial [*or Aerospace*] Surveillance
UAS Unusual Aerial Sighting (ADA)
UAS Upper Air Space (WDAA)
UAS Upper Atmospheric Sounder
UAS Upstream Activating Sequence [*Genetics*]
UAS Upstream Activation Site [*Genetics*]
UAS Urea-Ammonium Sulfate [*Fertilizer*]
UAS Urgent Action Service International [*British Library*]
UASANSW University Academic Staff Association of New South Wales [*Australia*]
UASB Upflow Anaerobic Sludge Blanket (EERA)
UASE Union of Arab Stock Exchanges
UASI United Air Specialists [*NASDAQ symbol*] (TTSB)
UASI United Air Specialists, Inc. [*NASDAQ symbol*] (SAG)
UASL User Agent Sublayer [*Telecommunications*] (OSI)
UASS Unmanned Aerial Surveillance System (MCD)
UASSS Underwater Acoustic Sound Source System
UAST Universal Association for Speech Tracing [*See also TPA*] (EAIO)
u-at-- Australia [*MARC geographic area code Library of Congress*] (LCCP)
UAT Ultraviolet Acquisition Technique
UAT Under Armor Tow (MCD)
UAT Underway Acceptance Trials (MCD)
UAT Uniform Asymptotic Theory (IAA)
UAT Union Aeromaritime de Transport [*Privately-owned French airline*]
UAT Universal Air Transport [*British*] [*FAA designator*] (FAAC)
UAT Until Advised by the Tower [*Aviation*] (FAAC)
UAT Up as Tolerated [*Medicine*] (DAVI)
UAT Urban Arts Theatre (EA)
UAT User Acceptance Test (MCD)
UATA Aralsk [*Former USSR ICAO location identifier*] (ICLI)
UATC United Artists Theatre Circuit, Inc.
UATE Universal Automatic Test Equipment
UATI Union de Asociaciones Tecnicas Internacionales [*Union of International Engineering Organizations - UIEO*] [*Spanish*] (ASF)
UATI Union des Associations Techniques Internationales [*Union of International Technical Associations - UITA*] (EAIO)
u-at-ne New South Wales [*MARC geographic area code Library of Congress*] (LCCP)
u-at-no Northern Territory [*Australia MARC geographic area code Library of Congress*] (LCCP)
UATP Universal Air Travel Plan [*Commercial airlines credit system*]
u-at-qn Queensland [*MARC geographic area code Library of Congress*] (LCCP)
UATR Chelkar [*Former USSR ICAO location identifier*] (ICLI)
u-at-sa South Australia [*MARC geographic area code Library of Congress*] (LCCP)
UATT Aktyubinsk [*Former USSR ICAO location identifier*] (ICLI)
u-at-tm Tasmania [*MARC geographic area code Library of Congress*] (LCCP)
UATV United Australian Television
u-at-vi Victoria [*MARC geographic area code Library of Congress*] (LCCP)
u-at-we Western Australia [*MARC geographic area code Library of Congress*] (LCCP)
UAU Underwater-to-Air-to-Underwater (IAA)
UAU Universities Athletics Union [*British*]
UAU Uterine Activity Unit [*Medicine*] (DMAA)
UAUM Underwater-to-Air-to-Underwater Missile [*Air Force*]
UAUOC United American Ukrainian Organizations Committee (EA)
UA/USA UNESCO Association/USA (EA)
UAuto Universal Automotive Industries, Inc. [*Associated Press*] (SAG)
UAV Ukrainian American Veterans (EA)
UAV United Aviation Ltd. [*New Zealand*] [*ICAO designator*] (FAAC)
UAV University of the Andes [*Merida*] [*Venezuela*] [*Seismograph station code, US Geological Survey*] (SEIS)
UAV Unmanned Aerial [*or Air*] Vehicle (RDA)
UAVC Univentricular Atrioventricular Connection [*Cardiology*] (DAVI)
UAV-CR Unmanned Aerial Vehicle-Close Range [*Military*]
UAV-SR Unmanned Aerial Vehicle - Short Range (DWSG)
UAW International Union, United Automobile, Aerospace, and Agricultural Implement Workers of America [*Also known as United Auto Workers*] (EA)
UAWB Universal Air Waybill [*Shipping*] (DS)
UAW-CAP United Auto Workers Community Action Program (EA)
UAWFA United Auto Workers, Family Auxiliary (EA)
UAWIU United Allied Workers International Union (EA)
UAWNO Union of Australian Women National Office
UAX Unit Automatic Exchange
UAZ East Hartford, CT [*Location identifier FAA*] (FAAL)
UAZ-EES University of Arizona-Engineering Experiment Station (PDAA)
UB Burma Airways Corp. [*Myanmar*] [*ICAO designator*] (ICDA)
UB Southall [*Postcode*] (ODBW)
Ub Ubertus de Bobio [*Flourished, 1214-37*] [*Authority cited in pre-1607 legal work*] (DSA)
UB Ultimobranchial [*Bodies*] [*Medicine*]
UB Umno Baru [*New Umno*] [*Malaysia*] [*Political party*]
UB Unaccompanied Baggage (MCD)
UB Underwater Battery [*Navy*]
UB Undistributed Budget (MCD)
UB Unemployment Benefits [*Unemployment insurance*] (OICC)
UB Unicbank [*Unique Bank*] [*Hungary*]
UB Uniform Billing
UB Union Bank [*British*] (ROG)
UB Unit Bond (SAA)
UB United Benefice
UB United Biscuits [*Commercial firm*] [*British*]
UB United Brands Co. (MHDW)
UB United Brethren in Christ
UB United Brotherhood [*Also written VC for secrecy*] [*Fenianism*] (ROG)
UB Unna's Boot (MEDA)
UB Unpaid Balance [*Business term*] (MHDB)
UB Upper Bench [*Legal*] [*British*] (ROG)
UB Upper Bound
UB Upper Brace (MCD)
UB Urea Briquettes [*Agronomy*]
UB Usage Block (MSA)
UB User Board (MHDB)
UB Utica-Bend (SAA)
UB Utility Bridge (NASA)
UB1 University of Connecticut, Stamford Branch, Stamford, CT [*OCLC symbol*] (OCLC)
UB2 University of Connecticut, Hartford Branch, West Hartford, CT [*OCLC symbol*] (OCLC)
UB3 University of Connecticut, Southeastern Branch, Groton, CT [*OCLC symbol*] (OCLC)
UB4 University of Connecticut, MBA Library, Hartford, CT [*OCLC symbol*] (OCLC)
UBA Myanmar Airways [*ICAO designator*] (FAAC)
UBA Uberaba [*Brazil*] [*Airport symbol*] (OAG)
UBA Ulan Bator [*Mongolia*] [*Geomagnetic observatory code*]
UBA Ulusal Basin Ajansi [*News agency*] [*Turkey*] (MENA)
UBA Unblocking Acknowledge [*Telecommunications*] (TEL)
UBA Undenatured Bacterial Antigen
UBA Underwater Breathing Apparatus [*Navy*] (CAAL)
UBA Union of Burma Airways
UBA United Baltic Appeal (EA)
UBA United Bank for Africa Ltd.
UBA United Breweries of America (EA)
UBA Universal Ballet Academy [*Washington, DC*]
UBA Universal Beer Agar [*Brewery bacteria culture medium*]
UBAEC Union of Burma Atomic Energy Centre
UBAF Union des Banques Arabes et Francaises [*Union of Arab and French Banks*] [*France*]
Ubal Ubaldus [*Authority cited in pre-1607 legal work*] (DSA)
U Balt University of Baltimore (GAGS)
UBAN Usbancorp, Inc. [*NASDAQ symbol*] (SAG)
UBARI Union of Burma Applied Research Institute
UBAT Ultrasonic Bioassay Tank [*Aerospace*]
UBATS Ultrasonic Bioassay Tank System [*Aerospace*]
UBB Union Bank of Bavaria
UBB Union of Burma Bank (DS)
UBB Universal Building Block
UBBA United Boys' Brigades of America [*Later, BGBA*] (EA)
UBBAWA United Beef Breeders' Association of Western Australia
UBBC Unsaturated (Vitamin) B_{12} Binding Capacity
Ub Bo Ubertus de Bobio [*Flourished, 1214-37*] (DSA)
UBBR University Bureaus of Business Research
UBC Ubiquitin-Conjugating [*Protein*]
UBC Unburned Carbon [*Fuel technology*]
UBC Undeb Bedyddwyr Cymru [*Baptist Union of Wales*] (EAIO)
UBC Uniform Broadband Channel [*Telecommunications*]
UBC Uniform Building Code (NRCH)
UBC United Black Christians (EA)
UBC United Bowhunters of Connecticut
UBC United Brotherhood of Carpenters and Joiners of America (EA)
UBC United Business Communications, Inc. [*Atlanta, GA*] [*Telecommunications*] (TSSD)
UBC Universal Bibliographic Control
UBC Universal Block Channel
UBC Universal Book Code (NITA)
UBC Universal Buffer Controller
UBC University of British Columbia [*Vancouver, BC*]
UBC University of British Columbia Library [*UTLAS symbol*]
UBC Used Beverage Can
UBCA United Black Church Appeal (EA)
UBCD UnionBancorp, Inc. [*NASDAQ symbol*] (SAG)
UBcGS Church of Jesus Christ of Latter-Day Saints, Genealogical Society Library, Brigham City South Branch, Brigham City, UT [*Library symbol Library of Congress*] (LCLS)
UBCHEA United Board for Christian Higher Education in Asia (EA)
UBcI National Indian Training Center, Brigham City, UT [*Library symbol Library of Congress*] (LCLS)
UBCIM Universal Bibliographic Control and International MARC

UBCIM .... Universal Bibliographic Control and International MARC [*IFLA Core Program*]
UBCIO .... University of British Columbia Institute of Oceanography [*Canada*] (MSC)
UBCJ .... United Brotherhood of Carpenters and Joiners of America
UBCL .... Union of Black Clergy and Laity of the Episcopal Church [*Later, UBE*] (EA)
UBCLN .... University of British Columbia. Legal News [*A publication*] (DLA)
UBC Notes ... University of British Columbia. Legal Notes [*A publication*] (DLA)
UBCP .... United Bancorp Ohio [*NASDAQ symbol*] (SAG)
UBcT .... Thiokol Chemical Corp., Utah Division, Brigham City, UT [*Library symbol Library of Congress*] (LCLS)
UBCW .... United Brick and Clay Workers of America [*Later, ABCWIU*] (EA)
UBD .... Bureau of Land Management, Billings, MT [*OCLC symbol*] (OCLC)
UBD .... Union for Liberation and Democracy [*Suriname*] [*Political party*] (EY)
UBD .... Universal Business Directory for the Pacific Islands [*A publication*]
UBD .... Universiti Brunei Darussalam
UBD .... User Brain Damage [*Computer hacker terminology*] (NHD)
UBD .... Utility Binary Dump [*Computer science*]
UBDA .... Uniform Brain Death Act [*National Conference of Commissioners on Uniform State Laws*]
UBDC .... Urban Bikeway Design Collaborative (EA)
UBDd .... You Be Darned [*Bowdlerized version*] (DSUE)
Ub de Bo ..... Ubertus de Bobio [*Flourished, 1214-37*] [*Authority cited in pre-1607 legal work*] (DSA)
UBDI .... Underwater Battery Director Indicator
UBDMA .... United Better Dress Manufacturers Association (EA)
UBE .... Union Bouddhique d'Europe [*Buddhist Union of Europe - BUE*] (EAIO)
UBE .... Union of Black Episcopalians [*Defunct*] (EA)
UBE .... Universal Bus Exercisor (NASA)
UBEA .... United Business Education Association [*Later, NBEA*]
UBeGS .... Church of Jesus Christ of Latter-Day Saints, Genealogical Society Library, Beaver Branch, Beaver, UT [*Library symbol Library of Congress*] (LCLS)
UBF .... Underground Baggage Facility [*Aviation*] (DA)
UBF .... Union Bank of Finland
UBF .... Universal Boss Fitting
UBF .... Universal Buddhist Fellowship (EA)
UBF .... Unknown Black Female (DAVI)
UBF .... Upstream Binding Factor [*Genetics*]
UBF .... Uterine Blood Flow [*Medicine*] (MAE)
UBFA .... United Black Fund of America (EA)
UBFC .... Underwater Battery Fire Control [*Navy*]
UBFCS .... Underwater Battery Fire Control System [*Navy*]
UBG .... Limon [*Honduras*] [*Airport symbol*] (AD)
UBG .... Newberg, OR [*Location identifier FAA*] (FAAL)
UBG .... Ultimobranchial Glands [*Endocrinology*]
UBG .... Underground Building [*National Security Agency*]
UBG .... Urobilinogen [*Medicine*] (MAE)
UBHC .... Unburned Hydrocarbon [*Also, UHC*] [*Fuel technology*]
UBHR .... User Block Handling Routine [*Computer science*] (IBMDP)
UBI .... Buin [*Papua New Guinea*] [*Airport symbol*] (OAG)
UBI .... Ultraviolet Blood Irradiation
UBI .... Understanding British Industry [*An association*] (ODBW)
UBI .... Unibus Interface (IAA)
UBI .... Universal Battlefield Identification
UBI .... Unrelated Business Income (DICI)
UBIC .... Universal Bus Interface Controller (NASA)
UBIP .... Ubiquitous Immunopoietic Polypeptide [*Immunochemistry*]
UBIT .... Unrelated Business Income Tax
UBITA .... Upper Bound of Information Translation Amount (MHDI)
UBITRON ..... Undulating Beam Interaction Electron Tube
UBJ .... Ube [*Japan*] [*Airport symbol*] (OAG)
UBJ .... Upper Ball Joint Suspension [*Automotive engineering*]
UBK .... Port Augusta [*South Australia*] [*Airport symbol*] (AD)
UBK .... Unbleached Kraft [*Pulp and paper processing*]
UBKA .... Universitaetsbibliothek Karlsruhe [*Karlsruhe University Library*] [*Information retrieval*]
UBL .... Unbleached (MSA)
UBL .... Unblocking [*Telecommunications*] (TEL)
UBL .... Undifferentiated B-Cell Lymphoma [*Medicine*]
UBL .... Unit Basic Load [*Army*]
UBL .... United Beverages [*Vancouver Stock Exchange symbol*]
UBLA .... Uniform Bill of Lading Act [*Legal shorthand*] (LWAP)
UBLDP .... Union Belge et Luxembourgeoise de Droit Penal [*Belgian and Luxembourg Association of Penal Law*] (EAIO)
UBLSLJ .... University of Botswana, Lesotho, and Swaziland Law Journal [*A publication*] (DLA)
UBLU .... United Building Labourers' Union [*British*]
UBM .... Ultrasonic Bonding Machine
UBM .... Unit Bill of Material (MHDW)
UBM .... University of Bridgeport, Bridgeport, CT [*OCLC symbol*] (OCLC)
UBM .... Unknown Black Male (DAVI)
UBMT .... United Financial [*NASDAQ symbol*] (TTSB)
UBMT .... United Savings Bank FA [*Great Falls, MT*] [*NASDAQ symbol*] (NQ)
UBMTA .... Uniform Biological Material Transfer Agreement [*National Institutes of Health*]
UBN .... United Business Network [*United Business Communications, Inc.*] [*Atlanta, GA*] [*Telecommunications*] [*Defunct*] (TSSD)
UBN .... United States Bank Note [*Printer of U.S. postage stamps*] (BARN)
UBN .... Universal Broadband Network [*Telecommunications*]
UBNK .... Union Bank [*NASDAQ symbol*] (SPSG)
UBNKZ .... UnionBanCal 8.375% Dep 'A' Pfd [*NASDAQ symbol*] (TTSB)
UBO .... Uinta Basin Array [*Utah*] [*Seismograph station code, US Geological Survey Closed*] (SEIS)
UBO .... Uinta Basin Observatory
UBO .... Undetermined Brain Opacities [*Magnetic Resonance Imaging*] (CPH)
UBO .... Unemployment Benefit Office [*British*]
UBO .... Unidentified Bright Object
UBOA .... United Bus Owners of America (EA)
U-BOOT .... Unterseeboot [*Submarine*] [*German*]
UBOT .... Unfavorable Balance of Trade (MHDW)
UBP .... Ubon Ratchathani [*Thailand*] [*Airport symbol*] (OAG)
UBP .... Ulusal Birlik Partisi [*National Unity Party*] [*Turkish Cyprus*] [*Political party*] (EY)
UBP .... Underwater Battery Plot [*Antisubmarine warfare*]
UBP .... Unit Beat Policing
UBP .... United Bahamian Party [*Political party*] (PPW)
UBP .... United Bermuda Party [*Political party*] (PPW)
UBP .... Upward Bound Programs [*Department of Labor*]
UBP .... Ureteral Back Pressure [*Medicine*] (MAE)
UBPC .... Utility Bill Performance Calculation (AAGC)
U-BPH .... Utah State Library Commission, Division of the Blind and Physically Handicapped,Salt Lake City, UT [*Library symbol Library of Congress*] (LCLS)
UBPLOT .... Underwater Battery Plotting Room [*Navy*] (NVT)
UBPR .... Uniform Bank Performance Report [*Federal Financial Institutions Examination Council*]
UB Pr .... Upper Bench Precedents Tempore Car. I [*A publication*] (DLA)
UBPVLS .... Uniform Boiler and Pressure Vessel Laws Society (EA)
UBR .... Uniform Business Rate [*Taxation*] [*British*]
UBR .... United Bison Resources [*Vancouver Stock Exchange symbol*]
UBR .... University Boat Race [*Cambridge and Oxford*] [*British*] (BARN)
UBR .... University of British Columbia Retrospective Conversion [*UTLAS symbol*]
UBR .... Upper Burma Rulings [*India*] [*A publication*] (DLA)
UBRD .... Usage Based Requirements Determination [*Army*] (DOMA)
UBRF .... Upper Branchial Filament
U Bridgeport ... University of Bridgeport (GAGS)
UBS .... Columbus [*Mississippi*] [*Airport symbol*] (AD)
UBS .... Columbus, MS [*Location identifier FAA*] (FAAL)
UBS .... Uniform Bearing Stress
UBS .... Union Bank of Switzerland
UBS .... Union Broadcasting System [*Fictitious broadcasting organization in film "Network"*]
UBS .... Unit Backspace Character [*Computer science*]
UBS .... Unit-Based Scheme (AIE)
UBS .... United Bible Societies [*Stuttgart, Federal Republic of Germany*] (EA)
UBS .... United Broadcasting System [*Network in TV series "America 2-Night"*]
UBS .... United States Biological Survey [*US Government*] (EERA)
UBS .... Universal Builders Supply Co.
UBS .... University of British Columbia, School of Librarianship, Vancouver, BC, Canada [*OCLC symbol*] (OCLC)
UBS .... U.S. Bioscience [*AMEX symbol*] (TTSB)
UBS .... US Bioscience, Inc. [*AMEX symbol*] (SPSG)
UBSA .... United Business Schools Association [*Later, AICS*] (EA)
UBSC .... Union Bankshares Ltd. [*NASDAQ symbol*] (SAG)
UBSH .... Union Bankshares [*NASDAQ symbol*] (TTSB)
UBSH .... Union Bankshares Corp. [*NASDAQ symbol*] (SAG)
UBSI .... United Bankshares [*NASDAQ symbol*] (TTSB)
UBSI .... United Bankshares, Inc. [*NASDAQ symbol*] (NQ)
UBSO .... Uinta Basin Seismological Observatory
UBST .... Unbonded Spool Type (DNAB)
UBS.WS .... U.S. Bioscience Wrrt [*AMEX symbol*] (TTSB)
UBT .... Ubatuba [*Brazil*] [*Airport symbol Obsolete*] (OAG)
UBT .... Universal Boattail Thor [*NASA*]
UBT .... Universal Book Tester [*Measures performance of binding*]
UB/TIB .... Universitatsbibliothek Hannover und Technische Informationsbibliothek [*University Library of Hannover and Technical Information Library*] [*Information service or system*] (IID)
UBTM .... United Bellows Tankage Module
UBV .... Ultraviolet-Blue-Visual [*Photometric system*]
UBVR .... Ultraviolet-Blue-Visible-Red [*Photometry*]
UBW .... Kuparuk, AK [*Location identifier FAA*] (FAAL)
UBW .... Unbewusste [*Unconscious Mind*] [*Psychology*]
UBW .... University of Connecticut, Waterbury Branch, Waterbury, CT [*OCLC symbol*] (OCLC)
UBWPS .... United Bargemen and Watermen's Protective Society [*A union*] [*British*]
UBWV .... United Bankshares, Inc. [*Associated Press*] (SAG)
UBX .... Cuba, MO [*Location identifier FAA*] (FAAL)
UBZ .... Upper Border Zone [*Geology*]
UC .... UC Television Network Corp. [*Associated Press*] (SAG)
UC .... Ulcerative Colitis [*Medicine*]
UC .... Uldall Catheter [*Medicine*] (MEDA)
UC .... Ultimate Collider [*Particle accelerator*]
UC .... Ultracentrifugal [*Biochemistry*] (MAE)
UC .... Umbilical Cable [*or Connector*]
UC .... Umbilical Cable Unit Cooler [*Aerospace*] (AAG)
UC .... Umbilical Connector
UC .... Unaccompanied Child [*Airline notation*]
UC .... Una Corda [*With one string or with the soft pedal*] [*Music*]
UC .... Unchanged (MAE)
UC .... Uncirculated Coins [*Numismatics*]
UC .... Unclassifiable [*Laboratory science*] (DAVI)
U/C .... Unclassified

UC ... Unclipping [*Medicine*]
UC ... Uncut Edges [*Bookbinding*]
UC ... Undeducted Contributions
U/C ... Under Carriage (MCD)
UC ... Under Charge
UC ... Under Construction
U/C ... Under Conversion (NATG)
U/C ... Under Cover (ADA)
U/C ... Under Current (NASA)
UC ... Undercut [*Technical drawings*]
UC ... Underfashion Club (EA)
UC ... Underwater Communications (MCD)
UC ... Undifferentiated Carcinoma [*Oncology*]
UC ... Unemployment Compensation
UC ... Unfair Competition (MHDW)
UC ... Unichannel
Uc ... Uniform, Coarse-Grained [*Soil*]
UC ... Union Caledonienne [*Caledonian Union*] [*Political party*] (PPW)
UC ... Union Camerounaise [*Cameroonese Union*] [*Political party*]
UC ... Union Constitutionelle [*Constitutional Union*] [*Morocco*] [*Political party*] (PPW)
UC ... Unitarian Church [*Australia*]
UC ... Unit Call [*Also known as CCS*] [*Telecommunications*]
UC ... Unit Chairman
UC ... Unit Clerk
UC ... Unit Cooler
UC ... Unit Cost
UC ... Unit Count (AFIT)
UC ... United Canada Insurance Co.
UC ... United Christian Party [*Australia Political party*]
UC ... United Companies Financial [*NYSE symbol*] (SAG)
uc ... United States Miscellaneous Caribbean Islands [*MARC country of publication code Library of Congress*] (LCCP)
UC ... Unity College [*London, England*]
UC ... University College
UC ... University Colleges [*Public-performance tariff class*] [*British*]
UC ... University of California
UC ... University of Chicago [*Illinois*] (PDAA)
UC ... University of Cincinnati [*Ohio*]
UC ... Unloader Coil (IAA)
UC ... Unoperated Control
UC ... Unsatisfactory Condition (NASA)
UC ... Untreated Controls [*Medicine*]
uc ... Up Center (WDMC)
UC ... Up Converter
UC ... Uplink Command
UC ... Upper Canada
UC ... Uppercase [*Typography*] (ADA)
UC ... Upper Characters (IAA)
UC ... Upper Control (IAA)
UC ... Upper Cylinder
UC ... Uranium Canada Ltd.
UC ... Uranium Carbide [*Inorganic chemistry*] (OA)
UC ... Urban Contemporary (WDMC)
UC ... Urban Council [*British*] (BARN)
UC ... Urbis Conditae [*From the Foundation of the City; that is, of Rome*] [*Latin*]
UC ... Urea Clearance [*Clinical chemistry*]
UC ... Urethral Catheterization [*Medicine*] (MAE)
UC ... Urinary Catheter [*Medicine*]
U/C ... Urine Culture [*Clinical chemistry*] (MAE)
UC ... Usable Control
UC ... Using Command
UC ... Usual Health-Care [*Medicine*]
UC ... Uterine Contraction [*Obstetrics*] (AAMN)
UC ... Utility Car [*British*]
UC ... Utility Cargo
UC ... Utility Corridor
UC ... Utilization Control
UC1 ... Underwater Control Rating 1st Class [*British military*] (DMA)
UC2 ... Underwater Control Rating 2nd Class [*British military*] (DMA)
UCA ... Champlain Enterprises, Inc. [*ICAO designator*] (FAAC)
UCA ... Rome-Utica [*New York*] [*Airport symbol*] (AD)
UCA ... Undefinitized Contractual Actions (DOMA)
UCA ... Under Color Addition [*Printing technology*]
UCA ... Uniform Chart of Accounts [*DoD*]
UCA ... United Carters' Association [*A union*] [*British*]
UCA ... United Chemists' Association Ltd. [*British*] (BI)
UCA ... United Collision [*Vancouver Stock Exchange symbol*]
UCA ... United Congressional Appeal (EA)
UCA ... United States Court of Appeals for the District of Columbia, Judges Library, Washington, DC [*OCLC symbol*] (OCLC)
UCA ... Unitized Component Assembly [*Aerospace*]
UCA ... Units Consistency Analyzer [*Computer science*]
UCA ... Universal Calibration Adapter
UCA ... Upper Control Area (NATG)
UCA ... User Computed Address [*Computer science*] (HGAA)
UCA ... Utah Code, Annotated [*A publication*] (DLA)
UCA ... Utica [*New York*] [*Airport symbol*] (OAG)
UCA ... Utility Communications Architecture [*Standardized computer program for utility companies*] (PS)
UCACEP ... United Council of Associations of Civil Employees of Pakistan
UCAE ... United Carters' Association of England [*A union*]
UCAE ... Universities Council for Adult Education [*British*]
UCAID ... University Corp. for Advanced Internet Development
UCAL ... Universal Cable Adapter (IAA)
U Cal (Berkeley) ... University of California at Berkeley (GAGS)
U Cal (Davis) ... University of California at Davis (GAGS)
U Cal (Irvine) ... University of California at Irvine (GAGS)
U Cal (Riverside) ... University of California at Riverside (GAGS)
U Cal (San Diego) ... University of California at San Diego (GAGS)
U Cal (San Francisco) ... University of California at San Francisco (GAGS)
U Cal (Santa Barbara) ... University of California at Santa Barbara (GAGS)
U Cal (Santa Cruz) ... University of California at Santa Cruz (GAGS)
UCAM ... United Campuses to Prevent Nuclear War (EA)
UCAN ... Union of Catholic Asian News [*Kwun Tong, Hong Kong*] (EAIO)
UCAN ... Utilities Conservation Action Now [*Federal Energy Administration*]
UCAN ... Utility Consumers Action Network
UC & P ... Uniform Customs and Practice for Documentary Credits [*International Chamber of Commerce*] [*A publication*] (DS)
UCapF ... United Capital Funding Partnership LP [*Associated Press*] (SAG)
UC App ... Upper Canada Appeal Reports [*A publication*] (DLA)
UC App (Can) ... Upper Canada Appeal Reports [*A publication*] (DLA)
UC App Rep ... Upper Canada Appeal Reports [*A publication*] (DLA)
UCar ... UCar International [*Associated Press*] (SAG)
UCAR ... United Carolina Bancsh [*NASDAQ symbol*] (TTSB)
UCAR ... United Carolina Bancshares Corp. [*NASDAQ symbol*] (NQ)
UCAR ... University Corp. for Atmospheric Research (EA)
UCAR ... Utilities Cost Analysis Report
UCarb ... Union Carbide Corp. [*Associated Press*] (SAG)
UCarBk ... United Carolina Bancshares Corp. [*Associated Press*] (SAG)
UCARCIDE ... Union Carbide Biocide [*Trademark*] [*Union Carbide Corp.*]
UCARS ... Uniform Cost Accounting and Reporting System
UCAS ... Uniform Cost Accounting Standards (MCD)
UCAS ... Union of Central African States (EY)
UCATA ... Uniform Contribution Among Tortfeasors Act [*National Conference of Commissioners on Uniform State Laws*]
UCATT ... Union of Construction, Allied Trades, and Technicians [*British*]
UCAV ... Uninhabited Combat Air Vehicle
$U_{Ca}V$ ... Urinary Calcium Excretion [*Laboratory science*] (DAVI)
UCAVJ ... Union Continentale Africaine des Villes Jumelees [*Continental African Union of Twin Cities*]
UCB ... Canadian Union Catalogue of Books [*National Library of Canada*] [*Information service or system*] (IID)
UCB ... UCB [*Belgium*] [*Research code symbol*]
UCB ... UCB Chemie [*Germany*] [*Research code symbol*]
UCB ... Unconjugated Bilirubin
UCB ... Union Chimique Belge [*Belgium*]
UCB ... Unit Control Block (MCD)
UCB ... United California Bank [*Los Angeles*] (IIA)
UCB ... United Cambridge Mines [*Vancouver Stock Exchange symbol*]
UCB ... United Commercial Bank Ltd. [*Bangladesh*]
UCB ... Universal Character Buffer
UCB ... University College Buckingham [*British*] (AIE)
UCB ... University of California, Berkeley
UCB ... University of California, Berkeley School of Library and Information Science, Berkeley, CA [*OCLC symbol*] (OCLC)
ucb ... Unless Caused by [*Insurance*] (BARN)
UCBC ... Parti de l'Unite et de la Communaute Belgo-Congolaise [*Political party*]
UCBEU ... Uniao Cultural Brasil-Estados Unidos [*Brazil-United States Cultural Union*] [*Brazil*] (EAIO)
UCBLL ... Language Laboratory [*Research center*] (RCD)
UCBR ... Unconjugated Bilirubin (MAE)
UCBSRP ... University of California, Berkeley, Sulfur Recovery Process
UCBT ... Union pour le Commerce des Bois Tropicaux dans la CEE [*Association for Trade in Tropical Woods in the EEC*] (ECED)
UCBT ... Universal Circuit Board Tester
UCBTAB ... User Control Block Table [*Computer science*] (MHDI)
UCBWM ... United Church Board for World Ministries (EA)
UCC ... Computing Center [*University of Rochester*] [*Research center*] (RCD)
UCC ... Uccle [*Belgium*] [*Seismograph station code, US Geological Survey*] (SEIS)
UCC ... Ultra Clean Coal (ERG)
UCC ... Umbilical Checkout Cable
UCC ... Unadjusted Contractual Changes
UCC ... Unified Classification Code (NITA)
UCC ... Uniform Classification Committee [*Later, NRFC*] (EA)
UCC ... Uniform Code Council (EA)
UCC ... Uniform Commercial Code [*National Conference of Commissioners on Uniform State Laws*]
UCC ... Uniform Credit Code
UCC ... Union Camp [*NYSE symbol*] (TTSB)
UCC ... Union Camp Corp. [*NYSE symbol*] (SPSG)
UCC ... Union Carbide Canada Ltd. [*Toronto Stock Exchange symbol*]
UCC ... Union Carbide Corp. (KSC)
UCC ... United Cancer Council (EA)
UCC ... United Church of Christ
UCC ... United Computer Corporation (NITA)
UCC ... Universal Checkout Console (NASA)
UCC ... Universal Copyright Convention
UCC ... University College, Cardiff [*Wales*]
UCC ... University College Computer [*London, England*] (DEN)
UCC ... University College, Cork [*Ireland*]
UCC ... University Computer Center [*University of Minnesota*] [*Research center*] (RCD)
UCC ... University Computer Center [*New Mexico State University*] [*Research center*] (RCD)
UCC ... University Computer Center [*San Diego State University*] [*Research center*] (RCD)

UCC University Computer Center [*Oklahoma State University*] [*Research center*] (RCD)
UCC University Computer Center [*North Dakota State University*] [*Research center*] (RCD)
UCC University Computing Co. [*International computer bureau*]
UCC University of Corpus Christi [*Texas*] [*Closed, 1973*]
UCC Upper Canada College
UCC Upper Control Center (NATG)
UCC Urgent Care Center [*Medicine*]
UCC Uruguay Collectors Club (EA)
UCC Utility Control Console
UCC Yucca Flat, NV [*Location identifier FAA*] (FAAL)
UCCA Ukrainian Congress Committee of America (EA)
UCCA Universities Central Council on Admission [*British*]
UCCATS Urban Combat Computer-Assisted Training System
UCCC Computing Center [*University of Cincinnati*] [*Research center*] (RCD)
UCCC Uniform Consumer Credit Code [*National Conference of Commissioners on Uniform State Laws*]
UCCC Unmarried-Catholics Correspondence Club (EA)
UCCCCWCS United Church of Christ Coordinating Center for Women in Church and Society (EA)
UCCCRJ United Church of Christ Commission for Racial Justice (EA)
UCCE Union des Capitales de la Communaute Europeenne [*Union of Capitals of the European Community*]
UCCE Universal Craftsmen Council of Engineers (EA)
UCCE Utah Council for Computers in Education (EDAC)
UCC/EMC Union Carbide and Carbon/Electric Metallurgical Co. (AAG)
UCCF United Campus Christian Fellowship [*Defunct*]
UC Ch Upper Canada Chancery Reports [*1849-82*] [*A publication*] (DLA)
UC Cham Upper Canada Chambers Reports [*A publication*] (DLA)
UC Chamb Upper Canada Chambers Reports [*1846-52*] [*A publication*] (DLA)
UC Cham (Can) Upper Canada Chambers Reports [*1846-52*] [*A publication*] (DLA)
UC Chan Upper Canada Chancery Reports [*A publication*] (DLA)
UC Ch (Can) Upper Canada Chancery Reports [*A publication*] (DLA)
UC Ch Rep Upper Canada Chancery Reports [*1849-82*] [*A publication*] (DLA)
UCCIS USAREUR [*United States Army, Europe*] Command and Control Information System
UCCJA Uniform Child Custody Jurisdiction Act (EDAC)
UCC Law Letter Uniform Commercial Code Law Letter [*A publication*] (DLA)
UCCL/GC United Church Coalition for Lesbian/Gay Concerns (EA)
UCC-ND Union Carbide Corp. - Nuclear Division (MCD)
UCCP Upper Canada Common Pleas Reports [*A publication*] (DLA)
UCCP (Can) Upper Canada Common Pleas Reports [*A publication*] (DLA)
UCCPD Upper Canada Common Pleas Division Reports [*Ontario*] [*A publication*] (DLA)
UCCPL United Citizens Coastal Protection League (EA)
UCCR Upper Canada Court Records [*Report of Ontario Bureau of Archives*] [*A publication*] (DLA)
UCCRC University of Chicago Cancer Research Center [*Research center*] (RCD)
UCC Rep Serv Uniform Commercial Code Reporting Service [*A publication*] (DLA)
UCCRL Union Carbide and Carbon Research Laboratories (AAG)
UCCRP Union College Character Research Project (EA)
UCCRS Underwater Coded Command Release System
UCCS Ultrasonic Chemical Cleaning System
UCCS United Cabinet and Chairmakers' Society [*A union*] [*British*]
UCCS Universal Camera Control System
UCCS University Classification and Compensation System
U-CD Companion Dog [*Prefix*]
UCD Unchanged Charge Distribution [*Fission*]
UCD Uniform Call Distribution [*Telephone system*]
UCD Union de Centro Democratico [*Union of the Democratic Center*] [*Spain Political party*] (PPE)
UCD United Canadian Shares Ltd. [*Toronto Stock Exchange symbol*]
UCD Universal Classification Decimal (ECII)
UCD University College, Dublin [*Ireland*]
UCD University of California, Davis
UCD Upper Critical Depth [*Oceanography*] (WDAA)
UCd Urine Cadmium Level
UCD Urine Collection Device [*NASA*] (MCD)
UCD Usual Childhood Diseases [*Medicine*]
UCD Utah Construction and Development Co., Inc. (AAGC)
UCDA University and College Designers Association (EA)
UC Davis L Rev University of California (Davis). Law Review [*A publication*] (DLA)
UCDC Ulster Constitution Defence Committee [*Northern Ireland*]
UCDC Uniado do Centro Democrata Cristao [*Union of the Christian Democratic Center*] [*Portugal Political party*] (PPE)
UCDCC Union Centro y Democratica Cristiana de Catalunya [*Union of the Center and Christian Democrats of Catalonia*] [*Spain Political party*] (PPE)
UCdE Emery County Library, Castle Dale, UT [*Library symbol Library of Congress*] (LCLS)
UCDEC Union Chretienne Democrate d'Europe Centrale [*Christian Democratic Union of Central Europe - CDUCE*] (EAIO)
UCdH Emery County High School, Castle Dale, UT [*Library symbol Library of Congress*] (LCLS)
UCDL Union Chretienne Democrate Libanaise [*Lebanese Christian Democratic Union*] [*Political party*] (PPW)
UCDMC University of California at Davis, Medical Center (DAVI)
UCDP Uncorrected Data Processor
UCDP Uncorrelated Data Processor (IAA)
UCDS Uniform Clinical Data Set
UCDS Unit Chemical Defense Study (MCD)
UCDWN Until Cleared Down [*Aviation*] (FAAC)
UCDWR University of California Division of War Research
U-CDX Companion Dog Excellent [*Prefix*]
UCE Union Canadienne des Etudiants
UCE Union Carbide Electronics (IAA)
UCE Unit Checkout Equipment
UCE Unit Control Error (IAA)
UCE Unit Correction Entry
UCE University of Central England
UCE Unsolicited Commercial E-Mail [*Computer science*]
UCE Upstream Control Element [*Genetics*]
UCE Ural Commodity Exchange [*Russian Federation*] (EY)
UCEA Uniform Conservation Easement Act [*National Conference of Commissioners on Uniform State Laws*]
UCEA Uniform Criminal Extradition Act [*National Conference of Commissioners on Uniform State Laws*]
UCEA Union Chimique Elf-Aquitaine [*France*]
UCEA University Council for Educational Administration (EA)
UCEA Used Clothing Exporters Association of America (EA)
UCE & A Upper Canada Error and Appeal Reports [*1846-66*] [*A publication*] (DLA)
UCEC Utility Commission Engineers Conference
UCeDe Union del Centro Democratico [*Union of the Democratic Center*] [*Argentina Political party*] (EY)
UCEMT University Consortium in Educational Media and Technology [*Later, UCIDT*]
U Cent Ark University of Central Arkansas (GAGS)
U Cent Okla University of Central Oklahoma (GAGS)
UCEP Upper Critical End Points [*Supercritical extraction*]
UCEPCEE Union du Commerce des Engrais des Pays de la Communaute Economique Europeenne [*Union of the Fertilizer Trade of Countries of the EEC*] [*Hasselt, Belgium*] (EAIO)
UCER Unit Cost Exception Report [*Army*]
UCER University Center for Energy Research [*Oklahoma State University*] [*Research center*] (RCD)
UC Err & App Upper Canada Error and Appeal Reports [*1846-66*] [*A publication*] (DLA)
UC Err & App (Can) Upper Canada Error and Appeal Reports [*1846-66*] [*A publication*] (DLA)
UCES University Center for Environmental Studies [*Virginia Polytechnic Institute and State University*] [*Research center*] (RCD)
UCET Universities Council for the Education of Teachers (AIE)
U Ceylon LR University of Ceylon. Law Review [*A publication*] (DLA)
UCF Ulster Cancer Foundation [*Northern Ireland*] (EAIO)
UCF Uniform Contract Format
UCF Union Culturelle Francais [*French Cultural Union*]
UCF Unit Control File [*Air Force*]
UCF United Cat Federation (EA)
UCF United Cooperative Farmers, Inc.
UCF University of Central Florida [*Orlando, FL*]
UCF Utility Control Facility
UCFA Uniform Comparative Fault Act [*National Conference of Commissioners on Uniform State Laws*]
UCFA Union pour la Communaute Franco-Africaine [*Union for the Franco-African Community*] [*Niger*]
UCFAC United Council of Filipino Associations in Canada
UCFC United Community Funds and Councils of America [*Later, UWA*] (EA)
UCFC United Companies Financial Corp. [*NASDAQ symbol*] (SAG)
UCFC United Cos. Financial [*NASDAQ symbol*] (TTSB)
UCFCMHPH Union Centrafricaine de la Fraternite Chretienne des Malades et Handicapes (EAIO)
UCFCP United Cos. Fin'l 6.75%'PRIDES' [*NASDAQ symbol*] (TTSB)
UCFE Unemployment Compensation, Federal Employees
UCFM United Christian Fellowship Ministry [*Australia*]
UCFML Union des Communistes de France Marxiste-Leniniste [*Marxist-Leninist Union of Communists of France*] [*Political party*] (PPW)
UCFRU Utah Cooperative Fishery Research Unit [*Utah State University*] [*Research center*] (RCD)
UCG Ultrasonic Cardiography [*Medicine*] (DMAA)
UCG Ultrasound Cardiogram (IAA)
UCG Underground Coal Gasification
UCG Unidirectional Categorical Grammar
UCG University College Galway [*Ireland*]
UCG Urinary Chorionic Gonadotrophin [*Endocrinology*]
UCGA University Center in Georgia, Inc. [*Library network*]
UCGF Undergraduate Computer Graphics Facility [*Stevens Institute of Technology*] [*Research center*] (RCD)
UCGIS University Consortium for Geographic Information Science
UCH University College Hospital [*British*] (DI)
UCH University of Connecticut, Health Center Library, Farmington, CT [*OCLC symbol*] (OCLC)
UCHCIS Urban Comprehensive Health Care Information System (PDAA)
UCHD Usual Childhood Diseases [*Medicine*]
UCHF Uncoupled Hartree-Fock [*Physical chemistry*]
UCHI Usual Childhood Illnesses (DAVI)
U Chicago [*The*] University of Chicago (GAGS)
UCHILS University of Chicago Law School (DLA)
UCHM Uniroyal Chemical [*NASDAQ symbol*] (TTSB)
UCHM Uniroyal Chemical Corp. [*NASDAQ symbol*] (SAG)
UCHS Uniting Church Historical Society [*Australia*]
UCHSC University of Colorado Health Sciences Center [*Denver*]
UCI Imperial Chemical Industries [*British*]

UCI .... Ultrasonic Contact Impedance [*Factory automation*] (BTTJ)
UCI .... Union Cycliste Internationale [*International Cycling Union*] [*Switzerland*] (EA)
UCI .... Unit Construction Index
UCI .... United Charity Institutions of Jerusalem (EA)
UCI .... Universite Cooperative Internationale [*International Cooperative University*]
UCI .... University of California at Irvine
UCI .... Updated Coordinating Instructions (DOMA)
UCI .... Urethral Catheter in [*Medicine*] (CPH)
UCI .... Urinary Catheter In [*or Input*] [*Medicine*]
UCI .... User Class Identifier (NITA)
UCI .... User-Communication Interface [*Telecommunications*]
UCI .... Usual Childhood Illnesses (DAVI)
UCI .... Utility Card Input
UCI .... Utility Communicators International (EA)
UCIA .... UCI Medical Affiliates [*NASDAQ symbol*] (TTSB)
UCIA .... UCI Medical Affiliates, Inc. [*NASDAQ symbol*] (SAG)
UCIB .... USAFE Command Intelligence Brief (MCD)
UCID .... Independent Democratic Union of Cape Verde [*Political party*] (PD)
UCID .... User Control Interface Device [*Army*]
UCIDT .... University Consortium for Instructional Development and Technology (EA)
UCIIM .... Unione Cattolica Italiana Insegnanti Medi
UCIMC .... University of California at Irvine, Medical Center (DAVI)
UCIMed .... UCI Medical Affiliates, Inc. [*Associated Press*] (SAG)
UCIMHPLD .... Union of Catholic Institutions for the Mentally Handicapped and Persons with Learning Disabilities [*Germany*] (EAIO)
UCIMT .... University Center for Instructional Media and Technology [*University of Connecticut*] [*Research center*] (RCD)
U Cincinnati ... University of Cincinnati (GAGS)
UCIP .... Union Catholique Internationale de la Presse [*International Catholic Union of the Press*] (EAIO)
UCIR .... University Center for International Rehabilitation [*Michigan State University*] [*Research center*] (RCD)
UCIS .... Unemployment Compensation Interpretation Service (DLA)
UCIS .... University Center for International Studies [*University of Pittsburgh*] [*Research center*] (IID)
UCIS .... University Computing and Information Services [*Villanova University*] [*Research center*] (RCD)
UCIS .... Uprange Computer Input System
UCISS .... Union Catholique Internationale de Service Social [*Catholic International Union for Social Service*] [*Brussels, Belgium*] (EAIO)
UCIT .... United Cities Gas [*NASDAQ symbol*] (TTSB)
UCIT .... United Cities Gas Co. [*NASDAQ symbol*] (NQ)
UCItGs .... United Cities Gas Co. [*Associated Press*] (SAG)
UCITS .... Undertakings for Collective Investment in Transferable Securities [*European Community*]
UCJ .... Unsatisfied Claim and Judgment [*State driver insurance*]
UCJG .... Alliance Universelle des Unions Chretiennes de Jeunes Gens [*World Alliance of Young Men's Christian Associations*]
UC Jur .... Upper Canada Jurist [*A publication*] (DLA)
UC Jur (Can) ... Upper Canada Jurist [*A publication*] (DLA)
UCK .... Union Culturelle Katangaise [*Katangan Cultural Union*]
UCK .... Unit Check (ECII)
UCKB .... Upper Canada King's Bench Reports, Old Series [*1831-44*] [*A publication*] (DLA)
UCKB (Can) ... Upper Canada King's Bench Reports, Old Series [*1831-44*] [*A publication*] (DLA)
UCL .... Ulnar Collateral Ligament [*Anatomy*]
UCL .... Unclamp (IAA)
UCL .... Uncomfortable Loudness [*Audiometry*]
UCL .... Uncomfortable Loudness [*Sound level*] (DAVI)
UCL .... Universal Computers Ltd. (NITA)
UCL .... Universal Consolidated Ltd. [*British*]
UCL .... University College of London (KSC)
UCL .... University of Calgary Library [*UTLAS symbol*]
UCL .... University of Connecticut, Law Library, West Hartford, CT [*OCLC symbol*] (OCLC)
UCL .... Unocal Corp. [*NYSE symbol*] (SPSG)
UCL .... Update Control List
UCL .... Upper Confidence Level [*Industrial engineering*] (IEEE)
UCL .... Upper Confidence Limit [*Statistics*]
UCL .... Upper Control Limit [*Nuclear energy*]
UCL .... Upper Cylinder Lubricant [*Automotive engineering*] (WDAA)
UCL .... Urea Clearance [*Test*] [*Medicine*]
UCL .... User Control List [*Computer science*] (HGAA)
UCLA .... University at the Corner of Lenox Avenue [*Nickname for "The Tree of Life," a Harlem bookstore*]
UCLA .... University of California, Los Angeles [*Databank originator*]
UCLA-Alaska L Rev ... UCLA [*University of California, Los Angeles*]-Alaska Law Review [*A publication*] (DLA)
UCLA Intra L Rev ... UCLA [*University of California, Los Angeles*] Intramural Law Review [*A publication*] (DLA)
UCLA J Envt'l L & Pol'y ... UCLA [*University of California, Los Angeles*] Journal of Environmental Law and Policy [*A publication*] (DLA)
UCLA Law Rev ... University of California at Los Angeles. Law Review [*A publication*] (DLA)
UCLA L Rev ... University of California at Los Angeles. Law Review [*A publication*] (DLA)
UCLAN .... User Cluster Language [*Computer science*] (MHDB)
UCLA Pac Basin LJ ... UCLA [*University of California at Los Angeles*] Pacific Basin Law Journal [*A publication*] (DLA)
UCLC .... Utah College Library Council [*Library network*]
UCLEA .... University and College Labor Education Association (EA)
UCLG .... United Cement, Lime, Gypsum, and Allied Workers International Union [*Formerly, CLGW*] (EA)
UCLJ .... University of California, La Jolla
UCLJ .... Upper Canada Law Journal [*1855-1922*] [*A publication*] (DLA)
UCLJ (Can) ... Upper Canada Law Journal [*A publication*] (DLA)
UCLJ NS .... Upper Canada Law Journal, New Series [*A publication*] (DLA)
UCLJ NS (Can) ... Upper Canada Law Journal, New Series [*A publication*] (DLA)
UCLJ OS .... Canada Law Journal, Old Series [*A publication*] (DLA)
UCLLL .... University of California Lawrence Livermore Laboratory (AAGC)
UCLM .... Unity of Czech Ladies and Men [*Later, CSA*] (EA)
UCLP .... Unilateral Cleft of Lip and Palate [*Medicine*] (DMAA)
UCLR .... University of Ceylon. Law Review [*A publication*] (DLA)
UCLRL .... University of California Lawrence Radiation Laboratory
UCLS .... Underwater Crash Locator System (MCD)
UCLT .... Until Cleared to Land by the Tower [*Aviation*] (FAAC)
UCM .... Can You Come and See Me
UCM .... Unicom Corp. [*Formerly, Commonwealth Edison*] [*NYSE symbol*] (SAG)
UCM .... Union des Croyants Malagaches [*Malagasy Christian Union*]
UCM .... Union of Catholic Mothers [*British*] (DI)
UCM .... Unit Control Module [*Computer science*] (ECII)
UCM .... Universal Cable Module (PCM)
UCM .... Universal Christian Movement (EA)
UCM .... Universal Church of the Master (IIA)
UCM .... Universal Communications Monitor
UCM .... University Christian Movement [*Formerly, NSCF*] [*Defunct*]
UCM .... Unresolved Complex Mixture
UCM .... User Command [*Computer science*] (PCM)
UCM .... User Communications Manager [*Audio-video*] (NTCM)
UCMAA .... University of Calcutta Medical Association of America
UCMAE .... United Carters' and Motormen's Association of England [*A union*]
UCMJ .... Uniform Code of Military Justice
UCML .... Unit Committed Munitions List
UCMP .... UniComp, Inc. [*NASDAQ symbol*] (NQ)
UCMS .... Unit Capability Measurement System (AFM)
UCMS .... United Christian Missionary Society (EA)
UCMSU .... United Chain Makers' and Strikers' Union [*British*]
UCMT .... Unglazed Ceramic Mosaic Tile [*Technical drawings*]
UCN .... Buchanan [*Liberia*] [*Airport symbol*] (AD)
UCN .... Ultracold Neutron
UCN .... Unemployment Compensation News [*James E. Frick, Inc.*] [*Information service or system*] (CRD)
UCN .... Uniform Control Number (NASA)
UCN .... Union Civica Nacional [*National Civic Union*] [*Dominican Republic*] [*Political party*] (PPW)
UCN .... Union del Centro Nacional [*Union of the National Center*] [*Guatemala*] [*Political party*]
UCN .... Urocortin [*Neurochemistry*]
UCNC .... Union Carbide Nuclear Corp.
UCNI .... Unclassified Controlled Nuclear Information [*Department of Energy*]
UCNI .... Unified Communications Navigation Identification
UCNS .... Universities Committee for Non-Teaching Staff [*British*]
UCNSW .... Unitarian Church of New South Wales [*Australia*]
UCNT .... Undifferentiated Carcinoma of Nasopharyngeal Type [*Oncology*]
UCNV .... University College of Northern Victoria [*Australia*]
UCNW .... University College of North Wales
UCNY .... Underfashion Club of New York [*Formerly, CBWC*] (EA)
UCO .... Union Corp. [*NYSE symbol*] (SPSG)
UCO .... United Commercial Bank [*India*] (EY)
UCO .... Universal Code [*Used for giving transport aircraft meteorological information in wartime*] (NATG)
UCO .... Universal Communications Object (PCM)
UCO .... Universal Weather Landing Code
UCO .... Urethral Catheter Out [*Medicine*] (MAE)
UCO .... Urinary Catheter Out [*or Output*] [*Medicine*]
UCO .... Utility Compiler
UCOD .... University Clearing Office for Developing Countries
UCOFT .... Unit Combat Fire Trainer [*Army*]
U-COFT .... Unit Conduct of Fire Trainer [*Army*]
UCOL .... Union des Colons du Katanga [*Settlers' Union of Katanga*]
U Colo .... University of Colorado (GAGS)
UCOM .... Unified Command [*DoD*]
UCOM .... Union Catalog of Medical Monographs and Multimedia [*Medical Library Center of New York*] [*No longer available online*] [*Information service or system*] (CRD)
UCOM .... United Currency Options Market [*Philadelphia Stock Exchange*] (ECON)
UCON .... Utility Control
UCONN .... University of Connecticut
UCOP .... Unit Cost of Production (MHDW)
UCOPOM .... Union Europeenne du Commerce de Gros des Pommes de Terre [*European Union of the Wholesale Potato Trade*] [*Common Market*]
UCOR .... UroCor, Inc. [*NASDAQ symbol*] (SAG)
UCOR .... UroCor Inc. [*NASDAQ symbol*] (TTSB)
UCORC .... University of California/Operations Research Center
UCOS .... Upper Canada King's Bench Reports, Old Series [*1831-44*] [*A publication*] (DLA)
UCOS .... Uprange Computer Output System
UCOSDDEEC ... Union of Cafe Owners and Soft Drink Dealers of the European Economic Community [*Paris, France*] (EAIO)
UCosF .... United Companies Financial [*Associated Press*] (SAG)
UCOSL .... University of Colorado School of Law (DLA)
UCOT .... Upper Critical Ordering Transition [*Polymer physics*]
UCount .... United Counties Trust Co. [*Associated Press*] (SAG)

UCOWR........ Universities Council on Water Resources (EA)
UCP............ New Castle, PA [*Location identifier FAA*] (FAAL)
UCP............ Ubiquitous Crystallization Process [*Photovoltaic energy systems*]
UCP............ Uncoupling Protein [*Biochemistry*]
UCP............ Unified Command Plan [*Military*] (AFM)
UCP............ Uniform Customs and Practice for Documentary Credits [*International Chamber of Congress*] [*A publication*]
UCP............ Uniform Customs Practices (AAGC)
UCP............ Uninterruptable Computer Power
UCP............ Union Comorienne pour le Progres [*Comorian Union for Progress*] (PD)
UCP............ Union of Coffee Planters [*Madagascar*] (EAIO)
UCP............ Unit Construction Practice (IAA)
UCP............ Unit Construction Principle (IAA)
UCP............ United Cerebral Palsy (DAVI)
UCP............ United Christian Party [*Australia Political party*] (ADA)
UCP............ United Country Party [*Australia Political party*]
UCP............ Universal Commercial Paper [*Investment term*]
UCP............ University of Connecticut, Health Center Library, Processing Center, Farmington,CT [*OCLC symbol*] (OCLC)
UCP............ Update Control Process [*Telecommunications*] (TEL)
UCP............ Urinary Coproporphyrin [*Urology*]
UCP............ Urinary C-Peptide [*Urology*]
UCP............ Utilities Conservation Program [*Navy*] (NG)
UCP............ Utility Control Program
UCPA.......... United Cerebral Palsy Associations (EA)
UCPA.......... University Counseling and Placement Association (AEBS)
UCPC.......... University of Connecticut Paleobotanical Collection
UCPE.......... Unit of Comparative Plant Ecology [*Natural Environment Research Council*] [*British*] (IRUK)
UCPF.......... United Church Peace Fellowship [*Defunct*] (EA)
UCPN.......... Union des Chefs et des Populations du Nord [*Union of Chiefs and Peoples of the North*] [*Togo*]
UCPN.......... United Communist Party of Nepal [*Political party*] (EY)
UCPP.......... Urban Crime Prevention Program [*Federal government*]
UCPR.......... Upper Canada Practice Reports [*A publication*] (DLA)
UC Pract...... Upper Canada Practice Reports [*1850-1900*] [*A publication*] (DLA)
UC Pr (Can)... Upper Canada Practice Reports [*A publication*] (DLA)
UCPREF....... United Cerebral Palsy Research and Educational Foundation (EA)
UC Pr R....... Upper Canada Practice Reports [*A publication*] (DLA)
UCPT.......... Urinary Coproporphyrin Test [*Urology*]
UCPTE......... Union pour la Coordination de la Production et du Transport de l'Electricite [*Union for the Coordination of the Production and Transport of Electric Power - UCPTE*] (EAIO)
UCPU.......... Universal Central Processor Unit [*Computer hardware*]
UCPU.......... Urine Collection and Pretreatment Unit (NASA)
UCQ............ University of Central Queensland [*Australia*]
UCQB.......... Upper Canada Queen's Bench Reports [*A publication*] (DLA)
UC QB OS.... Upper Canada Queen's Bench Reports, Old Series [*A publication*] (DLA)
UC QB OS (Can)... Upper Canada Queen's Bench Reports, Old Series [*A publication*] (DLA)
UCR............ Committee on Uniform Crime Records (EA)
UCR............ UCar International [*NYSE symbol*] (SAG)
UCR............ Unconditioned Reflex [*or Response*] [*Psychometrics*]
UCR............ Under-Color Removal [*Printing technology*]
UCR............ Uniform Crime Reports [*FBI*]
UCR............ Union Centriste et Radicale [*France Political party*] (EY)
UCR............ Union Civica Radical [*Radical Civic Union*] [*Argentina*] (PD)
UCR............ Unit Card Reader
UCR............ Unit Cost Report [*Military*] (RDA)
UCR............ University of California, Riverside (IID)
UCR............ Unsatisfactory Condition Report [*NASA*]
UCR............ Upper Canada Reports [*A publication*] (DLA)
UCR............ Upper Circulating Reflux [*Chemical engineering*]
UCR............ Upstream Control Region [*Biochemistry*]
UCR............ User Control Routine (MCD)
UCR............ Usual, Customary, and Reasonable (DAVI)
UCR............ Usual, Customary, and Reasonable Charges [*Medicine*]
UCR............ Utah Coal Route [*AAR code*]
UCRA.......... Universal Child Restraint Anchorage
UCRAO........ University of Calgary, Rothney Astrophysical Observatory [*Canada*] (IRC)
UCRB.......... Upper Circulating Reflux Bottom Section [*Chemical engineering*]
UCRC.......... Underground Construction Research Council
UCRC.......... Union Canadienne des Religieuses Contemplatives
UCRC.......... United Civil Rights Committee
UC Rep........ Upper Canada Reports [*A publication*] (DLA)
UCRG.......... Union des Clubs pour le Renouveau de la Gauche [*Union of Clubs for the Renovation of the Left*] [*France Political party*] (PPE)
UCRI........... Union Carbide Research Institute (KSC)
UCRI........... Union Civica Radical Intransigente [*Left-wing radical political party*] [*Argentina*]
U-CRIS........ Utah Computer Retrieval Information Service [*Utah State Office of Education*] (OLDSS)
UCRL........... University of California Radiation Laboratory (MCD)
UCRL........... University of California Research Laboratory (KSC)
UCRP.......... Uniform Crime Reporting Program [*FBI*]
UCRP.......... Union Civica Radical del Pueblo [*Moderate radical political party*] [*Argentina*]
UCR/PACE.... Usual, Customary, and Reasonable/Performance and Cost Efficiency [*Medicine*] (MEDA)
UCRS.......... Urban and Rural Commuter Service [*MOCD*] (TAG)
UCRT.......... Upper Circulating Reflux Top Section [*Chemical engineering*]
UCS............ Canadian Union Catalogue of Serials [*National Library of Canada*] [*Information service or system*] (IID)
UCS............ Southern Utah State College, Cedar City, UT [*Library symbol Library of Congress*] (LCLS)
UCS............ Unbalanced Current Sensing (MCD)
UCS............ Unclosed Contract Status [*Military*] (AFIT)
UCS............ Unconditioned Stimulus [*Psychometrics*]
UCS............ Unconfined Compressive Strength [*Rock mechanics*]
UCS............ Unconscious [*Medicine*]
UCS............ Uncontrolled Stimulus (HGAA)
UCS............ Underwater Cable System
UCS............ Underwater Communications System
UCS............ Underwater Conservation Society [*British*] (DI)
UCS............ Unican Security Systems Ltd. [*Toronto Stock Exchange symbol*]
UCS............ Uniform Chromaticity Scale [*Illuminant*]
UCS............ Uniform Communications System
UCS............ Union de Campesinos Salvadorcenos [*Peasant Union*] [*El Salvador*]
UCS............ Union of Catholic Students [*British*] (AEBS)
UCS............ Union of Concerned Scientists (EA)
UCS............ Unit Cost of Sales
UCS............ Unit-Count System
UCS............ United Carriers Systems, Inc. [*ICAO designator*] (FAAC)
UCS............ United Community Services
UCS............ United Computing Systems, Inc.
UCS............ United Concerned Students (EA)
UCS............ United States Army Corps of Engineers, Sacramento, Sacramento, CA [*OCLC symbol*] (OCLC)
UCS............ Unit of Coastal Sedimentation [*NERC*] [*British*]
UCS............ Universal Call Sequence
UCS............ Universal Camera Site (KSC)
UCS............ Universal Card Scanner [*Computer science*] (DIT)
UCS............ Universal Cargo Sling
UCS............ Universal Character Set [*Computer science*]
UCS............ Universal Classification System
UCS............ Universal Clothing System [*Software package*] (NCC)
UCS............ Universal Command System (KSC)
UCS............ Universal Communications Subsystem (NITA)
UCS............ Universal Component System [*Computer science*] (PCM)
UCS............ Universal Connector Strip
UCS............ Universal Control System (NASA)
UCS............ University College School [*British*] (BI)
UCS............ University Computer Services [*Ball State University*] [*Research center*] (RCD)
UCS............ University Computing Services [*University of Southern California*] [*Research center*] (RCD)
UCS............ University Computing Services [*State University of New York at Buffalo*] [*Research center*] (RCD)
UCS............ Urine Collection System [*NASA*] (KSC)
UCS............ User Control Store
UCS............ Utilities Control System [*NASA*] (KSC)
UCS............ Utility Consulting Services [*Petroleum Information Corp.*] [*Information service or system*] (IID)
UCSA.......... Ukrainian Canadian Servicemen's Association
UCSA.......... Uniform Conditional Sales Act [*Legal shorthand*] (LWAP)
UCSA.......... Uniform Controlled Substances Act [*National Conference of Commissioners on Uniform State Laws*]
UCSA.......... Union des Confederations Sportives Africaines [*Association of African Sports Confederations - AASC*] [*Yaounde, Cameroon*] (EAIO)
UCSA.......... United Chian Societies of America [*Later, CSA*] (EA)
UCSB.......... Universal Character Set Buffer [*Computer science*] (MHDB)
UCSB.......... University of California, Santa Barbara
UCSBS........ Ukrainian Catholic Soyuz of Brotherhoods and Sisterhoods (EA)
UCSC.......... University City Science Center [*Research center*] (RCD)
UCSC.......... University of California, Santa Cruz
UCSD.......... Universal Communications Switching Device
UCSD.......... University of California, San Diego
UCSD-p....... University of California at San Diego-p (NITA)
UC-SDRL..... University of Cincinnati Structural Dynamics Research Laboratory
UCSEL......... University of California Structural Engineering Laboratory (KSC)
UCSF.......... University of California, San Francisco
UCSJ........... Union of Councils for Soviet Jews (EA)
UCSL........... Unilever Computer Services Ltd. (NITA)
UCSL........... Union Congolaise des Syndicats Libres [*Congolese Union of Free Syndicates*] [*Leopoldville*]
UCSM.......... Utility Control Strategy Model [*Developed at Carnegie Mellon University for acid rain analysis*]
UCSMP........ University of Chicago School Mathematics Project (AEE)
UCSR.......... Ukrainian Center for Social Research (EA)
UCSR.......... Unionist Committee for Social Reform [*British*]
UCSS.......... Universal Communications Switching System (MCD)
UC/SSL....... University of California/Space Sciences Laboratory (KSC)
UCST.......... Upper Critical-Solution-Temperature
UCSTR........ Universal Code Synchronous Transmitter Receiver
UCSU.......... United Carters' and Storemen's Union [*British*]
UCSUR........ University Center for Social and Urban Research [*University of Pittsburgh*] [*Research center*] (RCD)
UCSUS........ Ukrainian Catholic Students of the United States [*Defunct*] (EA)
UCT............ Order of United Commercial Travelers of America [*Columbus, OH*] (EA)
UCT............ Ultrasonic Computed Tomography [*For examining interiors of solids*]
UCT............ Unchanged Conventional Treatment [*Medicine*]
UCT............ Underwater Construction Team [*Navy*] (NVT)
UCT............ Union Carbide Canada Equipment Trust Units [*Toronto Stock Exchange symbol*]

UCT............ Unite Centrale de Traitement [*Central Processing Unit - CPU*] [*French*]
UCT............ Units Compatibility Test
UCT............ Universal Coordinated Time
UCT............ University of Cape Town [*South Africa*]
UCT............ University of Connecticut [*Storrs*] [*Seismograph station code, US Geological Survey*] (SEIS)
UCT............ Urine Culture Tube [*Clinical chemistry*]
UCTA........... United Commercial Travellers Association of Great Britain and Ireland, Inc. (BI)
UCTA........... University and College Theatre Association (EA)
UCTA........... Urine Collection/Transfer Assembly [*Apollo*] [*NASA*]
UCTC........... Union Camerounaise des Travailleurs Croyants [*Cameroonese Union of Believing Workers*]
UCTC........... United Counties Trust Co. [*NASDAQ symbol*] (SAG)
UCTD........... Unclassifiable Connective Tissue Disease [*Medicine*] (DMAA)
UCTF........... Union Culturelle et Technique de Langue Francaise [*French-Language Cultural and Technical Union*] [*Paris, France*] (EA)
UCTGA.......... United Commercial Travellers' Guild of Australia
UCTL........... Up Control [*Aerospace*] (AAG)
UCTLIG......... Universities and Colleges Teaching, Learning, and Information Group [*Universities and Colleges Information Systems Association*] (AIE)
UCTN........... UC Television Network Corp. [*NASDAQ symbol*] (SAG)
UCTPA.......... United Coppersmiths Trade Protection Association [*A union*] [*British*]
UCTS........... United Chairmakers' Trade Society [*A union*] [*British*]
UCTS........... United Church Training School
UC TVNet..... UC Television Network Corp. [*Associated Press*] (SAG)
UCU............ University of California Union List, Berkeley, CA [*OCLC symbol*] (OCLC)
UCU............ UtiliCorp United [*NYSE symbol*] (TTSB)
UCU............ Utilicorp United, Inc. [*NYSE symbol Toronto Stock Exchange symbol*] (SPSG)
UCUE........... Udmurt Commodity Universal Exchange [*Russian Federation*] (EY)
UCUPrA......... UtiliCorp United $2.05 Pref [*NYSE symbol*] (TTSB)
UCUPrC......... UtiliCorp Capital 8.875%'MIPS' [*NYSE symbol*] (TTSB)
UCV............ Uncontrolled Variable
UCV............ Unimproved Capital Value [*Business term*] (ADA)
UCV............ United Confederate Veterans
UCW............ Union of Communications Workers [*British*] (ECON)
UCW............ Unit Control Word [*Computer science*] (BUR)
UCW............ United Church Women of the National Council of Churches (EA)
UCW............ University College of Wales
UCW............ University of Connecticut, Storrs, CT [*OCLC symbol*] (OCLC)
UCWA........... United Construction Workers Association (OICC)
UCWE........... Underwater Countermeasures and Weapons Establishment [*British*]
UCWR........... Universities Council on Water Resources (MCD)
UCWR........... Upon Completion Thereof Will Return To [*Air Force*]
UCWRE.......... Underwater Countermeasures and Weapons Research Establishment [*British militar y*] (DMA)
UCX............ Unemployment Compensation, Ex-Servicemen
UCX............ Urine Culture [*Urology*] (DAVI)
UCX............ Utility Jet Transport [*Air Force*]
UCY............ Union City, TN [*Location identifier FAA*] (FAAL)
UCY............ United Caribbean Youth
UCYM........... United Christian Youth Movement [*Defunct*] (EA)
UD............. Georgian Bay [*ICAO designator*] (AD)
UD............. lloyd Your Trans-Australian Airline [*ICAO designator*] (AD)
UD............. Ud Dictum [*As directed*] [*Pharmacy*] (DAVI)
UD............. Ulcerative Dermatitis [*Dermatology*] (DAVI)
UD............. Ulnar Deviation [*Medicine*]
UD............. Ultimate Dependability [*Automotive designation*]
UD............. Unable to Approve Departure for the Time Specified [*Aviation*] (FAAC)
UD............. Unavoidable Delay
UD............. Undated
U/D............ Under Deck (ADA)
UD............. Under Direct Vision (DAVI)
UD............. Underdrive [*Automotive engineering*]
UD............. Underground Distribution (MSA)
UD............. Underwater Demolition [*Navy*] (NVT)
UD............. Undesirable Discharge [*Military*]
UD............. Undetected Defect
UD............. Undifferentiated (BJA)
UD............. Undiluted
UD............. Unidentifiable (BJA)
UD............. Unidirectional
UD............. Uniflow Diesel [*Nissan-designed engine*]
UD............. Union Democratique [*New Caledonia*] [*Political party*] (EY)
UD............. Unit Designation
UD............. Unit Diary
UD............. Unit Director
UD............. Unit Dose [*Medicine*]
UD............. Unit Dose Package [*Pharmacy*] (DAVI)
UD............. Unity-and-Diversity World Council (EA)
UD............. Universal Dipole (DEN)
UD............. University of Denver [*Colorado*]
UD............. Unlawful Detainer [*Legal term for an eviction proceeding*]
UD............. Unplanned Derating [*Electronics*] (IEEE)
UD............. Update [*Computer science*] (NASA)
U/D............ Up/Down (KSC)
UD............. Upper Deck [*Naval*]
UD............. Urban District
UD............. Urban Education [*Educational Resources Information Center (ERIC) Clearinghouse*] [*Columbia University*] (PAZ)
UD............. Urethral Discharge [*Medicine*]
UD............. Uridine Diphosphate [*Biochemistry*] (AAMN)
UD............. Uroporphyrinogen Decarboxylase [*Also, UDase*] [*An enzyme*]
UD............. Usable Depth (MCD)
UD............. Usage Data
UD............. Ut Dictum [*As Directed*] [*Latin*]
UD............. Utility Dog [*Dog show term*]
UDA............ Pusdiklat Perhubungan Udara/PLP [*Indonesia*] [*ICAO designator*] (FAAC)
UDA............ Ulster Defence Association
UDA............ Ultrasonic Detergent Action
UDA............ Union for Democratic Action
UDA............ United Democratic Alliance [*European political movement*] (ECON)
UDA............ United States Department of the Interior, Alaska Resources, Anchorage, AK [*OCLC symbol*] (OCLC)
UDA............ Universal Detective Association [*Defunct*] (EA)
UDA............ Urban Development Agency [*British*]
UDA............ Urtica Dioica Agglutinin [*Biochemistry*]
UDAA........... Unlawfully Driving Away Auto
UDAC........... User Digital Analog Controller
UDACS.......... Underwater Detection and Classification System (IAA)
UDAG........... Urban Development Action Grant [*HUD*]
Udal........... Udal's Fiji Law Reports [*A publication*] (DLA)
UDAL........... United Distillers (Australia) Ltd. [*Commercial firm*]
U Dallas...... University of Dallas (GAGS)
UDAM........... Universal Digital Avionics Module (MCD)
UDAP........... Universal Digital Autopilot
UDAR........... Universal Digital Adaptive Recognizer (IEEE)
UDAS........... Unified Direct Access Standards (IAA)
UDAS........... Unified Direct Access System (BUR)
UDAS........... Universal Data Acquisition System
UDAS........... Universal Database Access Service [*Telecommunications*] (TSSD)
UDase.......... Uroporphyrinogen Decarboxylase [*Also, UD*] [*An enzyme*]
UDATS.......... Underwater Damage Assessment Television System (DNAB)
U Dayton...... University of Dayton (GAGS)
UDB............ Unified Data Base
UDB............ Union Democratique Bretonne - Unvaniezh Demokratel Breizh [*Breton Democratic Union*] [*France Political party*] (PPW)
UDB............ Universal Data Base (IAA)
UDB............ Unliquidated Dollar Balances (AAGC)
UDB............ Up-Data Buffer [*Computer science*]
UDC............ National Park Service, National Capital Region, Washington, DC [*OCLC symbol*] (OCLC)
UDC............ Ultrasonic Doppler Cardioscope [*Heartbeat monitor*]
UDC............ Underdeveloped Countries
UDC............ Underwater Decompression Computer [*Navy*] (CAAL)
UDC............ Uniao Democratica de Cabo Verde [*Democratic Union of Cape Verde*]
UDC............ Unidirectional Composite (MCD)
UDC............ Unidirectional Current (IAA)
UDC............ Union Delegates Committee [*Air carrier designation symbol*]
UDC............ Union Democratica Cristiana [*Christian Democratic Union*] [*Bolivia*] [*Political party*] (PPW)
UDC............ Union Democratique Centrafricaine [*Central African Democratic Union*] [*Political party*] (PPW)
UDC............ Union Democratique du Cameroun [*Political party*] (EY)
UDC............ Union Democratique du Centre [*Democratic Union of the Center*] [*Switzerland Political party*] (PPE)
UDC............ Union du Centre [*Mayotte*] [*Political party*] (EY)
UDC............ Union for Democratic Communications (EA)
UDC............ Union of Democratic Control [*British*]
UDC............ Union of the Democratic Centre [*Sahara*] [*Political party*] (PPW)
UDC............ Union pour la Democratie Congolaise [*Political party*] (EY)
UDC............ Unit Deployment of Containers (MCD)
UDC............ United Daughters of the Confederacy (EA)
UDC............ Unity-and-Diversity Council [*Later, UD*] (EA)
UDC............ Universal Decimal Classification [*Online database field identifier*]
UDC............ Universal Decimal Code (IAA)
UDC............ Universal Digital Control
UDC............ Universal Disk Controller [*Central Point Software*]
UDC............ University of the District of Columbia
UDC............ Up-Down Counter
UDC............ Upper Dead Center
UDC............ Urban Development Committee [*New South Wales, Australia*]
UDC............ Urban Development Corp. [*New York State agency*]
UDC............ Urban District Council [*British*]
UDC............ Ursodeoxycholate [*Biochemistry*]
UDC............ Ursodeoxycholic Acid
UDC............ User Designation Codes [*Navy*] (NG)
UDC............ User Dissemination Circuit [*Air Force Weather Center*]
UDC............ Usual Diseases of Childhood [*Medicine*]
UDCA........... Undesirable Discharge, Trial by Civil Authorities [*Navy*]
UDCA........... Union pour la Defense des Commercants et des Artisans [*Union for the Defense of Traders and Artisans*] [*France Political party*] (PPE)
UDCA........... Ursodeoxycholic Acid [*Pharmacology*]
UDCA........... US Deaf Cycling Association (EA)
UD-CCM......... University of Delaware Center for Composite Materials (RDA)
UDCCS.......... Uniform Data Classification Code Structure [*Navy*] (NG)
UDCD........... Unit Data and Control Diagram (IAA)
UDCI........... United Dental Care [*NASDAQ symbol*] (TTSB)
UDCI........... United Dental Care, Inc. [*NASDAQ symbol*] (SAG)
UDCS........... United Data Collection System (MCD)

UDCV .... Uniao Democratica de Cabo Verde [*Democratic Union of Cape Verde*]
UDD .... Bermuda Dunes, CA [*Location identifier FAA*] (FAAL)
UDD .... Bureau of Land Management, Denver, Denver, CO [*OCLC symbol*] (OCLC)
UDD .... Cuddapan [*Queensland*] [*Airport symbol*] (AD)
UDD .... Uddeholm [*Sweden*] [*Seismograph station code, US Geological Survey*] (SEIS)
UDD .... Ulster Diploma in Dairying
UDD .... Union Democratique Dahomeenne [*Benin*] [*Political party*]
UDD .... Union pour la Democratie et le Developpement [*Mali*] [*Political party*] (EY)
UDD .... Union pour la Democratie et le Developpement Mayumba [*Gabon*] [*Political party*] (EY)
UDDA .... Uniform Determination of Death Act [*National Conference of Commissioners on Uniform State Laws*]
UDDE .... Undesirable Discharge, Desertion without Trial [*Navy*]
UDDF .... Up and Down Drafts [*NWS*] (FAAC)
UDDIA .... Union Democratique pour la Defense des Interets Africains [*Democratic Union to Defend African Interests*]
UDDL .... Ultrasonic Dispersive Delay Line
UDDS .... Union para la Democracia y el Desarrollo Social [*Equatorial Guinea*] [*Political party*] (EY)
UDDS .... Urban Dynamometer Driving Schedule [*EPA engine test*]
UDE .... Underwater Detection Establishment [*British*] (MCD)
UDE .... Undetermined Etiology
UDE .... Union Douaniere Equatoriale [*Equatorial Customs Union*]
UDE .... United States Fish and Wildlife Service, Region 2, Albuquerque, NM [*OCLC symbol*] (OCLC)
UDE .... Universal Data Entry
UDE .... Universal Data Exchange [*Computer science*] (PCM)
UDE .... University Department of Education (AIE)
UDEAC .... Union Douaniere et Economique de l'Afrique Centrale [*Central African Customs and Economic Union*] (EAIO)
UDEAO .... Union Douaniere des Etats de l'Afrique et l'Ouest [*Customs Union of West African States*] [*Later, CEAO*]
UDEC .... Unitized Digital Electronic Calculator (MCD)
UDECMA-KMPT ... Parti Democratique Chretien Malgache [*Malagasy Christian Democratic Party*] [*Political party*] (PPW)
UDEFEC .... Union Democratique des Femmes Camerounaises [*Cameroonese Democratic Women's Union*]
U de J .... Ursulines of Jesus [*Roman Catholic women's religious order*]
U Del .... University of Delaware (GAGS)
UDENAMO ... Uniao Democratica Nacional de Mocambique [*Mozambican National Democratic Union*] [*Later, FRELIMO*] [*Political party*]
U Denver ..... University of Denver (GAGS)
UDET .... Universal Digital Element Tester (MCD)
UDETA .... Unsymmetric Diethyltrianine (MCD)
U Det L Rev ... University of Detroit. Law Review [*A publication*] (DLA)
UDETO .... Union Democratique Togolaise [*Togolese Democratic Union*]
U Detroit ...... University of Detroit Mercy (GAGS)
UDF .... Boise Interagency Fire Center, Boise, ID [*OCLC symbol*] (OCLC)
UDF .... Federation Guadeloupeenne de l'Union pour la Democratie Francaise [*Guadeloupe Federation of the Union for French Democracy*] [*Political party*] (PPW)
UDF .... Ulster Defence Force
UDF .... Unducted Fan [*Type of prop engine developed by General Electric Co.*]
UDF .... Union Defence Force [*British*]
UDF .... Union Democrata Foral [*Spain Political party*] (EY)
UDF .... Union of Democratic Forces [*Bulgaria*] [*Political party*]
UDF .... Union of Democratic Forces [*Mauritania*] [*Political party*] (EY)
UDF .... Union pour la Democratie Francaise [*Union for French Democracy*] [*France Political party*] (PPW)
UDF .... Union pour la Democratie Francaise [*Union for French Democracy*] [*Wallis and Futuna Islands*] [*Political party*] (EY)
UDF .... Union pour la Democratie Francaise [*Union for French Democracy*] [*Mayotte*] [*Political party*] (EY)
UDF .... Union pour la Democratie Francaise [*Union for French Democracy*] [*New Caledonia*] [*Political party*] (PPW)
UDF .... Union pour la Democratie Francaise [*Union for French Democracy*] [*Reunion*] [*Political party*] (PPW)
UDF .... Union pour la Democratie Francaise [*Union for French Democracy*] [*French Guiana*] [*Political party*] (PPW)
UDF .... Uniroyal, Dunlop, and Firestone [*Facetious translation of South African political party, United Democratic Front, which suppsedly executed dissenters with burning tires*]
UDF .... Unit Derating Factor [*Electronics*] (IEEE)
UDF .... Unit Development Folder (MCD)
UDF .... Unit Dining Facilities
UDF .... United Democratic Front [*South Africa*] [*Political party*] (PPW)
UDF .... United Democratic Front [*India*] [*Political party*] (PPW)
UDF .... Universal Disk Format (PCM)
UDF .... Upside-Down Flipper
UDF .... User-Defined Function [*Computer science*] (PCM)
UDF .... Utility and Data Flow (NASA)
UDFAA .... Upholstery and Decorative Fabrics Association of America [*Defunct*] (EA)
UDFAM .... User-Defined File Access Method [*Computer science*] (IT)
UDFE .... Undesirable Discharge, Fraudulent Enlistment [*Navy*]
UDFFC .... Unity-Displacement-Factor Frequency Changer (DICI)
UDFMA .... Upholstery and Drapery Fabric Manufacturers Association [*Later, UFMA*]
UDFP .... Union Democratique des Forces du Progres [*Benin*] [*Political party*] (EY)
UDFT .... Union Democratique des Femmes Tunisiennes [*Democratic Union of Tunisian Women*]
UDG .... National Fisheries Center, Kearneysville, WV [*OCLC symbol*] (OCLC)
UDG .... Unit Derated Generation [*Electronics*] (IEEE)
UD(G) .... United Distillers (Guiness) [*Commercial firm*]
UDG .... Uracil DNA [*Deoxyribonucleic acid*]
UDG .... Uracil DNA Glycosylase [*An enzyme*]
UDH .... National Park Service, Harpers Ferry Center, Harpers Ferry, WV [*OCLC symbol*] (OCLC)
UDH .... Universal Die Holder
UDH .... Unplanned Derated Hours [*Electronics*] (IEEE)
UDHS .... Unit Demand History Summary [*Military*] (AABC)
UDI .... Uberlandia [*Brazil*] [*Airport symbol*] (OAG)
UDI .... Udine [*Italy*] [*Seismograph station code, US Geological Survey*] (SEIS)
UDI .... Unilateral Declaration of Independence [*of Southern Rhodesia*]
UDI .... Union Democratica Independiente [*Independent Democratic Union*] [*Chile*] [*Political party*] (PPW)
UDI .... Union Democratique des Independants [*Democratic Union of Independents*] [*France Political party*] (PPE)
UDI .... Unique Data Item (MCD)
UDI .... United Dominion Indus [*NYSE symbol*] (TTSB)
UDI .... United Dominion Industries Ltd. [*NYSE symbol*] (SPSG)
UDI .... United States Department of the Interior, Natural Resources Library, Washington,DC [*OCLC symbol*] (OCLC)
UDI .... Universal Digital Instrument (IAA)
UDI .... Urban Development Institute [*Australia*]
UDI .... Utility Data Institute [*Information service or system*] (IID)
UDIA .... United Dairy Industry Association (EA)
UDICON .... Universal Digital Communications Network [*Computer science*] (PDAA)
UDID .... Unique Data Item Description (MCD)
UDIL .... University Directors of Industrial Liaison (PDAA)
U-Dink .... Upper Class - Double [*or Dual*] Income, No Kids [*Lifestyle classification*]
UDIR .... USAREUR Daily Intelligence Report (MCD)
UDIRL .... University of Durham Industrial Research Laboratories [*British*]
UDIT .... Union pour la Defense des Interets du Tchad [*Union for the Defense of Chadian Interests*]
UDITPA .... Uniform Division of Income for Tax Purposes Act
UDITS .... Universal Digital Test Set
UDJ .... Northern Prairie Wildlife Research Center, Jamestown, ND [*OCLC symbol*] (OCLC)
UDJM .... Union Democratique de la Jeunesse Marocaine [*Democratic Union of Moroccan Youth*]
UDJV .... Union Democratique de la Jeunesse Voltaique [*Voltaic Democratic Youth Union*]
UDK .... United States Fish and Wildlife Service, Alaska Area Office, Anchorage, AK [*OCLC symbol*] (OCLC)
UDK .... Upper Deck
UDK .... User Defined Key [*Computer science*] (HGAA)
UDL .... Bureau of Land Management, Boise District Office, Boise, ID [*OCLC symbol*] (OCLC)
UDL .... Ultrasonic Delay Line
UDL .... Underwater Data Link (MCD)
UDL .... Uniform Data Language
UDL .... Uniform Data Link
UDL .... Unit Designation List (DOMA)
UDL .... Unit Detail Listings [*Air Force*]
UDL .... Unit Document Listing (MCD)
UDL .... Universal Development Laboratory [*Computer debugger*] [*Orion Instruments*]
UDL .... Up-Data Link [*Computer science*]
UDL .... Urine Disposal Lock (DNAB)
UDLP .... United Defense Limited Partnership (RDA)
UDLP .... United Democratic Labour Party [*Trinidad and Tobago*] [*Political party*] (PPW)
UDLP .... United Dominica Labour Party [*Political party*] (PPW)
UDM .... National Mine Health and Safety Academy, Beckley, WV [*OCLC symbol*] (OCLC)
UDM .... Unassigned Direct Material [*Navy*] (DNAB)
UDM .... Unidimensional Drafting Manual
UDM .... Union Democratique Mauritanienne [*Mauritanian Democratic Union*] [*Political party*] (PD)
UDM .... Union of Democratic Mineworkers [*British*]
UDM .... Universal Drafting Machine Corp.
UDM .... Upright Drilling Machine
UDMA .... United Dance Merchants of America (EA)
UDMH .... Unsymmetrical Dimethylhydrazine [*Rocket fuel base, convulsant poison*]
UDMH/H .... Unsymmetrical Dimethylhydrazine Hydrazine Blend (NASA)
UDMU .... Universal Decoder Memory Unit (DNAB)
UDN .... Dnieproavia [*Ukraine*] [*FAA designator*] (FAAC)
UDN .... National Park Service, National Register Division, Washington, DC [*OCLC symbol*] (OCLC)
UDN .... Ulcerative Dermal Necrosis [*Medicine*]
UDN .... Underwater Doppler Navigation
UDN .... Uniao Democratica Nacional [*National Democratic Union*] [*Brazil*]
UDN .... Union Democrata Nacional [*National Democratic Union*] [*El Salvador*] [*Political party*] (PPW)
UDN .... Union Democratica Nicaraguense [*Nicaraguan Democratic Union*] [*Political party*] (PD)
UDO .... Undetermined Origin [*Medicine*] (AAMN)
UDO .... United States Fish and Wildlife Service, Billings, MT [*OCLC symbol*] (OCLC)

UDOFT......... Universal Digital Operational Flight Trainer [*Navy*]
UDOFTT....... Universal Digital Operational Flight Trainer Tool [*Navy*] (IAA)
UDom.......... United Dominion Realty Trust [*Associated Press*] (SAG)
UDomIn....... United Dominion Industries Ltd. [*Associated Press*] (SAG)
UDomR........ United Dominion Realty Trust, Inc. [*Associated Press*] (SAG)
UDOP.......... UHF [*Ultrahigh Frequency*] Doppler System
UDOP.......... Ultrahigh Doppler (NASA)
UDP............ National Park Service, Denver, Denver, CO [*OCLC symbol*] (OCLC)
UDP............ Ulster Diploma in Poultry Husbandry
UDP............ Undecyl Dodecyl Phthalate
UDP............ Uniao Democratica Popular [*Popular Democratic Unity*] [*Portugal*] [*Political party*]
UDP............ Unidad Democratica Popular [*Popular Democratic Unity*] [*Peru*] [*Political party*] (PPW)
UDP............ Unidad Democratica Popular [*Popular Democratic Unity*] [*Bolivia*] [*Political party*]
UDP............ Unification du Droit Prive
UDP............ Uniform Datagram Protocol [*Telecommunications*] (OSI)
UDP............ Uniform Delivered Price [*Business term*] (MHDB)
UDP............ Union pour la Democratie Populaire [*Union for People's Democracy*] [*Senegal*] [*Political party*] (PPW)
UDP............ Unitary Development Plan (EERA)
UDP............ United Data Processing (BUR)
UDP............ United Democratic Party [*Belize*] [*Political party*] (PD)
UDP............ United Democratic Party [*Basotho*] [*Political party*] (PPW)
UDP............ Universal Datagram Protocol [*Computer science*] (PCM)
UDP............ Urban Development Program [*University of Western Ontario*] [*Canada*] (IRC)
UDP............ Uridine Diphosphate [*Biochemistry*]
UDP............ User Datagram Protocol (BYTE)
UDPAG......... Uridine(diphospho)acetylglucosamine [*Biochemistry*]
UDPB.......... Union des Democrates et Patriotes Burkinabe [*Burkino Faso*] [*Political party*] (EY)
UDPC.......... UNIVAC Data Processing Center (HGAA)
UDPG.......... Uridine Diphosphate Glucose [*Biochemistry*]
UDPGA......... Uridine Diphosphate Glucuronic Acid [*Biochemistry*]
UDPgal........ Uridine Diphosphate Galactose [*Biochemistry*] (MAH)
UDPGDH........ Uridinediphosphoglucose Dehydrogenase [*An enzyme*]
UDPglu........ Uridine Diphosphate Glucose [*Biochemistry*] (DAVI)
UDPGT......... Uridine Diphosphate Glucuronosyltransferase [*An enzyme Biochemistry*]
UDPIA......... Uniform Disclaimer of Property Interests Act [*National Conference of Commissioners on Uniform State Laws*]
UDP/IP........ User Datagram Protocol/Internet Protocol [*Computer science*]
UDPK.......... United Democratic Party of Kurdistan [*Political party*] (BJA)
UDPL.......... United Dated Parts List [*Configuration listing*] (MCD)
UDPM.......... Union Democratique du Peuple Malien [*Mali People's Democratic Union*] [*Political party*] (PPW)
UDPPDU........ Unit Data Presentation Protocol Data Unit [*Telecommunications*] (OSI)
UDPS.......... Union pour la Democratie et le Progres Social [*Democratic Union of Social Progress*] [*Zaire*] [*Political party*]
UDPS.......... Union pour le Developpement et le Progres Social [*The Congo*] [*Political party*] (EY)
UDPT.......... Union Democratique des Populations Togolaises [*Democratic Union of Togolese People*]
UDQ............ Bureau of Land Management, Library, New Orleans, New Orleans, LA [*OCLC symbol*] (OCLC)
UDR............ Democratic Rural Union [*Brazil*]
UDR............ Udaipur [*India*] [*Airport symbol*] (OAG)
UDR............ Ulster Defence Regiment [*Military unit*] [*British*]
UDR............ Undersampling Ratio
UDR............ Union pour la Defense de la Republique [*Union for the Defense of the Republic*] [*France Political party*] (PPE)
UDR............ Union pour la Democratie Francaise [*Union for French Democracy*] [*Martinique*] [*Political party*] (PPW)
UDR............ United Dominion Realty Trust, Inc. [*NYSE symbol*] (SPSG)
UDR............ United Dominion Rlty Tr [*NYSE symbol*] (TTSB)
UDR............ United States Department of the Interior, Bureau of Reclamation, Denver, CO [*OCLC symbol*] (OCLC)
UDR............ Universal Digital Readout
UDR............ Universal Document Reader (BUR)
UDR............ Urgent Data Request [*GIDEP*]
UDR............ Usage Data Report
UDR............ Utility Data Reduction
UDRA.......... Uniform Divorce Recognition Act [*National Conference of Commissioners on Uniform State Laws*]
UDRA.......... United Drag Racers Association (EA)
UDRC.......... Utility Data Reduction Control (IAA)
UDRC.......... Utility Data Retrieval Control
UDRE.......... User Differential Range Error [*Navigation systems*]
UDRI.......... University of Dayton Research Institute [*Ohio*]
UDRN.......... Union pour la Democratie et la Reconstruction Nationale [*Benin*] [*Political party*] (EY)
UDRO.......... Utility Data Reduction Output (IAA)
UDRO.......... Utility Data Retrieval Output
UDRP.......... Uridine Diribose Phosphate [*Biochemistry*]
UDRPrA........ Utd Dominion Rlty 9.25% 'A' Pfd [*NYSE symbol*] (TTSB)
UDRPS......... Ultrasonic Data Recording and Processing System (NRCH)
UDRS.......... Union Democratique pour le Renouveau Social [*Benin*] [*Political party*] (EY)
UDRS.......... Universal Driver Rating System [*Harness racing*]
UDRT/RAD...... Union Democratique pour le Respect du Travail - Respect voor Arbeid en Democratie [*Democratic Union for the Respect of Labor*] [*Belgium Political party*] (PPW)
U/DRV......... Underdrive [*Automotive engineering*]
UDS............ Office of Surface Mining Reclamation and Enforcement, Region V, Denver, CO [*OCLC symbol*] (OCLC)
UDS............ Ultra-Doppler Sonography [*Radiology*] (DAVI)
UDS............ Ultramar Diamond Shamrock Corp. [*NYSE symbol*] (SAG)
UDS............ Ultraviolet Detector System
UDS............ Ultronic Data Systems (IAA)
UDs............ Undeliverables [*Fundraising*]
UDs............ Undeliverables [*Canadian*] [*Postal term*] (NFD)
UDS............ Unified Data System [*Computer science*]
UDS............ Union Democratique Senegalaise [*Senegalese Democratic Union*]
UDS............ Union pour la Democratie et la Solidarite Nationale [*Benin*] [*Political party*] (EY)
UDS............ Uniscope Display System (NITA)
UDS............ Unit Data System [*Military*]
UDS............ Universal Data Set (CMD)
UDS............ Universal Data System [*Army*]
UDS............ Universal Data Systems [*Hardware manufacturer*]
UDS............ Universal Digital Switch (MCD)
UDS............ Universal Distributed System [*UNIVAC*]
UDS............ Universal Documentation System [*NASA*]
UDS............ Unscheduled DNA Synthesis [*Genetics*]
UDS............ Urban Data Service [*International City Management Association*] (IID)
UDS............ Urban Decision Systems, Inc. [*Information service or system*] (IID)
UDS............ Urine Drug Screen [*Medicine*]
UDS............ Utility Data Systems [*Information service or system*] (IID)
UDS............ Utilization and Disposal Service [*Functions transferred to Property Management and Disposal Service*] [*General Services Administration*]
UDSG.......... Union Democratique et Sociale Gabonaise [*Gabonese Democratic and Social Union*]
UDSL.......... Union of Scientific Leisure Clubs [*France*] (EAIO)
UDSM.......... Union Departemental de Syndicats du Mungo [*Departmental Union of the Trade Unions of Mungo*] [*Cameroon*]
UDSM.......... Union des Democrates Sociaux de Madagascar [*Union of Social Democrats of Madagascar*]
UDSR.......... Union Democratique et Socialiste de la Resistance [*Democratic and Socialist Union of the Resistance*] [*France Political party*] (PPE)
UDSR.......... United Duroc Swine Registry (EA)
UDT............ Underdeck Tonnage
UDT............ Underwater Demolition Team [*Navy*]
UDT............ Unidirectional Transducer (IAA)
UDT............ Union Dominions Trust [*Commercial firm*]
UDT............ Union of Democratic Thais in the US (EA)
UDT............ United Detector Technology
UDT............ United States Fish and Wildlife Service, Science Reference Library, Twin Cities,MN [*OCLC symbol*] (OCLC)
UDT............ United Tire & Rubber Co. Ltd. [*Toronto Stock Exchange symbol*]
UDT............ Universal Dataflow and Telecommunication [*IFLA Core Program*]
UDT............ Universal Data Transcriber [*Navy*]
UDT............ Universal Documents Transfer [*Computer science*] (ECII)
UDT............ Universal Document Transport [*Computer science*] (OA)
UDT............ Upgraded Data Terminal (MCD)
UDT............ User Display Terminal
UDT............ Utility Dog Title with a Tracking Dog Title
UDT............ Utility Dog Tracker [*Degree of obedience training*]
UDTC.......... User-Dependent-Type Code
UDTD.......... Updated (MSA)
UDTDET........ Underwater Demolition Team Detachment [*Navy*] (NVT)
UDT/EOD....... Underwater Demolition Team/Explosive Ordnance Proposal [*Navy*] (MCD)
UDTI.......... Universal Digital Transducer Indicator
UDTPHIBSPAC... Underwater Demolition Teams, Amphibious Forces, Pacific Fleet [*Navy*]
UDTS.......... Universal Data Transfer Service [*ITT World Communications, Inc.*] [*Secaucus, NJ*] [*Telecommunications*] (TSSD)
UDTS.......... Universal Data Transmission System [*For international access*]
UDTUNIA....... Uniform Disclaimer of Transfers under Nontestamentary Instruments Act [*National Conference of Commissioners on Uniform State Laws*]
UDTV.......... Ultra-High Definition Television (DOM)
UDTX.......... Utility Dog and Tracking Excellent [*Degree of obedience training*]
UDTX.......... Utility Dog Title with a Tracking Dog Excellent Title
UDU............ National Maritime Museum, San Francisco, CA [*OCLC symbol*] (OCLC)
UDU............ Unabhaengige Demokratische Union [*Independent Democratic Union*] [*Austria Political party*] (PPE)
UDU............ Underwater Demolition Unit
UDU............ Union Democratique Unioniste [*Tunisia*] [*Political party*] (EY)
UDUAL......... Union de Universidades de America Latina [*Union of Latin American Universities*] [*Mexico*]
U Dubuque... University of Dubuque (GAGS)
UDucGS........ Church of Jesus Christ of Latter-Day Saints, Genealogical Society Library, Duchesne Branch, Stake Center, Duchesne, UT [*Library symbol Library of Congress*] (LCLS)
UDUF.......... Undesirable Discharge, Unfitness [*Navy*]
UDUPA......... Uniform Distribution of Unclaimed Property Act [*National Conference of Commissioners on Uniform State Laws*]
UDV............ Union Democratique Voltaique [*Voltaic Democratic Union*] [*Banned, 1974*]
UD-Ve......... Union Democratique pour la Cinquieme Republique [*Democratic Union for the Fifth Republic*] [*France Political party*] (PPE)
UDVST......... Utility Dog Title with a Variable Surface Tracking Title
UDW............ Ultradeep Water

UDW.......... Western Energy and Land Use Team, Fort Collins, CO [*OCLC symbol*] (OCLC)
UDX.......... Office of Surface Mining Reclamation and Enforcement, Washington, DC [*OCLC symbol*] (OCLC)
UDX.......... Utility Dog Excellent [*Dog show term*] [*Canada*]
UDY.......... USGS [*United States Geological Survey*] Water Resources Division, New York District, Albany, NY [*OCLC symbol*] (OCLC)
UDZ.......... United States Department of the Interior, Western Archeological Center, Tucson, AZ [*OCLC symbol*] (OCLC)
UE.......... Air La [*ICAO designator*] (AD)
UE.......... Ultrasonic Engineering (MCD)
UE.......... Uncertain Etiology Upper Esophagus [*Medicine*] (DAVI)
U/E.......... Unedged (DAC)
UE.......... Unemployment (GFGA)
UE.......... Unexpired (ADA)
UE.......... United Air [*ICAO designator*] (AD)
UE.......... United Electrical, Radio, and Machine Workers of America (EA)
UE.......... United Electrical, Radio, and Machine Workers of Canada [*See also OUE*]
UE.......... United Electrodynamics (AAG)
UE.......... United Empire [*Canada*]
UE.......... Unit Entry
UE.......... Unit Equipment [*as authorized to an Air Force unit*]
UE.......... Unit Establishment
UE.......... Unit Exception (CMD)
UE.......... Unit Exhausted [*Military*] (GFGA)
UE.......... Unity of Empire [*Award*] [*British*]
UE.......... University Extension
UE.......... Until Exhausted
UE.......... Update and Ephemeria (MUGU)
UE.......... Upper Entrance [*Theater*]
UE.......... Upper Epidermis [*Botany*]
UE.......... Upper Esophagus [*Medicine*] (DMAA)
UE.......... Upper Extremity [*Medicine*]
UE.......... Urinary Energy [*Nutrition*]
UE.......... User Element [*Telecommunications*] (OSI)
UE.......... User Equipment
UE.......... Uterine Epithelium [*Medicine*]
UE.......... Utility Expenditure (MHDW)
UEA.......... Graphic Arts Union Employers of America (EA)
UEA.......... Ulex europeus Agglutinin [*Immunology*]
UEA.......... Unattended Equipment Area
UEA.......... Union Europeenne de l'Ameublement [*European Furniture Manufacturers Federation*] (EAIO)
UEA.......... Union Europeenne des Aveugles [*European Blind Union - EBU*] (EAIO)
UEA.......... Union of European Abattoirs [*Belgium*] (EAIO)
UEA.......... United Egg Association (EA)
UEA.......... United Epilepsy Association [*Later, EFA*] (EA)
UEA.......... Universala Esperanto Asocio [*Universal Esperanto Association*] (EAIO)
UEA.......... University of East Anglia [*England*]
UEA.......... Uranium Enrichment Associates [*Bechtel Corp., Union Carbide Corp., Westinghouse Electric Corp.*]
UEAC.......... Union of Central African States
UEAC.......... United European American Club
UEAC.......... Unit Equipment Aircraft
UEAES.......... Union Europeenne des Alcools, Eaux de Vie et Spiritueux [*European Union of Alcohol, Brandies and Spirits*] [*EC*] (ECED)
UEAI.......... Ulex Europaeus Agglutinin I
UEAI.......... Union Europeenne des Arabisants et des Islamisants [*European Union of Arab and Islamic Studies - EUAIS*] [*Spain*] (EAIO)
UEAPME.......... Union Europeenne de l'Artisanat et des Petites et Moyennes Entreprises [*European Association of Craft, Small and Medium-Sized Enterprises*] [*EC*] (ECED)
U East LJ.......... University of the East. Law Journal [*Manila, Philippines*] [*A publication*] (DLA)
UEAtc.......... Union Europeenne pour l'Agrement Technique dans la Construction [*European Union of Agrement*] (EAIO)
UEAWG.......... Urban Export Advisory Working Group [*Australia*]
UEAWS.......... Union of European Associations of Water Suppliers [*Belgium*] (EAIO)
Ueb.......... Uebereinkommen [*Agreement*] [*German*] (ILCA)
UEB.......... Ultrasonic Epoxy Bonder
UEB.......... Unexploded Bomb
UEB.......... Union Economique BENELUX
UEB.......... Union of Evangelical Baptists (EAIO)
UEB.......... Upper Equipment Bay [*NASA*] (KSC)
UEBC.......... Union Espanola Benefica de California (EA)
UEC.......... Union des Etudiants Communistes [*France*]
UEC.......... Union Electric Co.
UEC.......... Union Europeenne de la Carrosserie [*European Union of Coachbuilders - EUC*] [*Belgium*]
UEC.......... Union Europeenne des Experts Comptables Economiques et Financiers [*European Union of Public Accountants*]
UEC.......... United Engineering Center
UEC.......... Unit Endurance Chamber (MCD)
UEC.......... Unmanned Equipment Cabinet
UEC.......... Upper Epidermal Cell [*Botany*]
UEC.......... Urban Elderly Coalition (EA)
UEC.......... Urban Environment Conference (EA)
UEC.......... USS Engineers & Consultants, Inc. [*Information service or system*] (IID)
UECA.......... Underground Engineering Contractors Association [*Later, ECA*] (EA)
UECA.......... Union Europeenne du Commerce Ambulant [*European Union of Door-to-Door Trade*] [*EC*] (ECED)
UECB.......... Union Europeenne des Commerces du Betail
UECBV.......... Union Europeenne du Commerce du Betail et de la Viande [*European Livestock and Meat Trading Union*] (EAIO)
UECL.......... Ultra Electronics Components Ltd. (IAA)
UECL.......... Union Europeenne des Constructeurs de Logements [*European Union of Independent Building Contractors*]
UECS.......... Unified Electronic Computer System [*Air Force*]
UECU.......... Union for Experimenting Colleges and Universities [*Later, UI*] (EA)
UECWA.......... Underwater Explorers' Club of Western Australia
UED.......... Air LA, Inc. [*ICAO designator*] (FAAC)
UED.......... Ultrafast Electron Diffraction [*Physics*]
UED.......... Ultrasonic Echo Detection (PDAA)
UED.......... United Electro Dynamics (IAA)
UED.......... Uranian Electrostatic Discharge [*Planetary science*]
UEDC.......... Union Europeenne Democrate Chretienne [*European Christian Democratic Union*]
UEDS.......... Uniao de Esquerda para a Democracia Socialista [*Left Union for Social Democracy*] [*Portugal Political party*] (PPE)
UEE.......... Queenstown [*Australia Airport symbol*] (OAG)
UEE.......... Unit Essential Equipment [*Military*] (NATG)
UEEA.......... Union Europeenne des Exploitants d'Abbatoirs [*European Abbattoirs Union*] [*EC*] (ECED)
UEEB.......... Union des Exploitations Electriques en Belgique
U/EECM.......... Unattended/Expendable Electronic Countermeasure
UEEJ.......... Union Europeenne des Etudiants Juifs [*European Union of Jewish Students - EUJS*] (EA)
UEF.......... Uniform Electric Field
UEF.......... Union Europaeischer Forstberufsverbaende [*Union of European Foresters*] [*Teningen-Heimbach, Federal Republic of Germany*] (EAIO)
UEF.......... Union Europeenne des Federalistes
UEF.......... Union Europeenne Feminine [*European Union of Women*]
UEF.......... Upper End Fitting [*Nuclear energy*] (NRCH)
UEFA.......... Union of European Football Associations [*Switzerland*] (EAIO)
UEFJA.......... Uniform Enforcement of Foreign Judgments Act [*National Conference of Commissioners on Uniform State Laws*]
UEFJM.......... Union of European Fashion Jewellery Manufacturers [*Italy*] (EAIO)
UEFS.......... United Enginemen's Friendly Society [*A union*] [*British*]
UEGO.......... Universal Exhaust Gas Oxygen Sensor [*Fuel systems*] [*Automotive engineering*]
UEHB.......... Uniform Effective Health Benefits
UEI.......... Union Energy [*Toronto Stock Exchange symbol*] (SPSG)
UEI.......... Union of Educational Institutions [*British*]
UEIC.......... United East India Co.
UEIC.......... Universal Electronics, Inc. [*NASDAQ symbol*] (SAG)
UEIC.......... Univl Electronics [*NASDAQ symbol*] (TTSB)
UEIL.......... Union Europeenne des Independants en Lubrifiants [*European Union of Independent Lubricant Manufacturers*] [*EC*] (ECED)
UEIS.......... United Engineering Information System
UEITP.......... Union Europeenne des Industries de Transformation de Pomme de Terre [*European Union of the Potato Processing Industries*]
UEJ.......... Unattended Expendable Jammer (MCD)
UEJDC.......... Union Europeenne des Jeunes Democrates-Chretiens [*European Union of Young Christian Democrats*]
UEK.......... Elmira, NY [*Location identifier FAA*] (FAAL)
UEL.......... Quelimane [*Mozambique*] [*Airport symbol*] (OAG)
UEL.......... Ultra Electronics Ltd. (IAA)
UEL.......... Underwater Environmental Laboratory [*General Electric Co.*]
UEL.......... United Empire Loyalist
UeL.......... University of East London (ECON)
UEL.......... UNIX Europe Ltd. (NITA)
UEL.......... Upper Earnings Limit (PDAA)
UEL.......... Upper Electrical Limit [*Nuclear energy*] (NRCH)
UEL.......... Upper Explosive Limit
UEL.......... Usage Exception List (MCD)
UE Law J.......... University of the East. Law Journal [*Manila, Philippines*] [*A publication*] (DLA)
UELF.......... Union des Editeurs de Langue Francaise (EAIO)
UELL.......... Chulman [*Former USSR ICAO location identifier*] (ICLI)
UELV.......... Ultralite Expendable Launch Vehicle [*NASA*]
UEM.......... Union Electrica Madrilena [*Spain*]
UEM.......... Union Europeenne de Malacologie [*European Malacological Union*]
UEM.......... Union Evangelique Mondiale [*World Evangelical Fellowship*]
UEM.......... United Engineers (Malaysia) Berhad (ECON)
UEM.......... Unite Electromagnetique [*Electromagnetic Unit*]
UEM.......... Universal Electron Microscope
UEM.......... University Extension Manuals [*A publication*]
UEMC.......... Unidentified Endosteal Marrow Cell [*Hematology*]
UEMN.......... Union des Ecrivains du Monde Noir [*World Union of Black Writers - WUBW*] (EAIO)
UEMO.......... Europaische Vereinigung der Allgemeinartze [*European Union of General Practitioners*] [*Denmark*] (EAIO)
UEMO.......... Union Europeenne des Medecins Omnipraticiens [*European Union of General Practitioners*] (EA)
UEMS.......... Unione Europea di Medicina Sociale [*European Union of Social Medicine - EUSM*] (EAIO)
UEMS.......... Union Europeenne des Medecins Specialistes [*European Society of Medical Specialists*] [*Belgium*] (SLS)
UEMTA.......... European Union for the Prevention of Cruelty to Animals (EAIO)
UEN.......... Unisave Energy Ltd. [*Vancouver Stock Exchange symbol*]
UENCPB.......... Union Europeenne des Negociants en Cuirs et Peaux Bruts [*European Association of Traders in Leather and Raw Hides*] [*EC*] (ECED)

UENDC......... Union Europeenne des Negociants Detaillants en Combustibles [*European Union of Merchant Dealers in Combustibles*] [*Switzerland*]
UEO............ Kume Jima [*Japan*] [*Airport symbol*] (OAG)
UEO............ Union de l'Europe Occidentale [*Western European Union - WEU*] (EAIO)
UEO............ Union of Electrical Operatives [*British*]
UEO............ Unit Emplaning Officer [*Military British*]
UEOA.......... Union des Etudiants Ouest Africains [*Union of West African Students*]
UEP............ Underwater Electric Potential
UEP............ Unequal Error Protection (IEEE)
UEP............ Uniform External Pressure
UEP............ Union Electric [*NYSE symbol*] (TTSB)
UEP............ Union Electric Co. [*NYSE symbol*] (SPSG)
UEP............ Union Europeenne de Pedopsychiatres [*European Union for Child Psychiatry*]
UEP............ United Egg Producers (EA)
UEP............ Unit Evolutionary Period
UEP............ Unplanned Event Pickup [*NASA*] (KSC)
UEP............ Unusual End of Program [*Computer science*]
UEPC.......... Union Europeenne des Promoteurs Constructeurs [*European Union of Developers and House Builders*] [*Belgium*] (EAIO)
UEPG.......... United European Power Grid (IAA)
UEPH.......... Unaccompanied Enlisted Personnel Housing [*Navy*] (DNAB)
UEPMD........ Union Europeenne des Practiciens en Medecine Dentaire [*European Union of Dental Medicine Practitioners*] (EAIO)
UEPPrA........ Union Electric, $3.50 Pfd [*NYSE symbol*] (TTSB)
UEPPrC........ Union Electric, $4.00 Pfd [*NYSE symbol*] (TTSB)
UEPPrD........ Union Electric, $4.50 Pfd [*NYSE symbol*] (TTSB)
UEPPrE........ Union Electric, $4.56 Pfd [*NYSE symbol*] (TTSB)
UEPPrG........ Union Electric, $6.40 Pfd [*NYSE symbol*] (TTSB)
UEPPrI......... Union Electric, $7.44 Pfd [*NYSE symbol*] (TTSB)
UEPR.......... Unsatisfactory Equipment Performance Report [*Military*] (AABC)
UEPS.......... Union Europeenne de la Presse Sportive [*European Sports Press Union*] (EAIO)
UEPS.......... Union Europeenne des Pharmacies Sociales [*European Union of the Social Pharmacies*] [*EC*] (ECED)
UEPS.......... United Elvis Presley Society (EAIO)
UER............ Union Europeenne de Radiodiffusion [*European Broadcasting Union - EBU*] (EAIO)
UER............ Unique Equipment Register (NASA)
UER............ Unite d'Enseignement et de Recherche [*Units of Teaching and Research*] [*University of Paris*]
UER............ Unit Equipment Report [*Marine Corps*] (DOMA)
UER............ Uniunea Evreilor Romani (BJA)
UER............ University Entrance Requirement [*British*] (DI)
UER............ Unplanned Event Record [*NASA*] (KSC)
UER............ Unsatisfactory Equipment Report
UER............ Ust-Elegest [*Former USSR Seismograph station code, US Geological Survey*] (SEIS)
UERA.......... Umbilical Ejection Relay Assembly (AAG)
UERA.......... Uniform Extradition and Rendition Act [*National Conference of Commissioners on Uniform State Laws*]
UERD.......... Underwater Explosives Research Division [*Navy*]
UERDC........ Underwater Explosion Research and Development Center [*Navy*] (CAAL)
UERE.......... Ultrasonic Echo Ranging Equipment
UERE.......... User Equivalent Range Error
UERG.......... Universitywide Energy Research Group [*University of California*] [*Research center*] (RCD)
UERL.......... Underwater Explosives Research Laboratory
UERL.......... Unplanned Event Record Log [*NASA*] (KSC)
UERMWA..... United Electrical, Radio, and Machine Workers of America
UERN.......... Utilities Emergency Radio Network (IAA)
UERP.......... Unione Europea di Relazioni Pubbliche [*European Union of Public Relations - International Service Organization - EURPISO*] (EAIO)
UERPIC....... Underground Excavation and Rock Properties Information Center (NITA)
UERPS........ Uniform Excess Reporting Procedures [*DoD*]
UERS.......... Unusual Event Recording System [*Jet transport*]
UERT.......... Union Explosivos-Rio Tinto [*Spain*]
UERT.......... Universal Engineer Tractor, Rubber-Tired [*Army*]
UES............ Snow College, Ephraim, UT [*Library symbol Library of Congress*] (LCLS)
UES............ Unified Energy System [*Russia*]
UES............ Uniform Emission Standard (DCTA)
UES............ United Engineering Societies (IAA)
UES............ United Engineering Steels [*Commercial firm British*]
UES............ Universal Environmental Shelter (KSC)
UES............ University Extension Series [*A publication*]
UES............ Upper Esophageal Sphincter [*Anatomy*]
UES............ Upstream Expression Sequence [*Genetics*]
UES............ Waukesha, WI [*Location identifier FAA*] (FAAL)
UESA.......... Ukrainian Engineers' Society of America (EA)
UESD.......... Uniao da Esquerda Socialista Democratica [*Union of the Socialist and Democratic Left*] [*Portugal Political party*] (PPW)
UESEG........ United Earth Sciences Exploration Group [*British*]
UESK.......... Unit Emergency Supply Kit
UESK.......... Unit Essential Spares Kit [*Military*] (AFM)
UESRG........ United Earth Sciences Research Group [*British*] (NUCP)
UEST.......... Institute of Urban and Environmental Studies [*Brock University*] [*Canada Research center*] (RCD)
UET............ Quetta [*Pakistan*] [*Airport symbol*] (OAG)
UET............ Unattended Earth Terminal
UET............ Underground Explosion Test (IAA)
UET............ United Engineering Trustees (EA)
UET............ Unit Equipment Table [*Military*]
UET............ Universal Emulating Terminal
UET............ Universal Engineer Tractor [*Later, BEST*] [*Army*]
UET............ Universal Expenditure Tax [*British*] (DI)
UET............ Ur Excavations: Texts [*London*] [*A publication*] (BJA)
UETA.......... Universal Engineer Tractor, Armored [*Army*]
UETP.......... University-Enterprise Training Partnership [*European Community*] (AIE)
UETRT........ Universal Engineer Tractor, Rubber-Tired [*Army*]
UETS.......... Universal Emulating Terminal System [*Computer science*] (MHDB)
U Evansville... University of Evansville (GAGS)
UEVP.......... Union Europeenne des Veterinaires Practiciens [*European Union of Practising Veterinary Surgeons*] (EAIO)
UEW........... United Electrical, Radio, and Machine Workers of America [*Also, UERMWA*] (NTCM)
UEW........... United Electrical Workers
UEWR.......... Upgraded Early Warning RADAR [*Military*]
UEWS.......... Ultimate Elastic Wall Stress [*Mechanical engineering*]
UEX............ Underexposed [*Photography*]
UEX............ Unit Exception (ECII)
UEX............ Ur Excavations [*A publication*] (BJA)
u/ext........... Upper Extremity [*Orthopedics*] (DAVI)
UF.............. Sydaero [*ICAO designator*] (AD)
UF.............. Ultrafilter [*or Ultrafiltration*]
UF.............. Ultrafine
UF.............. Ultrasonic Frequency (MSA)
UF.............. Unavailability Factor [*Electronics*] (IEEE)
UF.............. Uncertainty Factor [*Toxicology*]
UF.............. Under Frequency (DNAB)
UF.............. Underground Feeder
UF.............. Unemployed Father (OICC)
UF.............. Uni Air International [*France ICAO designator*] (ICDA)
UF.............. Unified Forces [*Military*]
UF.............. Union de Fribourg: Institut International des Sciences Sociales et Politiques [*Union de Fribourg: International Institute of Social and Political Sciences*] [*Fribourg/Pensier, Switzerland*] (EAIO)
UF.............. United Focus [*Later, Omni Learning Institute*] (EA)
UF.............. United Force [*Guyana*] (PD)
UF.............. United Foundation
UF.............. United Front [*Sri Lanka*] [*Political party*] (FEA)
UF.............. United States Facilities [*NYSE symbol*] (SAG)
UF.............. Uniterra Foundation (EA)
UF.............. Unit of Fire [*Military*] (MUGU)
UF.............. Universal Feeder [*Medicine*] (DMAA)
UF.............. Universities Funding Council [*British*]
UF.............. University of Florida [*Gainesville*]
UF.............. Unknown Factor
UF.............. Unofficial Funds [*British*]
UF.............. Uplink Frequency
UF.............. Upper Air Fallout [*Civil Defense*]
UF.............. Urea Formaldehyde
UF.............. Used For
UF.............. Used Fuel [*Nuclear energy*] (NUCP)
UF.............. Utility File
UF.............. Utilization Factor
UF6............ Uranium Hexafluoride
UFA............ State Flight Academy of Ukraine [*FAA designator*] (FAAC)
UFA............ Ukrainian Fraternal Association (EA)
UFA............ Unesterified Fatty Acid [*Biochemistry*]
UFA............ Uniformed Firefighters Association
UFA............ Uniform Firearms Act
UFA............ Union des Femmes d'Algerie [*Union of Algerian Women*]
UFA............ Union of Flight Attendants (EA)
UFA............ United Families of America (EA)
UFA............ United Fathers of America (EA)
UFA............ University Film Association [*Later, UFVA*] (EA)
UFA............ Universum-Film Aktien-Gesellschaft [*German motion picture company*]
UFA............ Unsaturated Fatty Acid [*Organic chemistry*]
UFA............ Until Further Advised
UFA............ Usable Floor Area [*Classified advertising*] (ADA)
UFA............ Use Frequency Analysis
UFAA.......... United Food Animal Association [*Defunct*] (EA)
UFAC.......... Unlawful Flight to Avoid Custody
UFAC.......... Upholstered Furniture Action Council (EA)
UFAED........ Unit Forecast Authorization Equipment Data (AFM)
UFAM.......... Universal File Access Method
UFAP.......... Ultrafine Ammonium Perchlorate (MCD)
UFAP.......... Union Francaise des Annuaires Professionels [*French Union for Professional Yearbooks*] [*Trappes*] [*Information service or system*] (IID)
UFAP.......... Universal-Fine Ammonium Perchlorate [*Organic chemistry*] (MCD)
UFAP.......... Unlawful Flight to Avoid Prosecution
UFAS.......... Unified Flight Analysis System [*NASA*]
UFAS.......... Uniform Federal Accessibility Standards [*Department of Housing and Urban Development*] (GFGA)
UFAT.......... Unlawful Flight to Avoid Testimony
UFAW.......... Universities Federation for Animal Welfare [*British*]
UFAWU........ United Fishermen and Allied Workers' Union [*Canada*]
UFB............ Unfit for Broadcast (WDMC)
UFBS.......... Union des Francais de Bon Sens [*Union of Frenchmen of Good Sense*] [*Political party*] (PPW)

UFBS .... United Friendly Boilermakers' Society [*A union*] [*British*]
UFC .... Unidirectional Filamentary Composite
UFC .... Unified Fire Control (MCD)
UFC .... Uniform Freight Classification
UFC .... Union des Facteurs du Canada [*Letter Carriers' Union of Canada - LCUC*]
UFC .... United Flight Classification
UFC .... United Flowers-by-Wire Canada
UFC .... United Free Church [*Scotland*]
UFC .... United Fruit Co. [*Railroad*] (MHDW)
UFC .... Unit Funded Costs (MCD)
UFC .... Universal Flight Computer
UFC .... Universal Foods Corp. [*NYSE symbol*] (SPSG)
UFC .... Universal Frequency Counter
UFC .... Universities Funding Council [*British*] (ECON)
UFC .... Univl Foods [*NYSE symbol*] (TTSB)
UFC .... Urinary Free Cortisol
UFCA .... Uniform Fraudulent Conveyance Act [*National Conference of Commissioners on Uniform State Laws*]
UFCA .... United Film Carriers Association [*Defunct*] (EA)
UFCA .... Urethane Foam Contractors Association [*Defunct*] (EA)
UFCC .... Underwater Fire Control Computer [*Navy*] (CAAL)
UFCC .... Uniform Freight Classification Committee
UFCE .... Union Federaliste des Communautes Ethniques Europeennes [*Federal Union of European Nationalities*]
UFCG .... Underwater Fire Control Group
UFCP .... Up-Front Control Panel (MCD)
UFCS .... UF-6 Chemical Feed Station [*Nuclear energy*] (NRCH)
UFCS .... Underwater Fire Control System
UFCS .... United Fellowship for Christian Service [*Later, BMMFI*] (EA)
UFCS .... United Fire & Casualty [*NASDAQ symbol*] (TTSB)
UFCS .... United Fire & Casualty Co. of Iowa [*NASDAQ symbol*] (NQ)
UFCS .... United Free Church of Scotland (DI)
UFCS .... Universal Fire Control System
UFCS .... Up-Front Control Set (MCD)
UFCT .... United Federation of College Teachers [*AFL-CIO*]
UFCW .... United Food and Commercial Workers International Union (EA)
UFCWIU .... United Food and Commercial Workers International Union (EA)
UFD .... Davis County Library, Farmington, UT [*Library symbol Library of Congress*] (LCLS)
UFD .... Ultrafast Detection
UFD .... Union des Forces Democratiques [*Union of Democratic Forces*] [*Mali*] [*Political party*] (EY)
UFD .... Union des Forces Democratiques [*Union of Democratic Forces*] [*France Political party*] (PPE)
UFD .... United Foods, Inc. [*AMEX symbol*] (SPSG)
UFD .... Unit Functional Diagram (IAA)
UFD .... Universal Firing Device [*Military*] (AABC)
UFD .... User File Directory (NASA)
UFD.A .... United Foods Cl'A' [*AMEX symbol*] (TTSB)
UFD.B .... United Foods Cv Cl'B' [*AMEX symbol*] (TTSB)
UFDC .... Union des Femmes Democratiques du Canada
UFDC .... Union des Forces Democratiques du Cameroun [*Union of Democratic Forces of Cameron*] [*Political party*] (EY)
UFDC .... United Federation of Doll Clubs (EA)
UFDC .... Universal Flight Director Computer
UFE .... Union des Feculeries de Pommes de Terre de la CE [*EC*] (ECED)
UFE .... Union des Francais a l'Etranger [*Union of French Citizens Abroad*] [*Political party*] (PPW)
UFE .... Union des Groupements Professionnels de l'Industrie de le Feculerie de Pommes deTerre [*Union of Professional Groups of the Potato Starch Industry*]
UFE .... Union of the Finance-Personnel in Europe [*EC*] (ECED)
UFE .... Universal Field Element (MCD)
UFedS .... United Federal Savings Bank [*Associated Press*] (SAG)
UFEM .... Ultrafem, Inc. [*NASDAQ symbol*] (SAG)
UFEM .... Ultrafem Inc. [*NASDAQ symbol*] (TTSB)
UFEMAT .... Federation Europeenne des Associations Nationales des Negociants en Materiaux deConstruction [*European Association of National Builders Merchants Associations*] (EAIO)
UFEMTO .... Union des Femmes du Togo [*Togolese Women's Union*]
UFER .... Mouvement International pour l'Union Fraternelle entre les Races et les Peuples [*International Movement for Fraternal Union among Races and Peoples*]
UFERI .... Union des Federalistes et Republicains Independants [*Zaire*] [*Political party*] (EY)
UFESA .... United Fire Equipment Service Association (EA)
UFET .... Unipolar Field-Effect Transistor (IAA)
UFF .... Ufficiale [*Official, Officer*] (EY)
UFF .... U-Landshjaelp fra Folk til Folk [*Development Aid From People to People*] [*Denmark*] (EAIO)
UFF .... Ulster Freedom Fighters
UFF .... Union et Fraternite Francaise [*French Union and Fraternity*] [*Political party*] (PPE)
UFF .... United Freedom Front [*Defunct*] (EA)
UF-F .... Universal Flip-Flop [*Computer science*]
UFF .... University Film Foundation (EA)
UFFCS .... IEEE Ultrasonics, Ferroelectrics, and Frequency Control Society (EA)
UFFI .... Urea-Formaldehyde Foam Insulation
UFFVA .... United Fresh Fruit and Vegetable Association (EA)
UFGCC .... Ultrafine Ground Calcium Carbonate [*Inorganic chemistry*]
UFH .... Ultra-Light Field Howitzer [*British*]
UFH .... Upper Facial Height [*Medicine*]
UFi .... Fillmore City Library, Fillmore, UT [*Library symbol Library of Congress*] (LCLS)
UFI .... Unifi, Inc. [*NYSE symbol*] (SPSG)
UFI .... Union des Foires Internationales [*Union of International Fairs*] (EAIO)
UFI .... Unit Fault Isolation (MCD)
UFI .... Universal Fermi Interaction
UFI .... Upstream Failure Indication (NITA)
UFI .... Usage Frequency Indicator
UFI .... User Friendly Interface
UFIB .... Union Federazioni Italiane Bocce [*Italian lawn bowling, or boccie, organization*]
UFIDA .... Union Financiere Internationale pour le Developpement de l'Afrique [*International Financial Union for the Development of Africa*]
UFIPTE .... Union Franco-Iberique pour la Coordination de la Production et du Transport de l'Electricite [*Franco-Iberian Union for Coordinating the Production and Transmission of Electricity*] (EAIO)
UFireC .... United Fire & Casualty Co. of Iowa [*Associated Press*] (SAG)
UFIRS .... Uniform Fire Incident Reporting System [*National Fire Protection Association*]
UFIRS .... Universal Far Infrared Sensor (MCD)
UFJC .... United Fund for Jewish Culture [*Defunct*] (EA)
UFL .... Underfull Employment [*Economics*]
UFL .... Upper Flammable Limit
U Fla .... University of Florida (GAGS)
UFLC .... Union Internationale des Femmes Liberales Chretiennes [*International Union of Liberal Christian Women*]
UFM .... Uganda Freedom Movement (PD)
UFM .... Union Fleuve de Mano [*Mano River Union - MRU*] (EAIO)
UFM .... United Financial Management Ltd. [*Toronto Stock Exchange symbol*]
UFM .... Universal Field Multiplexer [*Computer science*] (ECII)
UFM .... University for Man [*Manhattan, KS*]
UFM .... Unnormalized Floating Multiply (SAA)
UFM .... Upper Figure of Merit
UFM .... User to File Manager
UFMA .... United Fur Manufacturers Association (EA)
UFMA .... Upholstered Furniture Manufacturers Association (EA)
UFMA .... Upholstery Fabric Manufacturers Association [*Defunct*] (EA)
UFMCC .... Universal Fellowship of Metropolitan Community Churches (EA)
UFMG .... Universal Manufacturing [*NASDAQ symbol*] (SAG)
UFMG .... Univl Mfg [*NASDAQ symbol*] (TTSB)
UFMOP .... Unintentional Frequency Modulation on Pulse (MCD)
UFMT .... Urban Federation for Music Therapists [*Later, AAMT*] (EA)
UFN .... Union Franco-Nigerienne [*French-Nigerian Union*]
UFN .... Until Further Notice
UFNSHD .... Unfinished
UFO .... Ultralight Flight Organization (EA)
UFO .... Unflagged Order [*Laboratory science*] (DAVI)
UFO .... Unidentified Flying Object [*"Flying saucers"*] [*Facetious translation: "Undue Fuss Over"*]
UFO .... Unidentified Foreign Object [*Medicine*] (DAVI)
UFO .... Uniform Field Organization [*DoD*]
UFO .... United 510 Owners (EA)
UFO .... Unit Families Officer [*Military British*]
UFO .... Universal Fiber Optic (MCD)
UFO .... Unlimited Freak-Out [*Slang*] (DSUE)
UFO .... Unwanted Falling Objects (MCD)
UFO .... User Files On-Line [*Computer science*] (MHDI)
UFO .... User Friendly Operating System [*UFO Systems, Inc.*]
UFO .... Users Files on Line (IAA)
UFOA .... Union des Femmes de l'Ouest Africain [*West African Women's Union*]
UFOCAT .... UFO [*Unidentified Flying Object*] Catalog [*Center for Unidentified Flying Object Studies*]
UFOD .... Union Francaise des Organismes de Documentation (NITA)
UFOIN .... UFO Investigators Network [*British*]
UFOIRC .... Unidentified Flying Object Information Retrieval Center, Inc. (EA)
UFood .... United Foods, Inc. [*Associated Press*] (SAG)
UFOP .... Ultrafast-Opening Parachute (NG)
UFORDAT .... Umweltforschungsdatenbank [*Data Bank for Environmental Research Projects*] [*Deutsches Umweltbundesamt*] [*Germany*] [*Information service or system*] (CRD)
U format .... Unknown Format (NITA)
UFORQ .... Unidentified Flying Object Research Queensland [*Australia*]
UFOS .... Unacceptable Face of Socialism (DSUE)
UFOs .... United Flying Octogenarians (EA)
UFP .... Ultrafine Powder [*Materials processing*]
UFP .... Under Frequency Protector (MCD)
UFP .... Unemployed Full Pay [*Military British*]
UFP .... Union Frontier Police [*European Economic Community*] (ECON)
UFP .... United Federal Party [*Northern Rhodesia*]
UFP .... United Federation of Planets (EA)
UFP .... Universal Folded Plate [*Structural system*] (RDA)
UFP .... Utility Facilities Program [*Computer science*] (IBMDP)
UFPA .... University Film Producers Association [*Later, UFVA*] (EA)
UFPC .... United Federation of Postal Clerks [*Formerly, NFPOC*] [*Later, APWU*] (EA)
UFPDP .... Union des Forces Populaires pour la Democratie et le Progres [*Niger*] [*Political party*] (EY)
UFPI .... Universal Forest Products [*NASDAQ symbol*] (SAG)
UFPI .... Univl Forest Products [*NASDAQ symbol*] (TTSB)
UFP-ICP .... Ultrafine Particle Inductively Coupled Plasma [*Spectrometry*]
UFPO .... Underground Facilities Protective Organization (EA)
UFPS .... Uniform Federal Procurement System (AAGC)
UFPT .... UFP Technologies [*Commercial firm NASDAQ symbol*] (SAG)
UFP Tch .... UFP Technologies [*Commercial firm Associated Press*] (SAG)
UFR .... UF-6 Recovery Room [*Nuclear energy*] (NRCH)
UFR .... Ultrafiltration Rate [*Biomedicine*]

UFR .... Under Frequency Relay
UFR .... Unfinanced Requirement [*Army*]
UFR .... United Africa Airline (Liberia), Inc. [*ICAO designator*] (FAAC)
UFR .... Urine Flow Rate
UFRCC .... Uniform Federal Regional Council City
UFRM .... United Federal Savings & Loan of Rocky Mount [*NASDAQ symbol*] (NQ)
UFRM .... United Fed Svgs Bk Rocky Mt NC [*NASDAQ symbol*] (TTSB)
UFRWO .... United Federation of Russian Workers' Organizations of USA and Canada (EA)
UFS .... UFS, Inc. [*ICAO designator*] (FAAC)
UFS .... Ulster Folklife Society (EA)
UFS .... Ultimate Factor of Safety
UFS .... Under Frequency Sensing (MCD)
UFS .... United Farmers and Stockowners (EERA)
UFS .... United Features Syndicate [*Commercial firm*]
UFS .... United Feeder Service [*ICAO designator*] (FAAC)
UFS .... Universal Financial System (MHDW)
UFS .... Unnormalized Floating Subtract
UFSA .... Ukrainian Free Society of America (EA)
UFSD .... Union Free School District (BARN)
uFSH .... Urinary Follicle-Stimulating Hormone [*Medicine*] (DMAA)
UFSI-IWA .... Universities Field Staff International - Institute of World Affairs (EA)
UFSJ .... Unitarian Fellowship for Social Justice
UFSS .... Unified Flexible Spacecraft Simulation
UFSS .... Unmanned Free Swimming Submersibles (DNAB)
UFSSA .... United Farmers and Stockowners of South Australia
UFST .... United Federation of Canadian Star Trekkers
UFT .... Ultrasonic Frequency Transformer [*or Translator*]
UFT .... United Federation of Teachers [*New York*]
UFT .... United Fly Tyers (EA)
UFTA .... Uniform Fraudulent Transfer Act [*National Conference of Commissioners on Uniform State Laws*]
UFTAA .... Universal Federation of Travel Agents' Associations [*International Federa tion of Travel Agencies and Universal Organization of Travel Agents' Associations*] [*Formed by a merger of Australia*] (EAIO)
UFTR .... University of Florida Teaching Reactor
UFTS .... United Furnishing Trades Society [*A union*] [*British*]
UFU .... United Fishermen Union [*British*]
UFU .... Utility Flight Unit [*Navy*]
UFUA .... United Firefighters Union of Australia
UFUSA .... United Firefighters Union of South Australia
UFUWA .... United Firefighters Union of Western Australia
UFV .... Unsymmetrical Free Vibration
UFVA .... University Film and Video Association (EA)
UFVF .... University Film and Video Foundation (EA)
UFW .... United Farm Workers of America (EA)
UFW .... United Furniture Workers of America (EA)
UFW .... Urban Fighting Weapon (MCD)
UFWA .... United Farm Workers of America
UFWA .... United Furniture Workers of America
UFWDA .... United Four-Wheel Drive Associations (EA)
UFWOC .... United Farm Workers Organizing Committee [*Later, UFW*]
UFWU .... United Farm Workers Union
UFX .... Uniflex, Inc. [*AMEX symbol*] (SAG)
UG .... Norfolk Island Airlines [*Australia ICAO designator*] (ICDA)
UG .... Radio Frequency Connectors [*JETDS nomenclature*] [*Military*] (CET)
UG .... Uganda [*ANSI two-letter standard code*] (CNC)
ug .... Uganda [*MARC country of publication code Library of Congress*] (LCCP)
Ug .... Ugric [*Finno-Ugric Linguistic Family*] (BARN)
Ug .... Ugutio [*Huguccio*] [*Deceased, 1210*] [*Authority cited in pre-1607 legal work*] (DSA)
UG .... Uncertain Glory: Folklore and the American Revolution [*A publication*]
UG .... Undergarment
UG .... Undergoing (DNAB)
UG .... Undergraduate
UG .... Underground [*Technical drawings*]
Ug .... Uniform, Fine-Grained [*Soil*]
UG .... Union Guide (IAA)
UG .... United Guardian, Inc. [*AMEX symbol*] (SAG)
UG .... Unite Guyanaise [*Guyanese Unity*] [*Political party*] (PPW)
UG .... Universal Generalization [*Rule of quantification*] [*Logic*]
UG .... Universal Government
UG .... Upgrading Training [*Job Training and Partnership Act*] (OICC)
UG .... Urban Gorillas (EA)
UG .... Urogenital [*Medicine*]
UG .... User Group [*Computer science*]
UG .... US-North Africa (Gibraltar) Convoy [*World War II*]
UG .... Uteroglobin [*Physiology*]
UGA .... Uganda [*ANSI three-letter standard code*] (CNC)
UGA .... Uganda Airlines Corp. [*ICAO designator*] (FAAC)
uga .... Ugaritic [*MARC language code Library of Congress*] (LCCP)
UGA .... Ugashik [*Alaska*] [*Airport symbol*] (OAG)
UGA .... Ugashik, AK [*Location identifier FAA*] (FAAL)
UGA .... Under General Anesthesia (DAVI)
UGA .... Underwriters Grain Association (EA)
UGA .... United Golfers' Association (EA)
UGA .... Unity Gain Amplifier
UGA .... University of Georgia (PDAA)
UGA .... Unscreened Granulated Aluminate [*Inorganic chemistry*]
UGA .... Uracil Guanine Adenine [*Genetics*]
UGAA .... Untersuchungen zur Geschichte und Altertumskunde Aegyptens [*K. Sethe*] [*A publication*] (BJA)
UGAL .... Union des Groupements d'Achat Cooperatifs de Detaillants de l'Europe [*Association of Cooperative Retailer-Owned Wholesalers of Europe - ACROWE*] (EAIO)
UGAN .... Uganda
Ugan .... Uganda (VRA)
Uganda Leg Focus ... Uganda Legal Focus [*A publication*] (DLA)
Uganda LF ... Uganda Law Focus [*A publication*] (DLA)
Uganda LR ... Uganda Protectorate Law Reports [*1904-51*] [*A publication*] (DLA)
UGAQ .... United Graziers' Association of Queensland [*Australia*]
UGAQUE .... United Graziers' Association of Queensland Union of Employees [*Australia*]
UGB .... Pilot Point, AK [*Location identifier FAA*] (FAAL)
UGB .... Union de Guerreros Blancos [*White Warriors' Union*] [*El Salvador*] [*Political party*] (PD)
UGB .... Union Giovantu Benadir [*Benadir Youth Union*] [*Somalia*]
UGB .... United Gulf Bank [*Middle East*]
UGB .... Unity Gain Bandwidth
UGB .... Upper Guard Band
UGB .... Urban Growth Boundary
UGBW .... Unity Gain Bandwidth
UGC .... Ukrainian Gold Cross (EA)
UGC .... Ultrasonic Grating Constant
UGC .... United Gold Corp. [*Vancouver Stock Exchange symbol*]
UGC .... United Nations Food and Agriculture Organization Intergovernmental Committee [*World Food Program*]
UGC .... Unity Gain Crossover
UGC .... Universal Guided Column
UGC .... University Grants Commission [*India*]
UGC .... University Grants Committee [*British*]
UGC .... Urgench [*Former USSR Airport symbol*] (OAG)
UGCAA .... Union Generale des Cooperatives Agricoles d'Approvisionnement
UGCW .... United Glass and Ceramic Workers of North America
UGD .... United Greenwood [*Vancouver Stock Exchange symbol*]
UGDP .... University Group Diabetes Program [*Study group involving 12 medical schools*] [*Defunct*]
UGE .... Undergraduate Engineering Program [*Air Force*]
UGEAO .... Union Generale des Etudiants d'Afrique Occidentale [*General Union of West African Students*]
UGEC .... Union Generale des Etudiants Congolais [*General Union of Congolese Students*]
UGEE .... Yerevan/Zvartnots [*Former USSR ICAO location identifier*] (ICLI)
UGEED .... Union Generale des Etudiants et Eleves Dahomeens
U Gefl AWG ... Um Gefaellige Antwort Wird Gebeten [*The Favor of an Answer Is Requested*] [*Correspondence*] [*German*]
UGEG .... Union Generale des Etudiants Guineens [*General Union of Guinean Students*]
UGEM .... Union Generale des Etudiants du Maroc [*General Union of Moroccan Students*]
UGEMA .... Union Generale des Etudiants Musulmans d'Algerie [*General Union of Moslem Students of Algeria*]
U Georgia .... [*The*] University of Georgia (GAGS)
UGESP .... Uniform Guidelines on Employee Selection Procedures [*Equal Employment Opportunity Commission*] (GFGA)
UGET .... Union Generale des Etudiants Tunisiens [*General Union of Tunisian Students*]
UGF .... Unidentified Growth Factor
UGF .... United Givers Fund
UGF .... Unserviceable Generation Factor [*Military*]
UGF .... US-North Africa (Gibraltar) Convoy-Fast [*World War II*]
UGFNAB .... Ultrasound-Guided Fine-Needle Aspiration Biopsy [*Medicine*]
UGG .... Ugland Air AS [*Norway ICAO designator*] (FAAC)
UGGG .... Tbilisi/Novoalexeyevka [*Former USSR ICAO location identifier*] (ICLI)
UGGI .... Union Geodesique et Geophysique Internationale [*International Union of Geodesy and Geophysics*]
UGGSC .... Uggscombe [*England*]
UGH .... Uveitis, Glaucoma, and Hyphema Plus Vitreous Hemorrhage [*Syndrome*] [*Ophthalmology*] (DAVI)
UGH .... Uveitis-Glaucoma-Hyphemia [*Ophthalmology*]
UGHA .... United in Group Harmony Association (EA)
UGHP .... Undergraduate Helicopter Pilot Training [*Army*]
UGI .... Uganik [*Alaska*] [*Airport symbol*] (OAG)
UGI .... UGI Corp. [*Formerly, United Gas Improvement Co.*] [*NYSE symbol*] (SPSG)
UGI .... Union Geographique Internationale [*International Geographical Union*]
UGI .... Upper Gastrointestinal [*Medicine*]
UGIB .... Upper Gastrointestinal Bleeding [*Medicine*]
UGIH .... Upper Gastrointestinal Tract Hemorrhage [*Medicine*]
UGIS .... Upper Gastrointestinal Series [*Medicine*] (DAVI)
UgJ .... Uganda Journal [*A publication*]
UGJA .... United Galician Jews of America [*Defunct*] (EA)
UGL .... Inter-Island Air, Inc. [*ICAO designator*] (FAAC)
UGL .... Uglegorsk [*Former USSR Seismograph station code, US Geological Survey*] (SEIS)
UGL .... Utility General
UGLAS .... Uniform General Ledger Accounting Structure (NVT)
UGLE .... United Grand Lodge of England [*Masonry*]
UGLE .... Universal Graphics Language Executive (MCD)
Ug LF .... Uganda Law Focus [*A publication*] (DLA)
UGLI .... Universal Gate for Logic Implementation [*Computer science*] (MCD)
UGLIAC .... United Gas Laboratories Internally Programmed Automatic Computer
UGLJ .... University of Ghana. Law Journal [*A publication*]
UGLNSW .... United Grand Lodge [*Masons*] of New South Wales [*Australia*]
Ug LR .... Uganda Law Reports [*Africa*] [*A publication*] (DLA)
UGLRC .... Upper Great Lakes Regional Commission [*Department of Commerce*]

UGLY .... Ugly Duckling Corp. [*NASDAQ symbol*] (SAG)
UglyDck .... Ugly Duckling Corp. [*Associated Press*] (SAG)
UgM .... Ugaritic Manual [*A publication*] (BJA)
UG/M .... Umdrehungen je Minute [*Revolutions per Minute*] [*German*]
UGM .... Underwater Guided Missile [*DoD*] (MCD)
UGM .... Urogenital Mesenchyme [*Medicine*]
UGMA .... Uniform Gifts to Minors Act [*National Conference of Commissioners on Uniform State Laws*]
UGME .... Undergraduate Medical Education (HCT)
UGML .... Universal Guided Missile Launcher [*Navy*] (MCD)
UGMM .... Mukhrani [*Former USSR ICAO location identifier*] (ICLI)
UGN .... Waukegan, IL [*Location identifier FAA*] (FAAL)
UGNCO .... Unit Gas Noncommissioned Officer [*Army World War II*]
UGND .... Underground (AABC)
UGNE .... Unigene Laboratories [*NASDAQ symbol*] (TTSB)
UGNE .... Unigene Laboratories, Inc. [*NASDAQ symbol*] (NQ)
UGNEZ .... Unigene Labs Wrrt'B' [*NASDAQ symbol*] (TTSB)
UGO .... Uige [*Angola*] [*Airport symbol Obsolete*] (OAG)
UGO .... Unigesco, Inc. [*Toronto Stock Exchange symbol*]
UGO .... Unit Gas Offices [*Army World War II*]
UGO .... Unmanned Geophysical Observatory [*National Science Foundation*]
UGOC .... United Greek Orthodox Charities [*Defunct*] (EA)
UGOT .... Urine Glutamic-Oxaloacetic Transaminase [*An enzyme*]
UGP .... Union des Gaullistes de Progres [*Union of Progressive Gaullists*] [*France Political party*] (PPE)
UGP .... United Global Petroleum, Inc. [*Vancouver Stock Exchange symbol*]
UGPA .... Undergraduate Grade-Point Average [*Higher education*]
UGPCC .... Uniform Grocery Product Code Council [*Later, UPCC*] (EA)
UGPP .... Uridine Diphosphoglucose Pyrophosphorylase [*An enzyme*]
Ug Pr LR .... Uganda Protectorate Law Reports [*Africa*] [*A publication*] (DLA)
UGR .... Ultrasonic Grain Refinement
UGR .... United Gunn Resources [*Vancouver Stock Exchange symbol*]
UGR .... Universal Graphic Recorder [*Raytheon Co.*]
UGrdn .... United-Guardian, Inc. [*Associated Press*] (SAG)
UGRE .... Undergraduate Record Examination [*Education*]
UGRR .... Underground Railroad [*A smuggling system*] [*Criminal slang*]
UGS .... Unattended Ground Sensors
UGS .... Uniaxial Gyrostabilizer
UGS .... Union de la Gauche Socialiste
UGS .... Union des Guineens au Senegal [*Union of Guineans in Senegal*] [*Political party*] (PD)
UGS .... Union Graduate School [*Yellow Springs, Ohio*]
UGS .... United Grounders' Society [*A union*] [*British*]
UGS .... Upper Group Stop [*Nuclear energy*] (NRCH)
UGS .... Upper Guide Structure [*Nuclear energy*] (NRCH)
UGS .... Urogenital Sinus [*Anatomy*]
UGS .... Urogenital System [*Medicine*]
UGS .... US-North Africa (Gibraltar) Convoy-Slow [*World War II*]
UGSA .... Uniform Grain Storage Agreement (AAGC)
UGSA .... Union Generale des Syndicats Algeriens [*General Federation of Algerian Trade Unions*]
UGSP .... United Galaxy Sanitation Patrol [*In TV series "Quark"*]
UGSS .... Sukhumi [*Former USSR ICAO location identifier*] (ICLI)
UGSS .... Union of Girls' Schools for Social Service [*British*] (BI)
UgT .... Ugaritic Textbook [*A publication*] (BJA)
UGT .... Underground Test (MCD)
UGT .... Union General de Trabajadores de Espana [*General Union of Spanish Workers*] [*In exile*]
UGT .... United Bible Societies' Greek New Testament [*A publication*] (BJA)
UGT .... Upgraded Third-Generation Enroute Software Program [*Computer science*] (MCD)
UGT .... Upgrade Training [*Military*] (AFM)
UGT .... Urgent
UGT .... Urogenital Tract [*Medicine*]
UGT .... User Group Table [*Computer science*] (MHDB)
UGTA .... Union Generale des Travailleurs Algeriens [*General Union of Algerian Workers*]
UGTAN .... Union Generale des Travailleurs d'Afrique Noire [*General Union of Workers of Black Africa*]
UGTC .... Union Generale des Travailleurs Centrafricains [*General Union of Central African Workers*]
UGTC .... Union Generale des Travailleurs du Cameroun [*General Union of Workers of Cameroon*]
UGTCI .... Union Generale des Travailleurs de la Cote D'Ivoire [*General Union of Workers of the Ivory Coast*]
UGTD .... Uniform Geometrical Theory of Diffraction (MCD)
UGTD .... Union Generale des Travailleurs du Dahomey [*General Union of Workers of Dahomey*]
UGTK .... Union Generale des Travailleurs du Kamerun [*General Union of Workers of the Cameroon*]
UGTM .... Union Generale des Travailleurs de Mauritanie [*General Union of Workers of Mauritania*]
UGTM .... Union Generale des Travailleurs du Maroc [*General Union of Workers of Morocco*]
UGTS .... Union Generale des Travailleurs du Senegal [*General Union of Workers of Senegal*]
UGTT .... Union Generale de Travailleurs Tunisiens [*General Federation of Tunisian Workers*]
UGV .... Unmanned Ground Vehicle [*Military robotics*]
UGV/SJPO .... Unmanned Ground Vehicles/Systems Joint Project Office [*Army*] (RDA)
UGW .... United Garment Workers of America (EA)
UH .... Air-Cushion Vehicle built by Universal Hovercraft [*US*] [*Usually used in combination with numerals*]
UH .... Austin Airways [*ICAO designator*] (AD)
UH .... Ugaritic Handbook [*C. H. Gordon*] [*A publication*] (BJA)
UH .... Unavailable Hours [*Electronics*] (IEEE)
UH .... Underhatch
uH .... Unfractionated Heparin [*Anticoagulant*]
UH .... United Humanitarians (EA)
UH .... Unit Head
UH .... Unit Heater [*Technical drawings*]
UH .... Unit Hydrograph
UH .... University of Hawaii [*Honolulu, HI*]
UH .... Upper Half
UH .... Upper Hemispherical (MCD)
UH .... U.S. Home [*NYSE symbol*] (TTSB)
UH .... US Home Corp. [*NYSE symbol*] (SPSG)
UH .... Utah [*Obsolete*] (ROG)
UH .... Utility Helicopter [*Military*] (AABC)
UHA .... Ukrains'ka Halyts'ka Armiia
UHA .... Ultrahigh Altitude
UHA .... Unable Higher Altitude [*Aviation*] (FAAC)
UHA .... Unexpected Home Attack [*Medicine*]
UHA .... Union House of Assembly [*South Africa*] (DAS)
UHA .... United Homeowners' Association (EA)
UHA .... Universitets- och Hogskoleambetet [*National Board of Universities and Colleges*] [*Ministry of Education and Cultural Affairs*] [*Information service or system*] [*Sweden*] (IID)
UHA .... Upper Half Assembly
UHAA .... United Horological Association of America [*Later, AWI*]
UHAB .... Urban Homesteading Assistance Board (EA)
UHAC .... United Hellenic American Congress (EA)
UHAL .... AMERCO [*NASDAQ symbol*] (SAG)
U Hartford .... University of Hartford (GAGS)
U Hawaii .... University of Hawaii (GAGS)
UHB .... Ultra High Bypass [*Aviation*] (DA)
UHBI .... Upper Hemibody Irradiation [*Radiation Therapy*] (DAVI)
UHBP .... Ekimcham [*Former USSR ICAO location identifier*] (ICLI)
UHC .... Ultimate Holding Company
UHC .... Unburned Hydrocarbon [*Also, UBHC*] [*Fuel technology*]
UHC .... Unburned Hydrocarbons
UHC .... Under Honorable Conditions [*Military*]
UHC .... Unit Hardware Cost (MCD)
UHC .... University Hospital Consortium
UHC .... University of Houston at Clear Lake City, Houston, TX [*OCLC symbol*] (OCLC)
UHCC .... University of Houston Coastal Center [*Research center*] (RCD)
UHCMWIU .... United Hatters, Cap, and Millinery Workers International Union
UHCO .... Universal American Financial Corp. [*NASDAQ symbol*] (SAG)
UHCO .... Universal Holding Corp. [*NASDAQ symbol*] (NQ)
UHCO .... Univl Holding Corp. [*NASDAQ symbol*] (TTSB)
UHCOW .... Universal Hldg Wrrt [*NASDAQ symbol*] (TTSB)
UHCP .... United Heritage Corp. [*NASDAQ symbol*] (NQ)
UHCS .... Ultrahigh Capacity Storage
UHD .... Unstable Hemoglobin Disease [*Hematology*] (DAVI)
UHDDS .... Uniform Hospital Discharge Data Set [*National Center for Health Statistics*]
UHDODT .... Unable Higher Due Opposite Direction Traffic [*Aviation*] (FAAC)
UHDSDT .... Unable Higher Due Same Direction Traffic [*Aviation*] (FAAC)
UHDT .... Unable Higher Due Traffic [*Aviation*] (FAAC)
UHE .... Uherske Hradiste [*Former Czechoslovakia*] [*Airport symbol Obsolete*] (OAG)
UHE .... Ultimate Hour Estimate (MCD)
UHE .... Ultrahigh Efficiency [*Arc lamp*]
UHE .... Ultrahigh Energy
UHE .... Usual Home Elsewhere [*Bureau of the Census*] (GFGA)
U Health Sc (Chicago) ... University of Health Science Chicago Medicine School (GAGS)
UHF .... Ulster Historical Foundation (EA)
UHF .... Ultrahigh-Frequency [*Electricity of radio waves*]
UHF .... Uniform Heat Flux [*Engineering*]
UHF .... United Health Foundations [*Defunct*]
UHF .... Unrestricted Hartree-Fock [*Wave-Function*]
UHFDF .... Ultrahigh-Frequency Direction Finder
UHFF .... Ultrahigh-Frequency Filter
UHFG .... Ultrahigh-Frequency Generator
UHF/HF .... Ultrahigh-Frequency/High-Frequency (MCD)
UHFJ .... Ultrahigh-Frequency Jammer
UHFO .... Ultrahigh-Frequency Oscillator
UHFR .... Ultrahigh-Frequency Receiver
UHFRU .... Ultrahigh Frequency Radio Unit (MCD)
UHFS .... Unsteady Heat Flux Sensor
UHG .... Urban History Group [*Defunct*] (EA)
UHHH .... Khabarovsk/Novy [*Former USSR ICAO location identifier*] (ICLI)
UHHO .... Troitskoye [*Former USSR ICAO location identifier*] (ICLI)
UHI .... Upper Head Injection [*Nuclear energy*] (NRCH)
UHi .... Utah State Historical Society, Salt Lake City, UT [*Library symbol Library of Congress*] (LCLS)
UHJA .... United Hungarian Jews of America (EA)
UHK .... University of Hard Knocks [*West Virginia*] [*"University" founded by Jim Comstock and based on the expression "school of hard knocks"*]
UHL .... Unge Hoyres Landsforbund [*Norway Political party*] (EAIO)
UHL .... Universal Hypertrichosis Lanuginosa [*Medicine*] (MAE)
UHL .... User Header Label (CMD)
UHLCADS .... Ultra-High-Level Container Airdrop System [*Military*] (MCD)
UHLD .... Unholding Corp. [*NASDAQ symbol*] (TTSB)
UHLD .... Uni Holding Corp. [*NASDAQ symbol*] (SAG)

UHLI .... United Home Life Insurance Co. [*Greenwood, IN*] [*NASDAQ symbol*] (NQ)
UHlthCr .... United Healthcare Corp. [*Associated Press*] (SAG)
UHLVFD .... Ultra High Luminance Vacuum Fluorescent Display [*Automotive engineering*]
UHM .... Universal Host Machine [*Computer science*] (MHDI)
UHML .... Lavrentiya [*Former USSR ICAO location identifier*] (ICLI)
UHMR .... Beringovsky [*Former USSR ICAO location identifier*] (ICLI)
UHMS .... Ultrasonic Helmet Mounted Sight [*Army*] (MCD)
UHMS .... Undersea and Hyperbaric Medical Society (EA)
UHMW .... Ultrahigh Molecular Weight
UHMW-PE .... Ultrahigh Molecular Weight Polyethylene [*Organic chemistry*]
UHMWPE ..... Ultra High Molecular Weight Polythylene
UHN .... Uranyl Hexahydrate Nitrate (GFGA)
UHOS .... Universal Hospital Services [*NASDAQ symbol*] (SAG)
UHOS .... Univl Hospital Svcs [*NASDAQ symbol*] (TTSB)
U Houston ... University of Houston (GAGS)
UHP .... Ugaritic-Hebrew Philology [*Rome*] [*M. Dahood*] [*A publication*] (BJA)
UHP .... Ultra-High Performance [*in UHP Imposer, a product of Opti-Copy, Inc.*]
UHP .... Ultra High Performance [*Automotive engineering*]
UHP .... Ultra-High Porosity [*Materials science*]
UHP .... Ultrahigh Power
UHP .... Ultra-High Pressure [*Water cutting tools*]
UHP .... Ultrahigh Purity
UHP .... Undergraduate Helicopter Pilot Training [*Army*]
UHP .... United Air Service [*Nigeria*] [*ICAO designator*] (FAAC)
UHP .... University of Hawaii Press
UHPFB .... Untreated Hard Pressed Fiberboard
UHPMIS .... Urban Homesteading Program Management Information System [*Department of Housing and Urban Development*] (GFGA)
UHPr .... U.S. Home Cv Pfd [*NYSE symbol*] (TTSB)
UHPS .... Underground Hydro-Pumped Storage [*Room*]
UHPT .... Undergraduate Helicopter Pilot Training (MCD)
UHR .... Ultra High Reduction (NITA)
UHR .... Ultrahigh Resistance
uhr .... Ultrahigh Resistance (IDOE)
UHR .... Ultrahigh Resolution
UHR .... Underlying Heart Rhythm [*Medicine*] (DMAA)
UHR .... United Hearne Resources Ltd. [*Vancouver Stock Exchange symbol*]
UHR .... Upper Hybrid Resonance [*Spectroscopy*]
UHRA .... United Hunts Racing Association [*Later, NSHA*]
UHR-ESCA ... Ultrahigh-Resolution Electron Spectrometer for Chemical Analysis
UHRF .... Ultra High Resolution Facsimile (NITA)
UHrtg .... United Heritage Corp. [*Associated Press*] (SAG)
UHS .... Ultimate Heat Sink [*Nuclear energy*] (NRCH)
UHS .... Ultrahigh Speed
UHS .... Ulyanovsk Higher Civil Aviation School [*Former USSR*] [*FAA designator*] (FAAC)
UHS .... Unitarian Historical Society [*Later, UUHS*] (EA)
UHS .... United HIAS Service (EA)
UHS .... Unit Handling System
UHS .... Universal Health Services, Inc. [*NYSE symbol*] (NQ)
UHS .... Universalist Historical Society [*Later, UUHS*] (EA)
UHS .... University of Health Sciences - Chicago Medical School
UHS .... Univl Health Svs Cl'B' [*NYSE symbol*] (TTSB)
UHSA .... United Halsingian Society of America [*Defunct*] (EA)
UHSC .... University Health Services Clinic (DAVI)
UHS-CMS .... University of Health Sciences - Chicago Medical School
UHT .... Ultraheat Tested [*Milk*] (CDAI)
UHT .... Ultraheat Treated
UHT .... Ultrahigh Temperature
UHT .... Ultrasonic Hardness Tester
UHT .... Umbilical Handling Technician [*Computer science*] (IAA)
UHT .... Underheat
UHT .... United Hebrew Trades of the State of New York (EA)
UHT .... Unit Horizontal Tail
UHT .... Universal Hand Tool
UHT .... Universal Health Realty Income Trust [*NYSE symbol*] (SPSG)
UHT .... Universal Horizontal Tail [*Aviation*] (NG)
UHT .... Univl Health Realty [*NYSE symbol*] (TTSB)
UHTPB .... Unsaturated Hydroxyl-Terminated Polybutadiene [*Organic chemistry*]
UHTREX .... Ultrahigh-Temperature Reactor Experiment [*Nuclear energy*]
UHTS .... Universal Heights [*NASDAQ symbol*] (TTSB)
UHTS .... Universal Heights, Inc. [*NASDAQ symbol*] (SAG)
UHTSW .... Universal Heights Wrrt [*NASDAQ symbol*] (TTSB)
UHTV .... Unmanned Hypersonic Test Vehicle (MCD)
UHV .... Ultrahigh Vacuum
UHV .... Ultrahigh Voltage
UHV .... Under Hatch Valve
UHVA .... United Hellenic Voters of America (EA)
UHVC .... Ultrahigh Vacuum Chamber
UHV/CVD ..... Ultrahigh Vacuum Chemical Vapor Deposition [*Coating technology*] [*Semiconductor technology*]
UHVI .... Ultra High Viscosity Index
UHVS .... Ultrahigh Vacuum System
UH.WS .... U.S. Home Wrrt [*NYSE symbol*] (TTSB)
UI .... Flugfelag Nordurlands [*Northlands Air*] [*ICAO designator*] (AD)
UI .... Ultrasonic Industry (WDAA)
UI .... Underground Injection [*of wastes*]
U/I .... Under Instructions (ADA)
UI .... Understanding Industry (AIE)
UI .... Underwear Institute [*Later, NKMA*] (EA)
UI .... Undifferentiated Infiltrating [*Tumor*] [*Oncology*]
UI .... Unearned Income (MHDW)
UI .... Unemployment Insurance
UI .... Unexplained Infertility
U/I .... Unidentified
UI .... Union Institute (EA)
UI .... Union Interparlementaire [*Inter-Parliamentary Union*] (EAIO)
UI .... Union-Intersection [*Statistics*]
UI .... Unique Indentifier [*Computer science*]
UI .... United Inches
ui .... United Kingdom Miscellaneous Islands [*MARC country of publication code Library of Congress*] (LCCP)
UI .... Unit of Issue (KSC)
UI .... Universal Instantiation [*Rule of quantification*] [*Logic*]
UI .... Universal-International Studios (IIA)
UI .... Unix International [*Computer science*] (PCM)
UI .... Unnumbered Information [*Telecommunications*] (OSI)
UI .... Unreported Income [*IRS*]
UI .... Unsigned Integer [*Computer science*]
UI .... Uranium Institute [*British*] (EAIO)
UI .... Urban Initiatives (EA)
UI .... Urban Institute (EA)
UI .... Ureteral-Intestinal [*Medicine*] (DAVI)
UI .... Urinary Infection [*Medicine*]
UI .... Uroporphyrin Isomerase [*An enzyme*] (AAMN)
UI .... USE, Inc. [*Acronym is now organization's official name*] (EA)
UI .... User Interface
UI .... Ut Infra [*As Below*] [*Latin*]
UIA .... Uganda Investment Authority
UIA .... Uganda Investment Authority
UIA .... Ukrainian Institute of America (EA)
UIA .... Ultrasonic Industry Association (EA)
UIA .... Unemployment Insurance Act [*Canada*]
UIA .... Union Internationale Contre l'Alcoolisme
UIA .... Union Internationale des Architectes [*International Union of Architects*] (EAIO)
UIA .... Union Internationale des Avocats [*International Union of Lawyers*]
UIA .... Union Internationale des Syndicats des Industries Alimentaires
UIA .... Union of International Associations [*See also UAI*] [*Brussels, Belgium*] (EAIO)
UIA .... United Israel Appeal [*Australia*]
UIA .... Unit Identifier Applications (MCD)
UIA .... Universidad Iberoamericana, Mexico, DF, Mexico [*OCLC symbol*] (OCLC)
UIA .... Uranium Institute of America (EA)
UIA .... Urban Impact Analysis (EG)
UIA .... Usable Inside Area (MCD)
UIAA .... Chita/Kadala [*Former USSR ICAO location identifier*] (ICLI)
UIAA .... Union Internationale des Associations d'Alpinisme [*International Union of Alpine Associations*] [*Switzerland*]
UIAA .... Union Internationale des Associations d'Annonceurs [*International Union of Advertisers Associations*]
UIAA .... Union Internationale des Assureurs Aeronautiques
UIACM .... Union Internationale des Automobile-Clubs Medicaux [*International Union of Associations of Doctor-Motorists*]
UIAL .... United Italian American League (EA)
UIALC .... United Italian American Labor Council (EA)
UIAMS .... Union Internationale d'Action Morale et Sociale [*International Union for Moral and Social Action*]
UIAPME .... Union Internationale de l'Artisanat et des Petites et Moyennes Entreprises [*International Association of Crafts and Small and Medium-Sized Enterprises*]
UIAPPA .... Union Internationale des Associations de Prevention de la Pollution Atmospherique [*International Union of Air Pollution Prevention Associations*] (EAIO)
UIARVEP ...... Unione Italiana Agenti Rappresentati Viaggiatori e Piazzisti [*Italian Union of Agents and Travelers*]
UIAS .... Unified Information Access System [*California State University*]
UIAS .... Unified Information Access System
UIASPPA ...... Uniform Individual Accident and Sickness Policy Provisions Act [*National Association of Insurance Commissioners*]
UIAT .... Union Internationale des Syndicats des Industries de l'Alimentation et des Tabacs
UIATF .... United Indians of All Tribes Foundation (EA)
UIB .... Quibdo [*Colombia*] [*Airport symbol*] (OAG)
UIB .... Unidentified Infrared Band [*Astrophysics*]
UIB .... Unione Italiana Bancari [*Italian Union of Bank Employees*]
UIB .... Union Internationale des Maitres Boulangers [*International Union of Master Bakers*]
UIB .... United Independent Broadcasters (NTCM)
UIBB .... Bratsk [*Former USSR ICAO location identifier*] (ICLI)
UIBC .... Unsaturated Iron-Binding Capacity [*Clinical chemistry*]
UIBG .... Union Internationale de Banque en Guinee (EY)
UIBPIP .... United International Bureau for the Protection of Intellectual Property [*Superseded by WIPO*]
UIBWM .... Trade Unions International of Workers of Building, Wood, and Building Materials Industries
UIC .... U Interface Circuit (NITA)
UIC .... Ultraviolet Image Converter
UIC .... Underground Injection Control [*Environmental Protection Agency*]
UIC .... Unemployment Insurance Code (OICC)
UIC .... Unemployment Insurance Commission [*Canada*]
UIC .... Unidad de Izquierda Comunista [*Unity of the Communist Left*] [*Mexico Political party*] (PPW)
UIC .... Union Internationale de Cristallographie [*International Union of Crystallography*] (EAIO)

UIC............ Union Internationale des Chemins de Fer [*International Union of Railways*] (EAIO)
UIC............ Union Internationale des Chemins de Fer (EERA)
UIC............ Union of Independent Companies [*British*] (DBA)
UIC............ Union of International Conventions
UIC............ United Industrial [*NYSE symbol*] (TTSB)
UIC............ United Industrial Corp. [*NYSE symbol*] (SPSG)
UIC............ United Insulator Co. (IAA)
UIC............ Unit Identification Code [*Army*] (AABC)
UIC............ University of Illinois
UIC............ Upper Information Center [*Aviation*]
UIC............ Urban Information Center [*Milwaukee Urban Observatory*] [*Ceased operations*] [*Information service or system*] (IID)
UIC............ Urea Inclusion Compound [*Chemistry*]
UIC............ Urinary Immune Complex
UIC............ User Identification Code
UICA............ Union Internationale des Constructeurs d'Ascenseurs [*International Union of Elevator Constructors - IUEC*]
UICA............ Union of Independent Colleges of Art (EA)
UICANY............ United Irish Counties Association of New York (EA)
UICB............ Union Internationale des Centres du Batiment [*International Union of Building Centers*] [*British*]
UICC............ Union Internationale Contre le Cancer [*International Union Against Cancer*] [*Switzerland*]
UICC............ University of Illinois at Chicago Circle
UICGF............ Union Internationale du Commerce en Gros de la Fleur [*International Union for the Wholesale Flower Trade*]
UICI............ UICI [*Associated Press*] (SAG)
UICI............ United Insurance [*NASDAQ symbol*] (TTSB)
UICI............ United Insurance Companies, Inc. [*NASDAQ symbol*] (NQ)
UICIO............ Unit Identification Code Information Officer [*Military*] (AABC)
UICM............ Union Internationale Catholique des Classes Moyennes [*International Catholic Union of the Middle Classes*]
UICN............ Union Mondiale Pour la Nature (EERA)
UICNR............ Union Internationale pour la Conservation de la Nature et de ses Resources [*International Union for Conservation of Nature and Natural Resources*] [*Switzerland*] (EAIO)
UICO............ UNICO, Inc. Delaware [*NASDAQ symbol*] (NQ)
UICO............ Unico Inc. Oklahoma [*NASDAQ symbol*] (TTSB)
UICP............ Uniform Inventory Control Point
UICP............ Uniform Inventory Control Points System [*Military*]
UICP............ Union Internationale de la Couverture et Plomberie (EA)
UICPA............ Union Internationale de Chimie Pure et Appliquee [*International Union of Pure and Applied Chemistry*]
UICR............ Union Internationale des Chauffeurs Routiers [*International Union of Lorry Drivers - IULD*] (EAIO)
UICSM............ University of Illinois Committee on School Mathematics
UICT............ Union Internationale Contre la Tuberculose [*International Union Against Tuberculosis - IUAT*] (EAIO)
UICTMR............ Union Internationale Contre la Tuberculose et les Maladies Respiratoires [*International Union Against Tuberculosis and Lung Disease - IUATLD*] (EAIO)
UICWA............ United Infants' and Children's Wear Association (EA)
UID............ Selected Decisions by Umpire for Northern Ireland, Respecting Claims to Benefit [*A publication*] (DLA)
UID............ Unemployment Insurance Department
UID............ Universal Identifier (IAA)
UID............ Uno In Die [*Once daily*] [*Pharmacy*] (DAVI)
UID............ Usable Inside Depth (MCD)
UIDA............ Union Internationale des Organisations de Detaillants de la Branche Alimentaire [*International Federation of Grocers' Associations*]
UIDA............ United Indian Development Association (EA)
UIDAC............ Unione Italiana Dipendenti Aziende Commerciali ed Affini [*Italian Union of Commerical and Allied Workers*]
U Idaho............ University of Idaho (GAGS)
UIE............ UNESCO Institute for Education
UIE............ Union Internationale d'Editeurs [*International Publishers Association - IPA*] (EAIO)
UIE............ Union Internationale d'Electrothermie [*International Union for Electroheat*] (EAIO)
UIE............ Union Internationale des Editeurs [*International Union of Publishers*] (NTCM)
UIE............ Union Internationale des Etudiants [*International Union of Students - IUS*] (EAIO)
UIEA............ Union Internationale des Etudiants en Architecture [*International Union of Students in Architecture*]
UIEC............ Union Internationale de l'Exploitation Cinematographique [*International Union of Cinematographic Exhibitors*] (EAIO)
UIEIS............ Union Internationale pour l'Etude des Insectes Sociaux [*International Union for the Study of Social Insects - IUSSI*] [*Netherlands*]
UIEO............ Union of International Engineering Organizations
UIEP............ Union Internationale des Entrepreneurs de Peinture
UIES............ Union Internationale d'Education pour la Sante [*International Union of Health Education - IUHE*] [*Paris, France*] (EAIO)
UIES............ Union Internationale d'Etudes Sociales [*International Union for Social Studies*]
UIEV............ Universal Imagery Exploitation Viewer (DNAB)
UIF............ Ultraviolet Interference Filter
UIF............ Undegraded Insulin Factor [*Medicine*] (MAE)
UIF............ Unfavorable Information File [*Military*]
UIF............ Union Internationale de Ferrecarriles [*International Union of Railways*]
UIF............ Universal Intermolecular Force
UIF............ Unserviceable Items File
UIF............ USLIFE Income Fund [*NYSE symbol*] (TTSB)
UIF............ USLIFE Income Fund, Inc. [*NYSE symbol*] (SPSG)
UIFA............ Union Internationale des Femmes Architectes [*International Union of Women Architects - IUWA*] (EAIO)
UIFI............ Union Internationale des Fabricants d'Impermeables
UIFL............ Union Internationale des Federations de Detaillants en Produits Laitiers
uig............ Uigur [*MARC language code Library of Congress*] (LCCP)
UIG............ Uniform Inspection Guideline
UIG............ Uniglobe International Energy Corp. [*Vancouver Stock Exchange symbol*]
UIG............ User Instruction Group
UIGDC............ Unione Internazionale des Giovani Democratici Cristiana [*International Union of Young Christian Democrats*]
UIGSE............ Union Internationale des Guides et Scouts d'Europe [*International Union of European Guides and Scouts - IUEGS*] [*Chateau Landon, France*] (EAIO)
UIH............ Qui Nhon [*South Vietnam*] [*Airport symbol*] (AD)
UIH............ University of Iowa Hospitals (DAVI)
UIH............ Urban and Industrial Health (KSC)
UIHE............ Union Internationale de l'Humanisme et de l'Ethique
UIHI............ United International Holdings, Inc. [*NASDAQ symbol*] (SAG)
UIHIA............ United Intl Hldgs'A' [*NASDAQ symbol*] (TTSB)
UIHMSU............ Union Internationale d'Hygiene et de Medecine Scolaires et Universitaires [*International Union of School and University Health and Medicine - IUSUHM*] [*Brussels, Belgium*] (EAIO)
UIHPS............ Union Internationale d'Histoire et de Philosophie des Sciences
UII............ Unified Industries, Inc.
UII............ Universal Identification Interface [*Allen-Bradley Co.*]
UII............ Utila Island [*Honduras*] [*Airport symbol Obsolete*] (OAG)
UIIDE............ Union Internationale des Infirmieres Diplomees d'Etat [*International Union of Registered Nurses*] [*France*] (EAIO)
UIIG............ Union Internationale de l'Industrie du Gaz [*International Gas Union - IGU*] [*Paris, France*] (EAIO)
UIII............ Irkutsk [*Former USSR ICAO location identifier*] (ICLI)
UIII............ Urban Information Interpreters, Inc. (IID)
UIIO............ Ust-Ordynsky [*Former USSR ICAO location identifier*] (ICLI)
UIJA............ Union Internationale des Journalistes Agricoles [*International Union of Agricultural Journalists*]
UIJDC............ Union Internationale de Jeunesse Democrate Chretienne [*International Union of Young Christian Democrats*]
UIJPLF............ Union Internationale des Journalistes et de la Presse de Langue Francaise [*International Union of French-Language Journalists and Press - IUFLJP*] (EAIO)
UIJS............ Union Internationale de la Jeunesse Socialiste [*International Union of Socialist Youth*]
UIKB............ Bodaybo [*Former USSR ICAO location identifier*] (ICLI)
UIKK............ Kirensk [*Former USSR ICAO location identifier*] (ICLI)
UIKW............ Vitim [*Former USSR ICAO location identifier*] (ICLI)
UIL............ Quillayute, WA [*Location identifier FAA*] (FAAL)
UIL............ Unione Italiana del Lavoro [*Italian Union of Labor*]
UIL............ United Capital Funding Partnership LP [*NYSE symbol*] (SAG)
UIL............ United Illuminating [*NYSE symbol*] (TTSB)
UIL............ United Illuminating Co. [*NYSE symbol*] (SPSG)
UIL............ UNIVAC Interactive Language [*Computer science*] (IEEE)
UIL............ University of Iowa, School of Library Science, Iowa City, IA [*OCLC symbol*] (OCLC)
UIL............ User Interface Language (SSD)
UILA............ Unione Italiana Lavoratori Assicurazioni [*Italian Union of Insurance Workers*]
UILAM............ Unione Italiana Lavoratori Albergo e Mensa [*Italian Union of Hotel and Restaurant Workers*]
UILE............ Union Internationale pour la Liberte d'Enseignement [*International Union for the Liberty of Education*]
UIL-GAS............ Unione Italiana Lavoratori Aziende Gas [*Italian Union of Gas Workers*]
UILI............ Union Internationale des Laboratoires Independents [*International Union of Independent Laboratories*] [*Elstree, Hertfordshire, England*] (EAIO)
U Ill............ University of Illinois (GAGS)
U Ill (Chicago)... University of Illinois at Chicago (GAGS)
U Ill LB............ University of Illinois. Law Bulletin [*A publication*] (DLA)
U Ill L Bull... University of Illinois. Law Bulletin [*A publication*] (DLA)
UIllum............ United Illuminating Co. [*Associated Press*] (SAG)
UILPrA............ Utd Cap Fd LP.9.625% CapSec'A' [*NYSE symbol*] (TTSB)
UILU............ University of Illinois, Urbana
UIM............ Quitman, TX [*Location identifier FAA*] (FAAL)
UIM............ Ufficio Informazioni Militaire [*Office of Military Information*] [*Italian*]
UIM............ Ultra-Intelligent Machine
UIM............ Ultrasonic Interferometer Manometer [*Instrumentation*]
UIM............ Union Internationale des Magistrats [*International Association of Judges - IAJ*] (EAIO)
UIM............ Union Internationale des Metis [*International Union of Individuals of Mixed Parentage*]
UIM............ Union Internationale Monarchiste [*Weinsberg, Federal Republic of Germany*] (EAIO)
UIM............ Union Internationale Motonautique [*Union of International Motorboating*] (EAIO)
UIM............ Union of International Motorboating (EA)
UIMAS............ Ultrasound in Medicine - Australia Society
UIMC............ Union Internationale des Services Medicaux des Chemins de Fer [*International Union of Railway Medical Services*]
UIMI............ United Indian Missions, International (EA)
UIMJ............ Union Internationale des Maisons de Jeunesse [*Service de la FIJC*]
UIMP............ Union Internationale pour le Protection de la Moralite Publique [*International Union for the Protection of Public Morale*] [*France*]

UIMS .... User Interface Management System [*Computer science*]
UIMVT .... Union Internationale Contre les Maladies Veneriennes et les Treponematoses [*International Union Against the Venereal Diseases and the Treponematoses - IUVDT*]
UIN .... Quincy [*Illinois*] [*Airport symbol*] (OAG)
UIN .... Universal Internet Number
U Indianapolis... University of Indianapolis (GAGS)
UINF .... Union Internationale de la Navigation Fluviale [*International Union for Inland Navigation - IUIN*] (EAIO)
UINL .... Union Internationale du Notariat Latin [*International Union of Latin Notaries*]
UINN .... Nizhneudinsk [*Former USSR ICAO location identifier*] (ICLI)
UINP .... Unit of Insect Neurophysiology and Pharmacology [*University of Cambridge*] [*British*] (IRUK)
UIO .... Quito [*Ecuador*] [*Airport symbol*] (OAG)
UIO .... Union Internationale des Orientalistes [*International Union of Orientalists*]
UIO .... United Infertility Organization (EA)
UIO .... Units in Operation [*Business term*]
UIO .... Universal Input-Output [*Computer science*] (ECII)
UIO .... Utility Iterative Operation
UIOC .... Universal Input/Output Controller (NITA)
UIOD .... User Input/Output Devices [*Computer science*] (RDA)
UIOF .... Union Internationale des Organismes Familiaux [*International Union of Family Organizations - IUFO*] [*France*]
UIOGD .... Ut in Omnibus Glorificetur Deus [*That God May Be Glorified in All Things*] [*Latin*]
UIOOT .... Union Internationale des Organismes Officiels de Tourisme [*International Union of Official Travel Organizations*]
UIOVD .... Union Internationale des Ouvriers du Vetement pour Dames [*International Ladies' Garment Workers' Union - ILGW*]
U Iowa .... [*The*] University of Iowa (GAGS)
U Iowa L Rev... University of Iowa. Law Review [*A publication*] (DLA)
UIP .... Quimper [*France*] [*Airport symbol*] (OAG)
UIP .... Unallowable Items Program [*IRS*]
UIP .... Unfair Industrial Practice
UIP .... Unione Italiana Pescatori [*Italian Union of Fishermen*]
UIP .... Union Internationale d'Associations de Proprietaires de Wagons Particuliers [*International Union of Private Railway Truck Owners' Associations*] (EAIO)
UIP .... Union Internationale de Patinage [*International Skating Union - ISU*] [*Davos-Platz, Switzerland*] (EAIO)
UIP .... Union Internationale de Physique Pure et Appliquee [*International Union of Pure and Applied Physics*]
UIP .... Union Internationale des Publicitaires
UIP .... Union Interparlementaire
UIP .... United Ireland Party
UIP .... University of Illinois Press
UIP .... Usable in Place (MCD)
UIP .... Usual Interstitial Pneumonia [*Medicine*]
UIPA .... United Indian Planners Association [*Defunct*] (EA)
UIPC .... Underground Injection Practices Council (EA)
UIPC .... Union Internationale de la Press Catholique [*International Union of the Catholic Press*] [*France*]
UIPC .... Union Internationale de la Presse Catholique [*International Catholic Press Union*]
UIPCG .... Union Internationale de la Patisserie, Confiserie, Glacerie [*International Union of Bakers and Confectioners*]
UIPD .... Ulrich's International Periodicals Directory [*A publication*]
UIPE .... Union Internationale de Protection de l'Enfance [*International Union for Child Welfare - IUCW*] [*Geneva, Switzerland*] [*Defunct*] (EA)
UIPFB .... Union Internationale de la Propriete Fonciere Batie [*International Union of Landed Property Owners*]
UIPI .... Union Internacional de Proteccion a la Infancia [*International Union for Child Welfare*]
UIPI .... Union Internationale de la Propriete Immobiliere [*International Union of Property Owners*] [*Paris, France*] (EAIO)
UIPM .... Union Internationale de la Presse Medicale [*International Union of the Medical Press*]
UIPMB .... Union Internationale de Pentathlon Moderne et Biathlon [*International Union for Modern Pentathlon and Biathlon*] (EAIO)
UIPN .... Union Internationale pour la Protection de la Nature [*International Union for the Protection of Nature - IUPN*] [*Later, IUCN*]
UIPPA .... Union Internationale de Physique Pure et Appliquee [*International Union of Pure and Applied Physics*]
UIPPI .... Union Internationale pour la Protection de la Propriete Industrielle [*International Union for the Protection of Industrial Property*]
UIPRE .... Union Internationale de la Presse Radiotechnique et Electronique [*Freiburg, Federal Republic of Germany*] (EAIO)
UIPVT .... Union Internationale Contre le Peril Venerien et la Treponematose [*International Union Against the Venereal Diseases and the Treponematoses*]
UIQ .... Upper Inner Quadrant [*Anatomy*]
UIR .... Quirindi [*Australia Airport symbol Obsolete*] (OAG)
UIR .... Unidentified Infrared Band [*Spectroscopy*]
UIR .... Union Internacional de Radiodifusion [*International Broadcasting Union*] [*Also, IBU*] (NTCM)
UIR .... Union Internationale des Radioecologistes [*International Union of Radioecologists - IUR*] (EAIO)
UIR .... Union Internationale des Rembourreurs de l'Amerique du Nord [*Upholsterers' International Union of North America - UIU*] [*Canada*]
UIR .... Unitary Irreducible Representation
UIR .... United International Research, Inc.
UIR .... Unit Initial Range (MCD)
UIR .... University-Industry Research Program [*University of Wisconsin-Madison*] [*Information service or system*] (IID)
UIR .... Upper Information Region (NATG)
UIR .... Urban Intelligence Reports (CINC)
UIR .... User Instruction Register
UIR .... User Interface Requirement
UIRC .... Universal Interline Reservations Code
UIRD .... Union Internationale de la Resistance et de la Deportation [*International Union of Resistance and Deportee Movements*]
UIRR .... University-Industry Research Relationship
UIRV .... Universal Infrared Viewer (PDAA)
UIS .... Ulster-Irish Society (EA)
UIS .... Uncertain Inference System [*Logic*]
UIS .... Unemployment Insurance Service [*Department of Labor*]
UIS .... Union Internationale de Secours [*International Relief Union*]
UIS .... Union Internationale de Speleologie [*International Union of Speleology - IUS*] (EAIO)
UIS .... Union Internationale des Syndicats des Travailleurs des Transports [*Trade Unions International of Transport Workers*] (EAIO)
UIS .... Unisys Corp. [*NYSE symbol*] (SPSG)
UIS .... United Information Services, Inc. (IID)
UIS .... United Inventors and Scientists (IAA)
UIS .... Unit Identification System
UIS .... Universal Isolation Switch
UIS .... Unlimited Intermediate Storage [*Industrial engineering*]
UIS .... Upper Information Service (DA)
UIS .... Upper Internals Structure [*Nuclear energy*] (NRCH)
UIS .... Urban Information System (EERA)
UISA .... United Inventors and Scientists of America (EA)
UISAE .... Union Internationale des Sciences Anthropologiques et Ethnologiques [*International Union of Anthropological and Ethnological Sciences - IUAES*] (EAIO)
UISB .... Union Internationale des Sciences Biologiques [*International Union of Biological Sciences*]
UISC .... Unreported Interstate Shipment of Cigarettes
UISDC .... Unemployment Insurance Service Design Center [*Department of Labor*]
UISE .... Union Internationale de Secours aux Enfants
UISG .... Union Internationale des Superieures Majeures [*International Union of Superiors General*] [*Rome, Italy*] (EAIO)
UISIF .... Union Internationale des Societies d'Ingenieurs Forestiers [*International Union of Societies of Foresters - IUSF*] [*Ottawa, ON*] (EAIO)
UISJM .... Upper Internals Structure Jacking Mechanism [*Nuclear energy*] (NRCH)
UISM .... Union Internationale des Syndicats des Mineurs [*Miners' Trade Unions International*]
UISMM .... Union Internationale des Syndicats des Industries Metallurgiques et Mecaniques
UISMTE .... Union Internationale des Syndicats des Mineurs et des Travailleurs de l'Energie [*Trade Unions International of Miners and Workers in Energy - TUIMWE*] (EAIO)
UISN .... Union Internationale des Sciences de la Nutrition [*International Union of Nutritional Sciences - IUNS*] [*Wageningen, Netherlands*] (EA)
UISP .... Union Internationale des Societes de la Paix [*International Union of Peace Societies*]
UISP .... Union Internationale des Syndicats de Police [*International Union of Police Syndicates*] (EAIO)
UISPI .... Urethane Institute, Society of the Plastics Industry (EA)
UISPP .... Union Internationale des Sciences Prehistoriques et Protohistoriques [*International Union of Prehistoric and Protohistoric Sciences*]
UISPrA .... Unisys $3.75cm Cv A Pfd [*NYSE symbol*] (TTSB)
UISPTT .... Union Internationale Sportive des Postes, des Telephones, et des Telecommunications [*International Sports Union of Post, Telephone, and Telecommunications Services - ISUPTTS*] [*Switzerland*]
UISTABP ..... Union Internacional de Sindicatos de Trabajadores de la Agricultura, de los Bosques, y de las Plantaciones [*Trade Unions International of Agricultural, Forestry, and Plantation Workers*]
UISTAF .... Union Internationale des Syndicats des Travailleurs Agricoles et Forestiers et des Organisations des Paysans Travailleurs
UISTAFP ..... Union Internationale des Syndicats des Travailleurs de l'Agriculture, des Forets, et des Plantations [*Trade Unions International of Agriculture, Forestry, and Plantation Workers - TUIAFPW*] [*Prague, Czechoslovakia*] (EAIO)
UISTAV .... Union Internationale pour la Science, la Technique, et les Applications du Vide [*International Union for Vacuum Science, Technique, and Applications - IUVSTA*] (EAIO)
UISTC .... Union Internationale des Syndicats des Travailleurs du Commerce [*Trade Unions International of Workers in Commerce*]
UISTICPS .... Union Internationale des Syndicats des Travailleurs des Industries Chimiques du Petrole et Similaires
UIS Transport... Union Internationale des Syndicats des Travailleurs des Transports [*Trade Unions International of Transport Workers*] [*Hungary*] (EAIO)
UIT .... Jaluit [*Marshall Islands*] [*Airport symbol*] (OAG)
UIT .... Ultraviolet Imaging Telescope
UIT .... Union des Independants de Tananarive [*Union of Independents of Tananarive*]
UIT .... Union Internationale des Telecommunications [*International Telecommunication Union*] [*French United Nations*] (DUND)
UIT .... Union Internationale des Typographes [*International Typographical Union - ITU*]
UIT .... Union Internationale de Tir [*International Shooting Union*] [*See also IS*] [*Germany*] (EAIO)

UIT............ Unit Impulse Train
UIT............ Unit Investment Trusts [*Standard and Poor's Corp.*] [*Information service or system*]
UIT............ Utility Interim Tape (SAA)
UITA............ Union Internationale des Travailleurs de l'Alimentation et des Branches Connexes [*International Union of Food and Allied Workers Associations*]
UITA............ Union of International Technical Associations [*See also UATI*] [*ICSU*] [*Paris, France*] (EAIO)
UITAM......... Union Internationale de Mecanique Theorique et Appliquee [*International Union of Theoretical and Applied Mechanics*]
UITBB.......... Union Internationale des Syndicats des Travailleurs du Batiment, du Bois, et desMateriaux de Construction [*Trade Unions International of Workers of the Building, Wood, and Building Materials Industries*]
UITCA.......... International Union of Co-operative and Associated Tourism (EAIO)
Uitg............ Uitgave [*Edition*] [*Netherlands*] (ILCA)
UITP............ Union Internationale des Transports Publics [*International Union of Public Transport*] (EAIO)
UIU............ Universal Interactive Unit [*Telecommunications*]
UIU............ University of Illinois, Urbana, IL [*OCLC symbol*] (OCLC)
UIU............ Upholsterers' International Union of North America [*USWA*] [*Absorbed by*]
UIU............ Upper Iowa University [*Fayette*]
UIUC........... University of Illinois, Urbana-Champaign
UIUH........... Khorinsk [*Former USSR ICAO location identifier*] (ICLI)
UIUSD.......... Union Internationale Universitaire Socialiste et Democratique [*International Union of Social Democratic Teachers*]
UIUU........... Ulan-Ude/Mukhino [*Former USSR ICAO location identifier*] (ICLI)
UIV............ Union Internationale des Villes et Pouvoirs Locaux [*International Union of Local Authorities*]
UIW............ United Iron Workers
UIW............ Usable Inside Width (MCD)
UIWU........... United Israel World Union (EA)
UIWV........... United Indian War Veterans, USA (EA)
UIZ............ Utica, MI [*Location identifier FAA*] (FAAL)
UJ............. Air Sedona [*ICAO designator*] (AD)
UJ............. Union Jack
UJ............. Union Joint (MSA)
UJ............. Unique Jargon
UJ............. Uyoku Jiten [*A publication*]
UJA............ United Jewish Appeal (EA)
UJAFJP........ United Jewish Appeal - Federation of Jewish Philanthropies of New York (EA)
UJASU.......... Universal Jet Air Start Unit (DWSG)
UJB............ UJB Financial Corp. [*Formerly, United Jersey Banks*] [*NYSE symbol*] (SPSG)
UJB............ Umbilical Junction Box
UJB Fn......... UJB Financial Corp. [*Formerly, United Jersey Banks*] [*Associated Press*] (SAG)
UJC............ Union de la Jeunesse Congolaise [*Congolese Youth Union*]
UJC............ Union Jack Club [*British military*] (DMA)
UJC............ Union Junior College [*New Jersey*]
UJC............ Universal Japanese Coupe [*Automotive engineering*]
UJC............ Universal Japanese Custom [*Motorcycle design*]
UJC............ Urbana Junior College [*Ohio*]
UJC............ Urgency Justification Code [*Military*] (AFIT)
UJCC(M-L).... Union de la Jeunesse Communiste du Canada (Marxiste-Leniniste)
UJCD........... Union de la Jeunesse de la Cote d'Ivoire [*Ivory Coast Youth Union*]
UJCL........... Universal Job Control Language
UJCML.......... Union des Jeunesses Communistes Marxistes-Leninistes [*Union of Young Marxist-Leninist Communists*] [*France Political party*] (PPE)
UJD............ Ultriusque Juris Doctor [*Doctor of Either Law; i.e., Canon Law or Civil Law*] [*Latin*]
UJDG........... Union de la Jeunesse Democratique Gabonaise [*Union of Democratic Youth of Gabon*]
UJDK........... Union de la Jeunesse Democratique du Kongo [*Union of Democratic Youth of the Congo*]
UJE............ Universal Jewish Encyclopedia [*New York*] [*1939-1943*] [*A publication*] (BJA)
UJEKO.......... Union de la Jeunesse Congolaise [*Congolese Youth Union*]
UJF............ Unsatisfied Judgment Fund [*Insurance*]
UJH............ International Union of Journeymen Horseshoers of the United States and Canada
UJJ............ Ujjain [*India*] [*Geomagnetic observatory code*]
UJL............ Uninet Japan Ltd. [*Telecommunications*]
UJNR........... United States-Japan Cooperative Program on Natural Resources
U/JNT.......... Universal Joint [*Automotive engineering*]
UJS............ Universal Jamming System
UJSP........... United States-Japan Science Program (MSC)
UJT............ Ultrasonic Journal Tester
UJT............ Unijunction Transistor
UJTL........... Universal Joint Task List
UJTO........... Unijunction Transistor Oscillator (IAA)
UJTS........... United Jewish Teachers Seminary [*Montreal*] [*A publication*] (BJA)
UJW............ Union of Jewish Women [*Zimbabwe*] (EAIO)
UJWF........... United Jewish Welfare Fund (IIA)
Uk............. British Library, London, United Kingdom [*Library symbol Library of Congress*] (LCLS)
UK............. Pfizer Ltd. [*Great Britain*] [*Research code symbol*]
'Uk............ 'Ukzin (BJA)
UK............. Unabkoemmlich [*Indispensable, irreplaceable*] [*German military - World War II*]
UK............. Union Carbide [*NYSE symbol*] (TTSB)
UK............. Union Carbide Corp. [*Wall Street slang name: "Ukelele"*] [*NYSE symbol*] (SPSG)
UK............. Union Katangaise [*Katanga Union*]
UK............. Unit Check
uk............. United Kingdom [*MARC country of publication code Library of Congress*] (LCCP)
UK............. United Kingdom
UK............. University of Kansas [*Lawrence, KS*]
UK............. Unknown
UK............. Urinary Kallikrein [*Medicine*] (DMAA)
UK............. Urokinase [*An enzyme*]
UKA............ Air UK Ltd. [*British ICAO designator*] (FAAC)
UKA............ Ulster King-at-Arms
UKA............ United Kingdom Alliance
UKAACREG... United Kingdom Airways and Communication Region (IAA)
UkAc........... Accrington Public Library, Accrington, United Kingdom [*Library symbol Library of Congress*] (LCLS)
UKAC........... United Kingdom Automatic Control Council (ACII)
UKAC........... United Kingdom Automation Council [*London, England*]
UKADGE........ United Kingdom Air Defense Ground Environment
UKADR.......... United Kingdom NATO Air Defense Region (NATG)
UKAEA.......... United Kingdom Atomic Energy Authority [*London, England*] [*Databank originator and operator*] [*Research center*]
UKAEL.......... United Kingdom Association for European Law [*British*]
UKAFFP......... United Kingdom Association of Frozen Food Producers (DBA)
UKaGS.......... Church of Jesus Christ of Latter-Day Saints, Genealogical Society Library, KanabBranch, Stake Center, Kanab, UT [*Library symbol Library of Congress*] (LCLS)
UKAIRCCIS... United Kingdom Air Forces Command, Control, and Information System
UKAMBY....... United Kingdom Association of Manufacturers of Bakers Yeast (DBA)
U Kans......... University of Kansas (GAGS)
U Kans Med Ctr... University of Kansas Medicine Center (GAGS)
UKAPC.......... United Kingdom Agricultural Production Committee
UKAPE.......... United Kingdom Association of Professional Engineers [*A union*]
UKAPTD........ United Kingdom Alliance of Professional Teachers of Dancing (DBA)
UKARC.......... United Kingdom Agricultural Research Council
UKASE.......... University of Kansas Automated Serials
UKASS.......... United Kingdom Amalgamated Society of Shipwrights [*A union*]
UKASS.......... United Kingdom Association of Suggestion Schemes (DBA)
UKASTA........ United Kingdom Agricultural Supply Trade Association (DS)
UkAuI.......... Ashton-Under-Lyne Public Library, Ashton-Under-Lyne, United Kingdom [*Library symbol Library of Congress*] (LCLS)
UKAWG......... United Kingdom Asian Women's Conference [*British*]
UKAWPCM..... United Kingdom Association of Wood Packing Case Makers [*A union*]
UkB............ Birmingham Public Libraries, Birmingham, United Kingdom [*Library symbol Library of Congress*] (LCLS)
UKB............ United Kingdom Base [*World War II*]
UKB............ Universal Keyboard [*Computer science*] (AABC)
UKB............ Unvaniezh Kevredel Breizh [*Federalist Union of Brittany - FUB*] [*France*] (EAIO)
UKBB........... Kiev/Borispol [*Former USSR ICAO location identifier*] (ICLI)
UKBC........... United Kingdom Bomber Command (NATG)
UKBelQU....... Queen's University of Belfast, Belfast, United Kingdom [*Library symbol Library of Congress*] (LCLS)
UKBG........... United Kingdom Bartenders' Guild (BI)
UKBHU.......... United Kingdom Band of Hope Union (EAIO)
UkBl........... Blackpool Central Library, Blackpool, United Kingdom [*Library symbol Library of Congress*] (LCLS)
UkBIG.......... Blackpool Gazette & Herald Ltd., Blackpool, United Kingdom [*Library symbol Library of Congress*] (LCLS)
UkBoN.......... Bolton Evening News, Bolton, United Kingdom [*Library symbol Library of Congress*] (LCLS)
UkBot.......... Burton-On-Trent Public Library, Burton-On-Trent, United Kingdom [*Library symbol Library of Congress*] (LCLS)
UkBP........... Birmingham Post & Mail Ltd., Birmingham, United Kingdom [*Library symbol Library of Congress*] (LCLS)
UkBrP.......... Bristol Evening Post, Bristol, United Kingdom [*Library symbol Library of Congress*] (LCLS)
UKBS........... United Kingdom Base Section [*World War II*]
UKBSA.......... United Kingdom Board Sailing Association (DBA)
UkBU........... Birmingham University, Birmingham, United Kingdom [*Library symbol Library of Congress*] (LCLS)
UKC............ Air Ukraine Cargo [*FAA designator*] (FAAC)
UKC............ Ukrainian Gold Cross (EA)
UKC............ United Kennel Club (EA)
UKC............ Unit Kind Code [*Military*] (AFIT)
UKC............ University of Kansas City [*Later, University of Missouri at Kansas City*]
UKCA........... United Kingdom Coffee Association Ltd. (BI)
UKCC........... United Kingdom Central Council [*for Nursing, Midwifery, and Health Visiting*]
UKCC........... United Kingdom Commercial Corp.
UKCCD.......... United Kingdom Council for Computing Development (NITA)
UkCh........... Chelmsford Library, Chelmsford, United Kingdom [*Library symbol Library of Congress*] (LCLS)
UKCHH......... United Kingdom or Continent (Havre to Hamburg) (ROG)
UKCICC........ United Kingdom Commanders-in-Chiefs' Committee
UKCIS.......... United Kingdom Chemical Information Service [*University of Nottingham*] [*Nottingham, England Information broker, databank originator, and host*]
UKCMET....... United Kingdom Council for Music Education and Training (EAIO)
UkCoE.......... Essex County Newspapers Ltd., Colchester, United Kingdom [*Library symbol Library of Congress*] (LCLS)

UK/Cont (BH)... United Kingdom or Continent (Bordeaux-Hamburg) [*Shipping*] (DS)
UK/Cont (GH)... United Kingdom or Continent (Gibraltar-Hamburg) [*Shipping*] (DS)
UK/Cont (HH)... United Kingdom or Continent (Havre-Hamburg) [*Shipping*] (DS)
UKCOSA....... United Kingdom Council for Overseas Student Affairs (DS)
UkCoU......... University of Essex, Wivenhoe Park, Colchester, England [*Library symbol*] [*Library of Congress*] (LCLS)
UkCov.......... Coventry Corp., Coventry, United Kingdom [*Library symbol Library of Congress*] (LCLS)
UkCr............ Croydon Library, Croydon, United Kingdom [*Library symbol Library of Congress*] (LCLS)
UKCR........... United Kingdom Communication Region [*Air Force*] (MCD)
UkCrA.......... Croydon Advertiser, Croydon, United Kingdom [*Library symbol Library of Congress*] (LCLS)
UkCraT......... Cranfield Institute of Technology, Cranfield, Bedfordshire, United Kingdom [*Library symbol Library of Congress*] (LCLS)
UkCrC.......... Coulsdon Library, Croydon, United Kingdom [*Library symbol Library of Congress*] (LCLS)
UkCrP.......... Purley Library, Croydon, United Kingdom [*Library symbol Library of Congress*] (LCLS)
UKCS........... United Kingdom Continental Shelf
UKCSB......... United Kingdom Combat Support Boat
UKCSMA...... United Kingdom Cutlery and Silverware Manufacturers Association (BI)
UKCTA......... United Kingdom Commercial Travellers Association (DI)
UKCTRAIN... UK Catalogue Training (NITA)
UkCU........... Cambridge University, Cambridge, United Kingdom [*Library symbol Library of Congress*] (LCLS)
UkCU-P........ University of Cambridge, Scott Polar Research Institute, Cambridge, England [*Library symbol*] [*Library of Congress*] (LCLS)
UkCwN......... North Wales Weekly News, Conway, United Kingdom [*Library symbol Library of Congress*] (LCLS)
Uk-D............ British Library, Development and Systems Office, London, England [*Library symbol*] [*Library of Congress*] (LCLS)
UKD............. Unusual Killing Device [*Counterintelligence*]
UKDA........... United Kingdom Dairy Association (DBA)
UkDo............ Doncaster Public Library, Doncaster, United Kingdom [*Library symbol Library of Congress*] (LCLS)
UKDRC......... United Kingdom Dutch Rabbit Club (BI)
UkDw........... Dewsbury Central Library, Dewsbury, United Kingdom [*Library symbol Library of Congress*] (LCLS)
UkE.............. Edinburgh Public Library, Edinburgh, United Kingdom [*Library symbol Library of Congress*] (LCLS)
UKE.............. Ukelele (DSUE)
UKE.............. Uke Resources [*Vancouver Stock Exchange symbol*]
UKEA........... United Kingdom Energy Authority (DI)
UkEc............ Eccles Public Library, Central Library, Eccles, United Kingdom [*Library symbol Library of Congress*] (LCLS)
UKELA......... United Kingdom Environmental Law Association (DBA)
UKEMS........ United Kingdom Environmental Mutagen Society (EAIO)
UkENL.......... National Library of Scotland, Edinburgh, United Kingdom [*Library symbol Library of Congress*] (LCLS)
UkEPh.......... Pharmaceutical Society of Great Britain, Scottish Department, Edinburgh, United Kingdom [*Library symbol Library of Congress*] (LCLS)
UkERCP....... Royal College of Physicians, Edinburgh, United Kingdom [*Library symbol Library of Congress*] (LCLS)
UkERCS....... Royal College of Surgeons, Edinburgh, United Kingdom [*Library symbol Library of Congress*] (LCLS)
UKERNA....... United Kingdom Education and Research Networking Association (AIE)
UkES............ Scottish Central Library, Edinburgh, United Kingdom [*Library symbol Library of Congress*] (LCLS)
UkEU............ University of Edinburgh, Edinburgh, United Kingdom [*Library symbol Library of Congress*] (LCLS)
UKF.............. United Karate Federation (EA)
UKFA........... United Kingdom Fellmongers Association (BI)
UKFBPW...... United Kingdom Federation of Business and Professional Women (DI)
UKFC........... United Kingdom Fortifications Club (DBA)
UKFF........... Simferopol [*Former USSR ICAO location identifier*] (ICLI)
UKFO........... United Kingdom for Orders [*Shipping*]
UKFR........... United Kingdom Feline Register [*An association*] (DBA)
UkGM.......... Mitchell Library, Glasgow, United Kingdom [*Library symbol Library of Congress*] (LCLS)
UkGO........... George Outram & Co. Ltd., Glasgow, United Kingdom [*Library symbol Library of Congress*] (LCLS)
UkGP........... Royal Faculty of Procurators in Glasgow, Glasgow, United Kingdom [*Library symbol Library of Congress*] (LCLS)
UKGPA......... United Kingdom Glycerine Producers' Association (BI)
UkGU........... University of Glasgow, Glasgow, United Kingdom [*Library symbol Library of Congress*] (LCLS)
UkGUS......... University of Strathclyde, Andersonian Library, Glasgow, Scotland [*Library symbol*] [*Library of Congress*] (LCLS)
UKH............. Ukhta Airenterprise [*Former USSR*] [*FAA designator*] (FAAC)
UKH............. United Keno Hill Mines Ltd. [*Toronto Stock Exchange symbol*]
UkHA........... Atomic Energy Research Establishment, Didcot, Oxfordshire, United Kingdom [*Library symbol Library of Congress*] (LCLS)
UKHAD......... United Kingdom and Havre, Antwerp, and Dunkirk [*Shipping*] (DS)
UkHe............ Heywood Public Library, Heywood, Lancashire, United Kingdom [*Library symbol Library of Congress*] (LCLS)
UKHE........... Petrovskoye [*Former USSR ICAO location identifier*] (ICLI)
UKHEF......... United Kingdom Home Economics Federation [*British*]
UKHH........... United Kingdom and Havre-Hamburg [*Shipping*] (DS)
UKHT........... United Kingdom Housing Trust
UkHu............ Huddersfield Public Libraries, Huddersfield, United Kingdom [*Library symbol Library of Congress*] (LCLS)
UKI............... Ukiah [*California*] [*Seismograph station code, US Geological Survey*] (SEIS)
UKI............... Ukiah [*California*] [*Airport symbol*] (AD)
UKI............... Ukiah, CA [*Location identifier FAA*] (FAAL)
UKIAS.......... United Kingdom Immigrants Advisory Service
UKIBEK........ United Kingdom Insurance Brokers European Committee
UKII............. Kishinev [*Former USSR ICAO location identifier*] (ICLI)
UKing........... United Kingdom Fund [*Associated Press*] (SAG)
UKIP............ United Kingdom Import Plan
UKIPA.......... United Kingdom and Ireland Particleboard Association (EAIO)
UKIRT.......... United Kingdom Infrared Telescope
UKISC.......... United Kingdom Industrial Space Committee (DBA)
UKITO.......... United Kingdom Information Technology Organization
UKJATFOR... United Kingdom Joint Airborne Task Force [*British military*] (DMA)
UKJGA......... United Kingdom Jute Goods Association Ltd. (BI)
UkK.............. Keighley Central Library, Keighley, United Kingdom [*Library symbol Library of Congress*] (LCLS)
UKK............. Urho Kekkonen [*President of Finland*]
UkKi............. Kilmarnock Public Library, Central Library, Dick Institute, Kilmarnock, United Kingdom [*Library symbol Library of Congress*] (LCLS)
UKKK........... Kiev/Zhulyany [*Former USSR ICAO location identifier*] (ICLI)
UKKS........... Semyenovka [*Former USSR ICAO location identifier*] (ICLI)
UkKuK......... Knapp, Drewett & Sons Ltd., Kingston-Upon-Thames, United Kingdom [*Library symbol Library of Congress*] (LCLS)
UKL.............. Ukraine Airalliance [*FAA designator*] (FAAC)
UKL.............. Utashik Lake [*Alaska*] [*Seismograph station code, US Geological Survey*] (SEIS)
UkLA........... Associated Newspapers Ltd., London, United Kingdom [*Library symbol Library of Congress*] (LCLS)
UkLB........... Beaverbrook Newspapers Ltd., London, United Kingdom [*Library symbol Library of Congress*] (LCLS)
UkLBOA....... British Optical Association, London, United Kingdom [*Library symbol Library of Congress*] (LCLS)
UkLC........... Chemical Society, London, United Kingdom [*Library symbol Library of Congress*] (LCLS)
UkLCS......... Institute of Commonwealth Studies, London, United Kingdom [*Library symbol Library of Congress*] (LCLS)
UKLDS......... UK Library Database System (NITA)
UkLe............ Leeds City Library, Leeds, United Kingdom [*Library symbol Library of Congress*] (LCLS)
UKLF........... United Kingdom Land Forces [*Military*]
UkLG........... Guildhall Library, Aldermanbury, London, United Kingdom [*Library symbol Library of Congress*] (LCLS)
UkLH........... Hampstead Public Libraries, Central Library, London, United Kingdom [*Library symbol Library of Congress*] (LCLS)
UkLHu......... A. J. Hurley Ltd., London, United Kingdom [*Library symbol Library of Congress*] (LCLS)
UkLi............ Liverpool Public Libraries, Liverpool, United Kingdom [*Library symbol Library of Congress*] (LCLS)
UkLin.......... City of Lincoln Public Library, Lincoln, United Kingdom [*Library symbol Library of Congress*] (LCLS)
UkLIO......... India Office Library and Records, Foreign and Commonwealth Office, London, United Kingdom [*Library symbol Library of Congress*] (LCLS)
UkLIP.......... IPC Newspapers Ltd., London, United Kingdom [*Library symbol Library of Congress*] (LCLS)
UkLiP.......... Liverpool Daily Post & Echo Ltd., Liverpool, United Kingdom [*Library symbol Library of Congress*] (LCLS)
UkLiPE........ Liverpool Daily Post and Echo, Ltd., Liverpool, United Kingdom [*Library symbol*] [*Library of Congress*] (LCLS)
UkLiU.......... University of Liverpool, Liverpool, United Kingdom [*Library symbol Library of Congress*] (LCLS)
UkLJ........... Jews' College, London, United Kingdom [*Library symbol Library of Congress*] (LCLS)
UKLL........... Lvov [*Former USSR ICAO location identifier*] (ICLI)
UkLLA......... Library Association, London, United Kingdom [*Library symbol Library of Congress*] (LCLS)
UkLLT......... Lambeth Public Libraries, Tate Central Library, London, United Kingdom [*Library symbol Library of Congress*] (LCLS)
UkLMS........ Morning Star Co-Operative Society, London, United Kingdom [*Library symbol Library of Congress*] (LCLS)
UkLNAL....... National Art Library, Victoria and Albert Museum, London, United Kingdom [*Library symbol*] [*Library of Congress*] (LCLS)
UkLNw........ North West London Press Ltd., London, United Kingdom [*Library symbol Library of Congress*] (LCLS)
UkLPh......... Pharmaceutical Society of Great Britain, London, United Kingdom [*Library symbol Library of Congress*] (LCLS)
UkLPo......... H. Pordes, Publisher and Bookseller, London, United Kingdom [*Library symbol Library of Congress*] (LCLS)
UkLPR......... Public Record Office, London, United Kingdom [*Library symbol Library of Congress*] (LCLS)
UkLQ.......... Friends Reference Library, London, United Kingdom [*Library symbol Library of Congress*] (LCLS)
UKLR.......... University of Kansas. Law Review [*A publication*] (DLA)
UkLRCP....... Royal College of Physicians, London, United Kingdom [*Library symbol Library of Congress*] (LCLS)
UkLRCS....... Royal College of Surgeons of England, London, United Kingdom [*Library symbol Library of Congress*] (LCLS)
UkLRSM...... Royal Society of Medicine, London, United Kingdom [*Library symbol Library of Congress*] (LCLS)
UkLS........... Science Museum, London, United Kingdom [*Library symbol Library of Congress*] (LCLS)

UkLTh .... Thomasons Ltd., London, United Kingdom [*Library symbol Library of Congress*] (LCLS)
UkLU .... University of London, London, United Kingdom [*Library symbol Library of Congress*] (LCLS)
UkLuH .... Home Counties Newspapers Ltd., Luton, United Kingdom [*Library symbol Library of Congress*] (LCLS)
UkLU-K .... University of London, Kings College, London, United Kingdom [*Library symbol Library of Congress*] (LCLS)
UkLW .... Wellcome Historical Medical Library, London, United Kingdom [*Library symbol Library of Congress*] (LCLS)
UkLWa .... Wandsworth Borough News Co. Ltd., London, United Kingdom [*Library symbol Library of Congress*] (LCLS)
UKM .... UK MARC [*United Kingdom Machine-Readable Cataloging*] [*Source file*] [*UTLAS symbol*]
UKM .... United Kingdom Fund [*NYSE symbol*] (SPSG)
UKM .... Urea Kinetic Modeling [*Dialysis*] (CPH)
UkMa .... Manchester Public Libraries, Central Library, Manchester, United Kingdom [*Library symbol Library of Congress*] (LCLS)
UkMaG .... Guardian Newspapers Ltd., Manchester, United Kingdom [*Library symbol Library of Congress*] (LCLS)
UKMANZRA ... United Kingdom Manufacturers and New Zealand Representatives Association (BI)
UK MARC ..... UK [*British Library*] Machine Readable Catalogue [*Bibliographic database*]
UKMC .... University of Kentucky Medical Center [*Lexington, KY*]
UKMCA .... United Kingdom Module Constructors Association (DBA)
UkMe .... Public Libraries, Central Library, Merthyr-Tydfil, United Kingdom [*Library symbol Library of Congress*] (LCLS)
UKMF .... United Kingdom Mobile Force
UKMF(A) ...... United Kingdom Mobile Force (Air) [*British military*] (DMA)
UKMF(L) ...... United Kingdom Mobile Force (Land) [*British military*] (DMA)
UkMg .... Margate Public Library, Margate, United Kingdom [*Library symbol Library of Congress*] (LCLS)
UKML .... United Knitwear Manufacturers League (EA)
UKMO .... United Kingdom Meteorological Office
UKMO .... United Kingdom Meteorological Office [*Marine science*] (OSRA)
UKMOSS ...... United Kingdom Ministry of Supply Staff
UKMRC .... United Kingdom Medical Research Council
UKN .... Unknown (KSC)
UKN .... Waukon, IA [*Location identifier FAA*] (FAAL)
UKNCIAWPRC ... International Water Quality Association [*British*] (EAIO)
UKNCIAWPRC ... United Kingdom National Committee of the International Association on Water Pollution Research and Control (EAIO)
UkNcU .... University of Newcastle upon Tyne, Newcastle upon Tyne, United Kingdom [*Library symbol*] [*Library of Congress*] (LCLS)
UK/NL .... United Kingdom/Netherlands (MCD)
UKNND .... United Kingdom National Nutrient Databank [*Ministry of Agriculture and Royal Society of Chemistry*]
UkNr .... Norwich Public Libraries, Norwich, United Kingdom [*Library symbol Library of Congress*] (LCLS)
UKNR .... University of Kansas Nuclear Reactor
UkNrE .... Eastern Counties Newspapers Ltd., Norwich, United Kingdom [*Library symbol Library of Congress*] (LCLS)
UKNSDC ...... United Kingdom National Serials Data Centre [*Information service or system*] (IID)
UKO .... Unverhofft Kommt Oft [*The Unexpected Often Happens*] [*Motto of Franz, Duke of Pomerania (1577-1620)*]
UKOA .... United Kingdom Offshore Operators' Association
UKOBA .... United Kingdom Outboard Boating Association (BI)
UkoIn .... United Kingdom Office for Library Networking
UKOLUG .... United Kingdom On-Line User Group [*Information service or system*] (IID)
UKOO .... Odessa/Tsentralny [*Former USSR ICAO location identifier*] (ICLI)
UKOOA .... United Kingdom Offshore Operators' Association (DS)
UKOP .... United Kingdom Official Publications [*Information service or system*] (IID)
UK OSCA ..... United Kingdom Optical Sensors Collaborative Association (ACII)
UkOxU .... Oxford University, Bodleian Library, Oxford, United Kingdom [*Library symbol Library of Congress*] (LCLS)
UkOxU-AS .... Oxford University, All Souls College, Oxford, United Kingdom [*Library symbol Library of Congress*] (LCLS)
UkOxU-N ...... Oxford University, Nuffield College, Oxford, United Kingdom [*Library symbol Library of Congress*] (LCLS)
UkOxU-Rh .... Oxford University, Bodleian Library, Rhodes House, Oxford, United Kingdom [*Library symbol Library of Congress*] (LCLS)
UKP .... UK Home Office [*British ICAO designator*] (FAAC)
UKPA .... United Kingdom Patternmakers' Association [*A union*]
UKPA .... United Kingdom Pilots Association (DS)
UKPCA .... United Kingdom Postal Clerks' Association [*A union*]
UkPe .... Sandeman Public Library, Perth, United Kingdom [*Library symbol Library of Congress*] (LCLS)
UKPI .... United Kingdom Provident Institute [*Commercial firm*]
UKPIA .... United Kingdom Petroleum Industry Association
UKPMA .... United Kingdom Preserves Manufacturers Association (DBA)
UKPO .... United Kingdom Post Office [*Telecommunications*] (TEL)
UKPPD .... United Kingdom Paper and Packaging Directory [*A publication*]
UkPS .... Portsmouth & Sunderland Newspapers Ltd., Portsmouth, Hants, United Kingdom [*Library symbol Library of Congress*] (LCLS)
UKPTF .... United Kingdom Provision Trade Federation (DBA)
UKR .... Air Ukraine [*ICAO designator*] (FAAC)
UKR .... Mukeiras [*South Arabia*] [*Airport symbol*] (AD)
UKR .... Ukraine
ukr .... Ukrainian [*MARC language code Library of Congress*] (LCCP)
UKR .... Ukrainian Soviet Socialist Republic [*ISO three-letter standard code*] (CNC)
UKR .... UK Retrospective (NITA)
UKR .... United Kingdom Atomic Energy Authority Office at Risley (IAA)
UKR .... Uranian Kilometric Radiation [*Planetary science*]
UKRA .... United Kingdom Reading Association [*British*]
UKRA .... United Kingdom Renderers Association (DBA)
UKREP .... United Kingdom Permanent Representative [*EEC*] (DS)
UkRiH .... Richmond Herald Ltd., Richmond, Surrey, United Kingdom [*Library symbol Library of Congress*] (LCLS)
UKRK .... Ukrains'ka Kooperativna Rada Kanadi
UkRoS .... G. & A. N. Scott Ltd., Rochdale, United Kingdom [*Library symbol Library of Congress*] (LCLS)
UkrSSR .... Ukranian Soviet Socialist Republic
UKS .... United Kingdom Subsatellite
UKSA .... United Kingdom Settlers' Association [*Australia*]
UKSA .... United Kingdom Shipmakers' Association [*A union*]
UKSASS ...... United Kingdom Society of Amalgamated Smiths and Strikers [*A union*]
UKSATA ...... United Kingdom-South Africa Trade Association
UKSC .... United Kingdom Society of Coachmakers [*A union*]
UKSCC .... United Kingdom Spoon Collectors Club (DBA)
UKSG .... United Kingdom Serials Group
UkSh .... Sheffield City Libraries, Central Library, Sheffield, United Kingdom [*Library symbol Library of Congress*] (LCLS)
UkShU .... University of Sheffield, Sheffield, United Kingdom [*Library symbol Library of Congress*] (LCLS)
UKSIA .... United Kindgom Sugar Industry Association (DBA)
UKSIM .... United Kingdom Society of Information Management (DBA)
UkSlO .... Slough Observer Ltd., Slough, United Kingdom [*Library symbol Library of Congress*] (LCLS)
UKSMA .... United Kingdom Sugar Merchants' Association (BI)
UKSPA .... United Kingdom Science Park Association (DBA)
UkSsB .... John H. Burrows & Sons Ltd., Southend-On-Sea, United Kingdom [*Library symbol Library of Congress*] (LCLS)
UKST .... United Kingdom Schmidt Telescope
UkSta .... Stamford Public Library and Museum, Stamford, United Kingdom [*Library symbol Library of Congress*] (LCLS)
UKSTC .... United Kingdom Strike Command (NATG)
UKSTU .... United Kingdom Schmidt Telescope Unit
UkSw .... Swansea Public Library, Swansea, United Kingdom [*Library symbol Library of Congress*] (LCLS)
UKT .... Quakertown, PA [*Location identifier FAA*] (FAAL)
UKT .... United Kingdom Tariff (DS)
UKTA .... United Kingdom Tea Association (DBA)
UKTA .... United Kingdom Trade Agency
UKTD .... United Kingdom Treasury Delegation
UKTM .... UK [*United Kingdom*] Trade Marks [*The Patent Office*] [*British Information service or system*] (IID)
UKTOTC ...... United Kingdom Tariff and Overseas Trade Classification (DS)
UKTS .... United Kingdom Treaty Series [*A publication*]
UKTTSMA .... United Kingdom Timber Trade Shipowners Mutual Association Ltd. (DS)
UKU .... Nuku [*Papua New Guinea*] [*Airport symbol*] (OAG)
UKU .... Ukraine-Aviatrans [*FAA designator*] (FAAC)
UKUSA .... United Kingdom-United States Agreement [*Intelligence*] [*1947*]
U_kV .... Potassium-Excretion Rate [*Medicine*] (DAVI)
UKV .... Underground Keybox Vault (NATG)
UKW .... LVOV Airlines [*Ukraine*] [*FAA designator*] (FAAC)
UKW .... Ultrakurzwelle [*Ultrashort wave*] [*German*]
UkWC-A .... Windsor Castle, Royal Archives, Windsor, Berkshire, United Kingdom [*Library symbol*] [*Library of Congress*] (LCLS)
UkWE .... Eton College, Windsor, Berks, United Kingdom [*Library symbol Library of Congress*] (LCLS)
UKWE .... Ultrakurzwellenempfaenger [*Very-High-Frequency Receiver*] [*German*]
UkWg .... County Borough of Wigan Public Libraries, Central Library, Wigan, United Kingdom [*Library symbol Library of Congress*] (LCLS)
UKWGF .... United Kingdom Wool Growers Federation (DBA)
UkWoE .... Express & Star Ltd., Wolverhampton, United Kingdom [*Library symbol Library of Congress*] (LCLS)
UkWr .... Wrexham Public Library, Wrexham, United Kingdom [*Library symbol Library of Congress*] (LCLS)
UKY .... United Kingdom Energy [*Vancouver Stock Exchange symbol*]
UKY .... University of Kentucky (PDAA)
U Ky .... University of Kentucky (GAGS)
'Ukz .... 'Ukzin (BJA)
UL .... Air Lanka [*ICAO designator*] (AD)
UL .... Lansa, SRL [*Honduras*] [*ICAO designator*] (ICDA)
UL .... Ugaritic Literature [*C. H. Gordon*] [*A publication*] (BJA)
Ul .... Uldericus de Bamberg [*Flourished, 12th century*] [*Authority cited in pre-1607 legal work*] (DSA)
UL .... Ulitsa [*Street*] (EY)
UL .... Ultralinear
UL .... Ultralow
UL .... Unauthorized Launch
UL .... Uncontrolled (index) Language (NITA)
UL .... Underlay
U/L .... Underlever [*Rifles*] (DICI)
UL .... Underload (NASA)
UL .... Underwriters Laboratories (EA)
UL .... Undifferentiated Lymphoma [*Medicine*] (MAE)
UL .... Uniformly Labeled [*Compound, with radioisotope*] [*Also, U*]
UL .... Unilever ADR [*NYSE symbol*] (TTSB)
UL .... Unilever Ltd. [*NYSE symbol*] (SPSG)
UL .... Unionist Liberal [*British*] (ROG)
UL .... Union Liberal [*Liberal Union*] [*Spain Political party*] (PPW)

UL............... Union List
UL............... United Left [*Peru*] [*Political party*]
U/l............... United per Liter (DAVI)
U/L............... Unit Linked
UL............... Unit Load
UL............... Universala Ligo [*Defunct*] (EA)
UL............... Universal League (EAIO)
UL............... Universal Life [*Insurance*]
UL............... University Library (WDAA)
u/l............... Unlimited [*Water depth*]
UL............... Unterlafette [*Bottom carriage*] [*German military - World War II*]
UL............... Up Left [*The rear left portion of a stage*] [*A stage direction*]
UL............... Up Link [*Computer science*]
U/L............... UpLink
UL............... Upper Laterals [*Botany*]
UL............... Upper Left [*S-band antenna*] (NASA)
UL............... Upper Leg
UL............... Upper Level [*Nuclear energy*] (NRCH)
UL............... Upper Limb [*Upper edge of sun, moon, etc.*] [*Navigation*]
UL............... Upper Limit
UL............... Upper List (NITA)
UL............... Upper Lobe [*Anatomy*]
UL............... Urban League (MCD)
UL............... Usage List (MSA)
UL............... Useful Life (SAA)
UL............... User Language [*Computer science*] (DIT)
UL............... Utility Lead [*Telecommunications*] (TEL)
ULA............... San Julian [*Argentina*] [*Airport symbol*] (OAG)
ULA............... Ulamona Field Station [*New Britain*] [*Seismograph station code, US Geological Survey*] (SEIS)
ULA............... Uncommitted Logic Array [*Semiconductor technology*]
ULA............... Uniform Laws, Annotated [*A publication*] (DLA)
ULA............... Universal Logic Array [*Computer science*] (IAA)
ULA............... Upper Layer Architecture [*Telecommunications*] (OSI)
ULA............... Utah State University, Logan, UT [*Library symbol Library of Congress*] (LCLS)
ULA............... Zuliana de Aviacion [*Venezuela*] [*ICAO designator*] (FAAC)
ULAA............... Ukrainian Library Association of America (EA)
ULAA............... United Latin Americans of America (EA)
ULAB............... Unilab Corp. [*NASDAQ symbol*] (NQ)
ULAC............... Union Latinoamericana de Ciegos [*Latin American Blind Union - LABU*] [*Montevideo, Uruguay*] (EAIO)
ULAE............... Universal Limited Art Editions
ULAEY............... Union of Latin American Ecumenical Youth (EA)
ULAIDS............... Universal Locator Airborne Integrated Data System (MCD)
ULAJE............... Union Latino-Americaine des Jeunesses Evangeliques [*Union of Latin American Evangelical Youth*]
ULAJE............... Union Latinoamericana de Juventudes Ecumenicas [*Union of Latin American Ecumenical Youth - ULAEY*] (EAIO)
ULAK............... Kotlas [*Former USSR ICAO location identifier*] (ICLI)
ULANG............... User Language [*Computer science*]
ULAP............... Universitywide Library Automation Program (NITA)
ULAPC............... Union Latino-Americaine de la Presse Catholique
ULAS............... University of Louisville Archaeological Survey [*Research center*] (RCD)
ULASM............... Undersea Multichannel Large-Scale Scattering Meter [*NASA*] (MCD)
ULAST............... Union Latino Americana de Sociedades de Tisiologia [*Latin American Union of Societies of Phthisiology*]
U La Verne... University of La Verne (GAGS)
ULB............... Underwater Locator Beacon (MCD)
ULB............... Universal Logic Block (IEEE)
ULB............... University of Bradford
ULB............... Unlighted Buoy [*USCG*] (TAG)
ULBA............... Universal Love and Brotherhood Association [*Kyoto, Japan*] (EAIO)
ULBI............... ULtralife Batteries [*NASDAQ symbol*] (TTSB)
ULBI............... Ultralife Batteries, Inc. [*NASDAQ symbol*] (SAG)
ULBM............... Underlay Battle Manager
ULBW............... Ultralow Birth Weight [*Medicine*] (DMAA)
ULC............... Cache County Public Library, Logan, UT [*Library symbol Library of Congress*] (LCLS)
ULC............... Philippines Civil Liberties Union (PD)
ULC............... Ultra-Low Carbon [*Metallurgical engineering*]
ULC............... Underwriters' Laboratories of Canada
ULC............... Uniform Loop Clock
ULC............... Union de la Lutte Communiste [*Burkina Faso*] [*Political party*] (EY)
ULC............... Union Library Catalogue
ULC............... Unitary Launch Concept [*or Control*] (AAG)
ULC............... United Labor Congress [*Nigeria*]
ULC............... Unit Ledger Card [*Computer science*]
ULC............... Unit Level Code (AFM)
ULC............... Unit Level Computers [*Army*]
ULC............... Universal Life Church
ULC............... Universal Load Cell
ULC............... Universal Logic Circuit
ULC............... Unsafe Lane Change (WDAA)
ULC............... Upper and Lower Case (NITA)
ULC............... Upper Left Center [*The rear left center portion of a stage*] [*A stage direction*]
ULC............... Urban Libraries Council (EA)
ULC............... Utah State Library, Salt Lake City, UT [*OCLC symbol*] (OCLC)
ULCA............... Ukrainian Life Cooperative Association [*Defunct*] (EA)
ULCA............... Uncommitted Logic Array [*Semiconductor technology*] (EECA)
ULCA............... United Lutheran Church of America (WDAA)
ULCANS............... Ultra Light-Weight Camouflage Net System [*Air Force*] (RDA)
ULCANS............... Ultralightweight Camouflage Net System [*Army*]
ULCC............... Ulster Loyalist Central Coordinating Committee [*Ireland*]
ULCC............... Ultralarge Crude Carrier [*Oil tanker*]
ULCC............... Ultralow-Cement Castable [*Ceramics*]
ULCC............... University of London Computer Centre (NITA)
ULCE............... Unified Life Cycle Engineering (MCD)
ULCER............... Underwater Launch Control Energy Requirements
ULCER............... Underwater Launch Current and Energy Recorder
ULCHi............... Cache Valley Historical Society, Logan, UT [*Library symbol Library of Congress*] (LCLS)
ULCJ............... University Law College. Journal. Rajputana University [*India*] [*A publication*] (DLA)
ULCM............... United Lutheran Church Men [*Defunct*] (EA)
ULCP............... University Laboratory Cooperative Program
ULCRA............... Urban Land (Ceiling and Regulation) Act [*India*] (ECON)
ULCS............... Uniform Lightness and Chromaticity Scale (PDAA)
ULCS............... Unit Level Circuit Switch (CAAL)
ULCS............... Unit Level Computer Logistics System [*Army*]
ULD............... Ultralow Distortion [*Electronics*] (ECII)
ULD............... Ultrasonic Leak Detector
ULD............... Ultrasonic Light Diffraction
ULD............... Union pour la Liberte et le Developpement [*Benin*] [*Political party*] (EY)
ULD............... Unit Load Demand [*Nuclear energy*] (NRCH)
ULD............... Unit Load Device [*Shipping containers*]
ULD............... Unit Logic Device
ULD............... Universal Language Description [*Computer science*] (IAA)
ULD............... Upper Level Deck [*Cargo containers*]
ULD............... Upper-Limb Disorder [*Medicine*] (ECON)
ULDB............... Ultra-Light Displacement Boat (PS)
ULDEST............... Ultimate Destination [*Army*] (AABC)
ULDF............... United Left Democratic Front [*India*] [*Political party*] (PPW)
ULDMI............... Ultraprecise LASER Distance Measuring Instrument
ULDP............... Ulster Loyalist Democratic Party [*Northern Ireland*] [*Political party*] (PPW)
ULDS............... Union Liberale-Democratique Suisse [*Liberal Democratic Union of Switzerland*] [*Political party*] (PPE)
ULDT............... Unable Lower Due Traffic [*Aviation*] (FAAC)
ULE............... Leisure International Airways Ltd. [*British ICAO designator*] (FAAC)
ULE............... Sule [*Papua New Guinea*] [*Airport symbol*] (OAG)
ULE............... Ultralow Expansion [*Trademark, Corning Glass Works*]
ULE............... Unit Location Equipment (MCD)
ULEA............... University Labor Education Association [*Later, UCLEA*]
ULEAC............... University of London and East Anglia Consortium [*British*] (AIE)
ULEB............... Ultra-Low Emissions Bus [*Automotive engineering*]
ULECA............... Ultralow Energy Charge Analyzer [*Instrumentation*]
ULEE............... Ultra-Low Emissions Engine [*Automotive engineering*]
ULES............... University of Lancaster Engineering Services [*Research center British*] (IRUK)
ULET............... Ultra-Low Emissions Truck [*Automotive engineering*]
ULETE............... Ultra-Low Emissions Truck Engine
ULEV............... Ultra-Low-Emission Vehicle
ULew............... Lewiston Public Library, Lewiston, UT [*Library symbol Library of Congress*] (LCLS)
ULEWAT............... Ultralow-Energy Wide-Angle Telescope
ULF............... Ultralow Frequency
ULF............... United Labour Front [*Trinidad and Tobago*] (PD)
ULF............... United Left Front [*Nepal*] [*Political party*] (EY)
ULF............... University Labour Federation [*British*]
ULF............... Upper Limiting Frequency (ADA)
ULFA............... United Liberation Front of Assam [*India*] [*Political party*] (ECON)
ULFJ............... Ultralow-Frequency Jammer
ULFO............... Ultralow-Frequency Oscillator
ULG............... Upholstery Leather Group [*Later, AG*] (EA)
ULGCS............... United Lesbian and Gay Christian Scientists (EA)
ULGE............... Utility, Lawn, and Garden Engines
ULGS............... Church of Jesus Christ of Latter-Day Saints, Genealogical Society Library, CacheBranch, Logan, UT [*Library symbol Library of Congress*] (LCLS)
ULGX............... Urologix, Inc. [*NASDAQ symbol*] (SAG)
ULGX............... Urologix Inc. [*NASDAQ symbol*] (TTSB)
ULI............... ULI - the Urban Land Institute (EA)
ULI............... Ultra-Low Interstitial (PDAA)
ULI............... Underwriters Laboratories, Inc. [*Also, UL*]
ULI............... Uniono por la Linguo Internaciona Ido [*International Language Union*] (EA)
ULI............... Union pour la Langue Internationale Ido [*Union for the International Language Ido*]
ULI............... Universal Logic Implementer
ULI............... Unsigned Long Integer [*Computer science*]
ULI............... [*The*] Urban Land Institute [*An association*] (EAAP)
ULI............... Urban Law Institute of Antioch School of Law [*Defunct*] (EA)
ULIA............... Unattached List, Indian Army
ULIB............... Utility Library [*National Center for Atmospheric Research*]
ULICP............... Universal Log Interpretation Computer Program (PDAA)
ULIDAT............... Umweltliteraturedatenbank [*Data Bank for Environmental Literature*] [*Deutsches Umweltbundesamt*] [*Germany*] [*Information service or system*] (CRD)
ULIMO............... United Liberation Movement [*Liberia*] [*Political party*] (ECON)
ULIS............... Uniform Law on the International Sale of Goods
ULISC............... University Library and Information Services Committee [*Committee of Vice Chancellors and Principals*] [*British*] (AIE)
ULISYS............... Universal Library System (NITA)
ULJ............... Bedford, MA [*Location identifier FAA*] (FAAL)
ULL............... Savoonga, AK [*Location identifier FAA*] (FAAL)
ULL............... Ullage [*NASA*] (KSC)

ULL Uncomfortable Loudness Level (DAVI)

ULL Unitarian Laymen's League

ULL United States Department of Labor, Washington, DC [*OCLC symbol*] (OCLC)

ULL Unit Local Loading (AAG)

ULL University of London Library

ULL Upper Lip Length [*Medicine*]

ULLA Ultra-Low-Level Air-Drop [*British military*] (DMA)

ULLC Unit Level Learning Center

ULLDPE Ultra Linear Low-Density Polyethylene [*Plastics technology*]

ULLL Leningrad/Pulkovo [*Former USSR ICAO location identifier*] (ICLI)

UL-LL Upper-Limit, Lower-Limit (SAA)

UL-LLC Upper-Limit, Lower-Limit Comparator (SAA)

ULLNG Ultra-Large Liquified Natural Gas Carrier (PDAA)

ULLS Ultrasonic Liquid Level Sensor

ULLS Unit Level Logistics System [*Army*]

ULLV Unmanned Lunar Logistics Vehicle [*OMSF*]

ULM Meiji University, Maruzen Co. Ltd. [*UTLAS symbol*]

ULM Mine Safety and Health Administration, Denver, Denver, CO [*OCLC symbol*] (OCLC)

ULM New Ulm [*Minnesota*] [*Airport symbol Obsolete*] (OAG)

ULM Ultramar Capital Corp. [*Toronto Stock Exchange symbol*]

ULM Ultrasonic Light Modulator

ULM Undersea [*or Underwater*] Long-Range Missile [*Navy*]

ULM Universal Line Multiplexer

ULM Universal Logic Module

ULMA University Laboratory Managers Association [*Later, ALMA*] (EA)

ULMA Upper Level Management Advisor (IAA)

Ulm L Rec Ulman's Law Record [*New York*] [*A publication*] (DLA)

ULMS Undersea [*or Underwater*] Long-Range Missile System [*Redesignated "Trident"*] [*Navy*]

ULMS Union List of Montana Serials [*Library network*]

ULMS Unit Level Message Switch

ULN Ulan Bator [*Mongolia*] [*Airport symbol*] (OAG)

ULN United Lincoln Resources, Inc. [*Vancouver Stock Exchange symbol*]

ULN Unit Line Number (DOMA)

ULN University of Lowell, North Campus, Lowell, MA [*OCLC symbol*] (OCLC)

ULN Unlaunchable (IAA)

ULN Upper Limits of Normal [*Medicine*]

ULO Occupational Safety and Health Administration, Technical Data Center, Washington, DC [*OCLC symbol*] (OCLC)

ULO Unilateral Ovariectomy [*Gynecology*]

ULO United Labour Organization [*Burma*]

ULO Unmanned Launch Operations [*NASA*] (KSC)

ULO Unmanned Lunar Orbiter [*NASA*] (MCD)

ULO Unrestricted Line Officer [*Navy*] (DNAB)

ULOL Velikiye Luki [*Former USSR ICAO location identifier*] (ICLI)

ULOR Upward Light Output Ratio (PDAA)

ULOS Unliquidated Obligations (MCD)

ULOSSOM Union List of Selected Serials of Michigan [*Wayne State University Libraries*] [*Ceased*] [*Information service or system*] (IID)

ULOTC University of London Officer Training Corps [*British military*] (DMA)

U Louisville University of Louisville (GAGS)

ULOW Unmanned Launch Operations - Western Test Range [*NASA*] (KSC)

ULP Quilpie [*Australia Airport symbol*] (OAG)

ULP Ulster Petroleums Ltd. [*Toronto Stock Exchange symbol*]

ULP Ultra-Lightweight Panel (PDAA)

ULP Ultralow Chamber Pressure (MCD)

ULP Unfair Labor Practice [*Department of Labor*]

ULP Unfair Labor Practices (WYGK)

ULP Uniform Latex Particles

ULP Universal Logic Primitive (PDAA)

ULP University of London Press (DGA)

ULP Unleaded Petrol [*British*] (ADA)

ULP Upper Layer Protocol [*Telecommunications*] (OSI)

ULP Utilitaire Logique Processor [*Programming language*] [*Computer science French*]

ULP Utility Landplane [*Navy*]

ULPA Uniform Limited Partnership Act [*National Conference of Commissioners on Uniform State Laws*]

ULPA United Lightning Protection Association (EA)

ULPR Ultralow-Pressure Rocket

ULQ Tulua [*Colombia*] [*Airport symbol*] (OAG)

ULQ Upper Left Quadrant (AAMN)

ULR Uganda Law Reports [*A publication*] (DLA)

ULR Uganda Protectorate Law Reports [*1904-51*] [*A publication*] (DLA)

ULR Ultralinear Rectifier

ULR Ultra Long Range (DA)

ULR Ultramar Corp. [*NYSE symbol*] (SPSG)

ULR Underwater Locator Beacon

ULR Uniform Law Review [*A publication*] (DLA)

ULR Union Labor Report [*Bureau of National Affairs*] [*Information service or system*] (CRD)

ULR Union Law Review [*South Africa*] [*A publication*] (DLA)

ULR United Liberty Resources Ltd. [*Vancouver Stock Exchange symbol*]

ULR University Law Review [*United States*] [*A publication*] (DLA)

ULR Utilities Law Reporter [*A publication*] (DLA)

ULRA United Lithuanian Relief Fund of America (EA)

ULRF Urban Land Research Foundation (EA)

ULRGW Ultra-Long Range Guided Weapon (IAA)

ULRSA Union and League of Romanian Societies of America (EA)

ULS Carroll Air Service, Inc. [*ICAO designator*] (FAAC)

ULS ULS Capital Corp. [*Toronto Stock Exchange symbol*]

ULS Ultimatist Life Society (EA)

ULS Ultraviolet Light Stabilizer

ULS Ulysses, KS [*Location identifier FAA*]

ULS United Leukodystrophy Foundation (EA)

ULS United Limited Sprints [*Auto racing*]

ULS United Lutheran Society (EA)

ULS Unit Level Switchboard (MCD)

ULS University Libraries Section [*Association of College and Research Libraries*]

ULS University of Lowell, South Campus, Lowell, MA [*OCLC symbol*] (OCLC)

ULS Unsecured Loan Stock (DCTA)

ULS Upward-Looking SONAR

ULSA Ultralow Sidelobe Antenna [*Air Force*] (MCD)

ULSCS University of London Shared Cataloguing System (NITA)

ULSI Ultralarge-Scale Integration [*of circuits*] [*Semiconductor technology*]

ULSIA Uniform Land Security Interest Act [*National Conference of Commissioners on Uniform State Laws*]

ULSP Unified Legal Services Program

ULSS Underwater LASER Surveying System (MCD)

ULSSSHCL Union List of Serials in the Social Sciences and Humanities Held by Canadian Libraries [*National Library of Canada*] [*Information service or system*] (CRD)

ULSTD Union Label and Service Trades Department (of AFL-CIO) [*American Federation of Labor and Congress of Industrial Organizations*] (EA)

ULSV Unmanned Launch Space Vehicles [*NASA*] (KSC)

ULT Ultimate (AAG)

ULT Ultime [*Lastly*] [*Pharmacy*]

ult Ultimo [*In the Month Preceding the Present*] [*Latin*] (WGA)

ULT Ultrahigh Temperature (MAE)

ULT UltrAir, Inc. [*ICAO designator*] (FAAC)

ULT Ultralow Tar [*Cigarettes*] [*Tobacco industry*]

ULT Ultralow Temperature

ULT Ultramarine [*Philately*] (ROG)

ULT Ultramar Ltd. [*Toronto Stock Exchange symbol*]

ULT Uniform Low-Frequency Technique

ULT Unione per la Lotta alla Tubercolosi [*Union of Anti-Tuberculosis Association Workers*] [*Italy*]

ULT United Lodge of Theosophists (EA)

ULT Upper Layer Thickness [*Of ocean waters*] [*Oceanography*]

ULTA Uniform Land Transactions Act [*National Conference of Commissioners on Uniform State Laws*]

ULTC Urban Library Trustees Council [*Later, ULC*] (EA)

ULTD Ultradata Corp. [*NASDAQ symbol*] (SAG)

ULTD Ultradata Corp. [*NASDAQ symbol*] (TTSB)

ULTE Ultimate Electronics [*Commercial firm NASDAQ symbol*] (SAG)

UltElct Ultimate Electronics [*Commercial firm Associated Press*] (SAG)

ULTI Ultralow-Temperature Isotropic [*Carbon*]

ULTK Ultrak, Inc. [*NASDAQ symbol*] (NQ)

ULTO Ultimo [*In the Month Preceding the Present*] [*Latin*]

UltPac Ultra Pac, Inc. [*Associated Press*] (SAG)

ult praes Ultimum Praescriptus [*Last Prescribed*] [*Latin*] [*Pharmacy*] (DAVI)

ULT PRAESCR Ultimo Praescriptus [*The Last Ordered*] [*Pharmacy*] (ROG)

ULTR UltraData Systems [*NASDAQ symbol*] (TTSB)

ULTR UltraData Systems, Inc. [*NASDAQ symbol*] (SAG)

ULTRA Ultramarine [*Philately*] (ROG)

ULTRACOM Ultraviolet Communications

UltraD UltraData Systems, Inc. [*Associated Press*] (SAG)

UltraDt UltraData Systems, Inc. [*Associated Press*] (SAG)

Ultrafem Ultrafem, Inc. [*Associated Press*] (SAG)

ULTRAJ Ultrajectum [*Utrecht*] [*Imprint*] [*Latin*] (ROG)

Ultrak Ultrak, Inc. [*Associated Press*] (SAG)

Ultralife Ultralife Batteries, Inc. [*Associated Press*] (SAG)

UltramDS Ultramar Diamond Shamrock Corp. [*Associated Press*] (SAG)

Ultramr Ultramar Capital Corp. [*Associated Press*] (SAG)

UltraStp Ultratech Stepper, Inc. [*Associated Press*] (SAG)

ULTRA-X Universal Language for Typographic Reproduction Applications

Ultrdta Ultradata Corp. [*Associated Press*] (SAG)

ULTRW Ultradata Sys Wrrt'A' [*NASDAQ symbol*] (TTSB)

ULTSIGN Ultimate Assignment

ULTT Tallin [*Former USSR ICAO location identifier*] (ICLI)

ULU Gulu [*Uganda*] [*Airport symbol*] (OAG)

ULV Ultralow Volume

ULVA USS [*United States Ship*] Liberty Veterans Association (EA)

ULVZ Ultra Low Velocity Zone [*Seismology*]

ULW Unsafe Landing Warning

ULWA Union of Latin Writers and Artists [*Paris, France*] (EAIO)

ULWB Belozyorsk [*Former USSR ICAO location identifier*] (ICLI)

ULWC Ultra-Lightweight Coated [*Paper*]

ULWT Totma [*Former USSR ICAO location identifier*] (ICLI)

ULWW Vologda [*Former USSR ICAO location identifier*] (ICLI)

ULY Ulyanovsk [*Former USSR Airport symbol*] (OAG)

ULZP United Labor Zionist Party [*Later, LZA*] (EA)

UM Air Zimbabwe [*ICAO designator*] (AD)

um Micron (DAVI)

UM Ouguiya [*Monetary unit*] (ODBW)

UM Salt Lake County Library System, Midvale, UT [*Library symbol Library of Congress*] (LCLS)

UM Ugaritic Manual [*C. H. Gordon*] [*A publication*] (BJA)

UM Umbilical Mast [*NASA*] (KSC)

UM Umot Me'uhadot [*United Nations*] [*Hebrew*]

UM Unaccompanied Minor [*Airline passenger*]

UM Under-Mentioned [*i.e., mentioned later in a document*]

UM Underwater Mechanic

Um Uniform, Medium-Grained [*Soil*]

UM.............. Uninsured Motorists [*Insurance*]
UM.............. Unio Mallorquina [*Majorcan Union*] [*Political party*] (PPW)
UM.............. Unione Maniferro [*Somalia*]
UM.............. Union Movement Party [*British*]
UM.............. Unitas Malacologica [*An association Netherlands*] (EAIO)
UM.............. United States Minor Outlying Islands [*ANSI two-letter standard code*] (CNC)
UM.............. Unit of Measure (MCD)
UM.............. Universal Machine Gun (MCD)
UM.............. Universal Measuring Microscope
UM.............. Universal Monitor (MCD)
UM.............. University of Manitoba [*Canada*]
UM.............. University of Massachusetts [*Amherst, MA*]
UM.............. University of Miami [*Florida*]
UM.............. University of Miami, Florida [*USA*] [*Marine science*] (OSRA)
UM.............. University of Missouri Press
U/M.............. Unmanned (NASA)
UM.............. Unmarried
UM.............. Unpopular Magnetic Fields
UM.............. Unpriced Material
UM.............. Unscheduled Maintenance
UM.............. Upper Magazine [*Typography*]
UM.............. Upper Motor [*Neurons*] [*Medicine*]
UM.............. Uracil Mustard [*Antineoplastic drug*] (AAMN)
UM.............. Uromodulin
UM.............. Useful Method
UM.............. Use of Materials Bulletin [*Department of Housing and Urban Development*] [*A publication*] (GFGA)
UM.............. User Manual (MCD)
UM.............. Utilization Management (WYGK)
UMA.............. Lineas Aereas del Humaya, SA de CV [*Mexico*] [*FAA designator*] (FAAC)
UMA.............. Ultrasonic Manufacturers Association [*Later, UIA*] (EA)
UMA.............. Unified Memory Architecture [*Computer science*] (PCM)
UMA.............. Unified Memory Architecture (PCM)
UMA.............. Uniform - Memory - Access [*Computer science*]
UMA.............. Union de Mujeres Americanas [*United Women of the Americas*]
UMA.............. Union Mathematique Africaine [*African Mathematical Union - AMU*] (EA)
UMA.............. Union Medicale Arabe [*Arab Medical Union*] (EAIO)
UMA.............. Union Membership Agreement (DCTA)
UMA.............. Union Mondiale des Aveugles [*World Blind Union - WBU*] (EA)
UMA.............. United Maritime Administration
UMA.............. United Maritime Authority
UMA.............. United Methodist Association of Health and Welfare Ministries (EA)
UMA.............. Unit Mobilization Augmentation [*Army*] (DOMA)
UMA.............. Universal Measurement Assembly (MCD)
UMA.............. Universal Measuring Amplifier (KSC)
UMA.............. University of Mid-America [*Consortium of six midwestern universities*]
UMA.............. Unmanned Aircraft [*Aviation*]
UMA.............. Unscheduled Maintenance Action [*Military*] (AABC)
UMA.............. Upper Memory Area [*Computer science*]
UMA.............. Urinary Muramidase Activity [*Medicine*] (DMAA)
UMa.............. Ursa Major [*Constellation*]
UMAA.............. United Martial Arts Association (EA)
UMAA.............. University of Melbourne Alumni Association [*Australia*]
UMAB.............. University of Maryland at Baltimore
UMAC.............. UMI [*University Microfilms International*] Article Clearinghouse [*Information service or system*] (IID)
UMACHA...... Upper Midwest Automated Clearing House Association (MHDW)
UMAD.............. Umatilla Army Depot [*Oregon*] (AABC)
UMAH.............. Union Mondiale d'Avancee Humaine [*World Union for Human Progress*]
U Maine.......... University of Maine (GAGS)
U Maine L Rev... University of Maine. Law Review [*A publication*] (DLA)
U Maine (Portland-Gorham)... University of Maine at Portland-Gorham (GAGS)
UMaj.............. Ursa Major [*Constellation*]
UMan.............. Manti City Library, Manti, UT [*Library symbol Library of Congress*] (LCLS)
UMANA.............. Ukrainian Medical Association of North America (EA)
UMAP.............. United Methodist Associations of Preschools
UMAP.............. University of Michigan Assembly Program
UMARK.............. Unit Maintenance Aircraft Recovery Kit (MCD)
U Mary L Forum... University of Maryland Law Forum [*A publication*] (DLA)
UMASS.............. University of Massachusetts [*Amherst, MA*]
U Mass.............. University of Massachusetts Amherst (GAGS)
UMASS.............. Unlimited Machine Access from Scattered Sites [*Computer science*]
U Mass (Boston)... University of Massachusetts Boston (GAGS)
U Mass (Dartmouth)... University of Massachusetts Dartmouth (GAGS)
U Mass (Lowell)... University of Massachusetts Lowell (GAGS)
Umax.............. Maximum Solute Concentration [*Chemistry*] (DAVI)
Umax.............. Urinary Osmolality Maximum [*Physiology*] (MAH)
UMB.............. Ultramicrobacteria
Umb.............. Umbelliferyl [*Biochemistry*]
UMB.............. Umberatana [*Australia Seismograph station code, US Geological Survey*] (SEIS)
UMB.............. Umberto's Pasta Enterprises, Inc. [*Vancouver Stock Exchange symbol*]
UMB.............. Umbilical (MCD)
umb.............. Umbundu [*MARC language code Library of Congress*] (LCCP)
UMB.............. Umnak, AK [*Location identifier FAA*] (FAAL)
UMB.............. Union Medicale Balkanique [*Balkan Medical Union*] (EAIO)
UMB.............. Union Mondiale de Billard [*World Billiards Union - WBU*] [*Switzerland*]
UMB.............. United Merchant Bar [*Commercial firm British*]
UMB.............. Universal Masonic Brotherhood (EA)
UMB.............. Universal Missile Building (MCD)
UMB.............. Upper Memory Block [*Computer science*] (PCM)
UMBA.............. United Mortgage Bankers of America [*Philadelphia, PA*] (EA)
UM-BBD...... University of Minesota Biocatalysis/Biodegradation Database
UMBC.............. Umbilical Cord [*Aerospace engineering*]
UMBC.............. United Malayan Banking Corp.
UMBC.............. University of Maryland, Baltimore County
UMBF.............. UMB Financial [*NASDAQ symbol*] (TTSB)
UMBF.............. UMB Financial Corp. [*NASDAQ symbol*] (SAG)
UMB Fn.......... UMB Financial Corp. [*Associated Press*] (SAG)
UMBI.............. University of Maryland Biotechnology Institute
UMBL.............. Umbilical (AAG)
Umbr.............. Umbrian [*Language, culture, etc.*]
UMBR.............. Unclad-Metal Breeder Reactor
UMBR.............. Universal Multiple Bomb Rack (NG)
UMBS.............. University of Michigan Biological Station [*Research center*] (RCD)
UMBSM.............. University Marine Biological Station, Millport [*UK*] [*Marine science*] (OSRA)
UMB V.............. Umbilical Vein [*Anatomy*]
umb ven.......... Umbilical Vein [*Anatomy*] (DAVI)
UMC.............. Ukrainian Museum of Canada [*UTLAS symbol*]
UMC.............. Underwater Manifold Centre [*Shell Oil Co.*] [*British*]
UMC.............. Unibus Microchannel
UMC.............. Unidirectional Molding Compound (MCD)
UMC.............. Unified Management Corp. Database [*Information service or system*] (CRD)
UMC.............. Uniform Motion Coupling
UMC.............. Uniform Moving Charge
UMC.............. Uninsured Motorists Coverage [*Insurance*]
UMC.............. Union du Moyen-Congo [*Union of the Middle Congo*]
UMC.............. United Maritime Council
UMC.............. United Meridian Corp. [*NYSE symbol*] (SPSG)
UMC.............. United Methodist Church
UMC.............. United Microelectronics Corp. (NITA)
UMC.............. United Mining Corp. [*Vancouver Stock Exchange symbol*]
UMC.............. United Motor Courts
UMC.............. Unit Mail Clerk
UMC.............. Unit Mobility Center [*Military*] (AFIT)
UMC.............. Universal Match Corp.
UmC.............. Universal Microfilming Corporation, Salt Lake City, UT [*Library symbol Library of Congress Obsolete*] (LCLS)
UMC.............. University of Maryland, College Park, MD [*OCLC symbol*] (OCLC)
UMC.............. Unspecified Minor Construction Program [*Navy*] (DNAB)
UMCA.............. Ultra Marathon Cycling Association (EA)
UMCA.............. United Mining Councils of America (EA)
UMCA.............. Universities Mission to Central Africa [*Later, USPG*] [*British*]
UMCA.............. Uraba, Medellin & Central Airways, Inc.
UMCathA...... Young Men's Catholic Association (BARN)
UMCC.............. United Maritime Consultative Committee
UMCEES...... University of Maryland Center for Environmental and Estuarine Studies
UMCOM.............. United Methodist Communications [*Information service or system*] (IID)
UMCOR.............. United Methodist Committee on Relief (EA)
UMCP.............. Unit Maintenance Collection Point [*Army*] (INF)
UMCP.............. University of Maryland, College Park
UM/CR.............. Unsatisfactory Material/Condition Report (MCD)
UMCS.............. Unattended Multipoint Communications Station (MHDI)
UMD.............. Ultrasonic Material Dispersion
UMD.............. Union de Mouvements Democratiques [*Djibouti*] [*Political party*] (EY)
UMD.............. Unitized Microwave Devices
UMD.............. Unit Manning Document [*DoD*]
UMD.............. Unit Movement Data [*Military*]
UMD.............. University of Maryland [*College Park, MD*]
U Md.............. University of Maryland (GAGS)
UMD.............. University of Medicine and Dentistry of New Jersey
UMDA.............. Umatilla Depot Activity [*Army*]
UMDA.............. Uniform Marriage and Divorce Act [*National Conference of Commissioners on Uniform State Laws*]
UMDA.............. United Micronesia Development Association
U Md (Baltimore)... University of Maryland, Baltimore (GAGS)
UMDC.............. Union Mondiale Democrate Chretienne [*Christian Democratic World Union*]
UMDK.............. United Movement for Democracy in Korea [*Later, UMDUK*] (EA)
U Md LF.......... University of Maryland Law Forum [*A publication*] (DLA)
UMDNJ.............. University of Medicine and Dentistry of New Jersey [*Newark*]
UMDUK.............. United Movement for Democracy and Unification in Korea [*Defunct*] (EA)
UME.............. Ultramicroelectrode [*Electrochemical microscopy*]
UME.............. Umea [*Sweden*] [*Seismograph station code, US Geological Survey*] (SEIS)
UME.............. Umea [*Sweden*] [*Airport symbol*] (OAG)
UME.............. Underground Mine Engineer
UME.............. Uniform Manufacturers Exchange (EA)
UME.............. United Ministries in Education [*Later, HEMT/UMHE*] (EA)
UME.............. Unit Mission Equipment (AAG)
UME.............. Unit Mobility Equipment
UME.............. Unit Monthly Equipment (MSA)
UmE.............. University Music Editions, New York, NY [*Library symbol Library of Congress*] (LCLS)
UME.............. University of Maryland, Eastern Shore, Princess Anne, MD [*OCLC symbol*] (OCLC)
UME.............. Unpredictable Main Event
UME.............. Urethane Mixing Equipment

UMEA .... Universala Medicina Esperanto Asocio [*Universal Medical Esperanto Association*] (EAIO)
UMEB .... United Maritime Executive Board
UMEC .... Union Mondiale des Enseignants Catholiques [*World Union of Catholic Teachers*] [*Rome, Italy*]
UMED .... Unimed, Inc. [*NASDAQ symbol*] (NQ)
UMED .... Unimed Pharmaceuticals [*NASDAQ symbol*] (TTSB)
U Med Dent NJ ... University of Medicine and Dentistry of New Jersey (GAGS)
UMEJ .... Union Mondiale des Etudiants Juifs [*World Union of Jewish Students - WUJS*] (EAIO)
UMEMPA ..... Union of Middle Eastern and Mediterranean Pediatric Societies [*Greece*] (EAIO)
UMEMPS ..... Union of Middle Eastern and Mediterranean Pediatric Societies [*See also USPMOM*] [*Athens, Greece*] (EAIO)
UMER .... Ultrasonically-Modulated Electron Resonance (PDAA)
UMeridn ...... United Meridian Corp. [*Associated Press*] (SAG)
UMES .... United Mechanical Engineers' Society [*A union*] [*British*]
UMES .... University of Maryland, Eastern Shore
UmF .... National Cash Register Co., New York, NY [*Library symbol Library of Congress*] (LCLS)
UMF .... Ultramicrofiche
UMF .... Uniform Magnetic Field
UMF .... University of Maine at Farmington, Farmington, ME [*OCLC symbol*] (OCLC)
UMF .... User Message Format
UMF .... Users Master File (IAA)
UMFA .... United Mineworker's Federation of Australia (EERA)
UMFC .... United Methodist Free Churches
UMFCBMA ... United Male and Female Cardboard Box Makers' Association [*A union*] [*British*]
UMFDC .... Union Mundial de Mujeres Democrata Cristianas [*World Union of Christian Democratic Women*] [*Venezuela Political party*] (EAIO)
UMFP .... Unit Materiel Fielding Point [*Army*] (RDA)
Umfrev Off Cor ... Umfreville's Office of Coroner [*A publication*] (DLA)
UMFS .... United Mutual Fund Selector [*United Business Service Co.*]
UMG .... Universal Machine Gun (MCD)
UMG .... Universal Mercator Grid (NVT)
UMG .... US West [*NYSE symbol*] (SAG)
UMG .... US West Media Group [*NYSE symbol*] (TTSB)
$U_{Mg}V$ .... Magnesium Excretion [*Medicine*] (DAVI)
UMH .... United Mobile Homes [*AMEX symbol*] (TTSB)
UMH .... United Mobile Homes, Inc. [*AMEX symbol*] (SAG)
UMHE .... United Ministries in Higher Education [*Later, HEMT/UMHE*] (EA)
UMHK .... Union Miniere du Haut Katanga [*Mining Company of Upper Katanga*]
UMHP .... Union Mondiale des Societes d'Histoire Pharmaceutique [*World Organization of Societies of Pharmaceutical History*]
UMI .... Udruzena Metalna Industrija [*Belgrade, Yugoslavia*]
UMI .... Ukrainian Music Institute in America
UMI .... Ultra Microfiche (EECA)
UMI .... Underway Material Inspection [*Navy*] (NVT)
UMI .... Union de Melillenses Independientes [*Spanish North Africa*] [*Political party*] (MENA)
UMI .... Union Mathematique Internationale [*International Mathematical Union - IMU*] (EAIO)
UMI .... Union Mundial pro Interlingua (EA)
UMI .... United Methodist Information [*Database*] [*United Methodist Communications*] [*Information service or system*] (CRD)
UMI .... United States Minor Outlying Islands [*ANSI three-letter standard code*] (CNC)
UMI .... Unit Movement Identifier [*Army*] (AABC)
UMI .... University Microfilms, Inc. (WDMC)
UMI .... University Microfilms International [*Database producer*] (IID)
UMi .... Ursa Minor [*Constellation*]
U Miami (Fla) ... University of Miami (Florida) (GAGS)
U Mich .... [*The*] University of Michigan (GAGS)
UMICH .... University of Michigan [*Ann Arbor, MI*]
UMIFA .... Uniform Management of Institutional Funds Act [*National Conference of Commissioners on Uniform State Laws*]
UMII .... Vitebsk [*Former USSR ICAO location identifier*] (ICLI)
UMin .... Ursa Minor [*Constellation*]
UMINF .... United Movement of Iranian National Forces [*Defunct*] (EA)
U Minn .... University of Minnesota (GAGS)
UMIP .... Uniform Material Issue Priority [*Navy*]
UMIPS .... Uniform Material Issue Priority System [*Navy*] (NG)
UMIS .... Urban Management Information System
U Miss .... [*The*] University of Mississippi (GAGS)
U Miss (Med Cent) ... University of Mississippi Medicine Center (GAGS)
UMIST .... University of Manchester Institute of Science and Technology [*Databank or iginator and research institute*] [*British*]
UMIX .... User-Manufacturer Information Exchange
UMJL .... Union Mondiale pour un Judaisme Liberal
UMK .... Umanak [*Greenland*] [*Airport symbol*] (AD)
UMK .... University of Missouri at Kansas City, Kansas City, MO [*OCLC symbol*] (OCLC)
UMKC .... University of Missouri at Kansas City
UML .... Universal Mission Load [*Military*] (AABC)
UML .... University of Missouri, Columbia School of Library and Information Science, Co lumbia, MO [*OCLC symbol*] (OCLC)
UMLC .... Institute of Estate Planning, University of Miami Law Center (DLA)
UMLC .... Universal Multiline Controller
UMLC .... University of Miami Law Center (DLA)
UMLER .... Uniform Machine Language Equipment Register [*RSPA*] (TAG)
UMLER .... Universal Machine Language Equipment Register [*Association of American Railroads*] [*Information service or system*] (CRD)
UMM .... Summit, AK [*Location identifier FAA*] (FAAL)
UMM .... Union Mondiale du Mapam [*World Union of Mapam - WUM*] (EAIO)
UMM .... United Merchants & Manufacturers, Inc. [*NYSE symbol*] (SPSG)
UMM .... Universal Measuring Machine
UMM .... University of Manitoba Medical Library [*UTLAS symbol*]
UM-MaP ...... University of Maryland Mathematics Project
UMMC .... University of Michigan Medical Center (BABM)
UMMH .... Unscheduled Maintenance Manhours (MCD)
UMMIPS ...... Uniform Materiel Movement and Issue Priority System [*Military*] (AFM)
UMMIPS ...... Uniform Military Material Issue Priority System (DNAB)
UMMIS .... Uniform Material Movement and Issue Priority System [*Navy*] (ANA)
UMML .... Unione Medicale Mediterranea Latina [*Latin Mediterranean Medical Union - LMMU*] [*Mantua, Italy*] (EAIO)
UMML .... University of Miami Marine Laboratory [*Florida*]
UMMM .... Minsk/Loshitsa [*Former USSR ICAO location identifier*] (ICLI)
UMMMIPS ... Uniform Military Material Movement and Issue Priority System (DNAB)
UMMS .... Unit Maintenance Management System
UMMZ .... University of Michigan Museum of Zoology
UMN .... Monett, MO [*Location identifier FAA*] (FAAL)
UMN .... Union des Musiciens Nordiques [*Nordic Musicians' Union - NMU*] (EAIO)
UMN .... Union pour la Majorite Nouvelle [*Union for the New Majority*] [*France Political party*] (PPE)
UMN .... Unsatisfactory Material Notice (MSA)
UMN .... Upper Motor Neuron [*Medicine*]
UMN .... Urban Ministry Network [*Melbourne, Victoria, Australia*]
UMNB .... Upper Motor Neurogenic Bladder [*Neurology*] (DAVI)
UMNCF .... United Merchant Navy Christian Fellowship [*British*]
UMNL .... Upper Motor Neuron Lesion [*Neurology*]
UMNO .... United Malays National Organization [*Malaysia*] [*Political party*]
UMO .... Umbertino's Restaurant [*Vancouver Stock Exchange symbol*]
UMO .... Unconventional Military Operations (MCD)
UMO .... Unit Movement Officer [*Army*] (INF)
UMO .... University of Maine, Orono
UMO .... Unmanned Orbital [*NASA*] (NASA)
UMobH .... United Mobile Homes, Inc. [*Associated Press*] (SAG)
U MO B Law Ser ... University of Missouri. Bulletin. Law Series [*A publication*] (DLA)
U MO Bull L Ser ... University of Missouri. Bulletin. Law Series [*A publication*] (DLA)
UMOC .... Ugly Man on Campus [*Contest*]
U Mo (Columbia) ... University of Missouri at Columbia (GAGS)
UMOES .... Universal Masonic Order of the Eastern Star (EA)
UMOFC .... Union Mondiale des Organisations Feminines Catholiques [*World Union of Catholic Women's Organizations - WUCWO*] [*Canada*]
U Mo (KC) ... University of Missouri at Kansas City (GAGS)
UMOL .... Unmanned Orbital Laboratory
U MO L Bull ... University of Missouri. Law Bulletin [*A publication*] (DLA)
U Mont .... University of Montana (GAGS)
U Montevallo ... University of Montevallo (GAGS)
U Mo (Rolla) ... University of Missouri at Rolla (GAGS)
UMOS .... U-Grooved Metal Oxide Semiconductors (MCD)
UMOSBESL ... Union Mondiale des Organisations Syndicales sur Base Economique et Sociale Liberale [*World Union of Liberal Trade Union Organizations*]
UMOSEA ...... Union Mondiale pour la Sauvegarde de l'Enfance et de l'Adolescence [*World Union for the Safeguard of Youth*]
UMOST .... U-Groove Power Metal-Oxide Semiconductor Field Effect Transistor (IAA)
U Mo (St Louis) ... University of Missouri at St. Louis (GAGS)
UMP .... Umpire (DSUE)
UMP .... Uniformly Most Powerful Test [*Statistics*]
UMP .... Uninflated Movement Party [*Australia Political party*] (ADA)
UMP .... Union of Moderate Parties [*Vanuatua*] [*Political party*] (PPW)
UMP .... Universal Military Pod (VNW)
UMP .... Upper Mantle Project
UMP .... Upper Mantle Project [*Marine science*] (OSRA)
UMP .... Upper Merion & Plymouth Railroad Co. [*AAR code*]
UMP .... Upward Mobility Program
UMP .... Uracil Monophosphate [*Biochemistry*] (AAMN)
UMP .... Uridine Monophosphate [*Biochemistry*]
UMPAR .... Unit Mobilization Personnel Assignment Report [*Navy*] (DNAB)
UMPG .... University of Maine at Portland/Gorham
UMpGS .... Church of Jesus Christ of Latter-Day Saints, Genealogical Society Library, MountPleasant Branch, Stake Center, Mount Pleasant, UT [*Library symbol Library of Congress*] (LCLS)
UMPLIS .... Informations- und Dokumentationssystem Umwelt [*Environmental Information and Documentation System*] [*Berlin*] [*Information retrieval*]
UMPR .... Uniform Military Personnel Record (AFM)
UMPS .... Union Mondiale des Pioniers de Stockholm [*World Union of Stockholm Pioneers*] (EAIO)
UMPT .... Ultrahigh-Frequency Multi-Platform Transceiver [*Navy*] (MCD)
UMpW .... Wasatch Academy, Mount Pleasant, UT [*Library symbol Library of Congress*] (LCLS)
UMR .... Ultraviolet Mitogenic Radiation
UMR .... Unimar Indonesian Participating Units [*AMEX symbol*] (SPSG)
UMR .... Unimar Indonesian Ptc Units [*AMEX symbol*] (TTSB)
UMR .... Unipolar Magnetic Regions
UMR .... Unit Mail Room [*Air Force*] (AFM)
UMR .... Unit Manning Report [*Army*] (ADDR)
UMR .... University of Missouri at Rolla
UMR .... University of Missouri at Rolla, Library, Rolla, MO [*OCLC symbol*] (OCLC)

UMR .... Unsatisfactory Material Report [*Military*] (AABC)
UMR .... Upper Maximum Range
UMR .... Usual Marketing Requirement [*Business term*]
UMR .... Woomera [*Australia Airport symbol*] (OAG)
UMRAL .... University of Minnesota Rosemont Aeronautical Laboratories (SAA)
UMRB .... Upper Mississippi River Basin
UMRCC .... Upper Mississippi River Conservation Committee (EA)
UMREL .... Upper Midwest Regional Educational Laboratory, Inc.
UMREMP ..... Upper Mississippi River Environmental Management Program [*Federal government*]
UMRG .... Ergli [*Former USSR ICAO location identifier*] (ICLI)
UMRL .... Union Mondiale des Romains Libres [*World Union of Free Romanians - WUFR*] [*Creteil, France*] (EAIO)
UMRR .... Riga/Spilve [*Former USSR ICAO location identifier*] (ICLI)
UMRR .... University of Missouri Research Reactor
UMRW .... Ventspils [*Former USSR ICAO location identifier*] (ICLI)
UMS .... Ultrasonic Motion Sensor (MCD)
UMS .... Unattended Machinery Spaces (DS)
UMS .... Undersea Medical Society, Inc.
UMS .... Unfederated Malay States
UMS .... United Missionary Society
UMS .... Unit Manning System [*Army*] (RDA)
UMS .... Unity Management System [*Bytex Corp.*]
UMS .... Universal Maintenance Standards
UMS .... Universal Memory System [*Intel Corp.*]
UMS .... Universal Military Service
UMS .... Universal MODEM [*Modulate/Demodulate*] System (DWSG)
UMS .... Universal Multiprogramming System [*Computer science*] (MHDB)
UMS .... University of Missouri at St. Louis, St. Louis, MO [*OCLC symbol*] (OCLC)
UMS .... Unmanned Multifunction Satellite
UMS .... Upstream Modulation Sequence [*Genetics*]
UMS .... Urethral Manipulation Syndrome [*Urology*] (DAVI)
UMS .... Utilities Management Services (ACII)
UMSA .... United States Marine Safety Association (EA)
UMSA .... Utah-Manhattan-Sundt & Associates (AAG)
UMSDC .... Unscheduled Maintenance Sample Data Collection (MCD)
UMSE .... Unconditional Mean Square Error [*Statistics*]
UMSE .... Unit Maintenance Support Equipment [*Army*]
UMSE .... Unmanned Surveillance Equipment
UMSN .... Union Mondiale de Ski Nautique [*World Water Ski Union - WWSU*] [*Montreaux, Switzerland*] (EAIO)
UMSP .... Universal Microscope Spectro-Photometer
UMSP .... User Maintenance Support Plan (MCD)
UMSPA .... Uniform Metric System Procedure Act [*National Conference of Commissioners on Uniform State Laws*]
UMSR .... Universal Movement for Scientific Responsibility [*See also MURS*] (EAIO)
UMSSS .... UDAM [*Universal Digital Avionics Module*] Microprocessor Software Support System (MCD)
UMS/VS .... Universal Multiprogramming System/Virtual Storage (NITA)
UMT .... Ultrasonic Material Testing
UMT .... Umiat, AK [*Location identifier FAA*] (FAAL)
UMT .... Union Marocaine du Travail [*Moroccan Labor Union*]
UMT .... Unit Ministry Team [*Military*] (INF)
UMT .... Unit of Medical Time [*Each 4-hour period after 40-hour work week*] [*British*]
UMT .... Universal Microwave Trainer
UMT .... Universal Military Training [*Participants known as Umtees*] [*Post World War II*] [*Army*]
UMT .... Uranium Mill Tailings (GAAI)
UMTA .... Urban Mass Transportation Act [*1964*]
UMTA .... Urban Mass Transportation Administration [*Department of Transportation*]
UMTD .... Using Mails to Defraud
UMTE .... Unmanned Throat Emitter (DWSG)
UMTR .... Universal Movement Theater Repertory [*Defunct*]
UMTR .... University of Maryland Teaching Reactor (NRCH)
UMTRAP ...... Uranium Mill Trailings Remedial Action Program [*Department of Energy*]
UMTRCA ...... Uranium Mill Tailings Radiation Control Act (GFGA)
UMTRI .... University of Michigan Transportation Research Institute [*Research center*] (RCD)
UMTRIS .... Urban Mass Transportation Research Information Service [*National Academy of Sciences*] [*Database*] (IID)
UMTS .... Universal Military Training Service [*or System*] (GPO)
UMTS .... Universal Mobile Telecommunications Services
UMTSA .... Universal Military Training and Service Act
UMu .... Murray Public Library, Murray, UT [*Library symbol Library of Congress*] (LCLS)
UMU .... Umuarama [*Brazil*] [*Airport symbol*] (AD)
UMU .... Uplink Multiplexer Unit (MCD)
UMUS .... Unbleached Muslin
UMVF .... Union Mondiale des Voix Francaises [*World Union of French-Speakers - WUFS*] (EAIO)
UMVF .... Unmanned Vertical Flight [*NASA*] (NASA)
UMVS .... United Methodist Voluntary Services
UMVUE .... Uniformly Minimum Variance Unbiased Estimator (PDAA)
UMW .... Mumbwa [*Zambia*] [*Airport symbol*] (AD)
UMW .... Ultramicrowaves
UMW .... United Mine Workers [*Also, UMWA*] (CDAI)
UMW .... Upper Midwest
UMWA .... International Union, United Mine Workers of America [*Also known as UMW*] (EA)
UMWA .... United Machine Workers' Association [*A union*] [*British*]
UMWSF .... United Methodist Women in Switzerland and in France (EAIO)
UMWW .... Vilnius [*Former USSR ICAO location identifier*] (ICLI)
UN .... East Coast Airlines [*ICAO designator*] (AD)
UN .... Nephi Public Library, Nephi, UT [*Library symbol Library of Congress*] (LCLS)
UN .... Ulnar Nerve [*Anatomy*] (DAVI)
UN .... Unassigned [*Telecommunications*] (TEL)
UN .... Underworld Nobility [*Used by Walter Winchell to refer to mobsters in television series "The Untouchables"*]
UN .... UNESCO Statistical Yearbook [*A publication*]
UN .... Unico National (EA)
UN .... Unified (AAG)
UN .... Unilateral Neglect [*Neurology*] (DAVI)
UN .... Unilever NV [*NYSE symbol*] (SPSG)
UN .... Union (MSA)
UN .... Union
UN .... Union Flag [*Navy British*]
UN .... Union Nacional [*National Union*] [*Spain Political party*] (PPE)
UN .... Union Nationale [*National Union*] [*Canada Political party*]
UN .... Unit (AAG)
UN .... United
UN .... United Nations (EA)
UN .... United Nations [*Marine science*] (OSRA)
UN .... University
UN .... Unknown [*Telecommunications*] (TEL)
UN .... Untreated [*Medicine*]
UN .... Urea-Nitrogen [*Medicine*]
UN .... Urinary Nitrogen [*Medicine*] (DAVI)
U-N11 .... Unlicensed National Information Infrastructure (PCM)
UNA .... Ukrainian National Association (EA)
UNA .... Unable [*ICAO designator*] (FAAC)
UNA .... Unalaska [*Alaska*] [*Seismograph station code, US Geological Survey Closed*] (SEIS)
UNA .... Unattended Answering Accessory (MHDB)
UNA .... Underwear-Negligee Associates (EA)
UNA .... Unione Nazionale dell'Avicoltura [*Aviculture Union*] [*Italy*] (EY)
UNA .... United Nations Association
UNA .... United Native Americans (EA)
UNA .... United States Naval Academy, Annapolis, MD [*OCLC symbol*] (OCLC)
UNA .... Universair [*Spain ICAO designator*] (FAAC)
UNA .... Universal Network Achitecture [*Telecommunications*]
UNA .... Universal Night Answering [*Telecommunications*] (TEL)
UNA .... Universitats-Netz Austria [*Austrian University Network*] (TNIG)
UNA .... Urinary Nitrogen Appearance (DAVI)
UNa .... Urine Sodium [*Nephrology*] (DAVI)
UNA .... Use No Abbreviations (DNAB)
UNAAA .... Ukrainian National Aid Association of America (EA)
UNAAF .... Unified Action Armed Forces [*Military*]
UNAB .... Unabridged (ADA)
UNABOM ..... University/Airline Bomber [*FBI investigation*]
UNABR .... Unabridged
UNAC .... United Nations Africa Council
UNAC .... United Nations Appeal for Children
UNAC .... United Nations Association in Canada (EAIO)
UNAC .... United Nations Association of the Congo (EAIO)
UNACC .... Unaccompanied
UNACC .... United Nations Administrative Committee and Coordination (WDAA)
UNACOM ..... Universal Army Communication System
UNADA .... United Nations Atomic Development Authority (NUCP)
UNADE .... Union Nacional Democratica [*National Democratic Union*] [*Ecuador*] [*Political party*] (PPW)
UNADS .... UNIVAC Automated Documentation System [*Computer science*]
UNAEC .... United Nations Atomic Energy Commission [*Superseded by Disarmament Commission, 1952*]
UNAECC ...... United Nations Atomic Energy Control Commission
UNAF .... Universities National Antiwar Fund
UNAFEI .... United Nations Asia and Far East Institute for the Prevention of Crime and Treatment of Offenders
UNAFPA .... Union des Associations des Fabricants de Pates Alimentaires de la Communaute Economique Europeenne [*Union of Organizations of Manufacturers of Pasta Products in the European Economic Community*]
UNA-H .... United Nations Association of Hungary (EAIO)
UNAH .... Universidad Nacional Autonoma, Tegucigalpa [*Honduras*]
UNAIDS .... Joint United Nations Programme on Acquired Immune Deficiency Syndrome (ECON)
UNAIS .... United Nations Association International Service [*British*]
UNAKI .... Union des Colons Agricoles du Kivu [*Union of Agricultural Settlers of Kivu*] [*Congo - Leopoldville*]
UNALC .... User Network Access Link Control
UNALOT .... Unallotted (AABC)
UNALTD .... Unaltered (ROG)
UNAM .... Unico American [*NASDAQ symbol*] (TTSB)
UNAM .... Unico American Corp. [*NASDAQ symbol*] (NQ)
UNAM .... Universidad Nacional Autonoma de Mexico (CROSS)
UNAMACE .... Universal Automatic Map Compilation Equipment
UNAMAP ...... Users Network for Applied Modeling of Air Pollution [*Set of computer simulation models being developed by Battelle for EPA*]
UNA-MEX ..... United Nations Association of Mexico (EAIO)
UNAMI .... Uniao Nacional Africana de Mocambique Independente [*Mozambique*] [*Political party*]
UNAMIC .... United Nations Advance Mission in Cambodia (ECON)
UNAMIR .... United Nations Assistance Mission in Rwanda
UNAN .... Unanimous

UNANSD Unanswered (ROG)
UNAP Unable to Approve [*ICAO designator*] (FAAC)
UNAP Union Nationale Progressite [*National Progressive Union*] [*Burundi*]
UNAP United Nations Association of Poland (EAIO)
UNAPEC United Nations Action Program for Economic Cooperation
UNAPEI Union Nationale des Associations de Parents et Amis de Personnes Handicapees Mentales [*Formerly, Union Nationale des Associations de Parents d'Enfants Inadeptes*] [*France*] (EAIO)
Unapix Unapix Entertainment, Inc. [*Associated Press*] (SAG)
UNAPOC United National Association of Post Office Craftsmen [*Later, APWU*]
UNAPPD Unappointed (ROG)
UNAR Association for the United Nations in Russia (EAIO)
UNAR Unable to Approve Altitude Requested [*Aviation*] (FAAC)
UNAR Union Nationale Ruandaise [*Ruanda National Union*]
UNARU Union Nationale Africaine du Ruanda-Urundi [*African National Union of Ruanda-Urundi*]
UNAS Ukrainian National Academy of Sciences
UNAS United Nations Association of Sweden (EAIO)
UNASABEC Union Nationale des Syndicats Agricoles Forestiers, des Bois, de l'Elevage, et de la Peche du Cameroun [*National Union of Farmers, Fishermen, Forest Guards, and Timber Workers of Cameroon*]
UNASGD Unassigned (AABC)
UNASGN Unassigned [*Navy*] (NVT)
UNASL United Nations Association of Sri Lanka (EAIO)
UNASSAD Union Nationale des Associations de Soins et Service a Domicile [*Also, National Organisation for Home Care*] [*France*] (EAIO)
UNASSD Unassembled
UNAT Union Nationale des Agriculteurs Tunisiens [*National Union of Tunisian Farmers*]
UNAT United Nations Administrative Tribunal (EY)
UNAT United Nations Association of Turkey (EAIO)
UNATAC Union d'Assistance Technique pour l'Automobile et la Circulation Routiere [*Union of Technical Assistance for Motor Vehicle and Road Traffic*] [*Geneva, Switzerland*] (EAIO)
UNATNDD Unattended [*Aviation*] (FAAC)
UNATRACAM Union des Associations Traditionelles du Cameroun [*Union of Traditional Associations of Cameroon*]
UNATRACO Union Nationale des Travailleurs du Congo [*National Union of Workers of the Congo*]
UNATT Unattached (ROG)
UNATT Unattended (ADA)
UNATTRIB Unattributed
UNA-UK United Nations Association of Great Britain and Northern Ireland (EAIO)
UNAUS United Nations Association of the United States of America (AEBS)
UNA-USA United Nations Association of the United States of America (EA)
Unauth Unauthorized (DLA)
UNAUTHD Unauthorized (AABC)
$U_{Na}V$ Sodium Excretion [*Rate*] [*Medicine*] (DAVI)
$U_{Na}V$ Urine Sodium [*Medicine*] (DAVI)
$U_{Na}V$ Urine Sodium Excretion [*Medicine*] (DAVI)
UNAVBL Unavailable (FAAC)
UNAVCO University NAVSTAR Consortium
UNAVEM United Nations Angola Verification Mission
UNAVIC United Nations Audiovisual Information Center
UNB Fredericton [*New Brunswick*] [*Seismograph station code, US Geological Survey*] (SEIS)
UNB Kanab, UT [*Location identifier FAA*] (FAAL)
UNB Unbound (ROG)
unb Unbound (WDMC)
UNB Unexploded Booklet [*Philately*]
UNB United Nations Beacon
UNB Universal Navigation Beacon
UNB University of New Brunswick [*Canada*]
UNB University of New Brunswick Library [*UTLAS symbol*]
UNBAL Unbalanced [*Telecommunications*] (TEL)
UnBanCal UnionBanCal Corp. [*Associated Press*] (SAG)
UNBB Barnaul [*Former USSR ICAO location identifier*] (ICLI)
UNBC UnionBanCal Corp. [*NASDAQ symbol*] (TTSB)
UNBC UnionBanCal Corp. [*NASDAQ symbol*] (SAG)
UnBCal UnionBanCal Corp. [*Associated Press*] (SAG)
UnBCh United Board Chaplain [*British military*]
UNBCL University of Nebraska College of Law [*Lincoln, NE*] (DLA)
UNBD Unbound (WDAA)
Unbd Unbound (WDMC)
Un Bd Ch United Board Chaplain [*British military*] (DMA)
UNBIS United Nations Bibliographic Information System [*United Nations Headquarters*] (IID)
UNBJ United National Bancorp [*NASDAQ symbol*] (NQ)
UNBJ United Natl Bancorp [*NASDAQ symbol*] (TTSB)
UnBkCp Union Bankshares Corp. [*Associated Press*] (SAG)
unbld Unbleached [*Paper*] (DGA)
UNBLK Unblanking (MSA)
UNBLSJ University of New Brunswick. Law School. Journal [*A publication*] (DLA)
UNBNJ United National Bancorp [*Associated Press*] (SAG)
UnBnk Union Bank [*Associated Press*] (SAG)
UnBnOH United Bancorp Ohio [*Associated Press*] (SAG)
UNBRO United Nations Border Relief Operation
UNBSA United Nations Bureau of Social Affairs
UNBTAO United Nations Bureau of Technical Assistance Operations
UNC Uncertain (ADA)
UNC UNC, Inc. [*Formerly, United Nuclear Corporation*] [*NYSE symbol*] (SPSG)
UNC Uncirculated [*Numismatics*]
UNC Unclassified (KSC)
UNC Uncle (DSUE)
UNC Unconditional (IAA)
UNC Undercurrent (IAA)
UNC Unguia [*Colombia*] [*Airport symbol*] (AD)
UNC Unified Coarse [*Thread*]
UNC Unified National Coarse Thread (IAA)
UNC Union Nationale Camerounaise [*Cameroon National Union*]
UNC Union Nouvelle Caledonienne [*New Caledonia*] [*Political party*] (FEA)
UNC United Corporations Ltd. [*Toronto Stock Exchange symbol*]
UNC United Meridian [*NYSE symbol*] (TTSB)
UNC United National Convention [*Ghana*] [*Political party*] (PPW)
UNC United Nations Command
UNC United Network Co. [*TV broadcasting network*]
UNC United New Conservationists (EA)
UNC Universal Naming Convention [*Computer science*] (PCM)
UNC Universal Navigation Computer
UNC University of North Carolina [*Chapel Hill, NC*]
UNC University of Northern Colorado [*Formerly, Colorado State College*] [*Greeley*]
UNC Uranyl Nitrate Concentrate [*Nuclear energy*]
UNCA United Nations Correspondents Association (EA)
UNCA United Neighborhood Centers of America (EA)
UNCAA United Nations Centre Against Apartheid (EA)
UNCACK United Nations Civil Assistance Command, Korea
UNCAFE United Nations Commission for Asia and the Far East
UNCAH Union Nacional de Campesinas Autenticos de Honduras [*National Union of Authentic Peasants of Honduras*] (PD)
UnCap United Capital Corp. [*Associated Press*] (SAG)
UNCAST United Nations Conference on Applications of Science and Technology [*1963*]
UNCASTD United Nations Advisory Committee on the Application of Science and Technology to Development (ASF)
UNCAT Uncatalogued (ADA)
UNCB Uncle B Bakery, Inc. [*NASDAQ symbol*] (SAG)
UNCB Uncle B's Bakery [*NASDAQ symbol*] (TTSB)
UNCC Unable to Contact Company Radio [*Aviation*] (FAAC)
UNCC Union Nationale des Cheminots du Cameroun [*National Union of Railway Workers of Cameroon*]
UNCC United Nations Cartographic Commission (BARN)
UNCC United Nations Compensation Commission (ECON)
UNCC University of North Carolina at Charlotte
UNC-CH University of North Carolina at Chapel Hill
UNCCP United Nations Conciliation Commission for Palestine
UNCDF United Nations Capital Development Fund
UNCDF United Nations Capital Development Fund (EERA)
UNCDRP Universal Card Read-In Program (IAA)
UNCE Novokuznetsk [*Former USSR ICAO location identifier*] (ICLI)
UNCE United Nations Commission for Europe
UNCED United Nations Conference on Environment and Development
UNCED United Nations Conference on Environment and Development (EERA)
UNCERT Uncertainty [*Standard deviation*] [*Computer science*]
UNCF United Negro College Fund (EA)
UNCG Uncage
UNCG University of North Carolina, Greensboro
UNCHBP Center for Housing, Building, and Planning [*United Nations*]
UNCHE United Nations Conference on the Human Environment (MSC)
UNCHR United Nations Centre for Human Rights [*Switzerland*] (EAIO)
UNCHR United Nations Commission on Human Rights
UNCHR United Nations High Commissioner for Refugees (DLA)
UNCHS United Nations Center for Human Settlement [*Kenya*] [*Research center*] (IRC)
UNCI United Nations Committee on Information (EA)
UNCID Uniform Rules of Conduct for Interchange of Trade Data by Teletransmission [*ICC Publishing Co.*] [*A publication*]
UNCInc UNC, Inc. [*Formerly, United Nuclear Corp.*] [*Associated Press*] (SAG)
UNCIO United Nations Conference on International Organization [*San Francisco, 1945*]
UNCIP United Nations Commission for India and Pakistan
UNCIR Uncirculated (WDAA)
UNCIRC Uncircumcising Information Resources Center [*National Support Group*]
UNCITRAL United Nations Commission on International Trade Law (PDAA)
UNCIVPOL United Nations Civilian Police [*Peace-keeping force in Cyprus*]
UNCIWC United Nations Commission for Investigation of War Criminals
UNCL Kolpashevo [*Former USSR ICAO location identifier*] (ICLI)
UNCL Unified Numerical Control Language (IAA)
UNCLAS Unclassified (AABC)
unclass Unclassified (BARN)
UNCLE United Network Command for Law and Enforcement [*Fictitious intelligence organization in various television series*]
UncleB Uncle B Bakery, Inc. [*Associated Press*] (SAG)
UNCLOS United Nations Conference on the Law of the Sea
UNCLOS United Nations Convention on the Law of the Sea (EERA)
UNCLP Unclamp
UNCM User Network Control Machine
UNCMAC United Nations Command Military Armistice Commission
UNCMD United Nations Command
UnCmp Union Camp Corp. [*Associated Press*] (SAG)
UNCN United Nations Censorship Network
UNCOD United Nations Conference on Desertification
UNCOK United Nations Committee on Korea

UNCOL......... Universal Computer Oriented Language [*Programming language*] [*Computer science*]
UN Comm Int'l Trade LYB... United Nations Commission on International Trade Law. Yearbook [*A publication*] (DLA)
uncomp........ Uncompensated (MEDA)
uncomp........ Uncomplicated
uncon.......... Unconscious
UNCON........ Uncontainerable Goods [*Shipping*] (DS)
uncond......... Unconditioned
UNCONDL.... Unconditional (ROG)
UNCOND REF... Unconditioned Reflex [*Psychometrics*] (AAMN)
UNCONFD.... Unconfirmed (ROG)
Unconsol Laws... Unconsolidated Laws [*A publication*] (DLA)
UNCONSTAL... Unconstitutional [*Legal shorthand*] (LWAP)
UNCOPUOS... United Nations Committee on the Peaceful Uses of Outer Space
UNCOR........ Uncorrected (WGA)
uncorr.......... Uncorrected
Uncov.......... Uncover
UNCP.......... United Nations Conference of Plenipotentiaries
UNCR.......... United Nations Command (Rear)
UNCRD........ United Nations Center for Regional Development
UNCRD........ United Nations Centre for Regional Development (EERA)
UNCRO........ United Nations Confidence Restoration Operation (ECON)
Uncro.......... United Nations Confidence Restoration Operation in Croatia
unCS........... Unconditioned Stimulus [*Psychometrics*] (AAMN)
UnCS........... Uncorrected Stimulus [*Neurology*] (DAVI)
UNCSAT....... United Nations Conference on Science and Technology (BARN)
UNCSD......... United Nations Center for Science and Technology for Development (USDC)
UNCSF......... United Nations Command Security Force [*Military*] (INF)
UNCSTD....... United Nations Center for Science and Technology for Development [*Later, CSTD*] (EAIO)
UNCSTD....... United Nations Centre for Science and Technology for Development (EA)
UNCSTD....... United Nations Conference on Science and Technology Education for Development (AIE)
UNCT.......... Unctus [*Smeared*] [*Pharmacy*]
UNCT.......... Uncut (ROG)
UNCTAD....... United Nations Conference on Trade and Development
UNCTAD TDB... United Nations Conference on Trade and Development, Trade and Development Board
UNCTC......... United Nations Centre on Transnational Corporations (ECON)
UNCTD......... Uncoated
UNCTLD....... Uncontrolled (DA)
UNCURK....... United Nations Commission for the Unification and Rehabilitation of Korea
UNCW.......... Novy Vasyugan [*Former USSR ICAO location identifier*] (ICLI)
UND............ Kunduz [*Afghanistan*] [*Airport symbol Obsolete*] (OAG)
UND............ Undecaprenol [*Organic chemistry*]
UND............ Under (AAG)
und............. Undetermined [*MARC language code Library of Congress*] (LCCP)
Und............. Undivided (DLA)
UND............ Union Nacional Democratica [*El Salvador*] [*Political party*] (EY)
UND............ Union Nationale et Democratique [*National Democratic Union*] [*Monaco*] [*Political party*] (PPW)
UND............ Union Nigerienne Democratique [*Political party*] (EY)
UND............ Unit Derating [*Electronics*] (IEEE)
UND............ University of National Defense [*Formerly, Industrial College of the Armed Forces and National War College*]
UND............ University of North Dakota, Grand Forks, ND [*OCLC symbol*] (OCLC)
UND............ University of Notre Dame [*Indiana*] (KSC)
UND............ UNUM Corp. [*NYSE symbol*] (SAG)
UND............ UNUM Corp. 8.80% 'MIDS' [*NYSE symbol*] (TTSB)
UND............ Urgency of Need Designator [*Military*] (AFM)
UND............ User Need Date (KSC)
UNDA.......... International Catholic Association for Radio, Television and Audiovisuals [*Belgium*] (EAIO)
UNDA.......... Uniform Narcotic Drug Act [*National Conference of Commissioners on Uniform State Laws*]
Und Art Cop... Underwood on Art Copyright [*A publication*] (DLA)
UNDAT......... United Nations Development Advisory Team
UNDBK......... Undivided Back [*Deltiology*]
UNDC.......... Undercurrent
UNDC.......... Union Nationale pour la Democratie aux Comoros [*Political party*] (EY)
UNDC.......... United Nations Disarmament Commission [*Also, DC, DC(UN)*]
UNDCC......... United Nations Development Cooperation Cycle
Und Ch Pr... Underhill's Chancery Procedure [*1881*] [*A publication*] (DLA)
Und Conv.... Underhill on New Conveyancing [*1925*] [*A publication*] (DLA)
UNDD.......... Union Nationale pour la Democratie et le Developpement [*Madagascar*] [*Political party*] (EY)
UNDED......... Undereducated
UNDEF......... Undefined
UNDELORDCAN... Undelivered Orders Cancelled [*Military*]
UnDentC...... United Dental Care, Inc. [*Associated Press*] (SAG)
UNDERC....... University of North Dakota Energy Research Center [*Grand Forks, ND*] [*Department of Energy*] (GRD)
Underhill Ev... Underhill on Evidence [*A publication*] (DLA)
Under Nat.... Underwater Naturalist [*A publication*] (BRI)
UNDERPASS... Underpass [*Commonly used*] (OPSA)
UNDERSD...... Undersigned (ROG)
UNDERSECNAV... Under Secretary of the Navy
UNDERSTG... Understanding (ROG)
UNDERTG.... Undertaking (ROG)
Underw Nat... Underwater Naturalist [*A publication*]
UNDERWRTNG... Underwriting
UNDERWRTR... Underwriter
UNDET......... Undetermined
UNDETD....... Undetermined (WGA)
UNDETM....... Undetermined (AABC)
undet ori...... Undetermined Origin [*Medicine*] (DAVI)
Undet Orig... Undetermined Origin [*Medicine*] (CPH)
UNDEX......... Underwater Explosion [*Navy*]
UNDEX......... UN Documents Index (NITA)
UNDEX......... United Nations Index [*A publication*]
UNDF........... Underfrequency
UNDG........... Undergoing (AABC)
UNDG........... Unidigital, Inc. [*NASDAQ symbol*] (SAG)
UNDG........... Unidigital Inc. [*NASDAQ symbol*] (TTSB)
undglz.......... Underglaze (VRA)
UNDGRAD.... Undergraduate
UNDGRD...... Underground
UNDH.......... Unit Derated Hours [*Electronics*] (IEEE)
UNDHR........ United Nations Declaration of Human Rights (BJA)
UNDI........... United Nations Document Index
UNDIS.......... United Nations Documentation Information System (NITA)
Un Dk.......... Under Deck Tank [*on a ship*] (DS)
UNDK.......... Undock [*NASA*] (KSC)
UNDLD......... Undelivered (FAAC)
UNDLD......... Underload
UNDO.......... Ukrainian National Democratic Organization
UNDO.......... Union for National Draft Opposition
UNDOF......... United Nations Disengagement Observer Force [*Damascus, Syria*]
UNDP.......... Union Nationale pour la Democratie et le Progres [*The Congo*] [*Political party*] (EY)
UNDP.......... Union Nationale pour la Democratie et le Progres [*Cameroon*] [*Political party*] (EY)
UNDP.......... Union Nationale pour la Democratie et le Progres [*Benin*] [*Political party*] (EY)
UNDP.......... Union Nationals Democracy Party [*Myanmar*] [*Political party*] (EY)
UNDP.......... United Nations Development Program [*Marine science*] (OSRA)
UNDP.......... United Nations Development Programme (EA)
UNDP.......... University of Notre Dame Press
Und Part...... Underhill on Partnership [*10th ed.*] [*1975*] [*A publication*] (DLA)
UNDRC........ United Nations Disaster Relief Coordination
UNDRO........ United Nations Disaster Relief Office (EAIO)
UNDRO........ United Nations Disaster Relief Organization (EERA)
undsgd......... Undersigned (BARN)
UND SHER... Under Sheriff (DLA)
UnDsp.......... Universal Display Corp. [*Associated Press*] (SAG)
UNDTCD...... United Nations Department of Technical Cooperation for Development [*United Nations*] (GNE)
UNDTKR...... Undertaker (WGA)
Und Torts..... Underhill on Torts [*A publication*] (DLA)
Und Tr.......... Underhill on Trusts and Trustees [*A publication*] (DLA)
UNDV.......... Undervoltage
UNDW......... Underwater (KSC)
UNDWC....... Ultrasonically Nebulized Distilled Water Challenge
UNDWR....... Underwear
UNE............ Qacha's Nek [*Lesotho*] [*Airport symbol*] (OAG)
UNE............ Underground Nuclear Explosion
UnE............. Union Electric Co. [*Associated Press*] (SAG)
UNE............ United Nations European Headquarters [*Geneva, Switzerland*]
UNE............ Universal Nonlinear Element
UNE............ University of New England [*State*] (EERA)
UNE............ University of North Dakota, Law Library, Grand Forks, ND [*OCLC symbol*] (OCLC)
UNE............ Unst [*Shetland Islands, Scotland*] [*Airport symbol*] (AD)
UNE-A.......... University of New England - Armidale [*Australia*]
UNEASICO... Union des Etudiants et Anciens des Instituts Sociaux de Congo [*Congolese Union of Students and Former Students of Social Institutes*]
UN/EAT........ United Nations Electoral Assistance Team
U Neb.......... University of Nebraska (GAGS)
UNEBIF........ Union Europeenne des Fabricants de Bijouterie Fantaisie [*Union of European Fashion Jewelry Manufacturers*] [*Italy*] (EAIO)
U Neb (Kearney)... University of Nebraska at Kearney (GAGS)
U Neb (Omaha)... University of Nebraska at Omaha (GAGS)
UNEC.......... Union Nationale des Etudiants Camerounais [*National Union of Cameroonese Students*]
UNEC.......... United Nations Education Conference
UNECA........ United Nations Economic Commission for Africa (EA)
UNECE........ United Nations Economic Commission for Europe
UN-ECE....... United Nations Economic Commission for Europe (EERA)
UNE-CHC..... University of New England - Coffs Harbour Campus [*Australia*]
UNECLA....... United Nations Economic Commission for Latin America (BARN)
UNECO........ Union Economique du Congo [*Economic Union of the Congo*] [*Usumbura*]
UNECOLAIT... Union Europeenne du Commerce Laitier [*European Milk Trade Union*] [*Common Market*]
UNECOSOC... United Nations Economic and Social Council. Official Record [*A publication*] (DLA)
UNECTES..... Union Europeenne des Conseillers Techniques et Scientifiques [*European Union of Technical and Scientific Advisers*] [*EC*] (ECED)
UNEDA......... United Nations Economic Development Administration
UN/EDIFACT... United Nations Rules for Electronic Data Interchange for Administration, Commerce, and Transport
UNEEG......... Union Nationale des Eleves et Etudiants de la Guadeloupe [*National Union of Pupils and Students of Guadeloupe*] (PD)

UNEEM .... Union Nationale des Eleves et Etudiants du Mali [*National Union of Pupils and Students of Mali*] (PD)
UNEF .... Unified Extra Fine [*Thread*]
UNEF .... Unified National Extra Fine Thread (IAA)
UNEF .... United Nations Emergency Force [*to separate hostile forces of Israel and Egypt*]
UNEF .... United Nations Emergency Force in the Middle East
UNEF .... United Nations Environment Fund
UNEGA .... Union Europeenne des Fondeurs et Fabricants de Corps Gras Animaux [*European Union of Animal Fat Producers*] (EA)
UnEl .... Union Electric Co. [*Associated Press*] (SAG)
UnElec .... Union Electric Co. [*Associated Press*] (SAG)
UNEM .... Union Nationale des Etudiants du Maroc [*National Union of Moroccan Students*] (PD)
Unempl Ins Rep... Unemployment Insurance Reports [*Commerce Clearing House*] [*A publication*] (DLA)
Unempl Ins Rep (CCH)... Unemployment Insurance Reports (Commerce Clearing House) [*A publication*] (DLA)
UNEO .... United Nations Emergency Operation (PDAA)
UNEP .... United Nations Energy Planning [*A publication*]
UNEP .... United Nations Environment Program [*Marine science*] (OSRA)
UNEP .... United Nations Environment Programme [*Kenya*] [*Database originator*] (EAIO)
UNEP .... University of New England Press [*Australia*] (ADA)
UNEPCOM.... United Nations Commission of the USSR (EERA)
UNEP GC ..... United Nations Environment Program Governing Council
UNEP/IRS .... United Nations Environment Programme/International Referral System
UNEPNET-LAC... UNEP [*United Nations Environment Program*] Network for Latin America and the Carribean (EERA)
UNEPPA .... United Nations Environment Programme Participation Act of 1973
UNEPTA .... United Nations Expanded Program of Technical Assistance
UNERG .... United Nations Conference on New and Renewable Sources of Energy [*1981*]
UNESCAP ..... United Nations Economic and Social Commission for Asia and the Pacific
UNESCO .... United Nations Educational, Scientific, and Cultural Organization [*Databa se originator and operator*] [*France Research center*]
UNESCOR .... United Nations Economic and Social Council Official Record [*A publication*] (DLA)
UNESDA .... Union of EEC Soft Drinks Associations (EAIO)
UNESEM ...... Union Europeenne des Sources d'Eaux Minerales du Marche Commun [*European Union of Natural Mineral Water Sources of the Common Market*] (EAIO)
UNESOB .... United Nations Economic and Social Office in Beirut
UNETAS .... United Nations Emergency Technical Aid Service
UNETPSA ...... United Nations Educational and Training Program for Southern Africa
UNEV .... Unevaluated (MCD)
unev .... Uneven [*Quality of the bottom*] [*Nautical charts*]
U Nev .... University of Nevada at Reno (GAGS)
U Nev (Las Vegas)... University of Nevada at Las Vegas (GAGS)
U Newark L Rev... University of Newark. Law Review [*A publication*] (DLA)
U New Haven... University of New Haven (GAGS)
UNEWY .... United News & Media ADR [*NASDAQ symbol*] (TTSB)
UNEWY .... United News & Media PLC [*NASDAQ symbol*] (SAG)
UNEWY .... United Newspapers Public Ltd. Co. (MHDW)
UNEX .... Unexecuted
UNEXPL .... Unexplained
UNEXPL .... Unexploded
UNEXPL .... Unexplored
UNEXSO .... Underwater Explorers Society (EA)
UNF .... Unfinished [*Technical drawings*]
UNF .... Unfused (KSC)
UNF .... Unified Fine [*Thread*]
UNF .... Unified National Fine (IAA)
UNF .... Unifirst Corp. [*NYSE symbol*] (SPSG)
UNF .... Union Flight [*ICAO designator*] (FAAC)
UNF .... Union Freight R. R. [*AAR code*]
UNF .... United National Front [*Lebanon*] (BJA)
UNF .... Universal National Fine (MCD)
UNF .... University of North Dakota, Medical Library, Grand Forks, ND [*OCLC symbol*] (OCLC)
UNFA .... Union Nationale des Femmes Algeriennes [*Algeria*] [*Political party*] (EY)
UNFAO .... United Nations Food and Agriculture Organization
UNFAV .... Unfavorable
UNFB .... United Nations Film Board
UNFC .... United Nations Food Conference (BARN)
UNFCCC .... United Nations Framework Convention on Climate Change
UNFDAC .... United Nations Fund for Drug Abuse Control
UNFI .... Unfinished
UNFI .... Unifi, Inc. (MHDW)
UNFI .... United Natural Foods, Inc. [*NASDAQ symbol*] (SAG)
UNFICYP ...... United Nations Forces in Cyprus (DMA)
UNFICYP ...... United Nations Peacekeeping Force in Cyprus
UNFIN .... Unfinished
UNFN .... United Nations Fund for Namibia (EERA)
UNFO .... Unidentified Nonflying Objects
UNFP .... Union Nationale des Forces Populaires [*National Union of Popular Forces*] [*Political party Morocco*]
UNFP .... United National Federal Party [*Zimbabwe*] [*Political party*] (PPW)
UNFPA .... United Nations Fund for Population Activities
UNFR .... Uniforce Services [*NASDAQ symbol*] (TTSB)
UNFR .... Uniforce Services, Inc. [*NASDAQ symbol*] (SAG)
UNFR .... Uniforce Temporary Personnel, Inc. [*New Hyde Park, NY*] [*NASDAQ symbol*] (NQ)
UNFRM .... Uniform
UNFSSTD...... United Nations Financing System for Science and Technology for Development (EY)
UNFSTD .... United Nations Fund for Science and Technology Development (EERA)
UNFT .... Union Nationale des Femmes de Tunisie [*National Union of Tunisian Women*]
UNFTP .... Unified Navy Field Test Program (MCD)
UNFURNOTE... Until Further Notice [*Military*]
UNFY .... Unify Corp. [*NASDAQ symbol*] (SAG)
UNG .... Airung AEP [*Ukraine*] [*FAA designator*] (FAAC)
UNG .... Kiunga [*Papua New Guinea*] [*Airport symbol*] (OAG)
UNG .... Ungava [*Canada*]
UNG .... Unguentum [*Ointment*] [*Pharmacy*]
UNGA .... United Nations General Assembly (MCD)
UNGAOR ...... United Nations General Assembly Official Record [*A publication*] (DLA)
UNGEGN ...... United Nations Group of Experts on Geographical Names
unglz .... Unglazed (VRA)
UNGOMAP ... United Nations Good Offices Mission in Afghanistan and Pakistan [*Later, OSGAP*]
UNGT .... Unguentum [*Ointment*] [*Pharmacy*]
UN-GTDI ...... United Nations Guidelines for Trade Data Interchange
UNH .... United Healthcare [*NYSE symbol*] (TTSB)
UNH .... United Healthcare Corp. [*Minnetonka, MN*] [*NYSE symbol*] (NQ)
UNH .... United Homes, Inc. [*Vancouver Stock Exchange symbol*]
UNH .... University of New Hampshire (PDAA)
U NH .... University of New Hampshire (GAGS)
UNH .... Uranyl Nitrate Hexahydrate [*Inorganic chemistry*]
U_{NH4+} .... Urinary Ammonium (DAVI)
UNHC .... Unison HealthCare [*NASDAQ symbol*] (TTSB)
UNHC .... Unison HealthCare Corp. [*NASDAQ symbol*] (SAG)
UNHC .... United Nations High Commission (BJA)
UNHCC .... University of New Haven Computer Center [*Research center*] (RCD)
UNHCR .... United Nations High Commission [*or Commissioner*] for Refugees
UNHCR .... United Nations High Commission for Refugees (EERA)
UnHd .... Universal Holdings [*Associated Press*] (SAG)
UNHNOCY .... United Nations Headquarters Nongovernmental Organizations Committee on Youth (EA)
UNHQ .... United Nations Headquarters (DLA)
UNHRC .... United Nations Human Rights Commission (BJA)
UNHRD .... Unheard (FAAC)
UNI .... Athens/Albany, OH [*Location identifier FAA*] (FAAL)
uni- .... One (IDOE)
uni- .... Single (IDOE)
UNI .... Undistributed Net Income [*Banking*]
UNI .... Uniao da Vitoria [*Brazil*] [*Airport symbol*] (AD)
Uni .... Unicorn [*Record label*]
UNI .... Unicorp Canada Corp. [*Toronto Stock Exchange symbol*]
UNI .... Uniform (DSUE)
UNI .... Uni-Marts, Inc. [*AMEX symbol*] (SPSG)
UNI .... Union Island [*Windward Islands*] [*Airport symbol*] (OAG)
UNI .... Union Nationale des Independents [*National Union of Independents*] [*Monaco*] (PPE)
UNI .... Union Nationale pour l'Independence [*National Union for Independence*] [*Djibouti*] (PPW)
UNI .... Unite Australia Party [*Australia Political party*]
UNI .... United News of India Ltd. [*News agency*] (FEA)
UNI .... United States International Airways
UNI .... Unity Railways Co. [*AAR code*]
UNI .... University (ADA)
UNI .... University of Northern Iowa [*Cedar Falls, IA*] (OICC)
UNI .... User Network Interface [*Computer science*]
UNIA .... Universal Negro Improvement Association [*Organization led by Marcus Aurelius Garvey*]
UNIA & ACLW... Universal Negro Improvement Association and African Communities League of the World (EA)
UNIACT .... Unisex Edition of the American College Testing Program Interest Inventory (EDAC)
UNIADUSEC... Union Internationale des Associations de Diplomes Universitaires en Sciences Economiques et Commerciales
UNIATEC ...... Union Internationale des Associations Techniques Cinematographiques [*International Union of Technical Cinematograph Associations - IUTCA*] (EAIO)
UNIB .... University Bancorp, Inc. [*NASDAQ symbol*] (SAG)
UNIBANK ...... United City Bank [*Indonesia*] (EY)
UNIBI .... Unipolar Bipolar (IAA)
UNIBID .... UNISIST International Centre for Bibliographic Descriptions [*UNESCO*] [*Information service or system*] (IID)
UNIBORS ..... UNIVAC [*Universal Automatic Computer*] Bill of Material Processor Random System [*Computer science*] (IAA)
UNIBOSS ..... UNIVAC [*Universal Automatic Computer*] Bill of Material Processor Sequential System [*Computer science*] (IAA)
UNIBUS .... Universal Bus [*Digital Equipment Corp.*]
UNIC .... Union Internationale des Cinemas [*International Union of Cinemas*] (EAIO)
UNIC .... United International Club, Inc.
UNIC .... United Nations Information Centre
UNICA .... Asociacion de Universidades del Caribe [*Association of Caribbean Universities and Research Institutes*] (EA)
UNICA .... Union Internationale du Cinema Non Professionnel [*International Union of Amateur Cinema*] (EAIO)
UNICAP .... Universidade Catolica de Pernambuco [*Brazil*]

UNICCAP...... Universal Cable Circuit Analysis Program [*Bell System*]
UNICE.......... Union des Industries de la Communaute Europeenne [*Union of Industries of the European Community*] [*Belgium*]
UNICE.......... Union of Industrial and Employers' Confederations of Europe (EAIO)
UNICEF........ United Nations Children's Fund [*United Nations International Children's E mergency Fund*] [*Acronym is based on former name,*] (EA)
UNICEF-NZ... New Zealand National Committee for UNICEF (EAIO)
UNICHAL...... Union Internationale des Distributeurs de Chaleur [*International Union of Heat Distributors*] (EAIO)
UNICIS......... Unit Concept Indexing System
UNICLO......... United Nations Information Center and Liaison Office (PDAA)
UNICLO......... United Nations Information Centre and Liaison Office (PDAA)
UniCmp........ UniComp, Inc. [*Associated Press*] (SAG)
UNICO.......... Union pour les Interets du Peuple Congolais [*Union for the Interests of the Congolese People*]
UNICO.......... Universal Cooperatives (EA)
UnicoA......... Unico American Corp. [*Associated Press*] (SAG)
Unico Cp...... Unico Corp. [*Associated Press*] (SAG)
UNICOCYM... Union Internationale du Commerce et de la Reparation du Cycle et du Motocycle [*International Union of Cycle and Motocycle Trade and Repair*] [*Germany*]
UNICODE..... Unique Injector Concepts Development (MCD)
UNICOH....... Unidensity Coherent Light Recording (IAA)
UNICOL......... Union des Colons de la Province Orientale [*Union of Settlers in Orientale Province*]
UNICOL......... Universal Computer-Oriented Language (IAA)
UNICOM....... Underwater Integration Communication
Unicom........ Unicom Corp. [*Formerly, Commonwealth Edison*] [*Associated Press*] (SAG)
UNICOM....... Unidad Informativa Computable [*Computerized Information Unit*] [*Mexico Information service or system*] (IID)
UNICOM....... Unified Communications [*Radio station*]
UNICOM....... Universal Components [*Construction*]
UNICOM....... Universal Integrated Communication System [*Military*]
UNICOMP.... Universal Compiler (IEEE)
UNICON....... Unidensity Coherent Light Recording (IEEE)
UNICOR........ Federal Prison Industries (AAGC)
UNICORN..... Unilateral Arms Control
UNICRIM...... Uniform Crime Reporting System (PDAA)
UNICYP......... United Nations International Force, Cyprus
UNID............ Unidentified (DAVI)
unid............. Unidentified (VRA)
UNIDAHO..... Union des Independants du Dahomey [*Independents Union of Dahomey*]
UniDE........... Unico, Inc. Delaware [*Associated Press*] (SAG)
UNIDENT...... Unidentified
UNIDF.......... United Nations Industrial Development Fund
Unidig.......... Unidigital, Inc. [*Associated Press*] (SAG)
UNIDIR......... United Nations Institute for Disarmament Research [*Research center Switzerland*] (IRC)
UNIDO......... United Nations Industrial Development Organization [*Austria Also, an information service or system*] (IID)
UNIDROIT.... Institut International pour l'Unification du Droit Prive [*International Institute for the Unification of Private Law*] (EAIO)
Unidroit Yb... International Institute for the Unification of Private Law. Yearbook [*Rome, Italy*] [*A publication*] (DLA)
UNIEF.......... USEUCOM [*United States European Command*] Nuclear Interface Element Fastbreak (MCD)
UNIENET...... United Nations International Emergency Network [*Marine science*] (OSRA)
UNIEP.......... Union Internationale des Entrepreneurs de Peinture [*International Union of Master Painters - IUMP*] (EAIO)
Unif............. Unified (DLA)
UNIF............ Uniform (AFM)
UNIF............ Uniformity
UNIFAC........ Universal Functional Activity Coefficient [*Chemical engineering*]
UNIFE.......... Union des Industries Ferroviaires Europeennes [*Union of European Railway Industries*] (EA)
UNIFEM....... United Nations Development Fund for Women (EA)
UNIFET........ Unipolar Field-Effect Transistor
Unifi............ Unifi, Inc. [*Associated Press*] (SAG)
Unific LYB.... Unification of Law Yearbook [*A publication*] (DLA)
Unificyp....... United Nations Peacekeeping Force in Cyprus [*1964*]
UNIFIL......... United Nations Interim Force in Lebanon
UniFirst....... Unifirst Corp. [*Associated Press*] (SAG)
Unif L Conf... Proceedings, Uniform Law Conference of Canada [*A publication*] (DLA)
Unif L Conf Can... Uniform Law Conference of Canada [*A publication*] (DLA)
Uniflex......... Uniflex, Inc. [*Associated Press*] (SAG)
UNIFOM....... United Front of Political Movements [*Sierra Leone*] [*Political party*] (EY)
UNIFOR........ Unified Forces [*Military*]
UNIFORCE... United Defense Force [*Established by the Brussels Treaty*] (NATG)
Uniform City Ct Act... Uniform City Court Act [*A publication*] (DLA)
Uniform Dist Ct Act... Uniform District Court Act [*A publication*] (DLA)
Uniform L Rev... Uniform Law Review [*A publication*] (DLA)
Unifrce......... Uniforce Services, Inc. [*Associated Press*] (SAG)
Unifrce......... Uniforce Temporary Personnel, Inc. [*Associated Press*] (SAG)
UNI-FREDI... Universal Flight Range and Endurance Data Indicator
Unif Sys Citation... Uniform System of Citation [*Legal term*] (DLA)
UnifyCp........ Unify Corp. [*Associated Press*] (SAG)
UNIGABON... Union Interprofessionnelle du Gabon [*Inter-Trade Union of Gabon*]
Unigen.......... Unigene Labs, Inc. [*Associated Press*] (SAG)
Unign........... Unigene Labs, Inc. [*Associated Press*] (SAG)
UNIH............ United Healthcare Corp. (MHDW)
UNIHEDD..... Universal Head-Down Display [*Computer science*] (PDAA)
UNIHI........... University of Hawaii [*Honolulu, HI*] (NOAA)
UniHoldg..... UniHolding Corp. [*Associated Press*] (SAG)
UNII............. Unit Instruments [*NASDAQ symbol*] (TTSB)
UNII............. Unit Instruments, Inc. [*California*] [*NASDAQ symbol*] (SAG)
UNII............. Yeniseysk [*Former USSR ICAO location identifier*] (ICLI)
UNIIMOG..... United Nations Iran-Iraq Military Observer Group
UNIKOM....... United Nations Iraq/Kuwait Observer Mission
unil.............. Unilateral (DAVI)
Unilab.......... Unilab Corp. [*Associated Press*] (SAG)
Unilab.......... United Laboratories Inc. [*Philippines*]
UNILAC......... Universal Linear Accelerator
unilat........... Unilateral
Unilevr......... Unilever Ltd. [*Associated Press*] (SAG)
UNIMA......... Unione Nazionale Imprese di Meccanizzazione Agricola [*Agricultural Mechanization Enterprises Union*] [*Italy*] (EY)
UNIMA......... Union Internationale de Grands Magasins [*International Union of Department Stores*]
UNIMA......... Union Internationale de la Marionnette [*International Puppeteers Union*] [*France*]
Unimar......... Unimar Co. [*Associated Press*] (SAG)
UNIMARC.... Universal Machine Readable Cataloging (ADA)
Unimark........ [*The*] Unimark Group [*Associated Press*] (SAG)
UNIMA-USA... American Center of the Union Internationale de la Marionette (EA)
Unimed........ Unimed, Inc. [*Associated Press*] (SAG)
UNIMERC..... Universal Numeric Coding System [*Distilling industry*]
UNIMOD....... Unified Modular Plant [*Nuclear energy*]
UniMrt......... Uni-Marts, Inc. [*Associated Press*] (SAG)
UNINETT...... [*The*] University Network (TNIG)
Un Ins Co..... Unemployment Insurance Code [*A publication*] (DLA)
UNIO............ United Nations Information Organization
UNION.......... Union [*Commonly used*] (OPSA)
UnionA......... Union Acceptance Corp. Class A [*Associated Press*] (SAG)
Unionam...... Unionamerica Holdings PLC [*Associated Press*] (SAG)
UnionBc....... UnionBancorp, Inc. [*Associated Press*] (SAG)
UnionBsh..... Union Bankshares Ltd. [*Associated Press*] (SAG)
UnionC........ Union Corp. [*Associated Press*] (SAG)
Union C (Ky)... Union College (Kentucky) (GAGS)
Union C (NY)... Union College (New York) (GAGS)
UNION FLEURS... Union Internationale du Commerce de Gros en Fleurs [*International Union of the Wholesale Flower Trade*]
Union Pac LDB... Union Pacific Law Department. Bulletin [*A publication*] (DLA)
UNIONS....... Unions [*Commonly used*] (OPSA)
UNIP............ United National Independence Party [*Nigeria*] [*Political party*]
UNIP............ United National Independence Party [*Trinidad and Tobago*] [*Political party*] (PPW)
UNIP............ United National Independence Party [*Zambia*] [*Political party*] (PD)
UNIPAC........ Unified Prediction and Analysis Code (MCD)
UNIPAC........ Unit Packaging
UNIPAC........ Universal Payload Accommodation Capsule
UNIPAL........ Universities Educational Fund for Palestinian Refugees [*British*]
UNIPEDE...... Union Internationale de Producteurs et Distributeurs d'Energie Electrique [*International Union of Producers and Distributors of Electrical Energy*] [*France*]
Uniphase..... Uniphase Corp. [*Associated Press*] (SAG)
UNIPOCONGO... Union des Populations Rurales du Congo [*Union of Rural People of the Congo*]
UNIPOL........ Universal Problem-Oriented Language [*Computer science*] (MCD)
UNIPOL........ Universal Procedure-Oriented Language
UNIPON....... United Nations India-Pakistan Observer Mission (BARN)
UNIPRO....... Unite et Progres du Burundi [*Unity and Progress of Burundi*]
UNIPRO....... Universal Processor [*Computer science*]
UNIPZ.......... United National Independence Party of Zambia
uniq............. Unique (VRA)
UniqMbl....... Unique Mobility, Inc. [*Associated Press*] (SAG)
UNIQUAC..... Universal Quasichemical [*Chemical engineering*]
UNIQUE....... Uniform Inquiry Update and Edit (MHDI)
UNIQUE....... Uniform Inquiry Update Element
UNIR............ Unemployment Insurance Review [*A publication*]
UNIR............ Union de Izquierda Revolucionaria [*Union of the Revolutionary Left*] [*Peru*] [*Political party*] (PPW)
UNIR............ Union Nationale pour l'Initiative et la Responsabilite [*National Union for Initiative and Responsibility*] [*France Political party*] (PPW)
UNIR............ United Restaurants [*NASDAQ symbol*] (SAG)
UNIRAC........ Union Involved Racketeering [*FBI undercover investigation*]
UNIRAR........ Universal Radio Relay
UniroyC........ Uniroyal Chemical Corp. [*Associated Press*] (SAG)
UNIRW......... United Restaurants Wrrt'A' [*NASDAQ symbol*] (TTSB)
UNIRZ.......... United Restaurants Wrrt'B' [*NASDAQ symbol*] (TTSB)
UNIS............ Ukrainian National Information Service (EA)
UNIS............ Underwater Television and Inspection System
UNIS............ Unison
UNIS............ United Nations Information Service
UNIS............ United Nations International School
UNISA.......... University of South Africa
UniSA.......... University of South Australia
UNISAMS..... Universal Naval Integrated Surface-to-Air Missile System (DOMA)
UNISAP........ UNIVAC Share Assembly Program [*Sperry UNIVAC*] [*Computer science*] (IEEE)
UNISCAMTA... Union Territoriale des Syndicats de Cadres, Agents de Maitrise, Techniciens, et Assimiles du Senegal [*Territorial Union of Leaders, Supervising Personnel, and Related Workers of Senegal*]
UNISCAN..... United Kingdom and Scandinavia (NATG)

UNISCO........ Union des Interets Sociaux Congolais [*Congolese Union of Social Interests*]
UNISIST....... United Nations Information System in Science and Technology (NITA)
UNISIST....... United Nations Ingergovernmental System of Information in Science and Technology [*UNESCO*] [*Zagreb, Yugoslavia*]
UNISOM....... United Nations Force in Somalia [*Military*] (INF)
UNISOMI...... Universal Symphony Orchestra and Music Institute (AEBS)
Unison......... Unison Software, Inc. [*Associated Press*] (SAG)
UnisonH....... Unison HealthCare Corp. [*Associated Press*] (SAG)
UNISOR....... University Isotope Separator at Oak Ridge
UNISPACE.... United Nations Conference on the Exploration and Peaceful Uses of Outer Space
UNISPEC...... Universal Spectroscopy [*Trademark*] [*Kevex Corp.*]
Unisrce........ Unisource Worldwide, Inc. [*Associated Press*] (SAG)
UNISTAR...... UNIVAC Storage and Retrieval System [*Sperry UNIVAC*] [*Computer science*]
UNISTAR...... User Network for Information Storage, Transfer Acquisition, and Retrieval (MCD)
UNISTAT...... University Science Statistics Project [*Information service or system*] (IID)
UNISTOCK... Union Professionnelle des Stockeurs de Cereales dans la CEE [*Organization of Cereal Storage Firms in the European Economic Community*]
UNISWEP..... Unified Switching Equipment Practice (MCD)
Unisy........... Unisys Corp. [*Associated Press*] (SAG)
Unisys......... Unisys Corp. [*Associated Press*] (SAG)
UNISYS........ United Information Systems [*Burroughs Corp. and Sperry UNIVAC*] [*Formed by a merger of*]
UNISYS........ United Information Systems [*Marine science*] (OSRA)
UNIT............ Ultimate Network of Intelligent Tire Technology
UNIT............ Unitarian
Unit............. Unit Corp. [*Associated Press*] (SAG)
UNIT............ United Nations Information for Teachers [*Information service or system*] (AEBS)
UNIT............ Unitrin, Inc. [*NASDAQ symbol*] (SAG)
UNIT............ Universal Numerical Interchange Terminal
UNITA.......... Uniao Nacional para a Independencia Total de Angola [*National Union for the Complete Independence of Angola*] (AF)
UNITA.......... Union for the Total Liberation of Angola
UNITAR........ United Nations Institute for Training and Research [*New York*] [*ICSU*] [*Research center*]
UNITAS........ United International Antisubmarine Warfare
UnitC........... Unit Corp. [*Associated Press*] (SAG)
UNITE.......... User Network Interface to Everything [*A discussion list on the Internet*] (TNIG)
Unitech........ Unitech Industries, Inc. [*Associated Press*] (SAG)
UNITEL........ Universal Teleservice [*Satellite information service*]
UNITEL........ University Information Technology Corp. [*MIT-Harvard*]
UnitelV........ Unitel Video, Inc. [*Associated Press*] (SAG)
UNITIL......... UNITIL Corp. [*Associated Press*] (SAG)
UnitInd........ United Industrial Corp. [*Associated Press*] (SAG)
Unit Inst...... Unit Instruments, Inc. (California) [*Associated Press*] (SAG)
UNITNG........ Unit Training (NVT)
Unitog......... Unitog Co. [*Associated Press*] (SAG)
UNITOPOS... Unit to Which Ordered Will Operate in an Overseas Area a Contemplated ContinuousPeriod of One Year or More [*Military*]
UNITOR........ United Nations International TOKAMAK Reactor [*Proposed experimental fusion power plant*]
UNITRAC...... Universal Trajector Compiler (IEEE)
Unitrde........ Unitrode Corp. [*Associated Press*] (SAG)
UNITREP...... Unit Status and Identity Report [*DoD*]
Unitrin......... Unitrin, Inc. [*Associated Press*] (SAG)
UNITY.......... United National Indian Tribal Year (DICI)
UNITY.......... United National Indian Tribal Youth
UNIUM......... Union Nationale des Intellectuels et Universitaires Malgaches [*National Union of Intellectuals and University People of Madagascar*]
UNIV............ Universal (AFM)
UNIV............ Universal International, Inc. [*NASDAQ symbol*] (SPSG)
UNIV............ Universalist
UNIV............ University (AFM)
UNIV............ University
univ............. University (VRA)
UNIV............ Univl International [*NASDAQ symbol*] (TTSB)
UNIVAC........ Universal Automatic Computer [*Remington Rand Corp.*] [*Early computer*]
Univar.......... Univar Corp. [*Formerly, VWR United Corp.*] [*Associated Press*] (SAG)
UNIVAR........ Universal Valve Action Recorder
UnivAuto...... Universal Automotive Industries, Inc. [*Associated Press*] (SAG)
Univax......... Univax Biologies, Inc. [*Associated Press*] (SAG)
UnivBcp....... University Bancorp, Inc. [*Associated Press*] (SAG)
UniVBE........ Universal VESA [*Video Electronics Standards Association*] Bios Extension (CDE)
Univ Bkmn... University Bookman [*A publication*] (BRI)
Univ California Los Angeles L Rev... University of California at Los Angeles. Law Review [*Los Angeles, California*] [*A publication*] (DLA)
Univ D......... Doctor of the University
UNIVER........ Universal Inverter and Register (MCD)
UNIVERSE.... Universities Expanded Ring and Satellite Experiment (NITA)
UnivFor........ Universal Forest Products [*Commercial firm Associated Press*] (SAG)
Univ L Coll J... University Law College. Journal. Rajputana University [*India*] [*A publication*] (DLA)
Univ LR....... University Law Review [*A publication*] (DLA)
Univ L Rev... University Law Review [*A publication*] (DLA)
Univ NSW Law J... University of New South Wales. Law Journal [*A publication*]
Univ of Calif Davis L Rev... University of California at Davis. Law Review [*Davis, California*] [*A publication*] (DLA)
Univ of Ghana LJ... University of Ghana. Law Journal [*London, England*] [*A publication*] (DLA)
Univ of Manila L Gaz... University of Manila. Law Gazette [*Manila, Philippines*] [*A publication*] (DLA)
Univ of Richmond L Not... University of Richmond. Law Notes [*Richmond, Virginia*] [*A publication*] (DLA)
Univ of San Fernando Valley L Rev... University of San Fernando Valley. Law Review [*Sepulveda, California*] [*A publication*] (DLA)
Univ of Tas LR... University of Tasmania Law Review [*Australia A publication*]
Univ of Tulsa LJ... University of Tulsa. Law Journal [*Tulsa, Oklahoma*] [*A publication*] (DLA)
UNIVRSL...... Universal
Univ S Inst of Crim Proceeding... University of Sydney. Institute of Criminology. Proceedings [*Australia A publication*]
Univ Stud Hist Econ... University Studies in History and Economics [*A publication*]
Univ Stud W Aust Hist... University Studies in Western Australian History [*A publication*]
Univ Tas News... University of Tasmania. News [*A publication*]
UNJA.......... Union Nationale de la Jeunesse Algerienne [*Algeria*] [*Political party*] (EY)
UNJBS......... United Nations Joint Board of Strategy
UNJC.......... Unified National J Series Coarse [*Thread*]
UNJEF......... Unified National J Series Extra Fine [*Thread*]
UNJF.......... Unified National J Series Fine [*Thread*]
UNJS.......... Unified National J Series Special [*Thread*]
UNJSPF....... United Nations Joint Staff Pension Fund (ECON)
UN Juridical YB... United Nations Juridical Year Book [*A publication*] (DLA)
UN Jur YB... United Nations Juridical Year Book [*A publication*] (DLA)
UNK........... Unalakleet [*Alaska*] [*Airport symbol*] (OAG)
UNK........... Unknown (AFM)
unk............ Unknown (VRA)
UNK........... Unofficial (DAVI)
UNKA......... Abakan [*Former USSR ICAO location identifier*] (ICLI)
UNKI.......... Vanavara [*Former USSR ICAO location identifier*] (ICLI)
UNKK......... Krasnoyarsk [*Former USSR ICAO location identifier*] (ICLI)
UNKN......... Unknown
UNKO......... Sovetsky Rudnik [*Former USSR ICAO location identifier*] (ICLI)
UNKRA....... United Nations Korean Reconstruction Agency
UNKT......... Podkamennaya Tunguska [*Former USSR ICAO location identifier*] (ICLI)
UNK UNK.... Unknown Unknowns [*Design engineering*]
UNKW........ Baykit [*Former USSR ICAO location identifier*] (ICLI)
UNKWN...... Unknown
UNL........... United Leader Resources, Inc. [*Vancouver Stock Exchange symbol*]
UNL........... University of Nebraska - Lincoln
UNL........... University of New Brunswick Law Library [*UTLAS symbol*]
UNL........... Unleaded Fuel [*Automotive engineering*]
UNL........... Unlimited
UNL........... Unlisten (IAA)
UNL........... Unloading
UNLA......... Uganda National Liberation Army [*Political party*] (AF)
UNLCH....... Unlatch (MCD)
UNLD......... Unload (IAA)
UNLF......... Ugandan National Liberation Front [*Political party*] (PD)
UNLGTD..... Unlighted (FAAC)
UNLIM....... Unlimited
UNLIQ........ Unliquidated
UNLIS........ United National Life Insurance Society (EA)
UNLK......... Unlock
UNLKG....... Unlocking
UNLL......... United Nations League of Lawyers
UnINV........ Unilever NV [*Associated Press*] (SAG)
UNLOS....... United Nations Law of the Sea [*Conference*]
UNLR......... United Nations Law Reports [*A publication*] (DLA)
UNLTD....... Unlighted (DNAB)
UNLTD....... Unlimited
UNLV......... University of Nevada, Las Vegas
UNM.......... National University of Mexico [*Mexico*] [*Seismograph station code, US Geological Survey Closed*] (SEIS)
UNM.......... Unified Miniature
UNM.......... United National Movement [*Saint Christopher and Nevis*] [*Political party*] (EY)
UNM.......... United Nations Medal [*Military decoration*]
UnM.......... University Microfilms International, Ann Arbor, MI [*Library symbol Library of Congress*] (LCLS)
UNM.......... University of Nebraska, Medical Center, Omaha, NE [*OCLC symbol*] (OCLC)
UNM.......... University of New Mexico (PDAA)
UNM.......... Unmarried
UNM.......... UNUM Corp. [*NYSE symbol*] (SPSG)
UNMA........ Unified Network Management Architecture [*Computer science*]
UNMA........ Unified Network Management Architecture (TNIG)
UNMAC...... United Nations Mixed Armistice Commission
UNMC........ United Nations Mediterranean Command (BJA)
UNMC........ United Nations Mediterranean Commission
UNMC........ University of Nebraska Medical Center [*Omaha, NB*]
UNMCB...... Unscheduled Not Mission Capable Both [*Maintenance and supply*] (MCD)
UNMCM...... Unscheduled Not Mission Capable Maintenance (MCD)
UNMD........ Unmanned (KSC)
UNMEM..... United Nations Middle East Mission (EY)

U NMex....... [*The*] University of New Mexico (GAGS)
UNMG.......... [*The*] Unimark Group [*NASDAQ symbol*] (SAG)
Unmibh........ United Nations Mission in Bosnia and Herzegovina [*1995*]
Unmih.......... United Nations Mission in Haiti [*1993*]
UNMIH.......... United Nations Mission in Haiti (ECON)
UNMKD........ Unmarked
UnM-L......... University Microfilms Ltd., Penn, Buckinghamshire, United Kingdom [*Library symbol Library of Congress*] (LCLS)
UNMO.......... United Malays National Organisation [*Malaysia*] [*Political party*] (ECON)
UNMOGIP.... United Nations Military Observer Group for India and Pakistan (AABC)
Unmogip...... United Nations Military Observer Group in India and Pakistan [*1949*]
UNMON........ Unable to Monitor (FAAC)
Unmop......... United Nations Mission of Observers in Prevlaka [*Croatia, 1996*]
UNMO's....... United Nations Military Observers (BJA)
UNMSC........ United Nations Military Staff Committee (AABC)
UNMT.......... United Nations Multilateral Treaties [*A publication*] (DLA)
UNMTD........ Unmounted
UNNE.......... Universidad Nacional del Nordeste [*Argentina*]
UNNECY....... Unnecessary (ROG)
UNNEFO....... United Nations of the New Emerging Forces [*Indonesia*]
UNNN.......... Novosibirsk/Tolmachevo [*Former USSR ICAO location identifier*] (ICLI)
UNO............ Unicorn Resources [*Vancouver Stock Exchange symbol*]
UNO............ Unified Nimbus Observatory (MCD)
UNO............ Union Nacional Odriista [*Peruvian political party*]
UNO............ Union Nacional Opositora [*Electoral alliance*] [*Nicaragua*] (EY)
UNO............ United Nations Observer Corps (BJA)
UNO............ United Nations Organization [*ICSU*]
UNO............ United Nicaraguan Opposition
UNO............ University of Nebraska at Omaha
UNO............ University of New Orleans [*Louisiana*]
UNO............ Uno Restaurant Corp. [*NYSE symbol*] (TTSB)
UNO............ Uno Restaurants, Inc. [*NYSE symbol*] (SAG)
UNO............ Utility Night Observer
U No Ala...... University of North Alabama (GAGS)
UNOASD...... United Nations Outer Space Affairs Division (EERA)
UNOBSD...... Unobserved (ROG)
UNOC.......... Union Nationale des Ouvriers Congolais [*National Union of Congolese Workers*]
UNOC.......... United Nations Operation in the Congo
UNOCA......... United Nations Office Coordinating Humanitarian and Economic Aid to Afghanistan (ECON)
Unocal......... Unocal Corp. [*Associated Press*] (SAG)
UNO-CARA-PEN... Union Internationale pour la Cooperation Culturelle [*International Union for Cultural Co-operation*]
U No Car (Chapel Hill)... [*The*] University of North Carolina at Chapel Hill (GAGS)
U No Car (Greensboro)... [*The*] University of North Carolina at Greensboro (GAGS)
UNOCHA...... United Nations Office for the Coordination of Humanitarian Assistance to Afghanistan (ECON)
U No Colo.... University of Northern Colorado (GAGS)
U No Dak..... University of North Dakota (GAGS)
UNODIR....... Unless Otherwise Directed
UNOEOA...... United Nations Office for Emergency Operations in Africa [*Defunct*] (EA)
Unof............ Unofficial Reports [*A publication*] (DLA)
unoff........... Unofficial (CPH)
UNOFFL....... Unofficial (FAAC)
Un of Gh LJ... University of Ghana. Law Journal [*A publication*] (DLA)
U No Fla..... University of North Florida (GAGS)
UNOG.......... United Nations Organization - Geneva
UNOGIL....... United Nations Observer Group in Lebanon
UNOINDC..... Unless Otherwise Indicated
U No Iowa.... University of Northern Iowa (GAGS)
UNOLS......... University National Oceanographic Laboratory System [*Marine science*] (OSRA)
UNOLS......... University National Oceanographic Laboratory System [*National Science Foundation*]
Unomig........ United Nations Observer Mission in Georgia [*1993*]
UNOO.......... United Nations Oceanographic Organization
UNOP.......... Unopened (ADA)
UNOP.......... Unopposed
UNOPAR...... Universal Operator Performance Analyzer and Recorder
UNOPS......... [*The*] United Nations Office for Project Services (ECON)
UNORDCAN... Unexecuted Portion of Orders Cancelled
UNOREQ....... Unless Otherwise Requested (NVT)
U N Orleans... University of New Orleans (GAGS)
U N Orleans (Med Cent)... University of New Orleans Medicine Center (GAGS)
UnoRst......... Uno Restaurant Corp. [*Associated Press*] (SAG)
UNOS.......... United Network for Organ Sharing [*Database*] (EA)
UNOSOM...... United Nations Operation in Somalia (INF)
U No Tex...... University of North Texas (GAGS)
U Notre Dame... University of Notre Dame (GAGS)
UNP............ Uluru [*Ayers Rock - Mount Olga*] National Park (EERA)
UNP............ Unification National Party [*South Korea Political party*] (EY)
UNP............ Union Nacional Paraguaya [*Paraguayan political party*]
UNP............ Union Pacific [*NYSE symbol*] (TTSB)
UNP............ Union Pacific Corp. [*NYSE symbol*] (SPSG)
UNP............ United National Party [*Sri Lanka*] [*Political party*] (PPW)
UNP............ United Nations Philatelists (EA)
UNP............ United Northern Petroleum Corp. [*Vancouver Stock Exchange symbol*]
UNP............ University of Nebraska Press (DGA)
Unp............ Unnilpentium [*Chemical element*] (CDAI)
UNP............ Unpaged
UNP............ Unpostable [*Computer science*]
UNPA.......... Unione Nazionale Protezione Antiaere [*Italy*]
UNPA.......... United Nations Participation Act of 1945
UNPA.......... United Nations Postal Administration
UN-PAAERD... United Nations Programme of Action for African Economic Recovery and Development [*1986-1990*]
UnPac.......... Union Pacific Corp. [*Associated Press*] (SAG)
UNPAC......... Union Pacific Railroad Co.
UNPAD......... Universitas Negeri Padjadjaran [*Indonesia*]
UNPC.......... United Nations Palestine Commission
UNPCC......... United Nations Palestine Conciliation Commission (BJA)
UNPD.......... Unpaid (AABC)
UNPD-MSTR... Unpaid Master
UNPERF....... Unperformed [*Music*]
UNPERFD.... Unperformed (ROG)
UNPH.......... Uniphase Corp. [*NASDAQ symbol*] (SAG)
UNPIK......... United Nations Partisan Infantry Korea
UNPKD......... Unpacked (IAA)
UNPO.......... Unrepresented Nations and Peoples Organization
UNPOC......... United Nations Peace Observation Commission
Unpredep..... United Nations Preventive Deployment Force [*Macedonia*]
UNPROFOR... United Nations Protection Force [*Former Yugoslavia*] (ECON)
UNPROFOR... United Nations Protection Force in the Former Yugoslavia
UNPROFOR... United Nations Protective Forces
UnProp........ Union Property Investors, Inc. [*Associated Press*] (SAG)
UNPS.......... Unified Network Planning Study
UNPS.......... United Nations Philatelic Society [*Defunct*] (EA)
UNPS.......... Universal Power Supply
UNPUB......... Unpublished
Unpub......... Unpublished (AAGC)
UNPUBD....... Unpublished
Unpx........... Unapix Entertainment, Inc. [*Associated Press*] (SAG)
UNQ............ Providence, RI [*Location identifier FAA*] (FAAL)
UNQ............ Unique
UNQ............ Unique Resources Ltd. [*Vancouver Stock Exchange symbol*]
Unq............ Unnilquadium [*Chemical element*] (CDAI)
UNQTE......... Unquote
UNQUAL....... Unqualified (AABC)
unr............ Ukrainian Soviet Socialist Republic [*MARC country of publication code Library of Congress*] (LCCP)
UNR............ Ukrains'ka Natsional'na Rada
UNR............ Uniao Nacional Republicana [*National Republican Union*] [*Portugal Political party*] (PPE)
UNR............ Unicorp Resources Ltd. [*Toronto Stock Exchange symbol*]
UNR............ UNR Industries, Inc. [*Associated Press*] (SAG)
UNRAU......... Unified Numeric Representation Arithmetic Unit (PDAA)
UNRC.......... Unico Inc. [*NASDAQ symbol*] (TTSB)
UNRC.......... Unico, Inc. New Mexico [*NASDAQ symbol*] (SAG)
UNRCCFE..... United Nations Regional Cartographic Conferences on Asia and the Far East
UNRDBL...... Unreadable (FAAC)
UNREF......... United Nations Refugee Fund
UNREF......... Unreformed (ROG)
UNREL......... Unreliable
UNRELBL..... Unreliable (FAAC)
UNREP........ Underway Replenishment [*Military*]
Unrep Cr C... Bombay Unreported Criminal Cases [*1862-98*] [*India*] [*A publication*] (DLA)
Unrep NY Est TC... Unreported New York Estate Tax Cases [*Prentice-Hall, Inc.*] [*A publication*] (DLA)
Unrep Wills Cas... Unreported Wills Cases [*Prentice-Hall, Inc.*] [*A publication*] (DLA)
UN Res........ United Nations Resolutions [*A publication*] (DLA)
UNRF.......... Uganda National Rescue Front (PD)
UNRFNRE.... United Nations Revolving Fund for Natural Resources Exploration (EERA)
UNRGLTD.... Unregulated
UNRHCE...... United Nations Regional Housing Center for ESCAP [*Economic and Social Commission for Asia and the Pacific*] [*India*] (EAIO)
UNRI........... UNR Industries [*NASDAQ symbol*] (TTSB)
UNRI........... UNR Industries, Inc. [*NASDAQ symbol*] (NQ)
UNRIAA........ United Nations Reports of International Arbitral Awards [*A publication*] (DLA)
UNRIPS........ United Nations Regional Institute for Population Studies [*Legon, Ghana*] (EAIO)
UNRISD........ United Nations Research Institute for Social Development (EA)
UNROD......... United Nations Relief Operation in Dacca
UNRPR......... United Nations Relief for Palestine Refugees
UNRRA......... United Nations Relief and Rehabilitation Administration [*"United Nations" derives from the wartime alliance of this name, not from any affiliation with the postwar international organization*]
UNRRC......... United Nations Relief and Rehabilitation Conference
UNRS.......... Union pour la Nouvelle Republique Senegalaise [*Union for the New Senegalese Republic*] [*Political party*]
UNRSTD...... Unrestricted (FAAC)
UNRTD......... United Nations Resources and Transport Division
UNRWA........ United Nations Relief and Works Agency for Palestine Refugees in the Near East [*Austria*] (PD)
UNRWA........ United Nations Relief Works Agency (EERA)
UNRWAPR... United Nations Relief and Works Agency for Palestine Refugees in the Near East [*Austria*] (DLA)
UNRWAPRNE... United Nations Relief and Works Agency for Palestine Refugees in the Near East [*Pronounced: "Unwrap me"*] [*Austria*]
UnrylT......... Uniroyal Technology Corp. [*Associated Press*] (SAG)

UnrylTc........ Uniroyal Technology Corp. [*Associated Press*] (SAG)
UNS.......... Umnak, AK [*Location identifier FAA*] (FAAL)
UnS.......... Unconditioned Stimulus [*Psychometrics*] (AAMN)
UNS.......... Unified Numbering Systems [*for metals*] (MCD)
UNS.......... Unified Special [*Thread*]
UNS.......... Unions
UNS.......... Unions [*Postal Service standard*] (OPSA)
UNS.......... United News Shops [*British*]
UNS.......... Universal News Service [*British*]
UNS.......... Universal Night Sight
uns.......... Unsatisfactory (MAE)
uns.......... Unstable (IDOE)
uns.......... Unsymmetrical (IDOE)
UNS.......... Unsymmetrical
UNSAC........ United Nations Scientific Advisory Committee [*ICSU*]
UNSAT........ Unsatisfactory (AABC)
unsat........ Unsaturated [*Chemistry*]
UNSATFY....... Unsatisfactory
UNSBL........ Unseasonable [*NWS*] (FAAC)
UNSC......... United Nations Security Council
UNSC......... United Nations Social Commission
UNSCC........ United Nations Standards Co-Ordinating Committee
UNSCC........ University of Nevada System Computing Center [*Research center*] (RCD)
UNSCCUR.... United Nations Scientific Conference on the Conservation and Utilization of Resources
UNSCEAR.... United Nations Scientific Committee on Effects of Atomic Radiation (EERA)
UNSCEAR.... United Nations Scientific Committee on the Effects of Atomic Radiation
UNSCOB...... United Nations Special Committee on the Balkans [*Greece*]
UNSCOP...... United Nations Special Committee on Palestine
UNSD......... Unsweetened (ROG)
UNSDD........ United Nations Social Development Division
UNSDRI....... United Nations Social Defense Research Institute [*UN/Italy*]
UNSECNAV.... Under Secretary of the Navy
UNSERV....... Unserviceable (IAA)
UNSF......... United Nations Special Fund
UNSFH........ United Nations Security Forces, Hollandia (AABC)
UNSG......... United Nations Secretary General
UNSGD........ Unsigned (WGA)
UNSIS........ United Nations Statistical Information System (DUND)
UNSKED....... Unscheduled (FAAC)
UnSlf......... Universal Self Care, Inc. [*Associated Press*] (SAG)
UNSM......... United Nations Service Medal [*Military decoration*]
UNSN......... Unison Software [*NASDAQ symbol*] (TTSB)
UNSN......... Unison Software, Inc. [*NASDAQ symbol*] (SAG)
UNSO......... United Nations Statistical Office (EERA)
UNSO......... United Nations Sudano-Sahelian Office
UNSP......... Union Nationale pour la Solidarite et le Progres [*Benin*] [*Political party*] (EY)
UNSPDPM... United Nations Subcommission on the Prevention of Discrimination and the Protection of Minorities [*Geneva, Switzerland*] (EAIO)
UNSR......... United Nations Space Registry (BARN)
UNSS......... United Nations Sales Section [*for UN documents*]
UNSSOD....... United Nations Special Session on Disarmament (PDAA)
UNST......... Union Nordique pour la Sante et le Travail [*Nordic Union for Health and Work*] (EAIO)
UNSTAC....... United Nations Science and Technology Advisory Committee (AIE)
UNSTBL....... Unstable
UNSTD........ Union Nationale des Syndicats des Travailleurs du Dahomey [*National Federation of Workers' Unions of Dahomey*]
UNSTDY....... Unsteady
UNSTHV....... Union Nationale des Syndicats des Travailleurs de la Haute Volta [*National Federation of Workers' Unions of the Upper Volta*]
UNSU......... United Nations Staff Union (EA)
UNSU......... United Nations Study Unit [*Philatelic organization*] (EA)
UNSUB........ Unknown Subject [*FBI*] [*Acronym also used as title of television series*]
UNSUPPR.... Unsuppressed (MSA)
UNSVC........ Unserviceable (AABC)
UNSVC-RT-R... Unserviceable Return Rate
UNSVM........ United Nations Service Medal
UNSW......... Union Switch & Signal [*NASDAQ symbol*] (TTSB)
UNSW......... Union Switch & Signal, Inc. [*NASDAQ symbol*] (SAG)
UNSW......... University of New South Wales [*State*] (EERA)
UNSW......... University of New South Wales Australia
UNSWIL....... University of New South Wales Institute of Languages [*Australia*]
UnSwtch...... Union Switch & Signal, Inc. [*Associated Press*] (SAG)
UNSX......... Unisex
UNSYM........ Unsymmetrical
unsz c....... Unsized Canvas (VRA)
UNT.......... Undergraduate Navigator Training [*Air Force*] (AFM)
UNT.......... Underground Nuclear Test
UNT.......... Unit Corp. [*NYSE symbol*] (SPSG)
UNT.......... United Tariff Bureau, Inc., New York NY [*STAC*]
UNT.......... Unst [*Scotland*] [*Airport symbol*] (OAG)
unt.......... Untitled (VRA)
UNTA......... Union Nationale des Travailleurs Angolais [*National Union of Angolan Workers*]
UNTA......... United Nations Technical Assistance
UNTAA........ United Nations Technical Assistance Administration
UNTAC........ United Nations Transitional Authority in Cambodia (ECON)
UNTAF........ United Nations Technical Assistance Fellowship
UNTAG........ United Nations Transition Assistance Group
UNTAM........ United Nations Technical Assistance Mission (BARN)
UNTC......... Union Nationale des Travailleurs Congolais [*National Union of Congolese Workers*]
UNTC......... United Nations Trusteeship Council (BARN)
UNTCI........ Union Nationale des Travailleurs de Cote d'Ivoire [*National Union of Ivory Coast Workers*]
UNTCOK....... United Nations Temporary Committee on Korea
UNTCOR...... United Nations Trusteeship Council Official Record [*A publication*] (DLA)
UNTD......... First United Bancshares, Inc. [*El Dorado, AR*] [*NASDAQ symbol*] (NQ)
UNTD......... First United Bancshrs [*NASDAQ symbol*] (TTSB)
UNTD......... United
UNTD......... University Naval Training Division [*Canada*]
UNTDED....... United Nations Data Elements Directory [*A publication*]
UntdNat...... United Natural Foods, Inc. [*Associated Press*] (SAG)
UNTE......... Unit Corp. [*NASDAQ symbol*] (NQ)
UNTEA........ United Nations Temporary Executive Authority [*Supervised transfer of Netherlands New Guinea to Indonesia*]
UnTech....... United Technologies Corp. [*Associated Press*] (SAG)
UnTelev....... United Television, Inc. [*Associated Press*] (SAG)
untemp........ Untempered (VRA)
UNTEW........ Unit Corp. Wrrt [*NASDAQ symbol*] (TTSB)
UnTex......... Union Texas Petroleum [*Associated Press*] (SAG)
UNTFDPP...... United Nations Trust Fund for Development Planning and Projections
UNTFSD....... United Nations Trust Fund for Social Development
UNTG......... United Nations Theatre Group (EA)
UNTHD........ Unthreaded
UNTIS........ United Nations Treaty Information System (DUND)
UNTM......... Union Nationale des Travailleurs du Mali [*National Union of Malian Workers*]
UNTN......... Union Nationale des Travailleurs Nigeriens [*National Union of Nigerian Workers*]
Un Trav Dec... Unreported Travancore Decisions [*A publication*] (DLA)
UNTS......... Undergraduate Navigator Training System [*Air Force*]
UNTS......... Unilateral Nevoid Telangiectasia [*Medicine*] (DMAA)
UNTS......... Union Nationale des Travailleurs du Senegal [*National Union of Workers of Senegal*]
UNTS......... United Nations Treaty Series [*Project*] [*University of Washington*]
UNTSFA....... United Nations Trust Fund for Southern Africa (EERA)
UNTSO........ United Nations Truce Supervision Organization
UNTT......... Union Nationale des Travailleurs du Togo [*National Union of Togolese Workers*]
UNTT......... United Nations Trust Territory
UNTW......... Untwist
UNU.......... Juneau, WI [*Location identifier FAA*] (FAAL)
UNU.......... United Nations University [*Tokyo*]
UNU.......... United Nations University [*Marine science*] (OSRA)
UNU.......... Universidad de las Naciones Unidas [*United Nations University*] [*Spanish*] (DUND)
UNU.......... Universite des Nations Unies [*United Nations University*] [*French*] (DUND)
UNUIIST....... United Nations University International Institute for Software
UNU/INTECH... United Nations University/Institute of New Technologies
UNUM......... UNUM Corp. [*Associated Press*] (SAG)
UNUM25....... UNUM Corp. [*Associated Press*] (SAG)
UNUMO........ Universal Underwater Mobile [*Robot*]
UNUSBL....... Unusable
UNUSL........ Unusual (ROG)
UNU/WIDER... United Nations University / World Institute for Development Economics Research (DUND)
UNV.......... State College, PA [*Location identifier FAA*] (FAAL)
UNV.......... United Nations Volunteers (EAIO)
UNV.......... Unitel Video [*AMEX symbol*] (TTSB)
UNV.......... Unitel Video, Inc. [*AMEX symbol*] (SPSG)
UnvAm........ Universal American Financial Corp. [*Associated Press*] (SAG)
UnvAmr....... Universal American Financial Corp. [*Associated Press*] (SAG)
UnvDisp...... Universal Display Corp. [*Associated Press*] (SAG)
UnvElc....... Universal Electronics, Inc. [*Associated Press*] (SAG)
Unverd........ Unverified
UnvFd........ Universal Foods Corp. [*Associated Press*] (SAG)
UnvHgt....... Universal Heights, Inc. [*Associated Press*] (SAG)
UnvHld....... Universal Holdings [*Associated Press*] (SAG)
UnvHlt....... Universal Health Services, Inc. [*Associated Press*] (SAG)
UnvHR........ Universal Health Realty Income Trust [*Associated Press*] (SAG)
UnvHsp....... Universal Hospital Services, Inc. [*Associated Press*] (SAG)
UnvHt........ Universal Heights, Inc. [*Associated Press*] (SAG)
UnvInt....... Universal International, Inc. [*Associated Press*] (SAG)
UnvMfg....... Universal Manufacturing Co. [*Associated Press*] (SAG)
UnvSc........ Universal Security Instruments, Inc. [*Associated Press*] (SAG)
UnvSec....... Universal Security Instruments, Inc. [*Associated Press*] (SAG)
UnvSeis...... Universal Seismic Associates [*Associated Press*] (SAG)
UnvSelf...... Universal Self Care, Inc. [*Associated Press*] (SAG)
UnvslCp...... Universal Corp. [*Associated Press*] (SAG)
UnvsOut...... Universal Outdoor Holdings, Inc. [*Associated Press*] (SAG)
UnvStain..... Universal Stainless & Alloy Products [*Associated Press*] (SAG)
UnvStdM...... Universal Standard Medical Labs, Inc. [*Associated Press*] (SAG)
UNVX......... Univax Biologies [*NASDAQ symbol*] (SAG)
UNWCC........ Unions' Nation-Wide Coordinating Council for Oil and Allied Industries [*Defunct*] (EA)
UNWCC........ United Nations War Crimes Commission [*"United Nations" derives from the wartime alliance of this name, not from any affiliation with the postwar international organization*]
UNWG......... United Nations Women's Guild (EA)
UNWLA........ Ukrainian National Women's League of America (EA)

UNWMG....... Utility Nuclear Waste Management Group (EA)
UnwmK....... Unwatermarked [*Philately*]
UNWMKD.... Unwatermarked (WGA)
UNWR........ Unwritten (ROG)
UNWRAP..... United We Resist Additional Packaging [*Student legal action organization*]
UNX........... Underground Nuclear Explosion
UNX........... Univex Mining Corp. [*Vancouver Stock Exchange symbol*]
UNY........... San Antonio, TX [*Location identifier FAA*] (FAAL)
UNY........... United Nations of Yoga [*Stockholm, Sweden*] (EAIO)
UNY........... University of New York (ROG)
UNYB.......... United Nations Year Book [*A publication*] (DLA)
UNYFA........ Ukrainian National Youth Federation of America [*Later, Ukrainian Youth Association of America*] (EA)
UNYOM....... United Nations Yemen Observation Mission
u-nz--.......... New Zealand [*MARC geographic area code Library of Congress*] (LCCP)
UNZ............ Unzendake [*Japan*] [*Seismograph station code, US Geological Survey*] (SEIS)
UO.............. Direct Air [*ICAO designator*] (AD)
UO.............. Undelivered Orders [*Army*] (AABC)
U/O............ Under Observation (DAVI)
UO.............. Und Oefters [*And Often*] [*German*]
UO.............. Union Office (ROG)
UO.............. Union Railroad of Oregon [*AAR code*]
UO.............. Unit Operator (NRCH)
UO.............. University of Oxford (ROG)
UO.............. Ureteral Orifice [*Anatomy*] (MAE)
UO.............. Urinary Output [*Medicine*]
U/O............ Used On (MSA)
UO.............. Weber County Library, Ogden, UT [*Library symbol Library of Congress*] (LCLS)
UO2............ Uranium Dioxide
UOA............ Unattached Officers' Association [*A union*] [*British*]
UOA............ United Ostomy Association (EA)
UOA............ University of Arizona [*Seismograph station code, US Geological Survey Closed*] (SEIS)
UOA............ Used on Assembly
UOA............ Use of Other Automobiles [*Insurance*]
UOAQ.......... Unit Owners' Association of Queensland [*Australia*]
UOBTPS....... United Operative Bricklayers' Trade Protection Society [*A union*] [*British*]
UOC............ Ultimate Operating Capability
UOC............ Ultimate Operational Configuration (AAG)
UOC............ Unequilibrated Ordinary Chondrites
UOC............ Unilens Optical [*Vancouver Stock Exchange symbol*]
UOC............ Union de l'Ouest Cameroun [*Union of West Cameroon*]
UOC............ United Orpington Club (EA)
UOC............ Unit of Choice
UOC............ Universal Output Computer
UOC............ Unusual Occurrence Control
UOC............ Uranium Ore Concentrate
UOC............ Useable on Code (MCD)
UOCA.......... United Orpington Club of America [*Later, UOC*] (EA)
UOCB.......... Uncrossed Olivocochlear Bundle [*Otology*]
UOCMWD.... Union of Operative Card Makers and Wire Drawers [*British*]
UOCO.......... Union Oil Co.
UOD............ Ultimate Oxygen Demand [*Water conservation*] (WDAA)
UODDL........ User-Oriented Data Display Language [*Computer science*]
UODG.......... Underwater Ordnance Development Group
UOE............ Unit of Error (MCD)
u/o/e........... Unopened Edges [*Bookbinding*] (DGA)
UOEF.......... Union de Obreros Estivadores de Filipinos [*Union of Longshoremen of the Philippines*]
UOF............ Unplanned Outage Factor [*Electronics*] (IEEE)
UOF............ Unusual Order Form (MHDI)
U of A.......... University of Alaska [*Anchorage, AK*]
U of A.......... University of Arkansas [*Fayetteville, AR*]
U of D.......... University of Detroit [*Michigan*]
U of D.......... University of Dublin [*Ireland*]
U of I........... University of Illinois [*Urbana, IL*]
U of I........... University of Iowa [*Iowa City, IA*] (OICC)
U of Kansas L Rev... University of Kansas. Law Review [*A publication*] (DLA)
U of M.......... University of Michigan [*Ann Arbor, MI*]
U of MLB...... University of Missouri. Law Bulletin [*A publication*] (DLA)
U of Omaha Bull... Night Law School Bulletin. University of Omaha [*A publication*] (DLA)
UOFS.......... United States Forest Service, Intermountain Range and Experiment Station Library, Ogden, UT [*Library symbol Library of Congress*] (LCLS)
U of So........ University of the South (GAGS)
U of T.......... University of Toronto [*Ontario*]
U of T School of LR... School of Law. Review. Toronto University [*Canada*] [*A publication*] (DLA)
U of W......... University of Washington [*Seattle, WA*]
U of W......... University of Windsor [*Ontario*]
UOG............ Unit of Grading (MHDW)
UOGC.......... United Order of the Golden Cross [*Defunct*] (EA)
UOGF.......... Uranium Off-Gas Filter [*Nuclear energy*] (NRCH)
UOGS.......... Church of Jesus Christ of Latter-Day Saints, Genealogical Society Library, OgdenBranch, Ogden, UT [*Library symbol Library of Congress*] (LCLS)
UOH............ Unplanned Outage Hours [*Electronics*] (IEEE)
UOHC.......... Under Other than Honorable Conditions [*Discharge*] [*Military*]
UOI.............. Unit of Instruction
UOI.............. University of Illinois [*Record label*]
UOI.............. User On-Line Interaction [*Computer science*]
UOIW.......... United Optical and Instrument Workers of America
UOJC.......... Union of Orthodox Jewish Congregations of America (EA)
UOJCA........ Union of Orthodox Jewish Congregations of America (EA)
UOK............ University of Oklahoma [*Record label*]
U Okla......... [*The*] University of Oklahoma (GAGS)
UOL............ Underwater Object Locator
UOL............ Utility Octal Load
UOL............ Utility-Oriented Language (MCD)
UOLP.......... UOL Publishing, Inc. [*NASDAQ symbol*] (SAG)
UOL Pub...... UOL Publishing, Inc. [*Associated Press*] (SAG)
UOLS.......... Underwater Object Location and Search Operations [*Navy*] (NVT)
UOMCA........ United Orthodox Ministers and Cantors Association of America and Canada (EA)
UOME.......... Union des Opposants Malgaches Exterieurs [*Madagascar*] [*Political party*] (EY)
UOMGCU..... United Operative Masons' and Granite Cutters' Union [*British*]
UOMS.......... Union des Originaires de Mauritanie du Sud [*Union of Natives of South Mauritania*]
UOMS.......... Unmanned Orbital Multifunction Satellite
UON............ Muong Sai [*Laos*] [*Airport symbol*] (AD)
UON............ Unless Otherwise Noted (OA)
UON............ Urgency of Need (MCD)
UOO............ Unavailable, On Order [*Business term*] (NTCM)
UOO............ Undelivered Orders Outstanding [*Military*] (AFM)
UOO............ Upravleniye Osobykh Otdelov [*Armed Forces Counterintelligence-Directorate*] [*Former USSR*] (LAIN)
UOP............ Understanding of the Problem (MCD)
UOP............ Unit of Production (MHDW)
UOP............ Unit Operating Procedure (NRCH)
UOP............ University of the Pacific [*Stockton, CA*]
UOP............ Urine Output [*Physiology*]
UOP............ User Operations Panel (SSD)
UOPA.......... Uranium Ore Processing Association
UOPDP........ Union Ouvriere et Paysanne pour la Democratie Proletarienne [*Peasant and Worker Union for Proletarian Democracy*] [*France Political party*] (PPE)
UOPH.......... Unaccompanied Officer Personnel Housing [*Navy*]
UOPLF........ United Oromo People's Liberation Front [*Ethiopia*] [*Political party*] (EY)
UOQ............ Upper Outer Quadrant [*Anatomy*]
UOr............ Orem City Library, Orem, UT [*Library symbol Library of Congress*] (LCLS)
UOR............ Uniform Officer Record
UOR............ Unplanned Outage Rate [*Electronics*] (IEEE)
UOR............ Unusual Occurrence Report (NUCP)
UOR............ Urgent Operation Requirement
UORC.......... Used Oil Recycling Coalition [*Automotive lubricants*]
U Ore.......... University of Oregon (GAGS)
UORS.......... Unusual Occurence Report (IAA)
UOrUC........ Utah Valley Community College, Orem, UT [*Library symbol*] [*Library of Congress*] (LCLS)
UORUSC...... Union of Orthodox Rabbis of the US and Canada (EA)
UOS............ Sewanee, TN [*Location identifier FAA*] (FAAL)
UOS............ Ultraviolet Ozone Spectrometer (MCD)
UOS............ Undelivered Orders Schedule [*Army*]
UOS............ Underwater Ordnance Station [*Navy*]
UOS............ United Order of Smiths [*A union*] [*British*]
UOS............ University of the South [*Record label*]
UOS............ Unless Otherwise Specified (MSA)
UOS............ Unmanned Orbital Satellite
UOS............ User Operations Support (SSD)
UOSAT........ University of Surrey Satellite
UOSG.......... User Operations Support Group (SSD)
UOSM.......... Urinary Osmolarity [*Medicine*]
UOT............ Uncontrollable Overtime
UOT............ Union, SC [*Location identifier FAA*] (FAAL)
UOT............ Unit of Trading
UOT............ Upper Outer Tube
UOTASP....... United Order of the Total Abstaining Sons of the Phoenix (ROG)
UOTC.......... University Officers Training Corps [*British military*] (DMA)
UOTHC........ Under Other than Honorable Conditions [*Discharge*] [*Military*]
UOTS.......... United Order True Sisters (EA)
UOUT.......... Universal Outdoor Holdings, Inc. [*NASDAQ symbol*] (SAG)
UOV............ Union Ouvriere du Viet-Nam [*Vietnam Labor Union*] [*South Vietnam*]
UOV............ Unit of Value (MHDW)
UOV............ Units of Variance
UOW............ Weber State College, Ogden, UT [*Library symbol Library of Congress*] (LCLS)
UOX............ Oxford, MS [*Location identifier FAA*] (FAAL)
UOX............ University [*Mississippi*] [*Airport symbol*] (OAG)
UOZ............ Upper Outer Zone [*Also called upper outer quadrant*] [*Anatomy*] (DAVI)
UP.............. Bahamas Air [*ICAO designator*] (AD)
UP.............. Lab. UPSA [*France*] [*Research code symbol*]
UP.............. Oregon Short Line R. R. [*of Union Pacific Railroad Co.*] [*AAR code*]
UP.............. Oregon-Washington R. R. & Navigation [*of Union Pacific Railroad Co.*] [*AAR code*]
UP.............. Provo Public Library, Provo, UT [*Library symbol Library of Congress*] (LCLS)
UP.............. Ulster Parliament (DAS)
UP.............. Ultra Presse [*Press agency*] [*Colombia*]
UP.............. Umbilical Pin
UP.............. Uncertainty Principle [*Quantum mechanics*]

UP Uncertified Patient [*British*]
UP Uncovered Position (MHDW)
UP Undergraduate Program [*Subject area tests*]
UP Under-Proof [*Of spirituous liquors*] [*Distilling*]
UP Under Provisions Of [*Military*]
UP Unearned Premium [*Insurance*]
UP Unemployed Parent [*Department of Health and Human Services*]
UP Unified Programme [*Education*] (AIE)
UP Union del Pueblo [*Union of the People*] [*Mexico*] (PD)
UP Union Pacific Corp.
UP Union Patriotica [*Patriotic Union*] [*Spain Political party*] (PPE)
UP Union Patriotica [*Patriotic Union*] [*Colombia*] [*Political party*]
UP Union Popular [*Popular Union*] [*Uruguay*] (PD)
UP Uniprocessor
UP United Party [*Gambia*] [*Political party*] (PPW)
UP United Party [*Papua New Guinea*] [*Political party*] (PPW)
UP United Presbyterian
UP United Press [*Merged with International News Service to form UPI*]
UP United Provinces [*India*]
up United States Miscellaneous Pacific Islands [*MARC country of publication code Library of Congress*] (LCCP)
UP Unit Pack
UP Unit Price
UP Units Position (IAA)
UP Unity Party [*Liberia*] [*Political party*] (EY)
UP Unity Party [*Sierra Leone*] [*Political party*] (EY)
UP Universal Processor [*TRW, Inc.-Motorola, Inc.*] [*Computer science*]
UP University of the Philippines
UP University Partnership [*Australia*]
UP University Presses [*General term applied to presses of various universities*]
UP Unknown Precipitation [*ICAO*] (FAAC)
UP Unpostable [*Computer science*]
UP Unrealized Profit
UP Unrealized Profits (MHDW)
UP Unrotated Projectile [*Rocket*]
UP Unsaturated Thermoset Polyester [*Organic chemistry*]
UP Unsolicited Proposal (MCD)
UP Unstained Pollen [*Botany*]
UP Update [*Online database field identifier*] [*Computer science*]
UP Upper (ADA)
UP Upper Peninsula [*Michigan*]
UP Upper Proof (ROG)
UP Upright Posture (MAE)
UP Upset Price [*Business term*] (MHDB)
UP Urea Phosphate (OA)
UP Ureteropelvic [*Anatomy*]
UP Uridine Phosphorylase [*An enzyme*]
U/P Urine-Plasma Ratio [*Clinical chemistry*]
UP Uroporphyrin [*Biochemistry*]
UP Urticaria Pigmentosa [*Dermatology*]
UP User Program (MCD)
UP Uteropedvic [*Gynecology*] (DAVI)
UP Utility Path (IEEE)
UP Utility Program (MCD)
UP Utilizable Protein [*Biochemistry*] (DICI)
UPA Air Foyle Ltd. [*British ICAO designator*] (FAAC)
UPA Ukrains'ka Povstans'ka Armiia
UPA Ultimate Players Association (EA)
UPA Uncooled Parametric Amplifier
UPA Uniao das Populacoes de Angola [*Angolan People's Union*] [*Later, NFLA*]
UPA Uniform Partnership Act
UPA Union of Poles in America (EA)
UPA Union Panamericana [*Pan-American Union*] [*Washington, DC*]
UPA Union Postale Arabe [*Arab Postal Union*]
UPA Unique Product Advantage [*Advertising*]
UPA Unitary Pole Approximation
UPA United Patternmakers Association
UPA United Power Association (IAA)
UPA United Producers of America [*Motion picture company*]
UPA Units per Assembly [*Business term*] (MHDB)
UPA University Photographers Association of America
UPA University Press of America
UPA University Publications of America [*Database producer*] (IID)
UPA Unpressurized Aerosol [*Therapy*] [*Pharmacology*] (DAVI)
UPA Unwed Parents Anonymous (EA)
UPA Upala [*Costa Rica*] [*Airport symbol*] (AD)
UPA Urban Programme Authority [*Education*] (AIE)
UPA Urokinase Plasminogen Activator [*An enzyme*]
UPAA University Photographers Association of America (EA)
UPAC Ultra Pac [*NASDAQ symbol*] (TTSB)
UPAC Ultra Pac, Inc. [*NASDAQ symbol*] (SAG)
UPAC Unemployed and Poverty Action Council (EA)
UPAC Unificacion y Progreso [*Unification and Progress*] [*Mexico Political party*] (PPW)
UPAC United Parents of Absconded Children [*Defunct*] (EA)
U Pac University of the Pacific (GAGS)
UPacRs Union Pacific Resources Group, Inc. [*Associated Press*] (SAG)
UPACS Universal Performance Assessment and Control System
UPADI Union Pan-Americana de Asociaciones de Igenieros [*Pan American Federation of Engineering Societies*] [*Uruguay*] (EAIO)
up ad lib Up Ad Libitum [*Ambulatory*] [*Patient may walk*] (DAVI)
UPAE Union Postal de las Americas y Espana [*Postal Union of the Americas and Spain - PUAS*] (EAIO)
UPAEP Union Postal de las Americas, Espana, y Portugal [*Postal Union of the Americas, Spain, and Portugal*] [*Uruguay*] (EAIO)
UPAJ Union Panafricaine des Journalistes
UPAM United People's Association of Matabeleland [*Zimbabwe*] [*Political party*] (PPW)
UP & S Uniform Printing and Supply
UP & T Unit Personnel and Tonnage Table [*Military*]
UPANSW United Protestant Association of New South Wales [*Australia*]
UPAO University Professors for Academic Order (EA)
UPAP Union Pan Africaine des Postes [*Pan African Postal Union - PAPU*] (EAIO)
UPAP Urban Planning Assistance Program
UPAPH United Patients Association for Pulmonary Hypertension (EA)
UPAR Urokeinase Plasminogen Activator [*Biochemistry*]
UPAR Urokinase-Type Plasminogen Activator Receptor [*Biochemistry*]
U-PARC University of Pittsburgh Applied Research Center [*Research center*] (RCD)
UPARR Urban Park and Recreation Recovery
UPAS Underpass
UPAS Underpass [*Postal Service standard*] (OPSA)
UPAS Uniform Performance Assessment System [*Education*]
UPAT Union Panafricaine des Telecommunications [*Pan African Telecommunications Union - PATU*] (EAIO)
UPB Air Goyle Charter Ltd. [*British*] [*FAA designator*] (FAAC)
UPB Brigham Young University, Provo, UT [*Library symbol Library of Congress*] (LCLS)
UPB Union Patriotica Bonairiana [*Bonaire Patriotic Union*] [*Netherlands Antilles*] [*Political party*] (PPW)
UPB United Press of Bangladesh
UPB Universal Patents Bureau [*British*] (ROG)
UPB Upper Bound
UP/BA Unitary Payroll Benefit Accounting (MCD)
Up Ben Pr Upper Bench Precedents Tempore Car. I [*England*] [*A publication*] (DLA)
Up Ben Pre Upper Bench Precedents Tempore Car. I [*A publication*] (DLA)
UPB-L Brigham Young University, J. Reuben Clark Law Library, Provo, UT [*Library symbol Library of Congress*] (LCLS)
UPC Air Foyle Airways Ltd. [*British*] [*FAA designator*] (FAAC)
UPC Pennsylvania State University, Commonwealth Campuses, University Park, PA [*OCLC symbol*] (OCLC)
UPC Uganda People's Congress [*Suspended*]
UPC Underwater Pipe Cutter
UPC UNESCO Publications Center (WDAA)
UPC Uniform Plumbing Code (DAC)
UPC Uniform Practice Code
UPC Uniform Probate Code
UPC Union del Pueblo Canario [*Union of the Canarian People*] [*Spain Political party*] (PPE)
UPC Union des Populations Camerounaises [*Union of Cameroonian Peoples*] (PD)
UPC Unione di u Populu Corsu [*Union of the Corsican People*] [*France Political party*] (PPE)
UPC Union of the Corsican People [*France*]
UPC Union Planters [*NYSE symbol*] (TTSB)
UPC Union Planters Corp. [*NYSE symbol*] (CTT)
UPC Union pour le Progres Comorien [*Union for Comorian Progress*] [*Political party*] (PPW)
UPC Union Progressiste Congolaise [*Congolese Progressive Union*]
UPC United Pentecostal Church [*Australia*]
UPC United Poultry Concerns [*An association*] (EA)
UPC United Power Co. [*British*]
UPC United Presbyterian Church
UPC Unit of Packed Cells
UPC Unit of Processing Capacity
UPC Unit Processing Code (AFM)
UPC Unit Production Cost
UPC Universal Peripheral Controller
UPC Universal Postal Congress (IAA)
UPC Universal Product Code [*Inventory control*]
UPC Universal Product Code
UPC Unpostable Code [*Computer science*]
UPCA Uniform Planned Community Act [*National Conference of Commissioners on Uniform State Laws*]
UPCC Uniform Product Code Council [*Formerly, UGPCC*] (EA)
UPC-E Universal Product Code-Europe (NITA)
UPCHUK University Program for the Comprehensive Handling and Utilization of Knowledge [*Humorous*]
UPCI Union pour Construire l'Independence [*New Caledonia*] [*Political party*] (EY)
UPCO Union Progressiste Congolaise [*Congolese Progressive Union*]
UPCON Upgraded Constellation (MCD)
upconv Up Converter (IDOE)
UPCP Union Planters [*NASDAQ symbol*] (SAG)
UPCPO Union Planters 8% Cv'E'Pfd [*NASDAQ symbol*] (TTSB)
UPCS United Pastrycooks' and Confectioners' Society [*British*] (BI)
UPCS Universal Philatelic Cover Society
UPD Air Foyle Charter Airways Ltd. [*British*] [*FAA designator*] (FAAC)
UPD Underpotential Deposition [*Electrochemistry*]
UPD Union des Patriotes Democratiques [*Haiti*] [*Political party*] (EY)
UPD United Port District (WDAA)
UPD Unit Power Density [*Lighting*]
UPD Universally Programmable Digitizer Update (IAA)
UPD Unpaid (ADA)
UPD Update
UPD Urban Planning Directorate [*British*]

UPDA United Plastics Distributors Association [*Later, NAPD*] (EA)
UPDATE Universal Prefabricated Depot Automatic Test Equipment (DNAB)
UPDATE Unlimited Potential Data through Automation Technology in Education (IEEE)
UPDEA Union des Producteurs, Transporteurs, et Distributeurs d'Energie Electrique d'Afrique [*Union of Producers, Conveyors, and Distributors of Electric Power in Africa - UPDEA*] (EAIO)
UPDFT Updraft (MSA)
UPDMA United Popular Dress Manufacturers Association [*Later, LACA*] (EA)
UPDP Union des Patriotes Democrates et Progressistes [*Niger*] [*Political party*] (EY)
UPDRS Unified Parkinson's Disease Rating Scale
UPDT Update [*National Weather Service*] (FAAC)
UPE Union de Patriotas Espanoles [*Union of Patriots*] [*Spanish*]
UPE Union Panafricaine des Etudiants [*All Africa Students Union - AASU*] (EAIO)
UPE Unitary Pole Expansion
UPE Unit Proficiency Exercise
UPE Unsaturated Polyethylene [*Organic chemistry*]
UPE Upstream Promoter Element [*Genetics*]
UPEB Union de Paises Exportadores de Banano [*Union of Banana-Exporting Countries - UBEC*] (EAIO)
UPEBR Uncured Propellant End Burning Rocket (MCD)
UPECO Union Progressiste Congolaise [*Congolese Progressive Union*]
UPEI Union Petroliere Europeenne Independante [*Independent European Petroleum Union*] (EAIO)
UPEI University of Prince Edward Island [*Canada*]
UPEN Upper Peninsula Energy [*NASDAQ symbol*] (TTSB)
UPEN Upper Peninsula Energy Corp. [*NASDAQ symbol*] (NQ)
UPenE Upper Peninsula Energy Corp. [*Associated Press*] (SAG)
U Penn University of Pennsylvania (GAGS)
UPEP Undergraduate Preparation of Educational Personnel [*Office of Education*]
UPEP Urine Protein Electrophoresis [*Biochemistry*] (DAVI)
UPEPI Union of European Practitioners in Industrial Property [*EC*] (ECED)
UPEQUA Union Progressiste de l'Equateur [*Progressive Union of Equateur Province*] [*Congo - Leopoldville*]
UPES Ultraviolet Photoelectron Spectroscopy
UPET United Petroleum [*NASDAQ symbol*] (TTSB)
UPET United Petroleum Corp. [*NASDAQ symbol*] (SAG)
UPET Urokinase Pulmonary Embolism Trial
UPEU Uganda Public Employees' Union
UPF Uganda Popular Front [*Political party*] (PD)
UPF Ultrapherical Polynomial Filter (IAA)
UPF Union pour la France [*France Political party*]
UPF United Parkinson Foundation (EA)
UPF United Patriotic Front [*Defunct*] (EA)
UPF United People's Front [*Singapore*] [*Political party*] (PPW)
UPF United People's Front [*Nepal*] [*Political party*] (EY)
UPF Universal Proximal Femur [*Prosthesis*] [*Orthopedics*] (DAVI)
UPF Unofficial Personnel Folder
UPFAW United Packinghouse Food and Allied Workers [*Later, UFCWIU*] (EA)
UPFD United Pesticide Formulators and Distributors Association (EA)
UPFDA United Pesticide Formulators and Distributors Association
UPFF Universal Proutist Farmers Federation (EA)
UPFM Union Progressive des Femmes Marocaines [*Progressive Union of Moroccan Women*]
UPG Ujung Pandang [*Indonesia*] [*Airport symbol*] (OAG)
UPG Union des Populations de Guinee [*Guinea People's Union*] (PD)
UPG Union du Peuple Gabonais [*Political party*] (EY)
UPG Union Progressiste Guineenne [*Guinean Progressive Union*]
UPG United Pacific Gold [*Vancouver Stock Exchange symbol*]
UPG United Parents under God (EA)
UPG Unpaying Guest [*In a rooming or boarding house*]
UPG Upgrade [*Computer science*]
UPG Uroporphyrinogen [*Biochemistry*] (MAE)
UPGMA Unweighted Pair-Group Method with Arithmetic Means [*Phylogenetic analysis*]
UPGRADE University of Pittsburgh Generalized Recording and Dissemination Experiment
UPGRADE User-Prompted Graphic Data Evaluation [*US Council on Environmental Quality*]
UPGS Church of Jesus Christ of Latter-Day Saints, Genealogical Society Library, Utah Valley Branch, Provo, UT [*Library symbol Library of Congress*] (LCLS)
UPGS Unione Progressista della Gioventu Somala [*Progressive Union of Somali Youth*]
UPGWA International Union, United Plant Guard Workers of America (EA)
UPH Unaccompanied Personnel Housing [*Military*]
UPH Underground Pumped Hydro [*Energy storage*]
UPH Union of Platers Helpers [*British*]
UPH Union Patriotique Haitienne [*Haitian Patriotic Union*] (EA)
UPHA United Professional Horsemen's Association (EA)
UPHC United Party of Haitian Communists
UPHCI Undistributed Personal Holding Company Income
UPHD Uphold [*Law*] (ROG)
UPHD Upholstered
UPHEWA United Presbyterian Health, Education, and Welfare Association [*Later, PHEWA*] (EA)
UPHG Upholstering
UPHLR Upholsterer
UPHLSTG Upholstering (WGA)
UPHLSTRNG Upholstering
UPHLSTRY Upholstery
UPHOL Upholstery (WGA)
uphol Upholstry (VRA)
UPHPISEC Union for the Protection of the Human Person by International, Social, and Economic Cooperation [*Defunct*] (EA)
UPHSTR Upholster
UPI Fayetteville/Fort Bragg, NC [*Location identifier FAA*] (FAAL)
UPI United Press International (EA)
UPI Universal Personal Identifier (NITA)
UPI Universal Presentation Interface [*Uniface Corp.*]
UPI Upper Plenum Injection [*Nuclear energy*] (NRCH)
UPI Uteroplacental Insufficiency [*Medicine*]
UPI Uteroplacental Ischemia [*Obstetrics*] (DAVI)
UPIA Underwater Photography Instruction Association [*Defunct*] (EA)
UPIA Uniform Principal and Income Act [*National Conference of Commissioners on Uniform State Laws*]
UPIA United Press International Audio (NTCM)
UPIC Union Property Investors, Inc. [*NASDAQ symbol*] (SAG)
UPIC Universal Personal Identification Code (MHDI)
UPICV Uniao dos Povos das Ilhas do Cabo Verde [*Union of the Peoples of the Cape Verde Islands*]
UPICV-R Uniao do Povo para Independencia de Cabo Verde-Ressusitacao [*Cape Verde*] [*Political party*] (EY)
UPIF Universal Proutist Intellectual Federation (EA)
UPIGO Union Professionnelle Internationale des Gynecologues et Obstetriciens [*International Union of Professional Gynecologists and Obstetricians*]
UPIINS Uniform Procurement Instrument Identification Numbering System (MCD)
UPIN United Press International News-Features (NTCM)
UPIN United Press International Newspictures
UPIR Uniform Photographic Interpretation Report [*Military*] (AFM)
UPIRN United Press International Radio Network (NTCM)
UPITN United Press International Television News (NTCM)
U Pitt University of Pittsburgh (GAGS)
UPIU United Paperworkers International Union (EA)
UPJ Underwater Pump Jet
UPJ Ureteropelvic Junction [*Anatomy*]
UPJ Uteropelvic Junction [*Anatomy*] (DAVI)
UPK United Park City Mines Co. [*NYSE symbol*] (SPSG)
UPK United Park City Mns [*NYSE symbol*] (TTSB)
UPK Unpopped Kernel [*Popcorn*]
UPK Upkeep Period [*Navy*] (NVT)
UPkMn United Park City Mines Co. [*Associated Press*] (SAG)
UPL Unidentified Process Loss
UPL Union Populaire Locale [*Wallis and Futuna Islands*] [*Political party*] (FEA)
UPL Unit Personnel List [*Army*]
UPL Universal Programming Language [*Computer science*] (BUR)
UPL Universal Publications, London [*British*]
UPL Unusual Position of Limbs (DAVI)
UPL Upala [*Costa Rica*] [*Airport symbol Obsolete*] (OAG)
UPL Uplink
UPL Uranium Product Loadout [*Nuclear energy*] (NRCH)
UPL User Programming Language [*Burroughs Corp.*] [*Computer science*] (IEEE)
UPLAC Union des Producteurs de Levure-Aliment de la CEE [*Union of Dried Yeast Producers of the Common Market*]
UPLD Upland [*Plateau, highland*] [*Board on Geographic Names*]
UPLF Universal Payload Fairing [*NASA*] (KSC)
UPLF Universal Proutist Labour Federation (EA)
UPLG Union Populaire pour la Liberation de la Guadeloupe [*Popular Union for the Liberation of Guadeloupe*] (PD)
UPLI United Poets Laureate International (EA)
UPLK Uplink (NASA)
UPLM Uplink Logic Module
UPInt Union Planters Corp. [*Associated Press*] (SAG)
UPIntr Union Planters [*Associated Press*] (SAG)
UPLR Uganda Protectorate Law Reports [*1904-51*] [*A publication*] (DLA)
UPLR United Provinces Law Reports [*India*] [*A publication*] (DLA)
UPLR Unplanned Loss Report [*Navy*] (DNAB)
UPLT United Provinces Law Times [*India*] [*A publication*] (DLA)
UPLV Upper Leg Vein [*Anatomy*]
UPM Pennsylvania State University, University Park, PA [*OCLC symbol*] (OCLC)
UPM Uganda Patriotic Movement (PD)
UPM Ultrapure Metal
UPM Umdrehung per Minuten [*Revolutions per Minute*] [*German*]
UPM Union del Pueblo de Melilla [*Spanish North Africa*] [*Political party*] (MENA)
UPM Union du Peuple Malgache [*Malagasy People's Union*]
UPM Unione Politica Maltese [*Maltese Political Union*] [*Political party*] (PPE)
UPM Union Pontificale Missionnaire [*Pontifical Missionary Union - PMU*] [*Later, PMUPR*]
UPM Union Progressiste Mauritanienne [*Mauritanian Progressive Union*]
UPM Union Progressiste Melanesienne [*New Caledonia*] [*Political party*] (FEA)
UPM United People's Movement [*St. Vincent*] [*Political party*] (PPW)
UPM United People's Movement [*Antigua*] [*Political party*] (PPW)
UPM Unit Production Manager [*Filmmaking*]
UPM Universal Permissive Module [*Nuclear energy*] (IEEE)
UPM Unreached Peoples Mission (EA)
UPMC University of Pittsburgh Medical Center
UPMC Urban Planning Ministers Conference (EERA)

UPMI .... Union Progressiste Melanesienne [*Progressive Melanesian Union*] [*New Caledonia*] [*Political party*] (PPW)
UPMR .... Unit Personnel Management Roster
UPMS .... Under PM Services [*Computer science*] (PCM)
UPN .... Union del Pueblo Navarrese [*Union of the Navarrese People*] [*Spain Political party*] (PPW)
UPN .... Unique Project Number (SSD)
UPN .... United Paramount Network [*Television*]
UPN .... United Paramount Network
UPN .... United Party of Nigeria
UPN .... Uruapan [*Mexico*] [*Airport symbol*] (OAG)
UPNCA .... United Pants and Novelties Contractors Association [*Defunct*] (EA)
UPNE .... University Press of New England
UPNI .... Unionist Party of Northern Ireland [*Political party*] (PPW)
UP (Noth) .... Ueberlieferungsgeschichte des Pentateuch (M. Noth) [*A publication*] (BJA)
UPNS .... Ukrainian Philatelic and Numismatic Society (EA)
UPO .... Undistorted Power Output
UPO .... Unidentified Paleontological Object
UPO .... Unit Personnel Office [*or Officer*] [*Military*]
UPO .... Unstable Periodic Orbit
UPONF .... United Political Organization National Front [*Yemen*] (BARN)
UPOR .... Usual Place of Residence (MAE)
U Portland ... University of Portland (GAGS)
UPORVC ...... Upper Peninsula Off Road Vehicle Committee [*Michigan*]
UPOS .... Utility Program Operating System (IEEE)
UPOV .... International Union for the Protection of New Varieties of Plants (EERA)
UPOV .... Union Internationale pour la Protection des Obtentions Vegetales [*International Union for the Protection of New Varieties of Plants*] (EAIO)
UPP .... Hawi, HI [*Location identifier FAA*] (FAAL)
UPP .... Ultraprecision Parachute (NG)
UPP .... Undeducted Purchase Price
UPP .... UNESCO Publications and Periodicals
UPP .... Union del Pueblo Patriotico [*Ecuador*] [*Political party*] (EY)
UPP .... Unionist Progressive Party [*Egypt*] [*Political party*]
UPP .... United Papermakers and Paperworkers [*Later, UPIU*] (EA)
UPP .... United Peasants' Party [*Poland Political party*] (PD)
UPP .... United People's Party [*Sierra Leone*] [*Political party*]
UPP .... United People's Party [*Grenada*] [*Political party*] (PPW)
UPP .... United Press of Pakistan
UPP .... United Progressive Party [*Trinidad and Tobago*] [*Political party*] (PPW)
UPP .... United Progressive Party [*Zambia*] [*Political party*]
UPP .... Universal Procedure Pointer [*Computer science*]
UPP .... Universal PROM Programmer
UPP .... Universal Proximal Femoral Prosthesis [*Orthopedics*] (DAVI)
UPP .... University of Pennsylvania Press (DGA)
UPP .... University of Pittsburgh Press (DGA)
UPP .... Upolu Point [*Hawaii*] [*Airport symbol*] (OAG)
UPP .... Uppsala [*Sweden*] [*Seismograph station code, US Geological Survey*] (SEIS)
UPP .... Urea (Prilled) in Paper Packets [*Agronomy*]
UPP .... Urethral Pressure Profile [*Urology*] (DAVI)
UPP .... User Parameter Processing (NASA)
UPP .... Utility Print Punch
UPP .... Uvulopalatopharyngoplasty [*Otorhinolaryngology*] (DAVI)
UPP .... Uvulopalatoplasty [*Otorhinolaryngology*] (DAVI)
UPPA .... United People's Party of Arunachal [*India*] [*Political party*] (PPW)
UPPC .... Universal Pin Pack Connector
UPPE .... Ultraviolet Photometric and Polarimetric Explorer
UPPF .... United Presbyterian Peace Fellowship (EA)
UPPI .... Union des Pilotes Professionels Internationaux [*International Professio nal Drivers Union*] [*French*]
UPPN .... Union Postale des Pays du Nord [*Nordic Postal Union - NPU*] (EAIO)
UPPN .... United People's Party of Nigeria
UPPOE .... University of Pittsburgh Production Organization Exercise [*Simulation game*]
UPPP .... Uvulo-Palato-Pharyngoplasty [*Surgical procedure*] [*Initials are derived from the name of the problem the procedure cures*]
UPPR .... Upper
UPPS .... Ultimate Plant Protection System [*Nuclear energy*] (NRCH)
UPPS .... Unified Pilot Publication System [*American Chemical Society*]
UPR .... Ultraportable RADAR (MCD)
UPR .... Ultrasonic Parametric Resonance (IEEE)
UPR .... Ultraviolet Proton Radiation
UPR .... Unearned Premiums Reserve [*Finance*]
UPR .... Uniform Parole Reports [*Law Enforcement Assistance Administration*]
UPR .... Union des Populations Rurales [*Union of Rural People*] [*Lomela-Kasai*]
UPR .... Union Pacific Resources Group [*NYSE symbol*] (TTSB)
UPR .... Union Pacific Resources Group, Inc. [*NYSE symbol*] (SAG)
UPR .... University of Puerto Rico [*Mayaguez, PR*]
UPR .... Unsaturated Polyester Resin [*Organic chemistry*]
UPR .... Upper (AAG)
UPR .... Uranium Production Reactor [*Nuclear energy*]
UPR .... Urethral Profile at Rest [*Medicine*]
UPR .... Utility, Plant, and Reissue [*Patent applications*]
UPrB .... USAir Grp $4.375 Cv Dep Pfd [*NYSE symbol*] (TTSB)
UPRC .... Uranium Policy Review Committee [*Australia*]
UPrE .... College of Eastern Utah, Price, UT [*Library symbol Library of Congress*] (LCLS)
UPREAL .... Unit Property Record and Equipment Authorization List
UPREC .... Upon Receipt
UPREL .... Unit Property Record and Equipment List
UPRG .... Unit Personnel Records Group [*Air Force*] (AFM)
UPRGp .... Unit Personnel Records Group [*Air Force*] (AFM)
UPrGS .... Church of Jesus Christ of Latter-Day Saints, Genealogical Society Library, PriceBranch, Price, UT [*Library symbol Library of Congress*] (LCLS)
UPRI .... Uteroplacental Respiratory Insufficiency [*Gynecology*]
UPRICO .... University of Puerto Rico [*Mayaguez, PR*]
UPROCO ...... Union Progressiste du Congo [*Progressive Union of the Congo*] [*Niangara*]
UPRONA ...... Union pour le Progres National [*Union for National Progress*] [*Burundi*] [*Political party*] (PPW)
UPRP .... Union des Paysans Ruraux et Progressistes [*Union of Rural and Progressive Farmers*] [*Congo-Kasai*]
UPRR .... Union Pacific Railroad Co.
UPS .... Ultraviolet Photoemission Spectroscopy
UPS .... Uncontested Physical Searches [*CIA term for break-ins*]
UPS .... Underground Press Syndicate [*Later, APS*] (EA)
UPS .... Under Provisions of Section [*Military*]
UPS .... Underwater Photographic Society (EA)
UPS .... Uniform Procurement System
UPS .... Uninterruptable Power Source (DAVI)
UPS .... Uninterruptable Power Supply (ACII)
UPS .... Uninterruptable Power Supply (EERA)
UPS .... Uninterruptible AC [*Alternating Current*] Electric Power System (IAA)
UPS .... Uninterruptible Power Supply [*or System*]
UPS .... Union Progressiste Senegalaise [*Senegalese Progressive Union*] [*Political party*] (AF)
UPS .... United Parcel Service
UPS .... United Parcel Service Co. [*ICAO designator*] (FAAC)
UPS .... United Peregrine Society (EA)
UPS .... Unit Personnel Section [*Military*]
UPS .... Unit Price Standards (MCD)
UPS .... Unit Proficiency System (AAG)
UPS .... Universal Plotting Sheet
UPS .... Universal Polar Stereographic Grid
UPS .... Universal Press Syndicate Co.
UPS .... Universal Processing System
UPS .... Universities and Public Schools Battalions [*Military units*] [*World War I*] [*British*]
UPS .... Upper Sideband [*Telecommunications*] (EECA)
UPS .... Upright Perigee Stage [*Aerospace*] (MCD)
UPS .... Urethral Profile under Stress [*Medicine*]
UPS .... Uterine Progesterone System [*Contraceptive device*]
UPSA .... Ukrainian Political Science Association in the United States (EA)
UPSA .... Ukrainian Professional Society of America (EA)
UPSA .... Uniform Program Salary Administration (MCD)
UPSA .... Upper Peninsula Sportsmen's Alliance
UPSD .... Union pour le Progres Social et le Democratie [*The Congo*] [*Political party*] (EY)
UPSF .... Universal Proutist Student Federation (EA)
Upsher-S ..... Upsher-Smith [*Commercial firm*] (DAVI)
UPSI .... User Program Sense Indicator
UPSI .... User Program Switch Indicator [*Computer science*]
UPSIS .... United States Political Science Information Service [*University of Pittsburgh*] (IID)
UPSLP .... Upslope [*NWS*] (FAAC)
UPSN .... University Peace Studies Network (EA)
UPSNET .... United Postal Service Network [*National mobile data network*] [*Proposed*] (ECON)
UPSR .... Unit Proficiency System Requirements (AAG)
UPSS .... Ukrainska Partiia Samostiinykiv-Sotsiialistiv [*Ukrainian Party of Socialist-Independentists*] [*Russian Political party*] (PPE)
UPSS .... United Postal Stationery Society (EA)
UPSSL .... University of Puget Sound School of Law (DLA)
Ups Sto .... Upshur's Review of Story on the Constitution [*A publication*] (DLA)
UPSTAGE ..... Upper-Stage Guidance Experiment
UPSTARS ..... Universal Propulsion Stabilization, Retardation, and Separation [*Air Force*]
UPSTART ..... Universal Parachute Support Tactical and Research Target (NG)
UPSTEP ...... Undergraduated Pre-Service Teacher Education Program [*National Science Foundation*] (EA)
UPSTRM ...... Upstream [*Meteorology*] (FAAC)
UPT .... Undergraduate Pilot Training [*Air Force*]
UPT .... Upgrade Pilot Training
UPT .... Urgent Postal Telegram
UPT .... Urine Pregnancy Test [*Gynecology*] (DAVI)
UPT .... User Process Table
UPT .... US Platinum [*Vancouver Stock Exchange symbol*]
UPTA .... Uniform Perpetuation of Testimony Act [*National Conference of Commissioners on Uniform State Laws*]
UPTA .... United Parent-Teachers Association of Jewish Schools (EA)
UPTAS .... Utility Practical Transport Aircraft System [*Army*]
UPTC .... Union Panafricaine des Travailleurs Croyants [*Pan-African Union of Believing Workers*]
UPTD .... Unit Pulmonary Toxicity Dose [*Deep-sea diving*]
UPTE .... Ultra-Precision Test Equipment (PDAA)
UPTF .... Upper Plenum Test Facility [*Nuclear energy*] (NRCH)
UPT-H .... Undergraduate Pilot Training - Helicopter [*Air Force*]
UPTLM .... Up-Link Telemetry [*NASA*] (NASA)
Upt Mar W ... Upton on Maritime Warfare and Prize [*A publication*] (DLA)
UPTP .... Universal Package Test Panel
UPTS .... Undergraduate Pilot Training System (IAA)
UPTT .... Unit Personnel and Tonnage Table [*Military*] (AABC)
Upt Tr Mar ... Upton on Trade-Marks [*A publication*] (DLA)

UPU .... Union Postale Universelle [*Universal Postal Union*] [*Switzerland Also, an information service or system*] (IID)
UPU .... Universal Postal Union [*United Nations*] (MENA)
UPUC .... Unauthorized Publication or Use of Communications
UPUC .... Universal Postal Union Collectors (EA)
UPUC .... Universal Postal Union Convention
U Puerto Rico... University of Puerto Rico (GAGS)
U Puerto Rico, Mayaguez... University of Puerto Rico, Mayaguez (GAGS)
U Puget Sound... University of Puget Sound (GAGS)
UPUP .... Ulster Popular Unionist Party [*Northern Ireland*] [*Political party*] (PPW)
UPUP .... Ulster Progressive Unionist Party [*Northern Ireland*] [*Political party*] (PPW)
UPUP .... United Payors and United Providers, Inc. [*NASDAQ symbol*] (SAG)
UPUS .... United Public Utility Systems
UPUSA .... UPU [*Universal Postal Union*] Staff Association (EAIO)
U_pV .... Phosphate Excretion Rate [*Laboratory Science*] (DAVI)
UPV .... Unfired Pressure Vessel
UPV .... Universal Pre-Vent, Inc. [*Vancouver Stock Exchange symbol*]
UPV .... Upernavik [*Greenland*] [*Airport symbol*] (AD)
UPVC .... Unfired Pressure Vessel Code (AAG)
UPVC .... Unplasticized Polyvinyl Chloride
UPW .... Union of Post Office Workers [*British*] (DCTA)
UPW .... United Port Workers' Union [*Ceylon*]
UPW .... United Presbyterian Women (EA)
UPW .... United Public Workers of America
UPWA .... Union of Palestinian Women's Association in North America (EA)
UPWA .... Union of Polish Women in America (EA)
UPWA .... United Packinghouse Workers of America [*Later, UFCWIU*]
UPWA .... United Polish Women of America (EA)
UPWARD ..... Understanding Personal and Racial Dignity [*Navy program*]
UPWCA .... United Pest and Weed Control Association [*Australia*]
UPWD .... Upward (MSA)
UPWF .... Ukrainian Patriarchal World Federation (EA)
UPWP .... Unified Planning Work Program
UPWT .... Unitary Plan Wind Tunnel (KSC)
UPX .... Unapix Entertainment [*AMEX symbol*] (TTSB)
UPX .... Unapix Entertainment, Inc. [*AMEX symbol*] (SAG)
UPX.WS.B .... Unapix Enter Cl'B'Wrrt [*AMEX symbol*] (TTSB)
UPY .... Union of People's Youth [*Bulgaria*]
UPYF .... Universal Proutist Youth Federation (EA)
UPz .... Urkunden der Ptolemaerzeit [*U. Wilcken*] [*A publication*] (BJA)
UQ .... Fronte dell'Uomo Qualunque; Uomo Qualunque [*Common Man Front*] [*Italy Political party*] (PPE)
UQ .... Suburban Airlines [*ICAO designator*] (AD)
UQ .... Ubiquinone [*Also, CoQ, Q, U*] [*Biochemistry*]
UQ .... Ultraquick [*Flashing*] Light [*Navigation signal*]
UQ .... United African Airline [*Libya*] [*ICAO designator*] (ICDA)
UQ .... University of Queensland [*State*] (EERA)
UQ .... Upper Quadrant [*Anatomy*]
UQ .... Upper Quadrile
UQAC .... Universite du Quebec a Chicoutimi [*Canada*]
UQAH .... Universite du Quebec a Hull [*Canada*]
UQAM .... Universite du Quebec a Montreal [*Canada*]
UQAR .... Universite du Quebec a Rimouski [*Canada*]
UQB .... Universite de Quebec [*UTLAS symbol*]
UQC .... Underwater Telephone [*Navy*] (CAAL)
UQCP .... Uniform Quality Control Program
UQE .... Queen [*Alaska*] [*Airport symbol Obsolete*] (OAG)
UQGS .... Uniform Quality Grading System [*Tires*]
UQL .... Unacceptable Quality Level
UQM .... Unique Mobility [*AMEX symbol*] (TTSB)
UQM .... Unique Mobility, Inc. [*AMEX symbol*] (SAG)
UQOT .... Unquote (FAAC)
UQP .... Universities and the Quest for Peace [*An association*]
UQP .... University of Queensland Press [*Australia*]
UQS .... Nuiqsut Village, AK [*Location identifier FAA*] (FAAL)
Uqs .... 'Uqsin (BJA)
UQT .... User Queue Table
UQY .... Kansas City, MO [*Location identifier FAA*] (FAAL)
UR .... British International Helicopters [*ICAO designator*] (AD)
UR .... Empire Airlines [*ICAO designator*] (AD)
UR .... Lab. J. Uriach & Cia. SA [*Spain*] [*Research code symbol*]
UR .... Lloyd's Universal Register of Shipping [*British*] (ROG)
UR .... Red Carpet Airlines, Inc. [*ICAO designator*] (ICDA)
UR .... Uganda Rifles [*British military*] (DMA)
UR .... Ukraine [*International civil aircraft marking*] (ODBW)
UR .... Ullage Rocket (KSC)
UR .... Ultrared (IAA)
UR .... Unattended Repeater [*Telecommunications*] (OA)
UR .... Unconditioned Reflex [*Neurology*] (DAVI)
UR .... Unconditioned Response [*Psychometrics*]
U/R .... Underrange (IEEE)
UR .... Underreporter [*IRS*]
UR .... Under Review (MHDB)
UR .... Under the Rule [*Business term*]
UR .... Undulator Radiation [*High-energy physics*]
UR .... Unfinanced Requirement [*Army*] (AABC)
UR .... Unfractionated Reservoir [*Geology*]
UR .... Unfunded Requirement [*Military*] (AFIT)
UR .... Uniao Republicana [*Republican Union*] [*Portugal Political party*] (PPE)
UR .... Unidentified Remittance [*IRS*]
UR .... Uniform Regulations
UR .... Unitatis Redintegratio [*Decree on Ecumenism*] [*Vatican II document*]
UR .... Unit Real (IAA)
UR .... Unit Record [*Computer science*]
UR .... Unit Register
UR .... University of Rochester [*New York*] (KSC)
UR .... University Relations
UR .... Unprogrammed Requirements (MCD)
UR .... Unrelated (AAMN)
UR .... Unreleasable (MCD)
UR .... Unreliable
UR .... Unsatisfactory Report
UR .... Upper Rail
UR .... Upper Respiratory [*Medicine*]
UR .... Upper Right (MCD)
U/R .... Up Range [*NASA*] (KSC)
UR .... Up Right [*The rear right portion of a stage*] [*A stage direction*]
UR .... Uranium (ROG)
UR .... Urban Rat [*Virus*]
Ur .... Urdu [*Language*] (BARN)
UR .... Urgent Requirement (MCD)
UR .... Urinal (MSA)
UR .... Urine
UR .... Urology
Ur .... Uruguay
UR .... User Requirements [*Nuclear energy*] (NRCH)
ur .... USSR [*Union of Soviet Socialist Republics*] [*MARC country of publication code Library of Congress*] (LCCP)
UR .... Utility Room (MSA)
UR .... Utilization Review [*Preferred provider organization*] [*Medicine*]
UR .... Uti Rogas [*Be It as You Desire*] [*Used by Romans to express assent to a proposition*] [*Latin*]
URA .... Ugana Revenue Authority
URA .... Uniformly Redundant Array
URA .... United Red Army [*Japan*] (PD)
URA .... United Republicans of America
URA .... Universities Research Association (EA)
URA .... Upper Respiratory Allergy [*Medicine*]
Ura .... Uracil [*Biochemistry*]
URA .... Urakawa [*Japan*] [*Seismograph station code, US Geological Survey*] (SEIS)
URA .... Uralinteravia [*Russian Federation*] [*ICAO designator*] (FAAC)
Ura .... Urania [*Record label*] [*USA, Europe, etc.*]
URA .... Uranium Recycle Acid [*Nuclear energy*] (NRCH)
URA .... Urban Redevelopment Authority
URA .... Urban Renewal Administration [*of HHFA*] [*Terminated*]
URA .... Urine Receptacle Assembly [*NASA*] (MCD)
URA .... User Range Accuracy (SSD)
URA .... User Requirements Analysis
URA .... Utilization Review Agency [*Insurance*]
URAC .... Union des Republiques de l'Afrique Centrale [*Union of Central African Republics*]
URACTY .... Your Activity
URAD .... Unit for Research on Addictive Drugs [*University of Aberdeen*] [*British*] (IRUK)
URAEP .... University of Rochester Atomic Energy Project
URAF .... Unidentified Remittance Amount File [*IRS*]
URAI .... Universities Research Association, Inc.
URAM .... Association of Concern for Ultimate Reality & Meaning (AC)
URAM .... Unrelated Adult Man
Uran .... Uranus [*Astronomy*] (BARN)
ur anal .... Urine Analysis [*or Urinalysis*] [*Urology*] (DAVI)
UR & M .... Urinalysis-Routine and Microscopic [*Urology*] (DAVI)
UranRes ...... Uranium Resources, Inc. [*Associated Press*] (SAG)
URAPA .... Uniform Rendition of Accused Persons Act [*National Conference of Commissioners on Uniform State Laws*]
URARPAA .... Uniform Relocation Assistance and Real Property Acquisition Act [*1970*] (OICC)
URARPAPA... Uniform Relocation Assistance and Real Property Acquisition Policies Act of 1970
URARRED .... US Army Readiness Command (MCD)
URAS .... Union des Republicains d'Action Sociale [*Union of Republicans of Social Action*] [*France Political party*] (PPE)
URAUZ .... You Are Authorized (FAAC)
URAW .... Unrelated Adult Woman
URB .... Union Regionale de Bamileke [*Regional Union of Bamileke*] [*Cameroon*]
URB .... Unridable Bicycle
URB .... Urban
URB .... Urbana College, Urbana, OH [*OCLC symbol*] (OCLC)
URB .... Urbanization
URB .... Urban Shopping Centers [*NYSE symbol*] (SPSG)
URB .... Urubupunga [*Brazil*] [*Airport symbol*] (OAG)
Urb Aff Rep... Urban Affairs Reporter [*Commerce Clearing House*] [*A publication*] (DLA)
URBAMET .... Urbanisme, Amenagement, Equipments, et Transports [*Reseau URBAMET*] [*France Information service or system*] (CRD)
Urban Ed ..... Urban Education [*A publication*] (BRI)
URBANICOM... Association Internationale Urbanisme et Commerce [*International Association for Town Planning and Distribution*] (EAIO)
URBANK ...... Urban Development Bank
Urban Law Ann... Urban Law Annual [*A publication*] (ILCA)
Urban LJ ...... University of Detroit. Journal of Urban Law [*A publication*] (DLA)
Urban L Rev... Urban Law Review [*A publication*] (DLA)
URBC .... Uninfected Red Blood Cells [*Hematology*]
URBCOM ...... [*The*] Urban Communications Game
URBED .... Urban and Economic Development Ltd. (AIE)

Urb For........ Urban Forests [*A publication*]
URBK......... Union Rheinische Braunkohlen Kraftstoff [*West Germany*]
Urblaw......... Urban Law and Policy [*A publication*] (ILCA)
URBM......... Ultimate Range Ballistic Missile [*Air Force*]
URBN......... Urban Outfitters, Inc. [*NASDAQ symbol*] (SAG)
URBN......... Urban Outfittlers [*NASDAQ symbol*] (TTSB)
UrbnOut....... Urban Outfitters, Inc. [*Associated Press*] (SAG)
UrbnShp...... Urban Shopping Centers [*Associated Press*] (SAG)
URBOE......... Ultimatist Religious Bodies on Earth (EA)
URBPOP...... Urban Population File (MCD)
URC............ Uganda Railways Corp. (DCTA)
URC............ Ultrasonic Resin Cleaner [*Nuclear energy*] (NRCH)
URC............ Undersea Research Corp.
URC............ Uniform Resistance Capacitance [*Electronics*] (IAA)
URC............ Uniform Resource Characteristic [*Computer science*] (EERA)
URC............ Uniform Resource Citations [*Computer science*]
URC............ Uniform Rules for Collections
URC............ Union de Rassemblement et du Centre [*France Political party*] (ECON)
URC............ Union des Republicains du Cameroun [*Political party*] (EY)
URC............ Union du Rassemblement du Centre [*Mayotte*] [*Political party*] (EY)
URC............ United Racing Club [*Auto racing*]
URC............ United Ratepayers' Campaign [*British*] (BI)
URC............ United Reform Church [*Australia*]
URC............ United Reform Church in England and Wales
URC............ Unit Record Card
URC............ Unit Record Control
URC............ University Research Centre [*British*]
URC............ Upper Rib Cage [*Anatomy*]
URC............ Upper Right Center (WGA)
URC............ Ursuline College Library, Pepper Pike, OH [*OCLC symbol*] (OCLC)
URC............ Urumqi [*China*] [*Airport symbol*] (OAG)
URC............ Utility Radio Communication
URC............ Utilization Review Committee [*Medical records*] (DAVI)
URC A......... Uric Acid [*Laboratory science*] (DAVI)
URCC.......... University of Rochester Cancer Center [*Research center*] (RCD)
URCE.......... Union Restaurants Collectifs Europeens [*European Catering Association*] [*Germany*] (EAIO)
URCF.......... Unidentified Remittance Control File [*IRS*]
URCG.......... Uniform Rules for Contract Guarantees
URCLK......... Universal Receiver Clock
URCO.......... Union des Ressortissants du Congo pour la Defense et la Promotion du Congo [*Union of Congolese for the Defense and Promotion of the Congo*]
URCOT......... Urban Research Centre on Office Technology [*Australia*]
URCRM......... Urals Research Center for Radiation Medicine [*Russia*]
URCS.......... Uniform Railroad Cost System [*BTS*] (TAG)
URCS.......... Uniform Ration Cost System (MCD)
URC SP........ Uric Acid-Urine Spot [*test*] [*Laboratory science*] (DAVI)
URD............ New York, NY [*Location identifier FAA*] (FAAL)
URD............ Underground Residential Distribution [*Cable*]
URD............ Underground Rural Distribution (IAA)
URD............ Union Republicana Democratica [*Democratic Republican Union*] [*Puerto Rico, Venezuela*]
URD............ Unit Reference Designation [*Army*]
URD............ Upper Respiratory Disease [*Medicine*]
urd............ Urdu [*MARC language code Library of Congress*] (LCCP)
Urd............ Uridine [*Also, U*] [*A nucleoside*]
URD............ User Requirements Document (MCD)
URDA.......... Uniform Retirement Date Act [*National Conference of Commissioners on Uniform State Laws*]
URDA.......... Urban Resources Development Agency (OICC)
URDIS......... Your Dispatch [*Military*]
URDP.......... Ukrains'ka Revoliutsiino-Demokratychna Partiia
URDS.......... Unexplained Respiratory Distress Syndrome [*Medicine*]
URDS.......... Unknown Respiratory Stress Syndrome [*Medicine*]
URDS.......... User Requirements Data Base (MHDB)
URDU.......... Urban Regional Development Unit (EERA)
URE............ Undergraduate Record Examination [*Education*]
URE............ Unintentional Radiation Exploitation (AFM)
URE............ User Range Error
UREA.......... Urea Nitrogen [*Laboratory science*] (DAVI)
UREBA......... Union Revolutionnaire des Banques [*Burkina Faso*] (EY)
URED.......... Unable to Read [*Laboratory science*] (DAVI)
U Redlands... University of Redlands (GAGS)
UREHE......... Union for Research and Experimentation in Higher Education [*Later, UECU*]
UREKA......... Unlimited Resources Ensure Keen Answers
UREP.......... Unit Representative [*Military*] (INF)
UREP.......... University Research Expeditions Programs
URES.......... University Residence Environment Scale [*Student attitudes test*]
URESA......... Uniform Reciprocal Enforcement of Support Act
U-REST........ Universal Range, Endurance, Speed, and Time (NG)
ureth.......... Urethra [*Anatomy*]
Urethane...... Urethane Technologies, Inc. [*Associated Press*] (SAG)
URF............ Relaxin [*Medicine*] (DAVI)
URF............ Ukrainian Research Foundation [*Defunct*] (EA)
URF............ Unassigned Reading Frame [*Genetics*]
URF............ Unidentified Reading Frame [*Genetics*]
URF............ Unidentified Remittance File [*IRS*]
URF............ Union des Services Routiers des Chemins de Fer Europeens [*Union of European Railways Road Services*]
URF............ United Religious Front [*Israel*] (BJA)
URF............ United Republican Fund
URF............ Urfa [*Turkey*] [*Airport symbol*] (AD)
URF............ Uterine-Relaxing Factor [*Endocrinology*]
URFDA-NYC... United Retail Fish Dealers Association of New York City (EA)
UR-FST........ Urine - Fasting [*Urology*] (DAVI)
URG............ Air Urga [*Ukraine*] [*FAA designator*] (FAAC)
URG............ Underway Replenishment Group [*Military*]
URG............ United Rayore Gas [*Vancouver Stock Exchange symbol*]
URG............ Unit Review Group [*Nuclear energy*] (NRCH)
URG............ Universal Radio Group
URG............ Urban Regeneration Grant [*British*]
URG............ Urgent (AFM)
URG............ Urheberrechtsgesetz [*German Copyright Act*] (DLA)
URG............ Uruguaiana [*Brazil*] [*Airport symbol*] (OAG)
URGENT....... Universal Relevance Group Enterprise in a National Theater [*Theater workshop*]
URGI........... United Retail Group [*NASDAQ symbol*] (TTSB)
URGI........... United Retail Group, Inc. [*NASDAQ symbol*] (SAG)
URGNSW..... Underwater Research Group of New South Wales [*Australia*]
URGR........... Underway Replenishment Group [*Military*]
URHB........... Urban Renewal Handbook
U Rhode Island... University of Rhode Island (GAGS)
UR#HR......... Urine - Number of Hours/Glucose Tolerance [*The symbol is replaced with the correct numeral*] [*Endocrinology*] (DAVI)
URi............. Richmond City Library, Richmond, UT [*Library symbol Library of Congress*] (LCLS)
URI............. Unexpected Real Incapacitation (DNAB)
URI............. Uniform Resource Identifier [*Computer science*] (EERA)
URI............. Unintentional RADAR Interference (IAA)
URI............. Union Research Institute, Kowloon, Hong Kong [*Library symbol Library of Congress*] (LCLS)
URI............. United Research, Inc.
URI............. Universite Radiophonique Internationale [*International University of the Air*] (NTCM)
URI............. University of Rhode Island
URI............. University of Rhode Island, Kingston (USDC)
URI............. University Research Initiative [*DoD*] (RDA)
URI............. Unpublished Research Information [*Conducted by National Science Foundation*]
uri............. Unrelated (DAVI)
URI............. Upper Respiratory Infection [*Medicine*]
URI............. Upper-Respiratory-Tract Infection [*Medicine*] (DAVI)
URI............. Uranium Resources, Inc. [*Vancouver Stock Exchange symbol*]
URI............. Uribe [*Colombia*] [*Airport symbol Obsolete*] (OAG)
URI............. Utility Read-In Program (IAA)
URIA........... Universal Real-Time Information and Administration
URICA......... Universal Real-Time Information Control and Administration (MCD)
URICA......... University of Rhode Island Computer Access [*University of Rhode Island Library*] (OLDSS)
URICA......... Using Reading in Creative Activities
U Rich LN.... University of Richmond. Law Notes [*A publication*] (DLA)
U Richmond... University of Richmond (GAGS)
URifGS......... Church of Jesus Christ of Latter-Day Saints, Genealogical Society Library, Richfield Branch, Richfield, UT [*Library symbol Library of Congress*] (LCLS)
URII............ Ukrainian Research and Information Institute [*Defunct*] (EA)
URiL............ Richmond City Library, Richmond, UT [*Library symbol*] [*Library of Congress*] (LCLS)
URIMA......... University Risk and Insurance Managers Association [*Later, URMIA*] (EA)
URIN........... Random Urine [*Urology*] (DAVI)
URINT......... Unintentional Radiation Intelligence (MCD)
URIPS......... Undersea Radioisotope Power Supply
URIR........... Unified Radioactive Isodromic Regulator
URIS........... Urban and Regional Information System
URISA......... American Urban and Regional Information Systems Association (EERA)
URISA......... Urban and Regional Informations Systems Association
URISA......... Urban and Regional Information Systems Association (EA)
URIX........... Uranium Resources [*NASDAQ symbol*] (TTSB)
URIX........... Uranium Resources, Inc. [*NASDAQ symbol*] (NQ)
URIZR......... Your Recommendation is Requested (FAAC)
URJA........... United Roumanian Jews of America (EA)
Urk............. Urkunde [*Document, Deed, Instrument*] [*German*] (ILCA)
Urk............. Urkunden des Aegyptischen Altertums [*G. Steindorff*] [*Leipzig*] [*A publication*] (BJA)
URKK........... Krasnodar [*Former USSR ICAO location identifier*] (ICLI)
URL............. Uniform Resource Locator [*Telecommunications*]
URL............. Universal Reference Locator
URL............. Universal [*or Uniform*] Resource Locator [*Computer science*]
URL............. Universal Resource Locator [*Telecommunication*]
URL............. University of Regina Library [*UTLAS symbol*]
URL............. Unrequited Love [*Slang*]
URL............. Unrestricted Line Officer [*Navy*]
URL............. Upper Reference Limit [*Analytical chemistry*]
URL............. Uralavialy [*Russian Federation*] [*ICAO designator*] (FAAC)
URL............. User Requirements Language [*Computer science*]
URLA........... Uniform Reciprocal Licensing Act [*State law*] [*Insurance*]
Url Cl.......... Urling's Legal Guide for the Clergy [*A publication*] (DLA)
Url For Pat.... Urling on Foreign Patents [*A publication*] (DLA)
Url Trust...... Urling on the Office of a Trustee [*A publication*] (DLA)
URM............ Uncle Remus Museum (EA)
URM............ Uniform Reflectivity Mirror (PDAA)
URM............ University Reform Movement [*in Latin America*]
URM............ Unlimited Register Machine
URM............ Urban Renewal Manual
URM............ Uriman [*Venezuela*] [*Airport symbol*] (OAG)

URMD Uromed Corp. [*NASDAQ symbol*] (SAG)
URMIA University Risk Management and Insurance Association [*Madison, WI*] (EA)
URMIS Uniform Retail Meat Identity Standard [*Pronounced "er-miss"*]
URMK Kislovodsk [*Former USSR ICAO location identifier*] (ICLI)
UR M-L Uniao Revolucionaria, Marxista-Leninista [*Marxist-Leninist Revolutionary Union*] [*Portugal Political party*] (PPE)
URMM Mineralnye Vody [*Former USSR ICAO location identifier*] (ICLI)
URMS Universal Reproducing Matrix System (PDAA)
URN Covington/Cincinnati, OH [*Location identifier FAA*] (FAAL)
URN Turan Air [*Azerbaijan*] [*FAA designator*] (FAAC)
URN Ultrahigh Radio Navigation (NATG)
URN Uniform Random Numerator [*Computer science*]
URN Uniform Resource Name [*Computer science*] (EERA)
URN Uniform Resource Names [*Computer science*]
URN Union pour la Reconciliation Nationale [*Haiti*] [*Political party*] (EY)
URN Unique Record Number [*Computer science*] (ADA)
URN Unique Reference Number [*Customs*] (DS)
URN Urine (NASA)
URNF Unidentified Remittance Name File [*IRS*]
URNG Unidad Revolucionaria Nacional Guatemalteca [*Guatemalan National Revolutionary Unity*] [*Political party*] (PD)
URNM Uranium
URO United Restitution Organization
URO United Rink Operators [*Defunct*] (EA)
URO UROHEALTH Systems'A'(New) [*AMEX symbol*] (TTSB)
URO UROHEALTH Systems, Inc. [*AMEX symbol*] (SAG)
URO Urology
URO Urology
URO Uroporphyrin [*Biochemistry*]
URO Uroporphyrinogen [*Biochemistry*]
URO User Readout (MCD)
URO Ustredni Rada Odboru [*Central Council of Trade Unions*] [*Czechoslovakia*]
URO-2H Urobilinogen-2 Hour [*Gastroenterology*] (DAVI)
UROBA United Russian Orthodox Brotherhood of America (EA)
UROBIL Urobilinogen [*Medicine*] (DAVI)
UROC United Railroad Operating Crafts [*Defunct*]
U Rochester University of Rochester (GAGS)
UroCor UroCor, Inc. [*Associated Press*] (SAG)
UROEA UNESCO Regional Office for Education in Asia and Oceania [*Thailand*] (DLA)
uro-gen Urogenital [*Medicine*] (CPH)
UROGEN Uroporphyrinogen [*Biochemistry*]
Urohlt UROHEALTH Systems, Inc. [*Associated Press*] (SAG)
Urohlth UROHEALTH Systems, Inc. [*Associated Press*] (SAG)
UROL Urology
UROLA UNEP [*United Nations Environmental Programme*] Regional Office for Latin America (EAIO)
Urologix Urologix, Inc. [*Associated Press*] (SAG)
Uromed Uromed Corp. [*Associated Press*] (SAG)
UROP Undergraduate Research Opportunities Program [*Pronounced "your-op"*] [*Massachusetts Institute of Technology*]
UROQ UroQuest Medical Corp. [*NASDAQ symbol*] (SAG)
UroQst UroQuest Medical Corp. [*Associated Press*] (SAG)
UROS Uroporphyrinogen I Synthase [*An enzyme*]
URP Undergraduate Research Participation [*National Science Foundation project*] [*Defunct*] (EA)
URP Underreporter Program [*IRS*]
URP Union Republicaine du Peuple [*Benin*] [*Political party*] (EY)
URP Unique Radiolytic Product [*Food technology*]
URP United Reef Petroleums Ltd. [*Toronto Stock Exchange symbol*]
URP Unit Record Processor
URP University of Rochester, Department of Physics
URP Unmanned Recovery Platform [*Navy*] (NVT)
URP Upper-Stage Reusable Payload
URP Urban Renewal Project [*HUD*] (OICC)
URPC User Level Remote Procedure Call [*Computer science*]
URPE Union des Resistants pour une Europe Unie [*Union of Resistance Veterans for a United Europe*]
URPE Union for Radical Political Economics (EA)
URPE Union Revolucionaria Popular Ecuatoriana [*Ecuadorean Popular Revolutionary Union*] [*Political party*] (PPW)
URPG President's Urban and Regional Policy Group [*Terminated, 1978*] (EGAO)
URPIS Urban and Regional Planning Information Systems (EERA)
URPP Undergraduate Research Participation Program [*Formerly, URP*] (EA)
URQ Unsatisfactory Report Questionnaire
URQ Upper Right Quadrant [*Medicine*]
URR Ultra-Rapid Reader [*Computer science*]
URR Ultrareliable RADAR (MCD)
URR Unconstrained Requirements Report [*Army*]
URR Union Railroad Co. [*Pittsburgh, PA*] [*AAR code*]
URR United Redford Resources, Inc. [*Vancouver Stock Exchange symbol*]
URR Unit Readiness Report [*Army*] (AABC)
URR Universities Research Reactor [*British*]
URR Upstream Regulatory Region [*Genetics*]
URR Urea Reduction Ratio
URR Urrao [*Colombia*] [*Airport symbol*] (OAG)
URR Utilization Research Report
URRC Urological Rehabilitation and Research Center [*University of Alabama in Birmingham*] [*Research center*] (RCD)
URRM Morozovsk [*Former USSR ICAO location identifier*] (ICLI)
URRR Rostov-Na-Donu [*Former USSR ICAO location identifier*] (ICLI)
URS Ugurusu [*Japan*] [*Seismograph station code, US Geological Survey*] (SEIS)
URS Ultrasonic Renal Scanning [*Nephrology*] (DAVI)
URS Unate Ringe Sum [*Logic expression*] (IEEE)
Urs Underwriters [*Insurance*]
URS UNESCO Relations Staff
URS Uniformly Reflexive Structure (IAA)
URS Uniform Reporting System
URS Union of Railway Signalmen [*British*]
URS United Research Service (MCD)
URS Unit Readiness System
URS Unit Reference Sheet [*Military*] (AABC)
URS Universal Reference System
URS Universal Regulating System
URS University Research Support [*Department of Energy*]
URS Unmanned Repeater Station [*Telecommunications*] (OA)
URS Update Report System (TEL)
URS Urban Resource Systems (EA)
URS URS Corp. [*NYSE symbol*] (SPSG)
URS Ursinus College, Collegeville, PA [*OCLC symbol*] (OCLC)
URS User Readout Simulator [*Army*]
URS Utilization Reporting System (MCD)
URSA United Russia Societies Association [*London*]
URSA Unit Replacement System Analysis [*Military*]
URSA Urban and Rural Systems Associates
URSI Union Radio Scientifique Internationale [*International Union of Radio Science*] [*Also, ISRU*] [*Belgium*]
URSI Union Radio Scientifique Internationale (EERA)
URSIES Ultravariable Resolution Single Interferometer Echelle Scanner (PDAA)
URSNSC Union Regionale des Syndicats du Nyong-et-Sanaga
URSP Universal RADAR Signal Processor
URSS Sochi [*Former USSR ICAO location identifier*] (ICLI)
URSS Union des Republiques Socialistes Sovietiques [*Union of Socialist Soviet Republics; USSR*]
URSTM Unite de Recherche et de Service en Technologie Minerale de l'Abitibi-Temiscamingue [*University of Quebec at Abitibi-Temiscamingue*] [*Canada Research center*] (RCD)
URSW Union Regionale des Syndicats du Wouri [*Regional Union of Wouri Unions*]
URT Surat Thani [*Thailand*] [*Airport symbol*] (OAG)
URT Unit Recruit Training [*Army*] (AABC)
URT Universal RADAR Tracker
URT University Research and Training [*Programs*]
URT Upper Respiratory Tract [*Medicine*]
URT Upright (MSA)
Urt Urteil [*Judgment, Decision*] [*German*] (ILCA)
URT Utility Radio Transmitter
URTA University Resident Theatre Association (EA)
URTH Unreasonable Risk to Health [*Drinking water standards*] [*Environmental Protection Agency*]
URTI Universite Radiophonique et Televisuelle Internationale [*International Radio-Television University*]
URTI Upper Respiratory Tract Infection [*Medicine*]
URTIA Uniform Rights of the Terminally Ill Act [*National Conference of Commissioners on Uniform State Laws*]
UR-TIM Urine-Time [*Urology*] (DAVI)
URTNA Union des Radio-Televisions Nationales Africaines [*African National Radio-Television Union*] (AF)
URTRO Unloaded Radial Tire Run-Out
URTU United Road Transport Union [*British*] (DCTA)
URTWAE United Road Transport Workers' Association of England [*A union*]
URU Uruguay
Uru Uruguay (VRA)
URUC UNCTAD [*United Nations Conference on Trade and Development*] Reference UnitCatalogue [*Information service or system*] (DUND)
URV Undersea Research Vehicle [*or Vessel*]
URV Uraiavia [*Former USSR*] [*FAA designator*] (FAAC)
URVD Unilateral Renovascular Disease [*Nephrology*] (DAVI)
UR VOL Urine Volume [*Urology*] (DAVI)
URW Ultrasonic Ring Welder
URW United Racquetsports for Women (EA)
URW United Rubber, Cork, Linoleum, and Plastic Workers of America (EA)
URW Ural [*Former USSR*] [*FAA designator*] (FAAC)
URWA United Railroad Workers of America
URWC Urinal Water Closet (MSA)
URWRO Unloaded Radial Wheel Run-Out
URY Century Aviation, SA de CV [*Mexico*] [*FAA designator*] (FAAC)
URY Gurayat [*Saudi Arabia*] [*Airport symbol*] (OAG)
URY Union Railway of Memphis [*AAR code*]
URY Uruguay [*ANSI three-letter standard code*] (CNC)
URZ Uroozgan [*Afghanistan*] [*Airport symbol Obsolete*] (OAG)
US Luminosity (WDMC)
US Ubi Supra [*In the Place Mentioned Above*] [*Latin*]
US Ultrasonic (AAMN)
US Ultrasonic Spectroscopy
US Ultrasonography (DAVI)
US Ultrasound
U/S Unassorted (ROG)
US Uncle Sam
US Unconditional Selection
US Unconditional Stop (IAA)
US Unconditional Surrender
US Unconditioned Stimulus [*Psychometrics*]
US Underlying Stock [*Finance*]

US............ Under Secretary
U/S............ Underside
US............ Undersize (AAG)
US............ Underspeed (MSA)
US............ Underwater-to-Surface (IAA)
US............ Underwriters' Special Request
US............ Undistorted Signal (IAA)
US............ Uniform System
US............ Union Settlement Association (EA)
US............ Unitary Symmetry (MCD)
US............ United Serpents (EA)
US............ United Service
US............ United Sisters [*Defunct*] (EA)
US............ United States [*ANSI two-letter standard code*]
us............ United States [*MARC country of publication code Library of Congress*] (LCCP)
US............ United States
US............ United States Reports [*A publication*] (NTCM)
US............ United States Supreme Court Reports [*A publication*] (DLA)
US............ United States Supreme Court Reports [*A publication*] (AAGC)
US............ Unites States of America [*IYRU nationality code*] (IYR)
US............ Unit Secretary (MEDA)
US............ Unit Separator [*Control character*] [*Computer science*]
US............ Universal Service [*News agency*]
US............ Unknown Significance
US............ Unlike-Sexed
US............ Unregistered Stock [*Finance*]
US............ Unserviceable
U/S............ Unsorted
US............ Update State [*Online database field identifier*]
US............ Upper Stage (MCD)
US............ Uprighting Subsystem [*NASA*] (KSC)
US............ Up Stage [*Away from audience*] [*A stage direction*]
US............ Upstream (NTCM)
US............ USair Express [*ICAO designator*] (AD)
US............ US Ammunition Co. [*Vancouver Stock Exchange symbol*]
US............ Useless
US............ User Segment (SSD)
US............ US Supreme Court Reports (GPO)
US............ Uterine Stroma
US............ Utility Satellite (IAA)
us............ Ut Supra [*As Above*] [*Latin*] (WGA)
US 1 Inds.... US One Industries, Inc. [*Formerly, Transcom, Inc.*] [*Associated Press*] (SAG)
US3............ Unit Self-Sufficiency System (MCD)
USA............ INFO-DOC [*ACCORD*] [*UTLAS symbol*]
USA............ Liberty ALL-STAR Eqty [*NYSE symbol*] (TTSB)
USA............ Liberty All-Star Equity [*NYSE symbol*] (SPSG)
USA............ Ukiyo-E Society of America (EA)
USA............ Ullage Simulation Assembly (MCD)
USA............ Ultrasonic Agitation
USA............ Ultrastable Arc Lamp
USA............ Ultraviolet Spectral Analysis
USA............ Underwater Society of America (EA)
USA............ Underwriters Service Association
USA............ Unicycling Society of America [*Later, USA, Inc.*] (EA)
USA............ Uniform Sales Act [*Legal shorthand*] (LWAP)
USA............ Union of South Africa
USA............ Union Syndicale de l'Agriculture [*Union of Agricultural Workers*] [*Morocco*]
USA............ United Savers Association (EA)
USA............ United Scenic Artists (EA)
USA............ United Secularists of America (EA)
USA............ United Seniors Association, Inc.
USA............ United Shareholders Association (EA)
USA............ United Shareowners of America [*Defunct*] (EA)
USA............ United Shoppers Association
USA............ United Sidecar Association [*Later, USCA*] (EA)
USA............ United Soccer Association [*Later, NASL*]
USA............ United Socialist Alliance [*Sri Lanka*] [*Political party*]
USA............ United Spoilers of America [*Later, MERCPAC*] (EA)
USA............ United Sprint Association (EA)
USA............ United States [*ANSI three-letter standard code*]
USA............ United States Army
USA............ United States Attorney (EPA)
USA............ United States Automobile Association, San Antonio, TX [*OCLC symbol*] (OCLC)
USA............ United States of ACORN [*Publication of the Association of Community Organizations for Reform Now*]
USA............ United States of America
USA............ United States of America
USA............ United Steelworkers of America
USA............ United Stockcar Alliance [*Auto racing*]
USA............ United Student Aid Funds (EA)
USA............ United Students for America [*Defunct*] (EA)
USA............ United Support of Artists [*In USA for Africa, the chorus of American pop stars who recorded "We Are the World" to benefit famine victims in Africa*]
USA............ United Synagogue of America (EA)
USA............ Unit Services Assistant [*Administration*] (DAVI)
USA............ Unity for Safe Airtravel [*Program of Air Line Pilots Association*]
USA............ Universal Subject Access [*Librarianship*]
USA............ Unix Systems Association [*Defunct*] (EA)
USA............ Unsegmented Storage Analyzer [*Instrumentation*]
USA............ Urban Sanitary Authority [*British*]
USA............ US Air [*ICAO designator*] (FAAC)
USA............ Utility Shareholders Association (EA)
USAA.......... United Specialty Agents Alliance [*Also known as USA Alliance*] (EA)
USAA.......... United States Academy of Arms [*Defunct*] (EA)
USAA.......... United States Arbitration Act [*A publication*] (DLA)
USAA.......... United States Arbitration Act (AAGC)
USAA.......... United States Armor Association (EA)
USAA.......... United States Athletes Association (EA)
USAA.......... US Albacore Association (EA)
USAA.......... US Armbrust Association (EA)
USAA.......... US Armor Association (EA)
USAAA........ United States Army Audit Agency
USAAA........ US Amputee Athletic Association (EA)
USAAAVS..... United States Army Agency for Aviation Safety [*Formerly, USABAAR*] (AABC)
USAAAWR... United States Army Audit Agency, Washington Region
USAAB......... United States Army Aviation Board
USAABELCTBD... United States Army Airborne and Electronics Board [*Later, USAAESWBD*]
USA/ABF...... USA Amateur Boxing Federation (EA)
USAABMDA... United States Army Advanced Ballistic Missile Defense Agency (AABC)
USAABMU.... United States Army Aircraft Base Maintenance Unit (AABC)
USAABNAELCTBD... United States Army Airborne and Electronics Board (IAA)
USAABNSOTBD... United States Army Airborne and Special Operations Test Board (GFGA)
USAAC......... United States Army Administration Center [*Obsolete*] (AABC)
USAAC......... United States Army Air Corps
USAAC......... United States Army Aviation Center [*Fort Rucker*]
USAACDA...... United States Army Aviation Combat Developments Agency [*CDC*]
USAACEBD... United States Army Airborne Communications and Electronics Board
USAACS....... United States Army Armor Center and School
USAADASCH... United States Army Air Defense Artillery School
USAADAT..... United States Army Alcohol and Drug Abuse Team Training (MCD)
USAADB....... United States Army Air Defense Board
USAADCEN... United States Army Air Defense Center
USAADCENFB... United States Army Air Defense Center and Fort Bliss (AABC)
USAADCS.... United States Army Air Defense Center and School
USAADEA..... United States Army Air Defense Engineering Agency [*Formerly, USASADEA*] [*AEC*]
USAADMAC... United States Army Aeronautical Depot Maintenance Center
USAADS....... United States Army Air Defense School (AABC)
USAADTA..... United States Army Aircraft Development Test Activity
USAADTC..... United States Army Armor and Desert Training Center
USAADVCOM... United States Army Advance Command
USAAEFA..... United States Army Aviation Engineering Flight Activity [*Edwards Air Force Base, CA*]
USAAESWBD... United States Army Airborne, Electronics, and Special Warfare Board (AABC)
USAAF......... United States Army Air Forces
USAAFIME.... United States Army Air Forces in the Middle East
USAAFINO... United States Army Aviation Flight Information and Nav-Aids Office (AABC)
USAAFIO...... United States Army Aviation Flight Information Office
USAAFO....... United States Army Avionics Field Office [*Formerly, USASAFO*]
USAAFUK..... United States Army Air Forces in the United Kingdom
USAAGAR.... United States Army Advisor Group O - Army Reserve (AABC)
USAAGCDA... United States Army Adjutant General Combat Developments Agency (SAA)
USAAGDPSC... United States Army Adjutant General Data Processing Service Center (AABC)
USAAGNG.... United States Army Advisory Group (National Guard) (AABC)
USAAGPC.... United States Army Adjutant General Publications Center
USAAGS....... United States Army Adjutant General's School (AABC)
USAALS....... United States Army Aviation Logistics School (INF)
USAAMA...... United States Army Advent Management Agency (MUGU)
USAAMC...... United States Army Aeromedical Center
USAAMC...... United States Army Artillery and Missile Center
USAAMCCOM... United States Army Armament, Munitions, and Chemical Command
USAAML...... United States Army Aviation Materiel Laboratories
USAAMRDC... United States Army Air Mobility Research and Development Center
USAAMRDL... United States Army Air Mobility Research and Development Laboratory [*Also, AMR& DL, USAAMR & DL*]
USAAMS...... United States Army Artillery and Missile School [*Later, Field Artillery School*]
USAAPDT..... United States Army Aviation Precision Demonstration Team (AABC)
USAAPSA..... United States Army Ammunition Procurement and Supply Agency
USAARC...... United States Antiaircraft Replacement Center
USAARCOM... United States Army Armament Command
USAARDC.... United States Army Aberdeen Research and Development Center
USAARDEC... United States Army Armament Research Development and Engineering Center
USAARENBD... United States Army Armor and Engineer Board (AABC)
USAARL....... United States Army Aeromedical Research Laboratory [*Ft. Rucker, AL*] (AABC)
USAARMA.... United States Assistant Army Attache
USAARMBD... United States Army Armor Board
USAARMC... United States Army Armor Center [*Fort Knox, KY*]
USAARMHRU... United States Army Armor Human Research Unit [*Fort Knox, KY*] (AABC)
USAARMS.... United States Army Armor School
USAARTYBD... United States Army Artillery Board
USAARTYCDA... United States Army Artillery Combat Developments (SAA)
USAARU...... United States Army Aeromedical Research Unit

USAAS .... United States Army Air Services [*World War II*]
USAAS .... United States Army Armor Signals (IAA)
USAASC .... United States Army Air Service Command
USAASCFBH... United States Army Administrative School Center and Fort Benjamin Harrison (AABC)
USAASD .... United States Army Aeronautical Services Detachment
USAASD-E ... United States Army Aeronautical Services Detachment, Europe (AABC)
USAASD-LA... United States Army Aeronautical Services Detachment, Latin America (AABC)
USAASD-PAC... United States Army Aeronautical Services Detachment, Pacific (AABC)
USAASL .... United States Army Atmospheric Sciences Laboratory (RDA)
USAASO .... United States Army Aeronautical Services Office (AABC)
USAASTA ..... United States Army Aviation Systems Test Activity [*Also, AASTA*]
USAATBD ..... United States Army Arctic Test Board
USAATC .... United States Army Arctic Test Center
USAATCO ..... United States Army Air Traffic Coordinating Officer
USAATMS .... United States Army Air Traffic Management System
USAAVA .... United States Army Audio-Visual Agency (AABC)
USAAVCOM... United States Army Aviation Materiel Command (AABC)
USAAVLABS... United States Army Aviation Materiel Laboratories (AABC)
USAAVNBD... United States Army Aviation Board
USAAVNC ..... United States Army Aviation Center [*CONARC*]
USAAVNDTA... US Army Aviation Development Test Activity [*Fort Rucker, AL*] (GRD)
USAAVNHRU... United States Army Aviation Human Research Unit [*Ft. Rucker, AL*] (AABC)
USAAVNS .... United States Army Aviation School [*CONARC*]
USAAVNSC... United States Army Aviation Systems Command
USAAVNTA... United States Army Aviation Test Activity (AABC)
USAAVNTBD... United States Army Aviation Test Board
USAAVRADCOM... United States Army Aviation Research and Development Command
USAAVS .... United States Agency for Aviation Safety (MCD)
USAAVSCOM... United States Army Aviation Systems Command [*Obsolete*] (AABC)
USAB .... United States Activities Board (IAA)
USAB .... United States Air Base (AAG)
USAB .... United States Army, Berlin (AABC)
USAB .... USABancShares'A' [*NASDAQ symbol*] (TTSB)
USAB .... USABancshares, Inc. [*NASDAQ symbol*] (SAG)
USAB .... US Activities Board [*IEEE*]
USAB .... US Animal Bank (EA)
USABA .... US Association for Blind Athletes (EA)
USABAAR .... United States Army Board for Aviation Accident Research [*Later, USAAAVS*]
USABC .... United States Advanced Battery Consortium
USABD .... United States Army Air Defense Artillery Board
USABDA .... United States Amateur Ballroom Dancers Association (EA)
USABESRL... United States Behavioral Science Research Laboratory [*Obsolete*] (IEEE)
USABF .... United States Amateur Baseball Federation
USA-BIAC .... USA - Business and Industry Advisory Committee to the OECD [*Organization for Economic Cooperation and Development*] (EA)
USABIOLABS... United States Army Biological Laboratories (AABC)
USABnc .... USABancshares, Inc. [*Associated Press*] (SAG)
USABRDL ..... United States Army Biomedical Research and Development Laboratory [*Fort Detrick, MD*]
USABRL .... United States Army Ballistic Research Laboratories (AABC)
USABVAPAC... United States Army Broadcasting and Visual Activities, Pacific
USAC .... Union des Syndicats Autonomes Camerounais [*Federation of Cameroonese Autonomous Unions*]
USAC .... United States Activities Committee (IAA)
USAC .... United States Air Corps
USAC .... United States Alpine Club [*Defunct*]
USAC .... United States Apparel Council [*Defunct*] (EA)
USAC .... United States Archery Congress [*Defunct*] (EA)
USAC .... United States Army Corps (AABC)
USAC .... United States Auto Club (EA)
USAC .... United States of America Confederation [*Later, USAC/RS*] (EA)
USAC .... Universal Seismic Associates [*NASDAQ symbol*] (SAG)
USAC .... Univl Seismic Assoc [*NASDAQ symbol*] (TTSB)
USAC .... Urban Information Systems Inter-Agency Committee [*HUD Terminated*] (EGAO)
USAC .... US Aquaculture Council [*Defunct*] (EA)
USAC .... User Services Advisory Committee [*NERComP*]
USAC .... Utah State Agricultural College
USACA .... United States Advanced Ceramics Association
USACA .... United States Allied Commission Austria
USACA .... United States Army Civil Affairs [*World War II*]
USACA .... United States Army Communications Agency
USACA .... US A-Division Catamaran Association (EA)
USACAA .... United States Army Concepts Analysis Agency (AABC)
USACAC .... United States Army Combined Arms Center (AABC)
USACAC .... United States Army Continental Army Command [*CONARC*] [*Superseded by FORSCOM*]
USACACDA... United States Army Civil Affairs Combat Developments Agency (SAA)
USACAE .... United States Army Contracting Agency, Europe (AAGC)
USACAF .... United States Army Construction Agency, France
USACAG .... United States Army Combined Arms Group (SAA)
USACAK .... United States Army Construction Agency, Korea
US-ACAN ..... United States Advisory Committee on Antarctic Names [*1947-*]
USACAP .... United States Army Chemical Activity, Pacific (DOMA)
USACARA .... United States Army Civilian Appellate Review Agency (GFGA)
USACARMSCDA... United States Army Combined Arms Combat Developments Agency
USACAS .... United States Army Civil Affairs School
USACATB ..... United States Army Combat Arms Training Board (AABC)
USACBRWOC... United States Army Chemical, Biological, and Radiological Weapons Orientation Course (AABC)
USACBRWOCAAB... United States Army Chemical, Biological, and Radiological Weapons Orientation Course Academic Advisory Board (AABC)
USACC .... United States Army Communications Command (AABC)
USACC .... USA Convertible Club [*Defunct*] (EA)
USACC .... US-Arab Chamber of Commerce [*Defunct*] (EA)
USACC-A .... United States Army Communications Command - Alaska (AABC)
USACCA .... United States Army Congressional Correspondence Agency (AABC)
USACC-AMC... United States Army Communications Command - Army Materiel Command (AABC)
USACC COMMAGCY-HSC... United States Army Communications Command Communications Agency - Health Services Command (AABC)
USACC COMMAGCY-MTMC... United States Army Communications Command Communications Agency - Military Traffic Management Command (AABC)
USACC COMMAGCY-USACIDC... United States Army Communications Command Communications Agency - United States Army Criminal Investigation Command (AABC)
USACC COMMAGCY-USAINTC... United States Army Communications Command Communications Agency - United States Army Intelligence Center
USACC-CONUS... United States Army Communications Command - Continental United States (AABC)
USACCE .... United States Army Contracting Command, Europe (AAGC)
USACC-EUR... United States Army Communications Command - Europe (AABC)
USACC-FORCES... United States Army Communications Command - Forces (AABC)
USACCIA ...... United States Army Chemical Corps Intelligence Agency
USACCL .... United States Army Coating and Chemical Laboratory (AABC)
USACCO .... United States Army Commercial Communications Office
USACC-PAC... United States Army Communications Command - Pacific (AABC)
USACC-R/FMD... United States Army Communications Command Radio and Frequency Management Division
USACCSA ...... United States Army Command and Control Support Agency
USACC-SAFCA... United States Army Communications Command Safeguard Communications Agency
USACCSD .... United States Army Command and Control Support Detachment (AABC)
USACC SIG GP (AD)... United States Army Communications Command Signal Group (AD)
USACC-SO ... United States Army Communications Command - South (AABC)
USACC-T ...... United States Army Communications Command - Thailand (AABC)
USACCTC ...... United States Army Chemical Corps Technical Committee
USACC-TRADOC... United States Army Communications Command - Training and Doctrine Command (AABC)
USACD .... Arms Control and Disarmament Agency (AAGC)
USACDA .... United States Arms Control and Disarmament Agency
USACDA .... United States Army Catalog Data Agency (AABC)
USACDC .... United States Army Combat Developments Command
USACDCADA... United States Army Combat Developments Command Air Defense Agency [*Fort Bliss, TX*] (AABC)
USACDCAGA... United States Army Combat Developments Command Adjutant General Agency
USACDCARMA... United States Army Combat Developments Command Armor Agency [*Fort Knox, KY*] (AABC)
USACDCARTYA... United States Army Combat Developments Command Artillery Agency (AABC)
USACDCAVNA... United States Army Combat Developments Command Aviation Agency [*Fort Rucker, AL*] (AABC)
USACDCCA... United States Army Combat Developments Command Combined Arms Agency [*Fort Leavenworth, KS*]
USACDCCAA... United States Army Combat Developments Command Civil Affairs Agency [*Fort Gordon, GA*] (AABC)
USACDCCAG... United States Army Combat Developments Command Combat Army Group [*Fort Le avenworth, KS*] [*Obsolete*] (AABC)
USACDCCARMSA... United States Army Combat Developments Command Combat Arms Agency
USACDCCBRA... United States Army Combat Developments Command Chemical-Biological-Radiological Agency [*Fort McClellan, AL*] (AABC)
USACDCCEA... United States Army Combat Developments Command Communications-Electronics Agency [*Fort Monmouth, NJ*] (AABC)
USACDCCHA... United States Army Combat Developments Command Chaplain Agency [*Fort Lee, VA*] (AABC)
USACDCCOMSG... United States Army Combat Developments Command Combat Systems Group (AABC)
USACDCCONFG... United States Army Combat Developments Command Concept and Force Design Group (AABC)
USACDCCSG... United States Army Combat Developments Command Combat Support Group [*Fort Belvoir, VA*] [*Obsolete*] (AABC)
USACDCCSSG... United States Army Combat Developments Command Combat Service Support Group [*Fort Lee, VA*] [*Obsolete*] (AABC)
USACDCDPFO... United States Army Combat Developments Command Data Processing Field Office (AABC)
USACDCEA... United States Army Combat Developments Command Engineer Agency [*Later, USACDCENA*] [*Fort Belvoir, VA*] (AABC)
USACDCEC... United States Army Combat Developments Command Experimentation Center [*or Command*] [*Fort Ord, CA*]
USACDCENA... United States Army Combat Developments Command Engineer Agency [*Formerly, USACDCEA*] (AABC)

USACDCFAA... United States Army Combat Developments Command Field Artillery Agency [*Fort Sill, OK*] (AABC)
USACDCFINA... United States Army Combat Developments Command Finance Agency (AABC)
USACDCIA ... United States Army Combat Developments Command Infantry Agency [*Later, USACDCINA*] [*Fort Benning, GA*] (AABC)
USACDCIAS... United States Army Combat Developments Command Institute of Advanced Studies [*Carlisle Barracks, PA*] [*Obsolete*] (AABC)
USACDCICAS... United States Army Combat Developments Command Institute of Combined Arms and Support [*Fort Leavenworth, KS*] [*Obsolete*] (AABC)
USACDCIDDFO... United States Army Combat Developments Command Internal Defense and Development Field Office (AABC)
USACDCILC... United States Army Combat Developments Command Institute of Land Combat [*Alexandria, VA*] [*Obsolete*] (AABC)
USACDCINA... United States Army Combat Developments Command Infantry Agency [*Formerly, USACDCIA*] (AABC)
USACDCINCSG... United States Army Combat Developments Command Intelligence and Control Systems Group (AABC)
USACDCINS... United States Army Combat Developments Command Institute of Nuclear Studies [*Fort Bliss, TX*] [*Obsolete*] (AABC)
USACDCINTA... United States Army Combat Developments Command Intelligence Agency [*Fort Holabird, MD*] (MCD)
USACDCISA... United States Army Combat Developments Command Institute of Systems Analysis [*Fort Belvoir, VA*] [*Obsolete*] (AABC)
USACDCISS... United States Army Combat Developments Command Institute of Special Studies [*Fort Belvoir, VA*] [*Obsolete*] (AABC)
USACDCISSO... United States Army Combat Developments Command Institute of Strategic and Stability Operations [*Obsolete*] (AABC)
USACDCJAA... United States Army Combat Developments Command Judge Advocate Agency [*Charlottesville, VA*] (AABC)
USACDCMA... United States Army Combat Developments Command Maintenance Agency [*Aberdeen Proving Ground, MD*] (AABC)
USACDCMPA... United States Combat Developments Command Military Police Agency [*Fort Gordon, GA*] (AABC)
USACDCMSA... United States Army Combat Developments Command Medical Service Agency [*Fort Sam Houston, TX*] (AABC)
USACDCNG... United States Army Combat Developments Command Nuclear Group [*Fort Bliss, TX*]
USACDCNUA... United States Army Combat Developments Command Nuclear Agency (AABC)
USACDCOA... United States Army Combat Developments Command Ordnance Agency [*Aberdeen Proving Ground, MD*]
USACDCPALSG... United States Army Combat Developments Command Personnel and Logistics Systems Group (AABC)
USACDCPASA... United States Army Combat Developments Command Personnel and Administrative Services Agency [*Fort Benjamin Harrison, IN*] (AABC)
USACDCQA... United States Army Combat Developments Command Quartermaster Agency [*Fort Lee, VA*]
USACDCSA... United States Army Combat Developments Command Supply Agency [*Later, USACDCSUA*] [*Fort Lee, VA*] (AABC)
USACDCSAG... United States Army Combat Developments Command Systems Analysis Group [*Fort Belvoir, VA*] (AABC)
USACDCSOA... United States Army Combat Developments Command Special Operations Agency (AABC)
USACDCSSI... United States Army Combat Developments Command Strategic Studies Institute (AABC)
USACDCSUA... United States Army Combat Developments Command Supply Agency [*Formerly, USACDCSA*] (AABC)
USACDCSWA... United States Army Combat Developments Command Special Warfare Agency [*Fort Bragg, NC*] (AABC)
USACDCSWCAG... United States Army Combat Developments Command Special Warfare and Civil AffairsGroup [*Fort Belvoir, VA*]
USACDCSWG... United States Army Combat Developments Command Special Warfare Group
USACDCTA... United States Army Combat Developments Command Transportation Agency [*Fort Eustis, VA*] (AABC)
USACDEC..... United States Army Combat Developments Experimentation Command (GFGA)
USACE .... United States Army Corps of Engineers [*Merged with General Equipment Command*]
USACEBD..... United States Army Airborne Communications and Electronics Board (AABC)
USACECDA... United States Army Communications-Electronics Combat Developments Agency [*Fort Huachuca, AZ*]
USACECOM... United States Army Communications and Electronics Command
USACEEIA.... United States Army Communications-Electronics Engineering Installation Agency [*Fort Huachuca, AZ*] (AABC)
USACEEIA-PAC... United States Army Communications-Electronics Engineering Installation Agency-Pacific (RDA)
USACEEIA-WH... United States Army Communications-Electronics Engineering Installation Agency - Western Hemisphere (AABC)
USACEIBN.... United States Army Communications-Electronics Installation Battalion (AABC)
USACENCDCSA... United States Army Corps of Engineers National Civil Defense Computer Support Agency (AABC)
USACERCOM... United States Army Communications and Electronics Material and Readiness Command
USACERL..... US Army Construction Engineering Research Laboratory (RDA)
USACESSEC... United States Army Computer Systems Support and Evaluation Command
USACFSC..... United States Army Community and Family Support (AAGC)
USACFSC..... United States Army Community and Family Support Center (DOMA)
USACGSC .... United States Army Command and General Staff College
USACHB....... United States Army Chaplain Board
USACHS....... United States Army Chaplain School
USACI .... United States Advisory Commission on Information
USACIC........ United States Army Criminal Investigation Command (BARN)
USACICD...... United States Army Criminal Investigation Command [*Formerly, USACIDA*] (AABC)
USACIDA...... United States Army Criminal Investigation Division Agency [*Later, USACICD*] (AABC)
USACIECA.... United States Advisory Commission on International Educational and Cultural Affairs
USACII .... United States of America Standard Code for Information Interchange (NOAA)
USACIL .... United States Army Criminal Investigation Laboratory (AABC)
USACIR........ United States Army Criminal Investigation Repository
USACISO...... United States Army Counterinsurgency Support Office, Okinawa [*Obsolete*] (AABC)
USACIU........ United States Army Command Information Unit (AABC)
USACJE........ United Synagogue of America Commission on Jewish Education (EA)
USACM .... US Association for Computational Mechanics (EA)
USACMA ...... United States Army Club Management Agency (AABC)
USACMLC .... United States Army Chemical Center [*Later, United States Army Ordnance and Chemical Center and School*]
USACMLCB... United States Army Chemical Corps Board
USACMLCS... United States Army Chemical Center and School [*Later, United States Army Ordnance and Chemical Center and School*] (AABC)
USACMLCSCH... United States Army Chemical Corps School
USACMLRDL... United States Army Chemical Research and Development Laboratories
USACMLS..... United States Army Chemical School (AABC)
USACMR...... United States Army Court of Military Review (AABC)
USACMS....... United States Army Command Management School
USACOJE..... United Synagogue of America Commission on Jewish Education (EA)
USACOM...... United States Atlantic Command [*DoD*]
USACOMISA... United States Army Communications Management Information Systems Activity
USACOMZEUR... United States Army Communications Zone, Europe
USACOR ...... US Association for the Club of Rome (EA)
USACORADCOM... United States Army Communications Research and Development Command
USACPEB..... United States Army Central Physical Evaluation Board (AABC)
USACRAPAC... United States Army Command Reconnaissance Activities, Pacific Command
USACRC....... United States Army Crime Records Center (AABC)
USACRF....... United States Army Counterintelligence Records Facility (MCD)
USACRREL... United States Army Cold Regions Research and Engineering Laboratory (AABC)
USAC/RS...... United States Amateur Confederation of Roller Skating (EA)
USACRTC..... United States Army Cold Regions Test Center (INF)
USACS .... United States Army Combat Surveillance Agency (AAG)
USACS .... United States Army Courier Service (AABC)
USACSA....... United States Army Combat Surveillance Agency
USACSA....... United States Army Communications Systems Agency (AABC)
USACSA....... United States Army Contracting Support Agency (AAGC)
USACSC....... United States Army Computer Systems Command [*Fort Belvoir, VA*]
USACSG....... United States Army CINPAC Support Group
USACSLA..... United States Army Communications Security Logistics Agency (AABC)
USACSR....... United States Air Corps Specialist Reserve
USACSS....... United States Army Chief of Support Services
USACSS....... United States Army Combat Surveillance School (AABC)
USACSSAA... United States Army Computer Systems Selection and Acquisition Agency (AABC)
USACSSC..... United States Army Computer Systems Support and Evaluation Command (IEEE)
USACSSEA... United States Army Computer Systems Support and Evaluation Agency (AABC)
USACSSEC... United States Army Computer Systems Support and Evaluation Command
USACSTA..... United States Army Combat Systems Test Activity [*Aberdeen Proving Ground, MD*]
USACSTA..... United States Army Courier Station (AABC)
USACSTATC... United States Army Combat Surveillance and Target Acquisition Training Command
USACT .... United States Accident Containment Team [*Government agency in 1985 movie "Warning Sign"*]
USACTA .... US Army Central TMDE [*Test, Measurement, and Diagnostic Equipment*] Activity (RDA)
USACTC .... United States Army Clothing and Textile Center
USACTMC.... United States Army Clothing and Textile Materiel Center
USACWL...... United States Army Chemical Warfare Laboratory
USaD .... Deseret Medical, Inc., Sandy, UT [*Library symbol*] [*Library of Congress*] (LCLS)
USAD........... United States Army Dispensary (AABC)
USAD........... USA Detergents [*NASDAQ symbol*] (TTSB)
USAD........... USA Detergents, Inc. [*NASDAQ symbol*] (SAG)
USADA......... United States Amateur Dancers Association (EA)
USADAC...... United States Army Davison Aviation Command (GFGA)
USADACS .... United States Army Defense Ammunition Center and School (AABC)
USADAOA .... United States Army Drug and Alcohol Operations Agency
USADATCOM... United States Army Data Support Command
USADC......... United States Army Data Support Command
USADC......... United States Army Dental Clinic
USADCJ....... United States Army Depot Command, Japan (AABC)

USADEG....... United States Army Dependents' Education Group (AABC)
USADESCOM... United States Army Depot Support Command
USA Det....... USA Detergents, Inc. [*Associated Press*] (SAG)
USADIP........ United States Army Deserter Information Point (AABC)
USADJ.......... United States Army Depot, Japan (AABC)
USADOFL..... United States Army Diamond Ordnance Fuze Laboratory [*Later, HDL*]
USADP......... Uniform Shipboard Automatic Data Processing
USADPC....... United States Army Data Processing Center
USADPS....... Uniform Automatic Data Processing System [*Navy*]
USADRB...... United States Army Discharge Review Board (AABC)
USADSC....... United States Army Data Services and Administrative Systems Command
USA Dt......... USA Detergents, Inc. [*Associated Press*] (SAG)
USADTC....... United States Army Armor and Desert Training Center (AABC)
USAE........... United States Army Engineer (AABC)
USAEAGSC... United States Army, Europe, Adjutant General Support Center (AABC)
USAEARA..... United States Army Equipment Authorization Review Activity (AABC)
USAEARC..... United States Army Equipment Authorizations Review Center (AABC)
USAEB......... United States Army Engineer Board
USAEC......... United States Army Electronics Command [*Obsolete*]
USAEC......... United States Army Environmental Center (RDA)
USAEC......... United States Atomic Energy Commission
USAECA....... United States Army Electronics Command Computation Agency [*Obsolete*] (AABC)
USAECAV..... United States Army Engineer Construction Agency, Vietnam
USAECBDE... United States Army Engineer Center Brigade (AABC)
USAECDA..... United States Army Engineer Combat Developments Agency (SAA)
USAECFB..... United States Army Engineer Center and Fort Belvoir (AABC)
USAECOM.... United States Army Electronics Command [*Obsolete*]
USAECR....... United States Army Engineer Center Regiment (AABC)
USAECV(P)... United States Army Engineer Command, Vietnam (Provisional)
USAED......... United States Army Engineer District
USAEDE....... United States Army Engineer Division, Europe (AABC)
USAEDH....... United States Army Engineer Division, Huntsville (AABC)
USAEDLMV... United States Army Engineer Division, Lower Mississippi Valley (AABC)
USAEDM....... United States Army Engineer Division, Mediterranean (AABC)
USAEDMR.... United States Army Engineer Division, Missouri River (AABC)
USAEDNA.... United States Army Engineer Division, North Atlantic (AABC)
USAEDNC.... United States Army Engineer Division, North Central (AABC)
USAEDNE.... United States Army Engineer Division, New England (AABC)
USAEDNP.... United States Army Engineer Division, North Pacific (AABC)
USAEDOR.... United States Army Engineer Division, Ohio River (AABC)
USAEDPO.... United States Army Engineer Division, Pacific Ocean (AABC)
USAEDS....... US Atomic Energy Detection System (DOMA)
USAEDSA..... United States Army Engineer Division, South Atlantic (AABC)
USAEDSP..... United States Army Engineer Division, South Pacific (AABC)
USAEDSW.... United States Army Engineer Division, Southwestern (AABC)
USAEEA....... United States Army Enlistment Eligibility Activity (AABC)
USAEFMA.... United States Army Electronics Command Financial Management Agency [*Obsolete*] (AABC)
USAEGD....... United States Army Engineer, Gulf District
USAEGIMRADA... US Army Engineer, Geodesy, Intelligence, and Mapping Research and Development Agency (NOAA)
USAEHA....... United States Army Environmental Hygiene Agency [*Aberdeen Proving Ground, MD*] (AABC)
USAEHL....... United States Army Environmental Health Laboratory
USAEIGHT.... Eighth United States Army (CINC)
USAEIS........ United States Army Electronic Intelligence and Security (AABC)
USAEL......... United States Army Electronics Laboratories (IAA)
USAELCTPG... United States Army Electronic Proving Ground (IAA)
USAELRO.... United States Army Electronics Logistics Research Office
USAELRU.... United States Army Electronics Research Unit
USAEMA...... United States Army Electronics Materiel Agency [*Formerly, USASSA*]
USAEMAFHPO... United States Army Electronics Materiel Agency, Fort Huachuca Procurement Office
USAEMAFMPO... United States Army Electronics Materiel Agency, Fort Monmouth Procurement Office
USAEMAPICO... United States Army Electronics Materiel Agency, Plant Inventory Control Office
USAEMAWPO... United States Army Electronics Materiel Agency, Washington Procurement Office
USAEMC...... United States Army Engineer Maintenance Center (SAA)
USAEMCA.... United States Army Engineer Mathematical Computation Agency (AABC)
USAEMSA.... United States Army Electronics Materiel Support Agency [*Formerly, USASMSA*]
USAENGCOMEUR... United States Army Engineer Command, Europe (AABC)
USAENPG.... United States Army Engineer Power Group (RDA)
USAENPG-ED... United States Army Engineer Power Group Engineering Division [*Fort Belvoir, VA*]
USAEPA....... United States Army Electronics Command Patent Agency [*Obsolete*] (AABC)
USAEPG....... United States Army Electronic Proving Ground [*Fort Huachuca, AZ*]
USAEPMARA... United States Army, Europe, Personnel Management and Replacement Activity (AABC)
USAEPOC..... United States Army Engineer Procurement Office, Chicago
USAERA....... United States Army Electronics Command Logistics Research Agency [*Obsolete*] (AABC)
USAERADCOM... United States Army Electronics Research and Development Command (RDA)
USAERDA.... United States Army Electronic Research and Development Agency
USAERDAW... United States Army Electronics Research and Development Activity, White Sands [*New Mexico*] (AABC)
USAERDL..... United States Army Electronics Research and Development Laboratory [*Formerly, USASRDL*] (MCD)
USAERDL..... United States Army Engineer Research and Development Laboratories (IAA)
USAEREC..... United States Army Enlisted Records and Evaluation Center (MCD)
USAERG....... United States Army Engineer Reactor Group (AABC)
USAERLO..... United States Army Electronics Regional Labor Office
USAES......... United States Army Engineer School
USAES......... United States Association of Evening Students (EA)
USAESC....... United States Army Electronics Support Command (AABC)
USAESC....... United States Army Engineer Studies Center [*Fort Belvoir, VA*]
USAESEIA.... United States Army Electronic Systems Engineering Installation Agency (GFGA)
USAET & DL (ECOM)... United States Army Electronics Technology and Devices Laboratory (Electronics Command) (AABC)
USAETL........ United States Army Engineer Topographic Laboratories [*Fort Belvoir, VA*]
USAEU......... United States Army Exhibit Unit (AABC)
USAEUR....... United States Army, Europe (MCD)
USAEWES.... United States Army Engineer Waterways Experiment Station
USAF........... Under Secretary of the Air Force (AAGC)
USAF........... United States Aikido Federation (EA)
USAF........... United States Air Force [*Washington, DC*]
USAF........... United States Army Forces
USAF........... United Student Aid Fund
USAF........... United Students of America Foundation [*Defunct*] (EA)
USAF........... USA Foundation (EA)
USAF........... US Aquaculture Federation (EA)
USAFA......... United States Air Force Academy [*Colorado*]
USAFA......... USA Finn Association (EA)
USAFA......... US-Albania Friendship Association (EA)
USAFABD..... United States Army Field Artillery Board [*Fort Sill, OK*] (AABC)
USAFAC...... United States Army Finance and Accounting Center (AABC)
USAFACFS... United States Army Field Artillery Center and Fort Sill (AABC)
USAFACP.... United States Air Force Ammunition Control Point
USAFACS.... United States Air Force Air Crew School
USAFACS.... United States Army Field Artillery Center and School
USAFADS.... United States Air Force Air Demonstration Squadron
USAFADWC... United States Air Force Air Defense Weapons Center (MCD)
USAFAG...... United States Air Force Auditor General
USAFAGOS... United States Air Force's Air-Ground Operations School
USAFALCENT... United States Air Force Airlift Center
USAFAP....... United States Air Force Art Program
USAFAPC.... United States Air Force Airframe Production Contract
USAFAPS.... United States Air Force Air Police School
USAFAS...... United States Army Field Artillery School [*Fort Sill, OK*] (AABC)
USAFAS/MSL... United States Army Field Artillery School Morris Swett Technical Library Division [*Fort Sill, OK*]
USAFAVLO... United States Air Force Audiovisual Liaison Office
USAFB......... United States Army Field Band (AABC)
USAFBI....... United States Army Forces in the British Isles
USAFBMD.... United States Air Force Ballistic Missile Division
USAFBMS.... United States Air Force Basic Military School
USAFBS...... United States Air Force Bandsman School (AFM)
USAFBS...... United States Air Force Bombardment School
USAFCBI..... United States Forces, China, Burma, India [*World War II*]
USAFCBIT.... United States Forces, China, Burma, India Theater [*World War II*]
USAFCC...... United States Army Forces in Central Canada [*World War II*]
USAFCED.... United States Air Force Communications Electronics Doctrine (IAA)
USAF CMR... United States Air Force Court of Military Review (AFM)
USAFCO...... United States Air Force, Southern Command (MCD)
USAF CPT.... United States Air Force Cockpit Procedures Trainer
USAFCRL.... United States Air Force Cambridge Research Laboratories
USAFD........ United States Air Force Dictionary [*A publication*]
USAFE........ United States Air Force in Europe
USAFEC...... United States Army Forces in Eastern Canada [*World War II*]
USAFECI..... United States Air Force Extension Course Institute
USAF/EDA.... Society of United States Air Force Flight Surgeons (EA)
USAFEHL.... United States Air Force Environmental Health Laboratory
USAFEISC.... United States Air Forces in Europe Inspection and Safety Center
USAFEL........ United States Air Force Epidemiological Laboratory (AFM)
USAFEPC.... United States Air Forces in Europe Personnel Center
USAFESA.... United States Army Facilities Engineering Support Agency (AABC)
USAFESA-ED... United States Army Facilities Engineering Support Agency Engineering Division
USAFESA-RT... United States Army Facilities Engineering Support Agency Research and TechnologyDivision
USAFESA-RTD... United States Army Facilities Engineering Support Agency Research and TechnologyDivision
USAFESA-T... United States Army Facilities Engineering Support Agency Technology Support Division [*Fort Belvoir, VA*]
USAFESA-TS... United States Army Facilities Engineering Support Agency - Technology Support Division
USAFESA-TSD... United States Army Facilities Engineering Support Agency - Technology Support Division
USAFE-T...... United States Air Forces in Europe - Turkey
USAFETAC... United States Air Force Environmental Technical Applications Center [*Scott Air Force Base, IL*] (AFM)
USAFETC..... United States Air Force Environmental Technical Application Center [*Scott Air Force Base, IL*]
USAFETO..... United States Army Forces, European Theater of Operations [*World War II*]
USAFETPS.... United States Air Force Experimental Test Pilot School

USAFEURPCR... United States Air Force European Postal and Courier Region (AFM)
USAFEUSA... United States Army Forces (Korea), Eighth United States Army
USAFF... USA Film Festival (EA)
USAFFACG... United States Air Force Field Activity Group
USAFFACS... United States Air Force Field Activity Squadron
USAFFE... United States Army Forces, Far East [*World War II*]
USAFFGS... United States Air Force Flexible Gunnery School
USAFFSR... United States Air Force Flight Safety Research
USAFH... United States Air Force Hospital
USAFHA... USA Field Hockey Association (EA)
USAFHD... United States Air Force Historical Division
USAFHG... United States Air Force Honor Guard
USAFHRC... United States Air Force Historical Research Center
USAFI... United States Armed Forces Institute
USAFIA... United States Army Forces in Australia
USAFIC... United States Association of Firearm Instructors and Coaches (EA)
USAFICA... United States Army Forces in Central Africa [*World War II*]
USAFICPA... United States Army Forces in Central Pacific Area
USAFIFC... United States Air Force Instrument Flight Center (AFM)
USAFIGED... United States Armed Forces Institute Test of General Educational Development (AEBS)
USAFIK... United States Army Forces in Korea
USAFIL... United States Army Forces in Liberia [*World War II*]
USAFIME... United States Armed Forces in Middle East
USAFINCISCOM... United States Army Finance and Comptroller Information Systems Command (AABC)
USAFINTEL... United States Air Force Intelligence Publication
USAFINZ... United States Army Forces in New Zealand
USAFIP(NL)... United States Army Forces in the Philippines (Northern Luzon) [*World War II*]
USAFISA... US Army Force Integration Staff Agency (RDA)
USAFISPA... United States Army Forces in the South Pacific Area
USAFIT... United States Air Force Institute of Technology
USAFIWS... United States Air Force Interceptor Weapons School
USAFLANT... United States Air Forces, Atlantic (AABC)
USAFM... United States Air Force Manual [*A publication*] (AAGC)
USAFMC... United States Association of Former Members of Congress (EA)
USAFMD... United States Army Frequency Management Directorate (MCD)
USAFMEPCR... United States Air Force Mideast Postal and Courier Region (AFM)
USAFMEPCS... United States Air Force Mideast Postal and Courier Service (AFM)
USAFMIDPAC... United States Army Forces, Middle Pacific [*See AFMIDPAC*] [*World War II*]
USAFMPC... United States Air Force Military Personnel Center
USAFMTC... United States Air Force Marksmanship Training Center
USAFMTO... United States Army Forces, Mediterranean Theater of Operations [*World War II*]
USAF/NRD... United States Air Force, National Range Division
USAFNS... United States Air Force Navigation School
USAFO... United States Army Field Office (RDA)
USAFOB... USA Federation of Bocce (EA)
USAFOCA... United States Army Field Operating Cost Agency (AABC)
USAFOCS... United States Air Force Officer Candidate School
USAFOEHL... United States Air Force Occupational and Environmental Health Laboratory [*Brooks Air Force Base, TX*]
USAFOF... United States Army Flight Operations Facility (AABC)
USAFOMC... US Air Force Occupational Measurement Center [*Randolph Air Force Base, TX*] (GRD)
USAFOSR... United States Air Force Office of Scientific Research
USAFP... Uniformed Services Academy of Family Physicians (EA)
USAFPAC... United States Air Forces, Pacific
USAFPACPCR... United States Air Force Pacific Postal and Courier Region
USAFPCS... United States Air Force Postal and Courier Service
USAFPCS Eur-Me Rgn... United States Air Force Postal and Courier Service, Europe-Mideast Region (AFM)
USAFPCS LA Rgn... United States Air Force Postal and Courier Service, Latin American Region (AFM)
USAFPCS Pac Rgn... United States Air Force Postal and Courier Service, Pacific Region (AFM)
USAFPCS US Rgn... United States Air Force Postal and Courier Service, United States Region (AFM)
USAFPDC... United States Air Force Personnel Development Center
USAFPEB... United States Air Force Physical Evaluation Board (AFM)
USAFPLREP... United States Air Force Plant Representative Office
USAFPOA... United States Army Forces, Pacific Ocean Areas [*World War II*]
USAFPRO... United States Air Force Plant Representative Office
USAFPS... United States Air Force Pilot School
USAFR... Union of South Africa
USAFR... United States Air Force Representative (AFM)
USAFR... United States Air Force Reserve
USAFRD... United States Air Force Recruiting Detachment
USAFRED... United States Air Force Forces, Readiness Command
USAFRG... United States Air Force Recruiting Group
USAFRHL... United States Air Force Radiological Health Laboratory
USAFRO... United States Air Force Recruiting Office
USAFROTC... United States Air Force Reserve Officer Training Corps
USAFRR... United States Air Force Resident Representative (MCD)
USAFRS... United States Air Force Recruiting Service
USAFRSQ... United States Air Force Recruiting Squadron
USAFS... United States Army Finance School (AABC)
USAFSA... United States Army Forces in South America
USAFSA... United States Army Forces, South Atlantic [*World War II*]
USAFSAAS... United States Air Force School of Applied Aerospace Sciences (AFM)
USAFSACS... United States Air Force School of Applied Cryptologic Sciences (AFM)
USAFSAG... United States Air Force Special Activities Group
USAFSAM... United States Air Force School of Aerospace Medicine
USAFSAM/ED... Society of United States Air Force Flight Surgeons (EA)
USAFSAS... United States Air Force Special Activities Squadron
USAFSAWC... United States Air Force Special Air Warfare Center (AFM)
USAFSBSS... United States Air Force Standard Base Supply System
USAFSC... United States Army Food Service Center (AABC)
USAFSCHCS... United States Air Force School of Health Care Science
USAFSE... United States Air Force Supervisory Examination (AFM)
USAFSG... United States Army Field Support Group (AABC)
USAFSNCOA... US Air Force Senior Noncommissioned Officer Academy (DOMA)
USAFSO... United States Air Force Southern Air Division
USAFSO... United States Air Forces Southern Command (AABC)
USAFSOC... United States Air Force Special Operations Center (AFM)
USAFSOF... United States Air Force Special Operations Force (AFM)
USAFSOS... United States Air Force Special Operations School (AFM)
USAFSPA... United States Air Force Security Policy Academy
USAFSRA... United States Air Force Special Reporting Agency
USAFSS... United States Air Force Security Service [*Later, AFESC*]
USAFSTC... United States Air Force Special Treatment Center (AFM)
USAFSTC... United States Army Foreign Science and Technology Center (AABC)
USAFSTRIKE... United States Air Forces Strike Command (AABC)
USAFTAC... United States Air Force Technical Applications Center (MCD)
USAFTALC... United States Air Force Tactical Airlift Center (AFM)
USAFTARC... United States Air Force Tactical Air Reconnaissance Center (AFM)
USAFTAWC... United States Air Force Tactical Air Warfare Center (AFM)
USAF TESTPLTSCH... United States Air Force Test Pilot School
USAFTFWC... United States Air Force Tactical Fighter Weapons Center (AFM)
USAFTMCP... United States Air Force Tactical Missile Control Point
USAFTPS... United States Air Force Test Pilot School (MCD)
USAFTS... United States Air Force Technical School
USAFTTS... United States Air Force Technical Training School
USA FUNDS... United States Aid Funds [*An association*] (PAZ)
USAF-USPCR... United States Air Force - United States Postal Courier Region (AFM)
USAFWPLO... United States Air Force Water Port Logistics Office
USAFWPO... United States Air Force Water Port Liaison Office [*or Officer*] (AFM)
USAG... Underwater Sound Advisory Group [*Navy*]
USAG... United States Army Garrison (AABC)
USAG... United States Army in Greece
USAGA... United States of America Goju Association (DICI)
USAGEM... US Atlantic and Gulf Ports/Eastern Mediterranean and North African Freight Conference [*New York, NY*] (EA)
USAGETA... United States Army General Equipment Test Activity (AABC)
USAGF... United States Army Ground Forces (MUGU)
USAGG... United States Army Group, American Mission for Aid to Greece
USAGIMRADA... United States Army Geodesy Intelligence and Mapping Research and Development Agency (AABC)
USAGMPA... United States Army General Materiel and Petroleum Activity
USAGMPC... United States Army General Materiel and Parts Center (AABC)
USAGPC... United States Adjutant General Publications Center
USAGSC... United States Army General Supplies Commodity Center
USAH... United States Army Hospital
USAH... USA Harvest [*An association*] (EA)
USAHA... United States Animal Health Association (EA)
USAHAC... United States Army Headquarters Area Command
USAHC... United States Army Health Clinic (AABC)
USAHEL... United States Army Human Engineering Laboratories (AABC)
USAHI... United States Army History Institute (PDAA)
USAHOME... United States Army Homes [*Prefabricated houses, shipped overseas*]
USAHPSA... US Army Health Professional Support Agency (DOMA)
USAHS... United States Army Hospital Ship
USAHSC... United States Army Health Service Command
USAHSDSA... United States Army Health Services Data Systems Agency (AABC)
USAHTN... United States Army Hometown News Center (AABC)
USAI... US-Asia Institute (EA)
USAIA... United States Army Institute of Administration (AABC)
USAIA... United States Army Intelligence Agency (GFGA)
USAIAS... United States Army Institute of Advanced Studies (SAA)
USAIB... United States Army Infantry Board
USAIC... United States Army Infantry Center [*Fort Benning, GA*]
USAIC... United States Army Intelligence Center (IAA)
USAIC... United States Army Intelligence Command
USAICA... United States Army Interagency Communications Agency (AABC)
USAICS... United States Army Intelligence Center and School [*Fort Huachuca, AZ*] (AABC)
USAID... United States Agency for International Development [*Also, AID*]
USAIDR... United States Army Institute of Dental Research (AABC)
USAID/REDSO/WCA... [*The*] US Agency for International Development's Regional Economic Development Services Office for West and Central Africa (ECON)
USAIDSC... United States Army Information and Data Systems Command
USAIDSCOM... United States Army Information and Data Systems Command (AABC)
USAID/W... United States Agency for International Development, Washington (PDAA)
USAIG... United States Aircraft Insurance Group
USAIGC... United States Association of Independent Gymnastic Clubs (EA)
USAIIA... United States Army Imagery Interpretation Agency (AABC)
USAIIC... United States Army Imagery Interpretation Center (AABC)
USAILC... United States Army International Logistics Center
USAILCOM... United States Army International Logistics Command (AABC)
USAILG... United States Army International Logistics Group (AABC)

USAIMA .... United States Army Institute for Military Assistance [*Fort Bragg, NC*] (AABC)
USAIMC .... United States Army Inventory Management Center (AABC)
USAIMS .... United States Army Institute for Military Systems (AABC)
USAIN .... United States Agricultural Information Network
USA Inc .... Unicycling Society of America, Inc. (EA)
USAINFHRU... United States Army Infantry Human Research Unit [*Ft. Benning, GA*] (AABC)
USAINSB ...... United States Army Intelligence Security Board
USAINSBD ... United States Army Intelligence and Security Board (MCD)
USAINSCOM... United States Army Intelligence and Security Command
USAINTA ...... United States Army Intelligence Agency (AABC)
USAINTB ...... United States Army Intelligence Board
USAINTC ...... United States Army Intelligence Center
USAINTCA .... United States Army Intelligence Corps Agency
USAINTCDA... United States Army Intelligence Combat Developments (SAA)
USAINTELMDA... United States Army Intelligence Materiel Developments Agency (AABC)
USAINTS ...... United States Army Intelligence School
USAIPSG ...... United States Army Industrial and Personnel Security Group
USAIRA .... United States Air Attache
USAIRC .... United States Army Ionizing Radiation Center
UsairG .... United States Air Group [*Associated Press*] (SAG)
UsairG .... USAir Group, Inc. [*Associated Press*] (SAG)
USAIRLO ...... United States Air Liaison Officer (CINC)
USAIRMILCOMUN... United States Air Force Representative, UN Military Staff Committee
USAIRO .... United States Army Inventory Research Office [*Philadelphia, PA*]
USAIRR .... United States Army Investigative Records Repository (AABC)
USAIS .... United States Army Infantry School
USAISC .... Information Systems Command [*Army*] (AAGC)
USAISC .... United States Army Information Systems Command [*Fort Huachuca, AZ*]
USAISC-5th Sig Cmd... United States Army Information Systems Command - 5th Signal Command (GFGA)
USAISC-7th Sig Cmd... United States Army Information Systems Command - 7th Signal Command (GFGA)
USAISC-A .... United States Army Information Systems Command - Alaska (GFGA)
USAISC-AMC... United States Army Information Systems Command - Army Materiel Command (GFGA)
USAISC-FORSCOM... United States Army Information Systems Command - Forces Command (GFGA)
USAISC-HSC... United States Army Information Systems Command - Health Services Command (GFGA)
USAISC-INSCOM... United States Army Information Systems Command - Intelligence and Security Command (GFGA)
USAISC-MTMC... United States Army Information Systems Command - Military Traffic Management Command (GFGA)
USAISC-SO... United States Army Information Systems Command - South (GFGA)
USAISC-TRADOC... United States Army Information Systems Command - Training and Doctrine Command (GFGA)
USAISC-WESTCOM... United States Army Information Systems Command - Western Command (GFGA)
USAISD .... United States Army Intelligence School, Fort Devens (GFGA)
USAISESA .... United States Army Information Systems Engineering Support Activity [*Fort Huachuca, AZ*]
USAISMA ..... United States Army Information Systems Management Activity (GFGA)
USAISR .... United States Army Institute of Surgical Research [*Ft. Sam Houston, TX*] (AABC)
USAISSAA.... United States Army Information Systems Selection and Acquisition Activity (GFGA)
USAISSSC .... United States Army Information Systems Software Support Command (GFGA)
USA-ITA .... United States Association of Importers of Textiles and Apparel (EA)
USAITAC ...... United States Army Intelligence and Threat Analysis Center (AABC)
USAITAD ...... United States Army Intelligence Threat Analysis Detachment
USAITAG ...... United States Army Intelligence Threat Analysis Group
USAITC .... United States Army Intelligence Training Center
USAITFG ...... United States Army Intelligence Threats and Forecasts Group (AABC)
USAJAPA ..... United States Amateur Jai Alai Players Association (EA)
USAJFKCENMA... United States Army John Fitzgerald Kennedy Center for Military Assistance (AABC)
USAJFKCENSPWAR... United States Army John Fitzgerald Kennedy Center for Special Warfare [*Airborne*] (AABC)
USAJFKSWCS... US Army John F. Kennedy Special Warfare Center and School (RDA)
USAJHGSOWA... United States Army Joint Household Goods Shipping Office of the Armed Forces
USAJPG .... United States Army Jefferson Proving Ground (PDAA)
USAJSC .... United States Army Joint Support Command (AABC)
USAK .... USA Truck [*NASDAQ symbol*] (SAG)
USAKA .... US Army Kwajalein Atoll (DOMA)
USAKF .... USA Karate Federation (EA)
USA-KKA ...... USA-Korean Karate Association (EA)
USAKORSCOM... United States Army Korea Support Command (AABC)
US Al .... US Alcohol Testing of America, Inc. [*Associated Press*] (SAG)
USALA .... United States Amateur Lacrosse Association
USALAPA ..... United States Army Los Angeles Procurement Agency (AABC)
USALC .... United States Army Logistics Center
US Alc .... US Alcohol Testing of America, Inc. [*Associated Press*] (SAG)
USALCA .... United States Army Logistic Control Activity (AABC)
USALCJ .... United States Army Logistics Center, Japan (AABC)
USALDC .... United States Army Logistics Data Center
USALDJ .... United States Army Logistics Depot, Japan
USALDRHRU... United States Army Leadership Human Research Unit [*Presidio of Monterey, CA*] (AABC)
USALDSRA... United States Army Logistics Doctrine, Systems and Readiness Agency [*New Cumberland Army Depot, Harrisburg, PA*] (AABC)
USALEA .... United States Army Logistics Evaluation Agency (AABC)
USALGPM .... United States Army Liaison Group, Project Michigan
USALMC ...... United States Army Logistics Management Center [*Fort Lee, VA*]
USALOGC .... United States Army Logistics Center (AABC)
USALOGCTR... United States Army Logistics Center
USALS .... United States Army Language School
USALSA .... United States Army Legal Services Agency (AABC)
USALWL .... United States Army Limited War Laboratory (AABC)
USAM .... Unified Space Applications Mission (MCD)
USAM .... Uniformly-Sampled-Autoregressive Moving Average (PDAA)
USAM .... Union des Syndicats Autonomes de Madagascar [*Federation of Malagasy Autonomous Unions*]
USAM .... Unique Sequential Access Method
USAM .... United States Army Mothers Organization, National (EA)
USAM .... United States Automated Mail Service [*Telecommunications*] (TSSD)
USAM .... US Attorney's Manual [*A publication*] (DLA)
USAMAA ...... United States Army Memorial Affairs Agency (AABC)
USAM & TTC... United States Army Mechanical and Technical Training Center [*Also called MECHTECH*]
USAMANRRDC... United States Army Manpower Resources Research and Development Center (AABC)
USAMAPLA... United States Army Military Assistance Program Logistics Agency
USAMAPS .... United States Army Military Academy Preparatory School
USAMARDA... US Army Manpower Requirements and Documentation Agency
USAMB .... United States Army Maintenance Board (AABC)
USAMBRDL... United States Army Medical Bioengineering Research and Development Laboratory [*Fort Detrick, MD*] [*Later, USABRDL*] (AABC)
USAMBRL .... United States Army Medical Biomechanical Research Laboratory [*Walter Reed Army Medical Center*] (AABC)
USAMC .... United States Army Materiel Command [*Alexandria, VA*]
USAMC .... United States Army Medical Corps
USAMC .... United States Army Missile Command [*Obsolete*]
USAMC .... United States Army Mobility Command [*Later, Troop Support Command*]
USAMC .... United States Army Munitions Command [*Later, Armaments Command*]
USAMCALMSA... United States Army Materiel Command Automated Logistics Management Systems Agency (AABC)
USAMCC ...... United States Army Metrology and Calibration Center (AABC)
USAMCFG .... United States Army Medical Center, Fort Gordon (AABC)
USAMCFO .... United States Army Materiel Command Field Office (RDA)
USAMCFSA... United States Army Materiel Command Field Safety Agency (AABC)
USAMCI & SA... United States Army Materiel Command Installations and Service Agency (AABC)
USAMC-IRO... United States Army Materiel Command Inventory Research Office
USAMC-ITC... United States Army Materiel Command Intern Training Center
USAMCLDC... United States Army Materiel Command Logistics Data Center
USAMCLSSA... United States Army Materiel Command Logistic Systems Support Agency (AABC)
USAMCSFO... United States Army Materiel Command Surety Field Office
USAMD .... United States Army Missile Detachment (AABC)
USAMDAR ... United States Army Medical Depot Activity, Ryukyu Islands (AABC)
USAMDPC .... United States Army Maintenance Data Processing Center
USAMDW .... United States Army Military District of Washington (BARN)
USAMEAF .... United States Army Middle East Air Forces [*World War II*]
USAMEC ...... United States Army Mobility Equipment Command [*Obsolete*]
USAMECOM... United States Army Mobility Equipment Command [*Obsolete*] (AABC)
USAMEDCOMEUR... United States Army Medical Command, Europe (AABC)
USAMEDDBD... United States Army Medical Department Board (RDA)
USAMEDLAB... United States Army Medical Laboratory
USAMEDS .... United States Army Medical Service
USAMEDSVS... United States Army Medical Service Veterinary School (AABC)
USAMEDTC... United States Army Medical Training Center [*Ft. Sam Houston, TX*] (AABC)
USAMEERU... United States Army Medical Environmental Engineering Research Unit
USAMEOS .... United States Army Medical Equipment and Optical School (AABC)
USAMERCC... United States Army Middle East Regional Communications Command
USAMERDC... United States Army Mobility Equipment Research and Development Center (AABC)
USAMERDL... United States Army Medical Equipment Research and Development Laboratory (AABC)
USAMETA .... United States Army Management Engineering Training Activity [*Rock Island, IL*] (AABC)
USAMFSS .... United States Army Medical Field Service School (AABC)
USAMGIK .... United States Army Military Government in Korea
USAMHRC ... United States Army Military History Research Collection (AABC)
USAMICOM... United States Army Missile Command [*Obsolete*] (AABC)
USAMIDA .... United States Army Major Item Data Agency (AABC)
USAMIIA ..... United States Army Medical Intelligence and Information Agency (AABC)
USAML .... United States Army Medical Laboratory (AABC)
USAMMA .... United States Army Medical Materiel Agency (AABC)
USAMMAE ... United States Army Materiel Management Agency, Europe
USAMMAPAC... United States Army Medical Materiel Agency, Pacific (AABC)
USAMMC ..... United States Army Maintenance Management Center (AABC)
USAMMCE ... US Army Medical Material Center-Europe (DOMA)

USAMMCS ... United States Army Missile and Munitions Center School (AABC)
USAMMCSA... US Army Medical Material Center-Saudi Arabia (DOMA)
USA-MMDA... US Army Medical Materiel Development Activity (RDA)
USAMMT ..... United States Army Military Mail Terminal
USAMN........ United States Army Mothers, National [*Defunct*] (EA)
USAMOAMA... United States Army Medical Optical and Maintenance Activity
USAMOCOM... United States Army Mobility Command [*Later, Troop Support Command*]
USAMOMA... United States Army Medical Optical and Maintenance Agency (AABC)
USAMP .... United States Army Maintenance Plant
USAMP .... United States Army Mine Planter
USAMP .... United Stets Automotive Materials Partnership
USAMP & CS/TCTFM... United States Army Military Police and Chemical Schools/ Training Center and FortMcClellan
USAMPHIBFOR... United States Amphibious Forces (AABC)
USAMPS ...... United States Army Military Police School (AABC)
USAMPTAO... United States Army Military Personnel and Transportation Assistance Office (AABC)
USAMRAA.... United States Army Medical Research Acquisition Agency
USAMRDALC... US Army Medical Research, Development, Acquisition, and Logistics Command (RDA)
USAMRDC ... United States Army Medical Research and Development Command [*Fort Detrick, MD*]
USAMRICD... United States Army Medical Research Institute for Chemical Defense [*Aberdeen Proving Ground, MD*] (RDA)
USAMRIID ... United States Army Medical Research Institute of Infectious Diseases [*Fort Detrick, MD*] (AABC)
USAMRL....... United States Army Medical Research Laboratory [*Fort Knox, KY*] (AABC)
USAMRMC... US Army Medical Research and Materiel Command (RDA)
USAMRN...... United States Army Medical Research and Nutrition (MCD)
USAMRNL.... United States Army Medical Research and Nutrition Laboratory [*Denver, CO*] (AABC)
USAMRSA.... United States Army Material Readiness Support Activity
USAMRU...... United States Army Medical Research Unit [*Malaysia, Panama*] (AABC)
USAMRU-E... United States Army Medical Research Unit - Europe (INF)
USAMS .... United States Army Management School
USAMSAA.... United States Army Materiel Systems Analysis Agency
USAMSMADHS... United States Army Medical Service Meat and Dairy Hygiene School
USAMSSA.... United States Army Management Systems Support Agency
USAMTU..... United States Army Marksmanship Training Unit
USAMU .... United States Army Marksmanship Unit [*Fort Benning, GA*]
USAMU .... United States Army Medical Unit [*Frederick, MD*]
USAMUCOM... United States Army Munitions Command [*Later, Armaments Command*]
USAMUFD.... United States Army Medical Unit, Fort Detrick [*Maryland*] (AABC)
USAMV .... United States Association of Museum Volunteers [*Later, AAMV*] (EA)
USAN........... United States Adopted Name
USANA......... United States Army Nuclear Agency (AABC)
USANA......... USANA, Inc. [*Associated Press*] (SAG)
USANAFBA... United States Army, Navy, and Air Force Bandsmen's Association [*Defunct*]
USANAVEUR... United States Navy, Europe
USANC........ United States Army Nurse Corps
USANCA........ US Army Nuclear and Chemical Agency (RDA)
USANCG ...... United States Army Nuclear Cratering Group (AABC)
USANCSG .... United States Army Nuclear and Chemical Surety Group [*Formerly, USANWSG*] (AABC)
US&FCS....... United States and Foreign Commercial Service (AAGC)
US & FCS.... US and Foreign Commercial Service [*Department of Commerce*] (CROSS)
U San Diego... University of San Diego (GAGS)
USANDL....... United States Army Nuclear Defense Laboratory (AABC)
USANF......... United States Auxiliary Naval Force
U San Fernando Valley L Rev... University of San Fernando Valley. Law Review [*A publication*] (DLA)
U San Fernando VL Rev... University of San Fernando Valley. Law Review [*A publication*] (DLA)
U San Fran... University of San Francisco (GAGS)
USANG......... United States Army National Guard
USanGS....... Church of Jesus Christ of Latter-Day Saints, Genealogical Society Library, Santaquin Stake Branch, Santaquin, UT [*Library symbol Library of Congress*] (LCLS)
USANIBC...... United States Army Northern Ireland Base Command [*World War II*]
USANIF........ United States Army Northern Ireland Force [*World War II*]
USA-NLABS... United States Army Natick Laboratories
USANP......... United South African National Party
U Santa Clara... University of Santa Clara (GAGS)
USANWCG ... United States Army Nuclear Weapon Coordination Group
USANWSG ... United States Army Nuclear Weapon Surety Group [*Later, USANCSG*]
USANWTC.... United States Army Northern Warfare Training Center (AABC)
USAOAC....... United States Army Ordnance Ammunition Command [*Merged with Munitions Command, which later became Armaments Command*]
USAOC & S... United States Army Ordnance Center and School [*Later, United States Army Ordnance and Chemical Center and School*] (AABC)
USAOCBRL... United States Army Ordnance Corps Ballistic Research Laboratory
USAOCCCL... United States Army Ordnance Corps Coating and Chemical Laboratory
USAOCCS .... United States Army Ordnance-Chemical Center and School
USAOCDPS... United States Army Ordnance Corps Development and Proof Services
USAOD........ United States Army Ordnance District
USAOEC........ United States Army Officer Evaluation Center
USAOGMS ... United States Army Ordnance Guided Missile School
USAOMC...... United States Army Ordnance Missile Command [*Later, Missile Command*]
USAOMMCS... United States Army Ordnance Missile and Munitions Center and School
USAOMSA.... United States Army Ordnance Missile Support Agency (AAG)
USAORDCORPS... United States Army Ordnance Corps
USAORDMMCS... United States Army Ordnance Munitions and Missile Center and School
USAORP ...... United States Army Oversea Research Program
USAORRF .... United States Army Ordnance Rocket Research Facility
USAOSA....... United States Army Overseas Supply Agency (CINC)
USAOSANO... United States Army Overseas Supply Agency, New Orleans
USAOSANY... United States Army Overseas Supply Agency, New York
USAOSASF... United States Army Overseas Supply Agency, San Francisco
USAOSREPLSTA... United States Army Oversea Replacement Station
USAOSWAC... United States Army Ordnance Special Weapons-Ammunition Command
USAOTEA..... United States Army Operational Test and Evaluation Agency
USAOWC...... United States Army Ordnance Weapons Command [*Merged with Missile Command*]
USAP........... United States Antarctic Program [*National Science Foundation*]
US Ap.......... United States Appeals Reports [*A publication*] (DLA)
USAP........... Universal Stainless & Alloy Products [*NASDAQ symbol*] (SAG)
USAP........... Univl Stainless/Alloy Prods [*NASDAQ symbol*] (TTSB)
USAP........... USA Petites [*An association*] (EA)
USAPA......... United States Army Photographic Agency [*Obsolete*]
USAPACDA... United States Army Personnel and Administration Combat Developments Activity (AABC)
USAPAE........ United States Army Procurement Agency, Europe (AABC)
USAPATACE... United States Army Publications and Training Aids Center, Europe
USAPAV....... United States Army Procurement Agency, Vietnam
USAPC......... United States Army Petroleum Center
USAPC......... United States Army Pictorial Center
USAPCC....... United States Army Personnel Coordination Center
USAPDA....... United States Army Physical Disability Agency
USAPDC....... United States Army Property Disposal Center [*Merged with Defense Logistics Services Center*]
USAPDCE..... United States Army Petroleum Distribution Command, Europe (AABC)
USAPDSC..... United States Army Personnel Data Support Center (AABC)
USAPDSK .... United States Army Petroleum Distribution System, Korea (AABC)
USAPEB........ United States Army Physical Evaluation Board (AABC)
USAPEQUA... United States Army Productions Equipment Agency
USAPERSCEN... United States Army Personnel Center
USAPFS........ United States Army Physical Fitness School [*Army*] (INF)
USAPG......... United States Army Participation Group (AABC)
USAPHC....... United States Army Primary Helicopter Center (AABC)
USAPHS....... United States Army Primary Helicopter School
USAPIA........ United States Army Personnel Information Activity (AABC)
USAPIC........ United States Army Photointerpretation Center
USAPO......... United States Antarctic Projects Office
USAPO......... USA Plowing Organization (EA)
USAPOP....... United States Army Port Operations, Pusan (AABC)
US App....... United States Appeals Reports [*A publication*] (DLA)
USAPPA....... United States Army Publications and Printing Agency
USAPPC....... US Army Publications and Printing Command (DOMA)
USAPRC....... United States Army Physical Review Council (AABC)
USAPRDC .... United States Army Polar Research and Development Center
USAPRO ...... United States Army Personnel Research Office
USAPSG........ United States Army Personnel Security Group (AABC)
USAPT .... United States Army Parachute Team
USAPWA...... United Stone and Allied Products Workers of America [*Later, USWA*] (EA)
USAQMC....... United States Army Quartermaster Corps [*Merged with Supply and Maintenance Command*]
USAQMCDA... United States Army Quartermaster Combat Developments Agency (SAA)
USAQMCENFL... United States Army Quartermaster Center and Fort Lee (AABC)
USAQMCS.... United States Army Quartermaster Center and School
USAQMS....... United States Army Quartermaster School
USAQMTC.... United States Army Quartermaster Training Command
USAR........... Uniform Systems of Accounts and Reports for Certified Air Carriers [*Civil Aeronautics Board*]
USAR........... United States Aeronautical Reserve
USAR........... United States Army Reserve
USARA......... United States Air Racing Association [*Formerly, PRPA*] (EA)
USARA......... US Army Ranger Association (EA)
USARACS .... United States Army Alaska Communications Center
USARADABD... United States Army Air Defense Artillery Board [*Fort Bliss, TX*]
USARADBD... United States Army Air Defense Board
USARADCOM... United States Army Air Defense Command
USARADSCH... United States Army Air Defense School
USARADSCH... United States Army Research and Development School (AAG)
USARAE....... United States Army Reserve Affairs, Europe (AABC)
USARAL....... United States Army, Alaska
USARB......... United States Army Retraining Brigade (AABC)
USARBCO .... United States Army Base Command, Okinawa (AABC)
USARC......... United States Army Reserve Center (AABC)
USARCARIB... United States Army, Caribbean
USARCC....... US Association of Roller Canary Culturists (EA)
USA-RCEC ... USA-Republic of China Economic Council (EA)
USARCEN .... United States Army Records Center

USARCENT... United States Army Forces, Central Command
USARCPC .... United States Army Reserve Components Personnel Center (AABC)
USARCS....... United States Army Claims Service (AABC)
USARCSWIS... United States Army Claims Service Worldwide Information System (GFGA)
USARctBad... United States Army Recruiter Badge [*Military decoration*] (AABC)
USARDA ...... United States Army Regional Dental Activity (AABC)
USARDAISA... United States Army Research, Development, and Acquisition Information Systems Agency (AABC)
USARDL....... United States Army Research and Development Laboratories
USARDORAG... United States Army Research and Development Operational Research Advisory Group (AABC)
USARDSG-GE... United States Army Research, Development, and Standardization Group - Germany (RDA)
USARDSG-UK... US Army Research, Development, and Standardization Group - United Kingdom (RDA)
USAREC .... United States Army Recruiting Command (AABC)
USARECSTA... United States Army Reception Station
USARENBD... United States Army Armor and Engineer Board (RDA)
USAREPG .... United States Army Electronic Proving Ground
USAREREC... United States Army Enlisted Records and Evaluation Center
USARET-RSGSTA... United States Army Returnee - Reassignment Station
USAREUR .... United States Army, Europe
USAREURAGLO... United States Army, Europe, Adjutant General Liaison Office (AABC)
USAREURCSTC... United States Army, Europe, Combat Support Training Center (AABC)
USAREURORDCOM... United States Army European Ordnance Command
USARF .... United States Army Reserve Forces
USARFA........ United States of America Rugby Fives Association (EA)
USARFANT... United States Army Forces, Antilles
USARFEO..... United States Army Frequency Engineering Office (MCD)
USARFT....... United States Army Forces, Taiwan
USARFU....... United States of America Rugby Football Union (EA)
USARHAW... United States Army, Hawaii
USARIA........ United States Army Rock Island Arsenal
USARIBSS ... United States Army Research Institute for the Behavioral and Social Sciences (AABC)
USARIEM..... United States Army Research Institute of Environmental Medicine [*Natick, MA*] (AABC)
USARIOS ..... Association of Maritime Transport Users in the Central American Isthmus [*Guatemala*] (EAIO)
USARIS........ United States Army Information School [*Fort Slocum, New Rochelle, NY*]
USARJ .... United States Army, Japan
USARK......... United States Army, Korea (MCD)
USARLANT... United States Army Forces, Atlantic (AABC)
USARLT .... United States Army Reserve Losses Tally
USARMA...... United States Army Attache
USARMCOM... United States Army Armament Command
USARMIS...... United States Army Mission
USARMLO.... United States Army Liaison Officer
USARMY...... Uncle Sam Ain't Released Me Yet
USARNG ...... United States Army National Guard
USARO......... United States Army Research Office
USA-ROCEC... USA-Republic of China Economic Council [*Crystal Lake, IL*] (EA)
USAROD ...... United States Army Research Office (Durham)
USAROTC .... United States Army Reserve Officer Training Corps
USAROTCR... United States Army Reserve Officers' Training Corps Region (AABC)
USARP......... United States Army Research Program (IAA)
USARP......... US Antarctic Research Program (EA)
USARPA....... United States Army Publications Agency (GFGA)
USARPA....... United States Army Radio Propagation Agency (AABC)
USARPAC .... United States Army, Pacific
USARPACINTS... United States Army Pacific Intelligence School (AABC)
USARPERCEN... United States Army Reserve Personnel Center
USARR......... United States Army Readiness Regions (AABC)
USARRACL... United States Army Reserve Report Activity Control List
USARRADCOM... United States Army Armament Research and Development Command (RDA)
USARRED .... United States Army Forces, Readiness Command
USARS......... US Army Regimental System (INF)
USARS......... User Selected and Required Schedule (SAA)
USARSA....... United States Amateur Roller Skating Association [*Later, USAC/RS*] (EA)
USARSA....... United States Army School of the Americas [*Fort Benning, AR*] (INF)
USARSCV .... United States Army Support Command, Vietnam [*Obsolete*]
USARSG ...... United States Army Standardization Group
USARSO ...... United States Army Forces, Southern Command
USARSO-PR... United States Army Forces, Southern Command - Puerto Rico (AABC)
USARSOUTHCOM... United States Army Forces, Southern Command
USARSPACE... United States Army Space Command
USARSSO .... United States Army Safeguard Systems Office
USARSTRIKE... United States Army Forces Strike Command (AABC)
USARSUPTHAI... United States Army Support, Thailand (AABC)
USART......... Universal Synchronous/Asynchronous Receiver and Transmitter [*Computer science*]
USARTL .... United States Army Research and Technical Labs (MCD)
USARTLS..... United States Army Reserve Troop List by State
USARUCU.... United States Army Reserve Unit Commander Unit
USARV......... United States Army, Vehicle (SAA)
USARV......... United States Army Vietnam [*Obsolete*]
USARV/MACV... United States Army, Vietnam / Military Assistance Command, Vietnam (VNW)
USARYIS...... United States Army, Ryukyu Islands
USAS .... United States Air Service
USAS .... United States Airspace System (NOAA)
USAS .... United States Antarctic Service [*1939-41*] [*Navy*]
USAS .... United States of America Standard (IEEE)
USAS .... UNIVAC Standard Airline System (HGAA)
USAS .... US Aquatic Sports (EA)
USASA......... United States Army Security Agency
USASA......... Universities Staff Association of South Australia
USASAALA... United States Army Security Assistance Agency, Latin America (AABC)
USASAC....... United States Army Security Assistance Center
USASAC....... US Army Security Affairs Command (RDA)
USASACDA... United States Army Security Agency Combat Development Activity (AABC)
USASACDSA... United States Army Security Agency Command Data Systems Activity (AABC)
USASADEA... United States Army Signal Air Defense Engineering Agency [*Later, USAADEA*]
USASAE....... United States Army Security Agency, Europe (AABC)
USASAFLOG... United States Army Safeguard Logistics Command
USASAFO..... United States Army Signal Avionics Field Office [*Later, USAAFO*]
USASAFS..... United States Army Security Agency Field Station
USASAFSCOM... United States Army Safeguard System Command (AABC)
USASAGV.... US Army Security Agency Group, Vietnam (VNW)
USASAM...... United State Army School of Aviation Medicine (PDAA)
USASAPAC... United States Army Security Agency, Pacific (AABC)
USASASA..... United States Army Security Agency Systems Activity (AABC)
USASASA..... United States Army Small Arms Systems Agency
USASASSA... United States Army Security Agency Signal Security Activity (AABC)
USASATC & S... United States Army Security Agency Training Center and School (AABC)
USASATCOMA... United States Army Satellite Communications Agency (AABC)
USASATEC ... United States Army Security Agency Test and Evaluation Center (AABC)
USASATSA... United States Army Signal Aviation Test Support Activity
USASC......... United States Army Safety Center
USASC......... United States Army Signal Corps [*Merged with Communications and Electronics Command*]
USASC......... United States Army Subsistence Center
USASC......... United States Army Support Center
USASCA....... United States Army Safeguard Communications Agency (RDA)
USASCA....... United States Army Satellite Communications Agency (IAA)
USASCAF..... United States Army Service Center for the Armed Forces (AABC)
USASC & FG... United States Army Signal Center and Fort Gordon (AABC)
USASCC....... United States Army Strategic Communications Command
USASCH....... United States Army Support Command, Hawaii (AABC)
USASCHEUR... United States Army School, Europe [*Obsolete*] (AABC)
USASCII....... United States of America Standard Code for Information Interchange
USASCOCR... United States of America Standard Character Set for Optical Character Recognition [*Computer science*]
USASCR....... United States Army Support Center, Richmond (AABC)
USASCS....... United States Army Signal Center and School
USASCS....... United States Army Signal Corps School (IAA)
USASCSA..... United States Army Signal Communications Security Agency
USASCSOCR... United States of America Standard Character Set for Optical Character Recognition [*Computer science*]
USASCSOCR... United States of America Standard Character Set for Optical Characters (IAA)
USASCV....... United States Army Support Command, Vietnam [*Obsolete*]
USASD......... United States Army Student Detachment (AABC)
USASDC....... United States Army Strategic Defense Command
USASEA....... United States Army Signal Engineering Agency
USASEL....... United States Army Signal Engineering Laboratory (IAA)
USASESA..... United States Army Signal Equipment Support Agency (MCD)
USASESS..... United States Army Southeastern Signal School (AABC)
USASETAF ... United States Army Southern European Task Force
USASEUR .... United States Army School, Europe [*Obsolete*]
USASEXC..... United States Armed Services Exploitation Center (AABC)
USASF......... United States Army Special Forces (CINC)
USASFG....... United States Army Special Forces Group
USASFGV..... United States Army Special Forces Group, Vietnam
USASFV....... United States Army Special Forces, Vietnam [*Obsolete*]
USASG......... US Army Support Group (DOMA)
USASG(Aus)... United States Army Standardization Group (Australia)
USASG(Ca)... United States Army Standardization Group (Canada) (AABC)
USASG(UK)... United States Army Standardization Group (United Kingdom) (AABC)
USASGV....... United States Army Support Group, Vietnam [*Obsolete*]
USASI.......... United States of America Standards Institute [*Formerly, ASA*] [*Later, ANSI*]
USASIGC...... United States Army Signal Corps [*Merged with Communications and Electronics Command*]
USASIGENGLAB... United States Army Signal Engineering Laboratory (IAA)
USASIGRSCHUNIT... United States Army Signal Research Unit (IAA)
USASIGS...... United States Army Signal School (AABC)
USASIGTC.... United States Army Signal Training Center (IAA)
USASII......... United States of America Standard Code for Information Interchange (IAA)
USASIMSA... United States Army Signal Materiel Support Agency [*Later, USAEMSA*]
USASIS......... United States Army Strategic Intelligence School
USASLE........ Uniform Securities Agent State Law Examination [*Investment term*]
USASMA...... United States Army Sergeant Major Academy (AABC)
USASMC...... United States Army Supply and Maintenance Command
USASMC...... US Army Sergeants Major Course (INF)

USASMCOM... United States Army Supply and Maintenance Command (MUGU)
USASMSA.... United States Army Signal Materiel Support Agency [*Later, USAEMSA*]
USASMSA.... United States Army Signal Missile Support Agency (IAA)
USASMSG.... United States Army Signal Missile Support Group
USASOC....... US Army Special Operations Command (INF)
USASOPAC... United States Army Support Office, Pacific (AABC)
USASOS....... United States Army Services of Supply
USASPSAE... United States Army Special Services Agency, Europe (AABC)
USASPTAP... United States Army Support Activity, Philadelphia (AABC)
USASPTC.... United States Army Support Center (AABC)
USASPTCC... United States Army Support Command, Chicago
USASPTCM... United States Army Support Center, Memphis (AABC)
USASPTCP... United States Army Support Center, Philadelphia (AABC)
USASPTCR... United States Army Support Center, Richmond (AABC)
USASRDL .... United States Army Signal Research and Development Laboratory [*Later, USAERDL*]
USASRU ...... United States Army Surgical Research Unit (AABC)
USASSA....... United States Army Signal Supply Agency [*Later, USAEC*]
USASSAFMPO... United States Army Signal Supply Agency, Fort Monmouth Procurement Office
USASSAMRO... United States Army Signal Supply Agency, Midwestern Regional Office
USASSAUSAEPGPO... United States Army Signal Supply Agency, United States Army Electronic Proving Ground Procurement Office
USASSAWPO... United States Army Signal Supply Agency, Washington Procurement Office
USASSAWRO... United States Army Signal Supply Agency, Western Regional Office
USASSC....... United States Army Signal School and Center
USASSC & FBH... United States Army Soldier Support Center and Fort Benjamin Harrison (AABC)
USASSD....... United States Army Special Security Detachment
USASSDC .... United States Army Space and Strategic Defense Command
USASSG....... United States Army Special Security Group (AABC)
USASTAF ..... United States Army Southern European Task Force
USASTAF ..... United States Army Strategic Air Forces in the Pacific
USASTC....... United States Army Signal Training Center [*Fort Gordon, GA*]
USASTCEN... United States Army Signal Training Center (IAA)
USASTCFM... United States Army Signal Training Command and Fort Monmouth
USASTRATCOM... United States Army Strategic Communications Command [*Later, USACC*] (AABC)
USASTRATCOM-A... United States Army Strategic Communications Command - Alaska (AABC)
USASTRATCOM-CONUS... United States Army Strategic Communications Command - Continental United States (AABC)
USASTRATCOM-EUR... United States Army Strategic Communications Command - Europe (AABC)
USASTRATCOM-PAC... United States Army Strategic Communications Command - Pacific (AABC)
USASTRATCOM-SIGGP-T... United States Army Strategic Communications Command Signal Group - Thailand (AABC)
USASTRATCOM-SO... United States Army Strategic Communications Command - South (AABC)
USASTRATCOM-V... United States Army Strategic Communications Command - Vietnam [*Obsolete*] (AABC)
USASUPCOM-CRB... United States Army Support Command - Cam Ranh Bay [*Obsolete*] (AABC)
USASUPCOM-QN... United States Army Support Command - Qui Nhon [*Obsolete*] (AABC)
USASUPCOM-SGN... United States Army Support Command - Saigon [*Obsolete*] (AABC)
USASWCDA... United States Army Special Warfare Combat Developments Agency (SAA)
USASWL...... United States Army Signals Warfare Laboratory
USASWS...... United States Army Special Warfare School
USAT .... United States Army Transport
USATAC .... United States Army Terrain Analysis Center (MCD)
USATAC .... United States Army Training Center, Engineer [*Fort Leonard Wood, MO*]
USATACOM... United States Army Tank-Automotive Command [*Obsolete*]
USATAFO ..... United States Army Transportation Aviation Field Office
USATALS ..... United States Army Transportation and Aviation Logistics Schools (GFGA)
USATATSA... United States Army Transportation Aircraft Test and Support Activity
USATA(WH)... United States Army Transportation Agency (White House) (AABC)
USATB .... United States Army Training Board
USATC .... United States Air Target Chart
USATC .... United States Army Topographic Command
USATC .... United States Army Training Center
USATC .... United States Army Transportation Center and School
USATC .... United States Assault Training Center [*World War II*]
USATCA .... United States Army Terminal Command, Atlantic
USATCAD ..... United States Army Training Center, Air Defense
USATCARMOR... United States Army Training Center, Armor [*Fort Knox, KY*]
USATCBASIC... United States Army Training Center, Basic
USATCD .... United States Army Training Center, Air Defense
USATCEFLW... United States Army Training Center, Engineer, Fort Leonard Wood [*Missouri*] (AABC)
USATCENGR... United States Army Training Center, Engineer
USATCEUR... United States Army Terminal Command, Europe (AABC)
USATC FA.... United States Army Training Center, Field Artillery [*Fort Sill, OK*] (AABC)
USATCFE ..... United States Army Transportation Center and Fort Eustis (AABC)
USATCFLW... United States Army Training Center and Fort Leonard Wood (AABC)
USATCG....... United States Army Terminal Command, Gulf (AABC)
USATCINF.... United States Army Training Center, Infantry
USATCO....... Universal Satellite Corp. [*New York, NY*] [*Telecommunications*] (TSSD)
USATCO....... US Air Traffic Controllers Organization [*Defunct*] (EA)
USATCP....... United States Army Terminal Command, Pacific
USATCRTSA... United States Army Transportation Corps Road Test Support Activity
USATCS....... United States Army Transportation Center and School
USATDA....... United States Army Training Device Agency
USATDC....... United States Army Training and Doctrine Command (BARN)
USATDGL..... United States Army Terminal Detachment, Great Lakes (AABC)
USATEA....... United States Army Transportation Engineering Agency (AABC)
USATEC....... United States Army Test and Evaluation Command [*Obsolete*]
USATECOM... United States Army Test and Evaluation Command [*Obsolete*]
USATHAMA... United States Army Toxic and Hazardous Materials Agency (RDA)
USATIA........ United States Army Transportation Intelligence Agency
USATL......... United States Army Technical Library (DIT)
USATLA........ USA Toy Library Association (EA)
USATMACE... United States Army Traffic Management Agency, Central Europe (AABC)
USATMC...... United States Army Transportation Materiel Command
USATMC...... United States Army Troop Medical Clinic (AABC)
USATOPOCOM... United States Army Topographic Command (AABC)
USATOWA.... United States Amateur Tug of War Association (EA)
USATRADOC... United States Army Training and Doctrine Command
USATRASANA... United States Army TRADOC Systems Analysis Activity (AABC)
USATRC....... United States Army Transportation Research Command
USATRECOM... United States Army Transportation Research and Engineering Command
USATREOG... United States Army Transportation Environmental Operations Group (AABC)
USATRFSTA... United States Army Transfer Station
USA Trk....... USA Truck Co. [*Associated Press*] (SAG)
USATRML.... United States Army Tropical Research Medical Laboratory
USATROSCOM... United States Army Troop Support Command
USATS......... U.S. Air Traffic Service Corporation [*FAA*] (TAG)
USATSA....... United States Army Technical Support Activity (AABC)
USATSA....... US Army Troop Support Agency (DOMA)
USATSARCOM... United States Army Troop Support and Aviation Materiel Readiness Command [*St. Louis, MO*]
USATSC....... United States Army Terrestrial Sciences Center (AABC)
USATSC....... United States Army Training Support Center
USATSCH..... United States Army Transportation School
USATSG....... United States Army, the Surgeon General
USATSG....... United States Army TMDE [*Test, Measurement, and Diagnostic Equipment*] Support Group
USATT .... Union des Syndicats Autonomes des Travailleurs Tchadiens [*Federation of Autonomous Workers Unions of Chad*]
USATTAY ..... United States Army Transportation Test Activity, Yuma [*Arizona*] (AABC)
USATTB .... United States Army Transportation Terminal, Brooklyn
USATTC .... United States Army Transportation Training Command
USATTC .... United States Army Tropic Test Center (AABC)
USATTCA ..... United States Army Transportation Terminal Command, Atlantic
USATTCARC... United States Army Transportation Terminal Command, Arctic
USATTCG..... United States Army Transportation Terminal Command, Gulf
USATTCP..... United States Army Transportation Terminal Command, Pacific
USATTU....... United States Army Transportation Terminal Unit (AABC)
USATUC....... United States Army Terminal Unit, Canaveral (AABC)
US Av .... United States Aviation Reports [*A publication*] (DLA)
USAVA......... USA Victory Alliance (EA)
USAVC......... United States Army Vehicle Club [*British*] (DBA)
USAVETS..... United States Army Veterinary School
US Aviation Rep... United States Aviation Reports [*A publication*] (DLA)
US Avi Rep... United States Aviation Reports [*A publication*] (DLA)
US Av R....... United States Aviation Reports [*A publication*] (DLA)
USAW.......... Underwater Security Advance Warnings [*Navy*]
USAWC........ United States Army War College
USAWC........ United States Army Weapons Command [*Later, Armaments Command*]
USAWECOM... United States Army Weapons Command [*Later, Armaments Command*] (AABC)
USAWES...... United States Army Waterways Experiment Station (AABC)
USAWF........ United States Amateur Wrestling Foundation (EA)
USAWOA...... United States Army Warrant Officers Association (EA)
USA Wste.... USA Waste Services, Inc. [*Associated Press*] (SAG)
USB .... Unified S-Band (MCD)
USB .... United Society of Brushmakers [*A union*] [*British*]
USB .... United States Bases [*British World War II*]
USB .... United States Biochemical Corp. [*Chemistry*] (DAVI)
USB .... Universal Serial Bus [*Computer science*] (CDE)
USB .... Universal Serials and Book Exchange, Inc. [*ACCORD*] [*UTLAS symbol*]
USB .... Upflow Sludge Blanket [*Reactor, wastewater treatment*]
USB .... Upper Sideband
USB .... Upper Sternal Border [*Anatomy*] (DAVI)
USB .... Upper Surface Blown [*Jet flap*] [*Aviation*]
USB .... US Bass [*An association Defunct*] (EA)
USBA .... Union Syndicale des Bases Americaines [*Union of American Base Workers*] [*Morocco*]
USBA .... United States Badminton Association (EA)
USBA .... United States Bartenders Association (EA)
USBA .... United States Boardsailing Association (EA)
USBA .... United States Brewers Association [*Defunct*] (EA)

USBA .... US Base Association (EA)
USBA .... US Biathlon Association (EA)
USBA .... US Boomerang Association (EA)
USBATU ...... United States - Brazil Aviation Training Unit
USBBC .... United States Beef Breeds Council (EA)
USBBS .... United States Bureau of Biological Survey [*Terminated, 1940; later, Fish and Wildlife Service*]
USBBY .... US Board on Books for Young People (EA)
USBC .... United States Bureau of the Census (OICC)
USBC .... Universal Standard Book Code (PDAA)
USBC .... US Bancorp [*NASDAQ symbol*] (NQ)
USBCA .... United States Braille Chess Association (EA)
USBCC .... United States Border Collie Club (EA)
USBCJ .... US Business Committee on Jamaica [*Defunct*] (EA)
USBCODE .... Unipolar Straight Binary Code (IAA)
US BcOR ...... United States Bancorp [*Associated Press*] (SAG)
USBCP .... U.S. Bancorp 8.125%'A'Pfd [*NASDAQ symbol*] (TTSB)
USBE .... Unified S-Band Equipment
USBE .... United States Book Exchange (SAA)
USBE .... Universal Serials and Book Exchange, Inc. [*Acronym now used as official name of association*] (EA)
USBEP .... United States Bureau of Engraving and Printing
USBER .... United States Mission, Berlin
USBF .... United States Baseball Federation (EA)
USBF .... United States Bocce Federation (EA)
USBF .... United States Brewers Foundation [*Later, USBA*]
USBF .... United States Bureau of Fisheries [*Terminated*]
USBF .... US Bobsled and Skeleton Federation (EA)
USBFA .... US Bass Fishing Association [*Later, USB*] (EA)
USBFDC ...... United States Bureau of Foreign and Domestic Commerce
USBG .... United States Bartenders Guild [*Later, USBA*] (EA)
USBG .... United States Botanic Garden
USBG .... US Bridge Corp. [*NASDAQ symbol*] (SAG)
USBGA .... United States Blind Golfer's Association (EA)
USBGN .... United States Bureau on Geographical Names [*Terminated, 1947; later, Board on Geographical Names*]
USBIA .... United States Bowling Instructors Association (EA)
USBIA .... United States Bureau of Insular Affairs
USBIC .... United States Business and Industrial Council [*Washington, DC*] (EA)
US Bio .... United States Bioscience, Inc. [*Associated Press*] (SAG)
US Biosci ...... US Bioscience, Inc. [*Associated Press*] (SAG)
USBISS .... United Society of Boilermakers and Iron and Steel Shipbuilders [*A union*] [*British*]
USBJA .... United States Barrel Jumping Association (EA)
USBL .... United States Bureau of Lighthouses
USBLM .... United States Bureau of Land Management [*Department of the Interior*]
USBLS .... United States Bureau of Labor Statistics
USBM .... United States Bureau of Mines [*Department of the Interior*]
USBMG .... United States Berlin Mission in Germany
USBN .... United Sec Bancorp (WA) [*NASDAQ symbol*] (TTSB)
USBN .... United Security Bancorp (Washington) [*NASDAQ symbol*] (SAG)
US Bn .... United States Bancorp [*Associated Press*] (SAG)
USBN .... United States Bureau of Navigation
USBNP .... United States Bureau of Navy Personnel [*Terminated*]
USBP .... United States Border Patrol [*Department of the Treasury*]
USBPA .... United States Bicycle Polo Association (EA)
USBPa .... USbancorp, Inc. [*Associated Press*] (SAG)
USBPR .... United States Bureau of Public Roads
USBR .... United States Bureau of Reclamation [*Department of the Interior*] [*See also BOR*]
USBR .... U.S. Bridge of N.Y. [*NASDAQ symbol*] (TTSB)
USBR .... US Bridge on New York [*NASDAQ symbol*] (SAG)
USBrdge ...... US Bridge Corp. [*Associated Press*] (SAG)
USBrdgNY .... US Bridge of New York [*Associated Press*] (SAG)
US Brg .... US Bridge on New York [*Associated Press*] (SAG)
USBRO .... United States Base Requirements Overseas [*Military*] (AABC)
USBRW .... US Bridge of NY Wrrt [*NASDAQ symbol*] (TTSB)
USBS .... Unified S-Band System [*Radio*]
USBS .... United States Bureau of Standards
USBSA .... United States Beet Sugar Association (EA)
USBSA .... United States Boardsailing Association (EA)
USBSF .... US Bobsled and Skeleton Federation (EA)
USBSSW ...... United Society of Boilermakers, Shipbuilders, and Structural Workers [*A union*] [*British*]
USBT .... Upper Surface Blowing Technique [*Aviation*] (DA)
USBTA .... United States Board of Tax Appeals [*Later, the Tax Court of the United States*]
USBTC .... University-Small Business Technology Consortium [*Defunct*] (EA)
USBTC .... US Battery Trade Council
USBUC .... Upper Sideband Upconverter (IAA)
USBWA .... United States Basketball Writers Association (EA)
USC .... Ultrasonic Storage Cell
USC .... Under Secretaries Committee
USC .... Under Separate Cover
USC .... Unified Soil Classification (GNE)
USC .... Union of Sephardic Congregations (EA)
USC .... Union Sociale Camerounaise [*Cameroonese Social Union*]
USC .... Unitarian Service Committee [*Later, UUSC*] [*Post-World War II*]
USC .... United Satellite Communications [*Cable TV programming service*]
USC .... United Service Club [*Charter jet service to Europe for servicemen and dependents*]
USC .... United Sisters of Charity (EA)
USC .... United Somali Congress [*Political party*] (EY)
USC .... United States Canada [*Automobile content legislation*]
USC .... United States Catalog [*A bibliographic publication*]
USC .... United States Citizen
USC .... United States Code [*Legal term*]
USC .... United States Components (IAA)
USC .... United States Congress
USC .... United States Customs
USC .... United States Custom Service, Washington, DC [*OCLC symbol*] (OCLC)
USC .... United States of Colombia
USC .... United Strasser Club
USC .... United Survival Clubs (EA)
USC .... Universal Specimen Chamber
USC .... University of Santa Clara [*California*]
USC .... University of South Carolina [*Columbia, SC*]
USC .... University of Southern California [*Los Angeles*] [*Seismograph station code, US Geological Survey*] (SEIS)
USC .... University Scholarships of Canada
USC .... University Statistics Center [*New Mexico State University*] [*Research center*] (RCD)
USC .... Up Stage Center [*Away from audience*] [*A stage direction*]
USC .... U.S. Can [*NYSE symbol*] (TTSB)
USC .... US Can Corp. [*NYSE symbol*] (SAG)
USC .... US Check Airlines [*ICAO designator*] (FAAC)
USC .... User Service Center (MCD)
USC .... User Support Center (MCD)
USCA .... Under Secretary for Civil Aviation
USCA .... Uniformed Services Contingency Act
USCA .... United Sidecar Association (EA)
USCA .... United States Canoe Association (EA)
USCA .... United States Code Annotated [*Law*] [*Based on official USC*]
USCA .... United States Contract Awards (NITA)
USCA .... United States Copper Association [*Later, American Bureau of Metal Statistics*] (EA)
USCA .... United States Courts of Appeals
USCA .... United States Croquet Association (EA)
USCA .... United States Curling Association (EA)
USCA .... US Canola Association (EA)
USCAA .... United States Corporate Athletics Association (EA)
USCA App .... United States Code, Annotated, Appendix [*A publication*] (DLA)
USCAB .... United States Congressional Advisory Board (EA)
USCAC .... United States Continental Army Command [*Superseded by FORSCOM*]
USCAF .... United States Competitive Aerobics Federation
USCAGS ...... United States Coast and Geodetic Survey (IAA)
USCAL .... University of Southern California, Aeronautical Laboratory (MCD)
US Cal Sch L Tax Inst ... University of Southern California School of Law Tax Institute (DLA)
USCAM .... United States Civil Aviation Mission (AFM)
US Can .... US Can Corp. [*Associated Press*] (SAG)
USC & G ...... United States Coast and Geodetic Survey [*Later, National Ocean Survey*] (MUGU)
USCANS ...... Unified S-Band Communication and Navigation System [*NASA*]
USCANW ...... US Committee Against Nuclear War [*Defunct*] (EA)
USCAPP ...... Advanced Professional Programs, University of Southern California Law Center (DLA)
USC App ...... United States Code Appendix [*A publication*] (DLA)
USCAR .... United States Civil Administration, Ryukyu Islands
USCAR .... United States Council for Automotive Research [*General Motors, Ford, and Chrysler*] (ECON)
USCAR .... United States Council for Automotive Research
USCB .... United Saudi Commercial Bank
USCB .... United States Customs Bonded
USCBC .... US-China Business Council (EA)
USCBRA ...... United States CB Radio Association (EA)
USCC .... Union des Syndicats Croyants du Cameroun [*Federation of Cameroonese Believers' Unions*]
USCC .... United Society of Cork Cutters [*A union*] [*British*]
USCC .... United States Calorimetry Conference
USCC .... United States Camaro Club (EA)
USCC .... United States Capacitor Corp. (IAA)
USCC .... United States Catholic Conference (EA)
USCC .... United States Cellular Corp. [*Park Ridge, IL*] [*Telecommunications*] (TSSD)
USCC .... United States Chamber of Commerce
USCC .... United States Circuit Court
USCC .... United States Citizens' Congress [*Defunct*]
USCC .... United States Claims Court (AAGC)
USCC .... United States Commerical Co. [*World War II*]
USCC .... United States Cotton Commission
USCC .... United States Court of Claims [*Abolished, 1982*]
USCC .... United States Criminal Code
USCC .... United States Criminal Court
USCC .... United States Customs Court [*Later, United States Court of International Trade*]
USCC .... United Student Christian Council in United States
USCC .... US Cancellation Club (EA)
USCCA .... United States Circuit Court of Appeals
USCCA .... United States Circuit Court of Appeals Reports [*A publication*] (DLA)
USCCAN ...... United States Code Congressional and Administrative News [*A publication*]
USCCCA ...... United States Cross Country Coaches Association (EA)
USCCEC ...... United States Committee for Care of European Children [*Post-World War II*]
USCCHO ...... United States Conference of City Health Officers (EA)

USCCHSO....... United States Conference of City Human Service Officials (EA)
USCCPA....... United States Court of Customs and Patent Appeals [*Abolished, 1982*]
USCCSA....... US Corporate Council on South Africa (EA)
USCDC....... United States Civil Defense Council (EA)
USCEA....... US Council for Energy Awareness (EA)
USCEC....... University of Southern California, Engineering Center (MCD)
USCEF....... US-China Education Foundation (EA)
USCEFI....... United Social, Cultural, and Educational Foundation of India
USCEI....... United States - China Educational Institute (EA)
US Cell....... US Cellular Corp. [*Associated Press*] (SAG)
USCE/NPD... United States Army, Corps of Engineers, North Pacific Division (NOAA)
USCENTAF... United States Central Command - Air Forces
USCENTCOM... United States Central Command
US Cert Den... Certiorari Denied by United States Supreme Court [*Legal term*] (DLA)
US Cert Dis... Certiorari Dismissed by United States Supreme Court [*Legal term*] (DLA)
USCESS....... US Cultural Exchange and Sports Society (EA)
USCF....... United States Chess Federation (EA)
USCF....... United States Churchill Foundation [*Later, WCF*]
USCF....... United States Cycling Federation (EA)
USCG....... United States Coast Guard
USCG....... United States Consul General
USCGA....... United States Coast Guard Academy [*New London, CT*]
USCGA....... United States Coast Guard Auxiliary
USCGAD....... United States Coast Guard Air Detachment
USC-GARP... United States Committee for the Global Atmospheric Research Program [*Defunct*] (EA)
USCGAS....... United States Coast Guard Air Station
USCGASB.... United States Coast Guard Aircraft and Supply Base
USCGAUX.... United States Coast Guard Auxiliary (EA)
USCGB....... United States Coast Guard Base
USCG-B....... United States Coast Guard Office of Boating Safety
USCGB....... Uphill Ski Club of Great Britain (EAIO)
USCGC....... United States Coast Guard Cutter
USCG-C....... United States Coast Guard Office of Chief of Staff
USCGD....... United States Coast Guard Depot
USCG-E....... United States Coast Guard Naval Engineering Division
USCG-M....... United States Coast Guard Office of Merchant Marine Safety
USCG-MFSRS... United States Coast Guard Marine Fire and Safety Research Staff [*Groton, CT*]
USCG-N....... United States Coast Guard Office of Navigation
USC Govt'l Rev... University of South Carolina. Governmental Review [*A publication*] (DLA)
USCGR....... United States Coast Guard Reserve
USCGRC....... United States Coast Guard Receiving Center
USCGR(T).... United States Coast Guard, Reserve (Temporary)
USCGR(W).... United States Coast Guard, Reserve (Women)
USCGS....... United States Coast and Geodetic Survey [*Later, National Ocean Survey*]
USCGSCF.... United States Coast Guard Shore Communication Facilities
USCGTS....... United States Coast Guard Training Station
USCH....... University of South Carolina Herbarium
USCh....... US-China Industrial Exchange, Inc. [*Associated Press*] (SAG)
US Chlnd.... US-China Industrial Exchange, Inc. [*Associated Press*] (SAG)
USCHRB....... US Council for Human Rights in the Balkans (EA)
USCHS....... United States Capitol Historical Society (EA)
USCHS....... US Catholic Historical Society (EA)
USCI....... United Satellite Communications Inc.
USCI....... United States Catheter Instrument [*Commercial firm*] (DAVI)
USCI....... Universal Self Care [*NASDAQ symbol*] (TTSB)
USCI....... Universal Self Care, Inc. [*NASDAQ symbol*] (SAG)
USCI....... USCI, Inc. [*Associated Press*] (SAG)
USCIA....... United States Customs Inspectors' Association Port of New York (EA)
USCIAA....... United States Committee of the International Association of Art (EA)
USCIB....... United States Communications Intelligence Board [*Later, National Security Agency*]
USCIB....... United States Council for International Business (EA)
USCIB....... United States Council on International Banking (EA)
USCIB/IC.... United States Communications Intelligence Board Intelligence Committee [*Obsolete*]
USCICC....... United States Council of the International Chamber of Commerce [*Later, USCIB*] (EA)
USCICSW.... United States Committee of the International Council on Social Welfare (EA)
USCID....... US Committee on Irrigation and Drainage (EA)
USCIDFC....... US Committee on Irrigation, Drainage, and Flood Control [*Later, USCID*] (EA)
USCIGW....... Union of Salt, Chemical, and Industrial General Workers [*British*] (BI)
USCIIC....... United States Civilian Internee Information Center [*Army*] (AABC)
USCIIC(Br).... United States Civilian Internee Information Center (Branch) [*Army*] (AABC)
USCINCAFRED... United States Commander-in-Chief, Air Force Forces, Readiness Command
USCINCARRED... United States Commander-in-Chief, Army Forces, Readiness Command
USCINCCENT... Commander-in-Chief, United States Central Command
USCINCEUR... United States Commander-in-Chief, Europe
USCINCLANT... Commander-in-Chief, United States Atlantic Command
USCINCMEAFSA... United States Commander-in-Chief Middle East, Africa South of the Sahara, and Southern Asia (GFGA)
USCINCPAC... Commander-in-Chief, United States Pacific Command
USCINCRED... United States Commander-in-Chief, Readiness Command
USCINCREDCOM... Commander-in-Chief, US Readiness Command (MCD)
USCINCSO... United States Commander-in-Chief, Southern Command (AFM)
USCINCSOC... United States Commander in Chief, Special Operations Command (DOMA)
USCINCSOCOM... United States Commander in Chief, Special Operations Command (DOMA)
USCINCSOUTH... United States Commander-in-Chief, Southern Command
USCINCSPACE... United States Commander in Chief, Space Command (DOMA)
USCINCTRANSCOM... United States Commander in Chief, Transportation Command (DOMA)
USCINSTRAT... United States Commander in Chief, Strategic Command (DOMA)
US Cir Ct Rep DC... Hayward and Hazelton's United States Circuit Court Reports [*District of Columbia*] [*A publication*] (DLA)
USCISCO....... United States Counterinsurgency Support Office
USCIW....... Universal Self Care Wrrt'A' [*NASDAQ symbol*] (TTSB)
USCIZ....... Universal Self Care Wrrt'B' [*NASDAQ symbol*] (TTSB)
USCJ....... United Society of Carpenters and Joiners [*A union*] [*British*]
USCJE....... United Synagogue Commission on Jewish Education [*Later, USACJE*] (EA)
USCL....... United Society for Christian Literature [*British*]
USCL....... United States Coalition for Life (EA)
USCLA....... United States Club Lacrosse Association (EA)
USCLASS.... US Classifications (NITA)
USCLHO....... United States Conference of Local Health Officers (EA)
USCM....... United States Conference of Mayors (EA)
USCM....... Unit Simulated Combat Mission (AAG)
USCM....... USCI, Inc. [*NASDAQ symbol*] (SAG)
USCM....... USCI Inc. [*NASDAQ symbol*] (TTSB)
USCMA....... United States Catholic Mission Association (EA)
USCMA....... United States Cheese Makers Association (EA)
USCMA....... United States Court of Military Appeals
USCMA....... United States Crutch Manufacturers Association (EA)
USCMA Adv Op... United States Court of Military Appeals, Advance Opinions [*A publication*] (DLA)
USCMC....... United States Catholic Mission Council (EA)
USCMH....... United States Commission of Maritime History (MSC)
USCMI....... United States Commission on Mathematical Instruction
USCo....... Underwriters Salvage Company
USCO....... United States Committee for the Oceans (EA)
USCO....... US Commercial Office [*Department of Commerce, Department of State*] (IMH)
USCOA....... Uniformed Services Contingency Option Act
USCOB....... United States Commander, Berlin
US Code Cong & Ad News... United States Code Congressional and Administrative News [*A publication*] (DLA)
USCOLD....... United States Committee on Large Dams of the International Commission on Large Dams (EA)
USCOMEAST... United States Commander, Eastern Atlantic (MCD)
USCOMEASTLANT... United States Commander, Naval Forces, Eastern Atlantic (NATG)
US Comp St... United States Compiled Statutes [*A publication*] (DLA)
USCOMSUBGRUEASTLANT... United States Commander, Submarines Group, Eastern Atlantic (NATG)
USCONARC.... United States Continental Army Command [*Superseded by FORSCOM*]
US Cond Rep... Peters' Condensed United States Reports [*A publication*] (DLA)
US Const.... United States Constitution [*A publication*] (DLA)
USCP....... United States Capitol Police
USCP....... University of South Carolina Press (DGA)
USCP....... University of Southern California Press (DGA)
USCPAA....... United States Cerebral Palsy Athletic Association (EA)
USCPFA....... US-China Peoples Friendship Association (EA)
USCPSHHM... United States Committee to Promote Studies of the History of the Habsburg Monarchy [*Later, SAHH*] (EA)
USCR....... United States Committee for Refugees (EA)
USCR....... US Census Report [*Database*] [*Business Publishers, Inc.*] [*Information service or system*] (CRD)
USCRA....... United States Citizens' Rights Association (EA)
U Scranton... University of Scranton (GAGS)
USCS....... United States Coast Survey
USCS....... United States Code Service [*A publication*] (DLA)
USCS....... United States Commercial Standard
USCS....... United States Conciliation Service [*Functions transferred to Federal Mediation and Conciliation Service, 1947*]
USCS....... United States Customary System [*System of units used in the US*]
USCS....... United States Customs Service (MCD)
USCS....... Universal Ship Cancellation Society (EA)
USCS....... Urine Sampling and Collection System [*NASA*]
USCS....... US Commercial Service [*International Trade Administration*]
USCS....... USCS International, Inc. [*NASDAQ symbol*] (SAG)
USCSB....... United States Communications Security Board
USCSC....... United States Chefs Ski Club (EA)
USCSC....... United States Civil Service Commission [*Later, MSPB*]
USCSC....... United States Collegiate Sports Council (EA)
USCSC....... United States Cuban Sugar Council [*Defunct*] (EA)
USCSCV....... US Committee for Scientific Cooperation with Vietnam (EA)
USCSE....... United States Civil Service Examination
USC-SFI....... United States Committee-Sports for Israel (EA)
USCS Int....... USCS International, Inc. [*Associated Press*] (SAG)
USCSRA....... United States Cane Sugar Refiners' Association (EA)
USCSSB....... United States Cap Screw Service Bureau [*Later, Cap Screw and Special Threaded Products Bureau*] (EA)
usc sUPP.... United States Code Supplement (BARN)

USCT .... Union des Syndicats Confederes du Togo [*Federation of Confederated Unions of Togo*]
USCT .... United States Colored Troops [*Civil War*]
USCTA .... United States Combined Training Association (EA)
US Ct Cl .... United States Court of Claims (DLA)
US-CUES .... US Campaign for the University of El Salvador (EA)
USCUN .... United States Committee for the United Nations [*Later, UNA-USA*]
USCV .... Union Scientifique Continentale de Verre [*European Union for the Scientific Study of Glass - EUSSG*] (EAIO)
USCWC .... United States Chemical Warfare Committee
USCWCC .... United States Conference for the World Council of Churches (EA)
USCWF .... US Council for World Freedom (EA)
USC-WHO .... United States Committee for the World Health Organization (EA)
USD .... Ultimate Strength Design (IEEE)
USD .... Ultrasonic Separation Detector
USD .... Under Seas Defense Exposition (ITD)
USD .... Under Secretary of Defense [*DoD*] (RDA)
USD .... Unexplained Standard Deviation [*Statistics*]
USD .... Uniao Social Democratico [*Social Democratic Union*] [*Portugal Political party*] (PPE)
USD .... Unified School District
USD .... Union des Sociaux-Democrates [*Burkina Faso*] [*Political party*] (EY)
USD .... Union Social-Democrate [*Social Democratic Union*] [*The Ivory Coast*] [*Political party*] (EY)
USD .... Union Sociale Democratique [*Cameroon*] [*Political party*] (EY)
USD .... United Society of Drillers [*A union*] [*British*]
USD .... United States Dispensatory [*Pharmacology*]
USD .... United States Diving, Inc. (EA)
USD .... United States Dollars
USD .... United States Drone (SAA)
USD .... Universal Standard Data
USD .... University of San Diego
USD .... University of South Dakota, Vermillion, SD [*OCLC symbol*] (OCLC)
USD .... University Science Development [*National Science Foundation*]
USD .... Uranium Series Dating
USD .... Urban Sanitary District [*British*]
USD .... User-Supplied Data
USD(A) .... Under Secretary of Defense for Acquisition [*DoD*] (RDA)
USDA .... Uniform Simultaneous Death Act [*National Conference of Commissioners on Uniform State Laws*]
USDA .... United Square Dancers of America (EA)
USDA .... United States Department of Agriculture [*Washington, DC*] [*Database originator*]
USDA .... United States Disarmament Administration [*Transferred to US Arms Control and Disarmament Agency, 1961*]
USDA .... United States Duffers' Association [*Defunct*] (EA)
USDA .... US Darting Association (EA)
USDA .... US Disc Sports Association (EA)
USDA-APHIS-PP/Q... United States Department of Agriculture, Animal and Plant Health Inspection Service, Plant Protection and Quarantine Programs (PDAA)
USDA/CRIS... USDA Current Research Information System (NITA)
USDA-FS .... United States Department of Agriculture - Forest Service (PDAA)
USDA-FSVP... USDA-Forest Service Volunteers Program (EA)
USDAO .... United States Defense Attache Office [*or Officer*] (AABC)
USDA RDD... USDA [*United States Department of Agriculture*] Regional Document Delivery [*Library network*]
USDA-REA ... United States Department of Agriculture - Rural Electrification Administration (PDAA)
USDASL .... USDA [*United States Department of Agriculture*] Sedimentation Laboratory [*Research center*] (RCD)
USDATA .... United States Data Corp. (NITA)
USData .... US Data Corp. [*Associated Press*] (SAG)
USData .... USData Corp. [*Associated Press*] (SAG)
USDAW .... Union of Ship Distributive and Allied Workers [*British*] (DCTA)
Usdaw .... Union of Shop, Distributive, and Allied Workers [*British*] (ODBW)
USDB .... United States Disciplinary Barracks [*Military*]
USDC .... Underwater Search, Detection, Classification (AAG)
USDC .... United States Defense Committee (EA)
USDC .... United States Department of Commerce
USDC .... United States Display Consortium (PCM)
USDC .... United States District Court
USDC .... United States District of Columbia (DLA)
USDC .... USData Corp. [*NASDAQ symbol*] (SAG)
USDCFO .... United States Defense Communication Field Office (NATG)
USDC Haw... United States District Court, District of Hawaii (DLA)
USDC Haw... United States District Court, District of Hawaii, Reports [*A publication*] (DLA)
USDC Hawaii... United States District Court, District of Hawaii (DLA)
USDC Hawaii... United States District Court, District of Hawaii, Reports [*A publication*] (DLA)
USDD .... United States Department of Defense
USDE .... United States Department of Education
USDE .... United States Department of Energy (MCD)
USDEL .... United States Delegate (NOAA)
USDELIADB... United States Delegation, Inter-American Defense Board (AABC)
USDeliv .... US Delivery Systems, Inc. [*Associated Press*] (SAG)
US Dept Int... United States Department of the Interior (DLA)
US des AL ... Union Syndicale des Artistes Lyriques [*French*] (ROG)
USDESEA .... United States Dependent Schools, European Area [*Army*]
USDF .... United States Dressage Federation (EA)
USDFRC .... US Dairy Forage Research Center [*Research center*] (RCD)
USDGA .... United States Durum Growers Association (EA)
USDH .... United States Direct Hire [*Military*]
USDHE & W... United States Department of Health, Education, and Welfare
USDHUD .... United States Department of Housing and Urban Development
USDI .... United States Department of the Interior
USDia .... US Diagnostics Co. [*Associated Press*] (SAG)
US Diag .... US Diagnostics Co. [*Associated Press*] (SAG)
US Dig .... United States Digest [*A publication*] (DLA)
USDISBad .... United States Distinguished International Shooter Badge [*Military decoration*] (AABC)
U S Dist Ct... United States District Court (BARN)
US Dist Ct Haw... United States District Court District of Hawaii (DLA)
USDJ .... United States Department of Justice
USDJ .... United States District Judge
USDL .... United States Department of Labor
USDL .... U.S. Diagnostic Labs [*NASDAQ symbol*] (TTSB)
USDL .... US Diagnostics [*NASDAQ symbol*] (SAG)
USDLGI .... United States Defense Liaison Group, Indonesia [*Army*] (AABC)
USDNDR .... US Decade for Natural Disaster Reduction [*1990's*]
USDO .... United States Disbursing Officer
USDOC .... United States Department of Commerce
USDOCO .... United States Documents Officer (AFM)
USDOCOLANDSOUTHEAST... United States Document Office, Allied Land Forces, Southeastern Europe (AABC)
USDOD .... United States Department of Defense
USDOE .... United States Department of Energy [*Also, an information service or system*]
USDOI .... United States Department of the Interior (MCD)
USDOT .... United States Department of Transportation (MCD)
USD(P) .... Undersecretary of Defense for Policy (MCD)
USDP .... University of San Diego Press (DGA)
USDP .... University of South Dakota Press (DGA)
USDR .... United States Divorce Reform [*Defunct*] (EA)
USDRE .... Office of the Under Secretary of Defense for Research and Engineering
USDRO .... US Defense Representative Office (DOMA)
USDRP .... Unia Socjaldemokratyczna Rzeczypospolitej Polskiej [*Social Democratic Union of the Republic of Poland*] [*Political party*]
USDS .... United States Department of State
USDS .... US Disc Sports Association (EA)
USDSA .... United States Deaf Skiers Association (EA)
USDSEA .... United States Dependent Schools, European Area [*Army*] (AABC)
USDT .... United States Department of the Treasury
USDT .... United States Department of Transportation
USDTA .... United States Dental Tennis Association (EA)
USDTP .... Ukrainska Sotsial Demokraticheskaia Truda Partiia [*Ukrainian Social Democratic Labor Party*] [*Russian Political party*] (PPE)
USDW .... Underground Sources of Drinking Water
USE .... Encyclopedia of United States Reports [*A publication*] (DLA)
USE .... Underground Service Entrance
USE .... Undersea Scientific Expedition
USE .... Understanding Science in the Environment [*Australia*]
USE .... Unified S-Band Equipment
USE .... United States Economic Problems [*British World War II*]
USE .... United States Embassy
USE .... United States Envelope Co.
USE .... Unit Support Equipment
USE .... UNIVAC Scientific Exchange [*Later, UI, USE, Inc.*]
USE .... Universal Automatic Computer Scientific Exchange (IAA)
USE .... University of South Dakota, Law Library, Vermillion, SD [*OCLC symbol*] (OCLC)
USE .... University of Southern Europe [*Monaco*] (ECON)
USE .... University Space Experiments
USE .... Unmanned Surveillance Equipment
USE .... US English [*An association*] (EA)
USE .... User Support Environment (SSD)
USE .... Utilized Starch Equivalent (BARN)
USE .... Wauseon, OH [*Location identifier FAA*] (FAAL)
USEA .... Undersea (AABC)
USEASA .... United States Eastern Amateur Ski Association [*Later, ESA*]
USEC .... United State Enrichment Corporation
USEC .... United States Endurance Cup [*Car racing*]
USEC .... United States Enrichment Corporation (DOGT)
USEC .... United States Mission to European Communities [*Department of State*]
USEC .... United System of Electronic Computers (IEEE)
USEC .... Universal Security Instruments, Inc. [*NASDAQ symbol*] (NQ)
USEC .... Univl Security Instr [*NASDAQ symbol*] (TTSB)
USecBc .... United Security Bancorp (Washington) [*Associated Press*] (SAG)
USECC .... United States Employees' Compensation Commission [*Functions transferred to Federal Security Agency, 1946*]
USECOM .... United States Army Electronics Command [*Obsolete*]
USECOM .... United States Economic Mission [*Foreign aid*] (VNW)
USecWar .... Under Secretary of War [*Obsolete*]
USED .... Underwater Sound Explosive Devices Branch [*Naval Weapons Station*] [*Yorktown, VA*]
USEE .... United States Exploring Expedition [*1838-42*] [*Navy*]
USEEM .... United States Establishment and Enterprise Microdata Base [*Brookings Institution*]
USEES .... United States Naval Engineering Experiment Station [*Annapolis, MD*]
USEFP .... United States Educational Foundation in Pakistan
USEG .... U.S. Energy [*NASDAQ symbol*] (TTSB)
USEG .... US Energy Corp. [*NASDAQ symbol*] (NQ)
USEI .... United States Society of Esperanto Instructors [*Later, AATE*]
USEJ .... United States Society for Esperantists Youth (EA)
USELMCENTO... United States Element Central Treaty Organization (AFM)
USEM .... United States Egg Marketers (EA)
USEMA .... [*The*] United States Electronic Mail Association

USEMB United States Embassy (MCD)
USEME Undergraduate Science Engineering and Mathematics Education [*National Science Foundation*] (EGAO)
USEMS United Steam Engine Makers' Society [*A union*] [*British*]
USENET User Network (SSD)
US Enr United States Energy Corp. [*Associated Press*] (SAG)
US EnvS US Environmental Solutions, Inc. [*Associated Press*] (SAG)
USEO United States Employment Opportunities
USEO United States Engineer Office
USEORD Use Order [*Navy*] (NVT)
USEP United States Escapee Program
USEPA United States Environmental Protection Agency
US EPA United States Environmental Protection Agency
US EPA U.S. Environmental Protection Agency
US Eq Dig United States Equity Digest [*A publication*] (DLA)
USER Ultra-Small Electronics Research [*DoD*]
USER Unique-to-Site Equipment Review (SAA)
USER User System Evaluator [*Computer science*] (MHDB)
USER User Systems Ergonomics Research [*Computer science*]
USERC US Environment and Resources Council [*Defunct*] (EA)
USERDA United States Energy Research and Development Administration [*Superseded by Department of Energy, 1977*]
USERIA Ultrasensitive Enzymatic Radioimmunoassay [*Clinical chemistry*]
USERID User Identification [*Computer science*]
USER INC Urban Scientific and Educational Research, Inc. [*Defunct*] (EA)
USERP United Scientists for Environmental Responsibility and Protection (EERA)
USERRA Uniformed Services Employment and Re-employment Rights Act [*Military*]
USERS Uniform Socio-Economic Reporting System [*Financial reporting system for voluntary health and welfare organizations*]
USES United States Employment Service [*Department of Labor*]
US ES US Energy Systems, Inc. [*Associated Press*] (SAG)
USES U.S. Environmental Solutions [*NASDAQ symbol*] (TTSB)
USES US Environmental Solutions, Inc. [*NASDAQ symbol*] (SAG)
USESF United States Exchange Stabilization Fund
US-ESRIC US-El Salvador Research and Information Center (EA)
USESSA United States Environmental Science Services Administration (AABC)
US ESys US Energy Systems, Inc. [*Associated Press*] (SAG)
USET United South and Eastern Tribes (EA)
USET United States Equestrian Team (EA)
USEUCOM United States European Command
USEUCOM United States European Communications (SAA)
USExpInc United States Exploration, Inc. [*Associated Press*] (SAG)
USEY US Energy Systems, Inc. [*NASDAQ symbol*] (SAG)
USF Lommen Health Science Library, University of South Dakota, Vermillion, SD [*OCLC symbol*] (OCLC)
USF Und So Fort [*And So Forth*] [*German*]
USF Uniaxial Stress Field
USF United Scleroderma Foundation (EA)
USF United Socialist Front [*Thailand*] [*Political party*] (PD)
USF United Somali Front [*Political party*] (EY)
USF United States Filter Corp. [*NYSE symbol*] (SAG)
USF United States Fleet
USF United States Forces (CINC)
USF University of San Francisco [*California*]
USF Upstream Stimualtory Factor [*Genetics*]
USF U.S. Filter [*NYSE symbol*] (TTSB)
USF US Filter Corp. [*NYSE symbol*] (SPSG)
USFA United Sports Fans of America (EA)
USFA United States Fencing Association (EA)
USFA United States Fire Administration [*Federal Emergency Management Agency*] (GFGA)
USFA United States Forces in Austria
USFA United States Fuel Administration [*Terminated*]
USFA US Farmers Association (EA)
US Facil United States Facilities [*Associated Press*] (SAG)
US Facl United States Facilities Corp. [*Associated Press*] (SAG)
USFADTC United States Fleet Air Defense Training Center
USFAIRWINGMED United States Fleet Air Wing, Mediterranean (NATG)
USF & G United States Fidelity & Guaranty Co.
USFARS United States Federation of Amateur Roller Skaters [*Later, USAC-RS*] (EA)
USFBI United States Forces, British Isles [*World War II*]
USFC United States Foil Co.
USFC USFreightways [*NASDAQ symbol*] (TTSB)
USFC USFreightways Corp. [*NASDAQ symbol*] (SAG)
USFCA United States Fencing Coaches Association (EA)
USFCC United States Fire Companies Conference [*Defunct*] (EA)
USFCC US Federation for Culture Collections (EA)
USFCF USF Constellation Foundation (EA)
USFCT United States Forces, China Theater
USFET United States Forces, European Theater [*American headquarters for occupation of Germany after SHAEF was dissolved*] [*World War II*]
USFF United States Flag Foundation (EA)
USFFL United States Flag Football League (EA)
USFG USF & G Corp. [*Associated Press*] (SAG)
USFGC US Feed Grains Council (EA)
USFGP USF & G Pacholder Fund, Inc. [*Associated Press*] (SAG)
USFHA USA Field Hockey Association (EA)
USFHP Uniformed Services Family Health Plan [*DoD*]
USFI Unione Sindacale Ferrovieri Italiani [*National Union of Italian Railway Workers*]
USFIA United States Forces in Australia
US Filter United States Filter Corp. [*Associated Press*] (SAG)
USFIP United States Forces in the Philippines
USFIS United States Foundation for International Scouting (EA)
USFISC United States Foreign Intelligence Surveillance Court
USFIT User Standards Forum for Information Technology (NITA)
USFJ United States Forces, Japan (CINC)
USFK United States Forces, Korea
USFL US Football League [*Defunct*] (EA)
USFMG United States Fastener Manufacturing Group [*Defunct*] (EA)
USFMG United States Foreign Medical Graduate (DHSM)
USFMIA United States Fishmeal Importers Association [*Defunct*] (EA)
USFOA United States Forces, Occupation Austria [*World War II*]
USFOR United States Forces
USFORAZ United States Forces in Azores
USFORSCOM US Forces Command [*Specified*] (DOMA)
USFP Union Socialiste des Forces Populaires [*Socialist Union of Popular Forces*] [*Morocco*] [*Political party*] (PPW)
USFP United States Federation of Pelota (EA)
USFP United States Forces, Police
USFPS United States Forces, Police Squadron
USFR United States Fleet Reserve
US Frch US Franchise Systems, Inc. [*Associated Press*] (SAG)
USFreight USFreightways Corp. [*Associated Press*] (SAG)
USFS United Society of Fitters and Smiths [*A union*] [*British*]
USFS United States Foreign Service [*Department of State*]
USFS United States Forest Service
USFS United States Frequency Standard
USFS US Flywheel Systems [*Research center*] (ECON)
USFS US Franchise Systems, Inc. [*NASDAQ symbol*] (SAG)
USFSA United States Figure Skating Association (EA)
USFSPA Uniformed Services Former Spouse Protection Act [*Military*]
USFSS United States Fleet SONAR School
USFSS US Federation of Scholars and Scientists (EA)
USFTA United States Floor Tennis Association [*Defunct*] (EA)
USFTL US Flag and Touch Football League (EA)
USFU Unglazed Structural Facing Units [*Technical drawings*]
USFV United States Forces, Vietnam
USFVL Rev University of San Fernando Valley. Law Review [*A publication*] (DLA)
USFWS United States Fish and Wildlife Service [*Department of the Interior*]
USG Ultrasonic Space Grating
USG Ultrasonography
USG Ulysses Simpson Grant [*US general and president, 1822-1885*]
USG Underwater Systems Group [*Range Commanders Council*] [*White Sands Missile Range, NM*]
USG Union of Superiors General (EA)
USG United States Gallon (IAA)
USG United States Gauge
USG United States Government
USG User Support Group (NITA)
USG USG Corp. [*NYSE symbol*] (SPSG)
USG US Grant Mining [*Vancouver Stock Exchange symbol*]
USGA Ulysses S. Grant Association (EA)
USGA United States Golf Association (EA)
USGA US Green Alliance (EA)
USGAL United States Gallon (IAA)
USGC US Geodynamics Committee (EA)
USGCA US Government Contract Awards (NITA)
USGCC/A United States Group Control Council/Austria [*World War II*]
USGCC/G United States Group Control Council/Germany [*World War II*]
USGCLR United States-German Committee on Learning and Remembrance [*Defunct*] (EA)
USGCM United States Government Correspondence Manual
US/GCRP United States Global Change Research Program [*Marine science*] (OSRA)
USGCRP United States Global Change Research Program (BARN)
USGF United States Gymnastics Federation (EA)
USGIC United States Global-Positioning-Satellite Industry Council
USGIPU United States Group of the Inter-Parliamentary Union (EA)
USGL United States Gold Corp. [*NASDAQ symbol*] (SAG)
USGL U.S. Gold Corp. [*NASDAQ symbol*] (TTSB)
USGLI United States Government Life Insurance
USGlobal US Global Investors, Inc. [*Associated Press*] (SAG)
USGLW Union of Saddlers and General Leather Workers [*British*]
USGM United States Government Manual [*A publication*] (OICC)
US Gold United States Gold Corp. [*Associated Press*] (SAG)
USGP United States Grand Prix [*Auto racing*]
USGPM United States Government Purchasing Mission [*World War II*]
USGPO United States Government Printing Office
USGR United States Government Report (IEEE)
USGRA United States Government Report Announcements (IID)
USGRDR United States Government Research and Development Reports [*Later, GRA*]
USGRDR-I United States Government Research and Development Reports Index [*Later, GRI*]
USGRR United States Government Research Reports [*National Bureau of Standards publication*]
USGS United States Geological Survey [*Reston, VA*] [*Databank originator*]
USGS U. S. Geological Survey
USGSA United States Grain Standards Act (GFGA)
USGSA United States Grass Ski Association (EA)
USGSA United States Gymnastic Safety Association
USGSC United States Global Strategy Council (EA)
USGSG United States Government Standard Gage (IAA)
USGW Underwater-to-Surface Guided Weapon (MCD)
USG.WS USG Corp. Wrrt [*NYSE symbol*] (TTSB)

U SH .... Shilling [*Monetary unit in Uganda*]
USH .... United Scientific Holdings [*Defense equipment manufacturer*] [*British*]
USH .... Ushuaia [*Argentina*] [*Airport symbol*] (OAG)
USH .... USLIFE Corp. [*NYSE symbol*] (SPSG)
USHA .... United States Handball Association (EA)
USHA .... United States Housing Authority [*Functions transferred to Public Housing Commissioner, 1947*]
USHB .... Uniformed Services Health Benefits
USHBP .... Uniformed Services Health Benefits Program
USHC .... United States Housing Corp. [*Terminated, 1952*]
USHC .... U.S. Healthcare [*NASDAQ symbol*] (TTSB)
USHC .... US Healthcare, Inc. [*NASDAQ symbol*] (NQ)
USHCA .... US Horse Cavalry Association (EA)
USHCC .... US Hispanic Chamber of Commerce (EA)
USHDA .... United States Highland Dancing Association (EA)
USHDI .... United States Historical Documents Institute
USHE .... Upstream Heat Exchanger (AAG)
USHG .... United States Home Guard
USHG .... U.S. Home & Garden [*NASDAQ symbol*] (TTSB)
USHG .... US Home & Garden, Inc. [*NASDAQ symbol*] (SAG)
US HG .... US Home & Garden, Inc. [*Associated Press*] (SAG)
USHGA .... United States Hop Growers Association
USHGA .... US Hang Gliding Association (EA)
USHGW .... US Home & Garden Wrrt'A' [*NASDAQ symbol*] (TTSB)
USHH .... Khanty-Mansiysk [*Former USSR ICAO location identifier*] (ICLI)
USHIGEO .... United States National Committee for the History of Geology (EA)
USHL .... United States Hockey League
USHL .... United States Hydrograph Laboratory
USHL .... United States Hygienic Laboratory
US Hlth .... United States Healthcare, Inc. [*Associated Press*] (SAG)
USHm .... US Home Corp. [*Associated Press*] (SAG)
USHMAC .... United States Health Manpower Advisory Council
USHMC .... US Holocaust Memorial Council (EA)
USHmcr .... US HomeCare Corp. [*Associated Press*] (SAG)
USHme .... US Home Corp. [*Associated Press*] (SAG)
USHmGrd .... US Home & Garden, Inc. [*Associated Press*] (SAG)
USHO .... United States Hydrographic Office [*Later, Naval Oceanographic Office*]
USHO .... U.S. HomeCare [*NASDAQ symbol*] (TTSB)
USHO .... US HomeCare Corp. [*NASDAQ symbol*] (SPSG)
USHP .... United States Helium Plant [*Amarillo, TX*]
USHP .... U-Ship Inc. [*NASDAQ symbol*] (TTSB)
USHRA .... United States Hot Rod Association [*Auto racing*]
USHSLA .... US Hide, Skin, and Leather Association (EA)
USHTA .... United States Handicap Tennis Association (EA)
USHWA .... United States Harness Writers' Association (EA)
USHWC .... US Helsinki Watch Committee (EA)
USI .... Mabaruma [*Guyana*] [*Airport symbol*] (OAG)
USI .... Ultrasonic System [*Vancouver Stock Exchange symbol*]
USI .... Ultraviolet Spectroheliographic Instrument
USI .... Union of Students in Ireland (AIE)
USI .... United Schools International [*New Delhi, India*] (EAIO)
USI .... United Service Institution (BARN)
USI .... United Sons of Israel (EA)
USI .... United States Industries, Inc. [*NYSE symbol*] (SAG)
USI .... United States Industry
USI .... United States Information Agency, Washington, DC [*OCLC symbol*] (OCLC)
USI .... United States of Indonesia (BARN)
USI .... Universal Software Interface [*MRI Systems Corp.*]
USI .... University Systems, Inc. (AAGC)
USI .... Unlawful Sexual Intercourse
USI .... Unresolved Safety Issue [*Nuclear energy*] (NRCH)
USI .... Unsigned Short Integer [*Computer science*]
USI .... Update Software Identity (MCD)
USI .... Uranium Supply - Import Model [*Department of Energy*] (GFGA)
USI .... Urinary Stress Incontinence [*Urology*] (DAVI)
USI .... User Software Integration Subsystem [*Space Flight Operations Facility, NASA*]
USI .... User/System Interface
USI .... User System Interface (NITA)
USI .... US, Inc. (EA)
USI .... US Industries [*Subsidiary of the Hanson Group*] [*British*] (ECON)
USIA .... United States Information Agency [*Formerly called BECA, it later became known as ICA or USICA, then again as USIA*]
USIA .... US Inspection Agency (DOMA)
USIAC .... United States Inter-American Council [*Later, COA*] (EA)
USIAEA .... United States Mission to the International Atomic Energy Agency
USIAPR .... United States Information Agency Procurement [*A publication*] (AAGC)
USIB .... United States Intelligence Board [*Later, NFIB*] [*National Security Council*]
USIBA .... United States International Book Association (NTCM)
USIC .... Undersea Instrument Chamber [*Marine science*] (MSC)
USIC .... Union Sportive Interuniversitaire Canadienne
USIC .... United States Industrial Council (EA)
USIC .... United States Information Center [*Department of State*] (MCD)
USIC .... US Industrial Coalition [*For finding commercial use of nuclear technology*]
USICA .... United States International Communication Agency [*Also, ICA*] [*Formerly called BECA and USIA, it later became known again as USIA*]
USICC .... United States Industrial Chemical Co. (KSC)
USICC Rep .... United States Interstate Commerce Commission Reports [*A publication*] (DLA)
USICCVR .... United States Interstate Commerce Commission Valuation Reports [*A publication*] (DLA)
US ICDBL .... US Branch of the International Committee for the Defense of the Breton Language (EA)
USICF .... Union Sportive Interuniversitaire Canadienne Feminine
USICID .... United States National Committee, International Commission on Irrigation and Drainage
US/ICID .... US Committee on Irrigation and Drainage [*Formerly, USCIDFC*] (EA)
US/ICOMOS .... United States Committee of the International Council on Monuments and Sites (EA)
USIDF .... United States Icelandic Defense Forces (MCD)
USIFA .... US International Fireball Association (EA)
USIHR .... US Institute of Human Rights (EA)
USIITA .... United States Indian International Travel Agency, Inc.
USILA .... United States Intercollegiate Lacrosse Association (EA)
USIMC .... United States International Marketing Center [*American Embassy, London*] (CB)
USIMCA .... United States International Moth Class Association (EA)
USINCC .... United States International Narcotics Control Commission
US Inds .... United States Industries, Inc. [*Associated Press*] (SAG)
USINOA .... US Immigration and Naturalization Officers' Association (EA)
USINS .... United States Immigration and Naturalization Service (BARN)
USINT .... United States Interests Section [*Foreign Service*]
USIO .... Unidentified Submerged Illuminated Object (DNAB)
USIO .... United States Industrial Outlook [*A publication*]
USIO .... United States Institute of Oceanography (DNAB)
USIO .... Unlimited Sequential Input/Output
USIP .... United Solomon Islands Party (PPW)
USIP .... University of Stockholm Institute of Physics
USIP .... US Institute of Peace (EA)
USIPC .... Uniformed Services Identification and Privilege Card (AFM)
USIPU .... United States Inter-Parliamentary Union (EA)
USIRB .... United States Internal Revenue Bonded
USIS .... Ultraviolet Stratospheric Imaging Spectrometer (MCD)
USIS .... United States Information Service [*Name used abroad for USIA offices*]
USISA .... United States International Sailing Association (EA)
USISA .... United States International Skating Association
USISCA .... US Islands 17 Class Association [*Defunct*] (EA)
USISL .... United States Information Service Library (DIT)
USISSA .... United States International Speed Skating Association (EA)
US-ISY .... US International Space Year Association (EA)
USIT .... Unit Share Investment Trust
USITA .... United States Independent Telephone Association (EA)
USITA .... United States International Tempest Association (EA)
USITC .... United States International Trade Commission
USITC Pub .... United States International Trade Commission. Publication [*A publication*] (DLA)
USITE .... United States International Transportation Exposition (PDAA)
USITT .... United States Institute for Theatre Technology (EA)
USIU .... United States International University [*San Diego, CA*]
USJ .... Uniformed Services Journal [*A publication*]
USJ .... United States Jaycees (EA)
USJ .... United States Judo (EA)
USJ .... US Jet, Inc. [*ICAO designator*] (FAAC)
USJA .... United States Judo Association (EA)
USJAC .... US-Japan Culture Center (EA)
US JAYCEE .... United States Junior Chamber of Commerce [*Later, United States Jaycees*] (EA)
USJB .... Union Saint-Jean-Baptiste (EA)
USJBC .... US-Japan Business Council (EA)
USJCA .... United States Joint Communication Agency (NATG)
USJCB .... Unites States Joint Communication Board (IAA)
USJCC .... United States Junior Chamber of Commerce [*Later, United States Jaycees*] (EA)
USJCC .... US-Japan Culture Center (EA)
USJCIRPTE .... United States-Japan Committee on Industry Related Policies and Their Trade Effects [*Acronym pronounced "use-jay-krip-tee"*]
USJCS .... United States Joint Chiefs of Staff (NATG)
US-JCSC .... United States-Japan Committee on Scientific Cooperation [*Department of State*]
USJF .... United States Judo Federation (EA)
USJF .... United States Justice Foundation (EA)
USJNRP .... United States/Japan Natural Resources Panel
USJPRS .... United States Joint Publications Research Service
US-JTC .... United States-Japan Trade Council (EA)
USJTF .... United States Joint Task Force (AABC)
US Jur .... United States Jurist [*A publication*] (DLA)
USJUWTF .... United States Joint Unconventional Warfare Task Force (AABC)
USK .... Ultrasonic Kit
USK .... United States Forces, Korea
USKA .... United States Kart Association [*Defunct*] (EA)
USKBA .... United Strictly Kosher Butchers Association
USKBTC .... United States Kerry Blue Terrier Club (EA)
USKEC .... US-Korea Economic Council [*Later, KS*] (EA)
USKF .... United States Korfball Federation (EA)
USKOREA .... United States Forces Korea
USKOS .... US-Korea Society [*Later, KS*] (EA)
USl .... Salt Lake City Public Library, Salt Lake City, UT [*Library symbol Library of Congress*] (LCLS)
USL .... Underwater Sound Laboratory [*New London, CT*] [*Navy*]
USL .... Unemployed Supernumerary List [*Military British*]
USL .... Unique Suppliers List
USL .... United Satellites Ltd. [*London, England*] [*Telecommunications*] (TSSD)

USL............ United Soccer League (EA)
USL............ United States Laws (DLA)
USL............ United States Legation
USL............ Unit Spares List
USL............ Universal Sign Language (EERA)
USL............ Unix Systems Laboratory [*Computer science*]
USL............ Upper Specified Limit
USL............ Upper Square Law Limit (IAA)
USL............ Up Stage Left [*Away from audience*] [*A stage direction*]
USL............ Useless Loop [*Australia Airport symbol*] (OAG)
USL............ US Long Distance [*Vancouver Stock Exchange symbol*]
USL............ Usual (ROG)
USLA.......... United States Committee for Justice to Latin American Political Prisoners [*Defunct*] (EA)
USLA.......... United States Lifesaving Association (EA)
USLA.......... United States Luge Association (EA)
USL & H...... United States Longshoremen and Harborworkers Act
USLANT....... United States Atlantic Subarea [*NATO*]
USLANTCOM... US Atlantic Command [*Unified*] (DOMA)
US Law Ed... United States Supreme Court Reports, Lawyers' Edition [*A publication*] (DLA)
US Law Int... United States Law Intelligencer and Review [*Providence and Philadelphia*] [*A publication*] (DLA)
US Law Jour... United States Law Journal [*A publication*] (DLA)
US Law Mag... United States Law Magazine [*A publication*] (DLA)
USIC........... Church of Jesus Christ of Latter-Day Saints, Historian's Office, Salt Lake City,UT [*Library symbol Library of Congress*] (LCLS)
USLC........... United States Locals Collectors (EA)
USLCA......... United States Lacrosse Coaches' Association (EA)
USLCMBA.... US Letter Carriers Mutual Benefit Association [*Washington, DC*] (EA)
USID........... Daughters of Utah Pioneers Museum Library, Salt Lake City, UT [*Library symbol Library of Congress*] (LCLS)
USLD........... Ultrasonic Link Detector
USLD........... Union des Syndicats Libres du Dahomey [*Federation of Free Unions of Dahomey*]
USLD........... United States Long Distance [*NASDAQ symbol*] (SAG)
USLD........... US Long Distance [*NASDAQ symbol*] (SAG)
USLDMA...... United States Lanolin and Derivative Manufacturers Association [*Defunct*] (EA)
USLE........... Universal Soil Loss Equation [*Agricultural engineering*]
USL Ed........ Lawyers' Edition, United States Supreme Court Reports [*A publication*] (DLA)
USL Ed 2d... Lawyers' Edition, United States Supreme Court Reports, Second Series [*A publication*] (DLA)
UslfeF.......... USLIFE Income Fund, Inc. [*Associated Press*] (SAG)
USIGS.......... Church of Jesus Christ of Latter-Day Saints, Genealogical Society Library, Salt Lake City, UT [*Library symbol Library of Congress*] (LCLS)
USLH........... University of Southwestern Louisiana Herbarium
USLHS......... United States Lighthouse Society (EA)
USLI............ Ultra Large Scale Integration (NTCM)
USLIFE........ USLIFE Corp. [*Associated Press*] (SAG)
USLime........ United States Lime & Minerals Co. [*Associated Press*] (SAG)
USLJ........... United States Law Journal [*New Haven and New York*] [*A publication*] (DLA)
USIL............ Latter-Day Saints Museum, Salt Lake City, UT [*Library symbol Library of Congress*] (LCLS)
USLM........... US Lime & Minerals [*NASDAQ symbol*] (SPSG)
USL Mag..... United States Law Magazine [*A publication*] (DLA)
USLMRA...... United States Lawn Mower Racing Association
USLO........... United States Liaison Office [*or Officer*]
USLO........... University Students for Law and Order
USLOK........ US Liaison Office-Kuwait (DOMA)
US Long...... US Long Distance [*Associated Press*] (SAG)
US LongD.... United States Long Distance [*Associated Press*] (SAG)
USIOr.......... Oregon Short Line Law Department, Salt Lake City, UT [*Library symbol Library of Congress Obsolete*] (LCLS)
USLO SACA... United States Liaison Officer to Supreme Allied Commander, Atlantic (MUGU)
USLOT......... US Liaison Office-Tunisia (DOMA)
USIP............ Pioneer Memorial Museum, Salt Lake City, UT [*Library symbol Library of Congress*] (LCLS)
USLP........... United States Labor Party
USLS........... United States Lake Survey [*Marine science*] (MSC)
USLS........... United States Lighthouse Society (EA)
USLSA......... United States League of Savings Associations [*Later, USLSI*]
USLSA......... United States Livestock Sanitary Association [*Later, United States Animal Health Association*] (EA)
USLSI.......... United States League of Savings Institutions [*Chicago, IL*] (EA)
USLSO......... United States Logistics Support Office (AFM)
USIStM........ College of Saint Mary-of-the-Wasatch, Salt Lake City, UT [*Library symbol Library of Congress Obsolete*] (LCLS)
USIT............ Utah Technical College at Salt Lake, Salt Lake City, UT [*Library symbol Library of Congress*] (LCLS)
USLTA......... Uniform Simplification of Land Transfers Act (DICI)
USLTA......... United States Lawn Tennis Association [*Later, USTA*] (EA)
USLTC......... United States Lakeland Terrier Club (EA)
USLW.......... United States Law Week [*Bureau of National Affairs*] [*A publication*] (DLA)
USIW........... Westminster College, Salt Lake City, UT [*Library symbol Library of Congress*] (LCLS)
USM............ Underwater-to-Surface Missile [*Air Force*]
USM............ Uniform Staffing Methodologies [*DoD*]
USM............ United Securities Market [*British*] (CDAI)
USM............ United States Mail
USM............ United States Marine
USM............ United States Mint
USM............ United States Minutemen [*Defunct*] (EA)
USM............ United States Representative to the Military Committee Memorandum [*NATO*]
USM............ University of Southern Mississippi
USM............ Unlisted Securities Market [*London Stock Exchange*]
USM............ Unsaponifiable Matter [*Organic analytical chemistry*]
USM............ Unscheduled Maintenance
USM............ U.S. Cellular [*AMEX symbol*] (TTSB)
USM............ US Cellular Corp. [*AMEX symbol*] (SPSG)
UsM............ US Microfilm Corp., Jacksonville, FL [*Library symbol Library of Congress*] (LCLS)
USMA.......... Underfeed Stoker Makers' Association [*British*] (BI)
USMA.......... United States Maritime Administration
USMA.......... United States Military Academy [*West Point, NY*]
USMA.......... United States Military Attache
USMA.......... United States Monopoly Association (EA)
USMA.......... United Street Machine Association (EA)
USMA.......... US Maritime Academy (DOMA)
USMA.......... US Metric Association (EA)
USMA.......... US Military Academy (DOMA)
USMAC........ United States Marine Air Corps
USMAC........ United States Military Assistance Command
USMACSV.... United States Military Assistance Command, South Vietnam [*Obsolete*]
USMACTHAI... United States Military Assistance Command, Thailand [*Obsolete*] (AFM)
USMACV...... United States Military Assistance Command, Vietnam [*Obsolete*]
USMA/ESGS... United States Military Academy Department of Earth, Space, and Graphic Sciences [*West Point, NY*]
USMAG........ United States Military Advisory Group
USMAPS...... United States Military Academy Preparatory School
USMAPU...... United States Military Academy Preparatory Unit
USMARC...... Advisory Committee for the US Meat Animal Research Center [*Terminated, 1977*] (EGAO)
USMATS...... United States Military Air Transport Service [*Later, Military Airlift Command*]
USMB.......... United States Marine Barracks
USMB.......... United States Metric Board [*Terminated*]
USMBHA...... US-Mexico Border Health Association (EA)
USMBP........ US-Mexico Border Program (EA)
USMC.......... United States Marine Corps
USMC.......... United States Maritime Commission [*Functions transferred to Department of Commerce, 1950*]
USMCA........ United States Men's Curling Association [*Later, USCA*] (EA)
USMCA........ US Mariner Class Association (EA)
USMCA........ US Mirror Class Association (EA)
USMCAM..... United States Military Community Activity, Mannheim
USMCAS...... United States Marine Corps Air Station
USMCB........ United States Marine Corps Base (MCD)
USMCC........ United States Mint - Carson City (ROG)
USMCCCA.... US Marine Corps Combat Correspondents Association (EA)
USMCDIA.... United States Marine Corps Drill Instructors Association (EA)
USMCEB...... United States Military Communications Electronics Board (NVT)
USMCMG..... US Mine Countermeasures Group (DOMA)
USMCOC...... United States-Mexico Chamber of Commerce [*See also CCMEU*] (EA)
USMCP........ United States Military Construction Program (CINC)
USMCR........ United States Marine Corps Reserve
USMCR(AF)... United States Marine Corps Reserve (Aviation Fleet)
USMCR(AO)... United States Marine Corps Reserve (Aviation, Organized)
USMCR(AV)... United States Marine Corps Reserve (Aviation, Volunteer)
USMCR(F)... United States Marine Corps Reserve (Fleet)
USMCR(LS)... United States Marine Corps Reserve (Limited Service)
USMCR(NAV)... United States Marine Corps Reserve (Naval Aviators)
USMCR(NAVO)... United States Marine Corps Reserve (Graduate Aviation Cadets, Volunteer)
USMCR(NAVT)... United States Marine Corps Reserve (Aviation Specialist Transport Pilot, Volunteer)
USMCR(O)... United States Marine Corps Reserve (Organized)
USMCRTC.... United States Marine Corps Reserve Training Center
USMCR(V)... United States Marine Corps Reserve (Volunteer)
USMCR(VS)... United States Marine Corps Reserve (Volunteer Specialists)
USMCR(W)... United States Marine Corps Reserve (Women)
USMCSS...... United States Marine Corps Selective Service Selectee
USMCSSV.... United States Marine Corps Selective Service Volunteer
USMC(W).... United States Marine Corps (Women)
USMCWR..... United States Marine Corps Women's Reserve
USMD.......... U.S. Medical Products [*NASDAQ symbol*] (TTSB)
USMECBL.... United States Mission to the European Communities in Belgium and Luxembourg
USMEF......... United States Meat Export Federation (EA)
USMEMILCOMUN... United States Members, United Nations Military Staff Committee
USMEOUN.... United States Mission to the European Office of the United Nations
USMEPC...... United States Military Enlistment Processing Command
USMEPCOM... United States Military Entrance Processing Command
USMES........ Unified Science and Mathematics for Elementary Schools [*National Science Foundation*]
USMF.......... United States Sports Massage Federation (EA)
USMG.......... United States Medical Graduate
USMH.......... United States Marine Hospital
USMHS........ United States Marine Hospital Service

USMI .... Universal Software Market Identifier [*Technique Learning*] [*Information service or system*] (IID)
USMIAEAA... United States Mission to the International Atomic Energy Agency in Austria
USMICC .... United States Military Information Control Committee (AFM)
USMID .... Ultrasensitive Microwave Infrared Detector
USMILADREP... United States Military Advisor's Representative (CINC)
USMILADREPSMPO... United States Military Advisor's Representative, Southeast Asia Treaty Organization, Military Planning Office (CINC)
USMILATTACHE... United States Military Attache
USMILCOMUN... United States Delegation, United Nations Military Staff Committee
USMILLIAS... United States Military Liaison Office
USMILTAG... United States Military Technical Advisory Group (AFM)
USMITT....... United States Masters International Track Team [*Defunct*] (EA)
USML.......... United States Microgravity Laboratory [*NASA*]
USML.......... Universal Standard Medical Labs [*NASDAQ symbol*] (SAG)
USML.......... Univl Standard Medl Labs [*NASDAQ symbol*] (TTSB)
USML.......... US Munitions List (DOMA)
USMLM........ United States Military Liaison Mission (MCD)
USML Mag... United States Monthly Law Magazine [*A publication*] (DLA)
USMLMCINCGSFG... United States Military Liaison Mission to Commander-in-Chief, Group Soviet Forces, Germany (AABC)
USMLO .... United States Military Liaison Office
USMLS .... United States Museum Librarian Society (EA)
USMM .... Union Socialiste des Musulmans Mauritaniens [*Socialist Union of Mauritanian Moslems*]
USMM .... United States Merchant Marine
USMMA .... United States Merchant Marine Academy [*Kings Point, NY*]
USMMCC ..... United States Merchant Marine Cadet Corps
USMMVETS WW2... US Merchant Marine Veterans of World War II (EA)
USMNAM..... United States Military North African Mission [*World War II*]
USMO .... United States Marshals Office (BARN)
US Month Law Mag... United States Monthly Law Magazine [*A publication*] (DLA)
USMP .... United States Mallard Project [*Army*]
USMP .... United States Microgravity Payload [*NASA*]
USMP .... US Microgravity Payload [*NASA*]
USMPA .... United States Modern Pentathlon Association (EA)
USMPBA...... United States Modern Pentathlon and Biathlon Association [*Later, USMPA*] (EA)
USMPTC ...... United States Modern Pentathlon Training Center [*Military*] (AABC)
USMS .... Unattended Sensor Monitoring System
USMS .... United States Maritime Service
USMS .... United States Marshall Service [*Department of Justice*]
USMS .... United States Masters Swimming (EA)
USMS .... United States Mint - San Francisco (ROG)
USMSA .... United States Marine Safety Association (EA)
USMSA .... United States Military Sports Association
USMSGS...... United States Maritime Service Graduate Station
USMSMI ...... United States Military Supply Mission to India (AFM)
USMSOS...... United States Maritime Service Officers School
USMSR........ United States Military Specification Requirements (MCD)
USMSSB ...... United States Machine Screw Service Bureau [*Defunct*] (EA)
USMSTS ...... United States Maritime Service Training School
USMSTS ...... United States Maritime Service Training Ship
USMSTS ...... United States Maritime Service Training Station
USMT.......... United States Military Transport
USMTF........ United States Message Text Formating
USMTM........ United States Military Training Mission (MCD)
USMTMSA ... United States Military Training Mission to Saudi Arabia
USMWR....... United States Mission Weekly Report [*Military*]
USMWW ...... United Society of Mechanical Wood Workers [*A union*] [*British*]
USMX .... USMX, Inc. [*Formerly, US Minerals & Explorations Co.*] [*NASDAQ symbol*] (NQ)
USN .... Ultrasonic Nebulizer
USN .... Under Secretary of the Navy
USN .... Union des Scolaires Nigeriens [*Union of Nigerian Scholars*]
USN .... United States Industries, Inc. [*NYSE symbol*] (SAG)
USN .... United States Navy
USNA.......... United States National Army
USNA.......... United States Naval Academy [*Annapolis, MD*]
USNA.......... United States Naval Aircraft
USNA.......... United States Naval Attache (GFGA)
USNA.......... USANA, Inc [*NASDAQ symbol*] (SAG)
USNAAA....... United States Naval Academy Alumni Association
USNAAA....... United States Naval Academy Athletic Association
USNA ANNA... United States Naval Academy, Annapolis [*Maryland*]
USNAAS....... United States Naval Auxiliary Air Station
USNAB .... United States Naval Advanced Base [*World War II*]
USNAB .... United States Naval Amphibious Base
USNAC........ United States Naval Administrative Command
USNAC........ United States Naval Air Corps
USNAC........ United States of America National Committee of the International Dairy Federation (EA)
USNACC....... United States Naval Member of the Allied Control Commission [*Germany*]
USNADC ...... United States Naval Air Development Center
USNA-EPRD... United States Naval Academy Energy-Environment Study Group and Development Team
USNA-EW .... United States Naval Academy Division of Engineering and Weapons
USNAF......... United States Naval Avionics Facility
USNAG......... United States Navy Astronautics Group (SAA)
USNAHALO... United States NATO Hawk Liaison Office [*Missiles*] (NATG)
USNAMTC.... United States Naval Air Missile Test Center
USN & USMCRC... United States Navy and United States Marine Corps Reserve Center (DNAB)
USNARS ...... United States National Archives and Records Service (DIT)
USNAS......... United States Naval Air Service
USNAS......... United States Naval Air Station
USNATC....... United States Naval Air Training Center
USNATO....... United States Mission to the North Atlantic Treaty Organization [*Department of State*] (NATG)
USNATRA .... United States Naval Training
US Naval ..... United States Naval Postgraduate School (GAGS)
USNAVCENT... US Naval Forces, [*US*] Central Command (DOMA)
USNAVEUR... United States Naval Forces Europe (MCD)
USNAVFORCONAD... United States Naval Forces, Continental Air Defense Command (DNAB)
USNAVMILCOMUN... United States Navy Representative, Military Staff Committee, United Nations (DNAB)
USNAVPRO... United States Navy Plan Representative Office
USNAVREGDENCEN... United States Naval Regional Dental Center (DNAB)
USNAVREGMEDCEN... United States Naval Regional Medical Center (DNAB)
USNAVSO ..... United States Navy Forces Southern Command (AFM)
USNAVSOUTHC... United States Navy Southern Command
USNAVSOUTHCOM... United States Navy Southern Command
USNAVSUPACT... United States Naval Supply Activity (CINC)
USNAVWEASERV... United States Naval Weather Service
USNAVYMILCOMUN... United States Naval Representative, United Nations Military Staff Committee
USNB .... United States Naval Base (MUGU)
USNBS......... United States National Bureau of Standards (IAA)
USNC .... United States National Commission for UNESCO [*of the Department of State*]
USNC .... United States National Committee [*IEC*]
USNCB......... United States Naval Central Bureau
USNCB......... United States Naval Construction Battalion [*SEABEES*] [*BUDOCKS; later, FEC, NFEC*]
USNCBS....... US National Committee for Byzantine Studies (EA)
USNC/CIE..... US National Committee of the Commission Internationale de l'Eclairage [*International Commission on Illumination*] (EA)
USNC/DNDR... United States National Committee for the Decade for Natural Disaster Reduction
USNCEL .... United States Naval Civil Engineering Laboratory [*Port Hueneme, CA*] (SAA)
USNCEREL... United States Naval Civil Engineering Research and Evaluation Laboratory
USNCFID...... United States National Committee for Federation Internationale de Documentation
USNC/IBP .... United States National Committee for the International Biological Program [*Defunct*] (EA)
USNCIEC...... United States National Committee of the International Electrotechnical Commission
USNC-IGY .... United States National Committee for the International Geophysical Year
USNCIPS...... United States National Committee of the International Peat Society (EA)
USNCPNM ... United States National Committee for the Preservation of Nubian Monuments [*Defunct*] (EA)
USNCSCOR... US National Committee for the Scientific Committee on Oceanic Research (EA)
USNCSM & FE... United States National Council on Soil Mechanics and Foundation Engineering
USNC-STR ... United States National Committee for Solar-Terrestrial Research (MCD)
USNC/TAM... US National Committee on Theoretical and Applied Mechanics (EA)
USNC/UPSI... United States National Committee/International Union of Radio Science (MCD)
USNC-URSI... United States National Committee for the Union Radio Scientifique Internationale [*International Union of Radio Science*] (EA)
USNCWEC.... United States National Committee of the World Energy Conference (EA)
USNCWFD ... US National Committee for World Food Day (EA)
USNDC......... United States Nuclear Data Committee [*Nuclear Regulatory Commission*]
USNDD .... United States Naval Drydocks
USNEDS....... United States Navy Experimental Diving Station
USNEES .... United States Naval Engineering Experiment Station [*Annapolis, MD*] (SAA)
USNEL .... United States Naval Electronics Laboratory
USNELM ...... United States Naval Forces, Eastern Atlantic and Mediterranean (MCD)
USNFCLC..... US National Federation of Christian Life Communities (EA)
USNFEC ...... US National Fruit Export Council [*Defunct*] (EA)
USNFP .... US Nicaragua Friendship Project (EA)
USNFPN....... US Nuclear Free Pacific Network (EA)
USNFR......... United States Naval Fleet Reserve
USNG.......... United States National Guard
USNH.......... United States Naval Hospital
USNH.......... United States, North of Cape Hatteras [*Shipping*]
USNHO .... United States Navy Hydrographic Office [*Later, NOO*] (NATG)
USNI........... United States Naval Institute (EA)
USN-I.......... United States Regular Navy - Inductee
USN-I-CB ..... United States Regular Navy - Inductee - Construction Battalion
USNID......... United States National Institute of Dance (EA)
USN(I)(SA)... United States Navy (Inductee) (Special Assignment)
USNL.......... United States Navy League
USNLO......... United States Naval Liaison Officer
USNM.......... United States National Museum [*Smithsonian Institution*]
USNMATOEROF... United States Mission to the North Atlantic Treaty Organization and European Regional Organizations in France

USNMDL....... United States Navy Mine Defense Laboratory (MUGU)
USNMF........ United States Naval Missile Facility
USNMF........ United States Navy Memorial Foundation (EA)
USNMPS...... United States Naval Motion Picture Service (DNAB)
USNMR........ United States National Military Representative
USNMRC...... United States Naval Manpower Center (DNAB)
USNMSC...... United States Navy Medical Service Corps
USNMTC...... United States Naval Missile Test Center [*Point Mugu, CA*] (AAG)
USNO........... United Sabah National Organization [*Malaysia*] [*Political party*] (PPW)
USNO........... United States Naval Observatory
USNOA......... United States Norton Owners' Association (EA)
USNOADS.... United States Naval Observatory Automated Data Service [*Database*] [*Information service or system*] (CRD)
USNOBSY.... United States Naval Operating Bases System
USNOBSYSUBSTA... United States Naval Observatory, Time Service Sub-Station (DNAB)
USNODC...... United States National Oceanographic Data Center [*Marine science*] (OSRA)
USNOO........ United States Naval Oceanographic Office [*Marine science*] (MSC)
US (Noth).... Ueberlieferungsgeschichtliche Studien (M. Noth) [*A publication*] (BJA)
USNO-TS..... United States Naval Observatory Time Service Division [*Washington, DC*]
USNOTS....... United States Naval Ordnance Test Station
USNOWSP... United States National Ocean-Wide Survey Program (NOAA)
USNP........... United States Naval Prison
USNP........... United States Newspaper Program [*National Foundation on the Arts and the Humanities*] [*Information service or system*] (IID)
USNPACMISTESCEN... US Navy Pacific Missile Test Center
USNPG......... United States Naval Proving Ground
USNPGS...... United States Naval Postgraduate School (MUGU)
USNPS......... United States National Parks Service [*USA*] (EERA)
USNPS......... United States Naval Postgraduate School
USNR........... United States Naval Reserve
USNR........... United States Navy Regulations
USN-R......... United States Navy - Retired (DNAB)
USNR & SL... United States Navy Radio and Sound Laboratory [*San Diego, CA*]
USNRB......... United States Naval Repair Base
USNRC......... United States National Research Council [*Toxicology*]
USNRC......... United States Nuclear Regulatory Commission (NRCH)
USNRDL....... United States Naval Radiological Defense Laboratory
USNRDL....... United States Navy Research and Development Laboratory
USN(Ret)..... United States Navy (Retired)
USNRF......... United States Naval Reserve Force
USNRL......... United States Naval Research Laboratory
USNRM........ United States Merchant Marine Reserve
USNRM1...... United States Merchant Marine Reserve Seagoing
USNRM2...... United States Merchant Marine Reserve Coastal Defense
USNRO........ United States Organized Naval Reserve
USNRO1...... United States Organized Naval Reserve Seagoing
USNRO2...... United States Organized Naval Reserve Aviation
USN-ROTC... United States Navy - Reserve Officers Training Corps
USNRP......... United States National Reference Preparation [*Centers for Disease Control*]
USNR-R....... United States Naval Reserve - Retired (DNAB)
USNR-S....... United States Naval Reserve - Standby (DNAB)
USNRS......... United States Navy Recruiting Station
USNRSV...... United States Naval Reserve, Selective Volunteer
USNRTC...... United States Naval Reserve Training Center
USNRV........ United States Naval Reserve, Volunteer
USNR(W)..... United States Naval Reserve (Women's Reserve)
USNS........... United States National Committee on Standardization
USNS........... United States Naval Ship [*Civilian manned*]
USNS........... United States Naval Station
USNS........... United States NOTAM [*Notice to Airmen*] System [*Aviation*] (FAAC)
USNS........... Universal Stabilized Night Sight
USNSA......... United States National Student Association [*Later, USSA*]
USNSC......... United States Naval Safety Code
USNSCF....... United States Naval Shore Communication Facilities
USNSISSMFE... US National Society for the International Society of Soil Mechanics and Foundation Engineering (EA)
USNSMC...... United States Naval Submarine Medical Center
USNSMSES... United States Navy Ship Missile System Engineering Station
USNSO......... United States Navy Southern Command
USNSPO...... United States Navy Special Projects Office (DNAB)
USNSPS...... United States National Stockpile Purchase Specification [*for metals*]
USN-SV........ United States Regular Navy Selective Volunteer
USNTC......... United States Naval Training Center
USNTDC....... United States Naval Training Device Center
USNTI.......... United States Navy Travel Instructions
USNTPS....... United States Naval Test Pilot School
USNTS......... United States Naval Training School
USNUSL....... United States Navy Undersea Laboratory (IAA)
USNUSL....... United States Navy Underwater Sound Laboratory [*BUSHIPS; later, ESC, NESC*]
USNWC........ United States Naval War College
USNZC......... United States-New Zealand Council (EA)
USO............. Udaipur Solar Observatory [*India*]
USO............. Ultra Stable Oscillator [*Instrumentation*]
USO............. Under Secretary of the Navy's Office
USO............. Unidentified Submarine Object
USO............. Unidentified Superconducting Object (ECON)
USO............. Unilateral Salpingo-Oophorectomy [*Gynecology*] (MAE)
USO............. United Service Organizations, Inc. (EA)
USO............. United Siscoe Mines, Inc. [*Toronto Stock Exchange symbol*]
USO............. United States Outfitters
USO............. United States Outfitters
USO............. United States Overseas [*Facetious translation of United Services Organization*] (VNW)
USO............. Unit Security Officer (AAG)
USO............. Universal Service Order [*Bell System*] (TEL)
USO............. Unmanned Seismological Observatory
USO............. US 1 Indus [*NYSE symbol*] (TTSB)
USO............. US Office - UTLAS Corp. [*UTLAS symbol*]
USO............. US One Industries, Inc. [*Formerly, Transcom, Inc.*] [*NYSE symbol*] (SAG)
USOA........... Uniform System of Accounts [*Telecommunications*] (TEL)
USOA........... United States Olympic Association [*Later, USOC*]
USOA........... United States Othello Association (EA)
USOA........... United States Overseas Airlines
U So Ala...... University of South Alabama (GAGS)
USOAS......... United States Mission to the Organization of American States [*Department of State*]
USO-ASPCC... USO [*United Service Organizations*]-All Service Postal Chess Club [*Later, ASPCC*] (EA)
USOC........... Uniform Service Order Code [*Bell System*] (TEL)
USOC........... United States Olympic Committee (EA)
USOCA......... United States Office of Consumer Affairs
USOCA......... US 1 Class Association (EA)
USOCA......... US Out of Central America [*Defunct*] (EA)
U So Cal...... University of Southern California (GAGS)
U So Cal Tax Inst... University of Southern California Tax Institute (DLA)
U So Car...... University of South Carolina (GAGS)
USOCDC...... US Overseas Cooperative Development Committee (EA)
USO-CLAT.... US Relations Office of CLAT [*Central Latinoamericana de Trabajadores*] (EA)
USODA......... United States Organization for Disabled Athletes (EA)
U So Dak..... University of South Dakota (GAGS)
USOE........... United States Office of Education [*Later, USDE*]
USOECD...... United States Mission to the Organization for Economic Cooperation and Development [*Department of State*]
USOF........... United States Orienteering Federation (EA)
USOFA......... Under Secretary of the Army
US of A........ Under Secretary of the Army
US of AF...... Under Secretary of the Air Force
USOFAF....... Under Secretary of the Air Force
US OfcP...... US Office Products Co. [*Associated Press*] (SAG)
U So Fla...... University of South Florida (GAGS)
US of S........ Under Secretary of State
USOID......... United States Oversea Internal Defense [*Army*] (AABC)
USOLTA....... Uniform Simplification of Land Transfers Act [*National Conference of Commissioners on Uniform State Laws*]
USOM.......... United States Operations Mission [*Military*]
U So Maine... University of Southern Maine (GAGS)
USOMC........ United States Ordnance Missile Command
U So Miss... University of Southern Mississippi (GAGS)
USONIA........ United States of North America [*Name of a cooperative community in Pleasantville, NY designed by Frank Lloyd Wright*]
USONR......... United States Office of Naval Research
USOO........... United States Oceanographic Office (PDAA)
USOP........... United States of Poetry
USOPA......... United States Ordnance Producers Association [*Inactive*] (EA)
USOppS....... US Opportunity Search, Inc. [*Associated Press*] (SAG)
USOR........... US Order, Inc. [*NASDAQ symbol*] (SAG)
US Ord........ US Order, Inc. [*Associated Press*] (SAG)
USOS........... U.S. Opportunity Search [*NASDAQ symbol*] (TTSB)
USOS........... US Opportunity Search, Inc. [*NASDAQ symbol*] (SAG)
USOSP......... United States Ocean Survey Plan (NOAA)
U Southwestern La... [*The*] University of Southwestern Louisiana (GAGS)
USOVA......... United States Outdoor Volleyball Association (EA)
USp............. Springville City Library, Springville, UT [*Library symbol Library of Congress*] (LCLS)
USP............. Ultrasensitive Position (AFM)
USP............. Underwater Sound Projection
USP............. Uniform Specification Program (AAG)
USP............. Unique Selling Point
USP............. Unique Selling Proposition [*Advertising*]
USP............. Unique Selling Proposition [*Finance*]
USP............. United Socialist Party [*South Korea Political party*] (PPW)
USP............. United States Patent
USP............. United States Penitentiary
USP............. United States Pharmacopeia [*Following name of a substance, signifies substance meets standards set by USP*]
USP............. United States Pharmacopeial Convention [*Database producer*] (EA)
USP............. United States Postal Service Library, Washington, DC [*OCLC symbol*] (OCLC)
USP............. United States Property
USP............. Unit Stream Power [*Hydrology*]
USP............. Unit Support Plan (MCD)
USP............. Universal Signal Processor
USP............. Universal Systems Patching [*Mod-Tap System, Inc.*]
USP............. Unsuppressed Selling Price
USP............. Upper Sequential Permissive [*Nuclear energy*] (NRCH)
USP............. Upper Solution Point
USP............. Urban Studies Project
USP............. Usage Sensitive Pricing [*Telecommunications*]
USP............. US Precious Metals, Inc. [*Toronto Stock Exchange symbol Vancouver Stock Exchange symbol*]
USP............. Utility Seaplane [*Navy, Coast Guard*]
USP............. Utility Storage Print (SAA)

USP .... Utility Summary Program
USP70 .... US Patents 70 (NITA)
USP77 .... US Patents 77 (NITA)
USPA .... Uniformed Services Pay Act
USPA .... Uniform Single Publication Act [*National Conference of Commissioners on Uniform State Laws*]
USPA .... United States Parachute Association (EA)
USPA .... United States Passport Agency [*Department of State*]
USPA .... United States Pilots Association (EA)
USPA .... United States Polo Association (EA)
USPA .... United States Potters' Association (EA)
USPA .... US Patents (NITA)
USPA .... US Patents Alert [*Derwent, Inc.*] [*Database*]
USPA .... US Psychotronics Association (EA)
USPAACC .... United States PanAsian American Chamber of Commerce (EAIO)
USPACOM .... United States Pacific Command [*Military*]
USPAK .... US-Pakistan Economic Council (EA)
USP&FO .... United States Property and Fiscal Officer (AAGC)
USPAP .... Uniform Standards for Professional Appraisal Practice
US Pat Q .... United States Patent Quarterly [*A publication*] (DLA)
US Pat Quar .... United States Patent Quarterly [*A publication*] (DLA)
US Pat Quart .... United States Patent Quarterly [*A publication*] (DLA)
US Pawn .... United States Pawn, Inc. [*Associated Press*] (SAG)
USPC .... Union des Syndicats Professionels du Cameroun [*Federation of Professional Trade Unions of Cameroon*]
USPC .... United States Parole Commission [*Formerly, United States Parole Board*]
USPC .... United States Peace Corps (EA)
USPC .... United States Pharmacopoeial Convention
USPC .... United States Pony Clubs (EA)
USPC .... United States Privacy Council (EA)
USPC .... United States Procurement Committee
USPC .... United States Purchasing Commission
USPC .... US Peace Council (EA)
USPCA .... United States Police Canine Association (EA)
USPCC .... Utility and Support Programming Control Committee (SAA)
USPCF .... US Professional Cycling Federation [*Later, USPRO*] (EA)
USPCS .... US Philatelic Classics Society (EA)
USPCU .... US Postal Chess Union (EA)
USPD .... Unabhaengige Sozialdemokratische Partei Deutschlands [*Independent Social Democratic Party of Germany*] [*Political party*] (PPE)
USPD .... US Publicity Director [*A publication*]
USPDCA .... United States Professional Diving Coaches Association (EA)
USPDI .... United States Pharmacopeia Dispensing Information
USPDI .... United States Professional Development Institute
USPDO .... United States Property and Disbursing Officer
USPE .... United States Purchasing Exchange
USPE .... Unsatisfactory Specimen [*Laboratory science*] (DAVI)
USPEC .... United States Paper Exporters Council [*Defunct*] (EA)
USPEPA .... United States Poultry and Egg Producers Association (EA)
USPF .... US Powerlifting Federation (EA)
USPFO .... United States Property and Fiscal Officer [*Military*]
US/PFUN .... United States People for the United Nations [*Defunct*] (EA)
USPG .... Uniform System of Accounts Prescribed for Natural Gas Companies
USPG .... United Society for the Propagation of the Gospel [*Society for the Propaga tion of the Gospel in Foreign Parts and UMCA*] [*Formed by a merger of*] (EAIO)
USpGS .... Church of Jesus Christ of Latter-Day Saints, Genealogical Society Library, Springville Branch, Springville, UT [*Library symbol Library of Congress*] (LCLS)
USPh .... United States Pharmacopoeia
USPH .... U.S. Physical Therapy [*NASDAQ symbol*] (TTSB)
USPH .... US Physical Therapy, Inc. [*NASDAQ symbol*] (SAG)
USPHS .... United States Postal History Society [*Defunct*] (EA)
USPHS .... United States Public Health Service
USPHSR .... United States Public Health Service Reserve
USPHT .... United States Precision Helicopter Team
USPhys .... US Physical Therapy, Inc. [*Associated Press*] (SAG)
USPI .... Unione Stampa Periodica Italiana [*Press association*] (EY)
USPIN .... United States Pacific Issues Network [*Defunct*] (EA)
USPIRG .... US Public Interest Research Group (EA)
USPL .... Uniform System of Accounts, Public Utilities, and Licensees [*Federal Power Commission*]
USPL .... Unpriced Spare Parts List
USPLS .... United States Public-Land Surveys
USPLTA .... United States Professional Lawn Tennis Association [*Later, USPTA*] (EA)
USPM .... United Society of Pattern Makers [*A union*] [*British*]
USPMF .... US Patent Model Foundation (EA)
USPMOM .... Union des Societes de Pediatrie du Moyen-Orient et de la Mediterranee [*Union of Middle Eastern and Mediterranean Pediatric Societies - UMEMPS*] [*Athens, Greece*] (EAIO)
USPN .... United States Pawn, Inc. [*NASDAQ symbol*] (SAG)
USPN .... U.S. Pawn [*NASDAQ symbol*] (TTSB)
USPN .... US Pawn, Inc. [*NASDAQ symbol*] (NQ)
USPO .... United Sabah People's Organization [*Pertubuhan Rakyat Sabah Bersatu*] [*Malaysia*] [*Political party*] (PPW)
USPO .... United States Patent Office [*Department of Commerce*]
USPO .... United States Post Office [*Later, United States Postal Service*]
USPP .... United States Pacifist Party [*Political party*] (EA)
USPP .... United States Park Police [*Department of the Interior*]
USPP .... University Science Policy Planning [*Program*] [*National Science Foundation*]
USPPA .... United States Pulp Producers Association [*Later, API*] (EA)
USPPI .... United States Producer Price Index [*Database*] [*Department of Labor*] [*Information service or system*] (CRD)
USPPS .... US Possessions Philatelic Society (EA)
USPQ .... United States Patents Quarterly
USPRI .... USP Real Estate Investment Trust SBI [*Associated Press*] (SAG)
USPRO .... US Professional Cycling Federation (EA)
USPS .... United States Postal Service
USPS .... United States Power Squadrons (EA)
USPSA .... US Practical Shooting Association (EA)
USPSDA .... United States Private Security and Detective Association (EA)
USPSF .... United States Pigeon Shooting Federation [*Defunct*] (EA)
USPT .... United Societies of Physiotherapists (EA)
USPTA .... United States Physical Therapy Association (EA)
USPTA .... United States Pony Trotting Association [*Defunct*] (EA)
USPTA .... United States Professional Tennis Association (EA)
USPTA .... US Paddle Tennis Association (EA)
USPTO .... United States Patent and Trademark Office
USPTR .... United States Professional Tennis Registry (EA)
USPTS .... USP Real Estate Investment Trust SBI [*NASDAQ symbol*] (SPSG)
USPTS .... USP Real Est Inv Tr SBI [*NASDAQ symbol*] (TTSB)
USPWIC .... United States Prisoner of War Information Center [*Army*] (AABC)
USPWIC(Br) .... United States Prisoner of War Information Center (Branch) [*Army*] (AABC)
USQ .... Squeezed Files [*Computer science*] (MHDI)
USQMC .... United States Quartermaster Corps
USR .... Ukrainska Partiia Sotsialistov Revolyutsionerov [*Ukrainian Socialist Revolutionary Party*] [*Russian Political party*] (PPE)
USR .... Ultrasonic Radiation
USR .... Under Speed Relay (MCD)
USR .... Unheated Serum Reagin (Test) [*Clinical chemistry*] (AAMN)
USR .... United States [*Supreme Court*] Reports
USR .... United States Reserves
USR .... Unit Site Representative [*Army*]
USR .... Unit Status Report [*Army*]
USR .... Universal Series Regulator (IAA)
USR .... Up Stage Right [*Away from audience*] [*A stage direction*]
USR .... User Service Request
USR .... User Service Routine [*Digital Equipment Corp.*]
USR .... User Status Reporting (MCD)
USR .... Usher of the Scarlet Rod (ROG)
USR .... US Shoe Corp. [*NYSE symbol*] (SPSG)
USRA .... United Sportsman Racers Association [*Defunct*] (EA)
USRA .... United States Racquetball Association (EA)
USRA .... United States Railway Association [*In 1974, superseded United States Railroad Administration, which had been absorbed by the Department of Transportation in 1939*] [*Terminated in 1987*]
USRA .... United States Revolver Association (EA)
USRA .... United States Rowing Association (EA)
USRA .... United Street Rod Association [*Defunct*] (EA)
USRA .... Universities Space Research Association (EA)
USRA .... University Space Physics Association
USRAC .... US Repeating Arms Company
USRAD .... United States Fleet Shore Radio Station
USR-Borotbists .... Ukrainska Partiia Sotsialistov Revolyutsionerov-Borotbists [*Ukrainian Socialist Revolutionary Party-Fighters*] [*Russian Political party*] (PPE)
USRCMM .... US Region of Congregation of Mariannhill Missionaries [*Later, CMM*] (EA)
USRCPAC .... United States Reserve Components and Personnel Administration Center
USRCS .... United States Revenue Cutter Service
USRCSI .... United States Red Cedar Shingle Industry
USRD .... Underwater Sound Reference Detachment [*Orlando, FL*] [*Navy*]
US-RDA .... Union Soudanaise - Rassemblement Democratique Africain [*Mali*] [*Political party*] (EY)
USRDA .... US Recommended Daily Allowance [*Nutrition*]
USRD/NRL .... Underwater Sound Reference Division, Naval Research Laboratory
USRE .... US Facilities Corp. [*Costa Mesa, CA*] [*NASDAQ symbol*] (NQ)
USREC .... United States Environment and Resources Council [*Marine science*] (MSC)
USREDA .... United States Rice Export Development Association [*Later, RCMD*]
USREDCOM .... United States Readiness Command
US Reg .... United States Register [*Philadelphia*] [*A publication*] (DLA)
US Reh Den .... Rehearing Denied by United States Supreme Court [*Legal term*] (DLA)
US Reh Dis .... Rehearing Dismissed by United States Supreme Court [*Legal term*] (DLA)
US Rep .... United States Reports [*A publication*] (DLA)
US Rep (L Ed) .... United States Supreme Court Reports, Lawyers' Edition [*A publication*] (DLA)
USREPMC .... United States Representative to the Military Committee [*NATO*]
USREPMILCOMLO .... United States Representative to the Military Committee Liaison Office [*NATO*]
USREPMILCOMUN .... United States Representative, Military Staff Committee, United Nations
USREPOF .... United States Navy Reporting Office [*or Officer*]
US Rest .... US Restaurant Properties Ltd. [*Formerly, Burger King Investors*] [*Associated Press*] (SAG)
US Rev St .... United States Revised Statutes [*A publication*] (DLA)
USRFP .... US Requests for Proposals [*Washington Representative Service*] [*Information service or system Defunct*] (CRD)
USRL .... Laryak [*Former USSR ICAO location identifier*] (ICLI)
USRL .... Underwater Sound Reference Laboratory [*Navy*]
USRM .... United States Revenue Marine
USRN .... Nizhnevartovsk [*Former USSR ICAO location identifier*] (ICLI)

USRNMC...... United States Representative to NATO Military Committee (AABC)
USRO........... Ultrasmall Structures Research Office [*University of Michigan*] [*Research center*] (RCD)
USRO........... United States Mission to NATO and European Regional Organizations
USRO........... United States Navy Routing Office
US Robt....... United States Robotics, Inc. [*Associated Press*] (SAG)
USRP........... United States Refugee Program
USRPA......... United States Racing Pigeon Association [*Defunct*] (EA)
USRPHC...... US Real Property Holding Co.
USRR........... Surgut [*Former USSR ICAO location identifier*] (ICLI)
USRRC......... United States Road Racing Championship
USRR Lab Bd Dec... Decisions of the United States Railroad Labor Board [*A publication*] (DLA)
USRS........... United States Reclamation Service
USRS........... United States Revised Statutes
USRS........... United States Robotics Society (CSR)
USRS........... United States Rocket Society (EA)
USRS........... United States Rowing Society (EA)
USRSA......... United States Racquet Stringers Association (EA)
USRSG......... United States Representative, Standing Group [*Military*] (AABC)
USRT........... Universal Synchronous Receiver/Transmitter
USRTA......... United States Recreational Tennis Association (EA)
USRV........... US SerVis [*NASDAQ symbol*] (TTSB)
USRV........... US SerVis, Inc. [*NASDAQ symbol*] (SAG)
USRX........... United States Robotics Corp. [*NASDAQ symbol*] (SAG)
USRX........... U.S. Robotics [*NASDAQ symbol*] (TTSB)
USRX........... US Robotics, Inc. [*NASDAQ symbol*] (SPSG)
USS............. Shuttle, Inc. [*ICAO designator*] (FAAC)
USS............. Ultrasound Scanning
USS............. Ultraviolet Scanning Spectrometer
USS............. Underwater Sound Source
USS............. Unified S-Band System [*Radio*]
USS............. Union Syndicale Suisse [*Swiss Federation of Trade Unions*]
USS............. Unique Signal Switch
USS............. United Scholarship Service [*Later, NCAIAE, NCAIE*]
USS............. United Seamen's Service (EA)
USS............. United States Naval Vessel
USS............. United States Sellers [*Standard threads*] (DEN)
USS............. United States Senate
USS............. United States Ship
USS............. United States Standard
USS............. United States Steamer
USS............. United States Surgical Corp. [*NYSE symbol*] (SPSG)
USS............. United States Swimming, Inc. (EA)
USS............. United Swedish Societies (EA)
USS............. Universal Scheduling System (IAA)
USS............. Universities Superannuation Scheme
USS............. Unsmoked Sheets (PDAA)
USS............. Uptake Signal Sequence [*Genetics*]
USS............. USAF [*United States Air Force*] Security Service
USS............. Usage Sensitive Service [*Telecommunications*]
USS............. USAREUR [*United States Army, Europe*] Support System
USS............. User Services Support (SSD)
USS............. User Support System (MCD)
USS............. US Steel Canada, Inc. [*Toronto Stock Exchange symbol*]
USS............. US Steel Corp. [*Also, USSC*] [*Later, USX Corp.*]
USS............. U.S. Surgical [*NYSE symbol*] (TTSB)
USS............. Utility Support Structure (MCD)
USSA........... Underground Security Storage Association [*Defunct*]
USSA........... Uniaxial Split-Sphere Apparatus [*Mineralogy*]
USSA........... Union Suisse des Syndicats Autonomes [*Swiss Association of Autonomous Unions*]
USSA........... United Saw Service Association (EA)
USSA........... United States Salvage Association [*Defunct*] (EA)
USSA........... United States Security Authority [*for NATO affairs*]
USSA........... United States Ski Association (EA)
USSA........... United States Snowshoe Association (EA)
USSA........... United States Space Administration (IAA)
USSA........... United States Sports Academy (EA)
USSA........... United States Standard Atmosphere (KSC)
USSA........... United States Student Association (EA)
USSA........... United States Swimming Association (EA)
USSA........... United Sugar Samplers' Association [*Defunct*]
USSA........... US Sidewinder Association (EA)
USSA........... US Soling Association (EA)
USSAC......... United States Army Ambulance Service Association [*Defunct*] (EA)
USSAC......... United States Security Authority for CENTO Affairs (AABC)
USSAF......... United States Strategic Air Force [*Later, Strategic Air Command*]
USSAF......... US Sports Acrobatic Federation (EA)
USSAFE....... United States Strategic Air Forces in Europe
USSAG......... United States Support Activities Group [*Military*]
USSAG/7AF... United States Support Activities / Seventh Air Force [*Vietnam*] (VNW)
USSAH......... United States Soldiers' and Airmen's Home (AABC)
USSALEP..... US-South Africa Leader Exchange Program (EA)
USSAN......... United States Security Authority, NATO
USSAS......... United States Security Authority for SEATO Affairs (AABC)
USSatB........ United States Satellite Broadcasting Co. [*Associated Press*] (SAG)
USSB........... United States Satellite Broadcasting Co., Inc. [*Minneapolis, MN*] [*Telecommunications*] (TSSD)
USSB........... United States Savings Bond (WDAA)
USSB........... United States Shipping Board [*Terminated, 1933*]
USSB........... United States Shipping Board Decisions [*A publication*] (DLA)
USSB........... U.S. Satellite Broadcasting'A' [*NASDAQ symbol*] (TTSB)
USSBA......... United States Seniors Bowling Association [*Later, Seniors Division of the American Bowling Congress*] (EA)
USSBB......... United States Shipping Board Bureau Decisions [*A publication*] (DLA)
USSBD......... United States Savings Bonds Division [*Department of the Treasury*]
USSBF......... United States Skibob Federation (EA)
USSBIA....... United States Stone and Bead Importers Association (EA)
USSBL......... United States Stickball League (EA)
USSBS......... United States Strategic Bombing Survey [*Disbanded, 1946*]
USSC........... United States Sentencing Commission
USSC........... United States Servas Committee (EA)
USSC........... United States Strike Command [*Military combined Tactical Air Command and Strategic Army Command Force*]
USSC........... United States Supreme Court
USSC........... Upper-Sideband, Suppressed-Carrier (IDOE)
USSC........... US Steel Corp. [*Also, USS*] [*Later, USX Corp.*] (MCD)
USSC........... US Systems Corp. (EA)
USSCA......... US Ski Coaches Association (EA)
US-SCAN..... United States Special Committee on Antarctic Names [*1943-47*]
USSC Rep.... United States Supreme Court Reports [*A publication*] (DLA)
USSCS......... United States Soil Conservation Service (BARN)
USSCT......... United States Supreme Court
USSDP......... Uniformed Services Savings Deposits Program (AABC)
USSE........... Severouralsk [*Former USSR ICAO location identifier*] (ICLI)
USSE........... Ultrasonic Soldering Equipment
USSEA......... United States Scientific Export Association
USSEA......... United States Society for Education through Art (EA)
USSEA......... United States Space Education Association (EA)
USSECMILCOMUN... [*The*] Secretary, United States Delegation United Nations Military Staff Committee
USSEF......... United States Ski Educational Foundation (EA)
USSEI......... United States Society of Esperanto Instructors [*Later, AATE*] (AEBS)
USSerVis..... US SerVis, Inc. [*Associated Press*] (SAG)
USSES......... US Sheep Experiment Station [*University of Idaho*] [*Research center*] (RCD)
USSF........... Ulster Special Service Force [*British military*] (DMA)
USSF........... United States Soccer Federation (EA)
USSF........... United States Softball Federation
USSF........... United States Space Foundation (EA)
USSF........... United States Special Forces
USSF........... United States Steel Foundation
USSF........... United States Surfing Federation (EA)
USSF........... United States Swimming Foundation (EA)
USSFA......... United States Soccer Football Association [*Later, USSF*] (EA)
USSFFA....... United Soft Serve and Fast Food Association [*Later, NSSFFA*] (EA)
USSF LRRP... United States Special Forces Long Range Reconnaisance Patrol (VNW)
USSF(P)....... United States Special Forces (Provisional) (CINC)
USSFR......... US Scottish Fiddling Revival (EA)
USSG........... United States Standard Gauge
USSGA......... United States Seniors Golf Association [*Defunct*] (EA)
USSGREP.... United States Standing Group Representative [*NATO*]
USSH........... United States Soldiers' Home
USSHN......... Usher Syndrome Self-Help Network (EA)
USSI............ Ivdel [*Former USSR ICAO location identifier*] (ICLI)
USSI............ Ultrasonic Soldering Iron
USSI............ United States Strategic Institute (EA)
USSI............ USS Interphase (EA)
USSIA......... United States Shellac Importers Association (EA)
USSIAFCM... USS Intrepid Association of Former Crew Members (EA)
USSID......... United States Signal Intelligence Directive (AABC)
US-SIOP...... United States Single Integrated Operational Plan (NATG)
USSIS......... United States Signals Intellignce System (MCD)
USSLL......... United States Savings and Loan League [*Later, USLSI*] (EA)
USSMA......... US Spanish Merchants Association (EA)
USSNBA....... USS [*United States Ship*] Natoma Bay Association (EA)
USSOA......... USS [*United States Ship*] Oklahoma Association (EA)
USSOC......... United States Special Operations Command [*DoD*]
USSOCOM.... United States Special Operations Command [*DoD*]
USSOUTHCOM... United States Southern Command [*Air Force*]
USSP........... Unsuppressed Selling Price
USSP........... User Systems Support Plan
USSPA......... Uniformed Services Special Pay Act (DNAB)
USSPA......... United States Student Press Association [*Superseded by CPS*]
USSPACECOM... United States Space Command
USSPC......... US Student Pugwash Committee (EA)
USSPEI....... Union des Syndicats des Services Publics Europeens et Internationaux [*European and International Public Services Union*] [*Later, EUROFEDOP*] (EAIO)
USSPG......... United States Senate Press Photographers Gallery (EA)
USSPG......... US Sweetener Producers Group [*Later, ASA*] (EA)
USSPL......... United Ship Scrapers' Protection League [*A union*] [*British*]
USSPPG....... United States Senate Press Photographers Gallery (EA)
USSPrA........ U.S. Surgical $2.20 Dep'DECS' [*NYSE symbol*] (TTSB)
USSR........... State Music Trust [*Record label*] [*Former USSR*]
USSR........... Uninterrupted Sustained Silent Reading
USSR........... Union of Soviet Socialist Republics [*See also SSSR, CCCP*]
USSRA......... United States Squash Racquets Association (EA)
USSRCFT..... USSR State Committee for Foreign Tourism [*Defunct*] (EAIO)
US Srg......... United States Surgical Co. [*Associated Press*] (SAG)
USSRM......... State Music Trust [*78 RPM*] [*Record label*] [*Former USSR*]
USSRN......... Under Secretary of State for the Royal Navy [*British*]
USSS........... Sverdlovsk [*Former USSR ICAO location identifier*] (ICLI)
USSS........... Undersea Surveillance System (MCD)
USSS........... United States Secret Service [*Department of the Treasury*]
USSS........... United States Signals Intelligence System (MCD)

USSS .... United States Steamship
USSS .... Unmanned Sensing Satellite System
USSSA .... United States Slo-Pitch Softball Association (EA)
USSSA .... United States Snowshoe Association (EA)
USSSI .... United Stamp Society for Shut-Ins (EA)
USSSI .... United States Satellite Systems, Inc. [*Defunct*] (TSSD)
USSSI .... United States Synchronized Swimming, Inc. (EA)
USSSMA ...... US Shake and Shingle Manufacturers Association (EA)
USSSO .... United States Sending State Office [*Navy*]
USSST .... United States Sellers Standard Thread
USSS/UD ..... United States Secret Service Uniformed Division
USSTAF .... United States Strategic Air Force [*Later, Strategic Air Command*]
USSTAFE ..... United States Strategic Tactical Air Force, Europe
US Stat .... United States Statutes at Large [*A publication*] (DLA)
US St at L ... United States Statutes at Large [*A publication*] (DLA)
USSTRICOM... United States Strike Command [*Military combined Tactical Air Command and Strategic Army Command Force*]
USSTS .... US Student Travel Service (EA)
US St Tr ...... United States State Trials [*Wharton*] [*A publication*] (DLA)
US Sup Ct.... United States Supreme Court Reporter [*A publication*] (DLA)
US Sup Ct (L Ed)... United States Supreme Court Reports, Lawyers' Edition [*A publication*] (DLA)
US Sup Ct R... United States Supreme Court Reporter [*A publication*] (DLA)
US Sup Ct Rep... United States Supreme Court Reporter [*A publication*] (DLA)
US Sup Ct Reps... Supreme Court Reporter [*A publication*] (DLA)
US Surg .... United States Surgical Corp. [*Associated Press*] (SAG)
USSWA .... United States Ski Writers Association [*Later, NASJA*] (EA)
UST .... Ultrasonic Test
UST .... Ultrasonic Transducer [*Crystal*] [*Used in measuring human cardiac output*]
UST .... Unblocked Serial Telemetry (MCD)
UST .... Underground Storage Tank [*Environmental Protection Agency*]
UST .... Undersea Technology
UST .... Uniform Specification Tree
UST .... Union Senegalaise du Travail [*Senegalese Labor Union*]
UST .... Union Socialiste Tchadienne [*Chadian Socialist Union*]
UST .... United States Testing Co., Inc. (NASA)
UST .... United States Time
UST .... United States Treaties and Other International Agreements [*A publication*] (DLA)
UST .... Unit Security Technician
UST .... Universal Servicing Tool (NASA)
UST .... Universal Standard Time
UST .... Universal Subscriber Terminal (DNAB)
UST .... University of Saint Thomas [*Texas*]
UST .... User Symbol Table [*Computer science*] (MHDB)
UST .... Ustilago [*A fungus*]
UST .... UST, Inc. [*Formerly, US Tobacco*] [*NYSE symbol*] (SPSG)
UST .... Ustus [*Burnt*] [*Pharmacy*]
USTA .... Union des Syndicats des Travailleurs Algeriens [*Federation of Unions of Algerian Workers*]
USTA .... United States Telephone Association (EA)
USTA .... United States Tennis Association, Inc. (EA)
USTA .... United States Trademark Association (EA)
USTA .... United States Trotting Association (EA)
USTA .... United States Twirling Association (EA)
USTA .... Unlisted Securities Trading Act [*1936*]
USTA .... US Tornado Association (EA)
USTA .... US Triathlon Association [*Later, TRI-FED*] (EA)
USTA .... US Trivia Association [*Defunct*] (EA)
USTAF .... United States/Thai Forces
USTAG .... United States Technical Advisory Group (IAA)
USTA/NJTL... USTA [*United States Tennis Association*] National Junior Tennis League (EA)
UStatn .... United Stationers, Inc. [*Associated Press*] (SAG)
US Tax Cas... United States Tax Cases [*Commerce Clearing House*] [*A publication*] (DLA)
USTB .... United States Travel Bureau
USTB .... UST Corp. [*NASDAQ symbol*] (NQ)
USTBF .... United States Tenpin Bowling Federation (EA)
USTC .... Union Syndicale de Travail Centrafricaine [*Union of Central African Workers*] (EY)
USTC .... United States Tariff Commission [*Later, ITC*]
USTC .... United States Tax Cases [*Commerce Clearing House*] [*A publication*] (DLA)
USTC .... United States Testing Co., Inc.
USTC .... United States Tourist Council (EA)
USTC .... United States Transportation Commission [*Proposed commission to consolidate CAB, ICC, and FMC*]
USTC .... Universal Systems Technologies Corp.
USTC .... University of Science and Technology of China
USTC .... US-Tibet Committee (EA)
USTC .... US Trade Center [*Mexico*] (IMH)
USTC .... U.S. Trust [*NASDAQ symbol*] (TTSB)
USTC .... US Trust Corp. [*NASDAQ symbol*] (NQ)
USTCA .... United States Track Coaches Association [*Later, TFA/USA*]
USTC & TBA... US Tennis Court and Track Builders Association (EA)
UST Cp .... UST Corp. [*Associated Press*] (SAG)
USTD .... Union des Syndicats des Travailleurs du Dahomey [*Federation of Workers' Unions of Dahomey*]
USTD .... United States Treasury Department
USTD .... United States Treaty Development [*A publication*] (DLA)
USTDA .... United States Truck Drivers Association
USTDC .... United States Forces, Taiwan Defense Command (CINC)
USTDC .... US Travel Data Center (EA)
US Tech .... United States Technologies, Inc. [*Associated Press*] (SAG)
UStel .... UStel Co. [*Associated Press*] (SAG)
US TEL .... US Telephone, Inc. [*Dallas, TX*] [*Telecommunications*] (TSSD)
USTES .... United States Training and Employment Service [*Abolished, 1971*] [*Department of Labor*]
USTF .... Uniformed Services Treatment Facility [*DoD*]
USTF .... United States Tuna Foundation (EA)
USTFA .... United States Trout Farmers Association (EA)
USTFF .... United States Track and Field Federation [*Later, TFA/USA*]
USTFFA .... United States Touch and Flag Football Association (EA)
USTG .... Union Syndicale des Travailleurs de Guinee [*Guinean Federation of Workers*]
UStgD .... Dixie College, St. George, UT [*Library symbol Library of Congress*] (LCLS)
UStgGS .... Church of Jesus Christ of Latter-Day Saints, Genealogical Society Library, St. George Branch, St. George, UT [*Library symbol Library of Congress*] (LCLS)
UStgW .... Washington County Library, St. George, UT [*Library symbol Library of Congress*] (LCLS)
USTHF .... US Team Handball Federation (EA)
USTIIC .... United States Technical Industrial Intelligence Committee (MCD)
USTL .... UStel [*NASDAQ symbol*] (SAG)
USTL .... UStel Inc. [*NASDAQ symbol*] (TTSB)
USTMA .... United States Trademark Association (BARN)
USTOA .... United States Tour Operators Association (EA)
USTOL .... Ultrashort Takeoff and Landing [*Aviation*] (MCD)
USTOPS .... United States Travelers' Overseas Personalized Service [*Also known as TOPS*]
USTR .... United States Trade Representative [*Formerly, SRTN*] [*Executive Office of the President*]
USTR .... United Stationers [*NASDAQ symbol*] (TTSB)
USTR .... United Stationers, Inc. [*NASDAQ symbol*] (NQ)
USTRA .... United States Touring Riders Association [*Defunct*] (EA)
US Tran .... United States Transportation Systems, Inc. [*Associated Press*] (SAG)
US Tran .... United States Transportation Systems, Inc. [*Associated Press*] (SAG)
USTRANSCOM... United States Transportation Command
USTRC .... United States Transportation Research Command [*Army*]
US Treas Dept... United States Treasury Department (DLA)
US Treas Reg... United States Treasury Regulations [*A publication*] (DLA)
US Treaty Ser... United States Treaty Series [*A publication*] (DLA)
US Trn .... United States Transportation Systems, Inc. [*Associated Press*] (SAG)
US Trst .... US Trust Corp. [*Associated Press*] (SAG)
USTS .... Ultrahigh Frequency Satellite Terminal System (MCD)
USTS .... Union Syndicale des Travailleurs du Soudan [*Federation of Sudanese Workers*] [*Mali*]
USTS .... United States Time Standard [*National Institute of Standards and Technology*]
USTS .... United States Transmission Systems, Inc. [*Secaucus, NJ*] (TSSD)
USTS .... United States Travel Service [*Replaced by United States Travel and Tourism Administration*] [*Department of Commerce*]
USTS .... U.S. Transportation Sys [*NASDAQ symbol*] (TTSB)
USTS .... US Transportation Systems, Inc. [*NASDAQ symbol*] (SAG)
USTSA .... United States Trade Secrets Act (AAGC)
USTSA .... US Targhee Sheep Association (EA)
USTSA .... US Telecommunications Suppliers Association [*Later, TIA*] (EA)
USTTA .... United States Table Tennis Association (EA)
USTTA .... United States Travel and Tourism Administration [*Formerly, US Travel Service*] [*Department of Commerce*]
USTTA .... United States Travel and Tourism Administration (USGC)
U St Thomas... University of St. Thomas (GAGS)
USTTI .... US Telecommunications Training Institute [*Washington, DC*] [*Telecommunications*] (TSSD)
USTU .... Ultrasonic Test Unit
USTU .... US Taekwondo Union (EA)
USTU .... US Taxpayers Union (EA)
USTV .... Universal Subscription Television
USTV .... Unmanned Supersonic Test Vehicle (MCD)
USTVA .... United States Tennessee Valley Authority
USTW .... Sovetsky [*Former USSR ICAO location identifier*] (ICLI)
USTWA .... US Tennis Writers Association (EA)
USTZD .... Unsensitized
USU .... Ultimate Sampling Unit (GFGA)
USU .... Unbundled Stock Unit [*Investment term Obsolete*]
USU .... Uniformed Services University of the Health Sciences Library, Bethesda, MD [*OCLC symbol*] (OCLC)
USU .... United Stevedores' Union [*British*]
USU .... Usually
USU .... Utah State University (PDAA)
USUA .... United States Ultralight Association (EA)
USUARIOI .... Association of Maritime Transport Users in the Central American Isthmus [*Guatemala, Guatemala*] (EAIO)
USUB .... Unglazed Structural Unit Base [*Technical drawings*]
USUCA .... United Steel Workers' Union of Central Africa [*Rhodesia and Nyasaland*]
USUHS .... Uniformed Services University of the Health Sciences [*Bethesda, MD*] [*DoD*] (EGAO)
US/UK .... United States/United Kingdom
USUN .... United States United Nations Delegation (CINC)
USUNEP .... United States Committee for the United Nations Environment Program (EA)
USURP .... Usurpandus [*To Be Used*] [*Pharmacy*]
USUSA .... United Societies of the United States of America [*McKeesport, PA*] (EA)
USV .... United States Volunteers [*Civil War*]
USV .... Unmanned Strike Vehicle

USV .... U-Save Foods Ltd. [*Vancouver Stock Exchange symbol*]
USV .... U.S. Restaurant Properties [*NASDAQ symbol*] (TTSB)
USV .... US Restaurant Properties Ltd. [*Formerly, Burger King Investors*] [*NYSE symbol*] (SAG)
USVA .... United States Volleyball Association (BARN)
USVAAD .... United States Veteran's Administration Administrator's Decisions [*A publication*] (DLA)
USVAC .... United States Veterans' Assistance Center (OICC)
USvAd .... United Services Advisors, Inc. [*Associated Press*] (SAG)
USVB .... United States Veterans Bureau
USVBA .... United States Volleyball Association (EA)
USVBA .... US Venetian Blind Association (EA)
USVBDD ...... United States Veterans Bureau Director's Decisions [*A publication*] (DLA)
USvBk .... United Savings Bank FA [*Associated Press*] (SAG)
USVH .... United States Veterans Hospital
USVIP .... Uniformed Services Voluntary Insurance Program
USVMD .... Urine Specimen Volume Measuring Device
USVMS .... Urine Sample Volume Measurement System (MCD)
USVRU .... Ultra-Stable Voltage Reference Unit (PDAA)
USVS .... United Services Advisors, Inc. [*San Antonio, TX*] [*NASDAQ symbol*] (NQ)
USVSP .... United Svcs Advisor(Pfd) [*NASDAQ symbol*] (TTSB)
USVT .... Universal Stray Voltage Tester
USW .... Ultrashort Wave
USW .... Ultrasonic Welding
USW .... Undersea Warfare
USW .... Under Secretary of War [*Obsolete*]
USW .... United Steelworkers [*Trade union*] [*British*]
USW .... U S WEST Communic Grp [*NYSE symbol*] (TTSB)
USW .... US West, Inc. [*NYSE symbol*] (SPSG)
USW .... US Wheat Associates (EA)
USWA .... American Association for Study of the United States in World Affairs (EA)
USWA .... United Shoe Workers of America [*Later, ACTWU*] (EA)
USWA .... United States Wayfarer Association (EA)
USWA .... United Steelworkers of America [*Also known as USW*] (EA)
USWA .... United We Stand America
USWAB .... United States Warehouse Act Bonded
USWACC ...... United States Women's Army Corps Center
USWACS ...... United States Women's Army Corps School
USWAP .... United South West Africa Party [*Namibia*] [*Political party*]
USWAP .... United Steel Workers' Association of the Philippines
US Wats .... US Wats, Inc. [*Associated Press*] (SAG)
USWB .... United States Weather Bureau [*Later, National Weather Service*]
USWBC .... United States War Ballot Commission [*World War II*]
USWC .... US Wireless Corp. [*NASDAQ symbol*] (SAG)
USWCA .... United States Women's Curling Association (EA)
USWDIV .... Undersea Warfare Division [*Navy*] (DNAB)
USWest .... US West [*Associated Press*] (SAG)
USWF .... United States Weightlifting Federation (EA)
USWF .... United States Wrestling Federation (EA)
USWFA .... United States Water Fitness Association (EA)
USWGA .... United States Wholesale Grocers' Association [*Later, NAWGA*] (EA)
USWI .... United States West Indies
USWI .... US WATS [*NASDAQ symbol*] (TTSB)
USWI .... US Wats, Inc. [*NASDAQ symbol*] (SAG)
USWISOMWAGMOHOTM... United Single Women in Search of Men Who Aren't Gay, Married, or Hung-Up on Their Mothers [*Fictitious association*]
USWLA .... United States Women's Lacrosse Association (EA)
USWM .... US West [*Associated Press*] (SAG)
USWMS .... Uniform State Waterway Marking System (DICI)
USWP .... Ultrashort Wave Propagation Panel (IAA)
USWP .... United States Water Polo (EA)
USWPrA .... U.S.West Fin 7.96%'TOPrS' [*NYSE symbol*] (TTSB)
US WreCp .... US Wireless Corp. [*Associated Press*] (SAG)
USWSRA ...... United States Women's Squash Racquets Association (EA)
USWSSB ...... United States Wood Screw Service Bureau [*Defunct*] (EA)
USWst .... US West, Inc. [*Associated Press*] (SAG)
USWTCA ...... United States Women's Track Coaches Association (EA)
USWV .... United Spanish War Veterans (EA)
USX .... Ultrasoft X-Ray
USX .... US Express [*ICAO designator*] (FAAC)
USX .... US Steel Corp. [*Formerly, USS, USSC*]
USX .... USX-Marathon Group [*Associated Press*] (SAG)
USX Ca .... USX Capital LLC [*Associated Press*] (SAG)
USXDel .... USX Delhi Group [*Associated Press*] (SAG)
USXFS .... Ultrasoft X-Ray Fluroescence [*Spectroscopy*]
USXMar .... USX-Marathon Group [*Associated Press*] (SAG)
USXP .... United States Exploration, Inc. [*NASDAQ symbol*] (SAG)
USXP .... U.S. Exploration [*NASDAQ symbol*] (TTSB)
US Xprss ..... US Xpress Enterprises, Inc. [*Associated Press*] (SAG)
USXRS .... Ultrasoft X-Ray Spectroscopy
USXUSS .... USX US Steel Group [*Formerly, US Steel Corp.*] [*Associated Press*] (SAG)
USXX .... U.S. Technologies [*NASDAQ symbol*] (TTSB)
USXX .... US Technologies, Inc. [*NASDAQ symbol*] (NQ)
USY .... United Synagogue Youth (EA)
USY .... US Pay-Tel, Inc. [*Vancouver Stock Exchange symbol*]
USYC .... United States Youth Council [*Defunct*] (EA)
USYEC .... US Yugoslav Economic Council (EA)
USYRU .... US Yacht Racing Union (EA)
USYSA .... United States Youth Soccer Association (EA)
USZI .... United States Zone of the Interior
UT .... Conference Internationale pour l'Unite Technique des Chemins de Fer
UT .... Tooele Public Library, Tooele, UT [*Library symbol Library of Congress*] (LCLS)
UT .... Ultrasonic Test
UT .... Ultrathin
UT .... Umbilical Tower [*Aerospace*]
UT .... Unbound Testosterone [*Endocrinology*] (DMAA)
UT .... Uncontrolled Term [*Online database field identifier*]
UT .... Under the Tongue [*Pharmacy*]
U/T .... Under Training [*British military*] (DMA)
U/T .... Under Trust [*Legal term*] (DLA)
UT .... Underway Trials [*Shipbuilding*]
UT .... Unemployed Time [*Military British*]
UT .... Unexpired Term [*Real estate*] [*British*] (ROG)
UT .... Union Terminal Railway Co. [*AAR code*]
UT .... Union Territory [*India*] (BARN)
UT .... Unit (MCD)
UT .... Unitech (IAA)
UT .... United Technologies Corp.
UT .... United Territory
UT .... United Together [*An association Defunct*] (EA)
UT .... United TransNet [*NYSE symbol*] (TTSB)
UT .... Units Tens (IAA)
UT .... Unit Tester (NASA)
UT .... Unit Trust (ILCA)
UT .... Universal Time [*Astronomy*]
UT .... Universal Torpedo (MCD)
UT .... Universal Trainer
UT .... Universal Tube (IAA)
UT .... Universal Turret (MCD)
UT .... University of Tasmania [*State*] (EERA)
UT .... University of Tennessee
UT .... University of Texas
UT .... University of Toronto [*Ontario*]
UT .... University of Tulsa [*Oklahoma*]
UT .... Unspecified Temperature
UT .... Untested
U/T .... Untrained
UT .... Untreated [*Medicine*] (DAVI)
UT .... Upper Torso
UT .... Upper Tractor (ECII)
UT .... Up Through [*Parapsychology*]
UT .... Up Time
UT .... Urinary Tract [*Medicine*]
UT .... User's Terminal (MCD)
UT .... User Test
UT .... Using Television (WDMC)
UT .... Utah [*Postal code*]
Ut .... Utah (ODBW)
UT .... Utah Reports [*A publication*] (DLA)
UT .... Utah Territory [*Prior to statehood*]
UT .... Utendum [*To Be Used*] [*Pharmacy*] (ROG)
UT .... Uterus [*Anatomy*] (DAVI)
UT .... Utilitiesman [*Navy rating*]
UT .... Utility (BUR)
UT .... Utility Boat
UT .... Utility Player
UT1 .... Utilitiesman, First Class [*Navy rating*]
UT2 .... Utilitiesman, Second Class [*Navy rating*]
UT3 .... Utilitiesman, Third Class [*Navy rating*]
UTA .... Ultrasonic Thermal Action
UTA .... Umtali [*Zimbabwe*] [*Airport symbol*] (AD)
UTA .... Union des Transports Aeriens [*France ICAO designator*] (FAAC)
UTA .... Union de Transports Aeriens [*Air Transport Union*] [*Private airline*] [*France*] (EY)
UTA .... United Technologies Automotive
UTA .... United Typothetae of America [*Later, Printing Industries of America*]
UTA .... Unit Training Assembly [*Military*] (AABC)
UTA .... Unit Trust Association [*British*]
UTA .... University of Tasmania Association [*Australia*]
UTA .... University of Texas at Arlington
UTA .... Upper Terminal Area (NATG)
UTA .... Upper Testing Area (IAA)
UTA .... Urban Transportation Administration [*HUD*]
U_{TA} .... Urinary Titratable Acidity [*Laboratory science*] (DAVI)
UTA .... User Transfer Address
UTAC .... Union Tunisienne de l'Artisanat et du Commerce [*Tunisian Union of Artisans and Merchants*]
UTACV .... Urban Tracked Air-Cushion Vehicle [*Transit*] [*Department of Transportation*]
UTAD .... Utah Army Depot (AABC)
UTAEC .... University of Tennessee, Atomic Energy Commission (SAA)
UTAH .... Utah Railway Co. [*AAR code*]
Utah .... Utah Supreme Court Reports [*A publication*] (DLA)
Utah 2d .... Utah Reports, Second Series [*A publication*] (DLA)
Utah Admin Bull... State of Utah Bulletin [*A publication*] (DLA)
Utah Admin Code... Utah Administrative Code [*A publication*] (AAGC)
Utah Admin R... Administrative Rules of Utah [*A publication*] (DLA)
Utah Code Ann... Utah Code, Annotated [*A publication*] (DLA)
Utah IC Bull... Utah Industrial Commission. Bulletin [*A publication*] (DLA)
UtahMed .... Utah Medical, Inc. [*Associated Press*] (SAG)
Utah PUC ..... Utah Public Utilities Commission Report [*A publication*] (DLA)
Utah R .... Utah Reports [*A publication*] (DLA)
Utah St U ..... Utah State University (GAGS)

UTAL........... Upper Transition Altitude (SAA)
UT & E......... User Test and Evaluation [*Army*] (DOMA)
UT & GS...... Uplink Text and Graphics System (NASA)
UTAP........... Unified Transportation Assistance Program [*Proposed*]
UTAP........... Urban Transportation Assistance Program [*Canada*]
UTARS......... Utility Aircraft Requirements Study [*Army*] (DOMA)
UTAS........... Underwater Target-Activated Sensor (MCD)
UTASN......... University of Texas at Austin School of Nursing
UT/AT.......... Underway Trial/Acceptance Trial [*Navy*] (NVT)
UTATA......... Uniform Testamentary Additions to Trusts Act [*National Conference of Commissioners on Uniform State Laws*]
UTB............. Muttaburra [*Australia Airport symbol*] (OAG)
UTB............. Uni Taschenbuecher GmbH [*German publishers cooperative*]
UTB............. United Tariff Bureau
UTB............. University of Toronto Library, Brieflisted Records [*UTLAS symbol*]
UTB............. Utilitiesman, Boilerman [*Navy rating*]
UTBG........... Unbound Testosterone-Binding Globulin [*Immunology*] (DAVI)
UTBG........... Unbound Thyroxine Binding Globulin [*Endocrinology*] (AAMN)
UTBU........... Unhealthy to be Unpleasant [*Theatrical play*] (IIA)
UTC............. Coordinated Universal Time (USDC)
UTC............. Uncle Tom's Cabin [*Title of book by Harriet Beecher Stowe*]
UTC............. Underwater Training Centre [*British*]
UTC............. United Canso Oil & Gas Ltd. [*Toronto Stock Exchange symbol*]
UTC............. United States Tax Court, Library, Washington, DC [*OCLC symbol*] (OCLC)
UTC............. United Technologies Corp. [*Information service or system*] (IID)
UTC............. United Technology Center (IAA)
UTC............. United Telephone Cables (IAA)
UTC............. United Transformer Corp. (IAA)
UTC............. United Trust & Credit [*Finance group*] [*British*]
UTC............. Unit Test Cases (NASA)
UTC............. Unit Time Coding
UTC............. Unit Total Cost
UTC............. Unit Training Center [*Military*]
UTC............. Unit Type Code (AFM)
UTC............. Universal Test Console (KSC)
UTC............. Universal Time Code
UTC............. Universal Time Coordinated [*The universal time emitted by coordinated radio stations*]
UTC............. Universal Time Coordinated [*Marine science*] (OSRA)
UTC............. Universal Time Corrected (MCD)
UTC............. University of Tennessee at Chattanooga
UTC............. University Teachers Certificate
UTC............. University Training Corps [*British*]
UTC............. Urban Technology Conference
UTC............. Urban Training Center
UTC............. Utilitiesman, Chief [*Navy rating*]
UTC............. Utilities Telecommunications Council (EA)
UTC............. Utilities, Transportation, Communication
UTC............. Utility Tape Copy (SAA)
UTCA........... Constructionman Apprentice, Utilitiesman, Striker [*Navy rating*]
UTCAA......... Uncle Tom Cobley and All [*Refers to everyone*] [*Slang British*] (DSUE)
UTCC........... University of Tennessee at Knoxville Computer Center [*Research center*] (RCD)
UTCI............ Uniroyal Technology [*NASDAQ symbol*] (TTSB)
UTCI............ Uniroyal Technology Corp. [*NASDAQ symbol*] (SAG)
UTCIW......... Uniroyal Technology Wrrt [*NASDAQ symbol*] (TTSB)
UTCL............ Union des Travailleurs Communistes Libertaires [*Union of Libertarian Communist Workers*] [*France Political party*] (PPW)
UTCLK......... Universal Transmitter Clock
UTCM........... Utilitiesman, Master Chief [*Navy rating*]
UTCN........... Constructionman, Utilitiesman, Striker [*Navy rating*]
UTCPTT....... Union Internationale des Organismes Touristiques et Culturels des Postes et des Telecommunications [*International Union of Tourist and Cultural Associations in the Postal and Telecommunications Services*]
UTCS........... Urasenke Tea Ceremony Society (EA)
UTCS........... Urban Traffic Control System
UTCS........... Utilitiesman, Senior Chief [*Navy rating*]
UTCT........... Undermanned Tank Crew Test [*Military*] (MCD)
UTD............. Undetermined
UTD............. Uniform Theory of Diffraction (IAA)
UTD............. United
UTD............. United Air [*South Africa ICAO designator*] (FAAC)
UTD............. Universal Transfer Device
UTD............. University of Texas at Dallas (MCD)
UTD............. Up to Date (MAE)
UTD............. Uranium-Thorium Dating
UTD............. User Terminal and Display Subsystem [*Space Flight Operations Facility, NASA*]
UtdAHlt........ United American Healthcare Corp. [*Associated Press*] (SAG)
UtdAuto........ United Auto Group [*Associated Press*] (SAG)
UTDC........... Urban Transportation Development Corp. [*Canada*]
UtdCosF....... United Companies Financial [*Associated Press*] (SAG)
UTDD........... Dushanbe [*Former USSR ICAO location identifier*] (ICLI)
UTDF........... Universal Tracking Data Format (SSD)
UtdHmL........ United Home Life Insurance Co. [*Associated Press*] (SAG)
UT DICT....... Ut Dictum [*As Directed*] [*Latin*]
UtdIns.......... United Insurance Co., Inc. [*Associated Press*] (SAG)
UtdIntH........ United Inernational Holding, Inc. [*Associated Press*] (SAG)
UTDL........... United Leisure Corp. [*NASDAQ symbol*] (SAG)
UtdLeisr....... United Leisure Corp. [*Associated Press*] (SAG)
UTDLW......... United Leisure Wrrt'A' [*NASDAQ symbol*] (TTSB)
UtdMM......... United Merchants & Manufacturers, Inc. [*Associated Press*] (SAG)
UtdNews....... United News & Media PLC [*Associated Press*] (SAG)
UTDO........... Oktyabrsky [*Former USSR ICAO location identifier*] (ICLI)
UtdPay......... United Payors and United Providers, Inc. [*Associated Press*] (SAG)
UtdPetr........ United Petroleum Corp. [*Associated Press*] (SAG)
UtdPetrol...... United Petroleum Corp. [*Associated Press*] (SAG)
UtdR............ United Restaurants, Inc. [*Associated Press*] (SAG)
UtdRest........ United Restaurants, Inc. [*Associated Press*] (SAG)
UtdTst.......... United Trust, Inc. [*Associated Press*] (SAG)
UtdVideo...... United Video Satellite [*Associated Press*] (SAG)
UtdVs........... United Vision Group [*Associated Press*] (SAG)
UtdWis......... United Wisconsin Services, Inc. [*Associated Press*] (SAG)
UtdWste....... United Waste Systems [*Associated Press*] (SAG)
UTE............. Chandler, AZ [*Location identifier FAA*] (FAAL)
UTE............. Underwater Tracking Equipment (MCD)
UTE............. Union Technique de l'Electricite [*France*]
UTE............. Universal Test Equipment
UTE............. Utilization of Theoretical Energy
UTEA........... Unit Training Effectiveness Analysis [*Army*]
UTEC........... Universal Test Equipment Compiler (KSC)
UTEC........... Urethane Technologies [*NASDAQ symbol*] (TTSB)
UTEC........... Urethane Technologies, Inc. [*NASDAQ symbol*] (SAG)
UTEC........... Utah University Engineering College
UTED........... Dzhizak [*Former USSR ICAO location identifier*] (ICLI)
UTEELRAD... Utilization of Enemy Electromagnetic Radiation (MSA)
UTEK........... Ultratech Stepper [*NASDAQ symbol*] (TTSB)
UTEK........... Ultratech Stepper, Inc. [*NASDAQ symbol*] (SAG)
UTEND......... Utendus [*To Be Used*] [*Pharmacy*]
utend mor sol... Utendus More Solito [*To be Used in the Usual Manner*] [*Latin Pharmacy*] (MAE)
U Tenn......... University of Tennessee (GAGS)
U Tenn (Chattanooga)... University of Tennessee at Chattanooga (GAGS)
U Tenn (Martin)... University of Tennessee at Martin (GAGS)
U Tenn (Memphis)... University of Tennessee at Memphis (GAGS)
U Tenn (Oak Ridge)... University of Tennessee at Oak Ridge (GAGS)
UTEP........... University of Texas at El Paso
UTES........... Unit Training Equipment Site [*Military*] (AABC)
UTET........... Unione Tipografico-Editrice Torinese [*Publisher*] [*Italy*]
U Tex (Arlington)... [*The*] University of Texas at Arlington (GAGS)
U Tex (Austin)... [*The*] University of Texas at Austin (GAGS)
U Tex (Dallas)... [*The*] University of Texas at Dallas (GAGS)
U Tex (El Paso)... [*The*] University of Texas at El Paso (GAGS)
U Tex Health Sci Ctr (Houston)... University of Texas Health Science Center at Houston (GAGS)
U Tex Health Sci Ctr (San Antonio)... University of Texas Health Science Center at San Antonio (GAGS)
U Tex Med Br (Galveston)... University of Texas Medicine Branch at Galveston (GAGS)
U Tex Pan Amer... University of Texas Pan American (GAGS)
U Tex Perm Basin... University of Texas at Permian Basin (GAGS)
UTF............. Underwater Tank Facility
UTF............. Underwater Test Facility [*GE*]
UTF............. UNDEX [*Underwater Explosion*] Test Facility [*Navy*] (RDA)
UTF............. Unit Test Folder [*Military*]
UTF............. Unsuccessful Tenderers Fees
UTF............. Usual Throat Flora [*Medicine*] (DAVI)
UTF............. Valparaiso [*Chile*] [*Seismograph station code, US Geological Survey*] (SEIS)
UTFO........... Untouchable Force Organization [*Rap recording group*]
UTG............. United Tasmania Group [*Political party Australia*]
UTG............. University of Toronto Library, Government Documents [*UTLAS symbol*]
UTGA........... United Tobacco Growers Association [*Defunct*] (EA)
UTGT........... Under Thirty Group for Transit [*Defunct*] (EA)
UTH............. Udon Thani [*Thailand*] [*Airport symbol*] (OAG)
UTH............. Union Texas Petroleum [*NYSE symbol*] (TTSB)
UTH............. Union Texas Petroleum Holdings, Inc. [*NYSE symbol*] (SPSG)
UT-H........... University of Tasmania - Hobart [*Australia*]
UTH............. Upper Turret Half
UTHE........... Union des Associations des Etablissements Thermaux de la CE [*Union of Associations of Thermal Baths Establishments in the EC*] (ECED)
UTHSCSA..... University of Texas Health Science Center at San Antonio
UTI............. International Universal Time [*Telecommunications*] (TEL)
UTI............. Undistributed Taxable Income
UTI............. Union Telegraphique Internationale (MSC)
UTI............. United Transport International [*Bennett's Transport*] [*British*]
UTI............. Universal Text Interchange [*Computer science*] (PCM)
UTI............. Universal Trident Industries Ltd. [*Vancouver Stock Exchange symbol*]
UTI............. Urinary Tract Infection [*Medicine*]
UTI............. User Test Instrumentation [*Army*]
UTI............. UTI Energy [*AMEX symbol*] (TTSB)
UTI............. UTI Energy Corp. [*AMEX symbol*] (SPSG)
UTI............. Uttaradit [*Thailand*] [*Airport symbol*] (AD)
UTIA........... University of Toronto, Institute of Aerophysics (MCD)
UTIAS......... University of Toronto, Institute for Aerospace Studies [*Research center*] (MCD)
UTIC........... USAREUR Tactical Intelligence Center (MCD)
UTICI........... Union Technique des Ingenieurs Conseils [*French*]
UTICS......... University of Texas Institute for Computer Science (NITA)
UTI Eng........ UTI Energy Corp. [*Associated Press*] (SAG)
UT-IG........... University of Texas at Austin Institute for Geophysics [*Research center*] (RCD)
UTII............. Unitech Industries, Inc. [*NASDAQ symbol*] (SAG)
UTIL............ Utility [*or Utilization*] (AFM)
UtilC............ Utilicorp United, Inc. [*Associated Press*] (SAG)

UtiliCo .... Utilicorp United, Inc. [*Associated Press*] (SAG)
UTILIDOR .... Utility Corridor (SAA)
Util L Rep.... Utilities Law Reporter [*Commerce Clearing House*] [*A publication*] (DLA)
UTILN .... Utilitarian (AAG)
Util Sect Newl... Utility Section Newsletter [*A publication*] (DLA)
Utilx............ Utilx Corp. [*Associated Press*] (SAG)
UTIN .... United Trust [*NASDAQ symbol*] (TTSB)
UTIN .... United Trust, Inc. [*NASDAQ symbol*] (SAG)
UT INF .... Ut Infra [*As Below*] [*Latin*] (ADA)
UTIPS .... Upgraded Tactical Information Processing System [*Computer science*]
UTIRS .... United Tiberias Institutions Relief Society (EA)
UTJ .... Union for Traditional Judaism (EA)
UTJ .... Uterotubal Junction [*Medicine*]
UTK............. University of Tennessee, at Knoxville
UTK............. Uranium Tetrafluoride in Kiln [*Nuclear energy*] (NUCP)
UTK............. Utirik [*Marshall Islands*] [*Airport symbol*] (OAG)
UTK/PSL ...... University of Tennessee at Knoxville Plasma Science Laboratory
UTL.............. Ultratrace-Level [*Analytical chemistry*]
UTL.............. UNITIL Corp. [*AMEX symbol*] (SPSG)
UTL.............. Unit Transmission Loss
UTL.............. Unit Transmittal Letter [*Army*]
UTL.............. UnivEd Technologies Ltd. [*British*] (IRUK)
UTL.............. Universal Transporter Loader (MCD)
UT-L............ University of Tasmania - Launceston [*Australia*]
UTL.............. University of Toledo, College of Law, Toledo, OH [*OCLC symbol*] (OCLC)
UTL.............. University of Toronto Library [*UTLAS symbol*]
UTL.............. Up Telecommunications Switch
UTL.............. User Trailer Label (CMD)
UTL.............. Utila Island [*Honduras*] [*Airport symbol*] (AD)
UTLAS .... UTLAS International Canada [*Formerly, University of Toronto Library Automation System*] [*Library network*]
UTLB............ Unified Translation Lookaside Buffer [*Computer science*] (PCM)
UTLC............ University of Tennessee College of Law (DLA)
UtlCC .... Utilicorp Capital LP [*Associated Press*] (SAG)
UTLD .... Utah Test of Language Development [*Education*]
UTLM .... Up Telemetry (MCD)
UTLR .... University of Tasmania Law Review [*Australia A publication*]
UTLTY.......... Utility
UTLX............ UTILX Corp. [*NASDAQ symbol*] (SPSG)
UTLY............ Utility (BUR)
UTLZTN........ Utilization
UTM............. Union des Travailleurs de Mauritanie [*Union of Workers of Mauritania*]
UTM............. Union des Travailleurs de Mayotte [*Comoros*] (PD)
UTM............. Universal Testing Machine
UTM............. Universal Test Message
UTM............. Universal Transverse Mercator [*Cartography*]
UTM............. Universal Transverse Mercator Map Projection (EERA)
UTM............. Universal Turing Machine [*Mathematical model*] [*Computer science*] (BYTE)
UTM............. University of Tennessee at Martin
UTM............. Unsafe to Monitor (ACII)
UTMA........... Uniform Transfers to Minors Act [*National Conference of Commissioners on Uniform State Laws*]
UTMA........... United Tank Makers' Association [*A union*] [*British*]
UTMAWTU.... United Turners', Machinists', and Athletic Woodworkers' Trade Union [*British*]
UTMB........... University of Texas Medical Branch [*Galveston*]
UTMC........... United Technologies Microelectronics Center (NITA)
UTMCI .... Union des Travailleurs de la Moyenne Cote d'Ivoire [*Union of Middle Ivory Coast Workers*]
UTMC/K ...... University of Tennessee Medical Center/Knoxville
UTMD .... Utah Medical, Inc. [*NASDAQ symbol*] (NQ)
UTMD .... Utah Medical Products [*NASDAQ symbol*] (TTSB)
UTMDAH...... University of Texas, M. D. Anderson Hospital
UT/MI.......... Underway Trials and Material Inspection (MCD)
UTML........... Utility Motor Launch
UTMS........... Urban Transportation Modeling System [*TRB*] (TAG)
UTN .... University of Tennessee at Nashville
UTN .... Upington [*South Africa*] [*Airport symbol*] (OAG)
UTN .... Urban Telephone Network (OA)
UTN .... Utensil (MSA)
Utne R .... Utne Reader [*A publication*] (BRI)
UTNOTREQ... Utilization of Government Facilities Not Required as It Is Considered Such Utilization Would Adversely Affect Performance of Assigned Temporary Duty
UTNRS......... Underwater Terrain Navigation and Reconnaissance Simulator (MCD)
utnsl .... Utensil (VRA)
UTO .... Indian Mountain, AK [*Location identifier FAA*] (FAAL)
UTO .... United Telephone Organizations
UTO .... United Towns Organisation [*See also FMVJ*] [*Paris, France*] (EAIO)
UTO .... Upper Tibial Osteotomy [*Medicine*] (DMAA)
UTO .... Utopia Creek [*Alaska*] [*Airport symbol*] (OAG)
UTOA .... United Truck Owners of America (EA)
UTOA .... United TVRO [*Television Receive Only*] Owners Association [*Defunct*] (EA)
UTOC .... United Technologies Online Catalog [*United Technologies Corp.*] [*Information service or system*] (IID)
UTOCO......... Utah Oil Co.
UTOG .... Unitog [*NASDAQ symbol*] (TTSB)
UTOG .... Unitog Co. [*NASDAQ symbol*] (NQ)
UTOL .... Universal Translator Oriented Language
UTOLCL....... University of Toledo College of Law (DLA)
U Toledo...... [*The*] University of Toledo (GAGS)
U Toledo Intra LR... University of Toledo. Intramural Law Review [*A publication*] (DLA)
UTOP .... Utopian (WDAA)
UTOPIA........ Universal Terminalized Online Printing and Investigative Aid [*Bancroft-Parkman, Inc.*] [*Information service or system*]
U Tor L Rev... University of Toronto. School of Law. Review [*A publication*] (DLA)
U Toronto Sch L Rev... University of Toronto. School of Law. Review [*A publication*] (DLA)
UTP............. Unified Test Plan
UTP............. United Teaching Profession (MCD)
UTP............. United Trade Press (Holdings) Ltd. [*Commercial firm British*]
UTP............. Unit Territory Plan
UTP............. Unit Test Plan
UTP............. Universal Tape Processor
UTP............. Universal Test Point (CAAL)
UTP............. Unlisted Trading Privileges
UTP............. Unshielded Twisted-Pair [*Computer science*] (PCM)
UTP............. Upper Thames Patrol [*British military*] (DMA)
UTP............. Upper Trip Point
UTP............. Upper Turning Point
UTP............. Urban Transportation Planning [*Department of Transportation*] (GFGA)
UTP............. Uridine Triphosphatase [*An enzyme*]
UTP............. Uridine Triphosphate [*Biochemistry*]
UTP............. User Test Program [*Army*]
UTP............. Utapao [*Thailand*] [*Airport symbol Obsolete*] (OAG)
UTP............. Utility Tape Processor
UTPA .... Uniform Trustees' Powers Act [*National Conference of Commissioners on Uniform State Laws*]
UTPase........ Uridine Triphosphatase [*An enzyme*]
UTPE........... United Trekkers of Planet Earth [*An association*] (EA)
UTPL........... Urban Transportation Planning Laboratory [*University of Pennsylvania*] [*Research center*] (RCD)
UTPMS .... Unit Trust Portfolio Management Service [*Investment term British*]
UTPP .... Urban Transportation Planning Package [*Bureau of the Census*] (GFGA)
UTPS .... UMTA [*Urban Mass Transit Administration*] Transportation Planning System
UTPS .... Urban Transport Planning System [*Australia*]
UTQ .... Hinesville, GA [*Location identifier FAA*] (FAAL)
UTQG.......... Uniform Tire Quality Grade
UTQGS........ Uniform Tire Quality Grading Standards [*Department of Transportation*] (GFGA)
UTR .... Underwater Tracking Range
UTR .... Union Transportation [*AAR code*]
UTR .... Unitrode Corp. [*NYSE symbol*] (SPSG)
UTR .... Universal Torah Registry (EA)
UTR .... Universal Training Reactor [*Nuclear energy*] (GFGA)
UTR .... University of Toronto, Thomas Fisher Rare Book Library [*UTLAS symbol*]
UTR .... University Training Reactor
UTR .... Unprogrammed Transfer Register
UTR .... Untranslated Region [*Genetics*]
UTR .... Up Time Ratio
UTR .... Urticarial Transfusion Reaction [*Medicine*]
utra .... Uniform Trust Receipts Act [*Legal shorthand*] (LWAP)
UTRA .... Upper Torso Restraint Assembly
UTRANSRON... Utility Transport Squadron (DNAB)
UTRAO......... Radio Astronomy Observatory [*University of Texas at Austin*] [*Research center*] (RCD)
UTRC .... United Techniques Research Center [*Navy*] (DNAB)
UTRC .... United Technologies Research Centre
UTREP .... University of Tennessee Rehabilitation Engineering Program
UtRetail .... United Retail Group, Inc. [*Associated Press*] (SAG)
UTRF .... Update Training File [*IRS*]
UTRIP .... Universal Triangulation Program (IAA)
UTROAA...... Units to Round Out the Active Army
UTRON........ Utility Squadron [*Navy*]
UTRONFWDAREA... Utility Squadron, Forward Area [*Navy*]
UTRP .... Underwater Tactical Range, Pacific
UTRR .... University of Teheran Research Reactor
UTRTD........ Untreated
UTRWW....... Unitrode Corp. [*NASDAQ symbol*] (SAG)
UTRWW....... Unitrode Corp. Wrrt [*NASDAQ symbol*] (TTSB)
UTS............. Huntsville, TX [*Location identifier FAA*] (FAAL)
UTS............. Ullrich-Turner Syndrome [*Genetics*]
UTS............. Ultimate Tensile Strength [*or Stress*]
UTS............. Umbilical Test Set
UTS............. Underwater Telephone System
UTS............. Unified Transfer System [*Computer to translate Russian to English*]
UTS............. Union des Travailleurs du Senegal [*Senegalese Workers Union*]
UTS............. Union Theological Seminary
UTS............. United Tanners' Society [*A union*] [*British*]
UTS............. United Theological Seminary, Dayton, OH [*OCLC symbol*] (OCLC)
UTS............. United Tri-Star Resources Ltd. [*Toronto Stock Exchange symbol*]
UTS............. Unit Training Standard
UTS............. Unit Trouble Shooting
UTS............. Universal Terminal System [*Sperry UNIVAC*] [*Computer science*]
UTS............. Universal Test Station
UTS............. Universal Thrust Stand
UTS............. Universal Time Sharing [*Computer science*] (IEEE)
UTS............. Universal Timesharing System (NITA)
UTS............. Universal Time Standards (NG)

UTS .... Universal Treatment Standard [*Environmental protection agency*]
UTS .... University of Technology, Sydney [*Australia*] (ECON)
UTS .... University Tutorial Series [*A publication*]
UTS .... Unmanned Teleoperator Spacecraft (MCD)
UTS .... Update Transaction System (TEL)
UTS .... Urine-Transfer System [*Apollo*] [*NASA*]
UTS .... Utility Interim Table Simulation (SAA)
UTS .... Utility Tactical Support (SAA)
UTS .... Utsunomiya [*Japan*] [*Seismograph station code, US Geological Survey*] (SEIS)
UTSCC .... University of Texas System Cancer Center [*Houston, TX*] [*Research center*]
UTSE .... United Transport Service Employees [*Later, BRAC*] (EA)
UTS-FO .... Union Territoriale des Syndicats - Force Ouvrieres [*Territorial Federation of Trade Unions - Workers' Force*] [*French Somaliland*]
UTSI .... University of Tennessee Space Institute
UTSL .... University of Texas School of Law (DLA)
UTSL .... Use the Source, Luke [*Computer hacker terminology, used to parody commands to Luke Skywalker in the movie "Star Wars"*] (NHD)
UTSM .... Tamdy-Bulak [*Former USSR ICAO location identifier*] (ICLI)
UTS-M .... Universal Timesharing System for Mainframes (HGAA)
UTSMS .... University of Texas Southwestern Medical School
UTSN .... Used Truck Sales Network (EA)
UTSS .... Samarkand [*Former USSR ICAO location identifier*] (ICLI)
UTSS .... Universal Threat System for Simulators
UTS-S .... Universal Timesharing System for Superminis (HGAA)
UTST .... Termez [*Former USSR ICAO location identifier*] (ICLI)
UT SUP .... Ut Supra [*As Above*] [*Latin*]
UT SUPR ..... Ut Supra [*As Above*] [*Latin*]
UTSV .... Union Theological Seminary in Virginia
UTS/VS .... Universal Timesharing System/Virtual Storage (NITA)
UTT .... Umtata [*South Africa*] [*Airport symbol*] (OAG)
UTT .... Utility Tactical Transport (MCD)
UTT .... UT Technologies [*Vancouver Stock Exchange symbol*]
UTT .... Uttering [*FBI standardized term*]
UTTA .... United Thoroughbred Trainers of America (EA)
UTTAS .... Utility Tactical Transport Aircraft System [*Helicopter*] [*Military*]
UTT Avn .... Utility Tactical Transport Aviation Company [*US Army helicopters*] (VNW)
UTTC .... Universal Tape-to-Tape Converter
UTTCO .... Utility Tactical Transport Company [*US Army helicopters*] (VNW)
UTTL .... Uttlesford [*England*]
UTTO .... Universal Tractor Transmission Oil [*Lubricants*]
UTTR .... Utah Test and Training Range [*Air Force*]
UTTS .... Union Territoriale du Senegal des Travailleurs [*Senegalese Workers Union*]
UTTS .... Universal Target Tracking Station (MCD)
UTTT .... Tashkent/Yuzhny [*Former USSR ICAO location identifier*] (ICLI)
UTU .... Ulster Teacher's Union [*Ireland*] (AIE)
UTU .... Ultrasonic Test Unit
UTU .... Underway Training Unit
UTU .... United Transportation Union (EA)
UTU .... Ustupo [*Panama*] [*Airport symbol*] (OAG)
utu .... Utah [*MARC country of publication code Library of Congress*] (LCCP)
UTUC .... Uganda Trades' Union Congress
UTUC .... United Trades Union Congress [*India*]
U Tulsa .... [*The*] University of Tulsa (GAGS)
UTV .... Ulster Television [*Ireland*] (DI)
UTV .... Uncompensated Temperature Variation (TEL)
UTV .... Underwater Television
UTV .... Universal Test Vehicle [*Military*]
UTVI .... United Television, Inc. [*NASDAQ symbol*] (NQ)
UTVI .... United Televison [*NASDAQ symbol*] (TTSB)
UTW .... Queenstown [*South Africa*] [*Airport symbol*] (AD)
UTW .... Ultrathin Window [*Spectroscopy*]
UTW .... Under the Wing [*Aircraft*]
UTW .... Union of Textile Workers [*British*] (EAIO)
UTW .... United Telegraph Workers [*Later, C/UBC*] (EA)
UTW .... Utilitiesman, Water and Sanitation [*Navy rating*]
UTWA .... United Textile Workers of America (EA)
UTWG .... Utility Wing [*Navy*] (MUGU)
UTWING .... Utility Wing [*Navy*]
UTWINGSERVLANT .... Utility Wing, Service Force, Atlantic [*Navy*]
UTWINGSERVPAC ... Utility Wing, Service Force, Pacific [*Navy*]
UTX .... Jupiter, FL [*Location identifier FAA*] (FAAL)
UTX .... United Technologies [*NYSE symbol*] (TTSB)
UTX .... United Technologies Corp. [*NYSE symbol*] (SPSG)
UTZ .... Ultrasound [*Radiology*] (DAVI)
UU .... Reunion Air [*ICAO designator*] (AD)
UU .... Uglies Unlimited (EA)
UU .... Ulster Unionist Party
UU .... Ultimate User [*Nuclear energy*]
UU .... Unemployment Unit [*An association British*]
UU .... Unicorns Unanimous [*An association*] (EA)
UU .... Union University [*Tennessee*]
UU .... University of Utah, Salt Lake City, UT [*Library symbol Library of Congress*] (LCLS)
UU .... Urine Urobilin [*Clinical chemistry*] (DAVI)
UU .... Urine Urobilinogen [*Clinical chemistry*]
UU .... User Unit (MCD)
UUA .... Southern Utah State College, Cedar City, UT [*OCLC symbol*] (OCLC)
UUA .... Unitarian Universalist Society for Alcohol and Drug Education
UUA .... UNIVAC Users Association [*Later, AUUA*]
UUA .... Universal Automatic Computer Users' Association (IAA)
UUABCWG ... Unitarian Universalist Association Black Concerns Working Group (EA)
UUAC .... United Unionist Action Council [*Northern Ireland*]
UUARC .... United Ukrainian American Relief Committee (EA)
UUA/WO ...... Unitarian Universalist Association of Congregations-Washington Office (EA)
UUA/WOSC ... Unitarian Universalist Association-Washington Office for Social Concern [*Later,UUA/WOSJ*] (EA)
UUA/WOSJ ... Unitarian Universalist Association of Congregations-Washington Office for SocialJustice (EA)
UUB .... Brigham Young University, School of Library and Information Science, Provo, UT [*OCLC symbol*] (OCLC)
UUB .... UUB Financial [*Associated Press*] (SAG)
UUBCWG ..... Unitarian Universalist Black Concerns Working Group (EA)
UUBP .... Bryansk [*Former USSR ICAO location identifier*] (ICLI)
UUC .... Salt Lake County Library System, Salt Lake City, UT [*OCLC symbol*] (OCLC)
UUC .... Ulster University College (ACII)
UUC .... United University Club [*British*]
UUCA .... United Underwear Contractors Association [*Defunct*] (EA)
UUCD .... USA-USSR Citizens' Dialogue [*Defunct*] (EA)
UUCF .... Unitarian Universalist Christian Fellowship (EA)
UUCP .... Unix-to-Unix Call Procedure [*Telecommunications*] (OSI)
UUCP .... Unix-to-Unix Copy Program [*Computer science*]
UUCP .... UNIX-to-UNIX Copy Protocol (TNIG)
UUD .... Logan Public Library, Logan, UT [*OCLC symbol*] (OCLC)
U-UD .... Utility Dog [*Prefix*]
UUE .... University of Utah, Eccles Health Science Library, Salt Lake City, UT [*OCLC symbol*] (OCLC)
UUE .... Use until Exhausted
UUEE .... Moskva/Sheremetyevo [*Former USSR ICAO location identifier*] (ICLI)
UUEM .... Kalini/Migalovo [*Former USSR ICAO location identifier*] (ICLI)
UUEncode .... Binary to Text Encoding [*Computer science*]
UUEW .... United Unions for Employees and Workers [*Lebanon*]
UUFSJ .... Unitarian Universalist Fellowship for Social Justice (EA)
UUGS .... Unitarian and Universalist Genealogical Society [*Defunct*] (EA)
UUHS .... Unitarian Universalist Historical Society (EA)
UUID .... Universally Unique Identifier [*Computer science*]
UUIP .... Uppsala University Institute of Physics [*Sweden*]
UUK .... Kuparuk, AK [*Location identifier FAA*] (FAAL)
UU-L .... University of Utah, Law Library, Salt Lake City, UT [*Library symbol Library of Congress*] (LCLS)
UULGC .... Unitarian Universalist Lesbian Gay Caucus (EA)
UUM .... Underwater-to-Underwater Missile [*Air Force*]
UU-M .... University of Utah, Library of Medical Sciences, Salt Lake City, UT [*Library symbol Library of Congress*] (LCLS)
UUM .... University of Utah, Salt Lake City, UT [*OCLC symbol*] (OCLC)
UUMA .... Unitarian Universalist Ministers Association (EA)
UUMN .... Unitarian Universalist Musicians' Network (EA)
UUMP .... Unification of Units of Measurement Panel [*ICAO*] (DA)
UUMPS .... Unitarian Universalist Ministers' Partners Society (EA)
UUN .... Urinary Urea Nitrogen [*Clinical medicine*]
UUnet .... UUnet Technologies, Inc. [*Associated Press*] (SAG)
UUNT .... UUNET Technologies [*NASDAQ symbol*] (TTSB)
UUNT .... UUnet Technologies, Inc. [*NASDAQ symbol*] (SAG)
UUO .... Unimplemented User Operation [*Computer science*] (EECA)
UUO .... Weber State College, Ogden, UT [*OCLC symbol*] (OCLC)
UUOO .... Voronezh [*Former USSR ICAO location identifier*] (ICLI)
UUP .... Salt Lake City Public Library, Salt Lake City, UT [*OCLC symbol*] (OCLC)
UUP .... Uaupes [*Brazil*] [*Airport symbol*] (AD)
UUP .... Ulster Unionist Party [*British Political party*]
UUP .... Urine Uroporphyrin [*Medicine*] (MAE)
UUPP .... Unused Undeducted Purchase Price
UUR .... Under Usual Reserves
UURWAW .... United Union of Roofers, Waterproofers, and Allied Workers (EA)
UUS .... User-to-User Signaling [*Telecommunications*] (DOM)
UUS .... Utah State University, Logan, UT [*OCLC symbol*] (OCLC)
UUSAE .... Unitarian Universalist Society for Alcohol Education [*Later, UUA*] (EA)
UUSC .... Unitarian Universalist Service Committee (EA)
UUSS .... University of Utah Seismograph Stations [*Research center*] (RCD)
UUT .... Unit under Test
U Utah .... University of Utah (GAGS)
UUTI .... Uncomplicated Urinary Tract Infection [*Medicine*]
UUU .... Manumu [*Papua New Guinea*] [*Airport symbol*] (OAG)
UUUC .... United Ulster Unionist Coalition [*Northern Ireland*]
UUUM .... Moskva [*Former USSR ICAO location identifier*] (ICLI)
UUUM .... United Ulster Unionist Movement [*Northern Ireland*]
UUUP .... United Ulster Unionist Party [*Northern Ireland*] [*Political party*] (PPW)
UUUU .... Moskva [*Former USSR ICAO location identifier*] (ICLI)
UUUU .... Unidentified [*Marketing surveys*] (NTCM)
UUUU .... Unwilling, Led by the Unqualified, Doing the Unnecessary, for the Ungrateful [*Military slogan*] (VNW)
UUV .... Unmanned Undersea Vehicle [*Military robotics*]
UUV .... Untethered Underwater Vehicle (DOMA)
UUW .... Westminster College, Salt Lake City, UT [*OCLC symbol*] (OCLC)
UUWF .... Unitarian Universalist Women's Federation (EA)
UUWW .... Moskva/Vnukovo [*Former USSR ICAO location identifier*] (ICLI)
UUYEP .... US-USSR Youth Exchange Program (EA)
UUYT .... Ust-Kulom [*Former USSR ICAO location identifier*] (ICLI)
UUYY .... Syktyvkar [*Former USSR ICAO location identifier*] (ICLI)
UUZ .... Utah State Library, Processing Center, Salt Lake City, UT [*OCLC symbol*] (OCLC)
UV .... Air Kangaroo Island [*Airline code*] [*Australia*]

UV .... Ultra Vans (EA)
UV .... Ultraviolet [*Electromagnetic spectrum range*]
uv .... Ultraviolet (VRA)
UV .... Ultravisible
UV .... Umbilical Vein [*Medicine*]
UV .... Unabhaengige Volkspartei [*Independent People's Party*] [*Political party Germany*] (EAIO)
UV .... Unadilla Valley Railroad (IIA)
UV .... Under Voltage
UV .... Underwater Vehicle
UV .... Union Valdotaine [*Valdotaine Union*] [*Italy Political party*] (EAIO)
UV .... Union Valenciana [*Spain Political party*] (EY)
UV .... Universal Airways [*ICAO designator*] (AD)
uv .... Upper Volta [*MARC country of publication code Library of Congress*] (LCCP)
Uv .... Uppsala Virus [*Medicine*] (MAE)
UV .... Ureterovesical [*Urology*] (DAVI)
UV .... Urethrovesical [*Urology*] (DAVI)
UV .... Urinary Volume [*Physiology*]
UV .... Uterine Vein [*Anatomy*]
UV .... Uterine Volume
UV .... Utility Value [*Psychology*]
UVA .... Ultraviolet Absorption
UVA .... Ultraviolet A (Light)
UVA .... Ultraviolet Light, Long Wave
UVA .... Universal Airways, Inc. [*ICAO designator*] (FAAC)
UvA .... Universiteit van Amsterdam
UVA .... University of Virginia
UVA .... Ureterovesical Angle [*Urology*] (DAVI)
UVA .... Urethrovesical Angle [*Urology*] (DAVI)
UVA .... Uvalde, TX [*Location identifier FAA*] (FAAL)
UVAL .... Ultraviolet Argon LASER
UVAN .... Ukrainian Academy of Arts and Sciences of Canada
UVAR .... University of Virginia Reactor
UVAS .... Ultraviolet Astronomical Satellite (PDAA)
UVAS .... Unmanned Vehicle for Aerial Surveillance (MCD)
UVASER .... Ultraviolet Amplification by Stimulated Emission of Radiation
UVASERS .... Ultraviolet Amplification by Stimulated Emission of Radiation System
UVB .... Ultraviolet B [*or Ultraviolet light, midrange sunbeam, spectrum*] [*Dermatology*] (DAVI)
UV-B .... Ultraviolet Band
UV-B .... Ultraviolet-Biological (USDC)
UVB .... Ultraviolet B (Light)
UVB .... Ultraviolet Light, Midrange Sunbeam Spectrum [*Ultraviolet B*] [*Dermatology*] (DAVI)
UVBF .... Umbilical Vein Blood Flow
UVC .... Pennsylvania State University, Capitol Campus, Middletown, PA [*OCLC symbol*] (OCLC)
UVC .... Ullucus Virus C [*Plant pathology*]
UVC .... Ultrahigh Vacuum Chamber
UVC .... Ultraviolet Communications System
UVC .... Ultraviolet Light Cured
UVC .... Umbilical Venous Catheter [*Medicine*] (MEDA)
UVC .... Uniform Vehicle Code
UVCA .... Uniform Vehicle Code Annotated
UVCB .... Under-Voltage Circuit-Breaker [*Electronics*] (EECA)
UVCB .... Unknown or Variable Composition, Complex Reaction Products, and Biological Materials [*Chemical Abstracts Services*]
UVCE .... Unconfined Vapor Cloud Explosion
UVCS .... Ultraviolet Coronagraph Spectrometer [*Solar Physics*]
UVD .... Ultrasonic Vapor Degresser
UVD .... Ultraviolet Detector
UVD .... Undervoltage Device
UVD .... Unintegrated Viral DNA [*Deoxyribonucleic Acid*] [*Pathology*]
UVD .... Upper Vas Deferens [*Anatomy*]
UVDB .... Union des Verts pour le Developpement du Burkina [*Burkina Faso*] [*Political party*] (EY)
UVDC .... Urban Vehicle Design Competition
UVDIAL .... Ultraviolet Differential Absorption LIDAR [*Light Detection and Ranging*] (PDAA)
UVD-SV .... Upper Vas Deferens-Seminal Vesicle Complex [*Anatomy*]
UVE .... Ouvea [*Loyalty Islands*] [*Airport symbol*] (OAG)
UVEPROM .... Ultra-Violet Erasable Programmable Read Only Memory
UV-EPROMS .... Ultraviolet-Erasable Programmable Read-Only Memories [*Computer science*]
UVEROM .... Ultraviolet Eraseable Read Only Memory (PDAA)
UVF .... St. Lucia [*West Indies*] Hewanorra Airport [*Airport symbol*] (OAG)
UVF .... Ulster Volunteer Force
UVF .... Ultraviolet Filter
UVF .... Ultraviolet Floodlight (AAG)
UVF .... Underground Validation Facility [*Nuclear energy*] (NUCP)
UVF .... Unmanned Vertical Flight [*NASA*] (NASA)
UVFLT .... Ultraviolet Floodlight
UVFO .... Ultraviolet Fiber Optics
UVG .... UV [*Ultraviolet*] Spectrometry Group [*British*]
UVGS .... Church of Jesus Christ of Latter-Day Saints, Genealogical Society Library, Uintah Basin Branch, Vernal, UT [*Library symbol Library of Congress*] (LCLS)
UVH .... Univentricular Heart [*Cardiology*]
UVHFDS .... Ultraviolet Hydrogen Fire Detection System (DNAB)
UVI .... Ultraviolet Irradiation
UVI .... Uvira [*Zaire*] [*Seismograph station code, US Geological Survey Closed*] (SEIS)
UVIC .... University of Victoria [*British Columbia*]
UVICON .... Ultraviolet Image Converter (WGA)
UVIL .... Ultraviolet Inspection Light
UVIL .... Ultraviolet Ion LASER
UVIRSG .... Ultraviolet Infrared Scene Generator
UVJ .... Ureterovesical Junction [*Anatomy*] (MAE)
UVL .... New Valley [*Egypt*] [*Airport symbol*] (OAG)
UVL .... Ultraviolet Lamp
UVL .... Ultraviolet LASER
UVL .... Ultraviolet Light
UVL .... Universal [*Former USSR*] [*FAA designator*] (FAAC)
UVLI .... Ustav Vedeckych Lekarskych Informaci [*Institute for Medical Information*] [*Former Czechoslovakia Database operator*] [*Information service or system*] (IID)
UVLS .... Ultraviolet Light Stabilizer
UVM .... Ultraviolet Meter
UVM .... Universal Vendor Marking (WGA)
UVM .... Universitas Viridis Montis [*University of the Green Mountains; i.e., University of Vermont*]
UVM .... University of Vermont (PDAA)
UVM .... University of Vermont, Burlington (USDC)
UVMC .... United Voluntary Motor Corps (EA)
UVN .... Unionville [*Nevada*] [*Seismograph station code, US Geological Survey Closed*] (SEIS)
UVNO .... Ultraviolet Nitric-Oxide Experiment
UVO .... Uvol [*Papua New Guinea*] [*Airport symbol*] (OAG)
UVOH .... Union of Voluntary Organisations for the Handicapped [*British*] (DBA)
UVP .... Ultrahigh Vacuum Pump
UVP .... Ultrasound Vibration Potential [*Determination of electrokinetic potential*]
UVP .... Ultraviolet Photometry
UVP .... Under-Voltage Protection [*Electronics*] (EECA)
UVP .... Unified Vocational Preparation [*Manpower Services Commission*] [*British*]
UVPES .... Ultraviolet Photoelectron Spectroscopy
UVPJU .... Uganda Vernacular, Primary and Junior Secondary Teachers' Union
UVPROM .... Ultraviolet Programmable Read Only Memory
UVPS .... Ultrahigh Vacuum Pumping Station
UV-PSdA .... Unione Valdostana-Partito Sardo d'Azione [*Italy*] [*Political party*] (ECED)
UVR .... Uitenhage Volunteer Rifles [*British military*] (DMA)
UV-R .... Ultraviolet-Biological [*Marine science*] (OSRA)
UVR .... Ultraviolet Radiation
UVR .... Ultraviolet Radiometer (MCD)
UVR .... Ultraviolet Receiver
UVR .... Ultraviolet Resistant
UVR .... Ultraviolet Rocket
UVR .... Under Voltage Relay
UVR .... University of Virginia Reactor
UVR .... User Visible Resources
UVROM .... Ultraviolet Read Only Memory (IAA)
UVRR .... Ultraviolet Resonance Raman [*Spectroscopy*]
UVS .... Ultraviolet Spectrometer
UVS .... Under Voltage Sensing (MCD)
UVS .... Uninterruptable Voltage Source [*Electric power supply*]
UVS .... United Voluntary Services (EA)
UVS .... Universal Versaplot Software (IAA)
UVS .... Unmanned Vehicle System
UVSC .... Ultraviolet Solar Constant
UVSC .... Uranium Ventilation Scrubber Cell [*Nuclear energy*] (NRCH)
UVSG .... Ultra Violet Spectrometry Group [*British*] (DBA)
UVSG .... United Video Satellite [*NASDAQ symbol*] (SAG)
UVSGA .... United Video Satellite Gp'A' [*NASDAQ symbol*] (TTSB)
UVSL .... Universal Automotive Inds [*NASDAQ symbol*] (TTSB)
UVSL .... Universal Automotive Inds, Inc. [*NASDAQ symbol*] (SAG)
UVSLW .... Universal Auto Ind Wrrt [*NASDAQ symbol*] (TTSB)
UVSP .... Ultraviolet Spectral Photometer
UVT .... Ultraviolet Transmission
UVT .... Ultraviolet Tube
UVT .... Universal Voltage Tester
U Vt .... University of Vermont (GAGS)
UVT .... Usable Vector Table
UVTEI .... Ustredi Vedeckych, Technickych, a Ekonomickych Informaci [*Former Czechoslovakia*] [*Information service or system*] (IID)
UVV .... Universal Corp. [*NYSE symbol*] (SPSG)
UVV .... Univl Corp. [*NYSE symbol*] (TTSB)
UV-VIS .... Ultraviolet/Visible [*Spectroscopy*]
UVVO .... United Vietnam Veterans Organization (EA)
UVX .... Univar Corp. [*Formerly, VWR United Corp.*] [*NYSE symbol*] (SPSG)
UW .... Air Rwanda [*Rwanda*] [*ICAO designator*] (ICDA)
UW .... Perimeter Airlines [*ICAO designator*] (AD)
UW .... Ultimate Weapon (AAG)
UW .... Ultrasonic Wave
UW .... Unburned, Warmed [*Ecology*]
UW .... Unconventional Warfare [*Army*]
UW .... Underwater
UW .... Underwater Weapons [*British*]
U/W .... Underway (NVT)
U/W .... Under Will [*Legal term*] (DLA)
U/W .... Underwriter [*Insurance*]
UW .... Underwriter (DFIT)
UW .... Unique Word (IAA)
UW .... United Way (OICC)
UW .... United Weldors International Union
UW .... University of Washington [*Seattle, WA*]
UW .... University of Wisconsin [*Madison, WI*] (MCD)
UW .... Unladen Weight (BARN)

UW.............. Untere Winkelgruppe [*Angles up to 45*] [*German military - World War II*]
UW.............. Uppity Women [*An association*] (EA)
UW.............. Upset Welding
UW.............. Upwind [*Aviation*] (FAAC)
UW.............. Usable Width (MCD)
UW.............. USA Waste Service [*NYSE symbol*] (TTSB)
UW.............. USA Waste Services, Inc. [*NYSE symbol*] (SPSG)
U/W............. Used With
UW.............. Utility Water (AAG)
UWA............ Ukrainian Workingmen's Association [*Later, UFA*] (EA)
UWA............ United Way of America (EA)
UWA............ United Weighers Association (EA)
UWA............ United Women of the Americas (EA)
UWA............ United World Atheists (EA)
UWA............ University of Western Australia [*State*] (EERA)
UWA............ User Working Area
UWA............ Uwajima [*Japan*] [*Seismograph station code, US Geological Survey*] (SEIS)
UWA............ Ware, MA [*Location identifier FAA*] (FAAL)
UWAC.......... Ukrainian Women's Association of Canada
UWAGE........ Union Women's Alliance to Gain Equality [*Defunct*] (EA)
UWAL.......... Underwater Wide-Angle Lens
UWAL.......... University of Washington Aeronautical Laboratory (MCD)
UWARC........ United Whiteruthenian [*Byelorussian*] American Relief Committee (EA)
UWARS........ Universal Water-Activated Release System (DWSG)
U Wash........ University of Washington (GAGS)
U Wash L Rev... University of Washington. Law Review [*A publication*] (DLA)
UWASIS....... United Way of America Services Identification System
UWAT.......... User Written Application Test [*Computer science*]
UWATS........ Universal Weapons Assembly Test Standard (MCD)
UWATU........ Underway Training Unit
UWAVM....... Underwater Antivehicle Mine (MCD)
UWAVWA..... Union of West African Voluntary Workcamps Associations [*Ghana*] (EAIO)
UWAYTUNORVA... Underway Training Unit, Norfolk, Virginia (DNAB)
UWB............ Ultra-Wide Band
UWB............ Universal White Brotherhood [*An association France*] (EAIO)
UWBBR........ University of Wisconsin - Madison Bureau of Business Research [*Research center*] (RCD)
UWBS.......... Uniform Work Breakdown Structure
UWC............ Ulster Workers' Council
UWC............ Underwater Communications [*Navy*] (CAAL)
UWC............ Universal Water Charts [*Air Force*]
UWC............ Universal Winding Co. (MCD)
UWC............ University of the Western Cape [*South Africa*]
UWC............ Widener College, Chester, PA [*OCLC symbol*] (OCLC)
UWCCCM..... Union of Watch, Clock, and Clock Case Makers [*British*]
UWCE.......... Underwater Weapons and Countermeasures Establishment (BARN)
UWCS.......... Underwater Weapons Control System
UWCSEA...... United World College of South East Asia [*Singapore*] (ECON)
UWCSS........ Universal Weapon Control Stabilization System
UWD............ Underwater Weapons Department [*British military*] (DMA)
UWDD.......... Undersea Warfare Development Division [*Navy*] (MCD)
UWE............ University Women of Europe (EA)
UWE............ Uwekahuna [*Hawaii*] [*Seismograph station code, US Geological Survey*] (SEIS)
UWERT........ United World Education and Research Trust (EAIO)
UWF............ United World Federalists [*Later, World Federalists Association*] (EA)
UWF............ University of West Florida [*Pensacola*]
UWF............ Unknown White Female (DAVI)
UWFC.......... Underwater Fire Control [*Navy*] (CAAL)
UWFCS........ Underwater Fire Control System
UWFPC........ Union Wallisienne et Futunienne pour la Caledonie [*Wallisian and Futunian Union for Caledonia*] [*Political party*] (PPW)
UWG............ Gesetz Gegen den Unlauteren Wettbewerb [*Law Against Unfair Competition*] [*German*] (DLA)
UWGB.......... University of Wisconsin at Green Bay
UWH............ Underwater Habitat
UWH............ Underwater Welding Habitat [*Deep-sea diving*]
UWHAT........ Understanding without Heavy Acronym Training (AIE)
UW-HF......... Upset Welding-High Frequency
UWI............. Dalton, GA [*Location identifier FAA*] (FAAL)
UWI............. United Way International (EA)
UWI............. United Westburne Industries Ltd. [*Toronto Stock Exchange symbol*]
UWI............. University of the West Indies [*Jamaica*]
UW-I........... Upset Welding-Induction
UWICED....... University of the West Indies Centre for Environment and Development [*Barbados*]
U Windsor L Rev... University of Windsor. Law Review [*A publication*] (DLA)
UWIS........... University of Wisconsin (PDAA)
U Wis........... University of Wisconsin (GAGS)
U Wis (Eau Claire)... University of Wisconsin at Eau Claire (GAGS)
U Wis (La Crosse)... University of Wisconsin at La Crosse (GAGS)
U Wis (Milwaukee)... University of Wisconsin at Milwaukee (GAGS)
U Wis (Oshkosh)... University of Wisconsin at Oshkosh (GAGS)
U Wis (Platteville)... University of Wisconsin at Platteville (GAGS)
U Wis (River Falls)... University of Wisconsin at River Falls (GAGS)
U Wis (Stevens Point)... University of Wisconsin at Stevens Point (GAGS)
U Wis (Stout)... University of Wisconsin at Stout (GAGS)
U Wis (Superior)... University of Wisconsin at Superior (GAGS)
UWIST......... University of Wales Institute of Science and Technology [*British*]
U Wis (Whitewater)... University of Wisconsin at Whitewater (GAGS)
UWKD.......... Kazan [*Former USSR ICAO location identifier*] (ICLI)
UWL............ New Castle, IN [*Location identifier FAA*] (FAAL)
UWL............ Underwater Launch
UWL............ University of Winnipeg Library [*UTLAS symbol*]
UWL............ Utowana Lake [*New York*] [*Seismograph station code, US Geological Survey*] (SEIS)
UWLA Rev... University of West Los Angeles. School of Law. Law Review [*A publication*] (DLA)
UWM........... Uniform Wave Motion
UWM........... United World Mission (EA)
UWM........... University of Wisconsin at Milwaukee [*Seismograph station code, US Geological Survey*] (SEIS)
UWM........... Unknown White Male (DAVI)
UWMAK....... University of Wisconsin TOKAMAK
UWNDS........ Upper Winds [*Meteorology*] (FAAC)
UWNE.......... Brotherhood of Utility Workers of New England (EA)
UWNR.......... University of Wisconsin - Madison Nuclear Reactor Laboratory [*Research center*] (RCD)
UWO............ University of Western Ontario (MCD)
UWO............ University of Western Ontario Library [*UTLAS symbol*]
UWO............ University of Western Ontario, School of Library and Information Science, Lond on, ON, Canada [*OCLC symbol*] (OCLC)
UWOA.......... Unclassified without Attachment
UWOA.......... Unconventional Warfare Operations Area [*Army*] (AABC)
UWORDTECH... Underwater Ordnance Technician [*Navy*] (DNAB)
UWP............ Dominica United Workers' Party [*Political party*] (EY)
UWP............ United Workers' Party [*St. Lucia*] [*Political party*] (PPW)
UWP............ United Workers' Party [*Guyana*] [*Political party*] (EY)
UWP............ United Workers' Party [*Hungary Political party*] (PPW)
UWP............ Up with People (EA)
UWPC.......... United World Press Cooperative [*Later, The Peoples Media Cooperative*] (EA)
UWPP.......... Penza [*Former USSR ICAO location identifier*] (ICLI)
UWR............ Underwater Range (MUGU)
U/Wr........... Underwriter [*Insurance*] (DLA)
UWR............ Unexpected Wildlife Refuge (EA)
UWR............ United Water Res [*NYSE symbol*] (TTSB)
UWR............ United Water Resources [*Associated Press*] (SAG)
UWR............ United Water Resources, Inc. [*NYSE symbol*] (SPSG)
UWRA.......... Uniform Warehouse Receipts Act (LWAP)
UWRA.......... Urban Water Research Association (EERA)
UWRC.......... Urban Wildlife Research Center (EA)
UW-RF......... University of Wisconsin-River Falls
UWRR.......... University of Wyoming Research Reactor
UWS............ Undersea Weapon System
UWS............ University of Western Sydney [*State*] (EERA)
UWS............ Unmanned Weather Station
UWS............ User Work Station (NASA)
UWSAMBS... United Women's Societies of the Adoration of the Most Blessed Sacrament [*Later,NUWSAMBS*] (EA)
UWSDDMS... Underwater Weapons System Design Disclosure Management Systems (KSC)
UWSEC......... Underwater Weapons Systems Engineering Center [*Navy*] (DNAB)
UWS-M......... University of Western Sydney - Macarthur [*Australia*]
UWS-N.......... University of Western Sydney - Nepean [*Australia*]
UWSRD........ Underwater Weapons Systems Reliability Data (KSC)
UWST........... United Waste Systems [*NASDAQ symbol*] (SAG)
UWT............ Underwater Telephone
UWT............ Uniform Wave Train
UWT............ Union of Women Teachers [*British*] (DI)
UWT............ United World Education and Research Trust [*British*] (EAIO)
UWT............ Unit Weight (MSA)
UWTM.......... Underwater Team (MSA)
UWTR.......... Underwater (AABC)
UWTR.......... University of Washington Training Reactor
UWU............ Los Angeles, CA [*Location identifier FAA*] (FAAL)
UWU............ Utility Workers Union of America
UWUA.......... Utility Workers Union of America (EA)
UWW........... Unisource Worldwide, Inc. [*NYSE symbol*] (SAG)
UWW........... University without Walls [*Twenty-one-university consortium*]
UWWR......... Unpublished Scholarly Writings on World Religions (BJA)
UWWW........ Kuybyshev/Kurumoch [*Former USSR ICAO location identifier*] (ICLI)
UWY............ Upper Airway [*Aviation*] (DA)
U Wyo.......... University of Wyoming (GAGS)
UWZ............ United Wisconsin Services, Inc. [*NYSE symbol*] (SAG)
UWZ............ United Wisconsin Svcs [*NYSE symbol*] (TTSB)
UX.............. Air Illinois [*ICAO designator*] (AD)
UX.............. Unexploded (BARN)
ux.............. Uxor [*Wife*] [*Latin*] (WGA)
UXAA.......... Unexploded Antiaircraft [*Shell*]
UXAPB........ Unexploded Antipersonnel Bomb
UXB............ Unexploded Bomb
UXGB.......... Unexploded Gas Bomb
UXIB........... Unexploded Incendiary Bomb
UXL............ Laidlaw One 5.75% Ex Nts 2000 [*NYSE symbol*] (TTSB)
UXL............ Laidlaw One, Inc. [*NYSE symbol*] (SAG)
UXM........... Universal Extension Mechanism (KSC)
UXO............ Unexploded Ordnance
UXOI........... Unexploded Ordnance Incident
UXPLD........ Unexploded Bomb (SAA)
UXPM.......... Unexploded Parachuted Mine
UXS............ Unexploded Shell [*British military*] (DMA)
UXTGM........ Unexploded Type G Mine
UXW........... South Bend, IN [*Location identifier FAA*] (FAAL)
UY.............. Cameroon Airlines [*ICAO designator*] (AD)
UY.............. Unit Years [*Electronics*] (IEEE)

UY................ Universal Youth
UY................ Uruguay [*ANSI two-letter standard code*] (CNC)
uy................ Uruguay [*MARC country of publication code Library of Congress*] (LCCP)
UYA............ University Year for ACTION [*Refers to federal program, ACTION, which is not an acronym*]
UYA............ Yute Air Alaska, Inc. [*ICAO designator*] (FAAC)
UYC............ Cameroon Airlines [*ICAO designator*] (FAAC)
UYC............ Uxbridge Yeomanry Cavalry [*British military*] (DMA)
UYF............. London, OH [*Location identifier FAA*] (FAAL)
UYL............. Nyala [*Sudan*] [*Airport symbol*] (OAG)
UYLNA......... Ukrainian Youth League of North America [*Defunct*] (EA)
UYN............ Yulin [*China*] [*Airport symbol*] (OAG)
UYVDRA...... Upper Yarra Valley and Dandenong Regional Authority [*of Victoria*] [*State*] (EERA)
UZ................ Air Resorts Airlines [*ICAO designator*] (AD)
UZ................ Nefertiti [*ICAO designator*] (AD)
UZ................ Uhrzuender [*Clockwork fuze*] [*German military - World War II*]
UZ................ Upper Zone [*Geology*]
Uz................ Uzbek (BARN)
UZA............. Urbanized Area [*APTA*] [*FHWA*] (TAG)
U Zambia LB... University of Zambia. Law Bulletin [*A publication*] (DLA)
uzb.............. Uzbek [*MARC language code Library of Congress*] (LCCP)
UZB............. Uzbekistan Havo Jullary [*Uzbekistan Airways*] [*ICAO designator*] (FAAC)
UZH............ Uzhgorod [*Unuar*] [*Former USSR Seismograph station code, US Geological Survey*] (SEIS)
UZK............. Indianapolis, IN [*Location identifier FAA*] (FAAL)
UZM............ Unsaturated Zone Monitoring [*Environmental Protection Agency*] (ERG)
UZM............ Uoologisk Museum
uzr............... Uzbek Soviet Socialist Republic [*MARC country of publication code Library of Congress*] (LCCP)
UZRA........... United Zionist Revisionists of America [*Later, Herut - USA*] (EA)
UZU............ Curuzu Cuatia [*Argentina*] [*Airport symbol*] (OAG)
UZW............ Und Zwar [*That Is*] [*German*]

V
By Acronym

V.......... Abstracted Valuation Decisions [*A publication*] (DLA)
V.......... Base Value (IDOE)
V.......... Chest [*Anatomy*] (DAVI)
V.......... Coefficient of Variation [*Statistics*] (BARN)
V.......... Dead Space [*Medicine*] (DAVI)
V.......... Deflection of the Vertical
V.......... Digestum Vetus [*A publication*] (DSA)
V.......... Electric Potential [*Symbol*] [*IUPAC*]
V.......... Electromotive Force [*Symbol*] [*See also E, EMF Electrochemistry*] (DEN)
V.......... Five [*Roman numeral*]
V.......... Five Dollars [*Slang*]
V.......... Five-Year Sentence [*Criminal slang*]
V.......... Fixed-Wing Aircraft [*Navy symbol*]
V.......... Frequency [*Spectroscopy*]
V.......... Gas Volume [*in Gas Phase*] (DAVI)
V.......... Gas Volume per Unit Time [*Medicine*] (DAVI)
v.......... High Frequency (WDMC)
V.......... Minute Volume [*Laboratory science*] (DAVI)
v.......... Mixed Venous Blood [*Medicine*] (DAVI)
v.......... Potential (IDOE)
V.......... Potential Difference [*Symbol*]
V.......... Potential Energy [*Symbol*] [*IUPAC*]
V.......... Promotional Fare [*Also, K, L, Q*] [*Airline fare code*]
V.......... Quinque [*Five*] [*Latin*]
V.......... Ranger-Parachutist [*Army skill qualification identifier*] (INF)
V.......... Reluctivity (IDOE)
V.......... [*A*] Safe [*Criminal slang*]
V.......... Sanol Arzneimittel Dr. Schwarz [*Germany*] [*Research code symbol*]
V.......... Shape Descriptor [*V-sign, for example. The shape resembles the letter for which it is named.*]
v.......... Specific Volume [*Symbol*] [*IUPAC*]
V.......... Staff Transport [*When V is the first of two letters in a military aircraft designation*]
V.......... Swiss Volksbank [*Bank*]
V.......... Unusual Visibility
V.......... V3 London Gun [*British military*] (DMA)
V.......... Vacated [*Same case vacated*] [*Used in Shepard's Citations*] [*Legal term*] (DLA)
V.......... Vaccella [*Flourished, 12th century*] [*Authority cited in pre-1607 legal work*] (DSA)
V.......... Vaccinated [*Medicine*]
V.......... Vacuole
V.......... Vacuum (AAG)
V.......... Vacuum Tube (IAA)
V.......... Vagabond
V.......... Vagina [*Anatomy*] (DAVI)
V.......... Vale (ROG)
V.......... Valine [*One-letter symbol; see Val*]
V.......... Valley (ROG)
V.......... Value
V.......... Valve
V.......... Van
V.......... Vanadium [*Chemical element*]
V.......... Van Container [*Shipping*] (DS)
V.......... Vancouver Stock Exchange [*Canada*]
V.......... Vapor
V.......... Variable
V.......... Variable Region [*Immunochemistry*]
V.......... Variant [*Genetics*]
V.......... Variation
V.......... Variety Theatres and Shows [*Public-performance tariff class*] [*British*]
V.......... Varnish (AAG)
V.......... Varnish-Treated [*Insulation*] (MSA)
V.......... Varsity
V.......... Vascular Tissue [*Botany*]
V.......... Vatican City
V.......... Vector [*Mathematics*]
v.......... Vector (IDOE)
V.......... Veen, Publishers [*Holland*]
V.......... Vehicles (MCD)
V.......... Vein
V.......... Vel [*Or*] [*Pharmacy*]
V.......... Velocity
v.......... Velocity (IDOE)
V.......... Vendor (AAG)
V.......... Venerable
V.......... Venereology [*Medical Officer designation*] [*British*]
V.......... Venezuela [*IYRU nationality code*] (IYR)
V.......... Venous [*Medicine*]
v.......... Venous in the Blood Phase [*Medicine*] (DAVI)
V.......... Venstre [*Liberal Party*] [*Norway Political party*] (PPE)
V.......... Venstre (Liberale Parti) [*Liberal Party*] [*Denmark Political party*] (PPE)
V.......... Vent
V.......... Ventilation [*Medicine*] (DAVI)
V.......... Ventilator
V.......... Ventral
V.......... Ventur [*Quality of carburetor barrel*] [*Automotive engineering*]
V.......... Venturi [*Automotive engineering*]
V.......... Venue
V.......... Verapamil [*A coronary vasodilator*]
V.......... Verb
v.......... Verb (WDMC)
V.......... Verbal
V.......... Verbalize [*or Verbalization*] (DAVI)
V.......... Verbatim [*FAR clauses*] (AAGC)
V.......... Verdict [*Legal shorthand*] (LWAP)
V.......... Verfassung [*Constitution*] [*German*] (ILCA)
V.......... Verfuegung [*Order, Decree*] [*German*] (ILCA)
V.......... Vergeltung [*Retaliation*] [*German*]
V.......... Vermessung [*Survey*] [*German military*]
V.......... Vermiculite
V.......... Vermont Reports [*A publication*] (DLA)
V.......... Verordnung [*Decree, Regulation, Ordinance*] [*German*] (ILCA)
V.......... Verse
v.......... Verse (WDMC)
V.......... Versicle
V.......... Versiculo [*In Such a Way*] [*Latin*] (ROG)
V.......... Version
v.......... Version (WDMC)
v.......... Verso (WDMC)
V.......... Verso [*Left-hand page*] [*Latin*]
V.......... Versus [*Against*]
v.......... Versus (WDMC)
V.......... Vert [*Heraldry*]
V.......... Verte [*or Vertatur*] [*Turn Over*] [*Latin*]
V.......... Vertex
V.......... Vertical [*RADAR*]
v.......... Vertical (WDMC)
V.......... Vertical in Line [*Aircraft engine*]
V.......... Verticillium Wilt [*Plant pathology*]
V.......... Very
v.......... Very (WDMC)
V.......... Very High Frequency [*Also, VHF*] (DOAD)
V.......... Vespers
V.......... Veto (OICC)
V.......... Via [*By Way Of*] [*Latin*] (ADA)
V.......... Vibrio [*Microbiology*]
V.......... Vic [*Phonetic alphabet*] [*Pre-World War II*] (DSUE)
V.......... Vicar [*or Vicarage*]
V.......... Vice [*In a position or title*]
V.......... Vice
V.......... Vicinal [*Also, vic*] [*Chemistry*]
V.......... Victor [*Phonetic alphabet*] [*International*] [*World War II*] (DSUE)
V.......... Victoria
V.......... Victoria [*State*] (EERA)
V.......... Victory [*As in "the V campaign" in Europe, during World War II*]
V.......... Victualling [*British military*] (DMA)
V.......... Vide [*See*] [*Latin*] (WGA)
V.......... Video (SAA)
V.......... Video (VRA)
V.......... Viel [*Coarse*] [*Latin*] (DAVI)
V.......... View [*Computer science*] [*Telecommunications*]
V.......... Village
V.......... Vinblastine [*See VBL*]
V.......... Vincentius Hispanus [*Deceased, 1248*] [*Authority cited in pre-1607 legal work*] (DSA)
V.......... Vincristine [*Also, LCR, O, V, VC, VCR*] [*Antineoplastic drug*]
V.......... Vinegar [*Phonetic alphabet*] [*Royal Navy World War I*] (DSUE)
V.......... Vinyl
V.......... Violet

V ... Violin [*Music*]
V ... Virgin
V ... Virginia Reports [*A publication*] (DLA)
V ... Viridian Inc. [*TS symbol*] (TTSB)
V ... Virtual (HGAA)
V ... Virulent
V ... Virus
V ... Viscosity
V ... Viscount [*or Viscountess*]
V ... Vise Break Distance [*Stress test for steel*]
V ... Visibility
V ... Vision
V ... Visit
V ... Visiting Practice Only [*Chiropody*] [*British*]
V ... Visitor (DAVI)
V ... Visual
V ... Visual Acuity [*Also, VA*] [*Ophthalmology*]
V ... Visual Capacity (AAMN)
V ... Visual Magnitude [*When followed by a two-digit number*]
v ... Vitamin (MAE)
V ... Vivra, Inc. [*NYSE symbol*] (SPSG)
V ... Vixisti [*You Lived*] [*Latin*]
V ... Vixit [*He Lived*] [*Latin*]
V ... VMS Hotel (SPSG)
V ... Vocative
V ... Voce [*Voice*] [*Latin*]
V ... Voice
v ... Voice (WDMC)
V ... Voice Data [*NASA*]
V ... Void [*Decision or finding held invalid for reasons given*] [*Used in Shepard's Citations*] [*Legal term*] (DLA)
V ... Volcano (ROG)
V ... Volt [*Symbol*] [*SI unit of electric potential difference*]
V ... Voltage
v ... Voltage (IDOE)
V ... Voltare [*Turn Over*] [*Latin*] (ROG)
V ... Volti [*Turn Over*] [*Music*]
V ... Voltmeter
V ... Volts
V ... Volume [*Bibliography*]
V ... Volume [*Symbol*] [*IUPAC*]
v ... Volume (WDMC)
V ... Voluntary Aided School [*British*]
V ... Volunteer [*US Naval Reserve*]
V ... Vomiting [*Medicine*]
V ... Von [*Of, From*] [*German*]
V ... VOR [*Very-High-Frequency Omnidirectional Range*] Federal Airway [*Followed by identification*]
V ... Vous [*You*] [*French*] (ROG)
V ... Vowel
v ... Vowel (WDMC)
V ... VTOL [*Vertical Takeoff and Landing*] [*or STOL - Short Takeoff and Landing when V is the second or only letter in a military aircraft designation*]
V ... Vulgate [*Latin translation of the Bible*] [*A publication*] (BJA)
V ... Wrong Verb Form [*Used in correcting manuscripts, etc.*]
V_1 ... Fifth Cranial Nerve, Opththalmic Division (DAVI)
V_1 ... Takeoff Decision Speed [*Aviation*]
V-1 ... Vergeltungswaffe 1 [*Pilotless flying bomb employed by the Germans*] [*World War II*]
v1of ... Lift-Off Speed [*Aviation code*] (AIA)
V1S ... Vee One Side (DAC)
V2 ... Antigua [*International civil aircraft marking*] (ODBW)
V_2 ... Fifth Cranial Nerve, Maxillary Division (DAVI)
V_2 ... Takeoff Safety Speed [*Aviation*]
V-2 ... Vergeltungswaffe 2 [*Rocket bomb employed by the Germans during World War II*] [*Translation: Vengeance Weapon*]
V2S ... V-Groove on Two Sides [*Lumber*]
V3 ... Belize [*International civil aircraft marking*] (ODBW)
V_3 ... Fifth Cranial Nerve, Mandibular Division (DAVI)
V3 ... Takeoff Speed Over Screen [*Aviation code*] (AIA)
V4 ... Steady Initial Climb Speed [*Aviation code*] (AIA)
V4 ... St. Kitts and Nevis [*Aircraft nationality and registration mark*] (FAAC)
V8 ... Brunei Darussalam [*Aircraft nationality and registration mark*] (FAAC)
V_A ... Alveolar Gas Volume [*Medicine*] (DAVI)
VA ... Alveolar Ventilation
V_A ... Alveolar Ventilation per Minute [*Medicine*] (DAVI)
VA ... Alveolar Volume [*Clinical chemistry*] (AAMN)
VA ... Attack Squadron [*Symbol*] (MCD)
VA ... Avian Aircraft Ltd. [*Canada ICAO aircraft manufacturer identifier*] (ICAO)
VA ... Department of Veterans Affairs [*Pre-1989, Veterans Administration*] (AAGC)
VA ... Gilmer's Virginia Reports [*A publication*] (DLA)
VA ... University of Virginia, Charlottesville, VA [*OCLC symbol*] (OCLC)
Va ... Vacarius [*Flourished, 1144-70*] [*Authority cited in pre-1607 legal work*] (DSA)
Va ... Vaccella [*Flourished, 12th century*] [*Authority cited in pre-1607 legal work*] (DSA)
VA ... Vacuum Aspiration [*Medicine*]
VA ... Valentine (WGA)
Va ... Valid [*Decision or finding held valid for reasons given*] [*Used in Shepard's Citations*] [*Legal term*] (DLA)
VA ... Valium Anonymous (EA)
VA ... Valmet Corp. ADS [*NYSE symbol*] (TTSB)
VA ... Valproic Acid [*Anticonvulsant compound*]
VA ... Value (ECII)
VA ... Value Added (ADA)
VA ... Value Analysis
VA ... Value Analysis
Va ... Vanadium [*Chemical*] (EERA)
VA ... Variable Annuity
Va ... Variance (WGA)
va ... Variety (DAVI)
VA ... Variometer (IAA)
VA ... Vatican City [*ANSI two-letter standard code*] (CNC)
VA ... Vehicle Analyst (MCD)
VA ... Vehicular Accident [*British police*]
VA ... Velocity Aid
VA ... Velocity at Apogee (MCD)
VA ... Venezolana Internacional de Aviacion Sociedad Anonima (VIASA) [*Venezuela ICAO designator*] (ICDA)
VA ... Venoarterial [*Cardiology*] (DAVI)
VA ... Ventral Area [*Anatomy*]
VA ... Ventricular Aneurysm [*Cardiology*]
VA ... Ventricular Arrhythmia [*Cardiology*]
VA ... Ventriculoatrial [*Cardiology*] (WGA)
VA ... Verb Active
VA ... Verbal Adjective
VA ... VERLORT [*Very-Long-Range Tracking*] Azimuth [*NASA*]
VA ... Vermiculite Association (EA)
VA ... Verpflegungsausgabestelle [*Rations distributing point*] [*German military - World War II*]
VA ... Vertebral Artery [*Anatomy*]
VA ... Vertical Amplifier (IAA)
VA ... Vesicular-Arbuscular [*Mycorrhiza*] [*Botany*]
VA ... Veterans Administration (TDOB)
VA ... [*Department of*] Veterans Affairs (USGC)
VA ... [*Department of*] Veterans Affairs
V-A ... Vibroacoustic (NASA)
VA ... Vibroacoustic Test (NASA)
VA ... Vicar Apostolic
VA ... Vice Admiral [*Also, VADM, VADML*]
VA ... Vickers-Armstrong Gun
V-A ... Vickers-Armstrong Ltd.
VA ... Victims Anonymous (EA)
VA ... Victor Airways [*Aviation*] (FAAC)
VA ... Victoria and Albert Order [*British*]
VA ... Victualling Allowance [*British military*] (DMA)
VA ... Video Amplifier
V/A ... Video/Analog (NASA)
V/A ... Video/Audio [*Telecommunications*]
VA ... Vincent's Angina [*Medicine*]
VA ... Vinyl Acetate [*Organic chemistry*] (WDAA)
VA ... Viola [*Music*]
V-A ... Viper-Arrow (SAA)
VA ... Viral Antigen [*Medicine*] (DMAA)
VA ... Virginia [*Postal code*]
VA ... Virginia Reports [*A publication*] (DLA)
Va ... Virginia Reports [*A publication*] (AAGC)
VA ... Virginia Supreme Court Reports [*A publication*] (DLA)
VA ... Virtual Address
VA ... Virus-Antibody [*Immunology*]
VA ... Visual Acuity [*Also, V*] [*Ophthalmology*]
VA ... VisualAge
VA ... Visual Aid
VA ... Visual Arts [*US Copyright Office class*]
VA ... Visual Training Aid Specialist [*Navy*]
VA ... Vita Apollonii [*of Philostratus*] [*Classical studies*] (OCD)
VA ... Vital Area (NRCH)
VA ... Vixit Annos [*Lived a Certain Number of Years*] [*Latin*] (WDAA)
VA ... Voice Actuation (MCD)
VA ... Voice of America
VA ... Volcanic Ash [*ICAO*] (FAAC)
VA ... Voltage Amplifier (IAA)
VA ... Voltaire Alternative
VA ... Voltammeter (IAA)
V-A ... Volt-Ampere (AAG)
VA ... Volt-Ampere (IDOE)
V/A ... Volts per Ampere (IDOE)
VA ... Voluntary Aid (ADA)
VA ... Volunteer Artillery [*Military British*] (ROG)
VA ... Vorausabteilung [*Advance detachment*] [*German military - World War II*]
VA ... Vorderasien (BJA)
VA ... Vote America (EA)
VA ... Votre Altesse [*Your Highness*] [*French*]
V/A ... Voucher Attached [*Banking*]
VA ... Voyage Alliance [*Later, IVA*] (EA)
VA ... Vulnerability Assessment
VA ... Vulnerable Area (NATG)
VAA ... Vaasa [*Finland*] [*Airport symbol*] (OAG)
VAA ... Variable Attenuator Amplified
VAA ... Vegetarian Association of America [*Defunct*] (EA)
VAA ... Vehicle Assembly Area [*NASA*] (MCD)
VAA ... Venda Airways [*South Africa ICAO designator*] (FAAC)
VAA ... Venezuelan American Association of the United States (EA)
VAA ... Verticilliium albo-atrium [*A fungus*]
VAA ... Victorian Apiarists' Association [*Australia*]
VAA ... Victorian Athletics Association [*Australia*]

VAA Vietnamese American Association
VAA Viewpoint Adapter Assembly (NASA)
VAA Voice Access Arrangement
VAAC Vanadyl Acetylacetonate [*Organic chemistry*]
VAAC Vectored Thrust Aircraft [*Aviation*] (DA)
VA Acts Acts of the General Assembly, Commonwealth of Virginia [*A publication*] (DLA)
VAAH Ahmadabad [*India*] [*ICAO location identifier*] (ICLI)
VAAK Akola [*India*] [*ICAO location identifier*] (ICLI)
VAAL Vaal Reefs Exploration [*NASDAQ symbol*] (NQ)
VaalRf Vaal Reefs Exploration & Mining Co. Ltd. [*Associated Press*] (SAG)
VAALY Vaal Reefs Ex&Mng ADR [*NASDAQ symbol*] (TTSB)
VAAM Voice Actuated Address Mechanism (PDAA)
VA & I Verb Active and Intransitive (ROG)
VAAP Volunteer Army Ammunition Plant (AABC)
VA App Virginia Appeals [*A publication*] (DLA)
VAAR Veterans Administration Acquisition Regulation [*A publication*] (AAGC)
VAAR Vinyl Alcohol Acetate Resin [*NASA*] (KSC)
VAAS Vermont Academy of Arts and Sciences
VAAT Vibration and Acoustic Testing (IAA)
VAAT Victorian Animal Aid Trust [*Australia*]
VAAU Aurangabad [*India*] [*ICAO location identifier*] (ICLI)
VAAUS Venezuelan American Association of the United States (EA)
VAB Van Allen Belts
VAB Variable Action Button (NVT)
VAB Vehicle Assembly Building [*NASA*] (AFM)
VAB Vertical Assembly Building [*NASA*]
VAB Vertical Axis Bearing
VAB Victorian Artificial Breeders [*Australia*]
VAB Victorian Association of Bakers [*Australia*]
VAB Vinblastine, Actinomycin D, Bleomycin [*Antineoplastic drug regimen*]
VAB Voice Answer Back
VAB Vorderasiatische Bibliothek [*H. Winckler and A. Jeremias*] [*Leipzig*] [*A publication*] (BJA)
VABA Value Added by Advertising
VA Bar News Virginia Bar News [*A publication*] (DLA)
VABB Bombay [*India*] [*ICAO location identifier*] (ICLI)
VABCA Department of Veterans Affairs Board of Contract Appeals (AAGC)
VABCD Vinblastine, Adriamycin, Bleomycin, CCNU [*Lomustine*], Dacarbazine [*Antineoplastic drug regimen*]
VaBch Virginia Beach Federal Financial Corp. [*Associated Press*] (SAG)
VABD Van Allen Belt Dosimeter
VABF Bombay [*India*] [*ICAO location identifier*] (ICLI)
VABF Variety Artistes' Benevolent Fund [*British*] (ROG)
VABF Virginia Beach Federal Financial Corp. [*NASDAQ symbol*] (SAG)
VABF Virginia Beach Fed Finl [*NASDAQ symbol*] (TTSB)
VABI Bilaspur [*India*] [*ICAO location identifier*] (ICLI)
VAB-I Vinblastine, Actinomycin D [*Dactinomycin*], Bleomycin [*Antineoplastic drug regimen*]
VAB-II Vinblastine, Actinomycin D [*Dactinomycin*], Bleomycin, Cisplatin [*Antineoplastic drug regimen*]
VAB-III Vinblastine, Actinomycin D [*Dactinomycin*], Bleomycin, Cisplatin, Chlorambucil, Cyclophosphamide [*Antineoplastic drug regimen*]
VAB-IV Vinblastine, Actinomycin D [*Dactinomycin*] Bleomycin, Cisplatin, Cyclophosphamide, Chlorambucil, and Adriamycin [*Antineoplastic drug regimen*] (DAVI)
VABJ Bhuj [*India*] [*ICAO location identifier*] (ICLI)
VABM Belgaum [*India*] [*ICAO location identifier*] (ICLI)
VABM Value Added by Manufacturer [*Business term*] (MHDW)
VABM Vertical Angle Bench Mark
VABO Baroda/Vadodara [*India*] [*ICAO location identifier*] (ICLI)
VABP Bhopal [*India*] [*ICAO location identifier*] (ICLI)
VABPF Vice Admiral British Pacific Fleet
VABR Vehicle Assembly Building Repeater [*NASA*] (KSC)
VABS Vineland Adaptive Behavior Scale [*Psychology*] (EDAC)
VABV Bhaunagar [*India*] [*ICAO location identifier*] (ICLI)
VAB-V Vinblastine, Actinomycin D [*Dactinomycin*], Bleomycin, Cisplatin, and Cyclophosphamide [*Antineoplastic drug regimen*] (DAVI)
VAC AC [*Alternating Current*] Voltage (ACII)
VAC Alternating Current Volts
VAC Fifth Amphibious Corps
VAC Vacancy [*Real estate*] (ADA)
VAC Vacant (AFM)
VAC Vacate
VAC Vacation
vac Vacation (ODBW)
VAC Vacationair, Inc. [*Canada ICAO designator*] (FAAC)
Vac Vaccella [*Flourished, 12th century*] [*Authority cited in pre-1607 legal work*] (DSA)
VAC Vaccination [*or Vaccine*] [*Medicine*]
VAC Vacuolar Apical Compartment [*Cytology*]
VAC Vacuum (AABC)
vac Vacuum (IDOE)
VAC Value-Added Carrier [*Telecommunications*]
VAC Variable Air Capacitor
VAC Variance at Completion (MCD)
VAC Vector Analog Computer
VAC Vehicle Assembly and Checkout [*NASA*] (NASA)
VAC Ventriculoarterial Connections [*Cardiology*] (DAVI)
VAC Ventriculoatrial Conduction [*Cardiology*] (DAVI)
VAC Verified Audit Circulation [*Newspaper auditing firm*] [*Advertising*]
VAC Verified Audit Circulation Corp. (NTCM)
VAC Vertical Air Current
VAC Veterans Administration Center
VAC Veterans Affairs Canada [*See also AACC*]
VAC Vice-Admiralty Court [*British*]
VAC Victor Analog Computer [*Computer science*]
VAC Victorian Arts Council [*Australia*]
VAC Video Amplifier Chain
VAC Vidicon Alignment Coil
VAC Vincristine, Actinomycin D, Cyclophosphamide [*Antineoplastic drug regimen*]
VAC Vincristine, Adriamycin, Cyclophosphamide [*Also, VACY*] [*Antineoplastic drug regimen*]
VAC Visual Aid Console
VAC Visual Approach Chart [*Aviation*] (FAAC)
VAC Vital Area Center (CAAL)
VAC Voltage-Alternating Current (NITA)
VAC Volt-Ampere Characteristics [*Microwave emission*]
V_{ac} Volts AC (IDOE)
vac Volts AC (IDOE)
Vac Volts AC (IDOE)
VAC Volts Alternating Current
VAC Voluntary Action Center
VAC Volunteer Adviser Corps (EA)
VACA Victorian Amateur Canoe Association [*Australia*]
VACAA Victorian Autistic Childrens and Adults' Association [*Australia*]
VACAB Veterans Administration Contract Appeals Board
VACAPES Virginia Capes [*Navy*] (CAAL)
VACAR Vincristine, Adriamycin, Cyclophosphamide, and Actinomycin D [*Dactinomycin*] (DAVI)
VA Cas Virginia Cases (Brockenbrough and Holmes) [*A publication*] (DLA)
VA Cas Virginia Criminal Cases [*3-4 Virginia*] [*1789-1826*] [*A publication*] (DLA)
Vacc Vaccella [*Flourished, 12th century*] [*Authority cited in pre-1607 legal work*] (DSA)
vacc Vaccinate
VACC Value-Added Common Carrier [*Telecommunications*]
VAcC Visual Acuity with Spectacle Correction
VACCA Victorian Aboriginal Child Care Agency [*Australia*]
VACCAB Veterans Administration Construction Contract Appeals Board (AAGC)
VACCI Vaccine [*Medicine*]
VAcCL Visual Acuity with Contact Lens Correction
VAC DIST Vacuum Distilled (WDAA)
VacDry Vacu-Dry Co. [*Associated Press*] (SAG)
VACE Verification and Checkout Equipment
VACF Vietnamese-American Children's Fund [*Defunct*] (EA)
VACHA Virginias Automated Clearing House Association
VA Ch Dec Wythe's Virginia Chancery Reports [*1788-99*] [*A publication*] (DLA)
VA Cir Virginia Circuit Court Opinions [*A publication*] (DLA)
VACM Vector Averaging Current Meter [*Marine science*] (MSC)
VACM Vincristine, Adriamycin, Cyclophosphamide, Methotrexate [*Antineoplastic drug regimen*]
VA Col Dec Virginia Colonial Decisions (Randolph and Barrandall) [*A publication*] (DLA)
Va Commonwealth U Virginia Commonwealth University (GAGS)
VACR Variable Amplitude Correction Rack [*Telecommunications*] (OA)
VACR Visual Aircraft Recognition (MCD)
VACRPD Victorian Advisory Council on Recreation for People with Disabilities [*Australia*]
VACRS Vocational Assistance Commission for Retired Servicemen (CINC)
VACS Virtual Accounting Collecting System (MHDB)
VACSA Victorian Aboriginal Community Services Association [*Australia*]
VACSAT Vaccine Satellite Program (MCD)
VACSSS Veterans Affairs Cooperative Study of Systemic Sepsis
VACT Alternating Current Test Volts (MSA)
VACTERL Vertebral, Anal, Cardiac, Tracheosophageal, Renal, and Limb [*Defects*]
VACTL Vertical Assembly Component Test Laboratory
VACU Virtual Access Control Unit
VACURG Veterans Administration Cooperative Urological Research Group
VACVVD Vacuum and Vent Control Valve Distributor [*Automotive engineering*]
VACVVT Vacuum and Vent Control Valve Thermactor [*Automotive engineering*]
VACW Alternating Current Working Volts (MSA)
VACY Vincristine, Adriamycin, Cyclophosphamide [*Also, VAC*] [*Antineoplastic drug regimen*]
VAD Vacuum Arc Degassing [*Metal technology*]
VAD Vacuum Arc Degassing
VAD Val d'Or Explorations [*Vancouver Stock Exchange symbol*]
VAD Valdosta, GA [*Location identifier FAA*] (FAAL)
VAD Value Added and Data [*Communications network*]
VAD Value-Added Dealer [*Business term*]
VAD Value-Added Distributor
VAD Value-Added Driver [*Computer science*] (PCM)
VAD Vandenberg Addendum Document [*Air Force*] (NASA)
VAD Vapor Axial Deposition [*Optical fiber technology*]
VAD Vascular Access Device [*Cardiology*] (DAVI)
VAD Velocity-Azimuth Display
VAD Venous Access Device [*Cardiology*] (DAVI)
VAD Ventricle-Assist Device [*Cardiology*]
VAD Vereinigte Arbeitnehmerpartei Deutschland [*United Employees' Party of Germany*] [*Political party*] (PPW)
VAD Vertebral or Vascular Defects, Anorectal Malformation, Cardiac Anomaly, Tracheoesophageal Fistula, Renal Anomaly, Limb Anomaly [*Syndrome*] (DAVI)
VAD Veterans' Affairs Decisions, Appealed Pension and Civil Service Retirement Cases [*United States*] [*A publication*] (DLA)

VAD Veterans Against Drugs
VAD Vincristine, Adriamycin, Decadron [*Antineoplastic drug*] (CDI)
VAD Vincristine, Adriamycin, Dexamethasone [*Antineoplastic drug regimen*] (MEDA)
VAD Vitamin A Deficiency [*Medicine*] (DMAA)
VAD Voltmeter Analog-to-Digital Converter
VAD Voluntary Aid Detachment [*British World War I nursing unit*]
VAD Vought Aeronautics Division [*Ling-Temco-Vought*]
VAD Vulcan Air Defense (MCD)
VADA Versatile Automatic Data Exchange
VADA Victorian Abalone Divers' Association [*Australia*]
VADA Vincristine, Adriamycin, Cyclophosphamide, Actinomycin D [*Dactinomycin*] [*Antineoplastic drug regimen*] (DAVI)
VADAC Voice Analyzer Data Converter
VADC Victorian Association for Deserted Children [*Australia*]
VADC Video Analog to Digital Converter
VADC Voice Analyzer and Data Converter (MCD)
VADE Vandenberg Automatic Data Equipment [*Air Force*]
VADE Vandenberg Automatic Data Evaluation [*Air Force*]
VADE Versatile Automatic Data Exchange (MCD)
VADE Victorian Association for Drama in Education [*Australia*]
VADE Voice Analog to Digital Encoder
VA Dec Virginia Decisions [*A publication*] (DLA)
VADER Vacuum Arc Double-Electrode Remelting [*Metallurgy*]
VADF Vietnamese Air Defense Force (MCD)
VADG Victorian Antique Dealers' Group [*Australia*]
VADIC Vincristine, Adriamycin, DIC [*Dacarbazine*] [*Antineoplastic drug regimen*]
VADIS Voice and Data Integrated System [*Telecommunications*] (TEL)
VADM Vice Admiral [*Also, VA, VADML*]
VADM Virtual Axial Dipole Moment [*Geophysics*]
VADMS Voice-Analog-Digital Manual Switch (MCD)
VADN Victorian Association of Day Nurseries [*Australia*]
VADRC Vincristine, Adriamycin, Cyclophosphamide [*Antineoplastic drug regimen*] (DAVI)
VADS Value Added and Data Services
VADS Velocity-Aligned Doppler Spectroscopy
VADS Vendor Automated Data System (MCD)
VADS Verdix ADA Development System (NITA)
VADS Veterans Assistance Discharge System (MCD)
VADS Visual-Aural Digit Span Test [*Educational test*]
VADS Vulcan Air Defense Systems (MCD)
VAE Ciudad de Valles [*Mexico*] [*Airport symbol*] (AD)
VAE Vinta Exploration Ltd. [*Vancouver Stock Exchange symbol*]
VAE Vinyl Acetate - Ethylene [*Organic chemistry*]
VAE Votre Altesse Electorale [*Your Electoral Highness*] [*French*]
VAEC Variety and Allied Entertainments Council [*British*] (BI)
V_{A}eff Effective Alveolar Ventilation [*Medicine*] (DAVI)
VAEITB Victorian Arts and Entertainment Industry Training Board [*Australia*]
VAEP Variable, Attributes, Error Propagation (IEEE)
VaEP Virginia Electric & Power Co. [*Associated Press*] (SAG)
VAERS Vaccine Adverse Event Reporting System [*Food and Drug Administration*]
VAES Voice-Activated Encoding System
VAEVC Vinyl Acetate - Ethylene - Vinyl Chloride [*Organic chemistry*]
VAF Valence [*France*] [*Airport symbol*] (OAG)
VAF Vane Airflow Meter [*Automotive engineering*]
VAF Variety Artistes' Federation [*British*] (BI)
VAF Vendor Approval Form
VAF Vernacular Architecture Forum (EA)
VAF Vietnamese Air Force (MCD)
VAF Viral Antibody-Free [*Environment*]
VAF Volume Air Flow [*Automotive engineering*]
VAF Voluntary Application Fill (DNAB)
VAFA Victorian Amateur Football Association [*Australia*]
VAFAC Vincristine, Amethopterin [*Methotrexate*], Fluorouracil, Adriamycin, Cyclophosphamide [*Antineoplastic drug regimen*]
VAFB Vandenberg Air Force Base [*California*]
VAFC VESA [*Video Electronics Standards Association*] Advanced Feature Connector
VAFD Valley Federal Savings Bank [*NASDAQ symbol*] (NQ)
VAFD Valley Fed Svgs Bk Sheffield [*NASDAQ symbol*] (TTSB)
VAFF Variable Aperture Far Field
VAFI Victorian Association of Forest Industries [*Australia*]
VAFL Victorian Amateur Football League [*Australia*]
VaFst Virginia First Financial Corp. [*Associated Press*] (SAG)
VaFstSvg Virginia First Financial Corp. [*Associated Press*] (SAG)
VAFTAD Volcanic Ash Forecast Transport and Dispersion [*Model*] [*Marine science*] (OSRA)
VAFTAD Volcanic Ash Forecast Transport and Dispersion [*Model*] (USDC)
VAG Vagabond (DSUE)
VAG Vagar [*Faeroe Islands*] [*Airport symbol*] (AD)
VAG Vaginal [*Medicine*]
VAG Vaginitis [*Medicine*]
VAG Vagrancy [*FBI standardized term*]
VAG Vananda Gold [*Vancouver Stock Exchange symbol*]
VAG Vancouver Art Gallery [*Canada*]
VAG Varginha [*Brazil*] [*Airport symbol*] (OAG)
VAG Vernacular Architecture Group [*British*]
VAG Vertex Adjacency Graph (MHDI)
VAG Volkswagen Audi Group
VAGA Visual Artists and Galleries Association (EA)
Vag Hyst Vaginal Hysterectomy [*Gynecology*] (CPH)
VAGO Goa [*India*] [*ICAO location identifier*] (ICLI)
VAGP Victorian Academy for General Practice [*Australia*]
VAH Heavy Attack Squadron [*Symbol*] (MCD)
VAH Vaihoa [*Tuamotu Archipelago*] [*Seismograph station code, US Geological Survey*] (SEIS)
VAH Vertical Array Hydrophone
VAH Veterans Administration Hospital [*Later, VAMC*]
VAH Virilizing Adrenal Hyperplasia [*Medicine*]
VAH Vitiated Air Heater
VAHPA Victorian Allied Health Professionals Association [*Australia*]
VAHR Veterans Administration Hospital Representative [*Red Cross*]
VAHS Virus-Associated Hemophagocytic Syndrome [*Medicine*]
VAHT Vertical Axis Hydropower Turbine
VAI Vanimo [*Papua New Guinea*] [*Airport symbol*] (OAG)
VAI Vassar Attitude Inventory [*Education*]
VAI Ventilation Air Intake [*Hovercraft*]
VAI Video Arts International, Inc.
VAI Video-Assisted Instruction
VAI Visual Alignment Indicators [*Tire maintenance*]
VAI Vocational Awards International [*British*]
VAI Volleyball Association of Ireland (EAIO)
VAI Voluntary Action Indicated [*FDA*]
VAI Vorticity Area Index [*Meteorology*]
VA IC Ops Virginia Industrial Commission Opinions [*A publication*] (DLA)
VAID Indore [*India*] [*ICAO location identifier*] (ICLI)
VAIN Vaginal Intraepithelial Neoplasia [*Medicine*] (DAVI)
VAIO Video Audio Integrated Operation [*Computer science*]
VAIR Virginia Association for Institutional Research (EDAC)
Vaizey Vaizey's Law of Settlements [*1887*] [*A publication*] (DLA)
VAJ Vajont [*Belluno*] [*Italy*] [*Seismograph station code, US Geological Survey*] (SEIS)
VAJB Jabalpur [*India*] [*ICAO location identifier*] (ICLI)
VAJJ Bombay/Juhu [*India*] [*ICAO location identifier*] (ICLI)
VAJM Jamnagar [*India*] [*ICAO location identifier*] (ICLI)
VAK Aerial Refueling Squadron [*Navy symbol*] (DNAB)
VAK Chevak [*Alaska*] [*Airport symbol*] (OAG)
VAK Vak-Rosat [*Former USSR*] [*FAA designator*] (FAAC)
VAK Vertical Access Kit (NASA)
VAK Vertical Assembly Kit (NASA)
VAKD Khandwa [*India*] [*ICAO location identifier*] (ICLI)
VAKE Kandla [*India*] [*ICAO location identifier*] (ICLI)
VAKP Kolhapur [*India*] [*ICAO location identifier*] (ICLI)
VAKS Keshod [*India*] [*ICAO location identifier*] (ICLI)
VAKT Visual-Auditory-Kinesthetic-Tactile
VAKUME Visual Audio Kinetic Unit Multiples and Environments (PDAA)
VAL Light Attack Aircraft [*Symbol*] (MCD)
VAL Plattsburgh, NY [*Location identifier FAA*] (FAAL)
VAL University of Virginia, Law Library, Charlottesville, VA [*OCLC symbol*] (OCLC)
Val Valcausus [*Gualcosius*] [*Flourished, 11th-12th century*] [*Authority cited in pre-1607 legal work*] (DSA)
VAL Valentia [*Ireland*] [*Seismograph station code, US Geological Survey*] (SEIS)
val Valentine (BARN)
VAL Valid [*or Validation*] (KSC)
Val Valine [*Also, V*] [*An amino acid*]
val Valine [*An amino acid*] (DOG)
Val Valium [*A tranquilizer*] [*Roche Laboratories*] (DAVI)
VAL Valley (MSA)
Val Valley Girl [*Lifestyle classification*]
VAL Valspar Corp. [*NYSE symbol*] (SPSG)
VAL Valuation
VAL Value
val Value (IDOE)
VAL Value
VAL Value Investment Corp. [*Toronto Stock Exchange symbol*]
VAL Value-Oriented Algorithmic Language [*Computer science*] (PDAA)
VAL Valve
VAL Variable Angle Launcher
VAL Vehicle Authorization List [*Military*] (AFM)
VAL Vertical Assault Lift
VAL Vicarm Arm Language
VAL Victorian Athletic League [*Australia*]
VAL Vieques Air Link [*Caribbean airline*]
VAL Visual Approach and Landing Chart [*Aviation*]
VAL Vortex Arc LASER
VAL Voyageur Airways Ltd. [*Canada ICAO designator*] (FAAC)
VAL Vulnerability Assessment Laboratory [*White Sands Missile Range, NM*] [*Military*] (RDA)
Valassis Valassis Communications [*Associated Press*] (SAG)
VA Law J Virginia Law Journal [*Richmond*] [*A publication*] (DLA)
VALB Veterans of the Abraham Lincoln Brigade (EA)
VALCO Volta Aluminum Co. Ltd.
Val Com Valen's Commentaries [*A publication*] (DLA)
VALD Valued (ROG)
VALDEFD Value Defined (MHDW)
VA L Dig Virginia Law Digest [*A publication*] (DLA)
VALDN Validation
Valdosta St C Valdosta State College (GAGS)
VALE [*The*] Valley Railroad Co. [*AAR code*]
VALE Valley Systems [*NASDAQ symbol*] (TTSB)
VALE Valley Systems, Inc. [*NASDAQ symbol*] (SAG)
VALE Visual Acuity, Left Eye [*Ophthalmology*] (MAE)
Valero Valero Energy Corp. [*Associated Press*] (SAG)
ValFrg Valley Forge Corp. [*Associated Press*] (SAG)
VALH Value Holdings [*NASDAQ symbol*] (SAG)
Valhi Valhi, Inc. [*Associated Press*] (SAG)

ValHldg........ Value Holdings [*Associated Press*] (SAG)
ValHlth........ Value Health, Inc. [*Associated Press*] (SAG)
VALI........ Validate (AABC)
VALID........ Validation (NASA)
VALIPR........ Validation In-Process Review [*DoD*]
VA LJ........ Virginia Law Journal [*A publication*] (DLA)
VALL........ Vortex Arc LASER Light
Vallen........ Vallen Corp. [*Associated Press*] (SAG)
VALLEY........ Valley [*Commonly used*] (OPSA)
VALLEYS........ Valleys [*Commonly used*] (OPSA)
ValliCor........ ValliCorp Holdings, Inc. [*Associated Press*] (SAG)
ValLn........ Value Line, Inc. [*Associated Press*] (SAG)
VALLY........ Valley [*Commonly used*] (OPSA)
VallyRs........ Valley Resources, Inc. [*Associated Press*] (SAG)
VALM........ Valmont Indus [*NASDAQ symbol*] (TTSB)
VALM........ Valmont Industries, Inc. [*NASDAQ symbol*] (NQ)
Valmnt........ Valmont Industries, Inc. [*Associated Press*] (SAG)
VALN........ Vallen Corp. [*NASDAQ symbol*] (NQ)
VALN........ Valuation
VALNET........ Veterans Administration Library Network [*Veterans Administration Washington, DC*]
VALOR........ Veterans Administration Libraries Online Resources
VALOR........ Veterans Affairs Learning Opportunities Residency Program
VALP........ Vortex Arc LASER Pump
Valparaiso U... Valparaiso University (GAGS)
VALPO........ Valparaiso (DSUE)
VALRA........ Variable-Area Light-Reflecting Assembly [*Invented by T. C. Howard of Synergetics, Inc.*]
VA L Reg..... Virginia Law Register [*A publication*] (DLA)
VA L Reg NS... Virginia Law Register, New Series [*A publication*] (DLA)
Val Rep........ Valuation Reports, Interstate Commerce Commission [*A publication*] (DLA)
Val Rep ICC... Valuation Reports, Interstate Commerce Commission [*A publication*] (DLA)
Vals........ Valium [*A tranquilizer*] [*Roche Laboratories*] (DAVI)
VALS........ Value and Lifestyle [*Classifications*] [*Marketing*]
VALS........ Values and Lifestyles Program (WDMC)
VALS........ Victorian Aboriginal Legal Service [*Australia*]
VALSAS........ Variable Length Word Symbolic Assembly System (IEEE)
Valspar........ Valspar Corp. [*Associated Press*] (SAG)
VALT........ VTOL [*Vertical Takeoff and Landing*] Approach and Landing Technology [*Program*]
ValTech........ Valence Technology, Inc. [*Associated Press*] (SAG)
VALT(S)........ Vulnerability and Lethality Test (System) (MCD)
VALU........ Value Line [*NASDAQ symbol*] (TTSB)
VALU........ Value Line, Inc. [*NASDAQ symbol*] (NQ)
VALUE........ Validated Aircraft Logistics Utilization Evaluation [*Navy*]
VALUE........ Visible Achievement Liberates Unemployment [*DoD project for disadvantaged youth*]
ValueCty........ Value City Department Stores [*Associated Press*] (SAG)
ValueLn........ Value Line, Inc. [*Associated Press*] (SAG)
ValuePr........ Value Property Trust [*Associated Press*] (SAG)
ValuJet........ ValuJet Airlines, Inc. [*Associated Press*] (SAG)
VALUON........ Valuation
ValVis........ ValueVision International, Inc. [*Associated Press*] (SAG)
VA L Wk Dicta Comp... Virginia Law Weekly Dicta Compilation [*A publication*] (DLA)
VALY........ Vallicorp Holdings [*NASDAQ symbol*] (TTSB)
VALY........ Vallicorp Holdings, Inc. [*NASDAQ symbol*] (NQ)
ValySy........ Valley Systems, Inc. [*Associated Press*] (SAG)
VAM........ Ameravia [*Uruguay*] [*FAA designator*] (FAAC)
VAM........ Medium Attack Aircraft [*Navy symbol*] (NVT)
VAM........ University of Virginia, C. Moore Health Sciences Library, Charlottesville, VA [*OCLC symbol*] (OCLC)
VAM........ Vacuum-Assisted Molding [*Automotive technology*]
VAM........ Value Added Manufacture [*Program*]
VAM........ Value Added Market (MHDB)
VAM........ Value Aluminizing Machine
VAM........ Vamos [*Greece*] [*Seismograph station code, US Geological Survey*] (SEIS)
VAM........ Vector Airborne Magnetometer (IEEE)
VAM........ Vehiculos Automotores Mexicanos [*Commercial firm*]
VAM........ Vending and Affixing Machine
VAM........ Vesicular Arbuscular Mycorrhizae [*Botany*]
VAM........ Veterans Administration Matters [*FBI standardized term*]
VAM........ Vinyl Acetate Monomer [*Organic chemistry*]
VAM........ Virtual Access Method
VAM........ Vista Mines, Inc. [*Toronto Stock Exchange symbol*]
VAM........ Visual Approach Monitor [*Aviation*]
VAM........ Vogel's Approximation Method
VAM........ Voltammeter
VAM........ VP-16-213 [*Etoposide*], Adriamycin, Methotrexate [*Antineoplastic drug regimen*]
VAMA........ Vinyl Acetate Maleic Acid (DICI)
VAMAS........ Versailles Project on Advanced Materials and Standards
VAMC........ Veterans Administration Medical Center [*Formerly, VAH*]
VAMC........ Visual Approach Monitor Chart (PDAA)
VAMCO........ Village & Marketing Corp. [*Jamaica*]
VAMD........ Virginia & Maryland Railroad [*AAR code*]
VAME........ Victorian Association for Multicultural Education [*Australia*]
VAMFO........ Variable Angle Monochromatic Fringe Observation [*Film thickness determination*]
VAMHN........ Victorian Aboriginal Mental Health Network [*Australia*]
VAMIA........ Victorian Abattoir and Meat Inspection Authority [*Australia*]
VAMIS........ Versatile Automated Maintenance Information System (MCD)
VAMIS........ Virginia Medical Information System [*Library network*]
VAMOS........ Verified Additional Military Occupational Specialty
VAMOSC........ Visibility and Management of Operating and Support Costs [*Army*]
VAMP........ Value Analysis of Management Practices (MCD)
vamp........ Vampire (BARN)
VAMP........ Vandenberg Atlas Modification Program [*Air Force*] (MCD)
VAMP........ Variable [*or Visual*] Anamorphic Motion Picture [*Training device to provide realistic environment during simulated flight training*] (MCD)
VAMP........ Vector Arithmetic Multiprocessor [*Computer science*] (IEEE)
VAMP........ Vesicle-Associated Membrane Protein [*Biochemistry*]
VAMP........ Vietnam Ammunition Program (AFM)
VAMP........ Vincristine, Actinomycin, Methotrexate, Prednisone [*Antineoplastic drug regimen*]
VAMP........ Vincristine Amethopterin [*Antitumor agent*]
VAMP........ Vincristine, Amethopterin [*Methotrexate*], Mercaptopurine, Prednisone [*Antineoplastic drug regimen*]
VAMP........ Visual-Acoustic-Magnetic Pressure (IEEE)
VAMP........ Visual-Acoustic-Magnetic Program [*NOO*]
VAMP........ Visual Anamorphic Motion Picture (AIA)
VAMP........ Visual Approach for Management Planning (WDAA)
VAMP........ Volume, Area, and Mass Properties (PDAA)
VAMP........ Vulnerability Assessment Modeling Program [*Air Force*]
VAMR........ Vernon's Annotated Missouri Rule [*A publication*] (DLA)
VAMS........ Vernon's Annotated Missouri Statutes [*A publication*] (DLA)
VAMS........ Victor Airspeed Measuring System (MCD)
VAMS........ Visual Analog Mood Scale
VAMSI........ Visual Approach Multiple Slope Indicator [*Aviation*]
VAMT........ Vertical Assault Medium Transport (MCD)
van........ Advantage [*Tennis*] (BARN)
VAN........ Northern Virginia Community College, Springfield, VA [*OCLC symbol*] (OCLC)
VAN........ Value Added Network [*Computer science Telecommunications*]
VAN........ Van [*Turkey*] [*Airport symbol*] (OAG)
VAN........ Vance, SC [*Location identifier FAA*] (FAAL)
VAN........ Vandeno [*Race of maize*]
Van........ Vanguard [*Record label*]
VAN........ Vanguard Tracking Station [*NASA*] (NASA)
VAN........ Vanier College [*UTLAS symbol*]
VAN........ Vanilla (WDAA)
VAN........ Vannovskaya [*Former USSR Seismograph station code, US Geological Survey*] (SEIS)
VAN........ Vanwin Resources Corp. [*Vancouver Stock Exchange symbol*]
VAN........ Variable Area Nozzle
VAN........ Varotsos Alexopoulos Nomicos [*Authors of a technique for predicting earthquakes*]
VAN........ Vehicle Area Network [*Automotive engineering*]
VAN........ Vorlaeufige Arbeitsnormen
VANAC........ Veterans Affairs National Acquisition Center (AAGC)
VANC........ Vancouver [*Canada*] (WDAA)
Vand........ De Bello Vandalico [*of Procopius*] [*Classical studies*] (OCD)
VAND........ Nanded [*India*] [*ICAO location identifier*] (ICLI)
VAND........ Vacuum-Air-Nitrogen Distribution
VAND........ Van Den Bergh [*Liver function test*]
VAND........ Van Diemens Co. [*NASDAQ symbol*] (SAG)
V and A........ Valuable and Attractive [*A marking used by RAF on such supplies as watches and cameras*] [*British*]
V & A........ Victoria and Albert Museum [*London, England*]
V & B........ Vesey and Beames' English Chancery Reports [*35 English Reprint*] [*A publication*] (DLA)
V & DA........ Video and Data Acquisition (MCD)
V & DA........ Video and Data Processing Assembly (NASA)
V & E........ Vinethene and Ether
Vanderbilt LR... Vanderbilt Law Review [*A publication*] (DLA)
Vanderbilt U... Vanderbilt University (GAGS)
Vander L........ Vanderlinden's Laws of Holland [*A publication*] (DLA)
Vanderstr........ Vanderstraaten's Reports [*1869-71*] [*Ceylon*] [*A publication*] (DLA)
Vanderstraaten... Vanderstraaten's Decisions in Appeal, Supreme Court [*1869-71*] [*Sri L.*] [*A publication*] (DLA)
V & ET........ Verification and Evaluation Tests (MCD)
V & H........ Vertical and Horizontal [*Telecommunications*] (TSSD)
V & IA........ Victorian and Interstate Airways [*Australia*]
V & MM........ Vandalism and Malicious Mischief [*Insurance*]
V & P........ Vagotomy and Pyloroplasty [*Medicine*]
V & P........ Vendor and Purchaser [*Sales*] (ROG)
V & S........ Vernon and Scriven's Irish King's Bench Reports [*1786-88*] [*A publication*] (DLA)
V & T........ Vodka and Tonic
V & T........ Volume and Tension [*of pulse*]
VAND UNIV Q... Vanderbilt University Quarterly [*Tennessee*] [*A publication*] (ROG)
V & V........ Verification and Validation [*Computer science*]
VANFIS........ Visible and Near-Visible Frequency Intercept System [*Navy*]
VANFISH........ Victorian Adoption Network for Information and Self Help [*Australia*]
Van Fleet Coll Attack... Van Fleet on Collateral Attack [*A publication*] (DLA)
VangAir........ Vanguard Airlines, Inc. [*Associated Press*] (SAG)
VANGI........ Variable-Area Nozzle by Gas Injection (SAA)
VANHC........ Veterans Administration Nursing Home Care Program (GFGA)
Van Hey Eq... Van Heythuysen's Equity Draftsman [*2nd ed.*] [*1828*] [*A publication*] (DLA)
Van Hey Mar Ev... Van Heythuysen on Maritime Evidence [*A publication*] (DLA)
Van Hey Rud... Van Heythuysen's Rudiments of English Law [*A publication*] (DLA)
VANHP........ Virginia Natural Heritage Program [*Virginia State Department of Conservation and Historic Resources*] [*Information service or system*] (IID)
VANIS........ Volume Analysis Information System Software

Van K.......... Van Koughnet's Reports [*15-21 Upper Canada Common Pleas*] [*1864-71*] [*A publication*] (DLA)
Van K & H... Upper Canada Common Pleas Reports [*1864-71*] [*A publication*] (DLA)
Van L.......... Vander Linden's Practice [*Cape Colony*] [*A publication*] (DLA)
Van N.......... Van Ness' Prize Cases, United States District Court, District of New York [*A publication*] (DLA)
VAN N.......... Van Norden Magazine [*New York*] [*A publication*] (ROG)
Van Ness Prize Cas... Van Ness' Prize Cases, United States District Court, District of New York [*A publication*] (DLA)
VANP.......... Nagpur [*India*] [*ICAO location identifier*] (ICLI)
van pt.......... Vanishing Point (VRA)
VANR.......... Nasik Road [*India*] [*ICAO location identifier*] (ICLI)
VANS.......... Value Added Network Service [*Computer science Telecommunications*]
VANS.......... Vans, Inc. [*NASDAQ symbol*] (SPSG)
VANS.......... Vehicle Austere Night Sight [*Army*] (MCD)
Van Sant Ch J... Van Santvoord's Lives of the Chief Justices of the United States [*A publication*] (DLA)
Van Sant Eq Pr... Van Santvoord's Equity Practice [*A publication*] (DLA)
Van Sant Pl... Van Santvoord's Pleadings [*A publication*] (DLA)
Van Sant Prec... Van Santvoord's Precedents [*A publication*] (DLA)
VANT.......... Vibration and Noise Tester (SAA)
Vantive.......... Vantive Corp. [*Associated Press*] (SAG)
VANUSL.......... Vanderbilt University School of Law (DLA)
VANWACE.... Vulnerability Analysis of Nuclear Weapons in Allied Command, Europe [*Army*] (AABC)
VAO.......... Veterans Administration Office
VAO.......... Voting Assistance Officer
VAOKN.......... Visual Acuity by Optokinetic Nystagmus
VAOR.......... VHF [*Very-High-Frequency*] Aural Omnirange
VAOT.......... Victorian Association of Occupational Therapists [*Australia*]
VAP.......... Photographic Squadron (Heavy) [*Navy symbol*] (NVT)
VAP.......... Vaginal Acid Phosphatase [*An enzyme*]
VAP.......... Valence-Alternation Pair [*Solid-state physics*]
VAP.......... Value-Added Process [*Computer science*] (PCM)
VAP.......... Van Kam Am Cap Adv PA Mun [*NYSE symbol*] (TTSB)
VAP.......... Van Kampen Merritt Advantage Pennsylvania Municipal Income Trust [*NYSE symbol*] (SPSG)
VAP.......... Vaporization [*or Vaporizer*] (KSC)
VAP.......... Variant Angina Pectoris [*Cardiology*] (DAVI)
VAP.......... Vascular Adhesion Protein [*Biochemistry*]
VAP.......... Vehicle Antenna Position [*NASA*]
VAP.......... Velocity Analysis Program
VAP.......... Ventilator-Associated Pneumonia [*Medicine*]
VAP.......... Versatile Automatic Test Equipment Assembly Program [*Computer science*] (IAA)
VAP.......... Vertical Axis Pivots
VAP.......... Veteran Air Pilots
VAP.......... Vibrationally Adiabatic Potential [*Chemical physics*]
VAP.......... Video/Audio Participative [*Education*] (OA)
VAP.......... Videotex Access Point [*Computer science*] (IT)
VAP.......... Vinblastine, Actinomycin D [*Dactinomycin*], Platinol [*Cisplatin*] [*Antineoplastic drug regimen*]
VAP.......... Vincristine, Adriamycin, Prednisone [*Antineoplastic drug regimen*]
VAP.......... Vincristine, Adriamycin, Procarbazine [*Antineoplastic drug regimen*]
VAP.......... Viral Attachment Protein [*Biochemistry*]
VAP.......... Voluntary Assistance Program
VAP.......... Voting Age Population
VAP.......... Vulnerability Assessment Procedure (AAGC)
VAPA.......... Video Alliance for the Performing Arts (EA)
VAPC.......... Vector Adaptive Predictive Coding [*Telecommunications*]
VAPC.......... Veterans Administration Prosthetics Center [*Later, VAREC*]
VAP-Cyclo.... Vincristine, Adriamycin, Prednisolone, Cyclophosphamide [*Antineoplastic drug regimen*]
VAPH.......... Visual Acuity with Pin Hole
VAPI.......... Visual Approach Path Indicator [*Aviation*]
VAP-II.......... Vinblastine, Actinomycin D [*Dactinomycin*] Cisplatin (DAVI)
VAPLA.......... Victorian Amateur Power Lifting Association [*Australia*]
VAPO.......... Pune [*India*] [*ICAO location identifier*] (ICLI)
VAPO.......... Vaporizing Oil
Va Poly Inst... Virginia Polytechnic Institute and State University (GAGS)
VAPOX.......... Vapor Deposit Oxide (IAA)
VAPP.......... Vaccine-Associated Paralytic Poliomyelitis [*Medicine*]
VAPPRF.......... Vapor Proof (IAA)
VAPR.......... Porbandar [*India*] [*ICAO location identifier*] (ICLI)
VAPR.......... Veterans Administration Procurement [*or Purchase*] Regulations
VAPS.......... Virtual Avionics Prototyping System [*Virtual Prototypes, Inc.*]
VAPS.......... Volume, Article [*or Chapter*], Paragraph, Sentence [*Numbers*] [*Indexing*]
VAPS.......... V/STOL Approach System (MCD)
VAPSS.......... Victorian Association of Principals of Secondary Schools [*Australia*]
VaPw.......... Virginia Power Capital Trust I [*Associated Press*] (SAG)
VAQ.......... Tactical Electronic Warfare Squadron [*Navy symbol*] (DNAB)
VA/Q.......... Ventilation-Perfusion [*Ratio*] [*Radiology*] (DAVI)
VAQ.......... Visiting Airmen's Quarters [*Air Force*]
VAQ.......... Visual Air Quality
Va/Qc.......... Ventilation/Perfusion Quotient [*Medicine*] (MAE)
VAR.......... Corps of Volunteers Artillery Regiment [*British military*] (DMA)
VA R.......... Gilmer's Virginia Reports [*A publication*] (DLA)
VAR.......... Reactive Volt-Ampere
VAR.......... Vacuum Arc Remelting [*Steel alloy*]
VAR.......... Valet Air Services [*FAA designator*] (FAAC)
VAR.......... Validation Analysis Report [*Social Security Administration*]
VAR.......... Valley Air Services, Inc. [*ICAO designator*] (FAAC)
VAR.......... Value-Added Remarketer [*or Reseller or Retailer*] [*Business term*]
VAR.......... Value-Added Reseller
VAR.......... Varanasi [*India*] [*Seismograph station code, US Geological Survey*] (SEIS)
VAR.......... Variable (AFM)
Var.......... Variae [*of Cassiodorus*] [*Classical studies*] (OCD)
VAR.......... Varian Associates [*NYSE symbol*] (SPSG)
VAR.......... Variance Analysis Report (MCD)
VAR.......... Variant [*Numismatics*]
VAR.......... Variant (DAVI)
VAR.......... Variation
VAR.......... Variegated
var.......... Varietas [*Variety*] [*Biology*]
VAR.......... Variety
VAR.......... Variometer (WGA)
VAR.......... Various
VAR.......... Varistor [*Telecommunications*] (IAA)
VAR.......... Varitech Resources [*Vancouver Stock Exchange symbol*]
VAR.......... Varna [*Bulgaria*] [*Airport symbol*] (OAG)
VAR.......... Varnish [*Technical drawings*]
var.......... Varnish (VRA)
Var.......... Varsity [*Record label*]
VAR.......... Varying (IAA)
VAR.......... Vector Autoregressive Model [*Mathematics*]
VAR.......... Velocity Acceleration Relationship
VAR.......... Vendor Approval Request (AAG)
VAR.......... Verification Analysis Report (NASA)
VAR.......... Vertical Acceleration Ramp
VAR.......... Vertical Air Rocket (NATG)
VAR.......... Veterans Administration Regulations
VAR.......... Victorian Administrative Reports [*Australia A publication*]
VAR.......... Video-Audio Range [*Radio*]
VAR.......... Vintage Austin Register [*Ashover, Derbyshire, England*] (EAIO)
VAR.......... Virginia Register of Regulations [*A publication*] (AAGC)
VAR.......... Visual-Aural Range [*Radio*]
VAR.......... Voltage Adjusting Rheostat
VAR.......... Voltage Ampere Reactance [*AC electric motors*]
VAR.......... Voltage in Acceptable Range (MCD)
VAR.......... Volt-Ampere Reactive
VAR.......... Voluntary Auto Restraints [*Import quotas on automobiles*]
VAR.......... Volunteer Air Reserve [*Air Force*]
VAR.......... Votre Altesse Royale [*Your Royal Highness*] [*French*]
VAR.......... Vrij Anti-Revolutionaire Partij [*Free Anti-Revolutionary Party*] [*Netherlands Political party*] (PPE)
VARA.......... Vereinigung van Arbeiders Radio Amateurs
VARACTOR... Variable Reactor [*Electronics*] (EECA)
VARAD.......... Varying Radiation (IEEE)
VA R Ann.... Virginia Reports, Annotated [*A publication*] (DLA)
VARBLK.......... Variable Block [*Computer science*]
VARC.......... Variable Axis Rotor Control System [*Telecommunications*] (TEL)
VARC.......... Virginia Associated Research Campus [*Later, Continuous Electron Beam Accelerator Facility*] [*Research center*] (RCD)
VARCAP.......... Variable Capacitor (IAA)
Varco.......... Varco International, Inc. [*Associated Press*] (SAG)
Var Cond.......... Variable Condenser [*Radio*]
vard.......... Varied [*Quality of the bottom*] [*Nautical charts*]
VAR DIAL.... Various Dialects (WDAA)
VARE.......... Victorian Association for Religious Education [*Australia*]
VARE.......... Visual Acuity, Right Eye [*Ophthalmology*] (MAE)
VAREC.......... Veterans Administration Rehabilitation Engineering Center [*Formerly, VAPC*]
VAR ED & TR... Various Editions and Translations (WDAA)
Va Reg Regs... Virginia Register of Regulations [*A publication*] (AAGC)
VA Rep Anno... Virginia Reports, Annotated [*A publication*] (DLA)
VARES.......... Vega Aircraft RADAR Enhancing System [*FAA*]
VARG.......... Ratnagiri [*India*] [*ICAO location identifier*] (ICLI)
VARGUS.......... Variable Generator of Unfamiliar Stimuli [*Computer program*]
VARH.......... Volt-Ampere Reactive Hour (IAA)
VARHM.......... Var-Hour Meter [*Electricity*]
VARI.......... Vacuum-Assisted Resin Infusion (RDA)
VARI.......... Vacuum-Assisted Resin Injection
vari.......... Various (VRA)
VARI.......... Varityper
VARIA.......... Variamento [*In a Varied Style*] [*Music*] (ROG)
VARIAC.......... Variable Capacitor (IAA)
Varian.......... Varian Associates [*Associated Press*] (SAG)
VARICAP.......... Variable Capacitor
VARICC.......... Victorian Asbestos Removal Industry Consultative Committee [*Australia*]
Variflex.......... Variflex, Inc. [*Associated Press*] (SAG)
Vari-L Co.......... Vari-L Co. [*Associated Press*] (SAG)
VARIMU.......... Variable Mu Tube [*Electronics*] (IAA)
VARION.......... Variation (ROG)
VARISTOR... Variable Resistor
VARITRAN... Variable-Voltage Transformer (IEEE)
Varitrn.......... Varitronic Systems, Inc. [*Associated Press*] (SAG)
Varity.......... Varity Corp. [*Associated Press*] (SAG)
VARK.......... Rajkot [*India*] [*ICAO location identifier*] (ICLI)
VARL.......... Vari-L Co. [*NASDAQ symbol*] (SAG)
VARL.......... Vari-L Company [*NASDAQ symbol*] (TTSB)
VAR LECT.... Varia Lectio [*Variant Reading*] [*Latin*] (ROG)
Varlen.......... Varlen Corp. [*Associated Press*] (SAG)
VARM.......... Varmeter [*Engineering*]
VARN.......... Variation (FAAC)
VARN.......... Varnish

var nov .... Varietas Nova [*New Variety*] [*Biology*]
VARO .... Veterans Administration Regional Office (AFM)
VARP .... Raipur [*India*] [*ICAO location identifier*] (ICLI)
VARP .... Vietnam Asset Reconciliation Procedure [*Military*] (AABC)
VARPC .... Veterans Administration Records Processing Center
VARR .... Variable Range Reflector (IEEE)
VARR .... Visual-Aural Radio Range (MSA)
VARs .... Value-Added Remarketers (NITA)
VARS .... Variable Attribute Raster Scan System (NITA)
VARS .... Various (ROG)
VARS .... Varsity Spirit [*NASDAQ symbol*] (TTSB)
VARS .... Varsity Spirit Corp. [*NASDAQ symbol*] (SAG)
VARS .... Vertical Azimuth Reference System (NATG)
VARS .... Visual Aerial Reconnaissance and Surveillance [*Military*] (VNW)
VARS .... Vocational Adaptation Rating Scales [*Test*]
VARSITY .... University [*British*] (ROG)
VarSprt .... Varsity Spirit Corp. [*Associated Press*] (SAG)
VART .... Volunteer Air Reserve Training [*Air Force*]
VARTU .... Volunteer Air Reserve Training Unit [*Air Force*]
VARUNB .... Variable Unblocked (MHDB)
VAR/VAD .... Value-Added Reseller / Value-Added Dealer (BTTJ)
VARVS .... Variable Acuity Remote Viewing System (MCD)
VAS .... Aviatrans [*Former USSR ICAO designator*] (FAAC)
VAS .... Sivas [*Turkey*] [*Airport symbol*] (OAG)
VAS .... Validation System (SSD)
VAS .... Value-Added Service [*Telecommunications*] (TEL)
VAS .... Value-Added Service [*Medical benefits*]
VAS .... Value-Added Statement (ADA)
VAS .... Variable Angle Scatterometer (MCD)
VAS .... Vascular [*Cardiology*] (DAVI)
vas .... Vas Deferens [*Urology*] (DAVI)
VAS .... Vasectomy (WDAA)
VAS .... Vassijaure [*Sweden*] [*Seismograph station code, US Geological Survey Closed*] (SEIS)
VAS .... Vector Addition System
VAS .... Venomological Artifact Society (EA)
VAS .... Vesicle Attachment Sites [*Neurology*]
VAS .... Veterinary Assistant Surgeon [*British military*] (DMA)
VAS .... Vibration Analysis System
VAS .... Victorian Agricultural Strategy [*State*] (EERA)
VAS .... Videodisc Authoring System (NITA)
VAS .... Virtual Acoustic Synthesis [*Electronics*] (PS)
VAS .... Visible Atmospheric Sounder (MCD)
VAS .... VISSR [*Visible-Infrared Spin Scan Radiometer*] Atmospheric Sounder [*NASA*]
VAS .... Visual Analog [*Pain*] Scale
VAS .... Visual Analysis System [*Military*]
VAS .... Visual Attack System
VAS .... Visual Audit Sheet (DNAB)
VAS .... Visual Augmentation System
VAS .... Vortex Advisory System [*FAA*]
VASA .... Sihora [*India*] [*ICAO location identifier*] (ICLI)
VASA .... Victorian Ambulance Services Association [*Australia*]
VASA .... Viola d'Amore Society of America (EA)
VA SBA .... Virginia State Bar Association, Reports [*A publication*] (DLA)
VASC .... Vascular
VASC .... Verbal Auditory Screen for Children
VASC .... Vision and Autonomous Systems Laboratory, Carnegie Mellon University [*Research center*] (RCD)
VAsC .... Visual Acuity without Spectacle Correction [*Unaided*]
VASC .... Visual-Auditory Screen Test for Children (DAVI)
VASCA .... Electronic Valve and Semiconductor Manufacturers' Association (IAA)
VASCA .... Vacation and Senior Citizens Association (EA)
VASCAR .... Visual Average Speed Computer and Recorder [*Speed trap*]
VASCO .... Value-Added Supply Chain Optimization [*Automotive industry cost management*]
VASD .... Value-Added System Distributor (HGAA)
Vas Dis .... Vascular Disease (CPH)
VASE .... Variable Alternatively Spliced Exon [*Genetics*]
VASE .... Variable Angle Spectroscopic Ellipsometer
VASE .... Visualization Application Steering Environment [*Computer science*]
Vasenlisten ... Vasenlisten zur Griechischen Heldensage [*A publication*] (OCD)
VASG .... Songadh [*India*] [*ICAO location identifier*] (ICLI)
VASI .... Vertical Approach Slope Indicator
VASI .... Visual Approach Slope Indicator [*Aviation*]
VASI .... Volunteer Ambulance School of Instruction [*Military British*] (ROG)
VASIM .... Voltage and Synchro Interface Module
vasio-Para ... Veterans Administration Seating Interface Orthosis for Paraplegics (DAVI)
VASIS .... Visual Approach Slope Indicator System [*Aviation*]
VASL .... Sholapur [*India*] [*ICAO location identifier*] (ICLI)
VASO .... Vasomedical, Inc. [*NASDAQ symbol*] (SAG)
VASODIL .... Vasodilatation [*Physiology*] (AAMN)
VAS of GB ... Vasectomy Advancement Society of Great Britain
VASOG .... Veterans Administration Surgical Oncology Group
Vasomed .... Vasomedical, Inc. [*Associated Press*] (SAG)
VASP .... Value-Added Service Provider [*Agreement*] (IT)
VASP .... Variable Automatic Synthesis Program [*NASA*]
VASP .... Vasodilator-Stimulated Phosphoprotein [*Physiology*]
VASP .... Viacao Aerea Sao Paulo SA [*Airline*] [*Brazil*]
VAS RAD .... Vascular Radiology [*Medicine*] (DMAA)
VASRD .... Veterans Administration Schedule for Rating Disabilities (AABC)
VASS .... Van Allen Simplified Scoring [*Tennis*] (IIA)
VASS .... Variable Angle Sample Spinning [*Physics*]
VASS .... VAX Applicant Search System [*Science Applications International Corp.*]
VASS .... Victorian Architectural Students' Society [*Australia*]
VASS .... Visual Analysis Subsystem [*Military*]
VASS .... Visually Activated Switch System (MCD)
Vassar C .... Vassar College (GAGS)
VASSEL .... Validation of ASW [*Antisubmarine Warfare*] Subsystem Effectiveness Levels [*Navy*] (CAAL)
VASSS .... Van Alen Simplified Scoring System [*Tennis*]
VAST .... Vehicle Activity Status Transmission (PDAA)
VAST .... Vehicle Automatic State Transmitter (PDAA)
VAST .... Versatile Automatic Specification Tester
VAST .... Versatile Avionics Ship Test (IAA)
VAST .... Versatile Avionics Shop Test System (SAA)
VAST .... Versatile Avionics System Tester (GFGA)
VAST .... Virtual Archival Storage Technology [*Computer science*]
Vastar .... Vastar Resources, Inc. [*Associated Press*] (SAG)
VASTT .... Versatile Aerial Simulation TOW [*Tube-Launched, Optically Tracked, Wire-Guided (Weapon)*] Target (MCD)
Va St U .... Virginia State University (GAGS)
VASU .... Surat [*India*] [*ICAO location identifier*] (ICLI)
vas vit .... Vas Vitreum [*A Glass Vessel*] [*Latin Pharmacy*] (MAE)
VAS VITR .... Vas Vitreum [*A Glass Vessel*] [*Pharmacy*]
VAT .... Vacuum Arc Thrustor Program (MCD)
VAT .... Value-Added Tax
VAT .... Vane Air Temperature [*Automotive engineering*]
VAT .... Variable Area Turbine
VAT .... Variable Autotransformer (IAA)
VAT .... Variant Antigenic Type [*Genetics, immunology*]
VAT .... Varity Corp. [*NYSE symbol Toronto Stock Exchange symbol Vancouver Stock Exchange symbol*] (SPSG)
VAT .... Vatican
Vat .... Vatican (VRA)
VAT .... Vatican City [*ANSI three-letter standard code*] (CNC)
VAT .... Vatomandry [*Madagascar*] [*Airport symbol*] (OAG)
VAT .... Vatomandry [*Malagasy*] [*Airport symbol*] (AD)
VAT .... Ventricular Activation Time [*Cardiology*]
VAT .... Ventricular Activation Time (DAVI)
VAT .... Vernier Auto Track (IAA)
VAT .... Vertically Anchored Tire
VAT .... Veterinary Admissions Test (BARN)
VAT .... Veterinary Aptitude Test
VAT .... Vibration Acceptance Test
VAT .... Vibroacoustic Test (NASA)
VAT .... Village Assistance [*or Action*] Team (DNAB)
VAT .... Vincristine, Cytosine Arabinoside, 6-Thioguanine, Daunomycin [*Antineoplastic drug regimen*] (DAVI)
VAT .... Vineyards Association of Tasmania [*Australia*]
VAT .... Vinyl Asbestos Tile [*Technical drawings*]
VAT .... Virtual Address Translation
VAT .... Virtual Address Translator (NITA)
VAT .... Visibility, Amount, Height of Cloud Top, Base [*Weather*] [*DoD*]
VAT .... Visual Acquisition Technique
VAT .... Visual Action Time
VAT .... Visual Apperception Test [*Psychology*]
VAT .... Vitro Assistance Team
VAT .... Vocational Apperception Test [*Psychology*]
VAT .... Voice-Activated Transcription [*Machine*] (DAVI)
VAT .... Voice-Activated Typewriter
VAT .... Voice Activation Technology (NITA)
VAT .... Voltage Amplifier Tube
VAT .... Volt-Ampere Tester
VAT .... Vulnerability Analysis Team (MCD)
VATA .... Vertical Assembly and Test Area (SSD)
VATA .... Vibroacoustic Test Article (NASA)
Va Tax Rev ... Virginia Tax Review [*A publication*] (DLA)
VatBA .... Biblioteca Apostolica Vaticana, Vatican City, Vatican City [*Library symbol Library of Congress*] (LCLS)
VATD .... Vincristine, ara-C [*Cytarabine*], Thioguanine, Daunorubicin [*Antineoplastic drug regimen*]
VATE .... Vandenberg Automatic Test Equipment [*Air Force*]
VATE .... Versatile Automatic Test Equipment [*Computers*]
V-ATE .... Vertical Anisotropic Etch [*Raytheon Co.*]
VATER .... Vascular Tracheoesophageal-Limb-Reduction [*Endocrinology*]
VATER .... Vertebral, Anal, Tracheal, Esophageal, Renal
VATER .... Vertebral and/or Vascular Defects, Anorectal Malformation, Tracheoesophageal Fistula, Radial, Ray, or Renal Anomaly [*Syndrome*] [*Medicine*] (DAVI)
VATER .... Vertebral Defects, Imperforate Anus, Tracheoesophageal Fistula, Radial and RenalDysplasia [*Syndrome*] [*Medicine*] (DAVI)
VATERL .... Vertebral Defects, Imperforate Anus, Tracheoesophageal Fistula, Radial and RenalDysplasia, Limb Anomalies [*Syndrome*] [*Medicine*] (DAVI)
VATF .... Vibration and Acoustic Test Facility (NASA)
VAtf .... Visual Acuity with Trial Frame
VATH .... Vinblastine, Adriamycin, Thiotepa [*Antineoplastic drug regimen*]
VATH .... Vinblastine, Adriamycin, Thiotepa, Halotestin [*Fluoxymesterone*] [*Antineoplastic drug regimen*]
VATLIT .... Very Advanced Technology Light Twin (MCD)
VATLS .... Visual Airborne Target Locator System [*Military*]
VATOL .... Verical Altitude and Take-Off and Landing (PDAA)
VATP .... Vector Adaptive Transform Processing [*Computer science*] (PCM)
VATR .... Variable Aperture Target Recognition (MCD)
VATS .... Vehicle Acquisition and Tracking System (SAA)
VATS .... Vehicle Anti-Theft System [*General Motors Corp.*]

VATS .... Vehicle Automatic Test System
VATS .... Vernon's Annotated Texas Statutes [*A publication*] (DLA)
VATS .... Versatile Avionics Test [*or Tester*] Shop [*NASA*] (DNAB)
VATS .... Vertical-Lift Airfield for Tactical Support (NVT)
VATS .... Vibration Analysis Test Set (DWSG)
VATS .... Video-Assisted Thoracoscopic Surgery
VATS .... Video-Augmented Tracking System (MCD)
VATS/SNAP ... Video-Augmented Tracking System/Single Seat Night Attack Program (MCD)
VAT STA ...... Vatican State (WDAA)
VATT .... Vatican Advanced Technology Telescope [*At Mount Graham, AZ*]
Vatt .... Vattel's Law of Nations [*A publication*] (DLA)
Vattel .... Vattel's Law of Nations [*A publication*] (DLA)
Vattel Law Nat ... Vattel's Law of Nations [*A publication*] (DLA)
VATTR .... Value Added Tax Tribunal Reports [*A publication*]
VA/TVTA ...... Vibroacoustic/Thermal/Vacuum Test Article (NASA)
VAU .... Vertical Accelerometer Unit
VAU .... Vertical Arithmetic Unit
vau .... Virginia [*MARC country of publication code Library of Congress*] (LCCP)
VAU .... Volume Accumulator Unit
VAU .... Volunteer Air Units
VAUB .... Vehicle Authorization Utilization Board [*Military*]
VAUD .... Vaudeville
Vaug .... Vaughan's English Common Pleas Reports [*124 English Reprint*] [*A publication*] (DLA)
Vaugh .... Vaughan's English Common Pleas Reports [*124 English Reprint*] [*A publication*] (DLA)
Vaughan ...... Vaughan's English Common Pleas Reports [*124 English Reprint*] [*A publication*] (DLA)
Vaughan (Eng) ... Vaughan's English Common Pleas Reports [*124 English Reprint*] [*A publication*] (DLA)
Vaughn .... Vaughn's, Inc. [*Associated Press*] (SAG)
VAUS .... Value Added Utilisation System (EERA)
VAUSSI .... Veteran's Association of the USS [*United States Ship*] Iowa (EA)
VAUX .... Vauxhall [*Automobile*] (DSUE)
Vaux .... Vaux's Recorder's Decisions [*1841-45*] [*Philadelphia, PA*] [*A publication*] (DLA)
V AUX .... Verb Auxiliary [*Grammar*] (WDAA)
Vaux (PA) .... Vaux's Recorder's Decisions [*1841-45*] [*Philadelphia, PA*] [*A publication*] (DLA)
Vaux Rec Dec ... Vaux's Recorder's Decisions [*1841-45*] [*Philadelphia, PA*] [*A publication*] (DLA)
VAV .... Variable Air Volume
VAV .... Vava'u [*Tonga Island*] [*Airport symbol*] (OAG)
VAV .... Vaxjo [*Sweden*] [*Airport symbol*] (AD)
VAV .... Visicalc Advanced Version (HGAA)
VAV .... VP-16-213 [*Etoposide*], Adriamycin, Vincristine [*Antineoplastic drug regimen*]
VAVP .... Variable Angle, Variable Pitch
VAVS .... Veterans Administration Voluntary Service
VAW .... Carrier Airborne Early Warning Squadron [*Navy symbol*] (NVT)
VAW .... Vertical Arc Welder
VAWM .... Washim [*India*] [*ICAO location identifier*] (ICLI)
VAWP .... Voice-Activated Word Processor [*Computer science*]
VAWT .... Vertical Axis Wind Turbine [*Power generator*] [*See also VAWTG*]
VAWTG .... Vertical Axis Wind Turbine Generator [*Also, VAWT*]
VAX .... Alexandria Public Library, Alexandria, VA [*OCLC symbol*] (OCLC)
VAX .... Heavy Attack Aircraft, Experimental
VAX .... Vesta Airex [*Czechoslovakia*] [*ICAO designator*] (FAAC)
VAX .... Virtual Address Extension [*Computer science*]
VAX-L .... Aircraft Attack, Experimental-Light [*Navy*]
VAX/VMS ..... Virtual Address Extension/Virtual Memory System [*Computer science*] (DOM)
VAY .... Valandovo [*Yugoslavia*] [*Seismograph station code, US Geological Survey*] (SEIS)
Vayr .... Vayikra Rabba (BJA)
VAZ .... Voyageur Arizona Municipal Income Fund [*AMEX symbol*] (SPSG)
VAZ .... Voyageur Arizona Muni Income [*AMEX symbol*] (TTSB)
V_B .... Base Voltage (IDOE)
VB .... Birmingham European Airways [*Airline flight code*] (ODBW)
VB .... Birmingham European Airways [*ICAO designator*] (AD)
VB .... Bombing Plane [*Navy symbol*]
VB .... Dive Bomber Squadron [*Navy symbol*]
VB .... Vacancy Bit (IAA)
VB .... Valence Bond (DEN)
VB .... Valve Box
VB .... Van Buren [*Catheter*] [*Surgery*] (DAVI)
VB .... Vanity Bar [*Classified advertising*] (ADA)
VB .... Vapor Barrier [*Boots*] [*Army*] (INF)
VB .... Vascular Bundle [*Botany*]
VB .... Venous Blood [*Medicine*] (DMAA)
VB .... Ventrobasal Complex [*Brain anatomy*]
VB .... Verb
VB .... Vertebral-Basilar Arteries [*Anatomy*] (CPH)
VB .... Vertebral Body [*Anatomy*] (DAVI)
VB .... Vertical Beam [*of light*]
VB .... Vertical Bomb [*Air Force*]
VB .... Vertical Main Boiler [*on a ship*] (DS)
VB .... Veterinary Board [*Tasmania, Australia*]
VB .... Veterinary Bulletin [*Database*] [*Commonwealth Bureau of Animal Health*] [*Information service or system*] (CRD)
VB .... Viable Birth [*Medicine*]
VB .... Vibration (AAG)
VB .... Vibrator (IAA)
VB .... Vinblastine, Bleomycin [*Antineoplastic drug regimen*]
VB .... Vir Bonus [*A Good Man*] [*Latin*]
vb .... Virgin Islands, British [*MARC country of publication code Library of Congress*] (LCCP)
VB .... Visbreaker [*Petroleum technology*]
VB .... Visual Basic [*Computer science*] (PCM)
VB .... Vital Reaction [*on Autopsy*] [*Pathology*] (DAVI)
VB .... Viven and Bassiere [*Rifle grenade*]
VB .... Voelkischer Beobachter [*A publication*]
VB .... Voice Band [*Telecommunications*]
VB .... Voice Bank [*Telecommunications*] (TEL)
VB .... Voltage Board (IAA)
VB .... Voluntary Bankruptcy (MHDW)
VB .... Volunteer Battalion [*Military*]
VB .... Vorgeschobener Beobachter [*Forward Observer*] [*German military*]
VB .... Vulgate Bible
VB .... Westair Commuter Airlines [*ICAO designator*] (AD)
V-B1 .... Vitamin B_1 [*Also called thiamine*] (DAVI)
V-B6 .... Vitamin B_6 [*Also called pyridoxine*] (DAVI)
V-B12 .... Vitamin B_{12} [*Also called Cyanocobolamine*] (DAVI)
VBA .... Vagahova Ballet Academy [*Russia*]
VBA .... Variable Body Armor (INF)
VBA .... VB Anderson Co. [*BTAC*] (DAVI)
VBA .... Vegetarian Brotherhood of America [*Defunct*] (EA)
VBA .... Verbal Adjective (WDAA)
VBA .... Very Big Accelerator (PDAA)
VBA .... Veterans Benefits Administration [*Department of Veterans Affairs*]
VBA .... Vibrating Beam Accelerometer [*Inertial sensor*] (IEEE)
VBA .... Victorian Bar Association [*Australia*]
VBA .... Vincristine, BCNU [*Carmustine*], Adriamycin [*Antineoplastic drug regimen*]
VBA .... Visual Basic, Applications Edition [*Microsoft Corp.*] [*Computer macro language*] (PCM)
VBAA .... Vanilla Bean Association of America (EA)
VBAC .... Vaginal Birth After Caesarean [*Obstetrics*]
VBAI .... Vertebrobasilar Artery Insufficiency [*Medicine*]
VBAN .... Ann [*Myanmar*] [*ICAO location identifier*] (ICLI)
VBAN .... V Band Corp. [*NASDAQ symbol*] (NQ)
V Band .... V Band Corp. [*Associated Press*] (SAG)
VBAP .... Vincristine, BCNU [*Carmustine*], Adriamycin, Prednisone [*Antineoplastic drug regimen*]
VBAS .... Anisakan [*Myanmar*] [*ICAO location identifier*] (ICLI)
VBAS .... Von Braun Astronomical Society (EA)
VBAT .... Battery Voltage [*Automotive engineering*]
V_{BB} .... Base-Voltage Supply (IDOE)
vbb .... Volgens Bygaande Brief [*According to Accompanying Letter*] [*Correspondence*] [*Afrikaans*]
VBBM .... Bhamo [*Myanmar*] [*ICAO location identifier*] (ICLI)
VBBP .... Bokepyin [*Myanmar*] [*ICAO location identifier*] (ICLI)
VBBS .... Bassein [*Myanmar*] [*ICAO location identifier*] (ICLI)
VBC .... Bridgewater College, Bridgewater, VA [*OCLC symbol*] (OCLC)
VBC .... Variable Boost Control [*System*] [*Automotive engineering*]
VBC .... Velocity Bin Commanded
VBC .... Venetian Blind Council [*Formerly, VBI*]
VBC .... Versatile Base [*Bus*] Connector [*Electronics*] (BARN)
VBC .... Veterans Benefit Counselor [*Veterans Administration*] (GFGA)
VBC .... Victorian Bar Council [*Australia*]
VBC .... Vincristine, Bleomycin, Cisplatin [*Antineoplastic drug regimen*] (DAVI)
VBC .... Vinylbenzyl Chloride [*Organic chemistry*]
VBC .... Vogel-Bonner Citrate [*Growth medium*]
VBCI .... Coco Island [*Myanmar*] [*ICAO location identifier*] (ICLI)
VBCITC .... Victorian Building and Construction Industry Training Council [*Australia*]
VBD .... Vector-Borne Disease
VBD .... Veronal-Buffered Diluent
VBD .... Vertebrobasilar Dolichoectasia [*Medicine*]
VBD .... Vinblastine, Bleomycin, Diamminedichloroplatinum [*Cisplatin*] [*Antineoplastic drug regimen*]
VBD .... Voice Band Data (KSC)
VBDMA .... Vinylbenzyldimethylamine [*Organic chemistry*]
VBE .... Vernacular Black English (WGA)
VBE .... Vibrating Plate Extractor [*Chemical engineering*]
VBE .... Video BIOS [*Basic Input-Output System*] Extension [*Computer science*] (PCM)
VBE/AI .... VESA [*Video Electronics Standards Association*] BIOS Extension/ Audio Interface [*Basic Input-Output System*] (PCM)
VBEFA .... Vehicle Builders Employees Federation of Australia
VBF .... Bomber-Fighter Squadron [*Navy symbol*]
VBF .... Bombing-Fighting Aircraft [*Navy symbol*]
VBF .... Variable Bandwidth Filter
VBF .... Vibrated Fluid Bed [*Chemical engineering*]
VBF .... Vibratory Bowl Feeder
VBF .... Vinegar Brewers Federation [*British*] (DBA)
VBG .... Lompoc, CA [*Location identifier FAA*] (FAAL)
VBG .... Vein Aortocoronary Artery Bypass Graft [*Cardiology*] (AAMN)
VBG .... Vertical Banded Gastroplasty [*Medicine*] (MEDA)
VBGG .... Gangaw [*Myanmar*] [*ICAO location identifier*] (ICLI)
VBGH .... Volunteer Battalion Gordon Highlanders [*British military*] (DMA)
VBGQ .... Vacuum Brazed - Gas Quenched
VBGW .... Gwa [*Myanmar*] [*ICAO location identifier*] (ICLI)
VBHB .... Hmawbi [*Myanmar*] [*ICAO location identifier*] (ICLI)
VBHH .... Hebo [*Myanmar*] [*ICAO location identifier*] (ICLI)
VBHL .... Homalin [*Myanmar*] [*ICAO location identifier*] (ICLI)
VBHN .... Htilin [*Myanmar*] [*ICAO location identifier*] (ICLI)
VBI .... Venetian Blind Institute [*Later, VBC*] (EA)

VBI Vertebral-Basilar Insufficiency [*Medicine*] (CPH)
VBI Vertical Blanking Interval [*Telecommunications*]
VBI Video Bible Institute [*Defunct*] (EA)
VBI Vital Bus Inverter [*Computer science*] (IEEE)
VBIDB Victorian Building Industries Disputes Board [*Australia*]
V-BIG Ventricular Bigeminy [*Medicine*]
VBJ Vacuum Bell Jar
VBKG Kengtung [*Myanmar*] [*ICAO location identifier*] (ICLI)
VBKK Kutkai [*Myanmar*] [*ICAO location identifier*] (ICLI)
VBKM Kalemyo [*Myanmar*] [*ICAO location identifier*] (ICLI)
VBKP Kyaukpyu [*Myanmar*] [*ICAO location identifier*] (ICLI)
VBKU Kyauktu [*Myanmar*] [*ICAO location identifier*] (ICLI)
VBL BOCES [*Boards of Cooperative Educational Services*], Monroe 1, Penfield, NY [*OCLC symbol*] (OCLC)
VBL Vector Biology Laboratory [*University of Notre Dame*] [*Research center*] (RCD)
VBL Verbal
VBl Verordnungsblatt [*Official Gazette*] [*German*] (ILCA)
VBL Vertical-Blank [*Computer science*] (BYTE)
VBL Vinblastine [*Velban, Vincaleukoblastine*] [*Also, V, Ve, VLB*] [*Antineoplastic drug*]
VBL Voyager Biological Laboratory [*NASA*]
VBLK Loikaw [*Myanmar*] [*ICAO location identifier*] (ICLI)
VBLN Lonekin [*Myanmar*] [*ICAO location identifier*] (ICLI)
VBLO Langkho [*Myanmar*] [*ICAO location identifier*] (ICLI)
VBLS Lashio [*Myanmar*] [*ICAO location identifier*] (ICLI)
VBLS Voice-Based Learning System (EDAC)
V BLT Vee Built [*Ship classification term*] (DS)
VBLY Lanywa [*Myanmar*] [*ICAO location identifier*] (ICLI)
VBM BOCES [*Boards of Cooperative Educational Services*], Monroe 2, Orleans, Spencerport, NY [*OCLC symbol*] (OCLC)
VBM Valence Band Maximum [*Physics*]
VBM Valence Bond Maximum [*Physics*]
VBM Vincristine, Bleomycin, Methotrexate [*Antineoplastic drug regimen*]
VBMA Vacuum Bag Manufacturers Association [*Defunct*] (EA)
VBMAA Venetian Blind Manufacturers' Association of Australia
VBMH Mong-Hpayak [*Myanmar*] [*ICAO location identifier*] (ICLI)
VBMI Mongyai [*Myanmar*] [*ICAO location identifier*] (ICLI)
VBMK Myitkyina [*Myanmar*] [*ICAO location identifier*] (ICLI)
VBML Meiktila [*Myanmar*] [*ICAO location identifier*] (ICLI)
VBMM Moulmein [*Myanmar*] [*ICAO location identifier*] (ICLI)
VBMN Manaung [*Myanmar*] [*ICAO location identifier*] (ICLI)
VBMO Momeik [*Myanmar*] [*ICAO location identifier*] (ICLI)
VBMP Mong Pyin [*Myanmar*] [*ICAO location identifier*] (ICLI)
VBMR Ventilation Barrier Machine Room [*Nuclear energy*] (NRCH)
VBMS Mong-Hsat [*Myanmar*] [*ICAO location identifier*] (ICLI)
VBMS Victorian Business Migration Service [*Australia*]
VBMT Mong Tong [*Myanmar*] [*ICAO location identifier*] (ICLI)
VBMU Myauk U [*Myanmar*] [*ICAO location identifier*] (ICLI)
VBMW Magwe [*Myanmar*] [*ICAO location identifier*] (ICLI)
VBMWMO Vintage BMW [*Bavarian Motor Works*] Motorcycle Owners (EA)
VBN Verbal Noun
VBN Veterans Bedside Network (EA)
VBN Vrnjacka Banja [*Yugoslavia*] [*Airport symbol*] (AD)
VBNA Victorian Bush Nursing Association [*Australia*]
VBNC Viable but Not Culturable [*Microbiology*]
VBNJ Vista Bancorp [*NASDAQ symbol*] (SAG)
VBNK Village Bancorp [*NASDAQ symbol*] (SAG)
VBNM Naungmon [*Myanmar*] [*ICAO location identifier*] (ICLI)
VBNP Nampong [*Myanmar*] [*ICAO location identifier*] (ICLI)
VBNS Namsang [*Myanmar*] [*ICAO location identifier*] (ICLI)
vBNS Very High Speed Backbone Network System [*Computer science*]
VBNT Namtu [*Myanmar*] [*ICAO location identifier*] (ICLI)
VBNU Nyaung U [*Myanmar*] [*ICAO location identifier*] (ICLI)
VBO Oswego County BOCES [*Boards of Cooperative Educational Services*], Mexico, NY [*OCLC symbol*] (OCLC)
VBO Veterans Benefits Office
VBO Voltage Breakover (IAA)
VBOB Veterans of the Battle of the Bulge (EA)
V (Bomb) Vergeltungswaffe Bomb [*German "vengeance weapon"*]
VBOMP Virtual Base Organization and Maintenance Processor
VBOS Veronal-Buffered Oxalated Saline
VBot Verstreute Boghazkoei-Texte [*A. Goetze*] [*A publication*] (BJA)
VBP Vacuum Backing Pump
VBP Valid BIT [*Binary Digit*] Register [*Computer science*] (MHDB)
VBP Vinblastine, Bleomycin, and Platinol [*Antineoplastic drug regimen*] (MAE)
VBP Vinblastine, Bleomycin, Prednisone [*Antineoplastic drug*] (CDI)
VBP Virtual Block Processor
VBP Vortex Breakdown Position
VBPA Pa-An [*Myanmar*] [*ICAO location identifier*] (ICLI)
VBPB Phaungbyin [*Myanmar*] [*ICAO location identifier*] (ICLI)
VBPE Paletwa [*Myanmar*] [*ICAO location identifier*] (ICLI)
VBPF Variable Bandpass Filter
VBPG Pegu [*Myanmar*] [*ICAO location identifier*] (ICLI)
VBPI Pearl Island [*Myanmar*] [*ICAO location identifier*] (ICLI)
VBPK Pauk [*Myanmar*] [*ICAO location identifier*] (ICLI)
VBPL Pinlebu [*Myanmar*] [*ICAO location identifier*] (ICLI)
VBPP Papun [*Myanmar*] [*ICAO location identifier*] (ICLI)
VBPR Prome [*Myanmar*] [*ICAO location identifier*] (ICLI)
VBPT Putao [*Myanmar*] [*ICAO location identifier*] (ICLI)
VBPU Pakokku [*Myanmar*] [*ICAO location identifier*] (ICLI)
VBPW Palaw [*Myanmar*] [*ICAO location identifier*] (ICLI)
VBR Vacuum Bottoms Recycle [*Petroleum refining*]
VBR Valuation Board of Review [*Australia*]
VBR Variable BIT [*Binary Digit*] Rate [*Telecommunications*]
VBR Ventricle Brain Ratio [*Medicine*]
VBR Vinyl Bromide [*Organic chemistry*]
VBR Virginia Blue Ridge Railway [*AAR code*]
VBRA Sittwe [*Myanmar*] [*ICAO location identifier*] (ICLI)
VBRA Vehicle Builders and Repairers Association [*British*] (EAIO)
VBRK Vacation Break U.S.A. [*NASDAQ symbol*] (TTSB)
VBRK Vacation Break U.S.A., Inc. [*NASDAQ symbol*] (SAG)
VBRM Mandalay [*Myanmar*] [*ICAO location identifier*] (ICLI)
VBRN Mergui [*Myanmar*] [*ICAO location identifier*] (ICLI)
VBRR Rangoon/Mingaladon [*Myanmar*] [*ICAO location identifier*] (ICLI)
VBS Vacation Bible Schools (EA)
VBS Variable Ballast System
VBS Veronal-Buffered Saline
VBS Vertebral-Basilar System [*Medicine*] (CPH)
VBS Virtual Bragg Scattering [*Physics*]
VBS Vision Business Systems Ltd. (NITA)
VBSA Saw [*Myanmar*] [*ICAO location identifier*] (ICLI)
VBSA Value-Based Self-Assessment [*Model*] (AAGC)
VBS:FBS Veronal-Buffered Saline-Fetal Bovine Serum (MAE)
VBSK Sinkaling Khamti [*Myanmar*] [*ICAO location identifier*] (ICLI)
VBSL Salingyi [*Myanmar*] [*ICAO location identifier*] (ICLI)
VBSO Sidoktaya [*Myanmar*] [*ICAO location identifier*] (ICLI)
VBSS Visit, Board, Search, and Secure (DOMA)
VBST Shante [*Myanmar*] [*ICAO location identifier*] (ICLI)
VBSW Shinbweyang [*Myanmar*] [*ICAO location identifier*] (ICLI)
VBSY Sandoway [*Myanmar*] [*ICAO location identifier*] (ICLI)
VBT Bombing, Torpedo Plane [*Navy symbol*]
VBT Valence-Bond Theory [*Physical chemistry*]
VBT Variable Bandwidth Tuning
VBT Vertebral Body Tenderness [*Medicine*] (DAVI)
VBT Veterinary Board of Tasmania [*Australia*]
VBT Videos for Business and Training [*A publication*]
VBTA Vermont Business Teachers Association (EDAC)
VBTL Tachilek [*Myanmar*] [*ICAO location identifier*] (ICLI)
VBTN Tanai [*Myanmar*] [*ICAO location identifier*] (ICLI)
VBTV Tavoy [*Myanmar*] [*ICAO location identifier*] (ICLI)
VBTY Tanyang [*Myanmar*] [*ICAO location identifier*] (ICLI)
VBU Vibrating Bag Unloader
VBULE Vestibule [*Classified advertising*] (ADA)
VBUSA Vacation Break U.S.A., Inc. [*Associated Press*] (SAG)
VBV Vanuabalavu [*Fiji*] [*Airport symbol*] (OAG)
VBV Veterinary Board of Victoria [*Australia*]
VBVP Kawthaung [*Myanmar*] [*ICAO location identifier*] (ICLI)
VBW Air Burkina [*Burkina Faso*] [*ICAO designator*] (FAAC)
VBW Bridgewater, VA [*Location identifier FAA*] (FAAL)
VBW Video Bandwidth
VBWR Vallecitos Boiling Water Reactor
VBX Visual Basic Extension [*Computer science*]
VBY Visby [*Sweden*] [*Airport symbol*] (OAG)
VBYE Ye [*Myanmar*] [*ICAO location identifier*] (ICLI)
VC Acuity of Color Vision [*Ophthalmology*] (DAVI)
VC British Aircraft Corp. Ltd. [*ICAO aircraft manufacturer identifier*] (ICAO)
VC Capillary Volume [*Clinical chemistry*] (AAMN)
VC Circular Velocity
V_C Collector Voltage (IDOE)
VC Color Vision [*Ophthalmology*]
VC Composite Aircraft Squadron [*Navy symbol*]
VC Creditreform Databank [*Verband der Vereine Creditreform eV*] [*Information service or system*] (IID)
VC Cruise Speed [*Aviation*]
V_c Pulmonary Capillary Blood Volume [*Cardiology*] (DAVI)
VC St. Vincent and the Grenadines [*ANSI two-letter standard code*] (CNC)
VC Vacuolated Cell
VC Validity Check [*Data entry test program*] [*Computer science*] (IAA)
VC Valuable Cargo
VC Valuation Clause
VC Vanadium Carbide (PDAA)
VC Vaporizer Concentrate [*Nuclear energy*] (NRCH)
VC Variable Capacitor (DEN)
VC Variable Charge (DCTA)
VC Variable Cost (AAGC)
VC Varnished Cambric [*Insulation*]
VC Vascular Catheterization (CPH)
VC Vasoconstrictor [*Medicine*]
VC Vatel Club (EA)
vc Vatican City [*MARC country of publication code Library of Congress*] (LCCP)
VC Vector Character (NASA)
V/C Vector Control (KSC)
Vc Vecuronium [*A muscle relaxant*]
VC Vegetative Capability [*Biology*]
VC Vehicular Communications (MCD)
VC Velocity Character (MCD)
VC Velocity, Closing
VC Velocity Compounded
VC Velocity Counter (KSC)
VC Vena Cava [*Anatomy*]
VC Vencor, Inc. [*NYSE symbol*] (SAG)
VC Vendor Call (MCD)
VC Vendor Code (MCD)
VC Vendor Contact
VC Venereal Case [*Medical slang*]

VC Venice Committee (EA)
VC Venous Capacitance [*Clinical chemistry*] (AAMN)
VC Ventilated Containers [*Shipping*] (DCTA)
V/C Ventilation/Circulation Ratio [*Medicine*] (MAE)
VC Ventilatory Capacity [*Physiology*]
VC Ventricular Complex [*Cardiology*]
VC Ventricular Coupling [*Cardiology*]
VC Venture Capital [*or Capitalist*] [*Finance*]
VC VePesid, Carboplatin [*Antineoplastic drug*] (CDI)
VC Verb-Consonant [*Education of the hearing-impaired*]
VC Verbi Causa [*For Example*] [*Latin*]
VC Verification Condition
VC Vernair Flying Services [*British ICAO designator*] (ICDA)
VC Vernal Conjunctivitis [*Ophthalmology*]
VC Versatility Code
VC Vertical Center (SAA)
VC Vertical Circle (IAA)
VC Vertical Curve
VC Vertical Spacing (IAA)
VC Veterinary Corps [*Military*]
VC Vicar Choral
VC Vice Chairman [*or Chairperson or Chairwoman*]
VC Vice Chancellor
VC Vice-Chancellor's Courts [*England*] (DLA)
VC Vice Commodore [*Navy*] (NVT)
VC Vice Consul
VC Victoria Carriers [*Steamship*] (MHDB)
VC Victoria Cross [*British*]
VC Videocassette (DAVI)
VC Video Channel [*Auckland, NZ*]
VC Video Correlator
VC Videodisc Controller
VC Vietcong [*Vietnamese Communists*]
VC Vigilance Committee
VC Village of Childhelp (EA)
vc Vincentian Congregation (TOCD)
VC Vincentian Congregation (India) (TOCD)
VC Vincristine [*Also, LCR, O, V, VCR*] [*Antineoplastic drug*] (AAMN)
VC Vinyl Chloride [*Organic chemistry*]
VC Violoncello [*Music*]
VC Vir Clarissimus [*A Most Illustrious Man*] [*Latin*]
VC Virginia Central Railway [*AAR code*]
VC Virtual Circuit
VC Virtual Circuit [*Manager*] (TNIG)
VC Virtual Classroom [*Educational teleconferencing*]
VC Viscous Coupling [*Automotive engineering*]
VC Viscous Criterion
VC Visicalc (HGAA)
VC Vision Controllor [*Printer technology*]
VC Visiting Committee [*British*]
VC Visual Capacity [*Acuity*]
VC Visual Coincidence (SAA)
VC Visual Communication (WDAA)
VC Visual Cortex
VC Visum Cultum [*Seen Cultivated*] [*Botany*] (ROG)
VC Vital Capacity
VC Vitamin Capsule [*Pharmacy*] (DAVI)
VC Vitreous Carbon
VC Vitrified Clay [*Technical drawings*]
VC Vocal Cord
VC Voice Ciphony (CET)
VC Voice Circuit (SSD)
VC Voice Coil
VC Voice Coil of Speaker [*Computer hardware*] (IAA)
VC Voltage Changer (IAA)
VC Voltage Comparator [*or Compensator*] (DEN)
VC Volt-Coulomb (DEN)
VC Volume Control (DEN)
VC Volume of Compartment [*Technical drawings*]
VC Voluntary Closing [*Prosthesis*] [*Medicine*]
VC Volunteer Consultant [*Red Cross*]
VC Volunteer Corps
VC Voters for Choice [*Later, VFC*] (EA)
VC Voyage Charter
VC Vuelta de Correo [*Return Mail*] [*Spanish*]
VCA Vacant Code Announcement (DNAB)
VCA Valve Control Amplifier (MDG)
VCA Vancomycin-Colistin-Anisomycin [*Growth-inhibiting mixture*] [*Microbiology*]
VCA Vanished Children's Alliance (EA)
VCA Vegetarian Catering Association [*British*] (BI)
VCA Vehicle Checkout Area
VCA Venture Clubs of the Americas (EA)
VCA Vespa Club of America (EA)
VCA Veteran Corps of Artillery, State of New York, Constituting the Military Societyof the War of 1812 (EA)
VCA Victims of Crime Assistance Act
VCA Victims of Crime Association [*Australia*]
VCA Victorian Council of the Arts [*Australia*]
VCA Video Capture Adapter (PCM)
VCA Viewdata Corp. of America, Inc. [*Miami Beach, FL*] [*Telecommunications*] (TSSD)
VCA Vinchina [*Argentina*] [*Seismograph station code, US Geological Survey*] (SEIS)
VCA Vinylene Carbonate [*Organic chemistry*] (WDAA)
VCA Viral Capsid Antibody [*Hematology*]
VCA Viral Capsular Antigen [*Immunology*]
VCA Virtual City Associates Ltd. [*London, England*] [*Telecommunications*] (TSSD)
VCA Virtual Crystal Approximation (WDAA)
VCA Viscosity Control Agent
VCA Visual Course Adapter (MUGU)
VCA Vitrified China Association [*Defunct*]
VCA Voice Connecting Arrangement [*Telecommunications*] (TEL)
VCA Voltage-Controlled Amplifier (NTCM)
VCA Voltage Control of Amplification
VCA Voltage-Current Adapter (IAA)
VCAC Victorian Consumer Affairs Committee [*Australia*]
VCAD Vertical Contact Analog Display
VC Adm Victoria Reports, Admiralty [*A publication*] (DLA)
VCAI Veterinary Centers of America [*NASDAQ symbol*] (SAG)
VCAI Veterinary Ctrs of Amer [*NASDAQ symbol*] (TTSB)
VCAM Vascular Cell Adhesion Molecule [*Cytology*]
VCAM Vincam Group [*NASDAQ symbol*] (TTSB)
VCAM Volunteer Committees of Art Museums (EA)
VCAMCUS Volunteer Committees of Art Museums of Canada and the United States (EA)
VC & GCAssn Victoria Cross and George Cross Association [*British*] (DBA)
VCAP Vehicle Charging and Potential Experiment (NASA)
VCAP Vincristine, Cyclophosphamide, Adriamycin, Prednisone [*Antineoplastic drug regimen*]
VCAP-I VP-16[*Etoposide*], Cyclophosphamide, Adriamycin, Platinol [*Antineoplastic drug regimen*] (DAVI)
V-CAP III VP-16-213 [*Etoposide*], Cyclophosphamide, Adriamycin, Platinol [*Cisplatin*] [*Antineoplastic drug regimen*]
VCAR Vector Aeromotive [*NASDAQ symbol*] (TTSB)
VCAR Vector Aeromotive Corp. [*NASDAQ symbol*] (NQ)
VCARE Veterans Council for American Rights and Equality (EA)
VCARL Vector Aeromotive Wrrt [*NASDAQ symbol*] (TTSB)
VCARW Vector Aeromotive Wrrt [*NASDAQ symbol*] (TTSB)
VCAS Vice-Chief of the Air Staff [*British*]
VCAS Victorian Children's Aid Society [*Australia*]
VCASS Visually Coupled Airborne Systems Simulator (IEEE)
VCAT Veterinary College Admission Test (PGP)
VCB CBNU Learning Resources Center, Virginia Beach, VA [*OCLC symbol*] (OCLC)
VCB Construction Battalion [*USNR classification*]
VCB Vertical Location of the Center of Buoyancy
VCB Visual Control Board
VCBA Variable Control Block Area [*Computer science*]
VCBFE Vauxhall College of Building and Further Education [*London, England*]
VCBI Colombo/Katunayake [*Sri Lanka*] [*ICAO location identifier*] (ICLI)
V_{CC} Collector-Voltage Supply (IDOE)
VCC Vancouver Community College Library [*UTLAS symbol*]
VCC Variable Ceramic Capacitor
VCC Variable Characteristic Car (ADA)
VCC Variable Command Count (MCD)
VCC Variable Cycle Controller (IAA)
VCC Vasoconstrictor Center [*Physiology*]
VCC Vehicle Crew Chief [*NASA*] (KSC)
VCC Verification Code Counter (MCD)
VCC Vermilion Community College, Ely, MN [*OCLC symbol*] (OCLC)
VCC Versatile Corp. [*Toronto Stock Exchange symbol*]
VCC Vertical Centering Control
VCC Vertical Channel Computer (SAA)
VCC Veteran Car Club of Great Britain (BI)
VCC Vice-Chancellor's Courts (DLA)
VCC Video Coaxial Connector
VCC Video Compact Cassette [*Video recorder*] [*Philips*]
VCC Vietcong Captured
VCC Viet Cong Suspect Confirmed (VNW)
VCC Virginia Community College System
VCC Virtual Conference Center (PCM)
VCC Viscous-Damped Converter Clutch [*Automotive engineering*]
VCC Visual Communications Congress
VCC Vogelback Computing Center [*Northwestern University*] [*Research center*] (RCD)
VCC Voice Control Center [*NASA*] (KSC)
VCC Voice-Controlled Carrier [*Telecommunications*] (IAA)
VCC Voltage Coefficient of Capacitance
VCC Voltage-Controlled Capacitor
VCC Voltage-Controlled Clock (IAA)
VCC Voluntary Census Committee (EA)
VCC Volunteer Cadet Corps [*British*]
VCC Volunteer Capital [*NYSE symbol*] (TTSB)
VCC Volunteer Capital Corp. [*NYSE symbol*] (SPSG)
VCC Volvo Concept Car [*Automotive engineering*]
VCC Vuilleumier Cycle Cooler
VCCA Anuradhapura [*Sri Lanka*] [*ICAO location identifier*] (ICLI)
VCCA Victorian Credit Cooperative Association [*Australia*]
VCCA Vintage Chevrolet Club of America (EA)
VCCB Batticaloa [*Sri Lanka*] [*ICAO location identifier*] (ICLI)
VCCC Colombo/Ratmalana [*Sri Lanka*] [*ICAO location identifier*] (ICLI)
VCCC Vintage and Classic Car Club [*Australia*]
VCCC Vuilleumier Cycle Cryogenic Cooler
VCCCM Victorian Centre for the Conservation of Cultural Material [*Australia*]
VCCE Victorian Council of Christian Education [*Australia*]
VCCFT Victorian Council for Children's Films and Television [*Australia*]
VCCG Galoya/Amparai [*Sri Lanka*] [*ICAO location identifier*] (ICLI)

VCCI Victorian Chamber of Commerce and Industry [*Australia*]

VCCJ Jaffna/Kankesanturai [*Sri Lanka*] [*ICAO location identifier*] (ICLI)

VCCO Voltage-Controlled Crystal Oscillator (IAA)

VCCR Victorian Cervical Cytology Registry [*Australia*]

VCCR Vienna Convention on Consular Relations (EERA)

VCCS Video and Cable Communications Section of the ALA (NITA)

VCCS Visually Coupled Control System (MCD)

VCCS Voltage-Controlled Current Source [*Electronics*]

VCCT Trincomalee/China Bay [*Sri Lanka*] [*ICAO location identifier*] (ICLI)

VCCUS Venezuelan Chamber of Commerce of the United States

VCCW Wirawila [*Sri Lanka*] [*ICAO location identifier*] (ICLI)

VCD Value City Department Stores [*NYSE symbol*] (SPSG)

VCD Value City Dept Stores [*NYSE symbol*] (TTSB)

VCD Vapor Compression Distillation

VCD Variable-Capacitance Diode

VCD Variable Center Distance [*Computer science*] (OA)

VCD Verification Control Document (NASA)

VCD Vernier Engine Cutoff [*Aerospace*]

VCD Vibrational Circular Dichroism [*Spectrometry*]

VCD Victoria Diego Resource Corp. [*Vancouver Stock Exchange symbol*]

VCD Victoria River Downs [*Australia Airport symbol*]

VCD Visiting Card (BJA)

VCD Voltage Crossing Detector

VCDP Victorian Council of Deaf People [*Australia*]

VCDS Vapor Compression Distillation Subsystem (NASA)

VCDS Vice-Chief of Defence Staff [*British*]

VCDS(P & L) Vice Chief of Defence Staff Personnel and Logistics [*British*] (RDA)

VCE Vagina, Ectocervix, and Endocervix [*Medicine*] (DMAA)

VCE Vapor Cloud Explosion

VCE Vapor Compression Evaporation

VCE Variable Cycle Engine (MCD)

VCE Vehicle Condition Evaluation (MCD)

V_{CE} Velocity of Contractile Element (DAVI)

VCE Venice [*Italy*] [*Airport symbol*] (OAG)

VCE Vertical Centrifugal

VCE Vice

VCE Vinyl Chloride Ethylene [*Organic chemistry*]

VCE Virtual Coulomb Excitation (PDAA)

VCE Voice (NASA)

VCEA Victorian Congress of Employer Associations [*Australia*]

VCEL Vanguard Cellular Systems, Inc. [*NASDAQ symbol*] (NQ)

VCELA Vanguard Cellular Sys [*NASDAQ symbol*] (TTSB)

VCEMA Vinyl Chloride Ethylene Methyl Acrylate [*Organic chemistry*]

VcePw Voice Powered Tech International, Inc. [*Associated Press*] (SAG)

VC Eq Victoria Reports, Equity [*A publication*] (DLA)

VCF Vaginal Contraceptive Film [*Medicine*] (BARN)

VCF Vapor Chamber Fin

VCF Vapor Crystal Facility [*Materal processing center*] (SSD)

VCF Variable Crystal Filter (DEN)

Vcf Velocity of Circumferential Fiber Shortening [*Cardiology*]

VCF Venture Capital Fund [*Finance*]

VCF Verified Circulation Figure [*Advertising*]

VCF Victor Fly [*Italy ICAO designator*] (FAAC)

VCF Victorian Cycling Federation [*Australia*]

VCF Vietnam-Canada Foundation

VCF Vincristine, Cyclophosphamide, Fluorouracil [*Antineoplastic drug regimen*]

VCF Visual Comfort Factor

VCF Voltage-Controlled Filter

VCF Voltage-Controlled Frequency (IEEE)

VCF Voyageur CO Ins Muni Income [*AMEX symbol*] (TTSB)

VCF Voyageur Colorado Insured Municipal Income Fund [*AMEX symbol*] (SPSG)

VCF&L [*Department of*] Conservation, Forests and Lands of Victoria [*State*] (EERA)

VCFC Vik Chandler Fan Club (EA)

VCFGH Victorian Council on Fitness and General Health [*Australia*]

VCFL Victorian Country Football League [*Australia*]

VCFUSA Vietnamese Catholic Federation in the USA (EA)

VCG Calcutta Volunteer Guards [*British military*] (DMA)

VCG Vapor Crystal Growth [*Materials processing*]

VCG Vectorcardiogram [*Medicine*]

VCG Vehicle Control Group

VCG Verification Condition Generator

VCG Vertical Line Through Center of Gravity (IAA)

VCG Vertical Location of the Center of Gravity

VCG Vice-Consul General [*British*] (ROG)

VCG Video Command Generator (MCD)

VCG Voltage-Controlled Generator

VCGEN Verification Condition Generator (MHDB)

VCGS Vapor Crystal Growth System [*Materials processing*]

VCGS Vice Chief of the General Staff [*in the field*] [*Military British*] (RDA)

VCGS Victorian Clinical Genetics Services [*Australia*]

VCH Veterinary Convalescent Hospital

VCH Vichadero [*Uruguay*] [*Airport symbol Obsolete*] (OAG)

VCH Victoria County History [*Classical studies*] (OCD)

VCH Video Concert Hall

VCH Vinylcyclohexene [*Organic chemistry*]

VCHO Vicar Choral

VCHP Variable Conductance Heat Pipe

v-chr Vice-Chair of the Board (DD)

VCI Valassis Communcations [*NYSE symbol*] (TTSB)

VCI Valassis Communications, Inc. [*NYSE symbol*] (SPSG)

VCI Variety Clubs International (EA)

VCI Vegetation Condition Index [*for detecting and tracking droughts*] [*National Oceanic and Atmospheric Administration*]

VCI Vehicle Cone Index [*Engineering*] (OA)

VCI Velocity Change Indicator (NASA)

VCI Vibration Control Index

VCI Videtics International Corp. [*Vancouver Stock Exchange symbol*]

VCI Vietcong Infrastructure

VCI Virtual Circuit Identifier [*Computer science*]

VCI Visual Comfort Index

VCI Volatile Corrosion Inhibitor [*See also VPI*] [*Metallurgy*]

VCID Very Close in Defense

VCIGS Vice-Chief of the Imperial General Staff [*British*]

VCIM Varnished Cambric Insulation Material

VCINS Vietcong Infrastructure Neutralization System

VCIP Veterans Cost-of-Instruction Program [*Higher Education Act*]

VCIR Visual Communication and Image Representation [*Computer science*]

VCIS Voluntary Cooperative Information System [*American Public Welfare Association*] (EGAO)

V-CITE Vertical-Cargo Integration Test Equipment [*NASA*] (MCD)

VCJCS Vice Chairman, Joint Chiefs of Staff (DOMA)

VCJD Variant of Creutzfeldt-Jakob Disease [*Medicine*]

VC-K Eli Lilly & Co. [*Research code symbol*] [*Canada*]

VCK Video Camera Kit

VCK Vietcong Killed

VC KIA(BC) Vietcong Killed in Action (Body Count)

VC KIA(POSS) Vietcong Killed in Action (Possible)

VCKV Vacuum Control Check Valve [*Automotive engineering*]

VCL Vehicle Checkout Laboratory

VCL Vertical Center Line

VCL Violincello [*Music*]

VCL Visual Component Library [*Computer science*]

VCL Voice Communications Laboratory

VCL Voluntary College Letter [*British*]

VCLE Versicle

VCLF Vertical Cask-Lifting Fixture [*Nuclear energy*] (NRCH)

VCLK Video Clock [*Computer science*]

VCLLO Violoncello [*Music*]

VCLO Voltage-Controlled Local Oscillator

VCM Vacuum (AAG)

VCM Vacuum

VCM Vacuum Condensible Material [*Astronomy*] (OA)

VCM Vehicle Condition Monitor [*Automotive engineering*]

VCM Vehicle Control Module [*Automotive engineering*]

VCM Ventilation Control Module [*NASA*]

VCM Veracruz [*Mexico*] [*Seismograph station code, US Geological Survey*] (SEIS)

VCM Vertical Current Meter

VCM Vertical Cutter Motion

VCM Vibrating Coil Magnetometer

VCM Vibration Conditioning Monitoring (ACII)

VCM Victoria College of Music [*London*] (ROG)

VCM Victorian Chamber of Mines [*Australia*]

VCM Viking Continuation Mission [*NASA*]

VCM Vinyl Chloride Monomer [*Organic chemistry*]

VCM Virtual Circuit [*Call*] Manager (TNIG)

VCM Visual Countermeasure

VCM Volatile Combustible Material

VCM Volatile Condensable Material

VCM Voltage-Controlled Multivibrator

VCM Voorhees College, Denmark, SC [*OCLC symbol*] (OCLC)

VCMA Vacuum Cleaner Manufacturers Association (EA)

VCMA Vinyl Chloride Methyl Acrylate [*Organic chemistry*]

VCmax Maximum Viscous Response [*Medicine*]

VCMP Vincristine, Cyclophosphamide, Melphalan, Prednisone [*Antineoplastic drug regimen*]

VCMR Victorian Council for the Mentally Retarded [*Australia*]

VCMS Vehicle Cost Management System (NITA)

VCN Avcon, Aviation Consulting Ltd. [*Switzerland*] [*FAA designator*] (FAAC)

VCN Christopher Newport College, Newport News, VA [*OCLC symbol*] (OCLC)

VCN Millville, NJ [*Location identifier FAA*] (FAAL)

VCN Vancomycin-Colistin-Nystatin [*Growth-inhibiting mixture*] [*Microbiology*]

VCN Vancomycin Hydrochloride, Colistimethate Sodium, Nystatin, [*Medium*] [*Microbiology*] (DAVI)

VCN Vendor Contract Notice

VCN Verification Completion Notice (NASA)

VCN Vibrio cholerae Neuraminidase [*An enzyme*]

VCN Vinyl Cyanide [*Organic chemistry*]

VCN Visual Communications Network, Inc. [*Cambridge, MA*]

VCN Vulcan Resources [*Vancouver Stock Exchange symbol*]

VCNA VTAM Communications Network Application (NITA)

VCNB Ventura Cnty Natl Bancorp [*NASDAQ symbol*] (TTSB)

VCNB Ventura County National Bancorp [*NASDAQ symbol*] (SAG)

VCNC Voltage-Controlled Negative Capacitance (IAA)

VCNM Vice Chief of Naval Material Command

VCNO Vice Chief of Naval Operations

VCNR Voltage-Controlled Negative Resistance (IAA)

VCNS Vice-Chief of the Naval Staff [*British*]

VCNTY Vicinity (AFM)

VC/NVA Vietcong/North Vietnamese Army

VCO Aviacion Colombiana Ltd. [*Colombia*] [*ICAO designator*] (FAAC)

V_{co} Carbon Monoxide [*Endogenous production*] [*Medicine*] (DAVI)

VCO .... Glendale, AZ [*Location identifier FAA*] (FAAL)
VCO .... Variable Crystal Oscillator (IAA)
VCO .... Variable Cycle Operation
VCO .... Vehicle Control Officer [*Air Force*] (AFM)
VCO .... Verbal Concrete Object
VCO .... Verbit & Co., Consultants to Management [*Bala Cynwyd, PA*] [*Telecommunications*] (TSSD)
VCO .... Vertical Control Operator [*Military*]
VCO .... Viceroy's Commissioned Officer [*British military*] (DMA)
VCO .... Victorian College of Optometry [*Australia*]
VCO .... Vina Concha y Toro ADS [*NYSE symbol*] (TTSB)
VCO .... Vina Concha y Toro SA [*NYSE symbol*] (SAG)
VCO .... Voice Carry-Over [*Hearing-impaired technolgoy*]
VCO .... Voice Coder [*Telecommunications*] (IAA)
VCO .... Voice Controlled Oscillator [*Telecommunications*] (TEL)
VCO .... Voltage-Controlled Oscillator
VCO .... Voluntary Conservation Organisation (EERA)
VCO .... Volunteer Conservation Officers
VCO$_2$ .... Carbon Dioxide Production [*Medicine*] (DAVI)
VCOA .... Volkswagen Convertible Owners of America [*Defunct*] (EA)
VCoA .... Volvo Club of America (EA)
VCOD .... Vertical Carrier Onboard Delivery
VC of A .... Vizsla Club of America (EA)
VCOFGWBS ... Vietnamese Cross of Gallantry with Bronze Star [*Military decoration*] (AABC)
VCOFGWGS ... Vietnamese Cross of Gallantry with Gold Star [*Military decoration*] (AABC)
VCOFGWP ... Vietnamese Cross of Gallantry with Palm [*Military decoration*] (AABC)
VCOFGWSS ... Vietnamese Cross of Gallantry with Silver Star [*Military decoration*] (AABC)
VC of S .... Vice Chief of Staff
VC of SA ...... Vice Chief of Staff, Army [*Later, VCSA*] (AABC)
VCOI .... Veterans Cost-of-Instruction
VCOM .... VitalCom Inc. [*NASDAQ symbol*] (TTSB)
V Conv R ...... Victorian Conveyancing Cases [*Australia A publication*]
VCOP .... Variable Control Oil Pressure (MSA)
VCOS .... Vehicle Control and Operating System [*Army*]
VCOS .... Vice-Chiefs of Staff [*British*]
VCOS .... Visible Caching Operating System [*AT & T*]
VCOT .... Virtual Community of Tomorrow [*Internet resource*] [*Computer science*]
VCOV .... Volunteer Consultant for Office of Volunteers [*Red Cross*]
VCP .... Sao Paulo [*Brazil*] Viracopos Airport [*Airport symbol*] (OAG)
VCP .... Vacuum Condensing Point (IAA)
VCP .... Valosin-Containing Protein [*Biochemistry*]
VCP .... Variable Cam Phaser [*Automotive engineering*]
VCP .... Variable Cam Phasing [*Automotive engineering*]
VCP .... Vector Collecting Program [*Electronics design*] (IAA)
VCP .... Vector Correction Program (SAA)
VCP .... Vehicle Check Point [*Military*]
VCP .... Vehicle Collecting Point
VCP .... Velocity Control Programmer
VCP .... VERDAN [*Versatile Differential Analyzer*] Checkout Panel
VCP .... Veterinary Collecting Post [*British military*] (DMA)
VCP .... Veterinary Creolin-Pearson
VCP .... Victorian Centre for Photography [*Australia*]
VCP .... Video Cassette Player
VCP .... Vincristine, Cyclophosphamide, Prednisone [*Antineoplastic drug regimen*]
VCP .... Virtual Channel Processor [*Computer science*]
VCP .... Virtual Communication Path [*Computer science*] (IAA)
VCP .... Virtual Control Panel (NITA)
VCP .... Virtual Control Processor [*Computer science*] (IAA)
VCP .... Virtual Counterpoise Procedure [*Physical chemistry*]
VCP .... Virus Cancer Program [*National Cancer Institute*]
VCP .... Visual Comfort Probability (IAA)
VCP .... Voice Communication Panel
VCP .... Voluntary Cooperation Program [*World Meteorological Organization*] [*United Nations*]
VCP-1 .... [*Cisplatin*] VP-16[*Etoposide*], Cycophosamide, Platinol [*Cisplatin*] [*Antineoplastic drug regimen*] (DAVI)
VCPA .... Victorian Country Press Association [*Australia*]
VCPA .... Virginia-Carolina Peanut Association (EA)
VCPA .... Virginia Crab Packers Association [*Defunct*] (EA)
VCPI .... Virtual Control Program Interface [*Computer science*] (PCM)
VCPM .... Video-Enhanced Contrast Polarization Microscopy
VCPOR .... Vanguardia Comunista del Partido Obrero Revolucionario [*Bolivia*] [*Political party*] (PPW)
VCPP .... Virginia-Carolina Peanut Promotions [*An association*] (EA)
VCPS .... Velocity Control Propulsion Subsystem [*NASA*]
VCPS .... Video Copyright Protection Society [*British*]
VC PW .... Vietcong Prisoner of War
VCR .... Aviacor [*Former USSR*] [*FAA designator*] (FAAC)
VCR .... Go-Video [*AMEX symbol*] (TTSB)
VCR .... Go-Video, Inc. [*AMEX symbol*] (SPSG)
VCR .... Vacuum Contact Relay
VCR .... Valclair Resources Ltd. [*Vancouver Stock Exchange symbol*]
VCR .... Valuation by Components Rule (ADA)
Vcr .... Vancouver [*Canada*] (BARN)
VCR .... Variable Compression Ratio
VCR .... Vasoconstrictive [*Physiology*]
VCR .... Vertical Crater Retreat [*Mining technology*]
VCR .... Video Cartridge Recorder (IAA)
VCR .... Video Cassette Recorder
VCR .... Vincristine [*Also, LCR, O, V, VC*] [*Antineoplastic drug*]
VCR .... Visual Control Room
VCR .... Viva Cristo Rey [*Long Live Christ the King*] [*Spanish*]
VCR .... Vocal Character Recognition
VCR .... Voltage Coefficient of Resistance
VCR .... Voltage Control Resistor (IAA)
VCR .... Voluntary Content Rating System [*Solid Oak software*] [*Computer science*] (PCM)
VCRA .... Veterans Cycle Racing Association [*British*] (DBA)
VCRAS .... Office of Vice Chancellor for Research and Advanced Study [*University of Alaska*] [*Research center*] (RCD)
VCRC .... Vector Control Research Centre [*India*]
VCRC .... Voice Circuit Reconfiguration Confirmation (SSD)
VC Rep .... Vice-Chancellor's Reports [*English, Canadian*] [*A publication*] (DLA)
VCRI .... Verification Cross Reference Index
VCRO .... Validity Check and Readout (NITA)
VCRT .... Variable Contrast Resolution Test [*Optics*]
VCR.WS .... Go-Video Wrrts [*AMEX symbol*] (TTSB)
VCS .... Cruiser-Scouting Aircraft Squadron [*Navy symbol*]
VCS .... Vacuum Actuated Control Switch (IAA)
VCS .... Vacuum Control Switch
VCS .... Validation Control System
VCS .... Vane Control System (MCD)
VCS .... Vapor Coating System
VCS .... Vapor Cooling System
VCS .... Variable Correlation Synchronization
VCS .... Vasoconstrictor Substance [*Physiology*]
VCS .... Vehicular Communications System
VCS .... Velocity Cutoff System (KSC)
VCS .... Vent Collection System [*Engineering*]
VCS .... Ventilation Control System [*NASA*] (KSC)
VCS .... Ventricular Conduction System [*Cardiology*] (CPH)
VCS .... Verbal Communication Scales [*Educational testing*]
VCS .... Verification Control Sheet (NASA)
VCS .... Vernier Control System
VCS .... Version Control System [*Computer science*]
VCS .... Veterans Canteen Service [*Veterans Administration*]
VCS .... Veterinary Cancer Society (EA)
VCS .... Vice Chief of Staff
VCS .... Victorian Computer Society (IAA)
VCS .... Video Cassette System
VCS .... Video Clutter Suppression (CAAL)
VCS .... Video Communications System
VCS .... Video Compression Sampler [*Computer science*]
VCS .... Video Computer System [*Atari, Inc.*]
VCS .... Video Contrast Seeker
VCS .... Vietcong Suspect
VCS .... View Control System (HGAA)
VCS .... Viking Change Status [*NASA*]
VCS .... Virginia & Carolina Southern R. R. [*AAR code*]
VCS .... Visual Call Sign [*Communications*]
VCS .... Visually Coupled System (IEEE)
VCS .... Vocabulary Comprehension Scale [*Educational test*]
VC's .... Vocal Chords [*Musical slang*]
VCS .... Voice Command System [*Ground Communications Facility, NASA*]
VCS .... Voice Communication System
VCS .... Voice Control Switch [*NASA*]
VCS .... Voltage Calibration Set
VCS .... Voltage-Current-Sequence (MCD)
VCSA .... Vice Chief of Staff, Army [*Formerly, VC of SA*]
VCSA .... Victorian Catholic Schools Association [*Australia*]
VCSA .... Victorian Council for Sustainable Agriculture [*Australia*]
VCSA .... Vintage and Classic Sailing Association [*British*] (DBA)
VCSA .... Viral Cell Surface Antigen [*Medicine*] (DMAA)
VC/SAF .... Vice Chief of Staff, Air Force
VCSCT .... Vacuum Control Switch - Cold Temperature [*Automotive engineering*]
VCSDI .... Vacuum Control Switch - Deceleration Idle [*Automotive engineering*]
VCSEA .... Victorian Community Services Employers' Association [*Australia*]
VCSEL .... Vertical-Cavity Surface Emitting LASER
VCSFO .... Veterans Canteen Service Field Office [*Veterans Administration*]
VCSI .... Voice Control Systems [*NASDAQ symbol*] (TTSB)
VCSL .... Voice Call Signs List
VCSO .... Vice Chief of Staff [*Army*] (AAGC)
VCSP .... Voice Call Signs Plan
VCSR .... Voltage-Controlled Shift Register
VCSS .... Value Creation Study Society (CINC)
VCSS .... Victorian Council of Social Service [*Australia*]
VCSS .... Voice Communications Security System
VCT .... St. Vincent and the Grenadines [*ANSI three-letter standard code*] (CNC)
VCT .... Variable Cycle Technology
VCT .... Venous Clotting Time [*Clinical chemistry*]
VCT .... Victor (WGA)
VCT .... Victoria [*Texas*] [*Airport symbol*] (OAG)
VCT .... Victorian Conservation Trust [*Australia*]
VCT .... Video Contrast Tracker (PDAA)
VCT .... Vidicon Camera Tube
VCT .... Vintage Carriages Trust [*British*] (DBA)
VCT .... Vinyl Composition Tile
VCT .... Viscount Air Services, Inc. [*ICAO designator*] (FAAC)
VCT .... Vitrified Clay Tile [*Technical drawings*]
VCT .... Voice Code Translation (BUR)
VCT .... Voltage Clock Trigger (IAA)
VCT .... Voltage-Controlled Transfer (IAA)
VCT .... Voltage Control Transfer
VCT .... Voltage Curve Tracer

VCT Volume Control Tank [*Nuclear energy*] (NRCH)
VctA Vector Aeromotive Corp. [*Associated Press*] (SAG)
VCTA Victorian Commercial Travellers' Association [*Australia*]
VctAer Vector Aeromotive Corp. [*Associated Press*] (SAG)
VctAr Vector Aeromotive Corp. [*Associated Press*] (SAG)
VCTCA Virtual Channel to Channel Adapter
VCTD Vendor Contract Technical Data
VCTR Vector (NASA)
VCTR VECTRA Technologies [*NASDAQ symbol*] (SPSG)
VCTRY Victory
VCTS Vacuum Control Temperature Switch [*Automotive engineering*]
VCTS Variable Cockpit Training System (MCD)
VCTV Viewer Controlled Television (WDMC)
VCTY Vicinity (NVT)
VCU Variable Correction Unit (IAA)
VCU Very Close-Up [*Cinematography*] (NTCM)
VCU Video Combiner Unit (IAA)
VCU Video Control Unit (MCD)
VCU Videocystourethrography [*Medicine*]
VCU Virginia Commonwealth University
VCU Viscous Coupling Unit [*Automotive engineering*]
VCU Voiding Cystourethrogram [*Medicine*]
VCU Voltage Control Unit
VCUG Vesicoureterogram [*Urology*]
VCUG Voiding Cystourethrogram [*Medicine*]
VCV Clinch Valley College of the University of Virginia, Wise, VA [*OCLC symbol*] (OCLC)
VCV Vacuum Check Valve
VCV Vacuum Control Valve [*Automotive engineering*]
VCV Van Kam Am Cap CA Val Mun [*NYSE symbol*] (TTSB)
VCV Van Kampen Merritt California Value Municipal Trust [*NYSE symbol*] (SPSG)
VCV Variable Compression Vector (MHDI)
VCV Vicia Cryptic Virus [*Plant pathology*]
VCV Victorville, CA [*Location identifier FAA*] (FAAL)
VCV Vietnam Combat Veterans (EA)
VCVAC Vinyl Chloride Vinyl Acetate [*Organic chemistry*]
VCVDC Vinyl Chloride Vinylidene Chloride [*Organic chemistry*]
VCVS Vehicle Component Verification System [*Automotive engineering*]
VCVS Voltage-Controlled Voltage Source
VCW Victoria West [*South Africa*] [*Airport symbol*] (AD)
VCXO Voltage-Controlled Crystal Oscillator
VCY Valley City, ND [*Location identifier FAA*] (FAAL)
VCY Ventura County Railway Co. [*Army*]
VCY Vicinity [*Aviation*] (FAAC)
VCZ Vinylcarbazole [*Organic chemistry*]
VD Double Vibrations [*Cycles*]
V_D Drain Voltage (IDOE)
VD Leo Pharm. Products [*Denmark*] [*Research code symbol*]
VD Photographic Squadron [*Navy symbol*]
VD RTZ Services Ltd. [*British ICAO designator*] (ICDA)
VD Vacuum Distillation (PDAA)
VD Valuation Decisions [*A publication*] (DLA)
VD Vandyke [*Graphics*]
VD Vapor Density
VD Various Dates [*Bibliography*]
vd Various Dates (WDMC)
VD Vascular Disease [*Cardiology*] (DAVI)
VD Vasodilation [*Cardiology*] (DAVI)
VD Vasodilator [*Cardiology*] (DAVI)
VD Vault Door (AAG)
VD Venereal Disease
VD Ventilating Deadlight [*Technical drawings*]
VD Ventricular Dilator [*Neuron*] [*Medicine*]
VD Verbal Discrimination [*Psychology*]
VD Verbum Domini [*Rome*] [*A publication*] (BJA)
VD Vertical Deviation (DAVI)
VD Vertical Drive
VD Viceroy-Designate [*British*]
VD Victoria Docks [*British*] (ROG)
VD Victorian Decoration [*British*]
VD Video Decoder
VD Video Disk (BUR)
VD Video Display (IAA)
VD Violent Defectives [*British*]
VD Viral Diarrhea [*Medicine*] (DMAA)
VD Virtual Data
VD Visiting Dignitary
V/D Voice/Data (BUR)
VD Void (AAG)
VD Void [*Urology*] (DAVI)
VD Voltage Detector
VD Voltage Drop (MSA)
Vd Volume Dead Air Space (MAE)
VD Volume Deleted [*Finance*]
VD Volume Discount [*Investment term*]
VD Volume of Distribution
VD Volunteer Decoration [*British*]
V_DA Alveolar Dead-space Volume [*Medicine*] (DAVI)
VDA Valve Drive Amplifier
VDA Valve Driver Assembly (NASA)
VDA Variable Data Area (NASA)
VDA Variable Depth ASDIC (NATG)
VDA Vehicle Dynamics Area
VDA Velocity Dealiasing Algorithm (USDC)
VDA Velocity Dealiasing Algorithm [*Marine science*] (OSRA)
VDA Vendor Data Article
VDA Venous Digital Angiogram [*Cardiology*] (DAVI)
V_DA Ventilation of the Alveolar Dead-space [*Medicine*] (DAVI)
VDA Verbal Delay Announcement (NITA)
VDA Versatile Drone Autopilot (MCD)
VDA Vertical Danger Angle [*Navigation*]
VDA Victorian Docklands Authority [*Australia*]
VDA Video Dimension Analysis [*Sports medicine*]
VDA Video Distribution Amplifier
VDA Viola d'Amore [*Music*]
VDA Vision Distribution Amplifier (IAA)
VDA Visual Data Analysis
VDA Visual Discriminatory Acuity
VDA Volga-Dnepr [*Former USSR ICAO designator*] (FAAC)
VDA Volksbund fuer das Deutschtum im Ausland [*NAZI Germany*]
VDAC Vaginal Delivery after Caesarean [*Obstetrics*]
VDAC Vendor Data Article Control
VDAC Video Display Controller (IAA)
VDAC Voltage-Dependent, Anion-Selective Channels [*In the membrane of a mitochondrion*]
VDA/D Video Display Adapter with Digital Enhancement [*AT & T*]
VDAM Virtual Data Access Method (IEEE)
V_Dan Ventilation per Minute of the Anatomic Dead-space [*Medicine*] (DAVI)
V_Dan Volume of the Anatomic Dead-space [*Medicine*] (DAVI)
VDANL Vehicle Dynamics Analysis [*Computer simulation*] [*Automotive engineering*]
VDAS Vehicle Data and Acquisition System [*Automotive engineering*]
VDAS Vibration Data Acquisition System (KSC)
VDAS Video Data Acquisition System
VDAS Voltage-Dependent, Anion-Selective [*Proteins*] [*Biochemistry*]
VDB Brooklyn College, Brooklyn, NY [*OCLC symbol*] (OCLC)
VdB Van Den Bergh [*Liver function test*]
VDB Vector Data Buffer
VDB Vehicle Data Bus [*Automotive engineering*]
VDB Very Dear Brother [*Freemasonry*]
VDB Victor D. Brenner [*Designer's mark, when appearing on US coins*]
VDB Video Display Board
VDB Vrijzinnige-Democratische Bond [*Radical Democratic League*] [*Netherlands Political party*] (PPE)
VDBG Battambang [*Cambodia*] [*ICAO location identifier*] (ICLI)
VDBR Volume of Distribution of Bilirubin [*Medicine*] (MAE)
VDBS Vanguard Discount Brokerage Services [*Finance*]
VDC DC [*Direct Current*] Voltage (ACII)
VDC Vanadocene Dichloride [*Antineoplastic drug*]
VDC Variable Diode Circuit
VDC Variable Displacement Compressor [*Automotive engineering*]
VDC Vasodilator Center [*Physiology*]
VDC VDC Corp. Ltd. [*Associated Press*] (SAG)
VDC Vendor Data Control (MCD)
VDC Ventilation Duct Chase [*Nuclear energy*] (NRCH)
VDC Venture Development Corp. [*Natick, MA*] [*Telecommunications*] (TSSD)
VDC Verbum Dei Community (TOCD)
VDC Video Data Controller (NITA)
VDC Video Display Controller [*Computer science*] (MHDI)
VDC Video-Documentary Clearinghouse (EA)
VDC Vietnam Day Committee [*Antiwar group*] (VNW)
VDC Vocational Development Checklist (EDAC)
VDC Voltage-Direct Current (NITA)
VDC Voltage Doubler Circuit
VDC Voltage to Digital Converter
Vdc Volts DC (IDOE)
V_{dc} Volts DC (IDOE)
VDC Volts Direct Current
VDC Volunteer Defense Corps
VDC Volunteer Development Corps (EA)
VDCC Voltage-Dependent Calcium Channel [*Neurobiology*]
VDCE [*Department of*] Conservation and Environment, Victoria [*State*] (EERA)
VDCE Victorian Department of Conservation and Environment [*Australia*]
VDCLF VDC Corp. [*NASDAQ symbol*] (TTSB)
VDCLF VDC Corp. Ltd. [*NASDAQ symbol*] (SAG)
VDCP Video Data Collection Program
VDCT Direct-Current Test Volts
VDCT Viaduct [*Commonly used*] (OPSA)
VDCU Videograph Display Control Unit
VDCW Direct-Current Working Volts
VDD Verification Description Document (NASA)
VDD Version Description Document (KSC)
VDD Video Detector Diode
VDD Virtual Display Driver [*Computer science*]
VDD Visual Display Data
VDD Voice Digital Display
VDDI Voyager Data Detailed Index [*NASA*] (KSC)
VDDL Virtual Data Description Language [*Computer science*] (MHDB)
VDDL Voyager Data Distribution List [*NASA*] (KSC)
VDDP Video Digital Data Processing
VDDR Vitamin D-Dependent Rickets [*Medicine*]
VDDS Voice/Document Delivery System [*Computer science*]
VDDS Voyager Data Description Standards [*NASA*] (KSC)
VDE Vacuum Deposition Equipment
VDE Valverde [*Canary Islands*] [*Airport symbol*] (OAG)
VDE Variable Displacement Engine
VDE Variable Display Equipment

VDE............ Verband Deutscher Elektrotechniker [*Association of German Electrical Engineers*] (EG)
VDE............ Video Display Editor [*Computer science*] (CDE)
VDE............ Visual Development Environment [*Computer science*] (PCM)
VDE............ Voice Data Entry (NITA)
VDECS........ Vehicle Detector and Cueing System
V DEF......... Verb Defective [*Grammer*] (WDAA)
VDEF.......... Vie de France [*NASDAQ symbol*] (TTSB)
VDEF.......... Vie de France Corp. [*McLean, VA*] [*NASDAQ symbol*] (NQ)
VDEh.......... Verein Deutscher Eisenhuttenleute [*German Iron and Steel Engineers Association*] (IID)
VDEL.......... Variable Delivery
VDEL.......... Venereal Disease Experimental Laboratory
VDEM.......... Vasodepressor Material [*Physiology*] (MAE)
V DEP......... Verb Deponent [*Grammer*] (WDAA)
VDEQ.......... Virginia Department of Environmental Quality
VDEQ.......... Virginia Department of Environmental Quality (DOGT)
VDES.......... Voice Data Encoding System [*Telecommunications*] (IAA)
VDET.......... Voltage Detector (IEEE)
VDETS........ Voice Data Entry Terminal System
VDEV.......... "V" Device [*Military decoration*] (AABC)
VDF............ Ventricular Diastolic Fragmentation [*Medicine*] (DMAA)
VDF............ Very-High-Frequency Direction-Finding
VDF............ Vibration Damping Fastener
VDF............ Video Frequency
VDF............ Vinylidene Fluoride [*Organic chemistry*]
VDF............ Voice Data Fax [*Telecommunications*]
VDFB.......... Victorian Dried Fruits Board [*Australia*]
VDFG.......... Variable Diode Function Generator
VDG............ Royal Inniskilling Dragoon Guards [*Military unit*] [*British*]
VDG............ Vehicle Data Guide
VDG............ Venereal Disease Gonorrhea
VDG............ Vertical and Direction Gyro
VDG............ Vertical Display Generator (NG)
VDG............ Video Data Generator (NITA)
VDG............ Video Display Generator
vdg............ Voiding (MAE)
VdgB.......... Vereinigung der Gegenseitigen Bauernhilfe [*Mutual Farmers' Aid Society*] [*Germany*]
VDGI.......... Vietnamese Government Information Department (VNW)
VdGS.......... Viola da Gamba Society [*British*] (DBA)
VDGS.......... Visual Docking Guidance System [*Aviation*] (DA)
VdGSA........ Viola da Gamba Society of America (EA)
VDH............ Valvular Disease of the Heart [*Medicine*]
VDH............ Van Der Hout Associates Ltd. [*Toronto Stock Exchange symbol*]
VDH............ Variable Length Divide or Halt (SAA)
VDH............ Vickers Diamond Hardness (IAA)
VDI............ Variable Duration Impulse (IAA)
VDI............ Vat Dye Institute [*Later, American Dye Manufacturers Institute*] (EA)
VDI............ Vegetation Drought Index [*Agriculture*] (WDAA)
VDI............ Vendor Documentation Inventory (NASA)
VDI............ Verein Deutscher Ingenieure [*Society of German Engineers*]
VDI............ Vertical Direction Indicator (CAAL)
VDI............ Vertical Display Indicator (NG)
VDI............ Vidalia, GA [*Location identifier FAA*] (FAAL)
VDI............ Video Data Interrogator (SAA)
VDI............ Video Device Interface [*Computer science*] (PCM)
VDI............ Video Display Input
VDI............ Video Display Interface
VDI............ Virtual Device Interface [*Computer technology*]
VDI............ Visual Display Input
VDI............ Visual Doppler Indicator (IAA)
VDI............ Vocational Development Inventory (EDAC)
VDI............ Voluntary Data Inquiry
VDICAPP...... Verein Deutscher Ingenieure-Commission on Air Pollution Prevention (EAIO)
VDIEO........ Vendor Data Information Engineering Order (MCD)
VDIF.......... Video Display Information File (PCM)
VDIFF........ Visual Difference [*Computer science*] (NHD)
VDIG.......... Vertical Display Indicator Group
VDIKRL...... Verein Deutscher Ingenieure-Kommission Reinhaltung der Luft [*VDI - Commis sion on Air Pollution Prevention*] (EAIO)
VDI-N.......... VDI-Nachrichten [*VDI-Verlag GmbH*] [*Database*]
V disc.......... Victory Disc [*Music*] (WDMC)
VDISK.......... Virtual Disk [*Computer science*]
VDJ............ Variable-Diversity-Joining [*Genetics*]
VDK............ Vicinal Diketone [*Organic chemistry*]
VDKC.......... Kompong Cham [*Cambodia*] [*ICAO location identifier*] (ICLI)
VDKH.......... Kompong Chnang [*Cambodia*] [*ICAO location identifier*] (ICLI)
VDKT.......... Kratie [*Cambodia*] [*ICAO location identifier*] (ICLI)
VDL............ Van Diemen's Land [*Former name of Tasmania*]
VDL............ Variable Delay Line
VDL............ Vasodepressor Lipid [*Physiology*]
VDL............ Ventilating Deadlight
VDL............ VHF Digital Link [*FAA*] (TAG)
VDL............ Video Data Link (NVT)
VDL............ Vienna Definition Language [*1960*] [*Computer science*] (CSR)
VDL............ Visual Detection Level (MAE)
VDL............ Voice Direct Line
VDLF.......... Variable Depth Launch Facility (AAG)
VDLIB........ Virtual Disk Library [*Computer science*] (MHDI)
VDM............ Variable Direction Microphone
VDM............ Varian Data Machines
VDM............ Vasodepressor Material [*Physiology*]
VDM............ Vector Dominance Model [*Physics*]
VDM............ Vector Drawn Map
VDM............ Vehicle Deadlined for Maintenance (AFM)
VDM............ Verbi Dei Minister [*Minister, or Preacher, of the Word of God*] [*Latin*]
VDM............ Vibration Damping Mount
VDM............ Video Delta Modulation
VDM............ Viedma [*Argentina*] [*Airport symbol*] (OAG)
VDM............ Vienna Development Method [*Computer science*]
VDM............ Virtual Device Metafile [*Computer technology*] (DGA)
VDM............ Virtual Dipole Moment [*Geodesy*]
VDM............ Virtual DOS [*Disk Operating System*] Machine [*Computer science*] (PCM)
VDM............ Visual Display Module (EECA)
V_{DM}............ Volume of Mechanical Dead Space [*Medicine*] (DAVI)
VDME.......... Vibrating Dropping Mercury Electrode [*Electrochemistry*]
VDMID........ Victorian Department of Manufacturing and Industry Development [*Australia*]
VDMIE........ Verbum Domini Manet in Eternum [*The Word of the Lord Endureth Forever*] [*Latin*]
VDMK.......... Democratic Community of Vojvodina Hungarians [*Former Yugoslavia*] [*Political party*]
VDMO.......... Vinyl (dimethyl) Oxazolinone [*Organic chemistry*]
VDMOS........ Vertical Double Diffused Metal Oxide Semiconductor (MCD)
VDMS.......... Video Delta Modulation System
VDMS.......... Vocal Data Management System
VDMSC........ Volunteer Durham Medical Staff Corps [*British military*] (DMA)
VDN............ Varudeklarationsnamnden [*Labeling system*] [*Sweden*]
VDN............ Vedron Ltd. [*Toronto Stock Exchange symbol*]
VdN............ Voix des Notres [*Record label*] [*France*]
VDNCOA...... Veterans Division of the Non-Commissioned Officers Association of the USA (EA)
VDNCS........ Vapor-Deposited Noncrystalline Solid (PDAA)
VDNH.......... VD [*Venereal Disease*] National Hotline [*Later, NSTDH*] (EA)
VDNX.......... Videonics, Inc. [*NASDAQ symbol*] (SAG)
VDO............ Red Air, SA [*Belgium*] [*FAA designator*] (FAAC)
VDO............ Vadso [*Norway*] [*Airport symbol*] (AD)
VDO............ Videotron Groupe Ltee. SV [*Toronto Stock Exchange symbol*]
VDOP.......... Vertical Dilution of Precision
VD/OS........ Vacuum Distillation/Overflow Sampler [*Nuclear energy*] (NRCH)
VDOS.......... Vibrational Density of States [*Physics*]
VDP............ Vacuum Diffusion Pump
VDP............ Valle de la Pascua [*Venezuela*] [*Airport symbol*] (AD)
VDP............ Variable Length Divide or Proceed (SAA)
VDP............ Vehicle Deadlined for Parts
VDP............ Vehicle Development Process [*Automotive project management*]
VDP............ Venture Database Publisher [*Computer science*]
VDP............ Verenigde Democratische Partijen [*United Democratic Parties*] [*Surinam*] [*Political party*] (PPW)
VDP............ Vertical Data Processing
VDP............ Vertical Dipole (MCD)
VDP............ Vertical Director Pointer (SAA)
VDP............ Vibration Diagnostic Program
VDP............ Vibration-Dissociation Process
VDP............ Video Datagram Protocol [*Computer science*]
VDP............ Video Data Processor
VDP............ Videodisc Player [*RCA Corp.*]
VDP............ Vinblastine, Dacabazine, Cisplatin (CDI)
VDP............ Vincristine, Daunorubicin, Prednisone [*Antineoplastic drug regimen*]
VDP............ Visual Descent Point [*Aviation*] (FAAC)
VDP............ Visual Descent Point [*FAA*] (TAG)
VDP............ Volunteer Reservists in Drill Pay Status [*Navy*]
VDPA.......... Victorian Dairy Products Association [*Australia*]
VDPI.......... Vehicle Direction and Position Indicator
VDPI.......... Voyager Data Processing Instructions [*NASA*] (KSC)
VDPP.......... Phnom-Penh [*Cambodia*] [*ICAO location identifier*] (ICLI)
VDPS.......... Voice Data Processor System
VDPT.......... Pongtuk [*Cambodia*] [*ICAO location identifier*] (ICLI)
VDQ............ Visual Display of Quality
VDQS.......... Vins Delimites de Qualite Superieure [*Designation on French wine labels*]
VDR............ Validated Data Record
VDR............ Variable Deposit Requirement [*Business term*] (ADA)
VDR............ Variable Diameter Rotor
VDR............ Vehicle Data Recorder
VDR............ Vehicle Deselect Request [*NASA*] (KSC)
VDR............ Vendor Data Request
VDR............ Venous Diameter Ratio [*Cancer detection*]
VDR............ Video Disc Recorder
VDR............ Videodisk Recorder (WDMC)
VDR............ Videotape Recorder (IAA)
VDR............ Villa Dolores [*Argentina*] [*Airport symbol*] (AD)
VDR............ Vitamin D Receptor (DOG)
VDR............ Vitamin D Receptor [*Genetics*]
VDR............ Voice & Data Resources, Inc. [*Ashbury Park, NJ*] [*Information service or system Telecommunications*] (TSSD)
VDR............ Voice Digitization Rate
VDR............ Voltage-Dependent Resistor (DEN)
VDR............ Voyage Data Recorder
VDRA.......... Voice and Data Recording Auxiliary [*NASA*] (KSC)
V_{Drb}.......... Rebreathing Ventilation [*Medicine*] (DAVI)
VDRE.......... Vitamin D-Responsive Element [*Biochemistry*]
VDRG.......... Vendor Data Release Group (MCD)
V_{drive}........ Drive Voltage (IDOE)
VDRL.......... Venereal Disease Research Laboratory
VDRR.......... Vitamin D-Resistant Rickets [*Medicine*] (DMAA)
VDRS.......... Vehicular Disc Reproduction System (DICI)

VDRS Verdun Depression Rating Scale [Medicine] (MAE)
VDRT Venereal Disease Reference Test [of Harris]
VDRY Vacu-Dry Co. [NASDAQ symbol] (NQ)
VDS Vadso [Norway] [Airport symbol] (OAG)
VDS Van der Stratten [Auto racing team]
VDS Vapor Deposited Silica [Optical fiber technology]
VDS Vapor Detection System
VDS Variable Depth SONAR
VDS Variable Drop Size [Color printing]
VDS Vasodilator Substance [Physiology]
VDS Vehicle Description Summary [General Motors Corp.]
VDS Vehicle Descriptor Section
VDS Vehicle Dynamics Simulator [NASA] (NASA)
VDS Vendor Data Service
VDS Vendor Direct Shipment
VDS Venereal Disease Syphilis
VDS Vertical Display System [Navy]
VDS Victorian Deaf Society [Australia]
VDS Video Digitizer System (MCD)
VDS Vindesine [Also, E] [Antineoplastic drug]
VDS Viola d'Amore Society (EA)
VDS Virtual DMA [Direct Memory Access] Service [Computer science] (PCM)
VDS Visual Display System
VDS Visual Docking Simulator
VDS Voice Data Switch
VDS Volatile Dissolved Solids (MCD)
VDS Volunteer Development Scotland (AIE)
VDSA Veut Dieu Saint Amour [Knights Templar] [Freemasonry]
VDSM Internationaler Verband der Stadt-, Sport-, und Mehrzweckhallen [International Federation of City, Sport, and Multi-Purpose Halls] (EAIO)
VDSQ Video Data Sequence (NTCM)
VDSR Siem-Reap [Cambodia] [ICAO location identifier] (ICLI)
VDSS Variable Depth SONAR System
VDSS Volume of Distribution at Steady State
VDST Stung Treng [Cambodia] [ICAO location identifier] (ICLI)
VDSV Sihanouk [Cambodia] [ICAO location identifier] (ICLI)
VDT Van Doorne's Transmissie BV [Netherlands Automotive engineering]
VDT Varactor Diode Test
VDT Variable Data Table
VDT Variable Deflection Thruster [Helicopter]
VDT Variable Density Tunnel
VDT Variable Depth Transducer [Navy] (NVT)
VDT Variable Differential Transformer
VDT Vayudoot [India] [ICAO designator] (FAAC)
VDT Vehicle Data Table [NASA] (MCD)
VDT Vertical Deflection Terminal (IAA)
VDT Video Data Terminal [Computer science]
VDT Video [or Visual] Display Terminal [Computer science]
VDT Visual Display Terminal (EECA)
VDTA Vacuum Dealers Trade Association (EA)
VDTS Variable Display Training System
VDTS Vehicle Data Transmission System
VDTT Very Difficult to Test [Audiology]
VDU Refugio, TX [Location identifier FAA] (FAAL)
VDU Vacuum Distillation Unit [Petroleum technology]
VDU Variable Delay Unit (IAA)
VdU Verband der Unabhaengigen [League of Independents] [Dissolved, 1956] [Austria] (PPE)
VDU Video [or Visual] Display Unit [Computer science]
VDU Video Distribution Unit
VDU Visual Display Unit (OA)
VDUAC Victorian Drug Users' Advisory Committee [Australia]
VDUC VAS [VISSR Atmospheric Sounder] Data Utilization Center (USDC)
VDUC VDU Controller (NITA)
VDV Vacuum Differential Valve [Automotive engineering]
VDV Ventricular End-Diastolic Volume [Medicine] (MAE)
VDV Vojski Drzavne Varnosti [Yugoslavia]
VDV Vozdushno-Desantnye Voiska [Airborne Troops] [An autonomous command] [Former USSR]
VD-VF Vacuum Distillation - Vapor Filtration
VDVS Voeune Sai [Cambodia] [ICAO location identifier] (ICLI)
V_DV_T Physiologic Dead Space in Percent of Tidal Volume [Medicine] (DAVI)
VDW Venus Departure Window [NASA]
VDW Very Deep Water
VDWE Van der Waals Epitaxy [Physics]
VDX Vandorex Energy [Vancouver Stock Exchange symbol]
VDZ Valdez [Alaska] [Airport symbol] (OAG)
V_E Airflow per Unit of Time [Medicine] (DAVI)
Ve Biblioteca Nacional, Caracas, Venezuela [Library symbol Library of Congress] (LCLS)
V_E Emitter Voltage (IDOE)
V_E Environmental Variance (DAVI)
VE Minute Ventilation [Medicine] (DAVI)
V_E Respiratory Minute Volume [Medicine] (DAVI)
VE Vaginal Epithelium [Endocrinology]
VE Vaginal Examination [Medicine]
VE Value Effectiveness
VE Value Engineering [Military]
VE Value Engineering
VE Valve Engineer (WDAA)
VE Varicose Eczema [Medicine]
VE Vehicle Experimental (MCD)
Ve Velban [See VBL]
VE Velocity Equipment (MCD)
VE Velocity, Equivalent
VE Velocity Error
ve Venezuela [MARC country of publication code Library of Congress] (LCCP)
VE Venezuela [ANSI two-letter standard code] (CNC)
VE Venous Emptying [Cardiology] (DAVI)
VE Ventilating Equipment (MSA)
VE Ventilation [Medicine] (DAVI)
VE Ventricular Extrasystole [Cardiology] (DAVI)
VE Verbal Emotional (Stimuli) [Psychology]
V-E VERLORT [Very-Long-Range Tracking] Elevation [NASA]
VE Vernal Equinox
VE Vernier Engine [as a modifier] (AAG)
VE Vertex [Obstetrics] (DAVI)
VE Vertical Exaggeration [Geology]
Ve Vesey, Senior's, English Chancery Reports [27, 28 English Reprint] [A publication] (ILCA)
VE Vesicular Exanthema [Virus]
VE Veuve [Widow] [French] (ROG)
VE Vibration Eliminator (OA)
VE Victory in Europe [as in VE-Day]
VE Vidatron Enterprise Ltd. [Vancouver Stock Exchange symbol]
VE Vinyl Ester
VE Viral Encephalitis [Neurology] (DAVI)
VE Virtual Environment [Computer science] (ECII)
VE Visalia Electric Railroad Co. [AAR code]
VE Visual Efficiency
VE Visual Emissions [Environmental Protection Agency] (GFGA)
VE Visual Examination (MEDA)
VE Vocational Education (OICC)
VE Voltage (IAA)
VE Voltage Efficiency [Electrochemistry]
VE Volume Ejection [Medicine]
V_E Volume of Expired Gas [Medicine] (DAVI)
VE Voluntary Effort [A cost containment program established by AHA, AMA, and FAH]
VE Votre Eminence [Your Eminence] [French]
VEA Value Engineering Audit
VEA Value Engineers Association (BARN)
VEA Variable Energy Absorber (MCD)
VEA Vehicle Engineering Analysis
VEA Veliger Escape Aperture
VEA Ventricular Ectopic Activity [Cardiology] (MAE)
VEA Ventricular Ectopic Arrhythmia [Cardiology] (AAMN)
VEA Veterans Educational Assistance [Act]
VEA Victorian Exporters' Association [Australia]
VEA Viral Envelope Antigens [Immunology]
VEA Virtual Effective Address (NITA)
VEA Vocational Education Act [1963]
VEAG Vereinigte Energiewerke AG (ECON)
VEAMCOP Viking Error Analysis Monte Carlo Program [Computer science]
VEAN Along [India] [ICAO location identifier] (ICLI)
VE & B Vehicle Energy and Biotechnology (MCD)
Ve & B Vesey and Beames' English Chancery Reports [35 English Reprint] [A publication] (DLA)
VEAP Veterans Educational Assistance Program [DoD]
VEAT Agartala [India] [ICAO location identifier] (ICLI)
VEAZ Aizwal [India] [ICAO location identifier] (ICLI)
Veazey Veazey's Reports [36-44 Vermont] [A publication] (DLA)
VEB Variable Elevation Beam [RADAR]
VEB Vehicle Equipment Bay (MCD)
VEB Ventricular Ectopic Beats [Cardiology]
VEB Venus Entry Body [NASA]
VEB Vneshekonombank [State Bank for Foreign Economic Affairs] [Former USSR]
VEB Vocational Education Board (OICC)
VEB Volvo Engine Brake [Volvo AB] [Diesel engines]
VEBA Calcutta (Behala) [India] [ICAO location identifier] (ICLI)
VEBA Vereinigte Elektrizitaets und Bergwerks, AG [Holding company] [Germany]
VEBA Voluntary Employee Benefit Association [Type of trust established by a company, a union, or both to provide members with various insurance benefits]
VEBC Berachampa [India] [ICAO location identifier] (ICLI)
VEBD Baghdogra [India] [ICAO location identifier] (ICLI)
VEBG Balurghat [India] [ICAO location identifier] (ICLI)
VEBK Bokaro [India] [ICAO location identifier] (ICLI)
VEBL Barbil [India] [ICAO location identifier] (ICLI)
VEBR Visual Evoked Brain Response
VEBS Bhubaneswar [India] [ICAO location identifier] (ICLI)
VEBW Vacuum Electron Beam Welder
VEC Vacation Exchange Club (EA)
VEC Valence Electron Concentration (PDAA)
VEC Value Engineering Change
VEC Variable Energy Cyclotron (IEEE)
VEC Vector (KSC)
VEC Vector Control (MUGU)
VEC Venezolana Servicios Expresos de Carga Internacional CA [Venezuela] [ICAO designator] (FAAC)
VEC Vertical Electrical Chase [Nuclear energy] (NRCH)
VEC Vibration Exciter Control
VEC Video-Enhanced Contrast Technique [Microscopy]
VEC Visual Education Consultants, Inc. (AEBS)

VEC — Vocational Education Committee (ACII)
VEC — Voice Equivalent Channel (MCD)
VeCAL — Archivo del Libertador, Caracas, Venezuela [*Library symbol Library of Congress*] (LCLS)
VECAS — Vertical Escape Collision Avoidance System [*Aviation*]
VECC — Calcutta [*India*] [*ICAO location identifier*] (ICLI)
VECC — Value Engineering Control Committee [*Military*]
VECC — Variable Energy Content Curves (NOAA)
VECF — Calcutta [*India*] [*ICAO location identifier*] (ICLI)
VECG — Vector Electrocardiogram [*Cardiology*] (DAVI)
VECHCC — Voluntary Effort to Contain Health Care Costs (EA)
VECI — Vehicle Emission Control Information [*Automotive engineering*]
VECI — Vehicular Equipment Complement Index (IEEE)
VECIB — Vehicle Engineering Change Implementation Board (NASA)
VECK — Chakulia [*India*] [*ICAO location identifier*] (ICLI)
VECM — Vocational Education Curriculum Materials Database [*University of California, Berkeley*] [*Information service or system*] (CRD)
VECO — Cooch-Behar [*India*] [*ICAO location identifier*] (ICLI)
VECO — Veeco Instruments [*NASDAQ symbol*] (TTSB)
VECO — Veeco Instruments, Inc. [*NASDAQ symbol*] (SAG)
VECO — Vernier Engine Cutoff [*Aerospace*]
VECOS — Vehicle Checkout Set
VECP — Value Engineering Change Proposal [*Military*]
VECP — Visually Evoked Cortical Potential [*Neurophysiology*]
VECR — Vendor Engineering Change Request [*DoD*]
VECS — Videotex Editing Communications System (NITA)
VECS — Vocational Education Curriculum Specialists (OICC)
Vect — De Vectigalibus [*of Xenophon*] [*Classical studies*] (OCD)
V-ECT — Ventricular Ectopy
VECTAC — Vectored Attack [*Navy*] (NVT)
VECTAR — Value, Expertise, Client, Time, Attorney, Result [*Lawyer evaluation method*]
VectBk — Vectra Banking [*Associated Press*] (SAG)
VectraTc — Vectra Technologies [*Commercial firm Associated Press*] (SAG)
VECX — Car Nicobar [*India*] [*ICAO location identifier*] (ICLI)
VED — Vacuum Energy Diverter
VED — Vacuum Erection Device [*Medicine*]
VED — Ventricular Ectopic Depolarization
VED — Viscoelastic Damper
VED — Vitral Exhaustion and Depression (DAVI)
VED — Volumetric Energy Density [*of fuels*]
VEDA — Vestibular Disorders Association (EA)
VEDAR — Visible Energy Detection and Ranging
V-E (Day) — Victory in Europe Day [*World War II*]
VEDB — Dhanbad [*India*] [*ICAO location identifier*] (ICLI)
VEDC — Vitreous Enamel Development Council [*British*] (DI)
VEDIC — Video-Enhanced Differential Interference Contrast [*Microscopy*]
VEDILIS — Vehicle Discharge Lighting System
VEDR — Value Engineering Design Review
VEDS — Vehicle Emergency Detection System [*NASA*] (KSC)
VEDS — Vocational Education Data System
V Ed S — Vocational Education Specialist (PGP)
VEDZ — Deparizo [*India*] [*ICAO location identifier*] (ICLI)
V_{EE} — Emitter-Voltage Supply (IDOE)
VEE — Vagina, Ectocervix, and Endocervix [*Cytopathology*]
VEE — Vendee [*Legal shorthand*] (LWAP)
VEE — Venetie [*Alaska*] [*Airport symbol*] (OAG)
VEE — Venezuelan Equine Encephalomyelitis [*Virus*]
VEEAP — Vocational Education Evaluation and Assessment Process [*Pennsylvania*] (EDAC)
VEEC — Victorian Environmental Education Council (EERA)
VEECO — Vacuum Electronics Engineering Co. (MCD)
VeecoInst — Veeco Instruments, Inc. [*Associated Press*] (SAG)
VEEG — Vector Electroencephalograph
VEEGA — Venus-Earth-Earth-Gravity-Assist [*Spacecraft trajectory*]
VEEI — Vehicle Electrical Engine Interface [*NASA*] (NASA)
VEEI — Vehicle Electronics Engineering Institute
VEEITC — Victorian Electrical and Electronic Industry Training Committee [*Australia*]
VEEP — Vice President
VEER — Variable Emergence Electronically Rotated (MCD)
VEESS — Vehicle Engine Exhaust Smoke System [*Army*] (RDA)
VEF — Variable Electronic Filter
VEF — Ventricular Ejection Fraction [*Cardiology*] (DAVI)
VEF — Victorian Education Foundation [*Australia*]
VEF — Viscoelastic Fiber
VEF — Viscoelastic Flow
VEF — Vision Educational Foundation (EA)
VEF — Visually Evoked Field [*Neurophysiology*]
VEFCA — Value Engineering Functional Cost Analysis
VEFCO — Vertical Function Checkout
VEFV — Voice-Excitated Formant Vocoder (PDAA)
VEG — Maikwak [*Guyana*] [*Airport symbol*] (OAG)
VEG — Value Engineering Guideline
Veg — Vega [*Record label*] [*France*]
VEG — Vega Aircompany [*Russian Federation*] [*ICAO designator*] (FAAC)
VEG — Vegetable [*or Vegetation*] (KSC)
VEG — Vegetable
VEG — Vitreous Environmental Group
VEGA — Venera [*Venus*] and Gallei [*Halley*] [*Russian spacecraft*]
VEGANET — Vegetarian Awareness Network (EA)
VEGAS — Virtual-Egress Analysis and Simulation (ECON)
VEGEDINE — Association of Vegetarian Dietitians and Nutrition Educators (EA)
Veg Ex — Vegetable Exchange [*Dietetics*]
VEGF — Vascular Endothelial Growth Factor [*Biochemistry*]
VEGIL — Vehicle Equipment and Government-Furnished Infrared Locator
VEGK — Gorakhpur [*India*] [*ICAO location identifier*] (ICLI)
VEGL — Value Engineering Guideline
veg pcht — Vegetable Parchment [*Paper*] (DGA)
VEGT — Gauhati [*India*] [*ICAO location identifier*] (ICLI)
VEGY — Gaya [*India*] [*ICAO location identifier*] (ICLI)
VEH — Emory and Henry College, Emory, VA [*OCLC symbol*] (OCLC)
V_{EH} — Extrahepatic Distribution [*Gastroenterology*] (DAVI)
VEH — Valence Effective Hamiltonian [*Physical chemistry*]
VEH — Vehicle (AFM)
VEH — Veterinary Evacuation Hospital
VEHCAR — Cargo Loaded on Vehicles [*MTMC*] (TAG)
VEHDYN — Vehicle Dynamics
vehic — Vehicle (DAVI)
VEHIC — Vehicle
vehic — Vehiculum [*Vehicle*] [*Latin*] (MAE)
VEHID — Vehicle Identification [*NASA*] (MCD)
VEHK — Hirakud [*India*] [*ICAO location identifier*] (ICLI)
VEI — Value Engineered Indicator (NG)
VEI — Value Engineering Incentive [*Office of Federal Procurement Policy*]
VEI — Vehicle End Item (NASA)
VEI — Visual Exposure Indicator [*Advanced photo system*]
VEI — Volcanic Explosivity Index [*Measure of amounts of gas and ash that reach the atmosphere*]
VEIM — Imphal [*India*] [*ICAO location identifier*] (ICLI)
VEIS — Vocational Education Information System
VEITA — Vietnam Era Veterans Inter-Tribal Association (EA)
VEIX — VAALCO Energy [*NASDAQ symbol*] (TTSB)
VEJ — Aero Ejecutivos CA [*Venezuela*] [*ICAO designator*] (FAAC)
VEJH — Jharsuguda [*India*] [*ICAO location identifier*] (ICLI)
VEJP — Jeypore [*India*] [*ICAO location identifier*] (ICLI)
VEJS — Jamshedpur [*India*] [*ICAO location identifier*] (ICLI)
VEJT — Jorhat [*India*] [*ICAO location identifier*] (ICLI)
VEK — Veterana Esperantista Klubo [*Esperantist Club of Veterans - ECV*] (EAIO)
VEKH — Katihar [*India*] [*ICAO location identifier*] (ICLI)
VEKJ — Keonjhar [*India*] [*ICAO location identifier*] (ICLI)
VEKM — Kamalpur [*India*] [*ICAO location identifier*] (ICLI)
VEKN — Konark [*India*] [*ICAO location identifier*] (ICLI)
VEKR — Kailashahar [*India*] [*ICAO location identifier*] (ICLI)
VEKU — Silchar/Kumbhirgram [*India*] [*ICAO location identifier*] (ICLI)
VEKW — Khowai [*India*] [*ICAO location identifier*] (ICLI)
VEL — Vehicle Emissions and Fuel Economy Laboratory [*Texas A & M University*] [*Research center*] (RCD)
VEL — Vehicular Electronics Laboratory
Vel — Vela [*Constellation*]
VEL — Vellum
VEL — Velocity (AFM)
vel — Velocity (IDOE)
vel — Velvet (VRA)
VEL — Verified Encoded Logging (NTCM)
VEL — Vernal [*Utah*] [*Airport symbol*] (OAG)
VEL — Virginia Electric & Power Co. [*NYSE symbol*] (SPSG)
VEL — Virginia Power Capital Trust I [*NYSE symbol*] (SAG)
VELARC — Vertical Ejection Launch Aero-Reaction Control (MCD)
VELC — Velcro Industries NV [*NASDAQ symbol*] (NQ)
VELCF — Velcro Indus NV [*NASDAQ symbol*] (TTSB)
VELCOR — Velocity Correction
Velcro — Velcro Industries NV [*Associated Press*] (SAG)
VELCRO — Velour and Crochet [*Interlocking nylon tapes - one with tiny loops, the other with tiny hooks - invented as a reusable fastener by George de Mestral*]
VELES — Vibrational Energy Loss Electron Spectroscopy
VELF — Velocity Filter (IEEE)
VELG — Velocity Gain (AAG)
Vell Pat — Velleius Paterculus [*First century AD*] [*Classical studies*] (OCD)
VELOC — Velocity
VELPrE — Virginia El & Pwr $5 Pfd [*NYSE symbol*] (TTSB)
VELPrT — Va Pwr Cap Tr 1 8.05% Pfd [*NYSE symbol*] (TTSB)
VELR — Lilabari/North Lakhimpur [*India*] [*ICAO location identifier*] (ICLI)
vel sim — Vel Similis [*Or Similar*] [*Latin*] (WGA)
VEM — Eastern Mennonite College, Harrisonburg, VA [*OCLC symbol*] (OCLC)
VEM — Value Engineering Model (NG)
VEM — Vasoexcitor Material [*Physiology*]
VEM — Vector Element by Element Multiply (IAA)
VEM — Vendor Engineering Memorandum (MCD)
VEM — Versatile Exercise Mine [*Navy British*]
VEM — Vertical Extent of Mortality [*Intertidal organisms*]
VEM — Virtual Electrode Model (OA)
VEM — Voice E-Mail Messages [*Computer science*]
VEMASID — Vehicle Magnetic Signature Duplicator (MCD)
V_{Emax} — Maximum Flow Per Unit of Time [*Respiratory*] (DAVI)
VEMB — Victorian Egg Marketing Board [*Australia*]
VEMH — Malda [*India*] [*ICAO location identifier*] (ICLI)
VEMN — Mohanbari [*India*] [*ICAO location identifier*] (ICLI)
VEMP — Vincristine, Endoxan [*Cyclophosphamide*], 6-Mercaptopurine, Prednisone [*Antineoplastic drug regimen*] (DAVI)
VEMS — Vehicle and Equipment Maintenance System [*Software*]
VEMS — Vehicle Environment Management System [*Automotive engineering*]
VEMS — Versatile Exercise Mine System [*Military*] (PDAA)
VEMZ — Mazuffarpur [*India*] [*ICAO location identifier*] (ICLI)
VEN — Capital Aviation Services Ltd. [*Canada ICAO designator*] (FAAC)
VEN — Variable Exhaust Nozzle
Ven — Vendome [*Record label*] [*France*]

VEN............ Veneer (WDAA)
VEN............ Venerable
Ven............ Venerable (ODBW)
VEN............ Venereal (WDAA)
VEN............ Venetian
VEN............ Venezuela [*ANSI three-letter standard code*] (CNC)
VEN............ Venice [*Italy*] [*Seismograph station code, US Geological Survey Closed*] (SEIS)
VEN............ Venice [*Diocesan abbreviation*] [*Florida*] (TOCD)
VEN............ Venite [*95th Psalm*]
VEN............ Ventral (WDAA)
VEN............ Ventricle (WDAA)
VEN............ Venture Gold Corp. [*Vancouver Stock Exchange symbol*]
VEN............ Venture Stores [*NYSE symbol*] (TTSB)
VEN............ Venture Stores, Inc. [*NYSE symbol*] (SPSG)
VEN............ Venus (WDAA)
Ven............ Venus and Adonis [*Shakespearean work*]
VenAmCham... Venezuelan-American Chamber of Commerce and Industry (EA)
Ven & Ad..... Venus and Adonis [*Shakespearean poem*] (BARN)
Vencor......... Vencor, Inc. [*Associated Press*] (SAG)
VenCty......... Ventura County National Bancorp [*Associated Press*] (SAG)
VEND........... Vendor (KSC)
VEND........... Venerated
VENDAC....... Vendor Data Control
VENet.......... Vegetarian Education Network (EA)
VENET......... Venetian (ROG)
VEN EX........ Venditione Exponas [*Writ of Execution for Sheriff to Sell Goods*] [*Latin*] (ROG)
VENEZ......... Venezuela
Venez.......... Venezuela (VRA)
VEN FA........ Venire Facias [*Writ to Sheriff to Summon Jury*] [*Latin*] (ROG)
VENG........... Vengold, Inc. [*NASDAQ symbol*] (SAG)
VENGF......... Vengold Inc. [*NASDAQ symbol*] (TTSB)
Vengold........ Vengold, Inc. [*Associated Press*] (SAG)
VENP........... Nawapara [*India*] [*ICAO location identifier*] (ICLI)
VENP........... Vincristine, Endoxan [*Cyclophosphamide*], Natulan, Prednisone [*Procarbazine*] [*Antineoplastic drug regimen*]
VenPK.......... Venizelikon Phileleftheron Komma [*Venizelist Liberal Party*] [*Greek Political party*] (PPE)
VENPr.......... Venture Strs $3.25 Cv Dep Pfd [*NYSE symbol*] (TTSB)
VENR........... Veneer
VENS........... Versatile Exercise Mine System (DOMA)
VenSt........... Venture Stores, Inc. [*Associated Press*] (SAG)
VENT........... Ventilating
VENT........... Ventilation (AFM)
VENT........... Ventilator
VENT........... Ventricular [*Cardiology*]
VENT........... Ventriloquist
vent............ Ventriloquist (WDMC)
Vent............ Ventris' English Common Pleas Reports [*86 English Reprint*] [*A publication*] (DLA)
Vent............ Ventris' English King's Bench Reports [*A publication*] (DLA)
VENT........... Venturian Corp. [*NASDAQ symbol*] (NQ)
Vent (Eng)... Ventris' English Common Pleas Reports [*86 English Reprint*] [*A publication*] (DLA)
Vent (Eng)... Ventris' English King's Bench Reports [*A publication*] (DLA)
VENTEX........ Venting Experiment (USDC)
VENTEX........ Venting Experiment [*Marine science*] (OSRA)
VENT FIB..... Ventricular Fibrillation [*Also, VF, VFIB*] [*Cardiology*] (AAMN)
ventr........... Ventral
Ventr........... Ventris' English Common Pleas Reports [*86 English Reprint*] [*A publication*] (DLA)
ventric......... Ventricular
Ventricular Rhythm... Cardiology (DAVI)
Ventritx........ Ventritex, Inc. [*Associated Press*] (SAG)
VentSt.......... Venture Stores, Inc. [*Associated Press*] (SAG)
Venture........ Venture Seismic Ltd. [*Associated Press*] (SAG)
Venturn........ Venturian Corp. [*Associated Press*] (SAG)
Venul........... Venuleius Saturninus [*Flourished, 2nd century*] [*Authority cited in pre-1607 legal work*] (DSA)
VENUS......... Valuable and Effective Network Utility Services (BUR)
VENUS......... Variable and Efficient Network Utility Service (IAA)
VENUS......... Vertical Alignment Design by the Nodal-Tangent and Undulation System (PDAA)
VENUS......... Video-Enhanced User System [*Video conferencing*]
VENUS......... Vulcain Experimental Nuclear Study [*Nuclear reactor*] [*Belgium*]
VEO............ Value Engineering Organization
VEO............ Veronex Resources Ltd. [*Vancouver Stock Exchange symbol*]
VEO............ Visual Emission Observation [*Environmental Protection Agency*] (GFGA)
VEO............ Voluntary Environmental Organisation (EERA)
VEOP........... Veterans Education Outreach Program [*Department of Education*] (GFGA)
VEOS........... Versatile Electro-Optical System (MCD)
VEOXF......... Veronex Resources Ltd. (MHDW)
VEP............ Value Engineering Program
VEP............ Value Engineering Proposal [*Army*] (RDA)
VEP............ Vector Equilibrium Principle [*Crystallography*]
VEP............ Vertical Extrusion Press
VEP............ Veterans Education Project (EA)
VEP............ Visual Evoked Potential [*Electrophysiology*]
VEP............ Visually Evoked Potential [*Neurophysiology*]
VEP............ Vocational Exploration Program [*Office of Youth Programs*]
VEP............ Voter Education Project (EA)
VEPA........... Vincristine, Endoxan [*Cyclophosphamide*], Prednisone, Adriamycin [*Antineoplastic drug regimen*]
VEPA........... Vocational Education Planning Areas (OICC)
VEPB........... Port Blair [*India*] [*ICAO location identifier*] (ICLI)
VEPCO......... Virginia Electric & Power Co.
VEPG........... Pasighat [*India*] [*ICAO location identifier*] (ICLI)
VEPG........... Value Engineering Program Guideline
VEPH........... Panagarh [*India*] [*ICAO location identifier*] (ICLI)
VEPIS.......... Vocational Education Program Information System
VEPL........... Vendor Engineering Procurement Liaison (MCD)
VEPM........... Value Engineering Program Manager [*Military*] (AABC)
VEPN........... Phulbani [*India*] [*ICAO location identifier*] (ICLI)
VEPOL......... Vehicular Planimetric Dead Reckoning Computer Operating Language
VEPP........... Padampur [*India*] [*ICAO location identifier*] (ICLI)
VEPR........... Value Engineering Program Requirement [*Office of Federal Procurement Policy*] (NG)
VEPT........... Patna [*India*] [*ICAO location identifier*] (ICLI)
VEQ............ Variation in Estimated Quantity (AAGC)
VEQ............ Visiting Enlisted Quarters [*Army*] (AABC)
VEQ............ Vuelos Ejecutivos de Quertaro, SA de CV [*Mexico*] [*FAA designator*] (FAAC)
VER............ Boonville, MO [*Location identifier FAA*] (FAAL)
VER............ Vacuum Enhanced Recovery [*Computer science*]
VER............ Venus, SA [*Greece*] [*FAA designator*] (FAAC)
VER............ Veracruz [*Mexico*] [*Airport symbol*] (OAG)
VER............ Verandah [*Classified advertising*] (ADA)
VER............ Verapamil [*A coronary vasodilator*]
VER............ Vereda
VER............ Verein [*Association*] [*German*]
Ver............ Vereniging [*Association*] [*Dutch*] (ILCA)
VER............ Verge (ROG)
VER............ Verify (AFM)
Ver............ Veritas [*A publication*]
VER............ Vermifuge [*Destroying Worms*] [*Pharmacy*] (ROG)
VER............ Vermilion (ROG)
VER............ Vermillion Resources [*Vancouver Stock Exchange symbol*]
VER............ Vermont (ROG)
Ver............ Vermont Reports [*A publication*] (DLA)
VER............ Vernier [*Engine*] (AAG)
VER............ Verse
VER............ Version (ROG)
ver............ Version (VRA)
VER............ Vert [*Heraldry*]
VER............ Vertex (WGA)
VER............ Vertical (KSC)
VER............ Vertical Earth Rate
VER............ Vertical Ejector Rack (MCD)
VER............ Veterans Employment Representative [*Department of Labor*]
VER............ Visual Evoked Response
VER............ Voluntary Export Restraints
VERA........... Ranuna [*India*] [*ICAO location identifier*] (ICLI)
VERA........... Variable Eddington Radiation Approximation (MCD)
VERA........... Versatile Experimental Reactor Assembly (DEN)
VERA........... Veterans' Employment and Readjustment Act of 1972
VERA........... Vision Electric Recording Apparatus [*BBC*]
VERA........... Voluntary Early Retirement Authority [*DoD*]
VERAS......... Vehicule Experimental de Recherches Aerothermodynamique et Structurale [*Glider*] [*France*]
VERB........... Verbatim (MSA)
VERB........... Verbessert [*Improved*] [*German*]
verb............ Verbum [*Verb*] [*Latin*]
VERB........... Victor Electrowriter Remote Blackboard [*Educational device of Victor Comptometer Corp.*]
VERB........... Visual Electronic Remote Blackboard (PDAA)
VERB ET LIT... Verbatim et Literatim [*Word for Word, An Exact Copy*] [*Latin*] (ROG)
Verb Sap..... Verbum Sapienti Sat Est [*A Word to the Wise Is Sufficient*] [*Latin*]
VERC........... Ranchi [*India*] [*ICAO location identifier*] (ICLI)
VERC........... Vacation Eligibility and Request Card [*Military*]
VERC........... Vehicle Effectiveness Remaining Converter
Verc............ Vervet [*African green monkey*] [*Medicine*] (DMAA)
VERDAN....... Versatile Differential Analyzer
VERDAN....... Vertical Digital Analyzer (IAA)
VERDIN........ Antijam MODEM [*Modulate, Demodulate*], Very-Low Frequency (CAAL)
VERDT......... Verdict (ROG)
VERDUP....... Verify Duplication (DNAB)
VEREAD....... Value Engineering Retrieval of Esoteric Administrative Data (PDAA)
verfx........... Verifax (VRA)
VERG........... Rayaguda [*India*] [*ICAO location identifier*] (ICLI)
Verg............ Vergil [*First century BC*] [*Classical studies*] (OCD)
VERGL......... Vergleische [*Compare*] [*German*] (ROG)
Ver Hist...... Verae Historiae [*of Lucian*] [*Classical studies*] (OCD)
VERI........... Vineyard Environmental Research Institute [*Research center*] (RCD)
VERIC......... Vocational Education Resources Information Center
VERIF.......... Verification (MSA)
Verifne........ Verifone, Inc. [*Associated Press*] (SAG)
Verilink........ Verilink Corp. [*Associated Press*] (SAG)
VERIS.......... Vitamin E Research and Information Service (EA)
Veritas......... Veritas Music Entertainment, Inc. [*Associated Press*] (SAG)
VeritasSf...... Veritas Software Corp. [*Associated Press*] (SAG)
VeritCarit..... Veritatem in Caritate. Orgaan van de Protestanse Theologische Faculteit te Brussel [*A publication*] (BJA)
VeritDGC...... Veritas DGC, Inc. [*Associated Press*] (SAG)

Verity.......... Verity, Inc. [*Associated Press*] (SAG)
VERK.......... Rourkela [*India*] [*ICAO location identifier*] (ICLI)
VERL.......... Raxaul [*India*] [*ICAO location identifier*] (ICLI)
VERLORT..... Very-Long-Range Tracking [*NASA*]
VERLOT...... Very-Long-Range Tracking [*NASA*] (DNAB)
VERM.......... Vermilion (ROG)
VERM.......... Vermont
Verm.......... Vermont Reports [*A publication*] (DLA)
Vermont R... Vermont Reports [*A publication*] (DLA)
Vermont Rep... Vermont Reports [*A publication*] (DLA)
VermPu........ Vermont Pure Holdings [*Commercial firm Associated Press*] (SAG)
Vermt.......... Vermont Reports [*A publication*] (DLA)
VERN.......... Rangeilunda [*India*] [*ICAO location identifier*] (ICLI)
VERN.......... Vernacular (ADA)
VERN.......... Vernier [*Engineering*]
Vern.......... Vernon's English Chancery Reports [*23 English Reprint*] [*A publication*] (DLA)
Vern & S..... Vernon and Scriven's Irish King's Bench Reports [*1786-88*] [*A publication*] (DLA)
Vern & Sc.... Vernon and Scriven's Irish King's Bench Reports [*1786-88*] [*A publication*] (DLA)
Vern & Scr... Vernon and Scriven's Irish King's Bench Reports [*1786-88*] [*A publication*] (DLA)
Vern & Scriv... Vernon and Scriven's Irish King's Bench Reports [*1786-88*] [*A publication*] (DLA)
Vern & S (Ir)... Vernon and Scriven's Irish King's Bench Reports [*1786-88*] [*A publication*] (DLA)
VERNAV....... Vertical Navigation System
Vern (Eng)... Vernon's English Chancery Reports [*23 English Reprint*] [*A publication*] (DLA)
VERNITRAC... Vernier Tracking by Automatic Correlation [*Aerospace*]
Vernitrn....... Vernitron Corp. [*Associated Press*] (SAG)
Vernon's Ann CCP... Vernon's Annotated Texas Code of Criminal Procedure [*A publication*] (DLA)
Vernon's Ann Civ St... Vernon's Annotated Texas Civil Statutes [*A publication*] (DLA)
Vernon's Ann PC... Vernon's Annotated Texas Penal Code [*A publication*] (DLA)
Vernt.......... Vernitron Corp. [*Associated Press*] (SAG)
VERONICA... Very Easy Rodent-Oriented Net-Wide Index of Computerized Archives
VERP.......... Vertical Effective Radiated Power (MCD)
VERP.......... Viragen Europe Ltd. [*NASDAQ symbol*] (SAG)
VERP.......... Visitor Experience and Resource Protection [*Park tourism management*]
Verpl Cont... Verplanck on Contracts [*A publication*] (DLA)
Verpl Ev...... Verplanck on Evidence [*A publication*] (DLA)
Verr.......... In Verrem [*of Cicero*] [*Classical studies*] (OCD)
Ver Rep....... Vermont Reports [*A publication*] (DLA)
VERRP........ Voluntary Early Release and Retirement Program [*Army*]
VERS.......... Versed Sine [*Engineering*] (KSC)
vers.......... Versed Sine (IDOE)
VERS.......... Versicherung [*Insurance*] [*German Business term*]
VERS.......... Version (ROG)
Versa.......... Versa Technologies, Inc. [*Associated Press*] (SAG)
VERSACOMM... Versatile Contour Measuring Machine (MCD)
Versar.......... Versar, Inc. [*Associated Press*] (SAG)
VERSO........ Reverso [*Left-Hand Page of Open Book*] (ROG)
VERST........ Versatile
VERT.......... Venture Evaluation and Review Technique
Vert.......... Vermont Reports [*A publication*] (DLA)
Vert.......... Vertebra [*or Vertebral*] [*Anatomy*] (DAVI)
VERT.......... Vertebrate
VERT.......... Vertical (MCD)
vert.......... Vertical (IDOE)
vert.......... Vertical (WDMC)
Vert.......... Vertical Lights [*Navigation signal*]
VERT.......... Vertical Polarization (AFM)
VERT.......... Vertigo (WDAA)
VERT-2-EXP... Vertical Double-Expansion [*Engine*] (DNAB)
VERT-3-EXP... Vertical Triple-Expansion [*Engine*] (DNAB)
VERT-4-EXP... Vertical Quadruple-Expansion [*Engine*] (DNAB)
VERTAR....... Versatile Test Analysis RADAR (MCD)
VERTCL....... Vertical Clearance (DNAB)
VERTEB....... Vertebrate
VERTEX....... Vertical Transport and Exchange [*Oceanographic research program*]
VertexC....... Vertex Communications Corp. [*Associated Press*] (SAG)
Vertexl....... Vertex Industries, Inc. [*Associated Press*] (SAG)
VERTIC........ Verification Technology Information Centre [*British*] (CB)
VERTICAM... Vertical Camera (WDAA)
VERTIJET..... Vertical Takeoff and Landing Jet [*Aircraft*]
VERTIS........ Vehicle, Road, and Traffic Intelligence Society
VERTOL....... Vertical Takeoff and Landing [*Also, VTOL*]
VERTREP..... Vertical Replenishment [*Navy*] (NVT)
VertxPh....... Vertex Pharmaceuticals, Inc. [*Associated Press*] (SAG)
VERU.......... Rupsi [*India*] [*ICAO location identifier*] (ICLI)
veru.......... Verumontanum [*Anatomy*] (DAVI)
VERVIS........ Vertical Visibility [*Aviation*] (DA)
VerwG......... Verwaltungsgericht [*Administrative Court or Tribunal*] [*German*] (ILCA)
VES.......... Vacuum Evaporator System
VES.......... Vapor Extraction System [*Engineering*]
VES.......... Variable Elasticity of Substitution [*Industrial production*]
VES.......... Variable Explanation Sheet [*Army*]
VES.......... Vector Element by Element Sum (IAA)
VES.......... Vehicle Ecological System (AAG)
VES.......... Vehicle Engagement Simulator (MCD)
VES.......... Versailles, OH [*Location identifier FAA*] (FAAL)
Ves.......... Vesey, Senior's, English Chancery Reports [*27, 28 English Reprint*] [*A publication*] (DLA)
VES.......... Vesica [*Bladder*] [*Latin*] (ADA)
VES.......... Vesicula [*Blister*] [*Latin*] (ADA)
VES.......... Vesicular (AAMN)
VES.......... Vespere [*In the Evening*] [*Latin*] (ADA)
VES.......... Vessel (AABC)
ves.......... Vessel (VRA)
VES.......... Vestaur Securities [*NYSE symbol*] (TTSB)
VES.......... Vestaur Securities, Inc. [*NYSE symbol*] (SPSG)
VES.......... Vestry [*Ecclesiastical*] (WGA)
VES.......... Veterans Employment Service [*Later, VETS*] [*of USES*]
VES.......... Veterinary Evacuating Station [*British military*] (DMA)
VES.......... Victorian Era Series [*A publication*]
VES.......... Vieques Air Link, Inc. [*ICAO designator*] (FAAC)
VES.......... Vision Enhancement System
VES.......... Visual Effects Simulator (MCD)
VES.......... Visual Efficiency Scale
VES.......... Voluntary Euthanasia Society [*British*] (DBA)
VES.......... Vulcan Engagement Simulator (MCD)
VESA.......... Video Electronics Standards Association
VESA.......... Video Electronics Standards Association (ACII)
Ves & B....... Vesey and Beames' English Chancery Reports [*35 English Reprint*] [*A publication*] (DLA)
Ves & Bea... Vesey and Beames' English Chancery Reports [*35 English Reprint*] [*A publication*] (DLA)
Ves & Beam... Vesey and Beames' English Chancery Reports [*35 English Reprint*] [*A publication*] (DLA)
Ves & B (Eng)... Vesey and Beames' English Chancery Reports [*35 English Reprint*] [*A publication*] (DLA)
VESAT.......... Venus Environmental Satellite [*NASA, proposed*]
VESC.......... Vehicle Equipment Safety Commission
VESCAD....... Vehicle Electrical System Computer-Aided Design
VESCA(S)..... Vessels and Cargo
VESCF.......... Variable Eletronegativity Self-Consistent Field [*Physics*]
VESDA.......... Very Early Smoke Detection Alarm
VESE.......... Value Engineering Staff Engineer
VESG.......... Vocational Education Services Grant (OICC)
VESI.......... Victor Educational Services Institute [*Educational division of Victor Comptometer Corp.*]
VESIAC........ Vela Seismic Information Analysis Center (SAA)
Vesic.......... Vesicula [*Blister*] [*Latin*]
vesic.......... Vesicular
VESID.......... Vocational and Educational Services for Individuals with Disabilities
Ves Jr.......... Vesey, Junior's, English Chancery Reports [*30-34 English Reprint*] [*A publication*] (DLA)
Ves Jr (Eng)... Vesey, Junior's, English Chancery Reports [*30-34 English Reprint*] [*A publication*] (DLA)
Ves Jr Suppl... Supplement to Vesey, Junior's, English Chancery Reports, by Hovenden [*34 English Reprint*] [*A publication*] (DLA)
Ves Jun....... Vesey, Junior's, English Chancery Reports [*30-34 English Reprint*] [*A publication*] (DLA)
Ves Jun Supp... Supplement to Vesey, Junior's, English Chancery Reports, by Hovenden [*34 English Reprint*] [*A publication*] (DLA)
Ves Jun Supp (Eng)... Supplement to Vesey, Junior's, English Chancery Reports, by Hovenden [*34 English Reprint*] [*A publication*] (DLA)
VESMC.......... Vinyl Ester Sheet Molding Compound [*Plastics*]
VESO.......... Vocalization of the Egyptian Syllabic Orthography [*W. F. Albright*] [*A publication*] (BJA)
VESP.......... Value Engineering Supplier Program
Vesp.......... Vespae [*Wasps*] [*of Aristophanes*] [*Classical studies*] (OCD)
VESP.......... Vesper [*Evening*] [*Pharmacy*]
VESPER........ Vehicle Sizing and Performance (MCD)
VESR.......... Vallecitos Experimental Superheat Reactor
VESR.......... Value Engineering Study Request (MCD)
VESS.......... Vehicle Exhaust Smoke System (MCD)
VESS.......... Visual Environment Simulation System (MCD)
Ves Sen....... Vesey, Senior's, English Chancery Reports [*27, 28 English Reprint*] [*A publication*] (DLA)
Ves Sen Supp... Supplement to Vesey, Senior's, English Chancery Reports [*28 English Reprint*] [*A publication*] (DLA)
Ves Sr.......... Vesey, Senior's, English Chancery Reports [*27, 28 English Reprint*] [*A publication*] (DLA)
Ves Sr (Eng)... Vesey, Senior's, English Chancery Reports [*27, 28 English Reprint*] [*A publication*] (DLA)
Ves Sr Supp... Supplement to Vesey, Senior's, English Chancery Reports [*28 English Reprint*] [*1747-56*] [*A publication*] (DLA)
Ves Sr Supp (Eng)... Supplement to Vesey, Senior's, English Chancery Reports [*28 English Reprint*] [*A publication*] (DLA)
Ves Supp...... Supplement to Vesey, Junior's, English Chancery Reports, by Hovenden [*34 English Reprint*] [*1789-1817*] [*A publication*] (DLA)
VEST.......... Vertical Earth Scanning Test (SAA)
VEST.......... Vestibular [*Medicine*] (CPH)
VEST.......... Vestibule (MSA)
VEST.......... Vestro Natural Foods [*NASDAQ symbol*] (TTSB)
VEST.......... Vestro Natural Foods, Inc. [*NASDAQ symbol*] (NQ)
VEST.......... Vestry [*Ecclesiastical*] (ROG)
VEST.......... Volunteer Engineers, Scientists, and Technicians [*An association*]
VESTA.......... Vehicle Structure Analysis [*Automotive design*]
Vestalns....... Vesta Insurance Group [*Associated Press*] (SAG)
Vestro.......... Vestro Foods, Inc. [*Associated Press*] (SAG)
VestSe.......... Vestaur Securities, Inc. [*Associated Press*] (SAG)
VES UR........ Vesica Urinaria [*Urinary Bladder*]

VESV Vesicular Exanthema Swine Virus
VET Care Vet Pharmacy [*Vancouver Stock Exchange symbol*]
VET Value Engineering Training
VET Vehicle Elapsed Time (MCD)
VeT Ventilatory Threshold [*Cardiology*]
VET Verbal Test
VET Versatile Engine Tester
VET Vertical Test (SAA)
VET Vestigial Testes [*Anatomy*]
VET Veteran (AFM)
VET Veterans Administration, Somerville, NJ [*OCLC symbol*] (OCLC)
VET Veterinary (AFM)
VET Vibrational Energy Transfer [*LASER*] (MCD)
v et Vide Etiam [*See Also*] [*Latin*] (MAE)
VET Video Editing Terminal [*Computer science*]
VET Vidicon Electron Tube
VET Visual Editing Terminal (NITA)
VET Voice Entry Terminal (NITA)
VET Voluntary Early Transition [*Military*]
VET ADMIN Veterans Administration (WDAA)
VetAm Veterinary Centers of America, Inc. [*Associated Press*] (SAG)
VetCtAm Veterinary Centers of America, Inc. [*Associated Press*] (SAG)
VETDOC Veterinary Documentation (NITA)
VETDOC Veterinary Literature Documentation [*Derwent Publications Ltd.*] [*Bibliographic database London, England*]
VETF Vaccinia Early Transcription Factor [*Genetics*]
VETF Value Engineering Task Force
VETFR Veterans Transition Franchise Initiative Program
Vet Int Veteres Intrationes [*A publication*] (DLA)
VETJ Tezu [*India*] [*ICAO location identifier*] (ICLI)
VETK Tarakeshwar [*India*] [*ICAO location identifier*] (ICLI)
Vet MB Bachelor of Veterinary Medicine
Vet Med Veterinary Medicine (DAVI)
VETMIS Vehicle Technical Management Information System
VETMIS Vertical Technical Management Information System (MCD)
Vet Na B Old Natura Brevium [*A publication*] (DLA)
Vet N B Vetus Natura Brevium [*A publication*] (DSA)
Vet N Br Old Natura Brevium [*A publication*] (ILCA)
VETP Vandenberg Engineering Test Program (SAA)
VETRN Veterinarian
VETRNRY Veterinary
VETRONICS Vehicle Electronics [*Program*] [*Army*]
VETS Pet Practice [*NASDAQ symbol*] (TTSB)
VETS [*The*] Pet Practice, Inc. [*NASDAQ symbol*] (SAG)
VETS Tusra [*India*] [*ICAO location identifier*] (ICLI)
VETS Vehicle Electrical Test System (ADA)
VETS Venture Touring Society
VETS Vertical Engine Test Stand
VETS Veterans Adjustment Scale (MEDA)
VETS Veterans' Employment and Training Service [*Department of Labor*]
VetSci Veterinary Science
Vett Cens De Veterum Censura [*of Dionysius Halicarnassensis*] [*Classical studies*] (OCD)
VETX Vertex Industries [*NASDAQ symbol*] (TTSB)
VETX Vertex Industries, Inc. [*Clifton, NJ*] [*NASDAQ symbol*] (NQ)
VETY Vocabulary Etymology
VEU Very Extreme Ultraviolet (MCD)
VEUK Utkela [*India*] [*ICAO location identifier*] (ICLI)
VEUV Very Extreme Ultraviolet (MCD)
VEV Barakoma [*Solomon Islands*] [*Airport symbol*] (OAG)
VEV Vernier Engine Vibration [*Aerospace*]
VEV Vietnam Era Veterans (OICC)
VEV Vlaams Economisch Verbond
VEV Voice-Excited VOCODER
VEVA Vereingung der Europaischen Verbande des Automatenwirtschaft [*Federation of European Coin-Machine Associations*] (EAIO)
VEVERP Vietnam Era Veteran Recruitment Program
VEVITA Vietnam Era Veterans Inter-Tribal Association (EA)
VEVRA Vietnam Era Veterans Readjustment and Assistance Act of 1974 (WYGK)
VEVZ Vishakhapatnam [*India*] [*ICAO location identifier*] (ICLI)
VEWAA Vocational Evaluation and Work Adjustment Association (EA)
VEWS Very Early Warning System
VEWU Vietnam Educational Workers' Union [*North Vietnam*]
VEX Tioga, ND [*Location identifier FAA*] (FAAL)
VEXP Virtual Machine Experience
VEY Vestmannaeyjar [*Iceland*] [*Airport symbol*] (OAG)
Vez Vezey's [*or Vesey's*] English Chancery Reports [*A publication*] (DLA)
VEZO Zero [*India*] [*ICAO location identifier*] (ICLI)
VF British Air Ferries [*ICAO designator*] (AD)
VF Fighter Plane [*Navy symbol*]
VF Fighter Squadron [*Navy symbol*]
VF Flaps-Down Speed [*Aviation*]
VF Golden West [*ICAO designator*] (AD)
VF Vache Follet [*Mad Cow*] [*Deragatory term for French meat*]
VF Vacuum Fluorescent [*Graphic arts*] (DGA)
VF Valley Forge [*AMEX symbol*] (TTSB)
VF Valley Forge Corp. [*AMEX symbol*] (SPSG)
VF Value Foundation (EA)
VF Vanity Fair [*A publication*] (WDMC)
VF Vaporizer Feed [*Nuclear energy*] (NRCH)
VF Variable Factor [*Economics*]
VF Variable Frequency [*Electricity*] (MSA)
VF Variant Frequency [*Biology*]
VF Vector Field
VF Velocity Failure
VF Ventral Funiculus [*Anatomy*]
VF Ventricular Fibrillation [*Also, vent fib, VFIB*] [*Cardiology*]
VF Ventricular Fluid [*Cardiology*] (MAE)
VF Ventricular Flutter [*Cardiology*] (AAMN)
VF Verification of Function
VF Vertical File
VF Vertical Flight (NASA)
VF Very Fair
VF Very Fine [*Condition*] [*Antiquarian book trade, numismatics, etc.*]
VF Very Fine Soil [*Agronomy*]
VF VFW [*Vereinigte Flugtechnische Werke*]-Fokker [*Germany ICAO aircraft manufacturer identifier*] (ICAO)
VF Viane Francaise [*French Meat*]
VF Vicarius Foraneus [*Vicar-Forane*] [*Latin*]
VF Video Frequency
VF View Factor
VF Viewfinder [*Photography*]
VF Villers Foundation [*Later, Families USA Foundation*] (EA)
VF Vinyl Fabric [*Technical drawings*]
VF Vinylferrocene [*Organic chemistry*]
VF Virile Female Project [*RJ Reynolds Tobacco Co. marketing strategy for proposed Dakota brand*]
VF Virtual Floppy [*Computer science*] (PCM)
VF Viscosity Factor (IAA)
VF Vision Field [*Ophthalmology*] (DAVI)
VF Vision Foundation (EA)
VF Vision Frequency
VF Visiting Friends [*An association*] (EA)
VF Visual Field
VF Visual Field [*Ophthalmology*] (DAVI)
VF Vocal Fremitus
VF Voice Foundation (EA)
VF Voice Frequency [*Communications*]
VF Volcanic Front [*Geology*]
V/F Voltage to Frequency [*Converter*] [*Computer science*]
VF Volunteer Fireman
VF Vulcanized Fiber
VFA Variation Flow Analysis
VFA Victoria Falls [*Zimbabwe*] [*Airport symbol*] (OAG)
VFA Video Free America (EA)
VFA Video Frequency Amplifier
VFA Videotape Facilities Association (EA)
VFA Visual Flight Attachment [*Aviation*] (RDA)
VFA Volatile Fatty Acid [*Organic chemistry*]
VFA Volunteer Fire Alarm (TEL)
VFAM Vincristine, 5-Fluorouracil, Adriamycin, Mitomycin C [*Antineoplastic drug regimen*] (DAVI)
VFAS Vertical Force Accounting System
VFAS/TL Vertical Force Accounting System/Troop List (MCD)
VFAT Virtual File Allocation Table [*Computer science*] (CDE)
VFAT Visual Functioning Assessment Tool [*Educational test*]
VF AW Fighter Squadron - All Weather [*Navy symbol*] (MCD)
VFAW Victorian Fellowship of Australian Writers [*Australia*]
VFAX Heavier-than-Air Fighter/Attack/Experimental [*Aircraft*]
V_{FB} Feedback Voltage (IDOE)
VFB Fighter Bombing Plane [*Navy symbol*]
VFB Vertical Format Buffer
VFB Visual Form Builder [*Computer science*] (PCM)
VFC Ferrum College, Ferrum, VA [*OCLC symbol*] (OCLC)
VFC Variable File Channel
VFC Variable Frequency Clock (IAA)
VFC Variable Frequency Control
VFC Variable Frequency Crystal (IAA)
VFC Vector Function Chainer (MHDB)
VFC Ventricular Function Curve [*Cardiology*] (AAMN)
VFC Vertical Format Control
VFC Vertical Forms Control (MHDB)
VFC Very Fine Cognac
VFC V Fan Club (EA)
VFC VF Corp. [*NYSE symbol*] (SPSG)
VFC Video Film Converter (OA)
VFC Video Frequency Carrier [*or Channel*] (CET)
VFC Visual Field Control [*Aviation*]
VFC Voice Frequency Carrier [*or Channel*]
VFC Volatile Flavor Compound
VFC Voltage to Frequency Converter
VFC Volunteer Field Consultant [*Red Cross*]
VFC Vortex Flow Control
VFC Voters for Choice/Friends of Family Planning (EA)
VFC/FFP Voters for Choice/Friends of Family Planning [*Later, VFC*] (EA)
VFCG Voice Frequency Telegraph [*Telecommunications*] (OSI)
VF Cp VF Corp. [*Associated Press*] (SAG)
VFCP Voix des Femmes Canadiennes pour la Paix [*Canadian Voice of Women for Peace*] [*See also VOW*] [*Canada*] (EAIO)
VFCPC Victorian Federation of Catholic Parents' Clubs [*Australia*]
VFCS Vehicle Flight Control System
VFCT Voice Frequency Carrier [*or Channel*] Telegraph [*or Teletype*]
VFCTT Voice Frequency Carrier Teletype (MSA)
VFD Vacuum Fluorescent Display [*Computer science*]
VFD Value for Duty [*Business term*]
VFD Variable Frequency Drive [*Instrumentation*]
VFD Verified Free Distribution [*British*]
VFD Vocal Feedback Device [*Aid for stutterers developed at the University of Pittsburgh by Dr. George Shames*]

VFD Voltage Fault Detector [*Electronics*] (IAA)
VFD Volunteer Fire Department
VFDF Very Fast Death Factor
VFDF Victorian Football Development Foundation [*Australia*]
VFDM Vsemirnaia Federatsiia Demokraticheskoi Molodezhi [*World Federation of Democratic Youth*]
VFDMIS Vertical Force Development Management Information Systems
VFDR Variable-Flow Directed Rocket
VFE Vendor-Furnished Equipment (NASA)
VFEA Vacuum Freezing Ejector Absorption (PDAA)
VFEQT Voice Frequency Equipment [*Telecommunications*] (IAA)
VFER Veterans Federal Employment Representative [*Civil Service Commission*]
VFET Vertical Field Effect Transistor (IAA)
VFF Valence Force Field
VFF Victorian Farmers Federation (EERA)
VFF Voice Frequency Filter
VFF Volunteer Firefighter
VFFC Virginia First Financial [*NASDAQ symbol*] (TTSB)
VFFC Virginia First Financial Corp. [*NASDAQ symbol*] (SAG)
VFFDR Variable Fuel Flow Ducted Rocket (MCD)
VFFIA Victorian Farmers' Federation Industrial Association [*Australia*]
VFFT Voice Frequency Facility Terminal [*Telecommunications*] (TEL)
VFG Valley Fig Growers (EA)
VFH Vacuum Film Handling
VFH Vertical Flow Horizontal
VFHS Valley Forge Historical Society (EA)
VFHT Vacuum Film Handling Technique
VFI Valve Fuel Injection [*Automotive engineering*]
VFI Verification Flight Instrumentation (NASA)
VFI Verifone, Inc. [*NYSE symbol*] (SAG)
VFI VF RADAR Intercept Officer (DNAB)
VFI Vinyl Fabrics Institute [*Later, Chemical Fabrics and Film Association*] (EA)
VFI Visual Field Information [*Aviation*]
VFI Vocational Foundation, Inc. (EA)
VFI Volunteers for Israel (EA)
VFIB Ventricular Fibrillation [*Also, vent fib, VF*] [*Cardiology*]
VFIT Visual Field(s) Intact [*Ophthalmology*] (DAVI)
VFITC Victorian Fishing Industry Training Committee [*Australia*]
VFK Variable Function Key [*Computer science*] (ECII)
VFL LeMoyne College, Syracuse, NY [*OCLC symbol*] (OCLC)
VFL Variable Field Length (MCD)
VFL Variable Focal Length
VFL Ventricular Filling Pressure [*Cardiology*] (DAVI)
VFL Ventricular Flutter [*Cardiology*] (DAVI)
VFL Victorian Football League [*Receives television coverage in the US through the Entertainment and Sports Programming Network*] [*Australia*]
VFL Voice Frequency Line [*Telecommunications*] (TEL)
VFL Voyageur FL Insured Muni Inc. [*AMEX symbol*] (TTSB)
VFL Voyageur Florida Insured Municipal Income Fund [*AMEX symbol*] (SPSG)
VFLA Volume Folding and Limiting Amplifier
VFLC Video Fluorometric Detection Liquid Chromatograph
VFLX Variflex, Inc. [*NASDAQ symbol*] (SAG)
VF(M) Fighter Plane (Two-Engine) [*Navy symbol*]
VFM Vacuum Forming Machine
VFM Value for Money [*Accounting*]
VFM Van Kam Am Cap FL Qual Mun [*NYSE symbol*] (TTSB)
VFM Van Kampen Merritt Florida Quality Municipal [*NYSE symbol*] (SPSG)
VFM Variable Frequency Monitor [*Sony Corp.*]
VFM Vendor-Furnished Material (MCD)
VFM Vertical Flight Maneuver
VFM Volt Frequency Monitor (DNAB)
VFMED Variable Format Message Entry Device [*Computer science*] (MCD)
VF(N) Night Fighter Squadrons [*Navy symbol*]
VFN Verticillium Wilt, Fusarium Wilt, Nematode Resistance [*Tomato culture*]
VFNP Victorian Food and Nutrition Program [*Australia*]
VFO Vandenberg Field Office [*Air Force*] (MCD)
VFO Vaporized Fuel Oil [*Process*]
VFO Variable Frequency Oscillator
VFO Viking Flight Operations [*NASA*]
VFO Voice Frequency Oscillator (NITA)
VFOAR Vandenberg Field Office of Aerospace Research [*Air Force*] (PDAA)
VFON Volunteer Flight Officers Network
V-format Variable Length File Format (NITA)
V for V Volunteers for Vision [*Defunct*] (EA)
VFP Fighter Squadron, Photo [*Navy symbol*] (MCD)
VFP Vacuum Flash Pyrolysis
VFP Vacuum Fore Pump
VFP Variable-Factor Programming
VFP Variance Frequency Processor (MCD)
VFP Ventricular Fluid Pressure [*Cardiology*] (MAE)
VFP Vereenigde Feministiche Partij [*Belgium Political party*] (EY)
VFP Veterans for Peace (EA)
VFP Vitreous Fluorophotometry [*Ophthalmology*] (DAVI)
VFP Volatile Fission Product [*Nuclear energy*] (NUCP)
VFP Volunteers for Peace (EA)
VFP Vsemirnaja Federacija Profsojuzov [*World Federation of Trade Unions*]
VFPC Vertical Flight Performance Criteria
VFPR Via Flight Planned Route [*Aviation*] (FAAC)
VFR Vehicle Flight Readiness (KSC)
VFR Vehicle Force Ratio (MCD)
VFR Verein fuer Raumschiffahrt [*Society for Space Travel*] [*Germany*]
VFR Visiting Friends and Relatives [*Airlines*]
VFR Visual Flight Rules [*Aviation*]
VFR Volunteer Field Representative [*Red Cross*]
VFRA Volume Footwear Retailers of America [*Later, FDRA*]
VFRC Valley Forge Research Center [*University of Pennsylvania*] [*Research center*] (RCD)
VFRCTS Visual Flight Rules Control Tower Simulator [*Aviation*] (MCD)
VFS Vapor Feed System
VFS Variable Frequency Synthesizer [*Ariel Corp.*] [*Computer science*]
VFS Ventilated Flight Suit
VFS Video Frame Store (NITA)
VFS Virtual File Server [*Telecommunications*] (OSI)
VFS Virtual File Store [*Telecommunications*] (OSI)
VFS Visual Flight Simulator
VFS Voice from the Silence [*An association*] (EA)
VFS Volume Fraction of Solids in a Slurry
VFSB Verein der Freunde Schloss Blutenburg [*Association of Friends of Schloss Blutenburg-AFSB*] [*Germany*] (EAIO)
VFSC Vermont Financial Services Corp. [*NASDAQ symbol*] (NQ)
VFSC Vermont Fin'l Svcs [*NASDAQ symbol*] (TTSB)
VFSS Variable Frequency Selection System [*Aviation*] (DA)
VFSS Voice Frequency Signaling System
VFST Victorian Foundation for Survivors of Torture [*Australia*]
VFSW Variable Frequency Sine Wave
VFT Vacuum Form Tool (MCD)
VFT Vacuum Friction Test
VFT Velocity False Target [*Military*] (CAAL)
VFT Ventricular Fibrillation Threshold [*Cardiology*]
VFT Verbal Fluency Test [*Speech and language therapy*] (DAVI)
VFT Verification Flight Test (MCD)
VFT Vertical Flight Test (MCD)
VFT Very Fast Train (EERA)
VFT Viking Flight Team [*NASA*]
VFT Voice Frequency Telegraphy (NATG)
VFT Voice Frequency Terminal
VFTG Voice Frequency Telegraphy
VFTTA Visa for Travel to Australia (ADA)
VFU Van Wert, OH [*Location identifier FAA*] (FAAL)
VFU Vertical Format Unit (BUR)
VFU Vocabulary File Utility
VFUNDW Voluntary Fund for the United Nations Decade for Women (EA)
VFV Variable Fuel Vehicle [*General Motors Corp.*] [*Automotive engineering*]
VFV Venus Flyby Vehicle [*NASA*]
VFVC Vacuum Freezing, Vapor Compression [*Desalination*]
VFW Variable/Fixed Wavelength [*Electronics*]
VFW Verwaltungsamt fuer Wirtschaft [*Executive Committee for Economics*] [*Germany*]
VFW Veterans of Foreign Wars of the USA (EA)
VFW Veterans of Future Wars [*Facetious organization formed by Princeton students in 1930's*]
VFW Video for Windows [*Microsoft Corp.*] (PCM)
VFX Variable Frequency Mixer (IAA)
VFX Vector Float-to-Fix (IAA)
VFY Verify (AFM)
VG British Virgin Islands [*ANSI two-letter standard code*] (CNC)
VG City Flug [*ICAO designator*] (AD)
V_g Generator Voltage (IDOE)
V_g Generator Voltage (IDOE)
V_G Genetic Variance (DAVI)
VG Grundriss der Vergleichenden Grammatik der Semitischen Sprachen [*A publication*] (BJA)
VG Light Transport Plane [*Single-engine*] [*Navy symbol*]
VG Validity Generalization Testing (OICC)
VG Varga Aircraft Corp. [*ICAO aircraft manufacturer identifier*] (ICAO)
VG Variable Geometry [*Refers to an aircraft that is capable of altering the sweep of the wings while in flight*] (NATG)
VG Variable Geometry
VG Vector Generator [*Computer graphics*]
VG Vein Graft [*Cardiology*] (DAVI)
VG Velocity Gravity
VG Ventricular Gallop [*Cardiology*]
VG Ventrogluteal [*Anatomy*] (DAVI)
VG Verbi Gratia [*For Example*] [*Latin*]
VG Vertical Grain
V-G Vertical Gust (MCD)
VG Vertical Gyro (MCD)
VG Very Good [*Condition*] [*Antiquarian book trade, numismatics, etc.*]
VG Vibration Greatness
VG Vicarius Generalis [*Vicar-General*] [*Latin*]
VG Vice Grand [*Freemasonry*] (ROG)
VG Vinylguaiacol [*Biochemistry*]
VG Virgin (WDAA)
VG Viscosity Grade [*Automotive engineering*]
VG Vocational Guidance (ADA)
VG Voice Grade [*Telecommunications*] (TEL)
VG Volksgrenadier [*Title given to infantry divisions with distinguished combat records*] [*Germany*] [*World War II*]
VG Voltage Gain
VG Volunteer Guards [*British military*] (DMA)
VG Votre Grace [*Your Grace*] [*French*]
VG Votre Grandeur [*Your Highness*] [*French*]

Vg .... Vulgate [*Latin translation of the Bible*] (BJA)
VGA .... Air Vegas Airlines, Inc. [*FAA designator*] (FAAC)
VGA .... Vapor Generation Accessory [*Instrumentation*]
VGA .... Variable Gain Amplifier
VGA .... Vegetable Growers' Association [*Australia*]
VGA .... Vertical Gyro Alignment
VGA .... Very General Algorithm (KSC)
VGA .... Victorian Green Alliance [*Political party Australia*]
VGA .... Victorian Gymnastic Association [*Australia*]
VGA .... Video Graphics Adapter [*Computer science*]
VGA .... Video Graphics Array [*Computer technology*]
VGA .... Vijayawada [*India*] [*Airport symbol*] (OAG)
VGAA .... Vegetable Growers Association of America [*Defunct*] (EA)
VGAM .... Vector Graphics Access Method
VG & VF .... Vicar General and Vicar Foreign [*British*] (ROG)
VGAT .... Visual General Aviation Trainer
VGAU .... Victorian Government Advertising Unit [*Australia*]
VGB .... British Virgin Islands [*ANSI three-letter standard code*] (CNC)
VGBD .... Virtual Grain Boundary Dislocation
VGC .... Variable Gas Capacitor
VGC .... Velocity Gate Capture [*Military*] (CAAL)
VGC .... Verdstone Gold Corp. [*Vancouver Stock Exchange symbol*]
VGC .... Very Good Condition [*Doll collecting*]
vgc .... Very Good Condition (ODBW)
VGC .... Vesterheim Genealogical Center (EA)
VGC .... Victorian Grants Commission [*Australia*]
VGC .... Video Graphics Controller [*Apple Computer, Inc.*]
VGC .... Viscosity Gravity Constant
VGCA .... Voice Gate Circuit Adaptors [*Computer science*] (MCD)
VGCAC .... Victorian Government China Advisory Committee [*Australia*]
VGCB .... Cox's Bazar [*Bangladesh*] [*ICAO location identifier*] (ICLI)
VGCC .... Victorian Government Computing Centre [*Australia*]
VGCC .... Voltage-Gated Calcium Channel [*Neurophysiology*]
VGCF .... Vapor-Phase-Grown Carbon Fiber
VGCH .... Vent Gas Collection Header [*Nuclear energy*] (NRCH)
VGCL .... Vietnam General Confederation of Labor
VGCM .... Comilla [*Bangladesh*] [*ICAO location identifier*] (ICLI)
VGCO .... Virginia Gas Co. [*NASDAQ symbol*] (SAG)
V_{GD} .... Gate-Drain Voltage (IDOE)
VGD .... Valentine Gold [*Vancouver Stock Exchange symbol*]
VGD .... Valuer-General's Department [*Australia*]
VGD .... Vanguard Airlines, Inc. [*FAA designator*] (FAAC)
VGDC .... Victorian Geographic Data Committee [*State*] (EERA)
VGDIP .... Very God-Damned Important Person
VGE .... Air Service Vosges [*France ICAO designator*] (FAAC)
VGE .... Valery Giscard d'Estaing [*Former French President*]
VGE .... Video-Game Epilepsy [*Neurology*]
VGE .... Visual Gross Error
VGEG .... Chittagong [*Bangladesh*] [*ICAO location identifier*] (ICLI)
VGF .... Escort Fighter Squadron [*Navy symbol*]
VGF .... Vaccinia Growth Factor [*Biochemistry*]
VGF .... Vertical Gradient Freeze [*Crystal growing technique*]
VGF .... Virus Growth Factor [*Biochemistry*]
VGFR .... Dhaka [*Bangladesh*] [*ICAO location identifier*] (ICLI)
VGFTU .... Vietnam General Federation of Trade Unions [*North Vietnam*]
VGG .... Valhalla Gold Group [*Vancouver Stock Exchange symbol*]
VGG .... Video Graphics Generator
VGH .... Vancouver General Hospital
VGH .... Velocity, Normal Gravity, and Height
VGH .... Verlagsgruppe Georg von Holtzbrinck [*Commercial firm Germany*]
VGH .... Very Good Health [*Medicine*]
VGH .... Veterinary General Hospital
VGHN .... Vaughn Communications [*NASDAQ symbol*] (TTSB)
VGHN .... Vaughn's, Inc. [*NASDAQ symbol*] (NQ)
VGHQ .... Dhaka [*Bangladesh*] [*ICAO location identifier*] (ICLI)
VGI .... Variable Geometry Inlet
VGI .... Veiling Glare Index [*Vision research*]
VGI .... Vertical Gyro Indicator
VGIMU .... Velocity to Be Gained Related to IMU Orientation (MCD)
VGIN .... Visible Genetics, Inc. [*NASDAQ symbol*] (SAG)
VGIS .... Ishurdi [*Bangladesh*] [*ICAO location identifier*] (ICLI)
VGJR .... Jessore [*Bangladesh*] [*ICAO location identifier*] (ICLI)
VGLI .... Veterans Group Life Insurance
VGLIS .... Video Guidance, Landing, and Imaging System [*NASA*]
V/GLLD .... Vehicular/Ground LASER Locator Designator (MCD)
VGLM .... Lalmonirhat [*Bangladesh*] [*ICAO location identifier*] (ICLI)
VGM .... George Mason University, Fairfax, VA [*OCLC symbol*] (OCLC)
VGM .... Van Kam Am Cap Inv Gr Mun [*NYSE symbol*] (TTSB)
VGM .... Van Kampen Merritt Trust for Investment Grade Municipals [*NYSE symbol*] (SAG)
VGM .... Variable Grating Mode (PDAA)
VGM .... Ventriculogram [*A roentgenogram*]
VGM .... VGM Capital Corp. [*Formerly, Vestgron Mines Ltd.*] [*Toronto Stock Exchange symbol*]
VGM .... Vice Grand Master (BJA)
VGM .... Villa Grajales [*Mexico*] [*Seismograph station code, US Geological Survey Closed*] (SEIS)
VGML .... Vegetarian Meal [*Airline notation*]
VGMPU .... Victorian Government Major Projects Unit [*Australia*]
VGMU .... Vulcan Gunner Monitor Unit (MCD)
VGN .... Variable Geometry Nozzle
VGN .... Virginian Railway Co. [*AAR code*]
VGND .... Ground Velocity (GAVI)
vgnt .... Vignette (VRA)
VGO .... Vacuum Gas Oil [*Petroleum technology*]
VGO .... Vanderbilt Gold [*PC symbol*] (TTSB)
VGO .... Vereinigte Gruenen Oesterreich [*United Green Party of Austria*] [*Political party*] (EY)
VGO .... Vicar General's Office [*British*] (ROG)
VGO .... Vickers Gas Operated [*British military*] (DMA)
VGO .... Vigo [*Spain*] [*Airport symbol*] (OAG)
VGOR .... Vandenberg Ground Operations Requirement [*Air Force*] (NASA)
VGOR .... Vehicle Ground Operation Requirements [*NASA*] (NASA)
VGP .... Vehicle Ground Point [*NASA*] (NASA)
VGP .... Viral Glycoprotein [*Medicine*] (DMAA)
VGP .... Virtual Geomagnetic Pole [*Geophysics*]
VGPI .... Visual Glide Path Indicator
VGPI .... Visual Ground Position Indicator (NATG)
VGPO .... Velocity Gate Pulloff [*Military*] (CAAL)
VGPO .... Victorian Government Printing Office [*Australia*]
VGR .... Variable Gear Ratio [*Automotive steering systems*]
VGR .... Variable Geometry Rotor
VGR .... Vermont Government Register [*A publication*] (AAGC)
VGR .... Video Graphics Recorder (EECA)
VGR .... Vigoro Corp. [*NYSE symbol*] (SPSG)
VGR .... Virgin Gorda [*British Virgin Islands*] [*Airport symbol*] (AD)
VgrdCell .... Vanguard Cellular Systems, Inc. [*Associated Press*] (SAG)
VGRJ .... Rajshahi [*Bangladesh*] [*ICAO location identifier*] (ICLI)
VGS .... Escort-Scouting Squadron [*Navy symbol*]
V_{GS} .... Gate-Source Voltage (IDOE)
VGS .... Variable Geometry Structure
VGS .... Variable-Grade Gravity Sewer
VGS .... Vehicle Generating System
VGS .... Velocity Gate Stealer [*Military*] (CAAL)
VGS .... Vings [*Bulgaria*] [*ICAO designator*] (FAAC)
VGS .... Volunteer Gliding Schools [*British*]
VGSD .... Saidpur [*Bangladesh*] [*ICAO location identifier*] (ICLI)
VGSG .... Thakuragaon [*Bangladesh*] [*ICAO location identifier*] (ICLI)
VGSH .... Shamshernagar [*Bangladesh*] [*ICAO location identifier*] (ICLI)
VGSI .... Visual Glide Slope Indicator
VGSO .... Victorian Government Solicitor's Office [*Australia*]
VGSY .... Sylhet Osmani [*Bangladesh*] [*ICAO location identifier*] (ICLI)
VGT .... Las Vegas [*Nevada*] North Terminal [*Airport symbol*] (OAG)
VGT .... Las Vegas, NV [*Location identifier FAA*] (FAAL)
VGT .... National Victoria & Grey Trustco Ltd. [*Toronto Stock Exchange symbol*]
VGT .... Variable Geometry Turbocharger [*Automotive engineering*]
VGT .... Vehicle Ground Test [*NASA*] (NASA)
VGT .... Videographic Terminal
VGTE .... Vulcan Gunner Tracking Evaluation (MCD)
VGTJ .... Dhaka/Tejgaon [*Bangladesh*] [*ICAO location identifier*] (ICLI)
VGU .... Des Moines, IA [*Location identifier FAA*] (FAAL)
VGU .... Video Generation Unit (NITA)
VGV .... Vacuum Gate Valve
VGVT .... Vertical Ground Vibration Test (MCD)
VGW .... Variable Geometry Wing [*Aircraft*]
VGWA .... Variable Geometry Wing Aircraft (AAG)
VGWO .... Velocity Gate Walkoff [*Military*] (CAAL)
VGX .... Velocity to Be Gained [*Body X-Axis*] [*NASA*] (NASA)
VGY .... Velocity to Be Gained [*Body Y-Axis*] [*NASA*] (NASA)
VGZ .... Velocity to Be Gained [*Body Z-Axis*] [*NASA*] (NASA)
VGZ .... Vista Gold Corp. [*AMEX symbol*] (SAG)
VGZR .... Dhaka/Zia International [*Bangladesh*] [*ICAO location identifier*] (ICLI)
VH .... Air Burkina [*ICAO designator*] (AD)
VH .... Air Volta [*ICAO designator*] (AD)
VH .... Ambulance Plane [*Navy symbol*]
Vh .... Heater Voltage [*Electronics*] (OA)
V_H .... Hepatic Distribution Volume [*Gastroenterology*] (DAVI)
VH .... Rescue Squadrons [*Navy symbol*]
VH .... Vacuum Housing
VH .... Vaginal Hysterectomy [*Gynecology*]
VH .... Value Health, Inc. [*NYSE symbol*] (SAG)
VH .... Variable Heavy
VH .... Varia Historia [*of Aelianus*] [*Classical studies*] (OCD)
V/H .... Velocity/Height
VH .... Venice Hospital [*Venice, FL*]
VH .... Venous Hematocrit [*Medicine*] (MAE)
VH .... Vent Hole [*Technical drawings*]
VH .... Ventricular Hypertrophy [*Cardiology*] (DAVI)
VH .... Vertical Hook (IAA)
VH .... Very Hard (IAA)
VH .... Very Heavy [*Cosmic ray nuclei*]
VH .... Very High
VH .... Veterans Hospital
VH .... Vickers Hardness Number [*Also, HV, VHN*] (AAG)
VH .... Viral Hepatitis [*Medicine*]
VH .... Vir Honestus [*A Worthy Man*] [*Latin*]
VH .... Virtual Hospital [*University of Iowa*] [*Online database*]
VH .... Visually Handicapped [*Ophthalmology*] (DAVI)
VH .... Vitreous Hemorrhage [*Ophthalmology*] (DAVI)
V/H .... Vulnerability/Hardness [*Refers to a weapon system's weakness and capabilities in withstanding adverse operating environments*]
VH-1 .... Video Hits One [*Cable-television system*] [*Companion to MTV*]
VH1 .... Video Hits One [*Cable programming service*] (WDMC)
VHA .... Van Houten Associates [*Information service or system*] (IID)
VHA .... Variable Housing Allowance (MCD)
VHA .... Very High Accuracy (NITA)
VHA .... Very High Achievement [*Tertiary entrance*]
VHA .... Very High Altitude
VHA .... Very High Aluminum [*Rock composition*]

VHA Voluntary Hospitals of America (EA)
VHAA Very High Altitude Abort [*NASA*] (KSC)
VHAD Vehicle Headlight Aiming Device [*Automotive engineering*]
VHAP Volatile Hazardous Air Pollutant (EG)
VHB Buffalo and Erie County Public Library, Buffalo, NY [*OCLC symbol*] (OCLC)
VHB Very Heavy Bombardment [*Air Force*]
VHB Very High Bond Tape [*3M Co.*]
VHb Vitreoscilla Hemoglobin [*Genetics*]
VHBR Very High Burning Rate (MCD)
VHBW Very-High-Speed Black and White [*Photography*]
VHC Hollins College, Hollins College, VA [*OCLC symbol*] (OCLC)
VHC Saurimo [*Angola*] [*Airport symbol*] (OAG)
VHC Ventech Healthcare Corp., Inc. [*Toronto Stock Exchange symbol*]
VHC Vertical Hold Control
VHC Very High Contrast [*Liquid crystal display*]
VHC Very Highly Commended
VHCA Veterans Health Care Act (AAGC)
VHCC Very High Current Configuration [*Magnetic field*]
VHCH Cheung Chau [*Hong Kong*] [*ICAO location identifier*] (ICLI)
VHD Valvular Heart Disease
VHD Ventricular Heart Disease [*Cardiology*] (DAVI)
VHD Very High Density [*Computer science*] (CDE)
VHD Video High Density [*Television*]
VHD Viral Haemorrhagic Disease
VHD Viral Hematodepressive Disease (MAE)
VHDL Very-High Density Lipoprotein [*Biochemistry*]
VHDL VHSIC [*Very-High-Speed Integrated Circuit*] Hardware Description Language [*Computer science*]
VHDV Very High Dollar Value
VHE Very-High Energy
VHE Volatile Human Effluents
VH Eq Dr Van Heythuysen's Equity Draftsman [*2nd ed.*] [*1828*] [*A publication*] (DLA)
VHES Vitro Hanford Engineering Service [*Nuclear energy*] (NUCP)
VHF Vacuum Hydrogen Furnace
VHF Very-High-Frequency [*Electronics*]
VHF Visual Half-Field
VHF/AM Very-High-Frequency, Amplitude Modulated (NASA)
VHFC Van Halen Fan Club (EA)
VHF/DF Very-High-Frequency Direction-Finding
VHFF Very-High-Frequency Filter
VHF-FM Very-High-Frequency, Frequency Modulated (NOAA)
VHFG Very-High-Frequency Generator
VHFI Very-High-Frequency Indeed [*Ultrahigh frequency*] [*British*]
VHFJ Very-High-Frequency Jammer
VHFO Very-High-Frequency Oscillator
VHFOR Very-High-Frequency Omnirange (AFM)
VHFR Very-High-Frequency Receiver
VHFRT Very-High Frequency Radio Telephony (PDAA)
VHFS Vint Hill Farms Station [*Army*]
VHFT Very-High-Frequency Termination
VHHH Hong Kong/International [*Hong Kong*] [*ICAO location identifier*] (ICLI)
VHHK Hong Kong [*Hong Kong*] [*ICAO location identifier*] (ICLI)
VHI Valhi, Inc. [*NYSE symbol*] (SPSG)
VHI Vapro Hazard Index [*Environmental science*]
VHI Vehicle Heading Indicator
VHIC Vermont Health Care Information, Consortium
VHIP Vehicle Hit Indicator, Pyrotechnic
VHIS Vietnam Head Injury Study
VHKT Kai Tak [*Hong Kong*] [*ICAO location identifier*] (ICLI)
VHL Viceroy Homes Ltd. [*Toronto Stock Exchange symbol*]
VHL Von Hippel-Lindau Disease
VHLH Very Heavy Lift Helicopter
VHLL Very-High-Level Language
VHM Vibrating Head Magnetometer (IAA)
VHM Virtual Hardware Monitor [*Computer science*] (IEEE)
VHM Visitation Nuns [*Roman Catholic religious order*]
VHM Vista Hermosa [*Mexico*] [*Seismograph station code, US Geological Survey Closed*] (SEIS)
VHMCP Voluntary Home Mortgage Credit Program [*of HHFA*] [*Terminated*]
VHMWPE Very-High Molecular Weight Polyethylene (PDAA)
VHN Van Horn, TX [*Location identifier FAA*] (FAAL)
VHN Vickers Hardness Number [*Also, HV, VH*]
VHO Very High Output
VHO Vila Coutinho [*Mozambique*] [*Airport symbol Obsolete*] (OAG)
VHO Vista Hermosa [*Mexico*] [*Seismograph station code, US Geological Survey*] (SEIS)
VHO Volatile Halogenated Organic [*Analytical chemistry*]
VHOC Volatile Halogenated Organic Compound [*Environmental chemistry*]
VHOL Very-High-Order Language
VHP County of Henrico Public Library, Richmond, VA [*OCLC symbol*] (OCLC)
VHP Variable Horsepower
VHP Very High Performance
VHP Very High Polarization [*Raw sugar grade*]
VHP Very High Pressure
VHP Viral Hepatitis Panel [*Hematology*] (DAVI)
VHP Vooruitstrewende Hervormings Partij [*Progressive Reform Party*] [*Surinam*] [*Political party*] (PPW)
VHPA Vietnam Helicopter Pilots Association (EA)
VHPCC Very High Performance Computing and Communication (USDC)
VHPCC Very High Performance Computing and Communication [*Marine science*] (OSRA)
VHPIC Very-High Performance Integrated Circuit [*Electronics*] (PDAA)
VHR Very-Highly Repeated [*Genetics*]
VHR Very High Reduction (NITA)
VHR Very High Resistance (IDOE)
VHR Video-to-Hardcopy Recorder
VHRC Victoria Harness Racing Club [*Australia*]
VHRR Very High Resolution Radiometer [*NASA*]
VHRTG Veterans' Hospital Radio and Television Guild (EA)
VHRVM Very-High-Resistance Voltmeter (IDOE)
VHS Hampden-Sydney College, Hampden-Sydney, VA [*OCLC symbol*] (OCLC)
VHS Honorary Surgeon to the Viceroy of India
vHs Van Hove Singularities [*Physics*]
VHS Versatile High Speed [*Copier*]
VHS Vertical and Horizontal Spread [*Landfills*] (EG)
VHS Very High Speed [*Copier*]
VHS Victorian House of Studies
VHS Video Home System
VHS Viral Hemorrhagic Septicemia [*Medicine*]
VHS Virtual High School
VHS & RA Veterans Health Services and Research Administration [*Department of Veterans Affairs*]
VHSB Virtual Home Space Builder
VHS-C Video Home System - Compact
VHSD Very High Speed Data (LAIN)
VHSI Very-High-Speed Integrated [*Electronics*]
VHSIC Very-High-Speed Integrated Circuit [*Electronics*]
VHSK Sek Kong [*Hong Kong*] [*ICAO location identifier*] (ICLI)
VHSOC Very-High-Speed Optic Cable
VHST Very-High-Speed Transit
VHT Banyan Hotel Investment Fund [*Formerly, VMS Hotel Investment Fund*] [*AMEX symbol*] (SPSG)
VHT Banyan Hotel Inv Fund [*AMEX symbol*] (TTSB)
VHT Vehicle Hours Traveled [*MOCD*] (TAG)
VHT Vignetted Halftone [*Graphic arts*] (DGA)
VHTR Very-High-Temperature Reactor [*Nuclear energy*]
V/HUD Vertical/Heads-Up Display [*Aviation*] (MCD)
VHUP Veterinary Hospital of the University of Pennsylvania
VHV Very-High Voltage (IAA)
VHVI Very High Viscosity Index [*Petroleum oils*]
VHW Verband Hannoverscher Warmblutzuchter [*Germany*] (EAIO)
VHWG Vulnerability and Hardening Working Group
VHY Vess, Henry, Kansas City MO [*STAC*]
VHY Vichy [*France*] [*Airport symbol*] (AD)
V Hyst Vaginal Hysterectomy [*Gynecology*] (DAVI)
VI Congregation of the Incarnate Word and the Blessed Sacrament [*Roman Catholic women's religious order*]
VI In Bankruptcy or Receivership [*Investment term*] (DFIT)
VI Inertial Velocity
V_I Input Voltage (IDOE)
V_I Inspired Volume per Minute [*Medicine*] (DAVI)
VI Internal Velocity (SSD)
VI Six [*Roman numeral*] (DAVI)
VI St. Croix Island (VRA)
VI St. John Island (VRA)
VI St. Thomas Island (VRA)
VI Vaginal Irrigation [*Medicine*]
VI Value Included Entry [*Business term*]
VI Values Inventory [*Management test*]
VI Vancouver Island
VI Variable Intensity Light [*Aviation*] (DA)
VI Variable Interval [*Reinforcement schedule*]
VI Vasoinhibitory [*Medicine*]
VI Vastus Intermedius [*Muscle*] (DAVI)
VI Vector International (EA)
VI Vegetation Index
VI Velocity, Internal
VI Vendor Item [*Sales*] (AAG)
VI Vent Isolation [*Nuclear energy*] (NRCH)
VI Verb Intransitive
VI Vereniging Intercoop [*International Agricultural Society Intercoop*] [*Switzerland*] (EAIO)
VI Vermiculite Institute [*Defunct*]
VI Vertical Incidence (IAA)
VI Vertical Interval [*Mapmaking*]
VI Vested Interest [*Business term*] (MHDW)
VI Veterinary Inspector (ADA)
VI Vial
VI Vibration Institute (EA)
VI Victoria Institute [*British*] (DAS)
vi Vide Infra [*See Below*] [*Latin*] (WGA)
VI Video Integrator
VI Vieques Airlink [*ICAO designator*] (AD)
Vi Vincentius Hispanus [*Deceased, 1248*] [*Authority cited in pre-1607 legal work*] (DSA)
VI Vinegar Institute (EA)
VI Violet
Vi Virginia State Library, Richmond, VA [*Library symbol Library of Congress*] (LCLS)
VI Virgin Islands (IAA)
VI Virgin Islands of the US [*ANSI two-letter standard code*] (CNC)
VI Virgin Islands of the US [*Postal code*]
vi Virgin Islands of the US [*IYRU nationality code*] [*MARC country of publication code Library of Congress*] (LCCP)
VI Virgin Islands Reports [*A publication*] (DLA)
Vi Virginium (MAE)

VI .... Virgo Intacta [*Medicine*]
Vi .... Virulence [*Antigen*] [*Immunology*]
VI .... Viscosity Improver [*Element in multigrade engine oil*]
VI .... Viscosity Index
VI .... Visibility Impariment [*Environmental Protection Agency*]
VI .... Visual Identification
VI .... Visual Impairment
VI .... Visual Information
VI .... Visual Inspection
VI .... Visual Interface [*Computer science*] (NHD)
Vi .... Vivianus Tuscus [*Flourished, 13th century*] [*Authority cited in pre-1607 legal work*] (DSA)
VI .... Volume Index [*Medicine*] (DHSM)
VI .... Volume Indicator [*Radio equipment*]
VI .... Volume Investigation [*Three-dimensional imaging technology developed at The Toronto Hospital in Canada*]
VI .... Voluntary Indefinite [*Status*] [*Army*] (INF)
VI .... Voluntary Interceptor [*World War II British*]
VI .... Volunteers for Israel (EA)
VIA .... Arlington County Department of Libraries, Arlington, VA [*OCLC symbol*] (OCLC)
VIA .... Variable Income Annuity
VIA .... Versatile Interface Adapter [*Telecommunications*] (IAA)
VIA .... Viacom, Inc. [*AMEX symbol*] (SPSG)
VIA .... Viacom Inc Cl'A' [*AMEX symbol*] (TTSB)
VIA .... Viaduct
VIA .... Viaduct
VIA .... VIASA, Venezolana International de Aviacion SA [*Venezuela*] [*ICAO designator*] (FAAC)
VIA .... Victorian Importers' Association [*Australia*]
VIA .... Video Image Analysis
VIA .... Videotex Industry Association (EA)
VIA .... Videotex Industry Association Ltd. (NITA)
VIA .... Viral Interval Antigen [*Virology*]
VIA .... Virus Inactivating Agency [*Medicine*]
VIA .... Virus Infection Associated Antigen [*Immunology*]
VIA .... Vision Institute of America [*Later, VSP*] (EA)
VIA .... Visually Impaired Association (BARN)
VIA .... Vocational Interests and Vocational Aptitudes [*Psychology*]
VIA .... Voice Interactive Avionics [*Army*]
VIA .... Voluntary Insurance Association [*Australia*]
VIA .... Volunteers in Asia (EA)
VIA.B .... Viacom Inc. Cl'B' [*AMEX symbol*] (TTSB)
ViAb .... Washington County Public Library, Abingdon, VA [*Library symbol Library of Congress*] (LCLS)
ViAbC .... Virginia Highlands Community College, Abingdon, VA [*Library symbol*] [*Library of Congress*] (LCLS)
VIABLE .... Vertical Installation Automated Baseline [*Army*]
ViAc .... Eastern Shore Public Library, Accomac, VA [*Library symbol Library of Congress*] (LCLS)
Viac .... Viacom, Inc. [*Associated Press*] (SAG)
VIAC .... Vienna Allied Command [*British military*] (DMA)
ViacB .... Viacom, Inc. [*Associated Press*] (SAG)
Viacom .... Viacom, Inc. [*Associated Press*] (SAG)
VIADCT .... Viaduct [*Commonly used*] (OPSA)
VIADUCT .... Viaduct [*Commonly used*] (OPSA)
VIAFF .... Vancouver International Amateur Film Festival [*Canada*]
VIAG .... Agra [*India*] [*ICAO location identifier*] (ICLI)
VIAH .... Aligarh [*India*] [*ICAO location identifier*] (ICLI)
ViAl .... Alexandria Library, Alexandria, VA [*Library symbol Library of Congress*] (LCLS)
VIAL .... Allahabad [*India*] [*ICAO location identifier*] (ICLI)
ViAlA .... United States Army Material Command Headquarters, Technical Library, Alexandria,VA [*Library symbol Library of Congress*] (LCLS)
ViAlbS .... Southside Virginia Community College, Christanna Campus, Alberta, VA [*Library symbol Library of Congress*] (LCLS)
ViAlD .... Defense Technical Information Center, Cameron Station, Alexandria, VA [*Library symbol Library of Congress*] (LCLS)
ViAlDL .... Defense Logistics Agency, Cameron Station, Alexandria, VA [*Library symbol Library of Congress*] (LCLS)
ViAlP .... Jacob Simpson Payton Library, Alexandria, VA [*Library symbol Library of Congress*] (LCLS)
ViAlTh .... Protestant Episcopal Theological Seminary in Virginia, Alexandria, VA [*Library symbol Library of Congress*] (LCLS)
ViAm .... Amherst County Public Library, Amherst, VA [*Library symbol*] [*Library of Congress*] (LCLS)
ViAnGS .... Church of Jesus Christ of Latter-Day Saints, Genealogical Society Library, Annandale Branch, Annandale, VA [*Library symbol Library of Congress*] (LCLS)
ViAnN .... Northern Virginia Community College, Annandale, VA [*Library symbol Library of Congress*] (LCLS)
Viansa .... Vicky and Sam [*Sebastiani*] [*Brand name of wines made by the Sebastianis*]
VIAP .... Vanuatu Independent Alliance Party [*Political party*] (PPW)
VIAR .... Amritsar [*India*] [*ICAO location identifier*] (ICLI)
ViAr .... Arlington County Department of Libraries, Arlington, VA [*Library symbol Library of Congress*] (LCLS)
ViAr-A .... Arlington County Department of Libraries, Aurora Hills Branch, Arlington, VA [*Library symbol Library of Congress*] (LCLS)
ViArAL .... Center for Applied Linguistics, Arlington, VA [*Library symbol Library of Congress*] (LCLS)
VIARC .... Victorian Immigration Advice and Rights Centre Inc. [*Australia Commercial firm*]
ViAr-Ch .... Arlington County Department of Libraries, Cherrydale Branch, Arlington, VA [*Library symbol Library of Congress*] (LCLS)
ViAr-Cl .... Arlington County Department of Libraries, Clarendon Branch, Arlington, VA [*Library symbol Library of Congress*] (LCLS)
ViAr-F .... Arlington County Department of Libraries, Fairlington Branch, Arlington, VA [*Library symbol Library of Congress*] (LCLS)
ViAr-G .... Arlington County Department of Libraries, Glencarlyn Branch, Arlington, VA [*Library symbol Library of Congress*] (LCLS)
ViArHD .... United States Historical Documents Institute, Inc., Arlington, VA [*Library symbol Library of Congress*] (LCLS)
ViArM .... Marymount College, Arlington, VA [*Library symbol Library of Congress*] (LCLS)
ViArNG .... National Graduate University, Arlington, VA [*Library symbol Library of Congress*] (LCLS)
ViAr-W .... Arlington County Department of Libraries, Westover Branch, Arlington, VA [*Library symbol Library of Congress*] (LCLS)
VIAS .... Viasoft, Inc. [*NASDAQ symbol*] (SAG)
VIAS .... Voice Interference Analysis Set [*or System*]
VIASA .... Venezolana Internacional de Aviacion Sociedad Anonima [*Airline*] [*Venezuela*]
ViaSat .... ViaSat, Inc. [*Associated Press*] (SAG)
ViAsM .... Mobil Chemical Co., Industrial Chemicals Division, Ashland, VA [*Library symbol Library of Congress*] (LCLS)
Viasoft .... Viasoft, Inc. [*Associated Press*] (SAG)
ViAsR .... Randolph-Macon College, Ashland, VA [*Library symbol Library of Congress*] (LCLS)
Viatel .... Viatel, Inc. [*Associated Press*] (SAG)
VIATLS .... Visual Airborne Target Locator System [*Military*] (PDAA)
VIA WIS.E .... Viacom Inc.'99 Wrrt [*AMEX symbol*] (TTSB)
VIA WS.C .... Viacom Inc.'97 Wrrt [*AMEX symbol*] (TTSB)
VIB .... Vanilla Information Bureau (EA)
VIB .... Veal Infusion Broth [*Immunology*]
VIB .... Vertical Integration Building [*NASA*]
VIB .... Vibraphone [*Music*]
VIB .... Vibrate (AAG)
VIB .... Vibrator (IAA)
vib .... Vibrator [*Printing*] (DGA)
VIB .... Vitamin Information Bureau [*Defunct*] (EA)
VIB .... Vocational Interest Blank [*Psychology*] (DAVI)
VIB .... Volunteer Infantry Brigade [*British military*] (DMA)
VIBAC .... Vehicle Ice-Breaking Air Cushion (PDAA)
VIBG .... Vibrating (AAG)
VIBGYOR .... Violet, Indigo, Blue, Green, Yellow, Orange, Red [*Mnemonic for the colors of the spectrum*]
VIBH .... Banihal [*India*] [*ICAO location identifier*] (ICLI)
VIBI .... Virgini Immaculatae Bavaria Immaculata [*To the Immaculate Virgin Immaculate Bavaria*] [*Motto of the Order of St. George of Bavaria*] [*Latin*]
VIBK .... Bikaner [*India*] [*ICAO location identifier*] (ICLI)
VIBL .... Bakshi Ka Talab [*India*] [*ICAO location identifier*] (ICLI)
VIBL .... Variable Intensity Back Lighting (NITA)
ViBlbV .... Virginia Polytechnic Institute and State University, Blacksburg, VA [*Library symbol Library of Congress*] (LCLS)
ViBluC .... Bluefield College, Bluefield, VA [*Library symbol Library of Congress*] (LCLS)
VIBN .... Varanasi [*India*] [*ICAO location identifier*] (ICLI)
VIBN .... Vibration (AAG)
Vi-BPH .... Virginia State Library for the Visually and Physically Handicapped, Richmond, VA [*Library symbol Library of Congress*] (LCLS)
VIBR .... Kulu/Bhuntar [*India*] [*ICAO location identifier*] (ICLI)
VIBR .... Vibration
VIBRA .... Vehicle Inelastic Bending Response Analysis [*Computer program*]
VIBRAM .... Vitale Bramani [*Inventor of rubber soles for boots used in mountain climbing*]
ViBrC .... Bridgewater College, Bridgewater, VA [*Library symbol Library of Congress*] (LCLS)
VIBRECON .... Vibration-Recording Console (SAA)
VIBROT .... Vibrational-Rotational [*Spectra*] [*Computer science*]
ViBS .... Sullins College, Bristol, VA [*Library symbol Library of Congress*] (LCLS)
VIBS .... Vocabulatory, Information, Block Design, Similarities [*Psychology*]
ViBsgM .... Mountain Empire Community College, Big Stone Gap, VA [*Library symbol*] [*Library of Congress*] (LCLS)
VIBT .... Bhatinda [*India*] [*ICAO location identifier*] (ICLI)
VIBT .... Vibrator (IAA)
ViBV .... Virginia Intermont College, Bristol, VA [*Library symbol Library of Congress*] (LCLS)
VIBW .... Bhiwani [*India*] [*ICAO location identifier*] (ICLI)
VIBY .... Bareilly [*India*] [*ICAO location identifier*] (ICLI)
ViC .... McIntire Public Library, Charlottesville, VA [*Library symbol Library of Congress*] (LCLS)
VIC .... University of Victoria Library [*UTLAS symbol*]
VIC .... Value Incentive Clause [*General Services Administration*]
VIC .... Values Inventory for Children [*Attitude test*]
VIC .... Van Kam Am Cap InvGr CA Mun [*NYSE symbol*] (TTSB)
VIC .... Van Kampen Merritt Investment Grade California Municipal [*NYSE symbol*] (SPSG)
VIC .... Vapor Injection Curing [*Plastics technology*]
VIC .... Variable Instruction Computer
VIC .... Varnish Insulating Compound
VIC .... Vasoinhibitory Center [*Physiology*]
VIC .... Vehicle for Initial Crawling [*Physical therapy*] (DAVI)
VIC .... Vehicle Identification Code (SSD)
VIC .... Vehicle Intercommunications System (MCD)
VIC .... Very Important Cargo [*Shipping*]

VIC .... Very Important Contributors [*Political*]
VIC .... Very Important Customer
VIC .... Veterinary Investigation Centre [*Ministry of Agriculture, Fisheries, and Food*] [*British*]
VIC .... Vicar [*or Vicarage*]
VIC .... Vicenza [*Italy*] [*Airport symbol*] (AD)
VIC .... Vices [*Times*] [*Pharmacy*]
vic .... Vicinal [*Also, v*] [*Chemistry*]
vic .... Vicinalis [*Neighboring*] [*Latin*]
VIC .... Vicinity (AABC)
Vic .... Victor [*Record label*]
VIC .... Victoria [*British Columbia*] [*Seismograph station code, US Geological Survey*] (SEIS)
vic .... Victoria [*Platen Press*] (DGA)
VIC .... Victoria [*Diocesan abbreviation*] [*Texas*] (TOCD)
VIC .... Video Image Correlation
VIC .... Video Interface Controller [*Computer science*]
VIC .... Vienna International Centre [*United Nations*]
VIC .... Viking Integrated Change [*NASA*]
VIC .... Virginia Intermont College
VIC .... Virginia State Library, Richmond, VA [*OCLC symbol*] (OCLC)
VIC .... Virgin Islands Code [*A publication*] (DLA)
VIC .... Virgin Islands Corp. [*Intended to promote VI economic development, dissolv ed 1966*] [*Department of the Interior*]
VIC .... Virtual Interaction Controller
VIC .... Visibility of Intransit Cargo [*Shipping*]
VIC .... Visitor Information Center [*Kennedy Space Center*]
VIC .... Visitor Information Centre [*Australian National Botanic Gardens*]. (EERA)
VIC .... Visual Information Center [*Oldsmobile*] [*Automotive engineering*]
VIC .... Vortex in Cell [*Fluid Mechanics*]
VIC .... VSC Tech, Inc. [*Vancouver Stock Exchange symbol*]
VICA .... Vision Industry Council of America (EA)
VICA .... Vocational Industrial Clubs of America (EA)
Vic ACR .... Victorian Accident Compensation Reports [*Australia A publication*]
ViCAF .... United States Army, Foreign Science and Technical Center, Charlottesville, VA [*Library symbol Library of Congress*] (LCLS)
ViCAHi .... Abermarle County Historical Society, Charlottesville, VA [*Library symbol Library of Congress*] (LCLS)
Vical .... Vical, Inc. [*Associated Press*] (SAG)
VICAM .... Virtual Integrated Communications Access Method [*Sperry UNIVAC*]
VICANA .... Vietnamese Cultural Association of North America (EA)
VIC and ALB ... Victoria and Albert Museum [*London*] (DSUE)
Vic Ap .... Vicar Apostolic (BARN)
VICAP .... Violent Criminal Apprehension Program [*Quantico, VA*] [*National Center for the Analysis of Violent Crime Department of Justice*]
VICAR .... Video Image Communication and Retrieval
VIC C .... Victoria Cross (DSUE)
VICC .... Visual Information Control Console [*Telecommunications*] (IAA)
VICCC .... Victorian Indo-Chinese Community Council [*Australia*]
VICCI .... Voice-Initiated Cockpit Control and Integration [*Aviation*] (PDAA)
VICE .... Vast Integrated Communications Environment [*Carnegie Mellon University*] [*Pittsburgh, PA*]
VICE .... Vilnius Commodity Exchange [*Lithuania*] (EY)
VICE .... Virus Instructional Code Emulator [*Computer science*]
VICES .... Voice Internal Communications Equipment for Submarines (PDAA)
Vic Fam Alm ... Victorian Family Almanac [*A publication*]
VICG .... Chandigarh [*India*] [*ICAO location identifier*] (ICLI)
VICGEN .... Vicar General's Office [*British*]
ViChe .... Chesapeake Public Library, Chesapeake, VA [*Library symbol*] [*Library of Congress*] (LCLS)
ViCheC .... Tidewater Community College, Chesapeake, VA [*Library symbol*] [*Library of Congress*] (LCLS)
Vic His J .... Victorian Historical Journal [*A publication*]
Vic Hist J .... Victorian Historical Journal [*A publication*]
ViChT .... John Tyler Community College, Chester, VA [*Library symbol Library of Congress*] (LCLS)
VICI .... Vantage Information Consultants, Inc. [*Information service or system*] (IID)
VICI .... Velocity Indicating Coherent Integrator
VICI .... Ventures in Community Improvement Demonstration Project (EDAC)
VICI .... Video Console Indexing
VICI .... Video Isolation Channel Identifier (MCD)
VICI .... Voice Input Child Identicant [*Pronounced "Vicki"*] [*Young robot in television show "Small Wonder"*]
VICI .... Voice Input Code Identifier (MCD)
Vic Inst Ed Res Bull ... Victorian Institute of Educational Research. Bulletin [*A publication*]
VICK .... Vicksburg National Military Park
VICL .... Vical, Inc. [*NASDAQ symbol*] (SAG)
VICL .... Vienna International Centre Library [*Information service or system*] (IID)
ViClR .... Robbins Mills, Inc., Clarksville, VA [*Library symbol Library of Congress*] (LCLS)
VICO .... Virginia International Co.
VICO .... Volkswagen Insurance Co.
ViCoC .... Castle Hill Museum, Cobham, VA [*Library symbol Library of Congress*] (LCLS)
VICOED .... Visual Communications Education
VICOM .... Visual Communications Management
Vicon .... Vicon Industries, Inc. [*Associated Press*] (SAG)
VICON .... Visual Confirmation [*of voice takeoff clearing system*] [*Aviation*]
Vicor .... Vicor Corp. [*Associated Press*] (SAG)
VICORE .... Visual Conceptual Reading
Vicorp .... Vicorp Restaurants, Inc. [*Associated Press*] (SAG)
ViCou .... Walter Cecil Rawls Library and Museum, Courtland, VA [*Library symbol Library of Congress*] (LCLS)
ViCovI .... Industrial Rayon Corp., Covington, VA [*Library symbol Library of Congress*] (LCLS)
ViCovW .... West Virginia Pulp & Paper Co., Covington, VA [*Library symbol Library of Congress*] (LCLS)
ViCP .... Piedmont Virginia Community College, Learning Resources Center, Charlottesville,VA [*Library symbol Library of Congress*] (LCLS)
VICP .... [*National*] Vaccine Injury Compensation Program [*Established under the 1986 federal Childhood Vaccine Injury Act*] (PAZ)
VICP .... VINES [*Virtual Networking Software*] Interprocess Communications Protocol [*Computer science*] (PCM)
VICP .... Virtual Network System Internet Control Protocol [*Banyan Systems, Inc.*] [*Telecommunications*] (PCM)
VICPIC .... Victorian Prison Industries Commission [*Australia*]
VICR .... Vicor Corp. [*NASDAQ symbol*] (SPSG)
VICR .... Vicor Corp. [*NASDAQ symbol*] (TTSB)
ViCRA .... National Radio Astronomy Observatory, Charlottesville, VA [*Library symbol Library of Congress*] (LCLS)
VICS .... Variable Inertia Charging System [*Mazda Motor Co.*] [*Automotive engineering*]
VICS .... Vehicle Information and Communications System [*FHWA*] (TAG)
VICS .... Vehicle Information and Control System [*Highway traffic management*]
VICS .... Verbal Interaction Category System [*Student teacher test*]
VICS .... Vocational Information through Computer Systems [*Philadelphia School District*] [*Pennsylvania*] [*Information service or system*] (IID)
Vic's Res .... Victoria's Resources [*A publication*]
ViCT .... Institute of Textile Technology, Charlottesville, VA [*Library symbol Library of Congress*] (LCLS)
VICT .... Victoria Bankshares, Inc. [*NASDAQ symbol*] (NQ)
VICTA .... Valett Inventory of Critical Thinking Abilities [*Child development test*]
Vict Acts .... Victoria Acts of Parliament [*A publication*] (DLA)
VictBn .... Victoria Bankshares, Inc. [*Associated Press*] (SAG)
Vict CS .... Victorian Consolidated Statutes [*A publication*] (ILCA)
Vict L .... Victorian Law Journal [*A publication*] (DLA)
Vict L (Austr) ... Victorian Reports (Law)(Australia) [*A publication*] (ILCA)
Vict R .... Victorian Reports (Australian) [*A publication*] (DLA)
Victrm .... Victormaxx Technologies [*Associated Press*] (SAG)
Vict UL Rev ... Victoria University. Law Review [*A publication*] (DLA)
ViCVH .... Virginia Highway Research Council, Charlottesville, VA [*Library symbol Library of Congress*] (LCLS)
VICX .... Kanpur/Chakeri [*India*] [*ICAO location identifier*] (ICLI)
ViD .... Danville Public Library, Danville, VA [*Library symbol Library of Congress*] (LCLS)
VID .... Vaginal Intraepithelial Dysplasia [*Gynecology*] (DAVI)
VID .... Variable Intermittent Duty (IAA)
VID .... Vide [*or Videte*] [*See*] [*Latin*]
VID .... Video (AAG)
VID .... Video
VID .... Video-Data [*Computer graphics*] (BYTE)
VID .... Videodensitometry [*Laboratory science*] (DAVI)
VID .... Video Image Display Assembly [*Space Flight Operations Facility, NASA*]
Vid .... Vidian's Exact Pleader [*1684*] [*A publication*] (DLA)
VID .... Vidin [*Bulgaria*] [*Airport symbol*] (OAG)
vid .... Vidua [*Widow*] [*Latin*] (WGA)
VID .... Vienna Institute for Development (EAIO)
VID .... Virtual Image Display (MCD)
VID .... Visual Identification (CAAL)
VID .... Volunteers for International Development [*Later, Peaceworkers*] (EA)
ViDA .... Averette College, Danville, VA [*Library symbol Library of Congress*] (LCLS)
VIDA .... Ventricular Impulse Detector and Alarm [*Cardiology*]
VIDA .... VidaMed, Inc. [*NASDAQ symbol*] (SAG)
VIDAC .... Virtual Data Acquisition and Control [*Computer science*] (HGAA)
VIDAC .... Visual Information Display and Control
VidaMd .... VidaMed, Inc. [*Associated Press*] (SAG)
VIDAMP .... Video Amplifier
VIDAP .... Vibration Data Accuracy Program
VIDAR .... Velocity Integration, Detection, and Ranging (NG)
VIDAS .... Video Image Digitiser and Storage System [*Sirton Computer*] [*London, England*]
VIDAS .... Vitek ImmunoDiagnostic Assay System
VIDAT .... Visual Data Acquisition
ViDC .... Danville Community College, Danville, VA [*Library symbol Library of Congress*] (LCLS)
VIDC .... Virgin Islands Department of Commerce (EA)
VIDD .... Delhi/Safdarjung [*India*] [*ICAO location identifier*] (ICLI)
VIDD .... Vehicle Intrusion Detection Device
VIDD .... Vertical Interval Data Detector (NASA)
VidDsp .... Video Display Corp. [*Associated Press*] (SAG)
VIDE .... Video Display [*NASDAQ symbol*] (TTSB)
VIDE .... Video Display Corp. [*NASDAQ symbol*] (NQ)
VIDEC .... Vibration Analysis and Detection Concept (DNAB)
VIDEC .... Video Digitally Enhanced Compression (PCM)
VIDEM .... Vietnam Demonstration [*FBI security file*]
VIDEO .... Visual Data Entry On-Line [*Computer science*]
VIDEO .... VORTEX Interactive Data Entry Operation (NITA)
VideoL .... Video Lottery Technologies, Inc. [*Associated Press*] (SAG)
VideoLab .... VideoLabs, Inc. [*Associated Press*] (SAG)
VideoLan .... VideoLan Technologies, Inc. [*Associated Press*] (SAG)
Videonics .... Videonics, Inc. [*Associated Press*] (SAG)
VideoSen .... Video Sentry Corp. [*Associated Press*] (SAG)

Videotr........ Videotron Holdings PLC [*Associated Press*] (SAG)
VideoU........ Video Updates, Inc. [*Associated Press*] (SAG)
VideoUpd..... Video Updates, Inc. [*Associated Press*] (SAG)
VIDF............ Delhi [*India*] [*ICAO location identifier*] (ICLI)
VIDF............ Vertical Side of Intermediate Distribution Frame [*Telecommunications*] (TEL)
VIDF............ Video Frequency (IEEE)
VIDI............ Visual Input Detection Instrumentation (MCD)
VIDIAC........ Video Input to Automatic Computer (NITA)
VIDIAC........ Visual Information Display and Control (DGA)
VIDICODER... Video Interphone Communications System (SAA)
VidJuke........ Video Jukebox Network, Inc. [*Associated Press*] (SAG)
VidLan.......... VideoLan Technologies, Inc. [*Associated Press*] (SAG)
VIDN............ Dehra Dun [*India*] [*ICAO location identifier*] (ICLI)
VIDO............ Veterinary Infectious Disease Organization [*University of Saskatchewan*] [*Canada Research center*] (RCD)
VIDOC.......... Video Documentary (NTCM)
VIDOC.......... Visual Information Documentation [*Military*]
VIDP............ Delhi/Indira Gandhi International [*India*] [*ICAO location identifier*] (ICLI)
VIDPI........... Visually Impaired Data Processors International (EA)
VIDR............ Dadri [*India*] [*ICAO location identifier*] (ICLI)
ViDR............ Dan River Mills Co., Danville, VA [*Library symbol Library of Congress*] (LCLS)
VID-R........... Visual Information Display and Retrieval System [*Computer science*] (PDAA)
ViDS............ Stratford College, Danville, VA [*Library symbol Library of Congress*] (LCLS)
VIDS............ Vehicle Integrated Defense System [*Military*]
VIDS............ Vertical Instruments Display System (MCD)
VIDS............ Virtual Image Display System
VIDS............ Visual Information Display System (MCD)
VIDSEC......... Video Systems Exposition and Conference (PDAA)
VidServ........ VideoServer, Inc. [*Associated Press*] (SAG)
VIDS/MAF..... Visual Information Display System/Maintenance Action Form (NVT)
VIDT............ Variable Inductance Displacement Transducer (PDAA)
VidU............ Video Updates, Inc. [*Associated Press*] (SAG)
VIE.............. Vacuum Insulated Evaporator (PDAA)
VIE.............. Vampire Information Exchange (EA)
VIE.............. Vibration Isolation Equipment (RDA)
VIE.............. Vienna [*Austria*] [*Airport symbol*] (OAG)
VIE.............. Vienna [*Austria*] [*Seismograph station code, US Geological Survey*] (SEIS)
vie............... Vietnamese [*MARC language code Library of Congress*] (LCCP)
VIE.............. Vigilance, Initiative, Excellence [*Aerospace Defense Command's acronym for the Zero Defects Program*]
VIE.............. Villeneuve Resources [*Vancouver Stock Exchange symbol*]
VIE.............. Virtual Information Environment [*Computer science*] (PCM)
VIE.............. Visual Indicating Equipment [*Telecommunications*] (IAA)
VIE.............. Voluntary Import Expansion [*International trade*] (ECON)
VIE.............. Volunteers in Education
Vie deFr....... Vie de France Corp. [*Associated Press*] (SAG)
VIEEW.......... Video Enhanced Evaluation of Weathering [*Automotive paint durability*]
ViEIM........... Merck & Co., Inc., Stonewall Process Development Library, Elkton, VA [*Library symbol Library of Congress*] (LCLS)
ViEmoE........ Emory and Henry College, Emory, VA [*Library symbol Library of Congress*] (LCLS)
ViEmP.......... Greenville County Library, Emporia, VA [*Library symbol Library of Congress*] (LCLS)
VIEN............ Vienna [*Austria*] (WDAA)
Vien............ Viennola [*Record label*] [*Austria*]
VIEO............ Vendor's Item Engineering Order
VIERS.......... Virgin Islands Ecological Research Station
VIESA.......... Vocational Interest, Experience, and Skill Assessment [*Vocational guidance test*]
VIEW............ View [*Commonly used*] (OPSA)
VIEW............ Viewlogic Systems [*NASDAQ symbol*] (TTSB)
VIEW............ Viewlogic Systems, Inc. [*NASDAQ symbol*] (SPSG)
VIEW............ Virtual Interface Environment Workstation
VIEW............ Visible, Informative, Emotionally Appealing, Workable [*Package evaluation in marketing*]
VIEW............ Vital Information for Education and Work (OICC)
VIEW............ Vocational Information for Education and Work (AEBS)
Viewlg......... Viewlogic Systems, Inc. [*Associated Press*] (SAG)
VIEWS.......... VAST/IMA [*Versatile Avionics System Tester/Intermediate Maintenance Activity*] Effectiveness by Workload Simulation
VIEWS.......... Vibration Indicator Early Warning System (MCD)
VIEWS.......... Views [*Commonly used*] (OPSA)
VIEWS.......... Virtual Interactive Environment Workstation [*NASA*] (BYTE)
VIEWS.......... Vocational Information and Evaluation Work Samples [*Vocational guidance test*]
ViewT........... View Tech, Inc. [*Associated Press*] (SAG)
ViewTc......... View Tech, Inc. [*Associated Press*] (SAG)
ViF............... Fairfax County Public Library, Fairfax, VA [*Library symbol Library of Congress*] (LCLS)
VIF............... Vanier Institute of the Family [*Canada*]
VIF............... Variance Inflation Factor [*Statistics*]
VIF............... Vertical Infrared Fuze (CAAL)
VIF............... Video Information [*Winslow Associates*] [*No longer available*] [*Information service or system*] (IID)
VIF............... Virion Infectivity Factor [*Genetics*]
VIF............... Virus-Induced Interferon [*Cell biology*]
VIF............... Visual Image Formula [*of psychotherapist Joseph Bird's self-help theory*]
VIF............... Voice Interface Frame [*Telecommunications*] (IAA)
ViFarL.......... Longwood College, Farmville, VA [*Library symbol Library of Congress*] (LCLS)
VIFB............. Farrukhabad [*India*] [*ICAO location identifier*] (ICLI)
ViFbE........... United States Army Engineer School, Fort Belvoir, VA [*Library symbol Library of Congress*] (LCLS)
ViFbEM........ United States Army, Engineer Museum, Fort Belvoir, VA [*Library symbol Library of Congress*] (LCLS)
ViF-BPH....... Fairfax County Public Library, Services for the Blind and Physically Handicapped, Alexandria, VA [*Library symbol Library of Congress*] (LCLS)
VIFC............. VTOL [*Vertical Takeoff and Landing*] Integrated Flight Control
VIFD............. Faridkot [*India*] [*ICAO location identifier*] (ICLI)
ViFeAM........ United States Army, Air Mobility Research and Development Laboratory, Fort Eustis, VA [*Library symbol Library of Congress*] (LCLS)
ViFeAT......... United States Army Transportation School, Fort Eustis, VA [*Library symbol Library of Congress*] (LCLS)
ViFerF.......... Ferrum College, Ferrum, VA [*Library symbol Library of Congress*] (LCLS)
VIFF............. Vectoring in Forward Flight (MCD)
ViFGM.......... George Mason College [*Later, George Mason University*], Fairfax, VA [*Library symbol Library of Congress*] (LCLS)
VIFI............. Voyager Information Flow Instructions [*NASA*] (KSC)
VIFL............. Food Technology Service, Inc. [*NASDAQ symbol*] (SAG)
VIFL............. Food Technology Svc [*NASDAQ symbol*] (TTSB)
ViFIL............ United States Army Logistics Management Center, Fort Lee, VA [*Library symbol Library of Congress*] (LCLS)
ViFIQ........... Quartermaster Technical Library, Fort Lee, VA [*Library symbol Library of Congress*] (LCLS)
VIFM............ Video-Intensified Fluorescence Microscopy
ViFmTD........ United States Army, Training and Doctrine Command Library, Fort Monroe, VA [*Library symbol Library of Congress*] (LCLS)
ViFmTS........ United States Army Tralinet Systems Center, Fort Monroe, VA [*Library symbol Library of Congress*] (LCLS)
ViFmUS........ United States Army Field Forces Library, Fort Monroe, VA [*Library symbol Library of Congress*] (LCLS)
ViFmyA......... United States Army, Fort Meyer Post Library, Fort Meyer, VA [*Library symbol Library of Congress*] (LCLS)
ViFraC.......... Camp Manufacturing Co., Franklin, VA [*Library symbol Library of Congress*] (LCLS)
ViFraPC........ Paul D. Camp Community College, Franklin, VA [*Library symbol Library of Congress*] (LCLS)
ViFre............ Central Rappahannock Regional Library, Fredericksburg, VA [*Library symbol Library of Congress*] (LCLS)
ViFreJM........ James Monroe Memorial Foundation, Fredericksburg, VA [*Library symbol Library of Congress*] (LCLS)
ViFreM.......... Mary Washington College of the University of Virginia, Fredericksburg, VA [*Library symbol Library of Congress*] (LCLS)
ViFroA.......... American Viscose Co., Front Royal, VA [*Library symbol Library of Congress*] (LCLS)
VIFSC........... VTOL [*Vertical Takeoff and Landing*] Integrated Flight System Control
ViFvW.......... Woodrow Wilson Rehabilitation Center, Fishersville, VA [*Library symbol*] [*Library of Congress*] (LCLS)
VIFZ............. Ferojpur [*India*] [*ICAO location identifier*] (ICLI)
VIG.............. Vaccinia Immune Globulin [*Medicine*]
VIG.............. Van Kam Am Cap Inv Grade [*NYSE symbol*] (TTSB)
VIG.............. Van Kampen Merritt Investment Grade Municipal [*NYSE symbol*] (SPSG)
VIG.............. Video Image Generator
VIG.............. Video Integrating Group
Vig............... Vigente [*In Force*] [*Italian*] (ILCA)
VIG.............. Vigil (ROG)
VIG.............. Vigilant Identification (MCD)
VIG.............. Vignette (ADA)
VIG.............. Vigoroso [*With Vigor*] [*Music*] (ROG)
vig............... Vigorous (DAVI)
VIG.............. Visible Gold, Inc. [*Vancouver Stock Exchange symbol*]
VIGB............ Variable Inlet Guide Blades (MCD)
ViGcS.......... Scott County Library, Gate City, VA [*Library symbol Library of Congress*] (LCLS)
VIGIL........... Vertical Indicating Gyro Internally Lighted (MCD)
Vigl............. Viglius ab Ayta Zuichemus [*Deceased, 1577*] [*Authority cited in pre-1607 legal work*] (DSA)
VIGN........... Guna [*India*] [*ICAO location identifier*] (ICLI)
VIGORN....... Vigorniensis [*Signature of the Bishops of Worcester*] [*Latin*] (ROG)
Vigoro......... Vigoro Corp. [*Associated Press*] (SAG)
ViGpD.......... Deepsea Ventures, Inc., Gloucester Point, VA [*Library symbol Library of Congress*] (LCLS)
ViGpM.......... Virginia Institute of Marine Science, Gloucester Point, VA [*Library symbol Library of Congress*] (LCLS)
VIGR............ Gwalior [*India*] [*ICAO location identifier*] (ICLI)
VIGS............ Vertical Impact Guidance System [*Army*] (MCD)
VIGS............ Video Disc Gunnery Simulator [*Army*] (INF)
VIGS............ Video Interactive Gunnery System [*Military*] (INF)
VIGS............ Visual Glide Slope
VIH.............. Rolla/Vichy, MO [*Location identifier FAA*] (FAAL)
VIH.............. Velocity Impact Hardening
ViHa............ Charles H. Taylor Memorial Library, Hampton, VA [*Library symbol Library of Congress*] (LCLS)
ViHal........... Hampton Institute, Hampton, VA [*Library symbol Library of Congress*] (LCLS)
ViHal........... Halifax County-South Boston Regional Library, Halifax, VA [*Library symbol Library of Congress*] (LCLS)

ViHaNASA.... National Aeronautics and Space Administration, Langley Research Center, Hampton,VA [*Library symbol Library of Congress*] (LCLS)
ViHar.......... Rockingham Public Library, Harrisonburg, VA [*Library symbol Library of Congress*] (LCLS)
ViHarEM...... Eastern Mennonite College, Harrisonburg, VA [*Library symbol Library of Congress*] (LCLS)
ViHarT......... James Madison University, Harrisonburg, VA [*Library symbol Library of Congress*] (LCLS)
ViHaT.......... Thomas Nelson Community College, Hampton, VA [*Library symbol Library of Congress*] (LCLS)
ViHaV.......... United States Veterans Administration Center, Medical Library, Hampton, VA [*Library symbol Library of Congress*] (LCLS)
ViHdsC......... Hampden-Sydney College, Hampden-Sydney, VA [*Library symbol Library of Congress*] (LCLS)
ViHi............ Virginia Historical Society, Richmond, VA [*Library symbol Library of Congress*] (LCLS)
ViHo............ Hollins College, Hollins College, VA [*Library symbol Library of Congress*] (LCLS)
ViHop.......... Appomattox Regional Library, Hopewell, VA [*Library symbol Library of Congress*] (LCLS)
ViHopA........ Allied Corp., Hopewell, VA [*Library symbol Library of Congress*] (LCLS)
ViHopAT...... American Tobacco Co., Department of Research and Development, Hopewell, VA [*Library symbol Library of Congress*] (LCLS)
ViHopHC...... Hercules Powder Co. [*Later, Hercules, Inc.*], Cellulose Products Division, Hopewell, VA [*Library symbol Library of Congress*] (LCLS)
ViHopHV...... Hercules Powder Co. [*Later, Hercules, Inc.*], Virginia Cellulose Division, Hopewell, VA [*Library symbol Library of Congress*] (LCLS)
VIHR........... Hissar [*India*] [*ICAO location identifier*] (ICLI)
VII.............. Vacuum-Impregnated Inductor
VII.............. Vicon Indus [*AMEX symbol*] (TTSB)
VII.............. Vicon Industries, Inc. [*AMEX symbol*] (SPSG)
VII.............. Viscosity Index Improver [*for motor oil*]
VII.............. Vocational Interest Inventory [*Vocational guidance test*]
VIII-vwf........ Von Willebrand's Factor VIII [*Hematology*] (DAVI)
VIIS............ Virgin Islands National Park
Viisage........ Viisage Technology, Inc. [*Associated Press*] (SAG)
VIJ.............. Vera Institute of Justice (EA)
VIJ.............. Virgin Gorda [*British Virgin Islands*] [*Airport symbol*] (OAG)
VIJN............ Jhansi [*India*] [*ICAO location identifier*] (ICLI)
VIJO............ Jodhpur [*India*] [*ICAO location identifier*] (ICLI)
VIJP............ Jaipur [*India*] [*ICAO location identifier*] (ICLI)
VIJR............ Jaiselmer [*India*] [*ICAO location identifier*] (ICLI)
VIJU............ Jammu [*India*] [*ICAO location identifier*] (ICLI)
VIK............. Kavik River, AK [*Location identifier FAA*] (FAAL)
VIK............. Vik [*Iceland*] [*Seismograph station code, US Geological Survey Closed*] (SEIS)
VIK............. Viking International Airlines [*ICAO designator*] (FAAC)
VIKA........... Kanpur [*India*] [*ICAO location identifier*] (ICLI)
VIKA........... Viking Air Lines
VIKD........... Kud [*India*] [*ICAO location identifier*] (ICLI)
ViKeS.......... Southside Virginia Community College, John H. Daniel Campus, Keysville, VA [*Library symbol Library of Congress*] (LCLS)
Viking OP.... Viking Office Products, Inc. [*Associated Press*] (SAG)
VIKJ............ Khajuraho [*India*] [*ICAO location identifier*] (ICLI)
VIKO........... Kota [*India*] [*ICAO location identifier*] (ICLI)
VIL.............. Avia Airlines [*Ghana*] [*FAA designator*] (FAAC)
VIL.............. Dakhla [*Mauritania*] [*Airport symbol*] (OAG)
ViL.............. Jones Memorial Library, Lynchburg, VA [*Library symbol Library of Congress*] (LCLS)
VIL.............. University of Victoria Law Library [*UTLAS symbol*]
VIL.............. Vendor Item List [*Sales*] (AAG)
VIL.............. Vertical Injection Logic [*Computer science*]
VIL.............. Vertically Integrated Liquid (USDC)
VIL.............. Vertically Integrated Liquid [*Marine science*] (OSRA)
VIL.............. Very Important Ladies
VIL.............. Very Important Launch (MUGU)
VIL.............. Villa
VIL.............. Villa Cisneros [*Spanish Sahara*] [*Airport symbol*] (AD)
VIL.............. Village
VIL.............. Villa Mercy [*Maryland*] [*Seismograph station code, US Geological Survey Closed*] (SEIS)
Vi-L............ Virginia State Law Library, Richmond, VA [*Library symbol Library of Congress*] (LCLS)
VIL.............. Vivisection Investigation League (EA)
VIL.............. VTI Industries, Inc. [*Vancouver Stock Exchange symbol*]
VilagBcp....... Village Bancorp [*Associated Press*] (SAG)
ViLanAF....... United States Air Force, Langley Air Force Base Library, Langley AFB, VA [*Library symbol Library of Congress*] (LCLS)
Vil & Br....... Vilas and Bryant's Edition of the Wisconsin Reports [*A publication*] (DLA)
Vilas........... Vilas' Criminal Reports [*1-5 New York*] [*A publication*] (DLA)
ViLaw.......... Brunswick-Greensville Regional Library, Lawrenceville, VA [*Library symbol Library of Congress*] (LCLS)
ViLawS........ Saint Paul's College, Lawrenceville, VA [*Library symbol Library of Congress*] (LCLS)
ViLBW......... Babcock & Wilcox Co., Lynchburg, VA [*Library symbol Library of Congress*] (LCLS)
ViLC........... Lynchburg College, Lynchburg, VA [*Library symbol Library of Congress*] (LCLS)
ViLCV......... Central Virginia Community College, Lynchburg, VA [*Library symbol Library of Congress*] (LCLS)
VILD............ Ludhaiha [*India*] [*ICAO location identifier*] (ICLI)
VILIOR......... Vladimir Ilyich Lenin, Initiator of the October Revolution [*Given name popular in Russia after the Bolshevik Revolution*]
VILK............ Lucknow [*India*] [*ICAO location identifier*] (ICLI)
VILL............ Village
Vill............. Villandry Festival [*Record label*] [*France*]
VILLAG........ Village [*Commonly used*] (OPSA)
VILLAGE...... Village [*Commonly used*] (OPSA)
VILLAGES.... Villages [*Commonly used*] (OPSA)
Villanova U... Villanova University (GAGS)
ViLLB.......... Liberty Baptist College, Lynchburg, VA [*Library symbol*] [*Library of Congress*] (LCLS)
VILLE........... Ville [*Commonly used*] (OPSA)
VILLG.......... Village [*Commonly used*] (OPSA)
VillGr.......... Village Green Bookstore, Inc. [*Associated Press*] (SAG)
VillGrBk....... Village Green Bookstore [*Associated Press*] (SAG)
VillGrBk....... Village Green Bookstore, Inc. [*Associated Press*] (SAG)
VILLIAGE..... Village [*Commonly used*] (OPSA)
ViLoGH........ Gunston Hall Plantation Library, Lorton, VA [*Library symbol Library of Congress*] (LCLS)
VILP............ Lalitpur [*India*] [*ICAO location identifier*] (ICLI)
VILP............ Vector Impedance Locus Plotter
ViLRM......... Randolph-Macon Woman's College, Lynchburg, VA [*Library symbol Library of Congress*] (LCLS)
VilSpM......... Village Super Market, Inc. [*Associated Press*] (SAG)
VILTCH........ Verapamil, Imipramine, Lidocaine, Tamoxifen, Chlorpromazine, Haloperidol [*Antineoplastic drug regimen*]
ViLuV.......... Virginia Oak Tannery, Luray, VA [*Library symbol Library of Congress*] (LCLS)
ViLx............ Botetourt-Rockbridge Regional Library, Lexington, VA [*Library symbol Library of Congress*] (LCLS)
ViLxV.......... Virginia Military Institute, Lexington, VA [*Library symbol Library of Congress*] (LCLS)
ViLxW......... Washington and Lee University, Lexington, VA [*Library symbol Library of Congress*] (LCLS)
ViLxW-L...... Washington and Lee University, Law Library, Lexington, VA [*Library symbol Library of Congress*] (LCLS)
VIM............. Air-Via [*Bulgaria*] [*ICAO designator*] (FAAC)
VIM............. Vacuum Induction Melting [*Metallurgy*]
VIM............. Vacuum Induction Melting
VIM............. Van Kam Am Cap Ins Muni [*NYSE symbol*] (TTSB)
VIM............. Van Kampen Merritt Trust for Insured Municipals [*NYSE symbol*] (SAG)
VIM............. Variable Intake Manifold
VIM............. Vendor Independent Messaging [*Computer science*] (PCM)
VIM............. Vendor Initial Measurement [*Sales*]
VIM............. Ventral Intersegmental Muscles [*Anatomy*]
VIM............. Vertical Improved Mail [*Mail-delivery system for large buildings in which all tenants pick up their mail from lockboxes in a central mailroom*]
VIM............. Vibrational Microlamination (MCD)
VIM............. Vibration Isolation Module
VIM............. Video Intensified Microscopy
VIM............. Vinyl Insulation Material
VIM............. Vision Intensified Microscopy
VIM............. Visitor Impact Management [*Park tourism management*]
VIM............. Vocational Instructional Materials Section (EA)
VIM............. Voice Input Module [*Cascade Graphics Development Ltd.*] [*Software package*] (NCC)
ViMan.......... Ruffner-Carnegie Public Library, Manassas, VA [*Library symbol Library of Congress Obsolete*] (LCLS)
ViManCo...... Prince William County Public Library, Manassas, VA [*Library symbol Library of Congress*] (LCLS)
ViMarC........ Marion Junior College, Marion, VA [*Library symbol Library of Congress*] (LCLS)
ViMat.......... Mathews Memorial Library, Mathews, VA [*Library symbol Library of Congress*] (LCLS)
ViMcC.......... Central Intelligence Agency, McLean, VA [*Library symbol Library of Congress*] (LCLS)
VIMCOS....... Vehicle for the Investigation of Maintenance Control System (PDAA)
ViMelE......... Eastern Shore Community College, Learning Resources Center, Melfa, VA [*Library symbol Library of Congress*] (LCLS)
VIMEX.......... Visit Mexico [*Airline fares*]
VIMG........... Moga [*India*] [*ICAO location identifier*] (ICLI)
VIMHEX....... Venezuela International Meteorological and Hydrological Experiment [*Colorado State University project*]
ViMidL......... Lord Fairfax Community College, Learning Resources Center, Middletown, VA [*Library symbol Library of Congress*] (LCLS)
ViMiN.......... Notre Dame Institute, Middleburg, VA [*Library symbol Library of Congress*] (LCLS)
ViMiNS........ National Sporting Library, Inc., Middleburg, VA [*Library symbol Library of Congress*] (LCLS)
VIMIX........... Variable Intake and Mixture [*Fuel systems*] [*Automotive engineering*]
V IMP.......... Verb Impersonal [*Grammar*] (WDAA)
VIMP............ Vertical Impulse
V IMPER...... Verb Imperative [*Grammar*] (WDAA)
Vimrx........... VimRx Pharmaceuticals, Inc. [*Associated Press*] (SAG)
VIMS............ Mandasor [*India*] [*ICAO location identifier*] (ICLI)
VIMS............ Variable Integration Measurement System
VIMS............ Vehicle Integrated Management System
VIMS............ Verification Information Management System (DNAB)
VIMS............ Versatile Interior Multiplex System (PDAA)
VIMS............ Victorian Institute of Marine Science [*State*] (EERA)
VIMS............ Virginia Institute of Marine Science [*College of William and Mary*] [*Research center*]
VIMS............ Visible-Infrared Mapping Spectrometer [*Instrumentation*]

VIMS Visual Infrared Mapping Spectrometer
VIMSIS Victorian Institute of Marine Sciences Information System [*State*] (EERA)
VIMTPG Virtual Interactive Machine Test Program Generator
ViMtvL Mount Vernon Ladies' Association of the Union, Mount Vernon, VA [*Library symbol Library of Congress*] (LCLS)
ViMv Blue Ridge Regional Library, Martinsville, VA [*Library symbol*] [*Library of Congress*] (LCLS)
VIMVAR Vacuum Induction Melt, Vacuum Arc Remelt
ViMvD E. I. Du Pont de Nemours & Co., Martinsville, VA [*Library symbol Library of Congress*] (LCLS)
V_{in} Input Voltage (IDOE)
VIN Miami, FL [*Location identifier FAA*] (FAAL)
ViN Norfolk Public Library, Norfolk, VA [*Library symbol Library of Congress*] (LCLS)
VIN Vaginal Intraepithelial Neoplasia [*Gynecology*] (DAVI)
VIN Vehicle Identification Number
VIN Vendor Identification Number [*Sales*] (MCD)
VIN Victorian Industrial Notes [*A publication*]
VIN Vinair-Helicopteros Ltda. [*Portugal ICAO designator*] (FAAC)
VIN Vinbarbital [*A hypnotic and sedative*] (DAVI)
Vin Vincentius Hispanus [*Deceased, 1248*] [*Authority cited in pre-1607 legal work*] (DSA)
VIN Vineyard [*California*] [*Seismograph station code, US Geological Survey Closed*] (SEIS)
VIN Vinum [*Wine*] [*Pharmacy*] (ROG)
VIN Vinyl [*Technical drawings*]
VIN Voltage Input (TEL)
Vin Abr Supplement to Viner's Abridgment of Law and Equity [*England*] [*A publication*] (DLA)
Vin Abr (Eng) Viner's Abridgment of Law and Equity [*1741-53*] [*A publication*] (DLA)
VinaConc Vina Concha y Toro SA [*Associated Press*] (SAG)
ViNarC Celanese Corp., Narrows, VA [*Library symbol Library of Congress*] (LCLS)
ViNC Chrysler Art Museum, Jean Outland Chrysler Library, Norfolk, VA [*Library symbol Library of Congress*] (LCLS)
Vinc Vincentius Hispanus [*Deceased, 1248*] [*Authority cited in pre-1607 legal work*] (DSA)
Vinc Cr & Lib Vincent on Criticism and Libel [*A publication*] (DLA)
Vinc Cr L Vincent's Manual of Criminal Law [*A publication*] (DLA)
Vincent de Franch Vincentius de Franchis [*Deceased, 1601*] [*Authority cited in pre-1607 legal work*] (DSA)
Vin Comm Viner's Abridgment [*or Commentaries*] [*A publication*] (DLA)
VIND Vicarious Interpolations Not Desired
VIND Vindication (ROG)
ViNE Eastern Virginia Medical School, Norfolk, VA [*Library symbol Library of Congress*] (LCLS)
ViNe Newport News Public Library, Newport News, VA [*Library symbol Library of Congress*] (LCLS)
VINE Very Informal Newsletter (NITA)
ViNeA Southeastern Universities Research Association, CEBAF Library, Newport News, VA [*Library symbol*] [*Library of Congress*] (LCLS)
ViNeC Christopher Newport College, Newport News, VA [*Library symbol Library of Congress*] (LCLS)
ViNeM Mariners' Museum, Newport News, VA [*Library symbol Library of Congress*] (LCLS)
ViNeN Newport News Shipbuilding & Dry Dock Co., Newport News, VA [*Library symbol Library of Congress*] (LCLS)
Viner Abr Viner's Abridgment of Law and Equity [*1741-53*] [*A publication*] (DLA)
VINES Virtual Networking Software [*Banyan Systems*]
ViNeV Virginia Associated Research Center, Newport News, VA [*Library symbol Library of Congress*] (LCLS)
ViNEVM Eastern Virginia Medical School, Norfolk, VA [*Library symbol*] [*Library of Congress*] (LCLS)
VINF Vista Information Solutions, Inc. [*NASDAQ symbol*] (SAG)
VINF VISTA Info Solutions [*NASDAQ symbol*] (TTSB)
VINFA Volunteers in the National Forests Act [*1972*]
VINH Nuh [*India*] [*ICAO location identifier*] (ICLI)
VINI Viniculture (WDAA)
Vining Vinings Investment Properties Trust [*Associated Press*] (SAG)
VINITI Vsesoyuznyy Institut Nauchnoy i Tekhnicheskoy Informatsii [*All-Union Institute of Scientific and Technical Information*] [*Former USSR*]
VINL Naranaup [*India*] [*ICAO location identifier*] (ICLI)
Vinland Vinland Property Trust [*Associated Press*] (SAG)
ViNM Norfolk County Medical Society, Inc., Norfolk, VA [*Library symbol Library of Congress*] (LCLS)
ViNMoN Monsanto Chemical Co., Norfolk, VA [*Library symbol Library of Congress*] (LCLS)
Vinn ad Inst Vinnius' Commentary on the Institutes of Justinian [*A publication*] (DLA)
ViNO Old Dominion University, Norfolk, VA [*Library symbol Library of Congress*] (LCLS)
ViNott Nottoway County Library, Nottoway, VA [*Library symbol Library of Congress*] (LCLS)
Vin Palaeot Vincentius Palaeotus [*Deceased, 1498*] [*Authority cited in pre-1607 legal work*] (DSA)
ViNR F. S. Royster Guano Co., Norfolk, VA [*Library symbol Library of Congress*] (LCLS)
ViNS Norfolk State College, Norfolk, VA [*Library symbol Library of Congress*] (LCLS)
VINS Velocity Inertia Navigation System
VINS Very Intense Neutron Source [*Nuclear science*] (OA)
ViNSC United States Armed Forces Staff College, Norfolk, VA [*Library symbol Library of Congress*] (LCLS)
ViNSo Sovran Bank Corp. Library, Norfolk, VA [*Library symbol*] [*Library of Congress*] (LCLS)
Vin Supp Supplement to Viner's Abridgment of Law and Equity [*A publication*] (DLA)
ViNT Norfolk Testing Laboratories, Norfolk, VA [*Library symbol Library of Congress*] (LCLS)
VINT Video Integrate (NVT)
VInt Vie Intellectuelle [*A publication*] (BJA)
$VINT^2$ Vehicle Integrated Intelligence [*Army*]
Vint Can Law Vinton's American Canon Law [*A publication*] (DLA)
VintgPt Vintage Petroleum [*Associated Press*] (SAG)
ViNWe Virginia Wesleyan College, Norfolk, VA [*Library symbol Library of Congress*] (LCLS)
VIO Avionic Ltd. [*Greece*] [*FAA designator*] (FAAC)
VIO Verbal Intelligence Quotient (DAVI)
VIO Very Important Object (DCTA)
VIO Veterinary Investigation Officer [*Ministry of Agriculture, Fisheries, and Food*] [*British*]
VIO Video Input/Output
VIO Violet (AAG)
VIO Violino [*Violin*] [*Music*] (ROG)
VIO Vior Miniere d'Exploration Societe, Inc. [*Toronto Stock Exchange symbol*]
VIO Virtual Input/Output [*Computer science*] (IBMDP)
VIO Visual Intercept Officer [*Navy*]
VIOC Variable Input-Output Code
VIOL Viola [*Music*] (ROG)
viol Violaceus [*Purple*] [*Latin*] (WGA)
VIOLE Violone [*Double Bass*] [*Music*] (ROG)
VIOLENT Viewers Intent on Listing Violent Episodes on Nationwide Television [*Student legal action organization*]
VIOLO Violino [*Violin*] [*Music*] (ROG)
VION Vion Pharmaceuticals [*NASDAQ symbol*] (TTSB)
Vion Vion Pharmaceuticals, Inc. [*Associated Press*] (SAG)
VION Vion Pharmaceuticals, Inc. [*NASDAQ symbol*] (SAG)
VionPh Vion Pharmaceuticals, Inc. [*Associated Press*] (SAG)
VIONU Vion Pharmaceuticals Unit [*NASDAQ symbol*] (TTSB)
VIONW Vion Pharmaceuticals Wrrt'A' [*NASDAQ symbol*] (TTSB)
VIONZ Vion Pharmaceuticals Wrrt'B' [*NASDAQ symbol*] (TTSB)
ViOr Orange County Public Library, Orange, VA [*Library symbol Library of Congress*] (LCLS)
VIP Valuable-Items Policy [*Insurance*] (MHDI)
VIP Value Improving Products
VIP Value in Performance
VIP Variable Incentive Pay [*Military*] (NVT)
VIP Variable Individual Protection [*Insurance*]
VIP Variable Inductance Pickup
VIP Variable Information Processing [*Naval Ordnance Laboratory*] [*Information retrieval*]
VIP Variable Input Phototypesetter
VIP Variable Interest Plus [*Banking*]
VIP Variation in Price (MHDB)
VIP Vasoactive Inhibitory Principle [*Biochemistry*]
VIP Vasoactive Intestinal Peptide [*or Polypeptide*] [*Biochemistry*]
VIP Vasoinhibitory Peptide [*Medicine*] (MAE)
VIP Vector Inner Product (IAA)
VIP Vector Instruction Processor
VIP Vehicle Inspection Program
VIP Venous Impedance Plethysmography [*Medicine*] (DMAA)
VIP Ventilated Improved Pit [*Latrine*]
VIP Verification Integration Plan (SSD)
VIP Verifying Interpreting Punch (IAA)
VIP Verifying the Installation of Products [*Military*] (SAA)
VIP Vermont Information Processes, Inc. [*Information service or system*] (IID)
VIP Versatile Information Processor [*Computer science*]
VIP Very Important Passenger
VIP Very Important Patient (MAE)
VIP Very Important Person
VIP Very Important Poor
VIP Very Important Pregnancy [*In book title, "VIP Program"*]
VIP Vice President (AAG)
VIP Videodisc Innovation Project (NITA)
VIP Video Inertial Pointing [*System*] [*NASA*]
VIP Video Integrator and Processor
VIP Viewers in Profile [*A. C. Nielsen Co. reports for television industry*]
VIP Virgil Partch [*Cartoonist*]
VIP Virtual Image Processing [*Optics*]
VIP Virtual Instruction Package (IAA)
VIP Virtual Network System Internet Protocol [*Banyan Systems, Inc.*] [*Telecommunications*] (PCM)
VIP Viscosity-Index Improver [*for motor oil*]
VIP Visible Ink Press [*Publisher*]
VIP Vision Information Program (IID)
VIP Vision Inspection Processor (NITA)
VIP Visit-Investigate-Purchase [*Department of Commerce program*]
VIP Visitor Information Publications [*Defunct*] (EA)
VIP V-Isolation with Polysilicon Backfill (IAA)
VIP Visual Identification Point (AFM)
VIP Visual Image Processor (IAA)
VIP Visual Image Projection
VIP Visual Indicator Panel (IAA)
VIP Visual Information Processing

VIP.............. Visual Information Projection
VIP.............. Visual Input [*System*] [*AT & T*]
VIP.............. Visual Interactive Programming [*Computer science*]
ViP.............. Visual Programmer [*Computer science*] (PCM)
VIP.............. Vital Initial of Pregnancy [*In vitro fertilization*] (BABM)
VIP.............. Vital Initial of Pregnancy [*In vitro fertilization*] [*Obstetrics*] (DAVI)
VIP.............. Vocational Interviewing and Placement (DNAB)
VIP.............. Voice Information Processor
VIP.............. Voice Integrated Presentations [*Telecommunications*] (RDA)
VIP.............. Voice Intelligibility Processor [*Audio technology*] (ECON)
VIP.............. Voltage Impulse Protection (IAA)
VIP.............. Volume Inverse Pricing [*Business term*]
VIP.............. Voluntary Interruption of Pregnancy [*Obstetrics*] (MAE)
VIP.............. Volunteer Informant Program [*Navy*] (DNAB)
VIP.............. V-Shaped Isolation Regions Filled with Polycrystalline Silicon (IAA)
VIP.............. Vulcanized Interlinked Polyethylene [*Union Carbide Corp.*]
VIP.............. Vulcan Packaging, Inc. [*Toronto Stock Exchange symbol*]
VIPA.............. Volunteers in the Parks Act [*1969*]
VIPER.......... Verifiable Integrated Processor for Enhanced Reliability [*Computer science*] (BYTE)
VIPER.......... Video Processing and Electronic Reduction (IEEE)
VIPERSCAN... Viper Rocket with Scanner (SAA)
ViPet............ Petersburg Public Library, Petersburg, VA [*Library symbol Library of Congress*] (LCLS)
ViPetA.......... Allied Chemical Corp., Fibers Division, Technical Center Library, Petersburg, VA [*Library symbol Library of Congress*] (LCLS)
ViPetS.......... Virginia State College, Petersburg, VA [*Library symbol Library of Congress*] (LCLS)
VIPG............ VIP Global Capital [*NASDAQ symbol*] (SAG)
VIP Glbl....... VIP Global Capital [*Associated Press*] (SAG)
VIPI.............. Very Important Person Indeed
VIPI.............. Vinings Investment Properties Trust [*NASDAQ symbol*] (SAG)
VIPI.............. Volunteers in Probation, Inc. [*Later, VIP Division of National Council on Crime and Delinquency*] (EA)
VIPID........... Visual Information Processing Interface Device (MCD)
VIPK............. Pathankot [*India*] [*ICAO location identifier*] (ICLI)
VIPL............. Patiala [*India*] [*ICAO location identifier*] (ICLI)
ViPo............. Portsmouth Public Library, Portsmouth, VA [*Library symbol Library of Congress*] (LCLS)
ViPoN.......... Norfolk Naval Hospital, Portsmouth, VA [*Library symbol Library of Congress*] (LCLS)
ViPoVC........ Virginia Chemicals, Inc., Portsmouth, VA [*Library symbol Library of Congress*] (LCLS)
ViPoVS........ Virginia Smelting Co., Portsmouth, VA [*Library symbol Library of Congress*] (LCLS)
VIPP............. Variable Information Processing Package
VIPP............. Venda Independent People's Party [*Political party*] (PPW)
ViPrA........... American Cyanamid Co., Pigments Division, Piney River, VA [*Library symbol Library of Congress*] (LCLS)
VIPRA.......... Vest Individual Protective Reflective Adjustable [*System*] [*Military*] (INF)
VIPRE.......... Visual Precision (WDAA)
VIPRE FIRE... Visual Precision Fire Control [*Navy*] (DNAB)
VIPS............. Variable Induction Port System [*Automotive engineering*]
VIPS............. Variable Item Processing System
VIPS............. Verbal Instruction Programmed System
VIPS............. Versatile Isotope Power System (MCD)
VIPS............. Veterans in Public Service Act
VIPS............. Video Image Processing System
VIPS............. Video Interactive Processing System
VIPS............. Voice Information Processing System [*UNISYS Corp.*] [*Blue Bell, PA*] [*Telecommunications service*] (TSSD)
VIPS............. Voice Interruption Priority System
VIPSC........... Vinings Invstmt Prop [*NASDAQ symbol*] (TTSB)
VIPT............. Nainital (Pantnagar) [*India*] [*ICAO location identifier*] (ICLI)
VIPT............. Vinland Property [*NASDAQ symbol*] (NQ)
VIPTI............ Visually Impaired Piano Tuners International (EA)
VIPTS........... Vinland Property Tr SBI [*NASDAQ symbol*] (TTSB)
ViPur........... Purcellville Library, Purcellville, VA [*Library symbol Library of Congress*] (LCLS)
VIQ.............. Neillsville, WI [*Location identifier FAA*] (FAAL)
VIQ.............. Violetvale [*Queensland*] [*Airport symbol*] (AD)
VIQG............ Qazigund [*India*] [*ICAO location identifier*] (ICLI)
ViQM........... United States Marine Corps Schools, Quantico, VA [*Library symbol Library of Congress*] (LCLS)
ViQM-E........ United States Marine Corps Schools, Educational Center, Quantico, VA [*Library symbol Library of Congress*] (LCLS)
VIR.............. A. H. Robins Co., Richmond, VA [*OCLC symbol*] (OCLC)
VIR.............. Point Barrow, AK [*Location identifier FAA*] (FAAL)
ViR.............. Richmond Public Library, Richmond, VA [*Library symbol Library of Congress*] (LCLS)
VIR.............. Si Vires Permittant [*If the Strength Will Bear It*] [*Pharmacy*] (ROG)
VIR.............. Valve in Receiver (DICI)
VIR.............. Variable Interest Rate
VIR.............. Vendor Information Request [*Sales*]
VIR.............. Vendor Item Release [*Sales*]
VIR.............. Vertical Interval Reference [*Automatic color adjustment*] [*Television*]
VIR.............. Victoria Imperatrix Regina [*Victoria Empress and Queen*] (ILCA)
VIR.............. Victorian Industrial Reports [*A publication*]
VIR.............. Virco Manufacturing Co. [*AMEX symbol*] (SPSG)
VIR.............. Virco Mfg [*AMEX symbol*] (TTSB)
VIR.............. Virgin Atlantic [*British ICAO designator*] (FAAC)
Vir.............. Virginia Cases (Brockenbrough and Holmes) [*A publication*] (DLA)
VIR.............. Virgin Islands of the US [*ANSI three-letter standard code*] (CNC)
Vir.............. Virgin's Reports [*52-60 Maine*] [*A publication*] (DLA)
Vir.............. Virgo [*Constellation*]
VIR.............. Viridis [*Green*] [*Pharmacy*]
VIR.............. Virology
VIR.............. Virulent
VIR.............. Visible [*or Visual*] and Infrared Radiometer [*NASA*]
VIR.............. Vulcanized India Rubber
ViRa............ Radford College, Radford, VA [*Library symbol Library of Congress*] (LCLS)
ViRA............ Richmond Academy of Medicine, Richmond, VA [*Library symbol Library of Congress*] (LCLS)
VIRA............ Vehicular Infrared Alarm (MCD)
VIRA............ Venus International Reference Atmosphere [*Meteorology*]
VIRA............ Video Review Award
Vira-A.......... Vidarabine [*Also, ara-A*] [*Biochemistry*]
VIR AC.......... Viral Antibody, Acute [*Immunology*] (DAVI)
ViRACL........ Associates Catalog Librarians, Richmond, VA [*Library symbol*] [*Library of Congress*] (LCLS)
VIRAD.......... Virtual RADAR Defense [*Army*] (MCD)
Viragen........ Viragen, Inc. [*Associated Press*] (SAG)
ViRAM.......... Richmond Academy of Medicine, Richmond, VA [*Library symbol*] [*Library of Congress*] (LCLS)
VIR & Regs... Virgin Islands Rules and Regulations [*A publication*] (DLA)
ViRaP.......... Radford Public Library, Radford, VA [*Library symbol Library of Congress*] (LCLS)
ViRAV.......... Atlantic Varnish & Paint Co., Richmond, VA [*Library symbol Library of Congress*] (LCLS)
VIRB............ Raibarelli/Fursatganj [*India*] [*ICAO location identifier*] (ICLI)
ViRBG.......... Lewis Ginter Botanical Gardens, Inc., Richmond, VA [*Library symbol*] [*Library of Congress*] (LCLS)
ViRBL.......... Bryne Library Consulting, Richmond, VA [*Library symbol*] [*Library of Congress*] (LCLS)
ViRC............ Museum of the Confederacy, Richmond, VA [*Library symbol Library of Congress*] (LCLS)
ViRCC.......... [*The*] Computer Co., Richmond, VA [*Library symbol Library of Congress*] (LCLS)
ViRCCF........ Christian Children's Fund, Richmond, VA [*Library symbol*] [*Library of Congress*] (LCLS)
Virch PM..... Virchow on Post Mortem Examinations [*A publication*] (DLA)
Virco........... Virco Manufacturing Corp. [*Associated Press*] (SAG)
ViRCU.......... Virginia Commonwealth University, Richmond, VA [*Library symbol Library of Congress*] (LCLS)
ViRCU-A...... Virginia Commonwealth University, Academic Division, Richmond, VA [*Library symbol Library of Congress*] (LCLS)
ViRCU-H...... Virginia Commonwealth University, Health Sciences Division, Richmond, VA [*Library symbol Library of Congress*] (LCLS)
ViReA.......... American College of Radiology, Reston, VA [*Library symbol*] [*Library of Congress*] (LCLS)
ViREP.......... Virginia Electric & Power Co., Richmond, VA [*Library symbol Library of Congress*] (LCLS)
ViREx.......... Experiment, Inc., Richmond, VA [*Library symbol Library of Congress*] (LCLS)
ViRFR.......... Federal Reserve Bank of Richmond, Richmond, VA [*Library symbol Library of Congress*] (LCLS)
VIRG............ Reengus [*India*] [*ICAO location identifier*] (ICLI)
ViRG............ Richmond Guano Co., Richmond, VA [*Library symbol Library of Congress*] (LCLS)
VIRG............ Virgin
Virg............ Virgin's Reports [*52-60 Maine*] [*A publication*] (DLA)
Virg............ Virgo [*Constellation*]
Virg Cas...... Virginia Cases (Brockenbrough and Holmes) [*A publication*] (DLA)
VirgErp....... Viragen Europe Ltd. [*Associated Press*] (SAG)
VirgGas....... Virginia Gas Co. [*Associated Press*] (SAG)
VirgGs......... Virginia Gas Co. [*Associated Press*] (SAG)
Virgin.......... Virgin's Reports [*52-60 Maine*] [*A publication*] (DLA)
Virg LJ........ Virginia Law Journal [*Richmond*] [*A publication*] (DLA)
ViRGS.......... Church of Jesus Christ of Latter-Day Saints, Genealogical Society Library, Richmond Stake Branch, Richmond, VA [*Library symbol Library of Congress*] (LCLS)
VIRGS.......... VISSR [*Visible-Infrared Spin Scan Radiometer*] Image Registration and Gridding System (MCD)
ViRHC.......... Henrico County Public Library, Richmond, VA [*Library symbol Library of Congress*] (LCLS)
VIR IS.......... Virgin Islands (WDAA)
VIRIS.......... Visible/Infrared Intelligent Spectrometer
Vir LJ......... Virginia Law Journal [*A publication*] (DLA)
VIRM........... Variable-Interest-Rate Mortgage [*Real estate*]
ViRMu......... Virginia Museum of Fine Arts, Richmond, VA [*Library symbol Library of Congress*] (LCLS)
VIRNS.......... Velocity Inertia RADAR Navigation System
ViRo............ Roanoke Public Library, Roanoke, VA [*Library symbol Library of Congress*] (LCLS)
VIRO............ Virogroup, Inc. [*NASDAQ symbol*] (SAG)
ViRoA.......... American Viscose Co., Roanoke, VA [*Library symbol Library of Congress*] (LCLS)
ViRoC.......... Roanoke County Public Library, Roanoke, VA [*Library symbol*] [*Library of Congress*] (LCLS)
ViroGp........ Virogroup, Inc. [*Associated Press*] (SAG)
ViRoMH....... Roanoke Memorial Hospital, Roanoke, VA [*Library symbol*] [*Library of Congress*] (LCLS)
ViRoNW....... Norfolk & Western Railway Co., Roanoke, VA [*Library symbol Library of Congress*] (LCLS)
ViroPh......... ViroPharma, Inc. [*Associated Press*] (SAG)
ViRoV.......... Virginia Western Community College, Brown Library, Roanoke, VA [*Library symbol Library of Congress*] (LCLS)

ViRPM......... Philip Morris Research Center, Richmond, VA [*Library symbol Library of Congress*] (LCLS)
ViRPol......... W. P. Poythress Co., Richmond, VA [*Library symbol Library of Congress*] (LCLS)
ViRR........... Reynolds Metals Co., Richmond, VA [*Library symbol Library of Congress*] (LCLS)
VIRR........... Visible [*or Visual*] and Infrared Radiometer [*NASA*]
ViRRC.......... J. Sargeant Reynolds Community College, Downtown Campus, Richmond, VA [*Library symbol Library of Congress*] (LCLS)
ViRR-E......... Reynolds Metals Co., Executive Office Library, Richmond, VA [*Library symbol Library of Congress*] (LCLS)
ViRRob......... A. H. Robins Co., Richmond, VA [*Library symbol Library of Congress*] (LCLS)
ViRR-P......... Reynolds Metals Co., Packaging Research Division, Richmond, VA [*Library symbol Library of Congress*] (LCLS)
ViRR-T......... Reynolds Metals Co., Technical Information Services Library, Richmond, VA [*Library symbol Library of Congress*] (LCLS)
VIRS........... Vertical Interval Reference Signal [*Automatic color adjustment*] [*Television*] (IAA)
VIRS........... Visual Technology Research Simulator (MCD)
ViRSBF......... Southern Baptist Convention Foreign Mission Board, Richmond, VA [*Library symbol*] [*Library of Congress*] (LCLS)
ViRStM......... Saint Mary's Hospital, Health Sciences Library, Richmond, VA [*Library symbol*] [*Library of Congress*] (LCLS)
Virt........... De Virtutibus [*of Philo*] (BJA)
Virt........... Virtually (ILCA)
ViRU........... University of Richmond, Richmond, VA [*Library symbol Library of Congress*] (LCLS)
ViRUCA......... United States Circuit Court of Appeals, Fourth Circuit, Richmond, VA [*Library symbol Library of Congress*] (LCLS)
VirusRes....... Virus Research Institute, Inc. [*Associated Press*] (SAG)
ViRUT.......... Union Theological Seminary, Richmond, VA [*Library symbol Library of Congress*] (LCLS)
ViRUV.......... United Virginia Bankshares, Inc., Richmond, VA [*Library symbol Library of Congress*] (LCLS)
ViRV........... United States Veterans Administration Hospital, Richmond, VA [*Library symbol Library of Congress*] (LCLS)
ViRVal......... Valentine Museum, Richmond, VA [*Library symbol Library of Congress*] (LCLS)
ViRVB.......... Virginia Baptist Historical Society, University of Richmond, Richmond, VA [*Library symbol Library of Congress*] (LCLS)
ViRVI.......... Virginia Institute for Scientific Research, Richmond, VA [*Library symbol Library of Congress*] (LCLS)
ViRVM.......... Valentine Meat Juice Co., Richmond, VA [*Library symbol Library of Congress*] (LCLS)
ViRVU.......... Virginia Union University, Richmond, VA [*Library symbol Library of Congress*] (LCLS)
VIS............ Jet Servisx SA de CV [*Mexico ICAO designator*] (FAAC)
VIS............ Minority Vendor Information Service [*National Minority Supplier Development Council, Inc.*] (IID)
VIS............ Vaginal Irrigation Smear [*Medicine*] (MAE)
VIS............ Variable Induction System [*Automotive engineering*]
VIS............ Variable Inflation System
VIS............ Variance Index Score [*Statistics*]
VIS............ Vector Instruction Set [*Computer science*]
VIS............ Vegetarian Information Service (EA)
VIS............ Vehicle Indicator Section
VIS............ Vehicle Information System [*Automotive engineering*]
VIS............ Vehicle Interface Subsystem [*Army*] (RDA)
VIS............ Vehicular Intercommunications System
VIS............ Verification Information System (NASA)
VIS............ Veterinary Investigation Service [*Ministry of Agriculture, Fisheries, and Food*] [*British*]
VIS............ Vibration Isolation System
VIS............ Victim Impact Statement
VIS............ Video Imaging System
VIS............ Video Information System [*Tandy Corp.*] (DOM)
VIS............ Videotex Information System [*Radio Shack*] [*Information service or system*] (IID)
VIS............ Vietnamese Information Service
VIS............ Virtual Information Storage (BUR)
VIS............ Visalia [*California*] [*Airport symbol*] (OAG)
VIS............ Viscosity
VIS............ Viscount [*or Viscountess*]
VIS............ Viscount Resources Ltd. [*Vancouver Stock Exchange symbol*]
VIS............ Vishakhapatnam [*Andhra, Waltair*] [*India*] [*Seismograph station code, US Geological Survey*] (SEIS)
VIS............ Visible [*or Visibility*] (AFM)
VIS............ Vision (AAMN)
VIS............ Visit [*or Visitor*]
VIS............ Vista
VIS............ Vista
VIS............ Visual
VIS............ Visual Imagery System [*NASA*]
VIS............ Visual Information Storage
VIS............ Visual Information System
VIS............ Visual Instruction Set [*Computer science*]
VIS............ Visual Instrumentation Subsystem
VIS............ Visual Spectrophotometry
VIS............ VNR [*Van Nostrand Reinhold*] Information Services (IID)
VIS............ Voice Information Service [*Telecommunications*]
VIS............ Voice Interactive Subsystem (MCD)
VIS............ Voice Intercom Subsystem (MCD)
VIS............ Voltage Inverter Switch (IAA)
VIS............ Voters Information Service [*Provides congressional voting records*]
ViSa........... Salem Public Library, Salem, VA [*Library symbol Library of Congress*] (LCLS)
VISA........... Ventricular Inhibiting Synchronous with Atrium [*Cardiac pacemaker*] [*Trademark*]
VISA........... Vocational Interest and Sophistication Assessment [*Vocational guidance test*]
VISAM.......... Variable-Length Indexed Sequential Access Method [*Computer science*] (MHDB)
VISAM.......... Virtual Index Sequential Access Method (IAA)
VISAR.......... Velocity Interferometer System for Any Reflector (MCD)
VISAR.......... Velocity Interferometer System for any Reflector [*Instrumentation*]
ViSaRC......... Roanoke College, Salem, VA [*Library symbol Library of Congress*] (LCLS)
ViSaV.......... United States Veterans Administration Hospital, Salem, VA [*Library symbol Library of Congress*] (LCLS)
VISB........... Sikandrabad [*India*] [*ICAO location identifier*] (ICLI)
VISC........... Video Disc
visc........... Visceral
VISC........... Viscosity (AAG)
VISC........... Viscount [*or Viscountess*]
ViSC........... Visualization in Scientific Computing [*Computer science*] (EERA)
VISC........... Vitreous Infusion Suction Cutter [*Ophthalmology*]
VISCA.......... Video System Control Architecture [*Computer science*] (CDE)
VISCO.......... Visual Systems Corp.
VISCOM......... Visual Communications
VIS-COM-UK..... Visual Communications Exhibition and Conference, United Kingdom (ITD)
VISCT.......... Viscount [*or Viscountess*]
VISDA.......... Visual Information System Development Association (MHDB)
VisEd.......... Visual Edge Systems, Inc. [*Associated Press*] (SAG)
VisEdge........ Visual Edge Systems, Inc. [*Associated Press*] (SAG)
VISG........... Viisage Technology, Inc. [*NASDAQ symbol*] (SAG)
VisGene........ Visible Genetics, Inc. [*Associated Press*] (SAG)
Vishay......... Vishay Intertechnology, Inc. [*Associated Press*] (SAG)
VISI........... Volar Intercalated Segment Instability [*Orthopedics*]
VISIC.......... Visual Science Information Center (ECII)
VisiCalc....... Visible Calculation [*Electronic spreadsheet program brand*]
VISID.......... Visual Identification (MSA)
Visigenic...... Visigenic Software, Inc. [*Associated Press*] (SAG)
VisioCo........ Visio Corp. [*Associated Press*] (SAG)
VISIoN......... Victorian Information Services Network [*Australia*]
Vision......... Visioneer, Inc. [*Associated Press*] (SAG)
VISION......... Visual Imaging Systems in Origination Network (DGA)
VISION......... Volunteers in Service to India's Oppressed and Neglected (EA)
VisionSci...... Vision Sciences, Inc. [*Associated Press*] (SAG)
VISIT.......... Project VISIT - Vehicle Internal Systems Investigative Team (EA)
VISIT.......... Visual Information Systems for Image Transformation [*Air Force*]
VISITS......... Very Important Small Institution Travel Support
VISITT......... Vendor Information System for Innovative Treatment Technology [*Database*] [*Environmental Protection Agency*]
VISL........... Visual
VIS LAB........ Visibility Laboratory [*Research center*] (RCD)
VISM........... Simla [*India*] [*ICAO location identifier*] (ICLI)
VISMEM......... Visual Memory Task [*Neuropsychology test*]
VISMOD......... Visual Modifications [*Program*] [*Army*] (RDA)
VISMR.......... Viscometer [*Engineering*]
VISN........... Sight Resource [*NASDAQ symbol*] (TTSB)
VISN........... Sight Resources Corp. [*NASDAQ symbol*] (SAG)
VISN........... Vision Interfaith Satellite Network
VIS/NIR........ Visible and Near-Visible Infrared (MCD)
VISNZ.......... Sight Resource Wrrt [*NASDAQ symbol*] (TTSB)
VISP........... Saharanpur/Sarsawa [*India*] [*ICAO location identifier*] (ICLI)
VISP........... Vehicle Inspection by System Parameter [*Automotive diagnostics*]
VISPA.......... Virtual Storage Productivity Aid [*Computer science*] (MHDB)
VISPAC......... Videotex Information Service Providers Association of Canada [*Defunct*] (IID)
ViSpN.......... National Technical Information Service, Springfield, VA [*Library symbol Library of Congress*] (LCLS)
VISQI.......... Visual Image Quality Indicator (PDAA)
VISR........... Srinagar [*India*] [*ICAO location identifier*] (ICLI)
VISR........... Virginia Institute for Scientific Research [*University of Richmond*] [*Research center*] (MCD)
VISSR.......... Visible-Infrared Spin Scan Radiometer [*NASA*]
VIST........... Satna [*India*] [*ICAO location identifier*] (ICLI)
ViSt........... Staunton Public Library, Staunton, VA [*Library symbol Library of Congress*] (LCLS)
VIST........... Vista [*Commonly used*] (OPSA)
VIST........... Vista 2000, Inc. [*NASDAQ symbol*] (SAG)
VISTA.......... Variable Interlace System for Television Applications
VISTA.......... Variable (Stability) In-Flight Simulator Test Aircraft
VISTA.......... Varied Intelligent System Target Acquisition
VISTA.......... Verbal Information Storage and Text Analysis [*in FORTRAN computer language*]
VISTA.......... Very Intelligent Surveillance and Target Acquisition [*Army*] (RDA)
VISTA.......... Videodisc Interpersonal Skills Training and Assessment (INF)
VISTA.......... Viewing Instantly Security Transactions Automatically [*Wall Street*]
VISTA.......... Vista [*Commonly used*] (OPSA)
VISTA.......... Visual Information for Satellite Telemetry Analysis
VISTA.......... Visually Impaired Secretarial/Transcribers Association [*Indianapolis, IN*] (EA)
VISTA.......... Visual Storage Administrator [*Windows*] [*Computer science*] (PCM)
VISTA.......... Visual Talking [*Telecommunications*] (IAA)
VISTA.......... Volunteers in Service to America (EA)
Vista2000...... Vista 2000, Inc. [*Associated Press*] (SAG)
VISTAB......... Vistaril [*A central nervous system depressant*] (DAVI)

VistaBcP Bista Bancorp [*Associated Press*] (SAG)
VistaBcp Vista Bancorp [*Associated Press*] (SAG)
VistaG Vista Gold Corp. [*Associated Press*] (SAG)
VistaInf Vista Information Solutions, Inc. [*Associated Press*] (SAG)
ViSte Sterling Public Library, Sterling, VA [*Library symbol Library of Congress*] (LCLS)
VISTE Vista 2000 Inc. [*NASDAQ symbol*] (TTSB)
ViStM Mary Baldwin College, Staunton, VA [*Library symbol Library of Congress*] (LCLS)
VISTRAC Visual Target Reconnaissance and Acquisition (MCD)
ViStrR Robert E. Lee Memorial Association, Stratford Hall, Stratford, VA [*Library symbol Library of Congress*] (LCLS)
VISTTA Visibility Impairment for Sulfur Transformation and Transport in the Atmosphere [*Environmental Protection Agency*] (GFGA)
VIS-UV Visible Ultraviolet Spectrometer (MCD)
VIS/UV Visual/Ultraviolet (SSD)
ViSwC Sweet Briar College, Sweet Briar, VA [*Library symbol Library of Congress*] (LCLS)
VISWE Vista 2000 Wrrt'A' [*NASDAQ symbol*] (TTSB)
VISX VISX, Inc. [*NASDAQ symbol*] (SAG)
VIT Roanoke, VA [*Location identifier FAA*] (FAAL)
VIT Technical Research Centre of Finland
VIT Van Kam Am Cap Interm [*NYSE symbol*] (TTSB)
VIT Van Kampen Merritt Intermediate Term High Income Trust [*NYSE symbol*] (SPSG)
VIT Variable Impedance Tube
VIT Variable Inductive Transducer [*Automotive engineering*]
VIT Variable Injection Timing [*Diesel engines*]
VIT Vehicle Information Terminal
VIT Venom Immunotherapy [*Immunology*] [*Emergency medicine*] (DAVI)
VIT Vertical Interval Test [*Automatic color adjustment*] [*Television*] (IAA)
VIT Vertically Integrated Team [*Engineering*]
VIT Very Important Traveler
VIT Very Intelligent Terminal (IAA)
VIT Vibration Isolation Table
VIT Victoria Resources [*Vancouver Stock Exchange symbol*]
VIT Vineyard Telemeter [*California*] [*Seismograph station code, US Geological Survey Closed*] (SEIS)
Vit Vita [*of Josephus*] [*Classical studies*] (OCD)
Vit Vitae Parallelae [*of Plutarch*] [*Classical studies*] (OCD)
VIT Vital
VIT Vitamin
Vit Vitellius [*of Suetonius*] [*Classical studies*] (OCD)
vit Vitellus [*Yolk*] [*Latin Pharmacy*] (MAE)
VIT Vitoria [*Spain*] [*Airport symbol*] (OAG)
VIT Vitreous (AAG)
VIT Voice Interactive Technology
VITA Veterans Time Trial Association [*Bicycling*] (DICI)
VitA Vitamin A [*Used to indicate either dehydroretinol or retinol*] (DAVI)
VITA VMEbus International Trade Association (EA)
VITA Volunteer Income Tax Assistance Program [*Internal Revenue Service*]
VITA Volunteers for International Technical Assistance (IAA)
VITA Volunteers in Technical Assistance (EA)
VitA$_1$ Vitamin A$_1$ [*Also called retinol*] (DAVI)
VitA$_2$ Vitamin A$_2$ [*Also called dehydroretinal*] (DAVI)
VITAE Video Imaging Technique for Assessing Exposure [*to pesticides*]
VITAL Variably Initialized Translator for Algorithmic Languages [*Computer science*]
VITAL VAST [*Versatile Avionics Shop Test*] Interface Test Application Language
VITAL Verification of Interceptor Tactics Logic (SAA)
VITAL Virtual Image Takeoff and Landing [*Simulator*] (MCD)
VitalSgn Vital Signs, Inc. [*Associated Press*] (SAG)
Vita Luc Vita Lucani [*of Suetonius*] [*Classical studies*] (OCD)
VITAP Viking Targeting Analysis Program [*NASA*]
VITAS Visual Target Acquisition System [*Navy*] (MCD)
VITAS Vocational Interest, Temperament, and Aptitude System [*Aptitude test*]
Vit Auct Vitarum Auctio [*of Lucian*] [*Classical studies*] (OCD)
VitB Vitamin B [*A member of the vitamin B complex*] (DAVI)
VitB$_1$ Vitamin B$_1$ [*Also called thiamine*] (DAVI)
VitB$_2$ Vitamin B$_2$ [*Also called riboflavin*] (DAVI)
VitB$_3$ Vitamin B$_3$ [*Also called niacin and nicotinamide*] (DAVI)
VitB$_5$ Vitamin B$_5$ [*Also called calcium pantothenate and pantothenic acid*] (DAVI)
VitB$_6$ Vitamin B$_6$ [*Water-soluble substances including pyridoxine, pyridoxal, and pyridoxamine*] (DAVI)
VitB$_{12}$ Vitamin B$_{12}$ [*Also called cobalamin and cyanocobalamin*] (DAVI)
VitB$_{12b}$ VitaminB$_{12b}$ [*Also called hydroxycobalamin*] (DAVI)
VitB$_c$ Vitamin B$_c$ [*Also called folic acid*] (DAVI)
VITC Vertical Internal Time Code [*Electronic musical instruments*]
VITC Vertical Interval Time Code (NTCM)
VitC Vitamin C [*Also called ascorbic acid*] (DAVI)
vit cap Vital Capacity (MAE)
VitchAm Vitech America, Inc. [*Associated Press*] (SAG)
VitD Vitamin D [*Also called calciferol a collective name for several fat-soluble compounds*] (DAVI)
VitD$_2$ Vitamin D$_2$ [*Also called ergocalciferol*] (DAVI)
VitD$_3$ Vitamin D$_3$ [*Also called cholecalciferol and natural vitamin D*] (DAVI)
VitE Vitamin E [*Also called alpha-tocopherol*] (DAVI)
VITEAC Video Transmission Engineering Advisory Committee [*Army*] (PDAA)
VITEK Life Technology (MCD)
Vitel Vitellus [*Yolk*] [*Pharmacy*]
Vitesse Vitesse Semiconductor Corp. [*Associated Press*] (SAG)
VITG Vietnam Individual Training Group [*Deactivated in December, 1972*] [*Military*] (VNW)
VitG Vitamin G [*Also called riboflavin*] (DAVI)
VitH Vitamin H [*Also called biotin*] (DAVI)
VITIC Viticulture
VITIS-VEA VITIS-Viticulture and Enology Abstracts [*International Food Information Service*] [*Information service or system*] (IID)
VITK Futurebiotics, Inc. [*NASDAQ symbol*] (SAG)
VitK Vitamin K [*A group of fat-soluble vitamins that promote clotting of the blood*] (DAVI)
VitK$_1$ Vitamin K$_1$ [*Also called phytonadione*] (DAVI)
VitK$_2$ Vitamin K$_2$ [*Also called menaquinone*] (DAVI)
VITKW Futurebiotics Inc. Wrrt [*NASDAQ symbol*] (TTSB)
VITL Vital Signs, Inc. [*NASDAQ symbol*] (SAG)
VitL Vitamin L [*A factor necessary for lactation in rats*] (DAVI)
VitL$_1$ Vitamin L$_1$ [*A factor necessary for lactation in rats and found in beef-liver extract*] (DAVI)
VitInk Vitalink Pharmacy Services, Inc. [*Associated Press*] (SAG)
VitM Vitamin M [*Also called folic acid*] (DAVI)
Vit Ov Sol Vitello Ovi Solutus [*Dissolved in the Yolk of an Egg*] [*Pharmacy*]
VitPP Vitamin PP [*Also called nicotinamide and nicotinic acid*] (DAVI)
vitr Vitreous [*Ophthalmology*] [*Latin*] (DAVI)
VITR Vitreum [*Glass*] [*Latin*] (ADA)
Vitr Vitruvius [*First century BC*] [*Classical studies*] (OCD)
VITRAN Vibration Transient Analysis (MCD)
VitranCo Vitran Corp., Inc. [*Associated Press*] (SAG)
Vitro Vitro, Sociedad Anonima [*Associated Press*] (SAG)
VITROLAIN Vitreous Enamel Porcelain (IAA)
Vitronic Vitronics Corp. [*Associated Press*] (SAG)
Vitronic Vitronics Corp. [*Associated Press*] (SAG)
VITS Vertical Interval Test Signal (IEEE)
vit stat Vital Statistics (BARN)
VITT Vehicle Integration Test Team [*NASA*] (MCD)
VitU Vitamin U [*Also called antiulcer vitamin and cabagin vitamin*] (DAVI)
ViU University of Virginia, Charlottesville, VA [*Library symbol Library of Congress*] (LCLS)
VIU Vehicle in Use
VIU Video Interface Unit (MCD)
VIU Voice Intercommunications Unit
VIU Voice Interface Unit [*Telecommunications*] (TEL)
VIUD Udaipur [*India*] [*ICAO location identifier*] (ICLI)
ViU-ES University of Virginia, School of General Studies, Eastern Shore Branch, WallopsIsland, VA [*Library symbol Library of Congress*] (LCLS)
ViU-H University of Virginia Medical Center, Health Sciences Library, Charlottesville,VA [*Library symbol Library of Congress*] (LCLS)
ViU-L University of Virginia, Law Library, Charlottesville, VA [*Library symbol Library of Congress*] (LCLS)
ViU-Mu University of Virginia, Music Library, Charlottesville, VA [*Library symbol Library of Congress*] (LCLS)
VIURAM Video Interface Unit Random Access Memory
ViU-ST University of Virginia, Science/Technology Information Center, Charlottesville, VA [*Library symbol Library of Congress*] (LCLS)
VIV Variable Inlet Vane [*Nuclear energy*] (NRCH)
VIV Viajes Internacionales de Vacaciones SA [*Spain ICAO designator*] (FAAC)
VIV Vivace [*Lively*] [*Music*]
VIV Vivian, LA [*Location identifier FAA*] (FAAL)
VIV Vivid-Inventive-Vital [*Spring fashions*]
VIV Vivigani [*Papua New Guinea*] [*Airport symbol*] (OAG)
VIV Vlaamse Ingenieurs-Vereinigung
VIVA Viajes Internacionales de Vacaciones SA [*Spain ICAO designator*] (FAAC)
VIVA Victory in Vietnam Association
VIVA Virgin Islands Visitors Association
VIVA Visually Impaired Veterans of America (EA)
VIVA Voices in Vital America
ViVb Department of Public Libraries and Information, City of Virginia Beach, Reference Department, Virginia Beach, VA [*Library symbol Library of Congress*] (LCLS)
ViVbC CBN University, Virginia Beach, VA [*Library symbol*] [*Library of Congress*] (LCLS)
ViVbGS Church of Jesus Christ of Latter-Day Saints, Genealogical Society Library, Norfolk Virginia Stake Branch, Virginia Beach, VA [*Library symbol Library of Congress*] (LCLS)
ViVbRE Association for Research and Enlightenment, Virginia Beach, VA [*Library symbol Library of Congress*] (LCLS)
VIVED Virtual Visual Environment Display [*Helmet equipped with liquid crystal display screens viewed through wide-angle lenses*] [*NASA*]
Vivi Vivianus Tuscus [*Flourished, 13th century*] [*Authority cited in pre-1607 legal work*] (DSA)
VIVI Vivisection [*Medicine*] (WDAA)
Vivia Vivianus Tuscus [*Flourished, 13th century*] [*Authority cited in pre-1607 legal work*] (DSA)
VividTch Vivid Technologies, Inc. [*Associated Press*] (SAG)
Vivra Vivra, Inc. [*Associated Press*] (SAG)
Vivus Vivus, Inc. [*Associated Press*] (SAG)
ViW College of William and Mary, Williamsburg, VA [*Library symbol Library of Congress*] (LCLS)
ViWaR Rappahannock Community College, North Campus, Warsaw, VA [*Library symbol Library of Congress*] (LCLS)
ViWarUS United States Army, Post Library, Vint Hill Farms Station, Warrenton, VA [*Library symbol Library of Congress*] (LCLS)

ViWb........... Waynesboro Public Library, Waynesboro, VA [*Library symbol Library of Congress*] (LCLS)
ViWbD......... E. I. Du Pont de Nemours & Co., Benger Laboratory, Waynesboro, VA [*Library symbol Library of Congress*] (LCLS)
ViWbF......... Fairfax Hall Junior College, Waynesboro, VA [*Library symbol Library of Congress*] (LCLS)
ViWC........... Colonial Williamsburg, Inc., Williamsburg, VA [*Library symbol Library of Congress*] (LCLS)
ViWI............ Institute of Early American History and Culture, Williamsburg, VA [*Library symbol Library of Congress*] (LCLS)
ViWiN.......... United States National Aeronautics and Space Administration, Technical Library, Wallops Island, VA [*Library symbol Library of Congress*] (LCLS)
ViWis........... Lonesome Pine Regional Library, Wise, VA [*Library symbol*] [*Library of Congress*] (LCLS)
ViWisC......... Clinch Valley College of the University of Virginia, Wise, VA [*Library symbol Library of Congress*] (LCLS)
ViW-L.......... College of William and Mary, Law School, Williamsburg, VA [*Library symbol Library of Congress*] (LCLS)
ViWn............ Handley Library, Winchester, VA [*Library symbol Library of Congress*] (LCLS)
ViWnS.......... Shenandoah College and Conservatory of Music, Winchester, VA [*Library symbol Library of Congress*] (LCLS)
ViWR............ Williamsburg Regional Library, Williamsburg, VA [*Library symbol*] [*Library of Congress*] (LCLS)
ViWSC.......... National Center for State Courts, Williamsburg, VA [*Library symbol*] [*Library of Congress*] (LCLS)
ViWyC.......... Wytheville Community College, Wytheville, VA [*Library symbol Library of Congress*] (LCLS)
VIX.............. Vitoria [*Brazil*] [*Airport symbol*] (OAG)
VIX.............. Vixit [*He Lived*] [*Latin*]
VIY.............. Nashville, TN [*Location identifier FAA*] (FAAL)
ViYNW.......... United States Naval Weapons Station, Yorktown, VA [*Library symbol Library of Congress*] (LCLS)
VIZ.............. Videlicet [*Namely*] [*Latin*]
Viz............... Vizardinus [*Guizzardinus*] [*Deceased, 1222*] [*Authority cited in pre-1607 legal work*] (DSA)
VIZ.............. Vizianagram [*India*] [*Seismograph station code, US Geological Survey*] (SEIS)
VIZ.............. Vizmo [*Projection device*] (NTCM)
viz............... Vizmo (WDMC)
Vizar............ Vizardinus [*Guizzardinus*] [*Deceased, 1222*] [*Authority cited in pre-1607 legal work*] (DSA)
viz-code....... Visual Time Code (WDMC)
Viz Pr.......... Vizard's Practice of the Court in Banc [*A publication*] (DLA)
VJ................ Trans-Colorado [*ICAO designator*] (AD)
VJ................ Utility Plane [*Navy symbol*]
VJ................ Vacuum-Jacketed (KSC)
VJ................ Variable Joining [*Genetics*]
VJ................ Ventriculojugular [*Medicine*]
VJ................ Video Jockey [*Television version of disc jockey; originated on all-rock-music cable station MTV*]
VJ................ Visiting Judges [*British*]
VJ................ V-Joint [*Technical drawings*]
VJ................ Vogel: Johnson Agar [*Microbiology*] (DAVI)
VJA.............. Adelphi University, Garden City, NY [*OCLC symbol*] (OCLC)
VJA.............. V-8 Juice Agar [*Microbiology*]
VJA.............. ValuJet Airlines, Inc. [*ICAO designator*] (FAAC)
VJB.............. Verdan Junction Box
VJB.............. Victorian Judgements Bulletin [*Australia A publication*]
VJB.............. Vila de Joao Belo [*Mozambique*] [*Airport symbol*] (AD)
VJC.............. Vallejo Junior College [*California*]
VJC.............. Vermont Junior College
VJC.............. Virginia Junior College [*Minnesota*] [*Later, Mesabi Community College*]
V-J (Day)..... Victory over Japan [*Japanese surrender, World War II, 14 August 1945*]
VJET............ ValuJet Airlines [*NASDAQ symbol*] (TTSB)
VJET............ ValuJet Airlines, Inc. [*NASDAQ symbol*] (SAG)
VJH.............. Victorian Journal of History [*A publication*]
VJJ............... Johnson & Johnson Dental Products Co., Science Information Center, East Windsor,NJ [*OCLC symbol*] (OCLC)
VJMC........... Vintage Japanese Motorcycle Club (EA)
VJNRL......... Virginia Journal of Natural Resources Law [*A publication*] (DLA)
VJSW........... Voice Jamming Simulator, Weapons (SAA)
VJTA............ Veterans' Job Training Act
VJV.............. Van Kam Am Cap NJ Val Mun [*AMEX symbol*] (TTSB)
VJV.............. Van Kampen Merritt New Jersey Value Municipal, Inc. [*AMEX symbol*] (SPSG)
VJWI............ Velcro-Jumping while Intoxicated
VK................ Air Tungaru [*ICAO designator*] (AD)
VK................ Ventral Wall, Kidney [*Anatomy*]
VK................ Verbundkatalog Maschinenlesbarer Katalogdaten Deutscher Bibliotheken [*Deutsches Bibliotheksinstitut*] [*Germany Information service or system*] (CRD)
VK................ Vertical Keel
VK................ Vervet [*African green monkey*] [*Medicine*] (DMAA)
VK................ Volume Kill (WDAA)
VKA.............. Van Kam Am Cap Adv Muni [*NYSE symbol*] (TTSB)
VKA.............. Van Kampen Amer. Cap. Advantage Muni Income Trust [*NYSE symbol*] (SAG)
VKA.............. Van Kampen Merritt Advanced Municipal Income Trust [*NYSE symbol*] (SPSG)
VKA.............. Vienna-Kobenzl [*Austria*] [*Seismograph station code, US Geological Survey*] (SEIS)
VKA.............. Volatile Keying Assembly (AFM)
VKACBd....... Van Kampen Amer. Cap. Bond Fund [*Associated Press*] (SAG)
VKACCV....... Van Kampen Amer. Cap. Convertible Securities [*Associated Press*] (SAG)
VKACInc....... Van Kampen Amer. Cap. Income Trust [*Associated Press*] (SAG)
VKAdM2....... Van Kampen Amer. Cap. Advantage Muni. Income Trust I [*Associated Press*] (SAG)
VKAdPA........ Van Kampen Amer. Cap. Advantage PA Muni. Income [*Associated Press*] (SAG)
VKAdvM....... Van Kampen Amer. Cap. Advantage Muni. Income Trust [*Associated Press*] (SAG)
VKC.............. Canisius College, Buffalo, NY [*OCLC symbol*] (OCLC)
VKC.............. Van Kam Am Cap CA Muni [*AMEX symbol*] (TTSB)
VKC.............. Van Kampen Merritt California Municipal Trust [*AMEX symbol*] (CTT)
VKC.............. Vernal Keratoconjunctivitis [*Ophthalmology*] (DAVI)
VKCal........... Van Kampen Merritt California Municipal Trust [*Associated Press*] (SAG)
VKCAQ......... Van Kampen Merritt California Quality Municipal Trust [*Associated Press*] (SAG)
VKCAV......... Van Kampen Merritt California Value Municipal Trust [*Associated Press*] (SAG)
VKE.............. Von Karman Equation
VKF.............. Von Karman Gas Dynamics Facility [*Arnold Air Force Base, TN*] [*Air Force*]
VKFLO......... Van Kampen Merritt Florida Municipal Opportunity [*Associated Press*] (SAG)
VKFLQ......... Van Kampen Merritt Florida Quality Municipal Trust [*Associated Press*] (SAG)
VKG.............. Premiair [*Norway*] [*FAA designator*] (FAAC)
VKG.............. Scanair Ltd. [*Denmark ICAO designator*] (FAAC)
VKG.............. Viking
VKH.............. Vogt-Koyanagi-Harada [*Syndrome*] [*Ophthalmology*]
VKI............... Van Kam Am Cap Adv Mun II [*AMEX symbol*] (TTSB)
VKI............... Van Kampen Merritt Advanced Muncipal Income Trust II [*AMEX symbol*] (SPSG)
VKI............... Von Karman Institute (NATG)
VKIFD.......... Von Karman Institute for Fluid Dynamics [*Belgium*]
VKIGM......... Van Kampen Merritt Investment Grade Municipal Trust [*Associated Press*] (SAG)
VkingOP....... Viking Office Products [*Associated Press*] (SAG)
VKITH.......... Van Kampen Merritt Intermediate Term High Income Trust [*Associated Press*] (SAG)
VKL.............. Aerovekel SA [*Mexico ICAO designator*] (FAAC)
VKL.............. Van Kam Am Cap Sel Sec Mun [*AMEX symbol*] (TTSB)
VKL.............. Van Kampen Merritt Select Securities Municipal Trust [*AMEX symbol*] (SPSG)
VKLTH.......... Van Kampen Merritt Limited Term High Income Trust [*Associated Press*] (SAG)
VKMAd......... Van Kampen Merritt Advanced Municipal Income Trust [*Associated Press*] (SAG)
VKMAd2....... Van Kampen Merritt Advantage Municipal Income Trust 2 [*Associated Press*] (SAG)
VKMAPA...... Van Kampen Merritt Advantage Pennsylvania Municipal Income Trust [*Associated Press*] (SAG)
VKMAV........ Van Kampen Merritt Massachusetts Value Municipal [*Associated Press*] (SAG)
VKMIT.......... Van Kampen Merritt Municipal Income Trust [*Associated Press*] (SAG)
VKMM02...... Van Kampen Merritt Municipal Opportunity Trust 2 [*Associated Press*] (SAG)
VKMMO....... Van Kampen Merritt Municipal Opportunity Trust [*Associated Press*] (SAG)
VKMMT........ Van Kampen Merritt Municipal Trust [*Associated Press*] (SAG)
VKMOT........ Van Kampen Amer. Cap. Muni. Opportunity Trust [*Associated Press*] (SAG)
VKMOT2...... Van Kampen Amer. Cap. Muni. Opportunity Trust 2 [*Associated Press*] (SAG)
VKMTFL....... Van Kampen Merritt Trust for Investment Grade Florida [*Associated Press*] (SAG)
VKMTNJ....... Van Kampen Merritt Trust for Investment Grade New Jersey [*Associated Press*] (SAG)
VKMTNY...... Van Kampen Merritt Trust for Investment Grade New York [*Associated Press*] (SAG)
VKMTPA...... Van Kampen Merritt Trust for Investment Grade Pennsylvania [*Associated Press*] (SAG)
VKMuTr....... Van Kampen Amer. Cap. Muni. Trust [*Associated Press*] (SAG)
VKMVM....... Van Kampen Merritt Value Municipal Income Trust [*Associated Press*] (SAG)
VKN.............. Barre-Montpelier, VT [*Location identifier FAA*] (FAAL)
VKNG........... Viking Office Products [*NASDAQ symbol*] (SAG)
VKNJV......... Van Kampen Merritt New Jersey Value Municipal Income [*Associated Press*] (SAG)
VKNYQ........ Van Kampen Merritt New York Quality Municipal [*Associated Press*] (SAG)
VKNYV........ Van Kampen Merritt New York Value Municipal Income Trust [*Associated Press*] (SAG)
VKO.............. Moscow Vnukovo Airport [*Former USSR Airport symbol*] (OAG)
VKO.............. Vnukovo Airlines [*Former USSR*] [*FAA designator*] (FAAC)
VKOHQ........ Van Kampen Merritt Ohio Quality Municipal [*Associated Press*] (SAG)
VKOHV........ Van Kampen Merritt Ohio Value Municipal Income Trust [*Associated Press*] (SAG)
VKPAQ........ Van Kampen Merritt Pennsylvania Quality Municipal Trust [*Associated Press*] (SAG)

VKPAV .... Van Kampen Merritt Pennsylvania Value Municipal Trust [*Associated Press*] (SAG)
VKQ .... Van Kam Am Cap Mun Tr [*NYSE symbol*] (TTSB)
VKQ .... Van Kampen Merritt Municipal Trust [*NYSE symbol*] (SPSG)
VKR .... Video Kinescope Recording (PDAA)
VKS .... Van Kam Am Cap Str Sec Mun [*NYSE symbol*] (TTSB)
VKS .... Van Kampen Merritt Strategic Sector Municipal Trust [*NYSE symbol*] (SPSG)
VKS .... Vicksburg [*Mississippi*] [*Airport symbol*] (AD)
VKS .... Vicksburg, MS [*Location identifier FAA*] (FAAL)
VKSelS .... Van Kampen Merritt Select [*Associated Press*] (SAG)
VKStrS .... Van Kampen Merritt Strategic Sector Municipal Trust [*Associated Press*] (SAG)
VKT .... Vane Kindergarten Test [*Child development test*]
VKT .... Vehicle Kilometers Traveled (GFGA)
VKT .... Vehicle Kit Test
VKT .... Vilocity [*Former USSR*] [*FAA designator*] (FAAC)
VKTCA .... Van Kampen Merritt Trust for Investment Grade California [*Associated Press*] (SAG)
VKTFL .... Van Kampen Amer. Cap. Trust for Investment Grade FL [*Associated Press*] (SAG)
VKTIG .... Van Kampen Merritt Trust for Investment Grade Municipals [*Associated Press*] (SAG)
VKTIM .... Van Kampen Merritt Trust for Insured Municipals [*Associated Press*] (SAG)
VKTNJ .... Van Kampen Amer. Cap. Trust for Investment Grade NJ [*Associated Press*] (SAG)
VKTNY .... Van Kampen Amer. Cap. Trust for Investment Grade NY [*Associated Press*] (SAG)
VKTPA .... Van Kampen Amer. Cap. Trust for Investment Grade PA [*Associated Press*] (SAG)
VKV .... Van Kam Am Cap Value Muni [*NYSE symbol*] (TTSB)
VKV .... Van Kampen Merritt Value Municipal Income Trust [*NYSE symbol*] (SPSG)
VKValMu .... Van Kampen Amer. Cap. Value Muni. Income Trust [*Associated Press*] (SAG)
V_L .... Actual Volume of the Lung [*Medicine*] (DAVI)
VL .... Mid-South Commuter Airlines [*ICAO designator*] (AD)
VL .... Valmet OY [*Finland ICAO aircraft manufacturer identifier*] (ICAO)
VL .... Value Leader [*Automotive marketing*]
VL .... Value Line Investment Survey [*Finance*]
VL .... Vandalia Line [*Railroad*]
V-L .... Van Langenhoven [*Rifle*]
VL .... Vapor Return Line
V/L .... Vapor-to-Liquid
VL .... Variable Length
VL .... Variable Light [*Immunology*]
VL .... Varia Lectio [*Variant Reading*] [*Latin*]
VL .... Vario-Losser [*Electronics*]
VL .... Vector Length (MHDB)
VL .... Velar Lobe
VL .... Velocity Limit
VL .... Ventralis Lateralis [*Brain anatomy*]
VL .... Ventrolateral [*Anatomy*]
VL .... Vereinigte Linke [*United Left*] [*Germany Political party*] (PPW)
VL .... Vereniging Lucht [*Clean Air Society in the Netherlands-CLAN*] (EAIO)
VL .... Vertical Ladder [*Technical drawings*]
VL .... Vertical Landing (MCD)
VL .... Vestre Landsret [*Western Court of Appeal*] [*Denmark*] (ILCA)
VL .... Vice Lieutenant [*British*]
VL .... Videlicet [*Namely*] [*Latin*]
VL .... Vide Locum [*See the Place Indicated*] [*Latin*]
VL .... Video Logic (IEEE)
VL .... View Loss
VL .... Viking Lander [*NASA*]
VL .... Ville
VL .... Ville
VL .... Violation of Lawful [*Order*] [*Military*]
VL .... Violin [*Music*] (ROG)
VL .... Visceral Leishmaniasis
VL .... Visceral Leishmaniasis [*Medicine*]
VL .... Vision, Left Eye
VL .... Visual Laydown
VL .... Voltage-Logic [*Electronics*] (IAA)
VL .... Vraie Lumiere [*True Light*] [*Freemasonry*] [*French*] (ROG)
VL .... Vulgar Latin
VL .... Vulgar Latin [*Language*] (BARN)
VLA .... Vachel Lindsay Association (EA)
VLA .... Valhalla Energy Corp. [*Vancouver Stock Exchange symbol*]
VLA .... Vandalia, IL [*Location identifier FAA*] (FAAL)
VLA .... Vertical Landing Aid [*Military*] (CAAL)
VLA .... Vertical Launch ASROC [*Antisubmarine Rocket*]
VLA .... Vertical-Launched Antisubmarine Rocket (MCD)
VLA .... Vertical Line Array
VLA .... Very Large Airplane (PDAA)
VLA .... Very Large Antenna [*Telecommunications*] (IAA)
VLA .... Very Large Array [*Radioscope*]
VLA .... Very Late Activation Antigen [*Immunology*]
VLA .... Very Low Altitude
VLA .... Veterans' Land Act [*Canada*]
VLA .... Video Logarithmic Amplifier
VLA .... Viola [*Music*]
VLA .... Visual Landing Aid
VLA .... Vladivostok [*Russia*] [*Seismograph station code, US Geological Survey*] (SEIS)
VLA .... Voice of Liberty Association (EA)
VLA .... Volga [*Former USSR*] [*FAA designator*] (FAAC)
VLA .... Volume Limiting Amplifier
VLA .... Voluntary Licensing Authority [*Embryology*] [*British*]
VLA .... Volunteer Lawyers for the Arts (EA)
VLAB .... VideoLabs, Inc. [*NASDAQ symbol*] (SAG)
VLAC .... Vertical Lift Aircraft Council (EA)
VLAD .... Vertical Line Array DIFAR (MCD)
VLAD .... Vertical Line Array Directional
Vlad .... Vladivostok [*Russian port*] (BARN)
VLADD .... Visual Low-Angle Drogue Delivery (AFM)
VLAM .... Variable Level Access Method [*Computer science*]
VLAM .... Vlamertinghe [*City in Flanders*] [*World War I*] [*Army*] (DSUE)
VLAN .... Banyan Strategic Realty Trust [*NASDAQ symbol*] (SAG)
VLANS .... Banyan Strategic Realty Tr [*NASDAQ symbol*] (TTSB)
VLAO .... Vientiane [*Laos*] [*ICAO location identifier*] (ICLI)
VLAP .... Attopeu [*Laos*] [*ICAO location identifier*] (ICLI)
VLAP .... Vietnam Laboratory Assistance Program [*Naval Oceanographic Office*]
VLAPA .... Vietnam Laboratory Assistance Program, Army (RDA)
VLAT .... Very Large Array Telescope [*NASA*]
VLATME .... Very-Lighweight Air Traffic Management Equipment (MCD)
VLB .... Glider [*Special*] [*Navy symbol*]
VLB .... Vacuum Lens Blank
VLB .... Vertical Lift Bridge (BARN)
VLB .... Very Long Baseline
VLB .... Verzeichnis Lieferbarer Buecher [*List of Deliverable Books, i.e., books in print*] [*Germany*]
VLB .... VESA [*Video Electronics Standards Association*] Local Bus (PCM)
VLB .... Vincaleukoblastine [*Also, V, VBL, Ve*] [*Antineoplastic drug*]
VLB .... Visual LASER Beam
VLBA .... Very Long Baseline Array
VLBC .... Very Large Bulk-Cargo Carrier (PDAA)
VLBI .... Very Long Baseline Interferometer [*or Interferometry*]
VLBI .... Viking Lander Biological Instrument [*NASA*]
VLBR .... Very Low Birth Rate
VLBTI .... Very Long-Burning Target Indicator [*British military*] (DMA)
VLBW .... Very Low Birth Weight [*Medicine*]
VLC .... Valencia [*Spain*] [*Airport symbol*] (OAG)
VLC .... Valley Line Co. [*Steamship*] (MHDW)
VLC .... Variable-Length Coding [*Computer science*]
VLC .... Vehicle Launch Center [*Automotive industry project management*]
VLC .... Viking Lander Capsule [*NASA*]
VLC .... Violoncello [*Music*]
VLC .... Vital Load Center (MSA)
VLCBX .... Very Large Computerized Branch Exchange [*Computer science*] (MHDB)
VLCC .... Very Large Cargo [*or Crude*] Carrier [*Oil tanker*]
VLCD .... Very-Low-Calorie Diet
VLCD .... Very-Low-Cost Display (IAA)
VLCE .... Visible LASER Communication Experiment
VLCF .... Vectored Lift Cannon Fighter [*Air Force*] (MCD)
VLCF .... Victoria League for Commonwealth Fellowship [*British*]
VLCFA .... Very-Long-Chain Saturated Fatty Acid [*Organic chemistry*]
VLCFQ .... Victoria League for Commonwealth Fellowship in Queensland [*Australia*]
VLCFSA .... Victoria League for Commonwealth Fellowship in South Australia
VLCFV .... Victoria League for Commonwealth Fellowship in Victoria [*Australia*]
VLCHV .... Very-Low-Cost Harassment Vehicle (MCD)
VLCR .... Variable Length Cavity Resonance
VLCS .... Voltage-Logic-Current-Switching [*Electronics*]
VLCTY .... Velocity [*NWS*] (FAAC)
VLD .... Vacuum Leak Detector
VLD .... Valdez [*Alaska*] [*Seismograph station code, US Geological Survey Closed*] (SEIS)
VLD .... Valdosta [*Georgia*] [*Airport symbol*] (OAG)
VLD .... Vendor List of Drawings
VLD .... Very Low Density [*Biochemistry*] (DAVI)
VLD .... Village and Local Development
VLD .... Visual Laydown Delivery (AFM)
VLD .... Vulnerability/Lethality Division [*Ballistic Research Laboratory*] (RDA)
VLDB .... Very-Large Data Base (ADA)
VLDBS .... Very-Large Data Base System
VLDF .... Very-Long Delay Fuze [*Military*] (CAAL)
VLDL .... Very-Low-Density Lipoprotein [*Biochemistry*]
VLDLP .... Very-Low-Density Lipoprotein [*Biochemistry*] (DAVI)
VLDP .... Volunteer Leadership Development Program [*Canadian*] (NFD)
VLDP .... Volunteer Leadership Development Program [*Canada*]
VLDS .... Variable Length Distinguishing Sequence (IAA)
VLDS .... Verbal Language Development Scale [*Speech and language therapy*] (DAVI)
VLD-TG .... Very-Low-Density Lipoprotein Triglyceride [*Biochemistry*] (AAMN)
VLDTN .... Validation (AAG)
VLE .... Landing-Gear-Extended Speed [*Aviation*]
VLE .... Valle, AZ [*Location identifier FAA*] (FAAL)
VLE .... V & L Enterprises [*ACCORD*] [*UTLAS symbol*]
VLE .... Vapor-Liquid Equilibrium
VLE .... Vapour Levitation Epitaxy (NITA)
VLE .... Violone [*Violins*] [*Music*]
VLE .... Visible Light Emission
VLE .... Voice Line Expansion [*Telecommunications*] (IAA)
VLEA .... Very Long Endurance Aircraft (PDAA)
VLEASS .... Very Long Endurance Acoustic Submarine Simulator
VLED .... Visible Light-Emitting Diodes
VLF .... Valdresfly, AS [*Norway*] [*FAA designator*] (FAAC)

VLF .... Variable Length Field
VLF .... Vectored Lift Fighter (MCD)
VLF .... Vertical Launch Facility
VLF .... Very Low Flow
VLF .... Very-Low Fluence [*Physics*]
VLF .... Very-Low-Frequency [*Electronics*]
VLF .... Victoria Law Foundation [*Australia*]
VLFD .... Very-Low-Frequency Direct [*Electronics*] (IAA)
VLFD .... Via Low Frequency Direct [*Aviation*] (FAAC)
VlFdAla .... Valley Federal Savings Bank [*Associated Press*] (SAG)
VLFG .... Valley Forge Scientific [*NASDAQ symbol*] (TTSB)
VLFG .... Valley Forge Scientific Corp. [*NASDAQ symbol*] (NQ)
VLFJ .... Very-Low-Frequency Jammer [*Electronics*]
VLFR .... Very-Low-Frequency Receiver [*Electronics*]
VLFS .... Variable Low-Frequency Standard
VLFS .... Very Large Floating Structure [*Oceanography*]
VLG .... Maximum Landing Gear Operating Speed [*Aviation code*] (AIA)
VLG .... Trans Air Valtologia [*Moldova*] [*ICAO designator*] (FAAC)
VLG .... Valerie Gold Resources [*Vancouver Stock Exchange symbol*]
VLG .... Ventral Nucleus of the Lateral Geniculate Body [*Medicine*] (DMAA)
VLG .... Vertical Load Gun
VLG .... Village (MCD)
VLG .... Village
VLG .... Villa Gesell [*Argentina*] [*Airport symbol*] (OAG)
VLG .... Visible Light Generator
VLGE .... Village Super Market, Inc. [*NASDAQ symbol*] (NQ)
VLGEA .... Village Super Market'A' [*NASDAQ symbol*] (TTSB)
VLGM .... Vertical Loading Gun Mount (MCD)
VLGS .... Villages [*Commonly used*] (OPSA)
VLH .... Ventrolateral Nucleus of the Hypothalamus [*Neurology*] (DAVI)
VLH .... Very Large Herbivores
VLH .... Very Lightly Hinged [*Philately*]
VLH .... Volatile Liquid Hydrocarbon
VLHS .... Bane Houei Say [*Laos*] [*ICAO location identifier*] (ICLI)
VLI .... Port Vila [*Vanuata*] [*Airport symbol*] (OAG)
VLI .... Variable Life Insurance
VLI .... Very-Low Impedance (IAA)
VLI .... Very-Low Inertia
VLI .... Video Load Impedance
VLIA .... Virus-Like Infectious Agent [*Medicine*]
VLIS .... Viking Lander Imaging System [*NASA*]
VLIS .... Viking Library System [*Library network*]
VLIW .... Very Long Instruction Word [*Computer architecture*] [*Multiflow Computer, Inc.*]
VLJ .... Val Joyeux [*France*] [*Later, CLF*] [*Geomagnetic observatory code*]
VLK .... Viqueque [*Timor*] [*Airport symbol*] (AD)
VLKB .... Very Large Knowledge Base [*Computer science*]
VLKG .... Khong Island [*Laos*] [*ICAO location identifier*] (ICLI)
VLKT .... Kene Thao [*Laos*] [*ICAO location identifier*] (ICLI)
VLL .... Valladolid [*Spain*] [*Airport symbol*] (OAG)
VLL .... Valley SAR Training Unit [*British ICAO designator*] (FAAC)
VLLB .... Luang Prabang [*Laos*] [*ICAO location identifier*] (ICLI)
VLLC .... Very Long Linear Collider [*Proposed*] [*Former USSR*]
VLLD .... Vehicular LASER Locator Designator
VLLN .... Luong Nam Tha [*Laos*] [*ICAO location identifier*] (ICLI)
VLLO .... Violoncello [*Music*]
VLLW .... Very Low-Level Waste (BARN)
VLLY .... Valley [*Commonly used*] (OPSA)
VLM .... Variable Length Multiply
vlm .... Vellum (VRA)
VLM .... Virtual Loadable Module [*Computer science*]
VLM .... Visceral Larval Migrans [*Medicine*]
VLM .... Vlaamse Luchtransportmaatschappij NV [*Belgium ICAO designator*] (FAAC)
VLM .... Vortex Lattice Method
VLMB .... Vertical Launch Modular Booster (MCD)
VLMS .... Villa-Lobos Music Society (EA)
VLMS .... Vintage Light Music Society [*British*]
VLMTRC .... Volumetric
VLN .... Training Glider [*Navy symbol*]
VLN .... Valan Ltd. [*Moldova*] [*FAA designator*] (FAAC)
VLN .... Valencia [*Venezuela*] [*Airport symbol*] (OAG)
VLN .... Vanua-Lava [*Sola*] [*New Hebrides*] [*Seismograph station code, US Geological Survey*] (SEIS)
VLN .... Variable Length (IAA)
VLN .... Very Low Nitrogen [*Fuel technology*]
VLN .... Villebon Resources Ltd. [*Vancouver Stock Exchange symbol*]
VLN .... Violin [*Music*]
VLNC .... Valence Technology [*NASDAQ symbol*] (TTSB)
VLNC .... Valence Technology, Inc. [*NASDAQ symbol*] (SAG)
VLNT .... VideoLan Tech [*NASDAQ symbol*] (TTSB)
VLNT .... VideoLan Technologies, Inc. [*NASDAQ symbol*] (SAG)
VLNT .... Violent [*NWS*] (FAAC)
VLNTW .... Videolan Technologies Wrrt [*NASDAQ symbol*] (TTSB)
VLO .... Maximum Landing Gear of Operating Speed (GAVI)
VLO .... Maximum Speed to Extend or Retract Landing Gear [*Aviation code*] (AIA)
VLO .... Valero Energy [*NYSE symbol*] (TTSB)
VLO .... Valero Energy Corp. [*NYSE symbol*] (SPSG)
VLO .... Vereniging van Luguaart Onderhoudbedrywe [*Association of Aviation Maintenance Organizations*] (EAIO)
VLO .... Vertical Lockout
VLOF .... Lift-off Speed (GAVI)
VLOL .... Violating Local Option Law (WGA)
VLON .... Verwaltungslexikon [*Administration Dictionary*] [*NOMOS Datapool*] [*Information service or system*]
VLOOC .... Very Large Ore-Oil Carrier (PDAA)
VLOPr .... Valero Energy $3.125 Cv Pfd [*NYSE symbol*] (TTSB)
VLOS .... Oudomsay [*Laos*] [*ICAO location identifier*] (ICLI)
VLP .... Valparaiso [*Chile*] [*Seismograph station code, US Geological Survey*] (SEIS)
VLP .... Valpar Resources [*Vancouver Stock Exchange symbol*]
VLP .... Value Property Trust [*NYSE symbol*] (SAG)
VLP .... Vaporizing Liquid Plenum
VLP .... Vasopressin-Like Peptide [*Biochemistry*]
VLP .... Ventriculolumbar Perfusion [*Medicine*] (MEDA)
VLP .... Vertical Landing Point (AFM)
VLP .... Vertical Long Period
VLP .... Video Long Player [*Video disk system*] [*Philips/MCA*]
VLP .... Vincristine, L-Asparaginase, Prednisone [*Antineoplastic drug regimen*]
VLP .... Virus-Like Particle
VLP .... Volunteer Lawyers for the Poor [*An association*]
VLPD .... Very Long-Period Displacement [*Volcanology*]
VLPE .... Very Long Period Experiment [*Geophysics*]
VLPK .... Paksane [*Laos*] [*ICAO location identifier*] (ICLI)
VLPO .... Ventrolateral Preoptic
VLPP .... Very Low Pressure Pyrolysis
VLPS .... Pakse [*Laos*] [*ICAO location identifier*] (ICLI)
VLPS .... Vandenberg Launch Processing System [*Aerospace*] (MCD)
VLPV .... Phong Savanh [*Laos*] [*ICAO location identifier*] (ICLI)
VLR .... Randolph-Macon Woman's College, Lynchburg, VA [*OCLC symbol*] (OCLC)
VLR .... Transport Glider [*Navy symbol*]
VLR .... Valar Resources Ltd. [*Vancouver Stock Exchange symbol*]
VLR .... Vallenar [*Chile*] [*Airport symbol*] (AD)
VLR .... Variable Loan Rate [*Business term*]
VLR .... Vertical-Looking RADAR
VLR .... Very Long Range
VLR .... Very Low Range
VLR .... Very Low Resistance (IDOE)
VLR .... Violation of Law of Road [*Traffic offense charge*]
VLR .... Voice Logging Recorder (DWSG)
VLR .... Volare [*Russian Federation*] [*ICAO designator*] (FAAC)
VLR .... Voluntary Loss Rate [*of Air Force officers resigning before retirement*]
VLRSN .... Violation of Lawful Regulation Issued by the Secretary of the Navy
VLS .... Vacuum Loading System
VLS .... Valesdir [*Vanuata*] [*Airport symbol*] (OAG)
VLS .... Valsamata [*Kephallenia*] [*Greece*] [*Seismograph station code, US Geological Survey*] (SEIS)
VLS .... Valstieciu Liaudininku Sajunga [*Peasant Populist Union*] [*Lithuania*] [*Political party*] (PPE)
VLS .... Vandenberg Launch Site [*Air Force*]
VLS .... Vapor-Liquid-Solid
VLS .... Vertical Launch System [*Military*]
VLS .... Vertical Liquid Spring
VLS .... Very Long Shot [*A photograph or motion picture sequence taken from a considerable distance*]
VLS .... Very Low Speed
VLS .... Viking Lander System [*NASA*] (KSC)
VLS .... Village Voice Literary Supplement [*A publication*] (BRI)
VLS .... Virtual Linkage System [*or Subsystem*]
VLS .... Visible Light Sensors (MCD)
VLS .... Visual Lunacy Society (EA)
VLS .... Volume Loadability Speed (IEEE)
VLS .... Vry Langs Skip [*Free Alongside Ship*] [*Afrikaans*]
VLSB .... Sayaboury [*Laos*] [*ICAO location identifier*] (ICLI)
VLSB .... Very Low Surface Brightness [*Optics*]
VLSD .... Viscous Limited-Slip Differential
VLSI .... Very-Large-Scale Integration [*of circuits*] [*Electronics*]
VLSI .... VLSI Technologies [*Associated Press*] (SAG)
VLSI .... VLSI Technology [*NASDAQ symbol*] (TTSB)
VLSI .... VLSI Technology, Inc. [*NASDAQ symbol*] (NQ)
VLSIC .... Very-Large-Scale Integrated Circuit [*Electronics*]
VLSID .... Very Large Scale Integrated Device (SSD)
VLSIIC .... VLSI Implementation Centre [*Queen's University, Kingston*] [*Research center Canada*]
VLSIPS .... Very-Large-Scale Immobilized Polymer Synthesis [*Affymax Research Institute*] [*Organic chemistry*]
VLSK .... Savannakhet [*Laos*] [*ICAO location identifier*] (ICLI)
VLSM .... Vertical Launched Standard Missile (MCD)
VLSN .... Sam Neua [*Laos*] [*ICAO location identifier*] (ICLI)
VLSTRACK .... Vapor-Liquid-Solid Tracking [*Model*] [*Marine science*] (OSRA)
VLSTRACK .... Vapor-Liquid-Solid Tracking [*Model*] (USDC)
VLSV .... Saravane [*Laos*] [*ICAO location identifier*] (ICLI)
VLSW .... Vertical Launch SEAWOLF [*Military British*]
VLSW .... Virtual Line Switch
VLT .... Van Kam Am Cap Hi Inc. [*NYSE symbol*] (TTSB)
VLT .... Van Kampen Merritt Limited Term High Income Trust [*NYSE symbol*] (SPSG)
vlt .... Vault (VRA)
VLT .... Vault
VLT .... Vault Explorations, Inc. [*Vancouver Stock Exchange symbol*]
VLT .... Vehicle Licensing and Traffic [*British*]
VLT .... Very Large Telescope [*Proposed*] [*European Southern Observatory*]
VLT .... Very Low Titanium [*Geology*]
VLT .... Video Layout Terminal [*Computer science*]
VLT .... Video Lottery Terminal (ECON)

VLT .... Visible Light Transmittance
VLT .... Volute
VLTG .... Voltage (AAG)
VLTK .... Thakhek [*Laos*] [*ICAO location identifier*] (ICLI)
VLTP .... Variable Length Text Processor (MHDI)
VLTS .... Video Lottery Tech [*NASDAQ symbol*] (TTSB)
VLTS .... Video Lottery Technologies, Inc. [*NASDAQ symbol*] (SPSG)
VLTSV .... Virusoid Lucerne Transient Streak Virus
VLTT .... Vehicular Leger Toot Terrain [*Light All-Terrain Vehicle*] [*French*] (MCD)
VLU .... Vacuum Lifting Unit
VLU .... Vehicle Location Unit [*FTA*] (TAG)
VLU .... Video Logic Unit (MCD)
VLU .... Worldwide Value Fund [*NYSE symbol*] (SPSG)
VLV .... Valdivia [*Chile*] [*Seismograph station code, US Geological Survey*] (SEIS)
VLV .... Valera [*Venezuela*] [*Airport symbol*] (OAG)
VLV .... Valve (AAG)
VLV .... Vanguard Launch Vehicle (SAA)
VLV .... Velvet Exploration Co. Ltd. [*Vancouver Stock Exchange symbol*]
VLV .... Very-Low Volume
VLV .... Visna Lentivirus
VLVA .... Very-Large Low-Velocity Anomaly [*Seismology*]
v-LVN .... Ventral Lateral Ventricular Nerve [*Anatomy*]
VLVS .... Voltage-Logic-Voltage-Switching [*Electronics*]
VLVT .... Vientiane/Wattay [*Laos*] [*ICAO location identifier*] (ICLI)
VLW .... Village Level Workers [*India*]
VLW .... Washington and Lee University, Lexington, VA [*OCLC symbol*] (OCLC)
VLXG .... Xieng Khouang [*Laos*] [*ICAO location identifier*] (ICLI)
VLXK .... Xieng Khouang (Plaine Des Jarres) [*Laos*] [*ICAO location identifier*] (ICLI)
VLY .... Valley (MCD)
VLY .... Valley
VLY .... Valley National Bancorp [*NYSE symbol*] (SPSG)
VLY .... Valley Natl Bancorp [*NYSE symbol*] (TTSB)
VLY .... Valley Oil & Gas [*Vancouver Stock Exchange symbol*]
VLY .... Volley (DA)
VlyBcp .... Valley National Bancorp [*Associated Press*] (SAG)
VlyFrg .... Valley Forge Scientific Corp. [*Associated Press*] (SAG)
VLYS .... Valleys [*Postal Service standard*] (OPSA)
VLYS .... Valleys
VLZ .... Valdez [*Alaska*] [*Seismograph station code, US Geological Survey*] (SEIS)
VM .... Heading to a Manual Termination (GAVI)
VM .... Ocean Airways [*ICAO designator*] (AD)
VM .... Validation Material [*Social Security Administration*]
VM .... Valles Marineris [*A filamentary mark on Mars*]
VM .... Value Management
VM .... Vane Meter [*Automotive engineering*]
VM .... Vasomotor [*Physiology*]
VM .... Vastus Medialis [*A muscle*]
VM .... Vector Message
VM .... Velocity Meter
VM .... Velocity Modulation
VM .... Ventilation Management
VM .... Ventricular Muscle [*Cardiology*] (MAE)
VM .... Vertical Magnet
VM .... Vertical Meridian [*Optics, Eye anatomy*]
VM .... Verturi Mask [*Medicine*] (MEDA)
VM .... Vestibular Membrane [*Medicine*]
VM .... Victorian Museum [*State*] (EERA)
VM .... Victory Medal [*British*]
VM .... Vietminh (CINC)
vm .... Vietnam [*MARC country of publication code Library of Congress*] (LCCP)
VM .... Viomycin [*Antibiotic compound*] (AAMN)
VM .... Viral Myocarditis [*Medicine*]
VM .... Virgin and Martyr [*Church calendars*]
VM .... Vir Magnificus [*A Great Man*] [*Latin*]
VM .... Virtual Machine [*Computer science*]
VM .... Virtual Memory [*Computer science*] (MCD)
VM .... Virtual Multi-Access [*Computer science*] (IAA)
VM .... Viscosity Modifier [*Lubricants*]
VM .... V-Mail Specialists [*Navy*]
VM .... Voice Modulation
VM .... Volatile Matter
VM .... Volksmarine
VM .... Voltmeter
V/m .... Volts per Meter [*Also, VPM*]
V/m .... Volts per Meter (IDOE)
V/M .... Volts per Mil (DEN)
VM .... Vorigen Monats [*Of Last Month*] [*German*]
VM .... Votre Majeste [*Your Majesty*] [*French*]
VM .... Voyager Mars [*NASA*]
VM-26PP .... VM-26 [*Teniposide*], Procarbazine, Prednisone [*Antineoplastic drug regimen*]
VMA .... Marine Attack Squadron [*Navy symbol*] (NVT)
VMA .... Monmouth Airlines, Inc. [*ICAO designator*] (FAAC)
VMA .... Valid Memory Address [*Computer science*]
VMA .... Valve Manufacturers Association of America (EA)
VMA .... Vanillylmandelic Acid [*Also, HMMA*] [*Biochemistry*]
VMA .... Vehicle Maintenance Area
VMA .... Virtual Machine Assist [*IBM Corp.*]
VMA .... Virtual Memory Allocation
VMA .... Visual Maneuverability Aids (MCD)
VMA .... Voices of Multicultural America [*A publication*]
VMA .... Voids in Mineral Aggregate (DICI)
VMA .... Volume Merchandising Allowance (DOAD)
VMAAI .... Violin Makers Association of Arizona International (EA)
VMA(AW) .... Marine Attack Squadron (All-Weather) [*Navy symbol*] (NVT)
VMAD .... Vincristine, Methotrexate, Adriamycin, Actinomycin D [*Antineoplastic drug regimen*]
VMAD .... Virgin Mean Annual Discharge [*Of a river system*]
VMAI .... Veterinary Medical Association of Ireland (BI)
VM & P .... Varnish Makers' and Painters' Naphtha
VMAP .... Video Map Equipment
VMAPS .... Virtual Memory Array Processing System
VMAQ .... Marine Tactical Electronic Warfare Squadron [*Navy symbol*] (DNAB)
Vmark .... Vmark Software, Inc. [*Associated Press*] (SAG)
VMAT .... Marine Attack Training Squadron [*Navy symbol*] (DNAB)
VMAT .... Veterinary Medicine Aptitude Test (GAGS)
VMAT(AW) .... Marine All-Weather Attack Training Squadron [*Navy symbol*] (DNAB)
VMAVA .... Verdun-Meuse-Argonne Veterans Association (EA)
VMAX .... Maximum Velocity
VMAX .... Victormaxx Technologies [*NASDAQ symbol*] (SAG)
VMAXW .... Victormaxx Technologies Wrrt [*NASDAQ symbol*] (TTSB)
VMB .... Marine Medium and Heavy Patrol Bomber Squadron [*Land-based and seaplane*] [*Navy symbol*]
VMB .... Mary Baldwin College, Staunton, VA [*OCLC symbol*] (OCLC)
VMB .... Vermont Motor Rate Bureau Inc., Barre VT [*STAC*]
VMB .... Veterinary Medicines Board [*Tasmania, Australia*]
VMBA .... Victorian Medical Benevolent Association [*Australia*]
VMBC .... Vintage Motor Bike Club (EA)
VMBF .... Marine Fighter Bomber Squadron [*Navy symbol*]
VMBLOK .... Virtual Machine Control Block [*Computer science*] (IBMDP)
VMBR .... Visual Motor Behavior Rehearsal [*Psychology*]
VM/BSE .... Virtual Machine/Basic System Extension (NITA)
VMC .... James Madison University, Harrisonburg, VA [*OCLC symbol*] (OCLC)
VMC .... Minimum Control Speed with Critical Engine Out (GAVI)
VMC .... Variable Message Cycle
VMC .... Variable Mica Capacitor
VMC .... Vasomotor Center [*Physiology*]
VMC .... Vector Move Convert (IAA)
VMC .... Velocity Minimum Control (AAG)
VMC .... Veritable Master of Crewelwork
VMC .... Vermont Monitoring Cooperative [*Marine science*] (OSRA)
VMC .... Vermont Monitoring Cooperative (USDC)
VMC .... Vertical Machining Center [*Automotive manufacturing*]
VMC .... Vertical Motion Compensation (CAAL)
VMC .... VESA [*Video Electronics Standards Association*] Media Channel (PCM)
VMC .... Viet Montagnard Cong
VMC .... Villa Madonna College [*Kentucky*]
VMC .... Villa Maria College [*Erie, PA*]
VMC .... Ville Marie [*Quebec*] [*Seismograph station code, US Geological Survey Closed*] (SEIS)
VMC .... Virginia Medical College
VMC .... Visual Meteorological Conditions [*Aviation*]
VMC .... Vitramon Microwave Corp. (IAA)
VMC .... Void Metallic Composite
VMC .... VP-16 [*Etoposide*], Methotrexate, Citrovorum factor [*Antineoplastic drug regimen*] (DAVI)
VMC .... Vulcan Materials [*NYSE symbol*] (TTSB)
VMC .... Vulcan Materials Co. [*NYSE symbol*] (SPSG)
Vmca .... Minimum Control Speed in Air [*Aviation code*] (AIA)
VMCB .... Virtual Machine Control Block
VMCC .... Vintage Motor Cycle Club [*British*] (DBA)
VMCCA .... Veteran Motor Car Club of America (EA)
VMCF .... Virtual Machine Communication Facility
Vmcg .... Minimum Control Speed on the Ground [*Aviation code*] (AIA)
VMCG .... Vector Magnetocardiogram [*Medicine*] (DMAA)
VMCJ .... Marine Composite Reconnaissance [*Photo*] Squadron [*Navy symbol*]
Vmcl .... Minimum Control Speed for the Landing Approach [*Aviation code*] (AIA)
VMCM .... Vector-Measuring Current Meter [*Instrumentation*]
VM/CMS .... Virtual Machine/Conversational Monitor System [*Computer science*]
VMCP .... Vincristine, Melphalan, Cyclophosphamide, Prednisone [*Antineoplastic drug regimen*]
VMCR .... Volunteer Marine Corps Reserve
VMD .... Doctor of Veterinary Medicine
VMD .... Marine Photographic Squadron [*Navy symbol*]
VMD .... Vector Meson Dominance [*Particle physics*] (OA)
VMD .... Vertical Magnetic Dipole (IEEE)
VMD .... Vertical Main Distribution (IAA)
VMD .... Virtual Manufacturing Device [*Telecommunications*] (OSI)
VMD .... Volume Median Diameter [*Particle size*]
VMDA .... Veterinary Manufacturers' and Distributors' Association [*Australia*]
VMDF .... Vertical Side of Main Distribution Frame [*Telecommunications*] (TEL)
VMDI .... Vector Miss Distance Indicator
VMDP .... Veterinary Medical Data Program [*Association of Veterinary Medical Data Program Participants*] [*Information service or system*] (IID)
vMDV .... Virulent Marek Disease Virus [*Medicine*] (DMAA)
VME .... Aviacion Comercial de America, SA de DV [*Mexico*] [*FAA designator*] (FAAC)
VME .... British Columbia Ministry of Education [*UTLAS symbol*]
VME .... Villa Mercedes [*Argentina*] [*Airport symbol*] (OAG)
VME .... Vinyl Methyl Ether [*Organic chemistry*]
VME .... Virtual Machine Environment [*International Computers Ltd.*]
VME .... Virtual-Memory Environment [*Computer science*] (EECA)

VME............ Volve Marine Engines
VME............ Volvo Mechanical Equipment [*Auto industry supplier*]
VME............ Volvo, Michigan, Euclid [*In company name VME Americas, Inc.*]
VMEC.......... Vehicle Mounted Explosive Container (MCD)
VMEI........... Veritas Music Entertainment [*NASDAQ symbol*] (TTSB)
VMEI........... Veritas Music Entertainment, Inc. [*NASDAQ symbol*] (SAG)
VMEIW......... Veritas Music Entmt Wrrt [*NASDAQ symbol*] (TTSB)
VMF............ Marine Fighter Squadron [*Navy symbol*]
VMF............ Vacuum Melting Furnace
VMF............ Variable Message Formats (RDA)
VMF............ Vertical Maintenance Facility (NASA)
VMF............ Virtual Memory File [*Computer science*] (PCM)
VMFA.......... Marine Fighter Attack Squadron [*Navy symbol*] (NVT)
VMFAT......... Marine Fighter Attack Training Squadron [*Navy symbol*]
VMF(AW)..... Marine Fighter Squadron (All-Weather) [*Navy symbol*] (NVT)
VMFI........... Voltage Monitor and Fault Indicating
VMF(N)........ Marine Night Fighter Squadron [*Navy symbol*]
VMFP.......... Marine Tactical Reconnaissance Squadron [*Navy symbol*] (DNAB)
VMFPDET.... Marine Tactical Reconnaissance Squadron Detachment [*Navy symbol*] (DNAB)
VMG............ Banyan Mortgage Investment Fund [*Formerly, VMS Mortgate Investment Fund*] [*NYSE symbol*] (SPSG)
VMG............ Banyan Mortgage Inv Fund [*NYSE symbol*] (TTSB)
Vmg............ Velocity Made Good (WGA)
VMG............ Vickers Machine Gun [*British military*] (DMA)
VMG............ Video Mapping Group
VMG............ Video Micrographics (NITA)
VMG............ Video Mixer Group
VMG............ Voluntary Movement Group (EAIO)
VMGR.......... Marine Aerial Refueler/Transport Squadron [*Navy symbol*] (NVT)
VMGSE........ Vehicle Measuring Ground Support Equipment (KSC)
VMH............ Misericordia Hospital, Medical Library, Bronx, NY [*OCLC symbol*] (OCLC)
VMH............ Ventral Medial Hypothalamus [*Anatomy*]
VMH............ Victoria Medal of Honour
VMH............ Visual Maneuvering Height [*Aviation*] (DA)
VMHI........... Victorian Military History Institute [*Defunct*] (EA)
VMI............ Developmental Test of Visual-Motor Integration [*Beery & Buktenica*]
VMI............ Variable Moment of Inertia [*Nuclear physics*]
VMI............ Vertical Markets Information Database [*Amidon/Litman Associates*] [*Information service or system*] (CRD)
VMI............ Vertical Motion Index (PCM)
VMI............ Vibration Measurement Integrator
VMI............ Videodisc-Mouse Interface
VMI............ Video Mosaic Imaging [*Computer science*]
VMI............ Virginia Military Institute, Lexington, VA [*OCLC symbol*] (OCLC)
VMI............ Visual Maneuvering Indicator (MCD)
VMI............ [*Developmental Test of*] Visual-Motor Integration [*Also, Beery-Buktenica Test*] (PAZ)
VMI............ Voicemail International, Inc. [*Cupertina, CA*] [*Telecommunications*] (TSSD)
VMIA........... Vinyl Metal Industry Association [*Defunct*] (EA)
VMIAC......... Victorian Mental Illness Awareness Council [*Australia*]
VMIC........... Vermont Maple Industry Council (EA)
VMID........... Virtual Machine Identifier
VMIF........... Veterans' Mortgage Indemnity Fund [*Department of Veterans Affairs*]
VMII 1986.... Vertical Markets Information Index 1986 [*Amidon/Litman Associates*] [*A publication*]
V/mil........... Volts per Mil
VMIRL.......... VMI [*Virginia Military Institute*] Research Laboratories [*Research center*] (RCD)
VMJ............ Marine Utility Squadron [*Navy symbol*]
VMJ............ Vertical Multijunction [*Solar cell*]
VMK............ Vita-Metall-Keramik [*German dental material for crowns and bridgework*]
VMKey......... Voice Master Key
VML............ Marine Glider Squadron [*Navy symbol*]
VML............ Mohawk Valley Library Association, Schenectady County Public Library, Schenect ady, NY [*OCLC symbol*] (OCLC)
VML............ Valley Migrant League (EA)
VML............ Victorian Music Library [*Australia*]
VML............ Virtual Memory Linking [*Computer science*]
VML............ Virtual Microsystems Ltd. (NITA)
VMLB.......... Vertical Medium-Lead Burst [*Neuron*]
VMLH.......... Ventromedial and Lateral Hypothalami [*Neuroanatomy*]
VMLI........... Veterans Mortgage Life Insurance
VMLS/MLA... Veterinary Medical Libraries Section/Medical Library Association (EA)
VMM............ Vacuum Melting Module
VMM............ Vehicle Maintenance Monitor [*Automotive engineering*]
VMM............ Vehicle Model Movement
VMM............ Vertical Milling Machine
VMM............ Video Map Module
VMM............ Virtual Machine Manager [*Computer science*] (PCM)
VMM............ Virtual Machine Monitor [*Computer science*] (IEEE)
VMM............ Virtual Memory Manager [*Computer science*] (BYTE)
VMM............ Volunteer Missionary Movement [*London Colney, Hertfordshire, England*] (EAIO)
VMM............ Voyageur Minnesota Municipal Income Fund [*AMEX symbol*] (SPSG)
VMM............ Voyageur Minn Muni Income II [*AMEX symbol*] (TTSB)
VMMC.......... Macau [*Macau*] [*ICAO location identifier*] (ICLI)
VMMC.......... Veterans Memorial Medical Center
VMMPS........ Vehicle Management and Mission Planning System [*NASA*]
VMN............ Ventromedial Nucleus [*Brain anatomy*]
VMN............ Voyageur Minnesota Municipal Income Fund, Inc. [*AMEX symbol*] (SPSG)
VMN............ Voyageur Minn Muni Income [*AMEX symbol*] (TTSB)
VMO............ Marine Observation Squadron [*Navy symbol*]
VMO............ Maximum Operating Speed (MCD)
VMO............ Van Kam Am Cap Muni Opp [*NYSE symbol*] (TTSB)
VMO............ Van Kampen Merritt Municipal Opportunity Trust [*NYSE symbol*] (SPSG)
VMO............ Vastus Medialis Obliquus [*Muscle*]
VMO............ Velocity Max Operating (GAVI)
VMO............ Velocity-Modulated Oscillator
VMO............ Very Massive Object [*Astronomy*]
VMO............ Visiting Medical Officer (ADA)
VMO(AS)...... Marine Observation Squadron (Artillery Spotting) [*Navy symbol*]
VMOS.......... Vertical Metal-Oxide Semiconductor (IAA)
VMOS.......... V-Groove Metal-Oxide Semiconductor (MCD)
VMOS.......... Virtual Memory Operating System [*Sperry UNIVAC*] [*Computer science*] (IEEE)
VMOS.......... V-Type Metal Oxide Semiconductor (NITA)
VMOSFET.... Vertical Metal-Oxide-Semiconductor Field-Effect Transistor (IDOE)
VMOW.......... Vice Minister of War (MCD)
VMP............ Validation Master Plan [*Pharmaceutical processing*]
VMP............ Value as Marine Policy [*Insurance*] (DS)
VMP............ Variable Major Protein [*Genetics*]
VMP............ Vegetation Management Program [*of the Northern Territory*] (EERA)
vMP............ Ventral Midline Precursor [*Neuroanatomy*]
VMP............ Vertically Moored Platform [*Offshore drilling*]
VMP............ Visiting Medical Practitioner
VMPA.......... Vancouver Museums and Planetarium Association [*Canada*]
VMPE.......... Virtual Memory Performance Enhancement [*Computer science*] (MHDI)
VMPP.......... Vincristine, Melphalan, Prednisone, Procarbazine [*Antineoplastic drug regimen*]
VM/Prolog... Virtual Machine/Programming in Logic [*Computer science*] (HGAA)
VMR............ Marine Transport Squadron [*Navy symbol*]
VMR............ Variance to Mean Rate
VMR............ Vasomotor Rhinitis [*Medicine*]
VMR............ Victoria Mounted Rifles [*British military*] (DMA)
VMR............ Violation Monitor and Remover [*Bell System*]
VMR............ Volumetric Mixing Ratio
VMR............ Volunteer Military Rejectee (DNAB)
VMRA.......... Victorian Medical Record Association [*Australia*]
VMRB.......... Vereinigte Metallwerke Ranshofen-Berndorf [*AG*]
VMRC.......... Virginia Mason Research Center [*Virginia Mason Hospital and Mason Clinic*] [*Research center*] (RCD)
VMRI........... Veterinary Medical Research Institute [*Iowa State University*] [*Research center*] (RCD)
VMRK.......... VMARK Software [*NASDAQ symbol*] (TTSB)
VMRK.......... Vmark Software, Inc. [*NASDAQ symbol*] (SAG)
VMRMDS...... Vehicle-Mounted Road Mine Detector System
VMRO.......... Vnatresna Makedonska Revolucionerna Organizacija [*Internal Macedonian Revolutionary Organization (Known popularly among English-speaking nations as the IMRO)*] [*Former Yugoslavia*] [*Political party*] (PPE)
VMRO.......... Vutreshna Makidoniski Revoliutsionna Organizatsiia [*Internal Macedonian Revolutionary Organization*] [*Bulgaria*] [*Political party*] (PPE)
VMRO-DPMNE... Internal Macedonian Revolutionary Organization - Democratic Party for MacedonianNational Unity [*Political party*]
VMRO(U)..... Vnatresna Makedonska Revolucionerna Organizacija (Udruzena) [*Internal Macedonian Revolutionary Organization (United)*] [*Former Yugoslavia*] [*Political party*] (PPE)
VMRR.......... Vendor Material Review Report [*NASA*] (KSC)
VMRS.......... Vehicle Maintenance Reporting Standard [*American Trucking Association*]
VMRS.......... Vessel Movement Reporting System
VMRX.......... VimRx Pharmaceuticals [*NASDAQ symbol*] (SAG)
VMRX.......... VIMRx Pharmaceuticals [*NASDAQ symbol*] (TTSB)
VMRXZ........ VIMRx Pharma Wrrt'B' [*NASDAQ symbol*] (TTSB)
VMS............ Valve Monitoring System (IAA)
VMS............ Valve Mounting System
VMS............ Variable Magnetic Shunt [*Electronics*] (IAA)
VMS............ Variable Mass System
VMS............ Variable Memory System [*Computer science*] (IAA)
VMS............ Variable Message Sign
VMS............ Variable Message System
VMS............ Vehicle Management System
VMS............ Vehicle Monitoring System (RDA)
VMS............ Vehicle Motion Sensor
VMS............ Velocity Measurement System
VMS............ Vertical Market Structure (MHDB)
VMS............ Vertical Motion Simulator [*NASA*]
VMS............ Vibration Measuring System
VMS............ Vicinity Map Series [*Bureau of the Census*] (GFGA)
VMS............ Victorian Military Society (EAIO)
VMS............ Videofile Microwave System
VMS............ Video Modulation System
VMS............ Video Movie System [*For video recording tapes*]
VMS............ Viewfinder-Metering System (KSC)
VMS............ Virtual Memory Operating System [*Computer science*]
VMS............ Visual Management System (EERA)
VMS............ Visual Memory Scale [*Educational test*]
VMS............ Visual Motion Simulator (MCD)
VMS............ Voice Mail System [*Telecommunications*] (IAA)
VMS............ Voice Messaging System [*Telecommunications*]
VMS............ Volcanic-Associated Massive Sulphide [*Geology*]
VMS............ Vortex Magnetic Separation [*Ore processing*]

VMSB........ Marine Scout Bombing Squadron [*Navy symbol*]
VMSC........ Vineland Measurement of Social Competence [*Speech and language therapy*] (DAVI)
VM/SE........ Virtual Machine/System Extension (NITA)
VMSEA........ Vehicle Monitoring System Electronics Assembly (RDA)
VMSFRJ........ Variable-Mode Solid-Fueled Ramjet (MCD)
Vmsl........ Minimum Speed in a Stall [*Aviation code*] (AIA)
Vmso........ Minimum Speed in a Stall, Flaps Down [*Aviation code*] (AIA)
VM/SP........ Virtual Machine/System Product [*Operating system for large IBM mainframe computers*]
VMSP........ Volunteer Management Support Program [*ACTION*]
VMT........ Validate Master Tape
VMT........ Van Kam Am Cap Mun Inc. [*NYSE symbol*] (TTSB)
VMT........ Van Kampen Merritt Municipal Income Trust [*NYSE symbol*] (CTT)
VMT........ Variable Microcycle Timing
VMT........ Variable Mu Tube [*Electronics*]
VMT........ Vehicle-Miles Traveled
VMT........ Velocity-Modulated Transistor [*Solid-state physics*]
VMT........ Velocity-Modulated Tube
VMT........ Very Many Thanks
VMT........ Video Matrix Terminal
VMT........ Virtual Memory Technique [*Computer science*] (MDG)
VMT........ Virtual Method Table [*Computer science*] (PCM)
VMT........ Voltage-Modulated Transmission [*Electronics*]
VMT........ Von Mises Theory
VMT........ Vowel Matching Test [*Education*] (EDAC)
VMTB........ Marine Torpedo Bomber Squadron [*Navy symbol*]
VMTH........ Veterinary Medical Teaching Hospital [*University of California, Davis*]
VMTOL........ Very Many Takeoffs and Landings (MCD)
VMTP........ Versatile Message Transaction Protocol [*Computer science*]
VMTSS........ Virtual Machine Time-Sharing System [*Computer science*] (IEEE)
VMU........ Baimuru [*Papua New Guinea*] [*Airport symbol*] (OAG)
Vmu........ Minimum Unstick Speed [*Aviation code*] (AIA)
VMU........ Variable Match Unit (IAA)
VMU........ Vehicle Management Unit [*Powertrain*] [*Automotive engineering*]
VMU........ Velocity Measuring Unit (MCD)
VMU........ Voice Management Unit (DA)
VMV........ Van Kam Am Cap MA Val Mun [*AMEX symbol*] (TTSB)
VMV........ Van Kampen Merritt Massachusetts Value Municipal Trust [*AMEX symbol*] (SPSG)
VMV........ Vincristine, Methotrexate, VP-16 [*Etoposide*] [*Antineoplastic drug regimen*] (DAVI)
VMV........ Viola Mottle Virus
VMW........ Mary Washington College, Fredericksburg, VA [*OCLC symbol*] (OCLC)
VMW........ Vierteljahrschrift fuer Musikwissenschaft [*A publication*]
VMWWI........ Victory Medal World War I [*British*]
VMWWII........ Victory Medal World War II [*British*]
VMY........ York College of the City University of New York, Jamaica, NY [*OCLC symbol*] (OCLC)
VMZ........ Ventrolateral Marginal Zone [*Embryology*]
VN........ Hang Khong Vietnam [*ICAO designator*] (AD)
VN........ Training Plane [*Navy symbol*]
VN........ Vangold Resources, Inc. [*Vancouver Stock Exchange symbol*]
VN........ (Vanillyl)nonanamide [*Biochemistry*]
VN........ Van Ness' Prize Cases [*United States*] [*A publication*] (DLA)
VN........ Vegetative Nucleus [*Botany*]
VN........ Ventral Nerve [*Neuroanatomy*]
VN........ Ventral Nozzle
VN........ Verbal Noun
VN........ Verb Neuter
VN........ Verify Number If No Answer [*Telecommunications*] (TEL)
VN........ Vietnam [*ANSI two-letter standard code*] (CNC)
vn........ Vietnam, North [*vm (Vietnam) used in records cataloged after January 1978*] [*MARC country of publication code Library of Congress*] (LCCP)
VN........ VietNow (EA)
vn........ Vinyl (VRA)
VN........ Violin [*Music*]
VN........ Virus Neutralization
VN........ Visiting Nurse
VN........ Vladimir Nabokov [*In book title, "VN: The Life and Art of Vladimir Nabokov"*]
VN........ Vocational Nurse
VN........ Volatile Nitrogen (OA)
VN........ Vomeronasal [*Anatomy*]
VN........ Von Neumann [*Procedure*] [*Statistics*]
VN........ Vulnerability Number
VNA........ Air Viet-Nam
VNA........ Mercy Hospital, Library, Watertown, NY [*OCLC symbol*] (OCLC)
VNA........ Radio Hanoi [*North Vietnam radio programming which targeted US troops in South Vietnam*] (VNW)
VNA........ Very Narrow Aisle Truck (PDAA)
VNA........ Veterinary Nurses' Association [*Australia*]
VNA........ Vienna, GA [*Location identifier FAA*] (FAAL)
VNA........ Vietnamese National Army
VNA........ Vietnam News Agency
VNA........ Virtual Network Application [*Computer science*]
VNA........ Visiting Nurse Association
VNA........ Volatile Nitrosamine [*Organic chemistry*]
VNA........ Warbelow's Air Ventures, Inc. [*ICAO designator*] (FAAC)
VNAA........ Visiting Nurse Associations of America (EA)
VNAF........ Republic of Vietnam Air Force (VNW)
VNAF........ Vietnam Air Force
VNAF........ Vietnam Armed Forces
VNAF I & M... Vietnam Air Force Improvement and Modernization Program
VNAS........ Vehicle Navigation Aid System
VNAV........ Vertical Navigation Mode (IEEE)
V N B........ Vetus Natura Brevium [*A publication*] (DSA)
VNB........ Wadhams Hall Seminary College, Library, Ogdensburg, NY [*OCLC symbol*] (OCLC)
VNBG........ Bajhang [*Nepal*] [*ICAO location identifier*] (ICLI)
VNBJ........ Bhojpur [*Nepal*] [*ICAO location identifier*] (ICLI)
VNBL........ Baglung [*Nepal*] [*ICAO location identifier*] (ICLI)
VNBP........ Bharatpur [*Nepal*] [*ICAO location identifier*] (ICLI)
VNBR........ Bajura [*Nepal*] [*ICAO location identifier*] (ICLI)
VNBT........ Baitadi [*Nepal*] [*ICAO location identifier*] (ICLI)
VNBW........ Bhairawa [*Nepal*] [*ICAO location identifier*] (ICLI)
VNC........ North Country Reference and Research Resources Council, Union List of Serials, Canton, NY [*OCLC symbol*] (OCLC)
VNC........ Variable Neutralizing Capacitor
VNC........ Venice, FL [*Location identifier FAA*] (FAAL)
VNC........ Ventral Nerve Cord [*Neuroanatomy*]
VNC........ Victorian Naturalists' Club (EERA)
VNC........ Video Network Computer (PCM)
VNC........ Vietnamese Civilian (VNW)
VNC........ VNC Video Network [*Vancouver Stock Exchange symbol*]
VNC........ Voice Numerical Control
VNC........ Votes National Committee (EA)
VNCCI........ Volunteer - The National Center [*Later, NVC*] (EA)
VNCF........ Vietnam-Canada Foundation
VNCG........ Chandragarhi [*Nepal*] [*ICAO location identifier*] (ICLI)
VNCM........ Vietnam Campaign Medal [*Military decoration*]
VNCS........ Vietnam Christian Service [*Defunct*] (EA)
VND........ Jefferson Community College, Library, Watertown, NY [*OCLC symbol*] (OCLC)
VND........ Vanda [*Antarctica*] [*Seismograph station code, US Geological Survey*] (SEIS)
VNDG........ Dang [*Nepal*] [*ICAO location identifier*] (ICLI)
VNDH........ Dhangarhi [*Nepal*] [*ICAO location identifier*] (ICLI)
VNDNG........ Vending
VNDP........ Dolpa [*Nepal*] [*ICAO location identifier*] (ICLI)
VNDPT........ Visual Numerical Discrimination Pre-Test [*Medicine*] (DMAA)
VNDR........ Dhorpatan [*Nepal*] [*ICAO location identifier*] (ICLI)
VNDT........ Doti [*Nepal*] [*ICAO location identifier*] (ICLI)
VNE........ Ogdensburg Public Library, Ogdensburg, NY [*OCLC symbol*] (OCLC)
VNE........ Velocity Never to Exceed
VNE........ Verbal Nonemotional (Stimuli) [*Psychology*]
VNESE........ Vietnamese
VNET........ Virtual Networks [*Computer science*] (HGAA)
VNETF........ Vietnam Expediting Task Force [*Military*]
VNF........ Paul Smiths College, Library, Paul Smiths, NY [*OCLC symbol*] (OCLC)
VNF........ Vietnam Foundation (EA)
VNG........ Ventral Surface, Nephridial Gland [*Anatomy*]
VNG........ W. Alton Jones Cell Science Center Library, Lake Placid, NY [*OCLC symbol*] (OCLC)
VNGD........ Vanguard Airlines [*NASDAQ symbol*] (TTSB)
VNGD........ Vanguard Airlines, Inc. [*NASDAQ symbol*] (SAG)
VNGK........ Gorkha [*Nepal*] [*ICAO location identifier*] (ICLI)
VNHP........ Vermont Natural Heritage Program [*Information service or system*] (IID)
VNI........ Violini [*Violins*] [*Music*]
VNIC........ Voltage Negative Immittance Converter
VNIIMP........ Vsesoiuznyi Nauchno-Issledovatel'skii Institut Miasnoi Promyshlennosti [*All-Union Scientific Research Institute of the Meat Industry*]
VNIR........ Visible and Near Infrared (EERA)
VNIR........ Visible and Near-Visible Infrared (MCD)
VNIS........ Vehicle Navigation Information System [*Automotive engineering*]
VNJI........ Jiri [*Nepal*] [*ICAO location identifier*] (ICLI)
VNJL........ Jumla [*Nepal*] [*ICAO location identifier*] (ICLI)
VNJP........ Janakpur [*Nepal*] [*ICAO location identifier*] (ICLI)
VNJS........ Jomsom [*Nepal*] [*ICAO location identifier*] (ICLI)
VNKT........ Kathmandu/International [*Nepal*] [*ICAO location identifier*] (ICLI)
VNL........ Bogalusa, LA [*Location identifier FAA*] (FAAL)
VNL........ Variable Neodymium LASER
VNL........ Via Net Loss [*Telecommunications*]
VNLD........ Lamidada [*Nepal*] [*ICAO location identifier*] (ICLI)
VNLF........ Via Net Loss Factor (TEL)
VNLK........ Lukla [*Nepal*] [*ICAO location identifier*] (ICLI)
VNLT........ Langtang [*Nepal*] [*ICAO location identifier*] (ICLI)
VNM........ Van Kam Am Cap NY Qual Mun [*NYSE symbol*] (TTSB)
VNM........ Van Kampen Merritt New York Quality Municipal [*NYSE symbol*] (SPSG)
VNM........ Vietnam [*ANSI three-letter standard code*] (CNC)
VNMA........ Manang [*Nepal*] [*ICAO location identifier*] (ICLI)
VNMC........ Vietnam Marine Corps
VNMG........ Meghauli [*Nepal*] [*ICAO location identifier*] (ICLI)
VNMN........ Mahendranagar [*Nepal*] [*ICAO location identifier*] (ICLI)
VNN........ Eastern Virginia Medical Authority, Norfolk, VA [*OCLC symbol*] (OCLC)
VNN........ Mount Vernon, IL [*Location identifier FAA*] (FAAL)
VNN........ Vacant National Number [*Telecommunications*] (TEL)
VNN........ Van Nuys Byzantine [*Diocesan abbreviation*] [*California*] (TOCD)
VNN........ Vietnam Navy
VNNG........ Nepalgunj [*Nepal*] [*ICAO location identifier*] (ICLI)
VNO........ Cruising Speed [*Aviation code*] (AIA)
VNO........ Maximum Structural Cruising Speed (GAVI)
VNO........ Value Not Obtained

VNO .... Vilnius [*Former USSR Airport symbol*] (OAG)
VNO .... Vital National Objective (AAG)
VNO .... Vomeronasal Organ [*Anatomy*]
VNO .... Vornado Realty Trust [*NYSE symbol*] (SPSG)
VNODC .... Vietnamese National Oceanographic Data Center [*Marine science*] (OSRA)
VNP .... Vehicle Network Protocol [*Automotive engineering*]
VNP .... Venda National Party [*Political party*] (PPW)
VNP .... Vietnam Nationalist Party [*Political party*] (VNW)
VNPA .... Victorian National Parks Association [*Australia*]
VNPK .... Pokhara [*Nepal*] [*ICAO location identifier*] (ICLI)
VNPL .... Phaplu [*Nepal*] [*ICAO location identifier*] (ICLI)
VNQDD .... Viet Nam Quoc Dan Dang [*Political party*] (VNW)
VNR .... Van Nostrand Reinhold Co., Inc. [*Publisher*]
VNR .... Vanrook [*Queensland*] [*Airport symbol*] (AD)
VNR .... Variable Navigation Ratio
VNR .... Veneer [*Technical drawings*]
vnr .... Veneer (VRA)
VNR .... Video News Release [*A news release in the form of video tape*]
VNR .... Viennair Luftfahrt GmbH [*Austria ICAO designator*] (FAAC)
VNR .... Vietnam Reactor
VNR .... Vitronectin Receptor [*Biochemistry*]
VNR .... Voltage-[*Controlled Differential*] Negative Resistance [*Electronics*] (BARN)
VNRB .... Rajbiraj [*Nepal*] [*ICAO location identifier*] (ICLI)
VNRC .... Vegetarian Nutritional Research Center (PDAA)
VNRK .... Rukumkot (Chaurjhari) [*Nepal*] [*ICAO location identifier*] (ICLI)
VNRP .... Rolpa [*Nepal*] [*ICAO location identifier*] (ICLI)
VNRS .... Vietnamese National Railway System (CINC)
VNRT .... Rumjatar [*Nepal*] [*ICAO location identifier*] (ICLI)
VNS .... Norfolk State College, Norfolk, VA [*OCLC symbol*] (OCLC)
VNS .... Vagus Nerve Stimulation [*Physiology*]
VNS .... Varanasi [*India*] [*Airport symbol*] (OAG)
VNS .... Vasomotor Nervous System [*Physiology*]
VNS .... Vehicular Navigation System [*Military*]
VNS .... Ventral Nervous System [*Neuroanatomy*]
VNS .... Venus Air Services Ltd. [*Ghana*] [*ICAO designator*] (FAAC)
VNS .... Very North Shore [*Women's Wear Daily*]
VNS .... Vicarious Nucleophilic Substitution [*Organic chemistry*]
VNS .... Villonodular Synovitis [*Medicine*] (DAVI)
VNS .... Visiting Nurse Service
VNS .... Vladimir Nabokov Society (EA)
VNSB .... Syanboche [*Nepal*] [*ICAO location identifier*] (ICLI)
VnSc .... Florence Williams Public Library, Christiansted, St. Croix, VI [*Library symbol Library of Congress*] (LCLS)
VNSF .... Vietnamese Special Forces (CINC)
VNSI .... Simara [*Nepal*] [*ICAO location identifier*] (ICLI)
VNSK .... Surkhet [*Nepal*] [*ICAO location identifier*] (ICLI)
VNSL .... Variable Nozzle Slow Landing (MCD)
VNSM .... Kathmandu [*Nepal*] [*ICAO location identifier*] (ICLI)
VNSP .... Vacant Nozzle Shield Plug [*Nuclear energy*] (NRCH)
VNSR .... Safebagar [*Nepal*] [*ICAO location identifier*] (ICLI)
VnSt .... Saint Thomas Public Library, Charlotte Amalie, VI [*Library symbol Library of Congress*] (LCLS)
VNST .... Simikot [*Nepal*] [*ICAO location identifier*] (ICLI)
VnStC .... College of the Virgin Islands, St. Thomas, VI [*Library symbol Library of Congress*] (LCLS)
VNSWBAC .... Victoria/New South Wales Border Anomalies Committee [*Australia*]
VNT .... Compania Anonima Nacional Telefonos de Venezuela [*NYSE symbol*] (SAG)
VNT .... Variable-Nozzle Turbocharger [*Automotive engineering*]
VNT .... Ventora Resources Ltd. [*Vancouver Stock Exchange symbol*]
VNT .... Virus Neutralization Test [*Analytical biochemistry*]
VNTJ .... Taplejung [*Nepal*] [*ICAO location identifier*] (ICLI)
VNTP .... Tikapur [*Nepal*] [*ICAO location identifier*] (ICLI)
VNTR .... Tumlingtar [*Nepal*] [*ICAO location identifier*] (ICLI)
VNTR .... Variable Number of Tandem Repeats [*Genetics*]
VNTR locus ... Variable Number of Tandem Repeats Locus [*Genetics*] (DOG)
VNTS .... Vertical Nutrient-Solution Transport System [*i.e., plant stem*] [*Slang*]
VNTSC .... Volpe National Transportation Systems Center (BARN)
VNTV .... Vantive Corp. [*NASDAQ symbol*] (SAG)
VNTX .... Ventritex, Inc. [*NASDAQ symbol*] (SPSG)
VNU .... Verenigde Nederlandse Uitgeversbedrijven [*Publishing group*] [*Netherlands*]
VNV .... Van Kam Am Cap NY Val Mun [*NYSE symbol*] (TTBS)
VNV .... Van Kampen Merritt New York Value Municipal Income Trust [*NYSE symbol*] (SPSG)
VNV .... Vlaamsch Nationaal Verbond [*Flemish National League*] [*Dissolved*] [*Belgium*] [*Political party*] (PPE)
VNVO .... Verbal-Nonverbal Operation [*Psychometrics*]
VNVT .... Biratnagar [*Nepal*] [*ICAO location identifier*] (ICLI)
VNW .... Van Wert, OH [*Location identifier FAA*] (FAAL)
VNX .... Oceanographic Development Squadron [*Navy symbol*] (DNAB)
VNX .... Venexcargo (Transporte Aereo de Carga SA) [*Venezuela*] [*ICAO designator*] (FAAC)
VNX .... Vilanculos [*Mozambique*] [*Airport symbol*] (AD)
VNXL .... Vane Axial
VNY .... Van Nuys, CA [*Location identifier FAA*] (FAAL)
VO .... Battleship Observation Squadron [*Navy symbol*]
VO .... De Verborum Obligationibus [*A publication*] (DLA)
Vo .... Initial Velocity
VO .... Observation Plane [*Navy symbol*]
V_0 .... Output Voltage (IDOE)
VO .... [*The*] Seagram Co. Ltd. [*NYSE symbol Toronto Stock Exchange symbol Vancouver Stock Exchange symbol*]
VO .... Tyrolean Airways [*ICAO designator*] (AD)
VO .... Vacuum-Tube Oscillator (IAA)
VO .... Valuation Officer (WDAA)
VO .... Valve Oscillator (DEN)
VO .... Varying Order [*British*]
VO .... Vehicle Operations [*NASA*] (NASA)
VO .... Verbal Orders
VO .... Verbindungsoffizier [*Liaison Officer*] [*German military - World War II*]
VO .... Verb-Object [*Education of the hearing-impaired*]
VO .... Vernehmungsoffizier [*Interrogation Officer*] [*German military - World War II*]
VO .... Verpflegungsoffizier [*Mess Officer*] [*German military - World War II*]
VO .... Verso
VO .... Vertical Oculus
VO .... Vertical Output (IAA)
VO .... Very Old [*Wines and spirits*]
VO .... Veterinary Officer [*British*]
VO .... Victorian Order [*British*] (ROG)
VO .... Video Operator (NTCM)
VO .... Viking Orbiter [*NASA*]
VO .... Violation of [*Local*] Ordinance
VO .... Violino [*Violin*] [*Music*] (ROG)
VO .... Virtual Office
VO .... Visa Office [*Department of State*]
VO .... Vocal (AAG)
VO .... Voice (AAG)
VO .... Voice Over [*Commentary read over a program*] [*Television*]
VO .... Volatile Oil
VO .... Volcanic Origin (AAG)
VO .... Volt (ROG)
VO .... Volume
VO .... Voluntary Opening [*Prosthesis*] [*Medicine*]
VO .... Von Oben [*From the Top*] [*German*]
VO .... VOTEC, Servicos Aereos Regionais SA [*Brazil ICAO designator*] (ICDA)
VO .... Voucher (MCD)
VO_2 .... Volume Oxygen Consumption [*Medicine*] (DAVI)
VOA .... Vibrational Optical Activity [*Spectroscopy*]
VOA .... Voice of America [*United States Information Agency*]
VOA .... Volkswagen of America
VOA .... Volt-Ohm-Ammeter (IDOE)
VOA .... Volunteers of America (EA)
VOAEL .... Vocationally Oriented Adult Education and Literacy Program [*Australia*]
VO-AG .... Vocational Agriculture [*Education*]
VOAPA .... Vultee Owners and Pilots Association (EA)
VOARS .... Velocity over Altitude Ratio Sensor (MCD)
VOB .... Vacuum Optical Bench
VOB .... Volume over Bark [*Forestry*]
VOBANC .... Voice Band Compression (CET)
VOBG .... Bangalore [*India*] [*ICAO location identifier*] (ICLI)
VOBI .... Bellary [*India*] [*ICAO location identifier*] (ICLI)
VOBL BZ ...... Verordnungsblatt fuer die Britische Zone [*Official Gazette of the Former British Zone of Occupation*] [*German*] (ILCA)
VOBR .... Bidar [*India*] [*ICAO location identifier*] (ICLI)
VOBZ .... Vijayawada [*India*] [*ICAO location identifier*] (ICLI)
VOC .... Certificate of Vocational Preparation (AIE)
VOC .... Observation Spotter Squadron [*Navy symbol*]
VOC .... Onondaga Community College, Syracuse, NY [*OCLC symbol*] (OCLC)
VOC .... Variable Oil Capacitor
VOC .... Variable Output Circuit (DEN)
VOC .... Vehicle Observer Corps [*Road Haulage Association*] [*British*] (DCTA)
VOC .... Vehicle Out of Commission [*Army*] (AFIT)
VOC .... Verbal Orders of the Commander
VOC .... Victorian Olympic Council [*Australia*]
VOC .... Vincent Owners Club (EA)
VOC .... Virago Owners Club (EA)
VOC .... Vocabulary [*Linguistics*]
VOC .... Vocal (ADA)
VOC .... Vocational
VOC .... Vocative
VOC .... Voice of Calvary [*An association*]
VOC .... Voice of the Customer [*Business term*]
VOC .... Voice-Operated Coder
VOC .... Voice-Operated Control [*Telecommunications*] (IAA)
VOC .... Voice-Operated Relay Circuit (IAA)
VOC .... Voice Order Circuit (CET)
VOC .... Volatile Organic Chemical
VOC .... Volatile Organic Compound [*Environmental chemistry*]
VOC .... Volunteer Officer Candidate [*Army*]
VOCA .... Victims of Crime Act of 1984
VOCA .... Victims of Crime Association [*Australia*]
VOCA .... Visiting Orchestra Consultative Association [*British*] (DI)
VOCA .... Voice Communications Assembly [*Ground Communications Facility, NASA*]
VOCA .... Voice of China and Asia Missionary Society (EA)
VOCA .... Voice Output Communications Aid
VOCA .... Voltmeter Calibrator
VOCA .... Volunteers in Overseas Cooperative Assistance (EA)
VOCA .... VP-16 [*Etoposide*] Vincristine, Cyclophosphamide, Adriamycin [*Antineoplastic drug regimen*] (DAVI)
VOCAB .... Vocabulary
VOCAL .... Verification of On-Chip Chip Array Logic (NITA)
VOCAL .... Vessel Ordnance Allowance List

VOCAL......... Victims of Child Abuse Laws (EA)
VOCAL......... Victims of Crime and Leniency (EA)
VOCAL......... Vocabulary Language (MHDI)
VOCAL......... Voluntary Organisations of Communication and Language (DBA)
VOCAP......... , Cyclophosphamide, Adriamycin, Platinol [*Vincristine*] [*Cisplatin*] [*Antineoplastic drug regimen*]
VOCAT......... Vocational
VOCAT......... Vocative [*Grammar*] (ROG)
VOCB........... Coimbatore [*India*] [*ICAO location identifier*] (ICLI)
VOCC........... Cochin [*India*] [*ICAO location identifier*] (ICLI)
VOCCN......... Van Ommeren [*AM symbol*] (TTSB)
VOC-ED........ Vocational Education (OICC)
VOCED......... Vocational Education [*Database*] [*Australia*]
VOCG........... Verbal Orders of Commanding General
VOCL........... Calicut [*India*] [*ICAO location identifier*] (ICLI)
VOCLF......... VocalTec Ltd [*NASDAQ symbol*] (TTSB)
VOCM.......... St. John's, NF [*AM radio station call letters*]
VOCM.......... Vehicle Out of Commission for Maintenance [*Military*]
VOCM-FM.... St. John's, NF [*FM radio station call letters*]
VOCN........... Vocation
VOCNA......... Velocette Owners Club of North America (EA)
VOCNL......... Vocational
VOCO........... Verbal Orders of Commanding Officer
VOCODER.... Voice Coder (NITA)
VOCOM........ Voice Communications
VOCP........... Cuddapah [*India*] [*ICAO location identifier*] (ICLI)
VOCP........... Vehicle Out of Commission for Parts [*Military*]
VocRehab.... Vocational Rehabilitation (OICC)
VOCS........... Verbal Orders of the Chief of Staff
VOCSU......... Voice-Operated Carrier Switching Unit (IAA)
VOCTOR....... Void On Call to Operating Room (DAVI)
VOCX........... Carnicobar [*India*] [*ICAO location identifier*] (ICLI)
VOD............. Old Dominion University, Norfolk, VA [*OCLC symbol*] (OCLC)
VOD............. Vacuum Oxygen Decarburization [*Stainless-steel processing*]
VOD............. Vehicle On-Board Delivery
VOD............. Velocity of Detonation (IEEE)
VOD............. Veno-Occlusive Disease [*of the liver*]
VOD............. Verification of Deposit [*Finance*] (EMRF)
VOD............. Vertical On-Board Delivery [*Navy*] (NVT)
VOD............. Via Omni Direct [*Aviation*] (FAAC)
VOD............. Video on Demand (ECON)
VOD............. Vision, Right Eye
VOD............. Visio Oculus Dextra [*Vision, right eye*] [*Latin*] [*Ophthalmology*] (DAVI)
VOD............. Vodafone Group [*NYSE symbol*] (SPSG)
VOD............. Vodafone Group ADR [*NYSE symbol*] (TTSB)
VODACOM... Voice Data Communications
Vodafone..... Vodafone Group [*Associated Press*] (SAG)
VODARO...... Vertical Ozone Distribution from the Absorption and Radiation of Ozone (AAG)
VODAS......... Voice-Operated Device Antising (CET)
VODAT......... Voice-Operated Device for Automatic Transmission
Vodavi......... Vodavi Technology [*Associated Press*] (SAG)
VODC........... Viking Orbiter Design Change [*NASA*]
VODER......... Voice Coder
VODER......... Voice-Operated Demonstrator
VODG........... Dundigul [*India*] [*ICAO location identifier*] (ICLI)
VODIS.......... Voice Operated Database in Inquiry System (NITA)
VODK........... Donakonda [*India*] [*ICAO location identifier*] (ICLI)
VODK........... [*The*] Voice of Democratic Kampuchea [*Radio station of the Red Khmers*] (PD)
VODP........... Verbal Orders by Direction of the President
VODS........... Video Operator Distress Syndrome (HGAA)
VOE............. Venus Orbit Ejection [*NASA*] (MCD)
VOE............. Verificationof Employement (EMRF)
VOE............. Visual Order Error
VOE............. Vocational Office Education [*NASA employment program*]
VOEC........... Vegetable Oil Export Corp. (EA)
VOECRN....... Vietnamese Organization to Exterminate Communists and Restore the Nation (EA)
VOF............. Covington, GA [*Location identifier FAA*] (FAAL)
VOF............. Observation Fighter Squadron [*Navy symbol*]
VOF............. Van Kam Am Cap FL Mun Op [*AMEX symbol*] (TTSB)
VOF............. Van Kampen Merritt Florida Municipal Opportunity Fund [*AMEX symbol*] (SPSG)
VOF............. Variable Operating Frequency (NATG)
VOF............. Vennootschap Onder Firma [*Limited Partnership*] [*Dutch*] (ILCA)
VOF............. Victorian Overseas Foundation [*Australia*]
VOF............. Volatile Organic Fraction [*Automotive exhaust emission testing*]
VOF............. Volatile Organic Fractions
VOF............. Vsesoiuznoe Obshchestvo Filatelistov [*or Fizioterapistov*]
V of A......... Volunteers of America (EA)
V of R......... Vale of Rheidol Light Railway [*Wales*]
V of S......... Veterans of Safety (EA)
VOG............. Airvolga [*Former USSR*] [*FAA designator*] (FAAC)
VOG............. Observation Plane Squadron [*Navy symbol*]
VOG............. Vanguard Operations Group
VOG............. Vectoroculogram
VOG............. Vessel Off-Gas [*Nuclear energy*] (NRCH)
Vog............. Vogue [*Record label*] [*France*]
VOG............. Volgograd [*Former USSR Airport symbol*] (OAG)
VOGAA......... Voice-Operated Gain-Adjusting Amplifier [*NASA*]
VOGAD......... Voice-Operated Gain-Adjusting Device [*NASA*]
VOGAD......... Voice Operated Gain Adjustment Device (NITA)
VOGB........... Gulbarga [*India*] [*ICAO location identifier*] (ICLI)
VOGIN.......... Nederlandse Vereniging van Gebruikers van Online Informatie-Systemen [*Netherlands Association of Users of Online Information Systems*] (EAIO)
VOGOV......... Verbal Orders of the Governor
VOH............. Vohemar [*Madagascar*] [*Airport symbol*] (OAG)
VOHAP......... Volatile Organic Hazardous Air Pollutant [*Environmental Protection Agency*]
VOHCA......... Veterans Omnibus Health Care Act of 1976
VOHY........... Hyderabad [*India*] [*ICAO location identifier*] (ICLI)
VOI............. Vehicle Ordnance Installation
VOI............. Video Output Impedance
VOI............. Vocational Opinion Index (OICC)
VOI............. Voinjama [*Liberia*] [*Airport symbol*] (OAG)
VOICE.......... Victims of Incest Can Emerge (EA)
VOICE.......... Vocabulary of Intelligence Concept Expressions
VOICE.......... Vocal Output and Input-Controlled Environment
VOICE.......... Voice of Informed Community Expression
VOICE.......... Volunteer Oil Industry Communications Effort [*Program*] [*Phillips Petroleum Co.*]
VoiceC......... Voice Control Systems [*Associated Press*] (SAG)
VOICECON... Voice Telephone Conference
Voice It........ Voice It Woldwide, Inc. [*Associated Press*] (SAG)
VoicePw....... Voice Powered Tech International, Inc. [*Associated Press*] (SAG)
VOICES........ Victims of Institutionalised Cruelty, Exploitation and Supporters Inc. [*Australia*]
VOICES........ Voice-Operated Identification Computer Entry System (PDAA)
VOIR............ Venus Orbiting and Imaging RADAR [*NASA*]
VOIS............ Visual Observation Instrumentation Subsystem [*Lunar space program*]
VOIS............ Visual Observation Integration Subsystem (AAG)
VOIS............ Vocal Output for Industrial Systems (NITA)
VOIS............ Voice-Operated Inspection System [*Software*]
VOISC.......... Variable Orifice Idle Spark Control [*Automotive engineering*]
VOK............. Camp Douglas, WI [*Location identifier FAA*] (FAAL)
VOK............. Vry op Kaai [*Free on Quay*] [*Afrikaans*]
VOKM........... Khamampet [*India*] [*ICAO location identifier*] (ICLI)
VOKS........... Vsesoiuznoe Obshchestvo Kul'turnoi Sviazi s Zagranitsei [*All-Union Society for Cultural Relations with Foreign Countries*] [*Former USSR*]
VOL............. Variable Orientation Launcher (AAG)
VOL............. Video on Line [*Computer science*] [*Italy*]
VoL............. Voice of the Listener [*British*] [*An association*] (DBA)
Vol............. Volans [*Constellation*]
VOL............. Volante [*Lightly and Rapidly*] [*Music*] (ROG)
Vol............. Volar [*Anatomy*] (WGA)
vol............. Volatile [*Chemistry*] (DAVI)
VOL............. Volatilis [*Volatile*] [*Pharmacy*]
Vol............. Volcanic [*Quality of the bottom*] [*Nautical charts*]
VOL............. Volcano [*Maps and charts*]
VOL............. Volos [*Greece*] [*Airport symbol*] (AD)
vol............. Volume (VRA)
VOL............. Volume (EY)
vol............. Volume (IDOE)
VOL............. Volume
vol............. Volume (ODBW)
VOL............. Volume Label (IAA)
vol%........... Volume Percent (DAVI)
VOL............. Voluntary [*or Volunteer*] (AFM)
vol............. Volvendus [*To be rolled*] [*Latin*] (DAVI)
VOL............. Volvo AB [*Sweden ICAO designator*] (FAAC)
VOLA........... Volume, American Stock Exchange [*Selection symbol*]
vol adm....... Voluntary Admission [*Psychiatry*] (DAVI)
VOLAG......... Voluntary Agency [*Generic term for a charitable organization*]
VOLAR......... Volunteer Army [*Project, absorbed by MVA, 1972*]
Vol Ash........ Volcanic Ash [*Quality of the bottom*] [*Nautical charts*]
volc............ Volcanic (VRA)
VOLC........... Volcanics [*Lithology*]
VOLC........... Volcano
VOLCAL........ Volume Calculator (MHDI)
VOLCAS........ Voice-Operated Loss Control and Suppressor
VOLCAT........ Volume Catalog (IAA)
VolCC.......... Volunteer Capital Corp. [*Associated Press*] (SAG)
VOLCOM....... Value of Life Committee (EA)
VOLCUF....... Voluntary Organisations' Liaison Council for Under-Fives [*British*] (DI)
VOLERE........ Voluntary/Legal/Regulatory (IEEE)
VOLG........... Victorian Office of Local Government [*Australia*]
VOLID.......... Volume Identifier (MHDI)
VOLIR.......... Volumetric Indicating RADAR
VOLKS......... Volkswagen [*Automobile*] (DSUE)
VOLLIM........ Voltage Limiter (IAA)
VOLMET....... Meteorological Information for Aircraft in Flight [*ICAO*] (FAAC)
Voln............ Volans [*Constellation*]
VOLN........... Volume, New York Stock Exchange [*Selection symbol*]
VOLNTRY..... Voluntary
Volr............. Volunteer [*British military*] (DMA)
VOLRY......... Voluntary
VOLS........... Voluntary Overseas Libraries Service
VOLSCAN..... Volumetric Scanning RADAR
VOLSER....... Volume/Serial
volt............. Volatile [*Chemistry*] (DAVI)
VOLT........... Volt Information Sciences, Inc. [*NASDAQ symbol*] (NQ)
VOLT........... Volt Info Sciences [*NASDAQ symbol*] (TTSB)
VOLT........... Volume, Toronto Stock Exchange [*Selection symbol*]
VOLTAN....... Voltage Amperage Normalizer

VoltInf........ Volt Information Sciences, Inc. [*Associated Press*] (SAG)
VOLUM........ Volumetric (WDAA)
VOLV........ Volvendus [*To Be Rolled*] [*Pharmacy*] (ADA)
VOLV........ Volvo AB [*Sweden NASDAQ symbol*]
VOLVAR........ Volume-Variety (PDAA)
VOLVEND........ Volvendus [*To Be Rolled*] [*Pharmacy*]
Volvo........ Volvo AB [*Associated Press*] (SAG)
vol/vol........ Volume Ratio [*Volume per Volume*] [*Pharmacology*] (DAVI)
VOLVY........ Volvo AB 'B' ADR [*NASDAQ symbol*] (TTSB)
VOLWARE........ Volume-Weighted Averages of Realized Prices
VOLY........ Voluntary (ROG)
VOM........ Nux Vomica Strychnia [*Strychnine-producing plant*] [*Pharmacy*] (ROG)
VOM........ Vinyl Chloride Monomer [*Chemistry*] (DAVI)
VOM........ Voice of the Mediterranean [*Broadcasting service jointly owned by Maltese and Libyan Governments*] (EY)
VOM........ Volcano Resources Corp. [*Vancouver Stock Exchange symbol*]
VOM........ Volt Ohmmeter [*Electronics*] (IAA)
VOM........ Volt-Ohm Meter
VOM........ Volt-Ohm-Milliammeter
VOM........ Volt-Ohm-Milliampere Meter [*Electronics*] (IAA)
VOM........ Vomited (DAVI)
VOMA........ Volt-Ohm-Milliampere [*Electronics*] (IAA)
VOMD........ Madurai [*India*] [*ICAO location identifier*] (ICLI)
VOMD........ VAFB [*Vandenberg Air Force Base*] Operations and Maintenance Documentation (NASA)
VOMF........ Madras [*India*] [*ICAO location identifier*] (ICLI)
VOMG........ Magadi [*India*] [*ICAO location identifier*] (ICLI)
VOMH........ Mahad [*India*] [*ICAO location identifier*] (ICLI)
VOMI........ Volksdeutsche Mittelstelle [*NAZI Germany*]
VOML........ Mangalore [*India*] [*ICAO location identifier*] (ICLI)
VOMM........ Madras [*India*] [*ICAO location identifier*] (ICLI)
VOM URG........ Vomitione Urgente [*The Vomiting Being Troublesome*] [*Pharmacy*] (ROG)
VOMY........ Mysore [*India*] [*ICAO location identifier*] (ICLI)
VON........ Avon, CO [*Location identifier FAA*] (FAAL)
VON........ Victorian Order of Nurses
VON........ Voice on the Net [*A consortium of internet users, vested interests, and software companies*] (PCM)
VON........ Vons Companies [*NYSE symbol*] (SPSG)
VON........ Vons Cos. [*NYSE symbol*] (TTSB)
Von H Const Hist... Von Holst's Constitutional History of the United States [*A publication*] (DLA)
Von Ihr Str for L... Von Ihring's Struggle for Law [*A publication*] (DLA)
VONJY........ Elan Populaire pour l'Unite Nationale [*Popular Impulse for National Unity*] [*Malagascar*] [*Political party*] (PPW)
VONS........ Committee for the Defense of Persons Unjustly Persecuted [*Former Czechoslovakia*] [*Political party*] (PD)
VONS........ Nagarjunsagar [*India*] [*ICAO location identifier*] (ICLI)
Vons........ Vons Companies [*Associated Press*] (SAG)
VOO........ Ventricular Pacing, No Sensing, No Other Function [*Pacemaker*] [*Cardiology*] (MEDA)
VOofA........ Vasa Order of America [*Cranston, RI*] (EA)
Voorh Code... Voorhies' Code [*New York*] [*A publication*] (DLA)
Voorh Cr Jur... Voorhies' Criminal Jurisprudence of Louisiana [*A publication*] (DLA)
Voorh St........ Voorhies' Louisiana Revised Statutes [*A publication*] (DLA)
VOP........ Valued as in Original Policy [*Insurance*]
VOP........ Value of Production
VOP........ Value Option Package [*Automotive marketing*]
VOP........ Venous Occlusion Plethysmography [*Medicine*] (DMAA)
VOP........ Vertical Ozone Profile
VOP........ Very Old Pale [*Designation on brandy labels*]
VOP........ Viral Oncology Program [*National Cancer Institute*]
VOPA........ Verbal Order Purchase Agreement [*Sales*]
VOPAN........ Voice Pitch Analysis [*Consumer Response Corp.*]
VOPB........ Port Blair [*India*] [*ICAO location identifier*] (ICLI)
VOPB........ Voice of the People of Burma [*Radio station of the Burma Communist Party*] (PD)
VOPNAV........ Vice Chief of Naval Operations
VOPO........ Volkspolizei [*Also, VP*]
VOPP........ Veterinary Medicine, Optometry, Podiatry, and Pharmacy [*HEW program*]
VOPR........ Voice-Operated Relay
VOPT........ Voice of the People of Thailand [*Radio station of the Communist Party of Thailand*] (PD)
VOQ........ Van Kam Am Cap OH Qual Mun [*NYSE symbol*] (TTSB)
VOQ........ Van Kampen Merritt Ohio Quality Municipal [*NYSE symbol*] (SPSG)
VOQ........ Vehicle Owner's Questionnaire [*Auto safety research*]
VOQ........ Visiting Officers' Quarters [*Military*]
VOR........ Sunna Air Ltd. [*Iceland*] [*ICAO designator*] (FAAC)
VOR........ Vehicle Occupancy Rate [*MOCD*] (TAG)
VOR........ Vehicle off the Road [*British*]
VOR........ Vendor [*Legal shorthand*] (LWAP)
VOR........ Vertical Omnidirectional Radio
VOR........ Very-High-Frequency Omnidirectional Range
VOR........ Very-High-Frequency Omnirange (IDOE)
VOR........ Vestibulo-Ocular Reflex [*Neurology*]
VOR........ Visual Omnidirectional Range (DNAB)
VOR........ Visual Omnirange [*Directional Beacon*] [*Aviation*] (NG)
VOR........ Voice of Reason
VOR........ Voice of the Retarded [*An association*] (PAZ)
VOR........ Voice-Operated Relay
VORAD........ Vehicle On-board RADAR Accident Avoidance [*Automotive safety*]
VORAD........ Vehicular On-Board RADAR [*Automotive engineering*] (PS)
VOR/ATCS........ VHF [*Very-High-Frequency*] Omnidirectional Radio Beacon and Air Traffic Communications Station (SAA)
VORDAC........ VHF [*Very-High-Frequency*] Omnidirectional Range and Distance Measuring Equipmentfor Average Coverage (IAA)
VORDAC........ VHF [*Very-High-Frequency*] Omnidirectional Range/Distance-Measuring for AirCoverage
VORDME........ VHF [*Very-High-Frequency*] Omnidirectional Range/Distance-Measuring Equipment (CET)
VOR/DMET........ VHF [*Very-High-Frequency*] Omnidirectional Range/Distance-Measuring Equipment Compatible with TACAN
VOR-FIX........ Vestibuloocular Reflex with Fixation Light [*Ophthalmology*]
VORG........ Ramagundam [*India*] [*ICAO location identifier*] (ICLI)
VORG........ Victorian Ornithological Research Group (EERA)
VORLOC........ VHF [*Very-High-Frequency*] Omnirange Localizer (CET)
VORM........ Ramnad [*India*] [*ICAO location identifier*] (ICLI)
VORM........ Vormittags [*In the Morning*] [*German*]
Vornado........ Vornado Realty Trust, Inc. [*Associated Press*] (SAG)
VORR........ Raichur [*India*] [*ICAO location identifier*] (ICLI)
VORS........ Vestibulo-Ocular Reflex Suppression [*Ophthalmology*]
Vorsokr........ Fragmente der Vorsokratiker [*A publication*] (OCD)
VORTAC........ Combined VOR and TACAN Navigational Facility [*FAA*] (TAG)
VORTAC........ Variable Omnirange Tactical (NASA)
VORTAC........ VHF [*Very-High-Frequency*] Omnidirectional Range Collocated with TACAN [*Tactical Air Navigation System*] (IAA)
VORTAC........ VHF [*Very-High-Frequency*] Omnidirectional Range Tactical Air Navigation (IAA)
VORTAC........ VHF [*Very-High-Frequency*] Omnirange TACAN
VORTAL........ Vertical Ommi-Range, Take-Off, Approach, and Landing System (PDAA)
VORTAN........ Visual Omnirange/Tactical Air Navigation (MCD)
VORTEX........ Varian Omnitaste Real Time Executive [*Computer science*] (IAA)
VORTEX........ Venus Orbiter Radiometric Temperature Experiment [*NASA*]
VORTEX........ Verification of the Origins of Rotation in Tornadoes Experiment
VORTEX........ Versatile Omnitask Real-Time Executive (NITA)
VOR/VORTAC... Very High Frequency Omnidirectional Radio Range [*FAA*] (TAG)
VORY........ Rajahmundry [*India*] [*ICAO location identifier*] (ICLI)
VOS........ Observation Scout Plane [*Navy symbol*]
VOS........ Vacuum Oven Sublimation [*Automotive exhaust emission testing*]
VOS........ Vehicle on Stand (MCD)
VOS........ Vehicle Origin Survey [*R. L. Polk & Co.*] [*Information service or system*] (IID)
VOS........ Vertical Obstacle SONAR (IAA)
VOS........ Vessel of Opportunity [*Marine science*] (OSRA)
VOS........ Veterans of Safety (EA)
VOS........ Veterinary Orthopaedic Society (EA)
VOS........ Viking Orbiter System [*NASA*]
VOS........ Virtual Operating System
VOS........ Visicoder Oscillograph System
VOS........ Vision, Left Eye
VOS........ Vision on Sound (IAA)
VOS........ Visio Oculus Sinister [*Vision Left Eye*] [*Latin*] [*Ophthalmology*] (DAVI)
VOS........ Vitello Ovi Solutus [*Dissolved in yolk of egg*] [*Latin*] [*Pharmacology*] (DAVI)
VOS........ Vitello Ovi Solutus [*Dissolved in the Yolk of an Egg*] [*Pharmacy*] (ROG)
VOS........ Voice-Operated Switch [*or System*]
VOS........ Voluntary Observing Ship [*Marine science*] (OSRA)
VOS........ Voluntary Observing Ships [*Marine science*] (MSC)
VOS........ Volunteer Observing Ship [*Marine science*] (OSRA)
VOS........ Volunteer Observing Ship (EERA)
VOS........ Volunteer Observing Ship (USDC)
Vos........ Voskhod (BJA)
VOS........ Vostok [*Former USSR Geomagnetic observatory code*]
VOSA........ Variable Orifice Sound Attenuator [*System*] (DNAB)
VOSA........ Verbal Orders of the Secretary of the Army
VOSAF........ Verbal Orders of the Secretary of the Air Force
VOSC........ VAST [*Versatile Avionics Shop Test*] Operating System Code
VOSE........ Vacuum Operation of Spacecraft Equipment (IAA)
VOSH........ Volunteer Optometric Services to Humanity/International (EA)
VOSL........ Variable Operating and Safety Level (DNAB)
VO/SOT........ Voiceover/Sound on Tape [*Television*] (NTCM)
VOST........ Volatile Organic Sampling Train [*For air analysis*]
VOSW........ Very Old Scotch Whisky
VOT........ Valve Opening Time [*Nuclear energy*] (NRCH)
VOT........ Van Kam Am Cap Mun Opp II [*NYSE symbol*] (TTSB)
VOT........ Van Kampen Merritt Municipal Opportunity Trust 2 [*NYSE symbol*] (SPSG)
VOT........ Very Old Tawny [*Wines and spirits*]
VOT........ VHF [*Very-High-Frequency*] Omnitest
VOT........ Virtual Onsite Technology [*Telecommunications*]
VOT........ Visual Omnirange Test [*Aviation*] (IAA)
VOT........ Vocational Office Trainee
VOT........ Voice Onset Time
VOT........ Voice Output Terminal [*Computer science*] (WDMC)
VOT........ VOR [*Very-High-Frequency Omnidirectional Range*] Test Signal (CET)
vot........ Votic [*MARC language code Library of Congress*] (LCCP)
VOTA........ Vibration Open Test Assembly [*Nuclear energy*] (NRCH)
VOTACT........ Validation of Theoretical Automatic Checkout Techniques (MCD)
VOTAG........ Verbal Orders of the Adjutant General
VOTC........ Volume Table of Contents [*Computer science*]
VOTCA........ Victims of Terrorism Compensation Act
VO-TECH........ Vocational-Technical
VOTEM........ Voice-Operated Typewriter Employing Morse [*Telecommunications*] (IAA)

VOTERM ...... Voice Terminal (NITA)
VOTJ ...... Tanjore [*India*] [*ICAO location identifier*] (ICLI)
VOTM ...... Vacuum-Operated Throttle Modulator [*Automotive engineering*]
VOTP ...... Tirupeti [*India*] [*ICAO location identifier*] (ICLI)
VOTR ...... Tiruchchirappalli [*India*] [*ICAO location identifier*] (ICLI)
VOTS ...... VAX OSI [*Virtual Address Extension Open Systems Interconnection*] TransportService (TNIG)
VOTV ...... Trivandrum [*India*] [*ICAO location identifier*] (ICLI)
VOTX ...... Tambaram [*India*] [*ICAO location identifier*] (ICLI)
VOU ...... Visio Oculus Uterque [*Vision, Each Eye*] [*Ophthalmology*] [*Latin*] (MAE)
VOU ...... Voucher (AFM)
VOU ...... Vouglans [*France*] [*Seismograph station code, US Geological Survey*] (SEIS)
VOU DED ...... Voucher Deduction [*Military*] (DNAB)
V_{OUT} ...... Output Voltage (IDOE)
VOV ...... Van Kam Am Cap OH Val Mun [*AMEX symbol*] (TTSB)
VOV ...... Van Kampen Merritt Ohio Value Municipal Trust [*AMEX symbol*] (SPSG)
VOV ...... Very Old Version
VOV ...... Video Output Voltage
VOV ...... Voice of Vietnam [*Propaganda broadcast aimed at US POWs*] (VNW)
VOVB ...... Vikarabad [*India*] [*ICAO location identifier*] (ICLI)
VOVR ...... Vellore [*India*] [*ICAO location identifier*] (ICLI)
VOW ...... Canadian Voice of Women for Peace [*See also VFCP*]
VOW ...... Voice of Women
VOW ...... Voice Order Wire
VOWA ...... Warangal [*India*] [*ICAO location identifier*] (ICLI)
VOWF ...... Value-Operated Water Flash (DNAB)
VOWR ...... St. John's, NF [*AM radio station call letters*]
VOX ...... Audiovox Cl'A' [*AMEX symbol*] (TTSB)
VOX ...... Audiovox Corp. [*AMEX symbol*] (SAG)
VOX ...... Voice Controlled Relay
VOX ...... Voice-Operated Changeover
vox ...... Voice-Operated Control (IDOE)
VOX ...... Voice-Operated Keying [*Computer science*]
VOX ...... Voice-Operated Transmission
VOX ...... Voice Output Exchange
voxel ...... Volume Element (MAE)
Voxel ...... Voxel Co. [*Associated Press*] (SAG)
VOXL ...... Voxel [*NASDAQ symbol*] (SAG)
VOXLW ...... Voxel Wrrt [*NASDAQ symbol*] (TTSB)
VOX POP ...... Vox Populi [*Voice of the People*] [*Latin*]
VOXW ...... Voxware, Inc. [*NASDAQ symbol*] (SAG)
Voxware ...... Voxware, Inc. [*Associated Press*] (SAG)
VOY ...... Viceroy Resources Corp. [*Toronto Stock Exchange symbol Vancouver Stock Exchange symbol*]
VOY ...... Voice-Operated Relay (IAA)
voy ...... Voyage (DS)
VOYA ...... Voice of Youth Advocates [*A publication*] (BRI)
VoyAZ ...... Voyageur Arizona Municipal Income Fund [*Associated Press*] (SAG)
VoyCO ...... Voyageur Colorado Insured Municipal Income Fund [*Associated Press*] (SAG)
VoyFla ...... Voyageur Florida Insured Municipal Income [*Associated Press*] (SAG)
VoyMN ...... Voyageur Minnesota Municipal Income Fund, Inc. [*Associated Press*] (SAG)
VoyMN2 ...... Voyageur Minnesota Municipal Income Fund 2, Inc. [*Associated Press*] (SAG)
VoyMN3 ...... Voyageur Minnesota Municipal Income Fund 3, Inc. [*Associated Press*] (SAG)
VoyMO ...... Voyageur Missouri Municipal Income Fund [*Associated Press*] (SAG)
VP ...... All India Reporter, Vindhya Pradesh [*1951-57*] [*A publication*] (DLA)
VP ...... Patrol Plane [*Navy symbol*]
VP ...... Patrol Squadron [*Navy symbol*]
V_p ...... Pinchoff Voltage (IDOE)
V_p ...... Plasma Volume [*Laboratory science*] (DAVI)
V_p ...... Plate Volage (IDOE)
VP ...... Shore Based [*Navy symbol*]
VP ...... Vacant Property (ADA)
VP ...... Vacuum Packaged
VP ...... Vacuum Pickup
VP ...... Vacuum Pump
VP ...... Validation Parameter (DA)
VP ...... Validation Plan [*Social Security Administration*]
VP ...... Valve Pit (AAG)
VP ...... Valve Positioner
VP ...... Vanishing Point [*Term in art/drawing*]
VP ...... Vanuaaku Pati [*New Hebrides*] [*Political party*] (PD)
VP ...... Vanuatu Pati (PD)
VP ...... Vapor Pressure
VP ...... Variable Pitch [*as, an aircraft propeller*]
VP ...... Variable Procedure (AAG)
VP ...... Variable Property
VP ...... Variant Pinocytic [*Cell*] [*Medicine*]
VP ...... Variegate Porphyria [*Medicine*]
VP ...... Various Paging [*Bibliography*]
vp ...... Various Places [*MARC country of publication code Library of Congress*] (LCCP)
VP ...... Various Publishers [*Bibliography*]
VP ...... Vasopressin [*Endocrinology*]
VP ...... Vector Processor
VP ...... Vegetable Parchment [*Paper*] (DGA)
VP ...... Velocity of Propagation (IAA)
VP ...... Velocity Pressure
VP ...... Venereal Pamphlet [*Navy*]
VP ...... Venipuncture [*Medicine*] (MAE)
VP ...... Venous Pressure [*Medicine*]
VP ...... Vent-Clearing Pressure [*Nuclear energy*] (NRCH)
V-P ...... Ventilation-Perfusion Scintigraphy
VP ...... Vent Pipe [*Technical drawings*]
VP ...... Ventral Pioneer [*Neuron*]
VP ...... Ventral Posterior [*Anatomy*]
VP ...... Ventricular Premature [*beat*] [*Cardiology*] (DAVI)
VP ...... Ventriculoperitoneal [*Medicine*]
VP ...... Verb Passive
VP ...... Verb Phrase
VP ...... Verification Polarization (NASA)
VP ...... Verification Program [*Branch*] [*Marine science*] (OSRA)
VP ...... Verification Program [*Branch*] [*Forecast Systems Laboratory*] (USDC)
VP ...... Verifying Punch (CMD)
VP ...... Verstell Propeller (MCD)
VP ...... Vertex Processor
VP ...... Vertical Planning (NG)
VP ...... Vertical Polarization
VP ...... Vest Pocket
VP ...... Vice President
v-p ...... Vice-President (DD)
VP ...... Vice-Principal [*British*]
VP ...... Videoplayer
VP ...... Video Processor (NVT)
VP ...... Vietnam Press
VP ...... Viewpoint (NASA)
VP ...... Vincristine and Prednisone [*Antineoplastic drug regimen*]
VP ...... Vinylphenol [*Biochemistry*]
VP ...... Vinylpyrrolidinone [*Organic chemistry*]
VP ...... Viral Particle [*Medicine*]
VP ...... Viral Protein [*Biochemistry, genetics*]
VP ...... Virtual Control Program (NITA)
VP ...... Virtual Machine Control Program [*Computer science*] (IAA)
VP ...... Virtual Pitch [*Neurophysiology*]
VP ...... Virtual Processor
VP ...... Visa Petition
VP ...... Visitor's Passport [*British*]
VP ...... Vivre et Penser [*A publication*] (BJA)
VP ...... Voges-Proskauer [*Bacteriology*]
VP ...... Void in Part [*Decision or finding held invalid in part for reasons given*] [*Used in Shepard's Citations*] [*Legal term*] (DLA)
VP ...... Volkspartie [*People's Party*] [*Liechtenstein*] [*Political party*] (PPE)
VP ...... Volkspolizei [*Also, VOPO*]
VP ...... Volume-Pressure (MAE)
VP ...... Voluntary Patient [*British*]
VP ...... Vorposten [*Outpost*] [*German military*]
VP ...... Vossa Paternidade [*Yours Paternally*] [*Portuguese*]
VP ...... Voting Pool [*Said of disposition of stocks*]
VP ...... Vulnerable Period [*Physiology*]
VP ...... Vulnerable Point
VP-16-213 ...... Vepeside [*Etoposide*] [*Antineoplastic drug*]
VPA ...... Silver Plains [*Queensland*] [*Airport symbol*] (AD)
VPA ...... Valproic Acid [*Anticonvulsant compound*]
VPA ...... Value Purchase Agreement (HGAA)
VPA ...... Vascular Permeability Assay [*Clinical chemistry*]
VPA ...... Vegetable Protein Association [*British*] (DBA)
VPA ...... Vehicle Power Adapter
VPA ...... Vibration Pickup Amplifier
VPA ...... Victorian Psychologists' Association [*Australia*]
VPA ...... Videotape Production Association (EA)
VPA ...... Village Produce Association [*British*] (BI)
VPA ...... Virtual Population Analysis
VPA ...... Visual Packaging Association [*Defunct*] (EA)
VPA ...... Volatile Profile Analysis [*Food chemistry*]
VPA ...... Volume Purchase Agreement [*Sales*]
VPA ...... Vote Profile Analysis
VPAFA ...... Victorian Public Authorities Finance Agency [*Australia*]
VPAM ...... Verapamil [*Antineoplastic drug*] (CDI)
VPAM ...... Virtual Partitioned Access Method
VP and VLE ...... Vapour Pressures and Vapour Liquid Equilibria (NITA)
VPAP ...... Voluntary Petroleum Allocation Program [*Presidential*]
VPATH ...... Vertical Path (GAVI)
VPB ...... Medium and Heavy Patrol Bomber Squadron [*Land based and seaplane*] [*Navy symbol*]
VPB ...... Patrol-Bombing Plane [*Navy symbol*]
VPB ...... Vendors per Block [*Sales*]
VPB ...... Ventricular Premature Beat [*Cardiology*]
VPB ...... Vertical Plot Board [*Navy*]
VPB ...... Veteran Air [*Ukraine*] [*FAA designator*] (FAAC)
VPB ...... Vinblastine, Platinol [*Cisplatin*], Bleomycin [*Antineoplastic drug regimen*]
VPB ...... Virtually-Pivoted Beam LASER (IAA)
VPBA ...... Varipolarization Beacon Antenna
VPBA ...... Virginia Poultry Breeders Association (EA)
VPBC ...... Virginia Poultry Breeders Club [*Later, VPBA*] (EA)
VPB(HL) ...... Patrol Bomber, Four-Engine, Landplane [*Navy symbol*]
VPB(HS) ...... Patrol Bomber, Four-Engine, Seaplane [*Navy symbol*]
VPB(ML) ...... Patrol Bomber, Two-Engine, Landplane [*Navy symbol*]
VPB(MS) ...... Patrol Bomber, Two-Engine, Seaplane [*Navy symbol*]
VPC ...... La Vente par Correspondance [*Mail Order*] [*Business term French*]
VPC ...... Vaccines for Children [*Medicine*]
VPC ...... Vacuum Pump Chamber

VPC............. Vapor Permeation Curing [*Plastics technology*]
VPC............. Vapor-Phase Chromatography [*Medicine*] (DMAA)
VPC............. Variable Padder Capacitor
VPC............. Vehicle-Platform Center [*Ford Motor Co.*] (ECON)
VPC............. Vehicle Platform Center [*Automotive industry project management*]
VPC............. Ventricular Premature Contraction [*Cardiology*]
VPC............. Vertebrate Pests Committee (EERA)
VPC............. Vertical Path Computer (PDAA)
VPC............. Veterinary Products Committee [*British*]
VPC............. Victorian Psychological Council [*Australia*]
VPC............. Video Processor Control (MCD)
VPC............. Virginia Panel Corp. (IAA)
VPC............. Virtual Processor Complex [*Computer science*] (CDE)
VPC............. Visual Punch Card
VPC............. Voltage Phasing Control (DEN)
VPC............. Voltage to Pulse Converter
VPC............. Volume Packed Cells
VPC............. Volume Percent (MAE)
VPC............. Volume-Pulse-Charge
VPC............. Volunteer Program Consultant [*Red Cross*]
VPC............. Volunteers for Peaceful Change (EA)
VPC............. Vulval Precursor Cell [*Genetics*]
VPCA........... Video Prelaunch Command Amplifier
VPCDS......... Video Prelaunch Command Data System [*Air Force*]
VPCE........... Vapor-Phase Catalytic Exchange (MCD)
VPCF........... Vapor Pressure Correction Factor [*Nuclear energy*] (IAA)
VPCIS.......... Voice-Operated Computerized Identification System (PDAA)
VPCMF......... Vincristine, Prednisone, Cyclophosphamide, Methotrexate, Fluorouracil [*Antineoplastic drug regimen*]
VPCPr.......... Vincristine, Prednisone, Vinblastine, Chlorambucil, Procarbazine [*Antineoplastic drug regimen*]
VP/CSS........ Virtual Program/Conversation Software System (NITA)
VPD............. Vapor-Phase Deacidification [*of books and documents*]
VPD............. Vapor Phase Deposition [*Coating technology*]
VPD............. Vapor Pressure Deficit [*Meteorology*]
VPD............. Variable Power Drivetrain [*Automotive engineering*]
VPD............. Variation per Day [*Navigation*]
VPD............. Vehicle/Pedestrian Deviation [*FAA*] (TAG)
VPD............. Vehicle Performance Data
VPD............. Vehicle Propulsion Directorate [*Army and NASA joint operation*] (RDA)
VPD............. Vehicles per Day [*Military*] (AFM)
VPD............. Ventricular Premature Depolarization [*Cardiology*]
VPD............. Vertically Polarized Dipole (MCD)
VPD............. Victorian Parliamentary Debates [*A publication*]
VPD............. Vierte Partei Deutschlands [*Fourth Party of Germany*] [*Political party*] (PPW)
VPD............. Villa Park Dam [*California*] [*Seismograph station code, US Geological Survey*] (SEIS)
VPD............. Visual Pattern Discrimination (PDAA)
VPDB........... Vienna PeeDee Belemnite
VPDF........... Vacuum Pump Discharge Filter
VPE............. Vapor Growth Epitaxy [*Materials processing*] (IAA)
VPE............. Vapor-Phase Epitaxy
VPE............. Vehicle Positioning Equipment (MCD)
VPE............. Video Processing Equipment
VPE............. Visual Programming Environment
VPE............. Vulcanized Polyethylene (IAA)
VPELA.......... Victorian Planning and Environmental Law Association [*Australia*]
VP-F............ Falkland Islands [*International civil aircraft marking*] (ODBW)
VPF............. Vacuum Pump Filter
VPF............. Variable Parts Feeder
VPF............. Variable Phase Filter
VPF............. Vascular-Permeability Factor [*Medicine*]
VPF............. Vector Processing Facility (NITA)
VPF............. Vector Product Format
VPF............. Vertical Processing Facility [*NASA*] (MCD)
VPF............. Vibratory Pan Feeder
VPF............. Victorian Police Force [*Australia*]
VPF............. Victorian Protestant Federation [*Australia*]
VPF............. Viscoplastic Flow
VPFAS.......... Vice President of the Faculty of Architects and Surveyors [*British*] (DBQ)
VPFG........... Variable Phase Function Generator
VPG............. Vallentine Peace Group [*Political party Australia*]
VPG............. Variable-Rate Pulse Generator
VPG............. Vehicle Product Group
VPG............. Velopharyngeal Gap [*Medicine*] (DMAA)
VPGG........... Valine-Proline-Glycine-Glycine [*Biochemistry*]
VPGS........... Venous Pressure Gradient Support Stocking
VPGS........... Vice-President of the Geological Society [*British*]
VPGVG......... Valine-Proline-Glycine-Valine-Glycine [*Biochemistry*]
VPH............. Variation per Hour [*Navigation*]
VPH............. Vehicles per Hour [*Traffic*] (AFM)
V PH............ Vertical Photography (WDAA)
VPH............. Veterans of Pearl Harbor (EA)
VPH............. Vickers Pyramid Hardness Number (PDAA)
VPH............. Viewers Per Household [*Television ratings*] (DOAD)
VPH............. Volkspolizeihelfer
VPHD........... Vertical Payload Handling Device [*NASA*] (MCD)
VPHM........... ViroPharma, Inc. [*NASDAQ symbol*] (SAG)
VPI.............. Vacuum Pressure Impregnation (IEEE)
VPI.............. Valve Position Indicator (KSC)
VPI.............. Vapor-Phase Inhibitor [*See also VCI*] [*Chemical technology*]
VPI.............. Vehicle Performance Index [*Automobile technology*]
VPI.............. Vehicle Personality Module [*Automotive engineering*]
VPI.............. Velopharyngeal Insufficiency [*Medicine*] (MEDA)
VPI.............. Vendor Parts Index [*Sales*]
VPI.............. Vertical Point of Intersection [*Transportation*]
VPI.............. Very Promotable Item (WDMC)
VPI.............. Vessel Patentcy Index [*Medicine*]
VPI.............. Vintage Petroleum [*NYSE symbol*] (SPSG)
VPI.............. VIP Dynasty International Marketing Corp. [*Vancouver Stock Exchange symbol*]
VPI.............. Virginia Polytechnic Institute and State University [*Blacksburg*]
VPI.............. Virginia Polytechnic Institute and State University, Blacksburg, VA [*OCLC symbol*] (OCLC)
VPI.............. Vocational Preference Inventory [*Psychology*]
VPIC............ Victorian Prison Industries Commission [*Australia*]
VPJT............ Vertical Power Jump Test
VPK............. Military Industrial Commission [*Soviet-Russian*] (DOMA)
VPK............. Vehicle per Kilometer (AABC)
VPK............. Verdi Peak [*California*] [*Seismograph station code, US Geological Survey*] (SEIS)
VPK............. Vest Pocket Kodak [*Camera*]
VPK............. Volts Peak (NASA)
VPK............. Voyenno-promyshlennaya Komissiya [*Military Industrial Commission*] [*Former USSR*] (LAIN)
VPKA........... Volkspolizeikreisamt
VP(L)........... US Navy Patrol Squadron (Land) (CINC)
VPL............. Variable Pulse LASER
VPL............. Vendor Parts List (AAG)
VPL............. Ventral Posterolateral [*Anatomy*]
VPL............. Virginia Beach Public Library System, Virginia Beach, VA [*OCLC symbol*] (OCLC)
VPL............. Visible Panty Line [*In reference to clothing*]
VPL............. Voice-Programming Language [*Computer science*]
VPL............. Volunteer Prison League [*Defunct*] (EA)
VPL............. Vulcano Piano [*Lipari Islands*] [*Seismograph station code, US Geological Survey*] (SEIS)
VP-LA.......... Anguilla [*International civil aircraft marking*] (ODBW)
VPLCC.......... Vehicle Propellant Loading Control Center
VPLIC........... Victorian Public Library and Information Cooperative [*Australia*]
VP-LMA........ Montserrat [*International civil aircraft marking*] (ODBW)
VPLR........... Vacuum Pack Life Raft (DWSG)
VPLS........... Vice-President of the Linnaean Society [*British*]
VP-LV.......... Virgin Islands [*International civil aircraft marking*] (ODBW)
VPM............. Vacuum Pumping Module
VPM............. Variation per Minute [*Navigation*]
VPM............. Vascular Permeability Mediator [*Hematology*]
VPM............. Vehicle Project Manager [*NASA*] (NASA)
VPM............. Vehicles per Mile
VPM............. Velocity Preset Module (MCD)
VPM............. Vendor Part Modification (AAG)
VPM............. Versatile Packaging Machine
VPM............. Vertical Panel Mount
VPM............. Vertical Polarization Mode
VPM............. Vibrations per Minute
VPM............. Voice-Processing Module [*Computer science*]
VPM............. Voix du Peuple Murundi [*Voice of the Murundi People*]
VPM............. Volts per Meter [*Also, V/m*]
VPM............. Volts per Mil
VPM............. Volts per Mile (IAA)
VPM............. Volumes per Million [*Measure of gas contamination*]
VPMA........... Vegetable Parchment Manufacturers Association [*Later, API*] (EA)
VPMOS......... Verified Primary Military Occupational Specialty
VPMR........... Vanguard Party of the Malagasy Revolution
VPMS........... Virchow-Pirquet Medical Society (EA)
VPN............. Vendor Parts Number
VPN............. Vickers Pyramid Number [*Hardness test*]
VPN............. Virtual Page Number
VPN............. Virtual Private Network [*US Sprint Communications Co.*] [*Atlanta, GA*] (TSSD)
VPN............. Vopnafjordur [*Iceland*] [*Airport symbol*] (OAG)
VPNL........... Variable Pulse Neodymium LASER
VPO............. Vanadium Phosphate [*Inorganic chemistry*]
VPO............. Vanadium-Phosphorus Oxide [*Inorganic chemistry*]
VPO............. Vapor-Phase Oxidation [*Chemical processing*]
VPO............. Vapor Pressure Osmometer [*or Osmometry*] [*Analytical chemistry*]
VPO............. Vegetation Protection Ordinance [*Brisbane*] (EERA)
VPO............. Vienna Philharmonic Orchestra
VPO............. Viking Project Office [*NASA*] (KSC)
VPOC........... Variable Performance Optimizing Controller (IAA)
VPOF........... Vacuum-Processed Oxide Free
VPOP........... Vice Directorate for Production Office Procedure [*Defense Intelligence Agency*] (MCD)
VPP............. Vacuum Pickup Pencil
VPP............. Value Payable by Post
VPP............. Variable Pitch Propeller
VPP............. Variable Polarity Plasma [*Welding*]
VPP............. Vector Parallel Processor [*Computer science*]
VPP............. Vegetable Protein Products [*Food technology*]
VPP............. Velocity per Performance
VPP............. Velocity Prediction Program
VPP............. Vertebrate Pest Program (EERA)
VPP............. Vertical Pinpoint (AFM)
VPP............. Vertical Pouch Packager
VPP............. Very Public Person
VPP............. Vested Pension Plan (MHDB)
VPP............. Viral Porcine Pneumonia [*Veterinary medicine*]

VPP .... Virtual Pivot Point [*Suspension*] [*Tandem bike*]
VPP .... Viscous Plastic Processing [*Materials science and technology*]
VPP .... Vocational Preparation Programme (AIE)
V P-P .... Volt Peak-to-Peak (NASA)
VPP .... Voluntary Projects Programme [*British*]
VPP .... Voluntary Protection Program [*OSHA*]
VPP .... Volunteer Political Party [*Northern Ireland*]
VPPB .... Vendor Provisioning Parts Breakdown (AAG)
VPPD .... Vice Presidential Protective Division [*US Secret Service*]
VPPN .... Vampire Pen Pal Network [*Defunct*] (EA)
VPPPA .... Voluntary Protection Programs Participants' Association
VPPS .... Vehicle Parking Protection Services [*British*]
VPQ .... Van Kam Am Cap PA Qual Mun [*NYSE symbol*] (TTSB)
VPQ .... Van Kampen Merritt Pennsylvania Quality Municipal [*NYSE symbol*] (SPSG)
VPR .... Vacuum Pipette Rig (PDAA)
VPR .... Valveless Pulse Rocket
VPR .... Vaporize (MSA)
VPR .... Variable Parameter Record [*Statistics*] (IAA)
VPR .... Variable Parameter Regression [*Statistics*]
VPR .... Ventricle Pressure Response [*Cardiology*]
VPR .... Video Plankton Recorder [*Oceanography*]
VPR .... Virtual PPI [*Plan-Position Indicator*] Reflectoscope [*RADAR*]
VPR .... Virtual Processor Ratio [*Computer science*]
VPR .... Vital Pacific Resources Ltd. [*Vancouver Stock Exchange symbol*]
VPR .... Voice Position Report (DA)
VPR .... Voluntary Price Reduction (AABC)
VPRC .... Volume of Packed Red Cells [*Hematology*]
VPRES .... Vice-President
VPRESSVB ... Vice-Presidential Service Badge [*Military decoration*]
VPRF .... Variable Pulse Repetition Frequency (IEEE)
VPRGS .... Vice-President of the Royal Geographical Society [*British*]
VPRI .... Plant Research Institute, Burnley [*Victoria*] [*State*] (EERA)
VPRI .... Vice-President of the Royal Institute [*British*]
VPR-NMP .... Virtual PPI [*Plan-Position Indicator*] Reflectoscope with Navigational Microfilm Projector [*RADAR*]
VPRON .... US Navy Patrol Squadron (CINC)
VPRS .... Vice-President of the Royal Society [*British*]
VPRT .... Vector Pressure Ratio Transducer
VPS .... Eglin Air Force Base [*Florida*] [*Airport symbol*] (AD)
VPS .... Fort Walton Beach [*Florida*] [*Airport symbol*] (OAG)
VP(S) .... US Navy Patrol Squadron (Sea-Based) (CINC)
VPS .... Vacuum Pickup System
VPS .... Vacuum Pipe Still [*Chemical engineering*]
VPS .... Vacuum Pump System
VPS .... Valparaiso, FL [*Location identifier FAA*] (FAAL)
VPS .... Valvular Pulmonic Stenosis [*Cardiology*] (DAVI)
VPS .... Vanguard Planning Summary [*Air Force*]
VPS .... Vapor Phase Soldering (PDAA)
VPS .... Variable Parameter System
VPS .... Variable Power Supply (MCD)
VPS .... Vatican Philatelic Society (EA)
VPS .... Vectors Per Second (CDE)
VPS .... Vehicle Power Supply [*Automotive engineering*]
VPS .... Ventriculoperitoneal Shunt [*Neurology*] (DAVI)
VPS .... Vernier Propulsion System [*Aerospace*]
VPS .... Versatile Pacific Shipyards [*Shipbuilder*] [*Vancouver, Canada*]
VPS .... Vibrations per Second
VPS .... Vibrator Power Supply
VPS .... Video-Pac Systems Ltd. [*Hollywood, CA*] [*Telecommunications service*] (TSSD)
VPS .... Video Programme Service (NITA)
VPS .... Viewers-per-Set [*Television ratings*] (WDMC)
VPS .... Vinylpolysilane [*Organic chemistry*]
VPS .... Virtual Programming System (NITA)
VPS .... Visitor Program Service of Meridian House International (EA)
VPS .... Visual Programs Systems
VPS .... Voice Control Systems [*AMEX symbol*] (SAG)
VPS .... Voice Processing System [*Computer science*] (IT)
VPS .... Volcan Poas [*Costa Rica*] [*Seismograph station code, US Geological Survey*] (SEIS)
VPS .... Voluntary Product Standard [*National Bureau of Standards*]
VPSA .... Vice-President of the Society of Antiquaries [*British*]
VPSAB .... Victorian Post-Secondary Accreditation Board [*Australia*]
VPSB .... Veterans Placement Service Board [*Post-World War II*]
VPSS .... Vector Processing Subsystem
VPSSIHM ..... Volunteer Program of the Sisters, Servants of the Immaculate Heart of M ary (EA)
VPSS/VF ...... Vector Processing Subsystem/Vector Facility [*Computer science*] (HGAA)
VPSW .... Virtual Program Status Word
VPT .... Patrol Torpedo Plane [*Navy symbol*]
VPT .... Ventral Posterior Thalamic [*Electrode for stimulation*]
VPT .... Vibratron Pressure Transducer
VPT .... Video Pulse Termination
VPT .... Virtual Printer Technology [*Dataproducts Corp.*] (PCM)
VPT .... Voice plus Telegraph [*Telecommunications*] (TEL)
VPT .... Volume-Price Trend [*Finance*]
VPTAR .... Variable Parameter Terrain-Avoidance RADAR
VPTI .... Voice Powered Tech International [*NASDAQ symbol*] (SAG)
VPTI .... Voice Powered Tech Intl [*NASDAQ symbol*] (TTSB)
VPTIW .... Voice Powered Tech Intl Wrrt [*NASDAQ symbol*] (TTSB)
VPTR .... Value Pointer (MHDI)
VPTRM .... Viscous Partial Thermoremanent Magnetization [*Geophysics*]
VPU .... Pace University Library, Union List of Serials, New York, NY [*OCLC symbol*] (OCLC)
VPU .... Vacuum Penetration Unit
VPU .... Vibrator Power Unit (MSA)
VPUA .... Vibration Pickup Amplifier
VPUG .... Ventura Publisher User's Group (EA)
VPUR .... Vermont Pure Hldgs Ltd [*NASDAQ symbol*] (TTSB)
VPUR .... Vermont Pure Holdings [*NASDAQ symbol*] (SAG)
VPV .... Van Kam Am Cap PA Val Mun [*NYSE symbol*] (TTSB)
VPV .... Van Kampen Merritt Pennsylvania Value Municipal Income Trust [*NYSE symbol*] (SPSG)
VPVCPr .... Vincristine, Prednisone, Vinblastine, Chlorambucil, Procarbazine [*Antineoplastic drug regimen*]
VPVH .... Viewers-per-Viewing Household [*Television ratings*] (NTCM)
VPW .... Variable Pulse Width [*Automotive engineering*]
VPW .... Ventral Prostate Weight [*Medicine*]
VPW .... Vertically Polarized Wave
VPX .... Pineville, WV [*Location identifier FAA*] (FAAL)
VPY .... Vila Pery [*Mozambique*] [*Airport symbol*] (AD)
VPY .... Vinylpyridine [*Organic chemistry*]
VPZ .... Valparaiso [*Indiana*] [*Airport symbol*] (OAG)
VPZ .... Valparaiso, IN [*Location identifier FAA*] (FAAL)
VPZ .... Virtual Processing Zero
VPZS .... Vice-President of the Zoological Society [*British*]
VQ .... Fleet Air Reconnaissance Squadron [*Navy symbol*] (CINC)
VQ .... Oxley Airlines [*ICAO designator*] (AD)
VQ .... Vector Quantizer [*Computer science*]
V/Q .... Ventilation/Perfusion [*Quotient*] [*Medicine*]
VQ .... Very Quick [*Flashing*] Light [*Navigation signal*]
VQ .... Virtual Quantum
VQ .... Voluntary Quit [*Unemployment insurance*] [*Bureau of Labor Statistics*] (OICC)
VQA .... Al Sigl Center Library, Rochester, NY [*OCLC symbol*] (OCLC)
VQA .... Vendor Quality Assurance
VQAR .... Vendor Quality Assurance Representative [*Nuclear energy*] (NRCH)
VQB .... Bausch & Lomb, Inc., Library, Rochester, NY [*OCLC symbol*] (OCLC)
VQB .... Valuers' Qualification Board [*Victoria, Australia*]
VQB .... Visual Query Builder [*Computer science*] (PCM)
VQC .... Canandaigua Veterans Administration Medical Center Library, Canandaigua, NY [*OCLC symbol*] (OCLC)
VQC .... Van Kam Am Cap CA Qual Mun [*NYSE symbol*] (TTSB)
VQC .... Van Kampen Merritt California Quality Municipal Fund [*NYSE symbol*] (SAG)
VQC .... Variable Quartz Capacitor
VQC .... Vendor Quality Certification
VQD .... Center for Governmental Research Library, Rochester, NY [*OCLC symbol*] (OCLC)
VQD .... Vendor Quality Defect
VQE .... Colgate-Rochester Divinity School, Library, Rochester, NY [*OCLC symbol*] (OCLC)
VQE .... San Antonio, TX [*Location identifier FAA*] (FAAL)
VQF .... Convalescent Hospital for Children, Library, Rochester, NY [*OCLC symbol*] (OCLC)
VQG .... Eastman Dental Center, Basil G. Bibby Library, Rochester, NY [*OCLC symbol*] (OCLC)
VQH .... Eastman Kodak Co., KAD Library, Rochester, NY [*OCLC symbol*] (OCLC)
VQI .... Eastman Kodak Co., Business Library, Rochester, NY [*OCLC symbol*] (OCLC)
VQJ .... Eastman Kodak Co., Engineering Division, Library, Rochester, NY [*OCLC symbol*] (OCLC)
VQK .... Eastman Kodak Co., Health and Safety Laboratory, Library, Rochester, NY [*OCLC symbol*] (OCLC)
V Qk Fl .... Very-Quick Flashing Light
VQL .... Eastman Kodak Co., Photographic Technology Library, Rochester, NY [*OCLC symbol*] (OCLC)
VQL .... Variable Quantization Level [*Algorithm developed by Aydin Monitor Corp.*] [*Telecommunications*]
VQM .... Detroit, MI [*Location identifier FAA*] (FAAL)
VQM .... Eastman Kodak Co., Research Laboratories, Library, Rochester, NY [*OCLC symbol*] (OCLC)
VQMG .... Vice-Quartermaster-General
VQN .... General Railway Signal Co., Library, Rochester, NY [*OCLC symbol*] (OCLC)
VQO .... Genesee Hospital, Stabins Health Science Library, Rochester, NY [*OCLC symbol*] (OCLC)
VQO .... Provincetown, MA [*Location identifier FAA*] (FAAL)
VQP .... Highland Hospital, Williams Health Science Library, Rochester, NY [*OCLC symbol*] (OCLC)
VQQ .... Mixing Equipment Co., Library, Rochester, NY [*OCLC symbol*] (OCLC)
VQR .... Virginia Quarterly Review [*A publication*] (BRI)
VQS .... Isla De Vieques, PR [*Location identifier FAA*] (FAAL)
VQS .... Mobil Chemical Co., Plastics Division, Research Library, Macedon, NY [*OCLC symbol*] (OCLC)
VQS .... Valve Qualification Study
VQS .... Vieques [*Puerto Rico*] [*Seismograph station code, US Geological Survey Closed*] (SEIS)
VQS .... Vieques [*Puerto Rico*] [*Airport symbol*] (OAG)
VQT .... Monroe Community College, L. V. Good Library, Rochester, NY [*OCLC symbol*] (OCLC)
VQ-T .... Turks and Caicos Islands [*International civil aircraft marking*] (ODBW)
VQT .... Viewers for Quality Television (EA)
VQU .... Monroe Community Hospital, Medical-Nursing Library, Rochester, NY [*OCLC symbol*] (OCLC)

VQV .... Monroe County Department of Health, Library, Rochester, NY [*OCLC symbol*] (OCLC)
VQV .... Vacaville, CA [*Location identifier FAA*] (FAAL)
VQW .... Monroe Development Center, Library, Rochester, NY [*OCLC symbol*] (OCLC)
VQX .... Park Ridge Hospital, Medical Library, Rochester, NY [*OCLC symbol*] (OCLC)
VQY .... Pennwalt Corp., Pharmaceutical Division, Library, Rochester, NY [*OCLC symbol*] (OCLC)
VQZ .... R. T. French Co., Library, Rochester, NY [*OCLC symbol*] (OCLC)
VQZD .... Vendor Quality Zero Defects
VR .... Fleet Tactical Support [*Navy symbol*] (NVT)
VR .... Heading to a Radial (GAVI)
VR .... Relative Voltage
VR .... Takeoff Rotation Velocity (GAVI)
VR .... Transportes Aereos de Cabo Verde [*ICAO designator*] (AD)
VR .... Transport Plane [*Multiengine*] [*Navy symbol*]
VR .... Transport Squadron [*Navy symbol*]
VR .... Vagabonds Removed [*Prison van nickname used during reign of VR, Victoria Regina*] [*British*] (DSUE)
VR .... Vale of Rheidol Light Railway [*Wales*]
VR .... Validation and Recovery
VR .... Validation Report [*Army*]
VR .... Valley Resources [*AMEX symbol*] (TTSB)
VR .... Valley Resources, Inc. [*AMEX symbol*] (SPSG)
VR .... Valtionrautatiet [*Finnish State Railways*]
VR .... Valuation Reports, Interstate Commerce Commission [*A publication*] (DLA)
VR .... Valve Replacement [*Cardiology*]
VR .... Vanguardia Revolucionaria [*Revolutionary Vanguard*] [*Peru*] [*Political party*] (PPW)
VR .... Variable Rate [*Reinforcement*] [*Medicine*] (DAVI)
VR .... Variable Ratio [*Reinforcement*]
VR .... Variable Reluctance
VR .... Variable Resistance [*or Resistor*] (IAA)
VR .... Variant Reading
VR .... Variety Reduction (WDAA)
VR .... Varnishing Resistant [*Ink*] (DGA)
VR .... Vascular Resistance [*Medicine*] (MAE)
VR .... Vehicle Recovery
VR .... Velocity, Relative (MCD)
VR .... Vendor Rating [*Sales*]
VR .... Venous Reflux [*Medicine*] (DMAA)
VR .... Venous Return [*Medicine*]
VR .... Ventilation Rate
VR .... Ventral Root [*of a spinal nerve*] [*Anatomy*]
VR .... Ventricular Rate [*Cardiology*]
VR .... Verbal Reprimand (DAVI)
VR .... Verb Reflexive
VR .... Verification Receiver
V-R .... VERLORT [*Very-Long-Range Tracking*] Range [*NASA*]
VR .... Vermont Reports [*A publication*] (DLA)
VR .... Vertical Redundancy [*Telecommunications*] (IAA)
VR .... Vertical Resistance
VR .... Vertical Retort
VR .... Vertical Rule (DGA)
VR .... Very High Speed Radial Tire [*Automotive engineering*]
VR .... Very Respectfully [*Letter closing*]
VR .... Vested Right
VR .... Veterinary and Remount Service [*British military*]
V-R .... Vibrational-Rotational [*Chemical kinetics*]
VR .... Vicar Rural
VR .... Victoria Regina [*Queen Victoria*]
VR .... Video Recorder (NASA)
VR .... Virginia Register of Regulations [*A publication*] (AAGC)
V R .... Virtual Equal Real [*Computer science*] (MHDI)
VR .... Virtual Equals Real [*Computer science*] (IAA)
VR .... Virtual Reality
VR .... Virtual-Reality Machine [*Video technology*] (ECON)
VR .... Virtual Route [*Computer science*]
VR .... Viscous Response [*Medicine*]
VR .... Vision, Right Eye
VR .... Visit Request (AAG)
VR .... Visor
VR .... Visual Reconnaissance
VR .... Visual Resources [*A publication*]
VR .... Visual Route (DA)
VR .... Vital Records [*Genealogy*]
VR .... Vital Records [*Medical records*] (DAVI)
VR .... Vocal Resonance
VR .... Vocational Rehabilitation
VR .... Voice of Reason [*Later, Americans for Religious Liberty*] (EA)
VR .... Voltage Reference (DEN)
VR .... Voltage Regulator
VR .... Voltage Relay
VR .... Voltage Repair
Vr .... Volume of Relaxation [*Medicine*] (DMAA)
VR .... Volume Reduction [*Nuclear energy*] (NRCH)
VR .... Voluntary Returnees [*Immigration Service*]
VR .... Volunteer Regiment [*British military*] (DMA)
VR .... Volunteer Reserve (BJA)
VR .... Vox Reformata: Australasian Journal for Christian Scholarship [*A publication*] (APTA)
VR .... Voyage Repairs [*Navy*] (NVT)
Vr .... Vroom's Law Reports [*30-85 New Jersey*] [*A publication*] (DLA)
VR .... Vulcanized Rubber
VR .... Vulnerability Reduction [*Military*] (RDA)
VRA .... Radford College, Radford, VA [*OCLC symbol*] (OCLC)
VRA .... Rough-Air [*or Turbulence*] Speed [*Aviation*]
VRA .... Value Received Analysis (MHDW)
VRA .... Varadero [*Cuba*] [*Airport symbol*] (OAG)
VRA .... Vertical Reference Attitude
VRA .... Vertical Rising Aircraft
VRA .... Veterans Readjustment Appointment
VRA .... Veterans Readjustment Authority
VRA .... [*The*] Victorian Railways of Australia (DCTA)
VRA .... Victorian Rowing Association [*Australia*]
VRA .... Viking RADAR Altimeter [*NASA*]
VRA .... Vocational Rehabilitation Act [*1973*]
VRA .... Vocational Rehabilitation Administration [*Later, Social and Rehabilitation S ervice*] [*HEW*]
VRA .... Vocational Rehabilitation Association
VRA .... Voltage Reference Amplifier
VRA .... Voltage Regulator Alarm
VRA .... Voluntary Restraint Arrangement [*Import quotas*]
VRA .... Voluntary Restriction Agreement [*Pact between the US and Japan on automotive imports*]
VRA .... Voting Rights Act [*1965, 1970, 1975*]
VRAD .... Vertically Referenced Attitude Display
VRAH .... Vertical Receiving Array Hydrophone
VRAM .... Variable Random Access Memory [*Computer science*]
VRAM .... Variable Rate Adaptive Multiplexing [*Telecommunications*] (TEL)
VRAM .... Video Random Access Memory
VRAM .... Virtual Random Access Memory [*Computer science*]
VRAMHP .... Vancouver-Richmond Assoc. for Mentally Handicapped People
VR & C .... Vocational Rehabilitation and Counseling Service [*Veterans Administration*]
VR & E .... Vocational Rehabilitation and Education (MAE)
VRASS .... Voice Recognition and Synthesis System [*Aviation Navy*]
VRB .... Valve-Regulated Battery [*Energy source*]
VRB .... Variable
VRB .... Variable Reenlistment Bonus [*Military*] (AABC)
VRB .... Vehicle Retaining Board
VRB .... Vero Beach [*Florida*] [*Airport symbol*] (OAG)
VRB .... Vero Beach, FL [*Location identifier FAA*] (FAAL)
VRB .... VHF [*Very-High-Frequency*] Recovery Beacon [*NASA*] (KSC)
VRB .... Violet Red Bile [*Microorganism growth medium*]
VRB .... Visual Report Builder [*Computer science*] (PCM)
VRB .... Voice Rotating Beacon
VRB .... Volunteer Reenlistment Bonus
VRBA .... Veterans' Readjustment Benefits Act of 1966 (WYGK)
VRBA .... Violet Red Bile Agar [*Microorganism growth medium*]
VRBC .... Volume, Red Blood Cell [*Hematology*] (MAE)
VRBG .... Viceroy's Bodyguard [*British military*] (DMA)
vrbl .... Variable (BARN)
VRBM .... Variable Range Ballistic Missile [*DoD*] (MCD)
VRBQ .... Valuers' Registration Board of Queensland [*Australia*]
VRBT .... Valuers' Registration Board of Tasmania [*Australia*]
VR-C .... Cayman Islands [*International civil aircraft marking*] (ODBW)
VRC .... Fleet Tactical Support Squadron Carrier [*Navy symbol*] (CINC)
VRC .... Taxi Aereo de Veracruz [*Mexico ICAO designator*] (FAAC)
VRC .... Valve Remanufacturers Council (EA)
VRC .... Vampire Research Center (EA)
VRC .... Varco International, Inc. [*NYSE symbol*] (SPSG)
VRC .... Varco Int'l [*NYSE symbol*] (TTSB)
VRC .... Variable Reluctance Cartridge
VRC .... Vehicle Reference Controller [*Military*]
VRC .... Vehicle Research Corp.
VRC .... Vehicle Roadside Communications
VRC .... Vehicle-to-Roadside Communication [*Traffic management*]
VRC .... Vertical Redundancy Check [*Telecommunications*] (BUR)
VRC .... Vertical Ride Control (OA)
VRC .... Vibrating Reed Capacitor
VRC .... Victorian Relief Committee AT
VRC .... Victoria Rifles of Canada (DMA)
VRC .... Virac [*Philippines*] [*Airport symbol*] (OAG)
VRC .... Virginia Commonwealth University, Richmond, VA [*OCLC symbol*] (OCLC)
VRC .... Virtual Redundancy Check [*Computer science*]
VRC .... Viscometer Recorder-Controller
VRC .... Visible Record Computer (IAA)
VRC .... Visual Record Computer
VRC .... Voice Recognition Chip [*Electronics*] (EECA)
VRC .... Voice Recognition Control (MCD)
VRC .... Volunteer Rifle Corps [*Military British*] (ROG)
VRCA .... Voice Recording Assembly [*Ground Communications Facility, NASA*]
VRCAMS .... Vehicle-Road Compatibility Analysis and Modification System (RDA)
VRCCC .... Vandenberg Range Communications Control Center [*Air Force*] (MCD)
VRCI .... Variable Resistive Components Institute (EA)
VRC-LRC .... Vertical-Longitudinal Redundancy Check [*Electronics*] (ECII)
VRCM .... Variable Relay Control Module [*Cooling systems*] [*Automotive engineering*]
VR CON .... Viral Antibody, Convalescent [*Immunology*] (DAVI)
VRCR .... Vertical Redundancy Check Register [*Telecommunications*] (IAA)
VRCS .... Vector Reaction Control System (SSD)
VRCS .... Vehicle to Roadside Communication System
VRCS .... Vernier [*Engine*] Reaction Control System [*Aerospace*] (NASA)
VRCS .... Veterinary and Remount Conducting Section [*British military*] (DMA)
VRCTR .... Varactor (MSA)

VRD .... Vacuum-Tube Relay Driver
VRD .... Variable Ratio Divider (IAA)
VRD .... Vehicle Reception Depot [*British military*] (DMA)
VRD .... Victoria River District [*Region*] (EERA)
VRD .... Virtual Resource Unit, Deferred
VRD .... Voltage Regulating Diode
VRD .... Volunteer Reserve Decoration [*British*]
VRDCA .... Victoria River District Conservation Association (EERA)
VRDDO .... Variable Retention of Diatomic Differential [*Physics*]
VRDO .... Variable Rate Demand Obligation [*Finance*]
VRDS .... Vacuum Residuum Desulfurization [*Petroleum refining*]
VRDU .... Variable Range Delay Unit (PDAA)
VRDV .... Vacuum Retard Delay Valve [*Automotive engineering*]
VRE .... Vancomycin Resistant Enterococcus
VRE .... Vibrating Reed Electrometer
VRE .... Voltage Regulator-Exciter
VRE .... Volume Review Exercise (DNAB)
VREF .... Reference Velocity (GAVI)
VREF .... Reference Voltage [*Automotive engineering*]
V_{ref} .... Reference Voltage (IDOE)
VREFI .... Vanguard Real Estate Fund I [*Associated Press*] (SAG)
VREFII .... Vanguard Real Estate Fund II [*Associated Press*] (SAG)
V REFL .... Verb Reflexive [*Grammar*] (WDAA)
V/REG .... Voltage Regulator [*Automotive engineering*]
VREL .... Velocity, Relative (GFGA)
VRES .... Vacuum Reservoir [*Automotive engineering*]
VRES .... VICORP Restaurants [*NASDAQ symbol*] (TTSB)
VRES .... VICORP Restaurants, Inc. [*NASDAQ symbol*] (NQ)
VREST .... Vacuum Restrictor [*Automotive engineering*]
VR et I .... Victoria Regina et Imperatrix [*Victoria, Queen and Empress*]
V Rev .... Very Reverend
VRF .... Aircraft Ferry Squadron [*Navy*]
VRF .... Ferry Squadron [*Navy symbol*] (NVT)
VRF .... Vascular Research Foundation
VRF .... Versatile Repair Facility
VRF .... Vertical Random Format (NITA)
VRF .... Vertical Removal Fixture (NASA)
VRF .... Vietnam Refugee Fund (EA)
VRF .... Visual Recording Facility (MCD)
VRFI .... Voice Reporting Fault Indicator
VRFWS .... Vehicle Rapid-Fire Weapon System [*Army*]
VRFWSS .... Vehicle Rapid-Fire Weapons System Successor (IEEE)
VRFY .... Verify (MSA)
VR-G .... Gibraltar [*International civil aircraft marking*] (ODBW)
V-RG .... Vaccinia-Rabies Glycoprotein [*Medicine*]
VRG .... Veering (WGA)
VRG .... Vegetarian Resource Group (EA)
VRG .... Vertical Reference Gyro (DA)
VRG .... Viacao Aerea Rio-Grandense SA [*Brazil*] [*ICAO designator*] (FAAC)
VRG .... Visual Reference Gate [*Aviation*] (FAAC)
VRG .... Vocationally Related Annual Goal
VRGC .... Voucher Register and General Control [*Military*] (AABC)
VRGN .... Gan [*Maldives*] [*ICAO location identifier*] (ICLI)
VRGN .... Viragen, Inc. [*NASDAQ symbol*] (SAG)
VRH .... Var-Hour Meter [*Electricity*]
VRH .... Vertical Receiving Hydrophone
VR(HL) .... Transport, Four-Engine, Landplane [*Navy symbol*]
VRHMU .... Visor Rectical Helmet Mounted Unit [*Navy*] (MCD)
VR(HS) .... Transport, Four-Engine, Seaplane [*Navy symbol*]
VRHU .... Hanimaadhoo [*Maldives*] [*ICAO location identifier*] (ICLI)
VRI .... Aerotaxi Villa Rica, SA de CV [*Mexico*] [*FAA designator*] (FAAC)
VRI .... Varistor [*Telecommunications*] (TEL)
VRI .... Varitech Investors Corp. [*Toronto Stock Exchange symbol*]
VRI .... Vastar Resources [*NYSE symbol*] (TTSB)
VRI .... Vastar Resources, Inc. [*NYSE symbol*] (SAG)
VRI .... Vehicle Research Institute [*Society of Automotive Engineers*]
VRI .... Verbal Response Inventory
VRI .... Veterans Reopened Insurance
VRI .... Victoria Regina et Imperatrix [*Victoria, Queen and Empress*]
VRI .... Viral Respiratory Infection [*Medicine*]
VRI .... Visual Rule Instrument Landing (AAG)
VRI .... Vrincioaia [*Romania*] [*Seismograph station code, US Geological Survey*] (SEIS)
VRI .... Vulcanized Rubber Installation
VRIFS .... Vector Recurrent Iterated Function System [*Iterated Systems, Inc.*] [*Digital imaging*]
VRII .... Virus Research Institute, Inc. [*NASDAQ symbol*] (SAG)
VRIL .... Vendor Repairable Items List
VRIS .... Varistor [*Electronics*]
VRIS .... Vietnam Refugee and Information Services
VRISL .... Vancouver Island [*NWS*] (FAAC)
VRIV .... Vestibular Relay Neuron [*Neurology*]
VRK .... Varkaus [*Finland*] [*Airport symbol*] (OAG)
VRK .... Video Recorder Kit
VRK .... Viral Respiratory Kit [*Medicine*]
VRKD .... Kadhdhoo [*Maldives*] [*ICAO location identifier*] (ICLI)
VRL .... Validation Reject Listing (MCD)
VRL .... Vanterra Resources Ltd. [*Vancouver Stock Exchange symbol*]
VRL .... Vertical Recovery Line [*NASA*] (NASA)
VRL .... Vertical Reference Line [*Technical drawings*]
VRL .... Veterinary Research Laboratory [*Montana State University*] [*Research center*]
VRL .... Vibration Research Laboratory [*Stanford University*] (MCD)
VRL .... Victorian Rugby League [*Australia*]
VRL .... Vila Real [*Portugal*] [*Airport symbol*] (OAG)
VRL .... Virus Reference Laboratory
VRL .... Virus Reference Library (MAE)
VRL .... Voar Ltd. [*Angola*] [*FAA designator*] (FAAC)
VRLK .... Verilink Corp. [*NASDAQ symbol*] (SAG)
VRLN .... Varlen Corp. [*NASDAQ symbol*] (NQ)
VRLRA .... Victorian Rugby League Referees' Association [*Australia*]
VRLTRY .... Vale of Rheidol Light Railway [*Wales*]
VRLY .... Voltage Relay
VRM .... Randolph-Macon College, Ashland, VA [*OCLC symbol*] (OCLC)
VRM .... Van Riebeeck Medal [*British military*] (DMA)
VRM .... Variable Range Marker [*RADAR technology*]
VRM .... Variable-Rate Mortgage [*Real estate*]
VRM .... Variable Reluctance Microphone
VRM .... Vendor Receiving Memorandum [*Sales*]
VRM .... Venus RADAR Mapper [*Planetary exploration*]
VRM .... Vermiculite [*Technical drawings*]
VRM .... Virtual Resource Manager [*Computer science*] (IAA)
VRM .... Viscous Remanant Magnetization
VRM .... Visible Record Machine (NITA)
VRM .... Visual Resource Management
VRM .... Voice Recognition Module [*Computer science*]
VRM .... Voltage Regulator Module
VRM .... Volumetric Redox Measurement [*Analytical chemistry*]
VR(ML) .... Transport, Two-Engine, Landplane [*Navy symbol*]
VRML .... Virtual Reality Markup [*or Modeling*] Language [*Software program*]
VRML .... Virtual Reality Modeling Language
VRML .... Virtual Reality Modeling Language [*Computer science*]
VRMM .... Male/International [*Maldives*] [*ICAO location identifier*] (ICLI)
VR(MS) .... Transport, Two-Engine, Seaplane [*Navy symbol*]
VRMS .... Voltage Root Mean Square
VRN .... Vernier [*Engine*] (AAG)
VRN .... Verona [*Italy*] [*Airport symbol*] (OAG)
VRN .... Vessel Radiated Noise
VRN .... Voronezhavia [*Former USSR*] [*FAA designator*] (FAAC)
VRNA .... Viral Ribonucleic Acid [*Medicine*] (DMAA)
VRNF .... Von Recklinghausen Neurofibromatosis [*Medicine*]
VRNR .... Vernier [*Engine*] (NASA)
VRNT .... Vernitron Corp. [*NASDAQ symbol*] (SAG)
VRNTP .... Vernitron $1.20 Exch Pfd [*NASDAQ symbol*] (TTSB)
VRO .... Aerovitro SA de CV [*Mexico ICAO designator*] (FAAC)
VRO .... Roanoke College, Salem, VA [*OCLC symbol*] (OCLC)
VRO .... Vanguard Real Estate Fund I [*AMEX symbol*] (SPSG)
VRO .... Variable Ratio Oiling
VRO .... Verified Record Output [*Computer science*]
VRO .... Veterinary Research Officer [*British*]
VROC .... Vertical Rate of Climb [*Aviation*]
VROM .... Video ROM (NITA)
VROM .... Vocabulary Read-Only Memory [*Computer science*]
VRONY .... Videotron Hldgs Plc 'ADS' [*NASDAQ symbol*] (TTSB)
VRONY .... Videotron Holdings PLC [*NASDAQ symbol*] (SAG)
VROOM .... Vintage Racers of Old Motorcycles (EA)
Vroom .... Vroom's Law Reports [*30-85 New Jersey*] [*A publication*] (DLA)
VROOMM .... Virtual Real-Time Object-Oriented Memory Manager [*Computer science*]
Vroom (NJ) .... Vroom's Law Reports [*30-85 New Jersey*] [*A publication*] (DLA)
VROT .... Velocity, Rotation (MCD)
VROT .... Victorian Rare or Threatened Plants [*State*] (EERA)
VRP .... Richmond Public Library, Richmond, VA [*OCLC symbol*] (OCLC)
VRP .... Vapor Reheat Process
VRP .... Variable Reluctance Pickup
VRP .... Vector-to-Raster Processor [*Computer graphics terminology*]
VRP .... Vehicle Recycling Partnership [*Agreement involving General Motors Corp., Ford Motor Co., and Chrysler Corp.*]
VRP .... Vehicle Recycling Partnership
VRP .... Ventral Root Potential [*Neurophysiology*]
VRP .... Very Reliable Product (AAMN)
VRP .... Vestra Reverendissima Paternitas [*Your Very Reverend Paternity*] [*Latin*]
VRP .... Visual Record Printer
VRP .... Visual Reporting Point (DA)
VRP .... Visual Reporting Post (MCD)
VRP .... Visual Routine Processor [*Computer science*]
VR-PC .... Vanguardia Revolucionaria - Proletario Comunista [*Revolutionary Vanguard - Proletarian Communist*] [*Peru*] [*Political party*] (PPW)
VRPF .... Voltage-Regulated Plate Filament
VRPS .... Vintage Radio and Phonograph Society (EA)
VRPS .... Voltage-Regulated Power Supply
VRPSES .... Vocational Rehabilitation Program (EDAC)
VRR .... Rochester Regional Research Library Council, Rochester, NY [*OCLC symbol*] (OCLC)
VRR .... Validity, Repeatability, and Reliability [*Examination*]
VRR .... Valley Railroad
VRR .... Ventral Root Reflex [*Medicine*] (DMAA)
VRR .... Verification Readiness Review (NASA)
VRR .... Veterans Reemployment Rights
VRR .... Vibrating Reed Relay
VRR .... Visual Radio Range
vrr .... Visual Radio Range (IDOE)
VRR .... Visual Rapid Reorder (MCD)
VRRC .... Vehicle Radio Remote Control
VRRI .... Vocational and Rehabilitation Research Institute [*University of Calgary*] [*Research center*] (RCD)
VRRTFL .... Variable Reach Rough Terrain Forklift [*Military*]
VRS .... Rochester 3R's Union List of Serials, Rochester, NY [*OCLC symbol*] (OCLC)

VRS .... Vacuum Regulator Solenoid [*Automotive engineering*]
VRS .... Vacuum Relief System [*Nuclear energy*] (NRCH)
VRS .... Vehicle Registration System [*Army*]
VRS .... Vehicular RADIAC [*Radioactivity Detection, Indication, and Computation*] System
VRS .... Velocity Response Shape (CET)
VRS .... Veterinary and Remount Service [*British military*] (DMA)
VRS .... Vibration Reducing Stiffener [*Automotive engineering*]
VRS .... Video Reception System
VRS .... Video Relay System
VRS .... Virtual Reality and Simulation
VRS .... Visual Reference System
VRS .... Visual Response System
VRS .... Vocational Rehabilitation Services
VRS .... Voice Recognition System
VRS .... Voice Recording Subsystem
VRS .... Voice Response System (NITA)
VRS .... Voice Retrieval System (NITA)
VRS .... Volatile Reducing Substance (OA)
VRS .... Volume Reduction and Solidification [*Hazardous waste disposal*]
VRS .... Volunteer Reserve Section
VRS .... Vortex Rate Sensor
VRS .... Voter Research & Surveys [*Commercial firm*]
VRSA .... Versa Technologies [*NASDAQ symbol*] (TTSB)
VRSA .... Versa Technologies, Inc. [*NASDAQ symbol*] (NQ)
VRSA .... Voice Reporting Signal Assembly
VRSP .... Voltage Regulator Supervisory Panel (MCD)
VRSS .... Voice Reporting Signal System
VRSY .... Varitronic Systems, Inc. [*NASDAQ symbol*] (NQ)
VRT .... Vacuum Rectifying Tube
VRT .... Vanguard Real Estate Fd II [*AMEX symbol*] (TTSB)
VRT .... Vanguard Real Estate Fund II [*AMEX symbol*] (SPSG)
VRT .... Variable Reluctance Transducer
VRT .... Vehicle Reaction Time
VRT .... Vernon, TX [*Location identifier FAA*] (FAAL)
VRT .... Vibration-Rotation-Tunneling [*Spectroscopy*]
VRT .... Video Round Table [*American Library Association*]
VRT .... Visual Reaction Time (MHDB)
VRT .... Visual Recognition Threshold
VRT .... Vocational Rehabilitation Therapist
VRT .... Voltage Reduction Technology (PCM)
VRT .... Voltage Reference Tube
VRT .... Voltage Regulator Tube
VRT .... Volume-Rendering Technique [*Computer graphics*] (BYTE)
VRT .... Voluntary Reserve Training [*British military*] (DMA)
VRTC .... Vehicle Research and Test Center [*National Highway Traffic Safety Administration*] (GRD)
V-RTIF .... Vandenberg Real Time Interface (MCD)
VRTITC .... Victorian Road Transport Industry Training Committee [*Australia*]
VRT MOTN .... Vertical Motion [*NWS*] (FAAC)
VRTS .... VERITAS Software [*NASDAQ symbol*] (TTSB)
VRTS .... Veritas Software Corp. [*NASDAQ symbol*] (SAG)
VRTX .... Vertex Pharmaceuticals [*NASDAQ symbol*] (TTSB)
VRTX .... Vertex Pharmaceuticals, Inc. [*NASDAQ symbol*] (SPSG)
VRTX .... Virtual Real-Time Executive
VRTY .... Variety (MSA)
VRTY .... Variety
VRTY .... Verity, Inc. [*NASDAQ symbol*] (SAG)
VRU .... University of Richmond, Richmond, VA [*OCLC symbol*] (OCLC)
VRU .... Vehicle Reference Unit
VRU .... Velocity Reference Unit
VRU .... Vertical Reference Unit (MCD)
VRU .... Victorian Rugby Union [*Australia*]
VRU .... Virtual Resource Unit (MCD)
VRU .... Voice Read Out Unit [*Telecommunications*] (IAA)
VRU .... Voice Recognition Unit
VRU .... Voice Response Unit
VRU .... Voltage Readout Unit
VRU .... Vryburg [*South Africa*] [*Airport symbol*] (OAG)
VRV .... Vacuum Regulator Valve [*Automotive engineering*]
VRV .... Ventricular Residual Volume [*Cardiology*] (MAE)
VRV .... Viper Retrovirus
VRV .... Visual Range Visibility [*Aviation*] (MCD)
VRX .... Vestor Exploration [*Vancouver Stock Exchange symbol*]
VRX .... Virtual Resource Executive [*Software*] [*NCR Corp.*]
VRX-MP .... VRX-Multiprocessor (NITA)
VRY .... Fayetteville/Fort Bragg, NC [*Location identifier FAA*] (FAAL)
VRY .... Vaeroy [*Norway*] [*Airport symbol*] (OAG)
VRY .... Very [*Automotive advertising*]
VRYG .... Varying
VRZ .... Aero Veracruz SA de CV [*Mexico ICAO designator*] (FAAC)
VRZ .... Voronezh [*USSR*] [*Airport symbol*] (AD)
VS .... Air Antisubmarine Squadron [*Navy*]
VS .... Design Speed for Maximum Gust Intensity (GAVI)
VS .... Search Plane [*Navy symbol*]
VS .... Shore-Based Search Squadron [*Navy symbol*]
VS .... Single Vibrations [*Half cycles*]
VS .... Staging Velocity [*NASA*] (NASA)
VS .... Vaccination Scar [*Medicine*]
VS .... Vacuum Switch
VS .... Vagal Stimulation [*Medicine*] (DAVI)
VS .... Vaginal Stroma
VS .... Valley & Siletz Railroad Co. [*AAR code*]
VS .... Vapor Seal [*Technical drawings*]
VS .... Vapor Suppression [*Nuclear energy*] (NRCH)
VS .... Variable Speed (IEEE)
VS .... Variable Sweep (IEEE)
VS .... Variance Score [*Statistics*]
VS .... Vascular Strand [*Botany*]
VS .... Vascular System (SAA)
VS .... Vectoring Service
VS .... Vector Scan [*Digital imaging*] (IAA)
VS .... Vegan Society [*Oxford, England*] (EAIO)
VS .... Vehicle Station [*NASA*] (KSC)
VS .... Velocity Search (MCD)
VS .... Velocity, Staging
Vs .... Venae Sectio [*Venesection*] [*Latin Medicine*] (MAE)
V/S .... Vendor Supplier [*Sales*] (MCD)
VS .... Venerable Sage [*Freemasonry*] (ROG)
VS .... Venesection [*Medicine*]
VS .... Venstresocialisterne [*Left Socialists Party*] [*Denmark Political party*] (PPE)
VS .... Ventilation System [*NASA*]
VS .... Ventral Subiculum [*Brain anatomy*]
VS .... Ventricular Septum [*Cardiology*] (DAVI)
VS .... Vent Stack [*Technical drawings*]
VS .... Venture Capital/Special Situations [*Business term*]
VS .... Verbal Scale
VS .... Vergilian Society (EA)
VS .... Vermont Statutes [*A publication*] (DLA)
VS .... Vernacular Society (EA)
VS .... Verse
VS .... Versus [*Against*] [*Latin*]
vs .... Versus (WDMC)
VS .... Vertical [*Activity*] Sensor [*Physiology*]
VS .... Vertical Software [*AI Software*] [*Computer science*]
VS .... Vertical Sounding [*Telecommunications*] (OA)
VS .... Vertical Speed [*Aviation*]
VS .... Vertical Spread (MHDB)
VS .... Vertical Stereoscopic [*Photograph*]
VS .... Vertical Stripes [*Navigation markers*]
VS .... Vertical System [*Government arrangement*] (OICC)
VS .... Very Small Inclusions [*Diamond clarity grade*]
VS .... Very Soft (IAA)
VS .... Very Soluble
VS .... Very Special [*Age of the Cognac*]
VS .... Very Strong [*Spectral*]
VS .... Very Superior
VS .... Very Susceptible [*Plant pathology*]
VS .... Vesicular Sound [*in auscultation of chest*] [*Medicine*]
VS .... Vesicular Stomatitis [*Also, VSV*] [*Virus*]
VS .... Vestiarski Sisters (TOCD)
VS .... Vestigial Sideband (NITA)
VS .... Veterinary Surgeon
VS .... Vibration Seconds
VS .... Victorian Society (EA)
VS .... Victorian Studies [*A publication*] (BRI)
VS .... Video and Synchronization [*Telecommunications*] (IAA)
VS .... Video Selection
VS .... Vide Supra [*See Above*] [*Latin*]
vs .... Vietnam, South [*vm (Vietnam) used in records cataloged after January 1978*] [*MARC country of publication code Library of Congress*] (LCCP)
VS .... Vieux Style [*Old Style*] [*French*]
VS .... Villas
VS .... Villonodular Synovitis [*Medicine*] (MAE)
VS .... Vinyl Sulfone [*Organic chemistry*]
VS .... Violoncello Society (EA)
VS .... Virgil Society (EA)
VS .... Virgin Atlantic Airways [*ICAO designator*] (AD)
VS .... Virtual Storage [*Computer science*]
VS .... Virtual System
VS .... Visceral Sinus
VS .... Visible Supply
VS .... Visual Signaling [*Military*]
VS .... Visual Storage [*Computer science*]
VS .... Visum Siccum [*Seen in a Dried State*] [*Botany*] (ROG)
VS .... Vitae Sophistarum [*of Philostratus*] [*Classical studies*] (OCD)
VS .... Vital Signs [*Medicine*]
VS .... Vivisection
VS .... Vocal Students Practice Aid Records [*Record label*]
VS .... Vocal Synthesis
VS .... Voicespondence Club (EA)
VS .... Voice Stress (LAIN)
VS .... Voice Switching [*Telecommunications*] (IAA)
vs .... Voids [*Medicine*] (MAE)
VS .... Volatile Solids [*Environmental science*]
VS .... Voltage Switching (IAA)
VS .... Voltaire Society (EA)
VS .... Volti Subito [*Turn Over Quickly*] [*Music*]
VS .... Voltmeter Switch (MSA)
Vs .... Volt-Seconds [*Webers*] (IDOE)
VS .... Volumetric Solution
VS .... Voluntary School (AIE)
VS .... Voluntary Sterilization
VS .... Voorschrift [*Rule, Order*] [*Dutch*] (ILCA)
VS .... Voting Stock [*Investment term*] (MHDW)
VS .... Votre Seigneurie [*Your Lordship*] [*French*]
VS .... Vulcan Society (EA)
VS .... Without Glasses [*Ophthalmology*] (DAVI)

VS1 .... Virtual Storage One [*Computer science*] (HGAA)
VSA .... Vacuum Society of Australia
VSA .... Vacuum Swing Adsorption [*Chemical engineering*]
VSA .... Vancouver School of Art
VSA .... Variable Speed Assembly [*Mechanical powertrain*]
VSA .... Variable Stability Aircraft (NASA)
VSA .... Variant-Specific Surface Antigen [*Genetics, immunology*]
VSA .... Variation Simulation Analysis [*Automotive engineering*]
VSA .... Vegetarian Society of Australia
VSA .... Vehicle Security Association (EA)
VSA .... Vehicle Service Agreement [*Extended service contract*]
VSA .... Vehicle Service Assessment
VSA .... Velocity Sensor Antenna
VSA .... Verification Site Approval [*NASA*] (MCD)
VSA .... Vermont Statutes, Annotated [*A publication*] (DLA)
VSA .... Vernier Solo Accumulator [*Aerospace*] (AAG)
VSA .... Vertical Sensor Assembly
VSA .... Very Special Arts (EA)
VSA .... Vibrating String Accelerometer
VSA .... Victorian Society in America (EA)
VSA .... Victualling Store Allowance [*British military*] (DMA)
VSA .... Videocom Satellite Associates [*Dedham, MA*] [*Telecommunications*] (TSSD)
VSA .... Videographic Systems of America, Inc. [*Ceased operation*] [*Information service or system*] (IID)
VSA .... Villahermosa [*Mexico*] [*Airport symbol*] (OAG)
VSA .... Vintage Sailplane Association (EA)
VSA .... Violin Society of America (EA)
VSA .... Viscoelastic Stress Analysis
VSA .... Visual Skills Appraisal [*Child development test*]
VSA .... Voice-Stress Analyzer (ECII)
VSA .... Voltage-Sensitive Amplifier
Vs/A .... Volt-Seconds per Ampere [*Henrys*] (IDOE)
VSA/1800 ..... Volvo Sports America 1800 (EA)
vSAA .... Very Severe Aplastic Anemia [*Hematology*]
V/SABAC ...... Victoria/South Australia Border Anomalies Committee
V-SAC .... Vehicle Speed Activated Converter [*Automotive engineering*]
VSAD .... Vacuum Spark Advance Disconnect [*Auto air pollution control device*]
V/SAF .... Vulnerability and Survivability of the Armed Forces (MCD)
VSAG .... Viral Superantigen [*Immunochemistry*]
VSALS .... Vision Approach and Landing System [*Aviation*]
VSAM .... Variable, Spanned, and Undefined Mode (IAA)
VSAM .... Virtual Sequential Access Method
VSAM .... Virtual Storage Access Method [*Computer science*]
VSAM .... Virtual System Access Method
VS & A .... Veronis, Suhler & Associates, Inc. [*Telecommunications service*] (TSSD)
VSAT .... Very Small Aperture Terminal [*Telecommunications*] (TSSD)
VSAT .... ViaSat, Inc. [*NASDAQ symbol*] (SAG)
VSB .... Scout-Bombing Plane [*Navy symbol*]
VSB .... Sweet Briar College Library, Sweet Briar, VA [*OCLC symbol*] (OCLC)
VSB .... Venae Sectio Brachii [*Bleeding in the Arm*] [*Pharmacy*] (ROG)
VSB .... Vent and Supply Bay
VSB .... Verbal Substantive (WDAA)
VSB .... Vestigial Sideband [*Radio*]
VSB .... Vickers Ltd. [*British ICAO designator*] (FAAC)
VSB .... Video Source Book [*A publication*]
VSB .... Visible (BARN)
VSB .... Volunteer Services for the Blind [*Later, ASB*] (EA)
VSB-AM .... Vestigial Sideband - Amplitude Modulation
VSBF .... Vestigial Sideband Filter
VSBL .... Visible (MSA)
VSBNSW ...... Veterinary Surgeons' Board of New South Wales [*Australia*]
VSBNT .... Veterinary Surgeons' Board of the Northern Territory [*Australia*]
VSBQ .... Veterinary Surgeons' Board of Queensland [*Australia*]
VSBS .... Very Small Business System
VSBS .... Voluntary Standards Bodies (IAA)
VSBSA .... Veterinary Surgeons' Board of South Australia
VSBY .... Visibility (BARN)
VSBYDR .... Visibility Decreasing Rapidly [*NWS*] (FAAC)
VSBYIR .... Visibility Increasing Rapidly [*NWS*] (FAAC)
VSC .... Aerovias Especiales de Carga Ltda. [*Colombia*] [*ICAO designator*] (FAAC)
VSC .... Valdosta State College [*Georgia*]
VSC .... Variable Speech Control [*Device that permits distortion-free rapid playback of speech recorded on tape*]
VSC .... Variable Speed Chopper
VSC .... Varnville [*South Carolina*] [*Seismograph station code, US Geological Survey*] (SEIS)
VSC .... Vehicle Sectoring Code
VSC .... Vehicle System Control
VSC .... Vela Seismological Center [*Alexandria, VA*]
VSC .... Vendor Shipping Configuration (AAG)
VSC .... Ventral Spinal Cord [*Anatomy*]
VSC .... Vermont State College
VSC .... Vibration Safety Cutoff [*NASA*] (KSC)
VSC .... Victorian Safety Council [*Australia*]
VSC .... Vidicon Camera System (MCD)
V-S/C .... Viking Spacecraft [*NASA*]
VSC .... Vincentian Sisters of Charity [*Roman Catholic religious order*]
VSC .... Virginia State College [*Petersburg*]
VSC .... Virginia State College, Petersburg, VA [*OCLC symbol*] (OCLC)
VSC .... Virtual Subscriber Computer
VSC .... VirusScan Configuration [*Computer science*]
VSC .... Vocations for Social Change [*Employment clearinghouse*] [*Defunct*] (EA)
VSC .... Volatile Sulfur Compound [*Chemistry*]
VSC .... Voltage-Saturated Capacitor
VSC .... Volunteer Staff Corps [*British*] (ROG)
VSCA .... Vacation and Senior Citizens Association (EA)
VSCA .... Vietnamese Senior Citizens Association (EA)
VSCAN .... Vendor Scan
VSCAN .... Visual Scan
VSCC .... Vintage Sports Car Club [*Australia*]
VSCC .... Vintage Sports Car Club [*British*] (DBA)
VSCC .... Voltage-Sensitive Calcium Channel [*Physiology*]
VSCCA .... Vintage Sports Car Club of America (EA)
VSCCA .... Vintage Sports Car Club of Australia
VSCCSA .... Vintage Sports Car Club of South Australia
VSCDF .... Vatican's Sacred Congregation for the Doctrine of the Faith
VSCE .... Variable Stream Control Engine [*NASA*] (MCD)
VSCF .... Variable Speed Constant Frequency
VSCI .... Vision Sciences, Inc. [*NASDAQ symbol*] (SAG)
VSCI .... Vision-Sciences Inc. [*NASDAQ symbol*] (TTSB)
VSCNY .... Vedanta Society of the City of New York (EA)
VSCP .... Vital Statistics Cooperative Program [*Department of Health and Human Services*] (GFGA)
VSCS .... Voice Switch and Control System [*FAA*]
VSD .... Valve Solenoid Driver
VSD .... Variable Slope Delta
VSD .... Variable Speed Drive
VSD .... Vehicle Structures Directorate [*Army and NASA joint operation*] (RDA)
VSD .... Vendor's Shipping Document
VSD .... Ventral Septal Defect
VSD .... Ventricular Septal Defect [*Cardiology*]
VSD .... Versatile Signal Device
VSD .... Vertical Situation Display
VSD .... Video Subcarrier Detector
VSD .... Village Self-Development
VSD .... Virtually Safe Dose [*Toxicology*]
VSD .... Virus Search and Destroy [*Computer science*]
VSD .... Voter-Switch-Disagreement Detector (PDAA)
VSDA .... Video Software Dealers Association (EA)
VSD/ADI .... Vertical Situation Display/Attitude Director Indicator (MCD)
VSDI .... Voluntary Short-Term Disability Insurance
VSDM .... Variable Scope Delta Modulation (NITA)
VSDM .... Variable Slope Delta Modulation
VSDR .... Vieteljahrsheft zur Statistik des Deutschen Reichs [*Germany*]
VSDT .... Veterinary Surgeons' Disciplinary Tribunal [*New South Wales, Australia*]
VSE .... Steam Explosion in Vessel [*Nuclear energy*] (NRCH)
VSE .... Vancouver Stock Exchange [*Canada*]
VSE .... Variable Stroke Engine
VSE .... Vehicle Systems Engineer (SAA)
VSE .... Vessel (Reactor) Steam Explosion [*Nuclear energy*] (IEEE)
VSE .... Virtual Storage Extension [*IBM Corp.*] [*Computer science*]
VSE .... VSE Corp. [*Associated Press*] (SAG)
VSE .... Vuelos Asesorias y Representaciones SA de CV [*Mexico ICAO designator*] (FAAC)
VSE/AF .... Virtual Storage Exhibit/Advanced Function (NITA)
VSEC .... VSE Corp. [*NASDAQ symbol*] (NQ)
VSEIF .... Venture Seismic Ltd. [*NASDAQ symbol*] (SAG)
VSEL .... Vertical Surface Emitting LASER
VSEL .... Vickers Shipbuilding and Engineering Ltd. [*British*]
VSEN .... Video Sentry [*NASDAQ symbol*] (TTSB)
VSEN .... Video Sentry Corp. [*NASDAQ symbol*] (SAG)
VSEP .... Very Superior Extra Pale [*Designation on brandy labels*] (WGA)
VSEPR .... Valence-Shell Electron Pair Repulsion [*Theory of molecular structure*]
VSEPR .... Valence Shell Electron Pair Repulsion [*Model for molecular structure*]
VSERC .... Victorian Solar Energy Research Council [*Australia*]
VSES .... Victoria State Emergency Service [*Australia*]
VSEWF .... Venture Seismic Ltd. [*NASDAQ symbol*] (SAG)
VSEWF .... Venture Seismic Ltd Wrrt [*NASDAQ symbol*] (TTSB)
VSF .... Antisubmarine Fighter Squadron [*Navy*]
VSF .... Springfield [*Vermont*] [*Airport symbol*] (OAG)
VSF .... Springfield, VT [*Location identifier FAA*] (FAAL)
VSF .... Vestigial Sideband Filter
VSF .... VETRONICS [*Vehicle Electronics*] Simulation Facility [*Army*] (RDA)
VSF .... Vitreous Silica Fabric
VSF .... Voice Store and Forward [*Voice messaging*]
VSFC .... Vince Smith Fan Club (EA)
VSFP .... Venous Stop-Flow Pressure [*Medicine*]
VSFR .... Vertical Seismic Floor Response (IEEE)
VSFR .... Visibility Forecast (SAA)
VSFS .... Voice Store and Forward Messaging System [*Telecommunications*] (IAA)
VSG .... Variable Speed Gear (DEN)
VSG .... Variable [*or Variant*] Surface Glycoprotein [*Biochemistry*]
VSG .... Variant Surface Glycoprotein [*Immunology*]
VSG .... Vernier Step Gauge [*Aerospace*]
VSG .... Versatile Signal [*or Symbol*] Generator
VSG .... Vertical Sweep Generator [*Telecommunications*] (OA)
VSG .... Vibrating Structure Gyroscope
VSG .... Video Symbology Generator
VSG .... Viscous (USDC)
VSG .... Viscous Semi-Geostrophic [*Model*] [*Marine science*] (OSRA)
VSG .... Vulture Study Group [*South Africa*] (EAIO)
VSGN .... Visigenic Software, Inc. [*NASDAQ symbol*] (SAG)

VSH .... Village Self-Help
VSH .... Vishay Intertechnolgy [*NYSE symbol*] (TTSB)
VSH .... Vishay Intertechnology, Inc. [*NYSE symbol*] (SPSG)
VSH .... Vishnu Resources [*Vancouver Stock Exchange symbol*]
VSHPS .... Vernier Solo Hydraulic Power System [*Aerospace*] (AAG)
VSI .... College of Staten Island, St. George Campus Library, Staten Island, NY [*OCLC symbol*] (OCLC)
VSI .... Stalling Speed in a Specified Flight Configuration (GAVI)
VSI .... Variable Separation Incentive [*DoD*]
VSI .... Velocity and Steering Indicator (MCD)
VSI .... Vendor Shipping Instruction
VSI .... Vertical Sideband [*Radio frequency*] [*Telecommunications*] (IAA)
VSI .... Vertical Signal [*or Situation*] Indicator [*Helicopters*]
VSI .... Vertical Speed Indicator [*Aviation*]
VSI .... Very Seriously Ill [*Army*] (AABC)
VSI .... Videoconferencing Systems, Inc. [*Norcross, GA*] [*Telecommunications service*] (TSSD)
VSI .... Video Simulation Interface (NASA)
VSI .... Video Sweep Integrator
VSI .... Vinyl Siding Institute (EA)
VSI .... Virtual Screen Interface [*Computer science*] (HGAA)
VSI .... Virtual Storage Interrupt (NITA)
VSI .... Visual Simulator Interface (MHDI)
VSI .... Visual Site Inspection (GNE)
VSI .... Voluntary Separation Incentive [*DoD*]
VSI .... Voluntary Service International [*British*] (EAIO)
VSI .... Vuesenoria Ilustrisima [*Your Illustrious Ladyship (or Lordship)*] [*Spanish*]
VSIC .... Veterinary Surgeon's Investigation Committee [*New South Wales, Australia*]
VSI Ent .... VSI Enterprises [*Associated Press*] (SAG)
VS Ilma .... Vossa Senhoria Ilustrissima [*Your Illustrious Lordship*] [*Portuguese*]
VSIN .... VSI Enterprises [*NASDAQ symbol*] (SAG)
VSINC .... Virus Subcommittee of the International Nomenclature Committee [*Medicine*] (DMAA)
VSIO .... Visio Corp. [*NASDAQ symbol*] (SAG)
VSIP .... Valence State Ionization Potentials [*of atoms*]
VSIP .... Voluntary Separation Incentive Program [*DoD*]
VSIQ .... Verbal Scale Intelligence Quotient (EDAC)
VSIS .... V Channelled Substrate Inner Stripe (NITA)
VSJW .... Vise Jaw [*Tool*] (AAG)
VSL .... Special Libraries Cataloguing, Inc. [*UTLAS symbol*]
VSL .... State Library of Victoria [*State*] (EERA)
VSL .... Value of a Statistical Life [*Mortality rating*]
VSL .... Valve Signal Light
VSL .... Variable Safety Level
VSL .... Variable Specification List
VSL .... Ventilation Sampling Line (IEEE)
VSL .... Vermont State Department of Libraries, Montpelier, VT [*OCLC symbol*] (OCLC)
VSL .... Very Serious List [*Hospital administration*] (DAVI)
VSL .... Victorian School of Languages [*Australia*]
VSL .... Virtually Safe Level [*Toxicology*]
VSL .... Viscous Shock Layer
VSL .... Visual Software Library [*Computer science*]
VSL .... Volume of the Sacred Law [*Freemasonry*]
VSL .... VS Services Ltd. [*Toronto Stock Exchange symbol*]
VSLE .... Very Small Local Exchange [*Telecommunications*] (TEL)
VSLE .... Voiceband Subscriber Loop Emulator [*Telecom Analysis Systems, Inc.*]
VSLF .... Banyan Strategic Land Fd II [*NASDAQ symbol*] (TTSB)
VSLF .... Banyan Strategic Land Fund [*NASDAQ symbol*] (SAG)
VSLF .... Banyan Strategic Land Fund II [*NASDAQ symbol*] (SAG)
VSLI .... Veterans Special Life Insurance [*Veterans Administration*]
VSLS .... Very Slightly Soluble
VSM .... Vascular Smooth Muscle [*Anatomy*]
VSM .... Vehicle State Monitor
VSM .... Vestigial Sideband Modulation
VSM .... Vibrating Sample Magnetometer
VSM .... Video Switching Matrix (KSC)
VSM .... Vietnam Service Medal [*Military decoration*] (AFM)
VSM .... Virtual Storage Manager (BUR)
VSM .... Virtual Storage Memory [*Computer science*] (MCD)
VSM .... Voice Switch Monitor (MCD)
VSM .... Volcano System Monitor [*Marine science*] (OSRA)
VSMA .... Vibrating Screen Manufacturers Association (EA)
VSMC .... Vascular Smooth Muscle Cell [*Cytology*]
VSMF .... Vendor Specification Microfilm File (DNAB)
VSMF .... Visual Search Microfilm File [*Trademark*] [*Computer science*]
VSMF .... Visual Search on Microfilm (NITA)
VSMOS .... Verified Secondary Military Occupational Specialty
VSMOW .... Vienna Standard Mean Ocean Water
VSMPC .... Victorian School of Massage and Physical Culture [*Australia*]
VSMS .... Video Switching Matrix System
VSMS .... Vineland Social Maturity Scale [*Psychology*]
VSN .... Scout-Training Plane [*Navy symbol*]
VSN .... Video Switching Network (MCD)
VSN .... Vision
VSN .... Vision
VSN .... Vision Airways Corp. [*Canada ICAO designator*] (FAAC)
VSN .... Volume-Sequence-Number [*Computer science*]
VSN .... Volume Serial Number [*Computer science*] (IAA)
VSNKh .... Vysshego Soveta Narodnogo Khozyaystva [*Supreme Council of National Economy*] [*Former USSR*] (LAIN)
VSNL .... Videsh Sanchar Nigam Ltd. [*India*] [*Telecommunications service*] (TSSD)
VSN(M) .... Training Plane, 2-Engine [*Navy symbol*]
VSNP .... Viking Society for Northern Research [*British*]
VSNR .... Visioneer, Inc. [*NASDAQ symbol*] (SAG)
VSNR .... Visioneer Inc. [*NASDAQ symbol*] (TTSB)
VSNS .... Virgil C. Summer Nuclear Station (NRCH)
VSNY .... Vegetarian Society of New York [*Defunct*] (EA)
VSO .... Phuoc Long [*Vietnam*] [*Airport symbol*] (AD)
VSO .... Scout Observation Plane [*Navy symbol*]
VSO .... Stalling Speed in the Landing Configuration (GAVI)
VSO .... Valdosta Southern Railroad [*AAR code*]
VSO .... Verso (BJA)
VSO .... Very Special Old
VSO .... Very Stable Oscillator
VSO .... Very Superior Old [*Designation on brandy labels*]
VSO .... Victualling Stores Officer [*British military*] (DMA)
VSO .... Voltage-Sensitive Oscillator (IAA)
VSO .... Voluntary Service Overseas [*Military*]
VSO .... Voluntary Surgical Opinion [*Health insurance*] (GHCT)
VSOE .... Venice Simplon Orient-Express [*London-to-Venice train*]
VSOK .... Vital Signs Normal [*Medicine*] (MAE)
VSOK .... Vital Signs Okay [*on Physical Examination*] (DAVI)
VSOM .... Velocity Sensor, Oscillator, Multiplier (DNAB)
VSOP .... Very Long Baseline Interferometry [*Used in a space orbiting project*]
VSOP .... Very Superior Old Pale [*Designation on brandy labels. Facetious French translation is "Versez sans Oublier Personne," or "Pour without Forgetting Anyone"*]
VSOP .... VLBI [*Very Long Base-Line Interferometry*] Space Observatory Program [*Japan*]
VSOP .... VLBI [*Very Long BaselineInterferometry*] Space Observatory Programme
VSP .... Variable Size Parameter [*Thermodynamics*]
VSP .... Vectored Slipstream Principle
VSP .... Vehicle Scheduling Program [*Computer science*]
VSP .... Vehicle Synthesis Program [*Aerospace*]
VSP .... Vertical Seismic Profile [*Geology*]
VSP .... Viacao Aerea Sao Paulo SA [*Brazil*] [*ICAO designator*] (FAAC)
VSP .... Victorian Socialist Party [*Australia Political party*]
VSP .... Video Signal Processor
VSP .... Video System Processor [*Telecommunications*] (TSSD)
VSP .... Vikki's Special People (EA)
VSP .... Virtual Switching Point [*Telecommunications*] (TEL)
VSP .... Vision Service Plan National [*Defunct*] (EA)
VSP .... Visitor Services Project [*National Park Service*]
V SP .... Visum Sponanteum [*Seen Wild*] [*Botany*] (ROG)
V SP .... Visum Sporadicum [*Seen Wild*] [*Botany*] (ROG)
VSP .... Voiture sans Permis [*Car without license*] [*French*]
VSP .... Voltage-Stabilized Polyethylene (IAA)
VSPC .... Virtual Storage Personal Computing [*IBM Corp.*] [*Computer science*]
V/SPD .... Variable Speed
VSPEP .... Vehicle Sizing and Performance Evaluation Program (MCD)
VSPFT .... Vitalor Screening Pulmonary Function Test [*Medicine*] (DAVI)
VSPG .... Vehicle Speed Pulse Generator [*Automotive engineering*]
VSPI .... Visual Glide Path Indicator [*Aviation*] (FAAC)
VSPRITES .... Virtual Sprites [*Amiga computer hardware*]
VSPS .... Vernier Solo Power Supply [*Aerospace*] (AAG)
VSPX .... Vehicle Scheduling Program Extended [*Computer science*]
VSQ .... Very Special Quality
VSQC .... Veterinary Specialists' Qualification Committee [*Victoria, Australia*]
VSQG .... Very Small Quantity Generator [*Environmental science*]
VSR .... Vacuum Short Resid [*Petroleum technology*]
VSR .... Validation Summary Report
VSR .... Vallecitos Experimental Superheat Reactor (NRCH)
VSR .... Variable Length Shift Register [*Computer science*] (IAA)
VSR .... Venous Stasis Retinopathy [*Medicine*] (MEDA)
VSR .... Versar, Inc. [*AMEX symbol*] (SPSG)
VSR .... Vertical Size Ratio [*Ophthalmology*]
VSR .... Vertical Storage and Retrieval Systems
VSR .... Very Short Range
vsr .... Very Short Range (IDOE)
VSR .... Very Short Run [*Printing technology*]
VSR .... Very Special Reserve (ADA)
VSR .... Vibration Sensitive Relay
VSR .... Vietnam Supply Rate [*Military*] (MCD)
VSR .... Vincit Sapientia Robur [*Wisdom Overcomes Strength*] [*Motto of Johann Ernst, Duke of Saxony-Eisenach (1566-1638)*] [*Latin*]
VSR .... Visual Security Range (NATG)
VSR .... Voltage-Sensing Relay
VSRADS .... Very-Short-Range Air Defense Weapon System (MCD)
VSRADWS .... Very-Short-Range Air Defense Weapon System (NATG)
VSRBM .... Very-Short-Range Ballistic Missile
VSRC .... Vehicle Safety Recall Campaign
VSRGSR .... Very-Short-Range Ground Surveillance RADAR (MCD)
vsrs .... Voussoirs (VRA)
VSS .... Vampire Studies Society [*Defunct*] (EA)
VSS .... Vapor Saver System [*Automobile*]
VSS .... Vapor Suppression System [*Nuclear energy*] (IAA)
VSS .... Variable Slit Set
VSS .... Variable SONAR System
VSS .... Variable Stability System [*Aviation*]
VSS .... Vascular Surgical Society [*British*]
VSS .... Vassouras [*Brazil*] [*Geomagnetic observatory code*]
VSS .... Vector Scoring System [*Navy*] (MCD)
VSS .... Vehicle Speed Sensor [*Automotive engineering*]

VSS............ Vehicle Stability System [*Truck engineering*]
VSS............ Vehicle Surveillance System
VSS............ Vehicle System Simulator
VSS............ Velocity Sensor System
VSS............ Vented Suppressive Shielding
VSS............ Versions (ROG)
VSS............ Vertical Sounding System
VSS............ Vertical Spike Soderberg [*Pot*] [*Aluminum processing*]
VSS............ Vertical Support Structure
VSS............ Vessel Support System (MCD)
VSS............ Victim Support Scheme [*British*] (DI)
VSS............ Victor Scoring System
VSS............ Video Satellite Systems Inc. (NITA)
VSS............ Video Select Switch (MCD)
VSS............ Video Signal Simulator (NATG)
VSS............ Video Storage System [*or Subsystem*]
VSS............ Video Supervisory Signal
VSS............ Viet Cong Security Service (VNW)
VSS............ Virgin Islands Seaplane Shuttle, Inc. [*ICAO designator*] (FAAC)
VSS............ Virtual Storage System [*SEMIS*]
VSS............ Visual Sensor Set
VSS............ Visual Systems Simulator [*FAA*]
VSS............ Vital Signs Stable [*Medicine*]
VSS............ Vocabulary Switching System [*Computer science*]
VSS............ Voice Signaling System
VSS............ VoiceStation System [*Sydis, Inc.*] [*San Jose, CA*] (TSSD)
VSS............ Voice Storage System [*AT & T*]
VSS............ Volatile Suspended Solids [*Environmental science*]
VSS............ Voltage-Sensing Switch
VSS............ Voltage to Substrate and Sources [*Microelectronics*]
VSS............ Voyager Spacecraft Subsystem [*NASA*]
VSS............ V/STOL Support Ship
VSSC.......... Vedanta Society of Southern California (EA)
VS-SC......... Vestigial Sideband Suppressed Carrier (NITA)
VSSM.......... Video Scanner Switch Matrix
VSSP.......... Vendor Standard Settlement Program (AAG)
VSSSN......... Verification Status Social Security Number (AABC)
VST............ Banyan Short Term Income Trust [*Formerly, VMS Short Term Income Trust*] [*AMEX symbol*] (SPSG)
VST............ St. Thomas [*Virgin Islands*] [*Seismograph station code, US Geological Survey*] (SEIS)
VST............ Valve Seat (MSA)
VST............ Valve Setpoint Tolerance [*Nuclear energy*] (NRCH)
VST............ Vancouver School of Theology [*University of British Columbia*]
VST............ Vanstar Corp. [*NYSE symbol*] (TTSB)
VST............ Vanstates Resources Ltd. [*Vancouver Stock Exchange symbol*]
VST............ Variable Stability Trainer [*Aviation*]
VST............ Variable Surface Tracking
VST............ Vasteras [*Sweden*] [*Airport symbol*] (OAG)
VST............ Venom Skin Test [*Immunology*]
VST............ Very Small Truck (DICI)
VST............ Video Scroller Terminal [*Computer science*]
VST............ Video System Test
VST............ Visible Speech Translator (IAA)
VST............ Visit (NVT)
VST............ Vista [*Commonly used*] (OPSA)
VST............ Vocational Skills Training [*Funds*] [*Job Corps*]
VST............ Volume Sensitive Tariff [*Telecommunications*] (TEL)
VSTA.......... Virus-Serum-Toxin Act
VSTA.......... Vista [*Commonly used*] (OPSA)
VSTAG........ Vandenberg Shuttle Turnaround Analysis Group [*NASA*] (NASA)
VSTAR........ Variable Search and Track Air Defense RADAR
VSTBU........ Victorian State Building Trades Union [*Australia*]
VSTC.......... Vermont State Teachers College
VSTC.......... Very Short Time Constant (MCD)
VSTF.......... Very Short-Term Financing (MHDB)
vstib.......... Vestibule (VRA)
VSTM.......... Valve Stem (MSA)
vstmt.......... Vestment (VRA)
VSTNG........ Visiting
VSTO.......... Vertical/Short Takeoff [*and Landing*] (MCD)
V/STOL........ Vertical/Short Takeoff and Landing [*Aircraft*]
VSTP.......... Visual Satellite Tracking Program
VSTPT......... Vulcan-Stinger Troop Proficiency Trainer [*Army*]
VSTR.......... Ventral Striatum [*Neurology*]
VSTR.......... Visitor
VSTR.......... Volt Second Transfer Ratio
VSTSP........ Visit Ship in Port [*Navy*] (NVT)
VSTT.......... Variable Speed Tactical Trainer [*Air Force*] (MCD)
VSTT.......... Variable Speed Training Target
VSUH.......... Virginia State University Herbarium
VSUK.......... Vegetarian Society of the United Kingdom (DBA)
VSULA........ Vaccination Scar Upper Left Arm [*Medicine*] (MAE)
v-supt......... Vice-Superintendent (DD)
VSV............ Vacuum Switching Valve [*Automotive engineering*]
VSV............ Vesicular Stomatitis Virus [*Also, VS*]
VSVG.......... Vesicular Stomatitis Virus Glycoprotein [*Biochemistry*]
VSVR.......... VideoServer, Inc. [*NASDAQ symbol*] (SAG)
VSW............ Variable Sweep Wing
VSW............ Ventricular Stroke Work [*Cardiology*] (MAE)
VSW............ Vertrau Schau Wem [*Trust, but Be Careful Whom*] [*Motto of Johann Georg, Duke of Wohlau (1552-92)*] [*German*]
VSW............ Very Shallow Water (DOMA)
VSW............ Very Short Wave
VSW............ Visual Studies Workshop (EA)
VSW............ Vitrified Stoneware
VSW............ Voltage Standing Wave
VSWF.......... Voltage Standing-Wave Frequency (DNAB)
VSWR.......... Variable Standing Wave Ratio (MCD)
VSWR.......... Visual Standing Wave Ratio (NASA)
VSWR.......... Voltage Standing-Wave Ratio
VSX............ Navy Submarine Attack Airplane - Experimental (MCD)
VSYNC........ Vertical Synchronous [*Computer science*]
VSYNCH...... Vertical Synchronization [*Computer science*] (IAA)
VT.............. Air-Cushion Vehicle built by Vosper Thorneycroft [*England*] [*Usually used in combination with numerals*]
VT.............. Air Polynesie [*ICAO designator*] (AD)
Vt.............. State of Vermont, Department of Libraries, Montpelier, VT [*Library symbol Library of Congress*] (LCLS)
VT.............. Target-on-Threshold Speed [*Aviation*]
Vt.............. Tidal Volume [*Medicine*] (DAVI)
V_T.............. Tissue Volume [*Laboratory science*] (DAVI)
VT.............. Torpedo Plane [*Navy symbol*]
VT.............. Training Squadron [*Navy symbol*] (NVT)
VT.............. Vacuum Telegraphy [*Telecommunications*] (IAA)
VT.............. Vacuum Tube [*Electronics*]
vt.............. Vacuum Tube (IDOE)
VT.............. Vacuum Tuberculin [*Medicine*] (MAE)
VT.............. Validation Testing (MCD)
VT.............. Valitocin [*Endocrinology*]
VT.............. Vaportight (MSA)
VT.............. Variable Threshold (IAA)
VT.............. Variable Thrust
VT.............. Variable Time [*Fuse*] [*Also known as a "proximity fuse"*]
vt.............. Variable Time (IDOE)
VT.............. Variable-Time [*Proximity Fuse*] (DOMA)
VT.............. Variable Transformer
VT.............. Variable Transmission (ADA)
VT.............. Vascular Time
VT.............. Vasotocin
VT.............. Vat Petroleum [*Vancouver Stock Exchange symbol*]
VT.............. Vee-Twin [*Automotive engineering*]
VT.............. Vehicle Theft
VT.............. Vehicular Technology (MCD)
VT.............. Velocity, Target
V-T............ Velocity Time (MUGU)
VT.............. Venous Thrombosis [*Cardiology*] (DAVI)
VT.............. Vent (NASA)
VT.............. Ventricular Tachycardia [*Cardiology*]
VT.............. Verb Transitive
VT.............. Verfuegungstruppen (BJA)
VT.............. Vermont [*Postal code*]
VT.............. Vermont Reports [*A publication*] (DLA)
Vt.............. Vermont Reports [*A publication*] (AAGC)
VT.............. Verotoxin [*Biochemistry*]
VT.............. Vertical Tab [*Computer science*] (DOM)
VT.............. Vertical Tabulate (NITA)
VT.............. Vertical Tabulation [*or Tabulator*] [*Computer science*]
VT.............. Vertical Tabulator (ECII)
VT.............. Vertical Tail
VT.............. Vesalius Trust (EA)
VT.............. Vetus Testamentum [*Old Testament*] [*of the Bible*] [*Latin*]
V-T............ Vibrational-to-Translational [*Energy transfer*]
VT.............. Vibration Testing
VT.............. Victa Ltd. [*Aviation Division*] [*Australia ICAO aircraft manufacturer identifier*] (ICAO)
VT.............. Videotape
VT.............. Video Telemetry (CPH)
VT.............. Video Terminal
VT.............. Vinyl Tile [*Technical drawings*]
VT.............. Violet Tetrazolium (MAE)
VT.............. Virtual Terminal (BYTE)
VT.............. Virtual Terminal (DOMA)
VT.............. Viscous Traction [*Automotive engineering*] (PS)
VT.............. Viscous Transmission [*Automotive engineering*]
VT.............. Vision Test [*Ophthalmology*]
VT.............. Visual Telegraphy
VT.............. Visual Toss
VT.............. Vocational-Technical
VT.............. Voice Tube [*Technical drawings*]
VT.............. Volcano-Tectonic [*Earthquake*]
VT.............. Voltage Transformer (EECA)
VT.............. Voting Trust [*Investment term*]
VT2............ Virtual Tourist 2
VTA............ Air Tahiti [*France ICAO designator*] (FAAC)
V_TA............ Alveolar Tidal Volume [*Medicine*] (DAVI)
VTA............ Transport Aviation [*Soviet-Russian*] (DOMA)
VTA............ Vacuum-Tube Amplifier
VTA............ Variable Transfer Address
VTA............ Varnished Tube Association
VTA............ Ventral Tegmental Area [*Anatomy*]
VTA............ Vertex Time of Arrival [*FAA*] (TAG)
VTA............ Vertical Tracking Angle [*of a phonograph cartridge*]
VTA............ Vesta Insurance Group [*NYSE symbol*] (SPSG)
VTA............ Victorian Temperance Alliance [*Australia*]
VTA............ Video Trade Association [*British*] (DBA)
VTA............ Vision Test Apparatus [*Ophthalmology*]
VTA............ Vocational Training Authority [*Australian Capital Territory*]
VTA............ Vodka Trade Association [*British*] (DBA)
VTAADS...... Vertical the Army Authorization Document System

VTAB........... Vertical Tabulation Character [*Computer science*]
VTAC........... Victorian Transport Accident Commission [*Australia*]
VTAC........... Video Timing and Control
V-TACH........ Ventricular Tachycardia [*Cardiology*]
VT Admin Comp... Vermont Administrative Procedure Compilation [*A publication*] (DLA)
VTAJX.......... Navy Trainer Advanced Jet - Experimental (MCD)
VTAM........... Varian Telecommunication Access Method (IAA)
VTAM........... Virtual Telecommunications [*or Teleprocessing*] Access Method [*IBM Corp.*] [*Computer science*]
VTAM........... Virtual Terminal Access Method
VTAM........... VORTEX [*Varian Omnitask Real-Time Executive*] Telecommunications Access Method
VTAME......... Virtual Telecommunications Access Method Entry
V-TAS.......... Vericom Test Application System [*Vericom Ltd.*] [*Software package*] (NCC)
VTAS........... Visual Target Acquisition System [*Navy*]
VtB.............. Fletcher Free Library, Burlington, VT [*Library symbol Library of Congress*] (LCLS)
VTB.............. Torpedo-Bombing Plane [*Navy symbol*]
VTB.............. Vacuum Tower Bottoms [*Petroleum chemistry*]
VTB.............. Velocity Test Barrel
VtB.............. Verfahrenstechnische Berichte [*Process Technology Reports*] [*A publication*]
VtB.............. Verkehrswasserbaubibliothek [*Bundesanstalt fuer Wasserbau*] [*Database*]
VTB.............. Video Terminal Board [*Computer science*] (MHDB)
VTB.............. Vinyl T-Butylstyrene [*Organic chemistry*]
VTB.............. Visual Table Builder [*Computer science*] (PCM)
VTB.............. Vlaamsche Toeristenbond
VTB.............. Voltage Time to Breakdown (DEN)
VTB.............. Volunteer Talent Bank [*American Association of Retired Persons*]
VTBA........... Bangkok [*Thailand*] [*ICAO location identifier*] (ICLI)
VT BA.......... Vermont Bar Association Reports [*A publication*] (DLA)
VTBB........... Bangkok [*Thailand*] [*ICAO location identifier*] (ICLI)
VtBC........... Champlain College, Burlington, VT [*Library symbol Library of Congress*] (LCLS)
VTBC........... Chanthaburi [*Thailand*] [*ICAO location identifier*] (ICLI)
VTBD........... Bangkok/International [*Thailand*] [*ICAO location identifier*] (ICLI)
VTBE........... Saraburi [*Thailand*] [*ICAO location identifier*] (ICLI)
VtBef........... Rockingham Free Public Library, Bellows Falls, VT [*Library symbol Library of Congress*] (LCLS)
VtBenn......... Bennington Free Library, Bennington, VT [*Library symbol Library of Congress*] (LCLS)
VtBennC....... Bennington College, Bennington, VT [*Library symbol Library of Congress*] (LCLS)
VtBennM....... Bennington Museum, Inc., Bennington, VT [*Library symbol Library of Congress*] (LCLS)
VtBennP....... Putnam Memorial Hospital, Medical Library, Bennington, VT [*Library symbol Library of Congress*] (LCLS)
VTBF........... Chachoengsao/Phanom Sarakhan [*Thailand*] [*ICAO location identifier*] (ICLI)
VtBFB.......... Grand Lodge of Vermont, F & AM Library, Burlington, VT [*Library symbol Library of Congress*] (LCLS)
VTBG........... Kanchanaburi [*Thailand*] [*ICAO location identifier*] (ICLI)
VTBH........... Lop Buri/Sa Pran Nak [*Thailand*] [*ICAO location identifier*] (ICLI)
VTBI............ Prachin Buri [*Thailand*] [*ICAO location identifier*] (ICLI)
VTBJ............ Phetchaburi/Tha Yang [*Thailand*] [*ICAO location identifier*] (ICLI)
VTBK........... Nakhon Pathom/Kamphaeng Saen [*Thailand*] [*ICAO location identifier*] (ICLI)
VTBL........... Lop Buri [*Thailand*] [*ICAO location identifier*] (ICLI)
VTBM........... Phetchaburi/Maruk [*Thailand*] [*ICAO location identifier*] (ICLI)
VTBN........... Prachuap Khiri Khan/Pran Buri [*Thailand*] [*ICAO location identifier*] (ICLI)
VTBP........... Prachuap Khiri Khan [*Thailand*] [*ICAO location identifier*] (ICLI)
VTBR........... Ratchaburi [*Thailand*] [*ICAO location identifier*] (ICLI)
VtBran......... Brandon Free Public Library, Brandon, VT [*Library symbol Library of Congress*] (LCLS)
VTBR Case... Victorian Taxation Board of Review Case [*Australia A publication*]
VtBrt........... Brooks Memorial Library, Brattleboro, VT [*Library symbol Library of Congress*] (LCLS)
VtBrtS......... School for International Training, Brattleboro, VT [*Library symbol Library of Congress*] (LCLS)
VTBS........... Chon Buri/Sattahip [*Thailand*] [*ICAO location identifier*] (ICLI)
VTBT........... Chon Buri/Bang Phra [*Thailand*] [*ICAO location identifier*] (ICLI)
VtBT........... Trinity College, Burlington, VT [*Library symbol Library of Congress*] (LCLS)
VTBU........... Rayong/Utapao [*Thailand*] [*ICAO location identifier*] (ICLI)
VTBW........... Prachin Buri/Watthana Nakhon [*Thailand*] [*ICAO location identifier*] (ICLI)
VTC............. Vacuum Thermal Chamber (IAA)
VTC............. Vandenberg Test Center [*Air Force*]
VTC............. Variable Timing Control [*Intake subsystem*] [*Automotive engineering*]
VTC............. Variable Trimmer Capacitor
VTC............. Vehicular Traffic Control
VTC............. Veractor Tuned Microwave Cavity
VTC............. Vertical Trash Compactor (DWSG)
VTC............. Viable Titanium Composite
VTC............. Victorian Technology Centre [*Australia*]
VTC............. Video Tape Center [*Commercial firm British*]
VTC............. Video Teleconferencing
VTC............. Vidicon Television Camera
VTC............. Virtual Terminal Control [*Computer science*] (MHDB)
VTC............. Viscosity Temperature Coefficient (IAA)
VTC............. Vitronics Corp. [*AMEX symbol*] (SPSG)
VTC............. Volunteer Training Corps [*An organization for home defense*] [*World War I*] [*British*]
VTC............. Volvo Truck Corp.
VTC............. Voting Trust Certificate [*or Company*] [*Investment term*]
VTCA........... Chiang Rai/Chiang Khong [*Thailand*] [*ICAO location identifier*] (ICLI)
VTCA........... Vernon's Texas Codes, Annotated [*A publication*] (DLA)
VTCA........... Vintage Thunderbird Club of America [*Later, VTCI*] (EA)
VtCasT......... Castleton State College, Castleton, VT [*Library symbol Library of Congress*] (LCLS)
VTCB........... Chiang Rai/Ban Chiang Kham [*Thailand*] [*ICAO location identifier*] (ICLI)
VTCC........... Chiang Mai [*Thailand*] [*ICAO location identifier*] (ICLI)
VTCC........... Variable Temperature Compensation Capacitor
VTCCHE....... Tidewater Consortium, Librarians' Networking Committee [*Library network*]
VTCD........... Nan/Chiang Klang [*Thailand*] [*ICAO location identifier*] (ICLI)
VTCE........... Nan/Ban Pua [*Thailand*] [*ICAO location identifier*] (ICLI)
VTCE........... Vehicle Team Combat Exercise [*Army*] (INF)
VTCF........... Uttaradit (West) [*Thailand*] [*ICAO location identifier*] (ICLI)
VTCFITB....... Victorian Textile, Clothing and Footwear Industry Training Board [*Australia*]
VTCH........... Mae Hong Son [*Thailand*] [*ICAO location identifier*] (ICLI)
VTCH........... Vitech America, Inc. [*NASDAQ symbol*] (SAG)
VTCI............ Mae Hong Son/Pai [*Thailand*] [*ICAO location identifier*] (ICLI)
VTCI............ Vintage Thunderbird Club International (EA)
VTCK........... Mae Hong Son/Khun Yuam [*Thailand*] [*ICAO location identifier*] (ICLI)
VTCL........... Lampang [*Thailand*] [*ICAO location identifier*] (ICLI)
VTCN........... Nan [*Thailand*] [*ICAO location identifier*] (ICLI)
VTCP........... Phrae [*Thailand*] [*ICAO location identifier*] (ICLI)
VTCR........... Chiang Rai [*Thailand*] [*ICAO location identifier*] (ICLI)
VTCS........... Mae Hong Son/Mae Sariang [*Thailand*] [*ICAO location identifier*] (ICLI)
VTCS........... Variable Thermal Control Surface
VTCS........... Vega Target Control System [*Computer flight control of test vehicles*]
VTCS........... Vehicular Traffic Control System (IEEE)
VTCS........... Video Telemetering Camera Systems (AAG)
VTCT........... Vocational Training Charitable Trust [*British*]
VTD............. Aircraft (Training) [*Navy symbol*]
VTD............. Vacuum-Tube Detector (IAA)
VTD............. Variable Time Delay
VTD............. Variable Torque Distribution [*Automotive engineering*]
VTD............. Variable Torque Distribution
VTD............. Vertical Tape Display (IAA)
VTD............. Vision Testing Device [*Ophthalmology*]
VTDC........... Vacuum Tube Development Committee [*Columbia University*] (MCD)
VTDI............ Variable Threshold Digital Input
VTE............. Variable Thrust Engine
VTE............. Venous Thromboembolism [*Medicine*] (DAVI)
VTE............. Venous Thromboembolism [*Medicine*]
VTE............. Vertical Tube Effects [*Desalination*]
VTE............. Vertical Tube Evaporation [*Desalination*]
VTE............. Vibration Test Equipment
VTE............. Vicarious Trial and Error [*Psychology*]
VTE............. Vientiane [*Laos*] [*Airport symbol*] (OAG)
VTE............. Viscous Transonic Equation
VTE............. Visual Task Evaluation [*or Evaluator*] (MHDI)
VTEC........... Verotoxin-Producing Escherichia Coli
VTEC-E........ Variable Valve-Timing and Lift Electronic Control System - Economy [*Automotive technology*]
V-TECS........ Vocational Technical Education Consortium of States (OICC)
VTEK........... Vodavi Technology [*NASDAQ symbol*] (SAG)
VTEL........... Vtel Corp. [*NASDAQ symbol*] (SAG)
VTERL......... Veterinary Toxicology and Entomology Research Laboratory [*Department of Agriculture*] [*College Station, TX*] (GRD)
VTERM........ Variable Temperature Electrical Resistivity Measurement [*Physics*]
VTES........... Variable Thrust Engine System
VTES........... Vinyltriethoxysilane [*Organic chemistry*]
Vtesse......... Viscomtesse [*Vicountess*] [*French*] (BARN)
V-test.......... Voluter Test [*Radiology*] (DAVI)
VTEX........... Vertex Communications Corp. [*Kilgore, TX*] [*NASDAQ symbol*] (NQ)
VTEX........... Vertex Communic'ns [*NASDAQ symbol*] (TTSB)
VTF............. Vacuum Test Furnace
VTF............. Van Kam Am Cap InvGr FL Mun [*NYSE symbol*] (TTSB)
VTF............. Van Kampen Merritt Investment Grade Florida Municipal [*NYSE symbol*] (SPSG)
VTF............. Variable Time, Fragmentation [*Military*] (CAAL)
VTF............. Venezuelan Trust Fund [*Inter-American Development Bank*]
VTF............. Vertical Test Facility [*NASA*]
VTF............. Vertical Test Fixture
VTF............. Vertical Test Flight (MCD)
VTF............. Vertical Tracking Force [*of a phonograph cartridge*]
VTF............. Videotex Terminal Facility (NITA)
VTF............. Voltage Transfer Function
VTFE........... Vertical Tube Foam Evaporation [*Chemical engineering*]
VtFin........... Vermont Financial Services Corp. [*Associated Press*] (SAG)
VTFS........... Visual Technology Flight Simulator (MCD)
VTFT........... Value Task Force Team
VTG............. Vantage [*Washington*] [*Seismograph station code, US Geological Survey*] (SEIS)
VTG............. Vitellogenin [*Biochemistry*]
VTG............. Volume Thoracic Gas [*Medicine*]
VTG............. Voting [*Business term*]
VThB........... Vocabulaire de Theologie Biblique [*A publication*] (BJA)

VtHi .... Vermont Historical Society, Montpelier, VT [*Library symbol Library of Congress*] (LCLS)
VTI .... Statens Vag- och Trafikinstitut [*Swedish Road and Traffic Research Institute*] [*Linkoping*] [*Information service or system*] (IID)
VTI .... Valparaiso Technical Institute [*Indiana*]
VTI .... Vermont Telecommunications, Inc. [*Winooski, VT*] [*Telecommunications*] (TSSD)
VTI .... Vertical Technology Insertion [*Business term Army*] (RDA)
VTI .... Video Terminal Interface
VTI .... Vinton, IA [*Location identifier FAA*] (FAAL)
VTI .... VLSI Technology Inc. (NITA)
VTI .... Volume Thickness Index
VTI .... Voluntary Termination Incentive [*Business term*]
VTIP .... Visual Target Identification Point (AFM)
VTJ .... Johnson State College, Johnson, VT [*OCLC symbol*] (OCLC)
VTJ .... Van Kam Am Cap InvGr NJ Mun [*NYSE symbol*] (TTSB)
VTJ .... Van Kampen Merritt Investment Grade New Jersey Municipal [*NYSE symbol*] (SPSG)
VtJoT .... Johnson State College, Johnson, VT [*Library symbol Library of Congress*] (LCLS)
VTK .... Vertical Track Distance (GAVI)
VTK .... Virally-Encoded Thymidine Kinase [*Medicine*]
VTL .... Vacuum-Tube Launcher
VTL .... Variable Threshold Logic
VTL .... Vertical Turret Lathe
VTL .... Video Tape Lecture
VTL .... Virtual Tape Library
VTL .... Vittel [*France*] [*Airport symbol*] (AD)
Vt Law .... Vermont Law School (GAGS)
VTLC .... Virtual Terminal Line Controller [*Computer science*] (MHDB)
VTLK .... Vitalink Pharmacy [*NASDAQ symbol*] (TTSB)
VTLK .... Vitalink Pharmacy Services [*NASDAQ symbol*] (SAG)
VTLMB .... Victorian Tobacco Leaf Marketing Board [*Australia*]
Vt-LR .... Vermont Legislative Council, Montpelier, VT [*Library symbol Library of Congress*] (LCLS)
VTLS .... Virginia Technical Library System [*Virginia Polytechnic Institute and State University Center for Library Automation*] [*Information service or system*]
VtLyL .... Lyndon State College, Lyndonville, VT [*Library symbol Library of Congress*] (LCLS)
VTM .... Vacuum-Tube Module
VTM .... Vehicles to the Mile [*Military*]
VTM .... Vehicle Test Meter [*TACOM*] [*Army*] (RDA)
VTM .... Verification Test Matrix
VTM .... Verification Traceability Matrix
VTM .... Versatile Tracking Mount (MCD)
VTM .... Vibration Test Module (MCD)
VTM .... Vocal Tract Model (MHDI)
VTM .... Voltage Tunable Magnetron
vtm .... Voltage-Tuned Magnetron (IDOE)
VTM .... Volume Tidal Mechanical (MAE)
VtMan .... Mark Skinner Public Library, Manchester, VT [*Library symbol Library of Congress*] (LCLS)
VtMarC .... Marlboro College, Marlboro, VT [*Library symbol Library of Congress*] (LCLS)
VTMC .... Viable Titanium Matrix Composite
VtMiM .... Middlebury College, Middlebury, VT [*Library symbol Library of Congress*] (LCLS)
VtMiS .... Sheldon Art Museum, Middlebury, VT [*Library symbol Library of Congress*] (LCLS)
VTMO .... Voltage Tunable Microwave Oscillator
VtMor .... Morristown Centennial Library, Morrisville, VT [*Library symbol Library of Congress*] (LCLS)
VTMoV .... Velvet Tobacco Mottle Virus
VtMS .... Office of the Secretary of State, State Papers Division, Montpelier, VT [*Library symbol Library of Congress*] (LCLS)
VTMS .... Vehicle Thermal Management System
VTMS .... Vessel Traffic Management System (DS)
VTMS .... Vinyltrimethysilane [*Organic chemistry*]
VtMS-Ar .... Office of the Secretary of State, Vermont State Archives, Montpelier, VT [*Library symbol*] [*Library of Congress*] (LCLS)
VtN .... Brown Public Library, Northfield, VT [*Library symbol Library of Congress*] (LCLS)
VT(N) .... Night Torpedo Bomber Squadron [*Navy symbol*]
VTN .... Valentine, NE [*Location identifier FAA*] (FAAL)
VTN .... Van Kam Am Cap InvGr NY Mum [*NYSE symbol*] (TTSB)
VTN .... Van Kampen Merritt Investment Grade New York Municipal [*NYSE symbol*] (SPSG)
VTN .... Ventral Tegmental Nuclei [*Neuroanatomy*]
VTN .... Verification Test Network [*NASA*] (MCD)
VTN .... Video Tape Network [*Defunct*] (EA)
VTN .... Vitran Corp., Inc. [*Toronto Stock Exchange symbol*]
VTNA .... VTAM Telecommunications Network Architecture
VTNAF .... Vitran Corp. [*NASDAQ symbol*] (TTSB)
VTNAF .... Vitran Corp., Inc. [*NASDAQ symbol*] (SAG)
VTNF .... Variable Time Non-Fragmenting [*Military*] (CAAL)
Vtnm .... Vietnam (VRA)
VtNN .... Norwich University, Northfield, VT [*Library symbol Library of Congress*] (LCLS)
VTNS .... Voltage Tunable Noise Source
VTO .... Vacuum-Tube Oscillator (IAA)
VTO .... Vertical Takeoff
VTO .... Viable Terrestrial Organism
VTO .... Visual Training Officer [*Navy*]
VTO .... Vitro, Sociedad Anonima ADS [*NYSE symbol*] (SPSG)
VTO .... Vocational Training Officer [*Navy*]
VTO .... Voltage Tunable Oscillator
VTOC .... Volume Table of Contents [*Computer science*]
VTOF .... Voltage-to-Frequency (IAA)
VTOGW .... Vertical Takeoff Gross Weight
VTOHL .... Vertical Takeoff and Horizontal Landing
VTOL .... Vertical Takeoff and Landing [*Also, VERTOL*] [*Acronym used for a type of aircraft*]
VTOVL .... Vertical Takeoff Vertical Landing
VTP .... Valid Target Presentation [*Military*] (CAAL)
VTP .... Value Truck Package
VTP .... Vandenberg Test Program [*Air Force*]
VTP .... Van Kam Am Cap InvGr PA Mun [*NYSE symbol*] (TTSB)
VTP .... Van Kampen Merritt Investment Grade Pennsylvania Municipal [*NYSE symbol*] (SPSG)
VTP .... Vehicle Test Plan [*NASA*] (NASA)
VTP .... Vendor Test Procedure
VTP .... Verification Test Plan [*or Program*] (NASA)
vtp .... Videotape (VRA)
VTP .... VIEWDATA Terminal Program
VTP .... Virtual Terminal Protocol
VTP .... Visual Transmitter Power
VTP .... Voluntary Termination of Pregnancy [*Medicine*]
VTPA .... Vertical Turbine Pump Association [*Defunct*]
VTPA .... (Vinylthiazolidinylidene)phenylamine [*Organic chemistry*]
VTPH .... Prachuap Khiri Khan/Hua Hin [*Thailand*] [*ICAO location identifier*] (ICLI)
VTPI .... Nakhon Sawan/Takhli [*Thailand*] [*ICAO location identifier*] (ICLI)
VtPifi .... Free Library, Pittsfield, VT [*Library symbol Library of Congress*] (LCLS)
VTPL .... Pretchabun/Lom Sak [*Thailand*] [*ICAO location identifier*] (ICLI)
VtPlaG .... Goddard College, Plainfield, VT [*Library symbol Library of Congress*] (LCLS)
VTPM .... Tak/Mae Sot [*Thailand*] [*ICAO location identifier*] (ICLI)
VTPN .... Nakhon Sawan [*Thailand*] [*ICAO location identifier*] (ICLI)
VtPom .... Abbott Memorial Library, Pomfret, VT [*Library symbol Library of Congress*] (LCLS)
VtPouG .... Green Mountain College, Poultney, VT [*Library symbol Library of Congress*] (LCLS)
VTPP .... Phitsanulok [*Thailand*] [*ICAO location identifier*] (ICLI)
Vt-PR .... Vermont Public Records Library, Montpelier, VT [*Library symbol Library of Congress*] (LCLS)
VTPR .... Vertical Temperature Profile [*or Profiling*] Radiometer
VTPS .... Phitsanulok/Sarit Sena [*Thailand*] [*ICAO location identifier*] (ICLI)
VTPS .... Vibration Test Plotting System
VTPT .... Tak [*Thailand*] [*ICAO location identifier*] (ICLI)
VTPU .... Uttaradit [*Thailand*] [*ICAO location identifier*] (ICLI)
VtPuW .... Windham College, Putney, VT [*Library symbol Library of Congress*] (LCLS)
VTPY .... Tak/Sam Ngao [*Thailand*] [*ICAO location identifier*] (ICLI)
VTR .... Air Ostravia Ltd. [*Czechoslovakia*] [*FAA designator*] (FAAC)
VTR .... McGrath, AK [*Location identifier FAA*] (FAAL)
VTR .... Value of Time Research [*British*]
VTR .... Variable Takeoff Rating (GAVI)
VTR .... Variable Tandem Repetition [*Genetics*]
VTR .... Vehicle-Tracked Retriever [*An armored recovery vehicle*] [*Army*] (VNW)
VTR .... Vehicle Tracking Receiver
VTR .... Vehicle Track Recovery [*Military*]
VTR .... Vendor Trouble Report
VTR .... Verification Test Report (NASA)
VTR .... Vermont Railway, Inc. [*AAR code*]
VT R .... Vermont Reports [*A publication*] (DLA)
VTR .... Vertical Radial (MSA)
VTR .... Vertical Test Range
VTR .... Veto Resources Ltd. [*Vancouver Stock Exchange symbol*]
VTR .... Videotape Recorder [*or Recording*]
VTR .... Video-Tape Recording (IDOE)
VTR .... Vintage Triumph Register (EA)
VTR .... Vitkovice Air [*Czech Republic*] [*ICAO designator*] (FAAC)
VTR .... Voltage Transformation Ratio [*Physics*]
VTRA .... Vectra Banking [*NASDAQ symbol*] (SAG)
VTRAM .... Variable Topology Random Access Memory [*Computer science*] (PDAA)
VTRAN .... Vast Translator (KSC)
VTRAP .... Vectra Bkg 9.50%'A'Pfd [*NASDAQ symbol*] (TTSB)
VtRaStM .... Saint Mary's Seminary, Randolph, VT [*Library symbol Library of Congress*] (LCLS)
VTRB .... Variable Trim Reentry Body (MCD)
VT Rep .... Vermont Reports [*A publication*] (DLA)
V/TRK .... Vertical Track (GAVI)
VtRoc .... Rochester Public Library, Rochester, VT [*Library symbol Library of Congress*] (LCLS)
VTRR .... Visual Target RADAR Ranging
VTRS .... Videotape Recording System
VTRS .... Videotape Response System
VTRS .... Visual Technology Research Simulator (CAAL)
VTRU .... Variable Threshold Recently Used (MHDI)
VTS .... IEEE Vehicular Technology Society (EA)
VTS .... Vacuum Thermal Stability Test (MCD)
VTS .... Vandenberg Tracking Station [*Air Force*]
VTS .... Vanillin Thiosemicarbazone (IIA)
VTS .... Variable Time Step
VTS .... Variable Tracking Strategy (MCD)
VTS .... Vehicle Test Specification

VTS .... Vehicle Time Reproducer (SAA)
VTS .... Vehicle Tracking System [*Automotive engineering*]
VTS .... Venture Touring Society (EA)
VTS .... Veritas DGC, Inc. [*NYSE symbol*] (SAG)
VTS .... Versatile Training Systems (MCD)
VTS .... Vertical Test Site [*NASA*] (MCD)
VTS .... Vertical Test Stand [*NASA*] (KSC)
VTS .... Vertical Test System (NASA)
VTS .... Vertical Thrust Stand
VTS .... Vessel Traffic Service [*Harbor RADAR system*] [*Coast Guard*]
VTS .... Vibration Test Specification
VTS .... Vibration Test System
VTS .... Viewfinder Tracking System
VTS .... Viewscan Text System (NITA)
VTS .... Virginia Theological Seminary, Alexandria, VA [*OCLC symbol*] (OCLC)
VTS .... Virtual Terminal Service (TNIG)
VTS .... Virtual Terminal System [*Computer science*] (MHDB)
VTS .... Visual Typing System (MCD)
VTS .... Vitosha [*Bulgaria*] [*Seismograph station code, US Geological Survey*] (SEIS)
VTS .... Vocational Training Scheme [*British*]
VTS .... Vocational Training Service
VTS .... Vote Tally System
VTS .... Vulcan Training System (MCD)
VTSA .... Satun [*Thailand*] [*ICAO location identifier*] (ICLI)
VTSB .... Surat Thani [*Thailand*] [*ICAO location identifier*] (ICLI)
VTSC .... Narathiwat [*Thailand*] [*ICAO location identifier*] (ICLI)
VTSD .... Chumpon [*Thailand*] [*ICAO location identifier*] (ICLI)
VTSD .... Variable-Temperature Stepwise Desorption [*Chemical engineering*]
VTSE .... Vehicle Team Subcaliber Exercise [*Army*] (INF)
VTSH .... Songkhla [*Thailand*] [*ICAO location identifier*] (ICLI)
VtShelM .... Shelburne Museum, Inc., Research Library, Shelburne, VT [*Library symbol Library of Congress*] (LCLS)
VTsIK .... Vserossiyskiy Tsentral'nyy Ispolnitel'nyy Komitet [*All-Russian Central Executive Committee of the Congress of Soviets*] [*Former USSR*] (LAIN)
VTSK .... Pattani [*Thailand*] [*ICAO location identifier*] (ICLI)
VTS/MA .... Virtual Terminal Session/Multiple Access [*Computer science*] (HGAA)
VTSN .... Nakhon Si Thammarat [*Thailand*] [*ICAO location identifier*] (ICLI)
VTSO .... Surat Thani/Don Nok [*Thailand*] [*ICAO location identifier*] (ICLI)
VTSP .... Phuket [*Thailand*] [*ICAO location identifier*] (ICLI)
VTSPS .... Vsesoyuznyy Tsentral'nyy Sovet Professional'nykh Soyuzov [*All-Union Central Council of Trade Unions*] [*Former USSR*]
VTSR .... Ranong [*Thailand*] [*ICAO location identifier*] (ICLI)
VTSRS .... Verdun Target Symptom Rating Scale (MAE)
VTSS .... Songkhla/Hat Yai [*Thailand*] [*ICAO location identifier*] (ICLI)
VTSS .... Vitesse Semiconductor [*NASDAQ symbol*] (TTSB)
VTSS .... Vitesse Semiconductor Corp. [*NASDAQ symbol*] (SPSG)
VTST .... Trang [*Thailand*] [*ICAO location identifier*] (ICLI)
VTST .... Variational Transition State Theory [*Physical chemistry*]
VT Stat Ann... Vermont Statutes, Annotated [*A publication*] (DLA)
VtStjA .... St. Johnsbury Atheneum, St. Johnsbury, VT [*Library symbol Library of Congress*] (LCLS)
VtStjF .... Fairbanks Museum of Natural Science, St. Johnsbury, VT [*Library symbol Library of Congress*] (LCLS)
VTSU .... Virtual Terminal Support [*Computer science*] (IAA)
Vt-SWRL .... Vermont Department of Libraries, Southwest Regional Library, Rutland, VT [*Library symbol Library of Congress*] (LCLS)
VTSY .... Ya La [*Thailand*] [*ICAO location identifier*] (ICLI)
VTT .... Vacuum Thermal Testing
VTT .... Vacuum-Tube Transmitter
VTT .... Valtion Teknillinen Tutkimuskeskus [*Technical Research Center of Finland*] [*Espoo*] [*Information service or system*] (IID)
VTT .... Variable Threshold Transistor
VTT .... Vertolet Zhpa [*Ukraine*] [*FAA designator*] (FAAC)
VTT .... Video Teletraining [*Military*] (INF)
VTTC .... Video Tape Time-Code (NITA)
VTTeddy ...... Vermont Teddy Bear Co. [*Associated Press*] (SAG)
VTU .... Las Tunas [*Cuba*] [*Airport symbol*] (OAG)
VTU .... Oxnard, CA [*Location identifier FAA*] (FAAL)
VTU .... University of Vermont, Bailey Library, Burlington, VT [*OCLC symbol*] (OCLC)
VtU .... University of Vermont, Burlington, VT [*Library symbol Library of Congress*] (LCLS)
VTU .... Vehicle Tracking Unit [*Automated traffic management*]
vtu .... Vermont [*MARC country of publication code Library of Congress*] (LCCP)
VTU .... Vibrating Tie Under-Cutter (PDAA)
V + TU .... Voice plus Teleprinter Unit
VTU .... Volunteer Reserve Training Unit [*Coast Guard*]
VTU .... Volunteer Training Unit
VTUA .... Kalasin/Ban Na Khu [*Thailand*] [*ICAO location identifier*] (ICLI)
VTUB .... Bakhon Phanom/Mukdahan [*Thailand*] [*ICAO location identifier*] (ICLI)
VTUC .... Chaiyaphum [*Thailand*] [*ICAO location identifier*] (ICLI)
VTUD .... Udon Thani [*Thailand*] [*ICAO location identifier*] (ICLI)
VTUE .... Sakon Nakhon/Nam Phung Dam (North) [*Thailand*] [*ICAO location identifier*] (ICLI)
VTUF .... Sakon Nakhon/Nam Phung Dam (South) [*Thailand*] [*ICAO location identifier*] (ICLI)
VTUG .... Chaiyaphum/Phu Khieo [*Thailand*] [*ICAO location identifier*] (ICLI)
VTUH .... Nakhon Ratchasima/Pak Chong [*Thailand*] [*ICAO location identifier*] (ICLI)
VTUI .... Sakon Nakhon/Bankhai [*Thailand*] [*ICAO location identifier*] (ICLI)
VTUK .... Khon Kaen [*Thailand*] [*ICAO location identifier*] (ICLI)
VTUL .... Loei [*Thailand*] [*ICAO location identifier*] (ICLI)
VTUM .... Nongkhai [*Thailand*] [*ICAO location identifier*] (ICLI)
VtU-Med ...... University of Vermont, College of Medicine, Burlington, VT [*Library symbol Library of Congress*] (LCLS)
VTU(MMS)... Volunteer Training Unit (Merchant Marine Safety)
VTUN .... Nakhon Ratchasima [*Thailand*] [*ICAO location identifier*] (ICLI)
VTUP .... Nakhon Phanom [*Thailand*] [*ICAO location identifier*] (ICLI)
VTUR .... Roi Et [*Thailand*] [*ICAO location identifier*] (ICLI)
VTUS .... Sakon Nakhon [*Thailand*] [*ICAO location identifier*] (ICLI)
VTUT .... Ubon Ratchathani/Loeng Nok Tha [*Thailand*] [*ICAO location identifier*] (ICLI)
VTUU .... Ubon Ratchathani [*Thailand*] [*ICAO location identifier*] (ICLI)
VTUW .... Nakhon Phanom (West) [*Thailand*] [*ICAO location identifier*] (ICLI)
VtU-W .... University of Vermont and State Agricultural College, Wilbur Collection, Burlington, VT [*Library symbol Library of Congress*] (LCLS)
VTUZ .... Khon Kaen/Nam Phung Dam [*Thailand*] [*ICAO location identifier*] (ICLI)
VTV .... Vacuum Transmitting Valve [*Automotive engineering*]
VT(V) .... Vacuum-Tube (Voltmeter) (DEN)
VTV .... Value Television [*Television program*]
VTV .... Verification Test Vehicle [*Military*] (CAAL)
VtVe .... Bixby Memorial Free Library, Vergennes, VT [*Library symbol Library of Congress*] (LCLS)
VTVM .... Vacuum-Tube Voltmeter
VTW .... Variable Transmission Window
VTW .... Victorian Tapestry Workshop [*Australia*]
VtWeo .... Wilder Memorial Library, Weston, VT [*Library symbol Library of Congress*] (LCLS)
VtWinoS ...... Saint Michael's College, Winooski, VT [*Library symbol Library of Congress*] (LCLS)
VTX .... Vacuum-Tube Transmitter
VTX .... Ventex Energy [*Vancouver Stock Exchange symbol*]
VTX .... Vertex
VTX .... Videotex [*Telecommunications*]
VTX .... Vortex (AAG)
VTX .... VTX Electronics [*AMEX symbol*] (SPSG)
VTXTS .... Navy Jet Trainer (MCD)
VTY .... Vatovaky [*Madagascar*] [*Seismograph station code, US Geological Survey*] (SEIS)
VTZ .... Vishakhapatnam [*India*] [*Airport symbol*] (OAG)
VTZ .... Vitjaz [*Russian Federation*] [*ICAO designator*] (FAAC)
VU .... Air Ivoire [*ICAO designator*] (AD)
VU .... Utility Speed (GAVI)
VU .... Utility Squadron [*Navy symbol*] (MCD)
VU .... Validation Unit (AAG)
VU .... Vanity Unit [*Classified advertising*] (ADA)
VU .... Varicose Ulcer [*Medicine*]
VU .... Vaterlaendische Union [*Patriotic Union*] [*Liechtenstein*] [*Political party*] (PPE)
VU .... Vehicle Unit (KSC)
VU .... Vehicle Utility (MCD)
VU .... Velvet Underground [*Musical group*]
VU .... Very Urgent
VU .... Voice Unit [*Signal amplitude measurement*]
VU .... Volksunie [*People's Union*] [*Belgium Political party*]
VU .... Volksunite [*United People's Party*] [*Belgium*] [*Political party*]
VU .... Volume Unit [*Signal amplitude measurement*]
VU .... Von Unten [*From the Bottom*] [*German*]
VUA .... Valorous Unit Award [*Military decoration*]
VUA .... Verbal Underachievers [*Education*]
VUA .... Virtual Unit Address (BUR)
VUB .... Variational Upper Bound
VUB .... Vrije Universiteit Brussel [*Free University of Brussels*] [*Belgium*] [*Information service or system*] (IID)
VUCC .... Computer Center [*Vanderbilt University*] [*Research center*] (RCD)
VUCDT .... Ventilation Unit Condensate Drain Tank (IEEE)
VUCP .... Vietnamese Union Catalog Project, University of Michigan, Ann Arbor, MI [*Library symbol*] [*Library of Congress*] (LCLS)
VUCS .... Ventilation Umbilical Connector System
VUD .... Vertical Unit Displacement [*Military*] (INF)
VUE .... Upper Hudson Library Federation, Albany, NY [*OCLC symbol*] (OCLC)
VUE .... Visible/Ultraviolet Experiment
VUE .... Visual User Environment [*Military*]
VUEC .... Variable Underwater Experimental Community (PDAA)
VU-EVA .... Volksunie-Europese Vrije Alliante [*Belgium*] [*Political party*] (ECED)
VUF .... Vertical Upward Force
VUHZ .... Vyzkumny Ustav Hutnictvi Zeleza, Dobra [*Dobra Iron and Steel Research Institute*] [*Information service or system*] (IID)
VUI .... Video User Interface [*Computer science*] (DOM)
VUL .... Variable Universal Life [*Insurance*]
VUL .... Vulcan [*Taviliu*] [*New Britain*] [*Seismograph station code, US Geological Survey*] (SEIS)
VUL .... Vulcan International Corp. [*AMEX symbol*] (SPSG)
VUL .... Vulcan Int'l Corp. [*AMEX symbol*] (TTSB)
VUL .... Vulcanize (AAG)
VUL .... Vulgar (WDAA)
Vul .... Vulgate [*Version of the Bible*] (BARN)
VUL .... Vulnerary [*Medicine to heal wounds*] (ROG)
Vul .... Vulpecula [*Constellation*]
VULBS .... Virginia Union List of Biomedical Serials [*Library network*]
VULC .... Vanguard Unionist Loyalist Coalition [*Northern Ireland*] [*Political party*]

VULC .... Vulcanize
VULC .... Vulcanizing
VulcCp .... Vulcan International Corp. [*Associated Press*] (SAG)
VulcM .... Vulcan Materials Co. [*Associated Press*] (SAG)
VULCN .... Vulcanization
VULG .... Vulgar
VULG .... Vulgate [*Version of the Bible*]
Vulp .... Vulpecula [*Constellation*]
VULREP .... Vulnerability Report [*Navy*] (NVT)
VUMS .... Veterans of Underage Military Service (EA)
VUMS .... Vyzkumny Ustav pro Matematickych Stroju [*Research Institute for Mathematical Machines*] [*Czechoslovakia*]
VUN .... Air Ivoire Societe [*Ivory Coast*] [*ICAO designator*] (FAAC)
VUN .... Vunikawai [*Fiji*] [*Seismograph station code, US Geological Survey*] (SEIS)
VUNC .... Voice of United Nations Command
VUP .... Valledupar [*Colombia*] [*Airport symbol*] (OAG)
VUP .... Vela Uniform Platform
VUPD .... Video Updates, Inc. [*NASDAQ symbol*] (SAG)
VUPDA .... Video Update [*NASDAQ symbol*] (TTSB)
VUPDW .... Video Update Wrrt'A' [*NASDAQ symbol*] (TTSB)
VUPDZ .... Video Update Wrrt'B' [*NASDAQ symbol*] (TTSB)
VUPJ .... Victorian Union for Progressive Judaism [*Australia*]
VUPP .... Vanguard Unionist Progressive Party [*Northern Ireland*] [*Political party*]
VUQ .... Dayton, OH [*Location identifier FAA*] (FAAL)
VUR .... Vesicoureteral Reflex [*Nephrology*]
VUR .... Vesicoureteral Regurgitation [*Nephrology*] (MEDA)
VUS .... Versatile Upper Stage [*NASA*]
VUSA .... Visit USA [*Airline fare*]
VUT .... Union Theological Seminary Library, Richmond, VA [*OCLC symbol*] (OCLC)
VUTK .... View Tech, Inc. [*NASDAQ symbol*] (SAG)
VUTKW .... View Tech Wrrt [*NASDAQ symbol*] (TTSB)
VUTS .... Verification Unit Test Set (AFM)
VUU .... Virginia Union University [*Richmond*]
VUU .... Virginia Union University, Richmond, VA [*OCLC symbol*] (OCLC)
VUV .... Vacuum Ultraviolet
VUV .... Very Ultraviolet (SSD)
VUVM .... Voluntary Universal Marking Program (IAA)
VUW .... Eugene Isle, LA [*Location identifier FAA*] (FAAL)
VUW .... Victoria University of Wellington [*New Zealand*]
VUZ .... Birmingham, AL [*Location identifier FAA*] (FAAL)
VV .... First and Second Violins [*Music*] (ROG)
VV .... Semo Aviation [*ICAO designator*] (AD)
VV .... Vaccinia Virus
VV .... Vacuum Valve
V/V .... Validation/Verification (CAAL)
VV .... Valve Voltmeter (IAA)
VV .... Vanguard Ventures [*Vancouver Stock Exchange symbol*]
VV .... Variable Venturi [*Automotive engineering*]
VV .... Varicose Vein (MAE)
VV .... Veins [*Medicine*]
VV .... Velocity Vector (AAG)
VV .... Velocity-Volume
VV .... Venae [*Veins*] [*Latin*] [*Anatomy*] (DAVI)
vv .... Venerabiles [*Venerables*] [*Latin*] (WGA)
VV .... Venovenous [*Cardiology*] (DAVI)
VV .... Vent Valve
VV .... Verbs (ADA)
VV .... Verses
VV .... Vertebral Vein [*Anatomy*]
V/V .... Vertical Velocity
VV .... Vertical Visibility (DA)
VV .... Vesicovaginal [*Gynecology*] (DAVI)
V-V .... Vibrational-to-Vibrational [*Energy transfer*]
VV .... Vibrio Vulnificus [*A microorganism*]
VV .... Vice Versa
vv .... Vice Versa (WDMC)
vv .... Vice Versa (ODBW)
VV .... Victims for Victims [*Defunct*] (EA)
VV .... Vietnam Veterans (OICC)
VV .... Village Voice [*A publication*] (BRI)
VV .... Violini [*Violins*] [*Music*]
VV .... Viper Venom (MAE)
V V .... Virtual Equal Virtual [*Computer science*] (MHDI)
VV .... Visna Virus
VV .... Vista Ventures [*Commercial firm*] [*British*]
VV .... Visum Vivum [*Seen Alive*] [*Botany*] (ROG)
VV .... Viva Voce [*Spoken Aloud*] [*Latin*] (ADA)
VV .... Voices [*Music*]
VV .... Volume (NTCM)
v/v .... Volume of Solute per Volume of Solution [*Pharmacology*] (DAVI)
vv .... Volumes (ODBW)
V/V .... Volume/Volume
VV .... Vulva and Vagina [*Physiology*]
VVA .... Evaluation & Sale of Assets Agency
VVA .... Southern Adirondack Library System, Saratoga Springs, NY [*OCLC symbol*] (OCLC)
VVA .... Variable Valve Actuation [*Automotive engineering*]
VVA .... Venturi Vacuum Amplifier [*Automotive engineering*]
VVA .... Vietnam Veterans of America (EA)
VVAA .... Vietnam Veterans Association of Australia
VVAG .... Vietnam Veterans Arts Group [*Later, CTVWA*] (EA)
VV & A .... Verified, Validated, and Accredited (RDA)
VV & C .... Verification, Validation, and Certification (MHDB)
VVAOVI .... Vietnam Veterans Agent Orange Victims (EA)
VVAP .... Mouvement Socialiste Occitan - Volem Viure al Pais [*Occitanian Socialist Movement*] [*France Political party*] (PPW)
VVAW .... Vietnam Veterans Against the War (EA)
VVB .... Baruch College, New York, NY [*OCLC symbol*] (OCLC)
VVB .... Mahanoro [*Madagascar*] [*Airport symbol*] (OAG)
VVBAA .... Venetian and Vertical Blind Association of America [*Defunct*]
VVBM .... Buonmethuot/Chung Duc [*Viet Nam*] [*ICAO location identifier*] (ICLI)
VVC .... Colgate University, Hamilton, NY [*OCLC symbol*] (OCLC)
VVC .... Variable Vacuum Capacitor [*or Capacitance*]
VVC .... Variable Valve Control [*Automotive*]
VVC .... Variable Voltage Capacitor (IAA)
VVC .... Vertical Velocity Console
VVC .... Villavicencio [*Colombia*] [*Airport symbol*] (OAG)
VVC .... Volcano Veterinary Center [*Rwanda*]
VVC .... Voltage Variable Capacitor
VVCB .... Caobang [*Viet Nam*] [*ICAO location identifier*] (ICLI)
VVCC .... Victorian Vice-Chancellors' Committee [*Australia*]
VVCC .... Viri Clarissimi [*Most Illustrious Men*] [*Latin*]
VVCD .... Voltage Variable Capacitance Diode
VVCEC .... Voice and Video Control and Editing Components (MCD)
VVCS .... Conson [*Viet Nam*] [*ICAO location identifier*] (ICLI)
VVCS .... Vernier Velocity Correction System [*Aerospace*] (KSC)
VVCT .... Cantho [*Viet Nam*] [*ICAO location identifier*] (ICLI)
VVCUS .... Veteran Vespa Club, US [*Defunct*] (EA)
VVD .... Downstate Medical Center, SUNY [*State University of New York*], Brooklyn, NY [*OCLC symbol*] (OCLC)
VVD .... Valid Verifiable Defense [*Stamped on dismissed traffic tickets*]
VVD .... Valverde [*Canary Islands*] [*Seismograph station code, US Geological Survey*] (SEIS)
VVD .... Volkspartij voor Vrijheid en Democratie [*People's Party for Freedom and Democracy*] [*Netherlands Political party*] (EAIO)
VVD .... Voltage Variable Diode
VVDB .... Dienbienphu [*Viet Nam*] [*ICAO location identifier*] (ICLI)
VVDL .... Dalat/Lienkhuong [*Viet Nam*] [*ICAO location identifier*] (ICLI)
VVDN .... Danang [*Viet Nam*] [*ICAO location identifier*] (ICLI)
VVDS .... Video Verter Decision Storage
VVE .... Erie Community College-North, Buffalo, NY [*OCLC symbol*] (OCLC)
VVE .... Vertical Vertex Error (OA)
VVEJ .... Venus-Venus-Earth-Jupiter [*Trajectory*]
VVF .... New York Medical College, New York, NY [*OCLC symbol*] (OCLC)
VVF .... Veseco Vaginal Fistula [*Medicine*]
VVFR .... Vesicovaginal Fistula Repair [*Gynecology*] (DAVI)
VVG .... Aerovilla Ltda. [*Columbia*] [*FAA designator*] (FAAC)
VVG .... New York State Institute for Research in Mental Retardation, Staten Island, NY [*OCLC symbol*] (OCLC)
VVGF .... Vincent Van Gogh Foundation (EA)
VVGL .... Hanoi/Gialam [*Viet Nam*] [*ICAO location identifier*] (ICLI)
VVH .... Daemen College, Buffalo, NY [*OCLC symbol*] (OCLC)
VVH .... Very Very Heavy [*Cosmic ray nuclei*]
VVH .... Veterans Vigil of Honor (EA)
V/VH .... Viewers-per-Viewing Household [*Television ratings*] (NTCM)
VVHR .... Vibration Velocity per Hour
VVI .... Beth Israel Medical Center, New York, NY [*OCLC symbol*] (OCLC)
VVI .... Ventricular Pacing, Ventricular Sensing, Inhibited Mode [*Pacemaker*] [*Cardiology*] (MEDA)
VVI .... Vertical Velocity Indicator (MCD)
VVI .... Vice Viewers International (EA)
VVI .... Vietnam Veterans, Inc. [*Defunct*] (EA)
VVI .... Vietnam Veterans Institute [*Research center*] (RCD)
VVI .... Vocational Values Inventory [*Guidance in education*]
VVI .... Voltage Variation Indicator
VVIC .... Vietnam Era Veterans in Congress (EA)
VVID .... Vivid Technologies, Inc. [*NASDAQ symbol*] (SAG)
VVIP .... Very, Very Important Person
VVIR .... Voice and Vision of the Iranian Revolution [*Iranian television*]
VVIRA .... Vietnam Veterans Institute for Research and Advocacy (EA)
VVITA .... Vietnam Veterans Inter-Tribal Association (EA)
VVJ .... John Jay College of Criminal Justice, New York, NY [*OCLC symbol*] (OCLC)
VVK .... New York Academy of Medicine, New York, NY [*OCLC symbol*] (OCLC)
VVK .... Van Vleck [*Quantum mechanics*]
VVK .... Vastervik [*Sweden*] [*Airport symbol*] (OAG)
VVKP .... Kep [*Viet Nam*] [*ICAO location identifier*] (ICLI)
VVL .... Mount Sinai School of Medicine of the City University of New York, New York, NY [*OCLC symbol*] (OCLC)
VVLK .... Laokay [*Viet Nam*] [*ICAO location identifier*] (ICLI)
VV LL .... Variae Lectiones [*Variant Readings*] [*Latin*]
VVLP .... Vietnam Veterans Leadership Program [*ACTION*]
VVM .... Memorial Sloan-Kettering Cancer Center, New York, NY [*OCLC symbol*] (OCLC)
VVM .... Valve Voltmeter (IAA)
VVM .... Vector Voltmeter
VVM .... Velocity Vector Measurement
VVM .... Vietnam Veterans Memorial (VNW)
VVMC .... Voice and Video Monitoring Component (MCD)
vvMDV .... Very Virulent Marek Disease Virus [*Medicine*] (DMAA)
VVMF .... Vietnam Veterans Memorial Fund [*Defunct*] (EA)
VVMS .... Velocity Vector Measurement System
VVN .... Niagara University, Niagara University, NY [*OCLC symbol*] (OCLC)
VVNB .... Hanoi/Noibai [*Viet Nam*] [*ICAO location identifier*] (ICLI)
VVNS .... Nasan [*Viet Nam*] [*ICAO location identifier*] (ICLI)
VVNT .... Nhatrang [*Viet Nam*] [*ICAO location identifier*] (ICLI)

VVnW.......... Veterans of the Vietnam War (EA)
VVO.......... New York Medical College, Westchester Medical Center, Valhalla, NY [*OCLC symbol*] (OCLC)
VVO.......... Very Very Old [*Designation on brandy labels*]
VVO.......... Vladivostok [*USSR*] [*Airport symbol*] (AD)
VVOH.......... Vacuum Valve Operating Handle
VVOR.......... Visual-Vestibulo-Ocular Reflex [*Ophthalmology*] (DAVI)
VVP.......... Bard College, Annandale-On-Hudson, NY [*OCLC symbol*] (OCLC)
VVPB.......... Hue/Phubai [*Viet Nam*] [*ICAO location identifier*] (ICLI)
VVPK.......... Pleiku/Cu-Hanh [*Viet Nam*] [*ICAO location identifier*] (ICLI)
VVPP.......... Variable Volume Piston Pump
VVPQ.......... Phuquoc [*Viet Nam*] [*ICAO location identifier*] (ICLI)
VVQ.......... Roosevelt Hospital, Medical Library, New York, NY [*OCLC symbol*] (OCLC)
VVQ.......... Visualizer-Verbalizer Questionnaire (EDAC)
VVQN.......... Quinhon [*Viet Nam*] [*ICAO location identifier*] (ICLI)
VVR.......... Rockland Community College, Suffern, NY [*OCLC symbol*] (OCLC)
VVR.......... Vancouver Ventures [*Vancouver Stock Exchange symbol*]
VVR.......... Variable Voltage Rectifier
VVR.......... Vehicle Vapor Recovery [*Automobile*]
VVR.......... Viewdata/Videotex Report [*Link Resources Corp.*] [*Information service or system*] (CRD)
VVRG.......... Rachgia [*Viet Nam*] [*ICAO location identifier*] (ICLI)
VVRI.......... Veterinary Virus Research Institute [*New York State Veterinary College*]
VVRM.......... Vortex Valve Rocket Motor (MCD)
VVRS.......... Viscous Vortex Rate Sensor
VVS.......... Connellsville, PA [*Location identifier FAA*] (FAAL)
VVS.......... Sarah Lawrence College, Bronxville, NY [*OCLC symbol*] (OCLC)
VVS.......... Vein Ventures Ltd. [*Vancouver Stock Exchange symbol*]
VVS.......... Very Very Slightly Flawed [*Gems*]
VVS.......... Very, Very Small Inclusions [*Diamond clarity grade*]
VVS.......... Very Very Superior
VVS.......... Voenno-Vozdushnye Sily [*Army Air Forces*] [*Part of the MO*] [*Former USSR*]
VVS.......... Voice Verification System
VVSA.......... Velocity Vector Sensor Assembly
VVSO.......... Very, Very Superior Old [*Designation on brandy labels*]
VVSOP.......... Very, Very Superior Old Pale [*Designation on brandy labels*]
VVSS.......... Vertical Volute Spring Suspension [*Technical drawings*]
VVS-VMF..... Voenno-Vozdushnye Sily - Voenno-Morskogo Flota [*Naval Air Force*] [*Former USSR*]
VVT.......... Teachers College, Columbia University, New York, NY [*OCLC symbol*] (OCLC)
VVT.......... Variable Valve Timing [*Automotive*]
VVT.......... Velocity Variation Tube
VVT.......... Ventricular Pacing, Ventricular Sensing, Triggered Mode [*Pacemaker*] [*Cardiology*] (MEDA)
VVT.......... Venturi Vacuum Transducer [*Engineering*]
VVT.......... Visual-Verbal Test [*Psychology*]
VVTC.......... Vendor-Vendee Technical Committee
VVTS.......... Hochiminh/Tansonnhat [*Viet Nam*] [*ICAO location identifier*] (ICLI)
VVTV.......... ValueVision International, Inc. [*NASDAQ symbol*] (SAG)
VVTV.......... ValueVision Intl'A' [*NASDAQ symbol*] (TTSB)
VVU.......... New York University, Medical Center, New York, NY [*OCLC symbol*] (OCLC)
VVUS.......... Vivus, Inc. [*NASDAQ symbol*] (SAG)
VVV.......... Intercontinental Airlines Ltd. [*Nigeria*] [*ICAO designator*] (FAAC)
VVV.......... Ortonville, MN [*Location identifier FAA*] (FAAL)
VVV.......... Test Signal [*Telegraphy*] (IDOE)
VVV.......... Utica College of Syracuse University, Utica, NY [*OCLC symbol*] (OCLC)
VVV.......... Vacuum Vent Valve [*Automotive engineering*]
VVVH.......... Vinh [*Viet Nam*] [*ICAO location identifier*] (ICLI)
VVVT.......... Vungtau [*Viet Nam*] [*ICAO location identifier*] (ICLI)
VV/VTSHED... Variable Volume/Variable Temperature Sealed Housing for Evaporative Determination [*Automotive emissions testing*]
VVVV.......... Hanoi [*Viet Nam*] [*ICAO location identifier*] (ICLI)
VVW.......... Westchester Library System, Yonkers, NY [*OCLC symbol*] (OCLC)
VVWCA.......... Vintage Volkswagen Club of America (EA)
VV:WT.......... Vaccinia Virus: Wild Type [*Virology*]
VVX.......... Nassau Community College, Garden City, NY [*OCLC symbol*] (OCLC)
VVY.......... St. Luke's Hospital, Bolling Medical Library, New York, NY [*OCLC symbol*] (OCLC)
VVZ.......... Medical Library Center of New York, New York, NY [*OCLC symbol*] (OCLC)
VW.......... Air Concept [*Germany ICAO aircraft manufacturer identifier*] (ICAO)
VW.......... Ama-Flyg [*ICAO designator*] (AD)
VW.......... Early Warning Squadron [*Symbol*] (MCD)
Vw.......... Maximum Winch Launching Speed [*Gliders*] (AIA)
VW.......... Very Weak [*Spectral*]
VW.......... Very Worshipful
VW.......... Vessel Wall
VW.......... View (MCD)
vw.......... View (VRA)
VW.......... View
VW.......... Volkswagen [*German automobile*]
VW.......... Volts Working [*Electronics*] (ECII)
VW.......... Von Willebrand [*disease and Factor*] [*Hematology*] (DAVI)
VWA.......... Vacuum Window Assembly
VWA.......... Vendor Working Authority
VWA.......... Verband der Weiblichen Angestellten [*Association of Female Employees*] [*West Germany*]
VWA.......... Vintage Wireless Association [*British*]
VWA.......... Volkswagen of America (ECON)
VWA.......... Volume-Weighted Average [*Statistics*]
VWAC.......... Victorian Wheat Advisory Committee [*Australia*]
VWAM.......... Very Wide Area Mine (RDA)
VWB.......... Bronx Community College Library, Bronx, NY [*OCLC symbol*] (OCLC)
VWB.......... Visual Workbench [*Computer science*] (PCM)
VWC.......... Victorian Writers' Centre [*Australia*]
VWC.......... Villa Walsh College [*New Jersey*]
VWC.......... Vulcan Wheeled Carrier
VWCA.......... Volkswagen Club of America (EA)
VWCL.......... Volkswagen Caminhoes Limitada [*Brazil*]
VWD.......... Vereinigte Wirtschaftsdienste [*Press agency*] [*West Germany*]
VWD.......... Video-West Distributors Ltd. [*Vancouver Stock Exchange symbol*]
VWD.......... Vinyl Window and Door Institute (EA)
vWD.......... Von Willebrand's Disease [*Medicine*]
VWDU.......... Viewing Window Deicing Unit
VWE.......... Vanadium Wire Equilibration [*Nuclear energy*] (NRCH)
VWED.......... Vanadium Wire Equilibration Device [*Nuclear energy*] (NRCH)
VWF.......... Vehicle Work Flow
VWF.......... Vibration-Induced White Finger [*Medicine*]
vWf.......... Von Willebrand factor [*Also, vWF, VWF*] [*Hematology*]
VWFC.......... Very-Wide-Field Camera
VWG.......... Vibrating Wire Gauge (WDAA)
VWG.......... Vital Wheat Gluten [*Vegetable protein*]
VWGA.......... Vinifera Wine Growers Association (EA)
VWH.......... Vale of White Horse [*Hounds*]
VWH.......... Vertical Weld Head
VWHA.......... Vertical Weld Head Assembly
VWIA.......... Victorian Wine Industry Association [*Australia*]
VWL.......... College of William and Mary, Law School, Williamsburg, VA [*OCLC symbol*] (OCLC)
VWL.......... Variable Word Length
VWM.......... College of William and Mary, Williamsburg, VA [*OCLC symbol*] (OCLC)
VWM.......... Ventricular Wall Motion [*Cardiology*] (DAVI)
VWM.......... Volume-Weighted Mean [*Statistical technique*]
VWMP.......... Vietnam Women's Memorial Project (EA)
VWO.......... Valves Wide Open [*Nuclear energy*] (NRCH)
VWO.......... Woolsey, GA [*Location identifier FAA*] (FAAL)
VWOA.......... Veteran Wireless Operators Association (EA)
VWOA.......... Volkswagen of America
VWP.......... Variable Width Pulse
VWP.......... Vietnam Workers' Party [*Political party*] (PPW)
VWPI.......... Vacuum Wood Preservers Institute (EA)
VWQMN.......... Victorian Water Quality Monitoring Network [*State*] (EERA)
VWR.......... North Country Reference and Research Resources Council, Canton, NY [*OCLC symbol*] (OCLC)
VWR.......... Volkswirtschaftsrat [*Political Economy Bureau*] [*German*]
VWRF.......... Victorian Wheat Research Foundation [*Australia*]
VWRRC.......... Virginia Water Resources Research Center [*Virginia Polytechnic Institute and State University*] [*Research center*] (RCD)
VWRS.......... Vibrating Wire Rate Sensor
VWRSci.......... VWR Corp. [*Associated Press*] (SAG)
VWRX.......... VWR Corp. [*Seattle, WA*] [*NASDAQ symbol*] (NQ)
VWRX.......... VWR Scientific Products [*NASDAQ symbol*] (TTSB)
VWS.......... Valdez, AK [*Location identifier FAA*] (FAAL)
VWS.......... Variable Word Size
VWS.......... Ventilated Wet Suit (DNAB)
VWS.......... Views [*Postal Service standard*] (OPSA)
VWS.......... Virginia Woolf Society (EA)
VWS.......... Voice Warning System
vWS.......... Von Willebrand Syndrome [*Medicine*] (DMAA)
VWS.......... Vortex Wake System [*Aviation*] (DA)
VWSS.......... Vertical Wire Sky Screen (KSC)
VWSWCA..... Volkswagen Split Window Club of America (EA)
VWT.......... Victorian Women's Trust [*Australia*]
VWTA.......... Vintage White Truck Association (EA)
VW-TCA.......... Volkswagen Toy Collectors of America [*Defunct*] (EA)
VWU.......... Chincoteague Island, VA [*Location identifier FAA*] (FAAL)
VWV.......... Waterville, OH [*Location identifier FAA*] (FAAL)
VWW.......... Velocity of Wireless Waves
VWWI.......... Veterans of World War I of USA [*Defunct*] (EA)
VWY.......... Visway Transport, Inc. [*Toronto Stock Exchange symbol*]
VX.......... Aces [*ICAO designator*] (AD)
VX.......... Air Development Squadron [*Navy*]
VX.......... Experimental Squadron [*Symbol*] (MCD)
VX.......... Nerve Gas [*US Chemical Corps symbol*]
VX.......... Vanex Resources Ltd. [*Vancouver Stock Exchange symbol*]
VX.......... Vauxhall [*Automobile*] [*British*]
VX.......... Velocity along the X-Axis (NASA)
VX.......... Vertex [*Medicine*]
VX.......... Vivas, Care [*May You Live, Dear One*] [*Latin*]
VX.......... Voice
VX.......... Volume Unknown [*Medicine*]
VX-1.......... OPTEVFOR [*Operational Test and Evaluation Force*] Air Test and Evaluation Squadron One, Naval Air Station, Patuxent River, MD (CAAL)
VX-4.......... OPTEVFOR [*Operational Test and Evaluation Force*] Air Test and Evaluation Squadron Four, Naval Air Station, Pt. Mugu, CA (CAAL)
VX-5.......... OPTEVFOR [*Operational Test and Evaluation Force*] Air Test and Evaluation Squadron Five, Naval Weapons Center, China Lake, CA (CAAL)

VXA............ Harlem Hospital Center, Health Sciences Library, New York, NY [*OCLC symbol*] (OCLC)
VXC............ Lichinga [*Mozambique*] [*Airport symbol*] (OAG)
VXC............ Vila Cabral [*Mozambique*] [*Airport symbol*] (AD)
VXD............ New York University, College of Dentistry Library, New York, NY [*OCLC symbol*] (OCLC)
VxD............ Virtual Device Driver [*Computer science*] (PCM)
VXE............ Elmira College, Elmira, NY [*OCLC symbol*] (OCLC)
VXE............ Sao Vicente [*Cape Verde Islands*] [*Airport symbol*] (OAG)
VXF............ State University of New York, College of Environmental Science and Forestry, Syracuse, NY [*OCLC symbol*] (OCLC)
VXG............ New York Botanical Garden Library, Bronx, NY [*OCLC symbol*] (OCLC)
VXH............ Herkimer County Community College, Herkimer, NY [*OCLC symbol*] (OCLC)
VXI............ Iona College, New Rochelle, NY [*OCLC symbol*] (OCLC)
VXJ............ Jewish Theological Seminary of America, New York, NY [*OCLC symbol*] (OCLC)
VXL............ Albany Medical College, Schaffer Library of Health Sciences, Albany, NY [*OCLC symbol*] (OCLC)
VXM............ General Theological Seminary, St. Mark's Library, New York, NY [*OCLC symbol*] (OCLC)
VXN............ New York State Department of Health, Albany, NY [*OCLC symbol*] (OCLC)
VXO............ Houghton College, Houghton, NY [*OCLC symbol*] (OCLC)
VXO............ Variable Crystal Oscillator
VXO............ Vaxjo [*Sweden*] [*Airport symbol*] (OAG)
VXP............ State University of New York, College of Optometry, New York, NY [*OCLC symbol*] (OCLC)
VXR............ Rochester Museum and Science Center, Rochester, NY [*OCLC symbol*] (OCLC)
VXR............ Vertex Resources Ltd. [*Vancouver Stock Exchange symbol*]
VXT............ Tompkins-Cortland Community College, Dryden, NY [*OCLC symbol*] (OCLC)
VXU............ Chautauqua-Cattaraugus Library System, Jamestown, NY [*OCLC symbol*] (OCLC)
VXV............ Hudson Valley Community College, Troy, NY [*OCLC symbol*] (OCLC)
VXW............ Vassar College, Poughkeepsie, NY [*OCLC symbol*] (OCLC)
VXX............ Long Island University, C. W. Post Center, Greenvale, NY [*OCLC symbol*] (OCLC)
VXX............ Venturex Resources [*Vancouver Stock Exchange symbol*]
VXY............ Centro de Estudios Puertorriquenos, New York, NY [*OCLC symbol*] (OCLC)
VXZ............ Dowling College, Oakdale, NY [*OCLC symbol*] (OCLC)
VY............ Abelag Airways [*Belgium ICAO designator*] (ICDA)
VY............ Coral Air [*ICAO designator*] (AD)
VY............ Valley (ADA)
VY............ Various Years [*Bibliography*]
vy............ Various Years (WDMC)
VY............ Velocity along the Y-Axis (NASA)
VY............ Very (ROG)
VY............ Victualling Yard [*Obsolete Navy British*] (ROG)
VYA............ Molloy College, Rockville Centre, NY [*OCLC symbol*] (OCLC)
VYAN............ Victorian Youth Advocacy Network [*Australia*]
VYB............ St. Barnabas Medical Staff Library, Livingston, NJ [*OCLC symbol*] (OCLC)
VYB............ Vivian, Younger & Bond Ltd.
VYB............ Vyborg [*Former USSR Seismograph station code, US Geological Survey Closed*] (SEIS)
VYC............ Cornell University, Medical College, New York, NY [*OCLC symbol*] (OCLC)
VYC............ Yvic Airlines [*Nigeria*] [*ICAO designator*] (FAAC)
VYD............ Capital District Library Council, Troy, NY [*OCLC symbol*] (OCLC)
VYD............ Vryheid [*South Africa*] [*Airport symbol*] (OAG)
VYE............ Manhattanville College, Purchase, NY [*OCLC symbol*] (OCLC)
VYF............ Fordham University, Bronx, NY [*OCLC symbol*] (OCLC)
VYG............ Finger Lakes Library System, Ithaca, NY [*OCLC symbol*] (OCLC)
VYGS............ Vermont Yankee Generating Station [*Nuclear energy*] (NRCH)
VYI............ Kahului, HI [*Location identifier FAA*] (FAAL)
VYJ............ Martinsburg, WV [*Location identifier FAA*] (FAAL)
VYK............ Christ the King Seminary, East Aurora, NY [*OCLC symbol*] (OCLC)
VYK............ Colombia, SC [*Location identifier FAA*] (FAAL)
VYL............ Lehman College, Bronx, NY [*OCLC symbol*] (OCLC)
VYL............ Victorian Young Lawyers [*Australia*]
VYM............ United States Merchant Marine Academy, Kings Point, NY [*OCLC symbol*] (OCLC)
VYM............ Voyageur Minnesota Municipal Income [*AMEX symbol*] (SPSG)
VYM............ Voyageur Minn Muni Income III [*AMEX symbol*] (TTSB)
VYN............ Dallas-Fort Worth, TX [*Location identifier FAA*] (FAAL)
VYN............ Union Theological Seminary, New York, NY [*OCLC symbol*] (OCLC)
VYNP............ Vermont Yankee Nuclear Plant (NRCH)
VYNPS............ Vermont Yankee Nuclear Power Station (NRCH)
VYQ............ Upstate Medical Center, Syracuse, NY [*OCLC symbol*] (OCLC)
VYR............ Rome Air Development Center, Griffiss AFB, NY [*OCLC symbol*] (OCLC)
VyrexCp............ Vyrex Corp. [*Associated Press*] (SAG)
VYRX............ Vyrex Corp. [*NASDAQ symbol*] (TTSB)
VYRX............ Vyrex Corp. [*NASDAQ symbol*] (SAG)
VyrxCp............ Vyrex Corp. [*Associated Press*] (SAG)
VYRXU............ Vyrex Corp. Unit [*NASDAQ symbol*] (TTSB)
VYRXW............ Vyrex Corp. Wrrt [*NASDAQ symbol*] (TTSB)
VYS............ St. Bonaventure University, St. Bonaventure, NY [*OCLC symbol*] (OCLC)
VYS............ Visceral Yolk Sac [*Embryology*]
VYT............ Clarkson College of Technology, Potsdam, NY [*OCLC symbol*] (OCLC)
VYT............ Valley FTU [*British ICAO designator*] (FAAC)
VYTL............ Viatel, Inc. [*NASDAQ symbol*] (SAG)
VZ............ Aquatic Airlines [*ICAO designator*] (AD)
VZ............ Sisters of Charity of St. Vincent de Paul (TOCD)
VZ............ Varicella-Zoster [*Also, VZV*] [*A virus*]
V-Z............ Varicella-Zoster [*Antibody*] [*Immunology*] (DAVI)
VZ............ Velocity along the Z-Axis (NASA)
VZ............ Ventricular Zone [*Anatomy*]
VZ............ Virtual Zero
Vz............ Vizardinus [*Guizzardinus*] [*Deceased, 1222*] [*Authority cited in pre-1607 legal work*] (DSA)
Vz............ Zener Voltage [*Electronics*] (OA)
Vzar............ Vizardinus [*Guizzardinus*] [*Deceased, 1222*] [*Authority cited in pre-1607 legal work*] (DSA)
VZB............ State University of New York at Stony Brook, Health Sciences Library, Stony Brook, NY [*OCLC symbol*] (OCLC)
VZC............ Clinton-Essex-Franklin Library, Plattsburgh, NY [*OCLC symbol*] (OCLC)
VZD............ Vendor Zero Defect
VZE............ Mercy College, Dobbs Ferry, NY [*OCLC symbol*] (OCLC)
VZF............ St. Francis College, Brooklyn, NY [*OCLC symbol*] (OCLC)
VZG............ St. Joseph's College Library, Suffolk Campus, Patchogue, NY [*OCLC symbol*] (OCLC)
VZH............ Hartwick College, Oneonta, NY [*OCLC symbol*] (OCLC)
VZI............ Stony Brook Institute for Advanced Studies of World Religions, Stony Brook, NY [*OCLC symbol*] (OCLC)
VZIG............ Varicella-Zoster Immune Globulin
VZJ............ St. John Fisher College, Rochester, NY [*OCLC symbol*] (OCLC)
VZK............ King's College, Briarcliff Manor, NY [*OCLC symbol*] (OCLC)
VZL............ Pace University, Law Library, White Plains, NY [*OCLC symbol*] (OCLC)
VZL............ Vinzolidine [*Antineoplastic drug*]
VZM............ Margaret Woodbury Strong Museum, Rochester, NY [*OCLC symbol*] (OCLC)
VZM............ Von Zeipel Method
VZN............ College of New Rochelle, New Rochelle, NY [*OCLC symbol*] (OCLC)
VZO............ Coatesville, PA [*Location identifier FAA*] (FAAL)
VZP............ Pace University, New York, NY [*OCLC symbol*] (OCLC)
VZQ............ Pratt Institute, Brooklyn, NY [*OCLC symbol*] (OCLC)
VZR............ Roswell Park Memorial Institute, Buffalo, NY [*OCLC symbol*] (OCLC)
VZS............ Skidmore College, Saratoga Springs, NY [*OCLC symbol*] (OCLC)
VZS............ Valdez South [*Alaska*] [*Seismograph station code, US Geological Survey*] (SEIS)
VZT............ St. Joseph's College, Brooklyn, NY [*OCLC symbol*] (OCLC)
VZU............ Pace University, Pleasantville, Pleasantville, NY [*OCLC symbol*] (OCLC)
VZV............ College of Mount Saint Vincent, New York, NY [*OCLC symbol*] (OCLC)
VZV............ Varicella-Zoster Virus [*Also, VZ*]
VZW............ College of White Plains, White Plains, NY [*OCLC symbol*] (OCLC)
VZW............ Valdez West [*Alaska*] [*Seismograph station code, US Geological Survey*] (SEIS)
VZX............ Western New York Library Resources Council, Buffalo, NY [*OCLC symbol*] (OCLC)
VZY............ Montefiore Hospital, Bronx, NY [*OCLC symbol*] (OCLC)
VZZ............ International Museum of Photography, Eastman House, Rochester, NY [*OCLC symbol*] (OCLC)

W

By Acronym

W .... Acoustical Displacement (BARN)
W .... Angular Velocity (BARN)
W .... Climatic Data for the World [*A publication*]
W .... Coast Guard Ship [*When precedes vessel classification*] [*Navy symbol*]
W .... Dew [*Meteorology*] (BARN)
W .... Diameter of Driving-Wheel in Inches [*Railroad term*]
W .... Electrical Energy [*Symbol*] (DEN)
W .... Energy (IDOE)
w .... Flow Rate [*Heat transmission symbol*]
W .... Indefinite Ceiling [*Meteorology*] (BARN)
W .... Irradiance (BARN)
w .... Load per Unit of Length
W .... Mechanical Work of Breathing [*Medicine*] (DAVI)
W .... Microwatt (IAA)
W .... Requires an Engineer [*Search and rescue symbol that can be stamped in sand or snow*]
W .... Total Load
w----- .... Tropics [*MARC geographic area code Library of Congress*] (LCCP)
W .... Tryptophan [*One-letter symbol; see Trp*]
W .... Tungsten [*Chemical element*] (DOG)
W .... Underwater [*JETDS nomenclature*]
W .... Waffle [*Used in correcting manuscripts, etc.*]
W .... Wages [*Economics*]
W .... Waist (ADA)
W .... Wait Time [*Computer science*]
W .... Wales
W .... Walk [*Baseball*]
W .... Wall
W .... Wallace Laboratories [*Research code symbol*]
W .... Waltz [*Music*]
W .... Wander AG [*Switzerland*] [*Research code symbol*]
W .... Wanderer Books [*Publisher's imprint*]
W .... Wanting
W .... War
W .... Warden
w .... Wardrobe (WDMC)
W .... Wardroom [*Aerospace*]
W .... Warehouse
W .... Warhead [*Nuclear*] (NG)
W .... Warm
W .... Warner-Lambert Pharmaceutical Co. [*Research code symbol*]
W .... Warning [*Railroad signal arm*] [*British*]
W .... Warning Area [*Followed by identification*]
W .... Warrant [*A document entitling holder to purchase a given issue of stock*] [*Investment term*]
W .... Washington Reports [*1890-1939*] [*A publication*] (DLA)
W .... Waste
W .... Watch Time
W .... Water
W .... Waterloo [*Army British*] (ROG)
W .... Watermeyer's Cape Of Good Hope Supreme Court Reports [*A publication*] (DLA)
W .... Water Point [*British Waterways Board sign*]
W .... Water Vapor Content
W .... Watt [*Symbol*] [*SI unit of power*] (GPO)
w .... Watt (WDMC)
W .... Wattle [*Ornithology*]
W .... Watt Meter (IAA)
W .... Watt's Pennsylvania Reports [*A publication*] (DLA)
W .... Waveguide (SAA)
W .... Wave Height Correction
W .... Weak [*Spectral*]
W+ .... Weakly Positive [*Laboratory science*] (DAVI)
W .... Weather
W .... Weather Aircraft Equipped with Meteorological Gear [*Designation for all US military aircraft*]
W .... Weather Review [*A publication*]
W .... Web
W .... Weber [*Hearing test*] (MAE)
W .... Weber Fraction [*Psychology*]
W .... Wednesday
W .... Week
w .... Week (WDMC)
W .... Weekend Travel [*Also, Z*] [*Airline fare code*]
w .... Weekly
w .... Weekly (WDMC)
W .... Weekly Dose [*Medicine*]
W .... Weeping [*Shrub*]
W .... Wehnelt [*A unit of roentgen ray hardness*] (AAMN)
W .... Weight
w .... Weight (WDMC)
W .... Weld (DAS)
W .... Welding Program [*Association of Independent Colleges and Schools specialization code*]
W .... Welsh [*or Welch*]
W .... Wendell's Reports [*1826-41*] [*New York*] [*A publication*] (DLA)
W .... Wenig Fine [*Latin*] (DAVI)
W .... Wesleyan
W .... West [*or Western*]
W .... Westcoast Energy, Inc. [*Vancouver Stock Exchange symbol*]
W .... Westcoast Energy, Inc. [*Toronto Stock Exchange symbol*]
W .... Westerhout [*Astronomy*]
W .... Western Airlines (MHDW)
W .... Westinghouse [*as in "Group W"*]
W .... West Point, NY [*Mint mark when appearing on US coins*]
W .... Westvaco Corp. [*NYSE symbol*] (SPSG)
W .... Wet
W .... Wet Dew
W .... Wheaton's Reports [*14-25 United States*] [*A publication*] (DLA)
W .... Wheeled [*Vehicles*] (NATG)
W .... Whip
W .... Whiskey [*Phonetic alphabet*] [*International*] (DSUE)
W .... White [*Light, buoy, beacon*]
w .... White (VRA)
W .... White (DAVI)
W .... White Cell [*Medicine*] (AAMN)
W .... White Return [*Round trip fare for specified period*] [*British*]
W .... Whole [*Response*] [*Medicine*]
W .... Whole Word Designator [*Computer science*]
W .... Whorls and Compounds [*Fingerprint description*]
W .... Wicked (DAS)
W .... Wicket
w .... Wicket (ODBW)
w .... Wide (ODBW)
W .... Wide
w .... Wide (WDMC)
W .... Widow [*or Widower*]
W .... Widowed (DAVI)
W .... Width
w .... Width (WDMC)
w .... Wife (WDMC)
W .... Wife
W .... Wilderness [*State*] (EERA)
W .... Will Advise [*Business term*]
W .... Wille [*Will Factor*] [*Psychology*]
W .... Will Factor [*Psychology*]
W .... William [*Phonetic alphabet*] [*Royal Navy World War I Pre-World War II*] [*World War II*] (DSUE)
W .... William (King of England) (DLA)
W .... Wilson's [*or Willson's*] Reports [*Texas Civil Cases, Court of Appeals*] [*A publication*] (DLA)
W .... Win [*Sports*]
W .... Winch (DS)
W .... Wind [*In reference to wind velocity*]
W .... Window (NASA)
W .... Windward [*Botany*]
W .... Wins [*Sports*]
W .... Winter [*Vessel load line mark*]
W .... Wire
W .... Wireless [*Communication*] (IAA)
W .... Wisconsin Reports [*A publication*] (DLA)
W .... With
w .... With (WDMC)
w/ .... With (VRA)
W .... Withdrawal
W .... Within (WGA)
W .... Without Voice Facilities on Range or Radiobeacon Frequency
W .... Witwatersrand Local Division Reports [*South Africa*] [*A publication*] (DLA)
W .... Wolfram [*Tungsten*] [*Chemical element*]
W .... Woman (ADA)

W........ Women's Reserve, Unlimited Service [*USNR officer designation*]
W........ Won [*Sports statistics*]
W........ Won [*Monetary unit*] [*South Korea*]
W........ Wood
W........ Wooden [*Shipping*] (ROG)
W........ Woodfree [*Paper*] (DGA)
W........ Woody Plant [*Botany*]
W........ Word
W........ Word Fluency (DAVI)
W........ Work [*or w*] [*Symbol IUPAC*]
W........ Workmen's Compensation [*Insurance*]
W........ World
w........ WORLDSCALE [*Worldwide Tanker Nominal Freight Scale*] (DS)
W........ Worshipful [*Freemasonry*]
W........ Wright's Ohio Reports [*1831-34*] [*A publication*] (DLA)
W........ Write
W........ Writer Officer [*British military*]
W........ Wrong
W........ Wyoming Reports [*A publication*] (DLA)
W2........ Second Statute of Westminster [*A publication*] (DSA)
W-2........ Wage and Tax Statement [*IRS*]
W2........ William II [*German emperor and king of Prussia, 1888-1918*] (DSUE)
W 2d........ Washington State Reports, Second Series [*A publication*] (DLA)
W3........ WinWhatWhere (PCM)
W3........ World-Wide Web [*Information service*] [*European Organization for Nuclear Research*] (ECON)
W3C........ World Wide Web Consortium [*Internet*]
W-4........ Employee's Withholding Allowance Certificate [*IRS*]
W-4A........ Wage Withholding Form [*Revised version*] [*IRS*]
W4D........ Worth Four-Dot Test [*Ophthalmology*]
WA........ Appleton Public Library, Appleton, WI [*Library symbol Library of Congress*] (LCLS)
WA........ Independent Watchmen's Association
WA........ Wadsworth Athneneum [*Hartford, CT*]
WA........ Wage Record [*Social Security Administration*] (OICC)
WA........ Wagner Act of 1935 (WYGK)
WA........ Wainscot
WA........ Waiver
WA........ Walking Association (EA)
WA........ War Aims [*British*]
WA........ Warbirds of America [*Later, WB*] [*An association*] (EA)
WA........ Warm Air
W/A........ Warrant of Arrest
wa........ Wash (VRA)
WA........ Washer
WA........ Washington [*State*] [*Postal code*]
Wa........ Washington Reports [*A publication*] (DLA)
Wa........ Washington State Library, Olympia, WA [*Library symbol Library of Congress*] (LCLS)
WA........ Wassmer Aviation [*France ICAO aircraft manufacturer identifier*] (ICAO)
WA........ Water Agar [*Microbiology*]
WA........ Water Authority [*British*] (DCTA)
WA........ Watertown Arsenal [*Massachusetts*] [*Army*]
Wa........ Watts' Reports [*1890-1939*] [*A publication*] (DLA)
WA........ Wave Analyzer (IAA)
WA........ Waveform Analyzer
WA........ Weapon Armourer [*British military*] (DMA)
WA........ Weapons Analyst [*British military*] (DMA)
WA........ Weapons Assignment (NVT)
WA........ Weather Almanac [*A publication*]
WA........ Weather Atlas of the United States [*A publication*]
WA........ Wedge Action [*British military*] (DMA)
WA........ Weekly Announcements
WA........ Weighted Average [*Accounting*]
WA........ Weizmann Israel Archives [*Rehovoth*] (BJA)
WA........ Welfare Administration [*Became Social and Rehabilitation Service*] [*HEW*]
WA........ Wellness Associates (EA)
Wa........ Wellsiania [*An association*] (EA)
WA........ West Africa
WA........ Western Airlines, Inc. [*ICAO designator*]
WA........ Western Allegheny Railroad (IIA)
WA........ Western Approaches [*to Great Britain and Ireland*] [*Obsolete*]
WA........ Western Area
WA........ Western Australia [*State*] (EERA)
WA........ [*The*] Western Railway of Alabama [*AAR code*]
WA........ Westminster Abbey [*London*]
WA........ When Awake
WA........ While Awake (CPH)
WA........ Wide Angle [*Photography*]
WA........ Wide Angle (WDMC)
WA........ Wideband Amplifier
WA........ Will Adjust (AABC)
wa........ Will Advise (HGAA)
WA........ Williams Act [*1968*]
WA........ Wing Attack [*Netball*]
WA........ Wire Armored [*Cables*]
WA........ Wire Assembly (MSA)
WA........ Wire Association [*Later, WAI*]
WA........ With Answers
WA........ With Average [*Insurance*]
WA........ Withholding Agent (DLA)
WA........ Wohl Associates [*Bala Cynwyd, PA*] [*Telecommunications*] (TSSD)
WA........ Woman's Auxiliary (DAVI)
WA........ Women's Reserve, Aviation Nonflying Duties [*USNR officer designation*]
WA........ Womenwealth Ambika [*An association British*] (EAIO)
WA........ Woodfree Antique [*Paper*] (DGA)
WA........ Woolknit Associates (EA)
WA........ Woolwich Armstrong Gun
WA........ Word Add
WA........ Word After [*Message handling*]
WA........ Work Assignment (MCD)
WA........ Work Authorization (MCD)
WA........ Workers Anonymous [*Mythical organization created by columnist Arthur Hoppe that helps hard working individuals*]
WA........ Workmanship Assurance
WA........ Worksafe Australia
WA........ Workshop Assembly [*Torpedo*]
WA........ World Bank Atlas [*Monetary conversion rate*] (ECON)
WA........ Wright Aeronautical Corp. (KSC)
WA........ Writing Ability
WA........ Writing Academy (EA)
WA1........ Wongan Hills [*Australia Seismograph station code, US Geological Survey*] (SEIS)
WA2........ Wagin [*Australia Seismograph station code, US Geological Survey*] (SEIS)
Wa 2d........ Washington State Reports, Second Series [*A publication*] (DLA)
WA3........ Talbot Brook [*Australia Seismograph station code, US Geological Survey*] (SEIS)
WaA........ Aberdeen Public Library, Aberdeen, WA [*Library symbol Library of Congress*] (LCLS)
WAA........ Wabash Motor Freight Tariff Association, Springfield IL [*STAC*]
WAA........ Wales [*Alaska*] [*Airport symbol*] (OAG)
WAA........ Wales, AK [*Location identifier FAA*] (FAAL)
WAA........ War Assets Administration [*For disposal of US surplus war property*] [*Post-World War II*]
WAA........ Warden's Association of America [*Later, NAAWS*] (EA)
WAA........ Waris [*Papua New Guinea*] [*Seismograph station code, US Geological Survey*] (SEIS)
WAA........ Wartime Aircraft Activity (AFM)
Wa A........ Washington Appellate Reports [*A publication*] (DLA)
WAA........ Water-Augmented Air Jet
WAA........ Water Authorities Association [*British*] (ECON)
WAA........ Water Authorities Association (AIE)
WAA........ Watermark Association of Artisans (EA)
WAA........ Welded Aluminum Alloy
WAA........ West Australian Airways (ADA)
WAA........ Western Amateur Astronomers (EA)
WAA........ Western Awning Association [*Later, NPEA*] (EA)
WAA........ Wide-Aperture Array (MCD)
WAA........ Wien Air Alaska [*Air carrier designation symbol*]
WAA........ Women's Action Alliance (EA)
WAA........ Woolclassers' Association of Australia
WAA........ Worked All America [*Amateur radio*] [*Contacted at least one station in all counties*] (IAA)
WAA........ Worker Adjustment Assistance
WAA........ World Aluminum Abstracts [*Aluminum Association*] [*Information service or system A publication*] (IID)
WAA........ World Atlatl Association (EA)
WAA........ Writing Assistants' Association [*A union*] [*British*]
WAAA........ Ujung Pandang/Hasanuddin [*Indonesia*] [*ICAO location identifier*] (ICLI)
WAAA........ Walleye Anglers Association of America [*Defunct*] (EA)
WAAA........ Western Armenian Athletic Association (EA)
WAAA........ Winston-Salem, NC [*AM radio station call letters*]
WAA(A)........ Women's Action Alliance (Australia)
WAAA........ Women's Amateur Athletic Association [*British*] (DBA)
WAAB........ Bau Bau/Betoambari [*Indonesia*] [*ICAO location identifier*] (ICLI)
WAABI........ National Women's Association of Allied Beverage Industries (EA)
WAAC........ Valdosta, GA [*FM radio station call letters*]
WAAC........ War Artists' Advisory Committee [*British military*] (DMA)
WAAC........ West African Airways Corp.
WAAC........ Western Association for Art Conservation (EA)
WAAC........ Women's Army Auxiliary Corps [*Name later changed to WAC*] [*World War II*]
WAAC........ Women's Art Association of Canada [*1887, Lyceum Club and Women's Art Association from 1930*] (NGC)
WAAC........ Working Ampere Alternating Current (IAA)
WAAC........ World Academy of Arts and Culture (EA)
WAACC's Motor Ind... WAACC's [*Western Australian Automobile Chamber of Commerce*] Motor Industry [*A publication*]
WAACP........ Western Atlantic Airlift Command Post [*Navy*] (DNAB)
WAACS........ Western Airways and Air Communications Service (IAA)
WAAD........ Tice, FL [*FM radio station call letters*]
WAAD........ Westinghouse Air Arm Division
WAADA........ Western Australian Alcohol and Drug Authority
WAADS........ Washington Air Defense Sector [*ADC*]
WAAE........ World Association for Adult Education
WAAECG........ Western Australian Aboriginal Education Consultative Group
WAAE-FM........ New Bern, NC [*FM radio station call letters*] (RBYB)
WAAF........ Women's Auxiliary Air Force [*Functioned under direct command of RAF*] [*World War II British*]
WAAF........ Worcester, MA [*FM radio station call letters*]
WAAFB........ Walker Air Force Base (AAG)
WAAG........ Galesburg, IL [*FM radio station call letters*]
WaAG........ Grays Harbor College, Aberdeen, WA [*Library symbol Library of Congress*] (LCLS)
WAAG........ Malimpung [*Indonesia*] [*ICAO location identifier*] (ICLI)

WAAG.......... Western Australian Art Gallery
WAAGA........ Western Australian Asparagus Growers' Association
WAAH.......... Houghton, MI [*FM radio station call letters*]
WAAI........... Hurlock, MD [*FM radio station call letters*]
WAAI........... Malili [*Indonesia*] [*ICAO location identifier*] (ICLI)
WAAIC.......... Women's Association of the African Independent Churches
WAAJ........... Mamuju/Tampa Padang [*Indonesia*] [*ICAO location identifier*] (ICLI)
WAAJ........... Water-Augmented Air Jet
WAAJ-FM.... Benton, KY [*FM radio station call letters*] (RBYB)
WAAK.......... Dallas, NC [*AM radio station call letters*]
WAAL........... Binghamton, NY [*FM radio station call letters*]
WAAL........... Ponggaluku [*Indonesia*] [*ICAO location identifier*] (ICLI)
WaAlVA....... United States Veterans Administration Hospital, American Lake, WA [*Library symbol Library of Congress*] (LCLS)
WAAM.......... Ann Arbor, MI [*AM radio station call letters*]
WAAM.......... Masamba/Andi Jemma [*Indonesia*] [*ICAO location identifier*] (ICLI)
WAAM.......... Wide-Area Antiarmor Munitions [*Military*] (MCD)
WAAMA....... Woman's Auxiliary to the American Medical Association [*Later, AMAA*] (EA)
WAAMAC..... Weight, Alignment, and Mass Center Determination Equipment (AAG)
WAAMH....... Western Australian Association for Mental Health
WAAMMS.... Women's Auxiliary of the American Merchant Marine [*World War II*]
WaAn........... Anacortes Public Library, Anacortes, WA [*Library symbol Library of Congress*] (LCLS)
WAAN.......... West African Archaeological Newsletter [*A publication*]
WAAN.......... Wide-Area AppleTalk Network [*Telecommunications*]
WaAnH........ Island Hospital, Anacortes, WA [*Library symbol*] [*Library of Congress*] (LCLS)
WAAO.......... Andalusia, AL [*FM radio station call letters*]
WAAOT........ Western Australian Association of Occupational Therapists
WAAP.......... Burlington, NC [*Television station call letters*]
WAAP.......... Kolaka/Pomalaa [*Indonesia*] [*ICAO location identifier*] (ICLI)
WAAP.......... World Association for Animal Production [*Rome, Italy*] (EAIO)
WAAPA........ Western Australian Academy of the Performing Arts
WAAPC........ Western Australian Apple and Pear Council
WAAPM....... Wide-Area Antipersonnel Mine [*Military*]
WAAPM-CBU... Wide Area Antipersonnel Munition Cluster Bomb Unit (VNW)
WAAR.......... Raha/Sugi Manuru [*Indonesia*] [*ICAO location identifier*] (ICLI)
WAAR.......... Wartime Aircraft Activity Reporting [*System*]
WaArI.......... Indian Ridge Treatment Center, Staff Library, Arlington, WA [*Library symbol Library of Congress*] (LCLS)
WaArI-R....... Indian Ridge Treatment Center, Resident Library, Arlington, WA [*Library symbol Library of Congress*] (LCLS)
WAAS.......... Soroako [*Indonesia*] [*ICAO location identifier*] (ICLI)
WAAS.......... Warning and Attack Assessment (MCD)
WAAS.......... Wide-Area Active Surveillance [*Military*] (MCD)
WAAS.......... Wide-Area Augmentation System [*Navigation systems*]
WAAS.......... Women's Auxiliary Army Service [*British*]
WAAS.......... World Academy of Art and Science [*Solna, Sweden*] (EA)
WAASC........ Women's Auxiliary Army Service Corps [*British*]
WAAT.......... Makale/Pongtiku [*Indonesia*] [*ICAO location identifier*] (ICLI)
WAAT.......... Tiptonville, TN [*FM radio station call letters*]
WAATS........ Weights Analysis for Advanced Transportation Systems [*NASA*]
WaAu........... Auburn Public Library, Auburn, WA [*Library symbol Library of Congress*] (LCLS)
WAAU.......... Kendari/Wolter Monginsidi [*Indonesia*] [*ICAO location identifier*] (ICLI)
WaAuG........ Green River Community College, Auburn, WA [*Library symbol Library of Congress*] (LCLS)
WAAV.......... Leland, NC [*AM radio station call letters*]
WAAV-FM.... Leland, NC [*FM radio station call letters*] (RBYB)
WAAV-FM.... Leland, NC [*FM radio station call letters*] (RBYB)
WAAVP........ World Association for the Advancement of Veterinary Parasitology [*Thessaloniki, Greece*] (EAIO)
WAAW.......... Williston, SC [*FM radio station call letters*]
WAAX.......... Gadsden, AL [*AM radio station call letters*]
WAAY.......... Huntsville, AL [*Television station call letters*]
WAAZ.......... Crestview, FL [*FM radio station call letters*]
WAAZ.......... Ujung Pandang [*Indonesia*] [*ICAO location identifier*] (ICLI)
WAB............ Aero Industries, Inc. [*ICAO designator*] (FAAC)
WAB............ Wabag [*Papua New Guinea*] [*Seismograph station code, US Geological Survey*] (SEIS)
WAB............ Wabag [*New Guinea*] [*Airport symbol*] (AD)
WAB............ Wabash Railroad System [*AAR code Obsolete*]
WAB............ Waffenabwurfbehaelter [*Parachute Weapons Container*] [*German military - World War II*]
WAB............ Wage Adjustment Board [*World War II*]
WAB............ Wage Appeals Board [*Department of Labor*]
WAB............ Water-Activated Battery
WAB............ Weapons Allocation Branch (SAA)
WAB............ Western Actuarial Bureau [*Later, ISO*] (EA)
WAB............ Western Aphasia Battery [*Neuropsychology test*]
WAB............ Westinghouse Air Brake [*NYSE symbol*] (TTSB)
WAB............ Westinghouse Air Brake Co. [*NYSE symbol*] (SAG)
WAB............ When Authorized By
WAB............ Wine Advisory Board [*Later, WAG*] (EA)
WAB............ Work Allotment Board [*New Deal*]
WAB............ World Association for Buiatrics [*Hanover, Federal Republic of Germany*] (EAIO)
WABA.......... Aguadilla, PR [*AM radio station call letters*]
WABA.......... Welsh Amateur Boxing Association [*British*] (DBA)
WABA.......... Western Australian Bar Association
WABA.......... Women's American Basketball Association [*Defunct*] (EA)
Waban......... Waban, Inc. [*Associated Press*] (SAG)
Wabash....... Wabash National Corp. [*Associated Press*] (SAG)
WABASH VLY ALSA... Wabash Valley Area Library Services Authority [*Library network*]
WaBB........... Bellevue Community College, Bellevue, WA [*Library symbol Library of Congress*] (LCLS)
WABB.......... Biak/Frans Kaisiepo [*Indonesia*] [*ICAO location identifier*] (ICLI)
WABB.......... Mobile, AL [*AM radio station call letters*]
WABB-FM.... Mobile, AL [*FM radio station call letters*]
WaBC........... City University Library Resource Center, Bellevue, WA [*Library symbol*] [*Library of Congress*] (LCLS)
WABC.......... New York, NY [*AM radio station call letters*]
WABC.......... WestAmerica Bancorp [*NASDAQ symbol*] (SAG)
WABC.......... Westamerica Bancorporation [*NASDAQ symbol*] (TTSB)
WABC.......... Western Australian Ballet Company
WABC.......... Western Australian Bible College
WABCO........ Westinghouse Air Brake Co.
WABC-TV..... New York, NY [*Television station call letters*]
WABD.......... Fort Campbell, KY [*AM radio station call letters*]
WABD.......... Moanamani [*Indonesia*] [*ICAO location identifier*] (ICLI)
WABE.......... Atlanta, GA [*FM radio station call letters*]
WaBe........... Bellingham Public Library, Bellingham, WA [*Library symbol Library of Congress*] (LCLS)
WABE.......... Western Association of Broadcast Engineers [*Canada*]
WaBeAG...... Office of Attorney General, State of Washington, Bellingham Regional Office, Bellingham, WA [*Library symbol*] [*Library of Congress*] (LCLS)
WABEC........ Western Australian Business Education College
WaBeCo....... Whatcom County Public Library, Bellingham, WA [*Library symbol Library of Congress*] (LCLS)
WaBeCoL..... Whatcom County Law Library, Bellingham, WA [*Library symbol*] [*Library of Congress*] (LCLS)
WaBeSJ....... Saint Joseph Hospital, Bellingham, WA [*Library symbol Library of Congress*] (LCLS)
WaBeSL....... Saint Luke's Hospital, Bellingham, WA [*Library symbol Library of Congress*] (LCLS)
WaBeW........ Western Washington State College [*Later, WWU*], Bellingham, WA [*Library symbol Library of Congress*] (LCLS)
WABF.......... Fairhope, AL [*AM radio station call letters*]
WABF.......... Numfor/Jemburwo [*Indonesia*] [*ICAO location identifier*] (ICLI)
WaBfM........ Mission Creek Youth Camp, Staff Library, Belfair, WA [*Library symbol Library of Congress*] (LCLS)
WaBfM-R..... Mission Creek Youth Camp, Resident Library, Belfair, WA [*Library symbol Library of Congress*] (LCLS)
WABG.......... Greenwood, MS [*AM radio station call letters*]
WABG.......... Waghete [*Indonesia*] [*ICAO location identifier*] (ICLI)
WaBGS........ Church of Jesus Christ of Latter-Day Saints, Genealogical Society Library, Bellevue Branch, Bellevue, WA [*Library symbol Library of Congress*] (LCLS)
WABG-TV..... Greenwood, MS [*Television station call letters*]
WABH.......... Bath, NY [*AM radio station call letters*]
WABI........... Bangor, ME [*AM radio station call letters*]
WABI........... Nabire [*Indonesia*] [*ICAO location identifier*] (ICLI)
WABI........... Western Australian Biographical Index [*A publication*] (APTA)
WABI........... Windows Application Binary Interactive [*Computer science*]
WABI-TV...... Bangor, ME [*Television station call letters*]
WABJ........... Adrian, MI [*AM radio station call letters*]
WABK-FM.... Gardiner, ME
WABL........... Amite, LA [*AM radio station call letters*]
WABL........... Ilaga [*Indonesia*] [*ICAO location identifier*] (ICLI)
WABLC......... Wilmington Area Biomedical Libraries [*Library network*]
WABM.......... Birmingham, AL [*Television station call letters*]
WABN.......... Abingdon, VA [*AM radio station call letters*]
WABN.......... Kokonau [*Indonesia*] [*ICAO location identifier*] (ICLI)
WABN-FM.... Abingdon, VA [*FM radio station call letters*]
WABO.......... Serui/Sujarwo Condronegoro [*Indonesia*] [*ICAO location identifier*] (ICLI)
WABO.......... Waynesboro, MS [*AM radio station call letters*]
WaBODP...... Orcale Data Publishing, Bellevue, WA [*Library symbol*] [*Library of Congress*] (LCLS)
WABO-FM.... Waynesboro, MS [*FM radio station call letters*]
WaBOH........ Overlake Hospital, Medical Library, Bellevue, WA [*Library symbol Library of Congress*] (LCLS)
WaBoIS........ Info-Search/NW, Bothell, WA [*Library symbol*] [*Library of Congress*] (LCLS)
WaBP........... Puget Sound Power and Light Co., Bellevue, WA [*Library symbol Library of Congress*] (LCLS)
WABP.......... Timika/Tembagapura [*Indonesia*] [*ICAO location identifier*] (ICLI)
Wa-BPH....... Washington Regional Library for the Blind and Physically Handicapped, Seattle, WA [*Library symbol Library of Congress*] (LCLS)
WABQ.......... Cleveland, OH [*AM radio station call letters*]
WaBr........... Kitsap Regional Library, Bremerton, WA [*Library symbol Library of Congress*] (LCLS)
WABR.......... Tifton, GA [*FM radio station call letters*]
WABR.......... West Asia Blocking Ridge [*Meteorology*]
WaBrH......... Harrison Memorial Hospital, Bremerton, WA [*Library symbol Library of Congress*] (LCLS)
WaBrNP....... United States Navy, Puget Sound Naval Shipyard, Engineering Library, Bremerton, WA [*Library symbol Library of Congress*] (LCLS)
WaBrNR....... United States Navy, Naval Regional Medical Center, Bremerton, WA [*Library symbol Library of Congress*] (LCLS)
WaBrNS....... United States Navy, Naval Submarine Base, Bangor Library, Bremerton, WA [*Library symbol Library of Congress*] (LCLS)
WaBrO......... Olympic College, Bremerton, WA [*Library symbol Library of Congress*] (LCLS)

WaBrOC....... Olympic Center, Bremerton, WA [*Library symbol Library of Congress*] (LCLS)
WABS.......... Arlington, VA [*AM radio station call letters*]
WaBS........... Bellevue School District, Instructional Materials Center, Bellevue, WA [*Library symbol Library of Congress*] (LCLS)
WABSIH....... Society for Italic Handwriting, Western American Branch [*Later, WASIH*] (EA)
WABT........... Dundee, IL [*FM radio station call letters*]
WABT........... Enarotali [*Indonesia*] [*ICAO location identifier*] (ICLI)
WABT........... Western Aphasia Battery Test [*Speech and language therapy*] (DAVI)
WABTOC...... When Authorized by the Oversea Commander [*Military*]
WABU.......... Biak/Manuhua [*Indonesia*] [*ICAO location identifier*] (ICLI)
WABU.......... Boston, MA [*Television station call letters*]
WaBucR....... Rainier School, Staff Library, Buckley, WA [*Library symbol Library of Congress*] (LCLS)
WaBucR-R... Rainier School, Resident Library, Buckley, WA [*Library symbol Library of Congress*] (LCLS)
WABW......... Pelham, GA [*Television station call letters*]
WABW......... Waren [*Indonesia*] [*ICAO location identifier*] (ICLI)
WABY.......... Albany, NY [*AM radio station call letters*]
WABY-FM.... Ravena, NY [*FM radio station call letters*] (RBYB)
WABZ........... Albemarle, NC [*FM radio station call letters*]
WABZ........... Biak [*Indonesia*] [*ICAO location identifier*] (ICLI)
WAC............ Waca [*Ethiopia*] [*Airport symbol*] (OAG)
WAC............ Wage Analysis and Control (MHDB)
WAC............ Wagner Computer (IAA)
WAC............ Wake Analysis and Control (MCD)
WAC............ War Assets Corp. [*Post-World War II*] [*Succeeded by War Assets Administration*]
WAC............ Warnaco Group [*NYSE symbol*] (SPSG)
WAC............ Warnaco Group'A' [*NYSE symbol*] (TTSB)
WAC............ Washington Administrative Code [*A publication*] (AAGC)
WAC............ Waste Acceptance Criteria (GAAI)
WAC............ Weak Affinity Chromatography [*Analytical chemistry*]
WAC............ Weapon Arming Computer (MCD)
WAC............ Weapons Assignment Console
WAC............ Weber Aircraft Co.
WAC............ Weighted Average Coupon [*Finance*]
WAC............ Welsh Arts Council (EAIO)
WAC............ West Africa Command [*World War II*]
WAC............ West Africa Committee (EA)
WAC............ Western Archeological Center [*Department of the Interior*] (GRD)
WAC............ Western Athletic Conference (EA)
WAC............ Western Australian Club
WAC............ Wheat Advisory Committee (Western Australia)
WAC............ Wide-Open Throttle Air-Conditioning Cut-Off Switch [*Automotive engineering*]
WAC............ Wildlife Advisory Committee [*Tasmania, Australia*]
WAC............ Willys Air Cooled [*Automotive engineering*]
WAC............ Wolfe Angel Committee [*Defunct*] (EA)
WAC............ Women's Advisory Committee [*Trades Union Congress*] [*British*] (DCTA)
WAC............ Women's Aerobic Circuit [*Exercise regimen at some health spas*]
WAC............ Women's Army Corps [*Formerly, WAAC*] [*Abolished, 1978*] (GPO)
WAC............ Women's Auxiliary Corps [*British*] (DAS)
WAC............ Work Accomplishment Code [*Military*] (AFIT)
WAC............ Work Activities Center
WAC............ Work Assessment Course (AIE)
WAC............ Work Assignment Card (MCD)
WAC............ Worked All Continents [*Contacted at least one station on all continents*] [*Amateur radio*]
WAC............ Worked All Countries [*Contacted at least one station in all countries*] [*Amateur radio*] (IAA)
WAC............ Working Alternating Current (DEN)
WAC............ World Aeronautical Chart (FAAC)
WAC............ World Affairs Center for the United States [*Later, FPA*]
WAC............ World Air Network Co. Ltd. [*Japan ICAO designator*] (FAAC)
WAC............ World Archeological Congress
WAC............ World Area Code (MCD)
WAC............ World Assistance Corps [*Paris, France*] (EAIO)
WAC............ Wright Aeronautical Corp. (MCD)
WAC............ Write Address Counter
WaCa........... Camas Public Library, Camas, WA [*Library symbol*] [*Library of Congress*] (LCLS)
WACA.......... Walnut Canyon National Monument
WACA.......... West African Court of Appeal, Selected Judgments [*A publication*] (DLA)
WACA.......... Western Agricultural Chemicals Association (EA)
WACA.......... Winchester Arms Collectors Association (EA)
WACA.......... Women's Apparel Chains Associations [*Defunct*] (EA)
WACA.......... World Airlines Clubs Association [*Montreal, PQ*] (EAIO)
WACA.......... World Association of Center Associates (EA)
WACAAI....... Women's Africa Committee of the African-American Institute (EA)
WACAS........ Wave and Current Advisory Service [*British*]
WACASC...... West African Consolidated Administrative Service Center [*Foreign Service*]
WACB.......... Taylorsville, NC [*AM radio station call letters*]
WACB.......... Women's Army Classification Battery (AABC)
WACB.......... World Association for Christian Broadcasting (IAA)
WaCbC........ Clallam Bay Correctional Center, Clallam Bay, WA [*Library symbol*] [*Library of Congress*] (LCLS)
WACC.......... Hialeah, FL [*AM radio station call letters*] (RBYB)
WACC.......... Warning and Caution Computer [*Aviation*] (MCD)
WACC.......... Washing Corrosion Control (MCD)
WACC.......... Weighted Average Cost of Capital [*Accounting*] (ADA)
WACC.......... WestAmerica Corp. [*NASDAQ symbol*] (SAG)
WACC.......... World Africa Chamber of Commerce (EA)
WACC.......... World Association for Christian Communication
WACCC........ Worldwide Air Cargo Commodity Classification (DS)
WACCI......... Western Australian Chamber of Commerce and Industry
WACCM....... World Association for Chinese Church Music (EAIO)
WACE.......... Chicopee, MA [*AM radio station call letters*]
WaCeC......... Centralia College, Centralia, WA [*Library symbol Library of Congress*] (LCLS)
WaCeM........ Maple Lane School, Staff Library, Centralia, WA [*Library symbol Library of Congress*] (LCLS)
WACEO........ Western Australian Catholic Education Office
WaCeW........ Weyerhaeuser Co., Forestry Research Center, Centralia, WA [*Library symbol Library of Congress*] (LCLS)
WACF.......... Paris, IL [*FM radio station call letters*]
WACG.......... Augusta, GA [*FM radio station call letters*]
WACH.......... Columbia, SC [*Television station call letters*]
WACH.......... Wedge Adjustable Cushioned Heel [*Orthopedics*]
WACH.......... West African Clearing House [*Sierra Leone*]
WACH.......... Worship Arts Clearing House (EA)
WACHA........ Wisconsin Automated Clearing House Association
WaChehG.... Green Hill School, Staff Library, Chehalis, WA [*Library symbol Library of Congress*] (LCLS)
WaChehHS... W.F. West High School, Chehalis, WA [*Library symbol*] [*Library of Congress*] (LCLS)
WaChehYS... Washington State Twin City Center for Youth Services, Chehalis, WA [*Library symbol Library of Congress*] (LCLS)
WaChenE..... Eastern Washington State College, Cheney, WA [*Library symbol Library of Congress*] (LCLS)
Wachovia..... Wachovia Corp. [*Associated Press*] (SAG)
WACI........... Atlantic City, NJ [*Television station call letters*]
WACI........... Western Approaches Convoy Instructions [*British military*] (DMA)
WACI........... Women's Army Corps of India [*British military*] (DMA)
WACIID........ Winter Advanced Course for Immunology and Infectious Diseases [*Japan International Friendship and Welfare Foundation*]
WACJ........... Bowman, SC [*FM radio station call letters*]
WACK.......... Newark, NY [*AM radio station call letters*]
WACK.......... Wait and Acknowledge (IAA)
WACK.......... Wait before Transmitting Positive Acknowledgment
WackCor...... Wackenhut Corrections Corp. [*Associated Press*] (SAG)
WackhA....... Wackenhut Corp. [*Associated Press*] (SAG)
WackhB....... Wackenhut Corp. [*Associated Press*] (SAG)
WaCl............ Asotin County Library, Clarkston, WA [*Library symbol Library of Congress*] (LCLS)
WACL........... Wacoal Corp. [*Japan NASDAQ symbol*]
WACL........... Waycross, GA [*AM radio station call letters*]
WACL........... Worcester Area Cooperating Libraries [*Worcester, MA*] [*Library network*]
WACL........... World Anti-Communist League [*South Korea*] (EAIO)
WACLIM...... Climate Data Service for West Africa [*Marine science*] (OSRA)
WaClvSC..... Spruce Canyon Correctional Center, Staff Library, Colville, WA [*Library symbol Library of Congress*] (LCLS)
WaClvSC-R.. Spruce Canyon Correctional Center, Resident Library, Colville, WA [*Library symbol Library of Congress*] (LCLS)
WACLY........ Wacoal Corp. ADS [*NASDAQ symbol*] (TTSB)
WACM......... Western Association of Circuit Manufacturers
WACM......... West Springfield, MA [*AM radio station call letters*]
WACO......... Waco, TX [*AM radio station call letters*]
WACO......... World Air Cargo Organisation (PDAA)
WACO......... Written Advice of Contracting Officer [*Military*]
Wacoal........ Wacoal Corp. ADR [*Associated Press*] (SAG)
WACO-FM.... Waco, TX [*FM radio station call letters*]
WaCol......... Whitman County Library, Colfax, WA [*Library symbol Library of Congress*] (LCLS)
WACOTA...... Western Australian Council on the Ageing
WACPAC...... Whimsical Alternative Coalition Political Action Committee (EA)
WACQ......... Tallassee, AL [*AM radio station call letters*]
WACQ......... Tuskegee, AL [*FM radio station call letters*]
WACR......... Columbus, MS [*AM radio station call letters*]
WACRA....... World Association for Case Method Research and Application
WACRAL...... World Association of Christian Radio Amateurs and Listeners [*Hull, England*] (EAIO)
WACRES...... Women's Army Corps Reserve
WACR-FM.... Columbus, MS [*FM radio station call letters*]
WACRI........ West African Cocoa Research Institution
WACRRM..... Western Australian Centre for Remote and Rural Medicine
WACS......... Dawson, GA [*Television station call letters*]
WACS......... Warning and Caution System [*Aviation*] (MCD)
WACS......... Weather Analysis Computer System [*Accu-Weather, Inc.*]
WACS......... West African College of Surgeons [*See also COAC*] [*Nigeria*] (EAIO)
WACS......... Whole Angle Animal Cell Sorting
WACS......... Wide Angle Collimated Display System [*Aviation*] (DA)
WACS......... Wire Automated Check System (MCD)
WACS......... Women Associated with Crossdressers Communication Network (EA)
WACS......... Workshop Attitude Control System (MCD)
WACS......... World Association of Cooks Societies (EA)
WACSC....... Western Australian Coastal Shipping Commission
WACSEE..... Western Australian Centre for Self Esteem Education
WACSM...... Women's Army Corps Service Medal [*Military decoration*]
WACT......... Tuscaloosa, AL [*AM radio station call letters*]
WACT-FM.... Tuscaloosa, AL [*FM radio station call letters*]
WACU......... West African Customs Union
WACU......... Western Association of College and University Business Officers (AEBS)
WACV......... Montgomery, AL [*AM radio station call letters*]

WACVA .... Women's Army Corps Veterans Association (EA)
WACX .... Leesburg, FL [*Television station call letters*]
WACY .... Appleton, WI [*Television station call letters*] (RBYB)
WACY 2000... World Association for Celebrating the Year 2000 [*British*]
WAD .... Andriamena [*Madagascar*] [*Airport symbol*] (OAG)
WAD .... Waddy Lake Resources, Inc. [*Toronto Stock Exchange symbol Vancouver Stock Exchange symbol*]
WAD .... Washington Aqueduct Division [*Army*]
WAD .... Weapon Assignment Display [*Air Force*]
WAD .... Weapons Alert Designator [*Army*] (ADDR)
WAD .... Wide-Angle Optics Weapon Assignment Display [*DoD*]
WAD .... Wide-Area Display (MCD)
WAD .... William Addison Dwiggins [*American type designer and illustrator, 1880-1956*]
WAD .... Work Adjustment Program [*Education*]
WAD .... Work Authorization and Delegation
WAD .... Work Authorization Document [*NASA*]
WAD .... World Association of Detectives (EA)
WAD .... World Wide Military Command Control System Automated Data Processing
WAD .... Wright Aeronautical Division [*Curtiss-Wright Corp.*]
WAD .... WWMCCS [*Worldwide Military Command and Control System*] Architecture Division
WADA .... Shelby, NC [*AM radio station call letters*]
WADAAA...... Washington District Army Audit Agency (MUGU)
WADB .... Point Pleasant, NJ [*FM radio station call letters*]
WADB .... West African Development Bank [*Togo*] (EA)
WADC .... Parkersburg, WV [*AM radio station call letters*]
WADC .... Western Air Defense Command
WADC .... Wright Air Development Center [*Air Force*]
W ADD........ With Added [*Freight*]
WADD .... Wright Air Development Division [*Air Force*]
Wad Dig ...... Waddilove's Digest of Ecclesiastical Cases [*1849*] [*A publication*] (DLA)
WADE .... Wadesboro, NC [*AM radio station call letters*]
WADE .... World Association of Document Examiners (EA)
Wade Am Mining Law... Wade on American Mining Law [*A publication*] (DLA)
Wade Attachm... Wade on Attachment and Garnishment [*A publication*] (DLA)
WADEBR...... Wadebridge [*England*]
Wade Min.... Wade on American Mining Law [*A publication*] (DLA)
Wade Not .... Wade on the Law of Notice [*A publication*] (DLA)
Wade Retro L... Wade on Retroactive Laws [*A publication*] (DLA)
WADEX .... Words and Authors Index [*Computer-produced index*]
WADF .... Western Air Defense Force
WADFFU ...... Women's Association for the Defense of Four Freedoms for Ukraine (EA)
WADGPS...... Wide-Area Differential Global Positioning Satellite
WADH .... Wadham College [*Oxford University*] (ROG)
WADI .... Corinth, MS [*FM radio station call letters*]
WADILC ...... Western Australian Dairy Industry Liaison Committee
WADJ........ Somerset, PA [*AM radio station call letters*]
WADK .... Newport, RI [*AM radio station call letters*]
WADL .... Mount Clemens, MI [*Television station call letters*]
WADL .... Windshear Air Data Loader [*Aviation*]
WADM .... Decatur, IN [*AM radio station call letters*]
WADM .... Wide-Area Defense Missile (MCD)
Wad Mar & Div... Waddilove on Marriage and Divorce [*1864*] [*A publication*] (DLA)
WADN .... Concord, MA [*AM radio station call letters*]
WADO .... New York, NY [*AM radio station call letters*]
WADP........ World Association for Dynamic Psychiatry (EAIO)
WADQ .... Westport, NY [*FM radio station call letters*]
WADR .... Remsen, NY [*AM radio station call letters*]
WADR .... Waste Acid Detoxification and Reclamation [*Environmental science*]
WADR .... Weight Analysis Data Report
WADS .... Ansonia, CT [*AM radio station call letters*]
WADS .... Wide-Angle Display System
WADS .... Wide-Area Data Service [*Data transmission service*]
WADSEP ...... Walking and Dredging Self-Elevating Platform (PDAA)
WAD/SO...... Work Authorization Document/Shop Order (NASA)
WADT .... Brandon, VT [*FM radio station call letters*]
WADTF .... Western Atmospheric Deposition Task Force [*Environmental Protection Agency*] (GFGA)
WADU .... Norco, LA [*AM radio station call letters*]
WADU .... Reserve, LA [*FM radio station call letters*]
WADV .... Lebanon, PA [*AM radio station call letters*]
WADVBS...... World Association of Daily Vacation Bible Schools [*Later, VBS*] (EA)
WADW .... Pickford, MI [*FM radio station call letters*]
WAE........ Aoulef [*Algeria*] [*Airport symbol*] (AD)
WaE........ Everett Public Library, Everett, WA [*Library symbol Library of Congress*] (LCLS)
WAE........ Transportation Systems, Inc. [*FAA designator*] (FAAC)
WAE........ Weapon Aiming Error
WAE........ When [*or While*] Actually Employed [*Government short jobs*]
WAE........ Wills and Administration of Estates [*Law*]
WAE........ Worked All Europe [*Contacted at least one station in all European countries*] [*Amateur radio*] (IAA)
WAEA........ World Airline Entertainment Association
WaEawC ...... Canyon View Group Home, East Wenatchee, WA [*Library symbol Library of Congress*] (LCLS)
WaEawE ...... Eastmont High School, East Wenatchee, WA [*Library symbol*] [*Library of Congress*] (LCLS)
WAEB........ Allentown, PA [*AM radio station call letters*]
WAEB-FM .... Allentown, PA [*FM radio station call letters*]
WAEC........ Atlanta, GA [*AM radio station call letters*]
WAEC........ War Agricultural Executive Committee [*British*] (DAS)
Wa-Ec........ Washington State Library, Ecology Department, Olympia, WA [*Library symbol Library of Congress*] (LCLS)
WAEC........ West African Economic Community [*Ivory Coast, Mali, Mauritania, Niger, Senegal, Upper Volta*] (ASF)
WAEC........ Western Australian Electoral Commission
WAEC........ Wheel at Each Corner [*Automotive engineering*]
WAED .... Harkers Island, NC [*FM radio station call letters*]
WAED .... Westinghouse Aerospace Electrical Division
WaEdE........ Edmonds Community College, Edmonds, WA [*Library symbol Library of Congress*] (LCLS)
WAEDM ...... World Association for Emergency and Disaster Medicine [*Bristol, England*] (EAIO)
WaEE........ Everett Community College, Everett, WA [*Library symbol Library of Congress*] (LCLS)
WAEF........ Bedford, NH [*FM radio station call letters*]
WAEG .... Evans, GA [*FM radio station call letters*]
WaEG........ Everett General Hospital, Medical Library, Everett, WA [*Library symbol Library of Congress*] (LCLS)
WaEGS .... Church of Jesus Christ of Latter-Day Saints, Genealogical Society Library, Everett, Washington Stake Branch, Everett, WA [*Library symbol Library of Congress*] (LCLS)
WaEH........ Health Information Network Services, Everett, WA [*Library symbol*] [*Library of Congress*] (LCLS)
WaEHP .... Hewlett-Packard Co., Lake Stevens Instrument Division, Everett, WA [*Library symbol*] [*Library of Congress*] (LCLS)
WAEI........ Wautoma, WI [*FM radio station call letters*]
WAEJ........ Waynesboro, GA [*FM radio station call letters*]
WAEJ........ World Association of Esperanto Journalists [*See also TEJA*] [*Cittadella, Italy*] (EAIO)
WaEJP .... Washington State Office of Juvenile Parole Services, Everett, WA [*Library symbol Library of Congress*] (LCLS)
WaEl........ Ellensburg Public Library, Ellensburg, WA [*Library symbol Library of Congress*] (LCLS)
WAEL........ Maricao, PR [*FM radio station call letters*]
WAEL........ Mayaguez, PR [*AM radio station call letters*]
WaElC........ Central Washington State College, Ellensburg, WA [*Library symbol Library of Congress*] (LCLS)
WAEMA........ Western and English Manufacturers Association [*Denver, CO*] (EA)
WAEMB........ Western Australian Egg Marketing Board
WaEn .... Enumclaw Public Library, Enumclaw, WA [*Library symbol*] [*Library of Congress*] (LCLS)
WAEN .... Women's Alternative Economics Network [*An association*] (CROSS)
WaEp .... Ephrata Public Library, Ephrata, WA [*Library symbol Library of Congress*] (LCLS)
WAEP........ World Association for Element Building and Prefabrication [*Hamburg, Federal Republic of Germany*] (EAIO)
WAEPA .... War Agencies Employees Protective Association
WAEPA .... Western Australian Environmental Protection Agency
WAEPA .... Western Australian Environment Protection Authority (EERA)
WAEPA .... Worldwide Assurance for Employees of Public Agencies [*Falls Church, VA*] (EA)
WaEPH .... Providence Hospital, Everett, WA [*Library symbol Library of Congress*] (LCLS)
WaEpS........ Sunrise Group Home, Ephrata, WA [*Library symbol Library of Congress*] (LCLS)
WAER .... Syracuse, NY [*FM radio station call letters*]
WAER .... World Association for Educational Research [*See also AMSE*] [*Ghent, Belgium*] (EAIO)
WAES........ Teutopolis, IL [*FM radio station call letters*]
WAES........ Workshop on Alternative Energy Strategies
WAEV........ Savannah, GA [*FM radio station call letters*]
WAEW .... Crossville, TN [*AM radio station call letters*]
WAEY........ Princeton, WV [*FM radio station call letters*]
WaEYS........ Washington State Center for Youth Services, Everett, WA [*Library symbol Library of Congress*] (LCLS)
WAEZ........ Elizabethton, TN [*FM radio station call letters*] (RBYB)
WAF........ Flamenco Airways, Inc. [*ICAO designator*] (FAAC)
WAF........ Wafer (AAG)
Wa-F........ Washington State Film Library, Olympia, WA [*Library symbol Library of Congress*] (LCLS)
WAF........ West African Forces [*British military*] (DMA)
WAF........ Width across Flats (MSA)
WAF........ Wiring Around Frame (MSA)
WAF........ With All Faults [*i.e., to be sold as is*]
waf........ With All Faults (WDMC)
WAF........ Woman Activist Fund (EA)
WAF........ Women in the Air Force
WAF........ Women's Aglow Fellowship (EA)
WAF........ Women's Auxiliary Force [*World War I*] [*Later, Victory Corps*] [*British*]
WAF........ Word Address Format
WAF........ World AIDS Foundation
WAF........ World Apostolate of Fatima [*The Blue Army*] (EAIO)
WAF........ Wound Angiogensis Factor [*Biochemistry*]
WAF........ Wrap-Around-Fin (PDAA)
WAFA........ Western Australian Farmers' Association
WAFA........ Western Australian Football Association
WAFAC .... Western Australian Fruit Advisory Council
WAFAH .... West African Federation of Associations for the Advancement of Handicapped Persons [*See also FOAPH*] [*Bamako, Mali*] (EAIO)
WAFB........ Baton Rouge, LA [*Television station call letters*]
WAFB........ Warren Air Force Base [*Wyoming*] (AAG)
WAFB........ Whiteman Air Force Base (SAA)
WAFBB .... Western Australian Fire Brigade Board
WAFC........ Clewiston, FL [*AM radio station call letters*]

WAFC .... Wendel Adkins Fan Club [*Defunct*] (EA)
WAFC .... West African Fisheries Commission
WAFC .... Western Area Frequency Coordinator
WAFC .... Western Australian Football Commission
WAFC .... World Area Forecast Center [*Aviation*] (FAAC)
WAFC-FM .... Clewiston, FL [*FM radio station call letters*]
WAF/CP .... Women and Foundations/Corporate Philanthropy (EA)
WAFD .... Webster Springs, WV [*FM radio station call letters*]
WAFE .... Wives of the Armed Forces, Emeritus [*Defunct*] (EA)
WAFF .... Huntsville, AL [*Television station call letters*]
WAFF .... Wartime Fuel Factors
WAFF .... West African Frontier Force
WAFF .... Western Australian Farmers Federation (EERA)
WAFF .... Wrap-Around Folding Fin (MCD)
WAFFLE .... Wide-Angle Fixed-Field Locating Equipment
WAFG .... Fort Lauderdale, FL [*FM radio station call letters*]
WAFI .... Unadilla, GA [*FM radio station call letters*]
WAFIC .... Western Australian Fishing Industry Council
WAFIC .... Western Australian Furniture Industry Council
WAFITC .... Western Australian Forest Industry Training Council
WAFJ .... Belvedere, SC [*FM radio station call letters*]
WAFL .... Milford, DE [*FM radio station call letters*]
WAFL .... Write Anywhere File Layout [*Network Appliance Corp.*] [*Computer science*]
W Af LR .... West African Law Reports [*A publication*] (DLA)
WAFM .... Amory, MS [*FM radio station call letters*]
WaForC .... Clearwater Correctional Center, Staff Library, Forks, WA [*Library symbol Library of Congress*] (LCLS)
WaForC-R .... Clearwater Correctional Center, Resident Library, Forks, WA [*Library symbol Library of Congress*] (LCLS)
WAFP .... Woody Allen's Fall Picture [*Designation reflecting the filmmaker's reluctance to provide information about his movies in advance of their commercial release*] [*See also WASP*]
WAFR .... Tupelo, MS [*FM radio station call letters*]
W AFR .... West Africa
WAFR .... Wrap-Around Fin Rocket (MCD)
W Afr App .... West African Court of Appeal Reports [*A publication*] (DLA)
WaFrh .... San Juan Island Public Library, Friday Harbor, WA [*Library symbol*] [*Library of Congress*] (LCLS)
WAFRY .... Western Australian Federation of Rural Youth
WAFS .... Atlanta, GA [*AM radio station call letters*]
WAFS .... Women's Air Force Services [*British military*] (DMA)
WAFS .... Women's Auxiliary Ferrying Squadron [*Part of Air Transport Command*] [*World War II*]
WAFS .... Women's Auxiliary Fire Service [*British World War II*]
WAFS .... World Area Forecast System [*Meteorology*]
WAFS .... World Area Forecast System [*Marine science*] (OSRA)
WaFsWS ...... Western State Hospital, Staff Library, Fort Steilacoom, WA [*Library symbol Library of Congress*] (LCLS)
WAFT .... Valdosta, GA [*FM radio station call letters*]
WAFT .... Wichita Auditory Fusion Test
WaFtl .... United States Army, Fort Lewis Library System, Grandstaff Library, Fort Lewis, WA [*Library symbol Library of Congress*] (LCLS)
WAFV .... Wheeled Armoured Fighting Vehicle [*Military*]
WaFW .... Whatcom Community College, Ferndale, WA [*Library symbol Library of Congress*] (LCLS)
WAFWA .... Western Association of Fish and Wildlife Agencies (EA)
WaFwS .... Federal Way School District Central Library, Federal Way, WA [*Library symbol Library of Congress*] (LCLS)
WAFX .... Suffolk, VA [*FM radio station call letters*]
WAFY .... Middletown, MD [*FM radio station call letters*]
WAFZ .... Immokalee, FL [*AM radio station call letters*] (RBYB)
WAG .... The Gambia [*International civil aircraft marking*] (ODBW)
WAG .... Wagon (MSA)
WAG .... Walgreen Co. [*NYSE symbol*] (SPSG)
WAG .... Wanganui [*New Zealand*] [*Airport symbol*] (OAG)
WAG .... Warfare Analysis Group [*Navy*]
WAG .... Water-Alternating Gas [*Petroleum engineering*]
WAG .... Wellsville, Addison & Galeton Railroad Corp. [*AAR code*]
WAG .... Western Australian Green Party [*Political party*]
WAG .... Wiederaufbaugesellschaft fuer die Juedische Bevoelkerung der Bucovina [*A publication*] (BJA)
WAG .... Wild Aim Guess [*Bowdlerized version*]
WAG .... Wild-Assed-Guess Principle [*Military slang*] (VNW)
WAG .... Wild-Ass-Guess [*Aviation*]
WAG .... Wine Appreciation Guild (EA)
WAG .... Wireless Air Gunner [*British military*] (DMA)
WAG .... Worked All Goose (IAA)
WAG .... World Airline (Gambia) Ltd. [*ICAO designator*] (FAAC)
WAG .... World Area Grid (MCD)
WAG .... Writers' Action Group [*British*]
WAG .... WWMCCS [*Worldwide Military Command and Control System*] Action Group
WAGA .... Atlanta, GA [*Television station call letters*]
WAGA .... Welsh Amateur Gymnastic Association (DBA)
WaGal .... Intermediate School District 113, Instructional Materials Center, Galvin, WA [*Library symbol Library of Congress*] (LCLS)
WAGB .... Wildfowlers' Association of Great Britain
WAGBI .... Wildfowlers' Association of Great Britain and Ireland (BI)
WAGC .... Centre, AL [*AM radio station call letters*]
WaGc .... Grand Coulee Public Library, Grand Coulee, WA [*Library symbol Library of Congress*] (LCLS)
WAGC .... World Amateur Golf Council (EA)
WAGCOM ..... War Game Comparison (MCD)
WAGE .... Leesburg, VA [*AM radio station call letters*]
WAGE .... Union Women's Alliance to Gain Equality [*Defunct*] (EA)
Wage & Hour Rep ... Wage and Hour Reporter [*Bureau of National Affairs*] [*A publication*] (DLA)
WAGF .... Dothan, AL [*AM radio station call letters*]
WAGFEI .... Women's Action Group on Excision and Infibulation [*British Defunct*] (EAIO)
WAGF-FM .... Dothan, AL [*FM radio station call letters*] (RBYB)
WAGG .... Birmingham, AL [*AM radio station call letters*]
WAGGGS ..... World Association of Girl Guides and Girl Scouts [*See also AMGE*] [*British*] (EAIO)
WAGH .... Fort Mitchell, AL [*FM radio station call letters*]
WaGhP .... Purdy Treatment Center for Women, Gig Harbor, WA [*Library symbol Library of Congress*] (LCLS)
WAGI .... Gaffney, SC [*FM radio station call letters*]
WAGL .... Lancaster, SC [*AM radio station call letters*]
WAGL .... Western Australian Gould League
WAGM .... Presque Isle, ME [*Television station call letters*]
WAGN .... Menominee, MI [*AM radio station call letters*]
Wagner C ..... Wagner College (GAGS)
WAGO-FM .... Snow Hill, NC [*FM radio station call letters*] (RBYB)
WAGP .... Beaufort, SC [*FM radio station call letters*]
WAGP .... Women's Access Grant Program [*Australia*]
WAGR .... Lexington, MS [*FM radio station call letters*]
WAGR .... Lumberton, NC [*AM radio station call letters*]
WAGR .... Wald, Arnold, Goldberg, Rushton [*Test*] [*Statistics*]
WAGR .... Western Australian Government Railways (PDAA)
WAGR .... Wilms Tumor, Aniridia, Genitourinary Abnormalities, and Mental Retardation [*Syndrome*] [*Medicine*]
WAGR .... Windscale Advanced Gas-Cooled Reactor
WAGRC .... Western Australian Government Railways Commission
WAGRO .... Warsaw Ghetto Resistance Organization (EA)
WAGS .... Bishopville, SC [*AM radio station call letters*]
WAGS .... Washington Area Girls Soccer League (TAG)
WAGS .... Weighted Agreement Scores
WAGS .... Wireless Air Gunners School [*British military*] (DMA)
WAGS .... Worldwide Atmospheric Gravity Wave Study [*Ionospheric physics*]
Wag St .... Wagner's Missouri Statutes [*A publication*] (DLA)
Wag Stat ..... Wagner's Missouri Statutes [*A publication*] (DLA)
WAGT .... Augusta, GA [*Television station call letters*]
WAGUL .... West Australian Group of University Librarians
WAGV .... Harlan, KY [*Television station call letters*]
WAGX .... Manchester, OH [*FM radio station call letters*]
WAGY .... Forest City, NC [*AM radio station call letters*]
WAH .... Wage and Hour Division [*Department of Labor*] (IAA)
WAH .... Wahluke [*Washington*] [*Seismograph station code, US Geological Survey*] (SEIS)
WAH .... Womack Army Hospital Medical Library, Fort Bragg, NC [*OCLC symbol*] (OCLC)
WAHA .... Wide-Angle High Aperture (MCD)
WAHC .... Circleville, OH [*FM radio station call letters*]
WAHC .... West African Health Community (EA)
WAHC .... Western Australian Heritage Committee
WAHC .... World Airlines Hobby Club (EA)
WAHD .... Wilson, NC [*FM radio station call letters*]
WAHERE ...... Western Australian Herbarium Plant Specimen Database [*State*] (EERA)
WAHH-AM ... Wilmington, NC [*AM radio station call letters*] (RBYB)
WaHi .... Washington State Historical Society, Tacoma, WA [*Library symbol Library of Congress*] (LCLS)
WAHI-FM .... Augusta, IL [*FM radio station call letters*] (RBYB)
WaHJ .... Jefferson County Rural Library District, Hadlock, WA [*Library symbol*] [*Library of Congress*] (LCLS)
WAHL .... Ocracoke, NC [*FM radio station call letters*] (RBYB)
WAHLC .... World Association for Hebrew Language and Culture (EAIO)
Wahlco .... Wahlco Environment Systems, Inc. [*Associated Press*] (SAG)
WAHLI .... Indonesian Wildlife Forum [*Indonesia*] (EERA)
WAHO .... World Arabian Horse Organization [*Windermere, England*] (EAIO)
WAHQ .... Carolina, PR [*FM radio station call letters*]
WAHR .... Huntsville, AL [*FM radio station call letters*]
WAHS .... Auburn Hills, MI [*FM radio station call letters*]
WAHS .... World Airline Historical Society (EA)
WAHV-FM .... Owosso, MI [*FM radio station call letters*] (RBYB)
WAHVM .... World Association for the History of Veterinary Medicine [*Hanover, Federal Republic of Germany*] (EAIO)
WAI .... Antsohihy [*Madagascar*] [*Airport symbol*] (OAG)
WAI .... Wairiri [*Glentunnel*] [*New Zealand*] [*Seismograph station code, US Geological Survey*] [*Closed*] (SEIS)
WAI .... Walk Around Inspection
WAI .... Water Absorption Index [*Analytical chemistry*]
WAI .... Water Alcohol Injection (MCD)
WAI .... Western Atlas [*NYSE symbol*] (TTSB)
WAI .... Western Atlas, Inc. [*NYSE symbol*] (SAG)
WAI .... Wire Association International (EA)
WAI .... Worked All Italy [*Amateur radio*] (IAA)
WAI .... Work in America Institute (EA)
WAIABS .... Western Australian Institute of Applied Business Studies
WAIAL .... Western Australian Institute of Applied Linguistics
WAIB .... Tallahassee, FL [*FM radio station call letters*] (RBYB)
WAIC .... Springfield, MA [*FM radio station call letters*]
WAIC .... Western Australian Industrial Court
WAIC .... Western Australian International College
WAICA .... Women's Auxiliary of the ICA [*International Chiropractors Association*] (EA)
WAID .... Clarksdale, MS [*FM radio station call letters*]
WAID .... Wage and Information Documents [*IRS*]

WAIF .... World Adoption International Fund
WAIH .... Potsdam, NY [*FM radio station call letters*]
WAIHA .... Warm Autoimmune Hemolytic Anemia [*Medicine*]
WAII-FM ...... Hattiesburg, MI [*FM radio station call letters*] (RBYB)
WAIJ .... Grantsville, MD [*FM radio station call letters*]
WAIK .... Galesburg, IL [*AM radio station call letters*]
WAIL .... Key West, FL [*FM radio station call letters*]
WAIM .... Anderson, SC [*AM radio station call letters*]
WAIM .... Wide-Angle Impedance Matching (PDAA)
WAIN .... Columbia, KY [*AM radio station call letters*]
WAIN .... Wainwright Bank & Trust [*NYSE symbol*] (TTSB)
WAIN .... Wainwright Bank & Trust Co. [*NASDAQ symbol*] (CTT)
WainBk .... Wainwright Bank & Trust Co. [*Associated Press*] (SAG)
WAIN-FM ...... Columbia, KY [*FM radio station call letters*]
Wainoc .... Wainoco Oil Corp. [*Associated Press*] (SAG)
WAIOP .... Will Accept, If Offered, the Position [*Aviation*] (FAAC)
WAIP .... Worked All Italian Provinces [*Amateur radio*] (IAA)
WAIP .... World Association for Infant Psychiatry [*Later, WAIPAD*] (EA)
WAIPAD ...... World Association for Infant Psychiatry and Allied Disciplines (EA)
WAIQ .... Montgomery, AL [*Television station call letters*]
WAIR .... Atlanta, MI [*FM radio station call letters*]
WAIS .... Buchtel, OH [*AM radio station call letters*]
WAIS .... Wechsler Adult Intelligence Scale [*Education*]
WAIS .... West Antarctic Ice Sheet [*Geology*]
WAIS .... Wide Area Information Server [*Computer science*]
WAIS .... Wide Area Information Service [*or Server*] [*Telecommunications*]
WAIS-R .... Wechsler Adult Intelligence Scale-Revised [*Test*]
WAIT .... Crystal Lake, IL [*AM radio station call letters*]
WAIT .... Weighted Average Inlet Temperature [*Chemical engineering*]
WAIT .... Western Australia Institute of Technology (NITA)
Wait Act & Def ... Wait's Actions and Defences [*A publication*] (DLA)
Wait Co .... Wait's New York Annotated Code [*A publication*] (DLA)
Wait Dig .... Wait's New York Digest [*A publication*] (DLA)
WAITI .... Western Australian Institute of Translators and Interpreters
Wait L & P ... Wait's Law and Practice in New York Justices' Courts [*A publication*] (DLA)
Wait Pr .... Wait's New York Practice [*A publication*] (DLA)
WAITRO .... World Association of Industrial and Technological Research Organizations [*Arhus, Denmark*]
WAITS .... Wide Area Information Transfer System [*Computer science*] (PCM)
Waits Prac ... Wait's New York Practice [*A publication*] (DLA)
Wait St Pap ... Wait's State Papers of the United States [*A publication*] (DLA)
Wait Tab Ca ... Wait's New York Table of Cases [*A publication*] (DLA)
WAIV .... Spring Valley, IL [*FM radio station call letters*]
WAIZ .... Seneca, IL [*FM radio station call letters*] (RBYB)
WAJ .... Wajima [*Japan*] [*Seismograph station code, US Geological Survey*] (SEIS)
WAJ .... Water-Augmented Jet
WAJ .... World Association of Judges (EA)
WAJA .... Arso [*Indonesia*] [*ICAO location identifier*] (ICLI)
WAJA .... West African Journal of Archaeology [*A publication*]
WAJB .... Bokondini [*Indonesia*] [*ICAO location identifier*] (ICLI)
WAJCSC ...... W. Alton Jones Cell Science Center, Inc. [*Research center*] (RCD)
WAJD .... Gainesville, FL [*AM radio station call letters*]
WAJD .... Wakde [*Indonesia*] [*ICAO location identifier*] (ICLI)
WAJE .... New Albany, IN [*FM radio station call letters*] (RBYB)
WAJF .... Decatur, AL [*AM radio station call letters*]
WAJI .... Fort Wayne, IN [*FM radio station call letters*]
WAJI .... Sarmi/Orai [*Indonesia*] [*ICAO location identifier*] (ICLI)
WAJJ .... Jayapura/Sentani [*Indonesia*] [*ICAO location identifier*] (ICLI)
WAJK .... Kiwirok [*Indonesia*] [*ICAO location identifier*] (ICLI)
WAJK .... La Salle, IL [*FM radio station call letters*]
WAJL .... Lereh [*Indonesia*] [*ICAO location identifier*] (ICLI)
WAJL .... Pine Castle-Sky Lake, FL [*AM radio station call letters*]
WAJM .... Mulia [*Indonesia*] [*ICAO location identifier*] (ICLI)
WAJO .... Marion, AL [*AM radio station call letters*]
WAJO .... Oksibil [*Indonesia*] [*ICAO location identifier*] (ICLI)
WAJQ .... Alma, GA [*AM radio station call letters*]
WAJQ-FM ...... Alma, GA [*FM radio station call letters*]
WAJR .... Morgantown, WV [*AM radio station call letters*]
WAJR .... Waris [*Indonesia*] [*ICAO location identifier*] (ICLI)
WAJS .... Senggeh [*Indonesia*] [*ICAO location identifier*] (ICLI)
WAJS .... Tupelo, MS [*FM radio station call letters*] (RBYB)
WAJT .... Mount Vernon, IL [*FM radio station call letters*] (RBYB)
WAJU .... Ubrub [*Indonesia*] [*ICAO location identifier*] (ICLI)
WAJV .... Brooksville, MS [*FM radio station call letters*] (RBYB)
WAJW .... Chesterton, IN [*FM radio station call letters*] (RBYB)
WAJW .... Wamena [*Indonesia*] [*ICAO location identifier*] (ICLI)
WAJY .... New Ellenton, SC [*FM radio station call letters*]
WAJZ .... Jayapura Sector [*Indonesia*] [*ICAO location identifier*] (ICLI)
WAK .... Alaska Juneau Aeronautics, Inc. [*ICAO designator*] (FAAC)
WAK .... Ankazoabo [*Madagascar*] [*Airport symbol*] (OAG)
WAK .... Wackenhut Corp. [*NYSE symbol*] (SPSG)
WAK .... Wackenhut Corp. Cl'A' [*NYSE symbol*] (TTSB)
WAK .... Wait Acknowledge
wak .... Wakashan [*MARC language code Library of Congress*] (LCCP)
WAK .... Wakkanai [*Japan*] [*Seismograph station code, US Geological Survey*] (SEIS)
WAK .... Water Analyzer Kit
WAK .... Wearable Artificial Kidney
WAK .... Write Access Key
WAKA .... Akimuga [*Indonesia*] [*ICAO location identifier*] (ICLI)
WAKA .... Selma, AL [*Television station call letters*]
WAK B .... Wackenhut Corp. 'B' [*NYSE symbol*] (TTSB)
WAKB .... Wrens, GA [*FM radio station call letters*]
WAKC .... Akron, OH [*Television station call letters*]
WAKD .... Mindiptana [*Indonesia*] [*ICAO location identifier*] (ICLI)
WAKD .... Sheffield, AL [*FM radio station call letters*] (RBYB)
WAKE .... Bade [*Indonesia*] [*ICAO location identifier*] (ICLI)
WAKE .... Valparaiso, IN [*AM radio station call letters*]
Wake Forest Intra L Rev ... Wake Forest Intramural Law Review [*A publication*] (DLA)
Wake Forest U ... Wake Forest University (GAGS)
WaKeH .... Kennewick General Hospital, Kennewick, WA [*Library symbol*] [*Library of Congress*] (LCLS)
WaKel .... Kelso Public Library, Kelso, WA [*Library symbol Library of Congress*] (LCLS)
WaKeM .... Mid-Columbia Regional Library, Kennewick, WA [*Library symbol Library of Congress*] (LCLS)
WaKenS .... Saint Thomas Seminary, Kenmore, WA [*Library symbol Library of Congress*] (LCLS)
WAKG .... Agats [*Indonesia*] [*ICAO location identifier*] (ICLI)
WAKG .... Danville, VA [*FM radio station call letters*]
WAKH .... Abohoy [*Indonesia*] [*ICAO location identifier*] (ICLI)
WAKH .... McComb, MS [*FM radio station call letters*]
WAKI .... McMinnville, TN [*AM radio station call letters*]
WaKiE .... Evergreen General Hospital Library, Kirkland, WA [*Library symbol*] [*Library of Congress*] (LCLS)
WaKiN .... Northwest College, Kirkland, WA [*Library symbol Library of Congress*] (LCLS)
WAKJ .... DeFuniak Springs, FL [*FM radio station call letters*] (RBYB)
WAKK .... McComb, MS [*AM radio station call letters*]
WAKK .... Merauke/Mopah [*Indonesia*] [*ICAO location identifier*] (ICLI)
WAKM .... Franklin, TN [*AM radio station call letters*]
WAKN .... Primapun [*Indonesia*] [*ICAO location identifier*] (ICLI)
WAKN .... Winter Harbor, ME [*FM radio station call letters*] (RBYB)
WAKO .... Lawrenceville, IL [*AM radio station call letters*]
WAKO .... Okaba [*Indonesia*] [*ICAO location identifier*] (ICLI)
WAKO-FM ...... Lawrenceville, IL [*FM radio station call letters*]
WAKP .... Kepi [*Indonesia*] [*ICAO location identifier*] (ICLI)
WAKPAT ...... Walking Pattern (MHDI)
WAKQ .... Paris, TN [*FM radio station call letters*]
WAKR .... Akron, OH [*AM radio station call letters*]
WAKS .... Marysville, OH [*FM radio station call letters*]
WAKT .... Panama City Beach, FL [*FM radio station call letters*]
WAKT .... Tanah Merah [*Indonesia*] [*ICAO location identifier*] (ICLI)
WAKU .... Crawfordville, FL [*FM radio station call letters*]
WAKW .... Cincinnati, OH [*FM radio station call letters*]
WAKX .... Holland, MI [*FM radio station call letters*]
WAKY .... Greensburg, KY [*AM radio station call letters*]
WAKY-FM ...... Springfield, KY [*FM radio station call letters*] (RBYB)
WAL .... Chincoteague, VA [*Location identifier FAA*] (FAAL)
WAL .... Lawrence University, Appleton, WI [*Library symbol Library of Congress*] (LCLS)
WAL .... Sierra Leone [*International vehicle registration*] (ODBW)
WAL .... Wahlco Environment Systems [*NYSE symbol*] (SPSG)
WAL .... Wahlco Enviro Systems [*NYSE symbol*] (TTSB)
wal .... Walamo [*MARC language code Library of Congress*] (LCCP)
Wal .... Waldorf [*Record label*]
WAL .... Wallace [*Idaho*] [*Seismograph station code, US Geological Survey*] (SEIS)
WAL .... Walloon (ROG)
WAL .... Walnut (WGA)
wal .... Walnut (VRA)
WAL .... Walsh College, Canton, OH [*OCLC symbol*] (OCLC)
WAL .... Warfare Analysis Laboratory [*Johns Hopkins University/Applied Physics Laboratory*] (DOMA)
Wa-L .... Washington State Law Library, Olympia, WA [*Library symbol Library of Congress*] (LCLS)
WAL .... Waterloo Resources, Inc. [*Vancouver Stock Exchange symbol*]
WAL .... Watertown Arsenal Laboratory [*Massachusetts*] [*Army*]
WAL .... We Are Lost [*Army*]
WAL .... Weather Almanac [*A publication*]
WAL .... Western Airlines, Inc. [*Facetious translation: What an Airline*]
WAL .... Western Allegheny Railroad Co. [*AAR code*]
WAL .... Western American Literature [*A publication*] (BRI)
WAL .... Western Artic Air Ltd. [*Canada ICAO designator*] (FAAC)
W-AL .... Westinghouse-Astronuclear Laboratories
WAL .... Wide-Angle Lens
WAL .... World Association of Lawyers (EA)
WAL .... Wright Aeronautical Laboratories (MCD)
WALA .... Mobile, AL [*Television station call letters*]
Walach .... Walachian [*Romanian dialect*] (BARN)
WALB .... Albany, GA [*Television station call letters*]
WALB .... Walbro Corp. [*NASDAQ symbol*] (NQ)
Walbro .... Walbro Corp. [*Associated Press*] (SAG)
Wal by L .... Wallis' Irish Chancery Reports, by Lyne [*A publication*] (DLA)
WALC .... West African Lands Committee. Report [*A publication*] (ILCA)
WALC .... Worldwide Aviation Logistics Conference (RDA)
Wal Ch .... Walker's Michigan Chancery Reports [*A publication*] (DLA)
WalCS .... Wallace Computer Services, Inc. [*Associated Press*] (SAG)
Wald .... Walden [*Record label*]
WALD .... Walterboro, SC [*AM radio station call letters*]
Waldn .... Walden Residential Properties [*Associated Press*] (SAG)
WaldnRP ...... Walden Residential Properties [*Associated Press*] (SAG)
WALDO .... Wichita Automatic Linear Data Output
WALDO .... Winona Tri College University Library Network [*Library network*]
WALE .... Providence, RI [*AM radio station call letters*]
WALF .... Alfred, NY [*FM radio station call letters*]
Walf Cust .... Walford's Laws of the Customs [*1846*] [*A publication*] (DLA)

Walf Part Walford's Parties to Actions [*1842*] [*A publication*] (DLA)
Walf Railw Walford on Railways [*2nd ed.*] [*1846*] [*A publication*] (DLA)
WALG Albany, GA [*AM radio station call letters*]
Walgrn Walgreen Co. [*Associated Press*] (SAG)
WALH Mountain City, GA [*AM radio station call letters*]
WALI-FM Walterboro, SC [*FM radio station call letters*] (RBYB)
WALIP Western Australian Land Information Program [*State*] (EERA)
WALIS Western Australian Land Information System [*State*] (EERA)
WALJ Gordon, GA [*FM radio station call letters*]
WALK Patchogue, NY [*AM radio station call letters*]
WALK Walk [*Postal Service standard*] (OPSA)
WALK Walker Interactive Sys [*NASDAQ symbol*] (TTSB)
WALK Walker Interactive Systems [*NASDAQ symbol*] (SAG)
Walk Walker's Michigan Chancery Reports [*A publication*] (DLA)
Walk Walker's Pennsylvania Reports [*1855-85*] [*A publication*] (DLA)
Walk Walker's Reports [*96, 109 Alabama*] [*A publication*] (DLA)
Walk Walker's Reports [*22-25, 38-51, 72-88 Texas*] [*1-10 Civil Appeals Texas*] [*A publication*] (DLA)
Walk Walker's Reports [*1 Mississippi*] [*A publication*] (DLA)
Walk Am Law Walker's American Law [*A publication*] (DLA)
Walk Bank L Walker's Banking Law [*2nd ed.*] [*1885*] [*A publication*] (DLA)
Walk Ch Walker's Michigan Chancery Reports [*A publication*] (DLA)
Walk Chanc Rep Walker's Michigan Chancery Reports [*A publication*] (DLA)
Walk Ch Cas Walker's Michigan Chancery Reports [*A publication*] (DLA)
Walk Ch Mich Walker's Michigan Chancery Reports [*A publication*] (DLA)
Walk Com L Walker's Theory of the Common Law [*A publication*] (DLA)
Walk Eq Pl Walker's Equity Pleader's Assistant [*A publication*] (DLA)
Walker Walker's Michigan Chancery Reports [*A publication*] (DLA)
Walker Walker's Pennsylvania Reports [*1855-85*] [*A publication*] (DLA)
Walker Walker's Reports [*22-25, 38-51, 72-88 Texas*] [*1-10 Civil Appeals Texas*] [*A publication*] (DLA)
Walker Walker's Reports [*96, 109 Alabama*] [*A publication*] (DLA)
Walker Walker's Reports [*1 Mississippi*] [*A publication*] (DLA)
Walker's Ch R Walker's Michigan Chancery Reports [*A publication*] (DLA)
Walk Exec Walker and Elgood's Executors and Administrators [*6th ed.*] [*1926*] [*A publication*] (DLA)
WALK-FM Patchogue, NY [*FM radio station call letters*]
WalkInt Walker Interactive Systems, Inc. [*Associated Press*] (SAG)
Walk Int Walker's Introduction to American Law [*A publication*] (DLA)
Walk LA Dig Walker's Louisiana Digest [*A publication*] (DLA)
Walk (Mic) Ch Walker's Michigan Chancery Reports [*A publication*] (DLA)
Walk Mich Walker's Michigan Chancery Reports [*A publication*] (DLA)
Walk Michig Rep Walker's Michigan Chancery Reports [*A publication*] (DLA)
Walk Miss Walker's Reports [*1 Mississippi*] [*A publication*] (DLA)
Walk PA Walker's Pennsylvania Reports [*1855-85*] [*A publication*] (DLA)
Walk Pat Walker on Patents [*A publication*] (DLA)
WALKS Walks [*Commonly used*] (OPSA)
Walk Tex Walker's Reports [*22-25, 38-51, 72-88 Texas*] [*1-10 Civil Appeals Texas*] [*A publication*] (DLA)
Walk Wills Walker on Wills [*A publication*] (DLA)
WALL Middletown, NY [*AM radio station call letters*]
WALL Wall [*Postal Service standard*] (OPSA)
Wall Wallace's Nova Scotia Reports [*A publication*] (DLA)
Wall Wallace's Supreme Court Reports [*68-90 United States*] [*1863-74*] [*A publication*] (DLA)
Wall Wallace's United States Circuit Court Reports [*A publication*] (DLA)
Wall Wallace's United States Reports [*1863-74*] [*A publication*] (AAGC)
WALL Wallachian (ROG)
WALL Wall Data [*NASDAQ symbol*] (TTSB)
WALL Wall Data, Inc. [*NASDAQ symbol*] (SAG)
WALL Wallingford [*Municipal borough in England*]
Wall Wallis' Irish Chancery Reports [*A publication*] (DLA)
Wall Wallis' Philadelphia Reports [*1855-85*] [*Pennsylvania*] [*A publication*] (DLA)
WALL Walloon (ROG)
WALL Western Australian Law Libraries
Walla Walla C Walla Walla College (GAGS)
Wall CC Wallace's United States Circuit Court Reports [*A publication*] (DLA)
WallData Wall Data, Inc. [*Associated Press*] (SAG)
Wallis Wallis' Irish Chancery Reports [*A publication*] (DLA)
Wallis by L Wallis' Irish Chancery Reports, by Lyne [*1776-91*] [*A publication*] (DLA)
Wallis by Lyne Wallis' Irish Chancery Reports, by Lyne [*1766-91*] [*A publication*] (DLA)
Wallis (Ir) Wallis' Irish Chancery Reports [*A publication*] (DLA)
Wall Lyn Wallis' Irish Chancery Reports, by Lyne [*1776-91*] [*A publication*] (DLA)
Wall Pr Wallace's Principles of the Laws of Scotland [*A publication*] (DLA)
Wall Rep Wallace's Supreme Court Reports [*68-90 United States*] [*A publication*] (DLA)
Wall Rep Wallace's "The Reporters" [*A publication*] (DLA)
Wall SC Wallace's Supreme Court Reports [*68-90 United States*] [*A publication*] (DLA)
WallSDI Wall Street Deli Co. [*Associated Press*] (SAG)
WALM Albion, MI [*AM radio station call letters*]
WalMart Wal-Mart Stores, Inc. [*Associated Press*] (SAG)
WALN Carrollton, AL [*FM radio station call letters*] (RBYB)
WalnutF Walnut Financial Services, Inc. [*Associated Press*] (SAG)
WALO Humacao, PR [*AM radio station call letters*]
WaLo Longview Public Library, Longview, WA [*Library symbol Library of Congress*] (LCLS)
WaLoGS Church of Jesus Christ of Latter-Day Saints, Genealogical Society Library, Longview Stake Branch, Longview, WA [*Library symbol Library of Congress*] (LCLS)
WaLoL Lower Columbia College, Longview, WA [*Library symbol Library of Congress*] (LCLS)
WaLop Lopez Island Library District, Lopez, WA [*Library symbol*] [*Library of Congress*] (LCLS)
WALOPT Weapons Allocation and Desired Ground-Zero Optimizer [*Military*]
WaLoSH St. John's Hospital, Longview, WA [*Library symbol*] [*Library of Congress*] (LCLS)
WALP Weapons Assignment Linear Program
WALP World Association of Law Professors (EA)
Wal Prin Wallace's Principles of the Laws of Scotland [*A publication*] (DLA)
Walp Rub Walpole's Rubric of Common Law [*A publication*] (DLA)
WALQ Poughkeepsie, NY [*FM radio station call letters*] (RBYB)
WALR Athens, GA [*FM radio station call letters*]
WALR Atlanta, GA [*AM radio station call letters*] (RBYB)
WALR West African Law Reports [*Gambia, Ghana, and Sierra Leone*] [*A publication*] (DLA)
WaLrC Cedar Creek Youth Camp, Littlerock, WA [*Library symbol Library of Congress*] (LCLS)
WALRC Bull Western Australia Law Reform Commission. Bulletin [*A publication*]
WALRUS Water and Land Resources Use Simulation
WALRUS Water and Land Resource Utilization Simulation
WALS Oglesby, IL [*FM radio station call letters*] (RBYB)
WALS Walshire Assurance [*NASDAQ symbol*] (TTSB)
WALS Walshire Assurance Co. [*NASDAQ symbol*] (NQ)
WALS World Association of Law Students (EA)
Walsh Walsh's Irish Registry Cases [*A publication*] (DLA)
Walshr Walshire Assurance Co. [*Associated Press*] (SAG)
WALT Meridian, MS [*AM radio station call letters*]
WALT Warning Assessment Logic Terminal [*Air Force*]
WALT West's Automatic Law Terminal
WALTA Western Australian Lawn Tennis Association
Walter Walter Industries, Inc. [*Associated Press*] (SAG)
Walter Walter's Reports [*14-16 New Mexico*] [*A publication*] (DLA)
Walter C Walter's Code [*A publication*] (DLA)
Walt H & W Walton on Husband and Wife [*Scotland*] [*A publication*] (DLA)
Walt Lim Walter's Statute of Limitations [*4th ed.*] [*A publication*] (DLA)
WALTSTOW Walthamstow [*England*]
Wal US Rep Wallace's United States Reports [*A publication*] (DLA)
WALV Cleveland, TN [*FM radio station call letters*]
WALX Selma, AL [*FM radio station call letters*]
WALY Bellwood, PA [*FM radio station call letters*]
WALZ Machias, ME [*AM radio station call letters*] (RBYB)
WALZ-AM Machias, ME [*AM radio station call letters*] (RBYB)
WALZ-FM Machias, ME
WAM Ambatondrazaka [*Madagascar*] [*Airport symbol*] (OAG)
WAM Appleton Memorial Hospital, Appleton, WI [*Library symbol Library of Congress*] (LCLS)
WAM Emirates News Agency [*United Arab Emirates*] (MENA)
WAM Waitress-Actress-Model [*Lifestyle classification*]
WAM Walleye Measurements Program
WAM Wambrook [*Australia Seismograph station code, US Geological Survey*] (SEIS)
WAM Warburton Minerals [*Vancouver Stock Exchange symbol*]
WAM Wave Model (USDC)
WAM Wave Model [*Marine science*] (OSRA)
WAM Weapon Allocation Model
WAM Weight after Melt [*Metallurgy*]
WAM Weighted Average Maturity [*Finance*]
WAM Western Apparel Manufacturers Show (ITD)
WAM Western Associated Modelers (EA)
WAM Western Australian Mint
WAM Western Australian Museum
W AM White American Male (WDAA)
WAM Wide-Area Mine [*Military*] (MCD)
WAM Women in Advertising and Marketing (EA)
WAM Women's Action Movement
WAM Words a Minute
WAM Work Analysis and Measurement (WDAA)
WAM Working Association of Mothers [*British*] (DI)
WAM Worth Analysis Model (IEEE)
wam Writer of Accompanying Material [*MARC relator code*] [*Library of Congress*] (LCCP)
WAMA Galela/Gamarmalamo [*Indonesia*] [*ICAO location identifier*] (ICLI)
WAMA Tampa, FL [*AM radio station call letters*]
WAMA Watermarc Food Management Co. [*NASDAQ symbol*] (SAG)
WAMA Watermarc Food Mgmt [*NASDAQ symbol*] (TTSB)
WAMA Weight after Mars Arrival [*NASA*]
WAMACCR Western Australian Ministerial Advisory Council on Community Relations
WAMAP Watermarc Food Mgmt 9% Cv Pfd [*NASDAQ symbol*] (TTSB)
WaMaS Sno-Isle Regional Library, Marysville, WA [*Library symbol Library of Congress*] (LCLS)
WAMAW Watermarc Food Mgmt Wrrt'A' [*NASDAQ symbol*] (TTSB)
WAMB Donelson, TN [*AM radio station call letters*]
WAMB Kotamubagu/Mopait [*Indonesia*] [*ICAO location identifier*] (ICLI)
WAmBc WestAmerica Bancorp [*Associated Press*] (SAG)
WAMB-FM Donelson, TN [*FM radio station call letters*]
WAMC Albany, NY [*FM radio station call letters*]
WAMC Tentena [*Indonesia*] [*ICAO location identifier*] (ICLI)
WAMC Western Australian Meat Commission
WAMC Wide Area Mine Clearance [*Army*] (DOMA)
WaMcA McChord Air Force Base, Base Library, McChord Air Force Base, WA [*Library symbol*] [*Library of Congress*] (LCLS)
WAMCE Western Association of Minority Consulting Engineers (IAA)
WAMD Aberdeen, MD [*AM radio station call letters*]

WAMD Jailolo/Kuripasai [*Indonesia*] [*ICAO location identifier*] (ICLI)

WAMDII Wide-Angle, Michelson-Doppler Imaging Interferometer (SSD)

WAME Camden, SC [*AM radio station call letters*] (RBYB)

WaMeH Eastern State Hospital, Medical Lake, WA [*Library symbol Library of Congress*] (LCLS)

WaMeI Interlake School, Staff Library, Medical Lake, WA [*Library symbol Library of Congress*] (LCLS)

WaMeL Lakeland Village School, Medical Lake, WA [*Library symbol Library of Congress*] (LCLS)

WaMeP Pine Lodge Correctional Center, Staff Library, Medical Lake, WA [*Library symbol Library of Congress*] (LCLS)

WaMeP-R Pine Lodge Correctional Center, Resident Library, Medical Lake, WA [*Library symbol Library of Congress*] (LCLS)

WAMEX West African Monsoon Experiment [*Marine science*] (OSRA)

WAMF Tallahassee, FL [*FM radio station call letters*]

WAMFLEX Wave Momentum Flux Experiment [*National Science Foundation*]

WAMG Gorontalo/Jalaluddin [*Indonesia*] [*ICAO location identifier*] (ICLI)

WAMG Wauwatosa-Milwaukee, WI [*FM radio station call letters*] (RBYB)

WAMH Amherst, MA [*FM radio station call letters*]

WAMH Tahuna/Naha [*Indonesia*] [*ICAO location identifier*] (ICLI)

WAMI Opp, AL [*AM radio station call letters*]

WAMI Toli Toli/Lalos [*Indonesia*] [*ICAO location identifier*] (ICLI)

WAMI Washington, Alaska, Montana, and Idaho [*Program for states without medical schools*]

WAMI Wide-Angle Michelson Interferometer (PDAA)

WAMI World Association for Medical Informatics (IAA)

WAMI-FM Opp, AL [*FM radio station call letters*]

WaMiH Highline Community College, Midway, WA [*Library symbol Library of Congress*] (LCLS)

WaMil Milton Memorial Library, Milton, WA [*Library symbol*] [*Library of Congress*] (LCLS)

WAMIS Watershed Management Information System

WAMK Kao/Kuabang [*Indonesia*] [*ICAO location identifier*] (ICLI)

WAMK Kingston, NY [*FM radio station call letters*]

WAML Laurel, MS [*AM radio station call letters*]

WaMl Moses Lake Public Library, Moses Lake, WA [*Library symbol Library of Congress*] (LCLS)

WAML Palu/Mutiara [*Indonesia*] [*ICAO location identifier*] (ICLI)

WAML Watertown Arsenal Medical Laboratory [*Massachusetts*] [*Army*]

WAML Western Association of Map Libraries (EA)

WAML Work Authorization Material List (DNAB)

WAML Wright Aero Medical Laboratory [*Air Force*]

WaMlB Big Bend Community College, Moses Lake, WA [*Library symbol Library of Congress*] (LCLS)

WaMlGS Church of Jesus Christ of Latter-Day Saints, Genealogical Society Library, MosesLake Branch, Moses Lake, WA [*Library symbol Library of Congress*] (LCLS)

WAMM Bridgewater, VA [*FM radio station call letters*]

WAMM Manado/Sam Ratulangi [*Indonesia*] [*ICAO location identifier*] (ICLI)

WAMM Women Against Military Madness (EA)

WAMM Woodstock, VA [*AM radio station call letters*]

WAMMC Western Australian Meat Marketing Corp. [*Commercial firm*]

WAMN Green Valley, WV [*AM radio station call letters*]

WAMN Melangguane [*Indonesia*] [*ICAO location identifier*] (ICLI)

WAMO Pittsburgh, PA [*FM radio station call letters*]

WAMO-AM Pittsburgh, PA [*AM radio station call letters*] (RBYB)

WAMOC Women's Auxiliary to the Military Order of the Cootie (EA)

WaMonR Washington State Reformatory, Monroe, WA [*Library symbol Library of Congress*] (LCLS)

WaMonT Twin Rivers Correctional Center, Monroe, WA [*Library symbol Library of Congress*] (LCLS)

WAMOSCOPE Wave-Modulated Oscilloscope

WAMP Jackson, TN [*FM radio station call letters*] (RBYB)

WAMP Poso/Kasigunou [*Indonesia*] [*ICAO location identifier*] (ICLI)

WAMP Wire Antenna Modeling Program (PDAA)

WAMPUM Wage and Manpower Process Utilizing Machine [*Bureau of Indian Affairs*]

WAMPUM Wartime Availability of Medical Personnel upon Mobilization

WAMQ Bada [*Indonesia*] [*ICAO location identifier*] (ICLI)

WAMQ Great Barrington, MA [*FM radio station call letters*]

WAMR Morotai/Pitu [*Indonesia*] [*ICAO location identifier*] (ICLI)

WAMR Venice, FL [*AM radio station call letters*]

WAMRAC World Association of Methodist Radio Amateurs and Clubs

WAMR-FM Miami, FL [*FM radio station call letters*] (RBYB)

WAMRL Western Australian Marine Research Laboratory

WAMS Weapon Aiming and Mode Selector (MCD)

WAMS Wholesale Applications Management System (MHDB)

WAMS Women's Automotive Maintenance Staff

WAMSTAS Wide-Area Mine Seismic Target Acquisition Sensor [*Military*] (MCD)

WAMT Ternate/Babullah [*Indonesia*] [*ICAO location identifier*] (ICLI)

WAMT Titusville, FL [*AM radio station call letters*]

WAMT Women and Manual Trades [*British*] [*An association*] (DBA)

WaMtJF John Fluke Manufacturing Co., Mountlake Terrace, WA [*Library symbol Library of Congress*] (LCLS)

WAMTMC Western Area Military Traffic Management Command (DICI)

WAMTMTS Western Area, Military Traffic Management and Terminal Service (AABC)

WaMtv Mount Vernon Public Library, Mount Vernon, WA [*Library symbol Library of Congress*] (LCLS)

WaMtvGS Church of Jesus Christ of Latter-Day Saints, Genealogical Society Library, MountVernon Branch, Mount Vernon, WA [*Library symbol Library of Congress*] (LCLS)

WaMtvH Skagit Valley Hospital, Mount Vernon, WA [*Library symbol*] [*Library of Congress*] (LCLS)

WaMtvS Skagit Valley College, Mount Vernon, WA [*Library symbol Library of Congress*] (LCLS)

WAMU Washington, DC [*FM radio station call letters*]

WAMU Washington Mutual [*NASDAQ symbol*] (TTSB)

WAMU Washington Mutual, Inc. [*NASDAQ symbol*] (NQ)

WAMU Wuasa [*Indonesia*] [*ICAO location identifier*] (ICLI)

WAMUM Washington Mutual 7.60% 'E' Pfd' [*NASDAQ symbol*] (TTSB)

WAMUN Wash Mutual $6 Cv Per'D'Pfd [*NASDAQ symbol*] (TTSB)

WAMUO Washington Mutual $2.28'C'Pfd [*NASDAQ symbol*] (TTSB)

WA Mutl Washington Mutual, Inc. [*Associated Press*] (SAG)

WAMV Amherst, VA [*AM radio station call letters*]

WAMW Luwuk/Bubung [*Indonesia*] [*ICAO location identifier*] (ICLI)

WAMW Washington, IN [*AM radio station call letters*]

WAMW-FM Washington, IN [*FM radio station call letters*]

WAMX Saline, MI [*AM radio station call letters*]

WAMY Amory, MS [*AM radio station call letters*]

WAMY World Assembly of Muslim Youth [*Riyadh, Saudi Arabia*] (EAIO)

WAMZ Louisville, KY [*FM radio station call letters*]

WAMZ Menado Sector [*Indonesia*] [*ICAO location identifier*] (ICLI)

WAn Antigo Public Library, Antigo, WI [*Library symbol Library of Congress*] (LCLS)

WAN Wane Aviation Ltd. [*Kenya*] [*FAA designator*] (FAAC)

WAN Wanigan

WAN Wanliss Street [*New Britain*] [*Seismograph station code, US Geological Survey*] (SEIS)

WAN Waverney [*Queensland*] [*Airport symbol*] (AD)

WAN Western Air Navigation Ltd. [*Australia*]

WAN Wide Area Network [*Telecommunications*]

WAN Women's Aquatic Network (EA)

WAN Women's Royal Australian Naval Service [*World War II*] (DSUE)

WAN Work Authorization Number (NASA)

WANA Anniston, AL [*AM radio station call letters*]

WANA Woodworking Association of North America (EA)

WANAP Washington [*DC*] National Airport

WaNasY Naselle Youth Camp, Staff Library, Naselle, WA [*Library symbol Library of Congress*] (LCLS)

WaNasY-R Naselle Youth Camp, Resident Library, Naselle, WA [*Library symbol Library of Congress*] (LCLS)

WANB Waynesburg, PA [*AM radio station call letters*]

WANB-FM Waynesburg, PA [*FM radio station call letters*]

WANC Ticonderoga, NY [*FM radio station call letters*]

WANC Western Australian Naturalists' Club (EERA)

WAND Decatur, IL [*Television station call letters*]

WAND Milestone Scientific, Inc. [*NASDAQ symbol*] (SAG)

WAND Waveform Analysis for Nondestructive Evaluation [*Military computer software*] (RDA)

WAND Westinghouse Alphanumeric Display (IAA)

WAND Women and Development Unit (EA)

WAND Women's Action for New Directions [*An association*]

WAND Women's Action for Nuclear Disarmament (EA)

W & ACT Wey and Arun Canal Trust [*British*] (DBA)

WANDAH Writing-Aid and Author's Helper (EDAC)

W & B Walferstan and Bristowe's Election Cases [*1859-65*] [*A publication*] (DLA)

W & B Works and Building Services [*British military*] (DMA)

W & B Dig Walter and Bates' Ohio Digest [*A publication*] (DLA)

W & C Westmorland and Cumberland Yeomanry [*British military*] (DMA)

W & C Wilson and Courtenay's Scotch Appeal Cases [*A publication*] (DLA)

W & C Wire and Cable (NASA)

W & C Conv Wolstenholme and Cherry's Conveyancing Statutes [*13th ed.*] [*1972*] [*A publication*] (DLA)

W & D Wolferstan and Dew's English Election Cases [*1856-58*] [*A publication*] (DLA)

W&E [*CSIRO Division of*] Wildlife and Ecology [*Commonwealth*] (EERA)

WAND EF WAND [*Women's Action for Nuclear Disarmament*] Education Fund (EA)

Wandell Wandell's New York Reports [*A publication*] (DLA)

W & F Water and Feed

W & F Work and Flop [*Printing*] (WDMC)

W & F Work and Flop (WDMC)

WandGlt Wandel & Goltermann Technologies [*Associated Press*] (SAG)

W & H Wage and Hour Division [*Department of Labor*] (OICC)

W & I Weighing and Inspection

W&I World & I [*A publication*] (BRI)

W & IR Work and Inspection Record (SAA)

W & J Washington and Jefferson College [*Pennsylvania*] (IIA)

W & L Washington and Lee University [*Lexington, VA*]

W & L Weapon and/or Launcher

W & L Welshpool & Llanfair Light Railway [*Wales*]

W & L Westcott & Laurance Line [*Steamship*] (MHDW)

W & L Dig Wood and Long's Digest [*Illinois*] [*A publication*] (DLA)

W & LLR Welshpool & Llanfair Light Railway [*Wales*]

Wandlst Wanderlust Interactive, Inc. [*Associated Press*] (SAG)

Wandlust Wanderlust Interactive, Inc. [*Associated Press*] (SAG)

W & M War and Marine (DS)

W & M Washburn and Moen [*Wire gauge*]

W & M William and Mary [*King and Queen of England*] (ROG)

W & M Wilson & McLane, Inc. [*Information service or system*] (IID)

W & M Woodbury and Minot's United States Circuit Court Reports [*3 vols.*] [*A publication*] (DLA)

W & M GA Washburn and Moen Gauge (MSA)

W&M Q William and Mary Quarterly [*A publication*] (BRI)

W & N Weidenfeld & Nicolson [*Publisher*]

W & N Wharton & Northern [*Railroad*] (MHDB)

W & O Wills Wilgram and O'Hara on Wills [*A publication*] (DLA)

W & PH........ Wage and Purchase Hire
W & R........ Welfare and Recreation [*Navy*]
W & S........ Watts and Sergeant's Pennsylvania Reports [*1841-1845*] [*A publication*] (DLA)
W & S........ Whiskey and Soda
W & S........ Wilson and Shaw's Scotch Appeal Cases, English House of Lords [*A publication*] (DLA)
W & S App... Wilson and Shaw's Scotch Appeal Cases, English House of Lords [*A publication*] (DLA)
W & StP...... Winona & St. Peter Railroad
W & T......... Work-and-Turn [*Printing*] (WDMC)
W&T........... Work and Turn (WDMC)
W & T......... Wrightsville & Tennille Railroad (IIA)
W & T Eq Ca... White and Tudor's Leading Cases in Equity [*9 eds.*] [*1849-1928*] [*A publication*] (DLA)
W & TLC...... White and Tudor's Leading Cases in Equity [*9 eds.*] [*1849-1928*] [*A publication*] (DLA)
W & W........ De Witt and Weeresinghe's Appeal Court Reports [*Ceylon*] [*A publication*] (DLA)
W & W........ Wahlstrom & Widstrand [*Publisher*] [*Sweden*]
W & W........ White and Wilson's [*or Willson's*] Civil Cases, Texas Court of Appeals [*A publication*] (DLA)
W & W........ Williams & Wilkins [*Publishing company*]
W & WCC.... White and Wilson's [*or Willson's*] Civil Cases, Texas Court of Appeals [*A publication*] (DLA)
W & W Civ Cases Court of Appeals... White and Wilson's [*or Willson's*] Civil Cases, Texas Court of Appeals [*A publication*] (DLA)
W & W Con Cases... White and Wilson's [*or Willson's*] Civil Cases, Texas Court of Appeals [*A publication*] (DLA)
W & W Con Rep... White and Wilson's [*or Willson's*] Civil Cases, Texas Court of Appeals [*A publication*] (DLA)
W & WT...... Water and Waste Treatment
WANE.......... Fort Wayne, IN [*Television station call letters*]
WaNe.......... Pend Oreille County Library District, Newport, WA [*Library symbol*] [*Library of Congress*] (LCLS)
WANG.......... Wang Laboratories [*NASDAQ symbol*] (TTSB)
WANG.......... Wang Laboratories, Inc. [*NASDAQ symbol*] (SAG)
WangL.......... Wang Laboratories, Inc. [*Associated Press*] (SAG)
WangLab..... Wang Laboratories, Inc. [*Associated Press*] (SAG)
WANGW....... Wang Labs Wrrt [*NASDAQ symbol*] (TTSB)
WANL.......... Albany, GA [*AM radio station call letters*]
WANL.......... Westinghouse-Astronuclear Laboratories
WANM.......... Tallahassee, FL [*AM radio station call letters*]
WANN.......... Annapolis, MD [*AM radio station call letters*]
WANO.......... Pineville, KY [*AM radio station call letters*]
WANO.......... World Association of Nuclear Operators (ECON)
WANR.......... Warren, OH [*AM radio station call letters*]
WANS.......... Anderson, SC [*AM radio station call letters*]
WANST........ Wanstead [*England*]
WANT.......... Lebanon, TN [*FM radio station call letters*]
WANT.......... Wantage [*Urban district in England*]
WANT.......... Warrant Apprehension Narcotics Team [*In US Marshal Service's "Operation WANT"*]
WANTC........ Western Australian Nanny Training College
WANU-FM.... Lewistown, PA [*FM radio station call letters*] (RBYB)
WANX.......... Holly Hill, FL [*FM radio station call letters*] (RBYB)
WANY.......... Albany, KY [*AM radio station call letters*]
WANY-FM.... Albany, KY [*FM radio station call letters*]
WAO........... Outagamie County Hospital, Appleton, WI [*Library symbol Library of Congress*] (LCLS)
WaO........... Timberland Regional Library, Olympia, WA [*Library symbol Library of Congress*] (LCLS)
WAO........... Weapons Assignment Officer [*Air Force*] (AFM)
WAO........... Western Australian Opera
WAO........... Wet-Air Oxidation (PDAA)
WAO........... Women's American ORT (EA)
WAOA.......... Melbourne, FL [*FM radio station call letters*]
WaOAP........ Washington State Office of Adult Probation and Parole, Olympia, WA [*Library symbol Library of Congress*] (LCLS)
WaOAr........ State of Washington Department of General Administration, Division of Archives and Records Management, Olympia, WA [*Library symbol Library of Congress*] (LCLS)
WaOB.......... Washington State Department of Public Assistance, Ben Tidball Memorial Library, Olympia, WA [*Library symbol Library of Congress*] (LCLS)
WAOB.......... World Agricultural Outlook Board [*Department of Agriculture*] (GFGA)
WAOC.......... St. Augustine, FL [*AM radio station call letters*]
WAOC.......... Western Australian Olympic Council
WaOCA........ Washington State Court of Appeals, Olympia, WA [*Library symbol*] [*Library of Congress*] (LCLS)
WaOE.......... Evergreen State College, Olympia, WA [*Library symbol Library of Congress*] (LCLS)
WaOEd........ Washington State Department of Education, Olympia, WA [*Library symbol Library of Congress*] (LCLS)
WaOEng...... Washington State Energy Office, Olympia, WA [*Library symbol Library of Congress*] (LCLS)
WAOE-TV..... Peoria, IL [*TV station call letters*] (RBYB)
WAOF.......... Mount Juliet, TN [*FM radio station call letters*] (RBYB)
WaOGS........ Church of Jesus Christ of Latter-Day Saints, Genealogical Society Library, Olympia Branch, Olympia, WA [*Library symbol Library of Congress*] (LCLS)
WAOH.......... Outagamie County Health Center, Appleton, WI [*Library symbol*] [*Library of Congress*] (LCLS)
WAOHE........ Western Australian Office of Higher Education
WaOhNH...... United States Naval Hospital, Medical Library, Oak Harbor, WA [*Library symbol*] [*Library of Congress*] (LCLS)
WAOK.......... Atlanta, GA [*AM radio station call letters*]
WAOL.......... Ripley, OH [*FM radio station call letters*]
WaOLI.......... State of Washington Department of Labor and Industries Libraries, Olympia, WA [*Library symbol Library of Congress*] (LCLS)
WaOLN........ Washington Library Network, Olympia, WA [*Library symbol Library of Congress*] (LCLS)
WAOM.......... Morehead, KY [*Television station call letters*]
WaONR........ Washington State Department of Natural Resources, Division of Geology and Earth Resources, Olympia, WA [*Library symbol Library of Congress*] (LCLS)
WaOP.......... Washington State Patrol, Olympia, WA [*Library symbol*] [*Library of Congress*] (LCLS)
WAOP.......... Western Australian Opinion Polls
WaOPI.......... Washington Superindentent of Public Instruction, Olympia, WA [*Library symbol*] [*Library of Congress*] (LCLS)
WAOR.......... Niles, MI [*FM radio station call letters*]
WaOrc.......... Orcas Island Library, East Sound, WA [*Library symbol*] [*Library of Congress*] (LCLS)
WaOrtS........ Washington Soldiers' Home, Staff Library, Orting, WA [*Library symbol Library of Congress*] (LCLS)
WaOrtS-R..... Washington Soldiers' Home, Resident Library, Orting, WA [*Library symbol Library of Congress*] (LCLS)
WAOS.......... Austell, GA [*AM radio station call letters*]
WAOS.......... Welsh Agricultural Organisation Society (DBA)
WAOS.......... Wide-Angle Optical System
WaOSM........ Saint Martin's College, Olympia, WA [*Library symbol Library of Congress*] (LCLS)
WaOSP........ Saint Peter's Hospital, Olympia, WA [*Library symbol Library of Congress*] (LCLS)
WaOSPS...... South Puget Sound Community College Library, Olympia, WA [*Library symbol*] [*Library of Congress*] (LCLS)
WAOT.......... Kingstree, SC [*FM radio station call letters*] (RBYB)
WaOT.......... Washington State Department of Transportation, Olympia, WA [*Library symbol Library of Congress*] (LCLS)
WaOTC........ Olympia Technical Community College, Olympia, WA [*Library symbol Library of Congress*] (LCLS)
WAOU.......... Tawas City, MI [*FM radio station call letters*] (RBYB)
WaOUT........ Washington Utilities and Transportation Commission, Olympia, WA [*Library symbol*] [*Library of Congress*] (LCLS)
WAOV.......... Vincennes, IN [*AM radio station call letters*]
WAOW.......... Wausau, WI [*Television station call letters*]
WAOW.......... Women Against the Ordination of Women [*Australia*]
WAOX.......... Bryan, OH [*FM radio station call letters*] (RBYB)
WAOY.......... Saucier, MS [*FM radio station call letters*] (RBYB)
WAOZ.......... Cincinnati, OH [*AM radio station call letters*]
WAP............ Alto Palena [*Chile*] [*Airport symbol*] (AD)
WAP............ Institute of Paper Chemistry, Appleton, WI [*Library symbol Library of Congress*] (LCLS)
WAP............ Wandering Atrial Pacemaker [*Cardiology*]
WAP............ Wapentake [*Subdivision of some English shires*]
WAP............ Warner Audio Publishing
W Ap........... Washington Appellate Reports [*A publication*] (DLA)
WAP............ Waste Analysis Plan [*Environmental Protection Agency*] (GFGA)
WAP............ Wax Appearance Point [*Temperature at which waxy substances in fuel start to precipitate*]
WAP............ Weak Anthropic Principle [*Term coined by authors John Barrow and Frank Tipler in their book, "The Anthropic Cosmological Principle"*]
WAP............ Weatherization Assistance Program (GNE)
WAP............ Weekly Average Price
WAP............ Weight after Processing [*Metallurgy*]
WAP............ Whale Adoption Project (EA)
WAP............ Whey Acidic Protein
WAP............ White Anglo-Saxon Protestant (DAVI)
WAP............ Wide-Angle Panorama [*Photography*] [*NASA*]
WAP............ Wideband Acoustical Processor (CAAL)
WAP............ Wire Adhesion Promoter
WAP............ Wireless Application Protocol [*Computer science*]
WAP............ Women Against Pornography (EA)
WAP............ Women's Action Program [*HEW*]
WAP............ Work Activity Program
WAP............ Work Analysis Program [*Computer science*] (BUR)
WAP............ Work Assignment Procedure
WAPA.......... Amahai [*Indonesia*] [*ICAO location identifier*] (ICLI)
WaPa.......... Pasco Public Library, Pasco, WA [*Library symbol Library of Congress*] (LCLS)
WAPA.......... San Juan, PR [*AM radio station call letters*]
wapa........... Wall Paper (VRA)
WAPA.......... Western Area Power Administration [*Department of Energy*]
WAPA.......... White American Political Association (EA)
WaPaAp...... Washington State Office of Adult Probation and Parole, Pasco, WA [*Library symbol Library of Congress*] (LCLS)
WaPaC........ Columbia Basin College, Pasco, WA [*Library symbol Library of Congress*] (LCLS)
WaPaGS...... Church of Jesus Christ of Latter-Day Saints, Genealogical Society Library, PascoBranch, Pasco, WA [*Library symbol Library of Congress*] (LCLS)
WAPALS...... Workload and Productivity Analysis (MCD)
WAPA-TV.... San Juan, PR [*Television station call letters*]
WAPB.......... Bula [*Indonesia*] [*ICAO location identifier*] (ICLI)
WAPB.......... Murfreesboro, TN [*AM radio station call letters*] (RBYB)
WAPC.......... Appleton Post Crescent, Appleton, WI [*Library symbol*] [*Library of Congress*] (LCLS)

WAPC Banda [*Indonesia*] [*ICAO location identifier*] (ICLI)
WAPC Women's Auxiliary Police Corps [*British World War II*]
WAPCB West African Produce Control Board [*World War II*]
WAPC-FM Terre Haute, IN [*FM radio station call letters*] (RBYB)
WAPCOS Water and Power Development Consultancy Services
WAPD Dobo [*Indonesia*] [*ICAO location identifier*] (ICLI)
WAPD Western Air Procurement District
WAPD Western Australian Parliamentary Debates [*A publication*]
WAPDA Water and Power Development Authority (IAA)
WAPD-FM Campbellsville, KY [*FM radio station call letters*] (RBYB)
WAPE Jacksonville, FL [*FM radio station call letters*]
WAPE Mangole [*Indonesia*] [*ICAO location identifier*] (ICLI)
WAPE Windows Application Programming Environment [*Computer science*] (BTTJ)
WAPF McComb, MS [*AM radio station call letters*]
WAPF West African Pharmaceutical Federation [*Lagos, Nigeria*] (EAIO)
WAPG High-Endurance Coast Guard Cutter [*Later, WHEC*] (CINC)
WAPH Labuhu/Usman Sadik [*Indonesia*] [*ICAO location identifier*] (ICLI)
WaPH Pullman Memorial Hospital, Pullman, WA [*Library symbol*] [*Library of Congress*] (LCLS)
WAPI Birmingham, AL [*AM radio station call letters*]
WAPI Saumlaki [*Indonesia*] [*ICAO location identifier*] (ICLI)
WAPI World Aerial Photographic Index [*Meteorology*]
WAPJ-FM Torrington, CT [*FM radio station call letters*] (RBYB)
WAPL Appleton Public Library, Appleton, WI [*Library symbol*] [*Library of Congress*] (LCLS)
WAPL Appleton, WI [*FM radio station call letters*]
WAPL Langgur/Dumatubun [*Indonesia*] [*ICAO location identifier*] (ICLI)
WAPL Western Aerial Photography Laboratory [*Department of Agriculture*]
WaPIP Pacific Lutheran University, Parkland, WA [*Library symbol Library of Congress*] (LCLS)
WAPMA Western Australian Potato Marketing Authority
WAPME Writers and Artists for Peace in the Middle East (EA)
WAPN Holly Hill, FL [*FM radio station call letters*]
WAPN Sanana [*Indonesia*] [*ICAO location identifier*] (ICLI)
WAPO-FM Mount Vernon, IL [*FM radio station call letters*] (RBYB)
WaPoN North Olympic Library System, Port Angeles, WA [*Library symbol Library of Congress*] (LCLS)
WaPoP Peninsula College, Port Angeles, WA [*Library symbol Library of Congress*] (LCLS)
WAPOR World Association for Public Opinion Research (EA)
WAPP Ambon/Pattimura [*Indonesia*] [*ICAO location identifier*] (ICLI)
WAPP Berryville, VA [*FM radio station call letters*]
Wap Pr R Waples on Proceedings in Rem [*A publication*] (DLA)
WAPPS Work Aptitude Profile and Practice Set [*Test*]
WAPQ Crestline, OH [*FM radio station call letters*]
WAPR Namlea [*Indonesia*] [*ICAO location identifier*] (ICLI)
WAPR World Association for Psychosocial Rehabilitation (EAIO)
WAPR World Association for Psychosocial Rehabilitation - US Branch (EA)
WAPR-FM Selma, AL [*FM radio station call letters*] (RBYB)
WAPS Akron, OH [*FM radio station call letters*]
WAPS Selaru [*Indonesia*] [*ICAO location identifier*] (ICLI)
WaPS Washington State University, Pullman, WA [*Library symbol Library of Congress*] (LCLS)
WAPS Weighted Airman Promotion System [*Air Force*]
WAPS Women of the American Press Service [*Accredited American women war correspondents*] [*World War II*]
WAPS World Association of Pathology Societies
WA/PSF Work Authorization/Program Status Factor
WaPS-V Washington State University, Veterinary Medical Library, Pullman, WA [*Library symbol Library of Congress*] (LCLS)
WAPT Jackson, MS [*Television station call letters*]
WaPt Port Townsend Public Library, Port Townsend, WA [*Library symbol*] [*Library of Congress*] (LCLS)
WAPT Taliabu [*Indonesia*] [*ICAO location identifier*] (ICLI)
WAPT Weidels Auditory Processing Test [*Speech and language therapy*] (DAVI)
WAPT Wichita Auditory Processing Test [*Child development test*]
WAPT Wild Animal Propagation Trust [*Defunct*]
WAPT Work Area Pointer Table [*Computer science*]
WAPU-FM Colfax, IL [*FM radio station call letters*] (RBYB)
WaPuS Washington State University, Western Washington Research and Extension Center, Puyallup, WA [*Library symbol Library of Congress*] (LCLS)
WAPV-FM North Myrtle Beach, SC [*FM radio station call letters*] (RBYB)
WAPX Clarksville, TN [*FM radio station call letters*]
WAPZ Ambon Sector [*Indonesia*] [*ICAO location identifier*] (ICLI)
WAPZ Wetumpka, AL [*AM radio station call letters*]
WAQ Antsalova [*Madagascar*] [*Airport symbol*] (OAG)
WAQB-FM Brighton, NY [*FM radio station call letters*] (RBYB)
WAQC-FM Brunswick, GA [*FM radio station call letters*] (RBYB)
WAQE Rice Lake, WI [*AM radio station call letters*]
WAQE-FM Rice Lake, WI [*FM radio station call letters*]
WAQF-TV Batavia, NY [*TV station call letters*] (RBYB)
WAQG-FM Ozark, AL [*FM radio station call letters*] (RBYB)
WaQGS Church of Jesus Christ of Latter-Day Saints, Genealogical Society Library, Quincy Branch, Quincy, WA [*Library symbol Library of Congress*] (LCLS)
WAQI Miami, FL [*AM radio station call letters*]
WAQP Saginaw, MI [*Television station call letters*]
WAQX Manlius, NY [*FM radio station call letters*]
WAQY East Longmeadow, MA [*AM radio station call letters*]
WAQY Springfield, MA [*FM radio station call letters*]
WAQZ Milford, OH [*FM radio station call letters*]
WAR NZ Warbirds Association, Inc. [*New Zealand*] [*ICAO designator*] (FAAC)
WAR Warrant
WAR Warrenton Railroad Co. [*AAR code*]
WAR Warrior Industry Ltd. [*Vancouver Stock Exchange symbol*]
WAR Warsaw [*Poland*] [*Seismograph station code, US Geological Survey*] (SEIS)
WAR Warwickshire (ROG)
WAR Wassermann Antigen Reaction [*Test for syphilis*] [*Medicine*]
WAR Weapon Accuracy and Results [*Model*] (MCD)
WAR We Are Ridiculous [*Antiwar slogan*]
WAR West African Regiment [*Military unit*] [*British*]
WAR White Aryan Resistance (EA)
WAR Whiteruthenian American Relief (EA)
WAR With All Risks [*Insurance*]
WAR Women Against Rape [*An association*] (EA)
WAR Work Acquisition Routine
WAR Work Authorization Report [*or Request*] [*NASA*] (MCD)
WAR World Administrative Radio Conference for Space Communication
WAR World Affairs Report [*Database*] [*California Institute of International Studies*] [*Information service or system*] (CRD)
WARA Attleboro, MA [*AM radio station call letters*]
War Adv Att Warren's Adventures of an Attorney in Search of Practice [*A publication*] (DLA)
WARAMS Wartime Alignment of Reserve and Active Medical Systems
War Bell Ward on Belligerent and Neutral Powers [*A publication*] (DLA)
WARC Meadville, PA [*FM radio station call letters*]
WARC Washington Archaeological Research Center [*Washington State University*] [*Research center*] (RCD)
WARC Wharton Applied Research Center [*University of Pennsylvania*] [*Research center*] (RCD)
WARC World Administrative Radio Conference [*International Telecommunication Union*] (NTCM)
WARC World Alliance of Reformed Churches [*Alliance of the Reformed Churches th roughout the World Holding the Presbyterian System and International Congregational Council*] [*Formed by a merger of*] (EAIO)
WARCAD War Department - Civil Affairs Division [*Obsolete*]
WARCAT Workload and Resources Correlation Analysis Technique [*Army*]
WARC-BS World Administrative Radio Conference for Broadcast Satellite Service [*International Telecommunication Union*] (NTCM)
WARC-MAR World Administrative Radio Conference for Maritime Mobile Telecommunications
WARCO War Correspondent (DSUE)
War Cr L Warren's Ohio Criminal Law [*A publication*] (DLA)
WARC-ST World Administrative Radio Conference for Space Telecommunications
WARD Pittston, PA [*AM radio station call letters*]
Ward Warden's State Reports [*2, 4 Ohio*] [*A publication*] (DLA)
WARD Wardship
WARDA West Africa Rice Development Association
Ward & Sm Warden and Smith's State Reports [*3 Ohio*] [*A publication*] (DLA)
Warden Warden's State Reports [*2, 4 Ohio*] [*A publication*] (DLA)
Warden & Smith Warden and Smith's State Reports [*3 Ohio*] [*A publication*] (DLA)
Warden's Law & Bk Bull Warden's Weekly Law and Bank Bulletin [*Ohio*] [*A publication*] (DLA)
War Dept BCA United States War Department, Decisions of Board of Contract Adjustment [*A publication*] (DLA)
Ward Just Ward's Justice of the Peace [*A publication*] (DLA)
Ward Leg Ward on Legacies [*A publication*] (DLA)
Ward Nat Ward's Law of Nations [*A publication*] (DLA)
WARDS Welfare of Animals Used for Research in Drugs and Therapy
WaRe Renton Public Library, Renton, WA [*Library symbol Library of Congress*] (LCLS)
WARE Ware, MA [*AM radio station call letters*]
Ware Ware's United States District Court Reports [*A publication*] (DLA)
WaRedEM Eastside Medical Laboratory, Redmond, WA [*Library symbol*] [*Library of Congress*] (LCLS)
WaRedPC Physio-Control, Information Center, Redmond, WA [*Library symbol*] [*Library of Congress*] (LCLS)
WaRedSu Sundstand Data Control Corp., Sundstrand Corp., Redmond, WA [*Library symbol*] [*Library of Congress*] (LCLS)
WAREH Wareham [*Municipal borough in England*]
WARES Workload and Resources Evaluation System [*Navy*]
Ware's CC Rep Ware's United States District Court Reports [*A publication*] (DLA)
Ware's Rep Ware's United States District Court Reports [*A publication*] (DLA)
WaRetV Washington Veterans' Home, Medical Library, Retsil, WA [*Library symbol Library of Congress*] (LCLS)
WaRetV-R Washington Veterans' Home, Resident Library, Retsil, WA [*Library symbol Library of Congress*] (LCLS)
WaReVG Valley General Hospital, Renton, WA [*Library symbol Library of Congress*] (LCLS)
WAREX Warrant Issued for Extradite
WARF Jasper, AL [*AM radio station call letters*]
WARF Warfare (AFM)
WARF Warfarin [*Pharmacology*] (DAVI)
WARF Wartime Active Replacement Factors (AABC)
WARF Wartime Replacement Factors [*DoD*]
WARF Weekly Audit Report File [*IRS*]
WARF Wide-Aperture Research Facility [*For hurricane detection*]
WARFS Water Resources Forecasting System (USDC)
WARFS Water Resources Forecasting System [*Marine science*] (OSRA)
WARG Summit, IL [*FM radio station call letters*]
WARHD Warhead (AAG)

WARHUD ..... Wide-Angle Raster Head-Up Display (MCD)
WARI ..... Abbeville, AL [*AM radio station call letters*] (RBYB)
WaRi ..... Richland Public Library, Richland, WA [*Library symbol Library of Congress*] (LCLS)
WARI ..... Western Australian Agricultural Research Institute [*State*] (EERA)
WARI ..... Wheezing Associated with Respiratory Injections
WaRiAR ..... Atlantic Richfield Hanford Co., Richland, WA [*Library symbol Library of Congress*] (LCLS)
WaRiB ..... Battelle Memorial Institute, Pacific Northwest Laboratory, Richland, WA [*Library symbol Library of Congress*] (LCLS)
WaRiBN ..... Battelle-Northwest Hospital, Life Science Library, Richland, WA [*Library symbol Library of Congress*] (LCLS)
WaRiGS ..... Church of Jesus Christ of Latter-Day Saints, Genealogical Society Library, Richland Branch, Richland, WA [*Library symbol Library of Congress*] (LCLS)
WaRiHS ..... Hanford School Library, Richland, WA [*Library symbol*] [*Library of Congress*] (LCLS)
WaRiJ ..... Joint Center for Graduate Study, Richland, WA [*Library symbol*] [*Library of Congress*] (LCLS)
WaRiMC ..... Mid-Columbia Mental Health Center, Richland, WA [*Library symbol Library of Congress*] (LCLS)
WArl-R ..... Indian Ridge Treatment Center, Resident Library, Arlington, WA [*Library symbol Library of Congress*] (LCLS)
WARIS ..... Water Resources Information System [*New South Wales*] [*State*] (EERA)
WARIS ..... Western Arid Resource Information System [*Queensland*] [*State*] (EERA)
WaRit ..... Ritzville Public Library, Ritzville, WA [*Library symbol Library of Congress*] (LCLS)
WARITC ..... Western Australian Retail Industry Training Council
WARK ..... Hagerstown, MD [*AM radio station call letters*]
WARKS ..... Warwickshire [*County in England*]
WARL ..... Western Australian Rugby League
WARLA ..... Wide-Aperture Radio Location Array
WARLOCE ..... Wartime Lines of Communication, Europe (AABC)
WARLOG ..... Wartime Logistics (AABC)
War L St ..... Warren's Law Studies [*A publication*] (DLA)
WARM ..... Scranton, PA [*AM radio station call letters*]
WARM ..... Warranty [*Cost Effectiveness*] Model
WARM ..... Wartime Reserve Mode [*Military*]
WARM ..... Weapons Assignment Research Model [*Military*]
WARM ..... Wood and Solid Fuel Association of Retailers and Manufacturers (EA)
WARM ..... York, PA [*FM radio station call letters*]
WARMAPS ..... Wartime Manpower Planning System
WARMEDY ..... Warm, Family Comedy [*Type of television show*]
WARMER ..... World Action for Recycled Material and Energy from Rubbish (EERA)
WARN ..... Warning (NASA)
WARN ..... Weather Amateur Radio Network (NOAA)
WARN ..... Women of All Red Nations (EA)
WARN ..... Worker Adjustment and Retraining Notification (AAGC)
WARN ..... Worker Adjustment and Retraining Notification Act [*1988*]
WARNA ..... Worker Adjustment and Retraining Notification Act [*1988*]
Warnaco ..... Warnaco Group, Inc. [*Associated Press*] (SAG)
WarnL ..... Warner-Lambert Co. [*Associated Press*] (SAG)
WARNORD ..... Warning Order [*Military*] (INF)
Warntc ..... Warrantech Corp. [*Associated Press*] (SAG)
WARO ..... Naples, FL [*AM radio station call letters*]
WARO-FM ..... Naples, FL [*FM radio station call letters*] (RBYB)
War Op ..... Warwick's Opinions [*City Solicitor of Philadelphia, PA*] [*A publication*] (DLA)
WARP ..... Warp 10 Technologies, Inc. [*NASDAQ symbol*] (SAG)
WARP ..... Weather and Radar Processor [*FAA*] (TAG)
WARP ..... Wind Amplified Rotor Platform
WARP ..... Wind Amplifier Rotor Platform
WARP ..... Worldwide Ammunition Reporting Program (NG)
WARP ..... Worldwide AUTODIN [*Automatic Digital Information Network*] Restoral Plan (CET)
Warp10 ..... Warp 10 Technologies, Inc. [*Associated Press*] (SAG)
WARPAC ..... Wartime Repair Parts Consumption (MCD)
WARPATH ..... World Association to Remove Prejudice Against the Handicapped
WARPF ..... Warp 10 Technologies [*NASDAQ symbol*] (TTSB)
War Prof Dut ..... Warren. Moral, Social, and Professional Duties of Attorneys and Solicitors [*2nd ed.*] [*1851*] [*A publication*] (DLA)
WARQ ..... Columbia, SC [*FM radio station call letters*]
Warr ..... Warrant [*A document entitling holder to purchase a given issue of stock*] [*Investment term*]
WARR ..... Warranty (MSA)
WARR ..... Warrenton, NC [*AM radio station call letters*] (RBYB)
WARR ..... Waste Acid Release Reduction [*Environmental science*]
WARRAMP ..... Wartime Requirements for Ammunition, Materiel, and Personnel
WARRC ..... Western Aerospace Rescue and Recovery Center [*Air Force*]
Warren ..... Warren Bancorp, Inc. [*Associated Press*] (SAG)
Warren-T ..... Warren-Teed [*Commercial firm*] (DAVI)
WARRT ..... Warrant (ROG)
WARRTD ..... Warranted (WGA)
Wars ..... [*The*] Jewish Wars [*of Josephus*] [*A publication*] (BJA)
WARS ..... Warfare Analysis and Research System [*Navy*]
WARS ..... Wide-Area Remote Sensors
WARS ..... Worldwide Ammunition Reporting System [*Military*]
WARSCAP ..... Wartime Support Capability
WARSIC ..... Water Resources Scientific Information Center [*US Geological Survey*] [*Reston, VA Database originator*] (IT)
WARSIM ..... Warfighters' Simulation [*DoD*]
WARSL ..... War Reserve Stockage List (MCD)
WART ..... Weighted Average Remaining Term [*Finance*]
WART ..... Wenceslaus Anxiety Representation Taxonomy [*Satirical psychology term*]
WARTA ..... Western Australian Road Transport Association
Warth Code ..... West Virginia Code [*1899*] [*A publication*] (DLA)
WARU ..... Peru, IN [*AM radio station call letters*]
WARU-FM ..... Peru, IN [*FM radio station call letters*]
WARV ..... Warwick, RI [*AM radio station call letters*]
Warv Abst ..... Warvelle on Abstracts of Title [*A publication*] (DLA)
Warv El RP ..... Warvelle's Elements of Real Property [*A publication*] (DLA)
Warv V & P ..... Warvelle's Vendors and Purchasers of Real Property [*A publication*] (DLA)
WARW ..... Bethesda, MD [*FM radio station call letters*]
WARW ..... Warwickshire [*County in England*]
WARWICKS ..... Warwickshire [*County in England*]
Warwick's Op ..... Warwick's Opinions [*City Solicitor of Philadelphia, PA*] [*A publication*] (DLA)
WARWS ..... Warwickshire [*County in England*]
WARX ..... Hagerstown, MD [*FM radio station call letters*]
WARY ..... Valhalla, NY [*FM radio station call letters*]
WaS ..... Seattle Public Library, Seattle, WA [*Library symbol Library of Congress*] (LCLS)
WAs ..... Vaughn Public Library, Ashland, WI [*Library symbol Library of Congress*] (LCLS)
WAS ..... Wadley Southern Railway Co. [*AAR code Obsolete*]
WAS ..... Wallops Station [*Later, WFC*] [*NASA*]
WAS ..... Walsten Air Services [*Canada ICAO designator*] (FAAC)
WAS ..... War at Sea (NVT)
WAS ..... Ward Atmosphere Scale [*Psychology*]
WAS ..... Ware Resources Ltd. [*Vancouver Stock Exchange symbol*]
WAS ..... Warner & Swasey Co., Solon, OH [*OCLC symbol*] (OCLC)
WAS ..... Washington [*District of Columbia*] [*Airport symbol*] (OAG)
WAS ..... Washington [*District of Columbia*] [*Seismograph station code, US Geological Survey Closed*] (SEIS)
WAS ..... Washington Constr Grp [*NYSE symbol*] (TTSB)
was ..... Washo [*MARC language code Library of Congress*] (LCCP)
WAS ..... Waste-Activated Sludge
WAS ..... Waynesburg Southern [*AAR code*]
WAS ..... Weapons Alert System [*NORAD*] (MCD)
WAS ..... Weapons Application Study (SAA)
WAS ..... Weekly Arrival Schedule [*Military*] (AFIT)
WAS ..... Western Associated Schools [*Australia*]
WAS ..... Wide Analysis Sheet
WAS ..... Wide-Angle Sensor
WAS ..... Wide Area Surveillance [*Military*]
WAS ..... Wideband Antenna System
WAS ..... Wiskott-Aldrich Syndrome [*Immunology*]
WAS ..... Women's Addiction Service [*National Institute of Mental Health*]
WAS ..... Worked All States [*Contacted at least one station in all states*] [*Amateur radio*]
WAS ..... World Aquaculture Society (EA)
WAS ..... World Archaeological Society (EA)
WAS ..... World Around Songs (EA)
WAS ..... World Artifex Society (EAIO)
WAS ..... World Association for Sexology (EA)
WASA ..... Havre De Grace, MD [*AM radio station call letters*]
WaSA ..... Seattle Art Museum, Seattle, WA [*Library symbol Library of Congress*] (LCLS)
WASA ..... Wax Anti-Settling Additive [*Diesel fuel*]
WASA ..... West African Shippers Association [*British*] (DBA)
WASA ..... Western Australian Society of Arts
WASA ..... Women's All-Star Association (EA)
WaSAA ..... Catholic Archdiocese of Seattle, Archives, Seattle, WA [*Library symbol Library of Congress*] (LCLS)
WaSAB ..... Atomic Bomb Casualty Commission, Seattle, WA [*Library symbol Library of Congress*] (LCLS)
WASAC ..... Working Group of the Army Study Advisory Committee (AABC)
WaSAD ..... Alcohol and Drug Institute, Seattle, WA [*Library symbol*] [*Library of Congress*] (LCLS)
WASAG ..... Washington Special Action Group [*National Security Council*]
WASAL ..... Wisconsin Academy of Sciences, Arts, and Letters
WASAMA ..... Woman's Auxiliary to the Student American Medical Association (DAVI)
WASAR ..... Wide Application System Adapter
WASAW ..... Western Australian Sewerage and Waste Quality Infrastructure Program [*State*] (EERA)
WASB ..... Brockport, NY [*AM radio station call letters*]
WaSB ..... Pacific Northwest Bibliographic Center, Seattle, WA [*Library symbol Library of Congress*] (LCLS)
WASB ..... Steenkol/Bintuni [*Indonesia*] [*ICAO location identifier*] (ICLI)
WaSBa ..... Battelle Human Affairs Research Center, Seattle, WA [*Library symbol Library of Congress*] (LCLS)
WASB-FM ..... Brockport, NY [*FM radio station call letters*]
WaSBG ..... Bogle & Gates, Law Library, Seattle, WA [*Library symbol*] [*Library of Congress*] (LCLS)
WaSBH ..... Ballard Community Hospital Library, Seattle, WA [*Library symbol*] [*Library of Congress*] (LCLS)
WaSBo ..... [*The*] Boeing Co., Commercial Airplane Group, Technical Libraries, Seattle,WA [*Library symbol Library of Congress*] (LCLS)
WaSBo-A ..... [*The*] Boeing Co., Aerospace Division, Technical Library, Kent, WA [*Library symbol Library of Congress*] (LCLS)
WaSBo-B ..... Boeing Co., Technical Libraries, Bellevue, WA [*Library symbol*] [*Library of Congress*] (LCLS)
WaSBo-K ..... Boeing Co., Technical Libraries, Kent, WA [*Library symbol*] [*Library of Congress*] (LCLS)

WASC .... Ransiki/Abresso [*Indonesia*] [*ICAO location identifier*] (ICLI)
WaSC.......... Seattle Central Community College, Seattle, WA [*Library symbol Library of Congress*] (LCLS)
WASC .... Spartanburg, SC [*AM radio station call letters*]
WASC .... West Africa Supply Centre [*World War II*]
WASC .... Western Administrative Support Center (USDC)
WASC .... Western Administrative Support Center [*Marine science*] (OSRA)
WASC .... Western Association of Schools and Colleges (EA)
WASC .... Western Australian Shippers' Council
WASC .... White Anglo-Saxon Catholic
WASC .... Williams Awareness Sentence Completion [*Personality development test*] [*Psychology*]
WASCAL ...... Wide-Angle Scanning Array Lens Antenna
WaSC-D....... Seattle Central Community College, District Technical Services, Seattle, WA [*Library symbol*] [*Library of Congress*] (LCLS)
WASCL .... Western Australian Society for Computers and the Law
WaSC-N....... North Seattle Community College, Seattle, WA [*Library symbol Library of Congress*] (LCLS)
WaSCO .... Children's Orthopedic Hospital and Medical Center, Seattle, WA [*Library symbol Library of Congress*] (LCLS)
WASCO........ War Safety Council
WaSC-S .... South Seattle Community College, Seattle, WA [*Library symbol Library of Congress*] (LCLS)
WaSC-Sh ..... Shoreline Community College, Seattle, WA [*Library symbol Library of Congress Obsolete*] (LCLS)
WASD .... Wide-Angle Self-Destruct (MCD)
WASE........... Kebar [*Indonesia*] [*ICAO location identifier*] (ICLI)
WASE........... Radcliff, KY [*FM radio station call letters*] (RBYB)
WASE........... Saint Elizabeth Hospital, Appleton, WI [*Library symbol Library of Congress*] (LCLS)
WASEC .... Warner Amex Satellite Entertainment Co. [*Cable television*]
WaSelY........ Yakima Valley School, Selah, WA [*Library symbol Library of Congress*] (LCLS)
WaSEPA ...... United States Environmental Protection Agency, Region X Library, Seattle, WA [*Library symbol*] [*Library of Congress*] (LCLS)
WASES .... Western Australian State Emergency Service
WASEX .... War at Sea Exercise [*Navy*] (DOMA)
WASF........... Fak Fak/Torea [*Indonesia*] [*ICAO location identifier*] (ICLI)
WaSF .... Fircrest School, Staff Library, Seattle, WA [*Library symbol Library of Congress*] (LCLS)
WASF........... Water Authorities Superannuation Fund [*British*]
WASF........... Western Australian Sports Federation
WaSFC......... Firland Correctional Center, Staff Library, Seattle, WA [*Library symbol Library of Congress*] (LCLS)
WaSFC-R..... Firland Correctional Center, Resident Library, Seattle, WA [*Library symbol Library of Congress*] (LCLS)
WASFL......... Western Australian State Football League
WaSFP......... Foster, Pepper & Shefelman, Law Library, Seattle, WA [*Library symbol*] [*Library of Congress*] (LCLS)
WaSF-R....... Fircrest School, Resident Library, Seattle, WA [*Library symbol Library of Congress*] (LCLS)
WaSFRC ...... Federal Records Center, Seattle, WA [*Library symbol Library of Congress*] (LCLS)
WaSFSI........ Forest Service Information Network Northwest, University of Washington Campus, Seattle, WA [*Library symbol*] [*Library of Congress*] (LCLS)
WASG .... Atmore, AL [*AM radio station call letters*]
WaSG .... Seattle Genealogical Society, Seattle, WA [*Library symbol Library of Congress*] (LCLS)
WaSGAO...... United States General Accounting Office, Seattle Regional Office, Seattle, WA [*Library symbol*] [*Library of Congress*] (LCLS)
WaSGen ...... Genetic Systems Corp., Seattle, WA [*Library symbol*] [*Library of Congress*] (LCLS)
WASGFC...... Western Association of State Game and Fish Commissioners [*Later, Western Association of Fish and Wildlife Agencies*] (EA)
WaSGH .... Group Health Cooperative of Puget Sound, Medical Library, Seattle, WA [*Library symbol Library of Congress*] (LCLS)
WaSGH-H .... Group Health Cooperative of Puget Sound, Kathleen Hill Library, Seattle, WA [*Library symbol*] [*Library of Congress*] (LCLS)
WaSGS .... Church of Jesus Christ of Latter-Day Saints, Genealogical Society Library, Seattle North Branch, Seattle, WA [*Library symbol Library of Congress*] (LCLS)
WaSGS .... Good Samaritan Hospital, Seattle, WA [*Library symbol Library of Congress*] (LCLS)
WaSGSH...... Good Samaritan Hospital, Seattle, WA [*Library symbol*] [*Library of Congress*] (LCLS)
WaSh........... Shelton Public Library, Shelton, WA [*Library symbol Library of Congress*] (LCLS)
WaSH .... Virginia Mason Hospital, Medical Library, Seattle, WA [*Library symbol Library of Congress*] (LCLS)
WASH.......... Washer (AAG)
WASH.......... Washington (AAG)
Wash .... Washington (ODBW)
WASH.......... Washington, DC [*FM radio station call letters*]
Wash .... Washington Reports [*A publication*] (DLA)
Wash .... Washington's Reports [*1, 2 Virginia*] [*A publication*] (DLA)
Wash .... Washington's Reports [*16-23 Vermont*] [*A publication*] (DLA)
Wash .... Washington State Reports [*A publication*] (DLA)
Wash .... Washington's United States Circuit Court Reports [*A publication*] (DLA)
Wash .... Washington Territory Reports [*1854-88*] [*A publication*] (DLA)
WASH.......... Washington Trust Bancorp [*NASDAQ symbol*] (TTSB)
WASH.......... Washington Trust Bancorp, Inc. [*NASDAQ symbol*] (NQ)
Wash 2d...... Washington Reports, Second Series [*A publication*] (DLA)
Wash Admin Code... Washington Administrative Code [*A publication*] (DLA)
Wash Admin Reg... Washington State Register [*A publication*] (DLA)
Wash & Haz PEI... Washburton and Hazard's Reports [*Prince Edward Island, Canada*] [*A publication*] (DLA)
Wash & Lee U... Washington and Lee University (GAGS)
Wash App.... Washington Appellate Reports [*A publication*] (DLA)
Washb Easem... Washburn on Easements and Servitudes [*A publication*] (DLA)
Wash B News... Washington Bar News [*A publication*] (DLA)
Washb Real Prop... Washburn on Real Property [*A publication*] (DLA)
Washburn.... Washburn's Reports [*18-23 Vermont*] [*A publication*] (DLA)
Washburn U... Washburn University of Topeka (GAGS)
Wash C........ Washington College (GAGS)
WaShC......... Washington Correction Center, Staff Library, Shelton, WA [*Library symbol Library of Congress*] (LCLS)
WASHCAP.... Washington Operations Capabilities System
Wash CC..... Washington's United States Circuit Court Reports [*A publication*] (DLA)
Wash CCR ... Washington's United States Circuit Court Reports [*A publication*] (DLA)
WaSHCH...... Highline Community Hospital Library, Seattle, WA [*Library symbol*] [*Library of Congress*] (LCLS)
Wash Co...... Washington County Reports [*Pennsylvania*] [*A publication*] (DLA)
Wash Co (PA)... Washington County Reports [*Pennsylvania*] [*A publication*] (DLA)
Wash Co R... Washington County Reports [*Pennsylvania*] [*A publication*] (DLA)
Wash Co Repr... Washington County Reports [*Pennsylvania*] [*A publication*] (DLA)
WaSHCR...... Fred Hutchinson Cancer Research Center, Seattle, WA [*Library symbol Library of Congress*] (LCLS)
WaShC-R..... Washington Correction Center, Resident Library, Shelton, WA [*Library symbol Library of Congress*] (LCLS)
Wash Cr L.... Washburn on Criminal Law [*A publication*] (DLA)
Wash DC ..... Washington, D.C. (VRA)
Wash Dec.... Washington Decisions [*A publication*] (DLA)
Wash Dig..... Washburn's Vermont Digest [*A publication*] (DLA)
Wash Ease... Washburn on Easements and Servitudes [*A publication*] (DLA)
WashEn .... Washington Energy Co. [*Associated Press*] (SAG)
WashFed ..... Washington Federal, Inc. (Seattle) [*Associated Press*] (SAG)
Wash Fin Rep (BNA)... Washington Financial Reports (Bureau of National Affairs) [*A publication*] (DLA)
WashGs....... Washington Gas Light Co. [*Associated Press*] (SAG)
WashHm...... Washington Homes, Inc. [*Associated Press*] (SAG)
WaSHi .... Seattle Historical Society, Seattle, WA [*Library symbol Library of Congress*] (LCLS)
WaShIR .... ITT Rayonier, Inc., Olympic Research Center, Shelton, WA [*Library symbol Library of Congress*] (LCLS)
Wash Jur..... Washington Jurist [*A publication*] (DLA)
Wash Law Rep... Washington Law Reporter [*District of Columbia*] [*A publication*] (DLA)
Wash Legis Serv... Washington Legislative Service (West) [*A publication*] (DLA)
Wash LR (Dist Col)... Washington Law Reporter (District of Columbia) [*A publication*] (DLA)
Wash L Rep... Washington Law Reporter [*District of Columbia*] [*A publication*] (DLA)
Wash M....... Washington Monthly [*A publication*] (BRI)
WASHMIC.... Washington Military Industrial Complex
WashNt........ Washington Natural Gas [*Associated Press*] (SAG)
WashNt........ Washington Natural Gas [*Associated Press*] (SAG)
WASHO........ Western Association of State Highway Officials
Wash PUR.... Washington Public Utility Commission Reports [*A publication*] (DLA)
Wash Rev Code... Revised Code of Washington [*A publication*] (DLA)
Wash Rev Code Ann... Washington Revised Code, Annotated [*A publication*] (DLA)
Wash RP ..... Washburn on Real Property [*A publication*] (DLA)
Wash SBA ... Washington State Bar Association. Proceedings [*A publication*] (DLA)
Wash St...... Washington State Reports [*A publication*] (DLA)
Wash St Reg... Washington State Register [*A publication*] (AAGC)
Wash St U... Washington State University (GAGS)
WashSvg..... Washington Savings Bank FSB (MD) [*Associated Press*] (SAG)
WASH T....... Washington Territory (ROG)
Wash T........ Washington Territory Opinions [*1854-64*] [*A publication*] (DLA)
Wash T........ Washington Territory Reports [*1854-88*] [*A publication*] (DLA)
Wash Ter..... Washington Territory Opinions [*1854-64*] [*A publication*] (DLA)
Wash Ter..... Washington Territory Reports [*1854-88*] [*A publication*] (DLA)
Wash Ter NS... Allen's Washington Territory Reports, New Series [*A publication*] (DLA)
Wash Terr ... Washington Territory Opinions [*1854-64*] [*A publication*] (DLA)
Wash Terr ... Washington Territory Reports [*1854-88*] [*A publication*] (DLA)
WASHTO...... Western Association of State Highway and Traffic Officials
WashTrst..... Washington Trust Bancorp, Inc. [*Associated Press*] (SAG)
Wash Ty...... Washington Territory Opinions [*1854-64*] [*A publication*] (DLA)
Wash Ty...... Washington Territory Reports [*1854-88*] [*A publication*] (DLA)
Wash UJ Urb & Contemp L... Washington University. Journal of Urban and Contemporary Law [*A publication*] (DLA)
Wash UL Rev... Washington University. Law Review [*A publication*] (DLA)
Wash U (Mo)... Washington University (Missouri) (GAGS)
Wash VA...... Washington's Reports [*1, 2 Virginia*] [*A publication*] (DLA)
WashWtr..... Washington Water Power Co. [*Associated Press*] (SAG)
WASI .... Inanwatan [*Indonesia*] [*ICAO location identifier*] (ICLI)
WASI .... Whimbey Analytical Skills Inventory [*Educational test*]
WASIA .... Women's Armed Services Integration Act of 1948
WaSIF.......... International Fisheries Commission, Seattle, WA [*Library symbol Library of Congress*] (LCLS)
WASIH .... Western American Society for Italic Handwriting [*Formerly, WABSIH*] (EA)
WaSJB......... John Bastyr College of Naturopathic Medicine, Seattle, WA [*Library symbol*] [*Library of Congress*] (LCLS)
WASK .... Kaimana (Utarom) [*Indonesia*] [*ICAO location identifier*] (ICLI)

WaSK.......... King County Medical Society, Seattle, WA [*Library symbol Library of Congress*] (LCLS)
WASK.......... Lafayette, IN [*AM radio station call letters*]
WaSKC.......... King County Library System, Seattle, WA [*Library symbol Library of Congress*] (LCLS)
WASK-FM.... Battle Ground, IN [*FM radio station call letters*] (RBYB)
WaSKR.......... Keller, Rohrback, Law Library, Seattle, WA [*Library symbol*] [*Library of Congress*] (LCLS)
WaSKTK...... Karr, Tuttle, Koch, Campbell, Mawer, Morrow, & Sax, Seattle, WA [*Library symbol*] [*Library of Congress*] (LCLS)
WASL.......... Dyersburg, TN [*FM radio station call letters*]
WAsL.......... Vaughn Public Library, Ashland, WI [*Library symbol*] [*Library of Congress*] (LCLS)
WaSLP.......... Lane, Powell, Moss & Miller Library, Seattle, WA [*Library symbol*] [*Library of Congress*] (LCLS)
WAsM.......... Memorial Medical Center, Health Sciences Library, Ashland, WI [*Library symbol Library of Congress*] (LCLS)
WASM.......... Merdei [*Indonesia*] [*ICAO location identifier*] (ICLI)
WaSM.......... Mountaineers, Inc., Seattle, WA [*Library symbol Library of Congress*] (LCLS)
WASM.......... White Anglo-Saxon Male
WaSMA.......... Moss Adams Information Center, Seattle, WA [*Library symbol*] [*Library of Congress*] (LCLS)
WASMAC...... Western Australian Survey and Mapping Advisory Council [*State*] (EERA)
WASME.......... World Assembly of Small and Medium Enterprises [*See also AMPME*] [*India*] (EAIO)
WaSMH.......... Virginia Mason Hospital, Medical Library, Seattle, WA [*Library symbol*] [*Library of Congress*] (LCLS)
WaSMHI...... Museum of History and Industry, Seattle, WA [*Library symbol*] [*Library of Congress*] (LCLS)
WaSMo.......... Mountaineers, Inc., Seattle, WA [*Library symbol*] [*Library of Congress*] (LCLS)
WASN.......... Campbell, OH [*AM radio station call letters*]
WAsN.......... Northland College, Ashland, WI [*Library symbol Library of Congress*] (LCLS)
WasN.......... Washington National Corp. [*Associated Press*] (SAG)
WASN.......... Western Australian School of Nursing
WASNA.......... Western Apicultural Society of North America (EA)
WaSNH.......... Northwest Hospital, Effie M. Storey Learning Center, Seattle, WA [*Library symbol Library of Congress*] (LCLS)
WaSNPS...... United States National Park Service, Pacific Northwest Region, Seattle, WA [*Library symbol*] [*Library of Congress*] (LCLS)
WaSnqE.......... Echo Glen Children's Center, Staff Library, Snoqualmie, WA [*Library symbol Library of Congress*] (LCLS)
WaSnqE-R... Echo Glen Children's Center, Resident Library, Snoqualmie, WA [*Library symbol Library of Congress*] (LCLS)
WASO.......... Babo [*Indonesia*] [*ICAO location identifier*] (ICLI)
WASO.......... Covington, LA [*AM radio station call letters*]
WASO.......... Women's Association for Symphony Orchestras [*Later, AMSO*] (EA)
WASOG.......... World Association on Sarcoidosis and Other Granulomatous Disorders (EAIO)
WaSOnc.......... Oncogen Library, Seattle, WA [*Library symbol*] [*Library of Congress*] (LCLS)
WASP.......... Brownsville, PA [*AM radio station call letters*]
WASP.......... MARINALG International, World Association of Seaweed Processors (EA)
WASP.......... Oliver, PA [*FM radio station call letters*]
WaSp.......... Spokane Public Library, Spokane, WA [*Library symbol Library of Congress*] (LCLS)
WASP.......... Wafer Scale Associative String Processor (NITA)
WASP.......... Wafer Scale Systolic Processor (NITA)
WASP.......... Wait-and-See Parsing [*Computer science*] (BYTE)
WASP.......... War Air Service Program [*Department of Commerce*]
WASP.......... Water and Steam Program [*NASA*]
WASP.......... Weather-Atmospheric Sounding Projectile [*Research rocket*]
WASP.......... Weber Advanced Spatial Perception Test [*Vocational guidance test*]
WASP.......... Weed-Activated Spray Process [*Agriculture*]
WASP.......... Weightless Analysis Sounding Probe [*NASA*]
WASP.......... Westinghouse Advanced Systems Planning Group
WASP.......... White Anglo-Saxon Protestant
Wasp.......... White Anglo-Saxon Protestant (ODBW)
WASP.......... White Appalachian Southern Protestant [*Chicago slang*]
WASP.......... White Ashkenazi Sabra with Pull [*Israeli variation on White Anglo-Saxon Protestant*]
WASP.......... Wide Antiarmor Minimissile (MCD)
WASP.......... Wien Automatic Systems Planning [*Nuclear energy*] (NUCP)
WASP.......... Williams Aerial Systems Platform [*One-man flying platform*]
WASP.......... Wind-Assisted Ship Propulsion (DS)
WASP.......... Window Atmosphere Sounding Projectile [*NASA*]
WASP.......... Women's Airforce Service Pilots [*World War II*]
WASP.......... Woody Allen's Spring Picture [*Designation reflecting the filmmaker's reluctance to provide information about his movies in advance of their commercial release*] [*See also WAFP*]
WASP.......... Work Activity Sampling Plan
WASP.......... Workshop Analysis and Scheduling Programming
WASP.......... Workstation Automatic Script Processor (NITA)
WASP.......... World Association of Societies of Pathology - Anatomic and Clinical (EA)
WASP.......... World Associations for Social Psychiatry (EA)
WASP.......... Wrap-Around Simulation Program [*Military*] (CAAL)
WASPA.......... White Anglo-Saxon Protestant Ambulatory [*Extension of WASP; indicates the necessity of being able-bodied as an additional requirement for success*]
WaSPaM...... Pacific Medical Center, Seattle, WA [*Library symbol*] [*Library of Congress*] (LCLS)
WaSPATH.... PATH [*Program for Appropriate Technology in Health*] Library, Seattle, WA [*Library symbol*] [*Library of Congress*] (LCLS)
WaSpBM...... United States Bureau of Mines, Mining Research Center, Spokane, WA [*Library symbol Library of Congress*] (LCLS)
WaSpBMW... United States Bureau of Mines, Western Field Operations Center, Spokane, WA [*Library symbol Library of Congress*] (LCLS)
WaSPC.......... Seattle Pacific College, Seattle, WA [*Library symbol Library of Congress*] (LCLS)
WaSpCN...... Center for Nursing Education, Spokane, WA [*Library symbol Library of Congress*] (LCLS)
WaSpCo...... Spokane County Library, Spokane, WA [*Library symbol Library of Congress*] (LCLS)
WaSpD.......... Deaconess Hospital, School of Nursing, Spokane, WA [*Library symbol Library of Congress*] (LCLS)
WaSPe.......... Perkins, Coie, Stone, Olsen & Williams, Seattle, WA [*Library symbol Library of Congress*] (LCLS)
WaSpG.......... Gonzaga University, Spokane, WA [*Library symbol Library of Congress*] (LCLS)
WaSpGL...... Church of Jesus Christ of Latter-Day Saints, Genealogical Society Library, Spokane Branch, Spokane, WA [*Library symbol Library of Congress*] (LCLS)
WaSpG-L..... Gonzaga University, Law Library, Spokane, WA [*Library symbol Library of Congress*] (LCLS)
WaSpGS...... United States Geological Survey, Spokane, WA [*Library symbol Library of Congress*] (LCLS)
WaSpH.......... Holy Family Hospital, Spokane, WA [*Library symbol Library of Congress*] (LCLS)
WaSPH.......... United States Public Health Service Hospital, Medical Service Library, Seattle, WA [*Library symbol Library of Congress*] (LCLS)
WaSpHiE..... Eastern Washington State Historical Society, Museum Library, Spokane, WA [*Library symbol Library of Congress*] (LCLS)
WaSpIn.......... Intermediate School District 101, Professional Materials Library, Spokane, WA [*Library symbol Library of Congress*] (LCLS)
WaSpJ.......... Jesuit Archives of the Province of Oregon, Spokane, WA [*Library symbol Library of Congress*] (LCLS)
WaSpJP.......... Washington State Office of Juvenile Parole Services, Spokane, WA [*Library symbol Library of Congress*] (LCLS)
WaSpJS...... Jesuit Scholastic Library, Spokane, WA [*Library symbol Library of Congress*] (LCLS)
WaSPM.......... Providence Hospital, Medical Library and Learning Resource Center, Seattle, WA [*Library symbol Library of Congress*] (LCLS)
WaSpM.......... Spokane County Medical Library, Spokane, WA [*Library symbol Library of Congress*] (LCLS)
WASPM.......... Wide Area Side Penetrator Mine [*Army*] (ADDR)
WaSpMF...... Murphey Favre, Inc., Spokane, WA [*Library symbol Library of Congress*] (LCLS)
WaSpN.......... Fort Wright College, Spokane, WA [*Library symbol Library of Congress*] (LCLS)
WASP-NN.... White Anglo-Saxon Protestant Native Born of Native Parents
WaSPoD...... Population Dynamics, Seattle, WA [*Library symbol Library of Congress*] (LCLS)
WaSpPS...... Spokane Public Schools, Curriculum Library, Spokane, WA [*Library symbol Library of Congress*] (LCLS)
WaSPrM...... Providence Hospital, Medical Library and Learning Resource Center, Seattle, WA [*Library symbol*] [*Library of Congress*] (LCLS)
WASPRU...... West African Stored Products Research Unit
WaSPS.......... Seattle Public Schools, Library Technical Service, Seattle, WA [*Library symbol Library of Congress*] (LCLS)
WaSpS.......... Spokane Community College, Spokane, WA [*Library symbol Library of Congress*] (LCLS)
WASPS.......... Women's Agricultural Security Production Service [*British military*] (DMA)
WASPS.......... Women's Auxiliary Service Platoon
WaSpSC...... Spokane Community College, Spokane, WA [*Library symbol*] [*Library of Congress*] (LCLS)
WaSpSF...... Spokane Falls Community College, Spokane, WA [*Library symbol Library of Congress*] (LCLS)
WaSpSH...... Sacred Heart Medical Center, Spokane, WA [*Library symbol Library of Congress*] (LCLS)
WaSpSL...... Saint Luke's Hospital, Spokane, WA [*Library symbol Library of Congress*] (LCLS)
WaSpSL...... Spokane County Law Library, Spokane, WA [*Library symbol Library of Congress*] (LCLS)
WaSpStL...... Saint Luke's Hospital, Spokane, WA [*Library symbol*] [*Library of Congress*] (LCLS)
WaSpStM...... Saint Michael's Institute, Spokane, WA [*Library symbol Library of Congress*] (LCLS)
WaSPTS...... Preston, Thorgrimson, Shidler, Gates & Ellis, Seattle, WA [*Library symbol*] [*Library of Congress*] (LCLS)
WaSpVA...... United States Veterans Administration Hospital, Spokane, WA [*Library symbol Library of Congress*] (LCLS)
WaSpW.......... Whitworth College, Spokane, WA [*Library symbol Library of Congress*] (LCLS)
WASPWWII... Women Airforce Service Pilots WWII (EA)
WaSpYS...... Washington State Center for Youth Services, Spokane, WA [*Library symbol Library of Congress*] (LCLS)
WASR.......... Manokwari/Rendani [*Indonesia*] [*ICAO location identifier*] (ICLI)
WASR.......... Wolfeboro, NH [*AM radio station call letters*]
WaSS.......... Schick's Schadel Hospital, Medical Library, Seattle, WA [*Library symbol Library of Congress*] (LCLS)
WASS.......... Sorong/Jefman [*Indonesia*] [*ICAO location identifier*] (ICLI)
Wass.......... Wassermann [*Test for syphilis*]
WASS.......... Wavefront Analysis of Spatial Sampling [*Aircraft landing approach*]

WASS .... Wide-Angle Sun Seekers (SAA)
WASS .... Wide-Area Active Surveillance System [*Military*] (MCD)
WaSSB .... Washington State Office for the Services for the Blind, Seattle, WA [*Library symbol Library of Congress*] (LCLS)
WaSSC .... Saint Cabrini Hospital Library, Seattle, WA [*Library symbol*] [*Library of Congress*] (LCLS)
WaSSGB .... Schroeter, Goldmark & Bender, Seattle, WA [*Library symbol*] [*Library of Congress*] (LCLS)
WaSSh .... Shoreline Community College, Seattle, WA [*Library symbol Library of Congress*] (LCLS)
WaSSH .... Swedish Hospital Medical Center, Seattle, WA [*Library symbol Library of Congress*] (LCLS)
WaSSM .... Seattle Midwifery School, Seattle, WA [*Library symbol*] [*Library of Congress*] (LCLS)
WASSM .... WWMCCS [*Worldwide Military Command and Control System*] ADP System SecurityManager [*Automatic Data Processing*] (MCD)
WASSO .... WWMCCS [*Worldwide Military Command and Control System*] ADP System SecurityOfficer [*Automatic Data Processing*] (MCD)
WASSP .... Wallingford Storm Sewer Package [*Hydraulics Research*] [*Software package*] (NCC)
WASSP .... Wire Arc Seismic Section Profiler
WaSSRB .... Stoel, Rives, Bolly, Jones & Grey, Law Library, Seattle, WA [*Library symbol*] [*Library of Congress*] (LCLS)
WaSSW .... Shannon & Wilson, Inc., Seattle, WA [*Library symbol Library of Congress*] (LCLS)
WaSSwH .... Swedish Hospital Medical Center, Seattle, WA [*Library symbol*] [*Library of Congress*] (LCLS)
WAST .... Teminabuan [*Indonesia*] [*ICAO location identifier*] (ICLI)
WAST .... Western Alaska Standard Time (IAA)
WASTA .... Western Australian Science Teachers' Association
WASTAC .... Western Australian Satellite Technology Applications Consortium [*State*] (EERA)
WASTE .... Wisdom, Acclaim, and Status through Expenditures [*Fictional government agency in book "Alice in Blunderland"*]
WASTE .... World Association for Solid Waste Transfer and Exchange
WaSteM .... McNeil Island Correction Center, Steilacoom, WA [*Library symbol Library of Congress*] (LCLS)
WasteMI .... Waste Management International [*Associated Press*] (SAG)
WasteTc .... Waste Technology Corp. [*Associated Press*] (SAG)
WASTN .... Wireless Auxiliary Station [*Telecommunications*] (IAA)
WASU .... Boone, NC [*FM radio station call letters*]
WaSU .... Seattle University, Seattle, WA [*Library symbol Library of Congress*] (LCLS)
WaSUN .... United Nursing Homes, Seattle, WA [*Library symbol Library of Congress*] (LCLS)
WASV .... Asheville, NC [*Television station call letters*]
WaSVA .... United States Veterans Administration Hospital, Seattle, WA [*Library symbol Library of Congress*] (LCLS)
WASW .... Wasior [*Indonesia*] [*ICAO location identifier*] (ICLI)
WASWC .... World Association of Soil and Water Conservation (EA)
WaSWG .... West Seattle General Hospital, Seattle, WA [*Library symbol Library of Congress*] (LCLS)
WaSwH .... United General Hospital, Medical Staff Library, Sedro Woolley, WA [*Library symbol*] [*Library of Congress*] (LCLS)
WaSWK .... Williams, Kastner, Gibbs, Law Library, Seattle, WA [*Library symbol*] [*Library of Congress*] (LCLS)
WaSwN .... Northern State Multi-Service Center, Sedro Woolley, WA [*Library symbol*] [*Library of Congress*] (LCLS)
WASY .... Western Australian School of Yoga
WASZ .... Ashland-Lineville, AL [*FM radio station call letters*]
WaT .... Tacoma Public Library, Tacoma, WA [*Library symbol Library of Congress*] (LCLS)
WAT .... University of Waterloo Library [*UTLAS symbol*]
WAT .... Water [*Automotive engineering*]
Wat .... Waterford [*Crystal glassware*] (BARN)
Wat .... Watermeyer's Cape Of Good Hope Supreme Court Reports [*1857*] [*South Africa*] [*A publication*] (DLA)
WAT .... Waters Corp. [*NYSE symbol*] (SAG)
WAT .... Watertown Free Public Library, Watertown, MA [*OCLC symbol*] (OCLC)
WAT .... Watheroo [*Australia Seismograph station code, US Geological Survey Closed*] (SEIS)
WAT .... Weapons Assignment Technician (AFM)
WAT .... Web Action Time (MCD)
WAT .... Weeks after Treatment
WAT .... Weight, Altitude, and Temperature (IEEE)
WAT .... Weight Average Temperature [*Chemical engineering*]
WAT .... Wet Anode Tantalum
WAT .... White Adipose Tissue [*Physiology*]
WAT .... Wide-Angle Tail [*Galactic radio source*]
WAT .... Wide Area Telecommunications Service (NITA)
WAT .... Wideband Adapter Transformer
WAT .... Wings Air Transport Co. [*Sudan*] [*ICAO designator*] (FAAC)
WAT .... Word Association Test [*Psychology*]
WATA .... Boone, NC [*AM radio station call letters*]
WATA .... Western Australian Temperance Alliance
WATA .... Wisconsin Automatic Test Apparatus
WATA .... World Association of Travel Agencies (EAIO)
WaTAC .... Allenmore Community Hospital, Tacoma, WA [*Library symbol Library of Congress*] (LCLS)
WATAC .... Women and the Australian Church
WaTAH .... United States Army [*Madigan*] General Hospital, Tacoma, WA [*Library symbol Library of Congress*] (LCLS)
WATB .... Decatur, GA [*AM radio station call letters*] (RBYB)
WATBOL .... Waterloo COBOL [*Common Business-Oriented Language*] [*University of Waterloo*] [*Canada*]
WATC .... Atlanta, GA [*Television station call letters*]
WATC .... [*The*] Washington Terminal Co. [*AAR code*]
WATC .... Western Australian Tourism Commission
WATC .... Western Australian Tourist Centre
WATC .... Western Australian Treasury Corp. [*Commercial firm*]
WATC .... Wide-Area Traffic Control (PDAA)
WATC .... Women's Air Training Corps
WATC .... Women's Ambulance and Transportation Corps
WaTCC .... Tacoma Community College, Tacoma, WA [*Library symbol Library of Congress*] (LCLS)
Wat CGH .... Watermeyer's Cape Of Good Hope Reports [*South Africa*] [*A publication*] (DLA)
WaTCH .... Mary Bridge Children's Health Center, Tacoma, WA [*Library symbol Library of Congress*] (LCLS)
WATCH .... Watchers Against Television Commercial Harrassment [*Student legal action organization*]
WATCH .... Working Group on the Assessment of Toxic Chemicals [*British*]
WATCH .... World Against Toys Causing Harm
WATCHCON .... Watch Condition (DOMA)
WATCIM .... Waterloo Centre for Integrated Manufacturing [*University of Waterloo*] [*Canada Research center*] (RCD)
WaTCJ .... Cascadia Juvenile Diagnostic Center, Tacoma, WA [*Library symbol Library of Congress*] (LCLS)
WATCON .... Waterloo Concordance (NITA)
Wat Con .... Watkins on Conveyancing [*9th ed.*] [*1845*] [*A publication*] (DLA)
Wat Cop .... Watkins on Copyholds [*6th ed.*] [*1829*] [*A publication*] (DLA)
Wat Cr Dig .... Waterman's Criminal Digest [*United States*] [*A publication*] (DLA)
Wat Cr Proc .... Waterman's Criminal Procedure [*A publication*] (DLA)
WaTD .... Doctors Hospital, Tacoma, WA [*Library symbol Library of Congress*] (LCLS)
WATD .... Marshfield, MA [*FM radio station call letters*]
WATDOC .... Water Resources Document Reference Centre [*Canadian Department of Fisheries and the Environment*] [*Database*] (IID)
WATDOC .... Water Resources Document Reference System (NITA)
WATE .... Knoxville, TN [*Television station call letters*]
WATER .... Water Awareness Training Education and Recruitment
WATER .... Women's Alliance for Theology, Ethics, and Ritual (EA)
WATERF .... Waterford [*County in Ireland*] (ROG)
WATERFD .... Waterford [*County in Ireland*]
Waterhse .... Waterhouse Investor Services, Inc. [*Associated Press*] (SAG)
WATERLIT .... Water Literature (NITA)
Watermeyer .... Watermeyer's Cape Of Good Hope Reports [*South Africa*] [*A publication*] (DLA)
Watermrc .... Watermarc Food Management Co. [*Associated Press*] (SAG)
WATF .... Waterford Wedgwood Ltd. [*NASDAQ symbol*] (NQ)
WatfdW .... Waterford Wedgewood PLC ADR [*Associated Press*] (SAG)
WATFIV .... Waterloo FORTRAN [*Formula Translating System*] IV [*University of Waterloo*] [*Canada*] (HGAA)
WATFOR .... Waterloo FORTRAN [*University of Waterloo*] [*Canada*]
WaTFS .... Fort Steilacoom Community College, Tacoma, WA [*Library symbol Library of Congress*] (LCLS)
WATFY .... Waterford Glass Group PLC (MHDW)
WATFZ .... Waterford Wedgwood plcADs [*NASDAQ symbol*] (TTSB)
WaTG .... Tacoma Branch Genealogical Library, Tacoma, WA [*Library symbol Library of Congress*] (LCLS)
WATG .... Trion, GA [*FM radio station call letters*]
WATG .... Wave-Activated Turbine Generator (PDAA)
WaTGC .... Griffin College, Tacoma, WA [*Library symbol*] [*Library of Congress*] (LCLS)
WaTGH .... Tacoma General Hospital, Pierce County Medical Library, Tacoma, WA [*Library symbol Library of Congress*] (LCLS)
WaTGS .... Church of Jesus Christ of Latter-Day Saints, Genealogical Society Library, Tacoma Branch, Tacoma, WA [*Library symbol Library of Congress*] (LCLS)
WATH .... Athens, OH [*AM radio station call letters*]
WATJ .... Chardon, OH [*AM radio station call letters*]
WaTJP .... Washington State Office of Juvenile Parole Services, Tacoma, WA [*Library symbol Library of Congress*] (LCLS)
Wat Just .... Waterman's Justices' Manual [*A publication*] (DLA)
WATK .... Antigo, WI [*AM radio station call letters*]
Watk Con .... Watkins on Conveyancing [*A publication*] (DLA)
Watk Conv .... Watkins on Conveyancing [*A publication*] (DLA)
Watk Cop .... Watkins on Copyholds [*A publication*] (DLA)
Watk Copyh .... Watkins on Copyholds [*A publication*] (DLA)
Watk Des .... Watkins on Descents [*A publication*] (DLA)
WatkJn .... Watkins-Johnson Co. [*Associated Press*] (SAG)
WATL .... Atlanta, GA [*Television station call letters*]
WATLC .... Trades and Labour Council of Western Australia
WATLCC .... Western Australian Tripartite Labour Consultative Council
WaTLG .... Lakewood General Hospital and Convalescent Center, Tacoma, WA [*Library symbol Library of Congress*] (LCLS)
WATM .... Altoona, PA [*Television station call letters*]
WATN .... Watertown, NY [*AM radio station call letters*]
WaTO .... Oakridge Group Home, Tacoma, WA [*Library symbol Library of Congress*] (LCLS)
WATO .... Oak Ridge, TN [*AM radio station call letters*]
WaToH .... Heritage College, Toppenish, WA [*Library symbol*] [*Library of Congress*] (LCLS)
WATOX .... Western Atlantic Ocean Experiment (USDC)
WATOX .... Western Atlantic Ocean Experiment [*Marine science*] (OSRA)
WaToY .... Yakim Nation Library, Toppenish, WA [*Library symbol*] [*Library of Congress*] (LCLS)

WaTP.......... Pioneer Group Home, Tacoma, WA [*Library symbol Library of Congress*] (LCLS)
WaTPC......... Pierce County Library, Tacoma, WA [*Library symbol Library of Congress*] (LCLS)
WaTPG........ Puget Sound General Hospital, Tacoma, WA [*Library symbol Library of Congress*] (LCLS)
WaTPL......... Pierce County Law Library, Tacoma, WA [*Library symbol*] [*Library of Congress*] (LCLS)
WATPL......... Wartime Traffic Priority List (NATG)
WaTPM........ Pierce County Medical Library, Tacoma, WA [*Library symbol Library of Congress*] (LCLS)
WaTPS......... Tacoma Public Schools, Professional and Curriculum Library, Tacoma, WA [*Library symbol Library of Congress*] (LCLS)
WATR.......... Tetra Tech [*NASDAQ symbol*] (TTSB)
WATR.......... Tetra Tech, Inc. [*NASDAQ symbol*] (SPSG)
WATR.......... Water Attenuation by Tritium Relaxation [*Physics*]
WATR.......... Waterbury, CT [*AM radio station call letters*]
WATR.......... Waterville [*AAR code*]
WatrIn......... Waters Instruments, Inc. [*Associated Press*] (SAG)
WatrJ........... Water-Jel Technologies [*Associated Press*] (SAG)
WatrJel........ Water-Jel Technologies [*Associated Press*] (SAG)
Watrm.......... Watermarc Food Management Co. [*Associated Press*] (SAG)
WatrPnt........ Water Point Systems [*Associated Press*] (SAG)
WatrsCp....... Waters Corp. [*Associated Press*] (SAG)
WATS........... Sayre, PA [*AM radio station call letters*]
WATS........... Survey of Motor Freight Transportation and Public Warehousing [*BTS*] (TAG)
WATS........... Watson Pharmaceuticals [*NASDAQ symbol*] (TTSB)
WATS........... Watson Pharmaceuticals, Inc. [*NASDAQ symbol*] (SAG)
WAT's.......... Wide-Angle [*Galilean*] Telescopes
WATS........... Wide-Area Military Traffic Management and Terminal Service
WATS........... Wide-Area Telecommunications [*formerly, Telephone*] Service [*American Telephone & Telegraph Co. contract billing system*]
WATS........... Wide-Area Telephone Service [*Telecommunications*] (IAA)
WATS........... Wide Area Telephone Service
WATS........... Wide Area Transmission Service [*or System*]
WATS........... Women's Auxiliary Territorial Service [*British military*] (DMA)
WATS........... Women's Auxiliary Training Service
Wats Arb...... Watson on Arbitration [*A publication*] (DLA)
Watsc.......... Watsco, Inc. [*Associated Press*] (SAG)
Wats Cler Law... Watson's Clergyman's Law [*A publication*] (DLA)
Watsco......... Watsco, Inc. [*Associated Press*] (SAG)
Wats Com Man... Watson's United States Commissioners' Manual [*A publication*] (DLA)
Wats Comp Eq... Watson's Compendium of Equity [*A publication*] (DLA)
Wats Const Hist... Watson's Constitutional History of Canada [*A publication*] (DLA)
Wat Set-Off... Waterman on Set-Off [*A publication*] (DLA)
WatsGen...... Watson General Corp. [*Associated Press*] (SAG)
WaTSJ......... Saint Joseph Hospital, Tacoma, WA [*Library symbol Library of Congress*] (LCLS)
Wats Med Jur... Watson's Medical Jurisprudence [*A publication*] (DLA)
WatsnPh...... Watson Pharmaceuticals, Inc. [*Associated Press*] (SAG)
Watson........ Watson's Compendium of Equity [*2 eds.*] [*1873, 1888*] [*A publication*] (DLA)
Watson Eq... Watson's Compendium of Equity [*A publication*] (DLA)
Wats Part.... Watson on Partnership [*2nd ed.*] [*1807*] [*A publication*] (DLA)
Wats Sher... Watson's Office and Duty of Sheriff [*2nd ed.*] [*1848*] [*A publication*] (DLA)
WATSTORE... National Water Data Storage and Retrieval System [*US Geological Survey*] [*Information service or system*] (CRD)
WATT........... Cadillac, MI [*AM radio station call letters*]
WATTec....... Welding and Testing Technology Energy Conference [*Acronym is used as name of association*]
Wat Tres...... Waterman on the Law of Trespass [*A publication*] (DLA)
Watts........... Watts' Pennsylvania Reports [*1832-40*] [*A publication*] (DLA)
Watts........... Watts' Reports [*16-24 West Virginia*] [*A publication*] (DLA)
Watts & S.... Watts and Sergeant's Pennsylvania Reports [*1841-45*] [*A publication*] (DLA)
Watts & Serg... Watts and Sergeant's Pennsylvania Reports [*1841-45*] [*A publication*] (DLA)
Watts & S (PA)... Watts and Sergeant's Pennsylvania Reports [*1841-45*] [*A publication*] (DLA)
WattsInd...... Watts Industries [*Associated Press*] (SAG)
Watts (PA)... Watts' Pennsylvania Reports [*1832-40*] [*A publication*] (DLA)
WaTU........... University of Puget Sound, Tacoma, WA [*Library symbol Library of Congress*] (LCLS)
WATU.......... Western Approaches Tactical Unit [*Navy*]
WATV.......... Birmingham, AL [*AM radio station call letters*]
WATW......... Ashland, WI [*AM radio station call letters*]
WaTW.......... Weyerhaeuser Co., Tacoma, WA [*Library symbol Library of Congress*] (LCLS)
WATW......... Wood Awning Type Window
WaTWH....... Western State Hospital, Staff Library, Tacoma, WA [*Library symbol Library of Congress*] (LCLS)
WaTWH-R.... Western State Hospital, Resident Library, Tacoma, WA [*Library symbol Library of Congress*] (LCLS)
WaTW-T....... Weyerhaeuser Co., Technical Center, Tacoma, WA [*Library symbol Library of Congress*] (LCLS)
WATX........... Algood, TN [*AM radio station call letters*]
WATZ........... Alpena, MI [*AM radio station call letters*]
WATZ-FM.... Alpena, MI [*FM radio station call letters*]
WaU............. University of Washington, Seattle, WA [*Library symbol Library of Congress*] (LCLS)
wau.............. Washington [*MARC country of publication code Library of Congress*] (LCCP)
WAU............ Weapon Assignment Unit [*Military*] (CAAL)
WAU............ Women's Advisory Unit [*South Australia*]
WAUB.......... Auburn, NY [*AM radio station call letters*]
WAUC.......... Wauchula, FL [*AM radio station call letters*]
WAUD.......... Auburn, AL [*AM radio station call letters*]
WaU-D......... University of Washington, Drama Library, Seattle, WA [*Library symbol Library of Congress*] (LCLS)
WaU-EA....... University of Washington, East Asia Library, Seattle, WA [*Library symbol Library of Congress*] (LCLS)
WaU-FE....... University of Washington, Far Eastern Library, Seattle, WA [*Library symbol Library of Congress Obsolete*] (LCLS)
WAUG.......... New Hope, NC [*AM radio station call letters*]
WaU-HS....... University of Washington, Health Sciences Library, Seattle, WA [*Library symbol Library of Congress*] (LCLS)
WAUK.......... Waukesha, WI [*AM radio station call letters*]
WaU-L......... University of Washington, Law Library, Seattle, WA [*Library symbol Library of Congress*] (LCLS)
WaU-MC....... University of Washington, Harborview Medical Center Library, Seattle, WA [*Library symbol Library of Congress*] (LCLS)
WAUN.......... Kewaunee, WI [*FM radio station call letters*]
WAUR.......... Sandwich, IL [*AM radio station call letters*]
WAUS.......... Berrien Springs, MI [*FM radio station call letters*]
WAUS.......... World Association of Upper Silesians (EA)
WausauP..... Wausau Paper Mills [*Associated Press*] (SAG)
W Aust Hist Soc... Western Australian Historical Society. Journal [*A publication*]
W Austl R.... Western Australia Law Reports [*A publication*] (DLA)
W Aust Repr Acts... Reprinted Acts of Western Australia [*A publication*] (DLA)
WAUX.......... Lake Geneva, WI [*AM radio station call letters*] (RBYB)
WAUXCP...... West Auxiliary Airborne Command Post (MCD)
WaV............. Fort Vancouver Regional Library, Vancouver, WA [*Library symbol Library of Congress*] (LCLS)
WAV............. West-Avin Oy [*Finland ICAO designator*] (FAAC)
wav.............. Windows Sound File [*Computer science*]
WAV............. Wirtschaftliche Aufbau Vereinigung [*Economic Reconstruction Union*] [*Germany Political party*] (PPE)
WAVA.......... Arlington, VA [*FM radio station call letters*]
WAVA.......... World Association of Veteran Athletes (EAIO)
WAVA.......... World Association of Veterinary Anatomists (EA)
WAVAW....... Women Against Violence Against Women (EA)
WAVB.......... Lajas, PR [*AM radio station call letters*]
WaVC........... Clark College, Vancouver, WA [*Library symbol Library of Congress*] (LCLS)
WAVC.......... Duluth, MN [*FM radio station call letters*]
WAVD.......... Decatur, AL [*AM radio station call letters*]
WAVE........... Louisville, KY [*Television station call letters*]
WAVE........... Water-Augmented Vehicle
WAVE........... Weather Altimeter Voice Equipment
WAVE........... Westinghouse Audio Visual Electronics (IAA)
WAVE........... Women and Vocational Education [*Australia*]
Wavefrnt...... Wavefront Technologies, Inc. [*Associated Press*] (SAG)
WAVEGD..... Waveguide Standards (IAA)
Waver.......... Waverly Press, Inc. [*Associated Press*] (SAG)
WAVES........ Weight and Value Engineering System [*Computer science*]
WAVES........ Women Accepted for Volunteer Emergency Service [*US Navy Women's Reserve*] [*World War II and later*]
WAVES........ Women Appointed Volunteer Emergency Services [*British World War II*]
WAVES........ Worker and Visitor Entrance System [*Secret Service*] (GFGA)
WaveSys..... Wave Systems Corp. [*Associated Press*] (SAG)
WaveTec..... Wave Technologies International, Inc. [*Associated Press*] (SAG)
Wavetech.... Wavetech, Inc. [*Associated Press*] (SAG)
WAVF.......... Hanahan, SC [*FM radio station call letters*]
WAVFH........ World Association of Veterinary Food-Hygienists [*See also AMVHA*] [*Berlin, Federal Republic of Germany*] (EAIO)
WAVG.......... Louisville, KY [*AM radio station call letters*]
WAVH.......... Bay Minette, AL [*FM radio station call letters*]
WaVHS........ United States Park Service, Fort Vancouver National Historical Site, Vancouver, WA [*Library symbol Library of Congress*] (LCLS)
WAVI........... Christiansted, VI [*FM radio station call letters*]
WAVJ.......... Princeton, KY [*AM radio station call letters*]
WAVJ-FM.... Princeton, KY [*FM radio station call letters*] (RBYB)
WAVK.......... Marathon, FL [*FM radio station call letters*]
WAVL.......... Apollo, PA [*AM radio station call letters*]
WAVLD........ World Association of Veterinary Laboratory Diagnosticians (EAIO)
WAVM......... Maynard, MA [*FM radio station call letters*]
WaVMH....... Vancouver Memorial Hospital, Vancouver, WA [*Library symbol Library of Congress*] (LCLS)
WAVMI........ World Association of Veterinary Microbiologists, Immunologists, and Specialists in Infectious Diseases [*See also AMVMI*] [*Maisons-Alfort, France*] (EAIO)
WaVN.......... NERCO Minerals Co., Vancouver, WA [*Library symbol*] [*Library of Congress*] (LCLS)
WAVN.......... Southaven, MS [*AM radio station call letters*]
WAVO.......... Rock Hill, SC [*AM radio station call letters*]
WAVO.......... WavePhore, Inc. [*NASDAQ symbol*] (SAG)
WAVP.......... Avon Park, FL [*AM radio station call letters*]
WAVP.......... Western Australian. Votes and Proceedings [*A publication*]
WAVP.......... World Association of Veterinary Pathologists (EAIO)
WAVPM....... Women Against Violence in Pornography and Media (EA)
WAVQ.......... Inglis, FL [*FM radio station call letters*]
WAVR.......... Waverly Inc. [*NASDAQ symbol*] (TTSB)
WAVR.......... Waverly, NY [*FM radio station call letters*]
WAVR.......... Waverly Press, Inc. [*NASDAQ symbol*] (NQ)
WAVS.......... Davie, FL [*AM radio station call letters*]
WAVS.......... Wide Angle Visual System (MCD)

WaVSB .... Washington State School for the Blind, Vancouver, WA [*Library symbol Library of Congress*] (LCLS)
WaVSD .... Washington State School for the Deaf, Vancouver, WA [*Library symbol Library of Congress*] (LCLS)
WaVStJ .... Saint Joseph Community Hospital, Vancouver, WA [*Library symbol Library of Congress*] (LCLS)
WAVT .... Pottsville, PA [*FM radio station call letters*]
WAVT .... Wave Technologies Intl [*NASDAQ symbol*] (TTSB)
WAVT .... Wave Technologies Intl, Inc. [*NASDAQ symbol*] (SAG)
WAVU .... Albertville, AL [*AM radio station call letters*]
WAVV .... Marco, FL [*FM radio station call letters*]
WaVVA .... United States Veterans Administration Hospital, Vancouver, WA [*Library symbol Library of Congress*] (LCLS)
WAVW .... Vero Beach, FL [*FM radio station call letters*]
WAVX .... Thomaston, ME [*FM radio station call letters*]
WAVX .... Wave Systems'A' [*NASDAQ symbol*] (TTSB)
WAVX .... Wave Systems Corp. [*NASDAQ symbol*] (SAG)
WAVY .... Portsmouth, VA [*Television station call letters*]
WAVZ .... New Haven, CT [*AM radio station call letters*]
WAW .... University of Washington, School of Librarianship, Seattle, WA [*OCLC symbol*] (OCLC)
WaW .... Walla Walla Public Library, Walla Walla, WA [*Library symbol Library of Congress*] (LCLS)
WAW .... Ward's Auto World [*A publication*]
WAW .... Warsaw [*Poland*] [*Airport symbol*] (OAG)
WAW .... Waynesburg & Washington Railroad Co. [*Absorbed into Consolidated Rail Corp.*] [*AAR code*]
WAW .... Wings Airways [*ICAO designator*] (FAAC)
WAW .... Write-After-Write [*Computer science*]
WAWA .... Water Authority of Western Australia
WAWA .... West Africa Wins Again [*A reminder that visitors to this region must exercise caution if they wish to avoid bureaucratic harrassment and overcharging*]
WAWA .... Woolens and Worsteds of America [*Defunct*] (EA)
WaWAE .... U.S. Army Corps of Engineers, Walla Walla District, Walla Walla, WA [*Library symbol*] [*Library of Congress*] (LCLS)
WaWaW ...... Weller Public Library, Waitsburg, WA [*Library symbol*] [*Library of Congress*] (LCLS)
WAWB .... Ashland, VA [*Television station call letters*]
WAWC .... Syracuse, IN [*FM radio station call letters*]
WaWC .... Walla Walla College, College Place, WA [*Library symbol Library of Congress*] (LCLS)
WAWC .... West Africa War Council [*World War II*]
WAWC .... Western Australian Week Council
WaWCL .... Walla Walla County Rural Library, Walla Walla, WA [*Library symbol*] [*Library of Congress*] (LCLS)
WAWD .... Fort Walton Beach, FL [*Television station call letters*]
WaWeC .... Central Washington Hospital, Health Sciences Library, Wenatchee, WA [*Library symbol Library of Congress*] (LCLS)
WaWeN .... North Central Regional Library, Wenatche, WA [*Library symbol Library of Congress*] (LCLS)
WaWeW .... Wenatchee Valley College, Wenatchee, WA [*Library symbol Library of Congress*] (LCLS)
WaWeYS ..... Washington State Center for Youth Services, Wenatchee, WA [*Library symbol Library of Congress*] (LCLS)
WAWF .... William Allen White Foundation (EA)
WAWF .... World Arm Wrestling Federation (EA)
WAWF .... World Association for World Federation [*Netherlands*]
WAWG .... Where Are We Going
WAWHS .... Walla Walla High School, Walla Walla, WA [*Library symbol*] [*Library of Congress*] (LCLS)
WaWiS .... Wilbur Public Schools System, Wilbur, WA [*Library symbol Library of Congress*] (LCLS)
WAWK .... Kendallville, IN [*AM radio station call letters*]
WAWL .... Red Bank, TN [*FM radio station call letters*]
WaWnvGH ... Woodenville Group Home, Woodenville, WA [*Library symbol Library of Congress*] (LCLS)
WaWP .... Washington State Penitentiary, Walla Walla, WA [*Library symbol Library of Congress*] (LCLS)
WAWRC .... Western Australian Water Resources Council (EERA)
WAWS .... Jacksonville, FL [*Television station call letters*]
WAWV .... Sylacauga, AL [*FM radio station call letters*]
WaWV .... United States Veterans Administration Hospital, Walla Walla, WA [*Library symbol Library of Congress*] (LCLS)
WaWW .... Whitman College, Walla Walla, WA [*Library symbol Library of Congress*] (LCLS)
WaWWC ...... Walla Walla Community College, Walla Walla, WA [*Library symbol Library of Congress*] (LCLS)
WAWZ .... Zarephath, NJ [*FM radio station call letters*]
WAX .... Waxman Indus [*NYSE symbol*] (TTSB)
WAX .... Waxman Industries, Inc. [*NYSE symbol*] (SPSG)
WAX .... Weak Anion Exchanger [*Chemistry*]
WAX .... Weapon Assignment and Target Extermination
WAXB-FM .... Patterson, NY [*FM radio station call letters*] (RBYB)
WAXD .... Wide-Angle X-Ray Diffraction
WAXE .... Vero Beach, FL [*AM radio station call letters*]
WAXI .... Rockville, IN [*FM radio station call letters*]
WAXL-FM .... Santa Claus, IN [*FM radio station call letters*] (RBYB)
WAXM .... Big Stone Gap, VA [*FM radio station call letters*]
WAXM .... Waxman Industries, Inc. (MHDW)
Waxmn .... Waxman Industries, Inc. [*Associated Press*] (SAG)
WAXN-TV .... Kannapolis, NC [*TV station call letters*] (RBYB)
WAXO .... Lewisburg, TN [*AM radio station call letters*]
WAXQ .... New York, NY [*FM radio station call letters*]
WAXS .... Oak Hill, WV [*FM radio station call letters*]
WAXS .... Wide-Angle X-Ray Scattering
WAXS .... World Access, Inc. [*NASDAQ symbol*] (SAG)
WAXT .... Alexandria, IN [*FM radio station call letters*]
WAXX .... Eau Claire, WI [*FM radio station call letters*]
WAXY .... South Miami, FL [*AM radio station call letters*]
WAXZ .... Georgetown, OH [*FM radio station call letters*]
WAY .... Way [*Postal Service standard*] (OPSA)
WAY .... Waynesburg [*Pennsylvania*] [*Seismograph station code, US Geological Survey Closed*] (SEIS)
WAY .... Waynesburg, PA [*Location identifier FAA*] (FAAL)
WAY .... Wayne State College, Wayne, NE [*OCLC symbol*] (OCLC)
WAY .... Worked All Yokosuka [*Amateur radio*] (IAA)
WAY .... World Assembly of Youth [*Bronshoj, Denmark*] (EAIO)
WaY .... Yakima Valley Regional Library, Yakima, WA [*Library symbol Library of Congress*] (LCLS)
WAYA .... Spring City, TN [*FM radio station call letters*]
WaYacL .... Larch Mountain Correctional Center, Staff Library, Yacolt, WA [*Library symbol Library of Congress*] (LCLS)
WaYacL-R ... Larch Mountain Correctional Center, Resident Library, Yacolt, WA [*Library symbol Library of Congress*] (LCLS)
WAYB .... Graysville, TN [*FM radio station call letters*]
WAYB .... Waynesboro, VA [*AM radio station call letters*]
WAYC .... Bedford, PA [*AM radio station call letters*]
WAYE .... Birmingham, AL [*AM radio station call letters*]
WAYF .... West Palm Beach, FL [*FM radio station call letters*]
WAYG .... Sarasota, FL [*FM radio station call letters*]
WaYG .... Yakim Valley Genelogical Society, Yakima, WA [*Library symbol*] [*Library of Congress*] (LCLS)
WaYGS .... Church of Jesus Christ of Latter-Day Saints, Genealogical Society Library, Yakima Branch, Yakima, WA [*Library symbol Library of Congress*] (LCLS)
WAYJ .... Fort Myers, FL [*FM radio station call letters*]
WaYJP .... Washington State Office of Juvenile Parole Services, Yakima, WA [*Library symbol Library of Congress*] (LCLS)
WAYK-FM .... Kalamazoo, MI [*FM radio station call letters*] (RBYB)
WAYL .... St. Augustine, FL [*FM radio station call letters*]
WAYM .... Columbia, TN [*FM radio station call letters*]
WaYM .... Yakima Valley Memorial Hospital, Yakima, WA [*Library symbol Library of Congress*] (LCLS)
WAYMCA ..... World Alliance of Young Men's Christian Associations [*Geneva, Switzerland*] (EAIO)
WaYMHi ...... Yakima Valley Museum and Historical Association, Yakima, WA [*Library symbol Library of Congress*] (LCLS)
WAYN .... Rockingham, NC [*AM radio station call letters*]
WAYN .... Wayne Savings & Loan Co. [*NASDAQ symbol*] (SAG)
WAYN .... Wayne Svgs & Ln [*NASDAQ symbol*] (TTSB)
WayneB .... Wayne Bancorp, Inc. [*Associated Press*] (SAG)
Wayne St C (Neb)... Wayne State College (Nebraska) (GAGS)
Wayne St U... Wayne State University (GAGS)
WayneSv ...... Wayne Savings & Loan Co. [*Associated Press*] (SAG)
WAYQ .... Daytona Beach, FL [*Television station call letters*]
WAYR .... Orange Park, FL [*AM radio station call letters*]
WAYS .... Macon, GA [*FM radio station call letters*]
WAYS .... Ways [*Postal Service standard*] (OPSA)
WaYSE .... Saint Elizabeth Hospital, Health Sciences Library, Yakima, WA [*Library symbol Library of Congress*] (LCLS)
WAYT .... Wabash, IN [*AM radio station call letters*]
WAYV .... Atlantic City, NJ [*FM radio station call letters*]
WAYX .... Waycross, GA [*AM radio station call letters*]
WAYY .... Chippewa Falls, WI [*AM radio station call letters*]
WaYY .... Yakima Valley College, Yakima, WA [*Library symbol Library of Congress*] (LCLS)
WaYYS .... Washington State Center for Youth Services, Yakima, WA [*Library symbol Library of Congress*] (LCLS)
WAYZ .... Waynesboro, PA [*FM radio station call letters*]
WAZ .... Worked All Zones [*Contacted at least one station in all zones*] [*Amateur radio*] (IAA)
WAZF .... Yazoo City, MS [*AM radio station call letters*]
WAZL .... Hazleton, PA [*AM radio station call letters*]
WAZR .... Woodstock, VA [*FM radio station call letters*]
WAZS .... Summerville, SC [*AM radio station call letters*]
WAZU .... Santa Claus, IN [*FM radio station call letters*] (RBYB)
WAZU-FM .... Cincinnati, OH [*FM radio station call letters*] (RBYB)
WAZX .... Cleveland, GA [*FM radio station call letters*]
WAZX .... Smyrna, GA [*AM radio station call letters*]
WAZY .... Lafayette, IN [*FM radio station call letters*]
WAZZ .... Laurinburg, NC [*FM radio station call letters*]
W_B .... Base-Region Width (IDOE)
WB .... Wachovia Corp. [*NYSE symbol*] (SPSG)
WB .... Wage Board [*Civil Service classification*]
WB .... Wagon Box (MSA)
WB .... Wallboard
WB .... Wall Box (ROG)
WB .... Warbirds of America (EA)
WB .... Warehouse Book
WB .... Warner Brothers [*Television network*]
WB .... Washable Base (ADA)
WB .... Wash Basin
WB .... Wash Bucket
WB .... Waste Book (ROG)
WB .... Water Ballast [*Shipping*]
WB .... Water Board
W/B .... Water Boiler (KSC)
WB .... Water Bottle
WB .... Water Box

WB .... Waterproof Breathable [*Textile technology*]
WB .... Wave-Band (ADA)
WB .... Waybill [*Shipping*]
WB .... Weatherboard (ADA)
WB .... Weather Bomber [*Air Force*]
WB .... Weather Bureau [*Later, National Weather Service*] (EA)
Wb .... Weber [*Symbol*] [*SI unit of magnetic flux*]
WB .... Wechsler-Bellevue [*Psychological test*]
WB .... Wedge Biopsy [*Medicine*]
WB .... Weekly Boarding
WB .... Weekly Bulletin [*Army*] (AABC)
W/B .... Weight and Balance
WB .... Weight Bearing
WB .... Welded Base (DAC)
wb .... West Berlin [*MARC country of publication code Library of Congress*] (LCCP)
WB .... Westbound
WB .... Westbridge Computer Corp. [*Toronto Stock Exchange symbol*]
WB .... Western Blot [*Blood test*]
WB .... Westminster Biographies [*A publication*]
WB .... Wet Bulb [*Thermometer, of a psychrometer*] [*Meteorology*]
WB .... Whale Boat
WB .... Wheelbarrow (MSA)
WB .... Wheelbase
WB .... White Bag Propellant [*Army*] (ADDR)
WB .... White Balance [*Television*] (NTCM)
WB .... Whole Blood
WB .... Whole Body [*Medicine*]
WB .... Whole Body [*Nuclear energy*] (NRCH)
WB .... Whole Bow [*Music*] (ROG)
WB .... Wideband [*Radio transmission*]
WB .... Widebeam (NATG)
WB .... Will Be (AABC)
WB .... Willowbrook [*Virus*] (MAE)
WB .... Wilson Blair [*Agar*] (BABM)
WB .... Wilson Blair [*Agar*] [*Microbiology*] (DAVI)
WB .... Winchester Word Book [*A publication*]
WB .... Wingback [*Football*]
WB .... Winner's Bitch [*Dog show term*]
WB .... Wirebar [*Metal industry*]
W/B .... Wire Bundles (MCD)
WB .... Woerterbuch der Aegyptischen Sprache [*A publication*] (BJA)
WB .... Women's Bureau [*Department of Labor*]
WB .... Wood Base [*Technical drawings*]
WB .... Wood Burning [*Fireplace*] [*Classified advertising*]
WB .... Wool Back [*Knitting*]
WB .... Wool Bureau (EA)
WB .... Word Before [*Message handling*]
WB .... Workbench (AAG)
WB .... Work Book
WB .... World Bank
WB .... World Bank (EERA)
WB .... World Brotherhood
WB .... Write-Back [*Computer science*] (PCM)
WB .... Write Buffer
W/B .... Writing on Back [*Deltiology*]
WB2 .... Warramunga Array [*Australia Seismograph station code, US Geological Survey*] (SEIS)
WB3 .... Warramunga Array [*Australia Seismograph station code, US Geological Survey*] (SEIS)
WBA .... Washington Bay [*Alaska*] [*Airport symbol*] (AD)
WBA .... Wax Bean Agglutinin [*Biochemistry*]
WBA .... Weekly Benefit Amount [*Unemployment insurance*]
WBA .... Weekly of Business Aviation [*McGraw-Hill Information Services Co.*] [*Information service or system*] (CRD)
WBA .... West Coast Air [*Gambia*] [*ICAO designator*] (FAAC)
WBA .... Western Blot Assay [*Analytical biochemistry*]
WBA .... Whole Body Activity (DAVI)
WBA .... Wideband Amplifier
WBA .... Wire Bundle Assembly (MCD)
WBA .... Woman's Benefit Association [*Later, NABA*]
WBA .... Works and Building, High Priority [*British World War II*]
WBA .... World Boxing Association [*Later, WBO*] (EA)
WBA .... World Buffalo Association Ltd. Agricultural Association (EA)
WBA .... Worn by Astronaut [*NASA*] (KSC)
WBAA .... West Lafayette, IN [*AM radio station call letters*]
WBAA-FM .... West Lafayette, IN [*FM radio station call letters*]
WBAB .... Babylon, NY [*FM radio station call letters*]
WBAC .... Cleveland, TN [*AM radio station call letters*]
WBAD .... Leland, MS [*FM radio station call letters*]
WBAEA .... Wholesale Beer Association Executives of America (EA)
WBAF .... Barnesville, GA [*AM radio station call letters*]
WBAG .... Burlington-Graham, NC [*AM radio station call letters*]
WBAI .... New York, NY [*FM radio station call letters*]
WBAI .... Wesley Bull & Associates, Inc. [*Seattle, WA*] [*Telecommunications*] (TSSD)
WBAIS .... Walworth Barbour American International School in Israel (BJA)
WBAJ .... Blythwood, SC [*AM radio station call letters*]
WBAK .... Anduki/Seria [*Brunei*] [*ICAO location identifier*] (ICLI)
WBAK .... Terre Haute, IN [*Television station call letters*]
WBAL .... Baltimore, MD [*AM radio station call letters*]
WBAL-TV .... Baltimore, MD [*Television station call letters*]
WBAM .... Montgomery, AL [*FM radio station call letters*]
WBAMC .... William Beaumont Army Medical Center (AABC)
WBAN .... Rantoul, IL [*AM radio station call letters*]
WBAN .... Weather Bureau, Air Force, Navy [*Manuals*] [*Obsolete*]
WBAN .... West Coast Bancorp [*NASDAQ symbol*] (SAG)
WBANA .... Wild Blueberry Association of North America (EA)
WB & A .... Washington, Baltimore & Annapolis Railroad [*Nickname: Wobble, Bump, and Amble*]
WBANK .... Bank of Canada Weekly Financial Statistics [*I. P. Sharp Associates*] [*Information service or system*] (CRD)
WBAP .... Fort Worth, TX [*AM radio station call letters*]
WBAPTT .... Whole Blood Activated Partial Thromboplastin Time [*Hematology*] (DAVI)
WBAQ .... Greenville, MS [*FM radio station call letters*]
WBAR .... Bartow, FL [*AM radio station call letters*]
WBAR .... Lake Luzerne, NY [*FM radio station call letters*]
WBAR .... Wing Bar Lights [*Aviation*]
WBaraC .... Circus World Museum, Baraboo, WI [*Library symbol Library of Congress*] (LCLS)
WBaraHi .... Sauk County Historical Society, Baraboo, WI [*Library symbol Library of Congress*] (LCLS)
WBAS .... Weather Bureau Airport Station [*Obsolete*]
WBAS .... Woerterbuch der Aegyptischen Sprache [*A publication*] (BJA)
WBasR .... Randall Consolidated School, Bassett, WI [*Library symbol Library of Congress*] (LCLS)
WBAT .... Marion, IN [*AM radio station call letters*]
WBAT .... Weight-Bearing as Tolerated [*Orthopedics*] (DAVI)
WBAT .... Westport Bancorp [*NASDAQ symbol*] (TTSB)
WBAT .... Westport Bancorp, Inc. [*Westport, CT*] [*NASDAQ symbol*] (NQ)
WBAT .... Wideband Adapter Transformer
WBAU .... Garden City, NY [*FM radio station call letters*]
WBAV .... Charlotte, NC [*AM radio station call letters*]
WBAV .... Gastonia, NC [*FM radio station call letters*]
WBAW .... Barnwell, SC [*AM radio station call letters*]
WBAW-FM .... Barnwell, SC [*FM radio station call letters*]
WBAWS .... Weather, Briefing, Advisory, and Warning Service (AABC)
WBAX .... Wilkes-Barre, PA [*AM radio station call letters*]
WBAY .... Green Bay, WI [*Television station call letters*]
WBAZ .... Southhold, NY [*FM radio station call letters*]
WBB .... Beloit College, Beloit, WI [*Library symbol Library of Congress*] (LCLS)
WBB .... Stebbins [*Alaska*] [*Airport symbol*] (OAG)
WBB .... Stebbins, AK [*Location identifier FAA*] (FAAL)
WBB .... Webb [*Del E.*] Corp. [*NYSE symbol*] (SPSG)
WBB .... Wide Band Beam [*Physics*]
WBB .... Woodfree Bank and Bond [*Paper*] (DGA)
WBB .... World Bank Bond (MHDW)
WBBA .... Pittsfield, IL [*AM radio station call letters*]
WBBA .... Western Bird Banding Association (EA)
WBBA-FM .... Pittsfield, IL [*FM radio station call letters*]
WBBB .... Burlington, NC [*AM radio station call letters*]
WBBC .... Blackstone, VA [*FM radio station call letters*]
WBBCC .... Wide Bay Burnett Conservation Council (EERA)
WBBD-AM .... Wheeling, WV [*AM radio station call letters*] (RBYB)
WBBE-FM .... Gilford, FL [*FM radio station call letters*] (RBYB)
WBBF .... Rochester, NY [*AM radio station call letters*]
WBBG .... Youngstown, OH [*FM radio station call letters*]
WBBH .... Fort Myers, FL [*Television station call letters*]
WBBJ .... Jackson, TN [*Television station call letters*]
WBBK .... Blakely, GA [*AM radio station call letters*]
WBBK-FM .... Blakely, GA [*FM radio station call letters*]
WBBL .... Grand Rapids, MI [*AM radio station call letters*]
WBBM .... Chicago, IL [*AM radio station call letters*]
WBBM-FM .... Chicago, IL [*FM radio station call letters*]
WBBM-TV .... Chicago, IL [*Television station call letters*]
WBBN .... Taylorsville, MS [*FM radio station call letters*]
WBBP .... Memphis, TN [*AM radio station call letters*]
WBBQ .... Augusta, GA [*AM radio station call letters*]
WBBQ-FM .... Augusta, GA [*FM radio station call letters*]
WBBR .... New York, NY [*AM radio station call letters*]
WBBS .... Fulton, NY [*FM radio station call letters*]
WBBT .... Lyons, GA [*AM radio station call letters*]
WBBU .... Baker, LA [*FM radio station call letters*]
WBBV .... Vicksburg, MS [*FM radio station call letters*]
WBBW .... Youngstown, OH [*AM radio station call letters*]
WBBX .... Kingston, TN [*AM radio station call letters*]
WBBY .... Cedar Bluff, VA [*FM radio station call letters*]
WBBZ .... Ponca City, OK [*AM radio station call letters*]
WBC .... Bath, ME [*FM radio station call letters*] (RBYB)
WBC .... Warm-Blood Cardioplegia [*Medicine*]
WBC .... Washington, DC [*Location identifier FAA*] (FAAL)
WBC .... Water Binding Capacity [*Also, WHC*] [*Food industry*]
WBC .... Wayland Baptist College [*Texas*]
WBC .... Weather Bureau Central Office [*Obsolete*]
WBC .... Weather Bureau Communications [*Obsolete*]
WBC .... Weight and Balance Computer (GAVI)
WBC .... Weight-Bearing with Crutches [*Orthopedics*] (DAVI)
WBC .... Welsh Books Council
WBC .... Westbridge Capital [*NYSE symbol*] (SAG)
WBC .... Western Boundary Current [*Marine science*] (MSC)
WBC .... Westinghouse Broadcasting Co.
WBC .... Westpac Banking Corp. [*Australia Commercial firm*]
WBC .... White Blood Cell [*or Corpuscle*] [*Medicine*]
WBC .... White Blood Cell Count [*Medicine*]
WBC .... Whole Blood Cell Count [*Hematology*] (DAVI)
WBC .... Wideband Channel [*Telecommunications*]
WBC .... Wideband Coupler
WBC .... Wien Bridge Circuit [*Physics*]

WBC.......... Wilkes-Barre Connecting Railroad [*AAR code*]
WBC.......... Wilkes College Library, Wilkes-Barre, PA [*OCLC symbol*] (OCLC)
WBC.......... Wire Bridge Circuit
WBC.......... Women's Broadcasting Corp.
WBC.......... World Book Congress
WBC.......... World Boxing Council [*Information service or system*] (IID)
WBC.......... World Business Council [*Washington, DC*] (EA)
WBC.......... Wycliffe Bible Commentary [*A publication*] (BJA)
WBCA.......... Bay Minette, AL [*AM radio station call letters*]
WBCA.......... Welsh Black Cattle Association (EA)
WBCA.......... Welsh Black Cattle Society (DBA)
WBCA.......... Women's Basketball Coaches Association (EA)
WBCA.......... Wyandotte Bantam Club of America (EA)
WBCB.......... Levittown-Fairless Hills, PA [*AM radio station call letters*]
WBCC.......... Cocoa, FL [*Television station call letters*]
WBCC.......... White Blood Cell Count [*Hematology*] (DAVI)
WBCCI.......... Wally Byam Caravan Club International (EA)
WBCD.......... Chattahoochee, FL [*FM radio station call letters*]
WBCD.......... White Blood Cell Differential [*Hematology*]
WBCE.......... Wickliffe, KY [*AM radio station call letters*]
WBCF.......... Florence, AL [*AM radio station call letters*]
WBCG.......... Murfreesboro, NC [*FM radio station call letters*]
WBCG.......... Water Bird Conservation Group [*Australia*]
WBCH.......... Hastings, MI [*AM radio station call letters*]
WBCH-FM.......... Hastings, MI [*FM radio station call letters*]
WBC/HPF.......... White Blood Cells per High Power Field [*Hematology*] (MAE)
WBCI.......... WFS Bancorp [*NASDAQ symbol*] (TTSB)
WBCI.......... WFS Bancorp, Inc. [*NASDAQ symbol*] (SAG)
WBCI-FM.......... Bath, ME [*FM radio station call letters*] (RBYB)
WBCJ-FM.......... Spencerville, OH [*FM radio station call letters*] (RBYB)
WBCK.......... Battle Creek, MI [*AM radio station call letters*]
WBCL.......... Fort Wayne, IN [*FM radio station call letters*]
WBCM.......... Boyne City, MI [*FM radio station call letters*]
WBCN.......... Boston, MA [*FM radio station call letters*]
WBCO.......... Bucyrus, OH [*AM radio station call letters*]
WBCO.......... Wallace Barnes Co.
WBCO.......... Waveguide below Cutoff (IEEE)
WBCP.......... Urbana, IL [*AM radio station call letters*]
WBCR.......... Alcoa, TN [*AM radio station call letters*]
WBCR.......... Beloit, WI [*FM radio station call letters*]
WBCRR.......... Wilkes-Barre Connecting Railroad (MHDB)
WBCS.......... Boston, MA [*FM radio station call letters*]
WBCS.......... Wideband Communications Subsystem
WBCSC.......... Wide Band Cable Systems Committee (NITA)
WBCT.......... Grand Rapids, MI [*FM radio station call letters*]
WBCT.......... Whole-Blood Clotting Time [*Hematology*]
WBCT.......... Wideband Current Transformer
WBCU.......... Union, SC [*AM radio station call letters*]
WBCV.......... Bristol, TN [*AM radio station call letters*]
WBCV.......... Wideband Coherent Video (IEEE)
WBCW.......... Jeanette, PA [*AM radio station call letters*]
WBCX.......... Gainesville, GA [*FM radio station call letters*]
WBCY.......... Archbold, OH [*FM radio station call letters*]
WBD.......... Befandriana [*Madagascar*] [*Airport symbol*] (OAG)
WBD.......... Wallboard
WBD.......... Ward's Business Directory [*A publication*]
WBD.......... Washboard [*Musical instrument used in some jazz bands*]
WBD.......... Watts Bar Dam [*TVA*]
WBD.......... Webster's Biographical Dictionary [*A publication*]
WBD.......... Wideband Data
WBD.......... Wire Bound (IEEE)
WBD.......... World Business Directory [*A publication*]
WBDA.......... Wideband Data Assembly [*Ground Communications Facility, NASA*]
WBDC.......... Huntingburg, IN [*FM radio station call letters*]
WBDC-TV.......... Washington, DC [*Television station call letters*] (RBYB)
WBDDS.......... Weapons Bay Door Drive Subsystem [*Military*]
WBDF.......... Wideband Dicke-Fix (CET)
WBDFX.......... Wideband Dicke-Fix (MSA)
WBDG.......... Indianapolis, IN [*FM radio station call letters*]
WBDI.......... Wideband Data Interleaver (MCD)
WBDK.......... Algoma, WI [*FM radio station call letters*]
WBDL.......... Wideband Data Line [*or Link*]
WBDL-FM.......... Reedsburg, WI [*FM radio station call letters*] (RBYB)
WBDN.......... Brandon, FL [*AM radio station call letters*]
WBDNA.......... Women Band Directors National Association (EA)
WBdSJ.......... Saint Joseph's Hospital, Beaver Dam, WI [*Library symbol Library of Congress*] (LCLS)
WBDX.......... Trenton, GA [*FM radio station call letters*]
WBDX.......... Wideband Data Switch
WBDY.......... Bluefield, VA [*FM radio station call letters*]
WBE.......... Bealanana [*Madagascar*] [*Airport symbol*] (OAG)
WBE.......... Waterloo County Board of Education, Professional Education Library [*UTLAS symbol*]
WBE.......... West Bromwich [*England*] [*Seismograph station code, US Geological Survey Closed*] (SEIS)
WBE.......... Whole-Body Extract [*Immunology*]
WBE.......... Wideband Electronics
WBE.......... Women's Business Enterprise
WBEA.......... Montauk, NY [*FM radio station call letters*]
WBEA.......... Western Business Education Association (AEBS)
WBEB.......... Philadelphia, PA [*FM radio station call letters*]
WBEC.......... Pittsfield, MA [*AM radio station call letters*]
WBEC-FM.......... Pittsfield, MA [*FM radio station call letters*]
WBEE.......... Harvey, IL [*AM radio station call letters*]
WBEE.......... Rochester, NY [*FM radio station call letters*]
WB/EI.......... West Britain/East Ireland
WBEJ.......... Elizabethton, TN [*AM radio station call letters*]
WBEL.......... South Beloit, IL [*AM radio station call letters*]
WBelH.......... Holy Family Convent, Benet Lake, WI [*Library symbol Library of Congress*] (LCLS)
WBelSB.......... Saint Benedict's Abbey, Benet Library, Benet Lake, WI [*Library symbol Library of Congress*] (LCLS)
WBEM.......... Windber, PA [*AM radio station call letters*]
WBEN.......... Buffalo, NY [*AM radio station call letters*]
WBEP.......... Workplace Basic Education Project [*Australia*]
WBer.......... Berlin Public Library, Berlin, WI [*Library symbol Library of Congress*] (LCLS)
WBER.......... Rochester, NY [*FM radio station call letters*]
WBES.......... Dunbar, WV [*FM radio station call letters*]
WBET.......... Brockton, MA [*AM radio station call letters*]
WBEU.......... Beaufort, SC [*AM radio station call letters*]
WBEV.......... Beaver Dam, WI [*AM radio station call letters*]
WBEX.......... Chillicothe, OH [*AM radio station call letters*]
WBEY.......... Crisfield, MD [*FM radio station call letters*] (RBYB)
WBEZ.......... Chicago, IL [*FM radio station call letters*]
WBF.......... Whole Blood Folate [*Hematology*] (MAE)
WBF.......... Wood Block Floor [*Technical drawings*]
WBF.......... Wood-Burning Fireplace [*Classified advertising*] (WGA)
WBF.......... Workmen's Benefit Fund of the USA [*Carle Place, NY*] (EA)
WBF.......... World Batch Forum (ACII)
WBF.......... World Bridge Federation
WBFA.......... Western Bohemian Fraternal Association [*Later, WFLA*] (EA)
WBFC.......... Kota Kinabalu [*Malaysia*] [*ICAO location identifier*] (ICLI)
WBFC.......... Stanton, KY [*AM radio station call letters*]
WBFD.......... Bedford, PA [*AM radio station call letters*]
WBFF.......... Baltimore, MD [*Television station call letters*]
WBFH.......... Bloomfield Hills, MI [*FM radio station call letters*]
WBFI.......... McDaniels, KY [*FM radio station call letters*]
WBFI.......... Wild Bird Feeding Institute (EA)
WBFJ.......... Winston-Salem, NC [*AM radio station call letters*]
WBFJ-FM.......... Winston-Salem, NC [*FM radio station call letters*]
WBFL.......... Bellows Falls, VT [*FM radio station call letters*]
WBFM.......... Wideband Frequency Modulation
WBFM-FM.......... Sheboygan Falls, WI [*FM radio station call letters*] (RBYB)
WBFN.......... Quitman, MS [*AM radio station call letters*]
WBFO.......... Buffalo, NY [*FM radio station call letters*]
WBFP.......... Wood-Burning Fireplace [*Classified advertising*]
WBFR.......... Birmingham, AL [*FM radio station call letters*]
WBFS.......... Miami, FL [*Television station call letters*]
WBFX-TV.......... Lexington, NC [*TV station call letters*] (RBYB)
WBG.......... Webbing
WBG.......... Wichabai [*Guyana*] [*Airport symbol*] (AD)
WBGA.......... Long Atip [*Malaysia*] [*ICAO location identifier*] (ICLI)
WBGA.......... Waycross, GA [*FM radio station call letters*]
WBGB.......... Bintulu [*Malaysia*] [*ICAO location identifier*] (ICLI)
WBGB.......... Mount Dora, FL [*AM radio station call letters*]
WBGC.......... Belaga [*Malaysia*] [*ICAO location identifier*] (ICLI)
WBGC.......... Chipley, FL [*AM radio station call letters*]
WBGD.......... Brick Township, NJ [*FM radio station call letters*]
WBGD.......... Long Semado [*Malaysia*] [*ICAO location identifier*] (ICLI)
WBGE.......... Long Geng [*Malaysia*] [*ICAO location identifier*] (ICLI)
WBGE.......... Peoria, IL [*FM radio station call letters*]
WBGF.......... Belle Glade, FL [*FM radio station call letters*]
WBGF.......... Wholesale Buyers' Gifts Fair [*British*] (ITD)
WBGG.......... Fort Lauderdale, FL [*FM radio station call letters*]
WBGG.......... Kuching [*Malaysia*] [*ICAO location identifier*] (ICLI)
WBGJ.......... Limbang [*Malaysia*] [*ICAO location identifier*] (ICLI)
WBGK.......... Mukah [*Malaysia*] [*ICAO location identifier*] (ICLI)
WBGL.......... Champaign, IL [*FM radio station call letters*]
WBGL.......... Long Akah [*Indonesia*] [*ICAO location identifier*] (ICLI)
WBGM.......... Marudi [*Indonesia*] [*ICAO location identifier*] (ICLI)
WBGM-FM.......... New Berlin, PA [*FM radio station call letters*] (RBYB)
WBGN.......... Bowling Green, KY [*AM radio station call letters*]
WBGN.......... Sematan [*Indonesia*] [*ICAO location identifier*] (ICLI)
WBGO.......... Lio Matu [*Malaysia*] [*ICAO location identifier*] (ICLI)
WBGO.......... Newark, NJ [*FM radio station call letters*]
WBGP.......... Kapit [*Indonesia*] [*ICAO location identifier*] (ICLI)
WBGP.......... Waterborne Guard Post (NVT)
WBGQ.......... Bakelalan [*Malaysia*] [*ICAO location identifier*] (ICLI)
WBGR.......... Baltimore, MD [*AM radio station call letters*]
WBGR.......... Miri [*Indonesia*] [*ICAO location identifier*] (ICLI)
WBGS.......... Point Pleasant, WV [*AM radio station call letters*]
WBGS.......... Sibu [*Malaysia*] [*ICAO location identifier*] (ICLI)
WBGT.......... Staunton, VA [*FM radio station call letters*]
WBGT.......... Wet Bulb Globe Temperature
WBGT.......... Wet Bulb Globe Thermometer
WBGTI.......... Wet Bulb Globe Temperature Index (RDA)
WBGU.......... Bowling Green, OH [*FM radio station call letters*]
WBGU-TV.......... Bowling Green, OH [*Television station call letters*]
WBGV.......... Marlette, MI [*FM radio station call letters*]
WBGW.......... Fort Branch, IN [*FM radio station call letters*]
WBGW.......... Lawas [*Malaysia*] [*ICAO location identifier*] (ICLI)
WBGY.......... Simanggang [*Malaysia*] [*ICAO location identifier*] (ICLI)
WBGZ.......... Alton, IL [*AM radio station call letters*]
WBGZ.......... Bario [*Malaysia*] [*ICAO location identifier*] (ICLI)
WBH.......... Whole Blood Hematocrit [*Hematology*] (MAE)
WBH.......... Whole Body Hyperthermia [*Emergency medicine*] (DAVI)
WBHA.......... Hot Springs, VA [*FM radio station call letters*]
WBHB.......... Fitzgerald, GA [*AM radio station call letters*]
WBHC.......... Hampton, SC [*AM radio station call letters*]

WBHC-FM .... Hampton, SC [*FM radio station call letters*]
WBHF .... Cartersville, GA [*AM radio station call letters*]
WBHG .... Meredith, NH [*FM radio station call letters*]
WBHI .... Chicago, IL [*FM radio station call letters*]
WBHJ-FM .... Tuscaloosa, AL [*FM radio station call letters*] (RBYB)
WBHK-FM .... Warrior, AL [*FM radio station call letters*] (RBYB)
WBHL .... Florence, AL [*FM radio station call letters*]
WBHM .... Birmingham, AL [*FM radio station call letters*]
WBHN .... Bryson City, NC [*AM radio station call letters*]
WBHO .... Weather Bureau Hurricane Forecast Office [*Obsolete*]
WBHP .... Huntsville, AL [*AM radio station call letters*]
WBHQ .... Bloomfield, IN [*FM radio station call letters*]
WBHR .... Jackson, MI [*FM radio station call letters*] (RBYB)
WBHS .... Tampa, FL [*Television station call letters*]
WBHT .... Mountain Top, PA [*FM radio station call letters*]
WBHV .... State College, PA [*FM radio station call letters*]
WBHW-FM ... Loogootee, IN [*FM radio station call letters*] (RBYB)
WBHY .... Mobile, AL [*AM radio station call letters*]
WBHY-FM .... Mobile, AL [*FM radio station call letters*]
WBI .... Ward Behavior Inventory [*Psychology*]
WBI .... Washington Beverage Insight [*Wells & Associates*] [*Information service or system*] (IID)
WB-I .... Wechsler-Bellevue [*Test*] [*Psychiatry*] (DAVI)
WBI .... Whiskey Butte [*Idaho*] [*Seismograph station code, US Geological Survey Closed*] (SEIS)
WBI .... Will Be In (DAVI)
WBI .... Will Be Issued
WBI .... Wooden Box Institute [*Defunct*] (EA)
WBIB .... Centreville, AL [*AM radio station call letters*]
WBIC .... Royston, GA [*AM radio station call letters*]
WBIC .... Weather and Battle-Induced Contaminant (PDAA)
WBIF .... Wideband Intermediate Frequency (MCD)
WBIG .... Aurora, IL [*AM radio station call letters*]
WBIG .... Washington, DC [*FM radio station call letters*]
WBII .... Washington Business Information, Inc. [*Information service or system*] (IID)
WBIL .... Tuskegee, AL [*AM radio station call letters*]
WBIL-FM ..... Tuskegee, AL [*FM radio station call letters*]
WBIM .... Bridgewater, MA [*FM radio station call letters*]
WBIN .... Benton, TN [*AM radio station call letters*]
WBIN-FM ..... Benton, TN [*FM radio station call letters*]
WBINVD .... Write Back and Invalidate Data [*Cache*] [*Computer instruction*] (PCM)
WBIO .... Philpot, KY [*FM radio station call letters*]
WBIP .... Booneville, MS [*AM radio station call letters*]
WBIP .... Whitaker's Books in Print [*J. Whitaker & Sons Ltd.*] [*Information service or system*] (IID)
WBIP-FM ..... Booneville, MS [*FM radio station call letters*]
WBIQ .... Birmingham, AL [*Television station call letters*]
WBIR .... Knoxville, TN [*Television station call letters*]
WBIS-TV ...... New York, NY [*TV station call letters*] (RBYB)
WBIT .... Adel, GA [*AM radio station call letters*]
WBIT .... Wechsler-Bellevue Intelligence Test [*Psychology*] (WDAA)
WBIU .... Denham Springs, LA [*AM radio station call letters*]
WBIV .... Natick, MA [*AM radio station call letters*]
WBIW .... Bedford, IN [*AM radio station call letters*]
WBIZ .... Eau Claire, WI [*AM radio station call letters*]
WBIZ-FM ..... Eau Claire, WI [*FM radio station call letters*]
WBJB .... Lincroft, NJ [*FM radio station call letters*]
WBJC .... Baltimore, MD [*FM radio station call letters*]
WBJI .... Blackduck, MN [*FM radio station call letters*]
WBJJ-FM ..... Jackson, LA [*FM radio station call letters*] (RBYB)
WBJW-FM ... Albion, IL [*FM radio station call letters*] (RBYB)
WBJX .... Racine, WI [*AM radio station call letters*]
WBK .... Webb & Knapp (Canada) Ltd. [*Vancouver Stock Exchange symbol*]
WBK .... Westpac Banking ADS [*NYSE symbol*] (SPSG)
WBKA .... Semporna [*Malaysia*] [*ICAO location identifier*] (ICLI)
WBKB .... Alpena, MI [*Television station call letters*]
WBKC .... Painesville, OH [*AM radio station call letters*]
WBKC .... Westbank Corp. [*NASDAQ symbol*] (SAG)
WBKD .... Lahad Datu [*Malaysia*] [*ICAO location identifier*] (ICLI)
WBKE .... North Manchester, IN [*FM radio station call letters*]
WBKG .... Keningau [*Malaysia*] [*ICAO location identifier*] (ICLI)
WBKH .... Hattiesburg, MS [*AM radio station call letters*]
WBKJ .... Kosciusko, MS [*FM radio station call letters*]
WBKK .... Amsterdam, NY [*FM radio station call letters*]
WBKK .... Kota Kinabalu [*Malaysia*] [*ICAO location identifier*] (ICLI)
WBKL .... Labuan [*Malaysia*] [*ICAO location identifier*] (ICLI)
WBKN .... Brookhaven, MS [*FM radio station call letters*]
WBKO .... Bowling Green, KY [*Television station call letters*]
WBKP .... Pamol [*Malaysia*] [*ICAO location identifier*] (ICLI)
WBKP-TV ..... Calumet, MI [*TV station call letters*] (RBYB)
WBKR .... Owensboro, KY [*FM radio station call letters*]
WBKR .... Ranau [*Malaysia*] [*ICAO location identifier*] (ICLI)
WBKS .... Sandakan [*Malaysia*] [*ICAO location identifier*] (ICLI)
WBKT .... Kudat [*Malaysia*] [*ICAO location identifier*] (ICLI)
WBKV .... West Bend, WI [*AM radio station call letters*]
WBKW .... Tawau [*Malaysia*] [*ICAO location identifier*] (ICLI)
WBKY-FM .... Portage, WI [*FM radio station call letters*] (RBYB)
WBKZ .... Jefferson, GA [*AM radio station call letters*]
WBL .... Weak Black Liquor [*Pulp and paper technology*]
WBL .... Western Biological Laboratories
WBL .... White Bluff [*Washington*] [*Seismograph station code, US Geological Survey*] (SEIS)
WBL .... Wideband LASER
WBL .... Wideband Limiting (IEEE)
WBL .... Wissenschaftsgemeinschaft Blaue Liste
WBL .... Women's Basketball League [*Defunct*] (EA)
WBL .... Wood Blocking
WBL .... Work Based Learning (AIE)
WBLA .... Elizabethtown, NC [*AM radio station call letters*]
WBLB .... Pulaski, VA [*AM radio station call letters*]
WBLC .... Lenoir City, TN [*AM radio station call letters*]
WBLC .... Water-Borne Logistics Craft
WBLD .... Orchard Lake, MI [*FM radio station call letters*]
WBLE .... Batesville, MS [*FM radio station call letters*]
WBLF .... Bellefonte, PA [*AM radio station call letters*]
WBLG .... Smiths Grove, KY [*FM radio station call letters*]
WBLI .... Patchogue, NY [*FM radio station call letters*]
WBLJ .... Dalton, GA [*AM radio station call letters*]
WBLK .... Depew, NY [*FM radio station call letters*]
WBLL .... Bellefontaine, OH [*AM radio station call letters*]
WBLM .... Portland, ME [*FM radio station call letters*]
WBLMC .... Worldwide Branch Locations of Multinational Companies [*A publication*]
WBLN .... Murray, KY [*FM radio station call letters*]
WBLO .... Weak Black Liquor Oxidation [*Pulp and paper technology*]
WBLQ .... Block Island, RI [*FM radio station call letters*]
WBLR .... Batesburg, SC [*AM radio station call letters*]
WBLS .... New York, NY [*FM radio station call letters*]
WBLT .... Bedford, VA [*AM radio station call letters*]
WBLU .... Grand Rapids, MI [*FM radio station call letters*]
WBLV .... Twin Lake, MI [*FM radio station call letters*]
WBLX .... Fairhope, AL [*AM radio station call letters*]
WBLX .... Mobile, AL [*FM radio station call letters*]
WBLY .... Springfield, OH [*AM radio station call letters*]
WBLZ .... Mt. Vernon, IN [*FM radio station call letters*]
WBM .... Beloit Memorial Hospital, Beloit, WI [*Library symbol Library of Congress*] (LCLS)
WBM .... Wapenamanda [*Papua New Guinea*] [*Airport symbol*] (OAG)
WB M .... Weber Meter
WBM .... Wing Battle Manager [*Air Force*]
WBM .... Woerterbuch der Mythologie [*A publication*] (BJA)
WBM .... Women's Board of Missions
wb/m² .... Weber per Square Meter [*Chemistry*] (DAVI)
WBMA .... Western Building Material Association (EA)
WBMA .... Whirlpool Bath Manufacturers Association [*Defunct*] (EA)
WBMA .... Wirebound Box Manufacturers Association (EA)
WBMC .... McMinnville, TN [*AM radio station call letters*]
WBMC .... Weight before Mars Capture [*NASA*]
WBMCR .... Wideband Multichannel Receiver
WBMD .... Baltimore, MD [*AM radio station call letters*]
WBMG .... Birmingham, AL [*Television station call letters*]
WBMG .... Walter Bernard and Milton Glaser [*Founders of the magazine-design firm that bears their initials*]
WBMI .... West Branch, MI [*FM radio station call letters*]
WBMI .... Women's Board of Missions of the Interior
WBMJ .... San Juan, PR [*AM radio station call letters*]
WBML .... Macon, GA [*AM radio station call letters*]
WBMO .... Weather Bureau Meteorological Observation Station [*Obsolete*]
WBMQ .... Savannah, GA [*AM radio station call letters*]
WBMS .... Wilmington, NC [*AM radio station call letters*]
WBMS .... World Bureau of Metal Statistics [*British*] (EAIO)
WBMT .... Boxford, MA [*FM radio station call letters*]
WBMW .... Ledyard, CT [*FM radio station call letters*]
WBMX .... Boston, MA [*FM radio station call letters*]
WbMyth .... Woerterbuch der Mythologie [*A publication*] (BJA)
WBN .... Waban, Inc. [*NYSE symbol*] (SPSG)
WBN .... Well Behaved Net
WBN .... Wellborn Nursery [*Neonatology*] (DAVI)
WBN .... West by North
W Bn .... White Beacon
WBN .... Wide Band Noise (DAVI)
WBNA .... Louisville, KY [*Television station call letters*]
WBNC .... Conway, NH [*AM radio station call letters*]
WBNC-FM .... Conway, NH [*FM radio station call letters*] (RBYB)
WBND .... Westbound (FAAC)
W BNDR ...... With Binder [*Freight*]
WBNF .... Marianna, FL [*FM radio station call letters*]
WBNG .... Binghamton, NY [*Television station call letters*]
WBNH .... Pekin, IL [*FM radio station call letters*]
WBNI .... Fort Wayne, IN [*FM radio station call letters*]
WBNJ .... Cape May Court House, NJ [*FM radio station call letters*]
WBNK .... Christianburg, VA [*FM radio station call letters*]
WBNL .... Boonville, IN [*AM radio station call letters*]
WBNL .... Wideband Noise Limiting
WBNL-FM .... Boonville, IN [*FM radio station call letters*]
WBNM .... Gordon, GA [*AM radio station call letters*]
WBNN .... Union City, IN [*FM radio station call letters*]
WBNO .... Bryan, OH [*FM radio station call letters*]
WBNP .... Watts Bar Nuclear Plant (NRCH)
WBNQ .... Bloomington, IL [*FM radio station call letters*]
WBNR .... Beacon, NY [*AM radio station call letters*]
WBNS .... Columbus, OH [*AM radio station call letters*]
WBNS .... Water Boiler Neutron Source Reactor [*Nuclear energy*]
WBNS-FM .... Columbus, OH [*FM radio station call letters*]
WBNS-TV .... Columbus, OH [*Television station call letters*]
WBNT .... Oneida, TN [*FM radio station call letters*]
WBNU .... Charleston, SC [*Television station call letters*] (RBYB)
WBNV .... Barnesville, OH [*FM radio station call letters*]

WBNV .... Wideband Noise Voltage
WBNW .... Boston, MA [*AM radio station call letters*]
WB/NWRC ... Weather Bureau/National Weather Records Center [*Obsolete*] (KSC)
WBNX .... Akron, OH [*Television station call letters*]
WBNY .... Buffalo, NY [*FM radio station call letters*]
WBNZ .... Frankfort, MI [*FM radio station call letters*]
WBO .... Beroroha [*Madagascar*] [*Airport symbol*] (OAG)
WBO .... Weather Bureau Office [*Later, National Weather Service*]
WBO .... Western Buddhist Order [*British*] (EAIO)
WBO .... Wideband Oscilloscope
WBO .... Wideband Overlap
WBO .... Wien Bridge Oscillator [*Physics*]
W/BO .... With Blowout (MSA)
WBO .... World Boxing Organization (EA)
WBOB .... Galax, VA [*AM radio station call letters*]
WBOB .... Minneapolis, MN [*FM radio station call letters*]
WBOC .... Salisbury, MD [*Television station call letters*]
WBOD .... Waste Biochemical Oxygen Demand [*Oceanography*]
WBOG .... Tomah, WI [*FM radio station call letters*]
WBOK .... New Orleans, LA [*AM radio station call letters*]
WBOL .... Bolivar, TN [*AM radio station call letters*]
WBOM .... Danville, IL [*FM radio station call letters*] (RBYB)
WBOP .... Churchville, VA [*FM radio station call letters*]
WBOQ .... Gloucester, MA [*FM radio station call letters*]
WBOR .... Brunswick, ME [*FM radio station call letters*]
W/BOR .... White Border [*Deltiology*]
WBOS .... Brookline, MA [*FM radio station call letters*]
WBOW .... Terre Haute, IN [*AM radio station call letters*]
WBOX .... Bogalusa, LA [*AM radio station call letters*]
WBOX .... Varnado, LA [*FM radio station call letters*]
WBOY .... Clarksburg, WV [*Television station call letters*]
WBOZ .... San Juan, PR [*AM radio station call letters*] (RBYB)
WBOZ .... Woodbury, TN [*FM radio station call letters*]
WBP .... Wartime Basic Plan
WBP .... Water Bank Program [*Department of Agriculture*]
WBP .... Water Binding Potential [*of protein*]
WBP .... Weather- and Boil-Proof (IEEE)
WBP .... Women's Budget Program [*Australia*]
WBPA .... Elkhorn City, KY [*AM radio station call letters*]
WBPA .... Western Book Publishers Association (NTCM)
WBPAA .... Wine and Brandy Producers' Association of Australia
WBPASA .... Wine and Brandy Producers' Association of South Australia
WBPB .... Wideband Patch Bay [*Telecommunications*] (IAA)
WBPC .... Water-Based Polishing Compound
WBPCASA .... Wine and Brandy Producers' Cooperative Association of South Australia
WBPF .... World Bicycle Polo Federation (EA)
WBPH .... Bethlehem, PA [*Television station call letters*]
WBPM .... Kingston, NY [*FM radio station call letters*]
WBPP .... Strasburg, VA [*FM radio station call letters*]
WBPR .... Westernbank Puerto Rico [*NASDAQ symbol*] (SAG)
WBPR .... Worcester, MA [*FM radio station call letters*]
WBPS .... Dedham, MA [*AM radio station call letters*] (RBYB)
WBPT .... Wet-Bulb Potential Temperature (PDAA)
WBPTT .... Whole Blood Partial Thromboplastin Time [*Hematology*]
WBPV .... Charlton, MA [*FM radio station call letters*]
WBPW .... Presque Isle, ME [*FM radio station call letters*]
WBPZ .... Lock Haven, PA [*AM radio station call letters*]
WBQ .... Beaver [*Alaska*] [*Airport symbol*] (OAG)
WBQ .... Beaver, AK [*Location identifier FAA*] (FAAL)
WBQB .... Fredricksburg, VA [*FM radio station call letters*]
WBQN .... Barceloneta, PR [*AM radio station call letters*]
WBQQ .... Kennebunk, ME [*FM radio station call letters*]
WBR .... Water Boiler Reactor
WBR .... Weber
WBR .... Westbank Resources, Inc. [*Vancouver Stock Exchange symbol*]
WBR .... Wetboek van Burgerlijke Regtsvordering [*Code of Civil Procedure*] [*Dutch*] (ILCA)
WBR .... Whole Body Radiation
WBR .... Wideband Data Recorder
WBR .... Wideband Receiver
WBR .... Word Buffer Register (MSA)
WBR .... Workbench Rack (MCD)
WBRA .... Roanoke, VA [*Television station call letters*]
WBRB .... Mount Clemens, MI [*AM radio station call letters*]
WBRC .... Birmingham, AL [*Television station call letters*]
WBRC .... Walter Bagehot Research Council on National Sovereignty (EA)
WBRD .... Palmetto, FL [*AM radio station call letters*]
WBRD .... Wallboard
WBrE .... Elmbrook Memorial Hospital, Brookfield, WI [*Library symbol Library of Congress*] (LCLS)
WBRE .... Wilkes-Barre, PA [*Television station call letters*]
WBRF .... Galax, VA [*FM radio station call letters*]
WBRG .... Lynchburg, VA [*AM radio station call letters*]
W/BRG .... Wheel Bearing [*Automotive engineering*]
WBRH .... Baton Rouge, LA [*FM radio station call letters*]
WBRH .... Weather Bureau Regional Headquarters (FAAC)
WBRI .... Indianapolis, IN [*AM radio station call letters*]
WBrI .... International Foundation of Employee Benefit Plans, Information Center, Brookfield, WI [*Library symbol Library of Congress*] (LCLS)
WBRJ-FM .... Mount Sterling, IL [*FM radio station call letters*] (RBYB)
WBRK .... Pittsfield, MA [*AM radio station call letters*]
WBRM .... Marion, NC [*AM radio station call letters*]
WBRN .... Big Rapids, MI [*AM radio station call letters*]
WBRN-FM .... Big Rapids, MI [*FM radio station call letters*]
WBro .... Brodhead Memorial Public Library, Brodhead, WI [*Library symbol Library of Congress*] (LCLS)
WBRO .... Waynesboro, GA [*AM radio station call letters*]
WBRO .... Weather Bureau Regional Office [*Obsolete*]
W BRO .... Worshipful Brother [*Freemasonry*]
WBRQ .... Cidra, PR [*FM radio station call letters*]
WBRR .... Bradford, PA [*FM radio station call letters*]
WBRR .... Weather Bureau RADAR Remote [*Meteorology*]
WBRS .... Waltham, MA [*FM radio station call letters*]
WBRS .... Wideband Remote Switch (IEEE)
WBRS .... Wrought Brass (MSA)
WBRT .... Bardstown, KY [*AM radio station call letters*]
WBRT .... Weather Bureau Radiotheolite [*Meteorology*]
WBRT .... Whole-Blood Recalcification Time [*Hematology*]
WBRU .... Providence, RI [*FM radio station call letters*]
WBRV .... Boonville, NY [*AM radio station call letters*]
WBRV-FM .... Boonville, NY [*FM radio station call letters*]
WBRW .... Bridgewater, NJ [*AM radio station call letters*]
WBRX .... Patton, PA [*FM radio station call letters*]
WBRY .... Woodbury, TN [*AM radio station call letters*]
WBRZ .... Baton Rouge, LA [*Television station call letters*]
WBS .... Wage Board Staff
WB-S .... Wage Board, Supervisor [*Civil Service classification*]
WBS .... Walking Beam Suspension (WDAA)
WBS .... Wallace Barnes Steel [*Wallace Barnes Co.*]
WBS .... Washington Bibliographic Service [*Information service or system*] (IID)
WBS .... Waterloo County Board of Education [*UTLAS symbol*]
WBS .... WebChat Broadcasting Station
WBS .... Weight and Balance System (MCD)
WBS .... Welsh Bibliographical Society [*British*]
WBS .... West by South
WBS .... Western Base Section [*England*] [*World War II*]
WBS .... Western Conservative Baptist Theological Seminary, Portland, OR [*OCLC symbol*] (OCLC)
WBS .... Whole Blood Serotonin [*Biochemistry*]
WBS .... Whole Body Scan [*Medicine*] (DMAA)
WBS .... Whole Body Shower
WBS .... Wideband System [*Ground Communications Facility, NASA*]
WBS .... Wide Body STOL [*Short Takeoff and Landing*] [*Aviation*] (IAA)
WBS .... Withdrawal Body Shakes [*Medicine*] (DMAA)
WBS .... Without Benefit of Salvage
WBS .... Women's Budget Statement [*Australia*]
WBS .... Work Breakdown Sheets [*Army*]
WBS .... Work Breakdown Structure [*Computer science*]
WBS .... World Bird Sanctuary (EA)
WBS .... World Broadcasting System (NTCM)
WBSA .... Boaz, AL [*AM radio station call letters*]
WBSA .... Weather Bureau Synoptic and Aviation Reporting Station [*Obsolete*]
WBSB .... Brunei/International [*Brunei*] [*ICAO location identifier*] (ICLI)
WBSB-FM .... Anderson, IN [*FM radio station call letters*] (RBYB)
WBSC .... Bennettsville, SC [*AM radio station call letters*]
WBSC .... Wideband Signal Conditioner (NASA)
WBSC .... Work Breakdown Structure Code (MCD)
WBSCB .... Work Breakdown Structure Control Board [*Army*] (AABC)
WbsCtyF .... Webster City Federal Savings Bank [*Associated Press*] (SAG)
WBSD .... Burlington, WI [*FM radio station call letters*]
WBSF .... Melbourne, FL [*Television station call letters*]
WBSG .... Brunswick, GA [*Television station call letters*]
WBSH-FM .... Hagerstown, IN [*FM radio station call letters*] (RBYB)
WBSI .... Western Behavioral Sciences Institute [*Defunct*] (EA)
WBSIGSTA .... Weather Bureau Signal Station [*Obsolete*]
WBSJ-FM .... Portland, IN [*FM radio station call letters*] (RBYB)
WBSL .... Bay St. Louis, MS [*AM radio station call letters*]
WBSL .... Sheffield, MA [*FM radio station call letters*]
WBSL .... Wide Beam Special LASER (MCD)
WBSM .... New Bedford, MA [*AM radio station call letters*]
WBSM .... Weber per Square Meter (IAA)
WBSN .... New Orleans, LA [*FM radio station call letters*]
WBSP .... Western Beet Sugar Producers [*Defunct*]
WBSR .... Pensacola, FL [*AM radio station call letters*]
WBSS .... Millville, NJ [*FM radio station call letters*]
WBST .... Muncie, IN [*FM radio station call letters*]
WBST .... Webster Financial [*NASDAQ symbol*] (TTSB)
WBST .... Webster Financial Corp. [*Waterbury, CT*] [*NASDAQ symbol*] (NQ)
WbstFn .... Webster Financial Corp. [*Associated Press*] (SAG)
WBSU .... Brockport, NY [*FM radio station call letters*]
WBSV .... Venice, FL [*Television station call letters*]
WBSW-FM .... Marion, IN [*FM radio station call letters*] (RBYB)
WBSX .... Ann Arbor, MI [*Television station call letters*]
WBSY .... Rose Hill, NC [*FM radio station call letters*]
WBSZ .... Ashland, WI [*FM radio station call letters*]
WBT .... Charlotte, NC [*AM radio station call letters*]
WBT .... Wet Bulb Temperature
WBT .... Wichita Board of Trade [*Defunct*] (EA)
WBT .... Wideband Terminal (MCD)
WBT .... Wideband Transformer [*or Transmitter*]
WBT .... Windows-Based Terminal [*Computer science*]
WBT .... Women in Broadcast Technology (EA)
WBT .... Wycliffe Bible Translators (EA)
WBTA .... Batavia, NY [*AM radio station call letters*]
WBTA .... Wisconsin Board of Tax Appeals Decisions [*A publication*] (DLA)
WBTA-CCH Tax Reporter ... Wisconsin Board of Tax Appeals Decisions (Commerce Clearing House) [*A publication*] (DLA)

WBTB.......... Beaufort, NC [*AM radio station call letters*]
WBTC.......... Uhrichsville, OH [*AM radio station call letters*]
WBTC.......... Waterways Bulk Transportation Council (EA)
WBTE.......... Weapon Battery Terminal Equipment [*Air Force*]
WBTE.......... Windsor, NC [*AM radio station call letters*]
WBTF.......... Attica, NY [*FM radio station call letters*]
WBTF.......... Wrightsville Beach Test Facility [*Department of the Interior*] (NOAA)
WBT-FM...... Chester, SC [*FM radio station call letters*] (RBYB)
WBTG.......... Sheffield, AL [*AM radio station call letters*]
WBTG-FM.... Sheffield, AL [*FM radio station call letters*]
WBTH.......... Williamson, WV [*AM radio station call letters*]
WBTI.......... Lexington, MI [*FM radio station call letters*]
WBTM.......... Danville, VA [*AM radio station call letters*]
WBTM HYDRO... Weather Bureau Technical Memorandum: Hydrology [*Office of Hydrology*] [*Washington, DC*] [*A publication*]
WBTN.......... Bennington, VT [*AM radio station call letters*]
WBTO.......... Linton, IN [*AM radio station call letters*]
WBTQ.......... Buckhannon, WV [*FM radio station call letters*]
WBTR.......... Carrollton, GA [*FM radio station call letters*]
WBTS.......... Bridgeport, AL [*AM radio station call letters*]
WBTS.......... Waco, Beaumont, Trinity & Sabine Railway Co. [*AAR code*]
WBTS.......... Whereabouts [*Aviation*] (FAAC)
WBTS.......... Wideband Transmission System (KSC)
WBTT-FM.... Englewood, OH [*FM radio station call letters*] (RBYB)
WBTU.......... Kendallville, IN [*FM radio station call letters*]
WBTV.......... Charlotte, NC [*Television station call letters*]
WBTV.......... Weather Briefing Television (AFM)
WBTW.......... Florence, SC [*Television station call letters*]
WBTX.......... Broadway-Timberville, VA [*AM radio station call letters*]
WBTY.......... Homerville, GA [*FM radio station call letters*]
WBTZ-FM.... Plattsburgh, NY [*FM radio station call letters*] (RBYB)
WBU.......... Boulder [*Colorado*] [*Airport symbol*] (OAG)
WBU.......... Welsh Badminton Union (EAIO)
WBU.......... Welsh Baseball Union (DBA)
WBU.......... Wilberforce University, Wilberforce, OH [*OCLC symbol*] (OCLC)
WBU.......... World Billiards Union (EAIO)
WBU.......... World Blind Union (EA)
WBUB.......... North Charleston, SC [*FM radio station call letters*]
WBUC.......... Buckhannon, WV [*AM radio station call letters*]
WBUC.......... Western Boundary Undercurrent [*Atlantic Ocean*]
WBUC-FM.... Buckhannon, WV [*FM radio station call letters*]
WBUD.......... Trenton, NJ [*AM radio station call letters*]
WBUG.......... Amsterdam, NY [*AM radio station call letters*]
WBUG.......... Fort Plain, NY [*FM radio station call letters*]
WBUK.......... Fort Shawnee, OH [*FM radio station call letters*]
WBUL.......... Shepherdsville, KY [*AM radio station call letters*]
WBUQ.......... Bloomsburg, PA [*FM radio station call letters*]
WBUR.......... Boston, MA [*FM radio station call letters*]
WBur.......... Burlington Public Library, Burlington, WI [*Library symbol Library of Congress*] (LCLS)
WBurSFC..... Saint Francis College, Burlington, WI [*Library symbol Library of Congress Obsolete*] (LCLS)
WBURY........ Westbury [*England*]
WBUS.......... Kankakee, IL [*FM radio station call letters*]
WBUT.......... Butler, PA [*AM radio station call letters*]
WBUX.......... Doylestown, PA [*AM radio station call letters*]
WBUY.......... Holly Springs, MS [*Television station call letters*]
WBUZ.......... Delta, OH [*FM radio station call letters*]
WBV.......... Wideband Voltage
WBVB.......... Coal Grove, OH [*FM radio station call letters*]
WBVCO........ Wideband Voltage-Controlled Oscillator
WBVCXO...... Wideband Voltage-Controlled Crystal Oscillator
WBVE-FM.... Beulah, MI [*FM radio station call letters*] (RBYB)
WBVI.......... Fostoria, OH [*FM radio station call letters*]
WBVM.......... Tampa, FL [*FM radio station call letters*]
WBVN.......... Carrier Mills, IL [*FM radio station call letters*]
WBVP.......... Beaver Falls, PA [*AM radio station call letters*]
WBVP.......... Weeks Before Volume Production [*Automotive project management*]
WBVR.......... Bowling Green, KY [*FM radio station call letters*]
WBVRC........ West Bromwich Volunteer Rifle Corps [*British military*] (DMA)
WBVTR........ Wideband Video Tape Recorder
WBW.......... Wilkes-Barre, PA [*Location identifier FAA*] (FAAL)
WBW.......... Wilson Butte [*Washington*] [*Seismograph station code, US Geological Survey*] (SEIS)
WBW.......... World Bowling Writers (EA)
WBWB.......... Bloomington, IN [*FM radio station call letters*]
WBWC.......... Berea, OH [*FM radio station call letters*]
WBWI.......... West Bend, WI [*FM radio station call letters*]
WBWN.......... Le Roy, IL [*FM radio station call letters*]
WBWP.......... Warner Brothers Worldwide Publishing [*Commercial firm*]
WBWT.......... Wright Brothers Memorial Wind Tunnel [*Massachusetts Institute of Technology*] [*Research center*] (RCD)
WBWZ.......... New Paltz, NY [*FM radio station call letters*]
WBX.......... Wooden Box (MSA)
WBXB.......... Edenton, NC [*FM radio station call letters*]
WBXE.......... Baxter, TN [*FM radio station call letters*]
WBXL.......... Baldwinsville, NY [*FM radio station call letters*]
WBXQ.......... Cresson, PA [*FM radio station call letters*]
WBXR.......... Hazel Green, AL [*AM radio station call letters*]
WBXX.......... Battle Creek, MI [*FM radio station call letters*]
WBY.......... Wimberly Resources [*Vancouver Stock Exchange symbol*]
WBYA.......... Searsport, ME [*FM radio station call letters*]
WBYE.......... Calera, AL [*AM radio station call letters*]
WBYG.......... Point Pleasant, WV [*FM radio station call letters*]
WBYN.......... Boyertown, PA [*FM radio station call letters*]
WBYO.......... Sellersville, PA [*FM radio station call letters*]
WBYQ.......... Baltimore, MD [*FM radio station call letters*]
WBYR.......... Van Wert, OH [*FM radio station call letters*]
WBYS.......... Canton, IL [*AM radio station call letters*]
WBYS-FM.... Canton, IL [*FM radio station call letters*]
WBYT.......... Elkhart, IN [*FM radio station call letters*]
WBYU.......... New Orleans, LA [*AM radio station call letters*]
WBYW.......... Grand Rapids, MI [*FM radio station call letters*]
WBYY-FM.... Somersworth, NH [*FM radio station call letters*] (RBYB)
WBYZ.......... Baxley, GA [*FM radio station call letters*]
WBZ.......... Boston, MA [*AM radio station call letters*]
WBZ.......... Wadati-Benioff Zone [*Geology*]
WBZ.......... Works and Building, Low Priority [*British World War II*]
WBZA.......... Glens Falls, NY [*AM radio station call letters*]
WBZB.......... Selma, NC [*AM radio station call letters*]
WBZC.......... Pemberton, NJ [*FM radio station call letters*]
WBZE.......... Tallahassee, FL [*FM radio station call letters*]
WBZI.......... Xenia, OH [*AM radio station call letters*]
WBZK.......... York, SC [*AM radio station call letters*]
WBZN.......... Old Town, ME [*FM radio station call letters*]
WBZO.......... Bay Shore, NY [*FM radio station call letters*]
WBZQ.......... Greenville, NC [*AM radio station call letters*] (RBYB)
WBZR.......... Destin, FL [*AM radio station call letters*]
WBZS.......... Alexandria, VA [*AM radio station call letters*] (RBYB)
WBZT.......... West Palm Beach, FL [*AM radio station call letters*]
WBZ-TV...... Boston, MA [*Television station call letters*]
WBZU.......... Crewe, VA [*FM radio station call letters*] (RBYB)
WBZW.......... Loudonville, OH [*FM radio station call letters*]
WBZX.......... Columbus, OH [*FM radio station call letters*]
WBZY.......... New Castle, PA [*AM radio station call letters*]
WBZZ.......... Pittsburgh, PA [*FM radio station call letters*]
W_c.......... Collector-Region Width (IDOE)
WC.......... Cudahy Public Library, Cudahy, WI [*Library symbol Library of Congress*] (LCLS)
WC.......... Wage Change
WC.......... Wage Class (MHDI)
WC.......... Wages Council [*British*] (DCTA)
W/C.......... Waiver of Coinsurance [*Fire contract clause*]
WC.......... Walkways Center [*Defunct*] (EA)
WC.......... Walnut Council (EA)
WC.......... War Cabinet [*World War II*]
WC.......... War College
WC.......... War Communications
WC.......... Ward Clerk [*Medicine*]
WC.......... Warning Computer [*Aviation*]
WC.......... Watch Commanders
WC.......... Watch Committee [*British*] (ILCA)
WC.......... Water Chiller (DWSG)
WC.......... Water Closet [*A toilet*] [*Slang*]
WC.......... Water Cock (ROG)
wc.......... Watercolor (VRA)
WC.......... Water Column [*Mechanical engineering*]
WC.......... Water Content
WC.......... Water-Cooled (DEN)
WC.......... Watered Capital (MHDW)
WC.......... Waterfront Center (EA)
WC.......... Waterways Commission [*Western Australia*]
W/C.......... Watts per Candle [*Electricity*]
W/c.......... Watts per Candle (IDOE)
W/C.......... Wave Change
WC.......... WCN Investment [*Vancouver Stock Exchange symbol*]
WC.......... Weapon Carrier
WC.......... Weapons Command [*Later, Armaments Command*] [*Army*]
WC.......... Weapons Control [*or Controller*] (NVT)
WC.......... Weather Center [*Meteorology*] (DA)
WC.......... Weather Condition [*Nuclear energy*] (NRCH)
WC.......... We Care (EA)
W/C.......... Week Commencing (ADA)
WC.......... Wesleyan Chapel (ROG)
WC.......... Westbeth Corp. (EA)
WC.......... West Central [*Refers especially to London postal district*]
WC.......... West Coast Airlines, Inc.
WC.......... Western Cedar [*Utility pole*] [*Telecommunications*] (TEL)
WC.......... Western Central
WC.......... Western Civilization
WC.......... Western Classification
WC.......... Western Command
WC.......... Westminster College [*London, England*]
WC.......... Westminster Commentaries [*Oxford*] [*A publication*] (BJA)
WC.......... Wet Chemical System [*NFPA pre-fire planning symbol*] (NFPA)
WC.......... Whale Center (EA)
WC.......... Wheel Center (MSA)
WC.......... Wheelchair
WC.......... White Cell [*Medicine*]
WC.......... White Cell Cast [*Hematology*] (MAE)
W/C.......... White Clothing [*British military*] (DMA)
W/C.......... White Collar [*Worker*] (DCTA)
WC.......... White Confederacy [*Defunct*] (EA)
WC.......... White Count [*Hematology*]
WC.......... Whooping Complement (MAE)
WC.......... Whooping Cough [*Medicine*]
WC.......... Width Codes (AAG)
WC.......... Wien Air Alaska [*ICAO designator*] (AD)
WC.......... Wild Caught Animal [*Medicine*] (DMAA)
WC.......... Will Call

WC........ Wills Club (EA)
WC........ Willys Club (EA)
WC........ Wilshire Club [*Defunct*] (EA)
WC........ Wing Commander [*British military*]
WC........ Wings Club (EA)
WC........ Winston Cup
WC........ Wire Chief [*Test clerk*] [*Telecommunications*] (TEL)
WC........ Wireless Communication (IAA)
WC........ With Corrections [*Publishing*]
WC........ Without Charge
wc........ Without Charge (ODBW)
WC........ Woden's Coven [*Germany Defunct*] (EAIO)
W-C........ Women-Church: an Australian Journal of Feminist Studies in Religion [*A publication*] (APTA)
WC........ Women in Communications (EA)
WC........ Women's College [*University of Sydney*] [*Australia*]
WC........ Women's Reserve, Communications Duties [*USNR officer designation*]
WC........ Wood Casing
WC........ Wood Covers (DS)
WC........ Woodfree Coated [*Paper*] (DGA)
WC........ Woolwich College [*London, England*]
WC........ Word Count [*Computer science*]
WC........ Work Capacity (MAE)
WC........ Work Card (AAG)
WC........ Work Center (AFM)
WC........ Work Circle (AAG)
WC........ Work Control (AAG)
WC........ Working Capital
WC........ Working Circle [*Technical drawings*]
WC........ Working Current (IAA)
WC........ Workmen's Circle [*New York, NY*] (EA)
WC........ Workmen's Compensation [*Department of Health and Human Services*]
WC........ World Concern (EA)
WC........ World Coordinate
WC........ World's Classics [*A publication*]
WC........ Write and Compute
WC........ Written Component [*Qualification test*] [*Military*]
WCA........ Castro [*Chile*] [*Airport symbol*] (AD)
WCA........ Warm Cranking Amperes [*Battery*] [*Automotive engineering*]
WCA........ Warrant Claims Action [*Army*]
WCA........ Water Companies' Association [*British*]
WCA........ Weapon Control Area [*Military*] (CAAL)
WCA........ Weimaraner Club of America (EA)
WCA........ West Coast Airlines, Inc.
WCA........ West Coast Airlines Ltd. [*Ghana*]
WCA........ West Coast of Africa (ROG)
WCA........ Western Coal Association [*Australia*]
WCA........ Western College Association (EA)
WCA........ Who Cares, Anyway
WCA........ Whole Core Accident [*Nuclear energy*] (NRCH)
WCA........ Wholesale Confectioners Alliance Ltd. [*British*] (BI)
WCA........ Wideband Cassegrain Antenna
WCA........ Willys Club of America [*Later, WC*] (EA)
WCA........ Wind Correction Angle [*Aviation*] (DA)
WCA........ Windmill Class Association (EA)
WCA........ Wine Conference of America [*Defunct*] (EA)
WCA........ Winston S. Churchill Association [*Defunct*] (EA)
WCA........ Wireless Cable Association (TSSD)
WCA........ Wisco of Canada Ltd. [*Vancouver Stock Exchange symbol*]
WCA........ Women's Caucus for Art (EA)
WCA........ Women's Christian Association
WCA........ Women's Cricket Association [*British*]
WCA........ Wood Carver's Association [*British*] (DBA)
WCA........ Working-Capital Account (MHDW)
WCA........ Workmen's Compensation Act
WCA........ World Campus Afloat [*Cruise ship educational program*] (EA)
WCA........ World Christian Action [*Australia*]
WCA........ World Citizens Assembly [*Later, AWC*] (EA)
WCA........ World Communication Association (EA)
WCA........ Worst Case Analysis
WCAA........ West Coast Athletic Association (WDAA)
WCAA........ Window Coverings Association of America (EA)
WCAB........ Rutherfordton, NC [*AM radio station call letters*]
WCAB........ WorkCare Appeals Board [*Victoria, Australia*]
WCAB........ Working Committee of the Aeronautical Board
WCACTC........ West Coast Air Corps Training Center
WCAD........ San Juan, PR [*FM radio station call letters*]
WCAE........ Nekoosa, WI [*AM radio station call letters*]
WCAFS........ Wideband Cassegrain Antenna Feed System
WCAHI........ World Conference of Animal Health Industries [*Australia*]
WCAI........ Water Conditioning Association International [*Later, WQA*] (EA)
WCAI........ Wireless Cable Atlanta [*NASDAQ symbol*] (TTSB)
WCAI........ Wireless Cable of Atlanta, Inc. [*NASDAQ symbol*] (SAG)
WCAK........ Carlisle, KY [*FM radio station call letters*]
WCAL........ Northfield, MN [*FM radio station call letters*]
WCAM........ Camden, SC [*AM radio station call letters*]
WCAM........ Wisconsin Center for Applied Microelectronics [*University of Wisconsin - Madison*] [*Research center*] (RCD)
WCAN........ Canajoharie, NY [*FM radio station call letters*]
WCAN........ Worldwide Crisis Alerting Network (MCD)
WC & EL........ Workers' Compensation and Employers' Liability [*Insurance*]
WC & Ins (Eng)... Workmen's Compensation and Insurance Reports [*1912-33*] [*England*] [*A publication*] (DLA)
WC & Ins Rep... Workmen's Compensation and Insurance Reports [*1912-33*] [*England*] [*A publication*] (DLA)
WC & IR........ Workmen's Compensation and Insurance Reports [*1912-33*] [*England*] [*A publication*] (DLA)
WC & I Rep... Workmen's Compensation and Insurance Reports [*1912-33*] [*A publication*] (DLA)
WCANSW........ Workcover Authority of New South Wales [*Australia*]
WCAO........ Baltimore, MD [*AM radio station call letters*]
WCAP........ Lowell, MA [*AM radio station call letters*]
WCAP........ Westinghouse Commercial Atomic Power
WCAP........ Winfield Capital [*NASDAQ symbol*] (TTSB)
WCAP........ Winfield Capital Corp. [*NASDAQ symbol*] (SAG)
WCAP........ World Climate Applications Program [*WMO*] [*ICSU*]
WCAPW........ Winfield Capital Wrrt [*NASDAQ symbol*] (TTSB)
WCAR........ Livonia, MI [*AM radio station call letters*]
WCAR........ West Coast Formula Atlantic (Racing)
WCARU........ Western Carolina University (PDAA)
WCASP........ World Climate Applications and Services Program (EERA)
WCASS........ World Conference of Ashkenazi and Sephardi Synagogues
WCAT........ Athol, MA [*FM radio station call letters*]
WCAT........ Orange-Athol, MA [*AM radio station call letters*]
WCAT........ Weiss Comprehensive Articulation Test [*Education*]
WCAU........ Philadelphia, PA [*Television station call letters*]
WCAV........ Brockton, MA [*FM radio station call letters*]
WCAW........ Charleston, WV [*AM radio station call letters*]
WCAX........ Burlington, VT [*Television station call letters*]
WCAZ........ Carthage, IL [*AM radio station call letters*]
WCAZ-FM........ Carthage, IL [*FM radio station call letters*]
WCB........ War Communications Board [*World War II*]
WCB........ Warramunga Array [*Australia Seismograph station code, US Geological Survey*] (SEIS)
WCB........ Water Control Board
WCB........ Way Control Block
WCB........ Weekly Criminal Bulletin [*Canada Law Book, Inc.*] [*Information service or system*]
WCB........ Wellington County Board of Education [*UTLAS symbol*]
WCB........ West Africa Airlines Ltd. [*Ghana*] [*ICAO designator*] (FAAC)
WCB........ Will Call Back
WCB........ William C. Brown Publishers
WCB........ Workers' Compensation Board [*Australia*]
WCB........ Workmen's Compensation Board
WCBA........ Corning, NY [*AM radio station call letters*]
WCBA........ Washington Chinese Business Association
WCBA-FM........ Corning, NY [*FM radio station call letters*]
WCBB........ Augusta, ME [*Television station call letters*]
WCBC........ Cumberland, MD [*AM radio station call letters*]
WCBC........ Keyser, WV [*FM radio station call letters*]
WCBC........ World Candlepin Bowling Council
WCBD........ Charleston, SC [*Television station call letters*]
WCBG........ Chambersburg, PA [*AM radio station call letters*]
WCBH........ Casey, IL [*FM radio station call letters*]
WCBI........ Columbus, MS [*Television station call letters*]
WCBI........ Westco Bancorp [*NASDAQ symbol*] (TTSB)
WCBI........ Westco Bancorp, Inc. [*NASDAQ symbol*] (SAG)
WCBK........ Martinsville, IN [*FM radio station call letters*]
WCBL........ Benton, KY [*AM radio station call letters*]
WCBL........ World Council of Blind Lions [*Later, ACBL*] (EA)
WCBL-FM........ Benton, KY [*FM radio station call letters*]
WCBM........ Baltimore, MD [*AM radio station call letters*]
WCBN........ Ann Arbor, MI [*FM radio station call letters*]
WCBO........ West Coast Bancorp (Oregon) [*NASDAQ symbol*] (SAG)
WCBQ........ Oxford, NC [*AM radio station call letters*]
WCBR........ Arlington Heights, IL [*FM radio station call letters*]
WCBR........ Richmond, KY [*AM radio station call letters*]
WCBS........ New York, NY [*AM radio station call letters*]
WCBS........ World Confederation of Billiards Sports [*Malaysia*] (EAIO)
WCBS-FM........ New York, NY [*FM radio station call letters*]
WCBS-TV........ New York, NY [*Television station call letters*]
WCBSU........ West Coast Base Service Unit [*Navy*]
WCBT........ Roanoke Rapids, NC [*AM radio station call letters*]
WCBU........ Peoria, IL [*FM radio station call letters*]
WCBW........ Columbia, IL [*FM radio station call letters*]
WCBX........ Bassett, VA [*AM radio station call letters*]
WCBY........ Cheboygan, MI [*AM radio station call letters*]
WCBZ........ Williamston, NC [*FM radio station call letters*]
WCC........ Gerard P. Weeg Computing Center [*University of Iowa*] [*Research center*] (RCD)
WCC........ Sports Air Travel, Inc. [*ICAO designator*] (FAAC)
WCC........ Wales Craft Council (DBA)
WCC........ Wallace Communications Consultants [*Tampa, FL*] [*Telecommunications*] (TSSD)
WCC........ War Claims Commission [*Abolished, 1954*]
WCC........ War Cover Club (EA)
WCC........ War Crimes Commission (WDAA)
WCC........ Warfare Commanders Course (DOMA)
WCC........ Washington's United States Circuit Court Reports [*A publication*] (DLA)
WCC........ Waste Collection Containers
WCC........ Water-Cooled Copper
WCC........ Waters Computing Center [*Rose-Hulman Institute of Technology*] [*Research center*] (RCD)
WCC........ Watson Collectors Club (EA)
WCC........ Weapon Control Computer (MCD)
WCC........ Weapon Control Console [*Military*] (CAAL)
WCC........ Weapons Control Concept (MCD)

WCC .... Welsh Consumer Council [*British*] (ILCA)
WCC .... Westchester Community College [*Valhalla, NY*]
WCC .... Westchester Community College, Technical Services, Valhalla, NY [*OCLC symbol*] (OCLC)
WCC .... Western Canada Concept [*Political party*] (PPW)
WCC .... Western Carolina College [*Later, WCU*] [*North Carolina*]
WCC .... Westminster Choir College [*Princeton, NJ*]
WCC .... Whim Creek Consolidated [*Toronto Stock Exchange symbol*]
WCC .... White Cell Count [*Hematology*] (MAE)
WCC .... White Citizens' Council (WDAA)
WCC .... Whitney Communications Corp. [*New York, NY*]
WCC .... Widows Consultation Center [*Defunct*] (EA)
WCC .... Wildfire Coordinating Committee (EA)
WCC .... Wilson Cloud Chamber [*Physics*]
WCC .... Wingate Computer Center (HGAA)
WCC .... Women of the Church Coalition (EA)
WCC .... Women's Classical Caucus (EA)
WCC .... Women's College Coalition (EA)
WCC .... Women's Consultative Committee [*Ministry of Labour*] [*British World War II*]
WCC .... Work Center Code
WCC .... Work Control Center (AAG)
WCC .... Workmen's Compensation Cases [*Legal*] [*British*]
WCC .... World Cheerleader Council (EA)
WCC .... World Congress Centre [*Melbourne, Australia*]
WCC .... World Congress on Computing [*Trade show*]
WCC .... World Council of Christians [*Defunct*] (EA)
WCC .... World Council of Churches [*Geneva, Switzerland*]
WCC .... World Council of Clergy [*Defunct*] (EA)
WCC .... World Crafts Council (EA)
WCC .... World for Christ Crusade (EA)
WCC .... Worldwide Collectors Club [*Later, ISWSC*] (EA)
WCC .... Write Control Character [*Computer science*] (IAA)
WCCA .... Shallotte, NC [*FM radio station call letters*]
WCCA .... West Coast Crossarm Association [*Defunct*]
WCCA .... Whiteruthenian [*Byelorussian*] Congress Committee of America [*Later, Byelorussian Congress Committee of America*] (EA)
WCCA .... Whooping Crane Conservation Association (EA)
WCCA .... World Court Clubs Association [*Defunct*] (EA)
WCCA .... Worst Case Circuit Analysis
WCC&CRA ... World Championship Cutter and Chariot Racing Association (EA)
WCCB .... Charlotte, NC [*Television station call letters*]
WCCC .... Hartford, CT [*AM radio station call letters*]
WCCC .... Warwick China Collectors Club [*Defunct*] (EA)
WCCC .... Wayne County Community College [*Detroit, MI*]
WCCC .... Wisconsin Clinical Cancer Center [*University of Wisconsin*] [*Research center*] (RCD)
WCCC .... World Convention of Churches of Christ (EA)
WCCC-FM .... Hartford, CT [*FM radio station call letters*]
WCCD .... Parma, OH [*AM radio station call letters*]
WCCDBP ...... Weapon Control Computer Debug Program [*Military*]
WCCE .... Buie's Creek, NC [*FM radio station call letters*]
WCCE .... West Coast Commodity Exchange
WCCE .... World Conference on Computers in Education
WCCE .... World Council of Christian Education [*Later absorbed into Office of Education of World Council of Churches*]
WCCES .... World Council of Comparative Education Societies (EA)
WCCESSA .... World Council of Christian Education and Sunday School Association [*Later, WCCE*] (EA)
WCCF .... Punta Gorda, FL [*AM radio station call letters*]
WCCG .... Hope Mills, NC [*FM radio station call letters*]
WCCH .... Holyoke, MA [*FM radio station call letters*]
WCCI .... Savanna, IL [*FM radio station call letters*]
WCCI .... Western Country Clubs [*NASDAQ symbol*] (TTSB)
WCCI .... Western Country Clubs, Inc. [*NASDAQ symbol*] (SAG)
WCCI .... World Council for Curriculum and Instruction (EA)
WCCJ .... Harrisburg, NC [*FM radio station call letters*] (RBYB)
WCCK .... Calvert City, KY [*FM radio station call letters*]
WCCK .... Weapons Control Check (NVT)
WCCL .... New Orleans, LA [*Television station call letters*]
WCCLS .... Washington County Cooperative Library Services [*Library network*]
WCCM .... Lawrence, MA [*AM radio station call letters*]
WCCMORS ... West Coast Classified Military Operations Research Symposium
WCCN .... Neillsville, WI [*AM radio station call letters*]
WCCN-FM .... Neillsville, WI [*FM radio station call letters*]
WCC (NZ) .... Workers' Compensation Cases (New Zealand) [*A publication*] (DLA)
WCCO .... Minneapolis, MN [*AM radio station call letters*]
WCCON .... Whether Cleared Customs or Not [*Shipping*] (DS)
WCCO-TV ..... Minneapolis, MN [*Television station call letters*]
WCCP .... Clemson, SC [*AM radio station call letters*]
WCCP .... Woodward-Clyde Consultants, Pasadena [*California*]
WCCP-FM .... Clemson, SC [*FM radio station call letters*]
WCCPPS ...... Waste Channel and Containment Pressurization and Penetration System (IEEE)
WCCQ .... Crest Hill, IL [*FM radio station call letters*]
WCCR .... Clarion, PA [*FM radio station call letters*]
WCCR .... Washington's United States Circuit Court Reports [*A publication*] (DLA)
WCCRS .... Western Catholic Charismatic Renewal Services [*A publication*]
WCCS .... Homer City, PA [*AM radio station call letters*]
WCCS .... Window Contamination Control Number
WCCS .... Wireless Crew Communications System (LAIN)
WCCS .... World Chamber of Commerce Service (EA)
WCCSIS .... Westchester County Community Services Information System [*Westchester LibrarySystem*] [*Information service or system*] (IID)
WCCT .... Harwich, MA [*FM radio station call letters*]
WCCU .... Urbana, IL [*Television station call letters*]
WCC/US .... US Conference for the World Council of Churches (EA)
WCCV .... Arecibo, PR [*Television station call letters*]
WCCV .... Cartersville, GA [*FM radio station call letters*]
WCCW .... Traverse City, MI [*AM radio station call letters*]
WCCW-FM .... Traverse City, MI [*FM radio station call letters*]
WCCX .... Wackenhut Corrections Corp. [*NASDAQ symbol*] (SAG)
WCCX .... Waukesha, WI [*FM radio station call letters*]
WCCY .... Houghton, MI [*AM radio station call letters*]
WCCZ .... Pinckneyville, IL [*FM radio station call letters*] (RBYB)
WCD .... Weapons Classification Defects [*Navy*] (NG)
WCD .... Weather Card Data (IAA)
WCD .... We Can Do [*An association*] (EA)
WCD .... Western Canadian Mining [*Vancouver Stock Exchange symbol*]
WCD .... Wet Chemical Oxidation [*Chemistry*]
WCD .... Work Center Description (AFM)
WCD .... Workshop for Cultural Democracy (EA)
WCD .... Worse Case Difference (IAA)
WCDA .... Vorheesville, NY [*FM radio station call letters*]
WCDB .... Albany, NY [*FM radio station call letters*]
WCDB .... Wing Control During Boost
WCDB .... Work Control Data Base (NASA)
WCDC .... Adams, MA [*Television station call letters*]
WCDC .... West Coast [*Naval Publications*] Distribution Center
WC(DD)B ..... Worker's Compensation (Dust Diseases) Board [*Australia*]
WCDE .... Elkins, WV [*FM radio station call letters*]
WCDF .... World Children's Day Foundation (EA)
WCDFMA ..... Water Cooler and Drinking Fountain Manufacturers Association
WCDJ .... Truro, MA [*FM radio station call letters*]
WCDK .... Cadiz, OH [*FM radio station call letters*]
WCDL .... Carbondale, PA [*AM radio station call letters*]
WCDMP .... World Climate and Data Monitoring Program [*Marine science*] (OSRA)
WCDMP .... World Climate Data and Monitoring Program (EERA)
WCDO .... Sidney, NY [*AM radio station call letters*]
WCDO .... War Consumable Distribution Objective (AFM)
WCDO-FM .... Sidney, NY [*FM radio station call letters*]
WCDP .... Widows', Children's, and Dependents' Pension [*British*]
WCDP .... World Climate Data Program [*WMO*] [*ICSU*]
WCDPC .... War Control Data Processing Center (IAA)
WCDQ .... Sanford, ME [*FM radio station call letters*]
WCDR .... Cedarville, OH [*FM radio station call letters*]
W/Cdr .... Wing Commander [*British military*]
WCDS .... Glasgow, KY [*AM radio station call letters*]
WCDS .... West Coast Naval Publications Distribution Center (DNAB)
WCDT .... Westminster Centre for Design and Technology [*British*] (AIE)
WCDT .... Winchester, TN [*AM radio station call letters*]
WCDV .... Covington, IN [*FM radio station call letters*]
WCDX .... Mechanicsville, VA [*FM radio station call letters*]
WCDZ .... Dresden, TN [*FM radio station call letters*]
WCE .... Weapon Control Equipment
WCE .... West Coast of England [*Shipping*]
WCE .... Western Corporate Enterprises, Inc. [*Toronto Stock Exchange symbol*]
WCE .... Wiener Canonical Expansion [*Mathematics*]
WCE .... World Christian Encyclopedia [*A publication*]
WCEB .... Corning, NY [*FM radio station call letters*]
WCEC .... West Coast Entertainment [*NASDAQ symbol*] (TTSB)
WCEC .... West Coast Entertainment Corp. [*NASDAQ symbol*] (SAG)
WCED .... Du Bois, PA [*AM radio station call letters*]
WCED .... World Commission on Environment and Development (EA)
WCEE .... Mount Vernon, IL [*Television station call letters*]
WCEE .... Women's Council on Energy and the Environment (EA)
WCEF .... Ripley, WV [*FM radio station call letters*]
WCEG .... Middleboro, MA [*AM radio station call letters*]
WCEH .... Hawkinsville, GA [*AM radio station call letters*]
WCEI .... Easton, MD [*AM radio station call letters*]
WCEI-FM ..... Easton, MD [*FM radio station call letters*]
WCEL-FM .... Plattsburgh, NY [*FM radio station call letters*] (RBYB)
WCEM .... Cambridge, MD [*AM radio station call letters*]
WCEMA .... West Coast Electronic Manufacturers' Association [*Later, AEA*]
WCEM-FM ... Cambridge, MD [*FM radio station call letters*]
WCEN .... Mount Pleasant, MI [*AM radio station call letters*]
WCEN-FM .... Mount Pleasant, MI [*FM radio station call letters*]
WCER .... Canton, OH [*AM radio station call letters*]
WCER .... Wisconsin Center for Education Research [*Madison*]
WCES .... Wolfson Centre for Electrochemical Science [*British*] (CB)
WCES .... Women's Caucus of the Endocrine Society (EA)
WCES .... Wrens, GA [*Television station call letters*]
WCET .... Cincinnati, OH [*Television station call letters*]
WCET .... Weighted Common Examination Total (EDAC)
WCEU .... New Smyrna Beach, FL [*Television station call letters*]
WCEU .... World's Christian Endeavor Union (EA)
WCEV .... Cicero, IL [*AM radio station call letters*]
WCEZ .... Delaware, OH [*FM radio station call letters*]
WCf .... Chippewa Falls Public Library, Chippewa Falls, WI [*Library symbol Library of Congress*] (LCLS)
WCF .... Waste Calcination [*or Calcining*] Facility [*Nuclear energy*]
WCF .... Water Conditioning Foundation [*Later, WQA*] (EA)
WCF .... White Cathode Follower
WCF .... Winchester Center Fire [*Rifles*] (DICI)

WCF............ Winston Churchill Foundation (EA)
WCF............ Women's Campaign Fund (EA)
WCF............ Workers' Christian Fellowship [*British*] (BI)
WCF............ Working Capital Fund
WCF............ Workload Control File
WCF............ World Congress of Faiths - The Inter-Faith Fellowship [*British*] (EAIO)
WCF............ World Congress of Flight
WCF............ World Curling Federation [*British*] (EAIO)
WCFA.......... Wholesale Commission Florists of America [*Later, WF & FSA*]
WCFA.......... Wildlife Conservation Fund of America (EA)
WCFB.......... Daytona Beach, FL [*FM radio station call letters*]
WCFB.......... Webster City Federal Savings Bank [*NASDAQ symbol*] (SAG)
WCFB.......... Webster City Fed Svgs Bk [*NASDAQ symbol*] (TTSB)
WCFBA........ World Catholic Federation for the Biblical Apostolate [*Stuttgart, Federal Republic of Germany*] (EAIO)
WCFC.......... Chicago, IL [*Television station call letters*]
WCFC.......... Washington Capitals Fan Club (EA)
WCFE.......... Plattsburgh, NY [*FM radio station call letters*]
WCFE-TV..... Plattsburgh, NY [*Television station call letters*]
WCFF.......... Westinghouse Commercial Fuel Facility
WCFI........... Lajas, PR [*FM radio station call letters*]
WCFJ.......... Chicago Heights, IL [*AM radio station call letters*]
WCFL.......... Morris, IL [*FM radio station call letters*]
WCFN.......... Springfield, IL [*Television station call letters*]
WCfNC........ Northern Wisconsin Colony and Training School, Chippewa Falls, WI [*Library symbol Library of Congress*] (LCLS)
WCFPR........ Washington Center of Foreign Policy Research (MCD)
WCFR.......... Springfield, VT [*AM radio station call letters*]
WCFR.......... Washington Citizens for Recycling (EA)
WCFR-FM.... Springfield, VT [*FM radio station call letters*]
WCFRU........ Washington Cooperative Fishery Research Unit [*University of Washington*] [*Research center*] (RCD)
WCfSJ......... Saint Joseph's Hospital, Chippewa Falls, WI [*Library symbol Library of Congress*] (LCLS)
WCFT.......... Tuscaloosa, AL [*Television station call letters*]
WCFTB........ West Coast Freight Tariff Bureau
WCFW......... Chippewa Falls, WI [*FM radio station call letters*]
WCFX.......... Clare, MI [*FM radio station call letters*]
WCFY.......... Lafayette, IN [*AM radio station call letters*]
WCG............ War Crimes Group [*British*]
WCG............ Washington Calligraphers Guild (EA)
WCG............ Water-Cooled Garment
WCG............ Weapon Control Group [*Military*] (CAAL)
WCG............ West Coast Airlines Ltd. [*Ghana*] [*ICAO designator*] (FAAC)
WCG............ Willis Corroon Group ADS [*NYSE symbol*] (SPSG)
WCG............ Women of the Church of God (EA)
WCG............ Worldwide Church of God
WCGA.......... Woodbine, GA [*AM radio station call letters*]
WCGA.......... World Computer Graphics Association (EA)
WCGB.......... Juana Diaz, PR [*AM radio station call letters*]
WCGC.......... Belmont, NC [*AM radio station call letters*]
WCGL.......... Jacksonville, FL [*AM radio station call letters*]
WCGLJO...... World Congress of Gay and Lesbian Jewish Organizations (EA)
WCGM......... Writable Character Generation Memory (NITA)
WCGM......... Writable Character Generation Module [*Computer science*] (BUR)
WCGO.......... Chicago Heights, IL [*AM radio station call letters*]
WCGQ.......... Columbus, GA [*FM radio station call letters*]
WCGR.......... Canandaigua, NY [*AM radio station call letters*]
WCGR.......... Waterloo Centre for Groundwater Research [*University of Waterloo*] [*Canada*] (IRC)
WCGS.......... Western Collaborative Group Study [*University of California*] [*Psychology*]
WCGS.......... Wolf Creek Generating Station [*Nuclear energy*] (NRCH)
WCGTC........ World Council for Gifted and Talented Children (EA)
WCGV.......... Milwaukee, WI [*Television station call letters*]
WCGW......... Nicholasville, KY [*AM radio station call letters*]
WCGZ.......... World Confederation of General Zionists [*Later, WCUZ*] (EA)
WCH............ Chaiten [*Chile*] [*Airport symbol*] (AD)
WCh............ Chippewa Falls Public Library, Chippewa Falls, WI [*Library symbol Library of Congress Obsolete*] (LCLS)
WCH............ Weekly Contact Hours
WCH............ West Coast Handling
WCH............ Wichita [*Diocesan abbreviation*] [*Kansas*] (TOCD)
WCH............ Working Class Hero (EA)
WCHA.......... Chambersburg, PA [*AM radio station call letters*]
WCHA.......... Western Collegiate Hockey Association (EA)
WCHA.......... Wooden Canoe Heritage Association (EA)
WCHB.......... Taylor, MI [*AM radio station call letters*]
WCHB-FM.... Detroit, MI [*FM radio station call letters*] (RBYB)
WCHC.......... Worcester, MA [*FM radio station call letters*]
WCHE.......... West Chester, PA [*AM radio station call letters*]
WCHEN........ Western Council on Higher Education for Nursing
W'CHESTER... Winchester [*Borough in South England*] (ROG)
WCHF.......... Wet Crude Handling Facilities [*Petroleum engineering*]
WCHI........... Chillicothe, OH [*AM radio station call letters*]
WCHI........... Women's Council for the Histadrut in Israel (EA)
WCHI........... Workingmens Cap Hldgs [*NASDAQ symbol*] (TTSB)
WCHI........... Workingmens Capital Holdings, Inc. [*NASDAQ symbol*] (SAG)
WCHJ.......... Brookhaven, MS [*AM radio station call letters*]
WCHK.......... Canton, GA [*AM radio station call letters*]
WCHL.......... Chapel Hill, NC [*AM radio station call letters*]
WCHM......... Clarkesville, GA [*AM radio station call letters*]
WCHN.......... Norwich, NY [*AM radio station call letters*]
WCHO.......... Washington Court House, OH [*FM radio station call letters*]
WCHP.......... Champlain, NY [*AM radio station call letters*]
WCHQ.......... Camuy, PR [*AM radio station call letters*]
WCHQ-FM.... Camuy, PR [*FM radio station call letters*]
WCHR.......... Trenton, NJ [*FM radio station call letters*]
WCHR.......... Water Chiller
WCHR.......... Worldwide Creme Horse Registry (EA)
WCHS.......... Charleston, WV [*AM radio station call letters*]
WCHS-TV..... Charleston, WV [*Television station call letters*]
WCHT.......... Escanaba, MI [*AM radio station call letters*]
WCHV.......... Charlottesville, VA [*AM radio station call letters*]
WCHW......... Bay City, MI [*FM radio station call letters*]
WCHX.......... Lewistown, PA [*FM radio station call letters*]
WCHY.......... Savannah, GA [*AM radio station call letters*]
WCHY-FM.... Savannah, GA [*FM radio station call letters*]
WCHZ.......... Harlem, GA [*FM radio station call letters*]
WCI............. Waiting Calls Indicator (NITA)
WCI............. Washington International College, Washington, DC [*OCLC symbol*] (OCLC)
WCI............. Weapon Control Index [*Military*] (CAAL)
WCI............. White Cast Iron
WCI............. Wildlife Conservation International (EA)
WCI............. Workshop Computer Interface
WCIA........... Champaign, IL [*Television station call letters*]
WCIA........... Welsh Centre for International Affairs [*British*] (CB)
WCIB........... Falmouth, MA [*FM radio station call letters*]
WCIC........... Pekin, IL [*FM radio station call letters*]
WCID........... Friendship, NY [*FM radio station call letters*]
WCIE........... Lakeland, FL [*FM radio station call letters*]
WCIE........... Spring Lake, NC [*AM radio station call letters*]
WCIE........... World Center for Islamic Education (EA)
WCIF........... Melbourne, FL [*FM radio station call letters*]
WCIH........... Elmira, NY [*FM radio station call letters*]
WCII............ Spencer, NY [*FM radio station call letters*]
WCII............ Winstar Communications [*NASDAQ symbol*] (SAG)
WCIK........... Bath, NY [*FM radio station call letters*]
WCIL........... Carbondale, IL [*AM radio station call letters*]
WCIL-FM..... Carbondale, IL [*FM radio station call letters*]
WCIN........... Cincinnati, OH [*AM radio station call letters*]
WC Ins Rep... Workmen's Compensation and Insurance Reports [*1912-33*] [*A publication*] (DLA)
WCIP........... Weapon Control Indicator Panel [*Military*] (CAAL)
WCIP........... World Climate Impacts Program [*WMO*] [*ICSU*]
WCIP........... World Climate Impact Studies Program [*Marine science*] (OSRA)
WCIP........... World Council of Indigenous Peoples [*Ottawa, ON*] (EAIO)
WCIQ........... Mount Cheaha State Park, AL [*Television station call letters*]
WCIR........... Beckley, WV [*FM radio station call letters*]
WCIRP......... World Climate Impact Assessment and Response Strategies Program (EERA)
WCIS........... Morganton, NC [*AM radio station call letters*]
WCIS........... Wisconsin Career Information System [*Information service or system*]
WC-ISA........ Women's Commission of the Iranian Students Association (EA)
WCISP......... World Climate Impact Studies Program (EERA)
WCI Stl........ WCI Steel, Inc. [*Associated Press*] (SAG)
WCIT........... Lima, OH [*AM radio station call letters*]
WCIU........... Chicago, IL [*Television station call letters*]
WCIU........... Workshop Computer Interface Unit (MCD)
WCIV........... Charleston, SC [*Television station call letters*]
WCIW.......... [*The*] World Community of Al-Islam in the West
WCIY........... Canandaigua, NY [*FM radio station call letters*]
WCIY........... Westmorland and Cumberland Imperial Yeomanry [*British military*] (DMA)
WCIZ........... Watertown, NY [*FM radio station call letters*]
WCJ............. Caleta Josefina [*Chile*] [*Airport symbol*] (AD)
WCJA........... World Council of Jewish Archives (EAIO)
WCJB........... Gainesville, FL [*Television station call letters*]
WCJC........... Van Buren, IN [*FM radio station call letters*]
WCJC........... Webster City Junior College [*Iowa*]
WCJC........... Wharton County Junior College [*Texas*]
WCJCC......... World Confederation of Jewish Community Centers (EA)
WCJCS......... World Conference of Jewish Communal Service (EA)
WCJE........... World Council on Jewish Education
WCJM.......... West Point, GA [*AM radio station call letters*]
WCJM-FM.... West Point, GA [*FM radio station call letters*]
WCJO........... Jackson, OH [*FM radio station call letters*]
WCJU........... Columbia, MS [*AM radio station call letters*]
WCJW.......... Warsaw, NY [*AM radio station call letters*]
WCJX........... Five Points, FL [*FM radio station call letters*]
WCK............ Whiskey Creek Resources [*Vancouver Stock Exchange symbol*]
WCK............ Wilson Creek [*Kentucky*] [*Seismograph station code, US Geological Survey*] (SEIS)
WCKA.......... Sutton, WV [*FM radio station call letters*]
WCKB.......... Dunn, NC [*AM radio station call letters*]
WCKC.......... Cadillac, MI [*FM radio station call letters*]
WCKD.......... Madison, TN [*AM radio station call letters*] (RBYB)
WCKG.......... Elmwood Park, IL [*FM radio station call letters*]
WckhB......... Wackenhut Corp. [*Associated Press*] (SAG)
WCKI........... Greer, SC [*AM radio station call letters*]
WCKJ-FM.... St. Johnsbury, VT [*FM radio station call letters*] (RBYB)
WCKL.......... Catskill, NY [*AM radio station call letters*]
WCKM......... Lake George, NY [*FM radio station call letters*]
WCKM......... Saratoga Springs, NY [*AM radio station call letters*]
WCKN.......... Surfside Beach-Garden City, SC [*AM radio station call letters*] (RBYB)
WCKO.......... Norfolk, VA [*AM radio station call letters*] (RBYB)
WCKQ.......... Campbellsville, KY [*FM radio station call letters*]
WCKR.......... Hornell, NY [*FM radio station call letters*]

WCKS .... Fruithurst, AL [*FM radio station call letters*]
WCKT .... Lehigh Acres, FL [*FM radio station call letters*]
WCKW .... Garyville, LA [*AM radio station call letters*]
WCKW .... La Place, LA [*FM radio station call letters*]
WCKX .... London, OH [*FM radio station call letters*]
WCKY .... Cincinnati, OH [*AM radio station call letters*]
WCL .... Washington College of Law, Washington, DC [*OCLC symbol*] (OCLC)
WCL .... Water Coolant Line (MCD)
WCL .... Water Coolant Loop (MCD)
WCL .... WCI Canada Ltd. [*Toronto Stock Exchange symbol*]
WCL .... Weekly Cost Ledger (MCD)
WCL .... Western Carolinas League [*Baseball*]
WCL .... White Clip Level [*Video technology*]
WCL .... White Cross League [*British*]
WCL .... Wholesale Commodity Line (GFGA)
WCL .... Word Control Logic
WCL .... World Confederation of Labour [*See also CMT*] [*Brussels, Belgium*] (EAIO)
WCL .... Wright Center of Laboratories
WCLA .... Claxton, GA [*AM radio station call letters*]
WCLA .... West Coast Lumbermen's Association [*Later, WWPA*] (EA)
WCLA .... Workers' Compensation Legislation in Australia [*A publication*]
WCLA-FM .... Claxton, GA [*FM radio station call letters*]
WCL-ARS .... Agricultural Research Service Water Conservation Laboratory [*Tempe, AZ*]
WCLB-FM .... Fort Pierce, FL [*FM radio station call letters*] (RBYB)
WCLC .... Jamestown, TN [*AM radio station call letters*]
WCLC .... Watch Check List Completed [*Aviation*] (FAAC)
WCLC .... World Christian Life Community [*Italy*] (EAIO)
WCLC-FM .... Jamestown, TN [*FM radio station call letters*]
WCLCV .... White Clover Large Cryptic Virus [*Plant pathology*]
WCLD .... Cleveland, MS [*AM radio station call letters*]
WCLD .... Water-Cooled (AAG)
WCLD-AM .... Cleveland, MS [*AM radio station call letters*] (RBYB)
WCLD-FM .... Cleveland, MS [*FM radio station call letters*]
WCLE .... Calhoun, TN [*FM radio station call letters*]
WCLE .... Cleveland, TN [*AM radio station call letters*]
WCLF .... Clearwater, FL [*Television station call letters*]
WCLG .... Morgantown, WV [*AM radio station call letters*]
WCLG-FM .... Morgantown, WV [*FM radio station call letters*]
WCLH .... Wilkes-Barre, PA [*FM radio station call letters*]
WCLI .... Corning, NY [*AM radio station call letters*]
WClI .... Lakeshore Technical Institute, Educational Resource Center, Cleveland, WI [*Library symbol Library of Congress*] (LCLS)
WCLIB .... West Coast Lumber Inspection Bureau (EA)
WCLJ .... Bloomington, IN [*Television station call letters*]
WCLJ .... Workmen's Compensation Law Journal [*A publication*] (DLA)
WCLK .... Atlanta, GA [*FM radio station call letters*]
WCLL .... Wesson, MS [*FM radio station call letters*]
WCLM .... Highland Springs, VA [*AM radio station call letters*]
WCLMV .... White Clover Mosaic Virus [*Plant pathology*]
WCLN .... Clinton, NC [*AM radio station call letters*]
WCLN-FM .... Clinton, NC [*FM radio station call letters*]
WCLO .... Janesville, WI [*AM radio station call letters*]
WCLP .... Chatsworth, GA [*Television station call letters*]
WCLP .... Western Center on Law and Poverty (EA)
WCLP .... Women's Computer Literacy Project [*Commercial firm*] (EA)
WCLQ .... Wausau, WI [*FM radio station call letters*]
WCLR .... Piqua, OH [*FM radio station call letters*]
WCLR .... Workmen's Compensation Law Review [*A publication*] (DLA)
WCLS .... Oscoda, MI [*FM radio station call letters*]
WCLT .... Newark, OH [*AM radio station call letters*]
WCLT-FM .... Newark, OH [*FM radio station call letters*]
WCLU .... Glasgow, KY [*AM radio station call letters*]
WCLV .... Cleveland, OH [*FM radio station call letters*]
WCLW .... Eden, NC [*AM radio station call letters*]
WCLX .... Mio, MI [*FM radio station call letters*]
WCLX .... Wisconsin Central Trans [*NASDAQ symbol*] (TTSB)
WCLX .... Wisconsin Central Transportation Corp. [*NASDAQ symbol*] (SPSG)
WCLY .... Raleigh, NC [*AM radio station call letters*]
WCLZ .... Brunswick, ME [*AM radio station call letters*]
WCLZ-FM .... Brunswick, ME [*FM radio station call letters*]
WCM .... Warland Creek [*Montana*] [*Seismograph station code, US Geological Survey Closed*] (SEIS)
WCM .... Water Control Module (KSC)
WCM .... Weapon Control Module (MCD)
WCM .... Welded Cordwood Module
WCM .... Wesleyan Calvinistic Methodists (ROG)
WCM .... Wesley Central Mission [*Australia*]
WCM .... Wheat Curl Mite [*Entomology*]
WCM .... Whole Cow's Milk
WCM .... Winchester City Museum [*British*]
WCM .... Winkelmann Countermeasures, Inc. [*Vancouver Stock Exchange symbol*]
WCM .... Wired-Core Matrix
WCM .... Wired-Core Memory
WCM .... Word Combine and Multiplexer
WCM .... World-Class Manufacturing [*Management technique*]
WCM .... Writable Control Memory [*Computer science*] (BUR)
W/CM² .... Watts per Square Centimeter (CET)
W/cm² .... Watts per Square Centimeter (IDOE)
WCMA .... Corinth, MS [*AM radio station call letters*]
WCMA .... West Coast Mineral Association (EA)
WCMA .... Wisconsin Cheese Makers' Association (EA)
WCMA .... Working Capital Management Account [*Merrill Lynch & Co.*]
WCMB .... Harrisburg, PA [*AM radio station call letters*]
WCMC .... Westchester County Medical Center
WCMC .... Wildwood, NJ [*AM radio station call letters*]
WCMC .... World Conservation Monitoring Centre [*Information service or system*] (IID)
WCMD .... Advanced Certificate of the Welsh College of Music and Drama [*British*] (DBQ)
WCMD-FM ... Barre, VT [*FM radio station call letters*] (RBYB)
WCME .... Boothbay Harbor, ME [*FM radio station call letters*]
WCMF .... Rochester, NY [*AM radio station call letters*]
WCMF .... World Congress on Metal Finishing (PDAA)
WCMF-FM ... Rochester, NY [*FM radio station call letters*]
WCMG .... Marion, SC [*FM radio station call letters*]
WCMH .... Columbus, OH [*Television station call letters*]
WCMI .... Ashland, KY [*AM radio station call letters*]
WCMIA .... West Coast Metal Importers Association (EA)
WCMJ .... Cambridge, OH [*FM radio station call letters*]
WCMK .... Bolton, VT [*FM radio station call letters*] (RBYB)
WCML .... Alpena, MI [*FM radio station call letters*]
WCML .... Women's Caucus for the Modern Languages (EA)
WCML-TV .... Alpena, MI [*Television station call letters*]
WCMM .... Gulliver, MI [*FM radio station call letters*]
WCMN .... Arecibo, PR [*AM radio station call letters*]
WCMN-FM ... Arecibo, PR [*FM radio station call letters*]
WCMO .... Marietta, OH [*FM radio station call letters*]
WCMP .... Pine City, MN [*AM radio station call letters*]
WCMP-FM ... Pine City, MN [*FM radio station call letters*]
WCMQ .... Hialeah, FL [*FM radio station call letters*]
WCMQ .... Miami Springs, FL [*AM radio station call letters*]
WCMR .... Western Contract Management Region [*Air Force*]
WCMR .... World Conference on Missionary Radio [*Later, ICB*] (NTCM)
WCMS .... Norfolk, VA [*AM radio station call letters*]
WCMS-FM ... Norfolk, VA [*FM radio station call letters*]
WCMT .... Martin, TN [*AM radio station call letters*]
WCMT-FM ... Martin, TN [*FM radio station call letters*]
WCMU .... Mount Pleasant, MI [*FM radio station call letters*]
WCMU-TV .... Mount Pleasant, MI [*Television station call letters*]
WCMV .... Cadillac, MI [*Television station call letters*]
WCMV .... White Clover Mosaic Virus
WCMV .... Wild Cucumber Mosaic Virus [*Plant pathology*]
WCMW .... Harbor Springs, MI [*FM radio station call letters*]
WCMW .... Manistee, MI [*Television station call letters*]
WCMX .... Leominster, MA [*AM radio station call letters*] (RBYB)
WCMY .... Ottawa, IL [*AM radio station call letters*]
WCMZ .... Sault Ste. Marie, MI [*FM radio station call letters*]
WCN .... Walthard's Cell Nest [*Gynecology*] (AAMN)
WCN .... Washoe City [*Nevada*] [*Seismograph station code, US Geological Survey*] (SEIS)
WCN .... Wescan Energy Ltd. [*Vancouver Stock Exchange symbol*]
WCN .... Workload Control Number (MCD)
WCNA .... Potts Camp, MS [*FM radio station call letters*] (RBYB)
WCNB .... Connersville, IN [*AM radio station call letters*]
WCNC .... Charlotte, NC [*Television station call letters*]
WCNC .... Elizabeth City, NC [*AM radio station call letters*]
WCND .... Shelbyville, KY [*AM radio station call letters*]
WCNDT .... World Conference on Non-Destructive Testing (PDAA)
WCNG .... Murphy, NC [*FM radio station call letters*]
WCNI .... New London, CT [*FM radio station call letters*]
WCNJ .... Hazlet, NJ [*FM radio station call letters*]
WCNL .... Carlinville, IL [*FM radio station call letters*]
WCNN .... North Atlanta, GA [*AM radio station call letters*]
WCNO .... Palm City, FL [*FM radio station call letters*]
WCNR .... Bloomsburg, PA [*AM radio station call letters*]
WCNS .... Latrobe, PA [*AM radio station call letters*]
WCNU .... Crestview, FL [*AM radio station call letters*]
WCNW .... Fairfield, OH [*AM radio station call letters*]
WCNX .... Middletown, CT [*AM radio station call letters*]
WCNY .... Syracuse, NY [*FM radio station call letters*]
WCNY-TV .... Syracuse, NY [*Television station call letters*]
WCNZ .... Sheboygan, WI [*AM radio station call letters*]
WCO .... Columbia Helicopters, Inc. [*ICAO designator*] (FAAC)
WCO .... Coolullah [*Australia*] [*Airport symbol*] (AD)
WCO .... War Cabinet Office [*World War II*]
WCO .... Warrant Communication Officer [*British military*] (DMA)
WCO .... Waste Crankcase Oils
WCO .... Weapons Control Officer
WCO .... Weapons Control Order
WCO .... Western Coordination Office [*Later, WOO*] [*NASA*]
WCO .... Wet Chemical Oxidation [*Chemistry*]
WCOA .... Pensacola, FL [*AM radio station call letters*]
W Coast Rep... West Coast Reporter [*A publication*] (DLA)
WCOAT .... Wolfe Computer Operator Aptitude Test
WCOBL .... Wolfe Programming Language Test: COBOL
WCOD .... Hyannis, MA [*FM radio station call letters*]
WCOE .... La Porte, IN [*FM radio station call letters*]
WCOF .... St. Petersburg, FL [*FM radio station call letters*]
WCOF .... Women's Catholic Order of Foresters [*Later, NCSF*] (EA)
WCOH .... Newnan, GA [*AM radio station call letters*]
WCOJ .... Coatesville, PA [*AM radio station call letters*]
WCOK .... Sparta, NC [*AM radio station call letters*]
WCOL .... Columbus, OH [*AM radio station call letters*]
W (Colds) .... Whole Colds [*Medicine*]
WCOL-FM .... Columbus, OH [*FM radio station call letters*]
WCOM .... Bayamon, PR [*FM radio station call letters*] (RBYB)
WCOM .... WorldCom, Inc. [*NASDAQ symbol*] (SAG)

W Comm ..... Wing Commander [*British military*] (DMA)
WCOMMRGN... Western Communications Region [*Air Force*]
WCON .... Cornelia, GA [*AM radio station call letters*]
WCON-FM.... Cornelia, GA [*FM radio station call letters*]
WCOO .... New Bern, NC [*AM radio station call letters*] (RBYB)
WCOP .... Warner Robins, GA [*AM radio station call letters*]
WC Ops .... Workmen's Compensation Opinions, United States Department of Commerce [*A publication*] (DLA)
WCOR .... Lebanon, TN [*AM radio station call letters*]
WCOS .... Columbia, SC [*AM radio station call letters*]
WCOS-FM.... Columbia, SC [*FM radio station call letters*]
WCOT .... Jamestown, NY [*FM radio station call letters*]
WCOT .... Wall Coated Open Tubular [*Instrumentation*]
WCOTP .... World Confederation of Organizations of the Teaching Profession [*Internat ional Federation of Secondary Teachers and IFTA*] [*Formed by a merger of*] (EAIO)
WCOU .... Warsaw, NY [*FM radio station call letters*]
WCOU .... Wheelwrights and Coachmakers Operatives' Union [*British*]
WCOV .... Montgomery, AL [*Television station call letters*]
WCOW .... Sparta, WI [*FM radio station call letters*]
WCOX .... Camden, AL [*AM radio station call letters*]
WCOZ .... St. Albans, WV [*AM radio station call letters*]
WCP............. War Control Planners (EA)
WCP............. Warner Insurance Services [*NYSE symbol*] (SPSG)
WCP............. Waste Collector Pump (IEEE)
WCP............. Wayne County Public Library, Wooster, OH [*OCLC symbol*] (OCLC)
WCP............. Weapon Control Panel [*Aviation*]
WCP............. Weapon Control Processor [*Military*] (CAAL)
WCP............. Welder Control Panel
WCP............. Western Canada Party [*Separatist political party*]
WCP............. White Combination Potentiometer
WCP............. Wing Chord Plane [*Aviation*]
WCP............. Wing Command Post (MCD)
WCP............. Work Control Plan (AAG)
WCP............. World Climate Program [*WMO*] [*ICSU*]
WCP............. World Community Projects (EA)
WCP............. World Congress of Poets (EA)
WCP............. World Council of Peace (NATG)
WCPA .... Clearfield, PA [*AM radio station call letters*]
wc/pa .... Watercolor on Paper (VRA)
WCPA .... Western College Placement Association (AEBS)
WCPA .... World Centre for the Performing Arts
WCPA .... World Constitution and Parliament Association (EA)
WCPAB .... War Contracts Price Adjustment Board [*All functions dispersed, 1951*]
WCPB .... Salisbury, MD [*Television station call letters*]
WCPC .... Houston, MS [*AM radio station call letters*]
WCPD .... Waterloo Centre for Process Development [*University of Waterloo*] [*Research center*] (RCD)
WCPE.......... Raleigh, NC [*FM radio station call letters*]
WCPH .... Etowah, TN [*AM radio station call letters*]
WCPH .... World Congress of Professional Hypnotists (EA)
WCPI .... White Collar Productivity Improvement (MCD)
WCPM .... Cumberland, KY [*AM radio station call letters*]
WCPMEF...... Willa Cather Pioneer Memorial and Educational Foundation (EA)
WCPN.......... Cleveland, OH [*FM radio station call letters*]
WCPO .... Cincinnati, OH [*Television station call letters*]
WCPP .... Women of Color Partnership Program (EA)
WCPQ .... Havelock, NC [*AM radio station call letters*]
WCPR .... Coamo, PR [*AM radio station call letters*]
WCPR .... Weston, Clevedon & Portishead Railway [*British*]
WCPR-FM.... Wiggins, MS [*FM radio station call letters*] (RBYB)
WCPS .... Tarboro, NC [*AM radio station call letters*]
WCPS .... Women's Caucus for Political Science (EA)
WCPS .... World Confederation of Productivity Science (EAIO)
WCPSC .... Western Conference of Public Services Commissioners
WCPT.......... World Confederation for Physical Therapy [*British*] (EA)
WCPV .... Essex, NY [*FM radio station call letters*]
WCPX .... Orlando, FL [*Television station call letters*]
WCPZ .... Sandusky, OH [*FM radio station call letters*]
WCQA .... Fredonia, NY [*FM radio station call letters*]
WCQL .... Worst Cycle Quantity Level (PDAA)
WCQL .... York Center, ME [*FM radio station call letters*]
WCQM .... Park Falls, WI [*FM radio station call letters*]
WCQQ .... Cedar Key, FL [*FM radio station call letters*] (RBYB)
WCQR .... Fairlawn, VA [*AM radio station call letters*]
WCQR-FM.... Kingsport, TN [*FM radio station call letters*] (RBYB)
WCQS .... Asheville, NC [*FM radio station call letters*]
WCR .... Chandalar [*Alaska*] [*Airport symbol*] (OAG)
WCR .... Chandalar Lake, AK [*Location identifier FAA*] (FAAL)
WCR .... Walthard's Cell Rests [*Medicine*] (MEDA)
WCR .... Warm Core Ring [*Oceanography*]
WCR .... Water-Cooled Reactor
WCR .... Water-Cooled Rod
WCR .... Watercooler (AAG)
WCR .... Waterloo and City Railway (ROG)
WCR .... Western Communications Region [*Air Force*] (MCD)
WCR .... Willcrest Resources Ltd. [*Vancouver Stock Exchange symbol*]
WCR .... Wire Contact Relay
WCR .... Women's Council of Realtors [*of the National Association of Realtors*] (EA)
WCR .... Word Control [*or Count*] Register
WCR .... World Communication Report [*Database*] [*UNESCO*] (DUND)
WCRA.......... Effingham, IL [*AM radio station call letters*]
WCRA.......... Weather Control Research Association [*Later, Weather Modification Association*]
WCRA.......... Western College Reading Association (EA)
WCRA.......... Wet Crease Recovery Angle [*Textile technology*]
WCRB .... Waltham, MA [*FM radio station call letters*]
WCRC .... Effingham, IL [*FM radio station call letters*]
WCRC .... Water Conditioning Research Council [*Later, WQRC*] (EA)
WCRC .... Workers' Compensation and Rehabilitation Commission [*Western Australia*]
WCRD .... War Consumables Requirements Document [*Military*] (AFIT)
WCRE .... Cheraw, SC [*AM radio station call letters*]
WC Rep .... Workmen's Compensation Reports [*A publication*] (DLA)
WCRF .... Cleveland, OH [*FM radio station call letters*]
WCRF .... Weekly Collection Report File [*IRS*]
WCRF .... World Cancer Research Fund
WCRH .... Williamsport, MD [*FM radio station call letters*]
WCRJ.......... Jacksonville, FL [*AM radio station call letters*]
WCRK .... Morristown, TN [*AM radio station call letters*]
WCRL .... Oneonta, AL [*AM radio station call letters*]
WCRLA .... Western College Reading and Learning Association (EA)
WCRM .... Fort Myers, FL [*AM radio station call letters*]
WCRN .... Worcester, MA [*AM radio station call letters*]
WCRO .... Johnstown, PA [*AM radio station call letters*]
WCROS .... White Crossover Vote [*Political science*]
WCRP .... Guayama, PR [*FM radio station call letters*]
WCRP .... World Climate Research Program (EERA)
WCRP .... World Climate Research Programme [*WMO*] [*ICSU*]
WCRP .... World Conference on Religion and Peace (EAIO)
WCRP/USA... World Conference on Religion and Peace, USA Section (EA)
WCRQ .... Arab, AL [*FM radio station call letters*]
WCRR .... Rural Retreat, VA [*AM radio station call letters*]
WCRS .... Greenwood, SC [*AM radio station call letters*]
WC:RS .... Women's Caucus: Religious Studies [*Defunct*] (EA)
WCRSI .... Western Concrete Reinforcing Steel Institute [*Later, CRSI*] (EA)
WCRT .... Terre Haute, IN [*FM radio station call letters*]
WCRV .... Collierville, TN [*AM radio station call letters*]
WCRW .... Chicago, IL [*AM radio station call letters*]
WCRX .... Chicago, IL [*FM radio station call letters*]
WCRY .... Fuquay-Varina, NC [*AM radio station call letters*]
WCRZ .... Flint, MI [*FM radio station call letters*]
WCS............. Wallace Computer Services, Inc. [*NYSE symbol*] (SPSG)
WCS............. Wallace Computer Svc [*NYSE symbol*] (TTSB)
WCS............. Wang Computer System
WCS............. Waste Collection System [*NASA*] (MCD)
WCS............. Waste Compaction Station [*Nuclear energy*] (NRCH)
WCS............. Waste Control System (SSD)
WCS............. Watercolor Spectrometer (PDAA)
WCS............. Weak Calf Syndrome [*Veterinary medicine*]
WCS............. Weapon Control Station [*Military*] (CAAL)
WCS............. Weapon Control Status [*Military*] (INF)
WCS............. Weapons Control Status
WCS............. Weapons Control System
WCS............. Wedgwood Collectors Society [*Defunct*] (EA)
WCS............. Western Cover Society (EA)
WCS............. Wilkie Collins Society [*British*] (DBA)
WCS............. William Cobbett Society (EAIO)
WCS............. Woman Citizen Series [*A publication*]
WCS............. Work Control Station
WCS............. Work Control Status
WCS............. Work Control System (NASA)
WCS............. Work Core Storage
WCS............. World Congress on Superconductivity [*An association*]
WCS............. World Conservation Strategy (GNE)
WCS............. World Council of Synagogues (EA)
WCS............. Worm Community System [*Neurology database*]
WCS............. Writable Control Storage [*Computer science*]
WCSA .... Ripley, MS [*AM radio station call letters*]
WCSA .... West Coast of South America
WCSB .... Cleveland, OH [*FM radio station call letters*]
WCSB .... Weapon Control Switchboard [*Military*] (CAAL)
WCSB(G) ..... Weapon Control Switchboard (Gun)
WCSB(M)..... Weapon Control Switchboard (Missile)
WCSB(UB) ... Weapon Control Switchboard (Underwater Battery)
WCSC .... Charleston, SC [*Television station call letters*]
WCSC .... Weapon Control System Console
WCSC .... Weapons Control System Coordinator (NVT)
WCSC .... West Coast Switching Center [*Jet Propulsion Laboratory, NASA*]
WCSC .... World Correctional Service Center (EA)
WCSCV .... White Clover Small Cryptic Virus [*Plant pathology*]
WCSD .... Livingston, TN [*FM radio station call letters*]
WCSF.......... Joliet, IL [*FM radio station call letters*]
WCSFMA ..... Wisconsin Cheese and Specialty Food Merchants Association (EA)
WCSG .... Grand Rapids, MI [*FM radio station call letters*]
WCSG .... WWMCCS [*Worldwide Military Command and Control System*] Council Support Group (MCD)
WCSH .... Portland, ME [*Television station call letters*]
WCSI .... Columbus, IN [*AM radio station call letters*]
WCSI .... World Centre for Scientific Information
WCSICEC ..... Working Committee of the Scientific Institutes for Crafts in the EEC Count ries [*Munich, Federal Republic of Germany*] (EAIO)
WCSJ.......... Morris, IL [*AM radio station call letters*]
WCSK .... Kingsport, TN [*FM radio station call letters*]
WCSL.......... Cherryville, NC [*AM radio station call letters*]
WCSLEN ...... Wide Character String Length [*Computer science*] (PCM)
WCSM .... Celina, OH [*AM radio station call letters*]

WCSM .... World Congress of Sports Medicine
WCSM-FM ... Celina, OH [*FM radio station call letters*]
WCSMP .... World Climate System Monitoring Program [*Marine science*] (OSRA)
WCSN-FM.... Orange Beach, AL [*FM radio station call letters*] (RBYB)
WCSO .... Portland, ME [*FM radio station call letters*]
WCSP .... Wisconsin Cheese and Sausage Promotions (EA)
WCSPA .... West Coast Shrimp Producers Association (EA)
WCSR .... Hillsdale, MI [*AM radio station call letters*]
WCSRC .... Wild Canid Survival and Research Center - Wolf Sanctuary (EA)
WCSR-FM.... Hillsdale, MI [*FM radio station call letters*]
WCSS .... Amsterdam, NY [*AM radio station call letters*]
WCSS .... Weapons Control Subsystem (MCD)
WCSS .... Weapons Control System Simulator
WCSS .... West Coast Sound School [*Navy*]
WCST........... Berkeley Springs, WV [*AM radio station call letters*]
WCST........... Wescast Industries, Inc. [*NASDAQ symbol*] (SAG)
WCST........... Wisconsin Card Sorting Test [*Neuropsychology test*]
WCstB.......... West Coast Bancorp (OR) [*Associated Press*] (SAG)
WCstEnt....... West Coast Entertainment Corp. [*Associated Press*] (SAG)
WCSTF......... Wescast Industries'A' [*NASDAQ symbol*] (TTSB)
WCST-FM .... Berkeley Springs, WV [*FM radio station call letters*]
WCSU .... Western Connecticut State University [*Danbury*]
WCSU .... Wilberforce, OH [*FM radio station call letters*]
WCSUICA..... Women's Coalition to Stop US Intervention in Central America [*Later, WCSUICAC*] [*Defunct*] (EA)
WCSUICAC... Women's Coalition to Stop US Intervention in Central America and the Caribbean (EA)
WCSV .... Crossville, TN [*AM radio station call letters*]
WCSV .... Wheat Chlorotic Streak Virus [*Plant pathology*]
WCSW .... Shell Lake, WI [*AM radio station call letters*]
WCSX .... Birmingham, MI [*FM radio station call letters*]
WCSY .... South Haven, MI [*AM radio station call letters*]
WCSY-FM .... South Haven, MI [*FM radio station call letters*]
WCT............. Trinity Memorial Hospital, Cudahy, WI [*Library symbol Library of Congress*] (LCLS)
WCT............. War Crimes Tribunal [*Bertrand Russell*] [*Stockholm based pacifist organization founded during the Vietnam war*] (VNW)
WCT............. Water-Cooled Tube [*Nuclear energy*] (IAA)
WCT............. Waukesha County Institute, Pewaukee, WI [*OCLC symbol*] (OCLC)
WCT............. West Coast Travel [*Information service or system*] (IID)
WCT............. Westek Communications, Inc. [*Vancouver Stock Exchange symbol*]
WCT............. Wetlands Conservation Team
WCT............. World Championship Tennis, Inc.
WCT............. World Confederation of Teachers [*See also CSME*] [*Brussels, Belgium*] (EAIO)
WCT............. Worthy Chief Templar
WCTA........... Alamo, TN [*AM radio station call letters*]
WCTA........... Western Coal Transportation Association (EA)
WCTA........... Wholesale Confectionery and Tobacco Trade Alliance [*British*] (DBA)
WCTA........... World Committee for Trade Action [*See also CMAP*] [*Brussels, Belgium*] (EAIO)
WCTB........... Fairfield, ME [*FM radio station call letters*]
WCTB........... West Country Tourist Board [*British*] (DCTA)
WCTB........... Western Carriers Tariff Bureau
WCTC .... New Brunswick, NJ [*AM radio station call letters*]
WCTD .... Miami, FL [*Television station call letters*]
WCTD .... World Congress of Teachers of Dancing (EA)
WCTE........... Cookeville, TN [*Television station call letters*]
WCTEV......... White Clover Temperate Virus [*Plant pathology*]
WCTF........... Vernon, CT [*AM radio station call letters*]
WCTG .... Columbia, SC [*AM radio station call letters*]
WCTG .... Woodcutting (MSA)
WCTH .... Plantation Key, FL [*FM radio station call letters*]
WCTI .... New Bern, NC [*Television station call letters*]
WCTJ-AM .... Camp Lejeune, NC [*AM radio station call letters*] (RBYB)
WCTK........... New Bedford, MA [*FM radio station call letters*]
WCTL........... Union City, PA [*FM radio station call letters*]
WCTM.......... Eaton, OH [*AM radio station call letters*]
WCTN .... Potomac-Cabin John, MD [*AM radio station call letters*]
WCTP........... Wire Chief Test Panel [*Telecommunications*] (TEL)
WCTQ .... Venice, FL [*FM radio station call letters*]
WCTR .... Chestertown, MD [*AM radio station call letters*]
WCTR .... WCTU Railway Co. [*AAR code*]
WCTS........... Maplewood, MN [*AM radio station call letters*]
WCTS........... Weapon Cost Test Site [*Military*] (CAAL)
WCTS........... Weapons Controller Training Squadron
W Ct SA....... Union of South Africa Water Courts Decisions [*A publication*] (DLA)
WCTT .... Corbin, KY [*AM radio station call letters*]
WCTT .... Weapons Crew Training Test [*TCATA*] (RDA)
WCTT-FM .... Corbin, KY [*FM radio station call letters*]
WCTU .... National Woman's Christian Temperance Union (EA)
WCTU .... Tazewell, TN [*FM radio station call letters*]
WCTU .... Women's Connubial Temperance Union [*Satirical*]
WCTV .... Thomasville, GA [*Television station call letters*]
WCTV .... Westcott Communications [*NASDAQ symbol*] (SPSG)
WCTW .... Catskill, NY [*FM radio station call letters*]
WCTY........... Norwich, CT [*FM radio station call letters*]
WCTZ........... Clarksville, TN [*AM radio station call letters*]
WCu............. Cumberland Public Library, Cumberland, WI [*Library symbol Library of Congress*] (LCLS)
WCU .... Water Cooler Unit (AAG)
WCU .... Weapons Control Unit (MCD)
WCU .... Welsh Chess Union (DBA)
WCU .... West Coast University [*Los Angeles, CA*]
WCU .... Western Carolina University [*Cullowhee, NC*]
WCU .... Western Catholic Union (EA)
WCUB.......... Two Rivers, WI [*AM radio station call letters*]
WCUC.......... Clarion, PA [*FM radio station call letters*]
WCUE .... Cuyahoga Falls, OH [*AM radio station call letters*]
WCUG .... Cuthbert, GA [*AM radio station call letters*]
WCUH.......... Western Carolina University Herbarium
WCUK .... West Coast of the United Kingdom
WCUL .... Culpeper, VA [*FM radio station call letters*]
WCUM .... Bridgeport, CT [*AM radio station call letters*]
WCUMBS..... Western Canadian Universities Marine Biological Society
WCUNDDP... World Committee for the United Nations Decade of Disabled Persons (EA)
WCUP .... L'Anse, MI [*FM radio station call letters*] (RBYB)
WCUS .... Waterborne Commerce of the United States [*DoD/COE*] (TAG)
WCUW .... Worcester, MA [*FM radio station call letters*]
WCUZ .... Grand Rapids, MI [*AM radio station call letters*]
WCUZ .... World Confederation of United Zionists (EA)
WCUZ-FM .... Grand Rapids, MI [*FM radio station call letters*]
WCV............. Wafer Check Valve
WCV............. Winant and Clayton Volunteers (EA)
WCVA .... Culpeper, VA [*AM radio station call letters*]
WCVA .... Wales Council for Voluntary Action (DBA)
WCVB .... Boston, MA [*Television station call letters*]
WCVC .... Tallahassee, FL [*AM radio station call letters*]
WCVE........... Richmond, VA [*FM radio station call letters*]
WCVE-TV .... Richmond, VA [*Television station call letters*]
WCVF........... Fredonia, NY [*FM radio station call letters*]
WCVG .... Covington, KY [*AM radio station call letters*]
WCVH .... Flemington, NJ [*FM radio station call letters*]
WCVI .... Connellsville, PA [*AM radio station call letters*]
WCVJ............ Jefferson, OH [*FM radio station call letters*]
WCVK .... Bowling Green, KY [*FM radio station call letters*]
WCVL........... Crawfordsville, IN [*AM radio station call letters*]
WCVM .... Bronson, MI [*FM radio station call letters*]
WCVM .... Western College of Veterinary Medicine [*Canada*]
WCVN .... Covington, KY [*Television station call letters*]
WCVO .... Gahanna, OH [*FM radio station call letters*]
WCVP .... Murphy, NC [*AM radio station call letters*]
WCVP .... Robbinsville, NC [*FM radio station call letters*]
WCVQ .... Fort Campbell, KY [*FM radio station call letters*]
WCVR .... Randolph, VT [*FM radio station call letters*]
WCVS .... Virden, IL [*FM radio station call letters*]
WCVT........... Rossville, GA [*AM radio station call letters*]
WCVU .... Solana, FL [*FM radio station call letters*] (RBYB)
WCVV .... Belpre, OH [*FM radio station call letters*]
WCVW .... Richmond, VA [*Television station call letters*]
WCVY .... Coventry, RI [*FM radio station call letters*]
WCVZ........... Zanesville, OH [*FM radio station call letters*]
WCW .... Western College for Women [*Ohio*]
WCW .... Western College for Women, Oxford, OH [*Inactive*] [*OCLC symbol*] (OCLC)
WCW .... Wood Casement Window [*Technical drawings*]
WCW .... World Championship Wrestling
WCWA .... Toledo, OH [*AM radio station call letters*]
WCWB .... World Council for the Welfare of the Blind [*Later, WBU*] (EAIO)
WCWC .... Ripon, WI [*AM radio station call letters*]
WCWM .... Williamsburg, VA [*FM radio station call letters*]
WC/WO......... Working Committee on Weather Operations
WCWP .... Brookville, NY [*FM radio station call letters*]
WCWR........... Weil's Code of Wyoming Rules [*A publication*] (AAGC)
WCWS .... Wooster, OH [*FM radio station call letters*]
WCWT .... Centerville, OH [*FM radio station call letters*]
WCWV .... Summersville, WV [*FM radio station call letters*]
WCX............. Weak Cation Exchanger [*Chemistry*]
WCX............. Westmoreland Coal [*NYSE symbol*] (TTSB)
WCX............. Westmoreland Coal Co. [*NYSE symbol*] (SPSG)
WCXJ .... Braddock, PA [*AM radio station call letters*]
WCXL........... Kill Devil Hills, NC [*FM radio station call letters*]
WCXN .... Claremont, NC [*AM radio station call letters*]
WCXPrA....... Westmoreld Coal Cv Dep Ex Pfd [*NYSE symbol*] (TTSB)
WCXR .... Lewisburg, PA [*FM radio station call letters*] (RBYB)
WCXT........... Hart, MI [*FM radio station call letters*]
WCXU .... Caribou, ME [*FM radio station call letters*]
WCXX .... Madawaska, ME [*FM radio station call letters*]
WCY............. Viking Express, Inc. [*ICAO designator*] (FAAC)
WCY............. World Communications Year [*1983*]
WCYB .... Bristol, VA [*Television station call letters*]
WCYC .... Chicago, IL [*FM radio station call letters*]
WCYC .... Westmorland and Cumberland Yeomanry Cavalry [*British military*] (DMA)
WCYI .... Lewiston, ME [*FM radio station call letters*]
WCYJ............ Waynesburg, PA [*FM radio station call letters*]
WCYK .... Crozet, VA [*FM radio station call letters*]
WCYK-FM .... Crozet, VA [*FM radio station call letters*] (RBYB)
WCYN .... Cynthiana, KY [*AM radio station call letters*]
WCYN-FM.... Cynthiana, KY [*FM radio station call letters*]
WCYO .... Irvine, KY [*FM radio station call letters*]
WCYT........... Lafayette Township, IN [*FM radio station call letters*]
WCYY .... Biddeford, ME [*FM radio station call letters*]
WCZI............ Washington, NC [*FM radio station call letters*]
WCZQ .... Monticello, IL [*FM radio station call letters*]
WCZR .... Charleston, WV [*AM radio station call letters*]
WCZT........... Avalon, NJ [*FM radio station call letters*]
WCZX........... Hyde Park, NY [*FM radio station call letters*]
WCZY........... Mount Pleasant, MI [*FM radio station call letters*]

WD............ Decisions Won [*Boxing*]
WD............ General Warranty Deed [*Real estate*]
Wd............ Seaweed [*Quality of the bottom*] [*Nautical charts*]
WD............ Two-Conductor Cables [*JETDS nomenclature*] [*Military*] (CET)
WD............ Wallerian Degeneration [*Medicine*]
WD............ Ward
WD............ Ward Air [*ICAO designator*] (AD)
WD............ War Damage
WD............ War Department [*Created, 1789; became Department of the Army, 1947*]
WD............ Warehouse Distributor
w/d............ Warm and Dry (MEDA)
WD............ Warranted
WD............ Washington Decisions [*A publication*] (DLA)
WD............ Waste Disposal [*Nuclear energy*] (NRCH)
WD............ Water Damage (ADA)
WD............ Water Department (WDAA)
WD............ Water Desurger
WD............ Water Division [*Environmental Protection Agency*] (GFGA)
WD............ Watt Demand Meter (MSA)
WD............ Waveform Digitizer [*Telecommunications*] (IAA)
WD............ Waveform Distortion [*Telecommunications*] (IAA)
WD............ Wavelength Dispersive [*Spectrometry*]
WD............ Weapon Description (MCD)
WD............ Weapon Director [*SAGE*]
WD............ Weapons Data [*Navy*]
WD............ Weather Division [*Air Force*] (MCD)
WD............ Web Depth
WD............ Weed (WDAA)
WD............ Well Deck
W-D............ Well-Developed [*Medicine*]
WD............ Well Differentiated [*Medicine*]
WD............ Well-Drained [*Soil*]
WD............ West Division (ROG)
WD............ Westminster Dragoons [*British military*] (DMA)
WD............ Wet Dressing
WD............ Wheel Drive [*Engineering*]
WD............ When Directed
WD............ When Discovered
WD............ When Distributed [*Stock exchange term*] (SPSG)
WD............ White Dwarf [*Galactic science*]
WD............ White Dwarf [*Star*] (BARN)
WD............ Whitney Damon Dextrose [*Agar*] (BABM)
WD............ Whole Depth
wd............ Wide (VRA)
WD............ Widow
WD............ Width (MSA)
wd............ Width (VRA)
W/D............ Width-to-Diameter [*Ratio*] (KSC)
WD............ Wife's Divorce (ROG)
WD............ Will Dated [*Genealogy*] (ROG)
WD............ Williams Domain [*Computer science*] (IAA)
WD............ Wilson Dam [*TVA*]
WD............ Wilson's Disease [*Medicine*]
WD............ Wind (MSA)
WD............ Wind Deflection [*Ballistics*]
WD............ Wind Direction
WD............ Window Detector
WD............ Window Dimension [*Technical drawings*]
WD............ Wing Defence [*Netball*]
WD............ Winner's Dog [*Dog show term*]
WD............ Wired Discrete (NASA)
WD............ Wiring Diagram (IAA)
WD............ With Dependents (MCD)
WD............ With Disease (MAE)
W/D............ Withdrawal (DLA)
WD............ Withdrawn (AFM)
WD............ Wood (AAG)
wd............ Wood (VRA)
WD............ Wood Door [*Technical drawings*]
WD............ Word
WD............ Word Display
WD............ Work [*or Working*] Day (AFM)
WD............ Work Description (MCD)
WD............ Work Directive (MCD)
WD............ Working Distance [*Microscopy*]
WD............ Working Draft (OSI)
WD............ Works Department
WD............ Would
WD............ Wound (AAMN)
WD............ Wrist Disarticulation [*Medicine*]
WD............ Write Data
WD............ Write Direct
WD............ Writer's Digest [*A publication*]
WD............ Writer's Directory [*A publication*]
WD............ Wrongful Death [*Legal shorthand*] (LWAP)
WD............ Wrongful Detention [*British*]
WD............ Wydmar Developmental Corp. [*Vancouver Stock Exchange symbol*]
WD (2d)............ Washington Decisions, Second Series [*A publication*] (DLA)
WD 40............ WD-40 Co. [*Associated Press*] (SAG)
WDA............ Aram Public Library, Delavan, WI [*Library symbol Library of Congress*] (LCLS)
WDA............ Wadi Ain [*South Arabia*] [*Airport symbol*] (AD)
WDA............ Wallcovering Distributors Association (EA)
WDA............ Wardair Canada Ltd. [*ICAO designator*] (FAAC)
WDA............ Warehouse Distributors Association for Leisure and Mobile Products (EA)
WDA............ Waste Disposal Authority [*British*]
WDA............ Wave Data Analyzer [*Marine science*] (MSC)
WDA............ Weapons Defended Area
WDA............ Well Drillers' Association [*British*] (DBA)
WDA............ Welsh Development Agency [*British*] (DS)
WDA............ Western District Area [*Air Force*]
WDA............ Wheel Drive Assembly
WDA............ Wholesale Distributors Association (EA)
WDA............ Wildlife Disease Association (EA)
WDA............ Wilson's Disease Association (EA)
WDA............ Withdrawal of Availability [*Military*] (AFM)
WDA............ Women's Diocesan Association [*British*]
WDA............ World Aquathemes Ltd. [*Vancouver Stock Exchange symbol*]
WDA............ World Dance Alliance
WDA............ World Development Action [*An association British*]
WDA............ World Dredging Association (MSC)
WDA............ Wrongful Death Act (LWAP)
WDAB............ Travelers Rest, SC [*AM radio station call letters*]
WDAC............ Lancaster, PA [*FM radio station call letters*]
WDAD............ Indiana, PA [*AM radio station call letters*]
WDAE............ Tampa, FL [*AM radio station call letters*]
WDAF............ Kansas City, MO [*AM radio station call letters*]
WDAF............ Western Desert Air Force
WDAF-TV............ Kansas City, MO [*Television station call letters*]
WDAG............ Word Driver and Gate [*Computer science*] (IAA)
WDAHAC............ National Society Women Descendants of the Ancient and Honorable Artillery Company (EA)
WDAI............ Pawley's Island, SC [*FM radio station call letters*]
WDAK............ Columbus, GA [*AM radio station call letters*]
WDAL............ Dalton, GA [*AM radio station call letters*] (RBYB)
WDALMP............ Warehouse Distributors Association for Leisure and Mobile Products (EA)
WDAM............ Laurel, MS [*Television station call letters*]
WDAN............ Danville, IL [*AM radio station call letters*]
WDAO............ Dayton, OH [*AM radio station call letters*]
WDAP............ Huntingdon, TN [*AM radio station call letters*] (RBYB)
WDAP............ World Dictionary of Awards and Prizes [*A publication*]
WDAQ............ Danbury, CT [*FM radio station call letters*]
WDar............ Darien Public Library, Darien, WI [*Library symbol Library of Congress*] (LCLS)
WDAR-FM............ Darlington, SC [*FM radio station call letters*]
WDAS............ Philadelphia, PA [*AM radio station call letters*]
WDAS............ Western Dance Appreciation Society [*British*] (DBA)
WDAS-FM............ Philadelphia, PA [*FM radio station call letters*]
WDAV............ Davidson, NC [*FM radio station call letters*]
WDAY............ Fargo, ND [*AM radio station call letters*]
WDAY-FM............ Fargo, ND [*FM radio station call letters*]
WDAY-TV............ Fargo, ND [*Television station call letters*]
WDAZ............ Devils Lake, ND [*Television station call letters*]
WDB............ Westminster Dictionary of the Bible [*A publication*] (BJA)
WDB............ Wideband [*Radio*] (MCD)
WDB............ Wide Deadband [*NASA*]
WDB............ Winkelmann-Dibley Formula B [*Race car*]
WDB............ With Due Bills [*Stocks*] (MHDW)
WDB............ Word Driver BIT [*Binary Digit*] [*Computer science*] (MHDI)
WDB............ Working Data Base (MHDI)
WDB-1............ World Data Bank (NITA)
WDBA............ Du Bois, PA [*FM radio station call letters*]
WDBB............ Tuscaloosa, AL [*Television station call letters*]
WDBC............ Escanaba, MI [*AM radio station call letters*]
WDBCA............ War Department Board of Contract Appeals [*1942-50*] (AAGC)
WDBD............ Jackson, MS [*Television station call letters*]
WDBF............ Delray Beach, FL [*AM radio station call letters*]
WDBJ............ Roanoke, VA [*Television station call letters*]
WDBK............ Blackwood, NJ [*FM radio station call letters*]
WDBK............ Wordbook (ROG)
WDBL............ Springfield, TN [*AM radio station call letters*]
wdbl............ Woodblock (VRA)
WDBL-FM............ Springfield, TN [*FM radio station call letters*]
WDBM............ East Lansing, MI [*FM radio station call letters*]
WDBN............ Wrightsville, GA [*FM radio station call letters*]
WDBO............ Orlando, FL [*AM radio station call letters*]
WDBOR............ Wood Boring
WDBQ............ Dubuque, IA [*AM radio station call letters*]
WDBR............ Springfield, IL [*FM radio station call letters*]
WDBS-FM............ Bolingbroke, GA [*FM radio station call letters*] (RBYB)
WDBX-FM............ Carbondale, IL [*FM radio station call letters*] (RBYB)
WDC............ War Damage Commission [*British*]
WDC............ War Damage Corp. [*World War II*]
WDC............ War Department Constabulary [*British military*] (DMA)
WDC............ Washington [*Diocesan abbreviation*] [*District of Columbia*] (TOCD)
WDC............ Washington Document Center
WDC............ Waste Disposal Cask [*Nuclear energy*] (NRCH)
WDC............ Waste Disposal Code
WDC............ Water Data Center [*Department of Agriculture*] [*Information service or system*] (IID)
WDC............ Weapon Delivery Computer (MCD)
WDC............ Weapon Direction Computer [*Military*] (CAAL)
WDC............ Western Defense Command [*Army*]
WDC............ Western Digital [*NYSE symbol*] (TTSB)
WDC............ Western Digital Corp. [*NYSE symbol*] (SPSG)
WDC............ Westinghouse Defense Center

WDC ... Whiskeytown Dam [*California*] [*Seismograph station code, US Geological Survey*] (SEIS)
WDC ... Wideband Directional Coupler
WDC ... Women's Distance Committee (EA)
WDC ... Workers' Defence Committee [*Ghana*] [*Political party*] (PPW)
WDC ... Workers' Defense Committee [*Poland*] (PD)
WDC ... Working Direct Current (DEN)
WDC ... World Data Center [*National Academy of Sciences*] [*Data collection and exchange center*]
WDC ... World Data Centre on Micro-Organisms (EERA)
WDC ... World Data Centres (EERA)
WDC ... World Development Corp.
WDC ... World Disarmament Campaign (EAIO)
WDC ... World Disarmament Conference (NATG)
WDC ... World Druze Congress (EA)
WDC ... Write Data Check (CMD)
WDCA ... Washington, DC [*Television station call letters*]
WDC-A ... World Data Center A [*National Academy of Sciences*]
WDCA ... World Diving Coaches Association (EA)
WDCB ... Glen Ellyn, IL [*FM radio station call letters*]
WDC-B ... World Data Center B [*National Academy of Sciences*]
WDCC ... Sanford, NC [*FM radio station call letters*]
WDCC ... Well-Developed Collateral Circulation [*Medicine*] (DMAA)
WDCD ... Albany, NY [*AM radio station call letters*] (RBYB)
WDCE ... Richmond, VA [*FM radio station call letters*]
WDCF ... Dade City, FL [*AM radio station call letters*]
WDCG ... Durham, NC [*FM radio station call letters*]
WDCGG ... World Data Center for Greenhouse Gases [*Marine science*] (OSRA)
WDCI ... Bridgeport, WV [*FM radio station call letters*]
WDCL ... Somerset, KY [*FM radio station call letters*]
WDCM ... Cruz Bay, VI [*FM radio station call letters*]
WDCM ... World Data Centre on Microorganisms (EERA)
WDCMC ... War Department Classified Message Center [*Obsolete World War II*]
WDCN ... Nashville, TN [*Television station call letters*]
WDCO ... Cochran, GA [*FM radio station call letters*]
WDCO-TV ... Cochran, GA [*Television station call letters*]
WDCQ ... Pine Island Centre, FL [*AM radio station call letters*]
WDCR ... Hanover, NH [*AM radio station call letters*]
WDCS ... Cobleskill, NY [*AM radio station call letters*] (RBYB)
WDCS ... Weapons Data Correlation System (MCD)
WDCS ... Whale and Dolphin Conservation Society [*British*] (DBA)
WDCS ... Women's Division of Christian Service [*of the Board of Missions, The Methodist Church*]
WDCS ... Writable Diagnostic Control Store
WDCSA ... War Department Chief of Staff, US Army [*World War II*]
WDCSM ... Walt Disney Comic Strip Maker [*Apple computer software*]
WDCT ... Fairfax, VA [*AM radio station call letters*]
WDCT ... Woodcut (ROG)
wdct ... Woodcut (VRA)
WDCU ... Washington, DC [*FM radio station call letters*]
WDCV ... Carlisle, PA [*FM radio station call letters*]
WDCW ... Syracuse, NY [*AM radio station call letters*]
WDCX ... Buffalo, NY [*FM radio station call letters*]
WDCY ... Douglasville, GA [*AM radio station call letters*]
WDCZ ... Webster, NY [*FM radio station call letters*]
WDD ... Wave Dynamics Division [*US Army Corps of Engineers*]
WDD ... Western Development Division [*ARDC*]
WDD ... Word Description Drawing (SAA)
WDDA ... Wholesale Demand Deposit Accounting (DICI)
WDDB ... Wild Dog Destruction Board [*New South Wales, Australia*]
WDDC ... Portage, WI [*FM radio station call letters*]
WDDC ... Well Deck Debarkation Control [*Navy*] (CAAL)
WDDD ... Johnston City, IL [*AM radio station call letters*]
WDDD ... Marion, IL [*FM radio station call letters*]
WDDES ... World Digital Database for Environmental Sciences [*Marine science*] (OSRA)
WDDES ... World Digital Data for the Environmental Sciences (EERA)
WDDJ ... Paducah, KY [*FM radio station call letters*]
WDDK ... Greensboro, GA [*FM radio station call letters*]
WDDO ... Macon, GA [*AM radio station call letters*]
WDDQ ... Adel, GA [*FM radio station call letters*]
WDDT ... Greenville, MS [*AM radio station call letters*]
WDE ... Weapons Directing Equipment (NVT)
WDE ... Weapons Direction Evaluation (SAA)
wde ... Wood-Engraver [*MARC relator code*] [*Library of Congress*] (LCCP)
WDEA ... Ellsworth, ME [*AM radio station call letters*]
WDEB ... Jamestown, TN [*AM radio station call letters*]
WDEB-FM ... Jamestown, TN [*FM radio station call letters*]
WDEC ... Americus, GA [*AM radio station call letters*]
WDEC-FM ... Americus, GA [*FM radio station call letters*]
WDED ... Wounded [*Military*]
WDEE ... Reed City, MI [*AM radio station call letters*]
WDeep ... Western Deep Levels Ltd. [*Associated Press*] (SAG)
WDEF ... Chattanooga, TN [*AM radio station call letters*]
WDEF-FM ... Chattanooga, TN [*FM radio station call letters*]
WDEF-TV ... Chattanooga, TN [*Television station call letters*]
WDEH ... Sweetwater, TN [*AM radio station call letters*]
WDEH-FM ... Sweetwater, TN [*FM radio station call letters*]
WDEK ... De Kalb, IL [*FM radio station call letters*]
WDEL ... Weapons Development Effectiveness Laboratory (MCD)
WDEL ... Wilmington, DE [*AM radio station call letters*]
WDEMCO ... Walt Disney Educational Media Co.
WDEN ... Macon, GA [*AM radio station call letters*]
WDEN-FM ... Macon, GA [*FM radio station call letters*]
WDEOAT ... Wolfe Data Entry Operator Aptitude Test
WDEP ... Western Deep Levels Ltd. [*NASDAQ symbol*] (NQ)
WDEPY ... Western Deep Levels ADR [*NASDAQ symbol*] (TTSB)
WDEQ ... De Graff, OH [*FM radio station call letters*]
WDER ... Derry, NH [*AM radio station call letters*]
WDET ... Detroit, MI [*FM radio station call letters*]
WDEV ... Waterbury, VT [*AM radio station call letters*]
WDEV-FM ... Warren, VT [*FM radio station call letters*]
WDEX ... Monroe, NC [*AM radio station call letters*]
WDEZ ... Wausau, WI [*FM radio station call letters*]
WDF ... Wall Distribution Frame (MUGU)
WDF ... Wave Digital Filter (PDAA)
WDF ... Weapon Defense Facility (AAG)
WDF ... Weather Data Facility
WDF ... Western Desert Force [*World War II*]
WDF ... Winkelmann-Dibley Ford [*Race car*]
WDF ... Wood Door and Frame [*Technical drawings*]
WDF ... Woodruff
WDF ... World Darts Federation (EAIO)
WDF ... World Draughts (Checkers) Federation [*See also FMJD*] [*Dordrecht, Netherlands*] (EAIO)
WDFB ... Danville, KY [*FM radio station call letters*]
WDFB ... Junction City, KY [*AM radio station call letters*]
WDFC ... WD-40 Co. [*NASDAQ symbol*] (NQ)
WD/FE ... Water Dispenser/Fire Extinguisher [*Apollo*] [*NASA*]
WDFH ... Ossining, NY [*FM radio station call letters*]
WDFL ... Cross City, FL [*AM radio station call letters*]
WDFL-FM ... Cross City, FL [*FM radio station call letters*]
WDFM ... Defiance, OH [*FM radio station call letters*]
WDFM ... Wright Dust Feed Mechanism (PDAA)
WDFN ... Detroit, MI [*AM radio station call letters*]
WDFP ... World Day for Peace (EA)
WDFW ... Washingtons [*State*] Department of Fish and Wildlife
WDFX ... Cleveland, MS [*FM radio station call letters*]
WDFX-TV ... Ozark, AL [*Television station call letters*] (RBYB)
WDG ... Enid [*Oklahoma*] [*Airport symbol*] (OAG)
WDG ... Enid, OK [*Location identifier FAA*] (FAAL)
WDG ... Ministry of Agriculture Fisheries and Food [*British ICAO designator*] (FAAC)
WDG ... Wallace Dam [*Georgia*] [*Seismograph station code, US Geological Survey*] (SEIS)
WDG ... Weapons Display Generator (MCD)
WDG ... Winding (MSA)
WDG ... Wording (WGA)
WDG ... World Diplomatic Guide [*A publication*]
WDGC ... Downers Grove, IL [*FM radio station call letters*]
WDGE ... Wakefield-Peacedale, RI [*FM radio station call letters*] (RBYB)
WDGF ... War Department Ground Forces [*Obsolete*]
WDGF-FM ... Middletown, RI [*FM radio station call letters*] (RBYB)
WDGG ... Ashland, KY [*FM radio station call letters*] (RBYB)
WDGI ... Wholesale Dry Goods Institute [*Later, NATAD*]
W Dgns ... Westminster Dragoons [*British military*] (DMA)
WDGO ... War Department General Order [*Obsolete*]
WDGR ... Dahlonega, GA [*AM radio station call letters*]
WDGS ... War Department General Staff [*Obsolete*]
WDG TBA ... Wording to Be Agreed [*Insurance*] (AIA)
WDGY ... St. Paul, MN [*AM radio station call letters*]
WDH ... Watery Diarrhea, Hypokalemia [*Syndrome*] [*Medicine*]
WDH ... Windhoek [*Namibia*] [*Airport symbol*] (OAG)
WDH ... Winkelmann-Dibley Hillclimb [*Race car*]
WDH ... Wiring Data Handbook
WDHA ... Dover, NJ [*FM radio station call letters*]
WDHA ... Watery Diarrhea, Hypokalemia, Achlorhydria [*Medicine*]
WDHCB ... War Department Hardship Claims Board [*Obsolete*]
WDHC-FM ... Berkeley Springs, WV [*FM radio station call letters*] (RBYB)
WDHD ... Woodhead Indus [*NASDAQ symbol*] (TTSB)
WDHD ... Woodhead Industries, Inc. [*NASDAQ symbol*] (NQ)
WDHH ... Watery Diarrhea, Hypokalemia, Hypochlorhydria [*Syndrome*] [*Medicine*]
WDHHA ... Watery Diarrhea, Hypochlorhydria, Hypokalemia, and Alkalosis [*Medicine*]
WDHI ... Delhi, NY [*FM radio station call letters*]
WDHN ... Dothan, AL [*Television station call letters*]
WDHR ... Pikeville, KY [*FM radio station call letters*]
WDHS ... Iron Mountain, MI [*Television station call letters*]
WDHS ... Worldwide Dental Health Service (EA)
WDI ... Wardair, Inc. [*Toronto Stock Exchange symbol*]
WDI ... War Department Intelligence [*Obsolete*]
WDI ... Warfarin Dose Index
WDI ... Warhead Detection Indicator (AAG)
WDI ... Weapon Data Index [*Navy*] (MCD)
WDI ... Weapon Delivery Impairment (NVT)
WDI ... Web Depth Index
WDI ... Wind Direction Indicator [*ICAO*] (FAAC)
WDI ... Wood and Iron [*Freight*]
WDIA ... Memphis, TN [*AM radio station call letters*]
WDIC ... Clinchco, VA [*AM radio station call letters*]
WDICC ... War Department Intelligence Collection Committee
WDIC-FM ... Clinchco, VA [*FM radio station call letters*]
WDICPC ... War Department Intelligence Collection Planning Committee
WDIF ... Marion, OH [*FM radio station call letters*]
WDIF ... Women's Democratic International Federation (NATG)
W Dig ... New York Weekly Digest [*A publication*] (DLA)
WDIG ... Steubenville, OH [*AM radio station call letters*]
WDigitl ... Western Digital Corp. [*Associated Press*] (SAG)
WDIH ... Salisbury, MD [*FM radio station call letters*]

WDIO Duluth, MN [*Television station call letters*]
WDIP Weapon Data Insert Panel (MCD)
WDIQ Dozier, AL [*Television station call letters*]
WDIR Wind Direction
WDIR Working Directory (MHDI)
WDIRN What Do I Read Next [*A publication*]
WDIS Norfolk, MA [*AM radio station call letters*]
WDIV Detroit, MI [*Television station call letters*]
WDIY Allentown, PA [*FM radio station call letters*]
WDIZ Orlando, FL [*FM radio station call letters*]
WdJ Wissenschaft des Judentums [*A publication*] (BJA)
WDJB Columbia City, IN [*FM radio station call letters*]
WDJC-AM Birmingham, AL [*AM radio station call letters*] (RBYB)
WDJC-FM Birmingham, AL [*FM radio station*] (RBYB)
WDJL Huntsville, AL [*AM radio station call letters*]
WDJM Framingham, MA [*FM radio station call letters*]
WDJR Enterprise, AL [*FM radio station call letters*]
WDJS Mount Olive, NC [*AM radio station call letters*]
WDJT Milwaukee, WI [*Television station call letters*]
WDJW Somers, CT [*FM radio station call letters*]
WDJX Louisville, KY [*FM radio station call letters*]
WDJY Trenton, FL [*FM radio station call letters*]
WDJZ Bridgeport, CT [*AM radio station call letters*]
W Dk Weather Deck [*of a ship*] (DS)
WDKA Paducah, KY [*Television station call letters*]
WDKB De Kalb, IL [*FM radio station call letters*]
WDKC Covington, PA [*FM radio station call letters*]
WDKD Kingstree, SC [*AM radio station call letters*]
WDKM Adams, WI [*FM radio station call letters*]
WDKN Dickson, TN [*AM radio station call letters*]
WDKR-FM Maroa, IL [*FM radio station call letters*] (RBYB)
WDKX Rochester, NY [*FM radio station call letters*]
WDKY Danville, KY [*Television station call letters*]
WD KY United States District Court for the Western District of Kentucky (DLA)
WDL Warren Library Association and County Division, Warren, PA [*OCLC symbol*] (OCLC)
WDL Waveguide Directional Localizer
WDL Weapon Data Link (MCD)
WDL Weapons Density List (AABC)
WDL Well-Differentiated Lymphocytic [*Lymphoma classification*]
WDL Westdeutsche Luftwerbung [*Airline*] [*Germany*]
WDL Western d'Eldona Resources Ltd. [*Toronto Stock Exchange symbol*]
WDL Western Development Laboratories
WDL Wien Displacement Law [*Physics*]
WDL Wireless Data Link
WDL Workers' Defense League (EA)
WD LA United States District Court for the Western District of Louisiana (DLA)
WDLA Walton, NY [*AM radio station call letters*]
WDLA-FM Walton, NY [*FM radio station call letters*]
WDLB Marshfield, WI [*AM radio station call letters*]
WDLC Port Jervis, NY [*AM radio station call letters*]
WDLF Old Fort, NC [*FM radio station call letters*]
WDLF White-Dwarf Luminosity Function [*Galactic science*]
WDLI Canton, OH [*Television station call letters*]
WDLJ Indianola, MS [*FM radio station call letters*]
WDLK Dadeville, AL [*AM radio station call letters*]
WDLL Well-Differentiated Lymphatic [*or Lymphocytic*] Lymphoma [*Oncology*]
WDLM East Moline, IL [*AM radio station call letters*]
WDLM-FM East Moline, IL [*FM radio station call letters*]
WDLP Panama City Beach, FL [*AM radio station call letters*]
WDLR Delaware, OH [*AM radio station call letters*]
WDLS Dallas, PA [*FM radio station call letters*]
WDLT Chickasaw, AL [*FM radio station call letters*]
WDLX Washington, NC [*FM radio station call letters*]
WDLY Gatlinburg, TN [*FM radio station call letters*]
WDLY Widely (FAAC)
WDM Wavelength Division Multiplex [*or Multiplexing*] [*Telecommunications*]
WDM Weapon Delivery Model (PDAA)
WDM Weight after Departure from Mars [*NASA*]
WDM World Development Movement [*British*]
WDMA Wholesale Druggists Merchandising Association (EA)
WDMB War Department Manpower Board [*Obsolete*]
WDMCC Walt Disney Memorial Cancer Institute
WDMCI Walt Disney Memorial Cancer Institute
WDME-FM Dover-Foxcroft, ME [*FM radio station call letters*]
WDMET Wound Data Munitions Effectiveness Team (MCD)
WDMF Weak Disordered Magnetic Field
WDMG Douglas, GA [*AM radio station call letters*]
WDMG-FM Douglas, GA [*FM radio station call letters*]
WD Mich United States District Court for the Western District of Michigan (DLA)
WDMJ Marquette, MI [*AM radio station call letters*]
WDML Wiring Diagram Maintenance List
WDML Woodlawn, IL [*FM radio station call letters*]
WD MO United States District Court for the Western District of Missouri (DLA)
WDMO Weight before Departure from Mars Orbit [*NASA*]
WDMP Dodgeville, WI [*AM radio station call letters*]
WDMP-FM Dodgeville, WI [*FM radio station call letters*]
WDMS Greenville, MS [*FM radio station call letters*]
WDMT Eufaula, AL [*FM radio station call letters*]
WDMV Pocomoke City, MD [*AM radio station call letters*]
WDMX Vienna, WV [*FM radio station call letters*]
WDN Walden Residential Prop [*NYSE symbol*] (TTSB)
WDN Walden Residential Properties [*NYSE symbol*] (SAG)
WDN Wooden
WDNA Miami, FL [*FM radio station call letters*]
WDNC Durham, NC [*AM radio station call letters*]
WDNC United States District Court for the Western District of North Carolina (DLA)
WDNE Elkins, WV [*AM radio station call letters*]
WDNE-FM Elkins, WV [*FM radio station call letters*]
WDNG Anniston, AL [*AM radio station call letters*]
WDNH Honesdale, PA [*FM radio station call letters*]
WDNL Danville, IL [*FM radio station call letters*]
WDNO Laurel, DE [*FM radio station call letters*]
WDNOWRE Wooden Ware [*Freight*]
WDNR Chester, PA [*FM radio station call letters*]
WDNR Wisconsin Department of Natural Resources
WDNS Bowling Green, KY [*FM radio station call letters*]
WDNT Dayton, TN [*AM radio station call letters*]
WDNT-FM Dayton, TN [*FM radio station call letters*]
WDNX Olive Hill, TN [*FM radio station call letters*]
WDNY Dansville, NY [*AM radio station call letters*]
WDNY United States District Court for the Western District of New York (DLA)
WDNY-FM Dansville, NY [*FM radio station call letters*]
WDO Web Depth Order
WDO Widespread Depression Orchestra
WDO Window (MSA)
WDOC Prestonsburg, KY [*AM radio station call letters*]
WDOD Chattanooga, TN [*AM radio station call letters*]
WDOD-FM Chattanooga, TN [*FM radio station call letters*]
WDOE Dunkirk, NY [*AM radio station call letters*]
WDOE Washington Department of Ecology (DOGT)
WDOE Washington Department of Ecology
WDOG Allendale, SC [*AM radio station call letters*]
WDOG-FM Allendale, SC [*FM radio station call letters*]
WDOH Delphos, OH [*FM radio station call letters*]
WDOK Cleveland, OH [*FM radio station call letters*]
WD Okla United States District Court for the Western District of Oklahoma (DLA)
WDOL Englewood, OH [*FM radio station call letters*]
WDOM Providence, RI [*FM radio station call letters*]
WDOP Weighted Dilution of Precision
WDOPD War Department, Operations Division, General Staff [*World War II*]
WDOR Sturgeon Bay, WI [*AM radio station call letters*]
WDOR-FM Sturgeon Bay, WI [*FM radio station call letters*]
WDOS Oneonta, NY [*AM radio station call letters*]
WDOS Wooton Desk Owners Society (EA)
WDOV Dover, DE [*AM radio station call letters*]
WDOW Dowagiac, MI [*AM radio station call letters*]
WDOX Wildwood Crest, NJ [*FM radio station call letters*]
WDOY Fajardo, PR [*FM radio station call letters*]
WDOZ Dearborn, MI [*AM radio station call letters*]
WDP Weapons Direction Program
WDP Wenner Difference Potentiometer
WDP Women in Data Processing (EA)
WDP Wood Panel (AAG)
WDP Work Distribution Policy (AAG)
WD PA United States District Court for the Western District of Pennsylvania (DLA)
WDPA Wisconsin Dairy Products Association (EA)
WDPB Seaford, DE [*Television station call letters*]
WDPC Western Data Processing Center [*University of California, Los Angeles*]
WDPC-AM Dallas, GA [*AM radio station call letters*] (RBYB)
WDPG Greenville, OH [*FM radio station call letters*]
WDPMG-ID War Department Provost Marshal General, Investigation Division [*Obsolete*]
WDPN Alliance, OH [*AM radio station call letters*]
WDPR Dayton, OH [*FM radio station call letters*]
WDPS Dayton, OH [*FM radio station call letters*]
WDPT Water-Drop-Penetration Time [*Agriculture*]
WDQN Du Quoin, IL [*AM radio station call letters*]
WDQN-FM Du Quoin, IL [*FM radio station call letters*]
WDR Wardair International Ltd. [*Toronto Stock Exchange symbol Vancouver Stock Exchange symbol*]
Wdr Wardmaster [*British military*] (DMA)
WDR Westdeutscher Rundfunk [*Radio network*] [*West Germany*]
WDR Wide Dynamic Range
WDR Wider (WGA)
WDR Winder, GA [*Location identifier FAA*] (FAAL)
WDR Window Definition Record [*Computer science*]
WDR Winged Russia [*Russian Federation*] [*ICAO designator*] (FAAC)
WDR Withdrawal
WDR Women's Drug Research Project (EA)
WDR Write Drum
WDRB Louisville, KY [*Television station call letters*]
WDRC Hartford, CT [*AM radio station call letters*]
WDRC Women's Defence Relief Corps [*World War I*] [*British*]
WDRC-FM Hartford, CT [*FM radio station call letters*]
WDRE Garden City, NY [*FM radio station call letters*]
WDRG Danville, VA [*Television station call letters*]
WDRK Callaway, FL [*FM radio station call letters*]
Wdr L Wardmaster Lieutenant [*British military*] (DMA)
WDRM Decatur, AL [*FM radio station call letters*]

WDROP .... Water Distribution Register of Organic Pollutants [*National Institutes of Health*]
WDRP .... Windsor, NC [*FM radio station call letters*]
WDRQ-FM ... Detroit, MI [*FM radio station call letters*] (RBYB)
WDRR .... Sanibel, FL [*FM radio station call letters*] (RBYB)
Wdrst .... Woodroast Systems, Inc. [*Associated Press*] (SAG)
WDRT .... Water Detection Response Team [*DoD*]
WDRY .... Coinmach Laundry Corp. [*NASDAQ symbol*] (SAG)
WDRZ .... Etowah, TN [*FM radio station call letters*]
WDS .... Four Winds Aviation Ltd. [*ICAO designator*] (FAAC)
WDS .... Washington Document Service [*Information service or system*] (IID)
WD(S) .... Waste Disposal (System) [*Nuclear energy*] (NRCH)
WDS .... Wavelength Dispersive Spectrometer
WDS .... Weapon Delivery System
WDS .... Weapons Directing System [*Navy*]
WDS .... Wet Dog Shakes Syndrome [*Medicine*] (DMAA)
WDS .... Wire Data Service
WDS .... Wood Dye Stain
WDS .... Woodside [*California*] [*Seismograph station code, US Geological Survey*] (SEIS)
WDS .... Woodward's Ltd. [*Toronto Stock Exchange symbol Vancouver Stock Exchange symbol*]
WDS .... Word Discrimination Score
WDS .... World Deist Society (EA)
WDS .... Wounds
WDSC .... Dillon, SC [*AM radio station call letters*]
WDSD .... Dover, DE [*FM radio station call letters*]
WDSD .... Water Data Sources Directory [*US Geological Survey*] [*Information service or system*] (CRD)
WDSD .... Wisconsin School for the Deaf, Delavan, WI [*Library symbol Library of Congress*] (LCLS)
WDSE .... Duluth, MN [*Television station call letters*]
WDSI .... Chattanooga, TN [*Television station call letters*]
WDSK .... Cleveland, MS [*AM radio station call letters*] (RBYB)
WDSL .... Mocksville, NC [*AM radio station call letters*]
WDSM .... Superior, WI [*AM radio station call letters*]
WDSN .... Reynoldsville, PA [*FM radio station call letters*]
WDSO .... Chesterton, IN [*FM radio station call letters*]
WDSP .... Arlington, NY [*FM radio station call letters*]
WDSPR .... Widespread
WDSPRD ..... Widespread (FAAC)
WDSR .... Lake City, FL [*AM radio station call letters*]
WDSS .... War Department Special Staff [*Obsolete*]
WDSS .... Warning Decision Support System [*Marine science*] (OSRA)
WDSS .... Warning Decision Support System (USDC)
WDS SATSIM... Weapon Direction System Satellite Simulation [*Military*] (CAAL)
WDST .... Woodstock, NY [*FM radio station call letters*]
WD STL .... Wood or Steel [*Freight*]
WD STV .... Wood Stove [*Freight*]
WDSU .... New Orleans, LA [*Television station call letters*]
WDSY .... Pittsburgh, PA [*AM radio station call letters*]
WDSY-FM .... Pittsburgh, PA [*FM radio station call letters*] (RBYB)
WDT .... Warmth Detection Threshold
WDT .... Watch Dog Timer
WDT .... Wear Durability Trial
WDT .... Weight Data Transmitter (IAA)
WDT .... Weight Distribution Table
WDT .... Width
WDT .... Wiedemann Developed Template (MCD)
WDT .... World Cement Industries [*Vancouver Stock Exchange symbol*]
WDT .... Writers' Development Trust [*Canada*] (EAIO)
WDTC .... Western Defense Tactical Command (AAG)
WD Tenn ..... United States District Court for the Western District of Tennessee (DLA)
WD Tex .... United States District Court for the Western District of Texas (DLA)
WDTF .... Wetting-Drying and Temperature Fluctuation [*Geochemistry*]
WDTL .... Cleveland, MS [*FM radio station call letters*]
WDTM .... Selmer, TN [*AM radio station call letters*]
WDTN .... Dayton, OH [*Television station call letters*]
WDTR .... Detroit, MI [*FM radio station call letters*]
WDTRS .... Westinghouse Development Test Requirement Specification (IAA)
WDTU .... War Dog Training Unit [*British military*] (DMA)
WDTV .... Weston, WV [*Television station call letters*]
WDu .... Durand Free Library, Durand, WI [*Library symbol Library of Congress*] (LCLS)
WdU .... Wahlpartei der Unabhaengigen [*Electoral Party of Independents*] [*Austria Political party*] (PPE)
WDU .... Water Data Unit (DCTA)
WDU .... Weapons Director Unit (MCD)
WDU .... Window Deicing Unit
WDU .... Wireless Development Unit
WDU .... Workers' Defence Union [*British*]
WDUB .... Granville, OH [*FM radio station call letters*]
WDUF .... Duffield, VA [*AM radio station call letters*]
WDUK .... Havana, IL [*FM radio station call letters*]
WDUN .... Gainesville, GA [*AM radio station call letters*]
WDUQ .... Pittsburgh, PA [*FM radio station call letters*]
WDUR .... Durham, NC [*AM radio station call letters*]
WDUV .... Bradenton, FL [*FM radio station call letters*]
WDUX .... Waupaca, WI [*AM radio station call letters*]
WDUX-FM .... Waupaca, WI [*FM radio station call letters*]
WDUZ .... Green Bay, WI [*AM radio station call letters*]
WDV .... War Department Vehicle [*Obsolete*]
WDV .... Water Dilution Volume [*Environmental chemistry*] (FFDE)
WDV .... Western Diverging Volcanism [*Geology*]
WDV .... Wheat Dwarf Virus [*Plant pathology*]
WDV .... Winkelmann-Dibley Volkswagen [*Race car*]
WDV .... Worldwide Dollarvest Fund [*NYSE symbol*] (SAG)
WDV .... Written Down Value [*Accounting*]
WDVA .... Danville, VA [*AM radio station call letters*]
WD VA .... United States District Court for the Western District of Virginia (DLA)
WDVE .... Pittsburgh, PA [*FM radio station call letters*]
WDVI .... Dadeville, AL [*FM radio station call letters*]
WDVR .... Delaware Township, NJ [*FM radio station call letters*]
WDVX .... Clinton, TN [*FM radio station call letters*]
WDW .... Wholesale Dealer in Wines
WDW .... Window
WDW .... Wood and Wire [*Freight*]
WD Wash .... United States District Court for the Western District of Washington (DLA)
WDWG .... Atmore, AL [*FM radio station call letters*]
WD Wis .... United States District Court for the Western District of Wisconsin (DLA)
wdwk .... Woodwork (BARN)
WDWL .... Bayamon, PR [*Television station call letters*]
WDWN .... Auburn, NY [*FM radio station call letters*]
WDWN .... Well Developed - Well Nourished [*Medicine*]
WDWNBF .... Well-Developed Well-Nourished, Black Female (DAVI)
WDWNBM .... Well-Developed, Well-Nourished, Black Male (DAVI)
WDWNWF .... Well-Developed, Well-Nourished, White Female (DAVI)
WDWNWM ... Well-Developed, Well-Nourished, White Male (DAVI)
WDWRK .... Woodwork [*Freight*]
WDWS .... Champaign, IL [*AM radio station call letters*]
WDWT .... Dwight, IL [*FM radio station call letters*]
WDWZ-AM ... Lanett, AL [*AM radio station call letters*] (RBYB)
WDX .... Wavelength Dispersive X-Ray [*Spectrometer*]
WDXA .... Wave-Length Dispersive X-Ray Analysis
WDXC .... Pound, VA [*FM radio station call letters*]
WDXD-FM .... Holly Hill, FL [*FM radio station call letters*] (RBYB)
WDXE .... Lawrenceburg, TN [*AM radio station call letters*]
WDXE-FM .... Lawrenceburg, TN [*FM radio station call letters*]
WDXI .... Jackson, TN [*AM radio station call letters*]
WDXL .... Lexington, TN [*AM radio station call letters*]
WDXN .... Clarksville, TN [*AM radio station call letters*]
WDXR .... Golconda, IL [*FM radio station call letters*]
WDXR .... Paducah, KY [*AM radio station call letters*]
WDXRF .... Wavelength-Dispersive X-Ray Fluorescence
WDXRS .... Wavelength Dispersive X-Ray Spectrometry
WDXX .... Selma, AL [*FM radio station call letters*]
WDXY .... Sumter, SC [*AM radio station call letters*]
WDXZ .... Newberry, SC [*FM radio station call letters*] (RBYB)
WDY .... Phoenix Airline Services, Inc. [*ICAO designator*] (FAAC)
WDY .... Woody [*California*] [*Seismograph station code, US Geological Survey Closed*] (SEIS)
WDY .... Wordy [*Used in correcting manuscripts, etc.*]
WDYL .... Chester, VA [*FM radio station call letters*]
WDYN .... Chattanooga, TN [*FM radio station call letters*]
WDYT .... What Do You Think
WDYTYCIWSS... Why Don't You Take Your Change In War Savings Stamps [*Cashier's sign*] [*World War II*]
WDZ .... Decatur, IL [*AM radio station call letters*]
WDZ .... Werner Dahnz Co. Ltd. [*Toronto Stock Exchange symbol*]
WDZE .... Carolina, PR [*Television station call letters*]
WDZL .... Miami, FL [*Television station call letters*]
WDZQ .... Decatur, IL [*FM radio station call letters*]
WDZR .... Mount Clemens, MI [*FM radio station call letters*]
WDZS .... Darlington, SC [*AM radio station call letters*] (RBYB)
WDZZ .... Flint, MI [*FM radio station call letters*]
WE .... Eau Claire Public Library, Eau Claire, WI [*Library symbol Library of Congress*] (LCLS)
W_E .... Emitter-Region Width (IDOE)
WE .... Staff Meteorologist [*AFSC*]
WE .... Votec [*ICAO designator*] (AD)
WE .... Wage Earner [*Social Security Administration*] (OICC)
WE .... War Establishment
WE .... Watch Error [*Navigation*]
WE .... Watchman-Examiner [*A publication*] (BJA)
WE .... Water Equivalent (MCD)
We .... Watt Electric
WE .... WDL Flugdienst GmbH [*Germany ICAO designator*] (ICDA)
WE .... Weapons Electrical [*Navy British*]
WE .... Weapons Engineering [*Navy British*]
WE .... Weather Emergency
WE .... Webbing Equipment [*British military*] (DMA)
We .... Weber Number [*IUPAC*]
WE .... Wednesday
WE .... Weekend (ADA)
W/E .... Week Ending
WE .... Wescap Enterprises Ltd. [*Vancouver Stock Exchange symbol*]
WE .... Westcoast Energy [*NYSE symbol*] (TTSB)
WE .... Westcoast Energy, Inc. [*NYSE symbol*] (SPSG)
WE .... Western Electric Co. (AAG)
WE .... Western Encephalitis [*Medicine*] (MAE)
WE .... Western Encephalomyelitis [*Medicine*] (MAE)
We .... Western Tithe Cases [*England*] [*A publication*] (DLA)
We .... West's English Chancery Reports [*A publication*] (DLA)
We .... West's Reports, English House of Lords [*A publication*] (DLA)
WE .... White Edges (ADA)
WE .... Whole Economy [*Department of Employment*] [*British*]
W/e .... Width-to-Length [*Ratio*] (MDG)

WE .... Wing Elevon (MCD)
WE .... With Equipment (AABC)
WE .... Withholding Exemptions [*Army*] (AABC)
WE .... Women and Employment [*An association*] (EA)
WE .... Women Educators (EA)
WE .... Women Employed [*Chicago, IL*] (EA)
WE .... Women Entrepreneurs [*Defunct*] (EA)
WE .... Women Exploited (EA)
WE .... Women in Energy (EA)
WE .... Women in Enterprise [*British*] [*An association*] (DBA)
WE .... Women's Reserve, Engineering Duties [*USNR officer designation*]
WE .... Work Experience
WE .... World Ecologists Foundation [*Philippines*] (EAIO)
WE .... World Education, Inc.
WE .... World Evangelism (EA)
WE .... Write Enable [*Computer science*] (IEEE)
W/E .... Writer/Editor (MCD)
WEA .... Eastern Washington State College, Cheney, WA [*OCLC symbol*] (OCLC)
WEa .... East Troy Public Library, East Troy, WI [*Library symbol Library of Congress*] (LCLS)
WEA .... Royal West of England Academy
WEA .... Wall Effect Amplifier
WEA .... Warner-Eddison Associates, Inc. [*Information service or system*] (IID)
WEA .... Weak Equity Axiom
WEA .... Weather (AABC)
WEA .... Weatherford, TX [*Location identifier FAA*] (FAAL)
WEA .... Western Economic Association International (EA)
WEA .... Wilderness Education Association (EA)
WEA .... Women Employed Advocates (EA)
WEA .... Workers' Educational Association
WEA .... Workers Education Association (EERA)
WEAA .... Baltimore, MD [*FM radio station call letters*]
WEAAC .... Western European Airport Authorities Conference (MCD)
WEAAP .... Western European Association for Aviation Psychology (EA)
WEAB .... Adamsville, TN [*AM radio station call letters*]
WEAC .... Gaffney, SC [*AM radio station call letters*]
WEAC .... West European Advisory Committee [*Radio Free Europe*] (NTCM)
WEAC .... Winchester Engineering and Analytical Center [*Food and Drug Administration*] [*Winchester, MA*] (GRD)
WEACAP .... Weapon Capability (SAA)
WEADES .... Western Electric Air Defense Engineering Service (SAA)
WEADSC .... World Esperantist Association for Education, Science, and Culture [*Germany*] (EAIO)
WEAI .... Lynnville, IL [*FM radio station call letters*]
WEAI .... Western Economic Association International [*Later, WEA*] (EA)
WEAL .... Women's Equity Action League [*Defunct*] (EA)
WEAM .... Columbus, GA [*AM radio station call letters*]
WEA-N .... Westinghouse Engineers Association National [*Defunct*] (EA)
WE & FA .... Welsh Engineers and Founders Association (DBA)
W/E & SP .... With Equipment and Spare Parts
WEANSW .... Workers' Educational Association of New South Wales [*Australia*]
WEAO .... Akron, OH [*Television station call letters*]
WEAP .... Women's Economic Agenda Project [*An association*]
WEAP .... World Environment Action Plan (EERA)
WEAPD .... Western Air Procurement District
WEAQ .... Eau Claire, WI [*AM radio station call letters*]
WEAR .... Pensacola, FL [*Television station call letters*]
WEARCON .... Weather Observation and Forecasting Control System
WEARECONRON .... Weather Reconnaissance Squadron [*Air Force*] (DNAB)
WEARESFAC .... Weather Research Facility [*Navy*] (GFGA)
WEAS .... Savannah, GA [*AM radio station call letters*]
WEASA .... Workers' Educational Association of South Australia
WEASEL .... Weapon Selection (SAA)
WEASERVCOMM .... Weather Service Command [*Navy*]
WEAS-FM .... Savannah, GA [*FM radio station call letters*]
WEAT .... Weathertight
WEAT .... West Palm Beach, FL [*AM radio station call letters*]
WEAT-FM .... West Palm Beach, FL [*FM radio station call letters*]
WEAU .... Eau Claire, WI [*Television station call letters*]
WEAV .... Plattsburgh, NY [*AM radio station call letters*]
WEAX .... Angola, IN [*FM radio station call letters*]
WEAX .... En Route Weather Forecast [*Navy*] (NVT)
WEAZ .... Union Park, FL [*FM radio station call letters*] (RBYB)
WEB .... Wagner Earth Bridge
WEB .... War Engineering Board
web .... Web (VRA)
WEB .... Webbing (AAG)
WEB .... Webco Industries [*AMEX symbol*] (TTSB)
WEB .... Webco Industries, Inc. [*AMEX symbol*] (SAG)
WEBA .... Allendale, SC [*Television station call letters*]
WEBA .... Women Exploited by Abortion (EA)
WEBAstla .... World Equity Benchmark Shares [*Associated Press*] (SAG)
WEBAstr .... World Equity Benchmark Shares [*Associated Press*] (SAG)
WEBB .... Online System Svcs [*NASDAQ symbol*] (TTSB)
WEBB .... Waterville, ME [*FM radio station call letters*]
Webb .... Webb's Reports [*6-20 Kansas*] [*A publication*] (DLA)
Webb .... Webb's Reports [*11-20 Texas Civil Appeals*] [*A publication*] (DLA)
WEBB .... Writer's Electronic Bulletin Board [*Information service or system*] (IID)
Webb & D .... Webb and Duval's Reports [*1-3 Texas*] [*A publication*] (DLA)
Webb & Duval .... Webb and Duval's Reports [*1-3 Texas*] [*A publication*] (DLA)
Webb Cr Dig .... Webb's Digest of Texas Criminal Cases [*A publication*] (DLA)
WebbD .... Webb [*Del E.*] Corp. [*Associated Press*] (SAG)
WEB Bel .... World Equity Benchmark Shares [*Associated Press*] (SAG)
Webb Jud Act .... Webb on the Judicature Act [*A publication*] (DLA)
Webb Pl & Pr .... Webb's Kansas Pleading and Practice [*A publication*] (DLA)
Webb RR .... Webb's Railroad Laws of Maine [*A publication*] (DLA)
Webb Supr Ct Pr .... Webb's English Supreme Court Practice [*A publication*] (DLA)
WEBBW .... Online System Svcs Wrrt [*NASDAQ symbol*] (TTSB)
WEBC .... Duluth, MN [*AM radio station call letters*]
WEBCan .... World Equity Benchmark Shares [*Associated Press*] (SAG)
Webcolnd .... Webco Industries, Inc. [*Associated Press*] (SAG)
WEBE .... Western European Basic Encyclopedia (MCD)
WEBE .... Westport, CT [*FM radio station call letters*]
WEBELOS .... We'll Be Loyal Scouts [*Boy Scout slogan*]
WEBFra .... World Equity Benchmark Shares [*Associated Press*] (SAG)
WEBG-AM .... Loretto, PA [*AM radio station call letters*] (RBYB)
WEBGer .... World Equity Benchmark Shares [*Associated Press*] (SAG)
WEB HK .... World Equity Benchmark Shares [*Associated Press*] (SAG)
WEB Ita .... World Equity Benchmark Shares [*Associated Press*] (SAG)
WEBJ .... Brewton, AL [*AM radio station call letters*]
WEB Jpn .... World Equity Benchmark Shares [*Associated Press*] (SAG)
WEBK .... Killington, VT [*FM radio station call letters*]
WEB Mal .... World Equity Benchmark Shares [*Associated Press*] (SAG)
WEB Mex .... World Equity Benchmark Shares [*Associated Press*] (SAG)
WEBN .... Cincinnati, OH [*FM radio station call letters*]
WEB Net .... World Equity Benchmark Shares [*Associated Press*] (SAG)
WEBO .... Owego, NY [*AM radio station call letters*]
Web Pat .... Webster's New Patent Law [*4th ed.*] [*1854*] [*A publication*] (DLA)
Web Pat Cas .... Webster's Patent Cases [*1601-1855*] [*A publication*] (DLA)
Web PC .... Webster's Patent Cases [*1601-1855*] [*A publication*] (DLA)
WEBQ .... Eldorado, IL [*FM radio station call letters*]
WEBQ .... Harrisburg, IL [*AM radio station call letters*]
WEBR .... Washington, DC [*FM radio station call letters*] (RBYB)
WEBROCK .... Weather Buoy Rocket
WEBS .... Calhoun, GA [*AM radio station call letters*]
WEBS .... Weapons Effectiveness Buoy System
WEBS .... WebSecure, Inc. [*NASDAQ symbol*] (SAG)
Webs .... Webster's Patent Cases [*England*] [*A publication*] (DLA)
WEBS .... World Equity Benchmark Shares [*Investment term*]
WebSec .... WebSecure, Inc. [*Associated Press*] (SAG)
WEBSEC .... Western Beaufort Sea Ecological Cruise [*Coast Guard*]
WebSecr .... WebSecure, Inc. [*Associated Press*] (SAG)
WEB Sing .... World Equity Benchmark Shares [*Associated Press*] (SAG)
Webs Pat Cas .... Webster's Patent Cases [*England*] [*A publication*] (DLA)
WEB Spn .... World Equity Benchmark Shares [*Associated Press*] (SAG)
Webst Dict .... Webster's Dictionary [*A publication*] (DLA)
Webst Dict Unab .... Webster's Unabridged Dictionary [*A publication*] (DLA)
Webster in Sen Doc .... Webster in Senate Documents [*A publication*] (DLA)
Webster Pat Cas .... Webster's Patent Cases [*1601-1855*] [*A publication*] (DLA)
Webster Pat Cas (Eng) .... Webster's Patent Cases [*England*] [*A publication*] (DLA)
Webster U .... Webster University (GAGS)
Webst Int Dict .... Webster's International Dictionary [*A publication*] (DLA)
Webst New Int D .... Webster's New International Dictionary [*A publication*] (DLA)
WEB Swd .... World Equity Benchmark Shares [*Associated Press*] (SAG)
WEB Swz .... World Equity Benchmark Shares [*Associated Press*] (SAG)
WEBT .... Valley, Al [*FM radio station call letters*] (RBYB)
Web Tr .... Trial of Professor Webster for Murder [*A publication*] (DLA)
WEB UK .... World Equity Benchmark Shares [*Associated Press*] (SAG)
WEBX .... Tuscola, IL [*FM radio station call letters*] (RBYB)
WEBY .... Milton, FL [*AM radio station call letters*]
WEBZ .... Mexico Beach, FL [*FM radio station call letters*]
WEC .... District One Technical Institute, Eau Claire, Eau Claire, WI [*OCLC symbol*] (OCLC)
WEC .... Eau Claire County Hospital, Eau Claire, WI [*Library symbol Library of Congress*] (LCLS)
WEC .... Universal Airlines, Inc. [*ICAO designator*] (FAAC)
WEC .... Walking with Eyes Closed [*Equilibrium test*]
WEC .... Warhead Electrical Connector
WEC .... Water Export Control
WEC .... Weapon Engagement Console [*Military*] (CAAL)
WEC .... Weapon Engagement Controller [*Military*] (CAAL)
WEC .... Wescal Resources, Inc. [*Vancouver Stock Exchange symbol*]
WEC .... West European Container Liners [*Shipping*]
WEC .... Westinghouse Electric Corp.
WEC .... Wind Energy Conversion
WEC .... Wisconsin Energy Corp. [*NYSE symbol*] (SPSG)
WEC .... Women's Emergency Corps [*World War I*] [*British*]
WEC .... World Endurance Championship [*Auto racing*]
WEC .... World Energy Conference [*See also CME*] [*London, England*] (EAIO)
WEC .... World Energy Council
WEC .... World Environment Center (EA)
WEC .... World Environment Centre (EERA)
WEC .... Worldwide Evangelization Crusade (EA)
WECAF .... Western Central Atlantic Fisheries Commission [*Food and Agriculture Organization of the UN*]
WECAFC .... Western Central Atlantic Fisheries Commission [*Food and Agriculture Organization of the UN*] (EAIO)
WECB .... Seymour, WI [*FM radio station call letters*]
WECB .... Weapons Evaluation and Control Bureau [*USACDA*]
WECC .... St. Mary's, GA [*AM radio station call letters*]
WECC .... Western European Calibration Cooperation (ACII)
WECC .... White English Celtic Catholic
WECC .... Wyoming Educational Computing Council (EDAC)
WECEN .... Weather Center [*Air Force*]
WECI .... Richmond, IN [*FM radio station call letters*]
WECI .... WEC International (EA)
WECK .... Cheektowaga, NY [*AM radio station call letters*]
WECL .... Elk Mound, WI [*FM radio station call letters*]

WECM.......... Milton, FL [*AM radio station call letters*]
WECM.......... Warranted Existing Class Maintained (DS)
WECN.......... Naranjito, PR [*Television station call letters*]
WECO.......... Wartburg, TN [*AM radio station call letters*]
WECO.......... Western Electric Co. (MCD)
WECO.......... Westinghouse Electric Corp.
WECO-FM.... Wartburg, TN [*FM radio station call letters*]
WECOM....... Weapons Command [*Later, Armaments Command*] [*Army*]
WECON........ Weather Controlled Messages (NVT)
WECPNL...... Weighted Equivalent Continuous Perceived Noise Level
WECQ.......... Clyde, NY [*FM radio station call letters*]
WECR.......... Beech Mountain, NC [*FM radio station call letters*]
WECR-AM.... Newland, NC [*AM radio station call letters*] (RBYB)
WECS.......... Water-Glycol Evaporator Control System (SAA)
WECS.......... Willimantic, CT [*FM radio station call letters*]
WECS.......... Wind Energy Conversion System
WECST........ Waste Evaporator Condensate Storage Tank [*Nuclear energy*] (NRCH)
WECT.......... Wilmington, NC [*Television station call letters*]
WECU.......... Peoria, IL [*FM radio station call letters*]
WECV.......... Chippewa Valley Museum, Eau Claire, WI [*Library symbol Library of Congress*] (LCLS)
WECW.......... Elmira, NY [*FM radio station call letters*]
WECZ.......... Punxsutawney, PA [*AM radio station call letters*]
WED............ Walter Elias Disney [*These initials also identify the theme park division of Walt Disney Enterprises*]
WED............ War Emergency Dose (DEN)
WED............ Water Enforcement Division [*Environmental Protection Agency*] (EPA)
WED............ Weak Exchange Degeneracy [*Particle physics*] (OA)
WED............ Weapons Engineering Duty [*Navy*] (NG)
WED............ Wedau [*Papua New Guinea*] [*Airport symbol*] (OAG)
WED............ Wednesday (EY)
Wed............ Wednesday (ODBW)
WED............ West Delta Resources Ltd. [*Vancouver Stock Exchange symbol*]
WED............ Work Force Effectiveness and Development Group [*Office of Personnel Management*] (GRD)
WED............ World Environment Day
WEDA.......... Western Dredging Association (EA)
WEDA.......... Wholesale Egg Distributors' Association [*British*] (BI)
WEDA.......... Women's Enterprise Development Agency [*Established in 1987*] [*British*]
WEDAC........ Westinghouse Digital Airborne Computer
WEDC.......... Chicago, IL [*AM radio station call letters*]
WEDC.......... Wedco Technologies [*NASDAQ symbol*] (SAG)
Wedco.......... Wedco Technologies [*Associated Press*] (SAG)
WEDCOM..... Weapon Effects on D-Region Communications [*Computer code*]
WEDD-FM.... Englewood, FL [*FM radio station call letters*] (RBYB)
WEDG.......... Buffalo, NY [*FM radio station call letters*] (RBYB)
WEDG.......... Women's Education Group (AIE)
Wedg & Hom... Wedgwood and Homan's Manual for Notaries and Bankers [*A publication*] (DLA)
WEDGE........ Waterless Electrical Data Generating Effortless
WEDGE........ Weapon Development Glide Entry
WEDGE........ Western Education Development Group [*University of British Columbia*] [*Canada Research center*]
Wedg Gov & Laws... Wedgwood on American Government and Laws [*A publication*] (DLA)
Wedgw Dict Eng Etymology... Wedgwood's Dictionary of English Etymology [*A publication*] (DLA)
WEDH.......... Hartford, CT [*Television station call letters*]
WEDJ.......... Charlotte, NC [*FM radio station call letters*]
WEDM.......... Indianapolis, IN [*FM radio station call letters*]
WEDN.......... Norwich, CT [*Television station call letters*]
WEDO.......... McKeesport, PA [*AM radio station call letters*]
WEDO.......... Women's Environment and Development Organization
WEDR.......... Miami, FL [*FM radio station call letters*]
WEDS.......... Weapons Effect Display System [*AEC*]
Weds.......... Wednesday (ODBW)
WEDSS........ Whole Earth Decision Support System (EERA)
WEDU.......... Tampa, FL [*Television station call letters*]
WEDW.......... Bridgeport, CT [*Television station call letters*]
WEDW.......... Stamford, CT [*FM radio station call letters*]
WEDY.......... New Haven, CT [*Television station call letters*]
WEE............ Western Equine Encephalitis [*Virus*] (DAVI)
WEE............ Western Equine Encephalomyelitis [*Virus*]
WEE............ Wind Erosion Equation (EERA)
WEE............ Work Experience Education (DNAB)
WEEA.......... Women's Educational Equity Act [*1974*]
WEEB.......... Southern Pines, NC [*AM radio station call letters*]
WEEC.......... Springfield, OH [*FM radio station call letters*]
WEECN........ Women's Educational Equity Communications Network [*Defunct*]
WEED.......... Rocky Mount, NC [*AM radio station call letters*]
WEEF.......... Highland Park, IL [*AM radio station call letters*]
WEEF.......... Western Electric Educational Fund
WEEI.......... Boston, MA [*AM radio station call letters*]
WEEJ.......... Port Charlotte, FL [*FM radio station call letters*]
WEEK.......... Peoria, IL [*Television station call letters*]
Week Cin LB... Weekly Cincinnati Law Bulletin [*A publication*] (DLA)
Week Dig..... New York Weekly Digest [*A publication*] (DLA)
Week Dig (NY)... New York Weekly Digest [*A publication*] (DLA)
Week Jur..... Weekly Jurist [*Bloomington, IL*] [*A publication*] (DLA)
Week Law & Bk Bull... Weekly Law and Bank Bulletin [*A publication*] (DLA)
Week Law Bull... Weekly Law Bulletin and Ohio Law Journal [*A publication*] (DLA)
Week Law Gaz... Weekly Law Gazette [*Ohio*] [*A publication*] (DLA)
Week L Gaz... Weekly Law Gazette [*Ohio*] [*A publication*] (DLA)
Week L Mag... Weekly Law Magazine [*1842-43*] [*A publication*] (DLA)
Week LR...... Weekly Law Reports [*A publication*] (DLA)
Week L Rec... Weekly Law Record [*A publication*] (DLA)
Week L Record... Weekly Law Record [*A publication*] (DLA)
Week LR (Eng)... Weekly Law Reports (England) [*A publication*] (DLA)
Week L Rev... Weekly Law Review [*San Francisco*] [*A publication*] (DLA)
Weekly Cin Law Bull... Cincinnati Weekly Law Bulletin [*A publication*] (DLA)
Weekly Law B... Weekly Law Bulletin [*Ohio*] [*A publication*] (DLA)
Weekly L Bull... Weekly Law Bulletin [*England*] [*A publication*] (DLA)
Weekly LR... Weekly Law Reports [*England*] [*A publication*] (DLA)
Weekly NC... Weekly Notes of Cases [*Pennsylvania*] [*A publication*] (DLA)
Week No...... Weekly Notes of Cases [*Pennsylvania*] [*A publication*] (DLA)
Week No...... Weekly Notes of Cases (Law Reports) [*England*] [*A publication*] (DLA)
Week No Cas... Weekly Notes of Cases [*Pennsylvania*] [*A publication*] (DLA)
Week No Cas... Weekly Notes of Cases (Law Reports) [*England*] [*A publication*] (DLA)
Week Notes Cas... Weekly Notes of Cases (Law Reports) [*England*] [*A publication*] (DLA)
Week R........ Weekly Reporter [*1853-1906*] [*A publication*] (DLA)
Week R (Eng)... Weekly Reporter (England) [*A publication*] (DLA)
Week Rep.... Weekly Reporter [*England*] [*A publication*] (DLA)
Week Reptr... Weekly Reporter [*London*] [*A publication*] (DLA)
Week Reptr... Weekly Reporter [*Bengal*] [*A publication*] (DLA)
Weeks......... Weeks Corp. [*Associated Press*] (SAG)
Weeks Att at Law... Weeks on Attorneys at Law [*A publication*] (DLA)
Weeks DA Inj... Weeks' Damnum Absque Injuria [*A publication*] (DLA)
Weeks Dep... Weeks on Depositions [*A publication*] (DLA)
Weeks Min... Weeks on Mines and Mineral Law [*A publication*] (DLA)
Weeks Min Leg... Weeks' Mining Legislation of Congress [*A publication*] (DLA)
Week Trans Rep... Weekly Transcript Reports [*New York*] [*A publication*] (DLA)
Week Trans Repts... Weekly Transcript Reports [*New York*] [*A publication*] (DLA)
WEEL........... Shadyside, OH [*FM radio station call letters*]
WEEL........... Workplace Environmental Exposure Level [*A guide series published by the AIHA - American Industrial Hygiene Association*] [*A publication*]
WEEM.......... Pendleton, IN [*FM radio station call letters*]
WEEN........... Lafayette, TN [*AM radio station call letters*]
WEEP........... Women's Educational Equity Program (EA)
WEEP........... Work Experience on Employer's Premises [*Manpower Services Commission*] [*British*] (DI)
Weer............ Weerakoon's Appeal Court Reports [*Ceylon*] [*A publication*] (DLA)
WEER........... Welfare Entered Employment Rate [*Job Training and Partnership Act*] (OICC)
WEERC......... Western Electric Engineering Research Center (IAA)
WEETAG....... Women's Employment, Education, and Training Advisory Group (EERA)
WEEU........... Reading, PA [*AM radio station call letters*]
WEEX-AM..... Easton, PA [*AM radio station call letters*] (RBYB)
WEEZ........... Heidelberg, MS [*FM radio station call letters*]
WEF............. WAND [*Women's Action for Nuclear Disarmament*] Education Fund (EA)
WEF............. War Emergency Formula
WEF............. Waste Environmental Federation
WEF............. Water Emersion Facility
WEF............. Water Environment Federation (EAIO)
WEF............. With Effect From
WEF............. Women's Employment Federation [*British*] (BI)
WEF............. World Economic Forum (EAIO)
WEF............. World Education Fellowship (EA)
WEF............. World Evangelical Fellowship (EA)
WEF............. Write End of File (SAA)
WEFA........... Wharton Econometric Forecasting Association [*FAA*] (TAG)
WEFAX......... Weather Facsimile (EERA)
WEFAX......... Weather Facsimile Experiment [*Environmental Science Services Administration*]
WEFC........... Roanoke, VA [*Television station call letters*]
WEFC........... Weather Facsimile [*Environmental Science Services Administration*] (IAA)
WEFC........... Wells Financial [*NASDAQ symbol*] (TTSB)
WEFC........... Wells Financial Corp. [*NASDAQ symbol*] (SAG)
WEFG........... Whitehall, MI [*AM radio station call letters*]
WEFG-FM..... Whitehall, MI [*FM radio station call letters*]
WEFM........... Michigan City, IN [*FM radio station call letters*]
WEFR........... Erie, PA [*FM radio station call letters*]
WEFT........... Champaign, IL [*FM radio station call letters*]
WEFT........... Wings, Engines, Fuselage, Tail [*System for identifying aircraft*]
WEFX........... Norwalk, CT [*FM radio station call letters*]
WEG............. Washington Energy [*NYSE symbol*] (TTSB)
WEG............. Washington Energy Co. [*NYSE symbol*] (SPSG)
WEG............. Weapons Evaluation Group [*Military*]
WEG............. Wind Energy Generator
WEGA........... Vega Baja, PR [*AM radio station call letters*]
WEGC........... Sasser, GA [*FM radio station call letters*] (RBYB)
WEGE........... Crossville, TN [*FM radio station call letters*]
Wegenr........ Wegener Corp. [*Associated Press*] (SAG)
WEGG........... Rose Hill, NC [*AM radio station call letters*]
WEGK-FM..... Starview, PA [*FM radio station call letters*] (RBYB)
WEGL........... Auburn, AL [*FM radio station call letters*]
WEGM........... Hormigueros, PR [*FM radio station call letters*]
WEGO........... Concord, NC [*AM radio station call letters*]
WEGP........... Presque Isle, ME [*AM radio station call letters*]
WEGQ........... Lawrence, MA [*FM radio station call letters*]
WEGR........... Memphis, TN [*FM radio station call letters*]

WEGS .... Milton, FL [*FM radio station call letters*]
WEGS .... Western European Geological Survey (EERA)
WEGW .... Wheeling, WV [*FM radio station call letters*]
WEGX .... Dillong, SC [*FM radio station call letters*]
WEGZ .... Washburn, WI [*FM radio station call letters*]
WEH .... Walter and Eliza Hall Institute of Medical Research [*Australia*]
WE-H .... Weapons Employment Handbook [*DASA*] (MCD)
WEHC .... Emory, VA [*FM radio station call letters*]
WEHH .... Elmira Heights-Horseheads, NY [*AM radio station call letters*]
WEHM .... East Hampton, NY [*FM radio station call letters*]
WEHO .... Westwood Homestead Financial Corp. [*NASDAQ symbol*] (SAG)
WEHR .... Shepherdsville, KY [*FM radio station call letters*]
WEHS .... Aurora, IL [*Television station call letters*]
WEHT .... Evansville, IN [*Television station call letters*]
WEI .... Immanuel Lutheran College, Eau Claire, WI [*Library symbol Library of Congress*] (LCLS)
WEI .... Weapon Effectiveness Index (MCD)
WEI .... Weipa [*Australia Airport symbol*] (OAG)
WEI .... Western European Institute for Wood Preservation (EAIO)
WEI .... Women Employed Institute (EA)
WEI .... Wood Energy Institute [*Later, WHA*] (EA)
WEI .... Work Experience Instructor (OICC)
WEI .... World Education (EA)
WEI .... World Environment Institute
WEI .... Wound Elastomeric Insulation (MCD)
WEIB .... Northampton, MA [*FM radio station call letters*]
WEIC .... Charleston, IL [*AM radio station call letters*]
WEICO .... Westinghouse Electric International Co. (IAA)
Weight M & L ... Weightman's Marriage and Legitimacy [*1871*] [*A publication*] (DLA)
Weight Med Leg Gaz ... Weightman's Medico-Legal Gazette [*A publication*] (DLA)
WEI/IEO .... Western European Institute for Wood Preservation/Institut de l'Europe Occidentale pour l'Impregnation du Bois (EAIO)
WEIL .... Weil-Felix [*Test*] [*Laboratory science*] (DAVI)
WEIM .... Fitchburg, MA [*AM radio station call letters*]
WeinRI .... Weingarten Realty, Inc. [*Associated Press*] (SAG)
WEIO .... Eau Claire, WI [*AM radio station call letters*]
WEIQ .... Mobile, AL [*Television station call letters*]
Weir .... Weir's Criminal Rulings [*India*] [*A publication*] (DLA)
WEIR .... Weirton, WV [*AM radio station call letters*]
Weirt .... Weirton Steel Corp. [*Associated Press*] (SAG)
WEIS .... Centre, AL [*AM radio station call letters*]
WEIS .... World Event/Interaction Survey (DNAB)
WeisMk .... Weis Markets, Inc. [*Associated Press*] (SAG)
Weitek .... Weitek Corp. [*Associated Press*] (SAG)
WeitzrH .... Weitzer Homebuilders, Inc. [*Associated Press*] (SAG)
WEIU .... Charleston, IL [*FM radio station call letters*]
WEIU .... Women's Educational and Industrial Union (EA)
WEIU-TV .... Charleston, IL [*Television station call letters*]
WEI/WUV .... Weapons Effectiveness Indices/Weighted Unit Values [*Military*]
WEJ .... West Air Sweden AB [*ICAO designator*] (FAAC)
WEJC .... Lexington, NC [*Television station call letters*]
WEJE .... Churubusco, IN [*FM radio station call letters*] (RBYB)
WEJF .... Palm Bay, FL [*FM radio station call letters*]
WEJL .... Scranton, PA [*AM radio station call letters*]
WEJM .... Chicago, IL [*AM radio station call letters*]
WEJM .... Lansing, IL [*FM radio station call letters*]
WEJT .... Shelbyville, IL [*FM radio station call letters*]
WEJY .... Monroe, MI [*FM radio station call letters*]
WEJZ .... Jacksonville, FL [*FM radio station call letters*]
WEK .... Wewak [*Papua New Guinea*] [*Seismograph station code, US Geological Survey*] (SEIS)
WEKC .... Williamsburg, KY [*AM radio station call letters*]
WEKG .... Jackson, KY [*AM radio station call letters*]
WEKH .... Hazard, KY [*FM radio station call letters*]
WEKL .... Augusta, GA [*FM radio station call letters*]
WEKO .... Cabo Rojo, PR [*AM radio station call letters*]
WEKR .... Fayetteville, TN [*AM radio station call letters*]
WEKS .... Zebulon, GA [*FM radio station call letters*]
WEKT .... Elkton, KY [*AM radio station call letters*]
WEKU .... Richmond, KY [*FM radio station call letters*]
WEKW .... Keene, NH [*Television station call letters*]
WEKX .... Jellico, TN [*FM radio station call letters*]
WEKY .... Richmond, KY [*AM radio station call letters*]
WEKZ .... Monroe, WI [*AM radio station call letters*]
WEKZ-FM .... Monroe, WI [*FM radio station call letters*]
WEL .... Luther Hospital, Eau Claire, WI [*Library symbol Library of Congress*] (LCLS)
WEl .... Matheson Memorial Library, Elkhorn, WI [*Library symbol Library of Congress*] (LCLS)
WEL .... Warren Explorations Ltd. [*Toronto Stock Exchange symbol*]
WEL .... Weapons Effects Laboratory [*Army*] (RDA)
WEL .... Weapons/Equipment List
WEL .... Welfare
WEL .... Welkom [*South Africa*] [*Airport symbol*] (OAG)
WEL .... Wellcome Ltd. [*NYSE symbol*] (SPSG)
WEL .... Wellesley College, Wellesley, MA [*OCLC symbol*] (OCLC)
WEL .... Wellesley Hospital, Toronto [*UTLAS symbol*]
WEL .... Wellington [*New Zealand*] [*Seismograph station code, US Geological Survey*] (SEIS)
wel .... Welsh [*MARC language code Library of Congress*] (LCCP)
Wel .... Welsh's Irish Registry Cases [*A publication*] (DLA)
WEL .... Welt-Eis-Lehre [*Cosmic Ice Theory*] [*German*]
WELA .... East Liverpool, OH [*FM radio station call letters*]
WELAC .... Western European Laboratory Accreditation Co-operation (ACII)
WELB .... Elba, AL [*AM radio station call letters*]
WELC .... Welch, WV [*AM radio station call letters*]
WELC .... Welcome Home [*NASDAQ symbol*] (TTSB)
WELC .... Welcome Home, Inc. [*NASDAQ symbol*] (SAG)
WELC .... World Electrotechnical Congress (PDAA)
WELC-FM .... Welch, WV [*FM radio station call letters*]
WEICL .... Walworth County Law Library, Elkhorn, WI [*Library symbol Library of Congress*] (LCLS)
WELCO .... Westinghouse Electric Company
WelcomH .... Welcome Home, Inc. [*Associated Press*] (SAG)
WELD .... Fisher, WV [*AM radio station call letters*]
WELD .... Petersburg, WV [*FM radio station call letters*]
WELD .... Welding
Weldtrn .... Weldotron Corp. [*Associated Press*] (SAG)
WELE .... Ormond Beach, FL [*AM radio station call letters*]
WELF .... Dalton, GA [*Television station call letters*]
WelF .... Wells Fargo & Co. [*Associated Press*] (SAG)
WELF .... Woman's Education and Leadership Forum (EA)
Welfare L Bull ... Welfare Law Bulletin [*A publication*] (DLA)
Welfare L News ... Welfare Law News [*A publication*] (DLA)
Welf Eq .... Welford's Equity Pleadings [*1842*] [*A publication*] (DLA)
Welf News ... Welfare News [*A publication*]
WELG .... Rogers City, MI [*FM radio station call letters*] (RBYB)
WelGrd .... Wells-Gardner Electronics Corp. [*Associated Press*] (SAG)
WELH .... Luther Hospital, Eau Claire, WI [*Library symbol*] [*Library of Congress*] (LCLS)
WELH .... Providence, RI [*FM radio station call letters*]
WELI .... New Haven, CT [*AM radio station call letters*]
WELK .... Elkins, WV [*FM radio station call letters*]
WELL .... Battle Creek, MI [*AM radio station call letters*]
WEIL .... Lakeland Hospital, Elkhorn, WI [*Library symbol Library of Congress*] (LCLS)
WELL .... Marshall, MI [*FM radio station call letters*]
WELL .... Well [*Commonly used*] (OPSA)
WELL .... Wellcare Management Group [*NASDAQ symbol*] (SAG)
Well .... Wellington [*New Zealand*] (BARN)
WELL .... Whole Earth Lectronic Link [*Telecommunications*]
WEILC .... Lakeland Counseling Center, Elkhorn, WI [*Library symbol Library of Congress*] (LCLS)
Wellco .... Wellco Enterprises, Inc. [*Associated Press*] (SAG)
Wellcome .... Wellcome Ltd. [*Associated Press*] (SAG)
WELLE .... WellCare Management Group [*NASDAQ symbol*] (TTSB)
WellHall .... Wellington Hall Ltd. [*Associated Press*] (SAG)
Well High .... Wellbeloved on Highways [*1829*] [*A publication*] (DLA)
WellMgt .... Wellcare Management Group [*Associated Press*] (SAG)
Wellmn .... Wellman, Inc. [*Associated Press*] (SAG)
WELLS .... Wells [*Commonly used*] (OPSA)
WellsF .... Wells Fargo & Co. [*Associated Press*] (SAG)
WellsFn .... Wells Financial Corp. [*Associated Press*] (SAG)
Wells Inst Juries ... Wells on Instruction to Juries and Bills of Exception [*A publication*] (DLA)
Wells Jur .... Wells on the Jurisdiction of Courts [*A publication*] (DLA)
Wells L & F ... Well's Questions of Law and Facts [*A publication*] (DLA)
Wells Mar Wom ... Wells on the Separate Property of Married Women [*A publication*] (DLA)
Wells Rep .... Wells on Replevin [*A publication*] (DLA)
Wells Repl ... Wells on Replevin [*A publication*] (DLA)
Wells' Res Ad ... Wells' Res Adjudicata and Stare Decisis [*A publication*] (DLA)
Wellw Abr .... Wellwood's Abridgment of Sea Laws [*A publication*] (DLA)
WELM .... Elmira, NY [*AM radio station call letters*]
WELO .... Tupelo, MS [*AM radio station call letters*]
WelptHlt .... Wellpoint Health Networks [*Associated Press*] (SAG)
WELR .... Roanoke, AL [*AM radio station call letters*]
WELR-FM .... Roanoke, AL [*FM radio station call letters*]
WELS .... Kinston, NC [*AM radio station call letters*]
WELS .... Wisconsin Evangelical Lutheran Synod
WELS .... World-Wide Engineering Logistics Support [*Military*]
Welsb H & G ... Welsby, Hurlstone, and Gordon's English Exchequer Reports [*1848-56*] [*A publication*] (DLA)
Welsb Hurl & G ... Welsby, Hurlstone, and Gordon's English Exchequer Reports [*1848-56*] [*A publication*] (DLA)
Welsby H & G ... Welsby, Hurlstone, and Gordon's English Exchequer Reports [*1848-56*] [*A publication*] (DLA)
Welsby H & G (Eng) ... Welsby, Hurlstone, and Gordon's English Exchequer Reports [*1848-56*] [*A publication*] (DLA)
Welsf .... Wellsford Residential Property [*Associated Press*] (SAG)
Welsfd .... Wellsford Residential Property [*Associated Press*] (SAG)
Welsh .... Welsh's Irish Case at Siligo [*1838*] [*A publication*] (DLA)
Welsh .... Welsh's Irish Case of James Feighny [*1838*] [*A publication*] (DLA)
Welsh .... Welsh's Irish Registry Cases [*A publication*] (DLA)
Welsh Reg Cas ... Welsh's Irish Registry Cases [*A publication*] (DLA)
WELU .... Aguadilla, PR [*Television station call letters*]
WELV .... Ellenville, NY [*AM radio station call letters*]
WELW .... Willoughby-Eastlake, OH [*AM radio station call letters*]
WELX .... Callahan, FL [*AM radio station call letters*]
WELY .... Ely, MN [*AM radio station call letters*]
WELY-FM .... Ely, MN [*FM radio station call letters*]
WELZ .... Belzoni, MS [*AM radio station call letters*]
WEM .... War Eagle Mining Co. [*Vancouver Stock Exchange symbol*]
WEM .... Welfare of Enlisted Men [*Air Force*]
WEM .... Western European Metal Trades Employers Organization [*Cologne, Federal Republic of Germany*] (EA)
WeM .... Western Microfilm Ltd., Edmonton, AB, Canada [*Library symbol Library of Congress*] (LCLS)
WEM .... West Essex Militia [*British*]

WEM .... White European Male [*Lifestyle classification*] (ECON)
WEM .... Wireless and Electrical Mechanic [*British*] (DSUE)
WEM .... Workshops in Emergency Management [*RSPA*] (TAG)
WEM .... World's Epoch Makers [*A publication*]
WEM .... Woven Elastic Manufacturers Association [*Later, EFMCNTA*] (MSA)
WEMA .... Western Electronic Manufacturers Association [*Later, AEA*] (EA)
WEMA .... Winding Engine Manufacturers' Association [*British*] (BI)
WEMA .... Woven Elastic Manufacturers Association [*Later, EFMCNTA*] (EA)
WEMB .... Erwin, TN [*AM radio station call letters*]
WEMBA .... Weekend Executive Master of Business Administration (PGP)
WEMC .... Harrisonburg, VA [*FM radio station call letters*]
WEMD .... Western Electronics Maintenance Depot
WEMG .... Crete, IL [*FM radio station call letters*]
WEMG .... Knoxville, TN [*AM radio station call letters*]
WEMI .... Appleton, WI [*FM radio station call letters*] (RBYB)
WEMJ .... Laconia, NH [*AM radio station call letters*]
WEMM .... Huntington, WV [*FM radio station call letters*]
WEMOS .... International Women's Network on Pharmaceuticals [*Amsterdam, Netherlands*] (EAIO)
WEMP .... Milwaukee, WI [*AM radio station call letters*]
WEMR .... Tunkhannock, PA [*AM radio station call letters*]
WEMR .... Welding Equipment Maintenance and Repair [*UAW job classification*]
WEMR-FM .... Tunkhannock, PA [*FM radio station call letters*] (RBYB)
WEMSB .... Western European Military Supply Board [*NATO*] (NATG)
WEMT .... Greeneville, TN [*Television station call letters*]
WEMU .... Ypsilanti, MI [*FM radio station call letters*]
WEMX .... Ravena, NY [*FM radio station call letters*]
WEN .... Papa Westray [*Orkney Islands, Scotland*] [*Airport symbol*] (AD)
WEN .... Waive Exchange If Necessary
Wen .... Wendell's Reports [*New York*] [*A publication*] (DLA)
wen .... Wendic [*MARC language code Library of Congress*] (LCCP)
WEN .... Wendy's International, Inc. [*NYSE symbol*] (SPSG)
WEN .... Wendy's Intl [*NYSE symbol*] (TTSB)
WEN .... Wenkite [*A zeolite*]
WEN .... Wentworth Institute of Technology, Boston, MA [*OCLC symbol*] (OCLC)
WEN .... Wentworth Public Library [*UTLAS symbol*]
WEN .... Worldmark Encyclopedia of the Nations [*A publication*]
WEN .... Write Enable [*Computer science*] (IAA)
WENA .... Yauco, PR [*AM radio station call letters*]
WenBr .... Wendt Bristol Health Service [*Associated Press*] (SAG)
WENC .... Whiteville, NC [*AM radio station call letters*]
W/ENCL .... With Enclosure (DNAB)
WEND .... Salisbury, NC [*FM radio station call letters*] (RBYB)
Wend .... Wendell's Reports [*1826-41*] [*New York*] [*A publication*] (DLA)
WEND .... Wendover [*England*]
WENDB .... Water Enforcement National Data Base (GNE)
Wend Bl .... Wendell's Blackstone [*A publication*] (DLA)
Wendel .... Wendell's Reports [*New York*] [*A publication*] (DLA)
Wendell .... Wendell's Reports [*1826-41*] [*New York*] [*A publication*] (DLA)
Wendell Rep ... Wendell's Reports [*New York*] [*A publication*] (DLA)
Wendell's Rep ... Wendell's Reports [*New York*] [*A publication*] (DLA)
Wend (NY) ..... Wendell's Reports [*1826-41*] [*New York*] [*A publication*] (DLA)
Wend R .... Wendell's Reports [*New York*] [*A publication*] (DLA)
Wend Rep ...... Wendell's Reports [*New York*] [*A publication*] (DLA)
WENDS .... World Energy Data System [*Department of Energy*] [*Information service or system*] (IID)
Wendt .... Wendt's Reports of Cases [*Ceylon*] [*A publication*] (DLA)
WendtBr .... Wendt Bristol Health Service [*Associated Press*] (SAG)
Wendt Mar Leg ... Wendt's Maritime Legislation [*3rd ed.*] [*1888*] [*A publication*] (DLA)
Wendy .... Wendys International [*Associated Press*] (SAG)
Wendys .... Wendys International, Inc. [*Associated Press*] (SAG)
WENE .... Endicott, NY [*AM radio station call letters*]
WENELA .... Witwatersrand Native Labour Association [*Nyasaland*]
WENG .... Englewood, FL [*AM radio station call letters*]
WENH .... Durham, NH [*Television station call letters*]
WENK .... Union City, TN [*AM radio station call letters*]
WENN .... Birmingham, AL [*FM radio station call letters*]
WENO .... Nashville, TN [*AM radio station call letters*]
WENOA .... Weekly Notice to Airmen [*FAA*]
WENR .... Englewood, TN [*AM radio station call letters*]
WENS .... Shelbyville, IN [*FM radio station call letters*]
WENS .... World Electroless Nickel Society [*Defunct*] (EA)
WENT .... Gloversville, NY [*AM radio station call letters*]
W Ent .... Winch's Book of Entries [*A publication*] (DLA)
WENU .... Hudson Falls, NY [*FM radio station call letters*]
WENY .... Elmira, NY [*AM radio station call letters*]
WENY-FM .... Elmira, NY [*FM radio station call letters*]
WENY-TV .... Elmira, NY [*Television station call letters*]
WENZ .... Cleveland, OH [*FM radio station call letters*]
Wenz .... Wenzell's Reports [*60 Minnesota*] [*A publication*] (DLA)
WEO .... War Economic Operation [*World War II*]
WEO .... Warehouse Economy Outlet [*A & P Co.*]
WEO .... Weaco Resources Ltd. [*Vancouver Stock Exchange symbol*]
WEO .... Weapons Engineer Officer [*British military*] (DMA)
WEO .... Western Europe and Others [*United Nations*]
WEO .... Where Economy Originates [*A & P Co. marketing slogan, now obsolete*]
WEO .... World Energy Outlook [*International Energy Agency*]
WEOG .... Western European and Others Group [*United Nations*]
WEOK .... Poughkeepsie, NY [*AM radio station call letters*]
WEOL .... Elyria, OH [*AM radio station call letters*]
WEOS .... Geneva, NY [*FM radio station call letters*]
WEOS .... Water Extraction of Orange Solids [*Citrus processing*]
WEOW .... Key West, FL [*FM radio station call letters*]
WEOW .... Weapons Engineer Officer's Writer [*British military*] (DMA)
WEOZ .... Saegertown, PA [*FM radio station call letters*]
WEP .... War and Emergency Plan [*DoD*]
WEP .... Water Electrolysis Plenum
WEP .... Water Entry Point [*Navy*] (CAAL)
WEP .... Water-Extended Polyester
WEP .... Weak Equivalence Principle [*Gravity*]
WEP .... Weam [*Papua New Guinea*] [*Airport symbol*] (OAG)
WEP .... Weapon
WEP .... Weather Processor (MCD)
WEP .... Weekend Pass (DAVI)
WEP .... Windfall Elimination Provision (GFGA)
WEP .... Windows Entertainment Pack [*Computer science*]
WEP .... Wisconsin Experiment Package [*NASA*] (MCD)
WEP .... Women's Equity Program [*Defunct*] (EA)
WEP .... Work Experience Program [*Department of Labor*]
WEP .... World Economic Prospects (NITA)
WEP .... World Employment Program [*of the International Labour Organization*] [*Geneva, Switzerland*] [*United Nations*]
WEP .... Writing, Editing, and Publishing
WEPA .... Eupora, MS [*AM radio station call letters*]
WEPA .... Welded Electronic Packaging Association
WEPC .... Belton, SC [*FM radio station call letters*]
WEPC .... Weapons and Equipment Policy Committee [*British*] (RDA)
WEPCOSE .... Weapon Control Systems Engineering [*Navy*] (NG)
WEPEX .... Weapons Exercise [*Navy*] (NVT)
WEPG .... South Pittsburg, TN [*AM radio station call letters*]
WE/PGM .... Write Enable/Program [*Computer science*]
WEPH .... Weapon Phenomenology (RDA)
WEPM .... Martinsburg, WV [*AM radio station call letters*]
WEPOCS .... Western Equatorial Pacific Ocean Circulation Study (USDC)
WEPOCS .... Western Equatorial Pacific Ocean Climate Studies [*USA-Australia*] [*Marine science*] (OSRA)
WEPR .... Greenville, SC [*FM radio station call letters*]
WEPR .... Women Executives in Public Relations [*New York, NY*] (EA)
WEPREC .... West Pakistan Research and Evaluation Center
WEPS .... Elgin, IL [*FM radio station call letters*]
WEPS .... Weapons and Equipment Policy Statement [*Australia*]
WEPS .... Weapons System [*Navy*]
WEPSO .... Naval Weapons Services Office [*Also known as NAVWPNSERVO, NWSO*]
WEPTA .... War Excess Profits Tax Act [*1917*]
WEPTAC .... Weapons and Tactics Analysis Center [*Navy*] (MCD)
WEPTRAEX ...... Weapons Training Exercise (NVT)
WEPTU .... Weapons Reserve Training Units [*Navy*]
WEPU .... Weighted Elementary Pupil Unit [*Education*] (AEE)
WEPZA .... World Export Processing Zones Association [*Flagstaff, AZ*] (EA)
WEQ .... Wind Erosion Equation
WEQR .... Goldsboro, NC [*FM radio station call letters*]
WEQX .... Manchester, VT [*FM radio station call letters*]
WER .... Water Electrolysis Rocket
WER .... Weight Estimating Relationship (KSC)
WER .... Werombi [*Australia Seismograph station code, US Geological Survey*] (SEIS)
WER .... Whole Earth Review [*A publication*] (BRI)
WERA .... Plainfield, NJ [*AM radio station call letters*]
WERA .... Western Eastern Roadracers Association (EA)
WERA .... Western/English Retailers of America [*Defunct*] (EA)
WERA .... World Energy Research Authority
WERB .... Berlin, CT [*FM radio station call letters*]
WERC .... Birmingham, AL [*AM radio station call letters*]
WERC .... Warehousing Education and Research Council (EA)
WERC .... Waste Management Education and Research Consortium [*New Mexico State University*] [*Research center*] (RCD)
WERC .... Women's Education Resource Centre [*Women's Education Group*] [*British*] (CB)
WERC .... World Environment and Resources Council [*Louvain, Belgium*] (EAIO)
WERD .... East Point, GA [*AM radio station call letters*] (RBYB)
WERE .... Cleveland, OH [*AM radio station call letters*]
WERG .... Erie, PA [*FM radio station call letters*]
WERH .... Hamilton, AL [*AM radio station call letters*]
WERH-FM .... Hamilton, AL [*FM radio station call letters*]
WERI .... Water and Energy Research Institute of the Western Pacific [*University of Guam*] [*Guam*] [*Research center*] (RCD)
WERI .... Westerly, RI [*AM radio station call letters*]
WERK .... Muncie, IN [*AM radio station call letters*]
WERK-FM .... Muncie, IN [*FM radio station call letters*]
WERL .... Eagle River, WI [*AM radio station call letters*]
WERL .... Water Engineering Research Laboratory [*Cincinnati, OH*] [*Environmental Protection Agency*] (GRD)
WERM .... World Encyclopedia of Recorded Music, 1925-55 [*A publication*]
WERN .... Madison, WI [*FM radio station call letters*]
WERN .... Werner Enterprises [*NASDAQ symbol*] (TTSB)
WERN .... Werner Enterprises, Inc. [*Omaha, NE*] [*NASDAQ symbol*] (NQ)
Werner .... Werner Enterprises, Inc. [*Associated Press*] (SAG)
WERO-FM .... Washington, NC [*FM radio station call letters*] (RBYB)
WERP .... Women's Economic Rights Project (EA)
WERPG .... Western European Regional Planning Group [*NATO*] (NATG)
WERQ .... Baltimore, MD [*FM radio station call letters*]
WERR .... Utuado, PR [*FM radio station call letters*]
WERS .... Boston, MA [*FM radio station call letters*]
WERS .... War Emergency Radio Service
WERS .... Weapons Effect Reporting Station [*Civil defense*]

WERS .... Wing Equipment Repair Squadron
WERSI .... Committee on Women's Employment and Related Social Issues (EA)
WERT........... Paulding, OH [*FM radio station call letters*]
WERT........... Van Wert, OH [*AM radio station call letters*]
WERT........... Women's Economic Round Table (EA)
WERTS .... Writers' Ever-Ready Textual Service [*Rent-A-Script*] [*Satirical*]
WERU .... Blue Hill, ME [*FM radio station call letters*]
WERX .... Edenton, NC [*FM radio station call letters*]
WERZ........... Exeter, NH [*FM radio station call letters*]
WES............ Sacred Heart Hospital, Eau Claire, WI [*Library symbol Library of Congress*] (LCLS)
WES............ Warhead Electrical System
WES............ Washington Ethical Society (EA)
WES............ Water Electrolysis System
WES............ Waterways Experiment Station [*Army Corps of Engineers*] [*Vicksburg, MS*]
WES............ Weapon Electrical System
WES............ Weapon Engineering Station (MCD)
WES............ Weapons Effects Systems (MCD)
WES............ W. E. Schulz & Associates, Inc. [*Telecommunications service*] (TSSD)
WES............ Wesleyan [*A publication*]
WES............ West [*or Western*]
WES............ Westbury [*British depot code*]
WES............ Westcorp, Inc. [*NYSE symbol*] (SPSG)
WES............ Western Equestrian Soceity [*British*] (DBA)
WES............ Western Express Air Lines, Inc. [*Canada*] [*FAA designator*] (FAAC)
WES............ Westmills Carpets Ltd. [*Toronto Stock Exchange symbol*]
WES............ Weston [*Massachusetts*] [*Seismograph station code, US Geological Survey*] (SEIS)
WES............ Westport Public Library, Westport, CT [*OCLC symbol*] (OCLC)
WES............ Wind Electric System [*Telecommunications*] (TEL)
WES............ Wisdom of the East Series [*A publication*]
WES............ Women's Engineering Society (IAA)
WES............ Womens Engineering Society (ACII)
WES............ Work Environment Scale [*Test*]
WES............ World Economic Summit
WES............ Worldmark Encyclopedia of the States [*A publication*]
WES............ World-Wide Education Service [*Parents' National Educational Union*] [*British*]
WES............ Writing Equipment Society [*British*] (DBA)
WESA........... Charleroi, PA [*AM radio station call letters*]
WESA........... White Sands National Monument [*New Mexico*]
WESA........... Wind Energy Society of America [*Inactive*]
WESA........... Wind Energy Systems Act of 1980
WESA-FM...... Charleroi, PA [*FM radio station call letters*]
Wes Aust..... West Australian [*A publication*]
WESB........... Bradford, PA [*AM radio station call letters*]
Wesbanc...... Wesbanco, Inc. [*Associated Press*] (SAG)
WESC........... Greenville, SC [*AM radio station call letters*]
WESC........... Weapon Engagement Simulation Component (MCD)
WESC........... Whole Earth Software Catalog [*A publication*]
WESC........... Wire-Explosion-Spray Coating (PDAA)
WESCAR....... Western Carolines [*Navy*]
WESCARS..... West Coast Amateur Radio Service (PDAA)
WESCARSUBAREA... Western Carolines Subarea [*Navy*]
Wescast....... Wescast Industries, Inc. [*Associated Press*] (SAG)
WESC-FM..... Greenville, SC [*FM radio station call letters*]
Wes CLJ...... Westmoreland County Law Journal [*A publication*] (DLA)
WESCO........ Walnut Export Sales Co. (EA)
Wesco .... Wesco Financial Corp. [*Associated Press*] (SAG)
WESCO........ Westinghouse Corp.
WESCOBASESERVUNIT... West Coast Base Service Unit [*Navy*]
WESCOM..... Weapons System Cost Model
WESCOM..... Western Command [*Army*] (AABC)
WESCON...... Western Electronics Show and Convention [*IEEE*]
WESCOSOUNDSCOL... West Coast Sound School [*Navy*]
W/ESDC....... Weapons/Equipment System Designator Code
WESDET....... Wing Engineer Squadron Detachment (DNAB)
WESDEX...... Western Design Engineering Exposition (PDAA)
WESE........... Baldwyn, MS [*FM radio station call letters*]
WESE........... Wills Eye Society of Ex-Residents (EA)
WESED........ Weapons System Evaluation Division [*DoD*]
WESEG........ Weapons System Evaluation Group [*DoD*]
WESF........... Waste Encapsulation Storage Facility [*Nuclear energy*] (NRCH)
WESG........... Women Executives in State Government (EA)
WESH........... Daytona Beach, FL [*Television station call letters*]
WESIAC........ Weapons Effectiveness Systems Industry Advisory Committee (MCD)
Weskett Ins... Weskett's Complete Digest of the Theory, Laws, and Practice of Insurance [*A publication*] (DLA)
Wesk Ins..... Weskett's Complete Digest of the Theory, Laws, and Practice of Insurance [*A publication*] (DLA)
WESL........... East St. Louis, IL [*AM radio station call letters*]
Wesleyan U... Wesleyan University (GAGS)
WESM.......... Princess Anne, MD [*FM radio station call letters*]
WESN.......... Bloomington, IL [*FM radio station call letters*]
WESO.......... Southbridge, MA [*AM radio station call letters*]
WESO.......... Weapons Engineering Service Office [*DoD*]
WESOS........ Water-Extracted Soluble Orange Solids [*Citrus processing*]
WESP........... Dothan, AL [*FM radio station call letters*]
WESP........... War and Emergency Support Plan [*DoD*]
WESPAR...... Weapon Evaluation System Photographic Analog Recorder (MCD)
WESPEX...... War and Emergency Support Plan Exercise [*DoD*]
WESQ.......... Rocky Mount, NC [*FM radio station call letters*]
WESR.......... Onley-Onancock, VA [*AM radio station call letters*]
WESRAC...... Western Research Application Center [*University of Southern California*]
WESREP...... Weapon Engineering Station Representative (MCD)
Wes Res Law Jo... Western Reserve Law Journal [*A publication*] (DLA)
Wes Res Law Jrl... Western Reserve Law Journal [*Ohio*] [*A publication*] (DLA)
WESR-FM.... Onley-Onancock, VA [*FM radio station call letters*]
WESS........... East Stroudsburg, PA [*FM radio station call letters*]
WESS........... Weapons Effect Signature Simulator
WESS........... Weapons Engagement Scoring System
WESS........... Weapons System Status
WESS........... Western European Specialists Section [*Association of College and Research Libraries*]
WESSAS...... Wisconsin Elementary and Secondary School Accounting System (EDAC)
WESSEAFRON... Western Sea Frontier [*Navy*]
WEST........... Easton, PA [*AM radio station call letters*]
WEST........... Weapons Effectiveness Simulated Threat (MCD)
WEST........... Weapons Exhaust Study [*Military*] (MCD)
West............ Westbury's European Arbitration (Reilly) [*A publication*] (DLA)
West............ West Co., Inc. [*Associated Press*] (SAG)
WEST........... Western Earth Sciences Technologies [*Research center*] (RCD)
WEST........... Western Educational Society for Telecommunications [*Defunct*] (EA)
WEST........... Western Energy Supply and Transmission Associates [*Utility antipollution group*]
West............ Western's London Tithe Cases [*England*] [*A publication*] (DLA)
WEST........... Western Transportation Co. [*Later, WTCO*] [*AAR code*]
West............ Westminster [*Record label*]
West............ Westmoreland County Law Journal [*Pennsylvania*] [*A publication*] (DLA)
WEST........... West One Bancorp [*NASDAQ symbol*] (NQ)
West............ Weston's Reports [*11-14 Vermont*] [*A publication*] (DLA)
West............ West Publishing Co. (AAGC)
West............ West's English Chancery Reports [*A publication*] (DLA)
West............ West's Reports, English House of Lords [*A publication*] (DLA)
WEST........... Women's Enlistment Screening Test [*Military*]
WESTA......... White Sands Electromagnetic Pulse Systems Test Array [*New Mexico*] (RDA)
WestAB........ Westinghouse Air Brake Co. [*Associated Press*] (SAG)
WESTAF....... Western Transport Air Force
WESTAR....... Waterways Experiment Station Terrain Analyzer RADAR
WESTAR....... West Star (NITA)
Westbank..... Westbank Corp. [*Associated Press*] (SAG)
West Car U... Western Carolina University (GAGS)
West Ch....... West's English Chancery Cases [*25 English Reprint*] [*A publication*] (DLA)
West Ch (Eng)... West's English Chancery Cases [*25 English Reprint*] [*A publication*] (DLA)
West Chester U Pa... West Chester University of Pennsylvania (GAGS)
West Chy..... West's English Chancery Cases [*25 English Reprint*] [*A publication*] (DLA)
West Coast Rep... West Coast Reporter [*A publication*] (DLA)
WestcoB....... Westco Bancorp, Inc. [*Associated Press*] (SAG)
WESTCOM... Western Command [*Army*]
West Com.... Western's Commentaries on the Laws of England [*A publication*] (DLA)
WESTCOMMRGN... Western Communications Region [*Air Force*] (AFM)
West Conn St U... Western Connecticut State University (GAGS)
West Co Rep... West Coast Reporter [*A publication*] (DLA)
WestcotC..... Westcott Communications Co. [*Associated Press*] (SAG)
Westcp........ Westcorp, Inc. [*Associated Press*] (SAG)
WESTDIVNAVFACENGCOM... Western Division, Naval Facilities Engineering Command (DNAB)
Westd Zeit... Westdeutsche Zeitschrift fuer Geschichte und Kunst [*A publication*] (OCD)
WESTE......... Weapons Effectiveness and System Test Environment [*Air Force*] (AFM)
WESTEC....... Western Metal and Tool Exposition and Conference [*American Society for Metals*] (TSPED)
Westell........ Westell Technologies, Inc. [*Associated Press*] (SAG)
Westerfed.... Westerfed Financial Corp. [*Associated Press*] (SAG)
Western L Rev... Western Law Review [*Canada*] [*A publication*] (DLA)
Western Reserve LN... Western Reserve Law Notes [*A publication*] (DLA)
West Ext...... West on Extents [*1817*] [*A publication*] (DLA)
WestFidl...... Western Fidelity Funding, Inc. [*Associated Press*] (SAG)
Westfield St C... Westfield State College (GAGS)
WESTFORNET... Western Forestry Information Network [*Forest service*] [*Library network*]
West Ga C... West Georgia College (GAGS)
West HL...... West's Reports, English House of Lords [*A publication*] (DLA)
West II......... Second Statute of Westminster [*A publication*] (DSA)
West Ill U.... Western Illinois University (GAGS)
West Jur...... Western Jurist [*Des Moines, Iowa*] [*A publication*] (DLA)
West Ky U... Western Kentucky University (GAGS)
Westlake Int Private Law... Westlake's Private International Law [*A publication*] (DLA)
WESTLANT... Western Atlantic Area
West Law M... Western Law Monthly [*Ohio*] [*A publication*] (DLA)
West Law Mo... Western Law Monthly (Reprint) [*Ohio*] [*A publication*] (DLA)
West Law Month... Western Law Monthly [*Ohio*] [*A publication*] (DLA)
West Law Rev... Western Law Review [*Canada*] [*A publication*] (DLA)
WestLB........ Westdeutsche Landesbank [*West German bank*]
Westl Confl... Westlake's Conflict of Laws [*A publication*] (DLA)
West Legal Obser... Western Legal Observer [*A publication*] (DLA)
West Leg Obs... Western Legal Observer [*A publication*] (DLA)
West L Gaz... Western Law Gazette [*Cincinnati, OH*] [*A publication*] (DLA)

West LM...... Western Law Monthly [*Ohio*] [*A publication*] (DLA)
West L Mo... Western Law Monthly [*Ohio*] [*A publication*] (DLA)
West L Month... Western Law Monthly [*Ohio*] [*A publication*] (DLA)
Westl Priv Int Law... Westlake's Private International Law [*A publication*] (DLA)
West LR ...... Western Law Reporter [*Canada*] [*A publication*] (DLA)
West LR (Can)... Western Law Reporter [*Canada*] [*A publication*] (DLA)
West L Rev... Western Law Review [*A publication*] (DLA)
West LT....... Western Law Times [*Canada*] [*A publication*] (DLA)
Westly......... Westerly [*A publication*]
Westm......... Westmeath [*County in Ireland*] (WGA)
WESTM........ Westminster [*London*]
Westm......... Westmoreland County Law Journal [*Pennsylvania*] [*A publication*] (DLA)
Westmark.... Westmark Group Holdings, Inc. [*Associated Press*] (SAG)
WESTMD ..... Westmorland [*County in England*]
West Md C... Western Maryland College (GAGS)
Westm Hall Chron... Westminster Hall Chronicle and Legal Examiner [*1835-36*] [*A publication*] (DLA)
West Mich U... Western Michigan University (GAGS)
Westminster C... Westminster College (GAGS)
Westmk........ Westmark Group Holdings, Inc. [*Associated Press*] (SAG)
Westm LJ.... Westmoreland County Law Journal [*A publication*] (DLA)
Westmore Co LJ (PA)... Westmoreland County Law Journal [*Pennsylvania*] [*A publication*] (DLA)
Westmoreland... Westmoreland County Law Journal [*Pennsylvania*] [*A publication*] (DLA)
Westmoreland Co LJ... Westmoreland County Law Journal [*Pennsylvania*] [*A publication*] (DLA)
WESTN .... Western
WESTNAVELEX... Naval Electronics Systems Command, Western Division, Mare Island, Vallejo, California
WESTNAVFACENGCOM... Western Division, Naval Facilities Engineering Command
West NE C... Western New England College (GAGS)
West N Mex U... Western New Mexico University (GAGS)
WESTOMP... Western Ocean Meeting Point
Weston........ Weston [*Roy F.*], Inc. [*Associated Press*] (SAG)
Weston........ Weston's Reports [*11-14 Vermont*] [*A publication*] (DLA)
WestOne...... West One Bancorp [*Associated Press*] (SAG)
West Oregon St C... Western Oregon State College (GAGS)
WESTPAC.... Product Group for the Western Pacific (EERA)
WESTPAC.... Western Pacific [*Military*] (CINC)
WestPac...... Western Pacific Airlines, Inc. [*Associated Press*] (SAG)
WESTPACBACOM... Western Pacific Base Command [*Navy*]
WEST PACK... Western Packaging Exposition (TSPED)
WESTPACNORTH... Western Pacific North [*Navy*] (CINC)
WESTPACTRAMID... Western Pacific Training Program for Midshipmen [*Navy*] (DNAB)
West Pat...... West on Patents [*A publication*] (DLA)
WESTPO...... Western Governors Policy Office
West Pr Int Law... Westlake's Private International Law [*7th ed.*] [*1925*] [*A publication*] (DLA)
West R........ Western Reporter [*A publication*] (DLA)
WESTRAIL... Western Australian Government Railways Commission
WESTRAX.... Western Tropical Atlantic Experiment [*Marine science*] (OSRA)
WESTRAX.... Western Tropical Atlantic Experiment (USDC)
West Rep..... Western Reporter [*A publication*] (DLA)
West Res Coll... Western Reserve College
WESTS......... Women's Emergency Shelter and Training Scheme [*New South Wales, Australia*]
West School L Rev... Western School Law Review [*A publication*] (DLA)
WESTSEAFRON... Western Sea Frontier [*Navy*] (MUGU)
West's Op.... West's Opinions [*City Solicitor of Philadelphia, PA*] [*A publication*] (DLA)
West's Symb... West's Symboleographie [*Many eds.*] [*1590-1641*] [*A publication*] (DLA)
WESTT......... Weapon System Tactical Tester
West Tex St U... West Texas State University (GAGS)
West T H..... West's English Chancery Reports Tempore Hardwicke [*1736-39*] [*A publication*] (DLA)
West T Hard... West's English Chancery Reports Tempore Hardwicke [*1736-39*] [*A publication*] (DLA)
West T Hardw... West's English Chancery Reports Tempore Hardwicke [*1736-39*] [*A publication*] (DLA)
West Ti Cas... Western's London Tithe Cases [*1535-1822*] [*A publication*] (DLA)
West Tithe Cas... Western's London Tithe Cases [*England*] [*A publication*] (DLA)
West Va....... West Virginia Reports [*A publication*] (DLA)
West Va Col... West Virginia Graduate College (GAGS)
West Va L Rev... Western Virginia Law Review [*A publication*] (DLA)
West Va Rep... West Virginia Reports [*A publication*] (DLA)
West Va U... West Virginia University (GAGS)
Westvco....... Westvaco Corp. [*Associated Press*] (SAG)
West Wash St U... Western Washington State University (GAGS)
West Week (Can)... Western Weekly Notes (Canada) [*A publication*] (DLA)
West Week N... Western Weekly Notes [*Canada*] [*A publication*] (DLA)
West Week N (Can)... Western Weekly Notes (Canada) [*A publication*] (DLA)
West Week NS... Western Weekly, New Series [*Canada*] [*A publication*] (DLA)
West Week Rep... Western Weekly Reports [*Canada*] [*A publication*] (DLA)
West Wkly... Western Weekly Notes (Canada) [*A publication*] (DLA)
WESU.......... Middletown, CT [*FM radio station call letters*]
WESV.......... Richton, MS [*FM radio station call letters*]
WESX.......... Salem, MA [*AM radio station call letters*]
WESY.......... Leland, MS [*AM radio station call letters*]
WESYP........ Weapons System Plan [*Navy*] (NG)
WET............ Wagethe [*Indonesia*] [*Airport symbol*] (OAG)
WET............ Waste, Environment, and Technology [*Matrix*] [*Environmental Protection Agency*]
WET............ Waste Extraction Test
WET............ Water Exercise Technique [*In book title "The W.E.T. Workout"*]
WET............ Weapons Effectiveness Testing
WET............ Weighted Effective Temperature (IAA)
WET............ Western European Time (IAA)
WET............ Westfort Petroleums Ltd. [*Toronto Stock Exchange symbol*]
WET............ Westinghouse Electronic Tubeless
WET............ Wet Environment Trainer [*Navy*]
WET............ Wettzell [*Federal Republic of Germany*] [*Seismograph station code, US Geological Survey*] (SEIS)
WET............ Whole Earth Telescope [*Global network of telescopes*]
WET............ Whole Effluent Toxicity [*Environmental Protection Agency*]
WET............ Work Experience and Training
WETA.......... War Estate Tax Act [*1917*]
WETA.......... Washington, DC [*FM radio station call letters*]
WETAC........ Westinghouse Electronic Tubeless Analog Computer
WETAF........ Weather Task Force
WETARFAC... Work Element Timer and Recorder for Automatic Computing
WETA-TV..... Washington, DC [*Television station call letters*]
WETB.......... Johnson City, TN [*AM radio station call letters*]
WETC.......... Wendell-Zebulon, NC [*AM radio station call letters*]
WETD.......... Alfred, NY [*FM radio station call letters*]
WETF.......... Weightless Environment Training Facility (SSD)
WETH.......... Hagerstown, MD [*FM radio station call letters*]
WETH.......... Wetherley [*England*]
Weth........... Wethey's Reports [*Canada*] [*A publication*] (DLA)
Wethey........ Wethey's Reports, Upper Canada Queen's Bench [*A publication*] (DLA)
Weth UC...... Wethey's Reports, Upper Canada Queen's Bench [*A publication*] (DLA)
WE TIP........ We Turn in Pushers [*Organization combating drug traffic*]
WETK.......... Burlington, VT [*Television station call letters*]
WETL.......... South Bend, IN [*FM radio station call letters*]
WETM.......... Elmira, NY [*Television station call letters*]
WETM.......... Weather Team [*Air Force*] (AFM)
WETN.......... Wheaton, IL [*FM radio station call letters*]
WETNETNG... Wet-Net Training [*Navy*] (NVT)
WETO.......... Western Environmental Technology Office (ACII)
WETP.......... Work Experience Training Program (OICC)
WETR-AM.... Eden, NC [*AM radio station call letters*] (RBYB)
WETS.......... Johnson City, TN [*FM radio station call letters*]
WETS.......... Weapon Effects Training Simulator (MCD)
WETS.......... Week-End Training Site [*Military*] (AABC)
WetSeal....... Wet Seal, Inc. [*Associated Press*] (SAG)
WETSU........ We-Eat-This-Stuff-Up [*Mobile guerrilla force coded password*] [*Bowdlerized version*] (VNW)
WETT.......... Ocean City, MD [*AM radio station call letters*]
Wett........... Wettstein's Novum Testamentum Graecum [*A publication*] (BJA)
WETZ.......... New Martinsville, WV [*AM radio station call letters*]
WETZ-FM.... New Martinsville, WV [*FM radio station call letters*] (RBYB)
WEU............ University of Wisconsin-Eau Claire, Eau Claire, WI [*Library symbol Library of Congress*] (LCLS)
WEU............ Ward's Engine Update [*A publication*]
WEU............ Western Economic Union (DOMA)
WEU............ Western European Union [*Also, WU*] [*See also UEO*] (EAIO)
WEUC.......... Ponce, PR [*AM radio station call letters*]
WEUC-FM.... Ponce, PR [*FM radio station call letters*]
WEUL.......... Kingsford, MI [*FM radio station call letters*]
WEUP.......... Huntsville, AL [*AM radio station call letters*]
WEUP.......... Minor Hill, TN [*FM radio station call letters*]
WEUX.......... Chippewa Falls, WI [*Television station call letters*]
WEV............ Western European Vision
WEVA.......... Emporia, VA [*AM radio station call letters*]
WEVA.......... World Esperantist Vegetarian Association [*See also TEVA*] [*Dublin, Republic of Ireland*] (EAIO)
WEVA-FM.... Emporia, VA [*FM radio station call letters*]
WEVD.......... New York, NY [*AM radio station call letters*]
WEVE.......... Eveleth, MN [*AM radio station call letters*]
WEVE-FM.... Eveleth, MN [*FM radio station call letters*]
WEVH.......... Hanover, NH [*FM radio station call letters*]
WEVL.......... Memphis, TN [*FM radio station call letters*]
WEVN.......... Keene, NH [*FM radio station call letters*]
WEVO.......... Concord, NH [*FM radio station call letters*]
WEVR.......... River Falls, WI [*AM radio station call letters*]
WEVR-FM.... River Falls, WI [*FM radio station call letters*]
WEVS.......... Saugatuck, MI [*FM radio station call letters*]
WEVV.......... Evansville, IN [*Television station call letters*]
WEW............ St. Louis, MO [*AM radio station call letters*]
WEW............ Western Electronic Week
WEW............ West Wind Aviation, Inc. [*Canada ICAO designator*] (FAAC)
WEW............ Wewak [*Papua New Guinea*] [*Seismograph station code, US Geological Survey Closed*] (SEIS)
WEWAS........ Water Equipment Wholesalers and Suppliers [*Formerly, WEWSA*]
WEWM.......... Pentwater, MI [*FM radio station call letters*] (RBYB)
WEWO.......... Laurinburg, NC [*AM radio station call letters*]
WEWS.......... Cleveland, OH [*Television station call letters*]
WEWSA........ Water Equipment Wholesalers and Suppliers Association [*Later, WEWAS*] (EA)
WEX............ Business Science Experts [*NOMOS Datapool*] [*Germany Information service or system*] (CRD)
WEX............ Wexford [*County in Ireland*] (ROG)
WEX............ Wine Exchange [*Computer network*]
WEX............ Win-Eldrich Mines Ltd. [*Toronto Stock Exchange symbol*]

WEX............ Wings Express, Inc. [*ICAO designator*] (FAAC)
WEXC........... Greenville, PA [*FM radio station call letters*]
WEXF........... Wexford [*County in Ireland*] (ROG)
WEXFD......... Wexford [*County in Ireland*]
WEXI............ Huntington, IN [*FM radio station call letters*]
WEXITA........ Women Executives International Tourism Association [*Defunct*] (EA)
WEXL........... Royal Oak, MI [*AM radio station call letters*]
WEXS........... Patillas, PR [*AM radio station call letters*]
WEXT........... Wrist Extension [*Sports medicine*]
WEXY........... Wilton Manors, FL [*AM radio station call letters*]
WEY............. West Yellowstone, MT [*Location identifier FAA*] (FAAL)
Weyco.......... Weyco Group, Inc. [*Associated Press*] (SAG)
WEYE........... Surgoinsville, TN [*FM radio station call letters*]
Weyerh......... Weyerhaeuser Co. [*Associated Press*] (SAG)
WEYI............ Saginaw, MI [*Television station call letters*]
WEYM........... Weymouth [*Municipal borough in England*]
WEYS........... Key West, FL [*Television station call letters*]
WEYS........... Weyco Group [*NASDAQ symbol*] (TTSB)
WEYS........... Weyco Group, Inc. [*NASDAQ symbol*] (SAG)
WEYY........... Talladega, AL [*FM radio station call letters*]
WEYZ........... North East, PA [*AM radio station call letters*]
WEZ............. Weapon Engagement Zone [*Army*] (ADDR)
WEZB........... New Orleans, LA [*FM radio station call letters*]
WEZC........... Hickory, NC [*FM radio station call letters*]
WEZE........... Boston, MA [*AM radio station call letters*]
WEZF........... Burlington, VT [*FM radio station call letters*]
WEZG........... Jefferson City, TN [*FM radio station call letters*]
WEZI............ New Market, VA [*FM radio station call letters*]
WEZJ............ Williamsburg, KY [*AM radio station call letters*]
WEZJ-FM...... Williamsburg, KY [*FM radio station call letters*]
WEZK........... Knoxville, TN [*AM radio station call letters*]
WEZL........... Charleston, SC [*FM radio station call letters*]
WEZN........... Bridgeport, CT [*FM radio station call letters*]
WEZO........... Farmer City, IL [*FM radio station call letters*] (RBYB)
WEZQ........... Bangor, ME [*FM radio station call letters*]
WEZR........... Brillion, WI [*FM radio station call letters*]
WEZS........... Laconia, NH [*AM radio station call letters*]
WEZU........... Witterungseinfluesse und Zeitunterschied [*Weather factors and time difference*] [*German military - World War II*]
WEZV........... Brookston, IN [*FM radio station call letters*]
WEZW........... Augusta, ME [*AM radio station call letters*] (RBYB)
WEZX........... Scranton, PA [*FM radio station call letters*]
WEZY........... Racine, WI [*FM radio station call letters*] (RBYB)
WEZZ........... Clanton, AL [*FM radio station call letters*]
WF............... Four-Conductor Cables [*JETDS nomenclature*] [*Military*] (CET)
WF............... Wakefield [*Postcode*] (ODBW)
WF............... Wake Forest University [*North Carolina*]
WF............... Wallis and Futuna [*ANSI two-letter standard code*] (CNC)
wf................ Wallis and Futuna [*MARC country of publication code Library of Congress*] (LCCP)
WF............... Ward Foundation (EA)
WF............... Wash Fountain (AAG)
WF............... Water Filter
WF............... Water Finish [*Paper*]
WF............... Watershed Foundation (EA)
WF............... Waveform [*Telecommunications*] (IAA)
WF............... Wave Frequency [*Telecommunications*] (IAA)
W + F.......... Ways plus Filling [*Textile testing*]
WF............... Weatherproof Faience [*Tile*] (DICI)
WF............... Weighting Factor (EG)
WF............... Weil-Felix Reaction [*Medicine*] (MAE)
WF............... Welch Fusiliers [*British military*] (DMA)
WF............... Weld Fixture
WF............... Welfare Appointment Full Time [*Chiropody*] [*British*]
WF............... Wells Fargo & Co. [*Associated Press*] (SAG)
WF............... Western Front [*World War I*]
WF............... Westfair Foods Ltd. [*Toronto Stock Exchange symbol*]
WF............... West Feliciana Railroad (IIA)
WF............... Wet Film [*Radiology*] (DAVI)
WF............... White Falcon [*A publication*] (DNAB)
WF............... White Fathers [*Roman Catholic men's religious order*]
WF............... White Female
WF............... White Fir [*Botany*]
WF............... Wide Flange (DAC)
WF............... Wideros Flyveselskap [*ICAO designator*] (AD)
WF............... Wildfowl Foundation (EA)
WF............... Wind Finding RADAR (IAA)
WF............... Wind Force (WGA)
WF............... Window-Frame
WF............... Windstar Foundation (EA)
WF............... Wingfold
WF............... Wing Forward (WGA)
WF............... Wire Foundation (EA)
WF............... Wistar-Furth [*Rat strain*]
WF............... Withdrawn Failing [*Education*] (WGA)
WF............... Women's Firsts [*A publication*]
WF............... Won on Foul [*Boxing*]
WF............... Word Fluency [*Psychology*]
WF............... Work Function [*Physics*]
W/F............. Wow and Flutter
WF............... Write Fault (MHDB)
WF............... Write Forward
W/F............. Writing on Face [*Deltiology*]
WF............... Wrong Font [*Typesetting*] [*Proofreader's mark*]
wf................ Wrong Font [*Publishing*] (WDMC)

WFA............ War Food Administration [*Determined military, civilian, and foreign requirements for human and animal food, and for food used industrially*] [*Terminated, 1945*] [*World War II*]
WFA............ Wave Form Analyzer [*Instrumentation*]
WFA............ Weight-for-Age (ADA)
WFA............ Weightlifting Federation of Africa (EAIO)
WFA............ Western Fairs Association (EA)
WFA............ Western Falconry Association [*Defunct*] (EA)
WFA............ White Fish Authority [*MAFF*] [*British*]
WFA............ Wide-Frequency Antenna
WFA............ Winemakers' Federation of Australia
WFA............ Wire Fabricators Association [*Naperville, IL*] (EA)
WFA............ Women's Football Association [*British*]
WFA............ World Federalist Association (EA)
WFA............ World Federation of Advertisers [*See also FMA*] [*Brussels, Belgium*] (EAIO)
WFA............ World Footbag Association (EA)
WFA............ World Friendship Association
WFAA.......... Dallas, TX [*Television station call letters*]
WFAA.......... World Federation of Americans Abroad [*France*] (EAIO)
WFAB.......... Ceiba, PR [*AM radio station call letters*]
WFAC.......... World Federal Authority Committee [*Dundas, ON*] (EAIO)
WFACT........ Wildlife Foundation Australian Capital Territory
WFAD.......... Middlebury, VT [*AM radio station call letters*]
WFAE.......... Charlotte, NC [*FM radio station call letters*]
WFAFW....... World Federation of Agriculture and Food Workers (EA)
WFaH.......... Hoard Historical Museum, Fort Atkinson, WI [*Library symbol Library of Congress*] (LCLS)
WFAI........... Fayetteville, NC [*AM radio station call letters*]
WFALW....... Weltbund Freiheitlicher Arbeitnehmerverbande auf Liberaler Wirtschaftsgrundlage [*World Union of Liberal Trade Union Organisations - WULTUO*] [*Zurich, Switzerland*] (EAIO)
WFAM.......... Augusta, GA [*AM radio station call letters*]
WFAN.......... New York, NY [*AM radio station call letters*]
WF & EQ..... Wave Filters and Equalizers (MCD)
WF & FSA... Wholesale Florists and Florist Suppliers of America (EA)
WF & P....... Wabash, Frisco, and Pacific Association (EA)
WF & S....... Wichita Falls & Southern Railroad (IIA)
WFAOS........ World Federation of Associations of YMCA Secretaries [*Nigeria*] (EAIO)
WFAOSB...... World Food and Agricultural Outlook and Situation Board [*Department of Agriculture*]
WFAP.......... Women's Funding Assistance Project (EA)
WFAPS........ World Federation of Associations of Pediatric Surgeons [*Barcelona, Spain*] (EAIO)
WFAR.......... Danbury, CT [*FM radio station call letters*]
WFAS.......... White Plains, NY [*AM radio station call letters*]
WFAS.......... Women's Financial Advisory Service [*Australia*]
WFAS-FM..... White Plains, NY [*FM radio station call letters*]
WFAT.......... Portage, MI [*FM radio station call letters*]
WFAU.......... Gardiner, ME [*AM radio station call letters*]
WFAV.......... Fort Walton Beach, FL [*AM radio station call letters*]
WFAW.......... Fort Atkinson, WI [*AM radio station call letters*]
WFAW.......... World Federation of Agricultural Workers [*See also FMTA*] (EAIO)
WFAX.......... Falls Church, VA [*AM radio station call letters*]
WFAY.......... Fayetville, NC [*Television station call letters*]
WFAZ.......... Thomasville, NC [*FM radio station call letters*]
WFB............ Waferboard Corp. Ltd. [*Toronto Stock Exchange symbol*]
WFB............ Waterways Freight Bureau [*Defunct*] (EA)
WFB............ Wide Flange Beam [*Metal industry*]
WFB............ World Fellowship of Buddhists [*Bangkok, Tahiland*] (EAIO)
WFBA.......... Miami, FL [*AM radio station call letters*]
WFBB.......... Woodfree Bank and Bond [*Paper*] (DGA)
WFBBA........ World Federation of Bergen-Belsen Associations (EA)
WFBC.......... Greenville, SC [*AM radio station call letters*]
WFBC-FM.... Greenville, SC [*FM radio station call letters*]
WFBC-TV.... Anderson, SC [*Television station call letters*] (RBYB)
WFBE.......... Flint, MI [*FM radio station call letters*]
WFBF.......... Buffalo, NY [*FM radio station call letters*]
WFBG.......... Altoona, PA [*AM radio station call letters*]
WFBI........... Memphis, TN [*Television station call letters*]
WFBI........... Wood Fiber Blanket Institute [*Defunct*]
WFBL.......... Baldwinsville, NY [*AM radio station call letters*]
WFBMA....... Woven Fabric Belting Manufacturers Association (EA)
WFBQ.......... Indianapolis, IN [*FM radio station call letters*]
WFBR.......... Cambridge, MD [*FM radio station call letters*]
WFBSC........ World Federation of Building Service Contractors (EA)
WFBTMA..... World Federation of Baton Twirling and Majorette Associations (EA)
WFBY.......... World Fellowship of Buddhist Youth [*Bangkok, Thailand*] (EAIO)
WFBY-FM.... Clarksburg, WV [*FM radio station call letters*] (RBYB)
WFC............ Committee on the World Food Crisis [*Defunct*] (EA)
WFC............ Paul McCartney Fan Club [*British*] (EAIO)
WFC............ Wake Forest College [*Later, WFU*] [*North Carolina*]
WFC............ Walleye Filter Changer
WFC............ Wall Financial Co. [*Vancouver Stock Exchange symbol*]
WFC............ Wall Financial Corp. [*Toronto Stock Exchange symbol*]
WFC............ Wallops Flight Center [*Formerly, WS*] [*NASA*]
WFC............ Wanted for Cash (MHDW)
WFC............ War Finance Committee
WFC............ Water Facts Consortium [*Defunct*] (EA)
WFC............ Weld Flange Connection
WFC............ Wells Fargo [*NYSE symbol*] (TTSB)
WFC............ Wells Fargo & Co. [*NYSE symbol*] (SPSG)
WFC............ Wesleyan Free Church
WFC............ Western Football Conference

WFC............ Western Forestry Center (EA)
WFC............ West Florida Coast
WFC............ Wheat Foods Council (EA)
WFC............ Wide Field Camera
WFC............ Wolf First Class [*A philanderer*] [*Slang*]
WFC............ Women's Forage Corps [*World War I*] [*British*]
WFC............ World Food Council [*United Nations*] (EAIO)
WFC............ World Forestry Center (EA)
WFC............ World Friendship Centre (EA)
WFC............ World Fundraising Council (NFD)
WFC............ Worldwide Fiero Club (EA)
WFCA.......... Ackerman, MS [*FM radio station call letters*]
WFCA.......... Western Forestry and Conservation Association (EA)
WFCB.......... Chillicothe, OH [*FM radio station call letters*]
WFCC.......... Chatham, MA [*FM radio station call letters*]
WFCC.......... World Federation for Culture Collections (EAIO)
WFCE.......... World Federation of Czechoslovak Exile (EA)
WFCF.......... St. Augustine, FL [*FM radio station call letters*]
WFCG.......... Franklinton, LA [*AM radio station call letters*]
WFCH.......... Charleston, SC [*FM radio station call letters*]
WFCI........... Franklin, IN [*FM radio station call letters*]
WFCJ........... Miamisburg, OH [*FM radio station call letters*]
WFCL........... Clintonville, WI [*AM radio station call letters*]
WFCLC......... World Federation of Christian Life Communities [*See also FMCVC*] [*Rome, Italy*] (EAIO)
WFCM.......... Murfreesboro, TN [*FM radio station call letters*] (RBYB)
WFCMV........ Wheeled Fuel-Consuming Motor Vehicle
WFCNLM..... World Federation of the Cossack National Liberation Movement [*Later, WFCNLMC*] (EA)
WFCNLMC... World Federation of the Cossack National Liberation Movement of Cossackia (EA)
WFCO.......... Lancaster, OH [*FM radio station call letters*]
WFCO.......... Winton Financial [*NASDAQ symbol*] (TTSB)
WFCO.......... Winton Financial Corp. [*NASDAQ symbol*] (SAG)
WFCPrB....... Wells Fargo Adj Rt B Pfd [*NYSE symbol*] (TTSB)
WFCPrC....... Wells Fargo 9% 'C' Dep Pfd [*NYSE symbol*] (TTSB)
WFCPrD....... Wells Fargo 8.875% Dep Pfd [*NYSE symbol*] (TTSB)
WFCPrF....... Wells Fargo 9.875% Dep Pfd [*NYSE symbol*] (TTSB)
WFCPrG....... Wells Fargo 9% Dep Pfd [*NYSE symbol*] (TTSB)
WFCR.......... Amherst, MA [*FM radio station call letters*]
WFCS.......... New Britain, CT [*FM radio station call letters*]
WFCS.......... World's Fair Collectors Society (EA)
WFCT.......... Bradenton, FL [*Television station call letters*]
WFCV.......... Fort Wayne, IN [*AM radio station call letters*]
WFCY.......... World Federation of Catholic Youth
WFCYWG..... World Federation of Catholic Young Women and Girls [*Later, WFCY*]
WFD............ Avro International Aerospace [*British*] [*FAA designator*] (FAAC)
WFD............ Waveform Distortion [*Telecommunications*] (TEL)
WFD............ Westfield Minerals Ltd. [*Toronto Stock Exchange symbol Vancouver Stock Exchange symbol*]
WFD............ Women in Financial Development (NFD)
WFD............ Woodford BAE [*British ICAO designator*] (FAAC)
WFD............ Woods and Forests Department [*South Australia*]
WFD............ Wool Forward [*Knitting*]
WFD............ Work Function Difference [*Physics*] (IAA)
WFD............ World Fax Directory [*Information service or system*] (IID)
WFD............ World Federation of the Deaf [*Rome, Italy*]
WFD............ World Food Day [*October 16*]
WFD............ Worldwide Franchise Directory [*A publication*]
WFDA.......... Wholesale Floorcovering Distributors' Association [*British*] (BI)
WFDA.......... Wholesale Footwear Distributors' Association [*British*] (BI)
WFDA.......... World Fast-Draw Association (EA)
WFDD.......... Winston-Salem, NC [*FM radio station call letters*]
WFDF.......... Flint, MI [*AM radio station call letters*]
WFDF.......... World Flying Disc Federation (EAIO)
WFDFI......... World Federation of Development Financing Institutions [*See also FEMIDE*] [*Madrid, Spain*] (EAIO)
WFDL.......... Lomira, WI [*FM radio station call letters*]
WFDR.......... Manchester, GA [*AM radio station call letters*]
WFDRHL...... World Federation of Doctors Who Respect Human Life (United States Section) (EA)
WFDS.......... Warm Fog Dispenser System (MCD)
WFDS.......... Worthington Foods [*NASDAQ symbol*] (SAG)
WFDSA........ World Federation of Direct Selling Associations [*Washington, DC*] (EA)
WFDSC........ World Federation of Dark Shadows Clubs (EA)
WFDU.......... Teaneck, NJ [*FM radio station call letters*]
WFDW.......... World Federation of Democratic Women
WFDWRHL... World Federation of Doctors Who Respect Human Life [*Ostend, Belgium*] (EAIO)
WFDY.......... World Federation of Democratic Youth [*See also FMJD*] [*Budapest, Hungary*] (EAIO)
WFe............ Dwight T. Parker Public Library, Fennimore, WI [*Library symbol Library of Congress*] (LCLS)
WFE............ Williams Flexion Exercises [*Orthopedics*] (DAVI)
WFE............ Wiped Film Evaporation
WFE............ With Food Element
WFE............ World Federation of Europeans (By Birth or Descent) (EA)
WFEA.......... Manchester, NH [*AM radio station call letters*]
WFEA.......... World Federation of Educational Associations [*Later, WCOTP*] (EA)
WFEB.......... Sylacauga, AL [*AM radio station call letters*]
WFEB.......... Worcester Foundation for Experimental Biology
WFEN.......... Rockford, IL [*FM radio station call letters*]
WFEO.......... World Federation of Engineering Organizations [*Paris, France*]
WFES.......... Windshield Flight Environment Simulator (PDAA)
WFEWC........ World Federation of Estonian Women's Clubs (EA)
WFEX.......... Western Fruit Express
WFEZ.......... Williston, FL [*FM radio station call letters*]
WFF............ Wanderer Forum Foundation (EA)
WFF............ Wavy Vortex Flow [*Fluid mechanics*]
WFF............ Well-Formed Formula [*Logic*]
WFF............ Western Frontier Force [*British military*] (DMA)
WFF............ Whiting Field [*Milton*] [*Florida*] [*Seismograph station code, US Geological Survey*] [*Closed*] (SEIS)
WFF............ William Faulkner Foundation [*Defunct*] (EA)
WFF............ Wold Farm Foods [*Commercial firm British*]
WFF............ World Friendship Federation
WFFA.......... Women's Fashion Fabrics Association [*Defunct*] (EA)
WFFC.......... Ferrum, VA [*FM radio station call letters*]
WFFC.......... Women in Flavor & Fragrance Commerce Inc.
WFFF.......... Columbia, MS [*AM radio station call letters*]
WFFF-FM..... Columbia, MS [*FM radio station call letters*]
WFFF-TV...... Burlington, VT [*Television station call letters*] (RBYB)
WFFG.......... Marathon, FL [*AM radio station call letters*]
WFFI........... Western Fidelity Funding [*NASDAQ symbol*] (TTSB)
WFFI........... Western Fidelity Funding, Inc. [*NASDAQ symbol*] (SAG)
WFFL.......... World Federation of Free Latvians (EA)
WFFM.......... Ashburn, GA [*FM radio station call letters*]
WFFM.......... World Federation of Friends of Museums [*See also FMAM*] [*Paris, France*] (EAIO)
WFFN.......... Cordova, AL [*FM radio station call letters*]
WFFT.......... Fort Wayne, IN [*Television station call letters*]
WFFTH........ World Federation of Workers in Food, Tobacco, and Hotel Industries [*See also FMATH*] (EAIO)
WFFX.......... Tuscaloosa, AL [*FM radio station call letters*]
WFG............ Water Fog
WFG............ Waveform Function Generator
WFG............ Waveform Generator
WFGA.......... Women's Farm and Garden Association [*British*] (BI)
WFGA-FM.... Waycross, GA [*FM radio station call letters*] (RBYB)
WFGB.......... Kingston, NY [*FM radio station call letters*]
WFGC.......... Palm Beach, FL [*Television station call letters*]
WFGH.......... Fort Gay, WV [*FM radio station call letters*]
WFGI........... State College, PA [*FM radio station call letters*]
WFGL.......... Fitchburg, MA [*AM radio station call letters*]
WFGM.......... Fairmont, WV [*FM radio station call letters*]
WFGN.......... Gaffney, SC [*AM radio station call letters*]
WFGO.......... Erie, PA [*FM radio station call letters*]
WFGR.......... Grand Rapids, MI [*FM radio station call letters*]
WFGW.......... Black Mountain, NC [*AM radio station call letters*]
WFGX.......... Fort Walton Beach, FL [*Television station call letters*]
WFGY.......... Altoona, PA [*FM radio station call letters*]
WFGZ.......... Lobelville, TN [*FM radio station call letters*]
WFH............ World Federation of Hemophilia [*Montreal, PQ*] (EA)
WFHA.......... World Federation of Hungarian Artists (EA)
WFHAAVSC... World Federation of Health Agencies for the Advancement of Voluntary Surgical Contraception (EA)
WFHB.......... Bloomington, IN [*FM radio station call letters*]
WFHC.......... Henderson, TN [*FM radio station call letters*]
WFHE.......... Hickory, NC [*FM radio station call letters*]
WFHFF........ World Federation of Hungarian Freedom Fighters (EA)
WFHJ.......... World Federation of Hungarian Jews (EA)
WFHK.......... Pell City, AL [*AM radio station call letters*]
WFHL.......... Decatur, IL [*Television station call letters*]
WFHN.......... Fairhaven, MA [*FM radio station call letters*]
WFHQ.......... Pennsuco, FL [*FM radio station call letters*]
WFHR.......... Wisconsin Rapids, WI [*AM radio station call letters*]
WFHSLPAC... Water-Flooded Helical Screw Low-Pressure Air Compressor [*Navy*] (CAAL)
WFI............ Fianarantsoa [*Madagascar*] [*Airport symbol*] (OAG)
WFI............ Wait for It (DI)
WFI............ Water for Injection [*Pharmacy*]
WFI............ Westralian Forest Industries [*Australia Commercial firm*]
WFI............ Wheat Flour Institute [*Miller's National Federation*] [*Absorbed by*] (EA)
WFI............ Wishes and Fears Inventory [*Psychology*]
WFI............ Wood Flooring Institute of America [*Later, WSFI*] (EA)
WFI............ Wood Foundation Institute [*Defunct*] (EA)
WFI............ World Federation of Investors (EAIO)
WFI............ World Forest Institute (GNE)
WFI............ Worldwide Friendship International (EA)
WFIA........... Louisville, KY [*AM radio station call letters*]
WFIA........... Wells Fargo Investment Advisors (ECON)
WFIA........... Western Forest Industries Association (EA)
WFIC........... Collinsville, VA [*AM radio station call letters*]
WFICM........ World Federation of International Music Competitions [*Switzerland*] (EAIO)
WFID........... Rio Piedras, PR [*FM radio station call letters*]
WFIE........... Evansville, IN [*Television station call letters*]
WFIF........... Milford, CT [*AM radio station call letters*]
WFIL........... Philadelphia, PA [*AM radio station call letters*] (RBYB)
WFIM.......... World Federation of Islamic Missions [*Karachi, Pakistan*] (EAIO)
WFIMC........ World Federation of International Music Competitions [*See also FMCIM*] (EAIO)
WFIN........... Findlay, OH [*AM radio station call letters*]
WFIN........... Women and Food Information Network [*Defunct*] (EA)
WFIP........... Women's Financial Information Program [*American Association of Retired Persons*] (BARN)
WFIQ........... Florence, AL [*Television station call letters*]
WFIR........... Roanoke, VA [*AM radio station call letters*]

WFIS........... Fountain Inn, SC [*AM radio station call letters*]
WFIS........... World Federation of Iranian Students
WFIT........... Melbourne, FL [*FM radio station call letters*]
WFIU........... Bloomington, IN [*FM radio station call letters*]
WFIV........... Kissimmee, FL [*AM radio station call letters*]
WFIV........... White Light Fringe Image Velocimeter (PDAA)
WFIW........... Fairfield, IL [*AM radio station call letters*]
WFIW-FM.... Fairfield, IL [*FM radio station call letters*]
WFIX........... Rogersville, AL [*FM radio station call letters*]
WFJA........... Sanford, NC [*FM radio station call letters*]
WFJJ........... World Federation of Jewish Journalists [*Tel Aviv, Israel*] (EAIO)
WFK........... Frenchville [*Maine*] [*Airport symbol*] (OAG)
WFKJ........... Cashtown, PA [*AM radio station call letters*]
WFKN........... Franklin, KY [*AM radio station call letters*]
WFKS........... Palatka, FL [*FM radio station call letters*]
WFKX........... Henderson, TN [*FM radio station call letters*]
WFKY........... Frankfort, KY [*AM radio station call letters*]
WFKZ........... Plantation Key, FL [*FM radio station call letters*]
WFL........... Windflower Mining Ltd. [*Vancouver Stock Exchange symbol*]
WFL........... Within Functional Limits [*Physical therapy*] (DAVI)
WFL........... Woman's Freedom League
WFL........... Work Flow Language [*Computer science*] (BUR)
WFL........... World Football League [*Dissolved, 1975*]
WFL........... Worshipful [*Freemasonry*] (ROG)
WFL........... Wredemann-Frang Law
WFLA........... Tampa, FL [*AM radio station call letters*]
WFLA........... Western Fraternal Life Association (EA)
WFLA-TV..... Tampa, FL [*Television station call letters*]
WFLB........... Fayetteville, NC [*AM radio station call letters*]
WFLC........... Miami, FL [*FM radio station call letters*]
WFLD........... Chicago, IL [*Television station call letters*]
WFLD........... White Fine Lustre Double Weight [*Photographic paper*] (DGA)
WFLD........... Work/Family Life Database [*Database*]
WFLE........... Flemingsburg, KY [*AM radio station call letters*]
WFLE-FM.... Flemington, KY [*FM radio station call letters*]
WFLI........... Cleveland, TN [*Television station call letters*]
WFLI........... Lookout Mountain, TN [*AM radio station call letters*]
WFLK........... Geneva, NY [*FM radio station call letters*]
WFLM........... White City, FL [*FM radio station call letters*]
WFLN........... Philadelphia, PA [*FM radio station call letters*]
WFLO........... Farmville, VA [*AM radio station call letters*]
WFLO-FM.... Farmville, VA [*FM radio station call letters*]
WFLP........... Erie, PA [*AM radio station call letters*]
WFLQ........... French Lick, IN [*FM radio station call letters*]
WFLR........... Dundee, NY [*AM radio station call letters*]
WFLR-FM.... Dundee, NY [*FM radio station call letters*]
WFLRY........ World Federation of Liberal and Radical Youth [*Later, IFLRY*]
WFLS........... Fredericksburg, VA [*AM radio station call letters*]
WFLS-FM.... Fredericksburg, VA [*FM radio station call letters*]
WFLT........... Flint, MI [*AM radio station call letters*]
WFLW........... Monticello, KY [*AM radio station call letters*]
WFLX........... West Palm Beach, FL [*Television station call letters*]
WFLY........... Troy, NY [*FM radio station call letters*]
WFLZ........... Tampa, FL [*FM radio station call letters*]
WFM........... Water Flow Meter
WFM........... Waveform Monitor
WFM........... Waveguide Frequency Meter
WFM........... Weatherproof Faience Mosaics (DICI)
WFM........... Western Federation of Miners
WFM........... Westford [*Massachusetts*] [*Seismograph station code, US Geological Survey*] (SEIS)
WFM........... World Federalist Movement [*Netherlands*] (EAIO)
WFMA........... World Folk Music Association (EA)
WFMB........... Springfield, IL [*AM radio station call letters*]
WFMB........... World Federation of Merino Breeders [*Australia*]
WFMB-FM... Springfield, IL [*FM radio station call letters*]
WFMC........... Goldsboro, NC [*AM radio station call letters*]
WFMC........... Welding Filler Material Control [*Nuclear energy*] (NRCH)
WFMD........... Frederick, MD [*AM radio station call letters*]
WFME........... Newark, NJ [*FM radio station call letters*]
WFME........... West Milford, NJ [*Television station call letters*]
WFME........... World Federation for Medical Education (EA)
WFMF........... Baton Rouge, LA [*FM radio station call letters*]
WFMG........... Richmond, IN [*FM radio station call letters*]
WFMH........... Cullman, AL [*AM radio station call letters*]
WFMH........... World Federation for Mental Health (EA)
WFMH-FM... Cullman, AL [*FM radio station call letters*]
WFMI........... Brookfield, WI [*FM radio station call letters*] (RBYB)
WFMI........... Whole Foods Market [*NASDAQ symbol*] (TTSB)
WFMI........... Whole Foods Market, Inc. [*NASDAQ symbol*] (SAG)
WFMJ........... Youngstown, OH [*Television station call letters*]
WFMK........... East Lansing, MI [*FM radio station call letters*]
WFML........... Vincennes, IN [*FM radio station call letters*]
WFMLTA...... World Federation of Modern Language Teachers' Association (EA)
WFMO........... Fairmont, NC [*AM radio station call letters*]
WFMPT........ Wet-Fluorescence Magnetic Particle Technique [*Corrosion crack detection*]
WFMQ........... Lebanon, TN [*FM radio station call letters*]
WFMR........... Menomonee Falls, WI [*FM radio station call letters*]
WFMS........... Indianapolis, IN [*FM radio station call letters*]
WFMT........... Chicago, IL [*FM radio station call letters*]
WFMU........... East Orange, NJ [*FM radio station call letters*]
WFMU........... Weather and Fixed Map Unit [*FAA*]
WFMV........... South Congaree, SC [*FM radio station call letters*]
WFMW........... Madisonville, KY [*AM radio station call letters*]
WFMW........... World Federation of Methodist Women [*Seoul, Republic of Korea*] (EAIO)
WFMWNAA... World Federation of Methodist Women, North America Area (EA)
WFMX........... Statesville, NC [*FM radio station call letters*]
WFMY........... Greensboro, NC [*Television station call letters*]
WFMZ........... Allentown, PA [*FM radio station call letters*]
WFMZ-TV.... Allentown, PA [*Television station call letters*]
WFN........... Weapons and Facilities, Navy (NG)
WFN........... Well-Formed Net
WFN........... Westminster College, New Wilmington, PA [*OCLC symbol*] (OCLC)
WFN........... World Federation of Neurology (EA)
WFNA........... White Fuming Nitric Acid
WFNC........... Fayetteville, NC [*AM radio station call letters*]
WFNM........... Lancaster, PA [*FM radio station call letters*]
WFNMB........ World Federation of Nuclear Medicine and Biology (NUCP)
WFNMW...... World Federation of Trade Unions of Non-Manual Workers [*See also FMTNM*] [*Antwerp, Belguim*] (EAIO)
WFNN........... Villas, NJ [*FM radio station call letters*]
WFNO-AM.... Norco, LA [*AM radio station call letters*] (RBYB)
WFNP........... Rosendale, NY [*FM radio station call letters*]
WFNQ........... Forest City, NC [*FM radio station call letters*] (RBYB)
WFNR........... Blacksburg, VA [*AM radio station call letters*]
WFNS........... Plant City, FL [*AM radio station call letters*]
WFNS........... Women's Forum on National Security [*Defunct*] (EA)
WFNS........... World Federation of Neurosurgical Societies [*Nijmegen, Netherlands*] (EA)
WFNS........... Writers Federation of Nova Scotia [*Canada*] (WWLA)
WFNT........... Flint, MI [*AM radio station call letters*]
WFNW........... Naugatuck, CT [*AM radio station call letters*]
WFNX........... Lynn, MA [*FM radio station call letters*]
WFNZ........... Charlotte, NC [*AM radio station call letters*] (RBYB)
WFO........... Weather Forecast Office [*Marine science*] (OSRA)
WFO........... Weather Forecast Office (USDC)
WFO........... Western Fiordland Orthogneiss [*Geology*]
WFO........... Wide Field Optics
WF/O........... Wife Of [*Genealogy*]
WFO........... Wilbur's, Inc. [*ICAO designator*] (FAAC)
WFOB........... Fostoria, OH [*AM radio station call letters*]
WFOC........... Western Field Operations Center [*Bureau of Mines*] [*Spokane, WA*] (GRD)
WFOF........... Covington, IN [*FM radio station call letters*]
WFOF........... Wide Field Optical Filter
WFOG........... Suffolk, VA [*FM radio station call letters*]
WFOM........... Marietta, GA [*AM radio station call letters*]
WFon........... Fond Du Lac Public Library, Fond Du Lac, WI [*Library symbol Library of Congress*] (LCLS)
WFonM........ Marian College of Fond Du Lac, Fond Du Lac, WI [*Library symbol Library of Congress*] (LCLS)
WFonMM...... Mercury Marine, Fond Du Lac, WI [*Library symbol Library of Congress*] (LCLS)
WFonSA....... Saint Agnes Hospital, Fond Du Lac, WI [*Library symbol Library of Congress*] (LCLS)
WFont........... Fontana Public Library, Fontana, WI [*Library symbol Library of Congress*] (LCLS)
WFonU........ University of Wisconsin-Fond Du Lac, Fond Du Lac, WI [*Library symbol Library of Congress*] (LCLS)
WFOR........... Hattiesburg, MS [*AM radio station call letters*]
WFOR-TV.... Miami, FL [*Television station call letters*] (RBYB)
WFOS........... Cheasapeake, VA [*FM radio station call letters*]
WFOT........... World Federation of Occupational Therapists [*London, ON*] (EAIO)
WFOV........... Wide Field of View
WFOW-FM... Chatom, AL [*FM radio station call letters*] (RBYB)
WFOX........... Gainesville, GA [*FM radio station call letters*]
WFOY........... St. Augustine, FL [*AM radio station call letters*]
WFP........... Warm Front Passage [*NWS*] (FAAC)
WFP........... Water for People [*An association*] (EA)
WFP........... Wearout Failure Period
WFP........... Witness for Peace (EA)
WFP........... World Federation of Parasitologists [*Bilthoven, Netherlands*] (EAIO)
WFP........... World Food Programme [*Rome, Italy*] [*United Nations*]
WFP........... World Food Programs (EERA)
WFP........... Worldwide Fast for Peace [*An association Defunct*] (EA)
WFPA........... Fort Payne, AL [*AM radio station call letters*]
WFPA........... Washington Forest Protection Association (EA)
WFPA........... World Federation for the Protection of Animals [*Also known as FMPA, WTB*] [*Later, WSPA*]
WFPB-FM.... Falmouth, MA [*FM radio station call letters*] (RBYB)
WFPC........... Petersburg, IN [*FM radio station call letters*]
WFPC........... Wide Field/Planetary Camera
WFPFC........ Worldwide Fair Play for Frogs Committee (EA)
WFPG........... Atlantic City, NJ [*AM radio station call letters*]
WFPG-FM.... Atlantic City, NJ [*FM radio station call letters*]
WFPHA........ World Federation of Public Health Associations (EA)
WFPIS........... Whole Farm Plan Incentives Scheme [*of Victoria*] (EERA)
WFPK........... Louisville, KY [*FM radio station call letters*]
WFPL........... Louisville, KY [*FM radio station call letters*]
WFPLCA...... World Federation of Pipe Line Contractors Association (EA)
WFPMA........ World Federation of Personnel Management Associations [*Alexandria, VA*] (EA)
WFPMM...... World Federation of Proprietary Medicine Manufacturers
WFPP........... Whole Farm Planning Program [*of Tasmania*] (EERA)
WFPR........... Hammond, LA [*AM radio station call letters*]
WFPS........... Freeport, IL [*FM radio station call letters*]
WFPS........... Wild Flower Preservation Society (EA)
WFPT........... Frederick, MD [*Television station call letters*]

WFPT .... Welsh Figure Preference Test [*Psychology*]
WFPT .... World Federation for Physical Therapy
WFQS .... Franklin, NC [*FM radio station call letters*]
WFQX .... Front Royal, VA [*FM radio station call letters*]
WFR .... MEMC Electronic Materials [*NYSE symbol*] (TTSB)
WFR .... MEMC Electronic Materials, Inc. [*NYSE symbol*] (SAG)
WFR .... Wafer (MSA)
WFR .... Weight Flow Rate (SAA)
WFR .... Weil-Felix Reaction [*Medicine*] (MAE)
WFR .... Wharf Resources Ltd. [*Toronto Stock Exchange symbol*]
WFR .... Wheal and Flare Reaction [*Immunology*]
WFR .... Wide-Finding RADAR (MCD)
WFR .... Worcestershire and Sherwood Foresters Regiment [*Military unit*] [*British*]
WFRA .... Franklin, PA [*AM radio station call letters*]
WFRA .... Wharf Resources Ltd. [*NASDAQ symbol*] (NQ)
WFRAF .... Wharf Resources Ltd [*NASDAQ symbol*] (TTSB)
WFRA-FM .... Franklin, PA [*FM radio station call letters*]
WFRB .... Frostburg, MD [*AM radio station call letters*]
WFRBC .... Washed, Filtered Red Blood Cells [*Hematology*]
WFRB-FM .... Frostburg, MD [*FM radio station call letters*]
WFRC .... Columbus, GA [*FM radio station call letters*]
WFRC .... Western Fisheries Research Committee [*Australia*]
WFRD .... Hanover, NH [*FM radio station call letters*]
WFRE .... Frederick, MD [*FM radio station call letters*]
WFRG .... Utica, NY [*FM radio station call letters*]
WFRH .... Kingston, NY [*FM radio station call letters*]
WFRJ .... Johnstown, PA [*FM radio station call letters*]
WFRL .... Freeport, IL [*AM radio station call letters*]
WFRM .... Coudersport, PA [*AM radio station call letters*]
WFRM-FM .... Coudersport, PA [*FM radio station call letters*]
WFRN .... Elkhart, IN [*AM radio station call letters*]
WFRN-FM .... Elkhart, IN [*FM radio station call letters*]
WFRO .... Fremont, OH [*AM radio station call letters*]
WFRO-FM .... Fremont, OH [*FM radio station call letters*]
WFRQ .... Waynesboro, TN [*FM radio station call letters*]
WFRR-FM .... Walton, IN [*FM radio station call letters*] (RBYB)
WFRS .... Smithtown, NY [*FM radio station call letters*]
WFRS .... World Federation of Rose Societies [*Hurlingham, Argentina*] (EAIO)
WFRV .... Green Bay, WI [*Television station call letters*]
WFRW .... Webster, NY [*FM radio station call letters*]
WFRX .... West Frankfort, IL [*AM radio station call letters*]
WFRX-FM .... West Frankfort, IL [*FM radio station call letters*]
WFS .... Waterhouse-Friderichsen Syndrome [*Medicine*]
WFS .... Weapon Fire Simulator (MCD)
WFS .... Welfare Food Service [*British*]
WFS .... Women for Sobriety (EA)
WFS .... Women in Fire Service (EA)
WFS .... Wood Furring Strips [*Technical drawings*]
WFS .... Work Function Surface
WFS .... World Fertility Survey [*Program*]
WFS .... World Food Security [*FAO program*] [*United Nations*]
WFS .... World Future Society (EA)
WFSA .... Wash Frock Salesmen's Association (EA)
WFSA .... Wilhelm Furtwangler Society of America (EA)
WFSA .... World Federation of Societies of Anaesthesiologists [*Bristol, England*] (EAIO)
WFSB .... 1st Washington Bancorp [*NASDAQ symbol*] (TTSB)
WFSB .... Hartford, CT [*Television station call letters*]
WFSB .... Washington Federal Savings Bank [*NASDAQ symbol*] (NQ)
WFS Bcp .... WFS Bancorp, Inc. [*Associated Press*] (SAG)
WFSBP .... World Federation of the Societies of Biological Psychiatry (EA)
WFSC .... Franklin, NC [*AM radio station call letters*]
WFSE .... Edinboro, PA [*FM radio station call letters*]
WFSEC .... World Fellowship of Slavic Evangelical Christians (EA)
WFSF .... World Futures Studies Federation (EA)
WFS Fn .... WFS Financial, Inc. [*Associated Press*] (SAG)
WFS Fncl .... WFS Financial, Inc. [*Associated Press*] (SAG)
WFSG .... Panama City, FL [*Television station call letters*]
WFSG .... Wilshire Financial Services Group, Inc. [*NASDAQ symbol*] (SAG)
WFSGI .... World Federation of the Sporting Goods Industry (EAIO)
WFSH .... Valparaiso-Niceville, FL [*AM radio station call letters*]
WFSI .... Annapolis, MD [*FM radio station call letters*]
WFSI .... WFS Financial [*NASDAQ symbol*] (TTSB)
WFSI .... WFS Financial, Inc. [*NASDAQ symbol*] (SAG)
WFSICCM .... World Federation of Societies of Intensive and Critical Care Medicine (EAIO)
WFSJ-FM .... St. Augustine, FL [*FM radio station call letters*] (RBYB)
WFSK .... Nashville, TN [*FM radio station call letters*]
WFSL .... Washington Federal [*NASDAQ symbol*] (TTSB)
WFSL .... Washington Federal Savings & Loan Association of Seattle [*NASDAQ symbol*] (NQ)
WFSN-FM .... Port Charlotte, FL [*FM radio station call letters*] (RBYB)
WFSNSW .... Wine and Food Society of New South Wales [*Australia*]
WFSO-FM .... Olivebridge, NY [*FM radio station call letters*] (RBYB)
WFSP .... Kingwood, WV [*AM radio station call letters*]
WFSP-FM .... Kingwood, WV [*FM radio station call letters*]
WFSQ .... Tallahassee, FL [*FM radio station call letters*]
WFSR .... Harlan, KY [*AM radio station call letters*]
WFSS .... Fayetteville, NC [*FM radio station call letters*]
WFSS .... Welsh Folk Song Society [*British*]
WFST .... Caribou, ME [*AM radio station call letters*]
WFSt .... Wehrmachtfuehrungsstab [*Armed Forces Operations Staff*] [*German military - World War II*]
WFSU .... Tallahassee, FL [*FM radio station call letters*]
WFSU-TV .... Tallahassee, FL [*Television station call letters*]
WFSW .... Panama City, FL [*FM radio station call letters*]
WFSW .... World Federation of Scientific Workers [*See also FMTS*] [*ICSU*] [*British*] (EAIO)
WFSY .... Panama City, FL [*FM radio station call letters*]
WFT .... Warm Fluctuating Temperatures
WFT .... West Fraser Timber Co. Ltd. [*Toronto Stock Exchange symbol Vancouver Stock Exchange symbol*]
WFT .... Wildfowl Trust [*British*]
WFTA .... Fulton, MS [*FM radio station call letters*]
WFTA .... Winograd Fourier Transform Algorithm (MCD)
WFTA .... World Federation of Taiwanese Associations (EA)
WFTC .... Minneapolis, MN [*Television station call letters*] (RBYB)
WFTC .... Western Flying Training Command [*AAFWFTC*]
WFTD .... Marietta, GA [*AM radio station call letters*]
WFTD .... Women's Flying Training Detachment [*World War II*]
WFTE .... Salem, IN [*Television station call letters*]
WFTF .... Rutland, VT [*FM radio station call letters*]
WFTG .... London, KY [*AM radio station call letters*]
WFTH .... Richmond, VA [*AM radio station call letters*]
WFTI .... St. Petersburg, FL [*FM radio station call letters*]
WFTJW .... World Federation of Travel Journalists and Writers (EA)
WFTK .... Wake Forest, NC [*AM radio station call letters*]
WFTL .... Fort Lauderdale, FL [*AM radio station call letters*]
WFTM .... Maysville, KY [*AM radio station call letters*]
WFTM-FM .... Maysville, KY [*FM radio station call letters*]
WFTN .... Franklin, NH [*AM radio station call letters*]
WFTN-FM .... Franklin, NH [*FM radio station call letters*]
WFTO .... Fulton, MS [*AM radio station call letters*]
WFTP .... Weapons Fly-To Point [*Military*] (CAAL)
WFTR .... Front Royal, VA [*AM radio station call letters*]
WFTR-FM .... Front Royal, VA [*FM radio station call letters*]
WFTS .... Tampa, FL [*Television station call letters*]
WFTS .... Western Fish Toxicology Station [*Environmental Protection Agency*]
W FTTNGS .... With Fittings [*Freight*]
WFTU .... World Federation of Trade Unions [*See also FSM*] [*Prague, Czechoslovakia*] (EAIO)
WFTUNMW .... World Federation of Trade Unions of Non-Manual Workers [*Belgium*] (EY)
WFTV .... Orlando, FL [*Television station call letters*]
WFTVN .... Women's Film, Television, and Video Network (EAIO)
WFTW .... Fort Walton Beach, FL [*AM radio station call letters*]
WFTX .... Cape Coral, FL [*Television station call letters*]
WFTZ .... Manchester, TN [*FM radio station call letters*]
WFU .... Wake Forest University [*Winston-Salem, NC*]
WFU .... War Frauds Unit
WFUCA .... World Federation of UNESCO Clubs and Associations
WFUL .... West Florida Union List [*Library network*]
WFUM .... Flint, MI [*FM radio station call letters*]
WFUM-TV .... Flint, MI [*Television station call letters*]
WFUN .... Ashtabula, OH [*AM radio station call letters*]
WFUN .... Bethalto, IL [*FM radio station call letters*]
WFUNA .... World Federation of United Nations Associations (EA)
WFUPA .... World Federation of Ukrainian Patriarchal Associations (EA)
WFUR .... Grand Rapids, MI [*AM radio station call letters*]
WFUR-FM .... Grand Rapids, MI [*FM radio station call letters*]
WFUV .... New York, NY [*FM radio station call letters*]
WFUWO .... World Federation of Ukrainian Women's Organizations [*Toronto, ON*] (EA)
WFVA .... Fredericksburg, VA [*AM radio station call letters*]
WFVR .... Valdosta, GA [*AM radio station call letters*]
WFVT .... Rock Hill, SC [*Television station call letters*]
WFW .... Walden Forever Wild (EA)
WFW .... Windows for Workgroups [*Microsoft Corp.*]
WFW .... Word for Windows [*Computer science*]
WFWA .... Fort Wayne, IN [*Television station call letters*]
WFWC .... Walden Forever Wild Committee (EA)
WFWG .... Windows for Workgroups [*Microsoft Corp.*]
WFWI .... Fort Wayne, IN [*FM radio station call letters*]
WFWL .... Camden, TN [*AM radio station call letters*]
WFWM .... Frostburg, MD [*FM radio station call letters*]
WFXA .... Augusta, GA [*FM radio station call letters*]
WFXB-TV .... Myrtle Beach, SC [*TV station call letters*] (RBYB)
WFXC .... Durham, NC [*FM radio station call letters*]
WFXD .... Marquette, MI [*FM radio station call letters*]
WFXE .... Columbus, GA [*FM radio station call letters*]
WFXG .... Augusta, GA [*Television station call letters*]
WFXH .... Hilton Head Island, SC [*AM radio station call letters*] (RBYB)
WFXH-FM .... Hilton Head Island, SC [*FM radio station call letters*]
WFXI .... Morehead City, NC [*Television station call letters*]
WFXK .... Tarboro, NC [*FM radio station call letters*]
WFXL .... Albany, GA [*Television station call letters*]
WFXM .... Forsyth, GA [*FM radio station call letters*]
WFXN .... Milton, WV [*FM radio station call letters*] (RBYB)
WFXO .... Iuka, MS [*FM radio station call letters*]
WFXP .... Erie, PA [*Television station call letters*] (RBYB)
WFXQ .... Chase City, VA [*FM radio station call letters*]
WFXR .... Roanoke, VA [*Television station call letters*]
WFXS .... Soddy-Daisy, TN [*FM radio station call letters*]
WFXT .... Boston, MA [*Television station call letters*]
WFXU .... Live Oak, FL [*Television station call letters*]
WFXV .... Utica, NY [*Television station call letters*]
WFXW .... Geneva, IL [*AM radio station call letters*]
WFXX .... South Williamsport, PA [*AM radio station call letters*]
WFXY .... Middlesboro, KY [*AM radio station call letters*]

WFXZ-TV ..... Jacksonville, NC [*TV station call letters*] (RBYB)
WFY ..... World Federalist Youth [*Netherlands*]
WFYC ..... Alma, MI [*AM radio station call letters*]
WFYI ..... Indianapolis, IN [*FM radio station call letters*]
WFYI-TV ..... Indianapolis, IN [*Television station call letters*]
WFYN ..... Rocky Mount, VA [*AM radio station call letters*]
WFY/NIO ..... World Federalist Youth - Youth Movement for a New International Order [*Amsterdam, Netherlands*] (EAIO)
WFYR ..... Elmwood, IL [*FM radio station call letters*]
WFY-USA ..... World Federalist Youth - United States of America [*Later, Action for World Community: World Federalist Youth in the USA*] (EA)
WFYV ..... Atlantic Beach, FL [*FM radio station call letters*]
WFYZ ..... Ravenswood, WV [*FM radio station call letters*]
WFZ ..... Weapons Free Zone
WG ..... Grenada [*International vehicle registration*] (ODBW)
WG ..... Riker Laboratories Ltd. [*Research code symbol*] [*British*]
WG ..... Wage Garnishment (MHDB)
WG ..... Wage Grade [*Federal employee job classification*]
WG ..... Wartime Guidance [*Air Force*] (AFM)
WG ..... Waste Gas [*Nuclear energy*] (NRCH)
WG ..... Water Gauge
W/G ..... Water Glycol (KSC)
WG ..... Waveguide
WG ..... Weather Group [*Air Force*]
WG ..... Wedge (MSA)
WG ..... Wegener's Granulomatosis [*Medicine*]
WG ..... Weighing (ROG)
WG ..... Weight Guaranteed
WG ..... Welsh Guards [*Military unit*] [*British*]
WG ..... West German
WG ..... Window Guard (AAG)
WG ..... Wine Gallon
WG ..... Wing
WG ..... Wired Glass [*Technical drawings*]
WG ..... Wire Gauge
WG ..... With Grain
WG ..... Women for Guatemala (EA)
WG ..... Working Group
WG ..... World Goodwill (EA)
WG ..... Wright-Giemsa [*A stain*] [*Cytology*]
WG ..... Write Gate (MHDB)
WG ..... Writing [*Law*] (ROG)
WGA ..... Wagga Wagga [*Australia Airport symbol*] (OAG)
WGA ..... Waveguide Assembly
WGA ..... Weekly Government Abstracts [*National Technical Information Service*]
WGA ..... Weighted Guidelines Analysis [*Air Force*] (MCD)
WGA ..... Wells-Gardner Electr [*AMEX symbol*] (TTSB)
WGA ..... Wells-Gardner Electronics Corp. [*AMEX symbol*] (SPSG)
WGA ..... Western Golf Association (EA)
WGA ..... Western Growers Association (EA)
WGA ..... Wheat Germ Agglutinin [*Biochemistry*]
WGA ..... Wild Goose Association (EA)
WGA ..... Women Grocers of America (EA)
WGA ..... Working Group of Agriculture (EERA)
WGA ..... Writers Guild of Alberta [*Canada*] (WWLA)
WGA ..... Writers Guild of America, West (EA)
WGAA ..... Cedartown, GA [*AM radio station call letters*]
WGAB ..... Newburgh, IN [*AM radio station call letters*]
WGAC ..... Augusta, GA [*AM radio station call letters*]
WGAD ..... Gadsden, AL [*AM radio station call letters*]
WGAE ..... Writers Guild of America, East (EA)
WGAE-US ..... World Government of the Age of Enlightenment - US (EA)
WGAF ..... West Germany Air Force
WGAI ..... Elizabeth City, NC [*AM radio station call letters*]
WGAI ..... Working Group Agenda Item (SAA)
WGAJ ..... Deerfield, MA [*FM radio station call letters*]
WGAL ..... Lancaster, PA [*Television station call letters*]
WGAM ..... Greenfield, MA [*AM radio station call letters*]
WGAM ..... Working Group on Antarctic Meteorology [*Marine science*] (OSRA)
WGAN ..... Portland, ME [*AM radio station call letters*]
WG & L ..... Warren, Gorham & Lamont, Inc. [*Publisher*]
WGAO ..... Franklin, MA [*FM radio station call letters*]
WGAO ..... World Guide to Abbreviations of Organizations [*A publication*]
WGAP ..... Maryville, TN [*AM radio station call letters*]
WGAP-FM ..... Maryville, TN [*FM radio station call letters*]
WGAR ..... Cleveland, OH [*FM radio station call letters*]
WGARCR ..... Working Group against Racism in Children's Resources (AIE)
WGAS ..... South Gastonia, NC [*AM radio station call letters*]
WGAS ..... Wholesale Grocers' Association of Scotland (DBA)
WGAT ..... Gate City, VA [*AM radio station call letters*]
WGAU ..... Athens, GA [*AM radio station call letters*]
WGAW ..... Gardner, MA [*AM radio station call letters*]
WGAW ..... Writers Guild of America, West (EA)
WGAY-FM ..... Washington, DC [*FM radio station call letters*] (RBYB)
WGAZ ..... Goodman, WI [*FM radio station call letters*]
WGB ..... Weltgewerkschaftsbund [*World Federation of Trade Unions*]
WGBA ..... Green Bay, WI [*Television station call letters*]
WGBB ..... Freeport, NY [*AM radio station call letters*]
WGBC ..... Meridian, MS [*Television station call letters*]
WGBC ..... Waveguide Operating below Cutoff (IEEE)
WGBD ..... Attica, IN [*FM radio station call letters*]
WGBE-FM ..... Bryan, OH [*FM radio station call letters*] (RBYB)
WGBF ..... Evansville, IN [*AM radio station call letters*] (RBYB)
WGBF ..... Henderson, KY [*FM radio station call letters*]
WGBH ..... Boston, MA [*FM radio station call letters*]
WGBH-TV ..... Boston, MA [*Television station call letters*]
WGBI ..... Scranton, PA [*AM radio station call letters*]
WGBM ..... Mishicot, WI [*FM radio station call letters*]
WGBN ..... New Kensington, PA [*AM radio station call letters*]
WGBO ..... Joliet, IL [*Television station call letters*]
WGBQ ..... Galesburg, IL [*FM radio station call letters*]
WGBR ..... Goldsboro, NC [*AM radio station call letters*]
WGBS ..... Philadelphia, PA [*Television station call letters*]
WGBW ..... Green Bay, WI [*FM radio station call letters*]
WGBX ..... Boston, MA [*Television station call letters*]
WGBY ..... Springfield, MA [*Television station call letters*]
WGc ..... Genoa City Public Library, Genoa City, WI [*Library symbol Library of Congress*] (LCLS)
WGC ..... Waste Gas Compressor [*Nuclear energy*] (NRCH)
WGC ..... Waveguide Shutter
WGC ..... Western Gear Corp.
WGC ..... Western Governors Conference
WGC ..... West Georgia College [*Carollton*]
WGC ..... Winslow Gold Corp. [*Vancouver Stock Exchange symbol*]
WGC ..... World Games Council (EAIO)
WGC ..... World Gospel Crusades (EA)
WGC ..... Worthy Grand Chaplain [*Freemasonry*]
WGC ..... Worthy Grand Conductor [*Freemasonry*] (ROG)
WGCA ..... Quincy, IL [*FM radio station call letters*]
WGCA ..... Winegrape Growers' Council of Australia
WGCA ..... Wisconsin Gift Cheese Association (EA)
WGCB ..... Red Lion, PA [*AM radio station call letters*]
WGCB-FM ..... Red Lion, PA [*FM radio station call letters*]
WGCB-TV ..... Red Lion, PA [*Television station call letters*]
WGCC ..... World Games Coordination Committee [*Karsruhe, Federal Republic of Germany*] (EAIO)
WGCCD ..... Working Group on Climate Change Detection [*Marine science*] (OSRA)
WGCC-FM ..... Batavia, NY [*FM radio station call letters*]
WG/CDR ..... Wing Commander [*British military*] (NATG)
WGCDR ..... Working Group for Community Development Reform [*Defunct*] (EA)
WGCF-FM ..... Paducah, KY [*FM radio station call letters*] (RBYB)
WGCH ..... Greenwich, CT [*AM radio station call letters*]
WGCI ..... Chicago, IL [*AM radio station call letters*]
WGCI-FM ..... Chicago, IL [*FM radio station call letters*]
WGCL ..... Bloomington, IN [*AM radio station call letters*]
WGCL ..... Window Glass Cutters League of America [*Later, GBBA*] (EA)
WGCM ..... Gulfport, MS [*AM radio station call letters*]
Wg Cmdr ..... Wing Commander [*British military*] (DMA)
WGCM-FM ..... Gulfport, MS [*FM radio station call letters*]
WGCO ..... Midway, GA [*FM radio station call letters*]
WGCQ ..... Immokalee, FL [*FM radio station call letters*] (RBYB)
WGCR ..... Brevard, NC [*AM radio station call letters*]
Wg Cr ..... Wing Commander [*British military*] (DMA)
WGCS ..... Goshen, IN [*FM radio station call letters*]
WGCT ..... Ellettsville, IN [*FM radio station call letters*]
WGCTA ..... Watson-Glaser Critical Thinking Appraisal (EDAC)
WGCU-TV ..... Fort Myers, FL [*TV station call letters*] (RBYB)
WGCV ..... Petersburg, VA [*AM radio station call letters*]
WGCX ..... Fairhope, AL [*FM radio station call letters*]
WGCY ..... Gibson City, IL [*FM radio station call letters*]
WGD ..... Windshield Guidance Display
WGD ..... Working Group Director
WGD ..... Working Group on Data [*Marine science*] (OSRA)
WGD ..... Working Group on Data (USDC)
WGD ..... Worldwide Government Directory [*A publication*]
WGDA ..... Watermelon Growers and Distributors Association
WGDC ..... Waveguide Directional Coupler
WGDC ..... Working Group for Democracy in Chile (EA)
WGDHP ..... Working Group on Domestic Hunger and Poverty (EA)
WGDL ..... Lares, PR [*AM radio station call letters*]
WGDL ..... Waveguide Delay Line
WGDN ..... Gladwin, MI [*AM radio station call letters*]
WGDN-FM ..... Gladwin, MI [*FM radio station call letters*]
WGDR ..... Plainfield, VT [*FM radio station call letters*]
WGDS ..... Warm Gas Distribution System
WGDS ..... Waste Gas Disposal System [*Nuclear energy*] (NRCH)
WGDT ..... Waste Gas Decay Tank [*Nuclear energy*] (NRCH)
WGE ..... Walgett [*Australia Airport symbol*] (OAG)
WGE ..... World's Great Explorers [*A publication*]
WGEA ..... Geneva, AL [*AM radio station call letters*]
WGEE ..... Green Bay, WI [*AM radio station call letters*]
WGEE ..... Sturgeon Bay, WI [*FM radio station call letters*]
WGEEIA ..... Western Ground Electronics Engineering Installation Agency (AAG)
WGEIO ..... World Guide to Environmental Issues [*A publication*]
WGEL ..... Greenville, IL [*FM radio station call letters*]
WGEM ..... Quincy, IL [*AM radio station call letters*]
WGEM-FM ..... Quincy, IL [*FM radio station call letters*]
WGEM-TV ..... Quincy, IL [*Television station call letters*]
WGEN ..... Geneseo, IL [*AM radio station call letters*]
WGEN ..... Watson General Corp. [*NASDAQ symbol*] (SPSG)
WGEN-FM ..... Geneseo, IL [*FM radio station call letters*]
WGER ..... Saginaw, MI [*FM radio station call letters*]
W GER ..... West Germany (WDAA)
WGER ..... Working Group on Extraterrestrial Resources [*Defunct NASA*]
WGES ..... Oswego, NY [*FM radio station call letters*]
WGES ..... World's Greatest Environment Statement (EERA)
WGET ..... Gettysburg, PA [*AM radio station call letters*]
WGETS ..... Wayne George Encoder Test Set

WGEV .... Beaver Falls, PA [*FM radio station call letters*]
WGEZ .... Beloit, WI [*AM radio station call letters*]
WGF .... Waveguide Filter
WGF .... Western Goals Foundation (EA)
WGF .... Women's Gas Federation [*British*] (BI)
WGF .... Wound Glass Fiber
WGFA .... Watseka, IL [*AM radio station call letters*]
WGFA-FM .... Watseka, IL [*FM radio station call letters*]
WGFAR .... Wenner-Gren Foundation for Anthropological Research (EA)
WGFB .... Plattsburgh, NY [*FM radio station call letters*]
WGFC .... Floyd, VA [*AM radio station call letters*]
WGFD .... Wyoming Game and Fish Department
WGFG .... Branchville, SC [*FM radio station call letters*]
WGFL .... High Springs, FL [*Television station call letters*]
WGFM .... Cheboygan, MI [*FM radio station call letters*]
WGFN .... Glen Arbor, MI [*FM radio station call letters*]
WGFP .... Webster, MA [*AM radio station call letters*]
WGFR .... Glens Falls, NY [*FM radio station call letters*]
WGFS .... Covington, GA [*AM radio station call letters*]
WGFT .... Youngstown, OH [*AM radio station call letters*]
WGFX .... Gallatin, TN [*FM radio station call letters*]
WGG .... Warm Gas Generator
WGG .... Worthy Grand Guardian [*Freemasonry*]
WGG .... Worthy Grand Guide [*Freemasonry*]
WGGA .... Gainesville, GA [*AM radio station call letters*]
WGGB .... Springfield, MA [*Television station call letters*]
WGGB .... Writers' Guild of Great Britain (DCTA)
WGGC .... Glasgow, KY [*FM radio station call letters*]
WGGD .... Melbourne, FL [*FM radio station call letters*]
WGGG .... Gainesville, FL [*AM radio station call letters*]
WG-GGI .... Working Group on Geodesy and Geographic Information (EERA)
WGGH .... Marion, IL [*AM radio station call letters*]
WGGL .... Houghton, MI [*FM radio station call letters*]
WGGM .... Chester, VA [*AM radio station call letters*]
WGGN .... Castalia, OH [*FM radio station call letters*]
WGGN .... Sandusky, OH [*Television station call letters*]
WGGO .... Salamanca, NY [*AM radio station call letters*]
WGGR .... Greenwood, IN [*FM radio station call letters*]
WGGS .... Greenville, SC [*Television station call letters*]
WGGT .... Greensboro, NC [*Television station call letters*]
WGGY .... Scranton, PA [*FM radio station call letters*]
WGGZ .... Baton Rouge, LA [*FM radio station call letters*]
WGH .... Newport News, VA [*AM radio station call letters*]
WGH .... Warren Gamaliel Harding [*US president, 1865-1923*]
WGH .... Worthy Grand Herald [*Freemasonry*]
WGHB .... Farmville, NC [*AM radio station call letters*]
WGHC .... Clayton, GA [*AM radio station call letters*]
WGH-FM .... Newport News, VA [*FM radio station call letters*]
WGHI .... Westmark Group Hldgs [*NASDAQ symbol*] (TTSB)
WGHI .... Westmark Group Holdings, Inc. [*NASDAQ symbol*] (SAG)
WGHN .... Grand Haven, MI [*AM radio station call letters*]
WGHN-FM ... Grand Haven, MI [*FM radio station call letters*]
WGHP .... High Point, NC [*Television station call letters*]
WGHQ .... Kingston, NY [*AM radio station call letters*]
WGHR .... Marietta, GA [*FM radio station call letters*]
WGHT .... Pompton Lakes, NJ [*AM radio station call letters*]
WGHT .... Weight
WGI .... Waveguide Isolator
WGI .... Western Goldfields, Inc. [*Toronto Stock Exchange symbol*]
WGI .... Within-Grade Increase
WGI .... Word of God Institute [*Later, NIWG*] (EA)
WGI .... Work Glove Institute [*Later, WGMA*] (EA)
WGI .... World Geophysical Interval
WGI .... World Glacier Inventory (EERA)
WGIA .... Blackshear, GA [*AM radio station call letters*]
WGIB .... Birmingham, AL [*FM radio station call letters*]
WGIC .... Wheat Gluten Industry Council (EA)
WGIG .... Brunswick, GA [*AM radio station call letters*]
WGII .... Working Group on Internal Instrumentation [*NASA*]
WGIL .... Galesburg, IL [*AM radio station call letters*]
WGINC .... Wine Grape Industry Negotiating Committee [*Victoria, Australia*]
WGIQ .... Louisville, AL [*Television station call letters*]
WGIR .... Manchester, NH [*AM radio station call letters*]
WGIR-FM .... Manchester, NH [*FM radio station call letters*]
WGIX .... Gouverneur, NY [*FM radio station call letters*]
WGJ .... Worm Gear Jack
WGJB .... World's Greatest Jazz Band
WGK .... Wasser Gefahrdungsklasse [*Water hazard classification*] [*Germany*]
WGKA .... Atlanta, GA [*AM radio station call letters*]
WGKC-FM .... Mahomet, IL [*FM radio station call letters*] (RBYB)
WGKI .... Cadillac, MI [*Television station call letters*]
WGKP-FM .... Bensselaerville, NY [*FM radio station call letters*] (RBYB)
WGKR-FM .... Grand Gorge, NY [*FM radio station call letters*] (RBYB)
WGKS .... Paris, KY [*FM radio station call letters*]
WGKU .... Vanderbilt, MI [*Television station call letters*]
WGKX .... Memphis, TN [*FM radio station call letters*]
WGKY .... Wickliffe, KY [*FM radio station call letters*]
WGL .... Fort Wayne, IN [*AM radio station call letters*]
WGL .... Roanoke, IN [*FM radio station call letters*]
WGL .... Warangal [*India*] [*Seismograph station code, US Geological Survey*] (SEIS)
WGL .... Washington Gas Light Co. [*NYSE symbol*] (SPSG)
WGL .... Washington Gas Lt [*NYSE symbol*] (TTSB)
WGL .... Waveguide Load
WGL .... Weapons Guidance Laboratory
WGL .... Weighted Guidelines [*DoD*]
WGL .... Westar Group Ltd. [*Toronto Stock Exchange symbol Vancouver Stock Exchange symbol*]
WGL .... Western Guidance Laboratory [*Wright Air Development Center*] (MUGU)
WGL .... Westeuropaeische Gesellschaft fuer Luftfahrtpsychologie [*Western European Association for Aviation Psychology - WEAAP*] (EA)
WGL .... Wire Glass (AAG)
WGL .... Wire Grid Lens
WGL .... World Guide to Libraries [*A publication*]
WGL .... Wueste und Gelobtes Land [*A publication*] (BJA)
W GLAM .... West Glamorgan [*County in Wales*]
WGLB .... Port Washington, WI [*AM radio station call letters*]
WGLB-FM .... Port Washington, WI [*FM radio station call letters*]
WGLC .... Mendota, IL [*AM radio station call letters*]
WGLC-FM .... Mendota, IL [*FM radio station call letters*]
WGLD-FM .... Noblesville, IN [*FM radio station call letters*] (RBYB)
WGLE .... Lima, OH [*FM radio station call letters*]
WGLF .... Tallahassee, FL [*FM radio station call letters*]
WGLH .... La Follette, TN [*AM radio station call letters*] (RBYB)
WGLI .... Babylon, NY [*AM radio station call letters*]
WGLI .... Warren, Gorham & Lamont, Inc. (DLA)
WGLL .... Auburn, IN [*FM radio station call letters*] (RBYB)
WGLM .... West Lafayette, IN [*FM radio station call letters*]
WGLO .... Pekin, IL [*FM radio station call letters*]
WGLQ .... Escanaba, MI [*FM radio station call letters*]
WGLR .... Lancaster, WI [*AM radio station call letters*]
WGLR .... Wissenschaftliche Gesellschaft fuer Luft- und Raumfahrt [*Scientific Association for Air and Space Travel*] [*German*]
WGLR-FM .... Lancaster, WI [*FM radio station call letters*]
WGLS .... Glassboro, NJ [*FM radio station call letters*]
WGLS .... Weighted Guidelines System (AAGC)
WGLT .... Normal, IL [*FM radio station call letters*]
WGLU .... Johnstown, PA [*FM radio station call letters*]
WGLV .... Hartford, VT [*FM radio station call letters*]
WGLW .... Welsh Grand Lodge of Wales [*Freemasonry*]
WGLX .... Wisconsin Rapids, WI [*FM radio station call letters*]
WGLY .... Waterbury, VT [*FM radio station call letters*]
WGLZ .... West Liberty, WV [*FM radio station call letters*]
WGM .... Waveguide Meter
WGM .... Weighted Guidelines Method [*Navy*]
WGM .... Wilmington [*California*] [*Airport symbol*] (AD)
WGM .... World Gospel Mission (EA)
WGM .... Worthy Grand Marshal [*or Master*] [*Freemasonry*]
WGMA .... Spindale, NC [*AM radio station call letters*]
WGMA .... Washington Gallery of Modern Art
WGMA .... West Gulf Maritime Association (EA)
WGMA .... Wet Ground Mica Association [*Defunct*] (EA)
WGMA .... Work Glove Manufacturers Association (EA)
WGMA .... Working Group on Multilateral Assistance [*Department of the Treasury*]
WGMB .... Baton Rouge, LA [*Television station call letters*]
WGMC .... Greece, NY [*FM radio station call letters*]
WGMC .... West Germanic [*Language, etc.*]
WGMD .... Rehoboth Beach, DE [*FM radio station call letters*]
WGME .... Portland, ME [*Television station call letters*]
WGMF .... Watkins Glen, NY [*AM radio station call letters*]
WGMG .... Crawford, GA [*FM radio station call letters*]
WGMI .... Bremen, GA [*AM radio station call letters*]
WGMK .... Donalsonville, GA [*FM radio station call letters*]
WGML .... Hinesville, GA [*AM radio station call letters*]
WGMM .... Big Flats, NY [*FM radio station call letters*]
WGMO .... Shell Lake, WI [*FM radio station call letters*]
WGMP .... Philadelphia, PA [*AM radio station call letters*]
WGMR .... Tyrone, PA [*FM radio station call letters*]
WGMS .... Washington, DC [*FM radio station call letters*]
WGMS .... Working Group on Marine Sediments [*Marine science*] (OSRA)
WGMS .... World Glacier Monitoring Service [*of the International Union of Geodesy and Geophysics*] (EA)
WGMT .... Lyndon, VT [*FM radio station call letters*]
WGMX .... Marathon, FL [*FM radio station call letters*]
WGMZ .... Glencoe, AL [*Department of Commerce*]
WGN .... Chicago, IL [*AM radio station call letters*]
WGN .... Wagon
WGN .... White Gaussian Noise [*Random interference caused by movement of electricity in line*] [*Telecommunications*] (IAA)
WGN .... World's Greatest Newspaper [*Sometimes used in reference to Chicago Tribune*]
WGNA .... Albany, NY [*AM radio station call letters*]
WGNA-FM .... Albany, NY [*FM radio station call letters*]
WGNB .... Zeeland, MI [*FM radio station call letters*]
WGNC .... Gastonia, NC [*AM radio station call letters*]
WGNE .... Panama City, FL [*AM radio station call letters*]
WGNE .... Titusville, FL [*FM radio station call letters*]
WGNE .... Working Group on Numerical Experimentation [*Marine science*] (OSRA)
WGNI .... Wilmington, NC [*FM radio station call letters*]
WGNL .... Greenwood, MS [*FM radio station call letters*]
WGNL .... Waveguide Nitrogen Load
WGNM .... Macon, GA [*Television station call letters*]
WGNN-FM .... Fisher, IL [*FM radio station call letters*] (RBYB)
WGNO .... New Orleans, LA [*Television station call letters*]
WGNP .... Albany, GA [*FM radio station call letters*]
WGNR .... Monee, IL [*FM radio station call letters*]
WGNR .... Wegener Corp. [*NASDAQ symbol*] (NQ)

WGNRR .... Women's Global Network on Reproductive Rights [*Formerly, International Contraception, Abortion, and Sterilisation Campaign*] (EA)
WGNS .... Murfreesboro, TN [*AM radio station call letters*]
WGNT .... Portsmouth, VA [*Television station call letters*]
WGN-TV .... Chicago, IL [*Television station call letters*]
WGNU .... Granite City, IL [*AM radio station call letters*]
WGNV .... Milladore, WI [*FM radio station call letters*]
WGNX .... Atlanta, GA [*Television station call letters*]
WGNY .... Newburgh, NY [*AM radio station call letters*]
WGNY-FM .... Newburgh, NY [*FM radio station call letters*]
WGNZ .... Fairborn, OH [*AM radio station call letters*]
WGO .... Wehrmacht Graeberoffizier [*Armed forces graves registration officer*] [*German military - World War II*]
Wg O .... Wing Officer [*British military*] (DMA)
WGO .... Winnebago Indus [*NYSE symbol*] (TTSB)
WGO .... Winnebago Industries, Inc. [*NYSE symbol*] (SPSG)
WGOC .... Blountville, TN [*AM radio station call letters*]
WGOC .... World Government Organization Coalition (EAIO)
WGOCC .... World Government Organization Coordinating Council [*Later, WGOC*] (EA)
WGOD .... Charlotte Amalie, VI [*AM radio station call letters*]
WGOD-FM ... Charlotte Amalie, VI [*FM radio station call letters*]
Wg Offr .... Wing Officer [*British military*] (DMA)
WGOG .... Walhalla, SC [*AM radio station call letters*]
WGOG-FM ... Walhalla, SC [*FM radio station call letters*]
WGOH .... Grayson, KY [*AM radio station call letters*]
WGOJ .... Conneaut, OH [*FM radio station call letters*]
WGOK .... Mobile, AL [*AM radio station call letters*]
WGOL .... Lynchburg, VA [*FM radio station call letters*]
WGOM .... Marion, IN [*AM radio station call letters*]
WGOR .... Martinez, GA [*FM radio station call letters*]
WGOS .... High Point, NC [*AM radio station call letters*]
WGOT .... Merrimack, NH [*Television station call letters*]
WGOT .... Williams Grove Old Timers [*An association*] (EA)
WGOV .... Valdosta, GA [*AM radio station call letters*]
WGOW .... Chattanooga, TN [*AM radio station call letters*]
WGOX .... Inverness, FL [*Television station call letters*]
WGP .... Waingapu [*Indonesia*] [*Airport symbol*] (OAG)
WGP .... Wattle Grove Press
WGp .... Weather Group [*Air Force*] (AFM)
WGP .... Westgrowth Petroleums Ltd. [*Toronto Stock Exchange symbol*]
WGP .... William Grand Prix Racing Ltd. [*Cayman Islands*] [*ICAO designator*] (FAAC)
WGP .... Wire Grid Polarizer
WGPA .... Bethlehem, PA [*AM radio station call letters*]
WGPC .... Albany, GA [*AM radio station call letters*]
WGPC-FM .... Albany, GA [*FM radio station call letters*]
WGPH .... Vidalia, GA [*FM radio station call letters*]
WGPL-AM .... Portsmouth, VA [*AM radio station call letters*] (RBYB)
WGPM-FM ... Farmville, NC [*FM radio station call letters*] (RBYB)
WGPMS .... Warehousing Gross Performance Measurement System (AFM)
WGPR .... Detroit, MI [*FM radio station call letters*]
WGPR-TV .... Detroit, MI [*Television station call letters*]
WGPT .... Oakland, MD [*Television station call letters*]
WGPTDR ...... Danube Tourist Commission [*Formerly, Working Group for the Promotion of Tourism inthe Danube Region*] [*Austria*] (EAIO)
WGQR .... Elizabethtown, NC [*FM radio station call letters*]
WGr .... Brown County Library, Green Bay, WI [*Library symbol Library of Congress*] (LCLS)
WGR .... Buffalo, NY [*AM radio station call letters*]
WGR .... War Guidance Requirements (AFM)
WGR .... Water Graphite Reactor Experiment [*Nuclear energy*]
WGR .... Westbridge Resources Ltd. [*Vancouver Stock Exchange symbol*]
WGR .... Western Gas Resources [*NYSE symbol*] (SPSG)
WGR .... Women in Government Relations (EA)
WGR .... Working Group Report
WGRA .... Cairo, GA [*AM radio station call letters*]
WGRA .... Worksheet Global Recalculation Automatic [*Computer science*]
WGrB .... Bellin Memorial Hospital, Green Bay, WI [*Library symbol Library of Congress*] (LCLS)
WGRB .... Campbellsville, KY [*Television station call letters*]
WGrBC .... Brown County Hospital, Green Bay, WI [*Library symbol Library of Congress*] (LCLS)
WGRC .... Lewisburg, PA [*FM radio station call letters*]
WGRD .... Grand Rapids, MI [*AM radio station call letters*]
WGRD .... Working Group on Rural Development [*Department of Agriculture*] (EGAO)
WGRD-FM ... Grand Rapids, MI [*FM radio station call letters*]
WGRE .... Greencastle, IN [*FM radio station call letters*]
WGREPO ...... Western Governors Regional Energy Policy Office
WGRF .... Buffalo, NY [*FM radio station call letters*]
WGRF .... Working Group on Radiation Fluxes [*Marine science*] (OSRA)
WGRG .... Owego, NY [*FM radio station call letters*]
WGRIDA ...... World GRID Association (EA)
WGRK .... Greensburg, KY [*FM radio station call letters*]
WGRL .... Indianapolis, IN [*FM radio station call letters*]
WGRM .... Greenwood, MS [*AM radio station call letters*]
WGRM-FM ... Greenwood, MS [*FM radio station call letters*]
WGRN .... Greenville, IL [*FM radio station call letters*]
WGrN .... Northeastern Wisconsin Technical Institute, Green Bay, WI [*Library symbol Library of Congress*] (LCLS)
WGrnbg .... Greenburg [*William*] Jr. Desserts & Cafes, Inc. [*Associated Press*] (SAG)
WGrNM .... Neville Public Museum, Green Bay, WI [*Library symbol Library of Congress*] (LCLS)
WGRO .... Lake City, FL [*AM radio station call letters*]
WGRP .... Greenville, PA [*AM radio station call letters*]
WGRPr .... Western Gas Res$2.28 cm Pfd [*NYSE symbol*] (TTSB)
WGRPrA ..... Western Gas Res $2.625 Cv Pfd [*NYSE symbol*] (TTSB)
WGRQ .... Colonial Beach, VA [*FM radio station call letters*]
WGRR .... Hamilton, OH [*FM radio station call letters*]
WGRS .... Guilford, CT [*FM radio station call letters*]
WGrSM .... Saint Mary's Hospital, Green Bay, WI [*Library symbol Library of Congress*] (LCLS)
WGrSV .... Saint Vincent Hospital, Green Bay, WI [*Library symbol Library of Congress*] (LCLS)
WGRT-FM .... Port Huron, MI [*FM radio station call letters*] (RBYB)
WGrU .... University of Wisconsin-Green Bay, Green Bay, WI [*Library symbol Library of Congress*] (LCLS)
WGRV .... Greeneville, TN [*AM radio station call letters*]
WGrw .... Greenwood Public Library, Greenwood, WI [*Library symbol*] [*Library of Congress*] (LCLS)
WGRW-FM ... Anniston, AL [*FM radio station call letters*] (RBYB)
WGRX .... Westminster, MD [*FM radio station call letters*]
WGRY .... Grayling, MI [*AM radio station call letters*]
WGRY-FM .... Grayling, MI [*FM radio station call letters*] (RBYB)
WGRZ .... Buffalo, NY [*Television station call letters*]
WG(S) .... Waste Gas (System) [*Nuclear energy*] (NRCH)
WGS .... Waterford Generating Station [*Nuclear energy*] (NRCH)
WGS .... Water Gas Shift [*Chemical reaction*]
WGS .... Water Glycol Service Unit (MCD)
WGS .... Waveguide Glide Slope
WGS .... Weatherall Green Smith [*British*] (ECON)
WGS .... Web Guide System
WGS .... Work Group System [*Computer hardware*] (PCM)
WGS .... World Geodetic System (MUGU)
WGS .... World Government Sponsors
WGS .... Worthy Grand Sentinel [*Freemasonry*]
WGS84 .... World Geodetic Spheroid 1984 (EERA)
WGSA .... Working Group on Sustainable Agriculture [*Australia*]
WGSAT .... Working Group on Satellites [*Marine science*] (OSRA)
WGSB .... Mebane, NC [*AM radio station call letters*]
WGSC .... War Gaming and Simulation Center [*National Defense University*]
WGSC .... Wide Gap Spark Chamber [*Electronics*] (OA)
WGSE .... Myrtle Beach, SC [*Television station call letters*]
WGSF .... Bartlett, TN [*AM radio station call letters*] (RBYB)
WGSG .... Mayo, FL [*FM radio station call letters*]
WGSI .... Working Group on Sea Ice [*Marine science*] (OSRA)
WGSIM .... Working Group on Satellite Ionospheric Measurements [*NASA*]
WGSJ .... Worm Gear Screw Jack
WGSK .... South Kent, CT [*FM radio station call letters*]
WGSL .... Loves Park, IL [*FM radio station call letters*]
WGSM .... Huntington, NY [*AM radio station call letters*]
WGSN .... North Myrtle Beach, SC [*AM radio station call letters*]
WGSO .... New Orleans, LA [*AM radio station call letters*]
WGSP .... Charlotte, NC [*AM radio station call letters*]
WGSPR .... Working Group for Space Physics Research
WGSQ .... Cookeville, TN [*FM radio station call letters*]
WGSS-FM .... Kingstree, SC [*FM radio station call letters*] (RBYB)
WGST .... Atlanta, GA [*AM radio station call letters*]
WGST .... Canton, GA [*FM radio station call letters*]
WGST .... Waste Gas Storage Tank [*Nuclear energy*] (IEEE)
WGSU .... Geneseo, NY [*FM radio station call letters*]
WGSV .... Guntersville, AL [*AM radio station call letters*]
WGSY .... Phenix City, AL [*FM radio station call letters*]
WGT .... Water-Glycol Cooling Unit Technician (SAA)
WGT .... Wayne General and Technical College, Orrville, OH [*Inactive*] [*OCLC symbol*] (OCLC)
WGT .... Weapons Guidance and Tracking (SAA)
WGT .... Weight [*Shipping*] (DS)
wgt .... Weight (DAVI)
WGT .... Wet Globe Temperature (PDAA)
WGTA .... Summerville, GA [*AM radio station call letters*]
WGTA .... Wisconsin General Test Apparatus [*Psychology*]
WGTC .... New Carlisle, IN [*FM radio station call letters*]
WG-T-C ...... Waveguide-to-Coaxial [*Aerospace*] (AAG)
WGTC .... Working Group on Tracking and Computation [*NASA*]
WGT/COMB ... Weighter/Combiner (MCD)
WGTD .... Kenosha, WI [*FM radio station call letters*]
WGTE .... Toledo, OH [*FM radio station call letters*]
WGTE-TV .... Toledo, OH [*Television station call letters*]
WGTF .... Dothan, AL [*FM radio station call letters*]
WGTH .... Richlands, VA [*AM radio station call letters*] (RBYB)
WGTH-FM .... Richlands, VA [*FM radio station call letters*]
WGTI .... Wandel & Goltermann Tech [*NASDAQ symbol*] (TTSB)
WGTI .... Wandel & Goltermann Technologies [*NASDAQ symbol*] (SAG)
WGTK .... Middlebury, VT [*FM radio station call letters*]
WGTM .... Wilson, NC [*AM radio station call letters*]
WGTN .... Andrews, SC [*FM radio station call letters*]
WGTN .... Georgetown, SC [*AM radio station call letters*]
WGTO .... Cassopolis, MI [*AM radio station call letters*] (RBYB)
WGTQ .... Sault Ste. Marie, MI [*Television station call letters*]
WGTR .... Bucksport, SC [*FM radio station call letters*]
WGTS .... Takoma Park, MD [*FM radio station call letters*]
WGTT .... Alabaster, AL [*AM radio station call letters*]
WGTU .... Traverse City, MI [*Television station call letters*]
WGTV .... Athens, GA [*Television station call letters*]
WGTW .... Burlington, NJ [*Television station call letters*]

WGTX-AM.... Freeport, FL [*AM radio station call letters*] (RBYB)
WGTY.......... Gettysburg, PA [*FM radio station call letters*]
WGTZ.......... Eaton, OH [*FM radio station call letters*]
WGU........... Western Governors University
WGU........... Working Group on Untouchables (EA)
WGUC.......... Cincinnati, OH [*FM radio station call letters*]
WGUF.......... Marco, FL [*FM radio station call letters*]
WGUL.......... Dunedin, FL [*AM radio station call letters*]
WGUL-FM..... Dade City, FL [*FM radio station call letters*] (RBYB)
WGUN.......... Atlanta, GA [*AM radio station call letters*]
WGUS.......... North Augusta, SC [*AM radio station call letters*]
WGUSEASA... Working Group of US Overseas Educational Advisers in South America [*Defunct*] (EA)
WGUY.......... Dexter, ME [*FM radio station call letters*]
WGVA.......... Geneva, NY [*AM radio station call letters*]
WGVE.......... Gary, IN [*FM radio station call letters*]
WGVK.......... Kalamazoo, MI [*Television station call letters*]
WGVL-AM.... Greenville, SC [*AM radio station call letters*] (RBYB)
WGVM.......... Greenville, MS [*AM radio station call letters*]
WGVP.......... Valdosta, GA [*Television station call letters*]
WGVU.......... Allendale, MI [*FM radio station call letters*]
WGVU.......... Grand Rapids, MI [*Television station call letters*]
WGVU.......... Kentwood, MI [*AM radio station call letters*]
WGW........... Wallila Gap [*Washington*] [*Seismograph station code, US Geological Survey*] (SEIS)
WGW........... Waveguide Window
WGW........... Wedgewood Resources [*Vancouver Stock Exchange symbol*]
WGW........... Wheat Gluten World [*A publication*] (EAAP)
WGWC.......... Working Group on Waterborne Cryptosporidiosis [*Medicine*]
WGWC.......... Working Group on Weather Communications [*NATO*] (NATG)
WGWC.......... World Service Authority of the World Government of World Citizens (EAIO)
WGWD.......... Gretna, FL [*FM radio station call letters*]
WGWG.......... Boiling Springs, NC [*FM radio station call letters*]
WGWM-AM... London, KY [*AM radio station call letters*] (RBYB)
WGWP.......... Working Group on Weather Plans [*NATO*] (NATG)
WGXA.......... Macon, GA [*Television station call letters*]
WGXL.......... Hanover, NH [*FM radio station call letters*]
WGXM.......... Dayton, OH [*FM radio station call letters*]
WGY........... Schenectady, NY [*AM radio station call letters*]
WGYJ.......... Atmore, AL [*AM radio station call letters*]
WGYL.......... Vero Beach, FL [*FM radio station call letters*]
WGYV.......... Greenville, AL [*AM radio station call letters*]
WGZB.......... Corydon, IN [*FM radio station call letters*]
WGZS.......... Dothan, AL [*AM radio station call letters*]
WH............ China Northwest Airlines [*ICAO designator*] (AD)
WH............ Henry Wriothesley, Earl of Southampton; or Sir William Harvey; or William Hathaway; or William Herbert, Earl of Pembroke [*Possible identities of the W. H. to whom Shakespeare's sonnets were supposedly dedicated by publisher Thomas Thorpe in 1609*]
Wh............ Interrogative [*Linguistics*]
WH............ Southeastern Commuter Airlines [*ICAO designator*] (AD)
WH............ Wage and Hour Cases [*Bureau of National Affairs*] [*A publication*] (DLA)
WH............ Walking Hinge (KSC)
WH............ Wall Hung [*Technical drawings*]
WH............ Wall Hydrant [*NFPA pre-fire planning symbol*] (NFPA)
W-H........... Walsh-Healey Act [*Labor*]
WH............ Warhead
W/H........... Warheading Building (NATG)
WH............ Watchdog Title
WH............ Water Heater
WH............ Watt-Hour
WH............ We Have, Ready with Called Party [*Telecommunications*] (TEL)
WH............ Wehrmacht-Heer [*Marking on Army vehicles*] [*German military - World War II*]
WH............ Well Healed [*Medicine*] (AAMN)
WH............ Welsh Horse [*British military*] (DMA)
WH............ Western Hemisphere
WH............ Western Hemlock [*Utility pole*] [*Telecommunications*] (TEL)
WH............ Wharf
Wh............ Wharton's Pennsylvania Supreme Court Reports [*1835-41*] [*A publication*] (DLA)
Wh............ Wheaton's International Law [*A publication*] (DLA)
Wh............ Wheaton's Reports [*14-25 United States*] [*A publication*] (DLA)
Wh............ Wheeler's New York Criminal Reports [*3 vols.*] [*A publication*] (DLA)
WH............ Wheelhouse (MSA)
WH............ Wheeling-Charleston [*Diocesan abbreviation*] [*West Virginia*] (TOCD)
WH............ Where (AABC)
WH............ Which
Wh............ While (AIA)
WH............ Whispered (ADA)
WH............ White [*Thoroughbred racing*]
WH............ White
wh............ White (WDMC)
WH............ White Hornet [*Immunology*]
WH............ White House
WH............ Whitman Co. [*NYSE symbol*] (SPSG)
WH............ Whitman Corp. [*NYSE symbol*] (TTSB)
WH............ Who
WH............ Whore (DSUE)
WH............ Wildwood House [*Publisher*] [*British*]
WH............ William Heinemann [*Publisher*] [*British*]
WH............ Wing Half (WDAA)
WH............ Wings of Hope [*An association*] (EA)
WH............ Withholding (AFM)
WH............ Workable Hatch [*Shipping*] (DS)
WH............ Work Hour (KSC)
WH............ World Heritage (EERA)
WH2........... Whipple Mountains Number 2 [*California*] [*Seismograph station code, US Geological Survey*] (SEIS)
WHA........... Madison, WI [*AM radio station call letters*]
WHA........... Wadi Halfa [*Sudan*] [*Airport symbol*] (AD)
WHA........... Wahaula [*Hawaii*] [*Seismograph station code, US Geological Survey*] (SEIS)
WHA........... Walkaloosa Horse Association (EA)
WHA........... Walsh-Healey Public Contracts Act (AAGC)
WHA........... Washington Headquarters Association (EA)
WHA........... Weld Head Assembly
WHA........... Welsh Hockey Association (DBA)
WHA........... Western Hardwood Association (EA)
WHA........... Western History Association (EA)
WHA........... Western Horsemen's Association [*British*] (DBA)
wha........... Whale (VRA)
WHA........... W. H. Allen [*Commercial firm British*]
WHA........... Women's Hockey Association [*Australia*]
WHA........... Wood Heating Alliance (EA)
WHA........... Work Health Authority [*Northern Territory, Australia*]
WHA........... Work Hours Act of 1962 (WYGK)
WHA........... World Heritage Area [*Commonwealth*] (EERA)
WHA........... World Hockey Association
WHA........... Wounded by Hostile Action
WHAA.......... Madison, ME [*FM radio station call letters*]
WHAB.......... Acton, MA [*FM radio station call letters*] (RBYB)
WHAB.......... Westminster Historical Atlas to the Bible [*A publication*] (BJA)
WHAC.......... World Hemophilia AIDS [*Acquired Immune Deficiency Syndrome*] Center (EA)
WHACK........ Warhead Attack Cruise Killer (MCD)
WHAD.......... Delafield, WI [*FM radio station call letters*]
WHAG.......... Hagerstown, MD [*Television station call letters*]
WHAG.......... Halfway, MD [*AM radio station call letters*]
WHAG.......... Windows Help Authoring Guide [*Computer software*] [*Microsoft Corp.*] (PCM)
WHAI.......... Bridgeport, CT [*Television station call letters*]
WHAI.......... Greenfield, MA [*AM radio station call letters*]
WHAI.......... Walter Hinchman Associates, Inc. [*Telecommunications Defunct*] (TSSD)
WHAI-FM..... Greenfield, MA [*FM radio station call letters*]
WHAJ.......... Bluefield, WV [*FM radio station call letters*]
WHAK.......... Rogers City, MI [*AM radio station call letters*]
WHAL.......... Shelbyville, TN [*AM radio station call letters*]
WHAL.......... Wellington Hall Ltd. [*NASDAQ symbol*] (NQ)
WHAM.......... Rochester, NY [*AM radio station call letters*]
WHAM.......... Water Hammer
WHAM.......... Water Hydrogen Ammonia Methane
WHAM.......... Wayne Horizontal Acceleration Mechanism
WHAM.......... Winning the Hearts and Minds [*of the people*] [*Vietnam pacification program*]
WHAM.......... Wisconsin H-Alpha Mapper [*Astrophysics*]
WHAM.......... Women, Heritage, and Museums [*British*] [*An association*] (DBA)
WHAM.......... Women's Health Action and Mobilization (EA)
WHAM.......... Work Handling and Maintenance [*Navy*] (NG)
WHAN.......... Wellness and Health Activation Networks (EA)
WH & G....... Welsby, Hurlstone, and Gordon's English Exchequer Reports [*1848-56*] [*A publication*] (DLA)
WH & HSA... Welsh Hospitals and Health Services Association (DBA)
Wh & TLC.... White and Tudor's Leading Cases in Equity [*9 eds.*] [*1849-1928*] [*A publication*] (DLA)
Wh & Tud.... White and Tudor's Leading Cases in Equity [*9th ed.*] [*1928*] [*A publication*] (DLA)
WHAP.......... Hopewell, VA [*AM radio station call letters*]
WHAP.......... When [*or Where*] Applicable
WHAP.......... Women's Health and Abortion Project (EA)
WHAR.......... Clarksburg, WV [*AM radio station call letters*]
Whar........... Wharton's Pennsylvania Supreme Court Reports [*1835-41*] [*A publication*] (DLA)
WHAR.......... Whereafter [*Legal*] [*British*] (ROG)
WHAR.......... Wild Horses of America Registry (EA)
Whar Ag...... Wharton on Agency [*A publication*] (DLA)
Whar Am Cr L... Wharton's American Criminal Law [*A publication*] (DLA)
Whar & St Med Jur... Wharton and Stille's Medical Jurisprudence [*A publication*] (DLA)
Whar Confl Law... Wharton's Conflict of Laws [*A publication*] (DLA)
Whar Con Law... Wharton's Conflict of Laws [*A publication*] (DLA)
Whar Conv... Wharton on Principles of Conveyancing [*1851*] [*A publication*] (DLA)
Whar Cr Ev... Wharton on Criminal Evidence [*A publication*] (DLA)
Whar Cri Pl... Wharton's Criminal Pleading and Practice [*A publication*] (DLA)
Whar Cr Law... Wharton's American Criminal Law [*A publication*] (DLA)
Whar Cr Pl... Wharton's Criminal Pleading and Practice [*A publication*] (DLA)
Whar Dig..... Wharton's Pennsylvania Digest [*A publication*] (DLA)
Whar Dom.... Wharton on the Law of Domicile [*A publication*] (DLA)
Whar Ev...... Wharton on Evidence in Civil Issues [*A publication*] (DLA)
Wharf.......... Wharf Resources Ltd. [*Associated Press*] (SAG)
Wharfe........ Wharfedale [*Printing*] (DGA)
Whar Hom... Wharton's Law of Homicide [*A publication*] (DLA)
Whar Ind..... Wharton's Precedents of Indictments and Pleas [*A publication*] (DLA)
Whar Innk.... Wharton on Innkeepers [*1876*] [*A publication*] (DLA)
Whar Law Dic... Wharton's Law Lexicon [*14th ed.*] [*1938*] [*A publication*] (DLA)
Whar Leg Max... Wharton's Legal Maxims [*3rd ed.*] [*1903*] [*A publication*] (DLA)
Whar Neg.... Wharton's Law of Negligence [*A publication*] (DLA)

Whar Prec Ind... Wharton's Precedents of Indictments and Pleas [*A publication*] (DLA)
Whar St Tr... Wharton's United States State Trials [*A publication*] (DLA)
Whart.......... Legal Maxims with Observations by George Frederick Wharton [*A publication*] (DLA)
Whart.......... Wharton's Pennsylvania Supreme Court Reports [*1835-41*] [*A publication*] (DLA)
Whart Ag..... Wharton on Agency [*A publication*] (DLA)
Whart Am Cr Law... Wharton's American Criminal Law [*A publication*] (DLA)
Whart & S Med Jur... Wharton and Stille's Medical Jurisprudence [*A publication*] (DLA)
Whart Confl Laws... Wharton's Conflict of Laws [*A publication*] (DLA)
Whart Cr Ev... Wharton on Criminal Evidence [*A publication*] (DLA)
Whart Crim Law... Wharton's American Criminal Law [*A publication*] (DLA)
Whart Cr Law... Wharton's American Criminal Law [*A publication*] (DLA)
Whart Cr Pl & Prac... Wharton's Criminal Pleading and Practice [*A publication*] (DLA)
Whart Ev...... Wharton on Evidence in Civil Issues [*A publication*] (DLA)
Whart Hom... Wharton's Law of Homicide [*A publication*] (DLA)
Whart Homicide... Wharton's Law of Homicide [*A publication*] (DLA)
Whart Law Dict... Wharton's Law Dictionary [*or Lexicon*] [*A publication*] (DLA)
Whart Law Lexicon... Wharton's Law Lexicon [*A publication*] (DLA)
Whart Lex.... Wharton's Law Lexicon [*A publication*] (DLA)
Whart Neg... Wharton on Negligence [*A publication*] (DLA)
Wharton....... Wharton's American Criminal Law [*A publication*] (DLA)
Wharton....... Wharton's Law Lexicon [*A publication*] (DLA)
Wharton....... Wharton's Pennsylvania Supreme Court Reports [*1835-41*] [*A publication*] (DLA)
Wharton Crim Evidence... Wharton's Criminal Evidence [*A publication*] (DLA)
Wharton Crim Proc... Wharton's Criminal Law and Procedure [*A publication*] (DLA)
Whart PA..... Wharton's Pennsylvania Supreme Court Reports [*1835-41*] [*A publication*] (DLA)
Whart State Tr... Wharton's United States State Trials [*A publication*] (DLA)
Whart St Tr... Wharton's United States State Trials [*A publication*] (DLA)
WHAS.......... Louisville, KY [*AM radio station call letters*]
WHAS.......... Whereas
WHAS.......... Women's Health Advisory Service [*Australia*]
WHASA......... White House Army Signal Agency
WHAS-TV..... Louisville, KY [*Television station call letters*]
WHAT.......... Philadelphia, PA [*AM radio station call letters*]
WHAT.......... Wetland Habitat Alliance of Texas
WHAT.......... What A World [*NASDAQ symbol*] (TTSB)
WHAT.......... What A World, Inc. [*NASDAQ symbol*] (SAG)
WHAT.......... What's Here and There [*Australia A publication*]
WHAT.......... Windows Help Authoring Tools [*Computer software*] [*Microsoft Corp.*] (PCM)
WHAT.......... Winds, Heights, and Temperatures
WhatA.......... What A World, Inc. [*Associated Press*] (SAG)
WhatAW...... What A World, Inc. [*Associated Press*] (SAG)
WHATSR...... Whatsoever
WHA-TV...... Madison, WI [*Television station call letters*]
WHATW...... What A World Wrrt [*NASDAQ symbol*] (TTSB)
WHAV.......... Haverhill, MA [*AM radio station call letters*]
WHAV.......... When Available (KSC)
WHAW.......... Weston, WV [*AM radio station call letters*]
WHAY.......... Whitley City, KY [*FM radio station call letters*]
WHAZ.......... Troy, NY [*AM radio station call letters*]
WHB............ Kansas City, MO [*AM radio station call letters*]
WHB............ [*The*] Wandering Hand Brigade [*Men who are likely to take liberties with women*]
WHB............ Waste Heat Boiler [*Nuclear energy*] (CAAL)
WHB............ Weight-Bearing (DAVI)
WHB............ Wheel Bumpers [*Technical drawings*]
WhB............ Whole Blood [*Hematology*] (DAVI)
WHB............ Wire Harness Board (MCD)
WHBB.......... Selma, AL [*AM radio station call letters*]
WHBC.......... Canton, OH [*AM radio station call letters*]
WHBC-FM.... Canton, OH [*FM radio station call letters*]
WHBF.......... Rock Island, IL [*Television station call letters*]
WHBFC........ Wayne Hann Band Fan Club (EA)
WHBG.......... Harrisonburg, VA [*AM radio station call letters*]
WHBI........... Lake Worth, FL [*Television station call letters*]
WHBK.......... Marshall, NC [*AM radio station call letters*]
WHBL.......... Sheboygan, WI [*AM radio station call letters*]
WHBL.......... World Home Bible League [*Later, BL*] (EA)
WHBM.......... Park Falls, WI [*FM radio station call letters*]
WHBMA....... Wood Hat Block Manufacturers Association (EA)
WHBN.......... Harrodsburg, KY [*AM radio station call letters*]
WHBN-FM.... Harrodsburg, KY [*FM radio station call letters*]
WHBQ.......... Memphis, TN [*AM radio station call letters*]
WHBQ-TV.... Memphis, TN [*Television station call letters*]
WHBR.......... Pensacola, FL [*Television station call letters*]
WHBS.......... Eatonville, FL [*AM radio station call letters*]
WHBS.......... Waste Heat Boiler Survey (DS)
WHBT.......... Tallahassee, FL [*AM radio station call letters*]
WHBU.......... Anderson, IN [*AM radio station call letters*]
WHBX.......... Tallahassee, FL [*FM radio station call letters*]
WHBY.......... Kimberly, WI [*AM radio station call letters*]
WHBY.......... Whereby
WHBZ.......... Port Royal, SC [*FM radio station call letters*] (RBYB)
WHC............ Wackenhut Corrections [*NYSE symbol*] (TTSB)
WHC............ Wage and Hour Cases [*A publication*] (AAGC)
WHC............ Wages for Housework Committee (EA)
WHC............ Washington Hospital Center, Washington, DC [*OCLC symbol*] (OCLC)
WHC............ Water Holding Capacity [*Also, WBC*] [*Food industry*]
WHC............ Watt-Hour Meter with Contact Device
WHC............ Westinghouse Hanford Co. (NRCH)
WHC............ Whitehorse [*Yukon Territory*] [*Seismograph station code, US Geological Survey*] (SEIS)
WHC............ White House Conference
WHC............ Winchester Capital [*Vancouver Stock Exchange symbol*]
WHC............ World Hereford Council (EAIO)
WHC............ World Heritage Committee [*See also CPM*] (EAIO)
WHCA.......... War Hazards Compensation Act
WHCA.......... White House Communications Agency (AABC)
WHCA.......... White House Correspondents' Association (EA)
WHCA.......... Women's Health Care Association [*Australia*]
WHCA.......... World Hobie Class Association [*Later, IHCA*] (EA)
WH Cas....... Wage and Hour Cases [*Bureau of National Affairs*] [*A publication*] (DLA)
WHCB.......... Bristol, TN [*FM radio station call letters*]
WHCC.......... Waynesville, NC [*AM radio station call letters*]
WHCCY........ White House Conference on Children and Youth (EA)
WHCDHP..... Wainwright House Center for Development of Human Potential [*Later, WH*] (EA)
WHCDHR..... Wainwright House Center for Development of Human Resources [*Later, WH*] (EA)
WHCE.......... Highland Springs, VA [*FM radio station call letters*]
WHCF.......... Bangor, ME [*FM radio station call letters*]
WHCF.......... White House Conference on Families [*June 5-July 3, 1980*] (EGAO)
WHCG.......... Metter, GA [*FM radio station call letters*]
WHcGS........ Church of Jesus Christ of Latter-Day Saints, Genealogical Society Library, Milwaukee Branch, Hales Corners, WI [*Library symbol Library of Congress*] (LCLS)
WHCH.......... Munising, MI [*FM radio station call letters*]
wh ch.......... Wheel Chair [*Medicine*] (DMAA)
wh ch.......... White Child [*Medicine*] (DMAA)
WH Chron.... Westminster Hall Chronicle and Legal Examiner [*1835-36*] [*A publication*] (DLA)
WHCJ........... Savannah, GA [*FM radio station call letters*]
WHCL.......... Clinton, NY [*FM radio station call letters*]
WHCLIS....... White House Conference on Library and Information Services [*Washington, DC, 1979*]
WHCLIST..... White House Conference on Library and Information Services Taskforce
WHCM.......... Parkersburg, WV [*FM radio station call letters*]
WHCN.......... Hartford, CT [*FM radio station call letters*]
WHCO.......... Sparta, IL [*AM radio station call letters*]
WHCOA........ White House Conference on Aging
WHCOLIS..... White House Conference on Library and Information Services
WHCR.......... New York, NY [*FM radio station call letters*]
Wh Cr Cas... Wheeler's New York Criminal Cases [*3 vols.*] [*A publication*] (DLA)
Wh Crim Cas... Wheeler's New York Criminal Cases [*A publication*] (DLA)
WHcS........... Sacred Heart School of Theology, Hales Corners, WI [*Library symbol Library of Congress*] (LCLS)
WHCS.......... Well History Control System [*Later, Historical Well Data On-Line*] [*Petroleum Information Corp.*] [*Information service or system*] (IID)
WHCSA........ Welsh Health Common Services Authority
WHCT.......... Hartford, CT [*Television station call letters*]
WHCU.......... Ithaca, NY [*AM radio station call letters*]
WHCU.......... Window Heat Control Unit
WHCY.......... Blairstown, NJ [*FM radio station call letters*]
WHD............ Wage and Hour Division [*Department of Labor*]
WHD............ Warhead
WHD............ Western Hemisphere Defense
WHD............ Wheeler Dam [*TVA*]
WHD............ Wirlwind Resources Ltd. [*Vancouver Stock Exchange symbol*]
WHD............ Write Head Driver (SAA)
WHDB.......... Woods Hole Database, Inc. [*Information service or system*] (IID)
W-HDCS...... Wyeth Laboratories - Human Diploid Cell Strain [*Rabies vaccine*]
WHDG.......... Rhinelander, WI [*FM radio station call letters*]
WHDH.......... Boston, MA [*Television station call letters*]
WHDL.......... Olean, NY [*AM radio station call letters*]
WHDM.......... McKenzie, TN [*AM radio station call letters*]
WHDM.......... Watt-Hour Demand Meter
WHDQ.......... Claremont, NH [*FM radio station call letters*]
WHDS.......... Warhead Section [*Military*] (AABC)
WHE............ Water Hammer Eliminator
WHE............ Westland Helicopters Ltd. [*British ICAO designator*] (FAAC)
WHE............ Wheaton College, Norton, MA [*OCLC symbol*] (OCLC)
Wh e........... White Edges [*Bookbinding*] (DGA)
WHE............ Whole Human Embryo [*Type of cell line*]
Wheat.......... Wheaton's Reports [*14-25 United States*] [*A publication*] (DLA)
Wheat.......... Wheaton's United States Supreme Court Reports [*1816-27*] [*A publication*] (AAGC)
Wheat Cap... Wheaton on Maritime Captures and Prizes [*A publication*] (DLA)
Wheat El Int Law... Wheaton's Elements of International Law [*A publication*] (DLA)
WHEATH...... Wheathampstead [*England*]
Wheat Hist Law Nat... Wheaton's History of the Law of Nations [*A publication*] (DLA)
Wheat Int Law... Wheaton's Elements of International Law [*7th ed.*] [*1944*] [*A publication*] (DLA)
Wheat Int Law... Wheaton's International Law [*A publication*] (DLA)
Wheat Law of Nat... Wheaton's History of the Law of Nations [*A publication*] (DLA)
Wheaton...... Wheaton's Reports [*14-25 United States*] [*A publication*] (DLA)
WHEB.......... Portsmouth, NH [*FM radio station call letters*]
WHEC.......... High-Endurance Coast Guard Cutter [*Formerly, WAPG*] (CINC)
WHEC.......... Rochester, NY [*Television station call letters*]

WHEC .... Wildlife Habitat Enhancement Council (EA)
WHECON ...... Wheel Control (MCD)
WHEE .... Martinsville, VA [*AM radio station call letters*]
Wheel .... Wheeler's New York Criminal Cases [*A publication*] (DLA)
Wheel .... Wheelock's Reports [*32-37 Texas*] [*A publication*] (DLA)
Wheel Abr ... Wheeler's Abridgment of American Common Law Cases [*A publication*] (DLA)
Wheel Br Cas ... Wheeling Bridge Case [*A publication*] (DLA)
Wheel Cr C ... Wheeler's New York Criminal Cases [*A publication*] (DLA)
Wheel Cr Cas ... Wheeler's New York Criminal Cases [*A publication*] (DLA)
Wheel Cr Ch ... Wheeler's New York Criminal Cases [*A publication*] (DLA)
Wheel Cr Rec ... Wheeler's New York Criminal Recorder [*1 Wheeler's Criminal Cases*] [*A publication*] (DLA)
Wheeler Abr ... Wheeler's Abridgment [*A publication*] (DLA)
Wheeler Am Cr Law ... Wheeler's Abridgment of American Common Law Cases [*A publication*] (DLA)
Wheeler CC ... Wheeler's New York Criminal Cases [*A publication*] (DLA)
Wheeler Cr Cas ... Wheeler's New York Criminal Cases [*A publication*] (DLA)
Wheeler Cr Cases ... Wheeler's New York Criminal Cases [*A publication*] (DLA)
Wheeler Crim Cas ... Wheeler's New York Criminal Cases [*A publication*] (DLA)
Wheeler's Cr Cases ... Wheeler's New York Criminal Cases [*A publication*] (DLA)
Wheelock C ... Wheelock College (GAGS)
Wheel Slav ... Wheeler on Slavery [*A publication*] (DLA)
Wheel (Tex) ... Wheelock's Reports [*32-37 Texas*] [*A publication*] (DLA)
WHEI .... Tiffin, OH [*FM radio station call letters*]
WHEI .... Women's Heathy Eating and Living [*Medicine*]
WHEL .... Helen, GA [*FM radio station call letters*]
WHEM .... Eau Claire, WI [*FM radio station call letters*]
WHEN .... Syracuse, NY [*AM radio station call letters*]
WHENCESR ... Whencesoever [*Legal*] [*British*] (ROG)
WHEN-FM .... Syracuse, NY [*FM radio station call letters*]
WHENR .... Whenever [*Legal*] [*British*] (ROG)
WHENSR ...... Whensoever [*Legal*] [*British*] (ROG)
WHEO .... Stuart, VA [*AM radio station call letters*]
WHEP .... Foley, AL [*AM radio station call letters*]
WHEP .... Warhead Engagement Program [*Military*]
WHER .... Hattiesburg, MS [*FM radio station call letters*]
WHER .... Whether [*Legal*] [*British*] (ROG)
WHERER ...... Wherever [*Legal*] [*British*] (ROG)
WHERF .... Wood Heating Education and Research Foundation (EA)
WHES .... World Hunger Education Service (EA)
WHET .... Birnamwood, WI [*FM radio station call letters*]
WHETS .... Washington Higher Education Telecommunications System [*Washington State University*] [*Pullman*] [*Telecommunications service*] (TSSD)
WHEW-AM ... Franklin, TN [*AM radio station call letters*] (RBYB)
WHF .... Waveguide Harmonic Filter
WHF .... Wharf
Whf .... Wharfedale [*Printing*] (DGA)
WHF .... Women in Housing and Finance (EA)
WHF .... Women's Hall of Fame [*Later, NWHF*] (EA)
WHF .... World Heritage Fund [*UNESCO*]
WHFA .... Western Hemisphere Friendship Association (EA)
WHFB .... Benton Harbor, MI [*AM radio station call letters*]
WHFB-FM .... Benton Harbor, MI [*FM radio station call letters*]
WHFC .... Bel Air, MD [*FM radio station call letters*]
WHFD .... Lawrenceville, VA [*FM radio station call letters*]
WHFE .... Lakeland, GA [*FM radio station call letters*]
WHFG .... Wharfage [*Shipping*]
WHFH .... Flossmoor, IL [*FM radio station call letters*]
WHFI .... Lindside, WV [*FM radio station call letters*]
WHFI .... Wholesome & Hearty Foods [*NASDAQ symbol*] (TTSB)
WHFI .... Wholesome & Hearty Foods, Inc. [*NASDAQ symbol*] (SAG)
WHFM .... Southampton, NY [*FM radio station call letters*]
WHFM .... Wherefrom [*Legal*] [*British*] (ROG)
WHFMS .... Woman's Home and Foreign Mission Society (EA)
WHFORE ...... Wherefore [*Legal*] [*British*] (ROG)
WHFR .... Dearborn, MI [*FM radio station call letters*]
WHFR .... Wharfinger [*Shipping*] [*British*] (ROG)
WHFS .... Annapolis, MD [*FM radio station call letters*]
WHFT .... Miami, FL [*Television station call letters*]
WHFTB .... Waste Heat Fire Tube Boiler (DS)
WHFTBS ...... Waste Heat Fire Tube Boiler Survey (DS)
WHF-USA ... World Health Foundation, United States of America [*Defunct*] (EA)
WHFX .... Waycross, GA [*FM radio station call letters*]
WHGB .... WHG Bancshares [*NASDAQ symbol*] (TTSB)
WHGB .... WHG Bancshares Corp. [*NASDAQ symbol*] (SAG)
WHGBcs ...... WHG Bancshares Corp. [*Associated Press*] (SAG)
WHGC .... Bennington, VT [*FM radio station call letters*]
WHGDP .... World Hunger/Global Development Program [*Defunct*] (EA)
WHGE .... Wharfage [*Shipping*]
WHGG .... Roanoke Rapids, NC [*FM radio station call letters*]
WHGH .... Thomasville, GA [*AM radio station call letters*]
WHGL .... Canton, PA [*FM radio station call letters*]
WHGL .... Troy, PA [*AM radio station call letters*]
WHGR .... Houghton Lake, MI [*AM radio station call letters*]
WHGT .... Waynesboro, PA [*AM radio station call letters*]
WHH .... Hartford Memorial Hospital, Hartford, WI [*Library symbol Library of Congress*] (LCLS)
WHH .... Werthamar-Helfand-Hohenberg Theory [*Solid state physics*]
WHH .... William Henry Harrison [*US president, 1773-1841*]
WHHA .... White House Historical Association (EA)
WHHB .... Holliston, MA [*FM radio station call letters*]
WHHH .... Indianapolis, IN [*FM radio station call letters*]
WHHI .... Highland, WI [*FM radio station call letters*]
WHHK .... Galva, IL [*FM radio station call letters*] (RBYB)
WHHL .... Watanabe Hereditary Hyperlipidemic [*Rabbits*]
WHHM .... Henderson, TN [*FM radio station call letters*]
WHHO .... Hornell, NY [*AM radio station call letters*]
WHHS .... Havertown, PA [*FM radio station call letters*]
WHHT .... Cave City, KY [*FM radio station call letters*]
WHHV .... Hillsville, VA [*AM radio station call letters*]
WHHY .... Montgomery, AL [*AM radio station call letters*]
WHHY-FM .... Montgomery, AL [*FM radio station call letters*]
WHi .... State Historical Society of Wisconsin, Madison, WI [*Library symbol Library of Congress*] (LCLS)
WHI .... Washington Homes [*NYSE symbol*] (TTSB)
WHI .... Washington Homes, Inc. [*NYSE symbol*] (SPSG)
WHI .... Wave Height Indicator [*Oceanography*]
WHI .... Weekly Hospital Indemnity [*Insurance*]
WHI .... Western Highway Institute (EA)
WHI .... Whitney [*Hawaii*] [*Seismograph station code, US Geological Survey Closed*] (SEIS)
WHI .... Wild Horse Industry [*Vancouver Stock Exchange symbol*]
WHI .... Woman Health International [*Defunct*] (EA)
WHI .... Women's Health Initiative [*National Institutes of Health*]
WHIA .... Woolen Hosiery Institute of America [*Defunct*] (EA)
WHIC .... Hardinsburg, KY [*AM radio station call letters*]
WHIC .... Women's Health Information Centre [*British*] (CB)
WHID .... Green Bay, WI [*FM radio station call letters*] (RBYB)
WHIDDA ...... Wideband High-Density Data Acquisition (MCD)
WHIE .... Griffin, GA [*AM radio station call letters*]
WHIF .... Palatka, FL [*FM radio station call letters*]
WHIG .... Ward Howell International Group [*British*]
WHII .... Women's Health in Industry [*Australia*]
WHIJ .... Ocala, FL [*FM radio station call letters*]
WHIL .... Mobile, AL [*FM radio station call letters*]
WHIM .... West Warwick, RI [*AM radio station call letters*] (RBYB)
WHIM .... Wet High-Intensity Magnet [*for mineral processing*]
WHIM .... Women Happy in Minis [*Boise, Idaho, group opposing below-the-knee fashions introduced in 1970*]
WHIMS .... Wet High Intensity Magnetic Separation (PDAA)
WHIN .... Gallatin, TN [*AM radio station call letters*]
WHIN .... Wherein [*Legal*] [*British*] (ROG)
WHIO .... Dayton, OH [*AM radio station call letters*]
WHIO-TV ...... Dayton, OH [*Television station call letters*]
WHIP .... Mooresville, NC [*AM radio station call letters*]
WHIP .... Walks plus Hits Divided by Innings Pitched [*Baseball*]
WHIP .... Wideband High Intercept Probability
WHIPS .... Widebeam High-Density Pulsed Source (MCD)
WHIQ .... Huntsville, AL [*Television station call letters*]
WHIR .... Danville, KY [*AM radio station call letters*]
WHIR-FM ..... Danville, KY [*FM radio station call letters*] (RBYB)
WHIS .... Bluefield, WV [*AM radio station call letters*]
WHIS .... Whiskeytown-Shasta-Trinity National Recreation Area
WHIS .... Whistle [*Navigation*]
Whishaw ...... Whishaw's Law Dictionary [*A publication*] (DLA)
Whish LD ..... Whishaw's New Law Dictionary [*1829*] [*A publication*] (DLA)
WHISP .... Woods Hole In-Situ Pump [*Marine biology*] [*Instrumentation*]
WHIST .... Worldwide Household Goods Information System for Traffic Management [*Army*] (AABC)
WHIT .... Madison, WI [*AM radio station call letters*]
WHIT .... Whittman-Hart Inc. [*NASDAQ symbol*] (TTSB)
Whitak Liens ... Whitaker on Liens [*A publication*] (DLA)
WHITCH .... Whitchurch [*England*]
White .... White's Justiciary Court Reports [*3 vols.*] [*Scotland*] [*A publication*] (DLA)
White .... White's Reports [*10-15 West Virginia*] [*A publication*] (DLA)
White .... White's Reports [*31-44 Texas Appeals*] [*A publication*] (DLA)
White & Civ Cas Ct App ... White and Willson's Civil Cases, Texas Court of Appeals [*A publication*] (DLA)
White & TL Cas ... White and Tudor's Leading Cases in Equity [*A publication*] (DLA)
White & T Lead Cas Eq ... White and Tudor's Leading Cases in Equity [*England*] [*A publication*] (DLA)
White & T Lead Cas in Eq (Eng) ... White and Tudor's Leading Cases in Equity [*England*] [*A publication*] (DLA)
White & Tud LC ... White and Tudor's Leading Cases in Equity [*9th ed.*] [*1928*] [*A publication*] (DLA)
White & Tudor ... White and Tudor's Leading Cases in Equity [*A publication*] (DLA)
White & W ... White and Willson's Reports, Civil Cases, Texas Court of Appeals [*A publication*] (DLA)
White & W Civ Cas Ct App ... White and Wilson's [*or Willson's*] Civil Cases, Texas Court of Appeals [*A publication*] (DLA)
White & W Civil Cases Ct App ... Texas Civil Cases [*A publication*] (DLA)
White & Willson ... Texas Civil Cases [*A publication*] (DLA)
White & W (Tex) ... White and Willson's Reports, Civil Cases, Texas Court of Appeals [*A publication*] (DLA)
White Char ... Whiteford on Charities [*1878*] [*A publication*] (DLA)
White Coll ... White's New Collection of the Laws, Etc., of Great Britain, France, and Spain [*A publication*] (DLA)
Whitehl ...... Whitehall Corp. [*Associated Press*] (SAG)
White LL ...... White's Land Law of California [*A publication*] (DLA)
White New Coll ... White's New Collection of the Laws, Etc. of Great Britain, France, and Spain [*A publication*] (DLA)
Whit Eq Pr ... Whitworth. Equity Precedents [*A publication*] (ILCA)
Whit Eq Pr ... Whitworth's Equity Precedents [*A publication*] (DLA)
WhiteRvr ..... White River Corp. [*Associated Press*] (SAG)
White's Ann Pen Code ... White's Annotated Penal Code [*Texas*] [*A publication*] (DLA)

White's Rep... White's Reports [*10-15 West Virginia*] [*A publication*] (DLA)
White's Rep... White's Reports [*31-44 Texas Appeals*] [*A publication*] (DLA)
White Suppl... White on Supplement and Revivor [*A publication*] (DLA)
White W & M... Whiteley's Weights, Measures, and Weighing Machines [*1879*] [*A publication*] (DLA)
Whit Lien..... Whitaker's Rights of Lien and Stoppage in Transitu [*1812*] [*A publication*] (DLA)
Whitm Adopt... Whitemore on Adoption of Children [*A publication*] (DLA)
Whitman Pat Cas (US)... Whitman's Patent Cases [*United States*] [*A publication*] (DLA)
Whitm BL .... Whitmarsh's Bankrupt Law [*2nd ed.*] [*1817*] [*A publication*] (DLA)
WhitmE........ Whitman Education Group [*Associated Press*] (SAG)
Whitm Lib Cas... Whitman's Massachusetts Libel Cases [*A publication*] (DLA)
WhitmM......... Whitman Medical Corp. [*Associated Press*] (SAG)
Whitmn........ Whitman Corp. [*Associated Press*] (SAG)
Whitm Pat Cas... Whitman's Patent Cases [*United States*] [*A publication*] (DLA)
Whitm Pat Law... Whitman's Patent Laws of All Countries [*A publication*] (DLA)
Whitm Pat Law Rev... Whitman's Patent Law Review [*Washington, DC*] [*A publication*] (DLA)
Whitney....... Whitney's Land Laws [*Tennessee*] [*A publication*] (DLA)
WhitnyH....... Whitney Holding Corp. [*Associated Press*] (SAG)
Whit Pat ...... Whitman's Patent Laws of All Countries [*A publication*] (DLA)
Whit Pat Cas... Whitman's Patent Cases [*United States*] [*A publication*] (DLA)
WHITS .... Whitstone [*England*]
Whit Schol... Whitgift Scholar [*British*]
Whit St Tr.... Whitaker's Rights of Lien and Stoppage in Transitu [*1812*] [*A publication*] (DLA)
Whitt............ Whittlesey's Reports [*32-41 Missouri*] [*A publication*] (DLA)
Whittakr....... Whittaker Corp. [*Associated Press*] (SAG)
Whittier C.... Whittier College (GAGS)
WHITTL......... Whittlesey [*Urban district in England*]
Whittlesey ... Whittlesey's Reports [*32-41 Missouri*] [*A publication*] (DLA)
Whitworth C... Whitworth College (GAGS)
WHIY .... Moulton, AL [*AM radio station call letters*]
WHIZ .... Zanesville, OH [*AM radio station call letters*]
WHIZ-FM .... Zanesville, OH [*FM radio station call letters*]
WHIZ-TV ..... Zanesville, OH [*Television station call letters*]
WHJB........... Greensburg, PA [*AM radio station call letters*]
WHJC........... Matewan, WV [*AM radio station call letters*]
WHJE........... Carmel, IN [*FM radio station call letters*]
WHJJ .... Providence, RI [*AM radio station call letters*]
WHJM........... Knoxville, TN [*AM radio station call letters*]
WHJT .... Clinton, MS [*FM radio station call letters*]
WHJY .... Providence, RI [*FM radio station call letters*]
WHK .... Cleveland, OH [*AM radio station call letters*]
WHK .... Whakatane [*New Zealand*] [*Airport symbol*] (OAG)
WHKE .... Kenosha, WI [*Television station call letters*]
WHKN........... Millen, GA [*FM radio station call letters*]
WHKO........... Dayton, OH [*FM radio station call letters*]
WHKP .... Hendersonville, NC [*AM radio station call letters*]
WHKR........... Rockledge, FL [*FM radio station call letters*]
WHKS .... Port Allegany, PA [*FM radio station call letters*]
WHKW .... Corydon, IN [*FM radio station call letters*]
WHKW .... Louisville, KY [*AM radio station call letters*] (RBYB)
WHKY .... Hickory, NC [*AM radio station call letters*]
WHKY-TV..... Hickory, NC [*Television station call letters*]
WHKZ .... Cayce, SC [*FM radio station call letters*]
WHL............. Watt-Hour Meter with Loss Compensator (MSA)
WHL............. Western Hockey League
WHL............. Westland Helicopters Ltd. [*British*] (IRUK)
WHL............. Wheel (AAG)
WHL............. Wheel
whl.............. Wholesale (MHDB)
WHL............. Woodgate Air Services Ltd. [*Zambia*] [*FAA designator*] (FAAC)
WHL............. World Heritage List [*UNESCO*]
WHL............. World Heritage Listing
WHLA .... La Crosse, WI [*FM radio station call letters*]
WHLA-TV ..... La Crosse, WI [*Television station call letters*]
WHLB .... Virginia, MN [*AM radio station call letters*]
WHLC-FM .... Highlands, NC [*FM radio station call letters*] (RBYB)
WHLD .... Niagara Falls, NY [*AM radio station call letters*]
WHLD .... Wheeled
WHLE........... Byhalia, MS [*FM radio station call letters*]
WHLF........... South Boston, VA [*AM radio station call letters*]
WHLG .... Jensen Beach, FL [*FM radio station call letters*]
WHLI .... Hempstead, NY [*AM radio station call letters*]
WHLM .... Bloomsburg, PA [*FM radio station call letters*]
WHLN........... Harlan, KY [*AM radio station call letters*]
WHLO........... Akron, OH [*AM radio station call letters*]
WHLQ .... Louisburg, NC [*FM radio station call letters*]
WHLS .... Port Huron, MI [*AM radio station call letters*]
WHLS .... Wheels [*Automotive advertising*]
WHLT............ Hattiesburg, MS [*Television station call letters*]
WhlTech ...... Wheelabrator Technology [*Associated Press*] (SAG)
WHLV .... Hattiesburg, MS [*AM radio station call letters*]
WHLX .... Bethlehem, WV [*FM radio station call letters*]
WHLY .... South Bend, IN [*AM radio station call letters*]
WHLZ........... Manning, SC [*FM radio station call letters*]
WHM .... Watt-Hour Meter
WHM .... Weighmaster (WGA)
WHM .... Wickham [*Australia Airport symbol*]
WHM .... Wild Horse Parks [*Montana*] [*Seismograph station code, US Geological Survey Closed*] (SEIS)
WHMA .... Anniston, AL [*AM radio station call letters*]
WHMA .... Women's Home Mission Association
WHMAA....... Wool Hat Manufacturers Association of America (EA)
WHMA-FM... Anniston, AL [*FM radio station call letters*]
WH Man .... Wage and Hour Reference Manual [*Bureau of National Affairs*] [*A publication*] (DLA)
WHMB .... Indianapolis, IN [*Television station call letters*]
WHMC .... Conway, SC [*FM radio station call letters*]
WHMC .... Wilford Hall United States Air Force Medical Center [*Lackland Air Force Base, TX*] (GRD)
WHMC-TV.... Conway, SC [*Television station call letters*]
WHMD .... Hammond, LA [*FM radio station call letters*]
WHME .... South Bend, IN [*FM radio station call letters*]
WHME-TV .... South Bend, IN [*Television station call letters*]
WHMH .... Sauk Rapids, MN [*FM radio station call letters*]
WHMI .... Howell, MI [*AM radio station call letters*]
WHMI .... Whitman Mission National Historic Site
WHMI-FM .... Howell, MI [*FM radio station call letters*]
WHMIS .... Wage and Hour Management Information System [*Department of Labor*] (GFGA)
WHMIS .... Workplace Hazardous Materials Information System [*Canada*]
WHML .... Wellcome Historical Medical Library [*Burroughs Wellcome Co.*] (DAVI)
WHMM .... Washington, DC [*Television station call letters*]
WHMP .... Northampton, MA [*AM radio station call letters*]
WHMP-FM... Northampton, MA [*FM radio station call letters*]
WHMQ .... North Baltimore, OH [*FM radio station call letters*]
WHMS .... Champaign, IL [*FM radio station call letters*]
WHMS .... Well-Healed Midline Scar [*Surgery*] (DAVI)
WHMT .... Humboldt, TN [*AM radio station call letters*]
WHMV & NSSA... Woods Hole, Martha's Vineyard & Nantucket Steamship Authority (MHDB)
WHMX .... Lincoln, ME [*FM radio station call letters*]
WHN .... Wharton & Northern Railroad Co. [*Absorbed into Consolidated Rail Corp.*] [*AAR code*]
WHN .... Whonnock Industries Ltd. [*Toronto Stock Exchange symbol Vancouver Stock Exchange symbol*]
WHN .... Women's History Network (EA)
WHNC........... Henderson, NC [*AM radio station call letters*]
WHND........... Monroe, MI [*AM radio station call letters*]
WHNN........... Bay City, MI [*FM radio station call letters*]
WHNO........... New Orleans, LA [*Television station call letters*]
WHNPA......... White House News Photographers Association (EA)
WHNR........... Cypress Gardens, FL [*AM radio station call letters*]
WHNR........... Whenever [*Legal*] [*British*] (ROG)
WHNRC......... Western Human Nutrition Research Center [*Department of Agriculture*] [*Research center*] (RCD)
WHNS .... Asheville, NC [*Television station call letters*]
WHNS .... Wartime Host Nation Support
WHNSIMS.... Wartime Host Nation Support Information Management System (DOMA)
WHNSR......... Whensoever [*Legal*] [*British*] (ROG)
WHNT .... Huntsville, AL [*Television station call letters*]
WHNY .... McComb, MS [*AM radio station call letters*]
WHNZ .... Pinellas Park, FL [*AM radio station call letters*]
WHO .... Des Moines, IA [*AM radio station call letters*]
WHO .... War on Hunger Office [*Department of State*]
WHO .... Waterhouse Investor Service [*NYSE symbol*] (SPSG)
WHO .... Waterhouse Investor Svc [*NYSE symbol*] (TTSB)
WHO .... Western Heraldry Organization (EA)
WHO .... Westhill Resources [*Vancouver Stock Exchange symbol*]
WHO .... [*The*] White House Office
WHO .... World Health Organization [*The pronunciation "who" is not acceptable*] [*United Nations affiliate Databank originator*] [*Switzerland*]
WHO .... World Housing Organization
WHO .... Wrist-Hand Orthosis [*Medicine*]
WHOA........... Montgomery, AL [*Television station call letters*]
WHOA........... Walking Horse Owner's Association of America (EA)
WHOA........... Why Have Overages Afterwards [*DoD*]
WHOA .... Wild Horse Organized Assistance (EA)
WHOAA......... Walking Horse Owner's Association of America (EA)
WHOB .... Nashua, NH [*FM radio station call letters*]
WHOC .... Philadelphia, MS [*AM radio station call letters*]
WHOD .... Jackson, AL [*AM radio station call letters*]
WHOD-FM ... Jackson, AL [*FM radio station call letters*]
WHO/EPR .... World Health Organization/Panafrican Centre for Emergency Preparedness and Response [*United Nations*]
WHOER......... Whoever [*Legal*] [*British*] (ROG)
WHOF .... Whereof [*Legal*] [*British*] (ROG)
WHOF .... Wildwood, FL [*AM radio station call letters*]
WHOG........... Hobson City, AL [*AM radio station call letters*]
WHOG-FM ... Ormond-by-the-Sea, FL [*FM radio station call letters*] (RBYB)
WHOI .... Peoria, IL [*Television station call letters*]
WHOI .... Woods Hole Oceanographic Institution [*Woods Hole, MA*] [*Research center*]
WHOIRP .... World Health Organization International Reference Preparation (DAVI)
WHOK........... Lancaster, OH [*FM radio station call letters*]
WHOL........... Allentown, PA [*AM radio station call letters*]
WHOL........... Wholesale (WGA)
WHOL........... Wholesale
WholeFd .... Whole Foods Market, Inc. [*Associated Press*] (SAG)
WholHty........ Wholesome & Hearty Foods [*Associated Press*] (SAG)
WHOLIS......... World Health Organization Library Information System (IID)
WHOM........... Mount Washington, NH [*FM radio station call letters*]
WHON........... Centerville, IN [*AM radio station call letters*]

WHON .... Whereon [*Legal*] [*British*] (ROG)
WHOO .... Orlando, FL [*AM radio station call letters*]
WHOOPS ..... Washington Public Power Supply System (DFIT)
WHOP .... Hopkinsville, KY [*AM radio station call letters*]
WHOP-FM.... Hopkinsville, KY [*FM radio station call letters*]
WHOS .... Decatur, AL [*AM radio station call letters*]
WHOSOR ..... Whosoever [*Legal*] [*British*] (ROG)
WHOT-FM .... Youngstown, OH [*FM radio station call letters*]
WHO-TV ...... Des Moines, IA [*Television station call letters*]
WHOU-FM ... Houlton, ME [*FM radio station call letters*]
Whous .... Warehouse
WHOV .... Hampton, VA [*FM radio station call letters*]
WHOW .... Clinton, IL [*AM radio station call letters*]
WHOW-FM... Clinton, IL [*FM radio station call letters*]
WHOY .... Salinas, PR [*AM radio station call letters*]
WHOZ-AM.... Fairhope, AL [*AM radio station call letters*] (RBYB)
WHP .... Harrisburg, PA [*AM radio station call letters*]
WHP .... Los Angeles, CA [*Location identifier FAA*] (FAAL)
WHP .... Water Horsepower
WHP .... West Hartford Public Library, West Hartford, CT [*OCLC symbol*] (OCLC)
whp .... Whirlpool (MAE)
WHP .... White House Police [*Later, Executive Protective Service*]
WHP .... WOCE [*World Ocean Circulation Experiment*] Hydrographic Experiment (USDC)
WHP .... WOCE [*World Ocean Circulation Experiment*] Hydrographic Program [*Marine science*] (OSRA)
WHP .... World Hydrocarbon Program (NITA)
WHPA .... Hollidaysburg, PA [*FM radio station call letters*]
WHPB .... Belton, SC [*AM radio station call letters*]
WHPC .... Garden City, NY [*FM radio station call letters*]
WHPC .... Wage and Hour and Public Contracts Division [*Department of Labor*] [*Obsolete*]
WHPCA .... Walsh-Healey Public Contracts Act [*1936*] [*Labor*]
WHPCD .... Wage and Hour and Public Contracts Division [*Department of Labor*] [*Obsolete*]
WHPE .... High Point, NC [*FM radio station call letters*]
WHPE .... Windows Help Project Editor [*Microsoft Corp.*] (PCM)
WHPK .... Chicago, IL [*FM radio station call letters*]
WHPL .... West Lafayette, IN [*FM radio station call letters*]
whpl .... Whirlpool
WHPO .... Hoopeston, IL [*FM radio station call letters*]
WHPO .... White House Personnel Office [*Terminated, 1974*]
WHPO .... WOCE [*World Ocean Circulation Experiment*] Hydrologic Program Office [*Marine science*] (OSRA)
WHPP .... Waste Handling and Packaging Plant [*Department of Energy*] [*Oak Ridge National Laboratory*] (GAAI)
WHPR .... Highland Park, MI [*FM radio station call letters*]
WHPT .... Sarasota, FL [*FM radio station call letters*]
WHP-TV ...... Harrisburg, PA [*Television station call letters*]
WHPY .... Clayton, NC [*AM radio station call letters*] (RBYB)
WHQ .... War Headquarters (NATG)
WHQ .... Western Historical Quarterly [*A publication*] (BRI)
WHQO .... Skowhegan, ME [*FM radio station call letters*]
WHQQ .... Charleston, IL [*FM radio station call letters*]
WHQR .... Wilmington, NC [*FM radio station call letters*]
WHQT .... Coral Gables, FL [*FM radio station call letters*]
WHR .... Vail [*Colorado*] [*Airport symbol*] (OAG)
WHR .... Wage and Hour Reporter [*Bureau of National Affairs*] [*A publication*] (DLA)
WHR .... Waste Heat Removal
W-HR .... Watt-Hour (AAG)
WHR .... Western Hemisphere Reserve
WHR .... Western Humanities Review [*A publication*] (BRI)
WHR .... Whether
WHR .... Whirlpool Corp. [*NYSE symbol*] (SPSG)
WHR .... William H. Rorer [*Research code symbol*]
WHR .... Women and Health Roundtable (EA)
WHR .... Working Heart Rate [*Cardiology*]
WHRA .... Welwyn Hall Research Association (PDAA)
WHRA .... Western Historical Research Associates [*Defunct*] (EA)
WHRABTS.... Whereabouts [*Legal*] [*British*] (ROG)
WHRAS .... Whereas [*Legal*] [*British*] (ROG)
WHRAT .... Whereat [*Legal*] [*British*] (ROG)
WHRB .... Cambridge, MA [*FM radio station call letters*]
WHRC .... Norwell, MA [*Television station call letters*]
WHRC .... Washington Home Rule Committee [*Later, SDDC*] (EA)
WHRC .... White River [*NASDAQ symbol*] (TTSB)
WHRC .... White River Corp. [*NASDAQ symbol*] (SAG)
WHRC .... World Health Research Center
WHRD .... Huntington, WV [*AM radio station call letters*]
WHRF .... Bel Air, MD [*AM radio station call letters*]
WHRI .... Women's Health Research Institute
WHRIN .... Wherein
WHRK .... Memphis, TN [*FM radio station call letters*]
WHRL .... Albany, NY [*FM radio station call letters*]
Whrlpl .... Whirlpool Corp. [*Associated Press*] (SAG)
WHRM .... Watt-Hour Meter (IAA)
WHRM .... Wausau, WI [*FM radio station call letters*]
WHR Man .... Wage and Hour Reference Manual [*Bureau of National Affairs*] [*A publication*] (DLA)
WHRM-TV .... Wausau, WI [*Television station call letters*]
WHRO .... Hampton-Norfolk, VA [*Television station call letters*]
WHRO .... Norfolk, VA [*FM radio station call letters*]
WHRR .... Avon, NY [*FM radio station call letters*] (RBYB)
WHRR-FM ... Dennysville, ME [*FM radio station call letters*] (RBYB)
WHRS-FM.... Cookeville, TN [*FM radio station call letters*] (RBYB)
WHRT .... World Heart Corp. [*NASDAQ symbol*] (SAG)
WHRU .... Waste Heat Recovery Unit [*Chemical engineering*]
WHRV .... Norfolk, VA [*FM radio station call letters*]
WHRW .... Binghamton, NY [*FM radio station call letters*]
WHRY .... Hurley, WI [*AM radio station call letters*]
WHRZ .... Providence, KY [*FM radio station call letters*]
WHS .... Warehouse (AABC)
whs .... Warehouse (ODBW)
WHS .... Washington Headquarters Services [*Military*]
WHS .... Water Hydraulic Section
WHS .... Wesleyan Historical Society [*British*]
WHS .... Western Harvest Sea [*Vancouver Stock Exchange symbol*]
WHS .... Whalsay [*Shetland Islands*] [*Airport symbol*] (OAG)
WHS .... White Scale
WHS .... William Hunter Society (EA)
WHS .... Wolf-Hirschorn Syndrome [*Medicine*]
WHS .... Women's Health Study
WHS .... World Health Statistics Data Base [*World Health Organization*] [*Information service or system*] (IID)
WHS .... Wound Healing Society
WHSA .... Brule, WI [*FM radio station call letters*]
WHSB .... Alpena, MI [*FM radio station call letters*]
WHSC .... Hartsville, SC [*AM radio station call letters*]
WHSC .... White House Science Council
WHSC-FM.... Hartsville, SC [*FM radio station call letters*]
WHSCH .... Whitworth Scholar [*British*]
WHSD .... Hinsdale, IL [*FM radio station call letters*]
WHSD .... W. H. Smith Distributors [*British*]
WHSE .... Newark, NJ [*Television station call letters*]
WHSE .... Warehouse (AAG)
W/HSE .... Wheelhouse [*Automotive engineering*]
WHSG .... Monroe, GA [*Television station call letters*]
WHSH .... Marlborough, MA [*Television station call letters*]
WHSHS .... Wilbur Hot Springs Health Sanctuary (EA)
WHSI .... Smithtown, NY [*Television station call letters*]
WHSING ...... Warehousing
WHSL .... East St. Louis, IL [*Television station call letters*]
WHSLE .... Wholesale
WHSL-FM .... High Point, NC [*FM radio station call letters*] (RBYB)
WHSLR .... Wholesaler
WHSM .... Hayward, WI [*AM radio station call letters*]
WHSMAN...... Warehouseman [*Legal shorthand*] (LWAP)
WHSM-FM... Hayward, WI [*FM radio station call letters*]
WHSMN .... Warehouseman (AABC)
WHSN .... Bangor, ME [*FM radio station call letters*]
WHSNA .... Welsh Harp Society of North America (EA)
WHSNG........ Warehousing
WHSP .... Vineland, NJ [*Television station call letters*]
WHSR .... White House Situation Room (MCD)
WHSS .... Hamilton, OH [*FM radio station call letters*]
WHSS .... White House Signal Support
WHST .... Tawas City, MI [*FM radio station call letters*]
WHSUPA...... Wharton School, University of Pennsylvania (DLA)
WHSV .... Harrisonburg, VA [*Television station call letters*]
WHSV .... Weight-Hourly Space Velocity [*Fuel technology*]
WHSW .... Baltimore, MD [*Television station call letters*]
WHSY .... Hattiesburg, MS [*AM radio station call letters*]
WHT .... Watt-Hour Demand Meter, Thermal Type (IEEE)
WHT .... White (AAG)
WHT .... Whitehall Corp. [*NYSE symbol*] (SPSG)
WHT .... William Herschel Telescope
WHT .... William Howard Taft [*US president, 1857-1930*]
WHT .... Women's Health Trial [*Department of Health and Human Services*] (GFGA)
WHT .... Wometco Home Theatre [*Subscription television service*]
WHTA .... Fayetteville, GA [*FM radio station call letters*] (RBYB)
WHTA .... Walking Horse Trainers Association (EA)
WHTB .... Fall River, MA [*AM radio station call letters*]
WHTC .... Holland, MI [*AM radio station call letters*]
WHTD .... Three Lakes, WI [*FM radio station call letters*]
WHTE-FM .... Valley Station, KY [*FM radio station call letters*] (RBYB)
WhtePne ...... White Pine Software, Inc. [*Associated Press*] (SAG)
Whtewg .... Whitewing Labs, Inc. [*Associated Press*] (SAG)
Whtewng ..... Whitewing Labs, Inc. [*Associated Press*] (SAG)
WHTF .... Starview, PA [*FM radio station call letters*]
WHTG .... Eatontown, NJ [*AM radio station call letters*]
WHTG-FM.... Eatontown, NJ [*FM radio station call letters*]
WHTH .... Heath, OH [*AM radio station call letters*]
WHTJ .... Charlottesville, VA [*Television station call letters*]
WHTK .... Rochester, NY [*AM radio station call letters*]
WHTL .... Whitehall, WI [*FM radio station call letters*]
WHTM .... Harrisburg, PA [*Television station call letters*]
WHTM .... Wisconsin Hydrologic Transport Model
WHTN .... Murfreesboro, TN [*Television station call letters*]
WHTO .... Muncy, PA [*FM radio station call letters*]
WHTO .... Whereto [*Legal*] [*British*] (ROG)
WHTQ .... Orlando, FL [*FM radio station call letters*]
WHTR-FM.... Hudson Falls, NY [*FM radio station call letters*] (RBYB)
WHTS .... Rock Island, IL [*FM radio station call letters*] (RBYB)
WHTS .... Western Hemisphere Transmission System
WHTT .... Buffalo, NY [*AM radio station call letters*]
WHTT-FM .... Buffalo, NY [*FM radio station call letters*]
WHTZ .... Newark, NJ [*FM radio station call letters*]

WHU Well Head Unit
WHU Wild Horse [*Utah*] [*Seismograph station code, US Geological Survey*] (SEIS)
WHUB Cookeville, TN [*AM radio station call letters*]
WHUB-FM Cookeville, TN [*FM radio station call letters*]
WHUC Hudson, NY [*AM radio station call letters*]
WHud Hudson Public Library, Hudson, WI [*Library symbol Library of Congress*] (LCLS)
WHUD Peekskill, NY [*FM radio station call letters*]
WHudSO Hudson Star-Observer, Hudson, WI [*Library symbol Library of Congress*] (LCLS)
WHUG Jamestown, NY [*FM radio station call letters*]
WHUN Huntingdon, PA [*AM radio station call letters*]
WHUR Washington, DC [*FM radio station call letters*]
WHUS Storrs, CT [*FM radio station call letters*]
WHUT Anderson, IN [*AM radio station call letters*]
WHV Woodchuck Hepatitis Virus
WHVE Russell Springs, KY [*FM radio station call letters*] (RBYB)
WHVL Hinesville, GA [*FM radio station call letters*] (RBYB)
WHVN Charlotte, NC [*AM radio station call letters*]
WHVP Hudson, NY [*FM radio station call letters*]
WHVP Wedged Hepatic Venous Pressure
WHVR Hanover, PA [*AM radio station call letters*]
WHVS Wharves (WGA)
WHVT Clyde, OH [*FM radio station call letters*]
WHVW Hyde Park, NY [*AM radio station call letters*]
WHW Women Helping Women (EA)
WHWC Menomonie, WI [*FM radio station call letters*]
WHWC-TV Menomonie, WI [*Television station call letters*]
WHWD-AM Fort Wayne, IN [*AM radio station call letters*] (RBYB)
WHWE Howe, IN [*FM radio station call letters*]
WHWH Princeton, NJ [*AM radio station call letters*]
WHWK Binghamton, NY [*FM radio station call letters*]
WHWL Marquette, MI [*FM radio station call letters*]
WHWPNLA World Health Workers for Peace and NonIntervention in Latin America (EAIO)
WHWT Water and Hazardous Waste Team (GNE)
WHWTB Waste Heat Water Tube Boiler (DS)
WHWTBS Waste Heat Water Tube Boiler Survey (DS)
WHWTCA West Highland White Terrier Club of America (EA)
WHWTH Wherewith [*Legal*] [*British*] (ROG)
WHX Wheeling Pittsburgh Corp. [*Later, WHX Corp.*] [*NYSE symbol*] (SPSG)
WHX WHX Corp. [*NYSE symbol*] (TTSB)
WHX WHX Corp. Holding Co. [*Associated Press*] (SAG)
WHX Cp WHX Corp. Holding Co. [*Associated Press*] (SAG)
WHXPr WHX Corp.'A'Cv Pfd [*NYSE symbol*] (TTSB)
WHXPrB WHX Corp.'B'Cv Pfd [*NYSE symbol*] (TTSB)
WHXT Citronelle, AL [*FM radio station call letters*]
WHY Air Sorel Ltd. [*Canada ICAO designator*] (FAAC)
WHY What Have You [*British*] (ADA)
WHY World Hunger Year (EA)
WHYB Menominee, MI [*FM radio station call letters*]
WHYC Swanquarter, NC [*FM radio station call letters*]
WHYCOS World Hydrological Cycle Observing System [*Marine science*] (OSRA)
WHYDFTFT What Have You Done for the Fleet Today [*Navy*]
WHYFU Why Have You Forsaken Us? [*Fundraising*]
WHYFU Why Have You Forsaken Us [*Informal fundraising term*] (NFD)
WHYI Fort Lauderdale, FL [*FM radio station call letters*]
WHYL Carlisle, PA [*AM radio station call letters*]
WHYL-FM Carlisle, PA [*FM radio station call letters*]
WHYM Statesville, NC [*AM radio station call letters*]
WHYN Springfield, MA [*AM radio station call letters*]
WHYN-FM Springfield, MA [*FM radio station call letters*]
WHYS Bluefield, VA [*AM radio station call letters*]
WHYT Detroit, MI [*FM radio station call letters*]
WHYY Philadelphia, PA [*FM radio station call letters*]
WHYY Wilmington, DE [*Television station call letters*]
WHYZ Sans Souci, SC [*AM radio station call letters*]
WHZR Royal Center, IN [*FM radio station call letters*]
WHZT Mahomet, IL [*FM radio station call letters*]
WHZZ Lansing, MI [*FM radio station call letters*] (RBYB)
WI Oak Harbor, Whidbey Island, WA [*Naval base*]
WI Rottnest Airbus [*Airline code*] [*Australia*]
WI Swift-Aire Lines [*ICAO designator*] (AD)
WI Walk In (ADA)
WI Wallops Island [*Off coast of Virginia*]
WI Water Injection
WI Water Inlet (DAC)
WI Welding Institute [*Database originator and operator*] (EA)
WI Westerners International (EA)
WI West Indies [*Formerly, BWI*]
WI Wexas International [*Commercial firm British*] (EAIO)
WI When Issued [*Stock exchange term*] (SPSG)
WI White Information [*Banking*] [*British*]
WI Wilderness Inquiry [*An association*] (EA)
WI Wimpy International [*Commercial firm British*]
WI Windward Islands (WDAA)
WI Wine Institute (EA)
WI Winter [*Germany ICAO aircraft manufacturer identifier*] (ICAO)
WI Wire
wi Wire (VRA)
WI Wisconsin [*Postal code*]
WI Within
WI Women's Institute [*British*]
WI Women's Reserve, Intelligence Duties [*USNR officer designation*]
WI Word Intelligibility
WI World Impact (EA)
WI Worldwatch Institute (EA)
WI Wrought Iron
WIA Manitowoc Public Library, Manitowoc, WI [*OCLC symbol*] (OCLC)
WIA Waking Imagined Analgesia [*Medicine*]
WIA Watusi International Association (EA)
WIA Weather-Impacted Airspace (USDC)
WIA Weather-Impacted Airspace [*Marine science*] (OSRA)
WIA Weight Indicating Alarm [*Engineering*]
WIA Western Interpreters Association [*Later, NAI*] (EA)
WIA Wien-Auhof [*Austria*] [*Geomagnetic observatory code*]
WIA Windward Islands Airways International NV [*Netherlands ICAO designator*] (FAAC)
WIA Winward Islands Airways International [*Netherlands Antilles*] (EY)
WIA Women in Aerospace (EA)
WIA Women in Agribusiness [*An association*] (EA)
WIA Women in the Arts Foundation (EA)
WIA Wounded in Action [*Military*]
WIAA Interlochen, MI [*FM radio station call letters*]
WIAA Sabang [*Indonesia*] [*ICAO location identifier*] (ICLI)
WIAA Women's International Association of Aeronautics (IAA)
WIAB Banda Aceh/Maimun Saleh [*Indonesia*] [*ICAO location identifier*] (ICLI)
WIAC San Juan, PR [*AM radio station call letters*]
WIAC Women's International Art Club
WIAC Women's International Art Club, London [*1899*] (NGC)
WIAC-FM San Juan, PR [*FM radio station call letters*]
WIACLALS West Indian Association for Commonwealth Literature and Language Studies [*Jamaica*] (EAIO)
WIACO World Insulation and Acoustic Congress Organization (EA)
WIAG Menggala/Astrakestra [*Indonesia*] [*ICAO location identifier*] (ICLI)
WIAI Danville, IL [*FM radio station call letters*]
WIAJ Semplak/Atang Senjaya [*Indonesia*] [*ICAO location identifier*] (ICLI)
WIAK Margahayu/Sulaiman [*Indonesia*] [*ICAO location identifier*] (ICLI)
WIAL Eau Claire, WI [*FM radio station call letters*]
WIAM Tasikmalaya/Cibeureum [*Indonesia*] [*ICAO location identifier*] (ICLI)
WIAM Williamston, NC [*AM radio station call letters*]
WIAN Ishpeming, MI [*AM radio station call letters*]
WI & CTF Welsh Industry and Commerce Trade Fair (ITD)
WIAP Banyumas/Wirasaba [*Indonesia*] [*ICAO location identifier*] (ICLI)
WIAP Wartime Individual Augmentation Program [*Military*]
WIAP Westinghouse Industrial Atomic Power (MCD)
WIAR Leland, MI [*FM radio station call letters*]
WIAR Madiun/Iswahyudi [*Indonesia*] [*ICAO location identifier*] (ICLI)
WIAS Malang/Abdul Rachman Saleh [*Indonesia*] [*ICAO location identifier*] (ICLI)
WIAS West Indies Associated State
WIAS Whiteruthenian Institute of Arts and Science [*Later, BIAS*] (EA)
WIB Lawrence University, Appleton, WI [*OCLC symbol*] (OCLC)
WIB Wallcovering Information Bureau (EA)
WIB Wartime Information Board [*World War II Canada*]
WIB Weather Information Branch [*Air Force*] (MCD)
WIB When Interrupt Block (NASA)
WIB When-Issued-Basis [*Business term*]
WIB Wine Information Bureau [*Australia*]
WIB Women's Information Bank (EA)
WIBA Madison, WI [*AM radio station call letters*]
WIBA Welsh Indoor Bowls Association (DBA)
WIBA-FM Madison, WI [*FM radio station call letters*]
WIBB Fort Valley, GA [*FM radio station call letters*]
WIBB Pekanbaru [*Indonesia*] [*ICAO location identifier*] (ICLI)
WIBC Indianapolis, IN [*AM radio station call letters*]
WIBC Women's International Bowling Congress (EA)
WIBC World Institute of Black Communications (EA)
WIBD Dumai/Pinangkampai [*Indonesia*] [*ICAO location identifier*] (ICLI)
WIBF Jenkintown, PA [*FM radio station call letters*]
WIBFD Will Be Forwarded (NOAA)
WIBG Ocean City, NJ [*AM radio station call letters*]
WIBI Carlinville, IL [*FM radio station call letters*]
WIBIS Will Be Issued (NOAA)
WIBM Jackson, MI [*FM radio station call letters*]
WIBN Earl Park, IN [*FM radio station call letters*]
WIBNI Wouldn't It Be Nice If [*Computer hacker terminology*] (NHD)
WIBP Semilinang/Peranap [*Indonesia*] [*ICAO location identifier*] (ICLI)
WIBR Baton Rouge, LA [*AM radio station call letters*]
WIBR Sipora/Rokot [*Indonesia*] [*ICAO location identifier*] (ICLI)
WIBS Bengkalis/Sungai Pakning [*Indonesia*] [*ICAO location identifier*] (ICLI)
WIBS Guayama, PR [*AM radio station call letters*]
WIBS Wool Industry Bureau of Statistics [*British*] (CB)
WIBT Tanjung Balai/Sungai Bati [*Indonesia*] [*ICAO location identifier*] (ICLI)
WIBU Poynette, WI [*AM radio station call letters*]
WIBV Belleville, IL [*AM radio station call letters*]
WIBW Topeka, KS [*AM radio station call letters*]
WIBW-FM Topeka, KS [*FM radio station call letters*]
WIBW-TV Topeka, KS [*Television station call letters*]
WIBX Utica, NY [*AM radio station call letters*]
WIBZ Wedgefield, SC [*FM radio station call letters*]
WIC Medical College of Wisconsin, Milwaukee, WI [*OCLC symbol*] (OCLC)
WIC War Insurance Corporation
WIC Warning Information Correlation (MCD)
WIC Washington International Center (EA)

WIC............ Water Infiltration Course [*Army*]
WIC............ Wax Insulating Compound
WIC............ Wayfarer International Committee [*Axminster, Devonshire, England*] (EAIO)
WIC............ Weighted Ion Concentration [*Air pollution measure*]
WIC............ Welding Institute of Canada (EAIO)
WIC............ Welfare and Institutions Code (BARN)
WIC............ West India Committee [*British*] (EAIO)
WIC............ Wheat Industry Council (EA)
WIC............ Whitbread Investment Co. [*British*]
WIC............ Wick [*Scotland*] [*Airport symbol*] (OAG)
WIC............ WICOR, Inc. [*NYSE symbol*] (SPSG)
WIC............ WIC Western International Communications Ltd. [*Toronto Stock Exchange symbol Vancouver Stock Exchange symbol*]
WIC............ Wildlife Information Center (EA)
WIC............ Windsor Institute of Complementology [*Later, ICS*] (EA)
WIC............ Women in Cable (EA)
WIC............ Women in Communications
WIC............ Women in Crisis (EA)
WIC............ Women, Infants, and Children [*Supplemental food program*] [*Department of Agriculture*]
WIC............ Women's Interart Center (EA)
WIC............ Women's Issues Coordinator [*Australia*]
WIC............ Workplace Information Centre [*New South Wales, Australia*]
WIC............ Worksheet Inspection Card
WIC............ World Institute Council (EA)
WICA.......... Judgments of the West Indian Court of Appeal [*A publication*] (DLA)
WICA.......... While in Control Area [*Aviation*] (FAAC)
WICA.......... Wind Cave National Park
WICA.......... Witches International Craft Association (EA)
WICAT........ World Institute for Computer-Assisted Teaching (NITA)
WICB.......... Ithaca, NY [*FM radio station call letters*]
WICB.......... Women in Cell Biology (EA)
WICBC........ World Invitation Club Basketball Championships [*British*]
WICBE........ World Information Centre for Bilingual Education [*See also CMIEB*] [*Paris, France*] (EAIO)
WICC.......... Bridgeport, CT [*AM radio station call letters*]
WICC.......... Wisconsin Instructional Computing Consortium (EDAC)
WICC.......... Women's Inter-Church Council of Canada
WICD.......... Champaign, IL [*Television station call letters*]
WICE.......... World Industry Council for the Environment
WICEM........ World Industry Conference on Environmental Management
WICF.......... Women's International Cultural Federation [*See also FICF*] (EAIO)
WICH.......... Norwich, CT [*AM radio station call letters*]
WICHE........ Western Interstate Commission for Higher Education (AEE)
WICHE........ Western Interstate Commission for Higher Education (GAGS)
Wichita St U... Wichita State University (GAGS)
WichRO........ Wichita River Oil Corp. [*Associated Press*] (SAG)
WICI............ Sumter, SC [*FM radio station call letters*]
WICI............ Women in Communications, Inc. (EA)
WICK.......... Scranton, PA [*AM radio station call letters*]
WICK.......... Wicklow [*County in Ireland*] (ROG)
WICKF........ Wickford [*England*]
WICKL........ Wicklow [*County in Ireland*]
WickLu........ Wickes Lumber Co. [*Associated Press*] (SAG)
WICL.......... Work Inspection Characteristics List
WICN.......... Women in Chemistry Network [*Australia*]
WICN.......... Worcester, MA [*FM radio station call letters*]
WICO.......... Salisbury, MD [*AM radio station call letters*]
WICO.......... W. I. Carr Sons & Co. Overseas [*Stockbroker*] [*Hong Kong*]
WICO-FM..... Salisbury, MD [*FM radio station call letters*]
WICOMATIC... Wiring and Connective Device, Semiautomatic (DNAB)
WICOR.......... WICOR, Inc. [*Associated Press*] (SAG)
WICR.......... Indianapolis, IN [*FM radio station call letters*]
WICR.......... Wilson's Creek Battlefield National Park
WICS.......... Springfield, IL [*Television station call letters*]
WICS.......... Westinghouse Integrated Compiling System (NITA)
WICS.......... Women in Community Service (EA)
WICS.......... Worldwide Intelligence Communications System (MCD)
WICT.......... Grove City, PA [*FM radio station call letters*]
WICU.......... Erie, PA [*Television station call letters*]
WICY.......... Malone, NY [*AM radio station call letters*]
WICZ.......... Binghamton, NY [*Television station call letters*]
WICZ.......... While in Control Zone [*Aviation*] (FAAC)
WID............ University of Wisconsin, Madison Library School, Madison, WI [*OCLC symbol*] (OCLC)
WID............ Weekly Intelligence Digest [*Military*] (CINC)
WID............ West India Dock
WID............ Widow [*or Widower*]
WID............ Width
WID............ Window Identifier [*Computer science*]
WID............ Wind River Resources [*Vancouver Stock Exchange symbol*]
WID............ Women in Development [*Peace Corps*]
WID............ Women in Development [*Bureau of the Census*] [*A publication*] (GFGA)
WID............ Women's Interest Division [*Australia*]
WID............ World Institute on Disability (EA)
WIDA.......... Carolina, PR [*AM radio station call letters*]
WIDA-FM..... Carolina, PR [*FM radio station call letters*]
WIDE.......... Biddeford, ME [*AM radio station call letters*]
WIDE.......... Wide-Angle Infinity Display Equipment
WIDE.......... WideCom Group [*NASDAQ symbol*] (SAG)
WIDE.......... Wide-Field Infrared Explorer [*Satellite*]
WIDE.......... Wiring Integration Design (IEEE)
WideC.......... WideCom Group [*Associated Press*] (SAG)
WideCm........ WideCom Group [*Associated Press*] (SAG)
WIDEF.......... WideCom Group [*NASDAQ symbol*] (TTSB)
Widener U.... Widener University (GAGS)
WIDER.......... World Institute for Development Economics Research [*United Nations*]
WIDETRACK... Wideband Transmission Relay Acoustic Communications (MCD)
WIDF.......... Women's International Democratic Federation [*See also FDIF*] [*Berlin, German Democratic Republic*] (EAIO)
WIDG.......... St. Ignace, MI [*AM radio station call letters*]
WIDI............ Women in Design International [*Later, DI*] (EA)
WIDJET........ Waterloo Interactive Direct Job Entry Terminal System [*IBM Corp.*]
WIDL.......... Caro, MI [*FM radio station call letters*]
WIDOWAC.... Wing Design Optimization with Aerolastic Constraints [*Computer program*]
WIDP.......... Guayama, PR [*Television station call letters*]
WIDR.......... Kalamazoo, MI [*FM radio station call letters*]
WIDR.......... Widower [*Legal shorthand*] (LWAP)
WIDS.......... Russell Springs, KY [*AM radio station call letters*] (RBYB)
WIDS.......... Waterborne Intrusion Detection System (MCD)
WIDU.......... Fayetteville, NC [*AM radio station call letters*]
WIDU.......... Wireless Intelligence and Development Unit [*British military*] (DMA)
WIDW.......... WideCom Group [*NASDAQ symbol*] (SAG)
WIDWF........ WideCom Group Wrrt [*NASDAQ symbol*] (TTSB)
WIE............ University of Wisconsin-Superior, Jim Dan Hill Library, Superior, WI [*OCLC symbol*] (OCLC)
WIE............ Women in Education [*Australia*]
WIE............ Women in Engineering Centre (EAIO)
WIE............ Women in Entertainment [*British*]
WIE............ Women's Information Exchange (EA)
WIEB/WINB... Western Interstate Energy Board/Western Interstate Nuclear Board (EA)
WIEC.......... World Institute of Ecology and Cancer [*See also IMEC*] (EAIO)
WIEL.......... Elizabethtown, KY [*AM radio station call letters*]
Wien Stud... Wiener Studien [*A publication*] (OCD)
WIEU.......... Weekly Intelligence Estimate Update [*Vietnam*]
WIEZ.......... Lewistown, PA [*AM radio station call letters*]
WIF............ Mid-Wisconsin Federated Library System, Fond Du Lac, WI [*OCLC symbol*] (OCLC)
WIF............ Water Immersion Facility [*NASA*] (KSC)
WIF............ Weapons Integration Facility (MCD)
WIF............ West India Fruit & Steamship [*AAR code*]
WIF............ West Indies Federation
WIF............ Wideroe's Flyveselskap AS [*Norway ICAO designator*] (FAAC)
WIF............ Wildfire Resources Ltd. [*Vancouver Stock Exchange symbol*]
WIF............ Wilt-Inducing Factor [*Plant pathology*]
WIF............ Women in Film (EA)
WIF............ Worldview International Foundation (EAIO)
WIFA.......... Washington Institute of Foreign Affairs (EA)
WIFC.......... Wausau, WI [*FM radio station call letters*]
WIFE.......... Connersville, IN [*AM radio station call letters*]
WIFE.......... Women Involved in Farm Economics (EA)
WIFE.......... Women's Independent Film Exchange [*Defunct*] (EA)
WIFF.......... Auburn, IN [*AM radio station call letters*]
WIFF.......... Wang [*Laboratories, Inc.*] Image File Format [*Computer science*] (PCM)
WIFI............ Florence, NJ [*AM radio station call letters*]
WIFM.......... Elkin, NC [*AM radio station call letters*] (RBYB)
WIFM-FM..... Elkin, NC [*FM radio station call letters*]
WIFN.......... Marine City, MI [*AM radio station call letters*]
WIFNA........ White Inhibited Fuming Nitric Acid (SAA)
WIFO.......... Jesup, GA [*FM radio station call letters*]
WIFP.......... Women's Institute for Freedom of the Press (EA)
WIFR.......... Freeport, IL [*Television station call letters*]
WIFS.......... Work Injury Followback Survey [*Bureau of Labor Statistics and National Center for Health Statistics*] (GFGA)
WIFU.......... Western Interprovincial Football Union [*Canada*]
WIFX.......... Jenkins, KY [*FM radio station call letters*]
WIG............ Washington Information Group, Ltd. [*Research center*] (TSSD)
WIG............ Wiggins Airways [*ICAO designator*] (FAAC)
Wig............ Wigram on Loills [*A publication*] (DLA)
WIG............ Wing in Ground
WIG............ Wisconsin State Library, Processing Center, Madison, WI [*OCLC symbol*] (OCLC)
WIG............ Wolfram Inert Gas (MCD)
Wig Disc...... Wigram on Discovery [*2nd ed.*] [*1840*] [*A publication*] (DLA)
WIGE.......... Wax-Impregnated Graphite Electrode
WIGE.......... Wing-in-Ground Effect (PDAA)
Wig Ev.......... Wigram on Extrinsic Evidence [*A publication*] (DLA)
WIGG.......... Wiggins, MS [*AM radio station call letters*]
Wight.......... Wightwick's English Exchequer Reports [*145 English Reprint*] [*A publication*] (DLA)
Wight El Cas... Wight's Scottish Election Cases [*1784-96*] [*A publication*] (DLA)
Wightw........ Wightwick's English Exchequer Reports [*145 English Reprint*] [*A publication*] (DLA)
Wightw (Eng)... Wightwick's English Exchequer Reports [*145 English Reprint*] [*A publication*] (DLA)
WIGL.......... Orangeburg, SC [*FM radio station call letters*]
WIGM.......... Medford, WI [*AM radio station call letters*]
Wigm Ev...... Wigmore on Evidence [*A publication*] (DLA)
WIGM-FM..... Medford, WI [*FM radio station call letters*]
WIGO.......... What Is Going On [*Humorous definition of science*]
WIGORN...... Wigorniensis [*Signature of Bishop of Worcester*] [*British*] (ROG)
WIGS.......... Gouverneur, NY [*AM radio station call letters*]
Wig Wills.... Wigmore on Wills [*A publication*] (DLA)
WIGY.......... Madison, ME [*FM radio station call letters*] (RBYB)

WIH .... State Historical Society of Wisconsin, Madison, WI [*OCLC symbol*] (OCLC)
WIH .... Work in Hand (ILCA)
WIHC .... Newberry, MI [*FM radio station call letters*] (RBYB)
WIHN .... Normal, IL [*FM radio station call letters*]
WIHS .... Middletown, CT [*FM radio station call letters*]
WIHS .... Western Institute for Health Studies (EA)
WIHS .... Women's Interagency HIV [*Human Immuno Deficiency Virus*] Study [*Medicine*]
WII .... Beloit College Library, Beloit, WI [*OCLC symbol*] (OCLC)
WII .... Weatherford Enterra [*NYSE symbol*] (SAG)
WIIA .... Tangerang/Budiarto [*Indonesia*] [*ICAO location identifier*] (ICLI)
WIIAD .... Winrock International Institute for Agricultural Development (EA)
WIIB .... Bandung/Husein Sastranegara [*Indonesia*] [*ICAO location identifier*] (ICLI)
WIIB .... Bloomington, IN [*Television station call letters*]
WIIC .... Cirebon/Panggung [*Indonesia*] [*ICAO location identifier*] (ICLI)
WIID .... Jakarta/Kemayoran [*Indonesia*] [*ICAO location identifier*] (ICLI)
WIIFM .... What's In It For Me [*Electronic mail language*] [*Computer science*]
WIIFM .... What's in It for Me? [*Fundraising*]
WIIG .... Jakarta/Pulau Panjang [*Indonesia*] [*ICAO location identifier*] (ICLI)
WIIH .... Jakarta/Halim Perdanakusuma [*Indonesia*] [*ICAO location identifier*] (ICLI)
WIII .... Cortland, NY [*FM radio station call letters*]
WIII .... Jakarta/Cengkareng [*Indonesia*] [*ICAO location identifier*] (ICLI)
WIIJ .... Yogyakarta/Adi Sucipto [*Indonesia*] [*ICAO location identifier*] (ICLI)
WIIK .... Kalijati [*Indonesia*] [*ICAO location identifier*] (ICLI)
WIIL .... Cilacap/Tunggul Wulung [*Indonesia*] [*ICAO location identifier*] (ICLI)
WIIL .... Kenosha, WI [*FM radio station call letters*]
WIIN .... Ridgeland, MS [*AM radio station call letters*] (RBYB)
WIIP .... Jakarta/Pondok Cabe [*Indonesia*] [*ICAO location identifier*] (ICLI)
WIIP .... Waters Intelligent Information Processor
WIIQ .... Demopolis, AL [*Television station call letters*]
WIIR .... Pelabuhan Ratu [*Indonesia*] [*ICAO location identifier*] (ICLI)
WIIR .... Water-Insoluble Inorganic Residue (DICI)
WIIS .... Key West, FL [*FM radio station call letters*]
WIIS .... Semarang/Achmad Yani [*Indonesia*] [*ICAO location identifier*] (ICLI)
WIIS .... Wang Integrated Image System
WIIS .... Women in International Security (EA)
WIIT .... Tanjung Karang/Branti [*Indonesia*] [*ICAO location identifier*] (ICLI)
WIIU .... Worker's International Industrial Union
WIIW .... Wiener Institut fuer Internationale Wirtschaftsvergleiche [*Vienna Institute for Comparative Economic Studies*] [*Information service or system*] (IID)
WIIX .... Jakarta [*Indonesia*] [*ICAO location identifier*] (ICLI)
WIIZ .... Blackville, SC [*FM radio station call letters*] (RBYB)
WIIZ .... Jakarta [*Indonesia*] [*ICAO location identifier*] (ICLI)
WIJ .... Arrowhead Library System, Janesville Public Library, Janesville, WI [*OCLC symbol*] (OCLC)
WIJ .... Wit of the Jews [*A publication*]
WIJK .... Evergreen, AL [*AM radio station call letters*]
WIJY .... Hilton Head Island, SC [*FM radio station call letters*]
WIK .... Kenosha Public Library, Kenosha, WI [*OCLC symbol*] (OCLC)
WIK .... Waikato Aero Club, Inc. [*New Zealand*] [*ICAO designator*] (FAAC)
WIK .... Wien-Kobenzl [*Austria*] [*Geomagnetic observatory code*]
WIKB .... Batam/Hang Nadim [*Indonesia*] [*ICAO location identifier*] (ICLI)
WIKB .... Iron River, MI [*AM radio station call letters*]
WIKB-FM ...... Iron River, MI [*FM radio station call letters*]
WIKC .... Bogalusa, LA [*AM radio station call letters*]
WIKD .... Petes Brewing Co. [*NASDAQ symbol*] (SAG)
WIKD .... Tanjung Pandan/Bulu Tumbang [*Indonesia*] [*ICAO location identifier*] (ICLI)
WIKE .... Newport, VT [*AM radio station call letters*]
WIKI .... Carrollton, KY [*FM radio station call letters*]
WIKK .... Newton, IL [*FM radio station call letters*]
WIKK .... Pangkal Pinang [*Indonesia*] [*ICAO location identifier*] (ICLI)
WIKN .... Port Matilda, PA [*FM radio station call letters*]
WIKN .... Tanjung Pinang/Kijang [*Indonesia*] [*ICAO location identifier*] (ICLI)
WIKO .... Morehead, KY [*FM radio station call letters*]
WIKQ .... Greeneville, TN [*FM radio station call letters*]
WIKS .... New Bern, NC [*FM radio station call letters*]
WIKS .... Singkep/Dabo [*Indonesia*] [*ICAO location identifier*] (ICLI)
WIKS .... Wickes Lumber [*NASDAQ symbol*] (TTSB)
WIKS .... Wickes Lumber Co. [*NASDAQ symbol*] (SAG)
WIKX .... Punta Gorda, FL [*FM radio station call letters*]
WIKY .... Evansville, IN [*FM radio station call letters*]
WIKZ .... Chambersburg, PA [*FM radio station call letters*]
WIL .... Lakeland College, Sheboygan, WI [*OCLC symbol*] (OCLC)
WIL .... Nairobi-Wilson [*Kenya*] [*Airport symbol*] (OAG)
WIL .... St. Louis, MO [*FM radio station call letters*]
WIL .... Ward Indicator Light
WIL .... West Isle Air, Inc. [*FAA designator*] (FAAC)
WIL .... White Indicating Light [*or lamp*]
WIL .... Wilco Mining Co. Ltd. [*Toronto Stock Exchange symbol*]
WIL .... Wilkes [*Antarctica*] [*Seismograph station code, US Geological Survey Closed*] (SEIS)
WIL .... Wilmington [*Diocesan abbreviation*] [*Delaware*] (TOCD)
WIL .... Wilshire Technologies [*AMEX symbol*] (TTSB)
WIL .... Wilshire Technologies, Inc. [*AMEX symbol*] (SPSG)
WIL .... Windows Interface Language [*Computer science*] (PCM)
WIL .... Women in Leadership [*Project*]
WILA .... Danville, VA [*AM radio station call letters*]
Wilberforce... Wilberforce on Statute Law [*A publication*] (DLA)
Wilb Stat ..... Wilberforce on Construction and Operation of Statutes [*1881*] [*A publication*] (DLA)
WILC .... Laurel, MD [*AM radio station call letters*]
WILC .... West Central Illinois Library Cooperative [*Library network*]
Wilc Cond .... Wilcox's Condensed Ohio Reports (Reprint) [*1-7 Ohio*] [*A publication*] (DLA)
Wilc Cond Rep... Wilcox's Condensed Ohio Reports (Reprint) [*1-7 Ohio*] [*A publication*] (DLA)
Wilc Mun Corp... Wilcox on Municipal Corporations [*Ohio*] [*A publication*] (DLA)
WILCO .... Western Interstate Library Coordinating Organization
WILCO .... Will Comply [*Used after "Roger"*] [*Radio term*]
wilco .... Will Comply (ODBW)
WILCO .... Wiltshire Libraries in Cooperation (NITA)
Wilcox .... Wilcox's Lackawanna Reports [*Pennsylvania*] [*A publication*] (DLA)
Wilcox .... Wilcox's Reports [*10 Ohio*] [*A publication*] (DLA)
Wilcox Cond... Wilcox's Condensed Ohio Reports [*A publication*] (DLA)
WILD .... Boston, MA [*AM radio station call letters*]
WILD .... What I Like to Do [*Psychological testing*]
WILD .... Women's Independent Label Distribution Network (EA)
Wilde Conv... Wilde's Supplement to Barton's Conveyancing [*A publication*] (DLA)
Wilde Sup ... Wilde's Supplement to Barton's Conveyancing [*A publication*] (DLA)
Wildl A .... Wildlife in Australia [*A publication*]
Wildm Int L... Wildman's International Law [*A publication*] (ILCA)
Wildm Int Law... Wildman's International Law [*A publication*] (DLA)
Wildm Search... Wildman. Search, Capture, and Prize [*A publication*] (ILCA)
WildOats ...... Wild Oats Markets, Inc. [*Associated Press*] (SAG)
WILE .... Byesville, OH [*FM radio station call letters*]
WILE .... Cambridge, OH [*AM radio station call letters*]
Wiley .... John Wiley & Sons [*Publisher*] (AAGC)
WileyJA .... Wiley [*John*] & Sons [*Associated Press*] (SAG)
WileyJB .... Wiley, John & Sons class A [*Associated Press*] (SAG)
WILF .... Williamsport, PA [*Television station call letters*]
WILI .... Willimantic, CT [*AM radio station call letters*]
WILI-FM ...... Willimantic, CT [*FM radio station call letters*]
WILJ .... West Indian Law Journal [*Jamaica*] [*A publication*] (DLA)
WILK .... Wilkes-Barre, PA [*AM radio station call letters*]
Wilk .... Wilkinson, Owen, Paterson, and Murray's New South Wales Reports [*1862-65*] [*A publication*] (DLA)
Wilk .... Wilkinson. Texas Court of Appeals and Civil Appeals [*A publication*] (DLA)
Wilk & Mur... Wilkinson, Owen, Paterson, and Murray's New South Wales Reports [*1862-65*] [*A publication*] (DLA)
Wilk & Ow... Wilkinson, Owen, Paterson, and Murray's New South Wales Reports [*1862-65*] [*A publication*] (DLA)
Wilk & Pat... Wilkinson, Owen, Paterson, and Murray's New South Wales Reports [*1862-65*] [*A publication*] (DLA)
Wilkes C ...... Wilkes College (GAGS)
Wilk Funds... Wilkinson on Public Funds [*1839*] [*A publication*] (DLA)
Wilk Leg Ang Sax... Wilkins' Leges Anglo-Saxonicae Ecclesiasticae et Civiles [*A publication*] (DLA)
Wilk Lim ...... Wilkinson. Limitation of Actions [*A publication*] (ILCA)
Wilk P & M... Wilkinson, Paterson, and Murray's New South Wales Reports [*1862-65*] [*A publication*] (DLA)
Wilk Prec ..... Wilkinson on Precedents in Conveyancing [*4th ed.*] [*1890*] [*A publication*] (DLA)
Wilk Repl .... Wilkinson on Replevin [*1825*] [*A publication*] (DLA)
Wilk Sh .... Wilkinson's Office of Sheriff [*A publication*] (DLA)
Wilk Ship .... Wilkinson on Shipping [*1843*] [*A publication*] (DLA)
WILL .... Urbana, IL [*AM radio station call letters*]
Will .... Willes' English Common Pleas Reports [*125 English Reprint*] [*A publication*] (DLA)
Will .... William (King of England) (DLA)
Will .... Williams' Massachusetts Reports [*1 Massachusetts*] [*1804-05*] [*A publication*] (DLA)
Will .... Williams' Vermont Reports [*27-29 Vermont*] [*A publication*] (DLA)
Will .... Willson's Reports [*29-30 Texas Appeals*] [*1, 2, Texas Civil Appeals*] [*A publication*] (DLA)
WILL .... Workshop In Library Leadership [*Canada*]
WILL .... Workshop Institute for Living-Learning (EA)
Will Abr .... Williams' Abridgment of Cases [*1798-1803*] [*A publication*] (DLA)
Willamette U... Willamette University (GAGS)
Willamt .... Willamette Industries, Inc. [*Associated Press*] (SAG)
Will Ann Reg... Williams' Annual Register [*New York*] [*A publication*] (DLA)
Will Auct ..... Williams' Auctions [*5th ed.*] [*1829*] [*A publication*] (DLA)
Will Bankt ... Williams' Law and Practice of Bankruptcy [*19th ed.*] [*1977*] [*A publication*] (DLA)
Will-Bund St Tr... Willis-Bund's Cases from State Trials [*A publication*] (DLA)
Willc Const... Willcock's The Office of Constable [*A publication*] (DLA)
Willc Med Pr... Willcock's Medical Profession [*1830*] [*A publication*] (DLA)
Willc Mun Corp... Willcock's Municipal Corp. [*A publication*] (ILCA)
Willcock Mun Corp... Willcock's Municipal Corp. [*A publication*] (DLA)
Will Com ..... Williams on Rights of Common [*A publication*] (DLA)
Will Con Rep... Texas Civil Cases [*A publication*] (DLA)
WillCor .... Willis Corroon Ltd. [*Associated Press*] (SAG)
Will Cr L ...... Willan's Criminal Law of Canada [*A publication*] (DLA)
Will Eq Jur... Willard's Equity Jurisprudence [*A publication*] (DLA)
Will Eq Pl .... Willis on Equity Pleading [*1820*] [*A publication*] (DLA)
Willes .... Willes' English Common Pleas Reports [*125 English Reprint*] [*A publication*] (DLA)
Willes (Eng)... Willes' English Common Pleas Reports [*125 English Reprint*] [*A publication*] (DLA)
Will Ex .... Williams on Executors [*15th ed.*] [*1970*] [*A publication*] (DLA)
WILL-FM ...... Urbana, IL [*FM radio station call letters*]
Williams ...... Peere-Williams' English Chancery Reports [*A publication*] (DLA)
Williams ...... [*The*] Williams Companies [*Associated Press*] (SAG)
Williams ...... Williams' Reports [*1 Massachusetts*] [*A publication*] (DLA)
Williams ...... Williams' Reports [*10-12 Utah*] [*A publication*] (DLA)

Williams...... Williams' Vermont Reports [*27-29 Vermont*] [*A publication*] (DLA)
Williams & B Adm Jur... Williams and Bruce's Admiralty Practice [*3 eds.*] [*1869-1902*] [*A publication*] (DLA)
Williams & Bruce Ad Pr... Williams and Bruce's Admiralty Practice [*3 eds.*] [*1869-1902*] [*A publication*] (DLA)
Williams B Pr... Williams' Bankruptcy Practice [*17 eds.*] [*1870-1958*] [*A publication*] (DLA)
Williams C... Williams College (GAGS)
Williams Common... Williams on Rights of Common [*A publication*] (DLA)
Williams Ex'rs... Williams on Executors [*A publication*] (DLA)
Williams Ex'rs R & T Ed... Williams on Executors, Randolph and Talcott Edition [*A publication*] (DLA)
Williams P... Peere-Williams' English Chancery Reports [*1695-1736*] [*A publication*] (DLA)
Williams Pers Prop... Williams on Personal Property [*A publication*] (DLA)
Williams Real Prop... Williams on Real Property [*A publication*] (DLA)
Williams Saund... Williams' Notes to Saunders' Reports [*A publication*] (DLA)
Williams Seis... Williams on Seisin [*A publication*] (DLA)
William W Story's Rept... William W. Story's United States Circuit Court Reports [*A publication*] (DLA)
Willis Eq...... Willis on Equity Pleading [*1820*] [*A publication*] (DLA)
Willis Int..... Willis on Interrogatories [*A publication*] (DLA)
Williston...... Williston on Contracts [*A publication*] (DLA)
Williston...... Williston on Sales [*A publication*] (DLA)
Willis Trust... Willis on Trustees [*A publication*] (DLA)
Will Just...... Williams' Justice [*A publication*] (DLA)
Will LD........ Williams' Law Dictionary [*A publication*] (DLA)
Willm.......... Williams Companies [*Associated Press*] (SAG)
Willm25........ Williams Companies [*Associated Press*] (SAG)
Will Mass.... Williams' Reports [*1 Massachusetts*] [*A publication*] (DLA)
Will Mass Cit... Williams' Massachusetts Citations [*A publication*] (DLA)
Willms25........ Williams Companies [*Associated Press*] (SAG)
WillmVV...... Willamette Valley Vineyards, Inc. [*Associated Press*] (SAG)
Willm W & D... Willmore, Wollaston, and Davison's English Queen's Bench Reports [*1837*] [*A publication*] (DLA)
Willm W & H... Willmore, Wollaston, and Hodges' English Queen's Bench Reports [*1838-39*] [*A publication*] (DLA)
Will P.......... Peere-Williams' English Chancery Reports [*A publication*] (DLA)
Will Pet Ch... Williams' Petitions in Chancery [*1880*] [*A publication*] (DLA)
Will Real Ass... Williams' Real Assets [*1861*] [*A publication*] (DLA)
Will Real Est... Willard on Real Estate and Conveyancing [*A publication*] (DLA)
Will Real Pr... Williams on Real Property [*A publication*] (DLA)
Will Saund... Williams' Notes to Saunders' Reports [*A publication*] (DLA)
Wills Circ Ev... Wills on Circumstantial Evidence [*A publication*] (DLA)
Wills Cir Ev... Wills on Circumstantial Evidence [*A publication*] (DLA)
Will Seis..... Williams on Seisin of the Freehold [*1878*] [*A publication*] (DLA)
Wills Est & Tr (P-H)... Wills, Estates, and Trusts (Prentice-Hall, Inc.) [*A publication*] (DLA)
Wills Est Tr... Wills, Estates, Trusts [*Prentice-Hall, Inc.*] [*A publication*] (DLA)
Will Sett...... Williams on the Settlement of Real Estates [*A publication*] (DLA)
Willson........ Willson's Reports, Civil Cases [*29-30 Texas Appeals*] [*1, 2 Texas Court of Appeals*] [*A publication*] (DLA)
Willson Civ Cas Ct App... White and Willson's Civil Cases, Texas Court of Appeals [*A publication*] (DLA)
Willson's CC... Texas Civil Cases [*A publication*] (DLA)
Willson Tex Cr Law... Willson's Revised Penal Code, Code of Criminal Procedure, and Penal Laws of Texas [*A publication*] (DLA)
Will St L...... Williams on the Study of the Law [*A publication*] (DLA)
WILL-TV...... Urbana, IL [*TV station call letters*] (RBYB)
Will VT........ Williams' Vermont Reports [*27-29 Vermont*] [*A publication*] (DLA)
Will Woll & D... Willmore, Wollaston, and Davison's English Queen's Bench Reports [*1837*] [*A publication*] (DLA)
Will Woll & Dav... Willmore, Wollaston, and Davison's English Queen's Bench Reports [*1837*] [*A publication*] (DLA)
Will Woll & H... Willmore, Wollaston, and Hodges' English Queen's Bench Reports [*1838-39*] [*A publication*] (DLA)
Will Woll & Hodg... Willmore, Wollaston, and Hodges' English Queen's Bench Reports [*1838-39*] [*A publication*] (DLA)
WILM.......... Wilmington, DE [*AM radio station call letters*]
WILM.......... Wilmington Trust Co. [*NASDAQ symbol*] (NQ)
WILM.......... Wilmington Trust Corp. [*NASDAQ symbol*] (TTSB)
Wilm............ Wilmot's Notes and Opinions, King's Bench [*97 English Reprint*] [*A publication*] (DLA)
Wilm Burg... Wilmot's Digest of the Law of Burglary [*A publication*] (DLA)
WilmCS....... Williams Coal Seam Royalty Trust [*Associated Press*] (SAG)
WilmCtr....... William Controls, Inc. [*Associated Press*] (SAG)
Wilm Judg... Wilmot's Notes and Opinions, King's Bench [*97 English Reprint*] [*A publication*] (DLA)
Wilm Mort... Wilmot on Mortgages [*A publication*] (DLA)
Wilm Op...... Wilmot's Notes and Opinions, King's Bench [*97 English Reprint*] [*A publication*] (DLA)
Wilmot's Notes... Wilmot's Notes and Opinions, King's Bench [*97 English Reprint*] [*A publication*] (DLA)
Wilmot's Notes (Eng)... Wilmot's Notes and Opinions, King's Bench [*97 English Reprint*] [*A publication*] (DLA)
WilmTr........ Wilmington Trust Corp. [*Associated Press*] (SAG)
Wilm W & D... Willmore, Wollaston, and Davison's English Queen's Bench Reports [*A publication*] (DLA)
WILN........... Panama City, FL [*FM radio station call letters*]
WILO........... Frankfort, IN [*AM radio station call letters*]
WILP-AM..... West Hazleton, PA [*AM radio station call letters*] (RBYB)
WILPF.......... Women's International League for Peace and Freedom [*Switzerland*] (EAIO)
WILPF-US.... Women's International League for Peace and Freedom, US Section (EA)
WILQ........... Williamsport, PA [*FM radio station call letters*]
Wil Q........... Wilson Quarterly [*A publication*] (BRI)
WILS............ Lansing, MI [*AM radio station call letters*]
WILS............ Wang Interactive Learning System [*Computer science*] (HGAA)
WILS............ Western Illinois Library System [*Library network*]
Wils............. Wilson's English Chancery Reports [*37 English Reprint*] [*A publication*] (DLA)
Wils............. Wilson's English Common Pleas Reports, 3 [*95 English Reprint*] [*A publication*] (DLA)
Wils............. Wilson's English King's Bench Reports [*95 English Reprint*] [*1742-74*] [*A publication*] (DLA)
WILS............ Wisconsin Interlibrary Loan Service
Wils & Court... Wilson and Courtenay's Scotch Appeal Cases [*A publication*] (DLA)
Wils & S...... Wilson and Shaw's Scottish Appeal Cases [*1825-35*] [*A publication*] (DLA)
Wils & Sh.... Wilson and Shaw's Scottish Appeal Cases [*1825-35*] [*A publication*] (DLA)
Wils & S (Scot)... Wilson and Shaw's Scottish Appeal Cases [*1825-35*] [*A publication*] (DLA)
Wils Arb...... Wilson on Arbitrations [*A publication*] (DLA)
Wils Ch........ Wilson's English Chancery Reports [*37 English Reprint*] [*A publication*] (DLA)
Wils Ch (Eng)... Wilson's English Chancery Reports [*37 English Reprint*] [*A publication*] (DLA)
Wils CP....... Wilson's English Common Pleas [*A publication*] (DLA)
Wils (Eng)... Wilson's English Common Pleas Reports, 3 [*95 English Reprint*] [*A publication*] (DLA)
Wils Ent....... Wilson's Entries and Pleading [*3 Lord Raymond's King's Bench and Common PleasReports*] [*England*] [*A publication*] (DLA)
Wils Ex........ Wilson's English Exchequer Reports [*159 English Reprint*] [*1805-17*] [*A publication*] (DLA)
Wils Exch.... Wilson's English Exchequer Reports [*159 English Reprint*] [*A publication*] (DLA)
Wils Exch (Eng)... Wilson's English Exchequer Reports [*159 English Reprint*] [*A publication*] (DLA)
Wils Fines... Wilson on Fines and Recoveries [*A publication*] (DLA)
Wilshire....... Wilshire Financial Services Group, Inc. [*Associated Press*] (SAG)
WilshrO....... Wilshire Oil Co. of Texas [*Associated Press*] (SAG)
WilshTc....... Wilshire Technologies, Inc. [*Associated Press*] (SAG)
Wils Ind....... Wilson's Indiana Superior Court Reports [*A publication*] (DLA)
Wils Ind Gloss... Wilson's Glossary of Indian Terms [*A publication*] (DLA)
Wils Jud Acts... Wilson on the Judicature Acts, Etc. [*A publication*] (DLA)
Wils KB....... Sergeant Wilson's English King's Bench Reports [*1724-74*] [*A publication*] (DLA)
Wils Minn.... Wilson's Reports [*48-59 Minnesota*] [*A publication*] (DLA)
Wils Mod Eng Law... Wilson's History of Modern English Law [*A publication*] (DLA)
Wilson......... Wilson's English Chancery Reports [*37 English Reprint*] [*A publication*] (DLA)
Wilson......... Wilson's English King's Bench and Common Pleas Reports [*A publication*] (DLA)
Wilson......... Wilson's Exchequer in Equity Reports [*England*] [*A publication*] (DLA)
Wilson......... Wilson's Indiana Superior Court Reports [*A publication*] (DLA)
Wilson......... Wilson's Reports [*1-3 Oregon*] [*A publication*] (DLA)
Wilson......... Wilson's Reports [*48-59 Minnesota*] [*A publication*] (DLA)
Wilson & Shaw... Wilson and Shaw's Scottish Appeal Cases [*1825-35*] [*A publication*] (DLA)
Wilson's R... Wilson's Indiana Superior Court Reports [*A publication*] (DLA)
Wilson's Rev & Ann St... Wilson's Revised and Annotated Statutes [*Oklahoma*] [*A publication*] (DLA)
Wilson Super Ct (Ind)... Wilson's Indiana Superior Court Reports [*A publication*] (DLA)
Wils Oreg.... Wilson's Reports [*1-3 Oregon*] [*A publication*] (DLA)
Wils Parl L... Wilson's Parliamentary Law [*A publication*] (DLA)
Wils PC....... Wilson's English Privy Council Reports [*A publication*] (DLA)
Wils Super (Ind)... Wilson's Indiana Superior Court Reports [*A publication*] (DLA)
Wils Uses.... Wilson on Springing Uses [*A publication*] (DLA)
WILS/WLC... Wisconsin Interlibrary Loan Service - Wisconsin Library Consortium [*Library network*]
WILT-AM..... Mount Pocono, PA [*AM radio station call letters*] (RBYB)
WilTel.......... Williams Telecommunications Co. [*Tulsa, OK*] [*Telecommunications service*] (TSSD)
WILTS.......... Wiltshire [*County in England*]
Wilts............ Wiltshire [*County in England*] (ODBW)
WILUCL....... Willamette University College of Law (DLA)
WILX........... Onondaga, MI [*Television station call letters*]
WILY........... Centralia, IL [*AM radio station call letters*]
WIM............ Madison Public Library, Madison, WI [*OCLC symbol*] (OCLC)
WIM............ Waksman Institute of Microbiology [*Rutgers University*] [*Research center*] (RCD)
WIM............ Warm Ionized Medium [*Astrophysics*]
WIM............ Washington, Idaho & Montana Railway Co. [*AAR code*]
WIM............ Weigh in Motion
WIM............ Women in Management [*Chicago, IL*] (EA)
WIM............ Women in Medicine [*British*] [*An association*] (DBA)
WIM............ Women in Mining National (EA)
WIMA.......... Labuhan Bilik/Ajamu [*Indonesia*] [*ICAO location identifier*] (ICLI)
WIMA.......... Lima, OH [*AM radio station call letters*]
WIMA.......... Women's International Motorcycle Association (EA)
WIMA.......... World International Medical Association (EA)
WIMA.......... Writing Instrument Manufacturers Association (EA)
WIMB.......... Gunung Sitoli/Binaka [*Indonesia*] [*ICAO location identifier*] (ICLI)
WIMB.......... Wimborne Minster [*Urban district in England*]
WIMC.......... Crawfordsville, IN [*FM radio station call letters*]

WIMC.......... Whom It May Concern
WIME.......... Padang Sidempuan/Aek Godang [*Indonesia*] [*ICAO location identifier*] (ICLI)
WIMEA......... Wiretap, Investigation Monitoring, and Eavesdrop Activities (MCD)
WIMG.......... Ewing, NJ [*AM radio station call letters*]
WIMG.......... Padang/Tabing [*Indonesia*] [*ICAO location identifier*] (ICLI)
WIMG.......... Women in Municipal Government (EA)
WIMI.......... Ironwood, MI [*FM radio station call letters*]
WIMI.......... Warburg Investment Management International
WIMI.......... Watercraft Intensively Managed Items (AABC)
WIMIS......... Walk-In Management Information System [*Computer science*]
WIMK.......... Iron Mountain, MI [*FM radio station call letters*]
WIMK.......... Kisaran/Tanah Gambus [*Indonesia*] [*ICAO location identifier*] (ICLI)
WIML.......... Kisaran/Aek Loba [*Indonesia*] [*ICAO location identifier*] (ICLI)
WIMM.......... Medan/Polonia [*Indonesia*] [*ICAO location identifier*] (ICLI)
WIMM.......... Weapons Integrated Materiel Manager [*Military*]
WIMN.......... Stillwater, MN [*AM radio station call letters*]
WIMN.......... Women in Mining National (EA)
WIMO.......... Winder, GA [*AM radio station call letters*]
WIMP.......... Prapat/Sibisa [*Indonesia*] [*ICAO location identifier*] (ICLI)
WIMP.......... WARF [*Wartime Replacement Factors*] Intermediate Materiel Processor [*Military*]
WIMP.......... Weakly Interacting Massive [*or Integrated Magnetic*] Particle [*Astrophysics*]
WIMP.......... Windows, Icons, Mice, and Pointer [*Computer science*] (OSI)
WIMP.......... Windows, Icons, Mice, and Pucks [*Computer science*] (DGA)
WIMP.......... windows, icons, mouse and pull-down menus [*computers*]
WIMP.......... Windows/Icons/Mouse/Pull-Down-Menus [*Computer science*] (BYTE)
WIMP.......... Windward Island Passages Monitoring Program (USDC)
WIMP.......... Windward Island Passages Monitoring Program [*Marine science*] (OSRA)
WIMR.......... Pematang Siantar/Gunung Pamela [*Indonesia*] [*ICAO location identifier*] (ICLI)
WIMS.......... Michigan City, IN [*AM radio station call letters*]
WIMS.......... Sibolga/Pinang Sori [*Indonesia*] [*ICAO location identifier*] (ICLI)
WIMS.......... Wartime Instruction Manual for Merchant Ships [*For deck officers of the United States Merchant Marine; popularly known as the "Convoy Bible"*] [*World War II*]
WIMS.......... Waveguide Impedance Measuring Set
WIMS.......... Web Based Information Management System
WIMS.......... Wholesale Inventory Management System (MHDB)
WIMS.......... Winfrith Improved Multi-Group Scheme [*Nuclear energy*] (NUCP)
WIMS.......... Works Information and Management System [*M & E White Consultants Ltd.*] [*Software package*] (NCC)
WIMS.......... World Information Management System [*Air Force*] (GFGA)
WIMS.......... Worldwide Integrated Management of Subsistence
WIMSA......... Webster Institute for Mathematics, Science, and Arts [*Webster College*]
WIMSA......... Women in Military Service for America Memorial Foundation
WIMT.......... Lima, OH [*FM radio station call letters*]
WIMT.......... Tebing Tingci/Pabatu [*Indonesia*] [*ICAO location identifier*] (ICLI)
WIMZ.......... Knoxville, TN [*FM radio station call letters*]
WIMZ.......... Medan Sector [*Indonesia*] [*ICAO location identifier*] (ICLI)
WIN........... INELEC Library Project, Menomonie, WI [*Inactive*] [*OCLC symbol*] (OCLC)
WIN........... Irwin, Australia [*Spaceflight Tracking and Data Network*] [*NASA*]
WIN........... Warfighter Information Network [*Army*]
WIN........... Water-Insoluble Nitrogen [*Analytical chemistry*]
WIN........... Weapon Index Number [*Military*] (CAAL)
WIN........... Weapons Interception [*Military electronics*]
WIN........... Well Information Network [*Database*]
WIN........... Western Information Network
WIN........... Whip Inflation Now [*Slogan of President Gerald R. Ford's anti-inflation program, 1974*] [*Program discontinued March, 1975*]
WIN........... White-Indian-Negro
Win........... Winch's English Common Pleas Reports [*124 English Reprint*] [*A publication*] (DLA)
WIN........... Windhoek [*Namibia*] [*Seismograph station code, US Geological Survey*] (SEIS)
WIN........... Window [*Technical drawings*]
WIN........... Windsor Board of Education [*UTLAS symbol*]
Win........... Winer's Unreported Opinions, New York Supreme Court [*A publication*] (DLA)
WIN........... Winlink (St. Lucia) Ltd. [*ICAO designator*] (FAAC)
WIN........... Winn-Dixie Stores [*NYSE symbol*] (TTSB)
WIN........... Winn-Dixie Stores, Inc. [*NYSE symbol*] (SPSG)
WIN........... Winona [*Diocesan abbreviation*] [*Minnesota*] (TOCD)
Win........... Winston's North Carolina Reports [*1863-64*] [*A publication*] (DLA)
WIN........... Winter
WIN........... Winthrop Laboratories [*Research code symbol*]
WIN........... Winton [*Australia Airport symbol*] (OAG)
WIN........... Wireless In-Building Network [*Motorola, Inc.*] [*Computer science*]
WIN........... Wollongong Integrated Network (HGAA)
WIN........... Women's International Network (EA)
WIN........... Work Incentive Program [*Later, ETSC*] (EA)
WIN........... Workshop in Nonviolence (EA)
WIN........... World Information Network [*Information service or system*] (IID)
WIN........... WWMCCS [*Worldwide Military Command and Control System*] Intercomputer Network [*DoD*]
W/IN²......... Watts per Square Inch
Win 95........ Windows 95 [*Computer science*] (WDMC)
WINA.......... Charlottesville, VA [*AM radio station call letters*]
WINA.......... Webb Institute of Naval Architecture [*Glen Cove, NY*]
WINA.......... Witton Network Analyzer
WINAP......... Women's Information Network for Asia and the Pacific [*ESCAP*] [*United Nations*] (DUND)
WINB.......... Western Interstate Nuclear Board (NRCH)
WINBA......... World International Nail and Beauty Association (EA)
WINBAN........ Windward Islands' Banana Association
WINC.......... Western Interstate Nuclear Compact [*Later, WIEB/WINB*]
WINC.......... White Incumbent
WINC.......... Winchester, VA [*AM radio station call letters*]
WINC.......... Worldwide Integrated Communications [*Mohawk Data Sciences Corp.*] [*Parsippany, NJ*] [*Telecommunications*] (TSSD)
Win CE........ Windows Compact Edition [*Computer science*] (PCM)
WINC-FM....... Winchester, VA [*FM radio station call letters*]
WINCH......... Winchcombe [*England*]
WINCH......... Winchester [*City in England*] (ROG)
Winch......... Winch's English Common Pleas Reports [*124 English Reprint*] [*A publication*] (DLA)
Winch (Eng)... Winch's English Common Pleas Reports [*124 English Reprint*] [*A publication*] (DLA)
WINCMD........ [*A*] Windows Command [*Computer science*] (PCM)
WIND.......... Chicago, IL [*AM radio station call letters*]
WIND.......... Weather Information Network and Display
W IND......... West Indies (WDAA)
W Ind......... West Indies (VRA)
WIND.......... Wind River Systems [*NASDAQ symbol*] (TTSB)
WIND.......... Wind River Systems, Inc. [*NASDAQ symbol*] (SAG)
WIND.......... Windsor [*Municipal borough in England*]
WIND.......... Women in Distribution [*Commercial firm*]
WINDAV........ Wind Direction and Velocity Indicator [*Aviation*]
WINDEE........ Wind Tunnel Data Encoding and Evaluation [*System*] [*Boeing Co.*]
WIND I........ Windward Islands (WDAA)
WINDII........ Wind Imaging Interferometer
WinDix........ Winn-Dixie Stores, Inc. [*Associated Press*] (SAG)
WINDMG........ Wind Magnitude (GAVI)
Windmr........ Windmere Corp. [*Associated Press*] (SAG)
WINDO......... Wide Information Network Data Online [*Government Printing Office*]
WINDR......... Wind Direction (GAVI)
WindRivr...... Wind River Systems, Inc. [*Associated Press*] (SAG)
WindRvr....... Wind River Systems, Inc. [*Associated Press*] (SAG)
WINDS......... Weather Information Network and Display System [*NASA*]
Windsat....... Wind Satellite
WINE.......... Brookfield, CT [*AM radio station call letters*]
WINE.......... Canandaigua Wine Co., Inc. [*NASDAQ symbol*] (SAG)
WINE.......... Warning and Indications in Europe (MCD)
WINE.......... Webb Institute of Naval Engineering
WINEA......... Canandaigua Wine Cl'A' [*NASDAQ symbol*] (TTSB)
WINEB......... Canandaigua Wine Cl'B' [*NASDAQ symbol*] (TTSB)
Win Ent....... Winch's Book of Entries [*A publication*] (DLA)
Win Eq........ Winston's North Carolina Equity Reports [*A publication*] (DLA)
WINES......... World Integrated Nuclear Evaluation System [*Department of Energy*] (GFGA)
WINF.......... Staunton, VA [*AM radio station call letters*]
WINF.......... Winfrith [*England*]
Winfield...... Winfield Capital Corp. [*Associated Press*] (SAG)
Winfield Words & Phrases... Winfield's Adjudged Words and Phrases, with Notes [*A publication*] (DLA)
Winfld........ Winfield Capital Corp. [*Associated Press*] (SAG)
WING.......... Dayton, OH [*AM radio station call letters*]
Wing.......... Wingate's Maxims [*A publication*] (DLA)
WING-FM....... Springfield, OH [*FM radio station call letters*] (RBYB)
Wing Max...... Wingate's Maxims [*A publication*] (DLA)
WINGO......... Women's International Non-Government Organisation [*British*] (DI)
WINH-AM....... Winchester, KY [*AM radio station call letters*] (RBYB)
WinHEC........ Windows Hardware Engineering Conference
WinHEC........ Windows Hardware Engineering Conference [*Microsoft Corp.*] [*Computer science*]
WinHEC........ Windows Hardware Engineering Conference
WINI.......... Murphysboro, IL [*AM radio station call letters*]
WINJ.......... Pulaski, TN [*FM radio station call letters*]
WINK.......... Fort Myers, FL [*AM radio station call letters*]
WINK.......... Warning in Korea (MCD)
WINK.......... Winkleigh [*England*]
WINK-FM....... Fort Myers, FL [*FM radio station call letters*]
WINKS......... Women in Numerous Kitchens [*World War II*]
WINK-TV....... Fort Myers, FL [*Television station call letters*]
WINL.......... Linden, AL [*FM radio station call letters*]
WinInd........ Winland Electronics, Inc. [*Associated Press*] (SAG)
WINM.......... Angola, IN [*Television station call letters*]
WINN.......... North Vernon, IN [*FM radio station call letters*]
Winn.......... Winnipeg [*Canada*] (BARN)
WINN.......... Winston Hotels [*NASDAQ symbol*] (TTSB)
WINN.......... Winston Hotels, Inc. [*NASDAQ symbol*] (SAG)
Winnbg........ Winnebago Industries, Inc. [*Associated Press*] (SAG)
Winona St U... Winona State University (GAGS)
WINP.......... Water Insoluble Nonstarchy Polysaccharide [*Food composition*]
WINQ.......... Winchendon, MA [*FM radio station call letters*]
WINR.......... Binghamton, NY [*AM radio station call letters*]
WINR.......... Winthrop Resources [*NASDAQ symbol*] (TTSB)
WINR.......... Winthrop Resources Corp. [*NASDAQ symbol*] (SAG)
WINRA......... Women in the National Rifle Association
WinrEnt....... Winners Entertainment [*Commercial firm Associated Press*] (SAG)
WINS.......... New York, NY [*AM radio station call letters*]
WINS.......... Warehouse Industry National Standards Guidelines (ACRL)
WINS.......... Weapons and Integrated Navigation System (MCD)
WINS.......... Wideband Information Network Services [*Computer science*]
WINS.......... Windows - Internet Naming Service

WINS .... Winners Entertainment [*Commercial firm NASDAQ symbol*] (SAG)
WINS .... Winslow [*England*]
WINS .... Women in National Service [*Name given by Ladies' Home Journal to American housewives and their teen-age daughters, "the greatest reserve strength of America"*] [*World War II*]
WINS .... Women in Naval Service
WINS .... Women's Industrial and National Service Corps [*World War II British*]
WinsLoew.... WinsLoew Furniture, Inc. [*Associated Press*] (SAG)
WINSNAMS... Wind Indicating Systems for Navigation Aircraft in Missile Support
Winsock....... Windows Sockets [*Internet*]
Winst .... Winston's North Carolina Equity Reports [*A publication*] (DLA)
Winst .... Winston's North Carolina Law Reports [*A publication*] (DLA)
WINST .... Winstree [*England*]
WINSTAN..... Wings, Nonstraight-Taper Analysis (MCD)
Winstar........ Winstar Communications [*Commercial firm Associated Press*] (SAG)
Winst Eq...... Winston's North Carolina Equity Reports [*A publication*] (DLA)
Winst Eq (NC)... Winston's North Carolina Equity Reports [*A publication*] (DLA)
Winst L (NC)... Winston's North Carolina Law Reports [*A publication*] (DLA)
WinstonH..... Winston Hotels, Inc. [*Associated Press*] (SAG)
WinstRs....... Winston Resources Ltd. [*Associated Press*] (SAG)
WINT .... Crossville, TN [*Television station call letters*]
WINTEM ...... Forecast Upper Wind and Temperature for Aviation [*ICAO*] (FAAC)
WinterSpt .... Winter Sports, Inc. [*Associated Press*] (SAG)
WINTEX ...... Winter Exercise (MCD)
WinthpRs.... Winthrop Resources Corp. [*Associated Press*] (SAG)
Winthrop C... Winthrop College (GAGS)
Winton......... Winton Financial Corp. [*Associated Press*] (SAG)
Wint T .... [*The*] Winter's Tale [*Shakespearean work*] (BARN)
WINU.......... Highland, IL [*AM radio station call letters*]
WINV .... Inverness, FL [*AM radio station call letters*]
WINW .... Canton, OH [*AM radio station call letters*]
WINX .... Rockville, MD [*AM radio station call letters*]
WINX-FM..... Warrenton, VA [*FM radio station call letters*] (RBYB)
WINY .... Putnam, CT [*AM radio station call letters*]
WINZ .... Miami, FL [*AM radio station call letters*]
WIO .... Nashotah House, Nashotah, WI [*OCLC symbol*] (OCLC)
WIO .... Wilcannia [*Australia Airport symbol*] (OAG)
WIO .... Women's International ORT
WIOA .... San Juan, PR [*FM radio station call letters*]
WIOB .... Bengkayang [*Indonesia*] [*ICAO location identifier*] (ICLI)
WIOB .... Mayaguez, PR [*FM radio station call letters*]
WIOC .... Ponce, PR [*FM radio station call letters*]
WIOD .... Miami, FL [*AM radio station call letters*]
WIOG .... Bay City, MI [*FM radio station call letters*]
WIOG .... Nangapinoh [*Indonesia*] [*ICAO location identifier*] (ICLI)
WIOH .... Paloh/Liku [*Indonesia*] [*ICAO location identifier*] (ICLI)
WIOI .... New Boston, OH [*AM radio station call letters*]
WIOI .... Singkawang II [*Indonesia*] [*ICAO location identifier*] (ICLI)
WIOK .... Falmouth, KY [*FM radio station call letters*]
WIOK .... Ketapang/Rahadi Usman [*Indonesia*] [*ICAO location identifier*] (ICLI)
WION .... Ionia, MI [*AM radio station call letters*]
WION .... Natuna/Ransi [*Indonesia*] [*ICAO location identifier*] (ICLI)
WIOO .... Carlisle, PA [*AM radio station call letters*]
WIOO .... Pontianak/Supadio [*Indonesia*] [*ICAO location identifier*] (ICLI)
WIOP .... Putusibau/Pangsuma [*Indonesia*] [*ICAO location identifier*] (ICLI)
WIOQ .... Philadelphia, PA [*FM radio station call letters*]
WIOS .... Sintang/Susilo [*Indonesia*] [*ICAO location identifier*] (ICLI)
WIOS .... Tawas City, MI [*AM radio station call letters*]
WIOT .... Toledo, OH [*FM radio station call letters*]
WIOU .... Kokomo, IN [*AM radio station call letters*]
WIOV .... Ephrata, PA [*FM radio station call letters*]
WIOV .... Reading, PA [*AM radio station call letters*]
WIOZ .... Pinehurst, NC [*AM radio station call letters*]
WIOZ .... Pontianak Sector [*Indonesia*] [*ICAO location identifier*] (ICLI)
WIOZ .... Southern Pines, NC [*FM radio station call letters*]
WIP .... Philadelphia, PA [*AM radio station call letters*]
WIP .... Ripon College Library, Ripon, WI [*OCLC symbol*] (OCLC)
WIP .... Wartime Intelligence Plan (NATG)
WIP .... Weapon Indicator Panel [*Military*] (CAAL)
WIP .... Weapons Installation Plan [*Navy*] (NG)
WIP .... Women in Information Processing (EA)
WIP .... Women in Production (EA)
WIP .... Women's Issues Plan [*Australia*]
WIP .... Workgroup Indian Project [*Netherlands*]
WIP .... Work Incentive Program [*Department of Health, Education, and Welfare; Department of Labor*] (DLA)
WIP .... Working Group Indigenous Peoples [*Netherlands*] (EAIO)
WIP .... Work in Place (AABC)
WIP .... Work in Process
WIP .... Work in Progress (AFM)
WIPA .... Jambi/Sultan Taha [*Indonesia*] [*ICAO location identifier*] (ICLI)
WIPA .... Pittsfield, IL [*FM radio station call letters*]
WIPACE ...... Wartime Intelligence Plan, Allied Command Europe (NATG)
WIPB .... Muncie, IN [*Television station call letters*]
WIPC .... Lake Wales, FL [*AM radio station call letters*]
WIPC .... Rimbo Bujang [*Indonesia*] [*ICAO location identifier*] (ICLI)
WIPC .... Wool Industry Policy Council [*Australia*]
WIPC .... Writers in Prison Committee of International PEN [*British*] (EAIO)
WIPE........... Tanjung Enim/Bangko [*Indonesia*] [*ICAO location identifier*] (ICLI)
WIPF........... Kuala Tungkal [*Indonesia*] [*ICAO location identifier*] (ICLI)
WIPH .... Sungai Penuh/Depati Parbo [*Indonesia*] [*ICAO location identifier*] (ICLI)
WIPI............ Bungo Tebo/Pasir Mayang [*Indonesia*] [*ICAO location identifier*] (ICLI)
WIPI............ Easton, PA [*AM radio station call letters*]
WIPI............ Word Intelligibility by Picture Identification [*Artificial intelligence*]
WIPIS .... Who Is Publishing in Science [*An Institute for Scientific Information publication*] [*Trademark*]
WIPJ........... Jambi/Dusun Aro [*Indonesia*] [*ICAO location identifier*] (ICLI)
WIPL........... Bengkulu/Padang Kemiling [*Indonesia*] [*ICAO location identifier*] (ICLI)
WIPM........... Mayaguez, PR [*Television station call letters*]
WIPM........... West Indian People's Movement [*Netherlands Antilles*] [*Political party*] (EY)
WIPM........... Work in Process Measurement (MCD)
WIPO .... World Intellectual Property Organisation [*of United Nations*] (EERA)
WIPO .... World Intellectual Property Organization [*Switzerland*] (IID)
WIPP .... Palembang/Sultan Mahmud Badaruddin II [*Indonesia*] [*ICAO location identifier*] (ICLI)
WIPP .... Waste Isolation Pilot Plant [*Department of Energy*]
WIPP .... Work Isolation Pilot Project [*NASA*]
WIPPL .... Women in Political and Public Life [*British*] (DI)
WIPQ .... Pendoro [*Indonesia*] [*ICAO location identifier*] (ICLI)
WIPR .... Rengat/Japura [*Indonesia*] [*ICAO location identifier*] (ICLI)
WIPR .... San Juan, PR [*AM radio station call letters*]
WIPR-FM..... San Juan, PR [*FM radio station call letters*]
WIPR-TV...... San Juan, PR [*Television station call letters*]
WIPS .... Ticonderoga, NY [*AM radio station call letters*]
WIPS .... Washington Intelligence Data Processing System (SAA)
WIPS .... Women in Production Service [*A voluntary, semimilitary organization of women employees, primarily at the E. I. du Pont de Nemours & Co., at Richmond, Va.*] [*World War II*]
WIPS .... Word Image Processing System [*Datacopy Corp.*]
WIPTC .... Women's International Professional Tennis Council (EA)
WIPU .... Muko Muko [*Indonesia*] [*ICAO location identifier*] (ICLI)
WIPV .... Keluang [*Indonesia*] [*ICAO location identifier*] (ICLI)
WIPY .... Bentayan [*Indonesia*] [*ICAO location identifier*] (ICLI)
WIPZ........... Palembang Sector [*Indonesia*] [*ICAO location identifier*] (ICLI)
WIQ .... Appleton Public Library, Appleton, WI [*OCLC symbol*] (OCLC)
WIQB .... Ann Arbor, MI [*FM radio station call letters*]
WIQH .... Concord, MA [*FM radio station call letters*]
WIQO .... Covington, VA [*FM radio station call letters*]
WIQQ .... Leland, MS [*FM radio station call letters*]
WIQR .... Prattville, AL [*AM radio station call letters*] (RBYB)
WIR .... Racine Public Library, Racine, WI [*OCLC symbol*] (OCLC)
WIR .... War Information Report [*British military*] (DMA)
WIR .... Weapons Inspection Report [*Navy*] (NG)
WIR .... Weekly Intelligence Review
WIR .... Welfare in Review [*A publication*]
WIR .... Western Investment Real Estate Trust SBI [*AMEX symbol*] (SPSG)
WIR .... Western Inv RE Tr SBI [*AMEX symbol*] (TTSB)
WIR .... West Indian Reports [*A publication*] (DLA)
WIR .... West India Regiment
WIR .... Wildrose Petroleum Ltd. [*Vancouver Stock Exchange symbol*]
WIR .... Woman in Rock
WIR .... Work Injury Reports [*Human Resources*] (WYGK)
WIR .... Wuerttemberg Israelitische Religionsgemeinschaft [*A publication*] (BJA)
WIRA .... Fort Pierce, FL [*AM radio station call letters*]
WIRA .... Wool Industry Research Association [*British*] (DI)
WIRB .... Melbourne, FL [*Television station call letters*]
WIRC .... Hickory, NC [*AM radio station call letters*]
WIRC .... Women's Information and Referral Centre [*Australia*]
WIRC .... Women's International Resource Centre [*British*] (EAIO)
WIRD .... Lake Placid, NY [*AM radio station call letters*]
WIRDS......... Weather Information Remoting and Display System
WIRE .... Encore Wire Corp. [*NASDAQ symbol*] (SAG)
WIRE .... Lebanon, IN [*FM radio station call letters*]
WIRE .... Waseca Inter-Library Resource Exchange [*Library network*]
WIRE .... Weapons Interference Reduction Effort [*Navy*] (NG)
WIRE .... Wisconsin Information Resources for Education (EDAC)
WIRE .... Women's International Resource Exchange (EA)
Wireless...... Wireless Cable of Atlanta, Inc. [*Associated Press*] (SAG)
Wirelesst..... Wireless Telecom Group [*Formerly, Noise Com, Inc.*] [*Associated Press*] (SAG)
WirelssT...... Wireless Telecom Group [*Associated Press*] (SAG)
WireOne ...... Wireless One, Inc. [*Associated Press*] (SAG)
WIRES .... Women in Radio and Electrical Service [*World War II*]
WIRET .... Western Investment Real Estate Trust [*Associated Press*] (SAG)
WIRF .... Women's International Religious Fellowship (EA)
WIRG .... Wiring
WIRGA......... West Indian Royal Garrison Artillery [*British military*] (DMA)
WIRJ........... Humboldt, TN [*AM radio station call letters*] (RBYB)
WIRK .... West Palm Beach, FL [*FM radio station call letters*]
WIRL .... Peoria, IL [*AM radio station call letters*]
WIRL .... Wireless One [*NASDAQ symbol*] (TTSB)
WIRL .... Wireless One, Inc. [*NASDAQ symbol*] (SAG)
WIRMIT .... Women in RMIT [*Royal Melbourne Institute of Technology*] Group [*Australia*]
WIRN-FM..... Buhl, MN [*FM radio station call letters*] (RBYB)
WIRO .... Ironton, OH [*AM radio station call letters*]
WIRO .... Wyoming Infrared Observatory
WIRP-FM..... Pennsuco, FL [*FM radio station call letters*] (RBYB)
WIRQ .... Rochester, NY [*FM radio station call letters*]
WIRR .... Virginia-Hibbing, MN [*FM radio station call letters*]
WIRS .... Wage Information Retrieval System [*IRS*]
WIRS .... Workplace Industrial Relations Survey [*British*]
WIRS .... Yauco, PR [*Television station call letters*]
WIRT .... Hibbing, MN [*Television station call letters*]
WIRTSCH...... Wirtschaft [*Economy, Industry*] [*German*]

WIRV .... Irvine, KY [*AM radio station call letters*]
WIRX .... St. Joseph, MI [*FM radio station call letters*]
WIRY .... Plattsburgh, NY [*AM radio station call letters*]
WIS .... Central [*Wisconsin*] [*Airport symbol*] (AD)
WIS .... Columbia, SC [*Television station call letters*]
WIS .... University of Wisconsin, Stevens Point, Stevens Point, WI [*OCLC symbol*] (OCLC)
WIS .... Washington Inventory Service
WIS .... Washington Irving Society [*Defunct*] (EA)
WIS .... Wave Information Study [*US Army Corps of Engineers*]
WIS .... Weapon Interface Subsystem [*Army*] (INF)
WIS .... Weapon Interface Subsystem [*Army*]
WIS .... Weather Information Service [*Air Force*] (MCD)
WIS .... Wedgwood International Seminar (EA)
WIS .... Winchester Diversified [*Vancouver Stock Exchange symbol*]
WIS .... Wireless Interphone System (MCD)
WIS .... Wisconsin (AAG)
Wis .... Wisconsin (ODBW)
WIS .... Wisconsin Power & Light Co. [*AMEX symbol*] (SAG)
Wis .... Wisconsin Reports [*A publication*] (DLA)
Wis .... Wisdom [*Old Testament book*]
WIS .... Women in Sales Association (EA)
WIS .... Women in Soccer (EA)
WIS .... World Impact Services (EA)
WIS .... Worldwide Information System [*Navy*]
WIS .... Wright Investors' Service [*Information service or system*] (IID)
WIS .... WWMCCS [*Worldwide Military Command and Control System*] Information Systems
Wis 2d .... Wisconsin Reports, Second Series [*A publication*] (DLA)
WISA .... Isabela, PR [*AM radio station call letters*]
WISA .... West Indian Students Association (EA)
WISA .... West Indies Sugar Association [*Later, SAC*]
WISA .... Wholesale Interservices Support Agreement [*DoD*]
WISA .... Wholesale Interservice Supply Agreement [*Military*] (NG)
WISA .... Women's International Surfing Association (EA)
WISA .... Wormald International Sensory Aids (NITA)
Wis Admin Code... Wisconsin Administrative Code [*A publication*] (DLA)
WISA Law Rep... Western Indian States Agency Law Reports [*A publication*] (DLA)
WISALR .... Western Indian States Agency Law Reports [*A publication*] (DLA)
WISAP .... Waste Isolation Safety Assessment Program
WISARD .... Wideband System for Acquiring and Recording Data
Wisb .... Laws of Wisby [*Maritime law*] [*A publication*] (DLA)
WISB .... Wisbech [*Municipal borough in England*]
WISB .... Women in Show Business (EA)
Wis BA Bull... Wisconsin State Bar Association. Bulletin [*A publication*] (DLA)
Wis Bar Bull... Wisconsin State Bar Association. Bulletin [*A publication*] (DLA)
WIS B BULL... Wisconsin Bar Bulletin [*A publication*] (LWAP)
Wis BTA .... Wisconsin Board of Tax Appeals Reports [*A publication*] (DLA)
WISC .... Madison, WI [*Television station call letters*]
WISC .... Wang Information Services Corp. [*Telecommunications service*] (TSSD)
WISC .... Wechsler Intelligence Scale for Children [*Education*]
WISC .... Wisconsin (AFM)
Wisc .... Wisconsin Reports [*A publication*] (DLA)
WISC .... Women's Information and Study Centre
WISC .... Writable Instruction Set Computer [*Term coined by Phil Koopman, Jr.*] (BYTE)
WiscCt .... Wisconsin Central Transportation Corp. [*Associated Press*] (SAG)
WiscEn .... Wisconsin Energy Corp. [*Associated Press*] (SAG)
WISCII .... Wang International Standard Code for Information Interchange [*Pronounced "whiskey"*] [*Canada*]
WISCNET .... [*The*] Wisconsin Network [*Telecommunications service*] (TNIG)
WISCOM .... Wisconsin Information Science and Communications Consortium [*University of Wisconsin - Madison*] [*Research center*] (RCD)
WISC-R .... Wechsler Intelligence Scale for Children - Revised [*Education*]
Wisc Stud BJ... Wisconsin Student Bar Journal [*A publication*] (DLA)
WISD .... Wisdom [*Old Testament book*]
Wisd of Sol... Wisdom of Solomon [*Old Testament book*]
WISE .... Asheville, NC [*AM radio station call letters*]
WISE .... Wang Intersystem Exchange
WISE .... Wardens in the South East (AIE)
WISE .... Warning Indicators System Europe (MCD)
WISE .... Weapon Installation System Engineering
WISE .... Welsh Initiative for Specialised Employment
WISE .... Wheaton Information System for Education (IAA)
WISE .... Whirlwind I SAGE [*Semi-Automatic Ground Equipment*] Evaluation (SAA)
WISE .... Whistle-Blowers Integrity in Science and Education [*An association*]
WISE .... Wholesalers Institutional Service Extension [*Division of National American Wholesale Grocers Association*]
WISE .... Wicat Interactive System for Education (NITA)
WISE .... Women in Space Earliest (SAA)
WISE .... Women into Science and Engineering [*1984 campaign sponsored by the Equal Opportunities Commission and the Engineering Council*] [*British*]
WISE .... Women's Information Service, Inc.
WISE .... Women's Issues, Status, and Education (EA)
WISE .... WordPerfect Information System Environment [*Computer science*]
WISE .... World Information Service on Energy (EA)
WISE .... World Information Synthesis and Encyclopaedia [*Project of American Association for the Advancement of Science and American Society for Information Science*]
WISE .... World Information Systems Exchange [*Defunct*] (EA)
WISE .... World-Wide Information Service [*Information service or system*] (IID)
WISER .... Western Information System for Energy Resources [*Dataline, Inc.*] [*Canada Information service or system*]
WiserO .... [*The*] Wiser Oil Co. [*Associated Press*] (SAG)
WISF .... Women in Sport Foundation [*Australia*]
WISH .... Indianapolis, IN [*Television station call letters*]
WISH .... Women in the Senate and House [*Political fund-raising group*]
WISH .... Women's Interview Study of Health
WISH .... World Institute for Scientific Humanism [*Defunct*] (EA)
WISHA .... Washington Industrial Safety and Health Act (NUCP)
WISI .... Warner Insurance Svcs [*NASDAQ symbol*] (TTSB)
WISI .... World Index of Space Imagery [*Meteorology*]
WISI .... World Information System in Informatics (NITA)
Wis IC .... Wisconsin Industrial Commission Workmen's Compensation Reports [*A publication*] (DLA)
Wis Int'l LJ... Wisconsin International Law Journal [*A publication*] (DLA)
WISJMPO .... Worldwide Military Command and Control Information Systems, Joint Program Office
WISK .... Americus, GA [*AM radio station call letters*]
WISK-FM .... Americus, GA [*FM radio station call letters*]
WISL .... Shamokin, PA [*AM radio station call letters*]
WISL .... Westinghouse Information Systems Laboratory (IAA)
WISL .... Woven Integrated Structure Laminates [*Army*]
Wis Legis Serv... Wisconsin Legislative Service (West) [*A publication*] (DLA)
Wis Leg N... Wisconsin Legal News [*Milwaukee*] [*A publication*] (DLA)
WISL-FM .... Shamokin, PA [*FM radio station call letters*]
Wis LN .... Wisconsin Legal News [*Milwaukee*] [*A publication*] (DLA)
WISM .... Altoona, WI [*FM radio station call letters*]
WISN .... Milwaukee, WI [*AM radio station call letters*]
WISN-TV .... Milwaukee, WI [*Television station call letters*]
WISO .... Ponce, PR [*AM radio station call letters*]
WISP .... Holmes Beach, FL [*FM radio station call letters*]
WISP .... Warming Improvement Study Plan (MCD)
WISP .... Wartime Information Security Program (MCD)
WISP .... Waves in Space Plasma (SSD)
WISP .... Weapon Iterface Subsystem Processor [*Military*] (INF)
WISP .... Weaponization of Increased Speed Projectiles (MCD)
WISP .... Wide-Range Imaging Spectrophotometer [*Naval Oceanographic Office*]
WISP .... Winter Icing and Storms Project (USDC)
WISP .... Winter Icing and Storms Project [*Marine science*] (OSRA)
WisP .... Wisconsin Power & Light Co. [*Associated Press*] (SAG)
WISP .... Women in Scholarly Publishing (EA)
WISP .... Wyoming Infant Stimulation Program (EDAC)
WisPhrm .... Wisconsin Pharmacal Company, Inc. [*Associated Press*] (SAG)
WISPIT .... WISP [*Winter Icing and Storms Project*] Instrument Test (USDC)
WISPIT .... WISP [*Winter Icing and Storms Project*] Instrument Test [*Marine science*] (OSRA)
WISPr .... Wisc Pwr/Lt 4 1/2cm Pfd vtg [*AMEX symbol*] (TTSB)
Wis PSC .... Wisconsin Public Service Commission Reports [*A publication*] (DLA)
Wis PSC Ops... Wisconsin Public Service Commission Opinions and Decisions [*A publication*] (DLA)
WISQ .... Whitewater, WI [*FM radio station call letters*]
WISR .... Butler, PA [*AM radio station call letters*]
Wis R .... Wisconsin Reports [*A publication*] (DLA)
Wis RC Ops... Wisconsin Railroad Commission Opinions and Decisions [*A publication*] (DLA)
Wis RCR .... Wisconsin Railroad Commission Reports [*A publication*] (DLA)
Wis Rep .... Wisconsin Reports [*A publication*] (DLA)
WISS .... Berlin, WI [*AM radio station call letters*]
WISS .... Weapon Impact Scoring System [*Navy*] (MCD)
WISS .... Weekly Induction Scheduling System [*Navy*] (NG)
WISS .... World Institute of Sephardic Studies (BJA)
WISSA .... Wholesale Interservice Supply Support Agreements [*Military*]
Wis SBA Bull... Wisconsin State Bar Association. Bulletin [*A publication*] (DLA)
WISS-FM .... Berlin, WI [*FM radio station call letters*]
Wis Stat .... Wisconsin Statutes [*A publication*] (DLA)
Wis Stat Ann (West)... West's Wisconsin Statutes, Annotated [*A publication*] (DLA)
WissUnNT .... Wissenschaftliche Untersuchungen zum Neuen Testament [*Tuebingen*] [*A publication*] (BJA)
WIST .... Charlotte, NC [*AM radio station call letters*]
WIST .... Whitaker Index of Schizophrenic Thinking
Wis Tax App C... Wisconsin Tax Appeals Commission Reports [*A publication*] (DLA)
WIST-FM .... Waxhaw, NC FM radio station call letters (RBYB)
WISU .... Federation of Westinghouse Independent Salaried Unions
WISU .... Terre Haute, IN [*FM radio station call letters*]
WISW .... Columbia, SC [*AM radio station call letters*] (RBYB)
WISWAVE .... Wave Information Studies Wave Model [*Computer science*]
WISZ .... Rockford, MI [*AM radio station call letters*] (RBYB)
WIT .... Washington Institute of Technology [*Washington, DC*]
WIT .... Whitbread Investment Trust [*British*]
WIT .... Wicat Interactive Terminal (NITA)
WIT .... Wier-in-Tube Sensor (PDAA)
WIT .... Winnebago International Travelers (EA)
WIT .... Wiring Interface Tester (MCD)
WIT .... Wisconsin Institute of Technology
WIT .... Witco Corp. [*NYSE symbol*] (SPSG)
WIT .... Witness (AABC)
WIT .... Wittenberg University, Springfield, OH [*OCLC symbol*] (OCLC)
WIT .... Wittering FTU [*British ICAO designator*] (FAAC)
WIT .... Witteveen [*Netherlands*] [*Seismograph station code, US Geological Survey*] (SEIS)
WIT .... Women in Telecommunications [*Defunct*] (EA)
WIT .... Women in Transition (EA)
WIT .... Workflow Innovation Toolkit (PCM)

WIT .... World Ice Theory [*Hans Horbiger*]
WIT .... Worst Injection Timing (PDAA)
WITA .... Knoxville, TN [*AM radio station call letters*]
WITA .... Tapak Tuan/Teuku Cut Ali [*Indonesia*] [*ICAO location identifier*] (ICLI)
WITA .... Women in the Army (MCD)
WITA .... Women in the Arts [*Defunct*] (EA)
WITA .... Women's International Tennis Association (EA)
WITAG .... West Indies Trade Advisory Group [*British Overseas Trade Board*] (DS)
WITAMIR ..... Wisconsin Tandem Mirror
WITAN .... Wind-Time Analyzer
WITC .... Cazenovia, NY [*FM radio station call letters*]
WITC .... Meulaboh/Cut Nyak Dien [*Indonesia*] [*ICAO location identifier*] (ICLI)
WITCH .... Women Incensed over Traditional Coed Hoopla [*Feminist group*]
WITCH .... Women's Independent Cinema House [*British*]
WITCH .... Women's International Terrorist Conspiracy from Hell [*Feminist group*]
Witco .... Witco Corp. [*Associated Press*] (SAG)
WITF .... Harrisburg, PA [*FM radio station call letters*]
WITF .... What I Think and Feel (EDAC)
WITF .... Women's International Tennis Federation
WITF-TV ...... Harrisburg, PA [*Television station call letters*]
WITG .... Sinabang/Lasikin [*Indonesia*] [*ICAO location identifier*] (ICLI)
WITG .... Western International Trade Group [*Defunct*] (EA)
WITH .... Baltimore, MD [*AM radio station call letters*]
WITH .... Witheridge [*England*]
With Corp Cas... Withrow's American Corporation Cases [*A publication*] (DLA)
WITHDRL ...... Withdrawal (ROG)
Withrow .... Withrow's American Corporation Cases [*A publication*] (DLA)
Withrow .... Withrow's Reports [*9-21 Iowa*] [*A publication*] (DLA)
WITHT .... Without (ROG)
WITI .... Milwaukee, WI [*Television station call letters*]
WITI .... Women in Technology International
WITIS .... Weather Integration with Tactical Intelligence System (MCD)
WITK .... Warner Robins, GA [*AM radio station call letters*] (RBYB)
Witkin Cal Summary... Witkin's Summary of California Law [*A publication*] (DLA)
WITL .... Lansing, MI [*AM radio station call letters*]
WITL .... Lhok Sukon [*Indonesia*] [*ICAO location identifier*] (ICLI)
WITL-FM ...... Lansing, MI [*FM radio station call letters*]
WITM .... Whok Seumawe/Malikus Saleh [*Indonesia*] [*ICAO location identifier*] (ICLI)
WITN .... Washington, NC [*Television station call letters*]
WITNED .... Witnessed
WITNESS ...... Wire Installation Tester for Negating Errors by Sequencing and Standardization
WITNETH ..... Witnesseth [*Legal*] [*British*] (ROG)
WITNS .... Witness [*Legal*] [*British*] (ROG)
WITR .... Henrietta, NY [*FM radio station call letters*]
WITS .... Sebring, FL [*AM radio station call letters*]
WITS .... Seumayam [*Indonesia*] [*ICAO location identifier*] (ICLI)
WITS .... Wang Integrated Technology Show [*British*]
WITS .... Washington Interagency Telecommunications System [*GSA*]
WITS .... Weather Information Telemetry System [*Air Force*] (CET)
WITS .... West Integrated Test Stand [*NASA*]
WITS .... Women in Technical Service [*World War II*]
WITS .... Work Item Tracking System [*Nuclear energy*] (NRCH)
WITS .... Worldwide Information and Trade System
WITS .... Worldwide Interactive Trading System [*Information service or system*] (IT)
WITSEC .... Witness Security Program [*US government program for protection of witnesses whose lives are endangered by their testimony*]
WITSS .... Witnesses [*Legal*] [*British*] (ROG)
WITT .... Banda Aceh/Blangbintang [*Indonesia*] [*ICAO location identifier*] (ICLI)
WITT .... Wittenborn [*Psychiatric rating scale*] (DMAA)
Witthaus & Becker's Med Jur... Witthaus and Becker's Medical Jurisprudence [*A publication*] (DLA)
WITTL .... Wittlesford [*England*]
WITV .... Charleston, SC [*Television station call letters*]
WITW .... We Interrupt This Week [*Television program*]
WITX .... Beaver Falls, PA [*FM radio station call letters*]
WITY .... Danville, IL [*AM radio station call letters*]
WITZ .... Jasper, IN [*AM radio station call letters*]
WITZ-FM ...... Jasper, IN [*FM radio station call letters*]
WIU .... Warhead Interface Unit (MCD)
WIU .... Water Injection Unit
WIU .... Weather Intelligence Unit [*Army*] (MCD)
WIU .... Western Illinois University [*Macomb*]
WIU .... Western International University, Phoenix, AZ [*OCLC symbol*] (OCLC)
wiu .... Wisconsin [*MARC country of publication code Library of Congress*] (LCCP)
WIU .... Witu [*Papua New Guinea*] [*Airport symbol*] (OAG)
WIUAB .... Women's Inter-University Athletic Board [*British*] (BI)
WIUJ .... St. Thomas, VI [*FM radio station call letters*]
WIUM .... Macomb, IL [*FM radio station call letters*]
WIUP .... Indiana, PA [*FM radio station call letters*]
WIUS .... Macomb, IL [*FM radio station call letters*]
WIUV .... Castleton, VT [*FM radio station call letters*]
WIUW .... Warsaw, IL [*FM radio station call letters*] (RBYB)
Wiv .... [*The*] Merry Wives of Windsor [*Shakespearean work*]
WIV .... Waukesha Public Library, Waukesha, WI [*OCLC symbol*] (OCLC)
WIV .... WIC [*Women, Infants, and Children*] Income Verification Survey [*Food and Nutrition Service*] [*Department of Agriculture*] (GFGA)
WIVA .... Aguadilla, PR [*FM radio station call letters*]
WIVAB .... Women's Inter-Varsity Athletics Board [*British*] (DI)
WIVB .... Buffalo, NY [*Television station call letters*]
WIVH .... Christiansted, VI [*FM radio station call letters*]
WIVI .... Charlotte Amalie, VI [*FM radio station call letters*]
WiVik .... Windows Visual Keyboard [*Computer science*] (ECON)
WIVK .... Knoxville, TN [*AM radio station call letters*]
WIVK-FM ..... Knoxville, TN [*FM radio station call letters*]
WIVR .... Eureka, IL [*FM radio station call letters*]
WIVV .... Vieques, PR [*AM radio station call letters*]
WIVY .... Jacksonville, FL [*FM radio station call letters*]
WIW .... Marathon County Public Library, Wausau, WI [*OCLC symbol*] (OCLC)
WIW .... Wer Informiert Woruber [*Who Advises about What*] [*Gesellschaft fuer Informationsmarkt-Forschung - GIF Detmold, Federal Republic of Germany*] [*Information service or system*] (IID)
WIW .... Who's Inventing What [*A publication*]
WIW .... WI Wheels International [*Vancouver Stock Exchange symbol*]
WIW .... Wooded Island [*Washington*] [*Seismograph station code, US Geological Survey*] (SEIS)
WIWC .... Kokomo, IN [*FM radio station call letters*]
WIWHA .... Western International Walking Horse Association (EA)
WIWO .... Walk In, Walk Out (ADA)
WIWP .... World Institute for World Peace
WIWS .... Beckley, WV [*AM radio station call letters*]
WIX .... Steenbock Memorial Library, Madison, WI [*OCLC symbol*] (OCLC)
WIX .... Wait for Index (NASA)
WIX .... Whitman Education Group [*AMEX symbol*] (TTSB)
WIX .... Whitman Education Group [*AMEX symbol*] (SAG)
WIX .... Whitman Medical Corp. [*AMEX symbol*] (SAG)
WIX .... Windows Information Exchange [*Information service or system*] (IID)
WIX .... Winex Resources, Inc. [*Vancouver Stock Exchange symbol*]
WIXAMT .... Wixamtree [*England*]
WIXC .... Essexville, MI [*FM radio station call letters*]
WIXE .... Monroe, NC [*AM radio station call letters*]
WIXI .... Naples Park, FL [*FM radio station call letters*]
WIXK .... New Richmond, WI [*AM radio station call letters*]
WIXK-FM ...... New Richmond, WI [*FM radio station call letters*]
WIXN .... Dixon, IL [*AM radio station call letters*]
WIXN-FM ..... Dixon, IL [*FM radio station call letters*]
WIXO-FM ..... Bartonville, IL [*FM radio statio call letters*] (RBYB)
WIXQ .... Millersville, PA [*FM radio station call letters*]
WIXT .... Syracuse, NY [*Television station call letters*]
WIXV .... Savannah, GA [*FM radio station call letters*]
WIXX .... Green Bay, WI [*FM radio station call letters*]
WIXY .... Champaign, IL [*FM radio station call letters*]
WIXZ .... McKeesport, PA [*AM radio station call letters*]
WIY .... University of Wisconsin, Primate Research Center, Primate Library, Madison, WI [*OCLC symbol*] (OCLC)
WIYC .... Charlotte Amalie, VI [*FM radio station call letters*]
WIYD .... Palatka, FL [*AM radio station call letters*]
WIYN .... Deposit, NY [*FM radio station call letters*]
WIYY .... Baltimore, MD [*FM radio station call letters*]
WIZ .... Merlin Executive Aviation Group Ltd. [*British ICAO designator*] (FAAC)
WIZ .... Wiz Technology, Inc. [*AMEX symbol*] (SAG)
WIZA .... Savannah, GA [*AM radio station call letters*]
WIZA .... Workgroup for Indians in South America [*Netherlands*]
WIZB .... Abbeville, AL [*FM radio station call letters*] (RBYB)
WIZD .... Rudolph, WI [*FM radio station call letters*]
WIZE .... Springfield, OH [*AM radio station call letters*]
WIZ EC .... Wiz Technology [*ECM symbol*] (TTSB)
WIZF .... Erlanger, KY [*FM radio station call letters*]
WIZK .... Bay Springs, MS [*AM radio station call letters*]
WIZK-FM ..... Bay Springs, MS [*FM radio station call letters*]
WIZM .... La Crosse, WI [*AM radio station call letters*]
WIZM-FM ..... La Crosse, WI [*FM radio station call letters*]
WIZN .... Vergennes, VT [*FM radio station call letters*]
WIZO .... Franklin, TN [*AM radio station call letters*]
WIZO .... Women's International Zionist Organization [*Tel Aviv, Israel*] (EA)
WIZR .... Johnstown, NY [*AM radio station call letters*]
WIZS .... Henderson, NC [*AM radio station call letters*]
WIZT .... Wiztec Solutions Ltd. [*NASDAQ symbol*] (SAG)
WizTch .... Wiz Technology, Inc. [*Associated Press*] (SAG)
WiztecS .... Wiztec Solutions Ltd. [*Associated Press*] (SAG)
WIZTF .... Wiztec Solutions [*NASDAQ symbol*] (TTSB)
WIZY .... East Jordan, MI [*FM radio station call letters*]
WIZZ .... Streator, IL [*AM radio station call letters*]
WJ .... Joule [*Unit of work*] (ROG)
WJ .... Labrador Airways [*ICAO designator*] (AD)
WJ .... Torontair [*ICAO designator*] (AD)
WJ .... Wars of the Jews [*of Josephus*] [*A publication*] (BJA)
WJ .... Water Jacket (MSA)
WJ .... Watkins-Johnson [*NYSE symbol*] (TTSB)
WJ .... Watkins-Johnson Co. [*NYSE symbol*] (SPSG)
wj .... West Bank of the Jordan River [*MARC country of publication code Library of Congress*] (LCCP)
WJ .... Western Jurist [*United States*] [*A publication*] (DLA)
WJ .... Wood Jalousie
WJa .... Janesville Public Library, Janesville, WI [*Library symbol Library of Congress*] (LCLS)
WJA .... Women's Jewelry Association (EA)
WJA .... Woolen Jobbers Association (EA)
WJA .... World Jazz Association [*Defunct*] (EA)
WJA .... World Jurist Association (EAIO)
WJAA .... Austin, IN [*FM radio station call letters*]

WJaB .... Blackhawk Technical Institute, Janesville, WI [*Library symbol Library of Congress*] (LCLS)
WJAB .... Huntsville, AL [*FM radio station call letters*]
WJAC .... Johnstown, PA [*AM radio station call letters*]
WJAC-TV .... Johnstown, PA [*Television station call letters*]
WJAD .... Leesburg, GA [*FM radio station call letters*] (RBYB)
WJAG .... Norfolk, NE [*AM radio station call letters*]
WJAK-AM .... Jackson, TN [*AM radio station call letters*] (RBYB)
WJAL .... Hagerstown, MD [*Television station call letters*]
WJaM .... Mercy Hospital, Janesville, WI [*Library symbol Library of Congress*] (LCLS)
WJAM .... Orrville, AL [*FM radio station call letters*]
WJAN .... Sunderland, VT [*FM radio station call letters*]
WJAQ .... Marianna, FL [*FM radio station call letters*]
WJAR .... Providence, RI [*Television station call letters*]
WJaRH .... Rock County Health Care Center, Janesville, WI [*Library symbol Library of Congress*] (LCLS)
WJAS .... Pittsburgh, PA [*AM radio station call letters*]
WJaSDHi ..... Seventh Day Baptist Historical Society Library, Janesville, WI [*Library symbol*] [*Library of Congress*] (LCLS)
WJAT .... Swainsboro, GA [*AM radio station call letters*]
WJAT-FM .... Swainsboro, GA [*FM radio station call letters*]
WJAW .... McConnelsville, OH [*FM radio station call letters*]
WJAX .... Jacksonville, FL [*AM radio station call letters*]
WJAY .... Mullins, SC [*AM radio station call letters*]
WJAZ .... Summerdale, PA [*FM radio station call letters*]
WJB .... Wire Jig Board (MCD)
WJBB .... Haleyville, AL [*AM radio station call letters*]
WJBB-FM .... Haleyville, AL [*FM radio station call letters*]
WJBC .... Bloomington, IL [*AM radio station call letters*]
WJBC .... Winnipeg Jets Booster Club (EA)
WJBD .... Salem, IL [*AM radio station call letters*]
WJBD-FM .... Salem, IL [*FM radio station call letters*]
WJBF .... Augusta, GA [*Television station call letters*]
WJBI .... Batesville, MS [*AM radio station call letters*]
WJBK .... Detroit, MI [*Television station call letters*]
WJBL .... Ladysmith, WI [*FM radio station call letters*]
WJBM .... Jerseyville, IL [*AM radio station call letters*]
WJBO .... Baton Rouge, LA [*AM radio station call letters*]
WJBQ .... Fisher, WV [*FM radio station call letters*] (RBYB)
WJBR .... Wilmington, DE [*AM radio station call letters*]
WJBR-FM .... Wilmington, DE [*FM radio station call letters*]
WJBS .... Holly Hill, SC [*AM radio station call letters*]
WJBS .... West Jersey Bancshares [*NASDAQ symbol*] (TTSB)
WJBS .... West Jersey Bancshares, Inc. [*NASDAQ symbol*] (SAG)
WJBT .... Green Cove Springs, FL [*FM radio station call letters*]
WJBU .... William Jennings Bryan University [*Tennessee*]
WJBW .... Jupiter, FL [*FM radio station call letters*]
WJBX .... Fort Myers Beach, FL [*FM radio station call letters*]
WJBY .... Rainbow City, AL [*AM radio station call letters*]
WJBZ .... Seymour, TN [*FM radio station call letters*]
WJC .... Washington and Jefferson College [*Pennsylvania*]
WJC .... Washington Journalism Center (EA)
WJC .... Western Journalism Center
WJC .... William Jewell College [*Liberty, MO*]
WJC .... Wood Junior College [*Mathison, MS*]
WJC .... Worcester Junior College [*Massachusetts*]
WJC .... World Jewish Congress, American Section (EA)
WJC .... Worthington Junior College [*Minnesota*] [*Later, Worthington Community College*]
WJCB .... Norfolk, VA [*Television station call letters*]
WJCB .... World Jersey Cattle Bureau [*Jersey, Channel Islands, England*]
WJCC .... Western Joint Computer Conference
WJCC .... Women's Joint Congressional Committee (EA)
WJCC-FM .... Montgomery, AL [*FM radio station call letters*] (RBYB)
WJCD .... Norfolk, VA [*FM radio station call letters*] (RBYB)
WJCE .... Memphis, TN [*AM radio station call letters*]
WJCE .... Russellville, KY [*FM radio station call letters*]
WJCH .... Joliet, IL [*FM radio station call letters*]
WJCI-AM .... Rantoul,IL [*AM radio station call letters*] (RBYB)
WJCK .... Cedartown, GA [*FM radio station call letters*]
WJCL .... Savannah, GA [*FM radio station call letters*]
WJCL-TV ..... Savannah, GA [*Television station call letters*]
WJCM .... Sebring, FL [*AM radio station call letters*]
WJCO-FM .... Harwichport, MA [*FM radio station call letters*] (RBYB)
WJCP-FM .... Austin, IN [*FM radio station call letters*] (RBYB)
WJCR-FM .... Upton, KY [*FM radio station call letters*] (RBYB)
WJCS-FM .... Allentown, PA [*FM radio station call letters*] (RBYB)
WJCT .... Jacksonville, FL [*FM radio station call letters*]
WJCT-TV ..... Jacksonville, FL [*Television station call letters*]
WJCV .... Jacksonville, NC [*AM radio station call letters*]
WJCW .... Johnson City, TN [*AM radio station call letters*]
WJD .... Water Jet Drilling (PDAA)
WJD .... Welded Joint Design
WJDA .... Quincy, MA [*AM radio station call letters*]
WJDB .... Thomasville, AL [*AM radio station call letters*]
WJDB-FM .... Thomasville, AL [*FM radio station call letters*]
WJDF .... Orange, MA [*FM radio station call letters*] (RBYB)
WJDJ .... Burnside, KY [*FM radio station call letters*]
WJDK .... Morris, IL [*FM radio station call letters*]
WJDM .... Elizabeth, NJ [*AM radio station call letters*]
WJDQ .... Meridian, MS [*FM radio station call letters*]
WJDR .... Prentiss, MS [*FM radio station call letters*]
WJDS .... Jackson, MS [*AM radio station call letters*]
WJDT .... Rogersville, TN [*FM radio station call letters*]
WJDX .... Jackson, MS [*FM radio station call letters*]
WJDY .... Salisbury, MD [*AM radio station call letters*]
WJE .... Willis, Joyce, McMinnville OR [*STAC*]
WJEB .... Jacksonville, FL [*Television station call letters*]
WJEC .... Vernon, AL [*FM radio station call letters*]
WJEC .... Welsh Joint Education Committee [*British*]
WJED .... Dogwood Lakes Estate, FL [*FM radio station call letters*]
WJEF .... Lafayette, IN [*FM radio station call letters*]
WJEH .... Gallipolis, OH [*AM radio station call letters*]
WJEJ .... Hagerstown, MD [*AM radio station call letters*]
WJEL .... Indianapolis, IN [*FM radio station call letters*]
WJEM .... Valdosta, GA [*AM radio station call letters*]
WJEN .... Rutland, VT [*FM radio station call letters*]
WJEP .... Ochlocknee, GA [*AM radio station call letters*]
WJEQ .... Macomb, IL [*FM radio station call letters*]
WJER .... Dover-New Philadelphia, OH [*AM radio station call letters*]
WJER .... Dover, OH [*FM radio station call letters*]
WJersB .... West Jersey Bancshares, Inc. [*Associated Press*] (SAG)
WJES .... Johnston, SC [*AM radio station call letters*]
WJET .... Erie, PA [*FM radio station call letters*]
WJET-TV ..... Erie, PA [*Television station call letters*]
WJEZ .... Pontiac, IL [*FM radio station call letters*]
WJF .... Lancaster, CA [*Location identifier FAA*] (FAAL)
WJF .... Palmdale/Lancaster [*California*] Fox [*Airport symbol*] (OAG)
WJF .... White Jewish Female [*Classified advertising*]
WJF .... Widowed Jewish Female [*Classified advertising*]
WJFB .... Lebanon, TN [*Television station call letters*]
WJFC .... Jefferson City, TN [*AM radio station call letters*]
WJFC .... Waylon Jennings Fan Club (EA)
WJFD .... New Bedford, MA [*FM radio station call letters*]
WJFF .... Jeffersonville, NY [*FM radio station call letters*]
WJFFC .... Worldwide John Fogerty Fanclub (EAIO)
WJFI .... Women's Jazz Festival [*Defunct*] (EA)
WJFJ .... Women Judges' Fund for Justice (EA)
WJFK .... Baltimore, MD [*AM radio station call letters*]
WJFK .... Manassas, VA [*FM radio station call letters*]
WJFL .... Tennille, GA [*FM radio station call letters*]
WJFM .... Baton Rouge, LA [*FM radio station call letters*]
WJFP .... Fort Pierce, FL [*FM radio station call letters*]
WJFR .... Jacksonville, FL [*FM radio station call letters*]
WJFW .... Rhinelander, WI [*Television station call letters*]
WJFX .... New Haven, IN [*FM radio station call letters*]
WJGA .... Jackson, GA [*FM radio station call letters*]
WJGF .... Romney, WV [*FM radio station call letters*]
WJGG .... Lexington-Fayette, KY [*FM radio station call letters*]
WJGO .... World Jewish Genealogy Organization (EA)
WJGR .... Jacksonville, FL [*AM radio station call letters*]
WJHB .... Fair Bluff, NC [*AM radio station call letters*]
WJHD .... Portsmouth, RI [*FM radio station call letters*]
WJHG .... Panama City, FL [*Television station call letters*]
WJHL .... Johnson City, TN [*Television station call letters*]
WJHM .... Daytona Beach, FL [*FM radio station call letters*]
WJHO .... Opelika, AL [*AM radio station call letters*]
WJHR .... Flemington, NJ [*AM radio station call letters*]
WJHS .... Columbia City, IN [*FM radio station call letters*]
WJHU .... Baltimore, MD [*FM radio station call letters*]
WJIA .... Guntersville, AL [*FM radio station call letters*] (RBYB)
WJIB .... Cambridge, MA [*AM radio station call letters*]
WJIC .... Salem, NJ [*AM radio station call letters*]
WJIE .... Okolona, KY [*FM radio station call letters*]
WJIF .... Opp, AL [*FM radio station call letters*]
WJIG .... Tullahoma, TN [*AM radio station call letters*]
WJIK .... Binghamton, NY [*FM radio station call letters*]
WJIL .... Jacksonville, IL [*AM radio station call letters*]
WJIM .... Lansing, MI [*AM radio station call letters*]
WJIM-FM ..... Lansing, MI [*FM radio station call letters*]
WJIR .... Key West, FL [*FM radio station call letters*]
WJIS .... Bradenton, FL [*FM radio station call letters*]
WJIT .... Sabana, PR [*AM radio station call letters*]
WJIV .... Cherry Valley, NY [*FM radio station call letters*]
WJIZ .... Albany, GA [*FM radio station call letters*]
WJJA .... Racine, WI [*Television station call letters*]
WJJB .... Romney, WV [*FM radio station call letters*]
WJJC .... Commerce, GA [*AM radio station call letters*]
WJJD .... Chicago, IL [*AM radio station call letters*]
WJJF .... Hope Valley, RI [*AM radio station call letters*]
WJJG .... Elmhurst, IL [*AM radio station call letters*]
WJJH .... Ashland, WI [*FM radio station call letters*]
WJJJ-FM ..... Pittsburgh, PA [*FM radio station call letters*] (RBYB)
WJJL .... Niagara Falls, NY [*AM radio station call letters*]
WJJM .... Lewisburg, TN [*AM radio station call letters*]
WJJM-FM ..... Lewisburg, TN [*FM radio station call letters*]
WJJN .... Dothan, AL [*FM radio station call letters*]
WJJO .... Watertown, WI [*FM radio station call letters*]
WJJQ .... Tomahawk, WI [*AM radio station call letters*]
WJJQ-FM ..... Tomahawk, WI [*FM radio station call letters*]
WJJR .... Rutland, VT [*FM radio station call letters*]
WJJS .... Vinton, VA [*FM radio station call letters*]
WJJT .... Jellico, TN [*AM radio station call letters*]
WJJW .... North Adams, MA [*FM radio station call letters*]
WJJX .... Lynchburg, VA [*FM radio station call letters*]
WJJY .... Brainerd, MN [*FM radio station call letters*]
WJJZ .... Philadelphia, PA [*FM radio station call letters*]
WJKC .... Christiansted, VI [*FM radio station call letters*]
WJKE .... Stillwater, NY [*FM radio station call letters*]

WJKI .... Woodruff, SC [*AM radio station call letters*]
WJKK .... Vicksburg, MS [*FM radio station call letters*] (RBYB)
WJKL .... Elgin, IL [*FM radio station call letters*]
WJKM .... Hartsville, TN [*AM radio station call letters*]
WJKN .... Jackson, MI [*AM radio station call letters*] (RBYB)
WJKS .... Jacksonville, FL [*Television station call letters*]
WJKX .... Ellisville, MS [*FM radio station call letters*]
WJKY .... Jamestown, KY [*AM radio station call letters*]
WJLA .... Washington, DC [*Television station call letters*]
WJLB .... Detroit, MI [*FM radio station call letters*]
WJLC .... South Boston, VA [*FM radio station call letters*]
WJLC .... Wye Junction Latching Circulator
WJLCER .... Women's Joint Legislative Committee for Equal Rights [*Defunct*] (EA)
WJLD .... Fairfield, AL [*AM radio station call letters*]
WJLE .... Smithville, TN [*AM radio station call letters*]
WJLE-FM .... Smithville, TN [*FM radio station call letters*]
WJLF .... Gainesville, FL [*FM radio station call letters*]
WJLH .... Flagler Beach, FL [*FM radio station call letters*] (RBYB)
WJLK .... Asbury Park, NJ [*AM radio station call letters*]
WJLK-FM .... Asbury Park, NJ [*FM radio station call letters*]
WJLM .... Salem, VA [*FM radio station call letters*]
WJLR .... Austin, IN [*FM radio station call letters*]
WJLS .... Beckley, WV [*AM radio station call letters*]
WJLS-FM .... Beckley, WV [*FM radio station call letters*]
WJLU .... New Smyrna Beach, FL [*FM radio station call letters*]
WJLW-FM .... Allouez, WI [*FM radio station call letters*] (RBYB)
WJLY .... Ramsey, IL [*FM radio station call letters*]
WJM .... Waterjet Machining [*Factory automation*] (BTTJ)
WJM .... Widowed Jewish Male [*Classified advertising*]
WJMA .... Orange, VA [*AM radio station call letters*]
WJMA-FM .... Orange, VA [*FM radio station call letters*]
WJMC .... Rice Lake, WI [*AM radio station call letters*]
WJMC-FM .... Rice Lake, WI [*FM radio station call letters*]
WJMD .... Hazard, KY [*FM radio station call letters*]
WJMF .... Smithfield, RI [*FM radio station call letters*]
WJMG .... Hattiesburg, MS [*FM radio station call letters*]
WJMH .... Reidsville, NC [*FM radio station call letters*]
WJMI .... Jackson, MS [*FM radio station call letters*]
WJMJ .... Hartford, CT [*FM radio station call letters*]
WJMK .... Chicago, IL [*FM radio station call letters*]
WJML .... Petoskey, MI [*AM radio station call letters*]
WJMM .... Versailles, KY [*FM radio station call letters*]
WJMN .... Boston, MA [*FM radio station call letters*]
WJMN .... Escanaba, MI [*Television station call letters*]
WJMO .... Cleveland Heights, OH [*AM radio station call letters*]
WJMP .... Kent, OH [*AM radio station call letters*]
WJMQ .... Clintonville, WI [*FM radio station call letters*]
WJMR .... Peshtigo, WI [*FM radio station call letters*]
WJMS .... Ironwood, MI [*AM radio station call letters*]
WJMT .... Merrill, WI [*AM radio station call letters*]
WJMU .... Decatur, IL [*FM radio station call letters*]
WJMW .... Bloomsburg, PA [*AM radio station call letters*]
WJMX .... Cheraw, SC [*FM radio station call letters*]
WJMX .... Florence, SC [*AM radio station call letters*]
WJMZ .... Anderson, SC [*FM radio station call letters*]
WJNA-AM .... Boynton Beach, FL [*AM radio station call letters*] (RBYB)
WJNC .... Jacksonville, NC [*AM radio station call letters*]
WJNF .... Marianna, FL [*FM radio station call letters*]
WJNN .... North Cape May, NJ [*FM radio station call letters*]
WJNO .... West Palm Beach, FL [*AM radio station call letters*]
WJNR .... Iron Mountain, MI [*FM radio station call letters*]
WJNS .... Yazoo City, MS [*FM radio station call letters*]
WJNT .... Pearl, MS [*AM radio station call letters*]
WJNW .... Janesville, WI [*Television station call letters*]
WJNX .... Fort Pierce, FL [*AM radio station call letters*]
WJNY .... Watertown, NY [*FM radio station call letters*]
WJOB .... Hammond, IN [*AM radio station call letters*]
WJOC .... Chattanooga, TN [*AM radio station call letters*]
WJOD .... Galena, IL [*FM radio station call letters*]
WJOI .... Germantown, TN [*FM radio station call letters*]
WJOL .... Joliet, IL [*AM radio station call letters*]
WJON .... St. Cloud, MN [*AM radio station call letters*]
WJOR .... St. Joseph, TN [*FM radio station call letters*]
WJOX .... Birmingham, AL [*AM radio station call letters*]
WJOY .... Burlington, VT [*AM radio station call letters*]
WJP .... Water Jet Pump
WJPA .... Washington, PA [*AM radio station call letters*]
WJPA-FM .... Washington, PA [*FM radio station call letters*]
WJPB .... Woodcock-Johnson Psychoeducational Battery [*Psychology*] (DAVI)
WJPD .... Ishpeming, MI [*FM radio station call letters*]
WJPEB .... Woodcock-Johnson Psychoeducational Battery [*Educational test*]
WJPF .... Herrin, IL [*AM radio station call letters*]
WJPH .... Monticello, FL [*FM radio station call letters*]
WJPM .... Florence, SC [*Television station call letters*]
WJPR .... Lynchburg, VA [*Television station call letters*]
WJPS .... Evansville, IN [*AM radio station call letters*]
WJPS .... Newburgh, IN [*FM radio station call letters*]
WJPY .... Seaford, DE [*AM radio station call letters*]
WJPZ .... Syracuse, NY [*FM radio station call letters*]
WJQI .... Chesapeake, VA [*AM radio station call letters*]
WJQI .... Virginia Beach, VA [*FM radio station call letters*]
WJQK .... Zeeland, MI [*FM radio station call letters*]
WJQR .... St. Augustine Beach, FL [*FM radio station call letters*] (RBYB)
WJQZ .... Wellsville, NY [*FM radio station call letters*]
WJR .... Detroit, MI [*AM radio station call letters*]
WJR .... Wajir [*Kenya*] [*Airport symbol*] (OAG)
WJR .... World Jewish Register [*A publication*] (BJA)
WJRA .... Priceville, AL [*AM radio station call letters*]
WJRD .... Russellville, AL [*AM radio station call letters*]
WJRE .... Kewanee, IL [*FM radio station call letters*]
WJRH .... Easton, PA [*FM radio station call letters*]
WJRI .... Lenoir, NC [*AM radio station call letters*]
WJRM .... Troy, NC [*AM radio station call letters*]
WJRO .... Glen Burnie, MD [*AM radio station call letters*]
WJRQ .... Saluda, SC [*FM radio station call letters*]
WJRR .... Cocoa Beach, FL [*FM radio station call letters*]
WJRS .... Jamestown, KY [*FM radio station call letters*]
WJRT .... Flint, MI [*Television station call letters*]
WJRV .... Loretto, PA [*AM radio station call letters*]
WJRZ .... Manahawkin, NJ [*FM radio station call letters*]
WJRZ .... Toms River, NJ [*AM radio station call letters*]
WJS .... Wife's Judicial Separation [*Legal*] [*British*] (ROG)
WJSA .... Jersey Shore, PA [*AM radio station call letters*]
WJSA-FM .... Jersey Shore, PA [*FM radio station call letters*]
WJSB .... Crestview, FL [*AM radio station call letters*]
WJSC .... Johnson, VT [*FM radio station call letters*]
WJSE .... Petersburg, NJ [*FM radio station call letters*]
WJSG .... Hamlet, NC [*FM radio station call letters*]
WJSH .... Terre Haute, IN [*AM radio station call letters*]
WJSK .... Lumberton, NC [*FM radio station call letters*]
WJSL .... Houghton, NY [*FM radio station call letters*]
WJSM .... Martinsburg, PA [*AM radio station call letters*]
WJSM-FM .... Martinsburg, PA [*FM radio station call letters*]
WJSN .... Jackson, KY [*FM radio station call letters*]
WJSO .... Pikeville, KY [*FM radio station call letters*]
WJSP .... Columbus, GA [*Television station call letters*]
WJSP .... Warm Springs, GA [*FM radio station call letters*]
WJSQ .... Athens, TN [*FM radio station call letters*]
WJSR .... Birmingham, AL [*FM radio station call letters*]
WJST .... Fort Myers Villas, FL [*FM radio station call letters*] (RBYB)
WJSU .... Anniston, AL [*Television station call letters*]
WJSU .... Jackson, MS [*FM radio station call letters*]
WJSV .... Morristown, NJ [*FM radio station call letters*]
WJSZ .... Ashley, MI [*FM radio station call letters*]
WJT .... World Journal Tribune [*Defunct New York City afternoon newspaper*]
WJTA .... Kosciusko, MS [*FM radio station call letters*]
WJTB .... North Ridgeville, OH [*AM radio station call letters*]
WJTC .... Pensacola, FL [*Television station call letters*]
WJTD .... McArthur, OH [*FM radio station call letters*]
WJTF .... Panama City, FL [*FM radio station call letters*]
WJTG .... Fort Valley, GA [*FM radio station call letters*]
WJTH .... Calhoun, GA [*AM radio station call letters*]
WJTL .... Lancaster, PA [*FM radio station call letters*]
WJTM .... Frederick, MD [*FM radio station call letters*]
WJTN .... Jamestown, NY [*AM radio station call letters*]
WJTO .... Bath, ME [*AM radio station call letters*]
WJTP .... Newland, NC [*AM radio station call letters*]
WJTT .... Red Bank, TN [*FM radio station call letters*]
WJTV .... Jackson, MS [*Television station call letters*]
WJTW .... Joliet, IL [*FM radio station call letters*]
WJTY .... Lancaster, WI [*FM radio station call letters*]
WJu .... Juneau Public Library, Juneau, WI [*Library symbol Library of Congress*] (LCLS)
WJUB .... Plymouth, WI [*AM radio station call letters*]
WJUC .... Swanton, OH [*FM radio station call letters*] (RBYB)
WJUE .... Battle Creek, MI [*Television station call letters*]
WJUF .... Inverness, FL [*FM radio station call letters*] (RBYB)
WJUK .... Mt, Pleasant, SC [*FM radio station call letters*]
WJUL .... Lowell, MA [*FM radio station call letters*]
WJuMe .... Dodge County Mental Health Center, Juneau, WI [*Library symbol Library of Congress*] (LCLS)
WJUN .... Mexico, PA [*AM radio station call letters*]
WJUN-FM .... Mexico, PA [*FM radio station call letters*]
WJUS .... Fort Walton Beach, FL [*FM radio station call letters*]
WJUX .... Monticello, NY [*FM radio station call letters*] (RBYB)
WJVL .... Janesville, WI [*FM radio station call letters*]
WJVO .... South Jacksonville, IL [*FM radio station call letters*]
WJVP-FM .... Culebra, PR [*FM radio station call letters*] (RBYB)
WJVS .... Cincinnati, OH [*FM radio station call letters*]
WJW .... Cleveland, OH [*Television station call letters*]
WJWF .... Columbus, MS [*AM radio station call letters*]
WJWJ .... Beaufort, SC [*FM radio station call letters*]
WJWJ-TV .... Beaufort, SC [*Television station call letters*]
WJWN .... San Sebastian, PR [*Television station call letters*]
WJWS .... South Hill, VA [*AM radio station call letters*]
WJWV .... Fort Gaines, GA [*FM radio station call letters*]
WJX .... Wajax Ltd. [*Toronto Stock Exchange symbol*]
WJXA .... Nashville, TN [*FM radio station call letters*]
WJXB .... Knoxville, TN [*FM radio station call letters*]
WJXL .... Jacksonville, AL [*AM radio station call letters*] (RBYB)
WJXN .... Jackson, MS [*AM radio station call letters*]
WJXN .... Utica, MS [*FM radio station call letters*]
WJXQ .... Jackson, MI [*FM radio station call letters*]
WJXR .... Macclenny, FL [*FM radio station call letters*]
WJXT .... Jacksonville, FL [*Television station call letters*]
WJXY .... Conway, SC [*AM radio station call letters*]
WJXY-FM .... Conway, SC [*FM radio station call letters*]
WJY .... Westmoreland County Community College, Youngwood, PA [*OCLC symbol*] (OCLC)

WJYC ... Delhi Hills, OH [*FM radio station call letters*]
WJYE ... Buffalo, NY [*FM radio station call letters*]
WJYF ... Nashville, GA [*FM radio station call letters*]
WJYJ ... Fredericksburg, VA [*FM radio station call letters*]
WJYL ... New Washington, IN [*FM radio station call letters*]
WJYM ... Bowling Green, OH [*AM radio station call letters*]
WJYO ... Fort Myers, FL [*FM radio station call letters*]
WJYP ... South Charleston, WV [*FM radio station call letters*]
WJYR ... Myrtle Beach, SC [*FM radio station call letters*]
WJYS ... Hammond, IN [*Television station call letters*]
WJYY ... Concord, NH [*FM radio station call letters*]
WJYZ ... Albany, GA [*AM radio station call letters*]
WJZ ... Baltimore, MD [*Television station call letters*]
WJZA ... Columbus, OH [*FM radio station call letters*]
WJZB-FM ... Houston, MS [*FM radio station call letters*] (RBYB)
WJZD ... Long Beach, MS [*FM radio station call letters*]
WJZE ... Oak Harbor, OH [*FM radio station call letters*]
WJZF ... La Grange, GA [*FM radio station call letters*]
WJZI-FM ... Milwaukee, WI [*FM radio station call letters*] (RBYB)
WJZK-FM ... Charleston, SC [*FM radio station call letters*] (RBYB)
WJZM ... Clarksville, TN [*AM radio station call letters*]
WJZR ... Rochester, NY [*FM radio station call letters*]
WJZS ... Orangeburg, SC [*AM radio station call letters*]
WJZT-FM ... Midway, FL [*FM radio station call letters*] (RBYB)
WJZW ... Woodbridge, VA [*FM radio station call letters*]
WJZY ... Belmont, NC [*Television station call letters*]
WJZZ ... Detroit, MI [*FM radio station call letters*]
wk ... Wake Island [*MARC country of publication code Library of Congress*] (LCCP)
WK ... Warburg-Keilin System [*Cytochrome-cytochrome oxidase system*] [*Named for Otto Warburg and D. Keilin*]
WK ... Warehouse Keeper [*British*] (ROG)
WK ... Waylands Korongo [*Tanzania*]
WK ... Weak (DAVI)
WK ... Week (AFM)
wk ... Week (WDMC)
WK ... Well-Known
WK ... Wernicke-Korsakoff [*Syndrome*] [*Medicine*]
WK ... Western Alaska [*Airlines*] (OAG)
WK ... Westkuestenflug [*ICAO designator*] (AD)
WK ... Wetboek van Koophandel [*Commercial Code*] [*Dutch*] (ILCA)
WK ... Wilson-Kimmelstiel [*Disease*] (MAE)
WK ... Wit Kommando [*White Commando*] [*South Africa*]
WK ... Work
WK ... Worksheet [*Data format*]
Wk ... Wreck [*Nautical charts*]
WKa ... Kaukauna Public Library, Kaukauna, WI [*Library symbol Library of Congress*] (LCLS)
WKA ... Waffenkarren [*Weapons Cart*] [*German military - World War II*]
WKA ... Wkay Resources [*Vancouver Stock Exchange symbol*]
WKAA ... Ocilla, GA [*FM radio station call letters*]
WKAB ... Berwick, PA [*FM radio station call letters*]
WKAC ... Athens, AL [*AM radio station call letters*]
WKACC ... Work Accomplishment Code [*Navy*] (NG)
WKAI ... Macomb, IL [*FM radio station call letters*]
WKAJ-FM ... Saratoga Springs, NY [*FM radio station call letters*] (RBYB)
WKAK ... Albany, GA [*FM radio station call letters*]
WKAL ... Kalkaska, MI [*AM radio station call letters*]
WKAM ... Goshen, IN [*AM radio station call letters*]
WKAN ... Kankakee, IL [*AM radio station call letters*]
WKAP ... Allentown, PA [*AM radio station call letters*] (RBYB)
WKAQ ... San Juan, PR [*AM radio station call letters*]
WKAQ-FM ... San Juan, PR [*FM radio station call letters*]
WKAQ-TV ... San Juan, PR [*Television station call letters*]
WKAR ... East Lansing, MI [*AM radio station call letters*]
WKAR-FM ... East Lansing, MI [*FM radio station call letters*]
WKAR-TV ... East Lansing, MI [*Television station call letters*]
WKAS ... Ashland, KY [*Television station call letters*]
WKAT ... North Miami, FL [*AM radio station call letters*]
Wk Aust ... Weekend Australian [*A publication*]
WKAV ... Charlottesville, VA [*AM radio station call letters*]
WKAX ... Russellville, AL [*AM radio station call letters*]
WKAY ... Kannapolis, NC [*Television station call letters*]
WKAZ ... Miami, WV [*FM radio station call letters*]
WKB ... Warracknabeal [*Victoria, Australia*] [*Airport symbol*] (AD)
WKB ... Wentzel-Kramers-Brillouin Approximation [*Mathematics*]
WKBA ... Vinton, VA [*AM radio station call letters*]
WKBB ... West Point, MS [*FM radio station call letters*]
WKBC ... North Wilkesboro, NC [*AM radio station call letters*]
WKBC-FM ... North Wilkesboro, NC [*FM radio station call letters*]
WKBD ... Detroit, MI [*Television station call letters*]
WKBE ... Warrensburg, NY [*FM radio station call letters*]
WKBF ... Rock Island, IL [*AM radio station call letters*]
WKBG ... Martinez, GA [*FM radio station call letters*]
WKBH ... Holmen, WI [*AM radio station call letters*]
WKBH ... Trempealeau, WI [*FM radio station call letters*]
WKBI ... St. Mary, PA [*AM radio station call letters*]
WKBI-FM ... St. Mary, PA [*FM radio station call letters*]
WKBJ ... Milan, TN [*AM radio station call letters*]
WKBJ ... Wentzel-Kramers-Brillouin-Jeffreys [*Approximation or Method*] [*Physics*]
WKBK ... Keene, NH [*AM radio station call letters*]
WKBL ... Covington, TN [*AM radio station call letters*]
WKBL-FM ... Covington, TN [*FM radio station call letters*]
WKBM ... Coal City, IL [*FM radio station call letters*]
WKBN ... Youngstown, OH [*AM radio station call letters*]
WKBN-FM ... Youngstown, OH [*FM radio station call letters*]
WKBN-TV ... Youngstown, OH [*Television station call letters*]
WKBO ... Harrisburg, PA [*AM radio station call letters*]
WKBQ ... Jerseyville, IL [*FM radio station call letters*]
WKBQ ... St. Louis, MO [*AM radio station call letters*]
WKBR ... Manchester, NH [*AM radio station call letters*]
WKBS ... Altoona, PA [*Television station call letters*]
WKBT ... La Crosse, WI [*Television station call letters*]
WKBV ... Richmond, IN [*AM radio station call letters*]
WKBW ... Buffalo, NY [*Television station call letters*]
WKBX ... Kingsland, GA [*FM radio station call letters*]
WKBY ... Chatham, VA [*AM radio station call letters*]
WKBZ ... Muskegon, MI [*AM radio station call letters*]
WKBZ ... Whitehall, MI [*FM radio station call letters*]
WKC ... Walker Ridge [*California*] [*Seismograph station code, US Geological Survey*] (SEIS)
WKC ... Western Kenya Aircharters Co. Ltd. [*ICAO designator*] (FAAC)
WKC ... Westminster Kennel Club (EA)
WKCA ... Owingsville, KY [*FM radio station call letters*]
WKCB ... Hindman, KY [*AM radio station call letters*]
WKCB-FM ... Hindman, KY [*FM radio station call letters*]
WKCC ... Grayson, KY [*FM radio station call letters*]
WKCD ... Pawcatuck, CT [*FM radio station call letters*] (RBYB)
WKCE ... Maryville, TN [*AM radio station call letters*] (RBYB)
WKCF ... Clermont, FL [*Television station call letters*]
WKCG ... Augusta, ME [*FM radio station call letters*]
WKCH-FM ... Whitewater, WI [*FM radio station call letters*] (RBYB)
WKCI ... Hamden, CT [*FM radio station call letters*]
WKCJ ... Lewisburg, WV [*FM radio station call letters*]
WKCL ... Ladson, SC [*FM radio station call letters*]
WKCM ... Hawesville, KY [*AM radio station call letters*]
WKCM-FM ... Hawkesville, KY [*FM radio station call letters*]
WKCN ... Lumpkin, GA [*FM radio station call letters*]
WKCO ... Gambier, OH [*FM radio station call letters*]
WKCONSUPVR ... Work Control Supervisor [*Air Force*]
WKCQ ... Saginaw, MI [*FM radio station call letters*]
WKCR ... New York, NY [*FM radio station call letters*]
WKCS ... Knoxville, TN [*FM radio station call letters*]
WKCT ... Bowling Green, KY [*AM radio station call letters*]
WKCU ... Corinth, MS [*AM radio station call letters*]
WKCV ... Kingsport, TN [*AM radio station call letters*]
WKCW ... Warrenton, VA [*AM radio station call letters*]
WKCX ... Rome, GA [*FM radio station call letters*]
WKCY ... Harrisonburg, VA [*AM radio station call letters*]
WKCY-FM ... Harrisonburg, VA [*FM radio station call letters*]
WKD ... Weekday
WKD ... Wilson-Kimmelstiel Disease [*Medicine*] (DMAA)
WKDA ... Nashville, TN [*AM radio station call letters*]
WKDAY ... Weekday
WKDB ... Towson, MD [*AM radio station call letters*]
WKDD ... Akron, OH [*FM radio station call letters*]
WKDE ... Altavista, VA [*AM radio station call letters*]
WKDE-FM ... Altavista, VA [*FM radio station call letters*]
WKDF ... Nashville, TN [*FM radio station call letters*]
WKDI ... Denton, MD [*AM radio station call letters*]
WKDJ ... Clarksdale, MS [*FM radio station call letters*]
WKDK ... Newberry, SC [*AM radio station call letters*]
WKDL ... Silver Spring, MD [*AM radio station call letters*]
WKDM ... New York, NY [*AM radio station call letters*]
WKDN ... Camden, NJ [*FM radio station call letters*]
WKDO ... Liberty, KY [*AM radio station call letters*]
WKDO-FM ... Liberty, KY [*FM radio station call letters*]
WKDP ... Corbin, KY [*AM radio station call letters*]
WKDP-FM ... Corbin, KY [*FM radio station call letters*]
WKDQ ... Henderson, KY [*FM radio station call letters*]
WKDR ... Burlington, VT [*AM radio station call letters*]
WKDS ... Kalamazoo, MI [*FM radio station call letters*]
WKDU ... Philadelphia, PA [*FM radio station call letters*]
WKDV ... Manassas, VA [*AM radio station call letters*]
WKDW-AM ... Staunton, VA [*AM radio station call letters*] (RBYB)
WKDX ... Hamlet, NC [*AM radio station call letters*]
WKDZ ... Cadiz, KY [*AM radio station call letters*]
WKDZ-FM ... Cadiz, KY [*FM radio station call letters*]
WKE ... Wake [*Wake Island*] [*Seismograph station code, US Geological Survey Closed*] (SEIS)
WKEA ... Scottsboro, AL [*FM radio station call letters*]
WKED ... Frankfort, KY [*AM radio station call letters*]
WKED-FM ... Frankfort, KY [*FM radio station call letters*]
WKEE ... Huntington, WV [*AM radio station call letters*]
WKEE-FM ... Huntington, WV [*FM radio station call letters*]
WKEF ... Dayton, OH [*Television station call letters*]
WKEI ... Kewanee, IL [*AM radio station call letters*]
WKEL ... Myrtle Beach, SC [*AM radio station call letters*]
WKEN ... Dover, DE [*AM radio station call letters*]
WKen ... Gilbert M. Simmons Public Library, Kenosha, WI [*Library symbol Library of Congress*] (LCLS)
WKenA ... Armitage Academy Library, Kenosha, WI [*Library symbol Library of Congress*] (LCLS)
WKenC ... Carthage College, Kenosha, WI [*Library symbol Library of Congress*] (LCLS)
WKEND ... Weekend
WKenG ... Gateway Technical Institute, Kenosha, WI [*Library symbol Library of Congress*] (LCLS)

WKenG-E ..... Gateway Technical Institute, Elkhorn Campus, Elkhorn, WI [*Library symbol Library of Congress*] (LCLS)
WKenG-R ..... Gateway Technical Institute, Racine Campus, Racine, WI [*Library symbol Library of Congress*] (LCLS)
WKenHi .... Kenosha County Historical Association, Kenosha, WI [*Library symbol Library of Congress*] (LCLS)
WKenM .... Kenosha Memorial Hospital, Kenosha, WI [*Library symbol Library of Congress*] (LCLS)
WKenOS ...... Old Songs Library, Kenosha, WI [*Library symbol Library of Congress*] (LCLS)
WKenSC ...... St. Catherine's Hospital, Kenosha, WI [*Library symbol Library of Congress*] (LCLS)
WKenSD ...... Unified School District Number One, Media Center, Kenosha, WI [*Library symbol Library of Congress*] (LCLS)
WKenSD-B ... Unified School District Number One, Mary D. Bradford High School, Kenosha, WI [*Library symbol Library of Congress*] (LCLS)
WKenSD-R ... Unified School District Number One, Walter Reuther High School, Kenosha, WI [*Library symbol Library of Congress*] (LCLS)
WKenSD-T ... Unified School District Number One, Tremper High School, Kenosha, WI [*Library symbol Library of Congress*] (LCLS)
WKenU .... University of Wisconsin-Parkside, Kenosha, WI [*Library symbol Library of Congress*] (LCLS)
WKenU-A ..... University of Wisconsin-Parkside, Archives and Art Research Center, Kenosha, WI [*Library symbol Library of Congress*] (LCLS)
WKEQ .... Burnside, KY [*AM radio station call letters*]
WKES .... St. Petersburg, FL [*FM radio station call letters*]
WKET .... Kettering, OH [*FM radio station call letters*]
WKEU .... Griffin, GA [*AM radio station call letters*]
WKEW .... Greensboro, NC [*AM radio station call letters*]
WKEX .... Blacksburg, VA [*AM radio station call letters*]
WKEY .... Covington, VA [*AM radio station call letters*]
WKF .... Well-Known Factor
WKFD .... Wickford, RI [*AM radio station call letters*] (RBYB)
WKFE .... Yauco, PR [*AM radio station call letters*]
WKFI .... Wilmington, OH [*AM radio station call letters*]
WKFL .... Bushnell, FL [*AM radio station call letters*]
WKFM .... Huron, OH [*FM radio station call letters*] (RBYB)
WKFR .... Battle Creek, MI [*FM radio station call letters*]
WKFT .... Fayetteville, NC [*Television station call letters*]
WKFX .... Kaukauna, WI [*FM radio station call letters*]
WKG .... Working (MSA)
WKG .... Working
WKGA .... Zion, IL [*AM radio station call letters*]
WKGB .... Bowling Green, KY [*Television station call letters*]
WKGB .... Susquehanna, PA [*FM radio station call letters*]
WKGC .... Panama City Beach, FL [*AM radio station call letters*]
WKGC .... Panama City, FL [*FM radio station call letters*]
WKGF .... Arcadia, FL [*AM radio station call letters*]
WKGF-FM .... Arcadia, FL [*FM radio station call letters*]
WKGG .... Cape Vincent, NY [*FM radio station call letters*]
WKGM .... Smithfield, VA [*AM radio station call letters*]
WKGN .... Knoxville, TN [*AM radio station call letters*]
WKGO .... Cumberland, MD [*FM radio station call letters*]
WKGP .... Workgroup Technology [*NASDAQ symbol*] (TTSB)
WKGQ .... Milledgeville, GA [*AM radio station call letters*]
WKGR .... Fort Pierce, FL [*FM radio station call letters*]
WKGT .... Century, FL [*FM radio station call letters*]
WKGV .... Working Voltage (IAA)
WKGX .... Lenoir, NC [*AM radio station call letters*]
WKHA .... Hazard, KY [*Television station call letters*]
WKHB-FM .... Hartford, KY [*FM radio station call letters*] (RBYB)
WKHC-FM .... Dahlonega, GA [*FM radio station call letters*] (RBYB)
WKHG .... Leitchfield, KY [*FM radio station call letters*]
WKHI .... Pocomoke City, MD [*FM radio station call letters*]
WKHJ .... Mountain Lake Park, MD [*FM radio station call letters*]
WKHK .... Colonial Heights, VA [*FM radio station call letters*]
WKHL .... Stamford, CT [*FM radio station call letters*]
WKHM .... Brooklyn, MI [*FM radio station call letters*]
WKHM .... Jackson, MI [*AM radio station call letters*]
WKHQ .... Charlevoix, MI [*FM radio station call letters*]
WKHR .... Bainbridge, OH [*FM radio station call letters*]
WKHS .... Worton, MD [*FM radio station call letters*]
WKHT .... Bishopville, SC [*FM radio station call letters*]
WKHW-FM ... Pocomoke City, MD [*FM radio station call letters*] (RBYB)
WKHX .... Atlanta, GA [*AM radio station call letters*]
WKHX .... Marietta, GA [*FM radio station call letters*]
WKHY .... Lafayette, IN [*FM radio station call letters*]
WKi .... Kiel Public Library, Kiel, WI [*Library symbol Library of Congress*] (LCLS)
WKI .... Wankie [*Zimbabwe*] [*Airport symbol*] (AD)
WKIC .... Hazard, KY [*AM radio station call letters*]
WKID .... Vevay, IN [*FM radio station call letters*]
WKIG .... Glennville, GA [*AM radio station call letters*]
WKIG-FM ..... Glennville, GA [*FM radio station call letters*]
WKII .... Port Charlotte, FL [*AM radio station call letters*] (RBYB)
WKIK .... La Plata, MD [*AM radio station call letters*] (RBYB)
WKIM .... Augusta, GA [*AM radio station call letters*]
WKIN .... Kingsport, TN [*AM radio station call letters*]
WKIO .... Urbana, IL [*FM radio station call letters*]
WKIP .... Poughkeepsie, NY [*AM radio station call letters*]
WKIQ .... Eustis, FL [*AM radio station call letters*]
WKIS .... Boca Raton, FL [*FM radio station call letters*]
WKIS .... Wilson Knight Interdiscipline Society (EA)
WKISF .... Wilson Knight Interdiscipline Society and Foundation (EA)
WKIT .... Brewer, ME [*FM radio station call letters*]
WKIX .... Raleigh, NC [*FM radio station call letters*]
WKIY .... West Kent Imperial Yeomanry [*British military*] (DMA)
WKIZ .... Key West, FL [*AM radio station call letters*]
WKJ .... Wakkanai [*Japan*] [*Airport symbol*] (OAG)
WKJA .... Belhaven, NC [*FM radio station call letters*]
WKJB .... Mayaguez, PR [*AM radio station call letters*]
WKJB-FM ..... Mayaguez, PR [*FM radio station call letters*]
WKJC .... Tawas City, MI [*FM radio station call letters*]
WKJE .... Hertford, NC [*FM radio station call letters*]
WKJF .... Cadillac, MI [*AM radio station call letters*]
WKJF-FM ..... Cadillac, MI [*FM radio station call letters*]
WKJG .... Fort Wayne, IN [*Television station call letters*]
WKJK .... Salem, IN [*FM radio station call letters*]
WKJL .... Clarksburg, WV [*FM radio station call letters*]
WKJN .... Hammond, LA [*FM radio station call letters*]
WKJQ .... Parsons, TN [*AM radio station call letters*]
WKJQ-FM ..... Parsons, TN [*FM radio station call letters*]
WKJR .... Arcola, IL [*FM radio station call letters*] (RBYB)
WKJT .... Tryon, NC [*AM radio station call letters*]
WKJV .... Asheville, NC [*AM radio station call letters*]
WKJX .... Elizabeth City, NC [*FM radio station call letters*]
WKJY .... Hempstead, NY [*FM radio station call letters*]
WKJZ .... Hillman, MI [*FM radio station call letters*]
WKK .... Aleknagik [*Alaska*] [*Airport symbol*] (OAG)
WKK .... Aleknagik, AK [*Location identifier FAA*] (FAAL)
WKKB .... Key Colony Beach, FL [*FM radio station call letters*]
WKKC .... Chicago, IL [*FM radio station call letters*]
WKKD .... Aurora, IL [*AM radio station call letters*]
WKKD-FM ..... Aurora, IL [*FM radio station call letters*]
WKKE .... St. Pauls, NC [*AM radio station call letters*]
WKKG .... Columbus, IN [*FM radio station call letters*]
WKKI .... Celina, OH [*FM radio station call letters*]
WKKJ .... Chillicothe, OH [*FM radio station call letters*]
WKKL .... West Barnstable, MA [*FM radio station call letters*]
WKKM .... Harrison, MI [*FM radio station call letters*]
WKKN .... Cordele, GA [*FM radio station call letters*]
WKKO .... Toledo, OH [*FM radio station call letters*]
WKKP .... McDonough, GA [*AM radio station call letters*]
WKKQ .... Nashwauk, MN [*AM radio station call letters*]
WKKR .... Auburn, AL [*FM radio station call letters*]
WKKS .... Vanceburg, KY [*AM radio station call letters*]
WKKS-FM ..... Vanceburg, KY [*FM radio station call letters*]
WKKV .... Racine, WI [*FM radio station call letters*]
WKKW .... Clarksburg, WV [*FM radio station call letters*]
WKKX .... Granite City, IL [*FM radio station call letters*]
WKKY .... Geneva, OH [*FM radio station call letters*]
WKKZ .... Dublin, GA [*FM radio station call letters*]
WKL .... Waikoloa [*Hawaii*] [*Airport symbol*] (OAG)
WKLA .... Ludington, MI [*AM radio station call letters*]
WKLA-FM ..... Ludington, MI [*FM radio station call letters*]
WKLB .... Manchester, KY [*AM radio station call letters*]
WKLB-FM ..... Framingham, MA [*FM radio station call letters*] (RBYB)
WKLC .... St. Albans, WV [*FM radio station call letters*]
WKLD .... Oneonta, AL [*FM radio station call letters*]
WKLE .... Lexington, KY [*Television station call letters*]
WKLEERI ...... W. K. Lypynsky East European Research Institute (EA)
WKLF .... Clanton, AL [*AM radio station call letters*]
WKLG .... Rock Harbor, FL [*FM radio station call letters*]
WKLH .... Milwaukee, WI [*FM radio station call letters*]
WKLI .... Albany, NY [*FM radio station call letters*]
WKLJ .... Sparta, WI [*AM radio station call letters*]
WKLK .... Cloquet, MN [*AM radio station call letters*]
WKLK-FM ..... Cloquet, MN [*FM radio station call letters*]
WKLL .... Frankfort, NY [*FM radio station call letters*]
WKLM .... Millersburg, OH [*FM radio station call letters*]
WKLN .... St Augustine Beach, FL [*AM radio station call letters*]
WKLO .... Seymour, IN [*FM radio station call letters*] (RBYB)
WKLP .... Keyser, WV [*AM radio station call letters*]
WKLQ .... Holland, MI [*FM radio station call letters*]
WKLR .... Veedersburg, IN [*FM radio station call letters*] (RBYB)
WKLS .... Atlanta, GA [*FM radio station call letters*]
WKLT .... Kalkaska, MI [*FM radio station call letters*]
WKLV .... Blackstone, VA [*AM radio station call letters*]
WKLW .... Paintsville, KY [*AM radio station call letters*]
WKLW-FM .... Paintsville, KY [*FM radio station call letters*]
WKLX .... Rochester, NY [*FM radio station call letters*]
WKLY .... Hartwell, GA [*AM radio station call letters*]
WKLY .... Weekly
Wkly Cin Law Bul ... Weekly Cincinnati Law Bulletin [*Ohio*] [*A publication*] (DLA)
Wkly Dig ...... New York Weekly Digest [*A publication*] (DLA)
Wkly Law Bul ... Weekly Law Bulletin [*Ohio*] [*A publication*] (DLA)
Wkly Law Gaz ... Weekly Law Gazette [*Ohio*] [*A publication*] (DLA)
Wkly L Bul ... Weekly Law Bulletin [*Ohio*] [*A publication*] (DLA)
Wkly L Gaz ... Weekly Law Gazette [*Ohio*] [*A publication*] (DLA)
Wkly NC .... Weekly Notes of Cases [*Pennsylvania*] [*A publication*] (DLA)
Wkly Notes Cas ... Weekly Notes of Cases [*Pennsylvania*] [*A publication*] (DLA)
Wkly Notes Cas (PA) ... Weekly Notes of Cases [*Pennsylvania*] [*A publication*] (DLA)
Wkly Rep ..... Weekly Reporter [*London*] [*A publication*] (DLA)
WKLZ .... Petoskey, MI [*FM radio station call letters*]
WKM .... Hwange National Park [*Zimbabwe*] [*Airport symbol*] (OAG)
WKM .... State University of New York, Agricultural and Technical College, Cobleskill, Cobleskill, NY [*OCLC symbol*] (OCLC)
WKM .... Wankie Game Reserve [*Zimbabwe*] [*Airport symbol*] (AD)
WKMA .... Madisonville, KY [*Television station call letters*]

WKMB .... Stirling, NJ [*AM radio station call letters*]
WKMC .... Roaring Spring, PA [*AM radio station call letters*]
WKMG .... Newberry, SC [*AM radio station call letters*]
WKMI .... Kalamazoo, MI [*AM radio station call letters*]
WKMJ .... Louisville, KY [*Television station call letters*]
WKML .... Lumberton, NC [*FM radio station call letters*]
WKMM .... Kingwood, WV [*FM radio station call letters*]
WKMO .... Hodgenville, KY [*FM radio station call letters*]
WKMQ .... Winnebago, IL [*FM radio station call letters*]
WKMR .... Morehead, KY [*Television station call letters*]
WKMS .... Murray, KY [*FM radio station call letters*]
WKMT .... Kings Mountain, NC [*AM radio station call letters*]
WKMU .... Murray, KY [*Television station call letters*]
WKMX .... Enterprise, AL [*FM radio station call letters*]
WKMY .... Princeton, WV [*FM radio station call letters*]
WKMZ .... Martinsburg, WV [*FM radio station call letters*]
WKN .... Wakunai [*Papua New Guinea*] [*Airport symbol*] (OAG)
WKN .... Weaken
Wk N .... Weekly Notes of Cases [*Pennsylvania*] [*A publication*] (DLA)
WKNA .... Senatobia, MS [*FM radio station call letters*]
WKNB .... Clarendon, PA [*FM radio station call letters*] (RBYB)
WKNC .... Raleigh, NC [*FM radio station call letters*]
WKND .... Weekend
WKND .... Windsor, CT [*AM radio station call letters*]
WKNE .... Keene, NH [*AM radio station call letters*]
WKNE-FM .... Keene, NH [*FM radio station call letters*]
WKNG .... Tallapoosa, GA [*AM radio station call letters*]
WKNH .... Keene, NH [*FM radio station call letters*]
WKNI .... Lexington, AL [*AM radio station call letters*]
WKNJ .... Union Township, NJ [*FM radio station call letters*]
WKNK .... Edmonton, KY [*FM radio station call letters*] (RBYB)
WKNL .... Knoxville, TN [*AM radio station call letters*]
WKNL .... Walter Kidde Nuclear Laboratories, Inc. (MCD)
WKNN .... Pascagoula, MS [*FM radio station call letters*]
WKNO .... Memphis, TN [*FM radio station call letters*]
WKNO-TV .... Memphis, TN [*Television station call letters*]
WKNP .... Jackson, TN [*FM radio station call letters*]
WKNQ .... Dyersburg, TN [*FM radio station call letters*]
WKNR .... Cleveland, OH [*AM radio station call letters*]
WKNS .... Kinston, NC [*FM radio station call letters*] (RBYB)
WKNT .... Bowling Green, KY [*Television station call letters*]
WKNU .... Brewton, AL [*FM radio station call letters*]
WKNV .... Dublin, VA [*AM radio station call letters*]
WKNW .... Sault Ste. Marie, MI [*AM radio station call letters*]
WKNX .... Frankenmuth, MI [*AM radio station call letters*]
WKNY .... Kingston, NY [*AM radio station call letters*]
WKNZ .... Collins, MS [*FM radio station call letters*]
WKOA .... Lafayette, IN [*FM radio station call letters*]
WKOC .... Chesapeake, VA [*FM radio station call letters*] (RBYB)
WKOE .... Ocean City, NJ [*FM radio station call letters*]
WKOH .... Owensboro, KY [*Television station call letters*]
WKOI .... Richmond, IN [*Television station call letters*]
WKOK .... Northumberland, PA [*FM radio station call letters*]
WKOK .... Sunbury, PA [*AM radio station call letters*]
WKOL .... Plattsburgh, NY [*FM radio station call letters*] (RBYB)
WKOM .... Columbia, TN [*FM radio station call letters*]
WKON .... Owenton, KY [*Television station call letters*]
WKOO .... Jacksonville, NC [*FM radio station call letters*]
WKOP .... Binghamton, NY [*AM radio station call letters*]
WKOP .... Knoxville, TN [*Television station call letters*]
WKOR .... Columbus, MS [*FM radio station call letters*]
WKOR .... Starkville, MS [*AM radio station call letters*]
WKOS .... Kingsport, TN [*FM radio station call letters*]
WKOT .... Marseilles, IL [*FM radio station call letters*]
WKOV .... Wellston, OH [*FM radio station call letters*]
WKOW .... Madison, WI [*Television station call letters*]
WKOX .... Framingham, MA [*AM radio station call letters*]
WKOY .... Bluefield, WV [*AM radio station call letters*]
WKOZ .... Kosciusko, MS [*AM radio station call letters*]
WKP .... Wrotham Park [*Queensland*] [*Airport symbol*] (AD)
WKPA .... Lynchburg, VA [*AM radio station call letters*]
WKPB .... Henderson, KY [*FM radio station call letters*]
WKPC .... Louisville, KY [*Television station call letters*]
WKPD .... Paducah, KY [*Television station call letters*]
WKPE .... Orleans, MA [*AM radio station call letters*]
WKPE-FM .... Orleans, MA [*FM radio station call letters*]
WKPG .... Port Gibson, MS
WKPI .... Pikeville, KY [*Television station call letters*]
WKPK .... Gaylord, MI [*FM radio station call letters*]
WKPP .... Elizabethton, TN [*AM radio station call letters*] (RBYB)
WKPQ .... Hornell, NY [*FM radio station call letters*]
WKPR .... Kalamazoo, MI [*AM radio station call letters*]
WKPS .... State College, PA [*FM radio station call letters*] (RBYB)
WKPT .... Kingsport, TN [*AM radio station call letters*]
WKPT-TV .... Kingsport, TN [*Television station call letters*]
WKPV .... Ponce, PR [*Television station call letters*]
WKPW .... Knightstown, IN [*FM radio station call letters*]
WKPX .... Sunrise, FL [*FM radio station call letters*]
WKQB .... Southern Pines, NC [*FM radio station call letters*] (RBYB)
WKQDR .... Work Queue Directory
WKQH .... Marathon, WI [*FM radio station call letters*] (RBYB)
WKQI .... Detroit, MI [*FM radio station call letters*]
WKQL .... Jacksonville, FL [*FM radio station call letters*]
WKQQ .... Lexington, KY [*FM radio station call letters*]
WKQS .... Gifford, FL [*FM radio station call letters*]
WKQT .... Newport, NC [*FM radio station call letters*]
WKQV .... Olyphant, PA [*FM radio station call letters*]
WKQV-AM .... Pittston, PA [*AM radio station call letters*] (RBYB)
WKQW .... Oil City, PA [*AM radio station call letters*]
WKQW-FM .... Oil City, PA [*FM radio station call letters*]
WKQX .... Chicago, IL [*FM radio station call letters*]
WKQZ .... Midland, MI [*FM radio station call letters*]
WKR .... Walker's Cay [*Bahamas*] [*Airport symbol*] (OAG)
WKR .... Whittaker Corp. [*NYSE symbol*] (SPSG)
wkr .... Wicker (VRA)
WKR .... Worker
WKR .... Work Ranch [*California*] [*Seismograph station code, US Geological Survey*] (SEIS)
WKR .... World Koala Research [*Australia*]
WKR .... Wrecker (AAG)
WKRA .... Holly Springs, MS [*AM radio station call letters*]
WKRA-FM .... Holly Springs, MS [*FM radio station call letters*]
WKRB .... Brooklyn, NY [*FM radio station call letters*]
WKRC-TV .... Cincinnati, OH [*Television station call letters*]
WKRE .... Exmore, VA [*FM radio station call letters*]
WKRF .... Tobyhanna, PA [*FM radio station call letters*] (RBYB)
WKRG .... Mobile, AL [*Television station call letters*]
WKRJ .... New Philadelphia, OH [*FM radio station call letters*]
WKRK .... Murphy, NC [*AM radio station call letters*]
WKRL .... North Syracuse, NY [*AM radio station call letters*]
WKRL-FM .... North Syracuse, NY [*FM radio station call letters*]
WKRM .... Columbia, TN [*AM radio station call letters*]
WKRN .... Nashville, TN [*Television station call letters*]
WKRO .... Cairo, IL [*AM radio station call letters*]
WKRO-FM .... Edgewater, FL [*FM radio station call letters*] (RBYB)
WKRP .... Charleston, WV [*Television station call letters*]
WKRP .... North Vernon, IN [*AM radio station call letters*]
WKRQ .... Cincinnati, OH [*FM radio station call letters*]
WKRR .... Asheboro, NC [*FM radio station call letters*]
WKRS .... Waukegan, IL [*AM radio station call letters*]
WKRT .... Cortland, NY [*AM radio station call letters*]
WKRU-AM .... Burnettown, SC [*AM radio station call letters*] (RBYB)
WKRV .... Vandalia, IL [*FM radio station call letters*]
WKRW .... Wooster, OH [*FM radio station call letters*]
WKRX .... Roxboro, NC [*FM radio station call letters*]
WKRY .... Key West, FL [*FM radio station call letters*]
WKRZ .... Wilkes-Barre, PA [*FM radio station call letters*]
WKS .... Weeks Corp. [*NYSE symbol*] (SAG)
WKS .... Wernicke-Korsakoff Syndrome [*Chemical dependence*] (DAVI)
WKS .... Works
WKS .... Worksheet File [*Computer science*]
WKS .... Workshop (AAG)
WKSA .... Isabela, PR [*FM radio station call letters*]
WKSA .... Wernicke-Korsakoff Syndrome Association [*Defunct*] (EA)
WKSB .... Williamsport, PA [*FM radio station call letters*]
WKSC .... Kershaw, SC [*AM radio station call letters*]
WKSC .... Western Kentucky State College [*Later, WKSU*]
WKSD-FM .... Paulding, OH [*FM radio station call letters*] (RBYB)
WKSE .... Niagara Falls, NY [*FM radio station call letters*]
WKSF .... Asheville, NC [*FM radio station call letters*]
WKSG .... Cedar Creek, FL [*FM radio station call letters*]
WKSH .... Sussex, WI [*AM radio station call letters*]
WKSI .... Greensboro, NC [*FM radio station call letters*]
WKSJ .... Mobile, AL [*FM radio station call letters*]
WKSJ .... Prichard, AL [*AM radio station call letters*]
WKSK .... West Jefferson, NC [*AM radio station call letters*]
WKSL .... Greencastle, PA [*FM radio station call letters*]
WKSM .... Fort Walton Beach, FL [*FM radio station call letters*]
WKSN .... Jamestown, NY [*AM radio station call letters*]
WKSO .... Orangeburg, SC [*FM radio station call letters*]
WKSO .... Somerset, KY [*Television station call letters*]
WKSP .... Workshop
WKSQ .... Ellsworth, ME [*FM radio station call letters*]
WKSR .... Pulaski, TN [*AM radio station call letters*]
WKSS .... Hartford, CT [*FM radio station call letters*]
WKST .... Ellwood City, PA [*FM radio station call letters*]
WKST .... New Castle, PA [*AM radio station call letters*]
WKSU .... Kent, OH [*FM radio station call letters*]
WKSU .... Western Kentucky State University [*Formerly, WKSC*]
WKSV-FM .... Thompson, OH [*FM radio station call lettes*] (RBYB)
WKSW .... Urbana, OH [*FM radio station call letters*]
WKSX .... Johnston, SC [*FM radio station call letters*]
WKSY .... Marion, SC [*FM radio station call letters*]
WKSZ .... De Pere, WI [*FM radio station call letters*] (RBYB)
WKT .... Wicket
WKTA .... Evanston, IL [*AM radio station call letters*]
WKTC .... Goldsboro, NC [*FM radio station call letters*]
WKTE .... King, NC [*AM radio station call letters*]
WKTF .... Jackson, MS [*FM radio station call letters*]
WKTG .... Madisonville, KY [*FM radio station call letters*]
WKTI .... Milwaukee, WI [*FM radio station call letters*]
WKTJ .... Farmington, ME [*FM radio station call letters*]
WKTK .... Crystal River, FL [*FM radio station call letters*]
WKTL .... Struthers, OH [*FM radio station call letters*]
WKTM .... Soperton, GA [*FM radio station call letters*]
WKTN .... Kenton, OH [*FM radio station call letters*]
WKTO .... Samsula, FL [*FM radio station call letters*]
WKTP .... Jonesborough, TN [*AM radio station call letters*]
WKTQ .... South Paris, ME [*AM radio station call letters*]
WKTR .... Earlysville, VA [*AM radio station call letters*]

WKTS.......... Marathon, FL [*FM radio station call letters*] (RBYB)
WKTT.......... Cleveland, WI [*FM radio station call letters*]
WKTU.......... Ocean City, NJ [*FM radio station call letters*]
WKTV.......... Utica, NY [*Television station call letters*]
WKTX.......... Cortland, OH [*AM radio station call letters*]
WKTY.......... La Crosse, WI [*AM radio station call letters*]
WKTZ.......... Jacksonville, FL [*FM radio station call letters*]
WKU.......... Wakaura [*Wakayama Eri*] [*Japan*] [*Seismograph station code, US Geological Survey*] (SEIS)
WKU.......... Western Kentucky University [*Formerly, WKSC*] [*Bowling Green*]
WKUB.......... Blackshear, GA [*FM radio station call letters*]
WKUE.......... Elizabethtown, KY [*FM radio station call letters*]
WKUL.......... Cullman, AL [*FM radio station call letters*]
WKUN.......... Monroe, GA [*AM radio station call letters*]
WKUZ.......... Wabash, IN [*FM radio station call letters*]
WKVA.......... Lewistown, PA [*AM radio station call letters*]
WKVE.......... St. Marys, PA [*FM radio station call letters*]
WKVF.......... West Kent Volunteer Force [*British military*] (DMA)
WKVG.......... Jenkins, KY [*AM radio station call letters*]
WKVI.......... Knox, IN [*AM radio station call letters*]
WKVI-FM.......... Knox, IN [*FM radio station call letters*]
WKVM.......... San Juan, PR [*AM radio station call letters*]
WKVN.......... Levittown, PR [*FM radio station call letters*]
WKVN.......... Quebradillas, PR [*AM radio station call letters*]
WKVQ.......... Eatonton, GA [*AM radio station call letters*]
WKVR.......... Huntingdon, PA [*FM radio station call letters*]
WKVS.......... Lenoir, NC [*FM radio station call letters*]
WKVT.......... Brattleboro, VT [*AM radio station call letters*]
WKVT-FM.......... Brattleboro, VT [*FM radio station call letters*]
WKVX.......... Wooster, OH [*AM radio station call letters*]
WKWC.......... Owensboro, KY [*FM radio station call letters*]
WKWF.......... Key West, FL [*AM radio station call letters*]
WKWI.......... Kilmarnock, VA [*FM radio station call letters*]
WKWK.......... Wheeling, WV [*AM radio station call letters*]
WKWK-FM.......... Wheeling, WV [*FM radio station call letters*]
WKWL.......... Florala, AL [*AM radio station call letters*]
WKWM.......... Kentwood, MI [*AM radio station call letters*]
WKWN.......... Trenton, GA [*AM radio station call letters*] (RBYB)
WKWQ.......... Batesburg, SC [*FM radio station call letters*]
WKWS.......... Charleston, WV [*FM radio station call letters*]
WKWT.......... Union City, TN [*FM radio station call letters*]
WKWX.......... Savannah, TN [*FM radio station call letters*]
WKWZ.......... Syosset, NY [*FM radio station call letters*]
WKXA.......... Findlay, OH [*FM radio station call letters*]
WKXB.......... Burgaw, NC [*FM radio station call letters*]
WKXC.......... Aiken, SC [*FM radio station call letters*]
WKXD.......... Monterey, TN [*FM radio station call letters*]
WKXE.......... White River Junction, VT [*FM radio station call letters*]
WKXF.......... Eminence, KY [*AM radio station call letters*]
WKXG.......... Greenwood, MS [*AM radio station call letters*]
WKXI.......... Jackson, MS [*AM radio station call letters*]
WKXI.......... Magee, MS [*FM radio station call letters*]
WKXJ.......... South Pittsburg, TN [*FM radio station call letters*]
WKXK-FM.......... Chicago, IL [*FM radio station call letters*] (RBYB)
WKXL.......... Concord, NH [*AM radio station call letters*]
WKXL-FM.......... Concord, NH [*FM radio station call letters*]
WKXM.......... Winfield, AL [*AM radio station call letters*]
WKXM-FM.......... Winfield, AL [*FM radio station call letters*]
WKXN.......... Greenville, AL [*FM radio station call letters*]
WKXO.......... Berea, KY [*AM radio station call letters*]
WKXO-FM.......... Berea, KY [*FM radio station call letters*]
WKXP.......... Benton, PA [*FM radio station call letters*]
WKXQ.......... Rushville, IL [*FM radio station call letters*]
WKXR.......... Asheboro, NC [*AM radio station call letters*]
WKXT.......... Knoxville, TN [*Television station call letters*]
WKXV.......... Knoxville, TN [*AM radio station call letters*]
WKXW.......... Trenton, NJ [*FM radio station call letters*]
WKXX.......... Attala, AL [*FM radio station call letters*]
WKXY.......... Sarasota, FL [*AM radio station call letters*]
WKXZ.......... Norwich, NY [*FM radio station call letters*]
WKY.......... Oklahoma City, OK [*AM radio station call letters*]
WKY.......... Wakayama [*Japan*] [*Seismograph station code, US Geological Survey*] (SEIS)
WKY.......... Warwickshire Yeomanry [*British military*] (DMA)
WKY.......... West Kent Yeomanry [*British military*] (DMA)
WKY.......... Wistar-Kyoto [*Rat variety*]
WKYA-FM.......... Greenville, KY [*FM radio station call letters*] (RBYB)
WKYB.......... Hemingway, SC [*AM radio station call letters*]
WKYC.......... Cleveland, OH [*Television station call letters*]
WKYD.......... Andalusia, AL [*AM radio station call letters*]
WKYE.......... Johnstown, PA [*FM radio station call letters*]
WKYG.......... Parkersburg, WV [*AM radio station call letters*]
WKYI.......... Stamping Ground, KY [*FM radio station call letters*]
WKYK.......... Burnsville, NC [*AM radio station call letters*]
WKYL.......... Lawrenceburg, KY [*FM radio station call letters*]
WKYM.......... Monticello, KY [*FM radio station call letters*]
WKYN.......... Florence, KY [*AM radio station call letters*] (RBYB)
WKYO.......... Caro, MI [*AM radio station call letters*]
WKYQ.......... Paducah, KY [*FM radio station call letters*]
WKYR.......... Burkesville, KY [*AM radio station call letters*]
WKYR-FM.......... Burkesville, KY [*FM radio station call letters*]
WKYS.......... Washington, DC [*FM radio station call letters*]
WKYT.......... Lexington, KY [*Television station call letters*]
WKYU.......... Bowling Green, KY [*FM radio station call letters*]
WKYU-TV.......... Bowling Green, KY [*Television station call letters*]
WKYW.......... Frankfort, KY [*FM radio station call letters*]
WKYX.......... Paducah, KY [*AM radio station call letters*]
WKYY.......... Lancaster, KY [*AM radio station call letters*]
WKYZ.......... Gray, KY [*AM radio station call letters*]
WKZC.......... Scottville, MI [*FM radio station call letters*]
WKZD.......... Murrayville, GA [*AM radio station call letters*]
WKZE.......... Salisbury, CT [*FM radio station call letters*]
WKZE.......... Sharon, CT [*AM radio station call letters*]
WKZF.......... Bayboro, NC [*FM radio station call letters*]
WKZI.......... Casey, IL [*AM radio station call letters*]
WKZJ.......... Greenville, GA [*FM radio station call letters*]
WKZK.......... North Augusta, SC [*AM radio station call letters*]
WKZL.......... Winston-Salem, NC [*FM radio station call letters*]
WKZM.......... Sarasota, FL [*FM radio station call letters*]
WKZO.......... Kalamazoo, MI [*AM radio station call letters*]
WKZQ.......... Myrtle Beach, SC [*AM radio station call letters*]
WKZQ-FM.......... Myrtle Beach, SC [*FM radio station call letters*]
WKZR.......... Milledgeville, GA [*FM radio station call letters*]
WKZS.......... Auburn, ME [*FM radio station call letters*]
WKZT.......... Elizabethtown, KY [*Television station call letters*]
WKZT.......... Fulton, KY [*AM radio station call letters*]
WKZU.......... Ripley, MS [*FM radio station call letters*]
WKZV.......... Washington, PA [*AM radio station call letters*]
WKZW.......... Chillicothe, IL [*FM radio station call letters*] (RBYB)
WKZX.......... Cookeville, TN [*Television station call letters*]
WKZY.......... La Belle, FL [*FM radio station call letters*]
WKZZ.......... Douglas, GA [*FM radio station call letters*]
WL.......... Bursa Hava Yollari [*ICAO designator*] (AD)
WL.......... Wagons-Lits [*Railroad Sleeping or Pullman cars in Europe*] [*French*]
WL.......... Waiting List
WL.......... Wallenstein Laboratory [*Medium*] (BABM)
WL.......... Walther League (EA)
WL.......... War Legislation [*British World War II*]
WL.......... Warner-Lambert Pharmaceutical Co.
WL.......... Warning Light (SAA)
WL.......... Water Line
WL.......... Waterload Test [*Clinical chemistry*]
WL.......... Wavelength [*Electronics*]
WL.......... Weapons Laboratory (MCD)
WL.......... Wehrmacht-Luftwaffe [*Marking on Air Force vehicles*] [*German military - World War II*]
WL.......... Well
WL.......... Well [*Postal Service standard*] (OPSA)
WL.......... Western Larch [*Utility pole*] [*Telecommunications*] (TEL)
WL.......... Western League [*Baseball*]
WL.......... Westland Helicopters Ltd. [*British ICAO aircraft manufacturer identifier*] (ICAO)
WL.......... West Longitude (SSD)
WL.......... Westminster Library [*A publication*]
WL.......... Wheeler Laboratories, Inc. (MCD)
WL.......... Wheel Locks
WL.......... White Laboratories, Inc. [*Research code symbol*]
WL.......... White Leghorn [*Poultry*]
WL.......... White Light (MSA)
WL.......... Wideband Limiter
WL.......... Width-to-Length [*Ratio*] (IAA)
WL.......... Wiener Library [*London*] (BJA)
WL.......... Wind Load
WL.......... Wiring List
W-L.......... Wisconsin State Law Library [*Wisconsin State Library*], Madison, WI [*Library symbol Library of Congress*] (LCLS)
WL.......... With Restrictive Language (MCD)
WL.......... Women's Legion [*World War I*] [*British*]
WL.......... Women's Liberation (ADA)
WL.......... Women's Lobby [*Defunct*] (EA)
WL.......... Women's Reserve, Legal Specialist Duties [*USNR officer designation*]
WL.......... Wool
wl.......... Wool (VRA)
WL.......... Word in Life: Journal of Religious Education [*A publication*] (APTA)
WL.......... Word Length (IAA)
WL.......... Word Line
WL.......... Working Level
WL.......... Work Light
WL.......... Work Line (MSA)
WL.......... Workload (AABC)
WL.......... World List of Future International Meetings [*A publication*]
WL.......... Worldloppet (EA)
WL.......... World of Learning [*A publication*]
WL.......... Wyeth Laboratories [*Research code symbol*]
WL0.......... Water Line Zero (KSC)
WLA.......... Warner-Lambert [*NYSE symbol*] (TTSB)
WLA.......... Warner-Lambert Co. [*NYSE symbol*] (SPSG)
WLA.......... Wasteload Allocation [*Environmental science*] (FFDE)
WLA.......... Welsh Lacrosse Association (EAIO)
WLA.......... Wescosa Lumber Association [*Defunct*] (EA)
WLA.......... Western Lacrosse Association [*Canada*]
WLA.......... Western Literature Association (EA)
WLA.......... West London Aero Services Ltd. [*British ICAO designator*] (FAAC)
WLA.......... White Lung Association (EA)
WLA.......... Wire Line Adapter (MCD)
WLA.......... Wire Line Antenna
WLA.......... Wittsburg Lake [*Arkansas*] [*Seismograph station code, US Geological Survey Closed*] (SEIS)

WLA.......... Women's Land Army [*Part of the United States Crop Corps*] [*World War II*]
WLA.......... World Literary Academy (EAIO)
WLAB.......... Fort Wayne, IN [*FM radio station call letters*]
WLac.......... La Crosse Public Library, La Crosse, WI [*Library symbol Library of Congress*] (LCLS)
WLAC.......... Nashville, TN [*AM radio station call letters*]
WLAC.......... Watson Laboratories Air Materiel Command (SAA)
WLAC.......... Western Labour Arbitration Cases [*A publication*] (DLA)
WLAC-FM.......... Nashville, TN [*FM radio station call letters*]
WLacFW.......... United States Fish and Wildlife Service, Fish Control Laboratory, La Crosse, WI [*Library symbol Library of Congress*] (LCLS)
WLacL.......... La Crosse Lutheran Hospital, La Crosse, WI [*Library symbol Library of Congress*] (LCLS)
WLacSF.......... Saint Francis Hospital, La Crosse, WI [*Library symbol Library of Congress*] (LCLS)
WLacU.......... University of Wisconsin-La Crosse, La Crosse, WI [*Library symbol Library of Congress*] (LCLS)
WLacVC.......... Viterbo College, La Crosse, WI [*Library symbol Library of Congress*] (LCLS)
WLAD.......... Danbury, CT [*AM radio station call letters*]
WLadM.......... Mount Senario College, Ladysmith, WI [*Library symbol Library of Congress*] (LCLS)
WLAE.......... New Orleans, LA [*Television station call letters*]
WLAF.......... La Follette, TN [*AM radio station call letters*]
WLAF.......... World League of American Football [*1991*]
WLAG.......... La Grange, GA [*AM radio station call letters*]
WLag.......... Lake Geneva Public Library, Lake Geneva, WI [*Library symbol Library of Congress*] (LCLS)
WLagB.......... Badger Union High School District, Lake Geneva, WI [*Library symbol Library of Congress*] (LCLS)
WLagF.......... Franciscan Education Center, Lake Geneva, WI [*Library symbol Library of Congress*] (LCLS)
WLagSD.......... Joint School District Number One, Lake Geneva, WI [*Library symbol Library of Congress*] (LCLS)
WLAJ.......... Lansing, MI [*Television station call letters*]
WLAK.......... Huntingdon, PA [*FM radio station call letters*]
WLAL-AM.......... Cobleskill, NY [*AM radio station call letters*] (RBYB)
WLALW.......... World Laboratory Animal Liberation Week
WLAM.......... Gorham, ME [*AM radio station call letters*]
WLAM-FM.......... North Windham, ME [*FM radio station call letters*] (RBYB)
WLAN.......... Lancaster, PA [*AM radio station call letters*]
WLAN-FM.......... Lancaster, PA [*FM radio station call letters*]
WLANSW.......... Women Lawyers' Association of New South Wales [*Australia*]
WLAP.......... Lexington, KY [*AM radio station call letters*]
WLAQ.......... Rome, GA [*AM radio station call letters*]
WLAR.......... Athens, TN [*AM radio station call letters*]
WLAS.......... Jacksonville, NC [*AM radio station call letters*]
WLAT.......... Manchester, CT [*AM radio station call letters*]
WLAT.......... Women Lawyers' Association of Tasmania [*Australia*]
WLA/TMDL.......... Wasteload Allocation / Total Maximum Daily Load [*Environmental Protection Agency*] (EPA)
WLAU.......... Laurel, MS [*AM radio station call letters*]
WLAV.......... Will Advise (FAAC)
WLAV-FM.......... Grand Rapids, MI [*FM radio station call letters*]
WLAW.......... Fairhaven, MA [*AM radio station call letters*]
W Law Bul.......... Weekly Law Bulletin [*Ohio*] [*A publication*] (DLA)
WLAX.......... La Crosse, WI [*Television station call letters*]
WLAY.......... Muscle Shoals, AL [*AM radio station call letters*]
WLAY-FM.......... Muscle Shoals, AL [*FM radio station call letters*]
WLAZ-FM.......... Clermont, FL [*FM radio station call letters*] (RBYB)
WLB.......... National War Labor Board [*World War II*]
WLB.......... Seagoing Buoy Tender [*Coast Guard*] (NVT)
WLB.......... Wallboard (AAG)
WLB.......... Weapons Logbook [*Military*] (AABC)
WLB.......... Weekly Law Bulletin [*Ohio*] [*A publication*] (DLA)
W/L/B.......... White Letter [*or Line*] Block [*Typography*] (DGA)
WLB.......... Wilson Library Bulletin [*A publication*] (BRI)
WLBA.......... Gainesville, GA [*AM radio station call letters*]
WLBB.......... Carrollton, GA [*AM radio station call letters*]
WLBC.......... Muncie, IN [*AM radio station call letters*]
WLBC-FM.......... Muncie, IN [*FM radio station call letters*]
WLBE.......... Leesburg, FL [*AM radio station call letters*]
WLBF.......... Montgomery, AL [*FM radio station call letters*]
WLBG.......... Laurens, SC [*AM radio station call letters*]
WLBH.......... Mattoon, IL [*AM radio station call letters*]
WLBH-FM.......... Mattoon, IL [*FM radio station call letters*]
WLBI.......... Warrior, AL [*FM radio station call letters*]
WLBJ.......... Bowling Green, KY [*AM radio station call letters*]
WLBK.......... De Kalb, IL [*AM radio station call letters*]
WLBL.......... Auburndale, WI [*AM radio station call letters*]
WLBL-FM.......... Wausau, WI [*FM radio station call letters*] (RBYB)
WLBM.......... Wing-Level Bombing System (SAA)
WLBN.......... Lebanon, KY [*AM radio station call letters*]
WLBQ.......... Morgantown, KY [*AM radio station call letters*]
WLBR.......... Lebanon, PA [*AM radio station call letters*]
WLBR.......... Seagoing Buoy Tender Replacement Vessel [*USCG*] (TAG)
WLBT.......... Jackson, MS [*Television station call letters*]
WL Bull.......... Weekly Law Bulletin [*Ohio*] [*A publication*] (DLA)
WL Bull (Ohio)... Weekly Law Bulletin [*Ohio*] [*A publication*] (DLA)
WLBW.......... Fenwick Island, DE [*FM radio station call letters*]
WLBZ.......... Bangor, ME [*Television station call letters*]
WLC.......... Weapon-Launching Console (MCD)
WLC.......... Weapons Laboratory Civil Engineering Division [*Kirtland Air Force Base, NM*]
WLC.......... Wellco Enterprises [*AMEX symbol*] (TTSB)
WLC.......... Wellco Enterprises, Inc. [*AMEX symbol*] (SPSG)
WLC.......... Well Logging Cable
WLC.......... West London College [*England*]
WLC.......... White Light Coronagraph (KSC)
WLC.......... Wildcat
WLC.......... Wine Label Circle (EA)
WLC.......... Wisconsin Library Consortium (NITA)
WLC.......... World Literacy of Canada (EAIO)
WLCA.......... Godfrey, IL [*FM radio station call letters*]
WLCAC.......... Watts Labor Community Action Committee [*Los Angeles, CA*]
WLCB-TV.......... Leesburg, FL [*TV radio station call letters*] (RBYB)
WLCC.......... Luray, VA [*FM radio station call letters*]
WLCC.......... Walker-Lybarger Construction Co. [*Colorado*]
WLCE.......... White Light Coronagraph Experiment (KSC)
WLCH.......... Lancaster, PA [*FM radio station call letters*]
WLCK.......... Scottsville, KY [*AM radio station call letters*]
WL(CL).......... War Legislation, Civil Liabilities [*British World War II*]
WLCM.......... Charlotte, MI [*AM radio station call letters*]
WLCN.......... Madisonville, KY [*Television station call letters*]
WLCQ.......... Clarksville, VA [*FM radio station call letters*]
WLCS.......... North Muskegon, MI [*FM radio station call letters*]
WLCS.......... Workload and Cost Schedule [*Military*] (AABC)
WLCSS.......... Weapon Launch Console Switching Section (MCD)
WLCT.......... Lafayette, TN [*FM radio station call letters*]
WLCX.......... Farmville, VA [*FM radio station call letters*]
WLCY.......... Blairsville, PA [*FM radio station call letters*]
WLD.......... South African Law Reports, Witwatersrand Local Division [*A publication*] (DLA)
WLD.......... Warning Light Driver (IAA)
WLD.......... Water and Land Division [*Environmental Protection Agency*] (GFGA)
WLD.......... Weapon Loading Director (NVT)
WLD.......... Welded (MSA)
wld.......... Welded (VRA)
WLD.......... Weldotron Corp. [*AMEX symbol*] (SPSG)
WLD.......... Welsh Liberal Democrats [*Political party*] (EAIO)
WLD.......... West Longitude Date (AABC)
WLD.......... Wilderness Airline (1975) Ltd. [*Canada ICAO designator*] (FAAC)
WLD.......... Winfield/Arkansas City, KS [*Location identifier FAA*] (FAAL)
WLD.......... Women Liberal Democrat [*British Political party*] (EAIO)
WLD.......... World
WLD.......... World Technology Industry [*Vancouver Stock Exchange symbol*]
WLDA.......... Wholesale Leather Distributors Association [*British*] (BI)
WLDA.......... World Airways [*NASDAQ symbol*] (TTSB)
WLDA.......... World Airways, Inc. [*NASDAQ symbol*] (SAG)
WldAccep.......... World Acceptance Corp. [*Associated Press*] (SAG)
WldAcp.......... World Acceptance Corp. [*Associated Press*] (SAG)
WldAir.......... World Airways, Inc. [*Associated Press*] (SAG)
Wld Ch.......... World Champion (BARN)
WLDE.......... Fort Wayne, IN [*FM radio station call letters*]
WLDF.......... Women's Legal Defense Fund (EA)
WldFuel.......... World Fuel Services Corp. [*Associated Press*] (SAG)
WLDG.......... Welding (IAA)
WLDJ.......... Appomattox, VA [*FM radio station call letters*]
WLDLF.......... Wildlife
WLDMT.......... Weldment (MSA)
WLDN.......... Walden Bancorp [*NASDAQ symbol*] (TTSB)
WLDND.......... Wildland
WLDR.......... Traverse City, MI [*FM radio station call letters*]
WLDR.......... Welder (MSA)
WLDS.......... Jacksonville, IL [*AM radio station call letters*]
WLDS.......... Weldless
Wldtex.......... Worldtex, Inc. [*Associated Press*] (SAG)
WldwDlr.......... Worldwide Dollarvest Fund [*Associated Press*] (SAG)
WLDX.......... Fayette, AL [*AM radio station call letters*]
WLDY.......... Ladysmith, WI [*AM radio station call letters*]
WLE.......... Ward Lock Educational [*Publisher*] [*British*]
WLE.......... Wellore Energy, Inc. [*Toronto Stock Exchange symbol*]
WLEA.......... Hornell, NY [*AM radio station call letters*]
WLEC.......... Sandusky, OH [*AM radio station call letters*]
WLED.......... Littleton, NH [*Television station call letters*]
WLEE.......... Richmond, VA [*AM radio station call letters*]
WLEE-FM.......... Williamsburg, VA [*FM radio station call letters*] (RBYB)
WLEF.......... Park Falls, WI [*Television station call letters*]
WLEM.......... Emporium, PA [*AM radio station call letters*]
WLEN.......... Adrian, MI [*FM radio station call letters*]
WLEO.......... Ponce, PR [*AM radio station call letters*]
WLER.......... Butler, PA [*FM radio station call letters*]
WLES.......... Lawrenceville, VA [*AM radio station call letters*]
WLET.......... Toccoa, GA [*AM radio station call letters*]
WLET.......... Winland Electronics [*NASDAQ symbol*] (TTSB)
WLET.......... Winland Electronics, Inc. [*NASDAQ symbol*] (SAG)
WLET-FM.......... Toccoa, GA [*FM radio station call letters*]
WLEV.......... Easton, PA [*FM radio station call letters*]
WLEW.......... Bad Axe, MI [*AM radio station call letters*]
WLEW-FM.......... Bad Axe, MI [*FM radio station call letters*]
WLEX.......... Lexington, KY [*Television station call letters*]
WLEY.......... Cayey, PR [*AM radio station call letters*]
WLEZ.......... Terre Haute, IN [*FM radio station call letters*]
WLF.......... Walferdange [*Belgium*] [*Seismograph station code, US Geological Survey*] (SEIS)
WLF.......... Wallis and Futuna [*ANSI three-letter standard code*] (CNC)
WLF.......... Washington Legal Foundation (EA)
WLF.......... Welfare (AABC)
WLF.......... Whole Lithosphere Failure [*Geology*]

WLF .... Williams-Landel-Ferry [*Polymer physics*]
WLF .... Wolf River Resources Ltd. [*Vancouver Stock Exchange symbol*]
WLF .... Women's Law Fund (EA)
WLF .... Word of Life Fellowship (EA)
WLF .... Workload Factor (AFM)
WLF .... World Law Fund (EA)
WLFA .... Asheville, NC [*FM radio station call letters*]
WLFA .... West Lancashire Field Artillery [*Military unit*] [*British*]
WLFA .... Wildlife Legislative Fund of America (EA)
WLFB .... Bluefield, WV [*Television station call letters*]
WLFB .... Wolfeboro Railroad Co., Inc. [*AAR code*]
WLFC .... Findlay, OH [*FM radio station call letters*]
WLFC .... Washington Library Film Circuit [*Library network*]
WLFD .... World League for Freedom and Democracy [*South Korea*] (EAIO)
WLFE .... St. Albans, VT [*FM radio station call letters*]
WLFG .... Grundy, VA [*Television station call letters*]
WLFH .... Little Falls, NY [*AM radio station call letters*]
WLFI .... Lafayette, IN [*Television station call letters*]
WLFI .... WinsLoew Furniture [*NASDAQ symbol*] (TTSB)
WLFI .... WinsLoew Furniture, Inc. [*NASDAQ symbol*] (SAG)
WLFI .... Winslow Furniture, Inc. [*NASDAQ symbol*] (SAG)
WLFJ .... Greenville, SC [*FM radio station call letters*]
WLFL .... Raleigh, NC [*Television station call letters*]
WLFM .... Appleton, WI [*FM radio station call letters*]
WLFN .... La Crosse, WI [*AM radio station call letters*]
WLFPA .... World League for the Protection of Animals
WLFR .... Pomona, NJ [*FM radio station call letters*]
WLFX .... Ocean Pines, MD [*FM radio station call letters*]
WLFX .... Welding Fixture (AAG)
WLG .... Waldron Ledge [*Hawaii*] [*Seismograph station code, US Geological Survey*] (SEIS)
WLG .... Washington Liaison Group (AFM)
WLG .... Weekly Law Gazette [*Ohio*] [*A publication*] (ILCA)
WLG .... Wellington [*New Zealand*] [*Airport symbol*] (OAG)
WLG .... Work Learning Guide (AIE)
WL Gaz .... Weekly Law Gazette (Reprint) [*Ohio*] [*A publication*] (DLA)
WL Gaz (Ohio) ... Weekly Law Gazette (Ohio) [*A publication*] (DLA)
WLGC .... Greenup, KY [*AM radio station call letters*]
WLGC-FM .... Greenup, KY [*FM radio station call letters*]
WLGC-FM .... Greenup, KY [*FM radio station call letters*] (RBYB)
WLGI .... Hemingway, SC [*FM radio station call letters*]
WLGL .... Riverside, PA [*FM radio station call letters*]
WLGM .... Springfield, IL [*FM radio station call letters*] (RBYB)
WLGN .... Logan, OH [*AM radio station call letters*]
WLGN-FM .... Logan, OH [*FM radio station call letters*]
WLGO .... Lexington, SC [*AM radio station call letters*]
WLGP-FM .... Harkers Island, NC [*FM radio station call letters*] (RBYB)
WLGQ .... Gaston, NC [*FM radio station call letters*]
WLGX .... Carolina Beach, NC [*FM radio station call letters*]
WLH .... Society for the Study of Women in Legal History (EA)
WLH .... Walaha [*Vanuatu*] [*Airport symbol*] (OAG)
WLH .... Wealth Resources Ltd. [*Vancouver Stock Exchange symbol*]
WLH .... Wilhelmshaven [*Federal Republic of Germany*] [*Geomagnetic observatory code*]
WLHB .... Women's League of Health and Beauty (EAIO)
WLHE .... Water LASER Heat Exchange
WLHFP .... Women's Labor History Film Project (EA)
WLHM .... Logansport, IN [*FM radio station call letters*]
WLHN .... Elwood, IN [*FM radio station call letters*]
WLHN .... Wideband-Limiter-Heterodyne-Narrowband (PDAA)
WLHN .... Wolohan Lumber [*NASDAQ symbol*] (TTSB)
WLHN .... Wolohan Lumber Co. [*NASDAQ symbol*] (NQ)
WLHS .... West Chester, OH [*FM radio station call letters*]
WLHT .... Grand Rapids, MI [*FM radio station call letters*]
WLI .... Inland Buoy Tender [*USCG*] (TAG)
WLI .... Water Landing Impact (SAA)
WLI .... Wellesley Island [*New York*] [*Seismograph station code, US Geological Survey Closed*] (SEIS)
WLI .... Whole-Life Insurance (MHDB)
WLI .... Wilderness Leadership International (EA)
WLI .... Women's League for Israel (EA)
WLIB .... New York, NY [*AM radio station call letters*]
WLIC .... Construction Tender [*Coast Guard symbol*] (DNAB)
WLIC .... Frostburg, MD [*FM radio station call letters*]
WLIC .... Inland Construction Buoy Tender [*USCG*] (TAG)
WLIE .... Bridgehampton, NY [*FM radio station call letters*]
WLIF .... Baltimore, MD [*FM radio station call letters*]
WLIG .... Riverhead, NY [*Television station call letters*]
WLIH .... Whitneyville, PA [*FM radio station call letters*]
WLII .... Caguas, PR [*Television station call letters*]
WLIJ .... Shelbyville, TN [*AM radio station call letters*]
WLIK .... Newport, TN [*AM radio station call letters*]
WLIL .... Lenoir City, TN [*AM radio station call letters*]
WLIL-FM .... Lenoir City, TN [*FM radio station call letters*]
WLIM .... Patchogue, NY [*AM radio station call letters*]
WLIN .... Gluckstadt, MS [*FM radio station call letters*]
WLIO .... Lima, OH [*Television station call letters*]
WLIP .... Kenosha, WI [*AM radio station call letters*]
WLIQ .... Harriman, TN [*FM radio station call letters*]
WLIR .... Spring Valley, NY [*AM radio station call letters*]
WLIS .... Old Saybrook, CT [*AM radio station call letters*]
WLIT .... Chicago, IL [*FM radio station call letters*]
WLIU .... Lincoln University, PA [*FM radio station call letters*]
WLIV .... Livingston, TN [*AM radio station call letters*]
WLIW .... Garden City, NY [*Television station call letters*]
WLJ .... Willamette Law Journal [*A publication*] (ILCA)
WLJA .... Ellijay, GA [*AM radio station call letters*]
WLJA-FM ..... Ellijay, GA [*FM radio station call letters*]
WLJC .... Beattyville, KY [*FM radio station call letters*]
WLJC-TV ..... Beattyville, KY [*Television station call letters*]
WLJE .... Valparaiso, IN [*FM radio station call letters*]
WLJK .... Aiken, SC [*FM radio station call letters*]
WLJL .... Charlottesville, VA [*FM radio station call letters*]
WLJM-FM .... Lima, OH [*FM radio station call letters*] (RBYB)
WLJN .... Elmwood Township, MI [*AM radio station call letters*]
WLJN .... Traverse City, MI [*FM radio station call letters*]
WLJP .... Monroe, NY [*FM radio station call letters*]
WLJQ .... Colonial Heights, TN [*FM radio station call letters*]
WLJR .... Birmingham, AL [*FM radio station call letters*]
WLJS .... Jacksonville, AL [*FM radio station call letters*]
WLJT .... Lexington, TN [*Television station call letters*]
WLJY .... Marshfield, WI [*FM radio station call letters*]
WLJZ .... Mackinaw City, MI [*FM radio station call letters*] (RBYB)
WLK .... Selawik [*Alaska*] [*Airport symbol*] (OAG)
WLK .... Selawik, AK [*Location identifier FAA*] (FAAL)
wlk .... Wales [*MARC country of publication code Library of Congress*] (LCCP)
WLK .... Walk
WLK .... Westlake Industry [*Vancouver Stock Exchange symbol*]
WLK .... Wiest Lake [*California*] [*Seismograph station code, US Geological Survey*] (SEIS)
WLKA .... Canandaigua, NY [*FM radio station call letters*]
WLKC .... Henderson, NY [*FM radio station call letters*]
WLKE .... Bar Harbor, ME [*FM radio station call letters*]
WLKF .... Lakeland, FL [*AM radio station call letters*]
WLKG .... Lake Geneva, WI [*FM radio station call letters*]
WLKI .... Angola, IN [*FM radio station call letters*]
WLKK .... Erie, PA [*AM radio station call letters*]
WLKL .... Mattoon, IL [*FM radio station call letters*]
WLKM .... Three Rivers, MI [*AM radio station call letters*]
WLKM-FM ... Three Rivers, MI [*FM radio station call letters*]
WLKQ .... Buford, GA [*FM radio station call letters*]
WLKR .... Norwalk, OH [*FM radio station call letters*]
WLKS .... West Liberty, KY [*AM radio station call letters*]
WLKS-FM ... West Liberty, KY [*FM radio station call letters*]
WLKT-FM .... Lexington-Fayette, KY [*FM radio station call letters*] (RBYB)
WLKW .... Providence, RI [*AM radio station call letters*]
wlkwy .... Walkway (VRA)
WLKWY .... Walkway
WLKX .... Forest Lake, MN [*FM radio station call letters*]
WLKY .... Louisville, KY [*Television station call letters*]
WLKZ .... Wolfeboro, NH [*FM radio station call letters*]
WLL .... Williamstown [*Massachusetts*] [*Seismograph station code, US Geological Survey Closed*] (SEIS)
WLLA .... Kalamazoo, MI [*Television station call letters*]
WLLD .... Upper Arlington, OH [*FM radio station call letters*]
WLLE .... Raleigh, NC [*AM radio station call letters*]
WLLF .... Mercer, PA [*FM radio station call letters*]
WLLG .... Lowville, NY [*FM radio station call letters*]
WLLH .... Lowell, MA [*AM radio station call letters*]
WLLI .... Joliet, IL [*FM radio station call letters*]
WLLK .... Somerset, KY [*FM radio station call letters*]
WLLL .... Lynchburg, VA [*AM radio station call letters*]
WLLN .... Lillington, NC [*AM radio station call letters*]
WLLR .... East Moline, IL [*FM radio station call letters*]
WLLR .... Moline, IL [*AM radio station call letters*]
WLLS .... Hartford, KY [*AM radio station call letters*]
WLLS-FM .... Hartford, KY [*FM radio station call letters*]
WLLT .... Polo, IL [*FM radio station call letters*]
WLLV .... Louisville, KY [*AM radio station call letters*]
WLLW-FM ... Clyde, NY [*FM radio station call letters*] (RBYB)
WLLX .... Lawrenceburg, TN [*FM radio station call letters*]
WLLY .... Wilson, NC [*AM radio station call letters*]
WLLZ .... Detroit, MI [*FM radio station call letters*]
WLM .... Coastal Buoy Tender [*Coast Guard symbol*] (DNAB)
WLM .... Warning Light Monitor
WLM .... Wellman, Inc. [*NYSE symbol*] (CTT)
WLM .... Western Law Monthly [*Cleveland, OH*] [*A publication*] (DLA)
WLM .... Western Lumber Manufacturers [*Later, Western Timber Association*] [*An association*] (EA)
WLM .... Willow Mountain [*Alaska*] [*Seismograph station code, US Geological Survey Closed*] (SEIS)
WLM .... Wire Line MODEMS
WLM .... Working Level Month [*Nuclear energy*]
WLMA .... Greenwood, SC [*AM radio station call letters*]
WLMB .... Toledo, OH [*Television station call letters*]
WLMC .... Georgetown, SC [*AM radio station call letters*]
WLMD .... Bushnell, IL [*FM radio station call letters*]
WLME .... Cannelton, IN [*FM radio station call letters*]
WLMG .... New Orleans, LA [*FM radio station call letters*]
WLMH .... Morrow, OH [*FM radio station call letters*]
WLMI .... Kane, PA [*FM radio station call letters*]
WLML .... Montezuma, GA [*FM radio station call letters*]
WLMO .... Worldwide Logistics Management Office [*Army*]
WLMQ .... Monterey, TN [*FM radio station call letters*] (RBYB)
WLMR .... Chattanooga, TN [*AM radio station call letters*]
WLMR .... Coastal Buoy Tender Replacement Vessel [*USCG*] (TAG)
WLMR .... Wilmar Industries [*NASDAQ symbol*] (TTSB)
WLMS .... Lecanto, FL [*FM radio station call letters*]
WLMT .... Memphis, TN [*Television station call letters*]

WLMU .... Harrogate, TN [*FM radio station call letters*]
WLMW .... Manchester, NH [*FM radio station call letters*]
WLMX .... Rossville, GA [*FM radio station call letters*]
WLN .... Washington Library Network [*Washington State Library*] [*Olympia, WA*] [*Library network*]
WLN .... Welcome North Mines [*Vancouver Stock Exchange symbol*]
WLN .... Wellington [*British depot code*]
WLN .... Western Library Network [*Formerly, Washington Library Network*] [*Olympia, WA*] [*Database*] [*Library of Congress*]
WLN .... Wiswesser Line Notation [*Chemical structure*]
WLNA .... Peekskill, NY [*AM radio station call letters*]
WLNB .... Ligonier, IN [*FM radio station call letters*]
WLNC .... Laurinburg, NC [*AM radio station call letters*]
WLNE .... New Bedford, MA [*Television station call letters*]
WLNG .... Sag Harbor, NY [*AM radio station call letters*]
WLNG-FM .... Sag Harbor, NY [*FM radio station call letters*]
WLNH .... Laconia, NH [*FM radio station call letters*]
WLNI .... Lynchburg, VA [*FM radio station call letters*]
WLNL .... Horseheads, NY [*AM radio station call letters*]
WLNO .... New Orleans, LA [*AM radio station call letters*] (RBYB)
WLNR .... Kinston, NC [*AM radio station call letters*] (RBYB)
WLNS .... Lansing, MI [*Television station call letters*]
WLNT .... Winchester, KY [*AM radio station call letters*]
WLNX .... Lincoln, IL [*FM radio station call letters*]
WLNY-TV .... Riverhead, NY [*TV station call letters*] (RBYB)
WLNZ .... Lansing, MI [*FM radio station call letters*]
WLO .... Waterloo Railroad Co. [*AAR code*]
WLO .... Weapons Liaison Officer (NVT)
WLO .... Willowair Ltd. [*British ICAO designator*] (FAAC)
WLO .... Wilson [*Oklahoma*] [*Seismograph station code, US Geological Survey*] (SEIS)
WLO .... Working Layout (SAA)
WLOB .... Portland, ME [*AM radio station call letters*]
WLOC .... Munfordville, KY [*AM radio station call letters*]
WLOC-FM .... Munfordville, KY [*FM radio station call letters*]
WLOD .... Loudon, TN [*AM radio station call letters*]
WLOE .... Eden, NC [*AM radio station call letters*]
WLOG .... Logan, WV [*AM radio station call letters*]
WLOH .... Lancaster, OH [*AM radio station call letters*]
WLOI .... La Porte, IN [*AM radio station call letters*]
WLOJ .... New Bern, NC [*AM radio station call letters*]
WLOK .... Memphis, TN [*AM radio station call letters*]
WLOL .... Brooklyn Park, MN [*AM radio station call letters*]
WLON .... Lincolnton, NC [*AM radio station call letters*]
W Lon .... West Longitude
W long .... West Longitude (BARN)
WLOP .... Jesup, GA [*AM radio station call letters*]
WLOQ .... Winter Park, FL [*FM radio station call letters*]
WLOR .... Huntsville, AL [*AM radio station call letters*]
WLOS .... Asheville, NC [*Television station call letters*]
WLOT-FM .... Greer, SC [*FM radio station call letters*] (RBYB)
WLOU .... Louisville, KY [*AM radio station call letters*]
WLOV .... Washington, GA [*AM radio station call letters*]
WLOV .... West Point, MS [*Television station call letters*]
WLOV-FM .... Washington, GA [*FM radio station call letters*]
WLOW .... Bluffton, SC [*FM radio station call letters*]
WLOW .... Wicklow [*County in Ireland*] (ROG)
WLOX .... Biloxi, MS [*Television station call letters*]
WLP .... Wallops Island, NASA Center (MCD)
WLP .... Ways of Looking at People Scale [*Psychology*] (AEBS)
WLP .... Wellpoint Health Networks [*NYSE symbol*] (SPSG)
WLP .... Wellpoint Hlth Networks [*NYSE symbol*] (TTBS)
WLP .... Western Legal Publications [*Database*] [*Western Legal Publications Ltd.*] [*Information service or system*] (CRD)
WLP .... White Light Position
WLP .... Women's Law Project (EA)
WLPA .... Lancaster, PA [*AM radio station call letters*]
WLPAPER .... Wallpaper
WLPB .... Baton Rouge, LA [*Television station call letters*]
WLPB .... Woodcock Language Proficiency Battery [*Achievement test*]
WL/PD .... Warner-Lambert/Parke-Davis [*Computer files of chemical and biological data*]
WLPE .... Augusta, GA [*FM radio station call letters*]
WLPF .... Ocilla, GA [*FM radio station call letters*]
WLPF .... William L. Patterson Foundation [*Defunct*] (EA)
WLPG .... Florence, SC [*FM radio station call letters*]
WLPH .... Irondale, AL [*AM radio station call letters*]
WLPJ .... New Port Richey, FL [*FM radio station call letters*]
WLPM .... Suffolk, VA [*AM radio station call letters*]
WLPO .... La Salle, IL [*AM radio station call letters*]
WLPR .... Prichard, AL [*AM radio station call letters*]
WLPS .... Watermen and Lightermen's Protective Society [*A union*] [*British*]
WLPSA .... Wildlife Preservation Society of Australia
WLPT .... Jesup, GA [*FM radio station call letters*]
WLPT .... Wellington Properties Trust [*NASDAQ symbol*] (TTSB)
WLPW .... Lake Placid, NY [*FM radio station call letters*]
WLPX-FM .... Water Valley, MS [*FM radio station call letters*] (RBYB)
WLPZ .... Westbrook, ME [*AM radio station call letters*]
WLQE .... Moneta, VA [*AM radio station call letters*]
WLQE-FM .... Bedford, VA [*FM radio station call letters*] (RBYB)
WLQH .... Chiefland, FL [*AM radio station call letters*]
WLQH-FM .... Chiefland, FL [*FM radio station call letters*]
WLQI .... Rensselaer, IN [*FM radio station call letters*]
WLQM .... Franklin, VA [*AM radio station call letters*]
WLQM-FM .... Franklin, VA [*FM radio station call letters*]
WLQR .... Toledo, OH [*FM radio station call letters*]
WLQT .... Kettering, OH [*FM radio station call letters*]
WLQV .... Detroit, MI [*AM radio station call letters*]
WLQY .... Hollywood, FL [*AM radio station call letters*]
WLR .... River Buoy Tender, Large or Small [*Coast Guard symbol*] (DNAB)
WLR .... Wallisair Compagnie [*France ICAO designator*] (FAAC)
WLR .... Washington Law Reporter [*District of Columbia*] [*A publication*] (DLA)
WLR .... Water Level Recorder
WLR .... Weapons Locating RADAR (AABC)
WLR .... Weekly Law Reports [*British*]
WLR .... Weighted Linear Regression [*Mathematics*]
WLR .... Western Law Reporter [*Canada*] [*A publication*] (DLA)
WLR .... West London Railway (ROG)
WLR .... Wilanour Resources Ltd. [*Toronto Stock Exchange symbol*]
WLR .... World Law Review [*A publication*] (DLA)
WLR .... Wrong Length Record [*Computer science*]
WLRA .... Lockport, IL [*FM radio station call letters*]
WLRA .... Wagner Labor Relations Act (OICC)
WLRA .... World Leisure and Recreation Association [*Formerly, IRA*] (EA)
WLRB .... Macomb, IL [*AM radio station call letters*]
WLRC .... Walnut, MS [*AM radio station call letters*]
WLRC .... Women's Legal Resource Centre [*Sydney, New South Wales, Australia*]
WLRD .... St. Pauls, NC [*FM radio station call letters*]
WLRD .... Warning Light Relay Driver
WLRF .... WLR Foods, Inc. [*NASDAQ symbol*] (NQ)
WLR Fd .... WLR Foods, Inc. [*Associated Press*] (SAG)
WLR Fds .... WLR Foods [*Associated Press*] (SAG)
WLRH .... Huntsville, AL [*FM radio station call letters*]
WLRI .... Warner-Lambert Research Institute [*New Jersey*]
WLRI-FM .... Westhampton, NY [*FM radio station call letters*] (RBYB)
WLRN .... Miami, FL [*FM radio station call letters*]
WLRN-TV .... Miami, FL [*Television station call letters*]
WLRO .... Richmond, KY [*FM radio station call letters*] (RBYB)
WLRP .... San Sebastian, PR [*AM radio station call letters*]
WLRP .... Wandsworth's Legal Resource Project [*A publication*] (DLA)
WLRQ .... Cocoa, FL [*FM radio station call letters*]
WLRR .... Milledgeville, GA [*FM radio station call letters*]
WLRS .... Louisville, KY [*FM radio station call letters*]
wlrs .... Walrus (VRA)
WLRT .... Kankakee, IL [*FM radio station call letters*]
WLRV .... Lebanon, VA [*AM radio station call letters*]
WLRW .... Champaign, IL [*FM radio station call letters*]
WLRX .... Nappanee, IN [*FM radio station call letters*]
WLRZ .... Peru, IL [*FM radio station call letters*]
WLS .... Chicago, IL [*AM radio station call letters*]
WLS .... Livingston-Steuben-Wyoming BOCES [*Boards of Cooperative Educational Services*], Educational Communications Center, Geneseo, NY [*OCLC symbol*] (OCLC)
WLS .... Wallis Island [*Wallis and Futuna Islands*] [*Airport symbol*] (OAG)
WLS .... Water Lily Society (EA)
WLS .... Weighted Least Squares [*Statistics*]
WLS .... Wells
WLS .... Wells
WLS .... Welschbruch [*France*] [*Seismograph station code, US Geological Survey*] (SEIS)
WLS .... Welsh Language Society (EA)
WLS .... Westchester Library System [*Library network*]
WLS .... Westchester Public Library [*UTLAS symbol*]
WLS .... Western Launch Site [*Military*]
WLS .... Wet Lung Syndrome [*Medicine*] (DAVI)
WLS .... Williams Air, Inc. [*ICAO designator*] (FAAC)
WLS .... Winnefox Library System [*Library network*]
WLS .... World Listening Service (EA)
WLSA .... Louisa, VA [*FM radio station call letters*]
WLSA .... Wage and Labor Standards Administration (OICC)
WLSB .... Copperhill, TN [*AM radio station call letters*]
WLSC .... Loris, SC [*AM radio station call letters*]
WLSC .... West Liberty State College [*West Virginia*]
WLSD .... Big Stone Gap, VA [*AM radio station call letters*]
WLSE .... Wallace, NC [*AM radio station call letters*]
WLS-FM .... Chicago, IL [*FM radio station call letters*]
WLSH .... Lansford, PA [*AM radio station call letters*]
WLSI .... Pikeville, KY [*AM radio station call letters*]
WLSK .... Lebanon, KY [*FM radio station call letters*]
WLSL .... Walseal
WLSM .... Louisville, MS [*AM radio station call letters*]
WLSM-FM .... Louisville, MS [*FM radio station call letters*]
WLSN .... Greenville, OH [*FM radio station call letters*]
WLSO .... Sault Ste. Marie, MI [*FM radio station call letters*]
WLSP .... Lapeer, MI [*AM radio station call letters*]
WLSP .... World List of Scientific Periodicals [*A publication*] (DIT)
WLSQ .... Dyer, TN [*FM radio station call letters*]
WLSR .... Lima, OH [*FM radio station call letters*]
WLSS-FM .... Baton Rouge, LA [*FM radio station call letters*] (RBYB)
WLST .... Marinette, WI [*FM radio station call letters*]
WLS-TV .... Chicago, IL [*Television station call letters*]
WLSU .... La Crosse, WI [*FM radio station call letters*]
WLSV .... Wellsville, NY [*AM radio station call letters*]
WLSW .... Scottdale, PA [*FM radio station call letters*]
WLSY .... Jeffersontown, KY [*FM radio station call letters*]
WLSZ .... Humboldt, TN [*FM radio station call letters*]
WLT .... Waterload Test (DAVI)
WLT .... Weighing Less Than
WLT .... Western Law Times [*1890-95*] [*A publication*] (DLA)

WLT .... Wire Line Timing
WLT .... World Literature Today [*A publication*] (BRI)
WLTA .... Plymouth, IN [*FM radio station call letters*]
WLTA .... Welsh Lawn Tennis Association (DBA)
WLTAS .... Wingfoot Lighter-Than-Air Society [*Later, Lighter-Than-Air Society*] (EA)
WLTBU .... Watermen, Lightermen, Tugmen, and Bargemen's Union [*British*]
WLTC .... Gastonia, NC [*AM radio station call letters*]
WLTC .... Wimbledon Lawn Tennis Championship [*British*]
WLTD .... Pickens, MS [*FM radio station call letters*]
WLTE .... Minneapolis, MN [*FM radio station call letters*]
WLTE .... Warrant Loss to Enlisted Status [*Revocation of appointment*] [*Navy*]
WLTF .... Cleveland, OH [*FM radio station call letters*]
WLTG .... Panama City, FL [*AM radio station call letters*]
WLTH .... Gary, IN [*AM radio station call letters*]
WLTI .... Detroit, MI [*FM radio station call letters*]
WLTJ .... Pittsburgh, PA [*FM radio station call letters*]
WLTK .... Broadway, VA [*FM radio station call letters*]
WLTL .... La Grange, IL [*FM radio station call letters*]
WLTM .... Rantoul, IL [*FM radio station call letters*]
WLTN .... Lisbon, NH [*FM radio station call letters*]
WLTN .... Littleton, NH [*AM radio station call letters*]
WLTO .... Nicholasville, KY [*FM radio station call letters*] (RBYB)
WLTP .... Parkersburg, WV [*AM radio station call letters*]
WLTQ .... Milwaukee, WI [*FM radio station call letters*]
WLTR .... Columbia, SC [*FM radio station call letters*]
WLTR .... Walter Industries [*NASDAQ symbol*] (TTSB)
WLTR .... Walter Industries, Inc. [*NASDAQ symbol*] (SAG)
WLTS .... Slidell, LA [*FM radio station call letters*]
WLTT .... Shallotte, NC [*FM radio station call letters*]
WLTU .... Manitowoc, WI [*FM radio station call letters*]
WLTV .... Miami, FL [*Television station call letters*]
WLTW .... New York, NY [*FM radio station call letters*]
WLTX .... Columbia, SC [*Television station call letters*]
WLTY .... Norfolk, VA [*FM radio station call letters*]
WLTZ .... Columbus, GA [*Television station call letters*]
WLU .... Washington and Lee University [*Virginia*]
WLU .... Wesleyan University, Middletown, CT [*OCLC symbol*] (OCLC)
WLU .... Wilfrid Laurier University [*Canada*]
WLUA .... Westwood, KY [*FM radio station call letters*]
WLUC .... Marquette, MI [*Television station call letters*]
WLUC .... Women Life Underwriters Conference (EA)
WLUJ .... Petersburg, IL [*FM radio station call letters*]
WLUK .... Green Bay, WI [*Television station call letters*]
WLUM .... Milwaukee, WI [*FM radio station call letters*]
WLUN .... Lumberton, MS [*FM radio station call letters*]
WLUP .... Chicago, IL [*FM radio station call letters*]
WLUR .... Lexington, VA [*FM radio station call letters*]
WLUS .... Gainesville, FL [*AM radio station call letters*]
WLUS .... World Land Use Survey [*International Geographical Union*] (BARN)
WLUV .... Loves Park, IL [*AM radio station call letters*]
WLUV-FM .... Loves Park, IL [*FM radio station call letters*]
WLUW .... Chicago, IL [*FM radio station call letters*]
WLUX .... Islip, NY [*AM radio station call letters*] (RBYB)
WLUZ .... Bayamon, PR [*AM radio station call letters*]
WLV .... Lightship [*Coast Guard symbol*] (DNAB)
WLV .... Wolverine Tube [*NYSE symbol*] (TTSB)
WLV .... Wolverine Tube, Inc. [*NYSE symbol*] (SPSG)
WLVA .... Lynchburg, VA [*AM radio station call letters*]
WLVB .... Morrisville, VT [*FM radio station call letters*]
WLVC .... Fort Kent, ME [*AM radio station call letters*]
WLVE .... Miami Beach, FL [*FM radio station call letters*]
WLVF .... Haines City, FL [*AM radio station call letters*]
WLVF-FM .... Haines City, FL [*FM radio station call letters*]
WLVH .... Hardeeville, SC [*FM radio station call letters*]
WLVI .... Cambridge, MA [*Television station call letters*]
WLVJ .... Royal Palm Beach, FL [*AM radio station call letters*]
WLVK .... Fort Knox, KY [*FM radio station call letters*] (RBYB)
WLVL .... Lockport, NY [*AM radio station call letters*]
WLVM-AM .... Fairview, NC [*AM radio station call letters*] (RBYB)
WLVQ .... Columbus, OH [*FM radio station call letters*]
WLVR .... Bethlehem, PA [*FM radio station call letters*]
WLVS .... Lake Worth, FL [*AM radio station call letters*]
WLVT .... Allentown, PA [*Television station call letters*]
WLVU .... Dunedin, FL [*AM radio station call letters*]
WLVU .... Holiday, FL [*FM radio station call letters*]
WLVV .... Mobile, AL [*AM radio station call letters*]
WLVW .... Salisbury, MD [*FM radio station call letters*]
WLVY .... Elmira, NY [*FM radio station call letters*]
WLVZ-FM .... St. Mary's, OH [*FM radio station call letters*] (RBYB)
WLW .... Cincinnati, OH [*AM radio station call letters*]
WLW .... Weldwood of Canada Ltd. [*Toronto Stock Exchange symbol*]
WLW .... Willows, CA [*Location identifier FAA*] (FAAL)
WLW .... Women Library Workers [*Defunct*] (EA)
WLWC-TV .... New Bedford, MA [*TV station call letters*] (RBYB)
WLWH .... Workshop Library on World Humour (EA)
WLWI-FM .... Montgomery, AL [*FM radio station call letters*]
WLWL .... Rockingham, NC [*AM radio station call letters*]
WLWT .... Cincinnati, OH [*Television station call letters*]
WLWZ .... Easley, SC [*AM radio station call letters*]
WLXC .... Lexington, SC [*FM radio station call letters*]
WLXG .... Lexington, KY [*AM radio station call letters*]
WLXI .... Greensboro, NC [*Television station call letters*]
WLXN .... Lexington, NC [*AM radio station call letters*]
WLXR .... La Crosse, WI [*FM radio station call letters*]
WLXT .... Petoskey, MI [*FM radio station call letters*]
WLXV .... Cadillac, MI [*FM radio station call letters*]
WLXX .... Chicago, IL [*AM radio station call letters*] (RBYB)
WLXY .... Northport, AL [*FM radio station call letters*]
WLY .... Westerly
WLYC .... Williamsport, PA [*AM radio station call letters*]
WLYF .... Miami, FL [*FM radio station call letters*]
WLYH .... Lancaster, PA [*Television station call letters*]
WLYJ .... Clarksburg, WV [*Television station call letters*]
WLYK .... Lynchburg, VA [*FM radio station call letters*]
WLYN .... Lynn, MA [*AM radio station call letters*]
WLYT .... Haverhill, MA [*FM radio station call letters*]
WLYU .... Lyons, GA [*FM radio station call letters*]
WLYV .... Fort Wayne, IN [*AM radio station call letters*]
WLZA .... Europa, MS [*FM radio station call letters*]
WLZQ .... South Whitley, IN [*FM radio station call letters*]
WLZR .... Milwaukee, WI [*AM radio station call letters*]
WLZR-FM .... Milwaukee, WI [*FM radio station call letters*]
WLZS-FM .... Beaver Springs, PA [*FM radio station call letters*] (RBYB)
WLZW .... Utica, NY [*FM radio station call letters*]
WLZZ .... Montpelier, OH [*FM radio station call letters*]
WM .... Milwaukee Public Library, Milwaukee, WI [*Library symbol Library of Congress*] (LCLS)
WM .... Multiple-Conductor Cables [*JETDS nomenclature*] [*Military*] (CET)
WM .... Waldenstrom's Macroglobulinemia [*Medicine*]
WM .... Wall Motion (MEDA)
WM .... Ward Manager [*Medicine*]
WM .... War Memorial
WM .... Warming
WM .... Warrant Mechanician [*British military*] (DMA)
W/M .... Washing Machine [*Classified advertising*] (ADA)
WM .... Waste Management (NASA)
WM .... Waste Minimization
WM .... Watermark
WM .... Water Meter
WM .... Water Monitor (DS)
WM .... Watt Meter
WM .... Wave Meter
WM .... Ways and Means (DLA)
WM .... Weapon Mechanician [*British military*] (DMA)
WM .... Wehrmacht-Marine [*Marking on Navy vehicles*] [*German military - World War II*]
W/M .... Weight or Measurement
WM .... Welding Memorandum
WM .... Wesleyan Mission [*Australia*]
WM .... Western Microwave, Inc. (IAA)
WM .... West Midlands [*Metropolitan county in England*]
WM .... Wet Mount (MEDA)
WM .... Wheel-Made (BJA)
WM .... White Male
WM .... White Metal
WM .... Whitten's Medium [*for cell incubation*]
WM .... Whole Milk (MAE)
WM .... Whole Mount (AAMN)
Wm .... William (King of England) (DLA)
WM .... Windward Islands Airways International NV [*Netherlands ICAO designator*] (ICDA)
W/M .... Wing Main [*Airfield*] (NATG)
WM .... Wireless Manager (ACRL)
WM .... Wire Mesh
WM .... Without Margin
WM .... Woman (DAVI)
W/M .... Woman Marine (SAA)
WM .... Women in the Mainstream [*Defunct*] (EA)
WM .... Women Marines
WM .... Word Mark (BUR)
W/M .... Words per Minute (KSC)
WM .... Working Memory [*Psychology*]
WM .... Work Measurement [*Army*] (AABC)
WM .... Work of Mary [*An association*] (EAIO)
WM .... World Markets [*British investment firm*] [*Formerly, Wood Mackenzie*]
WM .... World Monitor [*Television program*]
WM .... Worshipful Master [*Freemasonry*]
W/M .... Wound, Missile [*Military*] (DAVI)
WM .... Wustite Magnetite [*Geology*]
W/M^2 .... Watts per Square Meter
W/(M^2 K) .... Watts per Square Meter Kelvin
W/(M^2 SR) .... Watts per Square Meter Steradian
WMA .... Alverno College, Milwaukee, WI [*Library symbol Library of Congress*] (LCLS)
WMa .... Madison Public Library, Madison, WI [*Library symbol Library of Congress*] (LCLS)
WMA .... Mandritsara [*Madagascar*] [*Airport symbol*] (OAG)
WMA .... Wallcovering Manufacturers Association (EA)
WMA .... Wall Motion Abnormality [*Cardiology*] (DAVI)
WMA .... Warfare Mission Area (DOMA)
WMA .... War Measures Act
WMA .... Washington Metropolitan Area (AFM)
WMA .... Waste Management Area [*NASA*]
WMA .... Waste Management Association [*Australia*]
WMA .... Waste Management Authority [*New South Wales, Australia*]
WMA .... Waterbed Manufacturers Association (EA)
WMA .... Weather Modification Association (EA)
WMA .... Welding Machine Arc
WMA .... Welding Manufacturers Association [*British*] (DBA)

WMA........... Wentworth Military Academy [*Lexington, MO*]
WMA........... West Mesa [*New Mexico*] [*Seismograph station code, US Geological Survey*] (SEIS)
WMA........... Wheelchair Motorcycle Association (EA)
WMA........... Wikalat Al-Maghreb Al-Arabi [*News agency*] [*Morocco*] (MENA)
WMA........... Wing Main Airfield (NATG)
WMA........... Women Marines Association (EA)
WMA........... Workers' Music Association [*British*]
WMA........... Working Mothers Association [*British*] (DBA)
WMA........... World Manx Association
WMA........... World Medical Association [*Ferney-Voltaire, France*]
WMA........... World Modeling Association (EA)
WMAA......... Bahau [*Malaysia*] [*ICAO location identifier*] (ICLI)
WMAA......... Warrant Master-at-Arms [*British military*] (DMA)
WMAA......... Whitney Museum of American Art [*New York, NY*]
WMAA......... World Martial Arts Association (EA)
WMaAR....... Wisconsin Alumni Research Foundation, Madison, WI [*Library symbol Library of Congress*] (LCLS)
WMAB......... Batu Pahat [*Malaysia*] [*ICAO location identifier*] (ICLI)
WMAB......... Mississippi State, MS [*FM radio station call letters*]
WMAB......... Weather Modification Advisory Board
WMaBR....... Wisconsin Department of Health and Social Services, Bureau of Research, Madison,WI [*Library symbol Library of Congress*] (LCLS)
WMAB-TV.... Mississippi State, MS [*Television station call letters*]
WMAC......... Alverno College, Milwaukee, WI [*Library symbol*] [*Library of Congress*] (LCLS)
WMAC......... Benta [*Malaysia*] [*ICAO location identifier*] (ICLI)
WMaC......... Central Wisconsin Colony, Staff Library, Madison, WI [*Library symbol Library of Congress*] (LCLS)
WMAC......... Metter, GA [*AM radio station call letters*]
WMAC......... Waste Management Advisory Council [*British*] (DCTA)
WMaCH....... Wisconsin Department of Health and Social Services, Community Health Service, Madison, WI [*Library symbol Library of Congress*] (LCLS)
WMACS....... AC Spark Plug Co., Electronics Division, Milwaukee, WI [*Library symbol Library of Congress*] (LCLS)
WMaCT........ Children's Treatment Center, Madison, WI [*Library symbol Library of Congress*] (LCLS)
WMaCW...... Central Wisconsin Colony, Staff Library, Madison, WI [*Library symbol*] [*Library of Congress*] (LCLS)
WMAD......... Bentong [*Malaysia*] [*ICAO location identifier*] (ICLI)
WMAD......... Sun Prairie, WI [*AM radio station call letters*]
WMAD-FM... Sun Prairie, WI [*FM radio station call letters*]
WMAE.......... Bidor [*Malaysia*] [*ICAO location identifier*] (ICLI)
WMAE.......... Booneville, MS [*FM radio station call letters*]
WMAE-TV.... Booneville, MS [*Television station call letters*]
WMAF.......... Madison, FL [*AM radio station call letters*]
WMaF.......... United States Forest Products Laboratory, Madison, WI [*Library symbol Library of Congress*] (LCLS)
WMAFPH..... World Medical Association for Perfect Health [*Also known as United States Association of Physicians*] (EA)
WMAG......... Dungun [*Malaysia*] [*ICAO location identifier*] (ICLI)
WMAG......... High Point, NC [*FM radio station call letters*]
WMaG......... Madison General Hospital, Madison, WI [*Library symbol Library of Congress*] (LCLS)
WMaG-N...... Madison General Hospital, School of Nursing, Madison, WI [*Library symbol Library of Congress*] (LCLS)
WMAH......... Biloxi, MS [*FM radio station call letters*]
WMAH......... Grik [*Malaysia*] [*ICAO location identifier*] (ICLI)
WMaH......... Wisconsin Division of Health Policy and Planning Library, Madison, WI [*Library symbol Library of Congress*] (LCLS)
WMAH-TV.... Biloxi, MS [*Television station call letters*]
WMAI.......... Gua Musang [*Malaysia*] [*ICAO location identifier*] (ICLI)
WMaJ.......... Jackson Clinic, Madison, WI [*Library symbol Library of Congress*] (LCLS)
WMAJ.......... Jendarata [*Malaysia*] [*ICAO location identifier*] (ICLI)
WMAJ.......... State College, PA [*AM radio station call letters*]
WMAK......... London, KY [*AM radio station call letters*]
WMAL.......... Kuala Krai [*Malaysia*] [*ICAO location identifier*] (ICLI)
WMAL.......... Washington, DC [*AM radio station call letters*]
WMaLS........ Wisconsin Division for Library Services, Bureau for Reference and Local Services, Madison, WI [*Library symbol Library of Congress*] (LCLS)
WMAM......... Langkawi [*Malaysia*] [*ICAO location identifier*] (ICLI)
WMAM......... Marinette, WI [*AM radio station call letters*]
WMaM......... Methodist Hospital School of Nursing, Madison, WI [*Library symbol Library of Congress*] (LCLS)
WMaMS....... Mendota Mental Health Institute, Madison, WI [*Library symbol Library of Congress*] (LCLS)
WMan.......... Manawa Public Library, Manawa, WI [*Library symbol Library of Congress*] (LCLS)
WMAN......... Mansfield, OH [*AM radio station call letters*]
Wm & M...... William and Mary (King and Queen of England) (DLA)
Wm & Mary Rev VA L... William and Mary Review of Virginia Law [*A publication*] (DLA)
WM & PHF... Waste Management and Personal Hygiene Facility [*NASA*] (KSC)
WM & S...... Work Methods and Standards
WMani......... Manitowoc Public Library, Manitowoc, WI [*Library symbol Library of Congress*] (LCLS)
WManiH...... Holy Family Hospital, Manitowoc, WI [*Library symbol Library of Congress*] (LCLS)
WManiHN.... Holy Family School of Nursing, Manitowoc, WI [*Library symbol Library of Congress*] (LCLS)
WMANT....... Wissenschaftliche Monographien zum Alten und Neuen Testament [*A publication*] (BJA)
WMAO......... Greenwood, MS [*FM radio station call letters*]
WMAO......... Kong Kong [*Malaysia*] [*ICAO location identifier*] (ICLI)
WMAO-TV.... Greenwood, MS [*Television station call letters*]
WMAP......... Kluang [*Malaysia*] [*ICAO location identifier*] (ICLI)
WMAP......... Monroe, NC [*AM radio station call letters*]
WMAP......... Pageland, SC [*FM radio station call letters*]
WMaPI........ Department of Public Instruction, Division for Library Services, Professional Library, Madison, WI [*Library symbol Library of Congress*] (LCLS)
WMaPI-CC... Department of Public Instruction, Division for Library Services, Cooperative Children's Book Center, Madison, WI [*Library symbol Library of Congress*] (LCLS)
WMaPI-PL... Department of Public Instruction, Division for Library Services, Public Library Services, Madison, WI [*Library symbol Library of Congress*] (LCLS)
WMaPI-RL... Department of Public Instruction, Division for Library Services, Reference and Loan Library, Madison, WI [*Library symbol Library of Congress*] (LCLS)
WMaPR....... Wisconsin Regional Primate Research Center, Madison, WI [*Library symbol Library of Congress*] (LCLS)
WMAQ......... Chicago, IL [*AM radio station call letters*]
WMAQ......... Labis [*Malaysia*] [*ICAO location identifier*] (ICLI)
WMAQ-TV.... Chicago, IL [*Television station call letters*]
WMAR......... Baltimore, MD [*Television station call letters*]
WMaR......... Raltech Scientific Services, Inc., Madison, WI [*Library symbol Library of Congress*] (LCLS)
WMAR......... West Marine [*NASDAQ symbol*] (TTSB)
WMAR......... West Marine, Inc. [*NASDAQ symbol*] (SAG)
WMaraS....... Saint Anthony Friary, Marathon, WI [*Library symbol Library of Congress*] (LCLS)
WMarC........ Marshfield Clinic, Marshfield, WI [*Library symbol Library of Congress*] (LCLS)
WMARC....... World Maritime Administrative Radio Conference (DS)
WMari.......... Stephenson Public Library, Marinette, WI [*Library symbol*] [*Library of Congress*] (LCLS)
WMarSJ....... Saint Joseph's Hospital, Marshfield, WI [*Library symbol Library of Congress*] (LCLS)
WMarW....... Wood County Hospital, Marshfield, WI [*Library symbol Library of Congress*] (LCLS)
WMAS......... Springfield, MA [*AM radio station call letters*]
WMaS.......... Student Association for the Study of Hallucinogens, Madison, WI [*Library symbol Library of Congress*] (LCLS)
WMAS-FM... Springfield, MA [*FM radio station call letters*]
WMaSM....... Saint Mary's Hospital, Doctors' Library, Madison, WI [*Library symbol Library of Congress*] (LCLS)
WMaSM-N... Saint Mary's Hospital, School of Nursing, Madison, WI [*Library symbol Library of Congress*] (LCLS)
WMAT.......... Lima Blas [*Malaysia*] [*ICAO location identifier*] (ICLI)
WMATA....... Washington Metropolitan Area Transit Authority (BARN)
WMaTC........ Madison Area Technical College, Madison, WI [*Library symbol Library of Congress*] (LCLS)
WMAU......... Bude, MS [*FM radio station call letters*]
WMau.......... Mauston Public Library, Mauston, WI [*Library symbol Library of Congress*] (LCLS)
WMAU......... Mersing [*Malaysia*] [*ICAO location identifier*] (ICLI)
WMAU......... Women's Martial Arts Union [*Defunct*] (EA)
WMaUCS..... University of Wisconsin-Center System, Madison, WI [*Library symbol Library of Congress*] (LCLS)
WMaUEx...... University of Wisconsin-Extension, Madison, WI [*Library symbol Library of Congress*] (LCLS)
WMAU-TV... Bude, MS [*Television station call letters*]
WMAV......... Muar [*Malaysia*] [*ICAO location identifier*] (ICLI)
WMAV......... Oxford, MS [*FM radio station call letters*]
WMaVA........ United States Veterans Administration Hospital, Madison, WI [*Library symbol Library of Congress*] (LCLS)
WMAV-TV.... Oxford, MS [*Television station call letters*]
WMAW......... Meridian, MS [*FM radio station call letters*]
WMaW......... Wisconsin Alumni Research Foundation Institute, Inc., Madison, WI [*Library symbol Library of Congress*] (LCLS)
WMAW-TV... Meridian, MS [*Television station call letters*]
WMAX......... Bay City, MI [*AM radio station call letters*]
WMAX......... Irondequoit, NY [*FM radio station call letters*]
WMAY......... Springfield, IL [*AM radio station call letters*]
WMAZ.......... Macon, GA [*AM radio station call letters*]
WMAZ.......... Segamat [*Malaysia*] [*ICAO location identifier*] (ICLI)
WMAZ-TV.... Macon, GA [*Television station call letters*]
WMB............ Walnut Marketing Board (EA)
WMB............ War Mobilization Board
WMB............ Warrnambool [*Australia Airport symbol*] (OAG)
WMB............ West Merchant Bank (ECON)
WMB............ Williamsburg Technical College, Kingstree, SC [*OCLC symbol*] (OCLC)
WMB............ [*The*] Williams Companies [*NYSE symbol*] (SPSG)
WMB............ Williams Cos. [*NYSE symbol*] (TTSB)
WMBA......... Ambridge, PA [*AM radio station call letters*]
WMBA......... Sitiawan [*Malaysia*] [*ICAO location identifier*] (ICLI)
WMBA......... Wire Machinery Builders Association [*Later, WISA*] (EA)
WMBB......... Panama City, FL [*Television station call letters*]
WMBB......... Sungei Patani [*Malaysia*] [*ICAO location identifier*] (ICLI)
WMBC......... Columbus, MS [*FM radio station call letters*]
WMBC......... Newton, NJ [*Television station call letters*]
WMBC......... Wisconsin Baptist State Convention, Milwaukee, WI [*Library symbol Library of Congress*] (LCLS)

WMBD .... Peoria, IL [*AM radio station call letters*]
WMBDA .... Wholesale Milk Buyers and Distributors' Association [*Australia*]
WMBD-TV .... Peoria, IL [*Television station call letters*]
WMBE .... Chilton, WI [*AM radio station call letters*]
WMBE .... Temerloh [*Malaysia*] [*ICAO location identifier*] (ICLI)
WMBF .... Ulu Bernam [*Malaysia*] [*ICAO location identifier*] (ICLI)
WMBG .... Williamsburg, VA [*AM radio station call letters*]
WMBH .... Joplin, MO [*AM radio station call letters*]
WMBH .... Kroh [*Malaysia*] [*ICAO location identifier*] (ICLI)
WMBI .... Chicago, IL [*AM radio station call letters*]
WMBI .... Taiping [*Malaysia*] [*ICAO location identifier*] (ICLI)
WMBI-FM .... Chicago, IL [*FM radio station call letters*]
WMBL .... Morehead City, NC [*AM radio station call letters*]
WMBL .... Wrightsville Marine Biomedical Laboratory
WMBM .... Miami Beach, FL [*AM radio station call letters*] (RBYB)
WMBN .... Petoskey, MI [*AM radio station call letters*]
WMBO .... Auburn, NY [*AM radio station call letters*]
WMBP .... Belpre, OH [*FM radio station call letters*]
WMBPrA ...... Williams Cos. $2.21 cm Pfd [*NYSE symbol*] (TTSB)
WMBR .... Cambridge, MA [*FM radio station call letters*]
WMBS .... Uniontown, PA [*AM radio station call letters*]
WMBT .... Pulau Pioman [*Malaysia*] [*ICAO location identifier*] (ICLI)
WMBT .... Shenandoah, PA [*AM radio station call letters*]
WMBTOPCITBWTNTALI ... We May Be the Only Phone Company in Town, but We Try Not to Act Like It [*Slogan*]
WMBU .... Forest, MS [*FM radio station call letters*]
WMBV .... Dixon's Mills, AL [*FM radio station call letters*]
WMBW .... Chattanooga, TN [*FM radio station call letters*]
WMC .... Concordia College, Milwaukee, WI [*Library symbol Library of Congress*] (LCLS)
WMC .... Memphis, TN [*AM radio station call letters*]
WMC .... War Manpower Commission [*Within the Office of Emergency Management*] [*World War II*]
WMC .... Waste Management Compartment [*NASA*] (KSC)
WMC .... Waste Minimization and Containment Services, Inc. (ECON)
WMC .... Ways and Means Committee [*House of Representatives*] (WDAA)
WMC .... Weapons and Mobility Command [*Army*]
WMC .... Weapons Monitoring Center
WMC .... Weapons Monitoring Console
WMC .... Western Maryland College [*Westminster*]
WMC .... Western Mining Corp. [*Commercial*] (EERA)
WMC .... Western Mining Corp. Holdings ADS [*NYSE symbol*] (SPSG)
WMC .... White Male Candidate [*Politics*]
WMC .... Wilmington College, Wilmington, OH [*OCLC symbol*] (OCLC)
WmC .... Windsor Microfilming Co., Windsor, ON, Canada [*Library symbol Library of Congress*] (LCLS)
WMC .... Winnemucca, NV [*Location identifier FAA*] (FAAL)
WMC .... Wisconsin Motor Carriers Association Inc., Madison WI [*STAC*]
WMC .... WMC Ltd ADS [*NYSE symbol*] (TTSB)
WMC .... Woodfree Machine-Coated Paper (DGA)
WMC .... Wool Manufacturers Council (EA)
WMC .... Working Men's Club [*British*] (BARN)
WMC .... World Meteorological Center [*World Meteorological Organization*]
WMC .... World Methodist Council (EA)
WMC .... World Ministries Commission (EA)
WMC .... World Missions to Children [*Later, WMF*] (EA)
WMC .... World Muslim Congress (BJA)
WMCA .... New York, NY [*AM radio station call letters*]
WMCA .... White Metal Casting Association [*British*] (DBA)
Wm Carey C ... William Carey College (GAGS)
WMCB .... Martinsville, IN [*AM radio station call letters*]
WMCC .... Concordia College, Milwaukee, WI [*Library symbol*] [*Library of Congress*] (LCLS)
WMCC .... Water Management Coordinating Committee [*Australia*]
WMCC-FM ... Munfordville, KY [*FM radio station call letters*] (RBYB)
WMCCMEC ... Women's Missionary Council of the Christian Methodist Episcopal Church (EA)
WMCCS .... Worldwide Military Command and Control System [*DoD*] (MCD)
WMCCSA ..... World Masters Cross-Country Ski Association (EA)
WMCD .... Statesboro, GA [*FM radio station call letters*]
WMCE .... Erie, PA [*FM radio station call letters*]
WMCF .... Montgomery, AL [*Television station call letters*]
WMC-FM ..... Memphis, TN [*FM radio station call letters*]
WMCG .... Milan, GA [*FM radio station call letters*]
WMCG .... Milwaukee County General Hospital, Milwaukee, WI [*Library symbol Library of Congress*] (LCLS)
WMCH .... Church Hill, TN [*AM radio station call letters*]
WMCH .... Columbia Hospital School of Nursing, Milwaukee, WI [*Library symbol Library of Congress*] (LCLS)
WMCHi .... Milwaukee County Historical Society, Milwaukee, WI [*Library symbol Library of Congress*] (LCLS)
WMCI .... Mattoon, IL [*FM radio station call letters*]
WMCJ .... Moncks Corner, SC [*AM radio station call letters*]
WMcK .... William McKinley [*US president, 1843-1901*]
WMCL .... McLeansboro, IL [*AM radio station call letters*]
WMCL .... Wideband Communications Line
WMCL .... William Mitchell College of Law [*St. Paul, MN*]
WMCM .... Milwaukee County Institutions, Mental Health Centers Libraries, Milwaukee, WI [*Library symbol Library of Congress*] (LCLS)
WMCM .... Rockland, ME [*FM radio station call letters*]
WMCN .... St. Paul, MN [*FM radio station call letters*]
WMCO .... New Concord, OH [*FM radio station call letters*]
WMCO .... William Controls, Inc. [*NASDAQ symbol*] (NQ)
WMCO .... Williams Controls [*NASDAQ symbol*] (TTSB)
WMCP .... Columbia, TN [*AM radio station call letters*]
WMCP .... Woman's Medical College of Pennsylvania
WMCR .... Oneida, NY [*AM radio station call letters*]
WMCR-FM ... Oneida, NY [*FM radio station call letters*]
WMCS .... Greenfield, WI [*AM radio station call letters*]
WMCSC .... Cardinal Stritch College, Milwaukee, WI [*Library symbol Library of Congress*] (LCLS)
WMCT .... Mountain City, TN [*AM radio station call letters*]
WMC-TV ..... Memphis, TN [*Television station call letters*]
WMCU .... Miami, FL [*FM radio station call letters*]
WMCW .... Harvard, IL [*AM radio station call letters*]
WMCW .... World Movement of Christian Workers [*See also MMTC*] [*Brussels, Belgium*] (EAIO)
WMCX .... West Long Branch, NJ [*FM radio station call letters*]
WMCZ .... Millbrook, AL [*FM radio station call letters*]
WMD .... Digital Equipment Corp., Westminster, Westminster, MA [*OCLC symbol*] (OCLC)
WMD .... Doctors Hospital, Milwaukee, WI [*Library symbol Library of Congress*] (LCLS)
WMD .... Mandabe [*Madagascar*] [*Airport symbol*] (OAG)
WMD .... Waste Management Division [*Environmental Protection Agency*] (GFGA)
WMD .... Water Management Division [*Environmental Protection Agency*] (GFGA)
WMD .... Weapon Mounted Display
WMD .... Weapons of Mass Destruction
WMD .... Wendt Bristol Health Service [*AMEX symbol*] (SAG)
WMD .... Wendt-Bristol Health Svcs [*AMEX symbol*] (TTSB)
WMD .... Wind Measuring Device
WMDA .... Woodworking Machinery Distributors Association (EA)
WMDAA .... Watch Material Distributors Association of America [*Later, WMJDA*] (EA)
WMDB .... Nashville, TN [*AM radio station call letters*]
WMDB .... Waste Management Database [*IAEA*] [*United Nations*] (DUND)
WMDC .... Hazlehurst, MS [*AM radio station call letters*]
WMDC-FM ... Hazlehurst, MS [*FM radio station call letters*]
WMDD .... Fajardo, PR [*AM radio station call letters*]
WMDe .... Deaconess Hospital, Milwaukee, WI [*Library symbol Library of Congress*] (LCLS)
WMDH .... New Castle, IN [*AM radio station call letters*]
WMDH-FM ... New Castle, IN [*FM radio station call letters*]
WMDI .... Bar Harbor, ME [*FM radio station call letters*]
WMDio .... Diocesan Library, Milwaukee, WI [*Library symbol Library of Congress Obsolete*] (LCLS)
WMDJ .... Allen, KY [*FM radio station call letters*]
WMDJ .... Martin, KY [*AM radio station call letters*]
WMDM .... Lexington Park, MD [*FM radio station call letters*]
WMDN .... Meridian, MS [*Television station call letters*]
WMDO .... Wheaton, MD [*AM radio station call letters*]
WMDR .... Augusta, ME [*AM radio station call letters*]
WMDR .... DePaul Rehabilitation Hospital Medical Library, Milwaukee, WI [*Library symbol Library of Congress*] (LCLS)
WMDT .... Salisbury, MD [*Television station call letters*]
WMDWS ...... Wendt-Bristol Health Wrrt [*AMEX symbol*] (TTSB)
WME .... Eaton Corp., Milwaukee, WI [*Library symbol Library of Congress*] (LCLS)
WMe .... Elisha D. Smith Public Library, Menasha, WI [*Library symbol Library of Congress*] (LCLS)
WME .... Waste Management International Ltd. ADS [*NYSE symbol*] (SPSG)
WME .... Waste Mgmt Intl plc ADS [*NYSE symbol*] (TTSB)
WME .... Window Meteoroid Experiment [*NASA*] (KSC)
WME .... Women and Mathematics Education (EA)
WME .... Worldwide Marriage Encounter (EA)
WMEA .... Biddeford, ME [*Television station call letters*]
WMEA .... Portland, ME [*FM radio station call letters*]
WMEA .... Welded Modules for Electronic Assemblies [*NASA*]
WMEB .... Orono, ME [*FM radio station call letters*]
WMEB .... West Midlands Enterprise Board [*British*] (ECON)
WMEB-TV .... Orono, ME [*Television station call letters*]
WMEC .... Eaton Corp., Milwaukee, WI [*Library symbol*] [*Library of Congress*] (LCLS)
WMEC .... Macomb, IL [*Television station call letters*]
WMEC .... Medium Endurance Cutter [*Coast Guard*] (NVT)
WMEC .... Western Military Electronics Center (KSC)
WMECO .... Western Massachusetts Electric Co.
WMED .... Calais, ME [*FM radio station call letters*]
WMed .... Medford Free Public Library, Medford, WI [*Library symbol*] [*Library of Congress*] (LCLS)
WMED .... Waste Management and Economics Division [*Environmental Protection Agency*] (EPA)
WMED-TV .... Calais, ME [*Television station call letters*]
WMEE .... Fort Wayne, IN [*FM radio station call letters*]
WMEF .... Fort Kent, ME [*FM radio station call letters*]
WMEG .... Guayama, PR [*FM radio station call letters*]
WMEH .... Bangor, ME [*FM radio station call letters*]
WMEI .... Arecibo, PR [*Television station call letters*]
WMEJ .... Proctorville, OH [*FM radio station call letters*]
WMEK .... Chase City, VA [*AM radio station call letters*]
WMEL .... Melbourne, FL [*AM radio station call letters*]
WMEM .... Presque Isle, ME [*FM radio station call letters*]
WMEM-TV ... Presque Isle, ME [*Television station call letters*]
WMEN .... Knoxville, TN [*AM radio station call letters*] (RBYB)
WMen .... Mabel Tainter Memorial Free Library, Menomonie, WI [*Library symbol Library of Congress*] (LCLS)
WMenM .... Memorial Hospital and Nursing Home, Menomonie, WI [*Library symbol Library of Congress*] (LCLS)

WMenofH .... Community Memorial Hospital, Health Science Library, Menomonee Falls, WI [*Library symbol Library of Congress*] (LCLS)
WMenU .... University of Wisconsin-Stout, Menomonie, WI [*Library symbol Library of Congress*] (LCLS)
WMeq .... Frank L. Weyenberg Library, Mequon, WI [*Library symbol Library of Congress*] (LCLS)
WMEQ .... Menomonie, WI [*AM radio station call letters*]
WMEQ-FM ... Menomonie, WI [*FM radio station call letters*]
WMeqW .... Wisconsin Lutheran Seminary, Mequon, WI [*Library symbol Library of Congress*] (LCLS)
WMER .... Meridian, MS [*AM radio station call letters*]
WMer .... T. B. Scott Free Library, Merril, WI [*Library symbol Library of Congress*] (LCLS)
WMET .... Gaithersburg, MD [*AM radio station call letters*]
WMeU .... University of Wisconsin-Green Bay, Fox Valley Campus, Menasha, WI [*Library symbol Library of Congress*] (LCLS)
WMEV .... Marion, VA [*AM radio station call letters*]
WMEV-FM .... Marion, VA [*FM radio station call letters*]
WMEW .... Waterville, ME [*FM radio station call letters*]
WMEX .... Boston, MA [*AM radio station call letters*]
WMEX-FM ... Westport, NY [*FM radio station call letters*] (RBYB)
WMEZ .... Pensacola, FL [*FM radio station call letters*]
WMF .... Maude Shunk Public Library, Menomonee Falls, WI [*OCLC symbol*] (OCLC)
WMF .... White Middle-Aged Female (MAE)
WMF .... Windows Metafile [*Vector file format*] [*Computer science*] (PCM)
WMF .... Windows Metafile Format [*Computer science*]
WMF .... Wire Mattress Federation
WMF .... Women's Motorcyclist Foundation (EA)
WMF .... Woodfree Machine-Finished Paper (DGA)
WMF .... World Mercy Fund (EA)
WMF .... World Missions Fellowship (EA)
WMF .... World Monuments Fund (EA)
WMFA .... Raeford, NC [*AM radio station call letters*]
WMFC .... Kuala Lumpur [*Malaysia*] [*ICAO location identifier*] (ICLI)
WMFC .... Monroeville, AL [*AM radio station call letters*]
WMFC-FM .... Monroeville, AL [*FM radio station call letters*]
WMFD .... Mansfield, OH [*Television station call letters*]
WMFD .... Wilmington, NC [*AM radio station call letters*]
WMFE .... Orlando, FL [*FM radio station call letters*]
WMFE-TV .... Orlando, FL [*Television station call letters*]
WMFG .... Hibbing, MN [*AM radio station call letters*]
WMFG-FM ... Hibbing, MN [*FM radio station call letters*]
WMFJ .... Daytona Beach, FL [*AM radio station call letters*]
WMFL .... Monticello, FL [*AM radio station call letters*]
WMFM .... Petal, MS [*FM radio station call letters*]
WMFM .... Wisconsin Scottish Rite Bodies AASR, Milwaukee, WI [*Library symbol Library of Congress*] (LCLS)
WMFN .... Zeeland, MI [*AM radio station call letters*] (RBYB)
WMFO .... Medford, MA [*FM radio station call letters*]
WMFP .... Lawrence, MA [*Television station call letters*]
WMFQ .... Ocala, FL [*FM radio station call letters*]
WMFR .... High Point, NC [*AM radio station call letters*]
WMFS .... Bartlett, TN [*FM radio station call letters*] (RBYB)
WMFX .... St. Andrews, SC [*FM radio station call letters*]
WMG .... Globe-Union, Inc., Milwaukee, WI [*Library symbol Library of Congress*] (LCLS)
Wmg .... Wilmington [*Delaware*] (BARN)
WMG .... Winchester Magnum (INF)
WMG .... Wire Measure Gauge
WMG .... Wire Metallizing Gun
WMG .... Working Mathematics Group (AIE)
WMGA .... Moultrie, GA [*AM radio station call letters*]
WMGa .... Wisconsin Gas Co., Milwaukee, WI [*Library symbol Library of Congress*] (LCLS)
WMGB .... Jeffersonville, GA [*FM radio station call letters*]
WMGC .... Binghamton, NY [*Television station call letters*]
WMGF .... Mount Dora, FL [*FM radio station call letters*]
WMGG .... Gallipolis, OH [*FM radio station call letters*]
WMGH .... Tamaqua, PA [*FM radio station call letters*]
WMGI .... Terre Haute, IN [*FM radio station call letters*]
WMGJ .... Gadsden, AL [*AM radio station call letters*]
WMGK .... Philadelphia, PA [*FM radio station call letters*]
WMGL .... Ravenel, SC [*FM radio station call letters*]
WMGL .... Wilmington Marine Geological Laboratory [*North Carolina*] (NOAA)
WMGM .... Atlantic City, NJ [*FM radio station call letters*]
WMGM .... Wildwood, NJ [*Television station call letters*]
WMGN .... Madison, WI [*FM radio station call letters*]
WMGO .... Canton, MS [*AM radio station call letters*]
WMGP .... Meridian, MS [*AM radio station call letters*]
WMGQ .... New Brunswick, NJ [*FM radio station call letters*]
WMGR .... Bainbridge, GA [*AM radio station call letters*]
WMGR .... Worm Gear [*Mechanical engineering*]
WMGR-FM ... Bainbridge, GA [*FM radio station call letters*]
WMGS .... Wilkes-Barre, PA [*FM radio station call letters*]
WMGT .... Macon, GA [*Television station call letters*]
WMGV-FM ... Newport, NC [*FM radio station call letters*] (RBYB)
WMGW .... Meadville, PA [*AM radio station call letters*]
WMGX .... Portland, ME [*FM radio station call letters*]
WMGY .... Montgomery, AL [*AM radio station call letters*]
WMGZ .... Sparta, GA [*FM radio station call letters*]
WMH .... Mountain Home [*Arkansas*] [*Airport symbol*] (OAG)
WMH .... WM Helijet [*Vancouver Stock Exchange symbol*]
WMH .... Women's Market Handbook [*A publication*]
WMHB .... Waterville, ME [*FM radio station call letters*]
WMHC .... South Hadley, MA [*FM radio station call letters*]
WMHD .... Terre Haute, IN [*FM radio station call letters*]
WMHG .... Muskegon, MI [*FM radio station call letters*] (RBYB)
WMHI .... Cape Vincent, NY [*FM radio station call letters*]
WMHK .... Columbia, SC [*FM radio station call letters*]
WMHN .... Webster, NY [*FM radio station call letters*]
WMHQ .... Schenectady, NY [*Television station call letters*]
WMHR .... Syracuse, NY [*FM radio station call letters*]
WMHS .... Wall-Mounted Handling System [*AEC*]
WMHS .... World Methodist Historical Society (EA)
WMHT .... Schenectady, NY [*FM radio station call letters*]
WMHT-TV .... Schenectady, NY [*Television station call letters*]
WMHW .... Mount Pleasant, MI [*FM radio station call letters*]
WMHX-FM ... Canandaigua, NY [*FM radio station call letters*] (RBYB)
WMHY .... World Mental Health Year [*1960*]
WMI .... War Materials, Inc.
WMI .... Washington Music Institute
WMI .... Waveguide Moisture Indicator
WMI .... Westmin Resources Ltd. [*Toronto Stock Exchange symbol Vancouver Stock Exchange symbol*]
WMI .... Wildlife Management Institute (EA)
WMI .... Wolfson Microelectronics Institute (NITA)
WMI .... Woodlands Mountain Institute (EA)
WMI .... Worker-Machine Interface
WMI .... Work Motivation Inventory [*Test*]
WMI .... World Manufacturer Identifier
WMI .... World Metal Index [*Sheffield City Libraries*] [*British Information service or system*] (IID)
WMI .... World Meteorological Intervals
WMIA .... Arecibo, PR [*AM radio station call letters*]
WMIA .... Woodworking Machinery Importers Association of America (EA)
WMIB .... Waste Management Information Bureau [*Atomic Energy Authority*] [*British Information service or system*] (IID)
WMIC .... Sandusky, MI [*AM radio station call letters*]
WMIC .... Western Microwave, Inc. [*NASDAQ symbol*] (NQ)
WMIC/CHCC ... Welsh Music Information Centre - Canolfan Hysbysrwydd Cerddoriaeth Cymru [*University College*] (CB)
WMicr .... Western Microwave, Inc. [*Associated Press*] (SAG)
WMicTc .... Western Micro Technology, Inc. [*Associated Press*] (SAG)
WMID .... Atlantic City, NJ [*AM radio station call letters*]
WMID .... Pleasantville, NJ [*FM radio station call letters*]
WMIE .... Cocoa, FL [*FM radio station call letters*]
WMIH .... Cleveland, OH [*AM radio station call letters*] (RBYB)
WMIK .... Middlesboro, KY [*AM radio station call letters*]
WMIK-FM .... Middlesboro, KY [*FM radio station call letters*]
WMIL .... Waukesha, WI [*FM radio station call letters*]
WMiltM .... Milton College, Milton, WI [*Library symbol Library of Congress*] (LCLS)
WMIM .... Mount Carmel, PA [*AM radio station call letters*] (RBYB)
WMIN .... Hudson, WI [*AM radio station call letters*]
WMin .... Waste Minimization (GAAI)
WMIN .... Words per Minute (IAA)
WMINST ...... Westminster [*England*]
WMIO .... Cabo Rojo, PR [*FM radio station call letters*]
WMIP .... Weapons Management Improvement Program [*Military*] (AABC)
WMIQ .... Iron Mountain, MI [*AM radio station call letters*]
WMIS .... Natchez, MS [*AM radio station call letters*]
WMIS .... Waste Management Information System
WMIT .... Black Mountain, NC [*FM radio station call letters*]
WMIU .... Water and Maritime Industry Union [*Australia*]
WMIW .... Atlantic Beach, SC [*AM radio station call letters*]
WMIX .... Mount Vernon, IL [*AM radio station call letters*]
WMIX-FM .... Mount Vernon, IL [*FM radio station call letters*]
WMIY .... Fairview, NC [*AM radio station call letters*]
WMIZ .... Vineland, NJ [*AM radio station call letters*]
WMJ .... Johnson Controls, Corporate Information Center, Milwaukee, WI [*Library symbol Library of Congress*] (LCLS)
WMJ .... World of Michael Jackson (EA)
WMJA .... Saginaw, MI [*FM radio station call letters*] (RBYB)
WMJB .... Evansville, WI [*FM radio station call letters*]
WMJC .... Smithtown, NY [*FM radio station call letters*]
WMJD .... Grundy, VA [*FM radio station call letters*]
WMJDA .... Watch Material and Jewelry Distributors Association [*Formerly, WMDAA*] (EA)
WMJE .... Clarkesville, GA [*FM radio station call letters*]
WMJH-AM .... Rockford, MI [*AM radio station call letters*] (RBYB)
WMJI .... Cleveland, OH [*FM radio station call letters*]
WMJJ .... Birmingham, AL [*FM radio station call letters*]
WMJK .... Pinconning, MI [*FM radio station call letters*] (RBYB)
WMJL .... Marion, KY [*AM radio station call letters*]
WMJL-FM .... Marion, KY [*FM radio station call letters*]
WMJM-FM ... Jeffersontown, KY [*FM radio station call letters*] (RBYB)
WMJQ .... Buffalo, NY [*FM radio station call letters*]
WMJR .... Hudson Falls, NY [*FM radio station call letters*]
WMJS .... Prince Frederick, MD [*FM radio station call letters*]
WMJT .... Moundsville, WV [*AM radio station call letters*]
WMJW .... Cleveland, MS [*FM radio station call letters*]
WMJX .... Boston, MA [*FM radio station call letters*]
WMJY .... Biloxi, MS [*FM radio station call letters*]
WMJZ .... Gaylord, MI [*FM radio station call letters*]
WMK .... Watermark
W/(M K) .... Watts per Meter Kelvin
WMK .... Weis Markets [*NYSE symbol*] (TTSB)
WMK .... Weis Markets, Inc. [*NYSE symbol*] (SPSG)

WMKA .... Alor Setar/Sultan Abdul Halim [*Malaysia*] [*ICAO location identifier*] (ICLI)
WMKB .... Butterworth [*Malaysia*] [*ICAO location identifier*] (ICLI)
WMKB .... Ridgebury, PA [*FM radio station call letters*]
WMKC .... Kota Bahru/Sultan Ismail Petra [*Malaysia*] [*ICAO location identifier*] (ICLI)
WMKC .... St. Ignace, MI [*FM radio station call letters*]
WMKD .... Kuantan [*Malaysia*] [*ICAO location identifier*] (ICLI)
WMKD .... Watermarked (WGA)
WMKE .... Kerteh [*Malaysia*] [*ICAO location identifier*] (ICLI)
WMKF .... Simpang [*Malaysia*] [*ICAO location identifier*] (ICLI)
WMKI .... Ipoh [*Malaysia*] [*ICAO location identifier*] (ICLI)
WMKJ .... Johore Bahru [*Malaysia*] [*ICAO location identifier*] (ICLI)
WMKJ .... Newnan, GA [*FM radio station call letters*]
WMKK .... Kuala Lumpur/International [*Malaysia*] [*ICAO location identifier*] (ICLI)
WMKM .... Inkster, MI [*AM radio station call letters*]
WMKM .... Malacca [*Malaysia*] [*ICAO location identifier*] (ICLI)
WMKN .... Kuala Trengganu/Sultan Mahmud [*Malaysia*] [*ICAO location identifier*] (ICLI)
WMKP .... Penang [*Malaysia*] [*ICAO location identifier*] (ICLI)
WMKR-FM ... Taylorville, IL [*FM radio station call letters*] (RBYB)
WMKS .... Kuala Lumpur [*Malaysia*] [*ICAO location identifier*] (ICLI)
WMKS .... Macon, GA [*FM radio station call letters*]
WMKT .... Charlevoix, MI [*AM radio station call letters*]
WMKV .... Reading, OH [*FM radio station call letters*]
WMKW-FM ... Crossville, TN [*FM radio station call letters*] (RBYB)
WMKX .... Brookville, PA [*FM radio station call letters*]
WMKY .... Morehead, KY [*FM radio station call letters*]
WMKZ .... Monticello, KY [*FM radio station call letters*]
WML .... Lakeside Laboratories, Milwaukee, WI [*Library symbol Library of Congress*] (LCLS)
WML .... Malaimbandy [*Madagascar*] [*Airport symbol*] (OAG)
WML .... Westar Mining Ltd. [*Toronto Stock Exchange symbol Vancouver Stock Exchange symbol*]
WMLB .... Cumming, GA [*AM radio station call letters*]
WMLC .... Monticello, MS [*AM radio station call letters*]
WMLC .... Way of Mountain Learning Center (EA)
WMLH .... Lutheran Hospital of Milwaukee, Milwaukee, WI [*Library symbol Library of Congress*] (LCLS)
WMLI-FM .... Sauk City, WI [*FM radio station call letters*] (RBYB)
WMLJ .... Summersville, WV [*FM radio station call letters*]
WMLM .... St. Louis, MI [*AM radio station call letters*]
WMLN .... Milton, MA [*FM radio station call letters*]
WMLO .... Havana, FL [*FM radio station call letters*]
WMLP .... Milton, PA [*AM radio station call letters*]
WMLQ .... Rogers City, MI [*FM radio station call letters*]
WMLR .... Hohenwald, TN [*AM radio station call letters*]
WMLT .... Dublin, GA [*AM radio station call letters*]
WMLV .... Ironton, OH [*FM radio station call letters*]
WMLZ .... Jupiter, FL [*AM radio station call letters*]
WMM .... Marquette University, Milwaukee, WI [*Library symbol Library of Congress*] (LCLS)
WMM .... Wall-Mounted Manipulator [*Nuclear energy*] (NRCH)
WMM .... White Middle-Aged Male (MAE)
WMM .... William Mitchell College of Law Library, St. Paul, MN [*OCLC symbol*] (OCLC)
WMM .... Willow Mixed Media (EA)
WMM .... Women Make Movies (EA)
WMM .... World Medical Mission (EA)
WMM .... World Movement of Mothers [*See also MMM*] [*Paris, France*] (EAIO)
WMMA .... Lebanon, OH [*FM radio station call letters*]
WMMA .... Waste Materials Management Act
WMMA .... Wood Machinery Manufacturers of America (EA)
WMMB .... Melbourne, FL [*AM radio station call letters*]
WMMB .... Milwaukee Blood Center, Inc., Milwaukee, WI [*Library symbol Library of Congress*] (LCLS)
WMMBC ...... Miller Brewing Co., Research Library, Milwaukee, WI [*Library symbol Library of Congress*] (LCLS)
WMMC .... Marshall, IL [*FM radio station call letters*]
WMMC .... Milwaukee Children's Hospital, Milwaukee, WI [*Library symbol Library of Congress*] (LCLS)
WMMCW ..... Medical College of Wisconsin, Medical-Dental Library, Milwaukee, WI [*Library symbol Library of Congress*] (LCLS)
WMME-FM ... Augusta, ME [*FM radio station call letters*]
WMMF .... Fond du Lac, WI [*Television station call letters*]
WMMG .... Brandenburg, KY [*AM radio station call letters*]
WMMG-FM ... Brandenburg, KY [*FM radio station call letters*]
WMMGIC ..... MGIC Investment Corp., Milwaukee, WI [*Library symbol Library of Congress*] (LCLS)
WMMH .... Misericordia Hospital, Milwaukee, WI [*Library symbol Library of Congress*] (LCLS)
WMMI .... Shepherd, MI [*AM radio station call letters*]
Wm Mitchell C Law ... William Mitchell College of Law (GAGS)
WMMJ .... Bethesda, MD [*FM radio station call letters*]
WMMK .... Destin, FL [*FM radio station call letters*]
WMM-L .... Marquette University, School of Law, Milwaukee, WI [*Library symbol Library of Congress*] (LCLS)
WMMM .... Westport, CT [*AM radio station call letters*]
WMMM-FM ... Verona, WI [*FM radio station call letters*] (RBYB)
WMM/MWS ... Western Material Management, Machinery, and Welding Show [*Canada*] (ITD)
WMMN .... Barrackville, WV [*FM radio station call letters*]
WMMN .... Fairmont, WV [*AM radio station call letters*]
WMM-N .... Marquette University, College of Nursing, Milwaukee, WI [*Library symbol Library of Congress*] (LCLS)
WMMO .... Orlando, FL [*FM radio station call letters*]
WMMP .... Wood Moulding and Millwork Producers [*Later, WMMPA*] (EA)
WMMPA ...... Wood Moulding and Millwork Producers Association (EA)
WMMQ .... Charlotte, MI [*FM radio station call letters*]
WMMR .... Philadelphia, PA [*FM radio station call letters*]
WMMRRI ..... Wyoming Mining and Mineral Resource Research Institute [*University of Wyoming*] [*Research center*] (RCD)
WMMS .... Cleveland, OH [*FM radio station call letters*]
WMMS .... Mount Sinai Hospital, Milwaukee, WI [*Library symbol Library of Congress*] (LCLS)
WMMt .... Mount Mary College, Milwaukee, WI [*Library symbol Library of Congress*] (LCLS)
WMMT .... Warm Month Mean Temperature [*Climatology*]
WMMT .... Whitesburg, KY [*FM radio station call letters*]
WMMus .... Milwaukee Public Museum, Reference Library, Milwaukee, WI [*Library symbol Library of Congress*] (LCLS)
WMMW .... Meriden, CT [*AM radio station call letters*]
WMMX .... Dayton, OH [*FM radio station call letters*]
WMMZ .... Spartanburg, SC [*AM radio station call letters*]
WMN .... Maroantsetra [*Madagascar*] [*Airport symbol*] (OAG)
WMN .... Winnemucca [*Nevada*] [*Seismograph station code, US Geological Survey Closed*] (SEIS)
WMN .... Women
WMNA .... Gretna, VA [*AM radio station call letters*]
WMNA-FM ... Gretna, VA [*FM radio station call letters*]
WMNB .... North Adams, MA [*FM radio station call letters*]
WMNC .... Morganton, NC [*AM radio station call letters*]
WMNC .... Whole Mononuclear Cell [*Biochemistry*]
WMNC-FM ... Morgantown, NC [*FM radio station call letters*]
WMNF .... Tampa, FL [*FM radio station call letters*]
WMNG .... Northwest General Hospital, Milwaukee, WI [*Library symbol Library of Congress*] (LCLS)
WMNI .... Columbus, OH [*AM radio station call letters*]
WMNJ .... Madison, NJ [*FM radio station call letters*]
WMNM .... Port Henry, NY [*FM radio station call letters*]
WMNN .... Minneapolis, MN [*AM radio station call letters*] (RBYB)
WMNR .... Monroe, CT [*FM radio station call letters*]
WMNS .... Olean, NY [*AM radio station call letters*]
WMNS .... William B. McGuire Nuclear Station (NRCH)
WMNT .... Manati, PR [*AM radio station call letters*]
WMNV .... Rupert, VT [*FM radio station call letters*]
WMNX .... Wilmington, NC [*FM radio station call letters*]
WMNY .... Elloree-Santee, SC [*AM radio station call letters*]
WMNZ .... Montezuma, GA [*AM radio station call letters*]
WMO .... White Mountain [*Alaska*] [*Airport symbol*] (OAG)
WMO .... White Mountain, AK [*Location identifier FAA*] (FAAL)
WMO .... Wichita Mountains Array [*Oklahoma*] [*Seismograph station code, US Geological Survey Closed*] (SEIS)
WMO .... Wing Maintenance Officer
WMO .... World Meteorological Office (NITA)
WMO .... World Meteorological Organization [*See also OMM*] [*Geneva, Switzerland*] [*United Nations*] (EAIO)
WMO .... World Monetary Organization
WMOA .... Marietta, OH [*AM radio station call letters*]
WMOA .... Waste Minimization Opportunity Assessment [*Environmental science*]
WMOB .... Mobile, AL [*AM radio station call letters*]
WMOD .... Bolivar, TN [*FM radio station call letters*]
W/MOD .... With Modification of Vertical Profile (GAVI)
WMOG .... Brunswick, GA [*AM radio station call letters*]
WMOH .... Hamilton, OH [*AM radio station call letters*]
WMOI .... Monmouth, IL [*FM radio station call letters*]
WMOK .... Metropolis, IL [*AM radio station call letters*]
WMoM .... Monroe Clinic, Monroe, WI [*Library symbol Library of Congress*] (LCLS)
WMON .... Montgomery, WV [*AM radio station call letters*]
WMOO .... Derby Center, VT [*FM radio station call letters*]
WMOP .... Ocala, FL [*AM radio station call letters*]
WMOQ .... Bostwick, GA [*FM radio station call letters*]
WMOR .... Morehead, KY [*AM radio station call letters*]
WmorC .... Westmoreland Coal Co. [*Associated Press*] (SAG)
WMOR-FM ... Morehead, KY [*FM radio station call letters*]
WMOS .... Quincy, IL [*FM radio station call letters*] (RBYB)
WMoS .... Saint Clare Hospital, Monroe, WI [*Library symbol Library of Congress*] (LCLS)
WMOT .... Murfreesboro, TN [*FM radio station call letters*]
WMOU .... Berlin, NH [*AM radio station call letters*]
WMOV .... Ravenswood, WV [*AM radio station call letters*]
WMOX .... Meridian, MS [*AM radio station call letters*]
WMP .... Mampikony [*Malagasy*] [*Airport symbol*] (AD)
WMP .... War and Mobilization Plan [*Air Force documents*]
WMP .... Waste Management Paper [*British*] (DCTA)
WMP .... Waste Management Plan (EERA)
WMP .... Weapon Monitor Panel (MCD)
WMP .... Weather Modification Program [*Boulder, CO*] [*Department of Commerce*]
WMP .... Wiener Mapping Procedure
WMP .... With Much Pleasure [*Meaning, "We accept the invitation"*]
WMP .... Women and the Military Project [*An association*] (EA)
WmP .... World Microfilms Publications, London, United Kingdom [*Library symbol Library of Congress*] (LCLS)
WMPA .... Wet Maximum Power Available (SAA)
WMPA .... Women's Military Pilots Association (EA)
Wm Paterson C NJ ... William Paterson College of New Jersey (GAGS)
WMPB .... Baltimore, MD [*Television station call letters*]
WMPC .... Lapeer, MI [*AM radio station call letters*]

WMPC .... War Manpower Commission [*Within the Office of Emergency Management*] [*World War II*]
WMPC .... War Materiel Procurement Capability (AFIT)
WMPCE......... World Meeting Planners Congress and Exposition [*Defunct*] (EA)
WMPCES(P)... War Manpower Commission Employment Stabilization (Plan) [*Terminated, 1945*]
WMPG .... Gorham, ME [*FM radio station call letters*]
WMPH .... Wilmington, DE [*FM radio station call letters*]
WMPI........... Scottsburg, IN [*FM radio station call letters*]
WMPI........... Women of the Motion Picture Industry, International [*Dallas, TX*]
WMPL.......... Hancock, MI [*AM radio station call letters*]
WMPL.......... Western Maryland Public Libraries Regional Resource Center [*Library network*]
WMPL.......... World Mission Prayer League (EA)
WMPM......... Smithfield, NC [*AM radio station call letters*]
WMPN .... Jackson, MS [*FM radio station call letters*]
WMPN-TV.... Jackson, MS [*Television station call letters*]
WMPO .... Middleport-Pomeroy, OH [*AM radio station call letters*]
WMPO .... Weather Modification Program Office [*Marine science*] (MSC)
WMPO-FM... Middleport-Pomeroy, OH [*FM radio station call letters*]
WMPR .... Jackson, MS [*FM radio station call letters*]
WMPRT....... Wartime Manpower and Personnel Readiness Team [*Military*]
WMPS .... Millington, TN [*AM radio station call letters*]
WMPT......... Annapolis, MD [*Television station call letters*]
WMPV .... Mobile, AL [*Television station call letters*]
WMPX .... Midland, MI [*AM radio station call letters*]
WMPZ.......... Ringgold, GA [*FM radio station call letters*] (RBYB)
WMQ .... Quarles & Brady, Law Library, Milwaukee, WI [*Library symbol Library of Congress*] (LCLS)
WMQ .... Westmount Public Library [*UTLAS symbol*]
WMQ .... Wulumuchi [*Republic of China*] [*Seismograph station code, US Geological Survey*] (SEIS)
WMQA .... Minocqua, WI [*AM radio station call letters*]
WMQA-FM... Minocqua, WI [*FM radio station call letters*]
WMQC .... Westover, WV [*FM radio station call letters*]
WMQQ .... Springfield, KY [*FM radio station call letters*]
WMQT .... Ishpeming, MI [*FM radio station call letters*]
WMQX-FM... Winston-Salem, NC [*FM radio station call letters*]
WMR .... Mananara [*Madagascar*] [*Airport symbol*] (OAG)
WMR .... Reinhart, Boerner, Van Deuren, Norris and Rieselbach, Law Library, Milwaukee, WI [*Library symbol Library of Congress*] (LCLS)
WMR .... Wake Measurements RADAR [*Army*] (MCD)
WMR .... War Maintenance Reserve [*British*]
WMR .... War Materiel Requirement (AFIT)
WMR .... Water Meter
WMR .... Water-Moderated Reactor
WMR .... Wideband Multichannel Receiver
WMR .... William and Mary Review of Virginia Law [*A publication*] (DLA)
WMR .... Wonder Marine Resources [*Vancouver Stock Exchange symbol*]
WMR .... Work Metabolic Rate (MAE)
WMR .... World Medical Relief (EA)
WMRA .... Harrisonburg, VA [*FM radio station call letters*]
WMRALC..... Western Metropolitan Regional Aboriginal Land Council [*Sydney, New South Wales, Australia*]
WMRB .... Columbia, TN [*AM radio station call letters*]
WMRC .... Milford, MA [*AM radio station call letters*]
WMRC .... War Minerals Relief Commission [*Department of the Interior*] [*Abolished, 1940*] (EGAO)
WMRD-AM... Middletown, CT [*AM radio station call letters*] (RBYB)
WMREI .... Waste Management Research and Education Institute [*University of Tennessee*]
WMRF .... Lewistown, PA [*FM radio station call letters*]
WMRH .... Waupun, WI [*AM radio station call letters*]
WMRI.......... Marion, IN [*FM radio station call letters*]
WMRK .... Selma, AL [*AM radio station call letters*]
WMRL .... Lexington, VA [*FM radio station call letters*]
WMRL .... Water Management Research Laboratory [*Fresno, CA*] [*Department of Agriculture*] (GRD)
WMRN .... Marion, OH [*AM radio station call letters*]
WMRN-FM... Marion, OH [*FM radio station call letters*]
WMRO .... Gallatin, TN [*AM radio station call letters*]
Wm Rob ...... William Robinson's English Admiralty Reports [*1838-52*] [*A publication*] (DLA)
Wm Rob Adm... William Robinson's English Admiralty Reports [*1838-52*] [*A publication*] (DLA)
WMRQ .... Waterbury, CT [*FM radio station call letters*] (RBYB)
WMRR .... Muskegon Heights, MI [*FM radio station call letters*]
WMRS .... Monticello, IN [*FM radio station call letters*]
WMRS .... White Mountain Research Station [*Research center*] (RCD)
WMRT .... Marietta, OH [*FM radio station call letters*]
WMRV .... Endicott, NY [*FM radio station call letters*]
WMRW .... Westhampton, NY [*FM radio station call letters*]
WMRX .... Beaverton, MI [*FM radio station call letters*]
WMRY .... Crozet, VA [*FM radio station call letters*] (RBYB)
WMS............ Wall-Motion Study (MEDA)
WMS............ Warehouse Material Stores (AAG)
WMS............ Waste Management System (MCD)
WMS............ Water Management Section [*Apollo*] [*NASA*]
WMS............ Watershed Modeling System
WMS............ Weapons Monitoring System
WMS............ Weather Mapping System
WMS............ Wechsler Memory Scale [*Neuropsychological test*]
WMS............ Wesleyan Missionary Society
WMS............ West Middle School [*South Carolina*] [*Seismograph station code, US Geological Survey*] (SEIS)
WMS............ Whaling Museum Society (EA)
WMS............ Wilderness Medical Society (EA)
WMS............ Willem Mengelberg Society (EA)
WMS............ William Morris Society [*Later, WMS/AB*] (EA)
WMS............ Wind Measuring System
WMS............ Wire Mesh Screen (OA)
WMS............ WMS Airways BV [*Netherlands ICAO designator*] (FAAC)
WMS............ WMS Industries [*Associated Press*] (SAG)
WMS............ WMS Industries, Inc. [*Formerly, Williams Electronics*] [*NYSE symbol*] (SPSG)
WMS............ Women for a Meaningful Summit (EA)
WMS............ Women in the Medical Service [*Army*]
WMS............ Women's Medical Specialist
WMS............ Women's Missionary Society, AME [*African Methodist Episcopal*] Church (EA)
WMS............ Workforce Management Staff [*Environmental Protection Agency*] (GFGA)
WMS............ Work Measurement System [*Postal Service*]
WMS............ World Magnetic Survey [*Defunct*]
WMS............ World Mariculture Society (EA)
WmS............ World Microfilms Division, Oyez Equipment Ltd., London, United Kingdom [*Library symbol Library of Congress*] (LCLS)
WMSA .... Massena, NY [*AM radio station call letters*]
WMSA .... Saint Anthony Hospital, Milwaukee, WI [*Library symbol Library of Congress*] (LCLS)
WMSA .... Woodworking Machinery Suppliers Association [*British*] (DBA)
WMS/AB ...... William Morris Society, American Branch (EA)
Wms Ann Reg... Williams' Annual Register [*New York*] [*A publication*] (DLA)
WMSC .... Upper Montclair, NJ [*FM radio station call letters*]
WMSC .... Weather Message Switching Center
WMSC .... White Mountain Scenic Railroad [*AAR code*]
WMSC .... Women's Medical Specialists Corps
WMSCMC .... Women's Missionary and Service Commission of the Mennonite Church (EA)
WMSCR .... Weather Message Switching Center Replacement (GAVI)
WMSE.......... Milwaukee School of Engineering, Walter Schroeder Library, Milwaukee, WI [*Library symbol Library of Congress*] (LCLS)
WMSE.......... Milwaukee, WI [*FM radio station call letters*]
Wms Ex .... Williams on Executors [*15th ed.*] [*1970*] [*A publication*] (DLA)
WMSF.......... Saint Francis Seminary, Milwaukee, WI [*Library symbol Library of Congress*] (LCLS)
WMSFH .... Saint Francis Hospital, Milwaukee, WI [*Library symbol Library of Congress*] (LCLS)
Wms flex ex... Williams flexion exercises [*Orthopedics*] (DAVI)
WMSFT........ Wormshaft
WMSG .... Oakland, MD [*AM radio station call letters*]
WMSH .... Sturgis, MI [*AM radio station call letters*]
WMSH-FM... Sturgis, MI [*FM radio station call letters*]
WMSI........... Jackson, MS [*FM radio station call letters*]
WMS-I .... Wechsler Memory Scale, Form I [*Psychology*] (DAVI)
WMSI........... Western Management Science Institute [*University of California*] (KSC)
WMSJ.......... Harpswell, ME [*FM radio station call letters*]
WMSJ.......... Saint Joseph's Hospital, Milwaukee, WI [*Library symbol Library of Congress*] (LCLS)
WMSK .... Morganfield, KY [*AM radio station call letters*]
WMSKF........ William Morris Society and Kelmscott Fellowship [*Kelmscott Fellowship and William Morris Society*] [*Formed by a merger of*] (EAIO)
WMSK-FM ... Morganfield, KY [*FM radio station call letters*]
WMSL.......... Athens, GA [*FM radio station call letters*]
WMSL.......... Saint Luke's Hospital, Milwaukee, WI [*Library symbol Library of Congress*] (LCLS)
WMSL.......... Wet Mock Simulated Launch [*NASA*] (KSC)
WMSL.......... Wichita Mountains Seismological Laboratory
WMSM......... Saint Mary's Hospital, Milwaukee, WI [*Library symbol Library of Congress*] (LCLS)
Wms Mass... Williams' Reports [*1 Massachusetts*] [*A publication*] (DLA)
WMSMi......... Saint Michael Hospital, Milwaukee, WI [*Library symbol Library of Congress*] (LCLS)
WMSMN ...... Saint Mary's School of Nursing, Milwaukee, WI [*Library symbol Library of Congress*] (LCLS)
WMSN .... Madison, WI [*Television station call letters*]
Wms Notes... Williams' Notes to Saunders' Reports [*England*] [*A publication*] (DLA)
WMSO .... Wichita Mountains Seismological Observatory
WMSP .... Montgomery, AL [*AM radio station call letters*] (RBYB)
Wms P.......... Peere-Williams' English Chancery Reports [*1695-1736*] [*A publication*] (DLA)
Wms Peere... Peere-Williams' English Chancery Reports [*A publication*] (DLA)
WMSQ .... Havelock, NC [*FM radio station call letters*]
WMSR .... Manchester, TN [*AM radio station call letters*]
WMSRG........ Weather-Modification Statistical Research Groups
WMSS .... Middletown, PA [*FM radio station call letters*]
WMSS .... Westinghouse Microscan System (IAA)
WmsSon....... Willams-Sonoma, Inc. [*Associated Press*] (SAG)
WMST.......... Mount Sterling, KY [*AM radio station call letters*]
WMST-FM ... Mount Sterling, KY [*FM radio station call letters*]
WMSU .... Starkville, MS [*FM radio station call letters*]
WMSV .... Starkville, MS [*FM radio station call letters*]
Wms VT....... Williams' Vermont Reports [*27-29 Vermont*] [*A publication*] (DLA)
WMSW .... Hatillo, PR [*AM radio station call letters*]
WMSWH....... Southeastern Wisconsin Health Systems Agency, Health Science Library, Milwaukee,WI [*Library symbol Library of Congress*] (LCLS)

WMSX .... Brockton, MA [*AM radio station call letters*]
WMSY .... Marion, VA [*Television station call letters*]
WMT .... Cedar Rapids, IA [*AM radio station call letters*]
WMT .... Wal-Mart Stores [*NYSE symbol*] (TTSB)
WMT .... Wal-Mart Stores, Inc. [*NYSE symbol*] (SPSG)
WMT .... Waste Monitor Tank (IEEE)
WMT .... Weighing More Than
WMT .... Western Motor Tariff Bureau, Los Angeles CA [*STAC*]
WMT .... West Meridian Time
WMT .... Wet Metric Ton [*Waste management*]
WMTA .... Central City, KY [*AM radio station call letters*]
WMTA .... Western Maquiladora Trade Association (CROSS)
WMTB .... Emmitsburg, MD [*FM radio station call letters*]
WMTB .... Western Motor Tariff Bureau
WMTBF .... Warranty Mean Time Between Failures [*Army*]
WMTC .... Milwaukee Technical College, Milwaukee, WI [*Library symbol Library of Congress*] (LCLS)
WMTC .... Vancleve, KY [*AM radio station call letters*]
WMTC .... Waste Management Technology Center [*Oak Ridge National Laboratory*]
WMTC-FM ... Vancleve, KY [*FM radio station call letters*]
WMTC-N ...... Milwaukee Area Technical College, North Campus Center Library, Mequon, WI [*Library symbol Library of Congress*] (LCLS)
WMTC-S ...... Milwaukee Area Technical College, South Campus Center Library, Oak Creek, WI [*Library symbol Library of Congress*] (LCLS)
WMTC-W ..... Milwaukee Area Technical College, West Campus Center Library, West Allis, WI [*Library symbol Library of Congress*] (LCLS)
WMTD .... Hinton, WV [*AM radio station call letters*]
WMTD-FM ... Hinton, WV [*FM radio station call letters*]
WMTE .... Manistee, MI [*AM radio station call letters*]
WMT-FM ...... Cedar Rapids, IA [*FM radio station call letters*]
WMTH .... Park Ridge, IL [*FM radio station call letters*]
WMTH .... Westmeath [*County in Ireland*] (ROG)
WMTI .... Morovis, PR [*AM radio station call letters*]
WMTI Exp Stn ... Manati, PR [*Radio expansion station*] (RBYB)
WMTJ .... Fajardo, PR [*Television station call letters*]
WMTK .... Littleton, NH [*FM radio station call letters*]
WMTL .... Leitchfield, KY [*AM radio station call letters*]
WMTM .... Moultrie, GA [*AM radio station call letters*]
WMTM-FM ... Moultrie, GA [*FM radio station call letters*]
WMTN .... Morristown, TN [*AM radio station call letters*]
WMTO .... Port St. Joe, FL [*FM radio station call letters*]
WMTR .... Archbold, OH [*FM radio station call letters*]
WMTR .... Morristown, NJ [*AM radio station call letters*]
WMTR .... Wheeled Mobility Test Rig [*Army*] (RDA)
WMTS .... Murfreesboro, TN [*AM radio station call letters*]
WMTS .... Western Manufacturing Technology Show and Conference (ITD)
WMTS-FM ... Murfreesboro, TN [*FM radio station call letters*] (RBYB)
WMTT .... Conklin, NY [*FM radio station call letters*] (RBYB)
WMTT .... Willamette Indus [*NASDAQ symbol*] (TTSB)
WMTT .... Willamette Industries, Inc. [*NASDAQ symbol*] (NQ)
WMTU .... Houghton, MI [*FM radio station call letters*]
WMTU .... Jackson, TN [*Television station call letters*]
WMTV .... Madison, WI [*Television station call letters*]
WMTW .... Poland Spring, ME [*Television station call letters*]
WMTX .... Clearwater, FL [*FM radio station call letters*]
WMTX .... Pinellas Park, FL [*AM radio station call letters*]
WMTY .... Greenwood, SC [*AM radio station call letters*]
WMTY-FM ... Greenwood, SC [*FM radio station call letters*]
WMTZ .... Johnston, PA [*FM radio station call letters*]
WMU .... Western Michigan University [*Kalamazoo*]
WMU .... West Mountain [*Utah*] [*Seismograph station code, US Geological Survey*] (SEIS)
WMU .... Woman's Missionary Union (EA)
WMU .... World Maritime University [*Sweden*] (DCTA)
WMUA .... Amherst, MA [*FM radio station call letters*]
WMUB .... Oxford, OH [*FM radio station call letters*]
WMUC .... College Park, MD [*FM radio station call letters*]
WMUF .... Paris, TN [*AM radio station call letters*]
WMUF .... Universal Foods Corp., Technical Information Services, Milwaukee, WI [*Library symbol Library of Congress*] (LCLS)
WMUF-FM ... Paris, TN [*FM radio station call letters*]
WMUH .... Allentown, PA [*FM radio station call letters*]
WMUK .... Kalamazoo, MI [*FM radio station call letters*]
WMUL .... Huntington, WV [*FM radio station call letters*]
WMUR .... Manchester, NH [*Television station call letters*]
WMUS .... Muskegon, MI [*AM radio station call letters*]
WMUSE .... World Markets for US Exports [*A publication*]
WMUS-FM ... Muskegon, MI [*FM radio station call letters*]
WMut .... Washington Mutual, Inc. [*Associated Press*] (SAG)
WMUU .... Greenville, SC [*AM radio station call letters*]
WMUU-FM ... Greenville, SC [*FM radio station call letters*]
WMUW .... Columbus, MS [*FM radio station call letters*]
WMUW .... University of Wisconsin-Milwaukee, Milwaukee, WI [*Library symbol Library of Congress*] (LCLS)
WMUZ .... Detroit, MI [*FM radio station call letters*]
WMV .... Madirovalo [*Malagasy*] [*Airport symbol*] (AD)
WMV .... Valuation Research Corp., Milwaukee, WI [*Library symbol Library of Congress*] (LCLS)
WMV .... War Munition Volunteers [*World War I*] [*British*]
WMV .... Watermelon Mosaic Virus
WMVA .... Martinsville, VA [*AM radio station call letters*]
WMV-E .... Watermelon Mosaic Virus E
WMVG .... Milledgeville, GA [*AM radio station call letters*]
WMVI .... Mechanicville, NY [*AM radio station call letters*]
WMVN .... Ishpeming, MI [*AM radio station call letters*]
WMVO .... Mount Vernon, OH [*AM radio station call letters*]
WMVP .... Chicago, IL [*AM radio station call letters*]
WMVR .... Sidney, OH [*AM radio station call letters*]
WMVR-FM ... Sidney, OH [*FM radio station call letters*]
WMVS .... Milwaukee, WI [*Television station call letters*]
WMVT .... Milwaukee, WI [*Television station call letters*]
WMVU .... Nashua, NH [*AM radio station call letters*]
WMVV .... Griffin, GA (RBYB)
WMVY .... Tisbury, MA [*FM radio station call letters*]
WMW .... Whyte & Hirschboeck, Law Library, Milwaukee, WI [*Library symbol Library of Congress*] (LCLS)
WMW .... Women's Media Workshop [*Defunct*] (EA)
WMWA .... Glenview, IL [*FM radio station call letters*]
WMWHL .... Wormwheel
WMWK .... Milwaukee, WI [*FM radio station call letters*]
WMWM .... Salem, MA [*FM radio station call letters*]
WMWN .... [*The*] Weatherford, Mineral Wells & Northwestern Railway Co. [*AAR code*]
WMWR-AM ... Macon, GA [*AM radio station call letters*] (RBYB)
WMWV .... Conway, NH [*FM radio station call letters*]
WMX .... Wamena [*Indonesia*] [*Airport symbol*] (OAG)
WMX .... Whirlpool, Massage, Exercise [*Medicine*]
WMX .... WMX Technologies [*NYSE symbol*] (SPSG)
WMXA .... Opelika, AL [*FM radio station call letters*]
WMXB .... Richmond, VA [*FM radio station call letters*]
WMXC .... Mobile, AL [*FM radio station call letters*]
WMXD .... Detroit, MI [*FM radio station call letters*]
WMXE .... Hudson, MI [*FM radio station call letters*] (RBYB)
WMXF .... Sauk City, WI [*FM radio station call letters*]
WMXH .... Olyphant, PA [*AM radio station call letters*]
WMXI-FM .... Laurel, MS [*FM radio station call letters*] (RBYB)
WMXJ .... Pompano Beach, FL [*FM radio station call letters*]
WMXK .... Morristown, TN [*FM radio station call letters*]
WMXL .... Lexington, KY [*FM radio station call letters*]
WMXM .... Lake Forest, IL [*FM radio station call letters*]
WMXN .... Stevenson, AL [*FM radio station call letters*] (RBYB)
WMXO .... Olean, NY [*FM radio station call letters*]
WMXP .... Peoria, IL [*FM radio station call letters*]
WMXQ .... Birmingham, AL [*FM radio station call letters*]
WMXR .... Woodstock, VT [*FM radio station call letters*]
WMXS .... Montgomery, AL [*FM radio station call letters*]
WMXT .... Pamplico, SC [*FM radio station call letters*]
WMX Tc .... WMX Technologies, Inc. [*Associated Press*] (SAG)
WMXU .... Starkville, MS [*FM radio station call letters*]
WMXV .... New York, NY [*FM radio station call letters*]
WMXW .... Vestal, NY [*FM radio station call letters*]
WMXX .... Jackson, TN [*FM radio station call letters*]
WMXY .... Hogansville, GA [*AM radio station call letters*]
WMXZ .... De Funiak Springs, FL [*FM radio station call letters*]
WMY .... Wakamiya [*Japan*] [*Seismograph station code, US Geological Survey Closed*] (SEIS)
WMYB .... Socastee, SC [*FM radio station call letters*]
WMYC .... Mobile, AL [*FM radio station call letters*]
WMYF .... Exeter, NH [*AM radio station call letters*]
WMYI .... Hendersonville, NC [*FM radio station call letters*]
WMYK .... Moyock, NC [*FM radio station call letters*]
WMYL-FM ... Salladasburg, PA [*FM radio station call letters*] (RBYB)
WMYM .... Cocoa, FL [*AM radio station call letters*]
WMYN .... Mayodan, NC [*AM radio station call letters*]
WMYQ .... Newton, MS [*AM radio station call letters*] (RBYB)
WMYQ-FM ... Newton, MS [*FM radio station call letters*] (RBYB)
WMYR .... Fort Myers, FL [*AM radio station call letters*]
WMYS .... Indianapolis, IN [*AM radio station call letters*]
WMYT .... Carolina Beach, NC [*AM radio station call letters*]
WMYU .... Sevierville, TN [*FM radio station call letters*]
WMYX .... Milwaukee, WI [*FM radio station call letters*]
WMYY .... Schoharie, NY [*FM radio station call letters*]
WMZ .... Williams Companies [*NYSE symbol*] (SAG)
WMZ .... Williams Cos. 9.60%'QUICS' [*NYSE symbol*] (TTSB)
WMZ .... Wlliams Companies [*NYSE symbol*] (SAG)
WMZK .... Merrill, WI [*FM radio station call letters*]
WMZQ .... Arlington, VA [*AM radio station call letters*]
WMZQ .... Washington, DC [*FM radio station call letters*]
WMZX .... Owosso, MI [*FM radio station call letters*]
WN .... Calcutta Weekly Notes [*A publication*] (DLA)
WN .... Neenah Public Library, Neenah, WI [*Library symbol Library of Congress*] (LCLS)
WN .... Southwest Airlines [*ICAO designator*] (AD)
WN .... Washington [*Obsolete*] (ROG)
Wn .... Washington Reports [*A publication*] (DLA)
WN .... WAVES [*Women Accepted for Volunteer Emergency Service*] National (EA)
WN .... Weekly Notes of English Law Reports [*A publication*] (DLA)
W/N .... Weight Note [*Tea trade*] (ROG)
W-N .... Well-Nourished [*Medicine*]
WN .... Weston [*George*] Ltd. [*Toronto Stock Exchange symbol Vancouver Stock Exchange symbol*]
WN .... White-Breasted Nuthatch [*Ornithology*]
WN .... White Noise
WN .... Will Not
WN .... Winch (AAG)
WN .... Wisconsin [*Obsolete*] (ROG)
WN .... Within (ROG)
WN .... Work Notice (AAG)

WN............ World Neighbors (EA)
WN............ Wrong Number [*Telecommunications*] (TEL)
WN............ Wynn's International, Inc. [*NYSE symbol*] (SPSG)
WN............ Wynn's Intl [*NYSE symbol*] (TTSB)
Wn 2d......... Washington Reports, Second Series [*A publication*] (DLA)
WNA........... Napaskiak [*Alaska*] [*Airport symbol*] (OAG)
WNA........... Napaskiak, AK [*Location identifier FAA*] (FAAL)
WNa........... Nashotah House, Nashotah, WI [*Library symbol Library of Congress*] (LCLS)
WNA........... Wa National Army [*Myanmar*] [*Political party*] (EY)
WNA........... Washington [*DC*] National Airport [*FAA*]
WNA........... Wedge Nozzle Assembly
WNA........... Welsh Netball Association (DBA)
WNA........... Winter, North Atlantic [*Vessel load line mark*]
WNA........... Wireless Network Access
WNA........... World Nature Association (EA)
WNAA.......... Greensboro, NC [*FM radio station call letters*]
WNAAA......... Women of the National Agricultural Aviation Association (EA)
WNAB.......... Nashville, TN [*Television station call letters*]
WNAB.......... Weekly Newspaper Advertising Bureau [*British*] (BI)
WNAC.......... Providence, RI [*Television station call letters*]
WNACFWB....... Woman's National Auxiliary Convention of Free Will Baptists (EA)
WNAE.......... Warren, PA [*AM radio station call letters*]
WNAF.......... Women's National Aquatic Forum (EA)
WNAH.......... Nashville, TN [*AM radio station call letters*]
WNAI.......... Word and Number Assessment Inventory [*Aptitude test*]
WNAK.......... Nanticoke, PA [*AM radio station call letters*]
WNAL.......... Gadsden, AL [*Television station call letters*]
WNAM.......... Neenah-Menasha, WI [*AM radio station call letters*]
WNAP.......... Indianapolis, IN [*FM radio station call letters*]
WNAP.......... Norristown, PA [*AM radio station call letters*]
WNAP.......... Washington [*DC*] National Airport
WNAR.......... Biometric Society, Western North American Region (EA)
WNAS.......... New Albany, IN [*FM radio station call letters*]
WNAT.......... Natchez, MS [*AM radio station call letters*]
WNAU.......... New Albany, MS [*AM radio station call letters*]
WNAV.......... Annapolis, MD [*AM radio station call letters*]
WNAW.......... North Adams, MA [*AM radio station call letters*]
WNAX.......... Yankton, SD [*AM radio station call letters*]
WNAX-FM....... Yankton, SD [*FM radio station call letters*]
WNAZ.......... Nashville, TN [*FM radio station call letters*]
WNB........... Will Not Be
WNB........... Winter Navigation Board
WNBA.......... Women's National Basketball Association [*Defunct*] (EA)
WNBA.......... Women's National Book Association (EA)
WNBA.......... World Ninepin Bowling Association [*Germany*] (EAIO)
WNBC.......... New York, NY [*Television station call letters*]
WNBF.......... Binghamton, NY [*AM radio station call letters*]
WNBH.......... New Bedford, MA [*AM radio station call letters*]
WNbH.......... New Berlin Memorial Hospital, New Berlin, WI [*Library symbol Library of Congress*] (LCLS)
WNBI.......... Park Falls, WI [*AM radio station call letters*]
WNBN.......... Meridian, MS [*AM radio station call letters*]
WNBP.......... Newburyport, MA [*AM radio station call letters*]
WNBR.......... Oriental, NC [*FM radio station call letters*]
WNBS.......... Murray, KY [*AM radio station call letters*]
WNBT.......... Wellsboro, PA [*AM radio station call letters*]
WNBT-FM....... Wellsboro, PA [*FM radio station call letters*]
WNBU.......... Concord, NH [*Television station call letters*] (RBYB)
WNBX-FM....... Lebanon, NH [*FM radio station call letters*] (RBYB)
WNBY.......... Newberry, MI [*AM radio station call letters*]
WNBY-FM....... Newberry, MI [*FM radio station call letters*]
WNBZ.......... Saranac Lake, NY [*AM radio station call letters*]
WNC........... Naval War College, Newport, RI [*OCLC symbol*] (OCLC)
WNC........... Wabash National [*NYSE symbol*] (TTSB)
WNC........... Wabash National Corp. [*NYSE symbol*] (SPSG)
WNC........... WAVES National Corp. [*An association*] (EA)
WNC........... Weak Neutral Current [*Chemistry*]
WNC........... Weekly Notes of Cases [*Pennsylvania*] [*A publication*] (DLA)
WNC........... Wencarro Resources Ltd. [*Vancouver Stock Exchange symbol*]
WNC........... Wenic Air Services [*Singapore*] [*ICAO designator*] (FAAC)
WNC........... Wilmington [*North Carolina*] [*Seismograph station code, US Geological Survey*] (SEIS)
WNC........... Women's National Commission [*British*] (EAIO)
WNCA.......... Siler City, NC [*AM radio station call letters*]
WN-CAELA...... Women's Network of the Council for Adult Education in Latin America [*See also RM-CEAAL*] [*Quito, Ecuador*] (EAIO)
WN (Calc)..... Calcutta Weekly Notes [*A publication*] (DLA)
WN Cas........ Weekly Notes of Cases [*Pennsylvania*] [*A publication*] (DLA)
WN Cas (PA)... Weekly Notes of Cases [*Pennsylvania*] [*A publication*] (DLA)
WNCB.......... Duluth, MN [*FM radio station call letters*]
WNCC.......... Barnesboro, PA [*AM radio station call letters*]
WNCCC......... Women's National Cancer Control Campaign [*British*]
WNCD.......... Niles, OH [*FM radio station call letters*]
WNCE-FM....... Palmyra, PA [*FM radio station call letters*] (RBYB)
WNCG.......... Clyde, OH [*FM radio station call letters*]
WNCI.......... Columbus, OH [*FM radio station call letters*]
WNCM.......... Atlantic Beach, FL [*AM radio station call letters*]
WNCM.......... Jacksonville, FL [*FM radio station call letters*]
WNCN.......... Goldsboro, NC [*Television station call letters*]
WNCO.......... Ashland, OH [*AM radio station call letters*]
WNCO-FM....... Ashland, OH [*FM radio station call letters*]
WNC (PA)...... Weekly Notes of Cases [*Pennsylvania*] [*A publication*] (DLA)
WNCQ.......... Morristown, NY [*FM radio station call letters*]
WNCQ.......... Watertown, NY [*AM radio station call letters*]
WNCR-AM....... Fair Bluff, NC [*AM radio station call letters*] (RBYB)
WNCS.......... Montpelier, VT [*FM radio station call letters*]
WNCT.......... Greenville, NC [*AM radio station call letters*]
WNCT-FM....... Greenville, NC [*FM radio station call letters*]
WNCT-TV....... Greenville, NC [*Television station call letters*]
WNCU.......... Durham, NC [*FM radio station call letters*]
WNCV.......... Niceville, FL [*FM radio station call letters*]
WNCW.......... Spindale, NC [*FM radio station call letters*]
WNCX.......... Cleveland, OH [*FM radio station call letters*]
WNCY-FM....... Neenah-Menasha, WI [*FM radio station call letters*] (RBYB)
WND........... Wind (KSC)
WND........... Windham [*New York*] [*Seismograph station code, US Geological Survey*] (SEIS)
WND........... Windmere Corp. [*NYSE symbol*] (SPSG)
WND........... Wound (MSA)
WNDA.......... Huntsville, AL [*FM radio station call letters*]
WNDB.......... Daytona Beach, FL [*AM radio station call letters*]
WNDC.......... Baton Rouge, LA [*AM radio station call letters*]
WNDC.......... Woman's National Democratic Club (EA)
WNDD.......... Silver Springs, FL [*FM radio station call letters*] (RBYB)
WNDE.......... Indianapolis, IN [*AM radio station call letters*]
WNDH.......... Napoleon, OH [*FM radio station call letters*]
WNDI.......... Sullivan, IN [*AM radio station call letters*]
WNDI-FM....... Sullivan, IN [*FM radio station call letters*]
WNDJ.......... White Stone, VA [*FM radio station call letters*]
WNDLS......... Windlass
WNDN.......... Salisbury, NC [*FM radio station call letters*]
WNDO.......... Weather Network Duty Officer [*Air Force*] (AFM)
WNDP.......... With No Down Payment [*Business term*] (WDAA)
WNDR.......... Syracuse, NY [*AM radio station call letters*]
WNDR.......... Winder
WNDR.......... Wonderware Corp. [*NASDAQ symbol*] (SAG)
WNDS.......... Derry, NH [*Television station call letters*]
WNDT-FM....... Alachua, FL [*FM radio station call letters*] (RBYB)
WNDU.......... South Bend, IN [*AM radio station call letters*]
WNDU-FM....... South Bend, IN [*FM radio station call letters*]
WNDU-TV....... South Bend, IN [*Television station call letters*]
wndw.......... Window (VRA)
WNDW.......... Window
WNDY.......... Crawfordsville, IN [*FM radio station call letters*]
WNDY-TV....... Marion, IN [*Television station call letters*] (RBYB)
WNDZ.......... Portage, IN [*AM radio station call letters*]
WNE........... Welsh National Eisteddfod (DAS)
WNE........... Western New England College, Springfield, MA [*OCLC symbol*] (OCLC)
WNE........... West Nile Encephalitis [*Medicine*] (DAVI)
WNEA.......... Newnan, GA [*AM radio station call letters*]
WNEB.......... Worcester, MA [*AM radio station call letters*]
WNEC.......... Henniker, NH [*FM radio station call letters*]
WNEC.......... Western New England College [*Springfield, MA*]
WNED.......... Buffalo, NY [*AM radio station call letters*]
WNED-FM....... Buffalo, NY [*FM radio station call letters*]
WNED-TV....... Buffalo, NY [*Television station call letters*]
WNEG.......... Toccoa, GA [*AM radio station call letters*]
WNEG-TV....... Toccoa, GA [*Television station call letters*]
WNEH.......... Greenwood, SC [*Television station call letters*]
WNEK.......... Springfield, MA [*FM radio station call letters*]
WNEL.......... Caguas, PR [*AM radio station call letters*]
WNelH......... New London Community Hospital, Health Science Library, New London, WI [*Library symbol Library of Congress*] (LCLS)
WNEM.......... Bay City, MI [*Television station call letters*]
WN (Eng)...... Weekly Notes of English Law Reports [*A publication*] (DLA)
WNEO.......... Alliance, OH [*Television station call letters*]
WNEP.......... Scranton, PA [*Television station call letters*]
WNEQ.......... Buffalo, NY [*Television station call letters*]
WNES.......... Central City, KY [*AM radio station call letters*]
WNET.......... Newark, NJ [*Television station call letters*]
WNEW.......... New York, NY [*FM radio station call letters*]
WNEX.......... Macon, GA [*AM radio station call letters*]
WNEZ.......... New Britain, CT [*AM radio station call letters*]
WNF........... Well-Nourished Female [*Medicine*]
WNF........... [*The*] Winfield Railroad Co. [*AAR code*]
WNFA.......... Port Huron, MI [*FM radio station call letters*]
WNFB.......... Lake City, FL [*FM radio station call letters*]
WNFC.......... Willie Nelson Fan Club (EA)
WNFGA......... Woman's National Farm and Garden Association (EA)
WNFK.......... Perry, FL [*FM radio station call letters*]
WNFL.......... Green Bay, WI [*AM radio station call letters*]
WNFM.......... Reedsburg, WI [*FM radio station call letters*]
WNFM.......... World Nuclear Fuel Market (NRCH)
WNFO.......... Ridgeland, SC [*AM radio station call letters*]
WNFQ.......... Newberry, FL [*FM radio station call letters*]
WNFR.......... Sandusky, MI [*FM radio station call letters*]
WNFR.......... Winifrede Railroad Co. [*AAR code*]
WNFT.......... Jacksonville, FL [*Television station call letters*]
WNFZ.......... Oak Ridge, TN [*FM radio station call letters*]
WNG........... Wang Laboratories, Inc., Lowell, MA [*OCLC symbol*] (OCLC)
WNG........... Warning (AFM)
WNG........... Washington Natural Gas Co. [*NYSE symbol*] (SPSG)
WNG........... Weighing
WNG........... West New Guinea
WNG........... Wing [*of a ship*] (DS)
WNG........... Wing Airways (Pty) Ltd. [*South Africa ICAO designator*] (FAAC)
WNG........... Wingst [*Federal Republic of Germany*] [*Geomagnetic observatory code*]

WNG .... Wiring (IAA)
WNGA .... Nashville, GA [*AM radio station call letters*]
WNGA .... Wholesale Nursery Growers of America (EA)
WNGC .... Athens, GA [*FM radio station call letters*]
WNGGA .... Welsh National Gymanfa Ganu Association (EA)
WNGM .... Athens, GA [*Television station call letters*]
WNGN .... Hoosick Falls, NY [*FM radio station call letters*]
WNGO .... Mayfield, KY [*AM radio station call letters*]
WNGPr .... Wash Nat'l Gas 7.45%Sr II Pfd [*NYSE symbol*] (TTSB)
WNGPrA .... Wash Nat'l Gas 8.50%Sr III Pfd [*NYSE symbol*] (TTSB)
WNGS .... Springville, NY [*Television station call letters*]
WNGX .... Fort Ann, NY [*FM radio station call letters*]
WNGZ .... Montour Falls, NY [*FM radio station call letters*]
WNH .... Western National [*NYSE symbol*] (TTSB)
WNH .... Western National Corp. [*NYSE symbol*] (SAG)
WNH .... Whiteface [*New Hampshire*] [*Seismograph station code, US Geological Survey*] (SEIS)
WNHA .... Concord, NH [*AM radio station call letters*]
WNHB .... Lake City, MI [*FM radio station call letters*] (RBYB)
WNHC .... New Haven, CT [*AM radio station call letters*]
WNHI .... Belmont, NH [*FM radio station call letters*]
WNHP .... Washington Natural Heritage Program [*Washington State Department of Natural Resources*] [*Olympia*] [*Information service or system*] (IID)
WNHP .... Wyoming Natural Heritage Program [*Wyoming State Department of Environmental Quality*] [*Cheyenne*] [*Information service or system*] (IID)
WNHQ .... Peterborough, NH [*FM radio station call letters*]
WNHU .... West Haven, CT [*FM radio station call letters*]
WNHV .... White River Junction, VT [*AM radio station call letters*]
WNHW .... Nags Head, NC [*FM radio station call letters*]
WNI .... Wang Institute of Graduate Studies, Tyngsboro, MA [*OCLC symbol*] (OCLC)
WNI .... Windkracht Nederland Information Centre [*Netherlands Wind Energy Information Centre*] [*Nethergy Ltd.*] [*Database producer*] (IID)
WNI .... Women's National Institute [*Defunct*] (EA)
WNIB .... Chicago, IL [*FM radio station call letters*]
WNIC .... Dearborn, MI [*FM radio station call letters*]
WNIC .... Wide Area Network Interface Co-Processor [*Communications adapter*] (PCM)
WNIE-FM .... Freeport, IL [*FM radio station call letters*] (RBYB)
WNIJ .... Rockford, IL [*FM radio station call letters*]
WNIK .... Arecibo, PR [*AM radio station call letters*]
WNIK-FM .... Arecibo, PR [*FM radio station call letters*]
WNIL .... Niles, MI [*AM radio station call letters*]
WNIM .... Wide-Area-Network Module [*Telecommunications*]
WNIN .... Evansville, IN [*FM radio station call letters*]
WNINTEL .... Warning Notice: Sensitive Intelligence Sources and Methods Involved (MCD)
WNIN-TV .... Evansville, IN [*Television station call letters*]
WNIO .... Niles, OH [*AM radio station call letters*] (RBYB)
WNIQ-FM .... Sterling, IL [*FM radio station call letters*] (RBYB)
WNIR .... Kent, OH [*FM radio station call letters*]
WNIS .... Norfolk, VA [*AM radio station call letters*]
WNIT .... South Bend, IN [*Television station call letters*]
WNIU .... De Kalb, IL [*FM radio station call letters*]
WNIV .... Atlanta, GA [*AM radio station call letters*]
WNIW-FM .... LaSalle, IL [*FM radio station call letters*] (RBYB)
WNIX .... Greenville, MS [*AM radio station call letters*]
WNIZ .... Zion, IL [*FM radio station call letters*]
WNJA .... Jamestown, NY [*FM radio station call letters*]
WNJB .... Bridgeton, NJ [*FM radio station call letters*]
WNJB .... New Brunswick, NJ [*Television station call letters*]
WNJC .... Washington Township, NJ [*AM radio station call letters*]
WNJM-FM .... Manahawkin, NJ [*FM radio station call letters*] (RBYB)
WNJN .... Atlantic City, NJ [*FM radio station call letters*]
WNJN .... Montclair, NJ [*Television station call letters*]
WNJP .... Sussex, NJ [*FM radio station call letters*]
WNJR .... Newark, NJ [*AM radio station call letters*]
WNJS .... Berlin, NJ [*FM radio station call letters*]
WNJS .... Camden, NJ [*Television station call letters*]
WNJT .... Trenton, NJ [*Television station call letters*]
WNJT-FM .... Trenton, NJ [*FM radio station call letters*]
WNJU .... Linden, NJ [*Television station call letters*]
WNJW .... Franklin Lakes, NJ [*FM radio station call letters*] (RBYB)
WNJX .... Mayaguez, PR [*Television station call letters*]
WNJY .... Delphi, IN [*FM radio station call letters*]
WNJZ-FM .... Cape May Court House, NJ [*FM radio station call letters*] (RBYB)
WNKC .... Kimberly-Clark Corp., Research and Engineering Library, Neenah, WI [*Library symbol Library of Congress*] (LCLS)
WNKI .... Corning, NY [*FM radio station call letters*]
WNKJ .... Hopkinsville, KY [*FM radio station call letters*]
WNKO .... Newark, OH [*FM radio station call letters*]
WNKR .... Williamstown, KY [*FM radio station call letters*]
WNKS-FM .... Charlotte, NC [*FM radio station call letters*] (RBYB)
WNKU .... Highland Heights, KY [*FM radio station call letters*]
WNKV .... St. Johnsbury, VT [*FM radio station call letters*]
WNKX .... Centerville, TN [*AM radio station call letters*]
WNKX-FM .... Centerville, TN [*FM radio station call letters*]
WNL .... Nicolet College, Learning Resources Center, Rhinelander, WI [*OCLC symbol*] (OCLC)
WNL .... Waveguide Nitrogen Load
WNL .... Windscale Nuclear Laboratories [*British*] (NUCP)
WNL .... Within Normal Limits [*Medicine*]
WNLA .... Indianola, MS [*AM radio station call letters*]
WNLA .... Witwatersrand Native Labour Association [*Nyasaland*]
WNLA-FM .... Indianola, MS [*FM radio station call letters*]
WNLC .... New London, CT [*AM radio station call letters*]
WNLE .... Fernadina Beach, FL [*FM radio station call letters*]
WNLK .... Norwalk, CT [*AM radio station call letters*]
WNLL .... Womens's National Loyal League [*Established by Elizabeth Cady Stanton and Susan B. Anthony*]
WNLN .... Western Nigeria Legal Notice [*A publication*] (DLA)
WNLR .... Churchville, VA [*AM radio station call letters*]
WNLR .... Weighted Nonlinear Regression [*Mathematics*]
WNLR .... Western Nigeria Law Reports [*A publication*] (DLA)
WNLS .... Tallahassee, FL [*AM radio station call letters*]
WNLSC .... Women's National Land Service Corps [*World War I*] [*British*]
WNLT .... Harrison, OH [*FM radio station call letters*]
WNM .... Warm Neutral Medium [*Astrophysics*]
WNM .... Washington National Monument
WNM .... Well-Nourished Male [*Medicine*]
WNM .... White Noise Making [*Psychology*]
WNMA .... Washington National Monument Association (EA)
WNMB .... North Myrtle Beach, SC [*FM radio station call letters*]
WNMC .... Traverse City, MI [*FM radio station call letters*]
WNMC .... Weather Network Management Center [*Air Force*] (AFM)
WNMH .... Northfield, MA [*FM radio station call letters*]
WN Misc .... Weekly Notes, Miscellaneous [*A publication*] (DLA)
WNMP .... Westwood Corp. [*NASDAQ symbol*] (SAG)
WNMT .... Garden City, GA [*AM radio station call letters*]
WNMU .... Marquette, MI [*FM radio station call letters*]
WNMU-TV .... Marquette, MI [*Television station call letters*]
WNMX-AM .... Charlotte, NC [*AM radio station call letters*] (RBYB)
WNMX-FM .... Waxhaw, NC [*FM radio station call letters*] (RBYB)
WNN .... World News Network [*In Muriel Dobbin's novel "Going Live"*]
WNNB .... Wayne Bancorp, Inc. [*NASDAQ symbol*] (SAG)
WNNC .... Newton, NC [*AM radio station call letters*]
WNND .... Fuquay Varina, NC [*FM radio station call letters*]
WNNE .... Hartford, VT [*Television station call letters*]
WNNH .... Henniker, NH [*FM radio station call letters*]
WNNI .... Christiansburg, VA [*AM radio station call letters*] (RBYB)
WNNJ .... Newton, NJ [*AM radio station call letters*]
WNNJ-FM .... Newton, NJ [*FM radio station call letters*]
WNNK .... Harrisburg, PA [*FM radio station call letters*]
WNNN .... Canton, NJ [*FM radio station call letters*]
WNNO .... Wisconsin Dells, WI [*AM radio station call letters*]
WNNO-FM .... Wisconsin Dells, WI [*FM radio station call letters*]
WNNR .... Sodus, NY [*FM radio station call letters*]
WNNS .... Springfield, IL [*FM radio station call letters*]
WNNT .... Warsaw, VA [*AM radio station call letters*]
WNNT-FM .... Warsaw, VA [*FM radio station call letters*]
WNNV .... Aguada, PR [*FM radio station call letters*]
WNNW .... Salem, NH [*AM radio station call letters*]
WNNX .... Atlanta, GA [*FM radio station call letters*]
WNNZ .... Westfield, MA [*AM radio station call letters*]
WNO .... Wa National Organization [*Myanmar*] [*Political party*] (EY)
WNO .... Welsh National Opera
WNO .... Wharton & Northern Railroad Co. [*Later, WHN*] [*AAR code*]
WNO .... Wrong Number [*Telecommunications*] (TEL)
WNOE-FM .... New Orleans, LA [*FM radio station call letters*]
WNOG .... Naples, FL [*AM radio station call letters*]
WNOG-FM .... Naples, FL [*FM radio station call letters*]
WNOI .... Flora, IL [*FM radio station call letters*]
WNOK .... Columbia, SC [*FM radio station call letters*]
WNOL .... New Orleans, LA [*Television station call letters*]
WNOO .... Chattanooga, TN [*AM radio station call letters*]
WNOP .... Newport, KY [*AM radio station call letters*]
WNOR .... Norfolk, VA [*AM radio station call letters*]
WNOR-FM .... Norfolk, VA [*FM radio station call letters*]
WNOS .... New Bern, NC [*AM radio station call letters*]
WNOV .... Milwaukee, WI [*AM radio station call letters*]
WNOW .... Mint Hill, NC [*AM radio station call letters*]
WNOX .... Loudon, TN [*FM radio station call letters*]
WNOZ .... Aguadilla, PR [*AM radio station call letters*]
WNP .... Naga [*Phillipines*] [*Airport symbol*] (OAG)
WNP .... Washington Nuclear Plant (NRCH)
WNP .... Welsh Nationalist Party (DI)
WNP .... Westland New Post [*Terrorist organization*] [*Belgium*] (EY)
WNP .... Will Not Proceed
WNP .... Will Not Process
WNP .... Wire Nonpayment
WNPB .... Morgantown, WV [*Television station call letters*]
WNPC .... Newport, TN [*AM radio station call letters*]
WNPC .... Women's National Press Club [*Later, WPC*] (EA)
WNPC-FM .... Newport, TN [*FM radio station call letters*]
WNPDL .... Windscale Nuclear Power Development Laboratories [*British*] (NUCP)
WNPE .... Watertown, NY [*Television station call letters*]
WNPI .... Norwood, NY [*Television station call letters*]
WNPL-FM .... Mount Juliet, TN [*FM radio station call letters*] (RBYB)
WNPQ .... New Philadelphia, OH [*FM radio station call letters*]
WNPR .... Norwich, CT [*FM radio station call letters*]
WNPT .... Linden, AL [*FM radio station call letters*]
WNPV .... Lansdale, PA [*AM radio station call letters*]
WNPW .... Wide, Notched P Wave [*Cardiology*]
WNQM .... Nashville, TN [*AM radio station call letters*]
WNR .... Weapons Neutron Research Facility [*Los Alamos*]
WNR .... Western NORAD Region
WNR .... Windorah [*Australia Airport symbol*] (OAG)
WNR .... World New Religion [*An association*] (EA)

WNRB .... Boston, MA [*AM radio station call letters*] (RBYB)
WNRC .... Dudley, MA [*FM radio station call letters*]
WNRC .... Washington National Records Center [*GSA*] (AABC)
WNRC .... Women's National Republican Club (EA)
WNRCEN .... Washington National Records Center [*GSA*]
WNRE .... Whiteshell Nuclear Research Establishment [*Atomic Energy of Canada Ltd.*] [*Research center*]
WNRG .... Grundy, VA [*AM radio station call letters*]
WNRI .... Woonsocket, RI [*AM radio station call letters*]
WNRJ .... Circleville, OH [*AM radio station call letters*]
WNRK .... Newark, DE [*AM radio station call letters*]
WNRM .... Women in Natural Resources Management Program (EERA)
WNRN-FM ...... Charlottesville, VA [*FM radio station call letters*] (RBYB)
WNRQ .... Pittsburgh, PA [*FM radio station call letters*] (RBYB)
WNRR .... Bellevue, OH [*FM radio station call letters*]
WNRS .... Herkimer, NY [*AM radio station call letters*]
WNRT .... Manati, PR [*FM radio station call letters*]
WNRV .... Narrows, VA [*AM radio station call letters*]
WNRX .... Tupelo, MS [*AM radio station call letters*] (RBYB)
WNRZ-FM ...... Dickson, TN [*FM radio station call letters*] (RBYB)
WNS .... Nawab Shah [*Pakistan*] [*Airport symbol*] (OAG)
WNS .... Women's News Service
WNS .... Worldwide News Service. Jewish Telegraphic Agency (BJA)
WNS .... Wren Resources Ltd. [*Vancouver Stock Exchange symbol*]
WNSA .... Woman's National Sabbath Alliance [*Defunct*]
WNSB .... Norfolk, VA [*FM radio station call letters*]
WNSC .... Rock Hill, SC [*FM radio station call letters*]
wnsct .... Wainscot (VRA)
WNSC-TV ...... Rock Hill, SC [*Television station call letters*]
WNSEA .... Wood Naval Stores Export Association
WNSH .... Beverly, MA [*AM radio station call letters*]
WNSI-AM ...... Jacksonville, AL [*AM radio station call letters*] (RBYB)
WNSL .... A. W. Wright Nuclear Structure Laboratory [*Yale University*] [*Research center*] (RCD)
WNSL .... Laurel, MS [*FM radio station call letters*]
WNSN .... South Bend, IN [*FM radio station call letters*]
WNSP .... Bay Minette, AL [*FM radio station call letters*]
WNSR .... Nashville, IL [*FM radio station call letters*]
WNSR .... West Nova Scotia Regiment (DMA)
WNSS-AM ...... Syracuse, NY [*AM radio station call letters*] (RBYB)
WNST .... Moncks Corner, SC [*FM radio station call letters*] (RBYB)
WNSW .... Brewer, ME [*AM radio station call letters*]
WNSX-FM ...... Poughkeepsie, NY [*FM radio station call letters*] (RBYB)
WNT .... Washington National [*NYSE symbol*] (TTSB)
WNT .... Washington National Corp. [*NYSE symbol*] (SPSG)
Wn T .... Washington Territory Reports [*1854-88*] [*A publication*] (ILCA)
WNT .... Waste Neutralization Tank [*Nuclear energy*] (NRCH)
WNT .... What's New in Travel [*CompuServe Information Service*] [*Information service or system*] (CRD)
WNT .... World News Tonight [*Television program*]
WNTA .... Rockford, IL [*AM radio station call letters*]
WNTC .... Chandler, IN [*FM radio station call letters*]
WNTC .... Theda Clark Memorial Hospital, Neenah, WI [*Library symbol Library of Congress*] (LCLS)
WNTE .... Mansfield, PA [*FM radio station call letters*]
WNTF .... Western Naval Task Force [*Navy*]
WNTH .... Winnetka, IL [*FM radio station call letters*]
WNTI .... Hackettstown, NJ [*FM radio station call letters*]
WNTJ .... Johnstown, PA [*AM radio station call letters*]
WNTK .... New London, NH [*FM radio station call letters*]
WNTK .... Newport, NH [*AM radio station call letters*]
WNTL .... Indian Head, MD [*AM radio station call letters*]
WNTM .... Mobile, AL [*AM radio station call letters*]
WNTN .... Newton, MA [*AM radio station call letters*]
WNTO-TV ...... Daytona Beach, FL [*TV station call letters*] (RBYB)
WNTPr .... Washington Natl $2.50 Cv Pfd [*NYSE symbol*] (TTSB)
WNTQ .... Syracuse, NY [*FM radio station call letters*]
WNTR .... Cumberland, MD [*AM radio station call letters*]
WNTS .... Beach Grove, IN [*AM radio station call letters*]
WNTT .... Tazewell, TN [*AM radio station call letters*]
WNTV .... Greenville, SC [*Television station call letters*]
WNTW .... Winchester, VA [*AM radio station call letters*]
WNTX .... Allegan, MI [*FM radio station call letters*] (RBYB)
WNTY .... Southington, CT [*AM radio station call letters*]
WNTZ .... Natchez, MS [*Television station call letters*]
WNU .... Western Newspaper Union
WNUA .... Chicago, IL [*FM radio station call letters*]
WNUB .... Northfield, VT [*FM radio station call letters*]
WNUC .... Wethersfield Township, NY [*FM radio station call letters*]
WNUR .... Evanston, IL [*FM radio station call letters*]
WNUS .... Belpre, OH [*FM radio station call letters*]
WNUT .... Walnut Financial Services [*NASDAQ symbol*] (TTSB)
WNUT .... Walnut Financial Services, Inc. [*NASDAQ symbol*] (SAG)
WNUU .... Garrison, KY [*FM radio station call letters*]
WNUV .... Baltimore, MD [*Television station call letters*]
WNUY .... Bluffton, IN [*FM radio station call letters*]
WNUZ .... Talladega, AL [*AM radio station call letters*]
WNV .... Wehrmachtnachrichtenverbindungen [*Armed Forces Signal Communications*] [*German military - World War II*]
WNV .... West Nile Virus
WNVA .... Norton, VA [*AM radio station call letters*]
WNVA-FM ...... Norton, VA [*FM radio station call letters*]
WNVC .... Fairfax, VA [*Television station call letters*]
WNVE .... South Bristol Township, NY [*FM radio station call letters*] (RBYB)
WNVL .... Nicholasville, KY [*AM radio station call letters*]
WNVR .... Vernon Hills, IL [*AM radio station call letters*]
WNVT .... Goldvein, VA [*Television station call letters*]
WNVY .... Cantonment, FL [*AM radio station call letters*]
WNVZ .... Norfolk, VA [*FM radio station call letters*]
WNW .... Superior Public Library, Superior, WI [*OCLC symbol*] (OCLC)
WNW .... Wenatchee [*Washington*] [*Seismograph station code, US Geological Survey*] (SEIS)
WNW .... West by North West [*Direction*] (EERA)
WNW .... West-Northwest
WNW .... Wingwork Aviation [*British ICAO designator*] (FAAC)
WNWC .... Madison, WI [*FM radio station call letters*]
WNWI .... Valparaiso, IN [*AM radio station call letters*]
WNWK .... Newark, NJ [*FM radio station call letters*]
WNWN .... Coldwater, MI [*FM radio station call letters*]
WNWN .... Portage, MI [*AM radio station call letters*] (RBYB)
WNWO .... Toledo, OH [*Television station call letters*]
WNWR .... Philadelphia, PA [*AM radio station call letters*] (RBYB)
WNWS .... Brownsville, TN [*AM radio station call letters*]
WNWS .... Jackson, TN [*FM radio station call letters*]
WnWste .... Western Waste Industries [*Associated Press*] (SAG)
WNWV .... Elyria, OH [*FM radio station call letters*]
WNWWD .... West-Northwestward (FAAC)
WNWZ .... Germantown, TN [*AM radio station call letters*]
WNXR .... Iron River, WI [*FM radio station call letters*] (RBYB)
WNXT .... Portsmouth, OH [*AM radio station call letters*]
WNXT-FM ...... Portsmouth, OH [*FM radio station call letters*]
WNY .... Burnie-Wynward [*Tasmania*] [*Airport symbol*] (AD)
WNY .... Washington [*DC*] Naval Yard
WNY .... Wilmington [*New York*] [*Seismograph station code, US Geological Survey*] (SEIS)
WNY .... Wynyard [*Australia Airport symbol*] (OAG)
WNYB .... Buffalo, NY [*Television station call letters*]
WNYC .... New York, NY [*AM radio station call letters*]
WNYC-FM ...... New York, NY [*FM radio station call letters*]
WNYC-TV ...... New York, NY [*Television station call letters*]
WNYE .... New York, NY [*FM radio station call letters*]
WNYE-TV ...... New York, NY [*Television station call letters*]
WNYG .... Babylon, NY [*AM radio station call letters*]
WNYHSL .... Western New York Health Science Librarians [*Library network*]
WNYK .... Nyack, NY [*FM radio station call letters*]
WNYLRC .... Western New York Library Resources Council [*Buffalo, NY*] [*Library network*]
WNYNRC .... Western New York Nuclear Research Center Reactor (NRCH)
WNYO .... Oswego, NY [*FM radio station call letters*]
WNYO-TV ...... Buffalo, NY [*TV station call letters*] (RBYB)
WNYQ-FM ...... Queensbury, NY [*FM radio station call letters*] (RBYB)
WNYR .... Waterloo, NY [*FM radio station call letters*]
WNYS .... Canton, NY [*AM radio station call letters*]
WNYS .... Syracuse, NY [*Television station call letters*]
WNYT .... Albany, NY [*Television station call letters*]
WNYU .... New York, NY [*FM radio station call letters*]
WNYV .... Whitehall, NY [*FM radio station call letters*]
WNYW .... New York, NY [*Television station call letters*]
WNZ .... Wairakei [*New Zealand*] [*Seismograph station code, US Geological Survey*] (SEIS)
WNZE .... Largo, FL [*AM radio station call letters*]
WNZK .... Dearborn Heights, MI [*AM radio station call letters*]
WNZN .... Lorain, OH [*FM radio station call letters*]
WNZR .... Mount Vernon, OH [*FM radio station call letters*]
WNZS .... Jacksonville, FL [*AM radio station call letters*]
WNZT .... Columbia, PA [*AM radio station call letters*]
WNZZ-AM ...... Montgomery, AL [*AM radio station call letters*] (RBYB)
WO .... Wait Order
WO .... Walkover
WO .... Walter Owen Bentley [*Automotive engineer*] [*British*]
WO .... Warning Order
WO .... War Office [*British*]
WO .... War Orientation [*Navy*]
WO .... Warrant Officer [*Usually in combination with numbers to denote serviceman's grade*] [*Military*]
WO .... Washington Office (FAAC)
WO .... Wash Out [*Medicine*]
W/O .... Water-dispersed-in-Oil [*emulsion*]
W/O .... Water-in-Oil
WO .... Water Outlet Gasket [*Automotive engineering*]
w/o .... Week Of (WDMC)
wo .... Weeks Old [*Medicine*] (MEDA)
WO .... Weeks Old [*Preceded by a number*] [*Neonatology*] (DAVI)
W/O .... Weight Percent (SAA)
WO .... Welfare Officer [*British military*] (DMA)
WO .... Welsh Office (DCTA)
WO .... Western Operation
W/O .... West Of [*In outdoor advertising*] (WDMC)
WO .... White Oval [*on Jupiter*]
WO .... Wind Offset
WO .... Wipe Out (MSA)
WO .... Wireless Operator
WO .... Without (AFM)
W/O .... Without (NITA)
w/o .... Without (IDOE)
wo .... Wollastonite [*CIPW classification*] [*Geology*]
WO .... Women
WO .... Women Outdoors (EA)
WO .... Women's Reserve, Ordnance Duties [*USNR officer designation*]
WO .... Woodfree Off-Machine Paper (DGA)

W/O .... Worked Off (DGA)
WO .... Working Overseer (ADA)
WO .... Work Order
WO .... World Airways (GAVI)
WO .... World Airways [*ICAO designator*] (AD)
W/O .... Write-Off [*Accounting*]
WO .... Write Once [*Computer science*] (CDE)
WO .... Write Only
WO .... Write Out
WO .... Writer Officer [*British military*] (DMA)
W/O .... Written Order [*Medicine*]
WO1 .... Warrant Officer One [*Army*]
WO3DC .... World Ozone Data Center [*Marine science*] (OSRA)
WOA .... Warrant Officers Association of the United States of America [*Defunct*] (EA)
WOA .... Washington Office on Africa (EA)
WOA .... Weapons Orientation Advanced (AFM)
WOA .... Web Offset Association (EA)
WOA .... Weight of Authority [*Legal shorthand*] (LWAP)
WOA .... Work Order Authorization (MCD)
WOA .... World Airways, Inc. [*ICAO designator*] (FAAC)
WOA .... WorldCorp., Inc. [*NYSE symbol*] (SPSG)
WOAB .... Ozark, AL [*FM radio station call letters*]
WOAC .... Canton, OH [*Television station call letters*]
WOAC .... Warrant Officer Advanced Course [*Army*] (INF)
WOAD .... Jackson, MS [*AM radio station call letters*]
WOAD .... World Offshore Accident Data
WOAH .... World Organization of Automotive Hobbyists
WOAI .... San Antonio, TX [*AM radio station call letters*]
WOAK .... La Grange, GA [*FM radio station call letters*]
WOAL .... Pippa Passes, KY [*FM radio station call letters*]
WOAM .... Peoria, IL [*AM radio station call letters*]
WO & HPS .... Wall Oven and Hot Plates [*Classified advertising*] (ADA)
WOAP .... Owosso, MI [*AM radio station call letters*]
WOAR .... Women Organized Against Rape
WOAS .... Ontonagon, MI [*FM radio station call letters*]
WOAS .... Wave-Off Advisory System [*Aircraft carrier*] [*Navy*]
WOASH .... Women Organised Against Sexual Harassment [*British*] (DI)
WOAY .... Oak Hill, WV [*AM radio station call letters*]
WOAY-TV .... Oak Hill, WV [*Television station call letters*]
WOAZ-FM .... Lowell, MA [*FM radio station call letters*] (RBYB)
WOB .... Walter Owen Bentley [*Automotive engineer*] [*British*]
WOB .... Washed Overboard [*Shipping*]
WOB .... Weight on Bit [*Drilling technology*]
WOB .... White on Black (DGA)
WOB .... Without Optical Brightener [*Biochemistry*]
WOB .... Woburn [*Parish in England*]
WOB .... Work of Breathing [*Medicine*] (DAVI)
WOB .... Work Order Bin (MCD)
WOBB .... Tifton, GA [*FM radio station call letters*]
WOBC .... Oberlin, OH [*FM radio station call letters*]
WOBC .... Waveguide Operating below Cutoff
WOBG .... Clarksburg, WV [*AM radio station call letters*]
WOBG .... Salem, WV [*FM radio station call letters*]
WOBL .... Oberlin, OH [*AM radio station call letters*]
WOBM .... Lakewood, NJ [*AM radio station call letters*]
WOBM .... Toms River, NJ [*FM radio station call letters*]
WOBN .... Westerville, OH [*FM radio station call letters*]
W O BNDR .... Without Binder [*Freight*]
WOBO .... Batavia, OH [*FM radio station call letters*]
W/OBO .... Without Blowout (MSA)
WOBO .... World Bottle [*Ecology*]
WOBO .... World Organization of Building Officials (EA)
WOBR .... Wanchese, NC [*AM radio station call letters*]
WOBR-FM .... Wanchese, NC [*FM radio station call letters*]
WOBS-AM .... Jacksonville, FL [*AM radio station call letters*] (RBYB)
WOBT .... Rhinelander, WI [*AM radio station call letters*]
WOC .... Davenport, IA [*AM radio station call letters*]
WOC .... Waiting on Cement
WOC .... Water-Oil Contact
WOC .... Wilshire Oil Co. of Texas [*NYSE symbol*] (SPSG)
WOC .... Wilshire Oil Texas [*NYSE symbol*] (TTSB)
WOC .... Wing Operations Center (CINC)
WOC .... Win Over Communism [*A fund-raising subsidiary of the Unification Church*]
WOC .... Without Compensation (ADA)
woc .... Without Compensation (ODBW)
WOC .... Women's Ordination Conference (EA)
WOC .... Woodfree Off-Machine Coated Paper (DGA)
WOC .... Woodfree Offset Cartridge Paper (DGA)
WOC .... Wood's Oriental Cases [*Malaya*] [*A publication*] (DLA)
WOC .... Work and Occupations [*A publication*] (BRI)
WOC .... Work Order Control (MCD)
WOC .... World Oceanographic Center (MSC)
WOCA .... Ocala, FL [*AM radio station call letters*]
WOCA .... Who Owns Corporate America [*A publication*]
WOCA .... World Outside Centrally Planned Economic Area [*Nuclear energy*] (NUCP)
WOCA .... World Outside Communist Areas
WOCAR .... Aviation Warrant Officer Career Course [*Army*]
WOCC .... Corydon, IN [*AM radio station call letters*]
WOCC .... Worldwide Operations Control Center [*United States Information Agency*]
WOCCI .... War Office Central Card Index [*British military*] (DMA)
WOccM .... Memorial Hospital at Oconomowoc, Oconomowoc, WI [*Library symbol Library of Congress*] (LCLS)
WOccR .... Redemptionist Seminary, Oconomowoc, WI [*Library symbol Library of Congress*] (LCLS)
WOCCU .... World Council of Credit Unions [*Madison, WI*] (EA)
WOCD .... Amsterdam, NY [*Television station call letters*]
WOCE .... World Ocean Circulation Experiment [*World Climate Research Programme*]
WOCE-IPO .... WOCE [*World Ocean Circulation Experiment*] International Project Office [*Marine science*] (OSRA)
WOCE-NEG .... WOCE [*World Ocean Circulation Experiment*] Numerical Experimentation Group [*Marine science*] (OSRA)
WOCE-SSG .... WOCE [*World Ocean Circulation Experiment*] Scientific Steering Group [*Marine science*] (OSRA)
WOCG .... Huntsville, AL [*FM radio station call letters*]
WOCIT .... We Oppose Computers in Tournaments [*A chess players' group, formed in 1983*]
WOCL .... De Land, FL [*FM radio station call letters*]
WOCL .... War Office Casualty List [*British military*] (DMA)
WOCLS .... World Ocean and Cruise Liner Society (EA)
WOCMDC .... Warrant Officer Candidate Military Development Course
WOCN .... Miami, FL [*AM radio station call letters*]
WOCN .... South Yamouth, MA [*FM radio station call letters*]
WOCO .... Oconto, WI [*AM radio station call letters*]
WOCO .... World Council of Service Clubs [*New Zealand*] (EAIO)
WOCO .... World Council of Young Men's Service Clubs (EA)
WOCO-FM .... Oconto, WI [*FM radio station call letters*]
WOCP .... World Organization of China Painters (EA)
WOCQ .... Berlin, MD [*FM radio station call letters*]
WOCR .... Olivet, MI [*FM radio station call letters*]
WOCS .... Work Order Control System (MCD)
WOCT .... Baltimore, MD [*FM radio station call letters*]
WOCT .... WAC [*Women's Army Corps*] Officer Candidate Test (AABC)
WOCU .... War on Community Ugliness [*Program*] [*Defunct*] (EA)
WOCV .... Oneida, TN [*AM radio station call letters*]
WOCW .... Parris Island, SC [*FM radio station call letters*]
WOD .... Washington & Old Dominion R. R. [*AAR code*]
WOD .... Wind over Deck (MCD)
WOD .... Without Dependents [*Military*] (AFM)
WOD .... Woodgate Air Services [*British ICAO designator*] (FAAC)
WODA .... World Organization of Dredging Associations (EA)
WODADIBOF .... Workshop on the Determination of Anti-Epileptic Drugs in Body Fluids
WODC .... Virginia Beach, VA [*FM radio station call letters*]
WODC .... Women's Olympic Distance Committee [*Later, WDC*] (EA)
WODC .... World Ozone Data Center [*Marine science*] (OSRA)
WODC .... World Ozone Data Centre (EERA)
WODCON .... World Dredging Conference
WODCON .... World Organization of Dredging Associations Proceedings of World Dredging Congress [*A publication*] (EAAP)
WODD .... Wave-Off Decision Device (MCD)
WODD .... World Oceanographic Data Display
WODDIN .... Worldwide On-Line Data and Document Intelligence System
WODE .... Easton, PA [*FM radio station call letters*]
WODECO .... Western Offshore Drilling & Exploration Co.
WODI-AM .... Brookneal, VA [*AM radio station call letters*] (RBYB)
WODJ .... Greenville, MI [*FM radio station call letters*]
WODL .... Birmingham, AL [*FM radio station call letters*]
WODS .... Boston, MA [*FM radio station call letters*]
WODT .... New Orleans, LA [*AM radio station call letters*] (RBYB)
WODX .... Marco Island, FL [*AM radio station call letters*]
WODY .... Fieldale, VA [*AM radio station call letters*]
WODZ .... Rome, NY [*AM radio station call letters*]
WODZ-FM .... Rome, NY [*FM radio station call letters*]
WOE .... Warhead Output Evaluation (MCD)
WOE .... Watchdogs on Environment
WOE .... Weapon Optical Effects
WOE .... Withdrawal of Enthusiasm [*Airline pilots objection to "Welcome aboard" talks*]
WOE .... Without Enclosure (MCD)
WOE .... Without Equipment
WOE .... Wound of Entry [*Medicine*]
W/OE & SP .... Without Equipment and Spare Parts
WOEC .... Warrant Officer Entry Course [*Military*] (INF)
WOEC-RC .... Warrant Office Entry Course, Reserve Component [*Army*] (INF)
WOEI .... Union City, IN [*FM radio station call letters*]
WOEL .... Elkton, MD [*FM radio station call letters*]
Woerner Adm'n .... Woerner's Treatise on the American Law of Administration [*A publication*] (DLA)
WOES .... Ovid-Elsie, MI [*FM radio station call letters*]
WOES .... Warrant Officer Education System
WOF .... Walk on Floor [*Ataxia*]
WOF .... Warmed-Over Flavor [*Food technology*]
WOF .... Widowed Oriental Female [*Classified advertising*]
WOF .... Work of Fracture [*Ceramic property*]
W of A .... [*The*] Western Railway of Alabama
WOFA .... Westinghouse Optimized Fuel Assembly [*Nuclear energy*] (NRCH)
WOFC .... Western Ohio Film Circuit [*Library network*]
WOFC .... Western Ohio Financial Corp. [*NASDAQ symbol*] (SAG)
WOFC .... Western Ohio Finl [*NASDAQ symbol*] (TTSB)
WOFE .... Rockwood, TN [*AM radio station call letters*]
WOFE-FM .... Rockwood, TN [*FM radio station call letters*]
WOFF .... Weight of Fuel Flow (MCD)
WOFI .... Wood Office Furniture Institute (EA)
WOFIWU .... World Federation of Industrial Workers' Unions

WOFL Orlando, FL [*Television station call letters*]
WOFL Wound Fluid [*Emergency Medicine*] (DAVI)
WOFM Mosinee, WI [*FM radio station call letters*]
WOFP Wearout Failure Period
WOFR Washington Court House, OH [*AM radio station call letters*]
WOFS Weather Observing and Forecasting System [*Air Force*] (MCD)
WOFT Warrant Officer Flight Training [*Army*] (INF)
W O FTTNGS Without Fittings [*Freight*]
WOFX Fairfield, OH [*FM radio station call letters*]
WOG Water-Oil-Gas (AAG)
WOG Weapon Order Generation [*Military*] (CAAL)
WOG Werner Oil & Gas Co. [*Vancouver Stock Exchange symbol*]
WOG Westernized Oriental Gentleman [*Singapore term for native following Western fashions*] [*Other translations include "Wily Oriental Gentleman" and "Wonderful Oriental Gentleman"*]
WOG With Other Goods [*Business term*]
wog With Other Goods (ODBW)
WOG Work Order Generator [*Military*]
WOG World Organization of Gastroenterology [*See also OMGE*] [*Edinburgh, Scotland*] (EAIO)
WOG Wrath of God [*Israeli counterterrorist group*]
WOGA Western Oil and Gas Association (EA)
WOGB-FM Kaukauna, WI [*FM radio station call letters*] (RBYB)
WOGK Ocala, FL [*FM radio station call letters*]
WOGL Philadelphia, PA [*FM radio station call letters*]
WOGO Hallie, WI [*AM radio station call letters*]
WOGR Charlotte, NC [*AM radio station call letters*]
WOGR-FM Salisbury, NC [*FM radio station call letters*] (RBYB)
WOGS Wrath of God Syndrome
WOGSC World Organisation of General Systems and Cybernetics [*Lytham St. Annes, Lancashire, England*] (EAIO)
WOGT East Ridge, TN [*FM radio station call letters*]
WOGX Ocala, FL [*Television station call letters*]
WOGY Germantown, TN [*FM radio station call letters*]
WOH War on Hunger [*Program*] (EA)
WOH Washington Office on Haiti (EA)
WOH Western Oklahoma Herbarium [*Southwest Oklahoma State University*]
WOH Wings of Hope [*An association*] (EA)
WOH Work on Hand [*Insurance*]
WOHC Chillicothe, OH [*FM radio station call letters*]
WOHC Warrant Officer Hospital Corps
WOHELO Work, Health, Love [*Camp Fire Girls slogan*]
WOHH Women's Organization of Hapoel Hamizrachi [*Later, EWA*] (EA)
WOHI East Liverpool, OH [*AM radio station call letters*]
WOHMA Waste Oil Heating Manufacturers Association (EA)
WOHP Portsmouth, OH [*FM radio station call letters*]
WOHP World Organization for Human Potential (EA)
WOHRC Women's Occupational Health Resource Center (EA)
WOHS Shelby, NC [*AM radio station call letters*]
WOHT Drew, MS [*FM radio station call letters*] (RBYB)
WOHZ Wheeling, WV [*AM radio station call letters*] (RBYB)
WOI Ames, IA [*AM radio station call letters*]
WOI Wealth of India [*A publication*]
WOI World of Invention [*A publication*]
WOI World Opportunities International (EA)
WOIC Columbia, SC [*AM radio station call letters*]
WOICE World Catalog of International Chemical Equipment [*A publication*]
WOI-FM Ames, IA [*FM radio station call letters*]
WOIO Shaker Heights, OH [*Television station call letters*]
WOIR Homestead, FL [*AM radio station call letters*]
WOIS Worn Out in Service [*Military*]
WOI-TV Ames, IA [*Television station call letters*]
WOIZ Guayanilla, PR [*AM radio station call letters*]
WOJAC World Organization for Jews from Arab Countries (EA)
WOJB Reserve, WI [*FM radio station call letters*]
WOJC Willys Overland Jeepster Club (EA)
WOJD World Organization of Jewish Deaf [*Tel Aviv, Israel*] (EAIO)
WOJG Bolivar, TN [*FM radio station call letters*]
WOJG Warrant Officer Junior Grade
WOJO Evanston, IL [*FM radio station call letters*]
WOJY Hampton, VA [*AM radio station call letters*]
WOK Kovar Air [*Czechoslovakia*] [*ICAO designator*] (FAAC)
WOK Wiener Oeffentlicher Kueche [*Viennese Open Kitchen*] [*Nonprofit temperance restaurant chain*] [*Austria*]
WOK Wokingham [*Municipal borough in England*]
WOK Wonken [*Venezuela*] [*Airport symbol*] (OAG)
WOKA Douglas, GA [*AM radio station call letters*]
WOKA-FM Douglas, GA [*FM radio station call letters*]
WOKB Winter Garden, FL [*AM radio station call letters*]
WOKC Okeechobee, FL [*AM radio station call letters*]
WOKF Folkston, GA [*FM radio station call letters*]
WOKH Bardstown, KY [*FM radio station call letters*]
WOKI Oak Ridge, TN [*FM radio station call letters*]
WOKK Meridian, MS [*FM radio station call letters*]
WOKN Southport, NY [*FM radio station call letters*]
WOKO Burlington, VT [*FM radio station call letters*]
WOKQ Dover, NH [*FM radio station call letters*]
WOKR Rochester, NY [*Television station call letters*]
WOKR Willys-Overland-Knight Registry (EA)
WOKS Columbus, GA [*AM radio station call letters*]
WOKT Cannonsburg, KY [*AM radio station call letters*]
WOKU-AM Hurricane, WV [*AM radio station call letters*] (RBYB)
WOKV Jacksonville, FL [*AM radio station call letters*]
WOKW Curwensville, PA [*FM radio station call letters*]
WOKX High Point, NC [*AM radio station call letters*]
WOKY Milwaukee, WI [*AM radio station call letters*]
WOKZ-FM Fairfield, IL [*FM radio station call letters*] (RBYB)
WOL Wainoco Oil [*NYSE symbol*] (TTSB)
WOL Wainoco Oil Corp. [*NYSE symbol*] (SPSG)
WOL War-Office Letter [*An order or an instruction*] [*British*]
WOL Washington, DC [*AM radio station call letters*]
WOL Wedge Opening Load
WOL Wharf Owner's Liability [*Insurance*]
WOL Wings Aviation Ltd. [*Guyana*] [*FAA designator*] (FAAC)
WOL Wiretap Online Library [*Online database*]
Wol Wolcott's Chancery Reports [*7 Delaware*] [*A publication*] (DLA)
Wol Wollaston's English Bail Court Reports [*A publication*] (DLA)
WOL Wollongong [*Australia Airport symbol*]
wol Wolof [*MARC language code Library of Congress*] (LCCP)
WOL Wolverton [*England*] [*Seismograph station code, US Geological Survey*] (SEIS)
WOLA Barranquitas, PR [*AM radio station call letters*]
WOLA Washington Office on Latin America (EA)
WOLAP Workplace Optimization and Layout Planning (MHDB)
WOLB Baltimore, MD [*AM radio station call letters*]
WOLC Princess Anne, MD [*FM radio station call letters*]
WOLD Marion, VA [*AM radio station call letters*]
WOLD-FM Marion, VA [*FM radio station call letters*]
WOLE Aguadilla, PR [*Television station call letters*]
WOLF Committee for Wildlife on the Last Frontier
WOLF Scranton, PA [*Television station call letters*]
WOLF Syracuse, NY [*AM radio station call letters*]
WOLF Wash-Off Line Film (DGA)
WOLF Wayne Oakland Library Federation [*Library network*]
WOLF Work Order Load Forecast (MCD)
Wolf & B Wolferstan and Bristow's English Election Cases [*1859-65*] [*A publication*] (DLA)
Wolf & D Wolferstan and Dew's English Election Cases [*1856-58*] [*A publication*] (DLA)
WolfHB Wolf [*Howard B.*], Inc. [*Associated Press*] (SAG)
WOLI-FM Easley, SC [*FM radio station call letters*] (RBYB)
WOLL Riviera Beach, FL [*FM radio station call letters*]
Woll Wollaston's English Bail Court Reports, Practice Cases [*1840-41*] [*A publication*] (DLA)
Woll BC Wollaston's English Bail Court Reports [*A publication*] (DLA)
WOLN Olean, NY [*FM radio station call letters*]
WOLO Columbia, SC [*Television station call letters*]
Wolohn Wolohan Lumber Co. [*Associated Press*] (SAG)
WOLR Lake City, FL [*FM radio station call letters*]
WOLS Florence, SC [*AM radio station call letters*]
WOLV Houghton, MI [*FM radio station call letters*]
WOLV Wolverton [*Urban district in England*]
WOLVES Wireless Operationally Linked Electronic and Video Exploration System
WolvTub Wolverine Tube, Inc. [*Associated Press*] (SAG)
WolvWW Wolverine World-Wide, Inc. [*Associated Press*] (SAG)
WOLW Cadillac, MI [*FM radio station call letters*]
Wolw Woolworth [*F.W.*] Corp. [*Wall Street slang name: "Five & Dime"*] [*Associated Press*] (SAG)
Wolwth Woolworth [*F.W.*] Corp. [*Wall Street slang name: "Five & Dime"*] [*Associated Press*] (SAG)
WOLX Baraboo, WI [*FM radio station call letters*]
WOLY Battle Creek, MI [*AM radio station call letters*]
WOLZ Fort Myers, FL [*FM radio station call letters*]
WOM Weapons Output Makeup
WOM Wideband Optical Modulation
WOM Widowed Oriental Male [*Classified advertising*]
WOM Wireless Operator Mechanic [*British*] (DSUE)
WOM Wise Old Men [*Term used to refer to group of US statesmen including Dean Acheson, Charles Bohlen, Averell Harriman, George Kennan, Robert Lovett, and John McCloy*]
WOM Woomera [*Australia*] (BARN)
WOM Word-of-Mouth (WDMC)
WOM Write Circuit for Queuing Messages [*Computer science*] (IAA)
WOM Write-Only Memory [*Computer science*]
WOM Write Optional Memory (IEEE)
WOMAD World of Music, Arts, and Dance [*Festival*] (PCM)
WOMAN World Organization of Mothers of All Nations
Woman Offend Rep Woman Offender Report [*A publication*] (DLA)
Woman's J Woman's Journal [*A publication*]
WOMB Courtney Foundation for the Welfare of Mother and Babies [*British*]
WOMBAT Waste of Money, Brains, and Time (NHD)
WOMBAT Waves on Magnetised Beams and Turbulence
WOMBAT Waves on Magnetized Beams and Turbulence [*Physics*] (ADA)
WOMC Detroit, MI [*FM radio station call letters*]
WOMC Woodfree Off-Machine Coated Paper (DGA)
WOMCB Woodfree Off-Machine Coated Board Paper (DGA)
WOMEN Women's Organization for Mentoring, Education and Networking Unlimited, Inc.
Women Labour Conf Pap Women and Labour Conference. Papers [*A publication*]
Women L Jour Women's Law Journal [*A publication*] (DLA)
Women's LJ Women's Law Journal [*A publication*] (DLA)
Women's L Rptr Women's Law Reporter [*A publication*] (DLA)
Women's Rights L Reptr Women's Rights Law Reporter [*A publication*] (ILCA)
WOMG-FM Columbia, SC [*FM radio station call letters*]
WOMI Owensboro, KY [*AM radio station call letters*]
WOMJEP [*A*] Woman in Jeopardy [*Screenwriter's lexicon*]
WOMP Bellaire, OH [*AM radio station call letters*]
WOMP Western Ocean Meeting Point (DMA)

WOMP .... World Order Models Project
WOMP-FM ... Bellaire, OH [*FM radio station call letters*]
WOMPI .... Women of the Motion Picture Industry, International (EA)
WOMR .... Provincetown, MA [*FM radio station call letters*]
Wom R Bks... Women's Review of Books [*A publication*] (BRI)
Womspk ...... Womanspeak [*A publication*]
WOMT .... Manitowoc, WI [*AM radio station call letters*]
WOMX-FM... Orlando, FL [*FM radio station call letters*]
WON .... Juan Air (1979) Ltd. [*Canada ICAO designator*] (FAAC)
WON .... Sports & Recreation, Inc. [*NYSE symbol*] (SAG)
WON .... Waiver of Notice [*Business term*] (MHDW)
WON .... Wondoola [*Queensland*] [*Airport symbol*] (AD)
WON .... Wool over Needle [*Knitting*]
WON .... Work Order Number (MCD)
WONA .... Winona, MS [*AM radio station call letters*]
WONAAC...... Women's National Abortion Action Coalition [*Defunct*]
WONA-FM.... Winona, MS [*FM radio station call letters*]
WONARD ..... Woman's Organization of the National Association of Retail Druggists (EA)
WONB .... Ada, OH [*FM radio station call letters*]
WONC .... Naperville, IL [*FM radio station call letters*]
WONCA........ World Organization of National Colleges, Academies, and Academic Associations ofGeneral Practitioners/Family Physicians [*Australia*] (EAIO)
WOND .... Pleasantville, NJ [*AM radio station call letters*]
Wondwre ..... Wonderware Corp. [*Associated Press*] (SAG)
WONE .... Akron, OH [*FM radio station call letters*]
WONE .... Dayton, OH [*AM radio station call letters*]
WONE .... Westwood One [*NASDAQ symbol*] (TTSB)
WONE .... Westwood One, Inc. [*Culver City, CA*] [*NASDAQ symbol*] (NQ)
WONF .... With Other Natural Flavors [*Food science*]
WONF .... Wonford [*England*]
WONG .... Canton, MS [*AM radio station call letters*]
WONG .... Weight on Nose Gear [*Aviation*] (MCD)
WONN .... Lakeland, FL [*AM radio station call letters*]
WONO .... Walterboro, SC [*FM radio station call letters*]
WONQ .... Oviedo, FL [*AM radio station call letters*]
Wont Land Reg... Wontner's Land Registry Practice [*12th ed.*] [*1975*] [*A publication*] (DLA)
WONU .... Kankakee, IL [*FM radio station call letters*]
WONW .... Defiance, OH [*AM radio station call letters*]
WONX .... Evanston, IL [*AM radio station call letters*]
WONY .... Oneonta, NY [*FM radio station call letters*]
WONZ .... Hammonton, NJ [*AM radio station call letters*]
WOO .... College of Wooster, Wooster, OH [*OCLC symbol*] (OCLC)
WOO .... Waiting on Orders
WOO .... Warrant Ordnance Officer [*Navy British*]
WOO .... Werke ohne Opuszahl [*Works without Opus Number*] [*Music*]
WOO .... Western Operations Office [*Later, WSO*] [*NASA*]
WOO .... Woodchopper, AK [*Location identifier FAA*] (FAAL)
WOO .... Woodstock [*Maryland*] [*Seismograph station code, US Geological Survey Closed*] (SEIS)
WoO .... Work without Opus Number (WGA)
WOO .... World Oceanographic Organization
WOO .... World of Outlaws [*Auto racing*]
WOOD .... Grand Rapids, MI [*AM radio station call letters*]
Wood .... Wood on Mercantile Agreements [*A publication*] (DLA)
Wood .... Wood's English Tithe Cases, Exchequer [*4 vols.*] [*A publication*] (DLA)
Wood .... Woods' United States Circuit Court Reports [*A publication*] (DLA)
WOOD .... Write Once Optical Disk (NITA)
Wood & M... Woodbury and Minot's United States Circuit Court Reports [*A publication*] (DLA)
Wood & Minot... Woodbury and Minot's United States Circuit Court Reports [*A publication*] (DLA)
Woodb & M... Woodbury and Minot's United States Circuit Court Reports [*A publication*] (DLA)
Woodb & Min (CC)... Woodbury and Minot's United States Circuit Court Reports, First Circuit [*A publication*] (DLA)
WoodBcp ..... Wood Bancorp [*Associated Press*] (SAG)
Wood Civ L... Wood's Institutes of the Civil Law of England [*A publication*] (DLA)
Wood Com L... Wood's Institutes of the Common Law [*A publication*] (DLA)
Wood Conv... Wood on Conveyancing [*A publication*] (DLA)
Wood Decr... Wood's Tithe Cases [*England*] [*A publication*] (DLA)
Wooddesson Lect... Wooddesson's Lecture [*A publication*] (DLA)
Woodd Lect... Wooddesson's Lectures on the Laws of England [*A publication*] (DLA)
Wood El Jur... Wooddesson's Elements of Jurisprudence [*A publication*] (DLA)
Woodf .... Woodfall on Landlord and Tenant [*25 eds.*] [*1802-1958*] [*A publication*] (DLA)
WOODF........ Woodford [*England*]
Woodf Cel Tr... Woodfall's Celebrated Trials [*A publication*] (DLA)
Woodf Landl & T... Woodfall on Landlord and Tenant [*25 eds.*] [*1802-1958*] [*A publication*] (DLA)
Woodf Landl & Ten... Woodfall on Landlord and Tenant [*25 eds.*] [*1802-1958*] [*A publication*] (DLA)
Woodf L & T... Woodfall on Landlord and Tenant [*28th ed.*] [*1978*] [*A publication*] (DLA)
WOOD-FM ... Grand Rapids, MI [*FM radio station call letters*]
Woodf Parl Deb... Woodfall's Parliamentary Debates [*A publication*] (DLA)
Wood H .... Hutton Wood's Decrees in Tithe Cases [*England*] [*A publication*] (DLA)
Woodhd .... Woodhead Industries, Inc. [*Associated Press*] (SAG)
Wood Inst.... Wood's Institutes of English Law [*A publication*] (DLA)
Wood Inst Com Law... Wood's Institutes of the Common Law [*A publication*] (DLA)
Wood Inst Eng L... Wood's Institutes of English Law [*A publication*] (DLA)
WOODL........ Woodleigh [*England*]
Wood Land & T... Wood on Landlord and Tenant [*A publication*] (DLA)
Wood Landl & Ten... Wood on Landlord and Tenant [*A publication*] (DLA)
Wood Lect... Wooddesson's Lectures on the Laws of England [*A publication*] (DLA)
Wood Lim.... Wood on Limitation of Actions [*A publication*] (DLA)
Wood Man... Wood on Mandamus [*A publication*] (DLA)
Woodman Cr Cas... Woodman's Reports of Thacher's Criminal Cases [*Massachusetts*] [*A publication*] (DLA)
Woodm & T For Med... Woodman and Tidy on Forensic Medicine [*A publication*] (DLA)
Wood Mast & Serv... Wood on Master and Servant [*A publication*] (DLA)
Wood Mayne Dam... Wood's Mayne on Damages [*A publication*] (DLA)
WOODMEM... Leonard Wood Memorial [*Later, LWM*] [*Also known as American Leprosy Foundation*] (EA)
Wood Nuis... Wood on Nuisances [*A publication*] (DLA)
Woodr.......... Woodroast Systems, Inc. [*Associated Press*] (SAG)
Wood Ry Law... Wood's Law of Railroads [*A publication*] (DLA)
Woods .... Woods' United States Circuit Court Reports [*A publication*] (DLA)
Woods CC.... Woods' United States Circuit Court Reports [*A publication*] (DLA)
Wood's Civ Law... Wood's Institutes of the Civil Law of England [*A publication*] (DLA)
Wood's Dig... Wood's Digest of Laws [*California*] [*A publication*] (DLA)
Woods Ins ... Wood on Fire Insurance [*A publication*] (DLA)
Woods Ins ... Wood's Institutes of English Law [*A publication*] (DLA)
Wood's Inst Civ L... Wood's Institutes of the Civil Law of England [*A publication*] (DLA)
Wood's Inst Com L... Wood's Institutes of the Common Law [*A publication*] (DLA)
Wood's R..... Wood's Manitoba Reports [*1875-83*] [*A publication*] (DLA)
Woods St Frauds... Wood's Treatise on the Statutes of Frauds [*A publication*] (DLA)
WOODST...... Wood Strength [*Botany*]
Wood Ti Cas... Wood's Tithe Cases [*1650-1798*] [*A publication*] (DLA)
Wood Tit Cas... Wood's Tithe Cases [*1650-1798*] [*A publication*] (DLA)
Wood Tr M... Wood on Trade Marks [*1876*] [*A publication*] (DLA)
WOOD-TV .... Grand Rapids, MI [*Television station call letters*]
Woodw .... Woodward's Decisions [*Pennsylvania*] [*A publication*] (DLA)
Woodw Dec... Woodward's Decisions [*1861-74*] [*Pennsylvania*] [*A publication*] (DLA)
Woodw Dec PA... Woodward's Decisions [*1861-74*] [*Pennsylvania*] [*A publication*] (DLA)
WOODWK .... Woodwork
WOODWKG... Woodworking
WOODWT..... Wood Weight [*Botany*]
WOOF .... Dothan, AL [*AM radio station call letters*]
Woof .... Well-Off, Older Folks [*Lifestyle classification*]
Woof .... Well-Off, Over Fifty [*Lifestyle classification*]
WOOF-FM.... Dothan, AL [*FM radio station call letters*]
WOOL .... Woolen
Wool .... Woolworth's United States Circuit Court Reports [*A publication*] (DLA)
Wool CC ...... Woolworth's United States Circuit Court Reports (Miller's Decisions) [*A publication*] (DLA)
Woolf Adult... Woolf on Adulterations [*1874*] [*A publication*] (DLA)
Wool Int ...... Woolsey's Introduction to Study of International Law [*6th ed.*] [*1888*] [*A publication*] (DLA)
Woolr Cert... Woolrych's Certificates [*1826*] [*A publication*] (DLA)
Woolr Com... Woolrych's Rights of Common [*2nd ed.*] [*1850*] [*A publication*] (DLA)
Woolr Cr L... Woolrych's Criminal Law [*1862*] [*A publication*] (DLA)
Woolr LW.... Woolrych's Law of Waters [*2nd ed.*] [*1851*] [*A publication*] (DLA)
Woolr PW.... Woolrych's Party Walls [*1845*] [*A publication*] (DLA)
Woolr Sew... Woolrych's Sewert [*3rd ed.*] [*1864*] [*A publication*] (DLA)
Woolr Waters... Woolrych's Law of Waters [*A publication*] (DLA)
Woolr Ways... Woolrych's Law of Ways [*2nd ed.*] [*1847*] [*A publication*] (DLA)
Woolr Wind L... Woolrych's Window Lights [*2nd ed.*] [*1864*] [*A publication*] (DLA)
Woolsey Polit Science... Woolsey's Political Science [*A publication*] (DLA)
Wools Int L... Woolsey's Introduction to Study of International Law [*6th ed.*] [*1888*] [*A publication*] (DLA)
Wools Pol Science... Woolsey's Political Science [*A publication*] (DLA)
Woolw .... Woolworth's Reports [*1 Nebraska*] [*A publication*] (DLA)
Woolw .... Woolworth's United States Circuit Court Reports [*A publication*] (DLA)
Woolworth... Woolworth's United States Circuit Court Reports [*A publication*] (DLA)
Woolworth's Cir Ct R... Woolworth's United States Circuit Court Reports [*A publication*] (DLA)
Woolw Rep... Woolworth's Reports [*1 Nebraska*] [*A publication*] (DLA)
Woolw Rep... Woolworth's United States Circuit Court Reports [*A publication*] (DLA)
WOOM .... Wives of Older Men [*An association*] (EA)
WOOMB .... World Organization of the Ovulation Method - Billings, USA [*Later, Families of the Americas Foundation*]
WOON .... Woonsocket, RI [*AM radio station call letters*]
WOOO .... Shelbyville, IN [*AM radio station call letters*]
WOOOL........ Words Out of Ordinary Language (WDAA)
Woopie .... Well-Off Older Person [*Lifestyle classification*]
WOOW .... Greenville, NC [*AM radio station call letters*]
WOOX .... Bedford, PA [*FM radio station call letters*]
WOOZ .... Harrisburg, IL [*FM radio station call letters*]
WOP .... Waiver of Premium [*Insurance*] (MHDW)
WOP .... War on Poverty (OICC)
WOP .... Wing Outer Panel [*Aviation*]
WOP .... Wireless Operator [*RAF slang*] [*World War II*]
WOP .... With Other Property (BARN)

WOP .... Without Pain (DAVI)
WOP .... Without Passport [*Immigration terminology*] [*Acronym often referred to early 20th century Italian immigrants*]
WOP .... Without Payment
W/O/P .... Without Penalty
WOP .... Without Personnel
WOP .... Without Preference [*Rating*]
WOP .... Without Priorities
WOP .... World Oil Project [*Massachusetts Institute of Technology*] [*National Science Foundation*] (IID)
WOPA .... War Overtime Pay Act [*1943*]
WOPAG .... Wireless Operator and Air Gunner [*British military*] (IAA)
W O PAR ...... Without Partition [*Freight*]
WOPAST ...... Work Plan Analysis and Scheduling Technique (MHDB)
WOPC .... World Oceanographic Data Processing and Services Center (MSC)
WOPD .... Warrant Officer Professional Development [*Military*] (MCD)
WOPE .... Without Personnel and Equipment
Wo Peo .... Work and People [*A publication*]
WOPI .... Bristol, VA [*AM radio station call letters*]
WOPP .... Opp, AL [*AM radio station call letters*]
WOPR .... War Operation Plan Response [*Pronounced "whopper"*] [*Name of NORAD computer in film "WarGames"*]
WOPR .... Woody's Office Power Pack [*Pinecliffe International*] [*Computer science*] (PCM)
WOPR .... Word for Windows Office Power Pack [*Computer program disk*] (PCM)
WOPTR .... Wireless Operator [*British military*] (IAA)
WOQ .... Wave Officers' Quarters
WOQ .... Wooroona [*Queensland*] [*Airport symbol*] (AD)
WOQI .... Ponce, PR [*FM radio station call letters*]
WOQT .... Warrant Officer Qualification Test [*Military*]
WOR .... New York, NY [*AM radio station call letters*]
WOR .... Water-Oil Ratio
WOR .... Wearout Rate (SAA)
WOR .... White and Orange [*Buoy*]
WOR .... White Owners Register (EA)
WOR .... Worcester [*Massachusetts*] [*Seismograph station code, US Geological Survey Closed*] (SEIS)
WOR .... Work Order Register (MCD)
WOR .... Work Order Release (MCD)
WOR .... Work Order Request
WOR .... Work Outline Retrieval (MCD)
WOR .... Worshipful
WORA .... Mayaguez, PR [*AM radio station call letters*]
WORAM .... Word-Oriented Random Access Memory [*Computer science*] (MCD)
WORA-TV ..... Mayaguez, PR [*Television station call letters*]
WORB .... Farmington Hills, MI [*FM radio station call letters*]
WORBAT ...... Wartime Order of Battle (NATG)
Wor Bib Leg... Worrall's Bibliotheca Legum [*A publication*] (DLA)
WORC .... Washington Operations Research Council (MCD)
WORC .... Worcester, MA [*AM radio station call letters*]
WORC .... Worcestershire [*County in England*]
Worcest Dict... Worcester's Dictionary [*A publication*] (DLA)
Worcester.... Worcester's Dictionary of the English Language [*A publication*] (DLA)
Worcester Poly Inst... Worcester Polytechnic Institute (GAGS)
Worcester St C... Worcester State College (GAGS)
WORCS .... Worcestershire [*County in England*]
WORCS .... Work Ordering and Reporting Communication System [*Army*]
WORD .... Pittsburgh, PA [*FM radio station call letters*]
WORD .... Spartanburg, SC [*AM radio station call letters*]
WORD .... Wechsler Objective Reading Dimensions [*Test*]
WORD .... Wind Oriented Rapid [*or Rocket*] Deployment (MCD)
Wor Dict ...... Worcester's Dictionary [*A publication*] (DLA)
Words Elect... Wordsworth's Law of Elections [*6th ed.*] [*1868*] [*A publication*] (DLA)
Words Elect Cas... Wordsworth's Election Cases [*England*] [*A publication*] (DLA)
Words JS ...... Wordsworth's Law of Joint-Stock Companies [*A publication*] (DLA)
Words Min.... Wordsworth's Law of Mining [*A publication*] (DLA)
Words Pat ... Wordsworth's Law of Patents [*A publication*] (DLA)
Words Ry & C... Wordsworth's Railway and Canal Companies [*A publication*] (DLA)
WORG .... Elloree, SC [*FM radio station call letters*]
WORI .... World Order Research Institute
WORK .... Barre, VT [*FM radio station call letters*]
WORK .... Widening Occupational Roles Kit (EDAC)
WorkCap ...... Workingmens Capital Holdings, Inc. [*Associated Press*] (SAG)
WORKHO ..... Workhouse [*British*] (ROG)
Workmen's Comp L Rep... Workmen's Compensation Law Reporter [*Commerce Clearing House*] [*A publication*] (DLA)
Workmen's Comp L Rev... Workmen's Compensation Law Review [*A publication*] (DLA)
Works Courts... Works on Courts and Their Jurisdiction [*A publication*] (DLA)
Works Pr ..... Works' Practice, Pleading, and Forms [*A publication*] (DLA)
WORL .... Christmas, FL [*AM radio station call letters*]
WORLD .... Women Organized to Respond to Life-Threatening Diseases (EA)
WorldC .... WorldCom, Inc. [*Associated Press*] (SAG)
WorldCm ..... WorldCom, Inc. [*Associated Press*] (SAG)
WORLDDIDAC... World Association of Manufacturers and Distributors of Educational Materials (EAIO)
World L Rev... World Law Review [*A publication*] (DLA)
WORLDS ...... Western Ohio Regional Library Development System [*Library network*]
WORLD SMART... World Sports Medicine Association of Registered Therapists
World Trade LJ... World Trade Law Journal [*A publication*] (DLA)
WorldV .... WorldViews: A Quarterly Review of Resources for Education and Action [*A publication*] (BRI)
WorldWIDE... World Women in the Environment [*Formerly, World Women in Defense of the Environment*] (EA)
WORM .... Savannah, TN [*AM radio station call letters*]
Worm .... White, Older Rich Man [*Lifestyle classification*]
WORM .... Write Once, Read Mainly [*or Many Times, or Mostly*] [*Computer science*]
WORM .... Write-Once, Read-Many [*Computer science*]
WORM .... Write-One Read Memory
WORM CD ... Write Once, Read Many Compact Disk (EERA)
WORM-FM... Savannah, TN [*FM radio station call letters*]
WORMS .... Warrant Officer Personnel Management System [*Army*]
WORMS .... World Organization to Restore Male Supremacy (EA)
WORN .... Write Once, Read Never [*Computer science*]
WORO .... Corozal, PR [*FM radio station call letters*]
WORO .... Weapons Operations Research Office
WOROM .... Write-Only Read-Only Memory [*Computer science*] (MDG)
WORP .... Word Processing [*Computer science*] (DCTA)
WORQ .... Green Bay, WI [*FM radio station call letters*]
WORSAMS... Worldwide Organizational Structure for Army Medical Support (AABC)
WORSE .... Word Selection (WDAA)
WORT .... Madison, WI [*FM radio station call letters*]
WORTAC ...... Westinghouse Overall RADAR Tester and Calibrator
WortFds .... Worthington Foods, Inc. [*Associated Press*] (SAG)
WorthFd .... Worthington Foods [*Associated Press*] (SAG)
Worthgtn ...... Worthington Industries [*Associated Press*] (SAG)
Worth Jur .... Worthington's Power of Juries [*1825*] [*A publication*] (DLA)
Worth Prec Wills... Worthington's General Precedent for Wills [*5th ed.*] [*1852*] [*A publication*] (DLA)
WORV .... Hattiesburg, MS [*AM radio station call letters*]
WORW .... Port Huron, MI [*FM radio station call letters*]
WORX .... Madison, IN [*AM radio station call letters*]
WORX-FM.... Madison, IN [*FM radio station call letters*]
WOS .... Warrant Officer Service [*Army*] (DOMA)
WOS .... Web Offset Section [*Later, WOA*] (EA)
WOS .... Wholly-Owned Subsidiary [*Business term*] (MHDW)
WOS .... Wilson Ornithological Society (EA)
WOS .... Winchester Financial [*Vancouver Stock Exchange symbol*]
WOS .... Worcester [*British depot code*]
WOSA .... Windows Open Services Architecture [*Microsoft Corp.*] (PCM)
WOSA .... Windows Open Systems Architecture [*Computer science*]
WOSA .... Workers' Organization for Socialist Action [*South Africa Political party*] (EY)
WOSAC .... Worldwide Synchronization of Atomic Clocks
WOSAPCON... World Safety and Accident Prevention Congress (PDAA)
WOSB .... War Office Selection Board [*British*]
WOSB .... Weather Observation Site Building (AABC)
WOSC .... Bethany Beach, DE [*FM radio station call letters*]
WOSC .... Warrant Officer Senior Course [*Army*] (DOMA)
WOSC .... Western Oklahoma State College
WOSC .... Western Oregon State College
WOSC .... World Organisation of Systems and Cybernetics (EAIO)
WOSD .... Weapons Operational Systems Development [*NORAD*]
WOSE-FM .... Coshocton, OH [*FM radio station call letters*] (RBYB)
WOSF .... Work Order Status File (MCD)
WOsh .... Oshkosh Public Library, Oshkosh, WI [*Library symbol Library of Congress*] (LCLS)
WOSH .... Oshkosh, WI [*AM radio station call letters*]
WOshM .... Mercy Hospital, Nursing Library, Oshkosh, WI [*Library symbol Library of Congress*] (LCLS)
WOshM-M ... Mercy Medical Center, Medical Library, Oshkosh, WI [*Library symbol Library of Congress*] (LCLS)
WOshU .... University of Wisconsin-Oshkosh, Oshkosh, WI [*Library symbol Library of Congress*] (LCLS)
WOSIC .... Watchmakers of Switzerland Information Center (EA)
WOSIN .... Wolters Kluwer Nv [*AM symbol*] (TTSB)
WOSL .... Women's Overseas Service League (EA)
WOSM .... Ocean Springs, MS [*FM radio station call letters*]
WOSN-FM.... Indian River Shores, FL [*FM radio station call letters*] (RBYB)
WOSO .... San Juan, PR [*AM radio station call letters*]
WOSP .... Portsmouth, OH [*FM radio station call letters*]
WOSQ .... Spencer, WI [*FM radio station call letters*]
WOSR .... Middletown, NY [*FM radio station call letters*]
WOSS .... Ossining, NY [*FM radio station call letters*]
WOSSU .... Women on Stamps Study Unit [*American Topical Association*] [*Defunct*] (EA)
WOST .... Block Island, RI [*Television station call letters*]
WOST .... World's Oldest Socketed Tool [*Refers to archeological discovery of a tool dated 2500 BC*]
WOSU .... Columbus, OH [*AM radio station call letters*]
WOSU-FM.... Columbus, OH [*FM radio station call letters*]
WOSUS .... Wang Office Systems User Society (CSR)
WOSU-TV .... Columbus, OH [*Television station call letters*]
WOSV .... Mansfield, OH [*FM radio station call letters*]
WOT .... Wide-Open Throttle
WOTAN .... Weather Observation Through Ambient Noise [*Marine science*] (OSRA)
WOTAN .... Weather Observation Through Ambient Noise (USDC)
WOTB .... Middletown, RI [*FM radio station call letters*]
WOTB .... Welfare of the Blind (EA)
WOTC .... Edinburg, VA [*FM radio station call letters*]
WOTCU .... Wave-Off and Transition Control Unit
WOTEC .... Waste Oil to Energy Converter
WOTF .... Writers of the Future [*Science fiction writing award*]

WOTJ.......... Morehead City, NC [*FM radio station call letters*]
WOTL.......... Toledo, OH [*FM radio station call letters*]
WOTO.......... Women on Their Own [*An association*] (EA)
WOTP.......... World Organization of the Teaching Professions [*Switzerland*]
WOTR.......... Lost Creek, WV [*FM radio station call letters*]
WOTR.......... Wolf Trap Farm Park [*National Park Service designation*]
WOTS.......... Kissimmee, FL [*AM radio station call letters*]
WOTS.......... Warrant Officer Training System [*Military*] (INF)
WOTS.......... Water Operations Technical Support [*US Army Corps of Engineers*]
WOTS.......... Wide-Open Throttle Switch [*Automotive engineering*]
WOTT.......... Wolves on the Track [*A group of philanderers looking for girls*] [*Slang*]
WOTTCS...... Warrant Officer Technical and Tactical Certification System [*Army*]
Wott Leg Wal... Wotton. Leges Wallicae [*A publication*] (DLA)
WOTV.......... Battle Creek, MI [*Television station call letters*]
WOU.......... Women's Outpatient Unit (AAMN)
WOU.......... Work Opportunities Unlimited
WOUB.......... Athens, OH [*AM radio station call letters*]
WOUB-FM.... Athens, OH [*FM radio station call letters*]
WOUB-TV.... Athens, OH [*Television station call letters*]
WOUC.......... Cambridge, OH [*FM radio station call letters*]
WOUC-TV.... Cambridge, OH [*Television station call letters*]
WOUDE........ Wait-on-User-Defined Event (MHDI)
WOUH.......... Chillicothe, OH [*FM radio station call letters*]
WOUI.......... Chicago, IL [*FM radio station call letters*]
WOUL.......... Ironton, OH [*FM radio station call letters*]
WOUR.......... Utica, NY [*FM radio station call letters*]
WOUZ.......... Zanesville, OH [*FM radio station call letters*]
WOV.......... Warren & Ouachita Valley Railway Co. [*AAR code*]
WOVI.......... Novi, MI [*FM radio station call letters*]
WOVK.......... Wheeling, WV [*FM radio station call letters*]
WOVO-FM.... Glasgow, KY [*FM radio station call letters*] (RBYB)
WOVO-FM.... Horse Cave, KY [*FM radio station call letters*] (RBYB)
WOW.......... Omaha, NE [*AM radio station call letters*]
WOW.......... Waiting on Weather [*Ocean storms*]
WOW.......... War on Want [*An association*] (EAIO)
WOW.......... War on Waste [*Navy*]
WOW.......... War on Words
WOW.......... Washington Opportunities for Women
WOW.......... Weight-on-Wheels (NASA)
WOW.......... Wider Opportunities for Women (EA)
WOW.......... Windows on Windows [*Computer software*] (CDE)
WOW.......... Winners on Wheels [*An association*] (PAZ)
WOW.......... Without Whiskers (IAA)
WOW.......... Woman Ordnance Worker
WOW.......... Women on Wheels (EA)
WOW.......... Women on Wine (EA)
WOW.......... Women Our Wonders [*Antifeminist men's group*]
WOW.......... Woodmen of the World (EA)
WOW.......... Word on the Way
WOW.......... World Ocean Watch [*Marine science*] (OSRA)
WOW.......... World of Winners [*A publication*]
WOW.......... World of Work [*Career-oriented course of study*]
WOW.......... Worlds of Wonder [*Electronic toy manufacturer*]
WOW.......... Worldwide Equities Ltd. [*Toronto Stock Exchange symbol*]
WOW.......... Worn-Out Wolf [*An aging philanderer*] [*Slang*]
WOW.......... Worst-on-Worst
WOW.......... Written Order of Withdrawal [*Banking*]
WO-WA........ Work Order-Work Authorization (SSD)
WOWAR........ Work Order and Work Accomplishment Record
WOWATE...... World War II Equivalent [*Three-year and eight-month unit of time measurement proposed by former Under Secretary of the Navy R. James Woolsey*]
WOWB.......... Little Falls, NY [*FM radio station call letters*]
WOWC.......... Jasper, AL [*FM radio station call letters*]
WOWE.......... Vassar, MI [*FM radio station call letters*]
WOW-FM...... Omaha, NE [*FM radio station call letters*]
WOWI.......... Norfolk, VA [*FM radio station call letters*]
WOWI.......... Women on Words and Images (EA)
WOWK.......... Huntington, WV [*Television station call letters*]
WOWL.......... Florence, AL [*Television station call letters*]
WOWLON...... Weight-on-Wheels Lock-On [*NASA*] (NASA)
WOWM.......... Write Once, Write Mostly [*Computer science*] (IAA)
WOWN.......... Shawano, WI [*FM radio station call letters*]
WOWN.......... Without Winch
WOWO.......... Fort Wayne, IN [*AM radio station call letters*]
WOWQ.......... DuBois, PA [*FM radio station call letters*]
WOWS.......... Wire Obstacle Warning System (IEEE)
WOWS.......... Women Ordnance Workers [*A national voluntary organization*] [*World War II*]
WOWT.......... Omaha, NE [*Television station call letters*]
WOWW.......... Pensacola, FL [*FM radio station call letters*]
WOWZ.......... Whitesboro, NY [*FM radio station call letters*] (RBYB)
WOXD.......... Oxford, MS [*FM radio station call letters*]
WOXF-FM.... Bedford, NH [*FM radio station call letters*] (RBYB)
WOXM.......... Oregon, IL [*FM radio station call letters*] (RBYB)
WOXO.......... Norway, ME [*FM radio station call letters*]
WOXR.......... Oxford, AL [*AM radio station call letters*]
WOXY.......... Oxford, OH [*FM radio station call letters*]
WOYE.......... Mayaguez, PR [*FM radio station call letters*]
WOYK.......... York, PA [*AM radio station call letters*]
WOYL.......... Oil City, PA [*AM radio station call letters*]
WOYL.......... Women of the Year Luncheon [*British*] (DI)
WOYS.......... Apalachicola, FL [*FM radio station call letters*]
WOZI.......... Presque Isle, ME [*FM radio station call letters*]
WOZK.......... Ozark, AL [*AM radio station call letters*]
WOZN.......... Key West, FL [*FM radio station call letters*]
WOZQ.......... Northampton, MA [*FM radio station call letters*]
WOZZ.......... New London, WI [*FM radio station call letters*]
WP.............. Aloha Islandair [*ICAO designator*] (AD)
WP.............. Pakistan Law Reports, West Pakistan Series [*A publication*] (DLA)
WP.............. Portage Free Public Library, Portage, WI [*Library symbol Library of Congress*] (LCLS)
WP.............. Princeville Airways [*ICAO designator*] (AD)
WP.............. Waiting Period (OICC)
WP.............. Waiver of Premium [*Insurance*]
WP.............. War and Peace Foundation (EA)
WP.............. Warming Pan [*Refers to a clergyman holding a job under a bond of resignation*] [*Obsolete Slang British*] (DSUE)
WP.............. Warm Pipe [*Nuclear energy*] (NRCH)
WP.............. Warm Pool [*Oceanography*]
WP.............. War Plans
WP.............. Warsaw Pact (NATG)
WP.............. Warsaw Pact Member (WDAA)
WP.............. Wastepaper
WP.............. Waste Pipe [*Technical drawings*]
WP.............. Water-Dispersible Powder [*Pesticide formulation*]
WP.............. Water Packed
WP.............. Water Plane (MSA)
WP.............. Water Point
W/P............ Water/Powder [*Ratio*] [*Pharmacology*] (DAVI)
WP.............. Waterproof
WP.............. Water Propeller (AAG)
WP.............. Water Pump (AAG)
WP.............. Way-Point
WP.............. Weakly Positive (MAE)
WP.............. Weapons Power
WP.............. Weapons Procurement (DOMA)
WP.............. Weather Permitting
WP.............. Weatherproof
WP.............. Weekly Premium [*Insurance*]
WP.............. Weight Penalty
WP.............. Welding Procedure [*Nuclear energy*] (NRCH)
WP.............. [*The*] Western Pacific Railroad Co. [*AAR code*]
WP.............. Western Pine [*Utility pole*] [*Telecommunications*] (TEL)
WP.............. West Point
WP.............. We the People [*Later, WPU*] (EA)
WP.............. Wet Pack [*Medicine*] (AAMN)
WP.............. Wet Process (MSA)
WP.............. Wettable Powder
WP.............. Wheel of Progress (EA)
WP.............. Whirlpool [*Medicine*]
WP.............. White Painted (BJA)
WP.............. White Paper (ADA)
WP.............. White Phosphorus [*Military*]
WP.............. Wide Pore [*Chromatography*]
WP.............. Wild Pitch [*Baseball*]
WP.............. Will Proceed To
WP.............. Will Proved [*Legal*] [*British*] (ROG)
WP.............. Windfall Profit
WP.............. Winning Pitcher [*Baseball*]
WP.............. Wire Payment
WP.............. Withdrawn Passing [*Education*] (WGA)
WP.............. Without Prejudice
WP.............. Wolfe Pack (EA)
WP.............. Wolseley Pattern [*British military*] (DMA)
WP.............. Woodfree Printing Paper (DGA)
WP.............. Woodfree Pulp Board (DGA)
WP.............. Wood Pattern (MSA)
WP.............. Word Processing [*Movement to improve secretarial/clerical function through a managed system of people, procedures, and modern office equipment*]
WP.............. Word Processor (ADA)
wp.............. Word Processor (ODBW)
WP.............. Word Punch
WP.............. Worker's Party [*Ireland*] [*Political party*]
WP.............. Working Paper
W/P............ Working Papers (AAGC)
WP.............. Working Party
WP.............. Working Point
WP.............. Working Pressure
WP.............. Work Package (NASA)
W/P............ Work Picture [*or Print*] [*Cinematography*]
WP.............. Work Preparation (AIE)
WP.............. Workprint [*Cinematography*] (NTCM)
WP.............. Work Procedure [*Nuclear energy*] (NRCH)
WP.............. Work Program (NATG)
WP.............. Workspace Pointer (MHDB)
WP.............. Workspace Register Pointer [*Computer science*] (IAA)
WP.............. World Peacemakers (EA)
WP.............. World Politics [*A publication*] (BRI)
WP.............. World Priorities (EA)
WP.............. Worship
WP.............. Worst Pattern (IAA)
WP.............. Worthy Patriarch
WP.............. Wrist Pitch (MCD)
WP.............. Write Permit (NITA)
WP.............. Write Protect
WP.............. Writers for Peace (EA)

WP3............ Working Party Three [*Economic Policy Committee of the Organization for Economic Cooperation and Development*]
WPA............ Puerto Aysen [*Chile*] [*Airport symbol*] (AD)
WPA............ Wagner-Peyser Act [*1933*] (OICC)
WPA............ Water Jet Propulsion Assembly (MCD)
WPA............ Water Pump Assembly
WPA............ Webb-Pomerene Act [*1918*]
WPA............ Wellhead Protection Area (GNE)
WPA............ Western Pacific Airservice [*Solomon Islands*] [*ICAO designator*] (FAAC)
WPA............ Western Pine Association [*Later, WWPA*] (EA)
WPA............ Western Pistachio Association (EA)
WPA............ Western Provident Association [*British*] (DI)
WPA............ Western Psychological Association (MCD)
WPA............ Wet-Process Phosphoric Acid [*Fertilizer*]
WPA............ Whale Protection Act 1980 [*Commonwealth Act*] (EERA)
WPA............ Wheelchair Pilots Association (EA)
WPA............ Whiskey Painters of America (EA)
WPA............ Whistleblower Protection Act of 1989 (WYGK)
WPA............ William Penn Association [*Pittsburgh, PA*] (EA)
WPA............ Wire Products Association [*British*] (BI)
WPA............ With Particular Average
WPA............ Women's Press Association (NTCM)
WPA............ Women's Prison Association (EA)
WPA............ Woody Point [*Australia Seismograph station code, US Geological Survey Closed*] (SEIS)
WPA............ Working Party on Aquaculture [*Australia*]
WPA............ Working People's Alliance [*Guyana*] (PD)
WPA............ Work Package Action (MCD)
WPA............ Work Package Address (MCD)
WPA............ Workshop of the Players Art [*New York City*]
WPA............ Works Progress Administration [*Later, Work Projects Administration*] [*Part of President Franklin D. Roosevelt's New Deal*]
WPA............ World Parliament Association
WPA............ World Pheasant Association [*Reading, Berkshire, England*] (EAIO)
WPA............ World Presbyterian Alliance
WPA............ World Psychiatric Association [*Copenhagen, Denmark*] (EAIO)
WPA............ Worst Possible Accident [*Nuclear safety*]
WPAA.......... Andover, MA [*FM radio station call letters*]
WPAAS........ Word Processing and Administrative Support System [*Computer science*] (HGAA)
WPAB.......... Ponce, PR [*AM radio station call letters*]
WPAB.......... Word Processing Aptitude Battery [*Test*]
WPAB.......... Word Processor Assessment Battery [*Selection and placement test*]
WPAC.......... Ogdensburg, NY [*FM radio station call letters*]
WPAC.......... Walden Pond Advisory Committee (EA)
WPAC.......... Western Pacific Airlines [*NASDAQ symbol*] (TTSB)
WPAC.......... Western Pacific Airlines, Inc. [*NASDAQ symbol*] (SAG)
WPAC.......... Working Program Advisory Committee [*DoD*]
W-PACC....... Wisconsin Procedure for Appraisal of Clinical Competence (EDAC)
WPAD.......... Paducah, KY [*AM radio station call letters*]
WPAE-FM.... Centreville, MS [*FM radio station call letters*] (RBYB)
WPAFB........ Wright-Patterson Air Force Base [*Ohio*]
WPAK.......... Farmville, VA [*AM radio station call letters*]
WPAL.......... Charleston, SC [*AM radio station call letters*]
WPAL.......... Walterboro, SC [*FM radio station call letters*]
WPAM.......... Pottsville, PA [*AM radio station call letters*]
WPAN.......... Fort Walton Beach, FL [*Television station call letters*]
WP & T........ War Plans and Training
WP&YR........ White Pass & Yukon Railway [*Nickname: Wait Patiently and You'll Ride*]
WPAP.......... Panama City, FL [*FM radio station call letters*]
WPAQ.......... Mount Airy, NC [*AM radio station call letters*]
WPAQ.......... Westra Preschool Assessment Questionnaire
WPAR.......... Hickory, NC [*FM radio station call letters*]
W PAR......... With Partition [*Freight*]
WP/AS......... Word Processing/Administrative Support [*Extension of Word Processing*]
WPAT.......... Atauro [*East Timor*] [*ICAO location identifier*] (ICLI)
WPAT.......... Paterson, NJ [*AM radio station call letters*]
WPAT.......... Wolfe Programming Aptitude Test
WPATC........ Western Pennsylvania Advanced Technology Center [*Research center*] (RCD)
WPAT-FM.... Paterson, NJ [*FM radio station call letters*]
WPA-USA.... World Pheasant Association of the USA (EA)
WPAW.......... Vero Beach, FL [*FM radio station call letters*] (RBYB)
WPAWA....... World Professional Armwrestling Association [*Defunct*] (EA)
WPAX.......... Thomasville, GA [*AM radio station call letters*]
WPAY.......... Portsmouth, OH [*AM radio station call letters*]
WPAY-FM.... Portsmouth, OH [*FM radio station call letters*]
WPAZ.......... Pottstown, PA [*AM radio station call letters*]
WPB............ Gunboat [*Coast Guard*] (NVT)
WPB............ Port Berge [*Madagascar*] [*Airport symbol*] (OAG)
WPB............ Wall Plate Box
WPB............ War Production Board [*World War II*]
WPB............ Wastepaper Basket [*or Bin*]
WPB............ Waste Processing Building [*Nuclear energy*] (NRCH)
WPB............ Whirlpool Bath [*Medicine*]
WPB............ Wide Pulse Blanking (MCD)
WPB............ Woodfree Pulp Board (DGA)
WPB............ World Peace Brigade (EA)
WPB............ Write Printer Binary
WPBA.......... Atlanta, GA [*Television station call letters*]
WPBA.......... Women Professional Bowlers Association (EA)
WPBA.......... Women's Professional Billiard Alliance (EA)
WPBC.......... Pittsfield, ME [*FM radio station call letters*]
WPBC.......... Western Pacific Base Command [*Marianas*] [*World War II*]
WPBCWS..... Waste Processing Building Chilled Water System [*Nuclear energy*] (NRCH)
WPBEF........ West Pakistan Bank Employees' Federation
WPBF.......... Tequesta, FL [*Television station call letters*]
WPBGP........ West Palm Beach Grand Prix [*Automobile racing event*]
WPBH.......... Port St. Joe, FL [*FM radio station call letters*]
WPBIC......... Walker Problem Behavior Identification Checklist [*Education*]
WPBL.......... Women's Professional Basketball League [*Defunct*] (EA)
WPBN.......... Traverse City, MI [*Television station call letters*]
WPBO.......... Portsmouth, OH [*Television station call letters*]
WPBQ.......... Flowood, MS [*AM radio station call letters*]
WPBR.......... Palm Beach, FL [*AM radio station call letters*]
WPBRL........ Warsaw Pact/Ballistic Research Laboratory (MCD)
WPBS.......... Conyers, GA [*AM radio station call letters*]
WPBSA........ World Professional Billiards and Snooker Association (BARN)
WPBT.......... Miami, FL [*Television station call letters*]
WPBX.......... Southampton, NY [*FM radio station call letters*]
WPBY.......... Huntington, WV [*Television station call letters*]
WPBZ.......... Indiantown, FL [*FM radio station call letters*]
WPC............ Walter P. Chrysler Club (EA)
WPC............ War Pensions Committee [*British military*] (DMA)
WPC............ Warrior Preparation Center [*Kaiserslautern, Federal Republic of Germany*] [*USAREUR*]
WPC............ Warsaw Pact Countries (MCD)
WPC............ Washington Press Club [*Formerly, WNPC*]
WPC............ Waste Product Costs [*Solid waste management*]
WPC............ Water Pollution Control
WPC............ Watt-per-Channel (IAA)
WPC............ Watts per Candle [*Electricity*]
Wpc............. Watts per Candle (IDOE)
WPC............ Webster's Patent Cases [*1601-1855*] [*A publication*] (DLA)
WPC............ Wedge Power Clamp
WPC............ Weldable Printed Circuit
WPC............ Wheat Protein Concentrate [*Food technology*]
WPC............ Whey Protein Concentrate [*Food technology*]
WPC............ William Paterson College [*Wayne, NJ*]
WPC............ William Penn College [*Oskaloosa, IA*]
WPC............ William Peterson College of New Jersey
WPC............ Wired Program Computer
WPC............ Wollaston's English Bail Court Reports, Practice Cases [*A publication*] (DLA)
WPC............ Woman Police Constable [*Scotland Yard*]
WPC............ Women's Political Caucus
WPC............ Wood-Plastic Combination [*or Composite*]
WPC............ Word Processing Center
WPC............ Workers Party of Canada
WPC............ Work Package Concept (MCD)
WP + C........ Work Planning and Control [*Computer science*]
WPC............ World Peace Congress
WPC............ World Peace Council [*See also CMP*] (EAIO)
WPC............ World Petroleum Congresses - a Forum for Petroleum Science, Technology, Economics, and Management (EAIO)
WPC............ World Philatelic Congress of Holy Land, Israel, and Judaica Societies (EA)
WPC............ World Planning Chart [*Aviation*]
WPC............ World Pooling Committee (MCD)
WPC............ World Power Conference [*Later, WEC*]
WPC............ World Print Council (EA)
WPC............ World Pumpkin Confederation (EA)
WPCA.......... Water Pollution Control Administration [*Department of the Interior*]
WPCA.......... Wool Pullers Council of America (EA)
WPCAA........ White Park Cattle Association of America (EA)
WP Cas........ Webster's Patent Cases [*1601-1855*] [*A publication*] (DLA)
WP Cas........ Wollaston's English Bail Court Reports, Practice Cases [*A publication*] (DLA)
WPCB.......... Greensburg, PA [*Television station call letters*]
WPCB.......... Western Pennsylvania Christian Broadcasting Co. [*A cable TV station*]
WPCC.......... Clinton, SC [*AM radio station call letters*]
WPCC.......... Wilson Pharmaceutical & Chemical Corp.
WPCC.......... World Paper Currency Collectors (EA)
WPCC.......... WPC [*Walter P. Chrysler*] Club (EA)
WPCC.......... Wright-Patterson Contracting Center [*Ohio*] [*Air Force*]
WPCD.......... Champaign, IL [*FM radio station call letters*]
WPCE.......... Portsmouth, VA [*AM radio station call letters*]
WPCF.......... Panama City Beach, FL [*FM radio station call letters*]
WPCF.......... Water Pollution Control Federation (EA)
WPCH.......... Atlanta, GA [*FM radio station call letters*]
WPCHLIJS... World Philatelic Congress of Holy Land, Israel, and Judaica Societies (EA)
WPCI........... Greenville, SC [*AM radio station call letters*]
WPCJ.......... Pittsford, MI [*FM radio station call letters*]
WPCM.......... Burlington, NC [*FM radio station call letters*]
WPCND........ Women's Patriotic Conference on National Defense (EA)
WPCO.......... Mount Vernon, IN [*AM radio station call letters*]
WPcom........ Write Precompensation [*Computer science*] (CDE)
WPCP.......... Ward's Private Companies Profiles [*A publication*]
WPCP.......... Water Polution Control Plant [*Environmental science*]
WPCR.......... Plymouth, NH [*FM radio station call letters*]
WPCR.......... Water Pollution Control Research [*Environmental Protection Agency*]
WPCS.......... Pensacola, FL [*FM radio station call letters*]
WPCS.......... Welsh Pony and Cob Society (DBA)
WPCSA........ Welsh Pony and Cob Society of America (EA)

WPCT.......... Panama City Beach, FL [*Television station call letters*]
WPCTS........ When Push Comes to Shove
WPCV.......... Winter Haven, FL [*FM radio station call letters*]
WPCX.......... Auburn, NY [*FM radio station call letters*]
WPD............ War Plan Division [*World War II*]
WPD............ Water Planning Division [*Environmental Protection Agency*] (EPA)
WPD............ Western Procurement Division [*Marine Corps*]
WPD............ Work Package Description [*NASA*] (NASA)
WPD............ World Pharmaceuticals Directory [*A publication*]
WPD............ Write Printer Decimal
WPDA.......... Jeffersonville, NY [*FM radio station call letters*]
WPDA.......... Writing Pushdown Acceptor
WPDA.......... Writing Push Down Acceptor (NITA)
WPDB.......... Suai [*East Timor*] [*ICAO location identifier*] (ICLI)
WPDC.......... Elizabethtown, PA [*AM radio station call letters*]
W/PDC........ Workers'/People's Defence Committee [*Ghana*] [*Political party*]
WPDE.......... Florence, SC [*Television station call letters*]
WPDES........ Waste Pollution Discharge Elimination System (IEEE)
WPDH.......... Poughkeepsie, NY [*FM radio station call letters*]
WPDJ.......... Huntington, IN [*AM radio station call letters*]
WPDL.......... Dili [*East Timor*] [*ICAO location identifier*] (ICLI)
WPDM.......... Potsdam, NY [*AM radio station call letters*]
WPDN.......... Wind Profiler Demonstration Network [*Marine science*] (OSRA)
WPDN.......... Wind Profiler Demonstration Network (USDC)
WPDOS........ WordPerfect for Disk Operating System [*Computer science*]
WP/DP........ Word Processing/Data Processing System (HGAA)
WPDQ.......... Jacksonville, FL [*AM radio station call letters*]
WPDR.......... Portage, WI [*AM radio station call letters*]
WPDT.......... Johnsonville, SC [*FM radio station call letters*] (RBYB)
WPDX.......... Clarksburg, WV [*AM radio station call letters*]
WPDX.......... Word Processing Document Exchange Program
WPDX-FM.... Clarksburg, WV [*FM radio station call letters*]
WPE............ Western Pacific Energy [*Vancouver Stock Exchange symbol*]
WPE............ Western Plastics Exposition [*HBJ Expositions and Conferences*] (TSPED)
WPE............ West Pittston-Exeter Railroad Co. [*AAR code*]
WPEA.......... Exeter, NH [*FM radio station call letters*]
WPEARS...... Working Papers Exhibits and Rate Schedules (AAGC)
WPEB.......... Philadelphia, PA [*FM radio station call letters*]
WPEC.......... Baucau [*East Timor*] [*ICAO location identifier*] (ICLI)
WPEC.......... Weapons Production Engineering Center [*Navy*]
WPEC.......... Western Power & Equip [*NASDAQ symbol*] (TTSB)
WPEC.......... Western Power & Equipment Corp. [*NASDAQ symbol*] (SAG)
WPEC.......... West Palm Beach, FL [*Television station call letters*]
WPEC.......... World Plan Executive Council [*Later, WGAE-US*] (EA)
WPECC........ Western Pacific Fisheries Consultative Committee [*Marine science*] (OSRA)
WPEG.......... Concord, NC [*FM radio station call letters*]
WPEH.......... Louisville, GA [*AM radio station call letters*]
WPEH-FM.... Louisville, GA [*FM radio station call letters*]
WPEK.......... Seneca, SC [*FM radio station call letters*] (RBYB)
WPEL.......... Montrose, PA [*AM radio station call letters*]
WPEL-FM.... Montrose, PA [*FM radio station call letters*]
WPEN.......... Philadelphia, PA [*AM radio station call letters*]
WPen.......... West Penn Power Co. [*Associated Press*] (SAG)
WPen25...... West Penn Power Co. [*Associated Press*] (SAG)
WPEO.......... Peoria, IL [*AM radio station call letters*]
WPEP.......... Taunton, MA [*AM radio station call letters*]
WPER.......... Asheboro, NC [*FM radio station call letters*] (RBYB)
WPES.......... Ashland, VA [*AM radio station call letters*]
WPET.......... Greensboro, NC [*AM radio station call letters*]
WPeW.......... Waukesha County Technical Institute, Pewaukee, WI [*Library symbol Library of Congress*] (LCLS)
WPEZ.......... Macon, GA [*FM radio station call letters*]
WPF............ War and Peace Foundation (EA)
WPF............ War Production Fund [*World War II*]
WPF............ Watcor Purification Systems, Inc. [*Vancouver Stock Exchange symbol*]
WPF............ Weather Profile Facility
WPF............ Weight, Power, Fulcrum
WPF............ Whale Protection Fund (EA)
WPF............ Work Process Flow [*NASA*] (NASA)
WPF............ World Peace Foundation (EA)
WPF............ World Prohibition Federation
WPF............ Worldwide Pen Friends (EA)
WPF............ Wright Peak Flow [*Medicine*] (DAVI)
WPFA.......... Wholesale Photo Finishers' Association [*British*] (BI)
WPFA.......... William Penn Fraternal Association [*Later, WPA*] (EA)
WPFA.......... Working Party on Feral Animals [*Australia*]
WPFB.......... Middletown, OH [*AM radio station call letters*]
WPFB-FM.... Middletown, OH [*FM radio station call letters*]
WPFC.......... Commission for Fisheries Research in the West Pacific
WPFC.......... Port Allen, LA [*AM radio station call letters*] (RBYB)
WPFC.......... Waterproof Fan Cooled (MSA)
WPFC.......... Westbeth Playwrights Feminist Collective [*Defunct*] (EA)
WPFC.......... William Perry Fan Club [*Defunct*] (EA)
WPFC.......... World Press Freedom Committee (EA)
WPFD.......... Fairview, TN [*AM radio station call letters*]
WPFF.......... Sturgeon Bay, WI [*FM radio station call letters*]
WPFILD....... West Point Fellowship in Leader Development [*US Military Academy*] (INF)
WPFJ.......... Franklin, NC [*AM radio station call letters*]
WPFL.......... Fuiloro [*East Timor*] [*ICAO location identifier*] (ICLI)
WPFL.......... West Pakistan Federation of Labor
WPFL.......... Worshipful (ROG)
WPFL-FM.... Century, FL [*FM radio station call letters*] (RBYB)
WPFM.......... Panama City, FL [*FM radio station call letters*]
WPFM.......... Wiping Form (AAG)
WPFM.......... Wright Peak Flow Meter [*Medicine*] (DAVI)
WPFMC........ Western Pacific Fishery Management Council [*National Oceanic and Atmospheric Administration*] (GFGA)
WPFTA........ White Plate Flat Trackers Association (EA)
WPFUL........ Worshipful
WPFW.......... Washington, DC [*FM radio station call letters*]
WPG............ Waterproofing (AAG)
WPG............ Weighted Pair Group
WPG............ West Point Graduate
WPG............ Wiping (MSA)
WPG............ Worcester Polytechnic Institute, Worcester, MA [*OCLC symbol*] (OCLC)
WPG............ WordPerfect Graphic [*Novell, Inc.*] [*File format*]
WPG............ Work Package Grouping [*NASA*] (NASA)
WPGA.......... Perry, GA [*AM radio station call letters*]
WPGA-FM.... Perry, GA [*FM radio station call letters*]
WPGA-TV..... Perry, GA [*Television station call letters*]
WPGC.......... Morningside, MD [*AM radio station call letters*]
WPGC-FM.... Morningside, MD [*FM radio station call letters*]
WPGD.......... Hendersonville, TN [*Television station call letters*]
WPGDY........ WPP Group PLC [*NASDAQ symbol*] (SAG)
WPGG.......... Evergreen, AL [*FM radio station call letters*]
WPGH.......... Pittsburgh, PA [*Television station call letters*]
WPGI.......... Horseheads, NY [*FM radio station call letters*] (RBYB)
WPGI.......... Western Publishing Group, Inc. [*New York, NY NASDAQ symbol*] (NQ)
WPGL.......... Pattersonville, NY [*FM radio station call letters*]
WPGM.......... Danville, PA [*AM radio station call letters*]
WPGM-FM.... Danville, PA [*FM radio station call letters*]
WPGS.......... Mims, FL [*AM radio station call letters*]
WPGT.......... Group Fore - Women's Pro Golf Tour (EA)
WPGU.......... Urbana, IL [*FM radio station call letters*]
WPGW.......... Portland, IN [*AM radio station call letters*]
WPGW-FM.... Portland, IN [*FM radio station call letters*]
WPGX.......... Panama City, FL [*Television station call letters*]
WPGY.......... Williamsport, PA [*FM radio station call letters*] (RBYB)
WPH............ West Pit [*Hawaii*] [*Seismograph station code, US Geological Survey Closed*] (SEIS)
WPH............ William Penn House (EA)
WPH............ WPL Holdings [*NYSE symbol*] (SPSG)
WPHB.......... Philipsburg, PA [*AM radio station call letters*]
WPHB-FM.... Philipsburg, PA [*FM radio station call letters*]
WPHC.......... Waverly, TN [*AM radio station call letters*]
WPHD.......... Tioga, PA [*FM radio station call letters*]
WPHE.......... Phoenixville, PA [*AM radio station call letters*]
WPHI........... Western Pennsylvania Horological Institute
WPHK.......... Blountstown, FL [*FM radio station call letters*]
WPHL.......... Philadelphia, PA [*Television station call letters*]
WPHM.......... Port Huron, MI [*AM radio station call letters*]
WPHN.......... Gaylord, MI [*FM radio station call letters*]
WPHOA........ Women Public Health Officer's Association [*British*]
WPHP.......... Wheeling, WV [*FM radio station call letters*]
WPHS.......... Warren, MI [*FM radio station call letters*]
WPHT-AM.... Philadelphia, PA [*AM radio station call letters*] (RBYB)
WPI............. Wall Paper Institute [*Later, Wallcovering Manufacturers Association*] (EA)
WPI............. Waxed Paper Institute [*Later, FPA*] (EA)
WPI............. Wedding Photographers International (EA)
WPI............. Western Personality Inventory [*Psychology*]
WPI............. Western Personnel Institute (AEBS)
WPI............. West Pride Industry [*Vancouver Stock Exchange symbol*]
WPI............. Whey Products Institute [*Later, ADPI*] (EA)
WPI............. Wholesale Price Index [*Economics*]
WPI............. Women and Priests Involved (EA)
WPI............. Women's Peace Initiative (EA)
WPI............. Worcester Polytechnic Institute [*Massachusetts*]
WPI............. Work Process Indicator (NASA)
WPI............. Work Progress Indicator [*NASA*] (NASA)
WPI............. World Patents Index [*Derwent Publications Ltd.*] [*Database*]
WPI............. World Peace One [*An association*] (EA)
WPI............. World Policy Institute (EA)
WPI............. World Press Institute (EA)
WPIB........... Bluefield, WV [*FM radio station call letters*]
WPIC........... Sharon, PA [*AM radio station call letters*]
WPIC........... Water Port Identifier Code
WPIC........... Western Psychiatric Institute and Clinic [*University of Pittsburgh*] [*Research center*] (RCD)
WPIC........... WPI Group [*NASDAQ symbol*] (TTSB)
WPIC........... WPI Group, Inc. [*NASDAQ symbol*] (SAG)
WPID........... Piedmont, AL [*AM radio station call letters*]
WPIE........... Trumansburg, NY [*AM radio station call letters*]
WPIG........... Olean, NY [*FM radio station call letters*]
WPI Grp....... WPI Group, Inc. [*Associated Press*] (SAG)
WPIK........... Summerland Key, FL [*FM radio station call letters*]
WPIM........... Martinsville, VA [*FM radio station call letters*]
WPIN........... Dublin, VA [*FM radio station call letters*]
WPINDEX..... Wholesale Price Index [*Data File*]
WPIO........... Titusville, FL [*FM radio station call letters*]
WPIO........... Waste Isolation Pilot Project Integration Office [*Department of Energy*] [*Albuquerque, NM*] (GAAI)
WPIP........... Winston-Salem, NC [*AM radio station call letters*]
WPIQ........... Brunswick, GA [*AM radio station call letters*]

WPIR .... Salem, VA [*FM radio station call letters*]
WPIS .... Wafer Parameter Identification System (IAA)
WPIT .... Pittsburgh, PA [*AM radio station call letters*]
WPIT .... Water Pressure Integrity Test [*For testing water filters*]
WPIX .... New York, NY [*Television station call letters*]
WPJ .... Weakened Plane Joint
WPJ .... Workers' Party of Jamaica [*Political party*] (EY)
WPJB .... Narragansett Pier, RI [*FM radio station call letters*]
WPJC .... Adjuntas, PR [*AM radio station call letters*]
WPJK .... Orangeburg, SC [*AM radio station call letters*]
WPJL .... Raleigh, NC [*AM radio station call letters*]
WPJM .... Greer, SC [*AM radio station call letters*]
WPJS .... Conway, SC [*AM radio station call letters*]
WPK .... Air-Lift Associates, Inc. [*ICAO designator*] (FAAC)
WPk .... Ward's Mechanical Tissue Pack [*Dentistry*] (BABM)
WPk .... Wet Pack [*Physical therapy*] (DAVI)
WPK .... Winpak Ltd. [*Toronto Stock Exchange symbol*]
WPK .... Wright Peak Flow [*Medicine*] (DAVI)
WPKE .... Elkhorn City, KY [*FM radio station call letters*]
WPKE .... Pikeville, KY [*AM radio station call letters*]
WPKM .... Scarborough, ME [*FM radio station call letters*]
WPKN .... Bridgeport, CT [*FM radio station call letters*]
WPKO .... Bellefontaine, OH [*FM radio station call letters*]
WPKO .... World Professional Karate Organization (DICI)
WPKQ-FM .... Berlin, NH [*FM radio station call letters*] (RBYB)
WPKR .... Omro, WI [*FM radio station call letters*]
WPKT .... Meriden, CT [*FM radio station call letters*]
WPKX .... Enfield, CT [*FM radio station call letters*]
WPKY .... Princeton, KY [*AM radio station call letters*]
WPKZ .... Elkton, VA [*FM radio station call letters*]
WPL .... Aeronaves del Peru SA [*ICAO designator*] (FAAC)
WPL .... War Plan, Long-Range (CINC)
WPL .... Warren Public Library, Warren, OH [*OCLC symbol*] (OCLC)
WPL .... Waste Pickle Liquor [*Industrial waste*]
WPL .... Wave Propagation Laboratory [*Boulder, CO*] [*National Oceanic and Atmospheric Administration*]
WPL .... Windows Personal Librarian [*Computer software*]
WPL .... Windows Portability Libraries [*Computer science*]
WPL .... Winnipeg Public Library [*UTLAS symbol*]
WPL .... Worshipful
WPL .... Worst Path Loss
WPLA .... Callahan, FL [*FM radio station call letters*] (RBYB)
WPLA-FM .... Callahan, FL [*FM radio station call letters*] (RBYB)
WPlaU .... University of Wisconsin-Platteville, Platteville, WI [*Library symbol Library of Congress*] (LCLS)
WPLB .... Greenville, MI [*AM radio station call letters*]
WPLB .... Lakeview, MI [*FM radio station call letters*]
WPLG .... Miami, FL [*Television station call letters*]
WPLH .... Tifton, GA [*FM radio station call letters*]
WPL H .... WPL Holdings [*Associated Press*] (SAG)
WPLJ .... New York, NY [*FM radio station call letters*]
WPLJ .... White Port and Lemon Juice [*Title of both song and drink*]
WPLK .... Palatka, FL [*AM radio station call letters*]
WPLL-FM .... Fort Lauderdale, FL [*FM radio station call letters*] (RBYB)
WPLM .... Plymouth, MA [*AM radio station call letters*]
WPLM-FM .... Plymouth, MA [*FM radio station call letters*]
WPLN .... Nashville, TN [*FM radio station call letters*]
WPLO .... Grayson, GA [*AM radio station call letters*]
WPLO .... Water Port Liaison Office [*or Officer*] [*Air Force*] (AFM)
WPLR .... New Haven, CT [*FM radio station call letters*]
WPLS .... Greenville, SC [*FM radio station call letters*]
WPLS .... Western Plains Library System [*Library network*]
WPLT .... Plattsburgh, NY [*FM radio station call letters*]
WPLTO .... Western Plateau [*NWS*] (FAAC)
WPLV-AM .... West Point, GA [*AM radio station call letters*] (RBYB)
WPLW .... Carnegie, PA [*AM radio station call letters*]
WPLX .... Germantown, TN [*AM radio station call letters*]
WPLY .... Media, PA [*FM radio station call letters*]
WPlyM .... Mission House Theological Seminary, Plymouth, WI [*Library symbol Library of Congress*] (LCLS)
WPLZ .... Petersburg, VA [*FM radio station call letters*]
WPM .... War Plan, Mid-Range
WPM .... War Planning Memorandum (NATG)
WPM .... Waterproof Membrane
WPM .... Western Premium [*Vancouver Stock Exchange symbol*]
WPM .... White Pine [*Michigan*] [*Seismograph station code, US Geological Survey*] (SEIS)
WPM .... Wipim [*Papua New Guinea*] [*Airport symbol*] (OAG)
WPM .... Wire-Wound Porous Material
WPM .... Wood Plastic Material
WPM .... Words per Minute
wpm .... Words per Minute (WDMC)
wpm .... Words per Minute (IDOE)
WPM .... Work Package Management (MCD)
WPM .... World Presbyterian Missions (EA)
WPM .... Write Program Memory [*Computer science*]
WPM .... Write Protect Memory
WPMA .... Wall Paper Merchants' Association of Great Britain (BI)
WPMA .... Waterproof Paper Manufacturers Association [*Later, API*]
WPMA .... Windows/Presentation Manager Association (EA)
WPMA .... Wood Products Manufacturers Association (EA)
WPMA .... Writing Paper Manufacturers Association [*Later, API*] (EA)
WPMB .... Vandalia, IL [*AM radio station call letters*]
WPMC .... Jellico, TN [*Television station call letters*]
WPMC .... Waxed Paper Merchandising Council [*Defunct*]
WPMCP .... Work Package Manpower and Cost Plan [*NASA*] (NASA)
WPME .... Women for Peace in the Middle East (EA)
WPMH .... Portsmouth, VA [*AM radio station call letters*]
WPMI .... Mobile, AL [*Television station call letters*]
WPMN .... Maliana [*East Timor*] [*ICAO location identifier*] (ICLI)
WPMR .... Mount Pocono, PA [*AM radio station call letters*]
WPMRR .... Work Package Milestone Progress Report (MCD)
WPMT .... York, PA [*Television station call letters*]
WPMW .... Mullens, WV [*FM radio station call letters*]
WPMX .... Statesboro, GA [*FM radio station call letters*] (RBYB)
WPMZ .... Providence, RI [*AM radio station call letters*] (RBYB)
WPN .... Weapon (AAG)
WPN .... Weapons Procurement, Navy (NVT)
WPN .... Wolverhampton [*British depot code*]
WPN .... World's Press News [*A publication*] (DGA)
WPN .... Write Punch [*Computer science*] (MCD)
WPNA .... Oak Park, IL [*AM radio station call letters*]
WPNA .... World Proof Numismatic Association (EA)
WPNC .... Plymouth, NC [*AM radio station call letters*]
WPNC-FM .... Plymouth, NC [*FM radio station call letters*]
WPNE .... Green Bay, WI [*FM radio station call letters*]
WPNE .... White Pine Software, Inc. [*NASDAQ symbol*] (SAG)
WPNE-TV .... Green Bay, WI [*Television station call letters*]
WPNFPT .... Weapon Fly-to-Point (NVT)
WPNG-FM .... Pearson, GA [*FM radio station call letters*] (RBYB)
WPNH .... Plymouth, NH [*AM radio station call letters*]
WPNH-FM .... Plymouth, NH [*FM radio station call letters*]
WPNR .... Utica, NY [*FM radio station call letters*]
WPNSTA .... Weapons Station
WPNT .... Chicago, IL [*FM radio station call letters*]
WPNTS .... War Plan Naval Transportation Service
WPNW .... Pawtucket, RI [*AM radio station call letters*] (RBYB)
WPNX .... Phenix City, AL [*AM radio station call letters*]
WPO .... War Plan Orange [*World War II*]
WPO .... Warsaw Pact Organization (MCD)
WPO .... Washington Post'B' [*NYSE symbol*] (TTSB)
WPO .... Washington Post Co. Class B [*NYSE symbol*] (SPSG)
WPO .... Water for Peace Office [*Department of State*]
WPO .... Water Programs Office [*Environmental Protection Agency*]
WPO .... West Pacific Ocean (SAA)
WPO .... Women's Project Officer
WPO .... World Packaging Organization [*See also OME*] [*Paris, France*] (EAIO)
WPO .... World Ploughing Organisation [*Carlisle, Cumbria, England*] (EAIO)
WPOA .... Western Pacific Orthopaedic Association (EA)
WPOB .... Plainview, NY [*FM radio station call letters*]
WPOC .... Baltimore, MD [*FM radio station call letters*]
WPOC .... Oecussi [*East Timor*] [*ICAO location identifier*] (ICLI)
WPoCC .... ICA [*International Co-Operative Alliance*] Working Party on Co-Operative Communications (EAIO)
WPoCP .... ICA [*International Co-Operative Alliance*] Working Party on Co-Operative Press [*Later, WPoCC*] (EAIO)
WPOD .... Water Port of Debarkation (AFM)
WPOE .... Water Port of Embarkation (AFM)
WPOE .... Word Processing and Office Equipment (MHDI)
WPOG .... Pease Oil & Gas [*NASDAQ symbol*] (TTSB)
WPOG .... Pease Oil & Gas Co. [*NASDAQ symbol*] (SAG)
WPOG .... Willard Pease Oil & Gas Co. [*NASDAQ symbol*] (NQ)
WPOGP .... Pease Oil & Gas $1 Cv'A'Pfd [*NASDAQ symbol*] (TTSB)
WPOK .... Pontiac, IL [*AM radio station call letters*]
WPOL .... Winston-Salem, NC [*AM radio station call letters*] (RBYB)
WPOM .... Riviera Beach, FL [*AM radio station call letters*]
WPON .... Walled Lake, MI [*AM radio station call letters*]
WPOP .... Hartford, CT [*AM radio station call letters*]
WPOR .... Portland, ME [*AM radio station call letters*]
WPOR-FM .... Portland, ME [*FM radio station call letters*]
WPOS .... Holland, OH [*FM radio station call letters*]
WP/OS .... Word Processing/Office Systems (HGAA)
WPOW .... Miami, FL [*FM radio station call letters*]
WPP .... Wage Pause Program [*Business term*] (ADA)
WPP .... Waterproof Paper Packing
WPP .... Water Pump Package (NASA)
WPP .... Weapon Position Preparation (MCD)
WPP .... Weapons Production Program
WPP .... Web Printing Press
WPP .... Wechsler Preschool Primary Scale of Intelligence [*Education*] (DAVI)
WPP .... Weibull Probability Paper [*Statistics*]
WPP .... Windward Passage Patrol [*Navy*] (NVT)
WPP .... Witness Protection Program (BARN)
WPP .... WordPerfect Presentations [*WordPerfect Corp.*] [*Computer science*] (PCM)
WPP .... Work Package Plan [*NASA*] (NASA)
WPP .... World Pen Pals (EA)
WPP .... Writing Proficiency Program [*Educational test*]
WPPA .... Pottsville, PA [*AM radio station call letters*]
WPPA .... West Point Protective Association [*Unofficial association of West Point graduates*] (VNW)
WPPB .... Boca Raton, FL [*Television station call letters*]
WPPC .... Penuelas, PR [*AM radio station call letters*]
WPPC .... Warning Point Photocell
WPPC .... West Penn Power Co.
WPPC .... West Point Parents Club (EA)
WPPD .... Whole-Powder-Pattern Decomposition [*Crystallography*]
WPPDA .... Welfare and Pension Plans Disclosure Act [*1958*] [*Department of Labor*]

WPPG .... WPP Group PLC [*NASDAQ symbol*] (SAG)
WPP Gp .... WPP Group PLC [*Associated Press*] (SAG)
WPP Grp ...... WPP Group PLC [*Associated Press*] (SAG)
WPPGY .... WPP Group ADS [*NASDAQ symbol*] (TTSB)
WPPI .... Carrollton, GA [*AM radio station call letters*]
WPP/IS .... Writing Proficiency Program/Intermediate System [*Educational test*]
WPPL .... Blue Ridge, GA [*FM radio station call letters*]
WPPM .... Weight Part per Million
WPPO .... Wood Products Purchasing Office [*Defense Construction Supply Center*] [*Defense Supply Agency*]
WPPR-FM .... Demorest, GA [*FM radio station call letters*] (RBYB)
WPPS .... Work Package Planning Sheet [*NASA*] (NASA)
WPPSI .... Wechsler Preschool and Primary Scale of Intelligence [*Education*]
WPPSS .... Washington Public Power Supply System [*Nicknamed "Whoops"*]
WPPW .... Association of Western Pulp and Paper Workers
WPQR .... Uniontown, PA [*FM radio station call letters*]
WPQR .... Welding Procedure Qualification Record [*Nuclear energy*] (NRCH)
WPR .... Auckland Regional Rescue Helicopter Trust [*New Zealand*] [*FAA designator*] (FAAC)
WPR .... Porvenir [*Chile*] [*Airport symbol*] (AD)
WPR .... Ward Pound Ridge [*New York*] [*Seismograph station code, US Geological Survey*] (SEIS)
WPR .... Wartime Personnel Requirements (NATG)
WPR .... Webster's Patent Reports [*England*] [*A publication*] (DLA)
WPR .... West Pakistan Railway
WPR .... White Puerto Rican
WPR .... Widescope Resources Ltd. [*Vancouver Stock Exchange symbol*]
WPR .... Witness Protection and Relocation [*Government agency in film "F/X"*]
WPR .... Woodpecker Repellent [*In company name, WPR Co.*]
WPR .... Working Party on Rationing [*Allied German Occupation Forces*]
WPR .... Working Pressure
WPR .... Write Permit Ring (NITA)
WPR .... Written Progress Report (HCT)
WPRA .... Mayaguez, PR [*AM radio station call letters*]
WPRA .... Waste Paper Recovery Association Ltd. [*British*] (BI)
WPRA .... Women's Professional Racquetball Association (EA)
WPRA .... Women's Professional Rodeo Association (EA)
WPRB .... Princeton, NJ [*FM radio station call letters*]
WPRC .... Lincoln, IL [*AM radio station call letters*]
WPRD .... Winter Park, FL [*AM radio station call letters*]
WPRE .... Prairie du Chien, WI [*AM radio station call letters*]
WPRE-FM .... Prairie du Chien, WI [*FM radio station call letters*]
WP (REI) ..... Wildlife Protection (Regulations and Exports and Imports) [*Act 1982*] (EERA)
WPRG .... Workers-Peasants Red Guards [*North Korea*]
WPRI .... Providence, RI [*Television station call letters*]
WPRI .... Wartime Pacific Routing Instructions [*Navy*]
WPRJ .... Coleman, MI [*FM radio station call letters*]
WPRK .... Winter Park, FL [*FM radio station call letters*]
WPRL .... Lorman, MS [*FM radio station call letters*]
WPRL .... Water Pollution Research Laboratory [*British*]
WPRM .... San Juan, PR [*FM radio station call letters*]
WPRN .... Butler, AL [*AM radio station call letters*]
WPRO .... Providence, RI [*AM radio station call letters*]
WPRO .... Wartime Personnel Replacement Operation [*Military*]
WPRO-FM .... Providence, RI [*FM radio station call letters*]
WPRP .... Ponce, PR [*AM radio station call letters*]
WPRR .... Altoona, PA [*FM radio station call letters*]
WPRS .... Paris, IL [*AM radio station call letters*]
WPRS .... War Powers Reporting System
WPRS .... Water and Power Resources Service [*Formerly, Bureau of Reclamation*] [*Department of the Interior Name changed back to Bureau of Reclamation, 1981*]
WPRS .... Wittenborn Psychiatric Rating Scale
WPRT .... Prestonsburg, KY [*AM radio station call letters*]
WPRT .... Waypoint Report [*Aviation*] (FAAC)
WPRV .... Fajardo, PR [*Television station call letters*]
WPRX .... Bristol, CT [*AM radio station call letters*]
WPRY .... Perry, FL [*AM radio station call letters*]
WPRZ .... Warrenton, VA [*AM radio station call letters*]
WPS .... International Association of Word Processing Specialists [*Formerly, NAWPS*] (EA)
WPS .... Warner Publishing Services
WPS .... War Planning Slate (CINC)
WPS .... War Plan, Short-Range
WPS .... Wartime Capability Play, Short Range (SAA)
WPS .... Waste Processing System [*Nuclear energy*] (NRCH)
WPS .... Watermen's Protective Society [*A union*] [*British*]
WPS .... Water Phase Salt [*of smoked food*]
WPS .... Water Pressure Switch
WPS .... Waterproof Shroud
WPS .... Water Purification System
WPS .... Watts per Steradian
WPS .... Waveform Processing System
WPS .... Wave Power Source
WPS .... Weapons Program Section
WPS .... Welding Procedure Specification [*Nuclear energy*] (NRCH)
WPS .... Wet Peridotite Solidus [*Geology*]
WPS .... White Power Structure
WPS .... Widowed Persons Service (EA)
WPS .... Windows Printing System [*Microsoft Corp.*] (PCM)
WPS .... Wind Power System
WPS .... Wireless Preservation Society [*British*]
WPS .... Wisconsin Physicians Service [*Army*]
WPS .... With Prior Service
WPS .... Women in Public Service (EA)
WPS .... Word Processing Society
WPS .... Word Processing System (BUR)
WPS .... Words per Second
WPS .... Workplace Shell [*IBM Corp.*] [*Computer science*] (PCM)
WPS .... Workstation Publishing Software
WPS .... World Photography Society (EA)
WPS .... World Politics Simulation
WPS .... World Population Society (EA)
WPS .... Worldwide Plug and Socket [*Proposed standard electrical plug for international use*] [*Pronounced "whoops"*]
WPS .... Worldwide Port System [*Army*] (RDA)
WPS .... WPS Resources [*NYSE symbol*] (TTSB)
WPS .... WPS Resources Corp. [*NYSE symbol*] (SAG)
WPSA .... Paul Smith's, NY [*FM radio station call letters*]
WPSA .... Welsh Pony Society of America [*Later, WPCSA*] (EA)
WPSA .... Wildlife Preservation Society of Australia (EERA)
WPSA .... World Professional Squash Association (EA)
WPSA .... World's Poultry Science Association [*See also AVI*] [*Celle, Federal Republic of Germany*] (EAIO)
WPSA .... World's Poultry Science Association, USA Branch (EA)
WPSB-FM .... Kane, PA [*FM radio station call letters*] (RBYB)
WPSC .... Shipping Control War Plan [*Navy*]
WPSC .... Wayne, NJ [*FM radio station call letters*]
WPSD .... Paducah, KY [*Television station call letters*]
WPSE .... Erie, PA [*AM radio station call letters*]
WPSG-TV .... Philadelphia, PA [*TV station call letters*] (RBYB)
WPSI .... Wahler Physical Symptoms Inventory [*Psychiatry*] (DAVI)
WPSI .... Word Processing Society, Inc. (EA)
WPSI .... World Poetry Society Intercontinental (EA)
WPSK .... Pulaski, VA [*FM radio station call letters*]
WPSL .... Port St. Lucie, FL [*AM radio station call letters*]
WPSL .... Western Primary Standard Laboratory
WPSM .... Fort Walton Beach, FL [*FM radio station call letters*]
WPSM .... Same [*East Timor*] [*ICAO location identifier*] (ICLI)
WPSN .... Westpoint Stevens [*NASDAQ symbol*] (SAG)
WPSO .... New Port Richey, FL [*AM radio station call letters*]
WPSP .... Royal Palm Beach, FL [*AM radio station call letters*] (RBYB)
WPSQ .... Wildlife Preservation Society of Queensland (EERA)
WPSR .... Evansville, IN [*FM radio station call letters*]
WPSR .... Weekly Performance Status Report (MCD)
WPS-RA .... World Pro Skiing-Racers Association [*Defunct*] (EA)
WPS Res ..... WPS Resources Corp. [*Associated Press*] (SAG)
WPST .... Trenton, NJ [*FM radio station call letters*]
WPSU .... State College, PA [*FM radio station call letters*]
WPSX .... Clearfield, PA [*Television station call letters*]
WPT .... Wapiti Aviation Ltd. [*Canada ICAO designator*] (FAAC)
WPT .... Warbled Pure Tone [*Speech and language therapy*] (DAVI)
WPT .... Waypoint [*ICAO*] (FAAC)
WPT .... Way Point (GAVI)
WPT .... Western Personnel Tests [*General intelligence test*]
WPT .... Windfall Profit Tax
WPT .... With Promotion To (NOAA)
WPT .... Wolfe Screening Test for Programming Aptitude
WPT .... Word Processing Test
WPT .... Workers' Party of Turkey
WPT .... Working Point [*Technical drawings*]
WPTA .... Fort Wayne, IN [*Television station call letters*]
WPTA .... Wooden Pail and Tub Association
WPTB .... Statesboro, GA [*AM radio station call letters*]
WPTB .... Wartime Prices and Trade Board
WPTD .... Dayton, OH [*Television station call letters*]
WPTE-FM .... Virginia Beach, VA [*FM radio station call letters*] (RBYB)
WPTF .... National Council for a World Peace Tax Fund (EA)
WPTF .... Raleigh, NC [*AM radio station call letters*]
WPTG .... West Point, VA [*FM radio station call letters*]
WPTH .... Olney, IL [*FM radio station call letters*]
WPTI .... Wildlife Preservation Trust International (EA)
WPTL .... Canton, NC [*AM radio station call letters*]
WPTLC .... World Peace through Law Center (EA)
WPTM .... Roanoke Rapids, NC [*FM radio station call letters*]
WPTN .... Cookeville, TN [*AM radio station call letters*]
WPTNG .... Weapons Training (NVT)
WPTO .... Oxford, OH [*Television station call letters*]
WPTR-FM .... Voorheesville, NY [*FM radio station call letters*] (RBYB)
WPTS .... Pittsburgh, PA [*FM radio station call letters*]
WPTT .... Pittsburgh, PA [*Television station call letters*]
WPTV .... West Palm Beach, FL [*Television station call letters*]
WPTW .... Piqua, OH [*AM radio station call letters*]
WPTX .... Lexington Park, MD [*AM radio station call letters*]
WPTY .... Memphis, TN [*Television station call letters*]
WPTZ .... North Pole, NY [*Television station call letters*]
WPU .... Puerto Williams [*Chile*] [*Airport symbol*] (AD)
WPU .... We the People, United (EA)
WPU .... Wet Pick Up (IAA)
WPU .... With Power Unit (NATG)
WPU .... Women's Protestant Union [*British*]
WPU .... Write Punch [*Computer science*]
WPUB .... Camden, SC [*FM radio station call letters*]
WPUC .... Waste-Paper Utilization Council [*Defunct*]
W/PUG .... Word Processing Users' Group
WPUL .... South Daytona, FL [*AM radio station call letters*]
WPUM .... Rensselaer, IN [*FM radio station call letters*]
WPUP .... Royston, GA [*FM radio station call letters*]
WPUT .... Brewster, NY [*AM radio station call letters*]

WPUV .... Pulaski, VA [*AM radio station call letters*]
WPVA .... Waynesboro, VA [*FM radio station call letters*]
WPVB .... Culpeper, VA [*FM radio station call letters*]
WPVG .... Funkstown, MD [*AM radio station call letters*]
WPVI .... Philadelphia, PA [*Television station call letters*]
WPVL .... Platteville, WI [*AM radio station call letters*] (RBYB)
WPVL-FM .... Platteville, WI [*FM radio station call letters*] (RBYB)
WPVO .... Princeton, WV [*AM radio station call letters*]
WPVQ .... Turners Falls, MA [*FM radio station call letters*]
WPVQ .... Viqueque [*East Timor*] [*ICAO location identifier*] (ICLI)
WPVR .... Roanoke, VA [*FM radio station call letters*]
WPW .... Wolff-Parkinson-White [*Syndrome*] [*Cardiology*]
WPWA .... Chester, PA [*AM radio station call letters*]
WPWB .... Byron, GA [*FM radio station call letters*]
WPWC .... Dumfries-Triangle, VA [*AM radio station call letters*]
WPWIN .... WordPerfect for Windows [*Computer science*]
WPWM .... Wide Pulse Width Modulation
WPWOD .... Will Proceed Without Delay
WPWP .... Western Pacific Warm Pod [*Oceanography*]
WPWP .... Western Pacific Warm Pool [*Oceanography*]
WPWR .... Gary, IN [*Television station call letters*]
WPWR .... World-Wide Plantation Walker Registry (EA)
WPWRA .... Wallcovering, Fabric, and Decor Retailers Association [*British*] (EAIO)
WPWT-AM ... Colonial Heights, TN [*AM radio station call letters*] (RBYB)
WPX .... Worked All Prefixes [*Amateur radio*] (IAA)
WPXC .... Hyannis, MA [*FM radio station call letters*]
WPXI .... Pittsburgh, PA [*Television station call letters*]
WPXN .... Paxton, IL [*FM radio station call letters*]
WPXT .... Portland, ME [*Television station call letters*]
WPXX .... Semora, NC [*FM radio station call letters*] (RBYB)
WPXY .... Rochester, NY [*FM radio station call letters*]
WPXZ .... Punxsutawney, PA [*FM radio station call letters*]
WPY .... White Pass & Yukon Corp. Ltd. [*Toronto Stock Exchange symbol Vancouver Stock Exchange symbol AAR code*]
WPY .... World Population Year [*1974*] [*United Nations*]
WPYB .... Benson, NC [*AM radio station call letters*]
WPYK .... Dora, AL [*AM radio station call letters*]
WPYX .... Albany, NY [*FM radio station call letters*]
WPZ .... Waipapa Point [*New Zealand*] [*Seismograph station code, US Geological Survey Closed*] (SEIS)
WPZ .... Western Plains Zoo [*Dubbo, New South Wales, Australia*]
WPZM .... Tullahoma, TN [*FM radio station call letters*] (RBYB)
WPZZ .... Franklin, IN [*FM radio station call letters*]
WQ .... Water Quenching (OA)
WQ .... Wings Airways [*ICAO designator*] (AD)
WQ .... Wotquenne Catalog [*Used to catalog music of C.P.E Bach*] (BARN)
WQA .... Water Quality Act (GFGA)
WQA .... Water Quality Association (EA)
WQA .... Weld Quality Assurance
WQAB .... Philippi, WV [*FM radio station call letters*]
WQAC .... Alma, MI [*FM radio station call letters*]
WQAD .... Moline, IL [*Television station call letters*]
WQAI .... Fernandina Beach, FL [*AM radio station call letters*]
WQAL .... Cleveland, OH [*FM radio station call letters*]
WQAM .... Miami, FL [*AM radio station call letters*]
WQAQ .... Hamden, CT [*FM radio station call letters*]
WQAU-P ...... Water Quality Analysis Unit - Purification [*Army*]
WQB .... Water Quality Based [*Environmental science*]
WQB .... Water-Quality Biological [*Survey*] [*Army*] (RDA)
WQBA .... Miami, FL [*AM radio station call letters*]
WQBB .... Knoxville, TN [*FM radio station call letters*]
WQBB .... Powell, TN [*AM radio station call letters*]
WQBC .... Vicksburg, MS [*AM radio station call letters*]
WQBE .... Charleston, WV [*AM radio station call letters*]
WQBE-FM .... Charleston, WV [*FM radio station call letters*]
WQBEL .... Water Quality-Based Effluent Limit [*Environmental Protection Agency*]
WQBH .... Detroit, MI [*AM radio station call letters*]
WQBJ .... Cobleskill, NY [*FM radio station call letters*]
WQBK .... Rensselaer, NY [*AM radio station call letters*]
WQBK-FM .... Rensselaer, NY [*FM radio station call letters*]
WQBN .... Temple Terrace, FL [*AM radio station call letters*]
WQBQ .... Leesburg, FL [*AM radio station call letters*]
WQBR .... Avis, PA [*FM radio station call letters*]
WQBS .... San Juan, PR [*AM radio station call letters*]
WQBX .... Alma, MI [*FM radio station call letters*] (RBYB)
WQBZ .... Fort Valley, GA [*FM radio station call letters*]
WQC .... Quinsigamond Community College, Worcester, MA [*OCLC symbol*] (OCLC)
WQC .... Water Quality Certification [*Nuclear energy*] (NRCH)
WQC .... Wheat Quality Council (EA)
WQCB .... Brewer, ME [*FM radio station call letters*]
WQCC .... La Crosse, WI [*FM radio station call letters*]
WQCD .... New York, NY [*FM radio station call letters*]
WQCH .... La Fayette, GA [*AM radio station call letters*]
WQCK .... Clinton, LA [*FM radio station call letters*]
WQCM .... Halfway, MD [*FM radio station call letters*]
WQCR .... Jackson, TN [*AM radio station call letters*]
WQCS .... Fort Pierce, FL [*FM radio station call letters*]
WQCT .... Bryan, OH [*AM radio station call letters*]
WQCY .... Quincy, IL [*FM radio station call letters*]
WQDK .... Ahoskie, NC [*FM radio station call letters*]
WQDQ .... Lebanon, TN [*AM radio station call letters*]
WQDR .... Raleigh, NC [*FM radio station call letters*]
WQDY .... Calais, ME [*AM radio station call letters*]
WQDY-FM .... Calais, ME [*FM radio station call letters*]
WQEC .... Quincy, IL [*Television station call letters*]
WQEC/C .... Weapons Quality Engineering Center, Crane [*Indiana*]
WQED .... Pittsburgh, PA [*FM radio station call letters*]
WQED-TV .... Pittsburgh, PA [*Television station call letters*]
WQEL .... Bucyrus, OH [*FM radio station call letters*]
WQEN .... Gadsden, AL [*FM radio station call letters*]
WQEQ .... Freeland, PA [*FM radio station call letters*]
WQEW .... New York, NY [*AM radio station call letters*]
WQEX .... Pittsburgh, PA [*Television station call letters*]
WQEZ .... Kennebunkport, ME [*FM radio station call letters*]
WQF .... Wider Quaker Fellowship (EA)
WQFE .... Brownsburg, IN [*FM radio station call letters*]
WQFL .... Rockford, IL [*FM radio station call letters*]
WQFM .... Milwaukee, WI [*FM radio station call letters*]
WQFN .... Walker, MI [*FM radio station call letters*]
WQFS .... Greensboro, NC [*FM radio station call letters*]
WQFX .... Gulfport, MS [*AM radio station call letters*]
WQGL .... Butler, AL [*FM radio station call letters*]
WQGN .... Groton, CT [*FM radio station call letters*]
WQHA .... Aquada, PR [*Television station call letters*]
WQHG .... Huntingdon, PA [*FM radio station call letters*]
WQHH .... Dewitt, MI [*FM radio station call letters*]
WQHK .... Decatur, IN [*FM radio station call letters*]
WQHK .... Fort Wayne, IN [*AM radio station call letters*]
WQHL .... Live Oak, FL [*AM radio station call letters*]
WQHL-FM .... Live Oak, FL [*FM radio station call letters*]
WQHQ .... Ocean City-Salisbury, MD [*FM radio station call letters*]
WQHR-FM ... Presque Isle, ME [*FM radio station call letters*] (RBYB)
WQHS .... Cleveland, OH [*Television station call letters*]
WQHT .... New York, NY [*FM radio station call letters*]
WQHY .... Prestonsburg, KY [*FM radio station call letters*]
WQI .... Water Quality Index
WQI .... Water Quality Instrument
WQIC .... Lebanon, PA [*FM radio station call letters*]
WQII .... San Juan, PR [*AM radio station call letters*]
WQIK .... Jacksonville, FL [*FM radio station call letters*]
WQIL .... Chauncey, GA [*FM radio station call letters*]
WQIO .... Mount Vernon, OH [*FM radio station call letters*]
WQIP .... Water Quality Incentive Program [*Department of Agriculture*]
WQIS .... Laurel, MS [*AM radio station call letters*]
WQIS .... Water Quality Indicator System [*Marine science*] (GFGA)
WQIS .... Water Quality Insurance Syndicate (EA)
WQIX .... Horseheads, NY [*FM radio station call letters*]
WQIX-AM .... Horseheads, NY [*AM radio station call letters*] (RBYB)
WQIZ .... St. George, SC [*AM radio station call letters*]
WQJU .... Mifflintown, PA [*FM radio station call letters*]
WQJY .... West Salem, WI [*FM radio station call letters*]
WQKC .... Seymour, IN [*AM radio station call letters*]
WQKI .... St. Matthews, SC [*AM radio station call letters*]
WQKK .... Ebensburg, PA [*FM radio station call letters*]
WQKL .... Ann Arbor, MI [*FM radio station call letters*]
WQKO .... Howe, IN [*FM radio station call letters*]
WQKR .... Portland, TN [*AM radio station call letters*]
WQKS .... Hopkinsville, KY [*AM radio station call letters*]
WQKT .... Wooster, OH [*FM radio station call letters*]
WQKX .... Sunbury, PA [*FM radio station call letters*]
WQKY .... Emporium, PA [*FM radio station call letters*]
WQLA-FM .... La Follette, TN [*FM radio station call letters*]
WQLC .... Watertown, FL [*FM radio station call letters*]
WQLE .... Kane, PA [*AM radio station call letters*]
WQLH .... Green Bay, WI [*FM radio station call letters*]
WQLJ .... Oxford, MS [*FM radio station call letters*]
WQLK .... Richmond, IN [*FM radio station call letters*]
WQLL .... Louisville, KY [*FM radio station call letters*]
WQLN .... Erie, PA [*FM radio station call letters*]
WQLN-TV .... Erie, PA [*Television station call letters*]
WQLR .... Kalamazoo, MI [*FM radio station call letters*]
WQLS .... Ozark, AL [*AM radio station call letters*]
WQLS-FM .... Ozark, AL [*FM radio station call letters*]
WQLT .... Florence, AL [*FM radio station call letters*]
WQLV .... Millersburg, PA [*FM radio station call letters*]
WQLW .... Eutaw, AL [*FM radio station call letters*]
WQLX .... Galion, OH [*FM radio station call letters*]
WQLZ .... Taylorville, IL [*FM radio station call letters*]
WQM .... University of Massachusetts, Medical Center, Worcester, MA [*OCLC symbol*] (OCLC)
WQM .... Water Quality Management
WQMA .... Marks, MS [*AM radio station call letters*]
WQMC .... Sumter, SC [*AM radio station call letters*]
WQMD .... Water Quantity Measuring Device
WQME .... Anderson, IN [*FM radio station call letters*]
WQMF .... Jeffersonville, IN [*FM radio station call letters*]
WQMG .... Greensboro, NC [*AM radio station call letters*]
WQMG-FM .... Greensboro, NC [*FM radio station call letters*]
WQMP .... Water Quality Management Project
WQMT .... Chatsworth, GA [*FM radio station call letters*]
WQMU .... Indiana, PA [*FM radio station call letters*]
WQMX .... Medina, OH [*FM radio station call letters*]
WQMZ .... Charlottesville, VA [*FM radio station call letters*]
WQNA .... Springfield, IL [*FM radio station call letters*]
WQNJ .... Ocean Acres, NJ [*FM radio station call letters*]
WQNN .... Artesia, MS [*FM radio station call letters*]
WQNS .... Waynesville, NC [*FM radio station call letters*]
WQNT-AM .... Charleston, SC [*AM radio station call letters*] (RBYB)

WQNX .... Aberdeen, NC [*AM radio station call letters*]
WQNY .... Ithaca, NY [*FM radio station call letters*]
WQNZ .... Natchez, MS [*FM radio station call letters*]
WQO .... Water Quality Office [*Later, OWP*] [*Environmental Protection Agency*]
WQOK .... South Boston, VA [*FM radio station call letters*]
WQOL .... Vero Beach, FL [*FM radio station call letters*]
WQON .... Roscommon, MI [*FM radio station call letters*] (RBYB)
WQOW .... Eau Claire, WI [*Television station call letters*]
WQOX .... Memphis, TN [*FM radio station call letters*]
WQP .... West Penn Power Co. [*NYSE symbol*] (SAG)
WQP .... West Penn Pwr 8.00% 'QUIDS' [*NYSE symbol*] (TTSB)
WQPM .... Princeton, MN [*AM radio station call letters*]
WQPM-FM .... Princeton, MN [*FM radio station call letters*]
WQPO .... Harrisonburg, VA [*FM radio station call letters*]
WQPR .... Muscle Shoals, AL [*FM radio station call letters*]
WQPT .... Moline, IL [*Television station call letters*]
WQPW .... Valdosta, GA [*FM radio station call letters*]
WQQB-FM .... Rantoul, IL [*FM radio station call letters*] (RBYB)
WQQK .... Hendersonville, TN [*FM radio station call letters*]
WQQL .... Springfield, IL [*FM radio station call letters*]
WQQQ .... Sharon, CT [*FM radio station call letters*]
WQQW .... Waterbury, CT [*AM radio station call letters*] (RBYB)
WQQZ .... Quebradillas, PR [*FM radio station call letters*]
WQRA .... Warrenton, VA [*FM radio station call letters*]
WQRB .... Bloomer, WI [*FM radio station call letters*]
WQRC .... Barnstable, MA [*FM radio station call letters*]
WQRC .... Water Quality Research Council (EA)
WQRF .... Rockford, IL [*Television station call letters*]
WQRI .... Bristol, RI [*FM radio station call letters*]
WQRK .... Bedford, IN [*FM radio station call letters*]
WQRL .... Benton, IL [*FM radio station call letters*]
WQRM .... Smethport, PA [*FM radio station call letters*]
WQRP .... Water Quality Research Program [*US Army Corps of Engineers*]
WQRP .... West Carollton, OH [*FM radio station call letters*]
WQRS .... Detroit, MI [*FM radio station call letters*]
WQRT .... Salamanca, NY [*FM radio station call letters*]
WQRX .... Valley Head, AL [*AM radio station call letters*]
WQSA .... Sarasota, FL [*AM radio station call letters*]
WQSB .... Albertville, AL [*FM radio station call letters*]
WQSC .... Charleston, NC [*AM radio station call letters*]
WQSE .... White Bluff, TN [*AM radio station call letters*]
WQSI .... Frederick, MD [*AM radio station call letters*]
WQSL .... Jacksonville, NC [*FM radio station call letters*]
WQSM .... Fayetteville, NC [*FM radio station call letters*]
WQSN .... Kalamazoo, MI [*AM radio station call letters*]
WQSR .... Catonsville, MD [*FM radio station call letters*]
WQSS .... Camden, ME [*FM radio station call letters*]
WQST .... Forest, MS [*AM radio station call letters*]
WQST-FM .... Forest, MS [*FM radio station call letters*]
WQSU .... Selinsgrove, PA [*FM radio station call letters*]
WQSV .... Ashland City, TN [*AM radio station call letters*]
WQSY .... Hawkinsville, GA [*FM radio station call letters*]
WQT .... Water Quench Test
WQTC .... Manitowoc, WI [*FM radio station call letters*]
WQTE .... Adrian, MI [*FM radio station call letters*]
WQTL .... Ottawa, OH [*FM radio station call letters*]
WQTM-AM .... Pine Hills, FL [*AM radio station call letters*] (RBYB)
WQTO .... Ponce, PR [*Television station call letters*]
WQTQ .... Hartford, CT [*FM radio station call letters*]
WQTU .... Rome, GA [*FM radio station call letters*]
WQTW .... Latrobe, PA [*AM radio station call letters*]
WQTY .... Linton, IN [*FM radio station call letters*]
WQUB .... Quincy, IL [*FM radio station call letters*]
WQUE-FM .... New Orleans, LA [*FM radio station call letters*]
WQUE-FM .... New Orleans, LA [*FM radio station call letters*] (RBYB)
WQUIS .... Water Quality Indicator System [*Marine science*] (MSC)
WQUL-FM .... West Frankfort, IL [*FM radio station call letters*] (RBYB)
WQUN-AM .... Hamden, CT [*AM radio station call letters*] (RBYB)
WQUT .... Johnson City, TN [*FM radio station call letters*]
WQVE .... Camilla, GA [*FM radio station call letters*]
WQVR .... Southbridge, MA [*FM radio station call letters*]
WQWK .... State College, PA [*FM radio station call letters*]
WQWQ .... Muskegon Heights, MI [*AM radio station call letters*]
WQXA .... York, PA [*AM radio station call letters*]
WQXA-FM .... York, PA [*FM radio station call letters*]
WQXB .... Grenada, MS [*FM radio station call letters*]
WQXC .... Otsego, MI [*AM radio station call letters*]
WQXC-FM .... Otsego, MI [*FM radio station call letters*]
WQXE .... Elizabethtown, KY [*FM radio station call letters*]
WQXI .... Atlanta, GA [*AM radio station call letters*]
WQXJ .... Clayton, GA [*FM radio station call letters*]
WQXK .... Salem, OH [*FM radio station call letters*]
WQXL .... Columbia, SC [*AM radio station call letters*]
WQXO .... Munising, MI [*AM radio station call letters*]
WQXQ .... Central City, KY [*FM radio station call letters*]
WQXR .... New York, NY [*FM radio station call letters*]
WQXY .... Hazard, KY [*AM radio station call letters*]
WQYK .... Seffner, FL [*AM radio station call letters*]
WQYK .... St. Petersburg, FL [*FM radio station call letters*]
WQYX .... Clearfield, PA [*FM radio station call letters*]
WQZK .... Keyser, WV [*FM radio station call letters*]
WQZQ .... Dickson, TN [*FM radio station call letters*]
WQZS .... Meyersdale, PA [*FM radio station call letters*]
WQZX .... Greenville, AL [*FM radio station call letters*]
WQZY .... Dublin, GA [*FM radio station call letters*]
WR .... Sutherland's Weekly Report [*India*] [*A publication*] (DLA)
WR .... Wagons-Restaurants [*Railroad dining cars in Europe*] [*French*]
WR .... Wall Receptacle (MUGU)
WR .... Wardrobe
WR .... Wardroom [*Navy*]
wr .... Ware (VRA)
WR .... Warehouse Receipt [*Often negotiable*]
WR .... Warner-Lambert Pharmaceutical Co. [*Research code symbol*]
WR .... War Reserve (AABC)
WR .... War Risk
WR .... War Risk Insurance Decisions [*United States*] [*A publication*] (DLA)
WR .... Wartime Report (MCD)
WR .... Wartime Requirements [*Air Force document*] (AFM)
WR .... Washout Rate
WR .... Washroom
W/R .... Was Received
WR .... Wassermann Reaction [*Test for syphilis*] [*Medicine*]
WR .... Water and Rail [*Transportation*]
WR .... Water Repellant [*Technical drawings*]
WR .... Water Retention (DAVI)
WR .... Water Rinse [*Photography*] (DGA)
W/R .... Water/Rock [*Ratio*] [*Geochemistry*]
WR .... Waveguide, Rectangular
WR .... Wave Retardation (DEN)
WR .... Weakly Reactive (MAE)
WR .... Weapon Radius (NVT)
WR .... Weapon Range (NATG)
WR .... Weapons Requirement [*DoD*]
WR .... Wear Resistant
WR .... Weather Reconnaissance
WR .... Weather Resistant (MSA)
WR .... Weekly Reporter [*Bengal*] [*A publication*] (DLA)
WR .... Weekly Reporter [*England*] [*A publication*] (DLA)
WR .... Weekly Reporter, Cape Provincial Division [*South Africa*] [*A publication*] (DLA)
WR .... Welfare Recipient (OICC)
WR .... Wendell's Reports [*1826-41*] [*New York*] [*A publication*] (DLA)
WR .... Western Resources [*NYSE symbol*] (TTSB)
WR .... Western Resources Capital I [*NYSE symbol*] (SAG)
WR .... Western Resources Capital II [*NYSE symbol*] (SAG)
WR .... Western Resources, Inc. [*Formerly, Kansas Power & Light Co.*] [*NYSE symbol*] (SPSG)
WR .... West's English Chancery Reports Tempore Hardwicke [*1736-39*] [*A publication*] (DLA)
WR .... Wet Runway [*NWS*] (FAAC)
WR .... Wheeler Flying Service [*ICAO designator*] (AD)
W/R .... White Room [*NASA*] (KSC)
WR .... Whiteshell Reactor [*Canada*]
WR .... Whole Rock [*Geology*]
WR .... Wide Range [*Nuclear energy*] (NRCH)
WR .... Wide Ratio [*Automotive engineering*]
WR .... Wide Receiver [*Football*]
WR .... Wildlife Reserve [*State*] (EERA)
WR .... Wild Rose Resources [*Vancouver Stock Exchange symbol*]
WR .... Willelmus Rex [*King William*]
WR .... Wilson Repeater (IEEE)
WR .... Wiping Reflex [*Physiology*]
WR .... Wire Recorder (DEN)
WR .... Wire Rope (AAG)
WR .... Wirral Railway [*British*] (ROG)
WR .... Wisconsin Reports [*A publication*] (DLA)
WR .... Wissenschaftsrat [*Science Council*] [*Germany*]
WR .... With Rights [*Securities*]
WR .... Wolf-Raye [*Star classification*]
WR .... Wolseley Register (EA)
WR .... Women's Reserve [*Navy*]
WR .... Women's Roundtable (EA)
WR .... Woodmen Rangers (EA)
WR .... Word Restoration
WR .... Working Register
WR .... Work Rate (AAMN)
WR .... Work Request (MCD)
WR .... Work Requirement (CAAL)
WR .... Workshop Reporting (IAA)
WR .... World Reporter [*World Council of Credit Unions*] [*A publication*]
WR .... World River [*Geology*]
WR .... Worthington Register [*Defunct*] (EA)
WR .... Wrap
WR .... Wreath (WGA)
WR .... Wrench (MSA)
Wr .... Wright [*Blood group*]
Wr .... Wright's Reports [*37-50 Pennsylvania*] [*A publication*] (DLA)
WR .... Wrist [*Medicine*]
WR .... Wrist Roll (NASA)
WR .... Write
WR .... Writer (MSA)
wr .... Wrong
WR2 .... Warramunga Array [*Australia Seismograph station code, US Geological Survey*] (SEIS)
WRA .... Walter Reed Army Medical Center, Washington, DC [*OCLC symbol*] (OCLC)
WRA .... Ward Room Attendant [*British military*] (DMA)
WRA .... Warramunga Array [*Australia Seismograph station code, US Geological Survey*] (SEIS)

WRA .... War Relocation Authority [*Within Office of Emergency Management*] [*To provide for the relocation of persons whose removal seemed necessary for national security, and for their maintenance and supervision*] [*World War II*]
WRA .... War Reserve Allowance (CINC)
WRA .... Waste Regulation Authority [*British*]
WRA .... Water Research Association [*British*] (DCTA)
WRA .... Weapons Replaceable [*or Replacement*] Assembly
WRA .... Western Railroad Association (EA)
WRA .... Western Range Association (EA)
WRA .... White River Air Services Ltd. [*Canada ICAO designator*] (FAAC)
WRA .... Whiteware Research Association [*Defunct*] (EA)
WRA .... Windarra Minerals Ltd. [*Vancouver Stock Exchange symbol Toronto Stock Exchange symbol*]
WRA .... Wind Restraint Area (SAA)
WRA .... With the Rule Astigmatism [*Ophthalmology*]
WRA .... Women's Rabbinic Alliance [*Later, WSA*] (EA)
WRA .... World Road Association [*Finland*] (EAIO)
WRA .... Wrinkle Recovery Angle (IAA)
WRAA .... Luray, VA [*AM radio station call letters*]
WRAB .... Arab, AL [*AM radio station call letters*]
WR/ABPR .... Weekly Record/American Book Publishing Record [*A publication*]
WRac .... Racine Public Library, Racine, WI [*Library symbol Library of Congress*] (LCLS)
WRAC .... Waste and Recycling Advisory Committee (EERA)
WRAC .... Water Resources Advisory Committee [*Australian Environment Council*] (EERA)
WRAC .... West Union, OH [*FM radio station call letters*]
WRAC .... Willow Run Aeronautical Center [*Michigan*] (MCD)
WRAC .... Women's Royal Army Corps [*British*]
WRacC .... Racine County Institutions Medical Library, Racine, WI [*Library symbol Library of Congress*] (LCLS)
WRacCL .... Racine County Law Library, Racine, WI [*Library symbol Library of Congress*] (LCLS)
WRacD .... DeKoven Foundation for Church Work, Racine, WI [*Library symbol Library of Congress*] (LCLS)
WRACELD .... Wounds Received in Action [*Incurred in*] Combat with the Enemy or in Line of Duty [*Army*] (AABC)
WRacGS ...... Girl Scouts of Racine County, Racine, WI [*Library symbol Library of Congress*] (LCLS)
WRacJ .... S. C. Johnson & Son, Inc., Racine, WI [*Library symbol Library of Congress*] (LCLS)
WRacSD ...... Racine Unified School District Number One, Racine, WI [*Library symbol Library of Congress*] (LCLS)
WRacSL .... Saint Luke's Memorial Hospital, School of Nursing, Racine, WI [*Library symbol Library of Congress*] (LCLS)
WRacSM .... Saint Mary's Hospital, Racine, WI [*Library symbol Library of Congress*] (LCLS)
WRacWa .... Walker Manufacturing Co., Racine, WI [*Library symbol Library of Congress*] (LCLS)
WRacWM ..... Wustum Museum of Fine Arts, Racine, WI [*Library symbol Library of Congress*] (LCLS)
WRacWP ..... Western Publishing Co., Inc., Racine, WI [*Library symbol Library of Congress*] (LCLS)
WRacY .... Young Radiator Co., Racine, WI [*Library symbol Library of Congress*] (LCLS)
WRAD .... Radford, VA [*AM radio station call letters*]
WRAF .... Toccoa Falls, GA [*FM radio station call letters*]
WRAF .... Women's Royal Air Force [*British*]
WRAFVR .... Women's Royal Air Force Volunteer Reserve [*British military*] (DMA)
WRAG .... Carrollton, AL [*AM radio station call letters*]
WRAH-AM ... Easley, SC [*AM radio station call letters*] (RBYB)
WRAIN .... Walter Reed Army Institute of Nursing (AABC)
WRAIR .... Walter Reed Army Institute of Research [*Washington, DC*] (MCD)
WRAIS .... Wide Range Analog Input Subsystem
WRAJ .... Anna, IL [*AM radio station call letters*]
WRAJ-FM ... Anna, IL [*FM radio station call letters*]
WRAK .... Williamsport, PA [*AM radio station call letters*]
WRAK-FM ... Salladasburg, PA [*FM radio station call letters*] (RBYB)
WRAL .... Raleigh, NC [*FM radio station call letters*]
WRALC .... Warner Robins Air Logistics Center [*Formerly, WRAMA*] (MCD)
WRAL-TV .... Raleigh, NC [*Television station call letters*]
WRAM .... Monmouth, IL [*AM radio station call letters*]
WRAM .... Water Resources Assessment Methodology [*Army Corps of Engineers*]
WRAM .... Wide-Range Recording and Monitoring [*System*] [*Radiation*]
WRAM .... Windows Random Access Memory (PCM)
WRAMA .... Warner Robins Air Materiel Area [*Later, WRALC*]
WRAMC .... Walter Reed Army Medical Center
WRANG .... Wrangler (ROG)
WRAP .... Warfighting Rapid Acquisition Program
WRAP .... Waste Reduction Always Pays [*Dow Chemical Co. antipollution program*]
WRAP .... Waste Reduction Assessments Program [*Environmental Protection Agency*]
WRAP .... Waste Reduction Audit Protocol
WRAP .... Water Reactor Analysis Program [*Nuclear energy*] (NRCH)
WRAP .... Weapons Readiness Achievement Program (MUGU)
WRAP .... Weapons Readiness Analysis Program [*Navy*]
WRAP .... Weapons Reliability Assurance Program [*Navy*] (DNAB)
WRAP .... Weighter Record Analysis Program [*Computer science*] (MHDI)
WRAP .... Women's Radical Action Project [*Feminist group*]
WRAP .... Woodland Resource Analysis Program [*Tennessee Valley Authority*]
WRAP .... Worker Readjustment Program [*Department of Labor*]
WRAP .... Workpackage Risk Analysis Procedure (AAGC)
WRAP .... Workpackage Risk Assessment Procedure (AAGC)
WRAP .... World Risk Analysis Package [*S. J. Rundt & Associates*] [*Information service or system*] (IID)
WRAPS .... Workload and Repair Activity Process Simulator (PDAA)
WRAQ .... Brevard, NC [*AM radio station call letters*]
WRAR .... Tappahannock, VA [*AM radio station call letters*]
WRAR-FM .... Tappahannock, VA [*FM radio station call letters*]
WRAS .... Atlanta, GA [*FM radio station call letters*]
WRAS .... Women's Reserve Ambulance Society [*World War I*] [*British*]
WRASPD ...... World Rehabilitation Association for the Psycho-Socially Disabled (EA)
WRAT .... Wide-Range Achievement Test
WRAT-FM .... Point Pleasant, NJ [*FM radio station call letters*] (RBYB)
WRATH .... Women Refusing to Accept Tenant Harassment (EA)
Wrat-R .... Wide Range Achievement Test-Revised
WRAW .... Reading, PA [*AM radio station call letters*]
WRAWG .... Water Resource Assessment Working Group [*Australia*]
WRAX-FM .... Trussville, AL [*FM radio station call letters*] (RBYB)
WRAY .... Princeton, IN [*AM radio station call letters*]
WRAY-FM .... Princeton, IN [*FM radio station call letters*]
WRAY-TV .... Wilson, NC [*Television station call letters*] (RBYB)
WRAZ .... Raleigh, NC [*Television station call letters*] (RBYB)
WRB .... Macon/Warner Robins, GA [*Location identifier FAA*] (FAAL)
WRB .... Walter Reed Army Medical Center, Post/Patient Library, Washington, DC [*OCLC symbol*] (OCLC)
WRB .... Wardrobe (MSA)
WRB .... Warramunga Array [*Australia Seismograph station code, US Geological Survey*] (SEIS)
WRB .... War Refugee Board [*Terminated, 1945*]
WRB .... Water Resources Board [*British*] (DCTA)
WRB .... Wide-Range Burner (DNAB)
WRBA .... Springfield, FL [*FM radio station call letters*]
WRBA .... World Robotic Boxing Association (EA)
WRBB .... Banjarmasin/Syamsuddin Noor [*Indonesia*] [*ICAO location identifier*] (ICLI)
WRBB .... Boston, MA [*FM radio station call letters*]
WRBC .... Batu Licin [*Indonesia*] [*ICAO location identifier*] (ICLI)
WRBC .... Lewiston, ME [*FM radio station call letters*]
WRBC .... Washed Red Blood Cells [*Hematology*] (DAVI)
WRBC .... Weather Relay Broadcast Center
WRBD .... Pompano Beach, FL [*AM radio station call letters*]
WRBE .... Lucedale, MS [*AM radio station call letters*]
WRBE-FM .... Lucedale, MS [*FM radio station call letters*]
WRBG .... Warner Robins, GA [*FM radio station call letters*] (RBYB)
WRBH .... New Orleans, LA [*FM radio station call letters*]
WRBI .... Batesville, IN [*FM radio station call letters*]
WRBI .... Pangkalan Bun/Iskandar [*Indonesia*] [*ICAO location identifier*] (ICLI)
WRBK .... Kotabaru/Setagen [*Indonesia*] [*ICAO location identifier*] (ICLI)
WRBL .... Columbus, GA [*Television station call letters*]
WRBM .... Muaratewe/Beringin [*Indonesia*] [*ICAO location identifier*] (ICLI)
WRBN .... Tanjung/Warukin [*Indonesia*] [*ICAO location identifier*] (ICLI)
WRBND .... Wire Bound
WRBP .... Hubbard, OH [*FM radio station call letters*]
WRBP .... Palangkaraya/Panarung [*Indonesia*] [*ICAO location identifier*] (ICLI)
WRBQ .... St. Petersburg, FL [*AM radio station call letters*]
WRBQ .... Tampa, FL [*FM radio station call letters*]
WRBR .... South Bend, IN [*FM radio station call letters*]
WRBR .... Wright Brothers National Memorial
WRBS .... Baltimore, MD [*FM radio station call letters*]
WRBS .... Sampit/H. Hasan [*Indonesia*] [*ICAO location identifier*] (ICLI)
WRBT .... Mt. Carmel, IL [*FM radio station call letters*]
WRBT .... Teluk Kepayang [*Indonesia*] [*ICAO location identifier*] (ICLI)
WRBU .... Buntok/Sanggau [*Indonesia*] [*ICAO location identifier*] (ICLI)
WRBW .... Orlando, FL [*Television station call letters*]
WRBX .... Reidsville, GA [*FM radio station call letters*]
WRBZ .... Banjarmasin Sector [*Indonesia*] [*ICAO location identifier*] (ICLI)
WRBZ .... Raleigh, NC [*AM radio station call letters*] (RBYB)
WRC .... War Resources Council [*Terminated*]
WRC .... Washed Red Cells [*Medicine*]
WRC .... Washington, DC [*Television station call letters*]
WRC .... Washington Research Council [*Research center*] (RCD)
WRC .... Water Research Centre [*Research center British*] (IRC)
WRC .... Water Resources Center [*University of Illinois*]
WRC .... Water Resources Congress (EA)
WRC .... Water Resources Council [*Inactive*]
WRC .... Water-Retention Coefficient
WRC .... Watson Research Center [*IBM Corp.*]
WRC .... Weapons Release Computer [*or Controller*]
WRC .... Weather Relay Center
WRC .... Weekly Readiness Check
WRC .... Welding Research Council (EA)
WRC .... Well to Right of Course [*Aviation*] (FAAC)
WRC .... Werewolf Research Center (EA)
WRC .... Whale Rescue Centre [*Australia*]
WRC .... Wheat Research Council [*Australia*]
WRC .... Wildland Resources Center [*University of California*] [*Research center*] (RCD)
WRC .... Wildlife Rehabilitation Council (EA)
WRC .... Williams Ranch [*California*] [*Seismograph station code, US Geological Survey Closed*] (SEIS)
WRC .... Williams Research Corp.
WRC .... Women's Relief Corps
WRC .... Women's Rights Committee (EA)
WRC .... Woodchip Research Committee [*Australia*]
WRC .... World Color Press [*NYSE symbol*] (TTSB)

WRC .... World Rally Championship
WRC .... World Relief Canada
WRC .... World Relief Corp. (EA)
WRC .... World Romani Congress
WRC .... W. R. Carpenter Airlines [*Australia*]
WRCA .... Waltham, MA [*AM radio station call letters*]
WRCA .... Western Red Cedar Association (EA)
WRCA .... W. R. Carpenter Airlines [*Australia*]
WR Calc ...... Sutherland's Weekly Reporter, Calcutta [*India*] [*A publication*] (DLA)
WRCB .... Chattanooga, TN [*Television station call letters*]
WRCB .... War Relief Control Board [*President's*]
WRCC .... Workers' Rehabilitation and Compensation Corp. [*South Australia*]
WRCCC .... Wheeler AFB Range Communications Control Center (MCD)
WRCC-FM ...... Marshall, MI [*FM radio station call letters*] (RBYB)
WRCCHE ...... Western Regional Consortium, Librarians' Networking Committee [*Library network*]
WRCD .... Honeyoye Falls, NY [*FM radio station call letters*]
WRCF .... Whale Research and Conservation Fund [*Defunct*] (EA)
WRCG .... Columbus, GA [*AM radio station call letters*]
WRCGR .... Women's Reserve of the Coast Guard Reserve
WRCH .... New Britain, CT [*FM radio station call letters*]
Wr Ch .... Wright's Ohio Reports [*1831-34*] [*A publication*] (DLA)
WRCHK .... Write Check [*Computer science*] (IAA)
WRCI .... Hillsboro, NH [*FM radio station call letters*]
WRCK .... Utica, NY [*FM radio station call letters*]
WRCKG .... Wrecking
WRCKR .... Wrecker
WRCLA .... Western Red Cedar Lumber Association (EA)
WRCM .... Wingate, NC [*FM radio station call letters*]
WRCN .... Riverhead, NY [*FM radio station call letters*]
WRCNS .... Women's Royal Canadian Naval Service [*World War II*]
WRCNSW .... Wheat Research Committee for New South Wales [*Australia*]
WRCO .... Richland Center, WI [*AM radio station call letters*]
WRCO-FM ...... Richland Center, WI [*FM radio station call letters*]
WRCP .... Providence, RI [*AM radio station call letters*]
WRCPATT .... World Rabbinic Committee for the Preservation of Ancient Tombs in Tiberias (EA)
WRCQ .... Dunn, NC [*FM radio station call letters*]
WRCQ .... Wheat Research Committee for Queensland [*Australia*]
WRCR .... Rushville, IN [*FM radio station call letters*]
WRCR .... Wife's Restitution of Conjugal Rights [*Law suit*] [*British*] (ROG)
WRCR .... Wisconsin Railroad Commission Reports [*A publication*] (DLA)
WRCS .... Ahoskie, NC [*AM radio station call letters*]
WRCS .... Weapons Release Computer Set [*or System*] (MCD)
WRCS .... Work Ordering and Reporting Communications System [*Army*] (MCD)
WRCSA .... Wheat Research Committee for South Australia
WRCT .... Pittsburgh, PA [*FM radio station call letters*]
WRCU .... Hamilton, NY [*FM radio station call letters*]
WRCV .... Wheat Research Committee for Victoria [*Australia*]
WRCV-AM ...... Grand Rapids, MI [*AM radio station call letters*] (RBYB)
WRCW .... Canton, OH [*AM radio station call letters*]
WRCWA .... Wheat Research Committee for Western Australia
WRCX .... Chicago, IL [*FM radio station call letters*]
WRCY .... Warrenton, VA [*FM radio station call letters*]
WRCZ .... Pittsfield, MA [*FM radio station call letters*]
WRD .... Warden [*Washington*] [*Seismograph station code, US Geological Survey*] (SEIS)
WRD .... Water Resources Division [*US Geological Survey*]
WRD .... Whole Rumen Digesta [*Dairy science*] (OA)
WRD .... Worm Runner's Digest [*A satirical publication*]
WRDA .... Water Resources Development Act (GFGA)
WRDB .... Reedsburg, WI [*AM radio station call letters*]
WRDB .... Worldwide Water Resources Database
WRDC .... Durham, NC [*Television station call letters*]
WRDC .... Western Rural Development Center [*Oregon State University*] [*Research center*] (RCD)
WRDC .... Westinghouse Research and Development Center (MCD)
WRDC .... White Rose Dollmakers Circle [*British*] [*An association*] (DBA)
WRDC .... Wool Research and Development Corp. [*Commonwealth*] (EERA)
WRDC .... Wright Research and Development Center [*Wright-Patterson Air Force Base*] (GRD)
WRDD .... Ebensburg, PA [*AM radio station call letters*]
WRDI .... We Remember Dean International (EA)
WRDIR .... Wrong Direction
WRDJ .... Roanoke, VA [*FM radio station call letters*]
WRDL .... Ashland, OH [*FM radio station call letters*]
WRDM .... Bloomfield, CT [*AM radio station call letters*]
WRDN .... Durand, WI [*AM radio station call letters*]
WRDN .... Warden
WRDN-FM .... Durand, WI [*FM radio station call letters*]
WRDO .... Fitzgerald, GA [*FM radio station call letters*]
WRDR .... Egg Harbor City, NJ [*FM radio station call letters*]
WRDS-FM .... Phoenix, NY [*FM radio station call letters*] (RBYB)
WRDU .... Wilson, NC [*FM radio station call letters*]
WRDV .... Warminster, PA [*FM radio station call letters*]
WRDW .... Augusta, GA [*AM radio station call letters*]
WRDW-TV ... Augusta, GA [*Television station call letters*]
WRE .... Washington Real Estate Investment Trust [*AMEX symbol*] (SPSG)
WRE .... Washington REIT SBI [*AMEX symbol*] (TTSB)
WRE .... Weapon Research Establishment
WRE .... Whangarei [*New Zealand*] [*Airport symbol*] (OAG)
WRE .... Whole Ragweed Extract (MAE)
WRE .... Winston Resources Ltd. [*Vancouver Stock Exchange symbol*]
WREA .... Dayton, TN [*AM radio station call letters*]
WREAFS ...... Waste Reduction Evaluation at Federal Sites [*Environmental Protection Agency*]
WREB .... Greencastle, IN [*FM radio station call letters*] (RBYB)
WREC .... Memphis, TN [*AM radio station call letters*]
WREC .... Wire Rope Export Conference [*British*] (DBA)
WRECISS ..... Weapons Research Establishment Camera Interception Single Shot
WRECS .... Weapon Radiation Effects on Communications Systems (MCD)
WRED .... Saco, ME [*FM radio station call letters*] (RBYB)
WREDAC ...... Weapons Research Establishment Digital Automatic Computer
WREDS .... Western Region Ethnic Disability Service [*Victoria, Australia*]
WREE .... Women for Racial and Economic Equality (EA)
WREF .... Ridgefield, CT [*AM radio station call letters*]
W REF .... With Reference To (WDAA)
WREFC .... We Remember Elvis Fan Club (EA)
WREG .... Memphis, TN [*Television station call letters*]
W/REG .... Window Regulator [*Automotive engineering*]
W REG .... With Regard To (WDAA)
WREI .... Women's Research and Education Institute (EA)
WREJ .... Richmond, VA [*AM radio station call letters*]
WREK .... Atlanta, GA [*FM radio station call letters*]
WREL .... Buena Vista, VA [*FM radio station call letters*]
WREL .... Lexington, VA [*AM radio station call letters*]
WREM-AM ... Monticello, ME [*AM radio station call letters*] (RBYB)
WREN .... Topeka, KS [*AM radio station call letters*] (RBYB)
WREN .... Women's Royal English Navy (IIA)
WRENACK .... WREN [*Women's Royal Naval Service*] Assistant Cook [*British military*] (DMA)
WRENAM ..... WREN [*Women's Royal Naval Service*] Air Mechanic [*British military*] (DMA)
WRENCINE(AB) ... WREN [*Women's Royal Naval Service*] Cinema Operator (Able) [*British military*] (DMA)
WRENCINE(ORD) ... WREN [*Women's Royal Naval Service*] Cinema Operator (Ordinary) [*British military*] (DMA)
WRENCK ...... WREN [*Women's Royal Naval Service*] Cook [*British military*] (DMA)
WRENDHYG ... WREN [*Women's Royal Naval Service*] Dental Hygienist [*British military*] (DMA)
WRENDSA ... WREN [*Women's Royal Naval Service*] Dental Surgery Assistant [*British military*] (DMA)
WRENEDUC ... WREN [*Women's Royal Naval Service*] Education Assistant [*British military*] (DMA)
WRENMET ... WREN [*Women's Royal Naval Service*] Meteorological Observer [*British military*] (DMA)
WRENMT ..... WREN [*Women's Royal Naval Service*] Motor Transport Driver [*British military*] (DMA)
WRENPHOT ... WREN [*Women's Royal Naval Service*] Photographer [*British military*] (DMA)
WRENQA ...... WREN [*Women's Royal Naval Service*] Quarters Assistant [*British military*] (DMA)
WREN(R) ..... WREN [*Women's Royal Naval Service*] (RADAR) [*British military*] (DMA)
WRENREG ... WREN [*Women's Royal Naval Service*] Regulating [*British military*] (DMA)
WRENREM ... WREN [*Women's Royal Naval Service*] Radio Electrical Mechanic [*British military*] (DMA)
WRENRO(M)1 ... WREN [*Women's Royal Naval Service*] Radio Operator (Morse) 1st Class [*British military*] (DMA)
WRENRO(M)2 ... WREN [*Women's Royal Naval Service*] Radio Operator (Morse) 2nd Class [*British military*] (DMA)
WRENS .... Women's Royal Naval Service [*Acronym is a phonetic reference to members of this British service branch*] [*Also, WRNS*]
WRENSA ...... WREN [*Women's Royal Naval Service*] Stores Accountant [*British military*] (DMA)
WRENS(C) ... WREN [*Women's Royal Naval Service*] Stores Assistant (Clothes) [*British military*] (DMA)
WRENS(S) ... WREN [*Women's Royal Naval Service*] Stores Assistant (Stores) [*British military*] (DMA)
WRENSTD ... WREN [*Women's Royal Naval Service*] Steward [*British military*] (DMA)
WRENS(V) ... WREN [*Women's Royal Naval Service*] Stores Assistant (Victualling) [*British military*] (DMA)
WRENTEL .... WREN [*Women's Royal Naval Service*] Telephonist [*British military*] (DMA)
WRENTSA .... WREN [*Women's Royal Naval Service*] Training Support Assistant [*British military*] (DMA)
WRENWA ..... WREN [*Women's Royal Naval Service*] Weapon Analyst [*British military*] (DMA)
WRENWTR(G) ... WREN [*Women's Royal Naval Service*] Writer (General) [*British military*] (DMA)
WRENWTR(P) ... WREN [*Women's Royal Naval Service*] Writer (Pay) [*British military*] (DMA)
WRENWTR(S) ... WREN [*Women's Royal Naval Service*] Writer (Shorthand) [*British military*] (DMA)
WREO .... Ashtabula, OH [*FM radio station call letters*]
W Rep .... West's English Chancery Reports Tempore Hardwicke [*1736-39*] [*A publication*] (DLA)
WREST .... Washington Regional Engineers, Scientists, and Technicians
WREST .... Wide Range Employability Sample Test
WRET .... Spartanburg, SC [*Television station call letters*]
WRET .... Work-Related Education and Training (AIE)
WREU .... Western Railway Employees' Union [*India*]
WREV .... Cambridge, MN [*FM radio station call letters*]
WREV .... Reidsville, NC [*AM radio station call letters*]
WREX .... Rockford, IL [*Television station call letters*]
WREX .... Wrexham [*City in Wales*]
WREY .... Millville, NJ [*AM radio station call letters*]

WREZ.......... Metropolis, IL [*FM radio station call letters*]
WRF.......... University of Wisconsin, River Falls, River Falls, WI [*OCLC symbol*] (OCLC)
WRF.......... Weak Radial Field
WRF.......... Weibull Reliability Function [*Statistics*]
WRF.......... Wheat Ridge Foundation (EA)
WRF.......... World Rehabilitation Fund (EA)
WRF.......... World Research Foundation (EA)
WRFB.......... Cocoa, FL [*AM radio station call letters*]
WRFC.......... Athens, GA [*AM radio station call letters*]
WRFCG.......... War Reserve Functional Coordinating Group [*DoD*]
WRFD.......... Columbus-Worthington, OH [*AM radio station call letters*]
WRFG.......... Atlanta, GA [*FM radio station call letters*]
WRFG.......... Wharfage [*Shipping*] (WGA)
WRFH.......... Marietta, PA [*FM radio station call letters*]
WRFK.......... California, MD [*FM radio station call letters*]
WRFL.......... Lexington, KY [*FM radio station call letters*]
WRFM-FM.......... Remsen, NY [*FM radio station call letters*] (RBYB)
WRFQ-FM.......... Mt. Pleasant, SC [*FM radio station call letters*] (RBYB)
WRFR.......... Franklin, NC [*FM radio station call letters*]
WRFS.......... Alexander City, AL [*AM radio station call letters*]
WRFT.......... Indianapolis, IN [*FM radio station call letters*]
WRfU.......... University of Wisconsin-River Falls, River Falls, WI [*Library symbol Library of Congress*] (LCLS)
WRFW.......... River Falls, WI [*FM radio station call letters*]
WRFX.......... Kannapolis, NC [*FM radio station call letters*]
WRFY.......... Reading, PA [*FM radio station call letters*]
WRG.......... Wearing (MSA)
WRG.......... Weather Reconnaissance Group [*Military*]
WRG.......... Westport Research Group [*Information service or system*] (IID)
WRG.......... White River [*Alaska*] [*Seismograph station code, US Geological Survey*] (SEIS)
WRG.......... Wire Routing Guide (MCD)
WRG.......... Wiring
WRG.......... Wrangell [*Alaska*] [*Airport symbol*] (OAG)
WRG.......... Wrangell, AK [*Location identifier FAA*] (FAAL)
WRG.......... Wrong [*Telecommunications*] (TEL)
WRGA.......... Rome, GA [*AM radio station call letters*]
WRGA.......... Western River Guides Association (EA)
WRGB.......... Schenectady, NY [*Television station call letters*]
WRGC.......... Sylva, NC [*AM radio station call letters*]
WRGG.......... Endwell, NY [*FM radio station call letters*]
WRGH.......... Walter Reed General Hospital (MCD)
WRGM.......... Ontario, OH [*AM radio station call letters*]
WRGN.......... Sweet Valley, PA [*FM radio station call letters*]
WRGO-FM.......... Cedar Key, FL [*FM radio station call letters*] (RBYB)
WRGP-FM.......... Homestead, FL [*FM radio station call letters*] (RBYB)
WRGR.......... Tupper Lake, NY [*FM radio station call letters*]
WRGR.......... Wringer
WRGS.......... Rogersville, TN [*AM radio station call letters*]
WRGT.......... Dayton, OH [*Television station call letters*]
WRGW.......... Somersworth, NH [*FM radio station call letters*]
WRGX.......... Briarcliff Manor, NY [*FM radio station call letters*]
WRh.......... Rhinelander Public Library, Rhinelander, WI [*Library symbol Library of Congress*] (LCLS)
WRH.......... Warnkenhagen [*German Democratic Republic*] [*Geomagnetic observatory code*]
WRH.......... William Randolph Hearst [*American newspaper publisher, 1863-1951*]
WRH.......... World Radio Handbook
WRHC.......... Coral Gables, FL [*AM radio station call letters*]
WRHD.......... Riverhead, NY [*AM radio station call letters*]
WRHI.......... Rock Hill, SC [*AM radio station call letters*]
WRHL.......... Rochelle, IL [*AM radio station call letters*]
WRHL.......... World Roller Hockey League
WRHL-FM.......... Rochelle, IL [*FM radio station call letters*]
WRHM.......... Lancaster, SC [*FM radio station call letters*]
WRHN.......... Rhinelander, WI [*FM radio station call letters*]
WRHO.......... Oneonta, NY [*FM radio station call letters*]
WRHQ.......... Richmond Hill, GA [*FM radio station call letters*]
wrhs.......... Warehouse (VRA)
WRHSE.......... Warehouse
WRHT.......... Morehead City, NC [*FM radio station call letters*]
WRHU.......... Hempstead, NY [*FM radio station call letters*]
WRHV.......... Poughkeepsie, NY [*FM radio station call letters*]
WRHY.......... Centre, AL [*FM radio station call letters*]
WRI.......... International Water Resources Institute [*George Washington University*] [*Research center*] (RCD)
WRI.......... War Resisters International [*British*]
WRI.......... War Risks Insurance [*British*]
WRI.......... Waterloo Research Institute [*University of Waterloo*] [*Research center*] (RCD)
WRI.......... Water Research Institute [*West Virginia University*] [*Research center*] (RCD)
WRI.......... Weatherstrip Research Institute
WRI.......... Weingarten Realty Investors, Inc. [*NYSE symbol*] (SPSG)
WRI.......... Weingarten Rlty SBI [*NYSE symbol*] (TTSB)
WRI.......... Welfare Research, Inc. (EA)
WRI.......... Western Research Institute [*Laramie, WY*] [*Department of Energy*] (GRD)
WRI.......... Winzen Research, Inc.
WRI.......... Wire Reinforcement Institute (EA)
WRI.......... Wire Rope Institute
WRI.......... World Research, Inc. [*San Diego, CA*] (EA)
WRI.......... World Resources Institute (EA)
WRI.......... Wrightstown, NJ [*Location identifier FAA*] (FAAL)
WRIA.......... Worked Republic of India Award [*Amateur radio*] (IAA)
WRIB.......... Providence, RI [*AM radio station call letters*]
WRIC.......... Petersburg, VA [*Television station call letters*]
WRIC.......... Richlands, VA [*AM radio station call letters*]
WRIC-FM.......... Richlands, VA [*FM radio station call letters*]
WRIE.......... Erie, PA [*AM radio station call letters*]
WRIF.......... Detroit, MI [*FM radio station call letters*]
WRIF.......... Water Resources Information File [*Terrain Analysis Center*] [*Army*]
WRIG.......... Schofield, WI [*AM radio station call letters*]
Wright.......... Wright's Ohio Reports [*1831-34*] [*A publication*] (DLA)
Wright.......... Wright's Reports [*37-50 Pennsylvania*] [*A publication*] (DLA)
Wright Ch.......... Wright's Ohio Reports [*1831-34*] [*A publication*] (DLA)
Wright Cr Cons... Wright's Criminal Conspiracies [*1873*] [*A publication*] (DLA)
Wright NP.......... Wright's Ohio Nisi Prius Reports [*A publication*] (DLA)
Wright (Ohio C)... Wright's Ohio Reports [*A publication*] (DLA)
Wright R.......... Wright's Ohio Reports [*A publication*] (DLA)
Wright's Rep... Wright's Ohio Reports [*A publication*] (DLA)
Wright St L... Wright's Advice on the Study of the Law [*A publication*] (DLA)
Wright St U... Wright State University (GAGS)
Wright Ten... Wright on Tenures [*A publication*] (DLA)
Wrigley.......... Wrigley [*Wm.*] Jr. Co. [*Associated Press*] (SAG)
WRIJ.......... Masontown, PA [*FM radio station call letters*]
WRIK.......... Brookport, IL [*AM radio station call letters*]
WRIK.......... Metropolis, IL [*FM radio station call letters*]
WRIL.......... Pineville, KY [*FM radio station call letters*]
WRIN.......... Rensselaer, IN [*AM radio station call letters*]
WRINS.......... Women's Royal Indian Naval Service [*British military*] (DMA)
WRIO.......... Ponce, PR [*FM radio station call letters*]
WRIOT.......... Wide Range Interest and Opinion Test
WRIP.......... Lake City, SC [*AM radio station call letters*]
WRipC.......... Ripon College, Ripon, WI [*Library symbol Library of Congress*] (LCLS)
WRIPS.......... Wave Rider Information Processing System [*Marine science*] (OSRA)
WRIPS.......... Wave Rider Information Processing System (USDC)
WRIPT.......... Wide Range Intelligence-Personality Test [*Personality development test*] [*Psychology*]
WRIQ.......... Radford, VA [*FM radio station call letters*]
WRIR-FM.......... Bethlehem, WV [*FM radio station call letters*] (RBYB)
WRIS.......... Roanoke, VA [*AM radio station call letters*]
WRIS.......... Water Resources Information System (NOAA)
WRISC.......... Western Regional Information Service Center [*University of California*] [*Information service or system Defunct*] (IID)
WRISE.......... Waste Reduction Institute for Scientists and Engineers [*Environmental Protection Agency*]
WRISE.......... Wisconsin Program for the Renewal and Improvement of Secondary Education (EDAC)
WRIST.......... Women's Repetition Injury Support Team [*Australia*]
WRIT.......... Bamberg-Denmark, SC [*AM radio station call letters*]
WRIT.......... Washington Real Estate Investment Trust [*Associated Press*] (SAG)
WRITAR.......... Waste Reduction Institute for Training and Applications Research [*Environmental Protection Agency*]
WRITE.......... Waste Reduction Innovative Technology Evaluation [*Environmental Protection Agency*]
WRITG.......... Writing (ROG)
WRIU.......... Kingston, RI [*FM radio station call letters*]
WRIU.......... Weather RADAR Interface Unit (MCD)
WRIU.......... Write Interface Unit
WRIV.......... Riverhead, NY [*AM radio station call letters*]
WRIX.......... Homeland Park, SC [*AM radio station call letters*]
WRIX.......... Honea Path, SC [*FM radio station call letters*]
WRJA.......... Sumter, SC [*FM radio station call letters*]
WRJA-TV.......... Sumter, SC [*Television station call letters*]
WRJB.......... Camden, TN [*FM radio station call letters*]
WRJC.......... Mauston, WI [*AM radio station call letters*]
WRJC-FM.......... Mauston, WI [*FM radio station call letters*]
WRJH.......... Brandon, MS [*FM radio station call letters*]
WRJL.......... Hanceville, AL [*AM radio station call letters*]
WRJM.......... Geneva, AL [*FM radio station call letters*]
WRJM-TV.......... Troy, AL [*Television station call letters*]
WRJN.......... Racine, WI [*AM radio station call letters*]
WRJO.......... Eagle River, WI [*FM radio station call letters*]
WRJQ.......... Appleton, WI [*AM radio station call letters*]
WRJS.......... Oil City, PA [*FM radio station call letters*]
WRJT.......... Royalton, VT [*FM radio station call letters*] (RBYB)
WRJW.......... Picayune, MS [*AM radio station call letters*]
WRJZ.......... Knoxville, TN [*AM radio station call letters*]
WRK.......... Wall & Redekop Corp. [*Toronto Stock Exchange symbol Vancouver Stock Exchange symbol*]
WRK.......... Wrecker
WRKA.......... Atambua/Haliwen [*Indonesia*] [*ICAO location identifier*] (ICLI)
WRKA.......... St. Matthews, KY [*FM radio station call letters*]
WRKB.......... Bajawa/Padhameleda [*Indonesia*] [*ICAO location identifier*] (ICLI)
WRKB.......... Kannapolis, NC [*AM radio station call letters*]
WRKC.......... Maumere/Wai Oti [*Indonesia*] [*ICAO location identifier*] (ICLI)
WRKC.......... Wilkes-Barre, PA [*FM radio station call letters*]
WRKD.......... Rockland, ME [*AM radio station call letters*]
WRKE.......... Ende/Ipi [*Indonesia*] [*ICAO location identifier*] (ICLI)
WRKE.......... Ocean View, DE [*FM radio station call letters*]
WRKF.......... Baton Rouge, LA [*FM radio station call letters*]
WRKF.......... Maskolen [*Indonesia*] [*ICAO location identifier*] (ICLI)
WRKG.......... Lorain, OH [*AM radio station call letters*]
WRKG.......... Ruteng/Satartacik [*Indonesia*] [*ICAO location identifier*] (ICLI)
WRKH-FM.......... Mobile, AL [*FM radio station call letters*] (RBYB)
WRKI.......... Brookfield, CT [*FM radio station call letters*]

WRKI .... Mbai [*Indonesia*] [*ICAO location identifier*] (ICLI)
WRKJ .... Mena [*Indonesia*] [*ICAO location identifier*] (ICLI)
WRKK .... Kupang/Eltari [*Indonesia*] [*ICAO location identifier*] (ICLI)
WRKK-AM.... Hughesville, PA [*AM radio station call letters*] (RBYB)
WRKL .... Larantuka/Gewayentana [*Indonesia*] [*ICAO location identifier*] (ICLI)
WRKL .... New City, NY [*AM radio station call letters*]
WRKM .... Carthage, TN [*AM radio station call letters*]
WRKM .... Kalabahi/Mali [*Indonesia*] [*ICAO location identifier*] (ICLI)
WRKN .... Brandon, MS [*AM radio station call letters*]
WRKN .... Naikliu [*Indonesia*] [*ICAO location identifier*] (ICLI)
WRKO .... Boston, MA [*AM radio station call letters*]
WRKP .... Moundsville, WV [*FM radio station call letters*]
WRKQ .... Madisonville, TN [*AM radio station call letters*]
WRKR .... Portage, MI [*FM radio station call letters*]
WRKR .... Rote/Lekunik [*Indonesia*] [*ICAO location identifier*] (ICLI)
WRKR .... Worker
WRKS .... New York, NY [*FM radio station call letters*]
WRKS .... Sabu/Tardanu [*Indonesia*] [*ICAO location identifier*] (ICLI)
WRKSHP...... Workshop
WRKT .... North East, PA [*FM radio station call letters*]
WRKU .... Skarpsville, PA [*FM radio station call letters*]
WRKX .... Ottawa, IL [*FM radio station call letters*]
WRKY .... Steubenville, OH [*FM radio station call letters*]
WRKZ .... Hershey, PA [*FM radio station call letters*]
WRKZ .... Kupang Sector [*Indonesia*] [*ICAO location identifier*] (ICLI)
WRl .... Rice Lake Public Library, Rice Lake, WI [*Library symbol Library of Congress*] (LCLS)
WRL .... War Resisters League (EA)
WRL .... Wellcome Research Laboratories [*Research center British*] (IRC)
WRL .... Western Reserve Law Review [*A publication*] (ILCA)
WRL .... Westinghouse Research Laboratories (KSC)
WRL .... Wien Radiation Law [*Physics*]
WRL .... Willow Run Laboratory [*NASA*] (KSC)
WRL .... Wing Reference Line [*Aviation*]
WRL .... Worland [*Wyoming*] [*Airport symbol*] (OAG)
WRL .... Worland, WY [*Location identifier FAA*] (FAAL)
WRLA .... Sangata [*Indonesia*] [*ICAO location identifier*] (ICLI)
WRLB .... Long Bawan/Juvai Semaring [*Indonesia*] [*ICAO location identifier*] (ICLI)
WRLB-FM.... Rainelle, WV [*FM radio station call letters*] (RBYB)
WRLC .... Bontang [*Indonesia*] [*ICAO location identifier*] (ICLI)
WRLC .... Williamsport, PA [*FM radio station call letters*]
WRLD .... Batu Putih/Talisayam [*Indonesia*] [*ICAO location identifier*] (ICLI)
WRLD .... Lanett, AL [*AM radio station call letters*]
WRLD .... Valley, AL [*FM radio station call letters*]
WRLD .... World Acceptance [*NASDAQ symbol*] (TTSB)
WRLD .... World Acceptance Corp. [*NASDAQ symbol*] (SPSG)
WrldAcc........ World Access, Inc. [*Associated Press*] (SAG)
WrldCp .... World Corp. [*Associated Press*] (SAG)
WrldHrt.......... World Heart Corp. [*Associated Press*] (SAG)
Wrldtalk........ Worldtalk Communication Corp. [*Associated Press*] (SAG)
WrldVl .... Worldwide Value Fund [*Associated Press*] (SAG)
WRLDWD...... Worldwide
WRLF.......... Fairmont, WV [*FM radio station call letters*]
WRLG .... Smyrna, TN [*FM radio station call letters*]
WRLG .... Tanjung Selor/Tanjung Harapan [*Indonesia*] [*ICAO location identifier*] (ICLI)
WRLH .... Richmond, VA [*Television station call letters*]
WRLH .... Tanah Grogot [*Indonesia*] [*ICAO location identifier*] (ICLI)
WRLI .... Southampton, NY [*FM radio station call letters*]
WRLI .... Tiong Chong [*Indonesia*] [*ICAO location identifier*] (ICLI)
WRLIS .... Wessex Regional Library and Information Service (NITA)
WRLK .... Columbia, SC [*Television station call letters*]
WRLK .... Tanjung Redep/Kalimarau [*Indonesia*] [*ICAO location identifier*] (ICLI)
WRLL.......... Balikpapan/Sepinggan [*Indonesia*] [*ICAO location identifier*] (ICLI)
WRLM .... Malinau [*Indonesia*] [*ICAO location identifier*] (ICLI)
WRLN .... Long Mawang [*Indonesia*] [*ICAO location identifier*] (ICLI)
WRLO .... Antigo, WI [*FM radio station call letters*]
WRLO .... Ongko Asa [*Indonesia*] [*ICAO location identifier*] (ICLI)
WRLP .... Russell, PA [*FM radio station call letters*]
WRLR .... Taraken [*Indonesia*] [*ICAO location identifier*] (ICLI)
WRLS .... Hayward, WI [*FM radio station call letters*]
WRLS .... Samarinda/Temindung [*Indonesia*] [*ICAO location identifier*] (ICLI)
WRLS .... Telular Corp. [*NASDAQ symbol*] (SAG)
WRLS .... Wireless [*Telecommunications*] (IAA)
WRLS .... Working Reference of Livestock Regulatory Establishments, Stations, and Officials [*A publication*]
WRLT .... Franklin, TN [*FM radio station call letters*]
WRLT.......... Tanjung Santan [*Indonesia*] [*ICAO location identifier*] (ICLI)
WRLU .... Sangkulirang [*Indonesia*] [*ICAO location identifier*] (ICLI)
WRLU .... Watermen and Riverside Labourers' Union [*British*]
WRLV .... Salyersville, KY [*AM radio station call letters*]
WRLV-FM.... Salyersville, KY [*FM radio station call letters*]
WRLW .... Muara Wahau [*Indonesia*] [*ICAO location identifier*] (ICLI)
WRLX .... West Palm Beach, FL [*FM radio station call letters*]
WRLX .... World Airways, Inc. [*Air carrier designation symbol*]
WRLZ-AM.... Eatonville, FL [*AM radio station call letters*] (RBYB)
WRM .... Wardroom (WGA)
WRM .... Warm [*NWS*] (FAAC)
WRM .... Warmifontaine [*Belgium*] [*Seismograph station code, US Geological Survey*] (SEIS)
WRM .... War Readiness Materiel [*Air Force*]
WRM .... War Reserve Mobilization (CINC)
WRM .... War Reserve Munitions
WRM .... Water Removal Mechanism
WRM .... West Rim Resources, Inc. [*Vancouver Stock Exchange symbol*]
WRM .... What Really Matters
WR(M).......... Wide Range (Monitor) [*Nuclear energy*] (NRCH)
WRM .... William Richard Morris [*Automobile industrialist*] [*British*]
WRM .... Worcester State College, Worcester, MA [*OCLC symbol*] (OCLC)
WRM .... Working Reference Material [*Nuclear energy*] (NRCH)
WRM .... World Rainforest Movement [*Penang, Malaysia*] (EAIO)
WRMA .... Fort Lauderdale, FL [*FM radio station call letters*]
WRMA .... Welded Ring Manufacturers Association [*Defunct*]
WRMAC .... Water Resources Management Advisory Committee [*Australia*]
WRMB .... Boynton Beach, FL [*FM radio station call letters*]
WRMC .... Middlebury, VT [*FM radio station call letters*]
WRMD .... St. Petersburg, FL [*AM radio station call letters*]
WRME .... Wood Raw Material Equivalent (EERA)
WRMF .... Palm Beach, FL [*FM radio station call letters*]
WRMF .... World Radio Missionary Fellowship (EA)
WRMFNT..... Warm Front [*NWS*] (FAAC)
WRMG .... Red Bay, AL [*AM radio station call letters*]
WRMJ .... Aledo, IL [*FM radio station call letters*]
WRMM .... Rochester, NY [*FM radio station call letters*]
WRMN .... Elgin, IL [*AM radio station call letters*]
WRMN .... Wireman (AABC)
WRMQ .... Orlando, FL [*AM radio station call letters*]
WRMR .... Cleveland, OH [*AM radio station call letters*]
WRMR .... War Reserve Materiel Requirement (AFIT)
WRMRATE.... War Readiness Materiel Rating [*Air Force*]
WRMRB........ War Reserve Materiel Requirement Balance (AFIT)
WRMRP........ War Reserve Materiel Requirement Protectable (AFIT)
WRMRS........ War Reserve Materiel Rating System
WRMS .... Beardstown, IL [*AM radio station call letters*]
WRMS .... War Reserve Materiel Stocks
WRMS .... Watts Root-Mean-Square
WRMS-FM.... Beardstown, IL [*FM radio station call letters*]
WRMSR........ Write Machine-Specific Register [*Computer science*]
WRMSTAT.... War Readiness Materiel Status [*Air Force*]
WRMT .... Rocky Mount, NC [*AM radio station call letters*]
WRMT .... Woodcock Reading Mastery Tests [*Educational test*]
WRMU .... Alliance, OH [*FM radio station call letters*]
WRMX .... Murfreesboro, TN [*FM radio station call letters*]
WRMY .... Rocky Mount, NC [*Television station call letters*]
WRN .... Warnaco of Canada Ltd. [*Toronto Stock Exchange symbol*]
WRN .... Warning (MSA)
WRN .... War Relief for Nicaraguans (EA)
WRN .... WCI Steel [*NYSE symbol*] (TTSB)
WRN .... WCI Steel, Inc. [*NYSE symbol*] (SAG)
WRN .... Western
WRN .... Women Returners Network (AIE)
WRN .... Wool Round Needle [*Knitting*]
WRN .... Wrangler Aviation, Inc. [*ICAO designator*] (FAAC)
WRNA .... China Grove, NC [*AM radio station call letters*]
WRNB .... Warren Bancorp [*NASDAQ symbol*] (TTSB)
WRNB .... Warren Bancorp, Inc. [*NASDAQ symbol*] (NQ)
WRND .... Manchester, NH [*FM radio station call letters*]
WRNE .... Pensacola, FL [*AM radio station call letters*]
WRNG .... Warning [*NWS*] (FAAC)
WRNI .... Wide-Range Neutron Indicator (IEEE)
WRNI .... Wide-Range Nuclear Instrument (IEEE)
Wrnlns .... Warner Insurance Services [*Associated Press*] (SAG)
WRNJ .... Belvidere, NJ [*FM radio station call letters*]
WRNJ .... Hackettstown, NJ [*AM radio station call letters*]
WRNL-AM.... Richmond, VA [*AM radio station call letters*] (RBYB)
WRNLR........ Western Region of Nigeria Law Reports [*A publication*] (DLA)
WRNN .... Murrell's Inlet, SC [*FM radio station call letters*]
WRNN-TV .... Kingston, NY [*Television station call letters*] (RBYB)
WRNO .... New Orleans, LA [*FM radio station call letters*]
WRNOA........ Washington Reef Net Owners Association (EA)
WRNQ .... Poughkeepsie, NY [*FM radio station call letters*]
WRNR .... Grasonville, MD [*FM radio station call letters*]
WRNR .... Martinsburg, WV [*AM radio station call letters*]
WRNR .... West Riding National Reserve [*British military*] (DMA)
WRNR .... Women's Royal Naval Reserve [*British military*] (DMA)
WRNS .... Kinston, NC [*AM radio station call letters*]
WRNS .... Women's Royal Naval Service [*Also, WRENS*] [*A member is familiarly called a "Wren"*] [*British*]
WRNS-FM.... Kinston, NC [*FM radio station call letters*]
WRNSR........ Women's Royal Naval Service Reserve [*British military*] (DMA)
WRNT .... Warrant (AABC)
WRNT .... Warrenton Railroad Co. [*Later, WAR*] [*AAR code*]
WRNVR........ Women's Royal Naval Volunteer Reserve [*British military*] (DMA)
WRNWCA .... Western Red and Northern White Cedar Association [*Later, WRCA*] (EA)
WRNWS........ Worldwide Radio Navigation Warning System [*Intergovernmental Maritime Consultative Organization*] (GFGA)
WRNX .... Amherst, MA [*FM radio station call letters*]
WRNY .... Rome, NY [*AM radio station call letters*]
WRNZ .... Lancaster, KY [*FM radio station call letters*]
WRO .... ARC [*Agricultural Research Council*] Weed Research Organization [*Research center British*] (IRC)
WRO .... War Records Office
WRO .... War Risks Only
WRO .... Water Rights Office [*Bureau of Indian Affairs*]
WRO .... Western Regional Office
WRO .... Wichita River Oil Corp. [*AMEX symbol*] (SPSG)
WRO .... Work Release Order (MCD)
WRO .... Worship Resources Office [*An association*] (EA)

WRO .... Wroclaw [*Poland*] [*Airport symbol*] (OAG)
WROA .... Gulfport, MS [*AM radio station call letters*]
WROB .... West Point, MS [*AM radio station call letters*]
WROC .... Rochester, NY [*Television station call letters*]
WROD .... Daytona Beach, FL [*AM radio station call letters*]
WROE .... Neenah-Menasha, WI [*FM radio station call letters*]
WROG .... Cumberland, MD [*FM radio station call letters*]
Wr Ohio .... Wright's Ohio Reports [*A publication*] (DLA)
WROI .... Rochester, IN [*FM radio station call letters*]
WROK .... Rockford, IL [*AM radio station call letters*]
WROL .... Boston, MA [*AM radio station call letters*]
WROM .... Rome, GA [*AM radio station call letters*]
WRON .... Ronceverte, WV [*AM radio station call letters*]
WRON-FM ... Ronceverte, WV [*FM radio station call letters*]
WROO .... Jacksonville, FL [*FM radio station call letters*]
WROQ .... Anderson, SC [*FM radio station call letters*]
WROR-FM ... Framingham, MA [*FM radio station call letters*] (RBYB)
WROS .... Jacksonville, FL [*AM radio station call letters*]
WROU .... West Carrollton, OH [*FM radio station call letters*]
WROV .... Martinsville, VA [*FM radio station call letters*]
WROV .... Roanoke, VA [*AM radio station call letters*]
WROW .... Albany, NY [*AM radio station call letters*]
WROX .... Cape Charles, VA [*FM radio station call letters*]
WROX .... Clarksdale, MS [*AM radio station call letters*]
WROY .... Carmi, IL [*AM radio station call letters*]
WROZ .... Lancaster, PA [*FM radio station call letters*]
WRP .... Water Resource Planning
WRP .... Water Resources Publications
WRP .... Weapons Release Programmer
WRP .... Weather Research Program [*Boulder, CO*] [*Department of Commerce*] (GRD)
WRP .... Wellsford Residential Property Trust [*NYSE symbol*] (SPSG)
WRP .... Wellsford Residential Prop Tr [*NYSE symbol*] (TTSB)
WRP .... Wiener Random Process [*Mathematics*]
WRP .... Wildlife Research Project
WRP .... Wing Reference Plan [*Aviation*]
WRP .... Women's Rights Project (EA)
WRP .... Workers' Revolutionary Party [*British*] (PPW)
WRPA .... Water Resources Planning Act [*1965*]
Wr PA .... Wright's Reports [*37-50 Pennsylvania*] [*A publication*] (DLA)
WRPA-FM .... Laporte, PA [*FM radio station call letters*] (RBYB)
WRPC .... San German, PR [*FM radio station call letters*]
WRPC .... Weather Records Processing Centers
WRPG .... Warping
WRPI .... Troy, NY [*FM radio station call letters*]
WRPJ .... Port Jervis, NY [*FM radio station call letters*]
WRPL .... Wadesboro, NC [*FM radio station call letters*]
WRPLS .... Western Regional Public Library System [*Library network*]
WRPM .... Poplarville, MS [*AM radio station call letters*]
WRPN .... Ripon, WI [*FM radio station call letters*]
WRPPD .... Wrapped
WRPPr .... Wellsford Res Prop'A'Cv Pfd [*NYSE symbol*] (TTSB)
WRPPrB .... Wellsford Res Prop Tr 9.65% Pfd [*NYSE symbol*] (TTSB)
WRPQ .... Baraboo, WI [*AM radio station call letters*]
WRPR .... Mahwah, NJ [*FM radio station call letters*]
WRPR .... Wrapper
WRPrA .... Western Res Cap 7.875%'QUIPS' [*NYSE symbol*] (TTSB)
WRPS .... Rockland, MA [*FM radio station call letters*]
WRPSM .... War Reserve Publication Shipment Memorandum
WRPT .... Write Protect [*Computer science*] (MHDB)
WRPT-AM .... Peterborough, NH [*AM radio station call letters*] (RBYB)
WRQ .... Westinghouse Resolver/Quantizer (IEEE)
WRQK .... Canton, OH [*FM radio station call letters*]
WRQM-FM ... Rocky Mount, NC [*FM radio station call letters*] (RBYB)
WRQN .... Bowling Green, OH [*FM radio station call letters*]
WRQO .... Monticello, MS [*FM radio station call letters*]
WRQQ .... Farrell, PA [*AM radio station call letters*]
WRQR .... Farmville, NC [*FM radio station call letters*]
WRQV-FM .... Avon, NY [*FM radio station call letters*] (RBYB)
WRQX .... Washington, DC [*FM radio station call letters*]
WRR .... Dallas, TX [*FM radio station call letters*]
WRR .... Warm Run Record
WRR .... Warrington, Inc. [*Toronto Stock Exchange symbol*]
WRR .... Water Resource Region [*Water Resources Council*]
WRR .... Water Resources Research [*A publication*] (NOAA)
WRR .... Woodmen Rangers and Rangerettes (EA)
WRR .... WRA, Inc. [*ICAO designator*] (FAAC)
WRRA .... Frederiksted, VI [*AM radio station call letters*]
WRRA .... Mataram/Selaparang [*Indonesia*] [*ICAO location identifier*] (ICLI)
WRRA .... Water Resources Research Act [*1964*]
WRRB .... Bima/Palibelo [*Indonesia*] [*ICAO location identifier*] (ICLI)
WRRC .... Lawrenceville, NJ [*FM radio station call letters*]
WRRC .... Water Resources Research Center [*University of Arizona*] (RCD)
WRRC .... Water Resources Research Center [*Purdue University*] (RCD)
WRRC .... Water Resources Research Center [*Indiana University*] (RCD)
WRRC .... Water Resources Research Center [*University of Minnesota of Minneapolis St. Paul*] (RCD)
WRRC .... Water Resources Research Center [*University of Massachusetts*] (RCD)
WRRC .... Water Resources Research Center [*University of Hawaii*] (RCD)
WRRC .... Western Rail Road Co. [*AAR code*]
WRRC .... Western Regional Research Center [*Albany, CA*] [*Department of Agriculture*] (GRD)
WRRC .... Western Regional Resource Center [*University of Oregon*] [*Research center*] (RCD)
WRRC .... Wildlife Refuge Reform Coalition (EA)
WRRC .... Willow Run Research Center [*Air Force*]
WRRC .... Women's Research and Resources Centre (EAIO)
WRRE .... Juncos, PR [*AM radio station call letters*]
WRRF .... Washington, NC [*AM radio station call letters*]
WRRG .... River Grove, IL [*FM radio station call letters*]
WRRH .... Hormigueros, PR [*FM radio station call letters*] (RBYB)
WRRI .... Alabama Water Resources Research Institute [*Auburn, AL*] [*Department of the Interior*] (GRD)
WRRI .... Water Resources Research Institute [*New Mexico State University*] [*Research center*] (RCD)
WRRI .... Water Resources Research Institute [*Oregon State University*] [*Research center*] (RCD)
WRRI .... Water Resources Research Institute [*Clemson University*] [*Research center*]
WRRK .... Braddock, PA [*FM radio station call letters*]
WRRL .... Rainelle, WV [*AM radio station call letters*]
WRRL-FM .... Rainelle, WV [*FM radio station call letters*]
WRRM .... Cincinnati, OH [*FM radio station call letters*]
WRRN .... Warren, PA [*FM radio station call letters*]
WRRNT .... Warrant
WRRO .... Warren, OH [*AM radio station call letters*]
WRRR .... Bali International/Ngurah Rai [*Indonesia*] [*ICAO location identifier*] (ICLI)
WRRR .... Rockford, IL [*AM radio station call letters*]
WRRR .... St. Marys, WV [*FM radio station call letters*]
WRRR .... Walter Reed Research Reactor [*Military*]
WRRS .... Sumbawa/Sumbawa Besar [*Indonesia*] [*ICAO location identifier*] (ICLI)
WRRS .... Wire Relay Radio System
WRRT .... Waikabubak/Tambolaka [*Indonesia*] [*ICAO location identifier*] (ICLI)
WRRV .... Middletown, NY [*FM radio station call letters*] (RBYB)
WRRW .... Waingapu/Mau Hau [*Indonesia*] [*ICAO location identifier*] (ICLI)
WRRX .... Micanopy, FL [*FM radio station call letters*]
WRRZ .... Bali [*Indonesia*] [*ICAO location identifier*] (ICLI)
WRRZ .... Clinton, NC [*AM radio station call letters*]
WRS .... Walter Reed Society (EA)
WRS .... Warning and Report System (CET)
WRS .... War Reserve Stocks (AABC)
WRS .... Warsak [*Pakistan*] [*Seismograph station code, US Geological Survey*] (SEIS)
WRS .... Wasabi Resources Ltd. [*Toronto Stock Exchange symbol Vancouver Stock Exchange symbol*]
WRS .... Washington Representative Services, Inc. [*Information service or system*] (IID)
WRS .... Water Recirculation System
WRS .... Water Recovery Subsystem [*NASA*] (KSC)
WRS .... Wave Radiometer System
WRS .... Weapons Recommendation Sheet (MCD)
WRS .... Weather RADAR Set [*or System*]
WRS .... Weather Reconnaissance Squadron [*Air Force*] (CINC)
WRS .... Western Massachusetts Regional Library System, Springfield, MA [*OCLC symbol*] (OCLC)
WRS .... Western Pacific Railroad Co. (MHDW)
WRS .... Wide-Range Sensor
WRS .... Winston Resources [*AMEX symbol*] (TTSB)
WRS .... Winston Resources Ltd. [*AMEX symbol*] (SPSG)
WRS .... Word Recognition System
WRS .... Working Transmission Reference System [*Telecommunications*] (TEL)
WRS .... Worse (FAAC)
WRS .... Write Strobe
WRSA .... Decatur, AL [*FM radio station call letters*]
WRSA .... War Reserve Stocks for Allies (MCD)
WRSA .... World Rabbit Science Association [*Cheltenham, Gloucestershire, England*] (EAIO)
WRSC .... Cepu/Ngloram [*Indonesia*] [*ICAO location identifier*] (ICLI)
WRSC .... State College, PA [*AM radio station call letters*]
WRSD .... Folsom, PA [*FM radio station call letters*]
WRSE .... Elmhurst, IL [*FM radio station call letters*]
WRSF .... Columbia, NC [*FM radio station call letters*]
WRSFA .... Western Reinforcing Steel Fabricators Association
WRSH .... Rockingham, NC [*FM radio station call letters*]
WRSI .... Greenfield, MA [*FM radio station call letters*]
WRSI .... Woodroast Systems [*NASDAQ symbol*] (TTSB)
WRSI .... Woodroast Systems, Inc. [*NASDAQ symbol*] (SAG)
WRSIC .... Water Resources Scientific Information Center [*US Geological Survey*] [*Reston, VA Database originator*]
WRSIW .... Woodroast Sys Wrrt [*NASDAQ symbol*] (TTSB)
WRSJ .... Bayamon, PR [*AM radio station call letters*]
WRSJ .... Surabaya/Juanda [*Indonesia*] [*ICAO location identifier*] (ICLI)
WRSK .... Slippery Rock, PA [*FM radio station call letters*]
WRSK .... War Readiness Spares Kit [*Air Force*] (AFM)
WRSL .... Stanford, KY [*AM radio station call letters*]
WRSL-FM .... Stanford, KY [*FM radio station call letters*]
WRSM .... Sumiton, AL [*AM radio station call letters*]
WRSN-FM .... Burlington-Graham, NC [*FM radio station call letters*] (RBYB)
WRSP .... Springfield, IL [*Television station call letters*]
WRSP .... Surabaya/Perak [*Indonesia*] [*ICAO location identifier*] (ICLI)
WRSP .... World Register of Scientific Periodicals
WRSQ .... Solo/Adi Sumarmo Wiryokusumo [*Indonesia*] [*ICAO location identifier*] (ICLI)
WRSq .... Weather Reconnaissance Squadron [*Air Force*] (AFM)
WRSR .... Two Harbors, MN [*FM radio station call letters*]
WRSR .... Water Reactor Safety Research [*Nuclear energy*] (NRCH)

WRSS San Sebastian, PR [*AM radio station call letters*]
WRSS Surabaya/Gedangan [*Indonesia*] [*ICAO location identifier*] (ICLI)
WRSSR White Russian Soviet Socialist Republic (IIA)
WRST Oshkosh, WI [*FM radio station call letters*]
WRST Sumenep/Trunojoyo [*Indonesia*] [*ICAO location identifier*] (ICLI)
WRSU New Brunswick, NJ [*FM radio station call letters*]
WRSUC Woodroast Systems, Inc. [*NASDAQ symbol*] (SAG)
WRSV Rocky Mount, NC [*FM radio station call letters*]
WRSV Wheat Rosette Stunt Virus [*Plant pathology*]
WRSW Warsaw, IN [*AM radio station call letters*]
WRSW-FM Warsaw, IN [*FM radio station call letters*]
WRT Warrior River Terminal Co. [*AAR code*]
WRT Water Round Torpedo (MSA)
WRT Westerra Resources Ltd. [*Vancouver Stock Exchange symbol*]
WRT With Reference To
WRT With Regard To (NHD)
WRT With Respect To (KSC)
WRT Wright Air Lines, Inc. [*ICAO designator*] (FAAC)
WRT Wright-Hargreaves Mines Ltd. [*Toronto Stock Exchange symbol*] (SPSG)
WRT Wrought
wrt Wrought (VRA)
WRT WRT Energy Corp. [*Associated Press*] (SAG)
WRTA Altoona, PA [*AM radio station call letters*]
WRTA Western Railroad Traffic Association (EA)
WRTB Wire Rope Technical Board (EA)
WRTC Hartford, CT [*FM radio station call letters*]
WRTC Working Reference Telephone Circuit [*Telecommunications*] (TEL)
WRTE WRT Energy Corp. [*NASDAQ symbol*] (SAG)
WRT En WRT Energy Corp. [*Associated Press*] (SAG)
WRTG Garner, NC [*AM radio station call letters*]
WRTH St. Louis, MO [*AM radio station call letters*]
WRTH World Radio TV Handbook [*A publication*]
WRTHG Worthing [*City in England*]
WRTI Philadelphia, PA [*FM radio station call letters*]
WRTK Youngstown, OH [*AM radio station call letters*] (RBYB)
WRTL Ephrata, PA [*FM radio station call letters*]
WRTM-AM Vicksburg, MS [*AM radio station call letters*] (RBYB)
WRTN New Rochelle, NY [*FM radio station call letters*]
WRTO Goulds, FL [*FM radio station call letters*]
WRTP Chapel Hill, NC [*AM radio station call letters*]
WRTQ Ocean City, NJ [*FM radio station call letters*]
WRTR Writer
WRTS Erie, PA [*FM radio station call letters*]
WRTTM Warhead Replacement Tactical Telemetry System (DWSG)
WRTU San Juan, PR [*FM radio station call letters*]
WRTV Indianapolis, IN [*Television station call letters*]
WRTX Dover, DE [*FM radio station call letters*]
WRTY Jackson Township, PA [*FM radio station call letters*]
WRU Watershed Research Unit [*Columbia, MO*] [*Department of Agriculture*] (GRD)
WRU Wave Run-Up
WRU Welsh Rugby Union [*British*] (DBA)
WRU Western Reserve University [*Later, Case Western Reserve University*]
WRU Who Are You [*Communication*]
WRUA Fajardo, PR [*Television station call letters*]
WRUC Schenectady, NY [*FM radio station call letters*]
WRUF Gainesville, FL [*AM radio station call letters*]
WRUF-FM Gainesville, FL [*FM radio station call letters*]
WRUL Carmi, IL [*FM radio station call letters*]
WRUM Rumford, ME [*AM radio station call letters*]
WRUN Utica, NY [*AM radio station call letters*]
WRUR Rochester, NY [*FM radio station call letters*]
WRUS Russellville, KY [*AM radio station call letters*]
WRUSS Western Reserve University Relay Searching Selector (SAA)
WRUV Burlington, VT [*FM radio station call letters*]
WRUW Cleveland, OH [*FM radio station call letters*]
WRV Water Relief Valve
WRV Water-Retention Value
WRV West Riding Volunteers [*British military*] (DMA)
WRV Winged Reentry Vehicle (IAA)
WRVA Richmond, VA [*AM radio station call letters*]
WRVC Huntington, WV [*AM radio station call letters*]
WRVC-FM Catlettsburg, KY [*FM radio station call letters*] (RBYB)
WRVD-FM Syracuse, NY [*FM radio station call letters*] (RBYB)
WRVE Schenectady, NY [*FM radio station call letters*]
WRVF Toledo, OH [*FM radio station call letters*] (RBYB)
WRVG Georgetown, KY [*FM radio station call letters*]
WRVH Richmond, VA [*AM radio station call letters*]
WRVI-FM New Albany, IN [*FM radio station call letters*] (RBYB)
WRVJ Watertown, NY [*FM radio station call letters*]
WRVK Mount Vernon, KY [*AM radio station call letters*]
WRVL Lynchburg, VA [*FM radio station call letters*]
WRVM Suring, WI [*FM radio station call letters*]
WRVN Utica, NY [*FM radio station call letters*]
WRVO Oswego, NY [*FM radio station call letters*]
WRVP Wedged Renal Venous Pressure [*Medicine*] (MAE)
WRVQ Richmond, VA [*FM radio station call letters*]
WRVR Memphis, TN [*FM radio station call letters*]
WRVS Elizabeth City, NC [*FM radio station call letters*]
WRVS Women's Royal Voluntary Service [*Formerly, WVS*] [*British*]
WRVT Rutland, VT [*FM radio station call letters*]
WRVU Nashville, TN [*FM radio station call letters*]
WRVV Harrisburg, PA [*FM radio station call letters*]
WRVX Mt. Carmel, TN [*AM radio station call letters*]
WRVY Henry, IL [*FM radio station call letters*]
WRVZ Pocatalico, WV [*FM radio station call letters*]
WR(W) War Reserve (Weapon)
WRW Weather Reconnaissance Wing [*Military*]
WRWA Dothan, AL [*FM radio station call letters*]
WRWB Harrogate, TN [*AM radio station call letters*]
WRWC Rockton, IL [*FM radio station call letters*]
WRWD Cornwall, NY [*AM radio station call letters*]
WRWD Highland, NY [*FM radio station call letters*]
WRWg Weather Reconnaissance Wing [*Air Force*] (AFM)
WRWH Cleveland, GA [*AM radio station call letters*]
WRWJ Murrysville, PA [*FM radio station call letters*]
WRWK Warwick Railway Co. [*AAR code*]
WRWO Montgomery, AL [*FM radio station call letters*] (RBYB)
WRWP Water-Repellent Wood Preservative (DICI)
WRWR San Juan, PR [*Television station call letters*]
WRX Western Refrigerator Line Co. [*AAR code*]
WRXB St. Petersburg Beach, FL [*AM radio station call letters*]
WRXC Shelton, CT [*FM radio station call letters*]
WRXK Bonita Springs, FL [*FM radio station call letters*]
WRXL Richmond, VA [*FM radio station call letters*]
WRXO Roxboro, NC [*AM radio station call letters*]
WRXQ Olive Branch, MS [*FM radio station call letters*]
WRXR Aiken, SC [*FM radio station call letters*]
WRXS Ocean City, MD [*FM radio station call letters*]
WRXT Roanoke, VA [*FM radio station call letters*]
WRXX Centralia, IL [*FM radio station call letters*]
WRXY Tice, FL [*Television station call letters*]
WRXZ Sylvester, GA [*FM radio station call letters*]
WRY Westray [*Scotland*] [*Airport symbol*] (OAG)
WRY Wheeling Railway
WRY World Refugee Year
WRYM New Britain, CT [*AM radio station call letters*]
WRYT Edwardsville, IL [*AM radio station call letters*]
WRZ Western Rift Zone [*Geology*]
WRZA-FM Kankakee, IL [*FM radio station call letters*] (RBYB)
WRZE Nantucket, MA [*FM radio station call letters*]
WRZI Vine Grove, KY [*FM radio station call letters*]
WRZK Tallahassee, FL [*FM radio station call letters*]
WRZN Hernando, FL [*AM radio station call letters*]
WRZQ Greenburg, IN [*FM radio station call letters*]
WRZX Indianapolis, IN [*FM radio station call letters*]
WRZZ Ravenswood, WV [*FM radio station call letters*]
WS Northern Wings [*ICAO designator*] (AD)
WS Single Conductor Cable [*JETDS nomenclature*] [*Military*] (CET)
WS Superior Public Library, Superior, WI [*Library symbol Library of Congress*] (LCLS)
WS Waardenburg's Syndrome [*Medicine*]
WS Wadley Southern [*Railroad*] (MHDW)
WS Wagner's Missouri Statutes [*A publication*] (DLA)
WS Wallops Station [*Later, WFC*] [*NASA*]
WS Wall Street
WS Ward Secretary [*Medicine*] (MEDA)
WS Ware Shoals Railroad Co. [*AAR code*]
WS Warm Shop [*Nuclear energy*] (NRCH)
WS War Scale (ADA)
WS War Service
WS War Substantive [*British military*] (DMA)
WS Warthin-Starry [*Silver impregnation stain*]
WS Washine Chemical Corp. [*Research code symbol*]
WS Wash Sale (MHDW)
WS Waste Stack [*Technical drawings*]
WS Waste System
WS Watchman Service (LAIN)
WS Watered Stock
WS Water Safety
WS Water Servicer (NASA)
WS Water Soluble
WS Water-Storage Cell [*Botany*]
WS Water Supply
WS Water Surface [*Elevation*]
WS Water Swallow [*Medicine*] (DMAA)
WS Water System
W S Watt Second
w/s Watt-Seconds
W/S Watts per Steradian (NG)
WS Waveform Synthesizer (IAA)
WS Wave Soldering
WS Weak Signals [*Radio*]
WS Weapons Specifications (NG)
W/S Weapons System
WS Weapon System
WS Weather Service
W/S Weather Ship (NATG)
WS Weather Squadron (MCD)
WS Weather Station
WS Weatherstripping (AAG)
WS Wedgwood Society [*Defunct*] (EA)
WS Wee Scots (EA)
WS Weirton Steel [*NYSE symbol*] (TTSB)
WS Weirton Steel Corp. [*NYSE symbol*] (SPSG)
WS Welsh Society (EA)
WS Werner's Syndrome [*Medicine*]

ws............... Western Samoa [*MARC country of publication code Library of Congress*] (LCCP)
WS............... Western Samoa [*ANSI two-letter standard code*] (CNC)
WS............... West Saxon [*Dialect of Old English*] [*Language, etc.*]
WS............... West Semitic (BJA)
W/S............... West Side [*In outdoor advertising*] (WDMC)
WS............... Wet Smoothed (BJA)
WS............... Wetted Surface
WS............... Wheat Straw
WS............... White Sisters [*Missionary Sisters of Our Lady of Africa*] [*Roman Catholic religious order*]
WS............... White Squire (MHDW)
WS............... White Sucker [*Ichthyology*]
WS............... White-Throated Sparrow [*Ornithology*]
WS............... Wide Shot [*Photography*]
W-S............... Wigner-Seitz [*Construction cell*] [*Solid state physics*]
WS............... Wilderness Society (EA)
WS............... [*The*] Wildlife Society
WS............... Williams Syndrome [*Medicine*]
WS............... Willow Society (EA)
WS............... Will Ship (MCD)
WS............... Winding Specification (IAA)
WS............... Wind Satellite (SSD)
WS............... Wind Shear [*Aviation*] (FAAC)
WS............... Wind Shield (NASA)
WS............... Windsonde (KSC)
WS............... Wind Speed
WS............... Wingspread (WGA)
WS............... Wing Station [*Aviation*]
WS............... Wireless Set (MCD)
WS............... Wireless Station (IAA)
WS............... Wire Send [*Telecommunications*] (TEL)
WS............... Wire Sound
WS............... Wirtschaft und Statistik [*Germany*]
Ws............... Wisdom [*Old Testament Book*] (BJA)
WS............... Withholding Statement (AAG)
W/S............... With Stock [*Business term*]
WS............... Women's Services [*Military British*]
WS............... Women's Shelter [*Australia*]
WS............... Women's Size
WS............... Women's Suffrage (ROG)
WS............... Wood-Sheathed Deck [*of a ship*] (DS)
WS............... WordStar [*Computer program*]
WS............... Word Sync
WS............... Working Space
WS............... Working Storage [*Computer science*] (MDG)
WS............... Worksheet (AAG)
WS............... Work Shop [*Military*]
WS............... Workshop Control (IAA)
WS............... Work Stand (MCD)
WS............... Work Statement (AAG)
W/S............... Work Station [*NASA*] (NASA)
WS............... Work Stoppage (AAG)
WS............... Worldscale
WS............... World Solidarity [*Belgium*] (EAIO)
WS............... Worldwide Searches (EA)
WS............... Worthy Sister (BJA)
WS............... Writer to the Signet [*British*]
WS............... Wrought Steel (MSA)
WSA............... Wagner Society of America (EA)
WSA............... War Shipping Administration [*Within Office of Emergency Management*] [*World War II*]
WSA............... War Supplies Agency (NATG)
WSA............... Water-Soluble Adjuvant [*Immunology*]
WSA............... Water Sports Australia
WSA............... Waveguide Slot Array
WSA............... Weapons Systems Analysis [*Army*] (AABC)
WSA............... Web Sling Association [*Later, WSTDA*] (EA)
WSA............... Wedgwood Society of Australia
WSA............... Weed Society of America [*Later, WSSA*] (EA)
WSA............... Westates Airlines [*ICAO designator*] (FAAC)
WSA............... Western Slavonic Association [*Later, WSA Fraternal Life*] (EA)
WSA............... Western Surfing Association (EA)
WSA............... Western Surgical Association (EA)
WSA............... West Sea Development [*Vancouver Stock Exchange symbol*]
WSA............... Wholesale Stationers' Association (EA)
WSA............... Wilderness Study Area [*Department of the Interior*]
WSA............... Williams-Steiger Act of 1970 (WYGK)
WSA............... Williams Syndrome Association (EA)
WSA............... Winter Soldier Archive [*Defunct*] (EA)
WSA............... Wisconsin Statutes Annotated [*A publication*] (DLA)
WSA............... Wolverine Society of America (EA)
WSA............... Women's Student Association (EA)
WSA............... Workers Solidarity Alliance (EA)
WSA............... Workplace Standards Administration [*Department of Labor*]
WSA............... Work Safety Analysis [*Engineering*]
WSA............... Work Sciences Association [*British*] (DBA)
WSA............... World Service Authority, District 5: Orient-Mediterranean Sea Coast [*Israel*] (EAIO)
WSA............... World Sign Associates (EA)
WSA............... Writers' Sodality of America [*Defunct*]
WSAA............... Waveguide Slot Array Antenna
WSAA............... Western States Angus Association (EA)
WSAAA............... Western States Advertising Agencies Association (EA)
WSAAS............... Western Sydney Area Assistance Scheme [*Australia*]
WSAC............... Louisa, KY [*FM radio station call letters*]
WSAC............... Washington State Apple Commission (EA)
WSAC............... Water Space Amenity Commission [*British*] (DCTA)
WSAC............... West of Scotland Agricultural College [*British*] (IRUK)
WSAD............... Weapon System Analysis Division [*Navy*]
WSAE............... Spring Arbor, MI [*FM radio station call letters*]
WSAF............... Trion, GA [*AM radio station call letters*] (RBYB)
WSAG............... Sembawang [*Singapore*] [*ICAO location identifier*] (ICLI)
WSAG............... Washington Special Action Group [*National Security Council*]
WSAI............... Cincinnati, OH [*AM radio station call letters*]
WSAJ............... Grove City, PA [*AM radio station call letters*]
WSAJ-FM............... Grove City, PA [*FM radio station call letters*]
WSAL............... Logansport, IN [*AM radio station call letters*]
WSAM............... Saginaw, MI [*AM radio station call letters*]
WSAM............... Weapon Systems Acquisition Management [*Navy*] (MCD)
WSAM............... Weapon Systems Acquisition Manager Program Naval Officers (AAGC)
W SAM............... Western Samoa (WDAA)
W Sam............... Western Samoa (VRA)
WSAN............... Vieques, PR [*FM radio station call letters*]
WSAO............... Senatobia, MS [*AM radio station call letters*]
WSAO............... Weapon System Analysis Office [*Navy*] (MCD)
WSAP............... Paya Lebar [*Singapore*] [*ICAO location identifier*] (ICLI)
WSAP............... Weapon Status and Approval Panel [*Military*] (CAAL)
WSAP............... Weapon System Acquisition Process (MCD)
WSAP............... Weighted Sensitivity Analysis Program [*Environmental Protection Agency*]
WSAQ............... Port Huron, MI [*FM radio station call letters*]
WSAR............... Fall River, MA [*AM radio station call letters*]
WSAR............... Singapore [*Singapore*] [*ICAO location identifier*] (ICLI)
WSAR............... Weekly Significant Action Report (AFIT)
WSAS............... Weapon System Acceptance Schedule (AAG)
WSAS............... Weather Service Airport (DA)
WSASSA............... Wholesale School, Art, and Stationery Supplies Association [*Later, WSA*] (EA)
WSAT............... Salisbury, NC [*AM radio station call letters*]
WSAT............... Tengah [*Singapore*] [*ICAO location identifier*] (ICLI)
WSAT............... Weapon Systems Accuracy [*formerly, Acceptance*] Trials [*Navy*] (NG)
WSATO............... War Shipping Administration Training Organization [*Terminated*]
WSAU............... Wausau Paper Mills [*NASDAQ symbol*] (TTSB)
WSAU............... Wausau Paper Mills Co. [*NASDAQ symbol*] (NQ)
WSAU............... Wausau, WI [*AM radio station call letters*]
WSAV............... Savannah, GA [*Television station call letters*]
WSAVA............... World Small Animal Veterinary Association [*See also AMVPA*] [*Hatfield, Hertfordshire, England*] (EAIO)
WSAW............... Wausau, WI [*Television station call letters*]
WSAWD............... White Sands Air Weather Detachment [*New Mexico*]
WSA-WGWC... World Service Authority of the World Government of World Citizens (EA)
WSAX............... West Saxon [*Dialect of Old English*] [*Language, etc.*]
WSAY............... Rocky Mount, NC [*FM radio station call letters*]
WSAZ............... Huntington, WV [*Television station call letters*]
WSB............... Atlanta, GA [*AM radio station call letters*]
WSB............... Steamboat Bay, AK [*Location identifier FAA*] (FAAL)
WSB............... Wage Stabilization Board [*Terminated, 1953*]
WSB............... [*The*] Washington Savings Bank [*AMEX symbol*] (SPSG)
WSB............... Washington Service Bureau [*Publisher*] (AAGC)
WSB............... Water-Soluble Base
WSB............... Water Spray Boiler (NASA)
WSB............... Weekly Statistical Bulletin [*Database*] [*American Petroleum Institute*] [*Information service or system*] (CRD)
WSB............... Wheat-Soya Blend (EA)
WSB............... Will Send Boat
WSB............... World Scout Bureau [*Geneva, Switzerland*] (EA)
WSBA............... York, PA [*AM radio station call letters*]
WSBB............... New Smyrna Beach, FL [*AM radio station call letters*]
WSBC............... Chicago, IL [*AM radio station call letters*]
WSBC............... Wesbanco, Inc. [*NASDAQ symbol*] (NQ)
WSbD............... Door County Library, Sturgeon Bay, WI [*Library symbol Library of Congress*] (LCLS)
WSBE............... Providence, RI [*Television station call letters*]
WSBF............... Clemson, SC [*FM radio station call letters*]
WSB-FM............... Atlanta, GA [*FM radio station call letters*]
WSBG............... Stroudsburg, PA [*FM radio station call letters*]
WSBI............... Static, TN [*AM radio station call letters*]
WSBK............... Boston, MA [*Television station call letters*]
WSBK............... Western Bank [*Coos Bay, OR*] [*NASDAQ symbol*] (NQ)
WSBL............... Selbyville, DE [*FM radio station call letters*]
WSBM............... Florence, AL [*AM radio station call letters*]
WSBM............... Wheat Soilborne Mosaic Virus
WSBMV............... Wheat Soilborne Mosaic Virus
WSBN............... Norton, VA [*Television station call letters*]
WSBP............... Western Society of Business Publications [*Defunct*] (EA)
WSBR............... Boca Raton, FL [*AM radio station call letters*]
WSBS............... Great Barrington, MA [*AM radio station call letters*]
WSBSA............... Weapon System Base Supply Account [*Military*] (AFIT)
WSBT............... South Bend, IN [*AM radio station call letters*]
WSBT-TV............... South Bend, IN [*Television station call letters*]
WSB-TV............... Atlanta, GA [*Television station call letters*]
WSBU............... St. Bonaventure, NY [*FM radio station call letters*]
WSBV............... South Boston, VA [*AM radio station call letters*]
WSBW............... Weddell Sea Bottom Water [*Oceanography*]
WSBY............... Salisbury, MD [*FM radio station call letters*]
WSBZ............... Miramar Beach, FL [*FM radio station call letters*] (RBYB)

WSC............ Washington Science Center [*Maryland*] [*Seismograph station code, US Geological Survey Closed*] (SEIS)
WSC............ Watered Silk Cloth (DGA)
WSC............ Water Soluble Carbodiimide [*Organic chemistry*]
WSC............ Water Studies Centre [*Australia*] [*Chisholm Institute of Technology*]
WSC............ Water Systems Council (EA)
WSC............ Weapons System Code
WSC............ Weapon System Computer (MCD)
WSC............ Weapon System Console [*Military*] (CAAL)
WSC............ Weapon System Contractor
WSC............ Weapon System Costing [*Navy*]
WSC............ Weber State College [*Ogden, UT*]
WSC............ Wesco Financial [*AMEX symbol*] (TTSB)
WSC............ Wesco Financial Corp. [*AMEX symbol*] (SPSG)
WSC............ Westech Resources Ltd. [*Vancouver Stock Exchange symbol*]
WSC............ Western Sahara Campaign for Human Rights and Humanitarian Relief (EA)
WSC............ Western Simulation Council
WSC............ Western Snow Conference (EA)
WSC............ White Sisters of Charity of St. Vincent de Paul [*Roman Catholic religious order*]
WSC............ Wideband Signal Conditioner (MCD)
WSC............ Wildcat Service Corp. (EA)
WSC............ Wilkinson Sword Company [*British military*] (DMA)
WSC............ William Shatner Connection (EA)
WSC............ Wind Sounding Capability
WSC............ Wing Security Control [*Air Force*] (AFM)
WSC............ Winona State College [*Later, Winona State University*] [*Minnesota*]
WSC............ Winston Spencer Churchill [*1874-1965*] [*British statesman and prime minister*]
WSC............ Wisconsin State College [*Later, University of Wisconsin*]
WSC............ Working Security Committee [*Navy*]
WSC............ World Series Cricket
WSC............ World Spanish Congress (EA)
WSC............ World Spiritual Council (EA)
WSC............ World Sportscar Championship [*Auto racing*]
WSC............ World Straw Conference
WSC............ Wrap-Spring Clutch
WSC............ Wright State, Celina Branch, Celina, OH [*OCLC symbol*] (OCLC)
WSC............ Writing Services Center
WSC-5........ Washington Science Center, Building 5 [*Marine science*] (OSRA)
WSC-5........ Washington Science Center, Building 5 (USDC)
WSCA......... Georgetown, SC [*FM radio station call letters*]
WSCA......... Weather Service Cooperating Agencies [*National Weather Service*] (NOAA)
WSCB......... Springfield, MA [*FM radio station call letters*]
WSCC......... Weapon System Configuration Control [*Navy*] (AAG)
WSCC......... Weather Service Communications Center [*National Weather Service*] (NOAA)
WSCC......... Western State College of Colorado [*Gunnison*]
WSCC......... Western Systems Coordinating Council [*Regional power council*]
WSCC......... Work Station Control Center [*NASA*] (NASA)
WSCCM....... Weapon System Configuration Control Manual [*Navy*] (NG)
WSCD......... Duluth, MN [*FM radio station call letters*]
WSCD......... Welfare and Service Conditions Department [*British military*] (DMA)
WSCF......... Vero Beach, FL [*FM radio station call letters*]
WSCF......... Waste Sampling and Characterization Facility
WSCF......... World Student Christian Federation (EA)
WSCH......... Aurora, IN [*FM radio station call letters*]
WSCH......... Weather Service Communications Handbook [*National Weather Service*] (NOAA)
WSCI......... Charleston, SC [*FM radio station call letters*]
WSCI......... Washington Scientific [*NASDAQ symbol*] (TTSB)
WSCI......... Washington Scientific Industries, Inc. [*NASDAQ symbol*] (NQ)
WSCL......... Salisbury, MD [*FM radio station call letters*]
WSCM......... Weapon System Compatible Munition [*Military*]
WSCMB....... Weapon System Configuration Management Board (MCD)
WSCMO....... Weather Service Contract Meteorological Observatory (FAAC)
WSCN......... Cloquet, MN [*FM radio station call letters*]
WSCO......... Suring, WI [*Television station call letters*]
WSCO......... Weber State College [*Odgen, UT*]
WSCOC....... Wills Sainte Claire Owners Club (EA)
WSCP......... Pulaski, NY [*FM radio station call letters*]
WSCP......... Sandy Creek-Pulaski, NY [*AM radio station call letters*]
WSCP......... Weapons System Control Point
WSCP......... Weapon System Stock Control Plan (SAA)
WSCQ......... West Columbia, SC [*FM radio station call letters*]
WSCR......... Chicago, IL [*AM radio station call letters*]
WSCS......... Waste Solidification and Compaction Station [*Nuclear energy*] (NRCH)
WSCS......... Weapon System Communications System (AAG)
WSCS......... Wide Sense Cyclo-Stationary [*Telecommunications*]
WSCS-FM.... New London, NH [*FM radio station call letters*] (RBYB)
WSCSR....... Weapons System Contract Status Report [*Navy*] (NG)
WSCT......... Springfield, IL [*FM radio station call letters*]
WSCT......... Wainscot [*Technical drawings*]
WSCV......... Fort Lauderdale, FL [*Television station call letters*]
WSCW......... South Charleston, WV [*AM radio station call letters*]
WSCY......... Moultonborough, NH [*FM radio station call letters*]
WSCZ......... Greenwood, SC [*FM radio station call letters*]
WSD........... Sheboygan County Federated Library System, Mead Public Library, Sheboygan, WI [*OCLC symbol*] (OCLC)
WSD........... Warfare Systems Directorate (MCD)
WSD........... Water Seal Drainage [*Medicine*] (MEDA)
WSD........... Water Supply and Destination
WSD........... Weapons System Demonstration (MCD)
WSD........... Weapon Support Detachment (MCD)
WSD........... Weapon System Designator
WSD........... Weapon System Development [*Military*] (CAAL)
WSD........... Weapon System Director
WSD........... White Sands, NM [*Location identifier FAA*] (FAAL)
WSD........... Wind Speed Detector
WSD........... Working Stress Design [*Nuclear energy*] (NRCH)
WSD........... World of Scientific Discovery [*A publication*]
WSD........... World Space Directory [*A publication*]
WSD........... World Systems Division [*of Communications Satellite Corp.*] [*Telecommunications*] (TEL)
WSDA......... Water and Sewer Distributors of America (EA)
WSDB......... World Studies Data Bank (IID)
WSDC......... Weapons System Designator Code (NVT)
WSDC......... Weapon System Design Criteria (AAG)
WSDC......... Wisconsin State Data Center [*Wisconsin State Department of Administration*] [*Madison*] [*Information service or system*] (IID)
WSDD......... Weapon Status Digital Display
WSDDS....... Western Suburbs Development Disability Service [*Sydney, New South Wales, Australia*]
WSDF......... Water-Soluble Dietary Fiber [*Medicine*]
WSDH......... Sandwich, MA [*FM radio station call letters*]
WSDI......... Wall Street Deli [*Formerly, Sandwich Chef*] [*NASDAQ symbol*] (SPSG)
WSDL......... Weapons System Development Laboratory
WSDL......... Weapons Systems Data Link (MCD)
WSDM......... Brazil, IN [*AM radio station call letters*]
WSDM......... Weapon System Data Module
WSDM-FM.... Brazil, IN [*FM radio station call letters*]
WSDP......... Plymouth, MI [*FM radio station call letters*]
WSDP......... Weapons System Development Plan
WSDQ......... Dunlap, TN [*AM radio station call letters*]
WSDR......... Sterling, IL [*AM radio station call letters*]
WSDS......... Salem Township, MI [*AM radio station call letters*]
WSDS......... Weighted Sum of Deviation Squared [*Statistics*]
WSDT......... Soddy-Daisy, TN [*AM radio station call letters*]
WSD/TD...... Weapon System Demonstration Test Directive (AAG)
WSE........... National Weather Service Employees Organization
WSE........... Weapons System Evaluator (MCD)
WSE........... Weapons Systems Effectiveness
WSE........... Weapon Support Equipment [*Navy*] (NG)
WSE........... Weapon System Engineering [*Navy*] (NG)
WSE........... Western Allenbee Oil & Gas Co. Ltd. [*Vancouver Stock Exchange symbol*]
WSE........... Western Society of Engineers
WSE........... West-Southeast (ROG)
WSE........... Winnipeg Stock Exchange (HGAA)
WSE........... Work Shop Equipment (SAA)
WSE........... Wound, Skin, Enteric [*Isolation*] [*Medicine*]
WSE........... WWMCCS [*Worldwide Military Command and Control System*] Systems Engineer (MCD)
WSEA......... Pawley's Island, SC [*FM radio station call letters*]
WSEB......... Englewood, FL [*FM radio station call letters*]
WSEC......... Jacksonville, IL [*Television station call letters*]
WSEC......... Washington State Electronics Council
WSEC......... Watt-Second (AAG)
WSECL....... Weapon System Equipment Component List
WSED......... Weapons Systems Evaluation Division [*DoD*] (WDAA)
WSED......... Weapon System Electrical Diagrams
WSEE......... Erie, PA [*Television station call letters*]
WSEES....... Weapon System Electromagnetic Environment Simulator (MCD)
WSEF......... Weapons System Evaluation Facility (MCD)
WSEF......... Weapons Systems Effectiveness Factors
WSEFGT..... Weapons System Evaluation Facility Group Test (MCD)
WSEG......... Brunswick, GA [*FM radio station call letters*]
WSEG......... Weapon System Evaluation Group [*DoD and Air Force*] (MCD)
WSEH......... Cumberland, KY [*FM radio station call letters*]
WSEI......... Olney, IL [*FM radio station call letters*]
WSEIAC...... Weapon System Effectiveness Industry Advisory Committee
WSEK......... Somerset, KY [*FM radio station call letters*]
WSEL......... Pontotoc, MS [*AM radio station call letters*]
WSEL......... Weapon System Engineering Laboratory
WSEL-FM.... Pontotoc, MS [*FM radio station call letters*]
WSEM......... Donalsonville, GA [*AM radio station call letters*]
WSEM......... Weapon System Evaluation Missile [*Air Force*] (AFM)
WSem......... West Semitic (BJA)
WSEN......... Baldwinsville, NY [*FM radio station call letters*]
WSEO......... Nelsonville, OH [*FM radio station call letters*]
WSEO......... Weather Service Evaluation Officer [*National Weather Service*]
WSEO......... WWMCCS [*Worldwide Military Command and Control System*] System Engineering Office (MCD)
WSEP......... Waste Solidification Engineering Prototype Plant [*Nuclear energy*]
WSEP......... Weapon System Evaluation Program [*Air Force*]
WSER......... Elkton, MD [*AM radio station call letters*]
WSES......... Waterford Steam Electric Station [*Nuclear energy*] (NRCH)
WSES......... Weapons System Evaluation Squadron
WSESA....... Weapon System and Equipment Support Analysis
WSET......... Lynchburg, VA [*Television station call letters*]
WSET......... Weapon System Evaluation Test [*Navy*] (NG)
WSET......... Writers and Scholars Educational Trust [*British*] (EAIO)
WSEV......... Sevierville, TN [*AM radio station call letters*]
WSEV......... Winged Surface Effect Vehicle (PDAA)
WSEW......... Sanford, ME [*FM radio station call letters*]
WSEY......... Mount Morris, IL [*FM radio station call letters*]

WSEZ.......... Paoli, IN [*AM radio station call letters*]
WSF.......... Wake Shield Facility [*NASA*]
WSF.......... Waste Shipping Facility [*Nuclear energy*] (NRCH)
WSF.......... Water/Sand Fillable
WSF.......... Water-Soluble Fraction
WSF.......... Water Supply Forecast (NOAA)
WSF.......... Wave Soldering Fixture (MCD)
WSF.......... Weapon System File (MCD)
WSF.......... Weather Support Force [*Military*] (AFM)
WSF.......... Week Second Feet
WSF.......... Well Spouse Foundation (EA)
WSF.......... Well-Springs Foundation (EA)
WSF.......... Western Sea Frontier [*Navy*]
WSF.......... William Shatner Fellowship [*Defunct*] (EA)
WSF.......... Women for a Secure Future (EA)
WSF.......... Women's Sports Foundation (EA)
WSF.......... Work Station Facility
WSF.......... World Salt Foundation (EA)
WSF.......... World Science Fiction [*France*] (EAIO)
WSF.......... World Scout Foundation [*Geneva, Switzerland*] (EAIO)
WSF.......... World Sephardi Federation [*See also FSM*] [*Geneva, Switzerland*] (EAIO)
WSF.......... World SF [*Science Fiction*] (EA)
WSF.......... World Space Foundation (EA)
WSF.......... World Strengthlifting Federation [*India*] (EAIO)
WSFA.......... Montgomery, AL [*Television station call letters*]
WSFB.......... Quitman, GA [*AM radio station call letters*]
WSFC.......... Somerset, KY [*AM radio station call letters*]
WSFC.......... Wallops Space Flight Center [*NASA*] (IAA)
WSFC.......... White Sands Field Center [*New Mexico*]
WSFC.......... Women's Solid Fuel Council [*British*] (DI)
WSFI.......... Wood and Synthetic Flooring Institute (EA)
WSFJ.......... Newark, OH [*Television station call letters*]
WSFL-FM.... New Bern, NC [*FM radio station call letters*]
WSFM.......... Southport, NC [*FM radio station call letters*]
WSFN.......... Muskegon, MI [*AM radio station call letters*]
WSFO.......... Weather Service Forecast Office [*National Weather Service*]
WSFP.......... Fort Myers, FL [*FM radio station call letters*]
WSFP.......... World Showcase Fellowship Program [*Walt Disney World*]
WSFP-TV..... Fort Myers, FL [*Television station call letters*]
WSFQ-FM.... Reshtigo, WI [*FM radio station call letters*] (RBYB)
WSFR-FM.... Corydon, IN [*FM radio station call letters*] (RBYB)
WSFS.......... World Science Fiction Society (EA)
WSFS.......... WSFS Financial [*NASDAQ symbol*] (TTSB)
WSFS.......... WSFS Financial Corp. [*NASDAQ symbol*] (SAG)
WSFT.......... Thomaston, GA [*AM radio station call letters*]
WSFU-FM.... Union Springs, AL [*FM radio station call letters*] (RBYB)
WSFW.......... Seneca Falls, NY [*AM radio station call letters*]
WSFW-FM.... Seneca Falls, NY [*FM radio station call letters*]
WSFX.......... Nanticoke, PA [*FM radio station call letters*]
WSFX.......... Wilmington, NC [*Television station call letters*]
WSFZ-AM.... Memphis, TN [*AM radio station call letters*] (RBYB)
WSG.......... International Wool Study Group [*Defunct*]
WSG.......... Wasaya Airways Ltd. [*Canada ICAO designator*] (FAAC)
WSG.......... Washington [*Pennsylvania*] [*Airport symbol*] (OAG)
WSG.......... Weapons Spectrum Generator (PDAA)
WSG.......... Wehrsportegruppe Hoffman Truppe [*Hoffman Paramilitary Troop*] [*Germany*]
WSG.......... Wells Gold Ltd. [*Vancouver Stock Exchange symbol*]
WSG.......... Wesleyan Service Guild [*Defunct*] (EA)
WSG.......... Western Suburbs Greens [*Political party Australia*]
WSG.......... White Smooth Glossy [*Photographic paper*] (DGA)
WSG.......... Winter Study Group
WSG.......... Wired Shelf Group [*Telecommunications*] (TEL)
WSG.......... Wire Strain Gauge
WSG.......... Worthiest Soldier in the Group
WSGA.......... Savannah, GA [*AM radio station call letters*]
WSGA.......... Water Soluble Gum Association (EA)
WSGA.......... Wine and Spirits Guild of America (EA)
WSGB.......... Sutton, WV [*AM radio station call letters*]
WSGC.......... Kaukauna, WI [*AM radio station call letters*]
WSGC.......... Ringgold, GA [*FM radio station call letters*]
WSGC.......... Williams-Sonoma [*NASDAQ symbol*] (TTSB)
WSGC.......... Williams-Sonoma, Inc. [*NASDAQ symbol*] (NQ)
WSGD.......... Carbondale, PA [*FM radio station call letters*]
WSGD.......... White Smooth Glossy Double Weight [*Photographic paper*] (DGA)
WSGE.......... Dallas, NC [*FM radio station call letters*]
WSGE.......... Western Society of Gear Engineers (MCD)
WSGF.......... Springfield, GA [*FM radio station call letters*] (RBYB)
WSGH.......... Lewisville, NC [*AM radio station call letters*]
WSGI.......... Springfield, TN [*AM radio station call letters*]
WSGL.......... Naples, FL [*FM radio station call letters*]
WSGM.......... Coalmont, TN [*FM radio station call letters*]
WSGN.......... Gadsden, AL [*FM radio station call letters*]
WSGO.......... Oswego, NY [*AM radio station call letters*]
WSGR.......... Port Huron, MI [*FM radio station call letters*]
WSGS.......... Hazard, KY [*FM radio station call letters*]
WSGS.......... White Smooth Glossy Single Weight [*Photographic paper*] (DGA)
WSGT.......... White Sands Ground Terminal [*NASA*] (MCD)
WSGT.......... WWMCCS [*Worldwide Military Command and Control System*] Standard Graphics Terminal (DOMA)
WSGU.......... Window Sash Glaziers' Union [*British*]
WSGW.......... Saginaw, MI [*AM radio station call letters*]
Wsh.......... Washington State Reports [*A publication*] (DLA)
WSH.......... Waste Shipping Facility [*Nuclear energy*] (NUCP)
WSH.......... Weather Service Headquarters (NOAA)
WSH.......... Western Star Trucks Hldg [*AMEX symbol*] (TTSB)
WSH.......... Western Star Trucks Holdings Ltd. [*AMEX symbol*] (SAG)
WsH.......... William S. Hein & Co., Inc., Buffalo, NY [*Library symbol Library of Congress*] (LCLS)
WSH.......... Wilshire Energy Resources, Inc. [*Toronto Stock Exchange symbol*]
WSH.......... Windows Scripting Host [*Computer science*]
WSha.......... Bringham Memorial Library, Sharon, WI [*Library symbol Library of Congress*] (LCLS)
WSHA.......... Raleigh, NC [*FM radio station call letters*]
WShawGS.... Church of Jesus Christ of Latter-Day Saints, Genealogical Society Library, Wisconsin East District Branch, Shawano, WI [*Library symbol Library of Congress*] (LCLS)
WSHC.......... Shepherdstown, WV [*FM radio station call letters*]
WSHD.......... Eastport, ME [*FM radio station call letters*]
WSHE.......... Fort Lauderdale, FL [*FM radio station call letters*]
WShe.......... Mead Public Library, Sheboygan, WI [*Library symbol Library of Congress*] (LCLS)
WSheL.......... Lakeland College, Sheboygan, WI [*Library symbol Library of Congress*] (LCLS)
WSheM.......... Sheboygan Memorial Hospital, Sheboygan, WI [*Library symbol Library of Congress*] (LCLS)
WSheSN...... Saint Nicholas Hospital, Sheboygan, WI [*Library symbol Library of Congress*] (LCLS)
WSHE-TV..... Martinsburg, WV [*TV station call letters*] (RBYB)
WSheU.......... University of Wisconsin Center-Sheboygan, Sheboygan, WI [*Library symbol Library of Congress*] (LCLS)
WSHF.......... Wives Self-Help Foundation (EA)
WSHF-FM.... Mexico Beach, FL [*FM radio station call letters*] (RBYB)
WSHFT.......... Wind Shift [*NWS*] (FAAC)
WSHG.......... Ridgeland, SC [*FM radio station call letters*]
WSHG.......... Washing (MSA)
WSHG.......... Washing
WSHGA.......... Washington State Holly Growers Association [*Defunct*] (EA)
WSHH.......... Pittsburgh, PA [*FM radio station call letters*]
WSHI.......... Walsh Intl [*NASDAQ symbol*] (TTSB)
WSHJ.......... Southfield, MI [*FM radio station call letters*]
WSHK.......... Russellville, AL [*FM radio station call letters*]
WSHL.......... Easton, MA [*FM radio station call letters*]
WSHLD.......... Windshield (AAG)
WSHN.......... Fremont, MI [*AM radio station call letters*]
WshNat.......... Washington National Corp. [*Associated Press*] (SAG)
WSHN-FM.... Fremont, MI [*FM radio station call letters*]
WshNt.......... Washington Natural Gas Co. [*Associated Press*] (SAG)
WSHO.......... New Orleans, LA [*AM radio station call letters*]
WSHP.......... Shippensburg, PA [*AM radio station call letters*]
WshPst.......... Washington Post Co. [*Associated Press*] (SAG)
WSHR.......... Lake Ronkonkoma, NY [*FM radio station call letters*]
WSHR.......... Washer (MSA)
WSHS.......... Sheboygan, WI [*FM radio station call letters*]
WshSci.......... Washington Scientific Industries, Inc. [*Associated Press*] (SAG)
WSHT.......... Wave Superheater Hypersonic Tunnel (IAA)
WSHU.......... Fairfield, CT [*FM radio station call letters*]
WSHV.......... South Hill, VA [*FM radio station call letters*]
WSHW.......... Frankfort, IN [*FM radio station call letters*]
WSHX.......... Danville, VT [*FM radio station call letters*]
WSHY.......... Shelbyville, IL [*AM radio station call letters*]
WSHZ-FM.... Muskegon, MI [*FM radio station call letters*] (RBYB)
WSI.......... Wafer-Scale Integration [*Microelectronics*]
WSI.......... WaferScale Integration, Inc.
WSI.......... Waingapu [*Sumba Island*] [*Seismograph station code, US Geological Survey*] (SEIS)
WSI.......... War Service Indefinite
WSI.......... War-Supporting Industry
WSI.......... Water Safety Instructor [*Red Cross*]
WSI.......... Water Ski Industry Association (EA)
WSI.......... Water Solubility Index [*Analytical chemistry*]
WSI.......... Water Stability Index [*Agronomy*]
WSI.......... Weapon System Integration (MCD)
WSI.......... Weather Services International Corp. [*Information service or system*] (IID)
WSI.......... Welfare State International [*Performance group*] [*British*]
WSI.......... Wind Speed Indicator
WSI.......... Wind Spirit Air, Inc. [*FAA designator*] (FAAC)
WSI.......... World Synoptic Interval
WSI.......... Writers and Scholars International [*British*] (EAIO)
WSIA.......... Staten Island, NY [*FM radio station call letters*]
WSIA.......... Water Ski Industry Association (EA)
WSIA.......... Water Supply Improvement Association [*Later, IDA*] (EA)
WSIA.......... Weapons Systems Integration Agent (MCD)
WSIB.......... Selmer, TN [*FM radio station call letters*]
WSIC.......... Statesville, NC [*AM radio station call letters*]
WSIC.......... Watchmakers of Switzerland Information Center (EA)
WSIE.......... Edwardsville, IL [*FM radio station call letters*]
WSIF.......... Wilkesboro, NC [*FM radio station call letters*]
WSIG.......... Mount Jackson, VA [*FM radio station call letters*]
WSIG.......... Weapons Support Improvement Group [*DoD*] (DOMA)
WSIIP.......... Weapons Installation Interrupted for Parts (DNAB)
WSIL.......... Harrisburg, IL [*Television station call letters*]
WSI/L.......... War Supporting Industries and Logistics (MCD)
WSIM.......... Water Separation Index, Modified
WSIM.......... Wooden Ships & Iron Men (PCM)
WSIP.......... Paintsville, KY [*AM radio station call letters*]
WSIP.......... Weapons System Improvement Program (DWSG)
WSIP-FM.... Paintsville, KY [*FM radio station call letters*]

WSIR .... White Sands Integrated Range [*New Mexico*] (AAG)
WSIR .... Winter Haven, FL [*AM radio station call letters*]
WSIT .... Washington State Institute of Technology (KSC)
WSIT .... Water Safety Instructor Trainer [*Red Cross*]
WSITC .... Western Sydney Information Technology Centre [*Australia*]
WSITS .... Weapon System Interface Trade Study [*Military*]
WSIU .... Carbondale, IL [*FM radio station call letters*]
WSIU-TV .... Carbondale, IL [*Television station call letters*]
WSIV .... East Syracuse, NY [*AM radio station call letters*]
WSIX .... Nashville, TN [*FM radio station call letters*]
WSIY .... West Somerset Imperial Yeomanry [*British military*] (DMA)
WSJ .... San Juan, AK [*Location identifier FAA*] (FAAL)
WSJ .... Wall Street Journal [*A publication*] (DFIT)
WSJ .... Wall Street Journal (Eastern Edition) [*A publication*] (BRI)
WSJ .... Worm Screw Jack
WSJB .... Standish, ME [*FM radio station call letters*]
WSJC .... Singapore [*Singapore*] [*ICAO location identifier*] (ICLI)
WSJD .... Princeton, IN [*FM radio station call letters*]
WSJI-FM .... Cherry Hill, NJ [*FM radio station call letters*] (RBYB)
WSJK .... Sneedville, TN [*Television station call letters*]
WSJL .... Cape May, NJ [*FM radio station call letters*]
WSJM .... St. Joseph, MI [*AM radio station call letters*]
WSJ-MW .... Wall Street Journal (Midwest Edition) [*A publication*] (BRI)
WSJN .... San Juan, PR [*Television station call letters*]
WSJP .... Murray, KY [*AM radio station call letters*]
WSJR .... Madawaska, ME [*AM radio station call letters*]
WSJS .... Winston-Salem, NC [*AM radio station call letters*]
WSJT-FM .... Lakeland, FL [*FM radio station call letters*] (RBYB)
WSJU .... San Juan, PR [*Television station call letters*]
WSJV .... Elkhart, IN [*Television station call letters*]
WSJW-FM .... Louisville, KY [*FM radio station call letters*] (RBYB)
WSJY .... Fort Atkinson, WI [*FM radio station call letters*]
WSJZ-FM .... Buffalo, NY [*FM radio station call letters*] (RBYB)
WSKB .... Westfield, MA [*FM radio station call letters*]
WSKE .... Everett, PA [*AM radio station call letters*]
WSKE-FM .... Everett, PA [*FM radio station call letters*]
WSKG .... Binghamton, NY [*FM radio station call letters*]
WSKG-TV .... Binghamton, NY [*Television station call letters*]
WSKI .... Montpelier, VT [*AM radio station call letters*]
WSKI .... Winter Sports [*NASDAQ symbol*] (TTSB)
WSKI .... Winter Sports, Inc. [*NASDAQ symbol*] (SAG)
WSKN .... San Juan, PR [*AM radio station call letters*]
WSKP .... Key West, FL [*FM radio station call letters*]
WSKQ .... New York, NY [*FM radio station call letters*]
WSKS .... Rome, NY [*FM radio station call letters*] (RBYB)
WSKT .... Spencer, IN [*FM radio station call letters*]
WSKV .... Stanton, KY [*FM radio station call letters*]
WSKW .... Skowhegan, ME [*AM radio station call letters*]
WSKX .... Hinesville, GA [*FM radio station call letters*]
WSKY .... Asheville, NC [*AM radio station call letters*]
WSKZ .... Chattanooga, TN [*FM radio station call letters*]
WSL .... Warren Spring Laboratory [*Research center British*] (DCTA)
WSL .... War Substantive Lieutenant [*British*]
WSL .... Water Science Laboratories Proprietary Ltd. [*Australia*]
WSL .... Weather Seal (AAG)
WSL .... Windscale
WSL .... Workstation Laboratory (PCM)
WSLA .... Slidell, LA [*AM radio station call letters*]
WSLB .... Ogdensburg, NY [*AM radio station call letters*]
WSLBRUC .... WS and LB Robinson University College [*Australia*]
WSLC .... Roanoke, VA [*AM radio station call letters*]
WSLC .... WOCE [*World Ocean Circulation Experiment*] Sea Level Center [*Marine science*] (OSRA)
WSLC .... WOCE [*World Ocean Circulation Experiment*] Sea Level Center (USDC)
WSLC .... World Shortwave Listeners Club (EA)
WSLD .... White Smooth Lustre Double Weight [*Photographic paper*] (DGA)
WSLD .... Whitewater, WI [*FM radio station call letters*]
WSLE .... Cairo, GA [*FM radio station call letters*]
WSLF .... Western Somali Liberation Front
WSLI .... Jackson, MS [*AM radio station call letters*]
WSL-INT .... Weltbund zum Schutze des Lebens [*World Union for the Protection of Life - WUPL-INT*] (EAIO)
WSLJ .... Watertown, NY [*FM radio station call letters*]
WSLK .... Saranac Lake, NY [*FM radio station call letters*]
WSLL .... Saranac Lake, NY [*FM radio station call letters*]
WSLM .... Salem, IN [*AM radio station call letters*]
WSLM-FM .... Salem, IN [*FM radio station call letters*]
WSLN .... Delaware, OH [*FM radio station call letters*]
WSLO .... Malone, NY [*FM radio station call letters*]
WSLO .... Weapon System Logistics Officer [*Air Force*] (AFM)
WSLQ .... Roanoke, VA [*FM radio station call letters*]
WSLR .... Weapon System Logistic Reviews [*Navy*] (NG)
WSLS .... Roanoke, VA [*Television station call letters*]
WSLT .... Clearwater, SC [*FM radio station call letters*]
WSLU .... Canton, NY [*FM radio station call letters*]
WSLV .... Ardmore, TN [*AM radio station call letters*]
WSLW .... White Sulphur Springs, WV [*AM radio station call letters*]
WSLX .... New Canaan, CT [*FM radio station call letters*]
WSLY .... York, AL [*FM radio station call letters*]
WSM .... Nashville, TN [*AM radio station call letters*]
WSM .... Weapon Support Manager [*Air Force*]
WSM .... Weapon System Manager [*Air Force*] (AFM)
WSM .... Weapon System Manual
WSM .... Western Samoa [*ANSI three-letter standard code*] (CNC)
WSM .... Western Society of Malacologists (EA)
WSM .... West-Mar Resources Ltd. [*Vancouver Stock Exchange symbol*]
WSM .... Wheat Streak Mosaic [*Plant pathology*]
WSM .... White Single Male [*Classified advertising*]
WSM .... Wigner-Seitz Method [*Solid state physics*]
WSM .... Windowing System Manager [*Computer science*] (PCM)
WSM .... Wiseman [*Alaska*] [*Airport symbol*] (OAG)
WSM .... Wiseman, AK [*Location identifier FAA*] (FAAL)
WSM .... Wisman Aviation [*ICAO designator*] (FAAC)
WSM .... Women's Suffrage Movement (ROG)
WSM .... Wright State University, Health Sciences Library, Dayton, OH [*OCLC symbol*] (OCLC)
WSMA .... Western States Meat Association (EA)
WSMA .... Window Shade Manufacturers Association (EA)
WSMAC .... Weapon System Maintenance Action Center
WSMaT .... Weapon System Management Team [*Army*] (RDA)
WSMB .... New Orleans, LA [*AM radio station call letters*]
WSMC .... Collegedale, TN [*FM radio station call letters*]
WSMC .... Weapons System Management Codes [*Navy*]
WSMC .... Western Space and Missile Center [*Vandenberg Air Force Base, CA*] [*Air Force*]
WSMC .... Western States Movers Conference
WSMD .... Mechanicsville, MD [*FM radio station call letters*]
WSME .... Sanford, ME [*AM radio station call letters*]
WSM-FM .... Nashville, TN [*FM radio station call letters*]
WSMG .... Greeneville, TN [*AM radio station call letters*]
WSMG .... Tusculum, TN [*FM radio station call letters*] (RBYB)
WSMH .... Flint, MI [*Television station call letters*]
WSMI .... Litchfield, IL [*AM radio station call letters*]
WSMI-FM .... Litchfield, IL [*FM radio station call letters*]
WSMIS .... Weapon Systems Management Information System [*Air Force*] (GFGA)
WSMK .... Buchanan, MI [*FM radio station call letters*]
WSML .... Graham, NC [*AM radio station call letters*]
WSML .... Saltfree Meal [*Airline notation*]
WSMN .... Nashua, NH [*AM radio station call letters*]
WSMO .... Weapon System Materiel Officer [*Air Force*] (AFM)
WSMO .... Weather Service Meteorological Observatory [*or Observations*] [*National Weather Service*] (NOAA)
WSMP .... Weapons System Master Plan [*Air Force*] (DOMA)
WSMP .... WSMP, Inc. [*Formerly, Western Steer Mom 'n' Pop's, Inc.*] [*NASDAQ symbol*] (SPSG)
WSMPA .... Western States Meat Association (EA)
WSMQ .... Bessemer, AL [*AM radio station call letters*]
WSMR .... White Sands Missile Range [*New Mexico*] [*Army*]
WSMS-FM .... Artesia, MS [*FM radio station call letters*] (RBYB)
WSMT .... Sparta, TN [*AM radio station call letters*]
WSMT .... Weapons System Maintenance Test (MCD)
WSMTC .... White Sands Missile Test Center [*New Mexico*]
WSMT-FM .... Sparta, TN [*FM radio station call letters*]
WSMTT .... White Star Mobile Training Teams [*Military*] (CINC)
WSMU .... North Dartmouth, MA [*FM radio station call letters*]
WSMV .... Nashville, TN [*Television station call letters*]
WSMV .... Wheat Streak Mosaic Virus
WSMX .... Winston-Salem, NC [*AM radio station call letters*]
WSMY .... Weldon, NC [*AM radio station call letters*]
WSMZ-FM .... Johnstown, Oh [*FM radio station call letters*] (RBYB)
WSN .... South Naknek [*Alaska*] [*Airport symbol*] (OAG)
WSN .... South Naknek, AK [*Location identifier FAA*] (FAAL)
WSN .... Spokane County Library, Spokane, WA [*Inactive*] [*OCLC symbol*] (OCLC)
WSN .... Wang System Networking (HGAA)
WSN .... Warm Springs [*Nevada*] [*Seismograph station code, US Geological Survey Closed*] (SEIS)
WSN .... Water-Soluble Nitrogen [*Analytical chemistry*]
WSN .... Western Co. of North America [*NYSE symbol*] (SPSG)
WSN .... Western Resources Technology [*Vancouver Stock Exchange symbol*]
WSN .... Western Society of Naturalists (EA)
WSNC .... Winston-Salem, NC [*FM radio station call letters*]
WSND .... Notre Dame, IN [*FM radio station call letters*]
WSNE .... Taunton, MA [*FM radio station call letters*]
WSNG .... Torrington, CT [*AM radio station call letters*]
WSNGT .... White Sands NASA Ground Terminal (MCD)
WSNI .... Thomasville, GA [*FM radio station call letters*]
WSNJ .... Bridgeton, NJ [*AM radio station call letters*]
WSNJ-FM .... Bridgeton, NJ [*FM radio station call letters*]
WSNN .... Potsdam, NY [*FM radio station call letters*]
WSNO .... Barre, VT [*AM radio station call letters*]
WSNP .... Water-Soluble Nonstarchy Polysaccharide [*Food composition*]
WSNQ .... Gaylord, MI [*AM radio station call letters*]
WSNR-AM .... Hartford, KY [*AM radio station call letters*] (RBYB)
WSNS .... Chicago, IL [*Television station call letters*]
WSNSCA .... Washable Suits, Novelties, and Sportswear Contractors Association (EA)
WSNT .... Sandersville, GA [*AM radio station call letters*]
WSNT-FM .... Sandersville, GA [*FM radio station call letters*]
WSNU .... Lock Haven, PA [*FM radio station call letters*]
WSNV .... Howland, ME [*FM radio station call letters*]
WSNW .... Seneca, SC [*AM radio station call letters*]
W/SNWS .... With Snow Tires [*Automotive advertising*]
WSNX .... Muskegon, MI [*FM radio station call letters*]
WSNY .... Columbus, OH [*FM radio station call letters*]
WSNY .... Wagner Society of New York (EA)
WSO .... Warrant Stores Officer [*Navy British*]
WSO .... Washabo [*Surinam*] [*Airport symbol*] (OAG)

WSO .... Washington Standardization Officers
WSO .... Water Service Operator (MCD)
WSO .... Watsco, Inc. [*NYSE symbol*] (SAG)
WSO .... Watsco, Inc. [*AMEX symbol*] (SPSG)
WSO .... Weapon System Officer [*or Operator*] [*Air Force*] (AFM)
WSO .... Weapon System Operator
WSO .... Weather Service Office [*National Weather Service*] (NOAA)
WSO .... Western Support Office [*Formerly, WOO*] [*NASA*]
WSO .... White Sands Operations [*New Mexico*] [*Formerly, White Sands Missile Operations*] [*NASA*]
WSO .... White Superficial Onychomycosis
WSO .... Wilcox Solar Observatory
WSO .... [*The*] WorkSheet Optimizer [*Laptop tool*] [*Brubaker Software*] (PCM)
WSO .... World Safety Organization [*United Nations*]
WSO .... World Simulation Organization
WSO .... WRAF [*Women's Royal Naval Air Force*] Staff Officer [*British military*] (DMA)
WSO(AG) ..... Weather Service Office for Agriculture [*National Weather Service*] (NOAA)
WSO(AV) ..... Weather Service Office for Aviation [*National Weather Service*] (NOAA)
WSO.B .... Watsco Inc. Cv Cl'B' [*AMEX symbol*] (TTSB)
WSOC .... Charlotte, NC [*FM radio station call letters*]
WSOC .... Weapon System Operational Concept (AAG)
WSOC .... Wider Share Ownership Council [*British*] (DBA)
WSOC-TV ..... Charlotte, NC [*Television station call letters*]
WSOE .... Elon College, NC [*FM radio station call letters*]
WSOEA .... Wholesale Stationery and Office Equipment Association [*Later, WSA*] (EA)
WSOF .... Madisonville, KY [*FM radio station call letters*]
WSO(FW) ..... Weather Service Office for Fire-Weather [*National Weather Service*] (NOAA)
WSOH-FM .... New Washington, IN [*FM radio station call letters*] (RBYB)
WSOJ .... Petersburg, VA [*FM radio station call letters*]
WSOJ .... Whole Blood Serum of a Patient with Obstructive Jaundice [*Hematology*] (DAVI)
WSOK .... Savannah, GA [*AM radio station call letters*]
WSOL .... San German, PR [*AM radio station call letters*]
WSOL-FM .... Brunswick, GA [*FM radio station call letters*] (RBYB)
WSOM .... Salem, OH [*AM radio station call letters*]
WSOM .... Weather Service Operations [*NWS*] (FAAC)
WSON .... Henderson, KY [*AM radio station call letters*]
WSON .... Worldwide Satellite Observing Network (MCD)
WSOO .... Sault Ste. Marie, MI [*AM radio station call letters*]
WSOP .... White Supercalendered Offset Paper [*Publishing*]
WSOR .... Naples, FL [*FM radio station call letters*]
WSOS .... St. Augustine, FL [*FM radio station call letters*]
WSOT .... Weapon System Operability Test [*Military*] (CAAL)
WSOU .... South Orange, NJ [*FM radio station call letters*]
WSOY .... Decatur, IL [*AM radio station call letters*]
WSOY .... Werner Soederstroem Osakeyhtio [*Book printer*] [*Finland*]
WSOY-FM .... Decatur, IL [*FM radio station call letters*]
WSP .... Ward's Sales Prospector [*A publication*]
W/SP .... Warheads and Special Projects Laboratory [*Picatinny Arsenal*]
WSP .... Washington School of Psychiatry
WSP .... Washington Square Press [*Publisher's imprint*]
WSP .... Waspam [*Nicaragua*] [*Airport symbol*] (AD)
WSP .... Watered Silk Paper (DGA)
WSP .... Water Spray Protection [*Shipping*] (DS)
WSP .... Water Supply Papers
WSP .... Water Supply Point
WSP .... Weapon Support Processor [*Military*] (CAAL)
WSP .... Weapon System Program (SAA)
WSP .... Weapon Systems Pouch (AFM)
WSP .... Weibull Shape Parameter [*Statistics*]
WSP .... West Penn Power Co. [*NYSE symbol*] (SPSG)
WSP .... Wheel Slide Protection (PDAA)
WSP .... White Star Parachute Flares [*Military*] (INF)
WSP .... Wideband Signal Processor
WSP .... Winspear Resources [*Vancouver Stock Exchange symbol*]
WSP .... Withdrawal Seizure-Prone [*Mouse strain*]
WSP .... Women Strike for Peace (EA)
WSP .... Working Steam Pressure
WSP .... Workshop (NATG)
WSP .... Work Simplification Program [*Military*]
WSP .... Work Study Program (OICC)
WSP .... Work Systems Package [*Navy underwater salvage operation*] (DICI)
WSP .... Worldwide Service Project
WSP .... Wright State University, Piqua Branch Campus, Piqua, OH [*OCLC symbol*] (OCLC)
WSpa .... Sparta Free Library, Sparta, WI [*Library symbol Library of Congress*] (LCLS)
WSPA .... Spartanburg, SC [*AM radio station call letters*]
WSPA .... World Society for the Protection of Animals [*WFPA and ISPA*] [*Formed by a merger of*] (EA)
WSPACS ...... Weapon Systems Planning [*or Programming*] and Control System
WSPA-FM .... Spartanburg, SC [*FM radio station call letters*]
WSPAT .... Wolfe-Spence Programming Aptitude Test
WSPA-TV ..... Spartanburg, SC [*Television station call letters*]
WSPB .... Sarasota, FL [*AM radio station call letters*]
WSPC .... Albemarle, NC [*AM radio station call letters*]
WSPC .... Weapons System Partnerships Committee [*NATO*] (NATG)
WSPC .... Weapons System Program Code [*Defense Supply Agency*]
WSPC .... World Sports Prototype Championship [*Auto racing*]
WSPD .... Toledo, OH [*AM radio station call letters*]
WSPD .... Weapons System Planning Data [*Navy*]
WSPD .... Weapon System Planning Document (NVT)
WSPDC .... Western Sydney Planning and Development Committee [*Australia*]
WSPF .... Watergate Special Prosecution Force [*Terminated, 1977*] [*Department of Justice*]
WSPG .... Wall Street Planning Group (EA)
WSPG .... Weapon System Phasing Group
WSPG .... Weapon System Purchasing Group
WSPG .... White Sands Proving Ground [*New Mexico*] [*Obsolete*]
WSPGL .... Weapon System Program Guide List
WSPI .... Mount Carmel, PA [*FM radio station call letters*]
WSP-I .... World Socialist Party - Ireland [*Political party*] (EAIO)
WSPK .... Poughkeepsie, NY [*FM radio station call letters*]
WSPL .... La Crosse, WI [*FM radio station call letters*]
WSPME .... Weavelength-Scanning Polarization-Modulation Ellipsometry (PDAA)
WSPN .... Saratoga Springs, NY [*FM radio station call letters*]
WSPNZ .... World Socialist Party of New Zealand [*Political party*] (EAIO)
WSPO .... Stevens Point, WI [*AM radio station call letters*]
WSPO .... Weapon System Project Office [*Air Force*]
WSPOP .... Weapon System Phase-Out Procedure [*Air Force*] (AFM)
WSPPD .... Weapons Systems Personnel Planning Data (MCD)
WSPPr .... West Penn Pwr 4 1/2%cmPfd [*NYSE symbol*] (TTSB)
WSPQ .... Springville, NY [*AM radio station call letters*]
WSPR .... Springfield, MA [*AM radio station call letters*]
WSPR .... Weapon System Program Review [*Army*]
WSPRD .... Weapons Systems Progress Reporting Data
WSPS .... Concord, NH [*FM radio station call letters*]
WSpS .... Saint Michael's Hospital, Stevens Point, WI [*Library symbol Library of Congress*] (LCLS)
WSPS .... Wire Strike Protection System (MCD)
WSPT .... Stevens Point, WI [*FM radio station call letters*]
WSPT-AM .... Stevens Point, WI [*AM radio station call letters*] (RBYB)
WSpU .... University of Wisconsin-Stevens Point, Stevens Point, WI [*Library symbol Library of Congress*] (LCLS)
WSPU .... Women's Social and Political Union [*British*]
WSPUS .... World Socialist Party of the United States (EA)
WSPY .... Plano, IL [*FM radio station call letters*]
WSPZ .... Tuscaloosa, AL [*AM radio station call letters*]
WSQ .... Wake Seeding and Quenching
WSq .... Weather Squadron [*Air Force*] (AFM)
WSQC .... Oneonta, NY [*FM radio station call letters*]
WSQE .... Corning, NY [*FM radio station call letters*]
WSQG .... Ithaca, NY [*FM radio station call letters*]
WSQN .... Scranton, SC [*FM radio station call letters*]
WSQR .... Sycamore, IL [*AM radio station call letters*]
WSQV .... Berwick, PA [*AM radio station call letters*]
WSQX .... Binghamton, NY [*FM radio station call letters*]
WSR .... Canadian Helicopters [*ICAO designator*] (FAAC)
WSR .... Warm Springs Repeater [*Nevada*] [*Seismograph station code, US Geological Survey Closed*] (SEIS)
WSR .... Warren & Saline River Railroad Co. [*AAR code*]
WSR .... War Service Regulation
WSR .... Wasior [*West Irian, Indonesia*] [*Airport symbol*] (AD)
W/sr .... Watts per Steradian
WSR .... Weak Signal Reception
WSR .... Weapons Spares Report [*Navy*]
WSR .... Weapons Status Report [*Navy*] (NG)
WSR .... Weapons System Review (NVT)
WSR .... Weapon System Reliability [*Air Force*] (AFM)
WSR .... Weapon Systems Requirement (MCD)
WSR .... Weather Search RADAR (MCD)
WSR .... Weather Surveillance RADAR
WSR .... Weekly Summary Report
WSR .... Wet Snow on Runway [*NWS*] (FAAC)
WSR .... Wild and Scenic Rivers Act
WSR .... Windsor Resources, Inc. [*Vancouver Stock Exchange symbol*]
WSR .... Wire Shift Register
WSR .... Withdrawal Seizure-Resistant [*Mouse strain*]
WSR .... Wood-Shingle Roof [*Technical drawings*]
WSR .... World Students Relief
WSR-88D ..... Weather Surveillance Radar [*Marine science*] (OSRA)
WSR-88D ..... Weather Surveillance Radar (USDC)
WSRA .... Wild and Scenic Rivers Act
WSRA .... Women's Squash Rackets Association [*British*] (BI)
WSRB .... Walpole, MA [*FM radio station call letters*]
WSRC .... Durham, NC [*AM radio station call letters*]
WSRCC .... War, Strikes, Riots, and Civil Commotions [*Insurance*] (AIA)
WSRCC .... Western Suburbs Regional Chamber of Commerce [*Sydney, New South Wales, Australia*]
WSRD .... Johnstown, NY [*FM radio station call letters*]
WSRE .... Pensacola, FL [*Television station call letters*]
WSRF .... Fort Lauderdale, FL [*AM radio station call letters*]
WSRG .... Sturgeon Bay, WI [*FM radio station call letters*] (RBYB)
WSRH .... Weather Service Regional Headquarters [*National Weather Service*] (NOAA)
WSRI .... Rochester, NH [*FM radio station call letters*] (RBYB)
WSRI .... World Safety Research Institute
WSRK .... Oneonta, NY [*FM radio station call letters*]
WSRL .... Water Supply Research Laboratory [*National Environmental Research Center*]
WSRL .... Wisconsin Survey Research Laboratory [*University of Wisconsin*] [*Research center*] (RCD)
WSRM .... Coosa, GA [*FM radio station call letters*]
WSRM .... Weather Surveillance RADAR Manual (NOAA)
W/(SR-M^2) ... Watt per Steradian Square Meter (WDAA)

WSRN .... Swarthmore, PA [*FM radio station call letters*]
WSRN .... Western Satellite Research Network (PDAA)
WSRO .... Marlborough, MA [*AM radio station call letters*]
WSRO .... Weapon System Replacement Operations (MCD)
WSRO .... Whole System Replacement Operation [*Army*] (INF)
WSRO .... World Sugar Research Organisation (EAIO)
WSRP .... Weapons System Requisitioning Procedure [*Military*] (AABC)
WSRQ .... Queensbury, NY [*FM radio station call letters*] (RBYB)
WSRR .... West Shore Railroad
WSRR-FM .... Millington, TN [*FM radio station call letters*] (RBYB)
WSRS .... Wildlife Sound Recording Society [*British*]
WSRS .... Worcester, MA [*FM radio station call letters*]
WSRT .... Mercersburg, PA [*FM radio station call letters*]
WSRT .... Weapons System Reliability Test (CINC)
WSRT .... Weapon System Readiness Test
WSRT .... Westerbork Synthesis Radio Telescope
WSRV .... Smyrna, DE [*FM radio station call letters*]
WSRW .... Hillsboro, OH [*AM radio station call letters*]
WSRW-FM ... Hillsboro, OH [*FM radio station call letters*]
WSRX .... Naples, FL [*FM radio station call letters*]
WSRZ .... Sarasota, FL [*FM radio station call letters*]
WSS .... Warfare Systems School [*Air Force*] (AFM)
WSS .... War Savings Staff
WSS .... Washington Strategy Seminar (EA)
WSS .... Weapon Support Systems
WSS .... Weapon System Specification (AAG)
WSS .... Weather Service Specialist [*National Weather Service*]
WSS .... Weekend Stress Syndrome [*Psychiatry*]
WSS .... Wheel Speed Sensor [*Automotive engineering*]
WSS .... Wheelwrights' and Smiths' Society [*A union*] [*British*]
WSS .... Wholesale Storage Site (DNAB)
WSS .... Wide Sense Stationary [*Telecommunications*] (IAA)
WSS .... Wind Shear Spike (SAA)
WSS .... Winston-Salem Southbound Railway Co. [*AAR code*]
WSS .... Women's Social Services [*Salvation Army*]
WSS .... Women's Studies Section [*Association of College and Research Libraries*]
WSS .... Workpack Scheduling System [*Industrial engineering*]
WSS .... Work Summarization System (MCD)
WSS .... World Ship Society [*Haywards Heath, West Sussex, England*]
WSS .... WWMCCS [*Worldwide Military Command and Control System*] Systems Specification (MCD)
WSSA .... Morrow, GA [*AM radio station call letters*]
WSSA .... Weapon System Support Activities (AAG)
WSSA .... Weed Science Society of America (EA)
WSSA .... Welsh Secondary Schools Association [*British*]
WSSA .... Western Social Science Association (EA)
WSSA .... White Sands Signal Agency [*New Mexico*] [*Military*] (MCD)
WSSA .... Wine and Spirits Shippers Association (EA)
WSSA .... World Secret Service Association [*Later, WAD*] (EA)
WSSAB .... Weller-Strawser Scales of Adaptive Behavior [*Educational test*]
WSSB .... Orangeburg, SC [*FM radio station call letters*]
WSSBA .... Western Single Side Band Association (EA)
WSSC .... Sumter, SC [*AM radio station call letters*]
WSSC .... Weapon System Support Center (AAG)
WSSC .... Weapon System Support Code [*Navy*] (NG)
WSSCA .... Welsh Springer Spaniel Club of America (EA)
WSSCA .... White Sands Signal Corps Agency [*New Mexico*] [*Military*] (AAG)
WSSCL .... Weapon System Stock Control List (AAG)
WSSD .... Chicago, IL [*FM radio station call letters*]
WSSD .... Weapon System Support Development (MCD)
WSSF .... National Weather Service Support FAcility (FAAC)
WSSF .... Weapons System Security Flight [*Military*]
WSSFN .... World Society for Stereotactic and Functional Neurosurgery (EA)
WSSG .... Goldsboro, NC [*AM radio station call letters*]
WSSG .... Weapon System Support Group (MCD)
WSSG .... WOCE [*World Ocean Circulation Experiment*] Scientific Steering Group [*Marine science*] (OSRA)
WSSH .... Lowell, MA [*FM radio station call letters*]
WSSI .... Carthage, MS [*AM radio station call letters*]
WSSI .... Women's Social Service for Israel (EA)
WSSIB .... WWMCCS [*Worldwide Military Command and Control System*] Standard System Information Base (MCD)
WSSI-FM ..... Carthage, MS [*FM radio station call letters*]
WSSJ .... Camden, NJ [*AM radio station call letters*]
WSSL .... Gray Court, SC [*FM radio station call letters*]
WSSL .... Seletar [*Singapore*] [*ICAO location identifier*] (ICLI)
WSSL .... Weapon System Stock List [*Army*]
WSSL .... Weapon System Stock/Support List [*Air Force*] (AFIT)
WSSL .... Western Secondary Standards Laboratory
WSSM .... Weapon System Staff Manager [*Army*] (RDA)
WSSM .... Weapon System Support Manager (AAG)
WSSMV .... Wheat Spindle Streak Mosaic Virus
WSSN .... Weston, WV [*FM radio station call letters*]
WSSO .... Starkville, MS [*AM radio station call letters*]
WSSO .... Weapon System Support Officer [*Army*] (RDA)
WSSP .... Goose Creek, SC [*FM radio station call letters*]
WSSP .... Weapon Systems Support Program [*Defense Supply Agency*]
WSSPM .... Weapons System Support Program Manager (AFIT)
WSSQ .... Sterling, IL [*FM radio station call letters*]
WSSR .... Georgetown, DE [*AM radio station call letters*]
WSSRAP ..... Weldon Spring Site Remedial Action Project [*Department of Energy*] [*Weldon Spring, MO*] (GAAI)
WSSRS .... Waksman Social Skills Rating Scale
WSSS .... Charlotte, NC [*FM radio station call letters*]
WSSS .... Singapore Changi [*Singapore*] [*ICAO location identifier*] (ICLI)
WSSS .... Weapon System Storage Site
WSSSFAF .... Wartime Standard Support System for Foreign Armed Forces (MCD)
WSSSG .... Wide-band Spread Spectrum Signal Generator
WSSSP .... Western States Small School Project
WSST .... Cordele, GA [*Television station call letters*]
WSSU .... National Weather Service Support Unit (FAAC)
WSSUS .... Wide Sense Stationary Uncorrelated Scattering [*Telecommunications*] (IAA)
WSSX .... Charleston, SC [*FM radio station call letters*]
WSSY .... Talladega, AL [*FM radio station call letters*]
WSSZ .... Greensburg, PA [*FM radio station call letters*]
WSt .... D. R. Moon Memorial Library, Stanley, WI [*Library symbol Library of Congress*] (LCLS)
WST .... Waste
WST .... Watch Station Trainer [*Military*] (DWSG)
WST .... Water Supply Tank
WST .... Weapon Safety Trainer
WST .... Weapon System Test
WST .... Weapon System Trainer [*Navy*]
WST .... Weightlessness Simulation Test
WST .... West Aviation AS [*Norway ICAO designator*] (FAAC)
WST .... West Co. [*NYSE symbol*] (TTSB)
WST .... West Co., Inc. [*NYSE symbol*] (SPSG)
WST .... Westerly [*Rhode Island*] [*Airport symbol*] (OAG)
WST .... Westerly, RI [*Location identifier FAA*] (FAAL)
WST .... Wholesale Sales Tax
WST .... Word Synchronizing Track (NITA)
WST .... World Satellite Terminal [*Telecommunications*] (IAA)
WST .... World Ship Trust [*Cambridge, England*]
WST .... World System Teletext (NTCM)
WST .... Write Symbol Table
WSTA .... Charlotte Amalie, VI [*AM radio station call letters*]
WSTA .... Weapon System Task Analysis (AAG)
WSTA .... White Slave Traffic Act
WstAmer ...... WestAmerica Corp. [*Associated Press*] (SAG)
WstAtlas ...... Western Atlas, Inc. [*Associated Press*] (SAG)
WSTB .... Streetsboro, OH [*FM radio station call letters*]
WstBeef ...... Western Beef [*Associated Press*] (SAG)
WstbPR .... Westernbank Puerto Rico [*Associated Press*] (SAG)
WstBrC .... Westbridge Capital [*Associated Press*] (SAG)
WSTC .... Stamford, CT [*AM radio station call letters*]
WSTC .... Weapons System Test Card (MCD)
WSTC .... Weapon System Total Complex
WSTC .... Willimantic State Teachers College [*Connecticut*]
WstCstFL ..... West Coast Bancorp Florida [*Associated Press*] (SAG)
WstCstOR .... West Coast Bancorp Oregon [*Associated Press*] (SAG)
WstctEg .... Westcoast Energy, Inc. [*Associated Press*] (SAG)
WSTD .... Standish, MI [*FM radio station call letters*]
WSTDA .... Web Sling and Tiedown Association (EA)
WSTE .... Ponce, PR [*Television station call letters*]
WSTE .... TransAmerican Waste Indus [*NASDAQ symbol*] (TTSB)
WSTE .... TransAmerican Waste Industries, Inc. [*NASDAQ symbol*] (SAG)
WSTEA .... Weapon System Training Effectiveness Analysis
WSTE MAT ... Waste Material [*Freight*]
W/STEP .... With Step Change in Altitude (GAVI)
WSTEW .... Transamerican Waste Inds Wrrt'A' [*NASDAQ symbol*] (TTSB)
WSTEZ .... Transamerican Waste Inds Wrrt'B' [*NASDAQ symbol*] (TTSB)
WSTF .... Andalusia, AL [*FM radio station call letters*] (RBYB)
WSTF .... Western Staff Services [*NASDAQ symbol*] (TTSB)
WSTF .... White Sands Test Facility [*New Mexico*] [*Military*]
WSTG .... Hampton, NH [*FM radio station call letters*] (RBYB)
WStG .... Wehrstrafgesetz [*Military Criminal Law*] [*German*] (ILCA)
WstG .... Western Gas Resources Co. [*Associated Press*] (SAG)
WstgEl .... Westinghouse Electric Corp. [*Associated Press*] (SAG)
WstGR .... Western Gas Resources [*Associated Press*] (SAG)
WSTH .... Alexander City, AL [*FM radio station call letters*]
WSTH .... Weapon System Tactical Handbook (MCD)
WSTI .... Quitman, GA [*FM radio station call letters*]
WSTI .... Welded Steel Tube Institute [*Later, STINA*] (EA)
WSTIB .... Woolen and Silk Textiles Industries Board [*New Deal*]
WSTJ .... St. Johnsbury, VT [*AM radio station call letters*]
WSTK .... Colonial Heights, VA [*AM radio station call letters*]
WSTL .... South Glens Falls, NY [*AM radio station call letters*]
WSTL .... Weapon System Test Laboratory
WSTL .... Westell Technologies'A' [*NASDAQ symbol*] (TTSB)
WSTL .... Westell Technologies, Inc. [*NASDAQ symbol*] (SAG)
WSTL .... Whistle (MSA)
WStL & P .... Wabash, St. Louis & Pacific Railway
WSTM .... Syracuse, NY [*Television station call letters*]
WSTM .... Western Micro Techn'gy [*NASDAQ symbol*] (TTSB)
WSTM .... Western Micro Technology, Inc. [*NASDAQ symbol*] (NQ)
WSTM .... White Sands Missile Range Transverse Mercator [*Army*] (AABC)
WstMar .... West Marine, Inc. [*Associated Press*] (SAG)
WstMn .... Western Mining Corp. [*Associated Press*] (SAG)
WstmorC ..... Westmoreland Coal Co. [*Associated Press*] (SAG)
WstmrC .... Westmoreland Coal [*Associated Press*] (SAG)
WSTN .... Western
WSTN .... Weston [*Roy F.*], Inc. [*West Chester, PA*] [*NASDAQ symbol*] (NQ)
WSTNA .... Weston(Roy F)'A' [*NASDAQ symbol*] (TTSB)
WSTN-AM .... Somerville, TN [*AM radio station call letters*] (RBYB)
WstnCC .... Western Country Clubs, Inc. [*Associated Press*] (SAG)
WstnGR .... Western Gas Resources [*Associated Press*] (SAG)
WstnNat ...... Western National Corp. [*Associated Press*] (SAG)
WstnOhF ..... Western Ohio Financial Corp. [*Associated Press*] (SAG)

WstnPb .... Western Publishing Group, Inc. [*Associated Press*] (SAG)
WstnPw .... Western Power & Equipment Corp. [*Associated Press*] (SAG)
WstnRes .... Western Resources, Inc. [*Associated Press*] (SAG)
WstnRs .... Western Resources [*Associated Press*] (SAG)
WSTO .... Owensboro, KY [*FM radio station call letters*]
WSTP .... Salisbury, NC [*AM radio station call letters*]
WSTP .... Wastewater Sewage Treatment Plant (GNE)
WSTP .... Weapon System Test Program
WstpBc .... Westport Bancorp, Inc. [*Associated Press*] (SAG)
Wstpc .... Westpac Banking Corp. [*Associated Press*] (SAG)
WSTPN .... Wrist Pin
WstptStv .... Westpoint Stevens Co. [*Associated Press*] (SAG)
WSTQ .... Streator, IL [*FM radio station call letters*]
WSTR .... Cincinnati, OH [*Television station call letters*]
WSTR .... Smyrna, GA [*FM radio station call letters*]
WSTR .... WesterFed Financial [*NASDAQ symbol*] (TTSB)
WSTR .... Westerfed Financial Corp. [*NASDAQ symbol*] (SAG)
Wstrbke .... Westerbeke Corp. [*Associated Press*] (SAG)
WstRes .... Western Resources Capital II [*Associated Press*] (SAG)
WSTRN .... Western
WSTRS .... Washington State Teachers Retirement System (EDAC)
WSTS .... Fairmont, NC [*FM radio station call letters*]
WSTS .... Weapon System Training Set (AFM)
WSTS .... World Semiconductor Trade Statistics [*Semiconductor Industry Association*] [*Information service or system*] (IID)
WSTSD .... Westside
WSTSHD .... Watershed
WstStr .... Western Star Trucks Holdings Ltd. [*Associated Press*] (SAG)
WSTT .... Thomasville, GA [*AM radio station call letters*]
WSTT .... Weather Scenario Test Tape [*Marine science*] (OSRA)
WSTT .... Weather Scenario Test Tape (USDC)
WstTleS .... West TeleServices Corp. [*Associated Press*] (SAG)
WstTr .... Western Transmedia, Inc. [*Associated Press*] (SAG)
WstTrns .... Western Transmedia, Inc. [*Associated Press*] (SAG)
WSTTWTR ... Wastewater
WSTU .... Stuart, FL [*AM radio station call letters*]
WSTV .... Steubenville, OH [*AM radio station call letters*]
WSTV .... World Service Television [*BBC*] (ECON)
WSTW .... Wilmington, DE [*FM radio station call letters*]
WstWatr .... Western Water Co. [*Associated Press*] (SAG)
Wstwd .... Westwood Corp. [*Associated Press*] (SAG)
WstwdF .... Westwood Financial Corp. [*Associated Press*] (SAG)
WstwdH .... Westwood Homestead Financial Corp. [*Associated Press*] (SAG)
WstWire .... Western Wireless Corp. [*Associated Press*] (SAG)
WstwOn .... Westwood One, Inc. [*Associated Press*] (SAG)
WSTX .... Christiansted, VI [*AM radio station call letters*]
WSTX-FM .... Christiansted, VI [*FM radio station call letters*]
WSTZ .... Vicksburg, MS [*FM radio station call letters*]
WSU .... University of Wisconsin-Superior, Superior, WI [*Library symbol Library of Congress*] (LCLS)
WSU .... Washington State University
WSU .... Wasu [*Papua New Guinea*] [*Airport symbol*] (OAG)
WSU .... Water Servicing Unit (NASA)
WSU .... Wayne State University [*Michigan*]
WSU .... Weighted Student Unit
WSU .... Wichita State University [*Kansas*] (PDAA)
WSU .... Windmill Study Unit [*American Topical Association*] (EA)
WSU .... Women on Stamps Unit [*American Topical Association*] (EA)
WSU .... Work Station Utility
WSU .... Wright State University, Dayton, OH [*OCLC symbol*] (OCLC)
WSUA .... Miami, FL [*AM radio station call letters*]
WSUB .... Groton, CT [*AM radio station call letters*]
WSUC .... Cortland, NY [*FM radio station call letters*]
WSUE .... Sault Ste. Marie, MI [*FM radio station call letters*]
WSUF .... Noyack, NY [*FM radio station call letters*]
WSUH .... Oxford, MS [*AM radio station call letters*]
WSUI .... Iowa City, IA [*AM radio station call letters*]
WSUL .... Monticello, NY [*FM radio station call letters*]
WSUN .... St. Petersburg, FL [*AM radio station call letters*]
WSUOPR ..... Washington State University, Open Pool Reactor
WSUP .... Platteville, WI [*FM radio station call letters*]
WSUR .... Ponce, PR [*Television station call letters*]
WSUS .... Franklin, NJ [*FM radio station call letters*]
WSU-SDL .... Washington State University Shock Dynamics Laboratory [*Pullman*]
WSUW .... Whitewater, WI [*FM radio station call letters*]
WSUX .... Seaford, DE [*FM radio station call letters*]
WSUY .... Charleston, SC [*FM radio station call letters*]
WSV .... Wall Street Ventures [*Vancouver Stock Exchange symbol*]
WSV .... Water Solenoid Valve
WSV .... Water-Soluble Vitamin
WSV .... Wheelchair Sports Victoria [*Australia*]
WSV .... Wooly-Monkey Sarcoma Virus [*Medicine*] (PDAA)
WSVA .... Harrisonburg, VA [*AM radio station call letters*]
WSVA .... Wang Software Vendors' Association [*Defunct*] (EA)
WSVE .... Jacksonville, FL [*AM radio station call letters*]
WSVG .... Mount Jackson, VA [*AM radio station call letters*]
WSVH .... Savannah, GA [*FM radio station call letters*]
WSVI .... Christiansted, VI [*Television station call letters*]
WSVM .... Valdese, NC [*AM radio station call letters*]
WSVN .... Miami, FL [*Television station call letters*]
WSVO-FM .... Staunton, VA [*FM radio station call letters*] (RBYB)
WSVS .... Crewe, VA [*AM radio station call letters*]
WSVY .... Portsmouth, VA [*AM radio station call letters*]
WSVY .... Windsor, VA [*FM radio station call letters*]
WSW .... Southwest Wisconsin Library System, Fennimore, WI [*OCLC symbol*] (OCLC)
WSW .... Wall Street Week [*Television program*]
WSW .... West by South West [*Direction*] (EERA)
WSW .... Western Shelf Water [*Oceanography*]
WSW .... West-Southwest
WSW .... White Sidewall [*Tires*]
WSWA .... Weed Society of Australia (EERA)
WSWA .... Wine and Spirits Wholesalers of America (EA)
WSWB .... Scranton, PA [*Television station call letters*]
WSWI .... Evansville, IN [*AM radio station call letters*]
WSWL .... Pensacola, FL [*AM radio station call letters*]
WSWL .... Warheads and Special Weapons Laboratory (MCD)
WSWMA ...... Water and Sewage Works Manufacturers Association [*Later, WWEMA*] (EA)
WSWMA ...... Western States Weights and Measures Association
WSWN .... Belle Glade, FL [*AM radio station call letters*]
WSWO .... Wilmington, OH [*FM radio station call letters*]
WSWP .... Grandview, WV [*Television station call letters*]
WSWR .... Shelby, OH [*FM radio station call letters*]
WSWRN ...... West-Southwestern (FAAC)
WSWS .... Opelika, AL [*Television station call letters*]
WSWT .... Peoria, IL [*FM radio station call letters*]
WSWV .... Pennington Gap, VA [*AM radio station call letters*]
WSWV-FM ... Pennington Gap, VA [*FM radio station call letters*]
WSWZ .... Lancaster, OH [*FM radio station call letters*]
WSX .... Wessex Air Services Ltd. [*British ICAO designator*] (FAAC)
WSY .... Airlie Beach [*Australia Airport symbol*]
WSY .... MAM Aviation Ltd. [*British ICAO designator*] (FAAC)
WSY .... West Somerset Yeomanry [*British military*] (DMA)
WSYB .... Rutland, VT [*AM radio station call letters*]
WSYC .... Shippensburg, PA [*FM radio station call letters*]
WSYC .... West Somerset Yeomanry Cavalry [*British military*] (DMA)
WSYD .... Mount Airy, NC [*AM radio station call letters*]
WSYE .... Houston, MS [*FM radio station call letters*]
WSYL .... Sylvania, GA [*AM radio station call letters*]
WSYM .... Lansing, MI [*Television station call letters*]
WSYN .... Georgetown, SC [*FM radio station call letters*]
WSYP .... White Sulphur Springs & Yellowstone Park Railway Co. [*AAR code*]
WSYR .... Syracuse, NY [*AM radio station call letters*]
WSYT .... Syracuse, NY [*Television station call letters*]
WSYW .... Indianapolis, IN [*AM radio station call letters*]
WSYW-FM ... Danville, IN [*FM radio station call letters*]
WSYX .... Columbus, OH [*Television station call letters*]
WSYY .... Millinocket, ME [*AM radio station call letters*]
WSYY-FM ... Millinocket, ME [*FM radio station call letters*]
WSZ .... Westport [*New Zealand*] [*Airport symbol*] (OAG)
WSZ .... Wheat-Sheep Zone [*Agriculture*]
WSZ .... Wood Supply Zone (EERA)
WSZ .... Wrong Signature Zero [*Nuclear science*] (OA)
WT .... Nigeria Airways [*ICAO designator*] (AD)
WT .... Three-Conductor Cables [*JETDS nomenclature*] [*Military*] (CET)
WT .... WAAC Ltd. - Nigeria Airways [*Nigeria*] [*ICAO designator*] (ICDA)
WT .... Waist Tether [*NASA*] (KSC)
WT .... Wait Time [*Computer order entry*]
W/T .... Walkie-Talkie
WT .... Wall Thickness [*Nuclear energy*] (NRCH)
WT .... Warm Tone [*Photography*]
WT .... Warning Tag (AAG)
WT .... Warrant
WT .... Warrant Telegraphist [*British military*] (DMA)
W-T .... Warren-Teed [*Commercial firm*] (DAVI)
WT .... War Tax
WT .... Wartime
WT .... War Transport [*British military*] (DMA)
WT .... Washington Territory [*Prior to statehood*]
WT .... Washington Territory Reports [*1854-88*] [*A publication*] (DLA)
WT .... Wash Trough
WT .... Waste Tank
WT .... Watchdogs of the Treasury (EA)
WT .... Watchdog Timer (MCD)
WT .... Watch Time
WT .... Water Tank
WT .... Water Tanker [*British*]
WT .... Water Tender [*Navy*]
WT .... Water Thermometer
WT .... Watertight
WT .... Water-Tube Boiler [*Naval*]
WT .... Watt (IAA)
WT .... Waveguide Transmission
WT .... Wealth Tax (PDAA)
WT .... Weapons Technician [*Air Force*] (AFM)
WT .... Weapons Tight [*Weapons will engage only objects identified as hostile*]
WT .... Weapon Test
WT .... Weapon Training (MCD)
WT .... Weight (AAG)
wt .... Weight (IDOE)
wt .... Weight (ODBW)
WT .... Weldwood Transportation Ltd. [*AAR code*]
WT .... Wellhead Tax [*Oil industry*]
WT .... Whiffle Tree [*Structural test*] (AAG)
WT .... Whistletip [*Catheter*] [*Urology*] (DAVI)
WT .... White (DAVI)
WT .... White Pennant [*Navy British*]

WT Wild Track [*Cinematography*]
WT Wild Type [*of a species*] [*Genetics*]
WT William Tell Gunnery Mate
WT Will Talk [*Telecommunications*] (TEL)
WT Wilms' Tumor [*Oncology*]
WT Wind Tunnel
WT Winterization Test (AAG)
WT [*The*] Winter's Tale [*Shakespearean work*]
WT Wireless Telegraphy [*or Telephony*]
WT Wireless Transceiver (ACRL)
WT Wireless Transmitter
WT Wireless Truck [*British*]
WT Wire Ticket [*NASA*] (NASA)
WT Wire Transfer [*Banking*]
WT Withholding Tax [*IRS*]
WT Without
WT With Tape
WT With Title [*Bibliography*]
WT Witness Terms (NITA)
WT Wood Threshold (MSA)
WT Word Target [*Psychology*]
WT Word Terminal
WT Word Type
WT Workshop Trains [*British*]
W/T Work Track [*Cinematography*]
WT Work Type (NITA)
WT Worldteam (EA)
WT World Trade (IAA)
WT Write Through [*Computer science*] (PCM)
WT Written Testimony (BJA)
WT Wyoming Territory
WTA Tambohorano [*Madagascar*] [*Airport symbol*] (OAG)
WTA Washington Technological Association (MCD)
WTA Water Transport Association [*Defunct*] (EA)
WTA Western Timber Association (EA)
WTA Wholesale Traders' Association [*British*] (DBA)
WTA Willingness-to-Accept [*Market research*]
WTA Willingness to Avoid (EERA)
WTA Window Test Apparatus
WTA Wire Traceability and Accountability [*NASA*] (NASA)
WTA Wissenschaftlich-Technischer Arbeitskreis fuer Denkmalpflege und Bauwerksanierung [*International Association for the Protection of Monuments and Restoration of Buildings*] (EAIO)
WTA Women's Tennis Association [*Later, WITA*] (EA)
WTA Women's Tricycle Association [*British*] (BI)
WTA World Teleport Association [*New York, NY*] [*Telecommunications*] (TSSD)
WTA Wyoming Trucking Association, Casper WY [*STAC*]
WTAB Tabor City, NC [*AM radio station call letters*]
WTAC Flint, MI [*AM radio station call letters*]
WTAC Waste Isolation Pilot Plant Technical Assistance Contractor [*Department of Energy*] (GAAI)
WTAC Water Technology Advisory Committee [*Australia*]
WTAD Quincy, IL [*AM radio station call letters*]
WTAD Wepman Test of Auditory Discrimination [*Speech and language therapy*] (DAVI)
WTAE Pittsburgh, PA [*AM radio station call letters*]
WTAE-TV Pittsburgh, PA [*Television station call letters*]
WTAG Worcester, MA [*AM radio station call letters*]
WTAI Melbourne, FL [*AM radio station call letters*]
WTAJ Altoona, PA [*Television station call letters*]
WTAK Hartselle, AL [*FM radio station call letters*]
WTAL Tallahassee, FL [*AM radio station call letters*]
WTAM-AM Cleveland, OH [*AM radio station call letters*] (RBYB)
WTAN Clearwater, FL [*AM radio station call letters*]
WTAO Murphysboro, IL [*FM radio station call letters*]
WTAP Parkersburg, WV [*Television station call letters*]
WTAQ La Grange, IL [*AM radio station call letters*]
WTAR Norfolk, VA [*AM radio station call letters*]
WTAT Charleston, SC [*Television station call letters*]
WTAU-AM Zion, IL [*AM radio station call letters*] (RBYB)
WT Aux B Water-Tube Auxiliary Boiler (DS)
WTAW College Station, TX [*AM radio station call letters*]
WTAX Springfield, IL [*AM radio station call letters*]
W/TAX Withholding Tax [*IRS*] (AAG)
W/Tax Withholding Tax (DFIT)
WTAY Robinson, IL [*AM radio station call letters*]
WTAZ Morton, IL [*FM radio station call letters*]
WTB Wales Tourist Board (DCTA)
WTB War Transportation Board [*World War II*]
WTB Water-Tube Boiler [*Naval*]
WTB Welttierschutzbund [*Also known as WFPA, FMPA*] [*World Federation for the Protection of Animals*]
WTB Where's the Beef [*Slogan created by the Dancer Fitzgerald Sample advertising agency for Wendy's International, Inc.*]
WTB Wilderness Trail Bike
WTB Willamette Tariff Bureau Inc., Portland OR [*STAC*]
WTB Woerterbuch [*Dictionary*] [*German*] (ROG)
WTB Write Tape Binary [*Computer science*] (IAA)
WTBA Water-Tube Boilermakers Association [*British*] (BI)
WTB & TS Watch Tower Bible and Tract Society
WTBB Bonifay, FL [*FM radio station call letters*]
WTBD Work to Be Done (ADA)
WTBF Troy, AL [*AM radio station call letters*]
WTBG Brownsville, TN [*FM radio station call letters*]
WTBH Chiefland, FL [*FM radio station call letters*]
WTBI Greenville, SC [*FM radio station call letters*]
WTBI Pickens, SC [*AM radio station call letters*]
WTBJ Oxford, AL [*FM radio station call letters*]
WTBK Manchester, KY [*FM radio station call letters*]
WTBK Westerbeke Corp. [*Avon, MA*] [*NASDAQ symbol*] (NQ)
WTBM Mexico, ME [*FM radio station call letters*]
WTBO Cumberland, MD [*AM radio station call letters*]
WTBQ Warwick, NY [*AM radio station call letters*]
WTBR War Trade Board Rulings [*United States*] [*A publication*] (DLA)
WTBS Atlanta, GA [*Television station call letters*]
WTBS Water-Tube Boiler Survey (DS)
WTBT New Port Richey, FL [*FM radio station call letters*] (RBYB)
WTBU Indianapolis, IN [*Television station call letters*]
WTBX Hibbing, MN [*FM radio station call letters*]
WTBY Poughkeepsie, NY [*Television station call letters*]
WTBZ Grafton, WV [*AM radio station call letters*]
WTBZ-FM Grafton, WV [*FM radio station call letters*]
WTC New York [*New York*] Battery Park [*Airport symbol*] (OAG)
WTC War Transport Council [*Later, ITWC*] [*World War II*]
WTC Waste Water Technology Centre [*Canada*] (ECON)
WTC Water Thermal and Chemical Technology Center [*University of California*] [*Research center*] (RCD)
WTC Waterton [*Colorado*] [*Seismograph station code, US Geological Survey Closed*] (SEIS)
WTC Well-Tempered Clavier [*Compositions of J. S. Bach*]
WTC Western Telecommunications Consulting Co. [*Los Angeles, CA*] [*Telecommunications*] (TSSD)
WTC Whole Tree Chips (PDAA)
WTC Wind Temperature Correction
WTC Wire Test Chamber
WTC Women's Talent Corps [*Later, CHS*] (EA)
WTC Women's Theater Council
WTC Woodford Flight Test Center [*British ICAO designator*] (FAAC)
WTC Workload Transaction Code [*Navy*] (NG)
WTC World Trade Center [*New York City*]
WTC World Trade Center of New Orleans [*New Orleans, LA*] (EA)
WTCA Plymouth, IN [*AM radio station call letters*]
WTCA Water Terminal Clearance Authority [*Army*] (AABC)
WTCA Welsh Terrier Club of America (EA)
WTCA Whole-Time Consultants' Association [*British*] (BI)
WTCA Wood Truss Council of America (EA)
WTCA World Tasar Class Association (EAIO)
WTCA World Trade Center Arhus [*Denmark*] (EAIO)
WTCA World Trade Centers Association (EA)
WTCAJ World Trade Center of Abidjan [*Ivory Coast*] (EAIO)
WTCARES Welsh Terrier Club of America Rescue Service (EA)
WTCB Orangeburg, SC [*FM radio station call letters*]
WTCB Water Tender Construction Battalion [*Navy*]
WTCC Springfield, MA [*FM radio station call letters*]
WTCC Water Turbine Closed Coupled (MSA)
WTCC Wet Tropics Consultative Committee (EERA)
WTCCC Wet Tropics Community Consultative Committee [*Australia*]
WTCCQ World Trade Center Club Chongqing [*China*] (EAIO)
WTCCY World Trade Centre - Cyprus (EAIO)
WTCE Fort Pierce, FL [*Television station call letters*]
WTCF Carrollton, MI [*FM radio station call letters*]
WTCGV World Trade Center Geneva [*Switzerland*] (EAIO)
WTCH Shawano, WI [*AM radio station call letters*]
WTCI Chattanooga, TN [*Television station call letters*]
WTCI Western Telecommunications, Inc. [*Englewood, CO*] [*Telecommunications*]
WTCIB Women's Travelers Center and Information Bank [*Later, WIB*] (EA)
WTCIS World Trade Center Istanbul [*Turkey*] (EAIO)
WTCJ Tell City, IN [*AM radio station call letters*]
WTCK World Trade Center Korea
WTCK-AM Greensboro, NC [*AM radio station call letters*] (RBYB)
WTCL Chattahoochee, FL [*AM radio station call letters*]
WTCM Traverse City, MI [*AM radio station call letters*]
WTCM Weld Timer Control Module
WTCM-FM Traverse City, MI [*FM radio station call letters*]
WTCMM World Trade Center Metro Manila [*Philippines*] (EAIO)
WTCN World Trade Center of Nigeria (EAIO)
WTCNJ World Trade Centre Nanjing [*China*] (EAIO)
WTCO Campbellsville, KY [*AM radio station call letters*]
WTCO Western Transportation Co. [*AAR code*]
WTCO World Trade Center Oslo [*Norway*] (EAIO)
WTCQ Vidalia, GA [*FM radio station call letters*]
WTCR Huntington, WV [*FM radio station call letters*]
WTCR Kenova, WV [*AM radio station call letters*]
WTCS Fairmont, WV [*AM radio station call letters*]
WTCS Windshield Temperature Control Systems
WTCSS West Coast Off-Shore Tactical Control Surveillance System [*Navy*] (DNAB)
WTCT Marion, IL [*Television station call letters*]
WTCV Weapon and Tracked Combat Vehicle (MCD)
WTCW Whitesburg, KY [*AM radio station call letters*]
WTCX Ripon, WI [*FM radio station call letters*]
WTCY Harrisburg, PA [*AM radio station call letters*]
WTD War Trade Department [*British World War II*]
WTD Watertight Door
WTD Water Turbine Direct (MSA)
WTD Weapons Training Detachment [*Military*]
WTD Weekly Total-to-Date
WTD Weighted Total Demerits [*Lubricating oil test*]

WTD............ West End [*Grand Bahama Island, Bahamas*] [*Airport symbol*] (AD)
WTD............ Whitland [*British depot code*]
WTD............ Wind Tunnel Data
WTD............ World Trade Directory [*Department of Commerce*] [*A publication*]
WTD............ Write Tape Decimal (IAA)
WTD............ WTD Industries, Inc. [*Associated Press*] (SAG)
wtdb............ Water-Tube Domestic Boiler (DS)
WTDF........... Wireless Telegraph Direction Finder (IAA)
WTDI........... WTD Industries [*NASDAQ symbol*] (TTSB)
WTDI........... WTD Industries, Inc. [*Portland, OR*] [*NASDAQ symbol*] (NQ)
WTDK........... Federalsburg, MD [*FM radio station call letters*] (RBYB)
WTDR........... Statesville, NC [*FM radio station call letters*]
WTDR........... Wireless Telegraphy Direction (IAA)
WTDR........... World Trade Directory Reports [*A publication Department of Commerce*]
WTDR........... World Traders Data Report (AAGC)
WTDY........... Madison, WI [*AM radio station call letters*]
WTE............ International Symposium on Wave and Tidal Energy (PDAA)
WTE............ Waste-to-Energy [*Resource recycling*]
WTE............ Wattle Tannin Equivalent [*Chemistry*]
WTE............ Westate Resources, Inc. [*Vancouver Stock Exchange symbol*]
WTE............ World Tapes for Education [*Defunct*]
WTE............ Worse than Expected [*Politics*]
WTE............ Wotje [*Marshall Islands*] [*Airport symbol*] (OAG)
W Teach...... Western Teacher [*A publication*]
WTEB........... New Bern, NC [*FM radio station call letters*]
WTEC........... Warrantech Corp. [*New York, NY NASDAQ symbol*] (NQ)
WTEK........... Waste Technology [*NASDAQ symbol*] (TTSB)
WTEK........... Waste Technology Corp. [*New York, NY NASDAQ symbol*] (NQ)
WTEL........... Philadelphia, PA [*AM radio station call letters*]
W Tel........... Warrant Telegraphist [*British military*]
WTEM........... Bethesda, MD [*AM radio station call letters*]
WTEN........... Albany, NY [*Television station call letters*]
W Ten........... Wright's Introduction to the Law of Tenures [*A publication*] (DLA)
W TER.......... Washington Territory
WTES........... West Tennessee Experiment Station [*University of Tennessee at Knoxville*] [*Research center*] (RCD)
WTEV-TV..... Jacksonville, FL [*TV station call letters*] (RBYB)
WTF............ Waste Treatment Facility [*Nuclear energy*] (IEEE)
WTF............ Waste Water Treatment Facility [*Nuclear energy*] (NRCH)
WTF............ Western Task Force [*Navy*]
WTF............ When Technology Fails [*A publication*]
WTF............ Will to Fire
WTF............ Wisconsin Test Facility [*Navy*]
WTF............ World Taekwondo Federation [*Seoul, Republic of Korea*] (EAIO)
WTF............ World Timecapsule Fund (EA)
WTFAA......... Washington Task Force on African Affairs [*Defunct*] (EA)
WTFDA......... Worldwide Television-FM DX Association (EA)
Wtff............ Waterford [*Glassware*] (BARN)
WTFM........... Kingsport, TN [*FM radio station call letters*]
WTFPA......... Wolf Trap Foundation for the Performing Arts (EA)
WTFU........... Women Teachers' Franchise Union (AIE)
WTFX........... Louisville, KY [*FM radio station call letters*]
WTG............ Waiting (MSA)
WTG............ Weighting (MSA)
WTG............ Williams Telecommunications Group [*Telecommunications service*] (TSSD)
WTG............ Wind Tape Generation
WTG............ Wind Turbine Generator
WTG............ Worker Trait Group
WTGA........... Thomaston, GA [*AM radio station call letters*]
WTGA-FM..... Thomaston, GA [*FM radio station call letters*]
WTGC........... Lewisburg, PA [*AM radio station call letters*]
WTGE........... Baton Rouge, LA [*FM radio station call letters*]
WTGF........... Milton, FL [*FM radio station call letters*]
WTGH........... Cayce, SC [*AM radio station call letters*]
WTGI........... Wilmington, DE [*Television station call letters*]
WTGL........... Cocoa, FL [*Television station call letters*]
WTGM........... Salisbury, MD [*AM radio station call letters*]
WTGN........... Lima, OH [*FM radio station call letters*]
WTGP........... Greenville, PA [*FM radio station call letters*]
Wtg P........... Writing Parchment (DGA)
WTGR........... Union City, OH [*FM radio station call letters*]
WTGS........... Hardeeville, SC [*Television station call letters*]
WTGV........... Sandusky, MI [*FM radio station call letters*]
WTGY........... Charleston, MS [*FM radio station call letters*]
WTGZ-FM..... Tuskegee, AL [*FM radio station call letters*] (RBYB)
WTH............ What the Heck [*Computer hacker terminology*] [*Bowdlerized version*] (NHD)
WTH............ Width (WGA)
WTHA-FM..... Boswell, GA [*FM radio station call letters*] (RBYB)
WTHB........... Augusta, GA [*AM radio station call letters*]
WTHC........... Seelyville, IN [*FM radio station call letters*]
WTHD........... Lagrange, IN [*FM radio station call letters*]
WTHE........... Mineola, NY [*AM radio station call letters*]
WTHE........... Workshop Test and Handling Equipment [*Military*] (CAAL)
WthfdEnt....... Weatherford Enterra [*Associated Press*] (SAG)
WTHG........... Worthington Indus [*NASDAQ symbol*] (TTSB)
WTHG........... Worthington Industries, Inc. [*NASDAQ symbol*] (NQ)
WTHI........... Terre Haute, IN [*AM radio station call letters*]
WTHI-FM..... Terre Haute, IN [*FM radio station call letters*]
WTHI-TV...... Terre Haute, IN [*Television station call letters*]
WTHK........... Hudson, NY [*FM radio station call letters*] (RBYB)
WTHL........... Somerset, KY [*FM radio station call letters*]
WTHM-FM.... Glen Arbor, MI [*FM radio station call letters*] (RBYB)
WTHN-FM.... Ellenville, NY [*FM radio station call letters*] (RBYB)
WTHO........... Thomson, GA [*FM radio station call letters*]
WTHPRF...... Weatherproof (MSA)
WTHQ........... Shelbyville, KY [*FM radio station call letters*]
WTHR........... Indianapolis, IN [*Television station call letters*]
WTHR........... Weather
WTHS........... Holland, MI [*FM radio station call letters*]
WTHT........... Lewiston, ME [*FM radio station call letters*]
WTHU........... Thurmont, MD [*AM radio station call letters*]
WTHV........... Hahira, GA [*AM radio station call letters*] (RBYB)
WTI............ Weapons Training Instruction (MCD)
WTI............ Western Telematic, Inc.
WTI............ West Texas Intermediate [*Crude oil*] (ECON)
WTI............ Wheelabrator Tech [*NYSE symbol*] (TTSB)
WTI............ Wheelabrator Technology [*NYSE symbol*] (SAG)
WTI............ Work Training in Industry
WTI............ World Trade Institute
WTI............ World Translations Index [*International Translations Centre*] [*Information service or system*]
WTIA........... Welding Technology Institute of Australia
WTIC........... Hartford, CT [*AM radio station call letters*]
WTIC........... World Trade Information Center (NITA)
WTICB......... Worldwide Travel Information Contact Book [*A publication*]
WTIC-FM..... Hartford, CT [*FM radio station call letters*]
WTIC-TV...... Hartford, CT [*Television station call letters*]
WTID........... Reform, AL [*FM radio station call letters*]
WTID........... World Travel Information Directory [*A publication*]
WTIE........... Wastewater Treatment Information Exchange [*National Small Flows Clearinghouse*]
WTIF........... Omega, GA [*FM radio station call letters*]
WTIF........... Tifton, GA [*AM radio station call letters*]
WTIG........... Massillon, OH [*AM radio station call letters*]
WTIK........... Durham, NC [*AM radio station call letters*]
WTIL........... Mayaguez, PR [*AM radio station call letters*]
WTIM........... Taylorville, IL [*AM radio station call letters*]
WTIN........... Ponce, PR [*Television station call letters*]
WTIQ........... Manistique, MI [*AM radio station call letters*]
WTIS........... Tampa, FL [*AM radio station call letters*]
WTIU........... Bloomington, IN [*Television station call letters*]
WTIV........... Titusville, PA [*AM radio station call letters*]
WTIX........... New Orleans, LA [*AM radio station call letters*]
WTIX-FM..... Galliano, LA [*FM radio station call letters*] (RBYB)
WTJ............ Wedge Type Jack
WTJ............ Wrin, T. J., San Francisco CA [*STAC*]
WTJA........... Jamestown, NY [*Television station call letters*]
WTJB........... Columbus, GA [*FM radio station call letters*]
WTJC........... Springfield, OH [*Television station call letters*]
WTJH........... East Point, GA [*AM radio station call letters*]
WTJP........... Gadsden, AL [*Television station call letters*]
WTJR........... Quincy, IL [*Television station call letters*]
WTJS........... Jackson, TN [*AM radio station call letters*]
WTJT........... Baker, FL [*FM radio station call letters*]
WTJU........... Charlottesville, VA [*FM radio station call letters*]
WTJX........... Charlotte Amalie, VI [*Television station call letters*]
WTJY........... Johnstown, OH [*FM radio station call letters*] (RBYB)
WTJZ........... Newport News, VA [*AM radio station call letters*]
WTK............ Noatak [*Alaska*] [*Airport symbol*] (OAG)
WTK............ Noatak, AK [*Location identifier FAA*] (FAAL)
WTKA........... Ann Arbor, MI [*AM radio station call letters*]
WTKB........... Huntingdon, TN [*FM radio station call letters*]
WTKC........... Kankakee, IL [*FM radio station call letters*]
WTKF........... Atlantic, NC [*FM radio station call letters*]
WTKI........... Huntsville, AL [*AM radio station call letters*]
WTKL........... New Orleans, LA [*FM radio station call letters*]
WTKM........... Hartford, WI [*AM radio station call letters*]
WTKM-FM.... Hartford, WI [*FM radio station call letters*]
WTKN........... Daleville, AL [*AM radio station call letters*]
WTKO........... Ithaca, NY [*AM radio station call letters*]
WTKR........... Norfolk, VA [*Television station call letters*]
WTKS........... Cocoa Beach, FL [*FM radio station call letters*]
WTKT........... Georgetown, KY [*FM radio station call letters*]
WTKU-FM.... Ocean City, NJ [*FM radio station call letters*] (RBYB)
WTKV-FM.... Oswego, NY [*FM radio station call letters*] (RBYB)
WTKW........... Bridgeport, NY [*FM radio station call letters*]
WTKX-FM.... Pensacola, FL [*FM radio station call letters*]
WTKY........... Tompkinsville, KY [*AM radio station call letters*]
WTKY-FM.... Tompkinsville, KY [*FM radio station call letters*]
WTKZ........... Allentown, PA [*AM radio station call letters*]
WTL............ Tuntatuliak [*Alaska*] [*Airport symbol*] (OAG)
WTL............ Western Canadian Land [*Vancouver Stock Exchange symbol*]
WTL............ Western Trunk Line Committee, Chicago IL [*STAC*]
WTL............ Wilms' Tumor Locus [*Genetics*] [*Oncology*]
WTL............ Wyle Test Laboratories
WTLA........... North Syracuse, NY [*AM radio station call letters*] (RBYB)
WTLB........... Utica, NY [*AM radio station call letters*]
WTLC........... Indianapolis, IN [*AM radio station call letters*]
WTLC........... Western Trunk Line Committee
WTLC-FM..... Indianapolis, IN [*FM radio station call letters*]
WTLG........... Starke, FL [*FM radio station call letters*]
WTLH........... Bainbridge, GA [*Television station call letters*]
WTLJ........... Muskegon, MI [*Television station call letters*]
WTLK........... Taylorsville, NC [*AM radio station call letters*]
WTLK........... Worldtalk Communication Corp. [*NASDAQ symbol*] (SAG)
WTLK........... Worldtalk Communications [*NASDAQ symbol*] (TTSB)
WTLK-FM..... Ponte Vedra Beach, FL [*FM radio station call letters*] (RBYB)

WTLK-TV ..... Rome, GA [*Television station call letters*]
WTLM-AM ... Pepperell, AL [*AM radio station call letters*] (RBYB)
WTLN .... Apopka, FL [*AM radio station call letters*]
WTLN-FM .... Apopka, FL [*FM radio station call letters*]
WTLO .... Somerset, KY [*AM radio station call letters*]
WTLQ-AM .... Pine Island Center, FL [*AM radio station call letters*] (RBYB)
WTLR .... State College, PA [*FM radio station call letters*]
WTLS .... Tallassee, AL [*AM radio station call letters*]
WTLS .... West Texas Library System [*Library network*]
WTLV .... Jacksonville, FL [*Television station call letters*]
WTLW .... Lima, OH [*Television station call letters*]
WTLZ .... Saginaw, MI [*FM radio station call letters*]
WTM .... Waitemata Aero Club, Inc. [*New Zealand*] [*ICAO designator*] (FAAC)
WTM .... Wind Tunnel Memorandum
WTM .... Wind Tunnel Model
WTM .... World Travel Market [*Trade show*] [*British*] (ITD)
WTMA .... Charleston, SC [*AM radio station call letters*]
WTMA .... Wood Tank Manufacturers Association (EA)
WTMA .... Wool Textile Manufacturers of Australia
WTMB .... Tomah, WI [*AM radio station call letters*]
WTMC .... Ocala, FL [*AM radio station call letters*]
WTMC .... Wet Tropics Ministerial Council [*Australia*]
WTMD .... Towson, MD [*FM radio station call letters*]
WTME .... Lewiston ME [*AM radio station call letters*]
WTMGE .... Wireless Telegraphy Message (IAA)
WTMH .... Watertight Manhole (WDAA)
WTMI .... Miami, FL [*FM radio station call letters*]
WTMJ .... Milwaukee, WI [*AM radio station call letters*]
WTMJ-TV ..... Milwaukee, WI [*Television station call letters*]
WTMM .... Richmond, VA [*AM radio station call letters*]
WTMN .... Portsmouth, NH [*AM radio station call letters*] (RBYB)
WTMP .... Temple Terrace, FL [*AM radio station call letters*]
WTMQ .... Columbus, GA [*AM radio station call letters*]
WTMR .... Camden, NJ [*AM radio station call letters*]
WTMS .... World Trade in Minerals Data Base System [*Computer science*]
WTMT .... Louisville, KY [*AM radio station call letters*]
WTMU .... Wildlife Trade Monitoring Unit (GNE)
WTMV .... Lakeland, FL [*Television station call letters*]
WTMW .... Arlington, VA [*Television station call letters*]
WTMX .... Skokie, IL [*FM radio station call letters*]
WTMX .... Wang Telephone Message Exchange [*Wang Laboratories, Inc.*] [*Telecommunications service*] (TSSD)
WTMY .... Sarasota, FL [*AM radio station call letters*]
WTMZ .... Dorchester Terrace-Brentwood, SC [*AM radio station call letters*]
WTN .... Warton BAE [*British ICAO designator*] (FAAC)
WTN .... Western Technical Net [*Air Force*]
WTN .... Wind Tunnel Note
WTN .... Witness
WTN .... Worldwide Television News Corp. (WDMC)
WTNA .... Wildfowl Trust of North America (GNE)
WtnBank ...... Western Bank [*Associated Press*] (SAG)
WTNC .... Thomasville, NC [*AM radio station call letters*]
WTND .... Grifton, NC [*FM radio station call letters*]
WTNE .... Trenton, TN [*AM radio station call letters*]
WTNH .... New Haven, CT [*Television station call letters*]
WTNI .... Hartsville, SC [*AM radio station call letters*]
WTNJ .... Mount Hope, WV [*FM radio station call letters*]
WTNL .... Reidsville, GA [*AM radio station call letters*]
WTNN .... Farragut, TN [*AM radio station call letters*]
WTNP .... Works Technical New Policy (EERA)
WTNR .... Waynesboro, TN [*AM radio station call letters*]
WtnRsC .... Western Resources Capital I [*Associated Press*] (SAG)
WTNS .... Coshocton, OH [*AM radio station call letters*]
WTNS .... Witness
WTNS-FM .... Coshocton, OH [*FM radio station call letters*]
WTNSTH .... Witnesseth [*Legal*] [*British*] (ROG)
WTNT .... Tallahassee, FL [*FM radio station call letters*]
WTNV .... Jackson, TN [*FM radio station call letters*]
WTNW .... Tuscaloosa, AL [*AM radio station call letters*]
WTNY .... Watertown, NY [*AM radio station call letters*]
WTNY .... Whitney Holding [*NASDAQ symbol*] (TTSB)
WTNY .... Whitney Holding Corp. [*NASDAQ symbol*] (SAG)
WTNY-FM .... Watertown, NY [*FM radio station call letters*]
WTNZ .... Knoxville, TN [*Television station call letters*]
WTO .... Warsaw Treaty Organization
WTO .... Westam Oil Ltd. [*Vancouver Stock Exchange symbol*]
WTO .... WESTPAC [*Western Pacific*] Transportation Office (CINC)
WTO .... Wireless Telegraphy Officer [*British military*] (DMA)
WTO .... Worked Three Oceans [*Amateur radio*] (IAA)
WTO .... World Tourism Organization [*Madrid, Spain*]
WTO .... World Trade Organisation (EERA)
WTO .... World Trade Organization [*Trade and tariff regulation*] (ECON)
WTO .... Wotho [*Marshall Islands*] [*Airport symbol*] (OAG)
WTO .... Write-to-Operator [*Computer science*] (IBMDP)
WTOB .... Winston-Salem, NC [*AM radio station call letters*]
WTOC .... Savannah, GA [*Television station call letters*]
WTOD .... Toledo, OH [*AM radio station call letters*]
WTOE .... Spruce Pine, NC [*AM radio station call letters*]
WTOEW .... Welcome to Our Elvis World (EA)
WTOF .... Canton, OH [*FM radio station call letters*]
WTOG .... St. Petersburg, FL [*Television station call letters*]
WTOH .... Mobile, AL [*FM radio station call letters*]
WTOH .... Western Ohio Railroad Co. [*AAR code*]
WTOJ .... Carthage, NY [*FM radio station call letters*]
WTOK .... Meridian, MS [*Television station call letters*]
WTOL .... Toledo, OH [*Television station call letters*]
WTOM .... Cheboygan, MI [*Television station call letters*]
WTON .... Staunton, VA [*AM radio station call letters*]
WTON-FM .... Staunton, VA [*FM radio station call letters*]
WTOP .... Washington, DC [*AM radio station call letters*]
WTOR .... Write-to-Operator with Reply [*Computer science*] (IBMDP)
WTOR-AM .... Youngstown, NY [*AM radio station call letters*] (RBYB)
WTOS .... Skowhegan, ME [*FM radio station call letters*]
WTOS .... Western Test Range Office of Safety [*Air Force*] (MCD)
WTOT .... Marianna, FL [*AM radio station call letters*]
WTOU .... Akron, OH [*AM radio station call letters*]
WTOV .... Steubenville, OH [*Television station call letters*]
WToVA .... United States Veterans Administration Hospital, Tomah, WI [*Library symbol Library of Congress*] (LCLS)
WTOW .... Washington, NC [*AM radio station call letters*]
WTOX .... Lincoln, ME [*AM radio station call letters*]
WTOY .... Salem, VA [*AM radio station call letters*]
WTP .... Warrant to Pollute
WTP .... Waste Water Treatment Plant [*Also, WWTP*]
WTP .... Water Treatment Plant [*Nuclear energy*] (NRCH)
WTP .... Weapons Testing Program (AAG)
WTP .... Wiggins Teape Paper [*Commercial firm British*]
WTP .... Willingness-to-Pay [*Market research*]
WTP .... Woitape [*Papua New Guinea*] [*Airport symbol*] (OAG)
WTP .... World Tape Pals (EA)
WTPA .... Mechanicsburg, PA [*FM radio station call letters*]
WTPA .... Wheelchair Tennis Players Association (EA)
WTPBC .... Wool Textiles Production Board of Control [*World War I*] [*British*]
WTPC .... Elsah, IL [*FM radio station call letters*]
WTPFT .... Weight per Foot (IAA)
WTPI .... Indianapolis, IN [*FM radio station call letters*]
WTPM .... Aguadilla, PR [*FM radio station call letters*]
WTPR .... Paris, TN [*AM radio station call letters*]
WTPR-FM .... McKinnon, TN [*FM radio station call letters*] (RBYB)
WTPS .... Quincy, FL [*FM radio station call letters*] (RBYB)
WTPS .... Water, Toxics, and Pesticides Staff [*Environmental Protection Agency*] (GFGA)
WTPX-FM .... Jupiter, FL [*FM radio station call letters*] (RBYB)
WTQR .... Winston-Salem, NC [*FM radio station call letters*]
WTQX .... Selma, AL [*AM radio station call letters*]
WTR .... Aquarion Co. [*NYSE symbol*] (SPSG)
WTR .... Waiter
WTR .... Warstar Resources, Inc. [*Vancouver Stock Exchange symbol*]
WTR .... War Tax Resistance [*An association Defunct*] (EA)
WTR .... Water
wtr .... Water (VRA)
WTR .... Water
WTR .... Waterford and Tranmore Railway [*British*] (ROG)
WTR .... Waters Associates, Milford, MA [*OCLC symbol*] (OCLC)
WTR .... Water Turnover Rate [*Physiology*]
WTR .... Waterville [*Colby College*] [*Maine*] [*Seismograph station code, US Geological Survey*] (SEIS)
WTR .... Weekly Transcript Reports [*New York*] [*A publication*] (DLA)
WTR .... Well to Right [*Aviation*] (FAAC)
WTR .... Western Test Range [*Formerly, Pacific Missile Range*] [*Air Force*]
WTR .... Westinghouse Test Reactor
WTR .... Winter
WTR .... Work Transfer Record (KSC)
WTR .... Work Transfer Request
WTR .... Wrightsville & Tennille R. R. [*AAR code*]
WTR .... Writer
WTRA .... Mayaguez, PR [*Television station call letters*]
WTRB .... Ripley, TN [*AM radio station call letters*]
WTRB-FM .... Ripley, TN [*FM radio station call letters*]
WTRC .... Elkhart, IN [*AM radio station call letters*]
WTRC .... Natchez, MS [*FM radio station call letters*]
WTRC .... Weapon Test Reports Committee [*AEC-DoD*]
WTRC .... Women's Training and Resources Corp.
WTRE .... Greensburg, IN [*AM radio station call letters*]
WTRF .... Wheeling, WV [*Television station call letters*]
WTRG .... Rocky Mount, NC [*FM radio station call letters*]
WTRG .... World Trade Resources Guide [*A publication*]
WTRI .... Brunswick, MD [*AM radio station call letters*]
WTRI-FM .... Mount Carmel, IL [*FM radio station call letters*] (RBYB)
WTRJ .... Troy, OH [*FM radio station call letters*]
WTRK .... Bay City, MI [*FM radio station call letters*]
WTRM .... Western Test Range Manual [*Air Force*] (MCD)
WTRM .... Winchester, VA [*FM radio station call letters*]
WTRN .... Tyrone, PA [*AM radio station call letters*]
WTRO .... Dyersburg, TN [*AM radio station call letters*]
WTRP .... La Grange, GA [*AM radio station call letters*]
WTRPP .... Water Pump Propeller [*on a ship*] (DS)
WTRPRF .... Waterproof (MSA)
WTRPRFG .... Waterproofing
WTRR .... Sanford, FL [*AM radio station call letters*]
WTRS .... Dunellon, FL [*FM radio station call letters*]
WTRS .... Waters Instruments [*NASDAQ symbol*] (TTSB)
WTRS .... Waters Instruments, Inc. [*NASDAQ symbol*] (NQ)
WTRSYS .... Water System (MCD)
WTRTT .... Watertight (MSA)
WTRV-FM .... LaCrosse, WI [*FM radio station call letters*] (RBYB)
WTRW .... Two Rivers, WI [*AM radio station call letters*]
WTRX .... Flint, MI [*AM radio station call letters*]
WTRY .... Troy, NY [*AM radio station call letters*]
WTRZ .... McMinnville, TN [*FM radio station call letters*]

WTRZ Winterize (AAG)
WTRZN Winterization (AAG)
WTS Tsiroanomandidy [*Madagascar*] [*Airport symbol*] (OAG)
WTS War Training Service [*of the Civil Aeronautics Administration*] [*Formerly Civilian Pilot Training*] [*World War II*]
WTS Watermen's Trade Society [*A union*] [*British*]
WTS Watts Industries [*NYSE symbol*] (SAG)
WTS Watts Industries'A' [*NYSE symbol*] (TTSB)
WTS Weapons Training Site [*Military*]
WTS Western Tariff Service Inc., Oakland CA [*STAC*]
WTS Westminister Theological Seminary, Philadelphia, PA [*OCLC symbol*] (OCLC)
WTS Whale Tumor Story [*Urban folklore term coined by Rodney Dale*]
WTS Windows-Based Terminal Server [*Microsoft Corp.*]
WTS Wind Tunnel Study
WTS Wing Tank Structure
WTS Winterswijk [*Netherlands*] [*Seismograph station code, US Geological Survey*] (SEIS)
WTS Wireless Telegraphy Station [*Telecommunications*] (IAA)
WTS Women's Transportation Seminar [*Later, WTSN*] (EA)
WTS Women's Transport Service [*British*]
WTS Word Terminal Synchronous
WT's Working Tools [*Freemasonry*]
WTS World Terminal Synchronous (IAA)
WTSA Brattleboro, VT [*AM radio station call letters*]
WTSA Wood Turners and Shapers Association [*Later, WPMA*] (EA)
WTSAC Wet Tropics Scientific Advisory Committee [*Australia*]
WTSA-FM Brattleboro, VT [*FM radio station call letters*]
WTSAP Wet Tropics Structural Adjustment Package (EERA)
WTSB Lumberton, NC [*AM radio station call letters*]
WTSB Wood Turners Service Bureau [*Later, WPMA*]
WTSC Potsdam, NY [*FM radio station call letters*]
WTSC West TeleServices Corp. [*NASDAQ symbol*] (SAG)
WTSC West Texas State College [*Later, WTSU*]
WTSC Wet Tantalum Slug Capacitor (NASA)
WTSDET Wing Transportation Squadron Detachment [*Navy*] (DNAB)
WTSF Ashland, KY [*Television station call letters*]
WTSFLW Women's Trade Society of Fancy Leather Workers [*A union*] [*British*]
WTSG-FM Carlinville, IL [*FM radio station call letters*] (RBYB)
WTSH Rockmart, GA [*FM radio station call letters*]
WTSH Rome, GA [*AM radio station call letters*]
WTSHRD Water and Toxic Substances Health Research Division [*Environmental Protection Agency*] (GFGA)
WTSJ Cincinnati, OH [*AM radio station call letters*]
WTSK Tuscaloosa, AL [*AM radio station call letters*]
WTSL Hanover, NH [*AM radio station call letters*]
WTSL Wet Seal, Inc. [*NASDAQ symbol*] (SAG)
WTSLA Wet Seal Cl'A' [*NASDAQ symbol*] (TTSB)
WTSM Western Transmedia [*NASDAQ symbol*] (TTSB)
WTSM Western Transmedia, Inc. [*NASDAQ symbol*] (SAG)
WTSMW Western Transmedia Wrrt [*NASDAQ symbol*] (TTSB)
WTSN Dover, NH [*AM radio station call letters*]
WTSN Women's Transportation Seminar-National (EA)
WTSNG Witnessing [*Legal*] [*British*] (ROG)
WTSO Madison, WI [*AM radio station call letters*]
WTSP St. Petersburg, FL [*Television station call letters*]
WTSPT Waterspout
WTSR Trenton, NJ [*FM radio station call letters*]
WTSS Scranton, PA [*AM radio station call letters*] (RBYB)
WTSU Troy, AL [*FM radio station call letters*]
WTSU West Texas State University [*Formerly, WTSC*]
WTSV Claremont, NH [*AM radio station call letters*]
WTSX Port Jervis, NY [*FM radio station call letters*]
WTT Warfare [*Commanders*] Team Training (DOMA)
WTT Weapon Tactics Trainer (MCD)
WTT Western Tank Truck Carriers' Conference Inc., Denver CO [*STAC*]
WTT Westmount Resources Ltd. [*Toronto Stock Exchange symbol*]
WTT Wind Tunnel Test
WTT Wireless Telecom [*AMEX symbol*] (TTSB)
WTT Wireless Telecom Group [*Formerly, Noise Com, Inc.*] [*AMEX symbol*] (SAG)
WTT Working Timetable (DCTA)
WTT World Team Tennis [*League*]
WTTA St. Petersburg, FL [*Television station call letters*]
WTTA Wholesale Tobacco Trade Association of Great Britain and Northern Ireland (BI)
WTTB Vero Beach, FL [*AM radio station call letters*]
WTTC Towanda, PA [*AM radio station call letters*]
WTTC Western Technical Training Command [*AAFWTTC*]
WTTC-FM Towanda, PA [*FM radio station call letters*]
WTTE Columbus, OH [*Television station call letters*]
WTTELE World Trade Telegraph (IAA)
WTTF Tiffin, OH [*AM radio station call letters*]
WTTF-FM Tiffin, OH [*FM radio station call letters*]
WTTG Washington, DC [*Television station call letters*]
WTTH Margate City, NJ [*FM radio station call letters*]
WTTI Dalton, GA [*AM radio station call letters*]
WTTK Kokomo, IN [*Television station call letters*]
WTTL Madisonville, KY [*AM radio station call letters*]
WTTM Trenton, NJ [*AM radio station call letters*]
WTTN Watertown, WI [*AM radio station call letters*]
WTTO Birmingham, AL [*Television station call letters*]
WTTR Westminster, MD [*AM radio station call letters*]
WTTS Bloomington, IN [*FM radio station call letters*]
WTTS Weak-Lined T Tauri Stars [*Astronomy*]
WTTT Amherst, MA [*AM radio station call letters*]
WTTU Cookeville, TN [*FM radio station call letters*]
WTTV Bloomington, IN [*Television station call letters*]
WTTW Chicago, IL [*Letters stand for "Windows to the World"*] [*Television station call letters*]
WTTX-FM Appomattox, VA [*FM radio station call letters*]
WTU Washington University, St. Louis, MO [*OCLC symbol*] (OCLC)
WTU Weekly TIF [*Taxpayer Information File*] Update [*IRS*]
WTU Whitetails Unlimited (EA)
WTU Williams Coal Seam Gas Realty [*NYSE symbol*] (SPSG)
WTU Williams Coal Seam Gas Rlty [*NYSE symbol*] (TTSB)
WTUA St. Stephen, SC [*FM radio station call letters*]
WTUC Tuckerton, NJ [*FM radio station call letters*]
WTUE Dayton, OH [*FM radio station call letters*]
WTUF Boston, GA [*FM radio station call letters*]
WTUG Tuscaloosa, AL [*FM radio station call letters*]
WTUK Harlan, KY [*FM radio station call letters*]
WTUL New Orleans, LA [*FM radio station call letters*]
WTUP Tupelo, MS [*AM radio station call letters*]
WTUR Upland, IN [*FM radio station call letters*] (RBYB)
WTURB Water Turbine (MSA)
WTURN White Turnout [*Political science*]
WTUS Mannington, WV [*FM radio station call letters*]
WTUX Meridian, MS [*FM radio station call letters*]
WTUZ Uhrichsville, OH [*FM radio station call letters*]
WTV Fowler [*Rick*] [*ICAO designator*] (FAAC)
WTV Water Tank Vessel [*Navy*]
WTV Wound Tumor Virus [*Plant pathology*]
WTVA Tupelo, MS [*Television station call letters*]
WTVA Wider Television Access [*British*]
WTVB Coldwater, MI [*AM radio station call letters*]
WTVC Chattanooga, TN [*Television station call letters*]
WTVD Durham, NC [*Television station call letters*]
WTVE Reading, PA [*Television station call letters*]
WTVF Nashville, TN [*Television station call letters*]
WTVG Toledo, OH [*Television station call letters*]
WTVH Syracuse, NY [*Television station call letters*]
WTVI Charlotte, NC [*Television station call letters*]
WTVJ Miami, FL [*Television station call letters*]
WTVK Naples, FL [*Television station call letters*] (RBYB)
WTVL Waterville, ME [*AM radio station call letters*]
WTVM Columbus, GA [*Television station call letters*]
WTVN Columbus, OH [*AM radio station call letters*]
WTVO Rockford, IL [*Television station call letters*]
wt/vol Weight per Volume [*Ratio*] [*Chemistry*] (DAVI)
WTVP Peoria, IL [*Television station call letters*]
WTVQ Lexington, KY [*Television station call letters*]
WTVR Richmond, VA [*AM radio station call letters*]
WTVR-FM Richmond, VA [*FM radio station call letters*]
WTVR-TV Richmond, VA [*Television station call letters*]
WTVS Detroit, MI [*Television station call letters*]
WTVT Tampa, FL [*Television station call letters*]
WTVU New Haven, CT [*Television station call letters*]
WTVW Evansville, IN [*Television station call letters*]
WTVX Fort Pierce, FL [*Television station call letters*]
WTVY Dothan, AL [*FM radio station call letters*]
WTVY-TV Dothan, AL [*Television station call letters*]
WTVZ Norfolk, VA [*Television station call letters*]
WTw Joseph Mann Library, Two Rivers, WI [*Library symbol Library of Congress*] (LCLS)
WTW Wall to Wall [*Technical drawings*]
WTW Washington Telecom Week [*A publication*]
WTW West Thumb [*Wyoming*] [*Seismograph station code, US Geological Survey*] (SEIS)
WTWA Thomson, GA [*AM radio station call letters*]
WTWA World Trade Writers Association [*New York, NY*] (EA)
WTWB Auburndale, FL [*AM radio station call letters*]
WTWB Johnstown, PA [*Television station call letters*]
WTWBIR Waste Isolation Pilot Plant Transuranic Waste Baseline Inventory Report [*Department of Energy*] (GAAI)
WTWC Tallahassee, FL [*Television station call letters*]
WTWL McKinnon, TN [*FM radio station call letters*]
WTWO Terre Haute, IN [*Television station call letters*]
WTWR Monroe, MI [*FM radio station call letters*]
WTWS New London, CT [*Television station call letters*]
wt/wt Weight per Weight [*Ratio*] [*Chemistry*] (DAVI)
WTWX Guntersville, AL [*FM radio station call letters*]
WTWZ Clinton, MS [*AM radio station call letters*]
WTX Worldtex, Inc. [*NYSE symbol*] (SPSG)
WTXF Philadelphia, PA [*Television station call letters*]
WTXL Tallahassee, FL [*Television station call letters*]
WTXT Fayette, AL [*FM radio station call letters*]
WTXX Waterbury, CT [*Television station call letters*]
WTXY Whiteville, NC [*AM radio station call letters*]
WTY Westley Mines Ltd. [*Toronto Stock Exchange symbol Vancouver Stock Exchange symbol*]
WTYD New London, CT [*FM radio station call letters*]
WTYE Robinson, IL [*FM radio station call letters*] (RBYB)
WTYF World Theosophical Youth Federation [*Porto Alegre, Brazil*] (EAIO)
WTYJ Fayette, MS [*FM radio station call letters*]
WTYL Tylertown, MS [*AM radio station call letters*]
WTYL-FM Tylertown, MS [*FM radio station call letters*]
WTYM Kittanning, PA [*AM radio station call letters*]
WTYR Soddy-Daisy, TN [*AM radio station call letters*]
W Ty R Washington Territory Reports [*1854-88*] [*A publication*] (DLA)

WTYS Marianna, FL [*AM radio station call letters*]
WTYX Jackson, MS [*FM radio station call letters*]
WTZ Western Trinity Resource [*Vancouver Stock Exchange symbol*]
WTZ Whakatane [*New Zealand*] [*Seismograph station code, US Geological Survey*] (SEIS)
WTZE Tazewell, VA [*AM radio station call letters*]
WTZE-FM Tazewell, VA [*FM radio station call letters*]
WTZQ Hendersonville, NC [*AM radio station call letters*]
WTZR Nanticoke, PA [*FM radio station call letters*]
WTZRA Weitzer Homebuilders'A' [*NASDAQ symbol*] (TTSB)
WTZRA Weitzer Homebuilders, Inc. [*NASDAQ symbol*] (SAG)
WTZX Sparta, TN [*AM radio station call letters*]
WU Netherlines [*ICAO designator*] (AD)
WU Rhine Air [*ICAO designator*] (AD)
WU University of Wisconsin, Madison, WI [*Library symbol Library of Congress*] (LCLS)
WU Washington University (PDAA)
WU Wash Up [*Printing*] (DGA)
WU Weapons and Utilities Maintenance [*Military*] (GFGA)
WU Weather Underground (EA)
WU Weight Unit [*Automobiles*]
WU Wesleyan University
WU Western European Union [*Also, WEU*] (NATG)
WU Western Union (NITA)
WU Western Union Telegraph Co. (TSSD)
WU Whitetails Unlimited (EA)
WU Window Unit (MSA)
WU Workshop Unit (MSA)
WU Work Unit [*Air Force*] (AFM)
w/u Work-Up
WU World Union [*Pondicherry, India*] (EA)
WU-A University of Wisconsin, Agricultural Library, Madison, WI [*Library symbol Library of Congress*] (LCLS)
WUA Weapon Utility Analysis
WUA Western Underwriters Association [*Later, ISO*]
WUA Work Unit Assignment [*Navy*] (NG)
WUAA Wartime Unit Aircraft Activity (AFM)
WUAB Lorain, OH [*Television station call letters*]
WUAG Greensboro, NC [*FM radio station call letters*]
WUAL Tuscaloosa, AL [*FM radio station call letters*]
WUAR Women United Against Rape
WUAT Pikeville, TN [*AM radio station call letters*]
WUAW Erwin, NC [*FM radio station call letters*]
WUB Woodfree Uncoated Boars [*Paper*] (DGA)
WUBE Cincinnati, OH [*AM radio station call letters*]
WUBE-FM Cincinnati, OH [*FM radio station call letters*]
WUBI Baxley, GA [*Television station call letters*]
WUBJ Jamestown, NY [*FM radio station call letters*]
WUBS South Bend, IN [*FM radio station call letters*]
WUBU South Bend, IN [*FM radio station call letters*]
WUBW World Union of Black Writers [*See also UEMN*] (EAIO)
WUBZ-FM Philipsburg, PA [*FM radio station call letters*] (RBYB)
WUC Western Union Corp.
WUC Work Unit Code
WUC Writers Union of Canada
WUC Wu-han [*Republic of China*] [*Seismograph station code, US Geological Survey*] (SEIS)
WU/CCM Washington University Center for Computational Mechanics [*St. Louis, MO*]
WU/CCR Washington University Center for Composites Research [*St. Louis, MO*]
WUCDU World Union of Christian Democratic Women [*Venezuela Political party*] (EAIO)
WUCF Orlando, FL [*FM radio station call letters*]
WUCF Work Unit Code File (NASA)
WUCM University Center, MI [*Television station call letters*]
WUCM Work Unit Code Manual
WUCO Marysville, OH [*AM radio station call letters*]
WUCOS Western European Union Chiefs of Staff (NATG)
WUCPS World Union of Catholic Philosophical Societies (EA)
WUCT World Union of Catholic Teachers
WUCU Western Union Computer Utilities (IAA)
WUCWO World Union of Catholic Women's Organizations [*Rosemere, PQ*] (EAIO)
WUCX Bay City, MI [*FM radio station call letters*]
WUCX-TV Bad Axe, MI [*Television station call letters*]
WUCZ Carthage, TN [*FM radio station call letters*]
WUDB Work Unit Data Bank
WU-DE University of Wisconsin, Center for Demography and Ecology, Madison, WI [*Library symbol Library of Congress*] (LCLS)
WUDO Western European Union Defense Organization (NATG)
WU-E University of Wisconsin, Engineering Library, Madison, WI [*Library symbol Library of Congress*] (LCLS)
WUE Water-Use Efficiency [*Agriculture*]
WUE Work Unit Engineer
WUEC Eau Claire, WI [*FM radio station call letters*]
WUEMI Western Union Electronic Mail, Inc. [*McLean, VA*] [*Telecommunications*] (TSSD)
WUEV Evansville, IN [*FM radio station call letters*]
WUEZ Christopher, IL [*FM radio station call letters*]
WUF Wattle-Urea-Formaldehyde [*Adhesive component*]
WUF Western United Front [*Fiji*] [*Political party*] (PPW)
WUF Where Used File [*Computer science*] (IAA)
WUF World Underwater Federation (ASF)
WUF World Union of Free Thinkers
WUF World University, Miami Learning Resource Center, Miami, FL [*OCLC symbol*] (OCLC)
WUFE Baxley, GA [*AM radio station call letters*]
WUFEC Western European Union Finance and Economic Committee (NATG)
WUFF Eastman, GA [*AM radio station call letters*]
WUFF-FM Eastman, GA [*FM radio station call letters*]
WUFI World United Formosans for Independence [*Political party*] (EY)
WUFK Fort Kent, ME [*FM radio station call letters*]
WUFL Sterling Heights, MI [*AM radio station call letters*]
WUFM-FM Columbus, OH [*FM radio station call letters*] (RBYB)
WUFN Albion, MI [*FM radio station call letters*]
WUFO Amherst, NY [*AM radio station call letters*]
WUFR World Union of Free Romanians [*See also UMRL*] [*Creteil, France*] (EAIO)
WUFS World Union of French-Speakers [*See also UMVF*] (EAIO)
WUFT Gainesville, FL [*FM radio station call letters*]
WUFT-TV Gainesville, FL [*Television station call letters*]
WUFTU World Union of Free Trade Unions
WUg Graham Public Library, Union Grove, WI [*Library symbol Library of Congress*] (LCLS)
WUG Wau [*Papua New Guinea*] [*Airport symbol*] (OAG)
WUGA Athens, GA [*FM radio station call letters*]
WUGN Midland, MI [*FM radio station call letters*]
WUGO Grayson, KY [*FM radio station call letters*]
WUgSC Southern Wisconsin Colony and Training School, Medical Library, Union Grove, WI [*Library symbol Library of Congress*] (LCLS)
WUH Wu-han [*Republic of China*] [*Seismograph station code, US Geological Survey*] (SEIS)
WUH Wuhan [*China*] [*Airport symbol*] (OAG)
WUHF Rochester, NY [*Television station call letters*]
WUHN Pittsfield, MA [*AM radio station call letters*]
WUI Western Union International [*Division of WUI, Inc.*]
WUI Workers' Union of Ireland (BI)
WUIS Springfield, IL [*FM radio station call letters*] (RBYB)
WUIS Water Use Information System [*Westinghouse Hanford Co.*] (IID)
WUIS Work Unit Information System [*Database*] [*DTIC*]
WUIV Icard Township, NC [*AM radio station call letters*]
WUJA Caguas, PR [*Television station call letters*]
WUJC University Heights, OH [*FM radio station call letters*]
WUJM Charleston, SC [*AM radio station call letters*]
WUJS World Union of Jewish Students [*Jerusalem, Israel*]
WUKO World Union of Karatedo Organizations [*Solna, Sweden*] (EAIO)
WUKY Lexington, KY [*FM radio station call letters*]
WU-L University of Wisconsin, Law Library, Madison, WI [*Library symbol Library of Congress*] (LCLS)
WUL Washington University, Law Library, St. Louis, MO [*OCLC symbol*] (OCLC)
WUL Workers Unity League [*Canada*]
WULA Eufaula, AL [*AM radio station call letters*]
WULA-FM Eufaula, AL [*FM radio station call letters*]
WULC West Virginia Union Catalog Interlibrary Loan Network [*Library network*]
WULDS Western Union Long Distance Service [*Western Union Telegraph Co.*] [*Upper Saddle River, NJ*] [*Telecommunications*] (TSSD)
WULF Hardinsburg, KY [*FM radio station call letters*] (RBYB)
WULS Broxton, GA [*FM radio station call letters*]
WU-LT University of Wisconsin, Land Tenure Center, Madison, WI [*Library symbol Library of Congress*] (LCLS)
WULTUO World Union of Liberal Trade Union Organisations [*See also WFALW*] [*Zurich, Switzerland*] (EAIO)
WU-M University of Wisconsin, School of Medicine, Madison, WI [*Library symbol Library of Congress*] (LCLS)
WUM Washington University, School of Medicine, St. Louis, MO [*OCLC symbol*] (OCLC)
WUM Women's Universal Movement [*Defunct*] (EA)
WUM Work Unit Manager
WUM World Union of Mapam [*See also UMM*] (EAIO)
WUMB Boston, MA [*FM radio station call letters*]
WUME Paoli, IN [*FM radio station call letters*]
WUMF Farmington, ME [*FM radio station call letters*]
WUMP Madison, AL [*AM radio station call letters*] (RBYB)
WUMP White, Urban, Middle Class, Protestant
WUMPS Women Umpires [*World War II*]
WUMR Memphis, TN [*FM radio station call letters*]
WUMS University, MS [*FM radio station call letters*]
WUMS Woman's Union Missionary Society of America [*Later, UFCS*] (EA)
WUMTPT World Union of Martyred Towns, Peace Towns (EAIO)
WUN Wiluna [*Australia Airport symbol*] (OAG)
WUN World Union of Nigerians
WUNA Ocoee, FL [*AM radio station call letters*]
WUNC Chapel Hill, NC [*FM radio station call letters*]
WUNC-TV Chapel Hill, NC [*Television station call letters*]
WUND Columbia, NC [*Television station call letters*]
WUNE Linville, NC [*Television station call letters*]
WUNF Asheville, NC [*Television station call letters*]
WUNG Concord, NC [*Television station call letters*]
WUNH Durham, NH [*FM radio station call letters*]
WUNI Needham, MA [*Television station call letters*]
WUNJ Wilmington, NC [*Television station call letters*]
WUNK Greenville, NC [*Television station call letters*]
Wunk WASP Funk [*1960's pop music*]
WUNL Winston-Salem, NC [*Television station call letters*]
WUNM Jacksonville, NC [*Television station call letters*]
WUNN Mason, MI [*AM radio station call letters*]
WUNO San Juan, PR [*AM radio station call letters*]

WUNP Roanoke Rapids, NC [*Television station call letters*]
WUNR Brookline, MA [*AM radio station call letters*]
WUNS World Union of National Socialists (EA)
WUNT Wissenschaftliche Untersuchungen zum Neuen Testament [*Tuebingen*] [*A publication*] (BJA)
WUNU Lumberton, NC [*Television station call letters*] (RBYB)
WUNV Albany, GA [*FM radio station call letters*]
WUNW Key West, FL [*FM radio station call letters*]
WUNX Harwichport, MA [*FM radio station call letters*] (RBYB)
WUNY Utica, NY [*FM radio station call letters*]
WUNZ Falmouth, MA [*FM radio station call letters*] (RBYB)
WUOC Warm-Up Oxidation Catalyst [*Automotive engineering*]
WU/OEL Washington University Optoelectronics Laboratory [*St. Louis, MO*]
WUOG Athens, GA [*FM radio station call letters*]
WUOK West Yarmouth, MA [*AM radio station call letters*]
WUOL Louisville, KY [*FM radio station call letters*]
WUOM Ann Arbor, MI [*FM radio station call letters*]
WUOSY World Union of Organizations for the Safeguard of Youth [*Later, UMOSEA*]
WUOT Knoxville, TN [*FM radio station call letters*]
WUOY Wilmington, NC [*FM radio station call letters*]
WUP Work Unit Plan [*Navy*] (NG)
WUPA Wupatki National Monument
WUPA-TV Atlanta, GA [*TV station call letters*] (RBYB)
WUPE Pittsfield, MA [*FM radio station call letters*]
WUPI Presque Isle, ME [*FM radio station call letters*]
WUPJ World Union for Progressive Judaism (EA)
WUPK Marquette, MI [*FM radio station call letters*]
WUPL Slidell, LA [*Television station call letters*] (RBYB)
WUPL-INT World Union for the Protection of Life [*See also WSL-INT*] (EAIO)
WUPM Ironwood, MI [*FM radio station call letters*]
WUPN Mexico, NY [*FM radio station call letters*] (RBYB)
WUPN-TV Greensboro, NC [*TV station call letters*] (RBYB)
WUPO World Union of Pythagorean Organizations [*Ivybridge, Devonshire, England*] (EAIO)
WUPPE Wisconsin Ultraviolet Photo-Polarimeter Experiment
WUPR Utuado, PR [*AM radio station call letters*]
WUPS Houghton Lake, MI [*FM radio station call letters*]
WUPS Westinghouse Uninterruptible Power System (IAA)
WUPS World Union of Process Servers
WUPW Toledo, OH [*Television station call letters*]
WUPX Marquette, MI [*FM radio station call letters*]
WUPY Ontonagon, MI [*FM radio station call letters*]
WUR World University Roundtable
WURB Western Utilization Research Branch (MCD)
WURB Windsor, NC [*FM radio station call letters*]
WURC Holly Springs, MS [*FM radio station call letters*]
WURD Philadelphia, PA [*AM radio station call letters*]
WURL Moody, AL [*AM radio station call letters*]
WURN Marietta, OH [*FM radio station call letters*] (RBYB)
WUS Woerterbuch der Ugaritischen Sprache [*A publication*] (BJA)
WUS Word Underscore Character [*Computer science*]
WUS World University Service [*See also EUM*] [*Geneva, Switzerland*] (EAIO)
WUSA Tampa, FL [*FM radio station call letters*]
WUSA Washington, DC [*Television station call letters*]
WUSA Waterfowl USA (EA)
WUSB Stony Brook, NY [*FM radio station call letters*]
WUSC Columbia, SC [*FM radio station call letters*]
WUSC Weather of US Cities [*A publication*]
WUSC World University Service of Canada [*See also EUMC*]
WUSCI Western Union Space Communications, Inc. (MCD)
WUSF Tampa, FL [*FM radio station call letters*]
WUSF-TV Tampa, FL [*Television station call letters*]
WUSG World Union Saint Gabriel [*Esher, Surrey, England*] (EAIO)
WUSI Olney, IL [*FM radio station call letters*]
WUSI-TV Olney, IL [*Television station call letters*]
WUSK Tomah, WI [*FM radio station call letters*]
WUSL Philadelphia, PA [*FM radio station call letters*]
WUSL Washburn University School of Law (DLA)
WUSL Women's United Service League [*British*]
WUSM Hattiesburg, MS [*FM radio station call letters*]
WUSN Chicago, IL [*FM radio station call letters*]
WUSO Springfield, OH [*FM radio station call letters*]
WUSP World Union of Stockholm Pioneers (EAIO)
WUSQ Winchester, VA [*FM radio station call letters*]
WUSR Scranton, PA [*FM radio station call letters*]
WU/SRL Washington University Semiconductor Research Laboratory [*St. Louis, MO*]
WUSS Atlantic City, NJ [*AM radio station call letters*]
WUST Washington, DC [*AM radio station call letters*]
WUS(UK) World University Service (United Kingdom) (DI)
WUS-US World University Service/USA (EA)
WUSW Oshkosh, WI [*FM radio station call letters*]
WUSX Portage, WI [*FM radio station call letters*]
WUSY Cleveland, TN [*FM radio station call letters*]
WUSY World Union for the Safeguard of Youth
WUSZ Virginia, MN [*FM radio station call letters*]
WUT Warm Up Time
WUT Washburn University of Topeka [*Kansas*]
WUT Woman Using Television (WDMC)
WUT Women Using Television (WDMC)
WUTA Washington University Technology Associates
WUTC Chattanooga, TN [*FM radio station call letters*]
WUTC Western Union Telegraph Co.
WUTELCO Western Union Telegraph Co.
WUTHH World Union of Tnuat Haherut Hatzorar [*Tel Aviv, Israel*] (EAIO)
WUTK Knoxville, TN [*AM radio station call letters*]
WUTK-FM Knoxville, TN [*FM radio station call letters*]
WUTM Martin, TN [*FM radio station call letters*]
WUTQ Utica, NY [*AM radio station call letters*]
WUTR Utica, NY [*Television station call letters*]
WUTS Sewanee, TN [*FM radio station call letters*]
WUTS Work Unit Time Standard [*Air Force*] (AFM)
WUTS Work Unit Tracking Subsystem (MCD)
WUTV Buffalo, NY [*Television station call letters*]
WUTWC Warm-Up Three-Way Catalyst [*Automotive engineering*]
WUU Wau [*Sudan*] [*Airport symbol*] (OAG)
WUUA World Union for a Universal Alphabet (EA)
WUUC West Ulster Unionist Council [*Northern Ireland*]
WUUN Women United for United Nations (EA)
WUUU Remsen, NY [*FM radio station call letters*]
WUV Weighted Unit Value (MCD)
WUV Wuvulu Island [*Papua New Guinea*] [*Airport symbol*] (OAG)
WUVA Charlottesville, VA [*FM radio station call letters*]
WUVCI Western Union VideoConferencing, Inc. [*Defunct*] (TSSD)
WUVR Lebanon, NH [*FM radio station call letters*]
WUVT Blacksburg, VA [*FM radio station call letters*]
WUW Wu-wei [*Republic of China*] [*Seismograph station code, US Geological Survey*] (SEIS)
WU-WA University of Wisconsin, Woodman Astronomical Library, Madison, WI [*Library symbol Library of Congress*] (LCLS)
WUWF Pensacola, FL [*FM radio station call letters*]
WUWM Milwaukee, WI [*FM radio station call letters*]
WUWU Cordele, GA [*AM radio station call letters*]
WUX Western Union Exchange [*Teleprinter*]
WUXA Portsmouth, OH [*Television station call letters*]
WUXP-TV Nashville, TN [*TV station call letters*] (RBYB)
WUZR Bicknell, IN [*FM radio station call letters*]
WV Diwag [*Germany*] [*Research code symbol*]
WV Midwest Aviation [*ICAO designator*] (AD)
WV Wall Vent [*Technical drawings*]
WV Water Valve (ROG)
wv Weave (VRA)
W/V Weight/Volume [*Concentration*] [*Chemistry*]
WV Westminster Version of the Bible [*A publication*] (BJA)
WV West Virginia [*Postal code*]
Wv West Virginia Library Commission, Charleston, WV [*Library symbol Library of Congress*] (LCLS)
WV West Virginia Reports [*A publication*] (DLA)
WV Whispered Voice
W/V Wind Vector [*or Velocity*] [*Navigation*]
WV Wireless Van [*British*]
WV Working Voltage (MSA)
WV World Vision [*An association*] (EA)
wv Woven (VRA)
WVA Alderson-Broaddus College, Philippi, WV [*OCLC symbol*] (OCLC)
WVA Alexandria [*Virginia*] [*Airport symbol*] (AD)
WVA H & D Aviation [*ICAO designator*] (FAAC)
WVA War Veterans Administration [*Canada*]
WVA Watervliet Arsenal [*New York*] [*Army*]
W VA West Virginia (AAG)
W Va West Virginia Supreme Court Reports [*A publication*] (DLA)
WVA Wool Valuers Association [*Australia*]
WVA World Veterinary Association [*See also AMV*] [*Madrid, Spain*] (EAIO)
WVA World Vision Australia
WVAA Burnettown, SC [*AM radio station call letters*]
W Va Acts Acts of the Legislature of West Virginia [*A publication*] (DLA)
WVAATS West Virginia Assessment and Tracking System (EDAC)
WVAB Virginia Beach, VA [*AM radio station call letters*]
WVAB War Veterans Allowance Board [*Canada*]
WVAC Adrian, MI [*FM radio station call letters*]
WvAC Concord College, Athens, WV [*Library symbol Library of Congress*] (LCLS)
WVAC Norwalk, OH [*AM radio station call letters*]
WVAC Working Voltage, Alternating Current (DEN)
W Va Code West Virginia Code [*A publication*] (DLA)
W Va Const West Virginia Constitution [*A publication*] (DLA)
W Va Crim Just Rev West Virginia Criminal Justice Review [*A publication*] (DLA)
WVAE Fairfield, OH [*FM radio station call letters*] (RBYB)
WVAF Charleston, WV [*FM radio station call letters*]
WVAH Charleston, WV [*Television station call letters*]
WVAL Sauk Rapids, MN [*AM radio station call letters*]
W Va Law Reports West Virginia Reports [*A publication*] (DLA)
W Va LQ West Virginia Law Quarterly [*A publication*] (DLA)
WVALSA Whitewater Valley Area Library Services Authority [*Library network*]
WVAM Altoona, PA [*AM radio station call letters*]
WVAN Savannah, GA [*Television station call letters*]
WVAO Staunton, VA [*FM radio station call letters*]
WVAO Waynesboro, VA [*AM radio station call letters*]
W Va PSCR West Virginia Public Service Commission Report [*A publication*] (DLA)
W Va PUR West Virginia Public Utility Commission Reports [*A publication*] (DLA)
WVAQ Morgantown, WV [*FM radio station call letters*]
WVAR Richwood, WV [*AM radio station call letters*]
Wv-Ar West Virginia Department of Archives and History, Charleston, WV [*Library symbol Library of Congress*] (LCLS)
W Va Reg West Virginia Register [*A publication*] (AAGC)
W Va Rep West Virginia Reports [*A publication*] (DLA)
WVAS Montgomery, AL [*FM radio station call letters*]

WVAS .... Wake Vortex Avoidance System [*FAA*]
WVAST .... Washer Visual Acuity Screening Technique [*Visual ability test*]
WVAX-AM .... Lincoln, IL [*AM radio station call letters*] (RBYB)
WVAY .... Wilmington, VT [*FM radio station call letters*]
WVAZ .... Oak Park, IL [*FM radio station call letters*]
WvB .... Beckley-Raleigh County Library, Beckley, WV [*Library symbol Library of Congress*] (LCLS)
WVB .... Bethany College, Bethany, WV [*OCLC symbol*] (OCLC)
WVB .... Walvis Bay [*Namibia*] [*Airport symbol*] (OAG)
Wv-B .... West Virginia Library Commission, Book Express Unit, Charleston, WV [*Library symbol Library of Congress*] (LCLS)
WVBA .... West Virginia Bowhunters Association
WVBA .... Wholesale Variety Bakers Association (EA)
WvBC .... Beckley College, Beckley, WV [*Library symbol Library of Congress*] (LCLS)
WVBC .... Bethany, WV [*FM radio station call letters*]
WVBEA .... West Virginia Business Education Association (EDAC)
WvBeC .... Bethany College, Bethany, WV [*Library symbol Library of Congress*] (LCLS)
WVBI .... Block Island, RI [*FM radio station call letters*]
WvBl .... Bluefield Public Library, Bluefield, WV [*Library symbol Library of Congress*] (LCLS)
WvBlS .... Bluefield State College, Bluefield, WV [*Library symbol Library of Congress*] (LCLS)
WVBO .... Oshkosh, WI [*FM radio station call letters*]
WVBR .... Ithaca, NY [*FM radio station call letters*]
WvBrA .... Appalachian Bible Institute, Bradley, WV [*Library symbol Library of Congress*] (LCLS)
WvBri .... Benedum Civic Center Public Library, Bridgeport, WV [*Library symbol Library of Congress*] (LCLS)
WVBS .... Burgaw, NC [*AM radio station call letters*]
WVBT-TV ..... Virginia Beach, VA [*TV station call letters*] (RBYB)
WVBU .... Lewisburg, PA [*FM radio station call letters*]
WvBu .... Stonewall Jackson Regional Library, Buckhannon, WV [*Library symbol Library of Congress*] (LCLS)
WvBuW .... West Virginia Wesleyan College, Buckhannon, WV [*Library symbol Library of Congress*] (LCLS)
WvBV .... United States Veterans Administration Hospital, Beckley, WV [*Library symbol Library of Congress*] (LCLS)
WvC .... Kanawha County Public Library, Charleston, WV [*Library symbol Library of Congress*] (LCLS)
WVC .... Western Veterinary Conference (EA)
WVC .... West Virginia Code [*1899*] [*A publication*] (DLA)
WvCA .... West Virginia Department of Agriculture, Charleston, WV [*Library symbol Library of Congress*] (LCLS)
WvCAE .... Appalachian Educational Laboratory, Inc., Charleston, WV [*Library symbol Library of Congress*] (LCLS)
WvCAP .... West Virginia Air Pollution Control Commission, Charleston, WV [*Library symbol Library of Congress*] (LCLS)
WVCB .... Shallotte, NC [*AM radio station call letters*]
WvCBHi .... West Virginia Baptist Historical Society Deposit, Department of Archives and History, Charleston, WV [*Library symbol Library of Congress*] (LCLS)
WVCC .... Linesville, PA [*FM radio station call letters*]
WvCCD .... West Virginia Department of Civil and Defense Mobilization, Charleston, WV [*Library symbol Library of Congress*] (LCLS)
WVCF .... Welsh Venture Capital Funds
WVCF-FM .... Eau Claire, WI [*FM radio station call letters*] (RBYB)
WvCFM .... West Virginia State Fire Marshal's Department, Charleston, WV [*Library symbol Library of Congress*] (LCLS)
WVCG .... Coral Gables, FL [*AM radio station call letters*]
WvCGH .... Charleston General Hospital, Charleston, WV [*Library symbol Library of Congress*] (LCLS)
WVCH .... Chester, PA [*AM radio station call letters*]
WvCH .... West Virginia Department of Health, Charleston, WV [*Library symbol Library of Congress*] (LCLS)
WvCheC .... Consolidated Gas Supply Corp., Chelyan, WV [*Library symbol Library of Congress*] (LCLS)
WvCHi .... West Virginia Department of Highways, Charleston, WV [*Library symbol Library of Congress*] (LCLS)
WvCl .... Clarksburg Public Library, Clarksburg, WV [*Library symbol Library of Congress*] (LCLS)
WvClC .... Consolidated Gas Supply Corp., Clarksburg, WV [*Library symbol Library of Congress*] (LCLS)
WvCM .... Morris Harvey College, Charleston, WV [*Library symbol Library of Congress*] (LCLS)
WvCMH .... West Virginia Department of Mental Health, Charleston, WV [*Library symbol Library of Congress*] (LCLS)
WvCMi .... West Virginia Department of Mines, Charleston, WV [*Library symbol Library of Congress*] (LCLS)
WvCNR .... West Virginia Department of Natural Resources, Charleston, WV [*Library symbol Library of Congress*] (LCLS)
WVCO .... Loris, SC [*FM radio station call letters*]
WVCP .... Gallatin, TN [*FM radio station call letters*]
WvCPS .... West Virginia Department of Public Safety, Charleston, WV [*Library symbol Library of Congress*] (LCLS)
WVCQ .... Brockway, PA [*AM radio station call letters*]
WVCR .... Loudonville, NY [*FM radio station call letters*]
WVCS .... California, PA [*FM radio station call letters*]
WVCT .... Keavy, KY [*FM radio station call letters*]
WvCTS .... West Virginia State Technical Services, Charleston, WV [*Library symbol Library of Congress*] (LCLS)
WVCV .... Boalsburg, PA [*FM radio station call letters*]
WvCVR .... West Virginia Division of Vocational Rehabilitation, Charleston, WV [*Library symbol Library of Congress*] (LCLS)
WVCX .... Tomah, WI [*FM radio station call letters*]
WVCY .... Milwaukee, WI [*FM radio station call letters*]
WVCY .... Oshkosh, WI [*AM radio station call letters*] (RBYB)
WVCY-TV .... Milwaukee, WI [*Television station call letters*]
WVD .... Dane County Hospital, Verona, WI [*Library symbol Library of Congress*] (LCLS)
WVD .... Davis and Elkins College, Elkins, WV [*OCLC symbol*] (OCLC)
WVD .... Waived (AABC)
WVD .... Wereldverband van Diamantbewerkers [*Worldwide Alliance of Diamond Workers*] (BARN)
WVdc .... DC Working Voltage (IDOE)
WVDC .... Working Voltage, Direct Current
WVDF .... Wolverhampton Volunteer Defence Force [*British military*] (DMA)
WVDP .... West Valley Demonstration Project [*Department of Energy*] [*West Valley, NY*] (GAAI)
WVDP .... West Valley Demonstration Project (DOGT)
WVE .... Water Vapor Electrolysis [*Cell*]
WVE .... Wind Velocity East (MCD)
WVEC .... Hampton, VA [*Television station call letters*]
WvED .... Davis and Elkins College, Elkins, WV [*Library symbol Library of Congress*] (LCLS)
WVEE .... Atlanta, GA [*FM radio station call letters*]
WVEE .... Wheeled Vehicle Experimental Establishment [*British*]
WVEH .... Wheel Vehicle (AABC)
WVEL .... Pekin, IL [*AM radio station call letters*]
WVEM .... Water Vapor Electrolysis Module [*NASA*]
WVEO .... Aguadilla, PR [*Television station call letters*]
WVEP .... Martinsburg, WV [*FM radio station call letters*]
WVER .... Rutland, VT [*Television station call letters*]
WVES .... Accomac, VA [*FM radio station call letters*]
WVEU .... Atlanta, GA [*Television station call letters*]
WVEZ .... Louisville, KY [*FM radio station call letters*]
WVF .... Fairmont State College, Fairmont, WV [*OCLC symbol*] (OCLC)
WvF .... Marion County Public Library, Fairmont, WV [*Library symbol Library of Congress*] (LCLS)
WVF .... United States Council, World Veterans Federation (EA)
WVF .... Wave Vector Filter
WVF .... World Veterans Federation [*See also FMAC*] [*Paris, France*] (EAIO)
WVF .... World Veterans Fund [*Defunct*] (EA)
WvFa .... Fayette County Public Library, Fayetteville, WV [*Library symbol Library of Congress*] (LCLS)
WVFB .... Celina, TN [*FM radio station call letters*]
WVFC .... McConnellsburg, PA [*AM radio station call letters*]
WVFC .... WVS Financial [*NASDAQ symbol*] (TTSB)
WVFC .... WVS Financial Corp. [*NASDAQ symbol*] (SAG)
WVFG .... Uniontown, AL [*FM radio station call letters*]
WVFJ .... Manchester, GA [*FM radio station call letters*]
WVFM .... Campton, NH [*FM radio station call letters*]
WvFMHi .... Marion County Historical Society, Fairmont, WV [*Library symbol Library of Congress*] (LCLS)
WVFN .... East Lansing, MI [*AM radio station call letters*]
WvFS .... Fairmont State College, Fairmont, WV [*Library symbol Library of Congress*] (LCLS)
WVFS .... Tallahassee, FL [*FM radio station call letters*]
WVG .... West Virginia State College/College of Graduate Studies, Institute, WV [*OCLC symbol*] (OCLC)
WVGB .... Beaufort, SC [*AM radio station call letters*]
WvGbN .... National Radio Astronomy Observatory, Green Bank, WV [*Library symbol Library of Congress*] (LCLS)
WvGlS .... Glenville State College, Glenville, WV [*Library symbol Library of Congress*] (LCLS)
WVGN .... Charlotte Amalie, VI [*FM radio station call letters*]
WVGO .... Richmond, VA [*FM radio station call letters*]
WVGR .... Grand Rapids, MI [*FM radio station call letters*]
WVGS .... Statesboro, GA [*FM radio station call letters*]
WVGV .... Lewisburg, WV [*Television station call letters*]
WVH .... Marshall University, Huntington, WV [*OCLC symbol*] (OCLC)
WVHA .... Wirtschaftsverwaltungshauptamt (BJA)
WvHB .... Pearl S. Buck Birthplace Museum, Hillsboro, WV [*Library symbol Library of Congress*] (LCLS)
WVHC .... Herkimer, NY [*FM radio station call letters*]
WVHF .... Clarksburg, WV [*FM radio station call letters*]
WvHfP .... United States Park Service, Harpers Ferry National Historical Park, Harpers Ferry, WV [*Library symbol Library of Congress*] (LCLS)
WVHI .... Evansville, IN [*AM radio station call letters*]
WVHM .... Benton, KY [*FM radio station call letters*]
WVHQ .... Dowagiac, MI [*FM radio station call letters*]
WVHR .... Huntingdon, TN [*FM radio station call letters*]
WvHu .... Cabell-Huntington Public Library [*Western Counties Regional Library*], Huntington, WV [*Library symbol Library of Congress*] (LCLS)
WvHuB .... Basic Systems, Inc., Huntington, WV [*Library symbol Library of Congress*] (LCLS)
WvHuE .... United States Army, Corps of Engineers, Huntington, WV [*Library symbol Library of Congress*] (LCLS)
WvHuG .... Huntington Galleries, Huntington, WV [*Library symbol Library of Congress*] (LCLS)
WvHuH .... Holland-Suco Color Co., Huntington, WV [*Library symbol Library of Congress*] (LCLS)
WvHuM .... Marshall University, Huntington, WV [*Library symbol Library of Congress*] (LCLS)
WvHuV .... United States Veterans Administration Hospital, Huntington, WV [*Library symbol Library of Congress*] (LCLS)
WVi .... Viroqua Public Library, Viroqua, WI [*Library symbol Library of Congress*] (LCLS)

WVI .... Watsonville, CA [*Location identifier FAA*] (FAAL)
WVI .... Work Values Inventory [*Psychometrics*]
WVI .... World Vision International
WVIA .... Scranton, PA [*FM radio station call letters*]
WVIA-TV .... Scranton, PA [*Television station call letters*]
WVIB .... Mount Kisco, NY [*FM radio station call letters*] (RBYB)
WVIC .... East Lansing, MI [*FM radio station call letters*]
WvIC .... West Virginia State College, Institute, WV [*Library symbol Library of Congress*] (LCLS)
WvICG .... West Virginia College of Graduate Studies, Institute, WV [*Library symbol Library of Congress*] (LCLS)
WVII .... Bangor, ME [*Television station call letters*]
WVIJ .... Port Charlotte, FL [*FM radio station call letters*]
WVIK .... Rock Island, IL [*FM radio station call letters*]
WVIL .... Virginia, IL [*FM radio station call letters*] (RBYB)
WVIM .... Coldwater, MS [*FM radio station call letters*]
WVIN .... Bath, NY [*FM radio station call letters*]
WVIO .... Blowing Rock, NC [*AM radio station call letters*]
WVIP .... Mount Kisco, NY [*AM radio station call letters*]
WVIQ .... Christiansted, VI [*FM radio station call letters*]
WVIR .... Charlottesville, VA [*Television station call letters*]
WVIS .... Christiansted, VI [*FM radio station call letters*]
WVIT .... New Britain, CT [*Television station call letters*]
WVIT .... West Virginia Institute of Technology
WVIV .... Pearl, MS [*FM radio station call letters*]
WVIX .... Vicksburg, MS [*AM radio station call letters*]
WVIZ .... Cleveland, OH [*Television station call letters*]
WVJC .... Mount Carmel, IL [*FM radio station call letters*]
WVJP .... Caguas, PR [*AM radio station call letters*]
WVJP-FM .... Caguas, PR [*FM radio station call letters*]
WVJS .... Owensboro, KY [*AM radio station call letters*]
WVK .... Kanawha County Public Library, Charleston, WV [*OCLC symbol*] (OCLC)
WvK .... Keyser-Mineral County Public and Potomac Valley Regional Library, Keyser, WV [*Library symbol Library of Congress*] (LCLS)
WVK .... Manakara [*Madagascar*] [*Airport symbol*] (OAG)
WVKC .... Galesburg, IL [*FM radio station call letters*]
WvKeFW .... Bureau of Sport Fisheries and Wildlife, Eastern Fish Disease Laboratory, Kearneysville, WV [*Library symbol Library of Congress*] (LCLS)
WVKM .... Matewan, WV [*FM radio station call letters*]
WVKO .... Columbus, OH [*AM radio station call letters*]
WvKP .... Potomac State College, Keyser, WV [*Library symbol Library of Congress*] (LCLS)
WVKR .... Poughkeepsie, NY [*FM radio station call letters*]
WVKS .... Toledo, OH [*FM radio station call letters*]
WVKV .... Hurricane, WV [*AM radio station call letters*]
WVKX .... Irwinton, GA [*FM radio station call letters*]
WVKY .... Louisa, KY [*AM radio station call letters*]
WVKZ .... Schenectady, NY [*AM radio station call letters*]
WVL .... Warfare Vision Laboratory [*Army*]
WVL .... Waterville [*Maine*] [*Airport symbol*] (OAG)
WVL .... Waterville, ME [*Location identifier FAA*] (FAAL)
WVL .... Wavelength [*Electronics*] (IAA)
WVL .... West Vancouver Laboratory [*Department of Fisheries and Oceans*] [*Canada*] (IRC)
Wv-L .... West Virginia State Law Library, Charleston, WV [*Library symbol Library of Congress*] (LCLS)
WVL .... Woodvale Aviation Co. Ltd. [*British ICAO designator*] (FAAC)
WVLA .... Baton Rouge, LA [*Television station call letters*]
WVLB .... Wheeled Vehicle Launched Bridge (MCD)
WVLC .... Mannsville, KY [*FM radio station call letters*] (RBYB)
WVLD .... Valdosta, GA [*AM radio station call letters*]
WvLe .... Greenbrier County Public Library, Lewisburg, WV [*Library symbol Library of Congress*] (LCLS)
WVLE .... Scottsville, KY [*FM radio station call letters*]
WvLeG .... Greenbrier College, Lewisburg, WV [*Library symbol Library of Congress*] (LCLS)
WVLI .... Kankakee, IL [*FM radio station call letters*] (RBYB)
WVLK .... Lexington, KY [*AM radio station call letters*]
WVLK-FM .... Lexington, KY [*FM radio station call letters*]
WVLN .... Olney, IL [*AM radio station call letters*]
WVLQ .... West Virginia Law Quarterly [*A publication*] (DLA)
WVLR .... Lynchburg, VA [*AM radio station call letters*]
WVLS .... Monterey, VA [*FM radio station call letters*]
Wv-LS .... West Virginia Library Commission, Library Science Department, Charleston, WV [*Library symbol Library of Congress*] (LCLS)
WVLT .... Vineland, NJ [*FM radio station call letters*]
WVLY .... Milton, PA [*FM radio station call letters*]
WvM .... Morgantown Public Library, Morgantown, WV [*Library symbol Library of Congress*] (LCLS)
WVM .... West Virginia Medical Center, Morgantown, WV [*Inactive*] [*OCLC symbol*] (OCLC)
WvMa .... Martinsburg-Berkeley County Public Library, Martinsburg, WV [*Library symbol Library of Congress*] (LCLS)
WVMA .... Women's Veterinary Medical Association [*Later, AWV*]
WvMaV .... United States Veterans Administration Center, Martinsburg, WV [*Library symbol Library of Congress*] (LCLS)
WV-MBC .... Walking Ventilation to Maximum Breathing Capacity Ratio [*Medicine*] (MAE)
WvMBM .... United States Bureau of Mines, Morgantown, WV [*Library symbol Library of Congress*] (LCLS)
WVMC .... Mansfield, OH [*FM radio station call letters*]
WvMc .... McMechen Public Library, McMechen, WV [*Library symbol Library of Congress*] (LCLS)
WvMDOE .... United States Department of Energy, Morgantown Energy Technology Center, Morgantown, WV [*Library symbol*] [*Library of Congress*] (LCLS)
WVMG .... Cochran, GA [*AM radio station call letters*]
WVMG-FM .... Cochran, GA [*FM radio station call letters*]
WVMH .... Mars Hill, NC [*FM radio station call letters*]
WVMI .... Biloxi, MS [*AM radio station call letters*]
WvMIL .... Institute for Labor Studies, Appalachian Center, Morgantown, WV [*Library symbol Library of Congress*] (LCLS)
WVMJ .... Blacksburg, VA [*FM radio station call letters*] (RBYB)
WVMM .... Grantham, PA [*FM radio station call letters*]
WVMN .... New Castle, PA [*FM radio station call letters*] (RBYB)
WvMNIO .... United States Public Health Service, National Institute for Occupational Safety and Health, Appalachian Laboratory for Occupational Safety and Health Library, Morgantown, WV (LCLS)
WvMo .... City-County Public Library, Moundsville, WV [*Library symbol Library of Congress*] (LCLS)
WvMonI .... West Virginia Institute of Technology, Montgomery, WV [*Library symbol Library of Congress*] (LCLS)
WVMR .... Frost, WV [*AM radio station call letters*]
WVMS .... Sandusky, OH [*FM radio station call letters*]
WVMT .... Burlington, VT [*AM radio station call letters*]
WVMV .... Wisteria Vein Mosaic Virus
WVMW .... Scranton, PA [*FM radio station call letters*]
WVMX .... Stowe, VT [*FM radio station call letters*]
WVN .... Water Vapor Nitrogen [*Nuclear energy*] (NRCH)
WVN .... West Virginia Northern Railroad Co. [*AAR code*]
WVN .... Wind Velocity North (MCD)
WVN .... Woven
WVNA .... Tuscumbia, AL [*AM radio station call letters*]
WVNA-FM .... Tuscumbia, AL [*FM radio station call letters*]
WVNC .... Canton, NY [*FM radio station call letters*]
WVNE .... Leicester, MA [*AM radio station call letters*]
WVNET .... West Virginia Network for Educational Telecomputing [*Research center*] (RCD)
WVNF .... Alpharetta, GA [*AM radio station call letters*]
WVNH .... Concord, NH [*FM radio station call letters*]
WVNI .... Nashville, IN [*FM radio station call letters*]
WvNiK .... West Virginia University, Kanawha Valley Graduate Center, Nitro, WV [*Library symbol Library of Congress*] (LCLS)
WVNJ .... Oakland, NJ [*AM radio station call letters*]
WvNmM .... Mobay Chemical Corp., Research Library, New Martinsville, WV [*Library symbol Library of Congress*] (LCLS)
WVNN .... Athens, AL [*AM radio station call letters*]
WVNO .... Mansfield, OH [*FM radio station call letters*]
WVNP .... Wheeling, WV [*FM radio station call letters*]
WVNR .... Poultney, VT [*AM radio station call letters*]
WVNS .... Claremont, VA [*AM radio station call letters*] (RBYB)
WVNS .... West Valley Nuclear Services Co. (GAAI)
WVNU .... Greenfield, OH [*FM radio station call letters*]
WVNV .... Malone, NY [*FM radio station call letters*]
WVNW .... Burnham, PA [*FM radio station call letters*]
WVNX .... Charlotte Amalie, VI [*FM radio station call letters*]
WVNY .... Burlington, VT [*Television station call letters*]
WVNY .... West Valley, New York [*Commercial waste site from 1963-81*] (GAAI)
WVNZ-AM .... Richmond, VA [*AM radio station call letters*] (RBYB)
WVOA .... DeRuyter, NY [*FM radio station call letters*]
WVOB .... Dothan, AL [*FM radio station call letters*]
WVOC .... Columbia, SC [*AM radio station call letters*]
WVOD .... Manteo, NC [*FM radio station call letters*]
WVOE .... Chadbourn, NC [*AM radio station call letters*]
WVOF .... Fairfield, CT [*FM radio station call letters*]
WVOG .... New Orleans, LA [*AM radio station call letters*]
WVOH .... Hazlehurst, GA [*AM radio station call letters*]
WVOH-FM .... Hazlehurst, GA [*FM radio station call letters*]
WVOI .... Toledo, OH [*AM radio station call letters*]
WVOJ .... Jacksonville, FL [*AM radio station call letters*]
WVOK .... Oxford, AL [*FM radio station call letters*]
WVOL .... Berry Hill, TN [*AM radio station call letters*]
WVOM .... Iuka, MS [*AM radio station call letters*]
WVON .... Cicero, IL [*AM radio station call letters*]
WVOP .... Vidalia, GA [*AM radio station call letters*]
WVOR .... Rochester, NY [*FM radio station call letters*]
WVOS .... Liberty, NY [*AM radio station call letters*]
WVOS-FM .... Liberty, NY [*FM radio station call letters*]
WVOT .... Wilson, NC [*AM radio station call letters*]
WVOV .... Danville, VA [*AM radio station call letters*]
WVOW .... Logan, WV [*AM radio station call letters*]
WVOW-FM .... Logan, WV [*FM radio station call letters*]
WVOX .... New Rochelle, NY [*AM radio station call letters*]
WVOZ .... Ponce, PR [*Television station call letters*]
WvP .... Carnegie Library of Parkersburg and Wood County, Parkersburg, WV [*Library symbol Library of Congress*] (LCLS)
WVP .... Water Vapor Permeability [*Physical chemistry*]
WVP .... Windscale Vitrification Plant [*British*] (NUCP)
WVP .... Women's Vote Project [*Defunct*] (EA)
WVPA .... World Veterinary Poultry Association [*See also AMVA*] [*Huntingdon, Cambridgeshire, England*] (EAIO)
WVPB .... Beckley, WV [*FM radio station call letters*]
WvPC .... Parkersburg Community College, Parkersburg, WV [*Library symbol Library of Congress*] (LCLS)
WVPE .... Elkhart, IN [*FM radio station call letters*]
WVPG .... Parkersburg, WV [*FM radio station call letters*]
WVPH .... Piscataway, NJ [*FM radio station call letters*]

WvPhA......... Alderson-Broaddus College, Philippi, WV [*Library symbol Library of Congress*] (LCLS)
WVPM......... Morgantown, WV [*FM radio station call letters*]
WVPN......... Charleston, WV [*FM radio station call letters*]
WvPO......... Ohio Valley College, Parkersburg, WV [*Library symbol Library of Congress*] (LCLS)
WVPO......... Stroudsburg, PA [*AM radio station call letters*]
WVPR......... Windsor, VT [*FM radio station call letters*]
WVPS......... Burlington, VT [*FM radio station call letters*]
WVPT......... Staunton, VA [*Television station call letters*]
WVPW......... Buckhannon, WV [*FM radio station call letters*]
WVPY-TV..... Front Royal, VA [*TV station call letters*] (RBYB)
WVQ......... Monongahela Power Co. [*NYSE symbol*] (SAG)
WVQ......... Monongahela Pwr 8% 'QUIDS' [*NYSE symbol*] (TTSB)
WVR......... Wakefield Volunteer Rifles [*British military*] (DMA)
WVR......... Wellington Volunteer Rifles [*British military*] (DMA)
Wv-R......... West Virginia Library Commission, Reference Department, WV [*Library symbol Library of Congress*] (LCLS)
WVR......... West Virginia Reports [*A publication*] (DLA)
WVR......... Within Visual Range [*Missile*] (MCD)
WVR......... Women's Volunteer Reserve [*World War I*] [*British*]
WVRAAM..... Within Visual Range Air-to-Air Missile
WVRB......... Wilmore, KY [*FM radio station call letters*] (RBYB)
WVRC......... Spencer, WV [*AM radio station call letters*]
WVRC......... Wabash Valley Railroad Co. [*AAR code*]
WVRC......... Wolverhampton Volunteer Rifle Corps [*British military*] (DMA)
WVRC-FM.... Spencer, WV [*FM radio station call letters*]
WVRD......... Belzoni, MS [*FM radio station call letters*]
WV Rep....... West Virginia Reports [*A publication*] (DLA)
WVRK......... Columbus, GA [*FM radio station call letters*]
WVRP......... Ripley, WV [*FM radio station call letters*]
WVRQ......... Viroqua, WI [*AM radio station call letters*]
WVRQ-FM.... Viroqua, WI [*FM radio station call letters*]
WVRRTC...... West Virginia Rehabilitation Research and Training Center [*West Virginia University*] [*Research center*] (RCD)
WVRT......... Jersey Shore, PA [*FM radio station call letters*] (RBYB)
WVRU......... Radford, VA [*FM radio station call letters*]
WVRV......... East St. Louis, IL [*FM radio station call letters*]
WVRY......... Waverly, TN [*FM radio station call letters*]
WVS......... Water Vapor Sensor
W-V(S)......... Women's Reserve, Emergency Duties [*USNR commissioned officer designation*]
WVS......... Women's Voluntary Services [*Coordinated work of women for national service*] [*Later, WRVS*] [*British*] [*World War II*]
WVSA......... Vernon, AL [*AM radio station call letters*]
WVSA......... Water-Vapor-Saturated Air (PDAA)
WVSA......... Weidingsvereniging van Suidelike Afrika [*Grassland Society of Southern Africa-GISSA*] (EAIO)
WvSaC......... Salem College, Salem, WV [*Library symbol Library of Congress*] (LCLS)
WVSC......... Somerset, PA [*AM radio station call letters*]
WVSC......... West Virginia State College
W-V(S) (CEC)... Women's Reserve, Civil Engineering Corps Duties [*USNR commissioned officer designation*]
WVSC-FM.... Somerset, PA [*FM radio station call letters*]
WvScU......... Union Carbide Corp., South Charleston, WV [*Library symbol Library of Congress*] (LCLS)
WVSD......... Itta Bena, MS [*FM radio station call letters*]
W-V(S) (DC)... Women's Reserve, Dental Corps Duties [*USNR commissioned officer designation*]
WVS Fn....... WVS Financial Corp. [*Associated Press*] (SAG)
WVSH......... Huntington, IN [*FM radio station call letters*]
WvSh......... Shepherdstown Public Library, Shepherdstown, WV [*Library symbol Library of Congress*] (LCLS)
W-V(S) (H)... Women's Reserve, Hospital Corps Duties [*USNR commissioned officer designation*]
WvShS......... Shepherd College, Shepherdstown, WV [*Library symbol Library of Congress*] (LCLS)
WVSM......... Rainsville, AL [*AM radio station call letters*]
W-V(S) (MC)... Women's Reserve, Medical Corps Duties [*USNR commissioned officer designation*]
WVSOM....... West Virginia School of Osteopathic Medicine
WVSR......... Charleston, WV [*AM radio station call letters*]
WVSR-FM.... Charleston, WV [*FM radio station call letters*]
WVSS......... Menomonie, WI [*FM radio station call letters*]
W-V(S) (SC)... Women's Reserve, Supply Corps Duties [*USNR commissioned officer designation*]
WVST......... Petersburg, VA [*FM radio station call letters*]
WVSU......... Birmingham, AL [*FM radio station call letters*]
WVSX-TV..... Lewisburg, WV [*TV station call letters*] (RBYB)
WVSY......... Ruckersville, VA [*FM radio station call letters*]
WVSZ-FM.... Chesterfield, SC [*FM station call letters*] (RBYB)
WVT......... Water Vapor Transmission
WVT......... Watervliet Arsenal [*New York*] [*Army*]
WVT......... West Virginia Institute of Technology, Montgomery, WV [*OCLC symbol*] (OCLC)
WVTA......... Windsor, VT [*Television station call letters*]
WVTB......... St. Johnsbury, VT [*Television station call letters*]
WVTC......... Randolph Center, VT [*FM radio station call letters*]
WVTF......... Roanoke, VA [*FM radio station call letters*]
WVTF......... Western Visayan Task Force [*World War II*]
WVTJ......... Pensacola, FL [*AM radio station call letters*]
WVTM......... Birmingham, AL [*Television station call letters*]
WVTR......... Marion, VA [*FM radio station call letters*]
WVTR......... Water Vapor Transmission Rate
WVTU......... Charlottesville, VA [*FM radio station call letters*]
WVTV......... Milwaukee, WI [*Television station call letters*]
WVTW-FM... Charlottesville, VA [*FM radio station call letters*] (RBYB)
WVTY......... Pittsburgh, PA [*FM radio station call letters*]
wvu......... West Virginia [*MARC country of publication code Library of Congress*] (LCCP)
WVU......... West Virginia University
WVU......... West Virginia University Library, Morgantown, WV [*OCLC symbol*] (OCLC)
WvU......... West Virginia University, Morgantown, WV [*Library symbol Library of Congress*] (LCLS)
WVUA......... Tuscaloosa, AL [*FM radio station call letters*]
WvU-AE....... West Virginia University, Agricultural Engineering Library, Morgantown, WV [*Library symbol Library of Congress*] (LCLS)
WVUB......... Vincennes, IN [*FM radio station call letters*]
WVUC......... Barrackville, WV [*FM radio station call letters*] (RBYB)
WVUD......... Newark, DE [*FM radio station call letters*]
WVUE......... New Orleans, LA [*Television station call letters*]
WvU-J......... West Virginia University, School of Journalism, Morgantown, WV [*Library symbol Library of Congress*] (LCLS)
WvU-L......... West Virginia University, College of Law, Morgantown, WV [*Library symbol Library of Congress*] (LCLS)
WVUM......... Coral Gables, FL [*FM radio station call letters*]
WvU-M......... West Virginia University, Medical Center, Morgantown, WV [*Library symbol Library of Congress*] (LCLS)
WvU-Mu....... West Virginia University, Music Library, Morgantown, WV [*Library symbol Library of Congress*] (LCLS)
WvU-P......... West Virginia University, Physical Sciences Library, Morgantown, WV [*Library symbol Library of Congress*] (LCLS)
WVUR......... Valparaiso, IN [*FM radio station call letters*]
WVUT......... Vincennes, IN [*Television station call letters*]
WVUV......... Leone, AS [*AM radio station call letters*]
WVV......... Volovan [*Malagasy*] [*Airport symbol*] (AD)
WVV......... Whole Virus Vaccine [*Immunology*]
WVVA......... Bluefield, WV [*Television station call letters*]
WVVC......... Utica, NY [*FM radio station call letters*]
WVVE......... Stonington, CT [*FM radio station call letters*]
WVVI......... Manassas, VA [*Television station call letters*]
WVVI......... Willamette Valley Vineyards, Inc. [*NASDAQ symbol*] (SAG)
WVVR......... Hopkinsville, KY [*FM radio station call letters*]
WVVS......... Valdosta, GA [*FM radio station call letters*]
WVVV......... St. Simons Island, GA [*FM radio station call letters*] (RBYB)
WVVW......... St. Marys, WV [*AM radio station call letters*]
WVVX......... Highland Park, IL [*FM radio station call letters*]
WvW......... Ohio County Public Library, Wheeling, WV [*Library symbol Library of Congress*] (LCLS)
WVW......... Westview Resources [*Vancouver Stock Exchange symbol*]
WvWaB......... Borg-Warner Corp., Borg-Warner Chemicals Technical Center, Washington, WV [*Library symbol Library of Congress*] (LCLS)
WVWC......... Buckhannon, WV [*FM radio station call letters*]
WVWC......... West Virginia Wesleyan College
WvWC......... Wheeling College, Wheeling, WV [*Library symbol Library of Congress*] (LCLS)
WvWelW....... West Liberty State College, West Liberty, WV [*Library symbol Library of Congress*] (LCLS)
WvWEPA....... United States Environmental Protection Agency, Wheeling Field Office, Wheeling, WV [*Library symbol Library of Congress*] (LCLS)
WvWH......... Wheeling Hospital, Medical Library, Wheeling, WV [*Library symbol Library of Congress*] (LCLS)
WVWI......... Charlotte Amalie, VI [*AM radio station call letters*]
WvWO......... Oglebay Institute, Wheeling, WV [*Library symbol Library of Congress*] (LCLS)
WVWV......... Huntington, WV [*FM radio station call letters*]
WVXC......... Chillicothe, OH [*FM radio station call letters*]
WVXD......... Chetek, WI [*FM radio station call letters*]
WVXF......... Charlotte Amalie, VI [*Television station call letters*]
WVXG......... Mount Gilead, OH [*FM radio station call letters*]
WVXM......... Manistee, MI [*FM radio station call letters*] (RBYB)
WVXR......... Richmond, IN [*FM radio station call letters*]
WVXU......... Cincinnati, OH [*FM radio station call letters*]
WVXW......... West Union, OH [*FM radio station call letters*] (RBYB)
WVYB......... Patterson, NY [*FM radio station call letters*] (RBYB)
WVYC......... York, PA [*FM radio station call letters*]
WVYH......... North Windham, ME [*FM radio station call letters*]
WVZA......... Herrin, IL [*FM radio station call letters*]
WVZC......... Montauk, NY [*FM radio station call letters*]
WVZD......... Dennysville, ME [*FM radio station call letters*]
WW......... Israel Aircraft Industries Ltd. [*ICAO aircraft manufacturer identifier*] (ICAO)
WW......... Scottish European Airways [*ICAO designator*] (AD)
WW......... Severe Weather Forecast [*National Weather Service*] (FAAC)
WW......... Trans-West [*ICAO designator*] (AD)
WW......... Walking Wounded (ADA)
WW......... Wall-to-Wall [*Carpeting*] [*Classified advertising*]
WW......... Walter Winchell [*American journalist*] (IIA)
WW......... Wardroom Window [*Aerospace*] (KSC)
WW......... Warehouse Warrant
WW......... Warm White (DAC)
WW......... Warrant Writer [*Navy British*]
WW......... Waste Watch [*Defunct*] (EA)
WW......... Waterwall (MSA)
WW......... Water Waste (NASA)
WW......... Water Watch (Program) [*Australia*]
WW......... Water-White

WW............ Waterworks
WW............ Watson Wyatt Worldwide [*Commercial firm*] (ECON)
WW............ Weather Wing (MCD)
WW............ Weather Working
w/w............ Weight of Solute in Weight of Solvent [*Chemistry*] (DAVI)
w/w............ Weight of Solute per Weight of Total Solution [*Chemistry*] (DAVI)
WW............ Weight Watchers [*An association*]
W/W............ Weight/Weight
WW............ Welfare Worker [*British military*] (DMA)
WW............ Well Water [*Nuclear energy*] (NRCH)
WW............ Western Waste Industries [*NYSE symbol*] (SPSG)
WW............ Westwater Industries Ltd. [*Toronto Stock Exchange symbol*]
W/W............ Wheel Well (MCD)
WW............ Whitewall Tire [*Automotive accessory*]
WW............ White Wyandotte [*Poultry*]
WW............ Wholesale Wine [*License*]
WW............ Who's Who [*A publication*]
WW............ Widow [*Genealogy*]
WW............ Wilderness Watch (EA)
W/W............ Wild Weasel [*Aerospace*]
WW............ Winchester & Western Railroad Co. [*AAR code*]
W/W............ Winding to Winding (MSA)
WW............ Wines of Westhorpe [*Commercial firm British*]
WW............ Winged Warriors/National B-Body Owners Association (EA)
WW............ Wire Way [*Technical drawings*]
WW............ Wire Wheel [*Automotive accessory*]
WW............ Wire-Wound
ww............ Wirewound (IDOE)
WW............ Wire Wrap (NASA)
WW............ Wirtschaftswoche-Datenbank [*Economic Week Data Bank*] [*Society for Public Economics*] [*Germany*] [*Information service or system*] (IID)
WW............ Wishing Well [*An association*] (EA)
WW............ With Warrants [*Stock exchange term*] (SPSG)
WW............ With Winch
WW............ Women in the Wind [*An association*] (EA)
WW............ Women to the World [*An association*] (EA)
WW............ Woodwind [*Instrument*] [*Music*]
WW............ Working Women (NTCM)
WW............ Working Women, National Association of Officeworkers (EA)
WW............ World War
WW............ Worldwide
WW............ Worldwide Equities Ltd. [*Toronto Stock Exchange symbol*]
WW............ Wound Width [*Forestry*]
WW............ Writers and Their Work [*British Council*]
WWA.......... Wallcovering Wholesalers Association [*Later, WDA*] (EA)
WWA.......... War Widows Association [*British*] (DBA)
WWa.......... Wauwatosa Public Library, Wauwatosa, WI [*Library symbol Library of Congress*] (LCLS)
WWA.......... Welsh Water Authority (DCTA)
WWA.......... Western Writers of America (EA)
WWA.......... Who's Wealthy in America [*A publication*]
WWA.......... Who's Who in America [*A publication*]
WWA.......... Who's Who in Art [*A publication*]
WWA.......... Who's Who in Australia [*A publication*]
WWA.......... With the Will Annexed
WWA.......... Woolens and Worsteds of America [*Defunct*]
WWA.......... World Warning Agency (MCD)
WWA.......... World Waterpark Association (EA)
WWA.......... World Watusi Association (EA)
WWA.......... World Wide Airlines, Inc.
WWA.......... Worldwide Aviation Services Ltd. [*Venezuela*] [*ICAO designator*] (FAAC)
WWAA........ Westfalen Warmblood Association of America (EA)
WWAA........ Who's Who Among Asian Americans [*A publication*]
WWAB........ Lakeland, FL [*AM radio station call letters*]
WWABCC..... World Wide Avon Bottle Collectors Club (EA)
WWABNCP... Worldwide Airborne Command Post [*Air Force*] (AFM)
WWABNRES... WWMCCS [*Worldwide Military Command and Control System*] Airborne Resources (DOMA)
WWAC........ Atlantic City, NJ [*Television station call letters*]
WWAC........ Walk with Aid of Cane (DAVI)
WWAC........ Western World Avon Club [*Defunct*] (EA)
WWAG........ McKee, KY [*FM radio station call letters*]
WWal.......... Walworth Memorial Library, Walworth, WI [*Library symbol Library of Congress*] (LCLS)
WWalPS...... Walworth Public Schools, Walworth, WI [*Library symbol Library of Congress*] (LCLS)
WWalSD...... North Walworth School District Number Five, Walworth, WI [*Library symbol Library of Congress*] (LCLS)
WWAM........ Jasper, TN [*AM radio station call letters*]
WWaMP...... Milwaukee Psychiatric Hospital, Wauwatosa, WI [*Library symbol Library of Congress*] (LCLS)
WW & D...... Willmore, Wollaston, and Davison's English Queen's Bench Reports [*1837*] [*A publication*] (DLA)
WW & H...... Willmore, Wollaston, and Hodges' English Queen's Bench Reports [*1838-39*] [*A publication*] (DLA)
WW & H (Eng)... Willmore, Wollaston, and Hodges' English Queen's Bench Reports [*1838-39*] [*A publication*] (DLA)
WW & IB..... Western Weighing and Inspection Bureau
WWAP........ Worldwide Asset Position [*Military*] (AABC)
WWAR........ Appomattox, VA [*AM radio station call letters*] (RBYB)
WWAS........ Williamsport, PA [*FM radio station call letters*]
WWAS........ World-Wide Academy of Scholars [*Defunct*] (EA)
WWAS........ World Wide Air Services [*Australia*]
WWaSC....... Saint Camillus Hospital, Wauwatosa, WI [*Library symbol Library of Congress*] (LCLS)
WWat.......... Watertown Free Public Library, Watertown, WI [*Library symbol Library of Congress*] (LCLS)
WWatf......... Waterford Public Library, Waterford, WI [*Library symbol Library of Congress*] (LCLS)
WWatfH....... Holy Redeemer College, Waterford, WI [*Library symbol Library of Congress*] (LCLS)
WWatN........ Northwestern College, Watertown, WI [*Library symbol Library of Congress*] (LCLS)
WWau.......... Waukesha Public Library, Waukesha, WI [*Library symbol Library of Congress*] (LCLS)
WWauC........ Carroll College, Waukesha, WI [*Library symbol Library of Congress*] (LCLS)
WWauH........ Waukesha Memorial Hospital, Waukesha, WI [*Library symbol Library of Congress*] (LCLS)
WWauHi...... Waukesha County Historical Society, Waukesha, WI [*Library symbol Library of Congress*] (LCLS)
WWauI......... Waukesha County Institution, Waukesha, WI [*Library symbol Library of Congress*] (LCLS)
WWaup........ Waupun Public Library, Waupun, WI [*Library symbol*] [*Library of Congress*] (LCLS)
WWaupa...... Waupaca Free Public Library, Waupaca, WI [*Library symbol Library of Congress*] (LCLS)
WWauU........ University of Wisconsin Center-Waukesha County, Waukesha, WI [*Library symbol Library of Congress*] (LCLS)
WWAV......... Santa Rosa Beach, FL [*FM radio station call letters*]
WWAX-FM... Hermantown, MN [*FM radio station call letters*] (RBYB)
WWAY......... Wilmington, NC [*Television station call letters*]
WWB........... Waterways Freight Bureau, Washington DC [*STAC*]
WWb........... West Bend Public Library, West Bend, WI [*Library symbol Library of Congress*] (LCLS)
WWB........... Wet Weight Basis [*Drying*] (DICI)
WWB........... Women's World Banking [*Financial organization*]
WWB........... Writers War Board
WWBA......... Walt Whitman Birthplace Association (EA)
WWBA......... Western Wooden Box Association (EA)
WWBA......... Who's Who among Black Americans [*A publication*]
WWBB......... Providence, RI [*FM radio station call letters*]
WWBB......... Wire-Wrapped Breadboard
WWBC......... Cocoa, FL [*AM radio station call letters*]
WWBD......... Bamberg, SC [*FM radio station call letters*]
WWBE......... Mifflinburg, PA [*FM radio station call letters*]
WWBF......... Bartow, FL [*AM radio station call letters*]
WWBF......... Woodrow Wilson Birthplace Foundation (EA)
WWBG......... Greensboro, NC [*AM radio station call letters*]
WWBH......... New Smyrna Beach, FL [*AM radio station call letters*]
WWBK......... Fredericktown, OH [*FM radio station call letters*]
WWBL......... Washington, IN [*FM radio station call letters*]
WWBN......... Tuscola, MI [*FM radio station call letters*]
WWBPU....... World Wide Baraca-Philathea Union (EA)
WWBR......... Trussville, AL [*FM radio station call letters*]
WWBT......... Richmond, VA [*Television station call letters*]
WWbU......... University of Wisconsin Center-Washington County, West Bend, WI [*Library symbol Library of Congress*] (LCLS)
WWBV......... Beaver Springs, PA [*FM radio station call letters*]
WWBX......... Bangor, ME [*FM radio station call letters*] (RBYB)
WWBZ......... McClellanville, SC [*FM radio station call letters*] (RBYB)
WWC........... Citizen's Library, Washington, PA [*OCLC symbol*] (OCLC)
WWC........... Walla Walla College [*Washington*]
WWC........... Warren Wilson College [*Swannan, NC*]
WWC........... Wastewater Coalition [*Environmental science*]
WWC........... Wavy Walled Cylinder
WWC........... Who's Who in Consulting [*A publication*]
WWC........... Wilkerson/Wilkinson Clearinghouse (EA)
WWC........... William Woods College [*Fulton, MO*]
WWC........... World's Wristwrestling Championship (EA)
WWC........... Worldways Canada Ltd. [*ICAO designator*] (FAAC)
WWC........... World Wide Company (MHDW)
WWC........... Woven Wire Cloth
WWCA......... Gary, IN [*AM radio station call letters*]
WWCA......... Western Wireless'A' [*NASDAQ symbol*] (TTSB)
WWCA......... Western Wireless Corp. [*NASDAQ symbol*] (SAG)
WWCA......... Women's Welsh Clubs of America (EA)
WWCB......... Corry, PA [*AM radio station call letters*]
WWCC......... Honesdale, PA [*AM radio station call letters*]
WWCC......... Western Wisconsin Communications Cooperative [*Independence, WI*] [*Telecommunications*] (TSSD)
WWCCIS...... World-Wide Command and Control Information System (MCD)
WWCD......... Grove City, OH [*FM radio station call letters*]
WWCH......... Clarion, PA [*AM radio station call letters*]
WWCICS...... Wolfe-Winrow CICS/VS Command Level Proficiency Test [*Computer science*]
WWCK......... Flint, MI [*AM radio station call letters*]
WWCK-FM... Flint, MI [*FM radio station call letters*]
WWCL......... Lehigh Acres, FL [*AM radio station call letters*]
WWCM......... Ypsilanti, MI [*AM radio station call letters*]
WWCN......... North Fort Myers, FL [*AM radio station call letters*]
WWCO......... Waterbury, CT [*AM radio station call letters*]
WWCP......... Clifton Park, NY [*FM radio station call letters*]
WWCP......... Johnstown, PA [*Television station call letters*]
WWCP......... Walking Wounded Collecting Post [*Military*]
WWCS......... Canonsburg, PA [*AM radio station call letters*]
WWCT......... Peoria, IL [*FM radio station call letters*]

WWCT Regt... Wellington, West Coast, and Taranaki Regiment [*British military*] (DMA)
WWCTU........ World's Woman's Christian Temperance Union [*Australia*] (EAIO)
WWCU......... Cullowhee, NC [*FM radio station call letters*]
WWCW......... Bedford, PA [*FM radio station call letters*]
WWD........... Cape May [*New Jersey*] [*Airport symbol*] (OAG)
WWd........... Kilbourn Public Library, Wisconsin Dells, WI [*Library symbol Library of Congress*] (LCLS)
WWD........... Weather Working Days [*Construction*]
WWD........... Wildwood, NJ [*Location identifier FAA*] (FAAL)
WWD........... Windward (KSC)
WWD........... Women's Wear Daily [*A publication*] (WDMC)
WWDB......... Philadelphia, PA [*FM radio station call letters*]
WWDC......... Washington, DC [*AM radio station call letters*]
WWDCFC..... World-Wide Dave Clark Fan Club [*Defunct*] (EAIO)
WWDC-FM... Washington, DC [*FM radio station call letters*]
WWDE......... Hampton, VA [*FM radio station call letters*]
WWdepSN.... Saint Norbert College, West De Pere, WI [*Library symbol Library of Congress*] (LCLS)
WWDF......... Richland, MS [*AM radio station call letters*] (RBYB)
wwdFHEx..... Weather Working Days, Fridays, and Holidays Excluded [*Shipping*] (DS)
WWDJ......... Hackensack, NJ [*AM radio station call letters*]
WWDL......... Scranton, PA [*FM radio station call letters*]
WWDM........ Sumter, SC [*FM radio station call letters*]
WWDMS....... Worldwide Data Management System
WWDMS....... Worldwide Standard Data Management System (MCD)
W Wdr......... Warrant Wardmaster [*British military*] (DMA)
WWDS......... Muncie, IN [*FM radio station call letters*]
WWDSA........ Worldwide Digital System Architecture
WWDSHEX... Weather Working Days, Sundays, and Holidays Excluded (DS)
WWDX......... St. Johns, MI [*FM radio station call letters*]
WWDZ......... Danville, IL [*FM radio station call letters*]
WWE........... Wide World of Entertainment [*TV program*]
WWE........... Worldwide Energy Corp. [*Toronto Stock Exchange symbol*] (SPSG)
WWea.......... West Allis Public Library, West Allis, WI [*Library symbol Library of Congress*] (LCLS)
WWeaJ........ Janlen Enterprises, West Allis, WI [*Library symbol Library of Congress*] (LCLS)
WWeaM....... West Allis Memorial Hospital, West Allis, WI [*Library symbol Library of Congress*] (LCLS)
WwE & Sp... Worldwide Entertainment & Sports Cp. [*Associated Press*] (SAG)
WwE & S un... Worldwide Entertainment & Sports Cp. [*Associated Press*] (SAG)
WWEB......... Wallingford, CT [*FM radio station call letters*]
WWEC......... Elizabethtown, PA [*FM radio station call letters*]
WWEE......... Spencer, TN [*FM radio station call letters*]
WWEF......... Working Women Education Fund (EA)
WWEG......... Mitchell, IN [*FM radio station call letters*]
WWEL......... London, KY [*FM radio station call letters*]
WWEMA...... Water and Wastewater Equipment Manufacturers Association (EA)
WWES......... Worldwide Entertainment & Sports Cp. [*NASDAQ symbol*] (SAG)
WWET......... Valdosta, GA [*FM radio station call letters*]
WWEV......... Cumming, GA [*FM radio station call letters*]
WWEZ......... Trenton, TN [*FM radio station call letters*]
WWF........... War/Watch Foundation (EA)
WWF........... Washington Workshops Foundation (EA)
WWF........... Welded Wire Fabric [*Technical drawings*]
WWF........... Whole Wheat Flour (OA)
WWF........... Widowed White Female [*Classified advertising*]
WWF........... Wire Wrap Fixture
WWF........... Wonder Woman Foundation [*Defunct*] (EA)
WWF........... WorldWide Fund for Nature (EA)
WWF........... World Wildlife Fund (EA)
WWFA......... Waterside Workers' Federation of Australia
WWFA......... World Wide Fund for Nature [*Australia*] (EERA)
WWFC......... Westwood Financial Corp. [*NASDAQ symbol*] (SAG)
WWFC......... Worldwide Fair Play for Frogs Committee
WWFD......... Key West, FL [*Television station call letters*]
WWFE......... Miami, FL [*AM radio station call letters*]
WWFG......... Ocean City, MD [*FM radio station call letters*]
WWFH-FM... Freeland, PA [*FM radio station call letters*] (RBYB)
WWFI.......... World Wildlife Fund International [*Later, Worldwide Fund for Nature*] (EAIO)
WWFM......... Trenton, NJ [*FM radio station call letters*]
WWFN......... Lake City, SC [*FM radio station call letters*]
WWFN......... World Wide Fund for Nature [*Australia*]
WWFNA....... World Wide Fund for Nature Australia
WWFO......... Lafayette, FL [*FM radio station call letters*] (RBYB)
WWFR......... Okeechobee, FL [*FM radio station call letters*]
WWFS......... West Wales Field Society [*British*]
WWF-US...... World Wildlife Fund - United States (EA)
WWFX......... Belfast, ME [*FM radio station call letters*]
WWG........... HSIA [*Halogenated Solvent Industry Alliance*] Water Work Group [*Defunct*] (EA)
WWG........... Warhead Working Group [*Military*]
WWG........... Warrington Wire Gauge (BARN)
WWg........... Weather Wing [*Air Force*] (AFM)
WWG........... Wiederwerbgesetz (BJA)
WWGA......... Georgiana, AL [*FM radio station call letters*]
WWGA......... War Widows Guild of Australia
WWGC......... Carrollton, GA [*FM radio station call letters*]
WWGL......... Lexington, NC [*FM radio station call letters*]
WWGM........ Alamo, TN [*FM radio station call letters*]
WWGN......... Ottawa, IL [*FM radio station call letters*]
WWGO-FM... Neoga, IL [*FM radio station call letters*] (RBYB)
WWGP......... Sanford, NC [*AM radio station call letters*]
WWGR......... Fort Myers, FL [*FM radio station call letters*]
WWGR......... Weil's Wyoming Government Register [*A publication*] (AAGC)
WWGS......... Tifton, GA [*AM radio station call letters*]
WWGT......... Vergennes, VT [*FM radio station call letters*]
WWGZ......... Lapeer, MI [*FM radio station call letters*]
W/WH......... With/Warhead [*Nuclear*]
WWH........... Women Working Home [*A publication*]
WWH........... W. W. Harrington's Reports [*31-39 Delaware*] [*A publication*] (DLA)
WWHA......... Welsh Women's Hockey Association (DBA)
WWHA......... Who's Who among Hispanic Americans [*A publication*]
WWHB......... Hampton Bays, NY [*FM radio station call letters*]
WWHC......... Oakland, MD [*FM radio station call letters*] (RBYB)
WWHE......... Woman Who Has Everything
WWHI.......... Muncie, IN [*FM radio station call letters*]
WWhiwSD... Whitewater Unified School District, Joint Number One, Whitewater, WI [*Library symbol Library of Congress*] (LCLS)
WWhiwU...... University of Wisconsin-Whitewater, Whitewater, WI [*Library symbol Library of Congress*] (LCLS)
WWHK......... Greenville, KY [*FM radio station call letters*]
WWHL......... Waterwheel
WWHN......... Joliet, IL [*AM radio station call letters*]
WWHO......... Chillicothe, OH [*Television station call letters*]
WWHP-FM... Farmer City, IL [*FM radio station call letters*] (RBYB)
WWHR......... Bowling Green, KY [*FM radio station call letters*]
WWHRAWAC... World Wide Horse Registry for the American White and the American Creme (EA)
WWHS......... Hampden-Sydney, VA [*FM radio station call letters*]
WWHS......... Western World Haiku Society [*Defunct*] (EA)
WWHT-FM... Syracuse, NY [*FM radio station call letters*] (RBYB)
WWI............ Weight Watchers International [*Commercial firm*] (EA)
WWI............ Whirlwind I
WWI............ Working Women's Institute [*Defunct*] (EA)
WWI............ World War I
WWI............ World Watch Institute (EERA)
WWIA......... Palm Bay, FL [*FM radio station call letters*]
WWI AERO... World War I Aeroplanes (EA)
WWIB......... Ladysmith, WI [*FM radio station call letters*]
WWIC......... Scottsboro, AL [*AM radio station call letters*]
WWiC......... Winnebago County Hospital, Winnebago, WI [*Library symbol Library of Congress*] (LCLS)
WWICS....... Woodrow Wilson International Center for Scholars (EA)
WWID......... Water & Wastewater Division (ACII)
WWIH......... High Point, NC [*FM radio station call letters*]
WWII.......... Shiremanstown, PA [*AM radio station call letters*]
WWII.......... Whirlwind II (SAA)
WWII.......... World War II
WWIIHSLB... World War II Honorable Service Lapel Button (AFM)
WWIII......... World War III
WWIIVM...... World War II Victory Medal [*Military decoration*]
WWil.......... Barrett Memorial Library, Williams Bay, WI [*Library symbol Library of Congress*] (LCLS)
WWIL.......... Wilmington, NC [*AM radio station call letters*]
WWIL-FM... Wilmington, NC [*FM radio station call letters*] (RBYB)
WWIMS....... Worldwide Indicators and Monitoring System (DOMA)
WWIMS....... Worldwide Integrated Management of Subsistence [*Military*] (NVT)
WWIN......... Baltimore, MD [*AM radio station call letters*]
WWIN......... Glen Burnie, MD [*FM radio station call letters*]
WWIO......... Brunswick, GA [*FM radio station call letters*]
WWIO......... Worldwide Inventory Objective (AABC)
WWiP......... Park View Health Center, Winnebago, WI [*Library symbol Library of Congress*] (LCLS)
WWIP......... Wabash, IN [*FM radio station call letters*]
WWIQ......... Gray, GA [*FM radio station call letters*]
WWIS......... Black River Falls, WI [*AM radio station call letters*]
WWiS......... Winnebago State Hospital, Winnebago, WI [*Library symbol Library of Congress*] (LCLS)
WWIS......... Worldwide Information Services
WWIS-FM.... Black River Falls, WI [*FM radio station call letters*]
WWIT......... Canton, NC [*AM radio station call letters*]
WWIT......... Who's Who in the Theatre [*A publication*]
WWITC....... Worldwide Improved Technical Control (MCD)
WWIVM....... World War I Victory Medal [*Military decoration*]
WWIZ......... Mercer, PA [*FM radio station call letters*]
WWJ........... Detroit, MI [*AM radio station call letters*]
WWJB......... Brooksville, FL [*AM radio station call letters*]
WWJC......... Duluth, MN [*AM radio station call letters*]
WWJCC....... Worldwide Joint Coordinator Center [*NATO*] (NATG)
WWJM......... New Lexington, OH [*FM radio station call letters*]
WWJO......... St. Cloud, MN [*FM radio station call letters*]
WWJQ......... Zeeland, MI [*AM radio station call letters*]
WWJR......... Sheboygan, WI [*FM radio station call letters*]
WWJ-TV...... Detroit, MI [*Television station call letters*] (RBYB)
WWJY......... Crown Point, IN [*FM radio station call letters*]
WWJZ......... Mount Holly, NJ [*AM radio station call letters*]
wwk........... Westwork (VRA)
WWK........... Wewak [*Papua New Guinea*] [*Airport symbol*] (OAG)
WWKA......... Orlando, FL [*FM radio station call letters*]
WWKB......... Buffalo, NY [*AM radio station call letters*]
WWKC......... Caldwell, OH [*FM radio station call letters*]
WWKC......... White Wolf-Kern Canyon [*Geological fault*]
WWKF......... Fulton, KY [*FM radio station call letters*]
WWKI.......... Kokomo, IN [*FM radio station call letters*]
WWKJ-FM... Mashpee, MA [*FM radio station call letters*] (RBYB)
WWKL......... Harrisburg, PA [*FM radio station call letters*]

WWKN-AM... Battle Creek, MI [*AM radio station call letters*] (RBYB)
WWKQ......... Kissimmee, FL [*FM radio station call letters*] (RBYB)
WWKS-FM... Cruz Bay, VI [*FM radio station call letters*] (RBYB)
WWKT......... Kingstree, SC [*FM radio station call letters*]
WWKX......... Woonsocket, RI [*FM radio station call letters*]
WWKY......... Louisville, KY [*AM radio station call letters*]
WWKZ......... New Albany, MS [*FM radio station call letters*]
WWL........... New Orleans, LA [*AM radio station call letters*]
WWL2M....... Women Who Love Too Much [*Title of book by Robin Norwood*]
WWLA......... Lewiston, ME [*Television station call letters*]
WWLC-FM... Balsam Lake, WI [*FM radio station call letters*] (RBYB)
WWLD-FM... Tallahassee, FL [*FM radio station call letters*] (RBYB)
WWLF......... Copenhagen, NY [*FM radio station call letters*]
WWLF......... Hazleton, PA [*Television station call letters*]
WWLG......... Baltimore, MD [*AM radio station call letters*]
WWLI.......... Providence, RI [*FM radio station call letters*]
WWLI.......... Whitewing Labs [*NASDAQ symbol*] (TTSB)
WWLI.......... Whitewing Labs, Inc. [*NASDAQ symbol*] (SAG)
WWLIS........ Woodmen of the World Life Insurance Society (EA)
WWLIW....... Whitewing Labs Wrrt [*NASDAQ symbol*] (TTSB)
WWLK......... Eddyville, KY [*AM radio station call letters*]
WWLO......... Gainesville, FL [*AM radio station call letters*]
WWLODS..... Wire and Wire-Like Object Detection System [*Helicopter*] (MCD)
WWLP......... Springfield, MA [*Television station call letters*]
WWLR......... Lyndonville, VT [*FM radio station call letters*]
WWLS......... Moore, OK [*AM radio station call letters*]
WWLT......... Manchester, KY [*FM radio station call letters*]
WWLTM....... Women Who Love Too Much [*Title of book by Robin Norwood*]
WWL-TV...... New Orleans, LA [*Television station call letters*]
WWLX......... Lawrenceburg, TN [*AM radio station call letters*]
WWM.......... Weizsaecker-Williams Method [*Physics*]
WWM.......... Welded Wire Matrix
WWM.......... Widowed White Male [*Classified advertising*]
WWM.......... Wire Wrap Machine
WWM.......... World-Wide Missions (EA)
WWM.......... Worldwide Monitor [*Vancouver Stock Exchange symbol*]
WWMB........ Florence, SC [*FM radio station call letters*]
WWMC........ Lynchburg, VA [*FM radio station call letters*]
WWMCCS.... Worldwide Military Command and Communications System [*Pronounced "wimex"*]
WWMCCS.... Worldwide Military Command and Control System [*DoD*]
WWMD........ Hagerstown, MD [*FM radio station call letters*]
WWME......... Worldwide Marriage Encounter (EA)
WWMG........ Shelby, NC [*FM radio station call letters*]
WWMJ......... Ellsworth, ME [*FM radio station call letters*]
WWML......... Wood, Wire, and Metal Lathers' International Union [*Later, UBC*] (EA)
WWMMP..... Western Wood Moulding and Millwork Producers [*Later, WMMPA*] (EA)
WWMMRD... Water and Waste Management Monitoring Research Division [*Environmental Protection Agency*] (EPA)
WWMO........ Eden, NC [*AM radio station call letters*]
WWMP........ Western Wood Moulding Producers [*Later, WMMPA*] (EA)
WWMR........ Rumford, ME [*FM radio station call letters*]
WWMS........ Oxford, MS [*FM radio station call letters*]
WWMS........ Water and Waste Management Staff [*Environmental Protection Agency*] (GFGA)
WWMS........ Water and Waste Management Subsystem [*NASA*] (KSC)
WWMT........ Kalamazoo, MI [*Television station call letters*]
WWMV........ Winter Wheat (Russian) Mosaic Virus [*Plant pathology*]
WWMX........ Baltimore, MD [*FM radio station call letters*]
WWN........... Washington Women's Network [*Defunct*] (EA)
WWN........... With Winch
WWNC......... Asheville, NC [*AM radio station call letters*]
WWNFF....... Woodrow Wilson National Fellowship Foundation (EA)
WWNH......... Madbury, NH [*AM radio station call letters*]
WWNH......... War Will Never Happen [*Philosophy attributed to the Defense Department by former Deputy Assistant Secretary of Defense John F. Ahearne*] [*1987*]
WWNJ......... Dover Township, NJ [*FM radio station call letters*]
WWNK......... Cincinnati, OH [*FM radio station call letters*]
WWNN......... Pompano Beach, FL [*AM radio station call letters*]
WWNO......... New Orleans, LA [*FM radio station call letters*]
WWNR......... Beckley, WV [*AM radio station call letters*]
WWNS......... Statesboro, GA [*AM radio station call letters*]
WWNS......... World Wide News Service (BJA)
WWNSS....... Worldwide Network of Standard Seismograph [*Stations*]
WWNSS....... Worldwide Network of Standard Seismograph Stations (PDAA)
WWNT......... Dothan, AL [*AM radio station call letters*]
WWNW........ New Wilmington, PA [*FM radio station call letters*]
WWNWS...... World-Wide Navigational Warning Service [*Marine science*] (OSRA)
WWNWS...... World Wide Navigational Weather Warning Service
WWNY......... Carthage, NY [*Television station call letters*]
WWNZ......... Orlando, FL [*AM radio station call letters*]
WWO........... Warrant Writer Officer [*British military*] (DMA)
WW/O......... Widow Of [*Genealogy*]
WWO........... Wing Warrant Officer [*RAF*] [*British*]
WWOD......... Lynchburg, VA [*AM radio station call letters*]
WWOF......... Camp Lejeune, NC [*AM radio station call letters*]
WWOF......... Willing Workers for Organic Farms [*Australia*]
WWOG......... Cookeville, TN [*FM radio station call letters*]
WWOJ......... Avon Park, FL [*FM radio station call letters*]
WWOL......... Forest City, NC [*AM radio station call letters*]
WWON......... Fenton, MI [*AM radio station call letters*]
WWOOF....... Working Weekends on Organic Farms [*British*] [*An association*] (DBA)
WWooH....... Howard Young Medical Center, Woodruff, WI [*Library symbol Library of Congress*] (LCLS)
WWOR......... Secaucus, NJ [*Television station call letters*]
WWoVA....... United States Veterans Administration Hospital, Wood, WI [*Library symbol Library of Congress*] (LCLS)
WWOW......... Conneaut, OH [*AM radio station call letters*]
WWOZ......... New Orleans, LA [*FM radio station call letters*]
WWP........... Walden Woods Project [*An association*] (EA)
WWP........... Washington Water Power Co. [*NYSE symbol*] (SPSG)
WWP........... Washington Water Pwr [*NYSE symbol*] (TTSB)
WWP........... Watchable Wildlife Program
WWP........... Water Wall (Peripheral Jet) (AAG)
WWP........... Weather Wing Pamphlet [*Air Force*] (MCD)
WWP........... Wire Wrap Panels (MCD)
WWP........... Workers World Party [*Political party*] (EA)
WWP........... Working Water Pressure
WWP........... World Weather Program [*National Science Foundation*]
WWPA......... Western Wood Products Association [*Australia*]
WWPA......... Williamsport, PA [*AM radio station call letters*]
WWPA......... Woven Wire Products Association (EA)
WWPB......... Hagerstown, MD [*Television station call letters*]
WWPB......... Worldwide Women Professional Bowlers (EA)
WWpC......... Central State Hospital, Waupun, WI [*Library symbol Library of Congress*] (LCLS)
WWPG......... Tuscaloosa, AL [*AM radio station call letters*]
WWPG......... Widows' War Pensions and Gratuities [*British*]
WWPH......... Princeton Junction, NJ [*FM radio station call letters*]
WWPLS....... World Wide Pet Lovers Society [*Defunct*] (EA)
WWPMU...... World-Wide Prayer and Missionary Union (EA)
WWPN......... Westernport, MD [*FM radio station call letters*]
WWPR......... Bradenton, FL [*AM radio station call letters*] (RBYB)
W/WPR........ Windshield Wiper [*Automotive engineering*]
WWPSA....... Western World Pet Supply Association (EA)
WWPT......... Westport, CT [*FM radio station call letters*]
WWPT......... Wet-Weather Parka and Trousers [*Army*] (INF)
WWPV......... Colchester, VT [*FM radio station call letters*]
WWQM........ Middleton, WI [*FM radio station call letters*]
WWQQ........ Wilmington, NC [*FM radio station call letters*]
WWr........... McMillan Memorial Library, Wisconsin Rapids, WI [*Library symbol Library of Congress*] (LCLS)
WWR........... Washington Weekly Report [*Independent Bankers Association of America*] [*A publication*]
WWR........... Washington Western [*AAR code*]
W/wr.......... Watts per Steradian (IDOE)
WWR........... Western Warner Oils [*Vancouver Stock Exchange symbol*]
WWR........... Western Weekly Reports [*Carswell Co. Ltd.*] [*Canada Information service or system*] (CRD)
WWR........... Widower [*Genealogy*]
WWR........... Wire-Wound Resistor
WWR........... Wisconsin Rapids, McMillan Library, Wisconsin Rapids, WI [*OCLC symbol*] (OCLC)
WWR........... Woodill Wildfire Registry (EA)
WWR........... Woodward, OK [*Location identifier FAA*] (FAAL)
WWRC......... Washington, DC [*AM radio station call letters*]
WWRC......... Wyoming Water Research Center [*University of Wyoming*] [*Research center*] (RCD)
WWRD......... Brunswick, GA [*FM radio station call letters*] (RBYB)
WWREC....... Western Washington Research and Extension Center [*Washington State University*] [*Research center*] (RCD)
WWRF......... Who's Who Resource File [*Minority Business Development Agency*] [*Database*]
WW/RGS...... Wind Shear Warning / Recovery Guidance System (DA)
WWRI.......... Worldwide Mobile Communications Routing Index (DNAB)
WWRK......... Elberton, GA [*AM radio station call letters*]
WWRK-FM... Elberton, GA [*FM radio station call letters*]
WWRL......... New York, NY [*AM radio station call letters*]
WWRM........ Tampa, FL [*FM radio station call letters*]
WWR (NS)... Western Weekly Reports, New Series [*Canada*] [*A publication*] (DLA)
WWRO......... Pensacola, FL [*FM radio station call letters*]
WWRQ......... Valdosta, GA [*FM radio station call letters*]
WWRR-FM... Brunswick, GA [*FM radio station call letters*] (RBYB)
WWRS......... Mayville, WI [*Television station call letters*]
WWRS......... Wash-Water Recovery System [*in a spacecraft*] [*NASA*]
WWRT......... Scotland Neck, NC [*FM radio station call letters*]
WWRV......... New York, NY [*AM radio station call letters*]
WWRX......... Westerly, RI [*FM radio station call letters*]
WWRZ-FM... Arcadia, FL [*FM radio station call letters*] (RBYB)
WWS........... Walker Wingsail Systems [*Shipbuilding*] [*British*]
WWS........... Wasawings AB [*Finland ICAO designator*] (FAAC)
WWS........... Water and Waste Subsystem [*Aerospace*] (MCD)
WWS........... Water Wall (Side Skegs) (AAG)
WWs........... Wausau Public Library, Wausau, WI [*Library symbol Library of Congress*] (LCLS)
WW(S)......... Well Water (System) [*Nuclear energy*] (NRCH)
WWS........... Wild Weasel Squadron [*Air Force*]
WWS........... Wind and Watermill Section [*of the Society for the Protection of Ancient Buildings*] (EA)
WWS........... Woman's Workshop [*Defunct*] (EA)
WWS........... Women's Welfare Service [*Defunct*] (EA)
WWS........... Working with Shortages (MCD)
WWS........... World Weather System
WWS........... World Wide Minerals Ltd. [*Toronto Stock Exchange symbol Vancouver Stock Exchange symbol*]

WWSA .... Walt Whitman Society of America [*Defunct*] (EA)
WWSA .... Who's Who in Saudi Arabia [*A publication*]
WWSA .... Women's War Service Auxiliary [*British military*] (DMA)
WWSB .... Sarasota, FL [*Television station call letters*]
WWSC .... Glens Falls, NY [*AM radio station call letters*]
WWSD .... Quincy, FL [*AM radio station call letters*]
WWSD .... Women's War Savings Division
WWSE .... Jamestown, NY [*FM radio station call letters*]
WWSF .... Andalusia, AL [*FM radio station call letters*] (RBYB)
WWSF .... World-Wide Stroke Foundation (EA)
WWSG .... Sylvester, GA [*FM radio station call letters*]
WWSH .... Pittston, PA [*FM radio station call letters*]
WWSJ .... St. Johns, MI [*AM radio station call letters*]
WWSK .... Mullins, SC [*FM radio station call letters*] (RBYB)
WWSL .... Philadelphia, MS [*FM radio station call letters*]
WWSM .... Annville-Cleona, PA [*AM radio station call letters*]
WWSMA ...... Wood Wool Slab Manufacturers Association [*British*] (DBA)
WWsMC .... Marathon Health Care Center, Wausau, WI [*Library symbol Library of Congress*] (LCLS)
WWSN .... Charlotte, NC [*FM radio station call letters*] (RBYB)
WWSN .... Worldwide Seismology Net [*National Bureau of Standards*]
WWSP .... Stevens Point, WI [*FM radio station call letters*]
WWSP .... Winter Weddell Sea Project [*Marine science*] (OSRA)
WWSP .... Worldwide Surveillance Program [*Military*] (NG)
WWSR .... St. Albans, VT [*AM radio station call letters*]
WWSRA .... Western Winter Sports Representatives Association (EA)
WWSSB .... World-Wide Software Support Branch (MCD)
WWSSN .... Worldwide Standardized Seismograph Network [*US Geological Survey*]
WWSSN .... World-Wide Standard Seismograph Network [*Earthquake detection*]
WWST .... Kams, TN [*FM radio station call letters*]
WWSU .... Dayton, OH [*FM radio station call letters*]
WWSU .... World Water Ski Union [*See also UMSN*] [*Montreux, Switzerland*] (EAIO)
WWSVA .... Worldwide Secure Voice Architecture (MCD)
WWSVCS ..... World-Wide Secure Voice Communications System (MCD)
WWSVCS ..... World-Wide Secure Voice Conference System (MCD)
WWSW .... Pittsburgh, PA [*AM radio station call letters*]
WWsW .... Wausau Hospitals, Inc., Wausau, WI [*Library symbol Library of Congress*] (LCLS)
WWSW-FM ... Pittsburgh, PA [*FM radio station call letters*]
WWsWV .... Wisconsin Valley Library Service, Wausau, WI [*Library symbol Library of Congress*] (LCLS)
WWSY-FM ... Sharpsville, PA [*FM radio station call letters*] (RBYB)
WWT .... Newtok [*Alaska*] [*Airport symbol*] (OAG)
WWT .... Newtok, AK [*Location identifier FAA*] (FAAL)
WWT .... Who's Who in Technology [*A publication*]
WWTA .... Marion, MA [*FM radio station call letters*]
WWTA .... Woollen and Worsted Trades Association [*British*] (BI)
WWTC .... Minneapolis, MN [*AM radio station call letters*]
WWTCA .... World War Tank Corps Association (EA)
WWTCIP ...... Worldwide Technical Control Improvement Program (MCD)
WWTE .... Lincoln, IL [*FM radio station call letters*]
WWTF .... Wastewater Treatment Facility
WWTI .... Watertown, NY [*Television station call letters*]
WWTK .... Lake Placid, FL [*AM radio station call letters*]
WWTK .... Weitek Corp. [*NASDAQ symbol*] (CTT)
WWTL .... Walkersville, MD [*AM radio station call letters*]
WWTM .... Worcester, MA [*AM radio station call letters*]
WWTN .... Manchester, TN [*FM radio station call letters*]
WWTO .... La Salle, IL [*Television station call letters*]
WWTP .... Waste Water Treatment Plant [*Also, WTP*]
WWTR .... Western Water [*NASDAQ symbol*] (TTSB)
WWTR .... Western Water Co. [*NASDAQ symbol*] (SAG)
WWTS .... Waste Water Treatment System
WWTT .... Worldwide Tapetalk [*An association*] (EA)
WWTV .... Cadillac, MI [*Television station call letters*]
WWU .... Water/Wastewater Utilities [*Environmental science*]
WWU .... Western Washington University
WWUC .... Union City, TN [*FM radio station call letters*]
WWUF .... Waycross, GA [*FM radio station call letters*]
WWUH .... West Hartford, CT [*FM radio station call letters*]
WWUI .... Working Women's United Institute [*Later, WWI*] (EA)
WWUN .... Clarksdale, MS [*FM radio station call letters*]
WWUP .... Sault Ste. Marie, MI [*Television station call letters*]
WWUS .... Big Pine Key, FL [*FM radio station call letters*]
WWV .... Walla Walla Valley Railway Co. [*AAR code*]
WWV .... Wheeling College, Wheeling, WV [*OCLC symbol*] (OCLC)
WWV .... World Wide Time [*National Bureau of Standards call letters*] (MUGU)
WWV .... World Wide Vermiculture [*An association*] (EA)
WWVA .... Wheeling, WV [*AM radio station call letters*]
WWVH .... World Wide Time Hawaii [*National Bureau of Standards call letters*] (MUGU)
WWVR .... West Terre Haute, IN [*FM radio station call letters*]
WWVR .... Wire-Wound Variable Resistor
WWVU .... Morgantown, WV [*FM radio station call letters*]
WWVZ-FM ... Braddock Heights, MD [*FM radio station call letters*] (RBYB)
WWW .... Who Was Who [*A publication*]
WWW .... [*The*] Who, What, or Where Game [*Also, 3W's*] [*Television show*]
WWW .... Wide Whitewall Tire [*Automotive accessory*]
WWW .... Wolverine World Wide [*NYSE symbol*] (TTSB)
WWW .... Wolverine World Wide, Inc. [*NYSE symbol*] (SPSG)
WWW .... World Weather Watch [*World Meteorological Organization*] [*Databank*] (IID)
WWW .... World Wide Wait [*Computer science*]
WWW .... Worldwide Warranty [*Canon USA, Inc.*]
WWW .... World-Wide Web [*Telecommunications*] (PCM)
WWW .... World Wide Web [*Software*] [*Computer science*] (EERA)
WWWB .... Greensboro, NC [*AM radio station call letters*]
WWWC .... Wilkesboro, NC [*AM radio station call letters*]
WWWC .... World without War Council (EA)
WWWCR ...... World Wide White and Creme Horse Registry (EA)
WWWE .... Cleveland, OH [*AM radio station call letters*]
WWWF .... Worldwide Wrestling Federation [*Later, WWF*]
WWWG .... Rochester, NY [*AM radio station call letters*]
WWWI .... Baxter, MN [*AM radio station call letters*]
WWWI .... Widows of World War I (EA)
WWWJ .... Who's Who in World Jewry [*A publication*] (BJA)
WWWK .... Ellenville, NY [*FM radio station call letters*]
WWWM .... Sylvania, OH [*FM radio station call letters*]
WWWN .... Vienna, GA [*AM radio station call letters*]
WWWO .... Hartford City, IN [*FM radio station call letters*]
WWWQ .... Glasgow, KY [*FM radio station call letters*]
WWWR .... Roanoke, VA [*AM radio station call letters*]
WWWS .... Buffalo, NY [*AM radio station call letters*]
WWWT .... Randolph, VT [*AM radio station call letters*]
WWWTTUTWTU... We Won't Write to Them until They Write to Us [*A servicemen's club*]
WWWV .... Charlottesville, VA [*FM radio station call letters*]
WWWV .... Women World War Veterans (EA)
WWWW .... Detroit, MI [*FM radio station call letters*]
WWWW .... Who's Who in the World of Women [*Australia A publication*]
WWWW .... Women Who Want to be Women [*An association*] (NTCM)
WWWY .... Columbus, IN [*FM radio station call letters*]
WWWZ .... Summerville, SC [*FM radio station call letters*]
WWX .... Warm White Deluxe (DAC)
WWX .... World Wide Exchange [*Commercial firm*] (EA)
WWXL .... Manchester, KY [*AM radio station call letters*]
WWXM .... Georgetown, SC [*FM radio station call letters*]
WWXQ .... Trinity, AL [*FM radio station call letters*] (RBYB)
WWY .... Warwickshire and Worcestershire Yeomanry [*British military*] (DMA)
WWY .... West Wyalong [*Australia Airport symbol*] (OAG)
WWY .... Wrigley [*Wm.*] Jr. Co. [*NYSE symbol*] (SPSG)
WWY .... Wrigley,(Wm) Jr [*NYSE symbol*] (TTSB)
WWYC .... Winchester, KY [*FM radio station call letters*]
WWYN .... McKenzie, TN [*FM radio station call letters*]
WWYO .... Pineville, WV [*AM radio station call letters*]
WWYZ .... Waterbury, CT [*FM radio station call letters*]
WWZ .... Willow Resources Ltd. [*Vancouver Stock Exchange symbol*]
WWZD .... New Albany, MS [*FM radio station call letters*]
WWZN .... Pine Hills, FL [*AM radio station call letters*] (RBYB)
WWZQ .... Aberdeen, MS [*AM radio station call letters*]
WWZQ-FM ... Aberdeen, MS [*FM radio station call letters*]
WWZZ-FM ... Waldorf, MD [*FM radio station call letters*] (RBYB)
WX .... Ansett Airlines of New South Wales [*ICAO designator*] (AD)
WX .... Ansett Express [*Airport symbol*]
WX .... Simplex Working [*Telecommunications*] (ADDR)
WX .... Wax
wx .... Wax (VRA)
WX .... Weather
WX .... Weather at Altitude [*Aviation*] (FAAC)
WX .... Weather Report (WDMC)
WX .... Westinghouse Elec [*NYSE symbol*] (TTSB)
WX .... Westinghouse Electric Corp. [*Wall Street slang name: "Wex"*] [*NYSE symbol*] (SPSG)
WX .... Wireless [*Communications*]
WX .... Women's Extra [*Size*]
WXAB .... McLain, MS [*FM radio station call letters*]
WXAC .... Reading, PA [*FM radio station call letters*]
WXAG .... Athens, GA [*AM radio station call letters*] (RBYB)
WXAH .... Orange Beach, AL [*FM radio station call letters*]
WXAJ .... Hillsboro, IL [*FM radio station call letters*]
WXAL .... Demopolis, AL [*AM radio station call letters*]
WXAM .... Buffalo, KY [*AM radio station call letters*]
WX-AM .... Weather and Air Movements (SAA)
WXAN .... Ava, IL [*FM radio station call letters*]
WxB .... Wax Bite [*Dentistry*]
WXBA .... Brentwood, NY [*FM radio station call letters*]
WXBB .... Kittery, ME [*FM radio station call letters*]
WXBC .... Hardinsburg, KY [*FM radio station call letters*]
WXBD .... Biloxi, MS [*AM radio station call letters*]
WXBM .... Milton, FL [*FM radio station call letters*]
WXBQ .... Bristol, VA [*AM radio station call letters*]
WXBQ-FM .... Bristol, TN [*FM radio station call letters*]
WXBX .... Rural Retreat, VA [*FM radio station call letters*]
WXC .... Westinghouse Canada, Inc. [*Toronto Stock Exchange symbol*]
WXCC .... Williamson, WV [*FM radio station call letters*]
WXCE .... Amery, WI [*AM radio station call letters*]
WXCF .... Clifton Forge, VA [*AM radio station call letters*]
WXCF-FM .... Clifton Forge, VA [*FM radio station call letters*]
WXCH .... Versailles, IN [*FM radio station call letters*]
WXCI .... Danbury, CT [*FM radio station call letters*]
WXCL .... Pekin, IL [*FM radio station call letters*]
WXCO .... Wausau, WI [*AM radio station call letters*]
WXCON .... Weather Reconnaissance Flight Pilot Report [*Aviation*] (FAAC)
WXCR-FM .... Ballston Spa, NY [*FM radio station call letters*] (RBYB)
WXCT .... Hamden, CT [*AM radio station call letters*]
WXCV .... Homosassa Springs, FL [*FM radio station call letters*]
WXCY .... Havre de Grace, MD [*FM radio station call letters*]
WXD .... Meteorological RADAR Station [*ITU designation*] (CET)

WXD .... Waxed
WXD .... Westrex Development Corp. [*Vancouver Stock Exchange symbol*]
WXDJ .... Homestead, FL [*FM radio station call letters*]
WXDU .... Durham, NC [*FM radio station call letters*]
WXDX .... Beaver Falls, PA [*FM radio station call letters*] (RBYB)
WXEC .... Nekoosa, WI [*FM radio station call letters*]
WXEE .... Welch, WV [*AM radio station call letters*]
WXEF .... Effingham, IL [*FM radio station call letters*]
WXEG .... Beavercreek, OH [*FM radio station call letters*] (RBYB)
WXEL .... West Palm Beach, FL [*FM radio station call letters*]
WXEL-TV .... West Palm Beach, FL [*Television station call letters*]
WXEM .... Buford, GA [*AM radio station call letters*]
WXER .... Plymouth, WI [*FM radio station call letters*]
WXEW .... Yabucoa, PR [*AM radio station call letters*]
WXEZ .... Yorktown, VA [*FM radio station call letters*]
WXFL .... Florence, AL [*FM radio station call letters*]
WXFM .... Mt. Zion, IL [*FM radio station call letters*]
WXFX .... Prattville, AL [*FM radio station call letters*]
WXG .... Warning (MUGU)
WXGA .... Waycross, GA [*Television station call letters*]
WXGC .... Milledgeville, GA [*FM radio station call letters*]
WXGI .... Richmond, VA [*AM radio station call letters*]
WXGJ-FM .... Apalachicola, FL [*FM radio station call letters*] (RBYB)
WXGL .... Topsham, ME [*FM radio station call letters*]
WXGM .... Gloucester, VA [*AM radio station call letters*]
WXGM-FM .... Gloucester, VA [*FM radio station call letters*]
WXGN-FM .... Egg Harbor Township, NJ [*FM radio station call letters*] (RBYB)
WXGO-AM .... Madison, IN [*AM radio station call letters*] (RBYB)
WXHC .... Homer, NY [*FM radio station call letters*]
WXHD .... Mt. Hope, NY [*FM radio station call letters*]
WXHL .... Christiana, DE [*FM radio station call letters*]
WXHT-FM .... York Center, ME [*FM radio station call letters*] (RBYB)
WXIA .... Atlanta, GA [*Television station call letters*]
WXIC .... Waverly, OH [*AM radio station call letters*]
WXID .... Mayfield, KY [*FM radio station call letters*]
WXII .... Winston-Salem, NC [*Television station call letters*]
WXIL .... Parkersburg, WV [*FM radio station call letters*]
WXIN .... Indianapolis, IN [*Television station call letters*]
WXIR .... Plainfield, IN [*FM radio station call letters*]
WXIS .... Erwin, TN [*FM radio station call letters*]
WXIT-AM .... Blowing Rock, NC [*AM radio station call letters*] (RBYB)
WXIX .... Newport, KY [*Television station call letters*]
WXIZ .... Waverly, OH [*FM radio station call letters*]
WXJB .... Harrogate, TN [*FM radio station call letters*]
WXJC .... Crystal River, FL [*FM radio station call letters*]
WXJJ .... Mt. Vernon, KY [*FM radio station call letters*]
WXJM .... Harrisonburg, VA [*FM radio station call letters*]
WXJN .... Lewes, DE [*FM radio station call letters*]
WXJX .... Washington, PA [*FM radio station call letters*]
WXKB .... Cape Coral, FL [*FM radio station call letters*]
WXKC .... Erie, PA [*FM radio station call letters*]
WXKE .... Fort Wayne, IN [*FM radio station call letters*]
WXKI .... Moulton, AL [*FM radio station call letters*]
WXKL .... Sanford, NC [*AM radio station call letters*]
WXKN .... Newburg, KY [*AM radio station call letters*]
WXKO .... Fort Valley, GA [*AM radio station call letters*]
WXKO .... Pana, IL [*FM radio station call letters*]
WXKQ .... Whitesburg, KY [*FM radio station call letters*]
WXKR .... Port Clinton, OH [*FM radio station call letters*]
WXKS .... Medford, MA [*AM radio station call letters*]
WXKS-FM .... Medford, MA [*FM radio station call letters*]
WXKW .... Renovo, PA [*FM radio station call letters*] (RBYB)
WXKX .... Parkersburg, WV [*FM radio station call letters*]
WXKZ .... Prestonsburg, KY [*FM radio station call letters*]
WXL .... Wix, Inc. [*Toronto Stock Exchange symbol*]
WXLA .... Dimondale, MI [*AM radio station call letters*]
WXLC .... Waukegan, IL [*FM radio station call letters*]
WXLE .... Mechanicville, NY [*FM radio station call letters*]
WXLG .... North Creek, NY [*FM radio station call letters*]
WXLH .... Blue Mountain Lake, NY [*FM radio station call letters*]
WXLI .... Dublin, GA [*AM radio station call letters*]
WXLJ-FM .... Spangler, PA [*FM radio station call letters*] (RBYB)
WXLK .... Roanoke, VA [*FM radio station call letters*]
WXLL .... Decatur, GA [*AM radio station call letters*]
WXLM-FM .... Eminence, KY [*FM radio station call letters*] (RBYB)
WXLN .... Eminence, KY [*FM radio station call letters*]
WXLN .... New Albany, IN [*AM radio station call letters*] (RBYB)
WXLO .... Fitchburg, MA [*FM radio station call letters*]
WXLP .... Moline, IL [*FM radio station call letters*]
WXLQ .... Gorham, NH [*FM radio station call letters*]
WXLR .... Harold, KY [*FM radio station call letters*]
WXLS .... Gulfport, MS [*FM radio station call letters*]
WXLT .... Carterville, IL [*FM radio station call letters*]
WXLU .... Peru, NY [*FM radio station call letters*]
WXLV .... Schnecksville, PA [*FM radio station call letters*]
WXLV-TV .... Winston-Salem, NC [*Television station call letters*] (RBYB)
WXLW .... Indianapolis, IN [*AM radio station call letters*]
WXLX .... Newark, NJ [*AM radio station call letters*] (RBYB)
WXLY .... North Charleston, SC [*FM radio station call letters*]
WXLZ .... Lebanon, VA [*FM radio station call letters*]
WXLZ .... St. Paul, VA [*AM radio station call letters*]
WXM .... Worcester Art Museum, Worcester, MA [*OCLC symbol*] (OCLC)
WXMC .... Parsippany-Troy Hills, NJ [*AM radio station call letters*]
WXMI .... Grand Rapids, MI [*Television station call letters*]
WXMJ .... Mount Union, PA [*FM radio station call letters*]
WXMK .... Dock Junction, GA [*FM radio station call letters*]
WXML .... Upper Sandusky, OH [*FM radio station call letters*]
WXMT .... Nashville, TN [*Television station call letters*]
WXMX .... Canaan, VT [*FM radio station call letters*]
WXMY .... Saltville, VA [*AM radio station call letters*]
WXNC .... Warrenton, NC [*FM radio station call letters*] (RBYB)
WXNR-FM .... Grifton, NC [*FM radio station call letters*] (RBYB)
WXNU .... Valley Station, KY [*FM radio station call letters*] (RBYB)
WXOD .... Winchester, NH [*FM radio station call letters*]
WXOF .... Beverly Hills, FL [*FM radio station call letters*]
WXOK .... Baton Rouge, LA [*AM radio station call letters*]
WXON .... Detroit, MI [*Television station call letters*]
WXOQ .... Selmer, TN [*FM radio station call letters*]
WXOR .... Ocean Springs, MS [*FM radio station call letters*]
WXOU .... Oakland, MI [*FM radio station call letters*]
WXOW .... La Crosse, WI [*Television station call letters*]
WXOX .... Bay City, MI [*AM radio station call letters*]
WxP .... Wax Pattern [*Dentistry*]
WXPC .... Horse Cave, KY [*FM radio station call letters*]
WXPH .... Harrisburg, PA [*FM radio station call letters*] (RBYB)
WXPL .... Fitchburg, MA [*FM radio station call letters*]
WXPN .... Philadelphia, PA [*FM radio station call letters*]
WXPR .... Rhinelander, WI [*FM radio station call letters*]
WXPS-FM .... Vergennes, VT [*FM radio station call letters*] (RBYB)
WXPW .... Wausau, WI [*FM radio station call letters*] (RBYB)
WXPX .... West Hazleton, PA [*AM radio station call letters*]
WXPZ .... Milford, DE [*FM radio station call letters*]
WXQK .... Spring City, TN [*AM radio station call letters*]
WXQL .... Baldwin, FL [*FM radio station call letters*]
WXQR .... Jacksonville, NC [*FM radio station call letters*]
WXQW-FM .... Meridianville, AL [*FM radio station call letters*] (RBYB)
WXQZ .... Canton, NY [*FM radio station call letters*]
WXR .... Radiosonde Station [*ITU designation*] (CET)
WXR .... Weather RADAR
WXRA .... Eden, NC [*FM radio station call letters*]
WXRC .... Hickory, NC [*FM radio station call letters*]
WXRCNSq .... Weather Reconnaissance Squadron [*Air Force*]
WXRECCO .... Weather Reconnaissance Flight [*Navy*] (NVT)
WXRF .... Guayama, PR [*AM radio station call letters*]
WXRG .... Gulfport, MS [*FM radio station call letters*]
WXRI .... Winston-Salem, NC [*FM radio station call letters*]
WXRK .... New York, NY [*FM radio station call letters*]
WXRL .... Lancaster, NY [*AM radio station call letters*]
WXRM-FM .... Naples Park, FL [*FM radio station call letters*] (RBYB)
WXRO .... Beaver Dam, WI [*FM radio station call letters*]
WXRQ .... Mount Pleasant, TN [*AM radio station call letters*]
WXRR .... Hattiesburg, MS [*FM radio station call letters*] (RBYB)
WXRS .... Swainsboro, GA [*AM radio station call letters*]
WXRS-FM .... Swainsboro, GA [*FM radio station call letters*]
WXRT .... Chicago, IL [*FM radio station call letters*]
WXRV .... Haverhill, MA [*FM radio station call letters*] (RBYB)
WXRX .... Belvidere, IL [*FM radio station call letters*]
WXRZ .... Corinth, MS [*FM radio station call letters*]
WXSR .... Quincy, FL [*FM radio station call letters*]
WXSS .... Memphis, TN [*AM radio station call letters*]
WXST .... Loudon, TN [*FM radio station call letters*]
WXTA .... Edinboro, PA [*FM radio station call letters*]
WXTB .... Clearwater, FL [*FM radio station call letters*]
WXTC .... Charleston, SC [*AM radio station call letters*]
WXTC-FM .... Charleston, SC [*FM radio station call letters*]
WXTK .... West Yarmouth, MA [*FM radio station call letters*]
WXTL .... Jacksonville Beach, FL [*AM radio station call letters*]
WXTN .... Lexington, MS [*AM radio station call letters*]
WXTQ .... Athens, OH [*FM radio station call letters*]
WXTR .... Waldorf, MD [*FM radio station call letters*]
WXTR-AM .... Frederick, MD [*AM radio station call letters*] (RBYB)
WXTRN .... Weak External Reference [*Computer science*] (BUR)
WXTS .... Toledo, OH [*FM radio station call letters*]
WXTU .... Philadelphia, PA [*FM radio station call letters*]
WXTV .... Paterson, NJ [*Television station call letters*]
WXTX .... Columbus, GA [*Television station call letters*]
WXTZ .... Noblesville, IN [*FM radio station call letters*]
WXUR .... Herkimer, NY [*FM radio station call letters*]
WXUS .... Fort Rucker, AL [*FM radio station call letters*]
WXUT .... Toledo, OH [*FM radio station call letters*]
WXVA .... Charles Town, WV [*AM radio station call letters*]
WXVA-FM .... Charles Town, WV [*FM radio station call letters*]
WXVE .... Spangler, PA [*FM radio station call letters*]
WXVI .... Montgomery, AL [*AM radio station call letters*]
WXVL .... Crossville, TN [*FM radio station call letters*]
WXVO .... Oliver Springs, TN [*FM radio station call letters*]
WXVQ .... De Land, FL [*AM radio station call letters*]
WXVS .... Waycross, GA [*FM radio station call letters*]
WXVT .... Greenville, MS [*Television station call letters*]
WXVU .... Villanova, PA [*FM radio station call letters*]
WXVW .... Jeffersonville, IN [*AM radio station call letters*]
WXVX .... Monroeville, PA [*AM radio station call letters*]
WXWX .... Easley, SC [*FM radio station call letters*]
WXWY .... Robertsdale, AL [*AM radio station call letters*]
WXWZ .... Greer, SC [*FM radio station call letters*] (RBYB)
WXXA .... Albany, NY [*Television station call letters*]
WXXI .... Rochester, NY [*AM radio station call letters*]
WXXI-FM .... Rochester, NY [*FM radio station call letters*]
WXXI-TV .... Rochester, NY [*Television station call letters*]
WXXK .... Newport, NH [*FM radio station call letters*]

WXXL Leesburg, FL [*FM radio station call letters*]
WXXP Anderson, IN [*FM radio station call letters*]
WXXQ Freeport, IL [*FM radio station call letters*]
WXXR Cullman, AL [*AM radio station call letters*]
WXXU Cocoa Beach, FL [*AM radio station call letters*]
WXXV Gulfport, MS [*Television station call letters*]
WXXW Webster, MA [*FM radio station call letters*]
WXXX South Burlington, VT [*FM radio station call letters*]
WXXZ-FM Grand Marais, MN [*FM radio station call letters*] (RBYB)
WXYB Indian Rocks Beach, FL [*AM radio station call letters*]
WXYC Chapel Hill, NC [*FM radio station call letters*]
WXYK Pascagoula, MS [*FM radio station call letters*]
WXYQ Manistee, MI [*FM radio station call letters*]
WXYT Detroit, MI [*AM radio station call letters*]
WXYV Baltimore, MD [*FM radio station call letters*]
WXYX Bayamon, PR [*FM radio station call letters*]
WXYZ Detroit, MI [*Television station call letters*]
WXZQ-FM Piketon, OH [*FM radio station call letters*] (RBYB)
WXZR East Lyme, CT [*FM radio station call letters*]
WXZX-FM Culebra, PR [*FM radio station call letters*] (RBYB)
WXZZ Georgetown, KY [*FM radio station call letters*] (RBYB)
WY Indiana Airways [*ICAO designator*] (AD)
WY Warwickshire Yeomanry [*British military*] (DMA)
WY Washington Yards [*Navy*]
WY Way (ADA)
WY Western Yiddish (BJA)
WY Wey [*Unit of weight*]
WY Weyerhaeuser Co. [*NYSE symbol*] (SPSG)
WY Wherry (ROG)
WY Woman's Year
WY Wrist Yaw (MCD)
Wy Wycliffe [*English cleric, translated Bible into English, 1320-1384*] (BARN)
WY Wyeth Laboratories [*Research code symbol*]
WY Wyoming [*Postal code*]
WY Wyoming Reports [*A publication*] (DLA)
Wy Wyoming State Library, Cheyenne, WY [*Library symbol Library of Congress*] (LCLS)
Wy Wythe's Virginia Chancery Reports [*1788-99*] [*A publication*] (DLA)
WyA Lincoln County Library, Afton Branch, Afton, WY [*Library symbol Library of Congress*] (LCLS)
WYA Whyalla [*Australia Airport symbol*] (OAG)
WYA Writers for Young Adults [*A publication*]
WYA Wyangala [*Australia Seismograph station code, US Geological Survey Closed*] (SEIS)
WyAGS Church of Jesus Christ of Latter-Day Saints, Genealogical Society Library, AftonBranch, Afton, WY [*Library symbol Library of Congress*] (LCLS)
WYAIO Will You Accept, If Offered, the Position Of [*Aviation*] (FAAC)
WYAJ Sudbury, MA [*FM radio station call letters*]
WYAK-FM Surfside Beach-Garden City, SC [*FM radio station call letters*]
WYAL Scotland Neck, NC [*AM radio station call letters*]
WYAM Hartselle, AL [*AM radio station call letters*]
Wy-Ar Wyoming State Archives and Historical Department, Cheyenne, WY [*Library symbol Library of Congress*] (LCLS)
Wyatt Prac Reg Wyatt's Practical Register in Chancery [*1800*] [*A publication*] (DLA)
Wyatt Pr R Wyatt's Practical Register in Chancery [*1800*] [*A publication*] (DLA)
WYAV Conway, SC [*FM radio station call letters*]
WYAY Gainesville, GA [*FM radio station call letters*]
WYBB Folly Beach, SC [*FM radio station call letters*]
WYBC New Haven, CT [*FM radio station call letters*]
WYBE Philadelphia, PA [*Television station call letters*]
WYBF Radnor Township, PA [*FM radio station call letters*]
WYBG Massena, NY [*AM radio station call letters*]
WYBL Western Young Buddhist League (EA)
WYBR Big Rapids, MI [*FM radio station call letters*]
WYBT Blountstown, FL [*AM radio station call letters*]
WyBu Johnson County Library, Buffalo, WY [*Library symbol Library of Congress*] (LCLS)
WYBZ Crooksville, OH [*FM radio station call letters*]
WyC Laramie County Library System, Cheyenne, WY [*Library symbol Library of Congress*] (LCLS)
WYC Warwickshire Yeomanry Cavalry [*British military*] (DMA)
WYC Wiley College, Marshall, TX [*Inactive*] [*OCLC symbol*] (OCLC)
WYC Wycombe [*England*]
WYC Wycombe Air Centre [*British ICAO designator*] (FAAC)
WYC Yes Bay [*Alaska*] [*Airport symbol*] (AD)
WYCA Hammond, IN [*FM radio station call letters*]
WyCa Natrona County Public Library, Casper, WY [*Library symbol Library of Congress*] (LCLS)
WyCaC Casper College, Casper, WY [*Library symbol Library of Congress*] (LCLS)
WyCaCH Wyoming State Children's Home, Casper, WY [*Library symbol Library of Congress*] (LCLS)
WyCaD Wyoming School for the Deaf, Casper, WY [*Library symbol Library of Congress*] (LCLS)
WyCaGS Church of Jesus Christ of Latter-Day Saints, Genealogical Society Library, Casper Branch, Casper, WY [*Library symbol Library of Congress*] (LCLS)
WYCB Washington, DC [*AM radio station call letters*]
WYCC Chicago, IL [*Television station call letters*]
WyCC Laramie County Community College, Cheyenne, WY [*Library symbol Library of Congress*] (LCLS)
WYCC Write Your Congressman Club (EA)
WYCD Detroit, MI [*FM radio station call letters*]
WyCDA Wyoming Department of Agriculture, Cheyenne, WY [*Library symbol Library of Congress*] (LCLS)
WyCDE Wyoming Department of Education, Cheyenne, WY [*Library symbol Library of Congress*] (LCLS)
WYCE Wyoming, MI [*FM radio station call letters*]
WYCF World Youth Crusade for Freedom (EA)
WYCFD World Youth Congress on Food and Development (EAIO)
WYCG Water Valley, MS [*FM radio station call letters*]
WyCGF Wyoming Game and Fish Commission, Cheyenne, WY [*Library symbol Library of Congress*] (LCLS)
WyCGS Church of Jesus Christ of Latter-Day Saints, Genealogical Society Library, Cheyenne Branch, Cheyenne, WY [*Library symbol Library of Congress*] (LCLS)
WyCHD Wyoming Highway Department, Cheyenne, WY [*Library symbol Library of Congress*] (LCLS)
WyCHS Wyoming Department of Health and Social Services, Cheyenne, WY [*Library symbol Library of Congress*] (LCLS)
WYCK Wilkes-Barre, PA [*AM radio station call letters*]
Wycl Wycliffe [*English cleric, translated Bible into English, 1320-1384*] (BARN)
WYCL-FM Pensacola, FL [*FM radio station call letters*] (RBYB)
WYCM Murfreesboro, NC [*AM radio station call letters*]
WyCMS Laramie County Medical Society, Cheyenne, WY [*Library symbol Library of Congress*] (LCLS)
WYCO Wausau, WI [*FM radio station call letters*]
WyCoB Buffalo Bill Museum, Cody, WY [*Library symbol Library of Congress*] (LCLS)
WyCoGS Church of Jesus Christ of Latter-Day Saints, Genealogical Society Library, Cody Branch, Cody, WY [*Library symbol Library of Congress*] (LCLS)
WYCQ Shelbyville, TN [*FM radio station call letters*]
WYCR York-Hanover, PA [*FM radio station call letters*]
WYCS Yorktown, VA [*FM radio station call letters*]
WyCSE State Engineer's Office, Cheyenne, WY [*Library symbol Library of Congress*] (LCLS)
WYCT Kentwood, LA [*FM radio station call letters*]
WYCV Granite Falls, NC [*AM radio station call letters*]
WyCV United States Veterans Administration Center, Cheyenne, WY [*Library symbol Library of Congress*] (LCLS)
WYCY Hawley, PA [*FM radio station call letters*]
WYD Wyandotte [*Queensland*] [*Airport symbol*] (AD)
Wy-D Wyoming State Documents, Cheyenne, WY [*Library symbol Library of Congress*] (LCLS)
WYDA-FM Graceville, FL [*FM radio station call letters*] (RBYB)
WYDC Corning, NY [*Television station call letters*]
WYDE Birmingham, AL [*AM radio station call letters*]
WYDH Atmore, AL [*FM radio station call letters*]
Wy Dic Wyatt's Dickens' Chancery Reports [*A publication*] (DLA)
Wy Dick Dickens' English Chancery Reports, by Wyatt [*A publication*] (DLA)
WYDIWYG What You Digitize Is What You Get
WYDN Worcester, MA [*Television station call letters*]
WyDo Converse County Library, Douglas, WY [*Library symbol Library of Congress*] (LCLS)
WYDO Greenville, NC [*Television station call letters*]
WYDP-TV Orange Park, FL [*TV station call letters*] (RBYB)
WYDS Decatur, IL [*FM radio station call letters*]
WYE Yengema [*Sierra Leone*] [*Airport symbol*] (OAG)
WYEA Sylacauga, AL [*AM radio station call letters*]
WYEP Pittsburgh, PA [*FM radio station call letters*]
WYER Mount Carmel, IL [*AM radio station call letters*]
WYES New Orleans, LA [*Television station call letters*]
WyEV Unita County Library, Evanston, WY [*Library symbol*] [*Library of Congress*] (LCLS)
WyEvGS Church of Jesus Christ of Latter-Day Saints, Genealogical Society Library, Evanston Branch, Evanston, WY [*Library symbol Library of Congress*] (LCLS)
WyEvSH Wyoming State Hospital, Evanston, WY [*Library symbol Library of Congress*] (LCLS)
WYEZ Bremen, IN [*FM radio station call letters*]
WYF World Youth Forum [*Defunct*] (EA)
WYFA Waynesboro, GA [*FM radio station call letters*]
WYFB Gainesville, FL [*FM radio station call letters*]
WYFC Clinton, TN [*FM radio station call letters*]
WYFD Decatur, AL [*FM radio station call letters*]
WYFE Tarpon Springs, FL [*FM radio station call letters*]
WyFEW United States Air Force, Francis E. Warren Air Force Base, Cheyenne, WY [*Library symbol Library of Congress*] (LCLS)
WyFEW-I United States Air Force Institute of Technology, Detachment 9, Francis E. WarrenAir Force Base, Cheyenne, WY [*Library symbol Library of Congress*] (LCLS)
WYFF Greenville, SC [*Television station call letters*]
WYFG Gaffney, SC [*FM radio station call letters*]
WYFH North Charleston, SC [*FM radio station call letters*]
WYFI Norfolk, VA [*FM radio station call letters*]
WYFJ Ashland, VA [*FM radio station call letters*]
WYFK Columbus, GA [*FM radio station call letters*]
WYFL Henderson, NC [*FM radio station call letters*]
WyFIL Fort Laramie Historic Site, Fort Laramie, WY [*Library symbol Library of Congress*] (LCLS)
WYFM Sharon, PA [*FM radio station call letters*]
WYFN Nashville, TN [*AM radio station call letters*]
WYFO Lakeland, FL [*FM radio station call letters*]
WYFQ Charlotte, NC [*AM radio station call letters*]
WYFS Savannah, GA [*FM radio station call letters*]

WYFT .... Luray, VA [*FM radio station call letters*]
WYFV .... Cayce, SC [*FM radio station call letters*]
WYFW .... Winder, GA [*FM radio station call letters*]
WYFX .... Boynton Beach, FL [*AM radio station call letters*]
WyG .... Campbell County Public Library, Gilete, WY [*Library symbol*] [*Library of Congress*] (LCLS)
WYG .... Wyoming Airlines Ltd. [*ICAO designator*] (FAAC)
WYGC .... Gainesville, FL [*FM radio station call letters*]
WYGE .... London, KY [*FM radio station call letters*] (RBYB)
WYGH .... Paris, KY [*AM radio station call letters*]
WYGINS .... What You Get Is No Surprise [*Pronounced "wiggins"*] [*Coined by Dave Tarrant, president of Lotus Development Corp.'s graphics products group*]
WYGL .... Elizabethville, PA [*FM radio station call letters*]
WYGL .... Selinsgrove, PA [*AM radio station call letters*]
WYGO .... Madisonville, TN [*FM radio station call letters*]
WYGR .... Wyoming, MI [*AM radio station call letters*]
WYGY .... Hamilton, OH [*FM radio station call letters*]
WYHC .... Charlotte, NC [*FM radio station call letters*]
WYHK .... Gibsonburg, OH [*FM radio station call letters*]
WYHS .... Hollywood, FL [*Television station call letters*]
WYHT .... Mansfield, OH [*FM radio station call letters*]
WYHY .... Lebanon, TN [*FM radio station call letters*]
WYII .... Williamsport, MD [*FM radio station call letters*]
WYIN .... Gary, IN [*Television station call letters*]
WYIQ .... Warner Robins, GA [*FM radio station call letters*]
WYIS .... McRae, GA [*AM radio station call letters*]
WYJB .... Albany, NY [*FM radio station call letters*]
WYJCA .... Wool Yarn Jobbers Credit Association [*Defunct*] (EA)
WYJS-FM .... Pickens, MS [*FM radio station call letters*] (RBYB)
WYJZ .... Pittsburgh, PA [*AM radio station call letters*]
WYKC .... Grenada, MS [*AM radio station call letters*]
WyKc .... Johnson County Library, Kaycee Branch, Kaycee, WY [*Library symbol Library of Congress*] (LCLS)
WyKe .... Lincoln County Library, Kemmerer, WY [*Library symbol Library of Congress*] (LCLS)
WYKK .... Quitman, MS [*FM radio station call letters*]
WYKM .... Rupert, WV [*AM radio station call letters*]
WYKO .... Sabana Grande, PR [*AM radio station call letters*]
WYKR .... Haverhill, NH [*FM radio station call letters*]
WYKR .... Wells River, VT [*AM radio station call letters*]
WYKS .... Gainesville, FL [*FM radio station call letters*]
WYKT .... Wilmington, IL [*FM radio station call letters*] (RBYB)
WYKX .... Escanaba, MI [*FM radio station call letters*]
WYKY .... Columbus, WI [*FM radio station call letters*]
WYKZ .... Beaufort, SC [*FM radio station call letters*]
WYL .... Laramie County Library System, Cheyenne, WY [*OCLC symbol*] (OCLC)
WYL .... Wyle Electronics [*NYSE symbol*] (TTSB)
WYL .... Wyle Electronics Co. [*Formerly, Wyle Laboratories*] [*NYSE symbol*] (SAG)
WYLA-FM .... Lacombe, LA [*FM radio station call letters*] (RBYB)
WyLan .... Fremont County Library, Lander, WY [*Library symbol Library of Congress*] (LCLS)
WyLanT .... Wyoming State Training School, Lander, WY [*Library symbol Library of Congress*] (LCLS)
WyLar .... Albany County Public Library, Laramie, WY [*Library symbol Library of Congress*] (LCLS)
WyLarBM .... United States Bureau of Mines, Laramie Petroleum Research Center, Laramie, WY [*Library symbol Library of Congress*] (LCLS)
WyLarHN .... Wyoming Health Science Network, University of Wyoming, Laramie, WY [*Library symbol Library of Congress*] (LCLS)
WyLarSh .... Sherwood Hall, Laramie, WY [*Library symbol Library of Congress*] (LCLS)
WyLarSM .... Saint Matthew's Cathedral, Laramie, WY [*Library symbol Library of Congress*] (LCLS)
WYLD .... New Orleans, LA [*AM radio station call letters*]
WYLD-FM .... New Orleans, LA [*FM radio station call letters*]
WYLE .... Florence, AL [*Television station call letters*]
WyleElec .... Wyle Electronics Co. [*Formerly, Wyle Laboratories*] [*Associated Press*] (SAG)
WYLF .... Penn Yan, NY [*AM radio station call letters*]
WYLI .... Marietta, OH [*FM radio station call letters*] (RBYB)
WYLIWYS .... Where You Look Is What You Select
WYLK-FM .... Folsom, LA [*FM radio station call letters*] (RBYB)
WYLL .... Des Plaines, IL [*FM radio station call letters*]
WyLoGS .... Church of Jesus Christ of Latter-Day Saints, Genealogical Society Library, Lovell Branch, Lovell, WY [*Library symbol Library of Congress*] (LCLS)
WYLR .... Glens Falls, NY [*FM radio station call letters*]
WYLS .... York, AL [*AM radio station call letters*]
WYLT-FM .... Bvbalia, MS [*FM radio station call letters*] (RBYB)
WyLu .... Niobrara County Library, Lusk, WY [*Library symbol Library of Congress*] (LCLS)
WYLV .... Alcoa, TN [*FM radio station call letters*]
WYLV .... Wheat Yellow Leaf Virus [*Plant pathology*]
WYM .... Wyoming Health Science Network, Laramie, WY [*OCLC symbol*] (OCLC)
Wyman .... Wyman-Gordon Co. [*Associated Press*] (SAG)
Wyman .... Wyman's Reports [*India*] [*A publication*] (DLA)
WYMB .... Manning, SC [*AM radio station call letters*]
WYMC .... Mayfield, KY [*AM radio station call letters*]
WYMG .... Jacksonville, IL [*FM radio station call letters*]
WYMJ .... Harrisburg, PA [*FM radio station call letters*] (RBYB)
WYMN .... Wyman-Gordon [*NASDAQ symbol*] (TTSB)
WYMN .... Wyman-Gordon Co. [*NASDAQ symbol*] (NQ)
WYMR .... Sebring, FL [*FM radio station call letters*] (RBYB)
WYMS .... Milwaukee, WI [*FM radio station call letters*]
WYMT .... Hazard, KY [*Television station call letters*]
WYMV .... Wheat Yellow Mosaic Virus [*Plant pathology*]
WYMX .... Greenwood, MS [*FM radio station call letters*]
WYN .... Walwyn, Inc. [*Toronto Stock Exchange symbol*]
WYN .... Wyndham [*Australia Airport symbol*]
WYN .... Wyndham Hotel [*NYSE symbol*] (TTSB)
WYNA .... Tabor City, NC [*FM radio station call letters*]
WYNC .... Yanceyville, NC [*AM radio station call letters*]
WYND .... De Land, FL [*AM radio station call letters*]
WYND .... Hatteras, NC [*FM radio station call letters*]
WYNE .... Wayne Bancorp, Inc. [*NASDAQ symbol*] (SAG)
WyNe .... Weston County Public Library, Newcastle, WY [*Library symbol Library of Congress*] (LCLS)
WyneB .... Wayne Bancorp, Inc. [*Associated Press*] (SAG)
WYNF .... Coral Cove, FL [*FM radio station call letters*]
WYNG .... Evansville, IN [*FM radio station call letters*]
WYNI .... Monroeville, AL [*AM radio station call letters*]
WYNI-FM .... Repton, AL [*FM radio station call letters*] (RBYB)
WYNK .... Baton Rouge, LA [*AM radio station call letters*]
WYNK-FM .... Baton Rouge, LA [*FM radio station call letters*]
WYNN .... Florence, SC [*AM radio station call letters*]
Wynne Bov .... Wynne's Bovill's Patent Cases [*A publication*] (DLA)
Wynne Eun .... Wynne's Eunomus [*A publication*] (DLA)
WYNN-FM .... Florence, SC [*FM radio station call letters*]
Wynns .... Wynn's International, Inc. [*Associated Press*] (SAG)
WYNR .... Darien, GA [*FM radio station call letters*]
WY/NRT .... Weidels Yes/No Reliability Test [*Speech and language therapy*] (DAVI)
WYNS .... Lehighton, PA [*AM radio station call letters*]
WYNT .... Upper Sandusky, OH [*FM radio station call letters*]
WYNU .... Milan, TN [*FM radio station call letters*]
WYNY .... Lake Success, NY [*FM radio station call letters*]
WYNZ .... Westbrook, ME [*FM radio station call letters*]
WYO .... Western Youth Orchestra [*Australia*]
WYO .... Write-Your-Own [*Insurance*] (MHDB)
WYO .... Wyoming (AAG)
Wyo .... Wyoming (ODBW)
WYO .... Wyoming Array [*Wyoming*] [*Seismograph station code, US Geological Survey*] (SEIS)
Wyo .... Wyoming Reports [*A publication*] (DLA)
WYOC .... High Springs, FL [*FM radio station call letters*]
WYOC .... Write-Your-Own-Company [*Insurance*] (MHDB)
WYOK .... Moss Point, MS [*FM radio station call letters*] (RBYB)
WYOM .... Wyoming (ROG)
Wyom .... Wyoming Reports [*A publication*] (DLA)
WYOO .... Springfield, FL [*FM radio station call letters*]
WYOR .... Brentwood, TN [*AM radio station call letters*]
Wyo Sess Laws .... Session Laws. Wyoming [*A publication*] (DLA)
WYOS-FM .... Chenango Bridge, NY [*FM radio station call letters*] (RBYB)
WYOU .... Scranton, PA [*Television station call letters*]
WYOW-TV .... Eagle River, WI [*TV station call letters*] (RBYB)
WYOY-FM .... Gluckstadt, MS [*FM radio station call letters*] (RBYB)
WYPC .... Wellston, OH [*AM radio station call letters*]
WyPdS .... Sublette County Library, Pinedale, WY [*Library symbol Library of Congress*] (LCLS)
WYPL .... Memphis, TN [*FM radio station call letters*]
WyPN .... Northwest Community College, Powell, WY [*Library symbol Library of Congress*] (LCLS)
Wy Pr R .... Wyatt's Practical Register in Chancery [*England*] [*A publication*] (DLA)
WYQE .... Naguabo, PR [*FM radio station call letters*]
WYR .... Waybo Resources Ltd. [*Vancouver Stock Exchange symbol*]
WYR .... [*The*] West Yorkshire Regiment [*Army British*]
WYRE .... Annapolis, MD [*AM radio station call letters*]
WyRi .... Fremont County Library, Riverton Branch, Riverton, WY [*Library symbol Library of Congress*] (LCLS)
WyRiC .... Central Wyoming Community College, Riverton, WY [*Library symbol Library of Congress*] (LCLS)
WYRK .... Buffalo, NY [*FM radio station call letters*]
WYRN .... Louisburg, NC [*AM radio station call letters*]
WYRQ .... Little Falls, MN [*FM radio station call letters*]
WYRS .... Manahawkin, NJ [*FM radio station call letters*]
WyRsW .... Western Wyoming College, Rock Springs, WY [*Library symbol Library of Congress*] (LCLS)
WYRU .... Red Springs, NC [*AM radio station call letters*]
WYRV .... Cedar Bluff, VA [*AM radio station call letters*]
WYRX .... Lima, OH [*FM radio station call letters*]
WYRY .... Hinsdale, NH [*FM radio station call letters*]
WYS .... West Yellowstone, MT [*Location identifier FAA*] (FAAL)
WYS .... Wyandotte Southern Railroad Co. [*AAR code*]
WYSA-FM .... Wauseon, OH [*FM radio station call letters*] (RBYB)
WYSBYGI .... What You See Before You Get It [*Computer science*]
WYSC .... McRae, GA [*FM radio station call letters*]
WYSH .... Clinton, TN [*AM radio station call letters*]
WyShCD .... Wheden Cancer Detection Foundation, Sheridan, WY [*Library symbol Library of Congress*] (LCLS)
WyShF .... Sheridan County Fulmer Public Library, Sheridan, WY [*Library symbol Library of Congress*] (LCLS)
WyShGS .... Wyoming Girls' School, Sheridan, WY [*Library symbol Library of Congress*] (LCLS)
WyShMH .... Northern Wyoming Mental Health Center, Sheridan, WY [*Library symbol Library of Congress*] (LCLS)

WyShS......... Sheridan College, Sheridan, WY [*Library symbol Library of Congress*] (LCLS)
WyShV......... United States Veterans Administration Hospital, Sheridan, WY [*Library symbol Library of Congress*] (LCLS)
WYSIAYG..... What You See Is All You Get
WYSIMOLWYG... What You See Is More or Less What You Get [*Pronounced "wizzi-mole-wig"*]
WYSIWYG.... What You See Is What You Get [*Pronounced "wizziwig"*] [*Indicates that video display on word processor bears a high-quality resemblance to printed page that will result*]
WYSIWYP.... What You See Is What You Print [*Computer science*]
WYSK.......... Spotsylvania, VA [*FM radio station call letters*]
WYSL.......... Avon, NY [*AM radio station call letters*]
WYSN.......... Central City, PA [*FM radio station call letters*]
WYSO.......... Yellow Springs, OH [*FM radio station call letters*]
WYSP.......... Philadelphia, PA [*FM radio station call letters*]
WYSR.......... Rotterdam, NY [*FM radio station call letters*] (RBYB)
WYSS.......... Sault Ste. Marie, MI [*FM radio station call letters*]
WYST.......... Detroit, MI [*FM radio station call letters*]
WYSU.......... Youngstown, OH [*FM radio station call letters*]
WYSY.......... Aurora, IL [*FM radio station call letters*]
WYSZ.......... Maumee, OH [*FM radio station call letters*]
WYT............ Wyandotte Terminal Railroad Co. [*AAR code*]
WYT............ Wyton FTU [*British ICAO designator*] (FAAC)
WYTE.......... Whiting, WI [*FM radio station call letters*]
WYTH.......... Madison, GA [*AM radio station call letters*]
Wythe.......... Wythe's Virginia Chancery Reports [*1788-99*] [*A publication*] (DLA)
Wythe Ch (VA)... Wythe's Virginia Chancery Reports [*1788-99*] [*A publication*] (DLA)
Wythes CC... Wythe's Virginia Chancery Reports [*1788-99*] [*A publication*] (DLA)
Wythe's R.... Wythe's Virginia Chancery Reports [*1788-99*] [*A publication*] (DLA)
Wythe's Rep... Wythe's Virginia Chancery Reports [*1788-99*] [*A publication*] (DLA)
Wythe (VA)... Wythe's Virginia Chancery Reports [*1788-99*] [*A publication*] (DLA)
WyThP......... Wyoming Pioneer Home, Thermopolis, WY [*Library symbol Library of Congress*] (LCLS)
WYTI........... Rocky Mount, VA [*AM radio station call letters*]
WYTL.......... Harbor Tug, Small [*Coast Guard symbol*] (DNAB)
WYTM.......... Buoy Tender [*Coast Guard symbol*] (DNAB)
WYTM.......... Fayetteville, TN [*FM radio station call letters*]
WYTM.......... Floating Workship [*Coast Guard symbol*] (DNAB)
WYTM.......... Freight Ship [*Coast Guard symbol*] (DNAB)
WYTM.......... Harbor Craft [*Coast Guard symbol*] (DNAB)
WYTM.......... Harbor Tug, Medium [*Coast Guard symbol*] (DNAB)
WYTM.......... Inshore Patrol Cutter [*Coast Guard symbol*] (DNAB)
WYTM.......... Lighthouse Tender [*Coast Guard symbol*] (DNAB)
WYTM.......... Patrol Boat [*Coast Guard symbol*] (DNAB)
WYTM.......... Revenue Cutter [*Coast Guard symbol*] (DNAB)
WYTM.......... Revenue Steamer [*Coast Guard symbol*] (DNAB)
WYTM.......... Seized Boat [*Coast Guard symbol*] (DNAB)
WYTM.......... Station Ship [*Coast Guard symbol*] (DNAB)
WYTM.......... Steam Derrick [*Coast Guard symbol*] (DNAB)
WYTN.......... Youngstown, OH [*FM radio station call letters*]
WyToE......... Eastern Wyoming College, Torrington, WY [*Library symbol Library of Congress*] (LCLS)
WyTs........... Washakie County Library, Ten Sleep Branch, Ten Sleep, WY [*Library symbol Library of Congress*] (LCLS)
WYTV.......... Youngstown, OH [*Television station call letters*]
WYTZ.......... Bridgman, MI [*FM radio station call letters*] (RBYB)
WyU............ University of Wyoming, Laramie, WY [*Library symbol Library of Congress*] (LCLS)
WYU............ University of Wyoming, Library, Laramie, WY [*OCLC symbol*] (OCLC)
wyu............. Wyoming [*MARC country of publication code Library of Congress*] (LCCP)
WyU-Ar........ University of Wyoming, Archive of Contemporary History, Laramie, WY [*Library symbol Library of Congress*] (LCLS)
WYUL.......... Chateaugay, NY [*FM radio station call letters*]
WyUp........... Weston County Public Library, Upton Branch, Upton, WY [*Library symbol Library of Congress*] (LCLS)
WYUS.......... Milford, DE [*AM radio station call letters*]
WYUU.......... Safety Harbor, FL [*FM radio station call letters*]
WYVC.......... Camden, AL [*FM radio station call letters*]
WYVE.......... Wytheville, VA [*AM radio station call letters*]
WYVN.......... Martinsburg, WV [*Television station call letters*]
WYWCA....... World Young Women's Christian Association (DI)
WyWo.......... Washakie County Library, Worland, WY [*Library symbol Library of Congress*] (LCLS)
WyWoI......... Wyoming Industrial Institute, Worland, WY [*Library symbol Library of Congress*] (LCLS)
WYWY......... Barbourville, KY [*AM radio station call letters*]
WYWY-FM... Barbourville, KY [*FM radio station call letters*]
WYXC.......... Cartersville, GA [*AM radio station call letters*]
WYXE.......... Gallatin, TN [*AM radio station call letters*] (RBYB)
WYXI........... Athens, TN [*AM radio station call letters*]
WYXL.......... Ithaca, NY [*FM radio station call letters*]
WYXR.......... Philadelphia, PA [*FM radio station call letters*]
WYXY-FM.... Lincoln, IL [*FM radio station call letters*] (RBYB)
WYXZ-FM.... Crestline, OH [*FM radio station call letters*] (RBYB)
WYYB.......... Dickson, TN [*FM radio station call letters*]
WYYC.......... West Yorkshire Yeomanry Cavalry [*British military*] (DMA)
WYYD.......... Amherst, VA [*FM radio station call letters*]
WYYS.......... Streator, IL [*FM radio station call letters*] (RBYB)
WYYU.......... Dalton, GA [*FM radio station call letters*] (RBYB)
WYYY.......... Syracuse, NY [*FM radio station call letters*]
WYYZ.......... Jasper, GA [*AM radio station call letters*] (RBYB)
WYZ............ Wyoming State Library, Cheyenne, WY [*OCLC symbol*] (OCLC)
WYZB.......... Mary Esther, FL [*FM radio station call letters*]
WYZD.......... Dobson, NC [*AM radio station call letters*]
WYZE.......... Atlanta, GA [*AM radio station call letters*]
WYZK.......... Valdosta, GA [*FM radio station call letters*]
WYZM.......... Waunakee, WI [*FM radio station call letters*]
WYZZ.......... Bloomington, IL [*Television station call letters*]
WZ.............. Berlin European [*ICAO designator*] (AD)
WZ.............. Trans Western Airlines of Utah [*ICAO designator*] (AD)
Wz.............. Warenzeichen [*Trademark*] [*German*]
WZ.............. War Zone
WZ.............. Wissenschaftliche Zeitschrift [*A publication*]
WZa............ Wide Zone Alpha (MAE)
WZAC.......... Danville, WV [*FM radio station call letters*]
WZAC.......... Madison, WV [*AM radio station call letters*]
WZAD.......... Wurtsboro, NY [*FM radio station call letters*]
WZAK.......... Cleveland, OH [*FM radio station call letters*]
WZAM-AM... Ishpeming, MI [*AM radio station call letters*] (RBYB)
WZAN.......... Portland, ME [*AM radio station call letters*]
WZAP.......... Bristol, VA [*AM radio station call letters*]
WZAR.......... Ponce, PR [*FM radio station call letters*]
WZAT.......... Savannah, GA [*FM radio station call letters*]
WZAZ.......... Jacksonville, FL [*AM radio station call letters*]
WZBB.......... Rocky Mount, VA [*FM radio station call letters*]
WZBC.......... Newton, MA [*FM radio station call letters*]
WZBD.......... Berne, IN [*FM radio station call letters*]
WZBG.......... Litchfield, CT [*FM radio station call letters*]
WZBH.......... Georgetown, DE [*FM radio station call letters*]
WZBN.......... Carthage, IL [*FM radio station call letters*] (RBYB)
WZBO.......... Edenton, NC [*AM radio station call letters*]
WZBQ.......... Carrollton, AL [*FM radio station call letters*] (RBYB)
WZBR.......... Kinston, NC [*FM radio station call letters*]
WZBS.......... Ponce, PR [*AM radio station call letters*]
WZBT.......... Gettysburg, PA [*FM radio station call letters*]
WZBU.......... Vineyard Haven, MA [*Television station call letters*]
WZBX.......... Sylvania, GA [*FM radio station call letters*]
WZBZ.......... Plattsburgh, NY [*AM radio station call letters*] (RBYB)
WZCH-FM.... Dundee, IL [*FM radio station call letters*] (RBYB)
WZCM.......... Young Harris, GA [*AM radio station call letters*]
WZCO-FM.... Crown Point, IN [*FM radio station call letters*] (RBYB)
WZCT.......... Scottsboro, AL [*AM radio station call letters*]
WZDM.......... Vincennes, IN [*FM radio station call letters*]
WZDQ.......... Humboldt, TN [*FM radio station call letters*]
WZDX.......... Huntsville, AL [*Television station call letters*]
WZEE.......... Madison, WI [*FM radio station call letters*]
WZEP.......... De Funiak Springs, FL [*AM radio station call letters*]
WZER.......... Jackson, WI [*AM radio station call letters*] (RBYB)
WZEW.......... East Brewton, AL [*FM radio station call letters*]
WZEZ-FM.... Madisonville, KY [*FM radio station call letters*] (RBYB)
WZFM.......... Narrows, VA [*FM radio station call letters*]
WZFX.......... Whiteville, NC [*FM radio station call letters*]
WZG............ Wissenschaftliche Zeitschrift fuer Juedische Geschichte [*A publication*] (BJA)
WZGC.......... Atlanta, GA [*FM radio station call letters*]
WZGO.......... Portage, PA [*AM radio station call letters*]
WZGO-FM.... Portage, PA [*FM radio station call letters*]
WZGX-FM.... San German, PR [*FM radio station call letters*] (RBYB)
WZHF-AM.... Arlington, VA [*AM radio station call letters*] (RBYB)
WZHR.......... Zephyrhills, FL [*AM radio station call letters*]
WZHT.......... Troy, AL [*FM radio station call letters*]
WZI............. Winzen International, Inc. [*Vancouver Stock Exchange symbol*]
WZID.......... Manchester, NH [*FM radio station call letters*]
WZIP........... Akron, OH [*FM radio station call letters*]
WZIQ.......... Smithville, GA [*FM radio station call letters*]
WZJM.......... Cleveland Heights, OH [*FM radio station call letters*]
WZJN.......... Jackson, NH [*FM radio station call letters*]
WZJS.......... Banner Elk, NC [*FM radio station call letters*]
WZJT........... Wissenschaftliche Zeitschrift fuer Juedische Theologie [*A publication*] (BJA)
WZJTh......... Wissenschaftliche Zeitschrift fuer Juedische Theologie [*A publication*] (BJA)
WZJY........... Mt. Pleasant, SC [*AM radio station call letters*]
WZJZ-FM.... Richwood, OH [*FM radio station call letters*] (RBYB)
WZKB.......... Wallace, NC [*FM radio station call letters*]
WZKD.......... Orlando, FL [*AM radio station call letters*] (RBYB)
WZKL........... Alliance, OH [*FM radio station call letters*]
WZKM.......... Montgomery, WV [*FM radio station call letters*]
WZKS.......... Union, MS [*FM radio station call letters*] (RBYB)
WZKX.......... Poplarville, MS [*FM radio station call letters*]
WZKY.......... Albemarle, NC [*AM radio station call letters*]
WZKZ-FM.... Alfred, NY [*FM radio station call letters*] (RBYB)
WZLA.......... Abbeville, SC [*FM radio station call letters*]
WZLE.......... Lorain, OH [*FM radio station call letters*]
WZLG.......... Hogansville, GA [*FM radio station call letters*] (RBYB)
WZLK.......... Virgie, KY [*FM radio station call letters*]
WZLM.......... Dadeville, AL [*FM radio station call letters*]
WZLQ.......... Tupelo, MS [*FM radio station call letters*]
WZLR.......... Xenia, OH [*FM radio station call letters*]
WZLS.......... Biltmore Forest, NC [*FM radio station call letters*]
WZLT.......... Lexington, TN [*FM radio station call letters*]
WZLX.......... Boston, MA [*FM radio station call letters*]
WZLY.......... Wellesley, MA [*FM radio station call letters*]
WZMB.......... Greenville, NC [*FM radio station call letters*]
WZMC.......... Colonial Heights, TN [*AM radio station call letters*]
WZMG.......... Opelika, AL [*AM radio station call letters*]
WZMP.......... Marion, MS [*FM radio station call letters*]

WZMQ .... Key Largo, FL [*FM radio station call letters*]
WZMT .... Hazleton, PA [*FM radio station call letters*]
WZMX .... Hartford, CT [*FM radio station call letters*]
WZNA .... Moca, PR [*AM radio station call letters*]
WZNF .... Rantoul, IL [*FM radio station call letters*]
WZNJ .... Demopolis, AL [*FM radio station call letters*]
WZNL .... Norway, MI [*FM radio station call letters*]
WZNN .... Rochester, NH [*AM radio station call letters*]
WZNO .... Pensacola, FL [*AM radio station call letters*] (RBYB)
WZNPS .... William H. Zimmer Nuclear Power Station [*Also, ZPS*] (NRCH)
WZNT .... San Juan, PR [*FM radio station call letters*]
WZNX .... Sullivan, IL [*FM radio station call letters*] (RBYB)
WZNY .... Augusta, GA [*FM radio station call letters*]
WZNZ .... Jacksonville, FL [*AM radio station call letters*]
WZO .... Wein Zollordnung [*Wine Duty Order*] [*German*]
WZO .... World Zionist Organization [*Israel*]
WZOA .... Women's Zionist Organization of America
WZOB .... Fort Payne, AL [*AM radio station call letters*]
WZOC-FM .... Plymouth, IN [*FM radio station call letters*] (RBYB)
WZOE .... Princeton, IL [*AM radio station call letters*]
WZOE-FM .... Princeton, IL [*FM radio station call letters*]
WZOK .... Rockford, IL [*FM radio station call letters*]
WZOM .... Defiance, OH [*FM radio station call letters*]
WZON .... Bangor, ME [*AM radio station call letters*]
WZOO .... Asheboro, NC [*AM radio station call letters*]
WZOO .... Edgewood, OH [*FM radio station call letters*]
WZOQ .... Wapakoneta, OH [*FM radio station call letters*]
WZOS .... Oswego, NY [*FM radio station call letters*]
WZOT .... Rockmart, GA [*AM radio station call letters*]
WZOU .... Lewiston, ME [*AM radio station call letters*]
WZOW .... Goshen, IN [*FM radio station call letters*]
WZOZ .... Oneonta, NY [*FM radio station call letters*]
WZPC-FM .... Shelbyville, TN [*FM radio station call letters*] (RBYB)
WZPK .... Berlin, NH [*FM radio station call letters*]
WZPL .... Greenfield, IN [*FM radio station call letters*]
WZPQ .... Jasper, AL [*AM radio station call letters*]
WZPR .... Meadville, PA [*FM radio station call letters*]
WZPT .... New Kensington, PA [*FM radio station call letters*]
WZQK .... Coeburn, VA [*FM radio station call letters*]
WZQQ .... Hyden, KY [*FM radio station call letters*]
WZQR .... Black Mountain, NC [*AM radio station call letters*]
WZR .... Wiser Oil [*NYSE symbol*] (TTSB)
WZR .... Wiser Oil Co. [*NYSE symbol*] (SAG)
WZRC .... New York, NY [*AM radio station call letters*]
WZRD .... Chicago, IL [*FM radio station call letters*]
WZRH .... Picayune, MS [*FM radio station call letters*]
WZRK .... Hancock, MI [*FM radio station call letters*]
WZRQ .... Ballston Spa, NY [*FM radio station call letters*]
WZRR .... Birmingham, AL [*FM radio station call letters*]
WZRS .... Smyrna, TN [*AM radio station call letters*]
WZRT .... Rutland, VT [*FM radio station call letters*]
WZRU .... Roanoke Rapids, NC [*FM radio station call letters*]
WZRW-FM ... Marion, MS [*FM radio station call letters*] (RBYB)
WZRX .... Jackson, MS [*AM radio station call letters*]
WZRZ-FM .... Mill Hall, PA [*FM radio station call letters*] (RBYB)
WZS .... Widespan Zoom Stereoscope (SAA)
WZSK .... Bethany Beach, DE [*FM radio station call letters*] (RBYB)
WZSR .... Woodstock, IL [*FM radio station call letters*]
WZST .... Signal Mountain, TN [*FM radio station call letters*]
WZT .... Wartegg-Zeichentest [*Wartegg Symbol Test*] [*German Psychology*]
WZTA .... Miami Beach, FL [*FM radio station call letters*]
WZTM-AM ... Largo, FL [*AM radio station call letters*] (RBYB)
WZTR .... Milwaukee, WI [*FM radio station call letters*]
WZTU .... Bear Lake, MI [*FM radio station call letters*]
WZTV .... Nashville, TN [*Television station call letters*]
WZTY .... Hartford, MI [*FM radio station call letters*] (RBYB)
WZTZ .... Elba, AL [*FM radio station call letters*]
WZVN .... Lowell, IN [*FM radio station call letters*]
WZVN-TV ..... Naples, FL [*Television station call letters*] (RBYB)
WZVU .... Long Branch, NJ [*FM radio station call letters*]
WZW .... Worcester Public Library, Worcester, MA [*OCLC symbol*] (OCLC)
WZWW .... Bellefonte, PA [*FM radio station call letters*]
WZWY .... Orlando, FL [*Television station call letters*]
WZWZ .... Kokomo, IN [*FM radio station call letters*]
WZXA .... Sturtevant, WI [*FM radio station call letters*]
WZXI .... Buffalo Gap, VA [*FM radio station call letters*] (RBYB)
WZXL .... Wildwood, NJ [*FM radio station call letters*]
WZXR .... South Williamsport, PA [*FM radio station call letters*]
WZXS .... Topsail Beach, NC [*FM radio station call letters*]
WZXV .... Palmyra, NY [*FM radio station call letters*]
WZY .... Nassau [*Bahamas*] [*Airport symbol*] (OAG)
WZYP .... Athens, AL [*FM radio station call letters*]
WZYQ .... Mound Bayou, MS [*FM radio station call letters*] (RBYB)
WZYX .... Cowan, TN [*AM radio station call letters*]
WZZA .... Tuscumbia, AL [*AM radio station call letters*]
WZZB .... Seymour, IN [*AM radio station call letters*]
WZZD .... Philadelphia, PA [*AM radio station call letters*]
WZZE .... Glen Mills, PA [*FM radio station call letters*]
WZZI-FM ..... Vinton, VA [*FM radio station call letters*] (RBYB)
WZZJ .... Pascagoula-Moss Point, MS [*AM radio station call letters*]
WZZK .... Birmingham, AL [*AM radio station call letters*]
WZZK-FM .... Birmingham, AL [*FM radio station call letters*]
WZZL .... Reidland, KY [*FM radio station call letters*]
WZZM .... Grand Rapids, MI [*Television station call letters*]
WZZN-FM .... Mount Kisco, NY [*FM radio station call letters*] (RBYB)
WZZO .... Bethlehem, PA [*FM radio station call letters*]
WZZQ .... Terre Haute, IN [*AM radio station call letters*] (RBYB)
WZZQ-FM .... Terre Haute, IN [*FM radio station call letters*]
WZZR .... Stuart, FL [*FM radio station call letters*]
WZZS .... Zolfo Springs, FL [*FM radio station call letters*]
WZZT .... Morrison, IL [*FM radio station call letters*]
WZZU .... Burlington-Graham, NC [*FM radio station call letters*]
WZZU-AM .... Babylon, NY [*AM radio station call letters*] (RBYB)
WZZW .... Milton, WV [*FM radio station call letters*]
WZZX .... Lineville, AL [*AM radio station call letters*]
WZZY .... Winchester, IN [*FM radio station call letters*]
WZZZ .... Fulton, NY [*AM radio station call letters*]

X

By Acronym

X .... Abscissa (IDOE)
X .... Abscissa of a Coordinate (BARN)
X .... Amino Acid, Unknown or Other [*Symbol*] [*Biochemistry*]
X .... Arithmetic Mean [*Statistics*]
x .... Axis [*of a cylindrical lens*] [*Ophthalmology*] (DAVI)
X .... By [*As in 9 x 12*]
X .... Central Drug Research Institute [*India*] [*Research code symbol*]
X .... Chile [*IYRU nationality code*] (IYR)
X .... Christus [*Christ*] [*Latin*]
X .... Closed at All Times (Except When in Actual Use) [*Ship's fittings classification*]
X .... Cross [*As in X-roads*]
X .... Cross [*Referring to sections*] [*Pathology*] (DAVI)
X .... Crossed With (DAVI)
X .... Crossmatch [*Hematology*] (DAVI)
X .... Crystal Cut [*Symbol*] (DEN)
X .... Decem [*Ten*] [*Latin*]
X .... Drill Sergeant [*Army skill qualification identifier*] (INF)
X .... Ecstasy [*Synthetic stimulant*]
X .... Ethnikon Agrotikon Komma Xiton [*National Agrarian Party "X"*] [*Political party*] (PPE)
X .... Examination [*Slang*]
X .... Except (DAVI)
X .... Exchange
X .... Exclusive [*Concession in a circus or carnival*]
X .... Exercise [*British military*] (DMA)
X .... Exhibitions [*Trade fairs, etc.*] [*Public-performance tariff class*] [*British*]
X .... Ex-Husband [*or Ex-Wife*] [*Slang*]
X .... Ex-Interest [*Without the right to interest*] [*Finance*]
X .... Exit [*Computer science*] [*Telecommunications*]
X .... Exophoria Distance [*Ophthalmology*]
X .... Experimental [*Military*] (AABC)
X .... Explosion [*Military*] (CAAL)
X .... Export [*Economics*]
X .... Extension (AAG)
X .... Extra
X .... Female Chromosome
X .... Frost
X .... Haploid Generation [*Biology*] (BARN)
X .... Hexadecimal [*Computer science*] (IAA)
X .... Horizontal Deflection [*Symbol*] (DEN)
X .... Index [*Computer science*]
X .... Kienboeck's Unit [*of x-ray dosage*] (AAMN)
X .... Kiss [*Correspondence*]
X .... Komma Xiton Ethnikis Antistasseos [*"X" National Resistance Party*] [*Political party*] (PPE)
X .... Lateral [*RADAR*]
X .... Location [*Symbol on map*]
X .... Midweek Travel [*Airline fare code*]
X .... Mistake [*or Error*] [*Symbol*]
X .... Multiplication (IDOE)
x .... Multiplication (IDOE)
X .... No Connection (IDOE)
X .... No Protest [*Banking*]
x .... Number of Carriers (IDOE)
X .... Parallactic Angle
%X .... Percentage of the Predicted Normal Value [*Indicated by the percent sign preceding the symbol*] [*Laboratory science*] (DAVI)
X .... Psychological Problem [*Classification system used by doctors on Ellis Island to detain, re-examine, and possibly deny entry to certain immigrants*]
X .... Raw Score [*Psychology*]
X .... Reactance [*Symbol*] [*IUPAC*] (AAG)
X .... Reactance [*Measurement and physics*] (DAVI)
X .... Removal of [*Surgery*] (DAVI)
X .... Research [*or Experimental*] [*Designation for all US military aircraft*]
X .... Respirations [*On anesthesia chart*] (DAVI)
x .... Roentgen [*Ray*] [*Radiology*] (DAVI)
X .... Simes [*Italy*] [*Research code symbol*]
X .... St. Andrew's Cross
X .... Start of Anesthesia (DAVI)
X .... Strike [*Bowling symbol*]
X .... Submersible Craft [*Self-propelled*] [*Navy ship symbol*]
x .... Takes [*As in K x B - King Takes Bishop*] [*Chess*]
X .... Ten [*Roman numeral*]
X .... Times [*Multiplication sign*] [*Mathematics*]
X .... Toilet [*Slang*]
X .... Transistor [*Symbol*] (DEN)
X .... Transmit
X .... Transverse [*Referring to sections*] [*Pathology*] (DAVI)
X .... Unknown Quantity (IDOE)
x .... Unknown Quantity (IDOE)
X .... USX Marathon [*NYSE symbol*] (SAG)
X .... USX US Steel Group [*Wall Street slang name: "Steel"*] [*NYSE symbol*] (SPSG)
X .... USX-U.S. Steel Group [*NYSE symbol*] (TTSB)
X .... Xanthosine [*One-letter symbol; see Xao*]
X .... X-Axis
X .... Xenon [*Chemical element*] (IAA)
X .... Xenopsylla [*A genus of fleas*] (DAVI)
X .... Xerxes [*Phonetic alphabet*] [*Royal Navy World War I*] (DSUE)
X+# .... Xiphoid Plus Number of Finger Breadths [*Height of fundus*] [*Obstetrics*] (DAVI)
X .... X-Ray (KSC)
X .... X-Ray [*Phonetic alphabet*] [*Pre-World War II International*] [*World War II*] (DSUE)
X .... X-Ray Assistant [*British military*]
X .... X Records [*Division of RCA-Victor*] [*Record label*]
X .... Xylem [*Botany*]
x .... Xylose [*As substituent on nucleoside*] [*Biochemistry*]
X_2t .... Chi-Squared Test [*Statistics*] (DAVI)
X3 .... Times Three [*Referring to orientation to time, place, and person*] [*Neurology*] (DAVI)
XA .... Auxiliary Amplifier (AAG)
Xa .... Chiasma [*Genetics*] (AAMN)
xa .... Christmas Island [*Indian Ocean*] [*MARC country of publication code Library of Congress*] (LCCP)
XA .... Exchange Access (ACRL)
XA .... Experimental (Air Force)
XA .... Extended Architecture [*Computer science*]
XA .... Transmission Adapter (MDG)
Xa .... Xanthine [*Biochemistry*]
XA .... Xanthurenic Acid [*Clinical chemistry*]
XAA .... Aeronautical Radio, Inc. [*ICAO designator*] (FAAC)
XAA .... American Municipal Income Portfolio [*NYSE symbol*] (SPSG)
XAA .... Amer Muni Income Portfolio [*NYSE symbol*] (TTSB)
Xaa .... Unknown Amino Acid [*Laboratory science*] (DAVI)
XAAM .... Experimental Air-to-Air Missile [*Air Force, NASA*]
XAC .... Air Charter World [*ICAO designator*] (FAAC)
XACIC .... X-Ray Attenuation Coefficient Information Center [*National Institute of Standards and Technology*]
XACT .... X Automatic Code Translation (IEEE)
XAD .... Certified Aircraft Dispatch, Inc. [*ICAO designator*] (FAAC)
XAD .... Experimental and Development
XAES .... X-Ray Induced Auger Electron Spectroscopy
XAF .... Executive Air Fleet [*ICAO designator*] (FAAC)
XAFH .... X-Band Antenna Feed Horn
XAFS .... X-Ray Absorption Fine Structure [*Organic chemistry*]
XAK .... Cargo Ship, Merchant Marine Manned
XAL .... Aerovias Xalitic SA de CV [*Mexico ICAO designator*] (FAAC)
XAL .... Xenon Arc Lamp
XALC .... Extended Assembler Language Coding [*Computer science*] (MHDI)
XAM .... AMR Combs, Inc. [*AMR Services, Inc.*] [*ICAO designator*] (FAAC)
XAM .... External Address Modifier [*Computer science*] (MHDI)
XAM .... Merchant Ship Converted to a Minesweeper [*Navy symbol Obsolete*]
X-A mixture.... Xylene-Alcohol [*Mixture*] [*An insecticide*] (DAVI)
Xan .... Xanthine [*Biochemistry*]
X & D .... Examination and Diagnosis (DAVI)
X & D .... Experiment and Development [*Flotilla*] [*Landing Craft*]
X & DFLOT... Experimental and Development Flotilla [*Navy*] (DNAB)
X & O .... Hug and Kiss (DAVI)
XANES .... X-Ray Absorption Near-Edge Structure [*Spectroscopy*]
XANST .... Xanthium strumarium [*Cocklebur*]
XANT .... Xanthochromic [*Neurology*] (DAVI)
xanth .... Xanthomatosis
XAO .... Airline Operations Services, Inc. [*ICAO designator*] (FAAC)
Xao .... Xanthosine [*Also, X*] [*A nucleoside*]
XAP .... Chapeco [*Brazil*] [*Airport symbol*] (OAG)
XAP .... Direct Air Inc. [*ICAO designator*] (FAAC)
XAP .... Merchant Transport [*Ship symbol*]
XAPC .... Merchant Coastal Transport, Small [*Ship symbol*]
XAPIA .... X.400 Application Program Interface Association (EA)

XAR .... Extended Attribute Record [*Computer science*] (DOM)
XARM .... Cross Arm (AAG)
XARO .... Artagraph Reproduction Technology [*NASDAQ symbol*] (SAG)
XAS .... Experimental Air Specification Weapons [*Navy*] (NG)
XAS .... PHH Aviation Systems, Inc. [*ICAO designator*] (FAAC)
XAS .... X-Band Antenna System
XAS .... X-Ray Absorption Spectroscopy
XASM .... Cross Assembler [*Computer science*] (MHDI)
XASM .... Experimental Air-to-Surface Missile [*Air Force, NASA*]
XAT .... AT & T Aviation Group [*ICAO designator*] (FAAC)
XAT .... X-Ray Analysis Trial
XATA .... XATA Corp. [*NASDAQ symbol*] (TTSB)
XATA .... XATA Corp. [*Associated Press*] (SAG)
XATA .... XATA Corp. [*NASDAQ symbol*] (SAG)
XAV .... Auxiliary Seaplane Tender [*Ship symbol*]
XAV .... Xavier University, Cincinnati, OH [*OCLC symbol*] (OCLC)
Xavier U (La)... Xavier University (Louisiana) (GAGS)
Xavier U (Ohio)... Xavier University (Ohio) (GAGS)
XavrCp .... Xavier Corp. [*Associated Press*] (SAG)
XAY .... Camp Atterbury, IN [*Location identifier FAA*] (FAAL)
XAY .... Xapuri [*Brazil*] [*Airport symbol*] (AD)
xb .... Cocos [*Keeling*] Islands [*MARC country of publication code Library of Congress*] (LCCP)
XB .... Crossbar [*Bell System*]
XB .... Crossbar Switch (NITA)
XB .... Experimental Bomber (MCD)
XB .... Exploding Bridge-Wire
XB .... International Air Transport Association (IATA) [*ICAO designator*] (ICDA)
XBAR .... Crossbar
XBASE .... Data Base Management Software Package (MHDI)
XBASIC .... Extension of BASIC [*Computer science*]
XBB .... Berne Public Library, Berne, IN [*OCLC symbol*] (OCLC)
XBC .... "B" Corp. [*Toronto Stock Exchange symbol*]
XBC .... External Block Controller
XBF .... Fort Wayne, IN [*Location identifier FAA*] (FAAL)
XBG .... Bogande [*Burkina Faso*] [*Airport symbol*] (OAG)
XBG .... City of Bangor, Maine [*FAA designator*] (FAAC)
XBIOS .... Extended BIOS [*Basic Input/Output System*] [*Operating system*]
XBK .... Xebeck [*Type of ship*] (ROG)
XBL .... Extension Bell [*Telecommunications*] (TEL)
XBLD .... Extrabold [*Typography*]
xbld .... Extrabold [*Type*] (WDMC)
XBM .... Extended BASIC Mode [*International Computers Ltd.*]
XBM .... State University of New York, College at Brockport, Brockport, NY [*OCLC symbol*] (OCLC)
XBM .... X-Window Bitmap [*For images*]
XBN .... Biniguni [*Papua New Guinea*] [*Airport symbol*] (OAG)
XBO .... Baseops International, Inc. [*ICAO designator*] (FAAC)
XBP .... Bancshare Portfolio Corp. [*Toronto Stock Exchange symbol*]
XBP .... X-Ray Bright Point [*Astronomy*]
XBR .... Brockville [*Canada*] [*Airport symbol*] (OAG)
XBR .... Experimental Breeder Reactor
XBR .... Ozark, AL [*Location identifier FAA*] (FAAL)
XBRA .... Cross Bracing (MSA)
Xbre .... December (BARN)
XBT .... Crossbar Tandem [*Telecommunications*] (TEL)
xbt .... Exhibit
XBT .... Expendable Bathythermograph [*Oceanography*]
XBT .... Expendable Bathythermograph (EERA)
XBTS .... Extract Bit String [*Computer science*] (PCM)
Xc .... Capacitive Reactance
XC .... Caribbean Air Transport [*ICAO designator*] (AD)
XC .... Cross-Clamp [*of carotid artery*]
XC .... Cross-Continent Auto Retailers, Inc. [*NYSE symbol*] (SAG)
XC .... Cross Country [*Also, XCY*]
xc .... Ex Capitalisation [*Finance*]
X-C .... Ex-Coupon [*Without the right to coupons, as of a bond*] [*Finance*]
XC .... Excretory Cystogram [*Medicine*] (MAE)
XC .... Expandable Case
XC .... Expendable Case (MCD)
XC .... Experimental Cargo Aircraft
xc .... Maldives [*MARC country of publication code Library of Congress*] (LCCP)
XC .... Mexico [*International civil aircraft marking*] (ODBW)
XC .... Xanthomonus Campestris [*Bacteriology*]
XC .... X-Chromosome
XC .... Xenotron Composer (DGA)
XC .... Xerox Copy
XC & UC .... Exclusive of Covering and Uncovering
XCB .... Extended Core Barrel [*Drilling technology*]
XCCE .... Extracapsular Cataract Extraction [*Ophthalmology*] (DAVI)
XCD .... Canadian Dollar [*Vancouver Stock Exchange symbol*]
XCE .... X-Band Cassegrain Experimental
XCED .... Water-Jel Technologies [*NASDAQ symbol*] (SAG)
XCEL .... Canterbury Corporate Services [*NASDAQ symbol*] (SAG)
XCEL .... Canterbury Corporate Svcs [*NASDAQ symbol*] (TTSB)
XcelNet .... XcelleNet, Inc. [*Associated Press*] (SAG)
XCG .... Experimental Cargo Glider
X-CGD .... X-Linked Chronic Granulomatous Disease [*Medicine*]
XCH .... Christmas Island [*Airport symbol*]
XCH .... Exchange (AAG)
X-chrom .... Female Sex Chromosome [*Genetics*] (DAVI)
XCI .... X-Chromosome Inactivation [*Genetics*]
XCID .... X-Linked Combined Immunodeficiency [*Immunology*]
XCIT .... Excitation (AAG)
XCIT .... Excite Inc. [*NASDAQ symbol*] (TTSB)
XCL .... Armed Merchant Cruiser [*Navy symbol*]
XCL .... Contel ASC [*ICAO designator*] (FAAC)
XCL .... Cross Claim [*Legal shorthand*] (LWAP)
XCL .... Excess Current Liabilities [*Insurance*]
XCL .... Excluded from General Declassification Schedule (MCD)
XCL .... Exploration Company of Louisiana, Inc. [*Later, XCL Ltd.*] [*AMEX symbol*] (SPSG)
XCL .... X-Cal Resources Ltd. [*Toronto Stock Exchange symbol*]
XCL .... XCL Ltd. [*Formerly, Exploration Company of Louisiana*] [*AMEX symbol*] (SAG)
XCL Ltd. .... XCL Ltd. [*Formerly, Exploration Company of Louisiana*] [*Associated Press*] (SAG)
XCMD .... External Command [*Computer science*]
XCMD .... External Command [*Computer science*] (CDE)
XCNGR .... Exchanger (AAG)
XCO .... Compuflight Operation Service, Inc. [*ICAO designator*] (FAAC)
XCO .... Cross Connection
XCOM .... CrossCom Corp. [*NASDAQ symbol*] (SAG)
XCOM .... CrossComm Corp. [*NASDAQ symbol*] (TTSB)
XCOM .... Exterior Communications [*Military*] (CAAL)
XCONN .... Cross Connection
XCP .... Ex-Coupon [*Without the right to coupons, as of a bond*] [*Finance*]
XCP .... Executive Control Program [*Computer science*] (MCD)
XCP .... Expendable Current Profiler [*Instrumentation, oceanography*]
XCPT .... Except (KSC)
XCR .... Little Falls, MN [*Location identifier FAA*] (FAAL)
XCS .... Cape Seppings, AK [*Location identifier FAA*] (FAAL)
XCS .... CompuServe, Inc. [*ICAO designator*] (FAAC)
XCS .... Cross-Country Skiing
XCS .... Ten Call Seconds [*Telecommunications*] (TEL)
XCS .... Xerox Computer Services [*Xerox Corp.*]
XCT .... Execute (IAA)
XCT .... X-Band Communications Transponder
XCTD .... Expendable Conductivity-Temperature-Depth [*Probe*] [*Marine science*] (OSRA)
XCTD .... Expendable Conductivity-Temperature-Depth Probe (USDC)
XCTD .... Expendable Current Temperature Density Profiler (EERA)
XCU .... Crosspoint Control Unit (NITA)
XCU .... Explosion Collapse, Underground Operations
XCU .... Extreme Close-Up [*Also, VCU*] [*Cinematography*] (NTCM)
XCVR .... Transceiver (AAG)
XCX .... Citibank NA [*ICAO designator*] (FAAC)
XCY .... Cross Country [*Also, XC*]
XD .... Bureau Veritas SA [*France ICAO designator*] (ICDA)
XD .... Crossed [*Telecommunications*] (TEL)
XD .... Examined (ROG)
XD .... Ex-Directory [*Telecommunications*] (TEL)
X-D .... Ex-Dividend [*Without the right to dividend*] [*Finance*] (SPSG)
X/D .... Ex Dividendum [*Without (or Exclusive) of Dividend*] [*Finance*] (ROG)
XD .... Executed (ROG)
XD .... Executive Development [*Civil Service Commission*]
XD .... Exploratory Development [*Military*] (MCD)
XD .... Extra Dense
XD .... X-Linked Dominant (MEDA)
XD .... Xylem Disease [*Plant pathology*]
XDA .... Bureau Veritas SA [*France ICAO designator*] (FAAC)
XDA .... X-Band Drive Amplifier
XDC .... Xylene-Dioxane-Cellosolve [*Scintillation solvent*]
XD/CO .... Ex-Directory/Calls Offered [*Telephone service*] (DI)
XDCR .... Transducer (AAG)
XDD .... Lockheed Duats [*ICAO designator*] (FAAC)
XDE .... Xylene-Dioxane-Ethanol [*Scintillation solvent*]
XDER .... Transducer
XDF .... Exchange Data Format [*Computer science*] (EERA)
XDF .... Extended Distance Feature (ACRL)
XDFLD .... Secondary Index Field [*Computer science*] (MHDI)
XDH .... Xanthine Dehydrogenase [*An enzyme*]
XDI .... Xylene Diisocyanate [*Organic chemistry*]
X-Dis .... Ex-Distribution
X-Div .... Ex-Dividend [*Without the right to dividend*] [*Finance*]
XDIVU .... Naval Experimental Diving Unit
XDM .... State University of New York, Agricultural and Technical College at Delhi, Delhi, NY [*OCLC symbol*] (OCLC)
XDM .... Xerox Dry Microfilm (NITA)
XDM .... X-Ray Density Measurement
XDMS .... Experimental Data Management System [*Computer science*] (MHDI)
XD/NC .... Ex-Directory/No Connections [*Telephone service*] (DI)
XDP .... Expendable Dissipation Profiler [*Oceanography*]
XDP .... Xanthine Diphosphate [*Biochemistry*] (DAVI)
XDP .... Xanthosine Diphosphate [*Biochemistry*]
XDP .... Xeroderma Pigmentosum [*Inherited, disfiguring syndrome*]
XDP .... X-Ray Density Probe
XDP .... X-Ray Diffraction Powder
XDPC .... X-Ray Diffraction Powder Camera
XDPS .... X-Band Diode Phase Shifter
XDPU .... Expanded Data Processing Unit (DNAB)
XDR .... Crusader (ROG)
XDR .... External Data Representation [*Computer science*]
XDR .... Transducer (AAG)
XDS .... Dispatch Services, Inc. [*ICAO designator*] (FAAC)
XDS .... Exoatmospheric Defense System [*DoD*]
XDS .... Xerox Data Systems [*Formerly, SDS*]
XDS .... X-Ray Diffraction System

XDT .... Data Transformation Corp. [*ICAO designator*] (FAAC)
XDT .... Xenon Discharge Tube
XDUCER .... Transducer
XDUP .... Extended Disk Utilities Program [*Computer science*]
XDY .... DynAir Services, Inc. [*ICAO designator*] (FAAC)
XDY .... Valdosta Moody Air Force Base, GA [*Location identifier FAA*] (FAAL)
XE .... Canadian Express Ltd. [*Toronto Stock Exchange symbol Vancouver Stock Exchange symbol*]
XE .... Experimental Engine [*NASA*]
XE .... South Central [*ICAO designator*] (AD)
Xe .... Xenon [*Chemical element*]
XEB .... Xylanolytic Enzyme Biodegradability [*Biochemistry*]
XEC .... Execute
XECF .... Experimental Engine - Cold Flow Configuration [*NERVA*]
Xechem .... Xechem International [*Associated Press*] (SAG)
Xechm .... Xechem International [*Associated Press*] (SAG)
XED .... Medford, OK [*Location identifier FAA*] (FAAL)
XEDS .... X-Ray Energy Dispersive System [*Microparticle analysis*]
XEF .... Excess Ejection Fraction [*Cardiology*] (DAVI)
XEF .... Xenon Fluoride (MCD)
XEG .... Xerox Education Group
XEG .... X-Ray Emission Gauge
XEIK .... Xeikon NV [*NASDAQ symbol*] (SAG)
Xeikon .... Xeikon NV [*Associated Press*] (SAG)
XEIKY .... Xeikon N.V. ADR [*NASDAQ symbol*] (TTSB)
XEL .... Excel Realty Trust [*NYSE symbol*] (TTSB)
XEL .... Excel Realty Trust, Inc. [*NYSE symbol*] (SPSG)
XEL .... Excelsior Life Insurance Co. [*Toronto Stock Exchange symbol*]
XEL .... Helicopteros Xel-Ha SA de CV [*Mexico ICAO designator*] (FAAC)
XELEDOP .... Transmitting Elementary Dipole with Optional Polarity (MCD)
Xen .... De Xenophane [*of Aristotle*] [*Classical studies*] (OCD)
XEN .... Xenia, OH [*Location identifier FAA*] (FAAL)
Xen .... Xenophon [*428-354BC*] [*Classical studies*] (OCD)
Xeno .... Xenometrix, Inc. [*Associated Press*] (SAG)
Xenomet .... Xenometrix, Inc. [*Associated Press*] (SAG)
XENOU .... Xenometrix, Inc. [*NASDAQ symbol*] (SAG)
Xenova .... Xenova Group Ltd. [*Associated Press*] (SAG)
XENOW .... Xenometrix Inc. Wrrt [*NASDAQ symbol*] (TTSB)
XEO .... Experimental Engineering Orders (DNAB)
XEOS .... Xerox Electro-Optical Systems
XEQ .... Execute
XER .... Xerox Corp., Xerox Library Services, Webster, NY [*OCLC symbol*] (OCLC)
XER .... Xerox Reproduction (AAG)
XERB .... Experimental Environmental Research Buoy [*Marine science*] (MSC)
XERG .... Xonics Electron Radiography [*Medical x-ray imaging equipment*]
xero .... Xeromammography [*Radiology*] (DAVI)
Xerox .... Xerox Corp. [*Associated Press*] (SAG)
XES .... X-Ray Emission Spectra
XES .... X-Ray Energy Spectrometry
XES .... X-Ray Exposure Study (NUCP)
XETA .... Xeta Corp. [*NASDAQ symbol*] (NQ)
XF .... Cobden Airways [*ICAO designator*] (AD)
XF .... Experimental Fighter
XF .... Extended Family [*Unitarian Universalist program*]
XF .... Extra Fine
xf .... Extremely Fine [*Philately*]
xf .... Midway Islands [*MARC country of publication code Library of Congress*] (LCCP)
XFA .... Cross-Field Acceleration
XFA .... X-Ray Fluorescence Absorption
XFC .... Extended Function Code
XFC .... Transfer Charge [*Telecommunications*] (TEL)
XFC .... Transferred Charge Call (NITA)
XFC .... X-Band Frequency Converter
XFCN .... External Function [*Computer science*] (CDE)
XFD .... Crossfeed (NASA)
XFD .... X-Ray Flow Detection
XFER .... Transfer (AAG)
XFES .... Xerox Family Education Services
XFH .... X-Band Feed Horn
XfL .... Cross in Front of Left Foot [*Dance terminology*]
XFLO .... Crossflow Engine [*Automotive engineering*]
XFLT .... Expanded Flight Line Tester
XFM .... Expeditionary Force Message [*Usually, EFM*] [*Low-rate cable or radio message selected from a list of standard wordings*]
XFM .... State University of New York, College at Fredonia, Fredonia, NY [*OCLC symbol*] (OCLC)
XFM .... X-Band Ferrite Modulator
XFMI .... Transformer Interface
XFMR .... Transformer (AAG)
xfmr .... Transformer (IDOE)
XFN .... Victoria, TX [*Location identifier FAA*] (FAAL)
xformer .... Transformer (IDOE)
XFQH .... Xenon-Filled Quartz Helix
XFR .... Transfer
XFRD .... Transferred (ECII)
XFRMR .... Transformer
XFS .... American Flight Service Systems, Inc. [*ICAO designator*] (FAAC)
XFS .... Fort Sill, OK [*Location identifier FAA*] (FAAL)
XFS .... Xenogenic Fetal Skin [*Medicine*]
XFS .... X-Ray Fluorescence Spectroscopy
XFSS .... Auxiliary Flight Service Station [*Aviation*] (FAAC)
XFT .... Xenon Flash Tube
XFX .... Airways Corp. of New Zealand Ltd. [*ICAO designator*] (FAAC)
XG .... Air North [*ICAO designator*] (AD)
XG .... Crossing
XG .... Xanthan Gum [*Chemistry*]
XGA .... Extended Graphics Adapter [*Computer science*] (DOM)
XGA .... Extended Graphics Array [*IBM Corp.*]
XGA .... General Aviation Terminal, Inc. [*Canada ICAO designator*] (FAAC)
XGAM .... Experimental Guided Air Missiles
XGDS .... Exempt from General Declassification Schedule (MCD)
Xge .... Exchange [*Business term*]
XGG .... Gorom-Gorom [*Burkina Faso*] [*Airport symbol*] (OAG)
XGG .... IMP Group Ltd. Aviation Services [*Canada ICAO designator*] (FAAC)
X-Gluc .... X-Glucuronide
XGP .... Experimental Geosynchronous Platform (SSD)
XGP .... Xanthogranulomatous Pyelonephritis [*Medicine*]
XGP .... Xerox Graphic Printer [*Xerox Corp.*]
XGPRT .... Xanthine-Guanine Phosphoribosyltransferase [*An enzyme*]
XGRAPHY .... Xylography [*Wood engraving*] (ROG)
XGS .... Global Systems, Inc. [*ICAO designator*] (FAAC)
XGW .... Global Weather Dynamics, Inc. [*ICAO designator*] (FAAC)
XH .... Experimental Helicopter
xh .... Niue [*MARC country of publication code Library of Congress*] (LCCP)
XH .... Sign-Filled Half-Word Designator [*Computer science*]
XH .... Special Handling Service for Aircraft [*ICAO designator*] (ICDA)
XHA .... Special Handling Service for Aircraft [*FAA designator*] (FAAC)
XHAIR .... Cross Hair (IEEE)
XHF .... Extra-High Frequency (NVT)
XHM .... X-Ray Hazard Meter
XHMO .... Extended Hueckel Molecular Orbit [*Atomic physics*] (IEEE)
xho .... Xhosa [*MARC language code Library of Congress*] (LCCP)
XHR .... Extra-High Reliability
XHS .... Indiana Historical Society, Indianapolis, IN [*OCLC symbol*] (OCLC)
XHST .... Exhaust (AAG)
XHV .... Extreme High Vacuum
XHVY .... Extra Heavy
X-I .... Ex-Interest [*Without the right to interest*] [*Finance*]
XI .... International Aeradio Ltd. [*British ICAO designator*] (ICDA)
xi .... St. Christopher-Nevis-Anguilla [*MARC country of publication code Library of Congress*] (LCCP)
XIA .... Irving Oil Ltd. [*Canada ICAO designator*] (FAAC)
XIA .... X-Band Inteferometer Antenna
Xian .... Christian (VRA)
XIB .... IBM Corp., Library Processing Center, White Plains, NY [*OCLC symbol*] (OCLC)
XIC .... Convent of Immaculate Conception Sisters of St. Benedict, Ferdinand, IN [*OCLC symbol*] (OCLC)
XIC .... Transmission Interface Converter
XIC .... Xichang [*China*] [*Airport symbol*] (OAG)
XIC .... X-Inactivation Centre [*Genetics*]
XICO .... Xicor, Inc. [*NASDAQ symbol*] (NQ)
Xicor .... Xicor, Inc. [*Associated Press*] (SAG)
XICS .... Xerox Integrated Composition System [*Xerox Corp.*] [*Computer typesetting system*]
XICTMD .... Xerox International Center for Training and Management Development [*Leesburg, VA*]
XID .... Exchange Identification
XIE .... Xieng Khouang [*Laos*] [*Airport symbol*] (AD)
XII .... Washington, DC [*Location identifier FAA*] (FAAL)
XII P .... Testaments of the Twelve Patriarchs [*Pseudepigrapha*]
Xilinx .... Xilinx, Inc. [*Associated Press*] (SAG)
XIM .... Ithaca College, Ithaca, NY [*OCLC symbol*] (OCLC)
XIM .... X-Ray Intensity Meter
XIN .... Ex-Interest [*Without the right to interest*] [*Finance*]
XING .... Crossing (MCD)
XING .... Crossing
XINT .... Ex-Interest [*Without the right to interest*] [*Finance*]
XI/O .... Execute Input/Output (DEN)
XIO .... Executive Input/Output (NITA)
XION .... Xionics Document Technologies, Inc. [*NASDAQ symbol*] (SAG)
XionDoc .... Xionics Document Technologies, Inc. [*Associated Press*] (SAG)
XIOX .... Xiox Corp. [*NASDAQ symbol*] (NQ)
XIP .... Execute-in-Place [*Computer science*]
XIP .... Xerox Individualized Publishing
XIPC .... Extended Interprocess Communications Facilities
XIQ .... Xique-Xique [*Brazil*] [*Airport symbol*] (AD)
XIRC .... Xircom, Inc. [*NASDAQ symbol*] (SAG)
Xircom .... Xircom, Inc. [*Associated Press*] (SAG)
XIRS .... Xenon Infrared Searchlight
XIS .... Xenon Infrared Searchlight
XIS .... Xerox Imaging System (PCM)
XIS .... X^PRESS Information Services (IID)
XIST .... Inactive Specific Transcriptase (BARN)
xistor .... Transistor (IDOE)
XIT .... Extra Input Terminal
XIWT .... Cross Industry Working Team
XJ .... Assistance Aeroportuaire de l'Aeroport de Paris [*France ICAO designator*] (ICDA)
XJ .... Experimental Jaguar [*Jaguar PLC*]
XJ .... Mesaba Aviation [*ICAO designator*] (AD)
xj .... St. Helena [*MARC country of publication code Library of Congress*] (LCCP)
XJA .... Assistance Aeroportuaire de l'Aeroport de Paris [*France*] [*FAA designator*] (FAAC)
XJM .... Schenectady County Community College, Schenectady, NY [*OCLC symbol*] (OCLC)
XJN .... Milwaukee, WI [*Location identifier FAA*] (FAAL)

XJP .... Jasper Public Library, Jasper, IN [*OCLC symbol*] (OCLC)
XJR .... Experimental Jaguar Racing
XK .... Agence pour la Securite de la Navigation Aerienne en Afrique et a Madagascar (ASECNA) [*ICAO designator*] (ICDA)
XK .... Experimental-Eleventh Generation [*Jaguar*] [*Automotive engineering*]
xk .... St. Lucia [*MARC country of publication code Library of Congress*] (LCCP)
XK .... X-Band Klystron
XKA .... Kavouras, Inc. [*ICAO designator*] (FAAC)
XKO .... Not Knocked Out (DAVI)
XKX .... Agence pour la Securite de la Navigation Afrique-Madagascar [*France*] [*FAA designator*] (FAAC)
XL .... Country Connection [*Airline code*] [*Australia*]
XL .... Cross-Reference List
XL .... Crystal
XL .... Excess Lactate
XL .... Execution Language [*Computer science*]
XL .... EXEL Limited [*NYSE symbol*] (TTSB)
XL .... EXEL Ltd. [*NYSE symbol*] (SPSG)
XL .... Existing Light [*Photography*] (NTCM)
XL .... Extra Large [*or Long*] [*Size*]
XL .... Extra Load [*Automotive engineering*]
XL .... Extra Long (WDMC)
X_L .... Inductive Reactance (IDOE)
xl .... St. Pierre and Miquelon [*MARC country of publication code Library of Congress*] (LCCP)
XL .... Telecomunicacoes Aeronauticas Sociedada Anonima (TASA) [*Brazil ICAO designator*] (ICDA)
XL .... Unmarried Lady [*Citizens band radio slang*]
XL .... X-Axis of Spacelab [*NASA*] (NASA)
XL .... Xylose-Lysine [*Agar base*] [*Microbiology*]
XLA .... X-Band Limiter Attenuator
XLA .... X-Linked Agammaglobulinaemia [*Medicine*]
XL & UL .... Exclusive of Loading and Unloading
XLATION .... Translation
XLB .... Xylem-Limited Bacteria [*Plant pathology*]
XLC .... Extra Large Capacity
XLC .... Extra Luxurious Chaparral
XLC .... Indiana University, School of Medicine, Medical Education Resources Program, Indianapolis, IN [*OCLC symbol*] (OCLC)
XLC .... USX Capital LLC [*NYSE symbol*] (SAG)
XLC .... Xenon Lamp Collimator
XLCnnSI .... XLConnect Solutions, Inc. [*Associated Press*] (SAG)
XLCPr .... USX Capital LLC 'MIPS' [*NYSE symbol*] (TTSB)
XLCT .... XLConnect Solutions, Inc. [*NASDAQ symbol*] (SAG)
XLD .... Experimental LASER Device (MCD)
XLD .... Jepenssen Data Plan, Inc. [*ICAO designator*] (FAAC)
XLD .... Xylose-Lysine-Deoxycholate [*Growth medium*]
XLDT .... Xenon LASER Discharge Tube
XLE .... Columbus, GA [*Location identifier FAA*] (FAAL)
XLF .... XL Food Systems Ltd. [*Toronto Stock Exchange symbol*]
XLF .... X-Ray Luminosity Function [*Cosmology*]
XLG .... Lockheed Air Terminal, Inc. [*Guam*] [*ICAO designator*] (FAAC)
XLGX .... Xylogics, Inc. [*NASDAQ symbol*] (NQ)
xlh .... Extra Large Hinge [*Philately*]
XLH .... X-Linked Hupophosphatemia [*Medicine*] (DMAA)
XLI .... Extra-Low Interstitial [*Alloy*]
XLISP .... Extension of LISP [*List Processor*] 1.5 [*Programming language*] (CSR)
XLIST .... Execution List (MCD)
XLL .... Extra Lightly Loaded (IAA)
XLM .... St. Lawrence University, Canton, NY [*OCLC symbol*] (OCLC)
XLMR .... X-Linked Mental Retardation [*Genetics*]
XLNT .... Excellent (WGA)
XLNX .... Xilinx, Inc. [*NASDAQ symbol*] (SAG)
XL/OS .... XL Operating System (NITA)
XLP .... Extended-Life Protection [*Automotive engineering*]
XLP .... Extra Large-Scale Packaging (MHDI)
XLP .... X-Linked Lymphoproliferative Syndrome [*Medicine*]
XLPE .... Cross-Linked Polyethylene [*Organic chemistry*] (NRCH)
XLPS .... Xenon Lamp Power Supply
XLPS .... X-Linked Lymphoproliferative Syndrome [*Medicine*]
XLR .... Experimental Liquid Rocket [*Air Force, NASA*]
XLR .... X-Linked, Lymphocyte-Regulated [*Genetics*]
XLRH .... X-Linked Recessive Hypophosphataemic [*Rickets*] [*Medicine*]
XLS .... Extra-Long Shot (WDMC)
XLS .... St. Louis [*Senegal*] [*Airport symbol*] (OAG)
XLS .... Xenon Light Source
XLS .... Xerox Learning Systems
XLSS .... Xenon Light Source System
XLT .... Telecomunicacoes Aeronauticas SA [*Brazil*] [*ICAO designator*] (FAAC)
XLT .... Xenon LASER Tube
XLTC .... Excel Technology [*NASDAQ symbol*] (TTSB)
XLTC .... Excel Technology, Inc. [*NASDAQ symbol*] (SAG)
XLTCP .... Excel Tech $0.40 Cv Pfd [*NASDAQ symbol*] (TTSB)
XLTCW .... Excel Technology Wrrt'B' [*NASDAQ symbol*] (TTSB)
XLTN .... Translation (NASA)
XLTR .... Translator (MSA)
XLWB .... Extra-Long Wheelbase
XM .... Christmas
XM .... Crossmatch (MAE)
XM .... Excitation Monochromator
XM .... Expanded Memory
XM .... Experimental Missile [*Air Force, NASA*]
XM .... Experimental Model
X_m .... Magnetic Susceptibility [*Physics*] (DAVI)
XM .... Research Missile [*NATO*]
XM .... Servicios a la Navegacion en el Espacio Aereo Mexicano (SENEAM) [*Mexico ICAO designator*] (ICDA)
xm .... St. Vincent [*MARC country of publication code Library of Congress*] (LCCP)
XMA .... Martin Aviation Services [*ICAO designator*] (FAAC)
XMAP .... Sweeper Device [*Navy symbol*]
XMAS .... Christmas
XMAS .... Expandable Machine Accounting System (IAA)
XMAS .... Extended Mission Apollo Simulation [*NASA*] (IEEE)
X-mat .... Crossmatch [*Hematology*] (DAVI)
XMBA .... Executive Master of Business Administration (GAGS)
X/MBR .... Cross Member [*Automotive engineering*]
XMC .... Borough of Manhattan Community College, New York, NY [*OCLC symbol*] (OCLC)
XMC .... Malacoota [*New South Wales, Australia*] [*Airport symbol*] (AD)
XmC .... Standard Microfilm Reproductions Ltd., Scarborough, ON, Canada [*Library symbol Library of Congress*] (LCLS)
XMD .... Ozark, AL [*Location identifier FAA*] (FAAL)
XME .... Medgar Evers College of the City University of New York, Brooklyn, NY [*OCLC symbol*] (OCLC)
XMFR .... Transformer (AAG)
XMG .... Mahendranagar [*Nepal*] [*Airport symbol*] (OAG)
XMH .... Manihi [*French Polynesia*] [*Airport symbol*] (OAG)
XMI .... Christmas Island [*Seismograph station code, US Geological Survey*] (SEIS)
XMI .... Masasi [*Tanzania*] [*Airport symbol*] (OAG)
XMI .... Seymour-Moss International Ltd. [*Vancouver Stock Exchange symbol*]
XMIM .... Transmitter Interface Module [*Army*]
xmission .... Transmission (IDOE)
xmit .... Transmit (IDOE)
XMIT .... Transmit [*or Transmitter*]
XMITR .... Transmitter (ADDR)
XMITTER .... Transmitter (NTCM)
xmitter .... Transmitter (IDOE)
XML .... Extensible Markup Language [*Computer science*]
XML .... Miles Laboratories, Inc., Miles Pharmaceutical Division, West Haven, CT [*OCLC symbol*] (OCLC)
XML .... Minlaton [*Australia Airport symbol Obsolete*] (OAG)
XMM .... Extended Memory Manager [*Computer science*] (PCM)
XMM .... Mamaia [*Romania*] [*Airport symbol*] (AD)
XMM .... State University of New York, Agricultural and Technical College at Morrisville,Morrisville, NY [*OCLC symbol*] (OCLC)
XMM .... Xaverian Missionary Society of Mary, Inc. (TOCD)
XMM .... Xeromammography [*Radiology*] (DAVI)
XMM .... X-Ray Multi-Mirror Mission [*Space observatory*]
xmn .... Transmission
X (Mode) .... Extraordinary Mode (MCD)
XMOS .... Cross Metal Oxide Semiconductor (NITA)
XMP .... Experimental Mathematical Programming System [*Computer science*] (MHDI)
XMP .... Marion Public Library, Marion, IN [*OCLC symbol*] (OCLC)
XMP .... Xanthosine Monophosphate [*Biochemistry*]
XMR .... Cape Canaveral, FL [*Location identifier FAA*] (FAAL)
XMS .... Experimental Development Specification [*Military*] (CAAL)
XMS .... Experimental Missile Specifications
XMS .... Extended Memory Specification [*Computer science*] (PCM)
XMS .... Xavier Mission Sisters [*Catholic Mission Sisters of St. Francis Xavier*] [*Roman Catholic religious order*]
XMS .... X-Band Microwave Source
XMS .... Xerox Memory System
XMSN .... Transmission (AAG)
XMT .... Exempt (NVT)
XMT .... Transmit (MSA)
xmt .... Transmit (IDOE)
XMT .... Transmit (WDMC)
XMT .... X-Band Microwave Transmitter
XMTD .... Transmitted (MCD)
XMTG .... Transmitting
Xmtl .... Experimental (DOMA)
XMTL .... Transmittal (IEEE)
XMTR .... Transmitter
xmtr .... Transmitter (IDOE)
XMT-REC .... Transmit-Receive (AAG)
XMTR-REC .... Transmitter-Receiver
XMX .... Servicios a la Navegacion en el Espacio Aereo Mexicano [*Mexico ICAO designator*] (FAAC)
XN .... Canadian National Telecommunications [*Canada ICAO designator*] (ICDA)
XN .... Christian
XN .... Ex-New [*Without the right to new stocks or shares*] [*Stock exchange term*] (SPSG)
XN .... Experimental (Navy)
XNA .... Xinhua News Agency [*China*]
XNB .... X-Band Navigation Beacon
XNC .... Canadian National Telecommunications [*FAA designator*] (FAAC)
XNC .... Nazareth College of Rochester, Rochester, NY [*OCLC symbol*] (OCLC)
XNE .... Xerox New Enterprises
XNET .... XcelleNet, Inc. [*NASDAQ symbol*] (SAG)
XNEW .... Ex New Issue [*Without the right to new stocks or shares*] [*Stock exchange term*]

XNG .... Crossing [*Aviation*] (FAAC)
XNG .... Quang Ngai [*Vietnam*] [*Airport symbol*] (AD)
XNL .... NELINET [*New England Library Information Network*], Newton, MA [*OCLC symbol*] (OCLC)
XNN .... Xining [*China*] [*Airport symbol*] (OAG)
XNO .... North, SC [*Location identifier FAA*] (FAAL)
XNOS .... Experimental Network Operating System
XNS .... Navtech Systems Support, Inc. [*Canada ICAO designator*] (FAAC)
XNS .... Xerox Network Services (NITA)
XNS .... Xerox Network Systems [*Telecommunications*]
XNT .... NOTAMS International, Inc. [*ICAO designator*] (FAAC)
XNTY .... Christianity
XNV .... TIGIN Ltd. [*ICAO designator*] (FAAC)
XNVA .... Xenova Group PLC [*NASDAQ symbol*] (SAG)
XNVAY .... Xenova Group ADS [*NASDAQ symbol*] (TTSB)
XNX .... Xenex Industries & Resources Ltd. [*Vancouver Stock Exchange symbol*]
XO .... 360 (Degrees) Communic [*NYSE symbol*] (TTSB)
XO .... Crystal Oscillator (IEEE)
XO .... Executive Officer [*Military*]
XO .... Expenditure Order [*Military*] (AABC)
XO .... Experimental Officer [*Also, EO, ExO*] [*Ministry of Agriculture, Fisheries, and Food*] [*British*]
XO .... Extra Old [*Designation on brandy labels*]
XO .... Rio Airways [*ICAO designator*] (AD)
XO .... Xanthine Oxidase [*Also, XOD*] [*An enzyme*]
XO .... X-Axis of Orbiter [*NASA*] (NASA)
XO .... Xylenol Orange [*An indicator*] [*Chemistry*]
XOB .... Xenon Optical Beacon
XOC .... Experimental On-Line Capabilities [*Computer science*]
XOD .... Xanthine Oxidase [*Also, XO*] [*An enzyme*]
XOFF .... Transmitter Off (BUR)
XOGP .... Xograph (VRA)
XOID .... Xyloid [*Woody*] (ROG)
XOMA .... XOMA Corp. [*NASDAQ symbol*] (SAG)
XOMD .... Xomed Surgical Products, Inc. [*NASDAQ symbol*] (SAG)
XomedS .... Xomen Surgical Products, Inc. [*Associated Press*] (SAG)
XON .... Cross-Office Highway [*Telecommunications*] (TEL)
XON .... Exxon Corp. [*NYSE symbol*] (SPSG)
XON .... Transmitter On (BUR)
XOP .... Extended Operation
XOP .... X-Ray Out of Plaster [*Radiology*] (DAVI)
XOR .... Exclusive Operating Room [*Medicine*] (MAE)
XOR .... Exclusive Operation [*Computer single-key cryptosystem*] (PCM)
XOR .... Exclusive Or [*Gates*] [*Computer science*]
XOS .... Cross-Office Slot [*Telecommunications*] (TEL)
XOS .... Extra Outsize [*Clothing*]
XOS .... Xerox Operating System
XOT .... Extra Output Terminal [*Computer science*] (MHDI)
xover .... Crossover (IDOE)
XOW .... Express Order Wire [*Telecommunications*] (TEL)
XOX C .... XOX Corp. [*Associated Press*] (SAG)
XOXC .... XOX Corp. [*NASDAQ symbol*] (SAG)
XP .... Avior [*ICAO designator*] (AD)
XP .... Exophoria [*Medicine*] (MEDA)
XP .... Expandable Processor [*IBM Corp.*] [*Computer science*]
XP .... Expansionist Party of the United States [*Political party*] (EA)
XP .... Express Paid
XP .... Express Parcel Systems [*Europe*]
XP .... Extra Person (WGA)
XP .... Fire Resistive Protected [*Insurance classification*]
XP .... Radio Aeronautica Paraguaya Sociedad Anonima (RAPSA) [*Paraguay*] [*ICAO designator*] (ICDA)
xp .... Spratly Islands [*MARC country of publication code Library of Congress*] (LCCP)
XP .... X-Axis of Payload [*NASA*] (NASA)
XP .... Xeroderma Pigmentosum [*Inherited, disfiguring syndrome*]
XPA .... Pama [*Burkina Faso*] [*Airport symbol*] (OAG)
XPA .... Pan Am Weather Systems [*FAA designator*] (FAAC)
XPA .... X-Band Parametric Amplifier
XPA .... X-Band Passive Array
XPA .... X-Band Planar Array
XPA .... X-Band Power Amplifier
XPAA .... X-Band Planar Array Antenna
XPARS .... External Research Publication and Retrieval System [*Department of State*]
XPC .... Christus [*Christ*] [*Latin*]
XPC .... Express Passenger Coach
XPC .... Morgan StanGp 7%CiscoSy'PERQS' [*AMEX symbol*] (TTSB)
XPC .... Morgan Stanley Group, Inc. [*AMEX symbol*] (SAG)
XPD .... Cross-Polarization Discrimination [*Telecommunications*]
XPD .... Expedient Demise [*Used as title of novel by Len Deighton*]
XPD .... Expedite (MUGU)
XPD .... X-Ray Photoelectron Diffraction
XPDR .... Transponder (MUGU)
XPDU .... X Protocol Data Unit (TNIG)
XPED .... Xpedite Systems [*NASDAQ symbol*] (TTSB)
XPED .... Xpedite Systems, Inc. [*NASDAQ symbol*] (SAG)
XPED .... X-Ray Photoelectron Diffraction
Xpedite .... Xpedite Systems, Inc. [*Associated Press*] (SAG)
XPF .... Explosion Release Factor [*Nuclear energy*] (NUCP)
XPG .... Southport Aerospace Centre [*Canada*] [*FAA designator*] (FAAC)
XPH .... Port Heiden, AK [*Location identifier FAA*] (FAAL)
XPHS .... Xylan Polyhydrogensulfate [*Antineoplastic drug*]
XPI .... Cross-Polarization Interference [*in radio transmission*]
XPL .... Explain [*or Explanation*] (IAA)
XPL .... Explosive (AAG)
XPLOR .... Xerox 9700 Users' Association (EA)
Xplor .... Xplor Corp. [*Associated Press*] (SAG)
XPLOS .... Explosive (FAAC)
XPLR .... Xplor Corp. [*NASDAQ symbol*] (NQ)
XPLR .... Xplor Corp. [*NASDAQ symbol*] (TTSB)
XPLT .... Exploit (MUGU)
XPM .... Expanded Metal [*Heavy gauge*]
XPM .... Xerox Planning Model [*A computerized representation of the Xerox Corp.'s operations*]
XPN .... Expansion (AAG)
XPN .... External Priority Number (ECII)
XPNDR .... Transponder (AAG)
XPONDER .... Transponder
xponder .... Transponder (IDOE)
X-POP .... X-Body Axis Perpendicular to Orbit Plane [*Aerospace*]
XPP .... Express Paid Letter (ROG)
XPP .... Xi Psi Phi [*Fraternity*]
XPP .... Xylem Pressure Potential [*Botany*]
XPPA .... X-Band Pseudopassive Array
XPPA .... X-Band Pulsed Power Amplifier
XPR .... Air-Rep [*FAA designator*] (FAAC)
XPR .... Ex-Privileges [*Without the right to privileges*] [*Finance*]
XPrA .... USX CORP 6.50% CV Pfd [*NYSE symbol*] (TTSB)
x pri .... Ex-Privileges [*Without the right to privileges*] [*Finance*] (DS)
XPRS .... US Xpress Enterprises, Inc. [*NASDAQ symbol*] (SAG)
XPRSA .... U.S. Xpress Enterprises'A' [*NASDAQ symbol*] (TTSB)
XPRT .... Expert Software [*NASDAQ symbol*] (TTSB)
XPRT .... Expert Software, Inc. [*NASDAQ symbol*] (SAG)
XPS .... Expert System [*Computer science*] (IAA)
XPS .... X-Band Phase Shifter
XPS .... XP International BV [*Netherlands ICAO designator*] (FAAC)
XPS .... X-Ray Photoelectron Spectroscopy (RDA)
XPS .... X-Ray Photoemission Spectroscopy
XPSW .... External Processor Status Word
XPT .... Crosspoint [*Switching element*] (MSA)
XPT .... Export
XPT .... Express Paid Telegraph
XPT .... External Page Table [*Computer science*] (BUR)
X PT .... Extra Point (WGA)
XPT .... X-Band Pulse Transmitter
XPT .... Xitron Portable Terminal (DGA)
XPU .... West Kuparuk, AK [*Location identifier FAA*] (FAAL)
XPW .... American Ex-Prisoners of War (EA)
XPX .... Phoenix Flight Operations Ltd. [*Canada ICAO designator*] (FAAC)
XQ .... Caribbean International [*ICAO designator*] (AD)
XQ .... Cross-Question [*Transcripts*]
XQ .... Experimental Target Drone [*Air Force, NASA*]
X/Q .... Relative Concentration [*Symbol*] (NRCH)
XQA .... Greenville, ME [*Location identifier FAA*] (FAAL)
XQH .... Xenon Quartz Helix
XQM .... Queens College, Flushing, NY [*OCLC symbol*] (OCLC)
XQP .... Quepos [*Costa Rica*] [*Airport symbol*] (OAG)
XR .... Cross Reference (MCD)
XR .... Empresa de Servicios Aeronauticos [*Cuba ICAO designator*] (ICDA)
XR .... Examiner (ROG)
XR .... Exchange Rate [*Economics*]
XR .... Export Reactor [*Nuclear energy*] (NRCH)
XR .... Ex-Rights [*Without Rights*] [*Investment term*]
XR .... Extended Range [*Film*] [*Briteline Corp.*]
XR .... Extended Response (WGA)
XR .... Extension Register
XR .... External Reset
XR .... Index Register
XR .... No Returns Permitted [*Business term*]
XR .... Roentgen Ray [*Radiology*] (DAVI)
XR .... RY II Financial Corp. [*Toronto Stock Exchange symbol*]
XR .... X-Ray
XRA .... X-Ray Assistant [*British military*] (DMA)
XRAY .... Dentsply International [*NASDAQ symbol*] (SAG)
XRB .... X-Band RADAR Beacon
XRB .... X-Ray Background [*Cosmology*]
XRC .... Xerox Research Centre of Canada Library [*UTLAS symbol*]
XRC .... X-Ray Centroid
XRCD .... X-Ray Crystal Density
XRD .... Crossroad [*Postal Service standard*] (OPSA)
XRD .... Crossroad
XRD .... X-Ray Diffraction [*or Diffractometer*]
XRDF .... X-Ray Radial Distance Function [*Surface chemistry analysis*]
XRDS .... Crossroads
X-REA .... X-Ray Events Analyzer (KSC)
X-REF .... Cross Reference (NG)
XRF .... Experimental Reproduction File [*Computer science*] (ECII)
XRF .... Experimental Reproduction Film (DIT)
XRF .... Explosion Release Factor [*Nuclear energy*] (NRCH)
XRF .... Extended Recovery Facility (NITA)
XRF .... Extended Reliability Feature (HGAA)
XRF .... Rockefeller Foundation, Library, New York, NY [*OCLC symbol*] (OCLC)
XRF .... X-Ray Fluorescence [*Spectrometry*]
XRFS .... X-Ray Fluorescence Spectrometer
XRG .... X-Ray Generator [*Instrumentation*]
XRGP .... Extended Range Guided Projectiles (MCD)
XRI .... Xenium Resources, Inc. [*Vancouver Stock Exchange symbol*]

XRII X-Ray Image Intensifier
XRIT X-Rite, Inc. [*NASDAQ symbol*] (NQ)
X-Rite X-Rite, Inc. [*Associated Press*] (SAG)
XRL Extended-Range Lance [*Missile*]
XRL X-Ray LASER
XRM External Relational Memory
XRM External ROM [*Read Only Memory*] Mode [*Computer science*] (IAA)
XRM Extra Range Multigrade [*Automotive engineering*]
XRM X-Ray Microanalyzer [*or Microscopy*] (IEEE)
XRMD X-Ray Microdiffraction [*Surface analysis*]
XRN RY NT Financial Corp. [*Toronto Stock Exchange symbol*]
XRN X-Linked Recessive Nephrolithiasis [*Medicine*]
XROAD Crossroad
XROI X-Ray Optical Interferometer
XRP X-Ray and Photofluorography Technician [*Navy*]
XRP X-Ray Polychromator
XRPM X-Ray Projection Microscope (IEEE)
XRS X-Ray Spectrometry
XRT Ex-Rights [*Without Rights*] [*Investment term*] (SPSG)
XRT Extended-Range TOW
XRT X-Ray Technician [*Navy*]
X-RT X-Ray Telescope (MCD)
XRT X-Ray Therapy [*or Treatment*]
XRTOW Extended-Range TOW [*Tube-Launched, Optically Tracked, Wire-Guided*] [*Weapon*] (MCD)
X-RTS Ex-Rights [*Without Rights*] [*Investment term*]
XRW Fort Campbell, KY [*Location identifier FAA*] (FAAL)
XRX Xerox Corp. [*NYSE symbol*] (SPSG)
XRY Jerez De La Frontera [*Spain*] [*Airport symbol*] (OAG)
XRY RY Financial Corp. [*Toronto Stock Exchange symbol*]
XRY Yakima, WA [*Location identifier FAA*] (FAAL)
XS Across Shoulder (WDMC)
XS Catholic Mission Sisters of St. Francis Xavier (TOCD)
XS Christus [*Christ*] [*Latin*]
XS Cross Section
XS Excess
XS Expenses
XS Extra Small
XS Extra Strong
XS Extremely Severe [*Rock climbing*]
X/S Over the Shoulder Shot [*Also, OS*] [*Cinematography*] (NTCM)
XS Societe Internationale de Telecommunications Aeronautiques, Societe Cooperative (SITA) [*ICAO designator*] (ICDA)
XS X-Axis of Solid Rocket Booster [*NASA*] (NASA)
XS Xerces Society (EA)
XS Xiphisternum [*Also called the xiphoid process*] [*Anatomy*] (DAVI)
XS3 Excess Three [*Code*]
XS-11 Excess Eleven [*1967 group of scientist-astronauts selected by NASA*]
XSA Cross-Sectional Area [*Cardiology*]
XSA Spectrum Air Service, Inc. [*ICAO designator*] (FAAC)
XSA X-Band Satellite Antenna
XSAES X-Ray Stimulated Auger Electron Spectroscopy (MCD)
XSAL Xenon Short Arc Lamp
XSAM Experimental Surface-to-Air Missile [*Military*] (IAA)
X-SAR Xband-Synthetic Aperture Radar (EERA)
XSB Smith Barney Holdings [*NYSE symbol*] (SAG)
XSB Xavier Society for the Blind (EA)
XSC Southampton Center of Long Island University, Southampton, NY [*OCLC symbol*] (OCLC)
XSC South Caicos [*British West Indies*] [*Airport symbol*] (OAG)
XSCID X-Linked Server Combined Immunodeficiency [*"Bubble Boy" disease*] [*Medicine*]
XSCR Xscribe Corp. [*NASDAQ symbol*] (NQ)
Xscribe Xscribe Corp. [*Associated Press*] (SAG)
XSD Southeast Dubois County, School Corp. Library, Ferdinand, IN [*OCLC symbol*] (OCLC)
XSD Tonopah, NV [*Location identifier FAA*] (FAAL)
XSE Sebba [*Burkina Faso*] [*Airport symbol*] (OAG)
XSECT Cross Section
xsect Cross Section (VRA)
X-section Cross Section (IDOE)
XSF Springfield, OH [*Location identifier FAA*] (FAAL)
XSF X-Ray Scattering Facility
X-SFA X-Ray Surface Forces Apparatus [*Imaging technique*]
XSL Experimental Space Laboratory
XS-LIM Exceeds Limits of Procedure (DAVI)
XSLR Crossed Straight Leg Raising [*Sign*] [*Neurology*] (DAVI)
XSM Experimental Strategic Missile
XSM Experimental Surface Missile
XSM X-Ray Stress Measurement
XSMDC Expanding Shielded Mild Detonating Cord (MCD)
XSN Stepheville Aviation Services [*Canada ICAO designator*] (FAAC)
XSOA Excess Speed of Advance Authorized [*Navy*] (NVT)
X-SONAD Experimental Sonic Azimuth Detector (MCD)
XSP Extended Set Processor [*Computer science*] (MHDI)
XSP Singapore-Seletar [*Singapore*] [*Airport symbol*] (OAG)
XSP Xi Sigma Pi [*Fraternity*]
XSP Xylem Sap Potential [*Botany*]
XSPV Experimental Solid Propellant Vehicle
XSR X-Band Scatterometer RADAR
XSRG X-Ray Standard Review Group [*Department of Health and Human Services*] (EGAO)
XSS Experimental Space Station [*NASA*]
XSS Xenon Solar Simulator
XSSM Experimental Surface-to-Surface Missile [*Military*] (IAA)
XST Experimental Stealth Tactical Demonstrator [*Air Force*]
XST Xylem Sap Tension [*Botany*]
XSTA X-Band Satellite Tracking Antenna
XSTD Expendable Salinity/Temperature/Depth Probe [*Oceanography*] (MSC)
XSTD X-Band Stripline Tunnel Diode
XSTDA X-Band Stripline Tunnel Diode Amplifier
XSTR Extra Strong (MSA)
XSTR Transistor (AAG)
XSTT Excess Transit Time
XSV Expendable Sound Velocimeter [*Oceanography*] (MSC)
XSW X-Ray Standing Wave [*Physics*]
XSWIS X-Ray Standing Wave Interference Spectroscopy
XSYS Xxsys Technologies [*NASDAQ symbol*] (SAG)
XsysTc Xxsys Technologies [*Associated Press*] (SAG)
XSYSW XXsys Technology Wrrt [*NASDAQ symbol*] (TTSB)
XT Christ
XT Cross Talk (IEEE)
XT Executive Transportation [*ICAO designator*] (AD)
XT Exotropia Near [*Ophthalmology*]
XT Extended
XT Extended Processor (NITA)
X(T) Intermittent Exotropia [*Ophthalmology*] (DAVI)
XT Servicos Auxiliares de Transportes Aereos (SATA) [*Brazil ICAO designator*] (ICDA)
X_T Total Reactance (IDOE)
X_t Total Reactance (IDOE)
XT X-Axis of External Tank [*NASA*] (NASA)
XT X-Ray Tube
Xta Chiasma [*Anatomy*] (DAVI)
XTA X-Band Tracking Antenna
XTAL Crystal
xtal Crystal (IDOE)
xtalk Crosstalk (IDOE)
XTALK Crosstalk [*Telecommunications*] (MSA)
XTASI Exchange of Technical Apollo Simulation Information [*NASA*] (IEEE)
XTB Experimental Test Bed [*Army*] (DOMA)
XTC Excess Three Code (IAA)
XTC Exco Technologies Ltd. [*Toronto Stock Exchange symbol*]
XTC External Transmit Clock
XTE X-Ray Timing Explorer
XTEL Cross Tell (IEEE)
XTEL XeTel Corp. [*NASDAQ symbol*] (TTSB)
XTEN Xerox Telecommunications Network [*Proposed*] (TSSD)
XTG Thargomindah [*Queensland*] [*Airport symbol*] (AD)
XTIAN Christian
XTJ Advance Aviation Services, Inc. [*ICAO designator*] (FAAC)
XTK Crosstrack [*Cross track error*] (GAVI)
XTLO Crystal Oscillator
XTM Experimental Test Model
XTM X-Ray Tomographic Microscope
XTN Christian (ROG)
XTN Qatn [*South Arabia*] [*Airport symbol*] (AD)
XTN XTree Tools for Networks [*XTree Co.*] [*Computer science*] (PCM)
XTND Extend [*or Extended*]
XTO Cross Timbers Oil [*NYSE symbol*] (TTSB)
XTO Cross Timbers Oil Co. [*NYSE symbol*] (SPSG)
XTO Taroom [*Queensland*] [*Airport symbol*] (AD)
XTO X-Band Triode Oscillator
XTON EXECUTONE Information Systems, Inc. [*NASDAQ symbol*] (SPSG)
XTON Executone Info Sys [*NASDAQ symbol*] (TTSB)
XTP Express Transfer Protocol (ACRL)
XTP Xanthosine Triphosphate [*Biochemistry*]
XTPA X-Band Tunable Parametric Amplifier
XTPS Xenotron Text Processing System (DGA)
XTR Sector Airlines [*Canada ICAO designator*] (FAAC)
XTR Tara [*Queensland*] [*Airport symbol*] (AD)
XTR X-Ray Transition Radiation
XTR XTRA Corp. [*NYSE symbol*] (SPSG)
XTRA Extra (ROG)
XTRA XTRA Corp. [*Associated Press*] (SAG)
XTRAN Experimental Translation Language (IAA)
XTRM Extreme
XTRY Extraordinary (ROG)
XTS Cross-Tell Simulator (IEEE)
XTV Xerox Team Vision [*Xerox Business Products and Systems Group*] [*El Segundo, CA*] (TSSD)
XTV Xerox Technology Ventures [*El Segundo, CA*] (ECON)
XTWA X-Band Traveling Wave Amplifier
XTWM X-Band Traveling Wave MASER
XTX New York Tax Exempt Income [*AMEX symbol*] (TTSB)
XTX New York Tax Exempt Income Fund [*AMEX symbol*] (SAG)
XTX X-Band Transmitter
XTY Christianity
XU Aerorepresentaciones Tupac Amaru [*Peru*] [*ICAO designator*] (ICDA)
XU Excretory Urogram [*Medicine*]
XU Fire Resistive Unprotected [*Insurance classification*]
XU Trans Mo Airlines [*ICAO designator*] (AD)
XU Xavier University [*Louisiana; Ohio*]
Xu X-Ray Unit [*Radiology*] (DAVI)
XU X Unit [*A unit of wavelength*]
XUB Circleville, OH [*Location identifier FAA*] (FAAL)
XUG Xyvision Users Group (EA)
XUM Xenium [*Gift*] (ROG)

XUPS .... Exide Electronics Group [*NASDAQ symbol*] (TTSB)
XUPS .... Exide Electronics Group, Inc. [*NASDAQ symbol*] (SAG)
XUS .... Americas Income Trust [*NYSE symbol*] (SPSG)
XUT .... Aerorepresentaciones Tupac Amaru [*Peru*] [*ICAO designator*] (FAAC)
XUV .... Extreme Ultraviolet
XV .... Mississippi Valley Airways [*ICAO designator*] (AD)
XV .... X-Ray Vision
XVA .... X-Ray Vidicon Analysis
XVC .... Xenotron Video Composer (DGA)
XVERS .... Transverse (AAG)
xVit .... Xenopus Vitellogenin
XVN .... Venice, FL [*Location identifier FAA*] (FAAL)
XVP .... Executive Vice President
XVP .... Xerox Virtual Printroom
XVR .... Exchange Voltage Regulator [*Telecommunications*] (TEL)
XVRC .... Xavier Corp. [*NASDAQ symbol*] (SAG)
XVT .... Extensible Virtual Toolkit [*Computer science*]
XVT .... Rome, NY [*Location identifier FAA*] (FAAL)
XVTR .... Transverter (AAG)
XW .... Crosswind [*Aviation*] (FAAC)
XW .... Experimental Warhead
XW .... Extra Wide [*Size*]
XW .... Ex-Warrants [*Without Warrants*] [*Finance*] (SPSG)
XW .... Walker's Cay Air Terminal [*ICAO designator*] (AD)
X-WARR .... Ex-Warrants [*Without Warrants*] [*Finance*]
XWAVE .... Extraordinary Wave (IEEE)
X-WAY .... Expressway
XWB .... Ozark, Fort Rucker, AL [*Location identifier FAA*] (FAAL)
XWC .... Wabash-Carnegie Public Library, Wabash, IN [*OCLC symbol*] (OCLC)
XWCC .... Expanded Water Column Characterization [*Oceanography*] (MSC)
XWS .... Experimental Weapon Specification
XWS .... Experimental Weapon System
XWS .... WSI Corp. [*ICAO designator*] (FAAC)
XWW .... World Weatherwatch [*Canada ICAO designator*] (FAAC)
XWY .... West Union, IA [*Location identifier FAA*] (FAAL)
XX .... Dos Equis [*Beer*] [*Standard Brands, Inc.*]
XX .... Doublecross Committee [*British military*] (DMA)
XX .... Double Excellent
XX .... Feminine Chromosome Pair
XX .... Heavy [*ICAO*] (FAAC)
xx .... No Place [*or Unknown*] [*MARC country of publication code Library of Congress*] (LCCP)
X-X .... Pitch Axis [*Aerospace*] (AAG)
XX .... Twenty Committee [*British espionage unit named after a "double-cross" operation it conducted during World War II*]
XX .... Valdez Airlines [*ICAO designator*] (AD)
XX .... Without Securities or Warrants [*Business term*]
XX .... Wrinkled Paper (BARN)
XXC .... University of South Dakota, Card Reproduction Project, Vermillion, SD [*OCLC symbol*] (OCLC)
XXC .... Xerox Canada, Inc. [*Toronto Stock Exchange symbol*]
XXH .... Double Extra Heavy (DAC)
XXL .... Extra-Extra Large [*Size*]
XXS .... Extra-Extra Strong
XXS .... Skyplan Services Ltd. [*Canada ICAO designator*] (FAAC)
XXSTR .... Double Extra Strong
XxsysTc .... Xxsys Technologies [*Associated Press*] (SAG)
XXV .... Administracion de Aeropuertos [*Bolivia*] [*ICAO designator*] (FAAC)
XXX .... Broken Paper (BARN)
XXX .... International Urgency Signal
XXX .... Peru, IN [*Location identifier FAA*] (FAAL)
XXX .... Triple Excellent
XXXX .... Quadruple Strength
XY .... Burma [*International civil aircraft marking*] (ODBW)
XY .... Masculine Chromosome Pair
XY .... Munz Northern [*ICAO designator*] (AD)
XY .... Myanmar [*Aircraft nationality and registration mark*] (FAAC)
XY .... Ryan Air (GAVI)
XY .... Spouse [*Citizens band radio slang*]
XY .... Xylography [*Wood engraving*] (ROG)
XYA .... X-Y Axis
XYA .... Yandina [*Solomon Islands*] [*Airport symbol*] (OAG)
XYAT .... X-Y Axis Table
XYBR .... Xybernaut Corp. [*NASDAQ symbol*] (SAG)
Xybrnaut .... Xybernaut Corp. [*Associated Press*] (SAG)
Xybrnt .... Xybernaut Corp. [*Associated Press*] (SAG)
XYC .... Aero Chasqui SA [*Peru*] [*ICAO designator*] (FAAC)
XYC .... Irvine, KY [*Location identifier FAA*] (FAAL)
XYD .... Daughter [*Citizens band radio slang*]
XYL .... Ex-Young-Lady [*Wife*] [*Amateur radio slang*]
XYL .... Xylocaine [*Topical anesthetic*] [*Astra trademark for lidocaine*]
XYL .... Xylophone [*Music*]
Xyl .... Xylose [*Also, x*] [*A sugar*]
XylanCp .... Xylan Corp. [*Associated Press*] (SAG)
XYLN .... Xylan Corp. [*NASDAQ symbol*] (TTSB)
XYLN .... Xylan Corp. [*NASDAQ symbol*] (SAG)
XYLO .... Xylophone [*Music*] (ADA)
Xylogic .... Xylogics, Inc. [*Associated Press*] (SAG)
XYM .... Husband [*Citizens band radio slang*]
XYP .... X-Y Plotter
XYR .... X-Y Recorder
XYrDev .... Ten-Year Device [*Military decoration*]
Xytron .... Xytronyx, Inc. [*Associated Press*] (SAG)
XYX .... Xytronyx, Inc. [*AMEX symbol*] (SPSG)
XYZ .... Examine Your Zipper
XYZ .... Extra Years of Zest [*Gerontology*]
XYZ .... Island Airlines [*ICAO designator*] (FAAC)
XZ .... Air Tasmania [*ICAO designator*] (AD)
XZ .... Myanmar [*Aircraft nationality and registration mark*] (FAAC)
XZY .... Philadelphia, PA [*Location identifier FAA*] (FAAL)

Y

By Acronym

Y .... Admittance [*Symbol*] [*IUPAC*]
Y .... Alleghany Corp. [*NYSE symbol*] (SPSG)
Y .... Closed at Sea (for High Degree of Emergency Readiness) [*Ship's fittings classification*]
Y .... Coach [*Airline fare code*]
Y .... Depth, Height, or Altitude [*Physics*] (BARN)
Y .... Doublecross [*i.e., to betray*] [*Criminal slang*]
Y .... Dry Air [*Meterology*] (BARN)
Y .... Except Sixth Form [*For the wearing of schoolgirls' uniforms*] [*British*]
Y .... Ex-Dividend and Sales in Full [*Investment term*] (DFIT)
Y .... Late Operating Contact [*Symbol*] (DEN)
Y .... Luminance
Y .... Male Chromosome
Y .... Nominal Gross National Product
y .... Ordinate (IDOE)
Y .... Pathfinder [*Army skill qualification identifier*] (INF)
Y .... Planck Function [*Symbol*] [*IUPAC*]
Y .... Prototype [*Designation for all US military aircraft*]
Y .... Pyrimidine [*Single-letter symbol*] [*Genetics*] (DOG)
Y .... [*A*] Pyrimidine Nucleoside [*One-letter symbol; see Pyd*]
Y .... Tanker [*Army symbol*]
Y .... Three-Phase Star Connection [*Symbol*] (DEN)
Y .... Transitional Testing [*Aircraft*]
Y .... Tyrosine [*One-letter symbol; see Tyr*]
Y .... Upsilon [*Symbol*] [*Quantum physics*]
Y .... Vertical Deflection [*Symbol*] (DEN)
Y .... Yacht (ADA)
Y .... Yankee [*Phonetic alphabet*] [*International*] (DSUE)
Y .... Yard [*Measure*]
y .... Yard (IDOE)
Y .... Yaw
Y .... Y-Axis
Y .... Yea [*Vote*]
Y .... Year
y .... Year (IDOE)
y .... Year (WDMC)
Y .... Yeates' Pennsylvania Reports [*1791-1808*] [*A publication*] (DLA)
Y .... Yellow [*Phonetic alphabet*] [*Royal Navy World War I*] (DSUE)
Y .... Yellow [*Horticulture*]
Y .... Yen [*Monetary unit in Japan*]
Y .... Yeoman
Y .... Yersinea [*A genus of bacteria*]
Y .... Yerushalmi [*Palestinian Talmud*] (BJA)
Y .... Yield [*Agriculture*] [*Stock exchange term*]
Y .... Yoke [*Phonetic alphabet*] [*World War II*] (DSUE)
Y .... Yorker [*Phonetic alphabet*] [*Pre-World War II*] (DSUE)
Y .... Yoshitomi Pharmaceutical Ind. Co. Ltd. [*Japan*] [*Research code symbol*]
Y .... You
Y .... Young (AAMN)
Y .... Younger [*or Youngest*]
Y .... Young Men's [*or Women's*] Christian Association [*Short form of reference, especially to the group's building or specific facility, as "the Y swimming pool"*]
Y .... Young's Modulus of Elasticity [*Symbol*] [*See also E, YME*]
Y .... Youngstown [*Diocesan abbreviation*] [*Ohio*] (TOCD)
Y .... Young Vic [*British theatrical company*]
Y .... Your
Y .... Y-Punch (IAA)
Y .... Yttrium [*Preferred form, but see also Yt*] [*Chemical element*]
Y .... Yugoslavia [*IYRU nationality code*] (IYR)
Y .... Yuppie [*As in Y-people*]
Y2K .... Year 2000
Y2Y .... Yellowstone to Canada's Yukon Territory
Y-12 .... Oak Ridge Y-12 Plant [*Department of Energy*] [*Oak Ridge, TN*] (GAAI)
YA .... Ash Lighter [*Navy symbol*]
YA .... Government Civil Aviation Authority [*ICAO designator*] (ICDA)
ya .... Yarn (VRA)
YA .... Yaw Axis
YA .... Year Authorized (NITA)
YA .... Yersinia Arthritis [*Medicine*] (DMAA)
YA .... Yet Another [*Computer hacker terminology*] (NHD)
Y/A .... York-Antwerp Rules [*Marine insurance*]
YA .... Yosemite Association (EA)
YA .... Young Achiever [*Australia*]
YA .... Young Adult [*Refers to books published for this market*]
YA .... Young Audiences (EA)
YAA .... Yachtsmen's Association of America (EA)
YAA .... Youth Ambassadors of America [*Later, YAI*] (EA)
YAAR .... Yacimientos Arqueologicos [*Database*] [*Ministerio de Cultura*] [*Spanish*] [*Information service or system*] (CRD)
YAB .... Yet Another BASIC [*Beginner's All-Purpose Symbolic Instruction Code*] [*Computer science*]
YABA .... Yacht Architects and Brokers Association (EA)
YABA .... Yet Another Bloody Acronym [*Computer hacker terminology*] (NHD)
YABA .... Young American Bowling Alliance (EA)
YABC .... Yesterday's Authors of Books for Children [*A publication*]
YABRI .... Young Adult Book Review Index [*A publication*]
YAC .... Yacuiba [*Bolivia*] [*Airport symbol*] (AD)
YAC .... Yeast Artificial Chromosome [*Genetics*] [*Biochemistry*]
YAC .... Young Adult Council of National Social Welfare Assembly (EA)
YAC .... Young Astronaut Council (EA)
YAC .... Youth Affairs Council [*Australia*]
YACC .... Yet Another Compiler-Compiler (MHDB)
YACC .... Yet Another Compiler-Complier (HGAA)
YACC .... Young Adult Conservation Corps
YACC .... Young America's Campaign Committee [*Later, FCM*] (EA)
YACE .... Yukon Alpine Centennial Expedition
Yacht .... Yachting [*A publication*] (BRI)
YACHT .... Youth and Christ Hang Together
YACP .... Young Adult Chronic Patient [*Medicine*] (MEDA)
YACTOFF .... Yaw Actuator Offset (KSC)
YACV .... Youth Accommodation Coalition of Victoria [*Australia*]
Yad .... Yadaim (BJA)
YAD .... Young's Nova Scotia Admiralty Decisions [*A publication*] (DLA)
YADH .... Yeast Alcohol Dehydrogenase [*An enzyme*]
YAEC .... Yankee Atomic Electric Co.
YAF .... Asbestos Hill [*Canada*] [*Airport symbol Obsolete*] (OAG)
YAF .... Yidishe Arbeter Froyen (BJA)
YAF .... Young Americans for Freedom (EA)
YAF .... Young America's Foundation (EA)
YAF .... Yugoslavian Air Force
YAG .... Fort Frances [*Canada*] [*Airport symbol*] (OAG)
YAG .... Miscellaneous Auxiliary [*Self-propelled*] [*Navy ship symbol*]
YAG .... Yagi [*Kashiwara*] [*Japan*] [*Seismograph station code, US Geological Survey*] [*Closed*] (SEIS)
YAG .... Young Actors Guild (EA)
YAG .... Yttrium-Aluminum Garnet [*LASER technology*]
YAGL .... Yttrium Aluminum Garnet LASER
YAGR .... Ocean RADAR Station Ship [*Navy symbol Obsolete*]
YAH .... Alfred University, Alfred, NY [*OCLC symbol*] (OCLC)
YAH .... Yahtse [*Alaska*] [*Seismograph station code, US Geological Survey*] (SEIS)
YAHOH .... Young Hard-of-Hearing Adults [*British*] (EAIO)
Yahoo .... Yahoo, Inc. [*Associated Press*] (SAG)
Yahoo .... Yet Another Hierarchically Officious Oracle [*World Wide Web*] (DOM)
YAI .... Young Adult Institute and Workshop (EA)
YAI .... Youth Ambassadors International (EA)
YAIC .... Young American Indian Council
YAIG .... Yttrium Alumnium Iron Garnet [*LASER technology*] (IAA)
YAK .... Yakima [*Diocesan abbreviation*] [*Washington*] (TOCD)
YAK .... Yakovlev [*Russian aircraft symbol; initialism taken from name of aircraft's designer*]
YAK .... Yakutat [*Alaska*] [*Airport symbol*] (OAG)
YAK .... Yakutsk [*Former USSR Seismograph station code, US Geological Survey*] (SEIS)
Yal .... Yalkut Shim'oni (BJA)
YAL .... Yalta [*Former USSR Seismograph station code, US Geological Survey Closed*] (SEIS)
YAL .... Youth Affairs Lobby (AIE)
YAL .... Yttrium Aluminum LASER
YALE .... Spreckels Industries [*NASDAQ symbol*] (TTSB)
Yale L & Pol'y Rev... Yale Law and Policy Review [*A publication*] (DLA)
Yale Rev Law & Soc Act'n... Yale Review of Law and Social Action [*A publication*] (DLA)
Yale Rev of L and Soc Action... Yale Review of Law and Social Action [*A publication*] (DLA)
Yale U .... Yale University (GAGS)
YalMakh .... Yalkut Makhiri (BJA)
YALSA .... Young Adult Library Services Association [*American Library Association*]

YAM............ American Museum of Natural History, New York, NY [*OCLC symbol*] (OCLC)
YAM............ Sault Ste. Marie [*Canada*] [*Airport symbol*] (OAG)
YAM............ Yamagata [*Japan*] [*Seismograph station code, US Geological Survey*] (SEIS)
YAM............ Yet Another MODEM [*Modulator-Demodulator*] [*Communications program*]
YAM............ Young Australian Male [*Lifestyle classification*]
YAN............ Yancey Railroad Co. [*AAR code*]
YAN............ Yangoru [*Papua New Guinea*] [*Seismograph station code, US Geological Survey*] (SEIS)
YANB.......... Yardville National Bancorp [*NASDAQ symbol*] (SAG)
YANB.......... Yardville Natl Banc [*NASDAQ symbol*] (TTSB)
YANCON...... Yankee Conference [*College sports*]
Y & C.......... Younge and Collyer's English Chancery Reports [*1841-43*] [*A publication*] (DLA)
Y & C.......... Younge and Collyer's English Exchequer Equity Reports [*1834-42*] [*A publication*] (DLA)
Y & CCC...... Younge and Collyer's English Chancery Cases [*62-63 English Reprint*] [*1841-43*] [*A publication*] (DLA)
Y & C Ch..... Younge and Collyer's English Chancery Reports [*1841-43*] [*A publication*] (DLA)
Y & C Ch Cas... Younge and Collyer's English Chancery Cases [*62-63 English Reprint*] [*1841-43*] [*A publication*] (DLA)
Y & C Ex...... Younge and Collyer's English Exchequer Equity Reports [*1834-42*] [*A publication*] (DLA)
Y & C Exch... Younge and Collyer's English Exchequer Equity Reports [*1834-42*] [*A publication*] (DLA)
Y & Coll...... Younge and Collyer's English Chancery Reports [*1841-43*] [*A publication*] (DLA)
Y & Coll...... Younge and Collyer's English Exchequer Equity Reports [*1834-42*] [*A publication*] (DLA)
Y & D.......... Bureau of Yards and Docks [*Later, NFEC*] [*Navy*]
Y & J.......... Younge and Jervis' English Exchequer Reports [*1826-30*] [*A publication*] (DLA)
Y & L.......... York and Lancaster Regiment [*Military unit*] [*British*] (DMA)
Y & LR........ York and Lancaster Regiment [*Military unit*] [*British*]
Y & MV........ Yazoo & Mississippi Valley Railroad Co.
Y & R.......... Young & Rubicam International [*Advertising agency*]
YANGPAT..... Yangtze Patrol, Asiatic Fleet [*Navy*]
YANK.......... Yankee (ROG)
YANK.......... Youth of America Needs to Know
YankEnS...... Yankee Energy Systems, Inc. [*Associated Press*] (SAG)
yao............. Yao (Bantu) [*MARC language code Library of Congress*] (LCCP)
YAO............ Yaounde [*Cameroon*] [*Airport symbol*] (OAG)
YAP............ Yap [*Caroline Islands*] [*Airport symbol*] (OAG)
YAP............ Yaw and Pitch
YAP............ Yield Analysis Pattern [*Computer science*]
YAP............ Young Americans in Prague [*Expatriot Americans in the 1990's*]
Yap............ Young Aspiring Professional [*In book title "YAP; the Official Young Aspir ing Professional's Fast-Track Handbook"*] [*Lifestyle classification*]
YAP............ Younger American Playwright [*Slang*]
YAPA.......... Youth Action Policy Association [*Australia*]
YAPA.......... Youth and Performing Arts [*Australia*]
YAPD.......... Young Americans of Polish Descent [*Defunct*] (EA)
YAPLO........ Yorkshire Association of Power Loom Overlookers [*A union*] [*British*] (DCTA)
Yappie........ Young Artist Professional [*Lifestyle classification*]
YAR............ Yemen Arab Republic
YAR............ York-Antwerp Rules [*Marine insurance*]
YARA.......... Young Americans for Responsible Action
Y-ARD......... Yarrow Admiralty Research Department [*Navy British*]
YARD.......... Youth Associated with the Restoration of Democracy [*Kenya*] [*Political party*] (EY)
YARDS........ Yard Activity Reporting and Decision System (PDAA)
YardvN........ Yardville National Bancorp [*Associated Press*] (SAG)
YARU.......... Yale Arbovirus Research Unit [*Yale University*] [*Research center*] (RCD)
YAS............ Yasodhara Ashram Society (EA)
YAS............ Yaw Attitude Sensor
YASD.......... Young Adult Services Division - of ALA [*American Library Association*] (EA)
YASGB........ Youth Association of Synagogues in Great Britain (BI)
YASIG......... Young Adult Special Interest Group [*Canadian Library Association*]
YASOQB...... Ye Anciente and Secret Order of Quiet Birdmen (EA)
YAT............ Attawapiskat [*Canada*] [*Airport symbol*] (OAG)
YAT............ Yaldymych [*Former USSR Seismograph station code, US Geological Survey Closed*] (SEIS)
Yate-Lee...... Yates-Lee on Bankruptcy [*3rd ed.*] [*1887*] [*A publication*] (DLA)
Yates Sel Cas... Yates' Select Cases [*1809*] [*New York*] [*A publication*] (DLA)
Yates Sel Cas (NY)... Yates' Select Cases [*1809*] [*New York*] [*A publication*] (DLA)
YATS.......... Youth Attitude Tracking Survey [*Navy*]
YAUI........... Yet Another User Interface [*Computer science*]
YAUN.......... Yet Another Unix Nerd [*Computer hacker terminology*] (NHD)
YAVIS......... Young, Attractive, Verbal, Intelligent, and Successful
YAWF.......... Youth Against War and Fascism (EA)
Yawnie........ Youngish Anglophone of Westmount and Notre-Dame-De-Grace [*Canadian Yuppie identified in Keith Harrison's novel "After Six Days"*] [*Lifestyle classification*]
YAWP.......... Yet Another Word Processor (BYTE)
YB............. Hyannis Aviation [*ICAO designator*] (AD)
YB............. Meteorological Operational Telecommunications Network Europe [*ICAO designator*] (ICDA)
YB............. Yard Bird [*Confined to camp*] [*Military slang*]
YB............. Yearbook
YB............. Yellowknife Bear Resources, Inc. [*Toronto Stock Exchange symbol*]
YB............. Yeshiva Benarroch. Tetuan (BJA)
YB............. Your Business [*A publication*] (ADA)
YB............. Your Business [*A publication*]
YB............. Youth Brigade [*Australia*]
YB............. Youth Bureau [*Australia*]
Yb............. Ytterbium [*Chemical element*]
Yb-169-DTPA... Ytterbium 169 Pentetate Sodium [*Chemistry*] (DAVI)
YBA............ Youth Basketball Association [*Joint program of NBA Players' Association and YMCA*]
YBAAA........ Yearbook. Association of Attenders of Alumni of the Hague Academy of Int ernational Law [*A publication*] (DLA)
YB Air & Space L... Yearbook of Air and Space Law [*A publication*] (DLA)
YB Ames...... Year Book. Ames Foundation [*A publication*] (DLA)
YBASL......... Yearbook of Air and Space Law [*A publication*] (DLA)
YBBFC......... Younger Brothers Band Fan Club [*Defunct*] (EA)
YBC............ Baie Comeau [*Canada*] [*Airport symbol*] (OAG)
YBC............ Yale Babylonian Collection (BJA)
YBCA.......... Yearbook of Commercial Arbitration [*A publication*] (DLA)
YBCO.......... Yttrium Barium Copper Oxide [*Inorganic chemistry*]
YBD............ Bowdock [*Navy symbol*]
YBD............ Yellow Band Resources [*Vancouver Stock Exchange symbol*]
YBD............ Young British Designers
YBDSA........ Yacht Designers and Surveyors Association (EAIO)
YBE............ Stewart Aviation Services, Inc. [*ICAO designator*] (FAAC)
YBE............ Uranium City [*Canada*] [*Airport symbol*] (OAG)
YBE............ York Borough Board of Education, Professional Education Library [*UTLAS symbol*]
YB Ed I........ Year Books of Edward I [*A publication*] (DLA)
YB Eur Conv on Human Rights... Year Book. European Convention on Human Rights [*A publication*] (DLA)
YB Europ Conv HR... Yearbook. European Convention on Human Rights [*The Hague, Netherlands*] [*A publication*] (DLA)
YBG............ Saguenay [*Canada*] [*Airport symbol*] (OAG)
YB Human Rights... Yearbook on Human Rights [*A publication*] (DLA)
YB Hum Rts... Yearbook on Human Rights [*A publication*] (DLA)
YBIA........... Youth Business Initiative Australia
YBICJ.......... Yearbook. International Court of Justice [*A publication*] (DLA)
YB Int L Comm... Yearbook. International Law Community [*A publication*] (DLA)
YB Int'l L Comm'n... Yearbook. International Law Commission [*A publication*] (DLA)
YB Int'l Org... Yearbook of International Organizations [*A publication*] (DLA)
YBJ............ Baie Johan Beetz [*Canada*] [*Airport symbol*] (OAG)
YBK............ Baker Lake [*Canada*] [*Airport symbol*] (OAG)
YBL............ Campbell River [*Canada*] [*Airport symbol*] (OAG)
YB League... Yearbook. League of Nations [*A publication*] (DLA)
YBM............ State University of New York, College at Buffalo, Buffalo, NY [*OCLC symbol*] (OCLC)
Y-BOCS........ Yale-Brown Obsessive-Compulsive Scale [*Psychology*]
Yb of Leg Stud... Year Book of Legal Studies [*Madras, India*] [*A publication*] (DLA)
Yb of the Eur Conv on Human Rights... Yearbook. European Convention on Human Rights [*The Hague, Netherlands*] [*A publication*] (DLA)
YBP............ Years before Present
YB P1 Edw II... Year Books, Part 1, Edward II [*A publication*] (DLA)
YBPC.......... Young Black Programmers Coalition (EA)
YBR............ Brandon [*Canada*] [*Airport symbol*] (OAG)
YBR............ Sludge Removal Barge [*Navy*]
YBR............ Yellow Brick Road [*Intelligence test*]
YBRA.......... Yellowstone-Bighorn Research Association (EA)
YB Rich II.... Bellewe's Les Ans du Roy Richard le Second [*1378-1400*] [*A publication*] (DLA)
YB (Rolls Ser)... Year Books, Rolls Series [*1292-1546*] [*A publication*] (DLA)
YB (RS)....... Year Books, Rolls Series [*1292-1546*] [*A publication*] (DLA)
YB (RS)....... Year Books, Rolls Series, Edited by Horwood [*1292-1307*] [*A publication*] (DLA)
YB (RS)....... Year Books, Rolls Series, Edited by Horwood and Pike [*1337-46*] [*A publication*] (DLA)
YBSC.......... Year Books, Selected Cases [*A publication*] (DLA)
YB Sch L..... Yearbook of School Law [*A publication*] (DLA)
YB (Sel Soc)... Year Books, Selden Society [*1307-19*] [*A publication*] (DLA)
YB (SS)........ Year Books, Selden Society [*1307-19*] [*A publication*] (DLA)
YBT............ Yale Oriental Series. Babylonian Texts [*New Haven, CT*] [*A publication*] (BJA)
YBT............ Youssef Ben Tachfine [*Morocco*] [*Seismograph station code, US Geological Survey*] (SEIS)
YBTV.......... Young Broadcasting, Inc. [*NASDAQ symbol*] (SAG)
YBTVA........ Young Broadcasting'A' [*NASDAQ symbol*] (TTSB)
YBUN.......... Yearbook of the United Nations [*A publication*] (DLA)
YBV............ Berens River [*Canada*] [*Airport symbol*] (OAG)
YBW............ Lehman Brothers, Inc. [*AMEX symbol*] (SAG)
YB World Pol... Yearbook of World Polity [*A publication*] (DLA)
YBX............ Blanc Sablon [*Canada*] [*Airport symbol*] (OAG)
YC............. Alaska Aeronautical Industries [*ICAO designator*] (AD)
Y/C............ Luminance, Color
YC............. Open Lighter [*Non-self-propelled*] [*Navy symbol*]
YC............. Rescue Coordination Center [*ICAO designator*] (ICDA)
YC............. Yacht Club
YC............. Yale College (ROG)
YC............. Yankee Conference [*College sports*]
YC............. Yard Craft [*Navy symbol*]
YC............. Yaw Channel
YC............. Yaw Coupling
YC............. Y-Chromosome
YC............. Yeomanry Cavalry [*Military British*]

YC .... Yesterday's Children (EA)
YC .... Yola Clay Loam [*A soil type*]
y/c .... Your Cable (DS)
YC .... Youth Clubs [*Public-performance tariff class*] [*British*]
YC .... Youth Conservative [*Political party*] [*British*]
YCA .... Yacht Charter Association [*British*] (DBA)
YCA .... Yachting Club of America (EA)
YCA .... Yale-China Association (EA)
YCA .... Yearbook of Construction Articles [*A publication*] (AAGC)
YCA .... Yield Component Analysis [*Botany*]
YCA .... Young Concert Artists (EA)
YCA .... Young Conservative Alliance of America [*Later, Campus Action Network*] (EA)
YCA .... Youth Camping Association [*British*] (BI)
YCAP .... Youth Committee Against Poverty
Y-CASP .... City of York Community & Agency Social Planning Council (AC)
YCB .... Cambridge Bay [*Canada*] [*Airport symbol*] (OAG)
YCB .... Yeast Carbon Base
YCB .... Yellow Creek Bluff [*Alaska*] [*Seismograph station code, US Geological Survey*] (SEIS)
YCC .... Computer Center [*Yale University*] [*Research center*] (RCD)
YCC .... Luma Chroma Chroma [*Photo CD channels*] (PCM)
YCC .... York Centre [*Vancouver Stock Exchange symbol*]
YCC .... Youth Civic Center
YCC .... Youth Conservation Corps (EA)
YCC .... Yuma City-County Public Library, Yuma, AZ [*OCLC symbol*] (OCLC)
YCCA .... National Youth Council on Civic Affairs [*Superseded by CCNYA*] (EA)
YCCA .... Yorkshire Canary Club of America (EA)
YCCIP .... Youth Community Conservation and Improvement Projects [*Department of Labor*]
YCD .... Fueling Barge [*Navy symbol Obsolete*]
YCD .... Nanaimo [*Canada*] [*Airport symbol*] (OAG)
YCD .... Youth Correction Division [*Department of Justice*]
YCEE .... Youth Cost per Entered Employment [*Job Training and Partnership Act*] (OICC)
YCF .... Car Float [*Non-self-propelled*] [*Navy symbol*]
YCF .... Yankee Critical Facility [*Nuclear energy*]
YCF .... Young Calvinist Federation (EA)
YCF .... Young Conservative Foundation [*Later, CAF*] (EA)
YCF .... Youth Citizenship Fund (EA)
YCG .... Castlegar [*Canada*] [*Airport symbol*] (OAG)
YCGS .... York County Genealogical Society (EA)
YCH .... Chatham [*Canada*] [*Airport symbol*] (OAG)
YCHT .... Yacht
YCI .... Year-Class Strength Index [*Pisciculture*]
YCI .... Young Communist International [*Dissolved, 1943*]
YCJCYAQFTJB .... Your Curiosity Just Cost You a Quarter for the Jukebox [*Tavern sign*]
YCK .... Aircraft Transportation Lighter [*Navy symbol*]
YCK .... Open Cargo Lighter [*Navy ship symbol*] [*Obsolete*]
YCL .... Charlo [*Canada*] [*Airport symbol*] (OAG)
YCL .... Yolk Cytoplasmic Layer [*Embryology*]
YCL .... Young Communist League of the United States of America (EA)
YCL .... Youth Counseling League (EA)
YCLA .... Young Circle League of America [*Later, Workmen's Circle*] (EA)
YCM .... State University of New York, College at Cortland, Cortland, NY [*OCLC symbol*] (OCLC)
YCM .... Yellow, Cyan, and Magenta [*Color model*] (WDMC)
YCM .... YMCA Camp [*Montana*] [*Seismograph station code, US Geological Survey Closed*] (SEIS)
YCM .... Young Christian Movement [*Formerly, YCW*] [*Defunct*]
YCMD .... Yaw Gimbal Command (KSC)
YCN .... Cochrane [*Canada*] [*Airport symbol*] (OAG)
YCND .... Youth Campaign for Nuclear Disarmament [*British*] (BI)
YCNP .... Yellow Creek Nuclear Plant (NRCH)
YCO .... Coppermine [*Canada*] [*Airport symbol*] (OAG)
YCP .... Yaw Coupling Parameter
YCp .... Yeast Centromere Plasmid [*Genetics*]
YCP .... York College of Pennsylvania, York, PA [*OCLC symbol*] (OCLC)
YCP .... Youth Challenge Program
YCPO .... Young Children: Priority One [*Kiwanis Club*]
YCR .... Cross Lake [*Canada*] [*Airport symbol*] (OAG)
YCS .... High School Young Christian Students (EA)
YCS .... Young Christian Student (AEBS)
YCS .... Young Collector Series [*A publication*]
YCS .... Youth Community Service [*ACTION project*]
YCSDS .... Young Children's Social Desirability Scale (EDAC)
YCSM .... Younger Christian Student Movement
YCTF .... Younger Chemists Task Force [*American Chemical Society*]
YCTSD .... Yugoslav Center for Technical and Scientific Documentation [*Information service or system*] (IID)
YCU .... Youth Clubs United
YCV .... Aircraft Transportation Lighter [*Non-self-propelled*] [*Navy symbol*]
YCV .... Young Citizens Volunteers [*14th (Service) Battalion, Royal Irish Rifles*] [*British military*] (DMA)
YCW .... Young Christian Workers [*Later, YCM*] (EA)
YCY .... Clyde River [*Canada*] [*Airport symbol*] (OAG)
YCY .... Rescue Co-Ordination Center [*FAA designator*] (FAAC)
YCZ .... Yellow Caution Zone [*Runway lighting*] [*Aviation*]
YD .... Ama Air Express [*ICAO designator*] (AD)
YD .... Authority Supervising the Aerodrome [*ICAO designator*] (ICDA)
YD .... Floating Crane [*Non-self-propelled*] [*Navy symbol*]
YD .... Floating Derrick [*Navy*]
YD .... People's Democratic Republic of Yemen [*ANSI two-letter standard code*] (CNC)
YD .... Yard [*Navy*]
YD .... Yard [*Measure*]
yd .... Yard [*Measure*] (ODBW)
YD .... Yaw Damper [*Aviation*] (MCD)
YD .... Yaw Deviation
YD .... Yoreh De'ah. Shulhan 'Arukh (BJA)
YD .... Yorkshire Dragoons [*British military*] (DMA)
YD .... Younger Dryas [*Geoscience*]
yd^2 .... Square Yard (CDAI)
YD^3 .... Cubic Yard
YDA .... Dawson City [*Yukon*] [*Airport symbol*] (AD)
YDA .... Young Democrats of America (EA)
YDA .... Youth Development Association [*British*] (DBA)
YDAW .... Dawson Public Library, Yukon [*Library symbol National Library of Canada*] (NLC)
YDAY .... Yesterday [*Business term*]
YDB .... Yield Diffusion Bonding
YDB .... Youth Development Bureau [*Department of Health and Human Services*]
YDC .... Yaw Damper Computer
YDC .... Yeast Extract - Dextrose Calcium Carbonate Agar [*Microbiology*]
YDC .... Yellow-Dog Contract (MHDB)
YDC .... Yiddish Dictionary Committee (EA)
YDC .... Youth for Development and Cooperation (EAIO)
YDCA .... Young Democratic Clubs of America [*Later, YDA*] (EA)
ydcw .... DC Working Voltage (IDOE)
YDCW .... Ymgyrch Diogelu Cymru Wledig [*Campaign for the Protection of Rural Wales*] [*See also CPRW*] (EAIO)
YDDPA .... Youth Development and Delinquency Prevention Administration [*Later, Youth D evelopment Bureau*] [*HEW*]
YDF .... Deer Lake [*Canada*] [*Airport symbol*] (OAG)
YDG .... District Degaussing Vessel [*Navy symbol*]
YDG .... Yarding (WGA)
YDI .... Yard Drain Inlet (WDAA)
YDI .... Youth Development, Inc. (EA)
YDM .... State University of New York, College of Ceramics at Alfred University, Alfred, NY [*OCLC symbol*] (OCLC)
YDN .... Dauphin [*Canada*] [*Airport symbol*] (OAG)
YDP .... Yeni Dogus Partisi [*New Dawn Party*] [*Turkish Cyprus*] [*Political party*] (EY)
YDPCK .... Klondike National Historic Site, Parks Canada [*Lieu Historique National Klondike, Parcs Canada*] Dawson City, Yukon [*Library symbol National Library of Canada*] (NLC)
YDPP .... Young Democratic Progressive Party [*Macedonia*] [*Political party*] (EY)
YDQ .... Dawson Creek [*Canada*] [*Airport symbol*] (OAG)
YDS .... Yards (MCD)
YDS .... Yorkshire Dialect Society [*British*] (DBA)
YDSD .... Yards and Docks Supply Depot [*Obsolete Navy*]
YDSO .... Yards and Docks Supply Office [*Navy*]
YDT .... Diving Tender [*Non-self-propelled*] [*Navy symbol*]
YDY .... Authority Supervising the Aerodrome [*FAA designator*] (FAAC)
YE .... Grand Canyon Airlines [*ICAO designator*] (AD)
YE .... Lighter, Ammunition [*Navy symbol*]
YE .... Pearson Aircraft [*ICAO designator*] (AD)
YE .... Year End
YE .... Yeast Enolase [*An enzyme*]
YE .... Yellow Edges
YE .... Yellow Enzyme [*Biochemistry*]
YE .... Yemen Arab Republic [*ANSI two-letter standard code*] (CNC)
ye .... Yemen Arab Republic [*MARC country of publication code Library of Congress*] (LCCP)
YE .... Yevreyskaya Entsiklopediya [*A publication*] (BJA)
YE .... Youth Enterprise (AIE)
YE .... Youth Entry [*British military*] (DMA)
YEA .... Yaw Error Amplifier
YEA .... Year of Energy Action
YEA .... Yeast Extract Agar [*Microbiology*]
Yea .... Yeates' Pennsylvania Reports [*1791-1808*] [*A publication*] (DLA)
YEA .... Youth Emotions Anonymous (EA)
YEA .... Youth Evangelism Association (EA)
Yearb P7 Hen VI .... Year Books, Part 7, Henry VI [*A publication*] (DLA)
Yeates .... Yeates' Pennsylvania Reports [*1791-1808*] [*A publication*] (DLA)
Yeates (PA) .... Yeates' Pennsylvania Reports [*1791-1808*] [*A publication*] (DLA)
Yeb .... Yebamoth (BJA)
YEB .... Young Engineers for Britain (ACII)
YEC .... Youngest Empty Cell
YEC .... Youth Employment Competency (OICC)
YEC .... Youth Exchange Centre [*Seymour Mews House*] [*British*] (CB)
YECP .... Yeast Extract-Casein Peptone [*Medium*]
YedNum .... Yedi'ot Numismatiyot be-Yisrael. Jerusalem (BJA)
YEDPA .... Youth Employment and Demonstration Projects Act of 1977
YEDTA .... Youth Employment and Demonstration Training Act [*Department of the Interior*]
Yeepie .... Youthful Energetic Elderly Person Involved in Everything [*Aging yuppie*] [*Lifestyle classification*]
YEER .... Youth Entered Employment Rate [*Job Training and Partnership Act*] (OICC)
Ye Et Rg Rt .... Yorkshire East Riding Regiment [*British military*] (DMA)
YEF .... Young Executives Forum [*Automotive Service Industry Association*]
YEG .... Edmonton [*Canada*] [*Airport symbol*] (OAG)
YEG .... Yeast Extract - Glucose [*Medium*]
YEH .... Yellow Enzyme, Reduced [*Biochemistry*]

YEIS .... Yamaha Energy Induction System
YEK .... Eskimo Point [*Canada*] [*Airport symbol*] (OAG)
YEL .... Elliot Lake [*Canada*] [*Airport symbol*] (OAG)
YEL .... Equitable Life Assurance Society of the United States, General Library, New York, NY [*OCLC symbol*] (OCLC)
YEL .... Yellow (AAG)
yel .... Yellow (VRA)
Yel .... Yelverton's English King's Bench Reports [*1603-13*] [*A publication*] (DLA)
YEL .... Young England Library [*A publication*]
YEL .... Youth Employment Lobby [*Canada*]
YELD .... Yeldham [*England*]
YELL .... Yellow (DAVI)
YELL .... Yellow Corp. [*NASDAQ symbol*] (SAG)
YELL .... Yellowstone National Park
YellowCp ..... Yellow Corp. [*Associated Press*] (SAG)
yelsh .... Yellowish [*Philately*]
Yelv .... Yelverton's English King's Bench Reports [*1603-13*] [*A publication*] (DLA)
Yelv (Eng) ... Yelverton's English King's Bench Reports [*1603-13*] [*A publication*] (DLA)
YEM .... Empire State College, Saratoga Springs, NY [*Inactive*] [*OCLC symbol*] (OCLC)
YEM .... Yemen (Sanaa) [*ANSI three-letter standard code*] (CNC)
YEN .... Ammunition Lighter [*Navy symbol*] (DNAB)
YEO .... Yeomanry
YEO .... Yeovil [*British depot code*]
YEO .... Young Entrepreneurs Organization [*Wichita, KS*] (EA)
YEO .... Your Eyes Only (PCM)
YEO .... Youth Employment Officer [*British*]
YEOM .... Yeomanry (WGA)
Yeomy .... Yeomanry [*British military*] (DMA)
YEp .... Yeast Episomal Plasmid [*Genetics*]
YEP .... Young Eucalypt Program (EERA)
YEP .... Your Educational Plan (AEBS)
YEPD .... Yeast Extract - Peptone Dextrose [*Medium*]
Yer .... Yerger's Tennessee Supreme Court Reports [*A publication*] (DLA)
YER .... Yerkesik [*Turkey*] [*Seismograph station code, US Geological Survey*] (SEIS)
Yer .... Yerushalmi [*Palestinian Talmud*] (BJA)
Yerg .... Yerger's Tennessee Reports [*9-18 Tennessee*] [*A publication*] (DLA)
Yerg (Tenn) ... Yerger's Tennessee Reports [*9-18 Tennessee*] [*A publication*] (DLA)
YES .... Yankee Energy System [*NYSE symbol*] (TTSB)
YES .... Yankee Energy System, Inc. [*NYSE symbol*] (SPSG)
YES .... Years of Extra Savings
YES .... Yeast Estrogen System [*Biochemistry*]
YES .... Yeast Extract Sucrose [*Cell growth medium*]
YES .... Yogurt Extra Smooth [*Trademark of the Dannon Co., Inc.*]
YES .... Young Entomologists' Society (EA)
YES .... Young Executive Society [*Automotive Warehouse Distributors Association*]
YES .... Youth Education Services [*Summer program*]
YES .... Youth Effectiveness Skills Program [*Australia*]
YES .... Youth Emergency Service
YES .... Youth Employment Service [*Department of Employment*] [*British*] (EA)
YES .... Youth Employment Support Volunteers Program [*ACTION*]
YES .... Youth Enquiry Service [*Australia*]
YES .... Youth Entering Service to America [*In YES Foundation, a volunteer organization proposed by the Bush administration*]
YES .... Youth Enterprise Scheme [*British*] (ODBW)
YES .... Youth Exhibiting Stamps [*US Postal Service*]
YES .... Youth for Environmental Sanity
YES .... Youths for Environment and Service [*Multinational association based in Turkey*] (EAIO)
YesClth .... Yes Clothing Co. [*Associated Press*] (SAG)
YesEn .... Yes Entertainment, Inc. [*Associated Press*] (SAG)
YesEnt .... Yes Entertainment, Inc. [*Associated Press*] (SAG)
Yeshiva U .... Yeshiva University (GAGS)
YES/MVS ..... Yorktown Expert System for Multiple Virtual Storage Environments [*Computer science*] (HGAA)
YESS .... Yes Entertainment [*NASDAQ symbol*] (TTSB)
YESS .... Yes Entertainment, Inc. [*NASDAQ symbol*] (SAG)
YEST .... Yesterday (DSUE)
YESTY .... Yesterday
YET .... Young Explorers Trust [*British*] (DBA)
YET .... Youth Effectiveness Training [*A course of study*]
YETI .... Youth Education and Training Innovators (AIE)
YETM .... Yetminster [*England*]
YETP .... Youth Employment and Training Programs [*Department of Labor*]
YEV .... Inuvik [*Canada*] [*Airport symbol*] (OAG)
Yev .... Yevamot (BJA)
YF .... Aeronautical Fixed Station [*ICAO designator*] (ICDA)
YF .... Covered Lighter [*Self-propelled*] [*Navy symbol*]
YF .... Wife [*Citizens band radio slang*]
yf .... Yarn to Front [*Knitting*] (BARN)
YF .... Yawmiyyaet Filastiniyya (BJA)
YF .... Yellow Fever [*Virus*] (MAE)
YF .... Yerushalmi Fragments [*A publication*] (BJA)
YF .... Young Filmakers Foundation (EA)
YF .... Youth Female [*International Bowhunting Organization*] [*Class Equipment*]
YFA .... Fort Albany [*Canada*] [*Airport symbol*] (OAG)
YFB .... Ferryboat or Launch [*Self-propelled*] [*Navy symbol*]
YFB .... First Boston Corp., New York, NY [*OCLC symbol*] (OCLC)
YFB .... Frobisher Bay [*Canada*] [*Airport symbol*] (OAG)
YFC .... Fredericton [*Canada*] [*Airport symbol*] (OAG)
YFC .... Yakima Firing Center (MCD)
YFC .... Young Farmers' Club [*British*]
YFC .... Youth for Christ [*Australia*]
YFCB .... Yonkers Financial [*NASDAQ symbol*] (TTSB)
YFCI .... Youth for Christ International [*See also JPC*] [*Singapore, Singapore*] (EAIO)
YFC/USA ...... Youth for Christ/USA (EA)
YFD .... Yard Floating Dry Dock [*Non-self-propelled*] [*Navy symbol*]
YFDC .... Youth Film Distribution Center (EA)
YFE .... Forestville [*Canada*] [*Airport symbol*] (OAG)
YFEC .... Youth Forum of the European Communities [*See also FJCE*] (EAIO)
YFED .... York Financial [*NASDAQ symbol*] (TTSB)
YFED .... York Financial Corp. [*York, PA*] [*NASDAQ symbol*] (NQ)
YFF .... Waltham, MA [*Location identifier FAA*] (FAAL)
YFFC .... Young Farmers Finance Council [*Australia*]
YFL .... Youth Forum Ltd. [*Australia Commercial firm*]
YFM .... State University of New York, Agricultural and Technical College at Farmingdale,Farmingdale, NY [*OCLC symbol*] (OCLC)
YFN .... Covered Lighter [*Non-self-propelled*] [*Navy symbol*]
YFNA .... Young Friends of North America (EA)
YFNB .... Large Covered Lighter [*Non-self-propelled*] [*Navy symbol*]
YFND .... Dry Dock Companion Craft [*Non-self-propelled*] [*Navy symbol*]
YFNG .... Covered Lighter (Special Purpose) [*Later, YFNX*] [*Navy symbol*]
YFNX .... Lighter (Special Purpose) [*Non-self-propelled*] [*Navy symbol*]
YFO .... Flin Flon [*Canada*] [*Airport symbol*] (OAG)
Y-FOS .... Y-Force Operations Staff [*Army World War II*]
YFP .... Floating Power Barge [*Non-self-propelled*] [*Navy symbol*]
YFR .... Refrigerated Covered Lighter [*Self-propelled*] [*Navy symbol*]
YFRN .... Refrigerated Covered Lighter [*Non-self-propelled*] [*Navy symbol*]
YFRT .... Covered Lighter (Range Tender) [*Self-propelled*] [*Navy symbol*]
YFS .... Fort Simpson [*Canada*] [*Airport symbol*] (OAG)
YFS .... Young Flying Service [*ICAO designator*] (FAAC)
YFT .... Torpedo Transportation Lighter [*Navy symbol Obsolete*]
YFTU .... Yugoslavia Federation of Trade Unions
YFU .... Harbor Utility Craft [*Self-propelled*] [*Navy symbol*]
YFU .... Why Have You Forsaken Us Letter [*Fundraising*]
YFU .... Yard Freight Unit
YFU .... Youth for Understanding (EA)
YFV .... Yellow Fever Virus [*Virology*]
YF/VA .... Young Filmakers/Video Arts [*Also known as Young Filmakers Foundation*] (EA)
YF(XYL) .... Wife (Ex-Young-Lady) [*Amateur radio slang*]
YG .... Garbage Lighter [*Self-propelled*] [*Navy symbol*]
YG .... Yankee Group [*Boston, MA*] [*Information service or system Telecommunications*] (TSSD)
YG .... Yard Gully
YG .... Year Group
YG .... Yellow-Green
YG .... Yellow-Green Beacon [*Aviation*]
YGA .... Gagnon [*Canada*] [*Airport symbol*] (OAG)
YGB .... Gillies Bay [*Canada*] [*Airport symbol*] (OAG)
YGC .... Yahweh and the Gods of Canaan [*A publication*] (BJA)
YGD .... Corporacion Centroamericana de Dervicios de Navagacion Aerea [*Mexico*] [*FAA designator*] (FAAC)
YGF .... General Foods Technical Center, White Plains, NY [*OCLC symbol*] (OCLC)
YGJ .... Yonago [*Japan*] [*Airport symbol*] (OAG)
YGK .... Kingston [*Canada*] [*Airport symbol*] (OAG)
YGL .... La Grande [*Canada*] [*Airport symbol*] (OAG)
YGL .... Yttrium Garnet LASER
YGM .... State University of New York, College at Geneseo, Geneseo, NY [*OCLC symbol*] (OCLC)
YGM .... Young Grandmother
YGN .... Garbage Lighter [*Non-self-propelled*] [*Navy symbol*]
YGO .... Gods Narrows [*Canada*] [*Airport symbol*] (OAG)
YGP .... Gaspe [*Canada*] [*Airport symbol*] (OAG)
YGQ .... Geraldton [*Canada*] [*Airport symbol*] (OAG)
YGR .... Iles De La Madeleine [*Canada*] [*Airport symbol*] (OAG)
YGR .... Magdalen Island [*Quebec*] [*Airport symbol*] (AD)
ygr .... Younger (VRA)
YGRT .... Yogurt
YGS .... Survey Craft [*Navy symbol*]
YGS .... Year of Grace Survey (DS)
YGS .... Young Guard Society [*Later, GS*] (EA)
YGT .... Target Service Task Craft [*Navy symbol*]
YGT .... Thunder Bay [*Ontario*] [*Airport symbol*] (AD)
YGTN .... Target Barge [*Navy symbol*]
YGV .... Havre Saint Pierre [*Canada*] [*Airport symbol*] (OAG)
YGW .... Great Whale [*Canada*] [*Airport symbol*] (OAG)
YGX .... Gillam [*Canada*] [*Airport symbol*] (OAG)
YH .... Lighter, Ambulance [*Navy symbol Obsolete*]
YH .... RADAR Beacon [*Maps and charts*]
YH .... Trans New York [*ICAO designator*] (AD)
YH .... Yorkshire Hussars [*British military*] (DMA)
YH .... Youth Hostel
YHA .... Youth Hostels Association
YHB .... House Boat [*Navy symbol*]
YHCFE .... Yorkshire and Humberside Council for Further and Higher Education [*British*] (AIE)
YHD .... Dryden [*Canada*] [*Airport symbol*] (OAG)
YHI .... Holman Island [*Canada*] [*Airport symbol*] (OAG)
YHIY .... Yorkshire Hussars Imperial Yeomanry [*British military*] (DMA)

YHJPCK....... Kluane National Park, Parks Canada [*Parc National Kluane, Parcs Canada*] Haines Junction, Yukon [*Library symbol National Library of Canada*] (NLC)
YHK............ Gjoa Haven [*Canada*] [*Airport symbol*] (OAG)
YHLC........... Salvage Lift Craft, Heavy [*Non-self-propelled*] [*Navy ship symbol*]
YHM............ Hamilton [*Canada*] [*Airport symbol*] (OAG)
YHM............ Hamilton College, Clinton, NY [*OCLC symbol*] (OCLC)
YHN............ Hornepayne [*Canada*] [*Airport symbol*] (OAG)
YHOO........... Yahoo, Inc. [*NASDAQ symbol*] (SAG)
YHOO........... Yahoo Inc. [*NASDAQ symbol*] (TTSB)
YHP............ Yokogawa Hewlett Packard Ltd. [*Japan*]
YHPA........... Your Heritage Protection Association (EA)
YHR............ Harrington Harbour [*Canada*] [*Airport symbol*] (OAG)
YHS............ Yukuharu Haiku Society [*Superseded by Yuki Teikei Haiku Society*] (EA)
YHT............ Heating Scow [*Navy symbol*]
YHT............ Young-Helmholtz Theory [*Physics*]
YHWH........... Yahweh [*Old Testament term for God*]
YHY............ Hay River [*Canada*] [*Airport symbol*] (OAG)
YHZ............ Halifax [*Canada*] [*Airport symbol*] (OAG)
YI............. Intercity [*ICAO designator*] (AD)
YI............. Young, Intact Animals [*Endocrinology*]
YIB............ Atikokan [*Canada*] [*Airport symbol*] (OAG)
YIBSV.......... Yam Internal Brown Spot Virus [*Plant pathology*]
yid............ Yiddish [*MARC language code Library of Congress*] (LCCP)
YIE............ Young Interference Experiment [*Physics*]
YIEPP.......... Youth Incentive Entitlement Pilot Projects [*Department of Labor*]
YIF............ St. Augustin [*Canada*] [*Airport symbol*] (OAG)
YIFCM.......... Yaw Integrated Flight Control Module (MCD)
YIG............ Yttrium Iron Garnet
YIGIB.......... Your Improved Group Insurance Benefits
YIH............ Yichang [*China*] [*Airport symbol*] (OAG)
YIIJS.......... Young Israel Institute for Jewish Studies [*Defunct*] (EA)
YIK............ Ivugivik [*Canada*] [*Airport symbol*] (OAG)
YIL............ Yahoo Internet Life [*Computer science*]
YIL............ Yellow Indicating Light (IEEE)
YILAG.......... Yidishe Landvirtshaftlekhe Gezelshaft [*A publication*] (BJA)
YILD........... YieldUp International Corp. [*NASDAQ symbol*] (SAG)
YILD........... YieldUP Intl [*NASDAQ symbol*] (TTSB)
YILDU.......... YieldUP Intl Unit [*NASDAQ symbol*] (TTSB)
YILDW.......... YieldUP Intl Wrrt'A' [*NASDAQ symbol*] (TTSB)
YILDZ.......... YieldUp Intl Wrrt'B' [*NASDAQ symbol*] (TTSB)
YIN............ Niagara County Community College, Sanborn, NY [*OCLC symbol*] (OCLC)
YIN............ Yingkow [*Republic of China*] [*Seismograph station code, US Geological Survey*] (SEIS)
YIN............ Yining [*China*] [*Airport symbol*] (OAG)
YIO............ Pond Inlet [*Canada*] [*Airport symbol*] (OAG)
YIP............ Willow Run Airport [*Michigan*] [*Airport symbol*]
YIp............ Yeast Integrating Plasmid [*Genetics*]
YIP............ Youth Initiative Project (AIE)
YIP............ Youth International Party [*Members known as "yippies"*]
YIPL........... Youth International Party Line [*Superseded by Technological American Party*]
YIPME.......... Youth Institute for Peace in the Middle East (EA)
Yippie......... Young Indicted Professional [*Lifestyle classification*]
YIR............ Yearly Infrastructure Report (NATG)
YIT............ Your Income Tax [*Computerized version of J. K. Lasser's book by the same name*]
YIT............ Youth in Transition [*Australia*]
YITB........... Yours in the Bond [*Motto of fraternity Tau Kappa Epsilon*]
YIV............ Island Lake [*Canada*] [*Airport symbol*] (OAG)
YIVO........... Yidisher Visnshaftlekher Institut [*Yiddish Scientific Institute*]
YIX............ Merrill Lynch & Co. [*AMEX symbol*] (SAG)
YJ............. Commodore [*ICAO designator*] (AD)
YJ............. RADAR Homing Beacon [*Maps and charts*]
YJ............. Vanuatu [*Aircraft nationality and registration mark*] (FAAC)
YJ............. Yellow Jacket [*Immunology*]
YJ............. Yuppie Jeep
YJA............ Yachting Journalists' Association [*British*] (DBA)
YJF............ Fort Liard [*Canada*] [*Airport symbol*] (OAG)
YJK............ Yellowjack Resources [*Vancouver Stock Exchange symbol*]
YJM............ Fulton-Montgomery Community College, Johnstown, NY [*OCLC symbol*] (OCLC)
YJS............ Yale Judaica Series [*A publication*] (BJA)
YJT............ Stephenville [*Canada*] [*Airport symbol*] (OAG)
YJV............ Yellow Jacket Venom [*Immunology*]
YK............. Cyprus Turkish Airways [*ICAO designator*] (AD)
YK............. RADAR Beacon [*Maps and charts*]
YK............. Yakovlev [*Former USSR ICAO aircraft manufacturer identifier*] (ICAO)
YK............. Yapi-Kredi Bank [*Turkey*] (ECON)
YK............. Yom Kippur (BJA)
YK............. York Antibodies [*Immunology*]
YKA............ Kamloops [*Canada*] [*Airport symbol*] (OAG)
YKA............ Yellowknife Array [*Northwest Territories*] [*Seismograph station code, US Geological Survey*] (SEIS)
YKB............ Yapi-Kredi Bank [*Turkey*]
YKB............ Yemen Kuwait Bank for Trade & Investment
YKB............ Yukon Bibliography [*Boreal Institute for Northern Studies*] [*Canada Information service or system Information service or system*] (CRD)
YKC............ Kingsborough Community College of the City University of New York, Brooklyn, NY [*OCLC symbol*] (OCLC)
YKC............ Yellowknife [*Northwest Territories*] [*Seismograph station code, US Geological Survey*] (SEIS)
ykc............ Yukon Territory [*MARC country of publication code Library of Congress*] (LCCP)
YKE............ Yankee Power, Inc. [*Vancouver Stock Exchange symbol*]
YKK............ Yoshido Kogyo Kabushiki-Kaishi [*Yoshida Industries Ltd.*] [*Japan*]
YKL............ Schefferville [*Canada*] [*Airport symbol*] (OAG)
YKM............ Corning Museum of Glass, Corning, NY [*OCLC symbol*] (OCLC)
YKM............ Yaak [*Montana*] [*Seismograph station code, US Geological Survey*] (SEIS)
YKM............ Yakima [*Washington*] [*Airport symbol*] (OAG)
YKM............ Young Kibbutz Movement [*Defunct*] (EA)
YKN............ Yankton [*South Dakota*] [*Airport symbol*] (OAG)
YKP............ Yeni Kibris Partisi [*New Cypus Party*] [*Turkish Cyprus*] [*Political party*] (EY)
YKQ............ Rupert House [*Canada*] [*Airport symbol*] (OAG)
YKR............ Yukon Revenue Mines [*Vancouver Stock Exchange symbol*]
YKS............ Yakushima [*Japan*] [*Seismograph station code, US Geological Survey Closed*] (SEIS)
YKS............ Yorkshire [*County in England*]
YKT............ Yakutat [*Alaska*] [*Seismograph station code, US Geological Survey Closed*] (SEIS)
YKU............ Fort George [*Canada*] [*Airport symbol*] (OAG)
YKU............ Yakutat [*Alaska*] [*Seismograph station code, US Geological Survey*] (SEIS)
YKUF........... Yiddisher Kultur Farband (EA)
YKW............ Yom Kippur War (BJA)
YKX............ Kirkland Lake [*Canada*] [*Airport symbol*] (OAG)
YKYBHTLW... You Know You've Been Hacking Too Long When [*Computer science*]
YKZ............ Toronto [*Canada*] Buttonville Airport [*Airport symbol*] (OAG)
YL............. Aircraft Accident Authority [*ICAO designator*] (ICDA)
YL............. Long Island Airlines [*ICAO designator*] (AD)
YL............. Montauk Caribbbean Airways and Ocean Reef Airways [*ICAO designator*] (AD)
YL............. Yad La-Kore. La-Safran ule-Pe'ile Tarbut (BJA)
YL............. Yawl (ROG)
YL............. Y-Axis of Spacelab [*NASA*] (NASA)
YL............. Yellow [*Maps and charts*]
YL............. Yellow Lamp (IAA)
YL............. Yield Limit (WDAA)
YL............. Young Lady [*Amateur radio slang*]
YL............. Young Life (EA)
YL............. Youth Liberation Press (EA)
YLA............ Open Landing Lighter [*Navy symbol*]
YLB............ Lac La Biche [*Canada Airport symbol*]
YLC............ Clinton Community College, Plattsburgh, NY [*OCLC symbol*] (OCLC)
YLC............ Youngest Living Child [*Medicine*] (DMAA)
YLC............ Young Labour Council [*Australia*]
YLC............ Young Life Campaign (EA)
YLCC........... Yellow Lamp Century Certificate (IAA)
YLD............ Chapleau [*Canada*] [*Airport symbol*] (OAG)
YLD............ High Income Advantage [*NYSE symbol*] (TTSB)
YLD............ High Income Advantage Trust [*NYSE symbol*] (SPSG)
YLD............ Yield [*Investment term*]
YLDG........... Yielding (ROG)
YIdUP.......... YieldUP International Corp. [*Associated Press*] (SAG)
YLE............ Yule Island [*New Guinea*] [*Airport symbol*] (AD)
YLF............ Young Leadership Forum [*Multinational association based in Israel*] (EAIO)
YLF............ Yttrium-Lithium-Fluoride [*Laser*]
YLH............ High Income Advantage III [*NYSE symbol*] (TTSB)
YLH............ High Income Advantage Trust III [*NYSE symbol*] (SAG)
YLH............ High-Income Advantage Trust III [*NYSE symbol*] (SPSG)
YLI............ [*The*] Yorkshire Light Infantry [*Military unit*] [*British*]
YLI............ Young Ladies Institute (EA)
YLJ............ Meadow Lake [*Canada*] [*Airport symbol Obsolete*] (OAG)
YLJ............ Yale Law Journal [*A publication*] (BRI)
YLL............ Lederle Laboratories, Pearl River, NY [*OCLC symbol*] (OCLC)
YLL............ Lloydminster [*Canada*] [*Airport symbol*] (OAG)
YLLC........... Salvage Lift Craft, Light [*Self-propelled*] [*Navy ship symbol*]
YLM............ Young Launderers' Movement [*British*] (BI)
YLMA........... Young Liberal Movement of Australia
YLP............ Mingan [*Canada*] [*Airport symbol Obsolete*] (OAG)
YLR............ YAG [*Yttrium Aluminum Garnet*] LASER Range-Finder
YLR............ York Legal Record [*Pennsylvania*] [*A publication*] (DLA)
YLRL........... Young Ladies Radio League
YLSN........... Young Lawyers Section Newsletter [*Australia A publication*]
YLSTN.......... Yellowstone (FAAC)
YLT............ High Income Advantage Trust II [*NYSE symbol*] (CTT)
YLT............ Yellow Light (MSA)
YLW............ Kelowna [*Canada*] [*Airport symbol*] (OAG)
YLW............ Yellow (ADA)
YLW............ Yellow
YLY............ Aircraft Accident Authority [*FAA designator*] (FAAC)
YM............. Dredge [*Self-propelled*] [*Navy symbol*]
YM............. Meteorological Office [*ICAO designator*] (ICDA)
YM............. Mountain Home Air Service [*ICAO designator*] (AD)
YM............. Prototype Missile (NATG)
YM............. Yacht Measurement
YM............. Yang Ming Line [*Shipping*] [*Taiwan*]
YM............. Yawing Moment (KSC)
YM............. Yearly Meetings [*Quakers*]
YM............. Yeast Extract - Malt Extract [*Medium*]
YM............. Yellow Man

YM ..... Yellow Metal
YM ..... Young Men's [*Christian Association*]
YMA ..... Mayo [*Canada*] [*Airport symbol*] (OAG)
YMA ..... Yarn Merchants Association [*Defunct*] (EA)
YMA ..... Yeast Morphology Agar (BABM)
YMA ..... Young Menswear Association (EA)
YMA ..... Youth Music Australia
YMB ..... Yeast Malt Broth
YMBA ..... Yacht and Motor Boat Association [*British*] (BI)
YMC ..... Moore-Cottrell Subscription Agencies, Inc., North Cohocton, NY [*OCLC symbol*] (OCLC)
YMC ..... Yeast Mold Count (OA)
YMC ..... Your Marketing Consultant [*An electronic publication*]
YMC ..... Youth and Music Canada
YMCA ..... National Counil of Young Men's Christian Associations [*British*] (DBA)
YMCA ..... Young Men's Christian Association
YMCAA ..... Young Men's Christian Association of Australia
YMCAIPS ..... YMCA [*Young Men's Christian Association*] International Program Services (EA)
YMCA-USA ..... Young Men's Christian Associations of the United States of America (EA)
YMCK ..... Yellow, Magenta, Cyan, Black (WDMC)
YMCU ..... Young Men's Christian Union
YMD ..... People's Democratic Republic of Yemen [*ANSI three-letter standard code*] (CNC)
YMDZAI ..... Young Men's Division - Zeirei Agudath Israel (EA)
YME ..... Matane [*Canada*] [*Airport symbol*] (OAG)
YME ..... Young's Modulus of Elasticity [*See also E, Y*]
YMF ..... Young Musicians Foundation (EA)
YMF ..... Youth Male Fingers [*International Bowhunting Organization*] [*Class Equipment*]
YMFS ..... Young Men's Friendly Society [*British*]
YMHA ..... Young Men's Hebrew Association [*Later, YM-YWHA*]
YMHSI ..... Yedi'ot ha-Makhon le-Heker ha-Shirah ha-'Ivrit. Jerusalem (BJA)
YMI ..... Young Men's Institute (EA)
YMISIG ..... Young Mensa International Special Interest Group [*Defunct*] (EA)
YML ..... Murray Bay [*Quebec*] [*Airport symbol*] (AD)
YML ..... Young Men's Lyceum
YMLC ..... Salvage Lift Craft, Medium [*Non-self-propelled*] [*Navy ship symbol*]
YMM ..... Fort McMurray [*Canada*] [*Airport symbol*] (OAG)
YMM ..... Yeast Minimal Medium [*Microorganism growth medium*]
YMM ..... Youngstown and Mahoning County Public Library, Youngstown, OH [*OCLC symbol*] (OCLC)
YMMV ..... Your Mileage May Vary [*E-Mail discussion*]
YMMY ..... Yedi'ot ha-Makhon le-Mada'ei ha-Yahadut. Jerusalem (BJA)
YMO ..... Moosonee [*Canada*] [*Airport symbol*] (OAG)
YMO ..... Yellow Magic Orchestra [*Musical group*] [*Japan*]
YMP ..... Motor Mine Planter [*Navy symbol*]
YMP ..... Yacht Materially Prejudiced [*Yacht racing*] (IYR)
YMP ..... Young Managing Printers [*British Printing Industries Federation*]
YMP ..... Young Master Printer (DGA)
YMP ..... Youth Mobility Program (OICC)
YMPA ..... Young Master Printers' Alliance (DGA)
YMPE ..... Year's Maximum Pensionable Earnings
YMR ..... Youth Male Release [*International Bowhunting Organization*] [*Class equipment*]
YMS ..... Auxiliary Motor Minesweeper [*Navy symbol*]
YMS ..... Yaw Microwave Sensor
YMS ..... Yield Measurement System
YMS ..... Yurimaguas [*Peru*] [*Airport symbol*] (OAG)
YMSCO ..... Yucca Mountain Site Characterization Office
YMSG ..... Your Message [*Aviation*] (FAAC)
YMSGD ..... Your Message Date [*Aviation*] (FAAC)
YMT ..... Chibougamau [*Canada*] [*Airport symbol*] (OAG)
YMT ..... Motor Tug [*Navy symbol*]
YMV ..... Manicouagan [*Quebec*] [*Airport symbol*] (AD)
YMV ..... Youcai Mosaic Virus [*Plant pathology*]
YMX ..... Montreal [*Canada*] Mirabel International Airport [*Airport symbol*] (OAG)
YMY ..... Meteorological Office [*FAA designator*] (FAAC)
YM-YWHA ..... Young Men's and Young Women's Hebrew Association (EA)
YN ..... International NOTAM Office [*ICAO designator*] (ICDA)
YN ..... Net Tender [*Navy symbol Obsolete*]
YN ..... Nicaragua [*International civil aircraft marking*] (ODBW)
YN ..... Night Coach [*Airline fare code*]
YN ..... Nor-East Commuter Airlines [*ICAO designator*] (AD)
YN ..... Yeoman [*Navy rating*]
YN ..... Yes-No [*Response prompt*]
Y/N ..... Yes/No (NITA)
YN ..... [*The*] Youngstown & Northern Railroad Co. [*AAR code*]
YN1 ..... Yeoman, First Class [*Navy rating*]
YN2 ..... Yeoman, Second Class [*Navy rating*]
YN3 ..... Yeoman, Third Class [*Navy rating*]
YNA ..... Naiashquan [*Canada*] [*Airport symbol*] (OAG)
YNA ..... Young Newspapermen's Association [*British*] (BI)
YNB ..... Yanbu [*Saudi Arabia*] [*Airport symbol*] (OAG)
YNB ..... Yeast Nitrogen Base
YNC ..... Paint Hills [*Canada*] [*Airport symbol*] (OAG)
YNC ..... Yeoman, Chief [*Navy rating*]
YNC ..... Yinchuan [*Republic of China*] [*Seismograph station code, US Geological Survey*] (SEIS)
YNCM ..... Yeoman, Master Chief [*Navy rating*]
YNCS ..... Yeoman, Senior Chief [*Navy rating*]
YND ..... Gatineau/Hull [*Canada*] [*Airport symbol*] (OAG)
YND ..... Yandina [*Solomon Islands*] [*Airport symbol*] (AD)
YNE ..... Norway House [*Canada*] [*Airport symbol*] (OAG)
YNG ..... Gate Craft [*Non-self-propelled*] [*Navy symbol*]
YNG ..... Young
YNG ..... Youngstown [*Ohio*] [*Airport symbol*] (OAG)
YNG ..... Youngstown State University, Youngstown, OH [*OCLC symbol*] (OCLC)
YNHA ..... Yosemite Natural History Association (EA)
YNHH ..... Yale-New Haven Hospital
YNK ..... Gagnon [*Quebec*] [*Airport symbol*] (AD)
YNM ..... Matagami [*Canada*] [*Airport symbol*] (OAG)
YNP ..... Young National Party [*Australia Political party*]
YNPA ..... Young National Party of Australia [*Political party*] (ADA)
YNPA ..... Young National Party of Australia [*Political party*]
YNPS ..... Yankee Nuclear Power Station (NRCH)
YNR ..... Yorkshire, North Riding [*County in England*] (ROG)
YNSA ..... Seaman Apprentice, Yeoman, Striker [*Navy rating*]
YNSN ..... Seaman, Yeoman, Striker [*Navy rating*]
YNT ..... Net Tender [*Tug Class*] [*Navy symbol Obsolete*]
YNT ..... Yellowstone National Travelers (EA)
YNTO ..... Yugoslav National Tourist Office [*Defunct*] (EA)
YNV ..... Yanov [*Later, LVV*] [*Former USSR Geomagnetic observatory code*]
YNW ..... International Finance Corp. [*AMEX symbol*] (SAG)
YO ..... Aeronautical Information Service Unit [*ICAO designator*] (ICDA)
YO ..... Fuel Oil Barge [*Self-propelled*] [*Navy symbol*]
YO ..... Heli-Air-Monaco [*ICAO designator*] (AD)
YO ..... Mayotte [*ANSI two-letter standard code*] (CNC)
YO ..... Yard Oiler [*Navy symbol*] (DICI)
YO ..... Yarn Over [*Knitting*]
YO ..... Y-Axis of Orbiter [*NASA*] (NASA)
YO ..... Year-Old
Y/O ..... Years Old (DAVI)
YO ..... Yes [*Citizens band radio slang*]
Yo ..... Yoma (BJA)
Yo ..... Younge's English Exchequer Equity Reports [*159 English Reprint*] [*A publication*] (DLA)
YO ..... Young Officer [*British military*] (DMA)
YOAN ..... Youth of All Nations (EA)
YOB ..... Year of Birth
YOB ..... Youth Opportunities Board
YoB ..... Yushodo Booksellers Ltd., Tokyo, Japan [*Library symbol Library of Congress*] (LCLS)
YOC ..... Old Crow [*Canada*] [*Airport symbol*] (OAG)
YOC ..... Youth Opportunity Campaign [*Civil Service Commission*]
YOC ..... Youth Opportunity Centers
YOC ..... Youth Opportunity Corps
YOCHINPROJ ..... Younger Chemists International Project [*American Chemical Society*]
YOCM ..... International Yogurt Co. [*NASDAQ symbol*] (NQ)
YOCM ..... Intl Yogurt [*NASDAQ symbol*] (TTSB)
YOD ..... Cold Lake [*Canada*] [*Airport symbol*] (OAG)
YOD ..... Year of Death
YOE ..... Year of Entry (MHDB)
YOG ..... Central Aviation, Inc. [*ICAO designator*] (FAAC)
YOG ..... Gasoline Barge [*Self-propelled*] [*Navy symbol*]
YOGN ..... Gasoline Barge [*Non-self-propelled*] [*Navy symbol*]
YOH ..... Oxford House [*Canada*] [*Airport symbol*] (OAG)
YOINK ..... Young, One Income, No Kids [*Lifestyle classification*]
YOJ ..... High Level [*Canada*] [*Airport symbol*] (OAG)
YOJ ..... Yonagunijima [*Ryukyu Islands*] [*Seismograph station code, US Geological Survey*] (SEIS)
YOK ..... Yokohama [*Japan*] [*Seismograph station code, US Geological Survey*] (SEIS)
YOL ..... Yola [*Nigeria*] [*Airport symbol*] (OAG)
YOM ..... State University of New York, College at Oswego, Oswego, NY [*OCLC symbol*] (OCLC)
YOM ..... Year of Marriage
Yom ..... Yoma (BJA)
YON ..... Fuel Oil Barge [*Non-self-propelled*] [*Navy symbol*]
YON ..... Yonago [*Japan*] [*Seismograph station code, US Geological Survey*] (SEIS)
YON ..... Yonkers School System, Yonkers, NY [*OCLC symbol*] (OCLC)
YONAH ..... Years of the North Atlantic Humpback [*Collaborative study*]
YONK ..... Younkers, Inc. [*NASDAQ symbol*] (SAG)
Yool Waste ..... Yool on Waste, Nuisance, and Trespass [*1863*] [*A publication*] (DLA)
YOP ..... Rainbow Lake [*Canada*] [*Airport symbol*] (OAG)
YOP ..... Youth Opportunities Programme [*British*] (DCTA)
YOR ..... Yale Oriental Research [*A publication*] (BJA)
YOR ..... Yoro [*Honduras*] [*Airport symbol*] (AD)
yor ..... Yoruba [*MARC language code Library of Congress*] (LCCP)
YORA ..... Younger-Onset Rheumatoid Arthritis [*Medicine*] (DAVI)
York ..... York Legal Record [*Pennsylvania*] [*A publication*] (DLA)
YORK ..... York Research [*NASDAQ symbol*] (TTSB)
YORK ..... York Research Corp. [*NASDAQ symbol*] (NQ)
York Ass ..... Clayton's English Reports, York Assizes [*A publication*] (DLA)
YorkFn ..... York Financial Corp. [*Associated Press*] (SAG)
YorkIn ..... York International [*Associated Press*] (SAG)
York Leg Rec ..... York Legal Record [*Pennsylvania*] [*A publication*] (DLA)
York Leg Record ..... York Legal Record [*Pennsylvania*] [*A publication*] (DLA)
York Leg Rec (PA) ..... York Legal Record [*Pennsylvania*] [*A publication*] (DLA)
YorkRs ..... York Research Corp. [*Associated Press*] (SAG)
YORKS ..... Yorkshire [*County in England*]
Yorks ..... Yorkshire [*County in England*] (ODBW)
YOS ..... Oil Storage Barge [*Non-self-propelled*] [*Navy symbol*]

YOS .... Years of Service [*Army*] (INF)
YOS .... Yosiwara [*Japan*] [*Seismograph station code, US Geological Survey Closed*] (SEIS)
YOSE .... Yosemite National Park
YOT .... Yale Oriental Texts [*A publication*] (BJA)
YOU .... Young [*Australia Seismograph station code, US Geological Survey*] (SEIS)
You .... Younge's English Exchequer Equity Reports [*159 English Reprint*] [*A publication*] (DLA)
YOU .... Youngman Oil & Gas [*Vancouver Stock Exchange symbol*]
YOU .... Young Officers' Union [*Philippines*]
YOU .... Youth Opportunities Unlimited [*Project*] (EA)
YOU .... Youth Organizations United
You & Coll Ch... Younge and Collyer's English Chancery Reports [*1841-43*] [*A publication*] (DLA)
You & Coll Ex... Younge and Collyer's English Exchequer Equity Reports [*1834-42*] [*A publication*] (DLA)
You & Jerv... Younge and Jervis' English Exchequer Reports [*A publication*] (DLA)
Young .... Young's Reports [*21-47 Minnesota*] [*A publication*] (DLA)
Young Adm... Young's Nova Scotia Admiralty Cases [*A publication*] (DLA)
Young Adm Dec... Young's Nova Scotia Vice-Admiralty Decisions [*A publication*] (DLA)
Young Adm Dec (Nov Sc)... Young's Nova Scotia Vice-Admiralty Decisions [*A publication*] (DLA)
YoungBd ...... Young Broadcasting, Inc. [*Associated Press*] (SAG)
Younge .... Younge's English Exchequer Equity Reports [*159 English Reprint*] [*A publication*] (DLA)
Younge & C Ch... Younge and Collyer's English Chancery Reports [*62-63 English Reprint*] [*A publication*] (DLA)
Younge & C Ch Cas (Eng)... Younge and Collyer's English Chancery Cases [*62-63 English Reprint*] [*A publication*] (DLA)
Younge & C Exch... Younge and Collyer's English Exchequer Equity Reports [*160 English Reprint*] [*A publication*] (DLA)
Younge & C Exch (Eng)... Younge and Collyer's English Exchequer Equity Reports [*160 English Reprint*] [*A publication*] (DLA)
Younge & Ch Cas... Younge and Collyer's English Chancery Cases [*62-63 English Reprint*] [*1841-43*] [*A publication*] (DLA)
Younge & Coll Ch... Younge and Collyer's English Chancery Reports [*62-63 English Reprint*] [*A publication*] (DLA)
Younge & Coll Ex... Younge and Collyer's English Exchequer Equity Reports [*160 English Reprint*] [*A publication*] (DLA)
Younge & J... Younge and Jervis' English Exchequer Reports [*148 English Reprint*] [*A publication*] (DLA)
Younge & Je... Younge and Jervis' English Exchequer Reports [*148 English Reprint*] [*A publication*] (DLA)
Younge & J (Eng)... Younge and Jervis' English Exchequer Reports [*148 English Reprint*] [*A publication*] (DLA)
Younge & Jerv... Younge and Jervis' English Exchequer Reports [*148 English Reprint*] [*A publication*] (DLA)
Younge Exch... Younge's English Exchequer Equity Reports [*159 English Reprint*] [*1830-32*] [*A publication*] (DLA)
Younge Exch (Eng)... Younge's English Exchequer Equity Reports [*159 English Reprint*] [*A publication*] (DLA)
Younge ML Cas... Younge's English Maritime Law Cases [*A publication*] (DLA)
Young ML Cas... Young's English Maritime Law Cases [*A publication*] (DLA)
Young Naut Dict... Young's Nautical Dictionary [*A publication*] (DLA)
Young VA Dec... Young's Nova Scotia Vice-Admiralty Decisions [*A publication*] (DLA)
Younker .... Younkers, Inc. [*Associated Press*] (SAG)
YOUR .... Your Own United Resources, Inc. (OICC)
YOUSA .... Youth Organizations USA (EA)
YOUTHS .... Youth Order United Toward Highway Safety (EA)
YouthSv .... Youth Services International, Inc. [*Associated Press*] (SAG)
YOW .... International Young Christian Workers [*Acronym is based on foreign phrase Belgium*]
YOW .... Ottawa [*Canada*] [*Airport symbol*] (OAG)
YOY .... Young-of-the-Year [*Conservation*]
YOYO .... You're on Your Own (DOMA)
YP .... Pagas Airlines [*ICAO designator*] (AD)
YP .... Patrol Craft [*Self-propelled*] [*Navy symbol*]
Yp .... Personal Disposable Income [*Economics*]
YP .... Yard Patrol
YP .... Y-Axis of Payload [*NASA*] (NASA)
YP .... Year of Publication (NITA)
YP .... Yeast Phase (AAMN)
YP .... Yellow Pine
YP .... Yield Point [*Ordinarily expressed in PSI*]
YP .... Yield Pressure (MAE)
YP .... Young People
YP .... Young Person (AIE)
YP .... Your Problem
YPA .... Port Authority of New York and New Jersey Library, New York, NY [*OCLC symbol*] (OCLC)
YPA .... Prince Albert [*Canada*] [*Airport symbol*] (OAG)
YPA .... Yaw Precession Amplifier
YPA .... Yearbook of Procurement Articles [*A publication*] (AAGC)
YPA .... Yearbook Printers Association (EA)
YPB .... Yeast Peptone Broth [*Microbiology*]
YPBF .... Yellow Sheet Price of Beef [*Business term*]
YPBYRB .... Youth Parole Board and Youth Residential Board [*Victoria, Australia*]
YPC .... Yangzi Petrochemical Industrial Corp. [*Commercial firm*] [*China*]
YPC .... Young Printers' Conference (DGA)
YPD .... Floating Pile Driver [*Non-self-propelled*] [*Navy symbol*]
YPD .... Parry Sound [*Canada*] [*Airport symbol*] (OAG)
YPD .... Yaw Phase Detector
YPD .... Yeast Extract-Peptones, Dextrose Medium [*Microbiology*]
YPD .... Yellow Pages Datasystem [*National Planning Data Corp.*] [*Database*]
YPDC .... Youth Policy Development Council [*Victoria, Australia*]
YPE .... Peace River [*Canada*] [*Airport symbol*] (OAG)
YPE .... Yoho Pitch Extractor
YPEC .... Young Printing Executives Club of New York (EA)
YPF .... Yacimientos Petroliferos Fiscales [*Argentinian oil company*] (ECON)
YPF .... Young Playwrights Festival [*Foundation of the Dramatists Guild*]
YPF .... YPF Sociedad Anonima [*NYSE symbol*] (SPSG)
YPF .... YPF Sociedad Anonima ADS [*NYSE symbol*] (TTSB)
YPF Soc .... YPF Sociedad Anonima [*Associated Press*] (SAG)
YPG .... Yuma Proving Ground [*Arizona*] [*Army*] (AABC)
YPH .... Port Harrison [*Canada*] [*Airport symbol*] (OAG)
YPI .... Youth Policy Institute (EA)
YPI .... Youth Pride, Inc. (EA)
YPK .... Pontoon Stowage Barge [*Navy symbol Obsolete*]
YPL .... Pickle Lake [*Canada*] [*Airport symbol*] (OAG)
YPL .... White Plains Public Library, White Plains, NY [*OCLC symbol*] (OCLC)
YPL .... York Public Library [*UTLAS symbol*]
YPL .... Young People's Literature [*A publication*]
YPLA .... Young People's LOGO Association (EA)
YPLB .... Yellow Sheet Price of Lamb [*Business term*]
YPLL .... Years of Potential Life Lost [*Epidemiology*]
YPM .... Saint Pierre [*Canada*] [*Airport symbol*] (OAG)
YPM .... State University of New York, College at Plattsburgh, Plattsburgh, NY [*OCLC symbol*] (OCLC)
YPM .... Yale Peabody Museum
YPM .... Yokefellowship Prison Ministry (EA)
YPN .... Port Menier [*Canada*] [*Airport symbol*] (OAG)
YPN .... Your Personal Network [*Information service or system*]
YPO .... Young Presidents' Organization (EA)
YPO .... Youth Programs Office [*Bureau of Indian Affairs*]
Y-POP .... Y-Body Axis Perpendicular to Orbit Plane [*Aerospace*]
YPPK .... Yellow Sheet Price of Pork [*Business term*]
YPQ .... Peterborough [*Canada*] [*Airport symbol*] (OAG)
YPR .... Prince Rupert [*Canada*] [*Airport symbol*] (OAG)
YPR .... Yanks Peak Resources [*Vancouver Stock Exchange symbol*]
YPR .... Youth Population Ratio (OICC)
YPS .... Yards per Second
YPS .... Yellow Pages Service [*Telecommunications*] (TEL)
YPSCE .... Young People's Society of Christian Endeavor
YPSL .... Young Peoples Socialist League [*Later, YSD*] (EA)
YPSSRB .... Yukon Public Service Staff Relations Board [*Canada*]
YPT .... Torpedo Retriever [*Navy symbol*] (DNAB)
YPVS .... Yamaha Power Valve System
YPW .... International Finance Corp. [*AMEX symbol*] (SAG)
YPW .... Powell River [*Canada*] [*Airport symbol*] (OAG)
YPW .... Putnam-Northern Westchester BOCES [*Boards of Cooperative Educational Services*], Yorktown Heights, NY [*OCLC symbol*] (OCLC)
YPX .... Povungnituk [*Canada*] [*Airport symbol*] (OAG)
YPY .... Collection Center [*FAA designator*] (FAAC)
YPY .... Fort Chipewyan [*Canada*] [*Airport symbol*] (OAG)
YPZ .... Young Poalei Zion (BJA)
YQ .... Lakeland [*ICAO designator*] (AD)
YQB .... Quebec [*Canada*] [*Airport symbol*] (OAG)
YQD .... The Pas, MB [*Canada*] [*Airport symbol*] (OAG)
YQF .... Red Deer [*Canada*] [*Airport symbol Obsolete*] (OAG)
YQG .... Windsor [*Canada*] [*Airport symbol*] (OAG)
YQH .... Watson Lake [*Canada*] [*Airport symbol*] (OAG)
YQI .... Yarmouth [*Canada*] [*Airport symbol*] (OAG)
YQJ .... Porquis Junction [*Ontario*] [*Airport symbol*] (AD)
YQK .... Kenora [*Canada*] [*Airport symbol*] (OAG)
YQL .... Lethbridge [*Canada*] [*Airport symbol*] (OAG)
YQM .... Moncton [*Canada*] [*Airport symbol*] (OAG)
YQQ .... Comox [*Canada*] [*Airport symbol*] (OAG)
YQR .... Regina [*Canada*] [*Airport symbol*] (OAG)
YQR .... Rochester Public Library, Rochester, NY [*OCLC symbol*] (OCLC)
YQT .... Thunder Bay [*Canada*] [*Airport symbol*] (OAG)
YQU .... Grande Prairie [*Canada*] [*Airport symbol*] (OAG)
YQV .... Yorkton [*Canada*] [*Airport symbol*] (OAG)
YQX .... Gander [*Canada*] [*Airport symbol*] (OAG)
YQY .... Sydney [*Canada*] [*Airport symbol*] (OAG)
YQZ .... Quesnel [*Canada*] [*Airport symbol*] (OAG)
YR .... Floating Workshop [*Non-self-propelled*] [*Navy symbol*]
YR .... Romania [*International civil aircraft marking*] (ODBW)
YR .... Scenic Airlines [*ICAO designator*] (AD)
YR .... Yale Review [*A publication*] (BRI)
YR .... Yaw Ring
Y-R .... Yaw-Roll (AAG)
YR .... Year [*Online database field identifier*] (EY)
yr .... Year (DAVI)
Yr .... Yearbook (BJA)
YR .... Yemeni Riyal (BJA)
YR .... Younger
yr .... Younger (ODBW)
YR .... Young Republican
YR .... Your (AAG)
yr .... Your (ODBW)
YR .... Youth Resources (EA)
YR .... Yukon Reports [*Maritime Law Book Co. Ltd.*] [*Canada Information service or system*] (CRD)
YRA .... Yacht Racing Association [*British*]
YRAC .... Yacht Racing Associations Council (EA)
YRAP .... Yellow Page Rate Base Analysis Plan [*Bell System*]

YRB .... Resolute [*Canada*] [*Airport symbol*] (OAG)
YRB .... Submarine Repair and Berthing Barge [*Non-self-propelled*] [*Navy symbol*]
YRB .... Yorbeau Resources, Inc. [*Toronto Stock Exchange symbol*]
YRBK .... Yearbook
YRBM .... Submarine Repair, Berthing, and Messing Barge [*Non-self-propelled*] [*Navy symbol*]
YRBM(L) ...... Submarine Repair, Berthing, and Messing Barge (Large) [*Navy symbol*]
YRBS .... Youth Risk Behavior Survey [*Medicine*]
YRC .... Submarine Rescue Chamber [*Navy symbol*]
YRC .... Yaw Ratio Controller (MCD)
YRDH .... Floating Dry Dock Workshop (Hull) [*Non-self-propelled*] [*Navy symbol*]
YRDM .... Floating Dry Dock Workshop (Machine) [*Non-self-propelled*] [*Navy symbol*]
YRDST .... Year-Round Daylight Saving Time
YRE .... Year Round Education (EDAC)
YRF .... Ross Bay [*Newfoundland*] [*Airport symbol*] (AD)
YRF .... Yoga Research Foundation (EA)
YRFC .... [*The*] Young and the Restless Fan Club (EA)
YRFLN .... Year Flown (MCD)
YRG .... Air Yugoslavia [*ICAO designator*] (FAAC)
YRGB .... Yellow Red Green Blue (IAA)
YRI .... Riviere-Du-Loup [*Canada*] [*Airport symbol Obsolete*] (OAG)
YRI .... Yri-York Ltd. [*Toronto Stock Exchange symbol*]
YRINY .... Youth Research Institute of New York (EA)
YRJ .... Roberval [*Canada*] [*Airport symbol Obsolete*] (OAG)
YRK .... York International [*NYSE symbol*] (TTSB)
YRK .... York International Corp. [*NYSE symbol*] (SPSG)
YRK .... York, KY [*Location identifier FAA*] (FAAL)
YRK .... York University Library [*UTLAS symbol*]
YRKG .... York Group [*NASDAQ symbol*] (TTSB)
YRL .... Covered Lighter (Repair) [*Navy symbol Obsolete*]
YRL .... Red Lake [*Canada*] [*Airport symbol*] (OAG)
yrl .... Yearling
YRL .... York University Law Library [*UTLAS symbol*]
YRLY .... Yearly (ROG)
YRM .... Rensselaer Polytechnic Institute, Troy, NY [*OCLC symbol*] (OCLC)
YRNF .... Young Republican National Federation (EA)
YRQ .... Trois Rivieres [*Quebec*] [*Airport symbol*] (AD)
YRR .... Radiological Repair Barge [*Non-self-propelled*] [*Navy symbol*]
YRR .... Scenic Airlines, Inc. [*ICAO designator*] (FAAC)
YRS .... Red Sucker Lake [*Canada*] [*Airport symbol*] (OAG)
YRS .... Yours
YRS .... Yugoslav Relief Society
YRSI .... Yves R. Simon Institute (EA)
YRST .... Salvage Craft Tender [*Non-self-propelled*] [*Navy ship symbol*]
YRT .... Rankin Inlet [*Canada*] [*Airport symbol*] (OAG)
YRT .... Yearly Renewable Term [*Insurance*]
YRT .... Yellowroot Tea [*Folk remedy, extract of buttercup root*]
YRX .... Rimouski [*Quebec*] [*Airport symbol*] (AD)
YS .... Aeronautical Station [*ICAO designator*] (ICDA)
YS .... Nihon Aeroplane Manufacturing Co. Ltd. [*Japan ICAO aircraft manufacturer identifier*] (ICAO)
YS .... San Juan Airlines [*ICAO designator*] (AD)
ys .... Southern Yemen (Aden) [*MARC country of publication code Library of Congress*] (LCCP)
YS .... Stevedoring Barge [*Navy symbol Obsolete*]
YS .... Yacht Service [*British military*] (DMA)
YS .... Yardstick
YS .... Yard Superintendent
YS .... Y-Axis of Solid Rocket Booster [*NASA*] (NASA)
YS .... Yellow-Bellied Sapsucker [*Ornithology*]
YS .... Yellow Spot
YS .... Yield Spread [*Investment term*]
YS .... Yield Strength [*Ordinarily expressed in PSI*]
YS .... Yield Stress
YS .... Yolk Sac (MAE)
YS .... Yoshida Sarcoma [*Medicine*]
YS .... Younger Son (ROG)
YS .... Young Soldier
YS .... Youngstown & Southern Railway Co. [*AAR code*]
YSA .... Young Socialist Alliance (EA)
YSA .... Youth Service America (EA)
YSAF .... Young Scientists of America Foundation [*Defunct*] (EA)
YSB .... Salomon Brothers Library, New York, NY [*OCLC symbol*] (OCLC)
YSB .... Sudbury [*Canada*] [*Airport symbol*] (OAG)
YSB .... Yacht Safety Bureau (EA)
YSB .... Yield Stress Bonding
YSC .... South Central Research Library Council, Ithaca, NY [*OCLC symbol*] (OCLC)
YSC .... Yearly Spares Cost (MCD)
YSC .... Yolk Sac Carcinoma [*Oncology, pathology, and pediatrics*] (DAVI)
YSCO .... Yes Clothing [*NASDAQ symbol*] (TTSB)
YSCO .... Yes Clothing Co. [*NASDAQ symbol*] (NQ)
YSD .... Seaplane Wrecking Derrick [*Self-propelled*] [*Navy symbol*]
YSD .... Young Social Democrats (EA)
YSDB .... Yield Stress Diffusion Bonding
YSDSA .... Youth Section of the Democratic Socialists of America (EA)
YSE .... Yaw Steering Error
YS/E .... Yield Strength to Elastic Modulus Ratio [*Dentistry*]
YSF .... Stoney Rapids [*Canada*] [*Airport symbol*] (OAG)
YSF .... Yield Safety Factor (IEEE)
YSG .... Young Solicitors' Group [*British*]
YSI .... Sans Souci [*Canada*] [*Airport symbol*] (OAG)
YSI .... Yellow Springs Instrument Co.
YSICSA .... Yellow Springs Institute for Contemporary Studies and the Arts (EA)
YSII .... Youth Services International, Inc. [*NASDAQ symbol*] (SAG)
YSII .... Youth Services Int'l [*NASDAQ symbol*] (TTSB)
YSJ .... Saint John [*Canada*] [*Airport symbol*] (OAG)
YSK .... Sanikiluaq [*Canada*] [*Airport symbol*] (OAG)
YSK .... Yokosuka [*Japan*] [*Seismograph station code, US Geological Survey Closed*] (SEIS)
YSL .... Saint Leonard [*Canada*] [*Airport symbol*] (OAG)
YSL .... Yolk Syncytial Layer [*Embryology*]
YSL .... Young Sowers' League [*British*]
YSL .... Yves Saint Laurent [*French couturier*]
Y-SLAV .... Yugoslavia
YSLF .... Yield Strength Load Factor (IEEE)
YSM .... Fort Smith [*Canada*] [*Airport symbol*] (OAG)
YSM .... State University of New York at Stony Brook, Stony Brook, NY [*OCLC symbol*] (OCLC)
YSM .... Yangtze Service Medal
YSM .... Young Socialist Movement
YSNC .... Youth Suicide National Center (EA)
YSO .... Young Stellar Object
YSP .... Pontoon Salvage Vessel [*Navy symbol*]
YSP .... Years Service for Severance Pay Purposes [*Military*]
YSP .... Yemen Socialist Party [*South Yemen*] [*Political party*] (PD)
YSR .... Nanisivik [*Canada*] [*Airport symbol*] (OAG)
YSR .... Sludge Removal Barge [*Non-self-propelled*] [*Navy symbol*]
YSR .... Years of Service Required
YSS .... Yuzhno-Sakhalinsk [*Russia*] [*Seismograph station code, US Geological Survey*] (SEIS)
YST .... Saint Therese Point [*Canada*] [*Airport symbol*] (OAG)
YST .... Yeast [*cells*] [*Laboratory science*] (DAVI)
YST .... Yolk Sac Tumor [*Oncology*]
YST .... Youngest
YST .... Yukon Standard Time (IAA)
YSTC .... Yorkshire Society of Textile Craftsmen [*A union*] [*British*] (DCTA)
YSU .... Summerside [*Prince Edward Island*] [*Airport symbol*] (AD)
YSV .... Yooralla Society of Victoria [*Australia*]
YSY .... Aeronautical Station [*FAA designator*] (FAAC)
YSY .... Sachs Harbour [*Canada*] [*Airport symbol*] (OAG)
YSZ .... Y-Stabilized Zirconia [*Physics*]
YSZ .... Yttria-Stablized Zirconia [*Materials science*]
YT .... Harbor Tug [*Navy symbol*]
YT .... Sky West [*ICAO designator*] (AD)
YT .... Telecommunication Authority [*ICAO designator*] (ICDA)
YT .... Yacht (ROG)
YT .... Yankee Team [*Phase of the Indochina bombing operation during US military involvement in Vietnam*]
YT .... Yard Tug [*NYSE symbol*] (DICI)
YT .... Yaw Trim (MCD)
YT .... Y-Axis of External Tank [*NASA*] (NASA)
yT .... Y-Matrix of Transistor (IDOE)
YT .... Yom Tov (BJA)
YT .... Youth Training (AIE)
Yt .... Yttrium [*See also Y*] [*Chemical element*]
YT .... Yukon Territory [*Postal code*] [*Canada*]
YTA .... Pembroke [*Canada*] [*Airport symbol*] (OAG)
YTA .... Yaw Trim Angle
YTA .... Yiddish Theatrical Alliance (EA)
YTB .... Large Harbor Tug [*Self-propelled*] [*Navy symbol*]
YTB .... Yard Tug Big [*Navy*]
YTB .... Yarn to Back [*Knitting*] (ADA)
YTB .... Yield to Broker [*Investment term*]
YTB .... Yuma Test Branch [*Yuma, AZ*] [*Army*]
YTC .... Yield to Call [*Investment term*]
YTC .... Yorkshire Trust Co. [*Toronto Stock Exchange symbol Vancouver Stock Exchange symbol*]
YTCA .... Yorkshire Terrier Club of America (EA)
YTD .... Year to Date (MCD)
YTD .... Year to Date (EERA)
YTD .... Young Tree Decline [*Plant pathology*]
YTE .... Cape Dorset [*Canada*] [*Airport symbol*] (OAG)
YTEC .... Yarsley Technical Centre Ltd. [*Research center British*] (IRC)
YTEP .... Youth Training and Employment Project
YTF .... Yad Tikvah Foundation (EA)
YTF .... Yarn to Front [*Knitting*] (ADA)
YTH .... Thompson [*Canada*] [*Airport symbol*] (OAG)
YTH .... Youth
YTHF .... Yours Till Hell Freezes [*Slang British*] (DI)
YTHJ .... Yeshivath Torah Hayim in Jerusalem (EA)
YTI .... Yeshiba Toledot Isaac. Tetuan (BJA)
YTJ .... Terrace Bay [*Canada*] [*Airport symbol*] (OAG)
YTL .... Big Trout Lake [*Canada*] [*Airport symbol*] (OAG)
YTL .... Small Harbor Tug [*Self-propelled*] [*Navy symbol*]
YTL .... Youth Tennis League (EA)
YTM .... Medium Harbor Tug [*Self-propelled*] [*Navy symbol*]
YTM .... State University of New York, College at Utica-Rome, Utica, NY [*OCLC symbol*] (OCLC)
YTM .... Yield to Maturity [*Investment term*]
YTP .... Youth Training Programme [*British*] (AIE)
YTRC .... Yokohama Technical Research Center [*Mazda Motor Corp.*]
YTRES .... Yankee Tractor Rocket Escape System (MCD)
YTS .... Timmins [*Canada*] [*Airport symbol*] (OAG)
YTS .... Youth Training Scheme [*British*]
YTS .... Yuma Test Station [*Missiles*]

YTT .... Torpedo Testing Barge [*Navy symbol Obsolete*]
YTTBT .... Yield Threshold Test Ban Treaty [*1976*]
YTTE .... Yield to Total Elation
YTV .... Yaw Thrust Vector
YTV .... Yorkshire Television [*British*]
YTX .... Planned District Craft [*Navy symbol*]
YTY .... Telecommunications Authority [*FAA designator*] (FAAC)
YTZ .... Toronto [*Canada*] [*Airport symbol*] (OAG)
YU .... Aerolineas Dominicanas [*ICAO designator*] (AD)
YU .... Yale Divinity School, New Haven, CT [*Inactive*] [*OCLC symbol*] (OCLC)
YU .... Yale University
YU .... Yeshiva University [*New York*]
YU .... Yugoslavia [*ANSI two-letter standard code*] (CNC)
yu .... Yugoslavia [*MARC country of publication code Library of Congress*] (LCCP)
YUA .... Youth for Understanding Australia
YUB .... Tuktoyaktuk [*Canada*] [*Airport symbol*] (OAG)
Yubbie .... Young Urban Baby [*Lifestyle classification*]
Yubbie .... Young Urban Breadwinner [*Lifestyle classification*]
YuBN .... Narodna Biblioteka Socijalisticke Republike Srbije, Beograd, Yugoslavia [*Library symbol Library of Congress*] (LCLS)
YUBO .... Yucca House National Monument
YUC .... Yucana Resources, Inc. [*Vancouver Stock Exchange symbol*]
YUC .... Yucatan
yuc .... Yucca (VRA)
Yuca .... Young Upwardly Mobile Cuban-American [*Lifestyle classification*]
Yucca .... Young Up-and-Coming Cuban American [*Lifestyle classification*]
YUCEE .... Youth Unit of the Council for Environmental Education (EAIO)
YUCI .... Yeshiva University Cumulative Index of Films of Jewish Interest [*A publication*] (BJA)
Yuckie .... Young Ultimate Creative Kitscher [*Lifestyle classification*]
Yuckie .... Young Urban Catholic [*Lifestyle classification*]
YUF .... Pelly Bay [*Canada*] [*Airport symbol*] (OAG)
Yuffie .... Young Urban Failure [*Lifestyle classification*]
YUG .... Yugawaralite [*A zeolite*]
YUG .... Yugoslavia [*ANSI three-letter standard code*] (CNC)
Yugo .... Yugoslavia (VRA)
Yugo L .... Yugoslav Law [*A publication*] (DLA)
Yugos .... Yugoslavia
YUK .... Youth Uncovering Krud [*Antipollution organization in Schenectady, New York*]
YUK .... Yuzhno-Kurilsk [*Former USSR Seismograph station code, US Geological Survey*] (SEIS)
Yuk Ord .... Yukon Ordinances [*Canada*] [*A publication*] (DLA)
Yuk Rev Ord ... Yukon Revised Ordinances [*Canada*] [*A publication*] (DLA)
YUL .... Montreal [*Canada*] [*Airport symbol*] (OAG)
YUL .... Yale University Library
Yullie .... Young Urban Laborer [*Lifestyle classification*]
YUM .... Yale Medical School, New Haven, CT [*Inactive*] [*OCLC symbol*] (OCLC)
YUM .... Yuma [*Arizona*] [*Airport symbol*] (OAG)
YUM .... Yuma Gold Mines Ltd. [*Vancouver Stock Exchange symbol*]
YUM .... Yumen [*Republic of China*] [*Seismograph station code, US Geological Survey*] (SEIS)
Yummie .... Young Upwardly Mobile Marxist [*Lifestyle classification*]
Yummie .... Young Upwardly Mobile Mountains [*Rocky Mountains*] [*Geological take-off on the abbreviation, Yuppie*] [*Canada*]
Yummie .... Young Urban Minister [*Lifestyle classification*]
Yummy .... Young Upwardly Mobile Mommy [*Lifestyle classification*]
Yumpie .... Young Upwardly Mobile Professional [*Lifestyle classification*]
Yumpy .... Young Upwardly Mobile Papa [*Lifestyle classification*]
YUN .... Yearbook of the United Nations [*A publication*] (DLA)
YUO .... Yuojima [*Bonin Islands*] [*Seismograph station code, US Geological Survey Closed*] (SEIS)
YUP .... Yale University Press (DGA)
Yuplis .... Young Upward Professional Library Information Specialist [*Lifestyle classification*]
Yuppie .... Young Urban Professional [*In book title "The Yuppie Handbook"*] [*Lifestyle classification*]
YUR .... Yuriko Resources [*Vancouver Stock Exchange symbol*]
Yurpie .... Young, Urban Republican Professional [*Lifestyle classification*]
YUS .... Yale University, New Haven, CT [*OCLC symbol*] (OCLC)
YUS .... Yushan [*Mount Morrison*] [*Republic of China*] [*Seismograph station code, US Geological Survey*] (SEIS)
YuSaN .... Narodne Biblioteka Bosne i Hercegovine [*National Library of Bosnia and Herzegovina*], Sarajevo, Yugoslavia [*Library symbol Library of Congress*] (LCLS)
YuSkN .... Nacionalna Biblioteka na Makedonija "Kliment Ohridaki", Skopje, Yugoslavia [*Library symbol Library of Congress*] (LCLS)
Yussie .... Young Unescorted Single [*Lifestyle classification*]
YUX .... Hall Beach [*Canada*] [*Airport symbol*] (OAG)
YUY .... Rouyn-Noranda [*Canada*] [*Airport symbol*] (OAG)
YuZU .... Nacionalna i Sveucilisna Biblioteka [*National and University Library of Croatia*], Zagreb, Yugoslavia [*Library symbol Library of Congress*] (LCLS)
YV .... Drone Aircraft Catapult Control Craft [*Navy symbol Obsolete*]
YV .... Mesa Aviation [*ICAO designator*] (AD)
YV .... Venezuela [*International vehicle registration and international civil aircraft marking*] (ODBW)
YV .... Yad Vashem [*An association Israel*] (EAIO)
YV .... Yield Value (IAA)
yV .... Y-Matrix of Vacuum Tube (IDOE)
YVA .... Moroni [*Comoro Islands*] [*Airport symbol*] (OAG)
YVA .... Yad Vashem Archives (BJA)
YVA .... Young Volunteers in ACTION
YVB .... Bonaventure [*Canada*] [*Airport symbol*] (OAG)
YVC .... Catapult Lighter [*Navy symbol*]
YVC .... Lac La Ronge [*Canada*] [*Airport symbol*] (OAG)
YVC .... Yellow Varnish Cambric
YVD .... Yaw Velocity Damping
YVM .... Broughton [*Canada*] [*Airport symbol*] (OAG)
YVO .... Onondaga Library System, Syracuse, NY [*OCLC symbol*] (OCLC)
YVO .... Val D'Or [*Canada*] [*Airport symbol*] (OAG)
YVP .... Fort Chimo [*Canada*] [*Airport symbol*] (OAG)
YVQ .... Norman Wells [*Canada*] [*Airport symbol*] (OAG)
YVR .... Vancouver [*Canada*] [*Airport symbol*] (OAG)
YVT .... Buffalo Narrows [*Canada*] [*Airport symbol Obsolete*] (OAG)
YVT .... Yakima Valley Transportation Co. [*AAR code*]
YVT .... Youth Visiting Team [*British military*] (DMA)
YW .... Military Flight Operational Control Center [*ICAO designator*] (ICDA)
YW .... Stateswest Airlines [*ICAO designator*] (AD)
YW .... Water Barge [*Self-propelled*] [*Navy symbol*]
YW .... Whitehorse Public Library, Yukon [*Library symbol National Library of Canada*] (NLC)
YW .... Yellow-White
YW .... Yellow Wove [*Paper*] (DGA)
YW .... Young Women of the Church of Jesus Christ of Latter-Day Saints (EA)
YW .... Young Women's [*Christian Association*]
YW .... Yreka Western Railroad Co. [*AAR code*]
YWA .... Yukon Archives, Whitehorse, Yukon [*Library symbol National Library of Canada*] (NLC)
YWAM .... Youth with a Mission (EA)
YWC .... Yukon College, Whitehorse, Yukon [*Library symbol National Library of Canada*] (NLC)
YWCA .... World Young Women's Christian Association (EAIO)
YWCA .... Young Women Committed to Action [*Feminist group*]
YWCAA .... Young Women's Christian Association of Australia
YWCA-USA ... Young Women's Christian Association of the United States of America (EA)
YWCJCLS .... Young Women of the Church of Jesus Christ of Latter-Day Saints [*Later, YW*] (EA)
YWCTU .... Young Women's Christian Temperance Union
YWDN .... Water Distilling Barge [*Non-self-propelled*] [*Navy symbol*]
YWED .... Department of Economic Development: Mines and Small Business, Government of the Yukon, Whitehorse, Yukon [*Library symbol National Library of Canada*] (NLC)
YWEEP .... Environmental Protection Service, Environment Canada [*Service de la Protection de l'Environnement, Environnement Canada*] Whitehorse, Yukon [*Library symbol National Library of Canada*] (NLC)
YWF .... Young World Federalists [*Later, World Federalist Youth*]
YWFD .... Young World Food and Development [*UN Food and Agriculture Organization*]
YWG .... Winnipeg [*Canada*] [*Airport symbol*] (OAG)
YWGASOYA ... You Won't Get Ahead Sitting on Your Afterdeck [*Slang Bowdlerized version*]
YWH .... Victoria [*Canada*] [*Airport symbol*] (OAG)
YWH .... Whalehead [*Quebec*] [*Airport symbol*] (AD)
YWHA .... Young Women's Hebrew Association [*Later, YM-YWHA*]
YWHHR .... Department of Health and Human Resources, Government of the Yukon, Whitehorse, Yukon [*Library symbol National Library of Canada*] (NLC)
YWHS .... Whitehorse Historical Society, Yukon [*Library symbol National Library of Canada*] (NLC)
YWHS .... Young Women's Help Society [*British*]
YWIN .... Northern Program, Indian and Northern Affairs Canada [*Programme du Nord, Affaires Indiennes et du Nord Canada*] [*Library symbol National Library of Canada*] (BIB)
YWK .... Wabush [*Canada*] [*Airport symbol*] (OAG)
YWL .... Williams Lake [*Canada*] [*Airport symbol*] (OAG)
YWL .... Yawl
YWL .... Yukon Law Library, Whitehorse, Yukon [*Library symbol National Library of Canada*] (NLC)
YWLL .... Young Workers Liberation League
YWLS .... Library Services Branch, Government of the Yukon, Whitehorse, Yukon [*Library symbol National Library of Canada*] (NLC)
YWM .... United States Military Academy, West Point, NY [*OCLC symbol*] (OCLC)
YWM .... Youth with a Mission [*Australia*]
YWN .... Ammunition Lighter [*Navy symbol*] (DNAB)
YWN .... Ammunition Pontoon [*Navy symbol*] (DNAB)
YWN .... Farm Scow [*Navy symbol*] (DNAB)
YWN .... Floating Crane [*Non-self-propelled*] [*Navy symbol*] (DNAB)
YWN .... Floating Pile Driver [*Non-self-propelled*] [*Navy symbol*] (DNAB)
YWN .... Lighterage Pontoon [*Navy symbol*] (DNAB)
YWN .... Pontoon [*Navy symbol*] (DNAB)
YWN .... Pontoon Barge [*Navy symbol*] (DNAB)
YWN .... Prison Ship [*Navy symbol*] (DNAB)
YWN .... Receiving Ship [*Navy symbol*] (DNAB)
YWN .... Sand Scow [*Navy symbol*] (DNAB)
YWN .... School Ship [*Navy symbol*] (DNAB)
YWN .... Transfer Barge [*Navy symbol*] (DNAB)
YWN .... Water Barge [*Non-self-propelled*] [*Navy symbol*]
YWN .... Winisk [*Canada*] [*Airport symbol*] (OAG)
YWN .... Yard Tug [*Navy symbol*] (DNAB)
YWOM .... [*The*] Old Log Church Museum, Whitehorse, Yukon [*Library symbol National Library of Canada*] (NLC)

YWP .... Sir Hugh Young's Working Party for Estimation of Civilian Relief Requirements [*World War II*]
YWPCN .... National Historic Sites, Parks Canada [*Lieux Historiques Nationaux, Parcs Canada*] Whitehorse, Yukon [*Library symbol National Library of Canada*] (NLC)
YWPG .... Young World Promotion Group [*UN Food and Agriculture Organization*]
YWR .... Yorkshire, West Riding [*County in England*] (ROG)
YWRR .... Department of Renewable Resources, Government of the Yukon, Whitehorse, Yukon [*Library symbol National Library of Canada*] (NLC)
YWS .... Young Wales Society
YWS .... Young Workers Scheme [*British*]
YWT .... Yard-Walk-Throughs [*Navy*] (NG)
YWTA .... Department of Territorial Affairs, Government of the Yukon, Whitehorse, Yukon [*Library symbol Obsolete National Library of Canada*] (NLC)
YWU .... Yiddish Writers Union (EA)
YWU .... Youth Work Unit [*National Youth Bureau*] (AIE)
YWY .... Military Flight Operational Control Centre [*FAA designator*] (FAAC)
YWY .... Wrigley [*Canada*] [*Airport symbol*] (OAG)
YX .... Midwest Express Airlines [*ICAO designator*] (AD)
YX .... Military Service or Organization [*ICAO designator*] (ICDA)
YX .... Societe Aeronautique Jurassienne [*ICAO designator*] (AD)
YXA .... National Airports Authority of India [*FAA designator*] (FAAC)
YXC .... Cranbrook [*Canada*] [*Airport symbol*] (OAG)
YXD .... Edmonton [*Canada*] Municipal Airport [*Airport symbol*] (OAG)
YXE .... Saskatoon [*Canada*] [*Airport symbol*] (OAG)
YXF .... Four County Library System, Binghamton, NY [*OCLC symbol*] (OCLC)
YXH .... Medicine Hat [*Canada*] [*Airport symbol*] (OAG)
YXJ .... Fort St. John [*Canada*] [*Airport symbol*] (OAG)
YXK .... Rimouski [*Canada*] [*Airport symbol*] (OAG)
YXL .... Sioux Lookout [*Canada*] [*Airport symbol*] (OAG)
YXO .... Houghton College, Buffalo Campus, West Seneca, NY [*OCLC symbol*] (OCLC)
YXP .... Pangnirtung [*Canada*] [*Airport symbol*] (OAG)
YXR .... Earlton [*Canada*] [*Airport symbol*] (OAG)
YXS .... Prince George [*Canada*] [*Airport symbol*] (OAG)
YXT .... Terrace [*Canada*] [*Airport symbol*] (OAG)
YXU .... London [*Canada*] [*Airport symbol*] (OAG)
YXX .... Abbotsford [*Canada Airport symbol*]
YXY .... Military Service [*FAA designator*] (FAAC)
YXY .... Whitehorse [*Canada*] [*Airport symbol*] (OAG)
YXZ .... Wawa [*Canada*] [*Airport symbol*] (OAG)
YY .... Robert Lynd [*American author, 1892-1970*] [*Pseudonym*]
Y-Y .... Yaw Axis (AAG)
YY .... Yedi'ot Yanai (BJA)
YYB .... North Bay [*Canada*] [*Airport symbol*] (OAG)
YYC .... Calgary [*Canada*] [*Airport symbol*] (OAG)
YYCI .... Youth-to-Youth Committee International (EA)
YYD .... Smithers [*Canada*] [*Airport symbol*] (OAG)
YYE .... Fort Nelson [*Canada*] [*Airport symbol*] (OAG)
YYF .... Penticton [*Canada*] [*Airport symbol*] (OAG)
YYG .... Charlottetown [*Canada*] [*Airport symbol*] (OAG)
YYH .... Spence Bay [*Canada*] [*Airport symbol*] (OAG)
YYJ .... Victoria [*Canada*] [*Airport symbol*] (OAG)
YYL .... Lynn Lake [*Canada*] [*Airport symbol Obsolete*] (OAG)
YYN .... Swift Current [*Saskatchewan*] [*Airport symbol*] (AD)
YYP .... Yarns of Yesteryear Project (EA)
YYP .... Yeshiva University, New York, NY [*OCLC symbol*] (OCLC)
YYQ .... Churchill [*Canada*] [*Airport symbol*] (OAG)
YYR .... Goose Bay [*Canada*] [*Airport symbol*] (OAG)
YYR .... Year of the Young Reader [*1989*] [*Library of Congress campaign*]
YYS .... Yo-Yo Stock [*Investment term*]
YYSCI .... Youth-to-Youth Sports Committee International [*Defunct*] (EA)
YYT .... St. Johns [*Canada*] [*Airport symbol*] (OAG)
YYU .... Kapuskasing [*Canada*] [*Airport symbol*] (OAG)
YYY .... Mont-Joli [*Canada*] [*Airport symbol*] (OAG)
YYY .... Organization Not Allocated Exclusive Designator [*FAA designator*] (FAAC)
YYY .... Yugntruf - Youth for Yiddish (EA)
YYZ .... Toronto [*Canada*] [*Airport symbol*] (OAG)
YZ .... Linhas Aereas da Guine-Bissau [*ICAO designator*] (AD)
YZ .... MET Databank [*ICAO designator*] (ICDA)
YZA .... Albany Law School, Albany, NY [*OCLC symbol*] (OCLC)
YZF .... Yellowknife [*Canada*] [*Airport symbol*] (OAG)
YZG .... Sugluk [*Canada*] [*Airport symbol*] (OAG)
YZP .... Sandspit [*Canada*] [*Airport symbol*] (OAG)
YZR .... Sarnia [*Canada*] [*Airport symbol*] (OAG)
YZS .... Coral Harbour [*Canada*] [*Airport symbol*] (OAG)
YZSZ .... Yarlung Zangbo Suture Zone [*Geophysics*]
YZT .... Port Hardy [*Canada*] [*Airport symbol*] (OAG)
YZV .... Sept-Iles [*Canada*] [*Airport symbol*] (OAG)
YZY .... Meteorological Data Bank [*FAA designator*] (FAAC)

Z
By Acronym

Z ... Administrative Aircraft [*When a suffix to Navy plane designation*]
Z ... Atomic Number [*Symbol*]
z ... Aza [*As substituent on nucleoside*] [*Biochemistry*]
Z ... Azimuth Angle
Z ... Characteristic Impedance (IDOE)
z ... Charge Number of a Cell Reaction [*Symbol*] [*Electrochemistry*]
Z ... Collision Number [*Symbol*] [*IUPAC*]
Z ... Compression Factor [*Symbol*] [*Thermodynamics*]
Z ... Contraction [*Medicine*]
Z ... Coriolis Correction
Z ... Dust Haze [*Meteorology*] (WDAA)
z ... Electrochemical Equivalent (IDOE)
Z ... Figure of Merit [*Symbol*] (DEN)
Z ... Glutamic Acid [*or Glutamine*] [*Also, Glx Symbol An amino acid*]
Z ... Haze [*Meterology*] (BARN)
Z ... Impedance [*Symbol*] [*IUPAC*]
Z ... Ionic Charge Number [*Chemistry*] (DAVI)
Z ... Normally Open [*Ship's fittings classification*]
z ... Partition Function, Particle [*Symbol*] [*IUPAC*]
Z ... Partition Function, System [*Symbol*] [*IUPAC*]
Z ... Planning [*Aircraft classification letter*]
Z ... Stadia [*Speedways, race tracks, etc.*] [*Public-performance tariff class*] [*British*]
z ... Standardized Device (DAVI)
Z ... Standard Score [*Psychology*]
Z ... Switzerland [*IYRU nationality code*] (IYR)
Z ... Weekend Travel [*Also, W*] [*Airline fare code*]
Z ... Woolworth Corp. [*Wall Street slang name: "Five & Dime"*] [*NYSE symbol Toronto Stock Exchange symbol*] (SPSG)
Z ... Zaire [*Monetary unit in Zaire*]
Z ... Zambon [*Italy*] [*Research code symbol*]
Z ... Z-Axis
Z ... Zebra [*Phonetic alphabet*] [*Royal Navy World War I Pre-World War II*] [*World War II*] (DSUE)
Z ... Zeitung [*Newspaper, Review*] [*German*] (ILCA)
Z ... Zenith
Z ... Zenith Distance [*Navigation*]
Z ... Zentralblatt [*Official Gazette*] [*German*] (ILCA)
Z ... Zentral-Sparkasse [*Banking Austria*] (ECON)
Z ... Zentrumspartei [*Center Party*] [*German Political party*] (PPE)
Z ... Zero
z ... Zero (WDMC)
z ... Zero (IDOE)
Z ... Zero Rate [*Valued added tax*]
Z ... Zerubbabel [*Freemasonry*] (ROG)
Z ... Zeta (NUCP)
Z ... Zimbabwe [*Aircraft nationality and registration mark*] (FAAC)
Z ... Zimmerman [*Used with a number in cataloging music of Henry Purcell*] (BARN)
Z ... Zinc [*Chemical symbol is Zn*]
Z ... Zionist
Z ... Zircon [*CIPW classification*] [*Geology*]
Z ... Zirconium [*Symbol is Zr*] [*Chemical element*] (ROG)
Z ... Zloty [*Monetary unit*] [*Poland*]
Z ... Zoen Tencararius [*Flourished, 13th century*] [*Authority cited in pre-1607 legal work*] (DSA)
Z ... Zoll [*Customs Duty*] [*German*]
Z ... Zone
z ... Zone (WDMC)
z ... Zone (IDOE)
Z ... Zone Code (IAA)
Z ... Zone Marker
Z ... Zone Meridian [*Lower or upper branch*]
Z ... Zuckung [*Contraction or spasm*] [*German Medicine*]
Z ... Zuender [*Fuze*] [*German military*]
Z ... Zuercher Bibel (BJA)
Z ... Zulu [*Phonetic alphabet*] [*International*] (DSUE)
Z ... Zulu Time [*Greenwich Mean Time*] (AFM)
(Z) ... Zusammen [*Together*] [*Chemistry*]
Z ... Zuse [*Calculator*] (HGAA)
Z ... Zwischenscheibe [*Disk*] [*Also, called intermediate disk, Z band, and Z line*] [*Laboratory science*] (DAVI)
Z ... Zyma AG [*Switzerland*] [*Research code symbol*]
Z8 ... Zilog Eight Bit One-Chip Microcomputer (HGAA)
Z80 ... Zilog Eight Bit Microprocessor (HGAA)
Z8000 ... Zilog Sixteen Bit Microprocessor (HGAA)
ZA ... Alpine Aviation [*ICAO designator*] (AD)
ZA ... Approach Control Office [*ICAO designator*] (ICDA)
ZA ... South Africa [*ANSI two-letter standard code*] (CNC)
Za ... Zabriskie's Reports [*21-24 New Jersey*] [*A publication*] (DLA)
za ... Zambia [*MARC country of publication code Library of Congress*] (LCCP)
ZA ... Zenith Angle [*Geophysics*]
ZA ... Zentralarchiv fuer Empirische Sozialforschung [*Central Archives for Empirical Social Research*] [*University of Cologne*] [*Information service or system*] (IID)
ZA ... Zero Adjuster (MSA)
ZA ... Zero and Add
ZA ... Zinc-Aluminum [*An alloy*]
ZA ... Zone of Action
ZAA ... Alice Arm/Kitsault [*Canada*] [*Airport symbol*] (OAG)
ZAA ... Zartman Association of America (EA)
ZAA ... Zeeman-Effect Atomic Absorption [*Spectrometry*]
ZAA ... Zero Angle of Attack
ZAAP ... Zero Antiaircraft Potential [*Missile*]
ZAB ... Albuquerque, NM [*Location identifier FAA*] (FAAL)
Zab ... Zabim (BJA)
ZAB ... Zabrze [*Poland*] [*Seismograph station code, US Geological Survey*] (SEIS)
ZAB ... Zinc-Air Battery
Zab Land Laws ... Zabriskie on the Public Land Laws of the United States [*A publication*] (DLA)
Zab (NJ) ... Zabriskie's Reports [*21-24 New Jersey*] [*A publication*] (DLA)
ZAC ... Zambia Airways [*ICAO designator*] (FAAC)
ZAC ... Zinc Aluminium Coater [*Metallurgy*]
ZAC ... Zinc Ammonium Chloride [*Organic chemistry*] (WDAA)
ZACH ... Zacharias [*Old Testament book*] [*Douay version*]
ZAD ... Zadar [*Former Yugoslavia*] [*Airport symbol*] (OAG)
ZAD ... Zenith Angle Distribution
ZADCA ... Zinc Alloy Die Casters' Association [*British*] (BI)
ZADCC ... Zone Air Defense Control Center (NATG)
ZADI ... Zentralstelle fuer Agrardokumentation und -Information [*Center for Agricultural Documentation and Information*] [*Databank originator*] [*Information service or system*] [*Germany*] (IID)
ZAED ... Zentralstelle fuer Atomkernenergie-Dokumentation beim Gmelin-Institut [*Central Agency for Atomic Energy Documentation of the Gmelin Institute*] [*Germany Database originator Also, AED*]
ZAF ... South Africa [*ANSI three-letter standard code*] (CNC)
ZAF ... Zero Alignment Fixture
ZAG ... Zagreb [*Croatia*] [*Seismograph station code, US Geological Survey*] (SEIS)
ZAG ... Zagreb [*Croatia*] [*Airport symbol*] (OAG)
ZAGI ... Zag Industries Ltd. [*NASDAQ symbol*] (SAG)
ZagIndus ... Zag Industries Ltd. [*Associated Press*] (SAG)
ZAH ... Zahedan [*Iran*] [*Airport symbol*] (OAG)
ZAHAL ... Z'va Hagana Le'Israel [*Israel Defense Forces*] [*Hebrew*]
ZAI ... Zaire Aero Service [*ICAO designator*] (FAAC)
ZAI ... Zeirei Agudath Israel (EA)
ZAI ... Zero Address Instruction
ZAK ... Zakamensk [*Former USSR Seismograph station code, US Geological Survey*] (SEIS)
ZAK ... Zero Administration Kit [*Computer science*]
ZAL ... State University of New York, Albany Library School, Albany, NY [*OCLC symbol*] (OCLC)
ZAL ... Valdivia [*Chile*] [*Airport symbol*] (AD)
ZAL ... Zionist Archives and Library (BJA)
ZALE ... Zale Corp. [*NASDAQ symbol*] (SAG)
ZaleCp ... Zale Corp. [*Associated Press*] (SAG)
ZALEW ... Zale Corp. Wrrt'A' [*NASDAQ symbol*] (TTSB)
ZALIS ... Zinc and Lead International Service
ZAM ... State University of New York, Agricultural and Technical College at Alfred, Alfred, NY [*OCLC symbol*] (OCLC)
ZAM ... Zambia (WDAA)
Zam ... Zambia (VRA)
ZAM ... Zamboanga [*Philippines*] [*Airport symbol*] (OAG)
ZAM ... Z-Axis Modulation
ZAM ... Zinc, Aluminium, Magnesium (PDAA)
Zambia LJ ... Zambia Law Journal [*A publication*] (DLA)
Zam LJ ... Zambia Law Journal [*A publication*] (DLA)
ZAMM ... Zen and the Art of Motorcycle Maintenance [*A novel*]
ZAMS ... Zero-Age Main Sequence [*Astronomy*]
ZAN ... Anchorage, AK [*Location identifier FAA*] (FAAL)

ZAN Zanderij [*Surinam*] [*Airport symbol*] (AD)
ZAN Zante [*Greece*] [*Seismograph station code, US Geological Survey*] (SEIS)
ZAN Zantop International Airlines, Inc. [*ICAO designator*] (FAAC)
Zan Zanzibar (BARN)
ZANA Zambia News Agency
ZANA Zanart Entertainment [*NASDAQ symbol*] (SAG)
ZANA Zanart Entmt [*NASDAQ symbol*] (TTSB)
Zanart Zanart Entertainment [*Associated Press*] (SAG)
ZANAU Zanart Entmt Unit [*NASDAQ symbol*] (TTSB)
ZANAW Zanart Entmt Wrrt'A' [*NASDAQ symbol*] (TTSB)
ZANC Zambia National Congress - Southern Rhodesia
Zane Zane's Reports [*4-9 Utah*] [*A publication*] (DLA)
ZANLA Zimbabwe African National Liberation Army (PD)
ZANU Zimbabwe African National Union [*Political party*] (PPW)
ZANU-PF Zimbabwe African National Union - Patriotic Front [*Political party*] (PD)
ZANZ Zanzibar
Zanz Zanzibar (VRA)
Zanzib Prot LR Zanzibar Protectorate Law Reports [*Africa*] [*A publication*] (DLA)
ZAP Zapata Corp. [*NYSE symbol*] (SAG)
ZAP Zapata Corp. [*NYSE symbol*] (TTSB)
ZAP Zaporozhe [*USSR*] [*Airport symbol*] (AD)
zap Zapotec [*MARC language code Library of Congress*] (LCCP)
ZAP Zero Ability to Pay [*Real estate*]
ZAP Zero and Add Packed
ZAP Zero Antiaircraft Potential [*Missile*] (MCD)
ZAP Zip Code Attachment Program [*Computer science*] (WDMC)
ZAP Znamenity Amerikansky Pisatel [*Famous American Writer*] [*Russian*]
ZAP Zone Axis Pattern (MCD)
ZAP Zoological Action Program [*Defunct*] (EA)
ZAP Zymosan-Activiated Plasma Rabbit [*Medicine*] (DMAA)
Zapata Zapata Corp. [*Associated Press*] (SAG)
ZAPB Zinc-Air Primary Battery
ZAPO Zimbabwe African People's Organization
ZAPP Zero Assignment Parallel Processor (NITA)
ZAPS Cooper Life Sciences [*NASDAQ symbol*] (TTSB)
ZAPS Cooper Life Sciences, Inc. [*NASDAQ symbol*] (NQ)
ZAPU Zimbabwe African People's Union
ZAR Zaire [*ANSI three-letter standard code*] (CNC)
ZAR Zairean Airlines [*Zaire*] [*ICAO designator*] (FAAC)
ZAR Zaria [*Nigeria*] [*Geomagnetic observatory code*]
ZAR Zaria [*Nigeria*] [*Airport symbol*] (AD)
ZAR Zero-G Antenna Range (SSD)
ZAR Zeus Acquisition RADAR [*Missile defense*]
Zaring Zaring Homes, Inc. [*Associated Press*] (SAG)
ZARP Zuid Afrikaansche Republick Politie [*South African Republic Police*] (DSUE)
ZAS Zaire Aero Service [*ICAO designator*] (FAAC)
ZAS Zarkani Air Services [*Egypt*] (EY)
ZAS Zas Airlines of Egypt [*FAA designator*] (FAAC)
ZAS Zero Access Storage
ZAS Zymosan-Activated Serum [*Immunology*]
ZAT Zantop Airways, Inc.
ZAT Zhaotong [*China*] [*Airport symbol*] (OAG)
ZAT Zinc Atmospheric Tracer
ZAT Zydowska Agencja Telegraficzna (BJA)
ZAU Chicago, IL [*Location identifier FAA*] (FAAL)
ZAV Zavalla [*Texas*] [*Seismograph station code, US Geological Survey Closed*] (SEIS)
Zav Zavim (BJA)
ZAW Zero Administration for Windows [*Microsoft Corp.*] [*Computer science*]
ZAW Zero Administration Initiative for Windows [*Microsoft Corp.*] [*Computer science*]
ZAZ Approach Control Office [*FAA designator*] (FAAC)
ZAZ Zaragoza [*Spain*] [*Airport symbol*] (OAG)
ZB Air Vectors [*ICAO designator*] (AD)
ZB Repetitive Flight Plan Office [*ICAO designator*] (ICDA)
ZB Zebra Body [*Medicine*] (DMAA)
ZB Zen Buddhism (BARN)
ZB Zero-Based (IAA)
ZB Zero Beat [*Radio*]
ZB Zimbabwe [*IYRU nationality code*] (IYR)
ZB Zimbabwe Banking Corp. Ltd.
ZB Zinc Borate [*Trademark for a flame retardant compound*] [*Humphrey Chemical Co.*]
ZB Zoom Back [*Cinematography*] (WDMC)
ZB Zuercher Bibel (BJA)
ZB Zum Beispiel [*For Example*] [*German*]
ZBA Z. Boskovic Air Charters Ltd. [*Kenya*] [*FAA designator*] (FAAC)
ZBA Zero Balance Accounts (TDOB)
ZBA Zero-Based Analysis (ADA)
ZBA Zero Based Analysis
ZBA Zero Bias Anomaly
ZBA Zero Bracket Amount [*IRS*]
ZBA Zoning Board of Approval [*Generic term*] (WGA)
ZBAA Beijing/Capital [*China*] [*ICAO location identifier*] (ICLI)
ZBB Zero-Base Budgeting
ZBBB Beijing City [*China*] [*ICAO location identifier*] (ICLI)
ZBC Zebec Resources [*Vancouver Stock Exchange symbol*]
ZBDC Zinc Dibutyldithiocarbamate [*Organic chemistry*]
ZBE Zinc Battery Electrode
ZBHH Huhhot [*China*] [*ICAO location identifier*] (ICLI)
ZBID Zero Bit Insertion/Deletion (NITA)
ZBL Brooklyn Law School, Brooklyn, NY [*OCLC symbol*] (OCLC)
ZBL Zero-Based Linearity
ZBLAN Zirconium, Barium, Lanthanum, Aluminum, Sodium Fluoride [*Molar composition of glass*] [*Chemistry*]
Zbl DDR Zentralblatt der Deutschen Demokratischen Republik [*A publication*] (DLA)
Zbl Soz Vers Zentralblatt fuer Sozialversicherung und Versorgung [*German A publication*] (DLA)
ZBM State University of New York, College at Oneonta, Oneonta, NY [*OCLC symbol*] (OCLC)
ZBMM Zenana Bible and Medical Mission [*British*] (DI)
ZBMP Zero-Base Media Planning
ZBN Brookhaven National Laboratory, Upton, NY [*OCLC symbol*] (OCLC)
ZBO Bowen [*Australia Airport symbol Obsolete*] (OAG)
ZBO Bowen [*Queensland*] [*Airport symbol*] (AD)
ZBO Zone of British Occupation [*Military*]
ZBOP Zero-Base Operational Planning and Budgeting (MHDB)
ZBOW Baotou [*China*] [*ICAO location identifier*] (ICLI)
ZBP Zero-Base Programming [*Military*]
ZBPE Beijing [*China*] [*ICAO location identifier*] (ICLI)
ZBR Chah-Bahar [*Iran*] [*Airport symbol*] (OAG)
ZBR Zero-Base Review
ZBR Zero Beat Reception [*Radio*]
ZBR Zero Bend Radius
ZBR Zone-BIT [*Binary Digit*] Recording [*Computer science*]
ZBRA Zebra Technologies'A' [*NASDAQ symbol*] (TTSB)
ZBRA Zebra Technologies Corp. [*NASDAQ symbol*] (SPSG)
ZBS Zivena Beneficial Society (EA)
ZBSB Zeitschriftenkatalog der Bayerischen Staatsbibliothek, Munchen [*Serials Catalogue of the Bavarian State Library, Munich*] [*Deutsches Bibliotheksinstitut*] [*Germany*] [*Information service or system*] (CRD)
ZBT Zeta Beta Tau [*Fraternity*]
ZBT Zion Bemishpat Tipadeh (Isaiah 1:27) (BJA)
ZBTJ Tianjin/Zhangguizhuang [*China*] [*ICAO location identifier*] (ICLI)
ZBTQM Zero-Based Tactical Quality Management [*Army*]
ZBTSI Zero Byte Time Slot Interchange (ACRL)
ZBV Zoological Board of Victoria [*Australia*]
ZBW Boston, MA [*Location identifier FAA*] (FAAL)
ZBY Sayaboury [*Laos*] [*Airport symbol*] (AD)
ZBYN Taiyuan/Wusu [*China*] [*ICAO location identifier*] (ICLI)
ZBZ Bureau des Plans de Vol Repetitifs [*FAA designator*] (FAAC)
ZC Royal Swazi National Airways [*ICAO designator*] (AD)
Z-C Zapalote-Chico [*Race of maize*]
Zc Zechariah (BJA)
ZC Ziegfeld Club (EA)
ZC Zinfandel Club [*British*] (EAIO)
ZC Zionist Congress [*Australia*]
ZC Zone Capacity
ZC Zonta Club [*Australia*]
ZCA Z Club of America (EA)
ZCAD Zycad Corp. [*NASDAQ symbol*] (NQ)
Z/CAL Zero Calibration (MCD)
ZCAV Zone Constant Angular Velocity [*Computer science*]
ZCB Chase Manhattan Bank, New York, NY [*OCLC symbol*] (OCLC)
ZCB Zinc-Coated Bolt
ZCC Zeppelin Collectors Club (EA)
ZCC Zirconia-Coated Crucible
ZCCFAR Zero Crossing Constant False Alarm Rate (IAA)
ZCCI Zippy Collectors Club [*Defunct*] (EA)
ZCD Zero Crossing Detector
ZCD Zone Controlled Deposition (IAA)
ZCG Impedance Cardiogram (NASA)
ZChN Zjednoczenie Chrzescijansko-Narodowe [*Christian National Union*] [*Poland Political party*] (EY)
ZCIC Zirconia-Coated Iridium Crucible
ZCL Zacatecas [*Mexico*] [*Airport symbol*] (OAG)
ZCM CM Preference Corp. [*Toronto Stock Exchange symbol*]
ZCM State University of New York, Agricultural and Technical College at Canton, Canton, NY [*OCLC symbol*] (OCLC)
ZCMI Zion's Cooperative Mercantile Institution [*Department store in Salt Lake City, UT*]
ZCN Zinc-Coated Nut
ZCO Temuco [*Chile*] [*Airport symbol*] (AD)
ZCO Zero Crossover (MHDB)
ZCO Ziegler Company, Inc. [*AMEX symbol*] (SAG)
ZCO Ziegler Cos. [*AMEX symbol*] (TTSB)
ZCON Zycon Corp. [*NASDAQ symbol*] (TTSB)
ZCON Zycon Corp. [*NASDAQ symbol*] (SAG)
ZCP Zinc Chloride Poisoning (DMAA)
ZCP Zinc Chromate Primer
ZCP Zonta Club of Perth [*Western Australia*]
ZCR Zero Crossing Rate
ZCR Zero-Temperature Coefficient Resistor
ZCR Zone of Correct Reading (IAA)
ZCRO Zero Cost Ration Option (TDOB)
ZCS Zero Code Suppression (ACRL)
ZCS Zinc-Coated Screw
ZCT Zero Count Table (IAA)
ZCW Zinc-Coated Washer
ZCZ Cazenovia College, Witherill Learning Center, Cazenovia, NY [*OCLC symbol*] (OCLC)
ZD Air Traffic Flow Control Unit [*ICAO designator*] (ICDA)
ZD Ross Aviation [*ICAO designator*] (AD)
ZD Zener Diode

ZD Zenith Description (WDAA)
ZD Zenith Distance [*Navigation*]
ZD Zero Defects
ZD Zero Discharge (DAVI)
ZD Ziff-Davis
ZD Zinc Deficiency (DMAA)
ZD ZIP Code Distribution
ZD Zone Description
ZDA Zinc Development Association [*British*] (EAIO)
ZDA/LDA/CA Zinc Development Association/Lead Development Association/ Cadmium Association [*Information service or system*] (IID)
Z (Day) Zero Day [*The date fixed for any important military operation*] [*British*]
ZDB Zeitschriftendatenbank [*German Union Catalog of Serials*] [*Deutsches Bibliotheksinstitut*] [*Germany*] [*Information service or system*] (CRD)
ZDBOP Ziff-Davis Benchmark Operation [*Computer utility tool*] (PCM)
ZDBOp Ziff-Davis Benchmark Operation (PCM)
ZDBT Zinc Dibenzyldithiocarbamate [*Organic chemistry*] (DICI)
ZDC Washington, DC [*Location identifier FAA*] (FAAL)
ZDC Zero Defects Council
ZDC Zeus Defense Center [*Missile defense*]
ZDC Zinc Dibenzyldithiocarbamate [*Rubber accelerator*]
ZDC Zinc Die Casting
ZDCTBS Zeus Defense Center Tape and Buffer System [*Missiles*] (IEEE)
ZDD Zero Delay Device
ZDDB Zip Code Demographic Data Base [*Demographic Research Co., Inc.*] [*Information service or system*] (CRD)
ZDDL Zero Deletion Data Link
ZDDP Zinc Dialkyldithiophosphate [*Organic chemistry*]
ZDE Zentralstelle Dokumentation Elektrotechnik [*Electrical Engineering Documentation Center*] [*Originator and database*] [*Germany Information service or system*] (IID)
ZDEC Zinc Diethyldithiocarbamate [*Organic chemistry*]
ZDF Zucker Diabetic Fatty [*Rat strain*]
ZDF Zweites Deutsches Fernsehen [*Television network*] [*West Germany*]
ZDG Corning Community College, Corning, NY [*OCLC symbol*] (OCLC)
ZDG Zinc-Doped Germanium
ZDI Ziff-Davis Interactive Co. [*Computer science*] (PCM)
ZDI Ziff Desktop Information [*Commercial firm*] (PCM)
ZDK Zen-Do Kai Martial Arts Association, International (EA)
ZDK Zonguldak [*Turkey*] [*Airport symbol*] (AD)
ZDMA Zinc Dimetylacrylate [*Plastics technology*]
Z DNA Deoxyribonucleic Acid, Zigzag [*DNA with left-handed helix*] [*Biochemistry, genetics*]
ZDO Zero Differential Overlap (DMAA)
ZDP Zero Defects Program
ZDP Zero Defects Proposal
ZDP Zero Delivery Pressure (IEEE)
ZDP Zimbabwe Democratic Party [*Political party*] (PPW)
ZDP Zinc Dialklydithiophosphate [*Automotive lubricants*]
ZDPA Zero Defects Program Audit
ZDPG Zero Defects Program Guideline
ZDPO Zero Defects Program Objective
ZDPR Zero Defects Program Responsibility
ZDR Zentraldeutsche Rundfunk [*Central German Radio*]
ZDR Zeus Discrimination RADAR [*Missile defense*]
ZDS Zenith Data Systems
ZDS Zilog Development System (NITA)
ZDS Zinc Depletion Syndrome [*Medicine*] (DMAA)
ZDS Zinc Detection System
ZDS Zung Depression Scale [*Psychiatry*] (DAVI)
Zdt Die Zoologie des Talmuds [*L. Lewysohn*] [*A publication*] (BJA)
ZDT Zero-Ductility Transition (IEEE)
ZDTP Zinc Dialklydithiophosphate [*Automotive lubricants*]
ZDV Denver, CO [*Location identifier FAA*] (FAAL)
ZDV Zero Dead Volume [*Chromatography*]
ZDV Zidovudine [*Antiviral*]
ZDWF Zentrale Dokumentationsstelle der Freien Wohlfahrtspflege fuer Fluechtlinge eV [*Germany*]
ZDX Zoladex [*Antineoplastic drug*] (CDI)
ZDZ Air Traffic Flow Control Unit [*FAA designator*] (FAAC)
ZE Air Caribe International [*ICAO designator*] (AD)
ZE Flight Information Database [*ICAO designator*] (ICDA)
ZE Pacific National [*ICAO designator*] (AD)
ZE Zenith Electronics [*NYSE symbol*] (TTSB)
ZE Zenith Electronics Corp. [*NYSE symbol*] (SPSG)
ZE Zero Balance Entry [*Banking*]
ZE Zero Effusion
ZE Zero Energy (BARN)
ZE Zeros Extended (IAA)
ZE Zollinger-Ellison [*Syndrome*] [*Medicine*]
ZE Zone Effect
ZE Zone Electrophoresis [*Analytical biochemistry*]
ZEA Zero Energy Assembly [*Nuclear energy*]
ZEA Zero Entropy Automorphism
Zeb Zebahim (BJA)
ZEB Zebra (ROG)
ZEB Zero-Emissions Bus
ZEBRA Zebra Energy Breeder Assembly
Zebra Zebra Technologies Corp. [*Associated Press*] (SAG)
ZEBRA Zero Balance, Reimbursable Account [*Year-end reclassification of taxable income*]
ZEBRA Zero Coupon Eurosterling Bearer or Registered Accruing Certificates (TDOB)
ZEBRA Zero Energy Breeder Reactor Assembly [*British*]
Zec Zechariah [*Old Testament book*]
ZEC Zero Energy Coefficient
ZEC Zinc-Electrochemical Cell
ZEC Zinsser-Engman-Cole [*Syndrome*] [*Medicine*] (DMAA)
ZEC Zurich Energy Corp. [*Vancouver Stock Exchange symbol*]
ZECC Zinc-Electrochemical Cell
ZECC Zonal Electric Comfort Council [*Defunct*] (EA)
Zech Zechariah [*Old Testament book*]
ZECM Zonal Elementary Circulative Mechanism
ZED Pakatoa [*New Zealand*] [*Airport symbol*] (AD)
ZED Zero Energy Deuterium [*Type of nuclear reactor*]
ZED Zero Express Dialing
ZEDRON Blimp Squadron [*Later separated into BLIMPRON and Blimp-HEDRON*] [*Navy*]
ZEEP Zero End Expiratory Pressure [*Medicine*]
ZEEP Zero Energy Experimental Pile [*Nuclear reactor*] [*Canada*]
ZEF Elkin, NC [*Location identifier FAA*] (FAAL)
ZEF Zero Extraction Force (EECA)
ZEG Senggo [*Indonesia*] [*Airport symbol*] (OAG)
ZEG Zero Economic Growth
ZEG Zero Energy Growth
ZEI Zeigler Coal Holding [*NYSE symbol*] (TTSB)
ZEI Zeigler Coal Holding Co. [*NYSE symbol*] (SAG)
ZEI Zero Environmental Impact
ZeigCoal Zeigler Coal Holding Co. [*Associated Press*] (SAG)
ZEKE Zero Kinetic Energy [*Physics*]
ZEL Bella Bella [*Canada*] [*Airport symbol*] (OAG)
ZEL Equitable Life Assurance Society of the United States, Medical Library, New Yor k, NY [*OCLC symbol*] (OCLC)
ZEL Zelovo [*Enthusiastically*] [*Music*] (ROG)
ZEL Zero-Length Launch [*Missiles*]
ZELL Zero-Length Launch [*Missiles*] (MCD)
ZELMAL Zero-Length Launch and Mat Landing [*Missiles*] (MCD)
ZEM East Main [*Canada*] [*Airport symbol*] (OAG)
ZEM Hobart and William Smith Colleges, Geneva, NY [*OCLC symbol*] (OCLC)
ZEM Zero Electrophoretic Mobility [*Analytical chemistry*]
Zemex Zemex Corp. [*Associated Press*] (SAG)
ZEMTR Zeus Early Missile Test RADAR [*Missile defense*] (AABC)
ZEN Zeitgeist, Enhancement, and Nonglare [*Camera lens finish developed by Sigma*]
zen Zenaga [*MARC language code Library of Congress*] (LCCP)
ZEN Zeneca Group [*NYSE symbol*] (SPSG)
ZEN Zeneca Group ADR [*NYSE symbol*] (TTSB)
ZEN Zenith (WDAA)
Zen Zenzelinus de Cassanis [*Deceased, 1334*] [*Authority cited in pre-1607 legal work*] (DSA)
ZEN Zero Effort Networking [*Novell*] [*Computer science*]
Zeneca Zeneca Group [*Associated Press*] (SAG)
ZENITH Zero Energy Nitrogen-Heated Thermal Reactor [*British*] (MCD)
ZenithE Zenith Electronics Corp. [*Associated Press*] (SAG)
Zenix Zenix Income Fund [*Associated Press*] (SAG)
ZEN-NOH National Federation of Agricultural Cooperative Associations [*Japan*] (EAIO)
ZenNtl Zenith National Insurance Corp. [*Associated Press*] (SAG)
Zenz Zenzelinus de Cassanis [*Deceased, 1334*] [*Authority cited in pre-1607 legal work*] (DSA)
ZEO Zeolite [*Chemistry*]
ZEOS Zeos International Ltd. [*NASDAQ symbol*] (NQ)
Zep Zephaniah [*Old Testament book*]
ZEP Zeppelin (DSUE)
Zeph Zephaniah [*Old Testament book*]
ZEPHYR Zero Energy Plutonium-Fueled Fast Reactor [*British*] (DEN)
ZEPI Zonal Echo Planar Imaging (DMAA)
ZEPL Zero Excess Propellants Line
ZEPS Zenith Energetic Particle Spectrometer (SSD)
ZER Pottsville, PA [*Location identifier FAA*] (FAAL)
Zer Zera'im (BJA)
ZER Zero Energy Reflection
ZERA Zero Energy Critical Assemblies Reactor [*British*] (DEN)
ZERC Zero Energy Reflection Coefficient
ZERLINA Zero Energy Reactor for Lattice Investigation and New Assemblies [*India*]
Zero Zero Corp. [*Associated Press*] (SAG)
Z-ERS Zeta Erythrocyte Sedimentation Rate [*Medicine*] (DMAA)
ZERT Zero Reaction Tool
ZES Zero Energy System [*Nuclear energy*]
ZES Zil Elwannyen Sesel [*Formerly, Zil Eliogne Sesel, then Zil Elwagne Sesel*]
ZES Zollinger-Ellison Syndrome [*Medicine*]
ZES Zone Electrophoresis System
ZES Zoo Education Service [*South Australia*]
Z-ESR Zeta Erythrocyte Sedimentation Rate [*Hematology*] (DAVI)
ZEST Zinc, E-Vitamin, Siberian Ginseng, Turnera [*Health product*] [*British*]
ZET Zero-Emissions Truck
ZET Zero-Gravity Expulsion Technique
ZETA Zero Energy Thermonuclear Apparatus [*or Assembly*] [*AEC*]
ZETR Zero Energy Thermal Reactor [*British*]
ZEUS Olympic Steel [*NASDAQ symbol*] (TTSB)
ZEUS Olympic Steel, Inc. [*NASDAQ symbol*] (SAG)
ZEUS Zero Energy Uranium System [*British*]
ZEV Zero Emissions Vehicle
ZEV Zero-Emission Vehicle [*Automotive engineering*] (PS)
Zev Zevahim (BJA)

ZevE ... Zeitschrift fuer Evangelische Ethik. Gutersloh [*A publication*] (BJA)
ZEvR ... Zeitschrift fuer die Evangelischen Religionsunterricht [*A publication*] (BJA)
ZEZ ... Flight information Data Base [*FAA designator*] (FAAC)
ZF ... Berlin U.S.A. [*ICAO designator*] (AD)
ZF ... Free Balloon [*Navy symbol*]
ZF ... Zahnradfabrik Friedrichshafen AG [*West Germany*]
ZF ... Zermelo-Fraenkel [*Set theory*] [*Mathematics*]
ZF ... Zero Frequency
ZF ... Ziegfeld Follies
ZF ... Zinc Finger [*Protein*] (DMAA)
ZF ... Zionist Federation [*British*] (DBA)
ZF ... Zona Fasciculata [*Of adrenal cortex*] [*Anatomy*]
ZF ... Zone Finder [*Telecommunications*] (OA)
ZF ... Zone of Fire [*Military*] (AAG)
ZF ... Zweig Fund [*NYSE symbol*] (SPSG)
ZFAL ... Zacherley Fans at Large (EA)
ZFB ... Signals Fading Badly
ZFC ... Zero Failure Criteria (IEEE)
ZFC ... Zero-Field Cooled [*Physics*]
ZFC ... Zipp-Forming Cells [*Immunology*]
ZFC ... Zirconia Fuel Cell
ZFDNMR ... Zero-Field Deuterium Nuclear Magnetic Resonance
ZFE ... Zone of Flow Establishment
ZFET ... Zionist Federation Educational Trust [*British*] (DI)
ZfG ... Zeitschrift fuer Geschichtswissenschaft [*A publication*]
ZFGBI ... Zionist Federation of Great Britain and Ireland (DI)
ZFL ... Zeitschrift fuer Luftrecht- und Weltraumrechtsfragen [*German A publication*] (DLA)
ZFM ... Community College of the Finger Lakes, Canandaigua, NY [*OCLC symbol*] (OCLC)
ZFM ... Fort McPherson [*Canada*] [*Airport symbol*] (OAG)
ZFMA ... Zip Fastener Manufacturers Association [*British*] (BI)
ZFMA ... Zip Fastener Manufacturers Association [*British*] (DBA)
ZFNMR ... Zero-Field Nuclear Magnetic Resonance
ZfP ... Dokumentation Zerstorungsfreie Pruefung [*Nondestructive Testing Documentation*] [*Federal Institute for Materials Testing*] [*Information service or system*] (IID)
ZFP ... Zinc Finger Protein (DMAA)
ZFP ... Zyglo-Fluorescent Penetrant
ZFPT ... Zyglo-Fluorescent Penetrant Testing
ZFS ... Zero Field Splitting
ZFS ... Zone Field Selection [*Physics*] (IAA)
ZFSC ... Zero-Field Splitting Constant [*Physics*]
Z f Schweiz Recht ... Zeitschrift fuer Schweizerisches Recht/Revue de Droit Suisse/Revista di Diritto Svizzero [*Basel, Switzerland*] [*A publication*] (DLA)
Z fur die Ost Gym ... Zeitschrift fuer die Oesterreichischen Gymnasien [*A publication*] (OCD)
ZFV ... Fort Severn [*Canada*] [*Airport symbol*] (OAG)
ZfV ... Zeitschrift fuer Versicherungswesen [*German A publication*] (DLA)
ZFW ... Fort Worth, TX [*Location identifier FAA*] (FAAL)
ZFW ... Zero Fuel Weight [*Aviation*]
ZG ... Air Traffic Control [*ICAO designator*] (ICDA)
ZG ... Silver State [*ICAO designator*] (AD)
Z-G ... Zapalote-Grande [*Race of maize*]
ZG ... Zap Gun
ZG ... Zero Gravity (IEEE)
ZG ... Zerstoerergeschwader [*Twin-engine fighter wing*] [*German military - World War II*]
ZG ... Zinc Gluconate [*Organic chemistry*]
ZG ... Zollgesetz [*Tariff Law*] [*German*]
ZG ... Zona Glomerulosa [*Of adrenal cortex*] [*Anatomy*]
ZG ... Zoological Gardens
Z/G ... Zoster Immune Globulin [*Immunology*] (MAH)
ZG ... Zymbal Gland [*Anatomy*]
ZGA ... Zero Grade Air
ZGB ... Zoological Gardens Board [*Western Australia*]
ZGCS ... Changsha/Datuopu [*China*] [*ICAO location identifier*] (ICLI)
ZGE ... Zero-Gravity Effect
ZGE ... Zero-Gravity Environment
ZGE ... Zero-Gravity Expulsion
ZGET ... Zero-Gravity Expulsion Technique
ZGF ... Grand Forks [*Canada*] [*Airport symbol Obsolete*] (OAG)
ZGF ... Zero Gravity Facility [*NASA*]
ZGG ... Zero-Gravity Generator
ZGGG ... Guangzhou/Baiyun [*China*] [*ICAO location identifier*] (ICLI)
ZGH ... Zonal Gravity Harmonic
ZGHK ... Haikou [*China*] [*ICAO location identifier*] (ICLI)
ZGI ... Gods River [*Canada*] [*Airport symbol*] (OAG)
ZGKL ... Guilin [*China*] [*ICAO location identifier*] (ICLI)
ZGL ... South Galway [*Queensland*] [*Airport symbol*] (AD)
ZGM ... City University of New York, Graduate School, New York, NY [*OCLC symbol*] (OCLC)
ZGM ... Ngoma [*Zambia*] [*Airport symbol*] (AD)
ZGM ... Zinc Glycinate Marker [*Immunochemistry*]
ZGMT ... Zu Gott Mein Trost [*In God My Comfort*] [*Motto of Ernst, Duke of Braunschweig-Luneburg (1564-1611)*] [*German*]
ZGN ... Zaghouan [*Tunisia*] [*Seismograph station code, US Geological Survey*] (SEIS)
ZGNN ... Nanning/Wuxu [*China*] [*ICAO location identifier*] (ICLI)
ZGOW ... Shantou [*China*] [*ICAO location identifier*] (ICLI)
ZGR ... Little Grand Rapids [*Canada*] [*Airport symbol*] (OAG)
ZGS ... Gethsemani [*Canada*] [*Airport symbol*] (OAG)
ZGS ... Zero Gradient Synchrotron [*AEC*]
ZGS ... Zero-Gravity Shower
ZGS ... Zero-Gravity Simulator
ZGS ... Zirconia Grain Stabilized [*Metal alloys*]
ZGS ... Zone Gradient Synchrotron [*Nickname: Ziggy*]
ZGT ... Zero-Gravity Trainer [*NASA*] (NASA)
ZGUA ... Guangzhou City [*China*] [*ICAO location identifier*] (ICLI)
ZGWBS ... Zero-Gravity Whole Body Shower
ZGWS ... Zane Grey's West Society (EA)
ZGZ ... Air Traffic Control [*FAA designator*] (FAAC)
ZGZJ ... Zhanjiang [*China*] [*ICAO location identifier*] (ICLI)
ZGZU ... Guangzhou [*China*] [*ICAO location identifier*] (ICLI)
ZH ... Helicopter Air Traffic Control [*ICAO designator*] (ICDA)
ZH ... Royal Hawaiian Airways [*ICAO designator*] (AD)
ZH ... Zinc Heads [*Freight*]
ZH ... Zonal Harmonic
ZH ... Zone Heater
zH ... Zu Haenden [*Attention Of, Care Of, To Be Delivered To*] [*German*] (GPO)
ZHA ... Zhangjiang [*China*] [*Airport symbol*] (OAG)
ZHCC ... Zhengzhou [*China*] [*ICAO location identifier*] (ICLI)
zHd ... Zu Haenden [*Attention Of, Care Of, To Be Delivered To*] [*German*]
ZHE ... Zero Headspace Extractor [*Environmental Protection Agency*] (ERG)
ZHF ... Zone Heat Flux
ZHHH ... Wuhan/Nanhu [*China*] [*ICAO location identifier*] (ICLI)
ZHL ... Hofstra University, Law School, Library, Hempstead, NY [*OCLC symbol*] (OCLC)
ZHM ... Hunter College of the City University of New York, New York, NY [*OCLC symbol*] (OCLC)
ZHM ... Shamshernagar [*Bangladesh*] [*Airport symbol*] (AD)
ZHN ... Honolulu, HI [*Location identifier FAA*] (FAAL)
ZHOM ... Zaring Homes [*NASDAQ symbol*] (TTSB)
ZHOM ... Zaring Homes, Inc. [*NASDAQ symbol*] (SAG)
Z HR ... Zero Hour (WDAA)
ZHR ... Zirconium Hydride Reactor
ZHSA ... Zeiss Historica Society of America (EA)
ZHU ... Houston, TX [*Location identifier FAA*] (FAAL)
ZHWH ... Wuhan [*China*] [*ICAO location identifier*] (ICLI)
ZHZ ... Helicopter Air Traffic Control [*FAA designator*] (FAAC)
ZI ... Flight Information Center [*ICAO designator*] (ICDA)
ZI ... Lucas Air Transport [*ICAO designator*] (AD)
ZI ... Zero Input
zi ... Zinc (VRA)
ZI ... Zinc Institute [*Defunct*] (EA)
ZI ... Zonal Index
ZI ... Zone of Interior [*Military*]
ZI ... Zonta International (EA)
Z/I ... Zoom In [*Cinematography and Video*]
ZI ... Zoom In [*Photography*] (NITA)
ZIA ... Zone of Interior Armies
ZIAX ... Zantop International Airlines, Inc. [*Air carrier designation symbol*]
ZIC ... Victoria [*Chile*] [*Airport symbol*] (AD)
ZIC ... Zirconia-Iridium Crucible
ZICON ... Zone of the Interior Consumers Network (MCD)
ZID ... Indianapolis, IN [*Location identifier FAA*] (FAAL)
ZID ... Zone of Initial Dilution [*Effluents*] (EG)
ZID(A) ... Zonta International Districts (Australia)
Zi de Cmo ... Ziliolus de Cremona [*Authority cited in pre-1607 legal work*] (DSA)
ZIE ... Zone Immunoelectrophoresis [*Analytical biochemistry*]
Ziegler ... Ziegler Co., Inc. [*Associated Press*] (SAG)
ZIF ... Zenix Income Fund [*NYSE symbol*] (SPSG)
ZIF ... Zero Insertion Force [*Electronics*]
ZIFT ... Zygote Intrafallopian Transfer [*Obstetrics*]
ZIFT ... Zygote Intrafallopian Tube Transfer [*Medicine*] (DMAA)
ZIG ... Zero Immune Globulin (WDAA)
zig ... Ziggurat (VRA)
ZIG ... Ziguinchor [*Senegal*] [*Airport symbol*] (OAG)
ZIG ... Zoster Immune Globulin [*Immunology*]
ZIGO ... Zygo Corp. [*NASDAQ symbol*] (NQ)
ZIH ... Hofstra University, Hempstead, NY [*OCLC symbol*] (OCLC)
ZIH ... Zihuatanejo [*Mexico*] [*Airport symbol*] (OAG)
ZIID ... Zentralinstitut fuer Information und Dokumentation [*Central Institute for Information and Documentation*] [*Germany Information service or system*] (IID)
ZII-ZD ... Zero Intersymbol Interference - Zero Derivative (PDAA)
ZIL ... Zigzag in Line [*Electronics*] (EECA)
ZIL ... Zork Interactive Language [*Computer science*]
ZILA ... Zila, Inc. [*NASDAQ symbol*] (NQ)
Zilla CD ... Zilla Court Decisions, Bengal, Madras, Northwest Provinces [*India*] [*A publication*] (DLA)
Zilog ... Zilog, Inc. [*Associated Press*] (SAG)
Zim ... Zimbabwe
ZIM ... Zimchurud [*Former USSR Seismograph station code, US Geological Survey Closed*] (SEIS)
ZIM ... Zi Mischari [*Merchant fleet*] [*Israel*]
ZIM ... Zonal Interdiction Missile (NVT)
ZIMB ... Zimbabwe (WDAA)
ZIMBANK ... Zimbabwe Banking Corp. Ltd.
ZIN ... Mount Zion Church [*South Carolina*] [*Seismograph station code, US Geological Survey Closed*] (SEIS)
zinco ... Zincograph (DGA)
ZinEB ... Zinc Ethylenebis(dithiocarbamate) [*Agricultural fungicide*]
ZING ... Zing Technologies [*NASDAQ symbol*] (TTSB)
ZING ... Zing Technologies, Inc. [*NASDAQ symbol*] (SAG)
Zink ... Zero Income, No Kids [*Lifestyle classification*]
Zinn Ca Tr ... Zinn's Select Cases in the Law of Trusts [*A publication*] (DLA)

ZIO .... Zinc Iodide-Osmium [*Biological staining procedure*]
Zion .... Zionism (BJA)
ZION .... Zions Bancorp [*NASDAQ symbol*] (TTSB)
ZION .... Zions Utah Bancorp [*NASDAQ symbol*] (SAG)
ZionBcP .... Zions Utah Bancorp [*Associated Press*] (SAG)
zip .... Archiving Utility [*Computer science*]
ZIP .... Zero Interest Payment [*Banking*]
ZIP .... Zigzag In-Line Package [*Wells American*] [*Computer science*]
ZIP .... Zinc Impurity Photodetector
ZIP .... Zone Improvement Plan [*Postal Service code*]
ZIP .... Zone Information Protocol (BYTE)
ZIP .... Zoster Immune Plasma [*Immunology*]
ZIPA .... Zimbabwe People's Army
ZIP Code .... National Zoning Improvement Plan Code [*US Postal Service*] (AAGC)
ZIPE .... Zentralinstitut Physik der Erde [*Potsdam*]
Zipp .... Zone of Inhibited Phage Plaques [*Immunology*]
ZIPRA .... Zimbabwe Independent People's Revolutionary Army (PD)
ZIR .... Zero Internal Resistance
ZIS .... Zone Information Socket (ACRL)
ZISS .... Zebulun Israel Seafaring Society (EA)
ZIT .... Zone Information Table [*Computer science*] (PCM)
Zitel .... Zitel Corp. [*Associated Press*] (SAG)
ZITF .... Zimbabwe International Trade Fair (ECON)
ZITL .... Zitel Corp. [*NASDAQ symbol*] (NQ)
ZIZ .... Flight Information Center [*FAA designator*] (FAAC)
Ziz .... Zizit (BJA)
ZJ .... Zipper Jacket
ZJC .... State University of New York, Central Administration, Albany, NY [*OCLC symbol*] (OCLC)
ZJX .... Jacksonville, FL [*Location identifier FAA*] (FAAL)
ZK .... Barrage Balloon [*Navy symbol*]
ZK .... Great Lakes Aviation [*ICAO designator*] (AD)
ZK .... New Zealand [*International civil aircraft marking*] (ODBW)
ZK .... Schering AG [*Germany*] [*Research code symbol*]
ZK .... Shavano Air [*ICAO designator*] (AD)
ZK .... Zachary Kurintner Books Ltd. [*British*]
ZK .... Zentralkommittee [*Central Committee*] [*of the Socialist Union Party of the German Democratic Republic*]
ZK .... Zera' Kodesh (BJA)
ZKB .... Bomber [*Russian aircraft symbol*]
ZKB .... Kasaba Bay [*Zambia*] [*Airport symbol*] (OAG)
ZKC .... Kansas City, MO [*Location identifier FAA*] (FAAL)
ZKC .... Keuka College, Lightner Library, Keuka Park, NY [*OCLC symbol*] (OCLC)
ZKE .... Kaschechewan [*Canada*] [*Airport symbol*] (OAG)
ZKEM .... Xechem International [*NASDAQ symbol*] (SAG)
ZKEM .... Xechem Intl [*NASDAQ symbol*] (TTSB)
ZKEMW .... Xechem Intl Wrrt [*NASDAQ symbol*] (TTSB)
ZKG .... Kegaska [*Canada*] [*Airport symbol*] (OAG)
ZKHH .... Hamhung [*North Korea ICAO location identifier*] (ICLI)
ZKIA .... Pyongyang [*North Korea ICAO location identifier*] (ICLI)
ZKKC .... Kimchaek [*North Korea ICAO location identifier*] (ICLI)
ZKKK .... Pyongyang [*North Korea ICAO location identifier*] (ICLI)
ZKL .... Steenkool [*West Irian, Indonesia*] [*Airport symbol*] (AD)
ZKM .... Sette Cama [*Gabon*] [*Airport symbol*] (AD)
ZKMDRVD .... Zmiesana Komisia Medzinarodnej Dohody o Rybolove vo Vodach Dunaja [*International Commission for Agreement on the Danube Fishing*] [*Former Czechoslovakia*] (EAIO)
ZKN .... Training Balloon [*Navy symbol*]
ZKO .... Observation Balloon [*Navy symbol*]
ZKPY .... Pyongyang/Sunan [*North Korea ICAO location identifier*] (ICLI)
ZKRVD .... Zmiesana Komisia o Rybolove vo Vodach Dunaja [*Joint Danube Fishery Commission - JDFC*] [*Zilina, Czechoslovakia*] (EAIO)
ZKSC .... Sunchon [*North Korea ICAO location identifier*] (ICLI)
ZKSR .... Sesura [*North Korea ICAO location identifier*] (ICLI)
ZKUJ .... Uiju [*North Korea ICAO location identifier*] (ICLI)
zkW .... Zero Kilowatt (IEEE)
ZKW .... Zi-ka-wei [*Republic of China*] [*Seismograph station code, US Geological Survey*] (SEIS)
zl .... Drizzle [*Meteorology*]
ZL .... Hazelton Airlines [*Airline code*] [*Australia*]
ZL .... Hazelton Air Services [*ICAO designator*] (AD)
ZL .... Z-Axis of Spacelab [*NASA*] (NASA)
ZL .... Zero Lift
ZL .... Zloty [*Monetary unit*] [*Poland*] (EY)
ZLA .... Los Angeles, CA [*Location identifier FAA*] (FAAL)
ZLAN .... Lanzhou City [*China*] [*ICAO location identifier*] (ICLI)
ZLB .... Balboa, Canal Zone [*Location identifier FAA*] (FAAL)
ZLC .... Salt Lake City, UT [*Location identifier FAA*] (FAAL)
ZLC .... Zero Lift Cord
ZLC .... Zinc, Lead, and Cadmium Abstracts [*Zinc Development Association/ Lead Development Association/Codmium Association*] [*British Defunct Information service or system*] (CRD)
ZLD .... Zero Level Drift
ZLD .... Zero Lift Drag
ZLD .... Zodiacal Light Device
ZLDI .... Zentralstelle fuer Luft- Raumfahrtdokumentation und Information [*Center for Documentation and Information in Aeronautics and Astronautics*] [*West Germany*] [*Information service or system*]
ZLE .... Zaba Lee Enterprises [*Vancouver Stock Exchange symbol*]
Z-LEV .... Zero-Level Emissions Vehicle
ZLG .... La Guera [*Morocco*] [*Airport symbol*] (AD)
ZLG .... Zero Line Gap
ZLG .... Zilog, Inc. [*NYSE symbol*] (SAG)
ZLH .... Lincoln Hospital, Bronx, NY [*OCLC symbol*] (OCLC)
ZLHW .... Lanzhou [*China*] [*ICAO location identifier*] (ICLI)
ZLIC .... Yinchuan [*China*] [*ICAO location identifier*] (ICLI)
ZLISP .... Zilog List Processor [*Programming language*] [*1979*] (CSR)
ZLJ .... Zambia Law Journal [*A publication*] (DLA)
ZLJM .... Zusters van Liefe Jezus en Maria [*Sisters of Charity of Jesus and Mary - SCJM*] [*Belgium*] (EAIO)
ZLJQ .... Jiuquan [*China*] [*ICAO location identifier*] (ICLI)
ZLK .... Zaleski, OH [*Location identifier FAA*] (FAAL)
ZLL .... Zero-Length Launch [*Missiles*]
ZLL .... Zero Lot Line [*Real estate*]
ZLL .... Zoned Lens Lamp
ZLLL .... Lanzhou/Zhongchuan [*China*] [*ICAO location identifier*] (ICLI)
ZLM .... State University of New York, College at New Paltz, New Paltz, NY [*OCLC symbol*] (OCLC)
ZLN .... Zwiazek Ludowo-Narodowy [*Populist-Nationalist Alliance*] [*Poland Political party*] (PPE)
ZLO .... Manzanillo [*Mexico*] [*Airport symbol*] (OAG)
ZLP .... Zongo [*La Paz*] [*Bolivia*] [*Seismograph station code, US Geological Survey*] (SEIS)
ZLR .... Zanzibar Law Reports [*1919-50*] [*A publication*] (DLA)
ZLR .... Zanzibar Protectorate Law Reports [*1868-1950*] [*A publication*] (DLA)
ZLS .... Zero-Gravity Locomotion Simulator [*NASA*] (PS)
ZLS .... Zero Level Sparing (MCD)
ZLSM .... Zeiss Light Section Microscope
ZLSN .... Xian [*China*] [*ICAO location identifier*] (ICLI)
ZLT .... La Tabatiere [*Canada*] [*Airport symbol*] (OAG)
ZLTO .... Zero-Length Takeoff (MCD)
Z-LV .... Z-Axis along Local Vertical (MCD)
ZLV .... Zero-Length Vector
ZLXN .... Xining [*China*] [*ICAO location identifier*] (ICLI)
ZLYA .... Yanan [*China*] [*ICAO location identifier*] (ICLI)
ZM .... Impedance Measuring Devices [*JETDS nomenclature*] [*Military*] (CET)
ZM .... Nike-Zeus at Point Mugu [*Missile defense*] (SAA)
ZM .... Trans-Central [*ICAO designator*] (AD)
ZM .... Zambia [*ANSI two-letter standard code*] (CNC)
ZM .... Zero Marker (MCD)
ZM .... Zoom/MODEM [*ZOOM Telephonics, Inc.*]
Z-M .... Zuckerman-Moloff [*Sewage treatment method*]
ZMA .... Miami, FL [*Location identifier FAA*] (FAAL)
ZMA .... Zinc Metaarsenite [*Insecticide, wood preservative*]
ZMAR .... Zeus Malfunction Array RADAR [*Missile defense*] (IAA)
ZMAR .... Zeus Multifunction Array RADAR [*Missile defense*]
ZMAR .... Zeus Multiple Array RADAR [*Missile defense*] (IAA)
ZMAR/MAR .... Zeus Multifunction Array RADAR / Multifunction Array RADAR [*Missile defense*] (SAA)
ZMB .... Zambia [*ANSI three-letter standard code*] (CNC)
ZMB .... Zero Moisture Basis [*Chemical analysis*]
ZMB .... Zinc Mercaptobenzimidazole [*Organic chemistry*]
ZMBH .... Zentrum fur Moleculare Biologie Heidelberg [*Center for Molecular Biology Heidelberg*]
ZMBT .... Zinc Mercaptobenzothiazole [*Organic chemistry*]
ZMC .... Manhattan College, Library, Bronx, NY [*OCLC symbol*] (OCLC)
ZMC .... Zero-Magnetostrictive Composition (PDAA)
ZMC .... Zygomatic [*Otorhinolaryngology*] (DAVI)
ZMC .... Zygomaticomaxillary Complex [*Otorhinolaryngology*] (DAVI)
ZMD .... Sao Madureira [*Brazil*] [*Airport symbol*] (AD)
ZMD .... Zung Measurement of Depression [*Scale*]
ZMDC .... Zinc Dimethyldithiocarbamate [*Organic chemistry*]
ZME .... Memphis, TN [*Location identifier FAA*] (FAAL)
ZMKR .... Zone Marker
ZML .... Medical Library Center of New York, Standardized Cataloging Service, New York, NY [*OCLC symbol*] (OCLC)
ZMM .... State University of New York, Maritime College, Bronx, NY [*OCLC symbol*] (OCLC)
ZMM .... Zone Melting Model
ZMMAS .... Zodiacal Microparticle Multiparameter Analysis System [*NASA*]
ZMMD .... Zurich, Mainz, Munich, Darmstadt [*A joint European university effort on ALGOL processors*]
ZMP .... Minneapolis, MN [*Location identifier FAA*] (FAAL)
zmphm .... Zoomorphism (VRA)
ZMR .... Zone-Melting Recrystallization [*Crystallography*]
ZMRI .... Zinc Metals Research Institute
ZMT .... Masset [*Canada*] [*Airport symbol*] (OAG)
ZMT .... ZIP [*Zone Improvement Plan*] Mail Translator [*Postal Service*]
ZMT .... Zoom Telephonics [*Vancouver Stock Exchange symbol*]
ZMUC .... Zoologisk Museum, University of Copenhagen [*Denmark*]
ZMX .... Zemex Corp. [*NYSE symbol*] (SPSG)
ZN .... Airship (Nonrigid) [*Navy symbol*]
ZN .... Tennessee Airways [*ICAO designator*] (AD)
Zn .... True Azimuth [*Symbol*] (MUGU)
ZN .... Zenith
ZN .... Ziehl-Neelsen [*A biological stain*]
Zn .... Zinc [*Chemical element*]
ZN .... Zone
ZNA .... Nanaimo [*Canada*] Harbour Airport [*Airport symbol*] (OAG)
ZNC .... New York City Technical College, Library, Brooklyn, NY [*OCLC symbol*] (OCLC)
ZNC .... Nyack, AK [*Location identifier FAA*] (FAAL)
ZNC .... Zone of Nonproliferating Cells [*Cytology*]
ZND .... Zinder [*Niger*] [*Airport symbol*] (OAG)
ZNE .... Newman [*Australia Airport symbol*] (OAG)
Zn Fl .... Zinc Flocculation [*Medical test*] (MAE)
ZNG .... Negginan [*Canada*] [*Airport symbol*] (OAG)
ZNG .... New Glasgow [*Nova Scotia*] [*Airport symbol*] (AD)

ZnG .... Zinc Gluconate [*Organic chemistry*]
ZNG .... Zoning [*Legal shorthand*] (LWAP)
ZNGI .... Zero Net Growth Isocline [*Ecological graph*]
ZNH .... Airship, Air-Sea Rescue [*Navy symbol*]
ZNJ .... Airship, Utility [*Navy symbol*]
ZNL .... Zero Memory Non-Linear (IAA)
ZNM .... Nioga Library System, Niagara Falls, NY [*OCLC symbol*] (OCLC)
ZNN .... Nonrigid Training Airship [*Navy symbol*]
ZNO .... Nonrigid Observation Airship [*Navy symbol*]
ZNO .... North Country Community College, Saranac Lake, NY [*OCLC symbol*] (OCLC)
ZNO .... Zenco Resources, Inc. [*Vancouver Stock Exchange symbol*]
ZnO .... Zinc Oxide [*Also, called white zinc*] [*Pharmacology*] (DAVI)
ZNOE .... Zinc Oxide-Eugenol [*Dental cement*]
ZNP .... Nonrigid Patrol Airship [*Navy symbol*]
ZNP .... Zanzibar Nationalist Party
ZnP .... Zinc Protoporphyrin [*Biochemistry*]
ZNP .... Zinc Pyrithione [*Antibacterial*]
ZNP .... Zion Nuclear Plant (NRCH)
ZNR .... Zinc Oxide Non-Linear Resistance (IAA)
ZNR .... Zinc Resistor
ZNRG .... Zydeco Energy [*NASDAQ symbol*] (TTSB)
ZNRG .... Zydeco Energy, Inc. [*NASDAQ symbol*] (SAG)
ZNRGW .... Zydeco Energy Wrrt [*NASDAQ symbol*] (TTSB)
ZNS .... Nonrigid Scouting Airship [*Navy symbol*]
ZnS .... Zinc Sulfide (BYTE)
ZNT .... Zenith National Insurance Corp. [*NYSE symbol*] (SPSG)
ZNT .... Zenith Natl Insurance [*NYSE symbol*] (TTSB)
ZNU .... Namu [*Canada*] [*Airport symbol Obsolete*] (OAG)
ZNXPO .... Zeus-Nike X Program Office [*Missiles*] (MCD)
ZNXS .... Zynaxis, Inc. [*NASDAQ symbol*] (SAG)
ZNY .... New York, NY [*Location identifier FAA*] (FAAL)
ZNZ .... Zanzibar [*Tanzania*] [*Airport symbol*] (OAG)
ZO .... Oceanic Air Traffic Control [*ICAO designator*] (ICDA)
ZO .... Trans-California [*ICAO designator*] (AD)
ZO .... Z-Axis of Orbiter [*NASA*] (NASA)
ZO .... Zero Output
Zo .... Zoen Tencararius [*Flourished, 13th century*] [*Authority cited in pre-1607 legal work*] (DSA)
ZO .... Zone (IAA)
ZO .... Zoological Origin
Z/O .... Zoom Out [*Cinematography*]
ZOA .... Oakland, CA [*Location identifier FAA*] (FAAL)
ZOA .... Zionist Organization of America (EA)
ZOA .... Zone of Avoidance [*Astronomy*]
ZOB .... Cleveland, OH [*Location identifier FAA*] (FAAL)
ZOBO .... Zongo [*La Paz*] [*Bolivia*] [*Seismograph station code, US Geological Survey*] (SEIS)
ZOC .... Zone of Convenience (ADA)
ZOC .... Zone of Convergence [*Aviation*] (DA)
ZOD .... Zero Order Detector (MCD)
ZOD .... Zodiac (ROG)
Zod .... Zodiac Records [*Record label*]
ZODIAC .... Zone Defense Integrated Active Capability (IEEE)
ZOE .... Zero Energy
ZOE .... Zinc Oxide-Eugenol [*Dental cement*]
ZOE .... Zone of Entry [*Military*] (AABC)
ZOE .... Zone of Exclusion (MCD)
ZOF .... Ocean Falls [*Canada*] [*Airport symbol Obsolete*] (OAG)
ZOF .... Zone of Fire [*Military*]
Z of C .... Zones of Communications [*Military*]
Z of I .... Zone of Interior [*Military*]
ZOG .... Paramaribo [*Suriname*] [*Airport symbol*]
ZOG .... Zeatin-O-Glucoside [*Biochemistry*]
ZOG .... Zionist Occupational Government
ZOH .... Zero Order Hold [*Telescope*]
ZOI .... Zero Order Interpolar (IAA)
ZOI .... Zone of Incorporation [*Environmental Protection Agency*] (ERG)
ZOL .... Zoladex (DMAA)
ZOLD .... Zeroth Order Logarithmic Distribution
ZOLL .... Zoll Medical [*NASDAQ symbol*] (TTSB)
ZOLL .... Zoll Medical Corp. [*NASDAQ symbol*] (SAG)
ZollMed .... Zoll Medical Corp. [*Associated Press*] (SAG)
ZOLT .... Zoltek Co. [*NASDAQ symbol*] (TTSB)
ZOLT .... Zoltek Companies [*NASDAQ symbol*] (SAG)
Zoltek .... Zoltek Cos. [*Associated Press*] (SAG)
ZOM .... Zomba [*Malawi*] [*Airport symbol*] (AD)
ZOMO .... Zmotoryzowane Oddzialy Milicji Obywatelskiej [*Motorized Units of People's Militia*] [*Poland's riot police*]
ZOMX .... Zomax Optical Media [*NASDAQ symbol*] (TTSB)
ZOMX .... Zomax Optical Media, Inc. [*NASDAQ symbol*] (SAG)
ZomxOpt .... Zomax Optical Media, Inc. [*Associated Press*] (SAG)
ZON .... Queenstown [*New Zealand*] [*Airport symbol*] (AD)
ZON .... Zonda [*Argentina*] [*Seismograph station code, US Geological Survey*] (SEIS)
ZON .... Zone Petroleum Corp. [*Vancouver Stock Exchange symbol*]
ZONA .... Zonagen, Inc. [*NASDAQ symbol*] (SAG)
Zonagen .... Zonagen, Inc. [*Associated Press*] (SAG)
Zonar .... Zonaras [*Twelfth century AD*] [*Classical studies*] (OCD)
ZONE .... Discovery Zone, Inc. [*NASDAQ symbol*] (SAG)
ZOO .... Minnesota Zoological Garden, Apple Valley, MN [*OCLC symbol*] (OCLC)
ZOO .... Zero on Originality (WDMC)
ZOOACT .... Zoological Action Committee [*Defunct*] (EA)
ZOOCHEM .... Zoochemistry (ROG)
ZOOGEOG .... Zoogeography (ROG)
ZOOL .... Zoological [*or Zoology*]
ZOOM .... Zoom Telephonics [*NASDAQ symbol*] (TTSB)
ZOOM .... Zoom Telephonics, Inc. [*NASDAQ symbol*] (SAG)
ZoomTI .... Zoom Telephonics, Inc. [*Associated Press*] (SAG)
zoopath .... Zoopathology (BARN)
ZOOPH .... Zoophytology (ROG)
ZOP .... Zero Order Predictor
ZOP .... Zinc Oxide Pigment
ZOPA .... Zinc Oxide Producers' Association [*European Council of Chemical Manufacturers Federations*] [*Belgium*] (EAIO)
ZOPFAN .... Zone of Peace, Freedom and Neutrality [*ASEAN*]
ZOPFAN .... Zone of Peace, Freedom and Neutrality Declaration (EERA)
ZOPI .... Zero Order Polynomial Interpolator
ZOPP .... Zero Order Polynomial Predictor
ZOR .... Zinc Oxide Resistor
ZOR .... Zone of Reconnaissance
ZOR .... Zorah Media Corp. [*Vancouver Stock Exchange symbol*]
Zoran .... Zoran Corp. [*Associated Press*] (SAG)
ZORRO .... Zero Offset Rapid Reaction Ordnance
ZOS .... Osorno [*Chile*] [*Airport symbol*] (AD)
ZOS .... Zapata Corp. [*NYSE symbol Toronto Stock Exchange symbol*]
ZOS .... Zone of Separation [*United Nations*] (INF)
ZOS .... Zoom Optical System
ZOTS .... Zoom Optical Target Simulator (OA)
Zouch Adm .... Zouche's Admiralty Jurisdiction [*A publication*] (DLA)
ZOW .... State University of New York, College at Old Westbury, Old Westbury, NY [*OCLC symbol*] (OCLC)
ZOX .... Ground Zero [*Nevada*] [*Seismograph station code, US Geological Survey Closed*] (SEIS)
ZOZ .... Oceanic Air Traffic Control [*FAA designator*] (FAAC)
ZP .... Air Traffic Services Reporting Office [*ICAO designator*] (ICDA)
ZP .... Patrol and Escort Aircraft [*Lighter-than-Air*] [*Navy symbol*] (MUGU)
ZP .... Revlon, Inc. [*Research code symbol*]
ZP .... Virgin Air [*ICAO designator*] (AD)
ZP .... Zadok Perspectives [*A publication*] (APTA)
ZP .... Z-Axis of Payload [*NASA*] (NASA)
ZP .... Zep Energy [*Vancouver Stock Exchange symbol*]
Zp .... Zephaniah (BJA)
ZP .... Zona Pellucida [*Embryology*]
ZP .... Zone Punch [*Computer science*] (IAA)
ZP .... Zweeppartij [*Whipping Party*] [*Political party Belgium*]
ZPA .... Zero Period Acceleration [*Nuclear energy*] (NRCH)
ZPA .... Zeus Program Analysis [*Missiles*]
ZPA .... Zone of Polarizing Activity [*Embryology, genetics*]
ZPapEpigr .... Zeitschrift fuer Papyrologie und Epigraphik [*A publication*] (BJA)
ZPAR .... Zeus Phased Array RADAR [*Missile defense*]
ZPB .... Z80A Processor Board [*North Star Computers*] (NITA)
ZPB .... Zinc Primary Battery
ZPC .... Zero Point of Charge
ZPC .... Zero Print Control (IAA)
ZPC .... Zinc-Phosphate Coating
ZPCA .... Zugzwang Postal Chess Association (EA)
ZPD .... Zero Path Difference
ZPDA .... Zinc Pigment Development Association [*British*] (BI)
ZPE .... Zero Point Energy
ZPE .... Zeta Phi Eta
ZPED .... Zeus Production Evaluation Program [*Missiles*] (MCD)
ZPEN .... Zeus Project Engineer Network [*Missiles*]
ZPFL .... Zanzibar and Pemba Federation of Labour
ZPG .... Airship Group [*Navy symbol*]
ZPG .... Zero Population Growth (EA)
ZPH .... Zephyrhills, FL [*Location identifier FAA*] (FAAL)
ZPH .... Zero-Phonon Hole [*Spectroscopy*]
ZPHGA .... Zimbabwe Professional Hunters & Guides Association
ZPI .... New York State Psychiatric Institute, Medical Library Center of New York, New York, NY [*OCLC symbol*] (OCLC)
ZPI .... Zone Position Indicator (IAA)
ZPID .... Zentralstelle fuer Psychologische Information und Dokumentation [*Center for Psychological Information and Documentation*] [*Database operator*] [*Germany Information service or system*] (IID)
ZPKM .... Kunming [*China*] [*ICAO location identifier*] (ICLI)
ZPL .... Zero-Phonon Line [*Physics*]
ZPL .... Zim Passenger Line (MHDB)
ZPLS .... Zimmerman Preschool Language Scale (DAVI)
ZPM .... State University of New York, College at Purchase, Purchase, NY [*OCLC symbol*] (OCLC)
ZPM .... Zero-Point-Motion [*Physics*]
ZPN .... Impedance Pneumograph [*Apollo*] [*NASA*]
ZPO .... Zeus Project Office [*Missiles*]
ZPO .... Zinc Peroxide [*Pharmacology*]
ZPO .... Zone Project Officer
ZPP .... Zimbabwe Progressive Party [*Political party*] (PPW)
ZPP .... Zinc Protophorphyrin [*Biochemistry*]
ZPPP .... Kunming/Wujiaba [*China*] [*ICAO location identifier*] (ICLI)
ZPPP .... Zanzibar and Pemba People's Party
ZPPR .... Zero Power Physics Reactor
ZPPR .... Zero Power Plutonium Reactor [*Nuclear energy*]
ZPR .... Zero Power Reactor [*Nuclear energy*]
ZPrA .... Woolworth Corp. $2.20 Cv Pfd [*NYSE symbol*] (TTSB)
ZPRF .... Zero Power Reactor Facility [*AEC*]
ZPRON .... Patrol [*Lighter-than-Air*] Squadron [*Navy symbol*]
ZPRSN .... Zurich Provisional Relative Sunspot Number [*NASA*]
ZPSS .... Zion Probabilistic Safety Study [*Nuclear energy*] (NRCH)

ZPT .... Zero Power Test
ZPT .... Zoxazolamine Paralysis Time [*In experimental animals*]
ZPV .... Zero-Point Vibration
ZPZ .... Air Traffic Services Reporting Office [*FAA designator*] (FAAC)
ZQ .... Ansett New Zealand [*ICAO designator*] (AD)
ZQ .... Ansett New Zealand [*Airline flight code*] (ODBW)
ZQC .... Queensborough Community College of the City University of New York, Library, Bayside, NY [*OCLC symbol*] (OCLC)
ZQC .... Zero Quality Control
ZQM .... State University of New York, College at Potsdam, Potsdam, NY [*OCLC symbol*] (OCLC)
ZQN .... Queenstown [*New Zealand*] [*Airport symbol*] (OAG)
ZQT .... Zero Quantum Transition [*Physics*]
ZR .... Area Control Center [*ICAO designator*] (ICDA)
ZR .... Freezing Rain [*Meterology*] (BARN)
ZR .... Rigid Airship [*Navy symbol*]
ZR .... Star Airways [*ICAO designator*] (AD)
ZR .... Zaire [*ANSI two-letter standard code*] (CNC)
ZR .... Zentralrat [*Central Board*] [*German*]
ZR .... Zero Coupon Issue (Security) [*In bond listings of newspapers*]
ZR .... Zimmerman Registry [*An association*] (EA)
Zr .... Zirconium [*Chemical element*]
ZR .... Zona Reticularis [*Of adrenal cortex*] [*Anatomy*]
ZR .... Zone of Responsibility
ZR .... Zone Refined
ZR .... Zoological Record Online [*Bio Sciences Information Service*] [*Information service or system*] (IID)
ZRA .... Zero Range Approximation [*Nuclear science*] (OA)
ZRA .... Zero Resistance Ammeter [*Instrumentation*]
ZRAN .... Zoran Corp. [*NASDAQ symbol*] (TTSB)
ZRAN .... Zoran Corp. [*NASDAQ symbol*] (SAG)
ZRBSC .... Zirconium Boride Silicon Carbide (PDAA)
ZRC .... Zenith Radio Corp.
ZRC .... Zurich Reinsurance Centre [*NYSE symbol*] (TTSB)
ZRC .... Zurich Reinsurance Centre Holdings [*NYSE symbol*] (SPSG)
ZRDI .... Zionic Research and Development Institute [*Defunct*] (EA)
ZRE .... Zaire [*International vehicle registration*] (ODBW)
ZRE .... Zero Rate Error (MCD)
ZREC .... Zoological Records [*BioSciences Information Service*]
ZRH .... Zurich [*Switzerland*] [*Airport symbol*] (OAG)
ZRI .... Serui [*Indonesia*] [*Airport symbol*] (OAG)
ZRIO .... Zimbabwe Rhodesian Information Office [*An association*] (EA)
ZRK .... Zona Receptor Kinase [*An enzyme*]
ZRL .... Zero Risk Level (GFGA)
ZRM .... Sarmi [*Indonesia*] [*Airport symbol*] (OAG)
ZRM .... Zone Reserved for Memory (NITA)
ZRN .... Rigid Training Airship [*Navy symbol*]
ZRN .... Zurn Indus [*NYSE symbol*] (TTSB)
ZRN .... Zurn Industries, Inc. [*NYSE symbol*] (SPSG)
ZRNO .... Freezing Rain Information Not Available [*NWS*] (FAAC)
ZRO .... Zero Corp. [*NYSE symbol*] (SPSG)
ZRO .... Zoological Record Outline
ZRP .... Rigid Patrol Airship [*Navy symbol*]
ZRP .... Zero Radial Play
ZRS .... Rigid Scouting Airship [*Navy symbol*]
ZRS .... Russell Sage College, Troy, NY [*OCLC symbol*] (OCLC)
ZRT .... Zero Reaction Tool
ZRV .... Zero-Relative Velocity
ZRZ .... Area Control Centre [*FAA designator*] (FAAC)
ZS .... Hispaniola Airways [*ICAO designator*] (AD)
Z/S .... Operational Display System
ZS .... Z-Axis of Solid Rocket Booster [*NASA*] (NASA)
ZS .... Zelena Slovenije [*Greens of Slovenia*] [*Political party*] (EY)
ZS .... Zellweger Syndrome [*Also, ZWS*] [*Medicine*]
ZS .... Zero and Subtract
ZS .... Zero Shift
ZS .... Zero State (IAA)
ZS .... Zero Sum [*Genetics*]
ZS .... Zero Suppress
ZS .... Zoological Society [*British*]
ZS .... Zoosporangia [*Botany*]
ZSA .... San Salvador [*Bahamas*] [*Airport symbol*] (OAG)
ZSA .... Southern Tier Library System, Corning, NY [*OCLC symbol*] (OCLC)
ZSA .... Zero-Set Amplifier (MSA)
ZSAM .... Xiamen [*China*] [*ICAO location identifier*] (ICLI)
ZSAT .... Zinc Sulfide Atmospheric Tracer
ZSB .... Zinc Storage Battery
ZSC .... Stauffer Chemical Co., Information Services, Dobbs Ferry, NY [*OCLC symbol*] (OCLC)
ZSC .... Zeeland Steamship Co. (MHDW)
ZSC .... Zero Subcarrier Chromaticity
ZSC .... Zinc Silicate Coat
ZSC .... Zose [*Republic of China*] [*Seismograph station code, US Geological Survey*] (SEIS)
Zschft f Ausl u Intl Privatr... Zeitschrift fuer Auslaendisches und Internationales Privatrecht [*Berlin and Tubingen, Germany*] [*A publication*] (DLA)
Zschft Luft- u Weltr-Recht... Zeitschrift fuer Luftrecht- und Weltraumrechtsfragen [*A publication*] (DLA)
Zschft Rechtsvergl... Zeitschrift fuer Rechtsvergleichung [*Vienna, Austria*] [*A publication*] (DLA)
ZSCN .... Nanchang [*China*] [*ICAO location identifier*] (ICLI)
ZSD .... Zebra Stripe Display
ZSD .... Zinc Sulfide Detector
ZSDS .... Zinc Sulfide Detection System
ZSE .... Seattle, WA [*Location identifier FAA*] (FAAL)
ZSEV .... Z Seven Fund [*NASDAQ symbol*] (TTSB)
ZSEV .... Z-Seven Fund, Inc. [*NASDAQ symbol*] (NQ)
Z Sevn .... Z-Seven Fund, Inc. [*Associated Press*] (SAG)
ZSF .... Zero Skip Frequency (IAA)
ZSFZ .... Fuzhou [*China*] [*ICAO location identifier*] (ICLI)
ZSG .... Zero-Speed Generator
ZSGZ .... Ganzhou [*China*] [*ICAO location identifier*] (ICLI)
ZSHA .... Shanghai [*China*] [*ICAO location identifier*] (ICLI)
ZSHC .... Hangzhou/Jianqiao [*China*] [*ICAO location identifier*] (ICLI)
ZSI .... Zero Size Image
ZSI .... Z Solar Inertial (MCD)
ZSI .... Zytec Systems, Inc. [*Toronto Stock Exchange symbol Vancouver Stock Exchange symbol*]
ZSJ .... St. John's University Library, Jamaica, NY [*OCLC symbol*] (OCLC)
ZSJ .... Zangri, S. J., Chicago IL [*STAC*]
ZSJA .... Jian [*China*] [*ICAO location identifier*] (ICLI)
ZSL .... Zero Sight Line (DNAB)
ZSL .... ZEROSLOTLAN [*Avatar Technologies, Inc.*] [*In Alliance ZSL, a PC network*]
ZSL .... Zjednoczone Stronnictwo Ludowe [*United Peasants' Party*] [*Poland Political party*] (PPW)
ZSL .... Zoological Society of London [*British*]
ZSM .... Zoologische Staatssammlung Muenchen
ZSN .... Zoological Station of Naples
ZSN .... Zurich Sunspot Number [*Astrophysics*]
ZSNJ .... Nanjing [*China*] [*ICAO location identifier*] (ICLI)
ZSOB .... Zinc-Silver-Oxide Battery (RDA)
ZSOF .... Hefei/Luogang [*China*] [*ICAO location identifier*] (ICLI)
ZSPG .... Zero-Speed Pulse Generator
ZSPS .... Zerex Saab Pro Series [*Auto racing*]
ZSQD .... Qingdao [*China*] [*ICAO location identifier*] (ICLI)
ZSR .... Zeta Sedimentation Rate [*Medicine*] (CPH)
ZSR .... Zinc Sedimentation Rate (MEDA)
ZS-RDS .... Zung Self-Rating Depression Scale [*Psychology*]
ZSRS .... Zung Self-Rating Scale [*For depression*]
ZSS .... Sassandra [*Ivory Coast*] [*Airport symbol*] (OAG)
ZSS .... Zen Studies Society (EA)
ZSS .... Zinc Sulfide System
ZSSA .... Shanghai City [*China*] [*ICAO location identifier*] (ICLI)
ZSSA .... Zoological Society of Southern Africa [*See also DUSA*] [*Port Elizabeth, South Africa*] (EAIO)
ZSSL .... Shanghai/Longhua [*China*] [*ICAO location identifier*] (ICLI)
ZSSS .... Shanghai/Hongqiao [*China*] [*ICAO location identifier*] (ICLI)
ZST .... Bratislava [*Czechoslovakia*] [*Seismograph station code, US Geological Survey*] (SEIS)
ZST .... Stewart [*Canada*] [*Airport symbol*] (OAG)
ZST .... Zentralabteilung Strahlenschutz [*Central Department for Radiation Protection*] [*Germany*]
ZST .... Zinc Sulfide Tracer
ZST .... Zone Standard Time
ZSTN .... Jinan [*China*] [*ICAO location identifier*] (ICLI)
ZSU .... San Juan, PR [*Location identifier FAA*] (FAAL)
ZSUP .... Zero Suppress (IAA)
ZSW .... Prince Rupert [*Canada*] [*Airport symbol Obsolete*] (OAG)
ZSZ .... Sarsat Center [*FAA designator*] (FAAC)
ZT .... Aerodrome Control Tower [*ICAO designator*] (ICDA)
ZT .... Training Aircraft [*Lighter-than-Air*] [*Navy symbol*] (MUGU)
ZT .... Zachary Taylor [*US president, 1784-1850*]
ZT .... Z-Axis of External Tank [*NASA*] (NASA)
ZT .... Zipper Tubing
ZT .... Zone Time [*Navigation*]
ZTA .... Zeta Tau Alpha [*Sorority*]
ZTAT .... Zero Turn-Around Time [*Microcomputer*] [*Hitachi Ltd.*]
ZTB .... Tete A La Baleine [*Canada*] [*Airport symbol*] (OAG)
ZTB .... Zone Telephony Box [*Telecommunications*] (ACRL)
Ztbl .... Zentralblatt [*Official Gazette*] [*German*]
ZTC .... Zero-Temperature Coefficient (MSA)
ZTEC .... Zytec Corp. [*NASDAQ symbol*] (SAG)
ZTH .... Zakinthos [*Greece*] [*Airport symbol*] (OAG)
ZTJWG .... Zeus Target Joint Working Group [*Missiles*] (AAG)
ZTK .... Stokmarknes [*Norway*] [*Airport symbol*] (AD)
ZTL .... Atlanta, GA [*Location identifier FAA*] (FAAL)
ZTL .... Touro Law Library, New York, NY [*OCLC symbol*] (OCLC)
ZTM .... Mid-York Library System, Utica, NY [*OCLC symbol*] (OCLC)
ZTN .... Zinc Tannate of Naloxone [*Opiate antagonist*]
ZTO .... Zero Time Outage [*Nuclear energy*] (NRCH)
ZTO .... Zone Transportation Officer [*Military*]
ZTP .... Zero-Temperature Plasma
ZTR .... Zweig Total Return Fd [*NYSE symbol*] (TTSB)
ZTR .... Zweig Total Return Fund, Inc. [*NYSE symbol*] (CTT)
ZTS .... Zoom Transfer Scope (OA)
ZTS .... Zymosan-Treated Serum [*Medicine*] (DMAA)
ZTSCHR .... Zeitschrift [*Review*] [*German*]
Z-TSP .... Zephiran-Trisodium Phosphate [*Medicine*] (DMAA)
ZTZ .... Aerodrome Control Tower [*FAA designator*] (FAAC)
ZU .... Upper Area Control Center [*ICAO designator*] (ICDA)
ZU .... Utility Aircraft [*Lighter-than-Air*] [*Navy symbol*] (MUGU)
ZU .... Zeitlich Untauglich [*Temporarily Unfit*] [*German military - World War II*]
ZU .... Zia Airlines [*ICAO designator*] (AD)
ZUA .... Agana, GU [*Location identifier FAA*] (FAAL)
ZUA .... Central New York Union List of Serials, Syracuse, NY [*OCLC symbol*] (OCLC)
ZUB .... Allied Chemical Corp., Library, Solvay, NY [*OCLC symbol*] (OCLC)

ZUC American Foundation for Management Research, Library, Hamilton, NY [*OCLC symbol*] (OCLC)
ZUCK Chongqing [*China*] [*ICAO location identifier*] (ICLI)
ZUD Ancud [*Chile*] [*Airport symbol*] (AD)
ZUD Bristol Laboratories, Library, Syracuse, NY [*OCLC symbol*] (OCLC)
ZUE Carrier Corp., Library, Syracuse, NY [*OCLC symbol*] (OCLC)
ZUE Zuni Energy [*Vancouver Stock Exchange symbol*]
ZUG Community-General Hospital, Staff Library, Syracuse, NY [*OCLC symbol*] (OCLC)
ZUG Zugdidi [*Former USSR Seismograph station code, US Geological Survey Closed*] (SEIS)
ZUGY Guiyang [*China*] [*ICAO location identifier*] (ICLI)
ZUH Education Opportunity Center of the State University of New York, Syracuse, NY [*OCLC symbol*] (OCLC)
ZUI General Electric Co., Electronics Park Library, Syracuse, NY [*OCLC symbol*] (OCLC)
ZUJ General Electric Co., Information Resources Library, Utica, NY [*OCLC symbol*] (OCLC)
ZUK United States Veterans Administration, Hospital Library, Syracuse, NY [*OCLC symbol*] (OCLC)
ZUL Agway, Inc., Library, Syracuse, NY [*OCLC symbol*] (OCLC)
ZUL Silfi [*Saudi Arabia*] [*Airport symbol*] (AD)
zul Zulu [*MARC language code Library of Congress*] (LCCP)
ZUL Zurich-Lageren [*Switzerland*] [*Seismograph station code, US Geological Survey*] (SEIS)
ZULS Lhasa [*China*] [*ICAO location identifier*] (ICLI)
ZUM Churchill Falls [*Canada*] [*Airport symbol*] (OAG)
ZUM Supreme Court, Fifth Judicial District, Law Library, Utica, NY [*OCLC symbol*] (OCLC)
ZUM Zeitschrift fuer Urheber und Medienrecht [*Journal for Copyright and Communication*] [*NOMOS Datapool*] [*Database producer*]
ZUM Zimbabwe Unity Movement [*Political party*] (ECON)
ZUM Zone Usage Measurement (WDAA)
ZUN Saint Joseph's Hospital, Health Center Library, Syracuse, NY [*OCLC symbol*] (OCLC)
zun Zuni [*MARC language code Library of Congress*] (LCCP)
ZUN Zuni Pueblo, NM [*Location identifier FAA*] (FAAL)
ZUO Utica Mutual Insurance Co., Library, New Hartford, NY [*OCLC symbol*] (OCLC)
ZUP Utica/Marcy Psychiatric Center, Utica Campus Library, Utica, NY [*OCLC symbol*] (OCLC)
ZUP Zone a Urbaniser en Priorite [*Priority Urbanization Zone*] [*French*]
ZUPO Zimbabwe United People's Organization [*Political party*] (PPW)
ZUQ Saint Luke's Memorial Hospital Center, Medical Library, Utica, NY [*OCLC symbol*] (OCLC)
ZUR Hancock Airbase Library, Hancock Field, NY [*OCLC symbol*] (OCLC)
ZUR Zurfund International Ltd. [*Vancouver Stock Exchange symbol*]
ZUR Zurich [*Switzerland*] [*Seismograph station code, US Geological Survey*] (SEIS)
ZURF Zeus Up-Range Facility [*Missiles*] (AAG)
ZurichR Zurich Reinsurance Centre Holdings [*Associated Press*] (SAG)
ZurnIn Zurn Industries, Inc. [*Associated Press*] (SAG)
ZUS Utica/Marcy Psychiatric Center, Marcy Campus Library, Utica, NY [*OCLC symbol*] (OCLC)
ZUS Zusammen [*Together*] [*Music*]
ZUT Maria Regina College, Library, Syracuse, NY [*OCLC symbol*] (OCLC)
ZUTRON Airship Utility Squadron [*Navy symbol*]
ZUU Masonic Medical Research Laboratory, Library, Utica, NY [*OCLC symbol*] (OCLC)
ZUUU Chengdu [*China*] [*ICAO location identifier*] (ICLI)
ZUW Munson-Williams-Proctor Institute, Library, Utica, NY [*OCLC symbol*] (OCLC)
ZUX Mohawk Valley Learning Resource Center, Utica Library, Utica, NY [*OCLC symbol*] (OCLC)
ZUY Special Metals Corp., Library, New Hartford, NY [*OCLC symbol*] (OCLC)
ZUZ Crouse-Irving Hospital, School of Nursing, Library, Syracuse, NY [*OCLC symbol*] (OCLC)
ZUZ Upper Area Control Centre [*FAA designator*] (FAAC)
ZUZZ Zug und Zerschneidezuender [*Pull-and-Cut Igniter*] [*German military - World War II*]
ZV Air Midwest [*ICAO designator*] (AD)
ZV Zoomed Video [*Toshiba*] (PCM)
ZV Zu Verfuegung [*At Disposal*] [*German*] [*Business term*]
ZVA Jervis Public Library, Rome, NY [*OCLC symbol*] (OCLC)
ZVA Miandrivazo [*Madagascar*] [*Airport symbol*] (OAG)
ZVA Zero Order Variable Aperture Nonredundant Point Transmitted [*Compression algorithm*] (MCD)
ZVB Syracuse Research Corp., Library, Syracuse, NY [*OCLC symbol*] (OCLC)
ZVC Utica Public Library, Utica, NY [*OCLC symbol*] (OCLC)
ZVD Supreme Court of New York, Library, Syracuse, NY [*OCLC symbol*] (OCLC)
ZVEI Zentralverband der Elektrotechnischen Industrie [*Electrical Equipment Industry Association*] [*Germany*] (EY)
ZVF Zero-Velocity Fading [*Aviation*] (AIA)
ZVfD Zionistische Vereinigung fuer Deutschaland [*Zionist Federation of Germany*]
ZVG Springvale [*Queensland*] [*Airport symbol*] (AD)
ZVK Savannakhet [*Laos*] [*Airport symbol*] (AD)
ZVM Mohawk Valley Community College, Utica, NY [*OCLC symbol*] (OCLC)
ZV Port Zoomed Video Port (PCM)
ZVR Zener Voltage Regulator
ZVRD Zener Voltage Regulator Diode
ZVS Zero Voltage Switch
ZVX Zygocactus Virus X [*Plant pathology*]
ZVZ Zavitz Technology, Inc. [*Toronto Stock Exchange symbol*]
ZW Air Wisconsin [*Airline code*]
ZW Air Wisconsin [*ICAO designator*] (AD)
ZW Nike-Zeus at White Sands [*Missile defense*] (SAA)
ZW Zero Wait [*Industrial engineering*]
ZW Zero Wear
ZW Zimbabwe [*ANSI two-letter standard code*] (CNC)
Zw Zwischensatz [*Interpolation*] [*Music*]
ZWA Andapa [*Madagascar*] [*Airport symbol*] (OAG)
ZWAK Aksu [*China*] [*ICAO location identifier*] (ICLI)
ZWC Zero Word Count
ZWC Zone Wind Computer
ZWE Zimbabwe [*ANSI three-letter standard code*] (CNC)
Zweig Zweig Fund [*Associated Press*] (SAG)
ZweigTl Zweig Total Return Fund, Inc. [*Associated Press*] (SAG)
ZWHM Hami [*China*] [*ICAO location identifier*] (ICLI)
ZWKC Kuqa [*China*] [*ICAO location identifier*] (ICLI)
ZWL Wollaston Lake [*Canada*] [*Airport symbol*] (OAG)
ZWL Zero Wavelength
ZWO Zuiver Wentenschappelijk Orderzock [*Netherlands*]
ZWOK Zirconium-Water Oxidation Kinetics (NRCH)
ZWP Zone Wind Plotter
ZWS Zellweger Syndrome [*Medicine*]
ZWS Zentralwohlfahrtsstelle der Juden in Deutschland [*A publication*] (BJA)
ZWS Zonal Wind Stress [*Meteorology*]
ZWSH Kashi [*China*] [*ICAO location identifier*] (ICLI)
ZWSt Zentralwohlfahrtsstelle der Juden in Deutschland [*A publication*] (BJA)
ZWTN Hotan [*China*] [*ICAO location identifier*] (ICLI)
ZWU Union College, Schenectady, NY [*OCLC symbol*] (OCLC)
ZWUQ Urumqi [*China*] [*ICAO location identifier*] (ICLI)
ZWV Zero Wave Velocity
ZWW Zonal Westerly Wind [*Climatology*]
ZWWW Urumqi/Diwopu [*China*] [*ICAO location identifier*] (ICLI)
ZWYN Yining [*China*] [*ICAO location identifier*] (ICLI)
ZX Air West Airlines [*ICAO designator*] (AD)
ZXC City College of New York, New York, NY [*OCLC symbol*] (OCLC)
ZXCFAR Zero Crossing Constant False Alarm Rate (MSA)
ZXMP Zero Transmission Power
ZXX Exxon Corp., Information Center, Technical Service Coordinator, New York, NY [*OCLC symbol*] (OCLC)
ZY Air Pennsylvania [*ICAO designator*] (AD)
Zy Zygion (DMAA)
ZYB Zionist Year Book [*A publication*] (BJA)
Zycad Zycad Corp. [*Associated Press*] (SAG)
ZYCC Changchun [*China*] [*ICAO location identifier*] (ICLI)
Zycon Zycon Corp. [*Associated Press*] (SAG)
ZydcoE Zydeco Energy, Inc. [*Associated Press*] (SAG)
ZydecoE Zydeco Energy, Inc. [*Associated Press*] (SAG)
ZYFV Zucchini Yellow Fleck Virus [*Plant pathology*]
zyg Zygotene (DMAA)
zyg Zygotene [*Deoxyribonucleic Acid*] [*Genetics*] (DOG)
ZYG Zygote Resources [*Vancouver Stock Exchange symbol*]
Zygo Zygo Corp. [*Associated Press*] (SAG)
ZYHB Harbin/Yanjiagang [*China*] [*ICAO location identifier*] (ICLI)
ZYL Sylhet [*Bangladesh*] [*Airport symbol*] (OAG)
ZYLA Hailar [*China*] [*ICAO location identifier*] (ICLI)
Zylo Zyloprim [*Burroughs Wellcome Co.*] [*Pharmacology*] (DAVI)
ZYMV Zucchini Yellow Mosaic Virus
Zynaxis Zynaxis, Inc. [*Associated Press*] (SAG)
ZYP Zefkrome Yarn Program [*Dow Chemical Co.*]
ZYQQ Qiqihar [*China*] [*ICAO location identifier*] (ICLI)
ZYSH Shenyang [*China*] [*ICAO location identifier*] (ICLI)
Zytec Zytec Corp. [*Associated Press*] (SAG)
ZYTL Dalian [*China*] [*ICAO location identifier*] (ICLI)
ZYU New York University, New York, NY [*OCLC symbol*] (OCLC)
ZYYY Shenyang/Dongta [*China*] [*ICAO location identifier*] (ICLI)
ZYZ Aerodrome Security Services [*FAA designator*] (FAAC)
ZZ Aircraft in Flight [*ICAO designator*] (ICDA)
ZZ Datum Position [*Arbitrary*] [*Navy British*]
ZZ Lighter-than-Air [*Aircraft*] [*Navy symbol*] (MUGU)
Z-Z Roll Axis [*Aerospace*] (AAG)
ZZ Zeitschrift fuer die Wissenschaft des Judentums [*Leopold Zunz*] [*A publication*] (BJA)
ZZ Zig-Zag
ZZ Zinziber [*Ginger*] [*Pharmacology*] (ROG)
ZZ Zugzuender [*Pull Igniter*] [*German military - World War II*]
ZZ Zu [*or Zur*] Zeit [*At This Time*] [*German*]
ZZA Zamak Zinc Alloy
ZZB Zanzibar [*Tanzania*]
ZZC Zero-Zero Condition
ZZD Zig-Zag Diagram
ZZM Agence Nationale des Aerodromes et de la Meteorologie [*Ivory Coast*] [*ICAO designator*] (FAAC)
ZZR Zig-Zag Rectifier
ZZR Zigzag Riveting (MSA)
ZZT Zu Zu [*Tennessee*] [*Seismograph station code, US Geological Survey Closed*] (SEIS)
ZZTFC ZZ Top Fan Club (EA)
ZZU Mzuzu [*Malawi*] [*Airport symbol*] (AD)
ZZV Zanesville [*Ohio*] [*Airport symbol*] (AD)
ZZV Zanesville, OH [*Location identifier FAA*] (FAAL)

ZZV .... Zero-Zero Visibility
ZZW .... Zero-Zero Weather
ZZZ .... Aircraft in Flight [*FAA designator*] (FAAC)